THE
CAMBRIDGE ITALIAN
DICTIONARY

THE CAMBRIDGE ITALIAN DICTIONARY

GENERAL EDITOR

BARBARA REYNOLDS

VOLUME I

ITALIAN—ENGLISH

CAMBRIDGE

AT THE UNIVERSITY PRESS

1962

PUBLISHED BY
THE SYNDICS OF THE CAMBRIDGE UNIVERSITY PRESS

Bentley House, 200 Euston Road, London, N.W. 1
American Branch: 32 East 57th Street, New York 22, N.Y.
West African Office: P.O. Box 33, Ibadan, Nigeria

©

CAMBRIDGE UNIVERSITY PRESS
1962

Printed in Great Britain at the University Press, Cambridge
(Brooke Crutchley, University Printer)

LIST OF CONTRIBUTORS

GENERAL EDITOR AND CHIEF EXECUTIVE

BARBARA REYNOLDS

B.A. (Hons. French), B.A. (Hons. Italian), Ph.D. (Italian)
(University of London)

GENERAL CONTRIBUTORS

C. P. Brand, M.A., Ph.D. (Cantab.)

Felicity Firth, M.A. (Cantab.)

T. Gwynfor Griffith, M.A. (Oxon., Dubl.), B.Litt. (Oxon.)

G. S. Purkis, B.A. (Hons.), M.A., Ph.D. (London)

Barbara Reynolds, B.A. (Hons.), Ph.D. (London)

Stanley Rundle, B.A. (Hons.), B.Sc. (Hons.), Ph.D. (London),
Dott. in Scienze (Milan)

Walter Shewring, M.A. (Oxon.)

SPECIALIST CONTRIBUTORS

Michael Cadwallader Adams, M.A. (Oxon.), Barrister-at-Law, Lincoln's Inn: *law (including administrative, bureaucratic, commercial and financial terms)*.

Commander H. C. Alexander, R.N.: *naval and military terms*.

Edward Allam, M.A. (Cantab.), D.Mus. (London), A.R.C.M.: *music*.

Marian Clegg, M.A. (Cantab.), F.R.G.S.: *geography, geology*.

H. Gilbert-Carter, M.A. (Cantab.), M.B., Ch.B. (Edin.): *botany*.

C. B. Goodhart, M.A., Ph.D. (Cantab.): *biology, zoology, etc.*

Anthony Lawrence, B.A. (Hons.) (London): *terms relating to broadcasting, sport, journalism*.

M. F. M. Meiklejohn, M.A. (Oxon.): *ornithology*.

G. S. Purkis, B.A. (Hons.), M.A., Ph.D. (London): *fine arts, theatre*.

Barbara Reynolds, B.A. (Hons.), Ph.D. (London): *archaic and dialect terms*.

Stanley Rundle, B.A. (Hons.), B.Sc. (Hons.), Ph.D. (London), Dott. in Scienze (Milan): *technology, industry, medicine, heraldry, etc.*

Walter Shewring, M.A. (Oxon.): *religion, philosophy, Greek and Roman literature, antiquities, prosody, rhetoric*.

SUPPLEMENTARY REVISION BY

R. H. Boothroyd, M.A. (Oxon.)

G. Carsaniga, Dott. in Lett. (Pisa, Scuola Normale Superiore)

Uberto Limentani, Dott. in Giurisp., Dott. in Lett. (Milan), Ph.D. (London)

Camilla Roatta, Dott. in Lett. (Bocconi University, Milan)

C. F. Turnbull, M.A. (Dunelm.)

FOREWORD

By E. R. VINCENT, C.B.E., Litt.D.
Professor of Italian in the University of Cambridge

The Italian Dictionary compiled by the late Alfred Hoare has been very extensively used since its first edition of 1915. Despite its many virtues, it had some deficiencies and, in any case, modern usage was inevitably leaving it behind. The present dictionary was first undertaken as a revision of its predecessor, but it was very soon realized that to meet the requirements, both of scholars and of those chiefly concerned with the current idiom, an entirely new work was needed. Anyone who takes the trouble to compare the two dictionaries will appreciate that in its completeness and accuracy the new Cambridge Dictionary stands alone. It can justly claim, indeed, to be the most complete dictionary in its field today. One feature of the older work has been omitted with regret, namely the inclusion of etymological derivations of Italian words. On consideration, it was felt that a bilingual dictionary was not the proper place for such information, particularly as dictionaries in Italy itself are in disagreement about the origins of many words.

The first practical step towards the composition of the present work was taken early in 1947 when a steering committee was formed of which I had the honour to be Chairman. A number of contributors were appointed, general principles were discussed and working procedures adopted. Perhaps the idea that has proved itself most fruitful over the years has been that specialist contributors should be asked to take responsibility for the translation and selection of any word that seemed to be beyond common parlance. As words occurred which fell into special categories (scientific, military, ecclesiastical, sporting, legal, archaic, etc.), they were written on cards of distinctive colours and sent to appropriate specialists. In this way a large number of completely new professional translations, which are not to be found elsewhere, have been incorporated in the dictionary.

As one who has not been directly concerned with the actual compilation of the dictionary, yet has watched its steady growth over the years, I am in a position to congratulate the contributors on the successful completion of their enormous task. Since this was team-work, a guiding mind was essential to co-ordinate and fashion into a consistent whole the numerous parts that were brought to the centre. Dr Barbara Reynolds, as General Editor and Chief Executive, has most admirably fulfilled this function and, with great persistence, has successfully overcome all difficulties.

It is a great satisfaction to all concerned with Italian studies in this University that such an important instrument for Anglo-Italian understanding has originated in Cambridge and goes out into the world under the imprint of the Syndics of the Cambridge University Press.

E. R. VINCENT

CORPUS CHRISTI COLLEGE
CAMBRIDGE
October 1961

INTRODUCTION

I. GENERAL PRINCIPLES

This Italian–English dictionary is the first of its kind. No comparative study of the two languages has been undertaken before on so comprehensive and so detailed a scale. It is hoped that the scholar, the student, the general reader, the translator, the scientist, the technician, the industrialist, the business man, the journalist, the diplomat, and all other potential users of this dictionary will find in it the assistance and verification which they require. Since it is in scope and intention a pioneer work, it is necessary to give some account of the principles on which it has been constructed and the functions which it is intended to fulfil.

First, and underlying all its criteria, is the fact that it has been compiled, selected and arranged from the point of view of the English-speaking user. That is to say, the primary object of this first volume of the *Cambridge Italian Dictionary* is to answer, by means of translation into English, the question, 'Che cosa vuol dire...?', 'What does this mean?' The second volume, the English–Italian dictionary, which is being compiled from the same point of view, will answer, by means of translation into Italian, the question, 'How does one say...?', 'Come si dice...?'[1] The standpoint, or 'orientation', of a bilingual dictionary affects not only the choice and arrangement of phrases but also the principles of selection governing the word-list. In an Italian–English dictionary, a particular aspect of the cultural relations between the two countries comes into play. For many English users, the chief purpose of an Italian–English dictionary is to provide guidance to the meaning of Italian words whether they are still in use or not. In view of the enduring interest taken by English readers in the cultural heritage of Italy, much obsolete or obsolescent Italian vocabulary has been included, not to exemplify usage but in order to meet the needs of readers of Italian texts of all periods.[2]

The 'telegraphic' nature of dictionary-language is such that it depends for its comprehension upon the maximum possible co-operation of the user. In this connexion also, the principle of orientation is influential. In the selection of English renderings, in the juxtaposition of synonyms or of near-synonyms, in the distinctions drawn between styles and categories, in the association of ideas serving to determine groupings, reliance has been placed on the English-speaking user's understanding of his own language.

A great deal of the contents of this dictionary will, however, prove serviceable to Italian as well as to English users. All the principal contributors possess English as their mother-tongue. The phrases and idioms chosen to convey the meaning and use of Italian vocabulary may, consequently, be relied upon as being devoid of that 'near-English' which characterizes, for the most part, the English renderings in bilingual dictionaries compiled by those to whom English is a foreign language. The guidance of Italian contributors, as well as the evidence of Italian unilingual dictionaries, has been drawn upon for the elucidation of meaning and illustration of usage, just as in the English–Italian volume it is being sought in the choice of Italian renderings of English words and phrases. It is hoped that by such means both English and Italian users of both volumes will find themselves benefited to the uttermost.

---

[1] It may be observed that if the two volumes of this dictionary had been compiled primarily from the point of view of the Italian-speaking user, they would answer the questions in reverse order.

[2] All obsolete words in the word-list are indicated as such by an obelus or dagger (†). See also under II (*l*).

A predecessor of the present work, also compiled from the point of view of the English user, and likewise published by the Cambridge University Press, was Alfred Hoare's *An Italian Dictionary*. The original version of this has long been out of print, and most users of what is called 'Hoare's Dictionary' know only the concise edition, in two volumes, entitled *A Short Italian Dictionary*. This gives very little idea of the range and quality, or even the character, of the original work, which was intended chiefly to be of service to English readers of the Italian classics, an aim which it very well fulfils. The author[1] began work on it in the autumn of 1906, at the age of 56, principally because, as a reader of Dante, he had not found the assistance he required in existing dictionaries. The first edition was published in 1915; a second and considerably revised edition appeared in 1925. This was followed five years later by *An Italian Phrase-Book*, also published by the Cambridge University Press, a small but useful compilation of Italian idiomatic phrases listed under English key-words. This little-known work was evidently intended to constitute a supplement to the English–Italian section of his dictionary which he had probably hoped to develop. He died eight years later in 1938, at the age of 88.

Hoare's principal authority was Policarpo Petrocchi's *Dizionario Universale della Lingua Italiana*, to which, in fact, his dictionary is very closely related, for it consists largely of translations of Petrocchi's definitions. In this resides one of the main defects of Hoare's work. Definitions, wholly appropriate in a unilingual dictionary, are either unnecessary or even actually misleading in a bilingual one.[2] The aim of the present dictionary is to provide, wherever possible, the English equivalents of Italian words and phrases, resorting to definitions and explanations only where this is unavoidable or advisable, as, for instance, with institutions, local customs, or national usages which differ between the two countries to such a degree that an attempted translation would be useless or virtually incomprehensible.

Elucidation by means of translation: this, then, is the primary service which the present dictionary aims to fulfil for the English-speaking user. If this aim is not best achieved by describing and defining the meaning of Italian words by paraphrasing them in English, neither is it adequately fulfilled by single-word translations. The ideal which the compilers of this dictionary have set themselves is the mapping out of the whole area of significance of Italian words by means of a series of equivalents, which not only serve to make the meaning and usage clear, but also provide, or failing that, suggest the exact or most appropriate translation for the context in which the user has seen or heard a word or phrase. In the case of 'key-words', such as *andare*, *albero*, *anima*, etc., which have widely and intricately ramifying meanings, and command a far-reaching area of usage, this is a very complex and

---

[1] Alfred Hoare was born on 4 November 1850, the fifth son of Henry Hoare, head of the historic banking family. From Eton, where he won the Tomline Prize for mathematics, he entered St John's College, Cambridge, as a scholar, graduating as 14th Wrangler in 1873. He later studied medicine and qualified as a surgeon, but never took his medical degree. Instead, he accepted partnership in the family business, Hoare's bank in Fleet Street, retiring 43 years later, in 1925. This famous firm had been carried on as a family business since 1673, handed down from father to son, and had banked for Samuel Pepys, John Evelyn, Narcissus Luttrell, Roger North, John Dryden, Harley, Halifax and Godolphin. For many years Alfred Hoare slept three nights a week at the bank, for the firm had kept up the old practice that one of the partners must sleep over the shop, opening the door in person for the morning's business. During his period as a lexicographer, it was his habit to keep half the dictionary in Fleet Street and half at his home, splitting in half from A to M and from N to Z the Italian source-books from which he was making his compilation. In his beautiful home, Charlwood House, near East Grinstead, he rose every morning at four and worked on the dictionary by a window overlooking the wooded and gently undulating Sussex landscape. It was an arduous but at the same time a leisured way of life, protected from the petty interruptions which beset most scholars under modern conditions of daily life. For fourteen years he worked at his self-imposed task, assisted only by a copyist and, in the preparation of the second edition, by his wife and his youngest daughter, Miss Sybil Hoare. It was an heroic undertaking and an important achievement, for its time, in the field of Anglo-Italian studies. (See J. M. Keynes, *The Economic Journal*, XLVIII, December 1938, pp. 753–7.)

[2] An example of an unnecessary paraphrase in Hoare is: *maglia*: 'closely knitted body-covering worn by dancers to simulate nudity.' The word required is 'tights'. An example of a misleading paraphrase is his definition of the musical term *puntato*: '(note) followed by a point, increasing its length by half.' What is required here is the English equivalent, (mus.) *dotted*, which needs no explanation.

variable task, and one in which, once again, the fundamental principle of orientation plays a decisive part.

It has been influential also in the selection of phrases. In order to make the dictionary as inclusive as possible, it was necessary to restrict the number of exemplifying phrases to reasonable proportions. The primary aim, in choosing them, has been to help the English-speaking user to understand the meaning of Italian words in terms of his own language, and to provide, or suggest, the special English rendering he seeks. Phrases are given especially where they show a meaning or shade of meaning which cannot adequately be conveyed by translation of the single word. A secondary, and often coincidental, aim has been to illustrate Italian usage, especially where Italian idiom differs significantly from English. Every care has been taken to give assistance, and to avoid ambiguity, on points of comparative syntax[1] and, although a dictionary is not a grammar, it has been thought advisable, in respect of grammatical indications, to err on the side of plenitude rather than the reverse.

In setting up the word-list, inclusiveness has been the first criterion. A scholar confronted with an unknown word requires, first of all, to know its meaning. Omission on grounds of rarity will tell him only that it is rare (which he probably knew already) and can hardly fail to exasperate him. On the other hand, a student of Italian, or a translator, requires guidance concerning the *usability* of words. In the comprehensive plan which has been devised for the *Cambridge Italian Dictionary* as a whole, it will be the primary function of the English–Italian volume to provide assistance in Italian usage; but in the present volume also care has been taken to indicate the range and limitations of usage both of the individual components of the word-list and of the exemplifying phrases. If the user will bear in mind the two basic aims of the present volume, namely inclusiveness and elucidation, he is unlikely to misinterpret the inclusion of a word or phrase as in every case an unqualified recommendation that he should use it. Further, a system of safeguards has been adopted whereby style or probable context is indicated within brackets, viz.: (colloq.), (poet.), (vulg.), (joc.), (fig.), (derog.), (slang), (iron.), etc. In addition, specialized words and phrases are sign-posted by appropriate abbreviations.[2] All obsolete words are marked by the obelus (†), but the user should note that the line of demarcation between obsolete, obsolescent, antiquated, old-fashioned, rare or literary words and those that are 'usable' is an exceedingly wavering one in Italian. Many words which do not yet qualify for an † have an antiquated, literary or pompous tone and would be inappropriate or even ludicrous if used today, especially by a foreigner, whether in written or verbal communication. It would have been possible, in order to meet the requirements, for instance, of students engaged in the academic exercise of prose composition, to put some conventional sign or warning by the side of such words, but a dictionary is not a classroom textbook and it is hoped that the temptation to indulge in undue pedagogy has been successfully resisted.[3]

Similarly, no barrier (except that of selection) has been erected against the many new words and expressions which have inundated Italian writing, advertising, and broadcasting

---

[1] See below, pp. xxiv–xxv.

[2] See 'List of Abbreviations used in the Dictionary', pp. xxix–xxxi.

[3] It may be noted that Bruno Migliorini, in his admirable *Vocabolario della Lingua Italiana*, attempts to 'rope off' certain categories of words by such indications as 'raro' or 'non comune'. But what is a rare or uncommon word? A word denoting a rare object? Or an uncommon word for a common object? And 'uncommon' or 'rare' in relation to what? Words like 'shubunkin' or 'leotard', for instance, in common use among children who keep goldfish or have lessons in ballet-dancing, are missing (presumed dead?) from the *Shorter Oxford English Dictionary*. A blunderbuss is an uncommon object now, but the word is not yet archaic, or even rare. There are many instances in Italian vocabulary of words which lexicographers, in relation to some usage, see fit to label 'raro'. But whose usage is to be the criterion? From the sub-title, which indicates that his dictionary has been compiled 'ad uso delle scuole', it is clear that Professor Migliorini had in mind the meaning of such indications in relation to students. The scope of the present dictionary is more extensive.

during the last few decades. There is a traditional resistance among Italian lexicographers to the introduction of neologisms, changes in syntax, and other manifestations of linguistic development. Fernando Palazzi, for instance, strongly disapproves of semantic change, and to many instances which he includes in his dictionary he attaches the condemnation, 'modo errato'. His avowed intention, in this respect, is to curb the development of the language. He says in his Introduction: 'Sotto la sigla in neretto (perchè bene spiccasse) M.E. (*Modi errati*) abbiamo registrato, in tutte le voci in cui il caso occorreva, i modi di dire errati o ripresi, a ciò che possano essere evitati da chi desidera scrivere o parlare italianamente; e a tal fine per ogni modo errato abbiamo dato le forme più schiette e più correttamente nostre.'[1] To other words and phrases he attaches derogatory labels such as 'brutto gallicismo' or 'modo inutile'. Such strictures are out of place in a dictionary. The function of a lexicographer, said Alessandro Manzoni,[2] is not to kill off words any more than the function of a compiler of a census is to kill off members of a population. But the century-old 'Questione della Lingua' is by no means settled in Italy and 'puristi' still exercise over Italian lexicographers an influence which they have in great part lost over usage.

The compiler of an Italian–English dictionary is not called upon to enter into such controversies; on the contrary, he should do what he can to avoid any appearance of attempting to arbitrate or to take sides. If a word or expression is currently used, an inclusive dictionary such as the present volume must record it and give its meaning. To attach to it some such indication as 'condemn. by pur.' serves little purpose. Condemned by which purists? On what grounds? At what period? There is no homogeneous category of words condemned by purists; each is an individual case and would involve special explanations beyond the terms of reference of a bilingual dictionary.

There is one aspect of the 'Questione della Lingua' to which the compiler of an Italian–English dictionary must pay heed. 'Standard Italian' is an even more elusive will o' the wisp than is 'standard English', but ever since the Renaissance recognition has been accorded to the authoritativeness of Tuscan. During the Fascist era, an official attempt was made to raise Roman pronunciation and forms of speech to a position at least equal to that of Tuscan.[3] Since the Second World War the industrial and commercial predominance of Milan, as well as the intellectual and cultural vitality of the north of Italy generally, have challenged, perhaps definitively, the age-old acceptance of Tuscan as the 'best' Italian. In the present dictionary pre-eminence, as is justly due, is given to Tuscan. Nevertheless, in accordance with the changing pattern of Italian social and economic life, a representative selection of the vocabulary, forms of speech, spelling and pronunciation current in the north of Italy and in Rome is also included. For similar reasons whenever a word or expression is limited in its usage to Tuscany, an indication to this effect is given.[4]

A language is more than a list of words; it is a mirror of the life of a community. Many words relating to institutions, customs and usages cannot comprehensibly be translated into, or even defined in terms of, another language without additional explanation. A dictionary is not an encyclopaedia, but there is some value, in a bilingual dictionary, in including information relating to national or local differences. Under **carta**, for instance, an explanation is given of the two main sorts of playing-cards in use in Italy; and under **regione** information is included concerning regional administration. Such entries, headed

---

[1] *Novissimo Dizionario della Lingua Italiana* (Milan, Ceschina, 7th edition, 1946, p. xii). There is an interesting example of his procedure to be found under the word *ambiente:* 'M.E. non è bello usarlo per indicare il luogo, le persone e le cose in mezzo a cui viviamo...*sebbene sia ormai entrato nell'uso*...', etc. (italics mine, Ed.).

[2] *Sentir Messa*, ed. Bulferetti (1923), p. 124.

[3] The recent prevalence of Roman actors, compères and comedians on television programmes has extended familiarity among the Italian public with the sound, and other characteristics, of 'romanesco', the dialect of the city of Rome, which is also a feature of many Italian neo-realist films and popular novels.

[4] For the principles governing the selection of regional and dialect words, see below under II (*l*).

by the word NOTE (in small capitals) are selected and worded from the point of view of the English-speaking user with the aim of assisting comprehension and translation, and of avoiding ambiguity. Explanatory definitions of this kind were already a feature of Hoare's dictionary and, although they there sometimes usurp the place of translations, their usefulness was such that it was decided in principle to retain and expand them.

A feature of Hoare's dictionary, on the other hand, which has not been retained is the inclusion of etymological derivations of Italian words. It is worth noting, in passing, that Hoare himself had not intended to include etymology and was only persuaded to do so, at a fairly late stage, by his friend, Professor W. W. Skeat. The suitability of giving derivations in a bilingual dictionary is at least questionable.[1] In a sense, they belong to the category of incidental information. Obvious derivations, such as *padre < patrem*, *madre < matrem*, seem scarcely worth the space they would occupy; a large number of etymologies affecting Italian are given in the *Oxford English Dictionary* and elsewhere,[2] an even greater number of words would have to be designated 'etym. dub.' or at the most, 'speculative'. On consideration, the purpose of including derivations in a bilingual dictionary was found to dwindle to one of function: would information about the origin of words help the user to understand or to translate them with greater clarity or precision; or would it constitute, for the most part, a 'luxury' feature, of value to a minority of users only? To philologists, it is of interest to know, for instance, that Italian *fegato* comes from the Latin *ficatum*, which stands for *iecur ficatum*, the liver of a fig-fattened goose, and that a similar farmyard and culinary custom is reflected in the relationship between modern Greek σικότι, liver and σύκον, a fig. But the proper place for such details is an Italian etymological dictionary. It might even be argued that to give such information under *fegato* in an Italian–English dictionary might blur the user's understanding of the word. Every care should be taken, for instance, to prevent a phrase such as 'olio di fegato di merluzzo', codliver oil, from conjuring up an image of figs.

Where, however, etymology serves to clarify meaning or to prevent ambiguity, derivations are given in the present work.[3] Etymology has been at work, also, behind the scenes, in the distinction of homonyms. It is important, for instance, that the user should be able to distinguish unequivocally, and at a glance, between *amante*, a lover, and *amante*, a halyard. Strangely enough, although Hoare usually draws on etymology to make such distinctions, he fails to do so in this instance and runs the two quite separate words together under one heading, namely: '**amante** *m.* 1. lover. 2. in bad sense, paramour. 3. (*mar.*) runner, tye, the length of chain or rope used to transmit the effort of a tackle to a yard; amante-taglia, runner and tackle; amante d'un pennone di gabbia, topsail tye; amante di panocchetto, fore topsail tye; amante di portelli, port-pendant; amante terzaruolo d'una vela, reef tackle pendant.' This is confusing to the user, who might easily be misled into imagining the nautical sense to be a metaphorical development of the meaning *lover*, whereas the origins of the two words are totally distinct, *amante*, a halyard, being derived from Greek ἱμάς, ἱμάντος, a leather strap. In Zingarelli's *Vocabolario della Lingua Italiana*,[4] the etymology is given but the two words are still grouped under a single heading. In the present dictionary, the etymology is omitted, but *amante*, a lover, is entered as a cross-reference to the headword *amare*, under which it is entered again and translated, while *amante*, a halyard, is given separately. Thus it may be seen that, although derivations are for the most part omitted, etymology has played an important part in determining the presentation of the word-list.

---

[1] They are not given, for instance, in J. E. Mansion's *French-English Dictionary*.

[2] Under **babbuccia**, for instance, Hoare gives: '(Persian *papoch*, from *pa*, foot, *poch*, to cover; this passed into Arabic, thence through Spanish *babuchas* into Italian).' The *Shorter Oxford English Dictionary* also gives, under BABOUCHE: '[a.F., ad(ult.) Pers *f.* pā, foot+pōsh, covering].'

[3] See, for instance, under †**abbaliare**[1] and †**abbaliare**[2].   [4] Bologna, Zanichelli, 1949.

The general principles governing the selection of the word-list have already been discussed. For the non-specialized vocabulary, the aim has been to make the dictionary as inclusive as possible. With specialized words, selection has of course had to operate. The intention has been to provide, on the one hand, a wide choice of such technical vocabulary as the layman is likely to meet in quasi-scientific or even general literature and, on the other hand, a reasonable quota of vocabulary that is of interest almost exclusively to specialists. Great care has been taken to ensure that not only obviously specialized words but also secondary specialized uses of general vocabulary have been dealt with by the specialists concerned. The usefulness of a dictionary depends in great measure upon the discernment of specialized uses of words; the subdivision of meaning has accordingly been scrutinized throughout with minute attention. Specialists have had individual control not only over the translation but also over the selection of vocabulary relating to their subjects. The working procedure adopted to this end ensured that, apart from the few exceptions which may have slipped through the net, all specialized words and specialized secondary meanings were referred separately to the specialists concerned, who were thus able to scrutinize them first in relation to the relevant subjects and subsequently in relation to adjacent entries. In consequence it may fairly be claimed that the interconnexion of general and specialized Italian vocabulary and the corresponding relationship between the English translations are here presented with unprecedented precision.

Since the criteria governing the selection and treatment of specialized terms are somewhat different for each category, a brief account of the methods followed by the various specialists is given below.

II. PRINCIPLES GOVERNING SPECIALIZED CATEGORIES

(a) Music

Since Italian is the universal language of musicians, many Italian musical terms in common use are best rendered by the same word in English. *Adagio* means 'adagio', and any standard English dictionary will provide a definition or explanation of this term. But, although *piano* means 'piano', a further explanation must be given in this case, because the general meaning of the Italian word may be either 'soft' or 'slow', whereas in music it always means 'soft' and never 'slow'. If, therefore, the user finds what appears to be inconsistency in the inclusion or omission of explanations, it may be that some such consideration has influenced the decision of the contributor or that juxtaposition with some general or other specialized meaning has necessitated a deviation from the rule.

One of the drawbacks of a universal language is that its usage may become corrupted by those who do not possess it as a mother-tongue. An example of musicians' 'lingua franca' is the well-known term *glissando*, which is not a genuine Italian word: it has been formed by non-Italians from an imaginary verb *glissare* on the analogy of the French *glisser*. An Italian composer usually prefers to write *strisciando* or *portamento*, but the usage has become so current as to lead even Italian composers, such as Busoni, to write *glissando*, and even such barbarous formations as *glissicando* and *glissicato* have been observed. To take another instance, it probably comes as a surprise to most English people to learn that *coloratura* has no musical application in Italian and that, even when referring to painting, Italian authors prefer the forms *colorazione* or *coloritura*. As it happens, the expression *bel canto* conveys to an Italian, in its connotation, all that an Englishman means by 'coloratura' and, to an Italian, *canto* without 'coloratura' is not singing at all.

Not all the musical terms included in the word-list of the present work occur in standard

Italian dictionaries. The word *cimbasso*, for instance, meaning 'ophicleide', occurs in the score of Verdi's *Un Ballo in Maschera* (1859), but is not elsewhere recorded. Room has been found also for a fairly representative number of expressions relating to recent musical inventions, such as *disco microsolco*, 'long-playing record', and to modern trends in composition, such as *serie dodecafonica*, 'twelve-note series', or 'tone-row', and *musica concreta*, 'concrete music', or, to use the commoner French expression, 'musique concrète'.

(*b*) *The fine arts*

What has been said concerning musical terms applies in general also to terms relating to the fine arts and to architecture. Many of these have been adopted into the English language, as for example, *chiaroscuro*, but the international use of such terms among artists is less well established than is the case in music. This means that the Italian word is probably used more extensively in Italian than in English, with the result that some additional phrase or explanatory note is usually required to indicate the extent of difference in the application of the corresponding terms. It is the habit also of Italian art critics to use terms rather loosely in describing aspects of painting and it has not been judged advisable to pinpoint such words by precise equivalents. Terms relating to architecture are more abundant in Italian than in English; consequently they cannot all be rendered by exact translations. Many of them in fact overlap with building terms and will be found rendered after the designation '(bldg.)'.

(*c*) *Religion*

In selecting and translating terms relating to religion, one important aim has been to make clear to the ordinary reader the normal activities of an Italian parish and the usual names of persons and things connected with the Church of Rome in Italy and abroad. Ignorance of these matters is widespread and is scarcely diminished by existing dictionaries. In the published translation of a novel by Fogazzaro, for example, the expression *direttore di coscienza*, 'spiritual director', has been rendered by 'conscientious business man'; and there are examples as bad even in works of learning. Hence it seemed inappropriate to introduce too many subtleties in this section. For instance, readers of Fucini's short stories need to know that a *priore* is not necessarily the prior of a religious house and is rather more likely to be a secular priest in charge of a parish. It is irrelevant to know whether this title is slightly less or slightly more honorific than *piovano* or *preposto*. In ordinary circumstances any of these three words may properly be rendered as 'parish priest'; exceptionally, the Italian word might be kept in italics. Again, those who are not themselves Roman Catholics may easily miss the flavour of some common expression, such as 'i fedeli'. This sometimes is equivalent to 'the faithful', but more often it means 'parishioners' or 'congregation'; and 'preti e fedeli' means 'clergy and laity' or 'priests and people'. It has been a principle in this dictionary to give assistance on such points, while excluding much of a more technical nature that would be more properly included in a specialized work of reference.

The names of church vestments which are used all over the world offer no difficulty, since they have fixed and simple English equivalents. Further explanation is usually not required, or (with other ecclesiastical information) may conveniently be sought in the *Oxford Dictionary of the Christian Church*. Italian dictionaries themselves are sometimes at fault in their definitions here. For instance, under *piviale*, Petrocchi gives: 'paramento sacerdotale fatto a mantello usato nel vespro e altre funzioni.' This misled Hoare, who translated and adapted this definition as follows: '*piviale*: pluvial, or cope, a sacerdotal robe worn at vespers and other functions, but not as a rule at mass.' This is inaccurate, because the cope, unlike the chasuble, is not reserved for the use of priests and may be worn by cantors who are not priests. In Roman Catholic usage it is never worn by the celebrant at mass, but may be worn there by other priests, though in Anglican usage it is sometimes worn by the celebrant. There are other points which a liturgist might bring out, but such a scale of detail is out of place in a bilingual dictionary. The entry under *piviale* in the present work reads, therefore, as follows: '(liturg.) cope, pluvial.' Under the derivative *pivialista*, an explanation has been added: '(liturg.) person wearing a cope (not necessarily a priest).' The question of clerical dress, as distinct from vestments, is more complicated. In this connexion, preference has been given to ordinary modern usage, words relating to local fashions in canons' tippets or past modes in shoe-buckles being for the most part omitted.

The divisions 'religious', 'ecclesiastical' and 'liturgical', which sometimes may overlap, are in principle distinguished thus: 'liturgical' is used with direct reference to services in church; but a term like 'rosary', given as one of the translations of *corona*, is preceded by the indication (rel.), i.e. 'religious', because its use is not confined to church; the term 'ecclesiastical' is used of the visible organization of the Church.

In church affairs, as in others, Italian usage shows a good deal of regional variation. There are a few differences in custom and many differences in names. A *curato* is normally a parish priest, especially in the country; but occasionally, as for instance in Liguria, he may actually be a curate attached to a large town church. A cassock is usually a *sottana*, but in Tuscany and elsewhere it is sometimes a *tonaca*. Every effort has been made to ensure that at least the most important of these variants have been recorded in the dictionary.

In connexion with the use in Italian authors of terms relating to church life and activities, it should be borne in mind that in Italy even Catholics are often indifferent to the niceties of church etiquette. *Frati*, for instance, a term which belongs to friars, is often used to refer to monks, for which the proper Italian word is *monaci*. Italian writers who are out of touch with the Church may carry confusion further. Not much liturgical precision is to be expected, for instance, from a novelist who makes Ascension Day fall on a Sunday.

In church history and archaeology, though a number of unimportant words have been omitted, room has been found for certain words which may be unfamiliar in English, but have some special Italian bearing. For instance, *acclamazione*, 'acclamation', as a particular kind of early Christian inscription, would be hard to trace in English books of reference but it might face the traveller in Rome on his first visit to the Catacombs.

Purely theological terms are usually best translated by one technical word, without further explanation. For example, in Hoare's dictionary, the three theological words, *dulia*, *iperdulia* and *latria* are translated as follows: '*dulia*: worship of saints and angels. *iperdulia*: idolatry of saints. *latria*: divine service.' The correct definitions of these terms are: '*dulia*: veneration paid to saints and angels in general. *iperdulia*: veneration paid to the Blessed Virgin Mary only. *latria*: veneration (worship) paid to God alone.' However interesting such definitions may be, they belong to an encyclopaedia or specialized work of reference, or, of course, to a unilingual dictionary, rather than to a bilingual work such as the present. The three words in question are therefore given as follows: '**duli·a** *f.* (theol.) dulia. **iperduli·a** *f.* (theol.) hyperdulia. **latri·a** *f.* (theol.) latria.' Sometimes however, it has been thought well to include a short explanatory note. For instance, the word *irregolarità*, in its ecclesiastical sense, is correctly translated 'irregularity', but without further warning the English word might well be taken by the non-specialist to signify a quite gentle censure. Accordingly, this meaning of *irregolarità* is given as follows: (eccl.) irregularity (bar to receiving or exercising holy orders).

With regard to religious terms other than Roman Catholic (those concerning the Orthodox or Protestant or non-Christian religions), every effort has been made to avoid renderings which would not be accepted by adherents of the religions concerned. If, as not seldom happens, instances have been found of mistaken usage by Italian writers who are themselves ill-informed on the subject, no note has been taken of them for the purposes of this dictionary.

(d) Philosophy

The translation of philosophic terms for the purposes of a dictionary does not offer many difficulties. The word *sostanza*, it is true, means a great variety of things to the philosophers of different schools, but the lexicographer's duty ceases when he has recorded 'substance' as the English equivalent, preceded, however, by the requisite indication that the word is used in a technical sense.

(e) Greek and Roman antiquity

In the selection of words belonging to Greek and Roman literature, history and antiquities, it was necessary to consider two contrasting factors. One was the real continuity linking Roman and Italian culture, which means that many words and ideas which are distant from the Englishman are near home for the Italian, or at least easily attachable to what is near home. The names of Aeneas, Cato, and Cicero have for a classically educated Italian not only the associations which they have for a similarly educated Englishman; they have also another kind of association, comparable to what the Englishman feels for the names of King Arthur, King Alfred, or the Venerable Bede. Many references, therefore, to classical antiquity which in England would be specialized or pedantic may reach a much wider public in Italy—may occur not only in popular history books but in fiction or films; hence an Italian dictionary ought to include more of such terms than its English equivalent. Moreover, certain Italian poets who were particularly at home in Greek and Latin (for example, Foscolo, Leopardi, Carducci, Pascoli) have no doubt sometimes given an Italian word a slight Greek or Latin turn which has not been recognized by dictionaries. On the other hand, side by side with the real Italian familiarity with certain classical words and notions, there is in some quarters an affected familiarity which does not bear close investigation. The prestige of Greek and Latin has often induced those who know little of either language to make a display of classical names and references which are in fact misleading. The Greek words which Zingarelli includes, for instance, are sometimes distorted by elementary errors, yet he goes out of his way to import a number of professedly classical words connected with minor antiquities—names of obscure local magistrates, strange parts of buildings, ships with an improbable number of banks of oars—which even if properly presented would be worth considering only in a quite specialized dictionary.

(f) Science, Technology, Industry

The first principle to be decided in connexion with vocabulary of these categories was the purpose it should serve in a comprehensive dictionary. Scientific and technical jargon has become so much a part of the normal currency of daily life among ordinary people that the need to include a representative proportion of it was apparent from the beginning. The schoolboy now talks of heterodynes and space capsules, his mother fears the effect of fall-out and radio-active strontium on her children, while her husband asks for a special viscosity index in his engine oil to put off the date of a re-bore. This last sentence contains no less than seven expressions which cannot be classified as other than scientific or technical, and no comprehensive dictionary which aims to serve the modern user can exclude them. Accordingly, it was decided to include all the scientific and technological words which the well educated general reader is likely to meet or use.

This decision casts the net much wider than might at first appear. What one person regards as 'highly technical jargon' is the everyday language of another. The man-in-the-street may jib at the noun 'wobbulation', derived from 'wobble', but to the electronics engineer it is no stranger than 'wow', 'tweeter' or 'woofer'. Or again—and this is perhaps the most difficult problem of all—ordinary, 'innocent-looking' words are frequently regarded in certain technical or scientific circles as denoting very clearly defined concepts. 'Fatigue' is a commonplace word enough, but to an engineer it has a specific meaning. 'To substitute' is an ordinary verb, but it has a special meaning in the eyes of the organic chemist. It is these technical uses of ordinary words which lexicographers find most elusive. And even when they have been duly caught in the net, it may often happen that a specialized entry in the dictionary will appear superfluous, in that the same use is made in both languages of the corresponding words. Nevertheless, inclusion of the technical meaning is still important, since the reader requires confirmation that such a similarity of usage does in fact occur.

In compiling the technical part of the present work, it was necessary to bear in mind the relative paucity of specialized Anglo-Italian dictionaries (as compared with those available in other languages, such as German, Russian and Japanese). Perhaps the best technical dictionaries available are the multi-lingual compilations, covering some half-dozen languages, but these are cumbersome to use and often too highly specialized to meet the average reader's requirements. The few bilingual English and Italian technical dictionaries available are intended mainly for Italian use, that is, they are designed to help Italian readers to understand American and English texts. Such dictionaries are mostly marred by the high proportion of bizarre and picturesque phrases, culled especially from American usage. There is at least one Italian–English engineering dictionary, for instance, which translates 'applicare la piena potenza' ('to turn on full power') by 'to give it the woiks'.

The shortage of reliable Anglo-Italian technical works of reference means that the user of a comprehensive Italian–English dictionary will be all the more dependent upon it for scientific and technological vocabulary. Consequently, the policy in respect of these categories has been to err on the side of inclusion rather than exclusion; even when it has not proved possible to do full justice to a term, it has been thought better to give the reader some guidance as to its probable meaning in a scientific or technological context, rather than exclude it altogether.

The inclusion of all the terms covered by the general principles enunciated above would have resulted in an unwieldy dictionary, greatly overweighted with technical words. Some system of pruning was called for. The following types of vocabulary have, for instance, been excluded:

(i) Highly specialized terms likely to be met only by a specialist within his own advanced field.

(ii) Terms which though enjoying a certain limited vogue at the time of compiling the dictionary had not yet been definitely accepted into the language.

(iii) Terms made up of obvious roots, especially instances in which parallel composite words are permissible in both Italian and English.

The following types of vocabulary have, on the other hand, been considered eligible for inclusion:

(i) Terms likely to be met in secondary or grammar-school education. Many people, for instance, who never become chemists in later life study chemistry for four or more years at school; the range of vocabulary relating to such subjects extends at least to the needs of such persons considered as general readers.

(ii) Terms which could easily be met in newspaper and (non-technical) magazine articles, wireless or television talks, etc.

(iii) Terms which serve as an indication of a mode of vocabulary construction. This is the counterpart of the third negative type mentioned above. There are many tens of thousands of scientific terms which are built up from smaller units. Every attempt has been made to ensure that all the main units, or 'building blocks', are included, and in positions where the user will find them or may be expected to look for them. Trouble has been taken to include enough examples of such composite words to enable the user to cope with other words he may meet which have been built up from the same elements.

Neologisms always constitute a problem for the lexicographer, but the problem is even more acute in regard to scientific and technical terms, because the development of science and technology is proceeding at so great a pace that language is often left lagging behind. As far as Italian is concerned, technical neologisms are increasing at a faster rate than in any other Romance language. French, for instance, is often content to borrow foreign terms where Italian, in a lively spirit of experimentation, invents new ones or makes creative use of new processes of word-building.

Such prolific growth, coupled with the state of flux characterizing the vocabulary of techniques which are still evolving, makes it especially difficult to fix the word-list, particularly in view of the fairly long interval which must perforce elapse between the preparation of the early stages of a large-scale dictionary and its final appearance in print. During the intervening years, many new words will have jostled with one another for a place in the language, some to emerge victorious, others to disappear for ever. By the very nature of the vocabulary, no word-list of technical terms in current use can be definitive.

The greater part of the vocabulary of these categories is derived from living sources, including standard text-books on all the relevant subjects. The English renderings are, in many instances, the fruit of some twenty years' comparative study of Italian and English texts dealing with various branches of industry. Whenever doubt arose, industrial firms and organizations were consulted, with the result that a high proportion of the technical terms and renderings have a live, on-the-spot authenticity.

(g) Zoology (including Entomology and Ichthyology)

The correct Latin scientific name is given wherever possible for all animal species, except for domestic animals and others where to do so is unnecessary and would be pedantic. If there is a genuine English vernacular name, this is given as the first translation, but where the only English name is an artificial one, not in ordinary use, it is usually omitted. Animals not occurring in Great Britain and having no genuine English name, but being related to some British species, are indicated by some such phrase as 'a kind of Sea Bream', or 'similar to a Grass Snake'. Such translations are adequate for many purposes, but warning is here given that they are not exact; if an exact identification is needed, the user will find it provided by the Latin name.

Sometimes dozens of Italian names can be found for a single species. This is especially true of edible fish[1] which, indeed, often have a large number of names in English as well. Here, names have been selected for inclusion if they are to be found in ordinary dictionaries or in other unspecialized source books, and also if they are dialect forms occurring in several

[1] Some idea of the magnitude of this problem may be gained from the following list of names for the Anchovy, *Engraulis encrasicholus*, given by Palombi and Santarelli, *Animali Commestibili dei mari d'Italia*: Acciuga, Aggiuva, Alece, Aliccia, Alice, Aliciastra, Aliciastruni, Amarou, Amplona, Amplouva, Amplova, Anchiò, Anciò, Ancioa, Ancioja, Anciona, Anciora, Anciova, Anciovillo, Anciva, Angiouvitta, Argentini, Azzuva, Bianchetti, Bianco mangiare, Gianchetti, Lilla, Magnana, Mascolini, Masculina, Masculinella, Mezz'alici, Nini, Nudini, Paranzoli, Sardela, Sardon, Sardone, Sfigghiata, Speronara.

regional dialects, especially if they are etymologically distinct from the standard forms, since dialect names of edible fish may well be used or understood by speakers of standard Italian in different parts of the country. Occasionally some of the different names for a single species may not be true synonyms but refer to different life stages, sexes, or colour varieties (for example, the Common Eel): for these, the exact English equivalents or, failing that, definitions, are given.

In Italian zoological writing, animal genera and species which have no genuine vernacular names often appear as italianized versions of the Latin scientific names. These have generally been omitted from the dictionary unless they are likely to be found in less specialized contexts (for example, agricultural pests), since they are usually easily recognized by anyone familiar with the Latin names and unlikely to be met by anyone else.

(h) Ornithology

In Italian, as in all languages, there are many bird-names which are applicable to more than one species or which are confined to certain dialect areas. Such names, when included in the dictionary, are translated into English but no attempt is made to identify them precisely, Latin scientific names being provided only for names which appear in standard modern ornithological works.

(i) Botany

What has been said above concerning zoological names applies also in the main to botany. In the selection of entries, for plants native to Italy reliance has been placed on Fiori and Paoletti's 'Dizionarietto dei nomi volgari' in their *Iconographica*. For all these, valid botanical names (i.e. Latin scientific names) are given and, wherever possible, English ones. For plants native to Britain, the botanical and English names in Clapham, Tutin and Warburg's *Flora of the British Isles* have been adopted. It was too late to make alterations in these names when Dandy's *List of British Vascular Plants* appeared in 1958 and Clapham, Tutin and Warburg's *Excursion Flora of the British Isles* in 1959. For cultivated and economic plants and those foreign to Italy and Britain, Bailey's *Manual*, Bedivian's *Dictionary* and Willis's *Flowering Plants and Ferns* have been consulted.

(j) Military and nautical terms

The mercenaries of medieval and Renaissance times, fortunately for the compilers of dictionaries, carried the names of their weapons and implements, as well as the jargon of their calling, all over central Europe. Consequently, the same words are used in most Latin countries with very rare changes in signification. The dialects of the provinces of Italy, likewise, produced comparatively few local variants of military terms and it has consequently proved possible to include a proportionately greater number of them than is strictly justified by the subject. It is hoped that they will be useful to the general reader, since, even when military terms become outmoded, they continue to live on in literary usage.

In attempting to give accurate but simple translations of nautical terms in general use, little difficulty arises. The vocabulary of seamen constituted a specialized lingua franca throughout the Mediterranean for many centuries, though a great number of words were corrupted and modified with use and the passage of time. Corsica, Sardinia and, to a lesser extent, Sicily formed meeting-places for navigators from western Europe, where they exchanged ideas and vocabulary. It must be remembered, however, that fishermen seldom moved beyond their own fishing grounds and, since the distance by sea separating Venice and Greece was such as to preclude any but the most occasional of contacts, the growth of dialect words and synonyms was enormous. Consequently, local variants, especially of fishing terms, have for the most part been omitted, since it would require a specialized dictionary to contain even a representative selection of them.

Some degree of complication is introduced by the mass of foreign nautical terms which the language has assimilated. Many of these were denounced under Mussolini's dictatorship as 'brutti gallicismi' and were officially replaced by 'good' Italian words. It thus occurred that archaic terms were resurrected and adapted to new meanings. Some of these have gained acceptance but many others have lapsed once more into oblivion.

(k) Law

The legal section is intended primarily for members of the English legal and associated professions, to help them to grasp and deal with the Italian side of matters involving Italian law or procedure within the field of the everyday, general law comprised in the four principal Italian Codes under the Constitution of 1947, namely, the Codice Civile of 1942 with its companion Codice di Procedura Civile of 1940, and the Codice Penale of 1930 with its companion Codice di Procedura Penale of 1930.

In the main, the general principles of the dictionary apply also to the legal section. When a departure is made, as in giving a series of English equivalents of an Italian legal term, the series is given in alphabetical order, not in any sort of order of importance. In such cases, the professional man, with his knowledge of English and of English law, will have no difficulty in choosing the appropriate one from any alphabetical series of English equivalents. Only exceptionally, as in the case, for example, of 'sentenza', where mistranslation ('sentence' instead of 'judgement') seems to have become habitual is a particular equivalent indicated as preferable.

In giving a series of English renderings, tautology has been avoided as far as possible, and so have paraphrases where the English word is exactly equivalent to the Italian, like 'quash' and 'cassare'.

Obscure English words whose meanings are to be found in the *Shorter Oxford English Dictionary* are not expounded.

Wherever possible, plain English, preferably Anglo-Saxon, is used rather than legal jargon, in homage to the practice of the English courts and legal profession, if not of the legislator.

While the context usually gives the user the key to the sense in which a given word is used in Italian legal writings, the same word is often used in a different sense, or has different shades of meaning, in the different fields of law. References have therefore been included in many entries, showing in which of the four Codes the particular usage occurs. All the references are positive; and it is not to be understood that the usage does not occur elsewhere.

The differences between the institutions, legal systems and jurisprudence of the two countries sometimes make it impossible to give a satisfactory simple translation. Then resort has to be had to definitions or explanatory notes in the attempt to convey the meaning accurately.

In the preparation of the legal section, it was especially necessary to consult living practitioners as well as works of reference. Deep indebtedness is here expressed to Avvocato Mario Fiore, a legal consultant to the British Embassy in Rome, Avvocato Ubaldo Benso, O.B.E., legal adviser to the British Consulate General, Genoa, the late Count Alessandro Savio, Judge of the Tribunal of San Remo, Avvocato Gianni Manca, of the Studio Graziadei, Rome, Avvocato Baron Enrico Sartorio of Turin, and to Avvocato Mario Matteucci, Counsellor of State, Secretary General of the International Institute for the Unification of

Private Law. Appreciation and gratitude must also be expressed to those who dealt with the legal, financial and commercial vocabulary in the early stages of the dictionary, namely Mr M. J. Prichard, Dr Uberto Limentani and Mr Franz Farrugia.[1]

(l) Obsolete and dialect words

Words of this category, potentially one of the largest, have been selected in accordance with literary rather than philological considerations. The main purpose of including archaisms has been to provide a select glossary of the principal Italian authors from the thirteenth century onwards. Similarly, the intention with regard to regional and dialect words[2] has been to meet the requirements of readers of regional writing of all periods rather than to exemplify local deviations from standard Italian or to provide a word-list of a linguistic atlas. A comparable bias is to be detected in the choice of obsolete terms relating to specialized categories such as music, the fine arts, zoology, botany, nautical and military terms and various technologies and crafts: the aim here has likewise been to meet the requirements of the general reader of literary, historical or quasi-technical writing rather than to provide a systematic list of specialized terminology of different centuries.

In translating obsolete and dialect words no attempt has been made, except in rare instances, to use period or regional English. The presence of the obelus or of some indication of regional limitation should be interpreted by the user as signifying 'in an archaic (or regional) text the word has the following meaning, or meanings'. It is not feasible, in translating words of this kind, to give a wide range of renderings, as for current general vocabulary, or to provide precise equivalents, as for current technical terms. Nevertheless, within these limitations, which are, in any event, implied by the nature and purpose of the dictionary, care has been taken to elucidate the meaning and to indicate divergence from normal Italian.

In regard to the pronunciation of obsolete words, indication is given only of main stress.[3] It would, of course, be possible, using etymological evidence and applying the rules of phonology, to show what the pronunciation of stressed e and o, and of s and z must have been at different periods. Since, however, the sounds given to these vowels and consonants are variable in modern Italian, there is a particular artificiality, above all in a bilingual dictionary, in attempting to 'standardize' the pronunciation of the past.

III. ARRANGEMENT

(a) Order

The word-list is presented in accordance with two main principles: (1) alphabetical sequence, and (2) subdivision into headwords and derivatives. For example, the verb *andare* is listed as a headword, being split into stem and termination by a tilde (~), and the derivatives *andamento, andante, andata*, etc. (indicated by means of their terminations, viz.

---

[1] The same principles have been followed in the compilation of the Commercial, Financial and Administrative sections, which all overlap the legal section.

[2] It may be helpful to make clear, for the benefit of the English user, the distinction between regional Italian and dialect. Nearly all Italians speak with the accent and use certain distinctive vocabulary of the region in which they were born or in which they have lived most of their lives. No social stigma attaches to this, as it sometimes does in England. Dialect, *dialetto*, on the other hand, is the term for the various regional *languages*. These are quite separate from Italian, to which they bear a relationship comparable to that of Lowland Scots to English. In certain regions, as, for instance, in Piedmont and in the Veneto, the aristocracy speak dialect amongst themselves. Among the middle classes, intellectuals also speak it and foster the literary use of it. The lower classes always speak dialect and, unless their work brings them into contact with Italian, they soon forget what they have learnt of it at school. In the lower middle classes a certain snobbery prevails and parents are careful to see that children speak only 'lingua' (i.e. Italian) and do not pick up dialect from servants. In moments of crisis or strong emotion, all Italians, even those who usually speak 'lingua', are likely to break out into 'dialetto' if they are among fellow-members of the same region.

[3] This is the practice also of the *Oxford English Dictionary*.

-amento, -ante, -ata) are entered, in alphabetical order in relation to each other, after the infinitive.[1] By this method the particular structure of the Italian language is appropriately displayed, derivatives are presented within the context of the parent-words, and the user is able to peruse each combined entry as an articulated and interrelated whole. For further convenience, derivatives are also entered separately, in alphabetical order in the word-list, cross-references being given to the headwords under which they are treated in full.

The order of the English renderings and phrases follows a recognizable but fairly flexible pattern. The primary and most general of the meanings in current use are given first, the less usual or less characteristic coming afterwards; figurative extensions of the general meanings precede specialized uses; obsolete meanings are given last and are marked by an obelus. The grouping of the phrases is, for the most part, associative, being finally determined by considerations of expediency and the convenience of the user. In the case of words commanding a wide area of usage and significance, such as **acqua**, **andare**, **carta**, **casa**, **dare**, etc., the various meanings, with their relevant phrases, have been subdivided and grouped under headings. In the organization of these major entries, the orientation of the dictionary has again been a determining influence. Distinctions and associations which are convenient or necessary for the English user may seem gratuitous or artificial from the Italian point of view, and *vice versa*.

(b) Derivatives

The whole question of Italian derivatives, especially of verbal substantives and participial adjectives, is one on which extensive and systematic research is required. Not even the *Dizionario Etimologico Italiano*, edited by Battisti and Alessio,[2] which is the fullest word-list in Italian to date, can be relied upon in this respect. Although it contains many derivatives which are not included by lexicographers such as Zingarelli, Palazzi, Migliorini or even Tommaseo, it also omits many which they do include or which are known to exist. Nor can it be said that such omissions are systematic or in any way significant. For instance, under *abbaccare*, *abbaccamento* is given but not *abbaccone*; under *abbacchiare*, *abbacchiato* and *abbacchiatura* are given, but not *abbacchiata* or *abbacchiamento*; from the long list of derivatives given under *abbacinare*, *abbacinante* (the most usual of all) is missing, although the less frequent *abbarbagliante* is given under *abbarbagliare*; *abbaìo* is not given under *abbaiare*, though verbal substantives in *-ìo* are included under other headwords, such as, for instance, *abbarbagliare* and *abbaruffare*. In view of the lack of co-ordination in Italian lexicography, the treatment of derivatives in the present work has had inevitably to rely in part on negative evidence. As far as general vocabulary is concerned, the omission of a verbal substantive or of a participial adjective is intended to signify that it is not recorded by Italian lexicographers nor known to be in current use. In specialized vocabulary selection has operated, with the result that omission of a specialized derivative does not imply its non-existence. The translation of a derivative implies that it is a 'live' word, in common or fairly common use; or else that its meaning, use, or most appropriate English equivalent cannot be deduced from adjacent entries. Derivatives of which the use is possible but infrequent are for the most part left untranslated, being entered in alphabetical order under the relevant headwords and enclosed in brackets.

(c) Suffixes

For economy of space, derivatives formed from nouns or adjectives by the addition of diminutive, augmentative, pejorative and other suffixes have been omitted, except for

---

[1] Adverbs are placed immediately after the adjectives from which they are derived. This sometimes involves breaking the alphabetical sequence in which derivatives are listed.

[2] Florence, Barbèra, 1950–7.

words in which some special use or anomaly is involved. For the convenience of the user, the principal groups of suffixes are given below, as follows:

Diminutive

Suffixes in this group, which correspond to English *-kin*, *-let*, convey a meaning of small-ness, sometimes combined with a suggestion of affection, approval, or condescension: -ello, -ellino; -etto, -ettino; -icello; -icino; -ino; -(u)olo.

Augmentative

Suffixes in this group, which are less numerous than the above, convey a meaning of bigness, sometimes combined with a suggestion of admiration, or, on the contrary, of distaste: -one; -otto (sometimes also diminutive; perhaps equivalent in effect to English *adv.* 'rather', 'somewhat', 'pretty').

It sometimes happens that a combination of a diminutive and an augmentative suffix is added to a noun, as for instance with *panettone, violoncello*, which have, of course, become permanent formations. It is also possible for a diminutive suffix to be added to an adjective denoting size, thereby bringing about an apparent contradiction, for example *grandicello*. This formation would be quite normal in a sentence such as: è già grandicello, he is already quite a big boy.

Pejorative

Suffixes in this group convey dislike or disapproval, sometimes combined with a sense of grudging admiration or even of affection: -accio; -uccio; -ucciolo, -ucciolino.

Italian grammarians and lexicographers distinguish a fourth group of suffixes which they term 'vezzeggiativo' ('affectionate', 'playful'). Among these may be listed *-ettino, -icino, -uccio, -ucciolino*, etc. The question of size is a psychological factor of some importance in relation to the emotions, and suffixes of this group are usually diminutives.

(d) Variants

Variants separated in the word-list by alphabetical sequence are entered individually, cross-references being given to the more authoritative or more usual form, for example *diman-dare*, see *domandare*; *abbate* see *abate*. For variants whose area of usage differs, translations and examples are given under each, together with a reciprocal cross-reference for purposes of comparison, as, for instance, under **arma**[1] and **arme**.

(e) Grammatical indications

(i) *Verbs*

All verbs are entered in the active infinitive form (that is, with the termination *-are*, *-ere*, *-ire* or *-urre*). The reflexive or passive form (that is, with the termination *-arsi*, *-ersi*, *-irsi* or *-ursi*) is not entered as a headword but is to be deduced, where relevant, from the active. All verbs are indicated as transitive (*tr.*), intransitive (*intr.*), reflexive (*rfl.*) or reciprocally reflexive (*recip. rfl.*). The auxiliaries of all intransitive verbs in current use are indicated, for example, **andare** *intr.* (*aux.* essere). Reflexive constructions in which the pronoun 'si' is in the dative are distinguished from those in which it is in the accusative, for example, **lav-are** *rfl.* (*acc.* of *prn.* 'si') -arsi, to wash oneself; to be washed; (dat. of *prn.* 'si') -arsi le mani, to wash one's hands. All verbs in current use are followed by a cipher in square brackets, for example, **andare** [A 8], referring to the comprehensive Verb Scheme by means of which the user will be able to supply the appropriate conjugation.[1]

[1] See pp. 885–97

(ii) *Nouns*

The gender of nouns, *m.* or *f.*, is shown at the beginning of the entry. All nouns ending in *-co* or *-go* form their plural in *-ci* or *-gi* unless otherwise indicated. (This also applies to the masculine plural of adjectives ending in *-co* or *-go*, the feminine plural being invariably *-che* or *-ghe*.) All nouns ending in *-à, -i, -ù* are indeclinable, that is, invariable, in the plural. Other nouns which are irregular or anomalous in the use or formation of the plural are shown with the appropriate indications.

Geographical and other proper nouns are included in the word-list.

(iii) *Prepositions*

The contractions of prepositions with the definite and indefinite article are shown at the beginning of each entry. Since the syntax governing prepositions cannot adequately be conveyed without examples, special use has been made of phrases illustrating the differences between Italian and English in this respect. The prepositions used in construction with intransitive verbs followed by an infinitive are shown in the individual entries and are also listed separately at the end of the Verb Scheme. Help is also given with the use of prepositions after transitive verbs and after adjectives wherever doubt is likely to arise or Italian usage differs markedly from English, for example *togliere a*, to take away from, *indipendente da*, independent of.

(f) *Pronunciation*

Indications as to the pronunciation of Italian words are here limited to the tonic accent (that is, main stress), the open or close pronunciation of stressed *e* and *o*, the voiced or voiceless (that is, 'dolce' or 'aspro') pronunciation of *s* and *z*, and as to whether or not the *g* is voiced in the group *gli*.

In obsolete words, that is, those marked with a dagger or obelus (†), the tonic accent only is shown. In all other cases, the following rules apply:

(i) Unless otherwise indicated, the tonic accent falls on the penultimate syllable, for example **mano, cappello**.

(ii) Words ending in a vowel with a written accent[1] bear the tonic accent on that vowel, for example, **città, virtù**.

(iii) Words in which the tonic accent falls on any but the ultimate or penultimate syllable, or concerning which doubt might arise, are marked by a mid-point, printed after the stressed vowel or syllable, for example **ta·vola, com·pito**. If the stressed vowel is a close *e* or *o*, the indication that this is so (that is, a dot beneath the vowel) also shows that the vowel bears the main stress, for example **sęmplice**. (Since unstressed *e* and *o* are always close, only stressed *e* and *o* need to be distinguished in respect of close or open pronunciation. See also below under iv.)

(iv) If a stressed *e* or *o* has the close pronunciation, it is marked with a sub-dot, for example **capęllo, cǫme**. A stressed *e* or *o* not marked with a sub-dot has the open pronunciation, for example **cappello, oro, o·spite, me·dico**. (See also above under iii.)

(v) An *s* or *z* pronounced with the so-called soft (that is, voiced) sound is marked with a sub-dot, for example **rǫsa, azzurro**. An *s* or *z* which has no such indication is pronounced with the so-called harsh (that is, voiceless) sound, for example **casa, zio**.

(vi) A *g* followed by *li* which is pronounced as in English *glee*, rather than as in the Italian definite article *gli*, is marked with a sub-dot, for example, **gli·cine, glifo**.

---

[1] See also 'Diacritic Marks used in the Dictionary', p. xxviii.

(vii) Foreign words imported into Italian from other languages either become Italianized or retain (a semblance of) their original pronunciation. In the latter case, an indication to that effect is given, for example **chic** (pron. as Fr.).

(g) *Typography*

All headwords and terminations of derivations are printed in bold type in their place of entry. A tilde (~) splits the headword either into stem and termination or into whatever divisions are convenient for the indication of stress or from the point of view of orthography. The Italian convention of syllabic division has not been followed, but care has been taken to avoid splitting such orthographical entities as *ch* and *gh*.[1]

The em-rule or dash (—) stands in every instance for the entire headword; derivatives are represented in phrases by the form in which they are printed in bold type.

The true hyphen (-) is used in the case of the relatively few Italian words in which it occurs.

Long entries are divided for the user's convenience into sections which are numbered and, where appropriate, introduced by headings printed in small capitals. Italic type is used only for grammatical and other indications which are abbreviated and for Latin scientific names of plants and animals. Both Italian and English phrases are printed in roman type, a departure from a long-standing convention which, in view of the wide columns, will, it is hoped, induce 'a reading glance', capable of taking in the inter-relationship of several renderings, rather than the swift spot-reference more appropriate to the consultation of a concise dictionary. Superior figures ([1], [2], [3], etc.) are used to distinguish homonyms or near homonyms one from another.

IV. FUTURE EDITIONS

The fact that this is a dictionary of two living languages means that, though completed, it cannot be complete. Italian in particular has recently undergone and is still undergoing rapid development, but the problem is not merely one of keeping pace with neologisms. A living language grows by changes in meaning and usage, as well as by additions to its vocabulary, and no dictionary, particularly no bilingual dictionary, can do more than present a static record of part of an ever-moving and elusive whole. Future editions of this dictionary will no doubt present a different cross-section, to meet different situations and requirements. There is, for instance, much progress still to be made in the comparative study of Italian and English. Translation depends for its accuracy not only on a knowledge of the meaning of words but also on an understanding of their subtleties in various contexts and associations. Wherever lexicography lends assistance on such points it ceases to be a science and becomes an art. There can be no absolute precision in questions of style. The translation of a zoological term such as *coniglio*, for instance, is 'rabbit, *Oryctolagus cuniculus*', and that is the end of the matter. A word like *andare*, on the other hand, can be translated in a great many different ways, according to the style, tone or purpose of the context.

In the arrangement of meanings and in the selection and translation of phrases, the lexicographer is faced with innumerable possibilities, and probably no two persons would make exactly the same decisions. The English renderings of words and phrases in this dictionary have all been carefully considered and many times revised, but it is not imagined that they could not be improved still further. Indeed, it is hoped that, once in use, the dictionary will serve to sharpen awareness of the distinctions between Italian and English forms of expression and that many suggestions for improvement in future editions will be communicated to the General Editor.

---

[1] Zingarelli also splits words into stem and termination, irrespective of syllabic division, and has no compunction even about beginning a termination with *h*, for example *brusc-a, -hetto, -hinare, -hino*.

ACKNOWLEDGEMENTS

It is with deep appreciation that I record my indebtedness to all the contributors who have co-operated with me in the compilation of this dictionary, as well as to Professor E. R. Vincent, whose advice as Chairman has been of great value. I wish also to thank the Syndics of the Cambridge University Press for all they have done to bring this work into being; to the Secretary, Mr R. J. L. Kingsford, I am especially grateful for his unfailing encouragement and support; to Mr Peter Burbidge, Assistant Secretary, and to Mr Oscar Watson who preceded him, I express heartfelt thanks for their help and guidance on innumerable points connected with the production of this work as a printed book. To Mr John Dreyfus who advised on the typography in the early stages, to Miss Margaret Hampton and to all the other members of the Press who have given secretarial and practical assistance, to Mr R. E. Britcher, the keyboard operator who set up almost the whole text, and to the proof-readers who gave it such care, I am most grateful. To the staff of the University Typewriting Office, Cambridge, in particular to Miss Dulcie Smith who typed and supervised the distribution of the first draft, I owe gratitude for the clarity and excellent co-ordination of the typescript. I am grateful also to the Syndics and staff of the Cambridge University Library for so kindly according house-room to the hundreds of thousands of index-cards which went to make up the work.

Among those who provided additional contributions and assistance I should like to thank especially Dr Brian Moloney, Mr Ronald Cosford, Mrs Valerie Minogue, and, for his expert filing of all the correspondence relating to the dictionary, Mr Adrian Thorpe.

To all these people, as well as to members of the Italian Institute, and to many others who have most kindly contributed information or answered inquiries, I here express my thanks.

BARBARA REYNOLDS

DEPARTMENT OF ITALIAN
UNIVERSITY OF CAMBRIDGE
October 1961

DIACRITIC MARKS
USED IN THE DICTIONARY

† **Obelus**   Obsolete.

· **Mid-point**   Indicates that the main stress (or tonic accent) falls on the preceding syllable, for example **me·dico**. *Note:* in words not marked with the mid-point, the main stress falls on the penultimate syllable, for example **cappello**.

. **Sub-dot**   (*a*) Appearing under **e** or **o** indicates that the vowel is close. **e** and **o** are marked thus only when they bear the main stress, since unstressed **e** or **o** is always close. The sub-dot appearing under **e** or **o** therefore serves two purposes: (i) it shows that the vowel so marked bears the main stress; (ii) it shows that the vowel is close, for example **rispọndere** (in which the vowel **o** bears the main stress and is close). Cf. **co·gliere** (in which **o** bears the main stress and is open).

(*b*) Appearing under **s** or **z** indicates that the consonant is soft, for example **roṣa, organiẓẓare**.

(*c*) Appearing under **g** in the group **gli** indicates that the **g** is pronounced as a separate consonant (as in English), for example, **g̣lifo**.

` **Grave accent**   This is the only accent used on Italian words in the dictionary and wherever it appears it is part of the word as written in Italian. *Note:* Italian typographers vary as to the style of accentuation they adopt; some use the acute accent for front vowels (close *e*, *i*, and *u*),[1] the grave for back vowels (*a*, open *e*, open *o*); others use the acute accent only for the close *e*. The use of the circumflex over *i*, instead of double *i*, is still found but is tending to become obsolete. In the face of such variation, it has been thought advisable to use only the grave accent, which indicates stress only. If the vowel so marked is close, a sub-dot indicates as much, for example **perchẹ̀**.

^ **Circumflex accent;** ´ **acute accent**   These accents are used only on French words in the dictionary.

[A I], **etc.**   See Verb Scheme.

[1] Close *o* never bears a written accent.

ABBREVIATIONS
USED IN THE DICTIONARY

Abbreviations are puzzling, but to puzzle is not their purpose. (FOWLER.)

abbrev.	abbreviation	*comm.*	commerce
abl.	ablative	*comp.*	comparative
abs.	absolute	*conj.*	conjunction
abstr.	abstract	*conjunct.*	conjunctive
acc.	accusative	*constr.*	construction
adj.	adjective	*contd.*	continued
admin.	administration	*contempt.*	contemptuous
adv.	adverb	*contr.*	contraction, contracted
aeron.	aeronautics	*corrupn.*	corruption
aesthet.	aesthetics	*Cors.*	Corsican
agric.	agriculture	*cost.*	costume
alp.	alpine, relating to alpinists, and mountain climbing	*C.P.*	Italian Penal Code
		C.P.P.	Italian Code of Penal Procedure
altern.	alternative, alternatively		
anat.	anatomy	*crit.*	criticism
antiphr.	antiphrasis	*cryst.*	crystallography
antiq.	in antiquity	*cul.*	culinary term
apocop.	apocopated	*cyt.*	cytology
appos.	(in) apposition		
archaeol.	archaeology	*dat.*	dative
archit.	architecture	*def.*	defective
art	relating to the visual arts	*def. art.*	definite article
artill.	artillery	*deriv(s).*	derivative(s)
astron.	astronomy	*derog.*	derogatory
athl.	athletics	*dial.*	dialect.
augm.	augmentative	*dim.*	diminutive
autom.	automobile engineering	*disjunct.*	disjunctive
aux.	auxiliary	*dressm.*	dressmaking
		dye.	dyeing
bibl.	biblical		
bibliogr.	bibliography	*eccl.*	ecclesiastical
biblioph.	bibliophily	*eccl. hist.*	ecclesiastical history
biochem.	biochemistry	*econ.*	economics
biol.	biology	*Egypt.*	Egyptology
bldg.	building	*electr.*	electricity
bookb.	bookbinding	*electron.*	electronics
bootm.	bootmaking	*encl.*	enclitic
bot.	botany	*eng.*	engineering
butcher.	butchering	*ent.*	entomology
B.V.M.	Blessed Virgin Mary	*equestr.*	equestrian
		esp.	especially
carpen.	carpentry	*etc.*	et cetera
C.C.	Italian Civil Code	*euphem.*	euphemism
C.C.P.	Italian Code of Civil Procedure	*excl.*	exclamation
		exist.	existentialist
ceram.	ceramics	*explos.*	explosives
cf.	compare	*expr.*	expression
chem.	chemistry		
chem. eng.	chemical engineering	*f.*	feminine
cinem.	cinematography	*fam.*	familiar
class.	classical	*fig.*	figurative
clockm.	clockmaking	*finan.*	financial, finance
colloq.	colloquial	*Florent.*	Florentine

Flor. hist.	Florentine history	*mech.*	mechanics
foll.	followed, following	*med.*	medical
fortif.	fortifications	*mediev.*	medieval
found.	foundry	*mens.*	mensuration
Fr.	French	*met., metall.*	metallurgy
		meteor.	meteorology
gen.	genitive	*mfr.*	manufacturing
geneal.	genealogy, genealogical	*mil.*	military
geog.	geography	*mil. comm.*	military command
geol.	geology	*min.*	mining
geom.	geometry	*miner.*	mineralogy
ger.	gerund	*motor.*	motoring
Gk.	Greek	*motorcycl.*	motorcycling
glass-m.	glass-manufacturing	*mount.*	mountaineering
govt.	government	*ms.*	manuscript
gramm.	grammatical term	*mus.*	music
gymn.	gymnastics	*myth.*	mythology
herald.	heraldry	*n.*	noun *or* used as a noun
hist.	history, historical	*naut.*	nautical
hortic.	horticulture	*naut. comm.*	nautical command
hosp.	hospital	*naut. hist.*	nautical history
hunt.	hunting	*Neap.*	Neapolitan
hydr., hydraul.	hydraulics	*needle-w.*	needle-work
hydr. eng.	hydraulic engineering	*neg.*	negative
		neol.	neologism
I.C.	Italian Constitution	*N. Ital.*	North Italian
ichth.	ichthyology	*no.*	number
illum.	illumination	*nos.*	numbers
imp.	imperative	*nom.*	nominative
impers.	impersonal	*numis.*	numismatics
indecl.	indeclinable		
indef.	indefinite	*obstet.*	obstetrics
indic.	indicative	*onom.*	onomatopoeic
industr.	industry	*opt.*	optics
inf.	infinitive	*orig.*	originally
infant.	baby language	*orn.*	ornithology
intens.	intensive form		
interr.	interrogative	*paint.*	painting
intr.	intransitive	*palaeog.*	palaeography
iron.	ironical	*palaeont.*	palaeontology
Ital. antiq.	Italian antiquity	*paperm.*	papermaking
		part.	participle (present or past)
joc.	jocular	*part. adj.*	participle used adjectivally
journ.	journalism	*partit.*	partitive
		patrist.	patristic term
km.	kilometre(s)	*pedagog.*	pedagogy
knitt.	knitting	*pejor.*	pejorative
		perh.	perhaps
lang.	language	*pers.*	person
Lat.	Latin	*pharm.*	pharmacy, pharmacology
leather-m.	leather-manufacturing	*philol.*	philology
leg.	legal term	*philos.*	philosophy
ling.	linguistic(s)	*phon.*	phonetics
lit. hist.	literary history	*photog.*	photography
lit.	literature	*phr.*	phrase
liturg.	liturgy	*phys.*	physics
Lomb.	Lombardy	*physiol.*	physiology
		Piedm.	Piedmont, Piedmontese
m.	masculine	*pl.*	plural
math.	mathematics	*poet.*	poetical

pol.	politics, political	*seis.*	seismology
pol. hist.	political history	*shoem.*	shoemaking
pop.	popular, popularly	*Sicil.*	Sicilian
poss.	possessive	*silkb.*	silkbreeding
pr.	proper	*sim.*	similar
pref.	prefix	*sing.*	singular
prep.	preposition	*sociol.*	sociology
prn.	pronoun	*sp.*	species
pr. n.	proper noun	*suff.*	suffix
procl.	proclitic	*superl.*	superlative
pron.	pronounced	*surg.*	surgery
prosod.	prosody	*syll.*	syllable
Prov.	Provençal		
provb.	proverb, proverbial	*tailor.*	tailoring
psychol.	psychology	*tan.*	tanning
		techn.	technical, technology
q.v.	quod vide	*teleph.*	telephonic
		telev.	television
radiol.	radiology	*text.*	textile
recip.	reciprocal	*text. ind.*	textile industry
rel.	religion	*theatr.*	theatrical
repet.	repetitive	*theol.*	theology
Repub.	Republic	*tr.*	transitive
rfl.	reflexive	*Tusc.*	Tuscan
rhet.	rhetoric	*typ.*	typography
rlwy.	railway		
Rom.	Roman	*Umbr.*	Umbrian
Romagn.	Romagnuolo	*usu.*	usually
Rom. antiq.	Roman antiquity		
		Ven.	Venetian
Sard.	Sardinian	*vet.*	veterinary
schol.	scholastic	*vulg.*	vulgar
scient.	scientific		
Scot.	Scottish	*zool.*	zoology
sculp.	sculpture		

A, a *f.*, *m.* the vowel A; the letter A; un'a maiuscola, a capital A; un'a minuscola, a small A; (fig.) beginning, outset; essere all'—, to have barely commenced, to be a beginner; dall'— alla zeta, from A to Z, from beginning to end; ricominciare dall'—, to begin all over again.

a¹ *prep.* (before another vowel sometimes **ad**; before another **a** preferably **ad**; *contr. with def. art.*: **al, allo, ai, agli, alla, alle**).

1. Motion towards (to): andare — scuola, to go to school; andiamo — casa, let's go home; va — Roma ogni anno, he goes to Rome every year; prendete — destra, turn to the right; — monte, upstream; — valle, downstream. 2. Place, Position (at, on, in, near, towards, facing): — scuola, at school; — casa, at home; — tavola, at table; — letto, in bed; — bordo, on board; sto — Roma, I live in Rome; al sole, in the sun; all'ombra, in the shade; Porta — San Giorgio, Gate near St George's, St George's Gate; — ponente, in the west, towards the west; finestra che dà — mezzogiorno, window facing south. 3. Distance: — dieci miglia da Firenze, ten miles from Florence; within ten miles of Florence; — tiro di fucile, within gun-shot; (fig.) — un dipresso, by and large. 4. Time (*a*) Moment, point of time (at, on, upon): alle cinque, at five o'clock; al tramonto, at sunset; allo spuntar del giorno, at daybreak; al primo del mese, on the first of the month; alla domenica, on Sundays; al giorno d'oggi, nowadays. (*b*) Interval of time: oggi — otto, a week from today; venerdì — otto, Friday week; addio — domani, goodbye until tomorrow. 5. Measurement, Quantity, Price (in, by, for): misurare — chili, to measure in kilos; vendere alla dozzina, to sell by the dozen; — cento lire, for a hundred lire; — buon mercato, cheaply; cinquanta mila lire al mese, fifty thousand lire a month; lavora otto ore al giorno, he works eight hours a day. 6. Method, means (with, by): battersi alla spada, to fight with swords; uccidere — tradimento, to kill by treachery; chiudere — chiave, to lock; campare — pane e acqua, to live on bread and water; — forza di, by dint of; vi riconosco alla voce, I know you by your voice; — quanto sembra, judging by appearances, as far as one can tell. 7. Result, consequence, extent: battersi — sangue, to fight until blood is drawn; ferito — morte, mortally wounded; — piena soddisfazione di, to the complete satisfaction of. 8. Construction, material, kind, form: costruire — mattoni, to build in brick; dipingere ad olio, to paint in oils; pittura ad olio, oil-painting; mulino — vento, wind-mill; pavimento — mattoni, brick floor; lavorato ad oro, worked in gold; fatto — rabeschi, ornamented in arabesques; cotto all'olio, cooked in oil; cotto al burro, cooked in butter; una casa — un solo piano, a one-storey house, a bungalow; reggersi — repubblica, to be constituted as a republic. 9. Manner, condition (as, like, in the style of, with, on): posa — poeta, he poses as a poet; una stanza accomodata — biblioteca, a room fitted up as a library; la nomina del Duca G. ad ambasciatore, the appointment of Duke G. as ambassador; all'inglese, in the English manner; alla Pompadour, Pompadour style; — braccia aperte, with open arms; ad occhi chiusi, with one's eyes shut; (fig.) blindfold, with complete confidence; — digiuno, on an empty stomach; — piedi, on foot; — cavallo, on horseback; (of a dog) al guinzaglio, on the lead; operare ad inganno, to act deceitfully; parlare — malizia, to speak spitefully; (mus.) — due, two voices together, two instruments together (see also **due, tre, piacere** for musical uses); — poco — poco, little by little; — due — due, two by two; — scapito di, to the detriment of; — bella posta, on purpose; — caso, at random; all'improvviso, unexpectedly; stare bene — soldi, to be well off; stare male — soldi, to be hard up, to be pushed for money. 10. Occasion (upon, at, for): — tali parole, upon these words; — prima vista, at first sight; destarsi al più piccolo rumore, to wake at the slightest noise; — prove effettuate, after testing. 11. Syntactical uses. (**i**) In Interjections: al ladro! al ladro!, thief! thief!; — voi, your turn, over to you. (**ii**) Followed by an infinitive: (*a*) expressing purpose after verbs of motion: andò — vedere, he went to look; andiamo — vedere, let's go and see; (*b*) representing a conditional clause: — parlar così ti farai detestare, if you talk like

that you will get yourself disliked; (*c*) corresponding to an English participle, esp. after **stare**: stavo — sedere, I was sitting; non staranno molto — tornare, they won't be long getting back; (*d*) with the historic infinitive: abbaiò il cane, e tutti — fuggire, the dog barked and off they all went; (*e*) after an adj.: facile — mentire, given to lying; bello — vedersi, lovely to look at; (*f*) with **essere**, replacing a relative clause: fu egli — dirmelo, it was he who told me so; (*g*) for verbs for which **a** serves as a junction with other infinitives, see list at end of Verb Scheme.

†a² *prep.* from.

à variant form of **ha**, for which see **avere**.

aaronita *adj.* (Bibl.) Aaronical; *n.m.* Aaronite.

abacà (Tusc. **abaca**) *f.* (bot.) abaca, a kind of banana plant of the Philippine Islands, *Musa textilis*; fibre from the abaca, Manilla hemp; (naut.) Manilla.

abac·chio *m.* See **abbacchio**.

abaceto *m.* (ent.) *Abacetus* sp., a carabid beetle.

a·ba·co *m.* (*pl.* **-chi, -ci**) abacus, calculating frame; (math.) graph, curve of a function; (archit.) abacus; (eng.) alignment chart.

aba·culo *m.* (archit.) abaculus, abaciscus.

Abaddon *pr.n.m.* (Bibl.) Abaddon, 'the angel of the bottomless pit'.

abadessa *f.* See **badessa**.

abadi·a *f.* See **abbazia** or **badia**.

abadillare [A I] (dial. Tusc. *intr.* (*aux.* avere)) to waste time, to idle.

abassi·a *f.* (med.) dyssynergia.

abate *m.* abbot; stare come un padre —, to be in clover; cleric, abbé.

†a·bav·o *m.* great-great-grandfather; *pl.* ancestors. **†-a** *f.* great-great-grandmother.

abazi·a *f.* See **abbazia** or **badia**.

abbac·are [A 2 S] *intr.* (*aux.* avere) to compute, to reckon; to day-dream; to let the thoughts wander; to be wool-gathering. **-amento** *m.* day-dreaming, dotage, wool-gathering; day-dream. **-one** *m.* day-dreamer.

abbaccare [A 2] *tr.* (dial. Tusc.) to leap, to jump over.

abbacchi-are [A 4] *tr.* to knock down (fruit, nuts) with a pole (from **bacchio¹**, q.v.); to beat down; to floor, to send sprawling; to humiliate; to bring down (price); to sell cheaply, to dispose of; — una ragazza, to marry a girl off; *rfl.* (Tusc.) to drowse, to drop off to sleep; to lose heart. **-amento** *m.* knocking-down; selling-off. **-ata** *f.* knocking-down; blow; all'-ata *adv.* heedlessly, blindly. **-ato** *part. adj.* knocked down; beaten; humbled; down-hearted, dejected. **-atura** *f.* knocking-down; selling-off.

†abbachier·e, **†-o** *m.* **† -a** *f.* See under **abbaco**.

abbachino *m. dim.* See under **abbaco**.

abbac·chi-o *m.* young lamb (slaughtered); lamb (on a menu); (fig.) fare — di, to sell off. **-aro** *m.* purveyor of lamb, butcher.

abbachista *m.* See under **abbaco**.

abbacin-are [A I, A I S] *tr.* to dazzle; to fascinate; to delude; to dim; to obscure; to outshine; (hist.) to abacinate, to blind. **-amento** *m.* dazzle, dazzling; fascination; dimming; obscuring; blinding. **-ante** *part. adj.* dazzling; fascinating; (fig.) blinding. **-ato** *part. adj.* dazzled; dazed, bemused; fascinated; faded, dim; outshone; (of eyesight) weak; (hist.) abacinated, blinded; (of marble, glass) dulled, dimmed; (paint.) subdued, dim; ombra -ata, deep shade, dimness; †brought low, reduced in circumstances, bereft. (**-atore** *m.* **-atrice** *f.*) **-io** *m.* (*pl.* **-ii**) continuous dazzling.

ab·ba·co *m.* (*pl.* **-chi**) elementary arithmetic book, primer; essere all'—, to be a beginner; ti ci vuol l'—, you can't add two and two together, you don't know the first thing about it; abacus, calculating frame (see also **abaco**); (mil.) artillery board; (dial. Siena) arithmetic; †school. **†-chiere**, **†-chiero** *m.*, **†-chiera** *f.* abacist, reckoner, calculator. **-chino** *m.* elementary sum book; primer; elementary class; far gli -chini (of children), to do simple sums. **-chista** *m.* abacist, reckoner, calculator, accountant; (iron.) poor mathematician.

abbacone *m.* See under **abbacare**.

abbadare¹ [A I]. See **badare**.

†abbadare² *intr.* to idle, to waste time.

abbadessa *f.* See **badessa**.

abbadi·a *f.* See **abbazia** or **badia**.

abbagli-are [A4] *tr.* to dazzle, to blind; to fascinate; to deceive; to delude; to astonish; *abs.* stile che -a, showy, flashy style; (paint.) to tone down, to soften; *rfl.* to be dazzled; to be deceived; to become bewildered; (of eyesight) to grow dim. -ag·gine *f.*, -amento *m.* glare, dazzle; dazzling, dazzlement; error, confusion; bewilderment. -ante *part. adj.* dazzling; glittering; fascinating; deceiving, confusing; faro anti-abbagliante, anti-dazzle lamp. †-anza *f.* dazzle; bewilderment; delirium. -ato *part. adj.* dazzled; fascinated; deluded; astonished; bewildered, confused; dim; toned down. -atamente *adv.* confusedly, dazedly, bewilderedly. -atore *m.* dazzler; deceiver. (-atrice *f.*).

abba·gli-o *m.* (*pl.* -i) dazzle, dazzling; glare; error, mistake, blunder, slip; prendere un —, to make a mistake, to blunder, to slip up; to be taken in, to be dazzled; per —, by mistake.

abbagl-ìo *m.* (*pl.* -ìi) continuous dazzle; spots before the eyes.

abbai-are [A4] *intr.* (*aux.* avere) to bark; to yelp; to bay; to howl; to snarl; è can che -a ma non morde, his bark is worse than his bite; (fig.) to shout, to rant, to rail; to make an outcry; (of a singer) to force, to yell; (colloq.) — dalla fame, to be ravenously hungry; — dalla sete, to be parched with thirst; (of an old maid) non trovare un cane che le abbai, to be left on the shelf. -amento *m.* barking; baying; howling. -ata *f.* bark, barking; baying; howling; (fig.) scolding; jeering, booing; (theatr.) 'the bird'. -atore *m.* barker; brawler. (-atrice *f.*) -atura *f.* barking; baying; howling. -one *m.* great talker; loud-mouthed individual; brawler.

abbaino *m.* sky-light; garret-window; (Lomb.) attic; (archit.) dormer-window, dormer.

abb-a·io *m.* (*pl.* -a·i) bark, way of barking.

abba-ìo *m.* (*pl.* -ìi) continuous, prolonged barking, howling.

†abbaire *intr.* to be dismayed, to quail; to marvel.

†abbaliare[1] *tr.* to put out to nurse (from Lat. ad and balia[2] *f.*, q.v.).

†abbaliare[2] *tr.* to wean (from Lat. ab and balia[2] *f.*, q.v.).

abball-are [A1] *tr.* to make up into parcels; to embale; to pack; to load; to stow; *intr.* (*aux.* avere) (fig.) to tell a tall story, to lay it on thick, to exaggerate. -inare [A1] *tr.* to roll up (a mattress, in airing a bed); †*intr.* to depart this life, to pack up. -ottare [A1] *tr.* to handle roughly, to bundle about; to jumble; *rfl.* (metall.) to go lumpy (of molten metal). -ottamento *m.*, -ottatura *f.* rough handling; jumble; (metall.) caking. -ottìo *m.* continuous rough handling; horse-play.

abbambinare [A1] *tr.* to trundle, to 'walk' (a heavy weight) along.

abbambolato *adj.* See **imbambolato**, under **imbambolare**.

abbanc-are [A2] *tr.* (naut.) to fit (a boat) with thwarts; (tan.) to spread on the table, to sleek. (-ato *part. adj.* -atura *f.*)

abbandon-are [A1c] *tr.* to abandon; to neglect; to desert; to forsake; to leave, to quit; to give up, to renounce; to do without; to forgo, to forfeit; to relinquish; to lay down (arms); to leave alone; to let fall, to drop; to let go, to loose; to slacken; to throw down; to cast away; (leg.) to waive; (naut.) — la nave, to abandon ship; *rfl.* to surrender, to yield; to resign oneself; to lose courage, to give in; to slack; to let oneself fall, to collapse; (*prep.* a) to give way (to); to be addicted (to); to become addicted (to); to indulge (in); -arsi alla gioia, to be transported with joy; †to take a risk, to commit oneself; †to plunge, to be lost. -amento *m.* abandoning, abandonment. -atario *m.* (leg.) underwriter to whom a ship is abandoned. -ato *part. adj.* abandoned; forsaken, deserted; relinquished; neglected; dismayed; despairing, unhappy; loose, slackened; obsolete, in disuse; addicted; -ato a cattiva vita, given over to a life of evil; una donna -ata, a forsaken woman; casa -ata, house left uninhabited; -ato dai medici, despaired of by the doctors; a briglia -ata, with slackened rein, full pelt; *n.m.* foundling, waif; Gli Abbandonati, foundling hospital formerly in Florence. -atamente *adv.* unreservedly; freely; passionately. -atore *m.* abandoner, deserter. (-atrice *f.*)

abbandono *m.* abandon, abandonment, neglect; lasciare in —, to abandon; tenere in —, to neglect; lasciare nell'—, to leave uncared for, to leave untidy; lasciare una casa nell'—, to let a house go to rack and ruin; desertion; deserted state, isolation; dereliction; relaxation, unconstraint; renouncement, relinquishing, giving up; l'— di un vizio, the relinquishing of a bad habit; (leg.) abandonment (to ship's underwriters); (rel. hist.) — al braccio secolare, handing over to the secular arm.

abbarbagli-are [A4] *tr.* to dazzle; to daze; to stupefy; *rfl.* to be dazzled; to be bewildered. -amento *m.* dazzle, dazzling. -ante

part. adj. dazzling. -ato *part. adj.* dazzled; (fig.) blinded, stupefied, bewildered. -atamente *adv.* confusedly, blindly, bewilderedly.

abbarba·gl-io *m.* (*pl.* -i) dazzling, dazzle; dizziness, giddiness; dimness, weakness (of sight).

abbarbagl-ìo *m.* (*pl.* -ìi) continuous, intense dazzling.

†abbarbare *vb.* and derivs. See **barbare** under **barba**.

abbarbic-are [A2s] *rfl.*, *intr.* (*aux.* avere) to strike root; to climb, to cling; (fig.) to take root, to be implanted; (of habit, emotion) to take hold. -amento *m.* taking root; clinging. -ato *part. adj.* rooted; clinging; (fig.) inveterate, fixed; entrenched.

abbarc-are [A2] *tr.* to heap, to pile (esp. sheaves of corn, from **barca**, stack, q.v.); (naut.) to bend (steel plates, etc.). -ato *part. adj.* stacked, heaped, piled up. -atura *f.* stacking; stack.

abbarrare [A1][1] and derivs. See **barrare**[1].

abbaruff-are [A1] *tr.* to rumple; to upset; to untidy; to embroil; †*rfl.* (of the sea) to roughen; *recip. rfl.* to come to blows, to scuffle; to quarrel, to squabble. -amento *m.*, -ata *f.* rumpling; scuffle, rumpus, rough and tumble. -ato *part. adj.* in disorder, untidy; dishevelled, ruffled; chaotic. (-atura *f.*) -ìo *m.* (*pl.* -ìi) confusion, disorder, chaos; continuous scuffling, fighting, squabbling.

abbass-are [A1] *tr.* to lower; to make lower; to let down; to take down; to pull down; to diminish the reputation of; — la voce, to drop one's voice; — il prezzo, to reduce the price; — la luce, to turn down the light; — i fari, to dip headlights; (naut.) — i fanali, to dim lights; — una perpendicolare, to drop a perpendicular; (typ.) — uno spazio, to push down a space; — un'equazione, to reduce an equation; to humble; to vilify; to degrade, to abase; — il capo, to bow one's head, (fig.) to resign oneself; — la cresta, to be humbled; — le armi, to lay down arms; *intr.* (*aux.* essere) to fall; to diminish; to lessen; to drop (of temperature); to sink (of sun, level of water); *rfl.* to humble oneself; to abase oneself; to stoop; to condescend; to diminish, to abate, to fall, to drop; to sag; to ebb; to decline, to slope. -a·bile *adj.* adjustable; detachable; capable of being lowered. -amento *m.* lowering, drop, fall, reduction, diminution; abatement; sagging, subsidence, settlement; humbling; abasement; (astron.) depression; (naut.) dip (of horizon). -ata *f.* lowering, reduction. -ato *part. adj.* lowered; down; abased; lower; diminished; (herald.) in base. -atore *m.* (anat.) -atore della lingua, tongue depressor. (-atura *f.*)

abbasso *adv.* down; below; downstairs; downwards; giù —, down below; stanze d'—, rooms on the ground floor; *excl.* — i tiranni! down with tyrants! (naut.) —!, below decks!; — da riva!, down from aloft!

abbastanza *adv.* enough; (iron.) averne —, to have had enough, to have had more than enough; rather, somewhat; pretty, fairly; sufficiently.

†abbastonare *vb.* and derivs. See **bastonare**.

abbastonato *adj.* (archit.) with rod-like mouldings; fusto di colonna —, column furnished with cable-mouldings.

abbatacchiare [A4] and derivs. See **sbatacchiare**.

abbat-e *m.* see **abate**. -essa *f.* see **badessa**.

abbat·t-ere [B1] *tr.* to knock down; to throw down; to pull down; to cut down; to reap; to bring down, to shoot down (an aeroplane); to floor; to overthrow; to demolish; to fell; to kill, to destroy; to slaughter (cattle); to defeat; to prostrate, to overcome; to allay; to abate; to confute; to dishearten; (miner.) to blast; (naut.) — in chiglia, to careen; *intr.* (*aux.* avere) (naut.) to cast, to veer; *rfl.* to descend; to swoop; to leap out; to break (of a storm); to lose heart; to fall, to collapse; -ersi in, to meet by chance, to run into; to come upon, to find by chance; -ersi bene, to fall on one's feet; è un -ersi, it's a matter of luck; †to happen, to occur; †to fight. -ifie·no *m.* trap-door (in a hay-loft). -imento *m.* dejection; prostration, weakness; knocking-down; overthrow; felling; combat; abating; mining, stoping, blasting; -imento idraulico, hydraulicking; (finan.) tax relief; †chance encounter; †per -imento, by chance. -itore *m.* killer; slaughterer; lumber-jack. (-itrice *f.*) -uta *f.* (naut.) search; (mil.) abattis. -uto *part. adj.* knocked down; felled; killed; reaped; stricken; (of an aeroplane) brought down; (fig.) cast down; dejected; prostrate; weakened.

abbattuffol-are [A1s] *tr.* to bundle together; to jumble; *recip. rfl.* to come to blows, to scuffle. -ato *part. adj.* jumbled, in confusion.

†abbavagliato *adj.* See **imbavagliato**, under **imbavagliare**.

abbaz-i·a *f.* abbey; abbacy; benefice. -iale *adj.* abbatial.

abbeceda·rio *m.* book; spelling book, primer; dictionary; encyclopaedia; †*adj.* alphabetical.

†**abbellare** *vb.* and derivs. See **abbellire**.

abbell-ire [D2] *tr.* to embellish; to beautify; to adorn; to enhance, to improve; to gild; (of a portrait) to flatter; — una notizia, to embroider a tale, to exaggerate an account; †*intr.* to please, to seem beautiful; *rfl.* to beautify oneself, to adorn oneself; to grow in beauty, to improve in looks; to become enhanced; (*prep.* di) to take what one wants, to help oneself (to); c'è di che -irsi, there's plenty. **-imento** *m.* embellishment; embellishing; improvement; (mus.) ornament. **-ito** *part. adj.* embellished, beautified; enhanced; improved in looks; adorned. **-itore** *m.* beautifier; *adj.* beautifying. (**-itrice** *f.*) **-itura** *f.* beautifying.

†**abbenchè** *conj.* See **benchè**.

†**abbendare** *tr.* to bind; to encircle, to surround.

†**abbent-are** *intr.* See **abentare**. †**-e**, †**-o** *m.* See under **abentare**.

†**abbergo** *m.* See **albergo**.

†**abbertescare** *tr.* (mil.) to fortify.

abbever-are [A1 SC] *tr.* to water (horses, cattle); — un prato, to irrigate a meadow; (fig.) to fill; to soak (a cask); (naut.) to flood (a tank); †to water (a ship); *rfl.* (of horses, cattle) to go to water, to drink. **-amento** *m.*, **-ata** *f.* watering. **-atic·cio** *m.* dregs. **-ato** *part. adj.* watered; quenched; filled; †sipped, tasted; †bene -ato, drunk; †*n.m.* dregs, drain. **-atoio** *m.* drinking-trough; horse-pond; drinking-bowl.

abbevicare [A2 S] and derivs. See **vivificare**.

†**abbì** *m.* alphabet.

abbi, ab·bia, abbiamo, ab·biano. See **avere**.

abbiabbe *m.* the early stages of reading; essere sempre all'—, to make no progress.

abbiadare [A1] *tr.* to put (a horse) on oats; to feed on oats.

abbia·tico *m.* (Lomb.) grandson. (See also **abiatico**.)

abbicare [A2] *tr.* to pile, to stack; *abs.* to stack the corn in sheaves; †*rfl.* to crouch, to huddle.

abbiccì *m. indecl.* the A B C; spelling book, primer; rudiments; essere all'—, to be a beginner; non sa l'— della medicina, he doesn't know the first thing about medicine.

†**abbientare** *tr.* to qualify.

abbiente *adj.* prosperous, well-to-do; †able, fit, skilful, qualified; *n.m.pl.* gli abbienti, the haves; i non abbienti, the have-nots.

†**abbiere** *vb.* and derivs. See **avere**.

abbiettare¹ [A4] and derivs. See **abiettare**.

abbiett-are² [A1 C] *tr.* to wedge. **-ato** *part. adj.* wedged.

abbietto *adj.* See **abietto**.

abbiezione *f.* See **abiezione**.

abbigli-are [A4] *tr.* to dress; to adorn; to ornament; *rfl.* to dress oneself; to dress smartly; to adorn oneself. **-amento** *m.* manner of dressing, style; clothes, dress, wear; attire, apparel; l'industria dell'-amento, clothing trade; ornament, adornment. **-ato** *part. adj.* dressed, attired. **-atoio** *m.* dressing-room. **-atura** *f.* dressing; robing; adorning; dress, attire.

abbin-are [A1] *tr.* to couple, to join, to combine; to sort into pairs. **-amento** *m.* combining, grouping, joining; collaboration, joint venture; (rlwy.) coupling (of points). **-ato** *part. adj.* coupled, combined.

abbindol-are [A1 S] *tr.* to wind (thread); (fig.) to pull the wool over (a person's) eyes, to humbug, to lead by the nose; *rfl.* to become twisted; (fig.) to become confused, to be perplexed. **-amento** *m.* confusion, perplexity; entanglement; trickery, fraud. **-ato** *part. adj.* (of thread) wound; (fig.) cheated, deceived. **-atore** *m.* trickster, fraud, cheat. (**-atrice** *f.*) **-atura** *f.* trickery, deceit; trick. (**-azione** *f.* **-eri·a** *f.*)

abbioccare [A2] *intr.* (*aux.* avere) (dial. Siena) to cluck; *tr.* (of a hen) to call (chickens); *rfl.* (colloq. Tusc.) to settle down to sleep, to go to roost.

abbiosciare [A3] *tr.* to dispirit; *rfl.* to collapse; to give in; to droop; to cower, to grovel.

abbisci-are [A3] *tr.* (naut.) to coil down, to snake down. (**-ato** *part. adj.*). **-atura** *f.* (naut.) stopper.

abbisogn-are [A5 C] *intr.* (*aux.* avere; *prep.* di) to have need (of); quel poverino -a di aiuto, that poor man needs help; *impers.* to be necessary; mi -a la tua collaborazione, I need your co-operation. **-evole**, **-oso** *adj.* needful, needy, in need.

abbitt-are [A1] *tr.* (naut.) to bitt (a cable). **-atura** *f.* bitting; -atura doppia, double bitting.

abbiurare [A1]. See **abiurare**, under **abiura**.

abbivaccare [A2] and derivs. See **bivaccare**, under **bivacco**.

abbocc-are [A2 C] *tr.* to snap up, to seize with the jaws; to bite; — l'esca, to swallow the bait (also fig.); to seize with pincers; to grip; to fill (a flask, cask) to the brim; — un chiodo, to fix a nail (before hammering it down); *intr.* (*aux.* avere) to bite, to nibble; — all'amo, to nibble at the hook; (fig. colloq.) il pesciolino ha -ato, he's fallen for it; (colloq.) to fit in, to go in; †(naut.) to go gunwale under; †— in mare, to sink; *rfl.* †(naut.) to fill and sink; *recip. rfl.* to parley, to confer, to meet. **-amento** *m.* interview; parley, talk; conference; †(mil.) encounter, combat; (med.) anastomosis. **-ato** *part. adj.* seized; bitten; nibbled; full to the brim; (of a flask) -ato e segnato, duly sealed and stamped; (of wine) sweet, sweetish; palatable; (of a person) è -ato, he's not particular what he eats; *n.m.* sweet flavour; (of wine) aver dell'-ato, to be somewhat sweet. **-atoio** *m.* (metall.) mouth of a furnace. **-atore** *m.* biter; nibbler; †contractor. **-atura** *f.* snapping up, seizing; swallowing; (of a person) è di facile -atura, he eats anything; opening up, broaching, mouth, opening; part of contents near top of flask or sack; part of loaf not baked through from having been too near the mouth of the oven; (of folding doors, casement windows) join, meeting of sections; †rim; †mouth (of river); (mus.) see **imboccatura**, under **imboccare**.

†**abbocche·vole** *adj.* (naut.) likely to capsize, unstable, tender.

abboccolato *adj.* (of hair) in ringlets, in cork-screw curls.

abbocconare [A1 C] *tr.* to cut up; to swallow in a mouthful.

†**abbominare** *vb.* and derivs. See **abominare**.

abbonacci-are [A3] *tr.* to calm; to appease, to placate; (paint.) to tone down; *rfl.* to grow calm; (of weather) to turn fine, to set fine. **-amento** *m.* calm; period of calm. **-ato** *part. adj.* calm; serene; placated; (of weather) è -ato, the wind has dropped. **-atamente** *adv.* calmly, tranquilly; quietly; placidly.

abbon-are¹ [A1] *tr.* to take out a subscription for; ho -ato mio figlio per un anno al *Times*, I've taken out a year's subscription to *The Times* for my son; to take out a season-ticket for; *rfl.* (*prep.* a) to subscribe (to); to take out a subscription (for); mi sono -ato al *Times*, I've taken out a subscription for *The Times*; to take a season-ticket (for). **-amento** *m.* subscription; subscription rate; agreement, contract; tessera d'-amento, season ticket. **-ato** *part. adj.* subscribing; subscribed; *n.m.* subscriber; season-ticket holder; consumer; (joc.) frequent visitor.

abbon-are² [A1 d] *tr.* to approve; to credit with; to believe of; non te l'abbuono, I don't believe it of you; (comm.) to allow a discount of; to reduce the price of. **-amento** *m.* crediting; -amento postale, composition for stamp duty. **-ato** *part. adj.* approved; credited. (Cf. **abbuono**.)

abbond-are [A1 C] *intr.* (*aux.* essere) to abound, to be plentiful; to be excessive; (*aux.* avere; *prep.* di, in) to abound (in), to have plenty (of); to be rich (in); †*tr.* — con parole, to overwhelm with a flood of words; †*abs.* to provide: -a Dio, God will provide. **-ante** *part. adj.* abounding; -ante di risorse naturali, abounding in natural resources; rich, fertile; abundant, plentiful, copious; un pasto -ante, a good meal; una pioggia -ante, a heavy fall of rain; tre miglia -anti, a good three miles. (**-antemente** *adv.*) **-anza** *f.* abundance; plenty; vino in -anza, plenty of wine; abbiamo tempo in -anza, we're in very good time; nuotare nell'-anza, to have plenty of everything, to be rolling in money; per -anza di cuore, out of the fullness of one's heart; provisions, victuals. †**-anziere** *m.* food-official. **-evole** *adj.* abundant, plentiful. (**-evolmente** *adv.*) **-evolezza** *f.* plentifulness, abundance, copiousness. †**-o** *adj.* abundant; †*n.m.* in-o, in abundance. **-one** *m.*, **-ona** *f.* gossip, chatterbox; wiseacre.

abbon-ire [D2] *tr.* to calm, to pacify; to appease; to cultivate, to improve (land); *tr., intr.* (*aux.* essere) to ripen; to mature; *rfl.* to grow calm; to be placated. **-imento** *m.* improvement (of land); cultivation; brightening (of weather). **-ito** *part. adj.* pacified; cultivated, improved; ripened, mature.

abbono *m.* See **abbuono**.

abbord-are [A1] *tr.* (naut.) to lay (a ship) alongside; to assault, to ram; (fig.) to approach; to open conversation with; to buttonhole; — un argomento, to broach a subject; *intr.* (*aux.* avere) (naut.) to land. **-a·bile** *adj.* accessible; approachable; affable; (of a subject) not too difficult. **-ag·gio** *m.* (naut.) collision; ramming; grounding; boarding (in a sea-fight). (**-atore** *m.*) **-o** *m.* (naut.) boarding; (fig.) di primo -o, first of all, at first sight; di facile -o, affable; of easy access; di molto -o, loquacious; impressive, taking. **-one** *m.* (colloq.) chatterbox; bore.

abborracci-are [A 3] *tr.* to bungle, to botch; to scamp; to put together hurriedly; to make a rough sketch of; †*rfl.* to talk indistinctly, to gabble; to gobble, to guzzle. **-amento** *m.* bungling, botching; a botched job. **-ato** *part. adj.* bungled; botched; scamped. **-atamente** *adv.* awkwardly; carelessly. **-atore** *m.*, **-atrice** *f.* bungler; careless worker. **-atura** *f.* bungling, botching. **-one** *m.*, **-ona** *f.* bungler.

abborraccio *m.* (Tusc.) perpetual hurry; confusion, rush; medley, jumble.

†**abborrare**[1] *tr.* to stuff with hair; to fill with flock; (fig.) to pad.

†**abborrare**[2] *intr.* See **aberrare**.

abborrire [D 2] and derivs. See **aborrire**.

†**abboscato** *adj.* leafy, in leaf.

abbottare[1] [A 1] *tr.* (dial. Rom.) to puff out, to swell (from **botta**, q.v.).

abbottare[2] [A 1 c] *rfl.* (dial. Rom.) to stuff oneself with food, to grow as round as a barrel (from **botte**, q.v.).

†**abbottin-are** *tr.* to plunder, to sack; to rouse to rebellion; *rfl.* (*prep.* da) to mutiny; to rebel (against), to desert; (*prep.* di) to be mutinous; to feel resentful (towards). †**-amento** *m.* plundering, sacking; rebellion, mutiny. †**-ato** *part. adj.* plundered, sacked; mutinous. †**-atore** *m.* plunderer.

abbotton-are [A 1 c] *tr.* to button, to button up; *rfl.* to button one's clothes; to button oneself up; (fig.) to become reserved; to be secretive. **-ato** *part. adj.* buttoned; (fig.) reserved; secretive; taciturn. **-atura** *f.* buttoning; buttons, row of buttons.

abbozzacchiare [A 4] and derivs. See **abbozzare**.

abbozzachire [D 2]. See **imbozzachire**.

abbozz-are[1] [A 1] *tr.* to sketch, to outline, to make a rough draft of; (sculpt.) to boast, to rough out; (naut.) to put on a slip, to stopper; (fig.) — un sorriso, to smile faintly; — un gesto, to make a tentative movement, to sketch a gesture. **-amento** *m.*, **-ata** *f.* sketching, roughing out, outlining; sketch, rough draft. **-ato** *part. adj.* roughed out, sketched; (archit.) built of rough-hewn stone. **-atamente** *adv.* roughly; sketchily. **-atic·cio** *adj.* sketchy, rough; *n.m.* rough outline; badly finished work. (**-atore** *m.* **-atrice** *f.*) **-atura** *f.* rough sketch.

abbozzare[2] [A 1] *intr.* (*aux.* avere) (dial. Rom.) to submit unwillingly; to stop, to leave off; *tr.* abbòzzala!, stop it!

abbozzato *adj.* (archit.) studded with bosses (from **bozza**,[2] q.v.).

abbozzo *m.* rough sketch, outline; quaderno per abbozzi, sketch-book; in —, in rough; un — d'uomo, an ungainly man; a deformed man; (zool.) 'anlage' of an organ in an embryo.

abbozzol-are [A 1 s] *rfl.* (of flour) to go lumpy; (ent.) to make a cocoon; (silkb.) to spin in. (**-ato** *part. adj.*)

abbracciabos-co, -chi *m. indecl.* (pop.) honeysuckle.

abbracci-are [A 3] *tr.* to embrace; to hug; to encompass; to encircle; to comprise; to include; to undertake; to espouse, to take up, to embrace (cause, ideal); — un consiglio, to follow advice; — con lo sguardo, to take in at a glance; *rfl.* (*prep.* a) to cling (to); to twine (round); *recip. rfl.* to embrace each other. **-a·bile** *adj.* embraceable. **-amento** *m.* embrace, hug; encompassing. **-ante** *part. adj.* embracing; comprising. **-ata** *f.* embrace, hug; un'-ata a tutti, love to all. **-ato** *part. adj.* embraced, hugged; encircled; comprised; undertaken; †-ato di, abundantly supplied with. **-atura** *f.* embrace, hug. **-atutto** *m., f. indecl.* busybody.

abbrac·cio *m.* embrace, hug.

†**abbracciare** *tr.* (fig.) to inflame, to incense; *rfl.* to burn with fervour.

†**abbragiare** *tr.* to kindle.

abbrancare[1] [A 2] *tr.* to seize (with claws); to grasp, to catch; to apprehend; to steal; *abs.* (naut.) to hold (of an anchor); *rfl.* (*prep.* a) to seize; *recip. rfl.* to come to grips, to fight tooth and nail (from **branca**, q.v.).

abbrancare[2] [A 2] *tr.* to collect in a drove, to herd together (from **branco**, q.v.).

abbrevare [A 1] *intr.* (*aux.* avere) (naut.) to shorten the stroke (in rowing).

abbrevi-are [A 4] *tr.* to abbreviate; to abridge; to shorten; to sum up; per -arla, to cut a long story short. **-amento** *m.* abbreviation, shortening; abridgement. **-ativo** *adj.* abbreviatory. **-ato** *part. adj.* abbreviated; shortened, cut short; abridged. (**-atamente** *adv.*) **-atore** *m.* abridger; (eccl.) abbreviator. (**-atrice** *f.*) **-atura** *f.*, **-azione** *f.* abbreviation; abridgement; shortening; contraction; sign of abbreviation.

†**abbrezzare** *rfl.* to shiver, to feel cold.

abbricca·gnolo *m.* See under **abbriccare**.

abbricc-are [A 2] *rfl.* to climb, to clamber; (of plants) to twine; *tr.* — un colpo, to deliver a blow. **-a·gnolo** *m.* hold (for climbing); (fig.) cavil, pretext, handle; (orn.) tree-creeper.

abbriv-are [A 1] *intr.* (*aux.* avere) (naut.) to get under way; abbriva!, full speed ahead! **-o** *m.* (naut.) way, course, headway; pigliare l'-o, to gather way; perdere l'-o, to lose way.

abbrividire [D 2]. See **rabbrividire**.

abbri·vio *m.* see **abbrivo**, under **abbrivare**.

abbronz-are [A 1 c] *tr.* to bronze; to scorch; to colour brown; to tan; to toast; *rfl.* to get brown, to become sunburnt. **-amento** *m.*, **-ata** *f.* bronzing; touch of brown; tan, sun-tan. **-atic·cio** *adj.* slightly bronzed, lightly tanned. **-ato** *part. adj.* sun-tanned; bronzed; tawny. **-atura** *f.* bronzing, scorching; sun-tan; sun-tan make-up; (bot.) plant-rust.

abbronz-ire [D 2] *intr.* (*aux.* essere) to become sun-tanned. **-ito** *part. adj.* sun-tanned, brown.

†**abbrostire** *tr.* to toast, to scorch, to roast.

abbruciacchiare [A 4] and derivs. See **bruciacchiare**.

abbruciare [A 3] and derivs. See **bruciare**.

abbrumare [A 1] *intr.* (*aux.* essere) (naut.) to become worm-eaten, to become foul-bottomed.

abbrun-are [A 1] *tr.* to darken; to colour brown, to turn black; to drape with black (for mourning); *rfl.* to grow dark; to put on mourning. **-amento** *m.* darkening, blackening; draping; putting on of mourning. **-ato** *part. adj.* darkened, browned; wearing mourning; hung with black; bandiera -ata, flag at half-mast; lettera -ata, black-edged letter.

abbrun-ire [D 2] *tr.* to bronze, to darken; il sole -isce la pelle, the sun darkens the skin; *rfl., intr.* (*aux.* essere) to darken; to become sun-tanned. **-imento** *m.* darkening; discoloration; sun-tan. **-ito** *part. adj.* darkened; discoloured; sun-tanned.

abbruscare [A 2] *tr.* (dial. Rom.) to toast; to scorch, to singe.

abbruschiare [A 4] *tr.* (dial. S. Italy) to toast; to scorch.

abbruschino *m.* toaster, toasting implement or machine.

abbrusti-are [A 4], **-care** [A 2 s] *tr.* (dial. Tusc.) to scorch, to singe.

†**abbrustire** *tr.* to toast; to scorch; to roast.

abbrustolacaffè *m. indecl.* See under **abbrustolare**.

abbrustol-are [A 1 s] *tr.* to toast (bread); to roast (coffee); to over-cook, to burn; to singe. **-acaffè** *m. indecl.* coffee-roasting machine. **-ato** *part. adj.* toasted; roasted; scorched; pane -ato, toast.

abbrustol-ire [D 2] *tr.* to toast; to roast; to burn, to over-cook; to singe. **-imento** *m.*, **-ita** *f.* toasting; roasting; singeing. **-ito** *part. adj.* toasted; roasted; scorched; pane -ito, toast.

abbrut-ire [D 2] *tr.* to brutalize; to coarsen; to degrade; *rfl., intr.* (*aux.* essere) to become degraded, to sink to the level of a brute. **-imento** *m.* brutalization; brutishness; sottishness; brutish dejection. **-ito** *part. adj.* brutal, cruel; brutish; sottish; stupefied, dazed.

abbruttire [D 2] and derivs. See **imbruttire**.

abbuffare [A 1] *rfl.* (slang) to stuff oneself, to eat fit to burst.

abbui-are [A 4] *tr.* to darken; to tarnish; (fig.) to obscure; to hush up; *rfl.* (of weather) to darken, to become overcast; (of a person) to lapse into melancholy; (of a countenance) to cloud, to darken, to grow menacing; (of sight) to grow dim. **-amento** *m.* darkening; tarnishing; obscuring; clouding. **-ato** *part. adj.* darkened; tarnished; obscured, obscure; gloomy, clouded; glowering.

abbuono *m.* handicap, advantage, start; (sport) advantage, allowance (on time taken or distance covered); (naut.) allowance on a charter; (comm.) allowance, discount; — per ammanco, allowance for underweight. (Cf. **abbonare**[2].)

abburatt-are [A 1] *tr.* to sieve, to sift, to bolt; to choose; (fig. joc.) to discuss, to ventilate, to sift thoroughly; — le parole, to choose one's words with care; *intr.* (*aux.* avere) to chatter unceasingly. **-amento** *m.* bolting; sifting; (med.) logorrhoea. **-ata** *f.* sifting; material sifted; sieve-full. **-ato** *part. adj.* sieved; sifted; (fig.) ventilated. (**-atore** *m.* **-atrice** *f.* **-atura** *f.*) **-one** *m.* (Tusc.) chatterbox.

abburare [A 1] *tr.* (dial. Tusc.) to burn.

abbuzzire [D 2] *tr.* to cram, to stuff; *intr.* (*aux.* avere) to suffer from indigestion; *rfl.* to over-eat, to stuff oneself.

abderit-a, -ano *adj.* wanting in intelligence; *n.m.* Abderite (from Abdera, a city in Thrace of which the inhabitants were held to be stupid).

abdic-are [A 2 s] *tr.*, to abdicate; to renounce, to waive; †to repudiate; †to disinherit; *intr.* (*aux.* avere; *prep.* a) to abdicate. **-ata·rio** *adj.* abdicating. **-ativo** *adj.* abdicative. **-atore** *m.* abdicator, abdicant. **-azione** *f.* abdication; abdicating.

†**abdito** *adj.* hidden, concealed.

abdolla·o *m.* (bot.) Egyptian melon, *Melo aegyptiacus minor.*

abduano *adj.* (poet., Foscolo) of the River Adda.

ab-ducente *adj.* (med.) abducent. **-duttore** *m.* abductor. **-duzione** *f.* (med.) abduction; (logic) abduction, apagoge.

abeceda·rio *m.* See **abbecedario**.

Abele *pr.n.m.* Abel.

abe·lia *f.* (bot.) *Abelia*, genus of ornamental shrubs.

abelmosco *m.* (bot.) musk-mallow, *Hibiscus Abelmoschus.*

†**abena** *f.* rein; bridle.

†**abent-are** *tr.* to calm, to quieten; to pacify; *intr.* to be calm, to be at rest. †**-e,** †**-o** *m.* calm, repose, rest.

Aberdonta *pr.n.f.* (geog.) Aberdeen.

abergo *m.* (dial. Tusc.). See **albergo**.

aberr-are [A I] *intr.* (*aux.* avere) to err; to go astray; to deviate; (techn.) to be out of true; (astron.; opt.) to aberrate. **-ante** (physiol.) aberrant. **-azione** *f.* aberration; error; (astron.; opt.) aberration.

abesperto *adv.* by experience, experientially.

abesto *m.* See **asbesto**.

abeta·ia *f.* See under **abete**.

abet-e *m.* (bot.) fir-tree; SPECIES OF FIR: — bianco, silver fir, *Abies alba;* — rosso, spruce fir, *Picea Abies;* — balsamifero, N. American balsam fir, *Abies balsamifera;* — bianco del Canadà, white spruce, *Picea glauca;* — del Canadà, hemlock fir, *Tsuga canadensis;* — nero, — americano, American black spruce, *Picea mariana;* (poet.) ship; mast; rudder; (naut.) — di rispetto, jury mast, reserve poles; **-a·ia** *f.* fir-forest; grove of firs. **-ella** *f.* fir pole; scaffold pole; pole for gymnastics. **-ina** *f.* grove of firs; fir pole. **-ino** *m. dim.* of abete; (ent.) *Hylobius abietis*, fir weevil.

abeto *m.* (Tusc.). See **abete**.

abezzo *m.* (dial. Tusc.). See **abete**.

abia·tico *adj.* (leg.) belonging to, or left by, a grandparent. See also **abbiatico**.

ab-ietato *m.* (chem.) abietate. **-ie·tico** *adj.* (chem.) abietic. **-ietina** *f.* (chem.) abietin(e). **-ietino** *adj.* smelling of fir resin.

abiett-are [A I] *rfl.* to become depraved. **-amento** *m.* depravation. **-ato** *part. adj.* depraved. **-azione** *f.* depravation; depravity.

abiett-o *adj.* despicable; mean, low, vile; depraved; degraded; abject, lowly. (**-amente** *adv.*) **-ezza** *f.* abjectness; baseness; vileness.

abiezione *f.* depravity; degradation; abjection; lowly estate; †low level (of water); †scarcity.

abi·ge-o *m.* (leg.) cattle-thief. **-ato** *m.* (leg.) cattle-stealing.

a·bil-e *adj.* able; capable; experienced; clever; skilful; talented; competent; suitable, fit; qualified, eligible; (mil.) — al servizio militare, fit for military service. **-mente** *adv.* skilfully; cleverly; wisely; †easily.

abilit-à *f.* (*prep.* a, per) ability, aptitude, skill; cleverness, adroitness; tact; permission, facility, access; fare — a, to permit; †suitability, opportuneness. **-are** [A I S] *tr.* to qualify, to pass; to train; to enable; (leg.) to empower, to make competent, fit, or legally entitled; *rfl.* to qualify, to become qualified; to become skilled, to train. **-ato** *part. adj.* qualified; enabled. **-azione** *f.* qualification; diploma, certificate; competency; diploma d'-azione all'insegnamento, teaching diploma.

abilmente *adv.* See under **abile**.

†**abindu-e, -o** *prn.* See **ambedue**.

abioge·nesi *f.* (biol.) abiogenesis.

abisse *m.* (dial. Tusc., Rom.). See **lapis**.

Abiss-i·nia *pr.n.f.* (geog.) *f.* Abyssinia. **-ino** *adj., n.m.* Abyssinian. (**-ina** *f.*)

abiss-o *m.* ocean deep; sea-bottom; whirlpool; abyss; gulf; chasm; bottomless pit; hell; (fig.) mine, treasure; vast quantity; un — d'iniquità, a monster of iniquity; †*adj.* deep, impenetrable. **-ale** *adj.* abysmal; deep (of colours); (zool.) fauna -ale, abyssal fauna. †**-are** *tr.* to submerge, to sink; *intr., rfl.* to sink; to decline; to fall.

abita·colo *m.* See under **abitare**.

abit-are [A I S] *tr.* to populate; to inhabit; to occupy; to haunt, to frequent; *intr.* (*aux.* avere) to live, to dwell, to reside. **-a·bile** *adj.* habitable, inhabitable; stanze -abili, living rooms. **-abilità** *f.* habitableness; **-a·colo** *m.* dwelling; (aeron.) -acolo del pilota, cockpit; (naut.) binnacle, compass box. †**-amento** *m.* dwelling-place; dwelling, inhabiting. **-ante** *part. adj.* inhabiting; †containing; *n.m.* inhabitant; resident; dweller; tenant. †**-anza** *f.*

dwelling-place, habitation; inhabiting, dwelling. **-ato** *part. adj.* inhabited; paese molto -ato, thickly populated country; *n.m.* inhabited district, houses, built-up area; village, hamlet. **-atore** *m.* inhabitant. (**-atrice** *f.*) **-azione** *f.* habitation; residence; dwelling, house; haunt; crisi delle -azioni, housing-problem. **-evole** *adj.* habitable.

a·bit-o¹ *m.* habit, custom; tendency; (med.) physical constitution, nature; (schol. philos.) habit, habitus.

a·bit-o² *m.* clothes, costume; gown; ceremonial garment; — militare, military attire; — da sera, evening dress; — da società, dress clothes (man's); — completo, suit of clothes, -i fatti, ready-made clothes; — su misura, suit made to measure; (eccl.) habit; vestire l'—, to enter the religious life; spogliare l'—, to leave the religious life; l'— non fa il monaco, 'all hoods make not monks'; (layfolk's) scapular; — talare, (priest's) cassock. **-ifi·cio** *m.* (neol.) clothing-firm, clothiers. **-ino** *m.* little dress; frock; (eccl.) scapular (as worn by layfolk).

abittare [A I] and derivs. See **abbittare**.

abitual-e *adj.* habitual, usual, customary; (theol.) grazia —, habitual grace; (med.) recurrent. **-mente** *adv.* habitually, usually. **-ità** *f.* habitualness; (leg.) habitual condition.

abitu-are [A 6] *tr.* to accustom, to inure; *rfl.* (*prep.* a) to accustom oneself (to); to get used (to). **-ato** *part. adj.* accustomed; inured; †clad, clothed, arrayed.

abitudina·rio *adj.* of fixed habits; *n.m.* person of fixed habits.

abitu·dine *f.* habit, custom; rule, practice; natural disposition, tendency; per —, out of habit, by habit.

abitura *f.* See **abituro**.

abituro *m.* hovel, poor cottage, hut; garret; †dwelling.

abiur-a *f.* (eccl.) abjuration. **-are** [A I] *tr.* to abjure; to renounce formally; to forswear. **-ante** *part. adj.* abjuring; *n.m., f.* abjurer. **-ato** *part. adj.* abjured; renounced. (**-atore** *m.* **-atrice** *f.* **-azione** *f.*)

†**ablasmare** *tr.* to blame.

ablativo *adj.* (gramm.) ablative; — assoluto, ablative absolute; (colloq.) essere ridotto all'— assoluto, to be penniless.

ablazione *f.* (geol.) erosion; (surg.) extraction, removal, ablation.

ablegato *m.* (eccl.) ablegate.

ablu-ente *adj.* (med.) abluent; *n.m.* abluent, abstergent. **-zione** *f.* washing, purification; (liturg.) ablution.

abneg-are [A 2] *tr.* to abnegate, to renounce. **-azione** *f.* abnegation, renunciation, sacrifice; self-denial; unselfishness, devotion.

abnorme *adj.* (scient.) abnormal.

abol-ire [D 2] *tr.* to abolish; to annul; to repeal; to abrogate. **-i·bile** *adj.* abolishable. **-endo** *adj.* (neol.) fit to be abolished; about to be abolished. **-imento** *m.* abolishment, abolition. **-itivo** *adj.* leggi -itive dell'usura, laws abolishing usury. (**-itore** *m.*) **-izione** *f.* abolition; cessation; repeal. **-izionismo** *m.* abolitionism. **-izionista** *m.* abolitionist. **-izioni·stico** *adj.* relating to abolitionism.

abolla *f.* (Rom. and Ital. antiq.) abolla, woollen cloak worn by soldiers and peasants.

abo·maso *m.* (vet.) abomasum.

abomin-are [A I S] *tr.* to abominate, to detest, to hold in horror. **-a·bile** *adj.* abominable, detestable, hateful. **-amento** *m.* abominating, detesting. **-ando** *adj.* to be abominated; hateful; nefarious; *n.m.* (eccl.) abominarium. **-a·rio** *m.* (eccl.) abominarium. **-ato** *part. adj.* abominated; abominable. **-azione** *f.* abomination; detestation; †repugnance, nausea. **-evole** *adj.* abominable. (†**-oso** *adj.*)

abomi·nio *m.* shame, disgrace, abomination; †abuse; †evil reputation.

†**abondare** *vb.* and derivs. See **abbondare**.

abori·g-eno, -ene, -ine *adj.* aboriginal; (bot.) indigenous, native; *n.m.pl.* aborigines, natives.

aborniello *m.* See **avorniello**.

†**aborrare** *vb.* and derivs. See **aberrare**.

aborr-ire [D I, D 2] *tr.* to abhor; to loathe; *intr.* (*aux.* avere; *prep.* da) to have a dread (of), to shrink (from), to feel repugnance (for), to abhor. **-ente** *part. adj.* (*prep.* da) abhorring; unwilling, reluctant. **-imento** *m.* abhorrence. **-ito** *part. adj.* abhorrent; abhorred, detested, loathed. **-itore** *m.* abhorrer. (**-itrice** *f.*)

abort-ire [D 2] *intr.* (*aux.* avere) (med.) to abort; to miscarry, to have a miscarriage; (bot.) to fail, to be blasted; (fig.) to miscarry, to fail. **-ivo** *adj.* (med.) abortive; arrested; abortifacient; (bot.) imperfect (of untimely fruit); (fig.) abortive, unfinished. **-o** *m.* (med.) abortion; miscarriage; (bot.) fruit that fails to ripen; (fig.) deformed person; unfinished work of art; failure; (tanning) slunk.

†**abo·scino**, †**abo·sino** *m.* plum.

abracadabra *m. indecl.* abracadabra; mumbo-jumbo; play on words.

abraccare [A 2] *tr.* (dial. Cors.) (naut.) to place (ships) alongside.

abra·dere [C 3] *tr.* to abrade.

Abramo *pr.n.m.* Abraham.

abraṣ-ivo *adj., n.m.* abrasive. **~iọne** *f.* abrasion; (leg.) erasure (C.C.).

abraṣo *part.* of **abradere**, q.v.

abraxe·o *adj.* (poet.) inscribed with the abraxas (a Cabalistic word inscribed on gems as a charm); *n.m.* talisman.

abrazite *f.* (miner.) abrazite, gismondite.

abreagire [D 2] *intr.* (*aux.* avere) (psychol.) to abreact.

†**abrego** *m.* S.W. wind.

abri·vio *m.* See **abbrivo**, under **abbrivare**.

abro *m.* (bot.) *Abrus*, tropical genus of Leguminosae; poison extracted from *Abrus precatorius*.

abrog-are [A 2 s] *tr.* (leg.) to revoke, to repeal, to abrogate. **-a·bile** *adj.* repealable. **-ato·rio** *adj.* (leg.) effecting an abrogation. **-aziọne** *f.* (leg.) repeal, reversal, abrogation.

abro·stine *m.* (bot.) foxgrape, *Vitis labrusca*.

abro·tane *f.* (bot.) — femmina, lavender-cotton, *Santolina chamae-cyparissus*.

abro·tano *m.* (bot.) southernwood, lad's love, old man, *Artemisia abrotanum*.

Abruzz-o *pr.n. m.,* **-i** *pr.n. m.pl.* (geog.) Abruzzi. **-ẹse** *adj.* of the Abruzzi; *n.m.,f.* native of the Abruzzi; *m.* dialect of the Abruzzi.

absentiṣmo *m.* See **absintismo**, under **absintio**.

ab·sid-e[1], **-a** *f.* (liturg.; archit.) apse.

ab·side[2] *m.* (geom.; astron.) apsis.

absintina *f.* oil of wormwood.

absint-io *m.* (bot.) *Absinthium*, wormwood. **~iṣmo** *m.* (med.) absinthism.

ab-uli·a *f.* (med.) abulia, loss of will-power. **-u·lico** *adj.* (med.) abulic, lacking in will-power.

abuṣ-are [A I] *intr.* (*aux.* avere, *prep.* di) to misuse, to abuse; to use to excess, to over-indulge in; to take advantage of; — del tempo di, to trespass upon (a person's) time; (with *inf., prep.* in) -a nel bere, he drinks too much; *rfl.* (*prep.* di) to take advantage (of). **-ato** *part. adj.* misused, abused; used to excess. (**-atọre** *m.* **-atrice** *f.*) †**-iọne** *f.* misuse; disuse, neglect; illusion, mistake; (gramm.) catachresis. **-iviṣmo** *m.* (neol.) improper use of a profession. **-ivo** *adj.* wrong, wrongful, improper; irregular; without authorization; excessive. (**-ivamẹnte** *adv.*) **-o** *m.* abuse; excessive use; misuse; ~o di confidenza, breach of confidence; per ~o, improperly, illicitly; wrongly; fare ~o di, to make excessive use of; fa ~o di caffè, he drinks too much coffee.

abuzza-go *m.* (*pl.* **-ghi**) (orn.) buzzard.

aca·cia *f.* (bot.) — comune bianca, acacia, *Robinia pseudacacia*; (in U.S.A.) locust tree; mimosa, Australian wattle (and various other species of *Acacia*); — ad ombrello, — di Costantinopoli, *Acacia Julibrissin*; — da fiori rosei, rose acacia, *Robinia hispida*; — spinosa, American honey-locust, *Gleditschia triacanthos*.

acagiù *m. indecl.* (bot.) cashew-nut, fruit of *Anacardium occidentale*; — da mobili, mahogany, wood of *Swietenia mahagoni*; — da farmacie, *Soymida febrifuga*; — della Nuova Olanda, *Eucalyptus robusta*.

†**acanino** *adj.* dear, beloved.

acanto *m.* (bot.) acanthus, bear's breech thistle, *Acanthus mollis*; (archit.) acanthus leaf.

acantoce·fali *m.pl.* (zool.) Acanthocephala, hookworms.

acant-otteri, **-otte·rigi** *m.pl.* (ichth.) Acanthopterygii, the spiny-finned fishes. **-uro** *m.* (ichth.) *Acanthurus* spp., surgeon fish.

acap·nia[1] *f.* dynamite powder.

acapni·a[2] *f.* (med.) lack of carbonic acid in the blood.

a·caro *m.* (zool.) mite; — dotto, *Cheyletus doctus*, book mite.

acaro·ide *f.* acaroid resin.

acarpo *adj.* (bot.) sterile, unfruiting.

acatafasi·a *f.* (med.) acataphasia.

acata-lessi·a *f.* (philos.; med.) acatalepsy; inability to relate ideas. **-let·tico**, **-letto** *adj.* (med.) suffering from acatalepsy; (philos.) acataleptic, not comprehensible; (prosod.) acatalectic.

acata·poṣi *f.* (med.) inability to swallow.

acatarsi·a *f.* (med.) acatharsia.

acate[1] *m.* See **agata[1]**.

Acate[2] *pr.n.m.* (myth.) Acates; (fig.) fido —, faithful companion.

†**acato** *m.* See **agata[1]**.

a(c)catto·lico *adj., n.m.* non-Catholic.

acca[1] *f., m.* the letter H; (fig.) a mere nothing; non vale un'—, it's not worth a fig; non ci capisco un'—, it's all Greek to me; (Tusc.) saper quattr'acche, to have a smattering.

†**acca[2]** *f.* horse.

accade·mia *f.* Academy; society; college, high school, institute; — aeronautica, flying school; formal recitation or performance; School of Art; Art Gallery; study from the nude; (joc.) senseless argument, empty words; far dell'—, to talk to no purpose; †(mus.) a private concert; †musical entertainment composed for a private concert.

accade·m-ico *adj.* academic; theoretic; alpinista —, member of the Club Alpino Accademico; *n.m.* academician; — d'Italia, member of the Italian Academy (now extinct); student at an academy. (**-icamẹnte** *adv.*) **-ista** *m.* member of a military school, cadet; pupil at an academy.

accad-ere [B 5] *intr.* (*aux.* essere) to happen, to occur; to befall; to come about, to chance; accada quel che accada, come what may; to be suitable, to be opportune; †to fall; (with *neg.* or *interrog.*) to be of importance, to be necessary: non accade, it is not necessary. †**-enza** *f.* occurrence, event. **-imento** *m.* event, happening, occurrence. **-uto** *part. adj.*; *n.m.* event, happening, occurrence; matter, case; accident.

†**accaffare** *tr.* to seize, to snatch.

†**accaggente** *adj.* opportune.

accagion-are [A I c] *tr.* to accuse, to impute, to inculpate; (*prep.* di) to charge (with), to blame (on). †**-amento** *m.* accusation. **-ato** *part. adj.* accused; charged. **-atọre** *m.* accuser. (**-atrice** *f.*) †**-e·vole** *adj.* blameworthy, culpable.

accagiù *m. indecl.* See **acagiù**.

accagli-are [A 4] *tr.* to curdle; to cause to coagulate; *rfl., intr.* (*aux.* avere) to curdle; to coagulate. **-amento** *m.* curdling; coagulating. **-ato** *part. adj.* curdled; coagulated. (**-atura** *f.*)

accalappiacani *m. indecl.* See under **accalappiare**.

accalappi-are [A 4] *tr.* to catch, to ensnare; to allure; to deceive; to trick; *rfl.* to get into difficulties. **-acani** *m. indecl.* dog-catcher. **-amento** *m.* ensnaring; (fig.) deceit, trickery; allurement. **-atọre** *m.* deceiver. (**-atrice** *f.*) **-atura** *f.* ensnaring; trickery.

accalc-are [A 2] *tr.* to crowd; to heap; *rfl.* to throng, to crowd, to bustle. **-amento** *m.* crowding; crowd, bustle. (**-ato** *part. adj.*)

accald-are [A I] *rfl.* to grow warm, to get over-heated; (fig.) to get excited, to get heated. **-ato** *part. adj.* warm, hot, over-heated; (fig.) excited, heated.

accallare [A I] *tr.* (dial. Lucca, Pistoia) to half-close, to leave ajar.

†**accalognare** *tr.* to calumniate, to slander.

accalor-are [A I c] *tr.* to excite; to incite; to warm up, to heat; *rfl.* to excite oneself; to become animated; to become exasperated; to work oneself into a fury. **-amento** *m.* excitement; animation; exasperation. **-ato** *part. adj.* excited, animated.

accalorire [D 2] and derivs. See **accalorare**.

†**accamiciare** *vb.* and derivs. See **incamiciare**.

accampamẹnto *m.* See under **accampare**.

accampan-are [A I] *tr.* (bot.) to train (a grape-vine) into the form of a bell. **-ato** *part. adj.* bell-shaped.

accamp-are [A I] *tr.* (mil.) to camp; to encamp; (fig.) to allege, to put forth, to assert (a right); to marshal, to set forth (pretexts); to set up (excuses); †to lead into battle; *rfl., intr.* (*aux.* avere) (mil.) to camp, to be encamped; to pitch one's tent; to go camping. **-amento** *m.* encampment, camp; camping; camping-site; il necessario per l'—amento, camping equipment. **-ato** *part. adj.* encamped, camped; alleged; asserted; marshalled.

accampion-are [A I c] *tr.* (leg.) to enter on the land-register; (comm.) to make a sample of. (**-ato** *part. adj.*)

accanalare [A I] *tr.* to channel; (archit.) see **scanellare**.

†**accan-are** *tr.* to set a dog upon. †**-ato** *part. adj.* pursued, hard-pressed; rabid, frenzied; †tenere ~ato, to hold in check. †**-eggiare** *tr.* to set a dog upon; to hound, to hunt; to pursue; to dun, to importune.

accan-ire [D 2] *tr.* to enrage; to infuriate; *rfl.* to become enraged; to be implacable; to work with feverish determination; to persist obstinately. **-imento** *m.* rage; bitterness; obstinacy, persistence. **-ito** *part. adj.* enraged, frenzied; bitter; dogged; inexorable; relentless; obstinate, persistent; un'-ita resistenza, a stiff opposition, a stubborn resistance. **-itamẹnte** *adv.* furiously; tenaciously, doggedly.

accannatoio *m.* (text.) rod for moving the stay of a loom.

accannell-are [A I] *tr.* (text.) to wind on to the spool; †(archit.) to flute. (-**amento** *m.* -**ato** *part. adj.*)

accanto *adv.* beside, near, by, nearby; †next, afterwards; *prep. phr.* — **a**, next to, beside.

accanton-are [A I C] *tr.* to set aside, to reserve; to put away; (euphem.) to 'eliminate', to 'put away'; to pigeon-hole, to shelve; to put on one side for the time being; (mil.) to quarter; (comm.) — una somma a riserva, to transfer an amount to a reserve fund. -**amento** *m.* reserving, setting on one side; pigeon-holing; (mil.) quartering; billet; cantonment. -**ato** *part. adj.* set aside, saved; pigeon-holed, shelved; (mil.) quartered; (herald.) -ato di, between.

accantonato *adj.* (archit.) angular, having corners.

accapacci-are [A 3] *rfl., intr.* (*aux.* essere) to feel heavy-headed; con questo sole c'è da —, this sun is too hot for one's head. (-**amento** *m.* -**ato** *part. adj.*) -**atura** *f.* touch of the sun.

†**accapare** *tr.* to bring to completion, to get to the end of.

accaparr-are [A I] *tr.* to engage, to book, to secure (by paying a deposit); to hoard; to corner; (fig.) to procure, to obtain, to gain; to seize. -**amento** *m.* (comm.) cornering; hoarding. (-**ato** *part. adj.*) -**atore** *m.* hoarder. (-**atrice** *f.*)

†**accapegliare** *vb.* See **accapigliare**.

accapezzare[1] [A I C] *tr.* to bring to completion, to terminate; (bldg.) to dress, to trim (stones).

†**accapezzare**[2] *tr.* to put a halter on.

accapì (neol.) H.P., i.e. British horse-power. The Italian horse-power is called **cavallo vapore**, abbreviated CV. (1 H.P. = 1·0139 CV.)

accapigli-are [A 4] *recip. rfl.* to scuffle, to tear each other's hair; to come to blows; to dispute, to argue; to squabble; †*tr.* to enrage, to incite. -**amento** *m.* scuffle, quarrel; contest; dispute. (-**atore** *m.* -**atrice** *f.*) -**atura** *f.* scuffling, quarrelling.

accappare [A I] *tr.* (Tusc., Umbr.) to choose, to pick.

accappatoio *m.* loose wrap; dressing-gown; dressing-jacket; bath-robe; beach-wrap.

accappi-are [A 4] *tr.* to catch in a noose, to lasso; to tie in a noose; (fig.) to ensnare. (-**ato** *part. adj.*) -**atura** *f.* slip-knot; noose, lasso. -**ettare** [A I C] to snare.

accapo *adv.* See under **capo**; *n.m. indecl.* beginning of a new paragraph.

accappon-are[1] [A I C] *tr.* to caponize, to castrate; *rfl.* (of flesh) to creep; mi si -a la pelle, my hair stands on end; *intr.* (infin. after fare) racconti che fanno — la pelle, stories which make one's flesh creep. -**ato** *part. adj.* castrated; pelle -ata, goose-flesh. -**atura** *f.* caponizing; creepy feeling.

accapponare[2] [A I C] *tr.* (naut.). See **capponare**[1], under **cappone**.

accappucci-are [A 3] *tr.* to put a hood on; *rfl.* to put on a hood, to cover one's head. -**ato** *part. adj.* hooded; (vet.) ewe-necked (of a horse).

accaprettare [A I C] (Tusc., Umbr.) *tr.* to tie the four feet together (as of lambs, goats).

†**accapricci-are** *tr.* to fill with horror; *rfl.* to feel horror, to shudder; to be capricious. †-**ato** *part. adj.* bristling, with hair on end.

†**accareggiare** *vb.* and derivs. See **accarezzare**.

accarezz-are [A I C] *tr.* to caress, to fondle; to stroke, to pat; to cherish, to nurse (illusion, resentment); to flatter; to smooth; (iron.) — le spalle con un bastone, to cudgel, to beat. -**amento** *m.* fondling; caress; cherishing. -**ativo** *adj.* amorous; caressing. -**ato** *part. adj.* caressed; cherished; (of a child) indulged, petted. -**atore** *m.* fondler; cherisher; flatterer. -**atura** *f.* caressing, caress; cherishing. -**evole** *adj.* caressing, soothing; flattering, coaxing; affectionate.

†**accarnare** *tr.* to wound, to pierce; to flesh; (fig.) to envisage, to grasp, to seize, to understand.

accarpionare [A I C] and derivs. See **carpionare**.

†**accartato** *adj.* (bibliogr.) numbered, paginated, paged.

accartocci-are [A 3] *tr.* to curl, to twist into a cone; to wrap up; to shrivel; (bot.) to cause to roll up (as of leaves); (archit.) to form into a scroll or cartouche; *rfl.* to curl up; to shrivel. -**amento** *m.* curling up; wrapping up; shrivelling; (archit.) frieze formed of scrolls, cartouches or corbels. -**ato** *part. adj.* curled up; wrapped up; shrivelled. -**atori** *m.pl.* (ent.) leaf-rollers. -**atura** *f.* curling, twisting.

accas-are [A I] *tr.* to settle, to marry off (a daughter); *rfl.* to marry, to settle down, to set up house. -**amento** *m.* settling down; marrying off. -**ato** *part. adj.* married; settled; †built-up, resi-

dential; *n.m.* (sport) racing-cyclist representing a cycling firm. (-**atore** *m.* -**atrice** *f.*)

†**accascare** *intr.* to occur, to happen; to be necessary.

accasci-are [A 3] *tr.* to weaken; to crush, to dispirit; *rfl.* to collapse; -arsi su una poltrona, to sink wearily into an armchair; to break down, to give way (to emotion); to lose strength; to lose courage; (naut.) to pound (of a ship aground). -**amento** *m.* dejection, despondency; moral collapse; crushing, weakening. -**ato** *part. adj.* dejected, dispirited; weakened; in a state of collapse.

accaserm-are [A I] *tr., rfl.* (mil.) to quarter in barracks. -**amento** *m.* (mil.) quartering, lodging in barracks. -**ato** *part. adj.* in barracks.

accastell-are [A I] *tr.* to pile, to heap up, to build up into a pyramid. -**amento** *m.* heaping up; heap, pile; (naut.) upper works (of a ship). -**ato** *part. adj.* heaped up; (naut.) nave -ata, ship having forecastle and poop.

accatarr-are [A I] *intr.* (*aux.* essere), *rfl.* to catch cold; to get catarrh. (-**amento** *m.*) -**ato** *part. adj.* suffering from a cold. (-**atura** *f.*)

accatast-are[1] [A I] *tr.* to heap, to pile up (wood). -**amento** *m.* stacking, piling; stack, pile. -**ato** *part. adj.* heaped, stacked.

accatast-are[2] [A I] *tr.* to register (property) for assessment. (-**amento** *m.*) -**ato** *part. adj.* registered for assessment.

†**accattamento** *m.* homage, reverence, obsequience, bow.

accatt-are[1] [A I] *tr.* to beg; to borrow; to scrounge; (fig.) — lodi, to look for praise; — pretese, to seek excuses; (math.) to borrow (in subtracting); *abs.* to go begging; to collect alms; essere ridotto ad —, to be reduced to beggary. -**abriga**, -**abrighe** *m. indecl.* quarrelsome person; mischief-maker; busybody. -**afieno** *m. indecl.* hay-gathering machine. -**aglimpacci** *m. indecl.* trouble-maker. -**amento** *m.* begging; borrowing. †-**amori** *f. indecl.* flirt. -**ano** *m.* (dial. Tusc.) collector for charity. -**apane** *m. indecl.* beggar, mendicant. -**arotto** *m.* (dial. Lucca) beggar. -**ato** *part. adj.* begged; borrowed. -**atore** *m.* beggar; borrower. (-**atrice** *f.*) -**atozzi** *m. indecl.* beggar. -**eri·a** *f.* begging; beggary. -**ino** *m.* (dial. Tusc.) collector for charity. -**o·lica** *f.* (joc.) begging, alms-collecting. -**onag·gio** *m.* begging; beggary. -**one** *m.* beggar, mendicant: vagrant; (fig.) è un -one di lodi, he's always on the lookout for praise.

†**accattare**[2] *tr.* to buy; to earn; to obtain.

accatto[1] *m.* begging; collecting of alms; amount collected, collection; loan; campar d'—, to live by begging; sapienza d'—, second-hand knowledge; derivation, borrowing; in questa poesia abbondanti sono gli accatti danteschi, there are numerous borrowings from Dante in this poem.

†**accatto**[2] *m.* purchase.

accavalcare [A 2] and derivs. See **cavalcare**.

accavalci-are [A 3] *tr.* to bestride. (-**ato** *part. adj.*) -**one**, -**oni** *adv.* astride.

accavall-are [A I] *tr.* to superimpose; to cross (one thing over another); — le gambe, to cross one's legs; to stagger, to space; (typ.) to inset; (text.) to skip (threads in weaving); — una maglia, to slip one stitch over another (in knitting); †to place on horse-back; *recip. rfl.* to pile on top of one another, to ride, to overlap; le onde si -ano, the waves form breakers; (med.) to be out of place (of nerves, muscles); to ride over one another (of broken ends of bone); †(naut.) le catene si sono -ate, the cable has got a cross in it. (-**amento** *m.*) -**ato** *part. adj.* crossed; overlapping. (-**atura** *f.*)

accavigli-are [A 4] *tr.* (text.) to wind on a bobbin; (naut.) to turn up, to take turns in. (-**ato** *part. adj.* -**atore** *m.* -**atrice** *f.*)

accec-are [A 2 d] *tr.* to blind; to dazzle; to obstruct, to block, to stop up; to wall up; to cancel, to blot, to scratch out; to mist, to blur; to darken; to countersink (the head of a nail, screw); (needle-w.) — un punto, to back-stitch; (bot.) to disbud, to prune; (naut.) to stop (a leak); *rfl., intr.* (*aux.* essere) to go blind; (of colours) to fade; (fig.) to become blind, to grow indifferent. -**amento** *m.* blinding; blindness; darkness; confusion, ignorance; obstruction; stoppage; walling-up. -**ante** *part. adj.* blinding, dazzling. -**ato** *part. adj.* blinded; -ato dall'ira, blind with rage; -ato dalla sua passione per, blinded by his love of; dazzled; blocked up; blotted out; misty, blurred. -**atoio** *m.* countersinking drill, rose bit. (-**atore** *m.* -**atrice** *f.*) -**atura** *f.* blinding; hollow (made by rose bit). (-**azione** *f.*) See also **acciecare**.

acce·dere [B I] *intr.* (*aux.* essere, *prep.* a) to accede; to assent, to agree; to adhere; to enter; to approach; (leg.) — a, to view, to carry out a judicial investigation on the spot; (eccl.) — a, to vote for by second choice at a papal election.

†**acceffare** *tr.* to seize with the jaws, to snap up.

accęggia *f.* (orn.) woodcock.

acceler-are [A I s] *tr., abs.* to accelerate, to hasten, to quicken; *rfl.* to become quicker, to hasten; (mus.) to quicken. **-amęnto** *m.* acceleration. **-ando** (mus.) accelerando. **-ativo** *adj.* accelerating; quickening. **-ato** *part. adj.* accelerated; quick; polso -ato, rapid pulse; treno -ato, slow train; marcia -ata, quick march. **-atamęnte** *adv.* acceleratedly; hastily; speedily. **-atore** *m.* accelerator; (cinem.) time-lapse camera. (**-atrice** *f.*) **-azione** *f.* acceleration; quickening, speeding-up. **-o·grafo** *m.* acceleration recorder. **-o·metro** *m.* accelerometer.

†**accellana** *f.* cloth of linen and wool.

accenciato *adj.* (Lucca) squatting; bundled out of the way.

accen·d-ere [C I] *tr.* to light, to kindle; to set fire to; (fig.) to inflame, to fire, to incite, to excite; to switch on; l'ora d'— le luci, lighting-up time; — la radio, to switch on the wireless; (joc.) — l'ombrello, to put up one's umbrella; (leg.) — un debito, to register a debt; — un'ipoteca, to raise a mortgage; (comm.) — un conto, to open an account; (naut.) — i fuochi, to raise steam; *rfl.* to be kindled, to light; to ignite; to light up; to catch fire; to become illumined; (fig.) -ersi d'amore per, to fall in love with; -ersi in volto, to blush; to flush, -ersi d'ira, to fly into a rage; *n.m.* (dial. S. Italy) match. **-ęvole** *adj.*, **-i·bile** *adj.* inflammable; combustible. **-ifuoco** *m. indecl.* fire-lighter. **-i·gliolo** *m.* faggot, fire-lighter. **-ilume** *m. indecl.* lamp-lighter. (**-imento** *m.*) **-ino** *m.*, **-isi·garo** *m. indecl.* cigarette-lighter. **-itoio** *m.* pilot-burner. **-itore** *m.* lighter; -itore automatico, cigarette-lighter. (**-itrice** *f.*)

accenn-are [A I c] *tr., intr.* (aux. avere, prep. a) to nod at, to point at, to indicate; to sign to; to beckon to; to hint at, to allude to; to mention; to show signs of; (art) to sketch lightly, to outline; (at cards) to announce; (slang) — l'asso, to be blind in one eye; — un pugno, to make as though to hit; (with *infin.*, *prep.* a, di); il tempo -a di calmarsi, the weather looks like clearing up; *recip. rfl.* to make signs to one another, to signal to one another. (**-amento** *m.*) **-ato** *part. adj.* indicated; su -ato, above-mentioned.

accęnno *m.* indication, hint, allusion; sign; brief outline; suggestion, air, taste; un — di, a touch of.

accensi·bile *adj.* ignitible, inflammable; excitable, irascible; touchy.

accensiǫne *f.* ignition, lighting; candela d'—, sparking plug; — a scintilla, spark ignition; flush, high colour; (med.) flushing; (of colours) brightness, vividness; (comm.) — di un conto, opening of an account.

accenso *adj.* (poet.). See **acceso**.

accent-are [A I] *tr.* to accent, to mark with an accent; to accentuate; to stress, to emphasize; (mus.) to accent. **-ato** *part. adj.* accented; written with an accent; stressed. **-atura** *f.*, **-azione** *f.* accenting, emphasizing, accentuation; emphasis.

accęnto *m.* accent, pronunciation; stress; emphasis; tone (of voice); (written) accent; (mus.) accent; (poet.) word, utterance, voice; *pl.* (poet.) strains.

accentorini *m.pl.* (eccl.) clerical singers in choir.

accentr-are [A I] *tr.* to centralize; to gather, to assemble, to collect; *rfl.* to become centralized; to assemble, to collect, to gather; to centre, to be focused: l'attenzione della stampa si -a su, the attention of the press is focused on. **-amento** *m.* centralizing; centralization. (**-ato** *part. adj.* **-atore** *m.* **-atrice** *f.*)

accentu-are [A 6] *tr.* to accentuate; to accent; to emphasize, to stress; (mus.) to play with expression. **-ale** *adj.* accentual. **-ato** *part. adj.* accentuated, marked, noticeable; emphasized, stressed. **-atamęnte** *adv.* markedly, noticeably; emphatically. **-azione** *f.* accentuation; stress, emphasis.

accepp-are [A I c] *tr.* (naut.) to fix the stock on (an anchor); to secure by the stock. (**-amento** *m.* **-ato** *part. adj.* **-atura** *f.*)

accerchi-are [A 4 c] *tr.* to encircle; to circumvent; to cheat; (mil.) to surround. **-amento** *m.* encircling; circuit, tour; politica d'-amento, policy of encirclement. (**-ato** *part. adj.*)

accerchiell-are [A I] *tr.* to wire (a packing case); to bind with hoops. **-ato** *part. adj.* wired; bound with hoops; (herald.) croce -ata, cross moline, cross recercely.

accerito *adj.* (Tusc.) frowning; †flushed, heated, rosy.

accerpellato *adj.* pock-marked, scarred.

†**accerrare** [A I] *tr.* (text.) to fringe, to make the selvage of.

accert-are [A I] *tr.* to ascertain, to verify; to check; to certify; to confirm, to assure; to assess; — la mira, to take careful aim; †*intr.* to hit the mark; to be successful; *rfl.* (*prep.* di) to make sure, to assure oneself; to seek confirmation; accèrtati, rest assured.

-a·bile *adj.* ascertainable; verifiable. **-amento** *m.* ascertaining; verification, check; assurance; confirmation; (finan.) tax assessment. **-ato** *part. adj.* ascertained, verified, checked; confirmed; certified. **-atamęnte** *adv.* assuredly.

accertello *m.* (orn.) lesser kestrel.

†**accerto** *m.* certainty.

accęs-o *part.* of **accendere**, q.v.; *adj.* alight, lit, kindled, burning; switched on; (herald.) with eyes; — d'amore, smitten, in love; — d'ira, furious, enraged; bright, vivid; lively; rosso —, fiery red; flushed; sparkling, brilliant; un radicale —, a violent Radical; (comm.) conto —, open account. **-amęnte** *adv.* ardently, fervently; passionately.

access-i·bile *adj.* accessible; approachable; affable; (of ideas) easily understood. **-ibilità** *f.* accessibility; affability. **-iǫne** *f.* (leg.) accession (to a treaty); accretion (to property) by natural causes; (med.) increase (of a fever), onset (of a disease); (astron.) new moon.

accessit *m.* (Lat.) honourable mention; proxime accessit; promotion.

accęsso *m.* access, entry, entrance; (min.) adit; admittance; accessibility; di facile —, affable; — d'ira, access of rage; (leg.) view, judicial inspection; (med.) fit; attack (of a recurrent disease); (eccl.) access, accessus.

accessǫr-io *m.* accessory; addition; appurtenance; *pl.* fittings; *adj.* additional, supplementary. **-amęnte** *adv.* additionally.

accest-ire [D 2] *intr.* (*aux.* avere) (bot.) to form a head (as cabbage, lettuce); to produce shoots in a cluster. (**-imęnto** *m.* **-ito** *part. adj.*)

accętt-a *f.* hatchet, chopper; battle-axe; adze; fatto con l'—, clumsily made; (of a person) rough, uncouth; darsi l'— sui piedi, to cook one's goose. **-ata** *f.* blow with a hatchet; (vet.) dip of the neck in a horse.

accett-are [A I] *tr.* to accept; to approve, to admit; to agree to; to receive, to welcome; to undertake; (leg.) — una cambiale, to accept a bill of exchange. **-a·bile** *adj.* acceptable, admissible. **-abilmęnte** *adv.* acceptably. **-ante** *m.* (leg.) acceptor; -ante per intervento, acceptor for honour. **-ato** *part. adj.* accepted; admitted; agreed; welcome. **-atore** *m.* acceptor. **-azione** *f.* acceptance; reception; (leg.) acceptance (of a bill of exchange); an accepted bill; mancata -azione, non-acceptance (of a bill). **-ęvole** *adj.* acceptable, pleasing, grateful. **-evolmęnte** *adv.* acceptably.

accettata *f.* See under **accetta**.

accettil-are [A I s] *tr.* (leg.) to release (from an obligation). **-azione** *f.* (leg.) release (from an obligation).

accętto *adj.* acceptable; dear, welcome, gratifying, valued; è bene — a tutti, he is universally liked; †*n.m.* adherent; †reception.

accezione *f.* accepted meaning; meaning, significance; acceptation; †partiality, favouritism; †exception.

acchet-are [A I] *tr.* to quiet; to appease, to pacify; to hush, to lull; to quell; *rfl.* to grow quiet; to be appeased. (**-a·bile** *adj.* **-amęnto** *m.* **-ato** *part. adj.*)

†**acchiantare** *tr.* to plant; *intr.* to take root.

acchiapp-are [A I] *tr.* to catch, to seize; to net; to lay hold of, to attack; (colloq.) to catch (a person) out, to catch red-handed; fare ad -arsi, to play tig. **-acani** *m. indecl.* dog-catcher. **-afarfalle** *m. indecl.* butterfly-net. **-amosche** *m. indecl.* (bot.) sticky catchfly, *Silene muscipula*; Venus's flytrap, *Dionaea muscipula*. **-arello** *m.* catch, tricky question. **-atoio** *m.* booby-trap; snare, plot. **-ino** *m.* tig; giuocare ad -ino, to play tig.

†**acchiavare** *tr.* to nail.

acchinare [A I] *tr.* (Tusc.) to cause to stoop, to humiliate.

acchiocciare [A 3] *rfl.* (of a hen) to go broody.

acchiocciol-are [A I s] *tr.* to coil up; to wind (a spring) on a drum or cylinder; *rfl.* to curl oneself up. **-amęnto** *m.* coiling up; winding on a drum. **-ato** *part. adj.* coiled, wound; curled up. **-atura** *f.* coiling; coil.

acchit-o *m.* (billiards) lead; (fig.) d'—, di primo —, at once; from the outset. **-are** [A I] *tr., rfl.* (billiards) to lead off; -are il pallino, to break.

acchiu·dere [C 3] *tr.* to enclose; †(mil.) to encircle, to surround.

ac·cia¹ *f.* spun hemp or flax.

ac·cia² *f.* axe; battle-axe.

acciabatt-are [A I] *tr.* to botch, to cobble; to patch; to bungle. (**-amęnto** *m.*) **-ato** *part. adj.* botched; bungled. **-ìo** *m.* continual bungling. **-ǫne** *m.*, **-ǫna** *f.* bungler. **-ura** *f.* bungling; bungled job.

acciacc-are [A 2] *tr.* to crush, to squash, to squeeze together; to pound; to bruise; to beat down; (fig.) to oppress, to crush.

acciacc-are (*cont.*)

-**amento** *m.* crushing, bruising; (vet.) Burdizzo's method of castration by compression. -**ata** *f.* bruising. -**ato** *part. adj.* crushed; bruised; broken down, ill; shattered. -**atura** *f.* crushing, bruising; (mus.) a very short grace-note; (typ.) wearing of the type-face.

acciaccin-are [A I] *rfl.* (colloq. Tusc.) to bustle about (with little result). -**ato** *adj.* bustling, flurried.

acciac-co *m.* (pl. -**chi**) infirmity; pain; burden; misfortune, tribulation; gli -**chi** della vecchiaia, the tribulations of old age; †insolence; †outrage. -**coso** *adj.* infirm, ailing.

acciai-are [A 4] *tr.* to convert (iron) into steel; (pharm.) to add steel or iron filings to (a medicinal preparation); (fig.) to steel, to harden. -**ato** *part. adj.* converted into steel; reinforced with steel; (fig.) steeled, braced; hardened. -**atura** *f.* conversion into steel; steel plating; (typ.) Garnier process.

acciaino *m.* steel (for sharpening); steel bead.

accia·i-o *m.* steel; (poet.) sword, weapon; — dolce, mild steel; — fucinato, wrought steel; — fuso, cast steel; — laminato, rolled steel; — stampato, pressed steel; — temperato, hardened steel; — inossidabile, stainless steel. -**eri·a** *f.* steel-works. -**oso** *adj.* ghisa -**osa**, 'wild steel'. -**uola** *f.* steel nib. -**uol(in)o** *m.* steel (for sharpening); steel for striking fire with flint.

acciambell-are [A I] *tr.* to roll, to coil; *rfl., intr.* (*aux.* essere) to curl up. -**ato** *part. adj.* coiled; curled up.

acciannare [A I]. See **acciaccinare**.

acciapin-are [A I] *rfl.* (colloq. Tusc.) to bustle about, to be very active; †*intr.* to tremble, to shake. -**ato** *part. adj.* bustling, rushed.

acciar-o *m.* (poet.) steel, sword. -**ino** *m.* steel (of a flint and steel or flint-lock musket); linch-pin; pistol (of a torpedo warhead). -**ito** *adj.* converted into steel; reinforced with steel.

acciarp-are [A I] *tr., intr.* (*aux.* avere) to bungle, to botch; to collect indiscriminately, to bundle together. -**amento** *m.* bungling; bundling together. -**ato** *part. adj.* bungled; bundled together. -**atore** *m.* bungler. (-**atrice** *f.*) -**io** *m.* continuous bungling. -**one** *m.*, -**ona** *f.* bungler.

accidem·poli *excl.* good Lord!; dash it! (euphem. for **accidenti**!, q.v.).

accident-e *m.* misfortune, casualty; apoplectic fit; accident; occurrence; unforeseen event; (of a person) essere un —, to be of a difficult temperament; (of a child) è un —, he is a little devil; (philos.) accident; (mus.) accidental; †*pl.* (gramm.) accidence. *excl.* accidente! (or accidenti!, the devil!, the deuce!; accidenti a lui!, the devil take him! -**ale** *adj.* accidental, fortuitous, incidental, not essential; casual; (mus.) accidental. -**almente** *adv.* accidentally; by chance; casually. -**alità** *f.* roughness, unevenness (of ground). †-**are** *intr.* to be struck by apoplexy. -**ato** *part. adj.* impotent; paralysed, suffering from the effects of a stroke; (of ground) uneven, broken, rough.

acciderba *excl.* good Lord!; dash it! (euphem. for **accidenti**!, q.v.).

acci·dere [C 3] *tr.* (dial. S. Italy) to kill.

acci·di-a *f.* indolence, laziness, sloth; exasperation; far venir l'—, to exasperate; (theol.) sloth as a deadly sin, accidie. -**are** [A 4] *intr.* (*aux.* avere) to fall into sloth, to live in sloth. -**ato** *part. adj.* slothful. -**osaggine** *f.* slothfulness. -**oso** *adj.* indolent, lazy, slack; slothful. -**osamente** *adv.* slothfully.

acciec-are [A 2 d] *tr.* (techn.) — chiodi, to caulk rivets. (-**ato** *part. adj.*) -**atura** *f.* (techn.) countersinking.

accigli-are [A 4] *rfl.* to frown; to knit one's brows; †*tr.* to sew up the eyes (of birds). -**amento** *m.* frown. -**ato** *adj.* frowning, stern, severe; gloomy, glowering, sullen; worried-looking. (-**atamente** *adv.*) -**atura** *f.* shape of the eyebrows; frown, stern expression.

acciglionare [A I c] *tr.* to fortify with a rampart; to bank (a road).

†**acci·gnere** *vb.* and derivs. See **accingere**.

accilecc-are [A 2 c] *tr.* to tempt, to allure, to entice; to trick, to deceive; to make (false) promises to. -**ato** *part. adj.* enticed; tricked.

†**accimare** *vb.* and derivs. See **azzimare**.

accincigli-are [A 4] *tr.* to ornament with fringes, to fringe. -**ato** *part. adj.* fringed.

accincignare [A 5]. See **incincignare** and derivs.

accin·gere [C 5] *tr.* to gird on; *rfl.* (fig.) to gird up one's loins, to roll up one's sleeves; accingersi al lavoro, to set to work.

accinto *part.* from **accingere** q.v.; *adj.* girt; prepared, ready, disposed.

accintolare [A I s] *intr.* (*aux.* avere) (text.) to attach a small strip of protecting material along the border of a piece of cloth where it is desired that it should not take the dye.

ac·cio *pej. suff., adj.* bad; questo vino non è tanto —, this wine isn't at all bad; *n.m.* bad hat; un dottoraccio, ma di quegli acci davvero, a quack, and a bad one at that.

acciò, acciocchè *conj.* in order that, so that.

acciocch-ire [D 2] *tr.* to make sleepy, to stupefy; *intr.* (*aux.* essere) to fall into a heavy sleep; to sleep like a log. -**ito** *part. adj.* sleepy, asleep; stunned, stupefied.

accioc-co *adj.* (*m.pl.* -**chi**) (bot.) tufted, clustered, bunch-flowered; viola -**ca**, wallflower, stock-gillyflower.

acciottol-are [A I s] *tr.* to pave with cobbles; to clatter, to rattle. -**ato** *part. adj.* cobbled; *n.m.* cobbled paving; una strada in -**ato**, a cobbled road. -**atura** *f.* cobbles, cobbled pavement; cobbling. -**io** *m.* (*pl.* -**ii**) clatter, rattle, clashing.

accipic·chia *excl.* good Lord!, dash it! (euphem. for **accidenti**!, q.v.).

accipigli-are [A 4] *rfl.* to frown. -**ato** *adj.* frowning; scowling, stern, angry.

accisa *f.* excise, accise, tax.

†**accismare** *tr.* to cut, to divide; to hack in pieces.

†**acciso**[1] = acceso.

acciso[2] *part.* of **accidere**, q.v.

acciucch-ire [D 2] *tr.* to stun, to stupefy; to astonish, to amaze; *intr.* (*aux.* essere) to be astonished. (-**ito** *part. adj.*)

acciuff-are [A I] *tr.* to seize by the hair; to seize, to lay hold of; to catch; *recip. rfl.* to seize each other by the hair; to scuffle, to come to blows. (-**ato** *part. adj.* rumpled.)

acciug-a[1] *f.* (ichth.) anchovy; pasta di acciughe, anchovy paste; (fig.) essere un'—, to be very thin; pigiati come acciughe, packed like sardines; aver cervello quanto un'—, to have no brains at all. -**ata** *f.* anchovy sauce; anchovies in oil.

acciug-a[2] *f.* (bot.) wild marjoram, *Origanum vulgare*. -**a·ria** *f.* (bot.) summer savory, *Satureja hortensis*.

acciu·ghero *m.* (bot.) wild marjoram.

acciugh-etta *f.*, -**ina** *f.* (ent.) silverfish, *Ctenolepisma* sp.

acciurmare [A I] *tr.* (naut.) to man (a ship).

†**accivanzare** *vb.* and derivs. See **civanzare**.

accivett-are [A I c] *tr.* (orn.) to lure (birds), using the little owl (civetta) as lure; (fig.) to charm, to flatter; to flirt with; to allure. -**ato** *adj.* (orn.) lured; (fig.) worldly-wise, shrewd, experienced.

†**accivire** *tr.* to obtain; to provide, to furnish; to achieve; to complete; *intr.* to be successful.

acclam-are [A I] *tr.* to acclaim; to applaud; to cheer; to proclaim; to declare; to elect unanimously; *intr.* (*aux* avere, *prep.* a) to approve, to applaud. -**ante** *part. adj.* acclaiming, applauding; vociferous; *n.m., f.* acclaimer. -**ato** *part. adj.* acclaimed; applauded, cheered; *n.m.* hero, idol. -**atore** *m.*, -**atrice** *f.* acclaimer. -**azione** *f.* acclamation; applause; per -**azione**, unanimously; (archaeol.) acclamation (in early Christian inscriptions).

acclar-are [A I] *tr.* to purify, to clarify; to liquefy; (leg.) to clarify, to make clear, to clear up. (-**ato** *part. adj.*)

acclim-are [A I], -**atare** [A I], -**atizzare** [A I] *tr.* to acclimatize; *rfl.* to acclimatize oneself, to become acclimatized. -**atazione**, -**azione** *f.* acclimatization; giardino di -**azione**, botanical garden for exotics.

acclin-e, -**o** *adj.* sloping downward; †(fig.) inclined.

accliv-e *adj.* sloping upward. -**ità** *f.* acclivity, ascent, upward slope.

acclu·dere [C 3] *tr.* (*prep.* a) to enclose (in a letter); cf. **acchiudere**.

acclus-a *f.* enclosure, letter enclosed. -**o** *part.* of **accludere**, q.v.; *adj.* enclosed; *n.m.* (leg.) enclosure.

accocc-are[1] [A 2] *tr.* to notch; to fit (an arrow) to the bowstring; (fig.) to let fly; — un colpo, to hit out; -**arla** a, to trick; *rfl.* (*prep.* a) to stick (to), to become attached (to). -**ato** *part. adj.* notched; *n.m.* notch.

accocc-are[2] [A 2] *tr.* to fold together the four corners (of a cloth). -**ato** *part. adj.* with the four corners brought together.

accoccol-are [A I s] *rfl.* to squat; to crouch. -**ato** *part. adj.* squatting; crouched.

accoccovare [A I s] and derivs. See **accoccolare**.

accod-are [A I c] *tr.* to fasten head to tail (of animals walking in line); to arrange in single file; to set in a row; †(naut.) to tow (ships or boats) in a long single line; to attach a feather to the tail of (a bird acting as lure); *rfl.* (*prep.* a) to follow closely, to tail after; to join a queue, to tag on, to fall in behind. (-**amento** *m.*) -**ato** *part. adj.* in single file, tagging along behind; (naut.) (of a headland) having a submerged reef extending from it. (-**atura** *f.*)

acco·gli-ere [B 7] *tr.* to receive; to accept; to contain; to welcome; to agree to; — una domanda, to grant a request; — un'opinione,

accogli-ere (*cont.*)
to adopt an opinion; (leg.) — una cambiale, to honour a bill of exchange; (poet.) to gather; †to catch, to seize. †-**atrice** *f.* See **levatrice.** -**ente** *part. adj.* hospitable, welcoming, cordial; comfortable; cosy. -**enza** *f.* reception; welcome; fare -enza a, to welcome; (leg.) honouring of a bill of exchange or note. -**mento** *m.* reception; acceptance; granting. -**tore** *m.,* -**trice** *f.* receiver.

accogliticcio *adj.* See **raccogliticcio.**

acco·lit-o *m.* (eccl.) acolyte; (fig.) devotee. -**ato** *m.* (eccl.) the order of acolytes.

accollacciato *adj.* wrapped up, muffled up; *adv.* vestire —, to wrap up carefully, to muffle oneself up.

accoll-are [A I] *tr.* (*prep.* di) to load; to charge; to yoke, to accustom (oxen) to the yoke; — un carro, to put the weight forward in a cart; (fig.) to burden, to lay on, to saddle (with); (leg.) to transfer (a debt or other liability) to; (bot.) to train (vine-stems); (naut.) to take aback; — una vela, to back a sail; — un canapo, to coil a rope; †to embrace; *intr.* (*aux.* avere) to come up high in the neck; (of a boot) to cover the ankle; *rfl.* to undertake, to assume responsibility for; (leg.) to transfer to oneself (a debt or other liability). (-**amento** *m.*) -**ata** *f.* accolade. -**ata·rio** *m.* (leg.) person who takes over, or to whom is transferred, a debt or other liability; (bldg.) contractor. †-**a·tico** *m.* (leg.) duty paid for use of yoked oxen. -**ato** *part. adj.* laden; yoked; (of a dress) high-necked; (of a boot) ankle-snug; close-fitting; (herald.) conjoined, in fesse; (eng.) sostegni idraulici -ati, continuous locks (in a canal). (-**atore** *m.* -**atrice** *f.*) -**atura** *f.* loading; yoking; (of a dress) neck-line, collar.

accollo *m.* weight, burden; (fig.) commitment; contract; (naut.) vela che fa —, sail taken aback; — di corda, coil of rope; (archit.) cornice, projection (supported by beams or corbels); (leg.) the act of taking over, or of transferring, a debt or other liability.

†**accolpare** *vb.* and derivs. See **incolpare.**

accolta *f.* assemblage, assembly, gathering; †reception, welcome.

accoltell-are [A I] *tr.* to knife, to stab; -**ato** *part. adj.* stabbed; (bldg.) laid edgeways (of bricks). -**atore** *m.* ruffian, cut-throat, murderer; †gladiator. (-**atrice** *f.*)

accolto *part.* of **accogliere,** q.v.; *adj.* caught; gathered; condensed; absorbed; draped, folded; sheltered, harboured; hit, struck; †*n.m.* reception, welcome.

†**accomandagione** *f.* protection; trusteeship; deposit (for valuables).

accomand-are [A I] *tr.* to recommend; to entrust; to lend; to fix, to secure; to send, to convey; *rfl.* to seek protection. -**ante** *m.* (leg.) limited partner (see **accomandita**). -**ata·rio** *m.* (leg.) general partner (see **accomandita**). -**ato** *part. adj.* recommended; *n.m.* protégé, protectee. -**i·gia** *f.* (hist.) pact by which one Commune placed itself under the protection of another.

accoman·dita *f.* (leg.) — semplice, limited partnership (a corporation in Italian law); — per azioni, a form of limited partnership constituted by share-holding (unknown in English law).

accomandolare [A I s] *tr.* (text.) to tie or take up (the broken threads of a warp).

accom(m)iat-are [A I] *tr.* to dismiss, to send away; *rfl.* to take one's leave; to say good-bye; -arsi da, to take leave of; *recip. rfl.* to part. (-**atore** *m.*) -**atura** *f.* dismissal; leave-taking, farewell.

acco·moda *m. indecl.* obliging person, one who is put upon, factotum; essere il ser Accomoda degli altri, to be at everyone's beck and call.

accomod-are [A I s] *tr.* to fix, to mend, to repair, to adjust, to put right; to patch up; to emend, to correct; to put in order, to tidy; to settle; to adorn, to deck out; to accommodate, to lodge, to put up; to place (a person) in service; to marry off; to reach agreement concerning; -arla, to get out of a scrape; — le uova nel panierino, to make the most of one's means; (iron. colloq.) to settle, to deal with: — pel dì delle feste, to beat; *intr.* (*aux.* avere) to be pleasing, to suit; to be convenient; to be obliging; *rfl.* to accommodate oneself; to make oneself comfortable; to take a seat; s'-i, do sit down, please come in, please come this way; to deck oneself out; to pose; *recip. rfl.* to come to terms, to come to an agreement. -**a·bile** *adj.* adjustable; alterable; la cosa è -abile, the matter can be settled. -**amento** *m.* agreement; compromise, arrangement; reconciliation; settlement; adjustment; adaptation; (comm.) -amento di conti, settlement of accounts. -**ante** *part. adj.* accommodating; peaceable, easy-going. -**atic·cio** *adj.* patched up; *n.m.* best of a bad job. -**ativo** *adj.* accommodating; convenient, adaptable. -**ato** *part. adj.* adjusted, fixed; suitable, opportune.

(-**atamente** *adv.*) -**atore** *m.,* -**atrice** *f.* mender, repairer. -**atura** *f.* mending, repairing; arrangement, settlement. -**azione** *f.* adaptation.

acco·modo *adj.* See **accomodato,** under **accomodare.**

accompagn-are [A 5] *tr.* to accompany; to attend; to wait upon; to escort, to come with, to go with; — a casa, to see home; — alla porta, to show out; to follow; to be a companion to; to couple, to pair, to marry; to match; to class together, to compare; to support, to keep from falling; (mus.) to accompany; — col cuore, to be with a person in spirit; — con l'occhio, to keep in view, to follow with one's gaze; Dio t'-i, God be with you; *rfl.* (*prep.* a) to keep company with, to follow, to join; to go with: questa salsa s'-a bene con la carne fredda, this sauce goes well with cold meat; (mus.) to accompany oneself; *recip. rfl.* to match, to be in keeping, to go well together. -**a·bile** *adj.* matchable. -**amento** *m.* accompaniment; procession, train, retinue, escort; attendance; -amento funebre, funeral procession; (mus.) accompaniment. -**ato** *part. adj.* accompanied; in company; escorted; *pl.* coupled; paired; (herald.) between. -**atore** *m.* companion, escort; (mus.) accompanist; (sport) team-manager; one in charge of athletics. (-**atrice** *f.*) -**atura** *f.* escort; matching, harmonizing; servire d'-atura, to serve as a fellow; essere d'-atura, to match, to suit; (eccl.) funeral fee for priest going with body to grave.

accompagno *adj. phr.* (admin.) lettera d'—, letter enclosed.

accomun-are [A I] *tr.* to join, to unite; to associate; to share in common; to make common, to throw open to all; to equalize, to put on a par, to level; to mingle; *rfl.* (*prep.* a, con) to be on equal terms (with); to join (with), to mingle (with); to fraternize (with). (-**a·bile** *adj.* -**amento** *m.*) -**ato** *part. adj.* joined; shared.

acconcezza *f.* See under **acconcio.**

acconci-are [A 3 c] *tr.* to arrange, to prepare, to put in order; to adorn, to attire: (iron. colloq.) to fix, to settle: — pel dì delle feste, to beat; to dress (skins); to pickle, to preserve; — lo stomaco, to settle the stomach; (fig.) — le uova nel paniere, to make the most of one's means; *rfl.* to deck oneself out; to adorn oneself; to resign oneself, to adapt oneself; to compose oneself. (-**a·bile** *adj.*) -**amente** *adv.* suitably; tidily, neatly. -**amento** *m.* arrangement; settlement; adaptation. -**ato** *part. adj.* arranged; settled; fixed; adorned. (-**atore** *m.* -**atrice** *f.*) -**atura** *f.* arrangement; hair-style; head-dress; attire.

acconcime *m.* (usu. *pl.*) minor repairs (of buildings); restoration.

accon·cio *part.* (apocop. form of **acconciato,** for which see **acconciare**); *adj.* fit, proper, right, suitable; opportune; seasonable; serviceable; *n.m.* suitability, opportuneness; venire in —, to be opportune; fish-trap, enclosure made with canes in a lagoon; †order, organization. -**cezza** *f.* suitability; opportuneness.

accondiscendere [C I] *intr.* (*aux.* avere, *prep.* a) to yield, to comply; to agree, to admit; to condescend.

accone *m.* flat-bottomed boat, barge.

†**acconigliare** *vb.* (naut.). See **conigliare.**

acconsent-ire [D I] *intr.* (*aux.* avere); to consent, to approve; to assent; (prov.) chi tace -e, silence gives consent; to concede; to admit; (of cloth) to stretch; to give, to yield to pressure; (of an argument) to be convincing, to get home; (of food) to comfort, to sustain; *tr.* to allow, to permit. -**imento** *m.* consent, approval; assent. -**ito** *part. adj.* permitted; approved.

acconsenziente *adj., n.m.* See **consenziente.**

†**accontare** *rfl.* to join; *recip. rfl.* to confer together, to parley; to reach agreement; *tr.* to get to know, to meet.

accontent-are [A I] *tr.* to meet the wishes of, to satisfy, to gratify; to content; *rfl.* (*prep.* di) to be content (with). (-**amento** *m.* -**ato** *part. adj.*) See also **contentare.**

acconto[1] *m.* (comm.) instalment; part payment; — dividendo, interim dividend; pagare in —, to pay on account.

†**acconto**[2] *m.* confidant, friend; representative; *adj.* well-known, familiar; friendly.

†**accontrare** *vb.* and derivs. See **incontrare.**

accopp-are [A I] *tr.* to kill, to 'bump off'; (slang) to catch, to cop; (archit.) to tile. (-**ato** *part. adj.*) -**atura** *f.* (dial. Neap.) top, top layer.

accoppi-are [A 4] *tr.* to couple, to pair; to match; to unite; to connect; to yoke; to combine; (colloq.) to join in marriage, to hitch; (text.) to double, to wind together before spinning; (naut.) to tow alongside; *recip. rfl.* (of animals) to mate; to copulate; (colloq.) to marry, to get hitched. -**a·bile** *adj.* matchable; capable of being joined together. -**amento** *m.* coupling; mating; matching, pairing; yoking; (eng.) coupling; connexion; -amento scorrevole, sliding

accoppi-are (*cont.*)
fit; -amento bloccato, drive fit; (electr.) connexion. -ata *f.* (sport) double (in horse- or dog-racing). -ato *part. adj.* coupled; yoked; combined; (eng.) matched (i.e. made to fit); (herald.) laced, tied. -atoio *m.* double-leash; (eng.) coupling; -atoio a labbro, flange joint; -atoio a manicotto, coupling-box. -atore *m.* coupler; *pl.* (hist.) magistrates of the Florentine Republic. -atrice *f.* (text.) doubling winder. -atura *f.* coupling; (text.) double winding.

accop·pio *m.* See **accoppiamento**, under **accoppiare**.

accor-are [A I d, A I] *tr.* to stab through the heart (in killing pigs); (fig.) to grieve, to pierce to the heart; *rfl.* to grieve, to distress oneself; to break one's heart, to be heart-broken. -amento *m.* grief, distress; heart-ache; heart-felt sentiment. -ante *part. adj.* heart-rending; -atag·gine *f.* grief. -ato *part. adj.* heart-broken; sad; una melodia -ata, a melancholy tune. -atamente *adv.* sorrowfully, sadly. -atezza *f.* grief. -atoio *m.* slaughterer's knife (for killing pigs). -azione *f.* grieving.

accorcare [A 2] and derivs. See **coricare**.

accorci-are [A 3 c] *tr.* to shorten; to curtail; to abbreviate; to abridge; (techn.) to cut to length; (mil.) — il fronte, to retreat; *rfl., intr.* (aux. essere) to become shorter; to shrink. -a·bile *adj.* capable of being shortened; reducible. -amento *m.* shortening, contraction, abbreviation. -ativo *adj.* capable of being shortened; reducible; *n.m.* shortened form, abbreviation; diminutive. -ato *part. adj.* shortened; abridged; shrunk. -atamente *adv.* briefly, shortly. -atoia *f.* short cut. -atoio *adj.* shortening; una via -atoia, a short cut. (-atore *m.* -atrice *f.*) -atura *f.* shortening; curtailing.

accord-are [A I] *tr.* to grant, to accord; to reconcile; to match (colours); (gramm.) to make agree; (mus.) to tune; (radio) to tune; *intr.* (aux. essere) to be in tune; *rfl.* -arsi per, to agree to; *recip. rfl.* to concur; to act in concert; to reach agreement; (gramm.) to agree; (mus.) to be in unison; to tune up. -a·bile *adj.* allowable; consistent; tuneable. -amento *m.* (mus.) tuning-up; †agreement, accord. -anza *f.* agreement, accord. -ato *part. adj.* agreed; matched, matching; (mus.) tuned; in tune. -atoio *m.* (mus.) tuning-key. -atore *m.* piano-tuner; tuner (of instruments). -atura *f.* (mus.) tuning.

accordell-are [A I] *tr.* to twist. -ato *part. adj.* twisted; *n.m.* ribbed cloth; (fig.) secret understanding, crooked business.

†**accor·dio**[1] *m.* See **accordo**.

accor·dio[2], **accor·dion** *m.* accordion.

accordo *m.* accord, agreement; essere d'—, to agree; andare d'—, to get on well together; vivere d'amore e d'—, to live happily together; d'—! agreed!; di comune —, by mutual consent; arrangement, convention; un — commerciale, a trade agreement; — fra gentiluomini, gentlemen's agreement; stare agli accordi, to stand by the agreement; in — con, in accordance with; unity, harmony; (mus.) chord; consort; d'—, in tune; (gramm.) agreement, concordance; (radio) tuning, syntonization.

accordon-are [A I c] *tr.* (archit.) to cable, to furnish with cable-mouldings; to lay a string-course. -ato *part. adj.* (archit.) cabled; having a string-course. -atura *f.* (archit.) cabling; (text.) twisting.

accore *m.* See **accoro**.

accor·g-ere [C 5] *rfl.* (prep. di) to perceive, to notice; to realize, to become aware (of); to be aware (of). -imento *m.* perception, shrewdness, sagacity; subtlety, cunning; expedient, contrivance, device.

accoro *m.* edge of a shoal, bank, or reef.

accorpamento *m.* (neol.) merging together of small allotments into larger units of cultivation (S. Italy).

accorpato *adj.* (of animals) with young; (archit.) (of a column) having entasis; (of a wall) bulging.

accorre [B 7]. See **accogliere**.

accorrere[1] [C 5 c] *intr.* (aux. essere) to run, to run up; to hasten; to run together; to run to help.

†**accor·rere**[2] *vb.* and derivs. See **occorrere**.

†**accorruomo** *excl.* help!; gridare —, to shout for help.

accorsato *adj.* (dial. S. Italy) thriving, flourishing (of a business, etc.).

accorse, accorsero, accorsi *3rd sing., 3rd pl., 1st sing. past def.* of **accorgere**, q.v.

accorse, accorsero, accorsi *3rd sing., 3rd pl., 1st sing. past def.* of **accorrere**[1], q.v.

accorso *part.* of **accorrere**[1], q.v.

accortamente *adv.* See under **accorto**.

†**accortare** *tr.* to shorten.

accortezza *f.* See under **accorto**.

†**accortinare** *tr.* to put curtains round, to curtain; (mil.) see **cortinare**.

accort-o *part.* of **accorgere**, q.v.; *adj.* shrewd, wise, sagacious, clever; wary, alert; suspicious; crafty; adroit; male — (malaccorto), unwary, incautious, silly; awkward, unskilful; fare — di, to caution against; stare —, to be on the alert. -amente *adv.* shrewdly, cautiously, wisely; adroitly; cunningly, astutely. -ezza *f.* shrewdness, sagacity; alertness, cunning; adroitness.

accosci-are [A 4] *rfl.* to squat; to crouch; †*intr.* (mil.) to retreat. -ato *part. adj.* squatting; crouched; †reclining.

accost-are [A I] *tr.* to bring close together, to bring near; to approach; — un tavolo al muro, to place a table against the wall; — un uscio, to set a door ajar; — una finestra, to half-close a window; to attend, to be in close attendance on; to frequent the company of, to approach; nessuno l'-a, no one will have anything to do with him; (naut.) — una nave, to come alongside a ship; *intr.* (aux. essere) to be close-fitting; questa porta non -a bene, this door does not shut properly; (of food) to be sustaining; (naut.) to alter course; to go alongside; *rfl.* (prep. a) to approach, to draw near; to resemble; to be intimate with; to adhere to (an opinion); -arsi a un partito, to belong to, to support a party; (eccl.) -arsi ai sacramenti, to approach the sacraments. -a·bile *adj.* approachable; affable. -amento *m.* bringing close, approach; juxtaposition; comparison; (sport) encounter, match, contest. -ante *part. adj.* sustaining, restorative; corroborative. -arello *m.* See **accostatore**. -ata *f.* (naut.) approach-angle. -atore *m.* (agric.) man who leads the cattle to the threshing floor to tread the corn. -evole *adj.* approachable; affable.

accosto *adv.* alongside, near at hand, nearby; la casa —, the house next door; d'—, close by; *prep.* — a, next to, near; *n.m.* supporter; support; *adj.* (Tusc.) neighbouring, adjoining.

accostol-are [A I s] *tr.* to cause (cloth) to wrinkle; (naut.) to fit (a ship) with ribs. -ato *part. adj.* wrinkled; (naut.) fitted with ribs; carcassa -ata, wreck (ribs only remaining); *n.m.* ribs of a ship. -atura *f.* wrinkle (in cloth).

accostum-are [A I] *tr.* to accustom; to inure; *rfl.* (prep. a) to accustom oneself; to get used (to); to get into the habit (of). -a·bile *adj.* adaptable. -atezza *f.* accustomedness. -ato *part. adj.* accustomed; well-bred; well-mannered. (-atore *m.*)

accoton-are [A I c] *tr.* to stuff or line with cotton, to comb cloth so as to give it a nap or covering of fine hairs combed out of its substance and lying smoothly in one direction, to fleecy-line. -atore *m.*, -atrice *f.* operative engaged in fleecy-lining.

accottimare [A I s] *tr.* (leg.) to take, or to give (a job) on piece-work.

accovacci-are [A 3] *rfl.* to crouch; to hide; to run into a lair; to curl up (of animals, for sleep). (-ato *part. adj.*) -olare [A I s] *rfl. dim.*

accovonare [A I c] *tr.* to bind into sheaves.

accozz-are [A I] *tr.* to jumble together; to amass, to heap; to gather together, to collect; to string together; to shuffle (cards); non poter — il desinare con la cena, to be unable to make both ends meet; (colloq. Tusc.) — i pentolini, to pool provisions, to mess together; *rfl.* to foregather, to meet; to crowd, to assemble; to conspire, to hatch mischief; to clash. -a·glia *f.* crowd, medley; hurly-burly. -amento *m.* jumble, muddle; heap; mixture, combination. -atic·cio *adj.* jumbled. (-atore *m.*) -atura *f.* jumbling; medley.

accozzo *m.* jumble, medley; combination.

accrebbe, accreb·bero, accrebbi *3rd sing., 3rd pl., 1st sing. past def.* of **accrescere**, q.v.

accredit-are [A I s c] *tr.* to credit; to confirm; to accredit; (comm.) to credit; *rfl.* to gain credit, to gain ground (of rumour). -a·bile *adj.* (comm.) to be credited. -amento *m.* crediting; accrediting; (comm.) credit entry. -ato *part. adj.* accredited; official, recognized, with credentials; reliable.

accresc-ere [B 9 c] *tr.* to increase, to augment, to amplify; †to raise, to bring up; †*intr.* to grow; *rfl.* to increase; to be increased; enlarged, augmented. (-enza *f.*) -imento *m.* increase; enlargement; enlarging. -itivo *adj., n.m.* (gramm.) augmentative. (-itore *m.* -itrice *f.*) -iuto *part. adj.* increased, enlarged, augmented.

accrespare [A I c] and derivs. See **increspare**.

accrezione *f.* (leg.) accretion.

†**accroccare** *tr.* to hook; to seize with a hook.

†**accrostell-are** *rfl.* (of blood) to congeal. -ato *part. adj.* congealed, clotted; crusted.

accu·bito *m.* (antiq.) accubation, the ancient posture of reclining at table; sofa, couch (on which the ancients reclined).

accucci-are [A3] *rfl.* (of a dog) to lie down, to curl up for sleep; to crouch; to sit. (**-ato** *part. adj.*) **-olare** [A1s] *rfl. dim.*

accud-ire [D2] *intr.* (*aux.* avere, *prep.* a) to attend (to); to be responsible (for); — alla casa, to see to the running of the house; to do the housework; (also *tr.*, but dial., S. Italy). **-ienza** *f.* (industr.) activity of caretaker, keeper or supervisor of industrial plant.

accul-are [A1] *tr.* to walk (a horse) backwards; to place (a horse, cart) with its back against a wall; — un carretto, to rest the body of a cart on the ground, with its shafts in the air; *rfl.* to sit on one's haunches; (of a dog) to sit; (iron.) to take up one's abode, to 'squat'; †(naut.). see **appoppare** *rfl.* **-amento** *m.* (naut.) curvature of ship's frames; †dipping of stern due to pitching.

acculattare [A1] *tr.* to pick (a child) up and plump down in a sitting position; — le panche, to sit idle (in school); (bookb.) to re-back.

accumul-are [A1s] *tr.* to accumulate; to heap, to pile, to amass; to store; *abs.* to make money, to put money by. **-a·bile** *adj.* accumulative. **-amento** *m.* accumulation, heap. **-ato** *part. adj.* accumulated; amassed. **-atore** *m.* hoarder; collector; (electr.) accumulator, battery; (eng.) accumulator. **-azione** *f.* accumulation, heap, mass; (rhet.) accumulation.

†**accupare**[1] *vb.* and derivs. See **occupare**.

†**accupare**[2] *vb.* See **accupire**.

accupire [D2] *rfl.* to grow sad; to become gloomy.

accur-ato *adj.* done with care; thorough; lavoro —, careful work, work done diligently; (of a person) meticulous, scrupulous, careful, diligent; well cared for, tidy, well groomed. **-atamente** *adv.* with care; diligently; scrupulously. **-atezza** *f.* diligence, care; thoroughness.

accusa *f.* charge, accusation; (leg.) charge, accusation; public prosecutor; prosecution of an offence; atto d'—, indictment; capo d'—, count; sezione d'—, section of Italian Court of Appeal which decides whether certain indictments should be proceeded with; sotto — di, on a charge of.

accus-are [A1] *tr.* (*prep.* di) to accuse, to charge; to blame; to declare, to confess; to show, to betray; to acknowledge; — il colpo, to acknowledge that the thrust has got home; to report; to complain of: il malato -a un dolore al lato sinistro, the patient complains of a pain on his left side; (at cards) to call; (leg.) to charge (with), to indict, to prosecute; (comm.) — ricevuta di, to acknowledge receipt of. **-a·bile** *adj.* chargeable; indictable. **-ata** *f.* (at cards) call, declaration. **-ato** *part. adj.* accused, charged; shown; complained of; *n.m.* **-ata** *f.* accused, prisoner at the bar. **-atore** *m.* accuser; (leg.) -atore pubblico, public prosecutor. (**-atrice** *f.*) **-ato·rio** *adj.* (leg.) accusatory, pertaining to the prosecution.

accusativo *adj.* (gramm.) accusative; *n.m.* accusative case.

ace·falo *adj.* acephalous; headless; lacking a beginning; *n.m.pl.* (eccl. hist.) Acephali; (zool.) Lamellibranchs.

acera·ia *f.* See under **acero**.

†**acerbare** *tr.* to make bitter; (fig.) to embitter; to aggravate, to intensify; *rfl.* to become embittered.

acerb-o *adj.* unripe; sour; bitter; tart, pungent; immature, young; green; severe, austere, harsh; grievous, tragic; (poet.) età -a, youth; morte -a, premature death; *n.m.* sour part; sourness; (fig.) immaturity; severity. **-amente** *adv.* sharply; bitterly; prematurely. **-etto** *adj. dim.* rather sour; sharp, pungent; †shy, coy. **-ezza** *f.*, **-ità** *f.* unripeness; sourness; (fig.) severity, harshness; bitterness; grievousness, gravity.

a·cero *m.* (bot.) maple-tree, *Acer campestre*; — di montagna, — bianco, sycamore, *Acer pseudo-platanus*; — da zucchero, American sugar maple, *Acer saccharum*; — della Virginia, American ash-leaved maple, box elder, *Acer negundo*. **-a·ia**, **-eta** *f.*, **-eto** *m.* maple-grove, maple plantation. **-oso** *adj.* maple-leaved, with maple-like foliage.

acerra *f.* (Rom. antiq.) incense-casket; incense-altar.

acer·rimo *adj. superl.* of **acre**, q.v.

acertello *m.* (orn.) See **accertello**.

acervo[1] *m.* heap, pile, mass.

†**acervo**[2] *adj.* See **acerbo**.

acesc-ente *adj.* turning acid; turning sour. **-enza** *f.* becoming acidic; souring.

aceta·bolo *m.* (archaeol.) acetabulum; (anat.) thigh-bone socket.

acetabula·ria *f.* (bot.) a Mediterranean seaweed, *Acetabularia mediterranea*.

ace·tico *adj.* acetic.

acet-o *m.* vinegar; pigliare l'—, to turn to vinegar; to go sour; (fig.) pigliare d'—, to be piqued; (Tusc. colloq.) una vecchietta dell'—, an old hag.

    1. DERIVS. RELATING TO VINEGAR, ACIDITY, ETC. **-are** [A1c] *tr.* to turn to vinegar, to make sour; to season with vinegar. **-a·rie** *f.pl.* greens for salad. **-ato** *part. adj.* sour; smelling of vinegar. **-ella** *f.* vinegar and water. **-ificare** [A2s] to acetify. (**-ificazione** *f.*) **-ino** *adj.* sour, vinegarish; *n.m.pl.* gherkins; pickles. **-ire** [D2] *intr.* (*aux.* avere) to turn sour. **-oliera** *f.* cruet-stand. **-o·lio** *m.* cruet. **-osa** *f.* fizzy lemonade. **-oso** *adj.* acid, sour. **-osità** *f.* acidity, sourness. **-ume** *m.* acidity, sourness; pickles. (See also **acetico**.)
    2. DERIVS. RELATING TO CHEM. USES. **-aldeide** *f.* acetaldehyde. **-am·mide** *f.* acetamide. **-anilide** *f.* acetanilide. **-arsenito** *m.* aceto-arsenite. **-ato** *m.* acetate. **-ilare** [A1s] *tr.* to acetylate; to acetylize. **-ilcolina** *f.* acetylcholine. **-ile** *m.* acetyl. **-ilene** *m.* acetylene. **-i·lico** *adj.* acetylic. **-iluro** *m.* acetylide. **-ofenone** *m.* aceto-phenone. **-olo** *m.* acetol. **-one** *m.* acetone. **-osella** *f.* sale di -osella, salts of lemon.

acetone *m.* (vet.) acetonaemia.

acetos-a *f.* (bot.) — coltivata, garden sorrel, *Rumex acetosa*; — romana, French sorrel, *R. scutatus*; — minore, sheep's sorrel, *R. acetosella*; wood sorrel, *Oxalis acetosella*. **-ella** *f.* (bot.) wood sorrel, *Oxalis acetosella*; -osella delle Indie, -osella sensitiva, sensitive plant, *Mimosa pudica*.

achelan·dia *f.* (naut. hist.) Mediterranean war galley (oars and sail) of the eighth and ninth centuries.

acheme·nio *adj.* (poet.) Achaemenian (from Achaemenes, the ancestor of the Persian kings).

ache·nio *m.* (bot.) achene.

acheo *adj.* (hist.) Achaean.

acherdo *m.* (bot.) wild pear.

Acher-onte *pr.n.m.* (myth.) Acheron. **-onte·o** *adj.* Acherontal. **-on·tico** *adj.* of Acheron; sepulchral (stone); funeral (rites).

†**achigiare** *intr.* to land, to reach the shore.

Achill-e *pr.n.m.* Achilles; l'— degli argomenti, the most cogent argument; il tallone d'—, la tendine d'—, Achilles' heel, Achilles' tendon. **-esco** *adj.* (*m.pl.* -eschi) Achillean.

achille·a *f.* (bot.) yarrow, milfoil, *Achillea millefolium*.

achilli *m. indecl.* (dial. Sicily) (ichth.) shagreen shark, *Oxynotus centrina*. See **pesce porco**.

achir-anto *m.* (bot.) a kind of amaranth, *Achyranthes aspera*. **-o·nia** *f.* (bot.) pink centaury, *Centaurium minus*.

achiro *m.* armless freak.

achiurgi·a *f.* surgical technique.

†**aciare** *intr.* to breathe.

aci·clic-o *adj.* acyclic; (electr.) dinamo -a, homopolar dynamo.

acicolare *adj.* (bot.) needle-shaped (of a leaf).

aci·cula *f.* (bot.) shepherd's needle, Lady's comb, *Scandix pecten-veneris*.

acida·lia *f.* (ent.) acidalia butterfly.

aci·dia *f.* See **accidia**.

acidific-are [A2s] *tr.* to acidify. (**-a·bile** *adj.* **-ato** *part. adj.* **-azione** *f.*)

a·cid-o *m.* sourness, acidity; (chem.) acid; — azotico, nitric acid; *adj.* acid, sour. **-ag·gio** *m.* (techn.) etching. **-are** [A1s] *tr.* to etch. **-imetri·a** *f.* acidimetry. **-i·metro** *m.* acidimeter. **-ezza** *f.* sourness. **-ità** *f.* acidity. **-ume** *m.* sour matter.

acidosi *f.* (med.) acidosis.

aci·dul-o *adj.* acidulous. **-are** [A1s] *tr.* to acidulate. **-ante** *part. adj.* acidulating. **-ato** *part. adj.* acidulated. **-azione** *f.* acidulation; acid scouring.

acifillo *adj.* (bot.) needle-leaved.

acin-esi·a *f.* (med.) akinesia, paralysis of the motor nerves. **-e·tico** *adj.* akinesic.

a·cin-o[1] *m.* pip, grape-stone; grape; berry; kernel. **-iforme** *adj.* resembling a bunch of grapes. **-oso** *adj.* with clustered fruit; with many fruit clusters.

a·cino[2] *m.* (bot.) basil-thyme, *Acinos arvensis*.

acirologi·a *f.* (rhet.) catachresis.

acisti·a *f.* (med.) acystia.

aclassista, aclassi·stico *adj.* (neol.) unrelated to the idea of social classes.

a·clid-e, -o *m.* (archaeol.) small javelin.

acme *f.* acme, highest point; (med.) crisis.

acmella *f.* (bot.) Asiatic plant, formerly used in medicine, *Spilanthes oleracea*.

acne *f.pl.*, *m.sing.* (med.) acne.

aco *m.* (dial. Ven.) (ichth.) See **aguglia**.[1]

aco·lito *m.* See **accolito**.

aconfession-ale *adj.* (rel.) undenominational; without sectarian religious bias. **-alità** *f.* (rel.) absence of religious allegiance.

aconitina *f.* (chem.) aconitine.

aco·nito *m.* (bot.) monkshood, blue aconite, *Aconitum napellus*; — europeo, wolfsbane, *A. vulparia*; — medicinale, medicinal aconite, *A. anthora*.

acon·zia *f.* (zool.) dart snake; (astron.) meteor.

a·core, aco·re *m.* (med.) achor, milk-crust.

a·coro *m.* (bot.) — aromatico, sweet flag, *Acorus calamus*; — falso, yellow water-iris, yellow flag, *Iris pseudacorus*.

acotile·done *f.* (bot.) acotyledon; *adj.* acotyledonous.

acqu-a *f.* **1.** WATER; — potabile, drinking water; — di conduttura, main water; — piovana, rain water; — di cisterna, water from a rain butt; — dolce, fresh water; soft water; — cruda, hard water; condotto d'—, water pipe; cassa d'—, water-tank; castello d'—, water-tower; — salsa, — salata, salt water; — salmastra, brackish water; — di mare, sea-water; — fina, pure water (see also under no. 2); — viva, — di sorgente, spring water; — cristallina, clear sparkling water; — pesante, flat water, stale water (see also under no. 6); — morta, flat water, stale water (see also under no. 4); — chiara, clear water; — spessa, cloudy water; — torbida, (Tusc.) — torba, muddy water (see also under no. 7); — pozza, contaminated water; getto d'—, spurt of water; scherzi d'—, giochi d'—, ornamental waterworks; — minerale, mineral water; — effervescente, fizzy water; — di seltz, soda-water; — santa, — benedetta, holy water; — lustrale, lustral water; passare le -e, to take the waters; stare a pane e —, to live on bread and water; †dare l'— alle mani, to wash the hands (before eating); †to come to table. **2.** RAIN; — del cielo, rain; — fina, fine rain, drizzle (see also under no. 1); — dirotta, — a dirotto, — a rovesci, — a orci, — a secchie, — a catinelle, — come Dio la manda, heavy rain, downpour; un rovescio d'—, a heavy shower; l'— vien giù, it's raining hard; prendere dell'—, to get caught in the rain; ho preso molt'—, I've got soaking wet; tetto a due -e, roof with a double slope; che non assorbe l'—, waterproof, rainproof. **3.** FLUID, LIQUID; andare in —, to turn to water; (joc.) il cervello gli va in —, he's going off his head, he's got softening of the brain; (of certain plants, e.g. cucumbers, mushrooms) juice; — di latte, whey; — lanfa, — nanfa, orange water; — di Colonia, eau-de-Cologne; — rosata, — di rosa, rose water (see also under no. 7); — antisterica, sal volatile; (Tusc. colloq.) — tinta, weak coffee, weak wine; (in Dante, *Inf.* VI, 10, — tinta, filthy water, *or* sleet); — panata, toast and water; sweat; andarsene in —, to sweat profusely; saliva; urine; fare —, to urinate, to make water; (med.) togliere l'— dal polmone, to draw fluid from the lung; (obstet.) le -e, the waters; (euphem.) — tofana, — di Perugia, poison. **4.** WATERS, SEA; CURRENT, STREAM; le -e, the waters, the deep; in grembo alle -e, in the bosom of the deep; -e territoriali, territorial waters; nelle -e di Genova, off the coast of Genoa; magistrato delle -e, local governmental department superintending waterworks and public works connected with canals and rivers; water board; specchio d'—, stretch of water, expanse of sea; filo d'—, weep, trickle; filo dell'—, direction of the current; filone dell'—, current; capo dell'—, source of the stream; contr'—, upstream; andare contr'—, to stem the tide; andare per —, to go by water, to go by sea; pelo dell'—, level of the water, water-surface; a fior d'—, on the surface of the water, level with the water; gettare in —, to throw overboard; sott'—, inundated, flooded out (see also under no. 7); — alta, deep water; high tide, springs; (Ven.) water at flood level; — di piena, flood water; — bassa, shallow water; low tide, neaps; (dial Sicil.) — manca, low tide; — morta, — stanca, — ferma, stagnant water, slack water (for — morta, see also under no. 1); — stabile, stationary water, tideless water; — viva, current, leak, springs; — cheta, sheltered waters, slick; still waters (see also under no. 7); a mezz'— (of divers, fish), some way below the surface (see also under no. 5). **5.** NAUTICAL USES: nave che prende molt'—, vessel of deep draught; nave che prende poca —, vessel of shallow draught; nave che non ha — a sufficienza, vessel which has insufficient water to float; a mezz'—, fra le due -e, awash (see also under nos. 4 and 7); far —, to leak; to take on water; aver — da correre, to be in open waters; mettersi all'—, to be launched; — delle murate,

water seeped into the bilges; — d'alimentazione, feed water; linea d'—, water-line. (For uses as to tides, see under no. 4). **6.** TECHNICAL AND SCIENTIFIC USES: — ossigenata, hydrogen peroxide; — ragia (acquaragia), turpentine; — pesante, heavy water (see also under no. 1); — forte (acquaforte), nitric acid; etching; — vite (acquavite), rough brandy; — vegeto-minerale, Goulard's extract, Goulard's water; †— arzente, spirits, alcohol; (of precious stones) water (see also under no. 7); (hydr.) — a monte, headwater; — a valle, tailwater; corpo d'—, volume of water per second. **7.** FIGURATIVE AND PROVERBIAL USES: — torbida, (Tusc.) — torba, troubled waters; intorbidire le -e, to make mischief; to complicate matters; lavorare sott'—, to work secretly, to go underground; — cheta, still waters; dark horse; l'— cheta rompe i ponti, still waters run deep; dripping water wears away a stone; stare fra le due -e, to have a foot in both camps; è un briccone della più bell'—, he's a rogue of the first water; innocente come l'—, as innocent as a new-born babe; lasciar andar l'— per la sua china, to let things take their course; è passata molt'— sotto i ponti, a lot of water has flowed under the bridges; portare — al mare, to carry coals to Newcastle; pestar l'— nel mortaio, to beat the air, to act to no purpose; essere un pesce fuor d'—, to be a fish out of water; rassomigliarsi come due gocce d'—, to be as like as two peas in a pod; è un Comunista all'— di rosa, he's a milk-and-water Communist (see also under no. 3); tirar l'— al proprio mulino, to bring grist to one's mill; buttarsi nell'— per, to cut off one's right hand for; aver l'— alla gola, to be at the eleventh hour; un buco nell'—, a damp squib; affogare in un bicchier d'—, to bungle a simple matter; to make a mountain out of a molehill; metter — sul fuoco, to pour oil on troubled waters; è come bere un bicchier d'—, it's as easy as falling off a log; il sangue non è — , blood is thicker than water; there's a limit to what one will put up with; fuggir l'— sotto le grondaie, out of the frying pan into the fire; navigare in basse -e, to pull the devil by the tail; l'— va al mare, money goes where money is; è una barca che fa — da tutte le parti, it's a very shaky concern; *excl.* — in bocca!, ssh!; don't tell a soul!; acqua! fuoco!, cold! hot! (used in guessing games); — alle funi!, help!

   -acotta *f.* (dial. Maremma) vegetable soup. **-ai(u)ola** *f.* water blister; (orn.) dipper; (dial. Neap.) water-vendor. **-ai(u)olo** *adj.* (orn.) merlo -aiuolo, dipper, *Cinclus cinclus*; bolla -aiuola, water blister; aquatic; *n.m.* water-vendor; water-carrier; man who waters the streets; (in fulling) finisher. **-arone** *m.* (Tusc.) rainy weather, period of rain. **-astrino** *adj.* waterlogged, soggy, sodden; *n.m.* marshy ground. **-ata** *f.* sudden storm, squall; cistern; (naut.) water supply; far l'-ata, (of ships) to water. **-a·tico** *adj.* aquatic. **-a·tile** *adj.* aquatic; (joc.) teetotal, on the water-wagon. **-ativo** *adj.* waterlogged, sodden. **-atura** *f.* (bldg.) camber, drainage slope. **-azzone** *m.* downpour, cloud-burst. **-azzonoso** *adj.* rainy, damp. **-erella** *f.*, **-eru·giola** *f.* light shower; fine rain, drizzle. **-etta** *f.* light shower; weak wine; poison; dare l'-etta a, to poison. **-icella** *f.* rivulet; fine rain. **-icina** *f.* light shower; fine rain, drizzle; flow of saliva; far venire l'-olina in bocca, to make one's mouth water. **-osità** *f.* wateriness. **-oso** *adj.* watery; similar to water; (chem.) aqueous.

acquacchi-are [A 4] *tr.* to humble; to override; *rfl.* to squat, to cower; to give way, to yield, to humble oneself. **-ato** *part. adj.* humbled, depressed, cast-down.

acquacedrat-a *f.* lemonade; lime-juice. **-a·io** *m.* lemonade-vendor.

acquadern-are [A I] *tr.* to make a note (of); (techn.) to fold (paper for book-making). (**-ato** *part. adj.*) **-atore** *m.* (techn.) folder.

acquafort-e *f.* (art) etching; (chem.) aquafortis, nitric acid. **-ista** *m.* (art) etcher.

acquafresca·io *m.* water-vendor.

†acquagliare *vb.* and derivs. See **accagliare**.

acqu-a·io *m.* kitchen sink; (fig.) gola d'—, voracious eater; mandar tutto per la gola dell'—, to live like fighting cocks, to lavish money on food; (agric.) water lead, shallow trench.

acquai(u)ol-a *f.*, **-o** *m.*, *adj.* See under **acqua**.

acquamarina *f.* aquamarine; beryl.

acquapendente *m.* slope, incline.

acquaplan-o *m.* surf-board. **-ista** *m.* surf-rider.

acquara·gia *f.* turpentine.

acquare [A 6] and derivs. See **innacquare**.

acquare·gia *f.* (chem.) aqua regia.

acquarellare [A I] and derivs. See **acquerellare**.

Acqu·ario[1] *pr. n. m.* (astron.) Aquarius.

acqua·rio[2] *m.* aquarium; (neol.) shade of green.

acquarone *m.* and other derivs. See under **acqua**.

acquartier-are [A I] *tr.* (mil.) to quarter; *rfl.* to quarter, to take up quarters, to be quartered. (-**amento** *m.*) -**ato** *part. adj.* (mil.) in quarters.

acquasant-iera *f.* (-**ino** *m.* dial. Lomb.) (eccl.) holy water stoup.

acquastrino *adj.*, **acquata** *f.*, **acquatico** *adj.*, **acquatile** *adj.*, **acquativo** *adj.* See under **acqua**.

acquatinta *f.* (art) aquatint.

acquatt-are [A I] *rfl.* to crouch, to cower; to squat; to hide. -**ato** *part. adj.* hidden, crouched; squatting; (agric.) bedded.

acquavit-e *f.* rough brandy. -**a·io** *m.* vendor of rough brandy, spirits-merchant.

acquazzone *m.* See under **acqua**.

acquedotto *m.* aqueduct; waterworks; water company; water main.

ac·queo *adj.* aqueous, watery; vapore —, steam.

†**acquere·cci-a** *f.*, †-**o** *m.* water-bottle; water jug, pitcher.

acquerell-are [A I] *tr.* to paint in water-colour. -**ista** *m.* painter in water-colour. -**o** *m.* water-colour painting; sour wine.

acqueru·giola *f.* See under **acqua**.

acquetare [A I] and derivs. See **acquietare**.

acquetta *f.*, **acquicella** *f.* See under **acqua**.

acquicoltura *f.* cultivation of edible fish and molluscs.

ac·quido *adj.* (poet.) watery, mixed with water.

†**acquidoc·cio** *m.* See **acquedotto**.

†**acquidoso** *adj.* watery; marshy.

acquie·sc-ere [B I] *intr.* (*aux.* avere; *prep.* a) to acquiesce; (leg.) to acquiesce (in). -**ente** *part. adj.* acquiescent, resigned. -**enza** *f.* acquiescence; (leg.) tacit renunciation of claim, right or possession.

acquiet-are [A I] *tr.* to quieten; to appease, to placate, to calm; to satisfy; to soothe; †to yield, to renounce; *rfl.* to become quiet, to calm oneself; to resign oneself; to be appeased; (of a storm) to die down. (-**a·bile** *adj.* -**amento** *m.*) -**ato** *part. adj.* appeased; calmed; placated.

acquirente *n.m.*, *f.* (comm.) purchaser, consumer; client.

acquis·ire [D 2] *tr.* (leg.) to acquire. -**itivo**, -**iti·zio** *adj.* acquisitive; (leg.) titolo -**itivo**, title to acquire. -**ito** *part. adj.* acquired, established; recognized; (leg.) diritto -**ito**, vested right; documento -**ito** agli atti, document entered in the file of court case; (med.) acquired, post-natal. -**itore** *m.* (econ.) commission agent, insurance agent. -**izione** *f.* acquisition.

acquist-are [A I] *tr.* to acquire, to obtain; to buy; (fig.) — tempo, to gain time; — terreno, to make headway; to win, to gain; to incur; *abs.* to make progress; to succeed; to develop, to improve; to gain ground; (leg.) capacità d'—, capacity to acquire. -**a·bile** *adj.* obtainable. -**ato** *part. adj.* acquired; gained; improved. -**atore** *m.* obtainer; purchaser; buyer. (-**atrice** *f.*)

acquist-o *m.* acquisition; purchase; profit, gain, advantage; increase; (poet.) conquest; far degli -**i**, to shop; — d'occasione, bargain; potere d'—, purchasing power; (comm.) addetto ufficio -**i**, buyer. (leg.) *pl.* after-acquired property.

acquitrin-o *m.* marshy ground; morass; bog, fen, marsh; water oozing from the ground, flush. -**oso** *adj.* boggy, marshy; sodden.

acquolina *f.*, **acquoso** *adj.* See under **acqua**.

acrale *adj.* (anat.) acral.

acr-e *adj.* (*superl.* **acerrimo**, used only in fig.) sharp, pungent; sour; bitter; acrid; harsh, strident; (fig.) severe, austere, biting; acrimonious; fierce, implacable. (-**emente** *adv.*) -**e·dine** *f.* sourness; bitterness; severity; (med.) acidity. -**ilato** *m.* (chem.) acrylate. -**i·lico** *adj.* (chem.) acrylic.

acrib-i·a *f.* accuracy, precision. -**ologi·a** *f.* precision of speech. -**o·metro** *m.* micrometer.

acri·d-io *m.* (ent.) locust; cricket. -**o·fago** *m.* (zool.) locust-eater.

acriflavina *f.* (med.; chem.) acriflavine.

acrimo·ni-a[1] *f.* acrimony; harshness; sourness. -**oso** *adj.* acrimonious.

acrimo·nia[2] *f.* (bot.). See **agrimonia**.

acro *m.* acre (4840 sq. yd. or 4046 sq. metres).

acroama·tico *adj.* (philos.) acroamatic, esoteric.

acroa·tico *adj.* (philos.) esoteric.

acro·b-ata *m.* acrobat; (fig.) clever, skilful person; one who stunts. -**a·tico** *adj.* acrobatic. (-**aticamente** *adv.*) -**atismo** *m.* acrobatics; fare dell'-**atismo**, to be an acrobat; (fig.) to stunt. -**azi·a** *f.* (also *pl.*) acrobatics; (fig.) è una vera -**azia**, it's a real tour de force; -**azie** di volo, stunt flying, aerobatics.

acrocera·unio *adj.* (poet., D'Annunzio) mountainous.

acro·c-oro, -**o·ro** *m.* plateau; summit. -**odi·nia** *f.* (med.) acrodynia. -**ofobi·a** *f.* (med.) acrophobia, fear of heights.

acro·gen-o, -**e** *adj.* (bot.) growing at extremity, as a fern.

acrografi·a *f.* etching.

acroleina *f.* (chem.) acrolein, acrylaldehyde.

acro·lito *m.* (archaeol.) acrolith.

acromani·a *f.* stark madness.

acrom-asi·a *f.* (phys.) achromatism. -**a·tico** *adj.* achromatic. -**atismo** *m.* achromatism. -**atopsi·a** *f.* (med.) acritochromacy, colour-blindness. -**iale** *adj.* (anat.) acromial. -**io·n** *m. indecl.* (anat.) acromial process, acromion.

acro·nico[1] *adj.* (astron.) acronychal.

acro·nico[2] *adj.* timeless.

acro·nimo *m.* name formed from the initial letters of several words, e.g. FIAT (Fabbrica Italiana Automobili Torino).

a·crono *adj.* seasonless.

acro·poli *f.* acropolis, citadel; (in Athens) Acropolis.

acro·pora *f.* (bot.) madrepore, lithophyte.

acro·stico *adj.*, *n.m.* acrostic.

acrote·rio *m.* (archit.) acroter; any ornament surrounding the pediment of a building.

acu-ire [D 2] *tr.* to sharpen, to make sharper; to make acute; to whet, to stimulate. -**ità** *f.* sharpness; acuteness; alertness, awareness; (opt.) -**ità** visiva, visual acuity. -**itivo** *adj.* stimulating, exciting. -**ito** *part. adj.* sharpened, sharp; aroused, alert.

acu·leo *m.* sharp point; sting; prickle; quill; thorn; goad; (fig.) incentive; stinging comment, sarcasm.

aculotta *f.* (dial. Sicily) (ichth.) black umber, *Johnius umber*. See **corvo**.

acume *m.* sharpness, acumen; perspicacity, discernment; penetration, insight.

acu·m-etro *m.* acoumeter. -**etri·a** *f.* acoumetry.

acumin-are [A I S] *tr.* to make pointed. -**ato** *part. adj.* pointed, ending in a point.

acusma *f.* acousma.

acu·stic-o *adj.* acoustic; corno —, ear-trumpet. -**a** *f.* acoustics.

acutan·golo *m.* (geom.) acute-angled triangle; *adj.* acute-angled.

acut-o *adj.* pointed, sharp; acute; shrewd, sharp-sighted; keen, eager; piercing, penetrating; high-pitched, shrill; freddo —, intense cold; male —, typhus; *n.m.* strong, unpleasant odour; (mus.) sharp; top note; begli -**i**, fine top notes; andare negli -**i**, to go very high; (archit.) arco a sesto —, pointed arch, ogive. -**amente** *adv.* acutely, shrewdly. -**ezza** *f.* acuteness; shrewdness; sharp-sightedness; acuity; -**ezza** d'ingegno, insight. -**izzare** [A I] *tr.* to make acute; *rfl.* to become acute (of illness).

acu·zie *f.* (med.) acute condition.

ad[1] *abbrev.* See **addietro** (naut.).

ad[2] *prep.* See **a** (prep.).

adacquare [A 6] and derivs. See **annacquare**.

adagi-are [A 3] *tr.* to lay, to set gently down; to make comfortable; to place in a reclining position; †to provide, to supply; *rfl.* to lie down; to stretch oneself out; to make oneself comfortable; -**arsi** sugli allori, to rest on one's laurels. -**a·bile** *adj.* adjustable. (-**amento** *m.*) -**ato** *part. adj.* comfortable; slow; well-to-do.

ada·gio[1] *adv.* slowly; softly, quietly; in a low voice; carefully; — Biagio! slow, Joe!, gently, Bentley!; (naut.) slow; orza —, starboard a little; (mus.) adagio; †*n.m.* ease, comfort; (mus.) adagio movement.

ada·gio[2] *m.* adage, proverb.

adamant-e[1] *m.* (poet.) adamant, impregnable hardness; diamond. -**ino** *adj.* adamantine.

†**adamante**[2] *m.* magnet.

Adam-o *pr.n.m.* Adam; i figli d'—, the sons of Adam, humanity; da — in qua, from time immemorial; quel d'—, human frailty, the old Adam; pomo d'—, Adam's apple. -**ismo** *m.* (neol.) school of literature which emphasizes man's primitive instincts. -**iti** *m.pl.* Adamites. -**i·tico** *adj.* pertaining to Adam; of the Adamites; primitive; in costume -**itico**, naked.

†**adarsen-a** *f.* (naut.). See **darsena**. †-**ale** (naut.). See **arsenale**.

†**ada·sio** *adv.* See **adagio**[1].

adastare[1] [A I] *tr.* to incite; to urge; *rfl.* to hurry.

†**adastare**[2] *rfl.* to stay, to remain, to tarry.

†**adastiare**[1] *tr.* to dislike; to envy; to antagonize; *recip. rfl.* to hate one another, to oppose one another.

†**adastiare**[2] *vb.* See **adastare**[1].

†**adastioso** *adj.* See **astioso**, under **astio**.

adatt-are [A I] *tr.* to adapt, to fit; to adjust; to apply; (radio) to match; *rfl.* (*prep.* a) to fit; to suit; to submit, to resign oneself; bisogna ~arci, we must make the best of it; to adapt oneself; to conform (to); ~arsi a qualunque lavoro, to turn one's hand to any work; (radio) to match. **-a·bile** *adj.* adaptable. **-abilità** *f.* adaptability. **-aménto** *m.* adaptation, arrangement; modification; capacità d'~amento, adaptability. (**-anza** *f.*) **-ato** *part. adj.* adapted; suitable, fit; opportune. **-ataménte** *adv.* suitably, appropriately. **-azióne** *f.* adaptation. **-évole** *adj.* adaptable; adjustable.

ad-atti·lia *f.* (med.) adactylia, congenital absence of fingers. **-at·tilo** *adj.* (med.) adactylous.

adatt-o *adj.* (*prep.* a) fit (for); qualified; suited; — al mare, seaworthy; suitable, proper, right; disposed. (**-aménte** *adv.*) **-ézza** *f.* aptness, suitability. **-o·metro** *m.* (med.; opt.) adaptometer.

addamascato *adj.* See **damascato**.

addanaiato *adj.* (herald.) spotted; †moneyed.

addare [A 8] *rfl.* (*prep.* di) to perceive, to notice, to become aware of; (*prep.* a) to begin; to be engaged (in); to devote oneself (to).

addaziare [A 4] *tr.* to tax, to put a tax on.

addebbiare [A 4] and derivs. See **debbiare**.

addębit-o *m.* accusation, imputation; (comm.) debit entry. **-are** [A I sc] *tr.* to accuse, to inculpate; (*prep.* di) to charge (with); (*prep.* a) to impute (to); (comm.) to debit. **-aménto** *m.* (comm.) debit entry. **-ato** *part. adj.* accused; imputed; debited.

†**addebolire** *vb.* and derivs. See **indebolire**.

addecim-are [A I s] *tr.* (hist.) to register for taxation; to exact a tenth as a tithe. (**-ato** *part. adj.* **-atóre** *m.* **-azióne** *f.*)

addendo *m.* sum, tot, figures to be added; addition to be made.

addens-are [A I] *tr.* to thicken; to make dense; to condense; (text.) to rub, to round; *rfl.* to grow thick, to thicken; to condense; to grow dense; to gather, to crowd. (**-aménto** *m.* **-ato** *part. adj.*)

addent-are [A I] *tr.* to seize with the teeth; to bite; to catch, to lay hold of; to attack, to injure; to dovetail, to mortise, to cog; to indent, to interlock; (fig.) to assail; to censure; to carp at. **-ato** *part. adj.* seized; bitten; attacked; dovetailed; cogged; indented, interlocked; (fig.) censured; †large-toothed, fanged. **-atura** *f.* bite; indentation, interlocking. **-ellare** [A I] *tr.* (archit.) to leave (the end of a wall) toothed; (eng.) to cog, to tooth. **-ellato** *part. adj.* (archit.) toothed; (fig.) unfinished, incomplete; indented; (text.) (of raw silk) with loose spiral end; *n.m.* (archit.) toothed wall-end; basis, groundwork; (eng.) denticulation; (fig.) stepping-stone, link; basis; pretext, hold; *pl.* gli ~ellati, things pertaining, kindred subjects.

addentr-are [A I c] *tr.* to thrust, to drive in; to put in; (naut.) to engage; †(naut.) -a a catena!, bring to!; *rfl.* to enter, to penetrate; to plunge (in); to study deeply, to become immersed. (**-aménto** *m.*) **-ato** *part. adj.* thrust, driven in; deep in; penetrating; immersed. **-atura** *f.* penetration; (naut.) joint; welding.

addéntro *adv.* inside, within; well in; deeply; vedere — a, to see deeply into; essere — in, to be in on, to have inside information about; to be well versed in, to be steeped in; (also **a dentro**).

†**addesiare** *vb.* and derivs. See **disiare**.

addestr-are [A I] *tr.* to train; to instruct; to inure; to discipline; to break in (a horse); (mil.) to drill; (naut.) to adjust (stern moorings); †to escort (on the right-hand side); *rfl.* (*prep.* a, in) to exercise; to practise; to train oneself; to go in for training; to become skilled. (**-a·bile** *adj.*) **-aménto** *m.* training; instruction; drilling. **-ato** *part. adj.* trained, skilled; instructed; accustomed, inured; disciplined; (herald.) on the dexter. **-atóre** *m.*, **-atrice** *f.* trainer.

addétto *adj.* employed, assigned, forming part, belonging; è — al reparto esportazioni, he has a job in the export department; given over; occupied; stanze -e all'amministrazione, rooms assigned to the management; *n.m.* attaché. — Stampa, Press attaché.

addì *adv.* on the day of, on; — 29 luglio, on the 29th of July.

addiacciare[1] [A 3] and derivs. See **agghiacciare**[1].

addiacciare[2] [A 3]. See under **addiaccio**.

addiac·ci-o *m.* sheep-pen, uncovered fold; dormire all'—, to sleep in the open; accampare all'—, to camp out. **-are** [A 3] *tr.* to keep (a herd, flock) out in the open for the night.

addiare [A 4] *rfl.* (dial.) to perceive, to become aware.

addiétro *adv.* behind, ago, before, previously; tempo —, some time ago; molti anni —, many years before; due pagine —, two pages

back; (naut.) aft (abbrev. **ad.**); dare —, to retreat; to draw back; to go backwards; to lapse, to get worse; in —, in days gone by; restar —, to make no progress; to be backward; lasciare —, lasciarsi —, to leave behind, to overtake; (of a clock) andare —, essere—, to be slow; *excl.* —!, keep back!; stand back!; *n.m.* rear, hind part; stern; past; per l'—, formerly.

addiettivo *m.* See **aggettivo**.

addimandare [A I] and derivs. See **domandare**.

addimesticare [A 2 s] and derivs. See **addomesticare**.

addimostrare [A I] and derivs. See **dimostrare**.

add-i·o *excl., n.m.* (*pl.* -ìi) good-bye; farewell; parting; parola d'—, parting word; adieu; lezione d'—, last lesson of the year; accademia d'—, serata d'—, farewell performance; dire — a, to say good-bye to, (fig.) to lose, to part with; to give up; voler dire —, to be on the point of death; fare —, to wave good-bye; e —, and that's that; ho mangiato due uova e —, I ate two eggs and that was all.

addipanare [A I] and derivs. See **dipanare**.

addire [B I O] *tr.* to dedicate, to assign, to destine; to allot; *rfl.* (*prep.* a) to be fitting, to be proper; to suit, to be becoming; to be to the taste (of); to dedicate oneself, to be destined.

addirittura *adv.* directly, immediately, without more ado; simply; quite, completely, absolutely; really; positively; downright, frankly.

addirizz-are[1] [A I] *tr.* to straighten; to put straight; to set up; to set right, to redress; to correct; to remedy; †(naut.) to fit out (a ship); — le gambe ai cani, to attempt the impossible, to waste one's time; *rfl.* to right oneself; to stand erect. (**-a·bile** *adj.*) **-aménto** *m.* straightening; redress. (**-ato** *part. adj.*) †**-atoio** *m.* comb. (**-atóre** *m.* **-atrice** *f.*) **-atura** *f.* straightening; redress; (of hair) parting.

addirizzare[2] [A I] and derivs. See **indirizzare**.

†**addi·scere** *tr., intr.* to learn.

addisciplinare [A I] and derivs. See **disciplinare**.

additaménto[1] *m.* addition; appendix; supplement.

additaménto[2] *m.* See under **additare**.

addit-are [A I] to indicate; to point out; to point at, to point to; to denote; to be indicative of; to show, to reveal, to disclose. **-aménto** *m.* indication; pointing out. (**-ato** *part. adj.*)

additivo *adj.* additive; *n.m.* additive; petrol additive.

ad·dito *m.* addition.

†**additto** *adj.* addicted; inclined; dedicated; destined.

addivenire [D 17] *intr.* (*aux.* essere) to become; to occur; to come (to), to reach; — ad un accordo, to reach an agreement; to consent (to).

addizión-e *f.* addition; total; supplement; (mech.) summation. **-ale** *adj.* additional; supplementary; (math.) pertaining to addition. (**-alità** *f.* **-alménte** *adv.*) **-are** [A I c] *tr.* to add up; to add; ~are di, to supplement with: ~are X di Y, to add Y to X. **-ato** *part. adj.* added up; added. ~ato di, supplemented with. **-atrice** *f.* adding machine.

addobb-are [A I] *tr.* to decorate; to adorn; to equip, to furnish; to dub; (tan.) to dress; (cul.) to garnish; †(naut.) to commission; †to arm; †— l'arme, to put on armour; *rfl.* to deck oneself out. **-aménto** *m.* decoration; furnishing. (**-ato** *part. adj.*) **-atóre** *m.*, **-atrice** *f.* decorator; upholsterer. **-o** *m.* ornament; decoration; (cul.) garnish; *pl.* hangings, bunting (e.g. in a church or town-hall).

addocciare [A 3 c] *tr.* (carp.) to rabbet, to groove, to channel.

addocilire [D 2] *tr.* (techn.) to soften, to mull (cloth), to stake (leather).

addog-are [A 2] *tr.* to stripe, to paint with stripes; to put staves round; (herald.) to bar. **-ato** *part. adj.* striped; with staves.

†**addogliare** *tr., rfl.* to grieve.

†**addolcare** *tr.* to soften; *intr.* (of weather) to grow milder.

addolc-ire [D 2] *tr.* to sweeten; (fig.) to soften; to soothe, to assuage; to quieten, to calm; to moderate; to make gentle, to civilize; to polish (manners); to alleviate; to allay; (paint.) to tone down; to temper (metals); *rfl.* to be sweetened; to become sweet; to soften; to be appeased, to relent; to grow mild; to be mitigated; to be assuaged. **-iménto** *m.* sweetening; softening; allaying, soothing; (archit.) chamfer, hollow chamfer, apophyge. **-itivo** *adj.* sweetening; appeasing, soothing; softening; (med.) demulcent, lenitive (also *n.m.*). (**-ito** *part. adj.* **-itóre** *m.* **-itrice** *f.*)

addolor-are [A I c] *tr.* to grieve, to sadden; to pain; to trouble, to afflict; *rfl.* (*prep.* di, per) to grieve; to mourn; to regret; to be sorry. **-ato** *part. adj.* sorrowful, grieved; sorry, regretful. l'—ata *f.* (eccl.) Our Lady of Sorrows, the Mother of Sorrows; her feast, church, picture, statue, or guild.

addomandare [A I] and derivs. See **domandare**

addo·m-e *m.* abdomen. **-inale** *adj.* abdominal.

addomestic-are [A2s] *tr.* to tame; to train; to domesticate; to refine; to bring into cultivation (of wild plants); to improve by cultivation; *rfl.* to become tame; to become sociable; -arsi con, to get to know, to become friendly with. (**-a·bile** *adj.* **-amento** *m.*) **-ato** *part. adj.* tamed, domesticated; tame; sociable; (iron.) prearranged: rivoluzione -ata, faked revolution. **-atore** *m.*, **-atrice** *f.* tamer, trainer. **-atura** *f.* cultivation of plants previously wild. **-azione** *f.* taming; training; domestication.

addomestichevol-e *adj.* tameable, capable of being domesticated. (**-ezza** *f.*)

addomestichire [D2] and derivs. See **addomesticare**.

†addo·mine *m.* See **addome**.

†addonare *intr.* to conform, to be adapted; to be subdued.

†addopare *rfl.* to hide, to conceal oneself.

addoppi-are [A4c] *tr.* to join (threads, strands), to use several thicknesses of; †see **raddoppiare**; †(naut.) See **doppiare**. (**-a·bile** *adj.* **-amento** *m.*) **-ato** *part. adj.* (of thread) double, joined. **-atoio** *m.* silk-winder, throwster's tool. (**-atore** *m.* **-atrice** *f.* **-atura** *f.*)

addoppio *m.* doubling (of thread); *adv.* doubly, in twos (of thread); †doubly, double, twice.

addore *m.* (dial.). See **odore**.

addorment-are [A1c] *tr.* to send to sleep, to make sleepy; to calm, to compose; — un bambino con le canzoni, to sing a child to sleep; to bore; to lull; to numb, to deaden; to beguile; to allay; to weaken; *abs.* to be boring: un libro che -a, a boring book; *rfl.* to go to sleep, to fall asleep; to grow numb; to be inactive; -arsi sugli allori, to rest on one's laurels; (colloq.) -arsi sull'arrosto, to miss an opportunity; -arsi nella pigrizia, to be sunk in apathy; -arsi nel Signore, -arsi nel bacio del Signore, to fall asleep in the Lord, to die a Christian death. **-atic·cio** *adj.* half asleep. (**-amento** *m.*) **-ativo** *adj.* soporific. **-ato** *part. adj.* asleep; numb; anaesthetized; calm; placated; lazy, indolent, slow; monotonous, dull; non far l'-ato, don't be stupid. **-atore** *m.* bore; wheedler, coax; -atore di serpenti, snake-charmer. (**-atrice** *f.*)

addormire [D1] and derivs. (poet.). See **addormentare**.

addoss-are [A1] *tr.* to put on (clothing); to pile, to heap; to load, to burden; to place with the back against; to place back to back; to build against; — le aiuole, to slope flower-beds southward by building up their northern edge; (bldg.) — i puntoni, to joint rafters; (fencing) to push (opponent) with back to the wall; (*prep.* a) to lay (upon), to put (upon); to attribute (to); to entrust (to); to accuse (of); — la colpa (a), to lay the blame (on); (comm.) — le spese (a), to charge expenses (to); *rfl.* (acc. of *rfl. prn.*, *prep.* a) to lean against; †(naut.) See **mettersi a ridosso**; (dat. of *rfl. prn.*) to take upon one's back; to undertake; to take on; to make oneself responsible for: -arsi un debito, to take over liability for a debt; *recip. rfl.* to stand back to back, to sit back to back; to crowd, to jostle. (**-amento** *m.*) **-ata** *f.* fitting, trying-on. **-ato** *part. adj.* on one's back; pick-a-back; (herald.) addorsed, back to back. **-atura** *f.* putting on; packing close; cramped writing.

addosso *prep., adv.* on, upon; on one's back; contiguous, close up against; avere —, to be burdened with; tirarsi —, to bring on oneself; mettersi —, to put on (clothing); portare —, to wear; non ho denaro —, I have no money on me; dare — a, to pitch into; to blame; gli furono subito —, they fell on him at once; dare — a, to attack; to blame; metter le mani — a, to lay hands on, to attack; to seize; stare — a, to stand over, to coerce; tagliare i panni — a, to speak ill of; (fig.) to tear to pieces; buttar la broda — a, to throw the blame on; stringer i panni — a, to corner; avere il diavolo —, to be restless, to be nervy; d'—, off; levarsi i panni d'—, to undress; non poteva levarsi d'— quel dolore, he couldn't get rid of the pain.

addotto¹ *m.* (ichth.) stone bass, *Polyprion cernium.* See **cerniola**.

addotto² *part.* from **addurre**, q.v.; *adj.* alleged; advanced, urged.

addottor-are [A1c] *tr.* to confer a university degree upon; (fig. iron.) to teach mischief to; *rfl.* to take a degree, to graduate. (**-amento** *m.*) **-ato** *part. adj.* graduated; holding a degree; è -ato in legge, he's a doctor of law.

addottrin-are [A1] *tr.* to instruct, to teach; to indoctrinate; *rfl.* to learn; to teach oneself; to become learned; (iron.) to become shrewd, to become cunning; *recip. rfl.* to instruct one another; to inform one another; to indoctrinate one another. (**-amento** *m.* **-ante** *part. adj.*) **-ato** *part. adj.* learned; indoctrinated; (iron.) shrewd, cunning. **-atura** *f.* instruction; indoctrination.

†addrappare *tr.* to clothe, to robe; *rfl.* to clothe oneself, to robe oneself.

†addrappellare *tr.* to draw up in a platoon.

†adduare *tr.* to couple, to combine; *rfl.* to double, to become double.

†adducere *vb.* and derivs. See **addurre**.

adduci·bile *adj.* (from **addurre**, q.v.); that may be alleged; adducible.

†addugliare *vb.* (naut.). See **cogliere**.

ad-durre [B2] *tr.* to allege; to quote, to cite; to adduce; to bring; to yield, to produce; to advance, to bring forward, to urge; (anat.) to adduct. **-duttore** *m.* (anat.) adductor muscle. **-duzione** *f.* (anat.) adduction.

Ade *pr.n.m.* (myth.) Hades.

adegu-are [A6c] *tr.* to equalize; to proportion; — le spese all'entrate, to keep within one's budget; to flatten, to smooth out; — al suolo, to raze to the ground; *rfl.* (*prep.* a) to become equal (to); to become adequate; to be compared; to become adjusted; (fig.) to rise (to). **-a·bile** *adj.* equalizable; proportionable. **-amento** *m.* equalizing; right relation, due proportion. **-atore** *m.* equalizer. (**-azione** *f.*)

adeguat-o *adj.* adequate; proportioned; suitable, fitting; right, fair; prezzo —, reasonable price. **-amente** *adv.* adequately; fairly.

Adel-e *pr.n.f.* Adela. **-ina** *pr.n.f.* Adeline.

Adelfi¹ *pr.n.m.pl.* the *Adelphi* (of Terence).

adelfi² *m.pl.* (bot.) adelphous plants.

adello *m.* (ichth.) a kind of sturgeon, *Acipenser huso.*

adempiere [D11], **ademp-ire** [D11] *tr.* to accomplish; to fulfil; to grant; to satisfy, to answer, to serve; to execute, to put into effect, to realize; †to make good, to compensate for; (leg.) — un contratto, to carry out a contract; *intr.* (aux. avere, *prep.* a) to fulfil, to carry out; (comm.) — ad un impegno, to meet an engagement, to meet an obligation; *rfl.* to be fulfilled, to come to pass. **-i·bile** *adj.* realizable. **-imento** *m.* fulfilment, realization, execution, accomplishment; performance. (**-itore** *m.* **-itrice** *f.*)

adempiuto *part.* of **adempiere**, q.v.; *adj.* accomplished; fulfilled.

adempri·v-io *m.* right to use pasture-land. **-ile** *adj.* (of land) subject to the right to be used as pasture.

aden-ite *f.* (med.) swollen glands, adenitis. **-o·ide** *f.* (usu. *pl.*), **-oidismo** *m.* adenoids. **-oma** *m.* glandular tumour. **-opati·a** *f.* adenopathy. **-oso** *adj.* adenose, glandulous.

adenocarpo *m.* (bot.) adenocarp.

adepto *m.* follower, disciple; †initiate in alchemy.

†adequazione *f.* equalizing, equalization; comparison.

†aderbare *tr.* to graze, to pasture.

aderen-te *adj.*, **-za** *f.* See under **aderire**.

ader·gere [C5] (poet.). See **ergere**.

ader-ire [D2] *intr.* (aux. avere, *prep.* a) to adhere, to stick, to cling; to follow, to be an adherent; to support, to join; to assent (to), to comply (with), to grant; — ad un invito, to write a formal acceptance of an invitation. **-ente** *adj.* sticking; adhesive; relevant; (of clothes) tight, close-fitting; *n.m.* adherent, supporter, partisan. **-enza** *f.* adherence; (motor.) wheel grip, grip on the road; (med.) adhesion; *pl.* connexions, contacts, influence. **-imento** *m.* adherence; assent.

†aderpicare *vb.* and derivs. See **inerpicare**.

†adesare *tr.* to arrange, to make ready, to prepare.

adesc-are [A2c] *tr.* to entice, to lure; to inveigle, to beguile; to bait; to decoy; (eng.) to prime (a pump). (**-a·bile** *adj.*) **-amento** *m.* enticement; flattery; bait; (eng.) priming. (**-ato** *part. adj.* **-atore** *m.* **-atrice** *f.*)

adesion-e *f.* adherence, adhesion; -i ad una società, supporters of a society; members of a society; approval, assent; support; formal acceptance (of an invitation); contact, meeting-point; (scient.) adhesion; cohesion; (leg.) parere d'—, corroborating opinion by senior legal adviser.

adesiv-o *adj.* adhesive; sticky; (leg.) parere —, see under **adesione**. **-ità** *f.* adhesiveness.

†adeso *adj.* adhered, attached.

ade·spot-a, -o *adj.* without an owner; anonymous, of unknown authorship.

adesso *adv.* now, at the present moment; ——, immediately, at once; è uscito —, he's just gone out; nowadays; uomini d'—, men of today; per —, for the present; — si spiega!, so that's it!

adetto *adj.* initiated, affiliated.

adiac-ente *adj.* (foll. by *prep.* a) adjacent, adjoining; nearby; contiguous. **-enza** *f.* adjacency; *pl.* vicinity, neighbourhood.

adia·fono *m.* (mus.) adiaphonon (keyboard instrument with tuning forks instead of strings).

adianto *m.* (bot.) genus of ferns, *Adiantum*, including the maidenhair, **capelvenere**, q.v.

adib-ire [D 2] *tr.* to destine; to reserve; to convert: — una stanza ad uso di cucina, to convert a room as a kitchen; (leg.) to produce (proof, witnesses). **-ito** *part. adj.* destined; seconded.

A·dice *pr.n.m.* poet. form of **Adige**, river of N. Italy.

†adiettivo *m.* See **aggettivo**.

adimare [A 1] *tr.* (poet.) to lower; *rfl.* to descend, to flow downwards.

adin·ami·a *f.* (med.) adynamia. **-a·mico** *adj.* adynamic.

a·dip-e *m.* fat, corpulence; *adj.* fat, corpulent. **-oce·ra** *f.* (med.) adipocere. **-osità** *f.* adiposity. **-oso** *adj.* adipose, fat.

a·dipso *m.* (bot.) liquorice plant, *Glycyrrhiza glabra*.

adir-are [A 1] *tr.* to enrage, to anger; to irritate; to vex; *rfl.* to get angry; to be exasperated; to take offence; to fly into a rage; *recip. rfl.* to quarrel, to fall out. **-amento** *m.* anger, wrath; passion, violence, transport, outburst. **-ato** *part. adj.* enraged, angry; fare l'-ato, to be angry, to sulk. **-atamente** *adv.* angrily. **-evole** *adj.* easily angered.

ad-ire [B 10] *tr.* (leg.) — un tribunale, to commence an action before a court; to apply to a court, to appear before a court; — le vie giudiziarie, to resort to legal proceedings; — un'eredità, to accept an inheritance. **-izione** *f.* (leg.) act of acceptance of an inheritance.

†adiroso *adj.* See **iroso**.

a·dito¹ *m.* entry; entrance, access; dare — a, to lead to; to give rise to; to permit entry to, to entitle to enter.

a·dito² *m.* (archaeol.) adytum.

†adiut-ore *m.* helper, assistant. **-o·rio** *m.* help; (anat.) humerus.

†adiuv-are *tr.* to help. **-ante** *part. adj.* (pharm.) adjuvant; (theol.) grazia -ante, actual grace.

adizione *f.* See under **adire**.

†adizzare *vb.* See **aizzare**.

admido·metro *m.* (phys.) atmometer, evaporimeter.

adnata *f.* (anat.) conjunctiva.

adnato *adj.* (anat.) adherent; (bot.) adnate.

adocchi-are [A 4] *tr.* to set eyes on; to catch a glimpse of, to espy; to glance at; to spot; to eye; to covet; (dial.) to put the evil eye on. (**-amento** *m.* **-ato** *part. adj.* **-atore** *m.* **-atura** *f.*)

adolesc-ente *adj.* adolescent; *n.m.* lad, youth; adolescent; *f.* girl, teenager; adolescent girl. **-entile** *adj.* of adolescence, youthful. **-enza** *f.* boyhood, girlhood, teenage, teens; adolescence.

†adole·scere *intr.* to enter adolescence, to become adolescent.

Adolfo *pr.n.m.* Adolphus.

adombr-are [A 1 c] *tr.* to shade; to darken; to conceal; to adumbrate; to represent; to symbolize, to suggest; to sketch, to outline; (paint.) to shade; *rfl.* (of horses) to shy; (of persons) to become suspicious, to be touchy, to take umbrage; to be afraid; to be in shadow. **-a·bile** *adj.* that can be shaded; (fig.) touchy; suspicious; (of a horse) skittish. (**-amento** *m.* **-ato** *part. adj.* **-atore** *m.* **-atrice** *f.* **-atura** *f.* **-azione** *f.*)

·†adonare *vb.* See **domare**.

†adonca *adv.* See **dunque**.

Adone¹ *pr.n.m.* Adonis; handsome youth; far l'—, to be a dandy; non è un —, he's no Adonis.

adone² *m.* (bot.) scarlet adonis, red pheasant's eye, *Adonis annua*.

adonestare [A 1] *tr.* to veil; to give the appearance of honesty to; to fake, to 'cook', to 'whitewash'.

ado·nico *m.* See **adonio**.

ado·nide *f.* See **adone²**.

ado·nio *adj., n.m.* (prosod.) Adonic.

adont-are [A 1 c] *tr.* to reproach; to affront; to offend; *rfl.* to take umbrage, to get annoyed; to take offence; *†intr.* to take umbrage; to feel ashamed. (**-amento** *m.*) **-oso** *adj.* touchy.

adop-erare [A 1 s], **adopr-are** [A 1] *tr.* to use, to make use of, to put to use, to employ; to engage the services of; to exert; to spend; *†intr.* to serve, to be of use; to be effective, to work; *rfl.* to exert oneself; -arsi per, to work for, to aim at; to strive, to endeavour. (**-a·bile** *adj.* **-amento** *m.* **-ativo** *adj.* **-ato** *part. adj.* **-atore** *m.* **-atrice** *f.*)

ador-are [A 1 c] *tr.* to adore; to love passionately; to revere; (rel.) to adore, to worship (God); to venerate (the Madonna, saints); to bow to (God's will); to do homage to (newly elected pope); *intr.* (*aux.* avere, *prep.* a) to pray to, to pay worship to. **-a·bile** *adj.*

adorable, lovable; charming; worthy of worship. (**-abilmente** *adv.* **-abilità** *f.*) **-ante** *part. adj.* adoring; worshipping; *n.m., f.* adorer; worshipper. **-ato** *part. adj.* adored, beloved; worshipped. **-atore** *m.* worshipper; admirer, swain. **-atrice** *f.* adorer; worshipper; *pl.* -atrici perpetue, nuns of the Perpetual Adoration. **-azione** *f.* adoration; worship, veneration; homage (of cardinals to new pope).

ado·reo *adj.* (poet.) wheaten, oaten.

†adorezzare *intr.* (Dante) to be shady, to be in shadow.

adorn-are [A 1 c] *tr.* to adorn, to decorate; to embellish, to set off, to enhance; to dress, to deck; †to provide, to furnish, to supply; †to dispose, to arrange; *rfl.* to adorn oneself; (fig.) to boast; (poet.) to grow beautiful. (**-a·bile** *adj.*) **-amento** *m.* adornment; ornament; decoration, trimming. (**-anza** *f.* **-ato** *part. adj.* **-atamente** *adv.* **-atore** *m.* **-atrice** *f.* **-atura** *f.*)

adorn-o *adj.* ornate; adorned, decorated, ornamented; bedecked; (poet.) beautiful; comely; con parola -a, with polished speech. **-ezza** *f.* ornateness.

†adotare *vb.* See **dotare**.

adott-are [A 1] *tr.* to adopt; to accept; to have recourse to; — una decisione, to take a decision. **-a·bile** *adj.* adoptable; acceptable, admissible. (**-amento** *m.* **-ante** *part. adj.*, *n.m., f.*) **-ativo** *adj.*, **-ato** *part. adj.* adopted, adoptive. (**-atore** *m.* **-atrice** *f.* **-azione** *f.*) **-ivo** *adj.* adopted, adoptive, by adoption; (bot.) growing on a graft.

†adovrare *vb.* See **adoperare**.

adoxa *f.* (bot.) town-hall clock, moschatel, *Adoxa moschatellina*.

adozion-e *f.* adoption; figliuolo d'—, adopted son; acceptance, choice. **-ismo** *m.* adoptionism. (**-ista** *m.*)

adracne *f.* (bot.) strawberry-tree, *Arbutus andrachne*; also *Andrachne telephioides*.

adragante *adj.* gomma —, gum tragacanth; *n.m.* (bot.) see **dragante**.

adrenalina *f.* (med.) adrenalin.

adri·aco *adj.* See **adriatico**.

Adriano *pr.n.m.* Hadrian; il Vallo d' —, Hadrian's Wall; Adrian.

adria·tico *adj., n.m.* (geog.) Adriatic; l'Alto —, the Upper Adriatic.

†adro *adj.* See **atro**.

adsorbimento *m.* (phys.) adsorption.

†adug·gere *tr.* to burn, to dry, to parch; to overshadow.

aduggi-are [A 3] *tr.* to overshadow; to darken; to stain, to sully; to sadden; to weary, to irritate; to stultify, to cramp, to hinder; to blight, to embitter; *rfl., intr.* (*aux.* essere) to be darkened; to grow sad; to be stultified; to become embittered. (**-amento** *m.*) **-ato** *part. adj.* shady, overshadowed; luogo -ato, sunless spot. (**-atore** *m.* **-atrice** *f.*)

adu·gli-a *f.* twist, turn; un'— di cavo, one turn of a cable; a coil of a cable. **-are¹** [A 4] *tr.* (naut.) to coil (a cable) into a spiral.

adugliare² [A 4] *tr.* (dial.) to anoint.

†adugnare *vb.* See **adunghiare**.

adul-are [A 1] *tr.* to adulate; to fawn upon; to flatter; *rfl.* to flatter oneself, to be conceited. (**-a·bile** *adj.*) **-ato** *part. adj.* flattered; (poet.) thronged with flatterers. **-atore** *m.*, **-atrice** *f.* flatterer, adulator; *adj.* flattering. **-ato·rio** *adj.* adulatory; complimentary; flattering. (**-atoriamente** *adv.*) **-azione** *f.* adulation, flattery.

adula·ria *f.* (miner.) adularia orthoclase.

adulazione *f.* See under **adulare**.

adulter-are [A 1 s] *tr.* to adulterate; to taint, to contaminate; to falsify; to debase; to counterfeit; to vitiate; to misrepresent, to distort; †*tr.* to corrupt, to commit adultery with; †*intr.* to commit adultery. (**-a·bile** *adj.* **-amento** *m.*) **-ato** *part. adj.* adulterated, contaminated; †adulterous. (**-atore** *m.* **-atrice** *f.*) **-azione** *f.* adulteration, contamination, falsification.

adulte·rio *m.* adultery; †sodomy; †rape.

adul·ter-o *m.* adulterer; *adj.* adulterous; †cuckold; †bastard; †incestuous; †adulterated; †false. **-a** *f.* adulteress. **-amente** *adv.* adulterously; in adultery. **-ino** *adj.* born of adultery, adulterine; †adulterous; †false.

adulto *adj.* adult; advanced; full-grown; *n.m.* adult, grown-up.

†adun(a) *adv.* together, at the same time.

adun-are [A 1] *tr.* to assemble, to gather together; to collect; to summon, to muster; to convoke, to convene; to amass; to contain, to comprise; *rfl.* to assemble, to meet, to gather, to congregate; to join together, to combine. (**-a·bile** *adj.* **-agione** *f.* **-amento** *m.*) **-anza** *f.* assembly, meeting; board; indire un'-anza, to call a meeting. **-ata** *f.* gathering, assembly; -ata in massa, mass-

adun·are (*cont.*) meeting; (mil.) parade, rally; fall-in. -**ato** *part. adj.* gathered together, assembled; *n.m.pl.* gli -**ati**, the assembly, those present. -**atore** *m.* gatherer; l'-**atore di nembi**, the cloud-gatherer, Zeus. (-**atrice** *f.*) -**o** *m.* meeting.

aduncinare [A I] *tr.* to seize with the claws; to tear.

adun·co *adj.* (*m.pl.* -**chi**) hooked; curved; crooked; naso —, hook nose, beaky nose; †perspicacious, wise.

adunghiare [A 4] *tr.* to claw, to clutch; to seize.

aduno *m.* See under **adunare**.

†**adu·rere** *tr.* to burn.

aduṣ·are [A I] *tr.* to accustom; *rfl.* to accustom oneself. -**ato** *part. adj.* accustomed. -**o** *adj.* accustomed

adust·o *adj.* scorched; dried up; sunburnt; sun-drenched; dry, thin, wiry; †inflammable; †tempo —, summer weather. -**are** [A I] *tr.* to parch, to dry up. -**ezza** *f.* dryness; aridity. (-**i·bile** *adj.*) -**ione** *f.* burning, scorching; combustibility; (med.) heated state of the blood. (-**ivo** *adj.*)

ae·do *m.* Greek poet; poet, bard.

aer·are [A I] *tr.* to air, to ventilate, to aerate. -**ag·gio** *m.* ventilation. -**ato** *part. adj.* airy, ventilated. -**azione** *f.* airing, ventilation. -**emoto** *m.* wind-storm, hurricane. -**o·foro** *m.* air-conditioner. -**oṣo** *adj.* airy.

a·ere *m.* (poet.) air; sky; atmosphere; — chiaro, daylight; — bruno, night; l'— cieco, the infernal regions; †disposition; †aspect, semblance; †essere di buon — verso, to be benevolent towards; †di buon —, joyful, benign.

ae·re·o *adj.* pertaining to air; similar to air; aerial, ethereal; airy, unsubstantial; light, graceful; (poet.) lofty, sublime; ferrovia -**a**, trazione -**a**, overhead railway; posta -**a**, air mail; per via -**a**, by air mail; forze -**e**, Air Force; (paint.) prospettiva -**a**, aerial perspective; *n.m.* aircraft; outdoor aerial.

ae·rio *adj.* (poet.). See **aereo**.

aer·i·fero *adj.* aeriferous. -**ificare** [A 2 s] *tr.* to aerify. (-**ificazione** *f.*) -**iforme** *adj.* aeriform; -**obus** *m. indecl.* passenger plane. -**oconvo·glio** *m.* air-convoy. -**odina·mica** *f.* aerodynamics. (-**odinamicità** *f.*) -**odina·mico** *adj.* aerodynamic; streamlined. -**o·dine** *f.* glider. -**o·dromo** *m.* aerodrome. -**oespresso** *m.* express air letter. -**ofotografi·a** *f.* air photography. -**ofonista** *m.* aircraft detector operator. -**o·fono** *m.* aircraft detector, listening post; (mus.) aerophone. -**o·foro** *m.* (mus.) aerophor (device for assisting breathing of wind instrument players). -**ografi·a** *f.* aerography. -**o·grafo** *m.* spray gun, airbrush. -**ogramma** *m.* air-letter. -**oidroscalo** *m.* seaplane base. -**oli·nea** *f.* air-line. -**olito** *m.* aerolite. -**ologi·a** *f.* aerology. -**o·logo** *m.* (*pl.* -**ologhi**) aerologist. -**omo·bile** *m.* aircraft. -**omodelliṣmo** *m.* model airplane flying. -**omodellista** *m.* model airplane enthusiast. -**ona·uta** *m.* pilot. -**ona·utica** *f.* aeronautics; air-force. -**ona·utico** *adj.* aeronautical. -**onave** *f.* airship. -**oplano** *m.* aeroplane; (slang) **carabiniere**, q.v. -**oporto** *m.*, -**oscalo** *m.* airport. -**osta·tica** *f.* aerostatics. -**osta·tico** *adj.* aerostatic. -**o·stato** *m.* aerostat.

aetite *f.* eagle-stone, aetites.

aetusa *f.* See **etusa**.

af·a *f.* sultriness; sultry weather; oppressive heat; breathlessness; boredom, tedium; nausea, disgust; fare — a, to smother; to bore; to arouse distaste; to sicken. -**ato** *adj.* stunted, withered. -**oṣo** *adj.* sultry, suffocating.

a·faca *f.* (bot.) yellow vetchling, *Lathyrus aphaca*.

a·fane *f.* (bot.) parsley piert, *Aphanes arvensis*.

afanite *f.* (miner.) aphanite.

afascista *m., adj.* non-Fascist.

afaṣi·a *f.* (med.) aphasia; (phil.) deliberate silence (of Sceptics).

afebbrile *adj.* (med.) apyretic, afebrile.

afe·lio *m.* (astron.) aphelion.

afe·resi *f.* (gramm.) aphaeresis; (surg.) amputation.

affa·bil·e *adj.* affable; agreeable, polite, courteous; kind. (-**ità** *f.*) -**mente** *adv.*)

affaccend·are [A I] *tr.* to give employment to, to occupy; *rfl.* to be busily occupied, to bustle about; to take trouble; (*prep.* a, dietro a) to busy oneself (with). (-**amento** *m.*) -**ato** *part. adj.* busy; bustling; fussy. -**io** *m.* continual bustling.

affaccettare [A I c] and derivs. See **sfacettare**.

affacchin·are [A I] *tr.* to overwork; to slave-drive; *rfl.* to labour, to toil, to drudge, to slog; to work like a black. (-**amento** *m.*)

-**ato** *part. adj.* weary; overworked; è tutto -**ato** dietro al suo lavoro, he's hard at it.

affacciare [A 3] *tr.* to hold up; to present, to show; (fig.) to put forward, to raise; *rfl.* to show oneself; to put in an appearance; to come forward, to stand forth; to bid (at an auction); affacciarsi alla finestra, to appear at the window; — allo specchio, to look at oneself in the mirror; (of an idea) to occur: mi si affacciò un'idea, an idea occurred to me; (of stars) affacciarsi appena, to peep, to begin to twinkle.

affagott·are [A I] *tr.* to roll up into a bundle; to bundle; to make into faggots; *rfl.* to bundle oneself up; to dress carelessly. -**ato** *part. adj.* bundled up; carelessly dressed.

†**affaitare** *rfl.* to adorn oneself; to conform.

affald·are [A I] *tr.* to pleat; to fold; *rfl.* to become wrinkled, to become creased. -**ato** *part. adj.* pleated; folded; wrinkled.

affaldellare [A I] *tr.* (text.) to separate (spun silk) into strands.

affam·are [A I] *tr.* to starve; to starve out, to reduce to hunger; *intr.* (*aux.* essere) to be hungry. (-**amento** *m.*) -**ato** *part. adj.* hungry, famished; voracious; (fig.) -**ato di**, eager for, greedy for; *n.m.pl.* gli -**ati**, the hungry, the poor. (-**atore** *m.* -**atrice** *f.*)

†**affamire** *intr.* to suffer hunger.

affann·are [A I] *tr.* to make breathless; to fatigue; to trouble, to distress; to vex; to make uneasy; †(naut.) to overload; *rfl.* to be breathless; to be tired; to be worried, to be preoccupied; to busy oneself; to toil, to strive, to do one's utmost; (*prep.* dietro a) to strive after. -**amento** *m.* anxiety; bustle. -**ante** *part. adj.* distressing; anxious; panting, short of breath. -**ato** *part. adj.* uneasy; panting; breathless; troubled, uneasy; distressed; exhausted. -**atamente** *adv.* with difficulty, breathlessly. (-**atore** *m.* -**atrice** *f.*) -**oṣo**. See under **affanno**.

affann·o *m.* heavy breathing; panting; palpitation; discomfort; difficulty, trouble; exertion; suffering, sorrow; darsi —, prendersi —, to trouble oneself, to take trouble. -**evole** *adj.* See -**oṣo**. -**one** *m.* (colloq.) busybody, meddler. -**oneri·a** *f.* meddling. -**oṣo** *adj.* (of breathing) troubled; painful; difficult; wearisome; oppressive; hurried; incessant; (fig.) feverish. -**oṣamente** *adv.* anxiously, breathlessly; feverishly.

affantocciare [A 3] *tr.* (agric.) to tie up the branches or tendrils of.

affarato *adj.* busy.

affardellare [A I] *tr.* to tie up into a bundle; to bundle together; to pack; (mil.) — lo zaino, to pack one's kit.

affar·e *m.* affair, matter; è — fatto, that's settled; un bell'—! a nice mess!; badate ai vostri -**i**, mind your own business; bargain; concludere un —, to strike a bargain; to conclude a matter of business; speculation; un — lucroso, a profitable transaction; è rimasto coinvolto in un — giudiziario, he has been involved in a lawsuit (or trial); — di cuore, love affair; importance, moment; persona di grand'—, a person of importance; impresa di gravoso —, undertaking of great moment; persona di mal —, a bad hat; donna di mal —, prostitute; thing, thingummy; cos'è quell' — lì?, what is that thingummy?; *pl.* business; gli -**i** sono gli -**i**, business is business; uomo d'-**i**, business man; mettersi negli -**i**, to go into business; -**i** commerciali, business transactions; -**i** esteri, foreign relations, foreign affairs; incaricato d'-**i**, chargé d'affaires. -**io** *m.* bustle, activity. -**iṣmo** *m.* speculation; sharp practice; ruthlessness in business affairs. -**ista** *m.* profiteer, shark. -**i·stico** *adj.* pertaining to business; dal punto di vista -**istico**, from the business angle. -**one** *m.* good bargain, good stroke of business. -**u·colo** *m.* trivial matter.

affare *vb.* See **confare**.

affaṣci·are [A 3] *tr.* to tie in bundles. (-**amento** *m.*) -**ato** *part. adj.* in bundles.

affascinare¹ [A I] *tr.* to make up into fascines.

affascin·are² [A I s] *tr.* to enchant, to bewitch; to fascinate, to delight, to charm; to attract. -**amento** *m.* fascination; seduction; evil eye; enchantment, spell. -**ante** *part. adj.* fascinating; attractive; bewitching, enchanting; charming, delightful. (-**ato** *part. adj.*) -**atore** *m.* lady-killer, charmer; sorcerer. -**atrice** *f.* femme fatale; enchantress. (-**azione** *f.*)

affastell·are [A I] *tr.* to tie into bundles; to heap up; to jumble, to confuse, to muddle. -**amento** *m.* piling up; heap; confusion, muddle. (-**ato** *part. adj.*) -**io** *m.* confusion, muddle, chaos.

†**affastidire** *tr.* to annoy.

†**affatappiare** *tr.* to bewitch, to cast an evil spell upon.

†**affatare** *tr.* to bewitch, to hold spellbound.

affatic-are [A 2] *tr.* to fatigue, to weary; to overwork; to strain; to weaken, to exhaust; to impoverish (land); (naut.) to buffet; *rfl.* to work hard, to toil, to strive; to grow weary, to tire. **-aménto** *m.* wearying; weariness. **-ante** *part. adj.* fatiguing; wearisome, tiresome. **-ato** *part. adj.* tired, weary; overworked; exhausted.

affatto *adv.* quite, entirely, wholly; absolutely; not at all; non — affatto, not…at all; niente —, nothing at all; not at all.

affattucchiare [A 4] and derivs. See **fattucchiare**.

affattur-are [A 1] *tr.* to bewitch, to cast a spell on; to enchant, to beguile; to delude; to adulterate, to concoct. (**-aménto** *m.* **-ato** *part. adj.* **-atore** *m.* **-atrice** *f.* **-azione** *f.*)

affazzolettato *adj.* (Carducci) folded like a handkerchief.

affazzonare [A 1 c]. See **raffazzonare**.

affè *excl.* truly! upon my word!, in faith!; — di Dio!, by God!

afferente *adj.* carrying, bearing; leading (to); concerning; (anat.) afferent.

afferm-are [A 1] *tr.* to affirm; to say; to state; to point out; to maintain; to establish; to confirm; †(naut.) to secure (the ensign); *rfl.* to prove oneself; to make a name for oneself; to become established; †to rally for defence. (**-abile** *adj.* **-ativa** *f.* assertion; affirmation; affirmative. **-ativaménte** *adv.* in the affirmative. **-ativo** *adj.* affirmative; positive; in caso -ativo, in the affirmative. (**-ato** *part. adj.* **-atore** *m.* **-atrice** *f.*) **-azione** *f.* affirmation, assertion; achievement, victory; una splendida -azione, a splendid performance; una -azione personale, a personal success.

affernante *adj.* (herald.) holding.

†afferrante *m.* war-horse.

afferr-are [A 1] *tr.* to seize, to take hold of, to grasp; to catch; to understand; — a volo, to catch on, to be quick in the uptake; (naut.) to secure (a ship) by anchoring or going alongside; to grapple; *abs.* (of an anchor) to hold; *rfl.* (*prep.* a) to get hold (of), to grasp; to cling (to); (bot.) to take root. (**-aménto** *m.* **-ante** *part. adj.*) **-atoio** *m.* pincers, grippers. (**-ato** *part. adj.* **-atore** *m.* **-atrice** *f.*)

affertilire [D 2]. See **infertilire**.

affett-are[1] [A 1] *tr.* to affect, to feign, to simulate; — un sorriso, to smirk; to assume, to pretend to; to influence, to have an effect on; †to desire, to covet. **-ato** *part. adj.* affected, mannered, insincere. (**-ataménte** *adv.* **-atézza** *f.* **-atore** *m.* **-atrice** *f.* **-atura** *f.*) **-azione** *f.* affectation; insincerity.

affett-are[2] [A 1 c] *tr.* to slice; to cut; (mil.) to cut down, to massacre; *rfl.* to be cut; to be thick enough to cut; nebbia che s' -a, a fog you could cut with a knife; (of clothing) to fall to pieces, to go into holes. **-aménto** *m.* slicing. **-asalumi** *m. indecl.* sausage-slicing machine. **-ato** *part. adj.* sliced; *n.m.* sliced sausage, salame, ham. **-atore** *m.* slicer; (fig.) -atore dell'aria, braggart. **-atrice** *f.* sausage-slicing machine. (**-atura** *f.*)

affetti·bil-e *adj.* modifiable, susceptible to modification. (**-ità** *f.*)

affett-o[1] *m.* affection; love; con —, with love; (mus.) with feeling; emotion; feeling, sentiment; inclination, desire; mozione degl — i, peroration; prendere — a, to take to, to become fond of; (med.) malady, disorder, affection, morbid state; (gramm.) case, inflexion; (mus.) †emotion; †the expression of an emotion in music; †passage expressing an emotion. **-ivo** *adj.* affective; emotional. (**-ività** *f.*) †**-uare** *rfl.* to become fond. **-uoso** *adj.* affectionate, loving; warm-hearted, tender; affecting; (mus.) *n.m.* a movement expressing tender feeling; †title assumed by some members of Italian musical academies. **-uosaménte** *adv.* affectionately. **-uosità** *f.* warm-heartedness, fondness.

affetto[2] *adj.* (*prep.* da) affected (by); suffering (from); afflicted (with); liked, loved: essere il bene — (a), to be well liked (by), to be the favourite (of); (leg.) encumbered; *n.m.* (math.) property.

affezion-are [A 1 c] *tr.* (*prep.* a) to attach, to bind, to make fond (of), to inspire affection (for); *rfl.* (*prep.* a) to become fond (of); to take a liking (to). (**-abile** *adj.* **-abilità** *f.* **-aménto** *m.*) **-atissimo** *adj.* (at end of letter) yours affectionately; yours very sincerely. **-ato** *part. adj.* affectionate; loving; faithful, devoted; -ato a, fond of; *n.m.* friend, dear friend. **-ataménte** *adv.* affectionately.

affezion-e *f.* affection, love; emotion, feeling; prezzo d'—, sentimental value; (math.) property; (med.) disorder, affection, morbid condition; (gramm.) inflexion. **-cella** *f.* passing attachment; (med.) slight morbid condition.

†affiammata *f.* brightly coloured cloth.

affianc-are [A 2] *tr.* to place side by side; to uphold, to support; to engage, to call in the assistance of; (mil.) to flank. **-ato** *part. adj.* flanked.

affiarare [A 1] *rfl.* (dial. Rom.) to hurl oneself.

affiat-are [A 1] *tr.* to harmonize; to train to work together; *rfl.* to adapt oneself, to adjust oneself; si è -ato coll'ambiente, he has adapted himself to his environment; ci vuole un po' di tempo per affiatarsi, it takes a little time to settle down; *recip. rfl.* to agree, to come to an understanding, to fall in with one another; (mus.) to achieve a good ensemble. **-aménto** *m.* working agreement, understanding; (mus.) good ensemble. **-ato** *part. adj.* agreeing, harmonizing; adjusted: non è ancora molto -ato, he's still rather new to it; bene -ati, working well together.

†affiato *adj.* in fief.

affibbi-are [A 6] *tr.* to buckle, to clasp; to do up; (fig.) to palm off; — un colpo, to deal a blow; — un soprannome (a), to nickname; — un incarico (a), to impose a task (on); — la colpa (a), to lay the blame (on); *rfl.* to buckle oneself up. †**-a·glio** *m.* brooch. (**-aménto** *m.*) **-ato** *part. adj.* buckled. **-atoio** *m.* buckle. **-atura** *f.* buckling; buckle; clasp; row of hooks and eyes; buttonhole.

affid-are [A 1] *tr.* to confide; to commit; to entrust; to assign; — alla memoria, to learn by heart; to assure, to guarantee; to protect; *rfl.* (*prep.* a) to rely (on), to trust (to, in). **-aménto** *m.* assurance, guarantee; dare -aménto, to assure, to inspire confidence, to show promise; fare -aménto su, to rely on. **-anza** *f.* confidence; familiarity, liberty. **-ato** *part. adj.* committed; entrusted. (**-ataménte** *adv.* **-atore** *m.* **-atrice** *f.*)

affien-are [A 1] *tr.* to put (a horse) on hay. **-ata** *f.* feed of hay. **-ato** *part. adj.* fed on hay. (**-atura** *f.*)

affienire [D 2] *intr.* (*aux.* essere) to turn to hay.

affievol-ire [D 2] *tr.* to weaken, to enfeeble; to soften; *intr.* (*aux.* essere) to grow weak; *rfl.* to weaken; to grow soft; (of sound) to diminish, to fade away; (fig.) to cool down. **-iménto** *m.* weakening; (radio) fading. **-ito** *part. adj.* enfeebled.

affig·gere [C 17] *tr.* to affix, to post up; to placard; to announce, to publish; — i propri sentimenti, to parade one's feelings; to fix (on); — gli occhi su, to stare at; *rfl.* to stop, to stand still; (*prep.* a) to gaze at.

affigliare [A 4] and derivs. See **affiliare**.

affigurare [A 1] and derivs. See **raffigurare**.

affilarato *adj.* (agric.) set with vines in rows.

affil-are[1] [A 1] *tr.* to sharpen, to whet; to make pointed; to taper; to grind; to hone; to strop; (fig.) — le spade, to prepare for battle. **-aménto** *m.*, **-ata** *f.* sharpening. **-ato** *part. adj.* sharpened; sharp; pointed; lingua -ata, bitter tongue; fare il viso -ato, to grow thin in the face. (**-atézza** *f.*) **-atoio** *m.* sharpener; razor strop. **-atrice** *f.* (eng.) sharpener, grinder, sharpening machine. **-atura** *f.* sharpening, grinding, honing; edge; (dial.) current of air, draught.

affilare[2] [A 1] *tr.* to place in rows (e.g. trees, plants); *rfl.* to form a line; †(naut.) to form line ahead.

affilatoio *m.* See under **affilare**[1].

affilett-are [A 1 c] *tr.* to point (a wall) with the point and edge of the trowel; *abs.* to lay nets. (**-atura** *f.*)

affili-are [A 4] *tr.* to affiliate; to associate; *rfl.* to become affiliated; to become a member; (dat. of prn.) -arsi un bambino, to adopt a child. **-ato** *part. adj.* affiliated; associated; *n.m.* member, supporter. (**-atura** *f.*) **-azione** *f.* adoption; fosterage.

affin-are[1] [A 1] *tr.* to refine; to thin; to sharpen; to improve; to purify; *rfl.* to become refined; to improve; to be tempered; to become sharper; (of weather) to set fine; †*intr.* to conclude, to have done. (**-aménto** *m.*) refining; sharpening. (**-ata** *f.*) **-ato** *part. adj.* refined; sharpened; purified; improved; matured. **-atoio** *m.* (met.) refining furnace. (**-atore** *m.*) **-atura** *f.*, **-azione** *f.*

†affinare[2] *vb.* See **finire**.

affinchè *conj.* in order that, so that; — non, lest.

affine[1] *conj.* (*prep.* di) in order to, for the purpose of, so as to; affin di bene, in a good cause; with the best intentions.

affin-e[2], **-o** *adj.* akin, kindred; allied, related; similar, alike; neighbouring, bordering; *n.m.* kinsman, relative; *f.* kinswoman; conoscenti ed -i, kith and kin. **-ità** *f.* similarity; affinity; relationship, connexion; (leg.) affinity; (eccl.) -ità spirituale, spiritual affinity; (chem.) affinity, chemical attraction.

†affinire *vb.* See **affinare**[1].

affinità *f.* See under **affine**[2] *adj.*

affiocare [A 2 c] and derivs. See **affiochire**.

affioch-ire [D 2] *tr.* to make hoarse; to weaken; to dim; *rfl., intr.* (*aux.* essere) to become hoarse; to grow weak; (of light) to grow dim; to burn low; (of sound) to die away. **-iménto** *m.* hoarseness; weakness. **-ito** *part. adj.* hoarse; faint; weak, dim.

†**affione** *m.* opium.

affior-are[1] [A 1 C] *tr.* to refine (flour). **-ato** *part. adj.* pane **-ato**, bread made of the finest flour.

affior-are[2] [A 1 C] *intr.* (*aux.* essere) (naut.) to appear (on the surface); (of a submarine) to surface; (fig.) to crop up; è **-ata** una notizia, the news has come through. **-amento** *m.* apparition; la crema di **-amento**, cream off the top of the milk; (geol.) outcrop. **-ato** *part. adj.* barely perceptible, emerging.

affiorato *adj.* flowered, worked with a floral pattern.

affisare [A 1]. See **affissare**.

affiss-are [A 1] *tr.* to fix with the eye; to fix; — gli occhi a, to stare fixedly at; — la mente a, to apply one's mind to, to consider; (**-amento** *part. adj.* **-azione** *f.*) **-ione** *f.* bill-posting; è proibita l'**-ione**, stick no bills; (pol.) ordinare l'**-ione** di un discorso, to order that the text of a speech made in (the Italian) parliament should be posted up on the notice boards in each Commune.

affiss-o *part. adj.* (from **affiggere**, q.v.) affixed, attached, fastened; *n.m.* bill, placard, poster; (gramm.) affix; enclitic; (pl.) fixtures (in a house); (Tusc.) shutters; †(naut.) ship's fixtures; †appellation, designation. **-ivo** *adj.* (gramm.) agglutinative.

affitt-are [A 1] *tr.* to let; to lease; to let out; to hire; to rent; stanze da —, rooms to let: affittasi, to let. (**-a·bile** *adj.* **-ato** *part. adj.*) **-aca·mere** *m., f. indecl.* lodging-house keeper; landlord; landlady. **-aiuo·lo** *m.* tenant. (**-amento** *m.*) **-ante** *m., f.* landlord; landlady; hirer, one who lets out on hire; one who hires; lessee, tenant. **-anza** *f.* tenancy. **-atore** *m.* **-atrice** *f.*) **-a·volo** *m.* see **-aiuolo**. **-uale** *m.* (Tusc.). **-ua·rio** *m.*, **-ua·ria** *f.* tenant; lessee.

affittire [D 2] *tr.* to thicken, to make thicker; *rfl., intr.* (*aux.* essere) to grow thicker; to grow darker.

affitt-o *m.* rent; hire; lease; dare in —, to let out; prendere in —, to hire; to rent; pagare l'—, to pay the rent; **-i** e prestiti, lend-lease. **-ua·rio** see under **affittare**.

†**afflare** *intr.* to breathe, to sigh.

afflato *m.* afflatus.

afflig·g-ere [C 17] *tr.* to afflict; to distress; to vex; to annoy; to chagrin; *rfl.* to grieve; to be sorry; to distress oneself; to worry; to mortify oneself. **-ente** *part. adj.* distressing; troublesome, vexatious.

afflitt-o *part. adj.* (from **affliggere**, q.v.) afflicted; hurt, affected; vexed, tormented; dejected; sorrowing; — da, suffering from; *n.m.* sufferer. (**-a** *f.*) **-ivo** *adj.* afflictive; (leg.) pena **-iva**, a punishment restricting personal freedom (as distinguished from a fine).

afflizióne *f.* affliction; suffering; sadness, misery, distress.

afflosciare [A 3] and derivs. See **affloscire**.

afflosc-ire [D 2] *tr.* to make flabby; to enervate; *rfl., intr.* (*aux.* essere) to become flabby; to weaken; to become soft; to become enervated. (**-iménto** *m.*) **-ito** *part. adj.* made flabby; enervated.

afflu-ire [D 2] *intr.* (*aux.* essere) (of a river) to be a tributary; to flow; to pour; to stream; to flock; to be in abundance. **-ente** *part. adj.,* *n.m.* tributary, affluent. (**-enteménte** *adv.*) **-enza** *f.* concourse; influx; abundance, affluence.

afflussionato *adj.* suffering from a cold in the head; suffering from catarrh.

afflusso *m.* (med.) afflux; (hydr.) inflow, influx.

affocalistiare [A 3] *tr.* (paint.) to blur (outlines), to scumble.

affoc-are[1] [A 2 d] *tr.* to inflame; to set fire to; to make red hot; to burn; (fig.) to fire; †to drown (see **affogare**); *rfl.* to become inflamed; to be made red hot; (fig.) to become enraged. **-amento** *m.* inflaming; kindling; (fig.) firing. **-ante** *part. adj.* burning, fiery. **-anteménte** *adv.* (D'Annunzio) ardently. **-ato** *part. adj.* red-hot; fiery-red; inflamed; enraged; ardent. (**-atore** *m.* **-atrice** *f.*)

affoc-are[2] [A 2 d] *tr.* to get in focus, to focus. **-ato** *part. adj.* in focus.

affog-are [A 2 c] *tr.* to suffocate, to smother, to stifle, to choke; to drown; to submerge; to inundate; to overwhelm; to quell, to silence; to poach (eggs); *intr.* (*aux.* essere) to drown; to suffocate; to be submerged; — in un bicchier d'acqua, to bungle a simple matter, to make a mountain out of a molehill; o bere o —, needs must when the devil drives; — nei debiti, to be up to the ears in debt; (naut.) to exceed the Plimsoll draught; *rfl.* to drown

oneself; to plunge; to lose oneself. (**-aménto** *m.*) **-ato** *part. adj.* suffocated, drowned; uovo **-ato**, poached egg. **-atóio** *m.* (colloq.) stiflingly hot place, oven; †extinguisher. (**-atóre** *m.* **-atura** *f.*)

affoll-are[1] [A 1] *tr.* to crowd, to crowd round; to throng; to crush; (fig.) to importune, to molest, to weary; *rfl.* to flock, to crowd; to eat greedily. **-aménto** *m.* crowd; crowding. **-ato** *part. adj.* (*prep.* di) crowded (with); overwhelmed; (naut.) **-ato** sulla costa, crowded on to a (lee) shore; *adv.* mangiare **-ato**, to eat greedily. **-ataménte** *adv.* tumultuously; precipitately, in haste.

†**affoll-are**[2] *intr.* to blow the bellows; *rfl.* to be breathless, to pant. †**-ato** *part. adj.* out of breath.

†**affoltare** *rfl.* to crowd, to flock; to speak hurriedly; *tr.* to attack, to oppress; (fig.) to overwhelm.

affoltire [D 2 c] *intr.* (*aux.* essere) to become thick.

†**affolto** *adj.* supported.

affond-are [A 1] *tr.* to sink; to send to the bottom; to founder; to submerge; to let go (anchor); — mine, to lay mines; — un pozzo, to sink a shaft, to sink a well; to thrust, to drive in; to embed; — una notizia, to print an item at the foot of the page; *rfl., intr.* (*aux.* essere) to sink; to founder; (naut.) to dive. **-aménto** *m.* (**-ato** *part. adj.*) **-atóio** *m.* (naut.) slipper. (**-atóre** *m.* **-atura** *f.*)

affóndo *adv.* at bottom, at the bottom (**a fóndo**); †*adj.* deep; *n.m.* (fencing) lunge; fare un —, to lunge.

afforc-are [A 2 c] *rfl.* (naut.) to moor with two anchors; †*tr.* to hang, to put to death by hanging. (**-atura** *f.*)

afforest-are [A 1] *tr.* to afforest. **-ato** *part. adj.* afforested.

†**affortificare** *vb.* See **fortificare**.

afforz-are [A 1] *tr.* to fortify, to strengthen, to reinforce; *rfl.* to gather strength; (mil.) to marshal forces. **-aménto** *m.* strengthening; (mil.) reinforcement; fortification. (**-ato** *part. adj.*)

†**affoscare** *vb.* See **offuscare**.

affoss-are [A 1] *tr.* to dig a moat round; to trench; to ditch; to excavate; *rfl.* (of eyes, cheeks) to become hollowed. **-aménto** *m.* ditching; excavation; sinking. **-ato** *part. adj.* surrounded by a moat; sunken, hollowed; occhi **-ati**, deep-set eyes. **-atura** *f.* ditching; ditch, trench, excavation.

affral-ire [D 2] *tr.* to weaken, to enfeeble; *rfl., intr.* (*aux.* essere) to grow weak. (**-iménto** *m.*) **-ito** *part. adj.* weakened, enfeebled.

affranc-are [A 2] *tr.* to liberate; to exempt; to redeem; to prepay; to stamp, to frank (a letter); (leg.) to free, to release (from a servitude or an incumbrance); †(naut.) to pump out bilges; *rfl.* to free oneself; to take courage; to gain confidence. (**-a·bile** *adj.* **-aménto** *m.*) **-ato** *part. adj.* free, liberated; exempt; redeemed; prepaid; (of a letter) stamped, franked. (**-atóre** *m.*) **-atrice** *f.* stamping-machine, franking-machine. **-atura** *f.* postage; postage-stamp. **-azióne** *f.* freeing; franking; (leg.) release; **-azione** del fondo enfiteutico, enfranchisement of long leasehold (C.C).

†**affranchire** *vb.* See **affrancare**.

affran·g-ere [C 5] *tr.* to break; to dishearten, to depress.

affrant-o *part.* from **affrangere**, q.v.; *adj.* disheartened, dismayed, dejected; crushed, overcome; un cuore —, a broken heart. †**-ura** *f.* dejection.

affratell-are [A 1] *tr.* to unite in comradeship; *rfl.* to fraternize. **-aménto** *m.* fraternizing; fraternization; intimacy. (**-anza** *f.*) **-ato** *part. adj.* fraternizing; united. (**-atóre** *m.* **-atrice** *f.*) **-évole** *adj.* fraternizing, friendly, comradely.

†**affreddare** *vb.* See **raffreddare**.

affrenare [A 1] and derivs. See **frenare**.

affrenellare [A 1] *tr.* (naut.) †to lash (the tiller or an oar); (in an ancient galley) to lash an oar with blade out of the water.

affrès-co *m.* (*pl.* **-chi**) (paint.) fresco. **-care** [A 2 c] *tr.* to paint in fresco. (**-ato** *part. adj.*) **-chista** *m.* fresco painter, painter in fresco.

affrett-are [A 1 c] *tr.* to hasten, to hurry; to quicken; — il passo, to quicken one's pace, to step out; to put forward, to anticipate; — un lavoro, to press for the completion of a work; *rfl., intr.* (*aux.* avere) to hurry, to make haste; affrettatevi!, hurry up! (**-a·bile** *adj.* **-aménto** *m.* **-anza** *f.*) **-ato** *part. adj.* hasty, hurried; lavoro **-ato**, careless, hurried work; (of fruit) forced. (**-ataménte** *adv.* **-atóre** *m.* **-atrice** *f.*) **-óso** *adj.* hurried; hasty.

africana *f.* (cul.) dessert, consisting of zabaione and chocolate.

africano *adj.* and derivs. See **africano**, under **Africa**.

affricato *adj.* (phon.) affricative, affricated.

af·frico *m.* south-west wind.

†**affricogno** *adj.* sharp, sour.

affrittell-are [A I] *tr.* to fry (eggs); to fry in batter; (colloq.) to kill. (-**ato** *part. adj.*)

affront-are [A I c] *tr.* to front; to confront; to defy; to face; to assail, to attack; — spese, to meet expenses; — la situazione, to deal with the situation; — battaglia, to give battle; — la morte, to risk one's life; to meet death with courage; (naut.) — la marea, to breast the tide; †to compare; †to be opposite to; †to meet, to greet; *rfl.* -arsi di, to take offence at; *recip. rfl.* to come face to face; to come to blows; to meet in battle. (-**a·bile** *adj.*) -**amento** *m.* encounter; confronting; assault. (-**ata** *f.*) -**ato** *part. adj.* confronted; defied; encountered; attacked; offended, assailed; (herald.) contra-rampant. (-**atore** *m.* -**atrice** *f.*) -**atura** *f.* (eng.) flush fitting.

affronto *m.* insult, affront; †meeting, encounter, †comparison, collation.

affruttato *adj.* planted with fruit-trees.

affumare *tr.* and derivs. See **affumicare**.

affumic-are [A 2 s] *tr.* to blacken with smoke; to fill with smoke; to smoke, to cure (ham, fish); to fumigate. (-**amento** *m.* -**ata** *f.*) -**ato** *part. adj.* blackened with smoke; smoked, cured; arringa -ata, kipper; fumigated; lenti -ate, sun-glasses. -**atura** *f.* smoking, curing.

affunare *tr.* (Tusc.) to bind with ropes.

affus-are [A I], -**ellare** [A I], -**olare** [A I s] *tr.* to make spindle-shaped; to taper. -**ato**, -**ellato**, -**olato** *part. adj.* tapering, slender.

affusione *f.* (chem.) pouring (liquid over other materials).

affusto *m.* (mil.) gun-carriage; (naut.) gun mounting, turret; (eng.) frame; barrel (of a tool).

Afg-a·nistan *pr.n.m.* (geog.) Afghanistan. -**ano** *adj.*, *n.m.* Afghan. (-**ana** *f.*)

a·fide, **afi·dio** *m.* (ent.) aphis, green-fly.

afill-ante *f.* (bot.) blue-flowered lily of the Riviera, *Aphyllanthes monspeliensis*; -**o** *adj.* (bot.) aphyllous, leafless (as the common rush).

aflogi·stico *adj.* (med.) aphlogistic.

af·nio *m.* (chem.) hafnium.

afo·n-ico, **a·fon-o** *adj.* (med.) aphonic, suffering from loss of voice; soundless; muted. -**i·a** *f.* (med.) aphony, loss of voice.

afor-isma, -**ismo** *m.* aphorism. -**i·stico** *adj.* aphoristic. (-**isticamente** *adv.*)

afoso *adj.* See under **afa**.

A·fric-a *f.* (geog.) Africa. -**anismo** *m.* Africanism; political activity or interest in Africa. (-**ani·stico** *adj.*) -**anista** *m.* student of African history or culture; African explorer. -**ano** *adj.* African; (colloq.) black in the face; *n.m.* African; south-west wind; marzipan sweet with chocolate icing. -**ana** *f.* African woman.

a·frico *m.* See **affrico**.

†**africogno** *adj.* slightly pungent.

afridosi *f.* (med.) adiaphoresis.

afr-o[1] *adj.* pungent, sharp (of smell or taste). -**ezza** *f.*, -**ore** *m.* pungency, strong odour. -**oso** *adj.* strong-smelling.

afro-[2] *adj. indecl.* African (in compounds): rapporti afro-europei, African-European relations.

afro[3] *m.* (dial. Piedm.) terror.

afrodisi·aco *adj.*, *n.m.* aphrodisiac.

afrodi·sio *adj.* sacred to Venus, aphrodisian.

Afrodite *pr.n.f.* Aphrodite.

afronitro *m.* (chem.) foam of nitre; saltpetre.

afta *f.* (med.) aphtha; thrush; (vet.) — epizootica, foot and mouth disease.

agalassi·a *f.* (med.) agalactia.

agal·(l)oco *m.* (bot.) East Indian shrub, *Aquillaria agallocha*, which yields aloe-wood.

Agamen·none *pr.n.m.* Agamemnon.

a·gami, **agamì** *m. indecl.* (orn.) trumpeter.

agam-i·a *f.*, -**oge·nesi** *f.* (biol.) agamogenesis.

agapanto *m.* (bot.) blue-flowered S. African liliaceous plant, *Agapanthus africanus*.

a·gape *f.* (eccl.) agape; (joc.) reunion, party.

agar-agar *m.* (med.) agar-agar.

aga·rico *m.* (bot.) agaric, gill-fungus, mushroom.

a·gat-a[1], -**e** *f.* agate; marmo —, agate marble, Strassburg marble.

agata[2] *f.* needle-ful.

A·gata *pr.n.f.* Agatha.

agatologi·a *f.* (philos.) doctrine, theory, of the Good.

a·gave *f.* so-called American aloe, *Agave americana*, frequently

planted in Italy; (text.) fibra dell'— americana, pita hemp, pita, henequen.

†**agazzare** *intr.* to become angry, to be annoyed.

age·min-a *f.* steel inlaid with gold or silver wire; lavoro all'—, inlaid steel work. -**are** [A I s] *tr.* to inlay with gold or silver wire. (-**ato** *part. adj.* -**atore** *m.* -**atura** *f.*)

agenda *f.* diary; appointment book; agenda.

agente *m.* agent; representative; — della Questura, policeman; — investigativo, police inspector, detective; — provocatore, agent provocateur; (comm.) broker; — di cambio, stockbroker; — di campagna, steward, land agent; — di trasporti, carrier; — marittimo, ship's agent; — delle tasse, tax-collector; (joc.) implement for extracting marrow from bones; *adj.* acting, active; †kind, courteous.

†**agenzare** *tr.* to embellish, to ornament; to satisfy; *intr.* to be pleasing.

agenzi·a *f.* (comm.) agency, branch office; agentship, stewardship; — di prestiti su pegno, pawnbroker's; — delle tasse, tax collector's office; — di viaggi, travel agency; — d'informazioni, enquiry office, information bureau; — di collocamento, employment agency.

age·rato *m.* (bot.) ageratum, blue moss-flower, sweet maudlin, *Achillea ageratum*.

†**agetto** *adj.* abject.

agevol-are [A I s c] *tr.* to facilitate; to assist; to alleviate; to cut through (red tape); (Tusc.) to tame; to further. (-**amento** *m.* -**ato** *part. adj.* -**atore** *m.* -**atrice** *f.* -**atura** *f.*) -**azione** *f.* facilitation; facility; concession; speciali -azioni, special facilities, special concessions.

agevol-e *adj.* easy; manageable; handy; moderate, mild; easy-going, compliant; conciliatory, affable; unconstrained; quick-witted; fluent; (of clothing) comfortable; (Tusc.) tame, docile; (of a horse) — di bocca, obedient to the rein. (-**mente** *adv.*) -**ezza** *f.* facility; ease; fluency; convenience; courtesy; (comm.) *pl.* facilities (as to payment, in price, for the extension of credit, etc.); usare -**ezze** con, to treat with consideration.

aggall-are [A I] *intr.* (*aux.* avere) (naut.) to surface. -**ato** *n.m.* (dial. Lucca) marshy ground.

agganci-are [A 3] *tr.* to hook; to hang upon a hook, to fasten; to couple; to hitch; (mil.) — il nemico, to grapple with the enemy. -**ato** *part. adj.* hooked; coupled; hook-shaped. -**atoio** *m.* fastening, catch. -**atore** *m.* (eng.) grip.

aggangherare [A I s] *tr.* to fasten with hook and eye; to hinge; *rfl.* to fasten, to be fastened; (fig.) to hold together.

aggarbare[1] [A I] *tr.* (naut.) to design and trace the lines of a hull.

†**aggarbare**[2] *vb.* See **garbare**.

aggatt-are [A I] *rfl.* to curl up like a cat, to climb like a cat. -**igliare** [A 4] *recip. rfl.* to scratch each other's eyes out, to fight like cats. -**onare** [A I c] *tr.* to stalk, to creep after (prey).

†**aggavignare** *tr.* to seize; to hold fast.

†**aggecch-ire** *rfl.* to be downcast; to humble oneself. †-**ito** *adj.* dejected; humbled.

aggeggiare [A 3 c] *tr.* (Tusc.) to titivate; to fiddle with; *intr.* (*aux.* avere) to fiddle about, to waste time; *rfl.* to deck oneself out.

aggeggio *m.* (Tusc.) thing, object of no value; — inutile, white elephant; thingummyjig; gimcrack, contraption, gadget; corruption, dirty work.

aggelare [A I]. See **gelare**.

aggeminare[1] [A I s]. See **geminare**.

aggeminare[2] [A I s]. See **ageminare**, under **agemina**.

aggentilire [D 2]. See **ingentilire**.

†**aggerare** *tr.* to accumulate, to pile up.

†**ag·gere** *m.* mound, rampart for attacking.

aggest-ione *f.* (geol.) deposit. -**ivo** *adj.* (geol.) thrown up by alluvial action.

aggettare [A I]. See under **aggetto**.

aggettiv-o *m.* adjective; *adj.* adjectival. -**amente** *adv.* as an adjective, adjectivally. -**are** [A I] *tr.* to adjective; to adjectival. (-**ato** *part. adj.* -**azione** *f.*)

agget-o[1] *m.* (bldg., etc.) projection; shoulder, overhang; (eng.) boss, lug. -**are** [A I] *intr.* (*aux.* essere) (archit.) to project, to jut out.

†**aggetto**[2] *adj.* abject.

†**agghermigliare** *tr.* to seize with claws.

aggheronato *adj.* (of garments) gored; (herald.) barred.

agghiacci-are[1] [A 3] *tr.* to congeal; to chill; to freeze; to ice; to terrify, to make the blood run cold; *intr.* (*aux.* essere) *rfl.* to freeze; to turn to ice; to congeal; to be terrified. (-**amento** *m.* -**ante** *part. adj.* -**ato** *part. adj.* -**atore** *m.* -**atrice** *f.*)

agghiacciare² [A3]. See **addiacciare**, under **addiaccio**.

agghiac·cio¹ *m.* sheep-cote.

agghiac·cio² *m.* (naut.) helm; steering gear.

†**agghiadare** *vb.* See **agghiacciare¹**.

agghiai-are [A4] *tr.* to cover with gravel, to gravel. **-ato** *part. adj.* gravelled; *n.m.* gravelled path, ground.

agghind-are [A1] *tr.* to dress up; to overdress; (naut.) †see **ghindare**; *rfl.* to dress oneself up. **-ato** *part. adj.* overdressed, decked out; artificial; stile **-ato**, stilted style.

agghiotta *f.* (dial. Sicil.) seaman's dish based on fish, onions and garlic.

aggiacc-are [A2] *tr.* to bend to the ground; to cut, to reap; to crumple. **-ato** *part. adj.* stretched out, reclining.

aggiac·cio *m.* See **agghiaccio¹**.

†**aggiacen-te** *adj.* See **adiacente**. **-za** *f.* see **adiacenza**.

aggiardinare [A1] *tr.* to cultivate, to make a garden of.

aggina¹ *f.* pasture.

†**aggina²** *f.* haste.

ag·gio¹ *m.* (comm.) premium; interest (on a loan); collector's profit; fare —, to command a premium; — sui fondi pubblici, stock-jobbing.

†**ag·gio²** *m.* age; date, year.

aggiog-are [A2c] *tr.* to yoke; to subject; to couple (oxen, horses); to link; (naut.) to place cross-beams athwartships in large rowing vessels. (**-a·bile** *adj.* **-amento** *m.*) **-ato** *part. adj.* yoked; coupled. (**-atore** *m.* **-atrice** *f.*) **-atura** *f.* yoking; coupling.

aggiogliato *adj.* See **alloggliato**.

aggiorn-are [A1c] *tr.* to fix (a day); to bring up to date; to adjourn, to postpone, to defer, to put off; *intr. impers.* (aux. essere) to become daylight; *rfl.* to get up to date; to become modernized. **-amento** *m.* bringing up to date; deferment; (leg.) adjournment. **-ato** *part. adj.* adjourned; up to date. (**-atore** *m.* **-atrice** *f.*)

aggio(t)t-ag·gio *m.* (comm.) agiotage, operation intended to produce a rise or a slump on the stock-exchange by unlawful means. **-atore** *m.* unscrupulous stock-jobber.

aggir-are [A1] *tr.* to revolve; to whirl; to go round; to surround; to trick; (mil.) to outflank; *rfl., intr.* (aux. avere) to revolve; to wander about, to perambulate; (*prep.* su) to have a bearing on, to concern, to be about, to deal with; (comm.) to rule at about: il prezzo si **-a** sulle duemila lire, the price rules at about two thousand lire. **-amento** *m.* revolving; circumvention; meandering; trickery, evasion, fraud; (mil.) outflanking; **-amento di parole**, circumlocution. **-ante** *part. adj.* encircling; outflanking. (**-ata** *f.* **-ato** *part. adj.*) **-atore** *m.* trickster, dodger. (**-atrice** *f.*)

aggiucch-ire [D2] *intr.* (aux. essere) to grow stupid. **-ito** *part. adj.* stupid.

aggiudic-are [A2s] *tr.* to adjudge; to adjudicate; to award; to assign; to allot; — un lotto a, to knock down a lot to (at an auction); — al petente le sue conclusioni, to give judgment for the plaintiff; *rfl.* (dat. of prn.) to win. (**-a·bile** *adj.* **-ante** *part. adj.* adjudicating; *n.m.* adjudicator. **-ata·rio** *m.* awardee; highest bidder at an auction. **-ativo** *adj.* (leg.) sentenza **-ativa**, judgment making an award (as opposed to a judgment on a point of procedure). (**-atore** *m.* **-atrice** *f.*) **-azione** *f.* adjudication; award; adjudgment.

aggiun·g-ere [C5] *tr.* to add; to subjoin; †*intr.* (*prep.* a) to reach; *rfl.* to be added; to join: molti si aggiunsero a noi, many people joined us. (**-imento** *m.* **-itore** *m.* **-itrice** *f.*)

aggiunta *f.* addition, increase; supplement; additional material; (text.) admixture; (eng.) angolo di —, clearance angle; (gramm.) adjunct; (leg.) rider.

aggiunt-are [A1] *tr.* to join, to piece together; (shoem.) to close. (**-atore** *m.* **-atrice** *f.*) **-atura** *f.* join, joint. **-ivo** *adj.* additional; (leg.) clausola **-iva**, rider; (gramm.) adjunctive. (**-ura** *f.*)

aggiunto *part.* from **aggiungere**, q.v.; *adj.* added; joined; *n.m.* adjunct; assistant; deputy; cassiere —, assistant cashier; — giudiziario, the lowest rank in the Italian judiciary; — di cancelleria, assistant to the clerk of a court.

aggiunzione *f.* addition; adding; †epithet.

aggiust-are¹ [A1] *tr.* to adjust, to adapt, to correct, to mend; to settle; to reconcile; to put in order; to arrange; to tidy; to deck out; (iron.) to fix, to settle; t'aggiusto io!, I'll settle you!; — per il dì delle feste, to trounce; (naut.) to trim (ship, sails, course); — la bussola, to set the compass; — la mira, to take careful aim; — di sale, to add the right amount of salt; (comm.) — un conto, to settle an account; — i conti, to settle accounts (also fig.); *rfl.* to adjust oneself; to make arrangements; to get ready; to

deck oneself out; to make oneself comfortable; il tempo si **-a**, the weather is improving; **-arsi coi creditori**, to settle with creditors. (**-a·bile** *adj.*) **-ag·gio** *m.* (eng.) fitting, adjustment; (typ.) compensation (of the line). (**-amento** *m.*) **-atezza** *f.* propriety, fitness; punctiliousness; good manners; accuracy, precision. **-ato** *part. adj.* tidy; spruce; precise, exact; *n.m.pl.* (lit. hist.) gli Aggiustati, members of the Academy of Treviso. **-atamente** *adv.* properly, rightfully. **-atore** *m.* adaptor; (eng.) fitter. (**-atrice** *f.* **-atura** *f.*)

†**aggiustare²** *rfl.* to place oneself beside.

†**aggiustare³** *tr.* †— fede, to believe.

agglob-are [A1] *tr.* to form into a globe. (**-ato** *part. adj.*)

agglomer-are [A1s] *tr.* to agglomerate; *rfl.* to crowd together. (**-amento** *m.*) **-ante** *part. adj.* agglomerating, agglomerative; *n.m.* (techn.) bonding agent. **-ato** *part. adj.* agglomerated; crowded; densely populated; *n.m.* built-up area; (geol.) agglomerate; agglomeration. **-azione** *f.* agglomeration.

†**agglo·mero** *m.* elbow.

agglutin-are [A1s] *tr., rfl.* to agglutinate; (techn.) to cake; (scient.) to gel. (**-amento** *m.*) **-ante** *adj.* agglutinant; agglutinative; *n.m.* (pottery, etc.) binder, cementing material. (**-ato** *part. adj.*) **-azione** *f.* agglutination. **-ina** *f.* (med.) agglutinin.

aggobbiato *adj.* gouge-shaped; scalpello —, gouge.

aggobbire [D2] *tr.* to make hunchbacked; *intr.* (aux. essere), *rfl.* to become hunchbacked; — sui libri, to swot; to be a bookworm.

aggomitol-are [A1s] *tr.* to wind; to roll up; to make up into a ball; *rfl.* to curl oneself up. (**-ato** *part. adj.* **-atore** *m.*) **-atrice** *f.* (text.) balling machine. (**-atura** *f.*)

aggott-are [A1c] *tr.* (naut.) to bail out; (bldg.) to pump out. **-atoio** *m.* bailer. (**-atura** *f.*)

aggrad-are [A1] *intr. impers. defect.* to be pleasing, to please; se ciò vi **-a**, if this is agreeable to you. (**-amento** *m.*) **-evole** *adj.* agreeable, pleasing; sweet. (**-evolezza** *f.* **-evolmente** *adv.*)

aggradire [D2] and derivs. See **gradire**.

aggraff-are [A1] *tr.* to seize; to catch; to claw; (eng.) to fold, to seam. (**-ato** *part. adj.*) **-atura** *f.* seizing; clawing; (eng.) seam (in a steel plate); **-atura ribaltata**, flat folded seam.

aggraff-iare [A4], **-ignare** [A5] *tr.* to seize; to catch; to claw.

aggrampare [A1] and derivs. See **aggrappare**.

aggranare [A1] *tr.* to granulate.

aggranchiare [A4]. See **aggranchire**.

aggranch-ire [D2] *tr.* to numb; *rfl., intr.* (aux. essere) to grow numb; to get cramp. **-ito** *part. adj.* numbed; numb; cramped; stiff.

†**aggrancire** [D2]. See **grancire**.

†**aggrandare** *vb.* See **aggrandire**.

aggrand-ire [D2] *tr.* to aggrandize; to enlarge; to extend; to magnify; to augment; to exaggerate; to raise; *rfl., intr.* (aux. essere) to grow large; to increase; to raise oneself, to grow powerful; to become elevated. **-imento** *m.* aggrandizement; increase; growth; enlargement; elevation; exaggeration. (**-ito** *part. adj.*)

aggranf-iare [A4], **-ignare** [A5] *tr.* to seize with the claws; to steal.

aggrapp-are [A1] *tr.* to seize, to grasp; to grapple; *abs.* (naut.) (of an anchor) to bite; *rfl.* (*prep.* a) to grasp at; to cling to. **-ato** *part. adj.* grasped; **-ato a**, clinging to.

aggrappo *m.* hold, clutch, grip.

aggrappol-are [A1s] *rfl.* to cluster. **-ato** *part. adj.* clustered.

aggraticci-are [A3] *tr.* to intertwine; to twist into trellis-work; *rfl.* to cling; to climb (of plants). (**-ato** *part. adj.*)

†**aggratigliare** *tr.* to imprison.

aggrav-are [A1] *tr.* to aggravate; to make worse; to make heavy; to burden; to overload; to oppress; to aggrieve; — la mano, (in writing) to press heavily, (fig.) to be severe; *rfl.* to become worse; to become aggravated; to grow heavy; to lean; to lean more heavily; to overburden oneself; to feel aggrieved. **-amento** *m.* aggravation; increase; surcharge. **-ante** *part. adj.* aggravating; *n.f.* (leg.) aggravating circumstance. **-ato** *part. adj.* aggravated; burdened; (mus.) in augmentation. (**-azione** *f.*)

aggra·vio *m.* weight; esser d'— a, to be a burden upon; wrong; injury; (econ.) charge, burden, expense; — fiscale, tax, duty, imposition; (leg.) incumbrance.

aggrazi-are [A4] *tr.* to make graceful, pretty; to make pleasing; to flavour pleasantly, to sweeten; *rfl.* (acc. of prn.) to ingratiate oneself; (dat. of prn.) to win over to oneself. **-ato** *part. adj.* graceful; pleasing; attractive; flavoured; medicina **-ata**, medicine pleasantly flavoured. (**-atamente** *adv.*) **-atura** *f.* (mus.) grace.

aggred·ire [D 2] *tr.* to attack; to assault; to go for, to round on. **-itrice** *f.* aggressor, assailant (cf. **aggressore**, under **aggressione**).

aggreg·are [A 2] *tr.* to aggregate; to unite; to associate; to admit; to enrol; *rfl.* to become united, joined; (*prep.* a) to join, to enrol. **(-a·bile** *adj.*) **-amento** *m.* association; company; assemblage; admission; mass; aggregation; aggregate. **(-anza** *f.*) **-ativo** *adj.* associative; cohesive. **-ato** *part. adj.* aggregated; united; joined, associated; *n.m.* aggregate; assemblage; amalgam; -ato di case, block of houses; deputy, stand-in; fellow, member; (geol.) aggregate. **-azione** *f.* aggregation; molecular attraction; coalition, tendency to coalesce.

aggreggiare [A 4 c] *tr.* to assemble in a herd; *rfl.* to form a herd.

aggress·ione *f.* aggression; assault, attack. **-ivo** *adj.* aggressive; *n.m.* weapon: -ivi chimici, poison gas, etc. **-ività** *f.* aggressiveness. **-ore** *m.* aggressor, assailant. (Cf. **aggreditrice**, under **aggredire**.)

aggrevare [A I]. See **aggravare**.

aggricciare [A 3] *tr.* to freeze; to terrify; *intr.*, *rfl.* to shudder, to shiver; to become stiff; to shrivel.

aggrinzare [A I]. See **aggrinzire**.

aggrinz·ire [D 2] *tr.* to wrinkle; to shrivel; to corrugate, to ripple; *rfl.* to become wrinkled; to shrivel; to ripple. **-ito** *part. adj.* wrinkled; shrivelled; rippling.

aggrommare [A I]. See **aggrumare**.

aggrond·are [A I c] *tr.* — le ciglia, to frown. **-ato** *part. adj.* frowning; gloomy, dejected. **-atura** *f.* frown.

aggropp·are[1] [A I] *tr.* to do up into a knot, to bundle; *rfl.* to amass, to accumulate. **(-amento** *m.* **-ato** *part. adj.* **-atura** *f.*) (From **groppo**, q.v.)

aggroppare[2] [A I] *tr.*, *rfl.* to bow, to bend (from **groppa**, q.v.).

aggrott·are [A I] *tr.* (agric.) to bank up; — le ciglia, to frown; to knit the brows. **-amento** *m.* frowning; (agric.) banking up.

aggrottesc·are [A 2 c] *intr.* (*aux.* avere) (art) to paint or carve grotesques. **(-ato** *part. adj.*)

aggrovigli·are [A 4] *tr.* to entangle; *rfl.* to become entangled; to intertwine; to become intricate; to curl up; to shrink; to get confused. **-amento** *m.* entanglement; confusion. **-ato** *part. adj.* entangled; intricate; involved, obscure, confused. **(-atura** *f.*)

aggrovigliolare [A I s]. See **aggrovigliare**.

aggrum·are [A I] *tr.* to curdle; *intr.* (*aux.* essere), *rfl.* to clot, to coagulate; to curdle; to crust. **(-ato** *part. adj.*)

aggrumolare [A I s] *rfl.* (bot.) to form a head, or heart (e.g. of lettuce, cabbage).

aggrupp·are [A I] *tr.* to gather together; to knot; to loop; to heap; (paint.) to group; *rfl.* to form groups, to gather together. **(-amento** *m.*) **-ato** *part. adj.* grouped; (herald.) leon -ato, lion sejant.

†aggruzzolare *vb.* See **raggruzzolare**.

agguagli·are [A 4] *tr.* to equalize; to level; to make smooth; — al suolo, to raze to the ground; to equal; to tally; to compare; (in straw plaiting) to sort; *rfl.* (*prep.* a) to compare oneself, to be compared (with); to be equal (to); to emulate. **(-a·bile** *adj.*) **-amento** *m.* equalizing; levelling; †equinox. **(-anza** *f.*) **-atoio** *m.* polisher. **-atora** *f.* (Tusc.) woman who sorts straws in hat-making industry. **(-ato** *part. adj.*) **-atore** *m.* equalizer; leveller; †equator. **(-atrice** *f.* **-atura** *f.* **-azione** *f.*) **-o** *m.* comparison.

agguant·are [A I] *tr.* to catch; to seize; to snatch; (colloq.) to steal, to 'lift'; to hit; gli tirò un pugno e l'-ò in un occhio, he hit out and got him in the eye; *intr.* (*aux.* avere) (naut.) to tack to windward; to claw off a lee shore; to hold on to (a rope); to bring to; (of a sail) to draw; agguanta!, order to 'hold water'. **-atore** *m.* snatcher; (naut.) good holding ground; foul bottom for fishing nets. **(-atrice** *f.*)

†agguardare *tr.* to regard, to consider.

†agguatare *tr.* to lie in wait for; to stare at.

agguato *m.* ambush; ambuscade; trap, snare; stare in —, essere in —, to lie in wait; to be on the alert; cadere in un —, to fall into an ambush; to fall into a trap.

†aggueffare *tr.* to wind into skeins; to add; to grasp.

agguerr·ire [D 2] *tr.* to train (for war); to inure; to strengthen, to fortify; *rfl.* to train; to become inured; to harden oneself. **(-imento** *m.*) **-ito** *art. adj.* trained; inured; hardened, seasoned.

agguindol·are [A I s] *tr.* to wind, to reel; (fig.) to twist, to cheat. **(-amento** *m.*) **-ato** *part. adj.* wound; tricked. **(-atore** *m.*)

agguin·dolo *m.* bobbin, reel.

†agherbino *m.* See **garbino**.

a·ghero *adj.* See **agro**.

aghętta *f.* litharge, lead oxide.

aghętto *m.* *dim.* of **ago**, q.v. shoe-lace; boot-lace; tag of a lace; (geog.) spicule.

aghifęrme *adj.* (chem.; bot.) needle-shaped, acicular.

aghiręne *m.* See **airone**.

†agiamento *m.* latrine.

†agiare *tr.* to make comfortable; — le ricchezze, to lay out one's wealth to advantage; *intr.* (*prep.* a) to be of service to; *rfl.* to lie down; to take one's ease.

agiat·o *adj.* well-to-do, comfortably off; di condizione -a, of independent means, well-off; slow, indolent; unhurried; †spacious; †loose-fitting; †suitable; *n.m.pl.* gli Agiati, the Academicians of Rovereto. **-amente** *adv.* comfortably; vivere -atamente, to be well off. **-ęzza** *f.* comfort; competency, comfortable means.

agiatoio *m.* latrine.

agi·bil·e *adj.* practicable, feasible; ready for use; in working order; (dial. Neap.) agile. **-ità** *f.* feasibility.

a·gil·e *adj.* agile, nimble; lithe; slender; alert; quick; skilful; (iron.) — di mano, light-fingered; libro —, light literature. **(-mente** *adv.*) **-ità** *f.* agility; (mus.) the playing or singing of rapid passages, as in: aria d'-ità; aptitude for doing this. **-izzare** [A I] *tr.* to make agile.

agilit·are [A I s] *tr.* to exercise, to make supple. **(-ato** *part. adj.*)

†agina *f.* haste.

a·gio *m.* ease; ad —, at ease; non trovarsi ad —, to be ill at ease; comfort; gli agi della vita, the comforts of life; vivere negli agi, vivere nell'—, to live in comfort; opportunity, time; se avrò —, if I have time; leisure: appena avrò un po' d'—, as soon as I have a little leisure; plenty of time: abbiamo —, we've plenty of time; convenience; a mio —, at my convenience; a bell'—, a tutt'—, ad —, at leisure, slowly. (See also **adagio**.)

agi·ografi·a *f.* hagiography. **-ogra·fico** *adj.* hagiographic(al). **-o·grafo** *m.* hagiographer; *pl.* (Bibl.) Hagiographa. **-olatri·a** *f.* hagiolatry. **-ologi·a** *f.* hagiology. **-olo·gico** *adj.* hagiologic(al). **-o·logo** hagiologist. **-o·nimo** *m.* saint's name.

agios·silo *m.* (bot.) Guaiacum tree, or wood, *Guaiacum officinale* and *G. sanctum*.

agire [D 2] *intr.* (*aux.* avere) to act; to behave; agir bene, to do good, to do right; agir male, to do wrong; — da, to act as; to proceed; to function, to work; to take action; (of a theatrical company) to act, to play; (leg.) to commence an action.

agit·are [A I s] *tr.* to agitate; to shake; to wave; to stir; to toss; (fig.) to stir up; to incite; to excite; to spur on, to urge forward; to disturb, to distress, to upset; to discuss, to air (a question); — lo spettro di, to hold up the bogey of; (leg.) — una lite, to carry on a lawsuit; *rfl.* to toss about; to run about; to fidget; to get excited; to get upset; (pol.) to agitate. **(-a·bile** *adj.*) **-a·colo** *m.* (chem.) stirring-rod. **(-amento** *m.*) **-ante** *part. adj.* agitating; upsetting; *n.m.* †actor. **(-ativo** *adj.*) **-ato** *part. adj.* shaken, tossed; agitated; excited; troubled; restless, fidgety; (of the sea) rough, storm-tossed; (mus.) agitato; *n.m.* violent maniac. **-atore** *m.* agitator; (chem.) stirring-rod; (industr.) beater, stirring gear; churn. **(-atrice** *f.*) **-azione** *f.* agitation; excitement; unrest; commotion; tumult; nausea.

agli. See under **a** (*prep.*).

aglia·ceo *adj.* See under **aglio**.

aglia·ia *f.* See **ghiaia**.

aglia·io, agliaro *m.* See under **aglio**.

agliata *f.* See under **aglio**.

a·glilo *m.* (chem.) acetylene.

a·gli·o *m.* — coltivato, common garlic, *Allium sativum*; — orsino, ramsons, wild garlic, *A. ursinum*; — delle vigne, — pippolino, crow garlic, *A. vineale*; — di serpe, rose-garlic, *A. roseum*; — napolitano, Naples garlic, *A. Neapolitanum*; — serpentino, spherical garlic, globe garlic, *A. Victorialis*; — dei fossi, pink-flowering rush, *Butomus umbellatus*; (fig.) mangiar l'—, to swallow one's rage; essere verde come un —, to look as pale as a ghost; consolarsi con l'aglietto, to make a virtue of necessity. **-a·ceo** *adj.* resembling garlic. **-aio** *m.* bed of garlic; garlic seller. **-aro** *m.* garlic seller. **-ata** *f.* garlic sauce. **-ola** *f.*, **-otta** *f.* (dial. Cors.) see **agghiotta**.

agliporro *m.* (bot.) rocambole, *Allium scorodoprasum*.

aglutizione *f.* (med.) aglutition, inability to swallow.

†agna *f.* ewe lamb.

agn·ato *m.* (leg.) agnate. **-a·tico, -ati·zio** *adj.* agnatic. **-azione** *f.* agnation.

agnell-o *m.* lamb; meek and mild individual; (theol.) — di Dio, Lamb of God; (bot.) — grasso, *Sedum dasyphyllum.* -**a** *f.* ewe lamb. -**a·io, -aro** *m.* butcher, vendor of lamb. -**atura** *f.* lambing; lambing season. -**ino** *m. dim.* lambkin, little lamb; (fig.) è un -ino, butter wouldn't melt in his mouth; (Tusc. bot.) valerian, *Valeriana officinalis.* -**otto** *m.* well-grown lamb; *pl.* dumplings.

Agnese¹ *pr.n.f.* Agnes.

agnese² *f.* (dial. Ven.) stupid individual, simpleton.

agnin-a *f.* lamb's fleece. -**o** *adj.* lamb's, lamb-like.

agnizione *f.* recognition scene in a play; (leg.) recognition.

†**agno¹** *m.* lamb.

†**agno²** *m.* swelling in the groin.

agnocasto *m.* (bot.) chaste-tree, *Vitex agnus-castus.*

agnolini *m.pl.* (cul.) a kind of ravioli.

†**a·gnol-o** *m.* angel; old French coin. (†-**a** *f.*)

agnolotti *m.pl.* (cul.) See **agnolini.**

†**agno·scere** *tr.* to recognize.

agnosi·a *f.* (med.) agnosia, loss of the faculty of recognition.

agno·stic-o *adj., n.m.* agnostic. -**i·smo** *m.* agnosticism.

agnusdei, agnus dei *m.* (eccl., fig.) Agnus Dei as wax disc (blessed by the Pope) with figure of lamb; far l'—, essere un —, parere un —, to look as if butter wouldn't melt in one's mouth; (liturg., mus.) Agnus (Dei) as part of the Mass or its musical setting; †the Blessed Sacrament.

ago *m.* (*pl.* **aghi**) needle; astuccio per aghi, needle-case; cruna d'—, eye of the needle; bodkin; — torto, crochet hook; — da calza, knitting needle; lavoro d'—, needlework; lavorare d'—, to do needlework; campare sull'—, to live by one's needle; hand (of a clock); stile, gnomon (of a sundial); tongue (of a balance, steel-yard); spire; compass; sting (of an insect); (bot.) needle (of pine-tree, etc.); (ichth.) *Belone acus*, garfish (see also **aguglia¹**); — di mare, *Syngnathus* spp., pipe-fish, horn eel.

†**Agob·bio** *pr.n.f.* (geog.) Gubbio.

†**agoc·chia** *f.* See **ago.**

ago·gica *f.* (mus.) tempo.

agogn-are [A 5 c] *tr.* to covet; to yearn for; *intr.* (*aux.* avere, *prep.* a) to long (for), to yearn (for). -**amento** *m.* longing. -**ato** *part. adj.* coveted; longed for. (-**atore** *m.* -**atrice** *f.*)

agone¹ *m.* (*augm.* of **ago**, q.v.) packing-needle; (ichth.) kind of fresh water shad found in the Lombardy Lakes, *Alosa lacustris.*

agon-e² *m.* circus, arena; athletic or gladiatorial combat; struggle, contest, competition; entrare nell'—, to enter the lists. -**ale** *adj.* agonistic; *n.m.pl.* (hist.) gli Agonali, athletic contests; -**ista** *m.* competitor; combatant. -**i·stica** *f.* athletics. -**i·stico** *adj.* sporting, competitive; athletic.

agonfosi *f.* (med.) agomphiasis.

agon-i·a *f.* death struggle; l'— fu lunga, the end came slowly; anguish, torment; agony; anxiety; suspense; longing. -**izzante** *adj., n.m., f.* dying; suffering. -**izzare** [A 1] *intr.* (*aux.* avere) to be at death's door, to be breathing one's last; to suffer anguish.

ago·nica *f.* (geog.) agonic line.

a·gono *adj.* (geom.) agonic, having or making no angle.

agopuntur-a *f.* (med.) acupuncture. (-**ista** *m.*)

a·gor-a¹, -à *f.* agora; market-place. -**afobi·a** *f.* (med.) agoraphobia. -**eta** *m.* orator.

†**a·gor-a²** *f.pl.* of **ago**, q.v. -**a·io** *m.* needle-case; †vendor of needles. †-**ato** pointed, sharp.

agostano *adj.* of August; fieno —, August hay.

agostaro *m.* coin of the time of Frederick II of Sicily.

agostinian-o *adj., n.m.* (eccl.) Augustinian (canon); *pl.* buildings or church of an Augustinian house. -**a** *f.* Augustinian (canoness).

Agostino¹ *pr.n.m.* Augustine.

agostino² *adj.* see **agostano**

agost-o¹ *m.* August; la Madonna di mezz'—, the Feast of the Assumption. -**ina** *f.* grape ripening in August. -**ino** *adj.* born in August; (of grapes) ripened in August.

†**agosto²** *adj.* See **augusto.**

agottare [A 1]. See **aggottare.**

ago·tile *m.* (orn.) nightjar.

agramente *adv.* See under **agro.**

agrafi·a *f.* (med.) agraphia.

agranulocit-o *m.* (med.) agranulocyte. -**o·si** *f.* (med.) agranulocytic anaemia, agranulocytosis.

agra·r-ia *f.* agriculture; science of agriculture; faculty of agriculture in a university. -**io** *adj.* agricultural; agrarian; i patti -i, farmers'

contracts; partito -io, agrarian (smallholders') party; *n.m.pl.* (hist.) junkers. -**i·smo** *m.* agrarianism.

agremà, agremani *m.pl.* See **agrimani.**

†**agremento** *m.* ink.

agreste *adj.* wild, uncultivated, agrestial; rustic.

agrest-o *adj.* sour; *n.m.* kind of grapes which do not ripen; verjuice. (-**a** *f.*) -**ata** *f.* verjuice. (-**ezza** *f.*) -**ino** *adj.* sour; *n.m.* sauce made from verjuice; unripened grapes. -**one** *m.* wild vine. (-**oso** *adj.* -**ume** *m.*)

agretto¹ *m.* watercress, *Nasturtium officinale.*

agretto² *adj. dim.* of **agro²**, q.v.

agrezza *f.* sourness; bitterness, irascibility; harshness; (metall.) harshness, brittleness; (med.) stomach acidity.

†**agri·cola** *m.* farmer, husbandman.

agri·colo *adj.* agricultural.

agri-coltore, -cultore *m.* farmer; agriculturist. -**coltura, -cultura** *f.* farming; agriculture; tillage.

agrifo·glio *m.* (bot.) holly, *Ilex aquifolium.*

Agrigent-o *pr.n.f.* (geog.) Girgenti. -**ino** *adj.* relating to Girgenti; (also *n.m.*). (-**ina** *f.*)

agrigno *adj.* sour, tart, sharp.

agrimani *m.pl.* decorations, trimmings, ornaments; diamonds set in silver.

agrimens-ore *m.* land-surveyor. (-**o·rio** *adj.*) -**ura** *f.* land-surveying.

agrimo·nia *f.* (bot.) agrimony, *Agrimonia eupatoria.*

agriotta *f.* (bot.) kind of bitter cherry.

agripni·a *f.* (med.) insomnia.

agrippa¹ *m.* (pharm.) salve, white ointment; †*f.* (obstet.) breech presentation.

Agrippa² *pr.n.f.* Agrippa.

agrippina *f.* chaise-longue, lounge-chair (Empire period).

agro¹ *m.* land round a city; l'—romano, the plain surrounding Rome; l'— pontino, the Pontine marshes.

agr-o² *adj.* sour; bitter; acid, tart; pungent; distasteful; harsh, severe; viso —, bitter, angry expression; parole -e, bitter words; †difficult; *n.m.* juice; l'— di limone, lemon-juice; (metall.) brittleness. -**amente** *adv.* bitterly; harshly; distastefully. (-**etto** *dim. adj.* -**igno** *adj.*) -**odolce** *adj., n.m.* aigre-doux; bitter-sweet; subacid. -**ore** *m.* sour taste.

agro·lo-go *m.* student of agrarian science. -**gi·a** *f.* agrarian science.

agro·n-omo *m.* scientific agriculturist, agronomist. -**omi·a** *f.* agronomy. -**o·mico** *adj.* agronomic.

agrore *m.* See under **agro².**

agrostemma *f.* (bot.) corncockle, *Agrostemma* (or *Lychnis*) *githago.*

agro·stide *f.* (bot.) bent-grass, *Agrostis.*

agrum-e *m.* citrus fruit; sour taste; *pl.* citrus fruits, lemons, oranges, limes. -**a·rio** *adj.* relating to citrus fruits. -**eto** *m.* land cultivated with citrus fruit-trees. -**icoltura** *f.* citrus cultivation.

aguacate *m.* (bot.) advocado pear, *Persea gratissima.*

†**aguaito** *m.* See **agguato.**

aguato *m.* See **agguato.**

aguc·chi-a *f.* needle. -**are** [A 4] *intr.* (*aux.* avere) to stitch; to sew; to knit.

agu-cella, -gella *f.* (paint.) needle (for scratching oil-paint).

agu·glia¹ *f.* (ichth.) kind of garfish, *Belone acus.*

†**agu·glia²** *f.* needle; obelisk; pinnacle; spire; (naut.) rudder pintle, sail needle.

†**agu·glia³** *f.* eagle.

†**agugliata** *f.* See **gugliata.**

†**aguto¹** *adj.* See **acuto.**

†**aguto²** *m.* nail.

aguzz-are [A 1] *tr.* to sharpen; to stimulate; to quicken; to excite; to goad; — l'appetito, to whet the appetite; — le labbra, to purse the lips; — l'ingegno, to sharpen one's wits; — l'occhio, to fix one's gaze intently; †— le ciglia, to look closely, to peer. -**amento** *m.*, -**ata** *f.*, -**atura** *f.* sharpening, whetting; point, edge. -**ato** *part. adj.* sharpened; pointed; (herald.) sharpened at each end. -**atore** *m.* sharpener; grinder. (-**atrice** *f.*) †-**etto** *m.* counsellor, adviser. (†-**etta** *f.*) -**ino** *m.* warder of galley slaves; torturer; executioner; jailer; (fig.) severe taskmaster, slave-driver, tyrant.

aguzzo *adj.* sharp; pointed; whetted; edged.

ah *excl.* ah!, ha! (expressing sorrow, pleasure, surprise, scorn, etc.).

ahi *excl.* alas; ah! (expressing grief); ow! (expressing pain).

ahimè *excl.* alack, woe is me; alas; ah, me; (joc.) **ahitè, ahilui, ahilei, ahinoi, ahivoi, ahiloro,** poor you, etc.

ai[1] unusual spelling of **hai**, 2nd pers. sing. pres. indic. of **avere**, q.v.

ai[2]. See under **a** *prep.*

ai[3] (colloq.) nè ai nè bai, nothing; senza dire nè ai nè bai, without more ado.

ai[4] *m.* (zool.) three-toed sloth, *Bradypus tridactylus.*

ai[5] *adv.* (dial. Lucca) yes.

ai[6] *excl., onomat.* expression of pain, or imitation of a cry.

a·i-a[1] *f.* threshing-floor; — per la tosatura, loft for shearing; †halo round the moon; menar il can per l'—, to beat about the bush; to spin out, to draw a red herring across the trail. **-ata** *f.* quantity of grain covering a threshing-floor.

a·ia[2] *f.* children's nurse, ayah; governess.

A·ia[3] *pr.n.f.* (geog.) L'—, The Hague; Tribunale dell'—, International Court of the Hague.

Aiac·cio *pr.n.f.* (geog.) Ajaccio.

Aiace *pr.n.m.* (myth.) Ajax.

†**aiato** *adv.* andare —, to stroll.

aiduco *m.* Haiduk, Bohemian or Hungarian soldier; outlaw; one of bodyguard of the Grand Dukes of Tuscany.

aierino *adj.* airy, of the air; *n.m.* sprite.

aigrette *f.* plume.

†**aigua** *f.* See **acqua**.

ailant-o *m.* (bot.) tree of Heaven, ailanthus, *Ailanthus altissima.* **-ina** *f.* flax from the ailanthus.

ailuro·fide *f.* (zool.) *Ailurophis vivax*, a kind of snake.

aimè *excl.* See **ahimè**.

†**ain-o** *m.* lamb. †**-ino** *adj.* lamb's, of lamb; carta **-ina**, parchment.

a·io *m.* tutor; †guardian.

aiola *f.* See **aiuola**.

aiolo *m.* See **aiuolo**.

aione, aioni *adv.* (colloq.) andare —, to stroll.

†**airare** *vb.* See **adirare**.

ai·re *m.* (colloq.) impulse; impetus; spring; push; direction, path; going; gait; prendere l'—, to set off; dare l'— a, to set going; †see **aria**.

airone *m.* (orn.) heron, *Ardea cinerea*; — guarda-buoi, cattle egret; — rosso, purple heron, *A. purpurea*; (neol.) type of bomber-plane.

ai·t-a *f.* (poet.) help; *excl.* aita!, help! **-are** [A I] *tr.* (poet.) to help. (**-atore** *m.* **-atrice** *f.*)

†**aitade** *f.* age.

†**aitale** *adj., prn.* See **tale**.

aitante *adj.* strong, vigorous; stout, hearty, robust.

a·iuga *f.* (bot.) common bugle, *Ajuga reptans.*

aiuola *f.* flower-bed; †threshing-floor; †small plot of earth.

aiuolo *m.* net for snaring birds; (Tusc. colloq.) tirare l'—, to kick the bucket.

aiut-are [A I] *tr.* to help; to assist; to tend, to succour; — la barca, to co-operate, to pull one's weight; to help business; *rfl.* to help oneself; to make an effort; aiùtati che Dio t'aiuta, God helps those who help themselves; (*prep.*) di) to avail oneself (of); to be improved: il terreno magro si -a con un buon concime, a poor soil is improved by good manure; to make do (with): m'-o con quel che c'è, I make do with what there is; *recip. rfl.* to help one another. (**-amento** *m.*) **-ante** *m.* assistant; (mil.) adjutant; -ante di campo, aide-de-camp; (naut.) warrant officer; -ante di bandiera, flag-lieutenant. (**-ativo** *adj.*) **-ato** *part. adj.* assisted; improved; *n.m.* assistantship. **-atore** *m.*, **-atrice** *f.* helper, helpmate; assistant. **-ato·rio** *adj.*; *n.m.* †assistant. **-evole** *adj.* helpful.

aiu·to *m.* help, assistance, aid; *excl.* aiuto!, help!; chiamare —, to call for help; assistant; second in command in a medical department of a university or in a department of a hospital; — professore, associate professor, lecturer; — compositore, assistant compositor; *pl.* aid, assistance, help; (mil.) auxiliaries; ancillaries.

aizz-are [A I] *tr.* to instigate, to incite; — un cane contro, to set a dog on. (**-amento** *m.* **-ato** *part. adj.* **-atore** *m.* **-atrice** *f.*) **-oso** *adj.* touchy, excitable.

al. See under **a**, *prep.*

al-a[1] *f.* (*pl.* **-i**, **-e**) wing; apertura d'-i, wing-span; star sulle -i, to hover; (fig.) to be on the point of departure; †battere le -i, to fly; in un batter d'-i, in a twinkling; alzare le -i, to go up in the world; abbassare le -i, to be humbled; tarpare le -i a, to clip the wings of; (fig.) colpo d'—, flight of imagination, heightening of poetic power, stroke of genius; spurt, awakening; fin; piece; tip, edge, line, row; (naut.) supporting or wing squadron; tip of propeller

blade, sail or rudder; stunsail; — di rispetto, reserve; — di scarroccio, leeboard; — di stivamento, internal subdivision of ship; ala!, (command) haul! (aeron.) — volante, tutt'—, tailless aircraft; *pl.* aircraft; (eng.) flange; — di onore, guard of honour; far —, to make way, to fall back, to line the path (of a procession or celebrity); (rugby) terza linea —, wing forward; tre quarti —, wing three quarter. **-a·rio** *adj.* pertaining to the wing; *n.m.* auxiliary soldier. **-ata** *f.* flap, beat of the wing. **-ato** *adj.* winged; uno stile -ato, winged words, an eloquent style; *n.m.pl.* gli -ati, the birds and winged animals. **-etta** *f.* iron support, bracket; (naut.) stunsail; (eng.) vane, fin (e.g. of cylinder block); pompa ad -ette, centrifugal pump; (aeron.) slat; -etta di compensazione, trim tab; (ichth.) fin; (ornith.) pinion; (anat.) ala. **-ettone** *m.* (naut.) bilge-keel; (aeron.) aileron; (ichth.) fin.

†**ala**[2] *f.* ale.

alabard-a *f.* halberd; †appoggiar l'—, to sponge on someone's hospitality, 'to hang up one's hat'. **-ata** *f.* blow with a halberd. **-ato** *adj.* bearing a halberd. **-iere** *m.* halberdier.

alabastr-o *m.* alabaster. **-a·io** *m.* worker in alabaster; vendor of alabaster. **-ino** *adj.* alabastrine. **-ite** *f.* imitation alabaster.

alac·cia *f.* (ichth.) *Sardinella aurita*, a small fish like a sprat.

a·lacr-e, ala·cre *adj.* active; industrious; willing; brisk; cheerful. (**-emente** *adv.*) **-ità** *f.* alacrity; eagerness.

Aladino *pr.n.m.* Aladdin; la lampada d'—, Aladdin's lamp.

†**Alagna** *pr.n.f.* (geog.) Anagni.

alag·gio *m.* (naut.) slipping, beaching (of a boat); towing, tow; tow-path; scalo d'—, dry-dock.

alalà *excl.* hurrah! (cf. **eia**).

alamanna[1] *f.* (bot.) muscatel grape, named after Alamanno Salviati.

†**alamanna**[2] *f.* See **alemanna**.

†**alamanna**[3] *f.* See under **alamanno**.

†**alamann-o** *adj., n.m.* German. †**-a** *f.* German woman.

alamaro *m.* braiding; loop; *pl.* frogs, loops, braided fastenings.

alambicco *m.* still, alembic.

alano *m.* bulldog; mastiff; boar-hound; wolf-hound.

alare[1] *m.* andiron; firedog (usu. *pl.*); iron support used in bending timber for boat-building; trestle.

alare[2] [A I] *tr.* to tow, to haul; (naut.) *intr.* (*aux.* avere) to sail close to the wind; to hoist on board to haul ashore; — a camminare, to haul walking away; — a cambiamano, to haul hand over hand; — per davanti, to haul without use of a leading block; — a segnaro, to haul hand over hand using a stopper.

alare[3] *adj.* (anat.) osso —, sphenoid bone; muscoli alari, dilator muscles of the nose.

alata *f., alato **adj.* See under **ala**.

ala·uda *f.* (poet. Carducci). See **allodola**.

alba[1] *f.* day-break; first light; dawn; aubade; — bianca, early dawn; — rossa, sunrise; (joc.) l'— dei tafani, midday, late in the morning.

alba[2] *f.* (liturg.) alb.

†**alba**[3] *f.* Venetian silver coin.

alba-gi·a *f.* pride, conceit; haughtiness. **-gioso** *adj.* vain; haughty.

†**albagio** *m.* coarse white woollen cloth; †*adj.* whitish.

albana *f.* (bot.) variety of white grape.

albanella *f.* (orn.) harrier; — col collare, marsh harrier; — minore, Montagu's harrier, *Circus pygargus*; — reale, hen-harrier, *C. cyaneus.*

Alban-i·a *pr.n.f.* (geog.) Albania. **-ese** *m., f.* Albanian; (hist.) light-cavalry soldier; †foreigner; *adj.* Albanian.

albano *m.* a white wine, made from **albana**, q.v.

albante *adj.* whitish, turning white.

albarde·ola *f.* (orn.) shoveller.

albarese *m.* See **alberese**.

alba·rio *adj.* (techn.) opera albaria, distemper mixed with white marble dust.

al·bar-o, -ello *m.* (bot.), silver poplar, *Populus alba*; †tree.

†**alba·sia** *f.* calm (at sea).

albaspina *f.* (poet.) hawthorn, whitethorn. (See also **biancospino**.)

albastrello *m.* (orn.) marsh sandpiper, *Tringa stagnatilis.*

albata *f.* aubade, dawn song.

alba·tico *m.* (bot.) dark grape, used to colour white wine.

al·batr-o *m., -a f.* (bot.) strawberry-tree, arbutus-tree; *Arbutus unedo.* **al·batro**[2] *m.* (orn.) albatross.

albe·dine *f.* whiteness; in alchemy, white principle, albedo.

albeggi-are [A 3 c] *intr.* (*aux.* essere), to dawn; to grow white; to tend towards white. (**-amento** *m.*)

albene *m.* kind of rayon.

†**alberag·gio** *m.* (comm., naut.) harbour dues; (naut.) see **alberatura**.

alber-are [A I s] *tr.* to plant with trees; to hoist; to set upright; (naut.) to step (a mast). **-a·glia** *f.* thicket of stunted, ill-grown trees. (**-amento** *m.*) **-ante** *m.* (naut.) look-out; topsman. (**-ata** *f.* **-ato** *part. adj.* **-atore** *m.*) **-atura** *f.* plantation of trees; (naut.) masts, yards, spars.

al·bera, alberella *f.* (bot.) aspen, *Populus tremula*.

alberello[1] *m.* big shrub; small tree; edible fungus which grows at roots of poplars, *Boletus scaber*; see **alberella**.

alberello[2] *m.* pot, jar; phial.

alberese *m.* kind of limestone, used for millstones; quarry of same.

alberet-a *f.*, **-o** *m.* grove of trees; plantation of poplars; avenue of poplars.

alberg-are [A 2] *tr.* to house; to shelter; (fig.) to harbour, to cherish; *intr.* (aux. avere) to put up at an inn, to lodge. (**-agione** *f.* **-amento** *m.* **-ante** *part. adj., n.m., f.*) **-aria** *f.* see **albergheria**. **-ato** *part. adj.* housed; inhabited; abounding in hotels. **-atore** *m.* hotel-keeper, innkeeper. **-atrice** *f.* landlady.

alber-gheri·a *f.* free lodging; right of free lodging. **-ghiero** *adj.* hotel-keeping, hotel; l'industria **-ghiera**, the hotel industry.

alber-go *m.* (*pl.* **-ghi**) hotel; inn; shelter; abode; hostel; — diurno, public baths, barber, hairdresser, etc., all in one; — per la gioventù, youth hostel; dare — a, to take in, to give shelter to; prendere —, to put up, to find accommodation; scendere ad un —, to put up at a hotel; dormire all'— delle stelle, to sleep rough, to sleep in the open; andare ad — (of birds), to go to roost; caccia all'—, taking birds at roost.

al·bero *m.* tree; — di Natale, Christmas tree; — genealogico, family tree, pedigree, genealogical tree. **1.** Botanical uses: poplar; wood from the poplar; — da aceto, smooth-leaved sumach, *Rhus glabra*; — di amore, — di Giuda, Judas tree, *Cercis siliquastrum*; — da burro americano, alligator pear, avocado tree, *Persea gratissima*; — del caffè, coffee tree, *Coffea arabica*; — della camfora, camphor tree, *Cinnamomum camphora*; — della cannella, cinnamon tree, *Cinnamomum zeylanicum*; — della china, Peruvian bark tree, quinine tree, *Cinchona officinalis*; — della cascariglia, *Croton eluteria*; — della cioccolata, cocoa tree, *Theobroma cacao*; — dei conciatori, tanners' tree, *Coriaria myrtifolia*; — da cucchiari, American mountain laurel, spoonwood, calico bush, *Kalmia latifolia*; — da foglie acide, American sourwood, *Oxydendron arboreum*; — da frange, — da neve, American fringe-tree, *Chionanthus virginicus*; — da frecce, Arrow-wood, *Viburnum dentatum*; — da garofani, clove-tree, *Eugenia aromatica*; — gigante della California, Giant redwood, *Sequoia gigantea*; — da gomma arabica, Gum arabic tree, *Acacia senegal*; — da gomma elastica, India-rubber tree, *Ficus elastica*; — di Linneo, lime tree, *Tilia*; — della mestizia, tree of sadness, *Nyctanthes arbor tristis*; — della mirra, Myrrh tree, *Commiphora molmol*; — della pagode, banyan tree, *Ficus indica* and *F. benghaliensis*; — del pane, breadfruit tree, *Artocarpus altilis*; — del Paradiso, tree of Heaven, *Ailanthus altissima* (see also **ailanto**); — della pazienza, Indian lilac, *Melia azedarach*; — da poponi, Papaw-tree, *Asimina triboba*; — a quaranta scudi, Ginkgo, maidenhair tree, *Ginkgo biloba*; — da sangue di dragone, Dragon's blood tree, *Dracaena draco*; — di Sant'Andrea, date plum; — del tè, tea tree, *Thea sinensis*; — da tulipani, Tulip-tree, *Liriodendron tulipiferum*; — del veleno di Giava, upas tree; — della vita, American white cedar (or) arbor vitae, *Thuja occidentalis*. **2.** Nautical uses: mast; — di trinchetto, foremast; — maestro, mainmast; — di mezzana, mizzenmast; — di bompresso, bowsprit; — di parrocchetto, foretopmast; — di pappafico, topgallant mast; — di gabbia, topmast (i.e. the middle section of a full-sized mast); — di fortuna, jury-mast; — a traliccio, trellice mast; — composto, composite mast; — di carico, stump mast; — dell'elica, propeller shaft. **3.** Engineering and Mechanical uses: shaft, spindle, axle, arbor; stem (of a valve); — a camme, camshaft; — a gomiti, crankshaft; — a doppio gomito, two-throw crankshaft; — base, standard shaft; — comando, drive shaft; — di propulsione, propeller shaft; — di rinvio, lay shaft, countershaft; — di trasporto, feed rod; — motore, driving shaft; —cavo, hollow shaft, quill; — oscillante, rocker shaft; — passante, through-shaft; — primario, main shaft; — secondario, driven shaft; — di sterzo, steering column; — ozioso, idler shaft; — porta pezzo, work arbor. **-etto** *m.dim.* of **albero**; (naut.) yard, spar.

albertite *f.* (miner.) albertite.

Alberto *pr.n.m.* Albert.

albescente *adj.* whitening, turning white.

†**Al·bia** *pr.n.f.* (geog.) the river Elbe.

albic-are [A 2 s] *intr.* to turn white. **-ante** *part. adj.* whitish, turning white.

albic·cio *adj.* whitish.

albicerato *adj.* colour of white wax, waxy, waxen.

albicocc-a *f.* apricot. **-o** *m.* apricot tree, *Prunus armeniaca*.

albicolore *adj. indecl.* white.

albific-are [A 2] *tr.* to whiten, to make white. (**-ato** *part.adj.* **-azione** *f.*)

albigese *adj.* Albigensian; *n.m., f.* Albigensian; *m.pl.* (hist.) Albigenses.

albi·glio *m.* (bot.) kind of vine.

albinag·gio *m.* (leg.) aubaine; escheat to the crown of the immovable estate of an alien.

albin-o *adj.* albino; whitish; *n.m.* albino. **-a** *f.* albiness. **-ismo** *m.* albinism.

Albione *pr.n.f.* (geog.) Albion; la perfida —, perfidious Albion.

albis *Lat.* (liturg.) Domenica in —, Low Sunday; la settimana in —, Easter week.

albite *f.* (miner.) albite, soda feldspar.

albo[1] *adj.* (poet.) white; (colloq.) tipsy.

albo[2] *m.* album; scrap-book; — dei medici, medical register; radiato dall' —, struck off the register; register; — comunale, — d'onore, roll of honour; public notice-board in a town hall; (Rom. hist.) — pretorio, album praetorium.

albogatto *m.* (bot.) poplar that grows beside watercourses.

albolite *f.* albolith.

albopale *m.* white opal.

albore *m.* whiteness; first light; dawn; gli -i della civiltà, the dawn of civilization.

†**a·lbore** *m.* See **albero**.

alborella *f.* (ichth.) *Leuciscus albidus*, fish resembling a chub.

alboro *m.* (ichth.) Spanish sea bream, *Pagellus erythrinus*.

†**alborotare,** †**albotorare** *rfl.* to rise in rebellion.

albuc·cio *m.* (dial.). See **albaro**.

albu·g-ine *f.* (med.) albugo, whiteness in the cornea of the eye. **-i·neo,** **-inoso** *adj.* albuginean.

album *m.* (*pl.* **albi**). See **albo**[2].

album-e *m.* albumen; white of egg. **-ina** *f.* albumin. **-inare** [A I] *tr.* (paperm.) to glaze with albumen. **-inato** *m.* (chem.) albuminate. **-inatura** *f.* (paperm.) glazing. **-inoide** *m.* albuminoid. **-inoso** *adj.* albuminous. **-inuri·a** *f.* (med.) albuminuria.

alburno *m.* sapwood.

alca *f.* (orn.) great auk, *Alca impennis*.

alca·ic-o *adj., n.m.* (prosod.) Alcaic (line). **-a** *n.f.* (prosod.) Alcaic ode.

al·cal-i *m. indecl.* (chem.) alkali. **-escente** *adj.* alkalescent, turning alkaline. **-escenza** *f.* alkalescence. **-i·geno** *adj.* alkaligenous. **-i·metro** *m.* alkalimeter. **-inità** *f.* alkalinity, basicity. **-ino** *adj.* alkaline, basic. **-i·nulo** *adj.* slightly alkaline. **-izzare** [A I] *tr.* to render alkaline. **-o·ide** *m.* alkaloid.

alcanna *f.* henna; (bot.) dyers' bugloss, *Alkanna tinctoria*; — vera degli Arabi, henna plant, *Lawsonia alba*; henna.

†**alcavala** *f.* tax.

alce *m.* (zool.) elk, moose, *Alces machlis*.

alce·a *f.* (bot.) hollyhock, *Althaea rosea*; marsh mallow, *A. officinalis*; hemp mallow, *A. cannabina*.

Alceo *pr.n.m.* Alcaeus.

alce·dine *f.* See **alcione**.

alchechengi *m.* (bot.) winter-cherry, Japanese lanterns, *Physalis alkekengi*; sleepy winter-cherry, *Withania somnifera*.

alchemilla *f.* (bot.) Lady's mantle, *Alchemilla*.

alch-ide *m.* (chem.) alkyd. **-i·dico** *adj.* (chem.) alkyd; resina -idica, alkyd resin.

alch-ile *m.* (chem.) alkyl. **-i·lico** *adj.* (chem.) alkyl.

alchi·m-ia, alchimi·a *f.* alchemy; deception. **-iare** [A 4] *tr.* to falsify. **-ista** *m.* alchemist. **-izzare** [A I] *intr.* (aux. avere) to alchemize.

alchimilla *f.* See **alchemilla**.

Alcina *pr.n.f.* Alcina, a character in Ariosto's *Orlando Furioso*; (fig.) enchantress.

alcion-e *m.* (orn.) kingfisher, halcyon; giorni dell'—, halcyon days; (neol.) type of Italian bomber plane. **-e·i** *m.pl.* (zool.) *Alcyonium digitatum*, 'dead men's fingers'.

alcio·nico, alcio·nio *adj.* halcyon.

alcma·nio *adj.* (prosod.) Alcmanian (metre).

al·col, al·cole *m.* and derivs. See **alcool**.

al·co-ol *m.* alcohol; — denaturato, methylated spirits, industrial spirit. **-olato** *m.* spirit solution, alcoholic solution. **-ole·metro, -olo·metro, -oli·metro** *m.* alcoholometer. (**-olemetri·a** *f.*) **-olicità** *f.* proof (of spirits), alcohol content. **-o·lico** *adj.* alcoholic; *n.m.pl.* wines and spirits; spaccio di -olici, wineshop, pub. **-olişmo** *m.* alcoholism. **-olista** *m.* alcoholic. **-oliti** *m.* (pharm.) spirit solutions. **-olizzare** [A I] *tr.* to alcoholize. **-olizzato** *part. adj.* alcoholized; *n.m.* (med.) alcoholic, habitual drunkard. (**-olizzazione** *f.* **-olomani·a** *f.*)

alcorano, alcorano *m.* Koran; (archit.) minaret.

alcov-a, alcova *f.* alcove, recess; bedroom; romanzi d'—, gallant novels. **-ista** *m.* (lit. hist.) frequenter of literary salons.

alcunchè *pron.* anything; something; a little.

alcun-o *adj.* (sing.) any (usu. in neg. context): non vedo -a ragione, I do not see any reason; senza -a spesa, without any expense; *pl.* some, a few; ha -i buoni quadri, he has some good pictures; *prn.* (sing.) anyone, anybody (usu. in neg. context): non c'è — che possa aiutarmi, there isn't anyone who can help me; se — mi vedesse, if anyone should see me; *pl.* some, some people; a few; -i dicono, some people say; quanti libri! me ne vorresti imprestare -i?, what a lot of books! would you lend me a few?; *adv.* alcun poco, a little, somewhat.

†**aldace** *adj.* See **audace**.

alde·ide *f.* (chem.) aldehyde.

ald-ino *adj.* (typ.) Aldine. **-o** *m.* book printed by Aldus or his successors.

†**aldire** *vb.* See **udire**.

aldolo *m.* (chem.) aldol.

a·le-a *f.* contingency, risk, hazard; correr l'—, to run the risk; game of chance. **-ato·rio** *adj.* (leg.) aleatory (of a contract or an undertaking), depending on chance; rashly speculative.

alea·tico *m.* a Tuscan grape; the wine made from it.

aleffe *m. indecl.* dire —, to begin.

aleggi-are [A 3 c] *intr.* (*aux.* avere) to flutter; to flit; to hover; to quiver; (fig.) to be in the air; *tr.* to have the air of, to suggest, to hint at. (**-amento** *m.*) **-ante** *part. adj.* fluttering, quivering.

aleggio *m.* (naut.) boat's plug; see also **alleggio**.

alemanna *f.* (mus.) allemande (also **allemanda**).

†**alemann-o** *adj.*; *n.m.* German. (†**-a** *f.*)

†**alen-a** *f.* breath; breathing; vigour, energy. †**-amento** *m.* breathing. †**-are** to breathe. †**-oso** *adj.* asthmatic; laboured in breathing.

†**alepardo** *m.* leopard.

alep-idosa·uro *m.* (ichth.) *Alepisaurus*, lancet-fish. **-oce·falo** *m.* (ichth.) *Alepocephalus*, smooth-head.

†**a·lere** *tr. def.* (3rd pers. sing. **ale** only recorded) to feed, to nourish.

alerione *m.* (herald.) alerion, eagle without beak and legs.

alerone *m.* (aeron.) aileron.

aleş-are [A I] *tr.* (eng.) to bore (out), to gouge, to ream, to broach, to enlarge with a reamer. **-ag·gio** *m.* bore, internal diameter; boring, reaming. **-atoio** *m.*, **-atore** *m.* reamer, broach. **-atrice** *f.* boring machine. **-atura** *f.* reaming, boring out; bore.

Alessandra *pr.n.f.* Alexandra.

Alessan·dr-ia *pr.n.f.* (geog.) Alessandria (Piedmont); — d'Egitto, Alexandria (Egypt). **-ino** *adj., n.m.* **-ina** *f.* Alexandrian.

alessandrin-o *adj., n.m.* (prosod.) Alexandrine; (hist.) Alexandrian. **-işmo** *m.* decadence in art.

Alessan·dro *p.n.m.* Alexander; — Magno, Alexander the Great.

aless-ifar·maco *m.* (pharm.) alexipharmic, antidote. **-ite·rio** *m.* antidote, counter-irritant.

Ales·sio *pr.n.m.* Alexis.

aletosco·pio *m.* an old form of stereoscope.

aletta *f.*, **alettone** *m.* See under **ala**.

alettato *adj.* (herald.) finned.

Aletto *pr.n.f.* (myth.) Alecto, one of the Furies; sonare la tromba d'—, to arouse discord.

aletto·ria *f.* (bot.) kind of lichen, *Alectoria*.

aleurone *m.* (chem.) aleuron.

ale·zano *adj.* (of a horse) chestnut.

alfa[1] *m.* Alpha; dall'— all'omega, from Alpha to Omega; (mech.) float-board.

alfa[2] *f.* (bot.) kind of esparto grass, *Stipa tenacissima*; the fibre obtained from it.

alfa-beto *m.* alphabet; code; — Morse, Morse code; — a cinque unità, five-unit code, Bandot code; per —, in alphabetical order; non sa l'— della medicina, he doesn't know the first thing about medicine; (colloq.) perder l'—, to talk nonsense. **-beta** *adj.* (joc.) literate. **-beta·rio** *m.* alphabet chart; set of toy letters; box of bricks with letters on them. **-be·tico** *adj.* alphabetical. **-beticamente** *adv.* alphabetically, in alphabetical order.

†**alfana** *f.* steed; horse; mare.

alfanetta *f.* (orn.) barbary falcon.

alfaromeişmo *m.* (neol.) speed-mania.

alfiere *m.* standard-bearer; ensign; (chess) bishop.

alfier-iano, -eşco (*m.pl.* **-eschi**) *adj.* Alfierian (from the name of Vittorio Alfieri, Italian dramatist).

alfine *adv.* finally, at last; after all; in the long run.

alfonsişmo *m.* procuring (from the play *Monsieur Alphonse*, by A. Dumas, fils).

Alfonso *pr.n.m.* Alphonse; procurer.

Alfredo *pr.n.m.* Alfred.

alg-a *f.* seaweed; (bot.) — di Chiana, — cornicolata, water tape grass, *Valisneria spiralis*; — marina dei vetrai, glass wrack, *Zostera marina*. **-oso** abounding in seaweed.

†**algari·a** *f.* ostentation.

al·gebr-a *f.* algebra. **-a·ico, -a·tico** *adj.* algebraical. (**-icamente** *adv.*) **-ista** *m.* algebraist.

alge·brico *adj.* See **algebraico**, under **algebra**.

algente *adj.* (poet.) cold, frozen.

†**alge·re** *intr. def.* to suffer intense cold; to freeze.

Alger-i *pr.n.f.* (geog.) Algiers. **-i·a** *f.* Algeria. **-ino** *adj., n.m.* Algerian. (**-ina** *f.*)

a·lgid-o *adj.* cold, frozen; (med.) algid. **-ità** *f.* algidity.

algore *m.* (poet.) intense cold; season of cold.

algorişmo, algoritmo *m.* algorism.

algoso *adj.* See under **alga**.

aliante *m.* (aeron.) glider.

ali-are [A 4] *intr.* (*aux.* avere) (poet.) to flutter; to fly; to flit. **-ante** *adj.* fluttering; flitting.

alibattente *m.* (aeron.) ornithopter.

alice[1] *f.* (ichth.) anchovy, *Engraulis encrasicholus*.

Alice[2] *pr.n.f.* Alice.

alicetta *f.* silver-fish, *Ctenolepisma* sp.

†**alicorn-a, -o** *m.* unicorn.

alidada *f.* (astron.) alidade.

a·lid-o *adj.* (Tusc.) dry; arid; carne -a, tough meat. (**amente** *adv.* **-ezza** *f.*) **-ire** [D I] *tr.* to dry; *rfl., intr.* (*aux.* essere) to become dry, hard. **-ore** *m.* dryness; drought; aridity. (**oso** *adj.*)

alidorato *adj.* (poet.) golden-winged.

alien-are [A I] *tr.* to alienate, to turn against; to estrange, to sever; (leg.) to alienate, to transfer; *rfl.* (*dat.* of *prn.*) to lose, to alienate from oneself; si è -ato l'affetto di tutti, he has turned everyone against him, he has lost everyone's affection. **-a·bile** *adj.* (leg.) alienable, transferable. **-abilità** *f.* (leg.) alienability. (**-amento** *m.*) **-ante** *part. adj.* alienating; (leg.) *n.m.*, *f.* transferor. **-ata·rio** *m.* (leg.) alienee, transferee. **-ato** *part. adj.* alienated; estranged; *n.m.* lunatic; ospizio per -ati, mental home. (**-ata** *f.*) (**-atore** *m.* **-atrice** *f.*) **-azione** (**-agione**) *f.* (leg.) alienation; transfer; mental derangement; (fig.) estrangement. **-ista** *m.* alienist, mental specialist, psychiatrist.

alienato *part. adj., n.m.* See under **alienare**.

alienista *m.* See under **alienare**.

alieno *adj.* (*prep.* da) averse, disinclined, reluctant: non sono — dal consentire, I am inclined to consent; extraneous, irrelevant; alien, foreign.

†**alie·utica** *f.* halieutics, the art or practice of fishing; a treatise on fishing.

alifa·tico *adj.* (chem.) aliphatic.

a·lig-a *f.*, **-oso** *adj.* See **alga** and derivs.

ali·gero *adj.* (poet.) winged.

alighiero *m.* (naut.) boat-hook.

aligusta *f.* See **aragosta**.

aliment-o[1] *m.* food, nutriment, aliment; subsistence; (fig.) nourishment, succour; *pl.* (leg.) alimony, maintenance; somministrare gli -i, corrispondere gli -i, to make an allowance for maintenance. **-are** *tr.* to feed, to nourish; to support, to maintain, to keep alive; to furnish with fuel, to stoke; (fig.) to cherish, to entertain (hopes); -are l'odio delle parti, to foster class-hatred; (leg.) to give

aliment-o (*cont.*)
alimony, or maintenance; to aliment. (**-amento** *m.*) **-are, -a·rio**
adj. alimentary; tubo, condotto **-are**, alimentary canal; nutritive;
prodotti **-ari**, foodstuffs; regime **-are**, diet; (leg.) pensione **-aria**,
alimony. **-arista** *m.* purveyor of foodstuffs. **-atore** *m.* nourisher;
(eng.) feeder. (**-atrice** *f.*) **-azione** *f.* feeding, nourishing, alimenta-
tion; (eng.) feed; supply; **-azione forzata**, pressure feed. (**-i·zio** *adj.*
-oso *adj.*)

†**alimento²** *m.* See **elemento**.

†**alimo·nia** *f.* (leg.) alimony.

ali·nea *f.* (leg.) paragraph.

alinevoso *adj.* (poet.) snowy-winged; snowy-sailed.

alioso *adj.* See **aliante**, under **aliare**.

aliosso *m.* (anat.) astragalus.

alio·tide *f.* (zool.) *Haliotis* sp., ear shell, ormer.

†**alipardo** *m.* leopard.

ali·pede *adj.* (poet.) wing-footed; *n.m.* wing-footed steed.

alipurpu·reo *adj.* (poet.) purple-winged.

alipta *m.* (sport) manager; (Gk. and Rom. antiq.) one who rubbed
the athletes down with oil.

ali·quot-o *adj.* (math.) aliquot. **-a** *f.* aliquot part; rate of taxation;
pagare l'**-a**, to lay out one's share of a payment; percepire l'**-a**,
to receive one's share of a payment.

alisciatoio *m.* See **alesatore**, under **alesare**.

alise·o *adj.* (geog.) venti alisei, trade winds; *n.m.pl.* gli alisei, trade
winds.

aliso *m.* (poet.) lily.

alisso *m.* (bot.) cruciferous genus, *Alyssum*.

alitare [A I S] *intr.* (*aux.* avere) to breathe; to blow softly; senz'**—**,
breathlessly, with wrapt attention.

alite *f.* (zool.) *Alytes obstetricans*, the midwife toad.

a·lit-o *m.* breath; exhalation; light breeze; puff; non ci spira un **—** di
vento, there's not a breath of wind; non si sente un **—**, there's
not a sound to be heard; lavoro fatto con l'**—**, exquisitely fine
work; **—** cattivo, **—** pesante, bad breath; riavere l'**—**, to recover
one's breath. **-oso** *adj.* suffering from halitosis.

aliveloce *adj.* (poet.) swift-winged.

ali·volo *adj.* (poet.) winged.

alizarina *f.* (techn.) alizarine; (chem.) alizarin.

alla¹ see under **a¹** (*prep.*).

Alla² *pr.n.m.* Allah.

†**alla³** *f.* ell.

†**alla⁴** *f.* covered market.

allalì *excl.* tally ho!, yoicks!

allacci-are [A 3] *tr.* to lace; to tie; to bind; to leash, to lasso;
allacciarsi le scarpe, to tie up one's shoes; to fasten; to entwine;
to buckle; to connect; **—** relazioni commerciali, to establish
business connexions; **—** le acque, to connect water by waterworks;
to ensnare, to entrap; to allure; (dial.) *intr.* to walk with long,
swift strides; †allacciarsela, to presume, to put on airs. **-amento** *m.*
lacing; linking; link; connexion; (rlwy.) branch-line; canalizing;
ligature; bandage; (fig.) deception, allurement. (**-ante** *part. adj.*
†**-ativo** *adj.* **-ato** *part. adj.* **-atore** *m.* **-atrice** *f.*) **-atura** *f.* tie, lace,
fastening; buttoning. (†**-e·vole** *adj.*) **-bottoni** *m. indecl.* button-
hook.

allag-are [A 2] *tr.* to inundate, to flood; to overflow; (fig.) to overwhelm; *rfl.*, *intr.* (*aux.* essere) to be inundated, to be flooded.
-amento *m.* inundation, flood; overflow, overflowing;
(naut.) flooding. **-ato** *part. adj.* flooded, inundated; under water.
(**-azione** *f.*)

allam-are¹ [A I] *intr.*, *rfl.* to become marshy. **-ato** *part. adj.* marshy.

allamare² [A I] *tr.* (dial. Lucca) to catch with a hook.

allamp-anare [A I S] *intr.* (*aux.* essere) to grow lean and pale;
— dalla fame, to be half-starved. **-ato** *part. adj.* lean, emaciated,
cadaverous; tall as a lamp-post, gangling.

allampare¹ [A I] *intr.* to be parched with thirst: ho una sete che
allampo, I have a raging thirst.

allampare² [A I] *intr.* (dial. Lucca) to disappear like lightning.

allapp-are¹ [A I] *tr.* to set (one's teeth) on edge; **—** la bocca, to make
the mouth dry. **-ante** *part. adj.* sour, pungent. (**-olare** [A I] *tr.*)

†**allappare²** *tr.* to blink; in un **—** d'occhio, in the twinkling of an eye.

allappicare [A 2 S] *rfl.* (Tusc.) to have forty winks.

allard-are [A I] *tr.* to lard, to grease. **-ato** *part. adj.* greased, larded;
greasy. **-ellare** [A I] *tr. dim.* to grease a little.

allarg-are [A 2] *tr.* to widen; to enlarge; to extend; to spread;

il pavone **-a** la coda, the peacock spreads its tail; **—** le braccia,
to open one's arms; **—** un vestito, to let out a dress; **—** una regola,
to relax a rule; **—** la mano, to be open-handed, to be liberal;
— il passo a, to make way for; **—** il freno, to slacken the reins;
— il respiro, to allow to breathe more freely; **—** il cuore a, to
comfort, to console, to lift a weight off one's mind; (mus.) **—** il
tempo, to broaden the tempo; to augment (in the contrapuntal
sense); *rfl.* to become wider, to widen; to grow large; to extend;
to spread; to spread out; to move into larger premises; (of weather)
to improve; **-arsi** sopra un argomento, to enlarge upon a subject;
gli si **-ò** il cuore, his heart was lightened; **-arsi con**, to open one's
heart to; (naut.) **-arsi** in mare, to make for the open sea; **-arsi**
nelle spese, to spend more. **-amento** *m.* enlarging; extending;
growth. **-ata** *f.* widening; stretching; dare un'**-ata** a, to stretch.
(**-ato** *part. adj.*) **-atoio** *m.* reamer. (**-atore** *m.* **-atrice** *f.* **-atura** *f.*)

allarm-e *m.* alarm; warning; air-raid signal, alert; il cessato **—**, the
'all clear'; call to arms; apprehension, agitation, alarm. **-ante**
part. adj. alarming. **-are** [A I] *tr.* to alarm, to frighten; *rfl.* to be
alarmed, to take fright. **-ato** *part. adj.* alarmed, aroused; frightened.
-ismo *m.* alarmist tendencies. **-ista** *m.* alarmist. **-i·stico** *adj.*
alarmist.

all'armi! *excl.* to arms!

allascare [A 2] *tr.* (naut.) to ease off, to pay out, to pay away (rope
or chain).

allato *adv.* (*prep.* di) beside; near; in comparison (with); non avere
denaro **—**, to have no money on one (also **a lato**).

allatt-are [A I] *tr.* to give suck to; **—** un bambino, to give a baby the
breast; to feed, to nurse; *intr.* (*aux.* avere) to suck, to suckle.
-amento *m.* suckling, feeding, nursing; periodo d'**-amento**,
lactation; **-amento** artificiale, bottle-feeding. **-atrice** *f.* nursing
mother; wet nurse. **-atura** *f.* lactation; suckling, feeding.

alle see under **a¹** (*prep.*).

allea *f.* (Piedm.) allée, avenue of trees.

alle-are [A I] *tr.* to unite, to ally; *rfl.* (*prep.* con) to ally oneself,
to form an alliance. **-anza** *f.* alliance; la Santa **-anza**, the Holy
Alliance; league; stringere un'**-anza** con, to enter into an alliance
with. **-ato** *part. adj.* allied; le forze **-ate**, the allied forces; *n.m.*
ally; *pl.* gli **-ati**, the allies.

†**alleccornire** *tr.* to tempt, to incite (appetite, desire).

alleg-are¹ [A 2] *tr.* (leg.) to allege, to assert, to bring in as evidence,
to plead as an excuse. **-ante** *part. adj.* (leg.) alleging; *n.m.,f.* party
who asserts. (**-ato** *part. adj.* **-atore** *m.* **-atrice** *f.*) **-azione** *f.* (leg.)
allegation, assertion, plea, adduction of evidence.

alleg-are² [A 2] *tr.* to alloy; †to bind; (fig.) **—** i denti, to set one's
teeth on edge; to enclose (in a letter); *intr.* (*aux.* avere) (of fruit,
when the blossom has fallen) to set; (of scissors) to be blunt:
queste forbici **-ano**, these scissors won't cut; (of teeth) to be set
on edge (also *rfl.*). (**-amento** *m.*) **-ata** *f.* letter enclosed. **-ato** *part.*
adj. joined; enclosed; accompanying; (of fruit) set; *n.m.* enclosure;
document enclosed, appendix; alloy. (**-azione** *f.*)

allegger-ire [D 2] *tr.* (*prep.* di) to lighten; to relieve; to ease, to
alleviate; to mitigate; **—** la mano, to be less heavy-handed;
(colloq.) to rob, to 'lift'; mi **-ì** del portafoglio, he relieved me of
my note-case; *rfl.* to be lightened; to become lighter; to be
relieved; to put on lighter clothes: d'aprile non t'alleggerire,
cast not a clout till May be out. **-imento** *m.* lightening; easing;
relieving; alleviation; diminution; relief. (**-ito** *part. adj.*)

alleggi-are [A 3 c] *tr.* (naut.) to lighten. **-amento** *m.* (aeron.) buchi
-amento, lighting holes. (**-ato** *part. adj.* **-atore** *m.* **-atrice** *f.*)

alle·ggio *m.* (naut.) lighter; spese d'**—**, lighterage.

alle-gori·a *f.* allegory; allegorical painting, sculpture. **-goreggiare**
[A 3 c] *intr.* (*aux.* avere) to allegorize to excess, to indulge in
allegory. **-go·rico** *adj.* allegorical. (**-goricamente** *adv.*) **-gorista**
m. allegorist. **-gorizzare** [A I] to allegorize. (**-gorizzamento** *m.*
-gorizzato *part. adj.* **-gorizzato** *part. adj.* **-gorizzatore** *m.*)

allegrare [A I c] and derivs. See **rallegrare**.

allegr-o *adj.* merry; cheerful; gay; lively; good-humoured; bright;
(colloq.) tipsy; (of a woman) giddy, fast; (herald.) unharnessed;
stare **-i**, to make merry; c'è poco da stare **-i**, there's not much to
be cheerful about; su, allegro!, cheer up!; (mus.) quick, vivacious;
n.m. (mus.) an allegro movement. **-amente** *adv.* cheerfully, gaily;
with a good grace; willingly, thoughtlessly; spendere **-amente**,
to spend heedlessly. **-etto** *adj.* (mus.) moderately quick, between
andante and allegro; *n.m.* (mus.) an allegretto movement. **-ezza** *f.*
cheerfulness; joy, gladness; gaiety, merriment; vividness (of

colour); demonstration of affection; jubilation. **-i·a** *f.* merriment, gaiety; vivere in -ia, to lead a gay life; far -ia a, to welcome with enthusiasm; stare in -ia, to have a good time.

allelomorfismo *m.* (biol.) allelomorphism.

allelu·i-a *m. indecl.* (rel.) alleluia, hallelujah; cantare l'—, to sing hallelujah; fino al dì dell'—, for ever; Eastertide. **-are** [A4] *intr.* (*aux* avere) to sing hallelujah.

allemanda *f.* (mus.) allemande (also **alemanna**).

†allemann-o *adj., n.m.* German. (**†-a** *f.*)

allen-are¹ [A1c] *tr.* to invigorate, to strengthen; (sport) to train, to coach; *rfl.* (sport) to train, to go into training. **-amento** *m.* training; practice; course of instruction. **-ato** *part. adj.* trained; fit, in good physical condition. **-atore** *m.* trainer, coach. (**-atrice** *f.*)

allenare² [A1c] *rfl.* to weaken, to become feeble; to lessen, to be diminished.

allen-ire [D2] *tr.* to weaken, to soften; to alleviate; *rfl.* to grow weak, to lose strength. (**-imento** *m.*) **-ito** *part. adj.* weak, faint; weakened; enfeebled.

allent-are [A1] *tr.* to relax, to slacken; to release; to loosen; to let go, to let slip; (naut.) to ease off; — il passo, to go more slowly; — una vite, to loosen a screw; — la stretta, to relax one's hold; (fig.) — la corda, to be less severe; — lo sdegno, to calm one's anger; — i cordoni della borsa, to be less tight-fisted; (mus.) — il tempo, to slacken the tempo; *rfl., intr.* (*aux.* avere) to slacken; to loosen; to work loose; to slow down; to relax; (of a slope) to become less steep; to loosen one's clothing; to rupture oneself. **-agione** *f.* See **allentatura**. **-amento** *m.* loosening; slackening; relaxation; decrease in speed; slack (of a rope). (**-ata** *f.*) **-ato** *part. adj.* slow; relaxed; slack; loosened up, softened. **-atura** *f.* (med.) hernia, rupture.

aller·g-ico *adj.* allergic. **-i·a** *f.* allergy.

allerione *m.* See **alerione**.

allerta *f.* warning (of danger); alert (air-raid).

allessare [A1c]. See **lessare**.

allesso *adv.* boiled; *n.m.* boiled meat; chi la vuole — e chi arrosto, it's all according to taste.

allest-ire [D2] *tr.* to prepare, to make ready; to equip, to rig out; (theatr.) — uno spettacolo, to stage a production, to put on a show; (naut.) — una nave, to fit out a ship; †— il passo, to hurry; *rfl.* to get ready; to prepare oneself; to get fitted out. **-imento** *m.* preparation; (theatr.) -imento scenico, production, scenery, costumes; (cinem.) art direction; (naut.) fitting out; (comm.) premio di -imento, dispatch money. **-ito** *part. adj.* prepared, ready; (naut.) fitted out. (**-itore** *m.* **-itura** *f.*)

alletamare [A1]. See **letamare**.

allettaiuo·lo *m.* decoy (bird).

allett-are¹ [A1] *tr.* to allure; to entice; to decoy; to attract; to charm, to flatter; to delight; †*rfl.* to be harboured, to be fostered. **-amento** *m.*, **-ativa** *f.* allurement; charm; attraction. **-ante, -ativo** *adj.* alluring; attractive; charming; seductive. **-ato** *part. adj.* allured; enticed; flattered. (**-atrice** *f.* **-azione** *f.*)

allett-are² [A1] *tr.* (of wind) to lay (crops) on the ground, to flatten; *rfl.* to take to one's bed; (of corn, etc.) to be flattened to the ground. (**-amento** *m.*) **-ato** *part. adj.* bedridden; confined to bed; (of crops) blown down, beaten down. **-atura** *f.* beating down, flattening.

allev-are [A1] *tr.* to breed; to rear; to bring up, to raise; — api, to keep bees; — polli, to keep hens; to give suck to, to feed. **-amento** *m.* breeding; rearing; bringing up, up-bringing; lactation; avere un -amento di, to breed, to go in for breeding, to be a breeder of; -amento di cavalli, stud farm; (sport) corsa di -amenti, race of one-year olds. **-ata** *f.* litter; fare un'-ata, to raise a litter. **-ativo** *adj.* valore -ativo, breeding value. **-ato** *part. adj.* bred; raised; brought up. **-atore** *m.* breeder; raiser. (**-atrice** *f.* **-atura** *f.*)

allevi-are [A4] *tr.* (*prep.* di) to alleviate; to lighten; to ease; to relieve, to allay, to mitigate; to soothe; *rfl.* to be relieved (of); †to give birth (to). **-amento** *m.* alleviation, mitigation; lightening, easing; relief, comfort. (**-ato** *part. adj.* **-atore** *m.* **-atrice** *f.* **-azione** *f.*)

allevimi *m.pl.* offspring, progeny (of sheep, goats).

allia·ria *f.* (bot.) garlic mustard, jack-by-the-hedge, *Alliaria petiolata*.

allibare [A1] (naut.). see **alleggiare**.

allibertare [A1] *rfl.* (Pirandello) to free oneself.

allib-ire [D2] *intr.* (*aux.* essere) to turn pale; to be dismayed; to be astounded; to be terrified. **-imento** *m.* confusion, consternation. **-ito** *part. adj.* pale; perturbed; confused; astounded; terrified.

allibr-are [A1] *tr.* to register, to enter, to book; †to tax. **-amento** *m.* registration, booking; certificato di -amento, statement that an entry has been made (e.g. in a banking or P.O. account). (**-ato** *part. adj.*) **-atore** *m.* (sport) bookmaker.

allicci-are¹ [A3] *tr.* (text.) to arrange (the warp-lines); to wind (the warp-lines) on the weaving staff; (techn.) — una sega, to set the teeth of a saw. **-amento** *m.* set (of the teeth of a saw). (**-ato** *part. adj.* **-atore** *m.* **-atura** *f.*)

allicciare² [A3] *intr.* (dial. Lucca) to run very fast, to run off.

†alli·cere *tr. def.* (3rd pers. sing. pres. indic. only recorded) to entice.

†alli·dere *tr.* to strike.

alliet-are [A1] *tr.* to cheer, to enliven; to gladden; to divert; to cheer up; *rfl.* to rejoice; to make merry; to become cheerful. **-ato** *part. adj.* cheered, enlivened; diverted; joyful, happy; rejoiced.

alliev-o *m.* pupil; schoolboy; student; apprentice; nursling; calf; foal; — ufficiale, officer cadet; (sport) corsa per -i, race reserved for apprentice jockeys. **-a** *f.* schoolgirl, pupil; student.

alligatore *m.* (zool.) alligator.

alligazione *f.* (math.) alligation, the Rule of Mixtures.

allign-are [A5] *intr.* (*aux.* essere, avere) to take root; to prosper, to flourish, to thrive; to grow (also fig.). (**-amento** *m.* **-azione** *f.*)

allile *m.* (chem.) allyl.

allind-are [A1] *tr.* to make tidy; to dress up; to adorn; to embellish; *rfl.* to tidy oneself; to adorn oneself. (**-ato** *part. adj.* **-atore** *m.* **-atura** *f.*)

alline-are [A6s] *tr.* to set in line, to line up; to range; to align; to draw up; *abs.* (typ.) — orizzontalmente, to straighten a line, to straighten lines; — verticalmente, to range; *rfl.* to form a line; (mil.) to dress. **-amento** *m.* ranging; alignment; direction, line; -amento difettoso, misalignment; (naut.; mil.) transit; (survey.) tracciare un -amento, to set out a straight line; (radio) -amento (di circuiti), gauging; -amento in fila, broadside array; -amento in linea, colinear array; (econ.) -amento monetario, monetary revaluation. **-ato** *part. adj.* in line; drawn up. (**-azione** *f.*)

alli·neo *m.* (sport) extension of arm (in fencing).

†allisione *f.* collision.

†alliso *part.* of **allidere**, q.v.

†allistare *tr.* to stripe, to streak; to adorn with bands.

†allitare *intr.* to land, to come to shore.

allit(t)era-zione *f.* alliteration; pun; tongue-twister; play on words. **-tivo** *adj.* alliterative.

allivell-are [A1] *tr.* (leg.) to rent land on a long or perpetual lease. **-azione** *f.* (leg.) long or perpetual lease of land.

allivid-ire [D2] *intr.* (*aux.* essere) to become livid; to turn pale. **-imento** *m.* turning livid; sudden pallor.

allo·bro-go (*pl.* **-ghi**) *adj., n.* Allobroge; rustic; (poet.) Savoyard, Piedmontese.

allocazione *f.* (sport) prize-money; stake.

alloc-co *m.* (*pl.* **-chi**) (orn.) owl, esp. the tawny owl, *Strix aluco*; (colloq.) fool, dolt, dupe, simpleton; fare l'—, to stand there like a fool. **-ag·gine** *f.* **-cherello** *m.* (orn.) owl. **-cheri·a** *f.* stupidity, tomfoolery. **-chire** [D2] *intr.* to play the fool.

allo-cro·ico *adj.* allochroic. **-cromasi·a** *f.* (med.) allochromasia. **-croma·tico** *adj.* allochromatic.

allocu·tore *m.* speaker; orator. **-zione** *f.* address, oration; solemn speech; exhortation; (eccl.) (papal) allocution.

†alloda *f.* See **allodola**.

allo·di-o *m.* (leg.) allodium. **-ale** *adj.* allodial. **-alità** *f.* allodial tenure.

allo·dola *f.* (orn.) lark; specchietto per le allodole, mirror for catching larks, (fig.) snare for the unwary or naïve.

allog-are [A2] *tr.* to place; to find a place for; to find employment for; to allocate; to assign; la biografia della regina fu -ata ad uno storico, a historian was commissioned to write the Queen's life; — fatiche, to expend effort; — una figlia, to marry off a daughter; — denari, to invest, to lay out money; (Tusc.) — una casa, to let a house; *rfl.* to find employment, to take a job; (colloq.) to get married. (**-amento** *m.* **-ato** *part. adj.*) **-atore** *m.* lessor, contractor. (**-atrice** *f.*) **-azione** *f.* lease; adjudication of contract work.

allo·geno *n.m.* alien-born citizen of a State, member of a population incorporated into a State but retaining different language and traditions (also *adj.*).

alloggi-are [A3] *tr.* to give lodging to; to house; to quarter; to billet; to accommodate, to put up; *intr.* (*aux.* avere) to lodge; (fig.)

alloggi-are (*cont.*)
to dwell; chi tardi arriva, male -a, first come first served. **-aménto** *m.* lodging; (mil.) camp; quarters; billet; (eng.) housing; slot. (**-ato** *part. adj.*) **-atóre** *m.* landlord; lodging-house-keeper. **-atrice** *f.* landlady.

allog·gio *m.* board, lodging; lodgings; prendere un —, to take lodgings; prendere — in, to put up at; vitto e —, board residence; — militare, billet; indennità di —, subsistence allowance.

allogliato *adj.* mixed with tares; †dazed, stupefied.

alloglott-o *adj.* speaking a different language; *n.m.* member of a linguistic minority. (**-a** *f.*)

allombato *adj.* (of an animal) strong in the loins.

allomerismo *m.* (chem., miner.) allomerism.

allo·nimo *adj.* (neol.) published under a pseudonym.

allontan-are [A I] *tr.* to remove; to separate; to withdraw; to send away; to dismiss; to dispel; to put off, to defer; to alienate; to estrange; — i sospetti, to avert suspicion; — l'influence against; *rfl.* (*prep.* da) to go away; to leave; to draw away; la nave si -a dal lido, the ship is pulling out from the shore; to lose touch, to become aloof; to become estranged; -arsi dal male, to renounce evil; to deviate, to swerve; -arsi dall'argomento, to wander from the subject; -arsi dalle intenzioni dell'amico, to differ from a friend in one's intentions. **-aménto** *m.* removal; separation; setting wider apart; distance, remoteness; dismissal; renouncing; alienation; estrangement. (**-ato** *part. adj.*)

allo·pati·a *f.* (med.) allopathy. **-pa·tico** *adj.* allopathic. (**-paticaménte** *adv.*)

alloppi-are [A 4] *tr.* to drug with opium; †to calm, to quieten; *rfl.* †to fall into a heavy sleep. (**-aménto** *m.* **-ato** *part. adj.*) **†-o** *m.* opium.

allóra *adv.* then, at that moment; at this; in that case; — —, at that very moment, just a moment before; per —, for the time being; fino ad —, up to then; d'— in poi, from then on; —?, well?; what then?; d'—, a moment ago, newly, freshly; fino da —, since then; — poi!..., if that's the case!....

†alloramai *adv.* See allora.

allorchè *conj.* when, at the time when, whilst; whenever.

allóro *m.* (bot.) bay laurel, *Laurus nobilis*; avocado pear, *Persea gratissima*; (fig.) laurel crown; victory, glory.

allorquando *conj.* when.

allo·trio *adj.* (Crocean philos.) l'—, the alien, extraneous, element (in poetry).

allotriofagi·a *f.* (med.) appetite for strange foods.

al-lotropi·a *f.* (chem.) allotropy. **-lotro·pico** *adj.* allotropic. **-lo·tropo** *m.* allotrope.

†allotta *adv.* See allora.

allott-are[1] [A I] *tr.* to put up to lottery. (**-ato** *part. adj.*)

allottare[2] (dial. S. Italy). See lottare.

allucchettare [A I c] *tr.* to padlock.

allucciato *adj.* bocca allucciata, mouth shaped like the mouth of a pike.

allucciol-ante, **-ato** *adj.* glittering, shimmering; spangled; moiré.

al·luce *m.* (anat.) great toe.

alluciare [A 3] *tr.* (Tusc. colloq.) to eye, to fix intently.

allucidare [A I s]. See lucidare.

allucignol-are [A I s] *tr.* (Tusc. colloq.) to crush, to crumple. (**-ato** *part. adj.*)

allucin-are [A I s] *tr.* to hallucinate; to dazzle; to deceive; to bewitch; to bewilder; *rfl.* to be dazzled; to be deceived. **-ato** *part. adj.* hallucinated; dazzled; aria -ata, haunted look; *n.m.* one suffering from hallucinations; madman. **-ata** *f.* madwoman. (**-atóre** *m.* **-atrice** *f.*) **-azióne** *f.* hallucination; bewilderment.

alluda *f.* alum leather.

allu·dere [C 3] *intr.* (*aux.* avere; *prep.* a) to allude (to); to refer (to); to hint (at).

allumac-are [A 2] *tr.* to mark with a slimy trail (as a snail). **-ato** *part. adj.* (of clothing) shiny with wear. **-atura** *f.* mark of a snail; shiny mark on clothing; (fig.) affectation in style.

†allumare[1] *tr.* to illumine; to eye, to set eyes on.

allum-are[2] *tr.* to alum, to treat with alum; (tanning) to taw; (dyeing) to mordant (with alum). **-ato** *part. adj.* treated with alum; (leather) alum-tawed. **-atura** *f.* (dye) mordanting with alum; (tanning) alum tawing.

allum-e *m.* alum. **-iera** *f.* alum mine.

allumina *f.* (chem.) alumina.

allumin-are[1] [A I s] *tr.* (poet.) to illuminate, to light up; †to illuminate (manuscripts); †to restore sight to; †to lend lustre to, to glorify. **-ato** *part. adj.* (poet.) lit up; †illuminated (of MSS.); †glorified; †sighted, seeing.

allum-inare[2] [A I s] *tr.* See allumare[2]. **-inato** *m.* (chem.) aluminate. **-(in)ite** *f.* (miner.) alumite. **-inóso** *adj.* aluminous.

allumi·ni·o *m.* aluminium. **-eri·a** *f.* aluminium-works.

allun-are [A I] *tr.* to shape like a half moon; (naut.) to camber. **-aménto** *m.* (naut.) camber (of deck); bellying (of a sail). **-ato** *part. adj.* curved like a half moon; (naut.) cambered. (**-atura** *f.* **-azióne** *f.*)

allunga *f.* (chem., eng.) adapter.

allungalapis *m. indecl.* pencil-holder.

allung-are [A 2] *tr.* to lengthen; — un vestito, to let down the hem of a dress; to elongate; to extend, to stretch; to hand: allungami quel libro, hand me that book; to eke out; to prolong; to defer, to postpone; to dilute, to thin, to water; to spin out: — il discorso, to be long-winded; — il passo, to step out, to quicken one's pace; — il muso, to pout, to pull a long face, to grow thin in the face; — il collo, to be obliged to wait, to kick one's heels, (slang) to be hanged, to hang, to 'swing'; — il collo a un pollo, to wring a chicken's neck; (colloq.) — un colpo, un ceffone, una pedata, to let fly a blow, a slap, a kick; — le braccia, to hold out one's arms; — la mano, to hold out one's hand, to stretch forth one's hand; to beg; — le mani, to be light-fingered, to steal; — gli orecchi, to prick up one's ears; (slang) — i piedi, to kick the bucket, to be pushing up the daisies; *rfl.* to grow longer, to lengthen; to stretch oneself; to grow tall; to expatiate; to extend; le giornate si -ano, the days are drawing out; s'-ò a parlare di cento cose, he talked on and on about this and that; †to remove oneself. **-a·bile** *adj.* extensible; capable of being lengthened. **-aménto** *m.* lengthening; elongation; prolonging; deferment; interval; distance; (text.) draught. (**-ativo** *adj.*) **-ato** *part. adj.* lengthened; un viso -ato, a long face; prolonged; deferred; diluted, let down, watered (down), thin, weak. (**-atóre** *m.* **-atrice** *f.*) **-atura** *f.* lengthening, elongation; piece added.

allungo *m.* (sport) pass (in football, basket-ball); spurt (athletics); extended lunge (fencing).

allunite *m.* See allumite, under alluminare[2].

allup-are [A I] *intr.* (*aux.* essere) to become wolf-like; to be as hungry as a wolf; — dalla fame, to be ravenous; *rfl.* to become wolf-like. **-ato** *part. adj.* famished; bitten by a wolf. **-atura** *f.* (tanning) crack in skins hung out to dry.

allus·ióne *f.* allusion, reference; hint; fare — a, to have reference to; to allude to; to hint at. **-ivo** *adj.* allusive. (**-ivaménte** *adv.*)

alluso *part.* of alludere, q.v.

alluvi-ale *adj.* (geol.) alluvial. **-ano** *adj.* see alluviale.

alluvión-e *f.* alluvion; alluvium; flood; (leg.) accessione per —, accretion by alluvion. **-ale** *adj.* relating to a flood. **-ato** *adj.* inundated, flooded; zona -ata, flood-area; *n.m.pl.* refugees from flood area.

alma *f.* (poet.) soul; spirit; (dial.) figlio d'—, adopted son.

Almagesto *pr.n.m.* Almagest, the treatise on geometry and astronomy compiled by Ptolemy.

almanac-co *m.* (*pl.* **-chi**) almanack; calendar; (fig., of a person) an original, an eccentric. **-care** [A 2] *intr.* (*aux.* avere) to build castles in the air; to daydream; to muse, to ponder; to puzzle one's head. **-caménto** *m.*, **-chìo** *m.* daydreaming, idle fancy. **-chista** *m.* writer of almanacks. **-cóne** *m.* idle dreamer. (**-cóna** *f.*)

†almanco *adv.* See almeno.

†almansore *m.* Saracen chief; †— del centro, Satan.

alme·a *f.* oriental dancing-girl, singing-girl.

almeno *adv.* at least; at the least; as much as.

†almir-a·glio, †**-ante** *m.* See ammiraglio.

almo[1] *adj.* (poet.) life-giving; vivifying; benign, kindly; dear, beloved; divine, sublime; noble, excellent; fertile.

†almo[2] *m.* soul.

almu·zia *f.* (eccl.) almuce (fur-lined tippet and hood).

†alna *f.* ell.

aln-o *m.* (bot.) alder tree, *Alnus*; — nero, alder buckthorn, *Frangula alnus*. **-éto** *m.* alder-grove.

Alò *pr.n.m.* Sant'Alò, Saint Eloi; (proverb. Tusc.) fare come Sant'Alò che lasciò il mondo come lo trovò; fare come Sant'Alò che prima morì e poi s'ammalò.

†aloda *f.* See allodola.

a·loe, **aloè** *m.* (bot.) various species of aloe; wood of **agalloco**, q.v.

alo·gen-o *m.* (chem.) halogen; *adj.* halogenous. **-azione** *f.* halogenation. **-uro** *m.* halide.

alo·idi *m.pl.* (chem.) haloids.

alone[1] *m.* halo; aura, effulgence.

alone[2] *m.* (mil.) lunette, or detached bastion in fortifications; side of cradle of a gun-carriage (from **ala**, q.v.).

alopeci·a *f.* (med.) alopecia, baldness.

alopecuro *m.* foxtail grass, *Alopecurus.*

alopia *f.* (ichth.) *Acanthias vulgaris*; spiny or piked dogfish, *Alopias vulpes*, thresher or fox shark.

†alore *m.* odour.

alosa *f.* (ichth.) shad.

al·pa(c)ca *m.* (zool.) alpaca, *Auchenia pacos*; wool of alpaca.

alpacca *f.* (metall.) white copper, Argentam, German silver, pack thong.

alpaga *f.* (text.) extract wool.

alp-e *f.* high mountain, alp; pasture; le Alpi, the Alps. **-eggiare** [A 3 c] *tr.* to lead (flocks) to summer pasture in the mountains. **-eggio** *m.* summer pasture in the mountains. **-estre** *adj.* mountainous; Alpine; wild; giardino -estre, rock garden. **-icare** [A 2 s] see **-eggiare**. (**-icazione** *f.*) **-igiano** *m.* inhabitant of alpine regions, or of the Alps; mountaineer. **-inismo** *m.* mountaineering. **-ino** *adj.* alpine; *n.m.* (mil.) member of the Alpine troops; *pl.* Alpine troops. **-ista** *m.*, *f.* mountaineer, mountain-climber. (**-i·stico** *adj.*)

alpiere *m.* Italian soldier of the Alpine troops who has had special training.

alpino *adj.*, *n.m.* See under **alpe**.

alquanto *adv.* somewhat, rather; considerably; *adj.* much, a good deal (of); ha mangiato — pane, he has eaten a good deal of bread; *prn.* (*foll. by* di, ne) presi — di carne, I took a fair amount of meat; *pl.* a good many, several.

Alsa·zi-a *pr.n.f.* (geog.) Alsace. **-ano** *adj.*, *n.m.* Alsatian. (**-ana** *f.*)

alsina *f.* chickweed, *Stellaria media*, and other similar plants.

alt! *excl.* halt!; *n.m. indecl.* halt, stop.

altalen-a *f.* seesaw; swing; (fig.) alternation, ups and downs; indecision; fare l' —; to swing to and fro, to swing up and down; (fig.) to alternate. **-are** [A 1 c] *intr.* (*aux.* avere), *rfl.* to swing; (fig.) to alternate. (**-io** *m.*) **†-o** *m.* (mil.) catapult; spring-board.

altamente *adv.* See under **alto**.

altana *f.* (archit.) broad terrace, loggia at the top of a house or tower (e.g. in Venice).

altano *n.m.* southerly wind.

†altanto *adj.* See **altrettanto**, under **altresì**.

altar-e *m.* (rel. and fig.) altar; (fig.) religion; — maggiore, high altar; — basso (laterale) side altar; l'Altare della Patria, altar in front of the monument to Victor Emmanuel II in Rome; condurre all'—, to lead to the altar, to marry; porre sugli -i, to raise to the altars, to canonize; (fig.) to raise to great honours; levar una cosa di sull'—, to commit sacrilege; scoprire un — per coprirne un altro, to rob Peter to pay Paul; scoprir gli -i (*usu.* -ini), to give away secrets, to reveal the skeleton in the cupboard; fare un contr'— (a), to compete (with), to set up a rival concern; (eng.) bridge (of a boiler or furnace). **-ino** *m.* little shrine (in private house); child's altar. **-ista** *m.* priest-in-charge of altar.

altaveła *f.* (ichth.) *Pteroplatea altavela*, butterfly ray.

altazimut *m.* (astron.) altazimuth.

altea *f.* (bot.) marsh mallow, *Althaea officinalis* and other malvaceous plants.

alter-are *tr.* [A 1 s] to alter, to change; to affect; to vary; to impair; to forge, to counterfeit; to adulterate; — i fatti, to misrepresent the facts; to alter matters; — la verità, to distort the truth; — un testo, to falsify a text; — il viso, to show anger; — lo stomaco, to turn the stomach; (mus.) to alter the pitch of (a note) by means of an accidental; *rfl.* to be altered, to alter; to vary; to be impaired; to get spoiled; to become angry; to become perturbed; to get slightly drunk. (**-a·bile** *adj.* **-abilità** *f.* **-amento** *m.* **-ativo** *adj.*) **-ato** *part. adj.* altered; impaired, spoiled, deteriorated; falsified, forged; perturbed, angered; -ato dal vino, intoxicated; vino -ato, adulterated wine; polso -ato, rapid pulse; (mus.) altered in pitch by means of an accidental. (**-atore** *m.* **-atrice** *f.*) **-azione** *f.* alteration; change; deterioration; falsification; debasement; discomposure; (mus.) alteration in pitch by means of an accidental.

alterc-are [A 2] *intr.* (*aux.* avere) to quarrel; to dispute; to wrangle, to bicker; to argue. (**-ativo** *adj.* **-atore** *m.* **-atorio** *adj.* **-atrice** *f.*) **-azione** *f.* altercation; quarrel, dispute; wrangle.

alter-co *m.* (*pl.* **-chi**) quarrel, row; avere un —, to have a row.

alterezza, alteri·gia *f.* See under **altero**.

altern-are *tr.*, *rfl.* [A 1] to alternate. **-amente** *adv.* alternately. (**-amento** *m.*) **-ante** *part. adj.* alternating; (electr.) corrente -ante, alternating current. (**-anza** *f.*) **-ativa** *f.* alternative; alternation; (eccl.) right of presentation alternating between two patrons. **-ativo** *adj.* alternative; **†***n.m.* (mus.) a dance movement alternating with a minuet, later called a trio. (**-ativamente** *adv.*) **-ato** *part. adj.* alternated; arranged alternately; (electr.) alternating multiphase. (**-atamente** *adv.*) **-atore** *m.* (electr.) alternator, generator. **-azione** *f.* alternation; rotation; permutation.

alterno *adj.* alternate; alternating; (geom.) alternate; (bot.) alternate (arrangement of leaves on stem).

alter-o *adj.* proud; haughty, arrogant; stately; lofty. **-amente** *adv.* proudly; arrogantly; haughtily; loftily. **-ezza** *f.* pride; arrogance. **-i·gia** *f.* haughtiness, arrogance, insolence.

altetto *adj.* See under **alto**.

altezz-a *f.* height; hill; eminence, grandeur; loftiness; Altezza, Highness; (geom.) altitude; (of material) breadth, width; thickness; loudness, volume; depth; (geog.) latitude; la nave era all'— di Genova, the ship lay off Genoa; (astron.) elevation; (hydr. eng.) — manometrica, pressure head; (typ.) — tipografica, type-height; (fig.) essere all'— di, to be equal to, to be up to the standard of, to be on a level with. **-oso** *adj.* proud, haughty, overbearing. (**-osamente** *adv.*)

al·tica *f.* (ent.) *Haltica* spp., flea-beetle.

altic·cio *adj.* See under **alto**.

altiero *adj.* See **altero**.

alt-imetri·a *f.* altimetry. **-ime·trico** *adj.* altimetric. **-i·metro** *m.* altimeter.

†altino *adj.* gentle breeze, zephyr; wind from the east.

altipiano *m.* (geog.) upland plain.

altisonante *adj.* high-sounding; loud-sounding; pompous.

†altisono *adj.* See **altisonante**.

altis·simo *adj.* superl. of **alto**, q.v.; *n.m.* l'Altissimo, the Almighty.

altista *m.*, *f.* (mus.) a male or female alto singer.

altitonante *adj.* loud-thundering; *n.m.* Jupiter, the Thunderer.

altitu·dine *f.* altitude; height.

altivolante *adj.* (poet.) high-flying.

alt-o[1] *adj.* high; lofty, elevated; tall; eminent; sublime; arduous, difficult; loud; deep; early, medieval: -a lirica d'amore, early love poetry; upper: Camera Alta, Upper House, House of Lords; (typ.) -a casa, upper case; (geog.) northern: l'Alt'Italia, northern Italy; — tradimento, high treason; (aeron.) -a quota, high altitude; (fig.) scrittore di -a quota, writer of the first rank; (mus.) high; loud; (equestr.) -a scuola, haute école; -a novità, latest fashion; ad -a voce, out loud; a notte -a, in the dead of night; a giorno —, when the sun is high in the sky; quest'anno la pasqua è -a, Easter is late this year; in — mare, on the high seas, in the open sea; (fig.) no nearer a solution, not out of the wood; -a marea, high tide; -e maree, spring tides; (naut.) una nave d'— bordo, a large ship; officiale d'— bordo, naval officer of high rank; *adv.* loudly; aloud; high up; parlare —, to speak in a loud voice; in —, on high, (fig.) in high place; dall'—, from above; far cascar una cosa dall'—, to give oneself importance about granting a thing; prendere una cosa dall'—, to begin a thing from the very beginning; tenersi —, to ask a stiff price; star —, to be haughty; — —, round about, as near as may be; ditemi così, — —, quanto può valere questo libro, tell me roughly how much you think this book is worth; guardare d'— in basso, to look down one's nose at; fare — e basso, to assume authority; levarsi in —, to stand on one's dignity; farsi da —, to begin all over again; (sport) salto in —, high-jump; *n.m.* height; top; summit; heaven; open sea, deep sea; (mus.) alto voice; (*pl.*) alti e bassi, ups and downs. **-amente** *adv.* highly, greatly; deeply, profoundly; remarkably; nobly. **-etto, -ic·cio** *adj.* tipsy, half-seas over, merry.

alto[2]**!** *excl.* (mil.) halt!; *n.m.* halt; fare —, to halt.

altoatesino *adj.* of the Alto Adige; also *n.m.*

altochiomato (poet.) long-haired.

altocinto *adj.* high-waisted.

alto-clarinetto *m.* (mus.) alto clarinet; basset horn.

altocu·mulo *m.* (meteor.) high cumulus.

altofọrno *m.* (*pl.* **altifọrni**) (met.) blast furnace; sacca dell'—, bosh.

altolà! *excl.* (mil.) who goes there?; halt!

altolocato *adj.* high-ranking, highly placed.

altomare *m.* open sea; in —, on the open sea, out at sea.

altomugghiante *adj.* loud-bellowing.

altoparlante *m.* (*pl.* **altoparlanti**) loudspeaker.

†**altopaˑscio** *m.* plenty, abundance of food; †morire di fame in —, to be idle.

altopiano *m.* See **altipiano**.

†**altore**¹ *m.* author.

†**altore**² *adj.* protective, nurturing; *n.m.* nourisher, life-giver.

altorilievo *m.* (sculp.) alto-relievo, high-relief.

altosonante *adj.* See **altisonante**.

altospumante *adj.* (of waves) tossing, spray-flinging.

altostrato *m.* (meteor.) altostratus.

altovolante *adj.* See **altivolante**.

altr-esì *adv.* also, too, likewise, as well. **-ettale** *adj.* similar; another such; equal. **-ettanto** *adj.* as much, of equal quantity, amount; as much again, as much more; *n.m.* the same; *pl.* as many, so many; *adv.* equally, likewise; so much, as much; tanti auguri! grazie e — (a voi), all the best! thank you and the same to you.

altri *indef. prn. indecl.* another person, someone else; anyone, anyone else; non dirlo ad — che al tuo amico, don't tell anyone but your friend about it.

†**altrice** *adj., f.* of **altore**², q.v.

altrieri *adv.* (l') the day before yesterday.

altrimẹnti *adv.* otherwise; or else; differently.

altr-o *adj.* other, different; tutt'-a persona, somebody completely different; another; next; more; non dico —, I say no more; further; un giorno o l'—, some day or other; volete dell'— caffè? will you have some more coffee?; datemi degli -i biscotti, give me some more biscuits; qualcos'—, something else; qualcun'—, somebody else; nessun —, nobody else; no other; dovemmo rinunziare a qualunque -a investigazione, we were obliged to give up all further enquiry; quest'—, next; quest'-a settimana, next week; l'-a settimana, last week; l'— ieri, the day before yesterday; the other day; (Tusc.) ier l'—, the day before yesterday; -a volta, previously, once before; -e volte, at other times; *n.m. indecl.* another thing; anything else; something else; ben —, much more than that, something quite different from that; ci vuol —, much more than that is needed; other things; pane, carne, e —, bread, meat and other things besides; avete — da dirmi? have you anything else to tell me?; (iron.) non ci mancava —, that's the limit; — è dire, — è fare, easier said than done; *adv. phrases*: senz'—, immediately, without more ado; without fail; tutt'—, not at all; on the contrary, far from it, quite the opposite; —! (or) — che!, yes, indeed!, rather!; — che pollo, — che collo! some chicken, some neck!; non chè —, let alone, to say the least; se non —, at least; per —, moreover; however; più che —, particularly, especially; dell'—, still more; d'uno in un —, all of a sudden; *prn.* another person, someone else; diventò un —, he changed completely; l'un l'—, each other, one another; l'uno o l'—, either; nè l'uno nè l'—, neither; *pl.* -i, others, other people; va a raccontare ad -i!, tell that to the marines!; noi -i Inglesi, we English; tra l'—, among other things. **-ọnde** *adv.* elsewhere; d'—, from another place, from elsewhere; however; besides, on the other hand. **-ọve** *adv.* elsewhere; essere -ove, aver il pensiero -ove, to be wool-gathering.

altru-i *prn. indecl. nom., acc., dat., abl.* another person; others; *gen.* another's; of others; la roba —, other people's property; †*n.m.* other people's belongings; †the Almighty; †people, mankind. **-iṣmo** *m.* altruism. **-iṣta** *m.* altruist. **-iˑstico** *adj.* unselfish; altruistic. (**-iṣticamẹnte** *adv.*)

altura *f.* eminence, rise, high ground; (poet.) open sea.

alturiere *m.* pilot; (aeron.) long-distance pilot.

aluˑcita *f.* (ent.) *Sitotroga cerealella*, grain moth.

aludello *m.* vessel for subliming sulphur.

alula *f.* (aeron.) slat.

alunite *f.* (miner.) alum-stone, alunite.

alunn-o *m.* pupil; schoolboy; student; disciple; scholar; apprentice. (**-a** *f.*) **-ato** *m.* apprenticeship; period of apprenticeship.

†**alvano** *m.* alder.

alveare¹ *m.* beehive; — umano, thickly populated district, swarming tenement house; *adj.* shaped like a beehive.

alveare² *vb.* See under **alveo**.

alˑv-eo *m.* river-bed; canal, conduit. **-eare** [A6] *tr.* to canalize. **-eolite** *f.* (med.) alveolar inflammation. **-eˑolo** *m.* cell (of a honey-comb); pod; (anat.) alveolus; (bot.) seed vessel.

Alverˑnia *pr.n.f.* (geog.) Auvergne.

alˑv-o *m.* belly; — materno, womb; (fig.) centre, heart. **-ino** *adj.* alvine.

alza-bicchieri *m. indecl.* toast. **-bọtti** *m. indecl.* barrel-rest, throll. **-cristalli** *m. indecl.* window regulator. **-valˑvole** *m. indecl.* valve lifter.

alzaˑia *f.* (naut.) tow-line; cable; hawser; strada —, tow-path.

†**alzana** *f.* See **alzaia**.

alz-are [A1] *tr.* to raise; to lift; — di peso, to lift bodily; to elevate; to set up, to construct; to heighten; to heave; to hoist; (fig.) **to exalt**; (colloq.) to 'lift', to 'pinch'; — le spalle, to shrug one's shoulders; — il gomito, to drink too much; — le carte, to cut the cards; (fig.) — la testa, — la cresta, — le corna, to stand up for oneself, to rebel; to become arrogant, to get puffed up; — la bandiera, to hoist the flag; (naut.) — la gran gala, to dress ship; — la mano, to put up one's hand; (fig.) to forgive, to condone; — le mani a, to raise one's hand to, to strike; — al cielo, to laud to the skies; la pentola -a il bollore, the saucepan is on the boil; *abs.* to clear the table, to clear away; *rfl.* to rise; to get up; to get up in the morning; to raise oneself; (of a wind) to blow up, to get up; -arsi in piedi, to stand up. (**-aˑbile** *adj.* **-amẹnto** *m.*) **-ata** *f.* lifting up, raising; rise; rising; -ata di mani, show of hands; elevation; embankment; fruit-stand; mirror, set of drawers (fixed to dressing-table); riser (of a step); -ata di spalle, shrug; -ata di scudi, rebellion; -ata d'ingegno, happy thought, brain wave; (archit.; eng.) elevation, front view. **-ato** *part. adj.* raised; (of skirts) shortened; up, out of bed; set up; heightened; hoist; exalted; (herald.) enhanced, in chief. (**-atore** *m.* **-atura** *f.*)

alzaˑvola *f.* (orn.) teal, *Anas crecca*.

alzo *m.* sight (of a gun); (artil.) dare l'—, to range; (bootm.) piece of leather fixed to a last to adjust the shape.

†**ama** *f.* nurse, governess.

amaˑbil-e *adj.* lovable; amiable; charming, gracious; (of wine) sweet. **-ità** *f.* amiability; sweetness; courtesy. **-mẹnte** *adv.* graciously.

amaca, aˑmaca *f.* hammock.

amadina *f.* (orn.) cut-throat finch, *Amadina fasciata*.

†**amadore** *m.* See **amatore**, under **amare**.

amadotta *f.* (bot.) October pear.

amadriˑade *f.* wood-nymph, hamadryad; (zool.) hamadryad, Arabian baboon, *Cynocephalus hamadryas*; king cobra, *Naja bungarus*.

†**amagˑgio** *m.* love, loving.

amaidi *m.pl.* (herald.) three bars couped.

amalˑgam-a *m.* amalgam. **-are** [A1s] *tr.* to amalgamate. **-ato** *part. adj.* amalgamated. (**-atore** *m.*) **-azione** *f.* amalgamation.

amandina *f.* (chem.) amandin.

†**amanˑdol-a** *f.* See **mandorlo**. **-ata** *f.* emulsion made from almonds.

amanit-e *f.* (bot.) Amanita, genus of fungi. **-ina** *f.* (chem.) amanitine.

amante¹ *m., f.* See under **amare**.

amant-e² *m.* (naut.) halyard. **-igliare** [A4] *tr.* to rig (ties). **-iˑglio** *m.* (naut.) tie.

amanuense *m.* amanuensis, copyist; †librarian (title of).

†**amanza** *f.* love; the loved one; the beloved object; desire.

Am-ara *pr.n.f.* (geog.) Amhara; *m. indecl.* Ethiopian. **-aˑrico** *adj.* of Amhara, Ethiopian.

amaracˑciola *f.* (bot.) broom, *Sarothamnus scoparius*.

amaˑrac-o *m.* (bot.) marjoram, *Origanum Majorana*. **-ino** *adj., n.m.* (unguent) containing marjoram.

amarant-o *m.* (bot.) amaranth, name of various members of the family Amarantaceae, and also of poke-weed, *Phytolacca americana*; (of colour) magenta; (chem.) amaranth; (sport) member of Leghorn football team. **-ino** *adj.* amaranthine.

amarasca *f.* (bot.) fruit of **amarasco** *m.*, sour or egriot cherry, from which maraschino is made.

am-are [A1] *tr.* to love; to be in love with; to be fond of; to like; to delight in, to take pleasure in; to want; (of plants) to require: è una pianta che -a l'ombra, it is a plant which needs shade; — meglio, to prefer; *abs.* to love; to be in love; *recipr. rfl.* to love each other; to love one another; †*n.m.* love. **-aˑbile** *adj.* and derivs. See separate entry. **-ante** *part. adj.* loving; fond; è molto -ante della musica, he's very fond of music; *n.m.* lover; †suitor; †swain; †devotee; *f.* mistress. **-ato** *part. adj.* loved, beloved;

am·are (*cont.*)
dear; liked; preferred; *n.m.* loved one. **-ata** *f.* loved one, sweetheart; lady-love, mistress. **-atore** *m.* amateur, connoisseur; admirer; lover. (†**-atrice** *f.*) **-ato·rio** *adj.* amatory; filtro -atorio, love philtre.

amareggiare [A 3 c]. See under **amaro**.

amareg·giola, amarella *f.* (bot.) common feverfew, *Chrysanthemum parthenium*; mugwort, *Artemisia vulgaris*.

amarezza *f.* See under **amaro**.

amarilli *f.* (bot.) *Amaryllis*; *pr.n.f.* (myth.) Amaryllis.

amar-o¹ *adj.* bitter; biting, harsh, sharp; painful, grievous, sad; galling; aver la bocca -a, to have a bitter taste in the mouth; (fig.) to be bitterly disappointed; to be unjustly treated; mandar giù un boccone —, to swallow an insult; una vita -a, a hard life; una critica -a, biting criticism; (S. Italy) wretched, unfortunate, unhappy; *n.m.* bitters; aperitif; (fig.) rancour, hatred, resentment; aver dell'— contro, to feel bitter towards; tra quei due c'è dell'—, there is a lot of ill feeling between those two; *pl.* bitters. (**amente** *adv.*) **-eggiare** [A 3 c] *tr.* to make bitter; (fig.) to embitter; to chagrin, to sadden, to vex; to afflict, to torment; *rfl.* to grieve, to fret, to take things to heart. (**-eggiamento** *m.*) **-etto** *adj.* slightly bitter; *n.m.* almond cake. **-ezza** *f.* bitterness; sorrow; pain; sharpness, harshness; rancour. **-icante** *m.* (med.) bitter tonic. **-is·simo** *adj. superl.* of **amaro**; *n.m.* (poet.; joc.) l'Amarissimo, the Adriatic. **-itu·dine** *f.* bitterness; grief. **-ognolo** *adj.* somewhat bitter. **-ore** *m.* bitterness; (agric.) disease affecting milk or wine. **-ulento** *adj.* (poet. D'Annunzio) bitter. **-ume** *m.* bitterness.

amaro² *m.* (slang) pedlars' slang.

amarra *f.* (naut.) mooring cable. See also **ammarrare**.

ama·și-o *m.* paramour. **-a** *f.* mistress.

amata *f.* See under **amare**.

†**amatista** *m.* See **ametista**.

†**amatita¹** *f.* See **matita**.

†**amatit-a²** *f.*, **-o** *m.* (min.). See **ematite**.

amato¹ *part. adj.*, *n.m.* See under **amare**.

†**amato²** *adj.* hook-shaped, hooked.

amatolo *m.* (chem.) amatol.

amatore *m.* See under **amare**.

amato·rio *adj.*, *n.m.* See under **amare**.

amatriciana *adv. phr.* (cul.) see **matriciana**.

amaur-oși *f.* (med.) amaurosis. **-o·tico** *adj.* amaurotic.

amașo·nia *f.* (orn.) Amazon parrot.

amaz·z-one *f.* Amazon; horsewoman; montare ad —, to ride side-saddle; vestito d'—, lady's riding-habit; (orn.) Amazon parrot; (geog.) il Rio delle Amazzoni, the Amazon (river). **-o·nico**, **-o·nio** *adj.* Amazon-like. **-onite** *f.* (min.) Amazonstone.

amba *f.* name given to certain mountains in Ethiopia which are the shape of a truncated pyramid.

ambag-e *f.*, *usu. pl.* circumlocution; evasion, ambages, subterfuge; senz' -i, plainly, in a few words; *sing.* circuitous path. (**-ioso** *adj.*)

ambarvali *m.pl.* (Rom. hist.) Ambarvalia (agricultural lustration ceremony).

ambasceri·a *f.* See under **ambasciata**.

amba·sci-a *f.* distress, anguish; difficulty in breathing, breathlessness. †**-are** *intr.* to suffer anguish; *tr.* to distress. **-ato** *part. adj.* anguished, distressed. (†**-oso** *adj.*)

ambasc-iata¹ *f.* embassy; ambassador's residence, headquarters; (fig.) commission, message, errand, negotiation; fare un'—, to bring a message. †**-iare** *intr.* to act as ambassador. **-iatore** *m.* ambassador; woman-ambassador; messenger. **-iatrice** *f.* wife of an ambassador, ambassadress. (**-iato·rio** *adj.*) **-eri·a** *f.* representation, embassy.

ambasciata² *f.* (dial. Rom.) herd of cattle.

ambasso *m.* (in dice, tric-trac, etc.) double ace.

†**ambe** *prn.pl.f.* See **ambedue**.

ambedue *prn.pl.*, *indecl.* both.

ambessa *m.* (poet. Pascoli) lion.

†**ambi** *prn.pl.m.* See **ambedue**.

ambi-are [A 4], **-atura** *f.* See under **ambio**.

ambidestr-o *adj.* ambidextrous; (fig.) astute. (**-ișmo** *m.*)

†**ambidue** *prn.pl.* See **ambedue**.

ambient-e *m.* surroundings, environment; habitat; setting; background; sphere, circle, society; (fig.) atmosphere; enclosed space:

vivere troppo in -i chiusi, to live too much indoors; room: appartamento di cinque -i, five-roomed flat; circumference; surrounding atmosphere; *adj.* surrounding, ambient; temperatura —, room temperature. (**-ale** *adj.*) **-are** [A I] *rfl.* to accustom oneself to one's surroundings, to settle down, to find one's level. **-ista** *m.* (neol.) photographer or painter of background.

ambige·nere *adj.* (gramm.) of either gender.

ambi·geno *adj.* hermaphroditic.

ambi·gu-o *adj.* ambiguous, equivocal, doubtful; dubious; obscure; persona -a, person of doubtful reputation; pianta ancora -a, plant not yet classified. (**-amente** *adv.*) **-ità** *f.* ambiguity, ambiguousness; †uncertainty, indecision.

ambilaterale *adj.* two-sided.

am·bi-o *m.* amble; andare all'—, to amble; (fig.) pigliar l'—, to take oneself off; dare l'— a, to dismiss. **-are** [A 4] *intr.* (*aux.* avere) to amble. (**-ante** *part. adj.* **-atore** *m.*) **-atura** *f.* ambling.

ambiopi·a *f.* (med.) diplopy.

amb-ire [D 2] *tr.* to covet; to thirst, to hanker after; to long for; to aspire towards; *intr.* (*aux.* avere) to aspire, to have ambitions, to be ambitious. **-ito** *part. adj.* desired, coveted, longed for; valued, sought after; (comm.) vostri -iti ordini, your esteemed order.

am·bito *m.* ambit; orbit; circuit, precincts; compass, circumference; range; span; limit, limits; nell'— del possibile, within the limits of possibility; competence: questo rientra nel nostro —, this lies within our competence; queste cose devono rimanere nell'— nostro, these things must not be allowed to go any further; striving, intrigue; (mus.) compass.

ambito *part.* of **ambire**, q.v.

ambival-ente *adj.* (psychol.) ambivalent. **-enza** *f.* ambivalence.

ambiz-ione *f.* ambition; desire for success; pretension; eagerness. **-iosag·gine** *f.* pretentiousness, foolish ambition. **-ioso** *adj.* ambitious; pretentious, aspiring; covetous; desirous, eager; *n.m.* ambitious person; careerist. (**-iosamente** *adv.*)

ambliopi·a *f.* (med.) amblyopia.

ambo *m. indecl.* both; *n.m.* pair; (iron.) un bell'—, a nice pair (of rogues); double (at lotto).

am·bolo *m.* (colloq. Tusc.) prender l'—, to go off coolly; dare l'— a, to sack.

ambone *m.* (liturg.; archit.) ambo.

ambr-a *f.* amber; — grigia, ambergris; — nera, jet. **-ato** *adj.* amber-coloured; smelling of ambergris. **-are** [A I] *tr.* to perfume with ambergris. **-etta** *f.* (bot.) common avens, herb bennet, *Geum urbanum*; -etta de' campi, field scabious, *Knautia arvensis*; -etta gialla, sweet sultan, *Centaurea moschata*; musk-seed plant, *Hibiscus abelmoschus*; (tanning) Russia leather.

ambrogetta *f.* small cube of marble or other substance for mosaic work; ornamental tile; majolica plaque.

Ambro·gio *pr.n.m.* Ambrose.

ambro·și-a *f.* ambrosia; (bot.) name of various aromatic plants. **-o** *adj.* ambrosial.

ambroș-iano *adj.* Ambrosian (rite, hymn); Milanese; (mus.) inno —, the Te Deum; la Biblioteca -iana, the Ambrosian Library; *n.m.* Milanese (man); -iana *f.* Milanese (woman); l'Ambrosiana, the Ambrosian Library. **-ianità** *f.* (neol.) drive and initiative of the Milanese. **-ino** *m.* (numism.) ambrosin.

ambulacro *m.* (archit.) ambulatory.

ambul-are [A I s] *intr.* (*aux.* avere) to walk; to ambulate; to walk off. **-antato** *n.m.* (neol.) commercial travelling. **-ante** *adj.* ambulating; itinerant; wandering; peripatetic; fare una vita -ante, to lead a wandering life; merciaio -ante, pedlar; un cadavere -ante, a walking ghost; una biblioteca -ante, a walking encyclopaedia; sonatore -ante, strolling musician; cattedra -ante, University department of which the teachers travel from place to place; *m.n.* mail train. **-antista** *m.* employee on a mail-train. **-anza** *f.* ambulance; first-aid post, field-hospital. **-ato·rio** *adj.* ambulatory; itinerant; *n.m.* cloister, covered walk; clinic; health-centre; out-patients' department; surgery.

am·bulo *m.* See **ambolo**.

Amburgo *pr.n.f.* (geog.) Hamburg.

ameba *f.* (zool.) amoeba.

amebe·o *adj.* amoebaean (verse, singing).

†**a·meda** *f.* aunt.

amello *m.* (bot.) wild aster, starwort, *Aster amellus*; fleabane, *Erigeron acer*.

amen *excl.* amen; *n.m.indecl.* in un —, in a twinkling; e —, and that's that.

†**amendue** *prn.pl.* See **ambedue**.

amen·o *adj.* droll, amusing; un capo —, a funny chap; un libro —, an amusing book; entertaining, delightful; agreeable, pleasant; paesaggio —, smiling landscape. **-amente** *adv.* pleasantly, agreeably. **-ità** *f.* pleasantness, agreeableness; pleasantry; urbanity.

amenorre·a *f.* (med.) amenorrhoea.

†**amentare** *tr.* to diminish.

†**amente** *adj.* half-witted, stupid.

†**amenticare** *vb.* See **dimenticare**.

ament·o *m.* (bot.) catkin. **-a·ceo** *adj.* catkin-like. **-i·fero** *adj.* catkin-bearing.

Ame·ric·a *pr.n.f.* (geog.) America; l'— del Nord, North America; l'— del Sud, South America; (fig.) trovare l'—, to find an El Dorado. **-ano** *adj.* American; truffa all'-ana, confidence trick; confronto all'-ana, identity parade; *n.m.* American; Italian who has lived in America; drink composed of vermouth, bitters, lemon-peel and soda-water. **-ana** *f.* American woman; slow-burning stove; American cigarette; -ana a coppia, American relay cycle race. **-anamento** *m.* Americanization. **-anata** *f.* lavish party; gigantic spectacle; sensational advertising stunt. **-anismo** *m.* Americanism; expansionist policy of the U.S.A.; (theol.) term applied by Leo XIII to certain doctrinal novelties (in *Testem Benevolentiae*, 1899). **(-ista** *m., adj.*) **-izzare** [A I] to Americanize. **(-izzamento** *m.*) **-izzato** *part. adj.* Americanized.

amerindiano, amerin·dio (neol.) *m., adj.* American Indian.

ametist·a *f.* amethyst. **-ino** *adj.* amethyst-hued, violet.

ameto·dico *adj.* unmethodical.

ametri·a *f.* lack of symmetry.

amfi·bolo *adj.* See **anfibolo**.

amfizion·i *m. pl.*, **-i·a** *f.* See **anfizioni, -ia**.

a·mia *f.* (dial. Ven.) aunt.

amianto *m.* asbestos.

amica *f.* See under **amico**.

amica·bile *adj.* See under **amicare**.

amic·are [A 2] *tr.* to inspire friendly feelings in; to reconcile; *rfl.* (dat. of prn.) -arsi (uno), to gain the allegiance of (someone); to make friends with (someone); *recip. rfl.* to make friends with one another; to become reconciled. **-a·bile** *adj.* amicable; (math.) numeri -abili, amicable numbers, numbers which are mutually equal to the whole sum of each other's aliquot parts. **-ale** *adj.* amicable. **-amente** *adv.* in a friendly spirit.

amichevol·e *adj.* friendly, amicable; amiable, affable; courteous; all'—, in an informal manner; as between friends, by private contract. **-ezza** *f.* friendliness; friendly action. **-mente** *adv.* in a friendly manner; amiably; by peaceful negotiations, peaceably, without litigation.

amici·zia *f.* friendship; amity; friendliness; affection, liking; per —, out of friendship; stringere — con, to make friends with; — di cappello, nodding acquaintance; congruity, similarity; affinity, sympathy; alliance; (euphem.) amorous relationship; in —, in confidence; *pl.* friends; friendships.

ami·c·o *m.* friend; well-wisher; sweetheart; lover; enthusiast; — di saluto, — di cappello, acquaintance; — del cuore, bosom friend; — interessato, fair-weather friend; -i in alto, influential friends; (joc.) l'—, quell'—, 'the gentleman in question', the party under discussion; quell'—, the Devil; — politico, one who shares one's political views; farsi — di, to get into the good graces of; tenersi — uno, to keep friends with someone; colori -i, colours that go well together; pianta -a dell'acqua, plant that needs a lot of water; *adj.* friendly; pleasing; dear, beloved; favourable, propitious. **-a** *f.* girl-friend, woman-friend; mistress. **-hetto** *m.* boy-friend. **-one** *m.*, **-ona** *f.* (joc.) good old friend, intimate friend.

a·mid·o *m.* starch; dare l'— a, to starch. **-a·ceo, -oso** *adj.* starchy.

amig·dal·a *f.* (anat.) tonsil. **-ina** *f.* (chem.) amygdalin. **-ite** *f.* tonsillitis.

amigdalo·ide *adj.* almond-shaped.

amilasi *f. indecl.* (chem.) diastase; any diastatic enzyme.

amil·e *m.* (chem.) amyl. **-ico** *adj.* amyl. **-oli·tico** *adj.* amylolitic. **-opsina** *f.* (chem.) diastase.

amiss·i·bile *adj.* (theol.) amissible (of grace); (leg.) see **ammissibile**. **-ione** *f.* (leg.) see **ammissione**, under **ammissibile**.

amist·à *f.* (poet.) friendship; love. †**-anza** *f.* familiarity, intimacy.

†**a·mita** *f.* aunt.

amitto *m.* (liturg.) amice.

Aml-eto *pr.n.m.* Hamlet; Italo —, Charles Albert of Savoy (so called by Carducci in *Piemonte*). **-e·tico** *adj.* hesitant, uncertain; mysterious.

ammacc·are [A 2] *tr.* to bruise; to contuse; to dent; to pound, to crush, to grind. **(-a·bile** *adj.*) **-amento** *m.* bruising; (colloq.) dense throng, crush. **(-ato** *part. adj.*) **-atura** *f.* bruise; dent; (sculp.) hollow; sunk relief; (paint.) hollow (represented by shading); (mech.) buckling.

†**ammacchiare** *rfl.* to go into hiding, to take to the maquis.

ammaestr·are [A I] *tr.* to teach, to instruct; to train; to tame. **-a·bile** *adj.* teachable; docile, manageable. **-amento** *m.* admonishment; teaching; training; precept; *pl.* upbringing. **(-ante** *part. adj., n.m., f.* **-anza** *f.* **-ativo** *adj.*) **-ato** *part. adj.* instructed; trained; tame. **-atore** *m.*, **-atrice** *f.* instructor; trainer; tamer. **(-atura** *f.*) **-azione** *f.* instruction; training. **(-evole** *adj.*)

ammagli·are¹ [A 4] *tr.* to cord, to cord up: — una valigia, to cord a trunk; to join (wool, in knitting); (chem.) to line with gauze. **(-ata** *f.* **-ato** *part. adj.* **-atura** *f.*)

ammagliare² [A 4] *rfl.* (of the eye) to form a white spot on the cornea (from **maglia**, q.v.).

ammagliare³ [A 4] *tr.* to hit with a mallet (from **maglio**, q.v.).

†**ammai·are** *tr.* to decorate with flowers and leaves; *rfl.* to adorn oneself with flowers and leaves. †**-ato** *part. adj.* (of a plant) leafy; in full flower; (joc., of a person) bedecked.

ammainare [A I] *tr.* (naut.) to furl, to take in; to reef; to strike, to haul down (flag, colour).

ammal·are [A I] *intr.* (aux. essere), *rfl.* to become ill, to fall sick; -arsi di morbillo, to get the measles; *tr.* to infect, to make ill. **-ato** *part. adj.* ill, sick, unwell; *n.m.* patient. **(-ata** *f.*)

ammalazz·are [A I] *intr.* (aux. essere) to become indisposed. **-ato** *part. adj.* sickly, off colour, not well.

ammali·are [A 4] *tr.* to bewitch, to fascinate, to charm; to enthral, to enchant; to practise sorcery on, to cast an evil spell on. **-amento** *m.* enchantment; bewitching. **-ato** *part. adj.* enchanted; bewitched. **-atore** *m.* enchanter, sorcerer. **(-atrice** *f.*) **-atura** *f.*, **-azione** *f.* enchantment; sorcery.

ammalincon·ire [D 2] *tr.* to depress, to make gloomy; to sadden; *abs.* to be dreary, to be depressing; *intr.* (aux. essere), *rfl.* to become melancholy; to grieve, to distress oneself. **(-ito** *part. adj.*)

ammalizi·are [A 4] *tr.* to teach mischief to; to make sly, to make cunning; to sharpen (wits); to dupe; *rfl., intr.* (aux. essere) to become sly; to sharpen one's wits. **-ato** *part. adj.* sly, cunning; sharp. **(-atore** *m.* **-atrice** *f.*)

ammalizzire [D 2] and derivs. See **ammaliziare**.

ammaltare [A I] *tr.* (bldg.) to cover with mortar; to plaster, to cement.

ammammol·are [A I S] *rfl.* to drop off to sleep, to nod. **-ato** *part. adj.* (of eyes) heavy with sleep.

ammanco *m.* (comm.) deficit; — di peso, underweight; — di cassa, leakage; colmare un —, to make good a deficit.

ammandorlato *adj.* latticed; diamond-shaped; *n.m.* lattice-work; (bldg.) opus reticulatum.

ammandriare [A 4] *tr.* to herd, to collect in droves.

ammanett·are [A I C] *tr.* to handcuff; to manacle, to shackle, to fetter. **(-ato** *part. adj.* **-atore** *m.* **-atrice** *f.*)

ammanier·are [A I] *tr.* to render affected; to embellish; — lo stile, to elaborate one's style. **(-amento** *m.*) **-ato** *part. adj.* affected, mannered, artificial; embellished; elaborate; *n.m.* (art) mannerist. **(-atura** *f.*)

†**ammannaiare** *tr.* to decapitate.

ammann·are¹ [A I] (Tusc.) *tr.* to make into sheaves; to bind in sheaves; *abs.* to bind; (fig.) to tell a tall story, to 'lay it on'. **(-amento** *m.*) **-ato** *part. adj.* in sheaves.

ammannare² *tr.* to prepare, to equip.

ammann·ire [D 2] *tr.* to prepare; — il pranzo, to get dinner ready; (paint.) to prime, to give a priming coat to. **-ime** *m.* (joc.) preparation, build-up. **-imento** *m.* preparation; cooking, dressing. **(-ito** *part. adj.*) **-itura** *f.* preparation; cooking, dressing; priming; priming coat (on paintwork).

ammansare [A I] and derivs. See **ammansire**.

ammans·ire [D 2] *tr.* to tame; to domesticate; to calm, to placate, to appease, to assuage; *rfl.* to grow calm, to be placated, to become subdued; to recover one's temper; to grow tame, to become docile; to become sociable; to abate, to subside. **(-imento** *m.*) **-ito** *part. adj.* tamed; tame, domesticated; appeased.

ammant-are [A I] *tr.* to cloak, to mantle; to cover, to wrap, to clothe; to disguise, to conceal; *rfl.* to wrap oneself in a cloak; to cover oneself, to wrap oneself round; -arsi nella propria virtù, to parade one's virtue; -arsi di, to be covered in, to become covered with; -arsi di onestà, to affect honesty; **-ato** *part. adj.* covered, mantled, cloaked; concealed; prati -ati di fiori, meadows carpeted with flowers; cielo -ato di stelle, sky studded with stars. **-atura** *f.* mantle, covering, wrap. **-ellare** [A I] *tr.*, *rfl.* to wrap in a mantle.

ammantigliare [A 4]. See amantigliare, under **amante²**.

ammanto *m.* (poet.) mantle; papale —, mantum, papal cope.

ammar-are *intr.* (*aux.* avere) to alight, to touch down (on water, of a seaplane). **-ag·gio**, **-amento** *m.*, **-ata** *f.* alighting (on water). **-ezzato** *adj.* (paperm.) marbled.

†**ammarcire** *vb.* See marcire.

ammarinare [A I] *tr.* (naut.) to man.

ammarr-are [A I] *tr.* (naut.) to fasten, to moor; *intr.* (*aux.* avere), to moor. **-ag·gio** *m.* (naut.) mooring.

ammartellare [A I] and derivs. See **martellare**.

†**ammascare** *tr.* to understand.

ammascatura *f.* riding strand (in a rope or cable).

†**ammascherare** *vb.* and derivs. See **mascherare**.

ammass-are [A I] *tr.* to amass; to hoard, to stockpile; to pile, to heap up; (mil.) to mass; *rfl.* to gather, to collect, to crowd together; to muster. **-amento** *m.* heap; hoard; crowd; meeting, gathering; (mil.) -amento di truppe, massing of troops, mustering of troops. **-ato** *part. adj.* amassed; piled up; dense. (**-atore** *m.* **-atrice** *f.*) **-ellare** [A I] *tr.* to pile up; to pack in a barrel.

ammassicci-are [A 3] *tr.* to mass, to pack; *rfl.* to form into a mass, to become solid; (of a cliff, hill) to tower, to overhang; (fig.) to become inured. **-ata** *f.* packing, massing. **-ato** *part. adj.* packed, massed; solid.

ammasso *m.* mass; bulk; heap; accumulation; (miner) mass; (econ.) stock-piling; buying up of goods; government stock-piling of rationed or price-controlled foodstuffs compulsorily purchased from producers; the government agency superintending the stock-piling.

ammatassare [A I] *tr.* to wind into a skein; (fig.) to confuse.

ammatt-are [A I] *tr.* (naut.) to rig (a ship); †*intr.* to signal. **-ato** *part. adj.* rigged.

ammatt-ire [D 2] *intr.* (*aux.* essere) to go mad; far —, to drive mad, to give endless trouble to; *rfl.* to cudgel one's brains; to be driven mad; to torment oneself. **-imento** *m.* annoyance; worry; embarrassment; difficulty; laborious task; vivere senza -imenti, to lead a carefree life. **-ito** *part. adj.* driven mad, harassed.

ammatton-are [A I c] *tr.* to pave with bricks. **-amento** *m.* brick-paving. **-ato** *part. adj.* paved with bricks; *n.m.* paving, pavement; brick floor. **-atura** *f.* brick-paving.

ammazz-are¹ [A I] *tr.* to kill; to murder; to slay; to slaughter; to overpower, to overwhelm; to bore, to weary; — il tempo, to kill time; (at cards) to beat by playing a higher card; — le parole, to clip one's words; *rfl.* to commit suicide; to kill oneself; to ruin one's health; to wear oneself out; *recip. rfl.* to kill one another; **-agatti** *m. indecl.* pop-gun. **-amento** *m.* killing, carnage; slaughter; murder; heavy labour. **-ante** *part. adj.* killing; boring. **-asette** *m. indecl.* braggart; giant-killer. **-atempo** *m. indecl.* idler; pastime. **-ato** *part. adj.* murdered; slaughtered; *n.m.* murdered man. (**-ata** *f.*) **-atoio** *m.* slaughterhouse; bludgeon; knock-out blow. (**-atore** *m.* **-atrice** *f.*) **-atura** *f.* tip to an assistant in a slaughterhouse.

†**ammazzare²** *tr.* to gather in bunches.

†**ammazzer-are** *tr.* to tie a weight to (a living creature) and fling into the water, to kill by drowning. †**-ato** *part. adj.* killed by drowning; soaked, sodden.

ammazzol-are [A I s] *tr.* to make up into nosegays; to bind; to gather (cards) up into a pack; †to hit with a club. (**-ato** *part. adj.*)

ammelm-are [A I c] *intr.* (*aux.* essere) to sink in the mud; *rfl.* to become muddy. **-ato** *part. adj.* muddy; stuck in the mud.

†**ammemorare** *vb.* See rammemorare.

ammen *excl.*, *n.m.* See amen.

ammenc-ire [D 2] *tr.* (colloq. Tusc.) to make flabby; *intr.* (*aux.* essere) to become flabby. **-ito** *part. adj.* flabby.

ammenda *f.* amends; correction; (leg.) fine for lesser crimes (e.g. 'contravvenzioni', misdemeanours).

ammend-are [A I] *tr.* to amend; to correct; to make amends for. (**-a·bile** *adj.*) **-amento** *m.* amending, amendment; (agric.) corrective

fertilizer. **-ato** *part. adj.* amended; corrected. (**-atore** *m.* **-atrice** *f.* **-azione** *f.*)

ammennni·colo *m.* cavil, pretext; hair-splitting argument; additional (tiresome) trifle; (leg.) specious argument; *pl.* sundries; l'affitto e tutti gli ammenicoli relativi, the rent and all the other sundry expenses.

ammensare [A I] *tr.* to add (a new item) to one's revenues (*usu.* of a bishop, but also of a community or public body).

†**ammentare** *vb.* and derivs. See rammentare.

†**ammenticare** *vb.* and derivs. See dimenticare.

†**ammesare** *tr.* to pay by the month.

†**ammessaro** *m.* stallion.

ammesso *part.* of ammettere, q.v.; *adj.* admitted; acknowledged; granted; received; allowed; — che, supposing that; — e non concesso, granted the possibility but the fact remains to be proved.

ammestare [A I] and derivs. See mestare.

ammestone *m.* intriguer.

ammetare [A I] *tr.* (poet. Pascoli) to pile up.

ammettere [C 20] *tr.* to admit; to permit; to be capable of; to acknowledge; to grant, to allow; to receive; — come cosa stabilita, — senz'altro, to take for granted. **-enza** *f.* (scient.) admittance.

ammezz-are¹ [A I] *tr.* to halve; to half-finish; to half-fill; to half-empty; to clip (words). (**-amento** *m.*) **-ato** *part. adj.* halved; half-done; *adv.* half: riempiere -ato, to half-fill; *n.m.* (Lomb.) entresol, mezzanine; watered wine.

ammezzare² [A I c] and derivs. See **ammezzire**.

ammezz-ire [D 2] *intr.* (*aux.* essere), *rfl.* (of fruit) to go soft, to become over-ripe. **-ito** *part. adj.* soft, over-ripe, 'sleepy'.

ammiccare [A 2] *intr.* (*aux.* avere) to wink; to beckon, to sign, to give the wink; (cards) to give a sign that certain cards are held.

ammic-co *m.* (*pl.* -chi) wink; winking; sign, nod.

amm-ina *f.* (chem.) amine. **-i·nico** *adj.* (chem.) amino; composti -inici, amino compounds.

amministr-are [A I] *tr.* to administer; to administrate; to manage, to direct; to conduct. (**-a·bile** *adj.* **-anza** *f.*) **-ativista** *m.* (neol.) specialist in administrative law. **-ativo** *adj.* administrative; governo -ativo, caretaker government; diritto -ativo, administrative law; anno -ativo, financial year; divisione -ativa dello stato, structure of provincial and local administration in a state; elezioni -ative, local-government elections. (**-ativamente** *adv.*) **-ato** *part. adj.* administered; *n.m.* citizen, inhabitant. (**-ata** *f.*) **-atore** *m.* administrator; manager; director; consiglio degli -atori, board of directors. (**-atrice** *f.*) **-azione** *f.* administration; management; directorship; consiglio di -azione, board of directors; -azione fiduciaria, mandate.

amminni·colo *m.* See ammennicolo.

†**amminuire** *vb.* See diminuire.

†**amminut-are, -ire** *tr.* to make minute; *intr.* to become minute.

ammira·bile *adj.* See under **ammirare**.

ammira·gli-o¹ *m.* admiral; Grande —, Admiral of the Fleet; — di Armata, Admiral; — di Squadra, Vice-Admiral; — di Divisione, Rear-Admiral; *adj.* ufficiale —, flag officer; nave -a, flagship. **-a** *f.* flagship.

†**ammira·glio²** *m.* mirror.

ammir-are [A I] *tr.* to admire; to gaze at in wonder; to wonder at; *abs.* to marvel, to admire. **-a·bile** *adj.* admirable; strange, wondrous. (**-abilmente** *adv.*) **-ando** *adj.* worthy of admiration, admirable. **-ativo** *adj.* admiring; punto -ativo, exclamation mark. **-ativamente** *adv.* admiringly. **-ato** *part. adj.* admired; lost in wonder. **-atore** *m.* admirer; suitor. (**-atrice** *f.*) **-azione** *f.* admiration; object of admiration. **-evole** *adj.* admirable.

ammiserire [D 2] *vb.* and derivs. See immiserire.

ammiss-i·bile *adj.* admissible; allowable. (**-ibilità** *f.*) **-ione** *f.* admission; admittance; tassa d'-ione, entrance fee; esame d'-ione, entrance examination; biglietto d'-ione, ticket of admission; (leg.) acknowledgement; admission; decision that a means of judicial proof is admissible; (eng.) inlet, intake; (of an electric motor) induction.

ammitto *m.* See amitto.

ammobi(g)li-are [A 4] *tr.* to furnish. **-amento** *m.* furnishing; furnishings. **-ato** *part. adj.* furnished; camere -ate, furnished rooms.

ammocete *m.* (ichth.) ammocoete.

ammodern-are [A I] *tr.* to modernize; to bring up to date; to refashion. **-amento** *m.* modernizing; refashioning. **-ativo** *adj.*

ammodern-are (*cont.*)
modernizing. **-ato** *part. adj.* modernized; brought up to date; refashioned. (**-atore** *m.* **-atrice** *f.*) **-atura** *f.* modernizing; refashioning; something brought up to date or refashioned.

ammodite *m.* (ichth.) *Ammodytes* sp., sand eel, launce; (zool.) *Vipera ammodytes*, horn-nosed viper.

ammodo *adv.* nicely; properly; with care; *adj. indecl.* nice, good, well-behaved; respectable, reliable; discreet, reserved, prudent, circumspect; 'comme il faut'.

ammo·fila *f.* (ent.) *Ammophila* spp., sand wasp.

ammogli-are¹ [A4c] *tr.* to find a wife for; (fig.) to unite, to combine, to match; *rfl.* to take a wife; †to mate. **-ato** *part. adj.* (of a man) married; *n.m.* married man. (**-atore** *m.*)

ammogliare² [A4] (dial. S. Italy). See **ammollare¹**.

†**ammoin-are¹** *tr.* to flatter, to coax; to fondle. (†**-amento** *m.*)

†**ammoinare²** *tr.* to annoy.

ammoll-are¹ [A1] *tr.* to steep, to soak, to wet, to dip; to soften; to slacken (a rope); to relax, to let go; to deal (a blow); to land (with), to fob off (with); *intr.* (*aux.* avere) to give way, to yield; *rfl.* to get soaked; to soften; to loosen, to slacken. **-amento** *m.* soaking; softening; slackening. **-ato** *part. adj.* soaked; softened; slackened. **-atore** *m.* (techn.) mulling agent.

†**ammollare²** *tr.* to furnish with springs (from **molla**, q.v.).

ammoll-ire [D2] *tr.* to soften; to mellow; to touch, to move (emotionally); to enervate; *rfl.* to become mellow, to soften; to become enfeebled. **-iente** *adj.*, *n.m.* emollient. **-imento** *m.* softening; effeminacy; -imento senile, senile decay. **-itivo** *adj.*, *n.m.* emollient. **-ito** *part. adj.* softened; enervated; weak in the head; *n.m.* imbecile. (**-ita** *f.*)

†**ammoncellare** *tr.* to heap up.

†**ammonestare** *tr.* to admonish.

ammoni·ac-a *f.* (chem.) ammonia. **-ale** *adj.* ammoniacal. **-ato** *adj.* ammoniated. **-o** *adj.* sale -o, sal ammoniac; *n.m.* gum ammoniac.

ammonimento *m.* See under **ammonire**.

ammo·n-io *m.* (chem.) ammonium. **-ico** *adj.* of ammonium.

ammon-ire [D2] *tr.* to reprimand; to admonish, to warn, to caution; to counsel, to advise; to enjoin; to forbid; (leg.) to caution (witnesses, experts); to inflict by administrative proceeding a measure involving specific restrictions (called 'ammonizione') on potential offenders; (hist. Florentine Repub.) to disqualify from office. **-imento** *m.* warning; admonition. **-itivo** *adj.* admonitory. **-ito** *part. adj.* warned; admonished; *n.m.* (leg.) person deemed potentially dangerous to society on whom a measure involving specific restrictions ('ammonizione') has been inflicted after administrative proceeding. **-itore** *m.* monitor; adviser; admonisher; (eccl.) admonitor. (**-itrice** *f.*) **-ito·rio** *adj.* admonitory. **-izione** *f.* warning; admonishment; reproof; (leg.) caution (to witnesses, experts); measure involving specific restrictions inflicted on potential offenders after administrative proceeding.

ammonite *f.* (geol.) ammonite.

ammont-are¹ [A1c] *tr.* to amass, to accumulate; to heap, to pile up; *intr.* (*aux.* essere, *prep.* a) to amount (to); *rfl.* to accumulate; *n.m.* amount, sum; (comm.) — complessivo, — globale, aggregate amount; — degli affari conclusi in un'annata, yearly turnover. **-amento** *m.* mass; heap. **-ato** *part. adj.* accumulated; heaped up. (**-atore** *m.*)

†**ammontare²** *tr.* (of a male animal) to mount (the female).

ammonticchi-are [A4] *tr.* to pile up, to heap; — il denaro, to count out one's money in little heaps; *rfl.* to accumulate, to pile up in small heaps; to gather together. (**-amento** *m.* **-ato** *part. adj.* **-atura** *f.*)

ammorb-are [A1] *tr.* to infect, to taint; to corrupt; to foul (the air); †to fall ill; to stink. (**-amento** *m.*) **-ante** *part. adj.*, **-ato** *part. adj.* foul, stinking. (**-atore** *m.* **-atrice** *f.*)

ammorbida-trice *f.* (text.) softener. **-tura** *f.* (text.) softening.

ammorbid-ire [D2] *tr.* to soften; to make supple; *rfl.* to become soft; to ripen. (**-imento** *m.*) **-ito** *part. adj.* soft; supple; softened up; ripe.

ammorchiato *adj.* full of dregs; muddy, turbid.

ammorire [D2] *intr.* (*aux.* essere) to become dark-skinned.

ammors-are¹ [A1] *tr.* to bite; to nibble. **-ato** *part. adj.* bitten; (archit.) crenellated. **-atura** *f.* bite, biting; (carp.) scarf (joint).

ammors-are² [A1] *tr.* to bit (a horse). **-ato** *part. adj.* (of a horse) wearing the bit.

ammorsellato *m.* dish of minced meat and eggs.

ammort-are [A1] *tr.* (comm.) to amortise, to redeem, to buy off; †to extinguish. **-amento** *m.* depreciation (of factory plant); (comm.) amortisation, redemption, extinction; fondo di -amento, sinking fund (reserve fund); fondo di -amento di obbligazioni o debito pubblico, redemption fund; piano di -amento, funding scheme; (naut.) wear and tear of hull and fittings.

ammort-ire [D2] *tr.* to deaden; to numb; to weaken; to parry (a blow), to break the force of; to soften (light); to tone down (colours); *intr.* (*aux.* avere) to fade; to faint; *rfl.* to be deadened; to fade; to faint. **-imento** *m.* deadening; weakening; (med.) numbness; mortification. **-ito** *part. adj.* deadened; weakened; acqua -ita, stagnant water.

ammortizz-are [A1] *tr.* to amortise, to redeem, to buy off; (mech.) to deaden, to dampen; — elasticamente, to cushion. **-a·bile** *adj.* redeemable. **-atore** *m.* shock absorber; -atore dello sterzo, steering damper. **-azione** *f.* amortisation, redemption, extinction; (mech.) deadening, dampening.

ammorvidire [D2] and derivs. See **ammorbidire**.

ammorz-are¹ [A1] *tr.* to extinguish; to weaken; *rfl.* to die down; to diminish; to grow faint, to weaken. (**-amento** *m.* **-ato** *part. adj.*) **-atore** *m.* (eng.) buffer, shock absorber.

ammorzare² [A1] *abs.* (dial. S. Italy) to breakfast.

ammosciare [A3c] and derivs. See **ammoscire**.

ammosc-ire [D2] *intr.* (*aux.* essere) to become flabby; to wither, to shrivel. **-ito** *part. adj.* flabby; withered, shrivelled.

ammost-are [A1c] *tr.* to tread, to press (grapes); *rfl.*, *intr.* (*aux.* essere) to ferment. **-atoio** *m.* plunger, winepress. **-atore** *m.* saccharifier. (**-atura** *f.*)

†**ammottare** *vb.* See **smottare**.

†**ammozzare** *tr.* to amass, to pile up.

ammucchi-are [A4] *tr.* to pile up; to heap; to cram, to huddle, to pack tightly together; *rfl.* to accumulate; to crowd; to huddle together. **-amento** *m.* piling, heaping; -amento compresso, packed heaping; -amento sciolto, loose piling. **-ato** *part. adj.* piled up, heaped; crowded, jumbled together. (**-atore** *m.* **-atrice** *f.*) **-ettare** [A1c] *tr.* to pile in little heaps.

ammucid-ire [D2] *intr.* (*aux.* essere), *rfl.* to grow musty. **-ito** *part. adj.* musty.

ammuffare [A1] and derivs. See **ammuffire**.

ammuff-ire [D2] *intr.* (*aux.* essere) to grow mouldy; (fig.) — sui libri, to pore over books; — in casa, to shut oneself up. **-ito** *part. adj.* musty, mouldy.

ammuin-are [A1] *intr.*, *rfl.* (dial. Neapol.) to exert oneself pointlessly, to fuss; to become upset. **-ato** *part. adj.* excited; upset; angry.

†**ammulinare** *vb.* See **mulinare**.

ammus-are [A1] *tr.* to nuzzle; *intr.* (*aux.* avere) to sulk, to pout; *rfl.* to sulk; *recip. rfl.* to nuzzle one another. **-ato** *part. adj.* pouting, sulky.

ammus-ire [D2] *intr.* (*aux.* essere), *rfl.* to sulk, to take offence. **-ito** *part. adj.* sulky.

ammuson-ire [D2] *intr.* (*aux.* avere) (colloq.) to sulk. **-ito** *part. adj.* sulky.

†**ammutare** *vb.* See **ammutolire**.

ammutin-are [A1s] *intr.* (*aux.* essere), *rfl.* to mutiny; to rebel; *tr.* to excite to revolt. **-amento** *m.* mutiny; sedition; revolt. **-ato** *part. adj.* mutinous; seditious; rebellious; *n.m.* mutineer; rebel. (**-atore** *m.* **-azione** *f.*)

ammutire [D2] and derivs. See **ammutolire**.

ammutol-ire [D2] *intr.* (*aux.* essere) to become dumb; to fall silent, to be reduced to silence. **-ito** *part. adj.* mute, speechless.

amnesi·a *f.* amnesia, loss of memory.

am·ni-o (anat.) amnion, caul. **-o·tico** *adj.* amniotic.

amnist-i·a *f.* amnesty; general pardon; (leg.) amnesty. **-iare** [A4] *tr.* (leg.) to grant an amnesty to. **-iato** *part. adj.* pardoned, under an amnesty; *n.m.* prisoner released under amnesty.

am-o *m.* fish-hook; (fig.) flattery; lure; tendere l'—, to bait the hook; pigliar l'—, to swallow the bait; rimanere all'—, to be caught fast.

amoe·rr-o, **-e** *m.* moiré silk.

amoral-e *adj.* amoral. **-ismo** *m.*, **-ità** *f.* amoralism.

amor-e *m.* love; love personified, Cupid, Eros; affection; fondness; friendship; passion; love-affair; — a prima vista, love at first sight; — non corrisposto, unrequited love; — interessato, cupboard love; pegno d'—, love-token; *pl.* love-affairs, amours, story of a love-affair: gli -i di Enea e Didone, the love-story of Dido and Aeneas; loved one, beloved object; lady-love;

amor-e (*cont.*)
essere l'— della mamma, to be a mother's darling; amore!, amor mio! my love!; portare — a, to love; essere tutto — per, to love dearly; fare all'—, to make love; fare all'— con, to make love to; (of animals) andare in —, to rut, to be in heat; (of land) in —, favoured for vegetation; amor proprio, self-respect, conscientiousness, thoroughness, pride in one's work; amor di sè, egoism; con —, eagerly, lovingly; per —, willingly; per — o per forza, willy-nilly, by hook or by crook; per l'amor di Dio!, for Heaven's sake!; fare una cosa per amor di Dio, to do a thing without thought of gain; gratis e amore Dei, free; d'— e d'accordo, in full agreement; per — di brevità, for the sake of brevity; lo farò per amor vostro, I will do it for your sake; quel disegno è un —, that drawing is a delight; che — di bambino!, what a lovely child!; (bot.) — nascosto, columbine, *Aquilegia vulgaris*. -azzo *m.* illicit love-affair. -etto *m.* flirtation. -evole *adj.* loving; kind, fond. -evolezza *f.* love; kindliness. -evolmente *adv.* lovingly; with solicitude. -ino *m.* (art) cupid; dear little thing, darling; flirtation; sofa for two, sociable, vis-à-vis; (bot.) mignonette, *Reseda odorata*. -oso *adj.* loving; affectionate; con -osa cura, with loving care; amorous; lettera -osa, love-letter; la vita -osa di. . ., the story of the love-affairs of. . .; *n.m.* (joc.) lover; fiancé; sweetheart, boy-friend; (theatr.) primo -oso, juvenile lead. (-a *f.*) -osamente *adv.* lovingly, affectionately.

amoreggi-are [A 3 C] *intr.* (*aux.* avere) to flirt; to philander. -amento *m.* flirtation; philandering; gallantry.

amorfo *adj.* shapeless, amorphous; fiammiferi amorfi, Swedish matches; (chem.) amorphous.

amoroso *adj.* See under amore.

amo·scino, amoscino *m.* (bot.) Damascene plum tree, *Prunus domestica* variety.

amovi·bil-e *adj.* removable; detachable; transportable; (admin.) temporary. (-ità *f.*)

ampel-ogi·a *f.*, **-ografi·a** *f.* treatise on grape-cultivation. -oterapi·a *f.* grape-cure.

ampelopraso *m.* (bot.) wild leek, *Allium ampeloprasum*.

ampèr-e *f.* ampère. -ag·gio *m.* amperage. -o·metro *m.* ammeter. -ora *f.* ampère-hour. -ora·metro *m.* ampère-hour metre. -spira *f.* ampère-turn.

am·pi-o *adj.* (*superl.* amplis·simo) ample; broad; wide; spacious; roomy; liberal, abundant; (of style) diffuse; large-hearted; easygoing. -amente *adv.* widely; amply; abundantly. -eggiante *adj.* una sottana -eggiante, a skirt cut rather full. -ezza *f.* spaciousness; largeness, width; breadth; range; capaciousness; (phys.) amplitude. (-oso *adj.*)

ampless-o *m.* embrace. -ica·ule *adj.* (bot.) amplexicaul.

ampli-are [A 4 S] *tr.* to enlarge; to expand; to increase; to amplify; *rfl.* to extend; to dilate; to grow larger. -amento *m.* enlargement; increase. -ativo *adj.* enlarging, amplifying. -ato *part. adj.* enlarged, amplified. (-atore *m.* -azione *f.*)

amplific-are [A 2 S] *tr.* to amplify; to enlarge; to extol; to laud to the skies. (-amento *m.*) -ativo *adj.* amplifying; stile -ativo, pompous style. -ato *part. adj.* amplified; overpraised. -atore *m.* (radio) amplifier. (-atrice *f.*) -azione *f.* amplification; enlargement; exegesis; (radio, etc.) amplification, gain.

ampli·fono *m.* (radio, etc.) pick-up.

ampl-o *adj.* wide. -is·simo *superl.* of ampio, q.v. -itu·dine *f.* amplitude.

ampoll-a *f.* phial; ampoule; *pl.* cruet (for oil and vinegar); avere il diavolo nell'—, to have the devil's own luck; bubble; blister; electric light bulb. -iera *f.* cruet-stand. -ina *f.* bulb of an hourglass; (liturg.) mass-cruet.

ampollos-o *adj.* bombastic, turgid, pompous; high-flown. (-amente *adv.*) -ità *f.* bombast, pomposity.

amput-are [A 1 S] *tr.* to amputate; — uno, to perform an amputation upon. (-a·bile *adj.*) -ato *part. adj.* amputated. -azione *f.* amputation.

amuleto *m.* amulet, charm; talisman.

amusi·a *f.* (psychol.) incapacity to understand music, lack of artistic sense.

ana *adv.* (pharm.) ana, equal quantities of each.

ana·basi *f. indecl.* anabasis; (mus.) succession of ascending sounds in ancient Greek music.

anabatt-ismo *m.* (rel.) Anabaptism. -ista *m.* Anabaptist. -i·stico *adj.* Anabaptist(ic).

anabbagliante *adj.* anti-dazzle.

anabolismo *m.* (biol.) anabolism, assimilation.

anabrosi *f. indecl.* (med.) corrosion of soft parts of the body by means of caustic.

anaca·mptico *adj.* (phys.) anacamptic, echoing.

anacar·d-io, -o *m.* (bot.) cashew-nut tree, *Anacardium occidentale*.

a·nace *m.* See anice.

anaciato *adj.* flavoured with aniseed.

anacoluto *m.* (gramm.) anacoluthon.

anaconda *m.* (zool.) Anaconda snake, *Eunectes murinus*.

anacor-eta *m.* (rel. and fig.) anchorite, hermit. -e·tico *adj.* anchoretish, hermit-like. (-eticamente *adv.*)

Anacre-onte *pr.n.m.* Anacreon. -on·teo *adj.* (prosod.) Anacreontic. -on·tica *f.* Anacreontic poem. -on·tico *adj.* Anacreontic. -ontizzare [A 1] *intr.* to write in the manner of Anacreon.

anacron-ismo *m.* anachronism. -i·stico *adj.* anachronistic.

anacrusi *f. indecl.* (prosod.) anacrusis; (mus.) anacrusis (that part of a melody which precedes the first accent).

anadema *f.* anadem, wreath, chaplet.

anadiomene *adj.* (poet.) Venere —, Venus arisen from the waves.

anadiplosi *f. indecl.* (rhet.) anadiplosis, reduplication.

anaero·bio *m.* (biol.) anaerobe, anaerobion.

ana·fora *f.* (rhet.) anaphora; repetition; (Eastern liturg.) anaphora; (med.) vomiting.

anafrodis-i·a *f.* (med.) anaphrodisia. -i·aco *adj.* anaphrodisiac.

anagal·lide *f.* (bot.) scarlet pimpernel (or blue), poor man's weatherglass, *Anagallis arvensis*.

anagiri *f.* (bot.) *Anagyris foetida*.

ana·glifo *m.* (archit.) anaglyph; (opt.) anaglyph, stereoscope.

anagnoste *m.* (Eastern eccl.) anagnost(es), lector.

anag-ogi·a *f.* (theol.) anagoge, anagogy. -o·gico *adj.* anagogic(al); mystical. (-ogicamente *adv.*)

ana·grafe *f.* register of births, deaths and marriages; register office; census; capo dell'ufficio d'—, registrar-general; ufficio d'—, registry.

anagramm-a *m.* anagram. -a·tico *adj.* anagrammatic. -atista *m.* anagrammatist. -atizzare [A 1] *tr.* to anagrammatize.

analabo *m.* (eccl.) analabus, a kind of scapular.

analcima *f.* (miner.) analcite.

analc-oo·lico, -o·lico *adj.* non-alcoholic.

†Analda *pr.n.f.* (geog.) province of Hainault; †all'—, after the fashion of Hainault.

anale *adj.* See under ano.

analessi *f.* (rhet.) anaphora, repetition.

analet·ti *m.pl.* analects.

analet·tic-a *f.* (med.) analeptic. -o *adj.* analeptic, restorative.

analfabet-a *adj.* illiterate; unlettered; *n.m.*, *f.* illiterate person. -ismo *m.* illiteracy.

anal-gesi·a *f.* analgesia. -ge·sico *adj.* analgesic; *n.m.* pain-killer.

an-a·lisi *f. indecl.* analysis; test; — del sangue, blood-test; (telev.) scanning; — tempi, time study (factory organization). -alista *m.* analyst; analyser; -alista tempi, time study engineer. -ali·tica *f.* analysis, principles of analysis; analytics. -ali·tico *adj.* analytic(al). (-aliticamente *adv.*)

analizz-are [A 1] *tr.* to analyse; to examine; (gramm.) to parse; (telev.) to scan. (-a·bile *adj.* -amento *m.* -ato *part. adj.*) -atore *m.* analyser, analyst; (telev.) scanner. (-atrice *f.*)

analo·gic-o *adj.* analogical; (leg.) applicazione -a, analogical interpretation.

ana·lo-go *adj.* (*m.pl.* -ghi) analogous; like, suitable, relevant, pertinent; respective; risposta -a, reply relevant to the question. -gamente *adv.* similarly, analogously; suitably; pertinently. -gi·a *f.* analogy. -gismo *m.* (philos.) argument by analogy. (-gista *m.*)

anamn-esi *f.* (med.) case-history. -e·stico *adj.* referring to the case history.

anamorfosco·pio *m.* (opt.) anamorphoscope.

anamorfo·si *f.* (opt.) anamorphosis, distorted image.

ananasso *m.* pineapple, *Ananas comosus*.

anan-che, -ke *f.* (poet.) fate, inevitability, violent end.

anandr-i·a *f.* effeminacy. -o *adj.* effeminate.

ana·nimo *adj.* ananym.

ana-pesto *m.* (prosod.) anapaest. -pe·stico *adj.* anapaestic.

ana-plasti·a *f.* plastic surgery, anaplasty. -pla·stico *adj.* anaplastic.

anapno·grafo *m.* (med.) anapnograph.

an-archi·a *f.* anarchy; (colloq.) tumult, chaos. -ar·chico *adj.* anarchic(al); *n.m.* anarchist. (-archicamente *adv.*) -archismo *m.* anarchism. -archista *m.* anarchist. -arco·ide *m.* near-anarchist; *adj.* verging on anarchy.

ana·rchici *m.pl.* (slang) beans.

†**anare** *m.* nostril.

anariano, ana·rio *adj.* non-Aryan; non-Indo-European.

ana·staşi *f.* (miner.) octahedrite.

Anasta·şia *pr.n.f.* Anastasia; (joc.) Madonna —, the Censorship.

anasta·tica *f.* (bot.) rose of Jericho, Resurrection-plant, *Anastatica hierochuntica.*

anasta·tico *adj.* (typ.; photog.) anastatic.

anastigma·tico *adj.* (opt.) anastigmatic.

ana-stomoşi *f. indecl.* (anat.) anastomosis. **-stomiẓẓare** [A I], **-stomoşare** [A I] *intr.* (anat.) to inosculate, to anastomose.

ana·strofe *f.* (rhet.) anastrophe.

anatem-a, ana·tem-a *m.* (rel. and fig.) anathema, excommunication, curse; accursed thing. **-atiẓẓare** [A I], **-iẓẓare** [A I] *tr.* to anathematize.

anatocişmo *m.* (leg.) compound interest.

Anato·l-ia *pr.n. f.* (geog.) Anatolia. **-ico** *adj.* Anatolian, oriental.

anat-omi·a *f.* anatomy. **-o·mico** *adj.* anatomic(al); sala -omica, dissecting room. (**-omicamẹnte** *adv.*) **-omista** *m.* anatomist. **-omiẓẓare** [A I] *tr.* to anatomize, to dissect.

a·natr-a *f.* (orn.) duck; *m.* drake; — maschio, drake; — dal piumino, eider duck; — di coda lunga, pintail; — d'inverno, white-headed duck; — marina, tufted duck; (fig.) of a person who waddles, è un'—. **-a·ia** *f.* covey of ducks. **-are** [A I] *intr.* (*aux.* avere) to quack. **-oc·colo** *m.*, **-otto** *m.* duckling.

†**anatrire** *vb.* See **nitrire**.

anc-a *f.* haunch; hip; thigh; side; leg, drumstick (of a bird); (naut.) quarter; battersi l'—, to wring one's hands; menar l'—, to stride; misura delle anche, hip measurement; ad ogni mover d'—, at every step; (sport) colpo d'—, side tackle in Graeco-Roman wrestling; *pl.* (of animals) hindquarters. **-acciuto** *adj.* wide-hipped. **-aione** *adv.* (of a horse) andare -aione, to limp. **-are** [A 2] *intr.* (*aux.* avere) to heave in breathing (of a horse). **-ata** *f.* stride, striding.

ancella *f.* (poet.; joc.) handmaid; maidservant.

ancestrale *adj.* ancestral.

anche *adv., conj.* and, too, also; likewise; still; even; quand'—, even though; — se, even if; e — e —, and even more; non —, not yet; per —, as yet; non s'è per — visto, he hasn't been seen yet; e — —, perhaps more, perhaps less; ce n'è —, there's some more left; fosse —, even if; nè —, not even.

anchegg-iare [A 3 C] *intr.* (*aux.* avere) to sway the hips (**-ìo** *m.*)

anchenne, †**anchina** *f.* (text.) nankeen.

anchi·loş-i *f. indecl.* (med.) anchylosis. **-are** [A I s] *rfl.* to become paralysed; to grow stiff. **-ato** *part. adj.* paralysed; stiff.

an·cia *f.* (mus.) reed (of a wind instrument).

an·ciolo *m.* (ichth.) *Heptranchias cinereus,* a kind of shark.

†**anci·dere** *tr.* to kill; to destroy; to torment.

ancile *m.* (Rom. hist.) ancile, sacred tutelary shield of Rome.

†**ancilla** *f.* See **ancella**.

ancillare *adj.* (joc.) relating to maidservants, ancillary.

anciolo *m.* (ichth.) *Notidanus cinereus,* comb-toothed shark.

anci·pite *adj.* amphibious; two-headed; uncertain, dubious.

anco[1] *adv., conj.* Tusc. form of **anche**, q.v.

†**anco**[2] *m.* measure of grain.

†**ancoi** *adv.* today, at the present time.

Ancọn-a[1] *pr.n.f.* (geog.) Ancona. **-itano** *adj.* of Ancona, from Ancona; *n.m.* inhabitant, native of Ancona. (**-itana** *f.*)

ancọna[2] *f.* (eccl. art) ancona, altar-piece; niche for statue; roadside shrine.

ancọna[3] *f.* (dial.) street-corner.

†**ancone**[1] *m.* (anat.) elbow.

†**ancone**[2] *m.* bay, gulf.

ancọr-a *adv.* still; yet; again; once more; more; further; even; also; per —, up to now; dammene —, give me some more; — una settimana, one week longer; — una volta, once more; ancor più, even more. **-chè** *conj.*, **-quando** *conj.* although, even if.

an·cor-a *f.* (naut.) anchor; — di posta, bower anchor; — di salvezza, — di speranza, sheet-anchor (also fig.); — galleggiante, sea anchor; — impegnata, — sporca, — incattivata, — impigliata, — inceppata, — ammarrata, foul anchor; stare sull'—, to lie at anchor; levare l'—, salpare l'—, to weigh anchor; dar fondo all'—, to cast anchor; (eng.) anchor, grappler; (electr.) keeper of a magnet; armature; — a doppio T, H-armature; (clockm.) pallet, lever, pallet fork; ruota d'—, escape wheel; albero d'—, pallet

staff; — montata, jewelled pallet fork and staff. **-ag·gio** *m.* (naut.) anchorage; dues; place of anchorage, berth. **-a·io** *m.* anchor-maker. **-are** [A I s] *tr.* to anchor; *rfl.* to come to anchor, to cast anchor. **-ato** *part. adj.* riding at anchor; (herald.) croce -ata, cross moline, cross scarcely. **-otto** *m.* kedge-anchor.

†**ancro·ia** *f.* old hag.

ancu·dine *f.* See **incudine**.

ancusa *f.* (bot.) borage, *Borago officinalis.*

anda *f.* (bot.) Brazilian tree, whose seeds yield medicinal oil, *Joannesia princeps.*

Andalu·ş-ia *pr.n.f.* (geog.) Andalusia. **-o** *adj.* Andalusian; (also *n.m.*).

†**andaluzzo** *m.* Andalusian breed of horse.

andamẹnto *m.* See under **andare**.

andana *f.* avenue between trees; (techn.) rope-walk; (naut.) line of ships moored side by side; (N. Italy) railway platform.

andante *part. adj.* See under **andare**.

and-are [A8] *intr.* (*aux.* essere).

1. To go (locomotion, travel); — a piedi, to walk; to go on foot; — di corsa, to run; (mil.) to go at the double; — al passo, (of a horse) to walk; (mil.) to march; — a cavallo, to ride; to go on horseback; — al trotto, to trot; — al galoppo, to gallop; — al galoppo sciolto, to canter; — in bicicletta, to ride a bicycle; to go for a bicycle ride; to go by bicycle; — in automobile, — in macchina, to go by car, to go by road; to go for a drive (see also under no. 11); — a cento all'ora, to do a hundred (km. an hour); — a rimorchio, to be on tow; — in treno, to travel in a train; — col treno, to go by train, to go by rail; — in barca, to go out in a boat; to go by boat; — per mare, to go by sea; — per terra, to go by land, to go over land (see also under no. 7).
2. To go away, to depart, to set out, to go; andiamo, let's go; off we go; andate con Dio! farewell!; vado e torno, I won't be a minute; andarsene, to go away; to take one's leave; (euphem.) to pass away, to depart this life; — nel mondo de' più, to pass over, to join the great majority; — verso il popolo, (of a politician) to identify oneself with the lower classes; — a Canossa, to eat humble pie, to go to Canossa; (colloq.) — a Patrasso, to kick the bucket, to go bust; — a Roma senza vedere il papa, to fail in an undertaking; — via in un sacco e tornare in un baule, to learn nothing from one's travels; — in pensione, to retire; — a nozze, to go to a wedding, to get married, to have a good time; per lui dare un esame è come — a nozze, for him taking an exam is just a piece of cake; — alla ventura, to go to seek one's fortune; to drift, to leave things to chance; — a servizio, to go into domestic service; — (a) soldato, to join up, to go for a soldier.
3. To arrive, to reach, to get, to land; — alle stelle, to rise to fame, to reach dizzy heights; (of prices) to soar; — a fondo di, to get to the bottom of, to make a thorough study of; (fencing) — a fondo, to lunge (see also under no. 19); — a un pelo da, to be a hairs-breadth from; — sotto un'automobile, to land under a car, to get run over; — a gambe all'aria, to tumble head over heels; to fall flat on one's back with one's legs in the air. 4. To go about, to proceed, to make one's way; — a zonzo, to stroll; — a braccetto, to walk arm in arm; va vestita in ghingheri, she goes about all dolled up; — per la propria strada, to go one's own way; — per i propri affari, to go about one's business; — in processione, to process, to take part in a procession; — di conserva, to keep in step (see also under no. 19); — a tempo, to keep time; — carponi, to get down on all fours, to crawl; — tastoni, to grope; — a rilento, to proceed at a snail's pace; to go carefully; — coi piedi di piombo, to go carefully; — di notte, to go about at night; peggio che — di notte, worse than ever; — per le lunghe, to take a long time, to be long-drawn-out; — a vapore, to rush (see also under no. 11). 5. To turn out, to end up, to prove, to go; — bene, to turn out well; to go right, to go well; purchè la vada! there's many a slip. . .; com'è -ata? how was it, how did you get on?; è -ata liscia, it went smoothly; gli è -ata liscia questa volta, he got away with it this time; com'è -ato a finire? what became of him?; — male, to turn out badly; to go wrong, to go badly; — di male in peggio, to go from bad to worse; (of food) — di traverso, to go down the wrong way (see also under no. 19); — al di sotto, — di sotto, — in giù, to come to grief, to go under; — giù, to go downhill (in health); — a rotoli, to fail, to miscarry; to go from bad to worse, to go downhill; to crash, to go bust; — in malora, to come to grief, to go to the bad, to fail, to crash (see also under no. 21); — a monte, — a vuoto, — all'aria, to

and·are (*cont.*)

come to nothing, to fall through, to fizzle out; — in disuso, to fall into disuse. **6.** To turn, to become, to grow, to go; — a male, to go bad; — in aceto, to turn to vinegar; — in fiele, (fig.) to turn to ashes; — in pezzi, to fall to pieces; — in bricioli, to crumble; — in fumo, to go up in smoke; — in sementa, to run to seed; — in piazza, to go bald; — tisico, to go into a decline; — in gangrena, to turn to gangrene; il cervello gli è -ato in acqua, he's off his head; — in collera, to be angry, to lose one's temper; — in bestia, to turn ugly, to lose all control; — in estasi, to go into ecstasy; (joc.) — in visibilio, to rave; (joc.) — in solluchero, — in brodo di giuggiole, to go into ecstasies; — in là cogli anni, to be growing old; — per i trenta, to be getting on for thirty. **7.** To go through it, to suffer; — per le mani di tutti, to be abused by all, to be the common butt; — di mezzo, andarne di mezzo, to suffer the consequences, to bear the brunt, to be the scapegoat; to be at stake; ne va di mezzo la vita, it's a matter of life and death; — per terra, to fall unheeded, to go by the wall (see also under no. 1). **8.** To serve, to pass, to do; può —, it will do, it will serve; va bene, that's all right, that will do; come va va, any old how, it's out of my hands now; questo andrà per le mille lire che mi devi, I'll take this in payment of the 1000 lire you owe me; (of coin) to be legal tender; to be acceptable, to be valid, to be good. **9.** To suit, to fit; — a capello, — a pennello, to suit to a t; (of clothes) to be a good fit; — bene, to suit; quest'abito non mi va bene, this dress does not suit me; — a genio, to please; to suit; — a contragenio, to go against the grain; — a fagiuolo, to be to one's liking, to be just the job; — in uggia, to be distasteful; mi va in uggia questo lavoro, I'm fed up with this work; — a noia, to be boring; to be displeasing; le è -ato a noia, she's taken a dislike to him. **10.** To act, to behave; — cauto, to act cautiously; — con le buone, to be kindly; to act in a kindly manner; — in oca, to act like a fool, to stupidly forget something; — d'accordo, to get on well together; to act in concert, to be hand in glove, to be in agreement. **11.** To function, to operate, to work, to run, to go, quest'orologio non va, this watch is not working properly; va bene il tuo orologio?, is your watch right?; — a vapore, to work by steam (see also under no. 4); — a elettricità, to run on electricity; — in orario, to run to time; (journ.) to appear, to come out, to be published: l'articolo andrà domani, the article will be in the paper tomorrow; (typ.) — di seguito, to run on; — in macchina, to go to press (see also under no. 1); come va questa musica?, how does this piece of music go?, how should this music be played?; così va il mondo, that's the way of the world. **12.** To frequent the company (of), to go (with); — insieme con, to keep company with; — appresso a una ragazza, to run after a girl; dimmi con chi vai e ti dirò chi sei, birds of a feather flock together; chi va con lo zoppo impara a zoppicare, evil communications corrupt good manners. **13.** To sell, to be saleable, to be sold; l'olio è un genere che va molto, oil is a commodity which is greatly in demand; — a ruba, to sell like hot cakes; — per la maggiore, to be in demand, to be popular; to be an authority; to be important and well known; — a peso, to be sold by weight; — a numero, to be sold by quantity; — all'asta, to go for auction, to be put up for auction; — in vendita, to go for sale, to be put up for sale; a quanto va il grano? what's the price of wheat? **14.** To be needed; a quest'opera ci andranno molti anni, it will take many years to finish this work; in questa giacca ci vanno cinque bottoni, there are five buttons to this jacket. **15.** To continue, to last; benone, finchè la va! very nice, as long as it lasts! **16.** To be contained, to go (into); quanto vino può — in questa botte? how much wine will this cask hold? **17.** Of Bodily Functions: to go to the lavatory; — di corpo, to have a motion of the bowels; — a femmine, to go with women; — in amore, — in calore, — in fregola, — in frega, to rut, to be on heat. **18.** Legal uses: — in appello, to appeal; — in Cassazione, to have recourse to the Supreme Court; — in diverso avviso, (of a judge) to reach a different opinion; — in desuetudine, to fall into abeyance. **19.** Nautical uses: — alla banda, to list, to heel over; — a fondo, to submerge (see also under no. 3); — all'ancoraggio, — alla fonda, to go to anchorage (in harbour); — alla deriva, — in deriva, to drift; — per occhio, to sink; — di conserva, to go side by side (see also under no. 4); — a traverso, — di traverso, to run before the wind (see also under no. 5); — in secco, to run

aground, to be stranded. **20.** In Games: (cards) vado, I pass; (poker) vado mille lire, I'll go a thousand lire; (draughts) — a dama, to get a king. **21.** Expletives: va a farti friggere!, va a mori' ammazzato! go to hell!; ma andiamo!, I say!; look here!; come on!; ma va là!, get on with you!, please do!, don't say that!, don't do that!; va a indovinarla!, who can tell?; va a fidarti!, look what comes of trusting someone!, don't trust them! **22.** Syntactical uses: (i) Followed by *prep.* a and an *infin.*: to be about to; -iamo a vedere, let's go and see; è -ato a mettersi in quei pasticci, he went and got himself in that mess. (ii) As an *infin.* after **lasciare**: lasciar —, to give up, to give over, to stop; lasciar — una pedata, to let fly a kick; lasciarsi —, to let oneself go, to neglect oneself; lasciarsi — a cattiva vita, to go to the bad; lasciarsi — a, to forget oneself so far as to. (iii) As an equivalent of **stare** or **essere**: come va? how are you?; come vanno gli affari?, how's business?; come va che...?, how is it that...?; va ben vestito, he dresses well; va da sè che..., it's perfectly obvious that, it follows naturally that; va pazzo per i libri, he is mad about books; — errato, to be mistaken; l'asta è -ata deserta, there were no bidders. (iv) As an *aux.* in a Passive Construction: tutte le carte -arono perdute, all the papers got lost; (with a sense of obligation) è una circostanza che non va taciuta, it is a circumstance which must not be hushed up; quel pezzo -rebbe suonato più presto, that piece ought to be played faster; la cosa -ava fatta diversamente, the thing ought to have been done differently. (v) With a Gerund conveying a sense of repetition: va gridando tutto il giorno, he never stops shouting all day long; -avamo leggendo Dante, we were reading Dante regularly.

   n.m. gait, walk; (poet.) proceeding, passing; manner, style; sull'— di, in imitation of; go, going, pace; a tutt'—, for all one is worth; il treno correva a tutt'—, the train was running at full speed; a lungo —, in the long run; al peggio —, at the worst; *pl.* pathways. -am̧ento *m.* proceeding; state; course; progress; tenor; movement; working-out; l'-amento di casa, the running of a house; l'-amento del mercato, the state of the market; l'-amento d'una malattia, the course of an illness; l'-amento dell'intreccio, the working-out of the plot; (mus.) an extended fugue-subject; progression; modulation. -ante *part. adj.* current, instant; il mese -ante, the current month; plain, everyday; cheap; (of a person) easy-going; (of work) steady; continuous, uniform, unbroken; fluent, facile, spontaneous; (mus.) neither quick nor slow; *n.m.* (mus.) an andante movement; *adv.* fluently. -antem̧ente *adv.* fluently, without interruption. -antȩzza *f.* fluency, spontaneity. -antino *m.* (mus.) an andantino movement; *adj.* (mus.) slightly quicker than andante. -ata *f.* going, journey; viaggio di -ata, outward journey; biglietto d'-ata e ritorno, return ticket; -ata di corpo, motion of the bowels, stool; a lunga -ata, in the long run. -ato *part. adj.* gone; done for, ruined; gone bad; gone off; mal -ato in salute, in very poor health; past; il mese -ato, last month. -atura *f.* gait; pace; walk, way of walking; fare l'-atura, to make the pace; going (in horse-racing); -atura pesante, heavy going. -azzo *m.* (bad) habit; (bad) practice; trend.

andeş-ina, -ite *f.* (miner.) andesite.

Ande *pr.n.f.* (geog.) Andes.

andicappare [A I] *tr.* (sport) to handicap.

andirivieni *m. indecl.* coming and going, bustle; labyrinth, maze; (fig.) meandering, aimless talk; (Tusc.) a kind of key.

an·dito *m.* passage, corridor; gallery; (mil. hist.) covered way running beneath a glacis.

Andracne *pr.n.f.* (myth.) Andrachne; (bot.) purslane, *Portulaca oleracea*; also *Andracne telephioides*.

Andre·a *pr.n.m.* Andrew.

andrena *f.* (ent.) *Andrena* sp., a kind of solitary bee.

†**andrienne** *f.* a wide-sleeved tea-gown (period 1703).

†**an·drio** *m.* an amphibious snake.

andriolo *m.* (bot.) macaroni, flint wheat, *Triticum durum*.

andr-iṣmo *m.* (med.) andrism, tendency towards masculinity in a woman. -ofobi·a *f.* (med.) androphobia, fear or dislike of the male sex. -ogini·a *f.* androgyny, hermaphroditism; (bot.) hermaphroditism, bisexuality. -o·gino *adj.* androgynous, hermaphroditic; (bot.) androgynous, having both male and female organs in the same flower. -omani·a *f.* nymphomania. -osace *f.* (bot.) *Androsace*, genus of the Primulaceae, mostly alpine. -osemo *m.* (bot.) tutsan, *Hypericum androsaemum*.

andrivello *m.* (naut.) whip; warp; kedge-anchor.

andro·ide *m.* automaton in human form, robot.

Andro·med-a *pr.n.f.* (myth.; astron.) Andromeda. **-e·idi** *f.pl.* (astron.) andromeds.

andrọne *m.* corridor; lobby, entrance-hall; pathway between trees; alley; (Eastern eccl.) andron.

aned·d-oto *m.* anecdote; *pl.* anecdota. **-o·tica** *f.* collection of anecdotes; anecdotage. **-o·tico** *adj.* anecdotal. (**-otismo** *m.* **-otista** *m.*)

anela·stico *adj.* (phys.) inelastic.

anel-are [A I] *intr.* (*aux.* avere) to pant; to gasp; *tr.* to long for, to desire. **-amẹnto** *m.* panting; longing. **-ante** *part. adj.* panting, gasping, breathless; eager, desirous. **-antemẹnte** *adv.* gaspingly; eagerly, ardently. (**-anza** *f.*) **-ato** *part. adj.* gasping, gasped out; desired. (**-atamẹnte** *adv.*) **-aziọne** *f.* panting; longing.

anelet-trico *adj.* anelectric.

ane·lito *m.* panting, gasping; sigh, sighing; yearning.

anel·lidi *m.pl.* (zool.) Annelida.

anell-o *m.* ring; circle, group (of people); — delle chiavi, key-ring; — fatato, wishing ring; — di fidanzamento, engagement-ring; — matrimoniale, — benedetto, — nuziale, wedding-ring; dare l'—, prendere l'—, to get married; — di catena, link; — per tovagliolo, napkin-ring; quoit: gioco degli -i, ring-quoits; tailor's thimble; ferrule; curl, ringlet (*pl.f.* le -a); (fig.) link, intermediary; — di congiunzione, missing link; (eccl.) l'— del pescatore, the Fisherman's ring; (mech.) race (of a ball bearing); — elastico d'arresto, circlip; — protettore, bead (of a tyre); (eng.) — di spessore, washer; (clockm.) bow; (anat.) sphincter; (archit.) *pl.* fillets (usually three, near ovolo moulding of Doric capital); (naut.) — d'ormeggio, mooring-ring. **†-are** *tr.* to wed. **-ato** *adj.* ringed; ring-shaped; (of hair) in ringlets; (herald.) ringed. **-ino** *m. dim.* of anello; (spinning, etc.) traveller. **-oso** *adj.* looped, in rings.

anelo *adj.* (poet.) panting, yearning; faint, weary.

an-emi·a *f.* anaemia; — perniciosa, pernicious anaemia. **-e·mico** *adj.* anaemic. **-emizzato** *adj.* suffering from loss of blood.

ane·mio *m.* blast-furnace.

anemocordo *m.* (mus.) Aeolian harp.

anem-o·file *f.pl.* (bot.) anemophilous (wind-pollinated) plants.

anem-ografi·a *f.* anemography. **-o·grafo** *m.* anemograph. **-ologi·a** *f.* anemology. **-ometri·a** *f.* anemometry. **-o·metro** *m.* anemometer; (aeron.) air speed indicator. **-ometro·grafo** *m.* anemometrograph. **-osco·pio** *m.* anemoscope, wind indicator.

ane·molo *m.* See anemone.

ane·mone *m.* (bot.) windflower, *Anemone*; (zool.) — di mare, sea anemone.

anepi·grafo *adj.* (of a MS.) without a title, lacking a heading.

aneritropsi·a *f.* (med.) anerythropsia; impaired colour perception of red.

aner-o·bio *m.* (biol.) anaerobe, micro-organism which lives without oxygen. **-o·bico** *adj.* anaerobic.

anero·ide *adj.* barometro —, aneroid barometer.

anest-esi·a *f.* anaesthesia. **-esi·metro** *m.* anaesthesimeter. **-esino** *m.* local anaesthetic. **-e·tico** *adj.*, *n.m.* anaesthetic. **-etista** *m.* anaesthetist. **-etizzare** [A I] *tr.* to anaesthetize, to put under an anaesthetic. **-etizzato** *part. adj.* under an anaesthetic.

aneste·tico *adj.* (philos.) non-aesthetic.

anẹt-o *m.* (bot.) dill, *Anethum graveolins*. **-ino** *adj.* made of dill, flavoured with dill.

anetolo *m.* (chem.) anethole, anise camphor.

aneuriṣm-a *f.* (med.) aneurism. **-a·tico** *adj.* aneurismal.

anfan-are [A I s] *intr.* (*aux.* avere) to bustle about; to talk wildly, to ramble. (**-amẹnto** *m.* **-atọre** *m.*) **-eggiare** [A 3 c] *intr.* (*aux.* avere) to be continually bustling about.

anfeṣibena *f.* (zool.) *Amphisbaena* sp., a kind of lizard; (myth.) amphisbaena.

anfiartrọṣi *f. indecl.* (med.) amphiarthrosis.

anfi·bio *adj.* amphibious; amphibian; (mil.) mezzi anfibi, amphibians; (fig.) untrustworthy; uncertain; *n.m.* (zool.) amphibian; (aeron.) amphibian plane; (neol.) waterproofed leather.

anfibolite *f.* (min.) actinolite.

anfi·bo-lo *adj.* ambiguous; (min.) hornblende; *adj.* (orn.) having outer toe reversible. **-logi·a** *f.* amphiboly; ambiguity. **-lo·gico** *adj.* ambiguous. (**-logicamẹnte** *adv.*)

anf-i·braco *m.* (prosod.) amphibrach. **-i·macro** *m.* (prosod.) cretic, amphimacer. **-iọsso** *m.* (zool.) Amphioxus, lancelet. **-i·podi** *m.pl.* (zool.) Amphipoda, sandhoppers.

anfigo·nico *adj.* (biol.) bisexual.

†an·fila *f.* See anfora.

†anfiṣbena *f.* See anfeṣibena.

anfiteatr-o *m.* amphitheatre. (**-ale** *adj.*)

Anfitriọne *pr.n.m.* (Gk. myth.) Amphitryon; (joc.) host, one who entertains on a lavish scale.

anfiziọn-i *m.pl.* (Gk. hist.) Amphictyons. **-i·a** *f.* Amphictyony.

an·fora *f.* amphora; jar; water-jar.

anfo·tero *adj.* (chem.) amphoteric.

anfratt-o *m.* winding path; sinuous crevice. **-uosità** *f.* sinuosity; *pl.* winding crevices, channels. **-uọso** *adj.* winding, sinuous.

an·gamo *m.* (naut.) dredge.

†angari·a *f.* See angheria.

angari-are [A 4] *tr.* to oppress, to torment; to vex, to harass; to over-tax. (**-amẹnto** *m.*) **-ato** *part. adj.* oppressed. (**-atọre** *m.* **-atrice** *f.*)

An·gela *pr.n.f.* Angela; see also under angelo[1].

ange·lic-o *adj.* angelic; (rel.) angelic (intellect, salutation, Doctor); (poet.) clear, pure, serene; *n.m.* l'—, the Dominican university in Rome; *f.* l'-a, the Augustinian library in Rome; *m.pl.* (eccl. hist.) Angelics (heretical sect); *f.pl.* (eccl. hist.) Angelicals of St Paul (nuns). **-a** *f. pr.n.f.* Angelica; (bot.) -a domestica, angelica, Holy Ghost, *A. archangelica*; -a selvatica, wild angelica, *A. silvestris*; pera -a, kind of pear. **-ale** *adj.* angelic, angelical. **-amẹnte** *adv.* angelically. **-ato** *adj.* in the form of an angel; angelic; idealized.

an·gelo[1] *m.* angel; cherub; darling; dead baby; suonare ad —, to ring (in a special way) for a child's funeral; è un — del Paradiso, he's a beautiful baby; cantare come un —, to sing divinely; è un — di bontà, he's as good as gold; he's the soul of kindness; essere l'— della casa, to be an angel about the house; — custode, guardian angel, (joc.) policeman; — cattivo, evil angel, devil; (numism.) angel; color d'—, pale pink; capelli d'—, a kind of pasta made in very fine strips; (mil.) angel-shot; (sport) fancy figure in skating; swallow-dive; (ichth.) monk fish, *Squatina squatina*.

An·gelo[2] *pr.n.m.* Angelo.

angeluṣdo·mini *m. indecl.* (rel.) angelus (prayer).

†an·gere *tr.* (poet.) to torment.

angevino *adj.* (hist.) Angevin, of the House of Anjou.

angheri·a *f.* oppression, tyranny; imposition; outrage; vexation; heavy taxation. (See also **angariare**.)

anghiere *m.* (naut.) boat-hook.

angin-a *f.* (med.) angina, quinsy; — pectoris, angina pectoris. **-oso** *adj.* suffering from angina; *n.m.* angina sufferer; sufferer from quinsy. (**-ọsa** *f.*)

angioino *adj.* See angevino.

An·giola *pr.n.f.* Angela; (agric.) kind of white grape.

an·giolo[1] *m.* See angelo[1].

an·giolo[2] *m.* (ichth.) See anciolo.

angiolọna *f.* kind of pear.

angiotomi·a *f.* (med.) angiotomy.

angiporto *m.* (poet.) blind alley; dead end; narrow lane.

anglesite *f.* (miner.) anglesite, native lead sulphate.

anglican-o *adj.* (rel.) Anglican; la Chiesa -a, the Anglican Church, the Church of England; *n.m.*, -a *f.* Anglican. **-iṣmo** *m.* Anglicanism.

an·glic-o *adj.* Anglo-Saxon; English. **-iṣmo** *m.* Anglicism. **-izzare** [A I] *tr.* to Anglicize. **-izzato** *part. adj.* Anglicized.

angl-o *pref.* Anglo; *n.m.pl.* (hist.) Angles. **-ofili·a** *f.* pro-English feeling. **-o·filo** *m.* anglophile. (**-o·fila** *f.*) **-ofobi·a** *f.* anglophobia, anti-English feeling. **-o·fobo** *m.* anglophobe. (**-o·foba** *f.*) **-o·mane** *m., f.* passionate admirer of the English. **-omani·a** *f.* Anglomania. **-osas·sone** *adj.* Anglo-Saxon; English-speaking (*n.m., f.*).

an·gol-o *m.* corner; nook; un posto d'—, a corner seat; centre, district: un — della città, a part of the town; — visuale, view point; un casa che fa —, a corner house; una strada che fa —, a street which is a turning off; (football) corner; calcio d'—, corner kick; (text.) — d'inserzione, shed; (geom.) angle; (mil.) — morto, safe retreat; — del tiro, angle of fire; — di elevazione, angle of elevation; — di depressione, angle of depression; (cinem.) — di presa, angle; *pl.* photo-fixers. **-are** *adj.* angular; pietra -are, corner-stone. (**-armẹnte** *adv.*) **-are** [A I s] *tr.* (cinem.; photog.) to take from a certain angle, to get an angle on. **-ato** *adj.* (cinem.; photog.) taken from a certain angle; (herald.) angled. **-aziọne** *f.* (cinem.; photog.) angle; (fig.) angle, point of view. **-ọso** *adj.* angular; (fig.) touchy. (**-osità** *f.*)

angọne *f.* (med.) globus hystericus, lump in the throat or feeling of suffocation during hysteria.

An·gora *pr.n.f.* (geog.) Ankara, Angora; gatto d'—, Persian cat; coniglio d'—, Angora rabbit; lana d'—, Angora wool.

†**angore** *m.* anguish; desire.

ango·sci-a *f.* anguish; pain; grief; travail; (med.) dyspnoea, distressed breathing. **-aménto** *m.* anguish. **-are** [A 3] *tr.* to distress, to grieve; to pain, to torment; *rfl.* to grieve; to torment oneself. **-ato** *part. adj.* anguished, stricken. **-oso** *adj.* grievous; painful; anguished. **-osaménte** *adv.* grievously; painfully.

angostura *f.* See **angustura**.

angrec-a *f.*, **-o** *m.* (bot.) *Angraecum fragrans*, tropical orchid whose leaves yield an aromatic infusion called Bourbon tea.

an·gu-e *m.* (zool.) *Anguis fragilis*, slow-worm, blindworm; (poet.) snake; (astron.) the constellation Draco. **-ichiomato**, **-icrinito** *adj.* (poet.) snake-haired, serpent-locked. **-iforme** *adj.* serpent-shaped, snake-like, anguiform.

anguella *f.* (ichth.) sand smelt, *Atherina hepsetus*.

anguill-a *f.* (ichth.) eel; (fig.) essere come un'—, sguizzare di mano come un'—, to be as slippery as an eel; (naut.) -e per ponti, deck girders; (paperm.) snailing. **-a·ia** *f.* eel-fishing ground. **-are** *adj.* eel-shaped; *n.m.* row of vines. **-eggiare** [A 3 c] *intr.* (*aux.* avere) to be evasive, to avoid committing oneself. **-iforme** *adj.* eel-shaped.

anguil·lula *f.* (zool.) eelworm.

anguina *f.* (bot.) snake or serpent melon, *Cucumis melo* var. *flexuosus*.

anguina·glia *f.* (poet.). See **anguinaia**.

anguina·ia *f.* (anat.) groin; (med.) tumour in the groin, bubo.

angui·neo *adj.* serpent-shaped, serpent-like.

angui·pede *adj.* (poet.) serpent-footed.

†**anguistara** *f.* carafe.

angu·ria *f.* (Lomb., Ven.) a kind of melon.

†**angustare** *tr.* to make narrow; *rfl.* to narrow.

angu·sti-a *f.* poverty, penury; want; anxiety; distress, pain, trouble; — di tempo, want of time; essere nelle -e, to be in difficulties. **-are** [A 4] *tr.* to distress; to afflict; *rfl.* to distress oneself; to be worried. **-ato** *part. adj.* worried; afflicted; anguished. (**-atóre** *m.* **-atrice** *f.*) **-oso** *adj.* worrying; annoying, aggravating. **-osaménte** *adv.* annoyingly; so as to cause worry or distress.

angust-o *adj.* narrow; limited; inadequate; petty; mean, stingy. **-aménte** *adv.* meanly; in a limited or petty way.

angustur-a *f.* (pharm.) angustura, bark of *Galipea cusparia*; — falsa, bark of *Strychnos nux vomica*. **-ina** *f.* (chem.) angusturine.

a·nice *m.* (bot.) anise, aniseed, *Pimpinella anisum*; — stellato, star anise, fruit of Asiatic aniseed-tree, *Illicium anisatum*.

anicino *m.* aniseed-ball.

anidr-ide *f.* (chem.) anhydride; — carbonica, carbon dioxide. **-ite** *f.* (miner.) anhydrite.

a·nidro *adj.* anhydrous.

anil, anile¹ *m.* (bot.) indigo plant, *Indigofera tinctoria*.

†**anile²** *adj.* like an old woman, senile.

anilina *f.* (chem.) aniline.

a·nim-a *f.* soul, spirit, breath of life; l'— del mondo, the Spirit that breathes o'er the world; esalar l'—, render l'— a Dio, to give up the ghost; la buon'— di mio padre, mio padre, buon'—, my father, God rest him; un'— buona, a kindly soul; darsi all —, to turn to spiritual things; essere l'— dannata di, to have an evil influence upon, to bring about the downfall of; to be the confederate, or follower, of (for evil designs); non c'è — viva, there's not a soul here; è una fatica che mi leva l'—, it's a soul-destroying job; dannarsi l'—, see **dannare**; conscience: aver sull'—, to have on one's conscience; (joc.) mettersi all'—, to account for, to be responsible for, to polish off; aver qualcuno sull'—, to be continually pestered by someone; cavare l'— a, to pester, to be a nuisance to; to nag; to get on the nerves of; giocare l'—, to bet one's last halfpenny; dare anche l'—, to give everything; mangiarsi l'—, rodersi l'—, to torment oneself, to eat one's heart out; essere un'— in pena, to be in great distress; reggere l'— coi denti, to be drained of strength; ci s'è messo — e corpo, he set to it heart and soul; era Carlo in corpo e —, it was Charles in person; essere corpo e — con, to be hand in glove with; esser l'— di, to be the life and soul of; ghost, spectre; person; è un'— lunga, he's a tall chap; *pl.* inhabitants; cura d'-e, cure of souls; stato d'-e, register of population; emotions, feeling, heart; — mia! my love!, dear heart!; passar l'—, arrivare all'—, to go to (one's) heart, to pierce (one's) heart; un bene dell'—, heartfelt love; courage; animation, liveliness, zest; senz'—, lifeless; leggere con —, to read with animation; centre, core; heart (of wood); kernel; seed; (of a football) bladder; (of an umbrella) shank; (eng.) core (in foundry); web (of rail); — metallica, mandrel; (bldg.) — delle scale, newel (of a staircase); (mil.) — di un cannone, tube; ad — liscia, smooth-bore; ad — rigata, rifle-bore; (mus.) sound-post (of violin). †**-ale** *adj.* spiritual. **-ella** *f. dim.* of **anima**; sweetbread; (eng.) sucker, clack, flap-valve (of a pump); core or stiffening of a cloth button. **-etta** *f. dim.* of **anima**; (liturg.) pall. **-ista** *m.* (eng.) core-maker.

animadversióne *f.* animadversion; †attention, concentration.

animal-e¹ *m.* animal; creature, dumb creature; brute, beast; (fig.) blockhead, imbecile; †*pl.* animai, creatures; *adj.* animal; physical; regno —, animal kingdom; funzioni -i, animal functions, physical functions. **-eri·a** *f.* bestial behaviour; collection of animals. **-ésco** *adj.* (*m.pl.* **-éschi**) animal; istinto -esco, animal instinct; bestial; vita -esca, bestial existence. (**-escaménte** *adv.*) **-étto** *m. dim.* of **animale**; (scient.) animalcule. **-iere** *m.* (paint.) animal-painter. **-ità** *f.* animality; animalism. **-óne** *m. augm.* of **animale**; dunderhead.

†**animale²** *adj.* See under **anima**.

animalizz-are [A 1] *tr.* to convert into animal substance, to animalize. **-ato** *part. adj.* animalized (**-azióne** *f.*)

anim-are [A 1 S] *tr.* to animate; to quicken; to enliven; to brighten; to give life to, to inspire, to encourage; — il commercio, to promote trade; (mech.) to actuate; to fan: un forte vento -ò le fiamme, a strong wind fanned the blaze; *intr.* (*aux.* avere) to develop, to come on well (of plants); *rfl.* to get excited, to become animated; to grow cheerful; to grow lively; to take courage. **-a·bile** *adj.* capable of being animated. **-ante** *part. adj.* animating. (**-atézza** *f.*) **-ativo** *adj.* animating, animative. **-ato** *part. adj.* animated; lively, sprightly; vivacious; disposed; animate; frequented; containing a core: bastone -ato, sword-stick; (mus.) with increased speed and animation; allegro -ato, quicker than allegro. (**-ataménte** *adv.*) **-atóre** *m.* animator; leading spirit; (cinem.) animator of cartoons; *adj.* animating, enlivening. (**-atrice** *f.*) **-azióne** *f.* animation; life, activity.

animavversióne *f.* See **animadversione**.

animella *f.* See under **anima**.

anim-ismo *m.* (philos.) animism. **-ista** *m.* animist. **-i·stico** *adj.* animistic.

animista *m.* (eng.). See under **anima**.

a·nimo *m.* mind; heart; nature; inclination, tendency; intention; courage; stato d'—, mood; avere in — di, to have a good mind to, to intend to; mettersi in — di, to make up one's mind to; aprire l'—, to speak frankly; aprire l'— a, to confide in; vi dirò l'— mio, I will open you my opinion, I will open my heart to you; guadagnarsi l'— di, to get into the good graces of; alienarsi l'— di, to fall out of favour with; avere — a, to have the courage to; non mi basta l'—, I haven't the courage; farsi —, to take heart; animo!, courage!; perdersi d'—, to lose heart; d'— gentile, of a kindly disposition; civilized, gentle; mal —, animosity, ill-will; star di buon —, to be serene; star di buon —, willingly, cheerfully; mettersi l'— in pace, to console oneself; to resign oneself; me lo diceva l'—, I had a presentiment; corse contro di lui con — di ucciderlo, he ran towards him intending to kill him; (leg.) intention.

animós-o *adj.* courageous, bold; spirited; fiery; ardent; †hostile. **-aménte** *adv.* with spirit; bravely; †with animus. **-ità** *f.* animosity, animus, rancour; †courage.

ani·mula *f.* (poet.) little soul, dear soul.

ani·one *m.* (chem.) anion. **-o·nico** *adj.* anionic.

anisétta *f.* aniseed cordial.

aniso·trop-o *adj.* anisotropic. **-i·a** *f.* anisotropy, allotropy.

a·nitra *f.* See **anatra**.

anitrella *f.* (herald.) duck.

anitrina *f.* (bot.) duckweed, *Lemna*.

anitrire [D 2] and derivs. See **nitrire**.

Ann-a *pr.n.f.* Anna, Anne. **-étta** *f.* Annie, Nan.

annacqu-are [A 6] *tr.* to water, to dilute; to temper, to moderate; to soften. **-aménto** *m.* watering. **-ata** *f.* sprinkling; light shower. **-ati·ccio** *adj.* watered down, watery; (paint.) soft, watery (tint). **-ato** *part. adj.* watered; diluted; weak; softened; (fig.) insincere; milk-and-water. (**-atóre** *m.* **-atrice** *f.*) **-atura** *f.* watering; (fig.) watered-down version.

annaffi-are [A 4] *tr.* to water, to sprinkle, to wet. **-aménto** *m.* watering,

annaffi-are (*cont.*) sprinkling. **-ato** *part. adj.* watered, sprinkled, wet. **-atoio** *m.* watering-can. (**-atore** *m.* **-atrice** *f.*) **-atura** *f.* watering, sprinkling.

†**annale** *adj.* annual; *n.m.* yearly tax.

annal-i *m.pl.* annals. **-ista** *m.* annalist.

†**annasare** *vb.* See **annusare**.

annasp-are [A I] *tr.* (text.) to wind (thread) on a reel; to reel; (fig.) to make a mess of; *intr.* (*aux.* avere) to grope blindly; to gesticulate wildly; to paw the air; to cudgel one's brains, to puzzle in vain. (**-amento** *m.*) **-atoio** *m.* (text.) reeler, reeling machine. (**-atura** *f.*) **-icare** [A 2 s] *intr.* (*aux.* avere) to become confused, to be tongue-tied. (**-ìo** *m.*) **-o** *m.* see aspo. **-one** *m.* busybody.

annat-a[1] *f.* year, the space of a year; the events of a year; numbers of a periodical published in a year; crop; income; le **-e** magre, the lean years; una buon'**—**, a good year, a good crop.

annata[2] *f.* See **adnata**.

annebbi-are [A 4 c] *tr.* to darken, to obscure; to cloud; to dim; to befog; to blight; *rfl.* to be obscured; to become foggy; (of sight) to grow dim; *intr.* (*aux.* essere) to become foggy (of atmosphere); (of plants) to be blighted. **-amento** *m.* obscuring, dimming; clouding of eyesight; black-out (esp. at high altitudes). **-ato** *part. adj.* obscured, dim; foggy; vague; clouded; viso **-ato**, countenance clouded with displeasure; (Tusc.) pale, white.

anneg-are[1] [A 2 c] *tr.* to drown; (bldg.) — nel calcestruzzo, to bury in concrete, to set in concrete; *intr.* (*aux.* essere) to drown, to be drowned; stare per —, to be drowning; *rfl.* to drown oneself. **-amento** *m.* drowning; submersion; ruin; — del carburatore, flooding of the carburettor. **-ato** *part. adj.* drowned; (naut.) bastimento **-ato**, a ship hull-down; *n.m.* drowned man. (**-ata** *f.*)

annegare[2] [A 2] and derivs. See **abnegare**.

anneghitt-ire [D 2] *tr.* to make lazy; to enervate; *intr.* (*aux.* essere), *rfl.* to grow lazy; to become inert. (**-imento** *m.*) **-ito** *part. adj.* enervated.

annegr-are [A I], **-ire** [D 2], **annerare** [A I c]. See **annerire**.

annerell-o *m. dim.* of anno, q.v.; (iron.) ha i suoi **-i**, he's not so young as he was.

anner-ire [D 2] *tr.* to blacken; to darken; to tarnish; il sole **-isce** la pelle, the sun gives one a tan; (fig.) to denigrate, to blacken; *intr.* (*aux.* essere), *rfl.* to become black; to grow dark; to become tarnished. **-imento** *m.* blackening; darkening. **-ito** *part. adj.* blackened; darkened; dark; **-ito** dal sole, sunburnt, tanned. **-itura** *f.* darkening; (shoe)-blacking.

annessione *f.* See under **annesso**.

annessite *f.* (med.) adnexitis, annexitis, inflammation of the uterine appendages.

anness-o *part.* of **annettere**, q.v.; *adj.* annexed; attached; conjoined; included, enclosed; *n.m.* annexe; outbuilding; appendage; (leg.) **-i** e connessi, appurtenances; (anat.) appendant, appendage, accessory part (of an organ). **-a** *f.* letter enclosed, enclosure. **-ione** *f.* annexation; addition. **-ionista** *m.* (pol.) annexationist.

annestare [A I] and derivs. See **innestare**.

anne·ttere [C 19] *tr.* to annex; to attach; to join; to enclose; — importanza, to attribute importance.

annetto *m.* See under **anno**.

Anni·bale *pr.n.m.* Hannibal.

annicchiare [A 4] and derivs. See **rannicchiare**.

annichil-are [A I s], **-ire** [D 2] *tr.* to annihilate; to destroy; to crush; to humble, to debase; *rfl.* to be annihilated; to be humiliated; to humble oneself, to cringe. **-amento**, **-imento** *m.* annihilation, destruction; humiliation. **-ato**, **-ito** *part. adj.* annihilated; destroyed; crushed. (**-atore** *m.* **-atrice** *f.* **-azione** *f.*)

annidare [A I] *tr.* to find a nook for; (fig.) to harbour, to cherish, to entertain; *rfl.* to nest; to nestle; to hide, to lie concealed.

annient-are [A I] *tr.* to annihilate; to defeat; to bring to nought; to destroy; to exterminate; *rfl.* (fig.) to humble oneself, to prostrate oneself; to come to nothing. (**-amento** *m.* **-ato** *part. adj.*)

†**anniffare** *intr.* to sulk.

†**annisti·a** *f.* See **amnistia**.

annitrire [D 2] and derivs. See **nitrire**.

anniversa·rio *adj., n.m.* anniversary; birthday; (liturg.) anniversary (requiem mass).

†**annizzare** *vb.* See **aizzare**.

ann-o *m.* year; (sometimes equiv. of **annata**: un — di stipendio, a year's salary, un buon —, a good harvest, a good year's work); (Tusc.) last year; — andai a Torino, last year I went to Turin; — per —, year after year; — bisestile, leap-year; — luce, light year; — santo, holy year; (fig.) mi tocca aspettare un — santo, I shall have to wait till doomsday; — emergente, year from which an era is counted; tredici mesi all'—, all the year round, continually; il primo dell'—, Capo d'—, New Year's Day; in capo all'—, at the end of the year; (comm.) — di gestione, — finanziario, financial year; *pl.* age; quanti **-i** hai?, how old are you?; pieno d'**-i**, old; ha trentacinque **-i** sonati, he is a good thirty-five; i verdi **-i**, youth; è morto nel fior degli **-i**, he was cut off in his prime; gli **-i** cadenti, old age; levarsi gli **-i**, to keep one's age back; sono cent'**-i** che non lo vedo, it's years since I've seen him; mi par mill'**-i** di tornare, I am longing to return; (joc.) **-i** domini, years and years ago; innanzi gli **-i**, before the proper time; (sport) un tre anni, a three-year-old (colt, filly). **-etto** *m. dim.* of anno; about a year, rather less than a year; (joc.) ha i suoi **-etti**, he's getting on in years. **-oso** *adj.* full of years, aged, elderly; hoary; una questione **-osa**, an age-old problem. **-osità** *f.* age (of plants); life-span (of animals).

ànno variant form of **hanno**, for which see **avere**.

annobil-ire [D 2] *tr.* to ennoble; to adorn; *intr.* (*aux.* essere) to become ennobled. **-imento** *m.* ennobling. (**-ito** *part. adj.*)

annoccare [A 2] *tr.* (bot.) to propagate (plants) by layering.

annod-are [A I] *tr.* to knot; to tie, to bind; — le scarpe, to tie up one's shoes; — relazioni, to form connexions; — un affare, to clinch an affair; *rfl.* to form a knot; to get entangled; gli si **-ò** la lingua in bocca, he was tongue-tied; il pianto gli si **-ò** in gola, he had a lump in his throat (with emotion). **-amento** *m.* knotting; knot; junction. **-ato** *part. adj.* knotted; tied; matrimonio **-ato**, marriage concluded, marriage arranged; (herald.) nowy. **-atore** *m.* (text.) knotter. **-atura** *f.* knotting; knot; joints (of body). (**-azione** *f.*) **-icchiare** [A 4] *tr.* to tie in little knots.

annoi-are [A 4] *tr.* to bore; to annoy; to tease, to trouble; to weary; *rfl.* to be bored; to be annoyed; to get weary; to get fed-up; **-arsi** da morire, to be bored to death. **-amento** *m.* boredom; annoyance. **-ato** *part. adj.* bored; annoyed; wearied; fed-up. (**-atore** *m.* **-atrice** *f.*)

annominazione *f.* play on words, pun, anagram.

annon-a *f.* food supply (of a municipality); supply of wheat; ufficio dell'—, food office, victualling-board. **-a·rio** *adj.* pertaining to provisions; leggi **-arie**, victualling laws; carta **-aria**, ration card.

annoso *adj.* See under **anno**.

annot-are [A I] *tr.* to annotate; to note, to jot down; to book. **-ato** *part. adj.* annotated; noted. **-atore** *m.* annotator. (**-atrice** *f.*) **-azione** *f.* annotation; entry; **-azione** in calce, footnote; (comm.) registration of mortgage or other encumbrance on National Debt certificate.

annottare [A I] *impers. intr.* (*aux.* essere) to grow dark; (of night) to draw on.

annottolare [A I s] *tr.* (Tusc.) to latch (a door).

†**annovale** *adj.* See **annuale**.

An·nover *pr.n.m.* (geog.) Hanover (prov.); *pr.n.f.* Hanover (town).

annover-are [A I s] *tr.* to enumerate; to include, to comprehend; to class; to number, to count. (**-a·bile** *adj.* **-amento** *m.* **-ante** *part. adj.*) **-ato** *part. adj.* enumerated; included. (**-atore** *m.* **-atrice** *f.*)

annual-e *adj.* annual, yearly; year-long; (bot.) annual; *n.m.* anniversary (esp. of public festivity). **-ità** *f.* salary, income; yearly instalment; annuity. **-mente** *adv.* annually, yearly; from year to year.

annua·rio *m.* year-book; annual; directory; list; †*adj.* annual.

†**annubilare** *vb.* See **annuvolare**.

annuenza *f.* See under **annuire**.

annugolare [A I s] (pop.). See **annuvolare**.

annu-ire [D 2] *intr.* (*aux.* avere, *prep.* a) to nod one's head in agreement; to assent, to agree; to consent (to). **-ente** *part. adj.* in agreement, consenting. **-enza** *f.* consent; agreement. **-ito** *part. adj.* agreed to, agreed upon.

annuità *f.* annuity.

annull-are [A I] *tr.* to annul; to nullify; to cancel; to annihilate; to undo; to undermine the authority of; to wipe, to wash (of tape recordings); (leg.) to annul, to cancel, to quash, to avoid, to declare void; *recip. rfl.* to cancel out, to cancel each other. **-a·bile** *adj.* annullable; (leg.) voidable. (**-abilità** *f.*) **-amento** *m.* annulment; cancellation. (**-ante** *part. adj.* **-ativo** *adj.*) **-ato** *part. adj.* annulled; cancelled; undone; undermined; (rugby) calcio **-ato**, touch-down. **-atore** *m.* annuller; (mech.) clearer, clearing lever; **-atore** tabulazione, tabulator clearance lever. (**-atrice** *f.* **-azione** *f.*) **-o** *m.* (admin.) cancellation (of a stamp).

annumer-are [A I s] *tr.* to enumerate; to include, to class. (-**ato** *part. adj.* -**azione** *f.*)

annunciare [A 3] and derivs. See **annunziare**.

annunzi-are [A 4] *tr.* to announce; to proclaim; to herald; to communicate; to indicate; to foretell, to prophesy; — sui giornali, to advertise. (-**amento** *m.*) -**ata** *f.* (eccl.) Our Lady of the Annunciation; her feast, church, picture or statue; (hist.) name of the highest Italian Order of Chivalry, instituted in 1362 by Amedeo VI of Savoy and renewed in 1515; collare dell'-ata, emblem of the Order of the Annunziata, member of the Order. (-**ante** *part. adj.*) -**ato** *part. adj.* announced; proclaimed; communicated; foretold; advertised. -**atore** *m.* harbinger; advertiser; (radio) wireless announcer; (eccl.) angelo -atore, angel of the Annunciation. (-**atrice** *f.*) -**azione** *f.* (eccl.) Annunciation; Lady Day (25 March).

annun·zio *m.* announcement; notice; information; presage; communication, news; — pubblicitario, advertisement.

an·nuo *adj.* annual, yearly.

annus-are [A I] *tr., abs.* to sniff, to smell, to suspect, to surmise; to nose out, to discover; (colloq.) fare — un pugno ad uno, to shake one's fist in a person's face; — tabacco, to take snuff; — una presa, to take a pinch of snuff. -**ata** *f.* sniff. (-**ato** *part. adj.* -**atore** *m.* -**atrice** *f.*) -**o** *m.* smell, sniff.

annuvol-are [A I s] *tr.* to darken, to cloud; to obscure; *intr.* (*aux.* essere), *rfl.* to grow cloudy; to darken; to become gloomy. -**amento** *m.* darkening; cloudiness; clouding over; mass of clouds; (meteor.) -amento notturno, night clouding. -**ato** *part. adj.* clouded; darkened; gloomy.

an-o *m.* (anat.) anus. -**ale** *adj.* anal; pinna -ale, anal fin.

ano·bio *m.* (ent.) *Anobium*, death-watch beetle.

ano·dino, anodino *adj., n.m.* (med.) anodyne.

a·n-odo *m.* (electr.) anode. -**o·dico** *adj.* anodic, anode; ossidazione -odica, anodizing; spazio -odico, anolyte.

†**anodone** *m.* (myth.) toothless serpent.

anodonta *f.* (zool.) freshwater mussel, swan mussel.

ano·fele *m., f.* (ent.) *Anopheles*, mosquito.

ano·ia *f.* (med.) madness; (philos.) irrationality.

anolita *m.* (electr.) anolyte.

ano·mal-o *adj.* anomalous; (leg.) erede —, an heir who is devoid of legal titles and is not an heir-at-law. -**i·a** *f.* anomaly; defect. -**i·stico** *adj.* (astron.) anomalistic.

anona *f.* (bot.) custard-apple, *Annona*.

ano·nim-o *adj.* anonymous; conservare l'—, to remain incognito; (leg.) società -a, limited company (in Italy the limited company is the only variety); *n.m.* one who is anonymous; l'Anonimo, the anonymous author of the MS. on which Manzoni's *I Promessi Sposi* is purported to be based. -**a** *f.* (leg.) limited company. -**ato** *m.*, -**i·a** *f.* anonymity.

anopisto·grafo *m.* MS. written on one side only of the papyrus or parchment.

anoplote·rio *m.* (geol.) anoplothere.

anopluri *m.pl.* (ent.) Anoplura, sucking lice.

anor·chide *adj.* (med.) without testicles.

anoressi·a *f.* (med.) anorexy, want of appetite.

anorga·nico *adj.* See **inorganico**.

anormal-e *adj.* abnormal; (euphem.) homosexual. -**ità** *f.* abnormality.

anortite *f.* (min.) anorthite.

anosmi·a *f.* (med.) anosmia, loss of the sense of smell.

ans-a¹ *f.* pot-handle; handle; (fig.) pretext, occasion, loophole; (anat.) loop (of intestine, nerve); (aeron.) — del carrello, under-carriage strut; (astron.) ansa, an end of Saturn's rings; (geog.) bend, loop (of river); creek. -**ato** *adj.* with handles.

Ansa² *pr.n.f.* (hist.) Hanse.

ans-are [A I] *intr.* (*aux.* avere) to pant; to gasp; to breathe heavily. -**amento** *m.* panting, gasping. -**ante** *part. adj.* panting, breathless; out of breath.

ansato *adj.* See under **ansa¹**.

ansea·tico *adj.* (geog., hist.) Hanseatic.

†**an·ser-a** *f.* goose. †-**ino** *adj.* pelle -ina, goose-flesh.

†**an·seri** *m.pl.* dried chestnuts.

an·si-a *f.* eager desire, longing, impatience; anxiety; vivere in —, to be on tenterhooks, to be anxious. (†-**ato** *adj.*) -**età** *f.* anxiety, trepidation. -**etato** *adj.* (D'Annunzio) filled with longing. -**oso** *adj.* eagerly awaiting, longing; anxious; wistful; desirous. -**osamente** *adv.* longingly; anxiously; desirously.

†**ansiare** *intr.* See **ansare**.

an·sim-a *f.*, -**o** *m.* shortness of breath. -**are** [A I s] *intr.* (*aux.* avere) to be short of breath. -**ante** *part. adj.* panting, gasping.

†**an·sio** *adj.* anxious; panting.

ansioso *adj.* See under **ansia**.

an·sito *m.* troubled breathing; gasping, panting.

anta¹ (dial. N. Italy) shutter (of a window); window-frame; door-frame; panel; ante scorrevoli, sliding doors.

anta² *f.*, *usu. pl.* (archit.) anta, kind of pilaster used in Greek and Roman architecture.

anta³ *m. indecl.* termination of numbers from 40 to 90, e.g. quaranta, etc.; (provb.) dagli anta in là mi dol qui e mi dol là; the story is told of the second wife of Alessandro Manzoni who on reaching the age of forty exclaimed: 'Uhi, Lisander! dervi (apro) l'anta'; and he replied, 'E mi serri (chiudo) la gelosia', cf. **anta¹**.

anta·cido *adj., n.m.* antacid.

antagon-ismo *m.* antagonism; rivalry; contest. -**ista** *m.* antagonist; adversary; rival; opponent; (anat.) antagonist, antagonistic muscle. -**i·stico** *adj.* (anat.) antagonistic.

antar·ti·co *adj.* (geog.) antarctic. -**de** *f.* (geog.) Antarctic.

antar·trico *adj.* (med.) anti-arthritic.

ante¹ *pref.* See **anti²**.

†**ante²** *adv.* before.

ante-ce·dere [C 19] *intr.* (*aux.* avere) to precede (in time). -**cedente** *part. adj.* preceding; previous, prior, antecedent; foregoing. -**cedentemente** *adv.* previously. -**cedenza** *f.* antecedence; priority. -**cessore** *m.* predecessor; ancestor. (-**cessora** *f.*)

antecursore *m.* See **anticursore**, under **anti²**.

antedetto *adj.* already mentioned, aforesaid.

†**antedire** *tr.* to foretell.

antefatto *m.* antecedent facts; previous history; all that has occurred before a play begins.

antefissa *f.* (archit.) antefix, antefixum; ornamented tile at top of cornice or eaves.

anteguerra *m.* pre-war period; la letteratura d'—, pre-war literature; *adj. indecl.* pre-war; prezzi —, pre-war prices.

antela *f.* See **antera**.

ante·lice *m.* (anat.) antihelix.

ante·lio *m.* (phys.) anthelion.

antelmin·tico *adj., n.m.* (med.) vermifuge.

ante-lucano *adj.* antelucan; preceding the dawn; splendori -lucani, first light. -**lunare** *adj.* antelunar; giorni -lunari, the first three days of the new moon.

antemar·cia *adv., adj. indecl.* (pol. hist.) previous to the march on Rome.

anteme·tico *adj.* See **antiemetico**, under **anti¹**.

antemettere [C 20] See **premettere**.

ante·mide *f.* (bot.) common camomile, *Anthemis nobilis*.

antemurale *m.* (hist.; mil. archit.) antemural, barbican, advanced defence work; (naut.) breakwater, sea wall.

antenat-o *m.* ancestor, forefather, progenitor. (-**a** *f.*)

†**antenito·rio** *m.* (pharm.) sublimation dish.

antenn-a *f.* (naut.) yard (on lateen-rigged ship); (zool.) antenna, feeler; (poet.) ship; lance; (radio) aerial; — interna, indoor aerial; (bldg.) spar, scaffolding standard; (electr. eng.) trolley pole. -**ale** *adj.* (naut.) towards the yard; *n.m.* (naut.) head (of a lateen sail, where it is attached to the yard). -**ato** *adj.* (zool.) provided with antennae.

Antenora *pr.n.f.* Antenora, the third division of Cocytus, the ninth circle of Dante's Inferno, named from Antenor of Troy who, according to medieval tradition, betrayed his city to the Greeks.

antenori *m.pl.* Paduans, inhabitants of Padua.

antenotato *adj.* already noted.

antepenul·timo *adj.* See **antipenultimo**, under **anti²**.

ante-porre [B 21] *tr.* to place before; to put at the head; to prefer; to give precedence to. (-**posto** *part. adj.*)

anteprima *f.* private view; (cinem.) preview.

anter-a, an·ter-a *f.* (bot.) anther. -**i·dio** *m.* (bot.) antheridium.

anterior-e *adj.* preceding; previous; prior; former; anterior; front, fore; (gramm.) futuro —, future perfect. -**ità** *f.* priority; precedence. -**mente** *adv.* formerly, previously; -mente a, prior to.

antero·tico *adj.* (med.) anaphrodisiac.

antescritto *adj.* aforementioned.

antesi *f.* (bot.) opening of flowers.

antesignano *m.* (Rom. hist.) standard-bearer; (fig.) leader, forerunner, apostle.

anteversiọne *f.* (med.) anteflexion of the uterus.

antevișiọne *f.* (cinem.) preview.

anti-[1] *pref.* against, counter, anti; *adj. indecl.* anti, opposed; anti-Fascist. **-abbagliante** *adj.* anti-dazzle; faro -abbagliante, dipped headlamp. **-a·cido** *adj.* antacid; acid-proof; *n.m.* antacid. **-ae·reo** *adj.* anti-aircraft; difesa -aerea, air-raid defence. **-alcalino** *adj.* alkali-proof; anti-alkaline. **-alcoo·lico** *adj.* teetotal, abstinent, abstemious. **-alo** *adj. indecl.* (photog.) anti-halation. **-alonicità** *f.* (photog.) antihalation. **-appannante** *adj.* non-fogging, anti-fogging (of glass, etc.). **-artri·tico** *adj.* anti-arthritic. **-asse** *adj. indecl.* (pol. hist.) anti-Axis. **-bac·chico**, **-bacchi·o** *m.* (prosod.) antibacchius. **-bilioso** *adj.* antibilious. **-bio·tic-o** *adj.*, *n.m.* antibiotic. **-bọmba** *adj. indecl.* rifugio -bomba, air-raid shelter. **-borghẹse** *adj. indecl.* anti-bourgeois, anti-middle-class. **-borsẹggio** *adj. indecl.* pickpocket proof. **-britan·nico** *adj.* anti-British. **-calca·reo** *m.* water-softener. **-cancerọso** *adj.* anticarcinomatous. **-cariọso** *adj.* anticarious. **-carrello** *m.* (of a lathe) apron. **-carro** *adj. indecl.* (mil.) anti-tank; cannone -carro, anti-tank gun. **-catarrale** *adj.* anticatarrhal. **-catto·lico** *adj.* anticatholic. **-ciclọne** *m.* anticyclone. **-ciclo·nico** *adj.* anticyclonic. **-clericale** *adj.*, *n.m.* anti-clerical. **-clericalișmo** *m.* anti-clericalism. **-clinale** *adj.* (geol.) anticlinal; piega -clinale, anticline. **-concettivo**, **-concezionale** *adj.*, *n.m.* contraceptive. **-congelante** *adj.*, *n.m.* anti-freeze. **-corpo** *m.* antibody. **-corrosivo** *adj.* anti-corrosive; *n.m.* corrosion-proofing. **-costituzionale** anti-constitutional. (**-costituzionalmente** *adv.*) **-cristo** *m.* Antichrist. **-cristiano** *adj.* antichristian. **-cristianẹșimo** *m.* antichristianism. **-cri·tica** *f.* counter-criticism. **-cri·tico** *adj.* contrary to the laws of criticism; *n.m.* critic of a critic. **-crittoga·mico** *adj.* fungicidal; *n.m.* fungicide. **-crollo** *adj. indecl.* 'quake-proof. **-crusca** *f.* (lit. hist.) l'—, the work of P. Beni against the Crusca Academy. **-cruscante** *adj.*, *n.m.* (lit. hist.) contrary to, opponent of, the Crusca Academy. **-cuore** *m.* heartburn, cardialgy; tumour in horses near the heart. **-dat·tilo** *m.* (prosod.) anapaest. **-deflagrante** *adj.* (of electric motor, etc.) flame-proof, explosion-proof. **-democra·tico** *adj.* anti-democratic. **-derapante** *adj.* see **-sdrucciolẹvole**. **-detonante** *adj.*, *n.m.* (motor.) anti-knock. **-diabe·tico** *adj.* anti-diabetic. **-diarro·ico** *adj.* anti-diarrhoea. **-difte·rico** *adj.* anti-diphtheria. **-distorsiọne** *f.* (teleph.) equalizing, compensation. **-eme·tico** *adj.*, *n.m.* antemetic. **-emorra·gico** *adj.*, *n.m.* haemostatic, styptic. **-emorroidale** *adj.* relieving piles. **-fascișmo** *m.* anti-Fascism. **-fascista** *adj.*, *n.m.*, *f.* anti-Fascist. **-febbrile** *adj.*, *n.m.* antifebrile, febrifuge. **-fecondativo** *adj.*, *n.m.* contraceptive. **-federale** *adj.* anti-federal. (**-federalișmo** *m.* **-federalista** *m.*) **-flogọși** *f.* treatment of inflammation. **-flogi·stico** *adj.* anti-phlogistic, counteracting inflammation. **-foni·a** *f.* see under **antifona**. **-fono** *m.* ear-plug. **-fosso** *m.* (mil.) ditch dug out in front of another. **-fra·stico** *adj.* see under **antifrasi**. **-frizione** *f.* (mech.) anti-friction; *adj. indecl.* metallo -frizione, Babbitt metal. **-furto** *adj. indecl.* burglar-proof, thief-proof; dispositivo -furto, burglar alarm. **-galat·tico** *adj.* antigalactic. **-gàs** *adj. indecl.* anti-gas, gas-proof; maschera -gas, gas-mask. **-gelo** *adj.*, *n.m.* anti-freeze. **-ghiac·cio** *m.* (aeron.) de-icer. **-gie·nico** *adj.* unhygienic. **-guerrẹsco** *adj.* anti-war. **-infortuni·stica** *f.* accident prevention. **-invecchiante** *m.* (chem.) age resister (added to rubber). **-lambda** *m.* (typ.) crow's-feet, French quotes. **-liberale** *adj.* anti-Liberal; reactionary. (**-liberalișmo** *m.*) **-logaritmo** *m.* anti-logarithm, anti-log. **-logi·a** *f.* antilogy. **-machiavellișmo** *m.* anti-Machiavellism. **-mala·rico** *adj.* anti-malarial. **-manifesto** *m.* counter-manifesto. **-miașma·tico** *adj.* anti-miasmatic, anti-malarial. **-militare** *adj.* anti-military. (**-militarișmo** *m.* **-militarista** *m.* **-militari·stico** *adj.*) **-ministeriale** *adj.* anti-ministerial. **-monar·chico** *adj.* antimonarchical. **-nazionale** *adj.* anti-national. **-ncendi** *adj. indecl.* fire-proof; autopompa -ncendi, fire truck. **-nefri·tico** *adj.* antinephritic. **-neuro·tico** *adj.* anti-neurotic. **-nevral·gico** *adj.* anti-neuralgia, pain-relieving. **-odontal·gico** *adj.* relieving toothache. **-ofi·dico** *adj.* antidote for snake-bite. **-ora·rio** *adj.* anticlockwise, counterclockwise. **-ossidante** *adj.* (chem.) anti-oxidation; *n.m.* anti-oxidizer. **-pal·lage** *f.* (rhet.) interchange of cases. **-papa** *m.* (rel. hist.) antipope. **-papale** *adj.* antipapal. **-papista** *m.* antipapist. **-parlamentare** *adj.* anti-parliamentary. **-patriot·tico** *adj.* anti-patriotic; unpatriotic. (**-patriottișmo** *m.*) **-peristalsi** *f. indecl.* antiperistaltic motion. (**-peristal·tico** *adj.*) **-pestilenziale** *adj.* antipestilential, anti-plague. **-petrarchișmo** *m.* (lit. hist.) reaction against the imitators of Petrarch. (**-petrarchista** *m.*) **-piega**, **-pieghe** *adj. indecl.* crease-resisting, uncrushable. **-piọmbo** *m.* (motor.) lead scavenger. **-pirina** *f.* (chem.) anti-pyrin, phenazone. **-pire·tico** *adj.* anti-pyretic. **-poe·tico** *adj.* (aesthet.) not conducive to poetry; commonplace. **-poli·tico** *adj.* anti-political. **-pso·rico** *adj.* anti-psoric, remedial against the itch. **-pu·trido** *adj.* anti-putrefactive. **-rab·bico** *adj.* anti-rabies. **-rachi·tico** *adj.* anti-rachitic, preventive of rickets. **-religiọso** *adj.* anti-religious. **-reuma·tico** *adj.* anti-rheumatic. **-riflettente** *adj.* (of a lens) reflexion-preventing. **-rolli·o** *m.* (aeron.) anti-rolling. **-rombo** *m.* sound-deadening; deadening mixture (paint for applying to a motor-car). **-rotazione** *f.* counter-rotation. **-rug·gine** *adj. indecl.* rustproof; rustless, stainless; *n.m.* rust preventer, rustproofing. **-schẹggia** *adj. indecl.* anti-splinter, non-splinterable. **-schiavista** *m.* abolitionist. **-scorbu·tico** *adj.* antiscorbutic. **-scottante** *adj.* (rubber indust.) anti-scorch. **-scriccholi·o** *m.* (mech.) antisqueak (e.g. for car bodies). **-sdrucciolẹvole** *adj.* anti-slip; (of a tyre) anti-skid. **-semita** *m.* anti-Semite. **-semi·tico** *adj.* anti-Semitic. **-semitișmo** *m.* anti-Semitism. **-sepsi** *f. indecl.* antisepsis. **-sepsia** *f.* (pharm.) disinfectant. **-set·tico** *adj.* antiseptic; disinfectant. **-sifili·tico** *adj.* antisyphilitic. **-sigma** *m.* (palaeog.) transposition mark. **-si·șmico** *adj.* aseismatic, 'quake-proof. **-sociale** *adj.* antisocial. **-spasmo·dico** *adj.* antispasmodic. **-statale** *adj.* contrary to the interests of the State. **-ste·rico** *adj.* antihysteric. **-teta·nico** *adj.* (med.) anti-tetanus. **-tos·sico** *adj.* antitoxic. **-tossina** *f.* antitoxin. **-u·mido** *adj.* damp-resisting; *adj. indecl.* shock-resistant. **-veleno** *m.* antidote. **-vene·reo** *adj.* antivenereal. **-ẓi·mico**, **-zimo·tico** *adj.* antizymic.

anti-[2] *pref.* ante. **-bagno** *m.* antechamber of a bathroom. **-bẹcco** *m.* (*pl.* -bẹcchi) (archit.) cutwater (of a bridge-pier). **-brac·cio** *m.* see **avambraccio**. **-ca·mera** *f.* antechamber, ante-room; fare -camera, to wait, to be kept waiting; to dance attendance; far fare -camera, to keep (someone) waiting. **-car·dio** *m.* anticardium, precordium, pit of the stomach. **-conọscere** [B9] *tr.* to have foreknowledge of; to foresee. **-conoscenza** *f.* foreknowledge, prescience. **-cọrte** *f.* courtyard. **-cursọre** *m.* pioneer; precursor, predecessor. **-data** *f.* antedate. **-datare** [A1] *tr.* to antedate. **-datato** *part. adj.* antedated. **-diluviano** *adj.* antediluvian; (joc.) out of date. **-let·tera** *f.* see **avantilettera**. **-meridiano** *adj.* antemeridian. **-mẹsso** *adj.* placed before; preferred. **-narrazione** *f.* preamble. **-parte** *f.* (leg.) share previously allotted to person entitled to preference. **-pastiera** *f.* hors-d'œuvre dish. **-pasto** *m.* hors-d'œuvre. **-penul·timo** *adj.* antepenultimate. **-porta** *f.* vestibule, entrance-hall; (mil.) fortification outside the gate of a city. **-porto** *m.* (archit.) hall; vestibule. **-purgatọrio** *m.* Ante-Purgatory, the four lower cornices of the Mountain of Purgatory in Dante's *Divina Commedia* (cf. **antinferno**). **-sala** *f.* antechamber. **-scalo** *m.* (naut.) slipway. **-spalto** *m.* (mil. archit.) glacis (properly a second one in front of the first). **-vedẹre** [B23] *tr.* to foresee. **-veggente** *part. adj.* foreseeing. **-veggenza** *f.* foresight. **-venire** [D17] see **prevenire**. **-vigi·lia** *f.* day before the eve; l'-vigilia di Natale, December 23; l'-vigilia di Pasqua, two days before Easter; (eccl.) day before a vigil.

†**anti[3]** *prep.* before.

antia·ride *f.* (bot.) upas-tree, *Antiaris toxicaria*.

antica·glia *f.* curiosity, antique; †ancient monument; (joc.) (of a person) wreck; *pl.* junk, lumber; negozio di anticaglie, old curiosity shop.

anticato *adj.* (poet.). See **antiquato**.

anticheggiare [A3c]. See under **antico**.

antichità *f.* antiquity; ancient times; age; antique; cattedra di —, chair in the Faculty of Arts in an Italian University relating to study of ancient monuments; *pl.* ancient monuments; epigraphy, etc.; negozio di —, antique shop.

anticip·are [A1s] *tr.* to anticipate; to forestall; to advance, to put forward (time or date); to make known in advance; to pay in advance, to put down (money); to antedate; *intr.* (aux. avere) to arrive before schedule; (of a train) to get in early; (of a watch) to be fast; *rfl.* to gain time, to get ahead of one's schedule. (**-amẹnto** *m.* **-ativo** *adj.*) **-ato** *part. adj.* anticipated; advanced; put forward; orario -ato, schedule altered to function from an earlier hour; anticipatory; premature; contatore a pagamento -ato, slot-meter. **-atamẹnte** *adv.* beforehand; in anticipation; in advance; before time. (**-atọre** *m.* **-atrice** *f.*) **-azione** *f.* anticipation; (comm.) advance; -azione su titoli depositati a garanzia, advance on securities deposited as a guarantee; (mus.) anticipation, a note which anticipates the succeeding harmony.

anti·cipo *m.* anticipation; advance (of money); earnest; in —, in advance, early; il treno arrivò con un — di sette minuti, the train got in seven minutes early; (motor.) — dell'accensione, spark lead, spark advance.

anti·co *adj.* (*m.pl.* **-chi**) ancient; old; long-standing; old-fashioned; obsolete; antique; l'—, the old days; antiquity; all'-ca, in an old-fashioned way, in the good old way; un uomo all'-ca, a loyal man, an honest man; in —, in ancient times; in the old days; un libro —, an early book; (poet.) l'-ca madre, Italy; la gran madre -ca, the Earth; *n.m.* antiquity; †ancestor; *pl.* gli -chi, the ancients; the classical authors. **-camente** *adv.* in ancient times; in the olden days; formerly. **-cheggiare** [A 3 c] *intr.* (*aux.* avere) to ape the manner of the ancients; to imitate the style of classical authors.

anti·creṣi *f.* (leg.) clause enabling creditor to retain income of pawned property (C.C.).

antic·tono *m.* one who lives at the antipodes (also *adj.*).

anti·dot·o *m.* antidote; preservative; (fig.) antidote; †redress. †**-a·rio** *m.* pharmacopoeia.

†**antifato** *m.* (leg.) jointure.

†**antifern·a** *f.* (leg.) gift from husband to wife on occasion of wedding. (†**-ale** *adj.*)

anti·fon·a *f.* (liturg., mus.) antiphon; verse; (fig.) capir l'—, to guess what (unpleasant thing) is coming next, to see how the land lies; l'— è più lunga del discorso, he takes a long time to come to the point. **-ale** *m.* (mus.) antiphoner; *adj.* antiphonal. **-a·rio** *m.* (eccl.) antiphonal, antiphonary; (mus.) antiphoner; a singer of antiphons. **-i·a** *f.* (mus.) antiphony.

anti·fr-aṣi *f.* (gramm.) antiphrasis. **-a·stico** *adj.* antiphrastic.

anti·gene *m.* (biol.) antigene.

anti·grafo *adj.* (of a manuscript) transcribed; *n.m.* copy; transcription.

†**antiguar·dia** *f.* See **avanguardia**.

anti·lope *m.* (zool.) antelope.

antim-o·nio *m.* antimony. **-onale** *adj.* containing antimony. **-oniato** *m.* antimonate. **-o·nico** *adj.* antimonic. **-onọṣo** *adj.* antimonious. **-onite** *f.* (min.) stibnite, grey antimony. **-onuro** *m.* (chem.) antimonide, stibnite.

antina *f.* window-sash frame.

antinomi·a *f.* (philos.) antinomy.

Antinferno *pr.n.m.* Ante-hell, a division of Dante's Inferno.

antiopa *f.* (ent.) *Vanessa antiopa*, Camberwell Beauty butterfly.

anti·pati·a *f.* antipathy, dislike. **-pa·tico** *adj.* unpleasant, displeasing; nasty; antipathetic.

anti·pod-e, -o *m.* one who lives at the Antipodes; *pl.* Antipodes; (fig.) essere agli -i (l'uno all'altro), to be poles apart.

antipo·for-a *f.* (rhet.) anthypophora. **-are** [A 1 s] *intr.* (*aux.* avere) to answer one's own (rhetorical) questions or objections.

antiqu-a·rio *adj.*, *n.m.* dealer in antiques; antiquarian; antiquary. **-a·ria** *f.* woman antiquarian; (abstr.) study of antiques, knowledge of antiques; †study of antiquity. **-ariato** *m.* antiquarian trade; second-hand book-trade.

antiquato *adj.* antiquated, old-fashioned; obsolete, archaic; †long-established; †inveterate.

†**anti·quo** *adj.* See **antico**.

antirrino *m.* (bot.) snapdragon, antirrhinum, *Antirrhinum majus*; lesser snapdragon, *A. orontium*.

antiste *m.* See **antistite**.

anti·stite *m.* (eccl.) cleric (of some importance, usu. bishop or other prelate).

anti·strofe *f.* antistrophe.

anti·t-eṣi *indecl.* antithesis. **-e·tico** *adj.* antithetic. (**-eticamente** *adv.*)

anti·trago *m.* (anat.) antitragus.

anto·cianina *f.* (chem.) anthocyanin. **-grafi·a** *f.* anthography; (typ.) floriated initials.

anto·logi·a *f.* anthology. **-lo·gico** *adj.* anthological.

antoniano *m.* (numism.) coin of the Antonines.

anto·nimo *m.* antonym.

Anto·nio *pr.n.m.* Anthony, Antony.

antono-maṣi·a *f.* (rhet.) antonomasia. **-ma·stico** *adj.* antonomastic. (**-masticamente** *adv.*)

antoptoṣi *f.* (bot.) petal drop.

antossanto *m.* (bot.) sweet-scented vernal grass, *Anthoxanthum odoratum*.

antozoi *m.pl.* (zool.) anthozoa.

antrac-e *m.* (med.) anthrax. **-ene** *m.* (chem.) anthracene. **-i·fero** *adj.* anthraciferous, yielding anthracite. **-ite** *f.* anthracite. **-o·metro** *m.*

anthracometer. **-oṣi** *f. indecl.* (med.) anthracosis, 'miners' lung'.

antrachinọne *m.* (chem.) anthraquinone.

antracografi·a *f.* (art) charcoal-drawing.

antreno *m.* (ent.) *Anthrenus museorum*, museum beetle.

antro¹ *m.* cave, cavern; den, lair; hovel; (anat.) cavity.

antro² *adj.* (dial. Centr. Italy). See **altro**.

antro·pico *adj.* anthropic, anthropical.

antro-pocen·trico *adj.* anthropocentric. **-po·fago** *adj.* (*m.pl.* **-po·fagi**, **-po·faghi**) man-eating, cannibal, anthropophagous; *n.m.* man-eater, cannibal. **-pofagi·a** *f.* anthropophagy, man-eating, cannibalism. **-pofobi·a** *f.* (med.) anthropophobia. **-pogeografi·a** *f.* human geography. **-po·glifo** (geol.) human fossil. **-pografi·a** *f.* anthropography. **-po·ide** *adj.*, *n.m.* (zool.) anthropoid. **-polite** *m.* anthropolite, fossil man. **-pologi·a** *f.* anthropology. **-polo·gico** *adj.* anthropological. (**-pologicamente** *adv.*) **-po·logo** *m.* (*pl.* **-po·logi**, **-po·loghi**) anthropologist. **-pomanzi·a** *f.* anthropomancy. **-pometri·a** *f.* anthropometry. **-pome·trico** *adj.* anthropometric. **-po·metro** *m.* anthropometer. **-pomorfi·a** *f.* similarity to the human body. **-pomor·fico** *adj.* anthropomorphic. **-pomorfiṣmo** *m.* anthropomorphism. **-pomorfita** *m.* anthropomorphite. **-pomorfo** *adj.* anthropomorphic; lettere -pomorfe, picture writing with human figures. **-poṣofi·a** *f.* anthroposophy; human wisdom. **-potomi·a** *f.* anthropotomy, human anatomy. **-po·zoico** *adj.* (geol.) neozoic.

anulare *adj.* ring-shaped; dito —, ring-finger, fourth-finger; (scient.) annular; eclisse —, annular eclipse; *n.m.* ring-finger.

†**a·nulo** *m.* See **anello**.

anulọṣo *adj.* (scient.) annulated.

anureṣi *f. indecl.* See **anuria**.

anuri *m.pl.* (zool.) anura, frogs and toads.

anu·ria *f.* (med.) anury.

Anversa *pr.n.f.* (geog.) Antwerp.

anzi *conj.* on the contrary; in fact, indeed; still more; or rather; fai bene, — benone, you're doing well, in fact very well; mi diede cento lire, — novanta cinque, he gave me a hundred lire, or rather 95; *prep.* before; — la mia morte, before my death; — tempo, before the expected time, early; †*adv.* before; — che, rather than; — che no, rather, somewhat. **-chè** *conj.* rather than. **-detto** *adj.* aforesaid, above mentioned. **-tutto** *adv.* above all; first of all.

anzian-o *adj.* aged; elderly; senior; retired; former; più —, older; *n.m.* elder; senior; alderman; third year student; *pl.* (hist.) senior officials in certain Italian Republics. †**-ato** office of senior official; term of office. **-ità** *f.* seniority; term of office, length of service; avanzamento ad -ità, promotion by seniority. **-otto** *dim. adj.* getting on in years.

anziate *adj.* (geog.) of Anzio.

anzichè, anzidetto, anzitutto. See under **anzi**.

anzipetto *m.* parapet.

aocchiare [A 4] to catch sight of, to set eyes on; to glance at; (agric.) to break up the clay with the eye of the hoe.

†**aombrare** *vb.* See **adombrare**.

ao·nio *adj.* (poet.) Aonian; le aonie sorelle, the Muses.

†**aorcare** *tr.* to put to death by hanging, to hang.

aoristo *m.* (gramm.) aorist tense.

†**aormare** *tr.* to track (game, prey).

aor·t-a *f.* (anat.) aorta. **-ico** *adj.* aortic. **-i·te** *f.* aortitis, inflammation of the aorta.

aostino *adj.* (geog.) of the valley of Aosta.

apagogi·a *f.* (philos.) apagoge, *reductio ad absurdum*.

a·pale *f.* (zool.) *Hapale*, marmoset.

apa·lidi *f.pl.* (zool.) marmoset family.

aparina *f.* (bot.) cleavers, goose-grass, *Galium aparine*.

aparti·tic-o *adj.* (neol. pol.) non-party; beyond parties. (**-icità** *f.*)

apati·a *f.* apathy; indifference; listlessness.

apa·t-ico *adj.* apathetic; indifferent; lackadaisical. (**-icamente** *adv.*) **-ista** *m.* apathetic individual; (lit. hist.) member of the Accademia degli Apatisti.

apatite *f.* (miner.) apatite.

ape *f.* (ent.) bee; — operaia, worker-bee; — regina, queen-bee; maschio dell'—, drone; — da miele, honey-bee.

apepsi·a *f.* (med.) apepsy.

apercre·dito *m.* (comm.) opening of credit; cf. **apertura di credito**, under **aperto**.

aperiente *adj.*, *n.m.* (med.) aperient.

aperio·dic-o *adj.* aperiodic. **-ità** *f.* aperiodicity.

aperitivo¹ *adj., n.m.* (med.) aperient.

aperitivo² *m.* apéritif; appetizer.

apert-o *part.* of **aprire**, q.v.; *adj.* open; spacious, roomy; obvious, clear; (fig.) è un libro —, one can read him like an open book; frank, sincere; parlarsi a cuore —, to have a heart-to-heart talk; alert, receptive; all'—, all'aria -a, in the open air, out of doors; giuochi all'aria -a, outdoor sports; (mil.) città -a, open city; battaglia -a, pitched battle; (paint.) light, bright (of colours); (mus.) open (as applied to organ-pipes, or to the unstopped notes of the horn); a libro —, at sight; allegro —, a slightly more deliberate tempo than allegro; organo —, full organ; (comm.) conto —, account which is still open; *adv.* openly, frankly; *n.m.* open space. **-a** *f.* opening; all'-a, at opening time (for shops, etc.); parlare all'-a, to speak openly. **-amente** *adv.* openly, frankly; clearly. **-ura** *f.* opening; ad -ura di libro, at the page where a book opens by chance; -ura lampo, zip-fastener; aperture, hole, chink, gap; breach, cleft; width; spread; (aeron.) -ura alare, wing span; inauguration; preliminary step; far qualche -ura, to make preliminary enquiries, to feel one's way; (pol.) approach, overture, opening; -ura verso la sinistra, overture to the Left; (rugby) pass; (of engine cylinder) port; -ura di sfogo, offtake (in blast furnace); (photog.) aperture, stop; -ura relativa, stop valve; -ura automatica, automatic release; (comm.) -ura di credito, opening of credit; (mus.) overture; (poker) 'the openers', the cards with which the original bet is made.

ape·talo *adj.* (bot.) apetalous, without petals.

api-a·io *m.* beekeeper, apiarist. **-a·ria** *f.* apiculture. **-a·rio** *m.* apiary.

a·pic-e *m.* apex; culminating point, height; all'— della gioia, in one's seventh heaven; (gramm.) dash indicating a long vowel; (math.) dash placed near a letter in geometry, as x'. **-ite** *f.* (med.) apical inflammation.

api·cio *m.* (joc.) good cook.

apicult-ore *m.* beekeeper, apiarist. **-ura** *f.* beekeeping, apiculture.

a·pi-o *m.* (bot.) celery, *Apium graveolens*. **-a·cee** *f.pl.* (bot.) certain umbellifers, including parsley and anise. **-oli·na** *f.* (bot.) common chamomile, *Anthemis nobilis*.

apione *m.* (ent.) *Apion*, a kind of weevil.

apireno *adj.* seedless.

apir-essi·a *f.* (med.) apyrexy. **-e·tico** *adj.* apyretic, free from fever.

a·pir-o *adj.* incombustible; infusible; apyrous. **-ite** *f.* type of smokeless gunpowder. **-o·tipi** *m.pl.* (typ.) non-cast printing type.

apis *m.* (dial.). See **lapis**.

api·stico *adj.* apistic, to do with bees.

aplisia *f.* (zool.) *Aplysia*, sea hare.

aplografi·a *f.* (palaeog.) haplography.

aplo·ide *f.* (biol.) haploid.

aplomb *m. indecl.* (sport) stance.

†aplustr-e, -o *m.* (poet.) curved stern of a ship with its ornaments.

apne·a *f.* (med.) apnœa, suspension or cessation of breathing.

apo *m.* (zool.) *Apus cancriformis*, a freshwater crustacean.

†a·poca *f.* (leg.) receipt.

apo-calisse, -calissi *f.* (Bibl.) Apocalypse, Revelation; (joc.) cavallo dell'—, gaunt-looking horse, jade. **-calit·tica** *f.* Apocalyptic writings. **-calit·tico** *adj.* apocalyptic.

apo-catarsi *f.* (med.) apocatharsis, purging. **-catar·tico** *adj.* (med.) apocathartic, purging.

apocata·stasi *f.* (philos.; med.; astron.) apocatastasis, return to previous condition or position.

apo·cop-e *f.* apocope. **-are** [A I s] *tr.* to apocopate. (**-ato** *part. adj.*)

apo·crifo *adj.* apocryphal; (eccl.) libri apocrifi, apocryphal books, apocrypha (not equivalent to A.V. 'Apocrypha').

apocroma·tico *adj.* (opt.) apochromatic.

apodite·rio *m.* (Rom. antiq.) apodyterium, dressing-room of a Roman bath.

apodit·tico *adj.* (philos.) apodeictic.

a·pod-o *m.* (zool.) apod. **-a·le** *adj.* apodal.

apo·dosi *f.* (rhet.) apodosis.

apo·fige *f.* (archit.) apophyge.

apofillite *f.* (miner.) apophyllite.

apo·fisi *f.* (anat.) apophysis.

apoft-egma, -emma *m.* apophthegm, maxim.

apo-ge·o¹ *m.* (astron.) apogee; (fig.) height, summit, climax; essere all'— della gloria, to be at the height of one's glory. **-giove** *m.* (astron.) apojove.

apoge·o² *m.* land wind.

apo·grafo *adj.* (of a manuscript) transcribed from a master-copy; *n.m.* apograph, exact transcript.

apo·lide *adj.* stateless; passaporto —, Nansen passport; *n.m., f.* person without a country, displaced person.

apoliti·a *f.* loss of citizenship.

apoli·tico *adj.* non-political.

Apol·line *pr.n.m.* (myth.) Apollo; mangiare in —, to be a guest at a sumptuous banquet.

Apoll-o *pr.n.m.* (myth.) Apollo; the sun; a handsome youth; (ent.) the Apollo or Parnassus butterfly. **-i·neo** *adj.* handsome; Apollonian; pertaining to Apollo. **-o·nicon** *m. indecl.* (mus.) apollonicon (an organ designed to imitate the orchestra).

apolog-i·a *f.* formal defence (written or spoken); justification; apologia. **-eta** *m.* apologist. **-e·tica** *f.* (theol.) apologetics. **-e·tico** *adj.* vindicatory; scritto -etico, apologia; *n.m.* apologia. **-ista** *m.* apologist; *pl.* (patrist.) apologists. (**-i·stico**.) **-i·ʒʒare** [A I] *intr.* (aux. avere) to write as an apologist.

apo·lo-go *m.* (*m.pl.* **-ghi**) apologue, fable.

aponeur-osi *f. indecl.* (anat.) aponeurosis. **-o·tico** *adj.* aponeurotic.

apo-plessi·a *f.* apoplexy. **-plet·tico** *adj.* apoplectic(al); *n.m.* sufferer from apoplexy, apoplectic.

aporema *m.* (Aristotelian philos.) aporeme (syllogism that 'reasons dialectically to a contradiction').

apo·stasi *f. indecl.* (med.) abscess.

apostasi·a *f.* (rel.; fig.) apostasy.

apo·stat-a *m., f.* apostate. **-are** [A I s] *intr.* (aux. avere) to apostatize. (**-atrice** *f.*)

†apostema *m.* (med.) abscess.

apo·st-olo *m.* apostle; propagandist; †wandering preacher; *pl.* (naut.) knight-heads; **-olato** *m.* apostolate. **-olicità** *f.* (rel.) apostolicity. **-o·lico** *adj.* apostolic; of the Apostles; of the Pope; †*n.m* the Pope. (**-olicamente** *adv.*).

apo·strof-e *f.* (rhet.) exclamatory address; (gramm.) apostrophe. **-o** *m.* (gramm.) apostrophe, omission mark; mettere un -o a, to mark with an apostrophe.

apostrof-are [A I s] *tr., abs.* to apostrophize; (gramm.) to mark with an apostrophe. **-ato** *part. adj.* apostrophized; (gramm.) marked with an apostrophe. (**-atura** *f.* **-azione** *f.*)

†apoteca *f.* (Gk. and Rom. antiq.) storehouse, storeroom; pharmacy.

apote·cio *m.* (bot.) apothecium, cup-like case of spores in certain fungi and lichens.

apot-egma, -emma *m.* See **apoftegma**.

apotema *m.* (math.) apothem.

apoteosi *f. indecl.* apotheosis; triumph; deification; (fig.) far l'— di, to laud to the skies.

ap-o·tesi *f. indecl.* (mus.) apothesis (final cadence). **-o·tome** *f.* (mus.) apotome, major semitone. **-oʒ·ʒema** *f.* (pharm.) apozem.

appaccare [A 2] and derivs. See **impaccare**.

appacchettare [A I c]. See **impacchettare**.

appaci-are [A 3] *tr.* to appease. **-amento** *m.* (neol. pol.) appeasement. **-ato** *part. adj.* appeased.

appacific-are [A 2 s] *tr.* to pacify; to reconcile; *rfl.* to reconcile oneself; *recip. rfl.* to make peace, to become reconciled, to bury the hatchet. **-ato** *part. adj.* pacified; reconciled.

appadiglion-are [A I c] *abs.* to pitch a tent; *rfl.* to go under canvas. **-ato** *part. adj.* pitched (tent, camp); (mil.) under canvas.

†appadronare *intr.* (leg.) to take possession of a landlord's reversion.

appag-are [A 2] *tr.* to satisfy; to content; to satiate; to gratify; to please; — la sete, to quench one's thirst; *rfl.* (*prep.* di) to satisfy oneself; to content oneself; to be satisfied, to rest content. (**-a·bile** *adj.*) **-amento** *m.* satisfying; gratification. (**-ante** *part. adj.*) **-ato** *part. adj.* satisfied; content. (**-atore** *m.* **-atrice** *f.*)

appagliaiare [A 4] *tr.* to stack (hay or straw), to form a rick.

appai-are [A 4] *tr.* to pair, to couple; to yoke; to match (colours); *rfl.* to form a pair; (colloq.) to get 'hitched'; (of colours, materials) to match. **-amento** *m.* coupling, pairing; yoking; (of colours, etc.) matching. **-ato** *part. adj.* coupled, paired; matching; rime -ate, couplets; (iron.) sono bene -ati, they're a nice pair. **-atoio** *m.* (orn.) breeding cage. (**-atura** *f.*)

appalancare [A I s] *tr.* to enclose in a palisade.

appaleşare [A I] and derivs. See **palesare**.

appallare [A I] *tr.* to make up into a ball.

appallottare [A I] and derivs. See **appallottolare**.

appallottol-are [A I s] *tr.* to make into pellets; — la neve, to make snowballs; — la lingua, to speak indistinctly; *rfl.* to curl up into a ball; (of milk) to curdle; (of wool) to get into a tangle; (techn.) to form lumps (e.g. of iron during smelting); to cake. **-ato** *part. adj.* made into pellets; rolled up into a ball; (of milk) curdled; (of wool) tangled; (techn.) gone lumpy, clinkered, caked.

appalmata *adj. f.* (herald.) appaumée, hand open.

appalpare [A I] *rfl.* (Tusc.) to fall asleep.

appalt-are [A I] *tr.* (leg.) to let out (public work or service) on contract; to undertake (public work or service) on contract; *rfl.* -arsi al teatro, to take out a season-ticket to a theatre **-atore** *m.* successful tenderer for a contract, contractor. (**-atrice** *f.*) **-o** *m.* giving out, allocation (of contract); undertaking; contract; the place of business where contract is fulfilled; tobacconist's shop; concorrere a un -o, to submit a tender for; ottenere in -o (in seguito a concorso), to be given a contract (after tender).

appaltone *m.* busybody; coxcomb.

appalugare [A 2] *rfl., intr.* (*aux.* avere) (Tusc.) to nod off, to have forty winks.

appan-are [A I] *tr.* (Tusc.) to make into loaves; (S. Italy) to cover with bread-crumbs. (**-atore** *m.* **-atrice** *f.* **-azione** *f.*)

†**appancacciare** *rfl.* to sit idle.

†**appanciollare** *rfl.* to loll, to take one's ease.

appanett-are [A I c] *tr.* to make into pats or slabs. (**-ato** *part. adj.*)

appanicare [A 2] *tr.* (orn.) to feed on millet seed.

appannag·gio *m.* appanage; Household List; (fig.) perquisite, prerogative; attribute.

appann-are [A I] *tr.* to dim, to blur, to mist; to tarnish; to frost (glass); to obscure, to veil; to hood, to cloak; †to entangle (birds) in a net; *rfl.* to tarnish, to darken; to mist over; (of sound) to drop, to die away; (of sight) to grow dim; †(fig.) -arsi nella sua ragna, to be caught in one's own trap. **-a·bile** *adj.* liable to tarnish. (**-amento** *m.* **-ante** *part. adj.*) **-ato** *part. adj.* obscured; tarnished; vetri -ati, windows steamed over. **-atoio** *m.* hood (for covering a horse's eyes, during breaking in); cloth used for giving horses a final rub-down. (**-atura** *f.*) **-ume** *m.* (bot.) green manure.

appannat-o *adj.* (Tusc. colloq.) stout; **-otto** *adj.* plump.

†**apparare**[1] *vb.* and derivs. See **parare**.

†**apparare**[2] *vb.* and derivs. See **imparare**.

apparat-o *m.* array, display; pomp, magnificence; decoration; discorso d'—, ceremonial address; (iron.) parade of eloquence; un conferenziere d'—, a showy lecturer; furnishings, fittings; — scenico, mise-en-scène, set; apparatus; — critico, *apparatus criticus*; (anat.) — digirente, digestive organs; (techn.) equipment, machinery; contrivance; (geog.) feature.

appara-tore *m.* decorator; (theatr.) stage-manager. (**-trice** *f.*)

apparecchi-are [A 4 c] *tr.* to prepare; to make ready; — la cena, to get supper ready; to dress (food); (text.) to dress (cloth); — la tavola, to lay the table; *abs.* devo apparecchiare? shall I lay the table?; (naut.) to prepare for sea; *rfl.* to prepare oneself; to get ready. **-amento** *m.* preparation; equipment, apparatus; (text.) dressing; †pomp; †fitting, furnishing; †vocabulary, glossary, reference-work. **-ato** *part. adj.* prepared; well provided for; (colloq.) andare a tavola -ata, to be on easy-street. **-atore** *m.* decorator. (**-atrice** *f.*) **-atura** *f.* apparatus; equipment, switchgear; preparation; (text.; industr.) finishing; (paint.) preparation (of surface).

apparecch-io *m.* preparation; arrangement; lay-out; (text.) dressing; stoffa con molto —, cloth with a lot of dressing in it; apparatus; machine; — radio, wireless set; outfit, equipment, gear; requisites; (med.) orthopaedic appliance; -i di guerra, war-effort, preparations for war; — Geiger, Geiger counter; (aeron.) plane; — da caccia, fighter plane; — da bombardamento, bomber; (paint.) preparation (of surface); (archit.) hewing, shaping (of stone for building).

†**appareggiare** *vb.* See **pareggiare**.

†**apparegliare** *vb.* See **apparecchiare**.

apparentamento *m.* (neol. pol.) coalition, agreement, political alliance (for election purposes).

†**apparentare** *vb.* See **imparentare**.

apparentato *adj.* (neol. pol.) forming a coalition (for election purposes).

apparente *part. adj.* See under **apparire**.

apparenza *f.* See under **apparire**.

†**apparere** *vb.* See **apparire**.

apparigli-are[1] [A 4] *tr.* to pair, to match (horses); (cards) in the game of scopa, to take (a card on the table) with a card of the same value; *rfl.* (joc.) to pair off; si sono -ati bene, they're well matched, they're a fine pair (of rogues). **-ato** *part. adj.* paired; (fig.) level, neck and neck.

†**apparigliare**[2] *vb.* See **pareggiare**.

appar-ire [D 3] *intr.* (*aux.* essere) to appear, to come into view; to turn up; to be visible; gli è -sa la Madonna, the Virgin appeared to him; to result, to turn out; to be apparent; to seem, to look; vuole — elegante, he likes to look well-dressed; vestita di nero -e più bella, black is more becoming to her; (astron.) to rise. **-ente** *part. adj.* apparent, seeming, ostensible; visible; evident, clear; morte -ente, catalepsy; †*n.m.* apparition, revenant. **-entemente** *adv.* seemingly, ostensibly, in appearance; at first sight; outwardly. **-enza** *f.* appearance; personal appearance; guise; aspect; look; form, shape; moving form, changing form; avere un'-enza solenne, to look grave; outward appearance; l'-enza inganna, appearances are deceptive; giudicare dalle -enze, to judge by appearance; sotto l'-enza di, under cover of; show, ostentation; per -enza, for the sake of show; per salvare l'-enza, for the sake of appearances; salvare l'-enza, to save face; sign, indication; nelle sue parole non c'è -enza di vero, there is not a shadow of truth in what he says; likelihood, probability: in -enza, apparently, to all appearance. †**-imento** *m.* appearing, appearance. **-ita** *f.* appearance, coming into view. **-itore** *m.* (eccl.) apparitor. **-izione** *f.* apparition; phantasm; (astron.) rising.

appariscen-te *adj.* visible; striking, conspicuous; showy; spectacular; pompous; flourishing; colori -ti, gaudy colours. **-za** *f.* appearance; striking appearance; impressiveness; conspicuousness; gaudiness.

apparizione *f.* See under **apparire**.

apparso *part.* of **apparire**, q.v.

appart-are [A I] *tr.* to set apart; to put on one side; to separate; *rfl.* to stand aloof; to withdraw; to retire; to lead a secluded life; to be of a retiring disposition. **-amento** *m.* setting on one side; (naut.) departure. **-ato** *part. adj.* set apart; separate; retired, retiring, withdrawn; secluded, solitary; remote; luogo -ato, remote spot, out-of-the-way place; †specific, particular. **-atamente** *adv.* separately, apart.

appartamento *m.* apartment, flat, living quarters; — da scapolo, bachelor flat.

apparten-ere [B 32] *intr.* (*aux.* avere, essere, *prep.* a) to belong; to pertain; to appertain; to be a member (of); to be in the service (of); to be related (to); to befit, to behove, to be the duty of (also *rfl.*). **-ente** *part. adj.* belonging; pertaining; concerning; befitting. **-enza** *f.*, *usu. pl.* belongings; accessories; (leg.) appurtenances; (in calendar) -enze dell'anno, moveable feasts and other special features of a given year. (†**-imento** *m.* **-uto** *part. adj.*)

†**appassare** *vb.* See **appassire** or **passare**.

appassimento *m.* See under **appassire**.

appassion-are [A I c] *tr.* to impassion; to move, to touch; to enamour; to interest; nulla lo -a, nothing interests him; *rfl.* (*prep.* a, di, per) to be enamoured (of), to be keen (on); si -a molto alla musica, he is very fond of music; (*prep.* per, di) to sorrow (over), to be deeply moved (by). **-amento** *m.* emotion; enthusiasm; sorrow. (**-atezza** *f.*) **-ato** *part. adj.* passionate; ardent; fond; è -ato per la musica, he adores music; broken-hearted, stricken; enamoured; emotional; prejudiced, subjective; partial, biased; (mus.) appassionato, impassioned. **-atamente** *adv.* passionately; ardently.

appass-ire [D 2] *tr.* to dry (fruit) in the sun; *intr.* (*aux.* essere), *rfl.* to fade; to wither; to droop; to decay. **-imento** *m.* drying; fading; withering. **-ito** *part. adj.* dry; dried-up; uva -ita, raisins; faded, withered. (**-itura** *f.*)

appassonare [A I] *tr.* (agric.) to tie up (cattle) in a pen.

appast-are [A I] *tr.* to make into a paste; *rfl.* to thicken to a paste. (**-ato** *part. adj.*)

appeggi *m.pl.* (bot.) Southern juniper, *Juniperus oxycedrus.*

appell-are [A I].
    1. LEGAL MEANINGS and derivs.: *intr.* (*aux.* avere), *rfl.* to appeal. **-a·bile** *adj.* subject to appeal. **-abilità** *f.* appealability. **-ante** *m.*, *adj.* appellant. **-ativo** *adj.* appellatory. **-ato** *part. adj.* appealed against; *n.m.* respondent in an appeal. **2.** POETIC AND FIG. USES and derivs.: *tr.* to call, to name, to designate; *rfl.* to be called, to be named; to appeal; (Tusc.) trovare da -arsi, to censure. **-ativo** *adj.* nome -ativo, common noun; *n.m.* designation, name, term. **-ato** *part. adj.* called, named. **-azione** *f.* appellation.

appello *m.* call; rispondere all'— della patria, to respond to the call of the fatherland; appeal; fare — a, to appeal to; — al popolo, plebiscite; (poet.) invocation; roll-call; fare l'—, to call the roll; — nominale, (in Italian Parliament) roll-call of members in alphabetical order for purposes of voting; votazione per — nominale, voting by this method; contr'—, second roll-call, check; (leg.) appeal; Corte d'Appello, Court of Appeal; ricorrere in —, to appeal; tribunale d'ultimo —, court of final resort; †challenge.

appena *adv.* as soon as; hardly, scarcely, barely, just; with difficulty; ce n'è — per tre, there's just enough for three; almost immediately; — . . .che, no sooner. . .than; non —, just as soon as; non — mi sarà possibile, just as soon as I possibly can; — saranno arrivati, as soon as they arrive; lo riconobbi — entrò, I knew him the minute he entered; — —, the very moment, hardly at all, the least little bit; with great difficulty (also **a pena**).

appenare [A I c] *tr.* to torment; *rfl.* to suffer; to distress oneself; to take trouble.

appen·d-ere [C I] *tr.* (*prep.* a) to suspend, to hang (on); — un ex-voto alla Madonna, to make an ex-voto offering to the Madonna; (poet.) to offer up; †to weigh **-ia·biti** *m. indecl.* coat-hanger.

append-ice *f.* appendix; supplement; attachment; annex; literary page (in a newspaper); romanzo d'—, serial story; (anat.) appendix; (aeron.) tailpiece. **-icista** *m.* journalist who writes for the literary section of a paper. **-ici·stico** *adj.* (neol.) characteristic of newspaper serial-stories. **-icite** *f.* appendicitis. **-icectomi·a** *f.* (surg.) removal of the appendix. **-icolare** *adj.* appendicular. **-i·zie** *f.pl.* (leg.) gift of farm produce from tenant of land to owner.

appennecchi-are [A 4 c] *tr., abs.* (text. ind.) to arrange the wool or cotton, etc., upon the distaff for spinning.

Appennino *pr.n.m.* (geog.) l'—, gli Appennini, the Apennines.

†**appensato** *m.* thought; *adj.* cautious, wary.

apper-cettivo *adj.* (philos.) apperceptive. **-cezione** *f.* (philos.) apperception.

appesantire [D 2] *tr.* (neol.) to make heavy; (fig.) to make dull.

appes-ire [D 2] *intr.* (*aux.* essere) to put on weight, to get heavier; (of a baby) to gain. **-ito** *part. adj.* heavier; (of a baby) gaining well.

appeso *part.* of **appendere**, q.v.; — a, hanging from.

appest-are [A I] *tr.* to infect; to taint; to contaminate, to pollute; (fig.) to corrupt; *abs.* to stink; †to catch the plague. **-ato** *part. adj.* infected; corrupted; plague-stricken; stinking; *n.m.* one sick of the plague; *adv.* (colloq.) esser caro **-ato**, to be shockingly expensive. (**-atore** *m.*)

appet-ire [D 2] *tr.* to hunger for; to desire; to long for; *intr.* (*aux.* essere, avere) to stimulate appetite, to be appetizing. **-ente** *part. adj.* appetizing; hungry for, in need of: **-ente** certi cibi, in need of certain foodstuffs; (fig.) **-ente** (di) gloria, eager for glory; (philos.) appetent. **-enza** *f.* appetite; inclination; longing; (philos.) appetence. (**-evole** *adj.*) **-i·bile** *adj.* desirable; appetizing, palatable; (philos.) appetible. (**-ibilità** *f.*) **-itivo** *adj.* appetitive, appetizing. (**-ito** *part. adj.*) **-itoso** *adj.* see under **appetito²**. **-itosamente** *adv.* see under **appetito²**.

appetito¹ *part.* of **appetire**, q.v.

appetit-o² *m.* appetite; hunger; inclination; avidity; sensuality, lust; stimolare l'—, to whet the appetite; l'— vien mangiando, l'appétit vient en mangeant; buon —!, a mode of salutation customary at meal-times (there is no English equivalent); avere un — da lupo, to be as hungry as a hunter; — di gloria, thirst for glory. **-oso** *adj.* appetizing; tempting; attractive; hungry. **-osamente** *adv.* hungrily; appetizingly.

appett-are [A I] *intr.* (*aux.* avere) (of a horse) to pull well; (of a wall) to bulge; (of a woman) to be large in the bust; †*tr.* to confront, to face. **-ata** *f.* (dial. S. Italy) steep hill.

appetto *prep.* (*foll. by* a) in comparison (with); opposite. (Also **a petto**.)

appezz-are [A I] *tr.* to patch, to piece together; to divide into pieces; to divide (land) into allotments. **-amento** *m.* small piece of land, lot, allotment, plot. **-ato** *part. adj.* patched, pieced together; divided up; in pieces, in bits. **-atura** *f.* piecing; piece joined on; join; division into pieces. **-ettare** [A I c] *tr.* to break to bits, to tear into small pieces.

appezzato *adj.* See **pezzato**.

Ap·pia *adj., n.f.* (Via) —, Appian Way.

appiaccicare [A 2 s] and derivs. See **appiccicare**.

appiacevolire [D 2] *tr.* to make pleasant; to soften, to mitigate; to cultivate (plants).

appiall-are [A I] *tr.* (techn.) to plane. **-ato** *part. adj.* planed.

appian-are [A I] *tr.* to level; to smooth; (fig.) to facilitate; to remove (difficulties). **-a·bile** *adj.* capable of being levelled; (fig.) removable; difficoltà facilmente **-abili**, difficulties that can easily be settled. **-amento** *m.* levelling; smoothing; settlement, settling (of difficulties). **-ato** *part. adj.* smooth; level; facilitated; settled. **-atoia** *f.* 'float', plasterer's smoothing board. **-atoio** *m.* garden-roller. **-atura** *f.* levelling; levelled ground. **-azione** *f.* levelling; smoothing; reduction of a curved surface to a plane in giving measurements of its area.

appiastr-are [A I] *tr.* to plaster; to stick; to glue; to daub; *rfl.* to stick (together), to adhere. (**-atura** *f.*) **-icciare** [A 3] *tr.* to plaster; to stick; to glue; **-icciare** le parole, to mumble; *rfl.* to stick (together); questo cibo s'**-iccia** in bocca, this food sticks to one's palate.

appiastro *m.* (bot.) lemon verbena, *Aloysia triphylla*; balm, *Melissa officinalis*.

appiatt-are [A I] *tr.* to flatten; to conceal, to hide; *rfl.* to crouch in hiding, to conceal oneself; to lie in wait; to cower; to squat; (fig.) to lurk. **-amento** *m.* crouching, hiding; concealment. **-ato** *part. adj.* flattened; crouched; hidden; lurking.

appiatt-ire [D 2] *tr.* to level, to flatten; *rfl.* to become flat; to be levelled. **-imento** *m.* levelling, levelling down. **-ito** *part. adj.* levelled, flattened.

appiccafuoco *m. indecl.* incendiary.

appicca·gnolo *m.* See under **appiccare**.

appicc-are [A 2] *tr.* to attach, to join; to hang up, to affix; to hang (by the neck); to fasten on; to palm off on; **-arla** a, to play a trick on; to pass on (a disease); — il fuoco a, to set fire to; — discorso, to open a conversation; — lite, to start a quarrel, to bring a lawsuit; — la battaglia, to give battle; *rfl.* to cling, to stick; **-arsi** alle vesti di, to cling to the skirts of (also fig.); to hang oneself; (of fire, disease) to spread; (bot.) to take root; (of a graft) to strike, to take. **-a·gnolo** *m.* hook, peg; (fig.) pretext, cavil. (**-amento** *m.*) **-ante** *part. adj.* adhesive, sticky; clammy; contagious. **-atic·cio** *adj.* sticky; contagious; (fig.) importunate. (**-ato** *part. adj.*) **-atoia** *f.* peg. **-atoio** *m.* peg; (bot.) stem of a fruit where it joins the bough. **-atura** *f.* join; adhesion.

appicci-are [A 3] *tr.* to attach; to kindle; to light; (Tusc.) to string (figs) together; *rfl.* to be kindled, to light. **-ante** *part. adj.* sticky, adhesive; clammy. **-ato** *part. adj.* attached; kindled. **-atura** *f.* attaching; kindling.

appiccic-are [A 2 s] *tr.* (*prep.* a) to paste; to stick; to palm off; (fig.) to stick on, to tack on (something extraneous); — uno schiaffo a, to slap; *intr.* (*aux.* avere) to adhere, to stick; *rfl.* to attach oneself; to cling; si **-a** come una sanguisuga, he sticks like a leech. **-atic·cio** *adj.* sticky; clammy; tacky; slimy; contagious; (of a work of art) patchy, thrown together, not forming an organic whole; *n.m.* sticky mess; hotch-potch. **-ato** *part. adj.* pasted; stuck; stuck on; (joc.) **-ato** collo sputo, stuck on with spit, insecure. **-atura** *f.* pasting, sticking; join; (paint.) daub. **-osità** *f.* stickiness; tackiness. **-oso** *adj.* sticky; adhesive.

appiccichino *m.* bore; hanger-on.

appiccinire [D 2] and derivs. See **impiccinire**.

appicciol-are [A I s], **-ire** [D 2] and derivs. See **impicciolire**.

appic-co *m.* (*pl.* **-chi**) pretext; handle, foothold; attachment; †dare — a, to lead on, to raise the hopes of.

appiccol-are [A I s], **-ire** [D 2] and derivs. See **impicciolire**.

appiè *prep.* (*foll. by* di) at the foot (of); *adv.* below, at the foot. (Also **a piè**.)

appied-are [A I] *tr.* (mil.) to cause (cavalry) to dismount; *intr.* (*aux.* essere) to dismount. (**-amento** *m.*) **-ato** *part. adj.* cavalleria **-ata**, cavalry (temporarily) dismounted.

appiede *prep., adv.* See **appiè**.

appieghettare [A I c] and derivs. See **pieghettare**.

appieno *adv.* fully, completely; thoroughly; quite.

appigion-are [A I] *tr.* to let; appigiònasi, house to let, room to let. **-amento** *m.* letting; rent. **-ante** *m., f.* person who lets rooms.

appigio·nasi *m. indecl.* the notice 'To let' (see under **appigionare**); mettere l'—, to sell up; (joc.) white head-band worn by widows; a lettere d'—, in large, bold writing.

appigli-are [A 4] *rfl.* (*prep.* a) to seize, to take hold (of); to take root; to adhere (to), to stick (to); **-arsi** a un pretesto, to resort to an excuse and doggedly stick to it; to choose and follow (a course of action); **-arsi** al partito di, to resolve to, to make up one's mind to.

appi·glio *m.* foothold, grip; (climbing) hold; attachment; pretext, cavil, excuse; dare — a, to provide a pretext for, to give occasion to.

appinzare [A I] and derivs. See **pinzare**.

appinzo *m.* sting (of an insect); sharp taste of wine gone sour.

ap·pio *m.* (bot.) — montano, lovage, *Levisticum officinale*; — palustre, — dolce, celery, *Apium graveolens*.

appiolina *f.* (bot.) common chamomile, *Anthemis nobilis*.

appiòmb-o *adv.* perpendicularly; cascare d'—, to arrive in the nick of time (also **a piombo**); *n.m.* plumb-line, perpendicular; (vet.) true or natural stance (of a horse); aplomb; confidence; balance; (of a dress, etc.) fall, line. **-are** [A I C] *tr.* to make perpendicular with a plumb-line; to plumb. **-atòio** *m.* (archit.) machicolation.

appiopp-are [A I C] *tr.* to plant with poplars; — la vite, to train the vine upon poplars; (colloq.) to plant, to palm off, to fob off; to give, to inflict, to administer: — una bastonata, to administer a beating; — sei mesi di carcere a, to sentence to six months' imprisonment; *rfl.* (*prep.* a) to hang round, to stick, to be always in the way.

appioriso *m.* (bot.) celery-leaved buttercup, *Ranunculus sceleratus*.

appiṣolare [A I S] *rfl.* to doze, to have forty winks, to take a cat nap; to feel drowsy.

appiuol-a *f.* (bot.) rennet apple. **-o** *m.* rennet apple tree, *Pirus malus apiana*.

applacidire [D 2] and derivs. See **implacidire**.

applaud-ire [D I or D 2] *tr.*, *intr.* (*aux.* avere, *prep.* a) to applaud; to clap; to cheer; to commend, to approve; to praise. **-ente** *part. adj.* applauding, admiring, approving. (**-i·bile** *adj.* **-iménto** *m.*) **-ito** *part. adj.* applauded; praised; commended; approved; celebrated. **-itóre** *m.* supporter, applauder, admirer. (**-itrice** *f.*)

appla·uso *m.* applause; clapping; cheering, cheers; approval; commendation; applausi scroscianti, thundering applause.

applic-are [A I S] *tr.* to apply; to lay on; to place close, to bring near; to attach, to stick; to adapt, to convert; to devote; to impose, to inflict; (joc.) — uno schiaffo, to administer a slap; — la legge, to apply the law; to enforce the law; — la pena, to enforce a penalty; (theol.) — la messa, to apply mass (to a particular intention); *rfl.* to apply oneself; to work industriously; to concentrate, to pay attention; to devote oneself. **-a·bile** *adj.* applicable, appropriate, suitable. **-abilità** *f.* applicability. **-aménto** *m.* applying, application. **-ata** *f.* (math.) applicate, ordinate. **-ataménte** *adv.* with application, attentively; intently. **-atézza** *f.* application, diligence. **-ato** *part. adj.* applied; matematica -ata, applied mathematics; attached; administered; adapted; intent, studious; *n.m.* low-grade civil servant or police officer employed on a temporary basis. **-azione** *f.* applying; attaching; diligence, application; appliqué trimming, decoration; scuola d'-azione, advanced technical school for officers or graduates in engineering, etc.; (comm.) -azione di fondi, appropriation of funds; (theol.) -azione della messa, application of mass; (text.) colori di -azione, stain for application by machine; *pl.* appliances; -azioni elettriche, electrical appliances.

†appo *prep.* near; in front of; in comparison with; after.

appoder-are[1] [A I C] *tr.* to portion out (land) into **poderi**, q.v.; to cultivate (land); to till; (fig.) to delegate, to authorize; *rfl.* (of a family) to settle on a **podere**, q.v.; to go into farming. **-aménto** *m.* division of land into farms. **-ato** *part. adj.* (of land) cultivated; tillable. (**-azione** *f.*)

†appoderare[2] *tr.* to dominate, to subjugate.

†appodi-are *tr.* (leg.) to enfeoff. **-atóre** *m.* feudal lord. **-azione** *f.* enfeoffment.

appoggi-are [A 3] *tr.* to lean; to rest; — nelle mani di, to entrust to; to prop, to support; to favour; to accept, to countenance; to reinforce; to stress; — una mozione, to second a motion; — la voce sopra una parola, to emphasize a word; — l'alabarda, to live at someone else's expense, to 'hang up one's hat'; — un colpo, to deliver a blow; (mus.) — la voce, to support the voice by means of an accompaniment; *rfl.* (*prep.* a) to lean (against); (*prep.* a, su) to base oneself (upon); to depend (on); to entrust oneself (to), to place confidence in. **-acapo** *m. indecl.* head-rest; antimacassar. **-amano** *m. indecl.* (paint.) mahlstick. **-aménto** *m.* laying; leaning; support; bannister; (paint.) mahlstick. **-apezzo** *m.* (eng.) workrest. **-ata** *f.* action of supporting, leaning; (naut.) heeling over. **-atesta** *m. indecl.* see **appoggiacapo**. **-ato** *part. adj.* supported; propped; leaning; based; aided, abetted, seconded;

†*n.m.* partisan, supporter. **-atòio** *m.* support, rest; prop; parapet; hand-rail, bannister, balustrade; head-rest; arm-rest. **-atura** *f.* supporting, leaning; (mus.) appoggiatura, a slow grace-note which delays the performance of the main note.

appòg·gio *m.* support; prop; balustrade; (archit.) buttress; corbel; (fig.) protection, favour; aid; (naut.) nave —, tender; (alp.) hold; gymn.) support used in arm-bending exercises; (eng.) bearing, (seat, seating; punto d'—, fulcrum; (leg.) diritto d'—, right of support; (comm.) pezza d'—, document in support (of); voucher.

†appoiare *vb.* See **appoggiare**.

appollaiare [A 4] *rfl.* to perch; to go to roost; (fig.) to make oneself at home; to settle, to take up one's abode.

†appomiciare *vb.* See **impomiciare**.

†appo·nere *vb.* See **apporre**.

apponitòio *m.* hook in a slaughterhouse.

appoppare [A I C] and derivs. See **impoppare**.

appòrre [B 2 I] *tr.* to affix; — la firma a, to sign; to append, to add; to set; to impute, to attribute; to censure; †to add; †to proffer, to administer; †to assign, to allot; *rfl.* to guess, to conjecture; to be in the right; se mal non mi appongo, if I am not mistaken.

apport-are[1] [A I] *tr.* to bring; to carry; to furnish, to produce; to bring about, to cause; — fortuna, to bring good luck; to cite, to adduce; †*intr.* to bring information. (**-ante** *part. adj.*) **-ato** *part. adj.* brought; caused; quoted. **-atóre** *m.* bringer; bearer; messenger; cause; -atore di buone notizie, bearer of good tidings; -atore di lutti, cause of sorrow. (**-atrice** *f.*)

†apportare[2] *intr.* to reach port.

apporto *m.* contribution; thing brought; (spiritualism) apport; (comm.) partner's share towards formation of capital.

appo·ṣit-o *adj.* suitable, proper, apposite; appropriate, respective; special, made to order; †placed; served, set out; †*n.m.* (gramm.) attribute. **-aménte** *adv.* suitably, appropriately; purposely, on purpose, expressly. **†-ivo** *adj.* appositive; artificial; fictitious. **†-i·zio** *adj.* artificial; fictitious.

appoṣizione *f.* (gramm.) apposition; addition; appending (of signature); (leg.) — dei sigilli, affixing of seals (in distraint) (C.C.P.); — di termini, placing of boundary markers (C.C.); †— di cuore, affection.

appoṣolare [A I S] *tr.* (Tusc.) to impose a heavy task upon, to burden.

apposta *adv.* on purpose; purposely, intentionally, deliberately; designedly, expressly; wilfully; — per voi, just for you; a farlo —, just at the right moment; (iron.) just to be awkward, to make matters worse; neanche a farlo —, as it happens, by sheer coincidence; *adj. indecl.* special, specially made. (Also **a posta**.)

appost-are [A I] *tr.* to lie in wait for; to waylay; to watch, to keep an eye on; to spy upon; (orn.) to lie in wait for; — un colpo, to deliver a blow; †to place, to set; †to recognize; †to reveal, to relate; *rfl.* to lie in wait; to lurk. **-aménto** *m.* ambush; -amento in calcestruzzo, pillbox; trap; lying-in-wait; mettersi in -amento, to lie in wait; †setting, placing. **-ato** *part. adj.* spied upon; ambushed; in ambush; †placed, set. (**-atóre** *m.* **-atrice** *f.*)

apposti·cio *adj.* false, artificial; fictitious.

apposto *part.* of **apporre**, q.v.

appozzare [A I C] *tr.* to make pools in, to reduce to puddles, to flood; (Tusc.) to overload (the stomach, with liquid); †to put into a well.

apprat-ire [A I] *tr.* (agric.) to grass over, to lay down (a field) to grass. (**-iménto** *m.*) **-ito** *part. adj.* grassed over, grassy.

appren·d-ere [C I] to learn; to hear; to apprehend; to be informed of; to know; to apprise, to inform; to teach; *rfl.* (*prep.* a) to take hold of; to cling to; to seize, to apprehend; to take root; †to cling; †to clot; †(of fire, emotion) to be kindled. **-ente** *n.m.* learner; apprentice; beginner. **-i·bile** *adj.* capable of being learnt. **-iménto** *m.* learning; knowledge; †apprehension. **-i(s)sag·gio** *m.* apprenticeship. **-ista** *m.* apprentice; learner. **-istato** *m.* apprenticeship. (**-itóre** *m.* **-itrice** *f.*)

apprens-i·bile *adj.* capable of being learnt, grasped; intelligible; apprehensive, anxious. (**-ibilità** *f.*) **-ione** *f.* apprehension, perception, comprehension; preoccupation, anxiety, nervousness. **-ionire** [D 2] *rfl.* to become apprehensive. **-iva** *f.* power of apprehension; †imagination, fantasy. **-ivo** *adj.* capable of learning; apprehensive, nervous; †intelligible.

appreṣo *part.* of **apprendere**, q.v.; †*adj.* clinging; †curdled; †taken; †learnt, taught; †kindled.

appress-are [A I] *tr.* to bring near, to move close; *rfl.* to draw near, to approach; to be near; to resemble. **-aménto** *m.* proximity;

appress-are (*cont.*)

approach; drawing nigh; approximation. **-ato** *part. adj.* near, close, at hand.

appress-o *adv.* near, close by, at hand; (fig.) stare — a, to tag on to, to stick to; (Rome, S. Italy) then, subsequently, afterwards; il giorno —, the day after; in —, subsequently; come —, as follows; *prep.* (sometimes foll. by a, di) in the presence of; in comparison with. **†-ochè** *conj.* as soon as.

apprest-are [A I] *tr.* to prepare; to equip; to supply; *rfl.* to prepare oneself, to get ready. **-amento** *m.* preparation; provision; supply; apparatus, equipment. **-ato** *part. adj.* prepared, ready; equipped; supplied. **†-o** *part.* see **apprestato**; **†***n.m.* see **apprestamento**. (**-atore** *m.* **-atrice** *f.*)

apprett-o *m.* (text.) finish, finishing, dressing; (leather; aeron.) finish, dope; finishing; dare l'— a, to size. **-are** [A I] *tr.* (industr.) to finish, to give a finish to. **-amento** *m.*, **-atura** *f.* finishing; dressing; sizing.

apprezz-are [A I] *tr.* to appreciate; to value; to judge; to appraise; to evaluate, to price. **-a·bile** *adj.* appreciable; considerable; valuable. **-abilmente** *adv.* appreciably; considerably. **-amento** *m.* appreciation; appraisement; valuation; judgment, criticism; fare -amenti intorno a, to comment on, to make remarks about; to judge, to criticize. **-ativo** *adj.* evaluating. **-ato** *part. adj.* appreciated, esteemed; valued; priced. **-atore** *m.* appreciator; judge; valuer. (**-atrice** *f.*)

†approc·ciare *intr.*, *rfl.* to approach; (mil.) to close in.

approc·cio *m.* (mil.) approach; (fig.) overtures; (naut.) approaches (to a good harbour); (fencing) advance in order to close with opponent.

approd-are[1] [A I] *intr.* (*aux.* essere) (naut.) to come alongside, to berth; to be down by the head; to land; (fig.) to lead (to), to come (to); *tr.* (agric.) to set boundaries to, to mark off by means of banks of earth; — la vite, to trail the vine along a bank. **-ante** *part. adj.* arriving, coming to shore. **-ato** *part. adj.* arrived; along shore. **-o** *m.* landing; landing-place.

approdare[2] [A I] *intr.* (*aux.* avere, *prep.* a) to be of use, to avail, to serve.

approfitt-are [A I] *rfl.*, *intr.* (*aux.* avere, *prep.* di) to profit (by); to take advantage (of); to avail oneself (of); — dell'occasione, to jump at the chance. **-ato** *part. adj.* benefited.

approfond-are [A I c] *tr.* to deepen; to investigate thoroughly; to dig down into. **-amento** *m.* deepening; investigation. (**-ato** *part. adj.*)

approfond-ire [D 2] *tr.* to examine carefully, to sift, to get to the bottom of; *rfl.* to go deeply into; to become learned in. **-imento** *m.* deepening; investigation; scrutiny. **-ito** *part. adj.* deepened; investigated; scrutinized; esame -ito, exhaustive examination.

appront-are [A I c] *tr.* to prepare, to make ready. (**-amento** *m.* **-ato** *part. adj.*)

†appropiare *tr.* to adapt; to make similar; *rfl.* to draw near; to conform.

appropinquare [A 6] *rfl.* to draw near, to approach; *intr.* to approach.

appropo·sito *adv.* à propos. See also under **proposito**.

appropri-are [A4] *tr.* to adapt; to adjust; to render suitable; — l'azione alla parola, to suit the action to the word; to apply; **†**to compare, to consider similar; **†**to assimilate; **†**to assert, to affirm; *rfl.* (*dat.* of *prn.*) to appropriate; to assimilate; (leg.) -arsi indebitamente, to embezzle. **-a·bile** *adj.* adaptable; appropriable. **-amento** *m.* adaptation; appropriation. **-atamente** *adv.* appropriately; suitably; precisely. **-ato** *part. adj.* appropriated; appropriate, proper, suitable. **-atore** *m.* appropriator; embezzler. (**-atrice** *f.*) **-azione** *f.* appropriation; suitability, applicability; (leg.) -azione indebita, embezzlement; misappropriation (C.P.).

approssim-are [A I s] *tr.* to bring near, to place beside; to approach; *rfl.* to approach, to draw near; to approximate. **-amento** *m.* approach; drawing near. **-ante** *part. adj.* approaching; near. **-ativamente** *adv.* approximately; at a rough guess. **-ativo** *adj.* approximate; un calcolo -ativo, a rough estimate; careless, inaccurate; indefinite. **-ato** *part. adj.* approximate; near; brought near. **-azione** *f.* approximation; approach; proximity; per -azione, by approximation; (math.) approximation; (aeron.) approach.

approv-are [A I] *tr.* to approve of; to praise, to commend, to approve; to countenance; to accept; to ratify, to sanction; to confirm; essere -ato agli esami, to pass one's examinations; — una legge, to pass a law; — un bilancio, to adopt a balance sheet; — una relazione, to adopt a report; — una proposta, to carry a resolution; **†**to experience; **†**to prove. **-a·bile** *adj.* commendable, praise-

worthy. **-amento** *m.* approbation, approval. (**-ante** *part. adj.*) **-ativo** *adj.* approbatory; approving. **-ato** *part. adj.* approved; praised; successful; elenco dei candidati -ati, pass-list. (**-atore** *m.* **-atrice** *f.*) **-azione** *f.* approbation; approval.

†approvecciare *rfl.* to avail oneself, to take advantage.

†approvveduto *adj.* See **provveduto**.

approvvigion-are [A I c] *tr.* to supply; to stock; to provision; to victual; (naut.) to rig, to fit out, to provision, to victual (a ship); *rfl.* to get in supplies. **-amento** *m.* provisionment; provisioning; supply; armaments. (**-ato** *part. adj.*)

appruato *adj.* (naut.) down by the head; (aeron.) nose-heavy.

†appulcrare *tr.* to beautify; to embellish.

appulso *m.* impulse; (astron.) appulse.

appuntamento *m.* appointment; dare — a, to make an appointment with; darsi —, to arrange to meet one another; non mancare ad un —, to keep an appointment; luogo di —, meeting-place, rendez-vous; secondo l'— prestabilito, according to schedule.

appunt-are [A I] *tr.* to sharpen, to make pointed; to stick into, to thrust; to point at, to turn on, to aim at; — gli occhi, to direct one's gaze; — lo sguardo su, to fix one's eyes on; — gli orecchi, to listen attentively; to press, to push; (fig.) — i piedi al muro, to dig one's toes in; to make notes on, to make a note of; to note as absent; to censure; to accuse (of); to stitch, to tack; to pin; to appoint, to fix, to determine; (eng.) — mediante scaldatura, to tack-weld; *rfl.* to be directed, to be focused; to be turned; to come to a point, to taper; to be sharpened; (dial. Rome) to be stagnant; **†**to cease, to terminate; **†**to stop, to rest; **†**to be obstinate. **-a·bile** *adj.* censurable, blameworthy; faulty. **-alapis** *m. indecl.* pencil-sharpener. (**-amento** *m.*) **-ata** *f.* rough sewing, tacking: dare un'-ata, to sew roughly, to tack; (fencing) remise made without previously bending arm by attacker whose first thrust has been parried against opponent delaying his riposte. **-atina** *f.* rough sewing, tacking; a stitch or two. **-atino** *adj.* narrow-minded, pedantic, over-precise. **-ato** *part. adj.* sharpened, pointed; pinned; noted, recorded, registered; fixed, determined; directed; precise, punctilious; affected; *adv.* scrivere -ato, to write correctly; parlare -ato, to speak correctly, to speak with precision; (herald.) in counterpoint; *n.m.* (mil.) lance-corporal of the Carabinieri. **-atamente** *adv.* precisely, accurately. **-atore** *m.* overseer, time-keeper, inspector (in a factory); glass-blower; marker; fault-finder. (**-atrice** *f.*) **-atura** *f.* pointing; sharpening; pinning; censure. **-ino** *adv.* nicely; carefully; with precision; *adj.* censorious, pedantic; *n.m.* fault-finder. (For **appuntino** *n.m. dim.*, see under **appunto**[1].)

appuntell-are [A I] *tr.* to support; to prop; to underpin; to shore up; (fig.) — coi polsi le ganasce, to sit idling. **-ata** *f.* propping; support, prop. **-ato** *part. adj.* supported; propped; shored up. **-atura** *f.* propping, supporting; prop for underpinning.

appuntito *adj.* sharp; pointed.

appunt-o[1] *m.* note; remark, comment; criticism; muovere un — a, to censure; fare -i a, to find fault with, to criticize; (paint.) note, sketch. **-ino** *m. dim.* brief note, jotting; (comm.) informal written acknowledgement of debt.

appunto[2] *adv.* precisely, exactly; just: parlavo — di ciò, I was speaking of that very thing; per l'—, precisely; as it happens; avrei invitato anche lui, ma per l'— oggi non c'è, I would have asked him too, but it just so happens he's away today; *n.m.* exact point; stare sull'—, to be a stickler for accuracy; *adj. indecl.* precise, impeccable, immaculate; elegant.

appur-are [A I] *tr.* to ascertain, to verify; to clear up; to wipe out (debt); (comm.) — un conto, to verify an account. (**-amento** *m.* **-ato** *part. adj.*)

appuzz-are [A I] *tr.* to pollute; to infect; (fig.) to taint, to corrupt. **-amento** *m.* stench. **-ato** *part. adj.* fetid; stinking.

apriballe *m. indecl.* (text.) bale-breaker.

apribarat·tolo *m. indecl.* tin-opener.

apribocca *m. indecl.* (med.) mouth-opener, gag.

†apricare *intr.* to dwell in the open.

†apricesso *m.* cypress.

apri-co *adj.* (*m.pl.* **-chi**) sunny; exposed to the sun; open, airy; bright; delightful, pleasing.

april-e *m.* April; nell'— degli anni, in the flower of youth; un pesce d'—, an April fool's trick, an April fool. **-ante** *adj.* (provb.) terzo -ante, quaranta dì durante, as the third of April so will the next forty days be. **-ino** *adj.* fresh, young; April-like.

†**aprimento** *m.* See **apertura**, under **aperto**.

apri·neo *adj.* See under **apro**.

aprior-iṣmo *m.* an *a priori* method of arguing. **-ista** *m.* one who argues *a priori.* **-i·stico** *adj. a priori,* aprioristic.

apripista *m. indecl.* bulldozer.

apr-ire [D 8] *tr.* to open; to begin; to inaugurate; to unlock; to cut open; to split; to expound; to disclose; to reveal, to manifest; — un mistero, to unveil a mystery; — un cadavere, to open up a body; — una buca, to make a hole; — un buco per tapparne un altro, to rob Peter to pay Paul; — uno spiraglio, to let in some light; (fig.) — gli occhi, to see the light; — gli occhi a, to put wise; — gli orecchi, to keep one's ears open; — le braccia, to receive with open arms; — la terra, to plough; — la radio, to switch on the wireless; — il rubinetto del gas, to turn on the gas; — un foglio di carta, to unfold a sheet of paper; — una processione, to head a procession; — le tende, to draw back the curtains; — un concorso, to hold a competition; — bottega, to set up shop; — casa, to set up house; — la casa, to hold receptions; — la porta, to open the door, to answer the door; (fig.) — una porta a, to give an opening to, to help; (comm.) — un conto, to open an account; (leg.) — un testamento, to read a will; (naut.) — le vele, to set (or unfurl) the sails; (mil.) — il fuoco, to open fire; *abs.* (poker) to open; *rfl.* to open; to lead (into); to begin; -irsi con alcuno, to confide in someone; to split, to crack; to be smashed; (of weather) to grow lighter, to clear up; to widen, to distend; (of flowers) to open, to unfold; (colloq.) apriti cielo!, Heavens above!, that's torn it!, now the fat'll be in the fire!; *intr.* (*aux.* essere) to gap, to gape. (**-i·bile** *adj.*) **-itivo** *adj.* laxative. **-itoio** *m.* (text.) opener, preparer; willow; -itoio a tamburo, cylinder opener; -itoio con tamburo a denti, porcupine opener. **-itore** *m.* opener; custodian. (**-itrice** *f.*) **-itura** *f.* opening; hiatus; throat, maw; (text.) opening.

apripalco *m., f. indecl.* attendant who conducts theatre-goers to a box.

aprisca·tole *m. indecl.* tin-opener.

apr-o *m.* (poet.) wild boar. **-i·neo** *adj.* relating to the wild boar.

ap·side *f.* See **abside**.

ap·tero *m.* (archit.) apteral temple; (zool.) apterous.

a·pua *f.* (ichth.) anchovy.

apuano *pr.n., adj.* (geog.) Apuan; Alpi apuane, Apuan mountains.

a·pulo *adj., n.m.* (poet.) Apulian.

aqua·rio *m.* See **acquario**.

aqua·tico *adj.* See **acquatico**.

a·queo *adj.* See **acqueo**.

aquifo·glio *m.* See **agrifoglio**.

a·quil-a *f.* (orn.) eagle; — anatraia, spotted eagle, *Aquila clanga;* — di mare, white-tailed eagle, *Haliaëctus alticilla;* — minore, booted eagle, *Hieraëtus pennatus;* — reale, golden eagle, *Aquila chrysaëtus;* (hist.) — bicipite, two-headed eagle, symbol of the Austrian Empire; (fig.) genius, outstanding intellect; (iron.) non è un'—, he's no genius; (astron.) the southern constellation Aquila; (herald.) eagle displayed. **-astro** *m.* (orn.) osprey; (poet.) eaglet. **-ino** *m. dim.* (orn.) eaglet; old Tyrolean silver coin; *adj.* aquiline. (**-inamente** *adv.*) **-otto** *m.* (orn.) young eagle; (aeron.) learner pilot; (herald.) eaglet.

aquile·gia *f.* (bot.) columbine, Venus' chariot, *Aquilegia vulgaris;* (herald.) columbine.

aqui·leo *adj.* (poet.) aquiline.

aquili·fero *m.* (Rom. hist.) standard-bearer; bearer of the Roman eagle.

aquilon-e[1] *m.* north wind. **-are** *adj.* northern; (of wind) from the north.

aquilone[2] *m.* kite; (herald.) aquilon.

aquimanale *m.* (archaeol.) ewer, containing water for washing the hands before eating.

Aquisgrana *pr.n. f.* (geog.) Aachen, Aix-la-Chapelle.

aquitana *f.* a French breed of cattle.

ara[1] *f.* (pagan) altar; (astron.) Ara.

ara[2] *f.* are, 100 sq. m.

ara[3] *f.* (orn.) macaw.

†**ara**[4] *f.* pig-sty.

ara·bile *adj.* See under **arare**.

a·r-abo *n.m.* Arab; Arabian; the Arabic language; Arabian steed; *adj.* Arab, Arabian, Arabic; l'-aba fenice, the phoenix, the Arabian bird. **-abescare** [A 2c] *tr.* to decorate with arabesques; *abs.* to doodle. **-abescato** *part. adj.* decorated with arabesques;

(typ.) swash (of lettering). **-abesco** *adj.* (*m.pl.* **-abeschi**) Arabic; Arabian; arabesque; *n.m.* Arab; *pl.* arabesques; scribbling, scrawl, illegible handwriting. **-a·bia** *f.* (geog.) Arabia; l'Arabia Saudiana, Saudi-Arabia. **-a·bico** *adj.* Arabian; Arabic; gomma -abica, gum arabic; †angry, enraged; †queer, fantastic. **-abina** *f.* (chem.) arabin. **-abiṣmo** *m.* Arabism. **-abista** *m.* Arabist.

ara·cee *f.pl.* (bot.) Araceae, arum family of plants.

†**arache** *f.* small poisonous snake.

ara·chide *f.* (bot.) peanut, monkeynut, groundnut, fruit of *Arachi hypogaea;* olio di —, groundnut oil.

aracneo *adj.* pertaining to the spider.

arac·nidi *m.pl.* (zool.) arachnida.

aracn-o·ide *f.* (anat.) arachnoid. **-oidi·te** *f.* inflammation of the arachnoid.

araga·ico *m.* (vet.) colic.

†**aragna** *f.* spider; net.

†**aragno** *m.* silkworm.

aragosta *f.* (zool.) *Palinurus vulgaris,* sea crayfish, crawfish, langouste; (pop.) lobster.

aralda *f.* (bot.) yellow mountain foxglove (the smaller species), *Digitalis lutea.*

ar-aldo *m.* herald; forerunner, harbinger. **-al·dica** *f.* heraldry. **-al·dico** *adj.* heraldic.

arama·ico, arame·o *adj., n.m.* Aramaic.

arance·to *m.* orange-grove.

aran·ci-a *f.* (bot.) orange (see also **arancio**); — forte, — amara, Seville orange, bitter orange; — sanguigna, blood-orange, Maltese orange; — bergamotta, small orange used for perfumery, but inedible, fruit of *Citrus bergamina;* — mandarina, mandarin or tangerine orange. **-a·ia** *f.*, **-a·io** *m.* orange-vendor. **-ata** *f.* orangeade. **-ato** *adj.* orange-coloured, orange; *n.m.* (chem.) -ato di metile, methyl orange. **-era** *f.* storehouse for oranges; greenhouse for orange-trees. **-o** *m.* (bot.) orange-tree; fiori d'-o, orange-blossom, (fig.) weddings; orange; spremuta d'-o, orange squash, orange juice; -o dolce, common orange-tree, *Citrus aurantium;* -o forte, Seville orange-tree, *C. vulgaris;* -o mandarino, mandarin orange-tree, *C. nobilis;* -o pompelmo, -o pomelo, grape-fruit, shaddock, *C. decumana;* acqua di -o, orange-flower water; *adj. indecl.* orange-coloured. **-one** *adj. indecl.* orange-coloured; *n.m.* orange colour.

ara·nea *f.* (anat.) arachnoid.

ara·neo *adj.* (med.) very weak (of the pulse).

ar-are [A 1] *tr.* to plough; *abs.* (fig.) — diritto, to go straight, to tread the straight and narrow path; (poet.) to voyage, to plough the furrows of the deep; — col bue e coll'asino, to do things at random; (naut.) to drag the anchor. **-a·bile** *adj.* arable. **-amento** *m.* ploughing. **-ati·o, -ativo** *adj.* arable. **-ato** *part. adj.* ploughed; lined, furrowed. **-atore** *m.* ploughman; ox for ploughing. **-ato·rio** *adj.* pertaining to ploughing. **-atrice** *f.* steam plough. **-atura** *f.* ploughing; land ploughed.

†**arato** *m.* See **aratro**.

aratr-o *m.* plough; (astron.) the Plough, Ursa Major; — multiplo, gang plough; — talpa, subsoil plough; — portato, direct-connected plough. **-ino** *m.* walking plough.

arauca·ria *f.* (bot.) monkey-puzzle tree, *Araucaria araucana.*

arazz-o *m.* arras; hanging, tapestry. **-ame** *m.* tapestry, hangings. **-eri·a** *f.* tapestry; tapestry factory; art of weaving tapestries. **-iere** *m.* tapestry-maker.

arbag·gio *m.* strip of cloth for protecting the skin in rope-making.

†**arbatraffa** *f.* long fat serpent.

arbi·trio *m.* judgment; caprice; authority; absolute power; fare a proprio —, to do as one likes; libero —, free will.

ar·bitr-o *m.* arbiter; judge; referee, umpire; adjudicator; master; (leg.) arbitrator. (**-a** *f.*) **-ag·gio** *m.* refereeing; umpiring; arbitration; (comm.) arbitrage. **-ale** *adj.* (leg.) arbitral; collegio -ale, board of arbitrators; patto -ale, arbitration clause. **-amento** *m.* (leg.) arbitration. (**-ante** *part. adj., n.m.*) **-are** [A 1 s] *intr.* (*aux.* avere) to arbitrate; to assume authority; to act on one's own authority; *tr.* to judge, to consider, to regard; (sport) to referee; *rfl.* to take the liberty, to assume the responsibility. **-a·rio** *adj.* arbitrary; (leg.) arbitral; (**-ariamente** *adv.*) **-ato** *m.* arbitration; arbitratorship; (hist.) magistrate empowered to reform laws and statutes in the Italian Communes; *part. adj.* arbitrated. **-atore** *m.* arbitrator, judge; one who takes matters into his own hands. (**-atrice** *f.*)

†**arbo** *adj.* unripe, sour.

ar·b-ore *m., f.* (poet.) tree; mast. †**-orare** *tr.* to plant with trees; (of a horse) to rear. **-orato** *adj.* planted with trees, thick with trees. **-oratura** *f.* plantation of trees. **-o·reo** *adj.* pertaining to trees; tree-like; arboreal, tree-haunting; branching; corna -oree, branching horns (e.g. of a stag). **-orescente** *adj.* (bot.) (of a shrub) arborescent, growing to the size of a (small) tree; forked (of lightning); branching, ramifying; (scient.) dendritic. **-orescenza** *f.* (bot.) arborescence; tendency to produce tree-shaped crystals; tree-like formation, branching. **-oreto** *m.* arboretum. **-oricoltore, -oricultore** *m.* arboriculturist. **-oricoltura, -oricultura** *f.* tree culture. **-ori·fero** *adj.* tree-growing (of soil or district). **-oriforme** *adj.* tree-shaped, arboriform. †**-orizzato** *adj.* (scient.) dendritic. **-orizzazione** *f.* (scient.) arborization. †**-oso** *adj.* thickly planted with trees.

arboscello *m.* small tree; shrub.

arbust-o *m.* shrub with several woody stems. **-ino** *adj.* (bot.) vite -ina, wild vine, *Vitis labrusca.*

ar·buto *m.* strawberry-tree, *Arbutus unedo.*

arc-a[1] *f.* tomb, sarcophagus; chest, coffer; l'— di Noè, Noah's ark; (zool.) several edible bivalves, including *Navicula noae* and *Arca barbata*; (Bibl.) — dell'Alleanza, — del testamento, Ark of the Covenant; (fig.) un'— di scienza, a walking encyclopaedia, a mine of learning, an eminent scholar; (zool.) a kind of clam, *Arca noae*. **-ac·cia** *f.* (naut.) stern-frame.

arca[2] *f.* band of Arabs.

ar·c-ade *adj., n.m.* Arcadian; member of the Arcadian Academy (founded in Rome, 1690); writer of Arcadian poetry. **-adessa** *f.* (joc.) woman member of Arcadia. **-a·dico** *adj.* Arcadian; affected; rhetorical; elegant; mawkish. (**-adicamente** *adv.*)

Arca·dia *pr.n.f.* Arcady; Arcadia, the Arcadian Academy, founded in Rome, 1690; (fig.) society in which empty speeches are made and conclusions never reached.

†**arcadore** *m.* archer.

†**arca·gnolo** *m.* See **arcangelo**.

arca·ic-o *adj.* archaic, obsolete; (geol.) archaean. (**-amente** *adv.*) **-ità** *f.* antiquity, great age. **-izzare** [A I] *intr.* (*aux.* avere) to affect archaisms (in speech and writing).

arca-ismo *m.* archaism. **-i·stico** *adj.* (of style) tending to affect archaisms. **-izzare** [A I] *intr.* (*aux.* avere) to affect archaisms.

arcale *m.* (archit.) arch of a doorway; centring; *pl.* rafters; (anat.) ensiform appendage of the breastbone.

†**arcaliffo** *m.* califf; successor.

†**arcame** *m.* carcass; skeleton.

arc-an·gelo, -an·giolo *m.* archangel.

arcan-o *adj.* secret, occult; mysterious; *n.m.* mystery, arcanum; secret; svelare l'—, to unravel the mystery. **-amente** *adv.* mysteriously, secretly. **-ista** *m.* (lit. hist.) writer of esoteric verse.

arc-are *tr.* to shoot (with bow and arrow); †to arch; †to dupe, to trick. **-ata** *f.* space of a bowshot; (archit.) arch, arched doorway (or other opening), vault; arcade; -ata finta, blind arcade; archway; span (of a bridge); (mus.) bow (i.e. one movement of a violin bow); bowing (i.e. the manner of moving a bow); bowstroke; (anat.) arch; (mil.) range; tirare in -ata, to fire at high elevation, to fire at long range; (fig.) indirect reference, hint; (fig.) tirare in -ata, to guess. **-ato** *adj.* arched, curved; tricked; colmo -ato, piled high; (mil.) tiro -ato, long range shot. **-atura** *f.* convexity.

arcarec·cio *m.* (bldg.) purlin; — a cerniera, pin-jointed purlin.

†**arca·rio** *m.* custodian.

†**arcaro** *m.* archer.

arcata *f.* arcade; archway; (mus.) bowing; †bowshot.

arca·vol-o *m.* great-great-grandfather; ancestor. (**-a** *f.*)

arce *f.* citadel; †summit.

†**arcella** *f.* cupboard; air-box of a furnace; (archaeol.) space below an altar leading to a tomb.

archeano *adj.* (geol.) Archaean.

archegg-io *m.* arching, curving; (mus.) bowing. **-io** *m.* arching; continual retching.

archeggi-are [A 3 c] *tr.* (mus.) to play (an instrument) with a bow; to winnow (corn) with a winnowing-fan; to bend to the shape of a bow. **-amento** *m.* (mus.) bowing. **-ato** *part. adj.* curved, arched; (archit.) having several tiers of arches. (**-atura** *f.*)

archeografi·a *f.* archeography.

arche-ologi·a *f.* archaeology. **-olo·gico** *adj.* archaeological. **-o·logo** *m.* (*pl.* **-o·logi, -o·loghi**) archaeologist.

arche·tipo *m.* archetype; master manuscript; model; *adj.* archetypal.

archetto *m.* small bow for archery; (mus.) bow; (orn.) bird trap made from bent twig; (archit.) small arch, lunette; archetti pensili, arcade; (med.) cradle for keeping the bedclothes off a patient's legs; drill-bow; a kind of file on a curved handle used by locksmiths and mosaic workers.

archi- *pref.* equiv. to English *pref.* arch-. **-acuto** *adj.* (archit.) Gothic, having pointed arches. **-atra, -atro** *m.* Court doctor, chief physician; physician to the Pope. **-cem·balo** *m.* (mus.) a large harpsichord. **-confrater·nita** *f.* see **arciconfraternita**. **-episcopale** *adj.* (eccl.) archiepiscopal. **-dia·cono** *m.* see **arcidia·cono**. **-dio·cesi** *f. indecl.* (eccl.) archdiocese. **-ginna·sio** *m.* title of the University of Bologna and the University of Rome. **-mandrita** *m.* (eccl.) archimandrite; (fig.) head, leader (of a literary or other group). †**-parente** *m.* the first parent, Adam. **-pen·dolo, -pen·zolo** *m.* mason's level. **-penzolare** [A I S] *tr.* to level. **-presbiterale** *adj.* (eccl.) archpriest's, archipresbyteral. **-presbiterato** *m.* (eccl.) archipresbyterate, deanship. **-sinagogo** *m.* (rel.) ruler, head, of a synagogue. **-trave** *m.* (archit.) architrave, epistyle, lintel. **-travata** *f.* (archit.) arrangement of arches or beams on columns or pillars. **-travato** *part. adj.* (archit.) architraved. (**-travatura** *f.*) **-triclino, -tricli·nio** *m.* (antiq.) president of a banquet. **-viola** *f.* (mus.) see **arciviola**. **-volto** *m.* (archit.) archway (over a street); archivolt; band of mouldings on an archivolt.

archibu·gi-o *m.* (mil.) arquebus. **-are** [A 3] *tr.* (mil.) to shoot; to shoot down with arquebus shots. **-ata** *f.* arquebus shot; arquebus wound. **-ere** *m.* soldier armed with an arquebus.

†**archibuso** *m.* See **archibugio**.

archifo·glio *m.* galena, lead sulphide.

archileo *m.* (Arezzo) old, cumbrous piece of furniture.

archilo·ch-io, -io *adj., n.m.* (prosod., literat.) Archilochian (verse, dicolon, satire).

architett-are [A I c] *tr.* (archit.) to make an architectural design of, to build; (fig.) to contrive, to devise; to machinate, to plot. **-amento** *m.* (archit.) designing, design, plan; (fig.) machination, plotting. **-ato** *part. adj.* (archit.) designed, planned; (fig.) contrived, plotted.

architett-o *m.* architect; (fig.) creator, author; il grande — dell'universo, the Great Architect of the Universe, God; — militare, military architect; — navale, naval architect, naval engineer. (In the Italian navy, architects may also be qualified engineers and serve at sea.) †**-o·nica** *f.* architecture. **-o·nico** *adj.* architectonic, architectural. †**-ore** *m.* architect, architectural draughtsman; (also *adj.*).

architettur-a *f.* architecture. (The word formerly had a wider application and covered all matters of construction and engineering which are now termed **ingegneria**. There is a modern tendency to restrict it to architecture and architectural design considered as an art); (paint.) architectural drawing, representation of buildings. **-ale** *adj.* architectural.

archi·v-io *m.* archive; archives; repository; learned publication relating to documents, as in title of periodicals, e.g. Archivio Storico Italiano; — di Stato, office in each Italian province where local and judicial records are kept; Archivio della Repubblica, National Record Office (in Rome). **-iare** [A 4] *tr.* to record, to register, to place in archives; (comm.) to file; (leg.) -iare una pratica, to close a criminal investigation by placing the papers in the archives. (**-iatura** *f.* **-iazione** *f.*) **-ista** *m.* archivist, custodian of archives; librarian; document officer. (**-i·stico** *adj.*)

arci- *pref.* equivalent to English *pref.* arch- (cf. **archi-**). **-beato** *adj.* blissfully happy. **-confrater·nita** *f.* (eccl.) archconfraternity. **-con·solo** *m.* (lit. hist.) former title of the President of the Accademia della Crusca (now **presidente**). **-consolare** *adj.* relating to the **arciconsolo**, q.v. **-consolato** *m.* office of president of the Accademia della Crusca; duration of such office. **-dia·cono** *m.* (eccl.) archdeacon. **-diaconale** *adj.* (eccl.) archidiaconal. **-diaconato** *m.* (eccl.) archidiaconate. **-dia·volo** *m.* archdevil; (bot.) nettle-tree, *Celtis australis.* **-dio·cesi** *f. indecl.* see **archidio·cesi**. **-duca** *m.* archduke. **-ducale** *adj.* archducal. **-ducato** *m.* archdukedom; archduchy. **-duchessa** *f.* archduchess. **-fallito** *adj.* utterly bankrupt. **-fan·fano** *m.* braggart; cock-of-the-walk. **-liuto** *m.* (mus.) archlute; theorbo. **-or·gano** *m.* (mus.) a large organ. **-pe·lago** *m.* (*pl.* **-pe·laghi**) archipelago. **-presso** *m.* (poet.) cypress. **-prete** *m.* (eccl.) archpriest, (rural) dean. **-pretale** *adj.* of an archpriest. **-pretato** *m.* archpriest's (term of) office, deanship. **-pretura** *f.* status of archpriest; archpriest's church, 'deanery church'. **-spedale** *m.* head hospital. **-ve·scovo** *m.* archbishop. **-vescovado, -vescovato** *m.* archbishop's house, palace; archbishopric, archdiocese. **-vescovile** *adj.* archbishop's, archiepiscopal. **-viola** *f.* (mus.) bass-viol. **-violato** *adj.* (mus.) lira -violata, a lyre similar to a viol.

arciera[1] *f.* loophole; embrasure; (mech.) vent.

arciera[2] *f.* See under **arciere**.

arcier-e *m.* archer, bowman; highwayman, robber; rogue; tipstaff; (astron.) the constellation Sagittarius. **-a** *f.* archeress.

arciero *m.* See **arciere**.

arcign-o *adj.* sour, vinegary; harsh; severe; frowning, surly, sullen; unpleasant. (**-amente** *adv.* **-ezza** *f.*)

arcile *m.* (dial. Lucca) chestnut-flour-bin; †chest for holding grain.

arcion-e *m.* saddle-bow; saddle; sapere tenersi in -i, to be able to ride; inforcar l'—, to mount into the saddle; voltar l'—, to fall from the saddle; reggersi in —, to stay in the saddle (also fig.); (archit.) rib (of a vault); *pl.* rockers (under a cradle). **-ato** *adj.* (of a saddle) constructed with saddle-bows; built-up.

ar-co *m.* (*pl.* **-chi**) bow (for shooting); tiro d'—, bowshot; a un trar d'—, a bowshot away; con le gambe ad —, bow-legged; (fig.) star con l'— teso, to be continually on the alert, to overlook nothing; archway; curve; l'— delle sopracciglia, the arch of the eyebrows; con l'— della schiena, with all one's might; (archit.) arch; — a tutto sesto, semicircular or round-headed arch; — a sesto acuto, pointed arch; — scemo, ribassato, four-centred (or other low) arch; — morto, closed arch; — di scarico, relieving arch; (mus.) bow; an indication to resume the bow after a pizzicato passage; the neck, or top part of a harp; *pl.* strings (of an orchestra); (theatr.) — scenico, proscenium; (geom.) arc: — voltaico, electric arc; lampada ad —, arc lamp; (anat.) arch; — di stomaco, effort of vomiting. **-cuc·cio** *m. dim.* of **arco**; †cradle, crib.

arcobaleno *m.* rainbow, iris; (mil.) crossbow; un — di colori, all the colours of the rainbow; (fig. joc.) passar sotto l'—, to change sex.

arcobal-estro *m.* crossbow; arbalest. **-ista** *m.* crossbowman.

arcola·io *m.* winder, a circular revolving frame to hold a skein of wool for winding; (fig.) girare come un —, to whirl, to reel; il capo mi gira come un —, my head is spinning; far l'—, (of children) to be always on the go; (mil.) ancient engine of war; †fare arcolai, to dream daydreams, to build castles in the air.

arcont-e *m.* (Gk. hist.) archon, magistrate of Athens. **-ato** *m.* archontate, archonship.

†**ar·cora** *f.pl.* of **arco**, q.v.

arcoreggiare [A3c] *intr.* (*aux.* avere) to retch, to vomit.

arcosa *m.* (geol.) arkose.

arcoso·lio *m.* (archaeol.) arcosolium.

†**arcostrale** *adj.* (poet.) bearing bow and arrow.

†**arcova** *f.* See **alcova**.

†**arcovata** *f.* arcade, series of arches, aqueduct.

†**arcover·gine** *f.* rainbow.

arcovolto *m.* See **archivolto**, under **archi**.

arctazione *f.* (med.) arctation, constriction, drawing up.

arcu-are [A6] *tr.* to arch, to curve, to bend. **-ato** *part. adj.* arched, curved; bent, bowed; cambered; gambe -ate, bow-legs. **-azione** *f.* (med.) arcuation, incurvation.

arcuc·cio *m.* See under **arco**.

ardeatino *adj.* (hist.) le fosse ardeatine, the Ardeatine caves.

Ardenne *pr.n.f.pl.* (geog.) the Ardennes.

ardente *adj.* burning, blazing; fiery; passionate; ardent, fervid; eager, earnest; shining, bright; scintillating; impetuous, hotheaded; spirited, courageous; (of a horse) mettlesome, frisky; (of hair) bright red, carroty; febbre —, high fever; (herald.) flaming at the top; face —, beacon flaming, beacon inflamed. cappella —, *chapelle ardente*, mortuary chapel (lit with tapers). **-entemente** *adv.* ardently, passionately; impetuously, with ardour; violently; zealously.

ar·d-ere [C3] *intr.* (*aux.* essere) to burn, to be on fire; to be parched, baked (of earth); to rage; -eva la mischia, the battle was raging; (of lights, stars) to shine; (fig.) to burn with love; — di sdegno, to be furiously angry; — di sete, to having a raging thirst; *tr.* to burn; to set fire to, to kindle, to dry up, to parch; (fig.) to inflame. **-enza** *f.* ardour; parching heat; (of horses) friskiness. **-ore** *m.* ardour; fervour; heat, warmth; †burning.

arde·sia *f.* slate; cava d'—, slate-quarry.

ardiglione *m.* prong of a buckle.

ard-ire [D2] *intr.* (*aux.* avere) to dare; to have the courage to; to have the impudence to; *abs., tr.* to venture: (provb.) chi nulla -isce, nulla fa, nothing venture, nothing gain; *n.m.* courage, temerity; boldness, daring; force of character; presumption, impudence, 'cheek'; prendere l'— di, to have the courage to; prendere —, to take courage. **-imentare** [A1c] *tr., intr.* (*aux.* avere) (neol.) to dare. **-imento** *m.* courage, boldness, temerity; hardihood. **-imentoso** *adj.* courageous, bold. (**-imentosamente** *adv.*) **-itamente** *adv.* boldly, courageously, fearlessly; impudently. **-itezza** *f.* boldness, courage; temerity; hardihood. **-ito** *part. adj.* bold, courageous, daring; presumptuous, impertinent; farsi —, to dare to; to take the liberty of; farsi -ito, to take courage; fare l'-ito, to swagger, to pretend to be brave; (Tusc.) peso -ito, overweight; salita -ita, steep incline; vino -ito, strong wine; *n.m.* early wheat; (mil.) member of the Arditi; *pl.* (mil.) gli Arditi, assault troops, shock troops.

ardore *m.* See under **ardere**.

ar·du-o *adj.* arduous; steep, uphill; inaccessible; difficult, perplexing, baffling; (poet.) high, elevated, lofty; †great, sublime, magnificent; †*n.m.* difficulty; misfortune. **-amente** *adv.* with difficulty, arduously. **-ità** *f.* arduousness, difficulty.

†**ardura** *f.* combustion, burning; (fig.) ardour.

†**are** *m.* See **aere**.

a·rea *f.* area; surface; region, zone; extent; ground; — da fabbricare, — fabbricabile, building plot; (fig.) patch; (geom.) area; field of a seal, the flat surface for the engraving; roasting-place in a metal refinery; (med.) — Celsi, area, bald patch on the head; (archit.) floor-space; building site (extent); (sport) — di rigore, penalty area; (rugby) — di meta, in-goal.

areca *f.* (bot.) genus of palms including the betelnut palm of India, *Areca catechu*.

arella *f.* pig-sty.

arem, aremme *m. indecl.* harem.

aren-a *f.* gravel; soil, earth; arena; stadium; ring; lists; open-air theatre; cockpit; dramma d'—, melodrama, blood-and-thunder drama; (med.) arena, deposits in the urine; (poet.) shore; †sand. **-a·ceo** *adj.* sandy; (scient.) arenaceous. **-a·io** *m.* sandpit. **-amento** *m.* silting up, stranding. **-are** [A1c] *tr.* to fill with sand; to clean with sand; (naut.) *intr.* (*aux.* essere), *rfl.* to run aground; to be stranded; (fig.) to be shelved, to get no further, to come to a standstill. **-a·ria** *f.* sandstone. **-a·rio** *adj.* cimiteri -ari, catacombs; *n.m.pl.* gladiators, combatants in the arena. **-ato** *part. adj.* stranded; aground; (fig.) shelved, at a standstill; (techn.) sanded, rubbed down; *n.m.* coarse limewash. **-azione** *f.* (med.) embedding (of a patient) in warm sand. **-ella** *f.* fine sand. **-ile** *m.* sandy waste; strand; sandpit. **-oso** *adj.* sandy, full of sand; arid; shifting, unstable. (**-osità** *f.*)

arenga[1] *f.* (bot.) one of the sago palms, yielding sugar, *Arenga saccharifera*.

†**arenga**[2] *f.* See **arringa**.

arenga·rio *m.* (hist.) medieval building where popular assemblies were held; (neol. pol.) balcony from which the mob is harangued.

arengo *m.* (hist.) popular assembly of Italian communes in the Middle Ages; lists, arena; (fig.) arena.

areni·cola *m.* (zool.) lugworm.

arenile *m.* See under **arena**.

arente *adj.* (poet.) arid, parched.

are·ola[1] *f.* (anat.) areola.

are·ola[2] *f.* (poet.). See **aiuola**.

areo·metro *m.* (phys.) araeometer, hydrometer.

areo·pag-o, areopa·g-o *m.* (Gk. hist.) Areopagus (court or hill at Athens). **-i·ta** *m.* Areopagite. **-i·tica** *f.* Areopagitic; Isocratean oration. **-i·tico** *adj.* Areopagitic.

areoplano *m.* See **aeroplano**.

areo·stilo *m.* (archit.) araeostyle, areostyle.

areotetto·nica *f.* (mil. archit.) areotectonics.

†**aresta** *f.* ear of corn.

†**aretag·gio** *m.* heritage.

†**areticare** *rfl.* to fly into a rage; to curse and swear.

aretina *f.* (mus.) a kind of dance.

aretin-o *adj.* (geog.) Aretine, of Arezzo; Aretine, pertaining to, characteristic of, Pietro Aretino (mus.) sillabe -e, syllables invented by Guido of Arezzo to denote the degrees of the scale; *pr.n.m.* l'—, the territory of Arezzo; Leonardo Bruni, fifteenth-century humanist; Pietro Aretino, sixteenth-century author.

arfasatto *m.* (Tusc.) worthless individual; cheat, cad; guy, laughing-stock.

ar·gan-o *m.* capstan; winch, windlass; (fig.) tirare con gli -i, to induce by great persuasion; a forza d'-i, with a great effort. **-ello** *m. dim.* of **argano**; turnstile; small mill. **-etto** *m. dim.* of **argano**, -etto idraulico, hydraulic turbine.

Argante *pr.n.m.* the pagan hero in Tasso's *Gerusalemme Liberata*; (theatr.) mobile lampstand for horizontal floodlighting; effects projector; table for stage properties.

arge·mone *f.* (bot.) Mexican poppy, yellow prickly poppy, *Argemone mexicana*.

argent-are [A I] *tr.* to silver-plate; see also **inargentare**. **-a·ria** *f.* (bot.) Illyrian knapweed, *Centaurea (Jacea) ragusina*. **-a·rio** *m.* silver-smith; *adj.* like silver; silvery; containing silver, argentine. **-ato** *part. adj.* silvered; silver-plated; volpe -ata, silver fox; silvery, gleaming like silver, argent. **-atore** *m.* silver-plater; (art) gilder or silverer (of statues); silversmith. **-atura** *f.* silver-plating. **-eri·a** *f.* silver plate, silverware. **-iera** *f.* silver mine. **-iere** *m.* silversmith; *adj.* argentiferous, silver-bearing. †**-iero** *m.* silver-smith. **-i·fero** *adj.* argentiferous, silver-bearing. **-i·metro** *m.* machine for measuring silver-plating. **-ina** *f.* (bot.) silverweed, *Potentilla anserina*; honesty, satin-flower, moonseed, *Lunaria annua*; (ent.) silver-fish, *Ctenolepisma* sp.; (ichth.) Argentine, *Argentina* sp.; silver lime; a white variety of mica. **-ino** *adj.* silvery; argentine; una voce -ina, a voice like a bell; *n.m.* (ichth.) *Alburnus lucidus*, bleak; nickel-silver, packtong; (see also under **Argentina**). **-one** *m.* packtong, nickel-silver.

argen·teo *adj.* silvery; like silver; (of a voice) bell-like; volpe argentea, silver fox.

Argent-ina *pr.n.f.* (geog.) Argentine. **-ino** *adj.*, *n.m.* Argentinian. **-ina** *f.* Argentinian woman; sports shirt.

argent-o *m.* silver; — battuto, wrought silver; — dorato, silver-gilt; — vivo, quicksilver, mercury; (fig.) aver addosso l'— vivo, to be like a cat on hot bricks; — rosso, pyrargyrite, native silver sulphide; — rosso arsenicale, proustite, native sulpharsenide of silver; nitrato d'—, silver nitrate; (pharm.) bacchetta di nitrato d'—, lunar caustic; silver coinage; †money; (herald.) argent; silverware, silver plate; silver colour, whiteness; white hair; d'—, silvery; silver, silvern; liquido d'—, clear water; raggio d'—, silvery beam, the moon's ray; nozze d'—, silver wedding; l'età d'—, the silver age; *pl.* silverware; (eccl.) ecclesiastical plate. †**-a·io** *m.* silversmith. **-ale** *adj.* like silver; silvery.

argentovivo *m.* quicksilver, mercury; *adj. indecl.* colour of quick-silver. (See also under **argento**.)

argeo *adj.* (poet.) Greek.

argill-a *f.* clay; — plastica, potter's clay; — cotta, terracotta; — magra, sandy clay; — grassa, rich clay; — saponifera, fuller's earth; (poet.) mortale —, dust of the earth, man, the body. **-a·ceo** *adj.* argillaceous, clayey. **-oschisto** *m.* (geol.) argilloschist. **-oso** *adj.* clayey, loamy; (geol.) argillaceous.

ar·gin-e *m.* bank, embankment; dyke; causeway; — di piena, flood dam; (fig.) obstacle, barrier; mettere — a, to put a stop to, to check, to stem; to hold back (crowd); rompere ogni —, to break all bounds; — traverso, dam; (naut.) mole, stone pier, jetty, breakwater; (mil.) parapet. †**-ale** *adj.* pertaining to an embankment; *n.m.* a long embankment. **-amento** *m.* embanking; embankments. **-are** [A I s] *tr.* to dam; to embank; (fig.) to stem, to check. **-ato** *part. adj.* dammed, embanked; *n.m.* embankment. **-atura** *f.* embankment; dykes. **-azione** *f.* embanking. **-ello** *m.* causeway; dam.

argin·nide *f.* (ent.) fritillary butterfly.

argironeta *m.* (zool.) water spider.

argnone *m.* See **arnione**.

Arg-o *pr.n.m.* (myth.) Argus; (fig.) spy; custodian; watchdog; (myth.) Argo, the ship of the Argonauts; (Gk. hist.) Argos; (ent.) Argus butterfly; (orn.) Argus pheasant; (astron.) Argus; (chem.) see **argon**. **-ivo** *adj.*, *n.m.* Argive, Greek. **-o·lico** *adj.* Argive, Greek. **-ona·uta** *m.* (myth.) Argonaut; (fig.) intrepid navigator; (zool.) nautilus.

†**argo·glio** *m.* See **orgoglio**.

†**argogna** *f.* resentment.

argoment-are [A I c] *tr.*, *abs.* to argue; to reason; to deduce, to infer, to conclude; †*rfl.* to contrive; †to exert oneself, to make an effort. **-a·bile** *adj.* deducible. **-ante** *m.* disputant. **-ativo** *adj.* explanatory, expository: prologo -ativo, prologue setting forth the subject of

a play. **-atore** *m.* arguer, reasoner; *adj.* reasoning. (**-atrice** *f.*) **-azione** *f.* argumentation, formal reasoning; arguing, argument.

argoment-o *m.* summary, exposition, synopsis, argument; theme, plot; subject, subject-matter; topic; insistere su un —, to dwell on a subject; un — scottante, a sore point; addurre un —, to put forward a point of view; — cornuto, dilemma; reason, proof; l'Achille degli -i, the most cogent argument; indication, sign; il suo silenzio è — di colpa, his silence argues his guilt; pretext, opportunity; dar —, to give cause; to give a pretext; †contrivance; †instrument, means †**-oso** *adj.* reasoned; astute, skilled; busy, industrious.

argon *m. indecl.* (chem.) argon.

argona·uta *m.* See under **argo**.

argu-ire [D 2] *tr.* to infer, to deduce, to gather, to conclude; to indi-cate, to suggest, to argue; *abs.* to argue; †to accuse, to charge. †**-ente** *part. adj.* accusing. **-ito** *part. adj.* deduced, inferred. (**-izione** *f.*)

ar·gulo *m.* (ent.) *Argulus* sp., carp louse.

argut-o *adj.* quick-witted, sharp; to the point; keen; penetrating; witty; humorous; subtle; occhio —, shrewd glance, penetra-ting expression; (of sound) sharp, acute, strident; (poet.) high, clear, ringing. **-amente** *adv.* sharply, keenly; wittily; humor-ously; subtly, acutely. **-ezza** *f.* sharpness, keenness; subtlety; wit.

argu·zia *f.* witticism, jest; humour, liveliness; subtlety, shrewdness; sharpness, keenness, acuteness.

a·ri-a *f.* air; (aeron.) Maresciallo dell'Aria, Air Marshal; — aperta, open air, fresh air; all'— aperta, in the open air; — chiusa, — colata, stale air, stagnant air; colpo d'—, sudden chill caused by a draught; corrente d'—, riscontro d'—, draught; soffio d'—, breath of air; sacca d'—, air-lock; camera d'—, air-space; inner tube (of a bicycle tyre); impermeabile all'—, air-tight; prender —, prender una boccata d'—, to take the air, to get some fresh air; dar — a una stanza, to air a room; non c'è un filo d'—, there's not a breath of air; fornito d'— condizionata, air-conditioned; aver paura dell'—, to be afraid of catching cold, (fig.) to be easily intimidated; cambiar —, to go away for a change of air; climate, weather; — gelata, cold, bitter weather; — fine, rarefied air; — vibrata, high altitude air; (fig.) qui non è — per lui, this is no place for him, (euphem.) he is not popular here; gli volevo parlar di quell'affare, ma vidi che non era —, I wanted to speak to him about the matter, but I saw that it was not a suitable moment; all'—, face upwards; mettersi a pancia all'—, to lie on one's back; mandare uno a pancia all'—, to knock a person flat on his back; buttare all'—, mandare all'—, to throw up, to put an end to; mandare all'— una stanza, to turn a room upside down; andare all'—, to come to nothing; andare a gambe all'—, to fall; (fig., colloq.) to go bust; saltare in —, to go up in smoke; (provb.) i cenci vanno all'—, the poor go to the wall; per —, in the air, in the sky; (fig.) in —, in the air; qualcosa in — c'è di sicuro, there's something in the air I feel certain; parlare in —, parlare a mezz'—, to hint; intendere a mezz'—, to take the hint; a mezz'—, in mid-air; intendere per —, to understand at once, to be quick in the uptake; non dire nemmeno all'—, to keep a secret; campar d'—, to live on air, to have nothing to eat, to eat very little; castelli in —, castles in Spain; camminare con la testa in —, to have one's head in the clouds; (mus.) aria: air, melody, tune; sull'— di, to the tune of; manner, air, demeanour: Carlo ha un po' l'— di Gigi mio fratello, Carlo reminds me rather of my brother Gigi; mi sta con una cert'—!, he stands there trying to lord it over me!; darsi delle -e, to put on airs; appearance, aspect; ha l'— di essere contento, he seems pleased; mi hai l'— di un galantuomo, you seem to me to be a good chap; giudicare ad —, to judge by appearances; (paint.) expression (of a face); colour representing the sky (or air); airiness; atmosphere; (archit.) ponte in —, suspension bridge; single-span arched bridge; gap; space, room: aria!, out of the way there!; †essere un poco d'—, to show off; †render — a, to resemble; †di buon'—, pleasantly, good-humouredly. **-etta** *f.* breeze; (mus.) a short aria; stanza intended to be sung (e.g. in the dramas of Metastasio). **-oso** *adj.* airy, well aired; graceful; light; attractive, pleasing; (joc.) pre-tentious; (mus.) tuneful; †(of weather) fine; †bold, impudent; †fatiguing; †bizarre; *n.m.* (mus.) arioso, a vocal composition in a style between aria and recitative.

Arianna *pr.n.f.* (myth.) Ariadne; il filo d'—, the clue to a difficulty.

arian-o[1] *adj.*, *n.m.* (eccl. hist.) Arian. **-ẹsimo, -ịsmo** *m.* (eccl. hist.) Arianism.

arian-o[2] *adj.*, *n.m.* (hist.) Aryan. **-ẹsimo, -ịsmo** *m.* (hist.) Aryanism.

aricina *f.* (chem.) aricine.

a·rid-o *adj.* arid, dry; barren; parched; (fig.) stile —, bald, unembellished style; un cuore —, a hard heart; un libro —, a dry, uninteresting book; *n.m.* aridity; dry substance; *pl.* dry goods, grain, etc. **-a** *f.* (poet.) l' -a, the earth. **-amẹnte** *adv.* aridly; drily; unemotionally. (**-ẹzza** *f.*) **-ità** *f.* aridity; barrenness; scarcity; lack of affection. **-ocultura** *f.* (agric.) dry farming.

arieggi-are [A3c] *tr.* to air, to ventilate; to resemble; (paint.) to suggest, to give an impression of; to resemble (in style); *intr.* (*aux.* avere, *prep.* a) to imitate, to ape, to assume the manner (of), to have an air (of). **-ato** *part. adj.* aired, ventilated; airy.

†**ariento** *m.* See **argento**.

ariet-e *m.* (zool.) ram; (astron.) Aries, the Ram; (mil.) battering ram; (eng.) ram; (hydraul.) colpo di —, water-hammer, air-lock; (naut.) warship used for ramming, sinker (of ships). **-are** [A1] *tr.* (mil.) to ram. **-ino** *adj.* (bot.) cece -ino, chick-pea, *Cicer arietinum.*

ariẹtta *f.* See under **aria**.

arillo *m.* (bot.) aril.

aringa *f.* herring; — affumicata, kipper; †see **arringa**.

a·rio *adj.* See **ariano**[1]; arioeuropeo, Indo-European.

†**ariolo** *m.* soothsayer; magician, seer.

ariọso *adj.* See under **aria**.

ariost-e·o, -ẹsco *adj.* (*m.pl.* **-ẹschi**) in the manner of Ariosto; pertaining to Ariosto; fantastic, improbable, far-fetched. **-eri·a** *f.* fantastic behaviour; improbability.

arisaro *m.* (bot.) friar's cowl, Italian Jack-in-the-pulpit, of the Arum family, *Arisarum vulgare.*

a·rista[1] *f.* (butcher.) chine of pork.

arista[2] *f.* (bot.) ear of corn; beard of the ear.

Aristarco *pr.n.m.* (Gk. lit.) Aristarchus, the Alexandrine critic; (fig.) pedantic or severe critic.

aristo·crate *m.*, *adj.* See **aristocratico**.

aristo-cra·tico *adj.* aristocratic; *n.m.* aristocrat; supporter of aristocratic form of government; one who apes the aristocracy. (**-craticamẹnte** *adv.*) **-crazi·a** *f.* aristocracy, nobility; haughtiness, condescension; l'-crazia dell'ingegno, the cream of the intelligentsia; (hist.) l'-crazia nera, the section of the Italian aristocracy which supported the temporal power of the Papacy; l'-crazia bianca, the aristocracy which supported the Kingdom of Italy. **-cratọne** *m.* (joc.) toff.

Aristo·fan-e *pr.n.m.* Aristophanes. **-ẹsco** *adj.* (*m.pl.* **-ẹschi**) Aristophanic, satirical.

aristol(o) *m.* (chem.) iodized thymol.

aristolo·chia *f.* (bot.) birthwort, *Aristolochia clematitis.*

a·riston *m. indecl.* (mus.) a kind of street-organ.

Aristo·t-ele, -ile *pr.n.m.* Aristotle. **-e·lico** *adj.* Aristotelian.

aritenọ·ide *f.* (anat.) arytenoid cartilage.

aritme·tic-a *f.* arithmetic; l'— non è un'opinione, facts are facts. **-amẹnte** *adv.* arithmetically; by means of arithmetic. **-o** *adj.* arithmetical; *n.m.* arithmetician.

a-ritmi·a *f.* want of rhythm; (med.) arrhythmy. **-rit·mico** *adj.* arrhythmic, lacking rhythm; (med.) arrhythmic.

†**aritmo** *m.* number.

aritmo·metro *m.* arithmometer, adding machine.

arlecchin-o *m.* harlequin, clown; buffoon; fool; (theatr.) Harlequin; (colloq.) cocktail; vestire da —, to dress in many colours. **-ata** *f.* buffoonery; clowning; volte-face. **-ẹsco** *adj.* (*m.pl.* **-ẹschi**) Harlequin-like; motley.

arli·a *f.* (dial. Lucca, Tusc.) superstition, delusion.

Arlotto *pr.n.m.* il piovano —, Arlotto Mainardi, a priest of the fifteenth century, famed for his wit, his untidy dress, and his illiteracy; (fig.) untidy individual; glutton.

arm *excl.* (mil.) spall'arm!, shoulder arms!; pied'arm!, ground arms!

arma[1] *f.* (*pl.* **armi, arme**) branch, arm (of a service); di che — è soldato?, what arm is he in?; regiment; l'— benemerita, the Carabinieri; service (army, navy, air-force); l'— azzurra, the Air-Force; l'— microbica, bacterial warfare branch; l'— chimica, chemical warfare branch; armi dotte, specialist arms. (See also **arme**.)

†**arma**[2] *f.* soul.

armacollo *adv.* ad —, slung diagonally across the shoulders; *n.m.* †gorget, neck-armour.

armadillo *m.* (zool.) armadillo, *Dasypus* spp.

arma·d-io *m.* wardrobe; cupboard; — farmaceutico, medicine cabinet; — a muro, wall cupboard. **-iẹtto** *m.* locker; cabinet; -ietto da spogliatoio, clothes locker. **-ino** *m.* show-case. **-iọne** *m.* *augm.* (fig.) essere un -one della scienza, to be a mine of learning.

†**armadura** *f.* See **armatura**, under **armare**.

armaiuo·lo *m.* armourer; gunsmith; naval ordnance staff.

armamenta·rio *m.* See under **armare**.

armamẹnto *m.* See under **armare**.

arm-are [A1] *tr.* to arm; to supply with arms; to enlist; to recruit; to man; to fortify; to strengthen; to reinforce (concrete); to put in order; to cock (a firearm); to lay (a railway line); — cavaliere, to knight, to dub; (eng.) to fit out; (archit.) to support with centring or props; (naut.) to commission, to store (a ship); to rig; (mus.) — la chiave, to write a key-signature after the clef; — uno strumento, to equip an instrument with strings or other fittings; *rfl.* to take up arms; to arm oneself; (fig.) -arsi di coraggio, to take courage; -arsi di pazienza, to be patient. **-amenta·rio** *m.* armoury; weapon case; (surg.) instrument case; (fig.) array, equipment; (joc.) goods and chattels, kit, paraphernalia. **-amẹnto** *m.* armament; arming; storing; (naut.) fitting out stores; industria dell'-amento, shipping industry; (rlwy.) superstructure; -amento ed inghiaiata, permanent way; (mining) timbering; -amento a quadri completi, square setting; *pl.* arming (of a nation); †arsenal; †fare -amento, to make preparations for war. **-ata** *f.* fleet; armada; army; corpo d'-ata, (army) corps; Generale d'-ata, General; Generale di corpo d'-ata, Lieutenant-General; -ata aerea, air force command. **-ato** *part. adj.* armed; a mano -ata, -ata mano, by force, with arms; armoured; strengthened; carro -ato, tank; (fig.) furnished, provided, equipped; (zool.) armoured; (bldg.) cemento -ato, reinforced concrete; volta -ata, vault strengthened with props or ridge-bands; (herald.) with claws, armed; *n.m.* armed man; soldier, man at arms; una schiera d'-ati, a band of armed men. **-atore** *m.* (mil.) fitter out; (naut.) -atore di una nave, owner or agent responsible for commissioning a ship; shipowner. **-atura** *f.* suit of armour; arms; warlike weapon; shelter, defence; (naut.) rig; (industr.) fittings; (bldg.) centring, falsework (of arch); reinforcement (of concrete); forms (for concrete); *pl.* scaffolding; (electr.) armature; magnet keep plate; plate (of condenser); armour (of cable); (mining) timbering; (text.) weave; -atura semplice, plain weave, taffeta weave; -atura spezzata, broken weave; (foundry) core spinale; gagger; spider; (mus.) fittings (e.g. bridge, soundpost, etc., of a violin); (dress-m.) stiffening; (tailor.) collar canvas; (orn.) trammel net.

†**arma·rio** *m.* See **armadio**.

armata *f.*, **armatura** *f.* See under **armare**.

arm-e *f.* (*pl.* **-i**) weapon; instrument of war; bayonet; sword; — da fuoco, firearm; — bianca, steel weapon; — a doppio taglio, double-edged weapon (also fig.); all'—!, to arms!; (hist.) gente d'—, soldiery; le -i, the armed forces; -i corte, side-arms; (fig.) ad -i corte, doggedly, bald-headedly; -i portatili, small-arms; piazza d'-i, drill ground, barrack-square; uomo d'-i, soldier, man at arms; essere sotto le -i, to be in the army, to be in the forces, to be doing one's national service; mestiere dell'-i, soldiering; (fig.) essere alle prime -i, to be a novice; il porto d'-i, licence to carry firearms; presentare le -i, to present arms; prendere le -i, to take up arms; abbassare le -i, to lay down arms; combattere ad -i pari, to fight on equal terms; passare per le -i, to execute; (fig.) fare il viso delle -i, to put on a severe expression; (fencing) sala d'-i, salle d'armes; (hist.) veglia di -i, vigil (before being knighted); prova delle -i, ordeal by weapons; †armour. (See also **arma**[1].)

armeggi-are[1] [A3c] *intr.* (*aux.* avere) to fight; to brandish weapons; †to prepare for war; to joust; (fig.) to bustle, to fuss, to fiddle (with); to become confused; to fumble; to contrive, to manœuvre, to intrigue, to pull strings. **-amẹnto** *m.* assault at arms; joust, tourney; jousting; (fig.) bustling; fumbling; manœuvring; procedure. **-ata** *f.* assault at arms; tourney. **-atore** *m.* jouster, tilter. **-ọne** *m.* busybody; fumbler; intriguer, wire-puller.

†**armeggiare**[2] *vb.* See **ormeggiare**.

armeggio *m.* (naut.) armament, equipment, rigging, rig.

armeggìo *m.* manœuvring; continual bustle, bustling; continual fumbling; jousting.

ar·mel *m. indecl.* (bot.) wild rue, *Peganum harmala.*

armellinata *adj.* (herald.) croce —, cross of four ermine spots.

†**armellino** *m.* See **ermellino**.

†**armene** *m.* reptile, serpent.

Arme·n·ia *pr.n.f.* (geog.) Armenia. **-o** *adj.*, *n.m.* Armenian. **-a** *f.* Armenian woman; (geol.) Armenian stone.

armẹnt-o *m.* herd, flock; drove; greggi e -i, sheep and cattle; (poet.) shoal (of fish), flock (of birds). **-a·rio** *adj.* pertaining to a herd; *n.m.* herdsman. **-iere** *m.* herdsman.

armeri·a *f.* museum of arms; armoury; arsenal; arms.

Armida *pr.n.f.* Armida, character in Tasso's *Gerusalemme Liberata*; enchantress; femme fatale.

armiere *m.* (mil.) gunner.

†**armiero** *m.* squire.

armi·gero *adj.* pugnacious, warlike, bellicose; martial, brave; (herald.) armigeral, armigerous; *n.m.* arms bearer; shield bearer; armiger.

armill-a *f.* (archaeol.) armilla, bracelet worn by Roman soldiers; small circle; bracelet. **-are** *adj.* armillary; (astron.) sfera -are, armillary sphere. **-ato** *adj.* wearing an armilla, decorated with an armilla.

armipotente *adj.* mighty in arms; armipotent.

armisti·zio *m.* armistice.

armo¹ *m.* (naut.) fitting out stores; crew (of a yacht); (sport) rowing crew; l'— di Cambridge, the Cambridge boat.

†**armo²** *m.* shoulder.

armo·fane *m.* (geol.) green crystalline corundum.

armoge, ar·moge *m.* (paint.) gradation of colours.

armoni·a *f.* (mus.) harmony; chord; an ensemble of wind instruments, or a composition for such; harmony (of words); sound-effect; — imitativa, onomatopoeia; (fig.) harmony; peace, agreement, concord; in — con, in keeping with; (anat.) false suture, conjunction by mere apposition.

armo·nic-a *f.* (mus.) harmonica, glass-harmonica, mouth organ; science of music (in ancient Greece); harmonic, overtone. **-o** *adj.* (mus.) harmonic; suoni -i, harmonics, overtones; (fig.) harmonious; proportionate; (joc.) capo -o, lively, amusing person; (math.) proporzione -a, harmonic proportion; *n.m.* (mus.) harmonic. (**-amẹnte** *adv.*)

armonicordo *m.* (mus.) harmonichord, an instrument resembling a pianoforte but whose strings are set in vibration by a revolving cylinder.

armonifono *m.* (mus.) harmoniphon(e), an instrument similar to a clarinet but furnished with a keyboard.

armo·nio *m.* harmonium.

armoniọs-o *adj.* harmonious; tuneful; proportionate. (**-amẹnte** *adv.*)

armon-ista *m.* harmonist; †musician (**-i·stico** *adj.*).

armoniẓẓ-are [A 1] *tr.* (mus.) to harmonize, to furnish with harmony; (fig.) to attune; to match (colours); to make agree; *intr.* (*aux.* avere) (mus.) to harmonize, to blend; (fig.) to live in harmony; to be in keeping, to be compatible; to be attuned. (**-amẹnto** *m.*) **-ato** *part. adj.* (mus.) harmonized; †set to music; (fig.) in harmony, in agreement, in accord; well proportioned. (**-aziọne** *f.*)

armoricano *adj.*, *n.m.* Armoric, Breton.

arnẹs-e *m.* tool, implement; borsa degli -i, tool-kit; attire, dress; male in —, poorly dressed; non posso presentarmi in quest'—, I can't appear in this get-up; rimettere uno in —, to fit a person out with new clothes, (fig.) to set a person on his feet; (hist.) suit of armour; (joc.) individual, type, good-for-nothing, down-and-out; un triste —, a bad lot; (colloq.) — da galera, jail-bird; (fam.) thingummajig, whatyoumaycallit; *pl.* -i di guerra, accoutrements of war; †fortress; †ornament, adornment; †(theatr.) property, prop, effect. †**-are** *tr.* to saddle, to harness. †**-a·rio** *m.* (theatr.) property-man, scene-shifter, scene-painter, stage-manager. †**-ato** *part. adj.* equipped.

ar·ni-a *f.* beehive. **-aio** *m.* apiary.

ar·nica *f.* (bot.) mountain arnica, mountain tobacco, *A. montana.*

arnigiano *adj.* See under **Arno**.

arniọne *m.* (butcher.) kidney.

Arn-o *pr.n.m.* (geog.) the River Arno. **-igiano** *adj.* of the Arno valley, from the Arno region.

arnoglossa *f.* (bot.) ribwort plantain, *Plantago lanceolata.*

Arnoldo *pr.n.m.* Arnold.

arnomanzi·a *f.* divination from a lamb.

aro¹ *m.* (bot.) wild arum, lords-and-ladies, wake robin, *Arum maculatum.*

†**aro²** *m.* See **ara.²**

Aroldo *pr.n.m.* Harold.

arom-a *m.* aroma, fragrance; *pl.* spices; aromatic herbs. **-ale** *adj.* (poet.) fragrant, aromatic. †**-a·rio** *m.* vendor of spices; vendor of aromatic herbs. **-aticità** *f.* fragrance; flavour; spiciness. **-a·tico** *adj.* aromatic; fragrant; spicy, savoury; (chem.) composto -atico, aromatic compound, compound containing one or more benzene rings; (fig.) fantastic, weird, strange. **-atite** *f.* kind of spiced wine. **-atiẓẓare** [A 1] *tr.* to spice. **-atiẓẓato** *part. adj.* spiced, aromatic. **-ato** *adj.* aromatic, fragrant; †*n.m.* aroma.

arp-a *f.* (mus.) harp; — eolia, — d'Eolo, Aeolian harp; — doppia, double harp; (zool.) *Harpa* spp., harp shell; (silk ind.) frame where cocoons are placed for the silkworms to become moths. **-anẹtta** *f.* (mus.) pointed harp (with two ranks of strings, one on either side of the sound-board). **-eggiare** [A 3 c] *intr.* (*aux.* avere) (mus.) to play the harp; to spread chords harpwise on a keyed instrument; (vet.) to suffer from stringhalt. **-eggiamẹnto** *m.* (mus.) harping. **-eggiato** *part. adj.* played in a harplike manner. (**-eggiatọre** *m.* **-eggiatrice** *f.*) **-eg·gio** *m.* (mus.) arpeggio. **-eggiọ** *m.* (mus.) strumming. **-icordo** *m.* (mus.) spinet, harpsichord. **-ista** *m., f.* (*pl.* gli -isti, le -iste) (mus.) harpist.

arpagọn-e¹ *m.* (naut.) grappling-iron. **-are** [A 1 c] *tr.* (naut.) to grapple.

Arpagọne² *pr.n.m.* Harpagon, from Molière's *L'Avare*; a miser.

†**arpare** *tr.* to steal; to snatch, to seize.

arpe¹ *f.* (poet.) crescent-shaped sword.

†**arpe²** *f.* See **arpa**.

arpeggiare [A 3 c] and derivs. See under **arpa**.

†**arpento** *m.* acre.

ar·pese, arpẹse *m.* (bldg.) clamp, tie iron.

arpi-a *f.* (myth.) harpy; (fig.) hag; (orn.) bearded vulture, *Gypaëtus barbatus*; (ent.) *Cerura vinula*, puss moth.

arpicare [A 2 s] *rfl.* to climb, to clamber; to scramble up; *intr.* (*aux.* avere) — col cervello, to rack one's brains.

arpicordo *m.* See under **arpa**.

†**arpignọne** *m.* See **arpagone¹**.

arpino *m.* boat-hook.

arpiọn-e *m.* hook; grapnel; hinge; (mech.) pawl; spike. **-iṣmo** *m.* (mech.) pawl and ratchet.

arpista *m., f.* See under **arpa**.

arpọne *m.* harpoon; (mech.) see **arpione**.

arra *f.* token; (comm.) pledge; guarantee; payment on account; earnest.

arrabattare [A 1] *rfl.* to strive, to endeavour to do one's best; to pull the devil by the tail, to be barely able to make both ends meet; (provb.) occhio non vede e cuore non s'arrabatta, what the eye doesn't see the heart doesn't grieve over.

arrabbi-are [A 4] *rfl.* to fly into a passion; to get angry; to get irritated; to be irritable; (of dogs) to become rabid, to catch rabies; *intr.* (*aux.* essere) to rage: non lo fate —, don't annoy him; — dalla sete, to have a raging thirst; (of dogs) to become rabid, to catch rabies; (bot.) (of cereal crops) to wither. **-amẹnto** *m.* anger, fury, rage; onset of rabies. **-atic·cio** *m.* (agric.) ground spoiled by untimely working. **-ato** *part. adj.* rabid, suffering from rabies; cross, angry; raging, furious; sembra un cane -ato, he's like a mad dog; enraged; desperate, frantic; madly enthusiastic, rabid; un fumatore -ato, a chain smoker; (med.) rabid, suffering from rabies; (culin.) rapidly braised; carne -ata nel tegame, meat burnt or toughened by being cooked too quickly; *adv.* secco -ato, frightfully thin; salato -ato, bitterly salt; *adv.* all'-ata, furiously; *n.m.pl.* (hist.) Gli Arrabbiati, the party opposed to Savonarola's religious reform in Florence. (**-atamẹnte** *adv.*) **-atura** *f.* rage, raging; prendere un'-atura, to fly into a rage.

arrabbire [D 2] and derivs. See **arrabbiare**.

arraffare *tr.* to seize, to snatch; (colloq.) to 'pinch', to 'lift'.

†**arraffiare** *vb.* See **arraffare**.

†**arramacciare** *tr.* to transport on a sledge; to bind together in branches.

†**arrampare** *vb.* See **arrampicare**.

arrampic-are [A 2 s] *rfl.* (*prep.* a, su) to climb, to clamber, to scramble; (of plants) to climb, to twine; (fig.) to get on in the world, to climb the social ladder; -arsi sugli specchi, to be pig-headed in argument, to go to fantastic lengths to uphold one's point of view. (**-amẹnto** *m.*) **-ante** *part. adj.* climbing, twining. **-ata** *f.* ascent, scramble; (sport) hill climbing (in motor-cycle racing). **-atọre** *m.* (sport) motor-cyclist who competes in scrambles; climber.

arranc-are[1] [A 2] *intr.* (*aux.* avere) to drag oneself along; to trudge; to hobble; to limp; (fig.) to strive; (naut.) to row hard; -a!, pull!, row! -**ata** *f.* (naut.) pull, hard pull (on the oars). -**ato** *adj.* lame, limping; (naut.) a voga -ata, pulling hard, rowing hard; *adv.* vogare -ato, to row hard.

†**arrancare**[2] *tr.* to uproot; to snatch.

arrancidire [D 2] and derivs. See **irrancidire**.

arrandellare [A 1] *tr.* to cudgel; to fling, to hurl; (fig. colloq. Tusc.) to 'give away' (to sell for very little); †to rope tightly.

arranf-are [A 1], **-iare** [A 4]. See **arraffare**.

arrangi-are *tr.* (colloq.) to adjust, to arrange; (fam.) — pel dì delle feste, to 'fix', to 'settle', (mus.) to arrange; *rfl.* to improvise; to get out of a fix as best one can; to make shift; to feather one's nest; to fend for one's self; arràngiati, do the best you can (by fair means or foul). (-**amento** *m.* -**atore** *m.* -**atura** *f.*).

arrangol-are [A 1 s] *rfl.* to strive, to take trouble. -**ato** *part. adj.* laborious.

arrapin-are [A 1] *tr.* to enrage; *rfl.* to fly into a rage; to exert oneself; to work like mad. -**ato** *part. adj.* bad-tempered; angry.

arrappare[1] [A 1] *tr.* to snatch.

†**arrappare**[2] *tr.* to wrinkle.

arraspare [A 1] *tr.* to rasp; to file; (fig.) to steal.

arrasso *adv.* (dial. S. Italy) far away.

†**arrazzare** *intr.* to shine, to send out a shower of sparks.

arrec-are [A 2] *tr.* to bring about, to occasion, to cause; — piacere, to be a source of pleasure; to cite; to allege; to produce, to furnish; to bring; †to induce, to persuade; †to reduce; †-arsi in braccio, †-arsi in collo, to pick up in one's arms. (See also **recare**.) (-**ante** *part. adj.*) -**atore** *m.* cause; †messenger, harbinger; †narrator. (-**atrice** *f.*)

arred-are [A 1] *tr.* to furnish; to equip; to fit out; (mil.) to furnish, to equip; (naut.) to rig out. -**amento** *m.* equipping, fitting out; equipment; rigging; interior decoration; (cinema, theatre) set decoration; *pl.* fittings, soft furnishings. (-**ato** *part. adj.* -**atore** *m.*) -**o** *m.* (often *pl.*) fittings, furnishings; equipment; outfit; (liturg.) -**i** (sacri), church 'ornaments' or furnishings (liturgical vessels, vestments and instruments).

arreggimentare [A 1 c] *tr.* to regiment.

arregidor-e *m.*, -**a** *f.* (dial. Emilian) manager (of a farm).

arremb-are[1] [A 1] *tr.* (naut.) to board. -**ag·gio** *m.* (naut.) boarding, assaulting, sacking. -**ata** *f.* naval assault. -**o** *m.* (poet.) see **arrembaggio**.

arremb-are[2] [A 1] *intr.* (*aux.* essere), *rfl.* to plod wearily, to drag oneself along: (of a horse) to go lame. (-**amento** *m.*) -**ato** *part. adj.* lagging, exhausted, worn out; low in funds; (of a horse) lame. (-**atura** *f.*)

arrenare [A 1 c] (Tusc.). See **arenare**, under **arena**.

arren-d-ere [C 1] *rfl.* to surrender; to yield, to give way; to give in, to throw in the sponge; to be flexible, to be supple, to give; †*tr.* to surrender. -**evole** *adj.* supple, pliant; docile, unresisting, compliant, biddable. (-**evolmente** *adv.*) -**evolezza** *f.* suppleness, pliability; docility. (-**ibilità** *f.* -**imento** *m.*)

†**arrengo** *m.* See **arringo**.

†**arrequiare** *intr.* to rest.

arrestabu·e *m. indecl.* (bot.) rest-harrow, *Ononis spinosa*.

arrest-are [A 1] *tr.* to arrest; to check; to stop; — istantaneamente, to bring to a stand; to place under arrest; to detain; (med.) to stanch (blood); (mil.) — il nemico, to halt the enemy; † — la lancia, to put one's lance in rest; *rfl.* to stop, to halt; to stop dead; to pull up, to draw up; to leave off; (of blood) to be stanched. -**amento** *m.* arrest; stopping; (med.) -amento del sangue, stanching. -**ato** *part. adj.* arrested; (herald.) statant. -**atoio** *m.* (naut.) capstan. (-**atore** *m.* -**atrice** *f.* -**azione** *f.*)

arresto *m.* (leg.) arrest; detention; pena dell'—, punishment by detention for lesser crimes listed as 'contravvenzioni' (misdemeanours); essere agli arresti, to be under arrest; arrest, stop; delay; standstill; (fencing) — in tempo, stop-hit; †decree, sentence; (mil.) — semplice, open arrest; — di rigore, close arrest; — in fortezza, close arrest (of officers only); (mech.) stop, catch; rubinetto d'—, stopcock; valvola d'—, cutoff valve; leva d'—, cutoff lever; — di fine corsa, limit stop; (of a furnace) damping down; (rugby) — al volo, fair-catch; (med.) — psichico, mental inhibition.

arret-are [A 1] *tr.* to net, to snare. -**ato** *part. adj.* netted, snared; covered with net; made of net; (fig.) lined, marked with a network.

arreticare [A 2 s] and derivs. See **arretare**.

arretr-are [A 1] *tr.* to move back, to draw back, to push back; *rfl.*, *intr.* (*aux.* essere, avere) to withdraw, to retire, to fall back; to recoil; to fall behind; (of a horse) to rear. -**amento** *m.* backing; (archit.) setback. -**ato** *part. adj.* behindhand; in arrears; numero -ato, back number; (of a child) backward; old-fashioned; behind the times; area -ata, depressed area; *n.m.* back number; (comm.) in -ato, in arrears, outstanding; -ati, arrears; back-payments; arrears (of work); remainders; essere in -ati, to be behindhand.

†**arrezzare** *tr.* to shade, to cast shadow upon.

arri *excl.* gee up!; — là, gee up there!; *n.m.pl. indecl.* (fig.) gli arri, encouragement, coaxing.

†**arriccare** *vb.* See **arricchire**.

arricch-ire [D 2] *tr.* to enrich; to endow; to make more abundant; to increase; to adorn; to embellish; (chem.; miner.) to concentrate; *intr.* (*aux.* essere), *rfl.* to grow rich; to prosper, to thrive; to be enriched, to be embellished. -**imento** *m.* enriching; enrichment; concentration; increase in wealth; (leg.) -imento indebito, undue enrichment. -**ito** *part. adj.* enriched; made wealthy; swollen with gain; adorned; *n.m.* nuovo -ito, nouveau-riche; -ito di guerra, profiteer. (-**itore** *m.* -**itrice** *f.*)

arricci-are [A 3] *tr.* to curl; -arsi i capelli, to curl one's hair; — i capelli, to make one's hair stand on end; — la fronte, to frown; — il naso, to turn up one's nose, to grimace, to pout; — le labbra, to curl one's lip (in disdain), (of an animal) to bare the fangs; — il pelo, (of an animal) to bristle up its hair; — il muro, to groove the plaster on a wall in preparation for whitewashing; *rfl.* (of hair) to curl, to be curly, to curl up; to stand on end; to bristle. -**aburro** *m. indecl.* tool for serving butter in curled portions. -**acapelli** *m. indecl.* curling-tongs; curler. -**amento** *m.* curling; frowning; †shuddering, horror. -**ato** *part. adj.* curled; on end; bristling; †(of material) richly worked, embroidered, brocaded; *n.m.* (bldg.) wall with the plaster grooved for whitewashing; †brocade. (-**atore** *m.* -**atrice** *f.*) -**atura** *f.* curling; hair-style; (bldg.) grooving for whitewashing or plastering; (text.) snarl (in spinning). -**olare** *tr.* to set (hair) in little curls; to frizz. -**olato** *part. adj.* (of hair) frizzy; in tight curls.

†**arricordare** *vb.* See **ricordare**.

arrid-are [A 1] *tr.* (poet., naut.) to set up (the stays or other ropes). -**atoio** *m.* rigging-screw, bottle-screw.

arri·dere [C 3] *intr.* (*aux.* avere, *prep.* a) to smile (upon); to be propitious (to), to be favourable (to); to assist, to favour; la fortuna vi arrida, may good fortune smile upon you; †*tr.* to fructify; †— un cenno, to consent smilingly.

arrière *m. indecl.* (rugby) full-back.

arriffare [A 1] *tr.* to raffle.

Arri·go *pr.n.m.* Harry.

†**Arrigobello** *pr.n.m.* clown who urged the crowds to come to a spectacle.

arring-a *f.* harangue; address; speech; (leg.) address by counsel. -**are** [A 2] *tr.* to harangue; to exhort; to address; (mil.) to array; to harangue; *intr.* (*aux.* avere) to make a speech; (leg.) to address a court. (-**amento** *m.*) -**ato** *part. adj.* harangued; exhorted. (-**atore** *m.* -**atrice** *f.*)

arrin-go *m.* (*pl.* -**ghi**) lists; arena; field; fight, contest; (fig.) scendere nell'—, to enter the lists.

†**arripare** *rfl.* to approach the shore.

arrischi-are [A 4] *tr.* to risk, to venture, to hazard; — la pelle, to risk one's life; *abs.* to dare; *rfl.* to venture; to run the risk; to run risks. (-**amento** *m.* -**ante** *part. adj.*) -**ato** *part. adj.* risky, hazardous; bold, rash. (-**atamente** *adv.* -**atore** *m.* -**atrice** *f.*) -**evole** *adj.* rash, venturesome, bold by nature. (-**evolmente** *adv.*) †-**o** *m.* risk.

arrisciare [A 3] (Tusc.) and derivs. See **arrischiare**.

arriva *adv.* (naut.) aloft; andare —, to go aloft; (command) —!, go aloft! (Also **a riva**.)

arriv-are *intr.* (*aux.* essere; *prep.* a) to arrive (at); to attain (to); to reach; to amount (to); to manage (to), to succeed (in); to be capable (of), to be up (to); to be sufficient; to be big enough, to be long enough, to be tall enough, to be strong enough; la fune è troppo corta, non ci -a, the rope is too short, it doesn't reach; le maniche non -ano, the sleeves are not long enough; non ci -o, I can't manage it, I can't understand it; piglia quel libro lassù, se ci -i, hand me down that book, if you can reach it; to go as far (as); -o al caffè e torno, I'm just going as far as the café and back; to be as tall as: mia figliuola mi -a fin quasi alle spalle, my daughter is almost up

arriv-are (*cont.*)

to my shoulder; — a dire, to go so far as to say; se -o a uscirne una buona volta, if once I manage to get out of this mess; — sopra a, to spring out on; *abs.* to arrive; — a proposito, to arrive at the right moment; (*provb.*) chi tardi -a male alloggia, first come first served; to occur, to befall; to succeed; to be a success, to get on in the world; — bene, to succeed, to turn out well; — male, to fail, to turn out badly; *tr.* to catch up with; to reach; l'-ò con una sassata, he threw a stone and hit him; to beat; to deliver (a blow); (*fig.*) to touch, to compare with: Maria non -a Francesca in bellezza, Mary doesn't compare with Frances for good looks. **-a·bile** *adj.* attainable; that can be reached. **-amento** *m.*, **-ata** *f.* arrival. **-ato** *part. adj.* ben -ato! welcome!; dare il ben -ato a, to welcome; -ato di cottura, ready, (of food) overcooked; *n.m.* successful man, success; jumped-up jack-in-office; one who has made good. (**-atura** *f.*) **-ismo** *m.* unscrupulous ambition, arrivism. **-ista** *m.* arriviste.

arriveder-ci, -la, -lo *excl.* good-bye; see you again soon.

arrivo *m.* arrival; al mio —, on my arrival; arrival platform; winning-post; (*comm.*) gli ultimi arrivi di merci, the latest supplies of goods.

†**arrizzare** *v.* See **rizzare.**

arrobbi-are [A4c] *tr.* (techn.). **-atura** *f.* (techn.).

†**arrocare** *vb.* See **arrochire.**

arrocc-are¹ [A2] *tr., abs.* (chess) to castle; (*mil.*) to move (troops) behind defence lines. **-amento** *m.* (chess) castling; (*mil.*) linea di -amento, road or railway behind defences. **-ato** *part. adj.* (*mil.*) fortified. (From **rocca,** q.v.)

arrocc-are² [A2c] (*text.*) to place (flax, etc.) on the distaff. (From **rocca,** q.v.)

arrocchettato *adj.* small, undersized; badly off.

arrocchi-are [A4] *tr.* to cut into blocks; (*fig.*) — un lavoro, to botch a job; *intr.* (*aux.* avere) to bungle, to work carelessly. **-one** *m.* bungler.

arrocci-are [A3] *rfl.* to remain stuck on the rock face during a mountain climb. (**-ato** *part. adj.*)

arroch-ire [D2] *tr.* to make hoarse; *intr.* (*aux.* essere), *rfl.* to become hoarse. **-imento** *m.* hoarseness. **-ito** *part. adj.* hoarse.

arrog-ante *adj.* arrogant, haughty, insolent, overbearing. (**-ante-mente** *adv.*) **-anza** *f.* arrogance; presumption, insolence; haughtiness.

arrog-are [A2] *tr.* (*leg.*) to adrogate, to adopt (a person not subject to anybody's paternal authority); *rfl.* to arrogate. **-ato** *part. adj.* (*leg.*) adopted; *n.m.* adoptive son. **-azione** *f.* arrogation; (*leg.*) adoption, adrogation.

†**arro·g-ere** *tr.* to add; *impers.* **-e, -i** add; besides, moreover.

arrol-are [A1d] *tr.* (*mil.*) to enrol, to recruit; *rfl.* (*mil.*) to enlist; to register. **-amento** *m.* recruiting; enlistment; enrolment. **-ato** *part. adj.* recruited. **-atore** *m.* recruiter, recruiting officer.

arronc-are [A2c] *tr.* (*bot.*) to trim with a billhook; to clear away (tangled growth, weeds, bushes, stumps). (**-amento** *m.* **-ato** *part. adj.*)

arroncigli-are [A4] *tr.* to catch with a hook, to seize; to curl (a moustache); *rfl.* to curl up. **-ato** *part. adj.* seized, hooked; baffi -ati, curling moustache.

arronz-are¹ [A1] *rfl.* to work hard, to slave, to wear oneself out. **-inare** [A1s] *rfl.* to work one's fingers to the bone.

arronzare² [A1] *tr.* to reprove, to 'tick off'.

†**arrorare** *tr.* to besprinkle, to bedew.

arrosare [A1] *rfl.* (*poet.*) to turn rosy; †*tr.* to water; to bedew.

arross-are [A1c] *tr.* to redden; (*chem.*) to turn red; *intr.* (*aux.* essere), *rfl.* to grow red. **-amento** *m.* reddening, turning red. **-ato** *part. adj.* reddened; (*chem.*) turned red (of litmus paper).

arrossente *adj.* (D'Annunzio) rusty-red.

arross-ire [D2] *intr.* (*aux.* essere) to blush; to flush, to flame; to turn red; to feel ashamed; fare — uno, to make a person blush. **-imento** *m.* blushing, blush; feeling of shame. **-ito** *part. adj.* blushing; reddened.

†**arrostare¹** *tr.* to wave; to beat off; *rfl.* to fan oneself.

†**arrostare²** *vb.* and derivs. See **arrostire.**

arrost-ire [D2] *tr.* to roast; to grill; to parch, to dry; (Tusc.) to toast; (joc.) to touch (for money); *intr.* (*aux.* essere), *rfl.* to become sunburnt, to sunbathe; — al sole, to roast in the sun. (**-imento** *m.* **-ito** *part. adj.* **-itura** *f.*)

arrosto *adv.* roasted, roast; uccelli arrosto, roast fowl; castagne

arrosto, roast chestnuts; cuocere —, to roast; morire —, to die in a fire; (*provb.*) chi la vuole allesso e chi —, tastes differ; *n.m.* roast meat; grill; — d'agnello, roast lamb; — morto, meat cooked in casserole; (*provb.*) più fumo che —, all show; (Tusc. colloq.) faux pas, brick, blunder; muddle.

†**arrot-a** *f.* addition. †**-o** *m.* addition; adjunct; assistant; *pl.* (Flor. hist.) officials appointed to scrutinize the ballot.

arrot-are [A1d] *tr.* to whet; to sharpen; — i denti, to grind one's teeth; to run over (with the wheels of a carriage); (Tusc.) — i panni, to wear one's clothes out; — le spade, to prepare for war; — la lingua, to talk spitefully; (hist.) to break on the wheel; *rfl.* (colloq.) to wear one's fingers to the bone; *recip. rfl.* (of wheels) to graze one against the other; (of persons) to be tightly wedged, to be squashed together (in a crowd). **-a·bile** *adj.* (techn.) capable of being re-ground. **-amento** *m.*, **-ata** *f.* whetting; sharpening. **-ato** *part. adj.* ground; sharpened; (of sound) sharp, harsh, piercing; pane -ato, hard-earned bread; (of a horse) dappled; (hist.) broken on the wheel; (*fig.*, of words) tortured, racked. **-atore** *m.* knife-grinder. **-atrice** *f.* grinder (machine); -atrice per sega, saw gummer. **-atura** *f.* sharpening, grinding; charge for grinding. **-ino** *m.* tinker, knife-grinder, scissors-grinder. **-io** *m.* continual grinding; wear and tear.

†**arroto** *m.* See under **arrota.**

arrotol-are [A1s] *tr., rfl.* to roll up; to furl; to curl up; — una sigaretta, to roll a cigarette. **-ato** *part. adj.* rolled up; curled up.

arrotond-are [A1c] *tr.* to make round, to round; to round off; (*fig.*) — lo stipendio, to add to, to eke out, to supplement one's salary; — un periodo, to round off a period, to polish the style of a paragraph; — una cifra, to make into a round figure; (*comm.*) — una somma, to make an amount a round figure; *rfl.* to become round; (*fig.*) to put on weight, to fill out. **-amento** *m.* rounding; rounding off; (*mech.*) -amento dello spigolo, corner radius. **-ato** *part. adj.* rounded; round.

arrotondire [D2] (Tusc.). See **arrotondare.**

arrovell-are [A1] *rfl., intr.* (*aux.* essere) to bother, to worry oneself; to get heated, to get angry; non ti —, don't bother, don't disturb yourself; *tr.* to rack, to torment; — il cervello, to rack one's brains. **-amento** *m.* agitation. **-ato** *part. adj.* vexed, agitated; heated; *adv.* brutto -ato, excessively ugly. (**-atamente** *adv.* **-io** *m.*)

arrovent-are [A1] *tr.* to make red hot; (metall.) to anneal; *rfl., intr.* (*aux.* essere) to grow red hot. (**-amento** *m.*) **-ato** *part. adj.* red hot. (**-atura** *f.*)

arroventire [D2] (Tusc.). See **arroventare.**

arrovesci-are [A3] *tr.* to overturn; to reverse; to upset; to spill; to pour; to turn out; to turn inside out; — le maniche, to roll up one's sleeves; (agric.) to turn underground (as in trenching); *rfl.* to overturn, to upset, to be overturned; to fall; si è -ato dal balcone, he fell from the balcony; (*fig.*) -arsi a, -arsi contro, to turn against. **-amento** *m.* overturning, upset; turning out; turning up. **-ato** *part. adj.* upset, overturned; turned out; turned up; le mani -ate sui fianchi, hands on hips; i baffi -ati all'insù, moustache curled upwards. **-atura** *f.* upsetting, overturning; reversal.

arrove·scio *adv.* See under **rovescio.**

arrozzire [D2] *tr.* to make rough, to make wild; to coarsen; *intr.* (*aux.* essere), *rfl.* to become rough; to roughen, to coarsen.

arrubin-are [A1] *tr.* (poet.) to make rosy red; †— un fiasco, to fill a flask with red wine; *rfl.* (poet.) to turn rosy red. **-ato** *part. adj.* rosy red.

arruff-are [A1] *tr.* to ruffle, to rumple; (of an animal) — il pelo, to ruffle up its coat; (of a person) -ò il pelo, his hair stood on end (with fear); to entangle; (*fig.*) — la matassa, to intrigue, to complicate matters, to act as a go-between; *rfl.* to become ruffled; to become entangled; (*fig.*) la matassa s'-a, the plot thickens. **-amatasse** *m. indecl.* intriguer, mischief-maker. **-amento** *m.* ruffling, rumpling, bristling, intriguing, entangling. **-apo·poli** *m. indecl.* demagogue, political agitator. **-ato** *part. adj.* ruffled, rumpled, bristling; dishevelled; entangled; encumbered. **-ata-mente** *adv.* in disorder; topsy-turvy. **-atore** *m.* intriguer, mischief-maker, swindler. (**-atrice** *f.*) **-atura** *f.* (text.) snarl. **-io** *m.* confusion, disorder; mischief-making. **-one** *m.* meddler; cheat; muddler; slap-dash individual.

arruffian-are [A1] *tr.* to procure for immoral purposes; (*fig.*) to 'put across', to show off, to cover up the faults of.

†**arrugare** *tr.* to make wrinkled; *rfl.* to become wrinkled.

arruggin-ire [D 2] *tr.* to make rusty, to rust; — i denti, to set the teeth on edge; *rfl.*, *intr.* (*aux.* essere) to rust, to become rusty; to get stale, to get out of practice; meglio logorarsi che arrugginire, it's better to wear out than rust out; (agric., of corn) to become infected with rust. ~ito *part. adj.* rusty; stale, out of practice.

†**arrugiadare** *tr.* to bedew, to sprinkle with dew.

arruolare [A I d] and derivs. See **arrolare**.

arruotare [A I d] and derivs. See **arrotare**.

arruvid-ire [D 2] *tr.* to make rough, to roughen; *intr.* (*aux.* essere), *rfl.* to become rough; to coarsen. ~ito *part. adj.* roughened; coarsened.

arruzzare [A I] and derivs. See **ruzzare**.

arruzzolare [A I s] and derivs. See **ruzzolare**.

arsanale *m.* See **arsenale**.

arsella *f.* (zool.) mussel, *Mytilus edulis*.

arsenal-e *m.* (naut.) arsenal; dockyard; arms factory; workshop; box-room, lumber-room; dump; glory-hole; (Tusc.) cheat, swindler. ~otto *m.* arsenal labourer; shipwright.

arseniato *m.* (chem.) arsenate.

arse·n-ico *m.* (chem.) arsenic; — giallo, yellow arsenic, orpiment; — rosso, red arsenic, realgar. ~icale *adj.* arsenical. ~ioso *adj.* (chem.) arsenious. ~iuro *m.* (chem.) arsenide. ~olite *f.* (min.) arsenolite, native white arsenic. ~opirite *f.* (min.) arsenopyrite, mispickel.

arsi *f.* (prosod.) arsis; (mus.) arsis; imitazione per — e tesi, imitation by contrary motion.

†**arsi·bile** *adj.* combustible.

arsina *f.* (chem.) arsine.

arsione. See under **arso**.

arsire [D I] *intr.* (*aux.* essere) (poet. Pascoli) to dry up, to shrivel.

ars-o *part.* from **ardere**, q.v.; *adj.* burnt; parched; dry; thirsty, athirst, thirsting. ~ic·cio *adj.* slightly burnt; singed; rather dry; parched; saper d'~iccio, to smell of burning, to give out a burnt smell. ~icciare [A 3] *tr.* to burn slightly, to singe; to parch. (~icciato *part. adj.* ~icciatura *f.*) ~ione *m.* (Tusc.) raging thirst; feverish heat; †conflagration. ~ura *f.* burning; raging thirst; feverish heat; dryness; †conflagration.

†**artagoticamente** *adv.* (Boccaccio) marvellously.

†**artalupo** *m.* antelope.

artat-o¹ *adj.* artificial; artful. †~amente *adv.* astutely, deceitfully; deliberately.

†**artato²** *adj.* obliged, coerced.

art-e *f.* art; l'— per l'—, art for art's sake; le belle ~i, the fine arts; ~i grafiche, graphic arts; le ~i liberali, the liberal arts; profession; — di governo, statesmanship; — di vendere, salesmanship; craft, handicraft; a regola d'—, according to the traditional rules of a craft; non avere nè — nè parte, to be bone idle; — mineraria, mining; — muraria, masonry; (hist.) guild; skill (esp. in painting, sculpture); artistry, craftsmanship; technique; opera d'—, work of art; (bldg.) constructional work; l'— del dire, l'— della parola, oratory, rhetoric; the stage; essere in —, to be on the stage; l'— muta, silent films; l'— bianca, baking; capacity, ability, knowledge, talent; artifice, cunning; ad —, deliberately; con —, skilfully; artfully; instinct; l'— delle api, the instinct of bees; far l'— di Michelaccio, to lead a life of idleness. ~efare [B 14] *tr.* to adulterate; to fake, to falsify. ~efatto *part. adj.* artificial; self-conscious; insincere; falsified; vino ~efatto, adulterated wine; *n.m.* artificial product.

artecrazi·a *f.* (neol.) autocracy of art.

artefice *m.* artificer; author; creator; Il Sommo Artefice, God, the Creator; egli stesso fu l'— della sua rovina, he wrought his own undoing; artist, artisan, craftsman.

arte·ri-a *f.* (anat.) artery; thoroughfare; main road; arterial road; main line (of railway). ~ale *adj.* arterial. ~ite *f.* (med.) arteritis. ~ologi·a *f.* arteriology. ~osclerosi *f.* (med.) arteriosclerosis, hardening of the arteries. ~oso *adj.* arterial; sangue ~oso, arterial blood. ~ostenosi *f.* (med.) arterial stenosis. ~otomi·a *f.* (surg.) arteriotomy.

artesiano *adj.* Artesian; pozzo —, Artesian well.

†**arte·tica** *f.* arthritis.

†**artezza** *f.* narrowness.

ar·tico *adj.* Arctic; northern; very cold, icy; circolo —, Arctic Circle.

articola·io *m.* See under **articolo**.

articol-are [A I s] *tr.* to articulate; to pronounce distinctly; to link; (gramm.) to combine (a preposition) with the def. art.; as in 'al', 'del', etc.; *rfl.* to be articulate; *adj.* articular, jointed. ~ato *part. adj.* articulate; clear, distinct (of pronunciation);

(gramm.) combined with the definite article (of prepositions); (anat.) articulate, articulated; (techn.) extending; adjustable: leggìo ~ato, adjustable reading desk; (fig.) adaptable, flexible (of ideas, etc.). ~atamente *adv.* articulately. ~azione *f.* articulation, clear pronunciation; (anat.) articulation; (mech.) articulation, joint, knuckle, link; ~azione sospesa, drag link; (fig.) flexibility.

arti·col-o *m.* article; subject, matter, point; item; material; requisite; (comm.) line, commodity; *pl.* goods, wares, articles; (gramm.) article; — determinativo, definite article; — indeterminativo, indefinite article; (anat.) joint, articulus; newspaper article; — di fondo, leading article, leader; subsection, sub-heading; (Tusc. colloq.) swindler, cheat; (leg.) article, section (of a law); ~i annessi al contratto di società, articles of partnership; ~i di un contratto, clauses of a contract; (comm.) article; ~i di prima necessità, necessities (of life); entry in an accountant's book; (theol., fig.) — di fede, article of faith; (fig.) sull'— onestà, nessuno può dir nulla contro di lui, in the matter of honesty, no one can say a word against him. ~a·io *m.* cheap journalist; †point, extremity; †point of time, juncture. ~essa *f.* low quality newspaper article. ~etto *m.* short article; paragraph. ~ista *m.* journalist, contributor to a newspaper, columnist. †~oso *adj.* wordy, verbose.

artiere *m.* artisan; craftsman; artificer; workman; (mil.) artisan, pioneer (road-works).

artifi·ci-o *m.* artifice; contrivance; trick; skill, art; artificiality; (art) technical skill; (mil.) device; fuochi d'—, fireworks; (mil.) pyrotechnics. ~ale *adj.* artificial; unnatural; imitation, synthetic; fuochi ~ali, fireworks. ~almente *adv.* artificially; artfully, deceitfully. ~ato *adj.* artificial; falsified, adulterated; †palla ~ata, fire-bomb. (~atamente *adv.*) ~ere *m.* (mil.) pyrotechnician. ~oso *adj.* artificial; contrived; artful, cunning, deceitful; false. (~osamente *adv.* ~osità *f.*)

artifi·zio *m.* (Tusc.). See **artificio**.

artigian-o *m.* artisan; craftsman; workman, operative; (fig.) architect, author, creator; *adj.* artisan; craft. ~ato *m.* class, etc. of artisans. ~esco *adj.* (*m.pl.* ~eschi) pertaining to the artisan class.

artigliare [A 4]. See under **artiglio**.

artigliere *m.* (mil.) artilleryman; gunner.

artiglier-i·a *f.* (mil.) artillery; piece; pezzo d'—, gun; cannon; ballistics; — a cavallo, horse artillery; — pesante campale, heavy field artillery; — da campagna, field artillery; — da assedio, siege artillery; — da costa, coast artillery; — da montagna, mountain artillery; — contro-aerei, antiaircraft artillery; — auto-campale, field mechanized artillery; — leggera, light artillery; — di marina, naval artillery; imboccare le ~ie, to put down counter battery fire; inchiodare le ~ie, to spike the guns; individuare le ~ie, to identify artillery.

arti·gli-o *m.* claw; (orn.) talon; (fig.) cadere negli ~i di, to fall into the clutches of. ~are [A 4] *tr.* (of a bird) to grip with talons; to clutch. ~ato *part.* of artigliare; *adj.* (orn.) armed with talons. (~oso *adj.*) ~uto *adj.* (poet.) with talons.

†**artimone** *m.* mainsail.

artiodat·tili *m.pl.* (zool.) *Artiodactyla*.

artist-a *m.* artist; performer, artiste; — di canto, singer, vocalist; — drammatico, — di prosa, actor; †(poet.) Creator.

arti·stic-o *adj.* artistic; tasteful; relating to art. ~amente *adv.* artistically; tastefully.

arto¹ *m.* (anat.) joint; limb.

arto² *adj.* narrow.

†**arto³** *m.* the North; the Great Bear.

Artofi·lace *pr.n.m.* (astron.) Boötes.

arto·grafo *m.* phototelegraph.

arto·o *adj.* (poet. Carducci) Northern.

artralgi·a *f.* pain in a joint.

artr-ite *f.* arthritis. ~i·tico *adj.* arthritic; *n.m.* sufferer from arthritis. ~i·tide *f.* see artrite. ~itismo *m.* arthritism. ~odat·tili *m.pl.* (zool.) artiodactyls. ~ologi·a *f.* arthrography. ~opla·stica *f.* (surg.) arthroplasty. ~o·podi *m.pl.* (zool.) Arthropoda.

Artù *pr.n.m.* (King) Arthur.

Artur-o *pr.n.m.* Arthur; (astron.) Arcturus; (poet.) the North; the guiding-star. ~iano *adj.*, *n.m.* Arthurian.

artusi *m. indecl.* cookery book (named after the author).

†**arunduco** *m.* reptile.

aru·sp-ice *m.* (Rom. hist.) haruspex, soothsayer. ~icare [A 2 s] *intr.* (*aux.* avere) to perform divination by inspection of entrails. ~icina *f.* haruspicy. ~i·cio *m.* haruspicy.

arvali *m.pl.* (Rom. hist.) Arval brethren (priests of agricultural cult).

arvi·cola *f.* (zool.) vole, *Microtus* sp.; hamster, *Cricetus frumentarius*.

arveiẓẓare [A 1] *tr.* (metall.) to Harveyize.

†**arzagogo** *adj.* foreign.

arza·gola, arza·vola *f.* (orn.) See **alzavola**.

†**arzanà** *m.* arsenal.

arz·ello, -e·glio *adj.* (of a horse) having white hind-feet; also *n.m.*

arẓente *m.* brandy; *adj.* (Tusc.) burning, biting.

ar·zica *f.* yellow (used by miniaturists).

arẓigo·gol-o *m.* quibble, cavil; fiddle-faddle; whim; circumlocution, meaningless verbiage. **-are** [A 1 s] *intr.* (aux. avere) to dream, to daydream; to quibble, to cavil; to rack one's brains; to split hairs. **-ǫne** *m.* quibbler, caviller.

arzilla *f.* (ichth.) various species of skate, *Raja* spp.; — chiodata, thornback ray, *R. clavata*; — ispidissima, shagreen ray, *R. fullonica*.

arzillo *adj.* sprightly, lively; vigorous; brisk; pungent; vino —, sparkling wine; (joc.) 'lit up', tipsy.

arzin-che, -ghe *f.pl.* crucible tongs; grooved tongs used in minting.

aṣbesto *m.* asbestos.

aṣbestoṣi *f.* (med.) asbestosis.

ascalabote *f.* (zool.) a kind of gecko.

asca·lafo *m.* (ent.) *Ascalaphus italianus* (Neuroptera).

a·scari *m. indecl.,* **a·scaro** *m.* ascari, a native soldier from Italian possessions in North and East Africa.

asca·ride *m.* (zool.) ascarid, round worm.

asce *f.* See **ascia**.

ascell-a *f.* (anat.) armpit, axilla; (bot.) axil. **-are** *adj.* axillary.

ascend-ere [C 1 c] *intr.* (aux. essere, avere) to ascend; — al trono, to ascend the throne; to climb, to mount; to rise; to go up; to amount; *tr.* to ascend, to climb up, to mount. **-entale** *adj.* ascendental; pertaining to ascent; (geneal.) linea -entale, ascending line. **-ente** *part. adj.* ascending, mounting; movimento -ente, upward movement; cronaca -ente, history of events told ascending from the present to the past; outward, outgoing: corsa -ente, outward journey; (scient.) ascendant, in the ascendant; *n.m.* ascendancy, influence; avere dell'-ente su, to have ascendancy over; *pl.* ancestors, ascendants; (astron.) ascendant. **-enza** *f.* relatives in the ascending line, ascendants, ancestors; genealogical tree; origin. (**-i·bile** *adj.*) **-imento** *m.* ascension, ascent.

Ascensa *pr.n.f.* (dial.) Ascension.

ascens-iǫne *f.* ascent; mounting; climb; (astron.) ascendant, elevation; (rel.) Ascension; (rarely) Assumption. **-ionale** *adj.* ascending, progressive. **-ionista** *m.* mountain-climber, alpinist. **-ioniṣmo** *m.* mountain-climbing. †**-o** *m.* step. **-ǫre** *m.* lift, elevator. **-orista** *m., f.* lift-attendant.

asceṣ-a *f.* ascent; climb; (aeron.) — statica, static rising. **-o** *part.* of **ascendere**, q.v.

asceṣi *f.* asceticism; mystic or ascetic exaltation.

ascesso *m.* abscess, gathering; — alla gengiva, gumboil.

asc-eta *m.* (rel.) ascetic; austere, abstemious or self-denying person. **-e·tica** *f.* ascetic theology. **-e·tico** *adj., n.m.* ascetic. **-etiṣmo** *m.* asceticism; (spiritual, moral, intellectual) self-discipline. **-ete·rio** *m.* monastery, cell.

†**a·schero** *m.* regret; anguish; (dial. Tusc.) desire.

†**a·schio** *m.* See **astio**.

a·sci-a *f.* axe, hatchet, chopper; adze; sax; (fig.) fatto coll'—, roughly, clumsily made; (herald.) doloire; maestro d'—, woodsman; carpenter; (naut.) shipwright. **-are** [A 3] *tr.* to hack; to rough-hew; to adze, to dress with an adze; to chop; to chop down. **-ata** *f.* stroke with an axe, chop with an adze. **-(u)olo** *m.* small billhook.

ascialǫne *m.* wooden carrier bolted to a scaffold pole to support a putlog; a movable piece for reducing the pressure of a vice where necessary; lashing.

asciare¹ [A 3]. See under **ascia**.

†**asciare²** *rfl.* to distress oneself, to worry.

asci·dia *f.* (zool.) ascidian, sea squirt.

†**a·scio¹** *adj.* casting no shadow (as when the sun is exactly overhead).

†**ascio²** *m.* See **agio**.

asciol·vere [C 14] *intr.* (aux. avere) to breakfast; *tr.* — il digiuno, to break one's fast; *n.m.* breakfast; †in meno d'un —, in a twinkling.

ascìsc *m. indecl.* See **hascisc**.

†**asciso** *adj.* deprived; lacerated, wounded.

ascissa *f.* (math.) abscissa; (survey.) longitude (of a point).

asc-ite *f.* (med.) ascites, dropsy of the abdomen. **-i·tico** *adj.* ascitic(al).

asciti·zio *adj.* accessory, derived from elsewhere.

asciug-are [A 2] *tr.* to dry; to dry up; to wipe; — le lagrime, to dry one's tears; (iron.) to be quickly consoled; to air; to drain (land); — un fiasco, to drink a bottle dry; (joc.) — uno, — le tasche a uno, to clean a person out, to leave him without a bean; *rfl.* to dry oneself; *rfl., intr.* (aux. essere) to get dry; mettere i panni ad asciugare, to hang out the clothes to dry. **-acapelli** *m. indecl.* hair-dryer. **-ag·gine** *f.* dryness, aridity. **-amano** *m.* (*pl.* -amani), **-amani** *m. indecl.* towel; hand-towel; -amano di spugna, Turkish towel. **-amento** *m.* drying. **-ante** *part. adj.* drying; carta -ante, blotting-paper. **-atina** *f.* wipe, quick wipe; dare un'-atina a, to wipe quickly. **-ato** *part. adj.* dried; wiped; dried up; drained; cleaned out. **-atǫio** *m.* towel; bath-towel; (industr.) dryer. **-atǫre** *m.* dryer; -atore a rullo, squeegee roller. **-atura** *f.* drying; drying-up; wiping.

asciutt-o *adj.* dry; thirsty; a occhi -i, with dry eyes, unmoved, without weeping; pasta -a, macaroni, etc.; pane —, dry bread; rimanere a bocca -a, rimanere a becco —, to go without food, to miss a meal; (fig.) to be disappointed, to fail to pull something off; persona -a, thin, wiry person; — di parole, terse, abrupt in manner; risposta -a, brusque reply; — di quattrini, penniless; rimanere all'—, to be penniless; *adv.* abruptly, tersely; drily; brusquely; *n.m.* dry climate; dry place; dryness, aridity; camminar sull'—, to walk where the path is dry. (**-amẹnte** *adv.*) **-are** (dial.) see **asciugare**. **-ẹzza** *f.* dryness, aridity; drought. **-ǫre** *m.* drought.

asclepiad-e·o *adj., n.m.* (prosod.) Asclepiad, Asclepiadean (metre). **-e·a** *f.* poem in Asclepiads.

†**ascolta¹** *f.* sentinel.

†**ascolta²** *f.* See **ascoltazione**, under **ascoltare**.

ascolt-are [A 1 c] *tr.* to listen to; to pay attention to, to heed; to give ear to; to overhear; — un consiglio, to follow advice; — la radio, to listen in; che la vostra preghiera sia -ata, may your prayer be heard; — la messa, to hear mass, to attend mass; (med.) to sound, to examine by auscultation; *intr.* (aux. avere) to listen; to pay attention; ascolta!, listen!; — dietro le porte, to eavesdrop. **-amẹnto** *m.* listening. **-ante** *part. adj.* listening, hearing; *n.m., f.* listener, hearer. **-ato** *part. adj.* heard. **-atǫre** *m.* listener; (acoustics) sound locator; *pl.* audience; listeners, public. (**-atrice** *f.*) **-aziǫne** *f.* (med.) auscultation, sounding.

ascǫlto *m.* listening; hearing; audience; dare —, to listen; mettersi, stare, in —, to be listening, to have one's ears pricked; prestare — a, to believe; prestare — ai consigli di, to follow the advice of; †see **ascoltazione**; †*part. adj.* see **ascoltato**.

ascǫnd-ere [C 1 1 c] *tr.* to hide, to conceal; *rfl.* to hide oneself, to hide; to be hidden. †**-arello** *m.,* **-i·glio** *m.* hiding-place. (**-imẹnto** *m.* **-itǫre** *m.*)

†**ascon·dito** *adj.* recondite.

†**asconsiǫne** *f.* hiding, concealment.

ascǫs-o *part.* from **ascondere**, q.v.; *adj.* hidden, secret; virtù -e, hidden virtues. **-amẹnte** *adv.* secretly. †**-to** see **ascoso**.

ascre-o *adj.* pertaining to or of Ascra in Boeotia, the birthplace of Hesiod; canto —, didactic poetry like Hesiod's; (poet.) le figliuole -e, the Muses.

ascritti·zio *adj.* (Rom. hist.) enrolled as citizen, colonist; (of a slave) attached to the soil and sold with the estate; (of a soldier) reservist, supernumerary; (of a god) created by apotheosis; also *n.m.*

ascritto *part.* from **ascrivere**, q.v.; *adj.* enrolled; ascribed, attributed.

ascri·vere [C 12] *tr.* to enrol, to inscribe, to register; to ascribe, to attribute; — ad onore, to consider an honour; — a lode, to single out as praiseworthy; — a biasimo, to single out as blameworthy; ascriversi la responsabilità, to assume the responsibility.

ascriziǫne *f.* enrolment; attribution.

asello *m.* (zool.) *Asellus aquaticus, A. terrestre,* woodlouse.

a·sepsi *f. indecl.* asepsis. **-set·tico** *adj.* aseptic.

asessu·ale *adj.* asexual. **-alità** *f.* asexuality. **-ato** *adj.* asexual.

asfa·lico *adj.* indelible.

asf·alto *m.* asphalt, bitumen; (paint.) bitumen (paint), Jew's pitch. **-altare** [A 1] *tr.* to asphalt. (**-altato** *part. adj.* **-altatura** *f.*) **-al·tico** *adj.* asphaltic, bituminous. **-altista** *m.* asphalt worker. **-altino** *adj.* of coal or other mineral, bituminous. **-altite** *f.* asphaltite.

asfiss-i·a *f.* asphyxia, suffocation; gassing. **-iare** [A 4] *tr.* to asphyxiate, to suffocate. **-iante** *part. adj.* asphyxiating.

asfit·tic-o *adj.* asphyxiated; asphyxial.

asfod-elo *m.* (bot.) asphodel, *Asphodelus*; *adj.* covered with asphodel; Elysian. **-illo** *m.* see **asfodelo**.

A·șia *pr.n.f.* (geog.) Asia; l'— Minore, Asia Minor.

a-și·aco *adj.* (poet.) Asiatic. **-șiano** *adj.* (poet.) Asiatic. **-șia·tico** *adj.* Asiatic; oriental; stile -siatico, ornate style; lusso -siatico, oriental splendour; Collegio -siatico, College of Oriental Languages (Naples); (med.) morbo -siatico, cholera.

așilo *m.* refuge, shelter; asylum; sanctuary; almshouse; — notturno, doss-house; (leg.) diritto d'—, right of asylum, right of sanctuary; school; — infantile, — d'infanzia, kindergarten, nursery-school; day-nursery; nave —, training ship for naval orphans.

†a·sim-a *f.* asthma. **†-are** *rfl.* to suffer from asthma; (fig.) to get out of breath, to wear oneself out.

asimboli·a *f.* (med.) asymbolia.

a-simmetri·a *f.* asymmetry; (math.) incommensurability. **-sim·metro**, **-simme·trico** *adj.* asymmetric; out of proportion; (math.) incommensurable.

†asinare *intr.* to travel on a donkey.

asincronișmo *m.* (cinem.) asynchronism.

asin·cron-o *adj.* asynchronous. **-a** *f.* (electr.) asynchronous machine.

asin-d-eto *m.* (rhet.) asyndeton. **-e·tico** *adj.* (rhet.) asyndetic.

asinf-oni·a *f.* dissonance. **-o·nico** *adj.* dissonant.

a·sin-o *m.* (zool.) ass, donkey; fool; pezzo d'—!, stupid creature!; — presuntuoso, conceited ass; dare dell'— a, to call (someone) an ass; — risalito, — d'oro, nouveau-riche, jack-in-office; (colloq.) fare l'— a, (of a man) to flirt with; — calzato e vestito, an out-and-out fool; lavare la testa all'—, to cast pearls before swine; il trotto dell'—, short-lived enthusiasm; il calcio dell'—, ingratitude; legar l'— dove vuole il padrone, to obey orders and wash one's hands of the responsibility; l'— di Buridano, Buridan's ass; qui mi casca l'—, here I come to grief, there's the rub; (provb.) dove l'— è cascato una volta, non ci casca più, a burned child dreads the fire; far come l'— del pentolaio, to gossip with everybody; il ponte dell'—, Pons Asinorum; (of a road) a schiena d'—, hog-backed; *pl.* (astron.) α and β Cancri. **-a** *f.* she-ass, female donkey. **-ag·gine** *f.* stupidity; silliness. **-a·ia** *f.* pasture for donkeys; stable for donkeys. **-a·io** *m.* donkey-driver. **-ello** *m.* little donkey; young ass; ass; (archit.) roof-tree, ridge-piece. **-eri·a** *f.* stupidity; dire delle -erie, to talk nonsense. **-ęsco** *adj.* (*m.pl.* **-ęschi**) stupid; asinine. (**-escamęnte** *adv.*) **-ino** *adj.* asinine; stupid; clumsy, graceless; tosse -ina, whooping cough. **-ità** *f.* stupidity; asinine behaviour.

asin-tote *f.* (math.) asymptote. **-to·tico** *adj.* asymptotic. **-toto** *m.* See **asintote**.

†a·sio *m.* See **agio**.

asi·șmico *adj.* 'quake-proof, aseismic.

așm-a *f.* asthma. **-a·tico** *adj.*, *n.m.* asthmatic(al). **†-oso** *adj.* see **asmatico**.

a·șol-a *f.* buttonhole; eyelet; buttonholing. **†-iere** *m.* belt.

așol-are [A I S] *intr.* (*aux.* avere) (of wind) to blow; to take the air; *tr.* to hang out to air; *rfl.* to take the air.

a·șolo *m.* breath of air, breather; light breeze; pigliare —, darsi —, to get a breath of air; dare — a, to hang out to air.

așo·pia *f.* (ent.) grain moth.

aspa *f.* See **aspo**.

†aspaldo *m.* parapet.

†aspalto *m.* See **asfalto**.

aspa·rag-o *m.* asparagus. **-ęto** *m.* asparagus-bed. **-ina** *f.* (chem.) asparagine.

asp-ata *f.*, **-atoio** *m.*, **-atrice** *f.*, **-atura** *f.* See under **aspo**.

aspe *m.* See **aspo**.

asperarte·ria *f.* (med.) trachea, windpipe.

asperella *f.* (bot.) horse-tail.

asper·g-ere [C4] *tr.* to sprinkle, to besprinkle; to strew; (liturg.) to sprinkle (with holy water). **-e** *m.*, **-es** *m.* (liturg.) Asperges (words or action); (holy water) sprinkler. (**-itore** *m.* **-itrice** *f.*)

asper·golo *m.* See **asperge, asperges**, under **aspergere**.

†a·spero *adj.* See **aspro**.

asperità *f.* asperity, roughness; unevenness; harshness.

asper·rimo *adj. superl.* of **aspro**, q.v.

aspers-o *part.* from **aspergere**, q.v.; *adi.* sprinkled, besprinkled; strewn. **-ione** *f.* sprinkling. **-o·rio** *m.* (liturg.) (holy water) sprinkler, aspergillum.

aspett-are [A I] *tr.* to wait for, to await; to expect (someone); egli ti -a, he is waiting for you; non vi -avo, I did not expect you;

---

to be in wait for; to look forward to; (fig.) — il Messia, to expect a miracle; qui t'-avo, I thought as much; I thought I'd catch you out on that; — la provvidenza, to wait upon Providence; — la palla al balzo, to wait for the right moment; chi ha tempo non -i tempo, strike while the iron is hot; -a che ti accomodo io!, you just wait!; chi la fa l'-i, you must take the consequences; (comm.) -ando una pronta risposta, awaiting a prompt reply; *intr.* (*aux.* avere) to wait; far — qualcuno, to keep someone waiting; farsi —, to be late for an appointment; *rfl.* to expect; non me l'-avo, I did not expect it; c'era da -arsela, it was only to be expected. **†-a·bile** *adj.* respectable, considerable. **-ante** *part. adj.* waiting, expecting; expectant; *n.m.* candidate for public office. **-anza** *f.* (poet.) awaiting, expectation. **-ativa** *f.* expectation; anticipation; hope; superare l'-ativa, to exceed all hopes; (mil.) essere in -ativa, to be temporarily discharged; to be on leave; to have leave of absence; (leg.) expectations. **-ato** *part. adj.* awaited, expected; desired, longed for. **†-atore** *m.* spectator; person waiting. **-azione** *f.* expectation; expectancy; rispondere all'-azione, to come up to expectation. **-ito** (sport) *adv. phr.* in -ito, in walk-over position (of athlete, or team).

aspetto[1] *m.* waiting; stare in —, to be waiting; sala d'—, waiting-room; (mus.) battuta d'—, bar's rest; (orn.) butt.

aspetto[2] *m.* look; mien; aspect; appearance; a primo —, at first sight; — esteriore, outward appearance; bell'—, good looks; di bell'—, good-looking; avere un brutt'—, to look ill; point of view; sotto quest'—, from this point of view; (astron.) aspect, relative position of the planets and stars; (techn.) drying frame; †observation, look, gaze; †look, power of sight.

a·spide[1] *m.* (zool.) asp; (fig.) viper, malevolent person.

†a·spide[2] *m.* shield.

aspidistra *f.* (bot.) aspidistra.

a·spio *m.* (ichth.) *Aspius alburnus*, a fish related to the bleak.

aspir-are [A I] *tr.* to inhale, to breathe in; to suck up; to aspirate; to favour, to be propitious to; *intr.* (*aux.* avere, *prep.* a) to aspire (towards); to aim (at); **-ante** *part. adj.* aspiring; inhaling; favourable, propitious; tromba -ante, suction inlet; intake funnel; pompa -ante, suction pump; *n.m.* candidate; applicant; suitor; aspirant; (mil.) warrant officer; (naut.) cadet (senior or seagoing). **-apolvere** *m. indecl.* vacuum cleaner. **-ata** *f.* (gramm.) aspirate. **-ato** *part. adj.* inhaled; aspirated; (gramm.) consonante -ata, aspirate; assisted; favoured. **-atamęnte** *adv.* pronunziare -atamente, to pronounce with the aspirate. **-atore** *m.* aspirator, suction pump; exhauster; vacuum cleaner. **-azione** *f.* inhalation; aspiration; ambition; yearning, desire; (Gk. gramm.) rough breathing; (phon.) aspiration; (eng.) suction, intake, induction; aspirate; (of a chimney) draught.

aspirina *f.* aspirin.

asp-o *m.* (text.) reel; winder; (naut.) winch handle, capstan bar. **-ata** *f.* (text.) winder-full (of silk). **-atoio** *m.* (text.) reeling frame; -atoio meccanico, power reel. **-atura** *f.* (silkb.) reeling.

asport-are [A I] *tr.* to remove; to take away; to transport; vino da —, wine for sale (to be taken away); (surg.) to extirpate, to remove; — con fiamma, to burn off (paint.). **-a·bile** *adj.* removable. **-azione** *f.* removal, carrying away, transporting; (surg.) extirpation, removal. **-o** *m.* (Tusc.) removal, transporting.

†asprare *vb.* See **aspreggiare**, under **aspro**.

asprì *m. indecl.* osprey trimming.

aspr-o *adj.* (*superl.* **asperrimo**) harsh; sharp; rough; rugged; una salita -a, a difficult ascent; uncouth; brusque; (of weather) biting, severe; (of wine) sharp; (of words) biting, harsh; (Gk. gramm.) spirito —, rough breathing. **-amęnte** *adv.* harshly; sharply. **-eggiare** [A 3] *tr.* to ill-treat, to treat harshly; *intr.* (*aux.* avere) to taste sour. **-eggiamęnto** *m.* ill-treatment. **-eggiato** *part. adj.* ill-treated. (**-eggiatore** *m.*) **-ętto** *adj.* (of persons) sharp in manner, terse; (of wine) rather sharp; *n.m.* sourness; questo vino ha preso l'-etto, this wine has gone rather sour. **-ęzza** *f.* asperity; roughness; harshness; sourness, sharpness. **-igno** *adj.* (of persons) sharp; (of fruit, wine, etc.) rather sour, tart; *n.m.* sour taste. **-ino** *adj.* rather sour; *n.m.*, **-i·nio** *m.* dry white wine of Aversa in Campania. (**-itu·dine** *f.*)

asprône *m.* (miner.) a black kind of tufa stone found near Rome.

assa[1] *f.* (bot.) See **assafetida**; — dolce, gum benzoin.

†assa[2] *f.* (also dial.). See **asse**[1].

assaett-are [A I C] (Tusc.) *tr.* to shoot with an arrow; *intr.* (*aux.* avere) (fig.) to be overpowering; to be excessively unpleasant: un puzzo

assaett-are (*cont.*)

che ~a, an overpowering stench; (colloq.) to come to a sudden death; ch'io ~i se non è vero!, so help me, it's true!; che ~i quel bugiardo! the liar! may the lie stick in his throat!; — dalla fame, to be dying of hunger; *rfl.* to wear oneself out. **-amẹnto** *m.* exhaustion. **-ante** *part. adj.* sharp; piquant. **-ato** *part. adj.* wounded, hit with an arrow; violent, extreme; *adv.* cursedly; caro -ato, damned expensive.

assafe·tida *f.* (bot.) asafoetida.

assaggi-are [A3] *tr.* to taste; to try; to sample; (iron.) gli ho fatto — la frusta, I gave him a taste of the whip; (scient.) to assay, to test. **-amẹnto** *m.* tasting, sampling; trial; taste. **-ato** *part. adj.* tasted, sampled. **-atọre** *m.* taster. (**-atrice** *f.*) **-atura** *f.* (met.) assaying, assay.

assag·gio *m.* tasting; sampling; trial, test; sample; (fig.) foretaste; (met.) assay; (mil.) foray, brush with the enemy.

assa·i *adv.* very; — ricco, very rich; much; very much; a great deal; plenty; quite; many; — buono, very nice, quite good; — più, much more, many more; — volte, many times; mi piace —, I like it very much; non c'entra nè pochi nè —, it's not a question of number; (colloq. antiphr.) m'importa —!, much I care!; so — io!, a fat lot I know (or care)!; enough; ne ho — di luì, I've had enough of him; vedere la terra gli era —, to see the land was all he asked; a far —, at the most.

assais·simo *adv. superl.* of assai, *q.v.*; more than enough.

†**assaldire** *tr.* to grant; to fulfil.

assale *m.* (eng.) axle; — anteriore, front axle; — posteriore, rear axle; tappo di —, axle cap; — fisso, axletree.

assal-ire [D4, D2] *tr.* to assail; to assault; to attack; to seize; (mil.) to assail, to attack, to assault, to invest; †to violate, to rape; †(of animals) to mount. (**-imẹnto** *m.* **-ita** *f.*) **-ito** *part. adj.* assailed, attacked; seized; ~ito da paura, seized with fear. **-itọre** *m.* assailant; attacker. (**-itrice** *f.*)

assalt-are [A1] *tr.* (mil.) to assail, to attack, to assault, to invest; (fig.) to attack, to assault. **-a·bile** *adj.* (mil.) capable of being assaulted. (**-amẹnto** *m.*) **-atọre** *m.* assailant, aggressor. (**-atrice** *f.*)

assalto *m.* (mil.) attack, assault; onslaught; onset; dare l' — (a), to attack; prendere d'—, to take by assault; respingere l'—, to repel an attack; sonare all'—, to sound the charge; — alla baionetta, bayonet attack; reparti di —, assault troops, spearhead troops; (fencing) match; bout; invasion, aggression lunge; (med.) onset, attack; (fig.) onslaught, attack; pigliarla d'—, to begin with great enthusiasm; di primo —, at first; pigliare d'—, to take by surprise.

†**assannare** *tr.* to seize with the fangs.

assaoritura *f.* See assauritura, under assaurire.

†**assapere** *tr.* fare —, to teach, to let know.

assapor-are [A1c] *tr.* to savour, to relish, to enjoy; †to season. **-amẹnto** *m.* relishing; tasting; relish, flavour, savour. (**-ato** *part. adj.* **-atọre** *m.* **-aziọne** *f.*)

assapor-ire [D2] *tr.* to season, to flavour; to give a relish to; to spice. (**-ito** *part. adj.*)

assa·rio *m.* (numism.) assary.

†**assassare** *tr.* to stone, to kill by stoning.

assassin-are [A1] *tr.* to assassinate; to murder; (fig.) to torment, to bore to death, to plague; to ruin, to spoil; filodrammatici che ~ano il Goldoni, amateur actors who murder Goldoni's comedies. **-amẹnto** *m.* assassination, murder; ruin; despoiling. **-atọre** *m.* assassin. (**-atrice** *f.*)

assassi·n-io *m.* (*pl.* -ii) assassination; murder; unjust condemnation; (colloq.) shockingly bad piece of work.

assassin-o *m.* murderer; assassin; evil genius, villain; incompetent bungler; quel pittore è un —, that painter is an absolute incompetent; (joc.) —!, wretch!; pezzo d'—!, murderer!; (hist.) hasish-eater, Moslem fanatic; *adj.* killing, fascinating; mosca ~a, patch (used by women in eighteenth century); occhiata ~a, killing glance; murderous; mano ~a, assassin's hand.

assaur-ire [D2] *tr.* (tanning) to sour. **-itura** *f.* (tanning) souring; acidification.

†**assavorare** *vb.* See assaporare.

ass-e¹ *f.* board, plank; — elastica, springboard; slab; — da stirare, ironing board; (baking) — da pane, peel. **-icella** *f. dim.* little board; sleeve-board; batten; lath.

asse² *m.* (scient., math.) axis; centre line; (opt.) — di collimazione, line of sight; (aeron.) — principale, zero-lift axis; — normale, yawing axis; (hist. pol.) l'— Roma-Berlino, the Rome-Berlin axis;

(mech.) axle, spindle; (naut.) axle fixed fore and aft; — diametrale, axle fixed thwartship; — longitudinale, axle parallel to the line of the keel; — trasversale, axle at right angles to the line of the keel; — verticale, vertical axle; — del timone, rudderstock.

asse³ *m.* (Rom. antiq.) as, copper coin; (leg.) — patrimoniale, estate; — ereditario, the estate of a deceased person; — sociale, the whole of a company's (or of a partnership's) assets; — demaniale, the whole of the real property belonging to the state; — ecclesiastico, church property taken over by the state.

asseccare [A1c], **assecchire** [D2] *intr.* (*aux.* essere) to become thin.

assẹcco *m.* (naut.) sump wheel.

assecond-are [A1c] *tr.* to support; to second; to favour; to assist; to uphold; to comply with.

†**assedere¹** *intr.* to sit down.

†**assedere²** *vb.* See assediare.

assedi-are [A4] *tr.* (mil.) to besiege, to lay siege to; to surround; (fig.) to encircle; to importune; — di domande, to badger with questions; to solicit. (**-amẹnto** *m.*) **-ante** *part. adj.* besieging; *n.m.* besieger. **-ato** *part. adj.* besieged; surrounded; *n.m.* una sortita degli -ati, a sortie. **-atọre** *m.* besieger. (**-atrice** *f.*)

asse·di-o *m.* (mil.) siege; porre l'— (a), to lay siege (to); levare l'—, rompere l'—, to raise siege; (hist. pol.) — economico, sanctions; (fig.) crowd; importunity.

†**asseg·gio** *m.* See assedio.

assegn-are [A3c] *tr.* to assign; to allot; to mete out; to award; to allow; to make an allowance of; to attribute; to ascribe; to appoint; to detail (a person to do a job); — un termine, to fix a term; (leg.) — gli alimenti, to award alimony; (aeron.) — la quota, to stack. **-a·bile** *adj.* assignable. **-amẹnto** *m.* allowance; allotment; assigning; attribution; reliance: far -amento su, to count on, to rely on; (comm.) guaranteed annuity. (**-ante** *part. adj.*, *n.m.*, *f.*) †**-atezza** *f.* restraint, control. **-atamẹnte** *adv.* particularly, precisely; †sparingly. **-ata·rio** *m.* assignee; grantee. **-ato** *part. adj.* assigned, allotted; attributed; appointed; parsimonious, thrifty; (comm.) to be paid on delivery; porto -ato, carriage forward, C.O.D.; *n.m.* (Fr. hist.) assignat. (**-atọre** *m.* **-atrice** *f.*) **-aziọne** *f.* assigning; allotting; granting; allowance, grant; (comm.) allotment.

assẹgno *m.* allowance; payment; — familiare, family allowance; (comm.) — bancario, cheque; — all'ordine, cheque to order; — al latore, cheque to bearer; — in bianco, blank cheque; — sbarrato, — chiuso, crossed cheque; — a vuoto, dud cheque; — circolare, banker's draft; libretto di assegni, cheque-book; emettere un —, to draw a cheque; contro —, cash on delivery.

†**asseguire** *vb.* See conseguire.

†**assembiare** *tr.* to assemble.

assemblag·gio *m.* (industr.) assembly, assembling; linea di —, assembly line.

†**assemblare** *tr.* to compare.

assemble·a *f.* assembly; meeting; conclave; congregation; (hunt.) meet; convocare un'—, to call a meeting; sciogliere un'—, to adjourn a meeting; — legislativa, legislative assembly, parliament; — costituente, constituent assembly; (comm.) convocare l'— degli azionisti, to call a meeting of the shareholders; (mil.) bugle or drum call for assembly; fall in; (naut.) hands fall in; divisions; both watches.

assembr-are¹ [A1] *tr.* to assemble, to collect, to muster; *rfl.* to assemble, to gather, to congregate, to flock. **-a·glia** *f.* gathering. **-amẹnto** *m.* assembling; crowd, assemblage, concourse.

†**assembrare²** *vb.* See sembrare.

†**assembre·a** *f.* See assemblea.

†**assem·p-io, -lo, -ro** *m.* example, model. †**-lare**, †**-rare** *tr.* to copy, to follow a model; to transcribe.

†**assenn-are**, †**-ire** *tr.* to teach sense to, to bring to one's senses.

assenn-ato *adj.* wise, sensible, judicious; wary, prudent, discreet. (**-atamẹnte** *adv.*) **-atẹzza** *f.* wisdom; good sense; prudence, discretion.

†**assensione** *f.* See ascensione.

assenso *m.* assent; approbation; consent; (leg.) official concurrence, sanction, assent.

assent-are¹ [A1] *rfl.* to absent oneself; to go away; to keep away; *tr.* to remove. **-amẹnto** *m.* absence. **-ato** *part. adj.* absent, away. (**-atọre** *m.*)

†**assentare²** *tr.* to flatter; to give way to.

†**assentare³** *rfl.* to sit down.

assent-e *adj.* absent; away; missing, wanting; absent-minded, wool-gathering; *n.m.* absentee; quanti sono gli -i?, how many are absent?; gli -i hanno sempre torto, those absent always bear the blame. **-eismo** *m.* absenteeism; (fig.) indifference. **-eista** *m.* absentee landlord.

assent-ire [D 1] *intr.* (*aux.* avere) to assent, to acquiesce; to approve. **-imento** *m.* assent; consent. **-ito** *part. adj.* accepted; approved. †sensible; †cautious. †-o *m.* see **assenso**. †-uto *adj.* cute, cunning, astute.

assenza *f.* absence; fare troppe -e, to be absent too often; — senza licenza, absence without leave; lack; — di scrupoli, lack of scruples; (leg.) non-appearance in Court; dichiarazione d'—, decree of a magistrate in respect of person unheard of for a given number of years; presunzione d'—, presumption applying to a person unheard of for a given number of years.

assenziente *adj.* assentient; willing; (also *n.m.*).

assen·z-io *m.* oil of wormwood, absinth; (fig.) bitterness. **-ina** *f.* (chem.) absinthin.

†**asserare** *intr.* to grow dark, to be nearing the evening.

asserella *f.* small board, plank.

†**asserenare** *tr.* to brighten; to gladden.

asser-ire [D 2] *tr.* to assert; to declare; to affirm; to state; to say; to maintain; to claim; (leg.) to assert. **-i·bile** *adj.* assertable. **-imento** *m.* asserting, assertion. **-ito** *part. adj.* asserted; claimed. (**-itore** *m.*)

as·sero *m.* shaft, axle; boarding-plank.

asserpentato *adj.* coiled, twisted.

asserpol-are [A 1 S] *tr.* to coil; *rfl.* to coil oneself; to become coiled; (naut.) see **abbisciare**. **-ato** *adj.* coiled, twisted like a serpent.

asserragli-are [A 4] *tr.* to barricade; *rfl.* to barricade oneself. **-amento** *m.* barricade. **-ato** *part. adj.* barricaded.

†**asserrare** *vb.* See **serrare**.

assert-o *adj.* asserted; affirmed; maintained; *n.m.* assertion; affirmation. **-iva** *f.* assertion. **-ivo** *adj.* assertive. (**-ivamente** *adv.*) **-ore** *m.* assertor; champion, defender; advocate. (**-rice** *f.*) **-o·rio** *adj.* assertive; (leg.) giuramento -orio, oath in support of a statement.

†**asservare** *tr.* to guard; to preserve.

asserv-ire [D 1] *tr.* to enslave; to enthral; to reduce to servitude. **-imento** *m.* enslavement; (mech.) follow-up link; **-ito** *part. adj.* enslaved; enthralled; subservient; essere -ito ad un partito, to be swayed by a political party, to observe its tenets blindly. (**-itore** *m.* **-itrice** *f.*)

asserzione *f.* assertion; statement; affirmation; (leg.) claim.

assessor-e *m., f.* member of the **giunta comunale**, elected from among the **consiglio comunale** of borough councillors; one of the citizens called upon to sit together with two judges in a criminal court (Corte d'Assise); assessor (one who sits as assistant, adviser to judge or magistrate). **-ato** *m.* office of member of **giunta comunale** or assessor; duration of same.

assest-are [A 1] *tr.* to adjust; to arrange; to settle; to set in order; (eng.) to bed; — un colpo, to deal a blow, to aim true; (comm.) — un bilancio, to strike a balance; — un conto, to balance an account; *rfl.* to settle down; to put one's affairs in order; to get organized. **-amento** *m.* arrangement; settlement; setting in order; (eng.) bedding; (bldg.) bond (in masonry); -amento incrociato, English cross bond; -amento inglese, modified English bond; -amento inglese normale, old English bond; -amento gotico, -amento polacco, double Flemish bond; (comm.) bilancio di -amento, supplementary estimate. **-atezza** *f.* orderliness; propriety. **-ato** *part. adj.* arranged, settled; orderly; neat; tidy; exact, precise. **-atamente** *adv.* tidily, neatly; in good order.

assesto *m.* order, orderliness; dar — a, to put in order.

asset-are [A 1 c] *tr.* to make thirsty; to deprive of water; (fig.) to fill with longing; l'esempio della vittoria lo -a di gloria, the sight of success arouses in him a thirst for glory. **-ato** *part. adj.* thirsty; dry; athirst; desirous; essere -ato di, to thirst for.

†**assetire** *vb.* See **assetare**.

assett-are[1] [A 1] *tr.* to arrange, to set in order; to adjust; — i capelli, to comb one's hair, to tidy one's hair; — una giovane, to marry a girl off; (liturg.) — l'altare, to prepare the altar; (mil.) to put on a war footing; (naut.) to trim; (naut. slang) to square off; †to sit down; *rfl.* to become settled; to settle; to tidy oneself, to take trouble with one's appearance; (of a building) to settle. **-amento** *m.* arrangement; setting in order; (archit.) laying of firm foundations; settlement. **-ato** *part. adj.* arranged; settled; orderly; in order; (of clothes, shoes) well-fitting; †seated. **-atamente** *adv.*

nicely; in good order. **-atino** *adj.* neat, tidy. **-atura** *f.* arranging; setting in order; arrangement; adjustment. **-atuzzo** *adj.* over-polished, slick.

assettare[2] [A 1] *tr.* to spay.

†**assettatore** *m.* follower, adherent.

assetto *m.* order; settled condition, settlement; arrangement; mettere in —, to set in order; in —, in bell'—, in readiness; (mil.) essere in — di guerra, to be on a war footing; to be in fighting trim; (naut.; aeron.) trim; (bldg.) see **assestamento**; †seat; †(fig.) dwelling, abode; †*part. adj.* see **assettato**.

†**assevare** *intr.*, *rfl.* to congeal; (fig.) to be faint with hunger, to long for food.

assever-are [A 1 S] *tr.* to assert; to affirm; to declare; to asseverate. **-amento** *m.* assertion; asseveration. **-ante** *part. adj.* assertive; dogmatic. **-antemente** *adv.* assertively; dogmatically. **-anza** *f.* assertiveness; firmness; assurance; asseveration; con -anza, firmly. **-atamente** *adv.* assertively; firmly. **-ativo** *adj.* affirmative; positive; assertive. **-ato** *part. adj.* asserted, affirmed, asseverated. **-azione** *f.* asseveration.

assiale *adj.* (mech.) axial; gioco —, axial play, end float; (hist. pol.) politica —, axis politics.

assibil-are [A 1 S] *tr.* (gramm., phon.) to assibilate; *rfl.* to become assibilated; †*intr.* to whistle; (onom.) to rustle, to swish. **-amento** *m.* assibilating, assibilation; rustling. **-ato** *part. adj.* assibilated. **-azione** *f.* assibilation; rustling.

†**assiccare** *vb.* See **seccare**.

assicella *f.* See under **asse**[1].

assicur-are [A 1] *tr.* to make secure; to secure; to fasten securely; (finan.) to insure; to assure, to convince; to affirm, to declare; to secure, to procure, to ensure; *rfl.* to make sure; to assure oneself; to fasten oneself; to tie oneself; (finan.) to insure oneself; -arsi di, to make sure of, to hold fast; (*dat.* of *prn.*) to secure for oneself. **-a·bile** *adj.* securable; insurable. **-amento** *m.* assurance; assuring; security; (finan.) insuring; insurance; assurance. **-ante** *part. adj., n.m.* assuring, reassuring; assurer; (finan.) insurer. **-anza** *f.* assurance. **-ativo** *adj.* (finan.) pertaining to insurance; ramo -ativo di una ditta, insurance branch of a firm. **-ato** *part. adj.* secured; assured; reassured; affirmed, declared; (finan.) insured, covered by insurance; *n.m.* l'assicurato, the assuree, the insured party; *f.* letter insured (for a specified amount). **-atamente** *adv.* assuredly, surely; with certainty. **-atore** *m.* insurer; underwriter; also *adj.* **-atrice** *f. adj.* compagnia -atrice, insurance company. **-azione** *f.* assurance; guarantee; security; pledge; (finan.) insurance; assurance; -azione contro gli incendi, fire insurance; -azione contro gli infortuni sul lavoro, industrial accident insurance; -azione contro la disoccupazione, unemployment insurance; — contro le malattie, health insurance; polizza d'-azione, insurance policy; polizza di -azione in caso di vita, endowment policy; -azione di rendita vitalizia, annuity insurance; -azione contro la responsabilità civile, third party insurance.

†**assidenza** *f.* presence.

assider-are [A 1 S] *intr.* (*aux.* essere), *rfl.* to become frozen; to be numb with cold; qui c'è da -arsi, you'll catch your death of cold here; *tr.* to freeze; to numb with cold, to chill. **-amento** *m.* frost-bite; morire per -amento, to freeze to death. **-ante** *part. adj.* freezing. **-ato** *part. adj.* frozen, chilled, benumbed; frost-bitten; frozen to death. **-azione** *f.* freezing; numbing; (agric.) withering.

assi·dere [C 3] *rfl.* to take one's seat; to be seated; *tr.* to besiege.

assi·du-o *adj.* assiduous; diligent; sedulous; regular (in attendance); uninterrupted, unbroken; (poet.) thronging, relentless, unending, unremitting; *n.m.* regular visitor. **-amente** *adv.* assiduously; continuously, without interruption. **-ità** *f.* assiduousness; regular attendance; diligence, constancy.

assiem-e *adv.* together; at the same time; jointly; — a, together with; mettere —, to put together, to save (money); stare —, to go well together, to agree; *n.m.* assembly; set. **-are** [A 1] *tr.* (eng.) to assemble. (**-ato** *part. adj.*)

assiep-are [A 1 d] *tr.* to fence, to hedge; to put a fence, hedge, round; to encircle; to throng, to crowd round; *rfl.* to crowd together, to mass; -arsi lungo i marciapiedi, to line the streets. **-amento** *m.* crowding. **-ato** *part. adj.* surrounded with a hedge; hedged round; crowded; crowding.

assile[1] *m.* See **asse**[1].

assile² *m.* (rlwy.) axle.

assillabazione *f.* series of words beginning with the same syllable; alliteration.

assill-are¹ [A I] *tr.* to goad, to incite, to spur on; to worry; -are di domande, to pester with questions; *intr.* (*aux.* avere) to be tormented, to suffer, to be in misery; — dalla sete, to be dying of thirst. **-ante** *part. adj.* tormenting, pestering. **-ato** *part. adj.* goaded, tormented, pestered.

assillare² *adj.* axillary.

assillo *m.* (ent.) *Asilus craboniformis*, robber fly; (fig.) torment; stimulus; sotto l'— della fame, goaded by hunger; painful thought; longing, desire.

†**assimigliare** *tr.* to compare; *intr.* to be similar; to become similar.

assimil-are [A I S] *tr.* to assimilate; to absorb; to compare, to consider similar; *rfl.* to be assimilated; (gramm.) to assimilate. **-a·bile** *adj.* assimilable. **-abilità** *f.* assimilability. (**-amento** *m.*) **-ativo** *adj.* assimilative. **-ato** *part. adj.* assimilated; made similar. (**-atore** *m.* **-atrice** *f.*) **-ato·rio** *adj.* assimilatory. **-azione** *f.* assimilation; absorption.

†**assincopare** *vb.* See **sincopare**.

assinite *f.* (miner.) axinite.

assintoto *m.* See **asintoto**.

assiolo *m.* See **assiuolo**.

assiom-a *m.* axiom; self-evident truth. **-a·tico** *adj.* axiomatic. (**-aticamente** *adv.*)

assio·metro *m.* (naut.) rudder indicator.

Assi·r-ia *pr.n.f.* (geog.) Assyria. **-iologi·a** *f.* Assyriology. **-io·logo** *m.* Assyriologist. **-o** *adj., n.m.* Assyrian. (**-a** *f.*)

assisa¹ *f.* uniform; livery.

†**assisa²** *f.* tax, duty.

assise *f.pl.* (leg.) Corte d'—, Italian criminal court empowered to judge the most serious crimes.

Assis·i *pr.n.f.* (geog.) Assisi. **-iate** *adj.* of Assisi; (also *n.m., f.*).

assiso *part.* from **assidere**, q.v.; *adj.* (poet.) seated; reclining; †situated.

assistae·reo *m.* (aeron.) homing beacon.

assi·st-ere [C 24] *tr.* to assist, to help, to aid; to look after, to nurse, to attend to; — i malati, to nurse the sick; to attend, to treat (medically); *intr.* (*aux.* avere, *prep.* a) to attend, to witness; to be present (at); — ad una conferenza, to attend a lecture. **-entato** *m.* (neol.) assistantship. **-ente** *part. adj.* assisting; present; *n.m., f.* assistant, helper; bystander, onlooker; -ente sociale, social worker; -ente sanitaria, district nurse; -ente universitario, assistant lecturer; (liturg.) assistant (priest). **-enza** *f.* assistance, help; prestare -enza, to assist; support; attendance, audience; care, treatment; -enza pubblica, public welfare services; -enza scolastica, public assistance services for schoolchildren; -enza sociale, welfare work, National Insurance and Health Services; -enza invernale, winter relief; diploma rilasciato dalla Scuola di -enza Sociale, diploma in social science; (naut.) -enza ostile, unneutral assistance. **-enziale** *adj.* pertaining to public assistance services: Opere -enziali del Regime (expression used particularly under Fascism), public assistance services. **-enzia·rio** *m.* relief centre, public welfare office. **-ito** *part. adj.* assisted; cared for, nursed; receiving relief, on the relief.

assit-are¹ [A I] (Tusc.) *tr.* (of a dog) to scent (the quarry); (fig.) to see through. **-ato** *part. adj.* evil-smelling.

†**assitare²** *rfl.* to acclimatize oneself, to become acclimatized.

assito *m.* (archit.; bldg.) partition; — intavolato, boarded wall or partition; — intelaiato, frame wall with brick nogging; hoarding, board fence; floor-board.

assiuolo *m.* (orn.) scops owl, *Otus scops*; (fig.) cuckold; capo d'—, ignoramus.

asso¹ *m.* ace, one (at cards, dice, dominoes); — di briscola, ace of trumps; (fig.) top-notcher; champion; — dell'aviazione, flying ace; — del volante, ace racing driver; essere l'—, to be unrivalled; essere l'— fisso in un luogo, to be a frequent visitor; — di bastoni, ace of clubs; (colloq.) beating.

asso² †*m.* dry place, dry part; *adv. phr.* lasciare in —, to leave in the lurch; rimanere in —, to be left high and dry.

associ-are [A 3] *tr.* (leg.) to entrust (cattle) to one who keeps part of produce in payment (cf. **soccida**). (**-amento** *m.*)

associ-are [A 3] *tr.* to associate; to combine, to unite; to take into partnership; — l'utile al dilettevole, to combine business with pleasure; (rel.) — un morto, to join in the funeral prayers for a dead person; *rfl.* to associate oneself; -arsi a, to join with; to enter into partnership with; to subscribe to; to join; *recipr. rfl.* to unite, to join in with one another; to form a partnership. **-a·bile** *adj.* compatible, associable. (**-abilità** *f.*) **-amento** *m.* associating; union. (**-ante** *part. adj.* **-ativo** *adj.*) **-ato** *part. adj.* associated; associate; *n.m.* associate; partner; member; subscriber. (**-atore** *m.* **-atrice** *f.*) **-azione** *f.* association; partnership; society; guild; subscription; (rel.) attendance at funeral prayers and ceremonies; Union, association; -azione fra la gente di mare, seamen's union; (leg.) diritto d'-azione, freedom of association; -azione a delinquere, conspiracy among five or more people for an unlawful purpose. **-azionismo** *m.* (philos.) associationism.

assod-are [A I] *tr.* to harden; — un uovo, to boil an egg hard; to consolidate; to make firm, to strengthen; l'esercizio -a le membra, exercise makes the muscles firm; to establish firmly; to confirm, to ascertain; *intr.* (*aux.* essere) to become hard, firm; *rfl.* to become solid; to become hard, firm; to boil hard (of eggs); (fig.) to gain experience, knowledge; -arsi di, to ascertain. **-amento** *m.* hardening; strengthening; consolidation; confirmation. **-ato** *part. adj.* firm, hardened; confirmed, certain; il fatto è oramai -ato, the fact is now established.

assogget-are [A I] *tr.* to subject; to subdue, to submit; to bind, to tie down; to subjugate; *rfl.* to subject oneself; to submit. **-a·bile** *adj.* subduable; capable of being subjugated, subjected. **-amento** *m.* subjugation, subjection; submission. (**-ante** *part. adj.* **-atore** *m.*)

assolare¹ [A I] *intr.* (*aux.* avere) (cards) to end with a singleton.

assol-are² [A I, 4] (agric.) *tr.* to spread out in layers, to spread out on the ground. (**-ato** *part. adj.*)

assol-are³ [A I] *tr.* to expose to the sun, to dry in the sun; *intr.* (*aux.* essere) (poet.) to dawn. **-ato** *part. adj.* sunny, exposed to the sun.

assolati·o *adj.* sunny.

assolc-are [A 2 C] *tr.* to furrow; to plough. **-ato** *part. adj.* furrowed.

assold-are [A I] *tr.* (mil.) to engage, to enrol, to enlist; *rfl.* to enlist, 'to take the shilling'. **-amento** *m.* (mil.) engaging, recruiting, enrolment, enlistment. **-ato** *part. adj.* engaged, enrolled, enlisted; *n.m.* strong-post. (**-atore** *m.*)

†**assolidare** *vb.* See **consolidare**.

†**assolo** *m.* (mus.) solo passage.

assolto *part.* of **assolvere**, q.v., *adj.* freed; exempt; (leg.) acquitted, absolved, cleared.

assolut-o¹ *adj.* absolute; hard and fast; positive; peremptory; unrestricted; unlimited; total, utter, complete; (scient.) zero —, absolute zero; (gramm.) ablativo —, ablative absolute; (mus.) soprano —, leading soprano; prima donna -a, leading lady; prima ballerina -a, prima ballerina in a ballet company (esp. attached to a State theatre); *n.m.* l'—, the absolute. **-amente** *adv.* absolutely; positively; definitely; at all costs; without restriction; unconditionally; generally. **-ezza** *f.* absoluteness; overstatement. **-ismo** *m.* absolutism. **-ista** *m.* absolutist; *adj.* absolutist; despotic.

assolut-o² *part.* of **assolvere**, q.v., *adj.* acquitted; absolved. **-ore** *m.* absolver, acquitter. (**-rice** *f.*) **-o·ria** *f.* (leg.) judgment or decree of acquittal. **-o·rio** *adj.* (leg.) absolutory.

assoluzione *f.* (leg.) acquittal, absolution; — con formula piena, full acquittal; — con formula dubitativa, acquittal for insufficiency of evidence; (theol., liturg.) absolution.

assol·vere [C 14] *tr.* (leg.) to acquit, to absolve; — da un debito, to waive a debt; (theol.) to absolve; to relieve, to release; to perform, to accomplish: — bene la propria parte, to acquit oneself well.

†**assomare** *tr.* to burden; to enslave.

assomigli-are [A 4] *tr.* (*prep.* a) to compare (with), to indicate resemblance (between); to make similar; *intr.* (*aux.* essere, avere) to be like; to be similar; *rfl. recip.* to resemble one another. **-amento** *m.* comparison. **-ante** *part. adj.* resembling, like; questo ritratto non è molto -ante, this portrait is not a very good likeness. **-anza** *f.* resemblance, likeness. **-ativo** *adj.* comparative. (**-ato** *part. adj.*) †**-o** *m.* double, image.

assommare¹ [A I C] *tr.* to add together, to add up; to combine; to conclude, to finish; †*intr.* (*aux.* essere) to amount to.

assommare² [A I] *tr.* (naut.) to surface (of a diver or submarine or any submerged object); to come up (from a hold or on deck); (naut. command) assomma! assomma!, get up aloft!

asson-are [A I d] *intr.* (*aux.* essere, avere) to correspond in sound, to assonate. **-ante** *part. adj.* assonant. **-anza** *f.* assonance, correspondence of sound.

assonn-are [A I c] *tr.* to send to sleep; *intr.* (*aux.* essere), *rfl.* to become sleepy; to fall asleep. **-acchiato** *adj.* sleepy, drowsy; half asleep. **-amento** *m.* sleepiness; falling asleep. **-ato** *part. adj.* sleepy, somnolent; asleep.

assonn-ire [D 2] *rfl.* to fall asleep. (**-imento** *m.*) **-ito** *part. adj.* drowsy, somnolent; dull-witted.

assono-metri·a *f.* (geom.) axonometry; — a sistema monometrico, isometric drawing. **-me·trico** *adj.* axonometric.

assop-ire [D 2] *tr.* to send to sleep; to lull; to soothe, to assuage; *rfl.* to nod off, to drowse; (of anger) to cool; (of violence) to be calmed. **-imento** *m.* dozing, doze; drowsiness. **-ito** *part. adj.* drowsy, dozing.

†**assor·bere** *vb.* See **assorbire**.

assorb-ire [D I, D 2] *tr.* to absorb; to take in, to imbibe; to dry up; to mop up; to suck up; to take up; to soak up; to engross; to swallow up, to engulf; to consume, to use up, to exhaust. **-ente** *part. adj.* absorbent; absorbing; engrossing; carta **-ente**, blotting-paper; *n.m.* absorbent; **-ente** acustico, soundproofing; **-ente** metallico, getter; **-enti** igienici, sanitary towels. **-imento** *m.* absorption. **-ito** *part. adj.* absorbed; dried up; sucked up; engrossed; engulfed. (**-itore** *m.* **-itrice** *f.*) **-ività** *f.* (phys.) absorptivity. **-ivo** *adj.* absorptive.

assord-are [A I c] *tr.* to deafen; to stun; *intr.* (*aux.* essere) to become deaf; to grow deaf; to be deafened. **-aggine** *f.* deafening row. **-amento** *m.* clamour, shouting; deafening; bewilderment. **-ante** *part. adj.* deafening; stunning. **-ato** *part. adj.* deafened.

†**assor·dio** *m.* poisonous spotted reptile.

assordire [D 2] and derivs. See **assordare**.

assorgere [C 5] *intr.* (*aux.* essere) to rise; to soar; to attain (to).

assort-ire[1] [D 2] *tr.* to sort; to grade; to stock (a shop); to select; to match, to combine. **-eri·a** *f.* assortment. **-imento** *m.* sorting; assortment; selection, range, stock; set (of tools, etc.); (miner.) screening. **-ito** *part. adj.* assorted; select, elect; matching, matched: il cappello **-ito** ai guanti, with hat and gloves matching; stocked, furnished, set up. **-itore** *m.* (industr.) sorter. **-itura** *f.* sorting, grading, classification.

†**assort-ire**[2] *tr.* to choose by lot. †**-ito** chosen by lot; (poet.) favoured by fortune; *n.m.* lucky man. †**-itore** drawer of lots.

assorto[1]: *adj.* (fig.) absorbed, preoccupied, immersed, distrait.

assorto[2] *part.* of **assorgere**, q.v.

assottigli-are [A 4] *tr.* to sharpen; to make pointed; — la mente, to sharpen the wits; to make thin; to disperse; to diminish; — il patrimonio, — la borsa, to spend lavishly; — le spese, to reduce expenditure; (med.) to thin (e.g. the blood); (mil.) — l'esercito, to reduce the strength of the army, to cut down the strength; *rfl.* to become sharp, fine, pointed; to grow thin; to fine down, to become slender; to taper; (fig.) to exert oneself; to sharpen one's wits. **-amento** *m.* sharpening, thinning; diminution, reduction; tapering. **-ata** *f.* sharpening; thinning. †**-ativo** *adj.* (hist. med.) that dilutes the humours. **-ato** *part. adj.* sharpened, pointed; thinned, rarefied. (**-atore** *m.* **-atrice** *f.*) **-atura** *f.* sharpening, thinning; rarefying.

†**assozzare** *tr.* to dirty.

assuccare [A 2] *tr.* (naut.) to taughten, to relace.

assuef-are [B 14] *tr.* to accustom; *rfl.* to accustom oneself, to become accustomed. **-atto** *part. adj.* used, accustomed; inured. **-azione** *f.* accustoming; custom, habit.

†**assuet-o** *adj.* see **consueto**. †**-u·dine** *f.* see **consuetudine**.

assu·m-ere [C8] *tr.* to take up; to assume; to engage, to appoint, to nominate; to raise, to elevate; to take; to undertake; to incur; — la responsabilità, to shoulder the responsibility; — informazioni, to make enquiries; — il servizio, to enter upon office; — in servizio, to take on, to engage; (leg.) — una prova testimoniale, to take the witnesses' evidence (in a civil case); (theol.) to assume, to take up (into Heaven); †to quote, to cite as evidence; *rfl.* (*dat.* of *prn.*) to take upon oneself. (**-i·bile** *adj.*)

assunt-o *part.* of **assumere**, q.v.; *adj.* assumed; raised; appointed, nominated; taken; undertaken; *n.m.* assumption; task, undertaking, enterprise; thesis, argument, hypothesis. **-a** *f.* (theol.) l'Assunta, Our Lady of the Assumption; (eccl.; art) feast, church or painting of the Assumption; *pr.n.f.* Assunta. **-ivo** *adj.* assumptive; (herald.) armi **-ive**, assumptive arms. †**-ore** *m.* contractor; employer.

assunzion-e *f.* assumption; assuming, undertaking; (theol.) Assump-tion; giorno dell'—, Assumption Day; raising; nomination, appointment; engagement (of an employee); — al trono, ascent to the throne; (leg.) — delle prove testimoniali, taking of witnesses' evidence. **-ista** *m.* (eccl.) Assumptionist, Augustinian of the Assumption.

assuolare [A I] and derivs. See **assolare**[2].

assurd-o *adj.* absurd, nonsensical; preposterous; unreasonable; extravagant, strange; *n.m.* absurdity; nonsense; absurdum; ragionamento per —, reductio ad absurdum. **-amente** *adv.* absurdly; preposterously. **-ità** *f.* absurdity; preposterousness.

assur·gere [C 5]. See **assorgere**.

ast-a *f.* lance, spear; staff; shaft, handle; leg (of pair of compasses); pole; stroke (in writing), pot-hook; (of a child) è ancora alle **-e**, he's just learning to write, he's still on pot-hooks and hangers; (anat.) penis; (sport) salto con l'—, pole-vault; (naut.) flag pole; awning stanchion; boom; — di fiocco, jib boom; — di contro-fiocco, outer jib-boom; (mech.) rod; — del cambio, gear selector rod; — di misurazione, dipstick; — articolata, trace; — di accoppiamento, drag link; — della punteria, tappet stem; — di guida, slide bar; (electr.) — di presa, trolley, collector; caliper; (comm.) auction; sale by auction; concorrere all'—, to bid at an auction; vendere all'—, to sell by auction; mettere all'—, to call for tenders; *pl.* (bldg.) trussing. **-aio** *m.* lance-maker. †**-a·rio** *m.* (mil. hist.) lance-bearer. **-ata** *f.* blow with a lance. **-ato** *adj.* armed with a lance; spear-shaped; *n.m.* lance-bearer. **-atore** *m.* auctioneer. **-icci(u)ola** *f.* dim. of **asta**; pen-holder; (archit.) metal tie; tie-beam; trussing; (ichth.) *Sudis hyalina.* **-icella** *f.* (metall.) **-icelle** di estrazione, lifting irons. **-icina** *f.* (electr.) filament holder, stem. **-ina** *f.* (of a pump) sucker rod. **-ista** *m.* (athl.) pole-vaulter.

a·staco *m.* (zool.) *Astacus fluviatilis*, crayfish; (pop.) lobster.

†**astallare** *vb.* See **installare**.

astant-e *adj.* attending, in attendance; attendant, assistant; medico —, doctor on duty (in a hospital); *n.m.* bystander; spectator, witness, onlooker; gli **-i**, those present. **-eri·a** *f.* (med.) reception ward of a hospital; first-aid post; staff on duty (at hospital).

†**astare** *intr.* to be present.

asta·tic-a *f.* (phys.) astatics. **-o** *adj.* (phys.) astatic.

astato *adj.* See under **asta**.

astatore *m.* See under **asta**.

†**aste** *f.* See **asta**.

asteggi-are [A 3 c] *intr.* (*aux.* avere) to make pot-hooks (in learning to write). **-atura** *f.* writing-exercise, making pot-hooks.

asteggio *m.* See **asteggiatura**, under **asteggiare**.

aste·mio *adj.* abstemious; *n.m.* abstainer, teetotaller.

asten-ere [B 32] *rfl.* (*prep.* da) to abstain; to refrain; to forbear; to abstain from voting; *tr.* to restrain. **-ente** *part. adj.* abstaining. **-imento** *m.* abstention. **-uto** *part. adj.* abstaining; *n.m.* abstainer, one who does not vote; gli **-uti** furono venti, twenty abstaining.

asten-i·a *f.* (med.) debility, asthenia. **-opi·a** *f.* (med.) asthenopia.

aste·nico *adj.* (med.) run down, out of sorts; asthenic.

astension-e *f.* abstention. **-ismo** *m.* abstentionism. **-ista** *m.* absten-tionist.

aster·g-ere [C 4] *tr.* to cleanse, to clean; to wipe; to dry; (med.) to absterge, to cleanse. **-ente** *part. adj.*, *n.m.* abstergent.

aste·ria *f.* (zool.) starfish; (miner.) asteria, asteriated sapphire, cymophane.

aster-isco *m.* (*pl.* **-ischi**) asterisk; star; segnato con —, starred, marked with an asterisk; (neol.) paragraph, brief note (in a newspaper). **-ismo** *m.* (astron.) constellation, asterism; (miner.) asterismus. **-oide** *m.* (astron.) asteroid; (math.) asteroid (cycloid where $r = R/4$); *pl.* (zool.) Asteroidea. **-ofoto·metro** *m.* see **astrofotometro**, under **astrochimica**. **-o·metro** *m.* see **astrometro**, under **astrochimica**.

asters-ione *f.* abstersion, cleansing; (scient.) abstersion. **-ivo** *adj.* cleansing, abrasive; abstersive.

asterso *part.* from **astergere**, q.v.; *adj.* cleansed; wiped.

Ast-i *pr.n.m.* (geog.) Asti, in Piedmont; an Italian red wine; — spumante, sparkling wine of Asti, Italian champagne. **-igiano** *adj.* of Asti; *n.m.* native of Asti; (poet.) il tragico **-igiano**, the dramatist, Vittorio Alfieri (1749–1803).

astiare [A 4]. See under **astio**.

asticci(u)ola *f.* See under **asta**.

a·stice *m.* (zool.). See **astaco**.

asticella, asticina *f.* See under **asta**.

astiera *f.* spear-sheathe.

†**astiere** *m.* lance-bearer.

astigiano *adj.* See under **Asti**.

astigma·t-ico *adj.* (med.) astigmatic; suffering from astigmatism. **-iṣmo** *m.* (med.) astigmatism.

astile *m.* spear-handle; †comma.

a·stilo *adj.* (archit.) without columns, astylar.

astimmaziọne *f.* See **astigmatismo**.

astina *f.* See under **asta**.

astin-ente *adj.* abstinent, abstemious; abstaining. **-enza** *f.* abstinence; moderation, restraint; (rel.) abstinence (esp. in relation to fasting): oggi fo -enza, I am abstaining today; fare -enza, to live an austere life.

a·sti-o *m.* grudge; resentment; grievance; rancour, envy, spite; avere — a (con, contro), to have a grudge against. **-are** [A4] *tr.* (Tusc.) to envy; to have a grudge against, to harbour resentment towards; *recip. rfl.* to envy one another, to nurse grievances against one another. **-oso** *adj.* envious, spiteful; resentful; grudging. **-osamẹnte** *adv.* resentfully, angrily. (**-osità** *f.*)

†**astivamente** *adv.* quickly, hastily.

†**asto¹** *m.* see **astuzia**; (dial. Umbr.) see **astio**.

†**asto²** *m.* haste.

astọre *m.* (orn.) goshawk, *Accipiter gentilis*.

astraca·n *m. indecl.* See **astrakan**.

astra·galo *m.* (anat.) ball of the ankle-joint, astragalus; knuckle-bone, huckle-bone, dib; (archit.) astragal, semi-circular moulding.

astraka·n *m. indecl.* (text.) astrakhan.

astrale *adj.* astral.

astrarre [B33] *tr.* to abstract; *intr.* (aux. avere) to prescind; *rfl.* to abstract oneself, to withdraw.

astratt-o *part.* from **astrarre**, q.v.; *adj.* abstracted, separated; abstract; inattentive, preoccupied; absent-minded; *n.m.* l'—, the abstract; in —, in the abstract. **-ag·gine** *f.* absent-mindedness, vagueness; inattention. **-amẹnte** *adv.* in the abstract; absent-mindedly. **-ẹzza** *f.* abstractness. **-iṣmo** *m.* abstraction; habit of dealing exclusively in abstractions; abstract art. **-ivo** *adj.* abstractive.

astraziọne *f.* abstraction; abstract concept; fare — da, to leave on one side, to abstract from; fatta — da, apart from, setting aside; preoccupation, vagueness, abstractedness; absent-mindedness.

Astre·a *pr.n.f.* (myth.) Astraea, symbol of law and justice; (astron.) Libra.

astrett-o *part.* from **astringere**, q.v.; *adj.* (fig.) constrained; compelled. **-ivo** *adj.* (med.) binding, astringent.

†**astri·fero** *adj.* starry.

astrin·g-ere [C10] *tr.* to constrain; to compel, to coerce; (med.) to bind, to constipate. **-ente** *part. adj.* astringent; (med.) binding; *n.m.* astringent. **-enza** *f.* astringency.

†**astri·tide** *f.* See **artritide**.

astr-o¹ *m.* star, heavenly body; l'— della sera, the evening star; l'— delle notti, the moon; luminary; — del cinema, film star (man); (ichth.) — marino, starfish. †**-oso** *adj.* fortunate, born under a lucky star.

astro² *m.* (bot.) aster.

astr-ochi·mica *f.* astrochemistry. **-odina·mica** *f.* astrodynamics. **-o·filo** *m.* enthusiast for astronomy. **-ofi·sica** *f.* astrophysics. **-ofi·sico** *adj.* astrophysical. **-ofobi·a** *f.* (med.) fear of storms. **-ofotometri·a** *f.* astrophotometry. **-ofoto·metro** *m.* astrophotometer. **-ografi·a** *f.* astrography. **-ola·bio** *m.* astrolabe. **-olatri·a** *f.* star-worship, astrolatry. **-ologare** [A2s] *intr.* (aux. avere) to astrologize, to read the stars; to make fantastic conjectures. **-ologi·a** *f.* astrology; †astronomy; (hist.) -ologia naturale, medieval meteorology. **-olo·gico** *adj.* astrological. (**-ologicamẹnte** *adv.*) **-o·logo** (*m.pl.* **-o·loghi, o·logi**) *m.* astrologer; †*adj.* astrological. **-ometeorologi·a** *f.* astro-meteorology. **-ometri·a** *f.* astrophotometry. **-o·metro** *m.* astrometer. **-ona·utica** *f.* interplanetary travel, astronautics. **-onomi·a** *f.* astronomy. **-ono·mico** *adj.* astronomical; (fig.) extreme, excessive; prezzi -onomici, astronomical prices. (**-onomicamẹnte** *adv.*) **-o·nomo** *m.* astronomer. **-osco·pio** *m.* astroscope.

astruṣ-o *adj.* abstruse; recondite; obscure; *n.m.* abstruseness. **-ag·gine** *f.* unnecessarily abstruse discourse or argument. **-amẹnte** *adv.* abstrusely, obscurely. **-eri·a** *f.* abstruseness; unnecessarily abstruse argument or exposition. **-ità** *f.* abstruseness.

astuc·ci-o *m.* case; box; sheath; container, holder; — per aghi, needle-case; — per gioielli, jewel case; (naut.) hounding (of a mast), mast casing; mast protection; propeller shaft casing; sail cover; locker; — dell'asse portaelica, propeller shaft casing.

-a·io *m.* case-maker; seller of cases. **-are** [A3] *tr.* (industr.) to pack, to put in containers. (**-ato** *part. adj.*)

Astu·rie *pr.n.f.pl.* (geog.) le —, the Asturias.

†**astutare** *vb.* See **attutire**.

astut-o *adj.* astute; wide awake, sharp, bright; cunning, sly; sagacious; artful. (**-amẹnte** *adv.*) **-ẹzza** *f.* astuteness; artfulness, slyness.

astu·zia *f.* astuteness; cunning; artfulness; guile; trickery; trick; conosco le tue astuzie, I know your tricks; (mil.) — di guerra, stratagem.

†**a·ṣuro** *m.* (ent.) vine grub or maggot.

atabale *m.* (mus.) atabal, a Moorish drum.

atalanta *f.* (ent.) Atalanta butterfly.

Atali·a *pr.n.f.* Athaliah.

Atana·sia¹ *pr.n.f.* Athanasia.

†**atana·sia²** *f.* (pharm.) electuary for liver and kidney troubles.

Atana·sio *pr.n.m.* Athanasius.

atarassi·a *f.* (philos.) ataraxy.

†**atare** *vb.* and derivs. See **aiutare**.

at-assi·a *f.* (med.) ataxy; — locomotrice, locomotor ataxy. **-as·sico** *adj.* ataxic.

†**atauto** *m.* bier; coffin.

a·t-avo *m.* great-great-grandfather; ancestor; (poet.) *adj.* ancestral. **-a·vico** *adj.* atavistic. **-avi·stico** *adj.* atavistic. **-aviṣmo** *m.* atavism.

†**atei·a** *f.* atheism.

ateiṣmo *m.*, **ateista** *m.* See under **ateo**.

ateli *m.pl.* (zool.) *Ateles* spp., spider monkeys, coaitas.

atellana *f.* (lit. hist.) farce of Oscan origin, named after the town of Atella in Campania.

Atena *pr.n.f.* (myth.) Athene.

Aten-e *pr.n.f.* (geog.) Athens. **-iese** *adj., n.m., f.* Athenian.

atene·o *m.* athenaeum; academy; university.

a·te-o *adj., n.m.* atheist. **-iṣmo** *m.* atheism. **-ista** *m., f.* atheist. **-i·stico** *adj.* atheistic.

aterina *f.* (ichth.) atherine, sand smelt, *Atherina hepsetus* and *A. boyeri*.

atermano *adj.* (phys.) opaque to radiant heat, athermanous.

ater·mico *adj.* (phys.) athermic.

ateroma *m.* (med.) atheroma.

atesino *adj.* pertaining to the River Adige, or to the region watered by that river; alto —, pertaining to the Upper Adige; *n.m.* inhabitant of the Adige region.

†**atezza** *f.* strength, robustness.

ati·pico *adj.* (scient.) atypic(al), not conforming to type.

At-lante *pr.n.m.* (myth.) Atlas; (astron.) le figlie d'—, Pleiades; (geog.) Mt Atlas; atlas, book of maps; book of plates; (anat.) atlas; (ent.) Atlas butterfly, *Attacus atlas*; (archit.) *pl.* atlantes. **-lan·tico** *adj.* Atlantean; (geog.) Atlantic; (neol. pol.) of, pertaining to, signatories of the Atlantic pact; †great; †wearisome; †of the size of an Atlas; *n.m.* Atlantic Ocean; (neol.) pilot who flies the Atlantic. **-lan·tide** *pr.n.f.* (myth.) Atlantis.

at-leta *m.* (*pl.* **-leti**) athlete; *f.* (*pl.* **-lete**) woman athlete. **-le·tica** *f.* athletics. **-le·tico** *adj.* athletic. (**-leticamẹnte** *adv.*) **-letiṣmo** *m.* athleticism.

atmos-fera *f.* atmosphere; mental or moral environment; (neol.) background; — pratica, 'generally used' atmosphere, 14·223 lb. per sq. in.; 1 kg. per sq. cm.; — teorica, atmosphere (760 mm. Hg at 0° C., 14·696 lb. per sq. in.); — tipo, standard atmosphere (760 mm. Hg at 15° C.). **-fe·rico** *adj.* atmospheric; *n.m.* (radio) atmospheric.

atollo *m.* (geog.) atoll.

a·t-omo *m.* (scient.) atom; (fig.) particle, bit, jot. **-o·mico** *adj.* atomic; (neol.) atomic-powered. **-omicità** *f.* (phys., chem.) atomicity. **-omiẓẓare** [A1] *tr.* to atomize, to vaporize. **-omiẓẓatọre** *m.* atomizer, vaporizer, spray. **-omiẓẓaziọne** *f.* atomization, vaporization.

aton-ale *adj.* (mus.) atonal. **-alità** *f.* (mus.) atonality.

atoni·a *f.* (med.) atony, languor, enervation, want of tone; (fig.) languor, depression.

a·tono *adj.* toneless; in una voce atona, in a toneless voice; (gramm.) atonic, unstressed; (med.) poor in tone, weak.

atos·sico *adj.* non-toxic.

atout *m. indecl.* (bridge) trumps; un senza —, one no trumps; battere gli —, to draw trumps.

atra-bile *f.* (med. hist.) black bile; melancholy, spleen. **-biliare** *adj.* moody, splenetic; umore -biliare, gloomy disposition, melancholy temperament; (med. hist.) atrabiliary.

†**atramento** *m.* ink.

a·tri-o *m.* atrium; entrance hall (of a hotel, law-courts, etc.); porch (of a church); lobby, vestibule; (biol.; anat.) atrium, auricle. **-en·se** *m.* (Rom. hist.) house-steward.

atro *adj.* (poet.) black; gloomy; fearful; lurid.

atrọc-e *adj.* atrocious; heinous, outrageous; terrible, cruel, ferocious; acute, severe, excruciating. (**-emẹnte** *adv.*) **-ità** *f.* atrociousness; odiousness; inhumanity, cruelty; atrocity.

atr-ofi·a *f.* (med.) atrophy; (text.) stunting. **-o·fico** *adj.* atrophous. **-ofizzare** [A I S] *tr.* to atrophy, to starve; *rfl.* to atrophy, to waste away. **-ofizzato** *part. adj.* atrophied.

atrop-ina *f.* (chem., pharm.) atropine. **-ịsmo** *m.* (med.) atropinism.

A·tropo *pr.n.f.* (myth.) Atropos, one of the Fates; (ent.) death's head hawk moth, *Acherontia atropos.*

attacc-are [A 2] *tr.* to attack, to set upon, to assail; to combat; to impugn, to inculpate; to broach, to begin; — discorso, to open a conversation; to strike up an acquaintance; — battaglia, to join battle; (mus.) to strike up; — un ballabile, to strike up a dance measure, to play the opening bars of a dance tune; (imper.) attacca subito, proceed to the next movement without pause; — un urlo, to let out a yell; — sonno, to drop off to sleep; — lite, to start a quarrel, to raise Cain; to fasten, to tie; to attach; to stick, to gum, to paste, to affix; to apply; to sew on, to stitch on; (colloq. fig.) — un bottone, to be extremely boring, to buttonhole; to hang up, to suspend; -ò il cappello a un chiodo, he hung his hat on a nail; (colloq.) — la voglia al chiodo, to resign oneself to disappointment; — fuoco a, to set fire to; — un cavallo, to harness a horse; — il pensiero a, to fix one's thoughts on; — la mano a, to seize; — il dente a, to get one's teeth into; — una malattia a, to pass on an illness to; (fig.) -arsela a un orecchio, to learn one's lesson; (chem.) to attack; to etch; *intr.* (aux. essere, *prep.* a) to stick well, to adhere; to begin; *abs.* (fig.) to catch on, to find favour; to be all the rage; to work, to be successful: non -a, it's no good, it doesn't work; *rfl.* to stick, to adhere; to cling; (of illness) to be contagious, to be infectious, to be catching; (foll. by *prep.* a) to become fond (of), attached (to); (foll. by *prep.* con) to come to blows (with); *recip. rfl.* to quarrel with one another, to have words. **-a·bile** *adj.* assailable; attachable. **-abottoni** *m., f. indecl.* bore, incessant talker. **-abrighe** *m., f. indecl.* wrangler, quarrelsome person. **-a·gnolo** *m.* peg, hook; (fig.) pretext. **-alite** *m., f. indecl.* quarrelsome, contentious person; one who goes to law at the slightest pretext. **-amẹnto** *m.* attachment; affection; -amento al denaro, stinginess. **-ante** *part. adj., n.m.* (football, rugby) forward. **-apanni** *m. indecl.* peg, hatstand. (**-atẹzza** *f.*) **-atic·cio** *adj.* sticky; contagious; boring, annoying, importunate; *n.m.* sticky mess; burned part of food that has stuck to the saucepan. **-ativa** *f.* adherence; sticking quality. **-ato** *part. adj.* attacked; attached; tied; stuck, gummed, pasted, affixed; fond, attached; stare -ato a, to give close attention to; careful with money, close. **-atamẹnte** *adv.* loyally, faithfully. **-atọio** *m.* hook, peg. **-atura** *f.* attaching; joining; juncture, join; (tanning) folding over on the flesh side; (paint.) junction (of limbs), articulation. **-hino** *m.* bill-poster, bill-sticker; quarrelsome person.

attac-co *m.* (*pl.* **-chi**) attack; assault; battle; juncture; attachment; team (of horses), turn-out; onset; connexion; cohesion, unity; affinity; pretext, opportunity; (Tusc.) tutto l'—, all accessories; (art) etching; (rlwy.) coupling; (radio) jack; (foundry) — di colata, ingate; (med.) attack; fit, access; (mech.) connexion; fastening, joint, attachment; (mil.) — a baionetta, bayonet base, bayonet socket; — alla baionetta, bayonet attack; — a sorpresa con rapido sganciamento, hit and run; (mus.) short fugue-subject; down-beat; (sport) forwards; centro —, centre-forward; — della roccia, part where the rock face begins; (fencing) thrust; — di botta dritta, straight thrust; *pl.* (ski.) footbindings.

attacconare [A I C] *intr.* (aux. avere) (shoem.) to attach the heel.

attagliare [A 4] *rfl.* (*prep.* a) to fit; to suit; to adapt oneself; *tr.* to adapt; to cut down; †to cut; †(fig.) to resolve, to cut through (difficulties).

†**attalentare** *tr.* to please, to delight.

†**attamente** *adv.* suitably.

†**attamo** *m.* See **attimo.**

attanagli-are [A 4] *tr.* to seize (with pincers); to clutch, to claw; (fig.) to hold fast, to get one's claws into; (hist.) to torture with red-hot pincers. (**-ato** *part. adj.*)

†**attanto** *adv.* See **intanto.**

attapin-are [A I] *rfl.* to be in poverty; to be in distress; to pull the devil by the tail; to be a poor wretch; to take great pains; †to hide oneself; *tr.* to make wretched. (**-amẹnto** *m.* **-ato** *part. adj.*)

attardare [A I] *rfl.* to stay behind, to dawdle, to dally, to tarry.

attarantato *adj.* bitten by the tarantula; *n.m.* sufferer from such a bite.

†**attare** *vb.* See **adattare.**

†**attassare** *tr.* to disturb; to terrify; to distress.

attast-are [A I] *tr.* to touch, to feel; to handle. **-ato** *part. adj.* †*n.m.* touch.

†**attatto** *m.* contact; touch.

†**attavolare** *rfl.* to sit down to table.

attecch-ire [D 2] *intr.* (aux. avere) to take root; to grow, to thrive; to sprout; to prosper; to succeed; to catch on; il vaccino non ha -ito, the vaccine has not taken. **-imẹnto** *m.* taking root; thriving; sprouting. **-ito** *part. adj.* thriving; prosperous.

attediare [A 4] and derivs. See **tediare.**

atteggi-are [A 3 c] *tr.* to pose; to compose, to arrange; to give an expression to: — le labbra al sorriso, to assume a smiling expression; — la voce, to modulate the voice; to represent (by gesture or expression); †to act (in dumb show); *rfl.* (*prep.* a) to assume an attitude (of), to pose (as); -arsi a martire, to pose as a martyr; si -a a critico, he sets himself up as a critic. (**-a·bile** *adj.*) **-amẹnto** *m.* attitude; pose; behaviour; policy; 'gait', air, characteristic movement (of style). (**-ante** *part. adj.*) **-ato** *part. adj.* posed; expressive, figurative; affected. **-atore** *m.* poseur. (**-atrice** *f.*) **-atura** *f.* pose; arrangement.

†**attelare** *tr.* (mil.) to deploy; *rfl.* to be deployed.

attemp-are [A I] *intr.* (aux. essere) to grow old; †*rfl.* **-ato** *adj.* elderly; old, aged. **-atello** *adj.* getting on in years.

attemperare [A I S] *tr.* (mus.) to tune, to temper; †see **temperare.**

attend-are [A I] *rfl.* to put up tents, to encamp; (mil.) to pitch camp. **-amẹnto** *m.* encampment, encamping; (mil.) tented camp. **-ato** *part. adj.* encamped; (mil.) under canvas; (joc.) given a shake-down, 'camped out'.

atten·d-ere [C I] *tr.* to wait for; to await; to expect (someone); to pay regard to; — la promessa, to keep one's promise; — con ansia, to look forward to; †to understand; *intr.* (aux. avere, *prep.* a) to mind, to look after, to care for; to attend (to), to pay attention (to); -eva ai fatti suoi, he was minding his own business; to apply oneself (to); attese allo studio della chimica, he applied himself to the study of chemistry; to wait: -i qui, wait here; *rfl.* (dat. of prn.) to expect: non me lo -evo, I didn't expect it; †to belong to, to be an adherent of. **-ente** *part. adj.* assisting; donna -ente a casa, domestic help; *n.m.* (mil.) batman; orderly. **-i·bile** *adj.* worthy of attention; authentic, valid, sound, well-founded; convincing; una fonte -ibile, a reliable source; (of experimental results) repeatable, consistent; *n.m.* (Ital. hist.) person suspected of Liberalist sympathies (Kingdom of Naples). **-ibilità** *f.* reliability, reliableness, authenticity, credibility. (**-imẹnto** *m.*) **-ịsmo** *m.* (neol. pol.) policy of 'wait and see'. (**-itore** *m.* **-itrice** *f.*)

atten-ẹre [B 32] *rfl.* (*prep.* a), *intr.* (aux. essere, *prep.* a) to concern; to be relevant (to); to be related (to); to belong (to); to abide (by); to follow, to stick (to), to adhere (to); ci si è -uti strettamente alle indicazioni, we kept strictly to the instructions; †to hold on carefully; †to hang on; †to be suspended; *tr.* to keep, to maintain (faith, promise). **-ente** *part. adj.* belonging; pertaining; adjoining. **-enza** *f.* appurtenance; appendage. (**-itore** *m.* **-itrice** *f.*)

attentamẹnte *adv.* See under **attento.**

attent-are [A I] *intr.* (aux. avere, *prep.* a) to commit an outrage (against); — alla vita di, to attempt, successfully or unsuccessfully, to assassinate; *rfl.* (*prep.* a, di) to dare; non si -ò di ripeterlo, he hadn't the courage to repeat it. **-ante** *part. adj.; n.m.* (leg.) person who attempts, successfully or unsuccessfully, to assassinate. **-ato** *part. adj.; n.m.* outrage, attack; attempt on someone's life. **-atore** *m.* person who has made an attempt upon the life of somebody. (**-atrice** *f.*) †**-atorio** *adj.* (leg.) pertaining to an attempt; directed against the authority of a magistrate. (**-azione** *f.*)

attent-o *adj.* attentive; alert; intent; diligent; careful; stare —, to pay attention; —!, look out!; — a non scivolare, mind you don't slip; -i al treno!, danger! keep a look out for trains; (mil.) mettersi sull' -i, to come to attention; stare sull'-i, to stand at attention; posizione di -i, at attention; (mil. command) attenti!, attention! **-amẹnte** *adv.* attentively; diligently; wistfully. **-ẹzza** *f.* attentiveness

attenu-are [A 5] *tr.* to attenuate; to weaken; to minimize; to

attenu-are (*cont.*)

extenuate; *rfl.* to weaken, to become weak; (radio) to fade. **-aménto** *m.* attenuation; extenuation; **-ante** *part. adj.* attenuating; extenuating; (leg.) extenuating; *n.f.* extenuating circumstance. **-ato** *part. adj.* attenuated, thin; extenuated; sigaro -ato, mild cigar; (**-atamente** *adv.*) **-atore** *m.* (electr.; teleg.) attenuator. **-azione** *f.* attenuation, diminution; extenuation; mitigation; (acoustics; math.) damping, deadening; (radio) -azione di inserzione, insertion loss; -azione di rumore, noise abatement.

attenzióne *f.* attention; notice; carefulness; heed, caution; fare —, to pay attention; richiamare l'—, to call attention; application; attenzione!, look out!; attention, please!; diligence; *pl.* attentions, courtesies, kindness.

at·teo *adj.* (poet.) Attic; Greek.

attepidire [D 2 d] and derivs. See **attiepidire**.

atterg-are [A 2] *tr.* (comm.) to endorse (a document) with a statement or a decision; to docket; †*rfl.* to turn one's back. **-ato** *part. adj.*; *n.m.* (finan.) transfer of registered stock or shares by endorsement of certificate; docket; endorsement of document.

at·t-eri *m.pl.* (zool.) aptera. **-e·rice**, **-e·rige** *f.* (orn.) kiwi, *Apteryx*.

atterr-are [A 1] *tr.* to knock down; to fell; to demolish; to throw down; to raze to the ground; to humble; — ogni difficoltà, to overcome every difficulty; †to lower (one's gaze); *intr.* (*aux.* avere) (naut.) to make landfall, to land; (aeron.) to land; (of birds) to alight; †*rfl.* to prostrate oneself, to humble oneself; †to become silted up. **-ag·gio** *m.* (aeron.) landing; pista d'-aggio, runway; -aggio forzato, forced landing; -aggio di fortuna, emergency landing; -aggio a piatto, pancake landing. **-aménto** *m.* knocking down; felling; demolition; overthrow; (aeron.) landing; †silting up. **-ata** *f.* arrival; landing. **-ato** *part. adj.* knocked down; felled; demolished; †humbled, brought low. (**-atore** *m.* **-atrice** *f.* **-azione** *f.*)

†**atterrenato** *adj.* cast low; cast down; dejected.

†**atterrimento**[1] *m.* See under **atterrire**.

†**atterrimento**[2] *m.* silting up.

atterr-ire [D 2] *tr.* to frighten, to terrify; *intr.* (*aux.* essere), *rfl.* to be frightened, to be terrified, to become frightened. **-imento** *m.* terror, fright; frightening. **-ito** *part. adj.* terrified. (**-itore** *m.*)

†**atterzare** *tr.* to reduce to a third; *intr.* to reach the third section.

attésa *f.* waiting; expectation; hope; delay; sala d'—, waiting-room; essere in — di, to be waiting for; con un'espressione di —, expectantly; in — dei vostri ambiti ordini, awaiting (the favour) of your esteemed orders.

attes-ismo *m.* (hist. pol.) policy of biding one's time (during Fascist era). **-ista** *m.* anti-Fascist who withdrew from politics.

attéso *part.* of **attendere**, q.v.; *adj.* awaited; expected; attentive; considering, taking into consideration: attesa la sua buona condotta, taking his good conduct into consideration; †— a, intent upon; *conj.* — che, considering that, seeing that; (leg.) — chè (attesochè) whereas, taking into consideration that.

attest-are[1] [A 1] *tr.* to testify; to affirm; to certify; to bear witness to; to vouch for; la presente è per — che, this is to certify that; *intr.* (*aux.* avere, *prep.* di) to vouch for: -o della verità di ciò, I vouch for the truth of that; to attest. to witness, to sign attestation papers, to make one's attestation. **-a·bile** *adj.* testifiable; verifiable. **-ato** *part. adj.* testified; affirmed; *n.m.* testimonial; evidence, token; certificate; -ato di nascita, birth certificate; evidence, token; in -ato di, in token of; attestation; *pl.* -ati di brevetto, letters patent. **-atore** *m.* testifier, witness. (**-atrice** *f.*) **-azione** *f.* attestation; affirmation; testimony; token; certificate.

attest-are[2] *rfl.* (mil.) to become entrenched; to meet with (the enemy). **-amento** *m.* (techn.) see **attestatura**; †(mil.) encounter. †**-ato** *part. adj.* head-on; †*n.m.* (mil.) encounter.

attestatura *f.* (archit.; carp.; mech. eng.) abutment.

†**attezza** *f.* aptness, suitability.

atticciato *adj.* (Tusc.) thick-set, heavily built; squat; stout; strong.

at·tic-o *adj.* Attic; sale —, Attic salt, wit; (archit.) Attic; piano —, Attic storey; *n.m.* (archit.) Attic storey, attic (in Roman and Italian styles); falso —, Attic storey consisting only of a dado, cornice or ogee; (neol.) pent-house flat on the top of a block of flats. **-amente** *adv.* in Attic style. **-ismo** *m.* Atticism. **-ista** *m.* Atticist. **-izzare** [A 1] *intr.* (*aux.* avere) to atticize. **-urgo** *adj.* (archit.) Attic.

attiepid-ire [D 2 d] *tr.* to cool, to make lukewarm; *rfl.*, *intr.* (*aux.* essere) to grow cool; (fig.) to cool off. **-ito** *part. adj.* cooled, lukewarm.

---

atti·gu-o *adj.* adjacent; adjoining; contiguous; la stanza -a, the next room. **-ità** *f.* adjacency; contiguity.

attill-are [A 1] *tr.* to dress up; to adorn, to deck; *rfl.* to dress (oneself) up, to deck oneself out. (**-amento** *m.*) **-atézza** *f.* affected elegance; style; (of clothes) good fit; close fit. **-ato** *part. adj.* decked out; beautifully dressed, 'not a hair out of place', elegant, smart; dressed-up; foppish; (of clothes) tight; well-fitting; fitted; waisted. (**-atamente** *adv.*) **-atura** *f.* dressing up, decking out; tightness of fit.

at·timo *m.* instant, moment; in un —, in the twinkling of an eye.

attin-ente *adj.* belonging; pertaining; relative, relating; related, connected. **-enza** *f.* relationship; affinity; relation, connexion; *pl.* relations; dependants.

attin·g-ere [C 5] *tr.* to derive, to obtain, to draw; — acqua, to draw water; — il vino dalla botte, to tap the wine-cask; — informazioni, to derive information; to reach, to arrive at, to attain. (**-imento** *m.*) **-itoio** *m.* (techn.) dipping vessel. (**-itore** *m.* **-itrice** *f.* **-itura** *f.*)

atti·nia *f.* (zool.) *Actinia* sp., a sea anemone.

att-inicità *f.* actinism. **-i·nico** *adj.* (phys.) actinic. **-i·nio** *m.* (chem.) actinium. **-inografi·a** *f.* actinograph. **-inolite** *f.* (miner.) actinolite, actinote. **-inometri·a** *f.* actinometry.

attinon *m. indecl.* (phys.) actinon.

attint-o *part.* of **attingere**, q.v.; *adj. indecl.* drawn; derived; †despoiled, pillaged, exhausted. **-ura** *f.* (vet.) spavin and/or curb.

attir-are [A 1] *tr.* to attract; to draw; — l'attenzione, to call attention; to lure; to entice; to win; *rfl.* (*dat.* of *prn.*) to draw upon oneself, to call down upon oneself; si -a la benevolenza di tutti, he is universally loved. †**-a·glio** *m.* (mil.) artillery equipment. **-anza** *f.* (neol.) attraction. **-ato** *part. adj.* attracted; lured, enticed.

†**attit-are** *tr.*, *intr.* (leg.) to begin legal proceedings; to litigate. †**-azione** *f.* (leg.) litigation.

attitu·din-e[1] *f.* aptitude, disposition, capacity, inclination, bent; liability, propensity, proneness; (psych.) — motoria, motor ability; †in —, potentially. **-ale** *adj.* (neol.) revealing of aptitude; esame -ale, examination to determine professional bent.

attitu·din-e[2] *f.* posture, position, attitude; pose. **-are** [A 1 s] *intr.* (*aux.* avere) (paint.) to pose. **-ato** *part. adj.* posed, posing.

attiv-are [A 1] *tr.* to bring into activity, to increase the activity of; to speed up; — una macchina, to start (*or*, to raise the rate of) an engine; — una miniera, to start work on (*or*, to raise the output of) a mine; (chem.) to activate. **-ato** *part. adj.* set going, started; (chem.) activated. **-atore** *m.* (chem.) activator. **-azione** *f.* bringing into activity; increasing of activity; (chem.) activation.

attivismo *m.* and derivs. See under **attivo**.

attività *f.* See under **attivo**.

attiv-o *adj.* active; working, effective; busy; industrious, diligent; energetic; (gramm.) active; (philos.; theol.) active (life, intellect); (comm.) profitable; azienda -a, profit-making business; partita -a, entry on credit side; conti -i, receivable accounts; cambiali -e, receivable bills; (chem.) active; activated; carbone —, activated charcoal; (in time study) productive; *n.m.* (comm.) assets, profits; la ditta è in —, the firm's assets exceed liabilities; il bilancio dell'annata è in —, the year's accounts show a profit; all'—, on the credit side (also fig.). **-amente** *adv.* actively, with activity, industriously; busily; (gramm.) in the active voice. **-ismo** *m.* (phil.) activism; hustle; activity for its own sake. **-ista** *m.*, *f.* voluntary helper; canvasser; un — del partito, an active member, a propagandist for, the party. **-i·stico** *adj.* (philos.) activistic. **-ità** *f.* activity, activeness; briskness, energy; enterprise, undertaking; volcano in fase di -ità, volcano in eruption; (mil.) essere in -ità di servizio, to be serving with the colours; *pl.* (comm.) assets; credit entries.

attizz-are [A 1] *tr.* to stir; — il fuoco, to poke the fire; to rake out (a boiler fire); to shake down (a furnace); (fig.) to stir up, to incite, to fan. **-aménto** *m.* stirring up, incitement. **-ato** *part. adj.* stirred up; incited. **-atoio** *m.* hook-poker; poker. **-atore** *m.* instigator, provoker. (**-atrice** *f.*) **-ino** *m.* trouble-maker, mischief-maker.

att-o[1] *m.* act, action, deed; (surg.) — operatorio, operation; mettere in —, to put into action; all'—, in practice; fu colto nell'—, he was caught in the act; essere in —, to exist; (rel.) act (of faith, hope, charity, contrition); expression, gesture; movement; manner, air, attitude; pose; act, division of a drama; sign, indication, token; fare — di presenza, to put in an appearance; per — di stima, in token of esteem; prendere — di, to take note of, to note; dare — di, to publish, to give notice of; (philos.) act, actuality; in —, in act, actualized; (leg.) deed; — pubblico, document under the seal of a public officer; — notarile, document

att-o (*cont.*)
under the seal of a notary; — d'ultima volontà, will; — d'accusa, indictment; dar — di, to acknowledge receipt of; to recognize the truth of, to admit the knowledge of; certificate; — di nascita, birth certificate; — di matrimonio, marriage certificate; — di morte, death certificate; *pl.* the documents in a legal case; procedere agli -i contro, to take legal proceedings against; mettere agli -i, to record, to enter in the records, to enter in the minutes; mettere in -i, to file among the documents of a legal case; passare una pratica agli -i, to end a case by placing its file in the archives; (comm.) all'—della consegna, on delivery; — di vendita, bill of sale.

atto² *adj.* apt, suitable, proper; fit, capable; (naut.) — alla navigazione, sea-worthy; (mil.) — alle armi, liable for military service; †agile, skilful.

†**attol·lere** *tr.* to raise.

atton-are [A I] *tr.* (med.) to tone up, to give tone to, to strengthen. **-ante** *part. adj., n.m.* tonic. **-ato** *part. adj.* toned up.

attond-are [A I c] *tr.* to make round, to round. (**-ato** *part. adj.* **-atura** *f.*)

attonimento *m.* (neol. Pirandello) astonishment, stupefaction.

atto·nit-o *adj.* astonished, amazed; stupefied, dumbfounded; (fig.) spellbound, hushed. (**-amente** *adv.*) **-ag·gine** *f.* astonishment, amazement, stupefaction.

attopare [A I] *rfl.* to hide.

attorare [A I] *tr.* (Tusc.) to mate (a cow), to bull.

attor·c-ere [C 5] *tr.* to twist, to twine; to wring. *rfl.* to twist, to writhe. (**-imento** *m.*) **-itura** *f.* (text.) doubling.

attorcigli-are [A 4] *tr., rfl.* to twist, to wind, to twine. (**-a·bile** *adj.* **-amento** *m.*) **-ato** *part. adj.* twisted; twined; (herald.) wreathed.

attor-e *m.* actor; attor comico, comedian; primo —, leading man; primo — giovane, juvenile lead; — promiscuo, character actor; (leg.) plaintiff; †agent, representative; †factor. †**-i·a** *f.* agency; administration.

attorni-are [A 4 c] *tr.* to surround, to encompass; (fig.) to beset; (colloq.) to hang upon, to hang round (a person); (mil.) — il nemico, to encircle the enemy; †to wander round, to go round; †to surround; †to trick, to deceive; †*intr.* to joust, to fight in a tournament. **-amento** *m.* surrounding, encompassing; environment; †snare; †siege. (**-ante** *part. adj.*) **-ato** *part. adj.* surrounded.

attorno *adv.* about; around; round; qui —, hereabout; andare —, to go round; to get about; tenersi — uno, to keep a person tied to one's apron strings; la madre se lo tiene attorno, his mother never lets him out of her sight; levarsi uno d'—, to get rid of someone; levatevi d'—!, get out of the way!; darsi d'—, to do one's utmost; to exert oneself, to bustle about; *prep.* — a, round; (fig.) stare — a, to hang round (a person).

attorrare [A I c] *tr.* to pile up, to stack.

attorta *f.* strand (of rope); twist of pastry.

attortigliare [A 4]. See **attorcigliare**.

attorto *part.* of **attorcere**, *q.v.*; *adj.* twisted; twined, twining; (archit.) colonna attorta, spiral column, spiral shaft.

attoscare [A 2 c] and derivs. (poet.). See **attossicare**.

†**attos-o** *adj.* affected, mannered. †**-ità** *f.* affectation.

attossic-are [A 2 s] *tr.* to poison; to infect; to pollute; (fig.) to embitter; to corrupt, to taint; to grieve, to distress. **-amento** *m.* poisoning, infection. **-ante** *part. adj.* poisonous. **-ato** *part. adj.* poisoned; toxic; corrupt, tainted; embittered, saddened. **-atore** *m.*, **-atrice** *f.* poisoner. **-azione** *f.* poisoning.

attrac-care [A 2] *tr.* (naut.) to secure; *intr.* (*aux.* avere) to go alongside. **-co** *m.* (*pl.* **-chi**) (naut.) berthing place.

attra-ente *part.* of **attrarre**, *q.v.*; *adj.* attractive; charming; alluring, seductive; flattering, pleasing; interesting. (**-entemente** *adv.*) **-enza** *f.* (neol.) attractiveness.

†**attraere** *vb.* See **attrarre**.

†**attrappare¹** *tr.* to catch; to trick.

†**attrappare²** *vb.* See **attrappire**.

attrappire [D 2] *rfl.* to contract, to shrink, to shrivel; to become stiff, to grow numb.

attrarre [B 33] *tr.* to attract; to draw; to capture; to appeal to, to please, to delight, to interest; *abs.* to be attractive; to appeal.

†**attrassare** *intr.* to delay.

attratt-o *part.* of **attrarre**, *q.v.*; *adj.* attracted, drawn, fascinated, allured; †contracted; †withered. **-iva** *f.* attraction; charm, allurement; draw, appeal; *pl.* charms. **-ività** *f.* power of attraction. **-ivo** *adj.* attractive. †**-ore** *adj.* attractive.

attravers-are [A I] *tr.* to cross, to traverse; to go through, to undergo; to pass through; to pierce; — a nuoto, to swim across; — un paese a cavallo, to ride through a country on horseback; to cross, to oppose, to impede, to thwart; — il passo a, to get in the way of; — i disegni a, to frustrate the plans of; to place across, to place crosswise; (bldg.) — con un arco, to span; (naut.) see **traversare** — il bastimento, to go right through the ship; — l'ancora, to cat; *rfl.* -arsi a, to cross, to oppose, to block. **-a·bile** *adj.* passable, traversable. **-amento** *m.* crossing; street-crossing; crossways; impediment, obstacle. **-ato** *part. adj.* placed crosswise; crossed, traversed; impeded, blocked; (herald.) debruised. (**-atore** *m.* **-atrice** *f.* **-atura** *f.*)

attraverso *prep.* across, athwart; through; — a, across; (before *pers. prn.*) — di, through, through the agency of; *adv.* wrongly; badly; ill, amiss; ungraciously; across; crosswise, obliquely; gli affari vanno —, business is going badly; il cibo è andato —, the food has gone down the wrong way; guardare —, to glower at; rispondere —, to reply crossly; pigliare una cosa —, to take a thing in bad part; passare —, to cross over, to go across; to pass through.

attrazione *f.* attraction; spectacle, show.

attrazz-o *m.* (Tusc.) useless object, white elephant; †(naut.) ship stores. †**-are** *vb.* and derivs. See **attrezzare**.

†**attrecciare** *vb.* and derivs. See **intrecciare**.

attrezz-are [A I c] *tr.* to equip; to fit out; to rig; (eng.) to tool; (naut.) to arm, to furnish, to commission. **-a·io** *m.* (neol.) repertory. **-amento** *m.* equipping; fitting out; (naut.) equipping, equipment. **-ato** *part. adj.* equipped; (naut.) -ato con (di) vele quadre, square rigged; ben -ato, well found. **-atoio** *m.* repertory. **-atore** *m.* (naut.) ship's chandler and outfitter. **-atura** *f.* plant; equipment; (naut.) complete equipment (sails, ropes, chains, etc.); method of rigging a ship; *pl.* fittings. **-eri·a** *f.* (poet.) see **-atura**. **-ista** *m.* (theatr.) property-man; scene-shifter; gymnast skilled in use of apparatus.

attrezzo *m.* implement, instrument, tackle; utensil; tool; fixture; (agric.) — operatore, implement (for attachment to tractor); — operatore trainato, trailing type implement; — operatore portato, mounted implement; *pl.* equipment; apparatus; ginnastica agli attrezzi, gymnastic exercises involving apparatus; hand-tools; (naut.) rig, complete outfit; (mil.) equipment (chiefly of artillery and bridging).

attribu-ire [D 2] *tr.* to attribute, to ascribe; to impute; to assign; to delegate; to award; — importanza, to attach importance; — a lode, to single out as praiseworthy; — a biasimo, to single out as blameworthy; *rfl.* (*dat.* of *prn.*) to take upon oneself; to arrogate to oneself; to assume. **-i·bile** *adj.* attributable; ascribable. **-imento** *m.* attribution, act of attributing. **-ito** *part. adj.* attributed, ascribed.

attribut-o *m.* attribute, quality, characteristic; sign, symbol; attribute; attributi di Dio, divine attributes; (gramm.) attribute, attributive adjunct. **-ivo** *adj.* attributive. (**-ivamente** *adv.*)

attribuzion-e *f.* attribution; function, responsibility, obligation; right, authority; delegated power; *pl.* (leg.) competence; jurisdiction; essere nell'ambito delle -i di un magistrato, to fall within a magistrate's jurisdiction. **-ismo** *m.* (art) attribution of anonymous works of art to probable authors.

attrice *f.* actress; prima —, leading lady. See also **attore**.

attrist-are [A I] *tr.* to sadden; to grieve; to afflict; *rfl.* to grow sad; to mope; *intr.* (*aux.* essere) to languish, to pine away. (**-amento** *m.*) **-ante** *part. adj.* saddening. **-ato** *part. adj.* saddened, sad; moping. (**-atore** *m.* **-atrice** *f.*)

attristire [D 2] and derivs. See **attristare**.

attrito¹ *m.* (scient.) friction; abrasion; (on a rail) traction; perdita per —, friction loss; privo di —, smooth, frictionless; (fig.) disagreement, discord, variance; attrition; in —, at variance.

attrito² *adj.* worn out; (theol.) having attrition, 'attrite'.

attrizione *f.* attrition, friction; (theol.) attrition; (fig.) friction, disagreement, difference of opinion.

attrozzare [A I] *tr.* (naut.) to sling (of a yard or topmast) using spectacle plates or chain or wire.

attrupp-are [A I] *tr.* to assemble; *rfl.* to collect together, to troop, to flock. **-amento** *m.* trooping; assembly; crowd, mob. **-ato** *part. adj.* assembled; trooped, trooping.

attua·bile *adj.* See under **attuare**.

attual-e *adj.* present, present-day, immediate, contemporary, current; storia —, current events; (philos.; theol.) actual. **-ismo** *m.* (philos.)

attual-e (*cont.*)

actualism. **-ista** *m.* (philos.) actualist. **-ità** *f.* actuality; reality; (the) present; novelty; un argomento di grande **-ità**, a subject of great topical interest; cose di **-ità**, recent events; le **-ità**, the news; cinema di **-ità**, news theatre; film di **-ità**, news film, newsreel. **-mente** *adv.* at present, nowadays; for the time being; in effect, in reality; effectively.

attu·are [A 5] *tr.* to carry out, to effect, to put into effect; to realize, to bring about; to actuate; to work; to operate; (philos.) to reduce to act, to make actual, to actualize; *rfl.* to come about, to come into effect, to be realized; to come true. **-a·bile** *adj.* practicable, feasible, possible, realizable. (**-abilità** *f.* **-amento** *m.* **-atore** *m.* **-atrice** *f.*) **-azione** *f.* bringing about; realization.

attua·ri·o *m.* actuary; †official recorder. **-ale** *adj.* actuarial. **-ato** *m.* office of actuary, function of actuary.

attuazione *f.* See under **attuare**.

attuffare [A I] and derivs. See **tuffare**.

attuire [D 2] *tr.* (dial. Lucca, Pistoia). See **attutire**.

attuọs-o *adj.* active, effective. (**-amente** *adv.* **-ità** *f.*)

†attutare *vb.* See **attutire**.

attut-ire [D 2] *tr.* to deaden; to quieten, to calm; to assuage, to mitigate; to subdue; †to quell; *rfl.* to grow calm, to control oneself; to be assuaged; to be deadened. (**-ito** *part. adj.*)

aubade *f.* (mus.; lit. hist.) aubade.

†aucchiare *vb.* See **agucchiare**.

†aucci·dere *vb.* See **uccidere**.

aucu·pio *m.* bird-catching, esp. with bird-lime.

aud-ace *adj.* audacious, daring, bold; rash, imprudent; essere — di, to dare to; *n.m.* gli **-aci**, the brave, the bold. (**-acemente** *adv.*) **-a·cia** *f.* (*pl.* **-a·cie**) audacity, boldness, daring; rashness, imprudence; act of boldness, act of rashness.

audibilità *f.* (acoustics) audibility; campo di —, audibility range.

†audienza *f.* See **udienza**.

audi·fono *m.* hearing aid.

audiofrequen-za *f.* (radio, etc.) audiofrequency. **-te** *adj.* relating to audiofrequency.

audiogramma *m.* (acoustics) audiogram.

audiola *f.* (neol.) wireless receiving apparatus.

audio·metro *m.* (phys.; med.) audiometer.

a·udion *m. indecl.* (radio) 3-electron thermionic valve.

†audire *vb.* See **udire**.

auditivo *adj.* auditive.

aud-itore *m.* listener, hearer; (leg. hist.) judge of certain tribunals; — di Rota, judge in the Rota. (**-itrice** *f.*) **-ito·rio** *m.* auditorium; (radio) studio; *adj.* auditory. **-izione** *f.* audition; hearing; **-izione** radiofonica, broadcast; (leg.) **-izione** dei testi, hearing or taking of witnesses' evidence.

au·f, **au·ffa** *excl.* expression of boredom or displeasure.

a·uge *m.* apogee; zenith; acme; apex, height, summit; essere in —, to be in great favour, to enjoy great reputation; venire in —, to find favour; (Tusc.) vivere in —, to be influential and well-to-do.

augello *m.* (poet.) bird.

†auggiare *vb.* See **aduggiare**.

Augi·a *pr.n.m.* (myth.) Augeas; le stalle d'—, the Augean stables.

augite *f.* (min.) augite.

augn-are [A 6] *tr.* to clutch, to seize; to claw. **-ato** *part. adj.* clutched; clawed. **-atura** *f.* clutching; clawing; mark of clawing.

†augument-are *tr.* See **aumentare**. **†-o** *m.* see **aumento**.

augurale *adj.* augural; auspicious.

augur-are [A I sa] *tr.* to wish: vi **-o** un felice anno nuovo, I wish you a happy New Year; — il malanno a, to curse, to wish ill to; to forebode; to augur; *rfl.* to wish, to hope, to desire; mi **-o** di rivederti presto, I hope to see you again soon; me lo **-o** ma ci credo poco, I hope for the best but I'm rather doubtful. **-a·bile** *adj.* desirable; è **-abile** che, it is to be hoped that. **-ato** *part. adj.* augured, foretold; wished for, desired; mal **-ato**, unfortunate; ill-omened (also **malaugurato**); for *n.m.* see under **augure**. **-atore** *m.* foreteller, harbinger; †augur. (**-atrice** *f.* **-azione** *f.*)

a·ugur-e *m.* augur. **-ato** *m.* augurate, augurship. **-ọso** *adj.* of good omen; of ill omen; ominous; significant; bene **-oso**, lucky; male **-oso**, unlucky. (**-osamente** *adv.*)

augu·rio *m.* wish; ti faccio l'— di una buona riuscita, I wish you success; gradite i miei sinceri auguri, accept my sincere good wishes; fare gli auguri, to greet, (e.g. on the occasion of a birthday); auguri!, good luck!, happy birthday!, etc.; indication,

portent, presage, sign; il cessar della febbre può essere — di pronta guarigione, the fall in temperature may be a portent of speedy recovery; il sale rovesciato porta cattivo —, spilt salt is a sign of bad luck; omen, augury: prendere gli auguri, to take auguries; uccello di mal —, bird of ill omen.

Augusta *pr.n.f.* Augusta; (geog.) Augsburg.

August-o *pr.n.m.* Augustus; Cesare —, Caesar Augustus. **-ale** *adj.* (Rom. hist.) imperial; *n.m.* (numism.) gold coin of time of Emperor Frederick II of Sicily. **-e·o** *adj.* Augustan; imperial; *n.m.* mausoleum of Emperor Augustus in Rome.

august-o *adj.* august, venerable, sacred; majestic. **†-are** *intr.* to become august.

a·ula *f.* hall, reception-room; — scolastica, schoolroom; — magna, great-hall, auditorium; (hist.) court, palace; (leg.) — giudiziaria, courtroom.

aul-edo, **-eta**, **-ete** *m.* (poet. hist.) aulos-player. **-e·tica** *f.* art of aulos-playing. **-e·tride** *f.* female aulos-player. (See also **aulo**.)

aulente *adj.* (poet.) fragrant, scented, sweet-smelling.

a·ulic-o *adj.* aulic; courtly; stately; regal; lingua **-a**, a courtly language (esp. with reference to Dante's theories in the *De Vulg. Eloq.*); (hist.) consigliere —, member of Aulic Council (esp. of council managing the war-department of Austrian Empire). (**-amente** *adv.*)

†aulire *intr.* to be fragrant, to smell sweet.

a·ulo *m.* (mus.) aulos, an ancient Greek reed instrument (often confused by poets with the flute).

aulope *m.* (ichth.) *Aulopus*, a deep-sea fish.

aulo·pide *f.* (poet. D'Annunzio) kind of elm.

auloroso *adj.* (poet. D'Annunzio) fragrant.

aument-are [A I c] *tr.* to augment, to enlarge; to enhance; to increase; to add to; to raise: — le spese, to increase expenditure; — gli stipendi, to raise salaries; (techn.) to boost; *intr.* (*aux.* essere) to increase; to rise; to grow; i prezzi **-ano**, prices are rising; il numero dei soci **-a**, the number of members is increasing; — di peso, to put on weight. **-a·bile** *adj.* augmentable; stipendario **-abile** a, salary rising to. **-ativo** *adj.* augmentative. **-ato** increased, augmented, raised; **-ato** del 10 %, increased by 10 %. (**-atore** *m.* **-atrice** *f.*) **-azione** *f.* increase; (mus.) augmentation.

aument-o *m.* increase; growth; enlargement; rise; advance (in price); essere in —, to be on the increase; (gramm.) augment. **-ista** *m.* (finan.) bull.

†aumiliare *vb.* See **umiliare**.

†a·una *f.* measure of length (1·19 metres); ell.

†aunare *vb.* See **adunare**.

†auncinare *vb.* See **uncinare**.

†aunghiare *vb.* See **augnare**.

†aunire *tr.* to dishonour, to insult.

a·ura *f.* (poet.) breeze; soft, light wind; zephyr; air; (fig.) atmosphere, emanation, air: un' — di candore, an air of frankness; favour, approbation: — popolare, popular favour; aura, halo; (med.) aura; (mus.) Jews' harp.

aurammina *f.* (chem.) auramine, diphenyl methane dye.

auran·zia *f.* (photog.) aurantia.

aurata *f.* (ichth.) gilt head, dorado, *Sparus auratus*.

aurato *adj.* (poet.) golden.

aure·a *f.* chemical cattle fodder.

aure·lia¹ *f.* (ent.) pupa, chrysalis, nymph; (zool.) jellyfish.

Aure·lia² *pr.n.f.* Aurelia.

a·ureo *adj.* gold; contenuto —, gold content; golden; massima aurea, golden rule; resplendent; precious, priceless, excellent; noble; numero —, golden number, the number of any year in the Metonic lunar cycle of 19 years; *n.m.* Roman gold coin.

aure·ola *f.* halo; glory; (electr.) aureole; (theol.) aureola; (rel. art) aureole, nimbus.

aureomicina *f.* aureomycin.

a·urica *f.* (naut.) square sail, trapezoid.

auri·col-a *f.* (anat.) auricle, auricula. **-are** *adj.* auricular; dito **-are**, little finger; (leg.) testimone **-are**, earwitness; *n.m.* little finger. **-ato** *adj.* auriculate.

auri·fero *adj.* auriferous; gold, yielding gold; terreni auriferi, gold-fields; (geol.) deposits of gold in sandy soil; (finan.) titoli auriferi, gold·mining shares.

auri·ga *m.* (*pl.* **-ghi**) charioteer; coachman; (astron.) the Wagoner.

aurina *f.* (chem.) aurine, pararosolic acid.

aurino *adj.* (poet.) gold, golden.

†au·rio *m.* See **augurio**.

aurito *adj.* eared, with ears; vaso —, large-handled pot; (poet.) listening, intent; †big-eared.

aˑuro *m.* (poet.) gold.

auror-a *f.* sunrise, dawn; daybreak; (fig.) earliest beginnings, dawn; (myth.) Aurora; — boreale, — polare, aurora borealis, Northern lights; — australe, Southern lights. **-ale** *adj.* auroral, pertaining to the dawn, like the dawn.

†ausare¹ *vb.* See **osare**.

†ausare² *vb.* See **adusare**.

auscult-are [A I] *tr.* (med.) to auscultate, to sound. **-azione** *f.* auscultation.

ausili-are *adj.* auxiliary; helpful, giving support; ancillary; (gramm.) verbo —, auxiliary verb; *n.m.* assistance, help; (gramm.) auxiliary. **-aˑrio** *adj.* (mil.) auxiliary; (mus.) nota **-aria**, auxiliary note; (admin.; mil.) funzionario in posizione **-aria**, official discharged (but not finally) from active service and not yet pensioned, on 'half-pay'; *n.m.* auxiliary. **-arità** *f.* (neol.) co-operation. **-atore** *m.* helper, protector. **-atrice** *f.* (rel.) Maria **-atrice**, Our Lady Help of Christians.

ausiˑlio *m.* succour; help.

†aˑuso *adj.* bold, courageous, daring.

Auşoˑni-a *pr.n.f.* (poet.) Italy. **-o**, **-co** *adj.* (poet.) Italic, Italian.

auspic-are [A 2 s] *tr., abs.* to prognosticate, to auspicate; to augur. **-aˑbile** *adj.* hoped for, to be hoped. **-ato** *part. adj.* under good auspices, fortunate, happy; hoped for, longed for; un'impresa male **-ata**, an undertaking ill begun; le **-ate** nozze, the marriage begun under happy auspices, the marriage to which all have looked forward. (**-atamente** *adv.* **-atore** *m.* **-atrice** *f.*)

aˑuspic-e *m.* protector, patron; promoter, supporter; l'impresa fu incominciata, — il Re, the undertaking was begun under the auspices of the King; (Rom. hist.) auspex. **-aˑle** *adj.* auspicious; (archit.) pietra **-ale**, foundation stone.

ausp-iˑcio, **-iˑzio** *m.* auspices, omen: di buon —, of good omen; protection, favour, patronage; sotto gli **-ici** di, under the auspices of; essere — di, to be a token of, to be a sign of.

austen-ite *f.* (metall.) austenite. **-iˑtico** *adj.* (of steel) austenitic.

auster-o *adj.* austere; severe, strict; unadorned; harsh to the taste, dry. (**-amente** *adv.*) **-ità** *f.* austerity; austereness; harshness; dryness (of taste).

austoˑrio *m.* sacrificial vase.

Australaˑşia *pr.n.f.* (geog.) Australasia.

australe *adj.* See under **austro**.

Austraˑli-a *pr.n.f.* (geog.) Australia. **-ano** *adj., n.m.* Australian. **-ana** *f.* Australian woman; (sport) **-ana** a coppie, Australian elimination cycle race.

Aˑustr-ia *pr.n.f.* (geog.) Austria. **-iacante** *m.* (Ital. hist.) supporter of Austria. **-iˑaco** *adj.* Austrian; *n.m.* Austrian. (**-iˑaca** *f.*)

aˑustr-o *m.* (poet.) south wind; south; auster. **-ale** *adj.* southern, south, austral.

aˑustro *pref.* Austro, Austrian; austro-ungarico, Austro-Hungarian.

autarca *m.* (philos. Croce) one who is constant to himself.

aut-archˑia *f.* autarchy; despotism; (philos.) self-sufficiency; (neol. pol.) economic self-sufficiency. **-arˑchico** *adj.* autarchic(al); self-sufficient; in pursuance of economic self-sufficiency; prodotto **-archico**, national product, home produce; false, unreliable, of poor quality.

†autare *m.* altar.

aut aut *m.* dilemma; porre un aut aut a, to place in a dilemma.

autentic-are [A 2 s] *tr.* to authenticate, to give validity to; (leg.) to affix the seal of a public officer to (signature, deed, or document). **-aˑbile** *adj.* verifiable. **-ato** *part. adj.* authenticated, authentic, valid. (**-atore** *m.* **-atrice** *f.*) **-azione** *f.* authentication; (leg.) affixing of seal of a public officer to signature, deed or document.

auten-tic-o *adj.* authentic; genuine; original; un imbroglione —, a real swindler; (leg.) authenticated by a public officer; copia **-a**, certified copy, copy of a document under the seal of a public officer; (mus.) modi **-i**, authentic modes; cadenza **-a**, authentic cadence, perfect cadence. **-a** *f.* authentication; proof, authentic evidence; *pl.* (hist.) Authentics, the new constitutions of Justinian collected by Irnerius. **-amente** *adv.* authentically, genuinely. **-ità** *f.* authenticity; genuineness; validity; (leg.) the character of a signature, deed or document bearing the seal of a public officer.

autiere *m.* (mil.) driver.

autista *m.* chauffeur, driver.

aˑuto-¹ *pref.* auto-, self-. (For derivatives in which the stress falls on the second syllable see separate headings, e.g. **autoˑgrafo**.) **-accensione** *f.* self-ignition (motor-cars). **-affondare** [A I C] *tr.* to scuttle. **-avviatore** *m.* (motor.) self-starter. **-biografiˑa** *f.* autobiography. **-biograˑfico** *adj.* autobiographic. **-bioˑgrafo** *m.* autobiographer. **-ceˑfalo** *adj.* autocephalous. **-centrante** *adj.* (eng.) self-centring. **-chiusura** *f.* self-locking device. **-clave** *f.* (industr.) autoclave; †*m.* (mus.) a kind of stringed instrument. **-collimatore** *m.* (opt.) autocollimator. **-collimazione** *f.* autocollimation. **-combustione** *f.* spontaneous combustion. **-compiacimento** *m.* self-complacence. **-consumo** *m.* (electr.) loss, wastage. **-coscienza** *f.* (philos.) self-consciousness. **-cromiˑa** *f.* (photog.) autochromy. **-cromo** *adj.* (photog.) autochrome. **-descante** *adj.* self-priming. **-decisione** *f.*, **-determinazione** *f.* (pol.) self-determination. **-didatta** *m., f.* self-taught man, or woman, autodidact. **-didatˑtico** *adj.* pertaining to self-teaching: metodo **-didattico** per la lingua italiana, 'teach-yourself-Italian', 'Italian without a master'. **-difesa** *f.* apologetic (written in the author's own defence). **-dina** *f.* (radio) autodyne, self-heterodyne. **-dinaˑmico** *adj.* (phys.) autodynamic. **-eccitazione** *f.* (electr.) self-excitation. **-elettroˑnico** *adj.* (phys.) autoelectronic. **-geˑneşi** *f.* (biol.) autogenesis. **-goal** *m. indecl.* (sport) goal scored against one's own team. **-goniˑa** *f.* (biol.) autogony. **-governo** *m.* self-government. **-grafiˑa** *f.* (typ.) autography (process of lithography). **-induzione** *f.* (electr.) self-induction. **-intossicazione** *f.* (med.) auto-intoxication. **-ipnoˑşi** *f.* (med.) auto-hypnosis, self-hypnosis. **-latriˑa** *f.* autolatry, worship of the self. **-lesione** *f.* (mil.) self-inflicted wound. (**-lesioniˑsmo** *m.* **-lesionista** *m.*) **-lubrificato** *adj.* (eng.) self-lubricating. **-mutilazione** *f.* (med.) self-mutilation. **-piano** *m.* pianola. **-pilota** *m.* (aeron.) automatic pilot, robot pilot. **-plastiˑa**, **-plaˑstica** *f.* (surg.) autoplasty. **-plaˑstico** *adj.* (surg.) autoplastic. **-reattore** *m.* (eng.) ram jet engine. **-recensione** *f.* review by an author of his own book. **-registratore** *adj.* (eng.) self-recording. **-regolatore** *adj.* (eng.) self-regulating. **-rete** *f. indecl.* (sport) goal scored against one's own team. **-ricottura** *f.* (metall.) self-annealing. **-ritratto** *m.* self-portrait. **-rivelatore** *m.* (radio) autocoherer, autodetector. **-rotazione** *f.* (eng.; aeron.) autorotation; windmilling. **-scaˑrica** *f.* (electr.) self-discharge. **-scatto** *m.* (photog.) automatic shutter release, delayed action release. **-sufficienza** *f.* conceit, self-satisfaction. **-suggestione** *f.* auto-suggestion; self-deception, self-delusion. **-suggestionare** [A I C] *rfl.* to delude oneself. **-suggestionato** *part. adj.* self-deluded, self-deceived. (**-suggestionatore** *m.*) **-temprante** *adj.* (metall.) self-hardening. **-tipo** *m.* autotype. **-tipografiˑa** *f.* autotypography. **-tomiˑa** *f.* (biol.) autotomy. **-trasformatore** *m.* (electr.) auto-transformer, balancing coil; **-trasformatore** a dispersione, leak transformer. **-ventilato** *adj.* self-ventilating.

aˑuto-² *pref.* auto-, motor-. (For derivatives in which the stress falls on the first or second syllable see separate headings, e.g. **aˑutobus**.) **-ambulanza** *f.* motor-ambulance. **-blinda** *f.*, **-blindata** *f.*, **-blindo** *f.* armoured fighting vehicle, armoured car. **-botte** *f.* water carrier; tank-wagon. **-bruco** *m.* tracked vehicle. **-carro** *m.* lorry; motor-van; **-carro** a cassone ribaltabile, tipping lorry, tipper. **-cisterna** *f.* tank-wagon. **-colonna** *f.* convoy (of lorries). **-corriera** *f.* country bus; post van; excursion bus; coach. **-drappello** *m.* (mil.) mobile detachment. **-fficina** *f.* (eng.) machine-shop truck. **-frigoriˑfero** *m.* refrigerator van. **-furgone** *m.* van; utility coach, shooting brake. **-garage** *m.* garage. **-gasoˑgeno** *m.* car running on producer gas. **-giro** *m.* autogiro, gyroplane, helicopter, rotaplane. **-gita** *f.* motor tour, excursion. **-innaffiatrice** *f.* motor sprinkler; street watering truck. **-lettiga** *f.* motor-ambulance. **-libro** *m.* book on motoring. **-mezzo** *m.* transport, vehicle. **-moˑbile** *f.* automobile, car; *adj.* self-moving, self-propelling. **-mobiliˑsmo** *m.* motoring. **-mobilista** *m.* motorist. **-mobiliˑstico** *adj.* motoring. **-montato** *adj.* (mil.) mechanized. **-motrice** *f.* rail car. **-noleggio** *m.* towing. **-parcheggio** *m.*, **-parco** *m.* (*pl.* **-parchi**) car-park. **-portato** *m.* carried by road. **-pompa** *f.* motor pump; **-pompa** antincendi, fire truck. **-postale** *f.* country post-van. **-pubˑblica** *f.* taxi. **-raˑdio** *f.* car radio. **-rimessa** *f.* garage. **-stazione** *f.* service station. **-strada** *f.* autobahn, trunk motor-road. (**-stradale** *adj.*) **-telaˑio** *m.* chassis. **-trainato** *adj.* truck-drawn. **-traˑino** *m.* haulage. **-traiˑno** *m.* trailer truck. **-trasporti** *m.pl.* road transport. **-trasporto** *m.* motor transport; **-trasporto** merci, freight motor transport; **-trasporto** passaggeri, passenger motor transport. **-treno** *m.* road train; trailer bus. **-veiˑcolo** *m.* mechanically-propelled vehicle, motor vehicle. **-vettura** *f.* motor vehicle.

a·uto³ *f.* car, auto, automobile.

a·uto⁴ *m.* autos, Spanish or Portuguese sacred drama.

†**au·to** *part. adj.* of **avere**, q.v.

a·utobus *m. indecl.* bus, motor-coach; — a due piani, — con imperiale, double-decker.

auto-casa *f.* (*pl.* auto-case) trailer-caravan.

auto·cr-ate, **-ata** *m.* autocrat. **-a·tico** *adj.* autocratic. (**-aticamente** *adv.*) **-azi·a** *f.* autocracy.

auto·cton-o *adj.* autochthonous; *n.m.*, *usu. pl.* aborigines, autochthones. **-i·a** *f.* autochthony. **-i·smo** *m.* autochthonism.

autodafè, **auto-da-fè** *m.* auto-da-fé.

auto·dromo *m.* motor-racing track.

auto·geno *adj.* autogenous; (eng.) soldatura autogena, autogenous welding.

auto·graf-o *adj.* in the author's handwriting, autograph; *n.m.* original MS.; autograph. **-ista** *m.* collector of autographs.

autom-a *m.* automaton. **-a·tico** *adj.* automatic; telefono **-atico**, dial system; involuntary, mechanical; *n.m.pl.* **-atici**, press-studs, snap fasteners. (**-aticamente** *adv.*) **-ati·smo** *m.* (philos.) automatism. **-azione** *f.* (industr.) automation.

†**auto·mato** *m.* See **automa**.

Automedonte *pr.n.m.* (myth.) Automedon, charioteer of Achilles; coachman; (joc.) chauffeur.

auto·nom-o *adj.* autonomous; self-contained; self-governing; independent; ente —, corporation; **-i·a** *f.* autonomy; independence; (aeron.) -ia di volo, range, endurance. **-ista** *m.* autonomist.

auto-oscillazione *f.* (radio) self-oscillation.

autopsi·a *f.* (med.) autopsy, post mortem.

autor-e *m.* creator, originator; father; -i del misfatto, perpetrators of the crime; author, writer; artist, painter; composer; artist with a well established reputation; diritti d'—, copyright, royalties; (leg.) predecessor in title. **-evole** *adj.* authoritative; reliable; commanding, imposing. **-evolmente** *adv.* authoritatively, with authority. **-evolezza** *f.* authoritativeness.

autorit-à *f.* authority; influence; persons in authority; expert; authoritative source; delegated power, sanction, permission; dare — a, to empower; (leg.) — giudiziaria, judicial authorities, judiciary; deferire all'— giudiziaria, to commit to the judicial authorities (for trial or for investigations leading to trial); — costituita, authorities set up and recognized by the law; fare —, to be authoritative: in materia di musica il suo libro fa —, his book is the authoritative work on music. **-a·rio** *adj.* autocratic; authoritative; dictatorial, overbearing. **-ativo** *adj.* authoritative. **-ativamente** *adv.* authoritatively.

autorizz-are [A I] *tr.* to authorize; to entitle. (**-ato** *part. adj.*) **-azione** *f.* authorization; permission; consent; delegated power, sanction, permission; per **-azione**, by authority.

autrice *f.* authoress, woman writer. See also **autore**.

autunn-o *m.* autumn, fall. **-ale** *adj.* autumnal, autumn.

auzion-e *f.* auction. **-ista** *m.* auctioneer.

†**auzzare** *vb.* See **aguzzare**.

ava *f.* See under **avo**.

†**avac·cio** *adj.* swift, speedy; hasty; *adv.* swiftly; hastily; *n.m.* speed, haste.

†**avagliare** *tr.* to equalize.

†**avale** *adv.* now.

avall-o *m.* (comm.) guarantee (by a third party backing a bill). **-ante** *m.* (comm.) guarantor. **-are** [A I] *tr.* (comm.) to back (a bill); (fig.) to confirm, to verify; to make valid, to legalize.

avalve *adj.* (eng.) valveless.

avam-becco *m.* (*pl.* **-becchi**) (bldg.) forestarling. **-brac·cio** *m.* forearm; (sport) strength in the wrists (of a jockey). **-paese** *m.* frontier territory. **-porto** *m.* (naut.) outer harbour. **-posto** *m.* (mil.) advance post; outpost.

Avana *pr.n.f.* (geog.) Havana; *n.m.* Havana cigar; *adj. indecl.* colour of Havana tobacco, tawny.

avan-ca·rica *f.* (mil.) muzzle loader. **-città** *f.* outskirts. **-corpo** *m.* (archit.) projection (usu. in the middle of a façade); (eng.) forepart. **-crogiuolo** *m.* (metall.) forehearth (of furnace). **-guar·dia** *f.* (mil.) advanceguard; vanguard; (fig.) forefront, fore; essere all'-guardia, to be a pioneer, to hold advanced views; letteratura d'-guardia, advanced literature. **-guardista** *m.* member of Fascist youth organization. **-scoperta** *f.* (mil.) reconnaissance, recce. **-sipa·rio** *m.* (theatr.) variety act before the drop-curtain. **-spetta·colo** *m.* (theatr.) curtain-raiser; a live act (in a cinema). **-treno** *m.* (mil.)

limber. **-vo·mere** *m.* (agric.) jointer (of a plough); **-vomere** a lama larga, skimmer.

avanera *f.* (mus.) habanera.

avani·a *f.* tax, burden; ill-treatment; insult, outrage.

avannotto *m.* (ichth.) fish fry; avannotti delle trote, young trout.

avanscoperta *f.* See under **avancarica**.

avanspetta·colo *m.* See under **avan-**.

†**avantare** *vb.* See **vantare**.

†**avante** *adv., prep.* See **avanti**.

avanti *prep.* before: — giorno, before day; — Cristo (*abbrev.* A.C.), B.C.; sooner than: vorrei morire — di mentire, I would die sooner than tell a lie; before, in the presence of; — a Dio, before God; — al sindaco, in the presence of the mayor; in front of; — all'uscio, in front of the door, outside the door; *adv.* before, in front; andare —, to go before, to precede (but cf. below); — c'è posto!, move along the car, please! (also joc.); beforehand; pensarci — per non pentirsi poi, look before you leap; ahead, forward; andare —, to proceed, to continue, to go ahead, to progress; — e indietro, to and fro; essere molto — negli studi, to be well advanced in one's work; il mio orologio è —, my watch is fast; mettere —, to put first, to prefer; tirare —, to get along as best one can, to move on; mandare — la famiglia, to find it difficult to make both ends meet, to pull the devil by the tail; tirarsi — per una professione, to study for, to go in for a profession; mettersi —, to push oneself forward; farsi —, to come into sight, to approach, to step forward; da qui in —, from here on; il mese —, the month before; in —, forward: piegarsi in —, to lean forward; d'ora in —, from now on; (rugby) fallo in —, knock-on; (rugby) passaggio in —, throw-forward; *excl.* —!, come in!; go ahead!; help yourself; (mil.) —!, forward!, advance!; (naut.)—a tutto vapore!, full steam ahead!; *n.m.* (football, rugby) forward.

†**avantichè** *conj.* before.

avantieri *adv.* the day before yesterday.

avantlet·tera *f.* (typ.) first incision of the metal; *adv., adj. indecl.* (fig.) before one's time; il Petrarca fu un romantico —, Petrarch was a Romantic born before his time.

avantreno *m.* See under **avancarica**.

avanz-are [A I] *tr.* to advance, to put forward; to promote; to surpass: mi -a di dottrina, he surpasses me in learning; lo -ò di un metro, he beat him by a metre; — danaro, to save money, to put money on one side; — tempo, to save time, to hurry; m'-a il crederlo, I can well believe it, I more than believe it; — denaro da, to be owed money by; (fig., iron.) quanto -i da me?, who do you think you are?; vorrei saper che -a da me quel signore, I'd like to know by what right he comes the high and mighty over me; — denaro a, to advance money to; — una domanda, to present an application; (eng.) to feed (forward); †to aggrandize; †to enrich; †to render superior; †to calm, to placate; *intr.* (*aux.* essere, avere) to advance, to proceed; to progress; to be in advance: il mio orologio -a, my watch is fast; to be left over, to remain; non -a nulla, nothing is left; dodici meno cinque, -a sette, five from twelve leaves seven; to be superabundant, to be excessive: in quella casa il mangiare -a, in that house food goes to waste; to be more than enough; ce n'ho una e me n'-a, I have one and that is more than enough; to be a survivor, to escape: solo venti soldati -arono alla strage, only twenty soldiers survived the massacre; *rfl.* to advance; to approach, to draw nigh; to hang over, to stand out. **-amento** *m.* advance; progress; development; promotion, advancement; -amento per anzianità, promotion by seniority; (eng.) feed; -amento ad immersione, plunge feed; -amento massimo, coarse feed. **-ante** *part. adj.* advancing; projecting, protruding. **-ata** *f.* (mil.) advance; sortie. **-atic·cio** *adj.* left over; *n.m.* remains, left-overs. **-ato** *part. adj.* advanced; a notte -ata, late in the night; -ato negli anni, advanced in years; left over, remaining: il pane -ato, the bread that is left over; a tempo -ato, in the time that remains; uomo -ato alla morte, man who has been at death's door; (mil.) posto -ato, advance post; sentinella -ata, advance sentry, forward sentry.

avanz-o *m.* remains, remainder; remnant; (comm.) — di cassa, cash in hand; surplus; mettere in —, to put on one side, to save; d'—, more than enough, excessive; to spare; quite enough; (Tusc.) lo credo d'—, I can well believe it; — di galera, gallows-bird; *pl.* ruins; left-overs; gli -i mortali, the mortal remains; (leg.) -i di acqua, residual water (C.C.) **-u·glio** *m.*, **-ume** *m.* residue; dregs.

avar·i·a *f.* damage; (comm.; leg.) loss or damage to ship, cargo or freight; average; — generale, general average; — particolare, particular average; franco d'— reciproca, free of average; liquidazione dell'—, adjustment of average; perito d'—, average surveyor; coperto da assicurazione solo in caso di — generale, free from particular average. **-iare** [A4] *tr.* (comm.) to damage. **-iato**, *part. adj.* damaged; nave -iata, ship which has suffered damage; merci -iate, damaged goods; reputazione -iata, damaged reputation; syphilitic.

avar·o *adj.* mean, miserly; close, stingy; avaricious; covetous; (fig.) — di parole, sparing of words; essere troppo — di sè, to be seen but rarely; gli -i risparmi, the hoard of savings; (poet.) avid, desirous, eager; *n.m.* miser, skinflint. **-amente** *adv.* avariciously; (poet.) avidly. **-eggiare** [A3c] *intr.* (aux. avere) to be avaricious, to be a miser. **-i·zia** *f.* avarice; cupidity, greed; miserliness, meanness; (joc.) crepi l'-izia!..., just once in a way....

avatara, avata·r *m.* (Indian rel.) avatar; (fig.) transformation, change.

ave *excl.* hail!; greetings!; *n.m., f.* (rel.) Hail Mary; in (men di) un —, in the twinkling of an eye.

avellana *f.* cob, filbert or hazel nut; (herald.) hazel nuts.

avellano *m.* nut-tree; hazel-nut tree.

†avel·lere *vb.* See svellere.

avello *m.* (poet.) tomb, sepulchre; (Tusc. vulg.) puzzare come un —, to stink.

avemmari·a, avemari·a, ave mari·a *f.* (rel.) the Hail Mary; *ave* bead, small bead (of rosary); the Angelus (prayer or bell), esp. that of evening or sunset; da un'— all'altra, from morn till eve; sunset, curfew time.

avena *f.* oats; farina d'—, oatmeal; (mus.) oaten pipe.

†avenante *adj.* See avvenente.

Aventin-o *pr.n.m.* Aventine, one of the seven hills of Rome; (fig. pol.) ritrarsi sull'—, to withdraw from the political scene, biding one's time. **-ismo** *m.* anti-Fascist movement.

av·ere [B3] *tr.* to have; to possess, to own; — fame, to be hungry; — sete, to be thirsty; — sonno, to be sleepy; — fretta, to be in a hurry; — paura, to be afraid; — vergogna, to be ashamed; — freddo, to be cold; — caldo, to be hot; — ragione, to be right; — torto, to be wrong; — moglie, to be married; ha la moglie malata, his wife is ill; quanti anni avete?, how old are you?; — indosso, to wear; (in *perf.*, *past def.* and *inf.*) to obtain, to get: ho avuto un podere per poco prezzo, I acquired a farm cheaply; ebbe il posto, he got the job; lo volli —, I wanted to get it (and I did); to consider: l'ho sempre avuto per un galant-uomo, I have always thought he was a decent chap; l'hanno per pazzo, they think he's mad; — a vile, to consider cowardly; — a schifo, to loathe; — in onore, to esteem; — in odio, to hate; — a caro, to like, to receive with pleasure; — a cuore, to have at heart; — a mente, to have in mind, to remember; — per certo, to know for certain; — a (foll. by *inf.*), to chance to: quand'ebbi a vederlo l'anno scorso, when I happened to see him last year; to have the misfortune to: quand'ebbe a perder la moglie, when he had the misfortune to lose his wife; to have to, to be obliged to; — da, to have the wherewithal: non ha da mangiare, he has nothing to eat; to have to, to be obliged to: ho da scrivere una lettera, I have a letter to write; to be: non v'ha motivo di crederlo, there is no reason for believing it; non v'ha pace per me, there is no peace for me; — del buono, to have good qualities; — dello stupido, to be rather stupid, to look stupid; avercela con, to be angry with; averne troppo, to have more than enough, to be fed up; non — nulla a che fare con, to have nothing to do with, to be quite dissimilar; — delle sue, to have troubles enough, to have troubles of one's own; aversene a male, to take offence at; *n.m.* property; wealth; (comm.) credit; il lato dell'—, credit side; quant'è il mio —, how much do you owe me?; *pl.* possessions, substance. **-ente** *part. adj., n.m.* (leg.) -ente causa, successor in title; -ente diritto, person who is entitled (to something). (**-uto** *part. adj.*)

averla *f.* (orn.) shrike, butcher-bird; — capirossa, woodchat, *Lanius senator*; — cenerina, lesser grey shrike, *L. minor*; — maggiore, great grey shrike, *L. excubitor*; — piccola, red-backed shrike, *L. collurio.*

Avern-o *pr.n.m.* (myth.) Avernus; hell. **-ale** *adj.* avernal, infernal.

averro-ismo *m.* (philos.) Averroism. **-ista** *m.* Averroist. **-i·stico** *adj.* Averroistic.

†aversier-a *f.* witch, she-devil. **†-e, -o** *m.* the Devil.

†ave·r-tere *tr.* to turn away, to distract. **†-sione** *f.* turning away. **†-so** *part. adj.* turned away.

avia·rio *m.* aviary.

avi-atore *m.* aviator; airman; tenente —, flight lieutenant; pilota —, flying officer; air pilot. **-ato·rio** *adj.* flying, aviation. **-atrice** *f.* woman pilot. **-azione** *f.* aviation, flying; air force; meccanico d'-azione, air-mechanic; ufficiale d'-azione, flying officer; -azione marittima, Fleet Air Arm. **-ere** *m.* aircraftman (Air Force rank).

avi·cula *f.* (zool.) *Avicola hirundo*, wing shell.

avicoltore *m.* and deriv. See avicultore.

avicult-ore *m.* bird fancier, aviculturist. **-ura** *f.* aviculture.

avicu·pio *m.* See aucupio.

a·vid-o *adj.* avid; greedy; eager. **-amente** *adv.* avidly; greedily; eagerly. **-ezza** *f.* see avidità. **-ità** *f.* avidity; greed; eagerness; l'-ità del denaro, greed for money; avariciousness.

avifa·una *f.* avifauna.

a·vio[1] *pref., adj. indecl.* air; — benzina, aviation petrol. **-getto** *m.* jet aircraft. **-lan·cio** *m.* parachute jump. **-li·nea** *f.* airline; airway. **-motore** *m.* aero-engine. **-rimessa** *f.* hangar. **-trasportato** *adj.* airborne. **-trasporto** *m.* air transport, air travel. **-ve·lico** *m.* (sport) gliding; *adj.* club -velico, glider club.

a·vio[2] *adj.* (poet.) impervious; inaccessible, remote.

av-o *m.* grandfather; forefather, ancestor. **-a** *f.* grandmother; ancestress. **-ito** *adj.* ancestral; inherited, hereditary.

avoc-are [A2s] *tr.* (leg.) to avocate, to call to a higher tribunal; — a sè, to arrogate to oneself, to take upon oneself; to undertake. **-azione** *f.* (leg.) arrogation, the calling of a case to a higher tribunal; arrogating assumption (of a task).

avocetta *f.* (orn.) avocet, *Recurvirostra avocetta.*

†avo·col-o *adj., n.m.* blind; blind man. **†-are** *tr.* to blind.

†avogad-ore, -ro *m.* (hist.) magistrate of the Venetian Republic.

a·vol-o *m.* grandfather; ancestor. **-a** *f.* grandmother; ancestress.

†avolterare *vb.* See adulterare.

avoltoio *m.* See avvoltoio.

avo·rio *m.* ivory; (paint.) nero d'—, ivory-black.

avorn-iello, -io, -o *m.* (bot.) laburnum; (poet.) ash.

avortone *m.* unborn lambskin; uterine vellum.

avosetta *f.* (orn.) See avocetta.

avuls-o *part.* of avellere, q.v.; *adj.* torn, rent; uprooted; (surg.) extirpated. **-ione** *f.* avulsion; (surg.) extirpation; (leg.) avulsion. **-ivo** *adj.* (phon.) suono -ivo, click.

†avun·colo *m.* maternal uncle.

†avuta *f.* receipt.

avuto *part.* of avere, q.v.

avvalere [B34] *rfl.* (prep. di) to make use (of), to avail oneself (of).

avvall-are [A1] *tr.* to lower; to debase; †to lean; *rfl., intr.* (aux. essere) to subside, to sink, to give way; to slope. **-amento** *m.* (of earth, building) sinking; depression; landslip; trough (of waves). **-ato** *part. adj.* sunken; sloping. **-atura** *f.* sinking; lowering.

avvalor-are [A1c] *tr.* to give value to, to make valuable; to increase the value of; to improve; to strengthen; to confirm, to bear out; to support; to temper; to invigorate; to test; *rfl.* to become stronger, to be strengthened; to increase in value. **-amento** *m.* increase in strength; rise in value; improvement. **-ato** *part. adj.* strengthened, reinforced, supported; made valuable. (**-atore** *m.* **-atrice** *f.* **-azione** *f.*)

avvamp-are [A1] *tr.* to set ablaze; to burn; to inflame; *rfl., intr.* (aux. essere) to blaze up; to burn, to blaze; to shine; (fig.) — di sdegno, to burn with indignation. **-amento** *m.* burning, blazing; blaze; flame. **-ante** *part. adj.* burning, blazing. **-ato** *part. adj.* burned, burning; inflamed.

†avvampire *vb.* See avvampare.

avvantaggi-are [A3] *tr.* to benefit, to favour; to endow; to improve, to ameliorate; *rfl.* (prep. di) to profit (by); to derive advantage (from); -arsi in un lavoro, to get ahead with one's work. **-amento** *m.* profit, advantage. **-ato** *part. adj.* benefited; (of measure) excessive, superabundant, too much; overweight: mezzo chilo -ato, a half kilo too much. **-atamente** *adv.* in excess; superabundantly.

avvantag·gio *m.* advantage; *adv.* d'—, more.

†avvantare *vb.* See vantare.

avved-ere [B23] *rfl.* (prep. di) to become aware (of), to notice, to perceive; senza -ersene, without meaning to, unconsciously, without ill intent. **-imento** *m.* discernment; understanding; shrewdness; sagacity; con -imento, wisely, shrewdly, cautiously.

avved-ere (*cont.*)

~**utęzza** *f.* shrewdness; discernment; astuteness; cunning. ~**uto** *part. adj.* aware; fare ~uto, to make aware, to warn; sagacious, discerning; wary, shrewd, astute. ~**utamęnte** *adv.* shrewdly, sagaciously; adroitly; artfully; on purpose, intentionally.

†**avvegnachè** *conj.* although.

†**avvelare** *vb.* and derivs. See **velare**.

avvelen-are [A I C] *tr.* to poison; to make poisonous; (fig.) to embitter; to sour; to sadden; *rfl.* to poison oneself, to take poison. ~**amẹnto** *m.* poisoning. ~**ato** *part. adj.* poisoned; morire ~ato, to die of poisoning. ~**atọre** *m.*, ~**atrice** *f.* poisoner.

avvelenire [D 2] and derivs. See **avvelenare**.

†**avvenante**[1] *adj.* See **avvenente**.

†**avvenante**[2] *adv.* all'—, in proportion; in comparison.

avven-ente *adj.* handsome, comely, personable, attractive; charming, prepossessing, gracious, agreeable, pleasant. (~**entemẹnte** *adv.*) ~**enza** *f.* attractiveness; good looks; charm of manner.

avven-ire [D 17] *intr.* (*aux.* essere) to happen, to occur; to take place; avvenne che, it came to pass that; avvenga che può, come what may; checchè avvenga, come what may; *rfl.* (*prep.* a) (Tusc.) to suit; †to meet with, to encounter; *n.m.* future; prospects; avere un grande —, to have a great future before one; *adj. indecl.* future, to come. ~**imẹnto** *m.* event, important occurrence; — al trono, accession to the throne; †arrival, coming; †advent; †increase, addition, multiplication. ~**irịsmo** *m.* (art) futurism; belief in future developments rather than in tradition; wagnerism. ~**irista** *m.* (art) futurist. ~**itic·cio** *adj.* see ~izio. ~**uto** *part.*, *n.m.* occurrence; l'~uto, what has occurred.

avvent-are [A I] *tr.* to hurl, to fling; (fig.) — un giudizio, to give a hasty opinion; *rfl.* to fling oneself, to hurl oneself; to rush; (Tusc.) *intr.* (*aux.* avere) to make a striking impression, to be loud, to be showy: un'opera che ~a, a showy piece of work; un colore che ~a troppo, a colour that is too loud. ~**amẹnto** *m.* hurling, flinging, fling; rushing. ~**ata** *adv.* all'~ata, precipitately, without due consideration. ~**atag·gine**, ~**atẹzza** *f.* rashness, recklessness; imprudence; impulsiveness. ~**ato** *part. adj.* reckless, rash; imprudent; impulsive; inconsiderate; ill-considered; giudizio ~ato, hasty judgment. ~**atamẹnte** *adv.* rashly, recklessly. (~**atọre** *m.* ~**atrice** *f.*)

avvent-o *m.* coming, advent; (rel.) Advent; arrival; — al trono, accession to the throne. ~**isti** *m.pl.* (rel.) Adventists. ~**i·zio** *adj.* adventitious; fortuitous; (bot.; orn.) adventitious; (econ.; comm.) guadagni ~izi, casual earnings; occasional profits; temporary; operaio ~izio, casual labourer; popolazione ~izia, fluctuating portion of population; (leg.) beni ~izi, sums or property received by way of advancement, as a gift, etc.; *n.m.* (comm.) temporary employee, apprentice. ~**iziato** *m.* (comm.) apprenticeship; temporary employment. ~**ọre** *m.* customer, client. (~**ọra** *f.*)

avventrinare [A I] *intr.* (*aux.* avere) (vet.) to suffer from blood, or tympany.

avventur-a *f.* adventure; love affair; per —, by chance; †good fortune. ~**are** [A I] *tr.* to venture, to risk; to adventure; *rfl.* to venture; to take a risk. ~**ato** *part. adj.* risked, ventured; fortunate, happy, lucky; male ~ato, unlucky. ~**atamẹnte** *adv.* fortunately; by chance. ~**iere**, ~**iero** *m.* adventurer; †soldier of fortune, freebooter, freelance. ~**iera** *f.* adventuress. ~**ọso** *adj.* adventurous; venturesome; enterprising; fortunate, lucky; blessed. ~**osamẹnte** *adv.* adventurously. ~**osità** *f.* adventurousness.

avver-are [A I C] *tr.* to verify; to establish, to confirm; to make valid; *rfl.* to be fulfilled, to come true, to come to pass; to take place, to occur; to make certain, to verify. (~**a·bile** *adj.*) ~**amẹnto** *m.* fulfilment; accomplishment; realization; verification. (~**atọre** *m.* ~**atrice** *f.*)

avver·bi-o *m.* adverb. ~**iale** *adj.* adverbial. ~**ialmẹnte** *adv.* adverbially.

avverd-ire [D 2] *tr.* to make green; to paint green; *intr.* (*aux.* essere) to grow green, to turn green. ~**ito** *part. adj.* green; viso ~ito dal dispetto, face green with envy.

avversamẹnte *adv.* See under **avverso**.

avvers-are [A I] *tr.* to oppose; to obstruct; to thwart, to frustrate. ~**ante** *part. adj.* contrary, opposing; hostile. ~**ativo** *adj.* (gramm.) adversative. ~**ato** *part. adj.* opposed, obstructed; †tidy, orderly, precise. ~**atọre** *m.* opponent, adversary. (~**atrice** *f.*) ~**azịọne** *f.* (gramm.) adversative formula, expression of contrast.

avvers-a·rio *m.* adversary; enemy; antagonist; opponent; (leg.) opposing party; †l'antico —, Satan; †~ari di Dio, doers of evil; †l'— d'ogni male, God; *adj.* opposing; contrary; hostile; (leg.) difesa ~aria, opposing counsel. ~**a·ria** *f.* (poet.) beloved; beloved enemy. †~**aro** *m.* see **avversario**. †~**iera** *f.* witch, she-devil. †~**iere** *m.* Satan.

avvers-o *adj.* adverse, unfavourable; contrary; opposite; averse; per —, on the contrary; (leg.) parte ~a, opposing party; †*prep.* versus, against. ~**amẹnte** *adv.* adversely, unfavourably. ~**iọne** *f.* aversion; dislike; hatred; ha ~ione a certi cibi, he has an aversion for certain foods; sente ~ione contro tutti, he has a grudge against everyone; prendere in ~ione, to conceive a dislike for; essere in ~ione a, to be disliked by; ~**ità** *f.*, *usu. pl.* adversity; misfortune; nelle ~ità si provano gli amici, a friend in need is a friend indeed.

avvert-ire [D I] *tr.* (*prep.* di) to warn, to caution (against); to admonish, to reprove (for); to point out: ti ~o di un errore che ti è sfuggito, I point out a mistake which you have overlooked; to inform: mi ~ì del suo ritorno, he informed me of his return; to remind: avvertilo che lo aspettiamo qui, remind him that we are waiting for him here; to feel; to notice, — un dolore, to feel a pain; *intr.* (*aux.* avere) to pay attention; to be on the alert; to try; ~i di parlar chiaramente, try to speak clearly. ~**entemẹnte** *adv.* with caution; carefully; prudently; considerately. ~**enza** *f.* caution; care, attention; usate ~enza! be careful!; fate ~enza di dirgli tutto, be sure to tell him everything; warning; direction, instruction; note; notice; foreword, short prefatory note. ~**i·bile** *adj.* noticeable. ~**imẹnto** *m.* warning; admonition; caution; attention; notice; prefatory note, advertisement. ~**ito** *part. adj.* warned; advised; aware; cautious, prudent; alert; (Tusc. provb.) uomo ~ito, mezzo munito, forewarned is forearmed; far ~ito, to warn. ~**itamẹnte** *adv.* carefully, with attention; knowingly, intentionally.

avvetrato *adj.* (Tusc.) icy, frozen hard.

avvezz-are [A I C] *tr.* to accustom; to train, to bring up; — bene, to bring up well; — male, to bring up badly, to spoil; *rfl.* to accustom oneself; to get accustomed, to get used. ~**amẹnto** *m.* training; habit. ~**ato** *part. adj.* accustomed; trained; hardened. ~**atura** *f.* becoming accustomed.

avvẹzzo *adj.* accustomed, used; trained; mal —, badly brought up, badly trained, ill-accustomed.

avvi-are [A 4] *tr.* to set going, to start; to send off; — il fuoco, to light the fire; — un ragazzo a una professione, to guide a boy in the early stages of a profession; — una corrispondenza, to open a correspondence; (knitt.) — una maglia, to cast on, to set up the work; (comm.) to set up, to get going (a shop, business, etc.); (eng.) to start; — alla manovella, to crank (a car); to route: i treni saranno ~ati sulla linea del Sempione, the trains will be routed on the Simplon line; (Tusc.) *intr.* (*aux.* avere, *prep.* a) to begin: ~a a piovere, it is beginning to rain; (comm.) to set up business; (typ.) to make-ready; *rfl.* to set off; to start; to go; ~arsi verso, to make off in the direction of, to set out towards; (fig.) to find one's feet; ~arsi male, to make a bad start; ~arsi per una professione, to begin training for a profession. ~**amẹnto** *m.* starting, start; direction; route to be followed, routing (of mail, transport); introduction, elements; introductory study; scuola di ~amento al lavoro, technical school, commercial school; ~amento allo studio del latino, first steps in Latin; (mech.) starting; ~amento a pedale, kick-start; manovella d'~amento, starting handle, crank; motorino d'~amento, self-starter; (electr.) corrente d'~amento, starting current; (comm.) goodwill; (typ.) make-ready. ~**ato** *part. adj.* begun, started; going, in motion; l'orologio è ~ato, the clock is going; essere bene ~ato, to be doing well; un negozio bene ~ato, a going concern. ~**atọre** *m.* one who teaches the groundwork of a subject, one who gives an introductory course of lessons; (motor.) starter; ~atore automatico, self-starter. (~**atrice** *f.*) ~**atura** *f.* work begun; first stages; fire-lighter; (knitt.) first row; dare l'~atura a, to start off, to get started.

avvicend-are [A I] *tr.* to alternate; *recip. rfl.* to alternate, to follow in succession, to succeed one another. ~**amẹnto** *m.* alternation; (agric.) rotation. ~**ato** *part. adj.* alternated, alternating.

avvicin-are [A I] *tr.* to bring near; to compare; to approach; — una persona, to walk up to a person; to frequent the company of; *rfl.* to approach; to draw near; to go near; la notte s'~a, night is drawing on; all'~arsi della morte, upon the approach of death; non è la traduzione esatta, ma ci si ~a, it is not an exact translation, but it is fairly close. ~**amẹnto** *m.* approach. ~**ante** *part. adj.* approaching; near; approximate; similar. (~**anza** *f.* ~**azịọne** *f.*)

avvign-are [A 5] *tr.* to plant with vines. (**-ato** *part. adj.*)

avvil-ire [D 2] *tr.* to debase; to lower; to humiliate; to demoralize; to depress, to discourage, to dishearten; to degrade; to dishonour, to disgrace; (econ.) to depreciate, to debase, to depress; — i prezzi, to bring prices down; — merci, to lower the market price of goods; *rfl.* to degrade oneself; to humiliate oneself; to lose courage, to become disheartened or depressed; to disgrace oneself; (econ.) questa moneta si -isce, this currency is depreciating. **-ente, -iente** *part. adj.* demoralizing; discouraging; humiliating. **-imento** *m.* dejection; discouragement; humiliation, degradation; disgrace; (econ.) -imento della valuta, depreciation of currency; -imento dei prezzi, fall in prices. **-itivo** *adj.* discouraging, degrading; †(gramm.) pejorative. **-ito** *part. adj.* dejected, downhearted, dispirited, discouraged; (econ.) depreciated, depressed, debased, lowered.

avvilupp-are [A I] *tr.* to envelop; to wrap up; to muffle up; to entangle; to complicate; to confuse, to bewilder; (mil.) — il nemico, to hem in the enemy; (flax dressing) — il manipolo, to lap the stick; *rfl.* to become enveloped; to get entangled. **-amento** *m.* envelopment; wrapping up; entanglement; (mil.) envelopment, encirclement. **-ante** *part. adj.* (mil.) manovra -ante, encirclement. **-ato** *part. adj.* enveloped; entangled; involved, complicated; bewildered, confused. **-atore** *m.* deceiver, cheat, swindler; entangler. (**-atrice** *f.*) **-atura** *f.* confusion; entanglement.

avvin-are [A I] *tr.* to soak in wine; to flavour with wine; to fill with wine; to season (casks) with wine. **-ato** *part. adj.* soaked in wine; wine-flavoured; (of casks) wine-seasoned; wine-coloured; (joc.) sozzled. **-azzare** [A I] *tr.* to make drunk; *rfl.* to drink too much wine, to get tipsy; (poet.) to flush rosy red. **-azzato** *part. adj.* tipsy, flushed with wine.

avvin·c-ere [C 5] *tr.* to bind, to tie; to embrace, to hug; to overwhelm; to fascinate. **-ente** *adj.* fascinating, winning; modi -enti, charming manners.

avvincigliare [A 4] *tr.* to bind; to twist.

avvincolare [A I s] *tr.* to clasp.

avvinghi-are [A 4] *tr.* to seize, to clasp, to grasp; *rfl.* -arsi, to clasp; †to encircle oneself, to ring oneself round; *recip. rfl.* to clasp one another. †-ata *f.* armful (measurement of circumference; as much as one's arms can hold). **-ato** *part. adj.* clasped.

avvinto *part.* of **avvincere**, q.v.; *adj.* bound; fascinated, held.

avvi·o *m.* (*pl.* **avvii**) beginning; dare l'— a, to start; prendere l'—, to begin; first steps; le scarpe d'—, a baby's first shoes.

avvisa·glia *f.* (mil.) skirmish, scrap, brush with the enemy; le prime avvisaglie, first contact; (fig.) conflict, set-to.

avvis-are[1] [A I] *tr.* to inform; to advise, to warn; to tell, to instruct, to remind; l'ho -ato di venire da te domani, I have told him (reminded him) to come and see you tomorrow; †to notice; †to observe; *rfl.* to consider, to believe, to think, to understand; *intr.* (*aux.* avere, *prep.* a) to think (about), to turn one's mind (to). **-amento** *m.* warning; information; †plan; ruse. (**-ante** *part. adj.*) **-ato** *part. adj.* informed; warned; shrewd, (provb.) uomo -ato, mezzo salvato, forewarned is forearmed; *adv.* intentionally, deliberately. **-atamente** *adv.* cautiously; judiciously; knowingly, intentionally. **-atore** *m.* announcer; informant; (theatr.) call-boy; (mil.) sentinel; †explorer; horn, siren; bell; -atore d'incendio, fire-alarm. (**-atrice** *f.*)

†avvisare[2] *tr.* to face, to encounter; *recip. rfl.* to come face to face.

avviso[1] *m.* notice, announcement; advertisement; (comm.) advice; — di convocazione dell'assemblea, notice of meeting; contro —, on notice; lettera d'—, letter of advice; — di consegna, notice of delivery, advice note; salvo contrario —, in the absence of notice to the contrary; in mancanza di —, in the absence of notice; come da —, as advised; — pubblicitario, placard, poster; advice, warning: ti serva d'— per un'altra volta, let it be a warning to you another time; star sull'—, to be on one's guard; opinion, belief: esser d'—, to be of the opinion; a mio —, in my view; (hist.) despatch.

avviso[2] *m.* (naut.) sloop, scout; patrol vessel.

avvist-are [A I] *tr.* to catch sight of, to come into sight of; (fig.) to recognize, to tell at a glance; to judge by first impressions; (naut.) to sight; — la terra, to make a landfall; †to exhibit, to put on show (at a fair, in a market, etc.) (**-amento** *m.*) **-ato** *part. adj.* sighted; perceived; alert, knowing; well-advised; †showy, vivid, gay.

avvisto *part.* of **avvedere**, q.v.

avvitaprigionieri *m. indecl.* (eng.) stud driver.

avvit-are [A I] *tr.* to screw, to screw down; to screw up; — a fondo, to screw tight, to tighten; *rfl.* (aeron.) to go into a spin; (ski.) to swing the body round. **-amento** *m.* screwing; (aeron.) spin; (naut.) winding (of a ship being turned end for end). (**-ata** *f.*) **-ato** *part. adj.* screwed down; tight-waisted. **-atrice** *f.* (eng.) wrench.

avviticchi-are [A 4] *tr.* to twine, to twist; *rfl.* (*prep.* a) to twine (round); to hang (upon), to cling (to). **-amento** *m.* twisting; twining. **-ante** *part. adj.* clinging. **-ato** *part. adj.* twisted, entwined; clinging.

avviticciare [A 3] *tr.* to twist, to twine.

avvit-ire [D 2] *tr.* to plant with vines. (**-ito** *part. adj.*)

avvittare [A I] *tr.* (admin.) to supply with food.

avvittolato *adj.* twisted, intertwined.

avviv-are [A I] *tr.* to enliven, to vivify; to invigorate; to give life to, to bring to life; to rekindle, to revive; *rfl.* to revive, to grow animated. **-amento** *m.* enlivenment; animation. **-ato** *part. adj.* enlivened; vivified; animated. **-atore** *m.* enlivener; animator; *adj.* animating. (**-atrice** *f.*)

avviziare [A 4] and derivs. See **viziare**.

avvizz-ire [D 2] *intr.* (*aux.* essere) to wither, to fade. **-imento** *m.* withering, fading. **-ito** *part. adj.* withered, faded.

†avvoc-are *tr.* to plead; to defend; *intr.* to carry on the profession of lawyer; to intercede. (**†-azi·a** *f.* **†-azione** *f.*)

avvocat-o[1] *m.* lawyer; member of the legal profession having right of pleading in courts (as solicitor and barrister); — dello stato, qualified lawyer employed by the state to conduct its legal cases; — rotale, lawyer having right of pleading in the Rota; — di cassazione, lawyer having right of pleading in the Supreme Court; elenco degli -i, roll of lawyers; ordine degli -i, college of lawyers; ottenere l'iscrizione nell'elenco degli -i, to be enrolled as a lawyer; (fig.) advocate, champion; — del diavolo, devil's advocate. **-a** *f.* (rel.) advocate (esp. of B.V.M.); patroness; (joc.) talkative woman; †woman lawyer. **-are** [A I] *tr.* to admit to the profession of lawyer. **-ato** *part. adj.* admitted to the profession of lawyer. **-eri·a** *f.* deed (or trick) worthy of a lawyer or typical of a lawyer. **-esco** *adj.* (*m.pl.* **-eschi**) worthy of a lawyer, typical of a lawyer; captious; (**-escamente** *adv.*) **-essa** *f.* woman lawyer; †lawyer's wife; protectress, patroness. **-ura** *f.* lawyer's profession; l'Avvocatura, the Bar; -ura erariale, -ura dello Stato, office of lawyers employed by the state to conduct its legal cases.

avvocato[2] *m.* (bot.) pero —, avocado pear.

†avvoggolare *tr.* to twist, to roll, to twirl.

avvogliato (Tusc.) *adj.* capricious, full of whims, fanciful.

avvol·g-ere [C 5] *tr.* to wind; to roll up; to wrap up; to entangle, to involve; to trick, to deceive; (text.) to wind, to wind on; *rfl.* to wrap oneself up; to become involved, to become implicated; to wind round; †to get confused; to be in error, to be deceived. **-i·bile** *adj.*; *n.m.* roller blind; roll shutter. **-imento** *m.* winding up; wrapping up; trickery, trick, deceit; fraudulent device, stratagem; (electr.) winding; -imento in parallelo, lap winding. **-itore** *m.* (text.) winding machine; (fig.) trickster, cheat, a person who pulls the wool over one's eyes. **-itrice** *f.* (text.) winding machine; (fig.) adventuress.

†avvolontato *adj.* willing.

†avvolpacchiare *tr.* to trick; *rfl.* to get confused, to become muddled; to be tricked.

avvolt-are [A I] *tr.* (Tusc.) to wind; to wrap up. **-atura** *f.* wrapping, wrapper. **-ic·chiare** [A 4] *tr.* to twist, to twine round.

avvolto *part.* of **avvolgere**, q.v.; *adj.* enveloped; rolled up; tricked.

avvoltoio *m.* (orn.) vulture, esp. the black vulture, *Ægypius monachus*.

avvoltol-are [A I s] *tr.* to roll up; *rfl.* to roll oneself up; to wallow, to roll. (**-ato** *part. adj.*) **-atura** *f.* rolling up; wallowing.

†avvoltore *m.* See **avvoltoio**.

azale·a *f.* (bot.) azalea.

azeotr-o·pico *adj.* (chem.) azeotropic; miscuglio —, constant-boiling mixture. **-opismo** *m.* (chem.) azeotropism.

aziend-a *f.* business, concern; — comunale, — governativa, manufacturing concern (frequently public utility concern owned and worked by borough or government); — industriale, manufacturing concern; — privata, private business, firm; direction, management; l'— della casa, the running of a house, the management of household affairs; difficult task, tedious occupation. **-ale** *adj.* pertaining to business or concern; conti -ali, accounts of business;

aziend-a (*cont.*)

   associazione -ale, association among workers of a single business; gita -ale, (annual) outing of the staff of a firm or business. **-a·ria** *f.* (neol.) business administration.

a·zimut *m. indecl.* (astron.) azimuth. **-ale** *adj.* azimuthic; cerchio -ale, horizontal circle (of theodolite).

az-ina *f.* (chem.) azine. **-i·nico** *adj.* (chem.) azo.

azion-e *f.* action; act, deed; uomo d'—, man of action; — chimica, chemical action; (pol.) partito d'—, Action Party; (theatr.) action, acting, movement; play; subject, theme; l'— si svolge a Venezia, the action takes place in Venice; unità d'—, unity of action; (sport) concerted movement (football, etc.); (fencing) attacking move; — di quarta, move carried out from a 'quarte' position; (mil.) action; (rel.) *usu. pl.* -i di grazie, thanksgiving; (comm.) share; — al portatore, bearer share; — nominativa, registered share; — di preferenza, preference share; — differita, deferred share; — di nuova emissione, newly issued share; — di vecchia emissione, share of an existing issue; — interamente versata, paid up share; certificato d'—, share warrant; -i tessili, textile shares; -i ferroviarie, railway shares; -i di miniere d'oro, gold shares; le -i sono state intestate al nome del proprietario, the shares have been registered in the owner's name; aprire la sottoscrizione di -i, open a subscription list; garantire l'emissione di -i, to underwrite an offer of shares to the public; fare il riparto delle -i, to allot shares; comunicazione formale dell'assegnazione di un riparto di -i, letter of allotment; comunicazione di mancata assegnazione di -i, letter of regret; emissione di -i, issue of shares; certificato provvisorio di — non interamente versata, scrip; strumento di trapasso di -i nominative, transfer; (leg.) action, action at law, legal process to establish claim or obtain remedy; — redibitoria, action for rescission (of a sale); — di risarcimento, action for damages; — cambiaria, action upon a protested bill of exchange; esercitare un'—, to bring an action; decadere da un'—, to cease to have a right of action; — prescritta, action brought out of time; reato di — pubblica, crime which is prosecuted irrespective of complaint by injured party. **-are** [A I c] *tr.* to actuate; to set going; (eng.) to drive, to power. **-a·bile** *adj.* (leg.) actionable. (**-amento** *m.*) **-ato** *part. adj.* actuated; -ato da un uomo, one-man. **-a·rio** *adj.* (comm.) capitale -ario, share capital. **-ista** *m.* shareholder; (pol.) member of the 'partito d'—'.

azocoloranti *m.pl.* (chem.) azo-dyes.

azo·ico *adj.* (geol.) azoic; archaeozoic, archaean.

az-oto *m.* nitrogen. **-otato** *adj.* nitrogenous. **-o·tico** *adj.* nitrogenous.

Azteco *pr.n.m., adj.* Aztec.

azza *f.* battle-axe.

azzampato *adj.* (of a dog) male —, cow-hocked; splay-footed; bene —, standing well, well-poised.

azzann-are [A I] *tr.* to seize with the teeth; to sink fangs into; to snap, to catch. **-amento** *m.* attack with fangs. **-ato** *part. adj.* bitten, mauled, savaged. (**-atore** *m.* **-atrice** *f.*) **-atura** *f.* wound from a fang or fangs.

azzard-o *m.* hazard, risk; giuoco d'—, game of chance; giuocare d'—, to gamble. **-are** [A I] *tr.* to hazard; to risk; to venture; *intr.* (*aux.* avere) to take risks; *rfl.* to dare, to venture. **-ato** *part. adj.* hazardous, risky; bold, daring; una congettura -ata, a flimsy conjecture. **-oso** *adj.* hazardous, risky; bold, daring, venturesome.

azzecc-are [A 2 c] *tr.* to hit, to strike; azzeccarla, to hit the mark, to get it right; azzeccarci, to guess right; non azzeccarne una, to be always wide of the mark, to be continually unsuccessful; to get, to draw (in a lottery): ho azzeccato due numeri al lotto, I have won a double on the lotto; azzeccammo una bella giornata per la nostra gita, we were lucky enough to hit a fine day for our trip. **-agarbu·gli** *m. indecl.* pettifogging lawyer, pettifogger (from the character in Manzoni's *I Promessi Sposi*). **-aprete** *m.* (ichth.) *Lepadogaster* sp., cling fish, sucker. **-ato** *part. adj.* completely successful, just right; born under a lucky star.

azzer-are [A I] *tr.* to put at zero. **-amento** *m.* zero setting. (**-ato** *part. adj.*)

†azzicare *tr.* to move gently; *rfl.* to stir, to budge.

azzim-are [A I s] *tr.* to deck, to dress ornately; *rfl.* to deck oneself out, to dress up. **-ato** *part. adj.* decked out, dressed up, gaudily dressed; -ato da festa, in one's Sunday clothes.

az·zim-o *adj.* unleavened; *n.m.* unleavened bread; gli -i, the feast of the Passover. **-a, -ella** *f.* unleavened bread. **-iti** *m.pl.* (rel. hist.) Azymites.

azzitt-are [A I], **-ire** [D 2] *tr.* to silence; *rfl.* to fall silent, to keep quiet.

azzollare [A I] *tr.* to stone.

azzopp-are [A I], **-ire** [D 2] *tr.* to lame, to render lame; *intr.* (*aux.* essere), *rfl.* to fall lame. **-imento** *m.* laming, falling lame. **-ato, -ito** *part. adj.* lame; lamed.

Azzorre *pr.n.f.pl.* (geog.) le —, the Azores.

azzuff-are [A I] *rfl.* (*prep.* con), *recip. rfl.* to come to blows; to scuffle. **-amento** *m.* scuffle, scrimmage, brawl, fight. **-atore** *m.* brawler, rioter. (**-atrice** *f.*)

†azzuolo *adj.* dark blue.

azzurite *f.* (miner.) azurite.

azzurr-o *adj.* azure; blue; sky-blue; Principe —, Prince Charming; — cupo, dark blue; — chiaro, light blue; arma -a, air force; *n.m.* blue, the colour blue; the azure; clear sky; (paint.) blue (all shades between ultramarine and sky-blue); — oltramarino, ultramarine; (sport) un —, an international; member of a team representing Italy in international sporting events; gli -i, the Italian team. **-a·bile** *adj., n.m.* (sport) in the running for colours, a 'probable' for colours. **-ag·gio** *m.* bluing (of laundry). **-are** [A I] *tr.* (laund.) to blue; (optics) to bloom (a lens). **-ato** *adj.* coloured blue, painted blue. **-eggiare** [A 3 c] *intr.* (*aux.* avere) to tend towards blue, to be bluish. **-i(g)no** *adj.* (paint.) pale blue, light blue. **-o·gnolo** *adj.* bluish.

B, b *f., m.* the letter B; una — maiuscola, a capital B; una — minuscola, a small b; essere segnato con —, to be hunchbacked, to be one-eyed, to be lame; somigliare un —, to be fat and dumpy; provare con A più B, to prove beyond doubt; (fig.) to be shrewd; non aver passato il B, U, Bu, to have learnt nothing.

ba *excl.* See **bah**.

babà¹ *m. indecl.* (cul.) baba, sponge-cake steeped in rum.

†babà² *m.* grandfather.

†babà³ *adv. phr.* apporre alla —, to grumble.

baba·u *m.* bogey, ogre; bugbear; (mil. slang) tank.

babbagigi *m.pl.* (bot.) a grass-like plant with edible tubers (rush-nuts), *Cyperus esculentus*; also peanuts, monkey-nuts, *Arachis hypogaea*.

babb-ale·o, -alocco (*m.pl.* **-alocchi**) **-ano, -e·o** *adj.* silly, stupid; dull; *n.m.* simpleton, blockhead, booby.

†babbilano *m.* man who is sexually impotent.

†bab·bi-o *m.* (**†-a** *f.*) dolt, simpleton.

babbione *m.* blockhead, dolt; simpleton; *adj.* stupid.

babbit *adj. indecl.* (eng.) metallo —, babbitt metal.

babb-o *m.* father, daddy; una cosa che non ha nè — nè mamma, a thing without rhyme or reason; prestare a — morto, to lend against expectations of an inheritance; un — morto, a contract made against such expectations. **-ino** *m. dim.* daddy, daddikins.

Babboriveggoli *m.* (Tusc.) the next world; andare a —, to 'pass over', to depart this world.

babbuasso *m.* fool, idiot, simpleton; clumsy fellow; *adj.* foolish, stupid.

babbuc·ci-a *f.* bedroom slipper; babouche. **-a·io** *m.* maker or seller of slippers.

babbuino *m.* (zool.) baboon; (fig.) dolt, fool, booby.

Bab-ele *f.* Babel; la torre di —, the tower of Babel; (fig.) confusion, bedlam; (poet.) the infidels, heathendom; the heathen. **-e·lico** *adj.* uproarious; chaotic.

Babil-o·nia *f.* Babylon; Babylonia; (fig.) place of corruption; turmoil, confusion; babel; crowd. **-onese, o·nico** *adj.* Babylonian; (fig.) in a state of turmoil, confused.

babord-o *m.* (naut.) port, side, larboard. **-ese** *adj.* (naut.) relating to port side, port.

†babulare *intr.* (of an owl) to hoot.

baca *f.* (Tusc.) pod.

baca·io *m.* See under **baco¹**.

bac-are [A 2] *intr.* (*aux.* essere), *rfl.* to become maggoty, to become worm-eaten; to decay, to go bad. (**-amento** *m.*) **-ato** *part. adj.* maggoty, worm-eaten; decayed, rotten, gone bad; (fig.) sick, unwell; physically unsound; morally corrupt; cervello -ato, unsound mind, diseased mind. **-atic·cio, -atino, -atuc·cio** *dim. adj.* (Tusc.) sickly, ailing. (**-atura** *f.*)

†bacarozzo *m.* bandit.

bacato¹ *m.* See under **baco¹**.

bacato² *part.* of **bacare**, q.v.

bacca[1] *f.* berry, fruit; — del cipresso, cone of the cypress; †jewel, pearl.

†**bacca**[2] *f.* Bacchante.

†**bacca**[3] *f.* See **vacca**.

baccagliare [A 4] *intr.* (*aux.* avere) to yell, to clamour, to set up a hullabaloo.

baccal-à *m. indecl.* dried salt cod; (fig.) blockhead; thin individual; irreligious person (cf. **baccalare**[1]). **-ara·io** *m.* (*pl.* **-ara·i**) dealer in dried cod, fishmonger.

baccalare[1] *m.* (iron.) fount of wisdom, mine of learning, know-all, wiseacre (cf. **baccelliere**); irreligious person.

baccalare[2] *m.* (naut. hist.) one of the timbers for supporting the outside platform or outriggers of a galley.

baccalaro *m.* stableboy, stableman.

†**baccala·uro** *m.* bachelor, graduate of a university.

baccalaureato *m.* baccalaureate, bachelorship of a university.

†**baccale** *adj.* belonging to Bacchus, Bacchic; †alla —, in the manner of the votaries of Bacchus, frenziedly.

†**baccaleri·a** *f.* status of bachelor; (fig.) pride, haughtiness, vanity.

baccàn *m. indecl.* (naut., Liguria) owner or 'master' of a ship.

baccanale *m.* Bacchanalian orgy; noisy revel, racket; row; *pl.* Bacchanalia; (mus.) Bacchanalian songs; *adj.* Bacchic, Bacchanal.

†**baccana·lia** *f.* loud revelry.

baccan-o *m.* uproar, hubbub; uproarious assembly; fare il —, to raise Cain; to riot about. **-a·ria** *f.* feast of Bacchus; (paint.) Bacchanal, Triumph of Bacchus. **-a·rio** *adj.* Bacchanal. **-ella** *f.* uproar; low tavern; (colloq.) rizzar -ella, to open shop. †**-ello** *m.* company of ribald merry-makers. †**-eri·a** *f.* Bacchanal.

baccant-e *f.* Bacchante; *adj.* frenzied. **-ina** *f.* little figure of a Bacchante.

bac·cara *f.* (bot.) Asarabacca, *Asarum europaeum.*

baccarà *m. indecl.* the game of baccarat; type of fine crystal glass (so called from Baccarat, a town in France famous for its manufacture).

†**bacc-are** *intr.* to take part in Bacchanalian orgies. †**-ato** *adj.* frenzied, wild as a Bacchante.

baccelleri·a[1] *f.* See under **baccello**[1].

†**baccelleri·a**[2] *f.* See **baccellierato**, under **baccelliere**.

baccellier-e *m.* (in an English or American university) holder of a bachelor's degree; (formerly in an Italian university) student who has completed the first two years; (hist.) squire to a knight. **-ato** *m.* bachelor's degree; bachelorship.

baccell-o[1] *m.* bean, i.e. pod with its beans; sgranare -i, to shell beans; apparire fiori e -i, to be well and affluent, (of a woman) to be young and blossoming; simpleton; penis. **-a·io** *m.* bean field; (joc.) padrone del -aio, monarch of all he surveys, cock of the walk; vendor of beans. **-atura** *f.* (ceram.) bean motif, decoration of bean-shaped design. **-eri·a** *f.* tomfoolery. **-ętto** *m. dim.* of **baccello**; (archit.) bean-shaped ornament. **-ino** *m. dim.* of **baccello**; *adj.* (bot.) pod-bearing, leguminous. **-one** *m. augm.* of **baccello**; simpleton; good-for-nothing; cheese eaten with beans.

baccello[2] *m.* (zool.) *Pharus legumen,* a shell-fish similar to the razor-shell.

baccheggi-are [A 3 c] *intr.* (*aux.* avere) to revel; to take part in Bacchic celebrations. **-ante** *part. adj.* revelling.

†**bacche·o** *adj.* Bacchic, Bacchanal.

bac·chera *f.* (bot.). See **baccara**.

baccherone *m.* sea-rocket, *Cakile maritima.*

bacchętt-a[2] *f.* rod, staff, staff of office; ramrod; drumstick; stick of a rocket; — del prestigiatore, conjuror's wand; — magica, wand; — divinatoria, divining-rod; (of spinning frame) faller; (in welding) — d'apporto, filler rod; (paint.) mahlstick; (mus.) drumstick, bowstick; — di direttore d'orchestra, conductor's baton; comandare a —, to be a martinet, to expect prompt obedience; passare sotto le -e, to run the gauntlet. **-ante** *m.* water-diviner. **-are** [A 1 c] *tr.* to thrash, to beat; (Tusc.) to sell at a very low price. **-ata** *f.* blow with a rod or stick. **-ina** *f.* wand; -ina fatata, fairy's wand. **-o** *m.* handle of a whip; holder for knitting-needles; large stick.

bacchętta[2] *f.* (zool.) baculum.

bacchetton-e *m.* ostentatiously religious person; devotee; pious humbug, hypocrite. **(-ona** *f.*) **-eri·a** *f.* churchiness; cant, hypocrisy. **-ęsco** *adj.* (*m.pl.* **-ęschi**) tiresomely pious. **-ismo** *m.* sanctimoniousness, irritating display of piety.

†**bacche·vole** *adj.* Bacchic, Bacchanal.

bachiano *adj.* (mus.) relating to Bach, of Bach, Bach.

bacchiare [A 4] and derivs. See under **bacchio**[1].

bac·chico *adj.* Bacchic, Bacchanal; canzone bacchica, drinking song.

bac·chie *f.pl.* red blotches on the face caused by excessive drinking.

bacchillone *m.* (Tusc.) man in his second childhood; idler, good-for-nothing.

bac·chi-o[1] *m.* pole; heavy stick, cudgel. **-are** [A 4] *tr.* to beat down (fruit, nuts, etc.) with a pole; to sell at a low price (cf. **abbacchiare**). **-ata** *f.* blow with a pole, stroke with a rod; cudgelling; (fig.) serious blow, setback. (**-atore** *m.*)

bacchi-o[2] *m.* (prosod.) bacchius.

Bac·co[1] *pr.n.m.* (myth.) Bacchus; wine; drinking, conviviality; *excl.* per — !, per — barile!, corpo di — !, by Jove! **-chetto** *m. dim.* small figure of Bacchus. **-chino** *m. dim.* (Tusc.) fat baby.

bacco[2] *m.* stepping-stone.

bac·cola *f.* myrtle berry; juniper berry; *pl.* (Tusc.) myrtle; juniper.

bacheca *f.* jeweller's showcase; glass case; †(fig.) charlatan, one who is all show.

bachelite *f.* See **bakelite**.

bacher-ello *m.* grub. **-ozzo, -oz·zolo** *m.* grub, maggot (esp. as bait for fishing); (fig.) unsavoury or importunate individual.

bacheri·a *f.* silkworm farm.

bachicolt-ore *m.* breeder of silkworms, silk grower, silk producer. **-ura** *f.* cultivation of silkworms, silkworm industry, silk growing.

bachicultore *m.* and derivs. See **bachicoltore**.

†**baciabasso** *m.* See under **baciare**.

baciamano *m.* See under **baciare**.

baci-are [A 3] *tr.* to kiss; to touch lightly; (of water) to wash against; — basso, to humiliate oneself; — la polvere, to bite the dust; — co' denti, to inflict an injury with a show of friendship; — il fiasco, to take a deep drink; — il chiavistello, to shake the dust from off one's feet, to go away for ever; *recip. rfl.* to kiss, to kiss one another. †**-abasso** *m.* deep bow with a kiss on the hand; (fig.) humiliation; obsequiousness. **-amano** *m.* hand-kissing; very polite salutation; compliment. **-amento** *m.* kiss, kissing; embrace. **-apile** *m. indecl.* pious humbug, hypocrite. **-apol·vere** *m. indecl.* hypocrite. **-asanti** *m. indecl.* pious humbug. **-ato** *part. adj.* kissed; kissing; (naut.) 'two blocks'; rima -ata, rhyme between consecutive lines; *adv.* a bocca -ata, a man -ata, with the utmost readiness. (**-atore** *m.* **-atrice** *f.*)

baciasca *f.* (Florent.) sink, tank; acquaio a una o due baciasche, single or double sink.

bacicci *m. pl.* (bot.) shrubby saltwort, *Salicornia fruticosa.*

Bacic·cia *pr.n.m.* (dial. Gen.) Baptiste; (fig.) fat, lazy man; (N. Ital.) Genoese.

baci·glia *f.* (bot.). See **bacicci**.

bacile *m.* basin; bowl; barber's bowl; wash-hand basin.

bacillo *m.* bacillus; bacterium, germ, microbe; (ent.) stick insect.

bacin-o[1] *m.* basin, bowl; pan; — oculare, eye-bath; (geog.) — di raccoglimento, catchment basin; — idrico, watershed; (geol.; geog.) basin; — carbonifero, coal bed; coalfield; — idrografico, catchment area; (naut.) dock; — di carenaggio, — di raddobbo, dry dock, graving dock; — di ricovero, shelter basin; — galleggiante, floating dock; — di marea, tidal dock; entrare in —, to dock; diritti di —, dock dues; (eng.) tank; firebox (of a boiler); (anat.) pelvis; (mus.) †*pl.* cymbals. **-ella, -ętta** *f.* enamel basin; copper kitchen vessel; (chem.) water-bath; (photog.) tray. **-ętto** *m. dim.*; †helmet, basinet.

bacino[2] *m. dim.* of **bacio**, q.v.

ba·ci-o *m.* kiss; mangiare coi baci, to devour with kisses; tempestare di baci, to shower kisses upon; — di Giuda, kiss of Judas, betrayal; addormentarsi nel — del Signore, to die at peace with God; *adv.* a —, osculating. **-one** *m. augm.*, **-ozzo** *m.* hearty kiss.

bacio *adj.* (Tusc.) shaded; having a northerly aspect; *adv.* a —, in the shade; *n.m.* shade, shady site, north outlook.

bacis·simo *m.* (neol., cinem.) long kiss, esp. close-up of.

baciucch-iare [A 4] *tr.* to kiss repeatedly. (**-iamento** *m.*) **-io** *m.* hurried kiss, peck. **-ìo** *m.* continual kissing.

baciucco *m.* See **bacicci**.

bac-o[1] *m.* (*pl.* **bachi**) (ent.) caterpillar, larva, grub; 'worm'; silkworm caterpillar; — da seta, silkworm; roundworm, *Ascaris* sp.; (fig.) defect, taint; secret ambition; avere un — nel cervello, to have a screw loose; †amorous desire; †avere il — con, to be

bac-o (*cont.*)
angry with, to hate; †fare — a, to frighten; †fare — —, to play peek-a-boo; †avere i bachi, to be melancholy. **-a·io** *m.* (*pl.* **-a·i**) breeder of silkworms, silk grower. **-ato** *m.* (Tusc.) raising of silkworms; quantity of silkworms raised. **-ologi·a** *f.* science of silkworm breeding. **-olo·gico** *adj.* relating to the science of silk-worm breeding. **-o·logo** *m.* expert in silkworm culture. **-oso** *adj.* likely to go maggoty.

baco² *m.* (*pl.* **bachi**) ferry-boat.

bacocco *m.* (*pl.* **bacocchi**) dolt; sciocco —, silly billy.

ba·cola *f.* pod.

ba·cole *f.pl.* myrtle berries; cf. **baccola**.

†ba·colo *m.* rod, staff; mace; — pastorale, crosier.

bacte·rio *m.* See **batterio**.

bactromanzi·a *f.* water-divining, rhabdomancy.

†bacucco¹ *m.* head-covering, hood.

bacucco² *adj.* stupid; vecchio —, dotard.

†ba·culo *m.* See **bacolo**.

bada¹ *adv. phr.* tenere a —, to hold at bay; to ward off, to check; to baffle; †*n.f.* delay, wait; heed, attention.

bada² *imper.*, *2nd pers. sing.* of **badare**, q.v.

†bada³ *f.* rhinoceros.

badag·gio *m.* delay, waiting; expectation.

†badal-ic·chio, -i·schio, -isco *m.* basilisk.

badaloc·care [A 2] *intr.* (*aux.* avere) to dally, to dawdle. **-co** *m.* (*pl.* **-chi**) trifle. gewgaw.

badalone *m.* choir lectern (in Florentine churches); pedestal; †lounger; †large fat individual.

†badalucc-o *m.* skirmish, delaying action; toy, plaything. **†-are** *intr.* to skirmish; to delay; to stand gaping.

badan-a·i *m. indecl.*, **-a·io** *m.* (Tusc., colloq.) noise of people chattering, hullabaloo.

bad-are [A 1] *intr.* (*aux.* avere) **1.** Before a noun or pronoun, with *prep.* a: to pay attention; -a a me, listen to me; — alle faccende di casa, to be a housewife, to stay at home, to run the house; -a alle tue faccende!, mind your own business!; to pay heed, to care; senza — a, regardless of; to look after; — ai figliuoli, to look after the children. **2.** Before an infin., with *prep.* di: to be careful; -a di non scivolare, mind you don't slip; also *abs.* badi, chè qui c'è una buca, look out, there's a hole here; bada!, look out!; bada, io non gli ho detto niente, mind you, I never said a word to him. **3.** Before an infin., with *prep.* a: to continue obstinately; -ano a ciarlare, they just go on gossiping; *rfl.* to be careful; -atevi!, look out!; to be on one's guard; bisogna -arsi da un tale pericolo, one has to be on one's guard against such a danger; *tr.* to tend, to watch; — le pecore, to tend the sheep; to keep an eye on, to superintend. **-atore** *m.* caretaker, guardian. **-atura** *f.* (Tusc.) watching of vineyards at night.

†baderl-a *f.* coquette. **†-are** *intr.* to loiter; to trifle.

baderna *f.* (naut.) sennit, a braid of 'foxes', small strands of rope wrapped round a cable at points where it is subject to friction (serving); (eng.) packing (for joints, etc.); premi —, gasket.

badessa *f.* abbess.

bad-i·a *f.* abbey; comfortable home; (naut.) open roadstead; †benefice. **-iale** *adj.* huge; comfortable; genial. **-ialmente** *adv.* in comfort.

†badiano *m.* herdsman.

†badigli-are *vb.* and derivs. See **sbadigliare**.

badil-e¹ *m.* shovel, spade. **-ante** *m.* navvy. **-ata** *f.* shovelful.

badile² *m.* (numis.) Austrian bilingual coin (Italian and German) coined in 1801.

badin-a, -e *f.* small whip, cane.

badin-age, -erie *f.* (pron. as Fr.) (mus.) badinerie.

badosce *f.* (mus.) a dance from the region of Valle d'Aosta.

bafarella *f.* nap, doze.

baffare [A 1] *tr., abs.* (slang) to eat.

baff-o *m.* (usu. *pl.*) moustache; -i all'americana, toothbrush moustache; (of animals) whiskers; ridere sotto i -i, to laugh up one's sleeve; rialzare i -i, to twirl one's moustache; cosa da leccarsi i -i, something to lick one's chops about; un'occasione coi -i, a gala occasion; (slang) questo mi fa un —, I don't give a damn about this; smudge, smear; un — d'inchiostro, a long smear of ink; wash of a ship's bows, bow wave; 'ship with a bone in its teeth'; (typ.) ornamental rule. **-ona** *f.* woman with

hairy upper lip. **-one** *m.* man with a large moustache. **-uto** *adj.* moustached, heavily moustached.

†baga¹ *f.* jewel.

†baga² *f.* leather sack, wineskin.

baga·gli-o *m.* luggage; fare i bagagli, to pack; — a mano, hand luggage; — pesante, heavy luggage; ufficio bagagli, luggage office; consegna dei bagagli, left luggage office, cloakroom; visita dei bagagli, customs examination; baggage; accoutrements; equipment; (fig.) burden; — di informazioni, store of information; (mil.) kit, pack; armi e bagagli, weapons and kit; (fig.) perdere armi e bagagli, to lose everything; passare in campo nemico con armi e bagagli, to go over to the enemy lock, stock and barrel. **-a·io** *m.* luggage-van; (aeron.) baggage compartment. **-era** *f.* (motor.) boot, luggage compartment. **†-one** *m.* baggage-master; wretch, low-down individual. **-ume** *m.* piles of luggage; paraphernalia.

baga·i *m. indecl.* (dial. Lomb.) boy.

bagarin-o *m.* (econ.) person who makes a corner in a commodity; ticket tout. **-ag·gio** *m.*, **-ismo** *m.* (econ.) cornering; touting (of tickets). **-are** [A 1] *tr.* (econ.) to corner, to make a corner in; to tout (tickets).

bagarozzo *m.* (dial. Rome) cockroach.

baga·sci-a *f.* prostitute, strumpet, whore. **-o** *m.*, **-one** *m.* male prostitute.

bagasse *m.* (sugar manuf.) bagasse.

bagat(t)ell-a *f.* bagatelle, trifle; sleight of hand trick; conjurer's apparatus; trinket; †fare le -e, to have a gay time, to make merry. **†-iere** *m.* jeweller; juggler.

bagattino *m.* (numis.) fourteenth-century small Venetian copper coin; †worthless individual, bad hat.

bagatto *m.* name of a card in a game played with the Tarot pack.

bagge·o *m.* booby, fool, dolt; *adj.* foolish.

baggian-a *f.* large bean; †idle story, fib. **-ata** *f.* foolish action; piece of nonsense; sono -ate, it's all nonsense. **-eri·a** *f.* tomfoolery. **-o** *m.* booby, simpleton; idiot; uncomplimentary nickname for a Milanese; *adj.* stupid.

bag·giol-o *m.* (Tusc.) supporting block placed under marble or stone slabs when arranged for storage or transport. **-are** [A 1 s] *tr.* (Tusc.) to support with blocks.

ba·gher-o¹ *m.* four-wheeled carriage. **-ino** *m.* two-wheeled carriage, trap.

ba·gher-o² *m.* (numis.) sixteenth-century small Venetian coin. **-one** *m.* (numis.) copper coin formerly in use in Emilia and Venetia.

baghetta *f.* clock (on a stocking).

bagigi *m. indecl.* peanut, ground-nut, *Arachis hypogaea*.

†ba·gio *m.* See **bacio**.

†baglì *m.* See **balì**.

ba·gli-o *m.* (*pl.* **ba·gli**) (naut.) ship's beam. **-etto** *m. dim.* (naut.) intermediate beam, one of the smaller beams that pass between the 'bagli' and with them support the deck.

bagliore *m.* dazzling flash; glare; beam, gleam; glow; un tenue — di speranza, a faint ray of hope; false splendour, mirage.

bagna *f.* (dial. Lomb., Piedm.) sauce, gravy; — cauda, hot sauce-like savoury served in communal dish. cooked on a brazier in the middle of a table, and containing oil and anchovy.

bagnai(u)olo *m.* See under **bagno**.

bagn-are [A 5] *tr.* to wet; to soak; to dip; to suffuse; to damp, to moisten; to bath; to bathe; (of the sea, rivers, etc.) to wash; ogni acqua lo -a, the least thing makes him ill; (colloq.) — la laurea, to throw a party to celebrate getting a degree; — i galloni, — le spalline, to celebrate promotion; *rfl.* to get wet, to get caught in the rain; to bathe; to take a bath. **-amento** *m.* dipping; (text.) damping; (wool) steeping. **-ante** *part. adj.*; *n.m.*, *f.* bather. **-apolvere** *m. indecl.* (rlwy.) spraying cock. **-asciuga** *m.* (naut.) motion of the ship placing the water line now under water now above; water line; al -asciuga, 'twixt wind and water; (geog.) strip of land alternately dry and under water; territory periodically inundated by Lake Trasimene; (joc.) il Bagnasciuga, nickname for Mussolini who used the word to mean the line along the shore to which the water reaches; discorso del -asciuga, the speech of 24 June 1943 in which Mussolini used the word. **-ata** *f.* dip (bathing); wetting, soaking. **-ato** *part. adj.* wet; strada -ata, wet road; soaked; -ato fino alle ossa, wet to the skin; -ato di sudore, dripping with sweat; -ato fradicio, wet through; parere un

bagn·are (*cont.*)

    pulcino ~ato, to be like a drowned duck; se non è zuppa è pan ~ato, it's much the same thing; piove sul ~ato, it never rains but it pours; (mil. slang) dandified. **-atore** *m.*, **-atrice** *f.* See **-ino**, **-ina**, under **bagno**. **-atura** *f.* bathing, bathe; course of baths; bathing season; steeping.

bagn·o *m.* bath; bath-tub; bathroom; stanza da —, bathroom; swimming bath; bathing establishment; watering-place, bathing-resort; andare ai ~i di mare, to go to the seaside; fare un —, to take a bath; fare il —, to bathe, to go for a bathe; essere in un —, di sudore, to be in a bath of perspiration; mettere a —, to put to soak; (industr.) molten metal in a furnace; (photog.) — di fissaggio, fixing-bath; — penale, convict prison. **-ai(u)olo** *m.* bath attendant. **-arola** *f.* bath-tub, bath. **-ino** *m.*, **-ina** *f.* bathing attendant, swimming-pool attendant. **-(u)olo** *m.* hot fomentation; (bldg.) slaking vat (for lime). **-omari·a** *m. indecl.* (cul.) bain-marie, steam cooker; cuocere a ~omaria, to cook in a double saucepan; (chem.) water-bath. **-osab·bia** *m. indecl.* (chem.) sand-bath.

ba·gola[1] *f.* (bot.) bilberry, whortleberry, blaeberry, fruit of *Vaccinium myrtillus*.

ba·gol-a[2] *f.* chatter. **-are** *m.*, **-one** *m.* braggart.

bagord-o *m.* (usu. *pl.*) revelry, merry-making; orgy; tavern, meeting-place of revellers; †lance for jousting. **-are** [A 1 c] *intr.* (*aux.* avere) to carouse, to make merry; †to joust.

bah *excl.* expression of wonder, disbelief, contempt, or resignation; bah!

bai (onom.) senza dire nè ai nè —, without a word; without warning.

ba·ia[1] *f.* bay, gulf; bight.

ba·ia[2] *f.* jest, joke; fu detto per —, it was said in fun; trick, prank; ridicule, chaff; dare la — a, to chaff; baie!, nonsense!, humbug!; son tutte baie, it's all nonsense.

baiadera *f.* Hindu dancing-girl, bayadère.

Baiante *pr.n.m.* essere tra — e Ferrante, to come to the same thing, to be much the same thing; (of two opponents) to be equally matched.

Baiardo *pr.n.m.* Bayard, the name of Rinaldo's horse in Ariosto's *Orlando Furioso*; horse, steed; †*adj.* (of a horse) bay; extraordinary, unusual.

†baiare *vb.* See **abbaiare**.

baiata *f.* uproar; derision, hoots of laughter.

bai·colo *m.* (Ven.) wafer-thin biscuit; (ichth.) common bass, *Morone labrax*.

baila·m, bailam·me *m. indecl.* See **bairam**; (Tusc.) uproar, hullabaloo.

ba·ilo *m.* (hist.) title of various officials, esp. of the Venetian ambassadors in Turkey and Syria; bailiff; †guardian; †tutor.

ba·io *adj.* bay (colour of a horse); *n.m.* bay horse.

baioc·co *m.* (*pl.* **-chi**) (numis.) copper coin, formerly in use in the Papal States, worth about 5 centesimi; non vale un —, it's not worth twopence; fifteenth-century silver coin; *pl.* riches, wealth.

baione *m.* wag, wit; fare il — a, to scold; *adj.* witty, jesting.

baionett-a *f.* bayonet; — in canna, with fixed bayonets; assalto alla —, bayonet attack; inastare la —, to fix bayonets; (mil.) baionett cann!, fix bayonets!; crociat ett!, charge swords!; levatt ett!, unfix bayonets!; (electr.) zoccolo a —, bayonet cap, Swan cap; †infantryman. **-ata** *f.* bayonet wound; bayonet thrust.

bairam(o) *m.* Bairam, the name of two Mohammedan festivals: il piccolo —, the Lesser Bairam, lasting three days, which follows the fast of Ramadan; il grande —, the Greater Bairam, seventy days later, lasting four days.

†baire *intr.* to be dismayed, to lose courage, to quail.

ba·ita *f.* Alpine hut; hut for mountain farmers during the summer months.

†ba·iulo *m.* standard-bearer; tutor, guardian.

bakelite *f.* bakelite; plastic.

balafò *m. indecl.* (mus.) balafo (a kind of Negro xylophone).

balala·ica *f.* (mus.) balalaika.

ba·lan-o *m.* (zool.) acorn barnacle, *Balanus* spp.; (anat.) glans. **-ino** *m.* (ent.) nut weevil, *Balaninus* spp. **-ite** *f.* (med.) balanitis.

bala·scio *m.* balas-ruby.

ba·lata *f.* balata; gomma —, balata gum.

bala·ustio *m.* (bot.) pomegranate-flower.

bala·usto *m.* (poet.) See **balaustio**.

balau·str-o *m.* baluster; small balustrade. **-a** *f.* (bldg.) banisters; elemento di ~a, banister; (liturg.) communion-rail; †balustrade. **-ata** *f.* balustrade; hand-rail; altar rail; (archit.) breastwork;

(naut.) guard rails. **-ato** *m.* balustrade; circular Masonic letter from the Supreme Council of 33; *adj.* balustraded. **-ino** *m.* (eng. drawing) bow compass, spring bow compass; ~ino di precisione, hair compasses.

balbett-are [A 1 c] *intr.* (*aux.* avere) to stammer; to stutter; to lisp; to prattle; to babble; (naut.) vela che ~a, thrashing sail; *tr.* — una lingua, to speak a language brokenly; — una scusa, to stammer out an excuse. **-ante** *part. adj.* stammering, stuttering; lisping, prattling; faltering; *n.m., f.* stammerer, stutterer. **-atore** *m.* stammerer, stutterer. (**-atrice** *f.*) **-io** *m.* constant stammering; prattle, babble. **-one** *m.* stammerer, stutterer.

balb-o *adj.* stammering, stuttering; †*n.m.* stammerer, stutterer. **†-are** *intr.* to cry (of an infant); to stammer.

balbutire [D 2] *intr.* (*aux.* avere) to stammer; to stutter; to lisp, to prattle.

balbu·zi-e *f. indecl.* stammer; stutter; lisp; stammering, stuttering. **-ente** *adj.* stammering; stuttering; lisping; *n.m., f.* stammerer; stutterer; lisping individual.

†balbuzz·are, **†-ire** *vb.* See **balbutire**.

Balc·ani *pr.n.m.pl.* (geog.) Balkans; Balkan Mts. **-a·nia** *f.* Balkan countries. **-a·nico** *adj., n.m.* Balkan; la penisola ~anica, the Balkan Peninsula.

†balco *m.* See **palco**.

balcon-e *m.* balcony; french window opening on to a balcony; shelter built on the roof of a house for drying washing. (**-cino** *m. dim.*) **-ata** *f.* gallery; railed balcony; (naut.) ~ata di poppa, stern walk.

baldacchino *m.* canopy; tester; (eccl.) baldacchino.

†baldacco *m.* Babylon; brothel.

Baldassar(r)e *pr.n.m.* Balthazar.

bald-o *adj.* bold, daring, fearless; gallant; confident; in good spirits; epithet of the Republic of San Marino: la Balda Repubblica di S. Marino. (**-amente** *adv.*) **-anza** *f.* boldness; self-assurance; impudence; rashness. **-anzeggiare** [A 3 c] *intr.* (*aux.* avere) to be bold, to be forward; to dare, to take a risk; to rejoice, to triumph. **-anzoso** *adj.* bold; self-confident, fearless; haughty. (**-anzosamente** *adv.*) **-ezza** *f.* boldness, courage. **†-ore** *m.* boldness; high spirits.

baldo·ria *f.* gaiety; merry-making; fare —, to make merry, to be rowdy, to spend recklessly; †firework; †bonfire.

†baldosa *f.* (mus.) a Provençal stringed instrument.

Baldovino *pr.n.m.* Baldwin, Baudouin; †fool, simpleton; †penis.

baldracca[1] *f.* harlot, prostitute, whore; slut, strumpet; †brothel.

†Baldracca[2] *pr.n.f.* Baghdad.

Bale·ari *pr.n.f.pl.* (geog.) Balearic Islands. **-a·rico** *adj.* Balearic.

balen-a *f.* whale; — dei baschi, *Balaena biscayensis*; stecca di —, whalebone; olio di —, whale-oil; (of a person) è una —, he's as fat as a pig; (astron.) Whale, the constellation Cetus; (geog.) Baia della —, Bay of Whales. **-iera** *f.* (naut.) whaler, whaling-ship. **-iere** *m.* whaler (person). **-ottera** *f.* rorqual, blue whale. **-otto** *m.* young whale, calf.

balen-are [A 1 c] *intr.* (*aux.* essere), *impers.* to flash with lightning, to lighten; in men che non ~a, in a flash; — a secco, to flash summer lightning; *pers.* to shine, to sparkle; mi ~ò un'idea, an idea came to me in a flash; to reel, to totter; †to be uncertain, to be undecided, to be irresolute; †*n.m.* lightning, flash of lightning. **-amento** *m.* flashes, flashing. **-ante** *adj.* flashing: il ~ante Giove, Jove the thunder-bearer; tottering, reeling. **-io** *m.* continual flashing, repeated flashes.

baleno[1] *m.* flash of lightning, thunderbolt; (provb.) dopo il — viene il tuono, these are no idle threats; in un —, in a flash, in an instant; come un —, as quick as lightning.

†baleno[2] *adj.* pesce —, whale. Cf. **balena**.

balera *f.* (N. Ital.) public dance-hall.

balestr-a *f.* crossbow; catapult; a un tiro di —, a stone's throw away; — furlana, see **furlana**; (eng.) leaf spring; carriage spring; appoggio della —, leaf spring seat; foglia di —, spring leaf; (motor.; rlwy.) molla a —, leaf spring; staffa della —, leaf spring clip; (naut.) starting lever; (ichth.) pesce —, trigger fish, *Balistes capriscus*. **†-aio** *m.* maker of crossbows; vendor of crossbows. **-are** [A 1] *tr., abs.* to shoot with a crossbow or catapult; to catapult; (fig.) to shoot (an official) into some distant locality; (naut.) to sweat up (a rope); (fig.) to harass. **-ata** *f.* shot from a crossbow or catapult; range of a crossbow or catapult; †measure of distance, bow-shot. **-ato** *part. adj.* wounded by a crossbow or

balestr-a (*cont.*)

catapult; (fig.) afflicted; dejected. †**-eri·a** *f.* place for keeping catapults or crossbows; company of crossbowmen. **-iera** *f.* loop-hole. **-iere** *m.* crossbowman. **-i·glia** *f.* Jacob's staff, a kind of astrolabe for observing the height of the sun (now replaced by sextant or theodolite). †**-o** *m.* See **balestra**. **-ọne** *m.* augm. of **balestra**; (naut.) sprit (for certain sails); (Arezzo) pane **-one**, cake similar to **panforte**, q.v. **-uc·cio** *m.* short curved piece of wood in a silk-winder over which the silk passes; gambe a **-uccio**, bow legs; dita a **-uccio**, fingers twisted by rheumatism; (orn.) house martin, *Delichon urbica*.

bal-ì *m. indecl.* (hist.) Knight Commander in certain orders of chivalry. **-iag·gio** *m.* grade or office of a **balì**. **-iato** *m.* rank or functions of a **balì**.

bal-i·a[1] *f.* power, authority; in — di, in the power of; in — delle onde, at the mercy of the waves; in sua —, at his own choice; in — di se stesso, uncontrolled; (hist.) Dieci di Balìa, the Florentine War Magistracy. †**-iare** *tr.* to rule. **-iọso** *adj.* bold; powerful; exuberant, vigorous.

ba·li-a[2] *f.* nurse; foster-mother; — da latte, wet-nurse; — asciutta, nurse to a young baby; mettere a —, dare a —, to put out to nurse; †midwife; (orn.) pied flycatcher, *Muscicapa hypoleuca*; — nera, collared flycatcher, *Muscicapa albicollis*. **-a·tico** *m.* wage paid to wet-nurse; period of wet-nursing; duty of wet-nursing; child out at nurse. **-o** *m.* husband of a wet-nurse; foster-father; †tutor, guardian; †obstetrician.

Balilla *pr.n.m.* nickname of a Genoese boy, G. B. Perasso, who by throwing a stone at some Austrian soldiers started the revolution which drove them out of Genoa in 1746; *m. indecl.* member of the Fascist youth organization, 'Opera Nazionale Balilla', for boys from 8 to 14 years old; trade name of the Fiat 1100, a small family motor-car of the 1930's; brand of beer in small bottles; small firework, cracker.

ba·lio[1] *m.* See under **balia**.[2]

†**ba·lio**[2] *m.* governor; high bailiff.

baliọso *adj.* See under **balia**.[1]

balipe·dio *m.* proving ground for artillery.

†**balire** *tr.* to rule, to govern; to coerce.

balista *f.* (mil. hist.) ballista.

bali·stic-a *f.* ballistics. **-o** *adj.* ballistic.

balistite *f.* (explos.) ballistite.

balivo *m.* (hist.) bailiff, governor.

balla[1] *f.* bale (of goods); package; a balle, in great quantity; †measure of weight (c. 200 kg.).

ball-a[2] *f.* ball; projectile; tall story; raccontare delle balle, to tell tall stories; *pl.* (N. Ital.) balls, testicles. **-ista** *m.* leg-puller, one who 'lays it on'.

ball-are [A I] *intr.* (aux. avere) to dance; far —, to make things hum; far — su un quattrino, to keep in order, to make toe the line; quando non c'è la gatta, i sorci **-ano**, when the cat's away the mice will play; quando siamo in ballo bisogna —, now we've begun we must go on; to bump up and down; to rock, to vibrate, to totter; to rattle; (of teeth) to be loose in one's head. **-a·bile** *adj.* suitable for dancing; *n.m.* piece of dance music; dance tune; attaccare un **-abile**, to strike up a dance tune; ballet in a play or opera; gli accordi di un **-abile**, the strains of a dance tune. **-amẹnto** *m.* dancing; ball, dance; bumping up and down; vibrating; rattling. **-ata** *f.* dance; song for a dance; poem set to dance music; ballade. **-erina** *f.* ballerina; ballet dancer; prima **-erina** assoluta, première danseuse; professional dancer; good dancer; (mech.) circular saw; (orn.) white wagtail, *Motacilla alba*; (bot.) wild rose hip; black nightshade, *Solanum nigrum*. **-erino** *m.* male ballet dancer; professional dancer; teacher of dancing; good dancer; (watchm.) sliding gear; pignone **-erino**, wig-wag pinion; (ichth.) *Pomatomus saltatrix*, a fish related to the horse mackerel; (bot.) hawthorn, white thorn, *Crataegus monogyna*; wild rose. **-ettare** [A I c] *intr.* (aux. avere) to walk with a dancing motion, to trip along; to bounce along; (of a horse) to curvet. **-ẹtto** *m.* dim. of **ballo**, q.v.; ballet.

ballast *m. indecl.* (rlwy.) ballast; — incassato, boxed-in ballast.

ballatọio *m.* circular gallery going round a building; platform; (theatr.) flies; (naut.) projection round forecastle or poop of warship; *pl.* perches in a birdcage.

ballista *m.* See under **balla**.[2]

ball-o *m.* dancing, dance, ball; ballet; corpo di —, corps de ballet;

maestro di —, dancing-master; festa da —, ball; — in costume, fancy-dress ball; — in maschera, — mascherato, masked ball; — per sottoscrizione, subscription dance; canzone a —, see under **canzone**.) (med.) — di San Vito, St Vitus's dance; (fig.) in —, in play, in action; essere in —, to be involved; sono in — dalla mattina alla sera, I'm on the go from morning till night; (provb.) chi è in —, deve ballare, you've made your bed, now you must lie on it; tirare in —, to drag in, to bring in; non mi tirare in —, don't bring me into it; (aeron.) bump; †battle, fray. **-onchiare** [A 4 c] *intr.* (aux. avere) to dance awkwardly. **-ọnchio** *m.* country dance; 'hop'. **-onzolare** [A 2 sc] *intr.* (aux. avere) to dance, to trip along; to romp; to bump about, to bounce; to swing about in the breeze. **-ọnzolo** *m.* country dance; 'hop'.

ballotta[1] *f.* ballot; shot.

ballotta[2] *f.* boiled chestnut.

ballottag·gio *m.* See under **ballottare**.

ballott-are[1] [A I] *tr.* to put to the vote; *intr.* (aux. avere) to cause a division; to vote. **-ag·gio** *m.* (*pl.* **-agi**) second vote to decide between a number of candidates who did not gain a sufficient majority in the first poll; inconclusive ballot; scrutinio di **-aggio**, additional ballot. **-atura**, **-azione** *f.* ballot, voting.

ballott-are[2] [A I] *tr.* to bump about, to bounce. **-ata** *f.* (equit.) ballottade, jump. **-ato** *m.* tossed hither and thither.

ballotto[1] *m.* (metall.) metal congealed.

ballotto[2] *m.* (bot.) N. African oak with edible acorns, *Quercus ballota*.

balne-are, **-a·rio** *adj.* pertaining to bathing; stagione **-are**, bathing season; stazione **-aria**, watering-place, seaside resort.

†**baloardo** *m.* See **baluardo**.

baloc-co *m.* (*pl.* **-chi**) toy; plaything; trifle; †*adj.* stupid, silly. **-care** [A 2] *tr.* to amuse, to keep amused; *rfl.* to play; to fiddle; to idle away the time. **-camẹnto** *m.* amusement. **-cheri·a** *f.* childishness. **-cọne** *m.* idler; booby; trifler.

balo·gio *adj.* unwell, out of sorts, indisposed; (of weather) heavy, overcast; uncertain.

balord-o *adj.* dull; slow-witted; stupefied, stunned; odd, foolish; pointless; è un'idea **-a**, it's a silly idea; *n.m.* dolt, simpleton. **-ag·gine** *f.* dullness (of mind); stupidity; stupid action; dire delle **-aggini**, to say stupid things. **-eri·a** *f.* stupidity; folly; stupid behaviour.

balsa *f.* balsa, balsa wood; raft or fishing-float of the Pacific coast of S. America.

balsamella *f.* (cul.). See **besciamella**.

balsa·mico *adj.* having healing properties, healing; sweet-smelling; (of air) balmy.

balsam-ina *f.* (bot.) balsam, *Impatiens Balsamina* and other species; a sweet black grape (cf. **-ino**). **-ino** *m.* (bot.) balsam tree, *Amyris balsamodendron*; vine growing in Emilia or the Marches, yielding a sweet black grape. **-ite** *f.* (bot.) costmary, alecost, *Chrysanthemum Balsamita*.

bal·sam-o *m.* balsam, balm; fragrance; (fig.) comfort, solace; ointment, resinous medicament; — della Maddalena, miraculous remedy; (eng.) cleaning paste.

†**balsimare** *tr.* to anoint with balsam; to embalm.

†**bal·simo** *m.* See **balsamo**.

balta *f.* (Tusc.) upset, overturning; collision, shock; dare —, dare di —, to overturn, to get knocked over; gli dette di — il cervello, he saw red; dare di — a, dare la — a, to squander; †dare la —, to pass the peak, to pass the zenith.

bal·teo *m.* baldric, sword-belt.

bal·t-ico *adj.* (geog.) Baltic; gli Stati **-ici**, the Baltic States. **-o** *adj.*, *pref.* Baltic; (philol.) lingue balto-slave, Balto-Slavonic languages.

†**baltresca** *f.* See **bertesca**.

baluardo *m.* bulwark; rampart, bastion; (fig.) defence.

balucano *m.* (Rom.) short-sighted.

baluginare [A I s] *intr.* (aux. essere) to flash into view for a moment, to blink; to be seen indistinctly; to loom, to loom up.

†**balusante** *adj.* short-sighted.

balusco *adj.* squinting.

balz-a[1] *f.* cliff, crag, precipice; rock. †**-ana** *f.* cliff.

balz-a[2] *f.* band of contrasting colour round a skirt; flounce; dado; white streak on a horse's fetlock, 'sock'; (naut.) casing (of human torpedo); †head-covering, coif; †veil. **-ana** *f.* See **balza**[2]; (hist.) flag of the Republic of Siena. **-anẹtta** *f.* book-marker.

balza[3] *f.* See **balsa**.

balzano *m.* horse with white markings, 'socks', on the fetlocks; *adj.* strange, unusual; un'idea balzana, a crack-brained idea; (of a horse) with white markings, 'socks', on the fetlocks.

balz-are [A 1] (*aux.* essere, avere) to bounce, to bound; to jump, to spring; to leap; — in piedi, to leap to one's feet; il cuore mi -ò nel petto per la gioia, my heart leapt for joy; (mil.) — fuori, to sally forth; *tr.* to bounce, to throw down; il cavallo lo -ò di sella, the horse threw him. **-ante** *part. adj.* bouncing. **-ellare** [A 1] *intr.* (*aux.* essere, avere) to hop, to skip, to leap; *tr.* to leap out upon, to stalk; (fig.) to catch 'on the hop'. **-ello** *m.* skip, jump; tax; heavy duty, crushing tax; run (where an animal usually passes). **-ellone** *m.* hop, skip; jump, start; andare a -elloni, to skip along. **-elloni** *adv.* hopping, skipping.

balzo¹ *m.* bound, bounce; rebound; dare un —, to give a start, to start up, to leap to one's feet; il cuore mi diede un —, my heart leaped; prendere la palla al —, to catch the ball on the bounce; (fig.) to seize an opportunity; di —, bouncing, on the bounce; andare a balzi, to hop along; d'un —, in one bound; (naut.) boatswain's chair.

balzo² *m.* small precipice, promontory; terrace; dry wall supporting a terrace; vigna a —, terraced vineyard; scala a —, staircase with landings; †turban-like hair-style (fourteenth century).

bamba·g-ia *f.* cotton, cotton wool, wadding, cotton waste; (fig.) di —, weak, frail; tenere nella —, to mollycoddle, to take great care of; †hand-made paper; (bot.) — coltivata, cotton-plant, *Gossypium.* †**-ello** *m.* cotton wool pad used for applying cosmetics. **-ina** *f.* cotton stuff. **-ino** *adj.* cotton; *n.m.* dimity. **-iona** *f.* (bot.) Yorkshire fog, *Holcus lanatus.* **-ione** *m.* fat, lazy fellow. (**-iona** *f.*) **-ioso** *adj.* soft, fleecy; flabby.

bambar-a *f.* a card game resembling 'primiera'. **-ina** *f.* a game of 'bambara'.

bamberot·tolo *m. dim.* fat, chubby little baby.

bambin-o *m.* baby, infant; child; little boy; boy; fare un —, to have a baby; fare il —, to behave childishly; Gesù Bambino, Infant Jesus; (mil. slang) unexploded bomb, 'dud'; *adj.* childish, child-like, infantile, puerile. **-a** *f.* baby girl; little girl; young girl; †childish action. **-ag·gine** *f.* childish action; childishness. **-a·ia** *f.* children's nurse, nursery governess. **-a·io** *m.* (*pl.* **-a·i**) person fond of children; *adj.* (*m.pl.* **-a·i**) fond of children. **-ata** *f.* babyish remark; babyish action. **-eri·a** *f.* childish action; puerility, childishness; childish talk. **-esco** *adj.* (*m.pl.* **-eschi**) of a child, childlike, proper to a child.

†**bambo** *m.* baby; child; *adj.* babyish; childish.

bamboc·ci-o *m.* plump, bonny child; fine baby; silly person; rag-doll. **-a·io** *m.* (*pl.* **-a·i**) rag-doll maker or seller. **-ata** *f.* childish trifle; childish action; childishness; (art) picture of low life in style of Peter Laar, nicknamed il Bamboccio. **-eri·a** *f.* childish action, childish behaviour.

bam·bol-a *f.* doll; (colloq.) pretty girl; giocare alle -e, to play with dolls; †glass of a mirror. **-eggiare** [A 3 c] *intr.* (*aux.* avere) to be babyish; to behave like a child; to play. **-eggiamento** *m.* childish behaviour; play; romping. **-eggiante** *part. adj.* babyish; playful. **-ifi·cio** *m.* doll factory. **-ina** *f. dim.* of **bambola**; (slang) home-made hand-grenade.

bam·bol-o *m.* baby; little child; (bookb.) device for spreading oil on leather before applying gold powder; *adj.* undeveloped, imperfect. **-one** *m.* plump baby; fat little boy; childish person; *adj.* childish, childlike; happy, gay. (†**-ona** *f.*)

bamb-ù *m. indecl.* bamboo plant; bamboo cane. **-usa·ia** *f.* bamboo plantation.

banal-e *adj.* commonplace, banal; trite; common. **-ità** *f.* commonplace, banality; triteness; commonness.

banan-a *f.* banana; (electr.) spina a forma di —, spring contact plug; *pl.* (slang) money, cash, 'dibs'. **-eto** *m.* banana-grove. **-icoltura** *f.* banana planting, cultivation of bananas. **-iera** *f.*, **-iero** *m.* banana-boat. **-o** *m.* banana-tree, *Musa paradisiaca.*

banato *m.* (hist.). See under **bano**.

bana·usico *adj.* (aesthet. Croce) banausic.

banc-a *f.* table, bench; sotto —, secretly; bench of galley slaves; (naut.) dugout; (mil.) pay office; bank, banking house, banking establishment; — succursale, branch bank; affari di —, banking business; biglietto di —, bank-note; — del sangue, blood-bank; (joc.) — dei Monchi, imaginary bank. **-a·bile** *adj.* (comm.) bankable, current. **-ac·cia** *f.* (naut.) sleeping berth for captain of a galley near the stern; berth for steersman of a galley. **-ale** *m.*

(eng.) bed; -ale del tornio, lathe bed; cloth; †covering for a bench; †rug. **-arella** *f.*, **-arello** *m.* barrow, stall for selling books. **-a·rio** *adj.* banking, bank; assegno -ario, bank draft; casa -aria, banking house; credito -ario, bank-credit; *n.m.* bank clerk. **-arotta** *f.* (leg.) bankruptcy; -arotta semplice, -arotta fraudolenta, bankruptcy with wilful default, with fraud (with discreditable implication); fare -arotta, to go bankrupt. **-arottiere** *m.* bankrupt. †**-arotto** *m.* banker in a lottery.

bancata *f.* (eng.; naut.). See under **banco**.

bancato *adj.* (naut.). See under **banco**.

banchetta *f.* (naut.) stretcher for the rowers' feet in a galley.

banchett-o *m. dim.* of **banco**, q.v.; cobbler's bench; stall; banquet; (fig. pol.) — delle Nazioni, place in the sun. **-are** [A 1 c] *intr.* (*aux.* avere) to feast, to banquet; *tr.* to give a banquet to, to give a banquet in honour of, to feast, to dine. **-ante** *part. adj.* banqueting; *n.m.* banqueter, guest.

†**bancherottolo** *m.* money-changer's bench.

banchiere *m.* banker.

banchi·glia *f.* See **banchisa**.

banchina *f.* slab forming a seat; garden seat; (naut.) wharf, quay; diritto di —, wharfage dues; (naut.) footboard to which galley slaves were chained; (mil.) raised piece of ground behind the parapet of a fort for firing from; fire step; (rlwy.) platform.

banchisa *f.* ice-floe, pack-ice; — polare, shelf-ice.

banchista *m., adj.* bank clerk.

banc-o¹ *m.* (*pl.* **banchi**) slab; writing table; desk; bench, form; seat, settle; row of desks (in a classroom); counter; roba di sotto —, under-the-counter goods; vendere sotto —, to sell under the counter; — di chiesa, pew; (pol.) bench; (leg.) — della difesa, defence counsel's seats; — degli accusati, dock; sedere a —, to sit in judgment; bank (in proper names, e.g. Banco di Roma, Bank of Rome; see also **banca**); — del lotto, State lottery-office; (in roulette, etc.) tenere il —, to be banker; far saltare il —, to break the bank; (naut.; geog.) bank, submarine elevation; reef; shoal; floe; — di nebbia, fog bank; (naut.) thwart; (techn.) bed (of a machine); (eng.) bench; — da lavoro, workbench; — di collaudo, test bench, test bed; — di prova, test bench; (fig.) the acid test; (text.) — a fusi, fly frame, speed frame; — in fino, roving frame; — a fusi in finissimo, — in sopraffino, jack frame; — a fusi in grosso, slubbing frame; (miner.) seam. **-ac·cio** *m. pej.* rough bench; settle; (chem. eng.) first charge of fuel in an alum furnace. **-acci(u)olo** *m.* (paperm.) pressure beam. **-ata** *f.* (eng.) main bearings (of an engine); (naut.) space between thwarts. **-ato** *adj.* (naut.) fitted with thwarts. **-ocrazi·a** *f.* economic domination of banks. **-ogiro** *m.* (comm.) transfer of a credit from one customer to another in the same bank; clearing transaction. †**-onota** *f.* bank-note. **-one** *m. augm.* bench. **-oniere** *m.*, **-onista** *m.* bar attendant; man behind the counter.

Banco² *pr.n.m.* Banquo; l'ombra di —, the ghost of Banquo.

band-a¹ *f.* side, part, sector; band, border; da — a —, through and through, right through; place, site; mettere da —, to leave behind; leaf of a folding door or shutter; (radio; electr.) band; — di frequenza, frequency band; larghezza di —, bandwidth; (cinem.) — sonora, sound-track; (herald.) bend; (naut.) broadside of a ship; mettere alla —, to careen a ship for the purpose of cleaning her hull; alla —!, pipe! (an order given when the crew are to muster for the reception of a visitor of high rank); capo di —, bulwark; falsa —, lapside; poggia alla —, hard down the helm; orza alla —, hard up the helm; *pl.* flashes, stripes on uniform. **-ella** *f. dim.* (book-trade) inside flap of a book-jacket; blurb.

band-a² *f.* band; gang, party, group; company; (hist.) Le Bande Nere, the troops captained by Giovanni de' Medici, so called when they went into mourning for Pope Leo X; (slang) -e nere, speculators on the stock-exchange; (mus.) band; — militare, military band; maestro di —, bandmaster; flag, pennant, banner, ensign; (eccl.) processional banner; cloth draped round processional cross. **-ista** *m.* (mus.) bandsman. **-i·stico** *adj.* (mus.) pertaining to a band; complesso -istico, band-combination; musica -istica, band-music.

band-a³ *f.* thin metal sheet or plate. **-ella** *f.* (metall.) strap, hoop-iron; -ella a cerniera, counterflap hinge; -ella a croce, T-hinge strap; -ella a cuore, hinge strap; (electr.) bus bar.

†**banda⁴** *adv.* a —, in abandon.

bandag·gio *m.* (electr.) binding; binding wire.

bandato *adj.* (herald.) bendy; — di otto pezzi, bendy of eight pieces.

†**bandeggiare** *tr.* to banish, to exile.

bandella[1] *f. dim.* see under **banda**[1].

bandella[2] *f. dim.* see under **banda**[3].

bandera·io *m.* vestment-maker; †flag-maker; † standard-bearer.

banderẹse *m.* (hist.) captain, commander of a troop; governor of Rome.

bander(u)ola *f.* pennant, streamer; vane, weathercock; (fig.) fickle person, time-server.

bandier-a *f.* flag, ensign, colours; issare la —, to hoist the flag; ammainare la —, to lower the flag, to strike the colours; battere — italiana, to fly the Italian flag; — a mezz'asta, flag at half-mast; (provb.) — vecchia onor di capitano, phrase expressing pride in tattered ensign, or well-worn tools (often joc.); andare sotto le -e, to be called to the colours; portare la —, to be pre-eminent; voltare —, to change sides, to be a turn-coat; a —, haphazard; a — spiegata, with flying colours; (herald.) banner; guidon; (naut.) aiutante di —, flag lieutenant; (aeron.) mettere in — (un'elica), to feather; messa in —, feathering; posizione in —, feathered position; (tailor.) remnant; (electr.) plate lug (of accumulator); (ichth.) — rossa, red band fish, *Cepola rubescens*; †troop. **-a·io** *m.* maker or seller of flags.

bandina *f.* almandine, a precious stone.

bandinella *f.* roller-towel; blind; (eccl.) lectern-cloth; processional banner.

band-ire [D2] *tr.* to publish; to announce from the pulpit; to proclaim; to give notice of, to notify; — un concorso, to advertise a competition or a competitive examination; to banish, to exile; to dispense with; — le cerimonie, not to stand on ceremony, to dispense with formalities; †— la croce, to preach a crusade, to proclaim a crusade; †— la guerra, to declare war. **-imẹnto** *m.* proclamation; banishment. **-ita** *f.* grounds where no trespassing, grazing, fishing, shooting or the like is allowed; preserves; (fig.) special privilege; preserves; †proclamation; †a -ita, publicly. **-ito** *part. adj.* proclaimed; banished; tenere corte -ita, to keep open house; *n.m.* bandit; criminal outlaw; †exile. **-itore** *m.* town crier; auctioneer; preacher (e.g. of a political ideology). (**-itrice** *f.*) **-izzare** [A1] *tr.* to proclaim, to announce by proclamation.

bandista *m.*, **bandi·stico** *adj.* See under **banda**[2].

bando *m.* proclamation; edict; bann; exile, banishment; mettere al —, to outlaw; — alle sciocchezze!, no more nonsense!; mettere in —, to put on one side, to disregard; (leg.) — di vendita, judicial order of sale (C.C.P.); (naut.) in —, running free; mollare in —, to let run.

bandol-a *f.* (mus.) cittern, bandore. **-on** *m. indecl.* (mus.) large cittern.

bandoliera *f.* shoulder belt; bandoleer; a —, slung across the shoulder; in a sling.

ban·dolo *m.* head or end of a skein of wool or silk; (fig.) trovare il —, trovare il — della matassa, to discover the key to the difficulty.

bandọne *m.* sheet iron; plate; — ondulato, corrugated iron; corrugated iron rolling shutter.

bandoneo·n *m. indecl.* (mus.) a large accordion (after Heinrich Band who put it on the market in 1840).

†**bandono** *m.* See **abbandono**.

bandura *f.* (mus.) See **bandola**.

banjo *m. indecl.* (pron. **ban·gio**) (mus.) banjo.

†**bannire** *vb.* See **bandire**.

†**banno** *m.* See **bando**.

ban-o *m.* (hist.) the Ban, the viceroy of certain military districts in Hungary, Slavonia and Croatia, who took command in time of war. **-ato** *m.* (hist.) Banate, Bannat.

bansa *f.* variety of white grape.

bao bao *onomat.* fare —, to play peep-bo.

bar[1] *m. indecl.* bar, coffee-house; cocktail cabinet.

bar[2] *m. indecl.* (phys.; meteor.) bar (unit of pressure), 1000 millibars.

bara *f.* bier; coffin; fino alla —, for ever; avere un piè nella —, to have one foot in the grave; †litter, stretcher; †barrow.

baraba·u *m. indecl.* bogey-man.

barabasso *m.* (bot.) mullein, high taper, *Verbascum thapsus*.

Barabba *pr.n.m.* Barabbas; (fig.) rogue.

baracan-e, -o *m.* barracan, a coarse waterproof cloth of wool or goat's hair.

baracc-a *f.* cabin, booth; hut; shed; stall; piantar — e burattini, to give something up lock stock and barrel; to wash one's hands

of an affair; (fig.) things in general; aiutare la —, to help things along; mandare avanti la —, to keep the home going; to keep a business going; (colloq.) far —, metter su —, to revel, to carouse. **-are** [A2] *intr.* (*aux.* avere) to revel. **-amẹnto** *m.* revelling; hutment; encampment of huts. **-ọne** *m. augm.* stall at a fair; roundabout; esibirsi nei -oni, to be on show at a fair. **-onista** *m.* attendant at a fair.

barracchiere *m.* stall keeper, stall attendant.

baracchino *m.* (mil.) mess-tin; mountain hut.

†**baraccame** *m.* See **baracane**.

baracelli *m.pl.* (Sardinia) watchmen, guards (on the land).

baraccolẹtta *f.* (ichth.) *Raja alba*, a kind of skate.

barag·g·ia *f.* (geog., Lomb., Piedm.) infertile, leached soil.

baraọnda *f.* confused medley of persons coming and going; confused mass of papers, books, etc.; disorder; hubbub of a noisy party; hurly-burly, hullabaloo.

bar-are [A1] *intr.* (*aux.* avere) to cheat at cards; †*tr.* to swindle, to dupe. **-ata** *f.* cheating; trick.

ba·ratro *m.* gulf, chasm; the Abyss, Hell; den of iniquity; mill-race.

†**baratta** *f.* conflict; dispute; deception, trickery, fraud.

baratt-are [A1] *tr.* to exchange; to barter; to exchange fraudulently; to mistake; to cheat; — quattro parole con, to exchange a word with, to chat with, to converse with; — le parole, not to abide by what one has said; — le carte in mano a uno, to twist what someone has said; *recip. rfl.* to exchange (with one another); -arsi delle ingiurie, to exchange insults. **-amẹnto** *m.* bartering; barter; exchange, business. **-ato** *part. adj.* bartered; exchanged; †scattered, routed. **-atọre** *m.* barterer. (**-atrice** *f.*) **-eri·a** *f.* corruption in public offices; (leg.; naut.) barratry; †gaming house, casino. **-iere** *m.* swindler, trafficker; embezzler; rogue, cheat; barrator. **-o** *m.* exchange; barter; fare -o, to make an exchange; in -o di, in exchange for; comprare a -o, to barter; swindling, fraud; smart trick; (typ.) passage to be re-set; (in a narrow street) room to pass; (Florence) part of a street where a tram track is doubled to allow two trams to pass.

†**barat·tola** *f.* (Pulci) a species of aquatic bird.

barat·tolo *m.* jar, gallipot; jam-pot; tin, can; medicine bottle; †theme, subject.

barb-a *f.* beard; di prima —, youthful; sapone da —, shaving soap, shaving-stick; farsi la — a, to shave (oneself); fare la — a, to shave (someone); fare la — e il contrappelo a, to be a severe critic of; servire di — e di capelli, to put in one's place; in — a, in spite of, in defiance of; alla — di, to the annoyance of, at the expense of; farla in — a, to do a thing in defiance of, to diddle, to get away with a thing under (a person's) very nose; dare di —, to be meddlesome, to stick one's nose in; notizia con tanto di —, hoary old tale, news as old as Adam; resolute individual; strength, valour; virility; cunning; una — d'uomo, a brave man, a determined man; non c'è — d'uomo che possa farlo, there's not a man alive who could do it; bore; che —!, how dull!, what a bore!; roba da far crescere la —, boring stuff; (dial. N. Ital.) uncle, 'grand-dad'; (zool.) vibrissa, whisker; (orn.) barb of a feather; (text.) tuft, fibre tuft; (bookb.) untrimmed edge; un esemplare con la —, an uncut copy; (paperm.) deckle-edge; carta con -e naturali, deckle-edged paper; (naut.) painter (or similar short hanging rope); ormeggio a — di gatto, mooring with two bower anchors; (mil.) artiglieria in —, guns placed in a raised position to fire over a parapet; (bot.) root; mettere le -e, to put out roots, to put down roots; (fig.) to settle down; — rossa, madder, *Rubia tinctorum*; — di cappuccini, stag's horn plantain, *Plantago coronopus*; — di capra, mountain spiraea, *Aruncus silvester*; herb christopher, baneberry, *Actaea spicata*; — caprina, meadowsweet, *Filipendula ulmaria*; drop wort, *F. vulgaris*; — di becco, salsify, purple goat's beard, *Tragopogon porrifolius*; yellow goat's beard, Johnny-go-to-bed-at-noon, *Tragopogon pratensis* and other related plants; — di Giove, house-leek, *Sempervivum*; Jupiter's beard, *Anthyllis Barba-Jovis*. **-are** [A1] *intr.* (*aux.* avere) to take root; to put down roots; *tr.* to plant, to set; (fig.) to play a trick on. **-atella** *f.* (agric.) sapling; sucker; rooted cutting. **-ato** *part. adj.* bearded; (bot.) bearded; well-rooted; (herald.) wattled. **-atoio** *adj.* (joc.) heavily bearded. **-ẹtta** *f. dim.* short beard; man with close-cropped beard; -etta a punta, goatee; small root; barb (fish-hook); tuft behind a horse's fetlock; (mil.) barbette, platform within a fortification on which guns are raised for firing

barb-a (*cont.*)
over the parapet; batteria a -etta, battery en barbette; (naut.) painter, rope at the bow of a boat; rope for hoisting the skiff on board; rope for drawing the bow-chaser to the bow of the ship. -**ẹtto** *m. dim.* razor-wiper; (Flor.) i Barbetti, Fathers of the Mission, Lazarists. -**i·cola** *f. dim.* short, stubbly beard; (bot.) fine root. -**icọne** *m. augm.* (bot.) taproot, main root. -**igliọni** *m.pl.* (vet.) mouth ulcers of a horse, esp. glanders. -**ina** *f. dim.* (text.) thread guide; *pl.* (hist. cost.) lady's bonnet strings; hat veils which tie under chin. -**ino** *m. dim.* goat's beard; razor-wiper; miser; cruel person; (text.) eyelet; filament guide; *adj.* stingy, mean, miserly; (Tusc.) unintelligent; fare una figura -ina, to lose face, to be made to look a fool, to look mean. -**ọne** *m. augm.* thick, long beard; bearded man, 'beaver'; poodle; (leather manuf.) ear; (numis.) eighteenth-century coin of Lucca; (dial. Milan) vagrant who lives by begging; (bot.) white bryony, *Bryonia dioica*; lizard orchid, *Himantoglossum hircinum*; (vet.) an infective disease of the throat, 'strangles' in horses and 'wooden tongue' in cattle. -**oncino** *m. dim.* of **barbone**, poodle puppy. -**ọso** *adj.* bearded; boring, long-winded. -**otta** *f.* (naut. hist.) a kind of Venetian warship protected with shaggy leather and armed with a spur for ramming (used in Siege of Tyre, 1187). -**ozza** *f.* chin groove of a horse; (hist.) the part of a helmet which protected the chin and cheeks. -**u·cola** *f. dim.* See -icola. -**uta** *f.* kind of helmet with beaver; beaver; soldier wearing a beaver. -**uto** *adj.* bearded; having a long, flowing beard; (of a comet) tailed.

barbabie·tola *f.* beet, beetroot, *Beta vulgaris*; — da zucchero, sugar beet; — da foraggio, mangel wurzel.

Barbablù *pr.n.m.* Bluebeard.

barbacane *m.* buttress; (bldg.) scarp wall; (road bldg.) cross-drain; (mil.) barbican.

barbaforte *m.* (bot.) horse-radish, *Armoracia rusticana*.

†**barba·gia** *f.* (geog.) barbarous hill country in Sardinia.

barbagiann-i *m. indecl.* (orn.) barn owl, *Tyto alba*; (fig.) stupid individual, dolt, blockhead. -**eri·a** *f.* party of barn owls. -**ẹsco** *adj.* (*m.pl.* -**ẹschi**) pertaining to the barn owl; owlish.

†**barbagliare**[1] *tr.* to dazzle.

†**barbagliare**[2] *intr.* to stammer, to stutter.

barba·glio *m.* dazzle, glare; dizziness.

†**barbagra·zia** *adv. phr.* in —, by special grace.

barba·ia *f.* See under **barbio**.

†**barbano** *m.* uncle.

Bar·bara[1] *pr.n.f.* Barbara; Santa —, St Barbara, patron saint of gunners and lexicographers; (naut.) la Santa —, magazine (on a warship).

†**bar·bara**[2] *f.* female barbarian. See also **barbaro**[1].

bar·bara[3] *f.* (log.) barbara, mnemonic for a syllogism, consisting of three universal affirmative (A type) propositions; argomento in —, argument set forth in this syllogistic form.

barbare [A 1]. See under **barba**.

barba·r-ico *adj.* barbaric, barbarian; uncivilized. -**ie** *f. indecl.* barbarity; brutality.

barbarina *f.* (numis.) Mantuan coin of the sixteenth century with the head of St Barbara on it.

bar·bar-o[1] *adj.* barbarous; barbaric; fierce; cruel; crude; uncouth; 'Le Odi -e', odes by Carducci, entitled 'barbaric' because though they partly imitate classical metres they are written in a non-classical language; *n.m.* barbarian, savage; cruel individual; †native of Barbary. -**eggiare** [A 3 c] *intr.* (*aux.* avere) to write or speak in barbarous language. -**ẹsco** *adj.* (*m.pl.* -**ẹschi**) semi-barbarous; uncouth; *n.m.* a red wine of Piedmont. -**ẹsca** *f.* (joc.) female barbarian. -**iṣmo** *m.* barbarism. -**ità** *f.* barbarity; cruelty. -**iẓẓare** [A 1] *intr.* (*aux.* avere) to use barbarisms.

†**bar·baro**[2] *m.* See **barbero**.

barbassoro *m.* wiseacre; know-all; bore; self-appointed authority; (hist.). See **valvassore**.

barbastelo *m.* (ichth.) flying fish, *Exocoetus volitans*; (zool.) barbastelle bat, *Synotus barbastellus*.

barbazzale *m.* curb-chain; (fig.) curb, check; non portare — a nessuno, to have no respect for anyone.

barbera *f.* a red Piedmontese wine of high alcoholic content.

barberẹsco *adj.* See under **Barberia**.

Barber-i·a *pr.n.f.* (hist. geog.) Barbary; organetto di —, barrel-organ. -**ẹsco** (*m.pl.* -**ẹschi**) *adj.* pertaining to Barbary; Barbaresque; Stati -eschi, the Berber States, Tunisia and Tripoli-

tania; cavallo -esco, Barbary steed; *n.m.* groom for Barbary horses.

barberina *f.* (numis.) seventeenth-century coin minted at Avignon, named after Maffeo Barberini.

bar·bero *m.* Barbary steed; *adj.* cavallo —, Barbary steed; (hist.) Corsa dei Barberi, race between Barbary horses let loose in Rome between the Piazza del Popolo and Piazza Venezia.

barbẹtta *f.*, **barbẹtti** *m.pl.* See under **barba**.

barbic-are [A 2 s] *intr.* (*aux.* avere) to take root. -**amento** *m.* rooting, taking root. -**ato** *part. adj.* rooted; (fig.) deep seated, inherent.

barbicella *f.* (orn.) barbicel.

barbi·cola *f.* See under **barba**.

barbicọne *m.* (bot.). See under **barba**.

barb-iere *m.* barber; barber's shop; †blood-letter, surgeon. -**iera** *f.* barber's wife. -**ieri·a** *f.* barber's shop; †woman barber; †loose woman.

barbificare [A 2 s] *intr.* (*aux.* avere) to take root; to put forth roots.

barbigi *m.pl.* (joc.) whiskers; (ichth.) barbels (cf. **barbio**).

barbi·glio *m.* fish-hook.

barbino *m.* See under **barba**.

bar·b-io *m.* (ichth.) barbel, *Barbus fluviatilis*. -**a·ia** *f.* fish trap for catching barbel and other fresh-water fish.

bar·bito *m.* (mus.) barbiton.

barbitonsọre *m.* (joc.) barber.

barbi-turato *m.* (chem.) barbiturate. -**tu·rico** *adj.* (chem.) barbituric; i -turici, the barbiturates; *n.m.* (med.; pharm.) barbiturate. -**turiṣmo** *m.* (med.) barbitalism.

barbo *m.* (ichth.). See **barbio**.

barbo·gio *adj.* senile, decrepit; *n.m.* old dodderer, dotard.

barboti·n *m. indecl.* (naut.) capstan lugs.

barbọne *m.* See under **barba**.

barbotta *f.* (naut. hist.). See under **barba**.

barbottare [A 1 c] *intr.* (*aux.* avere) to murmur; to mutter, to grumble under one's breath; to make a bubbling noise (e.g. of things boiling).

barbozza *f.* See under **barba**.

barbu·cola *f.* See under **barba**.

barbugli-are [A 4] *intr.* (*aux.* avere) to mumble; to splutter; to falter; *tr.* to stammer out. -**amento** *m.* mumbling; spluttering; faltering. -**ọne** *m.* mumbler; splutterer.

barbula *f.* (orn.) barbule.

bar·bule *f.pl.* (vet.) mouth ulcers of a horse.

barbut-a *f.*, **-o** *adj.* See under **barba**.

barc-a[1] *f.* boat; barge; launch; — a remi, rowing boat; — a vela, sailing boat; — peschereccia, — da pesca, fishing boat; — a motore, motor-boat; — fanale, lightboat; — di salvataggio, lifeboat; (hydr. eng.) — porta, caisson; (eccl.) — di Pietro, St Peter's bark, (zool.) 'by-the-wind sailor', *Velella spirans*; tirare i remi in —, to ship one's oars, (fig.) to retrench; è una — che fa acqua da tutte le parti, it's a very shaky concern; (slang) wide, sloppy shoe. -**a·ccia** *f. pej.* of **barca**; tub; (theatr.) double box; †box on a level with the stage. -**ag·gio** *m.* (Leghorn) fishing-net. -**ai(u)olo**, -**ar(u)olo** *m.* boatman; ferryman. †-**alà**, †-**ala·i** *excl.* (naut.) word of command to a boat to come alongside. -**amenare** [A 1 c] *rfl.* to keep afloat; to manage to get along; to steer a course between difficulties; saper -amenarsi, to be good at getting out of difficulties. -**arẹccio** *m.* (naut.) fleet of small boats. -**arizzo** *m.* (naut.) gangway, opening from the side of the ship. -**arola** *f.* (mus.) barcarolle, Venetian gondola song. -**ata** *f.* boatload; loads.

barc-a[2] *f.* stack; heap of corn (or other cereal) to be threshed; armful, pile; a barche, in large quantities, galore. -**o** *m.* (dial. N. Ital.) stack of corn; granary. -**ọne** *m. augm.* stack of corn; †large cloud.

Barcellọna *pr.n.f.* (geog.) Barcelona.

barcheggi-are [A 3 c] *intr.* (*aux.* avere) to go out in a boat, to go boating; to sail aimlessly, to be driven hither and thither; *rfl.* (fig.) to get through somehow, to manage. -**amento** *m.* boating; sailing aimlessly; (fig.) getting out of difficulties.

barchẹggio *m.* boats; ship to shore traffic; boating; (fig.) getting out of difficulties.

barcherẹccio *m.* fleet of small boats.

barcher(u)olo *m.* See **barcai(u)olo**, under **barca**.

barchẹssa *f.* shed, lean-to.

barchẹtta *f. dim.* of **barca**[1], q.v.; skiff, dinghy; net for trout-fishing.

barchino *m.* dim. of **barca**[1], q.v.; punt (for wild-fowl shooting); small motor-boat; midget submarine.

bar·co *m.* (*pl.* **-chi**) large boat; †embarkation; †see **parco**. **-cobe·stia** *m. indecl.* (naut., Gen.) barquentine, brigantine. **-co·ne** *m. augm.* barge; lighter.

barcoll-are [A I] *intr.* (*aux.* avere) to totter, to stagger; to reel; (fig.) to rock, to be precarious; to vacillate; to begin to give way. **-amento** *m.* tottering, staggering; precarious position. **-ante** *part. adj.* tottering, staggering; insecure. **-ìo** *m.* continual staggering. **-one** *m.* staggering gait, tottering; uscire a -oni, to stagger out. **-oni** *adv.* staggering, tottering.

barco·metro *m.* (leather manuf.) barkometer.

barcone[1] *m.* See under **barco**.

barcone[2] *m.* See under **barca**[2].

bard-a *f.* bard, a stuffed pack-saddle for ass or mule; bards, a covering of armour for the breast and flanks of a war-horse. **-a·glio** *m.* quilt or stuffed sack used instead of a saddle. **-are** [A I] *tr.* to fit (a horse) with bards; to harness (a saddle horse); †to deck. **-amento** *m.* harnessing; caparisoning. **-ato** *part. adj.* caparisoned; harnessed; (herald.) with saddle, bridle and trappers. **-atura** *f.* trappings of a horse; harness; togliere la -atura a, to unharness; -atura di guerra, governmental emergency measures taken during a war which have not been repealed. **-osso** *m.* quilt or stuffed sack used instead of a saddle; a -osso, bare-back, (fig.) roughing it.

bardana *f.* (bot.) — maggiore, burdock, *Arctium*; — minore, *Xanthium strumarium*; (wool indust.; leather manuf.) burr.

bardare [A I] and derivs. See under **barda**.

bardass-a *m.* urchin; *f.* loose woman. **-o** *m.* rogue, rascal. **-one** *m.* male prostitute.

bardell-a *f.* cattle-drover's or rancher's saddle with large front saddle bow; pack-saddle. **-are** [A I] *tr.* to saddle with a 'bardella'. **-one** *m.* large saddle used for breaking in young horses and mules; (bldg.) the bottom row of bricks in an arch.

bardi·glio *m.* white and blue streaked marble.

bard-o *m.* bard, poet; *adj.* (poet.) bardic. **-ito** *adj.* bardic; poesia -ita, bardic poetry.

bardolino *m.* wine from Bardolino on Lake Garda.

bardott-o *m.* hinny, the offspring of a she-ass by a stallion; animal ridden by a cattle drover; animal used to tow a barge; boy or man who tows a barge; beginner, apprentice, trainee; shop-boy; †passare a —, to sponge, to scrounge, to get out of paying one's share. **-a** *f.* female apprentice or trainee; shop-girl.

barege *m.* (text.) Barege, gauze; (Tusc.) alla —, carelessly, any old how.

bareggiare [A I c] *intr.* (*aux.* avere) to cheat.

barell-a *f.* hand-barrow; stretcher; portatore di —, stretcher-bearer; (eccl.) feretrum. **-are** [A I] *intr.* (*aux.* avere) to vacillate; to waver; to stagger; *tr.* to carry in a barrow; to carry on a stretcher. **-ata** *f.* barrow-load. **-iere** *m.* stretcher-bearer. **-one** *m.* staggerer; drunk, drunken man. **-oni** *adv.* staggering.

barena *f.* (geog., Ven.) grass-covered shoal in lagoon awash at high tide.

baren-are [A I c] *tr.* (eng.) to bore. **-atrice** *f.* boring machine.

bareri·a *f.* See under **baro**.

†bargagn-are *intr.* to bargain. **-o** *m.* bargain; agreement.

bargella[1] *f.* (Tusc.) basket slung on mule-back; *pl.* (joc.) spectacles.

bargella[2] *f.* See under **bargello**.

bargell-o *m.* (hist.) foreign officer commanding the troops which kept order in the ancient Italian republics; chief constable; policeman; temporary prison in police station; (Florence) the Bargello, a building formerly the residence of the bargello, subsequently a prison, now a museum. **-a** *f.* gossip; sly woman; informer. **-ato** *m.* the rank of bargello. **-esco** *adj.* (*m.pl.* **-eschi**) relating to the bargello. **-ino** *m. dim.* (hist.) one of seven officers serving under the bargello; (numism.) an old Florentine coin of 6 denari. **-one** *m.* insolent individual. **-ona** *f.* mischievous gossiper.

bar·gila *f.* dewlap; 'tassels' or 'doddles' of a goat.

bargi·gli-o, **-one** *m.* wattles of a cock or turkey. **-uto** *adj.* wattled.

bari-centro *m.* centre of gravity. **-cen·trico** *adj.* barycentric, pertaining to or passing through the centre of gravity; asse -centrico, axis of gravity.

ba·rico *adj.* (chem.) baric (cf. **bario**).

barigilione *m.* barrel; cask; tub.

baril-are [A I] *tr.* (eng.) to tumble. **-atrice** *f.* (eng.) tumbling barrel, rattler. **-atura** *f.* (eng.) tumbling.

baril-e *m.* barrel; cask; wine measure (34 litres in Sicily, 44 in Naples area, 60 in Lazio and 50 in Tuscany); scarica barili (also **scaricabarili**) *m. indecl.* game in which two children standing back to back with arms linked try to lift each other; (colloq.) fare a scarica barili, to 'pass the buck'; (numis.) Florentine coin of 12 soldi and 6 denari; †beehive. **-a·ia** *f.* store, rack or vault for empty casks. **-a·io** *m.* barrel-maker, dealer in barrels; cooper. **-ame** *m.* quantity of barrels. **-etta** *f. dim.* See **barletta**[1]. **-etto** *m. dim.* (watchm.) barrel (holding mainspring); (mus.) barrel-joint (of clarinet). **-otto** *m.*, **-ozzo** *m.* squat, capacious barrel; keg; bull's-eye of a target; fare -ozzo, to get a bull's-eye.

barilla *f.* (chem.) barilla (variety of potash), seaweed ash.

ba·r·io *m.* (chem.) barium. **-ite** *f.* (chem.) baryta. **-itina** *f.* (miner.; chem.) barytes, heavy spar, tiff.

barisfera *f.* the core of the earth, barysphere.

barista *m.* bartender; barman; *f.* barmaid.

baritina *f.* See under **bario**.

bari·ton-o *adj.*, *n.m.* (mus.) baritone; (Gk. gramm.) barytone. **-ale** *adj.* (mus.) baritone; (Gk. gramm.) barytone. **-eggiare** [A 3 c] *intr.* (*aux.* avere) to sing like a baritone, to imitate a baritone.

barlac·cio *adj.* (of an egg) bad; (of a person) not feeling up to the mark, seedy.

barletta[1] *f.* small cask; barrel-shaped flask to hang from a traveller's girdle; (orn.) red-footed falcon, *Falco vespertinus*.

Barletta[2] *pr.n.f.* (geog.) Barletta; (hist.) La Disfida di —, the Challenge of Barletta.

barletto *m.* (eng.) bench holdfast.

barloc·chio *adj.* weak-sighted; *n.m.* person with weak sight.

†barlott-a *f.*, **†-o** *m.* barrel, cask; ribaciare il -o, to have another drink; pettinare il -o, sollecitare il -o, to drink to excess.

barlume *m.* gleam, glimmer; (fig.) — di speranza, ray of hope; — di un'idea, shadow of an idea; — di ragione, atom of meaning.

barluzzo *adv. phr.* a —, in the gloaming.

barn *m. indecl.* (atom. phys.) barn (1 sq. cm. × 10⁻²⁴).

Barnabita *pr.n.m.* (eccl.) Barnabite.

†barnag·gio *m.* baronage; gathering of barons; action worthy of a baron; noble estate.

†barnocco *m.* blow on the head.

bar-o *m.* cheat, swindler (at cards). **-eri·a** *f.* cheating. **-esco** *adj.* (*m.pl.* **-eschi**) like a cheat, cheating, swindling.

baroc·c-io *m.* waggon; cart; tumbril; load; large quantity; waggon-load; cart-load. **-ia·io** *m.* waggoner; carter. **-iata** *f.* waggon-load; cart-load; a -iate, in quantity, in profusion. **-ina·io** *m.* hirer of trucks; barrow-boy. **-ino** *m.* truck; hand-cart; barrow.

baroc-co[1] *adj.* (*m.pl.* **-chi**) queer, grotesque, odd; over-ornate; (archit.) baroque; *n.m.* (arts) baroque (style); a baroque work. **-chi·smo** *m.* (archit., lit. etc.) baroque; (fig.) oddness, queerness. **-cume** *m. pej.* (archit.) a lot of baroque works; a baroque work.

†baroc-co[2], **-colo** *m.* usury; illicit gain.

bar-ociclono·metro *m.* (meteor.) barocyclonometer. **-o·grafo** *m.* (meteor.) barograph, aneroid barometer. **-ogramma** *m.* (meteor.) barogram. **-osco·pio** *m.* (phys.) baroscope.

Barolo *pr.n.m.* (geog.) Barolo, in Piedmont; red wine of the Alba district of Piedmont.

baro·m-etro *m.* barometer, glass; (fig.) — ambulante, an ailing person who feels every slight change in the weather. **-e·trico** *adj.* barometric.

baron-e[1] *m.* baron; (hist.) title associated esp. with southern Italy and Sicily, where 'i baroni' were the rich and powerful squirearchy; — dell'industria, captain of industry; †game played with dice. **-ag·gio** *m.* baronage; rank of baron. **-ale** *adj.* baronial. **-ato** *m.* barony. **-cello** *m. dim.* young baron; young sprig of nobility. **-cino** *m. dim.* son of a baron; young nobleman. **-esco** *adj.* (*m.pl.* **-eschi**) baronial. **-essa** *f.* baroness; dame: la -essa Margot Fonteyn, Dame Margot Fonteyn. **-essina** *f.* courtesy title given to the daughter of a baron. **-etto** *m.* baronet; il -etto John Gielgud, Sir John Gielgud. **-i·a** *f.* barony, rank of baron; baronage.

baron-e[2] *m.* scoundrel, rogue; baron cornuto, an out-and-out rogue. **-ag·gine** *f.* roguery. **-are** [A I c] *intr.* (*aux.* avere) to cheat; to live by one's wits. **-ata** *f.* knavery, scurvy trick. **-eri·a** *f.* deception, fraud, roguery. **-esco** *adj.* (*m.pl.* **-eschi**) roguish. **-cello** *m. dim.* young scamp.

barosco·pio *m.* (phys.) baroscope.

baro·stato *m.* (aeron.; eng.) barostat.

barotermo·grafo *m.* (phys.) barothermograph.

barr-a *f.* bar; — trasversale, cross-bar; rod; line; stroke; tre — quattro, three over four, $\frac{3}{4}$; — di direzione, steering-rod; (geog.) sand-bar at entrance to a harbour; dyke; dam; (naut.) helm, tiller; bit (for a horse). **-ẹtta** *f.* (techn.) strip, cutting (for testing); (text.) faller.

barramina *f.* (mining) steel, drill bit.

barranca *f.* gulf, chasm, gully; abyss.

barr-are[1] [A 1] *tr.* to bar; to block; to barricade; (comm.) see **sbarrare.** **-ato** *part. adj.* barred, blocked.

†barr-are[2] *tr.* to trick, to cheat, to swindle. **†-eri·a** *f.* trickery, swindling.

barre *m.* (Tusc.). See **bar**[1].

barricadiero *adj.* (hist.) revolutionary.

barr-icare [A 2 s] *tr.* to barricade; *rfl.* to barricade oneself. **-icata** *f.* barricade; city gate for excise duties.

barriera *f.* barrier; road-block; breakwater; level-crossing gate; — corallina, coral reef; — scalabile, stile; salto della —, horse jump; — transonica, — del suono, sound barrier; — di razza, colour bar.

barr-ire [D 2] *intr.* (*aux.* avere) to trumpet (like an elephant). **-ito** *m.* trumpeting (of elephants); (Rom. hist.) battle-cry.

barro *m.* bole, a kind of odoriferous clay used for making drinking cups; pottery.

barroc·cio *m.* and derivs. See **baroccio.**

barrotto *m.* (eng.) fire bar (of boiler).

Bartolome·o *pr.n.m.* Bartholomew; (fig.) blockhead.

barucca *f.* (Ven.) zucca —, roasted pumpkin.

baruccabà *m. indecl.* confusion, hullabaloo, brouhaha.

baruff-a *f.* squabble; scuffling; confusion; hurly-burly; far —, to squabble; to scuffle; to rag; to come to blows. **-are** [A 1] *intr.* (*aux.* avere) to squabble; to scuffle.

†barull-are[1] *tr., intr.* to roll. **†-o** *m.* tumble, roll.

†barull-are[2] *tr.* to buy wholesale and resell retail. **†-o** *m.* retailer.

barzellẹtt-a *f.* joke, witticism, funny story; comic or gay song; prendere uno in —, to pull someone's leg; dire -e, to tell jokes. **-are** [A 1 c] *intr.* to joke, to tell funny stories; *tr.* to make game of.

†basa *f.* See **base.**

basalte *m.* See **basalto.**

baṣ-alto *m.* (miner.) basalt. **-al·tico** *adj.* basaltic. **-altino** *adj.* basaltic; basalt-like.

baṣano *adj.* filthy, dirty; vulgar.

baṣ-are [A 1] *tr.* to base; to found; *rfl.* to base oneself; to be based, to be founded. **-amẹnto** *m.* basing; base; (archit.) base of a column; base of interior wall-decoration, base or footing of walls; (eng.) bed, base-plate; (motor.) crankcase. **-ato** *part. adj* based, founded, grounded.

†bascià *m.* See **pascià.**

†basciare *vb.* See **baciare.**

†ba·scio *m.* See **bacio.**

bas-co *adj.* (*m.pl.* **-chi**) (geog.) Basque; (mus.) tamburo —, tambourine; *n.m.* Basque; beret.

ba·scula *f.* (watchm.) yoke, clutch lever; molla della — per calibro a —, rocking bar spring.

basculla *f.* weighbridge; weighing-machine.

baṣ-e *f.* base, basis; foundation; senza —, groundless; a — di, based on; in — a, on the basis of; (finan.) — aurea, gold standard; — navale, naval base; — aerea, air base; tornare alla —, to return to base; (pol.) party membership, party masses; floor (at pol. meeting); (chem.) base, alkali; (in appos.) basic; il salario-base, basic salary. **-ale** *adj.* (neol.) basic, fundamental.

baṣẹtt-a *f.* (usu. *pl.*) side burns; (of an animal) whiskers. **-ino** *m. dim.* (orn.) bearded tit, *Panurus biarmicus.* **-ọne** *m. augm.* man with large side whiskers.

ba·ṣic-o *adj.* basic, fundamental; (chem.) basic, alkaline. **-ità** *f.* (chem.) basicity; alkalinity.

baṣilare *adj.* basic, serving as a basis; di importanza —, of fundamental importance.

Baṣile·a *pr.n.f.* (geog.) Bâle, Basel.

Baṣile·o *pr.n.m.* (hist.) Basileus.

baṣiliano *adj., n.m.* (eccl.) Basilian.

baṣi·lic-a *f.* (eccl., archit.) basilica. **-ale** *adj.* basilican. **†-ata** *f.* basilica.

Baṣilicata *pr.n.f.* (geog.) Basilicata, a province in Italy.

baṣi·lico *adj.* royal (of decrees, proclamations); (hist.) libri basilici, Basilics; *n.m.* (bot.) sweet basil, *Ocymum basilicum*; — selvatico, self-heal, *Prunella vulgaris.*

Baṣi·lio *pr.n.m.* Basil.

baṣil-isco *m.* (*pl.* **-ischi**) (zool.) iguanid lizard, *Basiliscus* spp.; (myth.) basilisk; (astron.) the star Regulus in the constellation of Leo; (Byz. hist.) Basiliskos; †heavy piece of artillery 22 feet long.

Baṣilissa *f.* Basilissa, Byzantine Empress.

baṣimento *m.* See under **basire.**

baṣino *m.* (text.) bombasine.

baṣ-ire [D 2] *intr.* (*aux.* essere) to swoon; to faint with hunger; to fade away; to fade away; to be terrified; to be struck dumb with horror; †to die; †to come to an end. **-imẹnto** *m.* fainting fit, swoon. **†-ito** *part. adj.* dead.

basket *m. indecl.* (sport) basket-ball.

baṣof·fia *f.* See **bazzofia.**

ba·ṣol-a *f.*, **-o** *m.* (S. Ital.) large paving-stone. **-ato** *m.* paving, pavement (e.g. in Naples, the pavements made of volcanic rock).

bassa[1] *f.* (geog.) plain; low ground; shoal; southern region; south (of Italy, or of an Italian province).

†bassa[2] *f.* a kind of dance for two or four people; the dance for two was called — gioiosa; the dance for four was called — delle ninfe, or — imperiale.

bassa[3] *f.* (mil.) pass.

†bassà *m.* See **pascià.**

bassacorte *f.* poultry-yard.

†bassadanza *f.* (mus.) basse danse.

bassanello *m.* (mus.) kind of bassoon (named after its inventor, Giov. Bassano, *c.* 1600).

†bassare *vb.* See **abbassare.**

bassa·rico *adj.* See **bacchico.**

bassa·ride *f.* female Bacchante.

bassẹtta[1] *f.* card game (cf. Eng. **basset**).

†bassett-a[2] *f.* skin of a new-born lamb. **†-are** *tr.* to kill, to do in.

bassẹtto[1] *adj.* See under **basso.**

bassẹtto[2] *m.* the name of various Italian breeds of hound.

bassẹtto[3] *m.* (mus.) a small bass viol; short score; figured bass; corno —, basset-horn.

bassẹzza *f.* lowness; baseness; vileness; base action; poverty; low altitude; depth.

bass-o *adj.* low; low-lying; short (in stature), stooping, bent; a occhi -i, with lowered gaze; tenere —, to keep under one's thumb; far man -a di, to loot; nether, lower; (geog.) — piano, lowland plain; la Bassa Italia, southern Italy; il Basso Egitto, Lower Egypt; (of water) shallow; (fig.) essere in acque -e, to be in low water, to be short of money; (of black espresso coffee) strong; humble, lowly; mean, base, inferior; vulgar; gente -a, lower classes; shameful, vile; -a macelleria, lights, offal; — latino, Vulgar Latin; Basso Impero, Late Roman Empire; -e ore, hours at the close of day; di -a stagione, out of season; (mil.) -a tenuta, undress uniform; (of metals) base; (of currency) depreciated; (eccl.) — clero, lower clergy; messa -a, low mass; altari -i, side altars; (mus.) low-pitched; *n.m.* the lower part, foot, base; depth; bottom, bed (of a river); (Naples) dwelling at street level; alti e -i, ups and downs; (mus.) bass (in all senses, viz. bass of harmony, bass instrument, bass singer, bass voice, double-bass); lowest string of an instrument; — cantante, bass voice of lighter quality; — cifrato, — numerato, figured bass; — continuo, thorough bass; — ostinato, ground bass; — profondo, deep bass voice; — baritono, bass baritone; chiave di —, bass clef; *adv.* low; low down; da —, downstairs; in —, down; downwards; below; at the bottom; a —!, down with...!; guardare d'alto in —, to look (a person) up and down, to look at with disdain and condescension. **-amẹnte** *adv.* basely; meanly; vilely; vulgarly; popularly; simply. **-ẹtto** *adj.* rather short, undersized; voce -etta, apologetic voice. **-ino** *adj.* (Flor.) at a low ebb, not up to standard; siamo -ini in letteratura in Italia, literature is in a bad way in Italy; rather short, stunted, stocky; *n.m.* dachshund; †dish of macaroni or rice cooked in the oven.

bassofondo *m.* (*pl.* **bassifondi**) (naut.) shoal, submarine sandbank; *pl.* (fig.) lowest level of society; underworld; slums.

bassone *m.* (mus.) robust bass voice; bassoon.

bassopiano *m.* (*pl.* **bassipiani**) low-lying plain, lowland.

Bassọra[1] *pr.n.f.* (geog.) Basra.

bassor-a[2] *f.* bassora gum. **-ina** *f.* (chem.) bassorin.

bassorilievo *m.* (*pl.* **bassorilievi, bassirilievi**) (sculpt.) bas-relief, low-relief.

bassotto *m.* basset hound; dachshund; short man.

bassoventre *m.* (anat.) lower abdomen.

bassura *f.* (geog.) lowland; low situation; (fig.) low condition.

basta[1] *f.* tuck; temporary hem.

basta[2] *excl.* that's enough!; nonsense!; silence! (cf. **bastare**).

†**basta**[3] *adv.* sufficiently, enough.

†**basta·gio** *m.* porter, bearer.

basta·io *m.* See under **basto**.

bastalena *adv. phr.* a —, with all one's might.

bast-ante *part. adj.*, **-anza** *f.* See under **bastare**.

bastard-o *m.* bastard; foundling; mongrel; (typ.) bastard type; (naut.) mainsail of a galley; *pl.* parrel-ropes; *adj.* bastard; illegitimate; mongrel; not genuine, spurious; hybrid; adulterated. **-a** *f.* illegitimate female, bastard daughter; (naut.) type of large galley; (mus.) lyra viol. **-ag·gine** *f.* illegitimacy; (fig.) spuriousness. **-ato** *adj.* degenerated. **-ella** *f. dim.* girl foundling; saucepan; earthenware stewing-pot. **-ello** *m. dim.* foundling; †register, record-book. **-i·gia** *f.* state of illegitimacy. **-ume** *m.* illegitimacy; number of bastard children; odd mixture of spurious things.

bast-are [A I] *intr.* (*aux.* essere) to suffice; to be enough, to be sufficient; to last; **-a!**, that's enough!; stop!; nonsense!; silence!; that'll do!; oh well!; più di quanto **-a**, more than enough; **-a** che, so long as, provided that; non mi **-a** l'animo di, I haven't the courage to; questo non **-erà** una settimana. this will not last a week. **-ante** *adj.* sufficient, enough. **-antemente** *adv.* sufficiently; quite. **-anza** *f.* sufficiency; a **-anza**, sufficiently (cf. **abbastanza**). **-evole** *adj.* sufficient. (**-evolmente**, *adv.*) **-evolezza** *f.* sufficiency.

†**basta·scio**, †**bastaso** *m.* See †**bastagio**.

baste·e *f.pl.* (naut.) rubbing strake.

basterna *f.* decorated cart; litter; †cart pulled by oxen.

ba·stia[1] *f.* See **basta**[1].

basti·a[2] *f.* stockade; fort.

Bastiano *pr.n.m.* (abbrev.) Sebastian; (Tusc.) fool, blockhead; (joc.) — contrario, contrary Joe.

†**bastiere** *m.* saddle-maker.

Basti·glia *pr.n. f.* (hist.) Bastille.

bastimento *m.* ship; vessel; ship-load; — cisterna, tanker; — di linea, steamship; — di guerra, warship. — a vela, sailing ship.

bastina *f.* See under **basto**.

†**bastingag·gio** *m.* (naut.) dressing ship (with flags).

bastion-e *m.* earthwork, bastion; rampart. **-are** [A I c] to fortify with bastions; to build up in the form of a rampart. **-ata** *f.* group of bastions. **-ato** *part. adj.* bastioned. **-atore** *m.* builder of earthworks.

†**bast-ire** *tr.* to build. †**-ita** *f.* fortification.

bast-o *m.* pack-saddle; cinghie di —, girths; cavallo da —, pack-horse; (fig.) heavy burden; essere da — e da sella, to be maid of all work; portare il —, to shoulder a burden; mettere in —, to break in, to subdue; non portar —, not to be subservient to anyone; — rovescio, a hollow drainage channel in the middle of a road; a — rovescio, describing a road with a central water channel (as opposed to one 'a schiena d'asino', hog-backed). **-a·io** *m.* pack-saddle maker. **-ina** *f. dim.* light pack-saddle without saddle-bows or stirrups; overall worn by peasants when carrying heavy loads; (slang) false bodice (worn for smuggling); †(Flor. hist.) tax on goods transported on horse- or mule-back.

baston-are [A I c] *tr.* to beat, to cudgel; to thrash, to cane; — di santa ragione, to beat soundly; (fig.) to flay with words; to sell cheaply; — il pianoforte, to play the piano badly, to strum; *recip. rfl.* to fight; to come to blows. **-amento** *m.* beating; thrashing. **-ata** *f.* blow with a stick; beating; thrashing. **-ato** *part. adj.* beaten; (fig.) whacked, tired out; come un cane **-ato**, very down in the mouth. (**-atore** *m.* **-atrice** *f.*) **-atura** *f.* beating; thrashing.

baston-e *m.* stick; walking-stick; cane; golf-club; — animato, sword-stick; — alpino, alpenstock; club; — di maresciallo, marshal's baton; perch (in a fowl-house); handle (e.g. of a broom); tirare di —, to play at single-stick; (herald.) baston; — scorciato, baston couped; (naut.) boom, bowsprit; — della bandiera, flag-staff; (fig.) support, prop, stay; harsh government; mettere i **-i** fra le ruote, to put a spanner in the works; *pl.* (cards) in the Venetian or tarocco pack the suits are: **bastoni, denari, coppe, spade**, instead of: **fiori, quadri, cuori, picche** (clubs, diamonds, hearts, spades) as in the French pack (see also under **carta**); asso di **-i**, ace of clubs, (joc.) beating, thrashing; accennare in coppe e dare in **-i**, to say one thing and do another; (bot.)

— d'oro, wallflower, *Cheiranthus cheiri*; — di San Giuseppe, flowering branch of oleander, *Nerium oleander.* **-cello** *m. dim.* rod; long stick of sweet bread with aniseed; (archit.) rod-moulding; (in flutings of a column) cable-moulding. **-cino** *m. dim.* stick, rod; splint; **-cino** di pane, French loaf; **-cini** da sci, ski-ing sticks; kind of rusk; (archit.) astragal.

bastorove·scio *m.* See 'basto rovescio' under **basto**.

†**bastracone** *m.* strong, powerful man.

†**ba·striga** *f.* rope to fasten bundles on an animal's back.

batac·chi-o *m.* stick, pole; clapper (of a bell); dolt, fool. **-are** [A 4] *tr.* to beat; to knock down. **-ata** *f.* blow with a stick; stroke of a clapper.

†**ba·talo** *m.* See **batolo**.

batano *adj.* (Tusc.) huge, enormous, gross. (cf. **patano**.)

†**batassare** *tr.* to shake; *intr.* to tremble, to shake.

†**bataste·o** *m.* conflict.

batata *f.* sweet potato, *Ipomoea batatas*.

batillo[1] *pr.n.m.* catamite, after Bathyllus, a youth celebrated by Anacreon.

batillo[2] *m.* (Pisa, agric.) wooden shovel used in winnowing.

bati·metro *m.* and derivs. See **batometro**.

batiscafo *m.* bathyscaphe; submersible vessel for deep-sea observation.

batisfera *f.* the ocean depths, the depths of the sea; bathysphere, deep diving bell.

batista[1] *f.* (text.) cambric, lawn, batiste.

batista[2] *m.* (dial. Lomb.) fool; simpleton.

Batiston *pr.n.m.* Baptiste, eighteenth-century carnival character.

bato *m.* (Hebr. measure) bath.

batoc·chio *m.* clapper of a bell; blind man's walking-stick.

batoc-co *m.* (*pl.* **-chi**) (mus.) popular two-part song of the Marche.

batolite *f.* (geol.) batholith.

ba·tolo *m.* doctor's or lawyer's hood; (eccl., chiefly Tusc.) kind of tippet or cape; underwater foundation of pier; platform.

bato·m-etro *m.* bathymeter; any sounding apparatus other than that of simply heaving the lead. **-etri·a** *f.* depth measurement, sounding, bathymetry. **-e·trico** *adj.* bathymetric.

batost-a *f.* severe blow; reverse, set-back, misfortune, stroke of ill-luck; (iron.) una bella —, a nice thing to happen; dispute, quarrel, skirmish. †**-are** *intr.* to fight; to squabble; to come to blows.

batrac-e *m.* (zool.) batrachian. **-omiomachi·a** *f.* Batrachomyomachy (the Greek mock-heroic poem *Battle of Frogs and Mice*); (fig.) useless polemics.

batra-co *m.* (*pl.* **-chi**). See **batrace**.

batta·gli-a *f.* battle; fight; fray; conflict, struggle; disagreement; (art) battle-scene; campo di —, battlefield; dare —, to give battle; finta —, mock battle; (fig. joc.) cavallo di —, hobby-horse, favourite topic; (of an actor) favourite part; (naut.) centre column; †duel; †(mil.) company; line; †in —, drawn up. **-are** [A 4] *intr.* (*aux.* avere) to fight, to battle, to war; to wrangle; to struggle. †**-era** *f.* fortification; woman warrior. **-ere**, **-ero** *adj.* warlike, combative; *n.m.* warrior; champion. †**-eresco** *adj.* quarrelsome, bellicose. †**-evole** *adj.* bellicose; martial. †**-evolmente** *adv.* in a warlike manner.

batta·glio *m.* clapper (of a bell); door-knocker; (herald.) clapper.

battagliole *f.pl.* (naut.) stanchions, berthing rails.

battaglione *m.* battalion; (fig.) multitude; †soldier in a battalion.

battaglista *m.* (art) painter of battle scenes.

battana *f.* (Ven.) flat-bottomed boat.

†**batteggiare** *vb.* See **battezzare**.

battell-o *m.* boat; — galleggiante, lightship; — pneumatico, rubber dinghy; — a remi, rowing-boat; — di salvataggio, lifeboat. **-ante** *m.* (neol.) boatman. **-ata** *f.* boatload. **-iere** *m.* boatman, waterman.

battello-porta *m. indecl.* (naut. eng.) caisson.

battente *m.* See under **battere**.

bat·t-ere [B I] *tr.*

1. To beat; — uno, to beat a person, to thrash someone; **-ersi** il petto, to beat one's breast; — il piede, to stamp one's foot; — le mani, to clap one's hands, to applaud; — il metallo, to beat metal; la pioggia **-e** i vetri, the rain lashes the window-panes; le onde **-ono** (contro) gli scogli, the waves beat against the rocks; un luogo **-uto** dal sole, a sun-drenched spot; dove non

bat·t-ere (*cont.*)

-e mai il sole, where the sun never reaches; — un tappeto, to beat a carpet; — il tempo, to beat time; — la musica, to conduct; (sport) — una campagna, to beat an area of country, to beat a covert (for shooting); (tennis) — la palla, to serve; (provb. uses) — la sella non potendo — il cavallo, — il cane invece del padrone, to take it out of someone who cannot answer back; — la solfa, to keep harping on the same string, to be the boss, to wear the trousers; — l'acqua nel mortaio, to flog a dead horse. **2.** To defeat, to vanquish, to beat, to take by assault: — il nemico, to defeat the enemy; — un avversario, to vanquish an adversary; — un concorrente, to beat a rival; ha -uto tutti, he has come out top. **3.** To strike, to hit, to knock, to tap, to clatter: — le ore, to strike the hours; sono -ute le sei, it has struck six; — moneta, to strike coins, to mint coins, (fig.) to lay hands on some ready money; — il capo nel muro, to knock one's head against the wall; non sapere dove — il capo, not to know which way to turn, to be in desperate straits, to see no way out of a difficulty; — un chiodo, to knock in a nail; — un malato, to sound a patient; — i tasti di una macchina da scrivere, to tap the keys of a typewriter; — a macchina, to type; — il tacco, to take to one's heels; — il naso in, to run into, to come across by chance; (provb. uses) — il ferro mentre è caldo, to strike while the iron is hot; la lingua -e dove il dente duole, tongue ever turns to aching tooth. **4.** To thresh: — il grano, to thresh the grain; — la canapa, to beat hemp; — il lino, to swingle flax. **5.** To tread, to traverse, to frequent, to tramp; — un luogo, to frequent a place; — una strada, to traverse the same path frequently; — le strade, (of a woman) to go on the streets; — una regione, (of a commercial traveller) to work a territory; — la campagna, to comb the district, (fig.) to digress; — una carriera, to make a career for oneself; — la via degli studii, to devote oneself to a life of study. **6.** To flutter, to knock together, to rattle, to bat: — le ali, to beat one's wings, to fly; in un batter d'ala, in the twinkling of an eye; hanno tanto freddo che -ono i denti, they are so cold their teeth are chattering; — gli occhi, to blink; — l'occhio, to wink; in un batter d'occhio, in the twinkling of an eye; non — ciglio, not to bat an eyelid, to gaze unwinkingly, not to flinch, to be unafraid, to be completely absorbed. **7.** To insist upon, to emphasize, to hammer home: — una parola, to emphasize a word; — una sillaba, to pronounce a syllable with particular distinctness; — un punto, — il chiodo, to hammer home a point, to drive home a point; — sempre su un tasto, to be continually harping on a subject; batti e ribatti, by dint of repeated insistence; (cards) — gli atout, to draw trumps. **8.** Military and Nautical Uses: (mil.) — l'assemblea, — l'attenti, bugle calls to summon for assembly and parade; (of artillery) to strafe, to pound; (naut.) — le ore, to strike the ship's bell; — bandiera italiana, to fly the Italian flag; — il mare, to flog the seas, interminably cruising. **9.** intr. (*aux.* avere, essere) to beat; il cuore gli -eva forte, his heart was beating fast; to pulsate; to palpitate; to tick; to twitch; to flap, to toss about; le tendine -evano al vento, the curtains were flapping in the wind; to jar; (of an engine) to pink; — a, to knock at, to knock on; — all'uscio, to knock at the door; — in, to frequent, to visit frequently; ci -o spesso, I'm a frequent visitor there; secondo come la -e, according to the way things turn out; -e giù di lì, it's almost there, nearly, not quite; non intendo dove vada a — questo discorso, I can't catch the drift of this speech, *or*, what he's driving at; *rfl.* (*acc. of prn.* si) to beat oneself; (*dat. of prn.* si) -ersela, to run away, to make off; -ersi il petto, to beat one's breast, (fig.) to repent; *recip. rfl.* to fight; to duel. **-ente** *m.* leaf of a folding door or shutter; porta a due -enti, double-leafed door; serrare a due -enti, to lock up securely; part of a frame of a mirror, picture, etc., into which the glass fits; clapper (of a bell); door-knocker; flap (of a desk); lid; (text.) sley, batten; (watchm.) hammer in a striking clock; -ente di suoneria, alarm clapper; (hydr.) -ente d'acqua, head of water; (naut.) hatch, combing, raised sill of a port, any aperture in a deck; -ente di boccaporto, washboard. **-entino** *m. dim.* (text.) trimming ribbon. (For compounds such as **battibecco**, etc. see under **battibaleno**.) **-erista** *m.* (mus.) percussion player, drummer. **-imento** *m.* beating; battering; hammering; (med.) -imento delle palpebre, involuntary twitching of the upper eyelids; (mus.) battery, i.e. a chord in arpeggio; il -imento dei trilli, the repercussions in making a shake; *pl.* (mus.; phys.) beats (produced

between notes of very similar but not identical pitch). **-itore** *m.* beater; scout; (sport) beater for game; (ball-games) server; batsman; (typ.) inker. **-itrice** *f.* (agric.) threshing-machine. **-itura** *f.* beating; thrashing; threshing; rabetting. **-otto** *excl.* (naut.) make it noon! **-uta** *f.* blow, stripe; act of beating or striking; clapping; stamping; beat of the pulse; stress (on a syllable); tick, ticking; -uta di ali, flapping of wings; in due o tre -ute, in two ticks; (naut.) stroke of an oar; (mus.) measure, bar; beat (of a conductor); cantare a -uta, to sing to the beat, to sing in time; -uta d'aspetto, bar's rest, (fig.) lull, pause; -uta in aria, up beat; -uta in terra, down beat; (sport) shooting party; beating of coverts; run of an animal; (tennis) service; (billiards) stuffing of the cushions; (theatr.) sentence which forms part of dialogue; cue; sally, quip, 'bon mot', witty remark; (carp.) ledge, shoulder; (topogr.) sight; part of a river where the current runs against the bank; beaten track; andare per la -uta, to keep to the beaten track. **-uto** *part. adj.* beaten; struck; frequented; la strada -uta, the beaten track; threshed; hammered; coined, minted; ferro -uto, wrought iron; oro -uto, beaten gold; a spron -uto, full pelt; *n.m.* (cul.) stuffing, forcemeat; roux; (bldg.) type of stone and cement flooring; (numis.) Tuscan coin of 8 denari.

batteri·a *f.* battery; (electr.) — di accumulatori, storage battery; (mech.) striking mechanism (of a clock); (naut.) battery, battery deck; — galleggiante, floating battery; (mil.) — di costa, coast battery; outfit, system, set; — di cucina, kitchen utensils, kitchen ware; (mus.) percussion-group, battery; (sport) heat; (fig.) scoprire le batterie, to give the show away, to let the cat out of the bag; avere le batterie scariche, to be run down in health.

batt-erio *m.* bacterium, bacillus. **-ericida** *m.* germicide. **-e·ridi** *m.pl.* microbes. **-eriologi·a** *f.* bacteriology. **-eriolo·gico** *adj.* bacteriological. **-erio·logo** *m.* bacteriologist.

batterista *m.* (mus.). See under **battere**.

battesim-o *m.* baptism, christening; blessing; nome di —, Christian name; tenere qualcuno a —, to stand as godparent to someone; — del fuoco, baptism of fire. **-ale** *adj.* baptismal; tenere al fonte -ale, to stand as godparent to.

†**battesmo** *m.* See **battesimo**.

battezz-are [A I C] *tr.* to baptize, to christen; to bless (bell, ship); to be godparent to; to name; (fig.) to misname; to wet, to soak; (colloq.) to water (wine); *rfl.* to be baptized; to undergo baptism; (fig.) to give oneself out as; to become initiated. **-amento** *m.* baptism; baptizing; christening. **-ando** *m.* person to be baptized. **-ato** *part. adj.* baptized, christened; named; (provb.) -ato in domenica, stupid; *n.m.* i -ati, the baptized. **-atoio**, **-ato·rio** *m.* baptistry, font. **-iere** *m.* (**-atore** *m.*) (Tusc.) priest baptizing (esp. in place of parish priest).

battiale *m.* (hatm.) crown press.

batti-baleno *adv. phr.* in un —, in an instant, in a flash. **-becco** *m.* (*pl.* -becchi) tiff, bickering, squabble; venire a -becco, to squabble. **-calcagno** *m.* (motor.) sill board. **-carne** *m. indecl.* mallet for pounding meat. **-coda** *f.* (orn.) wagtail. **-coffa** *m.*, *f.* (naut.) the tabling or lining, sewn on to a topsail where it is liable to fray against the top, top-lining. **-culo** *m.* (mil. hist.) part of the armour which protected the posterior; (naut.) mizzen; (joc.) tails of a dress jacket; the jacket itself. **-cuore** *m.* palpitation of the heart; heart-beat; (fig.) fear, fright, shock. **-ferro** *m.* mechanical hammer for beating iron. **-fianco** *m.* (*pl.* -fianchi) partition bar between horses in a stable where there are no fixed partitions. **-folle** *m.* citadel; fortification. **-fondo** *m.* a form of billiards in which one player plays against several others successively, undertaking to beat them all. †**-fredo** *m.* (mil. hist.) wooden tower. †**-fuoco** *m.* steel (for striking fire). **-gliuolo** *m.* flax cleaner. †**-lano** *m.* wool-carder. **-lastra** *m.* (eng.) panel-beater, sheet-metal worker. †**-lo·glia** *f.*, †**-lo·glio** *m.* coif. **-loc·chio** *m.* bonnet; veil; coif. **-loro** *m.* gold-beater. **-mano**, **-mani** *m. indecl.* clapping; applause. **-mare** *m.* (naut.) washboard, breakwater. **-mazza** *m. indecl.* blacksmith's mate. **-muro**, **-murino** *m.* boys' game of throwing coins against a wall. **-palla**, **-palle** *m.* head of a ramrod. **-palo** *m.* pile-driver. **-panni** *m. indecl.* rug-beater. **-petto** *m.* beating of the breast in sorrow, contrition. **-piastra** *m.* base-plate for beating. **-porta** *f.* double door; door-knocker. **-porto** *m.* hatchway. **-rame** *m.* coppersmith. **-scarpa** *adv. phr.* a -scarpa, in haste; mangiare a -scarpa, to eat standing up, to eat in a hurry. **-scopa** *adj. indecl.* (bldg.) zoccolo -scopa, skirting board (also *n.m.*). **-segola** *f.* (bot.) cornflower, *Centaurea cyanus*. **-soffia**, **-soffiola** *f.* sudden fright;

batti-baleno (cont.)
avere la -soffia, to be scared. **-spiag·gia** f. (naut.) revenue cutter. **-spolvere, -spolvero** m. (art) pounce. **-strada** m. indecl. outrider preceding a carriage; (joc.) far da -strada a uno, to go in front of someone as though to announce him; (fig.) fare da -strada, to smooth the way; pace-maker, tread (of a tyre); ricostruire il -strada a, to retread (a tyre); (rlwy.) locomotiva -strada, pilot engine. **-suo·cera** f. (bot.) see battisegola.

batti·gia[1] f. water-line on the shore, point to which the waves reach.

†**batti·gia**[2] f. epileptic fit; convulsions; illness.

bat·tima f. See battigia[1].

batt-io m. (pl.-ii) prolonged clapping of hands.

Battist-a pr.n.m. Baptiste; (Bibl.) the Baptist. **-ero, -e·rio,**† **-e·o** m. baptistry.

bat·tit-o m. pulsation; heart-beat; throb, throbbing; beating; tick, ticking; rattle; knocking; (motor.) — dello stantuffo, piston slap; (med.) quickened pulse; convulsive trembling; palpitation; (fig.) fear and trembling; that part of the beach washed by the waves. **-oia** f. (typ.) planer, wooden block for forcing down the type in a form and making the surface even. **-oio** m. rabbet of a door or window which when shut is in contact with the frame of the opening; projecting part of a cornice; beater; valve of a force-pump; (text.) willow; scutcher, beater; -oio cardatore, carding willow; †(mus.) conductor's baton; †battering-ram. **-ore** m., **-rice** f., see under battere. **-ura** f. succession of blows; -ura di Cristo, the scourging of Christ; threshing; the threshing season; imprint of the blow of a hammer; (techn.) the flakes of metal which come away during beating; (bldg.) tamping, ramming.

†**batto** m. boat.

bat·tol-a f. clack, clapper of a mill; (eccl.) clapper (as used in Holy Week); (metall.) rammer; (text.) beater arm; pl. facings on a magistrate's or lawyer's collar. **-are** [A1s] intr. (aux. avere) to chatter, to prattle. **-ona** f., **-one** m. noisy chatterbox.

battol-ogi·a f. battology, a needless repetition in speaking or writing. **-o·gico** adj. battological. **-ogizzare** [A1] intr. (aux. avere) to battologize.

battuta f. See under battere.

batuf·fol-o, batu·folo, batuffo m. little wad; — di cotone, little piece of cotton wool; (fig.) chubby baby; pl. padding, pads.

ba·tulo m. See batolo.

bau m. indecl. dog's bark; bow-wow; bogey, ogre, bogey-man; far — —, to play peep-bo. **-sette** m. bogey-man.

baubau m. (Tusc.). See babau.

†**bauc·co** m. porre al —, to ridicule; to reprove.

bauin·do m. (bldg.) bay-window.

bau·l-e m. travelling trunk; far il —, to pack, to pack up, to go away; viaggiare come i -i, to travel without seeing anything; disfare il —, to unpack; (fig. joc.) hunchback. **-etto, -ino** m. dim. travelling case, suitcase.

baussite f. See bauxite.

baut·ta f. black mantle with a hood worn by way of a mask, domino.

bauxite f. (miner.) bauxite, aluminium ore, aluminium hydroxide.

bav-a f. dribble, slaver, slobber; slime (of a snail); foam (at the mouth); con la — alla bocca, frothing at the mouth, in a great rage; (text.) floss-silk, the weak silk which is carded and spun like wool; (metall.) seam, fash, roughness on a casting due to cracks, etc., in the mould; (eng.) burr; togliere la —, to spud; (sculp.) thin ridge caused by plaster overflowing edge of mould; — di vento, puff of wind, catspaw. **-arello** m. workman in floss silk. **-ella** f. dim. floss silk. **-ellina** f. dim. material made from floss or inferior silk. **-etta** f. child's bib; (metall.) unevenness in a casting when it is withdrawn from the mould; pl. jabot. **-ettine** f.pl. dim. thin strips of macaroni for soup. **-osa** f. (ichth.) blenny, Blennius spp. **-oso** adj. slobbering; foaming. **-uc·cia** f. (metall.) irregularities on castings.

bava·gl-io m. bib; gag. **-ino** m. dim. baby's bib, feeder.

†**bavalisco, bavali·schio** m. basilisk.

ba·var-a f. (numis.) Bavarian coin. **-ese** adj., n.m. Bavarian; f. Bavarian woman; drinking milk chocolate; cream chocolate sweet. **-ina** f. lace modesty vest. **-o** m. Bavarian; †see bavero.

†**bava·rico** adj. See bavarese, under bavara.

ba·vera f. lady's cape; pelerine.

ba·vero[1] m. collar of a coat; cape of a greatcoat; — di pelo, fur collar.

ba·vero[2] adj., n.m. See bavarese, under bavara.

Baviera[1] pr.n.f. (geog.) Bavaria; Monaco di —, Munich.

baviera[2] f. visor.

ba·vio m. poetaster (from Bavius, a Latin poet).

baza·r indecl. bazaar.

bazz-a[1] f. piece of good luck; — a chi tocca, we shall see who is the lucky one; che —!, what a piece of luck!; what fun!; (cards, e.g. at 'calabresella') one point; (at 'trionfi') trick won without a trump or the number of cards won with each successive trick; cheap purchase; bargain.

bazz-a[2] f. long, protruding chin; (Flor.) chin. **-one** m., **-ona** f. person with a protruding chin; prognathous person.

bazzana f. bookbinding leather; sheepskin skiver; wash-leather.

bazza·r m. indecl. See bazar.

†**bazzarr-o**[1] m. bazaar; exchange, barter; shop. †**-are** intr. to barter; to deal.

†**bazzarro**[2] m. kind of leather.

bazze·cola f. trifle, bagatelle, gew-gaw.

†**bazze·o** adj. greenish; the colour of unripe fruit.

†**bazzesco** adj. rough, crude.

baz·zic-a[1] f. (cards) bezique; pool, a game of ninepins played on a billiard table. **-otto** m. three similar cards in the game of 'bazzica'. **-ottone** m. four similar cards in the game of 'bazzica'.

baz·zic-a[2] f. companion; company; conversation. **-are** [A1s] tr. to frequent; to haunt; to hang round; to associate with; -are cattive compagnie, to frequent bad company; intr. (aux. avere) to turn up, to be present, to be a frequenter. **-ature** f. pl. trifles.

†**bazzicheri·a** f. See bazzecola.

bazzof·fia f. strong, thick soup; (fig.) long involved composition; heap of papers; confused mass.

bazzotto adj. (of an egg) lightly boiled; (of fruit) unripe; (of a person) rather plump; (fig.) inexperienced, ill-prepared; 'half-baked'.

bè[1] excl. good!; well?

bè[2], **bee** (onomat.) baa; bleat.

beacione m. withy used for tying a vine to a poplar.

be-are [A6] tr. to make happy; rfl. to enjoy oneself; to rejoice; to be in one's seventh heaven; -arsi di, to delight in. **-ante** part. adj. cheering, conducive to good cheer; cheerful. **-ato** part. adj. made happy; rejoiced; rejoicing. (See also beato, adj.) †**-atore** m. one who brings happiness, one who gives joy. **-atrice** f. woman who makes blessed, woman who inspires happiness.

beante[1] part. adj. of beare, q.v.

beante[2] adj. (med.) open (of arteries).

†**beatanza** f. beatitude.

beati·fic-o adj. (theol.) beatific. **-a·bile** adj. (theol.) worthy of beatification. **-are** tr. [A2s] (theol.) to beatify. **-ato** part. adj. (theol.) beatified. (**-atore** m., **-atrice** f.) **-azione** f. (theol.) beatification.

†**beati·glia** f. kind of muslin.

beat-o[1] adj. happy, blessed; blissful; without a care; lucky; — lui!, the lucky man!; — te!, how lucky you are!; (eccl.) blessed; la -a Angela da Foligno, Blessed Angela of Foligno; (in address to the Pope) — Padre, Holy Father; n.m. blessed one; sanctimonious person; i -i, the blessed. (**-a** f.) **-amente** adv. happily; blissfully; blessedly; contentedly. †**-anza** f. power to render happy. †**-essa** f. sanctimonious woman. †**-ezza** f. happiness; success; prosperity. **-ina** f. dim. very pious woman. **-is·simo** adj. (eccl.) -issimo Padre, Most Holy Father (in formal address to the Pope). **-itu·dine** f. (theol.) beatitude, blessedness, bliss; le -itudini, the Beatitudes; (eccl. title) Vostra -itudine, (to the Pope) Your Holiness, (to a patriarch) Your Beatitude.

beato[2] part. of beare, q.v.

Beatrice[1] pr.n.f. Beatrice; (fig.) inspirer of a poet.

beatrice[2] f. See under beare.

bebè[1] m. indecl. baby.

bebè[2] m. indecl. little lamb.

†**bebù** m. bleat.

beca f. low peasant-woman; slut; country-lass.

becca f. corner of a handkerchief; cloth waistband; garter; turn-down; corner of a page in a book turned down to mark the place, dog-ear.

beccac·c-ia f. (orn.) woodcock, Scolopax rusticola; — di mare, oyster catcher, Haematopus ostralegus. **-ino** m. (orn.) snipe, Capella gallinago.

beccafi·co *m.* (*pl.* **-chi**) (orn.) garden warbler, *Sylvia borin*; any small bird for the table. **-cata** *f.* meal of beccafichi; (lit. hist.) annual banquet held by the Accademia della Crusca.

becca·io *m.* butcher; bad surgeon; murderer.

†**beccala·glio** *m.* children's game resembling blind-man's-buff.

becc-alite *m. indecl.* wrangler; quarrelsome person. **-amorti** *m. indecl.* (colloq.) gravedigger; undertaker; †(fig.) undoing, downfall. **-amoschino** *m.* (orn.) fan-tailed warbler, *Cisticola juncidis*. **-apesci** *m. indecl.* (orn.) sandwich tern, *Sterna sandivicensis*; **-apesci inglese**, gull-billed tern, *Gelochelidon nilotica*.

becc-are [A 2 c] to peck; to pick up in the beak; to nip, to bite; to show disapproval of; to win, to earn; to learn, to pick up, to get hold of; to catch, to nab, to pinch; **— una malattia**, to get an illness; *rfl.* (*dat.* of *prn.* **si**) to get, to 'collar'; to catch; **-arsi il cervello**, to rack one's brains; *recip. rfl.* to quarrel. (**-a·bile** *adj.*) **-amento** *m.* pecking; nipping; biting. **-ata** *f.* peck; beakful; (fig.) trifle. **-atella** *f.* a piece of meat thrown in the air to the hawk when it hovers over the net; (fig.) trifle. **-atello** *m.* (archit.) bracket to carry a balcony; corbel; peg of a hat-stand; (mus.) button, i.e. projection where the neck of a violin joins the body of the instrument. **-ato** *part. adj.* pecked; nipped; caught. **-atoio** *m.* bird's feeding trough; bird-table. **-atura** *f.* pecking; marks from a peck; bite, sting.

beccastrino *m.* (agric.) graft, narrow-bladed heavy spade for trenching.

beccheggi-are [A 3 c] *intr.* (*aux.* avere) (naut.) to pitch, to toss. **-ata** *f.* (naut.) pitch.

beccheggio *m.* (naut.; aeron.) pitching; (of a horse) 'star-gazing', 'chucking'.

beccheri·a *f.* See under **becco²**.

beccherini *m.pl.* (hist.) popular party at Perugia led by the Baglioni.

becchett-o *m. dim.* of **becco¹**, q.v.; point of a hood; flap of boot or shoe containing eyelets for laces. **-are** [A 1 c] to peck, to nip; to keep on pecking.

becchime *m.* bird-food.

becchincroce *m.* (orn.) crossbill, *Loxia curvirostra*.

becchino *m.* gravedigger; undertaker; (ent.) burying beetle, carrion beetle, *Necrophorus* sp.

†**bec·cia** *f.* nanny-goat.

becc-o¹ *m.* (*pl.* **becchi**) beak, bill; **metterci il —**, to chip in out of turn, to poke one's nose in; **ecco fatto il — all'oca**, that's done, that's the finishing touch; **dar di — in**, to eat; **aver paglia in —**, to be a partner to a secret; **metter il — in molle**, to drink; **non aver il — di un quattrino**, to be without a penny; **— giallo**, title of a humorous journal; prow (of a ship); spout; mouth, lip (of a jug, flask, etc.); neck (of funnel); burner; **— del gas**, gas-jet, gas-ring; (mus.) mouthpiece; (miner.) **— di stagno**, cassiterite, tin dioxide; (bot.) **barba di —**, see under **barba**. **-olare** [A 1 s] *tr.* to peck at; to eat slowly; to nibble. **-ucchiare** [A 4] *tr.* to keep pecking at. **-uc·cio** *m.* spout; mouth, lip of a jug; neck of bottle; (chem.) outlet of a retort, etc.; (foundry) tap hole. **-ume** *m.* bird food. **-uto** *adj.* beaked; with a beak. **-uzzare** [A 1] *tr.* to peck at.

becc-o² *m.* (*pl.* **-chi**) buck, he-goat, billy-goat; **— cornuto**, cuckold; **— contento**, mari complaisant, husband in a ménage à trois. **-cheri·a** *f.* butcher's shop; †slaughter-house; †slaughter. †**-cone** *m.* fool, dolt; *adj.* stupid.

beccofrosone, beccofrusone *m.* (orn.) waxwing, *Bombycilla garrulus*.

becer-o *m.* low blackguard; cad; Florentine uneducated speech (cf. Cockney in relation to English); **parlare proprio —**, to speak an uneducated form of Florentine Italian; **spirito —**, typical Florentine humour; †caddishness; †vulgarity. **-ata** *f.* caddish act. **-ume** *m.* bunch of blackguards; caddish behaviour; Florentine uneducated speech.

Beciua·nia *pr.n.f.* (geog.) Bechuanaland.

be·co *m.* (*pl.* **-chi**) bumpkin; cf. **beca**.

becolino *m.* (dial. Florence) little boat on the R. Arno.

bedale *m.* (N. Italy) stream, small canal.

†**bedano** *adj.* stupid; *n.m.* fool, dolt.

beduin-a *f.* opera cloak; †long cloak with a hood; opera cloak. **-o** *m.*, *adj.* Bedouin.

Beelzebù, Beelzebu·b *pr.n.m.* See **Belzebù**.

Beemo·t *pr.n.m.* (Bibl.) Behemoth.

†**befà** *m.* (mus.) B flat.

Befan-a *pr.n.f.* Epiphany; old woman who brings presents for children on the eve of Epiphany; present; presentation of gifts to children; old hag, funny old woman. **-esco** *adj.* (*m.pl.* **-eschi**) pertaining to 'Befana'. **-i·a** *f.* (poet.) Epiphany. **-o** *m.* ugly man. **-ona** *f.* ugly fat hag. **-one** *m.* ugly fat man; bogey-man.

beff-a *f.* derision, jest; practical joke; humiliating trick; **farsi -e di**, to mock, to make fun of, to ridicule; **restare col danno e con le -e**, to be insulted as well as injured; **mettere in —**, to jeer at. **-ardo** *adj.* mocking, bantering; scoffing; scornful; scolding; *n.m.* mocker, scoffer, ridiculer. **-ardamente** *adv.* mockingly; banteringly. **-are** [A 1] *tr.* to mock, to ridicule, to deride, to scoff; to rail at; *rfl.* (*prep.* di) to laugh (at); to make a fool (of); to play (with); not to take care (of); to trifle (with). **-a·bile** *adj.* laughable. **-amento** *m.* insult; derision. **-ato** *part. adj.* mocked. (**-atore** *m.* **-atrice** *f.*)

beff-eggiare [A 3 c] *tr.* to deride, to mock. **-eggiamento** *m.* mocking; derision. (**-eggiatore** *m.* **-eggiatrice** *f.*) †**-eggiato·rio** *adj.* mocking. †**-e·vole** *adj.* laughable.

be-ga *f.* dispute; wrangle; **trovare delle -ghe con**, to pick a quarrel with; unpleasant business, distasteful task; **avere delle -ghe**, to be in trouble, to have trouble. **-ghismo** *m.* (hist. Fascist) stirring up of discord.

begardi *m.pl.* (rel. hist.) Beghards.

beghin-a *f.* (eccl.) Béguine; dévote, 'church hen'. **-ag·gio** *m.* excessive piety. **-o** *m.* (rel. hist.) Beghard; sanctimonious person.

begli *adj. m.pl.* See **bello¹**.

beglio·mini, begliuo·mini *m.pl.* (bot.) garden balsam, *Impatiens Balsamina*; **— selvatici**, touch-me-not, *Impatiens noli-tangere*.

†**be·gol-e** *f.pl.* chatter; gossip. †**-ardo** *m.* gossip. †**-are** *intr.* to chatter; to gossip.

bego·nia *f.* (bot.) begonia.

begum *f. indecl.* begum; (colloq.) **fare la —**, to act like a lady of leisure.

beh *excl.* See **bè¹**.

Be·i¹, Bei *m. indecl.* Bey; governor.

be·i² *adj. m.pl.* See **bello¹**.

beige *adj. indecl.* (pron. as French) beige.

Bel¹ *pr.n.m.* (rel.) Bel, a Babylonian divinity.

bel² *m.* (phys., acoust.) bel.

bel³ *adj. m.* See **bello¹**.

bel-are [A 1] *intr.* (*aux.* avere) to bleat; (fig.) to whimper; to whine, to grizzle; to say stupid things. **-amento** *m.* bleating; bleat. **-ante** *part. adj.* bleating; *n.m.*, *f.* sheep. **-ato** *m.* bleat; bleating. (**-atore** *m.* **-atrice** *f.*) **-ecchiare** [A 4] *intr.* (*aux.* avere) to keep on bleating feebly. **-io** *m.*(*pl.* **-ii**) prolonged bleating; continual crying.

Belfego·r, Belfago·r *pr.n.m.* Baal Peor, a Syrian divinity; a devil, protagonist of a short story by N. Machiavelli.

belfigurino *m.* (bot.) *Coreopsis tinctoria*.

bel-ga *adj.* (*m.pl.* **-gi**) (geog.) Belgian; *n.m.* Belgian; (numis.) Belgian coin of 5 francs instituted in 1926; *f.* (*pl.* **-ghe**) Belgian woman.

bel·gico *adj.* (hist.) Belgic.

Bel·gio *pr.n.m.* (geog.) Belgium.

belgiuino *m.* See **belzoino**.

Belgrado *pr.n.f.* (geog.) Belgrade.

Be·lial *pr.n.m.* (Bibl.) Belial.

belic-ale *adj.* pertaining to a Bey or Beylic. **-ato** *m.* Beylic.

beliera *f.* Turkish armed vessel.

bella *f.*, *adj.* See **bello¹**.

belladama *f.* (ent.) painted lady butterfly, *Vanessa cardui*.

belladonna *f.* (bot.) deadly nightshade, dwale, *Atropa belladonna*.

†**bellagamba** *m.* fop; gallant.

bellamente *adv.* See under **bello¹**.

†**bell-are** *intr.* to fight. †**-atore** *m.* warrior; *adj.* fighting, combatant. †**-atrice** *f.* woman-warrior; *adj.* fighting, combatant; (astron.) star of the constellation of Orion.

bellave·dova *f.* (bot.) snake's head iris, widow iris, *Hermodactylus tuberosus*.

bellavita *f.* life of pleasure, life of idleness; (N. Italy) **in —**, in one's shirt-sleeves.

Bellerofo·nte *pr.n.m.* (myth.) Bellerophon; (astron.) constellation of Pegasus.

bellett-a *f.* slime, silt, dregs. **-one** *m.* land made of alluvial deposits. **-oso** *adj.* muddy, alluvial.

belletter-ista *m.* dilettante in belles lettres. **-i·stica** *f.* dilettantism in belles lettres.

bellett-o *m.* cosmetic, make-up, rouge, paint; darsi il —, to make up; (fig.) affectation; *adj.* pretty. **-iere** *m.*, **-iera** *f.* make-up expert.

bellezza *f.* beauty; good looks; (provb.) a lume spento ogni — è pari, when the candles are out all women are fair; che—!, how lovely!, how splendid!; è una — stare qui, it's delightful here; dorme ch'è una —, he sleeps beautifully; finire in —, to end with a flourish, to bring things to an end triumphantly; (fig.) large quantity; ha vissuto la — di cent'anni, he is turned a hundred; large sum; mi è costato la — di due milioni, it cost me a good two million; far del ben —, to indulge in prodigal expenditure; (bot.) — di Genova, Jerusalem cherry, *Solanum pseudocapsicum*; †— della Nencia, dimple.

bellichina *f.* (bot.) pimpernel, poor man's weather-glass, *Anagallis arvensis*.

belli-co[1] *m.* (*pl.* **-chi**) navel, umbilical; col — all'aria, idle; †centre, middle. **-conchio** *m.* umbilical cord. **-cone** *m.* fat person; large round-bellied drinking glass.

bel·lic-o[2] *adj.* relating to war; materiale —, war material; wartime; periodo —, war years. **-ista** *m.* militarist; warmonger; *adj.* warmongering. **-ismo** *m.* militarism. **-osità** *f.* pugnacity. **-oso** *adj.* bellicose; warlike. **-osamente** *adv.* martially; bravely.

belliger-o *adj.* warlike; belligerent. **-ante** *adj.*, *n.m.* belligerent. **-anza** *f.* belligerence.

bellimbusto *m.* fop, dandy, beau, coxcomb; fare il —, to play the beau.

Bellinzona *pr.n.f.* (geog.) Bellinzona.

bell-o[1] *adj.* (*m.s.* **bel** before consonant except **z** or impure **s**; **bello** before **z** or impure **s**; **bell'** before vowel; *m.pl.* **belli** as complement; **bei** before a consonant except **z** or impure **s**; **begli** before **z** or impure **s**; **begl'** before **i**.)

1. Beautiful; lovely; handsome; good-looking; fine; (N. Ital.) che —!, how lovely!; una -a signorina, a lovely young woman, a pretty girl; una -a donna, a good-looking woman; una gran -a donna, a very good-looking woman; un bell'uomo, a handsome man; un bel giovanotto, a good-looking young man; un bel bambino, a fine child; farsi —, to make oneself look attractive, to smarten oneself up, to dress in one's best bib and tucker; to improve in looks; col crescere si farà -a, she'll be pretty when she grows up; farsi — con le penne del pavone, to dress in borrowed plumes; farsi — della roba altrui, to take what doesn't belong to one; la -a stagione, Spring; i begli anni, youth, the springtime of life; il bel sesso, the fair sex; il Bel Paese, Italy; bel paese, a kind of cheese (also **belpaese**, q.v.); le -e arti, the fine arts; le -e lettere, belles lettres; facoltà di -e lettere, Faculty of Arts; una laurea in -e lettere, an Arts degree; è iscritto in -e lettere, he is reading for an Arts degree; (mus.) bel canto, *bel canto*, a style of singing cultivated and perfected by the best Italian singers; (provb.) non è — quel che è —, ma è — quel che piace, beauty is in the eye of the beholder. **2.** Good; nice; pleasant; admirable: una bell'azione, a good deed; avere un bel cuore, to have a good heart; questo è un bel pensiero, that's a good idea; cosa avete di — oggi?, what can you recommend (e.g. on a menu) today?; cosa c'è di — al cinema?, is there anything good on at the cinema?; stasera che fai di —?, doing anything this evening?; il bel mondo, high society, good society; un bel nome, a good name, a fine reputation; acquistarsi una -a fama, to make a name for oneself; -e maniere, nice manners, distinguished manners; fare una -a figura, to show up well, to cut a good figure; volevo fargli fare una -a figura, I wanted him to appear to advantage; un bell'ingegno, a first-class mind, an original mind, a talented and able person; un bel parlatore, a good talker; bel tempo, good weather, nice weather; darsi bel tempo, to lead a gay life; se è una -a giornata si va, altrimenti si rimanda, if it's a nice day we'll go, otherwise we'll put it off; fare il — e il brutto tempo, to have it in one's power to make or mar the atmosphere in a community; in quella casa è la cuoca che fa la pioggia e il bel tempo, in that household everything depends on what mood the cook is in; che bei tempi!, those were the days!; un bel giorno, one fine day, one of these days; a mio bell'agio, at my ease, in my own good time, when and how I like; fare una -a vita, to lead a life of luxury and idleness, to have a good time. **3.** Good-sized, considerable: una -a somma, a good sum; una -a eredità, a considerable inheritance; un bel vento, quite a strong wind; vien giù una bell'acqua, it's raining quite heavily; avere una bell'età, to be getting on in years. **4.** Precise, very: nel bel mezzo, right in the very middle; a -a posta, a — studio, on purpose, intentionally;

vale un bel nulla, it's worth precisely nothing; gli rispose un bel no, he said no and he meant it. **5.** Ironical uses: l'ho fatta -a!, I've gone and done it!; quest'è -a!, that's a good one!; ne ho viste delle -e, I've seen a few things in my time; ne fa sempre delle -e, he's always up to something; oh -a!, that's a nice thing!, how strange!; sei un bell'asino, you are an ass and no mistake. **6.** Intensification of *adj.* or *part.*: bell'e finito, already finished, quite finished; bell'e morto, dead as a doornail; bell'e buono, downright, out and out; è un furfante bell'e buono, he's an out and out rogue, he's a rogue and no mistake; è oro bell'e buono, it's real gold; (of clothing) bell'e fatto, ready-made; ho bell'e fatto, vengo subito, I'm coming, I've just finished. **7.** *adv. phrs.* bel bello, calmly, slowly, gradually, by degrees; alla -a e meglio, as best one can; di bel nuovo, all over again; ho avuto un bel dire, it was no use my saying; con tali prezzi si capisce è un bel vendere, with present prices naturally one can't sell a thing. **8.** *adv.* (Tusc. colloq.) beautifully; well; canta bello, he sings beautifully. **9.** *n.m.* beau; handsome man; fare il —, to go courting; sweetheart, love; beauty, that which is beautiful; non ha sentimento del —, he has no feeling for beauty; il — è, the funny thing is; ora viene il —, the cream of the jest is, the best of it is; sul più —, at the height of the excitement, when least expected, at the crucial point; c'è voluto del — e del buono per persuaderlo, we had an awful job to persuade him. **-a** *f.* beautiful woman; belle; sweetheart, girl-friend; ricopiare in -a, to make a fair copy of; (sport; cards) la -a, the last decisive round, the 'conqueror'; (iron.) fine thing, etc., see No. 5; (bot.) -a di giorno, dwarf morning glory and other day-blooming *Convolvulus* species, *Convolvulus tricolor*; -a di notte, Peruvian four o'clock plant, marvel of Peru, *Mirabilis Jalapa*; -a di undici ore, star of Bethlehem, *Ornithogalum umbellatum*. **-amente** *adv.* gently, gracefully; adroitly, skilfully; politely; smartly. **-ino** *adj.* pretty; far il -ino, to feign submissiveness; vederne di -ine, to witness some fine goings-on; *n.m.* (colloq.) penis. **-occio** *adj.* rather pretty and plump; rather good looking. **-ona** *f.* buxom woman; il cieco e la -ona, grotesque couple, or squalid Darby and Joan. †-**ore** *m.* beauty. †-**oso** *adj.* beautiful. **-uria** *f.* (Pistoia) beauty, beautiful appearance; ornamentation.

†**bello**[2] *m.* war.

belloc·chio *m.* (miner.) cat's-eye, a variety of chrysoberyl.

Bellona[1] *pr.n.f.* Bellona, Goddess of War.

bellona[2] *f.* See under **bello**[1].

bellosguardo *m.* viewpoint, belvedere; stare a —, to stand and stare.

bellospirito *m.* (*pl.* **begli spiriti**) wit, wag, would-be humorist.

†**belluin-o** *adj.* fierce, ferocious, wild, savage. †-**ità** *f.* ferocity; savagery.

bellumore *m.* (*pl.* **begli umori**). See **bellospirito**.

†**belo** *m.* bleat; bleating.

belpaese *m. indecl.* Belpaese, name of a cheese produced in Brianza.

beltà *f.* beauty; che —!, how lovely!; quella ragazza è una —, that girl is a beauty.

Beltramo *pr.n.m.* character in Bergamaske masks, pater familias.

†**beltresca** *f.* See **bertesca**.

Belucista·n *pr.n.m.* (geog.) Baluchistan.

beluga *f.* (ichth.) a kind of sturgeon, *Huso huso*; its caviare.

belv-a *f.* wild beast; big game; (fig.) brutal person, ferocious criminal. †-**acida** *m.* big game hunter.

belvedere *m.* look-out; turret; terrace; place commanding a fine view; *pr.n.m.* Vatican gardens and courtyard; (art) l'Apollo del —, the Belvedere Apollo; (rlwy.) vettura —, observation car; (naut.) mizzen-top-gallant sail; (bot.) summer cypress, *Kochia scoparia*.

Belzebù *pr.n.m.* Beelzebub.

belz-oa·r, **-ua·r** *m. indecl.* bezoar, bezoar-stone.

belz-oino, **-uino** *m.* (gum) benzoin.

†**bembe** *m.* (baby-language) drink.

bembè *excl.* (iron.) well! well!

bembesco *adj.* imitative of the writer, Pietro Bembo (1470–1547); (of style) affected, mannered.

†**bemì** *m.* (mus.) B natural.

bemoll-e *m.* (mus.) flat; doppio —, double flat. **-are** [A I], **-izzare** [A I] *tr.* (mus.) to flatten by means of an accidental.

ben-accetto *adj.* acceptable; desirable; welcome. **-accon·cio** *adj.* suitable. **-acconciamente** *adv.* suitably. **-affetto** *adj.* kindly disposed. **-allevato** *adj.* well brought up. **-alzato** *excl.* good morning!

ben·accetto (*cont.*)

-**amato** *adj.* well-beloved. †-**anche** *conj.* even if, no matter if. -**andare** *m.* the 'go-ahead', permission to proceed given by a foreman after inspecting a man's work; see **benandata**. -**andata** *f.* tip given to a servant by a departing guest; see **bonuscita**. †-**andato** *excl.* good-bye. -**arrivato** *excl.* welcome!; *n.m.* dare il -arrivato a, to welcome. -**augurante, -augurato** *adj.* auspicious. -**auguratamente** *adv.* auspiciously. -**avere** *m.* peace, tranquillity; lasciatemi un po' -avere, please do let me have a bit of peace. -**avveduto** *adj.* prudent, circumspect. -**avventurato, -avventuroso** *adj.* fortunate; lucky; successful. (-**avventurosamente** *adv.*) -**condizionato** *adj.* well-prepared. -**creato** *adj.*, †blessed, predestined to bliss. -**educato** *adj.* well brought up; well-bred; well-mannered. -**es·sere** *m.* comfort; well-being; prosperity; welfare. -**fare** *m.* good deeds, doing good. -**fatto** *adj.* well-made; handsome; well-done. -**godi** *m. indecl.* the land of plenty. -**guarito** *excl.* so glad you're better! -**intenzionato** *adj.* well-intentioned. -**inteso** *adj.* understood; taken for granted; agreed; -inteso le spese saranno a carica nostra, naturally all expenses will be charged to us; -inteso che, on the understanding that, provided that (cf. 'ben inteso' under **inteso**). -**levato** *phr.* dare il -levato a uno, to wish a person good-morning. -**montato** *adj.* well-mounted, on a good horse. -**nato** *adj.* well-born; †blessed. -**parlante** *adj.* well-spoken; *n.m.* person who speaks correctly. -**parlare** *m.* correct use of language, good speech. -**pasciuto** *adj.* well-fed, sleek, well-nourished. -**pensante** *adj.* 'right-thinking'; wise, judicious, sensible; orthodox; conventional, respectable; (also *n.m.*) -**portante** *adj.* hale and hearty; well-preserved; (also *n.m.*). †-**sa·i,** †-**sapete** *adv.* without doubt, of course, naturally. †-**sedente** *adj.* suitable. -**servito** *m.* certificate of character; testimonial; reference. -**sì** *adv.* certainly; but, on the contrary. -**tornato** *excl.* welcome!, welcome home! (also 'ben tornato!'); *n.m.* greeting, welcome, dare il -tornato a, to welcome, to greet. †-**tosto** *adv.* immediately, straightway. -**trovato** *excl.* well met! -**uscita** *f.* See **benandata**. -**veduto** *adj.* well thought of; liked; loved. †-**venga** *excl.* hail!, welcome!; *n.m.* greeting. †-**venuta** *f.* (mil.) extra pay. -**venuto** *adj.* welcome; *n.m.* person who is welcome (-**venuta** *f.*). -**visto** *adj.* See **benveduto**. -**volere** [B 3 b] *tr.* to love; to be fond of; to regard favourably; prendere a -volere uno, to become fond of someone; farsi -volere da tutti, to endear oneself to everyone; *n.m.* affection, goodwill. -**voluto** *adj.* much liked; well loved, much loved, beloved.

Bena·co *pr.n.m.* (geog.) Lake Garda.

ben be', *excl.* well! well!

benchè *conj.* although; il — minimo, even the very smallest.

bend·a *f.* band, bandage; fillet; headband; bandeau; kerchief; (fig.) avere la — agli occhi, to be blind, to be dazzled; gli cadde la — dagli occhi, the scales fell from his eyes; (rel.) sacre -e, veil (of nuns); fillet (of pagan priests); (naut.) tabling, parcelling (of a hawser). -**ag·gio** *m.* bandage, bandaging. -**one** *m.* (eccl.) lappet of a mitre.

bend·are [A I c] *tr.* to bind up, to bandage; (naut.) to serve (a rope); — (gli occhi a), to blindfold. -**ato** *part. adj.* bandaged; blindfold; †wearing a turban. -**atura** *f.* bandaging; bandages; blindfolding.

bendidi·o *m.* abundance; riches; fruits of the earth.

bendone *m.* See under **benda**.

ben·e *adv.*:

1. Well: fare —, to do well; to do right, to act rightly (cf. fare —, under No. 5); andare —, to go well, to be going well; to be on the right path; *impers.* va —, all right, very well, right you are, agreed; nascere —, to be well born; vestire —, to dress well, to dress smartly; ci si mangia —, the food is good there; morire —, to die a Christian death; parlare —, to speak well, to be a good speaker, (iron.) to have a smooth tongue; parlare — di, to speak well of, to praise; vedere —, to see well, to have good sight; vedere — uno, to think well of a person; pensare —, to be right-minded; — o male, somehow or other, by hook or by crook; per —, nicely, properly, gently, carefully (cf. per —, under No. 5); andare di — in meglio, to improve hand over fist, to get better and better. 2. Uses with **stare**: stare —, to be well, to be in good health; come stai?, sto —, grazie, how are you?, quite well, thanks; stare poco —, to be poorly, to be unwell; stia —!, good health!, look after yourself!; *impers.* stare —, to be right, to be proper; non sta — parlare così, it isn't right to talk like that; non sta — a una signorina uscire sola di notte, it isn't proper for a young girl to go out at night by herself; le sta —!, serve you right!; sta —, all right, very well, right you are, agreed (cf. 'va bene', under No. 1); stare — a, to suit, to become; ti sta — quel vestito, that dress is becoming to you; stare — a quattrini, to be well off, to have plenty of cash; stare — con, to be on good terms with. 3. Very, really, indeed (often shortened to **ben** before another word): è ben vero, that's very true, it is indeed true; era ben grande, it was very large; ben bene, really well, thoroughly, really nicely, properly; lo hanno sgridato ben bene, they scolded him good and proper; credo —, I do believe, I really believe, I should think so!; spero —che verrete, I do hope you'll come; lo spero —!, I should hope so! 4. Quite, at least (often shortened to **ben** before another word): l'ho visto ben quattro volte, I have seen him quite four times; ben mille lire, quite a thousand lire, at least a thousand lire; ben due mila, a good two thousand, quite two thousand, a cool two thousand; (iron.) gli ha dato ben due lire, he gave him quite two lire. 5. *n.m.* good; fare —, fare del —, fare il —, to do good; far — a, to be good for, to be good to; happiness; blessing; l'amore dei fanciulli è un gran —, the love of one's children is a great blessing; love, darling; caro mio —, my beloved; affection; il suo — per Nino, her love for Nino; il ben dell'intelletto, God (as the supreme goal of knowledge), (colloq.) reason, sense; (eccl.) opere di —, good works; non fiori ma opere di —, no flowers by request; fare un po' di — a un defunto, to say a few prayers for someone dead; (Tusc.) il — di maggio, May devotions; peace, quiet; non ha mai —, he's always restless; non ebbe — finchè non, he had no peace of mind until; voler — a, to love, to be fond of; dire — di, to speak well of, to praise; per —, a fin di —, with good intentions; gente da —, gente per —, straightforward, honest people; una persona per —, a decent individual, a well-thought of, law-abiding person; una signorina per —, a nicely brought up girl, a respectable girl; *pl.* (leg.; econ.) property, goods, wealth; -i dotali, dowry; -i mobili, personal property, personalty, movables; -i immobili, real property, real estate; sblocco di -i italiani in Gran Bretagna, release of Italian assets in U.K.; -i consumabili, -i di consumo, consumer goods; -i parafernali, paraphernalia; -i vacanti, bona vacantia, stray goods. -**accione** *m. augm.* (joc. Tusc.) great affection. -**ino** *adv. dim.* fairly well; quite nicely; not badly at all; per -ino, nicely, properly; star per -ino a tavola, to behave properly at table; accurately; primly; *adj. indecl.* prim and proper, old-maidish; una zitella per -ino, a prim old maid. -**is·simo** *adv. superl.* splendidly; excellently; certainly, perfectly well, quite well; si può -issimo dir così senza volere offendere, one can perfectly well say that without meaning to be insulting; *excl.* splendid!, excellent!, well done! -**one** *adv. augm.* (colloq.) very well indeed, splendidly, first class.

benedett·o¹ *part.* of **benedire**, q.v.; *adj.* blessed; holy; acqua -a, holy water; mani -e, skilful hands; parole -e, blessed words, timely words; l'anima -a di vostro padre, your father, God rest him; (colloq.) tiresome: quel — ragazzo, that blessed boy; sei un — uomo, con te è impossibile parlare, you're quite maddening, it's no use talking to you; *n.m.* slight convulsion, fit (in infants).

Benedett·o² *pr.n.m.* Benedict. -**a** *f.* (bot.) herb-bennet, avens, *Geum urbanum*; water-avens, *Geum rivale*. -**ino** *adj.* Benedictine; *n.m.* Benedictine (monk); Benedictine (liqueur); pazienza da -ino, patience of a saint.

bene·dicente *part.* of **benedire**, q.v.; *adj.* blessing, uttering praise. -**dicenza** *f.* praise. -**di·cite** *m.* grace before meals. -**di·cola** *f.* (joc.) little service in church.

†**benedi·cere** *vb.* See **benedire**.

bene·dire [B 10] *tr.* to bless; to consecrate; (iron.) mandare a farsi —, to send about one's business, to send packing; — con le pertiche, to thrash; quel ragazzo, che Dio lo -dica, non sta mai fermo, that blessed boy is never still a minute. -**dizione** *f.* benediction, blessing; Benediction (service).

beneducato *adj.* See under **benaccetto**.

benefacente *adj.* beneficent; beneficial.

†**bene-fare** *tr.* to benefit; *intr.* to do good. †-**fattivo** *adj.* beneficent. †-**fatto** *m.* church benefice.

benefatt·ore *m.* benefactor. -**rice** *f.* benefactress.

beneficare [A 2 s]. See under **benefico**.

beneficenza *f.* charity; beneficence, generosity, helpfulness; donation; (theatr.) serata di —, benefit night; istituto di — charitable institution.

benefici·are [A 3] *tr.* to benefit; *intr.* (*aux.* avere; *prep.* di) to benefit (by), to benefit (under). **-ata** *f.* theatrical benefit; lottery ticket on which is written the amount of the prize to be won. **-ato** *part. adj.* privileged; (eccl.) beneficed; (leg.) erede **-ato**, heir who disclaims liability for debts exceeding assets by requiring an inventory of the estate to be taken. **-a·rio** *m.* (leg.; eccl.) beneficiary.

benefici·o *m.* benefit; good office, kindness, courtesy; favour; chiedere a titolo di —, to ask as a favour; advantage; (econ.) profit, gain; (leg.) accettare un'eredità col — dell'inventario, to disclaim liability for debts exceeding assets by requiring an inventory to be taken when accepting an inheritance, (fig.) to take with a grain of salt; (eccl.) benefice, living; — semplice, sinecure. **-ale** *adj.* (eccl.) connected with a benefice. **-alista** *m.* expert in the laws of church livings.

bene·fic·o *adj.* beneficial; kindly; charitable; useful; è un burbero —, his bark is worse than his bite. (**-amente** *adv.*) **-are** [A 2 s] *tr.* to benefit; to do good to; to help; to be beneficial to; to favour. **-ativo** *adj.* helpful; beneficial. **-ato** *part. adj.* benefited; helped; favoured; *n.m.* beneficiary.

benefi·zio *m. and derivs.* (Tusc.). See **beneficio**.

†**benegno** *adj.* See **benigno**.

benemer-ente *adj.* meritorious, deserving; — di, that has deserved well of. **-enza** *f.* merit, good service; worth, deserts; in **-enza**, in recognition of good service; avere molte **-enze** verso la patria, to deserve well of one's country.

beneme·rit-o *adj.* deserving; praiseworthy; scrittore — della patria, a writer who has deserved well of the fatherland; (mil.) Arma **-a**, La **-a**, the Carabinieri, q.v.; *n.m.* merit. **-are** [A 1 s] *intr.* (*aux.* avere; *prep.* di) to be deserving (of).

†**benenanza** *f.* well-being.

benepla·cito *m.* approval, approbation; permission, consent; a — di, at the disposal of.

benes·sere *m.* See under **ben-accetto**.

benestante *adj.* comfortably off; di condizione —, living on a private income; *n.m.pl.* i benestanti, the well-to-do.

benestare *m.* comfort, prosperity; (iron.) gli è venuto a noia il —, he is tired of being well off (said of one who is compromising his position); (comm.; admin.) formal approval, consent; the 'go-ahead', 'O.K.'.

beneviso *adj.* looked upon favourably.

benevol-ente *adj.* benevolent; favourable. (**-entemente** *adv.*) **-enza** *f.* benevolence, indulgence; favour; goodwill.

bene·vol-o *adj.* benevolent, indulgent, benign; kind, kindly; well-disposed. **-mente** *adv.* benevolently; in a kindly way.

benfare [B 14] and derivs. See under **ben-accetto**.

Bengal-a *pr.n.m.* (geog.) Bengal; (*indecl.*, or *pl.* **-i**) Bengal light; firework; coloured flare. **-ese** *adj.* Bengali. **-ì** *m.* Bengali (language). **-ina** *f.* (text.) Bengal silk. **-ino** *m.* (orn.) Bengali (bird dealer's name for many small exotic cage-birds, especially the cordon bleu, *Uraeginthus bengalus*).

benga·lico *adj.* Bengali.

bengodi *m. indecl.*, **benguarito** *excl.* See under **ben-accetto**.

Beniam-ino *pr.n.m.* Benjamin; (fig.) favourite; favourite son; essere il — della mamma, to be a mother's darling. **-ina** *f.* favourite (of a girl), favourite daughter, pet. **-ita** *m.* Benjamite, descendant of the tribe of Benjamin; *adj.* of the tribe of Benjamin.

benign-o *adj.* kind; mild, benign; gracious; clima —, mild climate; (med.) light, mild, not dangerous. (**-amente** *adv.*) †**-anza** *f.* See **beninanza**. **-are** [A 5] *rfl.* to deign. **-ità** *f.* benignity, kindliness, mildness, clemency.

†**beninanza** *f.* well-being.

benino *adv.* See under **bene**.

benintenzionato *adj.* well-meaning, well-intentioned.

ben-inteso *adj.*, **-nato** *adj.* See under **ben-accetto**.

†**beni·volo** *adj.* See **benevolo**.

benna *f.* wickerwork carriage; builder's hod; grab (on a crane or excavator); (naut.) grab for raising wrecks, etc.

bennato *adj.* well-born; well-bred; well disposed; †blessed.

ben·nola *f.* (zool.) weasel, *Mustela nivalis*.

benone *adv.* See under **bene**.

ben-parlante *adj.*, **-pensante** *adj.*, **-portante** *adj.*, **-servito** *m.* See under **ben-accetto**.

bensì *adv.* See under **ben-accetto**.

bentamismo *m.* (philos.) Benthamism.

bentonite *f.* (miner.) bentonite.

bentornato, etc. See under **ben-accetto**.

benzalde·ide *f.* (chem.) benzaldehyde, artificial essential oil of almonds.

benzene *m.* (chem.) benzene.

benzin-a *f.* petrol, motor spirit; serbatoio della —, petrol-tank; bidone per —, petrol can; distributore della —, petrol-pump; far —, to fill up. **-a·io** *m.*, **-aro** *m.* petrol-pump attendant. (**-a·ia** *f.*)

benzoato *m.* (chem.) benzoate.

benz·o·e *m.* benzoin. **-o·ico** *adj.* (chem.) benzoic. **-oino** *m.* (bot.) Sumatra gum-tree, *Styrax benzoin*; (chem.) benzoin, bitter-almond-oil camphor. **-olina** *f.* benzine. **-olo** *m.* (chem.) benzene, benzol.

benzoile *m.* (chem.) benzoyl.

be·ola *f.* (geol.) a schistic variety of granite.

beone *m.* heavy drinker; winebibber.

beot-a *m.* Boeotian; (fig.) thick-headed person, dunce. **-ismo** *m.* dullness, stupidity.

beo·tico *adj.* Boeotian.

Beo·zia *pr.n.f.* (geog.) Boeotia.

bequadro *m.* (mus.) natural; †B natural.

ber·bero[1] *m.* (bot.) barberry-bush, *Berberis vulgaris*.

ber·bero[2] *adj.*, *n.m.* native of Barbary; Berber.

†**berbice** *f.* sheep.

berci-are [A 3] *intr.* (*aux.* avere) (Tusc.) to screech. **-ata** *f.* screech; screeching. **-one** *m.* screeching child.

ber·cio *m.* screech.

†**berciloc·chio** *m.* squint-eyed individual.

bere [B 4] *tr.* to drink; — a centellini, to sip; — a sazietà, to drink one's fill; — alla salute di, to drink to the health of, to propose the health of, to drink a toast to; to absorb; to suck up; (fig.) to believe; a me non lo dai a —, you can't expect me to swallow that; to drink in, to swallow; — con gli occhi, to drink in with one's eyes, to gaze at in rapture; uova da —, soft-boiled eggs; — un uovo, to swallow an egg raw; come — un uovo, as easy as falling off a log; — grosso, to be credulous; not to take account of details; berla, beversela, to swallow (something) hook, line and sinker; — d'un fiume, to live on the bank of a river; — del sangue, to get rich at the expense of others; — le distanze, to cover the ground at speed; beverseli tutti, to squander all one's inheritance in drink or riotous living; *abs.* to drink; to have something to drink; o — o affogare, sink or swim; (provb.) date da — al prete, chè il chierico ha sete, 'give the priest something to drink because the clerk is thirsty', quoted when receiving a request ostensibly for a third person but really for the benefit of the asker; (naut.) to ship water over the gunwale; (of a horse) — la briglia, — il morso, to swallow the bit; (billiards) to make a stroke which cancels a previous score.

Bere-cinto *m.* Berecyntus, a mountain in Phrygia, famed for the worship of Cybele. **-cin·tio** *adj.* Berecyntian; Phrygian, orgiastic.

beretta *f.* See **berretta**.

†**ber·fia** *adv. phr.* di —, secretly.

†**berga** *f.* dyke, bank.

bergamasc-o *adj.* from Bergamo, of Bergamo, Bergamask; *n.m.* native of Bergamo; †cloth from Bergamo. **-a** *f.* woman from Bergamo; (mus.) Bergomask.

bergamina[1] *f.* (N. Ital.) herd of cows famed for rich yield of milk.

bergamina[2] *f.* (Tusc.). See **pergamena**.

Ber·gamo *pr.n.f.* (geog.) Bergamo.

bergamott-a *f.* fragrant variety of pear; Bergamot orange, from the skin of which the perfume, 'olio di —', is derived. **-o** *m.* Bergamot orange-tree, *Citrus bergamina*.

†**bergantino** *m.* (naut.). See **brigantino**.

†**berghinella** *f.* loose woman, slut.

bergna *f.* peasant dress.

†**bergolare** *intr.* to chatter, to chat.

†**ber·golo** *adj.* light, volatile; yielding; unstable; simple-minded; rimanere —, to be mocked; *n.m.* (naut.) crank.

beri-beri *m.* (med.) beriberi.

beril·lio *m.* (chem.) beryllium, glucin(i)um.

berillo *m.* beryl.

beri(u)olo *m.* water-trough for a bird.

†**berleffe**[1] *m.* wound, injury.

berleffe[2] *m.* (slang) face; chin.

†**berlengo** *m.* dining-table.

Berlicche *pr.n.m.* (joc.) the devil, old Nick; far berlicche e berlocche, to break one's word; 'Lettere di Berlicche', 'The Screwtape Letters'.

berlina[1] *f.* pillory; stocks; 'stool of repentance', a parlour game in which one of the players sits in the middle to be criticized; mettere alla —, to pillory, to criticize, to deride.

berlina[2] *f.* (motor.) saloon, coupé; — sport, sports saloon; berlin, a luxurious coach; state-coach.

berlinga *f.* (numis.) old Milanese silver coin; cockpit.

berlingac·c·io *m.* (Tusc.) the last Thursday of the Carnival season. **-ino** *m. dim.* the last Thursday but one of the Carnival season.

†**berlingare** *intr.* to sit comfortably after a meal and chat.

berlingozz·a *f.* a kind of country dance. **-o** *m.* a large rich 'ciambella', ring-cake.

Berlin-o *pr.n.f.* (geog.) Berlin. **-ese** *adj.* Berlin; *n.m., f.* Berliner.

berlocca *f.* (naut.) dinner hour.

berlocche *m. indecl.* See **berlicche**.

berlusco *adj.* (Lomb., Ven.) squint-eyed.

berma *f.* enlarged base at the end of a pier; step half-way up an escarpment.

Bermude *pr.n.f.pl.* (geog.) Bermuda, the Bermudas.

bermudiana *f.* (bot.) Bermuda cedar, *Juniperus bermudiana*; — graminea, blue-eyed grass, *Sisyrinchium angustifolium*.

Berna *pr.n.f.* (geog.) Berne.

Bernabita *pr.n.m.* (eccl.). See **Barnabita**.

Bernardo *pr.n.m.* Bernard; (fig.) simpleton; — l'eremita, hermit crab.

bernecche *adv. phr.* essere in —, andare in —, to be drunk.

bern-eggiare [A 3 c], †**-ieggiare** *intr.* (*aux.* avere) to write after the style of Francesco Berni, burlesque poet of the sixteenth century. **-escante** *m.* author of burlesque poems in the style of Berni. **-esco** *adj.* (*m.pl.* **-eschi**) after the style of Berni; *adv.* alla **-esca**, in the style of Berni; *n.m.* prendere in **-esco**, to give a burlesque twist to, to read a double meaning into.

†**ber·nia** *f.* woman's dress shaped like a coat.

bernoc·col·o *m.* bump, protuberance either on the rind of a fruit, such as a cucumber, or on a person's head; prominence; swelling; (fig.) aver il — di, to have a talent for, to have a flair for; heavy mass of wood or stone. **-uto** *adj.* bumpy; knotted, gnarled.

bernusse *m.* burnous; large cloak with hood.

berrett-a *f.* cap; man's headgear; in —, wearing a cap; far di —, cavarsi la —, to touch one's cap, to raise one's hat; val più una — che cento cuffie, one man is worth more than a hundred women; (eccl.) biretta; — da prete, priest's hat, (bot.) spindlewood, skewerwood, *Euonymus europaeus*; (bot.) — di prete, bishop's hat, barren wort, *Epimedium alpinum*. **-a·io** *m.* seller or maker of caps; menar le mani come i **-ai**, to act speedily, to be quick. **-eri·a** *f.* hat shop. **-ifi·cio** *m.* cap factory. **-ino** *m. dim.* of **berretto**; child's cap; *adj.* greenish-grey; bad, malignant. **-o** *m.* cap with a peak or tassel; cardinal's hat; **-o** frigio, Phrygian cap, emblem of republicanism; **-o** a busta, forage cap; **-o** con visiera, peaked cap; **-o** basco, beret; **-o** da notte, nightcap. **-occo** *m.* (*pl.* **-occhi**) dunce's cap, foolscap. **-one** *m. augm.* professor's, judge's, doctor's cap; (zool.) **-one** di dragone, bonnet limpet, *Capulus hungaricus*.

†**berriuola** *f.* cap, skull-cap.

†**berro**[1] *m.* (mil.) gun-carriage.

†**berro**[2] *m.* glass, tumbler.

†**berrov·a·glia** *f.* troop of foot-soldiers. †**-iere** *m.* foot-soldier.

bersacca *f.* (dial. N. Italy) knapsack, rucksack, haversack.

bersaglier-e *m.* sharpshooter, Bersagliere; (slang) stump of a cigar; *pl.* the name of a crack corps of the Italian army; *adv. phr.* alla **-a**, like Bersaglieri, either in regard to uniform or to their characteristic rapid march; daringly, with dash; at full speed. **-ata** *f.* smack, slap, blow with the hand; blow on the head.

bersa·gli-o *m.* target; mark; shooting butts; shooting range; tiro al —, target practice; (fig.) butt; laughing-stock; †fight, encounter. **-are** [A 4] *tr.* to batter (with artillery); to fire upon; to shell; (fig.) to torment.

bersgrundo *m.* crevasse.

bersò *m. indecl.* summer house; arbour.

Berta[1] *pr.n., f.* 'Mrs Brown': the names Donna Berta and Ser Martino have long been used to denote ordinary people (as in Dante, *Par.* XIII, 139) and as such they occur in many sayings; e.g. non è più il tempo che Berta filava, it is not like it was in the good old days; al tempo della regina Berta, years and years ago;

joke, trick, trifle; raillery; dare la —, to play a trick; lace mantilla; (mil.) la grossa —, big Bertha; (orn.) shearwater; — maggiore, Mediterranean shearwater, *Puffinus kuhli*; — minore, Manx shearwater, *Puffinus puffinus*; jay, *Garrulus glandarius*. **-eggia-mento** *m.* bantering, chaff; joke, jest, trick. **-eggiare** [A 3 c] *tr.* to play a trick on; to mock. (**-eggiatore** *m.* **-eggiatrice** *f.*)

berta[2] *f.* pile-driver; rammer; drop hammer.

†**bertabello** *m.* See **bertuello**.

bertagnino *m.* small type of salt cod.

bertesc-a *f.* drawbridge between two turrets; bartisan, battlement tower; watchtower; tower drawn by elephants; scaffold platform for builders or decorators; †(naut.) castle. †**-are** *tr.* to fortify with turrets; *intr.* to strive, to exert oneself. †**-ato** *part. adj.* fortified with turrets; turreted.

bertina *f.* (orn.) jay, *Garrulus glandarius*.

†**bertino** *adj.* grey, ash-grey.

Berto *pr.n.m.* (abbrev. of **Alberto**) Bert.

bertoc·cio *m.* (naut.) small wooden ball; truck; parrel-truck.

bertoldo[1] *m.* simpleton, dunce (cf. 'Bertoldo, Bertoldino e Cacasenno' by G. C. Croce); *pl.* (joc.) beans.

†**bertoldo**[2] *m.* unfinished cloth.

†**bertolotto** *adv. phr.* a —, gratis, for nothing; mangiare a —, to live scot-free.

bertone[1] *m.* horse with cropped ears; (joc.) man with his hair cropped short; gigolo; (ichth.) gudgeon, *Gobio fluviatilis*.

†**bertone**[2] *m.* (naut.) large boat without masts.

bertovello *m.* See **bertuello**.

Bertrando *pr.n.m.* Bertrand.

†**bertresca** *f.* See **bertesca**.

bertuc·ci-a *f.* (zool.) Barbary ape, *Macacus inuus*; (fig.) ugly gossiping person; pigliar la —, to get drunk. **-ata** *f.* monkey-trick; act of foolishness. **-evole** *adj.* aping; foolish; **-one** *m. augm.* large male Barbary ape.

bertuell-o *m.* bow-net, eel-pot; a similar contrivance for catching birds; essere il — della gente, to be a laughing-stock. **-are** [A 1] *tr.* to trap.

†**beruse** *m.* amphibious reptile.

beruzzo, beruz·zolo *m.* (Tusc.) peasants' meal eaten out in the fields, snack.

†**berza** *f.* shin; levare le berze, to take to one's heels, to run fast.

†**berzagallo** *m.* poison made from arsenic and sulphur.

†**berza·glio** *m.* See **bersaglio**.

†**berzare** *tr.* to hit with an arrow.

berzelina *f.* (miner.) Berzelianite.

Beschidi *pr.n.m.m.pl.* (geog.) Beskidy (Mts.).

besciamella *f.* (cul.) Bechamel (sauce).

†**be·scio** *adj.* stupid.

†**bess-o** *adj.* stupid. †**-ag·gine**, †**-eri·a** *f.* stupidity.

†**bestegna** *f.* See **bestemmia**.

bestem·mi-a *f.* blasphemy; è una —!, it's blasphemy!; swearing; imprecation, oath, curse; invective; vulgar language; false criticism, false judgment. **-ante** *part. adj.* cursing; swearing; blaspheming; *n.m., f.* swearer; foul-mouthed person; blasphemer. **-are** [A 4 c] *intr.* (*aux.* avere) to swear; **-are** come un turco, to swear like a trooper; *tr.* to curse; to blaspheme; to grumble at; **-are** una lingua, to murder a language. **-ato** *part. adj.* cursed; accursed. **-atore** *m.* blasphemer. (**-atrice** *f.*) **-one** *m.* person who swears habitually.

be·sti-a *f.* beast, animal; creature (applied to birds, insects, fish, as well as to animals); *pl.* cattle; animals, animal kingdom; living creatures; — da soma, beast of burden; fool, ignoramus; irreligious person; andare in —, to fly into a rage; fur, fox-fur; game of chance played with cards; (ent.) — della vergine, ladybird, *Coccinella* spp. **-a·io** *m.* herdsman. **-ale** *adj.* bestial, brutish; brutal; beastly; stupid. **-almente** *adv.* in a bestial way; brutally. **-alità** *f.* bestiality; stupidity; dire della **-alità**, to talk nonsense; fare delle **-alità**, to do silly things; animality. **-ame** *m.* cattle; livestock; venti capi di **-ame**, twenty head of cattle. **-are** [A 4] *tr.* (slang) to insult, to call (someone) a fool. **-a·rio** *m.* bestiary; herdsman; (hist.) gladiator who fought with wild beasts. **-ola** *f.* little creature, little animal; fool; povera **-ola**!, poor creature! **-one** *m. augm.* ugly beast; dirty brute; ignoramus.

bet-a[1] *f.* beta, second letter of Greek alphabet. **-acismo** *m.* (ling.) mispronunciation of the consonant B.

Beta[2] *pr.n.f.* (Ven. dial.) la siora —, gossip, gossiping woman.

betaina *f.* (chem.) betaine.

Betani·a *pr.n.f.* (geog.) Bethany.

betaterapi·a *f.* (med.) betatherapy.

betatrone *m.* (atom. phys.) betatron, induction electron accelerator.

betizzare [A I] *intr.* (*aux.* avere) to be dull mentally; to be limp, to be flaccid.

Betlemme *pr.n.f.* (geog.) Bethlehem.

beton *m. indecl.* See **betone**.

beton-e *m.* (techn.) concrete. **-are** *tr.* [A I c] (techn.) to concrete, to cement. **-ata** *f.* construction in concrete. **-iera** *f.* cement-mixer.

beto·nica *f.* (bot.). See **bettonica**.

betta¹ *f.* (naut.) ship's boat; (Genoese) long boat; (Ven.) boat, lighter, hopper.

Betta² *pr.n.f.* (abbrev. of **Elisabetta**) Betty.

bet·tica *f.* (mil.) torpedo-thrower.

Bettina *pr.n.f.* Betsy; (dial. N. Ital.) la siora —, Death.

bettol-a *f.* jug-and-bottle shop, tavern; wine-shop; parole da —, vulgar language. **-are** [A I sc] *intr.* (*aux.* avere) to frequent low taverns; *n.m.* loud, vulgar talk. **-ante** *m.* tavern-keeper; pub-crawler; frequenter of taverns. **-iere** *m.* tavern-keeper. **-ina** *f.* (naut.) lighter, hopper. **-ino** *m.* (mil.) canteen, N.A.A.F.I. **-ìo** *m.* noisy talk.

betto·nica *f.* (bot.) betony, *Stachys officinalis*; conosciuto come la —, very well known; (provb.) avere più virtù della —, to be a cure-all.

betulla *f.* (bot.) birch-tree, *Betula*.

betulina *f.* (chem.) betulin.

bev-a *f.* time when a wine is fit to drink; beverage, drink; a buona —, fit to drink, worth drinking; essere nella sua —, to be in one's element. **-ace** *adj.* absorbent; porous. **-agna** *adv. phr.* (dial. Umbr.) andare a -agna, to go for a drink (pun on **Bevagna**, town in Umbria).

bevanda *f.* drink; beverage; i cibi e le bevande, food and drink; — alcoolica, alcoholic beverage.

bevatrone *m.* (phys.) bevatron.

bevazzare [A I] *intr.* (*aux.* avere) to guzzle.

bever-aggio *m.* drink (esp. for cattle); tip, pourboire; †(naut.) wine and water (equiv. of English 'grog'). †**-aglia** *f.* beverage, drink, potion.

bever-are [A I s]. See **abbeverare**. **-ato** *part. adj.* (poet.) that has drunk (of).

bever-atoio *m.* trough; horse-pond. **-eccio** *adj.* drinkable; delectable. **-ino** *m.* drinking bowl, trough (in a bird-cage). **-one** *m.* beverage; (for horses) bran mash; drenching, ducking; †poison.

be·vere [B 4] *tr.* See **bere**.

be·vero *m.* (zool.) beaver.

bev-i·bile *adj.* drinkable; reasonably pleasant to drink; (fig.) credible. **-icchiare** [A 4] *intr.* (*aux.* avere) to tipple; *tr.* to sip. †**-ilacqua** *m.* abstainer, water-drinker. †**-imento** *m.* drinking, drink; beverage, potion. **-itore** *m.* drinker; hard drinker, wine-bibber, tippler. (**-itrice** *f.*) †**-itorio** *m.* chalice, cup. **-ìtura** *f.* drink, drinking. **-one** *m.* heavy drinker, drunkard. **-ucchiare** *intr.* (*aux.* avere) to tipple; *tr.* to drink slowly, to sip. **-uta** *f.* drink, beverage; draught; act of drinking; drinking bout; (chem.) flask. **-uto** *part.* of **bere**, q.v.; *adj.* (N. Ital., colloq.) tipsy.

bey *m. indecl.* See **bei¹**.

bezioli *m.pl.* false spectacles to cure squint.

bezoar *m. indecl.* See **belzoar**.

bezzic-are [A 2 sc] *tr.* to peck at; to pick on; to tease; to quarrel with, to bicker with; to 'fleece' (of money); (mil.) to harass; *recip. rfl.* to bicker; to nag at one another. **-ata** *f.* peck; quarrel. **-atura** *f.* pecking, peck; bickering.

bezzo *m.* (numis.) a small Venetian coin; (fig.) essere senza un —, to be penniless; *pl.* money; avere dei bezzi, to be well off.

bezzoarre, bezzuardo *m.* See **belzoar**.

bi *m., f. indecl.* the letter B; *excl.* — e ro: the cry used by peasants to urge oxen on, 'ro' for the right-hand one which is usually red (rosso) and 'bi' for the left-hand one which is usually white (bianco).

biacc-a *f.* white lead; white make-up, wet white; whitewash. (**-oso** *adj.*)

biac-co¹ *m.* (*pl.* **-chi**) (zool.) *Zamenis gemonensis*, rat snake.

biac-co² *adj.* (*m.pl.* **-chi**) angry; venomous.

biac-co³ *adj.* (*m.pl.* **-chi**) weak, feeble, lacking in energy; *n.m.* coward, poltroon; fuggire come un —, to run away like a coward

biad-a *f.* corn; oats; (for horses) feed, fodder; le -e, the crops; †victuals, provisions. **-ai(u)olo** *m.* corn-merchant, corn-chandler. **-are** [A I] *tr.* to feed on oats; to feed with corn; to give fodder to. **-ato** *part. adj.* fed; cavallo ben -ato, well-fed horse. **-ume** *m.* corn; grain; cereal.

†**biado¹** *m.* See **biada**.

biad-o² *adj.* sky-blue. **-etto** *m. dim.* sky-blue; blue carbonate of copper.

Bia·gio *pr.n.m.* Blaise; (fig.) simpleton; adagio, —!, gently, Bentley!; slow, Joe!

Bianca¹ *pr.n.f.* Blanche.

bianc-a² *f.* See under **bianco**. †**-aiuola** *f.*, †**-agno** *adj.*, **-ana** *f.*, **-astro** *adj.* See under **bianco**.

Biancaneve *pr.n.f.* Snow White.

†**biancare** *vb.* and derivs. See **imbiancare**.

biancarossa *f.* (ent.) Spanish red scale insect, *Chrysomphalus dictyospermi*, a serious pest of citrus fruit.

biancheggi-are [A 3 c] *intr.* (*aux.* avere) to turn white; to show white; to look white; to shine with a white light; to blanch; (of hair) to go grey, to turn white; (of hills) to become snow-covered; *tr.* to bleach, to whiten. **-amento** *m.* blanching, turning white. **-ante** *part. adj.* whitening, lightening; whitish. **-atore** *m.* house-painter.

biancheri·a *f.* linen or cotton goods; laundry; — da tavola, table linen; — da letto, bed linen; — personale, underclothes; (leg.) — dotale, trousseau (C.C.).

bianchetta *f.* (text.) white lining cloth; (bot.) variety of wheat, *Triticum hibernum subaristatum*.

bianch-etto *adj.* whitish; pale; *n.m.* whitewash; bleach for clothes; blanco; (paint.) flake white; (theatr.) wet white; (ichth.) white-bait; (bot. Tusc.) See **bianchetta**. **-ezza** *f.* whiteness; dazzling white. **-iccio** *adj.* dingy white; off-white. **-ina** *f.* (slang) snow.

bianch-ire [D 2] *tr.* to bleach; to blanch; to whiten; to scour; to clean, to polish (metal); *intr.* (*aux.* essere) to bleach; to whiten. **-imento** *m.* bleaching; whitening; cleaning of silver; metal-polish. **-ito** *part. adj.* white; whitened; bleached; cleaned, polished (of metal).

biancic-are [A 2 s] *intr.* to turn white, to whiten; to show white, to gleam white. **-ante** *adj.* (poet.) whitish. **-ore** *m.* (poet.) whiteness.

bian-co (*m.pl.* **-chi**)

1. White: — come la neve, white as snow; — come il latte, milk-white; — come i gigli, lily-white; — come l'avorio, ivory-white; — come l'argento, silvery white; vino —, white wine; pane —, white bread; razza -ca, white race; bandiera -ca, white flag, flag of truce; carbone —, 'white coal', hydro-electric power; (fig.) segnare col carbone —, to mark with a white stone; l'arte -ca, the baking trade; una mosca -ca, a great rarity, a thing seen once in a blue moon, a unique person; un amico vero è una mosca -ca, true friends are few and far between; capelli -chi, white hair; mettere i capelli -chi, to go grey, to go white-haired; è cosa da far venire i capelli -chi, it's enough to turn one's hair grey; ci ho messo i capelli -chi, I grew old and hoary in its service; — e rosso, pink and white, in the pink of health; (geog.) il Monte Bianco, Mont Blanc; il Mar Bianco, the White Sea. 2. Pale, wan: — come un cencio, white as a sheet, pale as a ghost; fare il viso —, to turn pale, to look wan; (mus.) voce -ca, treble voice; (anat.) i canali -chi, the lymphatics. 3. Fair, shining, bright: carnagione -ca, fair complexion; vedere tutto —, to look on the bright side, to be optimistic, to see everything through rose-coloured spectacles; arma -ca, 'cold steel', bayonet, sword, etc. (not a firearm); attaccare all'arma -ca, to attack with bayonets; metallo —, silver, nickel, etc.; (poet.) — aprile, shining April; clear, evident. 4. Blank, empty; spazio —, blank space; foglio —, blank page; schede -che o nulle, voting papers left blank; dare carta -ca, to give carte blanche; sciopero —, stay-in strike; notte -ca, sleepless night; tavola -ca, dessert; rimanere —, to come off badly, to be made a fool of; (comm.) segno —, see **biancosegno**. 5. *n.m.* (i) white: — d'argento, fine white lead; — di cerussa, white lead; — d'Olanda, Flemish white; — di zinco, zinc white, zinc oxide, lithopone; mettere il nero sul —, mettere nero su —, to set it down in black and white, to put pen to paper; (art) artista in — e nero, black-and-white artist; fare del — nero, to do exactly the opposite in all respects; pigliare il — per nero, to misunderstand completely, to get a thing back to front; tra loro c'è la differenza che c'è tra il — e il nero, they

bian-co (*cont.*)

are as different as chalk from cheese; whitewash, limewash, distemper; dare di — a, dare il — a, to whitewash, (fig.) to blot out, to cancel, to wash out; il — dell'occhio, the white of the eye; guardare qualcuno nel — dell'occhio, to look a person straight in the eye; white of egg, albumen; vestire di —, to dress in white, to wear white; cucire di —, to mend linen; cucitrice in —, seamstress; (cul.) in —, seasoned with oil and lemon, or butter and cheese; pasta in —, macaroni served with butter and without sauce; pesce in —, boiled fish; (geog.) il Bianco, Mont Blanc; (naut.) untarred timber or hemp; — di balena, whale-fat. **(ii)** blank, blank space: in —, left blank, not written on; lasciare in —, to leave blank; firmare in —, to sign a blank document; (comm.) abuso di —, abuse of blank cheque; (typ.) — alla base, beard; (fig.) di punto in —, like a bolt from the blue. **(iii)** (hist.) i Bianchi, the Whites, a political party formed from among the Guelphs of Florence in 1300; (pol.) anti-clerical party in Rome. **(iv)** (numis.) silver coin. **-ca** *f.* white girl, white woman; fair girl, fair-haired woman; la tratta delle **-che**, white slave traffic; (agric.) **-ca** dei limoni, oleander scale; (typ.) stampare di **-ca** e volta, to print both sides of a page at the same time; (ent.) first moult of a silkworm; white woollen cloth used for linings; †(naut.) bunt whip. **-agno** *adj.* whitish. **-aiuola** *f.* linen maid in a convent. **-ana** *f.* (geog.) weathered infertile clay; vast tract of whitish barren countryside. **-arossa** *f.* (agric.) dictyospermum scale. **-astro** *adj.* whitish. **-olina** *f.* (ent.) second moult of a silk-worm. **-one** *adj. augm.* big and whitish, rather white; pallid; *n.m.* pale-complexioned person; (orn.) short-toed eagle, serpent eagle, *Circaetus gallicus*; (bot.) variety of white grape grown in Elba; (numis.) large silver coin of Modena; (art) il Biancone, the statue of Neptune in the Piazza della Signoria in Florence. **-onella** *f.* variety of white wine. **-ore** *m.* whiteness; pallor. **-oso** *adj.* whitish. **-ume** *m.* quantity of white things; mass of white; whitish substance.

Biancofiore[1] *pr.n.f.* Blanchefleur.

biancofior-e[2] *m.* kind of dance for two couples; (pol., slang) 'democristiano'. **-ito** *adj.* white-flowering.

biancomangiare *m.* blancmange.

bianconerista *m.* black-and-white artist.

biancoro·seo *adj.* pink, rose.

biancosegno *m.* (comm.) blank cheque; blank receipt.

biancospino *m.* (bot.) hawthorn, may-tree, whitethorn, *Crataegus oxyacantha*.

biancovestito *adj.* (poet.) white-clad, white-garbed.

†**biante** *m.* vagabond, vagrant.

bia·sci-a *f.* slobber, slaver; (on a horse) foam, froth. **-are** [A 3], **-icare** [A 2 s] *tr.* to chew with the gums (of a toothless person); to eat without appetite, to mix round in the mouth; to slobber over; to lisp, to murmur indistinctly, to mumble, to mouth; **-icare** paternostri, to mutter prayers; **-icarla** male, to suffer a thing with a bad grace, to do something unwillingly. **-amento**, **-icamento** *m.* mumbling. **-ntin·goli** *m. indecl.* good-for-nothing. **-amidolle** *m. indecl.* (joc.) toothless individual. **-amoc·coli**, **-anovene**, **-paternostri**, **-arosari** *m. indecl.* hypocritical devotee, religious humbug. **-asorbacerbe** *m. indecl.* wry-mouthed individual. **-icatura** *f.* mixing round in the mouth; mouthing, lisping, mumbling. **-cone** *m.* slobberer; lisper. **-cotto** *m.* spewed-out pellet or mouthful of food.

biasim-are [A I s] *tr.* to blame; to disapprove of; to censure; to reprove; to vituperate, to upbraid; *rfl.* to complain. **-a·bile** *adj.* blameworthy. **-amento** *m.* blame, disapproval, censure. (**-atore** *m.* **-atrice** *f.*) **-evole** *adj.* culpable, blameworthy, censurable, to blame; †disgusted, repelled. **-evolmente** *adv.* culpably, in a blameworthy manner.

bia·sim-o *m.* blame, censure; reproach; ill repute; fault; dare — a, to blame, to censure; avere —, to be blamed.

biasmo *m.* (poet.). See **biasimo**.

biassale, **bias·sico** *adj.* biaxial.

†**biato** *adj.* See **beato**.

biava *f.* (dial.). See **biada**.

†**biavo** *adj.* pale blue, light blue; faded.

†**bibace** *adj.* fond of wine; (fig.) absorbent.

biba·sico *adj.* (chem.) dibasic.

Bib·bi-a *f.* Bible; (fig.) gospel, gospel-truth; (joc.) long document or speech; fare la —, to sermonize; (paperm.) carta —, India paper. **-aro** *m.* vendor of the Protestant Bible.

bib·bio *m.* (orn.) widgeon, *Anas penelope*.

†**bi·bere** *vb.* See **bere**.

bibero·n *m. indecl.* baby's feeding bottle; allevato col —, bottle-fed, brought up on the bottle.

bi·bita *f.* soft drink; long, cool drink; draught, potion; — alcoolica, long alcoholic drink.

bi·bl-ico *adj.* biblical, relating to the Bible; solemn; prophetic. †*n.m.* expounder of the Bible. **-ista** *m.*, *f.* biblicist. **-i·stica** *f.* biblical study.

bibli-obu·s *m. indecl.* mobile library. **-ocromi·a** *f.* printing of a volume on coloured paper. **-ofili·a** *f.* bibliophily. **-ofilm** *m. indecl.* reproduction of a book in microfilm. **-o·filo** *m.* book-lover; bibliophile. **-ofoto** *m.* photographic apparatus producing microfilms. **-ogno·stica** *f.* knowledge of the value of books. **-ografi·a** *f.* bibliography. **-ogra·fico** *adj.* bibliographical. **-ografi-camente** *adv.* bibliographically. **-o·grafo** *m.* bibliographer. **-oia·trica** *f.* care and repair of books. **-olatri·a** *f.* bibliolatry, book-worship; blind faith in the letter of the Bible; fundamentalism. **-o·lito** *m.* (archaeol.) papyrus rolls carbonized by the eruption of Vesuvius and found at Herculaneum. **-ologi·a** *f.* bibliology; book-lore. (**-olo·gico** *adj.*) **-o·logo** *m.* bibliologist; student of books. **-omani·a** *f.* bibliomania. **-o·mane** *m.* bibliomaniac. **-omanzi·a** *f.* divination by consulting a text (e.g. the Bible or Virgil) at random. **-o·metro** *m.* book measure. **-ope·a** *f.* art of making books. †**-opega** *m.* bookbinder. †**-o·pola** *m.* bibliopole; bookseller. **-ota·fio** *m.* place where books are kept which are not to be read. **-o·tafo** *m.* person who jealously hides his books. **-ote·cnica** *f.* librarianship. **-oterapi·a** *f.* repair and restoration of books.

bibliotec-a *f.* library; series (of books); — circolante, circulating library; — pubblica di prestito, public lending library; (joc.) — ambulante, walking encyclopaedia. **-a·rio** *m.* librarian. **-ologi·a** *f.*, **-onomi·a** *f.* librarianship.

bi·bulo *adj.* absorbent; carta bibula, blotting paper; (geog.) watery.

bic-a *f.* stook; heap of sheaves; rick; heap of dung. **-one** *m. augm.* large stook; (fig.) fat clumsy person. (**-ona** *f.*)

bicamer-ale *adj.* (pol.) two-chamber. **-ismo** *m.* (pol.) system of political representation by two Houses.

bicarbonato *m.* (chem.) bicarbonate; — di soda, bicarbonate of soda, baking-powder.

bicchier-e *m.* drinking-glass; tumbler; cup; beaker; — di vino, glass of wine; — da vino, wine-glass; glassful; amico del —, friend of the bottle; (chem.) beaker; (fig.) wine drinking; — della staffa, stirrup cup; culi di —, sham diamonds; affogare in un — d'acqua, see under **acqua**; (bot.) potare a —, to trim trees to the shape of a cup; (bldg.) joint sleeve, socket (widened end of pipe section); (eng.) giunto a —, spigot-and-socket joint. †**-a·io** *m.* vendor of glassware; glass-blower; maker or vendor of wine-glasses. **-ata** *f.* glassful; round (of drinks); toast, health; wine-party, celebration. **-ino** *m. dim.* of **bicchiere**, q.v.; little drink, tot; posso offrirti un -ino?, won't you have a drop? †**-o** *m.* See **bicchiere**. **-otto** *m. augm.* largish glass.

†**biccaiacuto** *m.* two-edged chopper, twibil.

bicciare [A 3] *intr.* (*aux.* avere), *recip. rfl.* (Tusc.) to butt with the horns.

bic·cico *m.* (Arezzo) bruise, contusion.

†**biccicocca** *f.* See **bicocca**.

†**bicciu·ghera** *f.* restive wild animal.

bice[1] *adj.* (dial. Pisa) — sera!, good evening!; — notte!, good night!

Bice[2] *pr.n.f.* abbrev. of **Beatrice**.

bice·falo *adj.* two-headed, bicephalous.

bici *f. indecl.* (slang) bike.

bician·cole *f.pl.* see-saw.

bicicl-etta *f.* bicycle, cycle; andare in —, to ride a bicycle, to go by bicycle, to cycle; — a due posti, tandem; — da corsa, racing-bicycle; — da strada, roadster. **-ettare** [A I c] *intr.* (*aux.* avere) to cycle. **-ettina** *f. dim.* (child's) fairy cycle. **-ista** *m.*, *f.* cyclist. **-o** *m.* old-fashioned bicycle, 'penny-farthing'; *pl.* †pince-nez.

bicifurto *m.* stealing of bicycles.

bicimotore *m.* autocycle.

†**bici·nio** *m.* (mus.) bicinium.

bici·pit-e[1] *adj.* two-headed; l'aquila —, the two-headed eagle, symbol of the Austrian Empire; (poet.) il — monte, Parnassus. **-ale** *adj.* See **bicipite**.

bici·pite[2] *m.* (anat.) biceps.

bicloruro *m.* (chem.) dichloride.

†**bico** *adj.* oblique; *adv. phr.* a —, askew.

bicocca *f.* small fortress or castle on a hill; (hist.) la battaglia della —, the battle near Milan in which the French and Swiss were defeated, 1522; little tower or terrace built on to a house; hut, shanty (esp. on a steep hill).

bicolore *adj.* in two colours, two-coloured; (hort.) variegated; (pol.) governo —, two-party government (also *n.m.*).

bicomando *adj., indecl.* dual-control.

bicon·cavo *adj.* biconcave.

biconvesso *adj.* biconvex.

bicop·pia *f.* (electr.; teleg.) quad.

bicord-o *m.*, **-atura** *f.* (mus.) bichord; two strings in unison; double note; double stop.

bicorn-e *m.* (zool.) black rhinoceros, *Diceros bicornis*; *adj.* two-horned. **-ia** *f.* anvil with one horn square and the other round; bickern; (leather manuf.) moon knife. †**-o** *adj.* see **bicorne**; †*n.m.* priest's hat. **-uto** *adj.* two-horned, twin-horned; argomento -uto, dilemma.

bicromato *m.* (chem.) dichromate, bichromate.

bicr-omi·a *f.* two-colour illustration. (**-o·mico** *adj.*)

bicron *m. indecl.* (mens.) bicron.

bicu·spid-e *adj.* two-pointed; double-pointed, bicuspid. **-ale**, **-ato** *adj.* (archit.) having two cusps.

†**bidale** *m.* light-infantry soldier.

bidè *m. indecl.* bidet.

bidello *m.* beadle; usher; school-caretaker; janitor.

bidentale *m.* (Rom. hist.) bidental, spot struck by lightning and afterwards consecrated; *pl.* priests of a bidental.

bidentato *adj.* bidentate; bidental.

bidente *m.* two-year-old sheep; two-pronged fork; *adj.* (of a sheep) two-year-old.

†**bidetto** *m.* small horse, nag.

bidiodo *m.* (radio) duplex diode.

†**bidollo** *m.* (bot.). See **betulla**.

bidonare [A I C] *tr.* (football) to barge.

bidon-e *m.* can; drum; — per benzina, petrol tin; (naut.) tub used for issuing wine; (metall.) sheet bar; (slang) swindle, confidence trick; fare un —, to 'put one over'. **-ista** *m.* (slang) swindler, confidence trickster.

biduano *adj.* two-day-old.

bi·e *f.* (Pascoli) violence.

bie-co *adj.* (*pl.* **-chi**); askew; slanting; wrong; ugly; evil; sullen; fierce; grim; *adv.* guardar —, to look askance at, to look threateningly at, to glower at; †*n.m.* slant; incline. **-camente** *adv.* grimly; askance.

bie·gio *adj.* (Tusc.) weak, infirm.

biell-a (eng.) connecting rod; lever; (rlwy.) side rod; (motor.) testa di —, big end; piede di —, small end; (watchm.) connecting plate. **-etta** *f.* (eng.) link-rod. **-ismo** *m.* (eng.) linkage.

†**bieltà** *f.* See **beltà**.

bienn-e *adj.* two-year; two-year-old; (bot.) biennial. **-ale** *adj.* biennial, two-yearly, lasting two years or occurring every two years; *n.m., f.* event occurring every two years, esp. La Biennale, the International Art Exhibition held at Venice every two years.

bien·nio *m.* period of two years; two-year course of study.

†**bie·scio** *adj.* slanting; askew.

†**bieta** *f.* (bot.). See **bietola**.

bieticult-ore *m.* beet-grower. **-ura** *f.* beet-growing, cultivation of beet.

bie·tol-a *f.* beet, beetroot, *Beta vulgaris*, and other chenopodiaceous vegetables; — zuccherina, sugar beet. **-ag·gine** *f.* foolishness, silliness, stupidity. **-ina** *f. dim.* of **bietola** (bot.) dyer's rocket, *Reseda Luteola*. **-one** *m.* (bot.) orach, mountain-spinach, *Atriplex hortensis*; (slang) fool; booby; tearful individual.

biett-a *f.* wedge; (eng.) sunk key, feather key; — traversale, cotter; (fig.) mettere —, to drive a wedge, to cause discord; (typ.) wooden quoin; nut of a violin-bow. **-one** *m.* (joc.) large foot.

bi·fara *f.* (mus.) organ-stop with two pipes to each note, tuned so as to produce a tremulant effect, e.g. Vox Angelica.

bif-ase, **-a·sico** *adj.* (electr.) two-phase.

biff-a *f.* (survey.) sighting stake; (fig.) tirar la —, to use every possible means for attaining some purpose; glass cemented over a crack in a wall in order to see whether the crack gets bigger; white mark placed on a wall which is to be demolished. **-are** [A I] *tr.* to stake out; to mark with a white stake; to cross out.

†**biffo** *adj.* violet-coloured, lilac; *n.m.* violet, lilac (colour).

bi·fido *adj.* bifid, divided into two parts by a cleft or notch; forked.

bifilare *adj.* (electr.) bifilar; double-wire.

bifocale *adj.* (opt.) bifocal.

bifol-co *m.* (*pl.* **-chi**) ploughman; rough peasant; boor; (astron.) Boötes. **-ca** *f.* peasant girl; †variable agricultural measure (as much land as two oxen can plough in a day). **-cheri·a** *f.* art of ploughing; uncouth action, boorish behaviour.

bifonchiare [A 4 C]. See **bofonchiare**.

bi·fora *f.* (archit.) mullioned window with two lights (cf. **biforo**).

biforc-are [A 2 C] *tr.* to bifurcate, to divide into a fork; *rfl.* to branch off, to bifurcate, to fork. **-amento** *m.* fork; branch (railway, road, etc.); branching off. **-ato** *part. adj.* forked; bifurcate. **-atura** *f.* fork; join, junction. **-azione** *f.* bifurcation; branch; branching off, forking. †**-o** *m.* two-pronged fork. **-uto** *adj.* forked; cleft; cloven; (fig.) double-edged. **-uto** *adj.* forked; bifurcate

biforme *adj.* having two shapes, biform.

bi·foro *adj.* with two openings; with two lights; (archit.) finestra bifora, mullioned window with two lights. Cf. **bifora**.

bifronte *adj.* two-fronted, double-fronted; (fig.) double-faced, two-faced; Giano —, Janus, (fig.) two-faced person.

bifteck *m. indecl.* See **bistecca**.

biga *f.* (antiq., hist.) two-horsed racing chariot; (colloq.) horse and trap; *pl.* (naut.) shears.

†**bigallino** *m.* foundling cared for at the Bigallo foundlings' home in Florence.

bi·gam-o *adj.* bigamous; †twice married (legally); *n.m.* bigamist; †one who has married twice (legally); †spouse of such a person. (**-a** *f.*) **-i·a** *f.* bigamy.

bigato *m.* (numis.) ancient Roman silver coin.

bigatt-o *m.* (ent.) silkworm; corn weevil; (mech.) concealed worm spring; (fig.) clever, cunning individual. **-iera** *f.* silkworm house, hatching house. **-iere**, **-ino** *m.* silkworm breeder.

bigat·tolo *m.* See **bigatto**.

bigello *m.* See under **bigio**.

bigeminato *adj.* (bot.) bigeminal.

bigero·gnolo *adj.* See under **bigio**.

bighellare [A I] *intr.* (*aux.* avere), *rfl.* to idle about, to walk about doing nothing.

bighell-onare [A I C] *intr.* (*aux.* avere) to walk aimlessly, to lounge about, to idle. **-onag·gine** *f.*, **-onag·gio** *m.* idleness; vagrancy; lounging about. **-one** *m.* idler, loafer; lounger. **-oni** *adv.* idly; in idleness.

bi·gher-o *m.* lace; (herald.) laced ornamentation. **-a·io** *m.* lace-maker; lace-seller. **-ato** *part. adj.* laced; edged or trimmed with lace. **-ello** *m.* (naut.) hem (awning or sail). **-ino** *m.* lace; ornamentation like lace worked in straw; perforations in a shoe upper.

bi·gia¹ *f.* (orn.) garden warbler, *Sylvia borin*; — grossa, orphean warbler, *S. hortensis*; — padovana, barred warbler, *S. nisoria*.

†**bigia²** *f.* North wind.

bigiallo *adj., n.m.* bright yellow.

bigiarella *f.* (orn.) lesser whitethroat, *Sylvia curruca*.

bigino *m.* (school slang) crib.

bi·g-io *adj.* (*m.pl.* **-i**, *f.pl.* **-e**) grey; pane —, brown bread; dark; obscure; giornata -ia, dull day; scorgere il — dal nero, to be discerning; fare —, to obscure; (fig.) ill-disposed; evil; uncertain, irresolute. **-ello** *m.* coarse, grey cloth. **-ero·gnolo**, **-ic·cio**, **-ino**, **-io·gnolo** *adj.* greyish. **-ione** *m.* (orn.) garden warbler, *Sylvia borin*.

bigiott-eri·a *f.* (theatr.) costume jewellery; shop selling cheap trinkets. **-iere** *m.* cheap jeweller.

bi·gli-a *f.* billiard-pocket; billiard-ball. **-arda·io** *m.* manufacturer of billiard-tables, etc. **-ardo** *m.* billiards; giuocare al -ardo, to play billiards; billiard-table; billiard-room; palla da -ardo, billiard-ball; (joc.) la sua testa è una palla da -ardo, he's as bald as an egg.

bigliard-are [A I] *tr.* (naut.) to caulk. **-ata** *f.* (naut.) caulking-tool.

bigliettina·io *m.* See **bigliettaio**, under **biglietto**.

bigliett-o *m.* ticket; short letter, note; invitation card; — postale, letter card; — di andata e ritorno, return ticket; — di corsa semplice, single ticket; — d'ingresso, ticket of admission; (rlwy.) platform ticket; — di abbonamento, season ticket; — di coincidenza, transfer ticket; — di libero transito, free pass; fare un —, to take a ticket, to buy a ticket; — di (da) visita, visiting card; — augurale, greetings card; — di banca, bank-note; un — da mille,

bigliett-o (*cont.*)
a thousand-lire note; (mil.) — d'alloggio, billet; (naut.) — di uscita, clearance. **-a·io, -a·rio** *m.* ticket clerk; booking-office clerk; box-office attendant; conductor (on bus or tram). (**-a·ia** *f.*) **-eri·a** *f.* booking-office; ticket-office, box-office.

†bigliocco *m.* vagabond, down-and-out.

biglione¹ *m.* base silver.

biglione² *m.* (Tusc.) milking-pail; pail, bucket.

bigiù *m. indecl.* jewel; treasure; (fig.) pearl.

bignè *m. indecl.* (cul.) pastry horn filled with cream.

bigno·n-ia *f.* (bot.) trumpet-flower creeper, *Bignonia capreolata.*

bigodino *m.* hair-curler.

bi·goli *m.pl.* (N. Ital.) spaghetti.

bigol(l)o *m.* (Ven.) yoke (for carrying pails).

bigon·ci-a *f.* (*pl.* **bigonce**) bucket, tub; vat for pressing grapes; measure of 32 litres; a bigonce, in bucketsful; piove a bigonce, it's raining cats and dogs; reading desk, pulpit, rostrum; †essere in —, to be in a fix; †professorial chair. **-o** *m.* large tub with two of the staves longer than the others and perforated for slinging on a pole. **-(u)olo** *m.* pail, bucket.

†bigord-are *intr.* to joust. **†-o** *m.* lance.

bigotta¹ *f.* (naut.) dead-eye.

bigotta² *f.* See under **bigotto**.

bigott-o *m.*, **-a** *f.* over-devout person, over-zealous churchgoer, 'churchy' individual; vecchia -a, old 'church hen'; pious humbug, hypocrite. **-eri·a** *f.* sanctimonious attitude or behaviour. **-ismo** *m.* churchiness, sanctimoniousness, pious cant.

bigri·glia *f.* (radio) auxiliary grid.

bigutta *f.* iron cooking-pot; soup of the poor; heap, pile, mass; long, tedious address or lecture.

bilabi-ale *adj.* (phon.) bilabial. **-ato** *adj.* (bot.) bilabiate.

bilancella *f.* (naut.) each of two boats which operate a seine-net between them.

bilancere *m.* See **bilanciere**, under **bilancia**.

bilan·ci-a *f.* pair of scales; balance; dare il tracollo alla —, to weigh down the scales, to turn the scale; — a ponte, weighbridge; pesare una questione con la — dell'orafo, to weigh up a matter with the utmost care and precision; (mil.) portar l'arme in —, to carry the rifle at the trail; square fishing net operated by dipping; splinter-bar of a carriage to which the traces are fastened; the bar which is hooked on to the splinter-bar when an extra horse is attached; balance (of a watch); (astron.) Libra, the Scales; (econ.) — commerciale, — del commercio, balance of trade; **-a·io** *m.* scales maker; vendor of scales. **-are** [A3] *tr.* to balance, to weigh; to counterpoise; to equal; to ponder; *intr.* (*aux.* avere), *recip. rfl.* to balance, to counterbalance; to be in equilibrium. **-amento** *m.* balancing; balance. **-atamente** *adv.* in equilibrium. **-ato** *part. adj.* balanced; doubtful; ambiguous. **-atore** *m.* balancer; examiner. **-ere** *m.* balance; beam; pendulum; governor; pressa a -ere, beam press; (watchm.) balance. **-eri** *m.pl.* (ent.) halteres; (naut.) gimbals.

bilancino *m. dim.* of **bilancia**, q.v.; trace-horse, extra horse attached to a carriage at a steep hill; postilion who rides such a horse; bar to which the traces of the extra horse are attached; horse that sets the pace; (eng.) rocker arm; (fig.) extra hand in any job.

bilan·cio¹ *m.* (comm.) budget; balance; balance-sheet; — attivo, credit balance; — passivo, debit balance; — preventivo, budget estimate; — consuntivo, definitive budget; mettere in —, to estimate; — di verificazione, trial balance; rimettersi in —, to balance one's budget; commissione per il —, budget committee.

†bilan·cio², †bilancio *m.* undulation.

†bilanza *f.* See **bilancia**.

bilateral-e *adj.* bilateral; mutual; reciprocal. **-ità** *f.* bilateralism, reciprocity.

†bilbire *intr.* to gurgle.

bilbocchetto *m.* cup-and-ball game.

bil-e *f.* (med.) bile; atra —, blood in the stomach; anger; bad-temper; muovere la — a, fare della — a, to anger, to annoy, to upset; farsi della —, to be moved to anger; rodersi dalla —, to be gnawed by anger. **-iare** *adj.* (med.) biliary, bilious, pertaining to bile; calcoli -iari, gall-stones. **-ia·rio** *adj.* (med.) biliary, containing bile. **-ioso** *adj.* (med.) bilious; (fig.) sour, bad-tempered, peevish.

bilenco *adj.* crooked; bandy-legged (cf. **sbilenco**).

bi·li-a *f.*, **-ardo** *m.* See **biglia** and derivs.

bilic-are [A2s] *tr.* to balance; to put or maintain in equilibrium; †to ponder, to examine carefully, to weigh up; *rfl.* to swing; to see-saw. **-amento** *m.* balancing; see-sawing. **-ato** *part. adj.* balanced; **-azione** *f.* balancing; see-sawing; state of balance.

bi·lico¹ *m.* equilibrium; balance; (eng.) bascule; peso a —, platform scale; ponte a —, bascule bridge; (fig.) doubt; delicate poise; in —, precariously poised, in the balance; (fig.) irresolute.

†bilico² *m.* umbilicus, navel.

biliemme *m.* (dial. Flor.) hullabaloo; †plebs; common people of the quarter of S. Lorenzo.

bili·neo *adj.* having two lines; double-ruled; *n.m.* (geom.) two-line figure.

bilingu-e *adj.* bilingual; (fig.) double-tongued, two-faced. **-ismo** *m.* bilingualism.

bilione *m.* billion (1,000,000,000,000); rarely, thousand million (1,000,000,000).

†biliorsa *f.* bogey.

bilioso *adj.* See under **bile**.

biliottato *adj.* (herald.) covered with spots like drops.

billa *f.* (fam.) hen; bille-bille!, biddy! biddy! (call to bring the hens in).

†billera *f.* joke, jest; trick; cunning.

bil·leri *m.pl.* (bot.) milkmaids, cuckooflower, lady's-smock, *Cardamine pratensis*; — rossi, Venus's looking-glass, *Specularia Speculum-Veneris*.

billetta *f.* (metall.) billet.

†billi *m.pl.* game of ninepins; billing and cooing, lovey-dovey; *excl.* billi-billi!, cluck! cluck! (call to bring the hens in; cf. **billa**).

billo *m.* turkey; (fam.) chicken.

billocchetto *m.* gilding tool.

bilobato *adj.* (bot.) bilobate.

†biltà *f.* See **beltà**.

bilustre *adj.* (poet.) ten-years-old; ten-years-long; lasting ten years.

†bimadre *adj.* born of two mothers (epithet of Bacchus).

bimare *adj.* (poet.) washed by two seas.

bimbi *adv. phr.* (fam.) andare a —, to go walkies.

bimb-o *m.*, **-a** *f.* little child; baby.

bimembre *adj.* of a double nature (e.g. a Centaur).

bimensile *adj.* bi-monthly.

bimestr-e *m.* period of two months; bill for two months; fees for two months; *adj.* (agric.) ripening in two months. **-ale** *adj.* two-monthly.

bimetal·l-ico *adj.* (finan.) bimetallic. **-ismo** *m.* bimetallism. **-ista** *m.* bimetallist.

bimetic·cio *m.* (biol.) double hybrid; F_2 generation.

bimodale *adj.* (mus.) bimodal.

†bim(m)olle *m.* (mus.). See **bemolle**.

bimotore *m.* (aeron.) two-engined plane.

†binare *intr.* to give birth to twins.

bina·rio *adj.* binary; (mus.) tempo —, duple time; *n.m.* (rlwy.) line; track; il treno parte dal — 7, the train leaves from platform 7; — a doppio scartamento, double gauge line; — a scartamento ridotto, narrow gauge line; doppio —, double line track; — di corsa, main line; — cieco, — morto, dead-end, siding; — di scambio, shunting track; (fig.) stare in —, to toe the line.

†bina·sc-ere *intr.* to be born twins; (of fruit) to geminate. **-enza** *f.* birth of twins.

binato *adj.* double; coupled; twin; (archit.) colonne binate, coupled columns; †double-natured.

binatrice *f.* (text.) doubler, doubling machine.

binatura *f.* (text.) doubling.

binda¹ *f.* (mech.) any kind of jack used for lifting a heavy weight through a short space; — a martinicca, screw jack.

bind-a² *f.* (naut.) reef-band. **†-ella** *f.* ribbon. **-ellina** *f.* gold or silver braiding.

bindolare [A1s] and derivs. See **abbindolare**.

bin·dol-o *m.* chain-pump, an apparatus consisting of wheels and a drum with buckets attached for raising water for irrigation; apparatus for making skeins of silk; trickster, person full of dodges to evade his obligations. **-eri·a** *f.* dodge; trickery. **-esco** *adj.* (*m.pl.* **-eschi**) sly. **-one** *m.* cheat.

†bin-o *adj.* double; of a double nature. **†-ello** *m.* twin.

binoc·colo *m.* See **binocolo**.

bino·colo *m.* opera-glasses; field-glasses, binoculars.

binoculare *adj.* (opt.) binocular.

bino·culo *m.* See **binocolo**.

binomiale *adj.* (math.) binomial.

bino·mio *adj.* (math.) binomial; (biol.) nomenclatura binomia, binomial nomenclature, Linnaean system of classification; *n.m.* binomial; slogan or title involving two names: il — 'Dio e Popolo', the slogan 'God and the People'.

binormale *adj.* (math.) binormal.

bi·nubo *m.* widower who marries for a second time.

binucleare *adj.* binucleate.

biobba *f.* slush.

biocca *f.* broody hen.

bioc·col-o *m.* tuft of wool; flake (of snow); wisp, wreath (of smoke); candle-drip; raccattare i -i, to eavesdrop; tangle or small mass of any material. **-ume** *m.* wool sweepings. **-uto** *adj.* matted; (text.) lana -uta, pieces.

biocenọsi *f.* (geog.) adaptation to soil and climate.

biochi·mic-a *f.* biochemistry. **-o** *m.* biochemist; *adj.* biochemical.

biodo[1] *m.* (bot.) flowering rush, *Butomus umbellatus*; reed-mace, *Typha latifolia*; bulrush, chairmaker's rush, *Schoenoplectus lacustris*; bur-reed, *Sparganium*.

biodo[2] *m.* (radio) duodiode.

bioelettricità *f.* bio-electricity.

bio-fili·a *f.* instinct of self-preservation; love of life. **-fi·sica** *f.* biophysics. **-ge·nesi** *f.* biogenesis. **-gene·tico** *adj.* biogenetic. **-geni·a** *f.* biogeny.

bio·gr-afo *m.* biographer. **-afare** [A I S] *tr.* to write the biography of. **-afato** *part. adj.* written as a biography; made the subject of a biography; *n.m.* the subject of a biography. **-afi·a** *f.* biography. **-a·fico** *adj.* biographical.

biọlca *f.* (dial. Emilia) measure of area (cf. †**bifolca**, under **bifolco**).

biọlco *m.* (dial. N. Ital.). See **bifolco**.

bio·l-ogo *m.* biologist. **-ogi·a** *f.* biology. **-o·gico** *adj.* biological.

bioluminescenza *f.* bioluminescence.

†**biomba** *f.* screen.

biọnd-o *adj.* blond, fair-haired, flaxen; golden-haired; il — dio, Apollo; — rossiccio, tawny; — castagno, light chestnut; — metallo, gold; (poet.) — vino, golden wine; — grano, golden grain; il — Tevere, the tawny Tiber; *n.m.* fair-haired man or boy. **-a** *f.* blonde, fair-haired girl; fair-haired woman; type of silk lace; †hair bleach. **-ac·cio** *adj. pej.* mousy. **-are** [A I C] to bleach (the hair). **-astro** *adj.* fairish, inclined to be fair. **-eggiare** [A 3 C] *intr.* (aux. avere) to be blonde; il suo capo -eggia come l'oro, her hair has glints of gold; to turn blonde; to turn golden; to start to ripen (of corn). **-eggiante** *part. adj.* turning fair; golden; yellowish; i campi -eggianti di frumento, the fields golden with ripening corn; (of corn) ripening. **-ella** *f.* (bot.) pink centaury, *Centaurium minus*; dyer's rocket; dyer's yellow-weed, *Reseda luteola*; mezereon, *Daphne mezereon*. **-ẹzza** *f.* blondness; fairness; lightness; blonde hair, golden hair. **-ic·cio** *adj.* washed out, pale gold, fairish. **-ino** *m.* blonde, fair person.

biopsi·a *f.* (med.) biopsy.

bio·scia *f.* (Pistoia) slushy snow, slush; weak coffee; watery soup, 'dishwater'.

bio·scio *adj.* flabby, inert; †askew; oblique; †*adv.* a —, athwart.

bios·sido *m.* (chem.) dioxide, peroxide.

biotite *f.* (miner.) biotite, black mica.

biotto *adj.* (dial. N. Ital.) wretched; naked.

bip *m. indecl.* (onom.) pip; peep, cheep.

bipart-ire [D 2] *tr.* to divide into two; to separate; to part; to halve; *rfl.* to divide, to split; to branch off, to diverge. **-i·bile** *adj.* divisible into two; (bot.) bipartite. **-i·tico** *adj.* (neol. pol.) two-party, bipartisan. **-ito** *part. adj.* divided into two; separated; parted; halved; bipartite. **-izione** *f.* division into two parts, bipartition; halving.

bi·pede *m., adj.* (zool.) biped; (joc.) — implume, featherless biped, man.

bipenne *f.* (archaeol.) two-edged axe; battle-axe.

biplano *m.* (aeron.) biplane.

bipolare *adj.* (electr.) bipolar, dipole; cavo —, twin-core cable.

bipo·lide *adj.* having two nationalities; *n.m., f.* person who has two nationalities.

bipontina *f.* edition of classical texts published in the eighteenth century at Zweibrücken.

bipọsto *m., adj. indecl.* two-seater (car, aeroplane).

bipriṣma *m.* (opt.) biprism.

†**biq(q)uadro** *m.* (mus.). See **bequadro**.

biquadrato *m.* (maths.) the fourth power; *adj.* (raised) to the fourth power.

birac·chio *m.* rag; tatter; non saper —, to know nothing.

birb-a[1] *f.* lazy young fellow, rascal; scamp; young monkey; lazybones; una — matricolata, an out and out rascal; †fraud, knavery. **-acciọne** *m.* scoundrel. **-eri·a** *f.* rascality. **-ẹsco** *adj.* (*m.pl.* -ẹschi) rascally, roguish. **-o** *m.* rogue; bounder.

birba[2] *f.* open horse-carriage for two, trap.

birbant-e *m.* rogue, knave; scamp, rascal; scherzi da —, rascally tricks. **-ag·gine** *f.* roguery. †**-are** *intr.* to play the rogue; to live by begging. **-eggiare** [A 3 C] *intr.* (aux. avere) to be up to some roguery; to play mischievous tricks. **-eri·a** *f.* roguery, knavery; impudence. **-ẹsco** *adj.* (*m.pl.* -ẹschi) roguish; rascally. (**-esca·mẹnte** *adv.*) **-ina** *f.* battere la -ina, to clap one's arms round oneself to get warm.

birbo *m.* See under **birba**[1].

birbọn-e *m.* rascal, rogue, knave; scamp; †beggar, mendicant; (-a *f.*) *adj.* rascally; un tiro —, a dirty trick; (colloq.) fa un caldo —, it's terribly hot; ho una sete -a, I'm devilish thirsty. **-ag·gine** *f.* roguery. **-ai·a** *f.* bunch of rogues. **-a·io** *m.* rogue's meeting place; (fig.) noise, confusion. **-ata** *f.* scoundrelly action. **-eggiare** [A 3 C] *intr.* (aux. avere) to behave like a rogue, to behave knavishly. **-eri·a** *f.* roguery, knavery. **-ẹsco** *adj.* (*m.pl.* -ẹschi) roguish, rascally. (**-esca·mẹnte** *adv.*)

bir·cio *adj.* (Tusc.) short-sighted; squinting; (fig.) equivocal; *n.m.* one who casts furtive sidelong glances.

bireme *f.* (naut. hist.) bireme.

†**biribara** *m.* confusion.

biribiṣnonno *m.* (joc.) distant ancestor.

biribiss-i *m. indecl.* a game of chance with 36 numbered counters, some of which are drawn from a bag. **-a·ia** *f.* a blank piece which wins everything in the game of 'biribissi'. **-a·io** *m.* banker in the game of 'biribissi'; uproar; tumult.

birichin-o *m.* little rogue; scamp, rascal; cheeky youngster; rogue (of adult); *adj.* roguish; saucy. (-a *f.*) **-ata** *f.* prank, roguish trick; escapade. **-ẹsco** *adj.* (*m.pl.* -ẹschi) roguish, mischievous.

birifrangenza *f.* (phys.; opt.) double refraction; (phys.) — elettrica, Kerr effect.

birigna·o *m.* (theatr.) affected articulation; exaggeration of the final syllables in a drawling voice.

birilla *f.* marble (toy).

birillo *m.* skittle; ninepin; giuoco dei birilli, skittles, ninepins.

Birm-a·nia *pr.n.f.* (geog.) Burma. **-ano** *adj., n.m.* Burmese, Burman (-ana *f.*)

biroc·cio *m.* and derivs. See **baroccio**.

†**biroldo** *m.* black-pudding, sausage.

birr-a[1] *f.* beer; ale; — chiara, pale ale; lager; — in bottiglia, bottled beer; — alla spina, draught beer; fabbricare —, to brew beer; fabbrica di —, brewery; fabbricante di —, brewer. **-a·io** *m.* brewer. (-a·ia *f.*) **-eri·a** *f.* beer-shop, ale-house. **-ifi·cio** *m.* brewery. **-ọne** *m. augm.* strong beer.

birra[2] *f.* (sport) vigour, energy.

birrac·chio *m.* young calf (from birth to one year).

birra·glia *f.* See under **birro**[1].

birreri·a[1] *f.* See under **birra**[1].

†**birreri·a**[2] *f.* See under **birro**[1].

birr-o[1] *m.* policeman; police agent; copper's nark, police spy; any persecuting or obnoxious official or person; 'snooper'; (naut.) selvagee, an untwisted skein of rope-yarn matted together; wire strop. **-a·glia** *f.* gathering of police agents, etc. †**-eri·a** *f.* police-authority; troop of police; band of spies. **-ẹsco** *adj.* (*m.pl.* -ẹschi) pertaining to the police; policeman-like; aggressive; spying, snooping. (**-esca·mẹnte** *adv.*) **-ocra·tico** *m.* (satir., Giusti) police-official.

birro[2] *m.* (eccl.) mozzetta.

†**birro**[3] *adj.* red.

biruota *f.* penny-farthing bicycle.

bis *excl.* encore!; *adj. indecl.* treno —, relief train; pagina 25 —, page 25a; *n.m. indecl.* encore; dare il —, to encore; chiedere il —, to ask for an encore; concedere il —, to give an encore; quanti —!, what a lot of encores!; (colloq.) fare il —, to 'have another'; to be a great success.

biṣac·cia *f.* (*pl.* biṣacce) wallet; saddlebag; knapsack; agricultural unit of area (equivalent at Palermo to 43.65 ares).

†**bisacuto** *adj.* double-edged.

bisannuale *adj.* (bot.) biennial.

bisant-e *m.* (numis.) gold coin minted at Byzantium; Venetian copper coin; †sequin; (herald.) bezant; — di argento, plate (roundel argent); bisante-torta, roundel per fess; *pl.* (archit.) roundels used for decoration. **-ato** *adj.* (herald.) bezanty. **-ino** *adj.* Byzantine.

Bisan·zio *pr.n.m.* (geog.) Byzantium.

bisarca·vol-o *m.* great-great-grandfather. **-a** *f.* great-great-grand-mother.

bisatto *m.* (Ven.) little snake.

bis-avo *m.* great-grandfather. **-ava** *f.* great-grandfather. **-a·volo** *m.* great-grandfather; *pl.* ancestors, forefathers, forbears.

bisbe·tic-o *adj.* crabbed; ill-tempered, peevish; capricious; outlandish; waspish; shrewish; un nome —, a name difficult to pronounce. **-a** *f.* shrew; *La Bisbetica Domata, The Taming of the Shrew.* **-amente** *adv.* peevishly; capriciously; shrewishly.

bisbigli-are [A4] *intr.* (aux. avere) to whisper; *recip. rfl.* to whisper to one another. **-amento** *m.* whispering; whisper. **-ato** *part. adj.* whispered. (**-atore** *m.* **-atrice** *f.*) **-ato·rio** *m.* whispering gallery. **-one** *m.* constant whisperer; tell-tale-tit. (**-ona** *f.*)

bisbi·gl-io *m.* whisper; (radio) monkey chatter. **-io** *m.* continual whispering.

bisbocc-ia *f.* revelry, junketing, feasting; spree; fare —, to make merry, to go on the spree. **-iare** [A3] *intr.* (aux. avere) to have a gay time, to kick over the traces. **-ione** *m.* gay dog.

bisc-a *f.* gambling den; gambling house. **-ai(u)olo** *m.* frequenter of gambling dens; gambler.

Bisca·gl-ia *pr.n.f.* (geog.) Biscay; il Golfo di —, the Bay of Biscay. **-ina** *f.* (naut.) square-rigged sailing boat seen in the Bay of Biscay; rope ladder, Jacob's ladder, jumping ladder, sea gangway. **-ino** *adj.* pertaining to the Bay of Biscay; Basque; *n.m.* large rifle.

†**biscante**, †**biscanto**[1] *m.* (mus.) tune, air.

biscanto[2] *m.* double corner; corner with the point cut off; break in a straight line; (fig.) hiding place.

†**biscappa** *f.* short double hood for wear out of doors at night.

biscazz-a *f.* gambling den. **-are** [A1] *intr.* (aux. avere) to frequent gambling dens; *tr.* to gamble away. **-iere** *m.* billiard marker; gambler; owner or manager of gambling den.

†**bischenc-a** *f.*, †**-o** *m.* unpleasant practical joke.

bis·cher-o *m.* peg of a stringed instrument; (Tusc.) penis; dolt, simpleton; dishonest individual. **-ello**, **-etto** *m.* plug for closing a wineskin.

bischetto *m.* cobbler's bench.

†**bischizz-are** *intr.* to romance, to invent fantastic stories, to day-dream. †**-o** *m.* fantastic story; pun, play on words.

bi·scia *f.* snake; a —, zig-zag; (Tusc.) in abundance; (zool.) — dal collare, grass snake, *Tropidonotus natrix*; — viperina, a related snake, *Tr. viperina*; (herald.) serpent; (provb.) la — morde il ciarlatano, the biter bit.

bi·sciolo *adj.* lisping.

biscione *m. augm.* of biscia, q.v.; (herald.) viper, arms of the Visconti of Milan; *pl.* (sport) members of the 'Internazionale' football team.

bisciuola *f.* (vet.) liver fluke, *Fasciola hepatica.*

†**biscolore** *adj.* multicoloured; pied.

biscon·dola *f.* place sheltered from the wind.

biscott-o *m.* biscuit; rusk; (naut.) hard tack; mettersi in mare senza —, to set about a job without sufficient preparation; (joc.) boy-scout; *adj.* baked twice. **-are** [A1] *tr.* to bake like a rusk; to anneal; (fig.) to perfect. **-ato** *part. adj.* baked twice; annealed; (fig.) expert; well-trained. **-eri·a** *f.*, **-ifi·cio** *m.* biscuit-shop; biscuit-bakery; biscuits. **-ino** *m. dim.* little biscuit; sweet biscuit; snap of the fingers; (motor.) shackle, link.

biscroma *f.* (mus.) demisemiquaver.

biscugin-o *m.*, **-a** *f.* second cousin; distant cousin.

biscuit *m. indecl.* (pron. as Fr.) (ceram.) biscuit, unglazed ceramic ware fixed in a bisque oven; an ice-cream sweet.

†**biscurare** *vb.* and derivs. See **trascurare**.

bisdosso *adv. phr.* (equit.) a —, bareback; (naut.) with the yard of a lateen sail to windward of the mast, consequently with the sail bellied in two hollows fore and aft of the mast; aback.

bisdruc·ciolo *adj., n.m.* (word) accented on the last syllable but three, e.g. Eng. le·gionary, It. rico·verano.

bisec-are [A2c] *tr.* to bisect. **-ante** *part. adj.* bisecting. **-ato** *part. adj.* bisected.

bise·golo *m.* (shoem.) clams.

bisel·lio *m.* (Rom. hist.) seat of honour at public shows.

bisell-o *m.* (eng.; carp.) chamfer. **-atura** *f.* chamfering.

bisenso *m.* word bearing a double meaning; double-entendre.

bisessuale *adj.* (bot.) bisexual, monoecious, hermaphrodite.

bisest-o *m.* the day added to February in leap year; space of four years; *adj.* (Tusc.), see **bisestile**. †**-are** *intr.* (of leap year) to recur; quando —a, when it is leap year. **-ile** *adj.* bissextile; anno -ile, leap year.

bisettrice *f.* (math., geom.) bisector, bisecting line; (opt.) bisectrix.

bisettimanale *adj.* twice weekly; *n.m.* journal published twice a week, bi-weekly.

bisezione *f.* bisection.

†**bisge·nero** *m.* husband of one's granddaughter, grandson-in-law.

bisilicato *m.* (chem.) bisilicate, metasilicate.

bisiliere *m.* (poet. Pascoli) weaver of grey cloth.

bisil·l-abo *adj.* disyllabic; *n.m.* disyllable. **-a·bico** *adj.* disyllabic.

bislac-co *adj.* (m.pl. **-chi**) outlandish; queer, odd; fantastic; eccentric; una testa -ca, an odd fish; menti -che, eccentrics; (also *n.m.*). **-cheri·a** *f.* outlandishness; foolish or strange action; eccentricity.

†**bisleale** *adj.* disloyal.

†**bislessare** *tr.* to bring to the boil.

bislingua *f.* (bot.) leaf-under-leaf, *Ruscus hypoglossum* and *R. hypophyllum.*

bislungo *adj.* oblong; irregular in shape; †too long.

bismale *m.* (pharm.) preparation of bismuth.

bismalva *f.* (bot.) marsh mallow, *Althaea officinalis.*

bi·smarck *m. indecl.* kind of overcoat; *adv. phr.* (cul.) bistecca alla —, a steak with an egg and toasted cheese on top.

bism-uto *m.* (chem.) bismuth. **-u·tico** *adj.* bismuthic.

bisnipote *m.*, *f.* great-grandchild; great-grandson; great-grand-daughter; great-nephew; great-niece; *pl.* descendants, posterity.

bisnonn-o *m.* great-grandparent; great-grandfather; *pl.* ancestors, forefathers. **-a** *f.* great-grandmother.

bisogna *f.* business, work; accingersi alla —, to get down to work; affair; plight, need.

bisogn-are [A1c] *intr.* (aux. essere), *impers.* to be needed, to be needful; to be lacking; gli -a un po' di coraggio, he needs a bit more courage; to be obligatory; to be compulsory, to be necessary; -a, one must, it is necessary; -a bene, one simply must; non -a, one must not; più che non -a, more than is necessary; -a vedere!, we shall see!; -a vedere la gente che c'è fuori!, you ought to see how many people there are outside! **-ante** *part. adj.* in need; needy. **-anza** *f.* need, want; poverty. **-evole** *adj.* needful, necessary; poor, in need; †opportune; *n.m.* il -evole, the needful, what is required.

bisognata·rio *m.* (comm.) referee.

bisogn-o *m.* need; requirement; i -i della vita, the necessities of life; want; distress; poverty; aver — di, aver di —, to need; al —, if necessary; in caso di —, in case of need; trovarsi in —, to be needy; avere tutto il suo —, to have all one needs; non c'è — che venga, there's no need for him to come; (euphem.) aver un —, to want to go to the lavatory; fare i suoi -i, to go to the lavatory; †indigent soldier; †a un —, perchance. **-ino** *m. dim.* (provb.) biso-gnino fa l'uomo ingegnoso, necessity is the mother of invention; bisognino fa trottar la vecchia, needs must when the devil drives. **-oso** *adj.* needy; poor, indigent; *n.m.* pauper, destitute person. **-osamente** *adv.* vivere -osamente, to live in poverty, to be in dire need.

bisolf-ato *m.* (chem.) bisulphate. **-ito** *m.* (chem.) bisulphite. **-uro** *m.* (chem.) bisulphide, disulphide.

bisonte *m.* (zool.) aurochs, *Bison europaeus*; — d'America, bison, *B. americanus.*

bisquadro *m.* bevel.

bissare [A1] *tr.* to encore; to repeat; *intr.* (aux. avere) to call for an encore. (Cf. **bis**.)

bis·sino *adj.* made of fine linen; †*n.m.* See **bisso**.

bisso *m.* (text.) sea silk; (zool.) byssus; (industr.) beard (of wing shell).

bissolo *m.* (numis.) fifteenth-century Milanese coin, bearing the viper of the Visconti arms.

bissona *f.* eight-oared boat, decorated for regattas at Venice.

bista·bile *adj.* (telev.) flip flop.

†**bistante** *m.* interval, length of time; *adv. phr.* in bistanti, standing.

†**bistarda** *f.* bustard.

bistecca *f.* beefsteak; steak; — alla fiorentina, grilled veal cutlets.

†**bistent-o** *m.* delay; distress. **-are** *intr.* to delay; to dally.

bisticci-are [A 3] *intr.* (*aux.* avere) to wrangle, to quarrel, to argue; to have words; *rfl.* (*prep.* con) to quarrel (with); *recip. rfl.* to quarrel, to wrangle. **-amento** *m.* wrangle; wrangling, quarrelling. **-care** [A 2 s] *intr.* (*aux.* avere) to keep on wrangling.

bistic·cio *m.* pun; play on words, jingle; quarrel, wrangle.

bisticc·ìo *m.* (*pl.* **-ìi**) continual wrangling.

†**bistolfo** *m.* priest.

bistondo *adj.* not perfectly round; (colloq.) stupid.

bisto·nio *adj.* (poet.) Thracian.

bi·stori *m. indecl.* See **bisturi**.

†**bistornare** *tr.* to distort.

bistort-o *adj.* distorted; crooked; twisted, tortuous; malicious, evil. **-a** *f.* (bot.) snake root, bistort, *Polygonum bistorta*; †tortuousness; distortion.

bistoso *adj.* (text.) less than six months old (of wool).

bistrac·cola *f.* (dyeing) drying frame, straining board.

bistratt-are [A 1] *tr.* to treat badly, to ill-treat, to maltreat; to scold harshly; to bully; to snub. **-ato** *part. adj.* ill-treated, abused.

bistr-o *m.* bistre; eye-shadow. **-ato** *adj.* bistred.

bi·stur-i *m. indecl.*, **-ino** *m.* (surg.) scalpel, bistoury; bisturi elettrico, diathermy knife.

bisulco *adj.* forked; cleft; cloven-hoofed.

bisunto *adj.* greasy; unto e —, too oily; filthy; †*n.m.* cooked capon.

bisurata *f.* (chem.) bisurate of magnesia.

bitartarato *m.* — di potassa, cream of tartar.

bitema·tico *adj.* (mus.) bithematic.

bitont-ana *f.* a variety of pear from Bitonto in Apulia. **-one** *m.* a variety of fig.

bitorzol-o *m.* wart; pimple, spot; small protuberance. **-oso**, **-uto** *adj.* warty; pimply, spotty; swollen; (techn.) modular.

bitt-a *f.* (naut.) bitt; **-e da rimorchio**, towing bollards. **-are** [A 1] *tr.* to bitt (a cable). **-atura** *f.* turn of a cable round the bitts. **-oni** *m.pl.* (mooring) bitts; cleats.

bit·ter *m. indecl.* a bitter alcoholic drink, bitters.

bitterna *f.* bittern, the mother liquor which remains after the crystallization of salt.

bitum-e *m.* bitumen. **-inare** [A 1 s], **-are** [A 1] *tr.* to bituminate, to cover with bitumen; to tarmac. **-atrice** *f.* bitumen sprinkler. **-atura** *f.* bituminization. **-inoso** *adj.*, **-oso** *adj.* bituminous; carbone **-inoso**, soft coal.

†**biturro** *m.* butter.

†**biucco** *m.* (zool.) kind of poisonous snake.

biut-a *f.* greasy mixture; mixture of cow dung and clay; glazing for cakes and sweetmeats; †make-up, cosmetics. **-are** [A 1] *tr.* to glaze (confectionery). **-oso** *adj.* greasy.

biva *f.* (mus.) a kind of Japanese lute.

bivac-co *m.* (*pl.* **-chi**) (mil.) bivouac; (alp.) — fisso, tiny hut for rock-climbers. **-care** [A 2] *intr.* (*aux.* avere) to bivouac.

bivalen-te *adj.* (chem.) divalent, bivalent; dyad. **-za** *f.* (chem.) divalency, bivalency.

bivalv-e *adj.* (bot.; zool.) bivalve. **-olato** *adj.* (bot.) antera **-olata**, anther with two pores closed by valves.

†**bi·varo** *m.* See **bevero**.

bi·vio *m.* junction; road-fork; (rlwy.) frog; (fig.) parting of the ways; dilemma; trovarsi in un brutto —, to be between the devil and the deep blue sea.

bivoltino *adj.* (biol.) bivoltine, having two generations in a year.

bizantin-o *adj.* Byzantine; academic, theoretical, unrelated to practical conditions. **-eggiare** [A 3 c] *intr.* (*aux.* avere) to indulge in unpractical discourse or argument; to split hairs. **-eri·a** *f.*, **-ismo** *m.* hair-splitting. **-ista** *m., f.* Byzantine scholar.

bizona *f.* (neol. pol.) zone of occupation in Germany administered by two Western powers.

bizz-a *f.* caprice; waywardness; momentary bad temper, tantrum; andare in —, to fly into a rage, to fly off the handle; fare le **-e**, to be naughty, to be wayward, to be in a bad temper. **-oso** *adj.* wayward; naughty; freakish; irritable. **-osamente** *adv.* angrily.

bizzarr-o *adj.* bizarre, extraordinary, strange, odd, queer; whimsical, freakish; eccentric; capricious; cavallo —, spirited, mettlesome horse; †irritable, ill-tempered. **-amente** *adv.* oddly; queerly; freakishly. **-ia** *f.* oddity; eccentricity; grotesqueness; whimsicality; whim, caprice; †per **-ia**, angrily.

bizzeffe *adv. phr.* a —, in large quantities, galore.

†**bizzo-co** *m.* Franciscan tertiary; canting devotee. †**-cheri·a** *f.* smugly pious behaviour.

bizzoso *adj.* See under **bizza**.

†**bizzu-ca**, **-ga** *f.* tortoise.

black *m. indecl.* dishonest bookie.

blaga *f.* swaggering, boasting.

bland-ire [D 2] *tr.* to fondle; to blandish; to cajole; to soothe; to flatter, to entice. **-escente** *adj.*, **-iente** *part. adj.* blandishing, flattering; cajoling. **-imento** *m.* flattery, blandishment; seduction, wooing. **-itivo** *adj.* blandishing; soothing; winsome. **-ito** *part. adj.* blandished, flattered; won over. **-i·zie** *f.pl.* caresses; blandishments, flattery.

bland-o *adj.* bland; mild; pleasing, gentle; mellow; (of light, sound) subdued; un castigo —, a light punishment; (techn.) careful; apritura **-a**, a careful opening. **-amente** *adv.* mildly; gently, softly.

blan·dulo *adj.* light; frail, slight.

†**blasfema** *f.* blasphemy.

blasfem-are [A 1] *tr.*, *intr.* (*aux.* avere) to blaspheme. **-atore** *m.* blasphemer. **-o** *adj.* blasphemous; *n.m.* blasphemer.

†**blasmare** *vb.* and derivs. See **biasimare**.

blason-e *m.* heraldic drawing; heraldry; coat of arms; (fig.) nobility of birth; — popolare, popular saying. **-are** [A 1 c] *tr.* to blazon (heraldic arms). **-ato** *part. adj.* blazoned; armigerous; noble. **-ista** *m.* heraldic expert.

blaso·nico *adj.* relating to heraldry.

blastocele *m.* (zool.) blastocoel.

blater-are [A 1 s] *intr.* (*aux.* avere) to chatter; to gossip; to blether, to blather; to 'talk big', to 'shoot one's mouth off'. **-amento** *m.* chattering; blether. **-atore** *m.* bletherer. (**-atrice** *f.*) **-azione** *f.* blathering. **-one** *m.* bletherer; chatterbox.

blato·fago *m.* (ent.) pine bark beetle, *Myelophilus piniperda*.

blatta *f.* cockroach.

†**blavo** *adj.* pale blue, light blue.

bledone *m.* (bot.) blight, strawberry blight, *Amarantus Blitum*.

blef-a·rico *adj.* (med.) blepharal. **-arite** *f.* (med.) blepharitis. **-aroadenite** *f.* (med.) blepharadenitis. **-arocalasi** *f.* (med.) blepharochalasis. **-arofimosi** *f.* (med.) blepharophimosis. **-aropla·stica** *f.* (med.) blepharoplasty. **-aroplasto** *m.* (anat.) blepharoplast. **-aro·stato** *m.* (med.) blepharostat. **-arotomi·a** *f.* (med.) blepharotomy.

blenda *f.* (miner.) blende; — picea, pitchblende.

blenorragi·a *f.* (med.) blennorrhea.

bleso *adj.* lisping. *n.m.* lisper, lisping individual.

blind-a *f.* armament, reinforcement against gunfire. **-ag·gio**, **-amento** *m.* armouring; armour-plating. **-are** [A 1] *tr.* to armour. to fortify; to sheet (with metal); to lag; to sandbag. **-ato** *part. adj.* armoured; camera **-ata**, strongroom; (mil.) carro **-ato**, armoured car; armour-plated; lagged. **-atura** *f.* armouring; (aeron.) metal edging (of wooden propeller). **-o** *m.* machine gun.

blocc-are [A 2] *tr.* to block; to block up; — al traffico, to close to traffic; (mil.) to blockade; (eng.) to clamp; — a filo, to wire lock; (eng.) to jam, to lock; — i freni, to jam on the brakes; (typ.) to block; (billiards) to hole (the opponent's ball); (comm.) to block, to freeze; *intr.* (*aux.* avere) to join (with), to form a coalition (with); *rfl.* (eng.) to jam, to stick. **-ag·gio** *m.* locking, blocking; (eng.) clamping; ghiera di **-aggio**, locking ring. **-ato** *part. adj.* blocked; blocked up; blockaded; **-ato** dai ghiacci, icebound; (comm.) frozen; conto **-ato**, blocked account; credito **-ato**, frozen credit; (eng.) locked, gripped; **-ato** in posizione, locked in place; (if a defect) jammed. †**-atura** *f.* blockade.

bloc-co *m.* (*pl.* **-chi**) block; lump; bulk; log; in —, en bloc, in block, in bulk; writing-pad, block of paper; blockade; rompere il —, to run the blockade; lock, jam; (comm.) freeze; il — degli affitti, rent restriction; (motor. eng.) — cilindri, cylinder block; (rlwy.) sistema di —, block-system; sezione di —, block section of line; posto di —, road control point, police check; (athlet.) starting-block; (pol.) coalition, bloc; (typ.) block. **-chetto** *m.* block; **-chetto** di legno, block for road-making. **-chiera** *f.* machine for making cement blocks. **-chista** *m.* strategist in blockade. **-chi·stico** *adj.* relating to blockade.

blonda *f.* silk lace.

blouse *f.* (pron. as Fr.) blouse.

blu *adj. indecl.* blue; dark blue; — Madonna, Madonna blue; avere una paura —, to be in a blue funk. **-astro** *adj.* bluish.

bluff *m. indecl.* (the vowel is pron. like Fr. **eu**) bluff.

bluff-are [A I] (for pron. see above) *tr., intr.* (*aux.* avere) to bluff. **-atore** *m.* bluffer.

blumo *m.* (metall.) bloom; — rettangolare, slab.

blus-a, -e *f.* blouse; workman's blouse; smock. **-otto** *m. dim.* short-sleeved shirt.

†bo' *m.* See **bue**.

boa[1] *m. indecl.* (zool.) boa constrictor; lady's boa, feather boa.

boa[2] *f.* buoy; — d'ormeggio, mooring-buoy; — di salvataggio, life-buoy; giro di —, turning point in a sailing race (also fig.).

boari·a[1] *f.* (Emilia, Romagna) contract between landowner and farm-labourer by which the latter receives wages and the income from the farm belongs to the owner; (Ven.) farm.

boa·ria[2] *f.* (Tusc.) stall for work-cattle.

boarina *f.* (orn.). See **bovarina**.

bo-a·rio *adj.* pertaining to cattle; bovine; mercato —, cattle-market; foro —, cattle fair. **-aro** *m.* cattle-drover; cowherd; farm-labourer. **-attiere** *m.* cow-drover; cow-hand; cattle-dealer.

boato *m.* roar, bellow; lowing; reverberation, echoing, rumbling; hiatus.

boatta *f.* tin box.

bob *m. indecl.* bob-sleigh. **-ista** *m., f.* (*f.pl.* **-iste**) bob-sleigh rider.

boba[1] *f.* mixture; mess; (fig.) muddle.

boba[2] *f.* (ichth.). See **boga**.

bobba, bob·bia *f.* See **boba**[1].

bobin-a *f.* bobbin; spool, reel; (text.) cop; bobbin; (electr.) coil, solenoid; — di accensione, sparking coil, ignition coil; — d'arresto, choke (coil). **-are** [A I] *tr.* (electr.) to wind. **-ag·gio** *m.* (electr.) winding; -aggio di costa, strip-on-edge winding. **-atoio** *m.* (text.) winding-frame, porcupine box. **-atore** *m.* (text.) winder, spooler. **-atrice** *f.* (text.) winding frame; (female) spooler; (electr.) field-coil winding machine.

bobista *m., f.* See under **bob**.

bobò[1] *m. indecl.* (fam., nursery) pap, nipple.

bobò[2] *m. indecl.* (fam., nursery) pain, hurt.

†bobolca *f.* See **†bifolca**, under **bifolco**.

bocc-a *f.*

1. Mouth; (i) stare a — aperta, to gape, to stand open-mouthed; guardare a — aperta, to gape at; il cuore mi venne in —, my heart was in my mouth; torcere la —, to make a wry mouth; fare la — storta, to put on an expression of disgust; fare la — storta a, to turn up one's nose at; fare le bocche, to sneer; avere la schiuma alla —, to foam at the mouth; prendere una medicina per —, to take a medicine through the mouth; munizioni da —, victuals; (of a horse) — ardente, excessively tender mouth; tenere uno a — dolce, to lead someone up the garden path; duro di —, hard-mouthed; chiudere la — ad uno, to silence someone; (eccl.) chiudere la — a, aprire la — a, to close the mouth, to open the mouth of (a new cardinal); (provb.) a caval donato non si guarda in —, don't look a gift horse in the mouth; finchè uno ha denti in — non sa mai quel che gli tocca, life is full of surprises; in — chiusa non c'entrano mosche, silence is golden; in — al lupo!, good luck!. (ii) uses relating to taste and eating: fare la — a, to acquire a taste for, to get to like; rifarsi la —, to take something to take away an unpleasant taste; avere la — amara, to have a nasty taste in one's mouth, (fig.) to be embittered; lasciare la — cattiva, to leave a nasty taste in the mouth (also fig.); avere la — buona, to have a good palate; essere una buona —, essere di buona —, to be a hearty eater, to have a good appetite; avere la — gentile, to be able to eat only the choicest food; avere la — cattiva, to be no epicure, to have a poor digestion; avere sei bocche da mantenere, to have six to feed; essere una — inutile, to be idle, to eat one's head off; far venire l'acquolina in —, to make one's mouth water; fare a — e borsa, to 'go Dutch', to share expenses at a meal; non avere da mettersi in —, to have nothing to eat; restare a — asciutta, to be without food, (fig.) to come away empty-handed, to be left out in the cold, to come off badly; per i figli una madre si leverebbe il pan di —, for her children a mother would go short of food herself; quei pescecani si levano il pan di —, those sharks are at each other's throats; (mil.) munizioni di —, rations; (cul.) — di dama, almond sweet; — scelta, bonne bouche, dainty. (iii) uses relating to words, speech, utterance: a —, orally, by word of mouth; mettere in — a, to put into (a person's) mouth, to suggest to; dire a mezza —, to hint, to hint at; concedere a mezza —, to agree reluctantly,

to admit grudgingly; non aprire mai —, to keep silent, to sit tight, not to say a word; non gli si cava di — una parola, you can't get a word out of him; mi manca la parola in —, the word is on the tip of my tongue; ha sempre in — le solite scuse, he always makes the same excuses; parole che empiono la —, high-sounding words; mi è scappato di —, it slipped out, I let slip; essere sulla — di tutti, to be on everybody's lips; passare di in —, essere portato per —, to be discussed by all and sundry; tutti pendevano dalla sua —, they all hung on his words; lavarsi la — di, to speak ill of; avere alcuno in —, to be always talking of someone; mettere — in, to chip in on; essere largo di —, to be good at making promises; essere la — della verità, to be the soul of truth; essere una — sacrilega, essere una — d'inferno, to blaspheme, to swear, to be foul-mouthed; essere una — d'oro, to be eloquent, (iron.) to be a fount of wisdom; (mus.) a — chiusa, humming. **2.** Opening, orifice, aperture: la — di un salvadanaio, the slot of a money-box; plug-hole; muzzle (of a gun), throat (of a blast furnace); — da incendio, hydrant, fire-plug; — di accesso, manhole; (text. weaving) — d'inserzione, shed; (geog.) strait; (anat.) la — dello stomaco, the upper part of the stomach; (theatr.) — d'opera, proscenium; (naut.) — di granchio, fairlead; — di lupo, running bowline. **3.** (bot.) — di leone, snapdragon, *Antirrhinum majus*; — di leone gialla, yellow toadflax, butter-and-eggs, *Linaria vulgaris*; — di lupo, bastard balm, *Melittis melissophyllum*, snakeshead iris, widow iris, *Hermodactylus tuberosus*. **4.** (ichth.) — d'oro, — gialla, meagre, *Johnius hololepidotus*. **5.** (hist.) — del leone, secret denunciation, secret petition (Venice); — di verità, well-known Roman monument. **6.** †claw. **-ac·cia** *f. pej.* ugly mouth; grimace; essere una -accia, to be spiteful; far -acce, to pull faces. **-a·glio** *m.* nozzle. **-alepre** *m.* (orn.) flycatcher, *Muscicapa* spp. **-alino** *m.* (naut.) branch pipe; hose nozzle. **-alone** *m.* (orn.) nightjar, *Caprimulgus* spp. **-amele** *m.* (zool.) the Sardinian weasel, *Putorius nivalis* var. *boccamele*. **-anera** *f.* (ichth.) *Galeus melanostomus*, a kind of dogfish. **-are** [A 2c] *tr.* to nibble, to mouth; to eat. **-arola** *f.* (med.) herpes, cold-blisters. **-asacco** *m.* (milling) sack holder. **-ata** *f.* mouthful; prendere una -ata d'aria, to take a breather; -ata di fumo, puff of smoke; tirare delle -ate di fumo, to puff at one's pipe; slap in the mouth; non saperne una -ata, to know nothing about it; not to have a clue. **†-a·tica** *adv. phr.* amply, in abundance. **-atino** *m.* speaking-tube. **-ato** *part.* of **boccare**; *adj.* mouthed; nibbled; †wide-mouthed, large-mouthed. **†-atura** *f.* opening, mouth. **-uc·cia** *f.* finicky person; far -uccia, to turn up one's nose. **-uto** *adj.* wide-mouthed, large-mouthed.

boccacc-esco *adj.* (*m.pl.* **-eschi**) in the style of Boccaccio; licentious, broad. **-escamente** *adv.* in Boccaccio's style. **-evole** *adj.* See **boccaccesco**.

boccado·pera *f.* (theatr.). See 'bocca d'opera', under **bocca** (2).

boccadoro *m.* plausible, loquacious person; †St John Chrysostom; †money-bags; (ichth.). See 'bocca d'oro', under **bocca** (4).

boccal-e *m.* jug; tankard; pot; measure for wine or other liquids: equivalent to 2·2 litres at Perugia, 1·8 l. at Rome (2 l. oil), 1·4 l. at Ancona, 1·3 l. at Bologna, 1·2 l. at Udine, 1·1 l. at Florence and Modena, 0·8 l. at Milan, 0·7 l. at Brescia and Turin; scritto sui -i di Montelupo, extremely well known, known of old (from the old saws which used to be written on the terracotta vases of Montelupo). **-aio** *m.* jug seller. **-ino** *m.* jet. **-one** *m. augm.* big-mouthed person; loud-mouthed person.

boccaperta *m. indecl.* gaping fool.

boccaport-a *f.,* **-o** *m.* (naut.) hatchway; (eng.) mouth of firebox. **-ello** *m.* (naut.) coal-chute cover, ammunition hoist cover. **-ella** *f.* (naut.) coal-chute cover, ammunition hoist cover.

boccetta *f. dim.* See under **boccia**.

bocche *m. indecl.* bouquet.

boccheare [A 6] *intr.* (*aux.* avere) (Tusc.) to yawn.

boccheggi-are [A 3c] *intr.* to gasp; to open and shut one's mouth; (joc.) to eat. **-amento** *m.* gasping, breathlessness; mouthing. **-ante** *adj.* gasping; dying, moribund; at one's last gasp; *n.m., f.* person dying.

bocchello *m.* rivulet, weep; (civ. eng.) — d'efflusso, outlet, outflow.

bocchett-a *f. dim.* of **bocca**, q.v.; small aperture; opening, upper (of a shoe); striking plate (of a lock); — d'ispezione, soot door (of a chimney); (mus.) mouthpiece; (watchm.) pallet. **-ina** *f.,* *dim.* of **bocca**, q.v.; fare -ina a, to turn up one's nose at. **-one** *m.* union, pipe union, screw plug; pipe socket; -one di riempimento, filler cap (of petrol tank, etc.).

bocchętto m. reel, bobbin.

bocchi (Tusc. phr.) far — a, to turn up one's nose at, to scorn.

†bocchiduro adj. (of a horse) hard-mouthed.

bocchinista m. second-hand bookseller.

bocchin-o m. dim. of bocca, q.v.; fare il —, to pout, to purse one's lips; to try to look pretty or winsome; slap on the mouth; cigarette holder; cigar holder; mouthpiece of pipe; — (di) sughero, cork-tip; (mus.) mouthpiece. **-a·io** m. seller or maker of mouthpieces.

bocchipuz·zola f. See puzzola.

boc·c-ia f. (pl. -e) (bot.) bud; rose-hip; glass decanter; water-bottle; (techn.) flask; soap bubble; fare le -e, to be bubbly; ball used in the game of 'bocce', wood; giuoco delle -e, Italian game resembling bowls, bowls; fare una partita alle -e, to play a game of bowls; (electr.) — di Leida, Leyden jar; splash made by falling rain, 'little soldier'; boil, eruption on the skin; (joc.) head; gli gira la —, it has gone to his head. **-iare** [A3] tr. (in bowls) to blackball; (in a club) to blackball, to turn down for membership; intr. (aux. avere) to fail, to be failed; — a un esame, to fail an exam; — in una materia, to fail in a subject. **-iaro** m. maker of bowls. **-iato** part. adj. blackballed; failed, 'ploughed'. **-iatura** f. fail, failing; collision (between vehicles). **-ino** m. dim. the jack ball at bowls; (joc.) head. **-ętta** f. dim. little bottle; scent-bottle; medicine-bottle; phial; pl. game of billiards played with the hands. **-ettina** f. dim. small bottle, scent-bottle; phial.

bocciard-a f. (bldg.) bush-hammer; roughing roller, bush-roller; granulating hammer. **-are** [A1] tr. (bldg.) to bush-hammer; to granulate. **-atura** f. (bldg.) granulation (of stone); bush-hammering.

bocciardo m. male genital organ of an animal.

boccicata f. jot, iota; non saperne una —, not to know the first thing about it.

boccino[1] m. dim. See under boccia.

†boccino[2] m. calf; adj. bovine.

boc·c-io m. (pl. -i) (bot.) flower-bud, unopened calyx; (Rom.) elderly dandy, beau; †cocoon. **-ione** m. augm. large decanter made of dark glass. **-i(u)ola** f. rosebud. **-i(u)olo** m. bud; cocoon; internode of a cane; spout of a fountain; socket of a candlestick; (eng.) cam, lifter.

boccio·dromo m. bowling-green, bowling-alley.

boccio·filo adj. fond of the game of bowls; società bocciofila, bowling club; n.m. bowls enthusiast.

boccione m. augm. of boccia, q.v.; large decanter.

boc-co m. (pl. -chi) walnut or fruit-stone used as a missile by boys playing at 'nocino'; good-for-nothing boy; braggart, swaggerer; adj. stupid.

boccola f. buckle; ear-ring; boss; (eng.) bush, bushing, ferrule; mettere una —, to bush; (rlwy.) journal box, axle box, bearing box; grease box; (naut.) step (of a mast), socket; (text.) step, foot-step (of a loom).

bocco·lica f. (Tusc., joc.). See under buccolica.

bǫccolo m. curl; ringlet.

boccon-e m. mouthful; tutto in un —, in one mouthful; snack, bite; morsel, taste, little bit; (fig.) short spell; avere il — alla gola, to have just finished eating; contare i -i, to stint of food; — di cardinale, dish fit for a king; — del prete, the parson's nose; per un boccon di pane, for next to nothing, for a song; buon —, titbit; dare il — a, to poison; to corrupt; to bribe; un — amaro, a bitter pill; -i amari, humiliation; a -i, in bits, in penny numbers; fare una cosa a pezzi e a -i, to do a thing by fits and starts, to do a thing piecemeal; (bldg.) quarter (of a brick), quarter bat. **-ata** f. mouthful. **-cello** m. dim. mouthful, little taste; pill; -cello del complimento, scraps left on a person's plate, manners' bit. **-cino** m. dim. titbit; un -cino, just a little bit. **-i** adv., adj. indecl. lying face downwards; prone; cadere -i, to fall flat on one's face. **-otto** m. (cul.) pasty, pie.

boccuc·cia f. See under bocca.

boccuto adj. See under bocca.

†boce f. See voce.

bochinista m. See bocchinista.

boc-iare [A3c] intr. to bawl; to yell; to brawl; to shout; to denigrate. **-iato** part. adj. denigrated; infamous; of ill-repute. **-io** m. (pl. -ii) continued bawling. **-ione** m. bawler; brawler.

Bodano pr.n.m. (geog.) Lake Constance.

bo·dano m. tinned tunny-fish.

bodda f. (dial. Lucca). See botta[1].

bodino m. See budino.

bo·dola f. See botola.

bodonian-o adj., n.m. (typ., bookb.) Bodoni (from the name of Giambattista Bodoni, 1740–1813); rilegato alla -a, bound in boards.

boemme m. bohemian, artist; vita di —, vie de bohème; (poet.) Bohemia.

Boe·m-ia pr.n.f. (hist.) Bohemia. **-o** m., adj. Bohemian. **(-a** f.)

Boe·ro pr.n.m. Boer; Afrikander; la guerra dei Boeri, the Boer War; kind of sweet containing chocolate, liqueur and cherry.

Boe·zio pr.n.m. Boethius.

†boffetta f. slap.

bof·fic-e adj. soft, puffy, spongy; (cul.) puff; pane —, light bread; plump. **-ione** m. fat, plump person. **(-iona** f.)

bofonch-iare [A4c] intr. (aux. avere) to grumble, to moan; to snort. **-iello, -ino** m. grumbler.

bofonchio m. grumbler; (ent.) kind of hornet; (pop.) bumble-bee.

bog-a f. (ichth.) various species of sea bream, including 'bogasalpa', bogue, Box salpa; — ravaglio, Spanish bream, Pagellus bogaraveo; — comune, ox-eye, Box boops; (industr.) loop or ring for anchoring machine parts; †(naut.) buoy; †prison, chains. **-ara** f. special kind of set net used for catching bogues, and similar fish.

bogasalpa f. (ichth.). See under boga.

boghei m. indecl. (Piedm.) two-wheeled carriage, buggy.

bo·gia f. speck, blemish, pimple, spot on the skin.

bo·gio m. (Ven.) whirlpool; abyss.

†bogliente part. adj. See bollente, under bollire.

†bo·glio m. tablet, slab (of chocolate).

bo·gliolo adj. (of an egg) bad, gone bad.

bo·i-a m. indecl. executioner; hangman; (fig.) fare da —, to be cruel, to be ruthless; (of a woman) loose woman, good-for-nothing slut; (iron.) — mal pratico, said of a clumsy surgeon or dentist; è stato il mio —, he was a slave driver, it nearly killed me working under him; adj. indecl. fa un freddo —, it's cold as Hell. **-ata** f. a cruel or ruthless act; (vulg.) bungled performance.

boiacca f. (bldg.) cement grout.

boiard-o[1] m. (Russ. hist.) boyar, boyard. **-ismo** m. boyardism.

Boiard-o[2] pr.n.m. Boiardo, Matteo Maria, Italian poet (1441–94), author of Orlando Innamorato. **-ęsco** adj. (m.pl. -ęschi) in the style of Boiardo.

boiaro m. See boiardo[1].

boiata f. See under boia.

boicott-are [A1] tr. to boycott. **-ag·gio** m. boycott; boycotting; (leg.) i capi del -aggio, boycott ring-leaders (C.P.).

boina f. beret; (Sp. hist.) red cap worn by the soldiers of Franco's army.

†bo·ito adj. empty.

bolce·vico adj. See bolscevico.

†bolcione m. See bolzone.

boldo m. (slang) belly.

boldone m. (Arezzo) black pudding.

boldrò[1] m. indecl. (ichth.) angler fish, Lophius piscatorius.

boldrò[2] m. indecl. bulldog.

boldron-e m. fleece. **-a·io** m. fellmonger.

bolero m. (mus.) bolero; bolero jacket; hat with ribbons and one side turned up.

bolęto m. (bot.) cep, cepe, genus of tuber-bearing fungi, Boletus.

†bolge f. See bolgia.

bol·g-ia f. (pl. -e) one of the ten ditches of the eighth circle of Dante's Inferno; (fig.) pit, abyss; a place of chaos and disorder; †sack, bag; †pocket; †wallet; †bulge. **-ętta** f. dim. wallet; post-bag; portfolio. **†-iarolo** m. miner.

bolginello m. (Siena). See boncinello.

bo·lide m. (astron.) bolide, meteor, shooting star; fire-ball; (colloq.) fast car; passare come un —, to flash past.

bolimi·a f. See bulimia.

bolin-a f. (naut.) bowline; rope attached to a square sail; andare di —, to sail close hauled; nodo di — doppio, bowline on a bight. **-are** [A1s] tr., intr. (aux. avere) to haul to windward.

†bolino m. See bulino.

†bo·lio m. See bolo.

Boli·v-ia pr.n.f. (geog.) Bolivia. **-iano** adj., n.m. Bolivian. **(-iana** f.)

bǫll-a[1] f. bubble; fare le -e, to bubble; — d'aria, air-bubble, (foundry) gas pocket; livella a — d'aria, spirit level; — di sapone,

boll-a¹ (*cont.*)

soap-bubble; bleb, blister; (agric.) leaf curl (of a peach tree); bulb (of a thermometer); (Tusc. pop.) diphtheria. **-icella** *f. dim.* pimple; pustule. **-iciat·tola** *f.* boil; inflamed spot. **-oso** *adj.* spotty.

boll-a² *f.* seal; imprint; (eccl.; hist.) bull; — di scomunica, bull of excommunication. **-are** [A I C] *tr.* to seal, to stamp; to brand; to cheat, to rob by false pretences. **-a·rio** *m.* (eccl.) bullarium. **-ato** *part. adj.* (adm.; comm.) stamped; carta -ata, paper to be used for official documents bearing printed stamp which certifies that duty has been paid; fissato -ato, stockbroker's stamped statement of purchase or sale of stock or shares, contract note; valori -ati, all revenue stamps and paper bearing printed stamp which are used for the collection of stamp duty; †(fig., joc.) furbo -ato, proper scoundrel. **-atore** *m.* person who stamps or seals. **-atura** *f.* sealing; (admin.) stamping; branding. **-etta** *f. dim.* round-headed nail, stud; (comm.) bill; receipt; -etta del gas, gas bill; -etta delle imposte, tax demand notice; -etta doganale, bill of entry; -etta di sortita, shipping bill; -etta di accompagnamento in deposito, consignment note for warehousing; -etta di spedizione, advice note; (colloq.) essere in -etta, to be broke, to be hard-up. **-etta·rio** *m.* order book; receipt book; counterfoil book. **-ettato** *adj.* studded; †sealed. **-ettino** *m. dim.* of **bolletta**; bulletin; gazette; note; list; -ettino di ordinazione, order sheet; -ettino di spedizione, forwarding note; -ettino di consegna, delivery note; -ettino dei prezzi, price-list; -ettino dei cambi, exchange list; (joc.) -ettino del fante, -ettino della lavandaia, news that has leaked. **-ettone** *m. augm.* of **bolletta**; (shoem.) heel-peg.

Bollandisti *pr.n.m.pl.* (eccl.) Bollandists.

bollente *part. adj.* see under **bollire**.

bol·ler-o *m.* (tan.) plunger (for lime pits). **-are** [A I S] *tr.* to plunge (lime pits).

boll-etta *f.*, **-ettino** *m.* See under **bolla²**.

bolli bolli *m. indecl.* (Tusc., joc.) unrest; disquiet; 'bubble bubble, toil and trouble'.

bolli-care¹ [A 2 SC] *intr.* (*aux.* avere) to boil gently, to simmer. **-came** *m.* stream of molten lava. **-camento** *m.* simmering. **-chìo** *m.* continual bubbling, boiling, simmering.

bollicare² [A 2 SC]. See **brulicare**.

bollino *m.* See under **bollo¹**.

boll-ire [D I C] *intr.* (*aux.* avere) to boil; to be on the boil; la pentola -e, the saucepan's boiling; to bubble; to seethe; quel che -e in pentola, what is brewing, what is hatching; lasciar uno — nel suo brodo, to let someone stew in his own juice; sentirsi il sangue — nelle vene, to be boiling with anger, to feel full of vigour; qualcosa gli deve — in corpo, he always has a fire in his belly; *tr.* to boil; to bring to the boil; — adagio, to simmer. **-ente** *part. adj.* boiling; hot; hot-blooded; burning, fiery, ardent; impetuous. **-imento** *m.* boiling; boil; ebullition. **-ita** *f.* boiling; boil; dare una -ita a, to boil, to bring to the boil. **-itic·cio** *m.* sediment after boiling. **-ito** *part. adj.* boiled; stewed; cooked; *n.m.* boiled meat; stew. **-itore** *m.* boiler; pressure cooker; -itore elettrico, electric kettle. **-itura** *f.* boiling; time taken to bring to the boil; water in which a thing has been boiled; batch; (eng.) welding.

boll-o¹ *m.* seal; — a secco, embossed or impressed seal; — a umido, rubber stamp; (admin.) stamp; — postale, postmark; — dell'assegno, cheque stamp; — della cambiale, bill stamp; diritto di —, stamp duty; imposta (tassa) di —, stamp-tax; marca da —, revenue stamp; carta da —, paper to be used for official documents bearing printed stamp which certifies that duty has been paid; ufficio del — e del Registro, government office where certain duties are collected and certain public records kept; — di circolazione, road licence (on a car); *pl.* (eng.) dings. **-ino** *m. dim.* (N., Centr. Ital.) postage stamp; (food) coupon; bicycle licence (metal disk); token.

bollo² *m.* (S. Ital.) boiling.

bollo³ *m.* (Pisa) sweetmeat.

†bollone *m.* See **bullone**.

bollore *m.* boiling; boiling point; bubbling; essere in —, to be on the boil; (fig.) a —, at boiling point; dare un — a, to bring to the boil; levare il —, dare il primo —, to be on the boil; excessive heat of summer; ardour; fervour; heat, excitement; commotion, tumult.

bolo *m.* bole, a kind of clay used by artists and formerly used in medicine; dorare a —, to gild upon an under-surface of bole; bowl; (med.) bolus, a large pill.

Bologn-a *pr.n.f.* (geog.) Bologna; (miner.) sulphate of baryta found near Bologna; fosforo di —, Bologna phosphorus; oro di —, imitation gold; ecco la luna di —! (said of someone who rarely puts in an appearance); (cul.) kind of salame sausage. **-ese** *adj.*, *n.m., f.* Bolognan, Bolognese; (cul.) spaghetti alla -ese. spaghetti and minced meat seasoned with tomato sauce. **-ino** *m.* (numis.) old Bolognese copper coin.

bolo·metro *m.* (phys.) bolometer.

bolsce·v·ico, bolscev·i·co *adj., n.m.* (*pl.* **-ichi, -i·chi**) bolshevik. **-ismo** *m.* bolshevism. **-i·stica** *f.* study of bolshevik doctrines. **-izzare** [A I] *tr.* to bolshevize.

bols-o¹ *adj.* broken-winded (esp. of a horse); (fig.) weak, half-hearted (e.g. of style). **-ag·gine** *f.* broken-windedness, esp. of horses; weakness.

†bolso² *adj.* blunt.

bolz-one *m.* bolt, a sort of battering arrow with a lump of lead taking the place of the point; battering-ram; beam for moving a drawbridge; †coin. **†-ona** *f.* Tuscan silver coin of fourteenth century. **-ona·glia** *f.* copper coins. **-onare** [A I C] *tr.* to ram. **-onata** *f.* ram; blow with a battering-ram.

boma *f.* (naut.) boom; — di maestra, main boom; — della randa di mezzana, spanker boom.

bomb-a *f.* bomb; bomb-shell; gettar -e, to drop bombs; a prova di —, bomb-proof; (fig.) un alibi a prova di —, a watertight alibi; — a mano, hand grenade; — fetida, gas bomb; — fumogena, smoke bomb; — antisommergibile, depth charge; — atomica, atom bomb; — all'idrogeno, H bomb; (fig.) è scoppiata la —, the cat's out of the bag, the balloon's gone up; tall story, fib; che -e!, what nonsense; boast, bragging; (cul.) pastry puff; large drink; top-hat; 'base' or 'home' in boys' game like Prisoners' Base; tornare a —, to get back to the subject; discostarsi da —, to wander away from the subject; toccare —, to arrive and go away again immediately; †-abà *m.* drinking-song. **†-anza** *f.* pomp, boastfulness, bragging. **†-are** *tr.* to drink; to guzzle; *intr.* to reverberate. **-ire** [D 2] *intr.* (*aux.* avere) to reverberate. **†-ista** *m.* bomber, artillery-man; braggart. **†-itare** *intr.* to reverberate. **-o** *m.* reverberation, thundering; (fam., nursery) drink; (ent.) bumble bee, humble bee, *Bombus terrestris.* **-one** *m.* liar; boaster, braggart; †drunkard. (**-ona** *f.*)

Bomba·i *pr.n.f.* (geog.) Bombay.

bombarda *f.* (mil.) mortar; (naut.) two-masted vessel; small two-masted war-vessel; (mus.) bombard: bass reed-stop on the organ with 16-foot tone; euphonium.

bombard-are [A I] *tr.* to bombard; to bomb; to shell. **-amento** *m.* bombardment, bombing; shelling; apparecchio da -amento, bomber; -amento a picchiata, -amento a tuffo, dive-bombing; (phys.) bombardment. **-ata** *f.* bombing; shelling. **-atore** *m.* bomber; bombarder. **-iera** *f.* bomb embrasure; small vessel carrying artillery. **-iere** *m.* artilleryman; bombardier; tenor trumpet used in village bands; (aeron.) bomber; bomb-aimer; bomber-plane; (ent.) bombardier beetle, *Brachinus crepitans.* **-ino** *m.* (mus.) baritone saxhorn; †small pommer, shawm. **†-o** *m.* (mus.) pommer. **-one** *m.* (mus.) bombardon, contrabass saxhorn; †large pommer.

bomba·stico *adj.* bombastic, pompous.

bombat-o *adj.* rounded, arched, convex; (eng.) dished; (fam.) hunch-backed. **-atura** *f.* convexity; (eng.) swell, crowning (of a pulley); (roadm.) camber.

†bomberaca *f.* gum arabic.

bom·ber-o¹ *m.* fool, idiot; non fare il —, don't be silly; (Tusc.) bowler hat; *adj.* stupid.

bom·bero² *m.* See **vomero**.

bombetta *f.* bowler hat. (Cf. **bomba**.)

†bombettare *intr.* to drink heavily, to tipple.

bom·bice *m.* (ent.) silk moth, *Bombyx mori.*

bomb-ili, -i·lidi *m.pl.* (ent.) bee-flies, fam. *Bombylidae.*

bombire [D 2] *intr.* (*aux.* avere) (poet.) to buzz; to resound.

bom·bito *m.* resonance, reverberation; buzzing.

bombo *m.* See under **bomba**.

bom·bol-a *f.* water- or wine-jug; (techn.) gas cylinder; †bomb. **-etta** *f. dim.* round sausage. **-o** *m.* short, tubby person. **-one** *m.* (Flor.) doughnut; krapfen; (Rome) chubby baby.

bombone¹ *m.* See under **bomba**.

bombon-e² *m.* bonbon. **-eri·a** *f.* assortment of sweets, confectionery. **-iera** *f.* sweetmeat box, bonbonnière.

bompresso *m.* (naut.) bowsprit.

bonac·c-ia *f.* calm (at sea); — piena, dead calm; (fig.) smooth-running, plain-sailing; prosperity; †fine weather; †kindliness, good humour. -**iare** *vb.* See abbonacciare. -**ẹvole** *adj.* light (of a breeze). -**io** *adj.* favourable; well-disposed; favourably inclined. -**iọne** *adj.* kindly; easy-going; *n.m.* easy-going person; good-natured man; well-meaning person. (-**iọna** *f.*) -**iọso** *adj.* calm; fine; (fig.) well-disposed.

†**bonaccordo** *m.* (mus.). See buonaccordo.

bonaga *f.* (bot.) rest-harrow, *Ononis spinosa*.

bonagra·zia *f.* benevolence; *pl.* (**bonegra·zie**) curtain-fixtures (rail and brackets).

bonalana *f.* (*pl.* **bonelane**) contemptible scoundrel; (joc.) rogue (also **bona lana**).

bonamano *f.* (*pl.* **bonemani**) tip (esp. to drivers).

bonamorte *f.* (eccl.) Bona Mors (devotion or confraternity).

bona·nima *f.* the dear departed; spirit; mio padre, —, my father, God rest him.

Bonapart-e *pr.n.m.* (Napoleon) Bonaparte. -**ịsmo** *m.* Bonapartism. -**ista** *m., adj.* Bonapartist.

bonaerense *adj., n.m., f.* native of Buenos Aires.

bona·ri-o *adj.* good-natured; homely; friendly; benevolent; gentle; simple, credulous; un — accordo, an amicable agreement. -**amẹnte** *adv.* good-naturedly; in good faith; plainly, simply; in a homely manner. -**età** *f.* good nature; kindliness; affability; simplicity, candour, good faith.

bonatenen-te *m.* (hist., Naples) property-owner. -**za** *f.* (hist., Naples) property-tax payable by foreigners.

†**bonavo·glia** *m.* voluntary worker, unpaid assistant; (fig.) idler.

†**bonavventuroso** *adj.* fortunate.

boncerella *f.* a kind of sweet omelette with slices of apple; apple fritter.

†**bon·cia** *f.* cat.

bonciarella *f.* See boncerella.

boncinello *m.* bolt-staple for fixing a bolt so that it cannot be shot back.

†**bon·cio** *m.* (Pulci) unidentified fresh-water fish, perhaps a barbel or a roach.

boncuore *m.* good-heartedness.

bondiola *f.* (N. Ital.) kind of pork-sausage.

bondọne *m.* (N. Ital.) plug-hole of a barrel; plug, stopper.

bonello *m.* land formed by alluvium.

bonẹtta *f.* (naut.) stunsail, sprit; †bag, sack; †cloth.

bonẹtto *m.* forage cap; beret.

bongusta·io *m.* See buongustaio, under buonaccordo.

boni·fica *f.* reclamation (of land); drainage, irrigation; (leg.) — integrale, comprehensive land improvement or reclamation (C.C.); decontamination (after a gas attack).

bonific-are [A2s] *tr.* to improve or reclaim (land) by irrigation or drainage; to make good; (comm.) to allow, to grant an allowance or discount of, to reduce, — il 5 per cento, to grant an allowance of 5 per cent. -**a·bile** *adj.* reclaimable. -**amẹnto** *m.* reclaiming; reclamation; reclaimed land. -**ato** *part. adj.* reclaimed; allowed, granted, reduced. -**atọre** *m.* irrigation engineer. -**aziọne** *f.* (agric.) reclaiming; reclamation; (comm.) abatement, allowance, discount, reduction; -azione concessa dai grossisti ai dettaglianti, trade discount; -azione concessa per i pagamenti a pronti contanti, cash discount; tariffa a forfait con -azione, flat rate tariff.

bonifi·cio *m.* (comm.) discount, allowance.

bonimẹnto *m.* (showman's, quack's) patter; pretentious speech; hanky-panky.

bonis *phr.* stare in —, to be on good terms; (Neap.) to be well off, to be in the money; (Bologn.) essere in —, to be in the money.

bono *adj.* and derivs. See buono; *n.m.* good; cheque; bill; coupon.

bon-omi·a *f.* goodness of heart, bonhomie; affability, geniality. -**omo** *m.* easy-going person; simple fellow. -**peso** *m.* good weight; 'little bit for luck', make-weight. -**prò** *m. indecl.* advantage; pro (also **buon pro**). -**senso** *m.* good sense, common sense.

bontà *f. indecl.* goodness: specific excellence; inherent goodness; somma Bontà, God; virtue; kindness: — tua, in your kindness, as you are kind; quanta —!, how kind!; mi ha usato una vera —, he has been really kind to me; abbiate la — di ascoltarmi, be so good as to listen to me; avere la — di, to be so kind as to; good quality, goodness; la — del cibo, the excellence of the food; la — dell'aria di mare, the good sea air.

bontempọne *m.* cheerful fellow, gay companion; one who thinks only of having a good time.

bont-ò *m. indecl.* luxury, elegance, 'bon ton'. -**onista** *m.* dandy, beau.

bonturo *m.* swindler.

bonuomo *m.* See bonomo, under bonomia.

bonuscita *f.* payment for surrendering a lease or other rights; key money; leaving or retirement gratuity.

bọnzo¹ *m.* bonze, Buddhist priest in China or Japan.

†**bonzo²** *m.* tailor's goose (made of wool).

bon·zola *f.* (Tusc.) bladder.

Boote *m.* (astron.) Boötes, the Bearkeeper; Carro di —, the Great Bear, Ursa Major, the Plough, King Charles' Wain, the Dipper.

bora¹ *f.* very cold north-east or north-west wind blowing up suddenly in the Trieste area; (poet.) North.

bora² *m.* (Pulci) unidentified serpent, perhaps a python.

bor-ace *m., f.* borax; (miner.) — grezza, tincal. -**a·cico** *adj.* boracic, boric; acido -acico, boric acid. †-**aciere** *m.* pot, jar. -**aci·fero** *adj.* boraciferous. -**ato** *m.* (chem.) borate.

boracite *f.* (miner.) boracite, stassfurtite.

borasso *m.* (bot.) genus of palm-trees, including Palmyra palm, *Borassus flabellifer*; (naut.) coir rope.

borbogliare [A4] *intr.* (*aux.* avere) to murmur, to mutter; to grumble; to rumble; to gurgle.

borbo·gio *m.* rumbling (of the intestines).

borbog-ìo *m.* (*pl.* -**ìi**) murmuring; grumbling; rumbling; gurgling; hubbub.

Borb-ọne¹ *n.m.* (hist.) Bourbon. (-**onẹse**, -**oniano** *adj.*) -**o·nico** (hist.) *adj., n.m.* Bourbon. -**o·nidi** *m.pl.* (hist.) Bourbons. (-**o·nio** *adj.*)

Borbọne² *pr.n.m.* (geog.) Island of Bourbon; coffee from the island.

bọrbora *f.* (naut.). See burbera.

borborigmo *m.* intestinal rumblings.

borbott-are [A1] *tr., intr.* (*aux.* avere) to mutter; to grumble; to rumble; — l'inglese, to speak broken English; †to turn over ideas in the mind, to ruminate. -**amẹnto** *m.* muttering, mumbling; grumbling; rumbling; flatulence. -**atọre** *m.* mutterer, mumbler; grumbler. -**ino** *m.* long-necked bottle which gurgles when poured from. -**io** *m.* (*pl.* -**ii**) continued muttering; constant grumbling; rumbling in the bowels. -**ọne** *m.* mutterer, mumbler; grumbler. (-**ọna** *f.*)

bọrca *f.* (N. Ital.) fork in the road.

bor·chi-a *f.* ornamental button; metal disk; boss; escutcheon plate; horse brass; sequin; (bookb.) clasp; marble or stone disk to which the spout of a drinking fountain is fixed. -**a·io** *m.* maker of 'borchie'. -**ettato** *adj.* ornamented with brasses; studded.

bọrda *f.* (naut.) the second largest sail of a galley.

borda·glia *f.* mob, rabble, scum of the earth.

bordame *m.* (naut.) foot of a sail.

bord-are¹ [A1c] *tr.* to cudgel; to beat; to slave-drive; (naut.) to haul (sails), — a segno, to sheet close home; — la randa di mezzana, to haul out the spanker; †to plank; *intr.* (*aux.* avere) to joust; (pop.) to work like a slave. -**ata** *f.* (naut.) tack; board; broadside. -**ato** *part. adj.* cudgelled; hard worked; (naut.) made fast to board; planked; (herald.) fimbriated; croce -ata, cross fimbriated; (herald.) edged; *n.m.* (naut.) †planking. -**atura** *f.* (naut.) tacks; †planking.

bord-are² [A1c] *tr.* to border, to edge; (techn.) to rim; to bead. -**atino** *m.* striped cloth; tick, ticking. -**ato** *adj.* bordered, edged; *n.m.* striped cloth, tick, ticking. -**atọre** *m.* hammer (sewing machine accessory); (paperm.) apparecchio -atore, deckle strap. -**atura** *f.* hemming; (techn.) beading, skirt. -**atrice** *f.* (techn.) beading machine; flanging machine.

bordeggi-are [A3c] *intr.* (*aux.* avere) (naut.) to tack; to beat against the wind. -**amẹnto** *m.* -**ata** *f.* See bordeggio.

bordẹggio *m.* (naut.) tacking.

bordella *f.* young fat animal; (vulg.) fat woman.

†**bordellino** *m.* garment of striped cloth.

bordell-o¹ *m.* brothel, disorderly house; (fig.) uproar; far —, to kick up a shindy. †-**are** *intr.* to frequent a brothel; to whore, to go a-whoring. †-**eri·a** *f.* bagatelle, trifle. -**iere** *m.* frequenter of brothels; dissolute individual.

†**bordello²** *m.* lad; stable-boy; *adj.* fat, gross.

borderau *m. indecl.* (pron. as Fr.) memorandum of payment; account slip; waybill; (theatr.) counterfoils of tickets; returns, takings; budget for a single performance.

borderò *m. indecl.* See borderau.

bordi·gli-o *m.* thickness of thread. **-one** *m.* (text.) snarl, tangle in silk.

bordino *m.* flange (of tram or railway wheel); (eng.) flat band; — reggispinta, thrust collar.

†**bordi·zio** *m.* joust, tourney.

bordo¹ *m.* (naut.) side of a ship; board; a —, on board, aboard; franco a—, free on board; fuori —, overboard; giornale di —, log; virare di —, to alter course, to go about; viramento di —, going about; gente di —, crew; (fig.) nave di alto —, V.I.P., big shot.

bord-o² *m.* border, edge; rim, lip; brink; verge; — di marciapiede, kerb, kerb-stone.

Bordò *pr.n.m.* (geog.) Bordeaux; type of French wine, Bordeaux; Bordeaux colour, wine colour.

bordolęse *adj.* of Bordeaux; (agric.) mistura —, poltiglia —, Bordeaux mixture; *n.m.* claret.

bordona·io *m.* (naut.) sailors' rest (boarding-house).

†**bordonale** *m.* (naut.) ship's beam.

bordonaro *m.* (naut.) cod of tunny fisher's net.

bordonato *adj.* (herald.) pommelly; croce bordonata cross pommelly.

bordon-e¹ *m.* pilgrim's staff; piantare il —, to stay, to take up one's abode; (herald.) bourdon, pilgrim's staff.

bordone² *m.* (orn.) feather on a fledgling; *pl.* down, fluff; first hairs on a young man's face; fare venire i bordoni a uno, to make a person's hair stand on end.

bordon-e³ *m.* (mus.) burden; drone; tenor lute-string; bourdon (organ-stop of 16-foot tone); falso —, faburden, fauxbourdon; (fig.) tenere — a, to be the accomplice of, to egg on, to be in cahoots with. †**-izzare** *tr.* (mus.) to perform (a melody) with a drone-bass.

bordura *f.* border, margin; edge; decoration of left-hand margin of a page of MS.; (herald.) bordure.

bo·re-a *pr.n.m.* (poet.) Boreas; north wind; north. **-ale** *adj.* north, northerly, northern; aurora -ale, aurora borealis, Northern Lights.

borello *m.* (naut.) toggle.

†**borga** *f.* wicker basket used as a fish-trap or, filled with stones, to protect a river bank.

borgata *f.* village; scattered group of houses; township (cf. **borgo**).

borghęs-e *adj.* middle class, bourgeois; non-U; homely, plain; common; civilian; in —, in civilian dress, in mufti; *n.m.*, *f.* middle-class person; commoner; civilian; piccoli -i, lower middle-class people. **-i·a** *f.* middle classes, professional and business people; middle and upper classes; bourgeoisie; (army slang) civvy street; grassa -ia, wealthy shopkeepers, merchants; piccola -ia, lower middle class. **-ismo** *m.* middle-class way of life; middle-class outlook.

borghigiano *m.* See under **borgo**.

borgino *m.* fishing net.

borgiotto *m.* type of fig which ripens in September.

bor·gnola *f.* (Tusc.). See **borniola**, under **bornia¹**.

bor·go *m.* (*pl.* **-ghi**) group of houses; village; small country town; suburb outside the walls of a city; street (formerly outside the city walls). **-ghigiano** *m.* villager. **-gomastro** *m.* burgomaster.

Borgogn-a *pr.n.f.* (geog.) Burgundy; vino di —, Burgundy wine. **-ese**, **-one** *adj.* Burgundian; *n.m.* Burgundian; †porter, strong beer, stout.

borgognone¹ *adj.*, *n.m.* See under **Borgogna**.

borgognone² *m.* iceberg; ice shelf.

borgomastro *m.* See under **borgo**.

†**bor·gora** *pl.* of **borgo**, q.v.

†**bor·goro** *m.* See **borgo**.

bo·ri-a *f.* arrogance; vainglory, self-conceit; haughtiness; pride; ostentation; mettere su —, to put on airs; pieno di —, conceited. **-are** [A I] *intr.* (*aux.* avere), *rfl.* to swagger; to be conceited; to show off; to be arrogant or haughty. **-ata** *f.* conceited behaviour; ostentation; swagger. **-one** *m.* swaggerer. **-oso** *adj.* haughty, arrogant; conceited; swaggering; ostentatious. **-osamente** *adv.* conceitedly; arrogantly; haughtily; ostentatiously. **-osello** *m.* vain, swaggering person. **-osità** *f.* conceit; ostentatiousness; arrogance; haughtiness.

boric-co *m.* (*pl.* **-chi**) padding, stuffing; woollen cape.

bo·rico *adj.* (chem.) boric; cf. **borace**.

borina *f.* (naut.). See **bolina**.

borino *m. dim.* of **bora¹**, q.v.

boriọne *m.*, **boriọso** *adj.* See under **boria**.

bọrlo *m.* cylinder.

borne·olo *m.* (chem.) borneol, bornyl alcohol.

bor·ni-a¹ *f.* tall story; false judgment. **-ola** *f.* hasty judgment; contradiction of the truth.

bor·nia² *f.* (Lucca) (agric.) empty chestnut husk.

bor·nio¹ *m.* curbstone; spur-stone; projecting rock.

†**bor·nio²** *adj.* blind in one eye; squinting; (fig.) unjust.

bornite *f.* (miner.) bornite, erubescite, horseflesh ore, purple copper ore.

boro *m.* (chem.) boron.

borọsa *f.* (naut.) head earing, line which fastens the upper angle of a sail to the top of the yard.

borosilicato *m.* (chem.) borosilicate.

borotalco *m.* talcum powder.

bọrra¹ *f.* clippings and waste material for stuffing; shavings; packing; (text.) wool dropping; floss silk; (of a cartridge) wad; (naut.) tarred packing; — d'acqua, seaweed; (fig.) padding; idle words, chatter; essere —, to be worthless, to be mere padding; quel libro è tutta —, that book is all padding; †strength, 'guts'.

†**borra²** *f.* north wind; battere la —, to chatter one's teeth with cold.

†**borra³** *f.* See **borro**.

borrac·cia *f.* water-bottle; flask.

borraccina *f.* moss; (bot.) the moss, *Thuidium tamariscinum*.

borra·cio *m.* canvas.

borra·gine *f.* (bot.) borage, *Borago officinalis*; — selvatica, comfrey, comfort-root, *Symphytum officinale*; alkanet, *Anchusa italica*.

borrag·gio *m.* (miner.) stemming.

†**borrana** *f.* torrent; gulley; ditch; l'acqua corre alla —, each man follows his own bent.

borr-o *m.* deep ditch, drain; gully; watercourse. (**-one** *m. augm.*)

†**borrome·o** *m.* itinerant vendor of wool.

bọrs-a *f.* purse; (fig.) money; — di studio, scholarship, grant; mettere mano alla —, to 'put one's hand in one's pocket', to 'fork out'; pagare di propria —, to pay out of one's own pocket; toccare uno nella —, to touch a person for money; con la — degli altri, on other people's money; la — o la vita, your money or your life; tenere la — stretta, avere il granchio alla —, to be stingy; tenere i cordoni della —, to hold the purse-strings; fare — comune, to pool resources; bag; handbag; — d'acqua calda, hot water bottle; pouch; — da tabacco, tobacco pouch; -e agli occhi, bags under the eyes; (of material) bulge; (N. Ital.) briefcase; attaché case; (motor.) — utensili, tool kit; (liturg.) burse; (bot.) pod; (bot.) — di pastore, shepherd's purse, *Capsella bursa-pastoris*; (econ.) bourse, stock exchange; — grani, wheat market; — merci, commodity market; — nera, black market; contratti di —, stock exchange transactions (C.C.); listino di —, stock exchange quotations; (anat.) bursa. †**-a·io** *m.* maker or vendor of purses. **-ai(u)olo** *m.* pickpocket; bag-snatcher. †**-ale** *adj.* monetary. **-aro** *m.* profiteer; -aro nero, black marketeer. **-ata** *f.* purse-full. **-eggiare** [A 3 C] *tr.* to pick pockets. **-eggio** *m.* pocket-picking, theft. **-ellino** *m. dim.* money purse (for coins); (eccl.) collection-bag (on stick). **-etta** *f. dim.* (N. Ital.) woman's handbag; (bot.) -etta del muschio, musk pod. **-ettiere** *m.* manufacturer or vendor of handbags, etc. **-iere** *m.* bursar; treasurer. **-ista** *m.* (comm.) stockbroker, jobber; speculator; *m.*, *f.* holder of a scholarship, scholar. (**-i·stico** *adj.*) **-ite** *f.* (med.) bursitis; -ite prepatellare, housemaid's knee. **-otto** *m.* pouch for shot; large purse.

borsalino *m.* felt hat; trilby hat (manufactured by the firm of Borsalino in Alessandria, Piedmont).

borsanera *f.* See 'borsa nera' under **borsa**.

borsite *f.* (med.). See under **borsa**.

bortolino *m.* (Milan) native of Bergamo.

boruro *m.* (chem.) boride.

borusso *adj.*, *n.m.* (poet.) Prussian.

borzacchina *f.* (bot.). See 'borsa di pastore', under **borsa**.

borzacchino *m.* half boot.

boṣa *f.* (naut.) bull's-eye cringle, one of the rings to which the bowline bridles are attached.

bosca·glia *f.* See under **bosco**.

†**boscareccio** *adj.* See **boschereccio**, under **bosco**.

boscimano, bosci·mano *m.*, *adj.* (ethn.) bushman.

bos-co *m.* (*pl.* **-chi**) wood, forest; — ceduo, coppice, copse; portare legna al —, to carry coals to Newcastle; rimanere uccel di —, to keep out of prison; uomo da — e da campagna, versatile and experienced man; (silk-farming) spinning hut; (poet.) firewood.

bos·co (*cont.*)

†**-cag·gio** *m.* wood; forest. **-ca·glia** woodland, wooded country; thicket; undergrowth; (joc.) untidy hair, 'bird's nest'. **-cai(u)ola** *f.* woodman's wife. **-cai(u)olo** *m.* woodman, wood-cutter. **-cata** *f.* wooded tract. **-ato** *adj.* wooded. **-chereccio** *adj.* sylvan, woody; paesaggio **-chereccio**, woodland scenery; †rustic. **-chetto** *m. dim.* grove, thicket; shrubbery; place for snaring birds; the plants or shrubs which constitute part of the snare. †**-chiere** *m.* woodman, wood-cutter. **-chivo** *adj.* woody, wooded; terreno **-chivo**, forest-land; *n.m.* forester, woodman. **-coso** *adj.* wooded, well-wooded.

Boscoducale *pr.n.m.* (geog.) 's Hertogenbosch.

Bo·sforo *pr.n.m.* (geog.) the Bosphorus; †straits.

bosin-o *m.* peasant of Brianza. **-ata** *f.* poem in Milanese dialect, sometimes set to music, sung or recited by the 'bosini'.

Bo·sn·ia *pr.n.f.* (geog.) Bosnia. **-i·aco** *adj.*, *n.m.* Bosnian.

bosone *m.* (phys.) boson.

bosse *f.* (pron. as Fr.) aptitude, inclination, 'bump', flair.

bosso¹ *m.* (bot.) box-tree, *Buxus sempervirens*; African box-thorn, *Lycium afrum*; boxwood; siepe di —, box-hedge; (mus. poet.) flute (because made of boxwood); small wooden box; dice-box.

bosso² *m.* (neol.) boss, head, chief.

bos·sol-a *f.* nave-ring; horse-brush; lath or thin board used on a ceiling in making a seating for the plaster. **-ato** *adj.* lathed; balustraded.

bos·solo¹ *m.* (bot.). See **bosso¹**.

bos·sol-o² *m.* small box; powder-box; tin; cup for receiving alms; dice-box; — della cartuccia, cartridge case; ballot box; (in a flour-mill) wheelbox, the piece of timber or other material with a hole in the middle in which the beam of the wheel turns; compass box; (mil.) powder tube. **-ificio** *m.* cartridge factory. **-otto** *m.* poor-box, alms-box.

bo·strico *m.* (ent.) bark-beetle, *Bostrychus* spp.

bota·n-ica *f.* botany. **-ico** *adj.* botanical; orto **-ico**, giardino **-ico**, botanical gardens; *n.m.* botanist. (**-icamente** *adv.*) (†**-ista** *m.*)

†**botare** *tr.*, *rfl.* to empty.

bo·tola *f.* cellar-flap, trapdoor; manhole; manhole cover.

botolatura *f.* (techn.) tumbling.

bo·tolo *m.* small, snappish cur; bad-tempered dog; (fig.) bad-tempered individual.

botri *m. indecl.* (bot.) name of various aromatic plants.

botrite *f.* (met.) botryoid deposit of zinc or cobalt in a copper-smelting furnace; (miner.) a black semi-precious stone.

botro *m.* deep ditch; stagnant watercourse; steep slope.

botta¹ *f.* (zool.) common toad, *Bufo vulgaris*; (provb.) la — che non chiese non ebbe coda, faint heart never won fair lady; squat person; camminare a —, to hop; — scudellaia, tortoise.

bott-a² *f.* blow; thrust; bruise; smack, slap; dare le **-e** a, to spank; prendere le **-e**, to get a spanking, (fig.) to take a hard knock; jab; dab; (of a gun) kick; (fencing) hit; — dritta, straight thrust; quip, jibe; stroke of the pen; (mil.) — e risposta, attack and defence, (fig.) cut and thrust, quick repartee, tit for tat; la lezione è scritta a — e risposta, the lesson is in the form of questions and answers; fishing or hunting lamp; sudden bend or wind in a river; (paint.) dipingere a —, to dab with the brush (as in pointillism); (herald.) chabot; †attack, onslaught; †defeat; †discharge from a gun; †petto a —, armour protecting the chest. †a prova di —, †di tutta —, proof against attack; *pl.* cudgelling; **-e** da orbi, free for all, shindy, dust-up. **-ata** *f.* discharge of a gun; blow; quip; gibe; raillery; stroke of ill-luck, misfortune; fancy price.

bottacc-ino *m.*, **-i(u)olo** *m.* See under **botte**.

†**botta·glia** *f.* See under **botte**.

†**botta·glie** *f.pl.* leather boots.

botta·io *m.* See under **botte**.

bottal-e *m.* (tanning) drum. **-are** [A I] *tr.* to drum. **-atura** *f.* drumming.

bottana *f.* cheese cloth; lining.

bottarga *f.* botargo, dried smoked roe of the mullet or tunny.

bottata *f.* See under **botta²**.

botta·tico *m.* See under **botte**.

bottatrice *f.* (ichth.) burbot, *Lota lota*.

bott-e *f.* cask, barrel; in una — di ferro, fast, secure, (fig.) impregnable, cast-iron; essere il sedile di —, to carry the whole burden; culvert carrying a stream under a road; a mezza —, half-circle; (archit.) volta a —, volta a mezza —, barrel vault; (motor.)

— rimorchio, tank trailer; (provb.) dare un colpo alla — e uno al cerchio, to keep two things going at the same time, to run with the hare and hunt with the hounds; voler avere la — piena e la moglie ubriaca, to want to have one's cake and eat it; la — dà del vino che ha, the proof of the pudding is in the eating; nelle **-i** piccine ci sta il vino buono (said of a person of small stature). **-acciata** *f.* bottleful. **-accino** *m. dim.* small barrel; tub; short stout person. **-ac·cio** *m.* small barrel; bottle of wine given to the carter for each barrel carted; mill pond; (naut.) reinforcement to a ship's structure; *adj.* (orn.) tordo **-accio**, song thrush, *Turdus ericetorum*. **-acci(u)olo** *m.* gumboil; dwarf; squat person. †**-aglia** *f.* measure of liquid. **-aio** *m.* cooper. **-ame** *m.* quantity of casks. **-atico** *m.* (Tusc.) payment for hire of casks. **-icella** *f.* (Rome) cab, hired carriage. **-icello** *m. dim.* of **botte**; (techn.) drip feed. **-ino** *m.* See **bottino¹**.

botte·ga *f.* small shop; village store; workshop, studio; (joc.) place of business; tenere —, to keep a shop; mettere su —, aprire —, to set up shop; stare a —, to serve in the shop; chiudere —, to close down; chiudere la —, to shut up shop for the night; ferro di —, police spy; (joc.) aver la — aperta, to have one's flies undone; far —, to 'make a bit on the side'; ferri di —, implements of a trade; scarto di —, persons of disrepute; stare a uscio e —, to live near each other, to be close neighbours; sviar la —, to disgust customers; questo proviene dalla tua —, this is your doing. **-gaio** *m.* shopkeeper; small tradesman; provision dealer; (Tusc.) customer. (**-ga·ia** *f.*) **-gante** *m.* shopkeeper. **-gare** [A 2 c] *intr.* (*aux.* avere) to be in business, to keep a shop. **-ghina**, **-ghetta** *f. dim.* of **bottega**; pedlar's tray. **-ghino** *m. dim.* public lottery office; box-office; booth; pedlar's tray; place where illicit dealing is carried on. **-gone** *m. augm.* of **bottega**; large café; large store; (Flor.) name of a well-known bar.

bottell-o *m.* label; title sheet. **-ame** *m.* posters, handbills.

botticelliano *adj.* (art) in the style of, or pertaining to Sandro Botticelli (1447–1510).

botticello *m.* See under **botte**.

botticino *m.* white marble quarried near Lake Garda (used for the monument to Victor Emanuel II, Rome).

botti·gli-a *f.* bottle; jar; — di Leida, Leyden jar; mettere vino in —, to bottle wine; birra in —, bottled beer; verde —, bottle green; vetri a culo di —, bottle-glass windows. †**-ere** *m.* wine-waiter; cellarman. **-eri·a** *f.* wine-cellar; wine-shop; bar; assortment of wines.

bottin-o¹ *m.* cesspool; sewage; water-tank; settling tank; precipitation chamber. **-a·io** *m.* drain-cleaner, sewer-man. **-iere** *m.* settling-tank inspector.

bottin-o² *m.* booty; loot; prize, spoils; fare — di, to plunder; (mil.) mettere a —, to sack; (mil. slang) pack. †**-are** *tr.* to loot, to sack. **-atrice** *f.* worker bee.

†**bottino³** *m.* short boot.

botto¹ *m.* (zool.). See **botta¹**.

botto² *m.* blow; stroke, toll of a bell; di —, all at once, suddenly; †*adv.* — —, again and again (Cf. **botta²**).

bot·tola *f.* (ichth.) *Gobius martensii*.

botton-e¹ *m.* button; stud; pimple; contraceptive; stud ear-ring; long boring speech; attaccare un — a, to bore, to buttonhole, to subject to a long rambling discourse; sbagliare il primo —, to commit the initial error; — da collo, collar stud; **-i** gemelli, **-i** da polsino, cuff links; — automatico, — a pressione, press-stud; (text.) rote (of cotton); (eng.) — di una manovella, crank-pin; (bot.) rose-bud; button d'oro, buttercup; (fencing) — del fioretto, knob on the end of a foil; (zool.) — caudale, tail bud (of an embryo). **-a·io** *m.* button-maker; button-seller. **-ato** *adj.* (herald.) seeded. **-cino** *m. dim.* little button; stud; (bot.) bud. **-iera** *f.* row of buttons; buttonhole; posy (as buttonhole); machine for making buttons. **-iero** *adj.* button, button-making; l'industria **-iera**, the button industry. **-ificio** *m.* button factory. **-ista** *m.* (neol.) bore (cf. **attaccabottoni**).

†**bottone²** *m.* quip, jibe, witticism.

botulismo *m.* (med.) botulism.

bova¹ *f.* serpent; worm.

†**bova²** *f.* See **bove²**.

bova³ *f.* landslide, landslip.

bovarina *f.* (orn.) wagtail, *Motacilla* spp.

bovarismo *m.* social and cultural ambition; yearning for grandeur and romance (from Flaubert's *Madame Bovary*).

bov-e¹ *m.* (*pl.* **buoi**). See **bue**; occhio di —, bull's-eye window; occhi di —, big staring eyes, cow's eyes; (fig.) a person slow on the uptake; (eng., colloq.) hand shears. **-a·io**, **-aro** *m.* drover; cowherd, cowman. **-ile** *m.* cattle-stall, cowshed. **-ina** *f.* cow-dung. **-inità** *f.* passivity. **-ino** *adj.* bovine; (poet.) occhi -ini, large eyes; (med.) cuore -ino, cor bovinum; *n.m.pl.* cattle.

†bove² *f.pl.* bonds, chains.

bovindo *m.* (bldg.) bay window.

bovino *adj.* See under **bove¹**.

bovolento *m.* (geog.) whirlpool in the river Adige.

bo·volo *m.* (mech.) conic spiral.

bowdlerizzare [A I] *tr.* to bowdlerize.

boxe *f.* (pron. as Fr.) boxing, pugilism.

boxes *m.pl.* (pron. as Fr.) (motor.) pits.

boxeur *m.* (pron. as Fr.) boxer.

boycottare [A I] and derivs. See **boicottare**.

bozz-a¹ *f.* rough-hewn stone; draft, rough copy; pull; proof-sheet; -e (di stampa), proof(s); -e in pagina, -e impaginate, page-proof(s); -e in colonna, galley-proof(s), galleys; fare le -e, to pull (proof); correggere le -e, to proof-read, to correct proofs; (art) rough sketch; lavorare a —, to rough out. **-are** [A I] *tr.* to sketch; to rough out. **-ato** *part. adj.* sketched; roughed out; made of rough stone; *n.m.* rough sketch; rough cast.

bozz-a² swelling, protuberance; (archit.) corbel; boss; (naut.) stopper. **-are** [A I] *tr.* (naut.) to stopper.

bozzac·chi-o *m.* swollen, fungus-damaged plum; parasitic fungus which attacks plums. **-one** *m.* plum damaged by fungus. **-uto** *adj.* deformed, misshapen (of a person).

bozza-go *m.* (*pl.* **-ghi**) (orn.) buzzard, *Buteo buteo*.

bozzare¹ [A I]. See under **bozza¹**.

bozzare² [A I]. See under **bozza²**.

bozzell-o *m.* (naut.) block with one or more pulleys. **-ame** *m.* collection of pulley-blocks. **-eri·a** *f.* pulley-block store.

bozzetto *m. dim.* See under **bozzo²**.

boz·zim-a *f.* (text.) weaver's paste for softening the web on the loom; dressing, size; bran mash for fowls; soup, etc., spoilt, cooked into a paste; mess; (fig.) muddle, mix-up. **-are** [A I s] *tr.* (text.) to dress, to size.

bozz-o¹ *m.* pond. **-ale** *m.* puddle.

bozz-o² *m.* rough, rustic stone; rough sketch. **-ettismo** *m.* writing of short sketches. **-ettista** *m.* author of short sketches; designer. **-etto** *m. dim.* plan, design; model; sketch, short article; *pl.* (theatr.) designs for stage-set; designs for scenery and costumes.

†bozzo³ *m., adj.* cuckold; bastard.

†boz·zola¹ *f.* swelling, tumour.

†boz·zola² *f.* measure of liquid or grain; dazio della —, milling tax.

boz·zol-o¹ *m.* cocoon; (dye.) ladle; measure used by a miller in withdrawing from the meal the quantity to be retained by him as payment; *pl.* (bot.) -i di seta dei boschi, swallow-wort, *Vincetoxicum officinale*. **-ac·cio** *m.* empty cocoon after the moth has left it. **-a·ia** *f.* cocoon room (in silkworm culture). **-a·io** *m.* dealer in cocoons. **-are** [A I s] *tr.* to remove (a moth) from a cocoon.

boz·zol-o² *m.* boss; protuberance; lump. **-oso** *adj.* lumpy. **-uto** *adj.* slightly lumpy.

bozzone *m.* wether lamb; (typ.) galley, galley-proof; (Flor., colloq.) clumsy, foolish individual; silly-billy.

Bra *pr.n.m.* Piedmontese wine, named after the commune of Bra.

brabanzone *adj.* pertaining to Brabant.

bra-ca *f.* leg of a pair of breeches; baby's napkin, diaper; leather safety support worn by workmen when scaling buildings; *pl.* trunks, shorts, pants, knickers, drawers; (fig.) mi cascan le -che, I am losing heart; calare le -che, calarsi le -che, to give in shamefully, to yield with cowardice, to humble oneself; *sing.* (naut.) sling; (bldg., etc.) sling (for hoisting); chain or rope for lifting an object by means of a crane or pulley-block; strip of paper pasted on to mend a torn page; piece of gossip. **-calone** *m.* coarse, slovenly individual; overalls. **-caloni** *adv.* in a slovenly way; a -caloni, sloppy, slovenly; colle calze a -caloni, with one's socks falling down. **-care** [A 2] *intr.* (*aux.* avere) to pry; to gossip, to tattle. **-cato** *part. adj.* breeched, in breeches, wearing trousers; in long trousers; grasso -cato, very fat. **-cheri·a** *f.* gossip, prattle. **-chetta** *f. dim.* (hist. costume) front flap of breeches; (bookb.) guard. **-chino** *m.* gossiping person. **-coni** *m.pl. augm.* (hist.) trousers worn by halberdiers; overalls.

bracca *f.* of **bracco**, q.v.

bracc-are [A 2] *tr.* to follow by scent; to pursue, to hunt; (fig.) to nose out; to seek out; to fish (e.g. for compliments). **-ato** *part. adj.* hunted, pursued; at bay. **-atore** *m.* (of a dog) hunter; quel cane è un buon -atore, that dog has a good nose. **(-atora** *f.*)

bracc-etto *m.* (*pl.* **-etti** *m.*, **-ette** *f.*) *dim.* of **braccio**; bracket; overarm stroke (swimming); (naut.) topgallant and royal braces; *adv. phr.* a —, arm in arm; (fig.) andare a — con, to be great friends with.

braccheggiare [A 3 c]. See **braccare**.

braccheggio *m.* (sport) beating; searching; scenting out.

bracchiere *m.* See under **bracco**.

†bracciaiuola *f.* See under **braccio**.

braccial-e *m.* arm guard; armlet; arm-rest; toothed piece of wood fastened on the arm for playing 'pallone'; *pl.* large wrought iron rings seen on ancient buildings; bar to reinforce the inside of a door; bracelet; identity wristlet. **-ata** *f.* a blow with an arm guard. **-etto** *m. dim.* bracelet, wrist-band; metal wristlet for a watch.

bracci-are [A 3] *tr.* (naut.) to brace; — in croce, to square the yards; — di punta, to brace sharp up; — in ralinga, to brace by. **-ante** *m.* labourer, hand (esp. farm labourer paid daily). **-antato** *m.* social class of the farm labourers in Italy; -antato agricolo, agricultural labour pool. **-antile** *adj.* relating to farm labouring class. **-ata** *f.* armful; a -ate, in abundance; (swimming) armstroke; †embrace; †sweetheart. **-atella** *f.*, **-atello** *m.* ring cake, 'ciambella'. **-atura** *f.* measurement; arm's length; (naut.) sounding. **-ere** *m.*, **-esco** *adj.* See under **braccio**.

brac·ci-o *m.* (*pl.f.* **-a**. See also below for *pl.m.* **-i**) arm; a -a aperte, with open arms; prendere in —, to take up in one's arms; trasportare a -a, to lift bodily; prendere fra le -a, to take in ones' arms; avere qualcuno sulle -a, to have someone on one's hands, to have to support someone; avere un — al collo, to have one's arm in a sling; darsi in — a, to give oneself up to; avere le -a legate, to be bound by restrictions; col lavoro delle proprie -a, by one's own exertions; mi cascarono le -a, I lost heart, I gave in helplessly, I gave up all further attempt at explanation or persuasion; workman, 'hand'; tanto lavoro e poche -a!, so much to do and so few hands!; power, authority; avere — libero, to have unlimited power, to have a free hand; avere le -a lunghe, to have a lot of influence; il — secolare, the secular arm; yard, ell; dategli un dito e si prenderà un —, give him an inch and he'll take an ell; fathom; (mus.) viola da —, treble viol; (vet.) forearm of a horse; (herald.) — destro, dexter arm; — sinistro, sinister arm; (gymn.) — di ferro, arm exercise between two people (forearm against forearm, elbows supported on a table); (*pl.m.* **-i**) support; bracket; stand; (mech.) — della forza, leverage, purchase; — di bilancia, balance beam; (eng.) jib (of a crane); (text.) — del battente, sley sword; (carp.) brace; (naut.) fluke (of an anchor); branch; sector; ramification; wing (of a building); — di mare, inlet; — di terra, promontory; — di scale, flight of stairs. **†-aiuola** *f.* small shield. **-armi** *adv.* (mil.) shouldering arms. **-ere** *m.* escort, man giving his arm to a lady; squire. **-esco** *adj.* (*m.pl.* -eschi) (naut.) connected with squaring the yard; *n.m.* sailor in charge of squaring the yard. **-(u)olo** *m.* arm of an easy chair; sedia a -uoli, armchair; banister rail on stairs; (bldg.; eng.) pipe clip; *pl.* rafters forming the angle of a ridged roof; (naut.) knee; (Tusc.) measure of area; 0·3364 sq. metres.

brac-co *m.* (*pl.* **-chi**) name of various Italian breeds of gun-dogs resembling pointers; — da sangue, bloodhound; — da punta, pointer; — inglese, English pointer; — da fermo, setter; (fig.) police spy, 'snooper'; detective, sleuth. **-cheri·a** *f.* a number of gun-dogs; confusion of voices, babble. **-chiere**, **-chiero** *m.* kennelhand; man holding dogs in leash, man in charge of dogs.

braccon-aggio *m.* poaching. **-iere** *m.* poacher.

brac-e *f.* embers; live coal; charred wood; small pieces of smouldering charcoal; nero come la —, as black as soot; cadere dalla padella nella —, to fall out of the frying pan into the fire.

brache *f.pl.* See **braca**.

brach-eri·a *f.*, **-etta** *f.* See under **braca**.

brachetto *m.* red wine of Piedmont and Liguria.

brachettone *m.* wearing wide loose trousers; nickname of Domillo Racciarelli who covered the nudes in Michelangelo's *Last Judgment*; (archit.) ornamental mouldings on an archivolt.

brachiale *adj.* (anat.) brachial.

brachice·fal-o *adj.* brachycephalic. **-i·a** *f.* brachycephaly.

brachier-e *m.* (med.) truss; (fig.) tiresome person. **-a·io** *m.* truss-maker.

brachi-grafi·a *f.* shorthand; abbreviated writing. **-logi·a** *f.* brevity in speech. **-lo·gico** *adj.* stated with brevity.

brachiocefa·lico *adj.* (anat., of the arteries) brachyocephalic.

†bra·cia *f.* See **brace.**

bracia·i-o *m.* ashpit. **†-ola** *f.* ashpit in a smelting furnace.

bracier-e, -o *m.* brazier; charcoal burner; warming-pan.

bracino *m.* charcoal burner (person); (fig.) individual as black as soot.

braciol-a *f.* steak grilled on a low fire; cutlet; chump chop; — di maiale, pork chop; (colloq.) cut on the face in shaving. **-ina** *f.* *dim.* of **braciola**; -ina di vitello, veal chop.

†braco *m.* See **brago.**

braco·ni *m.pl.* See under **braca.**

bracotto *m.* (naut.) pendant, a strong piece of rope attached at one end to the clew of a staysail or jib and having a block at the other end through which a jib-sheet or staysail sheet is roved.

bra·dipo *m.* (zool.) three-toed sloth.

†bradire *intr.* to sing, to chirrup (of birds).

bradisi̇smo *m.* (geol.) bradyseism, earth-movement involving change of relative level of land and sea, change of base-level.

brad-o *adj.* (N. Ital.) running wild; grazing; pascolo —, free pasture; free; cavallo —, unbroken horse; untamed; *adv.* a —, running wild; free; grazing. **-ume** *m.* herd of wild cattle.

†bradone *m.* fold in the bosom or near the shoulder of a dress.

braga *f.* (naut.). See **braca.**

bragagn-a *f.* drag-net for fishing lagoons; boat from which such a net is used. **-o** *m.* dredger.

†brage *f.* See **brace.**

†braghetta *f.* See **brachetta**, under **braca.**

braghetta·rio *m.* (admin.) record book, register, file.

†bra·gia *f.* See **brace.**

brago *m.* mire; mud.

bragozzo *m.* (Ven.) fishing boat in the Adriatic.

brahmano *m.* and derivs. See **bramano.**

†bra·ido *adj.* active, lively.

†braire *intr.* to shout, to yell; to bray; to whinny.

†braitare *intr.* to shout, to yell.

bram-a¹ *f.* strong desire, yearning, longing; hankering; cupidity, greed; lust. **-a·bile** *adj.* desirable, longed-for. **-ante** *part. adj.* desirous of. **-are** [A I] *tr.* to wish, to desire, to yearn for, to long for passionately. **-ato** *part. adj.* desired, longed for; beloved. **†-eggiare** *intr.* to lust. **-osi·a** *f.* longing, eager desire; covetousness, avidity, greed. **-oso** *adj.* longing, desirous; eager; greedy; -oso di, desirous of. **-osame̜nte** *adv.* longingly; eagerly; ardently. **-osità** *f.* See **bramosia.**

brama² *f.* (ichth.) Ray's bream, *Brama rayi.*

bram-ano *m.* Brahman. **-a·nico** *adj.* Brahmanic. **-ani̇smo** *m.* Brahmanism. **-anista** *m.* Brahmanist.

bramante̜s-co *adj.* (*m.pl.* **-chi**) (archit.) in style of Donato Bramante of Urbino (1444–1514). **-ca** *f.* (archit.) external double staircase.

bramare [A I] and derivs. See under **brama.**

bramasangue *m.* blood-thirsty individual; *excl.* death!; *adv.* holding a sword poised horizontally.

†brameggiare. See under **brama.**

bramino¹ *m.* and derivs. See **bramano.**

bramino² *m.* instrument for removing outside covering from grains of rice.

bramire [D 2] *intr.* (*aux.* avere) to roar, to bellow; (of a stag) to bell.

bramito, bra·mito *m.* roar, bellow; bellowing.

bramma *f.* (metall.) slab, flat bloom.

bramoso *adj.* and deriv. See under **brama.**

bran-ca *f.* branch: una — dello scibile, a branch of knowledge; una — di scale, one of two flights of stairs; (bldg.; archit.) section; claw, talon; tentacle; *pl.* pliers, pincers; (naut.) fluke (of an anchor); (poet.) cluster; (anat.) ramus; (bot.) — ursina, acanthus, bear's breech, *Acanthus mollis*; (electr.) magnete con **-che**, magnet with salient poles. **-care** [A 2] *tr.* to seize with claws, to seize in the talons; (fig.) to clutch, to grasp. **-carella** *f.* See **brancherella. -cata** *f.* clawful; handful; group, band, set; blow with a claw or paw. **-coso** *adj.* clawed; branching.

brancherella *f.* (naut.) cringle.

bran·chi-a *f.* gill. **-ale** *adj.* branchial.

bran·chipo *m.* (zool.) *Branchipus stagnalis*, a small fresh-water crustacean.

brancic-are [A 2 s] *tr.* to fumble over; to maul, to paw. (**-ame̜nto** *m.* **-ato̜re** *m.*) **-atura** *f.* touch; fingermark. **-one** *m.* clumsy handler; mauler. (**-ona** *f.*).

branci-chino *m.* (of a child) toucher, fingerer; **-chìo** *m.* fingering; pawing, mauling.

bran-co *m.* (*pl.* **-chi**) flock (sheep, birds); drove, herd (cows, horses), troop (of persons); (fig.) andare in —, to go with the crowd; a -chi, in crowds.

brancol-are [A I s] *intr.* (*aux.* avere) to grope; to falter; to go unsteadily; (fig.) to be uncertain, to waver. **-ame̜nto** *m.* groping. **-ante** *part. adj.* groping; (fig.) uncertain, hesitant. **-oni** *adv.* groping, gropingly.

†branconi *adv.* See **brancoloni**, under **brancolare.**

brancorsina *f.* (bot.). See 'branca ursina', under **branca.**

brand-a¹ *f.* camp bed, folding bed; hammock. **-abbasso** *m.* (naut.) bunk parade.

†branda² *f.* a kind of rough brandy.

branda³ *m.* (hist. pol.) ultra-conservative, royalist, from the name of Branda dei Lucioni, head of the Piedmontese royalists in 1799.

brandano *m.* (Tusc.) slovenly individual.

brande̜ggi-o *m.* (artill.) traversing; act of training or slewing (a gun); congegno di —, slewing mechanism, training gear. **-are** [A 3 c] *tr.* (artill.) to train (gun or torpedo tubes).

brandello *m.* little piece, fragment, scrap; slip; tatter, shred; vestito a brandelli, dressed in rags; fare a brandelli, to tear to shreds.

brand-ire [D 2] *tr.* to seize in the hand; to brandish, to wave; *intr.* (*aux.* avere) (Tusc.) to shake; to oscillate. **-ime̜nto** *m.* brandishing; oscillation. **-ito** *part. adj.* brandished; shaken. (**-ito̜re** *m.*).

brand-o¹ *m.* (poet.) sword; brand, firebrand. **-istocco** *m.* boarding pike. **-one** *m.* firebrand.

†brando² *m.* movement, motion; leap; (mus.) branle, brawl, brantle.

brando̜ne¹ *m.* *augm.* of **brando¹**, q.v.

†brandone² *m.* strip; tatter.

brandy *m.* *indecl.* (pron. as Eng.) brandy.

bra·nia *f.* (Tusc.) furrow; strip of land built up on the flat against a slope, terrace.

†branla *f.* (mus.). See **brando².**

brano *m.* shred, scrap; fare a brani, to tear to pieces; cascare a brani, to fall to pieces; passage, extract; brani scelti, selected passages.

branta *f.* (orn.) brent goose.

branzino *m.* (ichth.) pike perch, *Lucioperca* sp.; sea bass, *Morone labrax* (in some dialects).

bras̜-are [A I] *tr.* to braise; (eng.) to braze. **-atura** *f.* (eng.) brazing.

brasca¹ *f.* small cabbage plant for transplanting.

bras-ca² *f.* small charcoal. **-chino** *m.* boy employed in an iron-works.

brasca³ *f.* wooden frame placed over a cart to increase its size.

†brascicare *tr.* to seize, to clutch.

Brasi̜l-e *pr.n.m.* (geog.) Brazil; noccioline del —, nocciole del —, Brazil nuts; (dye.) brazilwood; Brazilian snuff. **-e̜tto** *m.* (dye.) an inferior variety of brazilwood. **-iano** *adj., n.m.* (geog.) Brazilian. **-iana** *f.* Brazilian woman; topaz of Brazil. **-ina** *f.* (dye.) brazilwood extract.

bras·sica *f.* (bot.) *Brassica*, the cabbage genus or a plant belonging to it.

†bratta *f.* oil-dregs; (Gen.) mud.

bratt-are [A I] *intr.* (*aux.* avere) (naut.) to scull. **-o** *m.* sculling oar.

bratt-e·a *f.* (bot.) bract. **-ato** *adj.* bracteate. **-ifo̜rme** *adj.* shaped like a bract.

brava¹ *f.* See **bravo.**

†brava² *f.* seventeenth-century dance; the music of the same.

bravac·cio *m. pej.* See under **bravo.**

brav-are [A I] *tr.* to threaten, to menace; to challenge; to defy, to brave; *intr.* (*aux.* avere) to be threatening; to brag; to bluster. **-ata** *f.* menace, threat; act of bravado; bluff. **-ato̜re** *m.* swaggerer. **-ato·rio** *adj.* threatening. **-azzare** [A I] *intr.* (*aux.* avere) to swagger, to show off. **-azzata** *f.* bluster, bravado. **-azzo** *m.* swaggerer, blusterer. **-azzo̜ne** *m.* braggart. **-eggiare** [A 3 c] *intr.* (*aux.* avere) to bluster, to swagger; (of a horse) to frisk; to rear. (**-eggiato̜re** *m.* **-eggiatrice** *f.*).

braveri·a *f.* See under **bravo.**

†braviere¹ *m.* swaggerer.

†braviere² *m.* screech-owl.

†bravi·o *m.* prize.

brav-o *adj.* good, able, expert, capable; sei — ad aprire quella finestra, can you manage to open that window?; non è — a sgridare e far la voce grossa, it just isn't in him to rant and scold; non è — nemmeno a, he can't even manage to; è un brav'uomo, he's a decent chap; †not broken in (of animals); †(of a coast) rugged, rocky; *excl.* bravo!, well done!; *n.m.* good chap; vieni, da —, come along, like a good boy; fare il —, to show off; bravo, (hist.) hired cut-throat; desperado; *adv.* alla -a, boldly; in a slap-dash manner, roughly, crudely; quickly. **-acciata** *f.* bravado; swaggering act. **-ac·cio** *m. pej.* swaggerer; bully. **-amente** *adv.* bravely, courageously; stoutly, gallantly; skilfully, efficiently. **-eri·a** *f.* brave action, feat; boldness, bravado; gang of brigands. **-ura** *f.* ability, skill, expertise; courage; (iron.) bella -ura!, who would be afraid to do that!; (mus.) bravura. †**-u·ria** *f.* See **-ura**.

brecc-ia (*pl.* **-ie**, **-e**) breach; gap; (mil.) essere sulla —, to man the breach, (fig.) to be in full activity, to be active still; far — in, to force an entry through; aprire la —, to open a breach; (fig.) far —, to make an impression; broken stone, gravel; (miner.) breccia, agglomerate; **-e ossifere**, bone breccia, osseous breccia; rough plaster containing gravel. **-iame** *m.* road metal, broken stones for road-making. **-iato** *adj.* (geol.) brecciated. **-ioso** *adj.* stony, pebbly; (geol.) brecciated.

brefotro·fio *m.* foundling hospital.

bregm-a *f.* (anat.) bregma, sinciput. **-a·tico** *adj.* bregmatic.

bregno *m.* (agric.) wooden channel used for transferring grapes from one container to another.

Brema *pr.n.f.* (geog.) Bremen.

bremo *m.* plaited cord of esparto fibres.

bren·ciolo *m.* and derivs. (Tusc.). See **brendolo**.

bren·doli *m.pl.* (Tusc.) laburnum, *Cytisus laburnum.*

bren·dol-o *m.* tatter. **-are** [A I s] *tr.* to tear into tatters. **-one** *m.* ragamuffin; person in rags and tatters.

brenna[1] *f.* inferior horse or mare; 'screw', jade, nag, hack; (fig.) old hack, broken down individual.

†**brenna**[2] *f.* chaff, bran.

Bren·nero *pr.n.m.* (geog.) Brenner Pass.

brent-a[1] *f.* milk-churn; wine-keg; wine-measure (89·8 litres at Como, 75·8 l. at Reggio, 75·7 l. at Piacenza, 71·6 l. at Parma, 71·4 l. at Pavia, 70·5 l. at Verona, 70 l. at Bergamo, 47·4 l. at Cremona). **-atore** *m.* man who carries wine-kegs.

Brenta[2] *pr.n.m.* (geog.) R. Brenta.

brentana *f.* (Ven.) flood.

bren·tine *f.* (bot.) *Cistus*, rockrose, esp. *Cistus salvifolius*; *Filago*; *Helichrysum* spp.

bren·toli *m.pl.* (bot.) heather, ling, *Calluna vulgaris.*

†**brenu·zio** *m.* See **burnusso**.

†**bresa·ola** *f.* smoked beef.

bresca *f.* (poet.) honeycomb.

Bresci-a[1] *pr.n.f.* (geog.) Brescia; essere l'antichità di —, to be as old as Methuselah. †**-alda** *f.* strumpet, whore. **-ana** *f.* woman of Brescia; thin iron stake; strumpet, whore. **-ano** *adj.* pertaining to Brescia, of Brescia; *n.m.* native of Brescia; †cloth from Brescia.

brescia[2] *f.* (Tusc.) breeze.

brescianella *f.* plantation of trees up in the hills arranged for spreading nets to catch birds.

Breṣla·via *pr.n.f.* (geog.) Breslau, Wroclaw.

bressanella *f.* See **brescianella**.

Bretagna[1] *pr.n.f.* (geog.) Brittany; La Gran —, Great Britain.

bretagna[2] *f.* (bot.) double hyacinth.

bretella *f.* shoulder-strap; (eng.) brace; *pl.* braces; (foundry) bails.

bre·tone *adj.*, *n.m.*, *f.* Breton; Breton horse or mare.

Brettagna *pr.n.f.* See **Bretagna**[1].

bretelle *f.pl.* See **bretella**.

†**brettesca** *f.* See **bertesca**.

†**bret·tine** *f.pl.* reins.

†**bretto** *adj.* stupid, wretched; mean, sordid; (of soil, land) barren, bare; bleak.

bret·tone *adj.*, *n.m.*, *f.* See **bretone**.

†**bretto·nica** *f.* (bot.). See **bettonica**.

breun(n)erite *f.* (miner.) breunnerite.

brev-e *f.* (N. Ital.) cold wind of evening. **-ag·gio** *m.* (N. Ital.) strong wet wind from the East.

brev-e *adj.* short, brief; concise; (gramm.) short, unaccented; *n.m.* brief; (eccl.) brief; (rel.) small pouch with devotional objects sewn into it; (mus.) breve; alla —, twice as fast, taking the breve as time-unit; †(leg.) statute of a corporation; *adv.* in brief, briefly; *adv. phr.* fra —, shortly; per dirla in —, to make a long story short. **-emente** *adv.* briefly; shortly. **-ia·rio** *m.* summary, résumé; (eccl.) breviary; (leg. hist.) -iario di Alarico, compendium of Roman laws made at the request of Alaric II. **-ichiomato** *adj.* (poet.) short-haired. **-icino** *m.* (rel.) small pouch worn round the neck and containing medals, copies of prayers, etc. **-iloquente** *adj.* concise, of few words, laconic. **-iloquenza** *f.* conciseness; laconicism. **-ilo·quio** *m.* concision of speech; concise speaking. **-ità** *f.* brevity, shortness, conciseness; per -ità, for the sake of brevity; per -ità di spazio, for want of space.

brevetta *f.* hand-cart used by railway porters.

brevett-o *m.* patent; prendere un — per, to take out a patent on; (leg.) — d'invenzione, patent, letters patent; Ufficio dei Brevetti, Patent Office; diritto di —, patent right(s); concessionario di un —, patentee; licenziatario di un —, licensee of patent; decadenza di —, expiry of patent; violazione di —, infringement of patent (C.C.); brevet; warrant; diploma, certificate; licence; pilot's licence. **-a·bile** *adj.* patentable. **-are** [A I c] to patent; to license. **-ato** *part. adj.* patented; licensed.

brevi manu *adv.* (Lat.) dare — a, to pass by hand to, to give directly into the hands of.

brezz-a *f.* breeze. **-are** [A I] *tr.* — il grano, to winnow. **-eggiare** [A 3 c] *impers.*, *intr.* (*aux.* essere) to blow a breeze. **-olina** *f.* light breeze. **-olone** *m.* strong, cold wind.

†**bria** *adv. phr.* fuor di —, beyond measure.

bria-co *adj.* (*m.pl.* **-chi**). See **ubbriaco**. **-chella** *f.* drunkenness. **-chello** *m.* wine-bibber, toper. **-cone** *m.* drunkard.

briante·o *adj.* (poet.) of the Brianza.

brianzol-o *adj.* of the Brianza; *n.m.* native of Brianza. (**-a** *f.*)

Briare·o *pr.n.m.* Briareus; (fig.) glutton for work; overworked individual, one who takes too much work.

bricca[1] *f.* (Tusc.) she-ass (cf. **bricco**[2]).

†**bricca**[2] *f.* rocky place, precipice, ravine.

briccaldone *m.* (Lomb.) rogue, good-for-nothing.

bricchetta[1] *f.* brick.

bricchetta[2] *f. dim.* of **bricca**[1], *q.v.*

bricchetto[1] *m. dim.* of **bricco**[1], *q.v.*

bricchetto[2] *m. dim.* of **bricco**[2], *q.v.*

bricchetto[3] *m.* (N. Ital., slang) match; briquette.

bric·cic-a *f.* trifle; perdersi in **-che**, to waste time over trifles. **-are** [A 2 s] *intr.* (*aux.* avere) to trifle, to waste time.

bric-co[1] *m.* (*pl.* **-chi**) jug; tankard; — del latte, milk jug; — del tè, tea-pot; — del caffè, coffee-pot; — dell'acqua calda, hot water jug; kettle.

bric-co[2] *m.* (*pl.* **-chi**) (Romagna) donkey, ass.

bric-co[3] *m.* (*pl.* **-chi**) brick; squared stone for masonry.

bric·col-a[1] *f.* (mil. hist.) catapult; (Ven.) mooring post. **-are** [A I s] *tr.* to catapult, to hurl. (**-amento** *m.* **-ato** *part. adj.*)

†**bric·cola**[2] *f.* precipice (cf. **bricca**[2]).

briccolato *adj.* pock-marked.

briccon-e *m.. ,* **-a** *f.* rascal, scallywag; rogue, knave; un — matricolato, an out and out rascal; *adj.* roguish; rascally; knavish; †*adv.* alla -a, in a rascally way. **-ag·gine** *f.* rascality; roguery, knavery. **-ata** *f.* piece of rascality; roguery, knavish trick. **-cello** *m. dim.* little rascal. **-eggiare** [A 3 c] *intr.* (*aux.* avere) to be a rascal; to be up to tricks; to lead the life of a rogue; to cheat. **-eri·a** *f.* rascality, roguishness; roguery, knavery. **-esco** *adj.* (*m.pl.* **-eschi**) roguish; knavish.

†**bri·ci-a** *f.* crumb. †**-are** *tr.* to crumble.

bri·ciol-a *f.* crumb; tirar su a **-e** di pane, to bring up with all possible care and kindness; non ne saper —, to know nothing about it. **-are** [A I s] *tr.* to crumble. **-o** *m.* tiny piece, morsel, fragment; un -o!, just a drop!; fare a -i, to break to bits; (fig.) non ha un -o di giudizio, he hasn't a grain of sense.

bricolla *f.* rucksack or basket used by smugglers.

brida *f.* (mil. hist.) a grappling machine used in sieges; (eng.) clamp, yoke; (of a lathe) carrier, driving dog; †bridle.

bridgist-a *m.*, *f.* (*pl.m.* **-i**, *f.* **-e**) bridge-player.

†**brieve** *adj.* See **breve**.

†**briffalda** *f.* strumpet, whore.

brig-a *f.* trouble; worry; strife; obstacle, difficulty; annoyance, vexation; darsi — di, to go to the trouble of; accattar brighe, to pick a quarrel, to be looking for trouble; attaccare — con, to

brig-a (*cont.*)

quarrel with; †battle, fight; †war; †a —, scarcely, hardly; with great difficulty. **-are** [A2] *intr.* (*aux.* avere) to intrigue, to pull strings; to canvass; *rfl.* to attempt, to try, to make an effort; †*tr.* to search for, to look for; to use. †**-ari·a** *f.* controversy; wrangling, discord. **-atore** *m.* busybody; intriguer. **-oso** *adj.* quarrelsome; litigious; difficult, tiresome.

brigades *m.pl.* (hotel-keeping) staff on duty for service of breakfast.

brigadiere *m.* (mil.) (Carabinieri) sergeant.

brigant-e *m.* bandit, brigand; retainer, mercenary in the pay of a noble; (fig.) sharper, sly customer, rogue. **-aggio** *m.* brigandage; atti di -aggio, robbery. **-eggiare** [A3c] *intr.* (*aux.* avere) to live by brigandage. **-esco** *adj.* (*m.pl.* -eschi) brigand-like; relating to a brigand. **-essa** *f.* woman brigand. **-ina** *f.* coat of mail.

brigantina¹ *f.* See under **brigante**.

brigantina² *f.* See under **brigantino**.

brigantin-o *m.* (naut.) brig, two-masted ship with square rig; — a palo, barque, three-masted ship whose main and foremasts are square-rigged; — goletta, brigantine, ship with one square-rigged and one schooner-rigged mast. **-a** *f.* backsail, spanker.

brigare [A2]. See under **briga**.

brigat-a *f.* company, party of friends; un'allegra —, a merry crowd; di —, together; far —, to get together; (provb.) poca —, vita beata, two's company, three's a crowd; (mil.) brigade; generale di —, brigadier; — di marcia, column; (police) brigade; covey, flock of birds; †family, household; †multitude, great number. †**-are** *intr.* to band together.

brigatore *m.* See under **briga**.

brigge *m.* (cards) bridge.

Brighella *m.* one of the character-masks of the Italian theatre; he speaks in the Brescian or Venetian dialect, wears green and white clothes and a dark brown full mask, and is usually a servant and an intriguer (cf. **briga**; see also **maschera**); (fig.) clown; intriguer.

Bri·gida *pr.n.f.* Bridget; †pastry board.

brigidin-o *m.* small spiced wafer-like biscuit; cockade in a footman's hat; (hist.) il — tricolore, the cockade of red, white and green worn by Italian patriots during the Risorgimento; (Tusc.) Fascist emblem in enamel, worn in buttonhole. **-a·io** *m.* maker or vendor of 'brigidini'.

bri·glia *f.* bridle; rein; a — sciolta, at full gallop; a tutta —, quickly; dar la — sul collo, to let a horse have his head, (fig.) to allow freedom, to give rope; tenere in —, to rein in, (fig.) to restrain; tenere in — la lingua, to bridle one's tongue; voltar la —, to turn about; (fig.) tirar la —, to tighten the screw; (techn.) stay, support; reinforcements to prevent a landslide; (eng.) flange; (naut.) bobstay; martingale; strap; *pl.* brake.

Brigliadoro *pr.n.m.* Brigliadoro, Orlando's horse (Boiardo, Ariosto).

brigoletta *f.* (naut.) brigantine.

brigoso *adj.* See under **briga**.

brilla *f.* rice-mill, millstone made of marble with a cork bottom for grinding rice so as to remove the husk.

brillant-e *adj.* brilliant, shining, bright, sparkling, glittering; splendid, resplendent; menare una vita —, to lead a worldly, gay, social life; uno spirito —, a sparkling wit; una persona —, a lively, sparkling extrovert; una mente —, a lively, quick-witted mind; lana —, high-lustre wool; acqua —, tonic water; *n.m.* brilliant, cut diamond; (typ.) brilliant; (theatr.) actor specializing in light comedy roles. **-a·bile** *adj.* that may be cut (of a diamond). (**-emente** *adv.*) **-are** [A1] *tr.* to cut (a diamond); -are le unghie, to polish one's nails, to varnish one's nails; (cul.) to ice (cakes); to sprinkle (sweetmeats) with sugar crystals; (techn.) to furbish, to polish. (**-ato** *part. adj.*) **-atura** *f.* (techn.) furbishing, polishing. **-ina** *f.* brilliantine.

brill-are¹ [A1] *intr.* (*aux.* avere) to shine, to glitter, to glisten; to sparkle; to glare; (fig.) to be conspicuous, to shine, to distinguish oneself; — per l'assenza, to be conspicuous by one's absence; to go off (of a mine); far — una mina, to blow up a mine; *tr.* to husk (rice, etc.), to polish (cereals); to explode; — una mina, to blow up a mine. **-amento** *m.* shine; brilliance; glory; husking; blowing up; (min.) blasting. **-ante** *part.* of **brillare**; as *adj.* see **brillante. -anza** *f.* (phys.) brilliance. **-ato·io** *m.* husking machine. **-atura** *f.* husking; the price paid for it. **-ìo** *m.* glittering, glinting; sparkle; (cinem.) flickering.

brillare² [A1] *intr.* (*aux.* avere) to whirl round; to librate; (of a lark) to hover, to quiver; (naut.) to spin on a deep sea line (of divers).

brillo¹ *adj.* tipsy, merry; half-drunk.

brillo² *m.* quivering, hovering (of a bird in the air); aver il —, to quiver in mid-air; to spin, to twirl (of a ball).

brillo³ *m.* (bot.) osier, *Salix viminalis*.

†**brillo⁴** *m.* brilliant, imitation diamond.

†**brillo⁵** *m.* trill.

brilocche *f.* pendant, medallion, breloque.

brin-a *f.* hoar-frost; rime; (fig.) whiteness, pallor; white hairs, 'touch of white'. **-aiola** *f.* (bot.) stinking goosefoot, *Chenopodium vulvaria*. **-are** [A1] *impers.* to form hoar-frost; è —ato, there's been a fall of white frost. **-ata** *f.* fall of hoar-frost. **-ato** *part. adj.* hoary, frosty; (of hair) grizzled, turning grey. **-atoso** *adj.* hoary. **-oso** *adj.* frost-covered, frosted.

brincello *m.* (Tusc.) scrap; shred; morsel.

brin·cio *adj.* (Tusc.) turned down at the corners, drooping (of a mouth).

brinda·cola *f.* slattern, slut; gossip.

brind-are [A1] *intr.* (*aux.* avere; *prep.* a) to toast, to drink (to), to drink the health (of). †**-eggiare**, †**-ezzare** *vb.* See **brindare**.

brindell-o *m.* tatter; rag; a -i, in tatters. **-ato** *adj.* in tatters. **-one** *m.* person untidily dressed; tall but clumsily built person with awkward gait; cart covered with fireworks used in the ceremony of the 'scoppio del carro' which takes place in Florence on Holy Saturday).

brin·di·ṣi¹ *m. indecl.* toast to a person's health; music, etc., accompanying a toast; fare un — a, to drink a toast to, to toast. †**-e·vole** (joc.) worthy of a toast.

Brin·diṣi² *pr.n.f.* (geog.) Brindisi.

brinoso *adj.* See under **brina**.

bri-o *m.* vivacity, animation, liveliness; sprightliness; essere pieno di —, to be in high spirits, to be spirited; (mus.) con —, with fire, with energy. **-oso** *adj.* full of life, lively; sprightly; spirited. **-osamente** *adv.* with vivacity, spiritedly. **-osità** *f.* liveliness; sprightliness.

brioche *f. indecl.* (pron. as Fr.) brioche.

briografi·a, **briologi·a** *f.* bryology.

brio·nia *f.* (bot.) red-berried bryony, *Bryonia dioica*; — bianca, white bryony, *Bryonia alba*.

brio·scia *f.* See **brioche**.

brioso *adj.* See under **brio**.

brisa *f.* (bot.) *Boletus* spp.

brisato *adj.* (herald.) split, éclaté.

brisca *f.* (Piedm., Lomb.) a light carriage.

bri·scol-a¹ *f.* a card game for two or four, three cards being dealt to each player and one turned up which is the 'briscola' or trump, every card of that suit being also termed 'briscola'; — chiacchierina, the four-handed game when the partners may consult how to play; — muta, the game when no consultation is allowed; (fig.) contare come il due di —, to count for very little. **-ata** *f.* game of 'briscola'. **-ina** *f.*, **-ino** *m.* small card at 'briscola'. **-ona** *f.* ace or three at 'briscola'.

bri·scol-a² *f.* scolding; blow, beating; (fig.) che —!, what a blow! **-are** [A1s] *tr.* to beat, to thrash.

Briṣgo·via *pr.n.f.* (geog.) Breisgau.

brissa *f.* (bot.). See **brisa**.

bristol *m. indecl.* Bristol board, card; (aeron.) Bristol bomber.

Brit-an·nia *pr.n.f.* (Ancient) Britain; Britannia; Britannia metal. **-an·nico** *adj.* British; Britannic; Sua Maestà Britannica, Her Britannic Majesty; le Isole Britanniche, the British Isles; (bot.) erba -annica, marsh dock, *Rumex aquaticus*.

bri·vid-o *m.* shiver, trembling; shudder; thrill; avere dei -i, to shiver, to be shivering; mi fa venire i -i, it gives me the creeps, it gives me a thrill; storie del —, thrillers. **-io** *m.* (pl. -ii) continual shivering or shuddering.

brizzol-are [A1s] *tr.* to speckle; *rfl.* (of hair) to turn grey. **-ato** *part. adj.* speckled, mottled; (of hair) turning grey, grizzled. **-atura** *f.* speckled marking, mottling; (of hair) grizzling, greying; (mus.) yodelling; arcata di -atura, undulating tremolo.

†**brob·bio**, **brob·brio** *m.* See **obbrobrio**.

broc-ca¹ *f.* jug, pitcher; ewer; una — d'acqua, a jug of water. **-ca·io** *m.*, **-caro** *m.* maker or seller of jugs; potter. **-chetto** *m. dim.* wash-basin.

brocc-a² *f.* shoot (of a plant); cane split into parts at the end and spread out, used for gathering figs; bull's-eye of a target; dare in —, to set a bull's-eye; metal stud as ornament on binding or

brocc-a (*cont.*)
on upholstery; (text.; eng.) spindle. **-a·glio** *m.* iron rod with two points used for marking MSS. or material to be ruled with lines. **†-are** *tr.* to spur. **†-ata** *f.* touch of the spur.

broccardo[1] *m.* difficult legal problem.

†broccardo[2] *m.* gun.

†broccare[1] [A 2] *tr.* to brocade.

†broccare[2]. See under **brocca**[2].

broccat-o[1] *m.* brocade. **-ello** *m.* brocade; marble of Siena (peacock-blue and white), brocatelle.

broccato[2] *m.* (mil.) stockade.

brocchier-e, -o *m.* (mil. hist.) shield with a spike in the centre for attack or defence, buckler; protection.

broc·ci-a *f.* (eng.) broach. **-are** [A 3] *tr.* (eng.) to broach; †to spur. **-atrice** *f.* (eng.) broaching machine. **-atura** *f.* (eng.) broaching.

†broc·cio *m.* lance, spear.

broc·ciolo *m.* (Tusc.) a small fresh-water fish; blockhead.

brocc-o *m.* (*pl.* **brocchi**) shoot, sprout; stalk, stick; thorn; curl; unevenness in the surface of a textile; small nail, stud, tack pin; protruding tooth; bull's-eye; dare nel —, to hit the nail on the head; (slang, N. Ital. and Army) worn-out horse. **-oso** *adj.* sprouting; with protruding teeth. **-uto** *adj.* (of a plant) full of shoots; (of a person) with protruding teeth; *n.m.* (naut.) Plimsoll line.

broc·col-o *m.* broccoli; flower stalk of a turnip; (N. Ital.) cauliflower; (fig.) blockhead, nincompoop. **-one** *m. augm.* of **broccolo**; (fig.) utter fool. **-oso, -uto** *adj.* run to seed; having several flower stalks; knotted.

†broco *adj.* raucous, hoarse; lisping.

brod-a *f.* water in which vegetables have been boiled; thin soup, weak coffee, etc., or solid food which is too watery; dirty water; dish-water; rain; (fig.) insipid speech or writing; gettare la — addosso a, to put the blame on; andare in —, to liquefy, to turn to liquid; (agric.) — della concimaia, liquid manure. **-a·glia, -a·ia, -i·glia** *f.* thin broth.

brod-o *m.* broth; clear soup; water in which meat has been boiled; stock; soup-cube; — di bue, beef-tea; — lungo, weak broth; — ristretto, jelly broth; — secco, soup powder; tazza da —, soup-dish (with cover and handles, for individual portions); lasciare cuocere uno nel suo —, to let a person stew in his own juice; tutto fa —, it's all grist to one's mill, everything comes in handy; andare in —, to turn to liquid, (fig.) to come to grief; andare in — di giuggiole, to go into ecstasies. **-ai(u)olo** *m.* guzzler of soup. **-ame** *m.* food turned to liquid through over-cooking. **-etto** *m. dim.* broth with eggs beaten up in it, flavoured with lemon; fish soup; dish-water, bilge; antico quanto il -etto, as old as Adam. **-ic·chio** *m.* thin broth. **-olino** *m.* child that splashes itself with its food. **-olone** *m.* dirty eater; dirty, slovenly person. **-olona** *f.* slut. **-oloso** *adj.* dirty, greasy, soup-stained. **-oso** *adj.* with plenty of broth; minestra -osa, thin soup.

Bro·gio *pr.n.m.* shortened form of Ambrogio, q.v.; (fig.) fool, blockhead.

brogiotto *m.* See **borgiotto**.

brogli-are [A 4] *tr.* to embroil; *intr.* (*aux.* avere) to intrigue; †to move, to fidget; †to stir. **-ac·cio, -asso, -azzo** *m.* rough notebook; diary, journal; (comm.) day-book.

bro·glio *m.* intrigue, wangling; sharp practice; — elettorale, rigging of the election; †disorder, confusion.

†brogna *f.* horn used for calling pigs home.

broletto *m.* (hist.) Court House in the old Lombard towns.

†brollo *adj.* See **brullo**.

brolo[1] *m.* enclosure, garden; arbour; (N. Ital.) orchard; nursery garden; †garland.

brolo[2] *m.* See **broletto**; ambition, desire for preferment; intrigue (cf. **broglio**).

broma·lio *m.* (chem.; pharm.) bromal.

bromatol-ogi·a *f.* dietetics. **-o·gico** *adj.* relating to dietetics; *n.m.* dietetic expert.

brombolo *m.* (Romagna) vine tendril; (Istria) bubble on surface of water rising from decomposing matter.

brome·lia *f.* (bot.) *Bromelia*; (industr.) fibre della —, bromelia fibres.

brom-o *m.* (chem.) bromine. **-ato** *m.* bromate. **-idrina** *f.* (chem.) bromhydrin. **-irite** *f.* bromyrite, bromite, silver bromide. **-ismo** *m.* (med.) bromide. **-ofo·rmio** *m.* (chem.) bromoform. **-urazione** *f.* (chem.) bromination **-uro** *m.* (chem.) bromide; (photog.) carta al -uro d'argento, bromide paper.

bromo·lio *m.* (photog.) bromoil.

†bronca *f.* variety of pear; variety of lemon; vine-prop.

bron-chi[1] *m.pl.* (anat.) bronchi, bronchials. **-chiale** *adj.* bronchial. **-chite** *f.* bronchitis. **-cografi·a** *f.* (med.) bronchography. **-copleurite** *f.* bronchial pleurisy. **-copolmonite** *f.* bronchial pneumonia. **-cosco·pio** *m.* (med.) bronchoscope.

bronchi[2] *m.pl.* See **bronco**.

bronc-io *m.* grudge, ill-temper; sulks, pouting; pout, wry face; fare il —, to sulk, to pout; tenere il — a, to have a grudge against; *adj.* pouting; cross. **-ire** [D 2] *intr.* (*aux.* avere) to sulk, to pout.

bron-co *m.* (*pl.* **-chi**) trunk, stump, bough; *pl.* brushwood; †variety of pear tree; †variety of lemon tree. **-cone** *m.* large bough of a tree with many branches; stout vine-prop with cross-supports; (herald.) indentation.

bronco-grafi·a *f.*, **-pleurite** *f.*, **-polmonite** *f.*, **-sco·pio** *m.* See under **bronchi**[1].

bront-ofobi·a *f.* fear of thunderstorms. **-o·fobo** *m.* person who is afraid of thunderstorms.

brontol-are [A 1 sc] *intr.* (*aux.* avere) to grumble; to mutter; to rumble (of thunder); to gurgle. **-amento** *m.* grumbling, muttering; rumbling; gurgling. **-ìo** *m.* (*pl.* **-ìi**) continual grumbling; continual rumbling or gurgling. **-one** *m.* grumbler, moaner. (**-ona** *f.*) **-oso** *adj.* grumbling.

bronto-sa·uro *m.* brontosaurus. **-te·rio** *m.* brontothere.

bronza *f.* glowing heat of an oven which has to cool a little before it can be used.

bronzare [A 1 c] and derivs. See under **bronzo**.

bronzeo *adj.* bronze-coloured; bronze-like; made of bronze.

bronzina *f.* (eng.) bearing; bush.

bronz-o *m.* bronze; — da campane, bell metal; — duro, gun metal; — fosforoso, phosphor-bronze; (art) un —, a bronze; i sacri -i, church bells; avere un cuore di —, to have a heart of stone; avere una faccia di —, to be brazen-faced. **-are** [A 1 c] *tr.* to bronze. **-ato** *part. adj.* bronzed. **-atura** *f.* bronzing. **-ino** *adj.* bronze-coloured; sun-tanned; dark; (med.) pertaining to Addison's disease, supra-renal melasma; *n.m. dim.* bell; bronze vessel; (Tusc.) kind of cabbage. **-ista** *m.* worker in bronze, bronze founder. **-oluto** *adj.* (bot.) cavolo -oluto, a kind of cabbage (cf. **bronzino**). **-osonante** *adj.* (poet.) bronze-sounding.

bro·scia *f.* watery soup, slop.

brossura *f.* paper-covered book, paper-back; pamphlet, brochure; in —, unbound, in paper.

brosta *f.* (N. Ital.) scab.

brovatura *f.* (silk-manuf.) steaming.

†brucama·glia *f.* rabble, horde.

bruc-are [A 2] *tr.* to eat, to browse on; to nibble, to gnaw; to strip; †to weaken, to diminish; †to seek; *intr.* (*aux.* avere) to browse. **-ato** *part. adj.* maggot-eaten. **-atore** *m.* (Tusc.) olive gatherer; gatherer of mulberry leaves. (**-atura** *f.*) **-one** *m.* animal that does damage by stripping leaves off plants; defoliater.

bruc-co *m.* (*pl.* **-chi**) (ichth.) *Dasybatus brucco*, a kind of sting ray.

brucente *adj.* (Tusc.). See **bruciante**, under **bruciare**.

bruciacchi-are [A 4] *tr.* to scorch; (of frost) to blacken (plants). (**-ato** *part. adj.*) **-atura** *f.* scorch mark; blackening of plants by frost.

bruci-are [A 3] *tr.* to burn; to set on fire, to set fire to; to scald; to inflame; to scorch; to shirk; — la scuola, to play truant; — pagliaccio, to break one's word; — il paglione, to leave without paying, to 'welsh'; — i vascelli, to burn one's boats; — le tappe, to make lightning progress, to forge ahead; -arsi le cervella, to blow one's brains out; (med.) to cauterize; *intr.* (*aux.* avere) to burn; to be hot; to be on fire; to be scorching; to smart, to sting, to be too hot; — dal desiderio, to yearn, to long ardently, — della sete, to be parched with thirst; to be without money, (fam.) to discontinue playing after winning one's opponent's money; *rfl.* to burn oneself. **-abile** *adj.* inflammable, combustible. **-acaffè** *m. indecl.* coffee roaster. **-aculo** *m.* soreness after horse-riding. **-aglia** *f.* rubbish for burning. **-amento** *m.* burning; scalding. **-ante** *part. adj.* burning; scorching; smarting. **-apeli, -apelo** *adv. phr.* a -apelo, at close range, point-blank; (text.) macchina a -apeli, gassing machine; (fig.) suddenly, unexpectedly. **-aprofumi** *m. indecl.* ceramic jar with perforated lid in which

bru-ciare (*cont.*)

perfumes are burnt. **-ata** *f.* roast chestnut. **-ata·io** *m.* roast chestnut seller. **-atic·cio** *m.* remains of something burnt; smell of burning; sapere di -aticcio, to taste burnt. **-ato** *part. adj.* burnt; ora -ata, hot spell; -ato dal sole, sunburnt; puzzo di -ato, smell of burning; morello -ato, dark chestnut horse; (soc. hist.) la Generazione Bruciata, the Bright Young Things (after World War I), the Beat Generation (after World War II); (slang mil.) watched by the police (of a place). **-atore** *m.* (techn.) burner. **-atura** *f.* burn; burning; scald, scorch; (text.) singeing, gassing; (med.) cauterizing, cauterization. **-ore** *m.* burning sensation; smart; -ore di stomaco, heartburn; (fig.) burning desire. **-oretto** *m. dim.* (fig.) yearning, itch.

brucìo *m.* continual burning; constant itching.

bru-ciol-o[1] *m.* (ent.) grub, maggot. **-ato** *adj.* maggoty, worm-eaten.

bru·ciolo[2] *m.* (Tusc.) wood shaving (cf. truciolo).

bru·ciolo[3] *m.* (Tusc.) a variety of olive.

bru-co[1] *m.* (*pl.* **-chi**) grub, caterpillar; (eccl.) scroll part of book-marker.

bru-co[2] *adj. m.pl.* (**-chi**) destitute, in dire need; nudo —, without a rag to one's back, stark naked.

bru·colo *m.* boil, pustule.

brucone *m.* See under **brucare**.

bruf·folo *m.* pimple; spot; little boil; ragazzo con il viso pieno di bruffoli, boy with a spotty face.

brughiera *f.* (N. Ital.) moorland, heath; heather.

†**brugiare** *vb.* See **bruciare**.

†**brugiotto** *m.* See **borgiotto**.

bru·gliolo *m.* (Tusc.) pustule, pimple.

†**brugna** *f.* See **prugna**.

†**bruire** *intr.* to make a noise, to rustle, to stir; *n.m.* (poet.) rustling.

†**brul-asco**, †**-asso**, †**-azzo** *adj.* ill; unsound, unhealthy; pock-marked.

brulè *adj. indecl.* (of wine) mulled.

bruli-care [A 2 s] *intr.* (*aux.* avere) to swarm; to crawl; to teem; molti pensieri mi -ano nella mente, my mind is teeming with many thoughts; (*prep.* di) to be crawling (with). **-came** *m.* swarm, multitude; swarming. **-cante** *part. adj.* swarming; -cante di, swarming with. **-chìo** *m.* (*pl.* **-chii**) swarming, seething of multitude; -chìo di gente, swarm of people; commotion; shiver, shudder; rustling.

brullo *adj.* bare, stripped (e.g. of foliage); barren, bleak, desolate; scorched; (fig.) stripped, penniless.

brulotto *m.* fire-ship.

brum *m. indecl.* Brougham, carriage. **-ista** *m.* (N. Ital.) coachman, cabman.

brum-a[1] *f.* cold damp weather; depth of winter; fog. mist; †winter solstice; (poet., fig.) old age. **-a·ia** *f.* wintry weather. **-a·io** (hist.) *m.* Brumaire, the second month of the year in the French Revolutionary calendar (22 Oct.–21 Nov.). **-ale** *adj.* wintry; foggy. **-oso** *adj.* foggy, misty.

bruma[2] *f.* (zool.) ship worm, *Teredo navalis*.

bruma[3] *f.* sea-moss.

brumeggi-o *m.* (naut.) ground bait. **-are** [A 3 c] *intr.* (*aux.* avere) to throw bait into the sea.

brumista *m.* See under **brum**.

Bruna *pr.n.f.*; see also under **bruno**.

brunella *f.* (bot.) self-heal, *Brunella vulgaris*.

brun-ello *adj.*, **-etto** *adj.*, **-ezza** *f.* See under **bruno**[1].

brunice *f.* hot ash.

brun-ire [D 2] *tr.* to burnish; to polish. **-imento** *m.* burnishing; polishing. **-ito** *part. adj.* burnished; polished. **-itoio** *m.* polishing stick; burnisher; grindstone for giving the last finish in sharpening. (**-itore** *m.*) **-itrice** *f.* (eng.) burnishing machine. **-itura** *f.* polish, shine, burnish.

brunissure *f.* (agric.) discoloration of vine leaves owing to disease.

brun-o[1] *adj.* dark; brown; — di capelli, dark-haired; — di carnagione, swarthy; black; made of crape; vestimenti -i, mourning clothes; parare a —, to drape with black; notte -a, dark night; obscure, shaded; †gloomy; †evil; †un atto —, expression of distress or displeasure; *n.m.* brown; dark colour; dark man; mourning; — grave, full mourning; — leggiero, mezzo —, half mourning. **-a** *f.* dark girl, dark woman, brunette. **-astro** *adj.* darkish. **-eggiare** [A 3 c] *intr.* (*aux.* avere) to be brownish; to turn brown; to grow dark. **-ello** *adj.* brownish, *n.m.* (N. Ital.) prunella,

cloth. **-etto** *adj.* brownish; rather dark. **-ezza** *f.* brownness; dark colouring (of a person); darkness. **-otto** *adj.* deep brown; brownish.

Bruno[2] *pr.n.m.* Bruno.

brus-ca *f.* horse-brush; segmented ruler used in designing ships; breaming: material for burning near the side of a ship preparatory to tarring; (bot.) horse-tail, *Equisetum arvense*. **-care** [A 2] *tr.* to prune, to trim; to brush (a horse); (naut.) to bream; (Tusc.) to roast (coffee, almonds, etc.). **-carella** *f.* speck. **-chettino** *m.* (silkm.) agitating besom. **-chetto** *m.* horse-brush. **-chinare** [A 1] *tr.* to brush, to groom. **-chino** *m.* horse-brush; leather-dresser's brush; washerwoman's brush, floor-brush; (naut.) bottom brush.

bruscamente *adv.* See under **brusco**.

bruscello[1] *m.* (Tusc.) a kind of rustic play sung and danced along the street; a performer in such a play.

bruscello[2] *m.* ice or frost on a plant.

bruschette *f.pl.* drawing straws (a child's game).

brus-co[1] *adj.* (*m.pl.* **-chi**) sharp (in taste); brusque (in manner); blunt, curt; harsh; una -ca svolta, a sharp bend (in the road); -chi tempi, difficult times; un — risveglio, a sudden awakening; aria -ca, keen air; colle -che, brusquely, bluntly; lo licenziò colle -che, he sent him away with a flea in his ear; *n.m.* speck; (surg.) bone rasper; (bot.) butcher's broom, knee-holly, *Ruscus aculeatus*. **-camente** *adv.* brusquely; abruptly; sharply; bluntly. **-chetto** *adj. dim.* rather sharp and brusque; sourish, tart. **-chezza** *f.* brusqueness; sharpness, sourness. **-chino** *adj.* dark red.

brusco[2] *adv. phr.* fra lusco e —, at twilight; dimly.

bruscolini *m.pl.* salted and roasted melon seeds.

bru·scol-o *m.* speck; splinter, shaving; un — nell'occhio, something in one's eye; (joc.) slip of a thing (of a person); (fig.) defect, fault; doubt, suspicion; vedere i -i altrui e non le sue travi, to see the motes in other people's eyes but not the beam in one's own; (Tusc.) melon seed; *pl.* first drops of a shower. **-oso** *adj.* specked, blemished.

brus-io *m.* (*pl.* **-ii**) bustle, hum, confused noise of talking; stir; heap, large quantity. **-ire** [D 2] *intr.* (*aux.* avere) to make a noise, to make a stir; to hum; to rumble; to rustle.

Brusselle *pr.n.f.* (geog.) Brussels; cavolini, broccoletti di —, Brussels sprouts, *Brassica oleracea* var. *gemmifera*.

brut-o[1] *m.* brute, animal; man guilty of sexual offences against children; *adj.* brutal; brutish; irrational; unfeeling; forza -a, brute materia -a, inert matter. **-ale** *adj.* brutal, cruel, savage; bestial. **-almente** *adv.* brutally; brutishly. **-alità** *f.* brutality; bestiality; ferocity. **-alizzare** [A 1] *tr.* to treat brutally; to brutalize; *intr.* (*aux.* avere) to behave in a brutish way. †**-eggiare** *vb.* See **brutalizzare**.

Bruto[2] *pr.n.m.* Brutus.

brutta *f.* See under **brutto**.

bruttare [A 1] *tr.* to soil, to tarnish; to defile.

brutt-o *adj.* ugly; horrible; deformed; nasty; repellent; filthy; foul; mean; bad; -a notizia, bad news; — tempo, bad weather; -a copia, rough copy; — segno, bad omen, bad look-out; un — tipo, a nasty type, an unpleasant individual; un — muso, an arrogant person; il diavolo non è così — come lo si dipinge, the devil is not as black as he is painted; — tiro, dirty trick, stroke of bad luck; venire alle -e, to begin quarrelling; alle -e, at the worst; fare una -a figura, to cut a sorry figure, to lose face, to make out badly; avere dei -i modi, to be ill-mannered; con le -e, insistently, demandingly; rimanere —, to sulk; *n.m.* ugly man; evil man; ugliness; ora viene il — della faccenda, the worst of it is. **-a** *f.* ugly woman; evil woman; rough copy. (**-amente** *adv.*) **-eri·a** *f.* ugliness; filth. **-ezza** *f.* ugliness; filth; unpleasantness. **-ino** *adj.* plain, unprepossessing; quella ragazza è piuttosto -ina, that girl's rather plain. **-one** *m. augm.* ugly person; (Rome) lover, adulterer. **-i·zia** *f.* baseness, vileness, lowness, meanness, turpitude. **-ura** *f.* filth; ugliness; ugly thing; shocking thing; mean action; wicked action; group of low people.

bruum *excl.* bang!; boom! (noise of a fire-arm).

bruzza·glia *f.* rabble; rubbish.

bruz·zico *m.* (Tusc.) dawn, daybreak, morning twilight; levarsi a —, to rise at dawn.

bruz·zolo[1] *m.* light before sunrise, first light; twilight.

bruz·zolo[2] *m.* See **bruciolo**[2].

bu *excl.* (onom.) bu bu!, bow! wow!; boo!; brrr!

bua *f.* (fam., infant.) hurt, pain; farsi la —, to hurt oneself.

buac·cio *m.* and derivs., **buag·gine** *f.*, **buassag·gine** *f.* See under **bue**.

bu·balo *m.* (Tusc.). See **bufalo**.

bubare [A I]. See under **bubo**[1].

bubbo *m.* (Tusc., fam.) louse.

bub·bol-a[1] *f.* incredible story, romance, tall story; nonsense; raccontare -e, to tell fibs. **-are** [A I s] *tr.* to swindle, to cheat; *intr.* (*aux.* avere) to rumble, to roar. **-ata** *f.* pack of lies; foolish nonsense, silly talk. **-io** *m.* rumbling, roaring. **-one** *m.* romancer; hoaxer; leg-puller; teller of tall stories. (**-ona** *f.*)

bub·bola[2] *f.* (orn.) hoopoe, *Upupa epops*.

bub·bola[3] *f.* (bot.) various species of fungus, esp. *Lepiota* spp.

bubbolare[1] [A I s]. See under **bubbola**[1].

bubbol-are[2] [A I s] *intr.* (*aux.* avere) to tremble with cold, to shiver, to shudder. **-ini** *m.p.* (bot.) bladder campion, *Silene cucubalus*.

bub·bol-o *m.* (Tusc.) bell for a horse's or mule's collar; bell on a cat's collar; bell on a child's rattle. **-iera** *f.* horse's collar on to which the bells are fixed.

bubb-one *m.* (med.) bubo. **-oni** *m.pl.* (vet.) small pox. **-o·nico** *adj.* bubonic; la peste -onica, bubonic plague, (hist. 14th cent.) the Black Death. **-onocele** *m.* bubonocele, inguinal hernia.

bub-o[1] *m.* (Tusc., fam.) pigeon, dove. **-are** [A I] *intr.* (*aux.* avere) to coo.

bubo[2] *m.* pain; knock; bump.

bubolare [A I s] *intr.* (*aux.* avere) to hoot (like an owl).

†bubone *m.* owl.

bubo·nio *m.* (bot.) *Inula spiraeifolia*.

bubù *excl.* See **bu**.

†bubulca *f.* See **bifolca**, under **bifolco**.

buc-a *f.* opening, hollow; large hole; — delle lettere, post-box; letter-box (in a door); — del bigliardo, billiard-pocket; cavity, depression; narrow valley; pit; ditch; trench; grotto; (geog.) small depression; (fig.) grave; (theatr.) — del suggeritore, prompter's box; (golf) hole; fare —, to hole, (billiards) to pocket; turare le buche, to pay one's debts; (Florence, eccl.) underground chapel; (Florence) underground restaurant usually in the cellar of an old palazzo. **-acchiare** [A 4] *tr.* to perforate, to bore small holes in. **-are** [A 2] *tr.* to hole, to bore, to make a hole in; to puncture, to perforate, to pierce; to punch (e.g. tickets); to broach, to tap; to lance; (fig.) to penetrate, to open (up) to; to evade, to get past; — la palla, to drop a catch; *intr.* (*aux.* avere) to get a puncture; *rfl.* to prick oneself. **-ato** *part. adj.* pierced; holed; bored; riddled; aver le mani -ate, to spend money like water. **-atura** *f.* punching, perforating; hole; puncture. **-acuori** *m., f. indecl.* lady-killer; 'heart-throb'. **-afondi** *m. indecl.* borer for casks, esp. for making holes in the heads into which to fit the staves. **-neve** *m.* (bot.) snowdrop, *Galanthus nivalis*. **-pere** *m.* (ent.) *Cerambyx cerdo*, a species of Longicorn beetle.

bucanier-e, -o *m.* buccaneer, pirate.

bucar·dia *f.* (zool.) heart-shell, *Isocardia cor*.

bucato[1] *part.* of **bucare**, q.v.

bucat-o[2] *m.* washing, laundry; bleaching; il giorno di —, washing-day; mettere in —, to send to the laundry; fare il —, to do the washing, to wash clothes; di —, freshly laundered; panni di —, clean clothes; polvere da —, washing-powder; (fig.) fare il — in casa, not to wash one's dirty linen in public; lo scritto non si mette in —, what is writ can ne'er be washed out. **-a·ia** *f.* (Tusc.) washerwoman, laundress. **-a·io** *m.* wash-house; laundryman.

bucatura *f.* See under **buca**.

buc·caro *m.* See **bucchero**.

†buccella *f.* crust of bread (cf. **buccia**).

buccellato *m.* sort of ring-shaped sweet cake made at Lucca.

†bucceri·a *f.* butcher's shop.

buc·chero *m.* a scented, red-coloured earth used for making water-cooling vases, etc.; vase made from such earth; black clayey earth from which certain types of Etruscan vases were made.

buc·ci-a *f.* peel; crust; skin; rind; togliere la — a, to peel; bark; shell; (paint.: techn.) coating; — d'arancio, orange peel; slough (of a snake); (zool.) exuvium; (joc.) human skin; riveder le bucce a, to find fault with, to nag, to criticize adversely; la — gli preme, he's in fear of his life; di — dura, thick-skinned, tough; loose woman, prostitute. **-olina** *f.* cuticle. **-oso** *adj.*, **-uto** *adj.* thick-skinned.

buc·chio[1] *m.* (Tusc.) rabbit.

†buc·chio[2] *m.* curl.

†buc·chio[3] *m.* skin; outer covering.

buccicata *f.* (Tusc., fam.) nothing; damn-all; non ne so —. I haven't a clue.

†bucciere *m.* butcher.

buc·cin-a *f.* trumpet; shell used by Tritons and other sea-gods as a trumpet; (zool.) see **buccino**. **-are** [A I s] *intr.* (*aux.* avere) to play the trumpet, to sound the trumpet, to trumpet; *tr.* to shout (something) from the rooftops, to noise abroad, to proclaim. (**-amento** *m.* **-atore** *m.* **-atrice** *f.*) **-ato·rio** *m.* (anat.) buccinator. **-io** *m.* (*pl.* **-ii**) continual trumpeting; trumpet call

buc·cino *m.* (zool.) whelk, and related molluscs, *Buccinum undatum*, *Triton nodiferum*.

buc·cio *m.* (leather manuf.) grain, the outer or hair side of the skin.

bucciolina *f.* See under **buccia**.

bucci(u)olo *m.* See **bocciuolo**, under **boccio**.

bucciol-oso, -uto *adj.* See under **buccia**.

bucco *m.* (hist. theatr.) Roman mask character of the Fabulae Atellanae, buffoon.

buc·col-a *f.* curl; loop; drop ear-ring; †metal disk, boss. **-o** *m.* curl; loop. **-otto** *m.* ringlet.

bucco·lica *f.* see **bucolica**; (Tusc., joc.) gastronomy, good eating.

bucco·lico *adj.* See **bucolico**, under **bucolica**.

buccone *m.* See **bucco**.

Buce·falo *pr.n.m.* Bucephalus; (joc.) hack, nag.

†bucello *m.* calf.

Bucen·ta·uro, -toro, -to·rio *pr.n.m.* See **Bucintoro**.

bu·cero *m.* (orn.) hornbill.

buceto *m.* grazing for cattle.

†bucherame *m.* transparent cloth; colander.

bucher-are [A I s] *tr.* to pierce with holes; to riddle; *intr.* (*aux.* essere) to penetrate by underhand means, to sneak in, to 'gate-crash'; to intrigue for votes, to lobby. (**-amento** *m.*) **-atic·cio** *adj.* full of holes. **-ato** *part. adj.* pierced; full of holes; pointillé. **-ellare** [A I] *tr.* to make a lot of little holes in. **-ello** *m. dim.* little hole.

buci *excl.* (Tusc.) sh!

†buciac·chio *m.* calf.

bucicare [A 2 s] *tr., intr.* (*aux.* essere) to budge, to stir, to move slightly.

bucin-are [A I s] *tr.* to whisper abroad, to spread a report of; to murmur; si -a che abbia grossi debiti, it is rumoured that he is deeply in debt. **-amento** *m.* whispering; rumour. (**-ato** *part. adj.*) **-io** *m.* (*pl.* **-ii**) rumour; whispering.

bu·cine *m.* a conical-shaped fishing net or similar net for catching birds.

†bucino *m.* calf.

Bucintoro *pr.n.m.* Bucentaur, the state barge in which on Ascension Day the Doge of Venice went to wed the Adriatic by dropping a ring into it; royal pleasure boat.

buckyterapi·a *f.* (med.; radiol.) grenz-ray therapy.

bu-co[1] *m.* (*pl.* **-chi**) hole (usually smaller than **buca**); pit; pot-hole; cave; dimple; room, hiding-place; lair, den; — della chiave, — della serratura, keyhole; — degli orecchi, ear-hole; (colloq.) — della pancia, tummy-hole, navel; (naut.) — del gatto, lubber's hole; (mil.) — di lupo, fox-hole; manhole; (aeron.) — d'aria, air-pocket; (fig.) debt; tappare un —, to pay a debt; — nell'acqua, 'going round in circles', useless work; fare un — nell'acqua, to get nowhere, to make no impression, to fail; dare nel —, to hit the nail on the head; non ha cavato un ragno da un —, he didn't get anywhere, he failed completely; a —, exactly, precisely, in the nick of time; (provb.) non tutte le ciambelle riescono col —, things can't always turn out well. **-chino** *m. dim.* of **buco**; (Sicily) drawn-thread needlework. **-cuc·cio** *m. dim.* of **buco**; little cupboard, hidey-hole.

†buco[2] *m.* beehive.

buco·lic-a *f.* bucolic poem; pastoral poetry. **-o** *adj.* bucolic, idyllic, pastoral.

bucra·nio *m.* (archit.) ox-skull sculptured as an ornament, bucrane.

Buda[1] *pr.n.f.* (geog.) the old part of Budapest on the west bank of the Danube; (joc.) andare a —, to die, 'to peg out'; avere preso —, to have done something wonderful.

buda[2] *f.* (bot.) bulrush, *Schoenoplectus lacustris*.

Budd-a *pr.n.m.* Buddha. **-ismo** *m.* Buddhism. **-ista** *m., f.* Buddhist. **-i·stico** *adj.* Buddhist, relating to Buddhism.

buddle·ia *f.* (bot.) buddleia.

budell-o *m.* (*pl.f.* **-a**; in fig. uses, *m.* **-i**) bowel, gut, intestine; corde di —, catgut; slummy street; blind alley; (Tusc., vulg.) whore;

budell-o (*cont.*)

pl., entrails; stuffing, padding, filling. **-ame** *m.* guts; entrails. **-one** guzzler greedy-guts; †evil person.

budino *m.* pudding; black pudding; anything cooked in a sausage shape; roly-poly.

budriere *m.* sword-belt, baldric.

bu-e *m.* (*pl.* **buoi**) ox, bullock, steer; carne di —, beef; — salato, corned beef; grasso di piede di —, neat's foot oil; occhio di —, spotlight; *pl.* cattle; — marino, common seal, *Phoca vitulina*; (provb.) chiuder la stalla quando son scappati i buoi, to shut the stable-door after the horse is gone; (fig.) numskull; dunce, blockhead; — d'oro, wealthy ignoramus; mettere il carro innanzi ai buoi, to put the cart before the horse; imparare il — a memoria, not to learn anything; (archit.) occhio di —, bull's-eye window. **-accio** *m.* ignoramus, blockhead, dolt. **-acciolata** *f.* foolish deed or words. **-acciolo** *m.* young fool, silly ass. **-aggine** *f.* stupidity, slow-wittedness, doltishness. **-assag·gine** *f.* stupidity, dullness. **-essa** *f.* ignorant woman; †cow. **-ina** *f.* cow-dung.

bufa *f.* (naut.) spindrift.

bu·fal-o *m.* buffalo; (fig.) numskull. **-a·io, -a·ro** *m.* buffalo herdsman. †**-ata** *f.* (Florent. hist.) race run with buffaloes; song celebrating the occasion. **-otto** *m.* young buffalo.

bufare [A I] *impers.* (*aux.* essere) to snow with gusts of wind, to blow a blizzard.

bufera *f.* gale, wind-storm; squall; — di neve, snow-storm, blizzard; (fig.) sudden disaster.

buff-a *f.* (eccl.) hood worn by some religious guilds; cap covering the ears and part of the face, balaclava helmet; lower part of the visor of a helmet; (fig.) mask; blast, gust of wind; †mockery, jest. **-are** [A I] *intr.* (*aux.* avere) to blow, to puff; to say silly things; *tr.* to huff (at draughts). **-ata** *f.* gust; (draughts) huff. **-atore** *m.* glass-blower.

buffardello *m.* (Tusc.) sprite.

†**bufferanna** *f.* serpent.

buffè *m. indecl.*, (N. Ital.) **buffet** *m. indecl.* (pron. as Fr.) ball-supper, stand-up supper, refreshments; side-table, sideboard; buffet.

buffetto[1] *m.* occasional table.

buffetto[2] *m.* See under **buffo.**[1]

buff-o[1] *m.* squall of wind, gust; buffoon; singer in opera with low or broad comedy part; *adj.* funny, comic, droll; queer, odd; ridiculous, laughable; (N. Ital.) che —!, (Tusc.) com'è —!, how amusing!; (mus.) opera -a, an Italian form of comic opera; (mil.) la -a, the Infantry, 'the P.B.I.'. **-eri·a** *f.* trick, imposture. **-ettare** [A I c] *intr.* (*aux.* avere) to puff and blow. **-ettata** *f.* buffeting. **-etto** *m.* snap of the fingers; buffet, blow; stroke of fortune; *adj.* (of bread) very light. **-etteri·e** *f.pl.* (mil.) accoutrements. **-ettone** *m.* box on the ear.

buffo[2] *m.* (N., Centr. Ital.) debt.

†**buf·fola** *f.* folly; vanity.

buf·folo *m.* See **bufalo**.

buffon-e[1] *m.* buffoon; jester; (mus.) buffo tenor; fare il —, to play the fool. **-a** *f.* gay, foolish woman. **-aggine** *f.* See **buffonata**. **-are** [A I c] *intr.* (*aux.* avere) to act the fool. **-ata** *f.* piece of tomfoolery, buffoonery; slap-stick. **-eggiare** [A 3 c] *intr.* (*aux.* avere) to play the fool. **-eri·a** *f.* tomfoolery, buffoonery. **-esco** *adj.* (*m.pl.* **-eschi**) ridiculous, comical; jesting, facetious; clowning, clownish; waggish. (**-escamente** *adv.*) **-evole** *adj.* foolish. **-isti** *m.pl.* (theatr. hist.) Italian singers of *opéra bouffe*.

†**buffone**[2] *m.* short-necked, wide-bellied glass vessel.

bu·folo *m.* See **bufalo**.

bufonchiare [A 4] See **bofonchiare**.

bufon-e *m.* toad. **-ite** *f.* (miner.) batrachite, monticellite, toadstone.

bufo·nie *f.p.* (Gk. antiq.) bouphonia (Athenian sacrificial ceremony).

buftalmo *m.* (bot.) one of the yellow ox-eyes, *Buphthalmum* sp. and other similar plants.

buganvi·lia *f.* (bot.) bougainvillea.

buganza *f.* (N. Ital.) chilblain.

bug·ger-a *f.* trick, dodge, wangle; lie; tall story; waste of time. **-are** [A I s] *tr.* to trick, to humbug; *intr.* (*aux.* avere) to commit sodomy; *rfl.* **-arsene**, to be completely indifferent to.

bugi·a[1] *f.* lie, untruth, falsehood; (provb.) le -e hanno le gambe corte, truth will out; — pietosa, white lie (to protect someone else); white speck on the fingernail; white sore in the nose.

bugi·a[2] *f.* candle-stick with saucer-like base and a handle.

Bu·gia nen *pr.n.m.* (dial. Piedm.) nickname of a stubborn person who won't budge; die-hard.

bugiard-o *adj.* untruthful, lying, deceitful, false; *n.m.* liar; fibber storyteller; fare — a, to give the lie to. **-(u)olo** *m.* young liar. **-eri·a** *f.* pack of lies; untruthfulness, lying.

†**bugiare**[1] *tr.* to perforate, to pierce; to make a hole in.

†**bugiare**[2] *tr.* to deceive; *intr.* to tell lies, to lie.

bugigat·tolo *m.* cubby-hole, poky hole, dark recess; closet.

†**bu·gio** *adj.* pierced; empty; *n.m.* hole.

bu·glia[1] *f.* concourse, crowd.

bu·glia[2] *f.* (Tusc.) cavity, cave.

†**bugliare** *tr.* to fling down; *intr., rfl.* to move, to be restless; to become bewildered, to get lost.

buglione *m.* bouillon; broth; stew; mixture; conglomeration; bullion; trick, deceit; figment.

bugli(u)olo *m.* pimple, spot, blister; wooden or canvas bucket; earth closet.

buglossa *f.* (bot.) — volgare, Italian alkanet, *Anchusa officinalis*, and *A. italica*; — vera, borage, *Borago officinalis*; — selvatica, viper's bugloss, *Echium vulgare*.

bugn-a *f.* (archit.) boss, projection; rusticated ashlar; (naut.) clew; anti-torpedo net. **-ato** *adj.* (archit.) studded with bosses or with projecting stone surfaces; pietra -ata, rusticated ashlar; (also *n.m.*).

bugn-o *m.* beehive; confined space. **-one** *m.* thicket.

bu·gnol-a *f.* straw-plaited basket; teacher's desk, pulpit; dock (for a prisoner in court). **-ino** *m. dim.* lunch basket. **-o** *m.* small basket; †essere nel -o, to be in love; †entrare nel -o, to lose one's temper.

bu·gola *f.* (bot.) common bugle, *Ajuga reptans*.

bugrane *f.* buckram.

buina *f.* See under **bue**.

bu·i-o *adj.* dark; obscure; gatta -a, lock-up; *n.m.* darkness, dark; — pesto, pitch darkness; c'è — pesto fuori, it's inky black outside; (poker) 'blind'; *adv.* a —, at nightfall; al —, in the dark, (fig.) essere al — di, to be in the dark about. †**-ore** *m.* darkness. **-ose** *f.pl.* (Tusc., slang) prison.

bulbare *adj.* (med.) bulbar.

bulb-o *m.* bulb; root of hair; — dell'occhio, eyeball. **-iforme** *adj.* bulb-shaped. **-illo** *m.* (bot.) bulbil. **-oca·stano** *m.* (bot.) pig-nut, earth-nut, *Conopodium majus* and *Bunium bulbocastanum*. **-omani·a** *f.* (bot.) plant-disease, resulting in over-production of small bulbs. **-oso** *adj.* bulbous.

buldge *f. indecl.* (naut.) bulge.

†**buldriana** *f.* See **baldracca**.

buldrò *m. indecl.* bulldog.

bules·sia *f.* (vet.) coronet (of the hoof of a horse).

Bulgari·a *pr.n.f.* (geog.) Bulgaria

bul·gar-o *adj.* (geog.) Bulgarian; *n.m.* Bulgarian, Bulgar; Russia leather; (leg.) consuetudine di —, the widow's claim to a share of the deceased husband's estate. (**-a** *f.*)

bulic-are [A 2 s] *intr.* (*aux.* avere) to boil; to seethe; to bubble up. **-ame** *m.* boiling spring in the plain of Viterbo; seething crowd of people; seething mass.

†**bu·lima** *f.* crowd, multitude; rabble; assembly.

bulimaca *f.* (bot.) rest-harrow, *Ononis repens* or *spinosa*.

bulimi·a *f.* insatiable appetite.

bulin-o *m.* graving tool, burin; (fig.) the engraver's art; (eng.) centre punch. **-are** [A I] *tr.* to engrave; to chisel. **-atura** *f.* (eng.) centre pop. **-ista** *m.* engraver.

bulla[1] *f.* (Rom. antiq.) ornament worn by boys.

bulla[2] *f.* See **bolla**[2].

bullett-a *f.* ticket; chit; delivery note; consignment note; way bill; (shoem.) stud, hobnail; (carp.; eng.) tack; see also **bolletta**; *pl.* ear-rings. **-a·io** *m.* grindery merchant; mercer. **-ame** *m.* quantity of nails, tacks, tin-tacks, etc. **-a·rio** *m.* book of tickets with counterfoils. **-atura** *f.* the provision of tickets. **-ina·io** *m.* ticket-seller, booking clerk, box-office clerk. **-ino** *m.* bulletin; notice; summary of news; ticket; dressing placed on a wound. **-ona** *f.* hobnail, blakey. **-one** *m.* ornamental stud; large tack; upholsterer's tack; †register.

bullo *m.* (Rome) bully; flashy overbearing person; underworld character. (cf. **bulo**).

bullon-e *m.* bolt; rivet; (eng.) — da fondazione, rag bolt; — passante, through bolt. **-are** [A I c] *tr.* (eng.) to bolt. **-eri·a** *f.* (eng.) nuts and bolts.

bulo *m.* youngster, young shaver, young cub.

bulsino *m.* See **bolsaggine**, under **bolso**[1].

bum (onom.) bang!; boom!

bume·lia *f.* (bot.) iron wood, *Sideroxylon oxyacantha*.

bu·nio *m.* (bot.). See **bulbocastano**, under **bulbo**.

bunker *m. indecl.* (pron. as It.) bunker; blockhouse.

buon-accordo *m.* (mus.) small triangular spinet. **-brac·cio** *m.* (naut.) reach; soldiers' wind. **-acristiana** *f.* bon Chrétien, a variety of pear. **-giorno**, *excl.* good day!; †*n.m.* heavy-headed walking-stick. **-guar·dia** *excl.* (watchman's hail) all's well! **-gusta·io** *m.* gourmet, connoisseur. **-alana, -amano, -cuore.** See **bonalana**, etc.

buon-o[1] *adj.* (*m.s.* **buon**, before a vowel or consonant except impure s, z or gn; *f.s.* **buon'** before a vowel).
1. GOOD; Iddio è —, God is good; il buon Dio ti protegga, the good Lord protect you; il mio buon angelo, my good angel; è un buon padre, he is a good father; una -a figliuola, a good girl, a good-natured girl (cf. uses under No. 2); un uomo —, a good man (cf. 'un buon uomo', under No. 2); una donna -a, a good woman, a kind woman, a truly good and kind woman (cf. 'una -a donna', under No. 2); menare una vita -a, to lead a good life (cf. 'una -a vita', under No. 8); la -a volontà, good will; il buon costume, good behaviour, good morals; squadra del buon costume, vice squad; i -i proponimenti, good intentions. **2.** GOOD, kind, kindly; un'anima -a, a kind soul; la buon'anima di, the late lamented; dire una -a parola per, to put in a good word for, to say a kind word about; un buon signore, a kind gentleman; il suo buon cuore, his kind heart; — come il pane, angelically kind, really good; (with slight condescension): un buon figliuolo, a good lad; un buon uomo, a good-natured man, a kindly man, a good chap; venite qua, buon uomo!, come here, my good man!; un uomo tre volte —, a simpleton; un buon diavolo, a nice chap, a likeable fellow, a good sort; una -a donna, a kindly soul, a woman of easy virtue; -a gente, kindly people, simple souls; di buon umore, good-humoured; guardare di buon occhio, to look favourably upon, to view with sympathy; di -a voglia, willingly, ungrudgingly, energetically; di buon grado, with pleasure. **3.** GOOD, wholesome, enjoyable, palatable; buon cibo, good food; buon vino, good wine; c'è aria -a, the air is good here; il buon caffè pochi lo sanno fare, few people know how to make good coffee; -a questa pasta!, I'm enjoying this pasta! **4.** GOOD, sound, proper, adequate, sufficient; il buon gusto, good taste; il buon senso, common sense; di -a bocca, of good appetite; (of a horse) having a sensitive mouth; avere una -a cera, to look well, to have a good colour; le -e maniere, good manners; non è una -a ragione, that is not a good reason; fare —, to make good; fare — per. to credit with, to trust for. **5.** GOOD, of good quality, genuine; buon lavoro, good work, high-class work; questa penna è poco -a, this pen isn't much good; l'abito —, Sunday-best; un buon cane da guardia, a good house-dog; oro —, real gold; sono perle -e, they are genuine pearls; (finan.; comm.) valid; moneta -a, valid currency; -a società, high society, good society; di -a famiglia, of good family; un buon partito, an eligible partner for marriage; il buon secolo, the fourteenth century (for Italian language). **6.** GOOD, suitable, apt, fit, propitious; al momento —, in buon punto, at the right moment; coltello — a tagliare la carne, knife good for carving meat; — a nulla, good for nothing; una medicina -a per la bronchite, a medicine good for bronchitis; una donna -a a far di tutto, an all-round (daily) help, a competent housewife; è solo — a, he's only fit for; è solo — a parlare, all he can do is talk; cibo — a dare ai polli, food fit for pigs; questa è ora -a, this is a good moment, this is a convenient time (cf. under No. 8); è una -a occasione, it is a good opportunity; ammettere come —, to approve; menare -a una cosa a uno, to admit that a person is in the right about something; fare —, to pass as correct; far buon giuoco, to suffice for a purpose. **7.** GOOD, well-behaved, quiet, mild, gentle; buono buono, good as gold, quiet as a mouse; oggi i bambini sono stati -i, the children were good today; ieri il mare era —, the sea was calm yesterday; un clima —, a mild climate; sta lì zitto e —, he sits there quiet and good; -i, ragazzi!, quiet, children!; buon tempo, clement weather, nice weather (cf. 'darsi buon tempo' under No. 8); essere — con, to be gentle with, not to be hard on; star di buon animo, to be in good spirits; (leg.) il buon costume, moral behaviour (C.C., C.P.); cauzione di -a condotta, recognizance for good behaviour (C.P.). **8.** ADVANTAGEOUS, pleasing, enjoyable; un buon prezzo,

a good price (high or low, according to the point of view); l'ho avuto a buon prezzo, I got it cheap; una -a occasione, a bargain; a buon mercato, cheaply; di buon'ora, nice and early (cf. under Nos. 9 and 10); darsi buon tempo, to have a gay time (cf. under No. 7); menare una -a vita, to live well, to lead a life of pleasure (cf. under No. 1); siamo a buon punto, we've almost finished, the work is going on well; la -a stagione, spring and summer; essere in -e acque, to be doing well financially. **9.** GOOD (in measure), goodish; una buon'ora, un'ora -a, a good hour, at least an hour (cf. under Nos. 8 and 10); una -a dose di sale, a good dose of salts; stetti un buon tempo senza vederlo, it was a long time before I saw him; un buon tratto di strada, a good stretch of road; devo starmene un buon mese a letto, I shall have to stay in bed at least a month; di buon passo, at a good pace. **10.** IRON. OR EMPH. USES: quel buon Toni che ci credeva!, poor simple-minded Tony who fell for it!; farla -a, to drop a brick (cf. under No. 12); buon per te!, lucky for you!; una -a lavata di testa, a good scolding; finitela una -a volta!, have done, stop it once and for all!; alla buon'ora!, finally!, thank goodness for that! (cf. under Nos. 8 and 9); è un'impertinenza bell'e -a, that's a piece of impudence and no mistake! **11.** EXCL. USES: buon giorno!, good morning!, good-day!, how do you do?, good-bye!; -a notte!, good night!; (fig.) allora me ne vado e -a notte!, in that case I'll walk out and that will be the end of that!; -a sera!, good evening!, good afternoon!, how do you do?; buon Dio!, good Lord!; buon viaggio!, *bon voyage*!; -a permanenza!, have a nice time at home!; buon proseguimento!, all the best for the remainder of your journey!; (at New Year) may the New Year continue to be good!; buon lavoro!, good luck with your work!; -a fortuna!, good luck!; buon appetito! (a wish that a person may enjoy his meal: untranslatable); buon Natale!, happy Christmas!; buon divertimento!, have a good time!; buon riposo!, good night!, sleep well!; -a, questa!, that's a good one! (of a joke). **12.** WITH 'COSA', 'SORTE', ETC. UNDERSTOOD: averla avuta -a, to get off lightly; essere in -a, to be in a good humour; essere in -a con, to be on good terms with; sono di nuovo in -a, they've made it up, they're good friends once more; mettere in -a, to make a fair copy of; a farla -a, to be on the safe side, speaking broadly (cf. under No. 10); Dio ce la mandi -a!, let's hope for the best!; con le -e, politely, graciously, nicely ('maniere' are here understood); andarci con le -e, to go about a matter in a friendly and gracious manner; o con le -e o con le cattive, by fair means or foul, by hook or by crook, in a friendly way or with hostility and threats. **13.** ADV. PHR.: alla -a, simply, unpretentiously; in an unsophisticated way; sono gente alla -a, they're quite simple folk; una ragazza alla -a, an unsophisticated girl; a —, a lot, a good deal, really, very; è bella a —, she's a good-looker and no mistake!; piove a —, it's raining heavily; di —, seriously; dire di —, to speak seriously, to mean what one says; mettersi di buzzo — a, to put one's back into.

buon-o[2] *m.* **1.** GOOD; goodness; il vero, il bello, il —, truth, beauty, goodness; ha questo di — che, he has this point in his favour that; ogni cosa ha il suo — e il suo cattivo, there are two sides to every question, there's always a fly in the ointment; aver — in mano, to have a good amount in hand; questo è il —, qui viene il —, the beauty of it is, the best of it is; sul —, at the crucial moment; dare il — per la pace, to make some sacrifice for the sake of peace; c'è del — in questo libro, there are some parts in this book that are good; c'è voluto del bello e del — per persuaderlo, it was an awful job to persuade him; c'è poco di —, it's not much to write home about; quel poco di —, that rascal; un — a nulla, a good-for-nothing; fare del —, to do good; (of weather) mettersi al —, to turn fair; saper di —, to smell good; un bicchiere di quel —, a glass of good wine. **2.** GOOD MAN; fare il —, to be good; i -i, good people, virtuous people. **3.** (ECON.) order or promise to pay; government bond; — del tesoro, Treasury bond; bonus; coupon; policy; ticket; — di consegna, delivery note; voucher; — sconto, discount voucher; — d'acquisto, purchase voucher.

buon-peso, -prò, -senso, -tempone, -uomo, -uscita. See **bonpeso**, etc.

buranese *f.* variety of white grape; *adj.* of Burano.

burare [A I] *tr., intr.* (*aux.* avere) to burn away slowly, to smoulder.

burattin-o *m.* puppet; marionette; (fig.) person who acts on order from someone else, a spineless individual, a 'yes-man'; (fig.) fidgety child; castello dei -i, puppet stand. **-a·io** *m.* puppet-show-

burattin-o (*cont.*)
man. **-ata** *f.* puppet-like action; puppet-show; (fig.) foolish action. **-ęsco** *adj.* (*m.pl.* **-ęschi**) puppet-like.

buratt-o *m.* bolting cloth, sifter for bolting meal; straining cloth; bolter; (liter. hist.) the symbol of the Accademia della Crusca; (mil.) figure used as a target. **-aio** *m.* sifter, bolter. **-are** [A I] *tr.* to sift; to discuss (esp. literary or linguistic matters as in the Accademia della Crusca). **-ello** *m. dim.* bolting bag; bolting cloth.

burbanz-a *f.* offensive vanity, conceit; arrogance. **-ǫso** *adj.* conceited; haughty. **-osamęnte** *adv.* conceitedly; haughtily.

bur·ber-a *f.* windlass. **-ino** *m.* perforated bar at the back of a waggon through the holes in which pegs can be placed for twisting the bar so as to tighten the ropes which secure the load.

bur·bero *adj.* grumpy, crusty; gruff; *n.m.* grumpy person; è un — benefico, his bark is worse than his bite.

†bur·chia *f.* See **burchio**; *adv. phr.* alla —, carelessly; haphazard; andare alla —, to steal other people's ideas.

bur·chi-o *m.* barge. **-ello** *m. dim.* boat; wherry; barge.

burchiellęs-co *adj.* (*m.pl.* **-chi**) after the style of Domenico di Giovanni, a Florentine poet of the fifteenth century, called Burchiello because he had the sign of a barge over his barber's shop.

bure *m.* beam of plough.

burella[1] *f.* piebald horse.

burella[2] *f.* (herald.) bar.

†burella[3] *f.* underground passage; ditch; prison, dungeon.

burellato *adj.* (herald.) burely.

burello *m.* coarse cloth; (naut.) fid; toggle.

burętta *f.* (chem.) burette; (eng.) oil-can.

burga *f.* a conical frame containing clay, stones, etc. constructed as a protection for a river bank.

burgra·vio *m.* (hist.) Burgrave; (fig.) person who considers himself important.

buriana *f.* tempest; short, sharp storm, gale.

buriano *m.* (Tusc.) a white wine.

†buriasso *m.* trainer of knights in jousting; prompter.

buric-co *m.* (*pl.* **-chi**) (joc.) donkey, ass; sheepskin jacket.

burina *f.* See **bolina**.

burino *m.* See **bulino**; (Rom. dial.) peasant.

buristo *m.* black pudding.

burl-a *f.* practical joke; jest, prank, harmless trick; mettere in —, recare in —, to treat as a joke; per —, in fun; un re per —, a king in name only. **-are** [A I] *tr.* to play a joke on; to make a fool of; **†**to throw away; *intr.* (*aux.* avere) to joke; *rfl.* (*prep.* di) to laugh (at), to make a joke (of), to make light (of). **-atǫre** *m.* joker, banterer. (**-atrice** *f.*) **-ęsco** *adj.* (*m.pl.* **-ęschi**) jesting; farcical; burlesque. (**-escamęnte** *adv.*) **-ętta** *f. dim.* joke, farce; (theatr.) vaudeville; fare la **-etta**, to put up a pretence; fanno la **-etta**, they're putting on an act, it's a put-up job; *n.m.* burlesque. **-ęvole** *adj.* comic, laughable, farcical. (**-evolmęnte** *adv.*) **-ǫne** *m.* joker, jester (**-ǫna** *f.*).

burlanda *f.* brewer's grains.

†burlasco *adj.* ailing, infirm.

†burlętto[1] *m.* See **brolo**[1].

burlętto[2] *m.* (herald.) torse, crest-wreath.

burnitǫio *m.* See **brunitoio**, under **brunire**.

burnu·s *m. indecl.*, **burnusso** *m.* burnous.

†buro *adj.* See **buio**.

bur-o·crate *m.* bureaucrat. **-ocra·tico** *adj.* bureaucratic. (**-ocratica·męnte** *adv.*) **-ocrazi·a** *f.* bureaucracy; red tape.

burra·ia *f.* and other derivs. See under **burro**.

burrasc-a *f.* shower; squall; storm; blizzard; (fig.) buffeting of fate; misfortune. **-ǫso** *adj.* stormy; squally; tempestuous. (**-osamęnte** *adv.*)

†burrato *m.* See **burrone**.

burr-o *m.* butter; al —, cooked in butter; grease; (fig.) oiliness, flattery, 'soft soap'; dar del — a, to 'soft soap', to 'butter up'. **-a·ia** *f.* creamery, dairy. **-a·io** *m.* maker or seller of butter. **-ato** *adj.* buttered. **-ifi·cio** *m.* butter factory. **-ǫna** *adj. f.* soft (as applied to a pear or peach). **-ǫso** *adj.* buttery; creamy; (fig.) delicate, tender.

burrǫne *m.* (geog.) deep ravine.

busa *f.* (N. Ital.) animal droppings; cow-pat.

†busare *intr.* to tell lies, to lie.

†busb-o *m.* cheat; liar; fraud; swindler. **†-accare** *intr.* to cheat; to swindle. **†-accone** *m.* cheat; liar; fraud; swindler.

busc-a[1] *f.* quest, search; andare in — di, to go in search of; poaching; vivere alla —, to live on what one can pick up or steal; andare alla —, to leave for an unknown destination; olive basket. **-acchiare** [A4] *tr.* to seek, to hunt for; to poach, to forage.

†busca[2] *f.* See **bruscolo**.

buscalfana *f.* (joc.) poor thin horse.

buscalina *f.* (naut.) rope ladder.

busc-are [A2] *tr.* to seek, to hunt after; to get, to catch (esp. blame or punishment); **-arne**, to 'catch it', to get a beating, to get the worst of it; — la giornata, to get one's living; (of a dog) to retrieve, to fetch; *rfl.* (*dat.* of *prn.* si) to obtain, to procure, to get. (**-atǫre** *m.* **-atrice** *f.*)

buscher-are [A I S] *tr.* to waste, to squander, to throw away; to trick, to deceive, to cheat; to swindle. **-ata** *f.* nonsense, foolishness, stupid mistake; trick, deception. **-atura** *f.* deceit, fraud. **-ìo** *m.* noise, row; large quantity, great number.

†buscione *m.* thorn bush.

†busco *m.* See **bruscolo**.

busecca *f.* (Milan). See **busecchia**.

busęcch-ia *f.*, **-io** *m.* tripe; sausage-meat. **-ina** *f.* Bologna sausage; polony.

busilli(s) *m. indecl.* difficulty, snag; questo è il —, qui sta il —, here lies the difficulty, there's the rub.

bu·sina *f.* See **buccina**.

†busna *f.* See **buccina**.

buso *m.* See **buco**; **†***adj.* empty; useless, futile; stupid.

†busone *m.* a kind of trumpet.

buss-a *f.* smack, slap, blow, knock (usu. *pl.*); (fig.) loss, damage. **-are** [A I] *tr.* to slap; to hit; **-are** (alla porta), to knock (at the door); (fig.) — alla porta di, to call on (someone) for help. **-amento** *m.* knocking; beating. **-ata** *f.* knock, blow; request for help. **-atǫio** *m.* pole for driving fish. (**-atǫre** *m.*) **-o** *m.* blow; noise, turmoil; grumbling.

bussętto *m.* (shoem.) polisher, heel-stick, heel-ball, sleeker.

bus·sol-a *f.* (naut.) compass; rosa della —, compass card; (fig.) perdere la —, to lose one's bearings, to lose one's head; (fig.) criterion, standard; della prima —, of the best quality, first rate; della quinta —, of poor quality, fifth rate; (bldg.) decorative door; double-door; (eccl.) screened-off box from which the Pope hears sermons; (eng.) bush; sleeve; hub; (electr.) galvanometer; — dei seni, sine galvanometer; horse-brush. **-ante** *m.* (eccl.) member of the Pope's household who is with him in the 'bussola'. **-are** [A I S] *tr.* to curry (horses).

bussolotto *m.* wooden cup; dice shaker; jar; pot; giocatore di bussolotti, conjuror, thimble-rigger; giuoco di bussolotti, sleight of hand; (industr.) tin, can.

bust-a *f.* envelope; file-cover; — degli occhiali, spectacle case; small packet of cigarettes. **-apaga** *f. indecl.* pay-packet. **-arella** *f. dim.* tip, bribe. **-ina** *f. dim.* (mil.) forage cap.

bust-o *m.* bust; corset; bodice; (art) (herald.) bust. **†**corpse; **†**sepulchre, monument. **-a·ia** *f.* corsetière.

bu·stola *f.* See **pustola**.

bustrofedo *adj.* boustrophedonic; going alternately from left to right and from right to left; *n.m.* boustrophedon.

butan-o *m.* (chem.) butane. **-olo** *m.* (chem.) butanol, butyl alcohol.

butifiǫne *m.* puffed-up person.

butil-e *m.* (chem.) butyl. **-ene** *m.* (chem.) butylene.

buti·lico *m.* butyl; acetato —, butyl acetate.

but-irato *m.* (chem.) butyrate. **-i·rico** *adj.* (chem.) butyric.

butirr-o *m.* butter or similar substance (e.g. cocoa-butter). **-o·metro** *m.* butter fat tester. **-ǫso** *adj.* rich in butter. (Cf. **burro**.)

bu·trio *m.* a kind of bird snare.

butta-fuoco *m. indecl.* (mil.) flame-thrower. **-fuori** *m. indecl.* (theatr.) call-boy; (naut.) any projecting beam; outrigger; **-fuori** di briglia, dolphin-striker. **-sella** *m. indecl.* (mil.) signal for saddling. **-terra** *m. indecl.* (in alum works) man who throws the paste into the boiling pan.

buttagra, **butta·ghera** *f.* See **bottarga**.

buttalà *m. indecl.* clothes-rack, clothes-horse.

butt-are [A I] *tr.* to throw, to cast, to pitch; — sangue, to bleed; (fig.) to throw away, to waste; — via, to throw away; — la tonaca alle ortiche, to run away from one's monastery (convent); — giù, to gulp down, to jot down (on paper), to put on to

butt-are (*cont.*)
cook; — all'aria, to destroy, to throw up; — tutto all'aria, to turn everything upside down, to start all over again; *intr.* (*aux.* avere) to shoot (of plants); *rfl.* to throw oneself; -arsi allo sbarraglio, to risk one's life; -arsi giù, to lose heart, to become cast down. **-ata** *f.* throw; shoot (of a plant).

buttarola *f.* (eng.) set hammer.

but·ter-o *m.* pock-mark, scar from smallpox; (Maremma, Rome) cow-boy who rounds cattle in on horseback. **-are** [A I s] *tr.* to mark with pock-marks. **-ato** *part. adj.* pock-marked; scarred; (of metal) pitted. **-atura** *f.* (metall.) pitting; (found.) buckling.

†**butto** *m.* shoot (of a plant); *adv. phr.* di —, suddenly.

buyer *m. indecl.* (pron. as Eng.) foreign buyer at Italian trade-shows or fashion-shows.

buz·zi-co *m.* slight movement, rustle. **-care** [A 2 s] *intr.* (*aux.* avere) to budge, to stir; to rustle. **-chello** *m. dim.* slight noise, rustle. **-chìo** *m.* (*pl.* **-chìi**) continued whispering or rustling.

buzz-o *m.* paunch, belly; guts; di — buono, with a right good will; mettersi a lavorare di — buono, to get down to a job; *adj.* stormy (of weather); bad-tempered (of person). **-aio** *m.* tripe purveyor. **-ame** *m.* guts, entrails. **-one** *m.*, fat person, tub of guts; *adj.* (of weather) very stormy. (**-ona** *f.*)

buzzurro *m.* Swiss hawker of roast chestnuts and sweetmeats; (Rome) foreigner; Italian not born in Rome; (colloq.) boor.

Byron *pr.n.m.* Byron; collo alla —, Byronic collar. **-iano** *adj.* Byronic; in the manner of Byron.

C *f., m.* the letter C; in italiano il nome di Machiavelli si scrive con una — sola, Machiavelli's name is spelled with one c in Italian; un — maiuscolo, a capital C.

†**ca** *conj.* because; that.

ca' *f.* (Ven.) house (in names of Venetian palazzi or institutions, e.g. Ca' Pesaro, Ca' Foscari, etc.).

Ca(a)ba *pr.n.f.* Caaba.

ca·bal-a *f.* traditional Jewish interpretation of the scriptures; Cabbala; esoteric doctrine; quack spiritualism; Jewish clique, caucus; la — del lotto, the system of foretelling numbers in public lotteries; cabal, intrigue; far —, to conspire, to intrigue. **-are** [A I s] *intr.* (*aux.* avere) to indulge in fantastical dreams; to intrigue. **-ismo** *m.* cabbalism. **-ista** *m.* systematic player at lotteries; cabbalist. **-i·stico** *adj.* pertaining to the foretelling of numbers; cabbalistic; (fig.) incomprehensible. **-one** *m.* intriguer.

caballino *adj.* (poet.) fonte caballina, caballine fountain, the fountain Hippocrene.

cabarè, cabaret *m. indecl.* (pron. as Fr.) cabaret; trolley; tray.

cabaretti·stico *adj.* (neol.) pertaining to a cabaret; cantante —, cabaret singer.

cabasite *f.* (geol.) chabazite.

cab·bala *f.* See cabala.

cabessa *f.* variety of fine Indian silk.

cabestano *m.* (naut.) capstan.

†**cabigliò** *m.* codfish.

Cabil-a *pr.n.f.* Kabyle tribe. **-ano** *m.* member of the Kabyle tribe; *adj.* Kabyle.

cabin-a *f.* cabin; booth; — telefonica, telephone kiosk, call box; — da bagno, bathing hut; (motor.; eng.) cab (e.g. of a lorry); (rlwy.) cab; cage, car (funicular); — di blocco, — di manovra, — di segnalazioni, signal-box; (aeron.) cockpit; (cinem.) — di proiezione, projection booth. **-ista** *m.* (cinem.) projectionist.

Cab-iri *pr.n.m.pl.* (Gk. rel.) Cabiri, non-Hellenic deities worshipped in some parts of Greece. **-i·rie** *f.pl.* mysteries of the Cabiri.

cablag·gio *m.* (electr.; teleph.) wiring harness.

cabl-are [A I], **-ografare** [A I s] *tr.* to cable; *intr.* (*aux.* avere) to send a cable. **-ogramma** *m.* cable, cablegram.

cablotto *m.* (naut.) small anchor rope.

caboti n *m. indecl.* strolling player; quack, charlatan. **-ag·gio** *m.* life of a strolling player; charlatanism.

Caboto *pr.n.m.* (John *or* Sebastian) Cabot.

cabot(t)-ag·gio *m.* (naut.) coasting; coasting trade; piccolo —, coasting trade within the boundaries of a single country, (fig.) small-time trade; gran —, coasting trade on a wider scale. **-iere** *m.* captain of a coasting vessel. **-iero** *adj.* coasting, pertaining to coasting trade; *n.m.* coasting vessel.

cabr-are [A I] *intr.* (*aux.* avere) (aeron.) to fly tail-down, to cup. **-ata** *f.* tail-down flight. **-ato** *adj.* (aeron.) volo -ato, stall.

†**cabre·o** *m.* map, chart; account register.

cabriolè, cabriolet *m. indecl.* (pron. as Fr.) (motor.) closed two-seater, cabriolet, convertible, coupé.

†**caca·m, cacamme** *m.* rabbi; (Flor.) fare il —, to show off one's knowledge.

caca-o *m.* cocoa; (bot.) cacao. **-olina** *f.* butter substitute made from cocoa bean and palm oil.

cac-are [A 2] *intr.* (*aux.* avere) (vulg.) to stool, to shit. **-abasso** *m. indecl.* (vulg.) dwarf. †**-acciano** *m.* timid individual. †**-acciola** *f.* diarrhoea. **-adubbi** *m., f. indecl.* (vulg.) person who cannot make up his mind. **-afuoco** *m. indecl.* (joc.) shotgun. **-ai(u)ola** *f.* diarrhoea; dysentery; (fig.) terror; (vulg.) calzoni a -aiuola, trousers coming down; calze a -aiuola, socks not pulled up. †**-aloro** *m.* boaster, nouveau-riche. **-ani·dio** *m.* youngest bird of a brood. **-apensieri** *m., f. indecl.* (vulg.) one who spreads alarm and despondency; idler. **-arella** *f.* diarrhoea. **-asangue** *m. indecl.* dysentery; (fig.) misfortune. **-asenno** *m., f. indecl.* conceited individual, know-all. **-asentenze** *m., f. indecl.* pompous individual. **-asodo** *m., f. indecl.* self-important individual. **-astecchi** *m., f. indecl.* (vulg.) miser. **-ata** *f.* motion (of the bowels). **-atoio** *m.* (vulg.) privy, latrine. **-atura** *f.* excretion; (ent.) frass. **-azibetto** *m. indecl.* (vulg.) perfumed youth, fop, dandy. **-one** *m.* (vulg.) person who is loose in the bowels; (fig.) timid person.

cacato·a *m. indecl.* See cacatua.

cacatu·a *m. indecl.* (orn.) cockatoo.

cacca *f.* excrement; (fig.) anything dirty.

caccabal·dole *f.pl.* (Tusc.) wheedling, flattery.

cacca·o *m.* See cacao.

†**caccaro** *m.* (naut.) jackstaff.

cacchiatell-a *f.* bread made of the finest white flour (formerly used in making pap for babies) **-o** *m.* lump left in a mixture or beverage.

cac·chio[1] *m.* (agric.) first vine tendril.

cac·chio[2] *excl.* (euphem.) expression of wonder and surprise.

cacchion-e *m.* grub (of bee); maggot (of fly). **-oso** *adj.* maggoty; fly-blown.

cac·ci-a *f.* chase; hunting; shooting; netting; trapping; cane da —, sporting dog, gun-dog; leggi sulla —, game laws; — grossa, big-game hunting; dare la — a, to chase, to hunt, to track down; (fig.) to hunt for; — alle streghe, witch hunt; — del toro, bull fight; game caught, 'bag'; riserva di —, game preserve; (mus.) fourteenth-century vocal piece in canonic form; (naut.) pursuit; *m.* (naut.) for'ard bows; (abbrev. for **cacciasommergibile** and **cacciatorpediniere**) torpedo-boat destroyer; (aeron.) fighter aircraft; — da (a) reazione, jet fighter; — notturno, night fighter; (Flor.) goal in 'calcio storico' and several other old games. **-agione** *f.* see under cacciare. **-arella** *f.* wildfowling.

cac·cia-bombardiere *m.* (aeron.) fighter-bomber. **-bronzina** *m.* (mil.) tool for removing the bearing from a carriage wheel. **-botte** *f. indecl.* brassworker's chasing-hammer. **-buo·i** *m. indecl.* (rlwy.) cowcatcher. **-ccavallo** *m. indecl.* (naut.) fid, a bar which supports the weight of a topmast when erected. **-chiavette** *m. indecl.* (eng.) cottar. **-chiodo** *m. indecl.* extractor for drawing a nail out of a horse's hoof when the head of the nail is broken. **-cornac·chie** *f. indecl.* (mil. hist.) mortar for throwing stone projectiles. **-dia·voli** *m. indecl.* exorcist; (bot.) St John's Wort, *Hypericum perforatum* and *H. perfoliatum*. **-febbre** *f.* (bot.) common centaury, *Centaurium minus*. **-ffanni** *m. indecl.* amusement, pastime, distraction; *adj. indecl.* cheery, enlivening. **-luminello** *m. indecl.* (mil.) key for a match-lock. **-mazzetto** *m. indecl.* (naut.) metal rod for driving home the bristles of boiler tube brushes. **-mosche** *m. indecl.* fly-flap, fly-whisk. **-navetta** *m. indecl.* (text.) picker band. **-neve** *m. indecl.* see spazzaneve. **-nfuori** *m. indecl.* case-stake, a sort of gold-chaser's anvil. **-noce** *m. indecl.* (mil.) nut-driver. **-pas·sere** *m. indecl.* scarecrow. **-pensieri** *m. indecl.* see scacciapensieri. **-percussore** *m. indecl.* key for placing or removing the percussion caps of torpedoes or shells. **-perno** *m. indecl.* drive-bolt, riveting-setter, drift. **-sommergi·bili** *m. indecl.* submarine chaser. **-spoletta** *m. indecl.* (mil.) fuse-setter. **-tappo** *m. indecl.* tool for removing the pin of a torpedo. **-torpediniere** *m. indecl.* torpedo-boat destroyer. **-vite** *m. indecl.* screwdriver; -vite a pressione, spiral ratchet screwdriver.

cacci·are [A3] *intr.* (*aux.* avere) to go hunting; — alla volpe, to go fox hunting; to go shooting; — alle pernici, to go partridge shooting; — alle gonnelle, to run after women; *tr.* to pursue, to chase; to root out; — una cosa di tasca, to pull a thing from one's pocket; to hunt; to drive; to drive away; — un grido, to utter a cry; *rfl.* (*acc. of prn.* si) to put oneself; to hide oneself; to intrude oneself; to thrust oneself; to plunge; -arsi nei guai, to get into difficulties; (*dat. of prn.* si) -arsi in testa una cosa, to get something into one's head, to be obstinate about a thing. -**agione** *f.* game caught, 'bag'; venison. (-**amento** *m.*) -**ata** *f.* hunting; expulsion; driving away; hunting expedition; flush (of W.C.); cassetta per -ata, flush tank; (med.) -ata di sangue, blood-letting, bleeding. -**ato** *part. adj.* driven, chased; exiled. -**atoia** *f.* punch; (typ.) wedge (for holding the type). -**atoio** *m.* extractor for drawing a nail from a horse's hoof when the head of the nail is broken; marlin spike. -**atora** *f.* shooting-jacket; vestito alla -atora, coat cut in shooting-jacket style; (cul.) pollo alla -atora, chicken cooked in a frying-pan with tomatoes, stock, etc. -**atore** *m.* hunter, huntsman; (hist.) Gran Cacciatore, Master of the Royal Hunt; liveried groom, 'tiger'; (mil.) light infantryman; -atori a cavallo, light cavalry; (mil. hist.) Cacciatori, a Corps in the Piedmontese army, 1786; Cacciatori delle Alpi, civil militia organized by Garibaldi, 1859; (aeron.) fighter-plane; pilot of a fighter-plane; *pl.* (cul.) small salami sausages.

cacciù *m. indecl.* (bot.; med.; chem.) gum-catechu, from the areca palm.

cacciucco *m.* fish stew or chowder, made in the region of Leghorn, consisting of a great many different kinds of fish (sometimes up to seventeen varieties) and seasoned well with pepper and other spices.

†**cacciunde** *m.* See **cacciù**.

cac·col·a *f.* (vulg.) dirt and dried mucus in the nose, snot; rheum in the eye, 'sleepy dust'; dirt in sheep's wool; *pl.* gossip, idle talk. -**ino** *m.* nuisance; bore, tiresome person. -**one** *m.*, -**ona** *f.* snotty-nosed individual; nuisance. -**oso** *adj.* dirty, snotty; bleary-eyed.

cacher-ello *m.* droppings of mice, sheep, rabbits or any small animal. -**ellino** *m.* bird droppings; droppings of any very small animal. -**eri·a** *f.* flattery, 'soft soap'. -**oso** *adj.* given to flattery, wheedling.

cach-essi·a *f.* (med.) cachexy. -**e(t)·tico** *adj.* pertaining to cachexy.

cachet *m. indecl.* (pron. as Fr.) (med.) capsule; headache powder in a wafer container, cachet; colour-rinse at hairdresser's; professional fee (esp. for recitals, concerts, etc.); distinctive charm.

cachi[1] *m. indecl.* (bot.) Japanese persimmon, *Diospyros kaki*; fruit of same.

cachi[2] *adj. indecl.* khaki (colour).

cachi·grafo *m.* (joc.) person with a bad handwriting.

cachinn·o *m.* grotesque laugh, cackle; hollow, mirthless laugh. -**are** [A1] *intr.* (*aux.* avere) to cackle.

cachistocrazi·a *f.* (iron.) government by the worst elements.

cacia·io *m.* See under **cacio**.

cacic(c)o *m.* cacique, native chief or prince of W. Indies.

cacino *adj.* wretched; fare una figura cacina, to cut a sorry figure; vestito —, shabby dress.

ca·c·io *m.* cheese; una forma di —, a round cheese; (fig.) il — sui maccheroni, the finishing touch which makes something perfect, the high spot; esser pane e —, to be hand in glove; alto come un soldo di —, 'knee-high to a grasshopper'. -**ia·ia** *f.* cheese-room; woman cheese-maker. -**ia·io** *m.* cheese-maker. -**iai(u)olo** *m.*, -**iai(u)ola** *f.* cheese-seller; cheese-maker. -**iato** *adj.* sprinkled with cheese. -**impe·rio**, -**impero** *m. indecl.* cheese omelette. -**iocavallo** *m.* (*pl.* cacicavalli) hard Sicilian cheese, round or melon-shaped. -**iolo** *m.* see **caccio**. -**ioso** *adj.* cheesy, cheese-like. -**iotta** *f.* small soft cheese common in Central Italy. -**i(u)ola** *f.* flat round cheese; small new cheese; green cheese. -**i(u)olata** *f.* cheese and eggs, cheese-cake.

†**cacocerdo** *m.* person who lives on immoral earnings.

caco-crazi·a *f.* See **cachistocrazia**. -**de·mone** *m.* evil spirit. -**ete** *m.* chronic disease. -**foni·a** *f.* cacophony; clashing sounds. -**fo·nico** *adj.* cacophonous; harsh-sounding. -**grafi·a** *f.* bad spelling; bad handwriting. †-**grafizzare** *intr.* to make mistakes in spelling.

cacodile *m.* (chem.) cacodyl.

cacone *m.* See under **cacare**.

cacto *m.* See **cactus**.

cactus *m. indecl.* (bot.) cactus.

†**cacume** *m.* top, summit.

cacuminale *adj.* (ling.) consonante —, point consonant, dental consonant; (geog.) relating to rocks of crystalline massif.

cadauno *adj., prn.* See **ciascuno**.

cada·v·ere *m.* corpse, dead body. -**e·rico** *adj.* corpse-like, cadaverous; ghastly, deathly pale.

†**cadeni·glia** *f.* bandage.

cadenino *m.* (motor.) garnish strip, lining strip.

cadente *part.* see under **cadere**.

cadenz·a *f.* cadence; (mus.) cadenza; cadence, close; rhythm; — autentica, — semplice, authentic or perfect cadence; — intera, full close; mezza —, half-close; — d'inganno, — sfuggita, deceptive or interrupted cadence; — sospesa, imperfect cadence; — plagale, plagal cadence; ballare fuori di —, to dance out of time; (telev.) timing; (mil.) command given to a marching unit to check that men are keeping step. -**are** [A1] *tr.* (mus.) to mark the rhythm of; to furnish with cadenzas. -**ato** *part. adj.* (mus.) in regular rhythm; furnished with cadenzas; *adv.* parlare -ato, to talk in a sing-song voice.

cad·ere [C3] *intr.* (*aux.* essere) to fall; to drop; to decline; to sink, to set; to droop, to fail; to lapse, to flag; mi cadde l'animo, I became disheartened; — dalle nuvole, to be amazed, to be dumbfounded; — a proposito, to arise opportunely; — dalla padella nella brace, to jump from the frying-pan into the fire; (naut.) — sotto vento, to fall off. -**ente** *part. adj.* falling, setting; decadent, failing; enfeebled, decrepit; limp, weak; anno -ente, year nearing the end. -**evole** *adj.* falling; toppling; insecure; temporary, ephemeral. -**imento** *m.* falling, fall. -**uta** *f.* see below. -**uto** *part. adj.* fallen; ruined; broken, discredited; ogni speranza è -uta, all hope is lost.

cadetto *adj.* younger; *n.m.* younger son; younger brother; minor; junior; (mil.) cadet; (naut.) midshipman, cadet; (sport) footballer playing for B national team or for any second team.

cadì *m. indecl.* Qadi, Muslim judge.

Ca·dice *pr.n.f.* (geog.) Cadiz.

caditoi·a *f.* portcullis; machicolation. †-**o** *adj.* falling.

†**cadiva** *f.* epilepsy.

cadm-i·a *f.* (hist. chem.) cadmia. -**iare** [A4] *tr.* to cadmium plate, to cover with a thin layer of cadmium. -**iatura** *f.* cadmium plating. -**io** *m.* cadmium. -**opone** *m.* (paint mfr.) cadmium lithopone.

cad·mico *adj.* (chem.) relating to cadmium, of cadmium.

Cadmo *pr.n.m.* (myth.) Cadmus.

cad·o *m.* cask. -**ometri·a** *f.* mensuration of the capacity of casks, etc.

cadò *m. indecl.* (pop.) unexpected gift. (cf. Fr. 'cadeau').

cadolente *adj.* infirm; old and sad.

caduc-e·o *m.* caduceus, herald's wand; emblem of peace. -**eatore** *m.* (Rom. hist.) messenger bearing the caduceus. -**i·fero** *adj.* (myth.) caduceus-bearing.

cadu-co *adj.* (*pl.* -**chi**) short-lived, ephemeral; fleeting; windfallen (of fruit); deciduous (of leaves); (med.) mal —, epilepsy. (-**camente** *adv.*) -**cità** *f.* frailty; perishableness; decay; transience; (leg.) failure of a previously valid contract or will, owing to non-fulfilment of a condition, or to other supervening flaw or defect; †senility, old age.

caduno *adj., prn.* See **ciascuno**.

caduta *f.* fall, drop; collapse; downfall; (fig.) fault, failure; (econ.) slump; — dei prezzi, fall in prices; drape, 'hang' (of a curtain, etc.); (electr.) — di tensione, voltage drop; (hydraul.) head; (naut.) height of a sail.

caduto *part.* see under **cadere**.

†**caendo** *gerund.* andare —, to go in search of, to seek.

†**cafag·gi·a** *m.* preserve (hunting, fishing, etc.); †-**a·io**, †-**o** *m.* game-keeper; dairy-man.

cafardo *m.* depression, blues, *cafard*.

Cafar·nao, Cafarna·o *pr.n.m.* (geog.) Capernaum; (fig.) jumble, confusion; glory-hole, lumber-room; metter in —, to eat, to swallow; andare in —, to get lost, to get swallowed up.

†**caferaco** *m.* kind of serpent.

caff-è *m. indecl.* coffee; — ristretto, — espresso, — basso, very strong black coffee; (Tusc.) — alto, black espresso coffee of medium strength; (N. Italy) — lungo, weak coffee; macchinetta da —, percolator; macinino da —, coffee-grinder; coffee plant; coffee colour; di color —, coffee-coloured; coffee-house; café; (Lomb.) scolding. -**ea·rio** *adj.* relating to a café; l'industria -earia, the café business. -**eina** *f.* (chem.) caffeine. -**eismo** *m.* (med.)

caff-è (*cont.*)
caffeine poisoning. **-eista** *m.* coffee-drinker. **-ellatte** *m.* white coffee, café au lait; breakfast coffee; breakfast.

caffè-concerto *m.* (*pl.* **caffè-concerti**) café chantant.

caffettano *m.* caftan.

caffetteri·a *f.* food and drink served in cafés.

caffettier-e *m.* coffee-house keeper; café proprietor. **-a** *f.* wife of a proprietor of a coffee-house or café; coffee-pot; (joc.) old crock.

caff-o *adj.* odd, only, sole, unique; *n.m.* odd number; chance; nè pari nè —, neither one thing nor the other; pari e —, odd and even; giocare una cosa a pari e —, to play fast and loose with something; essere il — dei belli, to be one of the finest; essere il — dei brutti, to be one of the ugliest. **-etto** *m. dim.* stroke of luck.

cafioc, cafiocco *m. indecl.* (text.) fibre obtained from hemp (from **canapa**, abbrev., and **fiocco**).

†ca·fir *m.* unbeliever.

†cafi(s)so *m.* measure of grain (1¾ bushels); measure of oil.

cafon-e *m.* (S. Ital., Rom. Campagna) peasant; (fig.) boor, ill-mannered person; would-be elegant individual whose manners are insolent and boorish; bounder, cad. **-aggine**, **-a·ia** *f.* peasant class; boorish action; ill-mannered behaviour. **-ata** *f.* boorish action; ill-mannered behaviour. **-eri·a** *f.* See **cafonaggine**.

caforzo *m.* barley additive to coffee.

cafoscarino *adj.* relating to the Ca' Foscari Institute in Venice; *n.m.* graduate or student of the Ca' Foscari.

cafro *adj.* black; *n.m.* kaffir.

†cag·gere *vb.* and derivs. See **cadere**.

†caggiola *f.* cage.

†ca·gio *m.* See **cacio**.

cagion-e *f.* cause; occasion; reason; motive. **-are** [A 1 c] *tr.* to cause; to occasion; to give rise to; to produce. (**-amento** *m.*) **-ato** *part. adj.* caused; occasioned. (**-atore** *m.* **-atrice** *f.*) **-evole** *adj.* delicate, ailing; **-evole di salute**, not strong, susceptible to illness; salute **-evole**, poor health, ill-health. **-evolezza** *f.* frailty, weakness, sickliness. **-oso** *adj.* very delicate; infirm.

cagli-are¹ [A 4] *intr.* (*aux.* essere), *rfl.* to curdle; to clot; **-ata** *f.* curd.

cagliare² [A 4] *intr.* (*aux.* avere) to lose courage; to keep quiet.

Ca·gliar-i *pr.n.f.* (geog.) Cagliari. **-itano** *adj.*, *n.m.* native of Cagliari (**-itana** *f.*).

ca·glio *m.* rennet; coagulant; (bot.) — giallo, yellow bed-straw, cheese rennet, *Galium verum*; — bianco, white bed-straw, *Galium mollugo*; — porporino, purple bed-straw, *Galium purpureum*.

cagliostro *m.* adventurer, intriguer (from the name of the Count of Cagliostro, 1743–95).

cagn-a *f.* bitch, she-dog; tool for putting hoops on cartwheels; (rlwy.) jim crow, rail bender; (theatr.) woman vocalist of inferior voice; (N. Ital.) tall story. **-ac·cio** *m.* large dog; (ichth.) *Carcharias ferox*, a kind of shark. **-a·ia** *f.* barking of dogs; uproar, hubub; confusion. **-a·io** *m.* disorderly conduct. **-ara** *f.* see **cagnaia**. **-arotto** *m.* person who sets up an uproar. **-azzo** *m.* cur; *adj.* dog-like; ugly; livid; blue with cold. **†-eggiare** *intr.* to act cruelly. **-esco** *adj.* (*m.pl.* **-eschi**) dog-like; surly; *adv. phr.* guardare in **-esco**, to scowl at; stare in **-esco** con, to be cross with. **-etta** *f. dim.* bitch puppy; (mil. slang) cannon of 75 mm. **-etto** *m. dim.* dog puppy; (ichth.) blenny, *Blennius* spp. **-ina** *f.* (Cesena) name of a local wine. **-olino** *m.* puppy; dog puppy; little dog; lap-dog. **-(u)ola** *f.* bitch puppy; (naut.) cubby-hole. **-(u)olo** *m.* puppy, pup, whelp; cub; (vet.) turned in toe, pigeon-toe; quel cavallo ha un piede **-uolo**, that horse is pigeon-toed; (eng.) small clip or screw to prevent a wound-up spring from releasing. **-otta** *f.* (games) pool, kitty, pot. **-otto** *m.* hired bully, tool; hanger-on.

cago·ia *m.* abject coward.

caiaco *m.* (naut.) kayak.

caì caì (onom.) yelping of a puppy.

caicco *m.* (naut.) caique; (sport) small rubber canoe.

Caienna *pr.n.f.* (geog.) Cayenne; pepe di —, Cayenne pepper.

†caiera *f.* chair.

Caifasso *pr.n.m.* Caiaphas; (fig.) faccia di —, ugly mug.

caimano *m.* (zool.) caiman, *Caiman* spp.

Caina *pr.n.f.* Caina, the second division of the ninth circle of Dante's Hell where the betrayers of kindred are punished.

cainite *f.* (miner.) kainite.

Cain-o¹ *pr.n.m.* Cain; fratricide; murderer; assassin; traitor; offerta di —, treacherous offer. **†-ico** *adj.* relating to Cain; Cain-like. **-iti** *m.pl.* (rel.) Cainites.

caino² *m.* (pop.) far —, to howl like a dog.

cairo¹ *m.* coir.

Ca·iro² *pr.n.m.* (geog.) il —, Cairo.

cala *f.* inlet, bay; ship's hold.

calabrache *m. indecl.* submissive individual; person who is easily defeated; card game for two.

calabres-e *adj.* (geog.) Calabrian; (of a horse) constantly twitching its ears; *n.m.* Calabrian (also *f.*); wide-brimmed soft hat. **-ella** *f.* card game for three, in which two play against one.

Cala·bria *pr.n.f.* (geog.) Calabria; †S. Italy in general.

ca·labro *adj.*, *n.m.* See **calabrese**.

calabrone *m.* (ent.) hornet, *Vespa crabro*.

calabrosa *f.* (meteor.) rime; (geog.) opaque ice.

calafat-are [A 1] *tr.* (naut.) to caulk. **-aggio** *m.* act of caulking. **-ame** *m.* caulking. **-o** *m.* caulker; (aeron.) faying surface. **-ore** *m.* caulker. **-ura** *f.* caulking.

calamagna *f.* a variety of apple.

calama·io *m.* ink-well, inkstand; (fig.) avere i calamai agli occhi, to have shadows under one's eyes; (zool.) see **calamaro**.

†calamandra *f.* fine woollen cloth, calamanca.

calamar-o *m.* (zool.) squid, *Loligo vulgaris*. **-etto** *m.* young squid, used as food.

calambà *m. indecl.* calambac, a scented Chinese wood.

calambucco *m.* eagle wood; wood from either *Aloexylon agallochum* or the *Aquilaria agallocha* of Cochin China.

calameggiare [A 3 c]. See under **calamo**.

calamina *f.* (geol.) calamine, basic zinc silicate.

calamistr-o *m.* curling-iron, tongs. **-ato** *adj.* (of hair) curled.

calamit-a¹ *f.* magnet; lodestone; (fig.) attraction; essere la — di, to attract, to be the centre of. **-are** *tr.* [A 1] to magnetize. **-ato** *part. adj.* magnetized, magnetic. **-azione** *f.* magnetization.

calamita² *f.* (bot.) calamite.

calamit-à *f. indecl.* calamity. **-oso** *adj.* calamitous. (**-osamente** *adv.*)

ca·lam-o *m.* reed; pen; arrow, dart; (bot.) — aromatico, sweet flag, *Acorus calamus*. **-eggiare** [A 3 c] *intr.* (*aux.* avere) to flute, to pipe.

calanc-a *f.* (naut.) creek; (geog.) gully, furrow. **-o** *m.* (geol.) series of falls of land. **-oso** *adj.* friable; terreno **-oso**, territory where frequent falls of land occur.

calando *gerund*, *n.m.* See under **calare**.

calandr-a *f.* (orn.) calandra lark, *Melanocorypha calandra*; (ent.) grain weevil; (industr.) calender; (motor. slang) radiator cowling. **-aggio** *m.* (industr.) calendering. **-are** [A 1] *tr.* (industr.) to calender. **-atura** *f.* (industr.) calendering. **-ella** *f.* see **calandrino**. **-ino** *m.* (orn.) short-toed lark, *Calandrella brachydactyla*; (mech.) bevel, an instrument opening like a pair of compasses and constituting a kind of adjustable carpenter's square for measuring angles; †simpleton, from a character in Boccaccio's *Decameron*; far **-ino**, to take in, to deceive. **-o** *m.* (orn.) tawny pipit, *Anthus campestris*. **-one** *m.* (orn.) see **calandra**; (mus.) a rustic reed instrument, chalumeau.

calap·pio *m.* slip-knot; snare, gin, trap.

calapranzi *m. indecl.* service-lift, dumb waiter.

cal-are [A 1] *tr.* to lower, to drop; to let down; — il prezzo, to lower the price; **-arsi** le brache, to give in, to submit; — le ginocchia, to drop on one's knees, to kneel; — un colpo, to deliver a swinging blow, to bring one's sword down; (naut.) to strike; *intr.* (*aux.* essere) to drop, to get lower; to sink; to decline; to draw in, to get shorter; to descend; to ebb; to fall; to droop; to decay; (mus.) to drop in pitch; *rfl.* to drop, to let oneself down; **-arsi** in una buca, to let oneself down into a hole. **-ando** (mus.) *gerund*, *n.m.* becoming softer. **-ante** *part. adj.* waning, sinking, setting, falling; moneta **-ante**, coin under the proper weight; gobba a levante, luna **-ante**, gobba a ponente, luna crescente, when the bulge of the moon is in the east, the moon is waning, when the bulge is in the west, the moon is waxing. **-ata** *f.* lowering, fall, sinking, setting; dropping (e.g. of the voice); descent; la **-ata** dei barbari, the barbarian invasion; a **-ata** di sole, towards sunset; pigliarsela a un tanto la **-ata**, to do a thing at one's leisure; slope, declivity; type of dance; (naut.) quay, landing-place; (of nets) casting; (radio) aerial lead-in. **-ato** *part. adj.* dropped; lowered; diminished; shorter; down.

calastr-a *f.* seating for a cask or for a gun. **-ello** *m.* (bldg.) cross stiffening bracket; transom, jointing piece of a gun carriage.

calastrino *adj.* stony (of ground).

calato¹ *part.* see under **calare**.

†**ca·lato**[2] *m.* basket; vase for milk; (archit.) part of a Corinthian capital.

calatrone *m.* large bucket.

calaverna *f.* (naut.) batten, leather; (dial. Milan) mist, frost; icicle.

calaze *f.pl.* (zool.) chalazae.

calbi·gia *f.* a variety of wheat.

calca *f.* crowd, throng, press, crush; far — di, to make a point of.

calc-afogli *m. indecl.,* **-alet·tere** *m. indecl.,* etc. see under **calcare**.

calcagn-o *m.* (*pl.* -i; fig. uses, -a *f.*) heel; (vet.) point of the hock; fatto con le -a, very badly done; menare le -a, to run away; avere alle -a, to be closely pursued by. †-e *f.pl.* dare delle -e a, to spur on. **-are** [A5] *intr.* (*aux.* avere) (naut.) to touch bottom; †to take to one's heels. **-ata** *f.* kick with the heel. **-etto** *m.* heel (of a shoe). **-ino** *m. dim.* of calcagno; (hist. cost.) piece of wood placed inside a shoe to make the wearer look taller. **-(u)olo** *m.* (naut.) heel of a ship's keel; (sculp.) claw-tool.

calcaneale *adj.* relating to the heel; tendine —, Achilles tendon.

calcara *f.* lime kiln; (glassm.) calcar oven.

calc-are[1] [A2] *tr.* to trample upon, to tread; — l'uva, to tread grapes; to press down, to cram; to emphasize, to stress; — la voce, to speak with emphasis; — la mano, to be severe, to dot one's i's, to be emphatic; — la mano a uno, to force someone's hand; — le scene, to tread the boards, to go on the stage; — le orme di, to follow in the footsteps of; *intr.* (*aux.* avere) to trample, to mill. **-a·bile** *adj.* good for treading. **-afogli** *m. indecl.* paper-weight. **-alet·tere** *m. indecl.* letter-weight; clip, fastener (for papers). **-amento** *m.* trampling, treading. †-**astoppa** *f.* (naut.) caulking tool. **-ata** *f.* trampling; pressure; beaten track. **-ato** *part. adj.* trodden; (fig.) downtrodden, oppressed; exaggerated, overdone. **-atoio** *m.* (artill.) rammer. **-atore** *m.* one who tramples; oppressor; **-atrice** *f.* girl treading grapes; †cockatrice; poisonous serpent. **-atura** *f.* treading; trampling; pressing, milling.

calc-are[2] [A2] *tr.* to trace, to outline; to calk; to make a carbon copy of; (fig.) to copy, to imitate; (ling.) to transliterate. **-ato** *part. adj.* traced; calked, copied; imitated; (ling.) -ato su, on the model of. **-atoio** *m.* ivory-pointed pencil for tracing.

calcare[3] *m.* (geol.) calcareous rock; limestone; — concrezionato, calcareous deposits on the walls of a cave.

calca·r-eo, -io *adj.* calcareous.

calcato[1] *part.* of calcare[1], q.v.

calcato[2] *part.* of calcare[2], q.v.

calcatoio[1] *m.* See under calcare[1].

calcatoio[2] *m.* See under calcare[2].

calca-trep·pola *f.* (bot.) *Centaurea solstitialis*; — ametistina, *Eryngium amethystinum*; — marina, sea holly, *Eryngium maritimum*. **-trippa** *f.* (bot.) larkspur, *Delphinium ajacis*.

calce[1] *m.* heel of a lance; foot, bottom, lower part; in —, at the foot of a page.

calc-e[2] *f.* lime; calcium oxide; — viva, quicklime; — spenta, — estinta, slaked lime; (bldg.) bianco di —, whitewash; dare una mano di — a, to give a coat of whitewash to; (chem.) acqua di —, limewater. **-i·fero** *adj.* calciferous. **-i·metro** *m.* (chem.) calcimeter.

calcedo·ni-o *m.,* **-a** *f.* chalcedony. **-a·to** *adj.* like chalcedony (of marble).

calcedro *m.* metal bucket.

†**cal·ceo** *m.* (Rom. antiq.) half boot.

calceola·ria *f.* (bot.) — dei fioristi, calceolaria.

†**calcerello** *m.* See calcedro.

calcese *m.* (naut.) top of the mast of a lateen vessel or of a boat; principal block of a tackle, leading block.

calcestruzzo *m.* concrete; — battuto, tamped concrete; — precompresso, pre-stressed concrete; — armato, reinforced concrete.

calcetto *m.* slipper, pump, plimsoll; woollen footgear worn for trampling down snow; cavare altrui i calcetti, to extract secrets from people; mettere in un —, to confuse.

calchino *m.* engraving tool.

†**calciamento** *m.* boot, footwear, shoe; legging.

calci-are [A3] *intr.* (*aux.* avere) to kick; to kick out, to give kicks; (sport) — in porta, to shoot at goal; (techn.) to tread, to mill, to pound; *tr.* (sport) — la palla, to kick the ball. **-ante** *part. adj.* kicking. **-ato** *part. adj.* (sport) kicked, shot. **-atore** *m.* kicker; footballer (professional). †-care *intr.* to kick, to stamp.

cal·cico *adj.* containing calcium.

calci·cole *adj., f.pl.* (bot.) calciphytes, lime-loving plants.

cal·cide *f.* (ent.) chalcid wasp; †a kind of poisonous snake.

†**calcido·ni-a** *f.,* **-o** *m.* See calcidonio.

calci·fero *adj.* See under calce[2].

calcific-are [A2s] *tr.* to calcify. **-ante** *part. adj.* calcifying; (med.) cure -anti, the taking of waters containing lime. **-ato** *part. adj.* calcified. **-azione** *f.* calcification.

calci·metro *m.* See under calce[2].

calcin-a *f.* lime; limewash; mortar; — grassa, mortar with little sand; — magra, mortar with much sand; (text.) lana di —, fellmongered wool. **-ac·cio** *m.* bit of old mortar that breaks off a wall; flaked plaster; (in birds) hard excrement which causes constipation; (med.) tumour filled with lime-like deposit; *pl.* plaster rubble, masonry debris. **-a·io** *m.* pit for slaking lime; (tanning) lime-yard worker; -aio meccanico, lime wheel; fossa di -aio, lime-pit; *adj.* lime-bearing, calcareous. **-ai(u)olo** *adj.* containing lime; †*n.m.* builder, mason.

calcin-are [A1] *tr.* to burn, to calcine; to spread lime on, to dress with lime; (tanning) to lime; (chem.) to ignite; (industr.; glassm.) to frit, to calcine. **-a·bile** *adj.* suitable for calcination. **-ato** *part. adj.* calcined. **-atore** *m.* calciner. **-ato·rio** *adj.* (*m.pl.* -atorii) calcinatory, serving for calcination, used for calcining. **-atura** *f.* calcining; lime-dressing. **-azione** *f.* calcination; (tanning) liming. **-oso** *adj.* lime-bearing, calcareous. **-osità** *f.* calcareousness.

calcinello *m.* (zool.) wedge shell, *Donax* spp.

calcino *m.* (silkb.) lime disease, muscardine.

cal·ci-o[1] *m.* kick; fare a calci, to kick, to give kicks, to kick each other; (fig.) dar dei calci alla greppia, to return evil for kindness; dare un — a, to insult; tener sotto i calci, to oppress; tirare calci al rovaio, to be hanged; butt of a gun; (naut.) foot of a mast; (rlwy.) — dello scambio, heel of points; end of a branch nearest the tree; †foot; (sport) football (the game); (soccer) — d'inizio, kick-off; — d'angolo, corner kick; — di rinvio, goal-kick; — diretto, direct free kick; — indiretto, indirect free kick; — di rigore, penalty kick; — di punizione, penalty kick from outside goal area; (rugger) — di punizione, penalty kick; — piazzato, place kick; — franco, free kick; — al volo, punt; — di rimbalzo, drop-kick; — di rinvio, drop-out; — a seguire, punt ahead; — storico, — in costume, game of football played on special occasions in Florence in the costume and according to the rules of 1533. **-atore** *m.* see under calciare.

cal·cio[2] *m.* calcium. **-cianamide** *f.* calcium cyanamide fertilizer.

calciolo *m.* pistol grip; heelplate (of gun).

calci·stico *adj.* pertaining to football; società calcistica, football club.

calcistruzzo *m.* See calcestruzzo.

calcite *f.* (geol.) Iceland spar, calcite.

calcitr-are [A1s] *intr.* (*aux.* avere) to be recalcitrant. †-**oso** *adj.* recalcitrant.

cal·co *m.* (*pl.* -chi) take-off of a pencil drawing by pressing it upon another sheet, counter-drawing, calk; tracing; rubbing; carbon copy; imprint; the impress of a relief made on wax or other soft substance; cast; (linguist.) calk, model. **-cografi·a** *f.* copper engraving, steel engraving; engraving shop. **-cogra·fico** *adj.* pertaining to engraving. **-co·grafo** *m.* engraver; dealer in copper engravings. **-cotipi·a** *f.* copper engraving.

cal·col-a *f.* treadle (e.g. of a loom). **-ai(u)olo** *m.* weaver. †-**iere** *m.* weight used in weaving for keeping threads in position.

calcol-are [A1s] *tr.* to calculate; to reckon; to compute; to estimate; to count in, to allow for; to foresee; to count on; (comm.) — una perdita, to estimate a loss; — un profitto, to estimate a profit. **-a·bile** *adj.* that may be calculated, calculable. **-ato** *part. adj.* calculated; reckoned; estimated; allowed for. **-atore** *m.* calculator, computer; calculating person. **-atrice** *f.* calculator; calculating machine. **-azione** *f.* calculating; art of calculation; estimate.

†**calcoleri·a** *f.* See calcolazione, under calcolare.

cal·col-o[1] *m.* calculation; reckoning; computation; estimation; fare — su, to count on; (math.) calculus.

cal·col-o[2] *m.* (med.) calculus, stone; — alla vescica, stone in the bladder. **-osi** *f.* (med.) calculous condition. **-oso** *adj.* (med.) calculous; †stony.

calcomani·a *f.* See decalcomania, under decalcare.

calcopirite *f.* (miner.) chalcopyrite, yellow copper.

†**calcosa** *f.* road, path; battere la —, to travel, to journey.

calcosina *f.* (miner.) chalcosite.

calcotipi·a *f.* See under calco.

calda *f.* (metall.) heating, forging; far due chiodi a una —, to kill two birds with one stone; feverish cold; †southern slope of a mountain.

calda·i·a *f.* boiler, copper; copper-full; sala -e, stokehold; (mil.) dugout. **-ata** *f.* boiler-full, copper-full. **-one** *m. augm.* large boiler; great confusion. **-o** *m.* kettle; cauldron.

calda·ico *adj.* Chaldean.

caldaino *m.* dye-kettle.

caldallęss-a *f.* (*pl.* -e), **-o** *f. indecl.* boiled chestnut.

caldana *f.* heat; heat-wave; che — è oggi!, what a boiling hot day it is!; the hot time of the day; hot flush in the head; see **caldano**; (fig.) fit of rage; prendere una — per, to conceive a passion for.

caldan-o *m.* brazier; warm cupboard near the oven for allowing dough to rise. **-ino** *m. dim.* foot-warmer.

caldareri·a *f.* (eng.) boiler-making.

†caldaro *m.* copper vessel, cauldron.

caldarrost-a *f.* (*pl.* -e), **-o** *m. indecl.* roast chestnut. **-a·io**, **-aro** *m.* chestnut roaster, roast chestnut seller.

Cald-e·a *pr.n.f.* (geog. hist.) Chaldea. **-e·o** *adj.* Chaldean.

caldeggiare [A 3 c] *tr.* to favour; to support; to advocate; to plead warmly on behalf of; to do propaganda for.

calder-a·io *m.* boiler-maker; (N. Ital.) tinker; coppersmith; *pl.* (Risorg. hist.) association formed in opposition to the Carbonari. **-ina** *f. dim.* of **caldaia**, q.v.; auxiliary boiler; donkey boiler. **-one** *m.* cauldron; soup-kettle; melting-pot; (fig.) Gli Stati Uniti, -one di tante nazionalità, the United States, melting-pot of so many nationalities. **-otto** *m.* copper kettle.

calderino, *m.* see **cardellino**, under **cardello**.

calderu·gia *f.* (bot.) groundsel, *Senecio vulgaris*.

caldęzza *f.* See under **caldo**.

cald-o *adj.* hot; warm; battere il ferro finchè è —, to strike while the iron is hot; cibo —, hot food; tavola -a, snack bar; paese —, hot country; acqua -a, hot water; warm water; animali di sangue —, warm-blooded creatures; (fig.) heated, warm, impassioned, ardent; cuore —, warm heart, enthusiastic temperament; affetto —, warm affection; testa -a, impulsive nature, hot-head; un — discorso, an impassioned speech; le sue -e parole, his ardent words; a sangue —, in hot blood; piangere a -e lagrime, to weep scalding tears; — dal vino, flushed with wine; — d'amore, burning with love; tinte -e, warm colours; terreno —, parched earth; una notizia -a -a, hot news, the latest news; pigliarsela -a, to take it to heart; *n.m.* heat; (of weather) che —!, how hot it is!; oggi fa —, it's hot today; c'è troppo — qui dentro, it's too hot in here; (of a person) aver —, to be hot, to feel hot; questo pastrano mi fa —, I'm too hot in this overcoat; questa maglietta ti tiene —, this jersey keeps you nice and warm; non mi fa nè — nè freddo, I couldn't care less; i rimproveri non gli fanno nè — nè freddo, reproaches make no impression whatever on him; tenere in — la minestra, to keep the soup hot; (of animals) essere in —, to be on heat; nel — della discussione, in the heat of the discussion; nel — della battaglia, in the thick of the battle. **†-erno** *adj.* sunny, in the sun; warmed by the noonday sun. **-ęzza** *f.* hotness, heat, warmth; (fig.) vehemence, heat. **-ic·cio** *adj.* rather warm, hottish. **-ino** *m.* sunny place in the country; *adj.* rather warm. **-uc·cio** *adj.* warm and cosy; *n.m.* warmth; standosene al -uccio, keeping warm and cosy. **-ura** *f.* great heat of summer.

cale *vb. impers.* See **calere**.

†caleddalza *f.* (naut.) rope for raising and lowering a sail at will (cal'-ed-alza).

cale·done *adj., n.m.* Caledonian.

Caledo·nia *pr.n.f.* (hist. geog.) Caledonia.

†calefac(i)ente *adj.* warming, warmth-producing, calefacient.

calefazione *f.* (phys.; techn.) calefaction.

†caleff-are *tr.* to mock, to deride; to heat; to inflame; to excite. **†-atore** *m.* mocker.

†caleffo¹ *m.* mockery; trick, joke.

†caleffo² *m.* register of the Commune of Siena.

caleido-fo·nio *m.* (phys.) kaleidophone. **-sco·pico** *adj.* kaleidoscopic. **-sco·pio** *m.* kaleidoscope.

calemma *f.* (naut.) breaker; surf.

†calen *abbrev.* See **calende**, under **calendario**.

calend-a·rio *m.* calendar; giurare per tutti i santi del —, to swear by all the saints in the calendar; non aver uno nel —, not to have esteem or a liking for someone; — scolastico, school or university calendar; — sportivo, sporting calendar, fixtures. **-e** *f.pl.* Kalends; rimandare alle -e greche, to put off until doomsday. **-imag·gio** *m.* May Day.

calenz(u)ol-a *f.* (bot.) spurge; sun spurge, *Euphorbia helioscopia*; petty spurge, least spurge, *E. peplus*. **-o** *m.* (orn.) greenfinch.

calepino *m.* Latin dictionary; (hist.) the Latin dictionary first published in 1502 at Reggio by Ambrogio da Calepio.

calęre [def.] *intr. impers.* to matter; poco mi cale, it doesn't matter much to me; *adv. phr.* avere in non cale, to be indifferent about, not to care about.

calesce *m.* two-horse carriage.

caless-e *m.* gig, one-horse carriage. **-a·bile** *adj.* (of a road) suitable for a carriage. **-ata** *f.* carriage-load. **-ino** *m.* cab-horse.

calestro *m.* See **galestro**.

calętt-a *f.* dovetail; mortice and tenon; slice. **-amento** *m.* dovetailing; (electr.) -amento delle spazzole, brush position. **-are** [A 1 c] *intr.* (*aux.* avere) to make a close joint by dovetailing or otherwise; *tr.* to key; to dovetail; to fit flush; (eng.) -are a caldo, to shrink on; (electr.) -are le spazzole, to adjust the brushes. **-ato** *part. adj.* keyed; dovetailed; (eng.) -ato a caldo, shrunk on. **-atura** *f.* dovetailing, dovetail; (masonry) -atura a maschio e femmina, joggle.

calfat-are [A 1] *tr.* (naut.) to caulk. **-ag·gio** *m.* caulking.

cali·a *f.* chippings of gold or silver; old rubbish; something old-fashioned; trifle, useless bagatelle; worthless individual; ailing and querulous person; *adj. indecl.* fussy; che donna —!, what a tiresome, fussy woman!; *adv.* not at all, not in the least.

ca·libr-o, **calibr-o** *m.* calibre, bore, gauge; grossi -i, heavy guns, (joc.) big shots; (watchm.) watch; (eng.) gauge, caliper; — non passa, not-go gauge; — sagomato, template; (fig.) calibre; una persona di tutt'altro —, someone of quite another calibre. **-are** [A 1 s, A 1] *tr.* to calibrate, to gauge. **-ato** *part. adj.* **-atoio** *m.* calibrating device. **-atura** *f.* (eng.) gauging.

calicanto *m.* (bot.) Carolina allspice, strawberry shrub, *Calycanthus floridus*; — giapponico, Japan allspice, wintersweet, *Chimonanthus praecox*.

ca·lic-e *m.* chalice, goblet; champagne glass; (liturg.) chalice; (fig.) bere l'amaro —, to taste a bitter cup; (bot.) calyx. **-eot·tico** *m.* (zool.; embryol.) optic cup.

calicò *m. indecl.* calico.

calida·rio *m.* (Rom. antiq.) caldarium, hot room in the baths.

†ca·lid-o *adj.* see **caldo**. **†-ità** *f.* see **caldezza**, under **caldo**.

Calid-one *pr.n.f.* (hist. geog.) Calydon, capital of Aetolia. (**-o·nico**, **-o·nio** *adj., n.m.*)

calidra *f.* (orn.) sanderling, *Crocethia alba*.

†ca·life *m.* See **califfo**.

califf-o *m.* Caliph. **-ato** *m.* Caliphate.

ca·lig-a *f.* caliga, Roman soldier's boot. **-a·io**, **-a·ro** *m.* shoemaker, bootmaker.

†calig-are *intr.* to grow dark, to become misty, to become obscured with fog or smoke. **-amento** *m.* obscuring, befogging.

cali·gin-e *f.* mist, fog; thick vapour. **-are** [A 1 s] *intr., impers.* (*aux.* essere) to get dark, to grow foggy. **-oso** *adj.* misty; foggy. **-osità** *f.* mistiness; fogginess.

†caligo *f.* See **caligine**.

caliorna *f.* See **calorna**.

Calipso *pr.n.f.* (myth.) Calypso.

†caliss-a *f.*, **-e** *m.* woollen cloth, serge.

calla¹ *f.* (bot.) arum lily, *Zantedeschia aethiopica*.

†calla² *f.* narrow pass, defile; path; entrance; water-chute.

calla·i-a *f.* field path, footpath; opening in a hedge. **-(u)ola** *f.* small net for catching hares, etc. as they are running from the hounds.

†callare¹ *m.* See **callaia**.

†callare² *vb.* See **calare**.

call-e *m.* (poet.) path; country lane; way; *f.* (Ven.) alley-way, lane. **-ętta** *f.* sluice.

cal·lid-o *adj.* crafty. **-ità** *f.* craftiness.

calli·fu-go *m.* (*pl.* -ghi) corn plaster; pad for corns; remedy for corns.

call-igrafi·a *f.* handwriting; penmanship, calligraphy; (art) careful, over-stylized painting or drawing. **-igra·fico** *adj.* calligraphic; pertaining to handwriting; arte -igrafica, penmanship; (art) careful, over-stylized painting or drawing. (**-igraficamęnte** *adv.*) **-igrafismo** *m.* tendency towards over-stylization in painting or drawing. **-i·grafo** *m.* calligraph.; writing teacher; perito -igrafo, calligraph.

†**callira·fio** *m.* (Pulci) quadruped with striped coat.

callista *m.* See under **callo**[1].

callisteni·a *f.* callisthenics.

Callisto *pr.n.f.* (astron.) Callisto, Ursa Major.

call-o[1] *m.* corn, hard skin; far il — a, to become hardened to; tendon in cooked meat; (vet.) corn, bruise on the sensitive part of the horse's foot. **-ista** *m.* corn-curer, chiropodist. **-osità** *f.* horniness; corn; (fig.) callousness. **-oso** *adj.* having corns; hardened; horny; (fig.) callous.

callo[2] *m.* (numism.) coin of S. Ital. bearing imprint of a horse.

callone *m.* (naut.) passage through a bar.

†**callo·ria** *f.* see **galloria**.

calloso *adj.* and deriv. See under **callo**[1].

callotta *f.* See **calotta**.

Callott-o *pr.n.m.* Callot, French engraver and designer (1592–1635); figura del —, grotesque figure. **-esco** *adj.* (*m.pl.* **-eschi**) after the style of Callot.

callun-a *f.* (bot.) common heath, heather, or ling, *Calluna vulgaris.* **-eto** *m.* heathland.

calm-a *f.* calm, tranquillity; con —, calmly; (of the sea) essere in —, to be dead calm, (fig.) to be at rest; zona delle **-e**, doldrums; (econ.) — negli affari, stagnation. **-are** [A I] *tr.* to calm; to quieten; to soothe; *rfl.* to calm oneself; to grow calm; to abate. **-ante** *part. adj.* calming, soothing; *n.m.* (med.) sedative. †**-eri·a** *f.* (naut.) dead calm.

calmier-e *m.* (econ.) controlled price list; imporre un —, to impose a controlled price list; prezzo di —, controlled price. **-are** [A I] *tr.* to subject to price control. **-ativo** *adj.* relating to price control. **-i·stico** *adj.* price controlling.

calmo[1] *adj.* calm; tranquil, serene.

calmo[2] *m.* (hortic.) graft.

calmuc-co *adj.* (*m.pl.* **-chi**) (ethn.) Kalmuck, relating to a race of W. Mongolia; *n.m.* Kalmuck; coarse cloth; (fig.) rough, barbaric person.

calo *m.* drop, loss, waste; decadence; prendere a —, to hire an article and pay for the part of it which is consumed; (naut.) cast (nets, etc.); loss of cargo through leakage, etc.; †flow of a river.

calocaşia *f.* (bot.) taro, eddo, dasheen, kachehu, *Colocasia antiquorum.*

caloc·chia *f.* handle of a flail or thresher.

calo·faro *m.* (geog.) vortex in the Straits of Messina; †Charybdis.

calo·gero *m.* caloyer, monk in the Greek Church, esp. of the order of St Basil.

†**calogn-a**[1] *f.* calumny; offence. †**-are** *tr.* to calumniate; to offend. †**-oso** *adj.* calumniating; offending.

†**calogna**[2] *f.* See **carogna**.

calomelano *m.* (chem.) calomel, mercurous chloride.

†**calonizzare** *vb.* See **canonizzare**.

†**calon·nia** *f.* and derivs. See **calunnia**.

calor-e *m.* heat; warmth; ardour; fervour; heat-spots, rash; inflammation; in —, on heat (of a bitch). **-etto** *m. dim.* slight fever. **-i·a** *f.* (agric.) green manuring; field so dressed; (phys.) calorie; grande **-ia**, kilogramme calorie; piccola **-ia**, gramme calorie. **-ifera·io** *m.* heating engineer, hot-water engineer. **-i·fero** *m.* central heating apparatus, radiator. **-ificazione** *f.* the production of heat. **-i·fico** *adj.* calorific, heat-producing. **-imetri·a** *f.* (phys.) calorimetry. **-ime·trico** *adj.* (phys.) calorimetric. **-i·metro** *m.* (phys.) calorimeter. (**-osità** *f.*) **-oso** *adj.* heating, throwing out a good heat; (of a person) inclined to suffer from the heat, *or* tending not to feel the cold; (fig.) hot-tempered, heated; warm, cordial; *n.m.* hot-head; warm-hearted person; person who doesn't feel the cold. **-osamente** *adv.* heatedly; warm-heartedly.

calorna *f.* (naut.) strong tackle, double pulley-block; purchase.

†**caloro** *m.* See **calogero**.

caloroso *adj.* See under **calore**.

calo·scia *f.* galosh, over-shoe.

†**calo·scio** *adj.* soft; feeble, weak.

calosoma *m.* (ent.) a kind of carabid beetle.

calo·tipo *m.* (typ.) calotype, Talbotype.

calotta *f.* upper spherical section of any object; crown of a hat; (geog.) la — d'un monte, the rounded summit of a mountain; la — polare, the ice cap at the Poles; (watchm.) — di protezione, protecting cap; (eccl.) skull-cap; (geom.) segment; (anat.) top of the skull; (archit.) spherical or spheroidal vault; (mech.) depression, indentation, calotte; (eng.) cap, cover; (motor.) — del distributore, distributor cap.

calotterice *f.* (ent.) damsel fly, *Calopteryx* spp.

calpacco *m.* calpac, Greek fez.

calpest-are [A I c] *tr.* to trample upon; to tread underfoot; to stand on, to put one's foot on; (fig.) to ride roughshod over; to stamp on. **-amento** *m.* trampling; tread; stamping. **-ata** *f.* trampling; tread; stamping. **-ato** *part. adj.* trampled upon; (fig.) crushed; downtrodden. (**-atore** *m.* **-atrice** *f.*) **-atura** *f.* trampling; (fig.) oppression. **-io** *m.* noise of trampling. **-o** *apocop. part. adj.* (poet.) downtrodden.

†**calpicciare**, †**calpitare** *vb.* See **calpestare**.

calta *f.* (bot.) marigold, *Calendula;* — palustre, kingcup, marsh marigold, *Caltha palustris.*

†**caltela** *f.* See **cautela**.

calter-ire [D 2] *tr.* to scratch, to injure, to damage. **-ito** *part. adj.* crushed (e.g. olives); hardened; †shrewd. **-itura** *f.* damage.

calto[1] *m.* gully, ravine.

†**calto**[2] *m.* chest of drawers, chest.

†**caluco** *adj.* wretched, miserable.

calug·gine, **calu·gine** *f.* down; fine hairs.

calum-are [A I] *tr.* (naut.) to pay out (a cable, a rope); *rfl.* to lower oneself, to let oneself down. **-o** *m.* (naut.) that part of a rope or cable which is paid out; the length of the cable by which a ship rides to an anchor.

calun·ni-a *f.* calumny, slander. **-a·bile** *adj.* open to slander; open to misrepresentation. **-amento** *m.* slandering. **-are** [A 4] *tr.* to slander. (**-atore** *m.* **-atrice** *f.*) **-oso** *adj.* slanderous, calumnious; parole di lodi che sono **-ose**, damning with faint praise; (leg.) denunzia **-osa**, defamatory accusation (C.C.). (**-osamente** *adv.*)

calura *f.* (poet.) heat, warmth.

calutrone *m.* (atom. phys.) calutron.

†**calvare** *tr.* to make bald.

†**calva·ria** *f.* skull.

calva·rio *m.* Calvary; (eccl.) stazioni del —, (outdoor) stations of the Cross; (fig.) cross; è stato per me un — terribile, it was a terrible cross for me to bear.

calvell-o *m.*, **-a** *f.* beardless wheat.

calvezza *f.* See under **calvo**.

calvin-iano *adj.* pertaining to Calvin; *n.m.* see **calvinista**. **-işmo** *m.* Calvinism. **-ista** *m.*, *f.* Calvinist; (joc.) baldpate (cf. **calvo**). **-i·stico** *adj.* Calvinistic. **-izzare** [A I] *intr.* (*aux.* avere) to Calvinize; *tr.* to imbue with Calvinism.

calv-o *adj.* bald, hairless; (fig.) bleak, bare. **-ezza** *f.* baldness. **-i·zie** *f. indecl.* baldness. †**-i·zio** *m.* baldness.

calypso *m. indecl.* calypso dance; calypso song.

calz-a *f.* sock; stocking; hose; infilarsi una —, to pull on a sock; mettersi le **-e**, to put on one's stockings; (colloq.) farsi tirar le **-e**, to keep on refusing; tirar su le **-e** a, to worm a secret out of; tirar le **-e**, to 'peg out'; la — della Befana, stocking containing toys for children at Epiphany (equiv. to Eng. Christmas stocking); mettere la —, to hang up one's stocking; knitting; darning; far la —, to knit; to darn; cloth funnel for filtering wine, filter-bag; — del lume, lamp-wick; (electr.) braiding; piece of material tied to a bird's leg as a mark; †*pl.* trousers. †**-abraca** *f.* breeches and hose in one. **-ai(u)olo** *m.* hosier. **-etta** *f. dim.* sock; man's sock; (Tusc.) fine quality silk stocking. **-etta·io** *m.* vendor of stockings; stocking maker; (text.) knitter. **-ettone** *m.* thick woollen sock worn by skiers and mountaineers.

calz-are[1] [A I] *tr.* to wear (shoes, socks); to put on (shoes, socks, gloves); to shoe; to provide shoes for; to fit well; to fit closely; questo cappello non mi **-a** bene, this hat is too big for my head; — il coturno, to write tragedy; — il socco, to write comedy; to steady with a block or wedge (e.g. the legs of a piece of furniture); to scotch (a wheel, etc.); *intr.* (*aux.* avere) to be shod; to go shod; to be apt, to be appropriate; to fit, to fall pat; *rfl.* to go shod. †**-amento** *m.* footwear; hose; shoes and stockings. **-ante** *adj.* well-fitting; suitable; un paragone **-ante**, an apt comparison. **-ato** *part. adj.* shod; asino **-ato** e vestito, an ignorant fool; (herald.) chaussé. **-atura** *f.* footwear. **-aturifi·cio** *m.* shoe factory, boot and shoe factory.

calzar-e[2] *m.* boot; shoe; *pl.* footwear; (fig.) coi **-i** di piombo, with great caution and circumspection. **-etto** *m.* (herald.) legging, gaiter.

calzascarpe *m. indecl.* shoehorn.

calzastivali *m. indecl.* riding-boot jacks.

calzatoi-a *f.* wedge, scotch; (eng.; motor.) chock, chuck. **-o** *m.* shoehorn.

calzerotto *m.* short sock; legging, gaiter; foot pad (e.g. for a tripod).

calzętt·a *f.*, **-a·io** *m.*, **-ǫne** *m.* See under **calza**.

calzino *m.* (Tusc.) sock; man's sock; (colloq.) tirare il —, to 'peg out'.

calzo *m.* style of shoemaking; wedge, scotch.

calzol·a·io *m.*, **-a·ia** *f.* shoemaker; cobbler, shoe-repairer; keeper of a shoeshop. †**-aro** *m.* see **calzolaio**. **-eri·a** *f.* shoeshop.

calzǫne *m.* (cul.) Neapolitan dish resembling 'pizza'.

calzǫn-i *m.pl.* trousers; — corti, breeches; — a coscia, tights; — a campana, bell-bottom trousers; portare i —, to wear the trousers, to be the boss; seminare i —, to have one's trousers slipping down; *sing.* trouser-leg. **-cini** *m.pl.* knickers, knicker-bockers, shorts; pants. **-ętti** *m.pl.* pants.

calzuolo *m.* wedge, support, scotch; leather socket for carrying the butt of a flagstaff in procession; leather carrier or support for a carbine.

cama·glio *m.* (hist.) close-meshed mail armour round the neck; balaclava helmet.

†**cama·ido** *m.* See **camaglio**.

†**cama-ino**, †**-iuolo** *m.* cameo.

Camal·dol-i *pr.n.m.* (geog.) Camaldoli, in the Apennines near Arezzo; Camaldoli, near Naples; a district in Florence; di —, of low origin, plebeian. **-are** [A I S] *intr.* (*aux.* avere) to talk (the Italian equivalent of) Billingsgate. **-e(n)se** *adj.* pertaining to Camaldoli; belonging to the monastic order founded by St Romualdo of Camaldoli; Camaldolensian.

camaleǫne *m.* (bot.) star thistle, *Carlina acaulis*.

camaleǫnt-e *m.* (zool.) chameleon; (fig.) changeable, fickle person; turncoat; (chem.) mineral chameleon, green manganate of potash. **-eo** *adj.* chameleon-like; fickle. **-ęssa** *f.* (fig.) changeable, untrustworthy woman.

camall-are [A I] *tr.* (Lucca, Genoa) to hump (heavy loads), to carry on one's back. **-o** *m.* porter.

†**camangiare** *m.* pot herb; vegetables; salad; greens; food other than bread.

camarilla *f.* clique, camarilla.

camarlinga *f.* (eccl.) procuratrix (in a convent); †lady in waiting, maid of honour.

camarlingheri·a *f.* treasury.

camarling-o *m.* bursar, public treasurer; (eccl.) cardinale —, see **camerlengo**. **-ato** *m.* bursarship, treasurership. †**-one** *m.* see **camarlingo**. †**-ona** *f.* tall, powerful woman.

camarra *f.* martingale.

†**camat-o** *m.* carpet-beater; pole, rod. **-are** [A I] *tr.* to beat (carpets).

camatta *f.* See **casamatta**.

camauro *m.* (eccl.) camauro.

cambellotto *m.* See **cammellotto**, under **cammello**.

cambiadischi *m. indecl.* See under **cambiare**.

cambiale *f.* (comm.) bill of exchange; promissory note; — tratta, draft, bill of exchange; — a vista, bill payable at sight; avallare una —, to back a bill; girare una —, to indorse a bill; — pagabile all'estero, foreign bill; — pagabile all'interno, inland bill; — pagabile su piazza, local bill; cambiali in portafoglio, bills on hand; — a breve scadenza, short-term bill; — in sofferenza, unpaid bill; — di favore, kite.

cambi-are [A 4] *tr.* to change; to alter; to exchange; — consiglio, — opinione, to change one's mind; — un bambino, to change a baby's napkin, to change a baby; cambiar casa, to move house; cambiar aria, to go away for a change of air; cambiar vita, to mend one's ways, to turn over a new leaf; — aspetto, to take on a different appearance, to begin to look different; — le carte in tavola, to shift one's ground; (motor.) — marcia, to change gear; (naut.) — la barra, to put the helm over; — le scotte, to change tacks; — i fiocchi, to let draw on a new tack; — la rotta, to alter course; (comm., finan.) to change, to get change for; — un biglietto da mille, to change a thousand lire note; to exchange; to barter; *abs.* (motor.) to change gear; *intr.* (*aux.* essere) to change, to alter, to suffer change, to undergo alteration; tutto -a, everything is subject to change; niente è -ato, nothing has changed; il tempo accenna a —, the weather looks like changing; (*aux.* avere, *prep.* di) to change; ho -ato di parere, I have changed my mind, I have altered my opinion; voglio — di camera, I'd like to change my room, I'd like another room; *rfl.* (*acc.* of *prn.*) to change, to undergo change, to alter; ti sei molto -ato, you've changed a lot; to change one's clothes; vado a -armi, I'll just go and change; (*dat.* of *prn.*) -arsi le scarpe, to change one's shoes,

to put on another pair of shoes; -arsi il vestito, to change one's clothes; *recip. rfl.* to exchange with one another; -arsi l'indirizzo, to exchange addresses. **-a·bile** *adj.* changeable; exchangeable. **-adischi** *m. indecl.* record-changer. **-amęnto** *m.* changing, altering; change, alteration; (naut.) -amento di vire, -amento di rotta, going about, altering of course. **-ato** *part. adj.* changed, altered; different; exchanged; (mus.) nota -ata, changing note. †**-atore** *m.* money-changer. **-atura** *f.* (equit.) cavalcare a -atura, to change from one horse to another while riding; andare a -atura, to change horses at every posting-place; †change, changing. **-avalute** *m. indecl.* bureau de change; money-changer.

cam·bi-o *m.* change, exchange; in — di, instead of; (comm.; finan.) exchange of banknotes, coins or different currencies; corso del —, rate of exchange; agente di —, stockbroker, currency-broker; lettera di —, bill of exchange; seconda di —, duplicate of a lost bill of exchange, second of exchange; al tasso corrente del —, at the current rate of exchange; — marittimo, bottomry; contratto di prestito a — marittimo, bottomry bill; (hist.) Arte del Cambio, Bankers' Guild in medieval Florence; (naut.) — della marea, change of the tide; (eng.) gears; selettore del —, gearshift; — sincronizzato, synchromesh gears; scatola —, gearbox; senza —, single-gear; — della guardia, changing of the guard. **-a·rio** *adj.* (comm.) relating to exchange; vaglia -ario, promissory note; effetto -ario, bill of exchange; operazione -aria, exchange operation.

†**cambista** *m.* money-changer.

Cambo·gia *pr.n.f.* (geog.) Cambodia.

cambrętta *f.* (eng.; techn.) staple.

cambrì, cambri·c *m. indecl.* cambric; (med.) benda di —, elastic bandage.

cambr-iano, -ico *adj.* (geol.) Cambrian.

cambriglięne *m.* (shoem.) stiffener.

cambuş-a *f.* (naut.) victualling store. **-iere** *m.* (naut.) storekeeper on board ship under orders of the 'commesso ai viveri'.

came-ceparisso *m.* (bot.) lavender cotton, *Santolina chamaecyparissus*. **-ce·raso** *m.* (bot.) pink bush-honeysuckle, *Lonicera tatarica*. **-pi·zio** *m.* ground pine, *Ajuga chamaepitys*.

Camciatca *pr.n.f.* (geog.) Kamchatka.

came·lia *f.* (bot.) camellia, *Camellia japonica*.

camello *m.* See **cammello**.

camelopardo *m.* (zool.) giraffe (cf. Eng. †camelopard).

camena *f.* muse.

camepi·zio *m.* (bot.). See under **cameceraso**.

ca·mer-a *f.* bedroom; fare la —, to do the bedroom, to clean the bedroom; veste da —, dressing-gown; room, chamber; musica da —, chamber music; sonata da —, chamber sonata; — ardente, *chapelle ardente*, highly lit room where a body lies in state; debating chamber; legislative body; — alta, Upper House; — bassa, Lower House; — dei Deputati, Chamber of Deputies; fare un discorso alla —, to make a speech in the House; — elettiva, elective assembly; — vitalizia, parliament composed of life members; — di commercio, chamber of commerce; — di consiglio, judges' retiring-room or chambers, court's council chamber, court sitting in its council chamber; — del lavoro, trades union council; — di compensazione, Clearing House; — di custodia, safe vault; (techn.) chamber, space; — d'aria, air space, inner tube (of a tyre), (archit.) air cavity; (motor.) — di combustione, — di scoppio, combustion chamber; (eng.) firebox (of a boiler); explosion chamber (gun); — fotografica, camera; — oscura, *camera obscura*, (photog.) dark-room; camera (film, television); (theatr.) rivista da —, intimate revue; (eccl.) — apostolica, Apostolic Camera; chierico di —, clerk of the Apostolic Camera; (naut.) — del consiglio, Admiral's cabin; — di manovra, control room. **-ale** *adj.* relating to the Exchequer, belonging to the public treasury; imposta -ale, tax paid by members of the Chamber of Commerce; anno -ale, financial year. **-a·rio** *m.* gentleman of the bedchamber. **-ata** *f.* dormitory; 'year', 'term' of schoolboys; sharing quarters; †company; (mus. hist.) la Camerata dei Bardi, the Florentine Camerata, group of musicians and men of letters who, at the end of the sixteenth century, discussed the theory of the new music at the house of Count Bardi; *m.* (*pl.* -ati) comrade, friend, pal; un buon -ata, a good friend; (hist.) fellow Fascist (see also **compagno**). **-atęsco** *adj.* (*m.pl.* -atęschi) comradely. **-atescamęnte** *adv.* in a comradely manner. **-atişmo** *m.* comradeship. **-azzo** *m.* (Tusc. hist.) gentleman of the bedchamber. **-ella** *f. dim.* of

camer-a (*cont.*)

  camera; alcove; bed-curtains; (agric.) pod; cell of a honeycomb. **-ẹtta** *f. dim.* of **camera**; privy, toilet. **-iera** *f.* lady's maid; waitress; chambermaid; parlourmaid; housemaid; maidservant; (naut.) stewardess. **-iere** *m.* manservant; waiter; (naut.) steward; (eccl.) **-iere segreto**, Privy Chamberlain. **-ino** *m.* (theatr.) dressing-room; (theatr.) box office; manager's office; (naut.) cabin; stateroom; lavatory. **-ista** *f.* lady-in-waiting; (hist.) chambermaid. **-i·stico** *adj.* (mus.) pertaining to chamber music. **-otto** *m.* (naut.) cabin boy.

camerlengo *m.* (eccl.) **cardinale —**, Cardinal-Camerlengo. See also **camarlingo**.

camerlingo *m.* See **camarlingo**.

ca·mice *m.* dentist's or surgeon's white coat; (liturg.) alb.

cami·ci-a *f.* (*pl.* **cami·cie**) shirt; **in maniche di —**, in shirtsleeves; **rimboccarsi la —**, to roll up one's sleeves; (fig.) **rimetterci la —**, to lose one's last farthing; **rimanere in —**, to remain poor; **aver la — sudicia**, to feel guilty; **la — non gli tocca il fianco**, he is beside himself with joy; (vulg.) **essere culo e —**, to be thick as thieves; blouse; chemise; folder, file cover; **— di forza**, strait-jacket; (hist.) **camicie rosse**, redshirts, Garibaldini; **camicie nere**, blackshirts, Fascists; **camicie brune**, brownshirts, Nazis; (sculp.) investment; (mil.) brick outer casing of earthworks; (tech.) casing, outer casing; (eng.) jacket; **— di raffreddamento**, cooling jacket; (motor.) **— smontabile**, cylinder liner; (cul.) **uovo in —**, poached egg. **-a·io** *m. f.* shirtmaker. **-a·ia** *f.* violent sweat, making a change of shirt necessary; (mil. hist.) night attack, when a white shirt was worn over the armour so that the soldiers were visible to each other. **-ẹtta** *f. dim.* of **camicia**; blouse. **-(u)ola** *f.* vest; flannel waistcoat. **-ola·io** *m.* maker of flannel waistcoats. **-otto** *m.* workman's blouse; smock; porter's blouse.

camicino *m.* false shirt-front, dicky; lining (of a furnace).

Camilla *pr.n.f.* Camilla.

†**caminare** *vb.* and derivs. See **camminare**.

†**caminata** *f.* room heated by a stove.

camin-o *m.* fireplace; stove; chimney; funnel; (mount.) funnel-shaped gap between rocks. **-ẹtto** *m. dim.* fireplace; small stove for heating a room; mantelpiece, mantelshelf; (cards) 'chemin de fer'; (bldg.) fireplace. **-iera** *f.* fireguard; wood-bunker (for firewood); mantelpiece mirror.

ca·mio *m.* (Tusc.). See **camion**.

ca·mion, camiọn *m. indecl.* lorry, truck, van; lorry-load; **un — di carbone**, a load of coal. **-a·bile** *adj.* (of a road) suitable for lorries. **-ale** *adj.* pertaining to a lorry; *n.f.* name of an autostrada from Genoa to the Po valley. **-cino** *m. dim.* small van; light truck. **-ista** *m.* lorry driver, vanman.

camisac·cio *m.* sailor's blouse.

cam-i·ta *m., f.* Hamite. **-i·tico** *adj.* Hamitic.

camma *f.* (eng.) cam; **albero a camme**, camshaft.

cammell-o *m.* (zool.) camel; **pelo di —**, camel-hair; **color —**, buff, fawn; (eng.) camel. **-a** *f.* (zool.) she-camel. **-a·rio** *m.* camel driver. **-ato** *adj.* transported by camel. **-ẹtto** *m. dim.* of **cammello**; (mil. hist.) small cannon. **-iere** *m.* camel driver. **-ino** *adj.* camel-like; pertaining to camels. **-otto** *m.* camlet.

camm-e·o *m.* cameo. **-eista** *m.* cutter of cameos; connoisseur in cameos.

cammin-are [A I] *intr.* (*aux.* avere) to walk; to proceed; **— al sicuro**, to go carefully; **il treno -a forte**, the train is going fast; **la barca -a piano**, the boat is moving slowly; **la faccenda -a**, the affair is progressing; **lasciate che la cosa -i con i suoi piedi**, let the thing go its own sweet way; **— per un'età**, to be getting on for a certain age; **-a per i quaranta**, he's getting on for forty. **-a·bile** *adj.* passable; **la strada non è -abile**, the road isn't passable. **-amẹnto** *m.* walking, walk; (mil.) communication trench. **-ante** *part. adj.* walking; moving; *n.m.* traveller; *f.* (Neap.) see **pappina**. **-ata** *f.* walk, stroll; walk, gait; road. **-ato** *part. adj.* trodden. **-atura** *f.* gait.

cammino[1] *m.* journey; walk; stretch of road; way; **mettersi in —**, to set out; **cammin facendo**, while walking along; (fig.) course; path; **far molto —**, to make great progress; **tenere il — diritto verso una meta**, to keep on towards a goal; (atom. phys.) **— medio libero**, mean free-path; **nel mezzo del —**, half-way through life.

†**cammino**[2] *m.* See **camino**.

†**cammuccà** *m.* a kind of silk damask cloth, introduced into the West in the thirteenth century.

†**camo**[1] *m.* muzzle; bit; restraint, check.

†**camo**[2] *m.* cloth from Caen.

†**camoiardo** *m.* coarse haircloth.

camolino *adj.* (of rice) refined and polished.

camomill-a *f.* (bot.) **— comune**, wild camomile, *Matricaria chamomilla*; **— bastarda**, **— senza odore**, corn camomile, *Anthemis arvensis*; **— mezzana**, **— fetida**, stinking May weed, *Anthemis cotula*; **— nobile**, **—romana**, **— di Boemia**, camomile, *Anthemis nobilis*; **decotto di —**, camomile tea. **-ino** *adj.* pertaining to camomile.

†**camora** *f.* woman's gown.

camorr-a *f.* (hist. S. Ital.) rogues' secret society; tribute exacted by members of the society; (fig.) graft, palm-greasing, hush-money; (joc.) 'racket', swindle; (slang) **far —**, to kick up a disturbance (in school). **-ista** *m.* member of the 'camorra'; intriguer; racketeer; (slang) turbulent, undisciplined schoolboy. **(-i·stico** *adj.*)

camorro *m.* (Tusc.) person in failing health; troublesome person; worn-out object.

camoscino *adj.* made of chamois leather; soft, pliant, velvety.

camo·sci-o *m.* (zool.) chamois; chamois leather, shammy leather, oil-tanned leather, washleather; †*adj.* snub (nosed). **-are** [A 3] *tr.* to chamois, to oil-tan. (**-ato** *part. adj.*) **-atura** *f.* shammying, oil tanning, oil tannage.

camozza *f.* chamois doe; †slut (cf. **camoscio**).

campagn-a *f.* country, open country; **in —**, in the country; countryside; estate; **gente di —**, country people; period spent in the country; holidays, vacation; **buttarsi alla —**, to turn brigand; (naut.) period of voyage away from the home port; cruise; (mil.) campaign; **entrare in —**, to enter the war; **forno da —**, field oven; **artiglieria da —**, field artillery; (fig.) campaign; advocacy; plan of attack; **— di epurazioni**, political purge; (herald.) terrace in base; **-incalzata**, base embelif, per bend abased. **-(u)olo** *adj.* pertaining to the country; countrified; rural, rustic; (zool.) **topo -uolo**, field-vole, *Microtus agrestis*; *n.m.* countryman; rustic, peasant, yokel; (zool.) **-uolo della neve**, *Arvicola nivalis*.

camp-a·io *m.* country policeman; watchman. **-ai(u)olo** *adj.* pertaining to the fields. **-aro** *m.* See **campaio**.

campale *adj.* (mil.) in the field; **battaglia —**, decisive battle; **artiglieria —**, field artillery; **una giornata —**, a field day; (fig.) a heavy day, a crucial day's work; **in tenuta —**, in battledress and fully armed, (joc.) armed to the teeth.

campamẹnto *m.* See under **campare**.

campan-a *f.* bell; **a —**, bell-shaped (see also biol. and math. use); church bell; **dar nelle -e**, to start ringing the bells; (provb.) **non entra a messa la — e ognun ci chiama**, bells call others to church but go not themselves; (eccl.) **legare le -e**, to cease using bells (on Maundy Thursday); **sciogliere le -e, to ring them again** (on Holy Saturday); (mus.) bell (of wind instrument); **— in aria**, with bell up; (fig.) **sentire tutt'e due le -e**, **sentire l'altra —**, to hear both sides of the question; **fare —**, to cup the hand to the ear; **sordo come una —**, deaf as a post; **essere di -e grosse**, to be hard of hearing; any bell-shaped object; bell-shaped glass cover; **tenere sotto una — di vetro**, to mollycoddle; **— subacquea**, diving bell; cog wheel of a reel; variety of pear; (chem.) retort; (naut.) **— dell'argano**, drum of a capstan; (biol.; math.) **curva a —**, normal (gaussian) curve; (aeron.) whip stall; (techn.) gas-holder; (hydraul.) **— d'aria**, air-chamber. **-ac·cio** *m.* cow bell, sheep bell; earthenware bell for calling bees. **-a·io** *m.* bell ringer; bell founder. **-a·rio** *adj.* relating to bell founding; pertaining to bells; **torre -aria**, bell tower. **-aro** *m.* see **campanaio**. **-atura** *f.* (aeron.) rake (of propeller). **-ẹtto** *m.* cattle bell. **-ifọrme** *adj.* (bot.) bell-shaped. **-ino** *adj.* ringing; **marmo -ino**, marble from Pietrasanta in Tuscany which rings when worked. **-o** *m.* cow bell. †**-ò** *m.* festive ringing of bells.

campanell-a *f. dim.* of **campana**; (bot.) peach-leaved bellflower, *Campanula persicifolia*; *pl.* various bell-shaped flowers of the convolvulus family; ring (in a bull's nose); curtain ring; snaffle ring; gold earring; ring-shaped door knocker; (masonry) lewis; *pl.* (archit.) guttae. **-ina** *f.* (bot.) Spring snowflake, *Leucojum vernum*; a flower with small bells, e.g. lily-of-the-valley.

campanell-o *m.* door bell; harness bell; sleigh bell; electric bell; **star sotto il — di**, to be under the orders of; (vet.) a kind of bit; (butch.) a cut from the rump; *pl.* drops thrown up by heavy rain, 'little soldiers'.

campanil-e *m.* bell tower, campanile; **amor di —**, love of one's native town or village; **questioni di —**, matters concerning one's

campanil·e (*cont.*)
native district; sharp tower-like peak, esp. in the Dolomites. **-iṣmo** *m.* excessive and boastful love of one's native town or village; parochialism. **-ista** *m.* person inordinately proud of and concerned with his native town or village. (**-i·stico** *adj.*)

campano[1] *m.* See under **campana**.

campano[2] *adj.* of Campania; also *n.m.*

†**campanò** *m.* See under **campana**.

campa·nul-a *f.* (bot.) Canterbury bell; peach-leaved bellflower; — grande, Canterbury bell, *Campanula medium*; -e turchine selvatiche, harebell, bluebell (of Scotland), *C. rotundifolia*. **-ato** *adj.* bell-shaped.

camp-are [A I] *intr.* (*aux.* essere, avere) to get one's living; to live; to manage, to jog along; si -a, we're managing; tirare a —, to make a living as best one can; — d'aria, to live on air; — delle braccia, to live by the sweat of one's brow; — d'elemosina, to live on charity; -a ore, to live from hand to mouth; *tr.* to escape, to escape from; to save from danger; to maintain, to support, provide for; — la vita, to make a livelihood; (sculp.) to bring into relief, to set off; (paint.) to lay on (a flat wash or foundation colour). **-amento** *m.* livelihood, living; see †**accampamento**. **-ata** *f.* (archit.) abutment; (aeron.) wing panel; (electr.) length of cable between two pylons. **-ato** *part. adj.* safe from danger; alive and kicking; (sculp.) -ato in aria, deep-cut with perforations (of stone ornament); (fig.) ragioni -ate in aria, unfounded reasons; ragionamento -ato in aria, argument without foundation. **-ereccio** *adj.* prosperous, flourishing. **-erellare** [A I] *intr.* (*aux.* avere) to jog along, to manage. **-icchiare** [A 4], **-ucchiare** [A 4] *intr.* (*aux.* essere) to get along as best one can.

campeggi-are [A 3 c] *intr.* (*aux.* avere) to camp, to encamp, to be encamped; (fig.) to stand out (against a background); to be prominent; to spread oneself (in talking, etc.); *tr.* (mil.) to deploy; (paint.) — una pittura, to form the background (of a picture). **-amento** *m.* encampment; camping; deployment. **-ante** *m.*, *f.* camper. **-ato** *part. adj.* camped; deployed; in relief; (paint.) standing out against a background; *n.m.* (paint.) foundation colour; background.

campeggio[1] *m.* camping, camp; fare un —, to camp.

campeggio[2] *m.* (bot.) campeachy tree, logwood tree, *Haematoxylon campechianum*; (dye.) logwood, campeachy wood; haematin.

campereccio[1] *adj.* See **campestre**; †(of an animal) that grazes, grazing.

campereccio[2] *adj.* thriving, flourishing (cf. **campare**).

camp-estre *adj.*, **-ic·cio** *adj.* See under **campo**.

campicello *m. dim.* See under **campo**.

Campido·glio *pr.n.m.* (Rom. hist.) Capitol; the Capitoline Hill; (fig.) salire il —, to triumph, to come out top.

campiello *m. dim.* See under **campo**.

campi·geno *m.* physical training instructor.

campigiana *f.* (orn.) pintail; *Anas acuta*; large-sized floor-tile.

campignuolo *m.* (bot.) lycoperdon nut, a kind of truffle.

†**campi·o** *adj.* rustic, field.

campion-e *m.* (*f.* **-eṣsa**) champion; record-holder; — della libertà, champion of liberty; farsi — di, to champion; — da frode, unfair fighter; standard, norm; sample; specimen; pattern; (comm.) — di controllo, standard weight or measure for testing those of traders; — estratto in monte, sample from bulk, average sample; — senza valore, sample sent by post; trattare su —, to deal by sample; (leg.) day-book; register of taxpayers; record of costs in Clerk of the Court's office. **-ag·gio** *m.* (comm.) sampling. **-are** [A I c] *tr.* to sample; to produce as a sample; *tr.* (comm.) -are il carico, to sample the cargo. **-a·rio** *m.* collection of samples; pattern book; room where samples are kept; *adj.* referring to samples, sample; fiera -aria, sample fair, exhibition. **-ato** *m.* championship. **-atura** *f.* (comm.) sampling. **-cino** *m.* cutting, pattern.

campione-tipo *m.* (comm.) standard; — per contratti, futures standard.

campire[1] [D 2] *intr.* (*aux.* avere) (paint.) to paint the background.

†**campire**[2] *vb.* See **scampare**.

camp-o[1] *m.*:
   1. FIELD; — di grano, cornfield; — a patate, potato field; arare il —, to plough the field; i -i, the fields, the country, the countryside; la vita dei -i, country life, rural existence; fiori di —, wild flowers; torniamo ai -i! back to the land!; area of little less than an acre (Padua 38·63 ares, Treviso 54·4 ares); — aurifero, gold-

field; (geog.) -i carreggiati, clints, grykes. **2.** (MIL.) field; — di battaglia, battlefield; — di mine, minefield; a —, in the field; sul —, in the field, (fig.) on the spot; scendere in —, entrare in —, to enter the field (also fig.); tenere il —, to stand one's ground, to hold forth; cedere il —, to give way; mettere in —, to put into the field; — di Marte, place d'armes, parade ground, drill ground; (mil. hist.) — franco, place where fighting could be undertaken without fear of penalty, (fig.) free field; camp; mettere il —, to pitch camp; levare il —, to strike camp; passare al — avversario, to go over to the enemy's camp; cucina da —, field kitchen. **3.** GROUND; (sport) playing field; — da tennis, tennis court; — a terra battuta, hard court; — da golfo, golf course; (football) pitch; metà —, half-way line; — amico, home ground; il fattore — è importante in una partita di calcio, whether the match is played at home or away is an important factor; (horse racing) — pesante, heavy going; (naut.) — di regata, venue of rowing or sailing regatta; (aeron.) — d'aviazione, airfield; — di fortuna, emergency landing ground. **4.** SPHERE, range, field; — d'interesse, sphere of interest; — d'azione, sphere of action; — visivo, field of vision; — di visibilità, range of visibility; — magnetico, magnetic field; — di tiro, field of fire; (cinem.; telev.) fuori —, off screen; — medio, medium shot; — lungo, long shot; (opt.) — angolare, field of view; (techn.) — di misura, measuring range; (radio) — d'onda, waveband; (art) background; field (of a medal); (herald.) field. **5.** ROOM, space, occasion, opportunity; prendere — a, to find occasion to; dare — a, to give the opportunity to; datemi — di esaminare bene la cosa, give me leave to look into the matter carefully; nelle scienze c'è — per tutti, in the sciences there are opportunities for everybody. **6.** FIG. USES: essere in —, to be in question; to be actively engaged; mettere in —, portare in —, to put forward, to advance; perdere —, to lose ground; lasciare a uno correre il —, to let a person have a free hand; mettere tutto il — a rumore, to cause a commotion. **-erello** *m.* (agric.) smallholding. **-estre** *adj.* rural; wild; vita -estre, country life; †see **campale**. (**-estreṃente** *adv.*) **-ṭetto** *m. dim.* (sport) fare -etto, to ski on nursery slopes. **-ic·cio** *m.* coppice. **-icello** *m. dim.* little field; little bit of property. **-iere** *m.* field-watcher. **-orella** *adv. phr.* (Milan) andare in -orella, to go and make love in the fields.

camp-o[2] *m.* square, piazza; — di Siena, the main square in Siena. **-iello** *m.* (Ven.) small public square.

camposanto *m.* (*pl.* **camposanti**) cemetery, graveyard, churchyard.

camsi·n *m. indecl.* (naut.) Arabic Khamsin, hot wind, scirocco.

camuff-are [A I] *tr.* to muffle up; to disguise; to deceive; to conceal; *intr.* (*aux.* avere) to pretend; to set out to deceive; *rfl.* to muffle oneself up; to disguise oneself. **-amento** *m.* muffling; disguising; concealing. **-ato** *part. adj.* disguised, in disguise; pretended; *n.m.* impostor. **-atura** *f.* disguise; concealment. †**-azione** *f.* deception; disguise. †**-o** thief; impostor.

camuṣo *adj.* snub-nosed; *n.m.* snub-nosed person.

†**camuto** *m.* silk cloth.

Can[1] *pr.n.m.* Khan.

Can[2] *m.* See **cane**.

Can[3] *pr.n.m.* abbrev. for Can Grande della Scala.

Canad-à *pr.n.m.* (geog.) Canada; nel —, in Canada. **-eṣe** *adj.*, *n.m.*, *f.* Canadian.

cana·gli-a *f.* (*pl.* **-e**) rabble; scoundrel; (joc.) rascal. **-ata** *f.* blackguardly act. **-esco** *adj.* (*m.pl.* **-eschi**) blackguardly; belonging to the rabble; coarse. **-ume** *m.* mob, rabble.

cana·i-o *m.* dog-keeper, dog-breeder, kennelman; (Tusc.) hullabaloo; hurly-burly. **-(u)ola** *f.*, **-(u)olo** *m.* variety of black grape.

canal-e *m.* canal; Canal Grande, Grand Canal (in Venice); (archit.) ponte —, culvert, etc., built under a river or canal; channel; — di gronda, gutter; — di chiusa, sluice; (foundry) — di colata, runner, gate; (hydraul. eng.) — di scarico, tailbrace; groove; gulley, conduit; (anat.) canal, passage; (oceanog.) gully, passage; (surg.) leg-splint; (techn.) channel; (telev.) channel; (cinem.) — della pellicola, film track; (bookb.) — del libro, fore-edge; (fig.) -i gerarchici, official channels; mettere in —, to set in motion. †**-are** *vb.* (archit.) see **scanalare**. †**-atura** *f.* (archit.) see **scanalatura**. **-azzo** *m.* (Ven.) Grand Canal. **-ṭetta** *f.* (electr.) raceway. **-ṭetto** *m.* (archit.) hollow moulding. **-ino** *m. dim.* small mountain gorge. **-one** *m. augm.* steep mountain gorge.

canalizz-are [A I] *tr.* to canalize. (**-a·bile** *adj.*) **-ato** *part. adj.* canalized. **-azione** *f.* canalizing; (hydraul.) canalization; (electr.; bldg.) duct, raceway; (civ. eng.) sewers.

cana·ola f. (techn.) turnbuckle.

ca·nap-a f. hemp; hempen fibre; hempen twine; fibra di — sciolta, oakum; (bot.) hemp, *Cannabis sativa*; — acquatica, hemp agrimony, *Eupatorium cannabinum*; (text.) — di Bombay, Ambaree fibre; — bruna di Bengala, sunn, Indian hemp. **-ac·cia** f. (bot.) mugwort, *Artemisia vulgaris*. **-a·ia** f. hemp field; woman hemp worker; (fig.) tangle. **-a·io** m. hemp worker; hemp field; (naut.) cordage room. **-ella**, **-etta** f. a fine variety of hemp; hempen cloth. **-etto** m. hempen string. **-ifi·cio** m. hemp mill. **-ino** adj. hempen; n.m. hemp or flax comber; (joc.) white-haired person; pl. (tailor.) facing. **-uc·cia** f. hemp seed.

canapè m. indecl. sofa.

canaperino m. dim. of **canapè**; footstool.

canap-i·glia f. (orn.) gadwall, *Anas strepera*. **-ina** f. (poet.) see **canapino**. **-ino** m. (orn.) melodious warbler, *Hippolais polyglotta*; **-ino maggiore**, icterine warbler, *H. icterina*.

ca·nap-o m. hemp rope; cable-laid rope; (hist.) rope formerly used to stop the horses in the old riderless races down the Corso at Rome; (fig.) saltare il —, to overstep the bounds; (naut.) hawser. **-one** m. augm. rope cable; old man with flowing white hair; nickname of Leopold II, Grand-Duke of Tuscany.

canapule[1] m. hemp stalk stripped of bark.

†canapule[2] m. stiletto.

canaresi adj.f.pl. (geog.) Isole Canaresi, Canary Islands; pr.n.f.pl. (geog.) le Canaresi, the Canaries.

cana·ri-a f. (orn.) see **canarino**; (bot.) seed of *Phalaris canariensis* used for canary food. **-e** adj., f.pl. (geog.) Le Isole Canarie, the Canary Islands. **-o** m. (orn.) see **canarino**; a dance for two people; adj. canary coloured; canary.

canarino m. (orn.) canary; adj. canary coloured; giallo —, canary yellow.

canasta f. (cards) canasta; game of canasta; canasta party.

canata f. severe scolding; harsh rebuke; bestial action.

canato m. province ruled over by the khan (cf. **Can**[1]).

canavac·cio m. See **canovaccio**.

cancan m. indecl. can-can; noise, turmoil; scandal.

cancaneggiare [A3C] intr. (aux. avere) to make a fuss, to create a disturbance or scandal; cancaneggiandovi su, making a fuss about it.

can·caro m. See **canchero**.

can·cel m. indecl. cancellation (of a hotel-booking).

cancell-are[1] [A1] tr. to cancel; to annul; to obliterate; to erase, to rub out, to cross out; — il ricordo di, to wipe out the memory of; †to shut off by means of a gate. **-a·bile** adj. that can be rubbed out; cancellable. **-ato** part. adj. cancelled; annulled; rubbed out, crossed out; (herald.) fretty. **-atura** f. rubbing out; cancelling lines, crossings out; erasure; mark left by erasure; (leg.) tax due for cancellation of a deed, mortgage, etc. **-azione** f. cancellation, annulment, rescission; (telev.) blanking; (leg.) -azione di un'ipoteca, cancellation of a mortgage upon redemption; -azione di una causa dal ruolo, striking-out or withdrawal of an action (C.C.P.).

†cancellare[2] intr. to totter, to stagger; to topple; to falter; to weaken; to vacillate.

†cancellari·a f. See **cancelleria**.

cancellata f. See under **cancello**.

cancellato[1] part. adj. See under **cancellare**[1].

cancellato[2] m. See under **cancello**.

canceller-i·a f. chancellery; chancellorship; (leg.) office of a Clerk of the Court, Registry; stationer's shop; stationery; spese di —, clerical expenses. **-esco** adj. (m.pl. **-eschi**) pertaining to a Chancellor or chancellery; scrittura -esca, chancery hand; (fig.) pedantic. (**-escamente** adv.)

cancellier-e m. (leg.) Clerk of the Court, Registrar; — dello Scacchiere, Chancellor of the Exchequer. **-a** f. wife of a Chancellor. **-ato** m. office of Chancellorship.

cancell-o m. barred gate; iron railing; vendere a — chiuso, to sell lock, stock and barrel. **-ata** f. railings; (naut.) end of a contract or charter. **-ato** m. large iron fence. **-ino** m. wicket (gate).

canceroso adj. (med.) cancerous.

can·cher-o m. nuisance, annoyance, pest; (exclamation of annoyance) che il — ti venga!, blast you!; (pop.) cancer. **-oso** adj. annoying; (pop.) cancerous. **-usse!** excl. drat!

cancren-a f. (med.) gangrene, mortification. **-are** [A1] rfl. to go gangrenous. **-ato** part. adj. turned to gangrene. **-oso** adj. gangrenous.

cancr-o m. (med.) cancer, carcinoma; (vet.) — volante, anthrax, glossanthrax; (zool.) crab; (astron.) Cancer, the Crab; (geog.) tropico di —, tropic of Cancer. **-iforme** adj. crab-like.

†candari·a f. charm, magic portent.

candeggi-are [A3C] tr. to bleach. **-abilità** f. (techn.) bleaching capacity. **-ato** part. adj. bleached. **-atura** f. bleaching, bleach; (text.) bleaching croft.

candeggina f. bleach, bleaching powder, bleaching solution.

candeggio m. bleaching; dare il — a, to bleach.

candel-a f. candle; accendere una — a, to light a candle to (a saint, etc.); asta fino a estinzione di — vergine, auction the bidding at which is limited by the time taken for a new candle to burn out; essere al verde come una —, to be stony broke, to be at the end of one's resources (the bottom of a candle was formerly coloured green); il giuoco non vale la —, the game isn't worth the candle; (phys.) candle; watt; una lampadina da 50 -e, a fifty-watt bulb; (mech.) sparking-plug; (fig.) person who has grown thin through illness or worry; (surg.) gum catheter, bougie; (aeron.) venire giù a —, to do a pancake landing. **-abro** m. table candlesticks; -abro a muro, bracket candle-holder; candelabrum. **-a·ia** f., **-a·io** m. candle-maker. **-a·ra** f. (liturg.) Candlemas. **-etta** f. (surg.) gum catheter, bougie; pl. (naut.) any large tackle; †top burton tackles. **-(l)iere** m. candlestick; -iere alla Raffaella, candlestick with the stem carved in relief in the style of Raphael; -ieri accompagnati, a pair of candlesticks; essere sul -iere, to be very conspicuous; reggere il -iere, to aid and abet, to further by passive non-interference; metter sul -iere, to praise, to put on a pedestal; (naut.) stanchion. **-izza** f. (naut.) powerful lifting tackle. **†-o** m. see **candela**. **-ora** f. (liturg.) Candlemas. **-otto** m. short candle; candle or taper for use in processions; pl. a sort of pasta used for soup and made in the shape of thick tubes.

cand-ente adj. (poet.) lucent, shining, glowing. **-escente** adj. incandescent. **-ificare** [A2S] tr. to cause to glow.

†candi adj. indecl. candied.

Can·dia pr.n.f. (geog.) Candia; Crete; zucchero di —, sugar candy.

candidat-o m. candidate; aspirant. **-ura** f. candidature; fare atto di -ura, to stand for election; presentare la -ura di, to nominate; accettare la -ura, to accept nomination.

can·did-o adj. white; bright, shining; pure; candid; straightforward; frank. **-amente** adv. frankly. **-ezza** f. whiteness; brightness; purity. **†-ore** m. See **candore**.

candificare [A2S] see under **candente**.

cand-ire[1] [D2] tr. to candy; (fig.) to hoard, to treasure (useless objects). **-ito** part. adj. candied; n.m. candied fruit; candy.

†candire[2] tr. to make white hot.

candore m. whiteness, splendour, brilliance; candour; straightforwardness, forthrightness; honesty.

can-e m. (abbrev. to **can** in provb. expressions) dog; razza di —, breed of dog; — da caccia, gun-dog; — da guardia, house-dog, watch-dog; — da pagliaio, farm-dog, (fig.) braggart; — da poliziotto, police-dog, — da pastore, sheep-dog; — da punta, pointer; vita da —, dog's life; solo come un —, all alone; povero cane! poor devil!; darsi ai -i, to despair, to lose one's temper; essere come — e gatto, to lead a cat and dog life, to be at loggerheads; figlio d'un —, son of a gun; far spiritare i -i a, to scare; drizzare le gambe ai -i, to attempt the impossible; andare ai -i, to go to the dogs; menare il can per l'aia, to evade the issue; — non mangia —, there is honour among thieves; non stuzzicare il can che dorme, (to) let sleeping dogs lie; can che abbaia mai non morde, his bark is worse than his bite; faccia di —, ugly mug; beast, brute; quel — di marito, that beast of a husband; fare il —, to be cruel; dare il — a, to laugh at; — grosso, powerful man, 'big shot'; fortunato come un — in chiesa, unlucky in everything; non c'è un —, there's not a soul to be seen; fatto da —, appallingly badly done; il tenore è un —, the tenor is frightful; (artil.) firing pin, hammer, cock; hoop cramp, instrument used by coopers for lightening the hoops; (ichth.) tope, *Galeorhinus galeus*; (bot.) denti di —, dog tooth violet, adder's tongue, fawn lily, *Erythronium dens canis*; lingua di —, hound's tongue, ribwort plantain, *Plantago lanceolata*; capro di —, yellow foxglove, *Digitalis lutea*; (astron.) Canis. **-e·a** f. noise of barking; (fig.) uproar. **-ettiere** m. kennelman. **-ile** m. kennel; (fig.) hovel; adj. canine; doggy. **-ino**

can-e (*cont.*)
adj. canine; (fig.) tiresome, annoying; dente ~ino, eye-tooth; mosca ~ina, horse-fly; tosse ~ina, whooping-cough; severe cough; *n.m.* eye-tooth. **-ità** *f.* cruel act, act of brutality. **-izza** *f.* yelping of pack of hounds; (tanning) puer, liquor of dog dung. **-izzata** *f.* yelping of hounds.

Cane·fora *f.* (Gk. antiq.) Canephorus; (bot.) plants of the madder family.

canerino *m.* See **canarino**.

canęsca *f.* See **cane** (ichth.).

canestr-a *f.* fruit basket; washing basket; wicker basket with a handle at both ends; basket carriage; wicker cart. **-a·io** *m.* basket-maker. **-ata** *f.* basketful.

canestr-o *m.* flower basket; shopping basket; wicker basket with a single loop handle; (sport) goal at basket-ball; palla —, game of basket-ball. **-ello** *m. dim.* of **canestro**; (naut., aeron.) grommet; runner (on a sail, etc.); (zool.) ~ello di mare, *Chlamys opercularis* and *C. varia*, edible bivalves like small scallops.

canevac·cio *m.* See **canovaccio**.

can·for-a *f.* camphor. **-a·ta** *f.* (bot.) *Achillea ageratum*. **-a·to** *m.* (chem.) camphorate; *adj.* camphorated.

canfo·rico *adj.* (chem.) camphoric.

cang *m. indecl.* cangue, cang.

can·gia *f.* cangia, long, narrow barge on the Nile.

cangi-are [A 3] *tr.* (poet.) to change; — consiglio, to change one's mind, to think again. **-a·bile** *adj.* changeable, variable. **-amẹnto** *m.* changing; change. **-ante** *part. adj.* changing; iridescent; seta ~ante, shot silk. (**-ato** *part. adj.*)

cangia(r)ro *m.* Saracen dagger.

†**can·gio** *m.* see **cambio**; *adj.* see **cangiante**, under **cangiare**.

cangrena *f.* See **cancrena**.

canguro *m.* (zool.) kangaroo.

canic·cio *m.* and derivs. See **canniccio**.

cani·c-ola *f.* (astron.) Dog Star, Sirius; dog days; great heat; heat wave; hottest part of the day; sotto la —, in the midday sun. **-olare**, **-ulare** *adj.* pertaining to the dog days.

canile *m.*, **canino** *adj.* See under **cane**.

canipai(u)ola *f.* (orn.). See **canapino**, under **canapiglia**.

canistro *m.* can, petrol can.

canità *f.* See under **cane**.

cani·zie *f. indecl.* grey hairs, white hairs; hoary age, old age.

canizza *f.* See under **cane**.

cann-a *f.* cane; reed; (bot.) *Arundo donax*; — indica, — fiorita, flowering or garden Canna, *Canna indica*; — palustre, — di palude, — greca, — salvatica, reed, *Phragmites communis*; — d'India, Rattan cane, *Calamus rotang*; — da zucchero, sugar cane, *Saccharum officinale*; (paperm.) — palustre, *Arundo donax* cane, Spanish reed, Savannah grass, scriptural reed; (fig.) — fessa, broken reed; povero in —, poor as a church mouse; tremare come una —, to shake like a leaf; walking-stick, cane; cross-bar of a bicycle; portare in —, to carry on the cross-bar; rod; — da pesca, fishing-rod; drum-major's staff; giuocare a ~e, to play darts after the Spanish fashion with sharpened canes; a small tube or pipe; channel; (motor.) — di cilindro, cylinder liner; (anat.) — del polmone, windpipe, trachea; (mus.) organ-pipe; tube (of a wind instrument); bagpipe; — a lingua, reed-pipe; — aperta, open pipe; — chiusa, stopped pipe; — ad anima, flue-pipe; barrel (of a gun); fucile con la baionetta in —, rifle with fixed bayonet; glassblower's pipe; vent-pipe; stack (of a chimney); measurement of length, rod (varies in different regions between 2 and 6 metres); — quadrata, agricultural unit of area varying according to region (at Naples it is equivalent to 7 centiares and at Perugia to 30 centiares); misurare gli altri con la propria —, to judge other people according to one's own desires; prendersela a un tanto la —, not to give thought to oneself. **-a·io** *m.* weaver's tray containing spools of thread; shelf made of canes for drying fruit; eelpot. **-ai(u)ola** (orn.) reed warbler, *Acrocephalus scirpaceus*; — verdognola, marsh warbler, *Acrocephalus palustris*; cane or reed for making fruit shelves. **-ata** *f.* blow with a cane; lattice made of canes. **-ęto** *m.* cane-brake; fare il diavolo nel ~eto, to kick up a noise. **-ętta** *f.* small metal tube; swagger cane; pleating iron; (text.) pirn. **-ettiera** *f.* (text.) pirn-winding machine. **-izza** *f.* see **cannuccia**; (naut.) kind of raft used in the Abruzzi when fishing for squids. **-uc·cia** *f.* drinking-straw; stem of a tobacco-pipe; pipe of a quill; pen-holder; †marsh reed.

cannabișmo *m.* (med.) hashish poisoning.

cannacoro *m.* (bot.) Indian hemp, *Cannabis indica*.

†**cannamele** *f.* sugar cane.

cannarecciọne *m.* (orn.) great reed warbler, *Acrocephalus arundinaceus*.

cannarec·chia *f.* (bot.) Aleppo grass, *Sorghum halapense*.

cannata *f.* See under **canna**.

cannęggi-o *m.* measurement, survey. **-are** [A 3 C] *tr.* to measure (land). **-atọre** *m.* assistant to an engineer or surveyor in measuring.

cannęll-a *f.* small tube; tap in a barrel; spout (of a funnel, a fountain, etc.); tap; lavarsi alla —, to wash under a tap; round stick or billet (as of sulphur or charcoal); cinnamon; oil of cinnamon; (bot.) cinnamon tree, *Cinnamonum zeylanicum*. **-ato** *adj.* cinnamon-coloured; cinnamon-flavoured; (archit.) see **scanalato**. **-atura** *f.* (archit.) see **scanalatura**. **-ina** *f. dim.* of **cannella**; weaver's reel. **-ino** *adj.* cinnamon-like; cinnamon-flavoured; cinnamon-coloured.

cannęll-o *m.* internode, joint of a cane; piece of stalk (e.g. of hemp); weaver's reel; spool; penholder; pipe of a quill; — Bunsen, Bunsen burner; (eng.) welding torch; — ossidrico, blowlamp, blowpipe; — di gomma, small rubber tube; (archit.) cable, cable-moulding (in fluting on a column); stick (e.g. of sulphur, sealing-wax); (artil.) fuse tube; (eng.) taglio col —, gas-cutting. **-ętto** *m. dim.* of **cannello**; spout. **-ino** *m. dim.* of **cannello**; sort of sweet. **-ọne** *m. augm.* of **cannello**; *pl.* (cul.) pasta for soup in the shape of tubes nearly as thick as a finger and stuffed with meat or cheese. **-ọso** *adj.* reed-like; pipe-like, tubular.

cannereccione *m.* (orn.). See **cannareccione**.

cannęto *m.* See under **canna**.

canni·bal-e *m.* cannibal, man-eater; (fig.) fierce, cruel man; (skiing) ruthless and dangerous skier. **-ęsco** *adj.* (m.pl. ~ęschi) cannibalistic. **-ișmo** *m.* cannibalism.

cannic·chio *m.* firebrick lining of a furnace.

can(n)ic·ci-o *m.* tray made of reeds; floor or roof made of reeds; shelf of reeds for rearing silkworms or drying fruit. **-a·ia** *f.* shelf made of reeds used in drying chestnuts. **-ata** *f.* trayful, shelf-ful; palisade of canes.

cannizza *f.* See under **canna**.

cannocchiale *m.* telescope; spy-glass; (pop.) field-glasses.

cannoc·chio *m.* root-stock of a cane; cob of maize after the grain has gone.

cannolic·chio *m.* (zool.) razor shell, *Solen* spp.

cannolo *m.* (cul.) cream horn.

cannọn-e[1] *m. augm.* of **canna**, q.v.; cannon; carne da —, cannon fodder; (slang) essere un —, to be the cat's whiskers; ma sì, l'hai fatto benissimo: sei un —, you've done it frightfully well, you're a dab hand at it; reel for winding wool; water-pipe; pipe of a stove; conduit; a kind of gaiter or strap for a boot; ruff; (mus.) one of the larger organ-pipes. †**-are** *tr.* to shoot with cannon balls, to shell. **-ata** *f.* cannon shot; cannonade; (fig.) exaggeration; lie; (slang) è una ~ata! it's terrific! **-cętti** *m.pl.* strips of pasta for soup in the shape of pipes. **-cino** *m. dim.* small cannon; small pipe, small tube; stick; (cul.) pastry horn; †telescope; *pl.* strips of pasta for soup. **-cioni**, **-ciotti** *m.pl.* strips of pasta for soup. **-eggiare** [A 3 C] *tr., intr.* (*aux.* avere) to cannonade; to fire a cannon at frequent intervals. (**-eggiamẹnto** *m.*) **-iera** *f.* (mil.) embrasure; (naut.) porthole (for firing); (naut.) gunboat. **-iere** *m.* gunner.

†**cannọne**[2] *m.* (mus.) a kind of psaltery of oriental origin; mezzo —, a smaller 'cannone'.

†**cannono·bice** *m.* (mil. hist.) medium-sized cannon.

cannotto *m.* (eng.) the copper end of brass or steel boiler tubes.

cannuc·cia *f.* See under **canna**.

can·nula *f.* (med.) cannula.

cannulatura *f.* See **scannellatura**, under **scannellare**.

cannuti·glia *f.* See **canutiglia**.

†**cano** *adj.* white-haired.

can-o·a *f.* canoe. **-oìșmo** *m.* canoeing. **-oista** *m.* canoeist. **-ottag·gio** *m.* rowing. **-ottiera** *f.* wide-brimmed hard straw hat, boater; man's sleeveless vest, sports vest; tee-shirt. **-ottiere** *m.* rower, oarsman; member of rowing club; società dei ~ottieri, rowing and sculling club. **-ottiero** *adj.* pertaining to rowing. **-otto** *m.* skiff, ship's boat; speedboat; ~otto di gomma, rubber dinghy.

cano·chia *f.* (zool.) *Squilla mantis*, a crustacean.

canocchiale *m.* See **cannocchiale**.

ca·non-e *m.* (eccl.) canon (of a church council, of scripture, of the Mass, of saints, etc.); (fig.) basic rule, canon; *pl.* moral standards; (mus.) canon; — all'inverso, — per moto contrario, canon by contrary motion; — al sospiro, canon with entries at the distance of one beat; — a specchio, mirror canon; — enigmatico, riddle-canon; — infinito, — perpetuo, — circolare, infinite, perpetual, circular canon; — per aumentazione, canon by augmentation; — per diminuzione, canon by diminution; — per giusti intervalli, canon by exact intervals; — retrogrado, — cancrizzante, canon cancrizans, crab-canon; canone armonico, monochord; (leg.) rent; — d'affitto, rent; — enfiteutico, ground-rent (C.C.); (orn.) goldeneye, *Bucephala clangula.*

†canoni·a *f.* See **canonicato**, under **canonica**.

cano·n-ica *f.* (eccl.) priest's house, presbytery; canonry; canon law; canoness; †house for canons. **-icale** *adj.* (eccl.) of, suitable for, the canons of a chapter; messa **-icale**, capitular mass. **-icalmente** *adv.* in a manner befitting a canon. **-icamente** *adv.* in the manner prescribed by canon law; canonically. **-icato** *m.* (eccl.) canonry; (fig.) sinecure; chapter of canons. **-ichessa** *f.* (eccl.) canoness. **-icità** *f.* canonicity, canonicalness. **-ico** *adj.* canonical (books, impediments, hours); (joc.) l'ora **-ica**, the appointed hour; *adj.* (mus.) canonic; (leg.) diritto **-ico**, canon law; *n.m.* (eccl.) canon (of a chapter); vita da **-ico**, easy life; **-ici** regolari, Canons Regular. **-ista** *m.* (eccl.; leg.) canonist.

canonizz-are [A I] *tr.* to regularize; to give official approval to; to sanction; to recognize; to authenticate; to include among the authors officially quoted by the Accademia della Crusca; (eccl.) to canonize. **-ato** *part. adj.* regularized; sanctioned; canonized. **-azione** *f.* (eccl.) canonization.

Cano·po *pr.n.m.* (Egypt. antiq.) Canopus (town, and cult-name of a god); canopic vase; (astron.) Canopus, α Argonis.

canor-o *adj.* harmonious, melodious; singing; sweet; resonant; songful; uccelli **-i**, song-birds, songsters; (mus.) vocal; la classica tradizione **-a**, the classical tradition of singing; (poet.) Il — monte, Parnassus; cigno —, poet. (**-amente** *adv.*) **-ità** *f.* melodiousness, songfulness.

cano·sa *f.* (ichth.) *Squalus glaucus*, a kind of shark.

†cano·scere *vb.* and derivs. See **conoscere**.

Canoss-a *pr.n.f.* (hist.) Canossa, castle belonging to the Countess Matilda of Tuscany, where the Emperor, Henry IV, was humiliated before Pope Gregory VII in 1077; (fig.) andare a —, to humiliate oneself, to ask pardon, to eat humble pie. **-iane** *f.pl.* (eccl.) Daughters of Charity.

canotte *f.* (neol.) nightgown (abbrev. of 'camicia da notte').

canotto *m.* and derivs. See under **canoa**.

canov-a *f.* wine or provision shop; store, warehouse. **-aio**, **-aro** *m.* storekeeper.

canovac·cio *m.* canvas; (naut.) sail canvas; duster; hemp stalk left on the field; rough draft of a play; commedia a —, play in which the dialogue was improvised by the actors, as in the Commedia dell'arte.

canovo *m.* (naut.) hemp rope.

cans-are [A I] *tr.* to remove; to avoid; to throw away, to discard; *rfl.* to go away, to escape, to take refuge. **-ato** *part. adj.* removed; discarded; fled. **-ato·ia** *f.*, **-atoio** *m.* place of refuge.

cantalupo *m.* cantaloup.

cant-are [A I] *tr.* to sing; to intone, to chant; to stress, to emphasize; — vittoria, to exult, to count one's chickens before they are hatched; — le lodi di, to sing the praises of; — la solfa, to read the riot act; gliel'ho **-ata** chiara, I told him in no uncertain terms; *intr.* (*aux.* avere) to sing, to chant; **-a** che ti passa, cheer up and you'll get over it; to talk, to be eloquent; to be quite clear; lo scritto **-a** chiaro, the meaning of this document is quite plain; (naut.) to keep or give time for hauling a rope; (slang) to 'spill the beans', to 'squeal'; far — uno, to make a person talk, to make him reveal what he knows; (provb.) carta **-a** e villan dorme, the peasant with a written agreement of lease can sleep; to keep on chattering; to squeak; to crackle; to chirp; to crow; to ring (of glass); senti come **-a** questo cristallo, listen to the ring of this glass; botte che **-a**, empty barrel; *n.m.* singing. **-a·bile** *adj.* singable; (mus.) cantabile, in singing style, broadly melodious; *n.m.* (mus.) cantabile style (of singing or playing); passage written in cantabile style. **-afa·vola** *f.* long narrative; (fig.) long, improbable story. **†-afera** *f.* sing-song; long drawn-out tale. **†-afola** *f.* see **cantafavola**. **-ai(u)olo** *adj.* singing, chirping; *n.m.*

(orn.) decoy bird. **†-allu·scio** *m.* street-singer. **-ambancata** *f.* street act. **-ambanco** *m.* (*pl.* **-ambanchi**) strolling player, busker; charlatan. **-ando** *adj.* (mus.) in singing-style. **-ante** *adj.* singing; (mus.) see under **basso**; *n.m.*, *f.* singer. **-asto·rie** *m. indecl.* professional story-teller. **-ata** *f.* (mus.) cantata. **-atina** *f.* (mus.) short cantata. **-atista** *m.* (mus.) cantata composer. **-atore** *m.* (mus.) male singer. **-atrice** *f.* (mus.) see **cantante**. **†-ato·rio** *adj.* (mus.) singable, vocal (applied to melody).

cantarella *f.* (bot.) *Coronilla scorpioidea*; (ent.) see **cantaride**; (ichth.) *Spondyliosoma cantharus*, a kind of sea bream; decoy partridge; decoy whistle for partridges.

cantarellare [A I]. See **canterellare**.

canta·rid-e *f.* (ent.) Spanish-fly, *Lytta vesicatoria*, and various other cantharid beetles; *pl.* (pharm.) cantharides. **-ina** *f.* (chem.) cantharidin.

†cantaro *m.* measure of weight; (naut.) tonnage of ships.

can·taro¹ *m.* (ichth.) *Spondyliosoma orbicularis*, a kind of sea bream.

can·taro² *m.* drinking-cup, goblet, chalice; †chamber-pot.

cantasto·rie *m. indecl.* See under **cantare**.

cant-ata *f.*, **-atore** *m.*, **-atrice** *f.* See under **cantare**.

cante·o *m.* small beam or bar across the frame of a sawpit for supporting the timber to be sawn.

†can·tera *f.* drawer.

canter-ale, **-ano** *m.* chest of drawers.

canterella *f.* See **cantarella**.

canterell-are [A I] *tr.*, *intr.* (*aux.* avere) to hum, to sing to oneself. **-amento** *m.* humming; little song. **-io** *m.* constant humming.

canterello *m.* (bot.) chanterelle mushroom, *Cantharellus cibarius*; tinsel.

canterin-o *adj.* singing; uccello —, decoy bird; (bot.) orzo —, kind of barley; *n.m.* person fond of singing; (hist.) reciter of narrative. **-a** *f.* poor singer.

can·tero *m.* bed-pan; latrine.

can·tica *f.* poetic composition divided into cantos; each of the three parts of Dante's *Divine Comedy.*

canticchi-are [A 4] *tr.*, *intr.* (*aux.* avere) to sing softly, to hum. **-atore** *m.* person humming; mediocre versifier.

can·tico *m.* canticle, hymn; (Lat. comedy) canticum; Cantico dei cantici, Song of Songs; (mus.) — di Natale, Christmas carol.

cantiere *m.* yard, shed; shipyard; builder's works; worksite; (mining) stope; (naut.) mettere in —, to lay the keel, (fig.) to start on a job.

cantilen-a *f.* cradle song; lullaby; oft repeated song, old song, catch; long, dull poem or speech; sing-song kind of intonation; (fig.) è la solita —, always the same old story, always harping on the same string; (mus.) melodiousness; a melodious air; intonation (of a psalm-tone); sacred song; monotonous song. **-are** [A I] *tr.*, *intr.* (*aux.* avere) to sing-song; to hum; to drawl.

cantimban-co *m.* (*pl.* **-chi**). See **cantambanco**, under **cantare**.

cantimplora *f.* water-cooler, wine-cooler.

cantin-a *f.* cellar; giù in —, down in the cellar; wine-shop; dark gloomy place; (joc.) è in —, his voice is in his boots. **-ato** *m.* (bldg.) cellar, basement. **-ella** *f.* grape-vat. **-etta** *f.* wine-cooler, ice-bucket. **-iera** *f.* vivandière. **-iere** *m.* head butler; cellarman; manager of a wine-shop.

cantinella¹ *f.* See under **cantina**.

cantinella² *f.* ruler for marking positions, corner ruler.

cantino *m.* (mus.) E-string (of violin); chanterelle, treble-string (of any instrument); (fig.) rompere il — alla chitarra, to break off the conversation.

canto¹ *m.* song; chant; poem; canti popolari, folk-songs; canto; crowing of a cock; chirping of an insect; (mus.) singing; art of singing; soprano part (of harmony); treble-string; — ambrosiano, Ambrosian or Milanese chant; bel —, *bel canto*, a style of singing cultivated and perfected by the best Italian singers; canti carnascialeschi, carnival songs; — del cigno, swan-song; — fermo, plain-chant, *cantus firmus*; — figurato, florid melody; — gregoriano, Gregorian or Roman chant; (naut.) shanty.

cant-o² *m.* corner; side; a —, beside; levarsi da —, to get rid of; da — di mio padre, for my father's part; dal — mio, for my part; dall'altro —, on the other hand; †per —, across; obliquely.

canton-e *m.* part, side; corner; giuoco dei quattro **-i**, puss in the middle; mettere in un —, to put aside; to put out of mind; squared piece of artificial stone; slab of concrete; heap of rubble in the corner of a room; (geog.) Canton (of Switzerland); Lago

canton-e (*cont.*)

dei quattro ~i, Lake of Lucerne; (herald.) canton. **~ale** *adj.* cantonal; *n.m.* angle iron; (bldg.) fillet. **-ata** *f.* exterior corner of a building; prendere una ~ata, to bump into a corner; street corner; fare ~ata, to occupy a corner position, (fig.) to commit a great blunder. **-iera** *f.* corner cupboard; street-walker; (naut.) angle iron; casa ~iera, house of a road keeper who is responsible for the upkeep of a section of the road; (rlwy.) inspector's hut. **-iere** *m.* road keeper; (rlwy.) permanent-way inspector; †street-vendor, hawker, pedlar.

cantor-e *m.* singer; (eccl.) cantor; singer in (clerical) choir; poet; — di Ettore *or* di Achille, Homer; — di Enea, Virgil; — di Orlando, Ariosto; — di Beatrice, Dante; — di Goffredo, Tasso; — di Laura, Petrarch; — delle selve, nightingale. **-ato** *m.* (eccl.) office of cantor or precentor. **-i·a** *f.* (eccl.; archit.) singers' gallery; organ-loft. **-ino** *m.* (mus.) choir-book, manual of plain-song; (eccl.) young cantor, choirboy.

cantucchiare [A4.] See **canticchiare.**

cantuc·ci-o *m.* internal corner, corner of a room; mettere un bambino nel —, to stand a child in the corner; cubby hole; cosy corner; heel of the loaf; end bit of cheese; sugar biscuit. **-a·io** *m.* biscuit-maker. **-u·to** *adj.* angular.

cantula *f.* (text.) fibra dell'agave —, maguey fibre.

canuti·glia *f.* minute glass tubules used in making certain kinds of embroidery; tinsel; fringe or braid of gold or silver twist; (text.) bullion, purl.

canut-o *adj.* hoary, white-haired; old; wise, prudent, wary. **-ag·gine** *f.* senile action, behaviour of an elderly person. **-ezza** *f.* hoariness; age; shock of white hair. **-ire** [D2] *intr.* (aux. essere) to go white-haired. **-ola** *f.* (bot.) *Teucrium polium.*

canzona *f.* (mus.) song; Provençal troubadour-song; canzona, polyphonic composition for lute, organ, etc.; song-like instrumental piece.

canzon-are [A1c] *tr.* to make fun of; †to sing, to celebrate; *intr.* (aux. avere) to joke; †to write songs, to compose. (**-atore** *m.* **-atrice** *f.*) **-ato·rio** *adj.* teasing. (**-atoriamente** *adv.*) **-atura** *f.* joke, jest, leg-pull, take-off.

canzon-e *f.* song; a kind of lyric poem, canzone; ~i di gesta, chansons de geste; tiresome repetition; mettere in —, to jeer at. **-cino** *m.* dim. little song, ditty. **-ella** *f.* joke; mettere in ~ella, to make light of. **-etta** *f.* a kind of lyric poem; popular song, dance tune; (mus.) canzonet. **-etta·rio** *m.* song-writer. **-iere** *m.* poetry book; song book; all the lyric poems of an author; il Canzoniere di Dante, Dante's lyric poems. **-ettista** *m., f.* composer of popular songs. **-ista** *m.* song-writer.

†ca·o *m.* See **capo.**

caolino *m.* kaolin, china clay.

ca·os *m. indecl.* chaos; (fig.) state of confusion; medley.

cao·tico *adj.* chaotic.

†capac·cia *f.* annoyance.

capaccina *f.* heaviness in the head; headache.

capac·cio *m. pejor.* of **capo**, q.v.; dull, obtuse individual; obstinate, pig-headed person.

capacciuto *adj.* (of a plant) having a large top.

capac-e *adj.* capable, able; è — di fare una cosa simile, he's quite capable of doing a thing like that; far —, to persuade; (leg.) legally competent; — di agire, legally capable of transacting business, disposing of property, taking responsibilities, etc.; — di intendere e di volere, in full possession of one's faculties; capacious, capable of holding; questo vaso è — di, this vase holds; *impers.* è —, it is possible. **-ità** *f.* capacity; ability; skill; (phys.) ~ità termica, specific heat; (electr.) capacitance; ~ità elettrica, specific conductivity; (leg.) legal competency; ~ità di diritto, capacity to have rights; ~ità di stare in giudizio, capacity to plead; ~ità di testare, testamentary capacity.

capacit-are [A1s] *tr.* to convince, to persuade; to be acceptable, to please; *rfl.* to understand, to grasp, to conceive; non so ~armi come sia successo, I can't make out how it happened. **-a·bile** *adj.* comprehensible; reasonable, open to persuasion. **-amento** *m.* reasonableness. **-ante** *part. adj.* persuasive, convincing. **-anza** *f.* (electr.) capacitance. **-ato** *part. adj.* persuaded; convinced.

capacitivo *adj.* (electr.) capacitive.

†capaguto *m.* (mil. hist.) a kind of dagger.

capann-a *f.* shed, hut, barn; Festa delle ~e, Feast of Tabernacles; mountain hut; bathing hut; rough, improvised shelter; hood

of a chimney-piece; (of a roof) a —, lean-to, sloping. **-ella** *f. dim.* see **capannello**; le Capannelle, horse race-track near Rome. **-ello** *m. dim.* of **capanno**; small group of people, knot of persons; appena successo l'incidente si formò un ~ello di gente, as soon as the accident happened a little group collected; heap of wood, etc. for burning. **-o** *m.* hut for shelter when out shooting birds; andare al ~o, to go out shooting birds; summer-house, arbour. **-one** *m.* barn; ox-stall; large room; hangar; goods shed; (equit.) croupade. **-uc·cia** *f. dim.* of **capanna**; small Christmas crib (in private house). **-uc·cio** *m. dim.* of **capanno**; heap of brushwood for burning; (archit.) lantern (on a dome).

capannascondere *m.* (game of) hide-and-seek.

capar·bi-o *adj.* self-willed, obstinate, determined. (**-amente** *adv.*) *n.m.* self-willed person, stubborn person, pig-headed person. **-ag·gine** *f.* obstinacy, stubbornness, pig-headedness. **-eri·a** *f.* obstinacy; act of stubbornness. **-età** *f.* obstinacy, stubbornness, pig-headedness.

†capare *tr.* to choose.

caparello *m.* (ichth.) grey mullet, *Mugil cephalus.*

caparr-a *f.* (comm.) deposit; earnest, earnest-money; (leg.) — confirmatoria, deposit for due performance of contract (C.C.). **-are** [A1]. See **accaparrare.**

caparrone[1] *m.* one who obtains a contract by making himself out to be better than he is, intriguer.

†caparrone[2] *m.* See **caprone.**

capat-a *f.* bump on the head; dare una — in, to knock one's head against; (fig.) battere una —, to die; to go bankrupt, to be ruined; fare alle ~e, to run into something; †nod of the head; †shake of the head; †salutation. **-ina** *f. dim.* of **capata**; dare una ~ina in, to pop in.

capecchio *m.* tow; the rough part at each end of flax or hemp fibre; (bot.) wig tree, Venetian sumach, *Cotinus coggyria*; (dyeing) fustet.

capeggi-are [A3c] *tr.* to lead, to head, to be the head of; (naut.) — un paranco, to turn end for end. **-ato** *part. adj.* led, headed.

†capegli, capei *m.pl.* of **capello**, q.v.

†capella *f.* she-kid; (astron.) Capricorn.

capell-o *m.* hair (one single hair); non torcere un —, not to harm a hair (of a person's head); a —, exactly, precisely, to a 't'; spaccare un — in quattro, to split hairs; avere un diavol per —, to be in a dangerous mood; *pl.* hair, head of hair; ~i secchi, dry scalp; che bei ~i! what lovely hair!; pigliarsi per i ~i, to quarrel; tirare per i ~i, to compel; tirato per i ~i, far-fetched; si è salvato per un —, he escaped by the skin of his teeth; metter le mani nei ~i di, to take into one's power; fare rizzare i ~i in capo, to make one's hair stand on end; mettersi le mani nei ~i, to tear one's hair, to be at one's wit's end; averne fin sopra i ~i, to be fed up with something; è un signore fino alla punta dei ~i, he is a gentleman to his finger-tips; in ~i, bareheaded, uncovered; (cul.) ~i d'angelo, the thinnest possible type of pasta for soup; **-ame** *m.* head of hair; quantity of hair; colour of hair. **-atura** *f.* see **capigliatura**. **-iera** *f.* head of hair; †wig; †style of hair dressing. **-ini** *m.pl.* finest possible type of pasta for soup; (bot.) bent, *Agrostis*. †**-ino** *adj.* chestnut-coloured. **-uto** *adj.* hairy, hirsute; cuoio ~uto, scalp.

capelou *m. indecl.* (zool.) soft-shelled crab undergoing its moult.

capelve·nere *m.* (bot.) maidenhair fern, *Adiantum capillus-veneris.*

†capere *intr.* to be contained; to enter.

capestr-o *m.* halter; (fig.) brake, rein, check; cable, rope; girdle, cord (of a religious); rope for gallows; persona da —, gallows-bird; (fig.) scoundrel. **-eri·a** *f.* blackguardly act; freak; oddity.

capetin·gio *adj.* (hist.) Capetian, of the House of Capet.

capetto *m. dim.* of **capo**; naughty child.

†capevole *adj.* See under **capire.**

†capezza *f.* See **cavezza.**

capezz-ale *m.* bolster; al —, on the point of death, at the bedside (of a sick or dying person); (mining) bed on or against which the mineral vein rests. **-ata** *f.* (archit.) coping. **-iera** *f.* antimacassar, chair-back; (naut.) clews of a hammock.

capezzolo *m.* nipple.

†capiatur *m.* (leg.) capias, writ of arrest, warrant for arrest.

capido·glio *m.* (zool.) See **capodoglio.**

capienza *f.* capacity; quant'è la — del serbatoio? how much does the reservoir hold?; (leg.) extent to which an estate is capable of meeting liabilities.

capi-fosso *m.* main ditch, main drain. **-fuoco** *m.* (*pl.* **-fuochi**) andiron.

†capi·gli-a *f.*, **-o** *m.* brawl, scrap, rough-house.

capigliatura *f.* head of hair; tresses.

capilargo *adj.* top-heavy; wider at the top than at the bottom.

capillar-e *adj.* capillary. **-ità** *f.* capillarity; (paperm.) prova di assorbimento per -ità, mounting test.

capilli·fero *adj.* hair-growing.

†capilli·zio *m.* hair; (astron.) ring.

capimẹnto *m.* See under **capire**.

capinascọndere *m.* See **capannascondere**.

capinẹr-a *f.*, **-o** *m.* (orn.) blackcap, *Sylvia atricapilla*.

cap-ire [D 2] *tr.* to understand, to comprehend, to grasp; si -isce, naturally, of course; non -isce nulla, he's a fool; -irai che — of course you understand that; *intr.* (*aux.* essere) to be contained, to have place; to come in, to enter; non — in sè dalla gioia, not to contain oneself for joy. **†-evole** *adj.* capable; suitable, fit; intelligible; capacious; abundant; -evole di, deserving of; essere -evole, to be of importance, to signify. **-ito** *part. adj.* understood; hai -ito? do you understand? non ho -ito bene, I don't quite understand; -ito! right! -ito che, on the understanding that.

capirọsso *m.* (orn.) any bird with a red head; averla —, woodchat, *Lanius senator*.

†capirotto *m.* wounded man; broken pot, potsherd.

capitagna *f.* (agric.) uncultivated strip along the border of a field; (bldg.) plank along which to wheel a wheelbarrow.

capital-e *adj.* capital; supreme; principal, main; cardinal; (theol.) peccato —, capital sin, deadly sin; (naut.) nave —, capital ship; (leg.) sentenza -ale, death sentence; *n.f.* capital (city); capital (letter); *m.* (econ.; finan.) capital; — azionario, share capital; — circolante, circulating capital; — d'esercizio, working capital, trade capital; — ed interessi, principal and interest; per valorizzare un tal progetto ci vogliono dei forti -i, to develop a scheme like that you need vast capital; (fig.) fare — di, to make capital out of; buon —, bel —, wag, wit, merry person, scamp; (mil.) capital, an imaginary line bisecting the salient angle of a work. **-ẹtto** *m.*, **-ino** *m.* dim. of **capitale**; (fig.) bad type (of person). **-iṣmo** *m.* (econ.) capitalism. **-ista** *m.* capitalist; (econ.) entrepreneur. **-i·stico** *adj.* capitalistic. (**-isticamẹnte** *adv.*) **-iẓzare** [A I] *tr.* (finan.) to capitalize; to write with a capital. **-iẓzaziọne** *f.* (finan.) capitalization.

†capitana *f.* (naut.) flagship.

Capitanata *pr.n.f.* (hist.) region of S. Ital. under the domination of the Spaniards governed by a 'capitano'; (geog.) region now named Lucania.

capitan-o *m.* captain; (naut.) — di vascello, Captain; — di fregata, Commander; — di corvetta, Lieutenant-Commander; — del porto, — di porto, harbour master; — mercantile, master; — marittimo di gran cabotaggio, Merchant Captain holding Master's Ticket (coastal trade); — marittimo di lungo corso, Merchant Captain holding the equivalent of Extra Master's Ticket (N.B. The commanding officer of a warship is called **comandante**, whatever his rank); (mil.) leader; (poet.) general, commander; (hist.) il gran —, a term usually used to describe Consalvo di Cordoba; — di Stato Maggiore, officer of the General Staff; -i reggenti, Captains Regent, joint Heads of State of San Marino elected every half-year; (hist.) — del popolo, commander of the local militia in the Italian republics; Capitan Fracassa, braggart (originally a mask of the 'Commedia dell'Arte', representing a blustering soldier; he was a caricature of a Spanish soldier and usually spoke Spanish. The character may possibly have been influenced by reminiscences of the *Miles Gloriosus* of Plautus). **-a** *f.* woman leader; (naut.) nave -a, flagship; galea -a, leader of the line. **-anza** *f.* captaincy. **-are** [A I] *tr.* to command, to lead, to captain. **-ato** *part. adj.* captained, led, guided; *n.m.* rank of captain, captaincy; leadership. **-eggiare** [A 3 c] *tr.* to captain, to lead. **-eri·a** *f.* area of the jurisdiction of a captain; officer's residence; (naut.) coastal region under a naval officer's command; -eria di porto, harbour office. **-ẹssa** *f.* (hist.) woman captain, woman leader.

capit-are [A I s] *intr.* (*aux.* essere) to arrive; to turn up; to happen, to occur; mi -ò in mano, it came my way by chance; — bene, to fall on one's feet, to strike it lucky; — in mente a, to come into one's head; *†tr.* to conclude, to terminate. **-ato** *part. adj.* arrived by chance; (bot.) capitate; *†*concluded.

†capitazione *f.* capitation tax.

ca·pite *adj. phr.* in —, in chief; parola in —, headword; pro —, per head.

capitecenso *m.* a person counted only as an individual and not because of possessions; proletarian.

capitẹgole *m.* (archit.; archaeol.) antefix.

capitella *f.* the end of the wax thread used by shoemakers.

capitello *m.* (archit.) capital; (bookb.) strip of leather inside the spine; strong lye used in glassmaking; (chem.) receiving tube of a retort; receiver to catch the oil as it drips from the olive press; saw-handle; (bot.) head of composite flower; cover to protect a gun from the rain.

capitino *m.* knob of a flail-handle.

capito *part.* of **capire**, q.v.

capitol-are¹ [A I s] *intr.* (*aux.* avere) to capitulate; to make terms, to stipulate. **-ante** *part. adj.*, *n.m.f.* capitulant. **-ato** *part. adj.* paragraphed, divided into chapters, classified under heads; (leg.) divided into clauses, sections, chapters; *n.m.* terms; (techn.) specification; -ato d'oneri, specifications; articles and conditions (e.g. for a tender); (leg.) all the provisions of an agreement, treaty, etc.; all agreements, treaties, etc. between two contracting parties (cf. **capitolo**). **-azione** *f.* capitulation; *†*(leg.) capitulation, treaty, agreement; (hist.) le -azioni, the capitulations (or conventions) made by the Ottoman Turkish government granting extraterritorial privileges to certain governments and their nationals resident in Moslem countries.

capitolare² *adj.* (eccl.) capitular.

†capitolare³ *tr.* to divide into chapters.

capitolare⁴ *m.* (hist.) laws of the Frankish kings.

capi·tolo *m.* chapter, category, head; burlesque poetical composition in terza rima; (eccl.) chapter; (leg.) clause or article of an agreement or contract; chapter, heading or section of a law or statute; convention, pact; (econ.) — di spesa in un bilancio pubblico, expense item in a budget; *pl.* terms.

†capito·lio *m.* See **campidoglio**.

capitolino *adj.* Capitoline; Museo —, Capitoline Museum on the Campidoglio in Rome; Fasti Capitolini, marble tablets found at Rome in 1547 containing the names of the Roman consuls from 250 to 765 A.U.C.

capitọmbol-o *m.* headlong fall; tumble; (fig.) crash, collapse. **-are** [A I s] *intr.* (*aux.* essere) to fall headlong; (fig.) to crash. **-oni** *adv.* headlong.

†capiton·dolo *m.* See **capitombolo**.

†capitor·zolo *m.* pious humbug.

capitọne¹ *m.* (text.) uneven, lumpy silk thread.

capitọne² *m.* (ichth.) a large specimen of the common eel, *Anguilla anguilla*.

†capit·oso *adj.* stubborn, obstinate. **†-uto** *adj.* (of a plant) tufted, large-headed.

capitozz-a *f.* (hort.) pollard, pollarded tree. **-are** [A I] *tr.* (hort.) to pollard.

†capitu·dine *f.* (hist.) meeting of the heads of corporations of Italian communes; (Florence, Siena) meeting of guilds; head of a body of guilds; office and function of the 'Capitano del popolo' (see under **capitano**).

capivol·gere [C 5]. See **capovolgere**.

capo *m.*

1. HEAD; mettersi in — il cappello, to put on one's hat; andare a — nudo, to go bare-headed; a — chino, with bowed head, with downcast looks; a — all'ingiù, head downwards, head foremost; piegare il —, to bow one's head; tenere il — alto, to hold one's head high; scrollare il —, to shake one's head; da — ai piedi, from head to foot; non saper dove posare il —, to have nowhere to lay one's head; vino che dà al —, wine that goes to one's head; giramenti di —, dizzy turns, attacks of dizziness; pena del —, death penalty, capital punishment. 2. MIND, head; mettersi in —, to take (it) into one's head; mi saltò in — un'idea, I suddenly got an idea; aver altro per il —, to have something else to think about; far le cose col — nel sacco, to do things with one's eyes shut; aver il — nei piedi, to have one's head in the clouds; mettere il — a, to put one's mind to; mettere il — a partito, to acquire some sense; rompersi il —, to puzzle one's head. 3. CHIEF, head; Capo dello Stato, Head of the State; — della delegazione, head of delegation; delegato —, chief delegate; lui è —, he's the boss; il — di casa, the head of the house; — dei ladri, ringleader, leader of the gang of thieves; redattore —,

capo (*cont.*)

editor in chief; — indigeno, native chief. **4.** END, extremity, head; in — alla scala, at the head of the stairs; in — al ponte, on the further side of the bridge; sedere in — di tavola, sedere a — tavola, to sit at the head of the table; legare insieme i due capi dello spago, to tie the two ends of string together; infilare il — nella cruna, to thread the end through the needle; a — della pagina, at the head of the page; in — al mondo, at the other side of the world, to the ends of the world; fare — a, to lead to, to come to; le società che fanno — al gruppo, the companies which go to make up the group; in — a dieci anni, at the end of ten years; venire a —, to unravel, to solve; (provb.) cosa fatta ha, what's done is done, (or) it's no good crying over spilt milk. **5.** BEGINNING; Capo d'Anno, New Year's Day; da —, again, (typ.) new paragraph, (mus.) go back to the beginning; non ha nè — nè coda, there's neither rhyme nor reason in it. **6.** ITEM, head, chapter; — per —, one by one; un — di vestiario, an item of clothing; per sommi capi, in the main points; (leg.) — d'accusa, count, chief point, head of an indictment or charge; the evidence thereon. **7.** HEAD, individual, person; tanti capi di bestiame, so many head of cattle; dividere per capi, to share out per head; un — ameno, an amusing chap; un — scarico, an impetuous individual; — quadro, blockhead; — ricciuto, curly head. **8.** KNOB, top, head; — d'uno spillo, head of a pin; — d'un chiodo, head of a nail; — d'aglio, clove of garlic; (bot.) bulb; vine sprout; shoot left on a plant when pruning. **9.** (NAUT.) cable; — bianco, untarred cable; — vivo, cable under tension; — di fune, the standing end of a rope. **10.** (GEOG.) headland, ness, cape, end. **11.** (HERALD.) chief; — sostenuto, chief supported by a filet; — a destra, chief embelif.

capo·banda *m.* (*pl.* **capibanda**) ringleader; (mus.) bandmaster; (vet.) base of the neck (of a horse). **-bandito** *m.* (*pl.* **capobanditi**) brigand chief. **-barca** *m.* (*pl.* **capibarca**) master of a vessel (of less than 35 tons). **-brigante** *m.* (*pl.* **capobriganti**) brigand chief. **-cac·cia** *m.* (*pl.* **capicac·cia**) head gamekeeper. **-cannoniere** *m.* (sport) top goal-scorer (soccer). **-carderi·a** *m. indecl.* (text.) carding master. **-ca·rico** *m.* (*pl.* **capica·rico**) senior lower deck rating; -carico cannoniere, gunner's mate. **-cassa** *m.* (naut.) sailor entrusted with the key of the chest. **†-censo** *m.* capitation tax. **-centu·ria** *m.* (*pl.* **capicentu·ria**) (hist.) centurion; head of a section of the Fascist militia. **-cervo** *m.* withers. **-cielo** *m.* (liturg.) baldachin. **-classe** *m.* (*pl.* **capiclasse**) (schol.) class-captain, 'form-captain'. **-coffa** *m.* (*pl.* **†capicoffa**) (naut.) captain of a top. **-collo** *m.* (*pl.* **capocolli**) a cooked meat made from the neck and head of a pig, collared head. **-comicato** *m.* (theatr.) function and status of a capocomico, q.v. **-co·mico** *m.* (*pl.* **capoco·mici**) (theatr.) actor-manager; head of a theatre company who usually plays the lead; la Duse era -comico, Duse was the manager and leading actress of her company. **-convo·glio** *m.* (*pl.* **capiconvo·glio**) (naut.) leader of a convoy. **-corda** *m. indecl.* (electr.) cable terminal, lug. **-cordata** *m.* (*pl.* **capicordata**) climber at the head of the rope. **-cro·naca** *m.* (*pl.* **capicro·naca**) leading article, leader. **-cronista** *m.* (*pl.* **capocronisti**) leader-writer. **-cuoco** *m.* (*pl.* **capicuochi**) head cook, chef. **-depo·sito** *m.* (rlwy.) head of a goods depot. **-dibanda** *m.* (naut.) topside. **-dilatte** *m.* top of the milk, cream. **-diparti·mento** *m.* (*pl.* **capidipartimento**) head of a department, manager. **-divisione** *m.* (*pl.* **capidivisione**) head of a division. **-do·glio** *m.* (zool.) sperm whale, *Physeter macrocephalus*. **-fab·brica** *m.* (*pl.* **capifab·brica**) works manager; builder's foreman. **-fabbricato** *m.* (neol.) person responsible for a building (e.g. for air-raid precautions). **-facchino** *m.* (*pl.* **capifacchini**) foreman porter. **-fami·glia** *m.* (*pl.* **capifami·glia**) head of the family. **-fila** *m.* (*pl.* **capifila**) leader of a file (of horses, vessels, etc.). **-fitto** *adj.* (*m.pl.* **capofitti**) with head downwards; *adv.* a -fitto, head downwards, head first, headlong; *n.m.* (sport) header (dive). **-forna·io** *m.* head baker. **-fucina** *m.* (*pl.* **capifucina**) master smith. **-gabbiere** *m.* leading seaman. **-gatto** *m.* (vet.) staggers; (agric.) layer in horticulture. **†-girlo**, **†-gi·rolo** *m.* see capogiro. **-giro** *m.* (*pl.* **capogiri**) dizziness; (fig.) whim; (vet.) gid, sturdy, turnsick. **-giuoco** *m.* game leader. **-guar·dia** *m.* (*pl.* **capiguar·dia**) leader of a guard; chief warder. **-lan·cia** *m.* (naut.) sailor in charge of a launch. **-capolavori** *m.* masterpiece. **-lepre** *m.* (ichth.) *Tetraodon lagocephalus*, puffer fish. **-letto** *m.* (*pl.* **capoletti**) hangings between the head of a bed and the wall. **-li·nea** *f.* (of tram or bus service) terminus. **-lista** *m.* (*pl.* **capilista**) head of the list; (soccer) team at the head of

division. **-luogo** *m.* (*pl.* **capoluoghi**) town which is administrative centre of a district (cf. Eng.'county town'). **-mac·china** *m.* (paperm.) machine-man. **-macchinista** *m.* (*pl.* **capomacchinisti**) chief engineer. **-mae·stro** *m.* see capomastro. **-man·dria** *m.* chief herdsman. **-mani·polo** *m.* (mil.) squad leader; (Fasc. hist.) lieutenant in the Fascist militia. **-mastro** *m.* (*pl.* **capimastri**) master builder. **-mazzo** *m.* (tanning) top skin in a bale. **†-mese** *m.* first of the month. **-morto** *m.* (chem.) residue after distillation. **-movimento** *m.* (rlwy.) chief of traffic. **-mu·sica** *m.* (*pl.* **capimu·sica**) bandleader. **-pa·gina** *m.* (*pl.* **capipa·gina**) (typ.) ornamentation at the top of a page. **-palmetta** *m.* (naut.) captain of the heads. **-palo** *m.* (herald.) pale and chief. **-parte** *m.* (*pl.* **capiparte**) leader of a political faction. **-parto** *m.* (*pl.* **capoparti**) (med.) first menstruation after childbirth. **-pezzo** *m.* (mil.) the leading gun of a battery; (naut.) gunlayer. **†-piede** *adv.* upside down; *n.m.* mistake, blunder. **-po·polo** *m.* (*pl.* **capipo·polo, capopo·poli**) demagogue. **-posto** *m.* (*pl.* **capiposto**) (mil.) commander of a guard-post. **-prora** *m.* (naut.) chief forward watch. **-ra·is** *m. indecl.* boat from which the kill is made in tunny fishing. **-ran·cio** *m.* (naut.) head of a mess. **-razione** *m.* food controller. **-reparto** *m.* foreman; head of department. **†-ricciare** *intr.* (of hair) to stand on end. **†-ric·cio** *m.* shiver of fear (making one's hair stand on end). **-rione** *m.* (*pl.* **capirione**) (hist.) head of a 'rione', or region, in Rome; (*pl.* **caporioni**) ringleader; leader. **-riparto** *m.* (*pl.* **capiriparto**) head of a department. **-riverso** *adv.* head downwards. **-ronda** *m.* (*pl.* **capironda**) (mil.) conductor of a patrol. **-rove·scio** *adv.* head downwards. **-sala** *m. indecl.* (industr.) foreman. **-saldo** *m.* (*pl.* **capisaldi**) peg placed in the ground to indicate the level to which it must be raised or lowered; point of reference; main point, basis; (surv.) datum point; (mil.) strong point; (naut.) mooring post. **-scaglione** (herald.) chevron and over all a chief. **-scala** *m.* (*pl.* **capiscala**) landing; (naut.) metal or canvas hatch hood. **-scuola** *m.* (*pl.* **capiscuola**) founder of a school of thought or art. **-sesto** *m.* (naut.) foremost frame of a ship. **-setta** *m.* (*pl.* **capisetta**) leader of a sect. **-sezione** *m.* (*pl.* **capisezione**) head of a department. **-soldo** *m.* (mil.) extra pay. **-squadra** *m.* (*pl.* **capisquadra**) leader of a squad; charge hand, ganger. **-squadri·glia** *m.* (naut.) flotilla-leader. **-squadrone** *m.* squadron-leader. **-stanza** *m.* (*pl.* **capistanza**) head of a room, office-manager. **-stazione** *m.* (*pl.* **capistazione**) station-master. **-sti·pite** *m.* head of a clan; founder of a family. **-stiva** *m.* (*pl.* **capistiva**) (naut.) captain of the hold. **-storno** *m.* (vet.) gid (in sheep). **-stregone** *m.* (joc.) sorcerer-in-chief. **-tamburo** *m.* (*pl.* **capotamburi**) drum-major. **-tasto** *m.* (*pl.* **capotasti**) (mus.) capotasto, piece of ebony or ivory placed over the finger-board of a guitar so as to shorten the sounding-length of the strings; the left thumb of a 'cellist (when using thumb positions). **-ta·vola** *m.* (*pl.* **capita·vola**) person at the head of the table; a -tavola, at the head of the table. **-tec·nico** *m.* (*pl.* **capitec·nici**) chief technician. **-tela** *f.* (paperm.) breast-box. **-testa** *m.* (*pl.* **capitesta**) (naut.) end link. **†-timoniere** *m.* (naut.) warrant officer in charge of the navigating stores. **-torto** *m.* (orn.) wryneck. **-treno** *m.* (*pl.* **capitreno**) guard (of a train). **-truppa** *m.* leader of a troop. **-vacca·io** *m.* (orn.) Egyptian vulture, *Neophron percnopterus*. **-verde** *m.* (*pl.* **capoverdi**) (orn.) mallard. **-verso** *m.* (*pl.* **capoversi**) paragraph; sub-paragraph; beginning or end of a verse or paragraph; andiamo avanti fino al -verso, let's go to the end of the paragraph; (typ.) indent; †initial letter or word of a paragraph or line of verse. **-voga** *m.* (*pl.* **capivoga**) (naut.) stroke.

ca·poc *m. indecl.* kapok.

capoc·chi·a *f.* head of a pin or nail; knob of a club. **-eri·a** *f.* stubbornness, obstinacy. **-o** *m.* blockhead, dolt. **-ona** *f.* stupid woman. **-uto** *adj.* knobbly.

capoc·ci·a, **-o** *m.* (*pl.* **capocci**) head of a peasant house; patriarch; foreman; (joc.) person in authority, boss; leader. **-uto** *adj.* obstinate.

capoccione *m.* (ichth.) sand smelt, *Atherina boyeri*.

capolino *m. dim.* of capo, q.v.; far —, to peep; (bot.) head, capitulum.

ca·polo *m.* hilt of a sword; handle of a plough.

caponare [A I c]. See capponare, under cappone.

capon·e *m. augm.* of capo, q.v.; (fig.) blockhead, thickhead; large mask; (naut.; ichth.) see cappone. **-ag·gine** *f.* obstinacy, obduracy. **-eri·a** *f.* obstinacy, stubbornness.

caporal·e *m.* (mil.) corporal; ganger; porter (in a hospital); †head, leader; †*adj.* principal, chief. **-ato** *m.* rank of corporal, 'stripe'. **-etto** *m.* Il —, the little Corporal, Napoleon I.

†**caporano** *m.* leader, head, master.

caporchestra *m.* (mus.) conductor.

caporione *m.* See under **capo-banda**.

caporosso *m.* (orn.). See **capirosso**.

capot-are [A I] *intr.* (*aux.* avere) to overturn (of an aeroplane, car). -**amento** *m.* overturning, capsizing.

capo-te *m.*, -**tis** *m. indecl.* (motor.) hood.

capotorto *m.* (orn.). See under **capo-banda**.

capottare [A I] and deriv. See **capotare**.

capovol·g-ere [C 5] *tr.* to turn upside down; — la situazione, to reverse the situation; *rfl.* to capsize, to turn upside down. -**imento** *m.* capsizing, turning upside down.

capovoltare [A I] *tr.* See **capovolgere**.

capp-a¹ *f.* cape, cloak, hood; romanzo di — e spada, cloak and dagger novel; †cavarne — o mantello, to have done, to be rid of a thing by hook or by crook; (eccl.) cappa, kind of cope; (provb.) per un punto Martin perse la —, for want of a nail the horse was lost; (hist.) hooded cloak, esp. as worn by guilds; (naut.) heaving-to; essere (mettere, stare) alla —, to heave-to; alla —! lay-to! (joc.) nose; pyramid of four walnuts in the game of nocino; hood of a fireplace; (naut.) tarpaulin for protecting goods on deck; (poet.) vault, canopy; sotto la — del sole, under the canopy of high heaven, in this world. -**amagna** *f.* (eccl.) cappa magna; state robe, ceremonial robe; in -amagna, in all one's finery, in pomp and ceremony. †-**ato** *adj.* hooded; (herald.) chapé. -**etta** *f. dim.* of **cappa**¹; casing of sword-handle.

cappa² *f.* (zool.) bivalve molluscs of various species; — lunga, razor shell, *Ensis ensis*, or *Pinna nobilis*; — di dio, *Ensis ensis*; — chione, *Meretrix chione*, an edible bivalve; — gallina, *Chamelaea gallina*, an edible bivalve; — verrucosa, *Venus verrucosa*, an edible bivalve; — incrocicchiata, *Paphia decussata*, butter fish.

capp-a³ *f.* name of the letter K. -**acismo** *m.* (phon.) kappacism.

†**capp-are** *tr.* to choose, to pick. †-**ata** *f.* choice. †-**ato** *part. adj.* chosen; select; illustrious.

cap·paro *m.* (bot.). See **cappero**.

cappeggi-are [A 3 c] *intr.* (*aux.* essere) (naut.) to heave-to (in a storm). -**ato** *part. adj.* (naut.) lying-to.

cappeggio *m.* (naut.) lying-to.

cappell-a¹ *f.* (eccl.) chapel; — della Madonna, Lady chapel; — gentilizia, (formerly) family chapel (with tombs) in church; (now) family burial-place in cemetery; esser messo in —, to be taken into prison chapel before execution; (eccl.) chaplaincy; — ardente, *chapelle ardente*, brightly lit room where a body lies in state; (mus.) the singers or instrumentalists in a chapel choir; a —, voices unaccompanied; voices accompanied by organ only; tempo a —, see **alla breve**, under **breve**; maestro di —, choirmaster; musica a —, music in (pure) church style; (eccl.) service with music. -**ano** *m.* chaplain; curate; -ano militare, chaplain to the Forces. -**anato** *m.* chaplainship, chaplaincy. -**ani·a** *f.*, †-**aneri·a** *f.* (eccl.) chaplainship. -**one** *m. augm.* (pop. Flor.) the Spanish chapel in Santa Maria Novella.

cappella² *f.* head of a nail; cap of a mushroom; †little hood.

cappella·io *m.* See under **cappello**.

cappellano *m.* See under **cappella**¹.

cappell-o *m.* hat; head-gear, head covering; bonnet; — a cilindro, — a staio, — a tuba, top hat, silk hat; — a cilindro compressibile, opera hat, gibus; — a bombetta, — duro, bowler; — floscio, Trilby, felt hat; — morbido a tesa larga, soft broad-brimmed hat, slouch hat; mettersi il —, to put on one's hat; levarsi il —, to take off one's hat, to raise one's hat; far di — a, to take off one's hat to, to acknowledge, to bow to; amico di —, bowing acquaintance, nodding acquaintance; tanto di — a, hats off to; tenere il — sulle ventitré, to wear one's hat at a rakish angle; posare il —, to fall on one's feet, to strike it lucky; pigliare il —, prender il —, to depart, to take offence; (eccl.) — cardinalizio, cardinal's hat, red hat; ricevere il —, to be made a cardinal; top part, top, head; still-head; head of a fermenting liquid; lid; cover, covering; clouds covering a mountain-top; preface, preamble, introductory paragraph, foreword; (text.) flat (of carding machine); †garland; †crown. -**ac·cia** *f.* (orn.) crested lark, *Galerida cristata*. -**ac·cio** *m. pejor.* of **cappello**; (fig.) rebuke, reprimand; far -accio, to make a top fall instead of spinning it; tree covered with vines, left unpruned; *pl.* (bot.) burdock, *Arctium Lappa*. -**a·ia** *f.* milliner. -**a·io** *m.* hatter; (hawking) person who manages the hawk's hood. -**ata** *f.* hatful; quattrini a -ate, bags of money; swipe with a hat.

-**eri·a** *f.* hat shop (for men). -**etto** *m. dim.* of **cappello**; toe-cap of a sock or stocking; covering piece of waxed cloth at the top of an umbrella; cover for a retort; head of a nail; head of a screw; support for compass needle; leather helmet; *pl.* Venetian or Albanian mercenaries wearing leather helmets; (cul.) pasta stuffed with minced meat, for soup; (vet.) tumour in a horse's hock; a boys' game in which coins are shaken up and covered with a hat and a guess is made whether there are more heads or tails. -**iera** *f.* hat-box. †-**ina·io** *m.* hat-stand; pegs and hanging space in a cupboard. -**one** *m. augm.* of **cappello**; (mil. slang) raw recruit; *pl.* (bot.) Venus's navelwort, pennywort, *Umbilicus rupestris*; raw recruit; (joc. Florence) policeman. -**otto**, -**ozzo** *m.* percussion cap; (eng.) cap; -otto filettato, cap nut. -**uto** *adj.* crested, hooded (of bird, snake, etc.).

cappellone¹ *m.* See under **cappella**.

cappellone² *m.* See under **cappello**.

cap·peri *excl.* See **cappero**².

cap·per-o¹ *m.* (bot.) caper, *Capparis spinosa*; — falso, Syrian bean-caper, *Zygophyllum fabago*. -**eto** *m.* ground planted with capers.

cap·per-o², -**i** *excl.* Good Lord!; good gracious!

capper-one *m.* peasant's hood worn over the cap; jerkin. -**uc·cia** *f. pejor.* of **cappa**; (fig.) †in -uccia, secretly, hidden, without being observed. †-**uc·cio** *m.* hood; gutter, eave.

cappetoni *m.pl.* (hist.) pure-blooded Spaniards (in America).

†**cap·pia** *f.* horseshoe.

cap·pi-o *m.* slip-knot; tassel; halter; loop, eye.

cap·pita *excl.* See **caspita**.

cappon-e¹ *m.* capon; far venire la pelle di — a uno, to make one go goose flesh, to give one a cold shiver. -**a·ia** *f.* fattening coop. -**are** [A I c] *tr.* to castrate (a fowl), to caponize. -**ata** *f.* dish made from capons. -**atura** *f.* castration. (-**cino** *m. dim.*) -**essa** *f.* pullet spayed for fattening as a poularde.

cappone² *m.* (ichth.) gurnard, *Trigla* spp.; — ubriaco, *Tr. lineata*; — imperiale, *Tr. cuculus*; —organo, *Tr. lyra*; — gavotto, — barilotta, *Tr. obscuro*; — gallinella, *Tr. lucerna*; — gorno, *Tr. gurnardus*.

cappon-e³ *m.* (naut.) cat, tackle for raising the anchor to the cat head. -**are** [A I c] *tr.* (naut.) to cat.

capponiera *f.* (mil.) trench, slit-trench; (naut.) roof fitting in the cabin of a Venetian gondola.

cappott-a *f.* mantle; woollen hat, woman's hat; (motor.) hood. -**ata** *f.* (aeron.) ground loop. -**atura** *f.* (motor.) hooding; (eng.) cowling. -**o** *m.* overcoat; cloak; bridge coat; overcoat; (cards) capot; vincere a -o, to win all the tricks. -**ino** *m.* naval officer's uniform.

cappuccin-a *f.* (eccl.) Capuchin nun, Capuchiness; (mil.) first band on a rifle. -**o** *m.* (eccl.) Capuchin (friar); *pl.* i -i, church and buildings of a Capuchin house; barba di -o, salad of many small herbs; coffee with milk, white coffee; (bot.) fior -o, nasturtium, *Tropaeolum*; barba di -i, salad plants, chicory or endive; (naut.) standard of the head; *adj.* insalata -a, salad of small herbs; (orn.) falco —, marsh harrier.

cappuc·c-io *m.* hood of a cloak; *pl.* (hist.) popular party in Florence; (mil.) armour-piercing nose cap; (eng.) nipple; (bot.) fior —, garden delphinium, annual larkspur, *Delphinium ajacis*; fior — scempio, Venus's looking-glass, *Specularia speculum-Veneris*; (naut.) — subacqueo, plastic diving bell; *adj.* (of cabbage or lettuce) making a good head. -**etto** *m. dim.* little hood; Cappuccetto Rosso, Little Red Riding-Hood. -**iato** *adj.* (bot.) hooded (of petal or leaf).

capr-a *f.* goat; she-goat; nanny goat; luoghi da -e, mountainous places; cavalcar la —, to deceive oneself, to be mistaken; salvar — e cavoli, tenere l'orto salvo e la — sazia, to have the best of both worlds, to have one's cake and eat it, (tanning) goatskin, kid; trestle; three-legged hoisting tackle, shear-legs, sawing-horse; triangle for tying up a culprit to be flogged; *pl.* (naut.) sharp high rocks; †(astron.) α Aurigae. -**ag·gine** *f.* (bot.) goat's rue, *Galega officinalis*. -**a·ia** *f.* goat-girl; goatherd's wife; †goat-pen. -**a·io** *m.* goatherd. -**areccia** *f.* goat-pen. †-**ara** *f.*, †-**aro** *m.* See **capraia, capraio**. -**ata** *f.* dam made with timbers fixed into the earth like trestles. -**e·olo** *m.* two-pronged fork for digging; tendrils. -**etto** *m.* sucking kid, kid; guanti di -etto, kid gloves; *pl.* (astron.) two stars near the arm of Auriga. -**ettato** *adj.* speckled with black. †-**igno** *adj.* see **caprino**. †-**ile** *m.* stall, shelter for goats. -**ina** *f.* goat dung used for manure. -**ino** *adj.* goat-like; pertaining to a goat; barba

capr-a (*cont.*)

-ina, goatee; pelle ⁓ina, goatskin; questione di lana ⁓ina, a dispute about a trifle; *n.m.* smell of goats; goat manure. ⁓i·**pede** *adj.* goat-footed.

caprato *m.* (chem.) caprate.

†**capresto** *m.* See **capestro**.

†**caprezzo** *m.* shudder, shiver.

capriata *f.* (bldg.) roof truss, truss; — semplice, king post truss.

†**capricciare** *vb.* See **caporicciare**, under **capo**.

capric·c-io *m.* caprice, whim; cavare un —, to indulge a whim; brief amour; passing fancy; vagary; (of a child) fare i -i, to have tantrums, to cry for what one wants, to be naughty; a —, following one's fancy; (mus.) capriccio, caprice. ⁓**etto** *m. dim.* of **capriccio**; (mus.) short caprice. ⁓**ioso** *adj.* capricious; whimsical, fanciful; (of a child) spoilt; naughty; wilful; wayward; freakish; bizarre, odd; charming and original. (⁓**iosamente** *adv.*) ⁓**iosetto**, ⁓**iosino** *adj. dim.* rather whimsical. ⁓**iosità** *f.* capriciousness.

ca·prico *adj.* (chem.) capric.

Capricorno *pr.n.m.* (geog.; astron.) Capricorn.

caprifi-co *m.* (*pl.* ⁓**chi**) (bot.) wild fig, *Caprificus*. ⁓**care** [A 2] *tr.* (bot.) to caprificate, to cross (a fig) with a wild variety; *tr.* to cross (a fig) with the wild fig by hanging the fruit of the wild fig upon the branches of a fig tree, so that cross-fertilization by insects may occur. ⁓**cazione** *f.* cross-fertilization of figs and wild figs.

caprifo·glio *m.* (bot.) honeysuckle, *Lonicera periclymenum* and other species.

capr-ilo *m.* (chem.) capryl. ⁓**ilato** *m.* (chem.) caprylate. ⁓**i·lico** *adj.* (chem.) caprylic. ⁓**ilone** *m.* (chem.) product obtained by the distillation of barium caprylate.

caprimul-go *m.* (*pl.* ⁓**ghi**) goat-milker, goatherd; (orn.) nightjar, *Caprimulgus europaeus*.

caprina[1] *f.* (chem.) capric acid.

caprina[2] *f.* See under **capra**.

caprinella *f.* (bot.) European leadwort, *Plumbago europaea*; couch-grass, stroyle, *Agropyrum repens*.

caprino *adj.* See under **capra**.

ca·prio *m.* See **capri(u)olo**.

capri(u)ol-a *f.* somersault, cartwheel, caper; (of a horse) capriole; headlong fall; fare la —, to fall headlong; (naut.) to turn over end for end; (fig.) to fall from grace, to fall from power; volte-face (usually of political ideas); (zool.) doe of a roe deer. ⁓**are** [A I] *intr.* (*aux.* avere) to somersault, to cut capers.

capri(u)ol-o *m.* roe buck, *Capreolus capraea*; (cul.) venison; vine-shoot; (naut.) quoins; (herald.) chevron. ⁓**ato** *adj.* (herald.) chevronny.

capr-o *m.* (zool.) see **caprone**; (fig.) — emissario, — espiatorio, scapegoat.

capr-oato *m.* (chem.) caproate. ⁓**o·ico** *adj.* (chem.) caproic. ⁓**oileno** *m.* (chem.) caproylene. ⁓**oi·na** *f.* (chem.) caproin.

caprone *m.* (zool.) billy goat, he-goat.

Caproni *m. indecl.* warplane named after builder (G. Caproni).

caprug·gin-e *f.* chimb-notch, notch in a stave for fixing the bottom of a cask. ⁓**are** [A I S] *tr.* to notch (cask staves). ⁓**atoio** *m.* croze, a cooper's tool for making chimb-notches.

cap·sico *m.* (bot.) capsicum, plants of Solanum family, including Cayenne peppers.

cap·sul-a *f.* capsule; percussion cap; (chem.) evaporating dish. ⁓**are** *adj.* capsular; (ent.) verme ⁓are, boll-worm (of cotton); coleottero ⁓are, cotton boll weevil, *Anthonomus grandis*. ⁓**ismo** *m.* (eng.) rotary pump; compressore a ⁓ismo, rotary blower.

capt-are *tr.* (radio) to pick up; to capture. ⁓**a·bile** *adj.* (radio) that can be picked up, receivable. ⁓**azione** *f.* (techn.) fixation; (leg.) undue influence (e.g. over a testator). †⁓**ivo** *m.*, *adj.* captive. †⁓**ivare** *tr.* to take captive; to captivate.

†**captiv-are** *tr.* to capture. †⁓**o** *m.* captive.

Ca·pu-a *pr.n.f.* (geog.) Capua. ⁓**ano** *adj.*, *n.m.* Capuan.

capuc·c-io *m. dim.* of **capo**; head of threshing flail; obstinate person. ⁓**ac·cio** *m.* pig-headed person.

capzioso *adj.* captious, fraudulent; insidious. (⁓**amente** *adv.*)

cara[1] *f.* dear one; mia —, my dear girl; *adj. f.* see **caro**[1].

car-a[2] *f.* (bot.) stonewort, *Chara vulgaris* and other species.

†**cara**[3] *f.* aspect.

carabat·tole *f.pl.* odds and ends, trinkets; baubles; pigliar le —, to pack up one's traps and be off.

†**ca·rabe** *f.* yellow amber.

cara·bidi *m.pl.* (ent.) carabids (kinds of beetles).

carabin-a *f.* carbine. ⁓**ata** *f.* carbine-shot. ⁓**etta** *f.* tiro ⁓etta, prone position (rifle firing). ⁓**iere** *m.* carabiniere, member of an Army corps which is also a police force; (hist.) foot or horse soldier of an army of twenty legions raised by Victor Emmanuel I in 1814; (joc.) formidable woman, 'battle-axe'; cappello da ⁓iere, Napoleonic-type hat of the carabiniere uniform. †⁓**o** *m.* carabineer.

ca·rabo *m.* (ent.) various species of carabid beetles; — dorato, *Carabus auratus*; — violaceo, *C. violaceus*; (archaeol.) a Greek vessel.

carabottino *m.* (naut.) wooden grating.

caracalla *f.* (Rom. antiq.) long tunic.

caracca *f.* (naut.) carrack.

Caracci *pr.n.f.* (geog.) Karachi.

carace *m.* (ichth.) *Puntazzo puntazzo*, a kind of sea bream.

carachiri *m. indecl.* hara-kiri.

carac-ò, ⁓**ollo**[1] *m.* (bot.) caracol, fragrant bean, *Phaseolus caracalla*.

caracoll-are [A I] *intr.* (*aux.* avere) to caracol. ⁓**o** *m.* caracol; (mil.) movement of the first rank to the rear after firing a volley.

caracora *f.* (naut.) caracore, Malay boat.

caracu·l *m. indecl.* (tanning) Persian sheep.

caraff-a *f.* carafe; jug; water-jug, glass-jug; old liquid measure, equivalent to 8 decilitres at Naples and 4 decilitres at Palermo. †⁓**o** *m.* spurt, gush.

caragana *f.* (bot.) Siberian pea, *Caragana*.

cara·gnol-a *f.*, ⁓**o** *m.* (bot.). See **caracò**.

Car-a·ibi *pr.n.m.pl.* (geog.) Mar dei —, Caribbean Sea. ⁓**ai·bico** *adj.* (geog.) Caribbean.

caramba[1] *f.* (geol.) fissure.

caramba[2] *excl.* expression of surprise or wonder.

caram·bol-a *f.* a game like snooker; cannon (at billiards); (motor.) multiple collision. ⁓**are** [A I S] *intr.* (*aux.* avere) to cannon (at billiards). ⁓**ata** *f.*, ⁓**o** *m.* cannon (at billiards). ⁓**ista** *m.* player of 'carambola', snooker-player.

caramele *m.* caramel; crème brûlée; burnt sugar.

caramell-a *f.* sweet, boiled sweet, candy; toffee; monocle; (mus.) kind of bagpipe. ⁓**aio** *m.* sweet-vendor; keeper of a sweet-booth at a fair. ⁓**are** [A I] *tr.* to brown (sugar), to candy. ⁓**ato** *part. adj.* candied. ⁓**o** *m.* see **caramele**.

†**caramessa** *f.* kermesse.

†**caramo·gio** *m.* stunted person, dwarf.

caramus(s)ale *m.* (naut.) caramoussal, a Turkish or Moorish ship of burden.

carance *m.* (ichth.) horse mackerel, *Caranx trachurus*.

caran·col-a *f.* cavil; pretext. ⁓**are** [A I S] *intr.* (*aux.* avere) to cavil; to seek pretexts.

carantano *m.* (numism.) an old Austrian copper coin, so called after the province of Carinthia.

caranza *f.* (bot.) balsam-pear, *Momordica Charantia*.

carapace *m.* (zool.) carapace.

†**carapign-a** *f.* iced drink. †⁓**are** *tr.* to ice (a drink); *rfl.* ⁓**arsi** a, (fig.) to flatter, to hang round, to 'freeze on to'.

carapina *f.* carap oil.

carapuzza *f.* a kind of moorish armour.

caras·sio *m.* (ichth.) crucian carp, *Carassius carassius*; goldfish.

carata[1] *f.* (bot.) fruit of carob-tree, *Ceratonia Siliqua*.

†**carata**[2] *f.* See **carato**.

caratello *m.* a small cask, equal to the twenty-fourth part of an ordinary barrel.

carat-o *m.* carat; (naut.) one of the twenty-four parts into which a ship, its ownership and profits can be divided; (comm.) share in a commercial business. ⁓**are** [A I] *tr.* to weigh into carats; to examine minutely; (eng.) to gauge (a piece of mechanism) by the size of its most important part, such as the bore of a gun or the diameter of the cylinder of an internal combustion engine. ⁓**ista** *m.* (comm.) sharer; part-owner.

carat·ter-e *m.* character; disposition; type; nature; property; peculiarity; character part; commedia di —, comedy of character; style; literary portrait, sketch; letter, print, type, handwriting; scritto a -i di scatola, written in large block capitals; (typ.) type; fonderia di -i, type foundry; -i di testo, book-face; — gotico, black letter; — grassetto, bold-face; — schiacciato, worn type; (mus.) musica di mezzo —, music (in opera) which is neither serious nor comic; (theol.) character. ⁓**ista** *m.* (theatr.) character actor. ⁓**i·stica** *f.* characteristic, trait; feature; (math.) charac-

caratter-e (*cont.*)
teristic, the whole number in a logarithm; (eng.) performance; *pl.* (eng.) specification. **-i·stico** *adj.* characteristic, typical; full of character, individual, distinctive; atypical; picturesque, quaint; (mus.) nota **-istica**, characteristic note (of a mode or intonation); leading-note; (mil.) note **-istiche**, annual reports on the conduct of officers and soldiers. **-iẓẓare** [A I] *tr.* to characterize. **-olo·gico** *adj.* (psych.) characterological; prove **-ologiche**, character tests.

†carat·tola *f.* trifle, bagatelle.

caravana *f.* See **carovana**.

caravanserra·glio *m.* caravanserai.

caravẹlla *f.* (naut.) caravel; (zool.) — portoghese, Portuguese man o' war, *Physalia caravella*.

carb-ammato *m.* (chem.) carbamate. **-am·mico** *adj.* (chem.) carbamic. **-am·mido** *m.* (chem.) carbamide, urea.

†carba·sio *m.* easterly wind.

†car·baso *m.* veil; transparent cloth; linen mantle.

carb-azotato *m.* (chem.) picrate. **-azo·tico** *adj.* (chem.) picric.

carbinolo *m.* (chem.) methyl alcohol, methanol, wood spirit.

carboidrato *m.* (chem.) carbohydrate.

carboliṣmo *m.* (med.) phenol poisoning.

carbon·chio, carbọnchio *m.* carbuncle; (vet.) — maligno, anthrax; — sintomatico, blackleg, black quarter; (bot.) smut of wheat, *Ustilago nuda*; (herald.) escarbuncle, chabocle.

carboncino *m.* See under **carbọne**.

carbọn-e *m.* charcoal; carbon; coal; — forte, hard charcoal (from oak, chestnut); carbon dolce, soft charcoal (from willow, alder, poplar); carbon fossile, (mineral) coal; — animale, animal charcoal; **-i** agglomerati, coal bricks, ovals, boiler fuel; — bianco, 'white coal', hydroelectric power; carta —, carbon paper; — animato, cored carbon (for arc lamps); da segnare col — bianco, to be marked with a white stone; disegno a —, charcoal drawing; a misura di —, in plenty; nero come il —, black as soot; essere sui **-i** ardenti, to be on tenterhooks. **-a·ia** *f.* clearing in the woods where charcoal is burnt; charcoal kiln; charcoal store or cellar; dark dungeon; moat round a city wall; wood for burning into charcoal; charcoal burner's wife. **-a·io** *m.* charcoal burner; coal and charcoal seller; coalman, coal merchant; (naut.) collier. **-are** [A I c] *tr.* (naut.) to coal. **-ariṣmo** *m.* (Ital. hist.) the policy of the Carbonari. **-aro** *m.* see **carbonaio**; (Ital. hist.) member of the secret society of Carbonari formed in the early part of the nineteenth century for the liberation of Italy. **†-ata** *f.* salt pork grilled over a coal fire; (fig.) ridurre in **-ata**, to burn to a crisp. **-atazione** *f.* (techn.) carbonation. **-ato** *m.* (chem.) carbonate; dark brown or nearly black (as the colour of an animal's coat). **-cino** *m.* (art) charcoal stick, charcoal pencil; disegno al **-cino**, black chalk drawing. **-ella** *f.* small coal, ember; type of pear. **-era** *f.* (naut.) staysail. **-eri·a** *f.* (Ital. hist.) secret society of the Carbonari. **-ẹtto** *m.* dark-red coral. **-ic·cio** *adj.* blackish. **-iera** *f.* coal store, coal bunker; charcoal burner; (naut.) collier. **-iero** *m.* See **carbonaio**. **-i·fero** *adj.* (geol.) carboniferous. **-i·gia** *f.* charcoal dust. **-ile** *m.* coal bunker, coal tender; (chem.) carbonyl, ketone radical. **-ioṣo** *adj.* (geol.) carbonaceous. **-issag·gio** *m.* carbonization. **-iẓẓare** [A I] *tr.* to carbonize; to char. **-iẓẓato** *part. adj.* carbonized, charred. **-iẓẓazione** *f.* carbonization; charring. **-ometri·a** *f.* determination of the amount of carbon dioxide produced by a living organism. **-oṣo** *adj.* (chem.) containing carbon.

carbọ·nico *adj.* (chem.) carbonic; anidride **-ica**, carbon dioxide; (hist.) pertaining to the Carboneria, q.v. under **carbọne**.

carbo-nio *m.* (chem.) carbon; idrato di —, carbohydrate; ossido di —, carbon monoxide.

carborundo *m.* (eng.) carborundum; (chem.) silicon carbide.

carboss-ile *m.* (chem.) carboxyl. **-ilazione** *f.* (chem.) carboxylation. **-i·lico** *adj.* (chem.) carboxyl.

†carbun·co(lo) *m.* carbuncle; pustule; kind of soil.

carbur-o *m.* (chem.) carbide; — di calcio, calcium carbide, acetylene carbide. **-ante** *m.* motor fuel, vaporizing oil; il consumo del **-ante**, fuel consumption. **-are** [A I] *tr.* to carburet; to vaporize (fuel); (metall.) to carburize. **-ato** *part. adj.* carburetted; vaporized; (metall.) carburized. **-atore** *m.* (eng.; motor.) carburettor; annegamento del **-atore**, flooding of the carburettor; vaschetta del **-atore**, float-chamber. **-azione** *f.* (motor.) carburation; **-azione** ricca, rich mixture; **-azione** magra, weak mixture; (metall.) carburizing.

carcame[1] *m.* carcase; body of an animal after skinning and removal of the flesh; (naut.) wreckage of a hull.

†carcame[2] *m.* necklace of gold and gems; headdress of gold and gems worn as a garland.

carcare [A 2] and derivs. (poet.). See **caricare**.

carca·ria *f.* (ichth.). See **cagnaccio**, under **cagna**.

carcassa *f.* carcase; skeleton; smagrito fino alla —, reduced to skin and bone; the bones of the thorax; (fig.) physical wreck; broken-down machine, old crock; (naut.) hull; (mil.) grenade; (eng.) frame of a machine; casing; (electr.) yoke.

†carcasso *m.* quiver (for arrows).

carcer-are [A I s] *tr.* to imprison, to gaol, to send to prison, to put in prison. **-amẹnto** *m.* See **carcerazione**. **-ato** *part. adj.* imprisoned; *n.m.* prisoner; (fig.) fare una vita da **-ato**, to be tied to one's work. **-azione** *f.* imprisonment, incarceration.

car·cer-e *m., f.* (*pl.f.*) prison, gaol; imprisonment; direttore delle **-i**, prison governor; — duro, imprisonment with added punishment, such as hard labour; — preventivo, detention pending conviction or sentence, detention on suspicion (N.B. not English 'preventive detention', which aims at preventing further crime by habitual criminals); le **-i** giudiziarie, prison(s) where accused persons are held in custody pending trial. **-a·rio** *adj.* having to do with prison; guardie **-arie**, prison warders. **-iere** *m.* prison warder; gaoler.

carchedo·nico *adj.* Carthaginian.

car·cino *m.* (zool.) shore crab, *Carcinus maenas*.

carcin-oma *m.* (med.) carcinoma. **-oṣi** *f.* (med.) carcinosis.

carciof-o *m.* (bot.) globe artichoke, *Cynara scolymus*; — salvatico, wild artichoke, cardoon, *C. cardunculus*; — grasso, house leek, *Sempervivum tectorum*; (fig.) la politica del —, the policy of coping with enemies (or victims) one at a time; mangiare il —, to plod along patiently; (slang) homosexual; blockhead; (cul.) **-i** alla giudia, artichokes dipped in boiling oil. **-a·ia** *f.* artichoke bed. **-a·io** *m.* artichoke grower or seller; *adj.* artichoke producing. **-ẹto** *m.* artichoke bed. **-olata** *f.* dish or meal of artichokes. **-ọne** *m.* bearded artichoke.

†carci-o·fano, †-offo, †-o·folo *m.* see **carciofo**.

car-co *adj.* (*m.pl.* **-chi**) (poet.) loaded; laden, burdened (cf. **carico**); *n.m.* (poet.) weight, load.

carda *f.* (text.) card, carding machine.

carda·ria *f.* See under **cardo**.

carda·i-o *m.* (text.) carder. **-(u)olo** *m.* (text.) carder.

cardam-omo, -ọne *m.* (bot.) cardamom.

card-a·nico *adj.* pertaining to Cardano, mathematician of Pavia, 1501–76; sospensione **-anica**, Cardan suspension; (eng.) giunto —, universal joint. **-ana** *f.* gimbals for a compass. **-ano** *m.* joint or suspension according to Cardano's method (used for compasses, chronometers, etc.).

card-are [A I] *tr.* (text.) to card; (fig.) to backbite. **-ata** *f.* (text.) carding; una **-ata** di lana, quantity of wool carded. **-ato** *part. adj.* (text.) carded; (fig.) terse, precise, fine; *n.m.* (text.) type of woollen material (e.g. tweed, flannel). **-atore** *m.* carder. **-atrice** *f.* woman carder; carding machine. **-atura** *f.* carding; section of wool factory where carding is carried out. **-eggiare** [A 3 c] *tr.* (text.) to card; (fig.) to speak evil of; to misuse. **-eri·a** *f.* (text.) card room.

cardell-o *m.* (orn.) see **cardellino**; (agric.) fico —, kind of fig. **-ino** *m.* (orn.) goldfinch, *Carduelis carduelis*; *adj.* (geol.) pietra **-ina**, travertine stone quarried in Latium.

carde·nia *f.* (pop.). See **gardenia**.

carderi·a *f.* See under **cardare**.

cardẹto *m.* See under **cardo**.

cardi·aco *adj.* (med.) cardiac.

†cardina·io *m.* carder.

cardinal-e *adj.* cardinal; principal; numerali **-i**, cardinal numbers; virtù **-i**, cardinal virtues; mattoni **-i**, large bricks used for roofing ovens; (naut.) punti **-i**, cardinal points; *n.m.* (eccl.) cardinal; (cul.) boccone di —, Pope's nose; (orn.) cardinal, pine grosbeak, *Pinicola enucleator*; (bot.) nappe di —, cockscomb amaranth, *Celosia cristata*; †door-post, upright to which the hinges are affixed. **†-ano** *adj.* see **cardinalizio**. **†-a·tico** *m.* see **cardinalato**. **-ato** *m.* (eccl.) cardinalate. **-esco** *adj.* (*m.pl.* **-eschi**) cardinal-like; cardinal's; †bright red; *n.m.* bright red cloth. **-ista** *m.* (hist.) cardinalist. **-i·zio** *adj.* cardinalitial; cardinal's. **-ume** *m.* group of cardinals.

car·dine *m.* pintle, hinge; (fig.) pivotal point of an argument or theory; (naut.) ring and pintle of rudder; (astron.) cardinal point; (poet.) i cardini del mondo, the foundations of the earth.

cardino *m.* See under **cardo**.

car·dio *m.* (zool.) cockle, *Cardium* spp.

cardio-gramma *m.* (med.) cardiogram. **-palmo** *m.* palpitation of the heart.

cardioide *adj.* (radio; math.) cardioid.

card·o *m.* thistle, including many prickly plants belonging to various genera; (hist.) ordine del —, order of the thistle; (text.) carding tool for wool, consisting of two toothed iron plates; (archaeol.) main road running from south to north. **-a·ia** *f.* heap of thistles. **-ella** *f.* see **cardino**. **-ęto** *m.* field of thistles, patch of thistles. **-ino** *m.* brush with iron bristles. **-oncello**, **-oncino** *m.* (agric.) cuttings from old artichoke plants. **-oncione** *m.* (bot.) acanthus, *A. moltis*. **-one** *m.* cardoon, *Cynara cardunculus*. **-uc·cio** *m.* kind of thistle; thistledown.

carega *f.* (dial. Ven.) chair; (hist.) chariot.

†**careggiare** *tr.* to caress; to love; to hold dear; to indulge; to with-hold, to make appear desirable and cherished.

careggiativo *adj.* caressing; loving, fond.

†**carell-a** *f.* wooden frame for drying chestnuts. †**-o** *m.* cushion covered with chequerboard patterned cloth.

caren-a (Flor.), **caręn-a** (Rom.) *f.* keel, submerged part of the hull of a ship; (poet.) ship; dar — a, to careen; abbattere in —, to list for careening; (bot.) keel (of a flower). **-ag·gio** *m.* (naut.) careening; bacino di **-aggio**, dry dock; (aeron.) fairing. **-are** [A I, A I C] *tr.* (naut.) to careen; -are a secco, to dry dock; (motor. industr.; aeron.) to streamline, to fair. **-ato** *part. adj.* (naut.) careened; (aeron.) streamlined; (motor.) un profilo **-ato**, stream-line. **-atura** *f.* (naut.) careening; (aeron.) fairing, cowling.

carenza, *f.* privation; dearth; lack; — di vitamine, vitamin de-ficiency.

carest-i·a *f.* famine; dearth, shortage; avarice. **-ioso** *adj.* barren; pertaining to famine. †**-isi·a** *f.* see **carestia**. **-oso** *adj.* of famine; barren; anni **-osi**, lean years; high-priced (of a shop, etc.).

carętto[1] *m.* (bot.) caricetum.

carętto[2] *adj. dim.* of **caro**, q.v.; rather expensive.

caręzza[1] *f.* dearness of price, expensiveness; shortage; dearth.

caręzz-a[2] *f.* caress; kindness, act of kindness; affection; **-e asinine**, rude acts; clownish behaviour.

carezz-are [A I C] *tr.* to caress, to fondle; to stroke, to pat; — un'idea, to cherish an idea. **-ativo** *adj.* wooing, winning. **-ato** *part. adj.* caressed, fondled; illusioni **-ate**, cherished illusions. **-ęvole** *adj.* caressing; fondling; coaxing, wheedling; cuddly; soft, inviting caresses; la mia gattina è molto **-evole**, my kitten is very inviting to stroke. (**-evolmęnte** *adv.*) **-oso** *adj.* loving, affectionate.

†**carfagno** *adj.* (of colour) dull, subfusc; opaque, dark; (also *n.m.*).

car·fano *m.* (bot.) femmina, white water-lily, *Nymphaea alba*; *m.* — maschio, yellow water-lily, *Nuphar lutea*.

carfologi·a *f.* (med.) carphology, flocculation.

†**cargare** *vb.* and derivs. See **caricare**.

cari *m. indecl.* (cul.) curry.

cariag·gio *m.* See **carriaggio**.

cari-are [A4] *tr.* to cause to decay; *rfl.* to decay. **-ato** *part. adj.* decayed; very old, decrepit. **-azione** *f.* decaying; decay.

caria·tide *f.* (archit.) caryatid; (fig.) old, ugly person; far la —, to remain still and silent during a conversation.

cari·bico *adj.* (geog.). See **caraibico**, under **caraibi**.

†**caribo** *m.* roundelay, song to accompany dancing.

ca·rica *f.* charge; load; appointment, office; duties; nella — di consigliere, as a consultant, in an advisory capacity; essere in —, to be in office, to be in charge; entrare in —, to take office, to take charge; durata della —, term of office; instructions; care, custody; person holding office, officially; tornare alla —, to insist, to persist; (watchm.) winding; albero di —, winding stem; meccanismo di —, winding mechanism; (techn.) filler weighting; (rugger) tackle; (naut.) hoist; (mil.) charge; suonare la —, to sound the charge; a passo di —, at the double; refill (e.g. of a ball-point pen); (electr.) charge; entità di —, charging rate.

caric-abbasso *m.* (naut.) down-haul rope (of a sail). **-abolina** *f.* (naut.) leechline. **-abbugna** *f.* (naut.) clew-garnet. **-aggondo** *m.* (naut.) brail holding the bolt-rope. **-alcarro** *m.* (naut.) double brailing on lateen sails. **-ammezzo** *m.* (naut.) buntline. **-appęnna** *f.* brailing for the upper part of a sail.

caric-are [A2S] *tr.* (*prep.* di, con) to load; to heap (with), to pile up (with); to overload; — arsi lo stomaco, to overeat; — d'ingiurie, to heap abuse upon; to increase, to heighten, to deepen; — la

dose, to increase the dose; — le tinte, to paint in deeper colours, (fig.) to exaggerate, to lay it on thick; to bet heavily on; — un orologio, to wind up a clock; — una trappola di formaggio, to bait a mousetrap with cheese; -arla a, to set a trap for, to play a trick on; — la pipa, to fill one's pipe; — una penna, to fill a fountain pen; to get a refill for (a ball-point pen); — una macchina fotografica, to load a camera; — una pompa, to prime a pump; — una mina, to arm a mine; (electr.) to charge; (rugger) to tackle; (comm.) to charge; (techn.) to weight; (naut.) to heave taut; — a colletta, to load a mixed cargo; (mil.) — il nemico, to charge the enemy. **-a·bile** *adj.* (photog.) **-abile alla luce del giorno, daylight loading. **-amento** *m.* loading; charging; charge; (watchm.) a **-amento** automatico, self-winding. **-ato** *part. adj.* loaded; charged; (electr.) live. (**-atore** *m.* **-atrice** *f.*)

caricatur-a *f.* caricature. **-ista** *m.* caricaturist.

ca·rice *f.* (bot.) sedge, *Carex*.

ca·ri-co[1] *m.* (*pl.* **-chi**) load; fare il —, to load up; burden; weight; sobbarcarsi al — di, to shoulder the burden of; avere la famiglia a —, to have a family to support; — di coscienza, a load on one's conscience; heap, pile; un — di bugie, a heap of lies; un — di bastonate, a shower of blows; blame, accusation; far — a, dar — a, to blame; (leg.) accusation; charge; testimone a —, witness for the prosecution; (comm.) segnare a —, to debit; a — di, to the account of; a — mio, to my account, at my expense (also fig.); il trasporto sarà a — vostro, carriage forward; (econ.) — tributario, fiscal burden; (naut.) cargo, freight; shipment; loading, lading; polizza di —, lading bill; nave da —, freighter, cargo boat; (eng.) head (of water); (geol.) metamorfismo di —, static metamorphism; *pl.* (cards) in the game of 'briscola', the aces and the threes.

ca·ri-co[2] *adj.* (*m.pl.* **-chi**) loaded, laden, burdened; charged; — di anni, burdened with years; — di gloria, laden with glory; — di onori, heaped with honours; tinte **-che**, deep tones, warm colours; caffè —, strong coffee; cielo —, overcast sky; il fucile è —, the gun is loaded.

Cariddi *pr.n.f.* (myth.) Charybdis; essere tra Scilla e —, to be between Scylla and Charybdis.

ca·ri-e *f.* caries (in the bone, teeth); decay, dry rot; (bot.) decay in trees. **-oso** *adj.* carious, decayed.

cariello[1] *m.* latrine cover, lavatory seat.

cariello[2] *m.* lace trimming.

cariglione *m.* (mus.) carillon; musical box.

†**carina** *f.* See **carena**.

carino *adj. dim.* See under **caro**.

carioca *f.* carioca, S. American dance.

cario-cinęsi *f.* (biol.) karyokinesis. **-cine·tico** *adj.* (biol.) karyo-kinetic. **-die·resi** *f.* (biol.) nuclear division, esp. anaphase and telophase. **-fillina** *f.* (chem.) caryophyllin. **-gami·a** *f.* (biol.) fusion of pronuclei at fertilization. **-plasma** *m.* (biol.) karyo-plasm.

cariol-a *f.* wheelbarrow. **-ata** *f.* wheelbarrow-load.

cariolisi *f. indecl.* (med.) achromatolysis.

carios·side *f.* (bot.) caryopsis, a type of dry fruit characteristic of grasses.

carişm-a *m.* (*pl.* **carişmi**, **cari·şmati**) (theol.) charism, charisma. **-a·tico** *adj.* charismatic.

†**cari·stia** *f.* See †**carita**.

carit-à *f. indecl.* love; — di patria, love of country; charity; Suora di —, Sister of Charity; ospizio di —, almshouse; congregazione di —, charitable association; act of charity; kindness; gift; alms; opere di —, good works; — fiorita, real act of charity, wonder-fully kind action; benevolence; compassion; favour; (fam.) — pelosa, suspect generosity, apparent kindness with selfish motive; fatemi la — di star fermi, do please keep still! per —! please!; for pity's sake!; please don't suggest such a thing; most certainly not!; God forbid! **-atevole** *adj.* charitable; benevolent; compassionate. (**-atevolmęnte** *adv.*) **-ativo** *adj.* charitable.

†**carita** *f.* (Pulci) name of a bird which could fly through fire unharmed.

†**carit-ade, -ate** *f.* See **carità**.

Ca·riti *f.pl.* (myth.) the Graces.

cariuola *f.* See **cariola**.

†**cari·zia** *f.* famine, privation; dearth, lack; need (cf. **carestia**).

carizzo *m.* (ichth.) *Spicara alcedo*, an edible sea fish.

carlina *f.* (bot.) carline thistle, *Carlina vulgaris*, or *C. acaulis*.

carlinga *f.* (naut.) keelson; (aeron.) cockpit.

carlino[1] *m.* (numism.) name given to coins of various values formerly current in Naples and other Italian States; il resto del —, change from a coin; (fig.) the second half, the remainder; 'Il Resto del Carlino', name of a Bologna newspaper.

carlino[2] *m.* (ichth.) gilt head, *Sargus annularis*.

Carlo *pr.n.m.* Charles; Carlo Magno, Charlemagne; farne quanto — in Francia, to get into a lot of scrapes; (Tusc.) aver fatto quanto — in Francia, to have completed a Herculean task.

carlona *adv. phr.* alla —, carelessly, in a slapdash manner.

Carlotta *pr.n.f.* Charlotte; (cul.) timbale of fruit.

Carmagnola *pr.n.f.* (geog.) Carmagnola, in Piedmont; †name of a dress and a dance in vogue at the time of the French Revolution.

carme *m.* (poet.) poem, long and serious lyric; hymn; *pl.* poetry, poetic song, 'numbers'; (Rom. antiq.) *carmen*, solemn rhythmical utterance; esp. oracle or incantation.

carmel-itano, -ita, -i·tico *adj., pr.n.m.* (eccl.) Carmelite; i Carmelitani scalzi, the Discalced Carmelites.

Carmelo *pr.n.m.* (geog.) Monte —, Mount Carmel.

carmina *f.* See **carminio**.

carmin-are[1] [A I] *tr.* (text.) to card (wool); (fig.) to examine, to look into, to sift, to comb; †to cudgel, to belabour. **-ato** *part. adj.* (text.) carded; (fig.) combed.

carmin-are[2] *tr.* (med.) to relieve of wind. **-ativo** *adj.* (med.) carminative.

car·mine *m.* (eccl.) Carmel, Carmelite house or church.

carmi·n-(i)o *m.* carmine, the colouring matter of cochineal. **-ato** *adj.* stained with carmine.

carnacciuto *adj.* See under **carne**.

carnagione[1] *f.* complexion; — rosea, pink complexion; — delicata, delicate complexion; cure della —, care of the skin.

carnagione[2] *f.* (geol.) calcareous pink and white stone quarried in Umbria.

carn-a·io *m.* common burial ground; charnel house; (fig.) slaughter, massacre; (joc.) questa spiaggia è un vero —, this beach is strewn with bodies (sunbathers, etc.); †storehouse for meat. **†-aiuolo** *m.* butcher, slaughterer; purveyor of meat.

carnal-e *adj.* carnal; peccato —, carnal sin; of the flesh, sensual, bodily, physical; worldly; blood (of relationships); cugino —, first cousin; affectionate, tender. (**-mente** *adv.*) **-ità** *f.* carnality, sensuality; tenderness, affection. **†-itade, †-itate** *f.* see **carnalità**. **-one** *m.* mundane person. **†-oso** *adj.* bestial, animal, carnal.

carnallite *f.* (geol.) carnallite, potassium magnesium chloride.

carname *m.* See under **carne**.

†carnasciale *m.* carnival. **†-are** *intr.* to hold carnival; to make merry.

carnascial-esco *adj.* (*m.pl.* **-eschi**) pertaining to carnival, carnival; canti -eschi, songs sung in carnivals (esp. in Florence in the fifteenth century).

†carnassale *m.* See **†carnasciale**.

carnassiero *adj.* See under **carne**.

carnat-o *adj.* incarnate; of good complexion; †pink, flesh-coloured; †inherent, congenital; *n.m.* (Tusc.) good complexion. **†-ura** *f.* complexion.

carna·uba *f.* carnauba (wax).

carn-e *f.* **1.** FLESH; in — e ossa, incarnate, in the flesh; color di —, flesh-coloured; aver poca — addosso, to be thin; aver molta — addosso, to be plump; essere in —, to be well covered, (fig.) to be prosperous; — d'Adamo, human nature, human frailty; essere — ed unghia, to be inseparable; rimettersi in —, to put on flesh after an illness; a —, naked; (theol.) the flesh; flesh and blood; risurrezione della —, resurrection of the body; *pl.* complexion, skin; aver le -i morbide, to have a tender skin. **2.** MEAT; — grossa, flesh of the larger animals; — di bue, beef; — di castrato, mutton; — di maiale, pork; — di vitello, veal; — col becco, poultry; — in iscatola, tinned meat; — congelata, frozen meat; — del macellaio, butcher's meat; — stufata, stewed meat; — tritata, minced meat; (fig.) mettere troppa — al fuoco, to have too many irons in the fire; non è — per i suoi denti, it's too difficult for him, it's not his cup of tea; non c'è — senz'osso, there is no rose without a thorn, there's always a fly in the ointment; flesh of fish; non essere nè — nè pesce, to be neither fish, flesh nor fowl; — da cannone, cannon fodder. **3.** PULP, flesh of fruit. **-accioso** *adj.* meaty, fleshy. **-acciuto** *adj.* plump, well-covered. **†-ag·gio** *m.* edible meat; meal of meat; carnage, slaughter.

-ame *m.* carrion. **-assiero** *adj.* carnivorous. **†-eggiare** *intr.* to eat meat; to banquet; to commit carnal sin. **-ic·cio** *m.* (tanning) flesh side of a skin; (industr.) scrow, spetches (hide scraps for glue-making). **-icino** *adj.* flesh-coloured, pink. **-ificazione** *f.* (med.) carnification. **-ismo** *m.* (med.) excessive meat diet.

Carne·ade *pr.n.m.* Carneades, the Stoic philosopher; (joc.) an unknown person (in reference to Don Abbondio's inquiry, 'Carneade, chi era costui?' in Manzoni's *Promessi Sposi*).

carnecotta *f.* stewed tripe.

carnefic-e *m.* executioner; butcher, torturer. **-ina** *f.* torture; (fig.) butchery.

†carneggiare *vb.* See under **carne**.

car·neo *adj.* fleshy; of meat; alimentazione carnea, meat diet.

carne-salata *f.* pickled pork. **-secca** *f.* salted pork, cooked shoulder; (Tusc.) bacon; (joc.) old woman.

†carnesciale, carnessale *m.* and derivs. See **carnasciale**.

carneval-e *m.* carnival; revelry; merrymaking; far —, to make merry; aver parecchi -i sulle spalle, to be well on in years; effigy of carnival burnt on the last evening; fat cheery person. **-are** [A I] *intr.* (*aux.* avere) to keep carnival; to revel, to make merry. **-ata** *f.* carnival fun; prank; escapade. **-esco** *adj.* (*m.pl.* **-eschi**) of carnival, carnival. **-ino** *m.* first Sunday in Lent; (Milan) mid-Lent. **-one** *m.* (Milan) extension of carnival; jovial-looking person. NOTE: Carnival in Italy is a time of merrymaking before Lent, but its length and its manner of celebration have much varied with place and period. It is usually said to last from 7 January to Shrove Tuesday inclusively, but may begin as early as 26 December or again may be limited to Shrovetide or Shrove Tuesday itself (as often in older writers). The 'Ambrosian' Carnival at Milan includes Ash Wednesday and the three succeeding days.

carnic·cio *m.* See under **carne**.

carnico *m.* (geol.) middle trias.

carnier-a *f.*, **-e** *m.*, **†-o** *m.* poacher's pocket; game bag; shooting jacket.

carnificazione *f.* (med.). See under **carne**.

carnificina *f.* See **carneficina**, under **carnefice**.

carnismo *m.* (med.). See under **carne**.

carni·voro *adj.* carnivorous; *n.m.* carnivore; meat eater.

carnos-o *adj.* fleshy; meaty; (med.) carnous; (tanning) lato —, flesh side. **-ità** *f.* fleshiness; (paint.) softness; (med.) carnosity.

carnotite *f.* (miner.) carnotite.

†carnovale *m.* and derivs. See **carnevale**.

carn-ume *m.* (zool.) *Microcosmus sulcatus*, a large edible tunicate; excrescence. **-uta** *f.* (eccl.) box containing food for cardinals in conclave. **-uto** *adj.* fleshy; well-built, well-covered.

car-o[1] *adj.* dear, beloved; precious; well-loved; aver —, to prize, to love, to prefer; avere a —, to esteem; aver — di, to wish to, to long to; avrei — di parlargli un'ultima volta, I'd dearly like to talk to him once more; tener —, to take great care of; dear, expensive; costly; high (of a price); vendere a — prezzo, to sell dearly; *adv.* dear, dearly; gli costò —, it cost him dear; *n.m.* loved one; i miei -i, my loved ones, my family; — mio, my dear man; high price, expense; expensiveness; †scarcity, lack; †avere — di, to lack, to be in need of; — viveri, see **caroviveri**. **-ino** *adj.* pretty; lovely; nice.

caro[2] *m.* (bot.) caraway, *Carum carvi*.

car-o[3] *m.* coma. **-osi** *f.* coma. **-o·tico** *adj.* carotid.

carogn-a, carogn-a *f.* carrion; carcase; (vulg.) swine; slut; †corpse. **-(u)ola** *f.* (vulg.) wretched old woman.

carol-a *f.* dance accompanied by music and song; carol; tessere -e, intrecciar -e, to dance (usually round something). **-are** [A I] *intr.* (*aux.* avere) to dance (round).

Carolina[1] *pr.n.f.* Caroline.

carolina[2] *f.* a form of snooker played with five differently coloured balls.

carolin·gio *adj., n.m.* (hist.) Carolingian, Carlovingian.

carolino *adj.* (hist.) Carolingian; scrittura carolina, Carolingian minuscule.

carolo[1] *m.* (agric.) rust, a disease in rice.

ca·rolo[2] *m.* (numism.) coin of Charles VIII.

caronata *f.* (mil.). See **carronata**.

caron·cola *f.* wattle (of birds).

Caronte *pr.n.m.* (myth.) Charon; (fig.) severe-looking person.

caropane *m. indecl.* rise in price of bread; bread subsidy.

carosello m. merry-go-round, roundabout; pageant on horseback; tournament.

carot-a f. carrot; cock and bull story; hoax; (fig.) piantare -e, vendere -e, to tell cock and bull stories; (mining) core; estrattore per —, core lifter; (geog.) core-sample (of ocean floor). **-ag·gio** m. (mining) core boring. **-a·io** m. carrot-grower, carrot-seller; teller of tall stories. †**-are** intr. to tell tall stories, to romance. †**iere** m. (mining) core barrel; †one who tells tall stories, romancer, leg-puller. **-ina** f. (chem.) carotin.

caro·tide f. (anat.) carotid (artery).

carovan-a f. caravan; convoy; party, group, coachload; novitiate, apprenticeship; union of porters or stevedores. **-iera** f. caravan route. **-iere, -iero** m. caravan guide. **-ista** m. knight or squire of a military order (e.g. the Knights of Malta or the Pisan Knights of St Stephen).

carovell-o m. type of pear-tree. **-a** f. fruit of same (very fragrant pear).

carovita, carovi·veri m. indecl. rise in the cost of living bonus; (indennità di) —, cost of living bonus.

carpa f. (ichth.) carp, *Cyprinus carpio*.

carpacco m. See **calpacco**.

†**carpare** tr. to seize; to apprehend, to take prisoner (cf. **carpire**); intr. to crawl, to go on hands and knees, to scramble.

carpasfo·glia m., f. drag-net used for catching soles in the Adriatic.

Carpazi pr.n.m.pl. (geog.) Carpathians.

carpello m. (bot.) carpel.

carpent-eri·a f. carpentry, joinery; joiner's shop, wheelwright's shop, cartwright's shop; (bldg.) — in ferro, structural steel work. **-iere** m. joiner, carpenter, cartwright, wheelwright. **-o** m. (archaeol.) cart, waggon; cartload.

†**carpic·cio** m. shower of blows, a good few blows; a piece of one's mind.

car·pin-e, -o m. (bot.) hornbeam, *Carpinus betulus*; — nero, orientale, see **carpinella**. **-ella** f. (bot.) hop-hornbeam, *Ostrya carpinifolia*.

car·pi-o, -one m. (ichth.) *Salmo carpio*, a kind of large trout found only in Lake Garda. **-ionare** [A I c] tr. (cul.) to souse (fish) in vinegar to be eaten cold.

carpire [D 2] tr. to snatch; to seize; to obtain by fraud; †to surprise, to catch in the act. **-ito** part. adj. snatched; seized; dishonestly come by. (**-itore** m. **-itrice** f.)

†**carpita** f. bed covering of shaggy cloth.

carpo m. (anat.) carpus, wristbones. **-capsa** f. (ent.) codling moth, *Cydia pomonella*. **-logi·a** f. treatise on fruit.

carpo·liti m.pl. (geol.) carpolites.

carpon-i, -e adv. on all fours, crawling; andar —, to crawl on hands and knees.

carra[1] f. (Turin) measure of wine.

carra[2] f. stone, rock.

†**carra**[3] f. measure of area.

†**carra**[4] f.pl. of **carro**, q.v.

carr-adore m. carriage-builder; coachman. †**-a·ia** f. carriage road; (Florence) Ponte alla Carraia (formerly Ponte Nuovo), bridge which took its name from a main city-gate nearby. **-a·io** m. see under **carro**; adj. suitable for carriages; porta -aia, carriage entrance. **-areccia** f. carriageway; width between the wheels of a cart. **-areccio** adj. practicable for carriages; suitable for transport by cart. **-ata** f. see under **carro**.

carranco m. ravine.

Carrar-a pr.n.f. (geog.) Carrara; (geol.; sculp.) Carrara marble. **-ese** adj. relating to Carrara; n.m. inhabitant of Carrara; (numism.) old Paduan silver coin.

†**carratello** m. See **caratello**.

carravone m. (geog.) deep gully made by rain.

carrega f. (dial. N. Ital.) chair; armchair; old-fashioned carriage; fat old woman.

carreggi-are [A 3 c] tr. to cart; to travel (a road) by cart; intr. (aux. avere) to travel in a cart. **-a·bile** adj. (of a road) suitable for carts; strada -abile, cart-track; n.f. carriageway. †**-a·io** m. wheelwright. **-amento** m. carting; (geol.) erosion. **-ata** f. carriageway; rut; cart-track; track, gauge (of vehicle); width of wheelbase; andare per la -ata, to follow the beaten track; stare in -ata, to be on the right track; uscire di -ata, to wander from the point. **-ato** part. adj. carted, carried by cart; travelled over by cart. †**-atore** m. carter.

carreggio m. constant cart traffic; carting, cartage.

carrell-are [A I] tr. (cinem.; telev.) to track. **-ata** f. (cinem.) tracking shot, running shot, dolly shot. **-ato** part. adj. (cinem.) tracked; trailer-mounted, truck-mounted.

carrell-o m. (rlwy.) trolley; bogey; bogey-wheels; (aeron.) under-carriage; truck; (watchm.) — per cilindro, lower balance cock; (cinem.; telev.) — di camera, camera dolly; (typewriter) carriage; — porta-vivande, tea-trolley. **-ista** m. truck-driver.

carrett-a f. cart; tramp steamer; tirar la —, to be a drudge, to keep things going, to shoulder a burden; palio delle -e, the races that were formerly run in Florence on St John the Baptist's day (June 24); †coach; carriage; †plough. **-a·io** m. carter. †**-are** intr. to pull the plough. **-ata** f. cartload, truck-load. **-ella** f. dim. horse and trap for two persons. **-iere** m., **-iero** m. carter, cart-driver. (**-iera** f.) **-ino** m. dim. little cart; (provb.) se mia nonna avesse avuto le rotelle sarebbe stata un -ino, if all the world were bread and cheese, if pigs could fly. **-o** m. hand-truck, hand-barrow; hand-cart; stall; pulleys for hanging or changing the flies of a theatre. **-ona·io** m. driver, carter. **-onata** f. cartload, waggon-load. **-one** m. augm. waggon; cart, tipping cart; rough, communal hearse.

carriag·gio m. baggage waggon; baggage of an army as a whole.

carriega f. (naut.) docking.

carrier-a[1] f. full gallop; mettere un cavallo alla —, to let a horse have his head; prendere la —, to get the bit between its teeth; speed; a tutta —, di gran —, at full speed; career; profession; walk of life; (mil.) ufficiale di —, regular officer; fare —, to get on, to make a career for oneself; †course, route, path. **-ismo** m. careerism, ambition. **-ista** m. careerist. **-i·stico** adj. pertaining to a careerist; relating to careerism.

†**carriera**[2] f. stone quarry; metal quarry.

†**carrino** m. (mil. hist.) barricade formed of war-chariots.

carri(u)ola f. See **cariola**.

carriponte m. travelling crane.

carr-o m. waggon; cart; lorry; (rlwy.) truck; — cisterna, tank waggon; (mil.) — armato, tank; — spazzaneve, snowplough; — matto, flat, low truck, trolley; — funebre, hearse; (eng.) — di scorta, tender; (provb.) dura più un — rotto che uno nuovo, a creaking gate hangs longest; mettere il — avanti ai buoi, to put the cart before the horse; pigliare la lepre col —, to proceed too slowly and cautiously; la quinta (l'ultima) ruota del —, the least important person, the youngest, the most junior; — di Tespi, travelling theatre; (eng.) chassis; (astron.) — (di Boote), the Great Bear, the Plough, Ursa Major, King Charles's Wain; (hist.) chariot; — falcato, chariot armed with blades; (naut.) the lower and thicker of the two spars which form the forepeak of a lateen yard; (typ.) carriage; lo scoppio del —, set-piece of fireworks let off at Florence on Holy Saturday; waggon-load, cartload; †measure of wine or grain; †pillory. **-a·io** m. waggon-maker, cartwright; waggoner. †**-aro** m. see **carraio**. **-ata** f. waggon-load, cartload; a -ate, loads, in plenty; †chariot. **-icello** m. (dim.) rickety little waggon. **-ista** m. (mil.) tank-driver.

carroc·cio m. (hist.) ox-cart carrying an altar with the flag of a Commune into battle; campana del —, see **Martinella**.

carronata f. (mil.) carronade.

carrozz-a f. carriage; coach; — da nolo, — da noleggio, cab; andare in —, to drive in a carriage; andare in paradiso in, to be lucky in life; marciare in —, to lead a life of ease; (rlwy.) carriage; in —! all aboard!; — con buffet, buffet car; — letto, sleeper, sleeping car, wagon-lits; — ristorante, restaurant car, dining car; (naut.) small cabin protruding on the deck; waterproof hatch cover. **-a·bile** adj. suitable for vehicles; strada -abile, carriage road. **-a·io** m. coachbuilder. **-are** [A I] tr. (motor. industr.) to build or design the coachwork of. **-ata** f. carriage-load. **-ato** part. adj. (motor. industr.) designed; -ata da, coachwork by. **-atura** f. (motor.; rlwy.) coachwork, bodywork; body; -atura da corsa, racing body. **-eri·a** f. body of a car, coachwork; -eria fuori serie, coachwork to specification. **-iere** m. coachbuilder; coachman; designer and maker of specially built bodies for cars. **-ina** f. dim. of **carrozza**; perambulator, pram, baby-carriage. **-ino** m. dim. of **carrozza**; trap; perambulator; -ino della bambola, doll's pram; rather dishonest transaction; (motor.) sidecar. **-one** m. augm. of **carrozza**; illicit gains; hearse.

carrub-a f. (bot.) carob-bean, fruit of the **carrubo**, q.v. **-o** m. (bot.) carob-tree, locust-tree, *Ceratonia siliqua*.

carruc·cio m. child's buffer-chair.

carru·col-a *f.* pulley; (text.) wharve; (paperm.) bellows; -**e delle centiguide**, deckle pulleys; (naut.) see **puleggia**; (fig.) **ungere le -e**, to bribe, to grease the palm. -**are** [A I S] *tr.* to hoist with a tackle; (fig.) to trick.

carruga *f.* (ent.) grub of the cockchafer beetle, *Melolontha vulgaris.*

carrug·gio *m.* narrow alley-way.

car·sic-o *adj.* (geol.) pertaining to the Carso, the limestone plateau between the Eastern Alps and the mountains of Illyria. NOTE: The Carso has no system of valleys, nor surface hydrography, the ground being irregular and full of cavities large and small, either crater-shaped or like wells, locally termed Foibe, Busi, Doline, Dolazzi. Part is wooded, part arid and bare. There are many subterranean grottoes full of stalactites and stalagmites and twisting in every direction, due to the solvent action of the rains which form streams only underground. -**ismo** *m.* the geological phenomena of the Carso.

cart-a *f.*
1. PAPER; —**bambagina**, — **di bambagia**, — **di straccio**, rag paper; — **straccia**, waste paper, rough paper; — **da macero**, paper to be pulped; — **a mano**, handmade paper; — **a righe**, ruled paper; — **a formato protocollo**, foolscap; — **da lettere**, writing paper, notepaper; — **asciugante**, — **suga**, — **assorbente**, blotting paper; — **Bibbia**, India paper; — **da disegno**, drawing paper; — **a quadretti**, — **quadrettata**, squared paper, graph paper; — **pentagrammata**, music paper; — **da imballo**, wrapping paper; — **velina**, tissue paper; — **membranacea**, parchment, vellum; — **carbone**, carbon paper; — **crespata**, crepe paper, crinkly paper; — **oleata**, grease-proof paper; — **cerata**, waxed paper; — **igienica**, toilet paper; — **moschicida**, fly-paper; — **vetrata**, glass paper, sandpaper; — **di Francia**, — **da parato**, wallpaper; — **da giornali**, newsprint; **mettere in** —, to set down in black and white; **vergare** —, to write; (phot.) — **sensibile**, sensitized paper; (chem.) — **reattiva**, test paper; — **al tornasole**, litmus paper.
2. PAPER, document; -**e domestiche**, private papers; — **d'identità**, identity card; — **bollata**, — **da bollo**, stamped paper (i.e. with impressed Inland Revenue stamp, on which practically all public documents, deeds, etc., have to be written); — **libera**, document drafted on paper not subject to above tax; —**moneta**, paper money; **menu**; **mangiare alla** —, to choose a meal à la carte; **aver le -e in regola**, to have the requisite credentials, to have one's papers in order, (fig.) to be all in order, to have nothing to worry about, to be 'in the clear'; — **bianca**, *carte blanche*, full power to act; (naut.) -**e di bordo**, ship's papers; (provb.) — **canta e villan dorme**, when his lease is in written form the peasant can sleep in peace; †**letter**. 3. PAGE, sheet; **mandare uno a -e quarantotto**, to send someone to blazes; †**a -e 13**, on page 13; *pl.* (poet.) book, writing; **le Sacre Carte**, Holy Scripture. 4. DIPLOMA; statute; charter; **la Carta Atlantica**, the Atlantic Charter; **la Magna Carta**, Magna Carta. 5. CHART; — **geografica**, map; — **topografica**, plan (of a town); — **nautica**, — **idrografica**, nautical chart; — **celeste**, chart of the heavens; — **muta**, blank map; — **politica**, political map; — **fisica**, physical map. 6. CARD; — **da visita**, visiting card; — **da gioco**, playing card; **dare le -e**, to deal; **fare le -e**, to shuffle and deal; to tell fortunes by cards, to tell the cards; **quella signora mi ha fatto le -e e mi ha predetto delle cose che si sono poi avverate**, that woman told me the cards and predicted things which later came true; **cambiar le -e in tavola**, to shift one's ground; **tener le -e basse**, to keep one's cards out of sight, (fig.) to conceal one's intentions; **mettere le -e in tavola**, to put one's cards on the table; **scoprire la** — **più importante**, to play one's trump card. NOTE: Two different sorts of cards are used in Italy, the 'English' or 'French' poker cards (carte francesi, carte da poker) and the Italian cards (Carte napolitane, Carte venete). An Italian pack consists of forty cards in four suits: 'danari', 'coppe', 'spade' and 'bastoni' (coins, goblets, swords and clubs), the cards being figured with these instead of the variously shaped pips of French or English cards. The Italian names of the suits in a French pack are: 'cuori', hearts, 'quadri' (sometimes 'mattoni'), diamonds, 'picche', spades, and 'fiori', clubs. If a French pack is used as an Italian one, the eights, nines and tens are thrown out so as to reduce the number of cards in the pack to forty; the names of the suits are then: 'danari', for diamonds, 'coppe', for hearts, 'spade', for spades, and 'bastoni', for clubs. The Italian names of the suits in a French pack are indeclinable in form, but are used with the fem. article in the

singular and with the masc. in the plural: e.g. **hai i cuori?** have you got hearts?; **ho una quadri**, I have one diamond card; **i picche si sono divisi bene**, the spades were well distributed; cf. the refrain, 'la picche, la quadri, la fiori ce l'ho, dammi il tuo cuore, primiera farò'. -**ac·cia** *f. pejor.* of **carta**; waste paper; (paperm.) broke. †-**aia** *f.* paper mill. -**aio** *m.* paper manufacturer; card manufacturer; paperseller, stationer; paperhanger; dealer in a card game. †-**ara** *f.*, †-**aro** *m.* see **cartaio**. -**ata** *f.* a paper-full (e.g. of sweets); †**page**. -**iera** *f.* papermill.

carta-bello *m.* pamphlet. -**carbone** *f.* carbon paper. -**fac·cio** *m.* see **scartafaccio**. -**glo·ria** *f.* (*pl.* **cartegloglo·rie**) altar-card. -**pe·cora** *f.* (*pl.* **cartape·core**) parchment; (paperm.) vegetable parchment. -**pecorace·o** *adj.* parchment. -**pecorina** *f.* parchment. -**pęsta** *f.* papier mâché; **gente di -pesta**, spineless people. -**strac·cia** *f.* see 'carta straccia', under **carta**. -**suga** *f.* see 'carta sugante', etc., under **carta**. -**volta** *f.* reverse, back of a page, verso.

carta·ceo *adj.* (made of) paper; paper-like.

Carta·gin-e *pr.n.f.* (geog.) Carthage. -**ęse** *adj., n.m., f.* Carthaginian. †**Ca·rtagine** *pr.n.f.* (geog.) see **Cartagine**.

car·tam-o *m.* (bot.) safflower, *Carthamus tinctorius.* -**ina** *f.* Spanish red, China lake.

carteggi-are [A 3 C] *intr.* (*aux.* avere) to keep up a correspondence; — **con**, to correspond with; †(naut.) to chart work; *tr.* (carpen., etc.) to sand, to rub down; †to leaf through (papers, pages), to go through page by page. -**atura** *f.* (carpen., etc.) sanding, rubbing down.

cartęggio *m.* correspondence between two or more persons; collection of letters.

cartella *f.* portfolio; schoolbag, satchel; briefcase; file, folder; — **clinica**, hospital file; — **delle tasse**, tax assessment; lottery ticket; notice, notice-board placard; — **da scrittoio**, scribbling pad; page written on one side only; page of copy for printer; — **d'incanto**, conditions of sale (by auction); (archit.) tablet (for inscription); (mil.) lock-plate of a gun; (watchm.) plate where the pieces of the movement are attached; (comm.) bond-certificate, debenture certificate.

cartell-ame *m.*, -**are** [A I]. See under **cartello**.

cartell-o *m.* large public notice; placard; poster, bill; inscription; facia board; escutcheon, hatchment; name plate, name board (e.g. of a street); shop sign; book plate; — **indicatore**, road sign, traffic sign; **di** —, first class, famous; (theatr.) **tenere il** —, to run; (hist.) label tied round the neck, of a criminal with a list of his offences; — **(di sfida)**, challenge to a duel; (leg.) manufacturers' or producers' organization, monopoly; (Amer.) trust; cartel, temporary union of political parties, usually of the opposition; (comm.) cartel, combine; †libellous publication, broadsheet. -**ame** *m.* (archit.) series of tablets (for inscription). †-**are** *intr.* to publish pamphlets; to circulate broadsheets; *tr.* to challenge to a duel; *n.m.* challenge (to a duel), exchange of cards. -**a·rio** *m.* public archives. -**ętto** *m.* (archit.) small tablet or frieze for inscription. -**ino** *m.* label, ticket, tag; name-plate. -**iẓẓare** [A I] *tr.* to form into a cartel. -**iẓẓato** *part. adj.* organized as a cartel, syndicated. -**one** *m.* poster; placard; (theatr.) list of plays or operas for a season; (archit.) tablet (for inscription); sheet containing all the numbers, viz. from 1 to 90, used in playing at 'tombola'; † — **di cortesia**, 'lost' notice, offering a reward.

carter *m. indecl.* (eng.) gear-case; oil-bath (on a bicycle); crankcase; sump.

Cartesi-o *pr.n.m.* (René) Descartes, the philosopher (1596–1650). -**ano** *adj.* (philos.) Cartesian. -**anęsimo**, -**anismo** *m.* (philos.) Cartesianism.

carticino *m.* (typ.) signature, section; (typ.) imperfection, 'cancel'.

cartiera *f.* papermill; (naut.) chart table.

carti·gli-a *f.* (in games) small cards. -**o** *m.* scroll.

cartila·g-ine *f.* (anat.) cartilage. -**i·neo**, -**inoso** *adj.* cartilaginous.

cartina *f. dim.* of **carta**; small piece of paper, slip; small inset map; (cards) a low card; packet; — **di aghi**, packet of needles; (pharm.) small paper wrapping for a powder; dose; (chem.) — **al tornasole**, litmus paper.

cart-ismo *m.* (hist.) Chartism. -**ista** *m.* (hist.) Chartist.

cartoc·c-io *m.* (*pl.* -**i**) paper bag; wrapper or bag made by twisting a piece of paper into the form of a cone; the contents of such a wrapper; (archit.) volute; (mil.) cartridge for artillery; †*pl.* dried maize leaves used for stuffing mattresses. -**iame** *m.* (archit.) voluted ornaments. -**iata** *f.* bagful, twistful. -**ętto** *m. dim.* of **cartoccio**; curl-paper.

cart-ografi·a *f.* map-making, cartography; collection of maps or charts. **-ogra·fico** *adj.* pertaining to maps or cartography, cartographical. **-o·grafo** *m.* cartographer, map-maker, geographer.

cartol-a·io *m.* stationer; bookseller. NOTE: formerly 'cartolai' sold books as well as paper, and this custom lingers on in small towns. **-aro** *m.* (pop.) see **cartolaio**. **-eri·a** *f.* stationery shop, stationer's. **-ina** *f.* card, postcard; correspondence card; ticket, label; -ina illustrata, picture postcard; -ina vaglia, postal order; (pharm.) small paper wrapping for a powder; dose; (mil. slang) a type, a 'card', a funny chap, a character. **-inare** [A I] *tr.* to bind (a book) roughly.

†cartol-are¹ [A I s] *tr.* to number, to paginate. **-atura** *f.* numbering, pagination.

cartolare² *m.* folder, file; paper cover; diary, memo book, notebook; (naut.) ship's log.

cartoman-te *m., f.* fortune-teller by cards. **-zi·a** *f.* fortune-telling by cards, cartomancy.

carton-e *m.* cardboard, card, board; pasteboard; scatola di —, cardboard box; uomo di —, weak man; (art) cartoon; (cinem.) — e animato, cartoon. **-ag·gio** *m.* box-making; (paperm.) cartone per -aggio, boxboard. **-are** [A I C] *tr.* to bind with boards. **-ato** *adj.* bound with boards. **-cino** *m.* thin card; correspondence card; (paperm.) card, board; -cino patinato, art-board. **-feltro** *m.* (bldg.) feltpaper.

cartoso *adj.* similar to paper; (tanning) tinny.

cartuc·ci·a *f.* (*pl.* **cartucce**) cartridge; (typ.) insert or corrigenda slip; †scrap of paper; sheet of notepaper; ballot-paper. **-era** *f.* cartridge case; cartridge belt; cinghia reggi-cartucciere, cartridge belt.

cartula·rio *m.* (hist.) cartulary.

caruba *f.* and derivs. See **carruba**.

carun·col-a *f.* (anat.) caruncle. **-oso** *adj.* caruncular, carunculous.

caruso *m.* worker in the Sicilian sulphur mines.

carvi *m. indecl.* (bot.) see **caro²**; (industr.) essenza di —, caraway oil.

car·zia *f.* (numism.) Venetian copper coin formerly current in the Venetian colonies.

cas-a *f.* (for use as *m.* see under no. 2). 1. HOUSE; — d'abitazione, dwelling house; — colonica, farmhouse, peasant's house; — da giuoco, illicit gaming house; — chiusa, — di tolleranza, — di appuntamenti, brothel; l'uscio di —, the front door; — popolare, tenement house, block of cheap flats, council house; la Casa Bianca, the White House; — di Dio, — del Signore, house of God, church. 2. HOME, household, residence; in —, at home, indoors, in the house; in — la signora? is the lady of the house at home?; fatto in —, home-made; sto in — tutto il giorno, I'm at home all day long; non lo voglio in — mia, I don't want to see him in my house; stare a — del diavolo, to live at the back of beyond (BUT: *un casa del diavolo, a shindy, a racket; fare un casa del diavolo, to kick up a shindy, to raise hell*); a —, at home; andiamo a —, let's go home; tornare a —, to return home; a — mia, in my house, at home, where I live, (fig.) to my way of thinking, as I see it; avere il cervello a —, to have one's head screwed on the right way; tenere le mani a —, to keep one's hands to oneself; tenete a — la lingua, keep a civil tongue in your head; una donna di —, a woman fond of housekeeping, a housewife, a womanly woman; fuori di —, out, not at home; stare di —, to live, to reside; dove sta di —, Lei? where do you live?; mettere su —, to set up house; (provb.) casa mia, casa mia, per piccina che tu sia, tu mi sembri una badia, be it never so humble there's no place like home. 3. FAMILY, line, stock, house, dynasty; i miei di —, my family, my relatives; con lui si spegne la sua —, the family dies out with him, there is no heir to carry on his name; questi son fatti di — mia, these are family affairs of mine; essere di —, to feel at home, to be one of the family; amico di —, family friend; vado a colazione in — Rossi, I'm lunching with the Rossi family; Casa Savoia, House of Savoy; la Casa d'Austria, the Austrian Imperial Dynasty; la Casa Reale, the Royal Family. 4. INSTITUTION, home, firm, business house, headquarters; — di cura, nursing home; — di salute, convalescent home; — di correzione, house of correction, reformatory; — di pena, penitentiary; — dello studente, students' hostel; — editrice, publishing house, publishing firm; publisher; — bancaria, bank; (often used in names of shops, e.g. Casa dello Sport, Sport Emporium; cf. Scotch House);

religious house; — generalizia, religious house where the *pater generalis* resides; (Fasc. hist.) Casa del Fascio, local headquarters of Fascist party; Casa del Popolo, local headquarters of the Communist party. 5. (ASTRON.) house, one of the zodiacal regions. 6. (CHESS) see **casella**. **-ac·cia** *f. pejor.* wretched hovel. **-etta**, **-ina** *f. dim.* little house, pleasant little house. **-ona** *f.*, **-one** *m. augm.* great barracks of a house; block of flats. **-uc·cia** *f. dim. pejor.* shabby little house, suburban house; tumbledown house; shanty. **-u·cola** *f. dim.* little country cottage; shack. **-u·pola** *f. dim.* hut; humble little house, cot.

casac-ca *f.* cloak; voltare —, to turn one's coat, to change sides; *pl.* le -che, jockey's colours. **-chino** *m.* lady's cape.

casac·cio *m.* See under **caso**.

casal-e *m.* hamlet; group of houses; (Rom.) hovel. †**-ino** *m.* hut, hovel; house falling in ruins. **-one** *m. augm.* of **casale**; †castle falling into ruins.

casalinga *f.* housewife.

casalingo *adj.* domestic, household; home-made; home-loving; sedentary; cucina casalinga, good, plain home-cooking.

casamatt-a *f.* (*pl.* **casamatte**) (mil.) casement; pill-box; (mil. slang) glasshouse, cooler, clink. **-are** [A I] *tr.* (mil.) to fortify with casemates. **-ato** *part. adj.* (mil.) casemated.

casamento *m.* apartment house; inhabitants of an apartment house.

casanovismo *m.* way of life characteristic of Casanova (1725–98).

casarca *f.* (orn.) ruddy sheldrake, *Casarca ferruginea*.

casare¹ *tr.* to crown (a queen, in the game of backgammon).

†cas-are² *tr.* to marry off, to find a home for, to settle; *rfl.* to take a wife, to settle down.

casareccio *adj.* See **casereccio**.

casaro *m.* cheese or butter maker.

casat-a *f.* family, clan; family surname; †di —, in company, together. **-o** *m.* family name, surname; family; †see **caseggiato**.

†casa·tico *m.* house-tax.

cascag·gine *f.* sleepiness, muscular fatigue, drooping of the limbs, nodding of the head through sleepiness.

cascame *m.* offal; waste; remnants; (comm.) usable waste; by-product; scrap; cascami di ferro, scrap iron.

cascamort-o *m.* love-sick man; fare il —, to pretend to be madly in love. (**-a** *f.*)

cas·cara *f.* (pharm.) cascara; — sagrada, cascara sagrada.

casc-are [A 2] *intr.* (*aux.* essere) to fall; to drop; — in piè come le gatte, to fall on one's feet like a cat; to droop, to sag; — dalla fame, to be faint with hunger; — dal sonno, to be dog-tired; mi -ano le braccia, see under **braccio**; — dalle nuvole, to be struck with amazement; — di dosso, to hang loosely (of clothes); qui -a l'asino, here is the difficulty; (provb.) l'asino, dove è -ato una volta, non ci -a più, a burnt child dreads the fire; — ritto, to land on one's feet; fare — dall'alto una cosa, to make a thing seem unattainable; non -a il mondo!, the world won't come to an end (for a little thing like that)!; (naut.) — di prua, to be down by the bows; — di poppa, to be down by the stern. (**-amento** *m.*) **-ante** *adj.* falling; drooping, sagging, bent, round-shouldered; weak, fainting; età -ante, decrepitude, old age, senility. **-atic·cio** *adj.* ready to drop; ailing; liable to fall, precarious. **-ato** *part. adj.* fallen; down; dropped. **-atoio** *adj.* falling, drooping; susceptible. **-atura** *f.* droppings (esp. from a sieve).

cascata *f.* fall, drop; una — da cavallo, a fall from a horse; waterfall, cascade; (electron.) cascade; †frill, flounce, fringe, fold, drapery.

caschetto *m. dim.* See under **casco**.

caschimpetto *m.* jewel-pendant.

ca·scia *f.* (bot.). See **acacia**.

cascia·ia *f.* shelf for cheeses.

Cascimir *pr.n.m.* (geog.) Kashmir. **-(r)a** *f.* See **casimirra**.

cascin-a *f.* cowshed with dairy attached; cheese-press; peasant farmhouse; dairy-farm; thin board of beechwood used for making light boxes; Le Cascine, name of a public park in Florence. **-a·io** *m.* manager of a cheese factory. **-ale** *m.* see **cascina**. **-o** *m.* mould for shaping cheeses. **-otto** *m.* large trough.

ca·scio¹ *m.* (paperm.) deckle.

†ca·scio² *m.* See **cacio**.

casciotto *m.* (paperm.) vat, bleaching chest.

cas-co¹ *m.* (*pl.* **-chi**) helmet, casque; crash-helmet; hair-dryer; — coloniale, sun helmet.

cas-co² *m.* (*pl.* **-chi**) fall, drop; setback; fare un —, to suffer a setback; bunch; un — di banane, a bunch of bananas.

†**casco**³ *adj.* old, frail, drooping.

cas·cola *f.* (agric.) kind of wheat valued for its straw.

ca̧sea-rio *adj.* pertaining to the production of dairy foods; pertaining to cheese.

caseggiato *m.* group of houses; block of flats; block of houses and other buildings; inhabitants thereof; ha svegliato tutto il —, he woke the whole neighbourhood.

ca̧seifi·cio *m.*, **ca̧seina** *f.* See under **caseo**.

casell-a *f.* pigeon-hole, compartment; — postale, post box; cell; small square on ruled paper; (chess, draughts) square. **-ante** *m.* (rlwy.) signalman. **-a·rio** *m.* set of pigeon-holes; filing cabinet; -ario aperto, pigeon-hole; -ario chiuso, locker; (leg.) -ario giudiziario, card-index of criminal records. **-ina** *f.* (bot.) compartment in a pod. **-ista** *m.* (comm.) post-office box-holder. **-o** *m.* (rlwy.) track superintendent's house; signal-box.

ca̧se-o *m.* milk curds. **-ifi·cio** *m.* cheese factory. **-ina** *f.* (chem.) casein. **-i·nico** *adj.* (chem.) (of) casein; soluzione -inica, casein solution. **-o̧so** *adj.* (med.) cheesy, caseous.

casera *f.* (N. Ital.) mountain hut (used by herdsmen in summer).

caser-ȩccio *adj.* home-made; homely; domestic. **-ella** *f.* small house.

ca̧serm-a *f.* (mil.) barracks; quarters; consegnato in —, confined to barracks. **-ag·gio** *m.* (mil.) barrack furniture and fittings. **-iere** *m.* (mil.) barrack inspector. **-o̧ne** *m. augm. pejor.* big ugly block of flats.

casier-e *m.* caretaker. **(-a** *f.*)

casigliano *m.* fellow-lodger, fellow-inhabitant.

†**casile** *m.* hut, hovel.

ca̧simi(r)r-a *f.*, **-o** *m.* (text.) cashmere.

ca̧simi̧sde·o *m.* (pop.) trumped-up difficulty, unjustified opposition.

casino¹ *m.* casino; gaming house.

casino² *m.* house of ill-fame; (Tusc.) villa; — di caccia, hunting lodge.

casi·pola *f.* hut, hovel.

†**casi·pula** *f.* See **casipola**.

ca̧s-ista *m.* (eccl.) casuist; (fig.) over-cautious, over-scrupulous person. **-i·stica** *f.* casuistry; (theol.; leg.; med.) study of instructive cases; (med.) case histories.

ca̧s-o *m.* case; incident; accident; chance; occasion; opportunity; possibility; need; non è il — di offendersi, there's no need to get offended; non c'è — di, there's no possibility of; al —, should occasion arise; fare al —, to meet the case, to be just the job; a —, haphazardly, carelessly; per —, by chance; il — volle che, chance willed it that; mettiamo il — che, let us suppose that; — mai, in — che, should it so happen, if need be; non è il — di, there's no point in; non fa —, it doesn't matter; non ci faccia —! don't worry about it!; in ogni —, per ogni —, in tutti i -i, in any case; *pl.* events, deeds; i -i della vita, the ups and downs of life; (leg.; comm.) — di forza maggiore, act of God, unavoidable accident; (med.) case; due -i di polmonite, two cases of pneumonia; (eccl.) — di coscienza, case of conscience; (gramm.) case; (poet.) fate; acerbo —! cruel fate!; †disaster, accident; †sonare a —, to toll (a bell) in announcement of some disaster. **-ac·cio** *m. pejor.* bad case; *adv. phr.* a -accio, haphazardly, at random. **-o̧ne** *m.* nervous person. **-o̧so** *adj.* meticulous, scrupulous.

casolana *f.* (Tusc.) round, rosy apple; (also *adj., f.* qualifying **mela**).

casolare *m.* poor cottage; hovel; hut.

casolineri·a *f.* general grocer's, general stores.

cas-o̧na *f.*, **-o̧ne**¹ *m.* See under **casa**.

casonante *m.* (N. Ital.) superintendent of a waterway, lock-keeper.

ca̧sone *m.* See under **caso**.

casott-a *f.* rather large house. **-o** *m.* sentry-box; hut; kiosk; bathing hut; puppet box; small room; brothel; (naut.) cuddy; — del timone, wheelhouse; — di rotta, charthouse. **-a·io** *m.* bathing attendant.

caspa *f.* (agric.) pollarded tree.

Ca·spio *pr.n.m.* (geog.) il Mare —, the Caspian Sea.

ca·spita *excl.* good heavens! (expressing surprise or impatience).

cass-a *f.*

1. Box, case; packing-case; chest; bin; coffer; cupboard; — da morto, coffin; — dell'orologio, clock-case. 2. Container; tank; cavity, socket, chamber; butt of a gun; (eng.) steam chamber; stator (of a turbine); casing; caisson, frame (of a vehicle); inside of a railway carriage; — ingranaggi, gearbox; (anat.) — toracica,

chest cavity, thorax; — dell'occhio, eye-socket; (mus.) body, chest (of violin, etc.); — armonica, resonance chamber; — espressiva, swell-box (of organ); gran —, drum, bass drum; battere la gran —, to call people together; — rullante, tenor drum; (naut.) — d'acqua, freshwater tank; — d'aria, camel; — d'assetto, trimming tank; — d'ormeggio, mooring buoy; — a fumo, smoke box; — zavorra, ballast tank; (typ.) type-case. 3. Bank, fund, chest; — di risparmio, savings bank; — malattie, institution administering health insurance or sickness benefit; — infortuni, accident fund; — del Mezzogiorno, fund for the development of S. Italy; — di ammortamento, sinking fund; — degli invalidi della Marina mercantile, merchant seamen's pension fund; — ufficiali, officers' benevolent fund. 4. Cash; cash-register; cash-desk; libro di —, giornale di —, day-book, cash-book; si paga alla —, pay at the cash-desk; denaro in —, cash in hand; riserva di —, cash reserve; saldo di —, cash balance; ufficio —, cash department; tenere la —, to be cashier, to be banker; pagare a pronta —, to pay cash down; battere a —, bussare a —, to demand payment. **-a·io** *m.* case-maker; repairer of clock-cases.

cassa-banchi *m. pl.* (naut.) seat-lockers. **-fo̧rma** *f.* (techn.) mould, form; (bldg.) form. **-forte** *f.* (*pl.* **casseforti**) safe, strong-box. **-ma·dia** *f.* (*pl.* **cassema·die, cassama·die**) chest with a trough-shaped lid. **-misura** *f.* measuring box. **-panca** *f.* (*pl.* **cassapanche**) seat-locker; chest serving also as a seat; dormire come una -panca, to sleep like a log; fat, shapeless woman.

†**cassale** *adj.* mortal, deadly.

Cassandra *pr.n.f.* (myth.) Cassandra; (fig.; joc.) gloomy prophetess, person who has dire forebodings.

cass-are [A I] *tr.* to nullify; to abrogate; to annul; (leg.) to quash; to cancel, to erase; to strike out; to strike off the rolls; to dismiss, to cashier. **-amȩnto** *m.* annulling; cancelling; striking out. **-atic·cio** *m.* confused alteration in a manuscript. **-ato** *part. adj.* annulled; cancelled; struck out. **-ato̧io** *m.* eraser, knife for scratching out. **-atura** *f.* erasure, cancellation. **-azio̧ne** *f.* (mus.) cassation, instrumental serenade; (leg.) cassation; the act of quashing a conviction, reversing a judgement, annulling a decree; a legal decision of the last resort; Corte di -azione, Court of Cassation, the highest Italian Court of Appeal (Fr. law), competent to quash proceedings on legal or technical grounds only and, in proper cases, to order retrial; giurisprudenza della -azione, jurisprudence of cassation; precedents established in the Court of Cassation.

†**cas·saro** *m.* See **cassero**.

cassata *f.* ice-gâteau; (Sicily) cake with cream, etc.

cas·sera *f.* logan-stone.

cas·ser-o *m.* (naut.) quarterdeck; bridge; keep of a castle or fortress; old name of the principal street in Palermo; (hydr. constr.) caisson. **-ȩtto** *m.* (naut.) deck cabin.

casserola *f.* (pop. Tusc.). See **casseruola**.

casseruola *f.* saucepan.

cassȩtt-a *f. dim.* of **cassa**, q.v.; little box; drawer; collection box; — delle lettere, letter-box; cash-box; till; — di sicurezza, strong-box; — della spazzatura, dust-pan; — per caccia, W.C. cistern; box of a horse-drawn vehicle; montare a —, to mount the box; (fig.) stare a —, to be in control, to hold the reins; purse, money, account, income; (cinem.) — portapellicola, film magazine (of camera); (theatr.) box-office; successo di —, box-office success; fare —, to be good box-office; (mus.) peg-box of a violin; (naut.) doubling plate, sheath; ruota a —, water-wheel. **-a·io** *m.* box-maker. **-ata** *f.* drawerful, boxful. †**-atore** *m.* beggar.

cassе̧tt-o *m.* drawer (of a cabinet, desk, etc.); (eng.) valve, chamber, box; — girevole, rotary slide valve; — a stantuffo, piston valve; *pl.* edges of a cobbler's bench. **-o̧ne** *m.* chest of drawers; (archit.) cassette, coffer, panel; lacunaria; soffitto a -oni, wooden ceiling with beams crossing at right angles forming box-like squares; (hort.) raised flower-bed.

cas·sia *f.* (bot.) genus of leguminous plants; poets' cassia, *Osyris alba*; (fig.) dare l'erba di — a, to send away, to dismiss.

†**cas·side** *f.* helmet.

cassier-e *m.* cashier, treasurer; — ai pagamenti, paying teller; — alle riscossioni, receiving teller. **(-a** *f.*)

cassilag·gine *f.* (bot.) white henbane, *Hyoscyamus albus*.

cassina *f.* multiple farm.

ca(s)sine(n)se *adj. n.m.* (eccl.) Cassinese.

cassino *m.* small dust-cart; mould for cheese making; boards placed upright in a cart to hold the load; cassini di lana, flocks, wool for stuffing; duster, eraser (for a blackboard); (Tusc.) — dei cani, official dog-catcher.

cas·sio[1] *m.* purple of Cassius.

†**cas·sio**[2] *m.* (paperm.). See **cascio**[1].

Cassiope·a *pr.n.f.* (myth.; astron.) Cassiopeia.

cassiterite *f.* (geol.) cassiterite, tin dioxide.

casso[1] *apocop. part. adj.* See under **cassare**.

casso[2] *m.* (paperm.) deckle.

†**casso**[3] *m.* thorax, chest, upper part of the body down to the waist.

cassola *f.* See **cass(u)ola**.

cassone *m.* large case for transporting flour, etc.; linen chest, cassone; caisson; coffin; andare al —, to peg out; roba del —, trash; water-tank; (naut.) fore peak; cable locker; camel; foundation block in breakwaters, etc.; (slang) old tub; (motor.) body; (mil.) limber-box.

cas·sula *f.* (bot.) capsule.

cass(u)ola *f.* (chem.) evaporating dish.

cast *m. indecl.* (theatr.; cinem.) cast.

casta[1] *f.* caste.

casta[2] *adj.f., n.f.* See **casto**.

castagn-a *f.* chestnut; — domestica, Spanish chestnut, fruit of **castagno**, q.v.; farina di -e, chestnut flour; -e secche, roast, peeled chestnuts; castrare le -e, to slit the shells of chestnuts so that they do not explode in the fire; a scorza di —, reddish brown colour; cavare la — dal fuoco, to save the situation; cavare la — con lo zampino del gatto, to make a catspaw of someone; cogliere in —, to catch in the act; snap of the fingers; trifle, bagatelle; female genitals; (mech.) pawl; (vet.) chestnut, ergot; (naut.) wooden block to prevent a ship in the stocks from slipping towards the sea; -e dell'argano, capstan pawls. **-accia·io** *m.* vendor of 'castagnacci'. **-ac·cio** *m.* flat chestnut cake, made of chestnut flour and water, with chopped almond or walnut added and cooked in oil. **-a·io, -aro** *m.* chestnut-vendor. **-atura** *f.* chestnut harvest. **-eto** *m.* chestnut copse. **-etta** *f.* paper cracker; snap of the fingers; *pl.* (mus.) castanets. **-ic·cio** *adj.* chestnut (-coloured). **-ino** *adj.* chestnut-coloured; *n.m.* a game played with chestnuts. **-o** *m.* chestnut tree, Castanea sativa; -o amara, -o d'India, horse chestnut, fruit of Aesculus hippocastanum; -o d'acqua, water chestnut, fruit of Trapa natans; -o di terra, pig-nut, tuber of Bunium bulbocastanum; -o di terra minuta, tuber of Cyperus esculentus; wood from a chestnut tree; *adj.* chestnut, of chestnut wood; *adj.* chestnut-coloured; capelli -i, chestnut hair; cavallo -o, chestnut horse. **-oleta** *f.* chestnut plantation. **-(u)ola** *f.* firework cracker; (naut.) cleat. **-(u)olo** *m.* young chestnut tree; *adj.* (agric.) chestnut-coloured. **-uzza** *f.* (bot.) -uzza di terra, earthnut pigment; tuber of Conopodium majus.

castald-o *m.* (hist.) in the Lombard kingdom, the administrator of the royal demesnes; steward in a nobleman's household. **-a** *f.* steward's wife. †**-ella** *f.* (naut.) small, fast boat. **-eri·a** *f.* steward's office; farm. **-i·a** *f.* rank of a steward; residence of a steward. **-ire** [D2] *tr.* to administer.

cast-a·lio *adj.* Castalian, of the Parnassian spring. **-a·lidi** *pr.n.f.pl.* the Muses.

casta·neo *adj.* chestnut-coloured; capelli castanei, chestnut locks.

castano *adj.* chestnut-coloured; capelli castani, chestnut tresses.

†**castella** *f.pl.* of **castello**, q.v.

castell-o *m.* castle; mansion, palace; walled village or small town; (fig.) -i in aria, castles in Spain; fare -i in aria, to daydream; (eng.) pile-driver; (mil. hist.) wooden besieging tower; water-tower; (naut.) forecastle; (aeron.) — motore, engine mounting; wooden construction (box and stage) of a puppet show; wooden frame or slatted construction used for drying fruit, etc.; frame (e.g. of the works of a watch); a number of loose objects such as pins, needles, etc. **-ac·cio** *m. pejor.* of **castello**; castle ruins. **-ame** *m.* (mil. hist.) wooden tower borne upon an elephant. **-ana** *f.* châtelaine, mistress of a castle. **-aneri·a, -ani·a** *f.* office of the commander of a castle. **-ano** *m.* commander of a castle; owner of a castle; feudal lord; inhabitant of a town of which the name includes the word 'castello'; *adj.* pertaining to a castle, castle; le mura -ane, the castle walls. **-are** [A1] *intr.* (aux. avere) to encamp; †*n.m.* ruined castle. **-ata** *f.* wine cart. **-ato** *part. adj.* encamped. **-etto** *m. dim.* of **castello**; schedule of the gamesters'

ventures in the public lotteries, together with the amounts they stand to win; (finan.) credit register at a bank of the amounts up to which customers may overdraw; (techn.) a kind of frame used by goldsmiths. **-ina** *f.* small heap; una -ina di libri, a small pile of books; pile of four walnuts in a children's game.

castig-are [A2] *tr.* to chastise, to punish; to correct; to purify, to chasten; to tame, to bring under control, to master, to conquer; to beat; (provb.) chi ben ama ben -a, spare the rod and spoil the child; (agric.) to prune, to cut back; †to emend. **-a·bile** *adj.* punishable. **-amatti** *m. indecl.* stick formerly used for beating the insane; (joc.) aver bisogno di -amatti, to need coercion; (of a person) boss, tyrant, one who rules with a rod of iron; (joc.) spoil-sport; bogey-man. **-amento** *m.* punishment, chastisement. **-atezza** *f.* purity. **-ato** *part. adj.* punished; chastened; corrected; chaste; moderate; pure, pristine; (agric.) pruned. **-atamente** *adv.* moderately; modestly; restrainedly; correctly. **-atore** *m.* chastiser; corrector. (**-atrice** *f.*) †**-azione** *f.* castigation; emendation.

castiglian-o *adj., n.m.* Castilian. (**-a** *f.*)

†**castiglione** *m.* fortress, fortified town.

casti-go *m.* (*pl.* **-ghi**) punishment, chastisement; penalty; mettere un bambino in —, to punish a child; castigation; è un — di Dio, it is a judgement of God.

castimo·ni-a *f.* chastity, abstinence. **-ale** *adj.* pertaining to a life of chastity; *n.m.* sort of liqueur made from pears pickled in salt.

castità *f.* chastity; continence; abstinence; far voto di —, to take a vow of chastity; chasteness, purity; vivere in —, to live chastely.

†**castit-ade, -ate** *f.* See **castità**.

casto *adj.* chaste; continent; pure; virgin; innocent; menare una vita casta, to live a chaste life; (joc.) fare la casta Susanna, to pretend to be chaste (of a woman); fare il — Giuseppe, to pretend to be chaste (of a man).

castone *m.* bezel of a ring, the part which holds the stone; (watchm.) insetting.

castor-o *m.* (zool.) beaver; beaver-fur. **-eo** *m.* (pharm.) castor, an unction obtained from the inguinal glands of the beaver, castoreum. **-ina** *f.* (chem.) castorin. **-ino** *m.* (text.) material resembling beaver-fur. **-io** *m.* see **castoreo**.

†**castrametazione** *f.* encampment; entrenchment.

castr-are [A1] *tr.* to castrate, to emasculate. **-acani** *m. indecl.* gelder of dogs and other animals; small blunt knife. **-aporcelli, -aporci** *m. indecl.* pig-gelder; (fig.) a poor surgeon. **-atello** *m.* lamb; effeminate man. **-ato** *part. adj.* castrated; *n.m.* eunuch; gelding; mutton; (mus.) artificial male soprano or contralto. **-atoio** *m.* gelding knife. **-atore** *m.* gelder. **-atura** *f.* castration, gelding, emasculation. **-azione** *f.* castration; mutilation.

castrense *adj.* pertaining to military service; vescovo —, bishop to the Forces, chaplain general.

†**castrimagi·a** *f.* voracity, greed; ravenous hunger.

†**castrino** *m.* knife for slitting chestnuts; castrated kid; gelder.

†**castro** *m.* castle; fortress; fortified city; (dial. Pisa) pig-sty.

castron-e *m.* castrated colt; castrated wether; (fig.) blockhead. **-ag·gine** *f.* stupidity. **-eri·a** *f.* foolishness, stupidity; silly act.

castruc·cio *m.* (Tusc., agric.) pig-sty.

casual-e *adj.* casual, uncertain; hazardous, unintentional; occasional; un incontro —, a chance encounter; (finan.) guadagni -i, casual earnings. **-mente** *adv.* casually; by chance. **-ismo** *m.* (philos.) casualism. **-ità** *f.* chanciness, uncertainty; casualness; chance.

casua·rio *m.* (orn.) cassowary.

cas-uc·cia, -u·cola, -u·pola *f. dim.* see under **casa**.

casuista *m.* See **casista**.

†**casuro** *adj.* about to fall.

†**cata** *prep.* at, at the rate of; †otta cat'otta (ora per ora), every hour; (dial. Apulia) piede — piede, step by step.

cata·basi *f.* descent, way down; return.

cata-bo·lico *adj.* descending; curva -bolica, downward trend. **-bolismo** *m.* (biol.) catabolism. **-clisma** *m.* disaster, cataclysm; †flood. †**-clismo** *m.* see **cataclisma**. **-comba** *f.* catacomb, sepulchral tunnel. **-cresi** *f.* catachresis, abuse of a metaphor.

catacu·stica *f.* catacoustics, the science of reflected sounds.

catadiot·tric-a *f.* (phys.) catadioptrics. **-o** *adj.* (phys.) catadioptric(al).

catadiottro *m.* reflector, cat's eye.

†**catadupa** *f.* waterfall at the source of the Nile; cataract.

cata-falco *m.* catafalque. **-fa·scio** *adv. phr.* a -fascio, higgledy-piggledy; andare in -fascio, to go to pieces. **-filli** *m.pl.* (bot.) scale-leaves. **-foresi** *f.* (phys.) cataphoresis.

catafratt-a *f.* complete suit of armour, cataphract. **-o** *m.* completely armoured soldier; *pl.* (ichth.) armed gurnard, *Peristethus cataphractum.*

catagm-a *m.* (surg.) fracture. **-a·tico** *adj.* (surg.) catagmatic.

Cat-ai, -a·ia *pr.n.f.* (hist. geog.) Cathay. †**-aino** *adj.* Chinese.

catalan-ęsco *adj.* (*m.pl.* **-eschi**) after the Catalan fashion; uva **-esca**, white, hard kind of grape. **-o** *adj., n.m.* Catalan.

catalessi¹ *f.* (med.) catalepsy.

catalessi² *f.* (prosod.) catalexis.

catalessi·a *f.* (med.). See **catalessi**.

cataletti *m.pl.* short detached literary pieces, catalects.

catalet·tico¹ *adj.* (med.) cataleptic.

catalet·tico² *adj.* (prosod.) catalectic.

cataletto *m.* bier; portable bed, large stretcher.

cat-a·lişi *f.* (chem.) catalysis. **-ali·tico** *adj.* (chem.) catalytic. (**-aliticamęnte** *adv.*) **-alizzare** [A I] *tr.* (chem.) to catalyse. **-alizzatóre** *m.* (chem.) catalyst; (chem. eng.) catalyser.

catalog-are [A 2 s] *tr.* to catalogue. **-a·bile** *adj.* classifiable. **-ato** *part. adj.* catalogued. **-atóre** *m.* cataloguer, archivist, cataloguist.

Catalógna *pr.n.f.* (geog.) Catalonia; woollen covering.

catalógno *m.* (bot.) *Jasminum officinale* var. *grandiflorum.*

cata·lo·go *m.* (*pl.* **-ghi**) catalogue.

†**catalóne** *adv.* catalone catalone, as quiet as a mouse, on tiptoe.

catalpa *f.* (bot.) common catalpa, Indian bean, *C. bignonioides*; Western catalpa, *C. speciosa.*

cataluff-a *f.*, **-o** *m.* striped or flowered linen used for hangings, upholstery and vestments.

catameniale *adj.* (physiol.) catamenial, menstrual.

catana¹ *f.* shooting jacket; poacher's pocket.

catana² *f.* Japanese scimitar.

catana³ *f.* (Corsica) kind of pistol with a short barrel.

Cata·n-ia *pr.n.f.* (geog.) Catania. **-ęşe** *adj., n.m., f.* Catanian.

catapano *m.* (hist.) Catapan.

catapęcchia *f.* tumble-down hovel.

cata-plaşma *m.* (med.) poultice, cataplasm; (fig.) tiresome individual, bore; useless object. **-plaşmo** *m.* (pop.) see **cataplasma**. **-plessi·a** *f.* (med.) cataplexy.

catapult-a *f.* catapult; (mil. hist.; aeron.) catapult. **-are** [A I] *tr.* to catapult.

catapu·z-ia, -za *f.* (bot.) caper spurge, *Euphorbia lathyris*; castor-oil plant, *Ricinus communis.*

cataraf·fio *m.* (naut.) horsing iron, a special form of caulking iron.

cataratta *f.* See **cateratta**.

catarifrangente *adj.* reflecting (back); *n.m.* red reflector on back of a vehicle; reflector on a road-sign, cat's eye.

Catarina *pr.n.f.* See **Caterina**.

ca·tar-o¹ *m.* (rel. hist.) Catharist. **-işmo** *m.* (rel. hist.) Catharism.

cataro² *m.* — frangente, reflector (on bicycle, etc.).

catarr-o *m.* (med.) catarrh. **-ale** *adj.* catarrhal. **-óne** *m. augm.* of **catarro**; sufferer from catarrh. **-óso** *adj.* catarrhal.

cat-arsi *f.* (med.) catharsis, purging; (lit.) catharsis; (fig.) purification, expiation. **-ar·tico** *adj.* (med.) cathartic, purgative, purging; (lit.) cathartic.

catarzo *m.* coarse silk.

†**catascia·mito** *m.* silk cloth embroidered with gold and silver, formerly made at Lucca and Venice, samite.

catast-a *f.* (timber trade) pile of wood of specific size varying according to region; wood pile; pile of objects; funeral pyre; wooden grid for torturing a person by placing fire underneath; a kind of pillory or a stand for exposing a slave for sale, catasta. **-ale** *adj.* cadastral; imposta **-ale**, land tax; mappa **-ale**, land survey map; rendita **-ale**, annual value of, rents and profits of land; rilievo **-ale**, land tax relief; Ufficio **-ale**, Land Registry; *n.m.* beam for supporting casks in a cellar. **-o** *m.* (leg.) cadastre; land register; office where such register is kept.

cata·str-ofe *f.* catastrophe. **-o·fico** *adj.* catastrophic; disastrous; (of a person) inclined to over-dramatize. **-ofi·şmo** *m.* (pol.) radical change brought about suddenly.

catatoni·a *f.* (med.) a form of dementia praecox.

catatręppola *f.* (Tusc.) poky little hole; thingummajig; rough contrivance.

†**catau·no** *prn.* See **cadauno**.

catch *m. indecl.* (sport) all-in-wrestling.

catech-ęşi *f.* (eccl.) catechesis, catechizing. **-eta** *m.* eccl. catechist. **-e·tica** *f.* (eccl.) catechetics. **-işmo** *m.* (eccl. fig.) catechism. **-ista**

m. (eccl.) catechist. **-is·tico** *adj.* (eccl.) catechistic. **-iẓẓare** *tr.* [A I] (eccl.) to catechize; (fig.) to try to persuade, to argue into; lo sto **-izzando** perchè venga anche lui, I'm trying to get him to come too. (**-iẓẓante** *part. adj.* **-iẓẓato** *part. adj.* **-iẓẓatóre** *m.*)

catec-ù *m. indecl.* (chem.) catechu; (industr.) cutch, catechu; (also *adj.*). **-u·cico** *adj.* (chem.) catechuic.

catecu·men-o *m.* (eccl.) catechumen. **-ato** *m.* (eccl.) catechumenate.

†**ca·tedra** *f.* See **cattedra**.

categorema *m.* (philos.) categorem.

categ-ori·a *f.* category; group; class; le **-orie** sociali, the social classes. (**-amęnte** *adv.*) **-o·rico** *adj.* categorical; absolute; precise. (**-oricamęnte** *adv.*)

categoru·meno *m.* (philos.) categorem.

†**catelano** *m.* loose indoor coat.

†**catella¹** *f.* end of a skein.

†**catella²** *f.* little bitch, she-puppy.

catell-o¹ *m.* (paperm.) wooden pin forming part of the pulping apparatus; †little dog, puppy; †cub.

†**catello²** *m.* kind of camp bed.

catęn-a *f.* chain; (fig.) pazzo da —, raving mad; (geog.) range of mountains; (mus.) bass-bar (of violin); (text.) — d'ordito, warp; (eng.) ruota per —, sprocket; (bldg.) tie-iron, tie-beam, truss-rod; chain, measurement of land area; (naut.) — con traversini, studded cable; lunghezza di —, shackle (25 metres); **-ac·cio** *m.* door-bolt; deep scar in the face; *pejor.* (fig.) series, string. **-a·ria** *f.* (math.) catenary, catenary curve. **-ella** *f. dim.* small chain; watch-chain; light chain worn round the neck (usu. with a pendant); (paperm.) chain line, wire line; (shoem.) fair-stitching; chain-stitch; (text.) warp; orditura della **-ella**, warping. **-ello** *m.* cross-piece of a palisade, cross-beam of a set of rafters.

ca·tera *f.* almond eaten green.

cateratt-a *f.* cataract; (Bibl.) **-e** del Cielo, the floodgates of Heaven; piovere a **-e**, to rain buckets; sluice, sluice-gate; portcullis; any door which drops in this way; trap-door; shutter; cage door; (med.) cataract; operazione della —, operation for cataract. **-a·io** *m.* sluice-minder. **-ata** *adj.* (herald.) torre **-ata**, tower portcullised, castle portcullised.

†**cateratto** *m.* See **carattere**.

caterat·tola *f. dim.* of **cateratta**; hole in a door for an animal to pass through.

Caterin-a *pr.n.f.* Catherine, Catharine, Katharine; Santa —, St Catherine (of Siena). **-ętta** *pr.n.f. dim.* Kate, Kitty; (Turin) young unmarried apprentice in the dress trade; seamstress; ballo dalle **-ette**, working girls' ball. **-iniano** *adj.* relating to or characteristic of St Catherine of Siena.

caterva *f.* crowd, host, mob, herd.

cate·ter-e, cateter-e *m.* (surg.) catheter; — molle, rubber catheter. **-işmo** *m.* (surg.) catheterization.

cateto *m.* (math.) cathetus, a side of a right-angled triangle other than the hypotenuse.

cateto·metro *m.* (phys.) cathetometer, reading microscope.

catilina·ri-a *f.* invective (from Cicero's speeches against Catiline). **-o** *adj.* Catilinarian; ferocious (of a person).

catin-o¹ *m.* large basin; earthenware bowl; hollow; (archit.) (shallow) bowl-shaped vault; (metall.) receiver for molten metal from a furnace. **-a·io** *m.* seller or repairer of basins and bowls. **-ella** *f.* small basin; a **-elle**, in torrents; piovere a **-elle**, to rain cats and dogs; (provb.) cielo a pecorelle, acqua a **-elle**, fleecy clouds are a sign of rain. **-ellata** *f.* bowlful. **-ozza** *f.* barrel for salted meat.

†**catino²** *adj.* blue-green.

cati-óne *m.* (chem.; electr.) cation, electropositive ion. **-o·nico** *adj.* (chem.) cationic.

†**cato¹** *adj.* sharp, alert, cute, acute.

†**cato²** *m.* bucket.

cato·blepa *m.* (myth.) catoblepas.

cato-cala *f.* (ent.) underwing moth, *Catocala* spp.

ca·t-odo *m.* (chem.; electr.) cathode, negative electrode. **-o·dico** *adj.* pertaining to the cathode; raggi **-odici**, cathode rays.

catodonte *m.* (zool.). See **capidoglio**.

catolite *m.* (electr.) catholyte.

catollo *m.* large fragment of rock or metal.

Cat-ón-e *pr.n.m.* (hist.) Cato (the Censor); Cato (of Utica). **-eggiare** [A 3 c] *intr.* (*aux.* avere) to profess principles of Cato-like strictness; to be pompous, to hold forth; to be priggish. **-iano** *adj.* Catonian.

cator·bia *f.* (slang) prison, 'quod'.

cator·cio, catorzo *m.* bolt.

cator·zol-o *m.* stump left by pruning, snag; knot in wood. **-uto** *adj.* knotty, gnarled.

catot·tric-a *f.* (phys.) catoptrics, the science of reflection. **-o** *adj.* (phys.) catoptric(al).

†**catra-fosso** *m.* deep pit, chasm, abyss. †**-gi·moro** *m.* dizziness, vertigo.

catram-e *m.* tar, pitch; cement for sealing bottles. †**-are** and derivs. see **incatramare**. **-atrice** *f.* tar sprayer. **-ina** *f.* extract of tar. **-oso** *adj.* tarry.

†**catri·cola** *f.* palisade.

†**catriosso** *m.* (orn.) bird's skeleton, carcase.

†**cattano** *m.* lord of a manor, feudal lord; vavasour.

†**catt-are** *tr.* to obtain, to acquire; to gain. †**-atore** *m.* one who obtains; beggar.

Cat·taro *pr.n.m.* (geog.) Bocche di —, Kotor.

cat·tedr-a *f.* professorial chair; teaching post; sedere in —, to hold a chair, to be a professor; (eccl.) bishop's throne; St Peter's chair. **-ale** *adj.* pertaining to a (professorial) chair, professorial; doveri **-ali**, professorial duties. **-ante** *m.* professor, holder of a chair. **-a·tico** *adj.* professorial, academic; pedantic; pompous; tono **-atico**, pompous tone of voice; *n.m.* professor. (**-aticamente** *adv.*)

cattedral-e[1] *f.* cathedral; *adj.* pertaining to a cathedral; recinto —, cathedral close. **-ità** *f.* (eccl.) cathedral status.

cattedrale[2] *adj.* See under **cattedra**.

catti *adv. phr.* aver di — una cosa, to be thankful to have a thing.

cattivare [A I] and derivs. See under **cattivo**.

cattiv-o *adj.* bad; naughty; evil; wrong; vicious, dangerous (of an animal); wild, rough; mare —, rough seas; trovarsi in -e acque, to be in trouble, to be in difficulties; harmful; defective; con le -e, with threats and abuse; o con le buone o con le -e, by fair means or foul; †wretched; †captive. (**-amente** *adv.*); *n.m.* bad person; naughty child; †captive; †wretch; †widower. †**-aggio** *m.* captivity. †**-anza** *f.* captivity; imprisonment; negligence, neglect, carelessness; evil, bad behaviour; ill-will. †**-anzuola** *f.* evil action. **-are** [A I] *rfl.* (dat. of prn.) to win for oneself; **-arsi** il favore di, to win the favour of; **-arsi** le simpatie di, to enter into the good graces of; *tr.* to captivate; †to take prisoner, to capture; †*intr.* to beg, to live on charity, to lead an idle life. †**-eggiare** *intr.* to grieve, to be distressed; to lead a dissolute life. **-ello** *adj.* naughty, mischievous; *n.m.* naughty child; iron eye for hanging the clapper of a bell; †(fig.) slave, prisoner. **-e·ria, -eri·a** *f.* naughtiness, mischief, mischievousness; maliciousness, spite; badness. **-ezza** *f.* badness; naughtiness. **-ità** *f.* naughtiness; badness, bad disposition; slavery, captivity; †evil ways; †ribaldry; †idleness; †cowardliness; †vice, defect.

catto[1] *m.* (bot.). See **cacto**.

†**catto**[2] *part. adj.* from †**capere**, q.v.; captured, taken prisoner.

†**catto**[3] *m.* (mil. hist.). See under **gatto**.

catto·lic-o *adj.* (rel.) Catholic; universal, catholic; *n.m.* Catholic; †(med.) panacea, universal remedy. (**-a** *f.* **-amente** *adv.*) **-e·simo, -ismo** *m.* Catholicism; the Catholic world. **-ità** *f.* Catholicity; the Catholic world.

cattur-a *f.* capture; (leg.) capture, arrest, seizure; mandato di —, warrant for arrest; (phys.) capture. **-are** [A I] *tr.* to capture; (leg.) to capture, to seize. **-ato** *part. adj.* captured; (leg.) captured, seized.

catub-a *f.* (mus.) kind of cymbal; bass drum. **-are** [A I] *tr.* to bang with the fist.

Catull-o *pr.n.m.* Catullus. **-iano** *adj.* Catullian.

†**ca·tulo** *m.* puppy; cub.

†**Catuno** *pr.n.m.* See **cadauno**.

Ca·uc-aso *pr.n.m.* (geog.) Caucasus. **-a·sico, -a·seo** *adj., n.m.* Caucasian.

cauccìu *m. indecl.* rubber, indiarubber; (bot.) one of the tree species which yields indiarubber, *Ficus elastica*.

caud-ale *adj.* caudal, tail-like. **-ata·rio** *m.* (eccl.) train-bearer; (fig.) satellite. **-ato** *adj.* caudate, tailed.

ca·udice *m.* (bot.) tree-trunk.

caudine *adj. f.pl.* (hist.) Forche —, Caudine Forks; (fig.) passare sotto le Forche —, to suffer bitter humiliation.

†**ca·ula** *f.* flock, herd.

ca·ul-e, -o *m.* (bot.) stem of a plant, green or woody; †cabbage. **-i·colo** *m.* (archit.) caulicole (in a Corinthian capital).

†**caunoscenza** *f.* See **conoscenza**.

cauri *m.pl.* (zool.) cowrie shells, *Cypraea* spp.

†**cauro** *m.* See **coro**[2].

ca·us-a *f.* cause, motive, reason; a — di, per — di, because of, in consequence of; chiamare in —, to make reference to; chiamato direttamente in —, directly involved; (leg.) cause; action; suit; motive (of murder); — civile, civil action; civil proceedings; — commerciale, lawsuit; — determinante, motive (for a crime); — falsa, cause or title wrongly thought to be just or legal; — giudiziaria, lawsuit, case; — giusta, true and just cause; legal title; — lucrativa, an action that is purely gainful; — penale, criminal proceedings; gli aventi —, persons claiming under owner of a right, assigns; in — di, for the sake of; in — propria, for oneself; parlare con cognizione di —, to speak from experience; patrocinare una —, perorare una —, to argue a case in court, to plead a cause (also fig.); senza —, without just cause; intentare una —, fare —, muover — ad uno, to bring an action against someone; dare — vinta, to give in; — in appello, case in Court of Appeal; — in cassazione, case in Court of Cassation; — in pretura, case in the magistrate's court; — in tribunale, case in the Tribunal Court; — in ultima istanza, case in a court of last instance. **-ale** *adj.* causal; (leg.) causal, relating to a cause or action; *n.m.* (leg.) motive, reason, ground. **-almente** *adv.* (leg.) causally; from the cause of action. **-alità** *f.* (philos.; leg.) causality; (leg.) rapporto di **-alità**, relation of cause and effect (C.P.). **-ante** *adj.* causing, producing; *n.m.* cause. **-are** [A I S] *tr.* to cause; to bring about; to produce. **-ativo** *adj.* causative. **-ato** *part. adj.* caused; brought about; produced. (**-atore** *m.* **-atrice** *f.*) **-azione** *f.* (philos.) causation. **-i·dico** *m.* (leg.) pleader, advocate without professional qualifications.

causcìu *m. indecl.* See **cauccìu**.

ca·ustica *f.* (math.) caustic.

ca·ustic-o *adj.* caustic, burning; *n.m.* caustic. **-ità** *f.* causticity.

cautel-a *f.* caution; cautiousness, circumspection; warning; (leg.) caution money or similar security; — sociniana, choice allowed to legitimate heir in certain cases of insufficiency of testator's estate (C.C.). **-are** [A I] *tr.* to secure, to make safe; (leg.) to protect by means of caution money or similar security. **-ato** *part. adj.* prudent; secure. (**-atamente** *adv.*)

cautelare[1] [A I] see under **cautela**.

cautelare[2] *adj.* (leg.) precautionary; procedimenti cautelari, precautionary proceedings (C.C.P.)

cautere *m.* cautery burner.

cauter·io *m.* (surg.) cautery. **-izzare** [A I] *tr.* to cauterize. **-izzato** *part. adj.* cauterized. **-izzazione** *f.* cauterization.

ca·ut-o *adj.* cautious; careful; prudent; wary; secured against loss; mal —, incautious, imprudent; far —, to warn. **-amente** *adv.* cautiously; warily. **-ezza** *f.* cautiousness, prudence.

cauzion-e *f.* (leg.) bail; security; guarantee; recognizance; dare —, prestare —, to stand bail (C.P.) or security (C.C.); ammettere alla —, to admit to bail; offrire —, to offer bail; essere rilasciato dietro —, to be released on bail. **-ale** *adj.* (leg.) cautionary, by way of guarantee. **-are** [A I c] *tr.* (comm.) to guarantee.

cav-a *f.* pit; quarry, mine; — aperta, opencast mine; (eng.) slot, groove; †den, lair; †cave. **-ai(u)olo** *m.* quarryman. **-erella** *f. dim.* of **cava**.

cava-borra *m. indecl.* (mil.) charge-extractor. **-chiodi** *m. indecl.* nail-puller, nail-extractor. †**-denti** *m.* tooth-drawer, dentist. **-fango** *m. indecl.* (naut.) dredger. **-fascioni** *m. indecl.* (motor.) tyre-lever. **-fieno** *m. indecl.* (mil.) charge-extractor. **-fondi, -fondo** *m. indecl.* (naut.) dredger. **-loc·chio** *m.* (*pl.* cavalocchi) (ent.) stable fly, *Stomoxys calcitrans*; (fig.) quack lawyer; debt collector. **-mac·chie** *m., f. indecl.* cleaner (of clothing, etc.). **-pietre** *m. indecl.* quarryman. **-spolette** *m. indecl.* pin-remover for grenades. **-stivali** *m. indecl.* boot-jack. **-stoppa** *m. indecl.* (naut.) caulker's ripping iron; tool for removing old caulking. **-stracci** *m. indecl.* charge extractor. **-tappi** *m. indecl.*, **-tu·beri** *m. indecl.* (agric.) potato-lifter. **-turac·cioli** *m. indecl.* corkscrew.

cavaglione[1] *m.* (agric.) pile of fodder; haystack.

†**cavaglione**[2] *m.* purse or pocket attached to trousers.

cavagna *f.* (N.W. Ital.) See **cavagno**.

cavagn-o *m.* basket. **-(u)olo** *m.* basket-muzzle.

cavai(u)olo *m.* See under **cava**.

cavalc-are [A 2] *intr.* (*aux.* avere) to ride (horseback); *tr.* to ride; to straddle, to mount; to rise above, to overflow, to overtop; (of a road, etc.) to span. **-a·bile** *adj.* (of a horse) suitable for riding; (of a road) passable on horseback. **-amento** *m.* straddling; riding. **-ante** *part. adj.* riding; mounted; †*n.m.* mounted soldier, cavalry-man; †postilion; †driver of front pair of horses. **-ata** *f.* cavalcade; ride on horseback. **-ato** *part. adj.* ridden; †(mil.) mounted. **-atoio** *m.* mounting block. **-atore** *m.* rider; horseman. **-atrice** *f.* lady-rider; horsewoman. **-atura** *f.* riding-horse; mount; cost of hiring a mount; riding.

cavalcavi·a *f. indecl.* bridge over road or railway, road bridge; arch or bridge between two houses on opposite sides of a road; road that spans a railway or another road.

cavalcion-e, -i *adv.* astride; stare —— su, to bestride; tenere le gambe a ——, to sit with one's knees crossed.

cavalier-e *m.* rider, horseman; knight; member of an order of chivalry; nobleman; member of the nobility; fare ——, to knight; —— errante, knight errant; —— di ventura, knight errant, soldier of fortune; escort, male partner at a dance; (hist.) cavalier servente, married woman's escort, gentleman-in-waiting; —— d'industria, trickster, swindler; (joc.) —— del dente, scrounger; (techn.) rider on a precision balance; (mil.) cavalier, prominence; —— di Frisia, chevaux de Frise; a —— di, dominating (usu. two valleys); commanding (in situation); straddling; (ent.) silkworm; (orn.) —— d'Italia, blackwinged stilt, *Himantopus himantopus*; †(hist.) officer in service of a 'Podestà'; †executioner; †(chess) knight; *excl.* Tally-ho! †**-a** *f.* wife of a knight, lady; daughter of a knight. **-ato** *m.* knighthood. **-essa** *f.* lady, dame; wife of a knight; noblewoman. †**-o** *m.* see **cavaliere**.

cavall-a *f.* mare. **-etta** *f.* (naut.) mizzen staysail; (ent.) locust; (pop.) grasshopper; (agric. Lucca) sheaf of scythed grass; †tackle and pulley; †(fig.) trick, deception.

cavall-a·io *m.* horse-dealer. **-aro** *m.* teamster; leader of a packhorse; horseman; horse-dealer.

cavallante *m.* (dial. N. Ital.) driver, carter.

†**cavall-are** *tr.* to mount, to ride; *intr.* to go riding. †**-ata** *f.* yeomanry; mounted police. †**-ato** *m.* yeoman.

cavallegg(i)er-e, -o *m.* light cavalryman.

cavaller-i·a *f.* cavalry; chivalry; knighthood. **-esco** *adj.* (*m.pl.* **-eschi**) knightly; ordine -esco, order of knighthood; chivalrous; codice -esco, code of chivalry; gentlemanly; brave; generous; loyal; poema -esco, romantic epic. (**-escamente** *adv.*) †**-oso** *adj.* valiant, chivalrous.

cavallerizz-a *f.* riding school; manège, arena; equitation, art of riding, horsemanship; riding-instructress; horsewoman. **-o** *m.* riding-master; outrider; -o del Re, Master of the Horse.

cavalletta *f.* See under **cavalla**.

cavallett-o *m. dim.* of **cavallo**, q.v.; trestle, stand, tripod; strut of a roof; easel; (tanning) beam; (mil.) gun support; (mil.) barbed-wire entanglements, chevaux de Frise; instrument of torture; (agric.) sheaf; (mus.) bridge. **-ante** *m., f.* worker at a trestle or easel.

cavallin-a *f. dim.* of **cavalla**; filly, young mare; (fig.) correre la ——, to sow one's wild oats; †horse dung. **-o** *m. dim.* of **cavallo**, q.v.; colt, foal; pony; (Tusc.) cock-horse; (fig.) annoying individual; (eng.) donkey pump of a boiler; (naut.) -o di un ponte, fore and aft lift of deck; *adj.* equine; tosse -a, whooping cough; mosca -a, horse-fly; †libidinous.

cavall-o *m.* (sometimes **caval**, as in provbs. below) horse; —— di razza, —— puro sangue, thoroughbred; —— da caccia, hunter, —— da corsa, racehorse; —— di battaglia, warhorse, charger, (fig.) an artist's or an actor's forte, a work or part in which he excels; favourite subject, hobby-horse; —— da soma, packhorse; —— da tiro, draught horse, cart-horse; —— da noleggio, hack; —— da sella, saddle-horse; —— di San Francesco, shank's pony, walking-stick; —— a dondolo, rocking-horse; —— da giostra, vaulting-horse; salto al ——, vaulting; —— di legno, hobby-horse (toy); a ——, on horseback, mounted, astride; (fig.) essere ormai a ——, to have broken the back of a job, to be going strong, to be nearly at the end of a task; una febbre da ——, a raging temperature; (provb.) a caval donato non si guarda in bocca, don't look a gift horse in the mouth; caval che corre non ha bisogno di sprone, don't whip a willing horse; l'occhio del padrone ingrassa il ——, a business thrives when the proprietor keeps an eye on it; (slang) in roulette, counter placed between two numbers; (mil.) —— di Frisia, barbed-wire entanglements, chevaux de Frise; (mil. hist.) horse-soldier; (naut.) sandbar at the mouth of river or harbour; wave, breaker, 'white horse'; (chess) knight; (numism.) copper coin of reign of Ferdinand I (1458–94); (mech.) —— vapore, horse-power (abbrev. cv.; 1 H.P. = 1·0139 cv.); (bot.) coda di ——, mare's tail, *Equisetum arvense*; (meteor.) mare's tail; (bot.) ugna di ——, hornwort, *Ceratophyllum demersum*; (tailor.) —— dei pantaloni, crutch of trousers. **-one** *m. augm.* of **cavallo**; breaker, large wave. **-otto** *m.* fair-sized horse; (numism.) silver coin of c. 1413 to 1553 displaying figure on horseback. **-uccio** *m. pejor.* of **cavallo**, q.v.; nag, screw; a -uccio, pick-a-back; (Siena) a kind of honey-cake; (ichth.) -uccio marino, sea-horse, *Hippocampus* sp.; *pl.* -ucci e ricciarelli, little cakes, made of honey, sugar and flour.

cavaloc·chio *m.*, **cavamacchie** *m. indecl.* See under **cavaborra**.

cavana *f.* (geog.) underground stream.

cav-are [A I] *tr.* to excavate, to dig out; to extract; to obtain; non le ho -ato una parola di bocca, I couldn't get a word out of her; non —— un ragno da un buco, to make no headway, to be baffled, to be mystified; to take away, to remove; -arsi la voglia, to satisfy a desire; -arsi il cappello, to raise one's hat; -arsi i guanti, to take off one's gloves; -arsela, to get out of a difficulty, to manage fairly well; *intr.* (*aux.* avere) (fencing) to disengage. **-ata** *f.* extraction; -ata di sangue, blood-letting; (mus.) tone-production; brief arioso at the end of a recitative. **-atic·cio** *adj.* excavated; terra -aticcia, earth taken out along with the ore. **-atina** *f.* (mus.) cavatina, aria of one section without middle section or da capo; (fig.) ingenious ruse for getting out of a difficulty; cavil. **-atini** *m.pl.* (text.) short pieces of hemp or silk. **-ato** *part. adj.* excavated, extracted; obtained; hollow, concave; *n.m.* excavated place, cavity. **-atore** *m.* quarryman. **-atrice** *f.* (eng.) slotting machine. **-atura** *f.* removal; hollow, cavity. **-azione** *f.* (fencing) disengagement; finta di -azione, one, two; †excavation.

cavarella *f. dim.* of **cava**, q.v.

cava-stivali, -stracci, -tappi, -turaccioli, *m. indecl.* See under **cavaborra**.

ca·vea *f.* (archeol.) auditorium of the ancient Roman theatre; (archit.) rounded or horseshoe-shaped auditorium; una sala sistemata a ——, an auditorium in the shape of a horseshoe.

cavedagna *f.* (agric.) path bordering cultivated fields.

cave·d-ano *m.*, **-ine** *f.* (ichth.) chub, *Squalius cephalus*.

cave·dio *m.* (archeol.) entrance hall, atrium.

†**cavelle** *m.* something; a trifle; a bit; nothing; *adv.* in no way, not at all (cf. **covelle**).

†**cavello** *m.* See **capello**.

cavern-a *f.* cavern, cave; cavity. **-osità** *f.* cavernousness; (med.) cavity. **-oso** *adj.* cavernous; hollow; deep.

caverni·cola *m.* cave-dweller.

caveroz·zola *f.* scar left on a plant by pruning.

cavetto *m.* (archit.) cavetto, scotia; (naut.) small hawser; (electr.) small cable, lead.

cavezz-a *f.* halter; hangman's rope; pagare sulla ——, to pay on the nail; wretched man; cunning rogue; (of a horse) —— di moro, moor head, moor face. **-ale** *m.* path bordering cultivated fields. **-iera** *f.* cords suspending a hammock. **-ina** *f. dim.* small halter; reins. **-one** *m. augm.* halter with the addition of a noseband for refractory horses or for breaking horses in. **-(u)ola** *f. dim.* of **cavezza**, q.v.; ragamuffin.

ca·via *f.* (zool.) guinea pig (also fig.).

caviale[1] *m.* caviare.

caviale[2] *m.* (Tusc.) simpleton.

cavic·chi-a *f.* bolt; large peg. **-o** *m.* wooden pin; dow; hat-peg, peg; peg for string of an instrument; rung of a ladder; dibble or dibber for planting out seedlings; treenail; (fig.) pretext.

†**cavicciul-e, †-o** *m.* halter.

cavi·gli-a *f.* peg; bolt; (eng.) pin, cotter pin; dowel; (naut.) treenail; —— d'arresto, locking-pin; —— da dar volta, belaying-pin; —— da impiombare, marline spike; ankle; ankle-bone; —— slogata, sprained ankle; shin; (watchm.) —— del disco, roller jewel. **-atoio** *m.* (text.) throwing tool for silk; (naut.) peg hole of a capstan or helm. **-era** *f.* (naut.) rack for belaying pins. **-etta** *f. dim.* of **caviglia**; (watchm.) set arbor. **-o** *m.* large peg. **-otto** *m.* (naut.) cleat. **-(u)olo** *m.* peg, pin. **-one** *m.* (ichth.) *Lepidotriglia aspera*, a kind of gurnard; pocket, purse attached to trousers.

cavill-are [A I] *intr.* (*aux.* avere) to quibble, to cavil; *tr.* to criticize, to pick faults in. **-amento** *m.* quibbling; fault-finding. (**-atore** *m.*

cavill-are (*cont.*)
-**atrice** *f.*) -**azione** *f.* quibbling, cavilling; fault-finding. -**o** *m.* quibble, petty argument; chicane; cavil. -**oso** *adj.* of a quibbling nature. (-**osamente** *adv.*) -**osità** *f.* propensity to quibble.

cavità *f.* cavity; hollow, space, recess.

cavitazione *f.* (metall.) cavitation.

cavo[1] *adj.* hollow, concave; (anat.) vena cava; *n.m.* hollow, cavity; — di barca, interior of a boat; — dell'onda, trough of the wave; mould for casting; embroidery on canvas; (mil.) channel, moat.

cavo[2] *m.* cable; — telefonico, telephone line; — bianco, untarred cordage; — a rovescio, back-laid rope; — per le brande, hammock gant-line; — da ferro, drag-rope; — di primo tiglio, best quality hemp; — vegetale, hemp or grass hawser; — metallico, steel wire rope; — pilota, leader cable; (radio) — musicale, music line.

†**cavo**[3] *m.* reef, headland.

cavogramma *m.* See **cablogramma**.

ca·vol-o *m.* cabbage, *Brassica oleracea*; (N. Ital., Ven.) cauliflower; —verzotto, cabbage; — cappuccio, Savoy cabbage; — broccoluto, — romano, broccoli; — marino, sea-kale, *Crambe maritima*; non vale un —, it is not worth a rap; (vulg.) andare ad ingrassare i -i, to 'peg out'; essere andato a ingrassare i -i, to be 'pushing up the daisies'; salvare capra e -i, to manage to save two things, one of which seemed destined to be sacrificed; starci come i -i a merenda, to be out of place, to be like a fish out of water; — riscaldato, something renewed, e.g. a friendship after a quarrel; (colloq.) testa di —, blockhead. -**ac·cio** *m.* (bot.) butter bur, *Petasites hybridus*; (fig.) stupid person. -**a·ia** cabbage patch; cabbage vendor; (ent.) cabbage white butterfly, *Pieris brassicae*; -aia minore, *Pieris rapae*. -**a·io** *m.* gardener; cabbage patch. -**ata** *f.* dish of cabbage or of cabbage and lettuce. -**esco** *adj.* (*m.pl.* -**eschi**) cabbage-like. -**esse** *f.pl.* (bot.) -esse selvatiche, rock-cress, *Arabis hirsuta* and *Arabidopsis thaliana*. -**fiore** *m.* cauliflower. -**ino** *m. dim.* of **cavolo**; -ini Bruxelles, Brussels sprouts.

†**cavretto** *m.* See **capretto**, under **capro**.

cavri(u)ol-a, **cavrivuol-a** *f.* See **capri(u)ola**. -**o** *m.* see **capri(u)olo**.

cavurrino *m.* two-lire bank-note with an imprint of Cavour; type of cigar.

cazz-a *f.* crucible; ladle; (mil. hist.) instrument for charging a cannon. -**etta** *f.* ladle.

cazz-are [A I] *tr.* (naut.) to draw (a sheet) home. -**ame** *m.* (naut.) foot (of a sail).

cazzaruola *f.* See **casseruola**.

cazzascotte *f.* (naut.) kevel, extra-large cleat.

cazzeruol-a *f.*, -**o** *m.* See **casseruola**.

cazzo *m.* (vulg.) penis, male organ; simpleton.

cazzomatto *m.* idiot, fool.

cazzott-are [A I] *tr.* to punch. -**ata** *f.* punch, blow, thump. -**atura** *f.* punching. -**o** *m.* punch on the head; sly punch; fare a -i, to come to fisticuffs; (fig.) to be incompatible; a kind of pipe tobacco used in Sicily; (Naples) long French type of loaf.

cazzuol-a *f.* bricklayer's trowel; maestro della —, bricklayer; (zool.) tadpole; †*pl.* false promises; smooth words.

ce[1] *pers. prn.* form of **ci** used before lo, li, gli, la, le, ne.

†**ce**[2] *f.* name of the letter C (cf. **ci**[1]).

cec-a[1] *f.* (ichth.) elver, young eel. -**olina** *f.* the smallest stage of the eel, at which it first approaches the estuary.

Ceca[1] *pr.n.f.* (pol.) Cheka, Russian secret police (later renamed Ogpu).

cec-aggine *f.* blindness; heaviness (of the eyes), drowsiness. -**amente** *adv.* See **ciecamente**, under **cieco**. †-**are** *tr.* and derivs. See **accecare**.

cecc-a[1] *f.* (orn.) magpie; silly chattering woman; fare —, to misfire; to sing or play out of tune. -**ona** *f.* (mus.). See **ciaccona**.

Cecca[2] *pr.n.f.* abbrev. of **Francesca**, Frances.

ceccherino *m.* thin, scraggy chicken.

Cecchina *pr.n.f. dim.* of **cecca**[2], q.v.

cecchino *m.* (mil. slang) Austrian sniper (after Emperor Franz-Josef nicknamed Cecco-Beppe by the Italians); *pr.n.m. dim.* of **Cecco**, q.v.

Cecco *pr.n.m.* abbrev. of **Francesco**, Francis.

†**ceccosuda** *m.* busybody.

cec-e *m.* (bot.) chick-pea, *Cicer arietinum*; — (di) prete, star thistle, *Centaurea solstitialis* and *calcitrapa*; — selvatico, milk vetch, *Astragalus cicer*; — di terra, groundnut plant, *Arachis hypogaea*; (cul.) -i maritati, soup with pasta and lentils; (fig.) ministra di -i, poor man's soup; avere il — all'orecchio, to be deaf; fleshy

excrescence, e.g. on a swan's beak; charming little child or young girl; †non dare nè in tinche nè in -i, to come to nothing; to be inconclusive; to be irrelevant; to be neither flesh, fowl nor good red herring. -**erello** *m.* small yellowish stone. -**iato** *adj.* whitish. -**ina** *f.* attractive young woman. -**ino** *m.* dandy, pretty youth; small fleshy excrescence.

cecerello *m.* (bot.) caltrops, *Tribulus terrestris*; corn salad, lamb's lettuce, *Valerianella locusta*.

†**ce·c-ero**, †-**ino** *m.* (mute) swan.

†**cech-ezza**, †-**ità**, †-**itade**, †-**itate** *f.* See **cecità**.

cechino *m. dim.* of **cieco**, q.v.

ce·cia[1] *f.* small heater made of terracotta, suspended from a cage and used for warming beds.

†**ce·cia**[2] *m.* the north-east wind of Greece.

ceciarello *m.* (bot.). See **cecerello**; type of soil said to be favourable for growing corn.

†**ceciato** *adj.* of the colour of dried peas.

Ceci·lia *pr.n.f.* Cicely, Cecilia; (pop.) ladybird.

†**cecisbe·o** *m.* See **cicisbeo**.

cecità *f.* blindness; (med.) — serena, gutta serena, amaurosis; (med.) — nuvolosa, cataract.

ceco[1] *adj.* See **cieco**.

cèco[2] *adj.*, *n.m.* Czech.

cecolina *f.* See under **ceca**.

Cecoslov-ac·chia *pr.n.f.* (geog.) Czecho-Slovakia. -**acco** *adj.*, *n.m.* (*pl.* -**acchi**) Czecho-Slovak. (-**acca** *f.*)

cecro·pio *adj.* (poet.) seated in Athens.

ced-ere [B I] *intr.* (*aux.* avere) to yield, to give in; to submit, to surrender; to cave in; to subside; *tr.* to cede, to give up; to hand over; to make over; to renounce; to yield, to surrender; — il passo a, to make way for; — la destra a, to walk on the left of (someone); -erla a, to yield the palm to; (leg.) to transfer; to assign; to convey; to cede; to yield. -**ente** *part. adj.* yielding, pliable; obedient; biddable; *n.m.* (leg.) transferor, assignor. †-**enza** *f.* yielding; submission; capacity to yield, give. -**evole** *adj.* yielding, soft, flexible, pliable, pliant, supple; accommodating. -**evolezza** *f.* easy virtue; softness, suppleness, pliability. -**i·bile** *adj.* (leg.) transferable, assignable; non -ibile, non-transferable. -**imento** *m.* yielding; give, sag; giving way; -imento del terreno, subsidence; punto di -imento, yield point; (electr.) tensione di -imento, breakdown voltage. -**itore** *m.* (leg.) transferor, assignor. (-**itrice** *f.*)

†**cederno** *m.* See **cedro**[1].

cedi·glia *f.* (orthog.) cedilla.

cedimento *m.* See under **cedere**.

ce·dol-a *f.* (comm.) promissory note, coupon; — di banca, bank-note; voucher; — di commissione libraria, book-token. -**one** *m.* (eccl.) public notice of important church matter (e.g. summoning of a council, excommunication). -**otto** *m.* notice of decision by a diocesan council or church court.

†**cedo·nia** *f.* bridle, reins.

cedr-are [A I c] *tr.* to flavour with citron; to flavour with lemon. -**ata** *f.* citron-flavoured drink; lemonade. -**ato** *adj.* lemon-flavoured; citron-flavoured; *n.m.* ice-cream soda with lemon flavouring; (bot.) citron-tree, *Citrus medica*. See also **cedro**[1].

cedreleo *m.* lemon oil.

cedren-e, -**o** *m.* (chem.) cedrene.

ce·dria *f.* (bot.) cone of cedar of Lebanon, *Cedrus libani*.

cedrina *f.* (bot.) lemon-verbena, *Aloysia triphylla*.

cedrino[1] *adj.* See under **cedro**[1].

cedrino[2] *adj.* See under **cedro**[2].

cedri(u)olo *m.* (bot.). See **cetri(u)olo**.

cedr-o[1] *m.* (bot.) *Citrus*, genus of trees including orange, lemon, etc.; citron tree, *Citrus medica*; fruit of same, citron, — arancio, orange tree, *Citrus sinensis*; — arancio forte, Seville orange tree, *Citrus aurantium*; — limone, lemon tree, *Citrus limon*. -**ino** *adj.* lemon-coloured. -**one** *m.* citron; citron-juice, citron syrup; *adj.* lemon-coloured; (orn.) galle -one, capercaillie, *Tetrae urogallus*. -**oncella** (bot.) lemon balm, *Melissa officinalis*. -**onella** *f.* (bot.) see **cedroncella**; (ent.) brimstone butterfly, *Gonepteryx rhamni*.

cedr-o[2] *m.* (bot.) cedar, incl. *Cedrus* and other genera; — del Libano, Cedar of Lebanon, *Cedrus libani*. -**ino** *adj.* pertaining to cedar; (of) cedar.

ce·duo *adj.* (of a copse, etc.) suitable for cutting periodically for firewood; *n.m.* coppice.

cefagli·oli, **-ọni** *m.pl.* (bot.) European dwarf fan-palm, *Chamaeraps humilis*.

cefal-algi·a *f.* (med.) cephalalgy, headache. **-al·gico** *adj.* (med.) cephalalgic. **-e·a** *f.* violent headache. **-ografi·a** *f.* (med.) description of the head. **-ometri·a** *f.* craniometry. **-oplegi·a** *f.* (med.) paralysis of the neck muscles.

cefa·lico *adj.* cephalic.

ce·falo *m.* (ichth.) mullet; — vero, grey mullet, *Mugil cephalus*; — calamita, *Mugil capeto*; — musino, *Mugil saliens*.

cefalotorace *m.* (zool.) cephalothorax.

Ce·feo *pr.n.m.* (myth.; astron.) Cepheus.

ceff·o (Tusc.), **cẹff·o** (Rom.) *m.* snout, muzzle; ugly mug; sinister-looking person; guardare a — torto, to make a wry face at. **†-are** *tr.* to seize by the snout; to seize. **-ata** *f.* slap in the face. **†-autte** *m.* ugly face; grotesque mask or face sculptured on pottery. **-onare** [A I c] *tr.* to cuff, to slap, to clout. **-ọne** *m.* cuff, slap, clout. **-uto** *adj.* having a large snout.

†cefo *m.* a kind of ape.

Ce·ilan *pr.n.m.* (geog.) Ceylon.

Ceka *pr.n.f.* See **Ceca²**.

†ce·labro *m.* brain, brains.

celanẹse *m.* (text.) celanese.

cel-are¹ [A I] *tr.* to conceal; *rfl.* to hide, to hide oneself. **-amẹnto** *m.* concealment. **†-ata** *f.* ambush, ambuscade; underground passage. **-ato** *part. adj.* hidden, concealed; unrevealed; occult; †alla -ata, secretly; †*n.m.* confidant. (**-atamẹnte** *adv.*) **-atura** *f.* concealment.

†cel-are² *tr.* to chisel; to engrave; to sculpt. **†-ato** *part. adj.* chiselled; engraved. **-atura** *f.* chiselling; engraving.

celat-a¹ *f.* helmet without crest; †soldier wearing a 'celata'; †caul; nascere con la —, to be born with a caul. **-ina** *f.* helmet, cap. **-ọne** *m. augm.* of **celata**, q.v.; †a kind of telescope.

†celata² *f.* See under **celare¹**.

celeber·rimo *adj. superl.* of **celebre**, q.v.

celebr-are [A I s] *tr.* to celebrate; to solemnize; to praise; to extol; (leg.) — un contratto, to execute a formal contract; — un processo, to hold a trial. **-a·bile** *adj.* worthy of celebration. **-amẹnto** *m.* celebrating; celebration. **†-ando** *adj.* celebrated, worthy of renown. **-ante** *m.* (liturg.) celebrant. **-ato** *part. adj.* celebrated; famous, well-known, renowned. (**-atọre** *m.* **-atrice** *f.*) **-aziọne** *f.* celebration.

ce·lebr-e *adj.* celebrated, famous, distinguished, notable, well-known, renowned. (**-emẹnte** *adv.*) **-ẹvole** *adj.* worthy of celebration. **-ità** *f. indecl.* celebrity; fame; renown; celebrity, famous person; †celebration; †pomp; †solemnity; †concourse.

ce·lebret *m. indecl.* (eccl.) celebret.

†ce·lebro *m.* See **cerebro**.

celem·bolo *m.* (Gk. antiq.) hollow wedge (in tactics).

celenterati *m.pl.* (zool.) Coelenterates.

ce·ler-e *adj.* rapid, quick, fast, swift; (of a train) fast; *pr.n.f.* la Celere, branch of Italian police with jeeps called in to break up riots, disperse mobs, etc. **-mẹnte** *adv.* rapidly, quickly, swiftly, fast. **-imensura** *f.* tachymetry. **-i·metro** *m.* speedometer. **-ino** *m.* member of 'La Celere'. **-ità** *f.* celerity, speed, velocity, rapidity.

celesco·pio *m.* (surg.) small electric lamp for illuminating cavities.

celesta *f.* (mus.) celesta.

Celeste¹ *pr.n.m.*, *f.* Celeste.

celest-e² *adj.* celestial, heavenly; of the sky; divine; sotto la volta —, on earth; Impero —, China; (mus.) pedale —, damping pedal; blue, light blue, sky-blue; *n.m.* divinity; i -i, the gods; the colour blue, light blue, sky-blue. **-emẹnte** *adv.* divinely, in a heavenly manner. **-iale** *adj.* celestial, heavenly. **-ialmẹnte** *adv.* celestially. **†-riale** *adj.* see **celestiale**. **-ina** *f.* (miner.) celestine, celestite.

Celestino¹ *pr.n.m.* Celestine.

celestino² *m.* (eccl.) Celestine (monk).

celestino³ *adj.*, *n.m. dim.* of **celeste²**; pale blue.

celestite *f.* (geol.) celestite, celestine; strontium sulphate.

†celest-o, **†-re**, **†-ro** *adj.* See **celeste²**.

†celete *m.* racehorse; †(naut.) schooner, small brig.

cel-e·u(s)ma *m.* (Gk. antiq.) boatswain's call to rowers; sailors' song, sea shanty. **-e·uste** *m.* (Gk. antiq.) boatswain giving time to rowers.

ce·li-a¹ *f.* jest, joke; per —, in fun; reggere alla —, to stand a joke. **-are** [A 3] *intr.* (*aux.* avere) to joke. (**-atọre** *m.* **-atrice** *f.*) **-ọne** *m.* funny man, facetious person, man who loves a joke.

Ce·lia² *pr.n.f.* Celia.

celi·aco *adj.* (anat.) coeliac.

†celiarca *m.* See **chiliarca**.

ce·lib-e *adj.* unmarried; celibate; *n.m.* bachelor. **-ata·rio** *m.* celibatarian, confirmed bachelor. **-ato** *m.* celibacy; bachelorhood.

celi·cola *m.* inhabitant of heaven.

celido·nia *f.* (bot.) greater celandine, swallow-wort, *Chelidonium majus*; — minore, lesser celandine, *Ranunculus ficaria*.

cell-a¹ *f.* cell, small room; — frigorifera, cold room; (archaeol.) cella (of a temple); wine-cellar; storeroom. **-ẹtta** *f. dim.* little cell; small cavity; recess.

†cella² *f.* (numism.) coin minted in Aquila in 1420, in use up to 1480.

cell-a·io *m.* wine-cellar, store cupboard; buttery; †cellar-man. **†-a·rio** *m.* cellar. **†-era·io** *m.* cellar-man. **-era·(r)ia** *f.* cellar; (eccl.) cellaress. **-era·rio** *m.* (eccl.) cellarer. **-ereri·a** *f.* status of cellarer. **†-iere**, **†-iero** *m.* cell; cellar.

†cellamello *m.* (mus.). See **cennamella**.

cellofane, **cello·fane**, **cellofa·nia** *f.* cellophane; transparent paper.

†cel·lola *f.* See **cellula**.

†cello·ria *f.* (joc.) brains; intelligence; intellect; head, top-knot.

cell·lul-a *f.* cell; (phot.) — fotoelettrica, photo-electric cell, exposure meter; (naut.) compartment of double bottom. **-a·re** *adj.* cellular, divided into cells; canale -are, lumen, cell canal; (leg.) segregazione -are, solitary confinement; *n.m.* cluster of cells; prison; black Maria. **-ato** *adj.* cellular, composed of cells, containing cells. **-i·te** *f.* (med.) cellulitis; (pop.) excess weight. **-o·ide** *f.* celluloid; *adj.* cell-like, cellular. **-ọşa** *f.* (techn.) cellulose; wood pulp. **-o·şio** *m.* (chem.) cellulose. **-o·şico** *adj.* (of) cellulose. **-ọşo** *adj.* cellular, cell-like.

†celoce *m.* (naut.) small brig.

celoma *m.* (anat.; zool.) coelom.

celomo *m.* sea shanty.

†celone *m.* bedspread, bed covering; tablecloth.

celo·şia *f.* (bot.) cockscomb, *Celosia cristata*.

celotomi·a *f.* (surg.) celotomy.

†celsitu·dine *f.* (title) highness; eminence.

†celso *adj.* See **eccelso**.

celt-a *m.* Celt. **-i·bero** *m.* Celtiberian. **-izzare** [A I] *tr.* to Celticize; to Gallicize. **-izzato** *adj.* Celticized; Gallicized.

ce·ltico *adj.* Celtic; malattie celtiche, venereal diseases; lue celtica, syphilis.

celtoli·gure *adj.*, *n.m.* (ethn.) Celto-Ligurian.

cembalante *m.*, *f.* (mus.) harpsichordist.

†cembalare *tr.* (mus.) strike the timbrel.

cembala·ria *f.* (bot.) ivy-leaved toadflax, Kenilworth ivy, *Cymbalaria muralis*.

cẹmbalo¹ *m.* and derivs. See **clavicembalo**.

†cem·balo² *m.* (mus.) tambourine; (naut.) deck house; *pl.* (mus.) cymbals; (pop.) sonare il —, to steal skilfully, to be light-fingered.

†cembanell-a *f.* (mus.) rustic pipe. **†-o** *m.* (mus.) small tambourine or tabor.

†cembolism-a *f.*, **†-o** *m.* See **embolismo**.

†cem·bolo *m.* (mus.). See **cembalo¹,²**.

cembra *f.* (archit.) cimbia, fillet; scotia; (bot.) arolla pine, *Pinus cembra*.

cemẹnt-o *m.* cement; concrete; — romano, hydraulic cement; — armato, reinforced concrete; the carbon for converting iron into steel. **-are** [A I c] *tr.* to cement, to concrete; to submit (iron) to the steel-making process; to harden; (fig.) to reinforce, to strengthen, to cement. **-ato** *part. adj.* cemented; (fig.) strengthened. **-ato·rio** *adj.* suitable for cementing. **-aziọne** *f.* cementing, concreting; (metall.) hardening; rame di -azione, precipitated copper. **-eri·a** *f.*, **-ifi·cio** *m.* cement works. **-ista** *m.* cement-worker, cementer; cement-layer. **-ite** *f.* (metall.) cementite.

†cemmamella *f.* (mus.). See **cennamella**.

cempẹnn-a *m.*, *f.*, **-ọne** *m.*, **-ọna** *f.* (Tusc.) slow, inept individual; haverer. **-are** [A I c] *intr.* (*aux.* avere) (Tusc.) to walk with uncertain gait; to haver; to be ineffectual.

cen¹ (pop.) apocope for **cento** in compound numerals.

†cen² *contr.* of 'ce ne' (see **ci²**).

cẹn-a *f.* (N. Ital.) supper; (Tusc., S. Ital.) supper, dinner; non poter accozzare la — col desinare, to be unable to make both ends meet, to be pulling the devil by the tail; (eccl.) l'ultima —, la —, the Last Supper; — eucaristica, Holy Communion; — domini, Maundy Thursday; (in Protestant usage) santa —, the Lord's Supper. **-a·colo** *m.* (archaeol.) cenaculum; (rel.) the Upper Room;

cen-a (*cont.*)
small clique; (paint.) painting representing the Last Supper; il Cenacolo di Leonardo, Leonardo's 'Last Supper'. **-are** [A I c] *intr.* (*aux.* avere) to sup, to have supper. **-ata** *f.* a good supper. **-ato** *part. adj.* supplied with supper, having supped, having had supper, guest at supper; parasite. **-ato·rio** *adj.* pertaining to supper. **-erella**, **-ętta** *f. dim.* of cena. **-ọna** *f. augm.* of cena. **-ọne** *m.* supper on Christmas Eve, banquet, *réveillon.*

cena·brio *m.* See **cinabro.**

cenato[1] *part.* of cenare, q.v., under **cena.**

†cenato[2] *adj.* See under **ceno.**

cęnc-io *m.* (*pl.* -i) rag, cloth; duster; (paperm.) pasta di -i, rag-pulp; bianco come un — lavato, white as a sheet; capello a —, soft hat; i -i vanno sempre all'aria, it's always the poor that suffer; levare uno dai -i, to lift someone out of the gutter; cadere come un —, to flop, to collapse; useless person; person in a poor state of health; — molle, person of poor spirit; (cul.) kind of omelette. **-ia·ia** *f.* heap of rags. **-ia·io** *m.* rag picker, old-clothes man; (paperm.) rag-man. **-iai(u)olo** *m.* rag-man, old-clothes man. **-iame** *m.* pile of rags. **-iata** *f.* slap in the face with a wet clout; flick with a duster, a 'dust round'. **†-ierello** *m.* ragged beggar, man in rags. **-ieri·a** *f.* rags. **-iolano** *m.* (*pl.* cencilani) woollen cloth. **-iọso** *adj.* ragged; *n.m.* ragged man. **-iume** *m.* collection of rags.

cencro *m.* a kind of poisonous snake.

†cendado *m.* See **zendado.**

cendralina *f.* (Tusc.) slut.

cęner-e *f.* ash; *pl.* ashes; ashes of a cremated corpse; (poet.) mortal remains; (litург.) le -i, (blessed) ashes; le Ceneri, Ash Wednesday. **-ac·cio** *m.* the residue of ashes in a bucking cloth; ashes made up into a paste through which water is passed so as to make a lye for washing. **-ac·ciolo** *m.* cloth laid over a wash-tub on which ashes are placed; bucking cloth; ashes for making lye; goldsmith's crucible. **-a·io** *m.* dealer in ashes; ash-pan of a stove; ash-pit; (naut.) tubes for dumping cinders; garbage chute. **-an·dolo** *m.* dealer in ashes. **-a·rio** *adj.* cinerary; *n.m.* ash-pit; (naut.) see **ceneraio. -ata** *f.* ashes boiled in water for making lye. **-atọio** *m.* ash-pit. **†-ente** *adj.* ashen, ashy, ash-coloured. **-ic·cio** *adj.* ash-coloured, ashen. **-iera** *f.* ash-tray. **-i·gia** *f.* hot ashes. **-ina** *f.* ash not quite consumed; (ent.) second moult of silkworm. **-ino** *adj.* ash-coloured, ashen, grey. **-o·gnolo** *adj.* ashy pale. **-ọne** *m.* ashes in a bucking cloth; ash lye; manure in which ashes are an ingredient. **-ọso** *adj.* covered with ashes; soiled with ash. **†-u·giolo** *adj.* ash-coloured. **-ume** *m.* heap of ashes.

Ceneren·tola *pr.n.f.* Cinderella.

cenesteşi *f.* (psych.) coenaesthesis.

cęngi-a *f.*, **-o** *m.* (alp.) narrow ledge on a mountainside.

Ceni·sio *pr.n.m.* (geog.) Mont Cenis.

ceni·t *m. indecl.* See **zenit.**

cennamella *f.* (mus.) kind of bagpipe; †wind instrument; †bugle call.

†cen·namo *m.* (bot.) See **cinnamomo.**

cęnn-o *m.* sign; nod; gesture; hint; indication; brief explanation; signal, command, order; rough note, rough sketch; fare —, to signal, to give an indication; rendere —, to answer a signal; — di ricevuta, note of acknowledgement, -i su, notes on, outline of. **†-are** *vb.* See **accennare.**

†cen-o *m.* mud. **†-ato**, **†-olento** *adj.* muddy; filthy.

ceno·b-io *m.* monastery. **-iarca** *m.* (*pl.* -iarchi) abbot; head of a group or clique (in painting, writing, etc.). **-ita** *m.* monk (esp. of early centuries), cenobite. **-i·tico** *adj.* monkish, cenobitical. (**-iticamęnte** *adv.*)

cenọne *m. augm.* See under **cena.**

cenota·fio *m.* cenotaph.

cenozọ·ico *adj.* (geol.) cainozoic, tertiary.

cens-ire [D 2] *tr.* to take the census of; to assess; to tax. **-imęnto** *m.* census-taking; far il -imento, to take the census; modulo per il -imento, census paper. (**-ito** *part. adj.*)

censo *m.* census; (leg.) perpetual rentcharge or annuity (C.C.); (finan.) a —, in return for an annual payment; (fig.) money, wealth; moneyed classes; big business.

censọr-e *m.* censor. **†-are** *vb.* see **censurare. -ato** *m.* censorship.

censo·rio *adj.* censorial.

censu-ale *adj.* (econ.). **-are** [A 6] *tr.* (econ.). **-a·rio** *adj.* (econ.). **-ato** *part. adj.* **-azione** *f.*

censur-a *f.* censorship; censor; censure, reproof; pronunciare la —, to pass a vote of censure; police station; (eccl.) censure. **-a·bile**

adj. worthy of censure, blameworthy, censurable. **-are** [A I] *tr.* to censure, to reprove; to blame, to criticize; to disapprove (of). (**-atọre** *m.* **-atrice** *f.*)

†centarolo *m.* pig weighing 100 lb.

centa·urea, centaure·a *f.* (bot.) — minore, pink centaury, *Centaurium minus*; — nera, knapweed, hardhead, *Centaurea jacea, C. nigra*; — maggiore, great centaury, *C. centaurium.*

cent-a·uro *m.* (myth.) centaur; (astron.) Centaurus; (neol. slang) any motor-cyclist, not necessarily racing; racing motor-cyclist. **-a·ura, -auressa** *f.* female centaur. **-auręsco** (*m.pl.* -auręschi), **-a·urico, -a·uride** *adj.* pertaining to a centaur; (fig.) confused, muddled.

centellare [A I]. See **centellinare.**

centellin-are [A I] *tr.* to sip. **-o** *m.* sip; bere a -i, to drink in small sips.

centena *f.* (hist.) group of a hundred families among the ancient Germans.

centena·rio *adj.* centenarian, recurring every hundred years; *n.m.* centenary; centenarian.

cent-ennale *adj.* pertaining to a century; (leg.) prescrizione —, hundred-year period of prescription or limitation. **-enne** *adj.* lasting a hundred years; centennial. **-en·nio** *m.* a period of a hundred years, century; centennial.

centerbe *m. indecl.* liqueur of the Abruzzi flavoured with many herbs.

†cente·sima *f.* hundredth part; percentage; the difference between the astronomical year and the year of the Julian calendar, i.e. 13 minutes 36 seconds (Dante, *Par.* XXVII, 143).

cente·şim-o *adj.* hundredth; *n.m.* one-hundredth part; centime; cent; one-hundredth of a lira; †hundred; space of a hundred years, century. **-ale** *adj.* centesimal, referring to hundredths. NOTE: **centesimo** is compounded with other ordinal numbers, as centesimo primo, centesimo secondo, centesimo terzo, or else these numbers may be rendered centunesimo, centoduesimo, centotreesimo, and so on with -esimo to 109th, then centodecimo, centundecimo, after which centododicesimo (which, however, may be cento-duodecimo), centotredicesimo, etc.

†centesma *f.* See **centesima.**

centeşmo *m.* (poet.). See **centesimo.**

centiar-a *f.*, **-o** *m.* centiare, square metre.

centifọ·gli-o *m.* (bot.) chickweed, *Stellaria media*; **-a**, **-e** *f.* (bot.) cabbage rose, *Rosa centifolia.*

cent-i·grado *adj.* centigrade; il grado —, the Centigrade measure of heat. **-igramma, -igrammo** *m.* centigramme. **-ilag·gio** *m.* (psych.) intelligence quotient. **-i·litro, -ilitro** *m.* centilitre. **-i·metro** *m.* centimetre; tape-measure; ruler.

centiguida *f.* (paperm.) deckle strap; carrucole delle centiguide, deckle pulleys.

centilo·quio *m.* centiloquy.

centi·mano *adj. indecl.* hundred-handed.

centimbọcca *m.pl.* (cul.) fish fry.

centimor·bia *f.* (bot.). See **centinodia.**

cen·tin-a *f.* (archit.) centering, the temporary frame on which any vaulted work is constructed; curve in a bar; model or mould for giving a curve to a piece of work; (aeron.) each part of the frame-work of a wing; rib; small stitches like buttonhole stitches, esp. to keep a cut-out pattern from fraying; (bookb.) — del taglio concavo, fore-edge. **-are** [A I s] *tr.* (archit.) to arch, to bend into an arch; to construct the centering for. (**-amęnto** *m.*) **-ato** *part. adj.* scaloped, having a scaloped edge; (archit.) arched, vaulted, curved; *n.m.* (naut.) camber of a deck. **-atura** *f.* (archit.) arching, vaulting; centering; camber.

centin-a·io *m.* (*pl.f.* -a·ia) a quantity of a hundred; un —, about a hundred; per —, in groups of a hundred; †century.

†centinaro *m.* See **centinaio.**

centino *m.* (pop.) centime; cent; one-hundredth part of a lira.

centinọdi-a *f.*, **-o** *m.* (bot.) knotgrass, *Polygonum aviculare.*

centi·pede *adj.* having a hundred feet; *n.m.* (zool.) centipede, myriapod, millipede.

centista *m.* (sport) hundred-metre runner.

cent-o *num. adj. indecl.* hundred; one hundred; a hundred; per —, per cent; novantanove su —, ninety-nine cases out of a hundred. Sometimes, esp. in Tuscan usage, abbreviated to 'cen' in com-pound numerals like 'cencinquanta', 150. (NOTE: Each century after A.D. 1000 is usually referred to in Italian by the number of hundreds in the number of the year. Thus, the year 1360 is in the 'Trecento', or fourteenth century; likewise 'il Cinquecento'

cent-o (*cont.*)
is the sixteenth century, and so on.) **-o·cchio, -on·chio** *m.* (bot.) see **centifoglia. -ofo·glia, -ofo·glie** *f.* (bot.) yarrow, milfoil, *Achillea millefolium*; see **centifoglia. -ogambe** *m. indecl.* (zool.) see **centipedi**; (pop.) centipede. **-omila** *card. num.* hundred thousand; -omila volte, times without number, time and time again. **-omille·șimo** *ord. num.*, *adj. n.m.* hundred-thousandth. **-onovelle** *m. indecl.* book of a hundred tales. **-ope·lie** *f.* manyplies, omasum. **-opelle** *m.* omasum, honeycomb tripe. **-opiedi** *m. indecl.* (zool.) see **centipedi**.

centon-e¹ *m.* cento, a composition (of literature or music) formed by excerpts from different authors; miscellany; (hist.) rough garment stitched together from bits and pieces; (Rom. antiq.) slave's garment; (fig.) hotchpotch. **-ista** *m.* author or composer of a miscellany. **-ope·lie** *f.* (vet.) manyplies, omasum.

centone² *m.* (bot.). See **centifoglia**.

centrag·gio *m.* (eng.) centering.

central-e *adj.* central, centre, middle; chiesa a pianta —, round or octagonal church; *n.f.* main depot or works; main railway station; — elettrica, power station; — telefonica, telephone exchange; — del latte, depot where milk is pasteurized, bottled, etc., central dairy. **-inista** *m., f.,* **-ino** *m.,* **-ista** *m., f.* telephone operator; chiamare il -ino, to call the operator; switchboard. **-ità** *f.* centralness, centrality.

centralizz-are [A 1] *tr.* to centralize. **-ato** *part. adj.* centralized. (**-atore** *m.* **-atrice** *f.*) **-izzazione** *f.* centralization.

centranto *m.* (bot.) spur valerian, *Centranthus ruber*.

centr-are *tr.* [A 1] (sport) to centre (the ball); (eng.) to center; to true; to spot drill; *intr.* (*aux.* avere) to hit in the middle, to score a bull's eye; (fig.) to hit the nail on the head. **-ato** *part. adj.* (sport) centred; (herald.) banded. **-atrice** *f.* (eng.) centering machine.

centr-avanti *m. indecl.* **-attacco** *m.* (*pl.* **-attacchi**). See under **centro**.

cen·trico *adj.* (geom.) centric.

centr-ifugare [A 1 s] *tr.* to centrifuge. **-i·fuga** *f.* centrifuge; spin drier; extractor. **-ifugazione** *f.* centrifuging, separation of centrifuge. **-i·fugo** *adj.* (*m.pl.* **-i·fughi**) centrifugal.

centrina *f.* (ichth.) *Oxynotus centrina*, a kind of shark; the skin of *O. centrina*, used for rough polishing.

centri·peto *adj.* (phys.) centripetal.

centrista *m., adj.* (pol.) adherent of a centre party.

centr-o (Flor.), **centr-o** (Rom.) *m.* centre, middle; town centre; hub, heart; core; centre, club; institute; mid-point; fuori —, out of position, (eng.) out-of-center; essere nel suo —, to be in one's element; — da tavola, table centre, embroidered centre piece; — del bersaglio, bull's eye; — baricentrico, centre of gravity; (pol.) il Centro, the Centre party (of moderate views); (watchm.) pignone dei secondi al —, sweep second pinion; (naut.) amidships; (mil.) — di fuoco, artillery control position, battery emplacement; (football) — mediano, — sostegno, centre-half. **-oattacco** *m.* (*pl.* **-oattacchi**) (soccer, hockey) centre-forward. **-oavanti** *m. indecl.* (football) centre-forward. **-oe·urope·o** *adj.* Central European. **-osfera** *f.* (biol.) centrosphere. **-osoma** *m.* (biol.) centrosome.

†**centrongalli** *m.pl.* (bot.) seed of clary (*Salvia sclaria*), formerly used medicinally.

centum·vir-o *m.* (hist.) centumvir. **-ale** *adj.* centumviral. **-ato** *m.* centumvirate.

centuno *m.* (*f.* **centuna**, always qualifying a *sing.* noun) one hundred and one.

†**centu·pede** *m.* See **centipede**.

centuplic-are [A 2 s] *tr.* to centuplicate, to multiply a hundredfold. **-ato** *part. adj.* multiplied many times. (**-amente** *adv.*) **-azione** *f.* centuplication.

cen·tuplo *adj.* one hundred times greater.

†**centura** *f.* See **cintura**.

centu·ri-a *f.* (mil. hist.) ancient Roman century; company of three or four maniples; (Fasc.) company of 112 (three maniples) militiamen commanded by a captain; (eccl.) religious guild of a hundred members; collection of a hundred articles of a kind. **-are** [A 4] *tr.* to divide into bands of hundreds. **-ato** *part. adj.* divided into hundreds. **-onato** *m.* rank of centurion. **-one** *m.* centurion; (Fasc.) captain.

cenuro *m.* (zool.) *Coenurus cerebralis*, the cestode worm causing the disease of 'staggers' or 'gid' in sheep.

---

cepola *f.* (ichth.) red band fish, *Cepola rubescens*.

cepota·fio *m.* sepulchre in a garden; garden cemetery.

cepp-a *f.* underground part of the stem of a tree; trunk. **-aia** *f.* stump of a tree just above the ground; tenere a -aia, to keep (a copse) cut down for new growth; *pl.* underwood. **-ata** *f.* quantity of stumps; a living stump; (naut.) group of mooring posts. **-atella** *f.* sucker or cutting of a tree for transplanting. **-atello, -erello** *m.* (bot.) an edible fungus, *Ixocomus bovinus*. **-ato** *adj.* rooted. **-icone** *m.* (joc.) noddle.

ceppino *m.* (ichth.) shad, *Alosa alosa*.

ceppo *m.* root-stock, bole, trunk, stump; chopping block; execution block; brake block; support, base, rest; stock of a plough; (naut.) stock of an anchor; (geog.) bank of more or less coarse pebbles; (eccl.) block forming base of crucifix; log; Yule log; Christmas party; Christmas present; ardere il —, battere il —, custom of children in Tuscany when asking for Christmas presents; stock, family, race, line; source, origin; (of a word) etymology, root; *pl.* fetters, shackles; †wooden collecting box, alms box.

cer-a¹ *f.* complexion, air, mien, appearance; fare cattiva —, to look cross; fare buonissima — a, to welcome affably; †fare buona —, to eat heartily. **-ac·cia** *f. pejor.* ugly face, mug. **-ona** *f. augm.* round, open face. **-ozza** *f.* jovial, ruddy appearance. **-uc·cia** *f.* pale, sickly face.

cer-a² *f.* wax; — di Spagna, sealing-wax; (techn.) — fossile, ozokerito; — da scarpo, shoe polish, boot polish; — gialla, — vergine, unpurified wax; (fig.) essere di —, to be very delicate; parere di —, to be very pale; appiccato con la —, put together with spit; anything made of wax, e.g. candle, wax tablet, floor polish; (provb.) chi ha il capo di —, non vada al sole, people who live in glass houses shouldn't throw stones; †first matter, elements. **-ai(u)olo** *m.* wax chandler; sculptor in wax, maker of wax models. **-alacca** *f.* (*pl.* **ceralacche, cerelacche**) stick of sealing-wax; sealing-wax. **-ame** *m.* quantity of wax.

†**ceraldo** *m.* snake-charmer.

†**ceramella** *f.* (mus.). See **caramella**.

cera·m-ica *f.* pottery; ceramics; (metall.) sintering. **-ico** *adj.* ceramic, pertaining to pottery. **-ista** *m.* potter.

cer-are [A 1 c] *tr.* to wax. **-ato** *part. adj.* waxed; wax-impregnated; waterproofed; tela -ata, oilskin; carta -ata, waxed paper, greaseproof paper; *n.m.* (pharm.) scented ointment of wax and oil, cerate.

ceraș-a *f.*, **-o** *m.* See **ciliegi-a, -o**.

cerast-a *f.* (zool.) horned viper, *Cerastes cornutus*.

cerato *adj., n.m.* See under **cerare**.

cera·zia *f.* (astron.) a type of comet shaped like a horn.

cerazione *f.* (alchem.) ceration; fixation of mercury.

Cer·b-ero *pr.n.m.* (myth.; astron.) Cerberus; (joc.) person acting as a watchdog; guardian; concierge; (mus.) triple-necked theorbo. **-e·reo** *adj.* (poet.) relating to Cerberus.

cerba·ia¹ *f.* (Tusc.) deer-park.

cerba·ia² *f.* grove of Turkey oaks.

cer·bi-a *f.*, **-o** *m.* (zool.). See **cervo**.

cerbiatt-o *m.*, **-a** *f.* (zool.) fawn.

cerbone(c)a *f.* sour wine.

cerbottan-a *f.* blowpipe; pea-shooter; an early form of firearm; speaking-tube; ear-trumpet; sapere una cosa per —, to get to know of something indirectly. **-iere** *m.* (mil. hist.) soldier armed with a 'cerbottana'.

cerc-a *f.* quest, search, seeking; andare in — di, to look for, to seek, to be in search of; fare la —, to go begging; procession round the city by prisoners condemned to death; the fruits of begging, alms; (of a dog) — e riporto, fetching and retrieving; †visit, pilgrimage. †**-abrighe** *m.* quarrelsome person. **-afughe** *m. indecl.* leak detector. †**-amare** *m.* gunner in Knight of St John's galley. **-apersone** *m. indecl.* staff location equipment, 'paging' equipment. **-apoli** *m. indecl.* (electr.) pole indicator.

cerc-are [A 2 c] *tr.* to seek, to look for, to search (for); — qualcosa per mare e per terra, to look for something high and low; — qualcosa da qualcuno, to ask something of someone; — Maria per Ravenna, to seek something which is not there; to investigate, to look into, to examine, to scrutinize; to fetch; (*prep.* di, followed by *infin.*) to try (to), to endeavour (to), to attempt (to); †to encircle, to surround; †to go round. **-a·bile** *adj.* that may be sought after. **-amento** *m.* search, seeking. **-ante** *part. adj.* seeking; *n.m., f.* seeker; (eccl.) begging friar; beggar.

cerc-are (*cont.*)
-**ata** *f.* search, look; scrutiny. -**ato** *part. adj.* looked-for; sought-after, desired, in demand; examined. -**atore** *m.* seeker; investigator; (eccl.) begging friar; (rad.) detector; (rad.) -**atore a baffo di gatto**, cat's whisker. -**atora**, -**atrice** *f.* seeker; (eccl.) begging sister. -**oni** *adv.* looking, searching.

†**cercelli** *m.pl.* earrings.

cerchia *f.* circle, esp. of the walls of a city; sphere of interest or influence; confines; — **degli affari**, range of business; (geog.) — **morenica**, morainic arc.

cerchia·io *m.* See under **cerchio**.

cerchi-are [A4c] *tr.* to encircle, to go round; to ring; to hoop. -**amento** *m.* circlIng, ringing, encirclement. -**ata** *f.* trees trained or trimmed so as to form an arched passage; circling, ringing. -**ato** *part. adj.* enclosed; encircled, ringed round. -**atore** *m.* cooper; person who puts hoops on barrels, etc. -**atura** *f.* hooping, circling; collection of hoops, etc.

cerchi-o *m.* circle, ring; fare — **intorno a**, to cluster round, to form a ring round; hoop; crinoline; rim of a wheel; halo; (astron.) ring; (aeron.) fare il — **della morte**, to loop the loop; dare un colpo al — **e uno alla botte**, to keep two irons in the fire, to try to keep in with both parties; circle, group of people; meeting; orbit, range; (vet.) haminitis; (fencing) mezzo —, octave; (naut.) spectacle plate; thimble; — **azimutale**, azimuth plate; — **d'altezza**, position circle; †period, space of time. -**a·io** *m.* (*pl.* -**a·i**) hoop-maker. -**a·me** *m.* hoops, etc. in general. -**ello** *m. dim.* of **cerchio**; earring; box of a wheel; bearing. -**ettare** [A1c] *tr.* to ring with little hoops. -**olino** *m. dim.* of **cerchio**, q.v.; (vet.) see **cerchio**. -**one** *m. augm.* of **cerchio**, q.v.; large hoop; rim for wheels or barrels.

cercin-e *m.* round pad of cloth placed on the head for carrying loads; type of child's hat padded so as to give protection when he falls; swelling on the stem of a plant where it has been constricted; glass ring round the top of a wine bottle; (naut.) bolt-rope, edging-cord of a sail. -**ata** *f.* blow given with a 'cercine'; number of 'cercini'.

cerco¹ *adj. apocop.* (*m.pl.* **cerchi**). See **cercato**, under **cercare**.

†**cerco²** *m.* See **chierico**.

†**cerco³** *m.* See **cerchio**.

cercone *adj.* sour, bad-tasting (of wine); *n.m.* bad wine.

†**Cere** *pr.n.f.* (myth.). See **cerere**.

cere·a *excl.* (Piedm.) cheerio-oh!; goodbye!

cereal-e *adj., n.m.* cereal. -**icoltura** *f.* (agric.) corn growing.

†**cereatta** *m.* candelabrum.

cerebell-are *adj.* (anat.) cerebellar. -**o** *m.* (anat.) cerebellum. -**oso** *adj.* (anat.) cerebellic.

cerebr-ale *adj.* cerebral; (fig.) over-intellectual, sophisticated. -**alismo** *m.* intellectualism. -**are** [A1s] *intr.* (*aux.* avere) to cerebrate. -**azione** *f.* cerebration, brain action. -**iforme** *adj.* (anat.) cerebriform, encephaloid. -**ina** *f.* (chem.) cerebrin. -**ite** *f.* (med.) cerebritis.

ce·rebr-o *m.* brain. -**oso** *adj.* cerebric. -**ospinale** *adj.* (med.) cerebro-spinal.

†**ceremo·nia** *f.* See **cerimonia**.

ce·r-eo *adj.* waxy, waxen; (fig.) pale, haggard; *n.m.* candle (esp. Paschal); (eccl. art) (elaborate, carved) candlestick; (bot.) name applied to several cacti, especially to the giant cactus, *Carnegia gigantea*. -**eri·a** *f.* wax chandler's shop; wax refinery. -**etta** *f. dim.* of **cera**; polish; pomade. -**etta·io** *m.* polish maker. -**i·fero** *adj.* wax-producing.

Ce·rere *pr.n.f.* (myth.; astron.) Ceres; (fig.) corn.

cerfo·gli-o *m.* (bot.) garden chervil, *Anthriscus cerefolium*; — **selvatico**, wild chervil, *A. silvestris*; sweet Cicely, *Myrrhis odorata*; lock of untidy hair. -**one** *m. augm.* of **cerfoglio**; mop of hair.

ce·rico *adj.* (chem.). See under **cerio¹**.

cerigone *m.* opossum, *Didelphys* sp.

cerim·boli *m.pl.* (Umbr.) pork sausages flavoured with rosemary and fennel and smoked in the chimneypiece.

cerimo·ni-a *f.* ceremony, rite; pomp; formality, compliment; star **sulle** -**e**, to stand on ceremony. -**ac·cia** *f. pejor.* gratuitous compliment. -**ale** *adj.* ceremonial; (-**almente** *adv.*) *n.m.* ceremonial, rules at court, etiquette, protocol. †-**are** *intr.* to hold ceremonies; *n.m.* holding of ceremonies. -**ere** *m.* master of ceremonies.

cerimonios-o *adj.* ceremonious; *n.m.* ceremonious person. -**osamente** *adv.* ceremoniously; formally. -**osità** *f.* ceremoniousness.

cerin-o¹ *m.* small wax match; wax taper; tube of pomade. -**a·io** *m.* match-seller.

cerin-o² *m.* (slang) knife. -**ata** *f.* stab with a knife, knife wound.

cerint-a *f.*, -**e** *m.*, -**o** *m.* (bot.) honeywort, *Cerinthe major*.

ce·r-io¹ *m.* (chem.) cerium. -**ico** *adj.* (chem.) ceric. -**i·te** *f.* (miner.) cerite.

†**ce·rio²** *m.* See **cero**.

†**ceriuolo** *m.* cheat, trickster.

†**cerna¹** *f.* selection, sorting; (mil. hist.) soldier called up from a local region to satisfy military requirements; raw recruit.

cerna² *f.* (ichth.) a kind of sea perch, *Epinephelus gigas*.

cerna·glia *f.* (paperm.) retree; seconds; broke; **raccoglitore di** —, broke hustler.

†**cernecchiare** *vb.* and derivs. See **cernere**.

cernecchi-o *m.* lock of ruffled hair. -**one** *m.* person with ruffled hair. -**oso** *adj.* (of hair) rumpled, ruffled.

cer·n-ere [C28] *tr.* to separate, to select; to discern; to sift; to winnow; to sort. -**itore** *m.* sifter. -**itrice** *f.* (paperm.) rag-cutter. -**itura** *f.* sifting, separating, selection.

cer·nia *f.* (zool.). See **cerna²**.

†**cer·nida** *f.* division, selection; wandering bands of soldiers, groups of armed men.

cernier-a *f.* hinged clasp for shutting the mouth of a purse; frame of a handbag; **lampo a** —, zip fastener (round a handbag or case); (aeron.) **momento di** —, hinge moment; (geog.) crest of anticline, axial plane. -**ato** *adj.* hinged.

cerniere *m.* (naut.) drinking tank, drinking fountain.

cerniola *f.* (ichth.) stone bass, *Polyprion cernium*.

†**cernire** *vb.* and derivs. See **cernere**.

cer·nita *f.* choice, selection; (techn.) sorting, grading, classification; **fare la** — **di**, to grade.

cerni-tore *m.*, -**trice** *f.* See under **cernere**.

cer·o, cer·o *m.* large wax candle (used in churches); — **pasquale**, Paschal candle; (colloq.) gawky person; **bel** —, lout who gives himself airs. -**oe·no** *m.* (vet.) charge, soothing plaster (for a horse). -**oferario** *m.* (liturg.) candle-bearer. -**oma** *m.* (Gk. and Rom. antiq.) ointment of oil and wax used by wrestlers, ceroma. -**omanzi·a** *f.* ceromancy. -**omele** *m.* (pharm.) plaster of wax and honey, ceromel. -**ona** *f.* see under **cera¹**. -**one** *m. augm.* of **cero**; grease-paint. -**oplasta** *m.* wax-modeller. -**opla·stica** *f.* wax modelling, waxworks. -**o·sia** *f.* (techn.) cerosin. -**oso** *adj.* (techn.) waxen, cereous; (chem.) cerous. -**os·sila** *f.* (bot.) wax palm, *Ceroxylon andicola*. -**otato** *m.* (chem.) cerotate. -**oteno** *m.* cerotene. -**o·tico** *adj.* (chem.) cerotic. -**otina** *f.* cerotin, ceryl hydrate. -**otto** *m.* (pharm.) wax plaster; -**otto adesivo**, sticking plaster; -**otto plastico**, elastoplast; quack remedy; tiresome person, bore; person who is ailing, weakling; slipshod work; daub (in painting); †*dim.* of **cero**; thick, short candle. -**ot·tolo** *m.* see **cerotto**. -**ume** *m.* wax in the ears; (med.) cerumen; wax drippings from candles. -**uminoso** *adj.* ceruminous.

Cerokesi *m.pl.* (ethn.) Cherokees.

cerpellino *adj.* (of eyes) bloodshot; having the lids turned back.

cerpellone *m.* blunder, 'brick'; 'howler'; gross error.

†**cerpire** *tr.* to strip of foliage.

†**cerqua** *f.* See **quercia**.

cerra *f.* (bot.). See under **cerro¹**.

cerretano *m.* charlatan, quack, mountebank, impostor.

cerr-o¹ *m.* (bot.) turkey oak, *Quercus cerris*. -**a** *f.* (bot.) acorn of the turkey oak. -**a·ia** *f.*, -**eta** *f.*, -**eto** *m.* turkey oak plantation. -**osu·ghero** *m.* (bot.) hybrid oak, *Quercus hispanica*. †-**uto** *adj.* planted with turkey oak, bearing turkey oak trees.

cerr-o² *m.* mane, shock of hair. -**olino** *m.* fringe.

certaldese *adj., n.m.* native of Certaldo; **il** —, Boccaccio.

certame *m.* (poet.) combat; competition; **singolar** —, duel.

certamente *adv.* See under **certo**.

†**certan-o** *adj.* certain. †-**ità** *f.*, †-**za** *f.* certainty.

†**cert-are** *tr.* to fight; *intr.* to enter into combat; to be tried, to be proved. †-**ante** *m.* disputant. †-**azione** *f.* fight, contest, dispute.

certezza *f.* certainty, assuredness, certainness; proof; truth.

certific-are [A2s] *tr.* to certify, to prove, to demonstrate; to certificate; to affirm; to attest; *rfl.* to satisfy oneself. -**amento** *m.* certifying; demonstrating; attesting. -**ante** *part. adj.* certifying; attesting. -**ato** *part. adj.* made certain, ascertained, proved; certified; certificated; *n.m.* certificate, testimonial; (leg.) certi-

certific-are (*cont.*)
ficate; testimonial; rilasciare un -ato, to issue a certificate or testimonial; (naut.) -ato di classe, ship's certificate; -ato di stazza, tonnage certificate; -ato di sicurezza, safety certificate. **-azione** *f.* certification.

†**certitu·din-e** *f.* certainty. †**-almente** *adv.* with certainty; regularly, correctly.

cert-o *adj.* certain, sure; assured, persuaded; true; avere per —, to believe for certain; un — non so che, a certain something; definite; established, factual; any, some; un — uomo, a certain man; †factual, real; *n.m.* certainty; a thing that is certain; preferire il — all'incerto, to prefer the known to the unknown; *pl. prn.* some people; *adv.* certainly; doubtless; —! yes, indeed; di —, certainly. **-amente** *adv.* certainly; assuredly; with assurance.

certosa *f.* (eccl.) charterhouse, Carthusian house; chartreuse; (in regional usage) cemetery. †**-ano** *adj.*, *n.m.* see certosino. **-ino** *adj.* (eccl.) Carthusian; *n.m.* Carthusian monk; chartreuse; (Bologna) kind of cake. **-ina** *f.* Carthusian nun.

certuna[1] *f.prn.* (*pl.* **certune**) a certain woman.

certuna[2] *f.* (chem.) cilional.

certuno *m.prn.* (*pl.* **certuni**) a certain person, a certain individual, someone.

ceruc·cia *f.* See under **cera**[1].

†**ceru·lea** *f.* lapislazuli.

ceru·leo *adj.* blue; sky-blue, powder blue, pale blue.

ce·rulo *adj.* (poet.). See ceruleo.

cerum-e *m.*, **-inoso** *adj.* See under **cero**.

†**cer-usi·a**, **-u·sica** *f.* See **chirurgia**. †**-u·sico** *m.* See **chirurgo**, under **chirurgia**.

ceruss-a *f.* white lead; ceruse. **-ite** *f.* (miner.) cerussite.

cerva *f.* See under **cervo**.

cervato *adj.* dapple grey; *n.m.* (zool.) pelage countershaded as in a deer.

cervell-o *m.* (*pl.* **-a** *f.* when referring to human beings and animals; **-i** *m.* in other uses, esp. in all fig. senses) brain, brains; bruciarsi le —a, to blow one's brains out; lambiccarsi il —, to rack one's brains; dare volta al —, dare la balza al —, to go mad; a volta di —, as the whim takes one; essere in —, to be all there; mettere il — a partito, to come to see reason, to mend one's ways; mettere il — a partito a uno, to bring someone round to his senses; avere stoppa nel —, to be featherbrained; avere il — sopra il cappello, to have a topsy-turvy sort of mind; il vino gli ha dato al —, the wine has gone to his head; ha il — nella lingua, he talks without thinking; ha il — in processione, non ha il — a casa, he is miles away, he is daydreaming. **-ac·cio** *m. pejor.* bizarre intelligence. †**-ag·gine** *f.* odd caprice, freakish whim. **-a·io** *m.* seller of brains. **-ata** *f.* potted pigs' brains, Milanese sausage. **-etto** *m.* (anat.) cerebellum; odd habit, whim, caprice. **-iera** *f.* (mil. hist.) small steel helmet; hood worn beneath the helmet; coif worn by women; (provb.) chi ha -iera di vetro, non vada a battaglia di sassi, those who live in glass houses should not throw stones; vine producing large black grapes. **-iere**, **-iero** *m.* (mil. hist.) maker of small steel helmets. **-ino** *m. dim.* of cervello; silly individual; weak-minded person. **-inag·gine** *f.* stupid action. **-one** *m. augm.* of cervello; queer, stupid, obstinate man; know-all. **-onag·gine** *f.* stupid, obstinate trick. **-o·tico** *adj.* fantastic, overstrained, capricious; clever but impractical. (**-oticamente** *adv.*) **-uto** *adj.* brainy, bright, smart.

cer·via *f.* See under **cervio**.

cervic-e *f.* back of the neck, nape; (anat.) cervix; piegare la —, to bow the head; (fig.) to submit; to capitulate; di dura —, stiff-necked, obstinate, wayward. **-ale** *adj.* cervical.

cervier-e *m.* (zool.) lynx. †**-i** *m.* see cerviere. **-o** *adj.* lynx-like; occhio -o, lynx eye, eagle eye; (zool.) lupo -o, see cerviere.

†**cervi·gia** *f.* See cervogia.

cervino[1] *adj.* cervine; deer-like, pertaining to deer; (agric.) referring to hay reaped in the Alps and containing old grass along with the new; dapple-bay (colour of a horse); *n.m. dim.* of cervo, q.v.

Cervino[2] *pr.n.m.* (geog.) Matterhorn.

†**cer·vi-o** *m.* See cervo.

†**cerviona** *f.* See cervona.

cerv-o *m.* (zool.) stag, deer. **-a** *f.* hind; (ent.) — volante, stag beetle, *Lucanus cervus*; kite, observation kite; (mil. hist.) palings for defence of an area.

cervo·gia *f.* herb beer.

cervona *f.* strong glue; *adj.* colla —, fish glue.

cervone *m.* (zool.) *Coluber quatuorlineatus*, a harmless snake.

†**cervosa** *f.* See cervogia.

cerzior-are [A I c] *tr.* (leg.) to make certain of (a fact); (of a notary) — qualcuno, to inform someone of the nature of the deed he is executing; *rfl.* to satisfy oneself. **-ato** *part. adj.* (leg.) made certain. **-azione** *f.* (leg.) legal certainty.

cesa *f.* (agric. N. Ital.) hedge; copse.

Cesare (Flor.), **Ce·sare** (Rom.) *pr.n.m.* Caesar; emperor; avere un cuor di —, to have a heart of gold; o — o niente, either a man or a mouse; i Cesari, the Caesars; Giulio —, Julius Caesar.

cesa·r-eo *adj.* (hist.) Caesarian; imperial; poeta —, poet of the imperial court of Vienna; (med.) taglio —, Caesarian operation. **-iano** *adj.* (Rom. hist.) belonging to Julius Caesar's party. **-ismo** *m.* (pol.) Caesarism, absolute government.

cesa·rie *f. indecl.* hair, tresses, locks.

cesatura *f.* (agric.) green manuring.

cesell-are [A I] *tr.* to engrave, to chase; to chisel; (geog.) to erode. **-amento** *m.* engraving, chasing; chiselling; (geog.) erosion. **-ato** *part. adj.* engraved, chased; graven, cut; chiselled; (geog.) eroded. **-atore** *m.* engraver; chiseller. **-atura** *f.* engraving, chasing; chiselling.

cesello *m.* chisel, graving tool; art of engraving; engraved work.

cesena *f.* (orn.) fieldfare, *Turdus pilaris*.

ce·sio *m.* (chem.) caesium; *adj.* pale blue.

cesoi-a *f.* (eng.) shears; — a ghigliottina, squaring shears. **-e** *pl.* shears, cutters; scissors. **-ata** *f.* snip; (fig.) quell'uomo con due -ate si becca mille lire, that man makes a thousand lire by a couple of strokes. **-ette** *f.pl.*, **-ne** *f.pl.* scissors, snippers. **-one** *f.pl.* tailor's shears.

cesolfau·t *m. indecl.* (mus.). See **cisolfaut**.

ce·spit-e *m.* tuft; (leg.) capital asset, a specific source of income. **-oso** *adj.* tufty, tufted.

cespo *m.* tuft.

cespu·gli-o *m.* bush; thicket; clump (of shrubs, etc.); mass (of hair); †fare — di, to make a heap of, to pile up; †fare —, to be piled up. †**-ato** *adj.* heaped up, piled up. **-eto** *m.* (geog.) desert scrub, low bush. **-oso** *adj.* clumped, bushy. **-uto** *adj.* in clumps.

cessa *f.* cessation, respite; senza —, ceaselessly.

cess-are [A I] *intr.* (*aux.* avere) to cease, to stop, to come to an end, to leave off, to terminate, to end; — dal commercio, to retire from business; †to fail (in business), to go out of business; *rfl.* to take refuge, to keep out of the way; to flee; *tr.* to stop; — i pagamenti, to stop payment; to hold off; to remove; -i Dio! God forbid! **-ante** *part. adj.* ceasing, coming to an end; (leg.) lucro -ante, damage suffered by a person through being prevented from pursuing his usual occupation, such as loss of earnings or profit; †*n.m.* bankrupt. **-ato** *part. adj.* ended; past; -ato pericolo! all clear! **-azione** *f.* cessation; end; -azione di una società, discontinuance of a company, winding up of a company; -azione dei pagamenti, suspension of payments.

cessin-o *m.* manure from cesspools. **-atura** *f.* manuring with cesspool waste.

cession-e *f.* (leg.) cession; transfer; yielding up (e.g. of a benefice); assignment in bankruptcy (C.C.). **-a·rio** *m.* (leg.) assignee; grantee; transferee.

cesso[1] *m.* earth closet, latrine, (vulg.) rotter.

†**cesso**[2] *m.* cessation.

†**cesso**[3] *adj.* distant, remote; on one side.

†**cesso**[4] *adj.* yielded, surrendered, given in.

cest-a *f.* hamper, basket; wicker cart for transporting wine, etc.; wicker fish-trap; †carriage; *pl.* panniers. **-a·io** *m.* basket-maker; baker's boy. **-ella** *f. dim.* of cesta; wicker trap. **-one** *m. augm.* of cesta; large hamper; a -oni, in plenty; (metall.) a type of furnace.

cesta·ia *f.* See under **cesto**[1].

cestin-o *m. dim.* of cesta or cesto[2]; small basket; — da viaggio, meal in a paper bag sold on railway platforms; waste-paper basket; child's go-cart. **-are** [A I] *tr.* to put in the waste-paper basket; to reject; to scrap.

cestire. See under **cesto**[1].

cestista *m.* See under **cesto**[2].

cest-o[1] *m.* tuft, clump; head (of plants like cabbages, lettuces, etc.); fare —, to throw out shoots; (of corn) to tiller, to form a number of stems on the same root; (iron.) bel —, a man who thinks himself a gallant; †stump; †origin, race; †family tree. **-a·ia** *f.*

cest-o (*cont.*)

group of tufts. **-ire** [D 2] *intr.* (*aux.* avere) to throw out shoots. **-oso** *adj.* (agric.) well-tillered. **-uto** *adj.* having a good head (e.g. of a lettuce).

cest-o² *m.* basket, hamper (usu. smaller than 'cesta'); (sport) palla al —, basket-ball; (fig.) **-i e canestri**, one thing and another. **-ista** *m.* (sport) basket-ball player. **-istico** *adj.* (sport) pertaining to basket-ball.

cest-o³ *m.* (Rom. antiq.) cestus, glove used by ancient Roman boxers. **-iario** *m.* (Rom. antiq.) boxer.

cesto⁴ *m.* girdle of Venus, bridal knot; (zool.; med.) tapeworm.

cestoide-i, cesto-idi *m.pl.* (med.) cestoids.

cestola *f.* basket trap for birds.

cestone *m.* See under **cesta**.

cestr-o *m.* (paint.) stylus (used in encaustic painting). **-ote** *f.pl.* (paint.) figures painted by encaustic method. **-oto** *m.* encaustic painting.

cesura *f.* (prosod.) caesura.

ceta-ceo *m.* (zool.) cetacean.

†cete *f.* (zool.) whale.

ceter-a¹ *f.* (mus.). See **cetra**. **†-are** *intr.* to play the lyre. **-ante** *m.,f.,* **-atore** *m.* lyre-player. **-eggiare** [A 3 c] *intr.* to play upon the lyre. **†-ista** *m.* lyre-player.

ceter-a² *f.* the rest, etceteras; *pl.* **†entrare in -e**, to talk nonsense; to be confused, to become perplexed. **†-ato** *adj.* complete with all the usual etceteras. **†-atoio** *m.*: andarsene col **-atoio**, to go away empty-handed, to be put off with vain promises.

†ceter-a³ *f.* a kind of shield. **†-ato** *adj.* armed with a 'cetera', bearing a shield.

†ceterato *adj.* See under **cetera²**.

†ceterato *adj.* See under **cetera³**.

†cetina¹ *f.* pit in which charcoal is burned; field in which stubble has been burned; coppice in which brambles are burned to manure the soil.

cet-ina² *f.* (chem.) cetin, purified spermaceti. **-eno** *m.* (chem.) cetene. **-ilico** *adj.* cetyl. **-ile** *m.* cetyl (radio).

†cetino *m.* kind of wood from the East Indies.

ceto¹ *m.* class; — **medio**, middle classes; **†assembly**, gathering, re-union.

†ceto² *m.* whale.

cetra¹ *f.* (mus.) lyre; (fig.) poetry; **suonare la** —, to write poetry.

ce-tra² *f.* (hist.) buckler.

cetracca *f.* (bot.) rusty-back fern, *Ceterach officinarum.*

cetran-golo *m.* (bot.). See **cedrangolo**.

cetrarciero *adj.* (poet.) lyre- and bow-bearing (epithet of Apollo).

cetrina *f.* (bot.). See **cedrina**.

cetriolo *m.* cucumber, *Cucumis sativus*; (zool.) — **di mare**, sea cucumber, *Cucumaria* spp.; (colloq.) blockhead, foolish man.

†cetro¹ *m.* See **cetra²**.

†cetro² *m.* See **cedro**.

charivari *m. indecl.* hooting, booing, rattling of pots and pans in sign of public disapproval.

chassis *m. indecl.* (pron. as Fr.) (cinem.) reel, spool; — **debitore**, pay-out spool.

che¹ *rel. prn. indecl.* who; whom; which; that; what. (NOTE: The same form is used irrespective of the gender, number or case of the antecedent. Normally it is used only for nominative (subjective) or accusative (objective) cases, as: l'uomo che è venuto, the man who came; l'uomo che ho visto, the man whom I saw. Used also in popular speech for indirect cases, it sometimes stands for 'in cui': il giorno che lo salutai, the day when I greeted him; la pentola che ci si far il brodo, the saucepan in which the broth is made.) *interr. prn. indecl.* what?; *adj. indecl.* — **uomo?** what man?; *n.m. indecl.* something, a thing; **il** —, which, the which, which thing; **di** —, **con** —, of which thing, by which means; something to write home about, a fine thing; **non è un gran** —, it's not up to much, it's nothing to write home about; (iron.) **un bel** —, a nice thing; **un non so** —, an indefinable quality, 'un je ne sais quoi'; *excl.* — **uomo!** what a man! (expressing admiration or wonder); **ma — conte d'Egitto!** what Count! (suggesting there is no such Count); (pron. **che**, not **chè**) —!, **ma** —!, get away with you!, nonsense!; *conj.* that; sia —, whether; sempre —, provided that; **a** —, in order that; se non —, except that; quand'ecco, **è** — non è, si sente un rumore, when all of a sudden a noise is heard.

chè² *conj.* than, as; **tanto** —, as soon as; **altro** —! rather!, I should say so!

chè³ *conj.* because; **tanto—**, so much that.

checchè *prn. indecl.* whatever, no matter what.

checchessi-a *prn. indecl.* whatever it may be.

chec-c(h)ia *f.* (naut.) ketch.

check *m. indecl.* (pron. as Fr., *indef. art.* uno, *def. art.* lo) cheque.

†ched *prn.* See **che¹**.

cheddite *f.* an explosive.

cheilofagi-a *f.* the habit of biting the lips.

cheirospasmo *m.* writer's cramp.

chelan-dia *f.* (naut. hist.). See **achelandia**.

chele, cheli *f.pl.* (zool.) chelae; claws, nippers, pincers of a crab or lobster, or of a scorpion.

cheletomi-a *f.* (surg.) operation for strangulated hernia.

cheli *f. indecl.* (mus.) lyre.

che-l-ide *f.* (zool.) tortoise. **-idro** *m.* (zool.) water tortoise, *Emys orbicularis.*

chellerina *f.* (N. Ital.) barmaid.

chemio-terapi-a *f.* (med.) chemotherapy. **-tropismo** *m.* (biol.) chemotropism.

chenalo-pece *m.* (orn.) sheld-duck, shelduck.

chenisco *m.* (Gk. antiq.) figurehead shaped like a goose's head and neck.

cheno-lico *adj.* chenocholic.

†chente *adj., prn.* which, what; such; such as; how many; whoever; of what nature; whatever; **†— la cagion si sia**, whatever the reason may be; **— che**, whoever; whatever.

†chentechè *prn.* See 'chente che', under **chente**.

†chentunque *adj., prn.* whichever; whatever.

chepì *m. indecl.* military cap, képi.

cheppì *m. indecl.* See **chepì**.

cheppia *f.* (ichth.) shad, *Alosa fallax*; (colloq.) blockhead, dolt.

cheque *m. indecl.* (pron. as Fr., *indef. art.* uno, *def. art.* lo) cheque.

cherargi-rio *m.* See **cherargirite**.

cherargirite *f.* (miner.) cerargyrite, hornsilver, native silver chloride.

cherat-ina *f.* (chem.; zool.) keratin. **-ite** *f.* (med.) keratitis, inflammation of the cornea. **-oialina** *f.* (anat.) the hyaline layer of the skin. **-opla-stica** *f.* (surg.) keratoplasty.

cherca *f.* (poet.). See **chierica**.

cherco *m.* and derivs. (poet.). See **chierico**.

chercuto *adj.* (poet.). See **chiercuto**, under **chierica**.

†che-rere *tr.* to ask; to request; to require; to have need of; to desire; to seek; **— alla battaglia**, to challenge.

cherica *f.*, **cherico** *m.* See **chierica**, **chierico**.

chericuto *adj.* See **chiericuto**, under **chierica**.

†cherire *vb.* See **†cherere**.

†cherisi-a *f.* clergy.

cher-mes *m. indecl.* kermes; **— minerale**, mineral kermes, an artificial antimony sulphide of a brilliant red colour, kermesite. **-iş, -işi, -işì** *adj., n.m. indecl.*, **-işino** *adj., n.m.* crimson. **-işite** *f.* (miner.) kermesite.

chermessa *f.* kermis, kermesse.

†chernite *f.* chernites, a stone believed to have the property of preserving dead bodies.

cherosene *m.* kerosene.

†cherovana *f.* great quantity (cf. **carovana**).

†cherson-e-sio *adj.* peninsular. **†-eso** *m.* peninsula.

cheru-bico *adj.* cherubic, cherub-like; (theol., of intellectual power) cherubic, cherubinical.

cherubino *m.* cherub; **i Cherubini**, the Cherubim.

che-rubo, cherubo *m.* (poet.). See **cherubino**.

†chesta *f.* request; demand; search, quest.

chesterfield *m. indecl.* overcoat of check or variegated pattern.

†chetanza *f.* See **quietanza**.

chet-are [A 1 c] *tr.* to quieten, to silence, to calm; *rfl.* to be quiet; to fall quiet; to be hushed; (Tusc.) **chétati!** shut up! **-ato** *part. adj.* quietened; silenced; calmed down; hushed.

chetene *m.* (chem.) ketene, ethanone.

chetichella *adv. phr.* **alla** —, quietly; secretly.

chetmia *f.* (bot.) musk mallow, *Hibiscus syriacus.*

cheto *adj.* quiet, hushed, silent; tranquil, still; secret, not divulged; **l'acqua cheta rompe i ponti**, still waters run deep; dripping water wears away a stone; **è un'acqua cheta**, he's a deep one; (of a woman) **essere un'acqua cheta**, to be deceptively demure; **†quit,**

cheto (*cont.*)
freed of obligation; †exempt; *adv.* quietly, silently; di —, secretly. (**-amente** *adv.*)

chetone[1] *adj. augm.* of **cheto**, q.v.; silent, taciturn; *adv.* softly.

chetone[2] *m.* (chem.) ketone.

†**cheun·que** *prn.* whatever.

chi[1] *interr. prn. indecl.* who?; whom?; — sa?, I wonder, who knows?; — lo sa?, who can tell?; — è?, who's there?, who is it?, who is he?; *Chi e, Who's Who*; — ti dice che siano partiti per davvero?, how can you be sure they've really left?; — vive?, who goes there?; stare in sul — vive, to be on the qui vive; *indef. prn. indecl.* he who; they who; whoever; whosoever; some, some people; chi…chi, some…others; — che sia, anybody whatsoever, no matter who; †(naut.) a — primo, general chase.

chi[2] *m.* (gramm.) name of the Greek letter χ, chi.

chiac·chier-a *f.* chatter, gossip, idle talk; (colloq.) conversation, chat; trifle, thing of no consequence; fare quattro -e, to have a chat; a -e, all words (instead of deeds); stare sulle -e, to listen to gossip. **-amento** *m.* chattering, gossiping; rumour. **-are** [A 1 s] *intr.* (*aux.* avere) to chat, to talk; to chatter, to gossip; to backbite. **-ata** *f.* informal talk; chat; chattering, gossip; tedious rigmarole. **-atore** *m.*, **-atrice** *f.* chatterbox, gossip. **-evole** *adj.* chattering, talkative. †**-i·a** *f.* see **chiacchierata**. **-ic·cio** *m.* (*pl.* -ic·ci) chattering, chatter; confused babble of voices; ill-natured chatter, spiteful conversation. **-ina** *f. dim.* of **chiacchiera**; little chat, little talk; girl who is a chatterbox, gossiping girl. **-ino** *m.* gossip; chatterbox; (needlew.) tatting. **-io** *m.* (*pl.* -ii) constant chattering, murmur, confused babble. **-one** *m.*, **-ona** *f.* chatterbox, gasbag; person who cannot keep a secret.

†**chiacere** *vb.* and derivs. See **piacere**.

†**chia·ia**[1] *f.* See **ghiaia**.

†**chia·ia**[2] *f.* shore, strand.

†**chia·ito** *m.* intrigue; plot; obstruction.

chiama *f.* call; roll-call; fare la —, to call the roll.

chiam-are [A 1] *tr.* to call; to summon; to hail; to send for; to name; — al telefono, to ring up; — in disparte, to call aside; — in causa, to make reference to; (mil.) — (alle armi), to call up; (naut.) — la guardia, to call the relief; — a bordo, to recall to the ship; (leg.) — in giudizio, to sue, to bring an action against; to serve a summons on; *rfl.* to be called; come si -a Lei?, what is your name? **-ata** *f.* call; summons; -ata telefonica, telephone call; -ata interurbana, trunk call; -ata (alle armi), call-up; cross-reference; (typ.) catch-word; (theatr.) recall. **-ato** *part. adj.* called; named; invoked; invited. **-atore** *m.*, **-atrice** *f.* one who calls; announcer; call-boy. †**-azzo** *m.* clamour, commotion (cf. **schiamazzo**). †**-o** *m.* call, summons.

chiana *f.* swamp, marsh.

chianare [A 1] *tr.* to crush (coral).

chiancarella *f.* (geog. Bari) hard limestone used for building.

†**chiantare**[1] *intr.* to grumble, to complain, to raise a complaint.

†**chiantare**[2] *tr.* to 'catch', to trick; tu me l'hai chiantata, you've played a trick on me, you've caught me out.

chianti *m. indecl.* chianti, a Tuscan wine (red or white).

†**chiapin-o**, †**-etto** *m.* woman's shoe; slipper.

chiappa[1] *f.* seizing. catching; catch.

chiappa[2] *f.* buttock.

†**chiappa**[3] *f.* projecting rock.

chiappa-cani *m. indecl.* (pop.) see **accalappiacani**, under **accalappiare**. **-merli** *m. indecl.* simpleton. **-mosche** *f. indecl.* (bot.) Venus's fly-trap, *Dionaea muscipula*; sticky fleabane, *Inula viscosa*; other fly-catching plants; fly-trap, fly-catcher; fool, useless person; (orn.) fly-catcher. **-nu·vole**, **-nu·voli** *m. indecl.* conceited braggart.

chiapp-are [A 1] *tr.* to catch; to seize by surprise; to catch out; to trap; to hit (with a missile); to grab. **-ato** *part. adj.* caught; caught out; trapped; hit.

chiapp-arello, **-atello**, **-erello** *m.* trap, catch (in cross-questioning); acquisition.

chiappino *m. dim.* of **chiappo**[1], q.v.

chiapp-o[1] *m.* catch, object caught; trap; †group of people. **-ettino** *m. dim.* gain, catch. **-ino** *m. dim.* trap; catch, object caught; police spy.

chiapp-o[2] *m.* ring for attaching a rope. **-one** *m. augm.* ring bit; (naut.) mast wedge.

chiap·pol-a *f.* bagatelle; frivolous person; †buttock. **-are** [A 1 s] *tr.* to catch (a person) out; to appropriate. †**-eri·a** *f.* trifle, bagatelle.

†**-o** *m.* rubbish heap, dust heap; rimanere nel -o, to be forgotten; lasciare nel -o, to forget, to overlook; to neglect.

chiappone *m. augm.* of **chiappo**[2], q.v.

Chiara[1] *pr.n.f.* Clare; Clara.

chiar-a[2] *f.* raw white of egg; (paint.) light (in a picture); (astron.) star of the first magnitude; — della vergine, Spica; — delle guardie, the Great Bear. †**-are** *tr.* to reveal, to make clear; *rfl.* to lighten, to grow light, to clear. **-ata** *f.* (med.) dressing of tow, etc. steeped in white of egg; white of egg or a similar substance for clarifying wine, fining. †**-e·a** *f.* medicinal draught of brandy, cinnamon, cloves, sugar and water.

chiaramente *adv.* See under **chiaro**.

chiaranzana *f.* a kind of folk-dance; (naut.) loom.

chiareggiare [A 3 c]. See under **chiaro**.

chiarella[1] *f.* (text.) gap in cloth due to a faulty tooth in the comb.

chiarella[2] *f.* (bot.) — de' prati, meadow-sage, *Salvia pratensis*; — maggiore, clary, *S. sclarea*.

chiarelli *m.pl.* silkworms infected with the virus disease of 'Flacherie'.

chiarello *m.* wine diluted with much water.

†**chiarenna** *adv. phr.* essere in —, to be isolated at a great distance or height.

chiarentana *f.* See **chiaranzana**.

chiaretto *adj. dim.* of **chiaro**, q.v.; lightish; †tipsy; *n.m.* claret.

chiarezza *f.* clearness, clarity; lightness, brightness; nobility, distinction.

chiari·a *f.* brightness, lightness.

chiarific-are [A 2 s] *tr.* to clarify; to clear (up); †to glorify; †to exalt. **-ato** *part. adj.* clarified; cleared up; †glorified; †exalted; †in glory. (**-atore** *m.* **-atrice** *f.*) **-azione** *f.* clarification; †declaration, announcement; †glorification; †exalting.

†**chiarigione** *f.* clarification; explanation; declaration; deposition.

chiarin-a *f.*, **-o** *m.* (mus.) clarino, high-pitched trumpet; high trumpet-note.

chiar-ire [D 2] *tr.* to clarify; to make clear, to clear up; — un dubbio, to clear up a doubt; to illuminate, to lighten; (paint.) to lighten; *rfl.* to become clear; to make oneself clear; to assure oneself; to lose one's doubts; to gain information; (of the sky) to clear up, to clear. **-imento** *m.* explanation; clarification; clearing up; lightening. **-ito** *part. adj.* clarified; cleared; explained; freed of doubt; manifest; †resplendent; †of rare beauty; †well known, celebrated; †made known; †revealed, discovered. **-itoio** *m.* (*pl.* -itoi) apparatus for clarifying oil, etc.; warm place where oil is set to clear. (**-itore** *m.* **-itrice** *f.*) †**-itu·dine** *f.* splendour, brightness; †fame, renown. **-itura** *f.* clarification; clarifying.

chiarità *f.* brightness, splendour; clarity, clearness; †fame, illustriousness; †glory.

†**chiaritade**, †**chiaritate** *f.* See **chiarità**.

chiar-o *adj.* clear, bright; giorno —, broad daylight; light (of a colour); vestir di —, to wear light colours; transparent; pale; distinct, plain, evident; intelligible; fare —, to inform; famous, evident, renowned; †strong, robust; *n.m.* light; light colour; — di luna, moonlight; mettere in —, to make clear, to make plain; venire in — di, to come to an understanding about; avere in —, to decode; traduzione in —, decoding; white of egg; (paint.) light, high light; dare i -i, to paint in the light parts of a picture; *adv.* clearly, plainly; — e tondo, frankly, openly, straight from the shoulder. **-amente** *adv.* clearly, plainly; intelligibly. **-eggiare** [A 3 c] *tr.* to clear up, to make clear; to represent clearly; *intr.* (*aux.* avere) (paint.) to paint in the light parts of a picture.

chiarore *m.* light; luminescence; clearness; glimmer, gleam; il — dell'alba, the first light of dawn; (paint.) brightness, light; †nobility (of blood).

chiaroscur-o *m.* (*pl.* **chiaroscuri**) (paint.) light and shade (in one colour); chiaroscuro; (techn.) light-dark; (electr.) connessione a —, dimming circuit. **-are** [A 1] *tr.* (paint.) to shade; *intr.* (*aux.* avere) to accentuate light and shade.

chiarosonante *adj.* (poet.) sonorous, resonant, clear-sounding.

chiarovegg-ente *adj.* clear-sighted; far-seeing; clairvoyant. **-enza** *f.* clear-sightedness; clairvoyance.

†**chiarura** *f.* splendour, brightness.

chiasm-a, **-o** *m.* (rhet.) chiasmus; (anat.) chiasma, decussation, intercrossing.

chiassata *f.* See under **chiasso**.

chiass-o[1] *m.* shrill noise; babble of voices; rattle of plates, etc.;

chiass-o (*cont.*)
row; uproar; din; far —, to make a noise; to create a sensation; to become famous; fare il —, to joke. **-are** [A I] *intr.* (*aux.* avere) to make a noise. **-ata** *f.* noisy entertainment; disturbance, row; hubbub, din, racket. **-ett(in)o** *m. dim.* of **chiasso**; joke, jest. **-ino** *m. dim.* of **chiasso**; noise of children at play, rumpus; fare il -ino, (of small children) to play. **-oncello** *m.*, **-oncino** *m.* noisy child. **-one** *m.*, **-ona** *f.* noisy person. **-oso** *adj.* noisy; loud; colori -osi, loud colours. **-osamente** *adv.* noisily. **-ità** *f. indecl.* noisiness.

chiass-o² *m.* alley, narrow street; dar pei -i, to escape, to run away; brothel. **-ai(u)ola** *f.*, **-ai(u)olo** *m.* ditch in a field to collect rainwater. **-(u)olo** *m.* narrow street; narrow canal.

chia·stico *adj.* (rhet.) chiastic.

chiatt-a *f.* flat-bottomed boat, lighter; ponte di -e, pontoon bridge; — del passo, ferry. **-ai(u)olo** *m.* lighterman, ferryman, bargee. **-o** *adj.* flat; flattened; †(naut.) andare di -o, to be wrecked near the shore. **-one, -oni** *adv.* quietly; andare chiatton -oni, to creep along very quietly.

†**chiausso** *m.*

chiavac·cio *m.* large door-bolt; con tanto di —, well bolted, locked, bolted and barred.

chiava-cuore *m. indecl.* clasp, brooch; bodice. **-cuori** *m. indecl.* (joc.) lady-killer.

†**chiavagione** *f.* See under **chiavare²**.

chiava·i-o *m.* locksmith; keeper of the keys. **-(u)olo** *m.* locksmith; ironmonger.

chiavard-a *f.* bolt, screw-bolt; (archit.) tie; horse-brass. **-are** [A I] *tr.* to bolt. **-o** *m.* (vet.) sidebone.

†**chiavare¹** *tr.* to lock (from **chiave**, q.v.).

†**chiav-are²** *tr.* to nail; to fix; to pierce; to wound (from †**chiavo**, q.v.). **-agione** *f.* (naut.) act of nailing or bolting together the parts of a ship; †quantity of nails.

chiavare³ [A I] *tr.* (vulg.) to have sexual intercourse with; *intr.* (*aux.* avere) to have intercourse.

chiavare⁴ [A I] *tr.* (dial. S. Ital.) to deliver, to give (a blow).

†**chiavaro** *m.* See **chiavaio**.

chiav-e *f.* key; — maschia, — mascolina, key with a solid shaft; — femmina, key with a hollow shaft; — falsa, skeleton-key; — dello scatto, latch-key; — all'inglese, latch-key, key for a cylinder lock; yale key (see also — inglese, under techn. and eng.); — apritutto, — maestra, master-key; *pl.* (rel.) -i apostoliche, -i sante, -i somme, St Peter's keys; chiudere a —, to lock; chiuso a sette -i, safely locked away; locked, bolted and barred; tenere sotto —, to keep safely locked up, to guard jealously; sotto —, under lock and key; buco della —, keyhole; (techn.; eng.) key, spanner, wrench; — inglese, king-dick, adjustable wrench; (mus.) clef; — di violino, treble clef; — del basso, bass clef; key (tonality); fuori —, out of tune, in the wrong key; key (to a code, etc.); clue; romanzo a —, novel in which all the characters are real persons under fictitious names, *roman à clef*; (archit.) keystone; — di (della) volta, keystone (also fig.); tie; tie-bar; key, tap, cock, stopcock; (prosod.) key-rhyme, link-rhyme (in a canzone); verso di —, key-line, connecting line (between the two halves of a stanza); (fig.) le industrie-chiave, the key industries; (naut.) fid. **-etta** *f. dim.* of **chiave**; -etta della luce, electric-light switch; cock, tap; (eng.) splint, forelock, cotter; (watchm.) gib; -etta a vite, screw gib; -etta da orologio, watch-key.

chiavell-o *m.* nail, peg. †**-are** *tr.* to nail; to fix.

chiaverina *f.* (mil. hist.) javelin.

chia·vic-a *f.* sewer; short-line of a sewer, walled and covered in; sluice-gate; transverse road drain. **-are** [A 2 s] *tr.* to supply with a sluice or sewer.

†**chiavicarole** *f.pl.* eels fished from the Roman sewers, formerly highly prized as culinary delicacies.

†**chiaviere** *m.* porter, door-man, keeper of the door.

chiavistello *m.* iron bolt; door-bolt; window-bolt; tirare il —, to draw the bolt, to unbolt; mettere il —, to shoot the bolt, to bolt; (joc., of a burglar) tentare il polso ai -i, to try the locks; (fig.) rodere i -i, to fume with rage; baciare il —, to vow never to visit a place again, to shake the dust from off one's feet; ratchet.

†**chiavo** *m.* nail (cf. **chiavare²**).

chiazz-a¹ *f.* stain; large spot; fleck; (paperm.) grease spot. **-are** [A I] *tr.* to spot; to cover with spots. **-ato** *part. adj.* spotted; flecked. **-atura** *f.* spots; spottiness.

chiazza² *f.* (dial. S. Ital.). See **piazza**.

chic *m. indecl.* (pron. as Fr.) elegance; chic; che —! what elegance! how chic! **-aggine** *f.*, **-eri·a** *f.* (neol.) see **chic**.

chicc-a *f.* (infant.) sweetie, candy, sweetmeat. **-a·io** *m.* sweet-seller, confectioner.

chic·chera¹ *f.* small coffee cup; cup without handles; *pl.* (bot.) chicchere e rampicanti, climbers, cups-and-saucers, *Cobaea scandens.*

chic·chera² *f.* (dial. S. Ital.) pigliare una —, to make a blunder.

chicchessi·a *prn. indecl.* anybody whatsoever, no matter who.

chicchiri-chì *m. indecl.* the crow of a cock, cock-a-doodle-doo; (mil. slang) Bersagliere. **-are** [A4] *intr.* (*aux.* avere) to crow. **-ata** *f.* crowing, crow. †**-llare** *intr.* to joke, to play, to idle about.

chic-co *m.* (*pl.* **-chi**) grain (of corn); bean (of coffee); berry (of a bunch); bead on a rosary; un — d'uva, a grape; (knitting) — di pesce, one plain, one purl.

chie·d-ere [B 6] *tr.* to ask; to ask for; to beg; — perdono, to beg pardon; — scusa, to apologize; — un favore a qualcuno, to ask a favour of someone; — mille lire di qualcosa, to ask 1000 lire for something; — una ragazza in sposa, to ask a girl's hand in marriage, to propose to a girl; — il permesso, to ask permission; — l'elemosina, to ask for charity, to beg; — in prestito, to borrow, to ask for the loan of. **-ente** *part. adj.* asking; *n.m., f.* person asking; applicant. **-i·bile** *adj.* that may be asked for. (**-itore** *m.* **-itrice** *f.*) **-one** *m.* person who is always wanting something. (**-ona** *f.*)

†**chiedire** *vb.* See **chiedere**.

†**chiella** *f.* pride, arrogance; avere della —, to be proud; Tusc.) cunning.

chieppa *f.* See **cheppia**.

†**chierca** *f.* See **chierica**.

†**chie·rere** *vb.* and derivs. See **chiedere**.

†**chieresi·a** *f.* clergy.

chieric-a (Tusc.), **chie·ric-a** (Rom.) *f.* (eccl.) tonsure; clergy; (joc.) bald spot; baldness. **-uto** *adj.* (eccl.) tonsured; *n.m.* shaveling.

chie·ri-co (Tusc.), **chie·ri-co** (Rom.) *m.* (eccl.) cleric, ecclesiastic, esp. one in minor orders; student for the priesthood, seminarian; altar server; sacristan; †clerk, scholar, learned man. **-cato** *m.* clerical status; clergy; †clerical party. **-cheri·a** *f.* clerics, clergy.

chiericuto *adj.* See under **chierica**.

chies-a *f.* church, the whole community of Christians; la — militante, the Church Militant (on earth); la — purgante, the Church Suffering (in Purgatory); la — trionfante, the Church Triumphant (in Heaven); la Santa Madre Chiesa, Holy Mother Church; i padri della —, the Fathers of the Church; church (as building, sometimes with implication of parish or benefice); andare in —, to go to church, to be a churchgoer; (prov.) vicino alla —, lontano da Dio, the nearer to church, the farther from God. **-etta** *f. dim.* little church. **-ola** *f. dim.* little church; country church; faction, clique, coterie; (naut.) see **chiesuola**. **-uola** *f. dim.* little church; (naut.) binnacle.

chiesta *f.* request, petition; request for the hand of a girl in marriage; asking of a price.

chiesto *part.* of **chiedere**, q.v.; *adj.* asked, asked for; requested; begged; in demand.

chietin-o *m.* (eccl.) theatine; hypocrite. **-eri·a** *f.* hypocrisy.

†**chifare** *vb.* and derivs. See **schifare**.

chi·fel *m. indecl.*, **chi·fell-e**, **-o** *m.* small crescent-shaped roll, croissant.

chi·glia *f.* (naut.) keel; — di deriva, leeboard; — laterale, docking keel; per —, fore and aft.

chilalgi·a *f.* (med.) pain in the lips.

chili·a-gono *m.* (geom.) one-thousand-sided figure. **-arca** *m.* (*pl.* **-archi**) (hist.) commander of a thousand men. **-asmo** *m.* (theol.) chiliasm, millenarianism.

chi·lio *m.* (mus.). See **quilio**.

chil-o¹ *m.* (med.) chyle; the milky substance drawn from food in the intestines and passed into the blood; fare il —, to let one's food settle, to digest one's food, to rest after a meal. **-i·fero** *adj.* (med.) chyligerous. **-ificare** [A 2 s] *intr.* (*aux.* avere) (med.) to chylify. **-ificamento** *m.* chylification. **-ificante** *part. adj.* chylifactory. **-ificazione** *f.* chylification. **-osi** *f.* chylification.

chil-o² *m.* kilo, kilogramme. **-ampère** *m. indecl.* (last syll. pron. as Fr.) (electr.) kiloampere. **-ociclo** *m.* (radio) kilocycle. **-odina** *f.* (phys.) kilodyne. **-ogram·ma**, **-ogram·mo** *m.* kilogramme. kilo. **-ogram·metro** *m.* (phys.) kilogramme-metre. **-o·litro** *m.* one thousand litres. **-olu·men** *m.* (phys.) kilolumen. **-ometrag·gio** *m.*

chil-o (*cont.*)
(neol.) distance travelled in kilometres (equivalent to 'mileage'). **-o·metro** *m.* kilometre. **-ome·trico** *adj.* kilometric. **-oohmmetro** *m.* (electr.) meg-ohmmeter. **-ovatta** *f.* and deriv. see **chilowatt**. **-ovolt** *m. indecl.* (electr.) kilovolt. **-ovolt-ora** *m.* (electr.) kilovolt-hour. **-owatt** *m. indecl.* (electr.) kilowatt; — allasciati, connected kilowatt. **-owatt-ora** *m.* kilowatt-hour.

chilosi *f. indecl.* See under **chilo**[1].

chime·r-a *f.* (myth.) chimera; (fig.) wild supposition; foolish illusion. **-are** [A I] *intr.* (*aux.* avere) to make wild suppositions. **-i·stico** *adj.* given to fanciful daydreams, chimerical. **-izzare** [A I] *intr.* (*aux.* avere) to indulge in foolish illusions. **-izzamento** *m.* daydreaming, fanciful imagining. **-izzatore** *m.* daydreamer. (**-izzatrice** *f.*) **-oso** *adj.* see **chimerico**.

chime·ric-o *adj.* imaginary, fanciful; illusory; visionary; chimerical. (**-amente** *adv.*)

chi·mic-a *f.* chemistry. **-o** *adj.* chemical; *n.m.* chemist, research chemist (not in the Eng. sense of dispensing chemist, 'farmacista'). (**-amente** *adv.*)

chimificare [A 2 s] and derivs. See under **chimo**.

chimismo *m.* (biol.) all the chemical processes which take place in organic tissues, organs or liquids for a particular physiological function.

chimista *m.* (neol.). See **chimico**, under **chimica**.

chim-o[1] *m.* (biol.) chyme; sap. **-ificare** [A 2 s] *tr.* to turn into chyme, to chymify. **-ificazione** *f.* chymification. **-osi** *f.* chymification.

†**chimo**[2] *m.* fabulous sea fish.

chimo-grafo *m.* (phys.) kymograph.

chimono *m.* kimono.

chimosina *f.* (biol. chem.) chymosin, pepsin.

china[1] *f.* downward slope; alla —, downhill; a —, sloping; lasciar andare l'acqua alla —, to let things take their course; (fig.) downward path; mettersi su una brutta —, to start going wrong, to be going downhill (morally or physically); declining years.

china[2] *f.* double five (in dominoes or at dice).

China[3] *pr.n.f.* (geog.). See **Cina**; (paperm.) carta —, India paper; inchiostro di —, Indian ink.

chin-a[4] *f.* (bot.) Peruvian bark. **-achina** *f.* cinchona-tree, *C. officinalis*, and other species. **-ato** *adj.* (pharm.) containing quinine; containing Peruvian bark; vermouth -ato, vermouth with Peruvian bark added; *n.m.* (chem.) quinate; alcoholic drink containing Peruvian bark.

†**chin-amonte** *adv.* towards the hill, up on the hill. †**-avalle** *adv.* towards the valley, down in the valley.

chin-are [A I] *tr.* to bow, to bow down; — il capo, to bow one's head, (fig.) to submit; to lower; -ò gli occhi, he lowered his gaze; to incline; to let droop; *rfl.* to bow down; to bend; to stoop; to submit. **-ata** *f.* slope, descent. **-ato** *part. adj.* bowed down; bent; curved; inclined; leaning; -ato sul lavoro, bending over one's work; *n.m.* inclination, bow. **-atura** *f.* curvature; bending; bow. **-evole** *adj.* pliable. †**-evolmente** *adv.* reverently; humbly.

chinato[1] *adj., n.m.* See under **china**[4].

chinato[2] *part.* of **chinare**, q.v.

chinca·gli-e *f.pl.* knick-knacks; trinkets. **-ere** *m.* vendor of knick-knacks. **-eri·a** *f.* collection of knick-knacks; knick-knack shop.

†**chinche** *prn.* See **chiunque**.

†**chinchesi·a** *prn.* See **chicchessia**.

chine·a *f.* (hist.) the white horse which the Neapolitan kings presented annually to the Pope as their feudal lord; (joc.) sorry nag; andar di —, to amble along.

chinese *adj., n.m., f.* See **cinese**, under **cina**.

chineseri·a *f.* (neol.) Chinese puzzle; chinoiserie; (fig.) annoying bureaucratic evasions and obstruction.

chinesiter-api·a *f.* (med.) kinesitherapy, kinesiatrics. **-a·pico** *adj.* kinesitherapeutic.

chinetto *m.* (text.) a type of Flemish camlet.

chinevole *adj.* See under **chinare**.

chi·nico *adj.* (chem.) quinic.

chin-ina *f.* (pharm.) quinine. **-ino** *m.* (chem.) quinine, quinine preparation. **-oidina** *f.* quinoidine. **-oleina, -olina** *f.* (chem.) chinoline.

chino[1] *adj.* drooping, bent, bowed; a capo —, with bowed head; drooping.

†**chino**[2] *m.* See **china**.

chino[3] *m.* (techn.) gum kino.

chinon-a *f.,* **-e** *m.* (chem.) quinone.

chinotto *m.* type of bitter orange or tangerine; drink flavoured with this.

†**chintana** *f.* See **quintana**, under **quinto**.

chio *m.* (metall.) slate shutter at the side of a furnace to allow the molten metal to be drawn off.

chioca *f.* sewer.

†**chiocca**[1] *f.* blow; snap; crack (cf. **chioccare**).

†**chiocca**[2] *f.* lock of hair, tuft; quantity; a —, in —, in abundance.

chioc-care [A 2] *tr.* to crack (a whip); to snap (the fingers); *intr.* (*aux.* avere) (of a horse) to strike the hind and fore feet together. **-cata** *f.* crack; snap. **-co** *m.* (*pl.* **-chi**) crack of a whip.

chiocchiolìo *m.* See **chioccolio**, under **chioccolo**.

chiocc-ia *f.* (*pl.* **chiocce**) brooding hen or other bird; mother hen; far la —, to squat; to crouch; †ailing person, old crock. †**-ana** *f.* spiral staircase. **-are** [A 3] *intr.* (*aux.* avere) to cluck; to give a cracked sound (of pottery); to crouch round the fire. **-ata** *f.* clutch (of eggs or chicks).

chiocc-io *adj.* (*m.pl.* **-i**) hoarse, raucous.

chioc·ciol-a *f.* (zool.) snail, and any other gastropod with a snail-shaped shell; (mus.) scroll (of violin); mutare le noci in — e, to make a bad exchange; scala a —, spiral staircase; da —, worthless; stay-at-home; slow coach; dull dog; (mil.) movement of the front rank so as to allow the rear rank to fire; (eng.) female screw, nut; Archimedean screw; (anat.) the interior of the ear. **-aio** *m.* (*pl.* **-a·i**) snail dealer, vendor of snails; †kitchen-midden. **-ino** *m.* bun shaped like spiral, twist.

chiocco *m.* See under **chioccare**.

chio·ccol-o *m.* bird whistle; catching birds with decoy whistle. **-are** [A I S] *intr.* (*aux.* avere) to whistle (of birds); to gurgle (of water). **-io** *m.* (*pl.* **-ii**) whistling of birds.

chiò-chiò *m. indecl.* (orn.) dusky redshank, *Tringa erythropus.*

chio-dina *f.* sewer.

chiod-o *m.* nail; stud; ficcare un —, to hammer a nail down; attaccare un —, to knock in a nail, to put up a nail; — barbone, nail furnished with barbs so that it cannot be extracted; — a forcella, staple; — di garofano, clove; — da piastra, rivet; — a uncino, wall hook; (in a road) passaggio tracciato da -i, studded crossing; (provb.) — scaccia —, one evil gets rid of another; mettere i -i nel buco vecchio, to follow old customs; aver un — fisso, to have a bee in one's bonnet; attaccare una voglia al —, to put a wish aside, to resign oneself to not getting what one wants; roba da -i, rubbish, worthless thing or person; sono andata a vedere quella nuova commedia: roba da -i!, I went to see that new play: absolute trash!; quel suo marito, disonesto, ubriaco, roba da -i!, that husband of hers, drunk and dishonest, a downright rotter!; dice roba da -i di suo cugino, he hasn't a good word to say for his cousin; (fig.) very thin person; debt; piantar -i, to incur debts, to run up accounts; an acute headache in one spot; — solare, touch of the sun. †**-agione** *f.* quantity of nails, supply of nails. **-a·ia** *f.* tool for making nail-heads; tool used by watchmakers; (metall.) swage block. **-ai(u)olo** *m.* nail-maker, nail-seller; (joc.) person who runs up debts. **-ame** *m.* assortment of nails. **-are** [A I] *tr.* (eng.) to rivet; see also **inchiodare**. **-arello, -erello** *m. dim.* of **chiodo**; small nail; small debt, trifling sum owed. **-atrice** *f.* riveter, riveting machine. **-atura** *f.* (naut.) method of securing by nails, bolts or rivets; (eng.) riveting; riveted joint. **-eri·a** *f.* nail factory; assortment of nails. **-etto** *m. dim.* tack; (vet.) ringworm. **-iera** *f.* (metall.) swage block. **-ini** *m.pl. dim.* tiny nails, tacks; 'button' mushrooms. **-one** *m. augm.* big nail; hobnail.

chioggiota[1] *f.* See **chiozzotta**.

chioggiota[2] *f.* See **chioggioto**.

chioggioto *adj., n.m.* native of Chioggia.

chiom-a *f.* head of hair, tresses; mane; tail (of a comet); (astron.) — di Berenice, Coma Berenices; (poet.) foliage; †(naut.) tide; (Taranto) high water. **-ante** *adj.* with flowing hair; with mane. **-ato** *adj.* long-haired; with flowing hair; long-tailed (of a comet); (poet.) leafy. **-azzurro** *adj.* (poet.) blue-haired. **-indorato** *adj.* (poet.) golden-haired. **-inevoso** *adj.* (poet.) white-haired, hoary-haired. **-ispiovuto** *adj.* (poet.) with hair falling on to the shoulders. **-oso** *adj.* long-haired; (joc.) needing a haircut.

chionanto *m.* (bot.) fringe-tree, *Chionanthus virginica.*

chionzo *adj.* (Tusc.) squat; slow-witted.

chios-a *f.* explanatory note; comment; gloss; far le sue -e su di, to make one's comments about; dirty mark, stain; lead coin for children to play with. **-erella, -etta** *f. dim.* brief note.

chioṣ-are [A I] *tr.* to annotate; to explain; to comment; to gloss. **-amẹnto** *m.* annotating; glossing. **-ato** *part. adj.* commented; glossed. **-atọre** *m.* annotator; commentator; (fig.) backbiter. (**-atrice** *f.*)

chios-co *m.* (*pl.* **-chi**) kiosk; stall; bookstall; hut.

chiostra *f.* enclosed space; la — dei monti, the circle of the mountains, the encircling hills; an inhabited enclosure; (poet.) la — dei denti, 'the fence of one's teeth'.

chiostr-o *m.* cloister; (hist.) cathedral close; (fig.) monastic life, cloister; (poet.) enclosed space. **†-iere** *m.* (eccl.) 'cloisterer'.

chiotto *adj.* quiet, quiet as a mouse; *adv.* — —, silently; se ne andava — —, he went off on tiptoe without making a sound.

chio·vina *f.* See **chiodina**.

†chiovo *m.* and derivs. See **chiodo**.

chio·vola *f.* roller; joint.

chio·volo *m.* peg on a yoke by which the pole of the cart is attached; joint, articulation.

chiozza *f.* (agric.) grassy turf.

chiozẓo *m.* (ichth.) goby, *Gobius* spp.

chiozẓotta *f.* (naut.) a ship of 20–30 tons used for transporting fruit and vegetables from Chioggia to Venice.

chir-agra *f.* gout in the hands. **-a·grico** *adj.* pertaining to gout in the hands. **-agrọso** *adj.* suffering from gout in the hands.

chi·rie, chi·riele·ison, (pop.) **chirieleisonne** *m.* (liturg.; mus.) Kyrie (eleison).

chirin-tana, -zana *f.* See **chiaranzana**.

chir-ografa·rio *adj.* (leg.) creditore —, unsecured creditor under a written simple contract. **-o·grafo** *m.* (leg.) simple contract written and signed by the debtor.

chirologi·a *f.* talking with the hands; the 'deaf-and-dumb language'.

chirom-ante *m., f.* palmist, fortune-teller. **-an·tico** *adj.* relating to palmistry, chiromantic. **-anzi·a** *f.* palmistry, fortune-telling, chiromancy.

Chirọne *pr.n.m.* (myth.) Chiron; †(astron.) Sagittarius.

chironomi·a *f.* art of gesture; gesticulation.

chirosco·pio *m.* (scient.) chiroscope.

chiroteche *f.pl.* (liturg.) pontifical gloves.

chirot·teri *m.pl.* (zool.) chiroptera; bats.

chir-urgi·a *f.* surgery; — estetica, plastic surgery; cosmetic surgery; face-lifting. **-ur·gico** *adj.* surgical. (**-urgicamẹnte** *adv.*) **-urgo** *m.* (*pl.* **-urghi**) surgeon; -urgo estetico, plastic surgeon.

†chisciare¹ *tr.* (agric.) to rake.

chisciare² [A 3] (dial. S. Ital.) *rfl.* to take offence.

Chisciott-e *pr.n.m.* Don —, Don Quixote. **-ẹsco** *adj.* (*m.pl.* **-ẹschi**) see **donchisciottesco**.

chiserite *f.* (geol.) kieserite.

†Chisotto *pr.n.m.* see **Chisciotte**.

chissà *phr.* who knows? Heaven knows.

chissisi·a *prn.* (*indecl.* or *pl.* **chissisi·ano**) whoever it is; whoever he may be; *pl.* whoever they are.

†chitare *tr.* to quit, to leave; to abandon; to seek.

chitarr-a *f.* (mus.) guitar; — hawaiana, Hawaiian guitar. **†-eggiare** *intr.* to play the guitar. **-i·glia** *f.*, **-ino** *m.* small guitar. **-ista** *m.* guitar-player. **-ọne** *m.* large guitar; theorbo. **-onata** *f.* (mus.) guitar-playing; poem for reciting with guitar accompaniment; fat untidy woman, slattern.

†chite *m.* (Pulci) unknown bird which pecks its parents when they are old.

chitina *f.* (zool.) chitin.

chitọne *m.* (Gk. and Rom. antiq.) chiton, tunic.

chiù¹ *m. indecl.* (orn.) scops owl; the screech of the scops owl; (fam.) blockhead.

†chiù² *adv.* See **più**.

chiucchiupic·chio *m.* (orn.) chaffinch.

chiucchiurl-a·ia *f.* hooting; screeching. **-are** [A I] *intr.* (*aux.* avere) to hoot, to screech.

chiudenda *f.* fence, partition; enclosure; oven-door.

chiud-ere [B 3] to shut, to close; — a chiave, to lock; — la porta, to shut the door; — la finestra, to fasten the window, to shut the window; — le scuole, to close the schools; — bottega, to shut up shop, to finish work for the day; — casa, to shut up (the) house; to put away in a safe place; ho chiuso il denaro, I've shut the money away; — in carcere, to 'put away', to send to prison; — il pugno, to clench one's fist; — gli occhi, to shut one's eyes; — un occhio, to doze, to turn a blind eye, to be indulgent; non

poter — occhio, to be unable to sleep, not to get a wink of sleep; — le ali, to fold one's wings; — le forbici, to snap the scissors to; — un ventaglio, to close a fan; — la luce, to switch off the light; — il gas, to turn off the gas; hanno chiuso l'acqua, they've turned off the water; to stop up, to seal; — un buco, to block up a hole; — l'animo all'amore, to close one's heart to love; — in sè il rancore, to nurse one's resentment; to finish, to conclude, to end; — un discorso, to conclude a speech; molti -ono l'anno ubriacandosi, many people celebrate the close of the year by getting drunk; una compagnia di bersaglieri -eva la sfilata, a company of bersaglieri closed the column; to enclose, to confine; — un giardino, to build a wall round a garden, to build a boundary wall to a garden; *intr.* (*aux.* avere) to close, to shut; -ono la domenica, they shut on Sundays; Signori, si -e!, Time, gentlemen, please!; (cards, rummy, canasta) to go down; (bridge) to close the bidding; *rfl.* to shut oneself up; to shut oneself in; si chiuse in convento, he shut himself up in a monastery; to close; to be closed; to be concluded, to come to an end; il congresso si -e il 23 settembre, the congress ends on the 23rd September; (of a wound) to heal, to close up; (of the sky) to become overcast. **-imẹnto** *m.* closing; winding-up; closure; shutting up; imprisoning; imprisonment. (**-itọre** *m.* **-itrice** *f.*)

chiudẹtte *f.pl.* (agric.) apertures made in the banks of the small dykes in gardens and rice-fields to allow the water to pass from one dyke to another.

chiuino *m.* (orn.). See **chiù¹**.

†chiun-ca, †-che, †-qua *prn.* See **chiunque**.

chiunque *prn. indecl.* whoever; whomsoever; anyone, anybody; anyone who; anyone whom.

chiurl-o *m.* bird-catching with bird-lime and decoy owl or bird-call; (orn.) curlew, *Numenius arquata*; — piccolo, whimbrel, *Numenius phaeopus*; (fam.) fool, stupid man. **-a** *f.* silly woman. **-are** [A I] *intr.* (*aux.* avere) to hoot. **-ẹtto** *m.* (orn.) whimbrel, *Numenius phaeopus*. **-ì** *m. indecl.* (orn.) see **chiurlo**. **-otello** *m.* (orn.) slender-billed curlew, *Numenius tenuirostris*.

chiusa *f.* barrier, dam, lock-gate; water gate; (hydr. eng.) — a stramazzo, weir; enclosure, smallholding; enclosure, the shutting up of birds in the dark to prevent their singing; ending, close, conclusion; †barricade; †prison.

chiusino¹ *m.* stone lid; metal cover; manhole cover; secret drawer; furnace or oven door; partition.

chiusino² *adj., n.m.* native of Chiusi.

chius-o *part.* of **chiudere**, q.v.; *adj.* shut, closed; a porte -e, behind closed doors, in camera; a occhi -i, with one's eyes shut, (fig.) with the utmost confidence; turned off, switched off, off; enclosed; close, secret, taciturn, reserved; (of the sky) cloudy, overcast; (bookb.) foglio —, uncut edge; (paperm.) carta -a, well-closed paper; (naut.) porto —, blockaded or closed harbour; (mus.) a bocca -a, humming; canna -a, stopped pipe (organ); canone —, close canon; nota -a, adjacent note; organo —, quiet registration; suoni -i, stopped notes (natural horn); pezzi -i, separate numbers, detached movements; *n.m.* enclosed space, enclosure; pen, fold.

chiusura *f.* closure; sluice-gate; fastening; — lampo, zip fastener; l'ora di —, closing time; seduta di —, final sitting; discorso di —, closing speech; (comm.) corso di —, closing rate; data della — dei conti, settling-day; (cinem.) fase di —, dark interval; (electr.) closing; seal; — ermetica, hermetic seal.

chiusuranto *m.* (geog. Ven.) smallholder.

choc *m. indecl.* (pron. as Fr.) (med.) shock.

christofle *m.* (metall.) copper, zinc and nickel alloy, silver-plated.

cià¹ *m.* (onomat.) the sound of water running softly; the sound of a smack.

cià² *m. indecl.* (bot.) tea-plant, *Thea sinensis*.

†cià *adv.* See **qua**.

ci¹ *f., m.* name of the letter C.

ci² *pers. prn., 1st pl., acc., dat. conj.* (before lo, la li, le, ne: **ce**) us, to us; eccoci, here we are; *rfl. prn.* ourselves; *recip. rfl. prn.* each other, one another.

ci³ *adv.* (before lo, la, li, le, ne: **ce**). **1.** HERE; there; — siamo, here we are; there we are; c'è, there is; — sono, there are; c'è chi dice, there are some who say; c'era una volta, once upon a time there was; qui — sono stato due anni, I was here two years; non c'è, he's not here; c'è Luigi?, is Luigi there?; non ce n'è, there isn't any. **2.** REPLACING A NEUTER PRN.: to it, in it; by it; about it; it; — credo, I believe it; non — badate, don't worry about it; pay

ci (*cont.*)

no attention to it; pensarci, to think of it; to see about it; — penso io, I'll see to it; pensarci su, to think it over; — ho rimorso, I'm very sorry about it; — ho gusto, I'm delighted about it.   **3.** INSTEAD OF PERS. PRN. 3RD SING., PL., DAT. to him, with him; to her, with her; to them, with them; — parlo ora, I'm talking to him (her, them) now; con lui non — posso stare, I can't bear him.

ciab-a[1] *m.* chatterbox, jabberer; person who 'holds forth'. **-are** [A 1] *intr.* (*aux.* avere) to jabber, to chatter. **-one** *m.* chatterbox.

†**ciaba**[2] *m.* See **ciabattino**, under **ciabatta**.

ciabatt-a *f.* slipper with no upper at the heel; old bedroom-slipper with the upper trodden down at the back; worn-out shoe; essere in -e, to be in one's bedroom-slippers; essere nelle -e di uno, to be in someone else's shoes; (fig.) slovenly woman; slut. **-aio** *m.* (*pl.* -a·i) slipper-maker or -seller. **-are** [A 1] *intr.* (*aux.* avere) to shuffle along; to walk with the flapping noise of backless slippers; to botch. **-ata** *f.* blow with a slipper. **-eri·e** *f.pl.* cheap rubbish. †**-iere** *m.* shoemaker. **-ina** *f. dim.* of ciabatta; *f.* of ciabattino. **-ino** *m.* cobbler; bungler; (provb.) -ino parla sol del suo mestiere, let the cobbler stick to his last. **-inume** *m.* lot of bunglers. **-ona** *f.*, **-one** *m.* shambler; slovenly person; down-at-heel person; bungler. **-ure** *f.pl.* trifles, cheap rubbish.

ciabone *m.* See under **ciaba**.

ciac *m. indecl.* (cinem.) clap sticks.

ciacche (onomat.) the sound of smacking; the sound of crunching; the sound of the sea on shingle; the slap of waves.

ciac·cher-a *f.*, **-o** *m.* hoggish person; ragamuffin.

ciaccherandà *m.* (bot.) jacaranda-tree, *Jacaranda*.

ciacciare [A 3] *intr.* (*aux.* avere) to speak without being qualified; to be a know-all.

ciac-co *m.* (*pl.* -chi) hog; parasite; glutton; (Florence) *pr.n.m.* nickname for **Jacopo**, James; *adj.* dirty, filthy; hoggish.

ciac·col-a *f.* slut, sloven; (Ven.) chatter, gossip, idle talk; chat. **-are** [A 1 s] *intr.* (*aux.* avere) (Ven.) to chatter, to gossip; to chat.

ciacc-ona *f.* (mus.) chaconne, composition on a ground-bass; Spanish dance. **-otta** *f.* old Portuguese dance.

Ciad *pr.n.m.* (geog.) Lago —, Lake Chad.

†**ciaf·fero** *m.* policeman.

ciak *m. indecl.* (cinem.). See **ciac**.

†**cialabardone** *m.* careless individual, one who leaves things to chance; slovenly person.

cialamello *m.* (mus.). See **caramella**.

ciald-a *f.* large wafer; waffle; cockade. **-ona·io** *m.* (*pl.* -ona·i) seller of 'cialde' or 'cialdoni'. **-one** *m.* thin curled-up wafer, forming a tube or horn with which one scoops up cream; (cul., Flor.) panna e -oni, cream and 'cialdoni'.

cialtron-a *f.* loose woman; slut. **-aglia** *f.* group of idlers. **-ata** *f.* slovenly behaviour. **-e** *m.* lazy slovenly person. **-eri·a** *f.* slovenliness, untidiness; boorish manners; slatternly behaviour.

ciambell-a *f.* ring-shaped cake, coffee-cake; (provb.) non tutte le -e riescono col buco, things cannot always be expected to turn out well; baby's teething ring; lavatory seat; rubber ring for swimming; life-saver; air cushion; kiss-curl; (equit.) circular movement of a horse; knotted ring of cloth worn on the head when carrying a load; (watchm.) balance wheel; (joc.) gambe a —, bow legs; †(mil. hist.) kind of incendiary weapon made of rags covered with pitch, wax and oil. **-a·ia** *f.*, **-a·io** *m.* (*pl.* -a·i) pastrycook.

ciambellan-o *m.* chamberlain, steward, court official. **-ato** *m.* office of chamberlain.

†**ciambello** *m.* combat.

ciambellotto *m.* (text.) camlet.

ciamberlano *m.* See **ciambellano**.

†**ciamberlato** *adj.* (of a room) ornamented with arabesques, frescoes, intaglios, etc.

Ciambesi *pr.n.f.* (geog.) Zambesi.

ciam·bola *f.* low-bred woman; gossip.

ciambol-are [A 1 s] *intr.* (*aux.* avere) to prate, to prattle; to gossip. **-io** *m.* prating, prattling; gossiping; gossip. **-one** *m.*, **-ona** *f.* prating person; gossip.

†**ciambra** *f.* room, chamber.

†**ciammengola** *f.* trifle; object of no value; loose woman, slut.

ciamo *m.* (zool.) whale louse, *Cyamus ceti*.

ciamorro *m.* (vet.). See **cimurro**.

ciampanelle *f.pl.* dare in —, to make blunders; to behave foolishly, to behave as though drunk or mad.

†**ciampare** *vb* and derivs. See **inciampare**.

ciampi-care [A 2 s] *intr.* (*aux.* avere) to walk without lifting the feet properly, to shuffle along; to stumble; (fig.) to be a bad worker, to dawdle. **-chino** *m.*, **-china** *f.* slow, clumsy worker. **-cone** *m.*, **-cona** *f.* shuffler; dawdler.

cian-a[1] *f.* woman who speaks broad Florentine; woman of the Florentine slums; low woman; slut. **-a·io** *m.* (*pl.* -a·i) group of low women; piece of gossip. **-ata** *f.* ill-bred action or saying. **-esco** *adj.* (*m.pl.* -eschi) like a low woman, slatternly, sluttish. **-io** *m.* brawling; gossiping of low women. **-o** *m.* ruffian, low individual. **-ume** *m.* rabble, riff-raff.

†**ciana**[2] *f.* aunt.

cianamide *m.* (chem.) cyanamide; artificial fertilizer.

cianato *m.* (chem.) cyanate.

cian-ca *f.* (joc.) leg; gammy leg; shank. **-canella** *f.* rather bandy-legged person. **-chetta** *f. dim.* of cianca; thin leg; fare -chetta, to cut a caper; (ichth.) scald fish, *Arnoglossus grohmanni*, *A. laterna*.

†**ciancellare** *intr.* to totter.

cianc-ia *f.* (*pl.* -e) tittle-tattle, nonsense, gossip, stuff, idle talk; dare -e, to give promises (instead of payment); prendere a -e, to take lightly, to take as a joke; uscire a -e, to come to nothing. **-erella** *f.* small talk; toy. **-erello** *m.* chatterbox. **-eri·a** *f.* useless talk. **-etta** *f.* little word of flattery. **-iere**, **-iero** *adj.* prating; cackling, quacking. **-iolina** *f.* joke. **-ioso** *adj.* joking; †trifling, of no importance; †charming, delightful. (**-iosamente** *adv.*) †**-iume** *m.* nonsense; trifler, joker.

†**Ciancian·fera** *pr.n.f.* (joc.) name invented by Boccaccio (*Decam.* N. 79), 'La —', my Lady Tittle-tattle.

cianci-are [A 3] *intr.* (*aux.* avere) to prate, to chat, to gossip; to jest, to joke. **-afri·scola**, **-a(n)fru·scola** *f.* trifle, object of no importance; nonsense, pack of lies. **-amento** *m.* mere words, idle talk. (**-atore** *m.* **-atrice** *f.*) **-one** *m.*, **-ona** *f.* chatterbox.

cianc-icare [A 2 s] *intr.* (*aux.* avere) to mumble; to speak hesitantly; to do little and to do it badly; to eat slowly; to chew with the gums (of an old person). **-ichino** *m.*, **-ichina** *f.* mumbler. **-icone** *m.*, **-icona** *f.* bad mumbler; slow coach; old dodderer. **-iugliare** [A 4] *intr.* (*aux.* avere) to speak indistinctly; to lisp. **-iuglione** *m.*, **-iugliona** *f.* person who lisps or speaks indistinctly. **-iullare** [A 1 I] *intr.* (*aux.* avere) to keep prating.

cianesco *adj.* See under **ciana**.

†**cianfard-a** *f.* coat; cap. †**-one** *m.* low individual.

cianfrin-o *m.* caulking iron. **-atura** *f.* caulking.

†**cianfrogna** *f.* tittle-tattle, gossip; strange talk.

cianfrona *f.* slattern; untidily dressed woman.

cianfrugli-are [A 4] *tr.* to bungle; *intr.* (*aux.* avere) to idle; to do bad work. **-one** *m.*, **-ona** *f.* bungler; messy, untidy person.

cianfrusa·glia *f.* rubbish, junk; negozio di —, junk shop.

†**cianfrusca·glia** *f.* See **cianfrusaglia**.

cian·gol-a *f.* chatter; nonsense. **-are** [A 1 s] *intr.* (*aux.* avere) to chatter.

ciangott-are [A 1] *intr.* (*aux.* avere) to speak with an impediment, esp. when the difficulty concerns *l* or *r*; (of a child) to begin to talk, to lisp; (of a bird) to twitter, to tweet, to cheep. **-io** *m.* lisping; mispronunciation; twittering, cheeping. **-one** *m.* lisper, stutterer, indistinct speaker.

cia·nico *adj.* (chem.) cyanic.

cianite *f.* (chem.) corrosive sublimate, mercuric chloride.

cianizz-are [A 1] *tr.* to kyanise, to impregnate (timber). **-azione** *f.* (timber) kyanising.

ciano[1] *m.* See under **ciana**.

ci-an-o[2] *m.* blue colour; (bot.) — minore, cornflower, *Centaurea cyanus*; — maggiore, alpine cornflower, *C. montana*; — persico, sweet sultan, *C. moschata*. **-idrato** *m.* (chem.) cyanide. **-i·drico** *adj.* (chem.) hydrocyanic; acido -idrico, hydrocyanic acid, prussic acid. **-ina** *f.* (chem.) cyanin; (text.; chem.) cyanine. **-o·geno** *m.* cyanogen; di-cyanogen. **-ografi·a** *f.* blue print. **-ogra·fico** *adj.* for blue prints; carta -ografica, blue print paper. **-opati·a**, **-osi** *f.* (med.) cyanosis. **-o·tico** *adj.* (med.) cyanotic. **-otipa** *f.* (phot.) carta -otipa, Pellet paper, cyanotype paper. **-otipi·a** *f.* the making of blue prints. **-uro** *m.* (chem.) cyanide. **-urato** *m.* cyanurate. **-urazione** *f.* (metall.) cyaniding. **-u·rico** *adj.* cyanuric.

ciant-a *f.* old shoe used as a slipper. **-ella** *f. dim.* of cianta; slovenly woman. **-ellare** [A 1] *intr.* (*aux.* avere) to shuffle along.

ciantro *m.* (eccl.) precentor (in Sicilian churches).

cia·o *excl.* (fam.) hello!; goodbye!; so long!; e — ! and that's that!; and that was that!; you can say goodbye to that!; (of a child) fare — — con la manina, to wave goodbye.

ciappa *f.* loop in a strap for a buckle.

†ciapper-one *m.* head-covering, coif, cap (for women). **†-otto** *m.* hood, cloak.

ciap·pol-a *f.* graver, graving tool, small chisel. **-are** [A I S] *tr.* to grave, to carve. **-ato** *part. adj.* graven, carved.

ciar(a)fuglione *m.* bungler, dunderhead.

ciaramell-a *f.* (mus.) see **caramella**. **-are** [A I] *intr.* (*aux.* avere) to prate; *tr.* to embroil with words, to confound, to confuse, to obscure. **-io** *m.* babbling.

ciardoni *m.pl.* (Tusc.) corns on the feet.

ciarl-a *f.* gossip; loquacity; hearsay; tittle-tattle; fare quattro -e, to have a chat, to have a yarn; sono tutte -e, it's all gossip. **-are** [A I] *intr.* (*aux.* avere) to gossip, to chatter; to patter (of a cheap-jack). **-amento** *m.* talk, gossip; 'gas'; (pop. joc.) Parliament. **-ata** *f.* long, pointless talk. **-atore** *m.*, **-atrice** *f.* gossip; one who is all words and no deeds. **-eri·a** *f.* pointless discourse. **-iere, -iero** *m.*, **-iera** *f.* gossip, gossiping individual; gasbag. **-io** *m.* lot of gossip; pack of malicious lies. **-ivendolo** *m.* gossip-monger. **-one** *m.*, **-ona** *f.* great talker; gossip, gossiping individual.

ciarlatan-o *m.* charlatan, quack, impostor; mountebank; cheap-jack. **-ata** *f.* quackery. **-eri·a** *f.* charlatanism. **-esco** *adj.* (*m.pl.* **-eschi**) charlatanic, quack. **-ismo** *m.* charlatanism.

ciarlotta *f.* (cul.) charlotte.

ciarmott-a *f.*, **-ella** *f. dim.* (naut.) flat boat used on the Tiber.

ciarp-a *f.* scarf; neckerchief; sash; scrap, rubbish, lumber; pointless talk, verbiage. **-ame** *m.* junk; odds and ends; dried fallen leaves; lumber, clutter. **-are** [A I] *intr.* (*aux.* avere) to work quickly and carelessly. **-eri·a** *f.* lumber. **†-iere, †-iero** *m.*, **†-iera** *f.* busybody, interfering person; bungler. **-one** *m.* bungler. **-ume** *m.* lumber.

ciascheduno, ciascuno *prn.* each one, every one; each person; everyone; *adj.* each, every.

†ciato *m.* (archaeol.) small beaker or glass used for drawing wine; measure equal to one-twelfth of a sestarius; ten drachms.

†ciaus-ire *tr.* to choose; to select; to prefer. **†-imento** *m.* choice; compassion; clemency.

ciavatta *f.* See **ciabatta**.

cib-are [A I] *tr.* to feed; to nourish; di che cosa -i il tuo cane?, what do you feed your dog on?; — a forza, to feed forcibly; (fig.) — di speranza, to nourish the hopes of; *rfl.* to feed; -arsi di, to feed on; to eat; i gufi si -ano di topi, owls live on mice; -arsi di speranza, to live on hope. **-amento** *m.* feeding. **-ato** *part. adj.* fed; nourished, -ato di, fed on. **-azione** *f.* food; succour; spiritual nourishment.

ciba·ri-a *f.*, **-o** *adj.* See under **cibo**.

†cibeca *m.*, *f.* one who is difficult to please over food; stupid individual, fool, idiot.

cib-o *m.* food. **†-ac·cola** *f.* coarse foodstuff; object of no value, piece of rubbish. **-a·ia** *f.*, **-a·ria** *f.* victuals, food. **-a·rio** *adj.* pertaining to food, alimentary; nutritive; (hist.) legge -aria, sumptuary law to limit expenditure on feasts.

cibo·rio *m.* (archit.) canopy above the High Altar; (liturg.) ciborium (cup-shaped vessel containing the Blessed Sacrament).

†cibre·a *f.* sledge or dray for transporting hay, grain, etc.

cibre·o *m.* (cul.) fricassée of the giblets of chickens, with eggs; mixed sauce; mishmash, hotchpotch; long, inconclusive screed or speech.

cica¹ *f.* a mere nothing; non saperne —, to know nothing about it.

cica² *m.* Abyssinian chieftain.

cicada *f.* (poet.). See **cicala**.

cica·dee *f.pl.* (bot.) Cycads, family of palm-like trees.

cical-a *f.* (ent.) cicada; (zool.) — di mare (grande) *Scyllarides latus*, — di mare (piccola) *Scyllarus arctus*, edible crustaceans resembling lobsters; non valere una —, to be not worth a button; grattare il corpo alla —, to induce a person to speak and give information; chatterbox, parrot; (naut.) anchor ring; (electr.; teleg.) buzzer. **-a·io** *m.* (*pl.* **-a·i**) place of much chatter; buzz of gossip, hum of conversation. **-are** [A I] *intr.* (*aux.* avere) to chatter; *tr.* to repeat, to parrot. **-amento** *m.* much talk. **-ata** *f.* long speech with nothing in it; gossip, chatter. (**-atore** *m.* **-atrice** *f.*) **-ato·rio** *adj.* fond of talking. **-eccio** *m.* (*pl.* **-ecci**) chatter of many shrill voices. **-eggio** *m.* see **cicaleccio**. **-eri·a** *f.* chattering. **-ino** *m.* chatterbox, gasbag; (electr.; telegr.) buzzer. **-io** *m.* constant chattering. **-one**

m. a person who talks too much. **-ona** *f.* talkative woman; (orn.) gadwall.

cicatr-ice *f.* scar; (med.) cicatrix; †act of treachery; †low cunning. **-izzare** [A I] *tr.* to scar; to cicatrize; *rfl.* to form a scab; to heal. **-izzato** *part. adj.* scarred; cicatrized; healed. **-izzazione** *f.* cicatrization; healing.

cicc-a *f.* stub of a cigar; cigarette end; quid of tobacco; 'gasper'; non vale una —, it's not worth tuppence; **-ai(u)olo** *m.* man who picks up cigar- or cigarette-ends. **-are** [A 2] *intr.* (*aux.* avere) to chew tobacco; (fig.) to grumble.

†ciccanton-a *f.* prostitute. **-e** *m.* low-down individual, scoundrel; buffoon.

ciccerello *m.* See **cicirello**.

cicche ciacche (onomat.) sound of clapping, spanking.

cic·chera *f.* cup.

cicchett-o *m.* glass of brandy; (colloq.) reproof, scolding, telling off, dressing down; (motor.) priming. **-are** [A I c] *intr.* (*aux.* avere) to drink spirits; to tipple.

cic·ci-a *f.* (pop.) meat; (fam.) flesh; avere molta —, to be plump; di —, in the flesh, real. **†-a·io** *m.* butcher; butchery, slaughter. **†-alardone** *m.* glutton; one who gormandizes. **-one** *m.* fat man; (med.) inflammatory tumour in the skin. **-ona** *f.* fat woman. **-oso** *adj.* plump. **-otto** *m.* proud flesh. **-(u)olo** *m.* part of the gum close to the tooth. **-uto** *adj.* plump, fleshy.

cic·ciole *f.pl.* (bot.) edible fungus, *Pleurotus Eryngii*.

cic·ciolo *m.* fibrous residue after preparing lard; leaf; dare un — per ricavare un porco, to set a sprat to catch a mackerel; proud flesh, granulations in a wound; (techn.) greave.

ciccione *m.* See under **ciccia**.

†cicco, †cic·colo *adj.* little, tiny, small.

cicer·bita *f.* (bot.) sow-thistle, *Sonchus oleraceus*.

cicerch-ia *f.* (bot.) vetchling, *Lathyrus sativus*; — porporina, *L. articulatus*; sanguigna, Tangier pea, *L. tingitanus*. **-ione** *m.* (bot.) wild everlasting pea, *L. silvester*.

cicerello *m.* (ichth.). See **cicirello**.

ci·cero *m.* (typ.) a type first used in an edition of Cicero published at Rome in 1458 by Umberto Gallo and intermediate in size between 'Pica' and 'English'.

cicerona *f.* (fam.) blue stocking, learned woman.

Ciceron-e *pr.n.m.* Cicero; guide, cicerone; fare da —, to act as guide; (joc.) eloquent person. **-iano** *adj.* Ciceronian. **-ianamente** *adv.* in Ciceronian style.

ci ci (onomat.) whistling sound; *n.m. indecl.* (infant.) dicky-bird.

cicigna *f.* (zool.) *Seps chalcides*, a lizard with rudimentary legs, similar to a slow-worm; sharp-tongued woman.

†Cici·li-a *pr.n.f.* (geog.) see **Sicilia**. **†-ano** *adj.*, *n.m.* see **siciliano**.

cicilian-a *f.* (bot.) tutsan, *Hypericum androsaemum*; *adj.* gran -o, maize.

cicindela *f.* (ent.) tiger beetle, *Cicindela* spp.

cicirello *m.* (ichth.) sand-eel, *Ammodytes* spp.

cicisb-eo *m.* (hist.) cicisbeo, 'cavalier servente' the recognized gallant of a married woman; (fig.) lady-killer. **-ea** *f.* fast woman. **-eare** [A 6] *intr.* (*aux.* avere) to be a gallant, to go in for gallantry. **-eato** *m.* rank or status of a cicisbeo; cicisbeism. **-eatura** *f.* gallantry; gallant behaviour; courting, wooing.

cicla·bile *adj.* See under **ciclo**.

Ci·cladi *pr.n.f.pl.* (geog.) Cyclades Islands; (zool.) orb-shell, *Sphaerium* spp.

ciclamino *m.* (bot.) cyclamen; (mil.) — imboscato, evader of military service; coward.

ciclamoro *m.* (herald.) annulet.

ci·clica *f.* (astron.) apparent circle traversed by a star, path of a star.

ci·clico *adj.* cyclic, cyclical.

cicl-o *m.* cycle; il — solare, the solar cycle; — produttivo, cycle of production; group, collection, cycle; il — carolingio, the Carolingian cycle; — di una malattia, course of a disease; (colloq.) bike. **-a·bile** *adj.* fit for cycling (of a road). **-ismo** *m.* cycling, cycle racing. **-ista** *m.* cyclist. **-i·stico** *adj.* pertaining to cycling or cycle racing; giro -istico, cycling tour; gara -istica, cycle race. **-ocampestre** *f.* cross-country cycle racing. **-ocross** *m. indecl.* cross-country cycle racing. **-omotore** *m.* autocycle, power-assisted cycle. **-opista** *f.* cycle track. **-oturismo** *m.* pleasure cycling; tourist cycling. **-oturista** *m.* pleasure cyclist; tourist cyclist.

cicloesano *m.* (chem.) cyclohexane.

ciclo·grafo *m.* cyclograph.

ciclo·id-e *f.* (math.) cycloid. **-ale** *adj.* (math.) cycloidal.

cicl-one *m.* cyclone. **-o·nico** *adj.* cyclonic; area -onica, cyclone depression.

Cicl-ope *pr.n.m.* (myth.) Cyclops; (fig.) monster, one-eyed creature. **-o·pico, o·pio** *adj.* cyclopic.

ciclopista *f.* See under **ciclo**.

ciclorama *f.* cyclorama.

ciclostile *m.* duplicator, cyclostyle; carta per —, stencil (for duplicator).

cicl-otomi·a (surg.) cyclotomy. **-o·tomo** *m.* (surg.) cyclotome.

ciclotrone *m.* (atom. phys.) cyclotron.

cicogn-a *f.* (orn.) stork, esp. the white stork, *Ciceronia ciconia*; (mech.) beam which by its motion swings a bell; long lever; (naut.) fare —, to place a masthead lookout. **-are** [A5c] *tr.* (naut.) to peak (a yard), so as to use it as a crane for hoisting a heavy weight, or in token of mourning.

cico·rea *f.* (bot.). See **cicoria**.

cico·ria *f.* (bot.) endive, *Cichorium Endivia*; — salvatica, succory, wild chicory, *C. intybus*; coffee-substitute.

cicut-a *f.* (bot.) hemlock; either the hemlock of Socrates, *Conium maculatum*; or water hemlock, *Cicuta virosa*; — anglina, fool's parsley, *Aethusa cynapium*; — rossa, herb Robert, *Geranium Robertianum*; — acquatica, water dropwort, *Oenanthe crocata* or *O. aquatica*. **-a·ria** *f.* (bot.) rough chervil, *Chaerophyllum temulentum*. **-ina** *f.* (chem.) cicutine. **†-remma, †-renna** *f.* (mus.) hemlock pipe.

ci·dolo *m.* log sent floating down the Piave during the spring flood season.

cidoniato *m.* quince jam.

cieca *f.* (carp.) recess made to take the head of a screw or bolt, counter-sinking.

ciec-o *adj.* (*pl.* ciechi) blind; sightless; — da un occhio, blind in one eye; (fig.) odio —, blind hatred; -a ubbidienza, blind obedience; (fig.) unquestioning; inconsiderate; unobservant; alla -a, blindly, without care, without looking; dark, lightless, sunless; concealed; finestra -a, blocked-up window; vicolo —, blind alley; (anat.) l'intestino —, caecum; giocare a mosca -a, to play blindman's buff; *n.m.* blind person; ignorant person; (anat.) caecum; non aver da far cantare un —, to be stony broke; (provb.) nel paese dei ciechi beato chi ha un occhio solo, all things are relative; il — e la bellona, a grotesque couple, a squalid Darby and Joan. **-a** *f.* blind woman, blind girl. **-amente** *adv.* blindly; inconsiderately; unobservantly.

ciecolina *f.* (ichth.). See **cecolina**, under **ceca**[1].

†cie·lico *adj.* heavenly, celestial.

cielo *m.* sky; toccare il — con un dito, to be overjoyed; alzare al —, to praise to the skies; non stare nè in — nè in terra, to be fabulous; — a pecorelle, sky with little fleecy clouds; a ciel sereno, with a clear sky, (fig.) out of the blue; a — scoperto, a — aperto, in the open; — coperto, overcast sky; climate, atmosphere; (rel.) Heaven; per amor del Cielo, for heaven's sake; faccia il Cielo, heaven grant; santo Cielo!, for Heaven's sake!; andare ai sette cieli, to be in one's seventh heaven; top, roof, ceiling; tester, canopy (of bed); (motor.) crown (of piston).

ciera *f.* See **cera**[1].

†cieri·gio *m.* See **ciliegio**.

†ciesa *f.* hedge; bush.

†ciesora *f.* See **cesoie**.

†ci·fera *f.* See **cifra**.

cifolotto *m.* (orn.). See **ciuffolotto**.

cifosi *f.* (med.) cyphosis, curvature of the spine.

cifr-a *f.* cipher, figure, digit; in — tonda, in round figures; — indice, index number; code; secret writing; le -e di un nome, a monogram; sign (such as those denoting units of weight, money, etc.); (comm.) — di affari, turnover; — globale, aggregate amount; †zero, nought. **-are** [A1] *tr.* to code; to embroider with a monogram; †to sign, to mark (with initials). **-a·rio** *m.* code, cipher system. **-ato** *part. adj.* written in code; with initials, initialed.

ci·glia[1] *f.* (biol.) cilium.

ci·glia[2] *f.pl.* See **ciglio**.

ci·gli-o *m.* (*f.pl.* -a) eyelash; brow; (poet.) eye, face; aggrottare le -a, to frown; in un batter di —, in the twinkling of an eye; (*m.pl.* **cigli**) bank; brink; verge; rim; edge of a ditch or furrow. **†-a·io, †-are** *m.* see **ciglione**. **†-are** *tr.* (falconry) to sew up the eyelids of

(a falcon or hawk, in the process of taming it). **†-atura** *f.* (naut.) -atura del vento, eye of the wind. **-onare** [A1c] *tr.* to embank. **-one** *m.* embankment; bank; border, edge; (geog.) hill-brow, hill-side. **-uto** *adj.* with eyelashes.

cigna *f.* (pop.). See **cinghia**.

cignale *m.* (zool.). See **cinghiale**.

ci·gnere [C7] (pop. Tusc.). See **cingere**.

cigno *m.* (orn.) swan; — minore, Bewick's swan, *Cygnus bewickii*; — reale, mute swan, *Cygnus olor*; — selvatico, whooper swan, *Cygnus cygnus*; (astron.) Cygnus; (fig.) poet; musician; il — di Busseto, Giuseppe Verdi; canto del —, swansong.

cignone *m.* large strap, esp. one on which a carriage body is slung.

cign(u)olo *m.* small strap, riding strap.

cigol-are [A1s] *intr.* (*aux.* avere) to creak (of a waggon); to squeak; to rumble (of the intestines); to hiss (of burning wood); to twitter (of many birds). **-amento** *m.* creaking; groaning; rumbling; twittering. **-io** *m.* prolonged creaking or squeaking; hissing; constant groaning, etc.

†ci·golo, †ci·gulo *adj.* little, small, tiny; *n.m.* little one, child.

†cilamella *f.* (mus.). See **caramella**.

Cile *pr.n.f.* (geog.) Chile.

cilecca *f.* a 'sell', such as holding out a thing to a child and then taking it away; broken promise; a near-miss; a misfire; fare — alla morte, to escape death very narrowly; fare —, to fail; ho sparato e ho fatto —, I shot and missed.

†cilem-a, †-e *adv. phr.* in —, idle; stare in —, to be kicking one's heels; to be wasting one's time.

cilestr-o *adj.* (poet.) pale blue, sky-blue. **†-iale** *adj.* see **celestiale**. **-ino** *adj.* pale blue.

ciliare *adj.* (anat.) ciliary.

cili·cio *m.* hairshirt; sackcloth; (fig.) penance, torture, torment.

cilie·g-ia *f.* (*pl.* -ie) cherry; ratafia di -ie, cherry-brandy; (joc.) so-and-so; l'amico —, our friend (who shall be nameless). **-eto** *m.* cherry orchard. **-ia·io** *m.* (*pl.* -ia·i) cherry-seller. **-ine** *f.pl.* (bot.) winter cherry, ground cherry, *Physalis alkekengi*; cape gooseberry, *P. peruviana*. **-io** *m.* (*pl.* -i) (bot.) cherry-tree, *Prunus avium*. **-i(u)olo** *adj.* cherry-coloured; *n.m.* cherry-brandy.

cilin·dric-o *adj.* cylindrical. (**-amente** *adv.*)

cilindr-o *m.* cylinder; cappello a —, top hat; roller; calender, hot-press; barrel; drum; (watchm.) carrello per —, lower balance cock; (mus.) strumenti a —, valve-instruments. **-a·ia** *f.* (mining) crushing rolls. **-are** [A1] *tr.* to roll; to put through a roller; to mangle (clothes); -are una strada, to roll a road; (paperm.; text.) to calender. **-ata** *f.* (motor.) piston displacement, swept volume; cubic capacity; (paperm.) charge, furnish. **-ato** *part. adj.* rolled; calendered. **-atoio** *m.* (*pl.* -atoi) calender, roller. **-atura** *f.* calendering, rolling; printed sheet. **-o·ide** *m.* cylindroid.

cili·zio *m.* See **cilicio**.

cilus-co *adj.* (*m.pl.* -chi) (Tusc.) short-sighted; squint-eyed.

cim-a *f.* top, summit; peak; da — in fondo, from top to bottom; in —, on top; in — a, on top of; at the top of; highest point, highest degree; (fig.) eminent person; man of distinguished ability; genius; non è una —, he's not very bright, he's no genius; tree-top; tip of branch; albero da —, tree with the top not lopped off; tip, end; -e di rape, turnip tops; (bot.) cyme, inflorescence; (herald.) coupeaux; (naut.) hemp rope; end of rope; — buona, free end; — cattiva, inner end (of a coil); masthead; **-ai(u)olo** *m.* ridge.

cimandorlo *m.* (orn.) waterhen.

cim-are [A1] *tr.* to shear (cloth), to clip to an even surface; to poll (a tree), to trim (a shrub); to decapitate; †*rfl.* to unite, to be gathered together. **-ata** *f.* clipping; trimming, trim. **-ato** *part. adj.* trimmed; lopped; decapitated; (herald.) towered, with turrets; torre -ata, tower towered, tower with turrets. **-atore** *m.* trimmer. **-atrice** *f.* (text.) cutting machine; (agric.) hedge trimmer. **-atura** *f.* clippings, trimmings, shavings; trimming; cutting. **-eri·a** *f.* (text.) trimming shop.

cimasa *f.* (archit.) moulding on a cornice; (bldg.) coping.

cimba *f.* (naut.) boat; boat used for embarking officers and men; (poet.) craft, bark.

cimbal-a·ia, -a·ria *f.* (bot.) ivy-leaved toadflax, *Cymbalaria muralis*. **-iforme** *adj.* (bot.) cymbiform, boat-shaped.

cim·bal-o *m.* (mus.) cymbal; harpsichord; (fig.) essere in -i, to be joyful, to be merry (cf. **cimberli**). **†-a·io** *m.* (mus.) harpsichordist. **†-ante** *adj.* (mus.) cymbal-clashing.

cim·balon *m. indecl.* (mus.) cimbalom, dulcimer.

cimbasso *m.* (mus.) ophicleide.

cim·berli *m.pl.* (mus.) cymbals; (fig.) essere in —, to live merrily; to be in one's cups (cf. **cimbalo**).

†cim·bia *f.* (archit.) fillet, cincture (at the bottom of the shaft of a column).

†cimb-otto, †-ot·tolo *m.* tumble, fall; bump; fare dare un — a, to cause to fall with a bump, (euphem.) to bump off. **†-ottolare** *intr.* to tumble, to fall bump.

cimbrac·col·a *f.* (vulg.) slut. **-o** *m.* rag, tatter.

cime·lio *m.* precious object, museum piece, treasure; heirloom; relic; curio.

ciment-are [A I c] *tr.* to purify (gold, etc.); to assay; to put to the test; to try, to prove, *rfl.* to take a risk; to prove oneself; to put oneself to the test; to try one's strength; -arsi in, to venture upon. **-ato** *part. adj.* purified; assayed; tested; proved. **-atore** *m.* one who tests; one who takes a risk.

ciment-o *m.* hazardous trial or contest; testing, proving; tempting; tentare il — delle armi, to try the hazard of arms; — invernale, breaking the ice, open-air swimming in icy water; mixture of chemicals used in purifying metals; (hist.) Accademia del —, a seventeenth-century Florentine Academy of Sciences. **-oso** *adj.* dangerous, risky, hazardous; venturesome, bold, rash.

ci·mic-e *f.* (ent.) bed bug, *Cimex lectularis*; (Tusc.) drawing-pin; (joc.) Fascist badge worn in lapel; (ent.) — elegante, *Strachia ornata*, a pentatomid bug. **-ia·io** *m.* (*pl.* **-ia·i**) bug-ridden place. **-ia·ria** *f.* (bot.) baneberry, *Actaea spicata*. **-iat·tola** *f.* grape coloured like a bug. **-iat·tolo** *m.* the vine yielding it. **-ioso** *adj.* bug-ridden. **-iotto** *m.* (bot.) black horehound, *Ballotta nigra*.

cimiere *m.* See **cimiero**.

cimiero *m.* crest of a helmet; top part of a helmet; (poet.) helmet; swept-up hair-do; (herald.) crest.

†cimine·a *f.* See **ciminiera**.

ciminiera *f.* smokestack; factory chimney; funnel.

cimi·no, cimi-nio *m.* (bot.). See **comino**.

cimiter-o *m.* cemetery, graveyard; burial ground. **-iale** *adj.* pertaining to a cemetery. **-io** *m.* (poet.) See **cimitero**.

cimm-e·rico, -e·rio *adj.* Cimmerian, gloomy.

ci·molo *m.* young shoot of a plant; head of a lettuce.

cimo·metro *m.* (electr.) wavemeter, cymometer.

cim-ọsa, -ọssa *f.* (text.) selvedge, listing; rag for wiping a slate; blackboard eraser.

cimurro *m.* (vet.) nasal catarrh, referring also to glanders or strangles in horses and to distemper in dogs; (joc.) a cold in the head.

Cin-a *pr.n.f.* (geog.) China; inchiostro di —, Indian ink; (bot.) — gentile, China root, *Smilax china*. **-ẹse** *adj.* Chinese; *pr.n.m.* Chinaman; the Chinese language, Chinese; *f.* Chinese woman. **-eseri·a** *f.* chinoiserie.

cinabr-o *m.* cinnabar; sulphide of mercury; red ink; (poet.) the red colour of the lips. **-ẹse** *m.* ruddle, raddle, red ochre.

†cinam-olgo, †-o·logo, †-ulgo *m.* fabulous bird of Arabia.

cin·ci·a *f.* (orn.) titmouse; — alpina, willow tit, *Parus atricapillus*; — bigia, marsh tit, *P. palustris*; — dalmatina, sombre tit, *P. lugubris*; — mora, coal tit, *P. ater*. **-allegra** *f.* (orn.) great tit, *Parus major*. **-arella** *f.* (orn.) blue tit, *Parus coeruleus*. **-azzurra** *f.* see **cinciarella**.

cinci·glia *f.* (zool.) chinchilla; chincilla fur.

cinci·gli-o *m.* sort of sporran. **-ọne** *m.* heavy drinker, toss-pot.

cincilla *f.* (zool.). See **cinciglia**.

†cincinẹtto *m.* pillow; cushion.

Cincinnato¹ *pr.n.m.* Cincinnatus.

cincinnato² *part.* of **cincinnare**, q.v., under **cincinno**.

cincinn-o *m.* (poet.) curl, curly lock. **-are** [A I] *tr.* to curl (the hair). **-ato** *part. adj.* curled, curling, curly.

cincischi-are [A 4] *tr.* to gash (as with blunt scissors), to chop about; to clip (one's words); *intr.* (*aux.* avere) to mess about, to waste time. **-amento** *m.* gashing, chopping; wasting of time. **-ato** *part. adj.* cut about, gashed.

cincischìo *m.* continual or prolonged wasting of time, inconclusive activity.

cinci·schi-o *m.* gash, uneven cut. **-ọne** *m.* dawdler, person who wastes time in inconclusive activity.

cincọn-a *f.* (bot.) *Cinchona*, genus of plants which yield quinine. **-ina** *f.* (chem.) cinchonine. **-iṣmo** *m.* (med.) cinchonism.

cin-e *m. indecl.* (pop. abbrev.) cinema **-easta** *m.* (neol.) cinema expert; person professionally connected with films. **-edramma** *m.* (neol.) film drama. **-egiornale** *m.* (neol.) newsreel. **-elan·dia** *f.* cinema land. **-epresa** *f.* cine-camera. **-eromanzo** *m.* film love story. **-eteca** *f.* film library. **-etec·nica** *f.* motion-picture technique.

cinedo *m.* boy favourite, minion, catamite; (med.) homosexual.

cinefobi·a *f.* excessive fear of dogs.

cinege·tic-a *f.* sport, shooting, hunting (with dogs). **-o** *adj.* pertaining to hunting with dogs.

cine-giornale *m.*, **-lan·dia** *f.*, etc. See under **cine**.

cinell-e *f.pl.*, **-i** *m.pl.* (mus.) cymbals.

ci·nem-a *m. indecl.* cinema. **-ateca** *f.* film library. **-a·tica** *f.* kinetics; (naut.) -atica navale, study of nautical velocity. **-atiṣmo** *m.* (eng.) kinematic system. **-atografa·io** *m.* cinema worker, cinematographer. **-atografare** [A I S] *tr.* to take a moving picture of, to make a film of, to screen. **-atografi·a** *f.* cinematography; film; cinema show. **-atogra·fico** *adj.* cinematographic, pertaining to the cinema. **-ato·grafo** *m.* cinematograph, projector; cinema, picture theatre. **-u·sica** *f.* film-music.

cinera·ria *f.* (bot.) various native species of *Senecio*; — de' giardini, florists' cineraria, *Senecio cruenta*.

cinera·rio *adj.* cinerary.

cine·r-eo *adj.* ashy, ashen, grey; (astron.) luce -ea, earthshine. **-igno, -ino** *adj.* ashen, grey. **-i·zio** *adj.* ash-coloured, grey. **†-u·leo** *adj.* see **cinereo**.

cineromanzo *m.* See under **cine**.

cinẹse *adj., n.m., f.* See under **Cina**.

cineṣ-i·a *f.* (med.) kinesiatrics. **-iterapi·a** *f.* (med.) kinesitherapy, kinesiatrics. **-itera·pico** *adj.* kinesiatric.

cinest-eṣi·a *f.* kinaesthesia. **-e·tico** *adj.* kinaesthetic.

cine-teca *f.*, **-tec·nica** *f.* See under **cine**.

cin-e·tica *f.* kinetics. **-e·tico** *adj.* kinetic. **-etosco·pio** *m.* kinetoscope.

†cinfolare *intr.* to hiss.

Cingalẹse *adj.* Cingalese; *n.m.* native of Ceylon; Cingalese language; *f.* Cingalese woman.

cingallẹgra *f.* (orn.). See **cinciallegra**, under **cincia**.

cin·g-ere [C 5] *tr.* to gird; to girdle; to surround; — di una siepe, to fence; to embrace; to encompass; to wreathe; to border; — d'assedio, to besiege; to take up (arms, the sword, etc.); to put on (a crown, etc.); -erla a, to do evil to; (hist.) — la spada a, to dub knight; †to slash, to run through (with the sword); *rfl.* to gird oneself; to put on a belt; -ersi per i lombi, to gird up one's loins; (naut.) -ersi con la gomena, to foul the cable. **†-imento** *m.* girding; surrounding; girdle.

cin·ghi-a *f.* strap; belt; (naut.) serving; *pl.* braces; guiding reins; (of a child) essere sulle -e, to be beginning to stand. **-a·ia** *f.* (vet.) internal thoracic vein (of a horse). **-are** [A 4] *tr.* to lace up, to tie with a belt, to strap. **-ata** *f.* blow with a strap, belting; tying up, strapping up; play upon words. **-ato** *part. adj.* tied up; belted; strapped; (herald.) bridled. **-atura** *f.* tying with a strap, strapping up; girth of a saddle. **-ẹtta** *f.* dim. of **cinghia**; -etta per l'orologio, watchstrap. **†-o** *m.* circle; cornice. **-ọni** *m.pl.* straps on which a carriage body is slung.

cinghial-e *m.*, **-a** *f.* (zool.) wild pig, wild boar; pigskin. **-lessa** *f.* wild sow. **-ẹtto** *m.* young wild pig. **-ino** *m.* piglet.

†cin·ghio *m.* See under **cinghia**.

cingolato *adj.* (eng.) tracked, caterpillar.

cin·gol-o *m.* belt, girdle; (eng.) track, caterpillar track; suola di —, track shoe. **-ẹtta** *f.* small tracked vehicle.

cingottare [A I] and derivs. See **cinguettare**.

cinguett-are [A I c] *intr.* (*aux.* avere) to twitter, to chirp; to chatter, to prattle; to lisp, to speak indistinctly; *tr.* — una lingua, to speak a language badly. **-amento** *m.* chattering, twittering. **-ata** *f*, confused babble of voices. (**-atore** *m.* **-atrice** *f.*) **-eri·a** *f.* gossiping, chattering. **-iere, -iero, -ino** *m.* silly chatterbox. **-io** *m.* continual twittering, chirping; constant chattering. **-ọne** *m.* chatterbox.

ciniatri·a *f.* veterinary care of dogs; canine medicine.

ci·nic-o *adj.* cynical; *n.m.* cynic. **-amẹnte** *adv.* cynically.

†ci·nifo *m.* wild goat.

cini·gia *f.* smouldering ashes.

cini·glia *f.* (text.) chenille.

ci·nipe *m.* (ent.) cynipid; gall wasp.

ciniṣmo *m.* cynicism.

cinna·mico *adj.* (chem.) cinnamic.

cin·nam-o *m.* (bot.) see **cinnamomo**. -ato *m.* (chem.) cinnamate. -ene, -eno *m.* (chem.) cinnamene, styrol. -i·fero *adj.* cinnamon-producing.

cinnamomo *m.* (bot.) cinnamon-tree, *Cinnamomum zeylanicum*; bark of the same.

cino¹ *adj. indecl.* (abbrev. of **cinese**, q.v. under **cina**) cino-giapponese, Chino-Japanese.

cino² *m.* (bot.) hound's tongue, *Cynoglossum officinale*.

cin-oce·falo *m.* (zool.) baboon, *Cynocephalus* sp. -ofili·a *f.* love of dogs. -o·filo *m.* dog-fancier. -ofobi·a *f.* fear of dogs. -ogloss-a *f.* -olissa *f.* (vet.) rabies (in dogs). -omo·rio *m.* (bot.) Maltese fungus, *Cynomorium coccineum*. -oressi·a *f.* (med.) voracious appetite. -oṣura *f.* (astron.) Ursa Minor; (fig.) guide, attraction, cynosure.

†cinquadea *f.* kind of sword.

cinquant-a *card. num.* fifty; essere sui —, to be getting on for fifty. -are [A 1] *intr.* (aux. avere) to exaggerate. -ena·rio *m.* jubilee. -enne *adj.* fifty-year old; *n.m., f.* man or woman of fifty. -en·nio *m.* period of fifty years, half-century. -e·ṣimo *ord. num.* fiftieth. -ina *f.* set, group or batch of (about) fifty; essere sulla -ina, to be getting on for fifty years of age. -ino *m.* (bot.) a variety of maize which matures in fifty days; (numism.) silver coin worth fifty centesimi; (hist.) commander of fifty men. -otto *card. num.* fifty-eight; *m.* the year 1858.

cinqu-e *card. num.* five. -ecente·ṣimo *ord. num.* five-hundredth. -ecento *card. num.* five hundred; *n.m.* il -ecento, the sixteenth century. -ecentesco *adj.* (*m.pl.* -ecenteschi) relating to the sixteenth century; l'arte -ecentesca, sixteenth-century art. -ecentista *m.* writer or artist of the sixteenth century, cinquecentist; scholar specializing in the sixteenth century; *adj.* of the sixteenth century. -ecenti·stico *adj.* pertaining to the sixteenth century, typical of the sixteenth century; l'arte -ecentistica, sixteenth-century art. -ina *f.* a set of five; about five; a set of five numbers in a public lottery; five days' pay; (theatr.) actor's pay; (hist.) five citizens elected in Florence to impose a tax. -ino *m.* double five (at dice). -emila *card. num.* five thousand. -emille·ṣimo *ord. num.* five-thousandth.

†cinquedea *f.* See †cinquadea.

cinque-fo·glie *m.* (bot.) creeping cinquefoil, *Potentilla reptans*; (herald.) cinquefoil. -fo·glio *m.* (bot.) see **cinquefoglie**. -nervi, -nodi *m.* (bot.) plantain, *Plantago major, P. media*. -reme *f.* quinquereme.

cinta *f.* (mil.) perimeter defences; circuit; bounds; enclosure; — daziaria, barrier where local dues are collected on goods entering a town; entro la — delle vecchie mura, within the circle of the old walls; (naut.) wale, plank along the outer timbers of a ship's side; capo —, harping, the forepart of the wale surrounding the bow extensions of the rib-bands; — principale, sheer-strake; prima —, main wale; — di salvataggio, lifebelt; (herald.) orle, escutcheon voided; doppia —, tressure; (archit.) collarino (of a column). †girdle; †sword-belt.

†cinti·glio *m.* girdle; belt.

cintino *m.* (eccl.) kind of skirt used as substitute for a cassock.

cinto *part.* of **cingere**, q.v.; *adj.* girt; surrounded; fastened; *n.m.* belt; girdle; (med.) truss; (zool.) — di Venere, Venus's girdle, *Cestus veneris*; (astron.) halo.

cin·tol-a *f.* waist; waistline; waistband; star con le mani alla —, to be idle, to twiddle one's thumbs; tenersi alcuno a —, to have someone tied to one's apron-strings; type of money-bag; largo in —, generous; stretto in —, mean, stingy; †belt. -ino *m.* garter; stringere i -ini, to buck up, to 'pull one's socks up'. -o *m.* shoelace, bootlace; garter; list of broadcloth, strip along its edge to strengthen it. -one *m.* strap; sling of a gun or rifle.

cintraco *m.* (hist.) executive official in various Italian communes, esp. in Liguria.

cintur-a *f.* belt, girdle; sash; waist; waistband; middle; — porta-bretelle, suspender-belt, foundation garment; girdling; seizing round the waist; (wrestling) waist lock; largo di —, generous, indulgent; stretto di —, mean, grudging; stringere la —, to tighten one's belt; (naut.) strake; — di salvataggio, lifebelt; — corazzata, armoured belt; (med.) bendaggio a —, abanet; (zool.) — di Venere, see 'cinto di Venere', under **cinto**. -ini *m.pl.* band of knee breeches for buckling at the knee; (eccl.) flaps on clerical shoes. -ino *m.* sword-belt; †avere il -ino rosso, to be distinguished. -one *m.* belt; sling of a gun or rifle.

Cin·zia *pr.n.f.* Cynthia; (fig.) the moon; (zool.) *Cynthia papillosa*, a kind of ascidian.

ciò *prn. indecl.* that; this; a —, to which end; a — che, so that, in order that; — perchè, because of this; per — che, because, inasmuch as; con tutto —, for all that, in spite of all that; essere da —, to be up to it, to be able for it; — nonostante, — nondimeno, nevertheless, in spite of that; con —, therefore, consequently; oltre a —, besides that, moreover; †whatever; †con — sia cosa che, since, because; for all that, notwithstanding that.

cioc-ca *f.* lock of hair, tuft; bunch, cluster; branch; a -che, in great quantity. -chett(in)a, -colina *f. dim.* -ona *f. augm.* large bunch of flowers.

cioccare [A 2] *intr.* (aux. essere) (naut.) to veer handsomely.

ciocchè *prn. indecl.* that which; whatever.

ciocci-a¹ *f.* (fam.) nipple. -are [A 3 c] *intr.* (aux. avere) (of a baby) to suck.

cioc·ci-a² *m.* busybody, meddler; one who gives himself airs. -are [A 3] *intr.* (aux. avere) to interfere, to meddle in other people's affairs. -one *m.* busybody, interfering individual.

ciocciare¹ [A 3 c]. See under **cioccia¹**.

ciocciare² [A 3]. See under **cioccia²**.

cioc·cio *adj.* (of feet) disabled; avere i piedi ciocci, to have bad feet; to have a shambling gait.

cioc-co *m.* (*pl.* -chi) log; block; (fig.) blockhead. -chettone *m.* curved piece of wood for smoothing out clothes.

cioccolat-a *f.* chocolate; drinking chocolate, cocoa; — al latte, cocoa, milk chocolate. -ino *m.* a chocolate; vuoi un -ino? have a chocolate? -o *m.* chocolate; un pezzo di -o, a piece of chocolate. -a·io *m.* (*pl.* -a·i) chocolate maker. -iera *f.* jug for making chocolate; woman chocolate maker or seller. -iere *m.* chocolate manufacturer.

cio·ci-a *f.* (*pl.* -e) sandal with wrappings fastened round the legs like puttees formerly worn by agricultural labourers. -a·ro *m.*, -a·ra *f.* peasant or labourer wearing 'cioce'; peasant of the Roman campagna.

Ciociari·a *pr.n.f.* (geog.) district where 'cioce' were worn, i.e. south-east of Rome, in the Roman campagna.

cioè *adv.* that is, that is to say, i.e. namely.

cio(l)fo *m.* worthless person; vile individual.

†ciolla *f.* slut, slattern.

ciomp-o *m.* (Florentine hist.) wool-carder; il tumulto dei Ciompi, the revolt of the wool-carders in 1378; plebeian; (colloq.) fool, chump. -eri·a *f.* foolishness, stupidity. -esco *adj.* (*m.pl.* -eschi) foolish, stupid.

cionc-are¹ [A 2 c] *intr.* (aux. avere) to drink to excess, to tipple; *tr.* to guzzle; to gulp down. -atore *m.* tippler.

†cioncare² *vb.* See under **cionco**.

cion-co *adj.* (*m.pl.* -chi) broken; downcast; drooping; †truncated, cut off, †lopped off; †(fig.) lessened; †removed, †destroyed. †-are *tr.* to cut off, to chop off; to truncate; *rfl.* to be wounded, to fall (in battle). -one *m.* rough iron ingot for hammering or drawing out; slitting mill for cutting metal plates into strips.

ciondol-are [A 1 sc] *intr.* (aux. avere) to dangle; to sway; to stagger, to walk unsteadily; to loaf around, to hang about; *tr.* to dangle; to swing; to roll; to shake from side to side. -amento *m.* dangling; swaying; swinging; staggering. -ante *adj.* dangling; swaying; swinging; staggering.

ciondol-o *m.* drop-earring; dangling trinket; pendant; decoration; medal. -ino *m. dim.* little trinket; slovenly youth; boy with sloppy clothes. -one *m. augm.* large pendant; slovenly, careless person. -oni *adv.* dangling; with a swaying movement; swinging from side to side; carelessly.

†cionno *adj.* worthless; idle, slack; inept; stupid.

†cionta *f.* beating; cudgelling.

†cioppa *f.* flowing gown; full-length garment with a hood (worn by men and women).

ciortone *m.* (ichth.) common tunny, *Thunnus thynnus*.

ciospo *adj.* (Tusc.) butter-fingered; clumsy; awkward.

†ciota *f.* bowl (cf. **ciotola**).

cio·tol-a *f.* china or wooden bowl; wooden money-box; (anat.) socket of the hip-joint, acetabulum. -ata *f.* bowlful.

ciott-a¹ *m.*, -one *m.* busybody, meddler; bore.

†ciott-a² *f.* whiplash, blow with a whip. †-are *tr.* to whip, to lash.

ciotto¹ *adj.* lame; limping.

†ciotto² *m.* See **ciottolo**.

ciot·tol-o *m.* pebble; cobblestone; crock, piece of crockery. **-are** [A I S] *tr.* to pave with cobblestones. **-ata** *f.* blow with a stone. **-ato** *part. adj.* cobbled; paved; *n.m.* cobbled road; rough pavement; pebbled path; crazy pavement. **-oso** *adj.* pebbly, pebbled.

†**ciovetta** *f.* (orn.). See **civetta**.

cip *m. indecl.* (poker) chip.

cip cip (onomat.) tweet tweet; cheep cheep.

cipa·i *m. indecl.* sepoy.

ciparisso *m.* (bot.) cypress spurge, *Euphorbia cyparissias.*

ci·pero *m.* (bot.) sedge, *Cyperus esculentus* and other species of *Cyperus.*

cipi·gl-io *m.* (*pl.* **-i**) frown; angry expression; fare il —, to frown; to look angry. **-ioso** *adj.* frowning; easy to offend, touchy.

cipoll-a *f.* (bot.) onion, *Allium caepa;* — canina, — selvatica, — di serpe, plume hyacinth, *Muscari comosum;* — marina, — squilla, great sea squill; *Urginea* (*Scilla*) *maritima,* a bulb of Mediterranean shores; — di Catabonia, shallot, *Allium ascalonicum;* (fig.) mangiare pane e —, to live on poor fare; buccia di —, velo di —, onion-skin, (fig.) very thin paper or material; sottile come un velo di —, paper-thin; doppio come le —, treacherous; bulb; electric light bulb; suction strainer, rose; ball (e.g. of string, wool); campanile a —, bell tower surmounted by bulb-shaped summit; — da stirare, bulb for ironing the crown of a hat; (fam.) gizzard, crop; (joc.) large pocket watch, 'turnip'. **-ac·cio** *m.* (bot.) grape hyacinth, *Muscari botryoides;* -accio col fiocco, plume hyacinth, *Muscari comosum;* star-of-Bethlehem, *Ornithogalum umbellatum;* Narbonne star, *O. narbonense.* **-a·io** *m.* (*pl.* **-a·i**) onion bed; onion seller. **-ata** *f.* dish made of onions and pounded gourds; (fig.) (of a work of art) hotch-potch, mess. **-ato** *adj.* arranged in layers like an onion; (of wood) unworkable through having many large, glassy knots. **-atura** *f.* hard, glassy knot in timber, shake flakiness (in wood). **-etta** *f.,* **-ina** *f.* spring onion, young onion; -ine sott'aceto, pickled onions. **-ine** *f.pl.* (bot.) erbe -ine chives, *Allium Schoenoprasum.* **-ino** *m.* cipolin, a type of coloured marble mined in the mountains of Carrara. **-oso** *adj.* flaky.

cip·pero *m.* (bot.). See **cipero**.

cippettino *m.* friendly game of poker played at home.

cippo *m.* cippus, sepulchral pillar.

cipre·a *f.* (zool.) cowrie, *Cypraea* spp.

cipress-o *m.* (bot.) cypress, *Cupressus sempervirens; f.* — femmina, see **cipressa**. **-a** *f.* dwarf var. of cypress. **-a·ia** *f.,* **-eto** *m.* cypress grove. **-ino** *m.* tamarisk, *Tamarix gallica;* Lombardy poplar, *Populus italica.*

ci·pria *f.* face powder; toilet powder.

ci·pride *m.* (zool.) Cypris, cyprid.

Ciprigna *pr.n.f.* (myth.) Venus.

ciprigno[1] *adj.* of Cyprus.

†**ciprigno**[2] *adj.* harsh; angry; brusque.

ciprino *m.* (ichth.) carp-like fish, *Cyprinus* spp.

cipri-ota, -otto *adj., n.m.* See under **Cipro**.

cipripe·dio *m.* (bot.) an orchidaceous genus, lady's slipper, *Cypripedium.*

Cipr-o *pr.n.m.* (geog.) Cyprus; wine from Cyprus; face powder; (bot.) alkanet, *Alkanna tinctoria.* **-iota, -iotto** *adj., n.m.* Cypriot.

cirac·chio *m.* (Tusc.) rag; strip.

†**cira·gio** *m.* See **ciliegio**.

†**ciramella** *f.* (mus.). See **caramella**.

circa *adv.* about; more or less; approximately; nearly; — due mila, about two thousand, circa two thousand; in —, all'in —, a un bel —, more or less; *prep.* — a, about, regarding, as to, concerning.

circass-e *m.* (text.) a thin worsted fabric formerly known as Circassian. **-o** *adj., n.m.* (geog.) Circassian.

Circ-e *pr.n.f.* (myth.) Circe; (fig.) enchantress. **-e·a** *f.* (bot.) enchanter's nightshade, *Circaea lutetiana.*

circense *adj.* circensian.

†**circe·o** *m.* wind blowing off Circe's promontory (Gaeta).

†**cir·cino** *m.* perfect circle, circle drawn with a pair of compasses.

†**cir·cio** *m.* north-westerly wind.

†**circiuto** *m.* round (in a dance).

cir-co *m.* (*pl.* **-chi**) circus; — equestre, circus (entertainment); (geol.) cirque, corrie; — glaciale, basin where snows accumulate.

circol-are[1] [A I S] *intr.* (*aux.* avere, essere) to circulate; to move about; to keep moving; to move along; to travel; (of money) to be current; fare —, to put into circulation, to circulate, to send round; to give currency to; *tr.* to send round, to circulate. **-amento** *m.* circulation, rotation. **-ante** *adj.* circulating; moving; going round; biblioteca -ante, circulating library; (econ.) medio -ante, circulating medium. **-atoio** *m.* vessel in which liquid is kept circulating. **-atore** *m.,* **-atrice** *f.* circulator; †charlatan; †quack. **-ato·rio** *adj.* (*m.pl.* -atorii) circulatory. **-azione** *f.* circulation, rotation, going round; -azione stradale, road traffic; -azione rotataria, roundabout; -azione in senso unico, one-way traffic; vietata la -azione, no thoroughfare; tassa di -azione, road tax; (econ.) -azione monetaria, amount of currency in circulation; -azione cartacea, paper currency; (comm.) turnover, sales; effetti in -azione, outstanding bills; (mus.) modulation; modulation through all the keys.

circolar-e[2] *adj.* circular; biglietto —, circular ticket, tourist ticket; (comm.) assegno —, bank draft. **-mente** *adv.* round in a circle.

circolare[3] *f.* circular; mandare una — a, to circularize.

cir·colo *m.* circle; — massimo, great circle; — orario, — di declinazione, meridian; — di evoluzione, turning circle; (mus.) — armonico, circle of fifths; — mezzo, turn; circuit, region, area; (leg.) — delle Assise, territory in which certain courts are competent; club, society, group; — nautico, yacht club; *pl.* (herald.) concentric annulets.

circom-padano *adj.* (geog.) pertaining to territory surrounding the Po valley. **-polare** *adj.* circumpolar. **-pulsione** *f.* (eng.) circular propulsion.

circon-ci·dere [C3] *tr.* to circumcise. **-cisione** *f.* circumcision. **-ciso** *part. adj.* circumcised.

circond-are [A I C] *tr.* to surround; to encircle; to go round; to follow, to accompany. **-a·bile** *adj.* that may be surrounded. **-amento** *m.* surrounding. **-ato** *part. adj.* surrounded; accompanied. (**-atore** *m.* **-atrice** *f.*)

circonda·rio *m.* administrative district; tribunale di —, district court, county court.

circon-durre [B2] *tr.* to lead round; (fig.) to lead by the nose, to dupe, to lead a dance, to deceive. **-dotto** *part. adj.* led round; (fig.) duped, deceived. **-ducimento** *m.* leading round; (fig.) duping, deceiving. **-ferenza** *f.* circumference. **-ferenziale** *adj.* relating to the circumference. **-flessione** *f.* circumflexion. **-flesso** *part.* of **circonflettere**, q.v. *adj.* circumflex; verbi -flessi, (Gk.) contracted verbs; accento -flesso, circumflex accent; *n.m.* circumflex accent. **-flet·tere** [C19] *tr.* to circumflex, to put a circumflex accent on. **-fluenza** *f.* circumfluence. **-fluire** [D2] *intr.* (*aux.* avere) to flow round about. **-fondere** [C2] *tr.* to fuse together, to blend; to diffuse. **-ful·gere** [C5] *intr.* (*aux.* avere) to shine round about. **-fuso** *part.* of **circonfondere**, q.v.; *adj.* fused, blended; diffused. †**-gioviale** *adj.* (astron.) surrounding the planet Jupiter. **-locuzione** *f.* circumlocution. †**-lo·quio** *m.* See **circonlocuzione**. **-navigazione** *f.* See **circumnavigazione**, under **circumcingere**. See **circoscritto**, under **circoscrivere**. **-stanziare** [A4]. See **circostanziare**, under **circostante**. **-vallare** [A I] *tr.* to circumvallate; to run a road round, to by-pass. **-vallazione** *f.* circumvallation; route that runs right round a city; outer circle; spine-relief road; by-pass. **-venire** [D17] *tr.* to circumvent; to overreach; to outwit. **-venzione** *f.* circumvention. **-vicino** *adj.* circumjacent, round about. **-volare** [A I C] *intr.* (*aux.* avere) to fly round. **-volu·bile** *adj.* that may be rolled round. **-voluto** *adj.* rolled round; (of style) elaborate, involved. **-voluzione** *f.* convolution.

circo-scri·vere [C12] *tr.* to circumscribe, to restrict; to describe in minute detail. **-scritto** *part. adj.* circumscribed; (geom.) inscribed. **-scrizione** *f.* circumscription; (admin.; judicial) district; -scrizione elettorale, electoral ward.

circo-spetto *adj.* circumspect, wary, cautious, guarded. **-spettamente** *adv.* circumspectly, guardedly. **-spezione** *f.* circumspection.

circost-ante *adj.* nearby; neighbouring; surrounding; *n.m.,* *f.* bystander; person standing near; l'udirono appena i -anti, even those standing near could hardly hear him. **-anza** *f.* circumstance; occasion; alla -anza, if the opportunity arises, *or* according to circumstances; in quella -anza, on that occasion; dire alcune parole di -anza, to say a few words suitable to the occasion; (leg.) -anza aggravante, aggravating circumstance; -anza attenuante, extenuating circumstance. **-anziale** *adj.* circumstantial. **-anziare** [A4] *tr.* to circumstantiate. **-anziato** *part. adj.* circumstantiated; with all the circumstances set out. **-anziatamente** *adv.* circumstantially, in detail.

circu·ire [D 2] *tr.* to surround; to encircle; to circumvent; to entrap; to get round (a person), to wheedle, to coax. **-imento** *m.* surrounding; circumventing; getting round, wheedling, coaxing. †**-ità** *f.* circle; cycle. **-itazione** *f.* circulation. **-ito** *part. adj.* surrounded. **-izione** *f.* surrounding; round-about speech, circumlocution.

circu·ito¹ *m.* circuit; (electr.) chiudere il —, to connect the circuit; aprire il —, to break the circuit; — chiuso, close circuit; — aperto, open circuit; — corto, short circuit; circumlocution; round race; circuit; track (motor, motorcycle racing, cycling); (naut.) — di combattimento, action emergency circuit; — segnali, navigation circuits; †round (in a dance).

circuito² *part.* of **circuire**, q.v.

circulare [A 1 s]. See **circolare**.

circum·cin·gere [C 5] *tr.* to surround, to close in on, to circumscribe. **-circa** *adv.* about, more or less, near enough. **-navigazione** *f.* circum-navigation, sailing round. **-padano** *adj.* see **circompadano**. **-polare** *adj.* see **circompolare**, under **circompadano**.

Cirena·ica *pr.n.f.* (geog.) Cyrenaica.

Cirene *pr.n.f.* (geog.) Cyrene.

cirene·o *adj.* Cyrenian; *n.m.* one who labours for another's benefit or who suffers for another (from Simon the Cyrenian who carried Christ's cross).

ciribolla *f.* (Bologn. cul.) soup of beans and polenta.

cirie·gia *f.* (Tusc.). See **ciliegia**.

†**cirie·gio** *m.* See **ciliegio**.

cir(i)egiuolo *adj.* cherry-coloured; *n.m.* a variety of vine; a kind of liqueur.

cir·illiano, -il·lico *adj.* Cyrillic.

cirimbrac·cola *f.* See **cimbraccola**.

cirimo·ia *f.* (bot.) Peruvian custard apple, *Annona cherimolia.*

cirimo·nia *f.* See **cerimonia**.

cirindello *m.* little scrap.

ciri(u)ol·a *f.* (ichth.) young eel, elver. **-are** [A 1] *intr.* (aux. avere) to wriggle like an eel.

cirlo *m.* (orn.) cirl bunting.

cirmola *f.* (bot.). See **cirimoia**.

†**cirne·o** *adj.* Corsican; *n.m.* il Cirneo, Napoleon.

†**ciro** *m.* pig.

cirr·o¹ *m.* curl; tendril; (meteor.) cirrus, cirrus cloud, fleecy cloud. **-ato** *adj.* curly. **-i·fero** *adj.* (bot.) furnished with tendrils. **-iforme** *adj.* (bot.) tendril-shaped, cirriform. **-ocu·mulo** *m.* (meteor.) cirro-cumulus. **-ostrato** *m.* (meteor.) cirro-stratus.

cirr·o² *adj.* (med.) scirrhus. **-osi** *f.* (med.) scirrhosity.

cirrostrato *m.* See under **cirro¹**.

cirso·cele *f.* (med.) cirsocele. **-tomi·a** *f.* (surg.) cirsotomy.

†**cirugi·a**, †**cirurgi·a** *f.* See **chirurgia**.

cirus·co *adj.* (*m.pl.* **-chi**) (Tusc.) short-sighted; squinting, squint-eyed.

cisale *m.* (agric.) bank to mark the boundary of a field.

cisalpino *adj.* cisalpine, south of the Alps; (hist.) La Repubblica -a, the republic established by the French with capital at Milan and lasting from 1797–1804; *adv.* alla cisalpina, according to fashion current under the Cisalpine Republic; *n.f.* La Cisalpina, the Cisalpine Republic; *m.pl.* Cisalpini, soldiers of the Cisalpine Republic.

ciscrann·a *f.* armchair; seat-locker with moveable back; (colloq.) piece of lumber; (fam.) worn-out old woman. †**-o** *m.* bookshelf; bookshelves, bookcase.

†**cisello** *m.* See **cesello**.

ci·si·o *m.* (Rom. antiq.) *cisium,* light two-wheeled carriage. **-a·rio** *m.* (Rom. antiq.) driver of a *cisium.*

†**cisma** *f.* disagreement; essere in — con, to be at loggerheads with; averci della —, to be annoyed with.

cismarino *adj.* on this side of the sea; (geog. hist.) Pars cismarina, colonies between Sicily, Sardinia and Majorca.

cismontano *adj.* on this side of the mountain(s).

†**ciso·ie** *f.pl.* See **cesoie**.

cisolfaut, cisolfaut·te *m. indecl.* (mus.) C sol fa ut, middle C.

ciso·rio *m.* (vet.) trimming or cutting instrument.

cisp·a *f.* rheum in the eyes; blear-eyed person. **-ardo** *adj.*, **-ellino** *adj.* blear-eyed. **-icoso** *adj.* full of rheum. †**-o** *adj.* see **cisposo**. **-osità** *f.* ble*aredness; blear-eyed appearance. **-oso** *adj.* blear-eyed; bleary; l'età -osa, old age.

cispadan·o *adj.* south of the river Po; (hist.) Repubblica -a, the

Republic established in 1796 under Napoleon with Bologna as capital.

cisso·ide *f.* (math.) cissoid.

cist·a¹ *f.* (archaeol.) cist. **-o·fora** *f.* (archaeol.) cist-bearer.

cista² *f.* (in the game of macao) nought.

ciste *f.* (med.). See **cisti**.

cisterc(i)ense *adj.* Cistercian; *n.m.* Cistercian (monk).

cisterna *f.* cistern, tank, reservoir; acqua di —, rain-water; (naut.) water-tanker; nave —, tanker.

cisti *f.* (med.) cyst; (anat.) bladder.

cisticerco *m.* (biol.; med.) cysticercus, hydatid.

ci·stici *m.pl.* (zool.) cestodes.

ci·st·ico *adj.* (anat.; med.) cystic. **-ifelle·a, -ifel·lea** *f.* (anat.) gall-bladder. **-iflogi·a** *f.* (med.) inflammation of the bladder. **-ina** *f.* (chem.) cystine. **-ite** *f.* (med.) cystitis, inflammation of the bladder. **-oscopi·a** *f.* (med.) cystoscopy. **-osco·pio** *m.* (med.) cystoscope. **-otomi·a** *f.* (surg.) cystotomy, operation to remove gall stones.

ci·stide *f.* (med.). See **cisti**.

cisto, ci·stio *m.* (bot.) *Cistus,* white or pink-flowered shrubby rockrose.

cita·bile *adj.* See under **citare**.

citante *part. adj., n.m., f.* (leg.). See under **citare**.

ci·t·ara *f.* (mus.) cithara. **-aredi·a** *f.* singing to the accompaniment of the cithara. **-are·dico** *adj.* (mus.) citharoedic. **-aredo** *m.* (mus.) citharist, citharoedus. **-areggiare** [A 3 c] *intr.* (aux. avere) (mus.) to play the cithara. **-arino** *m.* (mus.) see **chitarrino**, under **chitarra**. **-arista** *m.* (mus.) citharist. **-ari·stica** *f.* (mus.) art of cithara-playing; art of string-playing; lyric poetry. **-ari·stico** *adj.* (mus.) citharistic, citharoedic. **-arizzare** [A 1] *intr.* (aux. avere) (mus.) to play the cithara, to citharize. **-arizzatore** *m.* (mus.) citharist. **-arodi·a** *f.* (mus.) solo singing to the cithara. **-aro·do** *m.* (mus.) one who sings to the cithara. **-arrino** *m.* (mus.) see **chitarrino**, under **chitarra**. **-era** *f.* (mus.) see **cetra¹**.

cit·are [A 1] *tr.* to quote; to cite; (leg.) to summon officially to appear in court of law as party or witness; to cite, to quote (an authority) as proof, precedent, etc. **-a·bile** *adj.* citable, quotable. **-ante** *part. adj., n.m., f.* (leg.) plaintiff. **-ato** *part. adj.* cited, quoted, adduced; (lit. hist.) autori -ati, authors whose works are accepted as standard texts by the Accademia della Crusca. **-azione** *f.* citation, quotation; (leg.) summons to appear; notificare una -azione a una persona, to serve a summons on a person.

Cite·r(e)a *pr.n.f.* (myth.) Cytherea, Venus.

citeriore *adj.* (geog.) hither, on this side, nearer.

†**citerna** *f.* See **cisterna**.

citillo *m.* (zool.) European ground squirrel, souslik, *Citellus citellus.*

citino *m.* (bot.) pomegranate flower; fruit of carob or tamarina; *Cytinus hypocistus,* parasite on roots of *Cistus.*

ci·tiso *m.* (bot.) laburnum, *Laburnum anagyroides* and *alpinum;* virgiliano, tree-medick, moon trefoil, *Medicago arborea.*

cito-die·resi *f.* (biol.) cleavage (of a cell). **-o·lisi** *f.* (biol.) cytolysis. **-ologi·a** *f.* cytology. **-olo·gico** *adj.* (biol.) cytological. **-opla·sma** *m.* (biol.) cytoplasm.

citofono *m.* internal telephone.

citra-conato *m.* (chem.) citraconate. **-co·nico** *adj.* (chem.) citraconic.

citrag·gine *f.* (bot.). See **cedroncella**, under **cedro¹**.

citramontano *adj.* on this side of the mountain(s), cismontane.

citr·ato *m.* (chem.) citrate; (pharm.) — di magnesio, a mild laxative, citrate of magnesia; (phot.) carta al —, aristo paper. †**-iata** *f.* drink flavoured with lemon, lime, or orange. **-ino** *adj.* lemon-yellow; *n.m.* (miner.) citrine, false topaz.

ci·trico *adj.* (chem.) citric.

citri(u)olo *m.* See **cetriuolo**.

citroniera *f.* glasshouse, greenhouse; conservatory.

citrull·o *adj.* stupid; *n.m.* silly-billy, fool. **-ag·gine** *f.*, **-eri·a** *f.* foolishness.

†**citta** *f.* lass; little girl (cf. **citto**).

città *f. indecl.* city, town; luce —, parking lights; — di mare, port; — giardino, garden city; — universitaria, University centre; — del Fiore, Florence; — del Naviglio, del panettone, Milan; — del Vespro, — dei Vespri, Palermo; — del Vesuvio, Naples; — della laguna, Venice; — delle Cinque Giornate, Milan; — degli studi, the University area of Milan (Science branch); — dei morti, cemetery; — Eterna, Rome; — Santa, Jerusalem; — del Capo, Cape Town; — del Lago Salato, Salt Lake City.

†**cittad-e** *f.* See **città**. †**-one** *m. augm.* large town or city.

cittadella *f.* citadel; stronghold.

cittadini *f. dim.* of **città**; small city; woman citizen; one-horse cab.

cittadin-o *adj.* belonging to the city, civic, city; vettura -a, one-horse cab; *n.m.* citizen; city-dweller, inhabitant of a city; — del mondo, citizen of the world, cosmopolite, cosmopolitan; †member of a nation; †subject; †official posted at the gate of a city. **-anza** *f.* body of citizens; citizenship; rights of citizenship; legal residence in a city or commune. †**-are** *tr.* to give rights of citizenship to; to naturalize. **-a·tico** *adj.* (leg.) pertaining to the rights of citizenship; *n.m.* legal right to citizenship. **-esco** *adj.* (*m.pl.* **-eschi**) civil; pertaining to city ways; townish, citified. (**-escamente** *adv.*) **-izzato** *part. adj.* made a citizen, granted citizenship; naturalized.

†**citt-o¹** *m.* lad; child. †**-a** *f.* lass; little girl. †**-olezza** *f.* childhood.

citto² *m.* (Tusc.). See **centesimo**.

ciuc-a *f.*, **-aggine** *f.* See under **ciuco**.

ciucca *f.* (N. Ital., slang) binge.

ciucchello *m.* (N. Ital., slang) dog.

ciuc·cio *m.* donkey, ass (cf. **ciuco**) (naut.) codline.

ciuci-are [A 3] *tr. intr.* (*aux.* avere) to hiss (in disapproval). **-ata** *f.* hiss, hissing. **-ato** *part. adj.* hissed; hissed off the stage.

ciu-co *m.* (*pl.* **-chi**) (pop.) donkey, ass; dunce, idiot; bad-mannered person; dunce's cap; (provb.) il — dà del bue all'asino, the pot calling the kettle black. **-ca** *f.* she-donkey. **-caggine** *f.* stupidity; stubbornness. **-ca·io** *m.* (*pl.* **-ca·i**) donkey-driver. **-cata** *f.* donkey ride; stupid action. **-carello, -cherello, -chetto** *m. dim.* of **ciuco**. **-cheri·a** *f.* stupidity; stubbornness. **-chesco** *adj.* (*m.pl.* **-cheschi**) asinine. **-chino** *adj.* asinine; *n.m. dim.* of **ciuco**.

ciuff-o *m.* tuft; forelock; quiff; tassel; cluster; bunch. †**-agno** *adj.* (of a falcon) skilled at seizing prey. **-are** [A I] *tr.* to seize. **-ata** *f.* seizing; grasping. **-ettino** *m.* child with a forelock; *pr.n.m.* character of the Italian puppet stage. **-etto** *m.* child with a forelock; slap, smack; dare un **-etto** a, to slap; (orn.) sgarza **-etto**, squacco heron, *Ardeola ralloides*. **-one** *m. augm.* of **ciuffo**; person with long, untidy hair.

ciuf·fol-e *f.pl.* trifles. **-o** *m.* tuft; (bot.) robin's cushion, bedeguar, ragged robin (produced on rose bushes by an insect, *Rhodites* sp.).

ciuffolotto *m.* (orn.) bullfinch, *Pyrrhula pyrrhula*; — scarlatto, scarlet grosbeak.

†**ciullo¹** *m.* child; *adj.* stupid.

†**ciullo²** *adj.* experienced, wise; clever; witty; astute.

ciurl-are [A I] *intr.* (*aux.* avere) to shift; — nel manico, to be shifty, to be unreliable, to waver; to fail to fulfil a pledge. **-etto** *m.* (orn.) small wading bird, esp. little stint. **-o** *m.* twirl; (orn.) — marino, glossy ibis; *adj.* tipsy; infatuated. **-one** *m.* blow with the fist which sends the victim spinning. **-otto** *m.* cuff, punch, clout.

ciurm-a¹ *f.* a poor crew, rabble; — scapola, the rowers of a galley who were not chained to the oars. **-a·glia** *f.* rabble, crew, crowd.

†**ciurma²** *f.* See under **ciurmare**.

ciurm-are [A I] *tr.* to charm, to render secure by enchantment; to cheat by charming; to swindle; *rfl.* to get drunk. †**-a** *f.* enchantment, dream, illusion. **-ato** *part. adj.* charmed; bearing a charmed life. **-atore** *m.* charmer; swindler; charlatan, quack. (**-atrice** *f.*) **-ato·rio** *adj.* cheating, swindling, deceitful. **-eri·a** *f.* imposture, trick; winning with soft words; rascally crowd of people.

†**ciu·schero** *adj.* tipsy, 'lit up', 'tight'.

civad-a *f.* (naut.) spritsail. **-iera** *f.*, **-iero** *m.* (naut.) spritsail gaff.

civa·i-a *f.* (usu. *pl.*) leguminous vegetables; †vote. **-(u)olo** *m.* greengrocer.

civanz-o *m.* advantage, saving; gain, profit. †**-a** *f.* see **civanzo**. **-are** *tr.* to provide; *rfl.* to secure, to obtain; to provide for oneself, to look after one's welfare; **-arsi di**, to take advantage of.

civ-are [A I] *tr.* to prime (a gun). **-ato** *part. adj.* primed.

†**cive** *m.* citizen; member of society.

civett-a *f.* (orn.) little owl, *Athene noctua*; caccia alla —, shooting with little owl as lure; (naut.) nave —, decoy ship, Q-boat; (zool.) civet, civet cat; (fig.) flirt; †fare alla —, to duck one's head, to dodge a blow. **-are** [A I] *intr.* (*aux.* avere) to shoot with the little owl as lure; to flirt. **-eri·a** *f.* coquettishness, flirting. **-ino** *m.* young owl; (orn.) scops owl; (fig.) young dandy. **-ìo** *m.* (*pl.* **-ìi**) coquettishness. **-ismo** *m.* dandyism; coquettishness. **-ona** *f.* coquette, flirt. **-one** *m.* dandy, gallant, flirt; coquette, flirt. **-uolo** *adj.* coquettish; fetching; winsome.

ci·vico *adj.* civic, municipal; befitting a good citizen.

civil-e *adj.* civil; well-behaved, well-bred; persona —, gentleman, lady; civilized; (leg.) diritto —, civil law; diritti -i, civil rights; human rights; a person's private (as distinguished from political, etc.) rights and remedies; morte —, civil death, legal death (carrying loss of civil and political rights and standing); tribunale —, civil-law court; codice —, civil code; causa —, civil action, suit (as distinct from, e.g., criminal); azione —, civil action; parte —, party joining in criminal proceedings to claim civil relief, such as damages, against the accused; Stato —, civil status; Ufficio dello Stato —, office of Registrar of Births, Deaths and Marriages; Lista —, Civil List; matrimonio —, register-office marriage; frutti -i, fruits of a pecuniary nature (C.C.); trasporto —, burial without religious rites; abito —, civilian dress; lay dress; colore —, quiet colour (of clothes); coraggio —, moral courage. **-mente** *adv.* civilly; in a well-bred manner. **-ista** *m.* (leg.) lawyer versed in civil law; civil (as distinguished from a criminal) lawyer; middle-class person.

civilizz-are [A I] *tr.* to civilize. **-ato** *part. adj.* civilized. (**-atore** *m.* **-atrice** *f.*) **-azione** *f.* civilization.

civiltà *f.* civility, good manners; civilization.

†**civilt-ade**, †**-ate** *f.* See **civiltà**.

†**civire** *tr.* to provide; to obtain; to get.

civismo *m.* good citizenship, patriotism, civic spirit.

†**ci·vita** *f.* city (still used in place-names, e.g. **Civitavecchia**).

†**civo** *m.* see **cibo**; (mil. hist.) priming, gunpowder placed in the pan of a firearm.

ci·volo *m.* (aeron.) platform for launching seaplanes.

†**cizza** *f.* nipple; breast.

clacchettista *m.* (theatr.) tap-dancer.

clacson *m. indecl.* (motor.) horn.

†**clade** *f.* slaughter.

†**clam-are** *intr.* to shout; to call out. †**-anza** *f.*, †**-azione** *f.* shout; call; crying out.

cla·mid-e *f.* (archaeol.) cloak, chlamys. **-ato** *adj.* wearing a cloak.

clamor-e *m.* clamour; outcry; din, noise. **-oso** *adj.* clamorous; noisy; sensational; è un successo -oso, it's a *succès fou*, it's a sensational success; *n.m.* noisy person. **-osamente** *adv.* noisily.

clampa *f.* (miner.) clamp.

clan *m. indecl.* (pron. as Fr.) clan; coterie.

clandestina *f.* (bot.) toothwort, *Lathraea squamaria*.

clandestin-o *adj.* clandestine, secret; underground. **-amente** *adv.* clandestinely, in secret, secretly, under cover.

†**clan·gere** *intr.* to sound the trumpet; to sound the clarion.

clangore *m.* sound of a trumpet; metallic noise, clang.

claque¹ *f.* (pron. as Fr.) claque; capo della —, paid ringleader of a claque.

†**claque²** *f.* over-shoe, galosh.

claretto *m.* claret; (mus.) see **clarino**.

clarificare [A 2s] and derivs. See **chiarificare**.

clarin-o *m.* (mus.) clarino, high-pitched trumpet; clarinet. **-etto** *m.* (mus.) clarinet. **-ettista** *m.* clarinettist. **-ista** *m.* clarino-player.

Clarissa¹ *pr.n.f.* Clarissa.

clarissa² *f.* (eccl.) Poor Clare.

†**claro** *adj.* and derivs. See **chiaro**.

clarone *m.* (mus.) bass clarinet.

classare [A I] and derivs. See under **classe**.

class-e *f.* class; di —, high-class; fuori —, unequalled; è un fuori —, he's in a class on his own, there's no one to touch him; (mil.) year; (archaeol.) fleet. **-are** [A I] *tr.* to class. **-atore** *m.* (industr.) screen; (paperm.) chip screen. **-azione** *f.* classing, classification. **-ia·rio** *m.* (Rom. hist.) marine. **-ismo** *m.* (pol.) tendency to seek support from a social class.

clas·sic-o¹ *adj.* classic, classical; libro —, standard work; classic; questa è -a! that's a good one!; vino —, wine of guaranteed excellence, 'appellation contrôlée'; *n.m.* classic. **-amente** *adv.* classically. **-ismo** *m.* classicism; (liter. hist.) classical school of writers, classicism. **-ista** *m.* classicist, classic. **-ità** *f. indecl.* quality of a classic; classical tendencies. **-izzare** [A I] *intr.* (*aux.* avere) to tend towards classicism.

clas·sico² *m.* (Rom. antiq.) trumpet-call; trumpet.

classi·fica *f.* (sport) classified results; (at school) mark; (in an exam.) class-list; sorting, classification.

classific-are [A 2 s] *tr.* to classify; to assess, to mark. **-a·bile** *adj.* classifiable. **-ato** *part. adj.* classified; assessed, marked. **-atore** *m.* classifier. (**-atrice** *f.*) **-azione** *f.* classification; marking.

classismo *m.* See under **classe**.

cla·stico *adj.* (geol.) clastic.

clatro *m.* gate; (bot.) genus of fungi.

†**cla·udere** *vb.* and derivs. See **chiudere**.

Cla·udia *pr.n.f.* Claudia; *f. adj.* susina —, greengage.

claudic-are [A2s] *intr.* (*aux.* avere) to limp. **-azione** *f.* limping; affection of the lower limbs.

†**cla·udo** *adj.* lame, limping.

cla·usola *f.* clause, proviso; (rhet.) close of a sentence, rhythmical cadence, clausula; — aggiuntiva, — addizionale, rider; — scappatoia, escape clause; (mus.) cadence.

claustr-o *m.* (poet.) cloister, enclosure. **-ale** *adj.* claustral, of the cloister, monastic; *n.m.pl.* i -ali, monks and nuns (esp. of enclosed orders). **-ofili·a** *f.* love of confined spaces. **-ofobi·a** *f.* claustrophobia.

cla·usula *f.* See **clausola**.

clausura *f.* (eccl.) monastic or conventual enclosure; religious house with strict enclosure; prohibition of entry.

clav-a *f.* club; policeman's truncheon. †**-adura** *f.* nailing; piercing; wound made with nails. **-iforme** *adj.* club-shaped; (bot.) clavate.

clavi-cem·balo *m.*, †**-cim·balo** *m.* (mus.) harpsichord; Il — ben temperato, The Forty-Eight (Preludes and Fugues of Bach). **-cembalista** *m.* (mus.) harpsichord-player. **-cor·dio**, **-cordo** *m.* (mus.) clavichord. **-or·gano** *m.* (mus.) claviorganum, an instrument combining harpsichord and organ.

clavi·col-a *f.* (anat.) clavicle, collar-bone. **-a·re** *adj.* clavicular.

claviforme *adj.* See under **clava**.

clavi·gero[1] *m.* key-bearer (e.g. St Peter).

clavi·gero[2] *adj.* armed with a club; *n.m.* club-bearer (e.g. Hercules).

clavior·gano *m.* (mus.). See under **clavicembalo**.

clavo[1] *m.* (med.) callus, usu. on the sclera; fungus disease of olive trees; (naut.) tiller.

†**clavo**[2] *m.* nail; stud; (bot.) clove; (Rom. antiq.) lato —, laticlave (stripe on Senator's dress).

clefta *m.* klepht, Greek brigand.

cleidomastoide·o *adj.* (anat.) cleido-mastoid.

clem-a·tide *f.* (bot.) wild clematis, traveller's joy, old man's beard, *Clematis flammula, C. vitalba,* and other species, including garden hybrids. **-atite** *f.* twig prepared for a graft.

clement-e[1] *adj.* mild, clement; benign. (**-emente** *adv.*)

Clemente[2] *pr.n.m.* Clement.

Clementina *pr.n.f.* Clementine.

clementino[1] *adj.* (eccl. hist.) Clementine.

clementino[2] *m.* (agric.) clementine.

Clementino[3] *pr.n.m.* Clementine.

clemenza *f.* clemency; mildness; tolerance; leniency; atti di —, provisions by which prisoners may be set free or pardoned.

clepsidra *f.* See **clessidra**.

clepte *f.pl.* (ent.) cuckoo wasps, *Cleptes* spp.

clept-o·mane *adj., n.m., f.* kleptomaniac. **-omani·a** *f.* kleptomania. **-osco·pio** *m.* periscope.

clergyman *m. indecl.* (pron. as Eng.) Anglican clergyman; (neol.) Anglo-Saxon clerical dress (black suit and reversed collar as against cassock, religious habit, etc.).

clerical-e *adj.* (eccl.; pol.) clerical; *n.m.* member of clerical party; (pol.) person favourable to political influence of Church and clergy. (**-mente** *adj.*) **-eggiare** [A3c] *intr.* (*aux.* avere) (pol.) to side with the clerical party. **-ismo** *m.* (pol.) clericalism.

†**cle·rico** *adj.* See **chierico**.

clero[1] *m.* (eccl.) clergy.

†**clero**[2] *adj.* See **chiaro**.

cleromanzi·a *f.* cleromancy, divination by lots.

†**cle·sia** *f.* See **chiesa**.

clessidra *f.* clepsydra, water-clock; hour-glass.

†**clibana·rio** *m.* cavalry soldier wearing armour.

cliché *m. indecl.* (pron. as Fr.) (typ.) block; illustration; cliché, commonplace.

clidono·grafo *m.* (electr.) klydonograph.

client-e *m.* client, customer. **-ela** *f.* customers, clientele; patronage. †**-olo**, †**-ulo** *m.* hanger-on, partisan, adherent.

clima *m.* climate; zone; (naut.) — marittimo, coastal climate having a temperature range of under 15° C.

†**climat-e**, **-o** *m.* See **clima**.

climate·rico *adj.* climacteric.

clim-a·tico *adj.* climatic; stazione climatica, health resort; fare una cura climatica, to go to a health resort. **-atologi·a** *f.* climatology.

cli·max *m. indecl.* (rhet.) climax.

clime·n-io, **-o** *m.* (bot.) everlasting pea, *Lathyrus latifolius*.

†**climo** *m.* See **clima**.

cli·nic-a *f.* clinic, practical teaching of medicine at the bedside; (in University or teaching hospitals) department, section; nursing-home. **-o** *adj.* clinical; l'occhio -o, experienced doctor's ability to diagnose illness at a glance; (fig.) expert eye; experienced eye; *n.m.* doctor teaching at a University, clinical professor; (eccl.) sick person given 'clinical' baptism.

clino *m.* (ichth.) — argentato, *Cristiceps argentatus*, a kind of blenny.

clin-o·grafo *m.* (mining) clinograph. **-o·metro** *m.* clinometer; spirit level.

clinopo·dio *m.* (bot.) wild basil, *Clinopodium vulgare*.

clio *f.* (myth.) Clio, muse of History.

cli·pe-o *m.* (Rom. antiq.) clipeus, shield. **-ato** *adj.* armed with a clipeus, bearing a shield.

clisce *m. indecl.* See **cliché**.

cliso·pompa *f.* (med.) injection apparatus.

cliste·re *m.* (med.) enema, douche.

clistron *m. indecl.* (electron.) klystron.

clito·rid-e *f.* (anat.) clitoris. **-e·o** *adj.* (anat.) pertaining to the clitoris.

clivag·gio *m.* (chem.; miner.) cleavage.

clivo *m.* hill, rise, slope.

cli·zia *f.* (bot.) common sunflower, *Helianthus annuus*.

cloa·ca *f.* sewer; — massima, main drain; (zool.) cloaca.

clodiense *adj.* (geog.) of, relating to, Chioggia.

clo·nico *adj.* (med.) clonic.

clor-ale, **-a·lio** *m.* (chem.) chloral. **-ite** *f.* (miner.) chlorite.

clo·rico *adj.* (chem.) chloric.

clor-o *m.* (chem.) chlorine. **-ato** *adj.* chlorinated; *n.m.* (chem.) chlorate. **-idrato** *m.* hydrochloride. **-i·drico** *adj.* hydrochloric. **-ite** *f.* (miner.) chlorite. **-obromuro** *m.* (photogr.) carta al -obromuro, gaslight paper. **-ofilla** *f.* chlorophyll. **-ofor·mio** *m.* chloroform. **-oformizzare** *tr.* to chloroform. **-oformizzatore** *m.* assistant giving chloroform. **-omicetina** *f.* (pharm.) chloromycetin, chloramphenicol. **-osi** *f.* (med.) chlorosis. **-o·tico** *adj.* chlorotic; anaemic. **-urare** [A1] *tr.* to chlorinate. **-urazione** *f.* chlorination. **-uro** *m.* (chem.) chloride.

club *m. indecl.* (pron. clœb) club; society; — nautico, yacht club; — alpino, Alpine Club.

clune *m., f.* buttock.

cluniacense *adj.* (eccl.) Cluniac.

†**co**[1] *prep.* See **con**.

†**co**[2] *adv.* See **come**.

†**co**[3] *m.* head; (of rivers) mettere — a, to flow into; end, foot; in — del ponte, at the foot of the bridge; in — dell'anno, at the end of the year.

co' *prep.* (Tusc.). See **coi**, under **con**.

coabit-are [A1s] *intr.* (*aux.* avere) to cohabit, to live together. (**-atore** *m.* **-atrice** *f.*) **-azione** *f.* cohabitation, living together.

coaccade·mico *m.* member of the same academy; colleague, fellow.

coaccusato *m.* (leg.) co-defendant (in criminal proceedings).

coacerv-are [A1] *tr.* to heap up; to accumulate. (**-ato** *part. adj.*) **-azione** *f.* heaping; heap. **-o** *m.* medley; heap, pile; (finan.) -o degli interessi, accumulation of interest; aggregate; aggregated value; (chem.) coacervate.

coad-erire [D2] *intr.* (*aux.* avere) to cohere. **-erente** *adj.* coherent. **-esione** *f.* cohesion; adhesion.

coadiut-ore *m.* assistant, coadjutor, fellow-helper; (eccl.) coadjutor; curate. (**-rice** *f.*) **-orato** *m.*, **-ori·a** *f.* coadjutorship.

coadiuv-are [A1s] *tr.* to assist. **-ante** *part. adj.* assisting; *n.m.* (techn.) -ante della filtrazione, filtration aid. (**-ato** *part. adj.*)

coadun-are [A1] *tr.* to conjoin. (**-ato** *part. adj.* **-azione** *f.*)

coagolare *vb.* See **coagulare**.

coagul-are [A1s] *tr.* to (cause to) coagulate; *rfl.* to coagulate; (of milk) to curdle; (of blood) to clot. (**-a·bile** *adj.* **-amento** *m.*) **-ativo** *adj.* coagulative. **-ato** *part. adj.* coagulated. **-azione** *f.* coagulation.

coa·gulo *m.* curds, coagulum; coagulation; rennet.

coaiutore *m.* See **coadiutore**.

coalescenza *f.* coalescence.

coal-ire [D2] *intr.* (*aux.* avere) to join together, to unite. **-izione** *f.* (pol.) coalition; governo di -izione, coalition government. **-izzare** [A1] *intr.* (*aux.* avere), *rfl.* to form a coalition; *tr.* to form into a coalition. (**-izzato** *part. adj.*)

coallievo *m.* fellow-pupil; fellow-disciple.

coalterno *adj.* (math.) alternate with another (of angles).

coamministratore *m.* joint-manager, co-director.

coapo·stolo *m.* (rel.) co-apostle, fellow-apostle.

coart-are [A I] *tr.* to constrain, to coerce; to compress; to restrict. (**-ato** *part. adj.*) **-azione** *f.* coercion.

†coaso *m.* (zool.) polecat.

coassiale *adj.* (techn.) coaxial.

coattazione *f.* knitting together (of bones).

coatt-o *adj.* (leg.) compulsory; forced; domicilio —, internment; liquidazione -a amministrativa, compulsory winding-up and dissolution (C.C.). **-ivo** *adj.* coercive.

coautore *m.* co-author, joint author; joint perpetrator.

coazione *f.* coercion; compulsion.

cobalt-o *m.* (chem.; miner.) cobalt. **-ina** *f.* see **cobaltite. -ite** *f.* (miner.) cobaltite.

cob·bola *f.* (prosod.) cobla (in Provençal verse); stanza.

cobe·a *f.* (bot.) cups-and-saucers (an ornamental climber), *Cobaea scandens.*

cobice *m.* (ichth.) Adriatic sturgeon, *Acipenser naccarii.*

cobite *m.* (ichth.) — barbatello, *Cobitis barbatula,* — fluviale, *C. taenia,* two species of roach.

cobla, co·bola *f.* (prosod.). See **cobbola.**

coboldo *m.* kobold, brownie, pixie, gnome.

cobra *f.* (zool.) cobra.

Coburgo *pr.n.f.* (geog.) Coburg; Sassonia-Coburgo, Saxe-Coburg.

coca[1] *f.* (pop.). See **cuoca.**

coc-a[2] *f.* (bot.) coca, a Peruvian shrub, *Erythroxylon coca,* which yields cocaine. **-ai·na** *f.* cocaine. **-ainismo** *m.,* **-ainomani·a** *f.* addiction to cocaine. **-aino·mane** *m.* cocaine addict.

coc-ca[1] *f.* notch in an arrow for the cord of the bow; flap; turned-up corner of a handkerchief, napkin, tablecloth, etc.; knot, kink; top, point; far le -che, to snap one's fingers; (naut. hist.) ship, usu. three-master, of medieval times; square sail; (text.) bead, button or knot at either end of a spindle to prevent the thread flying off; †summit, hill-top. **†-care** *vb.* see **accoccare. -china** *f. dim.* (naut.) spare sail. **-cone** *m. augm.* (naut.) storm sail.

†cocca[2] *f.* See **cocco.**

coccarda *f.* cockade; plait of ribbons of national colours; favour, ribbon or rosette worn as sign of support.

†coccare[1] *vb.* See **accoccare.**

†coccare[2] *tr.* to mock, to make fun of; to hoax.

coccerello *m. dim.* See under **coccio.**

coc·chia *f.* (naut.) trawl net.

cocchier-e *m.* coachman. **†-essa** *f.* coachman's wife.

cocchino *m.* cheat.

coc·chio *m.* (Rom. antiq.) chariot; two-wheeled carriage.

cocchium-e *m.* bung; bung-hole. **-are** [A I] *tr.* to plug, to close with a bung; to trick. **-atoio** *m.* bung-borer.

coc·c-ia *f.* (*pl.* -e) hilt, guard of a sword; sabre, foil, épée; swelling, protuberance; ornamentation on the butt of a pistol; bowl of a pipe; shell of a tortoise or mollusc; (colloq.) head, topknot; aver la — dura, to be pig-headed. **-iare** [A 3] *tr.* to butt, to bump into with one's head.

coccia·i-a *f.,* **-o** *m.* See under **coccio.**

cocciare[1] [A 3]. See under **coccia.**

cocciare[2] [A 3]. See under **coccio**[1].

coc·c-ige *m.* (anat.) coccyx. **-i·geo** *adj.* (anat.) coccygeal.

Coccincina *pr.n.f.* (geog.) Cochin-China; (bot.) clove-bark tree, *Dicypellium caryophyllatum.*

coccinella *f.* (ent.) ladybird beetle.

coccinello *m.* (naut.) toggle.

†cocci·neo *adj.* dark red.

coccini·glia *f.* (ent.) cochineal insect; cochineal (dye).

coccino[1] *m.* scarlet cloth.

coccino[2] *m.* See under **coccio**[1].

coc-c-io[1] *m.* (*pl.* -i) potsherd; cracked pot; fragment of pottery; *pl.* broken, chipped or cracked crockery; attento a non far -i! mind you don't drop (or break) the china; pigliar i -i, to lose one's temper; (provb.) chi rompe paga e i -i sono suoi, what's done is ended; shell of a mollusc; husk, outer covering of a seed; hand-warmer; delicate, ailing person. **-erello** *m.* (Tusc.) delicate, ailing person. **-iac·cio** *m.* hand-warmer, small brazier; delicate person. **-ia·ia** *f.* crockery cupboard. **-ia·io** *m.* crockery-seller; potter. **-iare** [A 3] *intr.* (*aux.* avere) to be fond of huddling over the fire;

to sit holding a charcoal brazier for warmth. **-ione** *m.,* **-ino** *m.* (Tusc.) mollycoddle, one who huddles over the fire.

coc·cio[2] *m.* (ichth.) *Trigla lyra* and *T. lucerna,* kinds of gurnard.

cocciola[1] *f.* (zool.) cockle, *Cardium edule,* and various other edible bivalves; — zizza, heart shell, *Isocardium cor.*

cocci(u)ola[2] *f.* small swelling caused by an insect bite.

cocciut-o *adj.* pig-headed, stubborn; stiff-necked, proud. **-ag·gine** *f.* pig-headedness; pride.

cocco[1] *m.* kermes, cochineal; coccus; scarlet cloth.

coc-co[2] *m.* (*pl.* -chi) (infant.) egg, 'chucky egg'; (term of endearment) 'ducky'; — di mamma, mother's darling.

coc-co[3] *m.* (*pl.* -chi) (bot.) — malefico, poisonous fungus, fly agaric, *Amanita muscaria.*

coc-co[4] *m.* (*pl.* -chi) (bot.) coconut palm, *Cocos nucifera;* noce di —, coconut; (text.) coco; fibra di —, coir, coconut hair.

coc-co[5] *m.* (*pl.* -chi) (bacter.) coccus.

coccodè *m. indecl.* (onomat.) the cackle of a hen after she has laid an egg.

coccodrillo *m.* (zool.) crocodile.

coc·cola *f.* (bot.) globular fruit of various plants; hoary cress, *Cardaria draba;* (joc.) head, 'knob'; *pl.* (bot.) coccole di Levante, fruits of *Anamirta cocculus;* (pop.) berries and small cones of various plants; trinkets, odds and ends.

†coccolina *f.* (med.) chill, cold.

coc·col-o *m.* delicious treat; sort of pastry; cuddly baby; (term of endearment) — mio! my love! **-are** [A I s] *tr.* to cuddle; *rfl.* to nestle; to mollycoddle oneself. **-ato** *part. adj.* spoilt, mollycoddled. **-one** *m.* (pop.) apoplectic fit; (fig.) gli è venuto un -one, he had a fit, he was dumbfounded; (orn.) see **croccolone;** *adj.* cuddlesome; *adv.* see **coccoloni. -oni** *adv.* squatting.

†coc·colo[2] *m.* cochineal, coccus.

coccon-e *m.* (naut. hist.) galleon; (mil. hist.) wooden wad used in a mortar for throwing stones. **-etto** *m.* (cards) a variety of 'tressette', q.v.

†coccoveg·gia *f.* (orn.). See **civetta.**

coccoveggiare [A 3 c] *intr.* (*aux.* avere) to flirt; to hoot like an owl; *tr.* to mock, to make fun of.

coc-ente *adj.* scorching, searing, burning; ardent; intense; pungent; violent. (**-entemente** *adv.*) **-imento** *m.* roasting; cooking. **-iore** *m.* burning; heat. **-itoio** *adj.* easy to cook, good for cooking. **-itore** *m.* baker's assistant; assistant salt-boiler. (**-itrice** *f.*) **-itura** *f.* cooking. **-iucchiare** [A 4] *tr.* to cook slightly. **-iuto** *part. adj.* displeased, upset; †cooked; †(fig.) chewed over.

†cochi·glia, †cochilla *f.* See **conchiglia.**

Cocincina *pr.n.f.* (geog.) Cochin-China.

co·cle-a *f.* spiral staircase; screw; Archimedean screw; (anat.) cochlea. **-ato** *adj.* spiral, winding.

co·clide *f.* (archit.) spiral column.

cocò *f.* (slang) cocaine, 'coke'.

co·cola *f.* (bot.). See **coccola.**

cocoll-a *f.* (eccl.) cowl; (bot.) an edible fungus, *Amanita curtipes.* **-ato** *adj.* (eccl.) cowled, wearing a cowl.

cocomer-o *m.* (bot.) water-melon, *Citrullus vulgaris;* — asinino, — salvatico, squirting cucumber, *Ecballium elaterium;* (colloq.) avere un — in corpo, to have a skeleton in one's cupboard. **-aio** *m.* water-melon bed; water-melon seller. **-ata** *f.* feed of water-melon. **-ello, -ino** *m. dim.* of cocomero; stud; nail. **-uzzo** *m.* stud; nail.

cocorita *f.* (orn.) green parakeet, *Bolborhyncus monachus.*

cocoruzzo *m.* (geog.) summit shaped like a pear.

cocotte *f.* (pron. as in Fr.) prostitute, street-walker.

cocuzz-a *f.* (fam.) pumpkin, head; far la — a uno, to cut off someone's head; *excl.* **-e!** bless my soul!

cocuz·zolo *m.* crown (of the head or of a hat); top of a mountain; topknot; very top, tip; heel of a loaf.

cod-a *f.* tail; avere la — di paglia, to have good reason to be afraid, to have a weak case; con la — fra le gambe, (of a dog) with its tail between its legs; (provb.) botta che non chiese, non ebbe — who doesn't ask, doesn't get; non aver nè capo nè —, (of a speech) to be rambling, to make no sense, to be incoherent; a — di rondine, dovetailed, (of a coat) swallow-tailed; far di testa —, to about turn; sapere dove il diavolo ha la —, to know how many beans make five; queue; fare la —, to queue (up); (mus.) coda, concluding passage; tail (of a note); pianoforte a —, grand piano; pigtail; — di cavallo, pony-tail (hair-style); parrucca

cod-a (*cont.*)

con la —, reactionary person; aver la —, to have reactionary views; (fig.) reactionary; train (of a dress, etc.); (prosod.) coda; sonetto con la —, caudated sonnet; bottom (e.g. of a table); corner (of the eye); fanale di —, tail-light, rear light; (radio) down-lead (of aerial); (photog.) leader (of film); (aeron.) piani di —, empennage; (herald.) queue, tail; — forcata, queue fourchy; (bot.) — del grappolo (stalk of a bunch of grapes); — di cavallo, — cavallina, — equina, horse-tail, *Equisetum arvense, E. telmateia*; — acquatica, mare's tail; *Hippuris vulgaris*; hornwort, *Ceratophyllum demersum*; — di prato, — di topo, meadow foxtail, *Alopecurus pratensis*; — di sorcio, mousetail, *Myosurus minimus*; — di lepre, hare's tail, *Lagurus ovatus*; — di leone, mullein, *Verbascum*; -e russe, prince's feathers, *Amarantus hybridus* var. *hypochondriacus*; (comm.) — della cambiale, allonge; (ichth.) — del prelato, sting ray, *Dasybatius violaceus*. **-ato** *adj.* tailed, having a tail. †**-azza** *f.* tail end; rearguard. **-azzo** *m.* train of people (paying court to some personage). **-etta** *f. dim.* of **coda**; cedilla placed under a Latin *e* to show that it represents a diphthong; in official or business letters, the name and titles of the addressee written on the left of the first page; lash of a whip; (bootm.) the ends of the vamp which are sewn to the quarters; *pl.* disease of silkworms; tailings of flour; (naut.) warp attached from the stern to a kedge-anchor for bringing a vessel broadside on; stern line; rope's end, tail; tail of a column; cod of a net; -etta di bandiera, fly of a flag; -etta del gavitello, swifter; -etta di porco, perruque of tobacco; -etta di ratto, bock splice; -etta di topo, pointing; -etta di vacca, frayed rope's end; (mus.) short coda; codetta, short phrase following the end of a fugue-subject. **-ina** *f. dim.* of **coda**. **-ino** *m.* pigtail; reactionary. **-one** *m. augm.* of **coda**; rearguard; tail-piece (of a gun, etc.); tail-strap (of harness). **-uto** *adj.* tailed, having a tail; (orn.) pin-tail, *Anas acuta*.

codaga·pala *f.* (bot.) conessi bark, bark of *Holarrhena antidysenterica*.

codalunga *f.* (ichth.) thresher or fox shark, *Alopias vulpinus*.

codard-o *adj.* cowardly; (herald.) leone —, lion coward, lion with its tail between its legs; *n.m.* coward. (**-a** *f.*) **-amente** *adv.* in a cowardly manner. **-i·a** *f.* cowardliness, cowardice. †**-i·gia** *f.* cowardice.

codatre·mola *f.* (orn.). See **coditremola**, under **codirosso**.

code *f.pl.* (bot.) Love-lies-bleeding, *Amarantus caudatus*.

codeina *f.* (chem.) codeine.

code·sto *prn., adj.* See **cotesto**.

codiare *tr.* [A4] to tail, to trail, to follow.

codibu·gnolo *m.* (orn.) long-tailed tit, *Ægithalos caudatus*.

†**codicalca** *f.* (joc.) train (of a garment).

co·dic-e *m.* codex; manuscript; code; inciampare nel —, to fall foul of the law; (naut.) — internazionale, international code; (leg.) code; the body of the law on a given subject, or in a given field, reduced into a settled text; — civile, civil code; — militare, military code; — commerciale, commercial code; — penale, penal code, criminal code; — napoleonico, Code Napoléon. †**-o** *m.* see **codice**.

codicillo *m.* (leg.) codicil.

codific-are [A2s] *tr.* to codify. **-ato** *part. adj.* codified. **-atore** *m.* codifier. **-azione** codification.

codi·glio *m.* (cards) codille, defeat of the player who is 'Ombra' at the game of ombre.

codimozzo *adj.* short-tailed, having a docked tail.

codi-rosso *m.* (orn.) redstart, *Phœnicurus phœnicurus*; — maggiore, rock thrush; — moretto, — spazzacammino, black redstart, *Phœnicurus ochrurus*. **-rossone** *m.* (orn.) rock thrush, *Monticola saxatilis*. **-tremola** *f.* (orn.) wagtail.

codinzin·zola *f.* (orn.) grey wagtail.

codin·zolo *m. dim.* of **coda**, q.v.; dimenare il —, to wag its tail.

codione *m.* (orn.) rump.

co·dole *f.pl.* (bot.). See **code**.

co·dolo *m.* tang, the part of a knife that goes into the haft; the corresponding part of a fork or spoon that has no separate haft; (mus.) tail (of a violin); tail-pin; metal bar for making horse-shoes.

codona *f.* (orn.). See **codibugnolo**.

codone *m.* See under **coda**.

codon·zolo *m.* See **codinzolo**.

codr-ione *m.* (orn.). See **codione**.

codulo *m.* (eng.) shaft (of a tool, bit, etc.).

coe·fere *f.pl.* (Gk. antiq.) *choephori*, libation-bearers, as in the play of Aeschylus (458 B.C.).

coeffici-ente *m.* (math., scient.) coefficient; (naut.) — di finezza, coefficient of fineness; (fig.) factor, contributory cause. **-enza** *f.* co-factor.

coegual-e *adj.* co-equal. (**-mente** *adv.*) **-ità** *f.* co-equality.

coeletto *adj.* elected jointly with another.

coenzione *f.* (hist.) coemption.

coepi·scop-o *m.* (eccl.) coadjutor (bishop). **-ato** *m.* (eccl.) coadjutor-ship.

coequale *adj.* See **coeguale**.

coerc-i·bile *adj.* coercible; (phys.) compressible. **-itivo** *adj.* coercive; compressible; resistant (to magnetization). **-izione** *f.* restriction, compression.

coere·d-e *m.* (leg.) co-heir; *f.* co-heiress. **-ità** *f.* (leg.) co-inheritance; inheritance in common.

coer-ente *adj.* coherent; consistent. (**-entemente** *adv.*) **-enza** *f.* coherence; consistence; integrity; unswerving loyalty.

coeserci·zio *m.* (comm.) joint working.

coesione *f.* (phys.) cohesion; (fig.) oneness of mind or will.

coesi·st-ere [C24] *intr.* (aux. essere) to co-exist. **-ente** *adj.* co-existent. **-enza** *f.* co-existence.

coesivo *adj.* cohesive.

coesore *m.* (radio) coherer.

coessenziale *adj.* co-essential.

coesten·dere [C1] *rfl.* to co-extend.

coet·a·neo *adj.* contemporary; of the same age; of the same generation; *n.m.* contemporary; è un mio —, he is the same age as I am; he is of my generation. (**-a·nea** *f.*)

coeten-o *adj.* (theol.) co-eternal. **-ità** *f. indecl.* (theol.) co-eternity.

coe·vo *adj.* coeval, contemporaneous, of the same epoch.

†**cofac·cia** *f.* See **focaccia**.

co·fan-o *m.* jewel-case; casket; ammunition box; (motor.; aeron.) bonnet; (eng.) boiler casing; (mil.) defensive work built in a trench; (ichth.) trunk fish, cow fish, *Ostracion* spp.; (zool.) Noah's ark shell, *Arca* spp.; †basket. **-etto** *m. dim.* jewel-case, trinket box; -etto pic-nic, picnic hamper.

coffa *f.* (naut.) crow's nest; top, platform originally giving splay to the topmast shrouds and suitable for a lookout position; — militare, fighting top, gun control position; †basket; (Calabria) eel-trap.

†**cof·foro** *m.* coffer, chest.

†**co·fino** *m.* basket.

co·ft-ico *adj.* Coptic. **-o** *adj.* Coptic; *n.m.* Copt.

cogit-are [A1s] *intr.* (aux. avere) to cogitate; *tr.* to cogitate upon; to think over; to think up. **-abondo** *adj.* pondering, thoughtful, pensive, meditative. **-ativa** *f.* thinking faculty. **-ativo** *adj.* relative to thought. **-ato** *part. adj.* thought over, pondered; *n.m.* thought. **-azione** *f.* thinking, reasoning, cogitation. **-oso** *adj.* pensive.

cogli *prep. contr.* See under **con**.

cogli-a *f.* scrotum; (vulg.) coxcomb, fop. **-arella** *f.* dandy, gallant. **-ata** *f.* foppishness. **-eggiare** [A3c] *intr.* (aux. avere) to play the gallant. **-onare** [A1c] *tr.* (vulg.) to make a fool of; to hoax; to scorn. **-onatura** *f.* (vulg.) derision. **-oncello** *m.* (vulg.) fool. **-one** *m.* testicle; (vulg.) fool. **-onella** *f.* hoax; pigliare in -onella, to hoax. **-oneri·a** *f.* foolish act; trifle; stupidity. **-uto** *m.* ram lamb (uncastrated), tup.

co·gl-iere [B27] *tr.* to gather, to pluck, to pick; to grasp, to seize; — l'occasione per, to take the opportunity of; — la palla al balzo, to be quick off the mark, to seize a sudden chance; to collect; to take, to surprise; to meet, to run into; — nel segno, to hit the mark, the target; — nel fallo, to catch in the act; (naut.) to coil; — manovre, to haul taut; — alla pescatora, to coil ready for running; — alla festa, to coil decoratively; *intr.* (aux. essere) to happen, to succeed; s'ei coglie, colga, if it works it works; ben gliene colse, it was well for him, it was a good thing for him. (**-itore** *m.*) **-itura** *f.* gathering, plucking.

cogna·c, **co·gnac** *m. indecl.* brandy, cognac.

cognacchino *m.* See **cognac**.

cogn-ata *f.* sister-in-law. **-ati·zio** *adj.* by marriage (of a relationship). **-ato** *m.* brother-in-law; cognate; *adj.* cognate. **-azione** *f.* relationship (esp. by marriage; cognation).

co·gnito *adj.* well-known, known; — di, acquainted with.

cognizione f. knowledge, judgement; cognition; cognizance; notion; item of knowledge; avere buone cognizioni di, to have a good knowledge of; (leg.) prendere — di, to obtain knowledge of (C.P.); il processo di —, stage, in process of administration of justice, in which Court becomes seised of facts of matter and applies law (C.C.P.).

cogn-o m. (pl. f. **-a**) quantity of oil or wine taken by the owner of an oil or wine press in payment for its use; a wine measure of from four to ten barrels at different times; †basket.

cognolo m. (industr.) fare i cognoli (in an alum-works), to set out the raw material ready for processing.

cogno·me m. surname; †nickname; †name.

cognomin-are [A I S] tr. to give a surname to; †to nickname, to dub; rfl. to take a surname. **-ato** part. adj. surnamed; †nicknamed. **-azione** f. surname; surnaming.

†cogno·scere vb. and derivs. See **conoscere**.

co·gol-o m. pebble. **-a·ria** f. large fishing net with aperture that can be slowly closed.

coguaro m. (zool.) puma, cougar, Felis concolor.

coherer m. (electr.) coherer.

coi contr. See under **con**.

coi-a·io m. leather-dresser; leather-seller. **-ame** m. quantity of leather, skins, hides. **-at·tolo** m. leather scrap, leather chip. **-eri·a** f. leather store. **-etto** m. leather jerkin. **-uc·cia** f. (miner.) pudding-stone.

coib-ente adj., n.m. bad conductor, non-conductor (of heat, electricity, etc.), insulator; adj. non-conducting; insulating; (industr.; bldg.) carta —, sheathing paper, insulating paper. **-entazione** f. insulation, insulating material. **-enza** f. (phys.) resistance.

coinci·d-ere [B I] intr. (aux. avere) to coincide; to correspond. **-enza** f. coincidence; combining; point of intersection; overlapping; clashing, clash (on a time-table); (of trains) connection.

coinquilino m. fellow-tenant.

†coinquinare tr. to soil; to contaminate.

cointeress-are [A I] tr. to implicate, to involve (esp. financially); to share. **-ato** part. adj. implicated, involved; associated (with a firm or business enterprise). **-anza** f., **-enza** f. participation, association (esp. in a business enterprise).

coinvol·gere [C 5] tr. to implicate, to drag in.

coire [def.] intr. (aux. essere) to have sexual intercourse; to copulate.

†coitare vb. See **cogitare**.

co·ito m. coitus, sexual intercourse; copulation; (astron.) conjunction.

coke, coks m. indecl. (pron. **coc**) coke.

cokeri·a f. (chem. industr.) coke plant, coke oven; gas di —, coke oven gas.

col contr. See under **con**.

Cola[1] pr.n.m. short for **Nicola**, q.v.; (fig.) stupid person, clown.

cola[2] f. (bot.) tropical African tree, Cola acuminata, producing nut chewed by natives and used as an ingredient in soft drinks.

cọla[3] f. sieve, filter, strainer.

colà adv. there, over there; yonder; così —, so so, middling.

colabrina f. (bot.) good King Henry, Chenopodium Bonus Henricus.

cọla-brodo m. indecl. broth strainer, sieve. **-pasta** m. indecl. utensil for straining pasta.

†colafizzare tr. to slap; (fig.) to offend.

colag·gio m. See under **colare**.

colaggiù adv. down there.

†colago·go m. (pharm.) medicine favouring the flow of bile from gall-bladder to intestine.

colame m. (foundry) sprue.

colapasta m. See under **colabrodo**.

col-are [A I C] tr. to strain, to sift, to filter; to pour; (naut.) — a picco, to sink; -ammo a picco tre unità nemiche, we sank three enemy ships; intr. (aux. essere) to trickle, to leak, to run; to drip; to flow; (of a canal) to gutter; (foundry) to pour, to cast, to run, to teem; (naut.) — a picco, — a fondo, to sink. **-ag·gio** m. (comm.) leakage (of liquid goods in transport); (techn.) casting. **-amento** m. dripping, dropping, running, leaking. **-ata** f. (metall.) casting, pouring; tap; (naut.) time during which a breeze blows steadily; (geol.) deposit of cooled lava; (geog.) low mound; flow, flowing, running, trickling; (dial. S. Ital.) washing, laundry. **-atic·cio** m. dregs which remain after straining; (metall.) dross (from a metal). **-ato** part. adj. fused, melted; refined, purified; strained, sifted;

melted down; aria **-ata**, air which has come in by an indirect route; close-fitting; n.m. straining, filtering, dripping; mode in which a thing occurred, rationale of the occurrence. **-atoio** m. sieve, filter; colander; crucible; (foundry) sprue, gate; (leg.) gutter (C.C.). **-atore** m. drainage channel. **-atura** f. straining, filtration; strained liquid; filtrate; candle-drippings; dregs; (geog. Lomb.) canal which collects water from irrigated meadow; **†-atura d'acqua**, stalactite.

colascion-e m. (mus.) two- or three-stringed Neapolitan lute played with a plectrum (played by wandering ballad-singers); (fig.) poesia da —, doggerel. **-ata** f. doggerel verse.

colassù adv. up there, up yonder.

colata f. See under **colare**.

colazion-e f. (Tusc., S. Ital.) breakfast; (N. Ital.) lunch; prima —, breakfast; fare —, to have lunch (or breakfast). **†-are** intr. to breakfast; to lunch, to have lunch. **-cina** f. dim. of **colazione**; snack; light breakfast; light lunch.

colbac(co) m. (mil. hist.) a form of cap worn by light cavalry; busby, bearskin helmet.

†colcare intr., rfl. to go to bed; to lie down; to rest, to take one's ease.

col·chic-o m. (bot.) meadow-saffron. **-ina** f. (chem.) colchicine.

colcos m. indecl. Russian collective farm; collective farming.

colcota·r m. indecl. (chem.) colcothar, red iron oxide.

colecistite f. (med.) cholecystitis.

cole·doco m. (anat.) bile duct, choledoch.

colei pers. prn. f. (pl. **coloro**) she; her; that woman.

col-elologi·a f. chololology. **-e·lito** m. (med.) cholelith, gall-stone.

†colendis·simo adj. superl. of **colendo**; most revered, most esteemed (in titles).

†colendo adj. venerable; reverend.

†colente part. adj. of **colere**, q.v.; inhabiting, frequenting.

coleot·tero m. (ent.) coleopteron, beetle; (text.) — capsulare, boll weevil (of cotton).

col-era f. (med.) cholera. **-e·rico** adj. choleric. **-eriforme** adj. choleriform. **-erina** f. (med.) cholerine. **-eroso** adj. affected with cholera; dead as a result of cholera.

co·lere [def.] tr. (poet.) to revere; to venerate.

colesterina f. (chem.) cholesterin, cholesterol.

colett-o m. sieve for corn. **-are** tr. [A I C] to sift (threshed corn).

†colezione f. See **colazione**.

†colfo m. See **golfo**.

co·lia f. (ent.) clouded yellow butterfly, Colias spp.

coli-ambo m. (prosod.) choliamb(us), scazon. **-am·bico** adj. (prosod.) choliambic.

†colibeto m. suggestive talk, scurrilous conversation; double-meaning.

colibrì, co·libri m. indecl. (orn.) humming-bird.

co·lic-a f. colic. **-o** adj. colic(al); (chem.) cholic.

colimbo m. (orn.) diver, grebe; — maggiore, great crested grebe; — massimo, great northern diver; — minore, — piccolo, dab-chick; — orecchiuto, — turco, black-headed grebe.

colina f. (chem.) choline.

col-ino m. dim. of **colo**[1]; small strainer. **-ìo** m. constant dripping, drips.

Colise·o pr.n.m. (pop.). See **Colosseo**.

colite f. See under **colon**.

†colizione f. See **colazione**.

cọlla[1] contr. See under **con**.

colla[2] f. glue, gum, paste; — d'amido, starch paste; (fig.) — che non attacca, friendship that will not last; (paperm.) size; dare la — a, to size; — di pesce, isinglass; (paint.) — di rosso d'uovo, tempera; colori a —, gouache.

†coll-a[3] f. rope; (naut.) stare alla —, (of a ship) to be charging or discharging; (hist.) torture. **†-are** tr. to torture.

collabor-are [A I] intr. (aux. avere) to collaborate, to co-operate. **-atore** m. **-atrice** f. collaborator, colleague; contribution. **-azione** f. collaboration, co-operation. **-azionismo** m. (neol. pol.) collaborationism. **-azionista** m. (neol. pol.) collaborationist.

collacrim-are [A I S] intr. (aux. avere) to weep together, to mourn together.

collageno m. (biol.; tanning) collagen.

collag·gio m. See under **collare**[2].

collana f. necklace; series, collection; — di salsicce, string of sausages; (naut.) running noose used in cablework.

collar-e¹ *m.* collar for dog, horse or draught animal; dog-collar necklace; riband worn round neck; neck-band; (eng.) collar; (eccl.) clerical stock or collar; prendere il —, to begin a clerical career; gettare il —, to abandon a clerical career; collar of order of Knighthood (e.g. — dell'Annunziata); Knight of such an order; lady's fur collar; (sport) grip round opponent's neck; (naut.) hoop, fender, rubbing strake. **-ẹssa** *f.* wife of a knight (esp. of the Annunziata); collar for draught-animals. **-ẹtto** *m.* lady's collar; cloak collar; (archit.) band between the shaft and the capital of a column; †(mil.) steel necklet of helmet. **-ina** *f.* clerical collar. **-inato** *adj.* (herald.) collared. **-ino** *m.* clerical stock; (archit.) collarino, neck of a column (esp. in Roman Doric and Tuscan orders); band at the bottom of a capital.

coll-are² [A I] *tr.* (paperm.) to size; *rfl.* (techn.) to cake together. †See **incollare¹**. **-ag·gio** *m.* (paperm.) size. **-ante** *part. adj.* carbone -ante, caking coal; *n.m.* (techn.) binder. **-atura** *f.* (text.) dressing.

collargolo *m.* (chem.) colloidal silver.

collarinato *adj.* (herald.). See under **collare**.

collasso *m.* (med.) collapse.

collata *f.* blow on the neck; (hist.) accolade.

collater-ale *adj.* collateral; (-almẹnte *adv.*) *n.m.* a collateral kinsman; (hist.) type of magistrate appointed in Venice after 1509; deputy-mayor. †-ali·a *f.* see **collaterato**. **-ato** *m.* deputy-mayoralty.

collat-o¹ *adj.* bestowed, given. **-ọre** *m.* (eccl.) patron of a benefice; (naut.) lanyard.

collato² *part.* of **collare**, q.v.

collatta·neo *m.* milk-brother, foster-brother.

collaud-are [A I S] *tr.* to approve officially; to test; to try; to inspect. **-ato** *part. adj.* approved; (mech.) tested. **-atore** *m.* (industr.) tester; inspector; (aeron.) pilota -atore, test pilot. **-aziọne** *f.* official approval.

colla·udo *m.* approval (of work done or contract fulfilled); certificate authorizing payment for work done; (eng.) test; testing; inspection; banco di —, test-bench.

collaziọn-e *f.* comparison of a copy with an original; textual criticism; collation; (eccl.) gift (of benefice); conferment (of holy orders); (leg.) collation, comparison of a copy with the original; hotchpot; †colloquium; †conference. **-amẹnto** *m.* collating. **-are** [A I C] *tr.* to compare, to contrast (e.g. texts); to collate. **-atura** *f.* collation; collating.

coll-e¹ *m.* hill (not so high as a **collina**); (sport) ascensione di una montagna in —, climbing up one side of a mountain and down the other; (geog.) col, saddle. **-ẹtto**, **-icẹllo** *m. dim.* of **colle**.

colle² *prep. contr.* See under **con**.

colle-ga *m.,f.* (*m.pl.* -ghi, *f.pl.* -ghe) colleague. **-ganza** *f.* colleagueship.

colleganza¹ *f.* See under **collega**.

colleganza² *f.* See under **collegare**.

colleg-are [A 2] *tr.* to unite, to put together; to join; to act as liaison between; to link. **-amẹnto** *m.* union; connexion, liaison; comitato di -amento, liaison committee; linking, uniting; (radio; telev.) relay, link-up; network; in -amento Eurovisione, by the Eurovision network. **-ante** *part. adj.* linking, joining. **-anza** *f.* link, union, liaison. **-ativo** *adj.* connective. **-ato** *part. adj.* united; joined; linked, connected. (-atamẹnte *adv.* **-atore** *m.* **-atrice** *f.*) **-atura** *f.* linkage, joint, connexion. **-aziọne** *f.* link, connexion, tie.

collegata·rio *m.* (leg.) co-legatee.

colle·gi-o *m.* college; corporation; body (of like people, e.g. professors, doctors); guild; (iron.) clique; boarding-school; the students of a college; (eccl.) sacro —, sacred college (of cardinals); †monastery, religious house; (leg.) il — degli avvocati, the Bar (in partic. sense); il — degli avvocati di Roma, the Rome Bar (cf. **avvocatura**); il — dei giudici, the Bench (in partic. sense, cf. **magistratura**); il — giudicante, the bench, the court; la costituzione del — giudicante delle corte di appello, the composition of the bench (or, of the court) in the Court of Appeal; il — di difesa, the lawyers for the defence; — arbitrale, court of arbitration; — elettorale, constituency; — uninominale, single-member constituency; — plurinominale, multi-member constituency. **-ale** *adj.* collegiate; done in collaboration; (leg.) adunanza -ale, assembly or body of judges; *n.m.* collegiate; boy at boarding school. **-almẹnte** *adv.* in collaboration. **-alità** *f. indecl.* all the collegians of a college; the rights and duties of a collegian; (eccl.) collegiate status; (pol.) group loyalty. †-are *intr.* to consult together, to confer (of doctors). **-ata** *f.* (eccl.) collegiate church. **-ato** *adj.* collegiate.

†**colleppolare** *tr.* to shake; to masticate; to steal, to carry off; *intr.* to prance; to leap about; *rfl.* to rejoice; to dance for joy; to wriggle; to shake oneself.

col·ler-a *f.* anger, rage, ire; andare in —, montare in —, to fly into a rage. †-oso *adj.* see **collerico**.

colle·ric-o *adj.* angry, enraged; choleric. (-amẹnte *adv.*)

coll-etta, **-ẹtta** *f.* collection (for charitable purposes); (liturg.) special collect; (naut.) picking up of cargo here and there; (comm.) caricare a —, to load a mixed cargo; †assembly, gathering; †confiscation, sequestration.

collettame *m.* railway parcels.

collett-ivo *adj.* collective; televisione -iva, community television, piped television; (comm.) società in nome —, general partnership; firma -iva, joint signature. **-ivamẹnte** *adv.* collectively; jointly. **-ivismo** *m.* collectivism. **-ivista** *m.* collectivist. **-ività** *f. indecl.* collectivity; the social community; all and sundry; l'opinione della -ità pubblica, public opinion; nell'interesse della -ità, in the general interest. **-izio** *adj.* collected together anyhow; esercito -izio, hastily collected army.

collẹtto¹ *m.* collar; (mil.) leather jerkin; (orn.) ferruginous duck.

collẹtto² *m. dim.* See under **colle**.

†**collẹtto³** *m.* bundle of merchandise, bale.

†**collẹtto⁴** *adj.* collected, gathered.

collett-ọre *m.* collector; (electr.) commutator; (motor.) manifold; (boiler) header; (hydraul.) main sewer. **-ori·a** *f.* collector's office.

colleziọn-e *f.* collection; †assembly; †gathering; †tax, imposition. **-are** [A I C] *tr.* to collect, to be a collector of. **-cella**, **-cina** *f. dim.* of collezione. **-ista** *m.* collector.

†**collicare** *vb.* See **coricare**.

collicello *m. dim.* See under **colle¹**.

collidere [C 3] *intr.* [*aux.* avere] to collide; (prosod.) to elide; *rfl.* to collide (with); (prosod.) to elide (with).

†**colligare** *vb.* See **collegare**.

colligiano *adj.* dwelling in the hills; *n.m.* hill-dweller.

collilungo *adj.* long-necked.

collim-are [A I] *intr.* (*aux.* avere) to have a common aim, to harmonize; to agree; to match, to correspond; to concur; (eng.; opt.) to collimate, to centre. **-atore** *m.* collimator; sight. **-aziọne** *f.* collimation.

collin-a *f.* hill. Note: a 'collina' usually has an altitude of not more than 500 or 600 metres, and is still within the zone of cultivation; quella zona è tutta —, that region is all hills (or, hilly); in —, in the hills; a me la — piace più del mare, I prefer hills to the sea. **-oso** *adj.* hilly.

collino *m. dim.* See under **collo**.

coll-i·rio *m.* (med.) eyewash. **-i·rico** *adj.* (med.) pertaining to eyewash.

colliş·iọne *f.* collision; contrast; hiatus. **-ivo** *adj.* collisive.

collo¹ *prep. contr.* See under **con**.

coll-o² *m.* neck; narrow part of bottle, flask or vessel, neck; throat; — del piede, instep; — dell'utero, neck of the womb; narrow handle; opening in a garment for the neck; — di una camicia, neck of a shirt; — di una scarpa, part of a shoe which grips the instep; tirare il — a, to wring the neck of, (fig.) to seize (a good opportunity); rompersi l'osso del —, to break one's neck; fiaccarsi il —, to break one's neck, (fig.) to come off badly, to be ruined, to be verging on disaster; a fiacca —, a rotta di —, a scavezza —, headlong, at breakneck speed, (fig.) downhill, verging on disaster; lasciare la briglia sul —, to let a horse have its head, (fig.) to go at full speed; essere nei debiti fino al —, to be up to one's eyes in debt; giocarsi l'osso del —, to gamble the shirt off one's back; avere il braccio al —, to have one's arm in a sling; allungare il —, to stretch one's neck to see above the crowd, to be curious, to be kept waiting for one's meal; fare allungare il — a uno, to keep a person waiting; tenere in —, to hold in one's arms; mettere il piede sul —, to keep (a person) down; to dominate, to treat like a slave; cascare di —, to fall from favour; prendere per il —, to seize by the throat, (fig.) to take advantage of, to overcharge; tra capo e —, unexpectedly, out of the blue; (of a cart) aver troppo in —, to be overloaded on the shafts; (geog.) col; (archit.) neck (of a column); (mech.) — d'oca, crank-shaft; (naut.) round turn; hank; coil; prendere un —, to take a turn; doppio —, clove hitch; mezzo —, half turn; — tondo, full turn; — d'oca, gooseneck, fireman standpipe, ramshorn hook; vele a —, sails aback; sotto —, separate loading of a ship (mixed cargo). **-icino** *m. dim.* thin neck; child's neck. **-ino** *m.* neck of a shirt.

collo³ *m.* package, bundle; item of luggage; viaggio con tre colli, più l'ombrello e la borsa, I'm travelling with three pieces of luggage, plus my umbrella and handbag; — postale, parcel.

colloc·are [A 2 s] *tr.* to place; to find employment for; — a riposo, to pension off; — una ragazza, to marry a girl off; (comm.) to place, to dispose of; — denari, to invest money; *rfl.* to settle down. **-a·bile** *adj.* employable; marketable. **-amento** *m.* placing; situation, position, post; employment; ufficio di -amento, employment exchange; agenzia di -amento, employment agency. **-ato** *part. adj.* placed; in employment; settled. (**-atore** *m.* **-atrice** *f.*) **-azione** *f.* collocation, classification (of books); placing; marriage, marrying off (of a daughter); arrangement of words in a sentence; (paint.) grouping.

collocas·sia *f.* (bot.). See colocasia.

collocut-ore *m.* collocutor, one who takes part in a dialogue. **-o·rio** *m.* (eccl.) parlour.

collo·d-io *m.* (chem.) collodion, nitrocellulose. **-iare** [A 4] *tr.* (chem.) to collodionize. **-ione** *m.* (chem.) see collodio.

collo·id-e *adj., n.m.* (chem.) colloid. **-ale** *adj.* (chem.) colloidal.

colloquinta *f.* (bot.). See coloquinta.

collo·quio *m.* interview; conference; conversation; colloquium; discussion group; (eccl.) parlour.

†col·lora *f.* See collera.

collorosso *m.* (orn.) pochard.

collos-o *adj.* sticky, gummy, gluey; glutinous; tacky. **-ità** *f.* stickiness, gumminess, glueyness.

collotorto *m.* (*pl.* **collitorti**) hypocrite; (orn.) wryneck; (bot.) polyanthus narcissus, *Narcissus tazetta*.

collot·tola *f.* nape of the neck; thick neck; far —, to grow fat.

colloverde *m.* (*pl.* **colliverdi**) (orn.) mallard.

collu·dere [C 3] *intr.* (*aux.* avere) (leg.) to collude, to commit collusion.

collus·ione *f.* (leg.) collusion. **-ivo** *adj.* (leg.) collusive. **-ivamente** *adv.* (leg.) collusively.

colluto·rio *m.* (med.) mouthwash.

collutt-are [A 1] *intr.* (*aux.* avere) to struggle; to wrestle; to fight; *rfl.* to fight with one another. **-azione** *f.* struggle; struggling; wrestling; fight.

collu·vi-e *f. indecl.* cesspool; mass of filth; (fig.) heap; horde. **-a·rio** *m.* vent (of water-main).

colma *f.* (naut.) high water; high water spring; extra high tide, surge.

colm-are [A 1 c] *tr.* to fill to the brim; — il sacco, to go right to the very limit (of evil things, misfortunes, etc.); — uno di gloria, di onori, to load one with glory, honours; — uno di gentilezze, to overwhelm one with kindness; — un vuoto, — una lacuna, to fill a need, to supply a want, to supply what is lacking; — una strada, to give a road a proper camber; *abs.* to deposit silt on land by introducing flood-water. **-ata** *f.* banking up; depositing silt; filling up; grading of an incline; (geog.) warp-land. **-ato** *part. adj.* filled; overflowing; laden; overwhelmed; cambered. **-atura** *f.* fullness to the brim; top, summit; (archit.) space at the top of an arch.

colmeggiare [A 3 c] *intr.* (*aux.* avere) to rise slightly in the centre, to camber.

colmigno *m.* ridge (of a roof).

colm-o¹ *m.* top, summit; peak; arrivare al —, to get to the top; crown; the full (of water); high tide; prime (of life); è il —! it's the limit!; al —, to the utmost; crown (of a road); (archit.) roof-tree; ridge of a roof; (naut.) — dell'anca, turn of a ship's hull. **-ello** *m.* ridge of a roof. **-etto** *m.* main beam of a roof.

colmo² *apocop. part.* of colmare, q.v.; *adj.* full, brimful, full to the brim, overflowing; convex, curved, arched.

colo¹ *m.* sieve.

colo² *m.* (anct. rhet.) phrase, part of a period; colon (as structural unit in prose or verse).

co·lob¹ *m. indecl.* (zool.) colobus monkey.

colo·bio *m.* (archaeol.) colobium.

coloca·sia *f.* (bot.) taro, eddo, *Colocasia esculenta*.

colocintina *f.* (chem.) colocynthin.

colofo·nia *f.* colophony, rosin.

cologaritmo *m.* (math.) cologarithm.

colomb-a *f.* (orn.) dove; — migratrice, passenger pigeon, *Ectopistes migratorius*; — sassarola, rock dove; la — della pace, the dove of peace; docile, loving woman; (iron.) loose woman; (naut.) keel. **-ella** *f.* (orn.) stock dove, *Columba œnas*; pure young girl; a ball game; a -ella, falling perpendicularly (of a ball). **-ellare**

[A 1] *intr.* (*aux.* avere); to play at 'colombella'. **-ina** *f. dim.* of **colomba**; Easter egg; Easter cake; (iron.) prude; pigeon dung; fuse for setting fire to fireworks; variety of grape; (chem.) columbin; *pr.n.f.* (theatrical hist.) Columbine, originally in Neapolitan comedy, mistress of Pulcinella, later of Arlecchino; 'servetta' (soubrette) character in various comedies by Goldoni.

colomb-a·ia *f.* dovecote; sviare la —, to turn away all comers; tirar sassi in —, to foul one's own nest; stare in —, to live at the top of the house. **-ana** *f.* variety of large, white, sweet grape. **-ano** *m.* vineyard of 'colombana' grapes; Lombard wine. **†-ara** *f.* see colombaia. **-a·ria** *f.* (liter. hist.) Florentine Academy. **-a·rio** *m.* pigeon-holes; vault for cinerary urns, columbarium; niche for cinerary urns; (naut.) holes through which the oars pass. **-iere** *m.* (naut.) masthead. **-ina** *f. dim.* of **colomba**, q.v. **-ino** *m. dim.* of **colombo**, q.v.; vineyard of 'colombina' grapes; lover; *adj.* dove-like; dove-grey; (geol.) sasso -ino, variety of limestone.

Colo·mbia *pr.n.f.* (geog.) Columbia.

colombier *m. indecl.* (paperm.) Colombier (format of drawing paper; English size is $34\frac{1}{2} \times 24$ in., but Italian is 90×63 cm.).

colomb-io *m.* (chem.) niobium. **-ico** *adj.* (chem.) niobic; tantalic. **-ite** *f.* (min.) columbite, niobite.

Colombo¹ *pr.n.m.* Columbus.

colomb-o² (orn.) pigeon; — gozzuto, pouter pigeon; — messaggero, carrier pigeon; — pavoncello, fantail pigeon; — torraiolo, semi-domesticated pigeon, rock dove; — viaggiatore, homing pigeon; — di gesso, clay pigeon; — da pelare, a bad player; i due -i, a courting couple, sweethearts; -i fuggitivi, an eloping couple; (pharm.) radice di —, calumbin; (ichth.) — di mare, — vescovo *Pteromyleus bovina*; also the eagle ray, *Myliobatis aquila*. **-ac·cio** *m.* (orn.) wood pigeon, *Columba palumbus*.

co·l-on *m. indecl.* (anat.) colon. **-ite** *f.* (med.) colitis.

colonetto *m.* (paperm.) rib (of mould).

Colo·ni-a¹ *pr.n.f.* (geog.) Cologne; acqua di —, eau-de-Cologne.

colo·n-ia² *f.* colony; school camp and similar institutions; (leg.) agricultural lease on a profit-sharing basis; — agricola (penal) Agricultural Settlement (C.P.); — penale, — penitenziale, penal settlement. **-iale** *adj.* colonial; casa -iale, farmhouse; casco -iale, sun-helmet; *n.m.pl.* groceries (from the colonies) such as coffee, tea, etc. **-ista** *m., f.* child at a school camp.

colo·nico *adj.* having to do with the tenant or the farm under an agricultural lease on a profit-sharing basis; casa colonica, farmhouse.

coloniz̧z̧-are [A 1] *tr.* to colonize. **-a·bile** *adj.* colonizable. **-ato** *part. adj.* colonized. **-atore** *m.* colonizer. (**-atrice** *f.*) **-azione** *f.* colonization.

colonn-a, (Rom.) **colonn-a** *f.* column; pillar; — di cifre, column of figures; (typ.) galley; bozze in —, galley-proofs; — vertebrale, spinal column; (mil.) column; (naut.) column; — della bitta, drum of the bits; — d'ormeggio, bollard; vertical height of a sail; — di cavo, mast pendant; — di paranco, tail of a block; captain's emergency fund; (mus.) pillar (of harp); (cinem.) — sonora, sound track; — visiva, picture, mute; (watchm.) ruota a -e, pillar wheel; (paperm.) rib (of mould); (leg.) an old form of maritime contract; outlay for fitting out a ship for a voyage. **†-ale** *adj.* column-shaped, column-like. **-are** *adj.* columnar. **†-ata** *f.* see colonnato. **-ato** *m.* colonnade; (numism.) old Spanish coin; *adj.* having columns, pillared. **-etta** *f. dim.* of **colonna**; tombstone; bedside table; (eng.) stud bolt; (bldg.) post (of railings, etc.). **-ina** *f. dim.* -ina spartitraffico, equiv. to a traffic sign marked 'keep left' in England. **-ino** *m. dim.* of **colonna**; baluster, wooden prop; (paperm.) rib (of mould).

colonnell-o¹ *m.* colonel. **-a** *f.* colonel's wife.

†colonnello² *m. dim.* of **colonna**, q.v.

colono *m.* (leg.) agricultural tenant under a form of lease called 'colonia', q.v.

coloquint-a, -ida *f.* (bot.) colocynth, *Citrullus colocynthis*.

color-are [A 1 c] *tr.* to colour, to give colour to; to simulate; *rfl.* to paint one's face, to make-up. **-a·bile** *adj.* that may be coloured. **-amento** *m.* colouring. **-ante** *part. adj.* colouring; materie -anti, colouring matter, dyes; potere -ante, dyeing capacity; *n.m.* (chem.; techn.) dye, dyestuff, colouring material. **-ato** *part. adj.* coloured; dyed, stained. (**-atamente** *adv.*) **-atura** *f.* colouring; (mus.) coloratura, a term used by English but not by Italian writers to denote a style of singing demanding great vocal agility. **-azione** *f.* coloration, colouring; pigmentation.

color·e *m.* colour; tint; un abito di —, a coloured dress; un uomo di —, a coloured man; — fondamentale, — primitivo, primary colour; ~i solidi, fast colours; scatola dei ~i, paint-box; — locale, local colour; semblance; un — di verità, a semblance of truth; sotto — di timidizza, with a show of timidity; cambiar —, to change colour, to turn pale, to blush, (fig.) to change sides; vedere tutto color di rosa, to see everything through rose-coloured spectacles; dipingere con ~i smaglianti, to paint in glowing colours; farne di tutti i ~i, to be up to all sorts of mischief; dye, stain; paint; — a olio, oil paint; (poker) 'flush'; (journ.) pezzo di —, write-up of the background of an event. **-ifi·cio** *m.* paint-factory. **-imetri·a** *f.* (techn.) colorimetry. **-ina** *f.* madder extract. **-ino** *m. dim.* delicate, light shade of colour. **-one** *m. augm.* loud colour; strong colour. **-uc·cio** *m. pejor.* washed-out colour; sickly colour.

colori·metro *m.* colorimeter, tintometer.

color-ire [D 2] *tr.* to colour, to paint; — un disegno, to put a plan into effect; (paint.) to paint. **-ista** *m.* (paint.) colourist; (fig.) vivid writer; (industr.) colour-matcher. **-ito** *part. adj.* coloured, tinted; painted; highly coloured (also fig.); *n.m.* colour (in a painting); manner of using colour; *n.m.* colouring, tint; expression; complexion. **-itore** *m.* (paint.) colourist. **-itura** *f.* colour wash. **-izzazione** *f.* (chem.) coloration.

coloro *prn.* they, those; them.

Colosseo *pr.n.m.* Colosseum.

coloss-o *m.* colossus. **-ale** *adj.* colossal, enormous. **-esco** *adj.* (*m.pl.* **-eschi**) pertaining to a colossus.

colostro *m.* (med.) colostrum; (agric.) beest, beestings, beastlings.

colpa *f.* guilt; fault; essere in —, to be in the wrong; è — mia, it's my fault; dir sua —, to own one's guilt; buttar la — addosso a, to lay the blame on; — default; fault; guilt without criminal intent (cf. **dolo**); riconoscere la propria —, to confess one's guilt; far — ad uno di, to charge someone with.

†colpa·bile *adj.* See **colpevole**.

colpabilità *f.* culpability; imputability; (leg.) guilt; guiltiness.

†colpare¹ *tr.* to blame; to inculpate; *intr.* to be guilty.

†colpare² *tr.* to hit (cf. **colpire**); to cut.

colpevol-e *adj.* culpable; guilty; (leg.) dichiararsi —, to plead guilty; *n.m., f.* culprit. **-mente** *adv.* culpably; guiltily. **-ezza** *f.* guilt.

colp-ire [D 2] *tr.* to hit, to strike; — nel segno, to get a bull's eye; — nel vivo, to hit the mark, to get (someone) on the raw, to cut to the heart, touch to the quick; (finan.) — una forma di reddito, to impose a tax upon a source of revenue; una tassa che ~isce i prodotti agrari, a tax affecting agricultural profits; (fig.) to make an impression on, to strike. **-ito** *part. adj.* struck, hit; impressed; surprised. (**-itore** *m.* **-itrice** *f.*)

colp-o *m.* blow, thrust, hit; di un sol —, at a single blow; (fig.) blow, tragedy, disappointment; è stato un gran —, it's been a great blow; (naut.) — di mare, heavy sea shipped on board; stroke (single motion); (eng.) — dello stantuffo, stroke of the piston; il motore sta perdendo ~i, the engine is missing; — di timone, a sudden movement of the rudder; — del pennello, brush-stroke; — d'ala, see under **ala**; single, separate act; un — di telefono, a telephone call, a 'ring'; sudden, unexpected move, coup; — di stato, *coup d'état*; — d'occhio, glance; wide view, prospect, panorama; che — d'occhio!, what a magnificent view!; tutto d'un —, di —, all at once; sul —, immediately; — di fortuna, stroke of luck; — di mano, *coup de main*; a — sicuro, unhesitatingly; shot; (naut.) smart operation; — di grazia, *coup de grâce*, finishing stroke; ferir di —, to hit the mark; successful stroke; (med.) stroke; fit; — di apoplessia, apoplectic fit; un — di sole, a touch of the sun, sunstroke; un — d'aria, a chill from a draught; — di pressione, divers' disease, bends (after a person has been in an atmosphere of higher pressure); fall, downfall; (billiards) the force behind a stroke; (mus.) — di timpano, drumstroke; — d'arco, bowstroke; (tennis) — dritto, forehand; — rovescio, backhand; — schiacciato, smash; — d'arresto, — smorzato, drop-shot; — nullo, let.

colpos-o *adj.* (leg.) culpable but without criminal intent; omicidio —, manslaughter, culpable homicide. **-amente** *adv.* (leg.) culpably (without malice aforethought; cf. **dolosamente**).

colt-a *f.* harvesting, gathering; mill-pond; pond, tank; (naut.) trimming; †tax, imposition; †task; †blow; †far —, to strike, to hit.

coltel *m. indecl.* See **coltello**.

coltell-a *f.* large kitchen knife. **-ina** *f.* filleting knife.

coltellac·cio *m.* See under **coltello**

coltell-o *m.* (sometimes **coltel**, as in provb. below) knife; blade; — a molla, — a cric, — a serramanico, clasp-knife; prendere il — per la lama, to hurt oneself; avere il — per il manico, to have the whip-hand; avere il — alla gola, to be hard pressed; servire di —, to serve humbly; fumo fitto da tagliarsi col —, smoke thick enough to cut with a knife; (provb.) chi di coltel ferisce, di coltel perisce, he who takes the sword will perish by the sword; azione da —, base act; guerra a —, war to the death; (of a machine) cutter; edge; jointer (of a plough); (bldg.) mattoni a —, mattoni per —, bricks laid on edge, with the largest face vertical; (eng.) sopporto a —, knife-edge bearing; *pl.* (orn.) primaries; †weapon; †sword; †vivere in —, to live by the sword. **-ac·cio** *m. pejor.* of **coltello**; hunting knife; sort of scimitar; cutlass; (naut.) studding sail (pron. 'stuns'l'); ploughshare; (bot.) bur-reed, *Sparganium ramosum*; yellow water-iris, *Iris pseudacorus*; corn-gladiolus, *Gladiolus segetum*. **-accino** *m. dim.* (naut.) upper studding sail. **-ame** *m.* cutlery. **-ata** *f.* knife wound; finire a -ate, to end up in quarrels; (fig.) sorrow, anguish; (bldg.) top of a wall where the bricks have been laid on edge. **-ato** *adj.* built with the bricks standing on edge. **-atore** *m.* see **accoltellatore**. **-esca** *f.* sheath for a knife. **-iera** *f.* knife-stand; knife-box, knife-case, cutlery cabinet. **-ina·io** *m.* cutler. **-inata** *f.* penknife wound. **-ino** *m.* pocket-knife, penknife; (bot.) iris. **-otto** *m.* medium-sized knife.

coltiv-are [A I sc] *tr.* to cultivate, to till; to tend. **-a·bile** *adj.* cultivable, cultivatable; arable; tillable. (**-abilità** *f. indecl.*) **-amento** *m.* cultivating; cultivation; culture. **-ato** *part. adj.* cultivated, tilled, tended; *n.m.* cultivated land. **-atore** *m.* cultivator; grower; -atore diretto, farmer who cultivates his own land; (fig.) instigator. (**-atrice** *f.*) **-azione** *f.* cultivation; (mining) stoping.

coltivo *adj.* cultivable; cultivated; arable, fit for tillage.

colto¹ *m.* cultivated land; cultivation; religious rite, cult; *adj.* cultured; well-mannered; well-educated; †venerated, worshipped; †overdressed, dandified, foppish.

colto² *part.* of **cogliere**, q.v.

coltrare [A I]. See under **coltro**.

coltr-e *f.* pall; bed-cover (usu. quilted); (Lucca) measure of 40·9 ares. **-ino** *m.* strong sheet with handles for transporting a patient or a dead body. **-oncino** *m.* light quilt; quilted skirt. **-one** *m. augm.* quilt; quilted curtain hanging at the door of a church.

coltret·tola *f.* (orn.). See **cutrettola**.

coltric-e *f.* feather bed, mattress. **-ia·io** *m.* feather-bed maker.

coltr-o *m.* (agric.) coulter, the upright fore-iron of a plough; ploughshare for throwing the earth to one side; (naut. hist.) a special bulkhead in old vessels. **-are** [A I c] *tr.* (agric.) to plough with a coulter. **-atura** *f.* (agric.) ploughing to one side. **-ina** *adv. phr.* (bldg.) muro a -ina, wall built of bricks laid on the flat and on edge in alternate layers.

coltur-a *f.* cultivation; farming; raising; gran —, farming on a large scale, mechanized agriculture; — intensiva, intensive cultivation; la rotazione di -e, l'alternarsi delle varie -e, the rotation of crops; (bacter.) culture (cf. **cultura**); †cultivated ground; †religious cult, veneration.

colubrin-a *f.* (mil. hist.) large arquebus; culverin, a long cannon, generally an eighteen-pounder; (bot.) bryony, *Bryonia dioica*; dragon arum, *Dracunculus vulgaris*. **-ata** *f.* (mil. hist.) culverin shot. **-ato** *adj.* (mil. hist.) shaped like a culverin; long (of a cannon).

co·lubro, colubro *m.* (zool.) — d'Esculapio, *Coluber longissimus*, — liscio, *Coronella austriaca*, harmless snakes resembling the grass-snake; — lacertino, *Coelopeltis monspessulanus*, a poisonous, but not dangerous, snake; (poet.) snake.

colu·i *pers. prn.* he; that person; — che, he who, the one who; †of him, his.

Colum·bia *pr.n.f.* Columbia; (geog.) — Britannica, British Columbia.

coluro *m.* (astron.) colure.

colza *f.* (bot.) rape, *Brassica campestris oleifera*; olio di —, colza oil, rape oil.

†com' *adv.* See **come**.

coma¹ *m.* (med.) coma; (telev.) coma.

†com-a² *f.* see **chioma**. **†-ato** *adj.* see **chiomato**.

†coma³ *f.* comma.

comand-are [A I] *tr.* to command; to be in charge; to control; chi è che -a qui? who is in charge here?; — a bacchetta, to rule with a high hand; to order; ~i! yes, sir! your order, sir?; (Ven.) what

comand·are (*cont.*)
did you say?; (eng.; techn.) to control; — a distanza, to remote-control. **-ante** *m.* commandant; commander; (naut.) captain; — di bandiera, flag captain; — in secondo, executive officer. **-ata** *f.* (mil.) fatigue duty; le -ate, horses kept in readiness at a railway station or elsewhere for the convenience of royal or other important travellers; (naut.) working party; night watch; prima -ata, first watch (from 1600 hrs. to midnight); seconda -ata, middle watch; ufficiale di -ata, stand-by officer. †**-ata·rio** *m.* agent; trustee. †**-ativo** *adj.* commanding; demanding; (gramm.) imperative. **-ato** *part. adj.* ordered, commanded; controlled; seconded; -ato a distanza, remote-controlled; (eccl.) feste -ate, holidays of obligation; giorni -ati, fasting days. (**-atore** *m.* **-atrice** *f.*) †**-gia** *f.* recommendation; trust.

†**coman·dita** *f.* commission; trust; avere in —, to hold on commission, to have on trust.

comando *m.* command; order; al —, in command, in charge; prendere il — di, to take command of; (mil.) command; headquarters; (naut.) executive command; — di guardia, duty officer, officer of the watch; ponte di —, bridge; (aeron.) barra di —, joystick; *pl.* (eng.) control; drive; — a mano, manual control, hand drive; — a distanza, remote control.

coman·dolo *m.* (text.) hank of thread wound on a bobbin at the bottom of a weaver's frame, for fastening any threads of the warp which come undone in weaving.

comar·e¹ *f.* godmother; (pop.) gossip, 'mother', neighbour; (euph.) Death; giuoco delle -i, children's game of pretending to go on a visit to a friend who has had a baby; tazza della —, large cup with pedestal, usu. two-handled; (Ven., Lomb., Romagna) midwife. **-oc·cia**, **-ozza** *f.* plump little woman. **-uc·cia** *f.* pejor. vulgar, low-class woman.

†**comare²** *tr.* to deceive; to gloss over.

comas·co *adj.* (*m.pl.* **-chi**) (geog.) pertaining to Como in N. Italy.

comasta *m.* (hist.) reveller.

comatoso *adj.* (med.) comatose.

coma·tula *f.* (zool.) feather star, *Antedon rosacea.*

comba *f.* (geog.) coomb; (geol.) cwm.

combaci·are [A 3] *intr.* (*aux.* avere) to meet at a point, to fit together exactly; to coincide; (eng.) to mate; †*recip. rfl.* to kiss each other; to meet flush; to be osculant. **-amento** *m.* point of coincidence; fitting together; (eng.) mating; -amento imperfetto, mismating.

†**combagiare** *vb.* and derivs. See **combaciare**.

†**combar·bio** *m.* cross-roads, meeting of the ways.

combat·t-ere [C I] *intr.* (*aux.* avere) to fight; *tr.* to fight, to combat; to assail. **-ente** *adj.* fighting, combatant; *n.m.* combatant; serviceman, ex-serviceman; (orn.) ruff, reeve, *Philomachus pugnax.* **-enti·stico** *adj.* (neol.) 'ex-service' (as applied to organizations). †**-e·vole** *adj.* attacking, fighting. †**-iere** *m.* fighting-man, soldier. **-imento** *m.* combat, fight; struggle, travail; (mil.) indecisive battle. **-itore** *m.*, **-itrice** *f.* fighter; combatant; warrior; †athlete, champion. **-ivo** *adj.* bellicose, of a fighting nature, combative. **-ività** *f.* fighting spirit. **-uto** *part. adj.* hard-fought, hard-won; assailed; (fig.) much argued about, much disputed; -uto fra, 'torn between'.

†**combiat·are** *tr.* to dismiss; to send away. †**-o** *m.* dismissal; leave, departure.

†**combib·bia** *f.* drinking party, carousal; conviviality; league; friendship; agreement; plot, intrigue, machination.

combin·are [A I] *tr.* to arrange; to bring into agreement; to combine; to settle; *intr.* (*aux.* avere) to be in agreement, to agree; to match, to 'go with'; to happen, to chance; *recip. rfl.* to come to an agreement; to coincide. **-a·bile** *adj.* combinable; compatible. **-abilità** *f. indecl.* compatibility, affinity. **-amento** *m.* combining. **-ata** *f.* (sport) -ata alpina, ski-event consisting of slalom coupled with free descent trial; -ata nordica, ski-event consisting of distance trial coupled with ski-jump. **-atore** *m.* combiner; negotiator; (teleph.) sequence switch; (electr.; rlwy.) equipaggiamento -atore, controller equipment. **-azione** *f.* combination; chance; per -azione, by chance; per pura -azione, by sheer coincidence; ma guarda che -azione! what a coincidence!; per -azione non avresti una gomma da imprestarmi? you wouldn't happen to have a rubber would you, by any chance?; *pl.* combinations (article of clothing).

combric·col-a *f.* gang; gang of rogues; merry party of friends; coterie, clique. **-a·io** *m.* member of a gang or party. **-are** [A I S] *intr.* (*aux.* avere) to gang together. **-one** *m.* member of a gang.

combu·glio *m.* confusion; medley, hotch-potch.

†**combu·r-ere** *tr.* to burn. †**-ente** *m.* fuel. †**-enza** *f.* combustibility.

combust-i·bile *adj.* combustible; *n.m.* fuel; quanto brucia di — al giorno questa caldaia? how much fuel does this boiler burn a day?; quali -ibili adopera in casa? what kinds of fuel do you use in the house? **-ibilità** *f.* combustibility. **-ione** *f.* combustion; (med.) burn; (fig.) confusion, revolt. **-ivo** *adj.* burnable, suitable as fuel. **-o** *adj.* burned; set on fire; (astron.) Via -a, Milky Way.

combutta *f.* crowd, gang; conspiratorial group; tangled mass, confusion; in —, all together, in a gang, conspiring; (joc.) quei due sono in —, those two are hand in glove; che cosa fate lì in —?, what are you plotting there?

come *adv.* how; in what way: —?, — dici?, what did you say?; ma —!, how can that be?, surely not!; as; like; in the same way as; to the same extent as; in the capacity of; (poet.) as if.

come(c)che *conj.* in whatever way, no matter how, however; although. **-si·a** *adv.* anyhow.

†**come·dia** *f.* See **commedia**.

comentare [A I C] and derivs. See **commentare**.

comentari(u)olo *m.* note-book, memorandum.

comento¹ *m.* and derivs. See **commento**.

comento² *m.* (naut.) seam.

†**comenzare** *vb.* See **cominciare**.

†**comere** *tr.* to decorate, to embellish, to adorn.

comet-a, (Rome) **comet-a** *f.* (astron.) comet; a card game, formerly known as comet in England; white patch on a horse's head, blaze, star. **-a·rio** *adj.* (astron.) cometary. **-i·cola** *m.* (myth.) comet-dweller. **-o·ide** *f.* (astron.) comet-like body.

comiato *m.* See **commiato**.

co·mica¹ *f.* woman comedian (cf. **comico**).

†**co·mica²** *f.* (theatr.) skill in acting; dramatic art.

co·mic-o *adj.* comic, comical; funny; (theatr.) relating to comedy; dramatic; (liter. hist.) stile —, lowly style; *n.m.* (theatr.) comedian, comic actor; actor; Capo —, actor manager; Capo comica, woman actor-manager. **-amente** *adv.* comically; funnily; as befits comedy. **-ità** *f. indecl.* (theatr.) comedy, comic quality; burlesque.

comi·gnolo *m.* (bldg.) ridge of a roof; roof-tree; ridge-tile; top of a stack.

†**comincia·glia** *f.* beginning, commencement.

cominci·are [A 3] *tr.*, *intr.* (*aux.* essere, avere) to begin, to commence, to start; (in telegrams, etc.) -a,...finisce, quote...unquote; una parola che -a per elle, a word beginning with L; *n.m.* beginning; opening; al —, at the outset; al cominciar del giorno, at daybreak. **-amento** *m.* beginning, start; outset; fin dal -amento, right from the outset. (**-ante** *part. adj.*) **-ato** *part. adj.* begun, started, commenced; †*n.m.* beginning, start. (**-atore** *m.* **-atrice** *f.*) **-atura** *f.* (text.) bare place in cloth. †**-o** *apocop. part. adj.* see **cominciato**.

cominiano *adj.* pertaining to the editions of Giuseppe Comino of Padua in the eighteenth century.

comin-o *m.* (bot.) cumin, *Cuminum cyminum*, or its seed; — nostrale, *Ammi majus*; — tedesco coltivato, common caraway, *Carum carvi*. **-ella** *f.* (bot.) love-in-the-mist, *Nigella sativa*.

†**comissare** *intr.* to revel.

comitagi *m.pl.* (hist.) comitadji.

comitale *adj.* pertaining to a count or earl.

comitato *m.* committee; — ad interim, interim committee; — di collegamento, liaison committee; — consultivo, advisory committee; — di designazione, nominations committee; — di esperti, committee of experts; — direttivo, steering committee; — per l'ospitalità, reception committee; — d'onore, patrons; — di redazione, drafting committee; sotto —, sub-committee; (leg.) — dei creditori, Committee of Inspection (C.C.); (hist.) country, province (e.g. of Hungary); †company, band, group.

†**co·mite** *m.* (hist.) companion to the Emperor; companion to a Governor; Count.

comitiva *f.* party, group of persons; band.

co·mit-o, **-e** *m.* boatswain; — di fischietto, boatswain's mate.

comi·zi-o *m.* meeting; reunion; rally; — elettorale, electoral meeting or assembly; tenere un —, to hold a meeting; indicare un —, to call a meeting. **-ale** *adj.* (leg.) having to do with an assembly or meeting; comitial. †morbo -ale, epilepsy.

†**comizzare** *intr.* to revel.

comm-a *m.* (leg.) parenthetic clause; clause, subsection; (mus.) comma; †(gramm.) comma.

†**commacerare** *tr.* to pulverize, to macerate thoroughly.

†**commacolare** *tr.* to stain; to blemish.

†**commaginazione** *f.* vivid imagination, fancy.

commallevadore *m.* (leg.) surety, jointly and severally with another.

commando *m.* (naut.) nettlestuff, second quality general-purpose light tarred hemp; serving (of a hawser).

†**commasticare** *tr.* to masticate thoroughly; (fig.) to chew over, to ponder.

†**commeato** *m.* provisions, victuals.

comme·di·a *f.* (theatr.) comedy; play; — di carattere, comedy of character; — d'intreccio, comedy of intrigue; — a tesi, problem play; — storica, historical play; — dell'arte, a kind of play common in Italy in the sixteenth and following centuries, in which the plot and the stock characters ('maschere') only were provided, the dialogue being improvised by the actors; (fig.) make-believe, deception; recitare la —, to act (esp. in sense of feigning joy, grief or other emotion), 'to put it on'; far più parti in —, to contradict oneself, to change one's mind; mettere in —, to make fun of. **-a·io** *m.* (*pl.* **-a·i**) (joc.) playwright. **-ona** *f.* great comedy, magnificent play. **-one** *m.* heavy comedy.

commedi-are [A4] *tr.* to put in a comedy, to write a comedy about. **-a·bile** *adj.* suitable for comedy. **-ante** *m., f.* comedian, comédienne; actor, actress; (fig.) hypocrite, one who feigns emotion. **-ato** *part. adj.* made into a comedy, written as a comedy. **-o·grafo** *m.* playwright, author of comedies.

commemor-are [A I s] *tr.* to commemorate; (liturg.) to commemorate. **-a·bile** *adj.* commemorable. †**-amento** *m.* commemoration. **-ativo** *adj.* commemorative; (med.) anamnestic. **-azione** *f.* commemoration; (liturg.) commemoration.

commenda *f.* a title, rights or stipend (if any) belonging to a member of an Order of Chivalry; (eccl.) *commendam*; dare in —, to commend, to give in *commendam*; †(leg.) contratto di —, maritime contract of agency, for trade of goods on consignment.

commend-are [A I] *tr.* to commend; †to recommend; †to entrust; †— alla memoria, to commit to memory. **-a·bile** *adj.* commendable. †**-amento** *m.* commendation; praise. **-ata·rio** *m.* (eccl.) commendator. **-ati·zia** *f.* letter of recommendation. **-ati·zio** *adj.* recommending. **-ato** *part. adj.* commended; praised. **-atore** *m.* one who commends; Knight of an order of chivalry (see **ordine**); (joc.) prosperous-looking elderly man. (**-atrice** *f.*) **-azione** *f.* commendation. **-evole** *adj.* commendable, praiseworthy. (**-evolmente** *adv.*)

commensale *m., f.* table-companion; messmate; fellow-guest; (zool.) commensal.

commensur-are [A I s] *tr.* to compare, to set beside, to measure (against). **-a·bile** *adj.* commensurable, commensurate. **-abilità** *f. indecl.* commensurability. **-ato** *part. adj.* compared as to measurements. **-azione** *f.* commensuration.

comment-are [A I c] *tr.* to comment upon, to remark upon; to commentate, to edit, to annotate. **-ato** *part. adj.* commented upon; commentated, annotated. **-atore** *m.* commentator. (**-atrice** *f.*)

comment-o¹ *m.* comment, remark; commentary, exposition; far -i, to make remarks (usu. disparaging). **-a·rio** *m.* commentary, summary, résumé, digest.

commento² *m.* (naut.). See **comento²**.

commerci-are [A3] *tr.* (econ.) to market, to sell; *intr.* (*aux.* avere) to trade; to deal, to hold dealings. **-a·bile** *adj.* saleable; marketable; negotiable. **-abilità** *f.* saleability. **-ante** *part. adj.* trading; *n.m.* business man; merchant; trader; dealer; tradesman; -ante in olio, oil dealer; -ante all'ingrosso, wholesaler; -ante al minuto, retailer.

commer·ci-o *m.* commerce; business; trade; Camera di —, Chamber of Commerce; codice di —, commercial law; fuori di —, not on the market; essere in —, to be on sale; metter in —, to put on the market; — all'ingrosso, wholesale trade; — al minuto, retail trade; — di esportazione, export trade; — nazionale, home trade; — bancario, banking business; traders, commercial class; business people; darsi al —, to go in for trade; far — di, to trade in, (fig.) to trade on. **-ale** *adj.* commercial. **-almente** *adv.* commercially.

†**commerite·vole** *adj.* in proportion to the merit; as deserved.

commescol-are [A I sc] *tr.* to mix together, to commingle, to blend. **-ato** *part. adj.* commingled, blended, mixed together.

commessa *f.* shop girl; female clerk; order; a —, bespoke, jobbing; (naut.) offshore purchase.

†**commess-a·rio** *m.* see **commissario**. †**-ione** *f.* see **commissione**.

†**commessazione** *f.* overeating, gluttony.

commesso¹ *part.* of **commettere¹**, q.v.; *adj.* committed; commanded; imposed; pledged; perpetrated; *n.m.* clerk; assistant; — di negozio, shop assistant; substitute, deputy; representative; — viaggiatore, commercial traveller; (naut.) — ai viveri, warrant victualling officer; †ward.

commess-o² *part.* of **commettere²**, q.v.; *adj.* put together, joined side by side; *n.m.* stone for mosaic; mosaic work; splicing; (naut.) art and method of rope-making. **-ura** *f.* junction; (paint.) joint (e.g. knee, elbow).

commesti·bile *adj.* eatable; edible; *n.m.* food, comestible.

commestione *f.* (eccl.) the one full meal allowed on fast days; †meal.

commett-ere¹ [C I] *tr.* to commit, to entrust; — un incarico a, to entrust a task to; to commission; to devote; to perpetrate, to commit; — un errore, to commit an error; †to use, to employ; †— la questione a, to put a matter to, to consult about a matter; †— pace, to make peace; †— battaglia, to open battle, to begin hostilities; †— zuffa, to start to fight; *rfl.* to commit oneself; -ersi al pericolo, to expose oneself to danger. (**-itore** *m.* **-itrice** *f.*)

commett-ere² [C I] *intr.* (*aux.* avere) to fit together; to meet properly; *tr.* to fit together, to join together. **-imale** *m., f. indecl.* mischief-maker. **-itura** *f.* union; fitting together; mosaic; (in rope-making) working up of a hauser, lay.

†**commezz-amento** *m.*, †**-o** *m.* division into two equal parts; point at which the horizon is cut by the southern or northern meridian.

commiat-o *m.* leave-taking; prendere — da, to take leave of; dismissal; discharge; permission to withdraw; repulse; (prosod.) envoi. †**-are** *tr.* to dismiss, to send away; *rfl.* to take one's leave.

commilitone *m.* fellow-soldier.

commin-are [A I] *tr.* (leg.) to comminate; to threaten with a penalty. **-ato·ria** *f.* (leg.) notice or warning in which a penalty is threatened. **-ato·rio** *adj.* (leg.) threatening with or warning of a penalty; termine -atorio, time limit, failure to observe which may entail penalty (as distinguished from 'termine perentorio', an absolute time limit). **-azione** *f.* (leg.) threat, commination.

†**comminuire** *tr.* to diminish, to reduce.

commin-uto *adj.* (med.) comminuted. **-uzione** *f.* (med.) comminution, crushing (of a bone).

commiser-are [A I s] *tr.* to commiserate, to condole with, to have compassion on. **-a·bile** *adj.* commiserable (**-abilmente** *adv.*). **-ando** *adj.* deserving of sympathy. **-ativo** *adj.* sympathetic; commiserating. **-ato** *part. adj.* pitied, sympathized with. **-azione** *f.* commiseration. **-evole** *adj.* deserving of sympathy; wretched; pathetic.

†**commiso** *adj.* See **commesso¹**.

commissa·r-io *m.* commissar; commissioner; minister; inspector; member of a commission; delegate; commissary; (naut.) — di bordo, ship's paymaster; Legal Commissioner (of San Marino). **-iato** *m.* commissariat; commissionership; -iato di polizia, divisional police station; quartermaster-general's office; corpo di -iato military, Army Service Corps.

commission-e *f.* commission; order; errand; deputation; committee; costituire una —, to set up a committee; nominare una —, to appoint a committee; — mista, — paritaria, joint committee; — per il regolamento, standing orders committee; — per la verifica dei conti, auditing committee; — per la verifica dei poteri, credentials committee; — d'esami, body of examiners; — d'inchiesta, committee of inquiry; (leg.) commission; committee; (naut.) — di disciplina, board of inquiry, disciplinary court; — delle prede, prize court. **-are** [A I c] *tr.* to order; to commission; to send on an errand. **-a·rio** *m.* (comm.) commission agent; selling agent. **-ato** *part. adj.* ordered; commissioned.

commist-ione *f.* mixture; (leg.) commingling (C.C.). **-o** *adj.* mixed together. **-ura** *f.* mixture. **-urato** *adj.* mingled.

commisur-are [A I] *tr.* to compare in size; to measure together. **-ato** *part.* compared in size; *adj.* commensurate, commensurable. **-azione** *f.* proportion; proportioning.

committente *m.* one who orders or commissions; purchaser, customer; orderer; (leg.) employer (C.C.).

commo *m.* (Gk. trag.) commos, kommos.

†**com·modo** *adj.* and derivs. See **comodo**.

commodoro *m.* commodore.

commor-are *intr.* to abide; to dwell together. **-ante** *m., f.* dweller. **†-azione** *f.* (rhet.) the dwelling on some important point.

com-mosso *part.* of **commovere**, q.v.; *adj.* moved, touched; irritated, annoyed; ruffled; piqued, riled; †moved, buffeted, swayed, tossed. **†-moto** *adj.* see **commosso**. **†-motivo** *adj.* moving, touching; emotive.

commo·v-ere [C15] *tr.* to move, to affect, to touch; to excite; to disturb; to displace; to shake, to stir; *rfl.* to be moved; to be affected, to be touched; to become agitated; to rebel, to rise. **-ente** *part. adj.* moving, affecting, touching. **-imento** *m.* shock, push, shake; perturbation. (**-itore** *m.* **-itrice** *f.*)

commozione *f.* perturbation; agitation; emotion; (med.) physical injury through impact; — cerebrale, concussion; upheaval; — tellurica, earthquake; †rebellion, tumult.

†commune *adj.* and derivs. See **comune** (1, 2, or 3).

commu·nio *m.* (liturg.; mus.) communion (antiphon).

communire [D2] *tr.* to confirm, to corroborate; to back up.

commuo·vere [C15]. See **commovere**.

commut-are [A1] *tr.* to change, to alter; (leg.) to commute; (electr.) to commutate, to switch over. **-a·bile** *adj.* commutable. (**-abil-mente** *adv.*) **-amento** *m.* commuting; commutation. **-ativo** *adj.* commutative; (leg.) giustizia -ativa, commutative justice, the justice of mutuality of consideration. **-atore** *m.* (electr.) commutator; switch. **-atrice** *f.* (electr.) rotary converter. **-azione** *f.* commutation; switching; (leg.) commutation of a penalty to one less severe.

†como¹ *adv.* See **come**.

†como² *m.* banquet; revelry.

Como³ *pr.n.f.* (geog.) Como; il lago di —, Lake Como.

comò *m. indecl.* chest of drawers; commode.

comod-are [A1S] *tr.* to lend, to furnish, to favour, to accommodate; *intr.* (aux. avere) to suit. **-ata·rio** *m.* (leg.) person who receives the free loan of an article (see **comodato**). **-ato** *part. adj.* lent; furnished; accommodated; *n.m.* (leg.) commodatum (Roman law), free loan of an article. **-atamente** *adv.* easily, comfortably, conveniently. **-atore** *m.* person who lends an article (see **comodato**).

comodino *m.* pedestal cupboard, bedside cupboard; (theatr.) drop-scene; (fam.) fare da —, to make oneself useful in some questionable way.

comodità *f. indecl.* convenience; comfort; opportunity; †benefit, advantage; †fare — a, to help, to assist, to give assistance to; †commode, privy.

co·mod-o *adj.* convenient, comfortable; stia —!, don't get up!, don't trouble!; prendersela -a, to take one's time, to be in no hurry, to take it easy; venite su -i, come up slowly, don't hurry yourselves; commodious; willing, prepared, ready, amenable; *n.m.* convenience, comfort; di —, for convenience; faccia il suo —, you are welcome to do as you please; (iron.) faccia il — suo, have everything your own way; essere in —, to be prepared, to be willing; *pl.* means; (naut.) battere bandiera di —, to fly a flag of convenience (e.g. U.S. liner registered under a Panamanian flag and carrying liquor without tax). (**-amente** *adv.*) **-ac·cio** *m. pejor.* a person's 'own way'; the convenience of one person regardless of the needs of others; fare il -accio suo, to do as one pleases. **-ona** *f.*, **-one** *m.* person who likes to have or do everything his or her own way.

com-padrone *m.* co-proprietor, joint-owner. **-paesano** *m.* fellow-villager; person from the same district.

†compage *f.* density, thickness; structure.

compagin-are¹ [A1S] *tr.* to put (parts) together, to assemble. (**-ato** *part. adj.*)

compagin-are² [A1S] *tr.* to make up into pages, to page. **-ato** *part. adj.* paged. (**-atore** *m.*) **-atura** *f.* (typ.) make-up; paging. **-azione** *f.* paging.

compa·gine *f.* union, closely-fitting joint, connexion; internal structure; (fig.) structure, framework; (sport) team.

compagna¹ *f.* (woman) companion, (woman) friend; partner in a game.

†compagna² *f.* company; guide, companion; tenere — con, to support, to be of the party of; (mil.) company; (Rom. hist.) division of the Roman people, curia.

†compagna³ *f.* (naut.) ship's galley; victualling store.

compagni·a *f.* company; Dama di —, Damigella di —, Lady-in-Waiting; tener — a uno, to keep someone company; (provb.) per — prese moglie un frate, (said of a person who will do any-

thing to be in the swim); (fam.) e —, and co., the whole bunch; e — bella, and all the rest, Uncle Tom Cobley and all; (mil.) company; (hist.) — di ventura, company of mercenaries; (eccl.) confraternity, guild; guild chapel; — di Gesù, Society of Jesus; (finan.; comm.) company; joint-stock company.

compagn-o *m.* companion; friend; comrade; mate; partner in a game; school-fellow, class-mate; (pol.) comrade, fellow Communist; (eccl.) padre —, father *socius*; *adj.* alike, belonging to one another. **-ac·cio** *m.* pal; *pl.* (hist.) a political sect in Florence which opposed Savonarola. **-esco** *adj.* (m.pl. **-eschi**) pertaining to companions; guerra -esca, civil war. **-essa** *f.* (joc.) female companion. **-evole** *adj.* sociable; friendly. (**-evolmente** *adv.*) **-is·simo** *adj. superl.* most friendly; -issimo di, most friendly with, the great friend of. **-one** *m. augm.* of **compagno**; boon companion; accomplice; †equal, fellow; †soldier in the same company; †*adj.* companionable.

†companag·gio *m.* See **companatico**.

compana·tico *m.* food to be eaten with bread (usu. workman's lunch or other picnic meal).

compar- †**ag·gio** *m.,* **-a·tico** *m.* See under **compare**.

compar-are [A1S, A1] *tr.* to compare; †to acquire; †to buy. **-a·bile** *adj.* comparable. (**-abilmente** *adv.*) †**-agione** *f.* see **comparazione**. **-ante** *adj.* comparing; *n.m.* standard of comparison. **-ativo** *adj.* comparative. (**-ativamente** *adv.*) **-ato** *part. adj.* compared; comparative; grammatica -ata, comparative grammar; anatomia -ata, comparative anatomy. (**-atamente** *adv.*) **-atore** *m.* (opt.; techn.) comparator; gauge; -atore pneumatico, air gauge. **-azione** *f.* comparison; a -azione, in comparison; similarity.

compar-e *m.* godfather; sponsor at baptism or confirmation; rimaner —, to make a loan which is not repaid; 'gossip' (one's child's father); witness at wedding, groomsman (comparable to the 'best man' but the relationship is more lasting in Italian ceremonies, approximating to that of godfather); (pop., S. Ital.) friend, comrade, crony; accomplice, confederate (in conjuring or in shady deal). †**-ag·gio** *m.,* **-a·tico** *m.* status of godfather. **-ino** *m.* godson. **-one** *m.* chum, pal.

†comparere *vb.* See **comparire**.

compar-ire [D2] *intr.* (aux. essere) to appear; le comparve un angelo, an angel appeared before her; to make an appearance; non mi -isca più davanti!, don't let me set eyes on you again!; to put in an appearance; to arrive; to turn up; (leg.) — in giudizio, to appear in Court; to appear, to seem; — gran signore, to put on important airs; tutto -iva giusto e regolare, everything seemed fair and square; to show up, to be conspicuous; è cosa fine, non -isce, it's too fine, it doesn't show up; le piace di —, she likes to make a conspicuous appearance. **-ente** *part. adj.* appearing. †**-igione** *f.* (leg.) see **comparizione**. **-iscente** *part. adj.* showy; striking; apparent, obvious. **-ita** *f.* appearing, appearance. **-ito** *part. adj.* appearing. **-izione** *f.* (leg.) appearance, ordine di -izione, sub poena; mandato di -izione, summons to appear before investigating magistrate for a criminal offence.

compars-a *f.* appearance; fare —, to show up, to be noticeable; fare una magnifica —, to look a magnificent figure; (leg.) appearance; mandato di —, summons to appear; la — di risposta, the Defence in civil action; — conclusionale, pleadings in a civil action (similar to the Statement of Claim and the Defence and Counter-claim); *pl.* summons; (mil.) review, parade; tourney; (theatr.) stage-set; walking-on part; stage-extra; film-extra; (fig.) fare da —, to be merely an onlooker, (or) to put in an appearance.

comparso *part.* of **comparire**, q.v.

compart-ecipe *adj.* participating. **-ecipare** [A1sc] *intr.* (aux. avere) to participate; -ecipare ad un'impresa, to share in an undertaking. **-ecipazione** *f.* participation; (comm.) -ecipazione agli utili, profit-sharing; in -ecipazione, in joint account. †**-e·fice** *adj.* see **compartecipe**.

compart-ire [D1, D2] *tr.* to divide, to share; to bestow. **-imento** *m.* compartment, division; -imento stagno, watertight compartment; (fig.) una mente a -imenti stagni, a watertight compartment mind; (geog.) département (of France); (naut.) -imento marittimo, coastal sector (divided into 37 commands in Italy). **-ito** *part. adj.* distributed; divided; bestowed. (**-itore** *m.* **-itrice** *f.*) **-itura** *f.* division into compartments; sharing; distribution. **-izione** *f.* division into compartments; distribution; administrative division.

compascuo *m.* common grazing land.

compass-are *tr.* to measure with compasses; (fig.) to measure; — bene ogni mossa, to work out carefully every move. **-ato** *part. adj.* measured with compasses; (fig.) measured, carefully thought out; slow, dignified and formal; parlare -ato, measured, balanced way of talking; maniere -ate, formal, correct manners. (**-atamente** *adv.*)

†**compassi·bile** *adj.* sympathetic, compassionate.

compassion-are [A I C] *tr.* to have compassion on. †**-a·bile** *adj.* worthy of compassion. **-amento** *m.* pity, compassion, having compassion. **-evole** *adj.* pitiable, piteous; pitiful; compassionate, sympathetic. (**-evolmente** *adv.*)

compassione *f.* compassion; pity; sympathy.

compasso *m.* pair of compasses, dividers; — a grossezze, calipers, compasses bent inwards at the points for measuring the diameter of solid objects; — a vite, screw gauge; (eng.) — ballerino, inside caliper; (fig.) col —, with measured care; avere il — negli occhi, to be a good judge of distances; †section; †subdivision; †compartment.

compastor-e *m.*, **-ella** *f.* fellow-member of the Arcadia Academy.

compat-ire [D 2] *tr.* to pity, to have pity on, to sympathize with; to regard with indulgence, to pardon, to excuse; -itemi se sbaglio, I ask your indulgence if I am mistaken; farsi —, to make a pitiful exhibition of oneself; †*intr.* — a, to be sorry for; to be fellow-sufferers; *recip. rfl.* to put up with one another. **-i·bile** *adj.* deserving of pity; excusable. (**-ibilmente** *adv.*) **-ibilità** *f.* compatibility. **-imento** *m.* sympathy; indulgence; tolerance.

compatriot-a *m.*, *f.* compatriot, fellow-countryman. **-o** *m.* (pop.) see **compatriota**.

compatron-o *m.*, **-a** *f.* (eccl.) joint patron (saint or other).

compattezza *f.* compactness; conciseness.

compatto *adj.* compact; concise; *n.m.* (typ.) close type.

compaziente *adj.* compassionate, sympathetic.

compendi-are [A 4] *tr.* to abridge, to make a précis of, to summarize. **-ato** *part. adj.* abridged, in précis form. **-atamente** *adv.* in brief. **-atore** *m.* précis-writer, abridger.

compen·di-o *m.* compendium, abridgment, précis, summary; shortened version; in —, in brief, in précis form; (leg.) il — del furto, the substance of the theft, the stolen goods; — ereditario, summary of statement of the estate of a deceased person. **-ario** *adj.* in abridged form. **-oso** *adj.* shortened, abbreviated, abridged, summarized; †via -osa, short cut, quickest way. (**-osamente** *adv.*) **-osità** *f.* shortness, conciseness.

compenetr-are [A I S] *tr.* to interpenetrate, to permeate, to infiltrate into. **-a·bile** *adj.* capable of interpenetration. **-abilità** *f. indecl.* capability of or liability to interpenetration. **-ato** *part. adj.* permeated; mi sento -ato da gran rispetto, I am filled with respect. **-azione** *f.* interpenetration, permeation, infiltration.

compens-are [A I] *tr.* to compensate, to make up for, to make good; to reward. **-a·bile** *adj.* that may be compensated. **-abilità** *f. indecl.* capability of being compensated. **-amento** *m.* compensation. **-ativo** *adj.* compensating. **-ato** *part. adj.* compensated; legno -ato, plywood; (paperm.) cartone -ato a quattro strati, four-sheet. **-atore** *m.* compensator; -atori di derivazione, correcting magnets. **-azione** *f.* compensation; (leg.) compensation; satisfaction; (finan.) stanza di -azione, clearing house; (mech.) pendulum, governor; (naut.) compass correction.

compenso *m.* compensation; making good; remuneration; reward; in —, in compensation; talvolta non scrive nulla per un mese, in — poi manda due letters di fila, sometimes he doesn't write for a month, then, on the contrary (or, to make up for it) he writes two letters straight off; (naut.) substitute or assistant frame; — di costruzione, building subsidy; — di navigazione, seagoing subsidy; — di stallio, demurrage; (comm.) settlement of account in Stock Exchange; prezzi di —, settlement prices; (leg.) set-off; †uomo di molti -i, resourceful man, cunning man.

compera *f.* See **compra**.

comper-are [A I S] and derivs. See **comprare**. **-a·bile** *adj.* purchasable.

†**compesare** *vb.* See **compensare**.

compet-ente *adj.* suitable; apt; mancia —, adequate tip, generous tip; (leg.) competent, qualified; *n.m.* †competitor; *pl.* (eccl. hist.) competentes. **-entemente** *adv.* competently; suitably. **-enza** *f.* competence; sphere of competence; qualifications; questo non è di tua -enza, this is not part of your duties; (leg.) competence; jurisdiction; oltrepassare i limiti della -enza, to be 'ultra vires'; *pl.* fees; allowances; terms of equality.

compe·t-ere [C I def.] *intr.* to compete; to dispute; (leg.) to be, or to lie, within the jurisdiction; non -e a questo foro, it is not within the jurisdiction of this court. **-itore** *m.* competitor, rival. (**-itrice** *f.*) **-izione** *f.* competition.

compiac-ente *adj.* obliging; tolerant, complaisant; indulgent; willing. (**-entemente** *adv.*) **-enza** *f.* satisfaction; complaisance; courtesy, kindness, goodness; abbia la -enza di, be good enough to; †adulation.

compiac-ere [B 20] *intr.* (*aux.* avere; *prep.* a) to give pleasure (to), to please; to satisfy; to fall in with the whims (of); *rfl.* to feel satisfaction; -ersi con, to congratulate; -ersi di, to take pleasure in; mi compiaccio di avervi conosciuto, I am so glad to have met you; to be pleased to; *tr.* to please, to satisfy, to pacify, to placate; †to grant, to concede. **-evole** *adj.* pleasing, satisfying; flattering. **-imento** *m.* pleasure, satisfaction, delight (esp. of an august or superior person); consent, approval.

†**compia·gnere** *vb.* See **compiangere**.

compian·gere [G 5] *tr.* to pity; to lament, to mourn; *rfl.* (*prep.* di, per) to complain (of); to lament, to mourn.

compianto *part.* of **compiangere**, q.v.; *adj.* lamented, mourned, late; il — Benedetto Croce, the late lamented Benedetto Croce; *n.m.* mourning, lament.

compicciare [A 3] *tr.* (colloq.) to put together, to finish, to get through; — bugie, to tell lies; non — nulla, to be unable to do a thing; con questo caldo non mi riesce — nulla, I can't do a thing in this heat.

compiegare [A 2] *tr.* to fold together; to enclose.

compiere [D I I]. See **compire**.

compieta, compieta *f.* (liturg.) compline; (fig.) eventide (of life).

†**compietare** *tr.* to commiserate with, to sympathize with.

†**compi·glio** *m.* hive.

compil-are [A I] *tr.* to compile; to put together, to compose, to write; — un modulo, to fill in a form. **-ato** *part. adj.* compiled; put together, composed; filled in. (**-atore** *m.* **-atrice** *f.*) †**-atura** *f.* compilation; compiling; completion. **-azione** *f.* compilation; compiling; work compiled.

†**compinto** *adj.* moved, stirred; stimulated, incited.

comp-ire [D I] *tr.* to fulfil, to accomplish; to execute, to carry out; to complete; — gli anni, to have a birthday; oggi mia figlia -ie nove anni, my daughter is nine years old today; †to fill; †to satisfy; †to see to the needs of; †to supply; †— a, to satisfy; *rfl.* to come to pass. †**-ita** *f.* see **compimento**. **-imento** *m.* conclusion; perfection; completion; consummation, execution; complement, supplement. **-itezza** *f.* politeness, good manners. **-ito** *part. adj.* supplied, fulfilled, adequate, perfect; accomplished, well-mannered, polite, gentlemanly; -ita, ladylike. **-itamente** *adv.* adequately; in a finished manner; perfectly; with polish, politely. (**-itore** *m.*)

compital-e *adj.* (Rom. antiq.) compital; divinità —, guardian of the crossways. **-i·zio** *adj.* (Rom. antiq.) compital.

compit-are [A I SC] *tr.* to spell out, to pronounce syllable by syllable; †to compute. **-ato** *part. adj.* spelled out; †written out in full, not abbreviated. **-azione** *f.* spelling.

compito[1], **com·pito** *m.* task, duty, job; task set as homework; *pl.* homework, prep; a —, carefully, thoughtfully; †account, sum.

compito[2] *adj.*, *part.* of **compire**, q.v.

compiut-o *part.* of **compiere**, q.v.; *adj.* completed, perfected; fatto —, fait accompli; luna -a, full moon; †fully grown; †adult, mature. **-amente** *adv.* completely, fully.

†**complacenza**. See **compiacenza**.

†**complantato** *adj.* natural, innate, inherent.

complato·nico *adj.* (philos.) fellow-Platonist.

compleanno *m.* birthday; anniversary.

complement-o *m.* complement, supplement; (math.) complement; (gramm.) complement; (mil.) ufficiale di —, officer not in the regular army. **-are** *adj.* complementary; scuola -are, school for children of over 11 who continue practical instruction (handicrafts, etc.) for three or four years after the 'scuola elementare'; (finan.) imposta -are, tassa -are, direct tax on income.

complession-e *f.* constitution; è di sana —, he has a strong, healthy constitution; disposition; †combination of elements, complex. **-are** [A I C] *tr.* to form, to build, to give a structure or constitution to. **-ato** *part. adj.* formed, having a certain constitution; bene -ato, having a good constitution; male -ato, having a weak constitution. **-cella**, **-cina** *f. dim.* delicate constitution. **-uc·cia** *f.* very weak constitution.

compless-ivo *adj.* comprehensive; aggregate; l'ammontare —, the aggregate amount; entrata -iva, gross income; studio —, survey; un giudizio — di un libro, a considered opinion on a book as a whole; *n.m.* (eng.) assembly, unit; assembly drawing. **-ivamente** *adv.* comprehensively, on the whole. **-ità** *f.* complexity.

complesso *adj.* complex; (math.) numero —, complex number (referring to quantities expressed in non-decimal systems, as pounds, shillings and pence); robust, sturdy; *n.m.* complex; mass, aggregate; in —, on the whole; votare sul —, to vote on the motion as a whole; assembly, unit, set; (mus.) opera company, ballet company; ensemble; combination; (psych.) complex; (comm.) group, chain, combine; (industr.) large works; (leg.) — delle leggi, body of laws; †embrace.

complet-are [A I] *tr.* to complete. **-amento** *m.* completing; completion. **-ato** *part. adj.* completed; -ato con, furnished with, complete with, together with.

complet-o *adj.* complete, entire; finished, done; full up; al —, entirely; siamo al —?, are we all here?; — di, complete with, containing, including; *n.m.* suit (of jacket, waistcoat and trousers). **-amente** *adv.* completely. **-ivo** *adj.* complementary. **-orio** *adj.* supplementary.

†complet·tere *tr.* to include, to implicate.

complic-are [A 2 s] *tr.* to complicate; †to combine; *rfl.* to become complicated; la faccenda si -a, the plot thickens; (med.) la malattia s'è -ata, complications have set in. **-anza** *f.* complication (complicating circumstance); increased difficulty. **-atezza** *f.* complicatedness, complication. **-ato** *part. adj.* complicated; complex; involved; †intertwined, interlocked, linked. **-azione** *f.* complication.

com·plic-e *m.* (leg.) accomplice; associate; accessory; un — nella congiura, a party to the conspiracy. **-ità** *f. indecl.* (leg.) complicity or participation in a crime.

compliment-are [A I c] *tr.* to compliment; to congratulate. **-ato** *part. adj.* complimented; congratulated.

compliment-o *m.* compliment, wish, salutation; far -i, to stand on ceremony, to be coy about accepting; non faccia -i, senza -i, don't stand on ceremony, make yourself at home; senza -i, without flattery; senza -i, ti dico, I tell you frankly; senza tanti -i, without preamble, forthwith, brusquely; †completion; †complement. **-ac·cio** *m. pejor.* back-handed compliment. **-oso** *adj.* full of compliments, obsequious; flattering; ceremonious; on one's best behaviour. (**-osamente** *adv.*)

†complire *intr.* to exchange compliments.

complott-o *m.* plot, conspiracy; (naut.) mutiny in merchant navy by three members of crew or more up to the number of one-third. **-are** [A I] *tr.* to plot against; *intr.* (aux. avere) to plot.

complu·vio *m.* (Rom. antiq.) compluvium; (bldg.) juncture at the bottom of two sloping roofs where rainwater is collected.

compon-ente *adj.* component, conciliatory; *n.m.* component, constituent; — di una commissione, member of a committee; i -enti di una ditta, the members or partners of a firm. **-icchiare** [A 4] *intr.* (aux. avere) to dabble in composing. **†-ista** *m.* composer. **-itore** *m.* composer (of differences), conciliator; †author. (**-itrice** *f.*) **†-itura** *f.* composition.

†compo·nere *vb.* and derivs. See **comporre**.

componimento *m.* composition; essay; literary work; conciliation; agreement; (leg.) composition; settlement; arrangement; †temperance, moderation.

comporre [B 21] *tr.* to compound; to make up; to compose; — un cadavere, to lay out a body; (mus.) to compose; (leg.) to settle by negotiation, to make an accommodation; — una causa, to compromise an action; (typ.) to compose; to set (type); †to reconcile; †to prearrange, to agree upon; *rfl.* to be composed; to behave correctly.

comport-are [A I] *tr.* to tolerate, to put up with, to stand, to bear; to imply; to involve; — ingenti spese, to involve enormous expense; prezzi che non -ano riduzioni, prices on which no reduction can be made; *rfl.* to behave; to contain oneself. **-a·bile** *adj.* tolerable, bearable. **-abilmente** *adv.* tolerably; -abilmente con, in conformity with. **-amentismo** *m.*, **-ameti·stica** *f.* (psych.) behaviourism. **-amento** *m.* behaviour; action, actions; (leg.) deportment (C.C.). **†-ativo** *adj.* long-suffering, tolerant. **-ato** *part. adj.* tolerated, borne; implied; involved. **-evole** *adj.* tolerable, bearable; convenient. (**-evolmente** *adv.*)

comporto *m.* tolerance; grace; tregi orni di —, three days grace;

(rlwy.) the length of time a train will wait if a connecting train is late.

com·pos *Lat. phr.* — sui, of sound mind, *compos mentis*.

compositivo *adj.* synthetic.

compo·sito *adj.* compound; (archit.) composite.

composito·io *m.* (typ.) composing-stick.

composit-ore *m.* composer; (mus.) composer; (typ.) compositor; type-setter; composing-stick. **-rice** *f.* woman composer; (typ.) typesetting machine. **†-ura** *f.* see **composizione**.

composizione *f.* composition; (mus.) composition (in both senses, viz. the act of composing, or a piece of music which has been composed); (comm.) composition fee; (typ.) composition, setting; †reconciliation; †temperance, moderation.

compossess-o *m.* (leg.) possession in common. **-ore** *m.* (leg.) possessor in common.

†compossi·bile *adj.* compatible.

compost-a *f.* compote; oatmeal, chopped hay, etc. mixed with water as a cattle food; compost. **-iera** *f.* compote dish.

compost-o, **compost-o** *part.* of **comporre**, q.v.; *adj.* compound, compounded; combined; composed, collected; neat and tidy; (opt.) lente -a, compound lens; (bldg.) trave -a, built-up beam; trave a doppio T —, girder, compound H-beam; (naut.) albero —, composite mast; (mus.) intervallo —, compound interval; movimento per intervalli -i, conjunct movement; (herald.) compony, gobony; *n.m.* compound; fruit juice and syrup or milk, eggs and syrup; †fare — con, to agree with, to match, to be in conformity with. **-amente** *adv.* in ordered fashion; composedly; †in entirety, as a whole, generally. **-ezza** *f.* calmness; correctness, orderliness; modesty.

compotazione *f.* banquet.

compound *m. indecl.* (eng.) compound steam engine.

com·pra, **compra** *f.* purchase; — a pagamento rateale, hire purchase; fare le compre, to shop.

compr-are [A I, A I c] *tr.* to buy, to purchase; — a contanti, to buy for cash; — a credito, — a respiro, to buy on easy terms, to buy on hire-purchase; — a buon mercato, to buy cheaply; — di seconda mano, to buy second-hand; (fig.) — e non vendere, to hear without repeating, to listen and say nothing; venderla come s'è -ata, to tell something just as it was heard; to buy over, to bribe. **†-abrighe** *m.* see **accattabrighe**, under **accattare**. **-atore** *m.* purchaser; buyer (esp. in fashion or textile trades). (**-atrice** *f.*) **-avendita** *f.* (leg.) agreement for sale and purchase; compromesso di -avendita, contract and conditions of sale and purchase; atto di -avendita, conveyance on sale.

compren·d-ere [C I] *tr.* to comprise; to embrace; to include, to cover; to understand, to comprehend; to make out; †to reach, to attain to; †to surprise, to apprehend; †to intend. **-i·bile** *adj.* comprehensible, understandable. **-imento** *m.* comprehension, understanding; †circuit, circumference (of an area); †area of land.

comprend-o·nio *m.*, **-o·nia** *f.* (fam.) nous, power of understanding; duro di —, 'slow on the uptake'. **-o·nico** *m.* judgement, intellect.

comprens·i·bile *adj.* understandable, comprehensible. (**-ibilmente** *adv.*) **-ibilità** *f.* understandableness, comprehensibility. **-ione** *f.* comprehension, understanding; sympathy; (theol.) comprehension (in the Beatific Vision). **-iva** *f.* faculty of understanding. **-ivo** *adj.* sympathetic; understanding; comprehensive. (**-ivamente** *adv.*) **-ore** *m.* (theol.) comprehensor. **-o·rio** *m.* (leg.) -orio di bonifica, area comprised in land-improvement or reclamation scheme (C.C.).

compres-o *part. adj.* comprised, included, embraced; tutto —, all included, all in; contained; understood, comprehended; taken up, occupied; — di meraviglia, filled with wonder; — della sua autorità, filled with a sense of his authority; †possessed (by a demon); †apprehended; *adv.* including; inclusively; *n.m.* circuit, area, district. **†-a** *f.* district, area, environs.

compress-a *f.* (med.) compress (dressing); (pharm.) compress, tablet. **-i·bile** *adj.* compressible. **-ibilità** *f.* compressibility; (techn.) compressibility. **-ione** *f.* compression; (med.) compression; — cerebrale, compression of the brain; (med.) compress, dressing; disposition (cf. **complessione**). **-ivo** *adj.* compressing.

compress-o[1] *part.* of **comprimere**, q.v.; *adj.* compressed, pressed together; concise; oppressed. **-ore** *adj.* compressing; rullo -ore, steam-roller; *n.m.* (anat., med.; eng.) compressor; (motor.) supercharger; (motor-racing, etc.) con -ore, supercharged; roller; -ore stradale, street-roller.

†compresso² *adj.* robust, sturdy.

comprima·rio *adj.* (theatr.; mus.) pertaining to a secondary role; *n.m.* (theatr.; mus.) actor or singer cast for a secondary role in an opera; le parti di —, supporting roles; (med.) a doctor who shares controlling duties with a 'primario', q.v.

comprim·ere [c18] *tr.* to compress; to restrain; to repress; †to oppress; †to violate; †to draw forth, to suck out. **-imento** *m.* compressing, restraining.

†compriso *adj.* See **compreso.**

compro¹ *apocop. part.* of **comprare,** q.v.

†compro² *m.* See **compra.**

†comprobare *vb.* See **comprovare.**

compromesso *part.* of **compromettere,** q.v.; *adj.* compromised; *n.m.* (leg.) compromise; agreement to go to arbitration; conditional contract; — di compravendita, contract and conditions of sale and purchase.

compromettere [c20] *tr.* to compromise; (leg.) to compromise; to go or to refer to arbitration; *rfl.* to compromise oneself, to be compromised; to become committed.

compromiss·a·rio *m.* (leg.) arbitrator; umpire. **-o·rio** *adj.* (leg.) having to do with compromise or arbitration; clausola **-oria,** arbitration clause.

compromissione *f.* compromise.

compropriet·à *f. indecl.* joint-ownership. **-a·rio** *m.* joint-owner, part-owner.

comprotettore *m.* joint protector (e.g. a patron saint).

comprov·are [a1] *tr.* to prove, to confirm absolutely; †to approve; †*rfl.* to be tested. **-a·bile** *adj.* provable, that may be proved. **-ato** *part. adj.* proved; confirmed. **-azione** *f.* proof, confirmation; approval.

comprovinciale *adj.* belonging to the same province; belonging jointly to more than one province (e.g. a hospital, etc.).

†compto *adj.* adorned.

comptometrista *m.* comptometer operator.

compuls·are [a1] *tr.* to consult; to examine; to compare; to check; to inspect; to look through (papers, documents); to flip through (pages of a book). **-ione** *f.* compulsion; restriction; (eng.) propulsion by several forces.

compun·gere [c5] *tr.* to sting, to cause pain to; (rel.) to prick (of conscience), to cause remorse to; *rfl.* to feel remorse.

compunto *part.* of **compungere,** q.v., *adj.* remorseful, grieved; demure; wearing an expression of sorrow; (rel.) contrite, remorseful; †pricked; †urged.

compunzione *f.* compunction; demureness.

comput·are [a1] *tr.* to compute, to reckon, to count; to take into account; (leg.) to calculate, to count; — il sofferto, to take into account the time spent in custody or under arrest; *rfl.* to be computed; to be reckoned; (leg.) i giorni festivi si **-ano** nel termine, Sundays and Bank Holidays are counted in the period. **-a·bile** *adj.* calculable, that may be reckoned. **-ato** *part. adj.* computed, calculated, worked out; tutto **-ato,** when all has been taken into account, all things considered. **-azione** *f.* computation, calculation, reckoning, taking into account.

comput·ista *m.* accountant. **-isteri·a** *f.* accountancy; book-keeping; accountant's office. **i·stico** *adj.* relating to accountancy and book-keeping.

com·puto *m.* calculation, computation; (eccl.) computus, table of movable feasts; (leg.) calculation (of periods, etc.); il — dei termini di prescrizione, the calculation of periods of limitation or prescription.

†comuna *f.* See **comune.**

comunal·e *adj.* belonging to the commune, municipal, civic, public; communal, belonging to, having to do with the municipality; Teatro —, Municipal Theatre (in Florence); (pertaining to) town, parish; palazzo —, town hall, guildhall; commonplace, ordinary; †accommodating; †lenient; †affable, benign. **-mente** *adv.* communally; generally.

comunardo *m.* (hist.) Paris commune of 1871.

comunanza *f.* community; society; fellowship; in —, in common; — d'interessi, community of interests, interests in common.

†comunare *vb.* See **accomunare.**

†comunche *adv.* however (cf. **comunque**); *conj.* when; as.

comun·e¹ *adj.*

    1. COMMON, ordinary, plain; commonplace, trite, undistinguished; l'uomo —, the ordinary man, the man in the street;

anno —, ordinary year (not leap year); vino —, ordinary, table wine; un luogo —, a commonplace, a trite remark, a platitude (or, a public place, see no. 2); maniere molto **-i,** vulgar manners; (mil.) soldato —, private soldier; (naut.) marinaio —, ordinary seaman; marinaio — di prima classe, able seaman. **2.** COMMON, shared, mutual; diritto —, common law; — a tutti, common to all, shared by all; un luogo —, a public place, a place open to all (or, a commonplace, see no. 1); (provb.) mal — mezzo gaudio, when everyone is in the same boat it is easier to bear the hardship; il nostro — amico, our mutual friend; fare vita —, to live a life in common, to live together; (comm.) conto —, joint-account; (gramm.) genere —, common gender; nome —, common noun (but cf. under no. 3); (leg.) delitti di — pericolo, crimes to the common danger (C.P.); *adv. phr.* in —, in common, communally; avere in —, to share; vivere in —, to live together; comprare una casa in —, to share in the purchase of a house. **3.** COMMON, usual, habitual, general; una malattia — ai vecchi, an illness common in old people; Rossi è un nome molto —, Rossi is a very common (usual) name; senso —, meaning generally understood; questa frase non fa senso —, this sentence does not make sense; un'abitudine —, a general habit; †popular; †affable, benign; †lenient; †impartial, neutral. **-emente** *adv.* commonly; generally; usually; in common. **†-e·vole** *adj.* communal; †-o *adj.* see **comune.**

comun·e² *m.* generality; the general run; il — degli uomini, most people; levarsi dal —, to rise above the common level; civic centre, municipal offices or buildings; urban district; administrative area presided over by a mayor; frazione di un —, village, hamlet or group of houses at some distance from the town in whose municipal area it is; commune; local government (mayor and town council); Palazzo del Comune, town hall, guildhall; dirla al popolo e al —, to tell all and sundry; la Camera dei Comuni, i Comuni, the (British) House of Commons; ai Comuni, in the Commons; (liturg.) common; (hist.) commune; (mil.) private soldier. **-ella** *f. dim.* small party, group; far **-ella,** to band together; master-key (e.g. to rooms in a hotel). **-ello** *m. dim.* small, rural commune.

comun·e³ *f.* generality, the general run; la — dei lettori, most readers; (Tusc.) town hall, guildhall, municipal offices (but usu. **comune²,** q.v.); (hist.) the communes of Paris in 1792 and 1871; (theatr.) principal door in a stage-set.

comunic·are [a2s] *tr.* to communicate, to impart; (eccl.) to give Holy Communion to; *intr.* (aux. avere) to communicate; to be in touch; to live together; to have things in common; *rfl.* to be made common; (eccl.) to make one's communion, to go to Holy Communion. **-a·bile** *adj.* communicable, that may be imparted; †affable, accessible. **-abilità** *f.* communicableness, communicability. (**-amento** *m.*) **-ando** *m.,* **-anda** *f.* (eccl.) communicant (esp. one making First Communion). **-ante** *adj.* communicating; due camere **-anti,** two bedrooms with a communicating door; *n.m.* (eccl.) (priest) giving Holy Communion; person receiving Holy Communion, communicant; *pl.* (eccl. hist.) (Anabaptist) communicantes. **†-anza** *f.* communication; community; resemblance, connection. **-ativa** *f.* faculty of imparting knowledge, aptitude for teaching; gift of establishing contact or 'getting across' to an audience. **-ativo** *adj.* communicative; (med.) catching. **-ato** *part. adj.* communicated, imparted; *n.m., f.* (rel.) communicant; communiqué; bulletin; **-ato stampa,** press release. (**-atore** *m.* **-atrice** *f.*) **-ato·rio** *m.* (eccl.) communion grille. **-azione** *f.* communication; means of communication; message; **-azione telefonica,** telephone call; non riesco ad avere la **-azione,** I can't get through on the phone; c'è una **-azione** per Lei, you're wanted on the phone; mettere in **-azione,** to put through (on the phone); togliere la **-azione,** to cut off; **-azione intercomunale,** trunk call; strada di grande **-azione,** main road, trunk road. †Communion.

comunichino *m.* (eccl.) small host; communion cloth; communion grille.

comun·ione *f.* communion; community; (theol.) communion (of the faithful), Communion (of Saints); (liturg.) (the) communion as part of the Mass; (mus.) Communion antiphon; (eccl.) Holy Communion (as given in church or taken to the sick and dying); è passata ora la —, the priest has just gone by with the Blessed Sacrament; (leg.) — degli acquisti, community of after-acquired property (C.C.); (fam.) botte, pugni, da —, blows, beating,

comun·ione (*cont.*)
enough to make one send for a priest, enough to bring one to death's door.

comun·ismo *m.* communism. **-ista** *m.*, *f.* (*m.pl.* **-isti**, *f.pl.* **-iste**) communist.

comunit·à *f.* community; fellowship; association; commonwealth; la — Britannica, the British Commonwealth; (rel.) community; town hall, civic offices, municipal buildings. **-ativo** *adj.* municipal.

†comuno *m.* See **comune**².

comunqu·e *adv.*, *conj.* in whatever manner; although; however; anyhow, all the same; †when, as soon as. **†-emente** *adv.* however, in whatever manner.

con¹ *prep.* (*contr.* with *def. art.*: **col**, **colla**, **coi**, **cogli**, **colle**) with; in company with, accompanied by; by means of; viaggiare col treno, to travel by train; leggere cogli occhiali, to wear glasses for reading; studiare —, to study under; — l'alba, at dawn; combattere col nemico, to fight against the enemy; si picchiò col fratello, he had a fight with his brother; partirono — un freddo invernale, it was as cold as winter when they left; gentile — tutti, charming to everyone; — tutto ciò, nevertheless, all the same; in spite of, notwithstanding; — tanti denari non è felice, with all his money, he's not happy; (rowing) due —, a coxed pair.

†con² *conj.* See **come**.

conato *m.* effort, attempt; (scient.) conatus, nisus; conati di vomito, retching.

conc·a *f.* large earthenware washing-pot; any kind of large open vessel; basin, hollow container; (geog.) small basin, depression; lock; reservoir; cavity; (oceanog.) cauldron; (fig.) — fessa, sickly, ailing person; (provb.) dura più una — fessa che una sana, a creaking gate hangs longest; (geog.) large hollow surrounded by hills; la Conca d'Oro, name of the environs of Palermo; (med.) concha, hollow of the external ear; (zool.) conch-shell; (hydraul.) lock-chamber; (of a canal) a —, furnished with locks; (archit.) concha, conch, shell (of a vault); (naut.) unprotected anchorage surrounded by lowland. **-ata** *f.* tubful, basinful.

concamer·are [A I s] *tr.* (archit.) to concamerate, to vault. (**-ato** *part. adj.*) **-azione** *f.* (archit.) concameration; (phys.) curve of a sound-wave.

concapitano *m.* fellow-captain.

concaten·are [A I c] *tr.* to link together; to connect, to join; (fig.) — le idee, to trace or establish a connexion between one idea and another. **-amento** *m.* linking together. **-ato** *part. adj.* linked together; concatenate(d). **-atura** *f.* link, linkage. **-azione** *f.* linking together; concatenation; manca la -azione tra queste idee, there is no connexion between these ideas.

concattedrale *f.* (eccl.) con-cathedral (church).

conca·us·a *f.* joint cause; contributory cause, concause; (leg.) pre-existing cause as a result of which a crime has an unusually serious effect. **-ale** *adj.* acting as a contributing cause, concausal; (leg.) operating as a 'concausa'; *n.f.* (leg.) see **concausa**. **-are** [A I] *tr.* to help to cause, to contribute towards.

concavità *f.* concavity, concaveness; cavity.

con·cavo *adj.* concave; *n.m.* hollow.

conce·d·ere [C 19] *tr.* to grant, to concede; to accord; -etemi un po' di tempo, give me a little time; -o che sia un po' pigro, I admit he's rather lazy; — di, to allow of; *rfl.* (*acc.* of *prep.* **si**) to yield; to give oneself up; (*dat.* of *prep.* **si**) to allow oneself; mi sono finalmente concesso una piccola vacanza, I finally allowed myself a brief holiday. **-ente** *part. adj.*, *n.m.* (leg.) grantor. **-i·bile** *adj.* that may be granted, admissible. **-imento** *m.* concession. (**-itore** *m.* **-itrice** *f.*) **-uto** *part. adj.* see **concesso**.

concento *m.* (mus.) harmony of voices and instruments; harmoniousness, concent; dolce —, sweet harmony.

concentr·are [A I] *tr.* to concentrate; to gather in one place; *rfl.* to concentrate; -arsi in un pensiero, to fix one's mind on a thought. **-amento** *m.* concentrating, concentration; campo di -amento, concentration camp. **-ato** *part. adj.* concentrated, gathered in one place; una soluzione -ata, a concentrated solution; condensed; pomodoro -ato, tomato purée; capable of mental concentration. **-azione** *f.* concentration; (pol.) coalition.

concen·tric·o *adj.* concentric. **-amente** *adv.* concentrically.

†conce·pere *vb.* See **concepire**.

concep·ire [D 2] *tr.* to conceive; — un bambino, to conceive a baby; — un poema, to conceive a poem; — stima per, to conceive esteem for; to engender, to create; to imagine, to envisage; to conceive of; to understand; to form, to formulate; — sospetti, to entertain suspicions; *abs.* to conceive, to become pregnant. **-i·bile** *adj.* conceivable. **-ibilità** *f.* conceivability, conceivableness. **-imento** *m.* conceiving; conception. **-ito** *part. adj.* conceived; thought of, considered; imagined, envisaged; understood; formed, formulated; worded, phrased.

conceri·a *f.* tannery; tanning, leather dressing.

concer·n·ere [C def.] *tr.* to concern, to have to do with, to relate to, to regard; questo non ti -e, this is no concern of yours. **-ente** *part. prep.* concerning, regarding, about, with regard to, relating to.

concert·are [A I] *tr.* to concert; to plan; to plot, to hatch; to arrange, to adjust; to agree; (mus.) to conduct; to rehearse; to orchestrate, to score. **-amento** *m.* (mus.) ensemble; arrangement; act of rehearsing. **-ante** *n.m.*, *f.* (mus.) performer in a concert; concerted part. **-ato** *part. adj.* concerted; planned; plotted, hatched; arranged, adjusted; agreed; (mus.) concerted; orchestrated, scored; *n.m.* (mus.) concerted piece. **-atore** *m.* plotter; arranger; (mus.) opera coach. (**-atrice** *f.*) **-azione** *f.* (mus.) arrangement; orchestration, score.

concert·o *m.* (mus.) concert; concerto; ensemble; — grosso, grand concerto (in which the concertino of solo parts is contrasted with the full body of strings); piano da —, concert grand-piano; agreement, concerted action; fare —, to go well together; di — in agreement. **-ina** *f.* (mus.) concertina. **-ino** *m.* short concerto; concertino, the solo parts in a concerto grosso. **-ismo** *m.* concert-giving. **-ista** *m.*, *f.* recitalist; musician of soloist calibre; performer in a concert. **-i·stico** *adj.* relating to a concert; società -istiche concert societies.

concess·ione *f.* concession; permission; permit; (leg.) government licence; — di pesca, fishing licence. **-iona·rio** *m.* (leg.) holder of a concession or privilege or grant, concessionaire; agent; -ionario di brevetto, patentee; -ionario di licenza, licensee. **-ioncella** *f.* *dim.* slight concession. **-ivo** *adj.* (gramm.) concessive. (**-ivamente** *adv.*) **-ore** *m.* (leg.) grantor.

concesso *part.* of **concedere**, q.v.; *adj.* granted, conceded; allowed; admitted; dato e non —, granted for the sake of argument.

concett·o¹ *m.* concept, notion, idea; opinion; estimate; reputation; essere in buon —, to have a good reputation; (verbal, literary) conceit; lavoro di —, (in business or admin.) work involving judgement and capacity to use initiative and make decisions; elemento femminile di —, female assistant engaged for work involving judgement, initiative and decision; elemento maschile di —, male assistant engaged for such work. **†**See **concepimento**, under **concepire** or **concezione**. **-ino** *m.* *dim.* of **concetto**; quaint idea; silly or rather clever, literary conceit. **-ivo** *adj.* full of ideas. **-izzare** [A I] *intr.* (*aux.* avere) to indulge in literary conceits. **-one** *m.* *augm.* (joc.) brilliant idea, brainwave. **-oso** *adj.* succinct; full of conceits; full of laboured conceits. (**-osamente** *adv.*) **-osità** *f.* *indecl.* succinctness; conceited style. **-uale** *adj.* conceptual, ideal, relating to mental conception. **-ualismo** *m.* conceptualism (in medieval philosophy). **-ualista** *m.* conceptualist. **-uc·cio**, **-uzzo** *m.* *pejor.* silly, frivolous notion.

†concetto² *part.* of **concepire**, q.v.

concezion·e *f.* conception; axiom; principle; (theol.) l'Immacolata Concezione, the Immaculate Conception; feast or church of this title. **-ale** *adj.* conceptional. **-ismo** *m.* conceptualism (in modern philosophy).

conchi·fero *adj.* (geol.) conchiferous.

conchi·gl·ia *f.* (zool.) shell (of a mollusc); (zool.) — dei pellegrini, — di S. Jacopo, scallop, *Pecten jacobaeus*; (archit.) conch-shaped ornament; (foundry) chill; (herald.) escallop, scallop; — di San Giacomo, vannet. **-ia·ceo** *adj.* (zool.) shell-like. **-iforme** *adj.* shell-shaped. **-iologi·a** *f.* conchology.

†conchile *m.* See **conchiglia**.

conchiu·dere [C 3] See **concludere**.

conchiusione *f.* See **conclusione**.

conci·a *f.* (*pl.* **conce**) trade or science of tanning; tan, tanning material; tanyard; dye-bath for dyeing clothes; fragrance; perfume; doctoring (of wine); treatment, pickling (of olives, and tobacco for snuff); fish-pickling; (text.) lana di —, fellmongred wool. **-a·ia** *f.* tan-pit; manure-pit. **-ai(u)olo** *m.* tanyard hand.

conci·are [A 3 c] *tr.* to tidy up, to dress, to 'do' (e.g. hair); to adorn; to tan; — al cromo, to chrome tan; to dress; to prepare, to dress (tobacco for snuff, flax for spinning, etc.); (fig.) to ill-use, to knock

conci-are *(cont.)*
about; to spoil, to disfigure; — uno per le feste, to give someone a good thrashing, to deal with severely; to treat (wine); to castrate (pigs, calves, etc.); to cut (diamonds); (med.) to set (fractures); to replace (dislocations); to trim; *rfl.* (colloq.) to get oneself up; to get oneself dirty and untidy; guarda come s'è -ato!, look how he has got himself up!, *or* look what a state he's in! **-abrocche** *m. indecl.* kettle-mender, tinker. **-acalda·ie** *m. indecl.* tinker. **-alana** *m. indecl.* mattress-maker. **-apelli** *m. indecl.* leather-dresser. **-ateste** *m. indecl.* (joc.) person who tries to put other people right. **-ato** *part. adj.* dressed; tidied; (techn.) dressed; (colloq.) dressed up to the nines; dirty and untidy. **-atọra** *f.* tanner's wife. **-atọre** *m.* tanner, leather dresser; dresser; -atore alla scorza, bark tanner; -atore al cromo, chrome tanner; -atore in bianco, alum tanner; -atore di scamosciato, chamois leather dresser. **(-atrice** *f.*) **-atura** *f.* dressing, tanning; make-up; titivating; heap of articles dressed, tanned, treated, etc.; mixture for feeding birds. **-ero** *m.* correction, rubbing-out, alteration.

concil-ia·bile *adj.* reconcilable. **(-iabilmẹnte** *adv.*) **-iabilità** *f. indecl.* reconcilableness.

concilia·bolo *m.* furtive gathering of subversive or shady characters; (joc.) people whispering or conferring together; (eccl.) council unlawfully assembled.

conciliare¹ *adj.* See under **concilio**.

concili-are² [A 4] *tr.* to reconcile; to conciliate; — il sonno, to induce slumber, to make one sleepy; — la fame, to arouse hunger; questo ti -erà l'appetito, this will give you an appetite; — l'allegria, to excite merriment; to conclude (an arrangement); *rfl.* (*dat.* of *prn.* **si**) -arsi uno, to make friends with someone, to propitiate someone. **-amẹnto** *m.* conciliation. **-ante** *part. adj.* conciliating; conciliatory. **-ativo** *adj.* conciliative. **-atọre** *m.* conciliator, peacemaker; (leg.) conciliator; giudice -atore, local magistrate (with limited civil jurisdiction); arbitro -atore, referee. **(-atrice** *f.*) **-aziọne** *f.* conciliation; (leg.) conciliation; reconciliation; conciliation court; il giudice procede al tentativo di -azione, the judge proceeds to seek a settlement between the parties; la -azione dei coniugi, the reconciliation of husband and wife; Commissione di Conciliazione, Conciliation Commission.

conci·li-o *m.* (eccl.) council, synod; (fig.) assembly, gathering. **-are** *adj.* conciliar. **(-armẹnte** *adv.*)

concim-e *m.* manure, fertilizer. **-a·ia** *f.*, **-a·io** *m.* manure-heap. **-are** [A 1] *tr.* to manure, to spread fertilizer upon. **-atọre** *m.*, **-atrice** *f.* one who manures, muck-spreader. **-atura** *f.* dressing with fertilizer, manuring, muck-spreading; manure. **-aziọne** *f.* dressing with fertilizer or manure.

concinn-are [A 1] *tr.* to render elegant, to concinnate. **-ità** *f. indecl.* harmoniousness of language, studied elegance of style, concinnity. **-o** *adj.* harmonious, elegant, stylish, concinnate.

concino *m.* (industr.) tan.

conci-o *apocop. part.* of **conciare**, q.v.; *adj.* tanned, dressed; worked; (archit.) pietra -a, hewn stone; knocked about, 'the worse for wear'; mal —, in a bad way, in a poor condition; knocked about; shabby and down-at-heel; spoiled, ruined; *n.m.* manure, muck; stuff gone bad; venire in —, to come in handy; in —, in order, ready; ornament, make-up, decoration; (archit.) hewn stone; †agreement, accord; †peace. **-olino** *m.* stew. **-ume** *m.* (industr.) tan.

†concio-fossecosachè, **†-siachè**, **†-siacosachè** *conj.* provided that; for all that; for the reason that, since; notwithstanding that, although.

conciọn-e *f.* harangue, declamatory speech; (hist.) council of state. **-ale** *adj.* pertaining to a council or harangue. **(-almẹnte** *adv.*) **-are** [A 1 c] *intr.* (*aux.* avere) to harangue, to 'hold forth'. **(-atọre** *m.* **-atrice** *f.*) **-ato·rio** *adj.* referring to speech-making.

†conci·pere *vb.* See **concepire**.

concis-iọne *f.* conciseness; concision. **-o** *adj.* concise, brief. **(-amẹnte** *adv.*)

concist-oro, †-o·rio *m.* (eccl.) consistory; (fig., joc.) any group of talking people. **-oriale** *adj.* (eccl.) consistorial.

concit-are [A 1 s] *tr.* to stir up, to arouse, to provoke. **-ato** *part. adj.* excited, moved, agitated, provoked, aroused; (mus.) lo stile -ato, agitated style (used by Monteverdi to describe a vocal style with rapid notes). **(-atamẹnte** *adv.* **-atọre** *m.* **-atrice** *f.*) **-aziọne** *f.* excitement, agitation; emotion.

con-cittadino *adj.*, *n.m.* fellow-citizen. **-cittadinanza** *f.* citizenship of the same place. **-cive** *m.* citizen; fellow-citizen, neighbour.

conclam-are [A 1] *tr.* to call in a loud voice; (of a crowd), to acclaim. **-ato** *adj.* acclaimed; universally acknowledged; (med.) obvious, apparent. **-aziọne** *f.* acclamation; (Rom. antiq.) conclamation.

conclav-e *m.* (eccl.) conclave. **†-io** *m.* conclave; inner room. **-ista** *m.* (eccl.) conclavist.

conclud-ẹnte *part.* of **concludere**, q.v.; *ad.* conclusive; effective; purposeful. **(-entemẹnte** *adv.*) **-ẹnza** *f.* conclusiveness; effectiveness.

conclu·d-ere [C 3] *tr.* to conclude; to bring to a conclusion; to clinch; to carry out, to effect; to include, to comprise, to embrace; *intr.* (*aux.* avere) to be conclusive; to conclude, to come to a conclusion, to end; to succeed; to get something done; non -e niente, he never achieves anything. **-imẹnto** *m.* concluding; conclusion. **(-itọre** *m.* **-itrice** *f.*)

conclusiọn-e *f.* conclusion; senza —, inconclusive; ineffectual; useless; *pl.* (leg.) conclusions; concluding summary statement, by counsel, in the pleadings or at the trial, of the verdict, judgement or relief sought by the party he represents. **-ac·cia** *f. pejor.* wrong conclusion. **-ale** *adj.* (leg.) having to do with, or comprising, the 'conclusioni'; la comparsa -ale, the pleadings in a civil action similar to the Statement of Claim and the Defence and Counterclaim; *n.f.* (leg.) see 'comparsa conclusionale'.

conclus-iva *f.* conclusion. **-ivo** *adj.* conclusive. **-ivamẹnte** *adv.* conclusively. **-o** *part.* of **concludere**, q.v.; concluded; clinched; *adj.* carried out, effected; †enclosed; *n.m.* conclusion.

concocimẹnto *m.* digestion.

conco·id-e *f.* (math.) conchoid curve; (miner.) frattura —, conchoidal fracture. **-ale** *adj.* conchoidal.

concolọre *adj.* (poet.) similarly coloured, of similar hue.

concomit-ante *adj.* concomitant; (theol.) grazia —, co-operating grace; (leg.) concomitant. **-anza** *f.* concomitance; (theol.) concomitance.

†concorda *f.* See **concordia**.

concord-are [A 1] *tr.* to reconcile, to make agree; to settle; to agree upon; — un prezzo, to agree a price; (mus.) to bring (sounds) into harmony; to tune; *intr.* (*aux.* avere, *prep.* con) to agree (with), to be in agreement (with); (mus.) to agree harmoniously; *recip. rfl.* to become reconciled to one another; son due indoli che mal si possono -are, those two are incompatible in temperament. **-a·bile** *adj.* that may be made to agree, reconcilable; compatible. **(-abilmẹnte** *adv.*) **-amẹnto** *m.* agreement. **-ante** *part. adj.* agreeing; agreeable, willing, consenting. **(-antemẹnte** *adv.*) **-anza** *f.* agreement; concordance; studiare le -anze, to study the basic rules of grammar; (mus.) concord; concordance; (aeron.) filleting; filetto di -anza, fillet. **-ata·rio** *adj.* matrimonio -atario, marriage which in a Roman Catholic country is valid in civil law by virtue of a Concordat with the Vatican. **†-ativo** *adj.* leading to agreement; capable of concordance. **-ato** *part. adj.* agreed, in agreement; reconciled; *n.m.* pact, concordat; (leg.) agreement between the Holy See and a secular government; arrangement; composition between debtor and creditor; -ato fallimentare, scheme of arrangement; -ato fallimentare preventivo, composition with creditors (C.C.). **-atọre** *m.*, **-atrice** *f.* conciliator. **-ẹvole** *adj.* liable to agree; reconcilable. **(-evolmẹnte** *adv.*)

concord-e *adj.* in accord; plauso —, unanimous applause; — con, in accordance with; siamo -i, we are in agreement. **-emẹnte** *adv.* in agreement; unanimously; in concord. **-ẹvole** *adj.* see **concordabile**, under **concordare** or **concorde**. **†-iamente** *adv.* see **concordemente**. **-ità** *f. indecl.* agreement, concord; conformity; harmony.

concor·d-ia *f.* agreement, concord; unanimity; peace, harmony, good will; (leg.) concord; consensus; mutual agreement; (bot.) spotted orchis, *Orchis maculata*. **†-iare** *tr.* to reconcile; to make peace between; *recip. rfl.* to make peace.

†concorporale *adj.* of one body, of the same body.

concọrr-ere [C 5] *intr.* (*aux.* avere) to assemble, to come together; to flow together; (geom.) to meet, to pass through the same point; to converge; to combine; — alla spesa, to contribute towards the expense; to co-operate, to strive together; to participate; to concur; to compete; — ad un posto, to put in for a job, to apply for a job; — ad un premio, to go in for a prize. **-ẹnte** *part. adj.* concurrent; competing; (eng.) taglio -ente, climb cut; (geom.) meeting, converging; †occurring; †recurrent; *n.m.* competitor; rival aspirant; applicant; candidate; (comm.) competitor. **-ẹnza** *f.* concurrence; concourse; una gran -enza di spettatori, a great concourse of spectators; competition; rivalry; sleale -enza,

concorr·ere (*cont.*)
unfair competition; vuol fare -enza a tutti, he tries to vie with everybody; (comm.) competition; -enza protetta, dumping; (finan.) fino alla -enza di, to the extent of. **-iménto** *m.* running together; competition. (**-itóre** *m.* **-itrice** *f.*)

concórs·o[1] *m.* competition; competitive examination; (comm.) call for tenders; concourse; coming together; — ippico, horse-show; — di vocali, hiatus; (geom.) meeting point; point of intersection of several lines; (leg.) — di cause, concurrence of causes (C.P.); — tra creditori, ranking of creditors in bankruptcy for dividend (C.C.).

concorso[2] *part.* of concorrere, q.v.

conc-otto *adj.* digested, assimilated. **-ozióne** *f.* digestion, assimilation.

concre-are [A6c] *tr.* to create together. **-ato** *part. adj.* created together; innate, inborn, congenital; un sentimento -ato con l'uomo, a sentiment innate in man.

†concre·dere *tr.* to believe implicitly; *intr.* to have faith in common; concredendo di fare bene, with the utmost good faith.

concresc-enza *f.* (med.) concretion. **-i·bile** *adj.* concrescible.

concret-are [A1] *tr.* to bring to a concrete conclusion; to realize; to put into effect; *intr.* (*aux.* avere) to come to a conclusion; to achieve something definite; si discute, si discute e non si -a nulla, they talk and talk and nothing ever comes of it. **-ato** *part. adj.* realized, effected.

concret-o *adj.* concrete; substantial; real; factual; nel caso —, in the case in point; in —, in actual fact; actual, practical; finora non c'è nulla di —, there's nothing definite yet; (mus.) musica -a, *musique concrète*, concrete music. **-ezza** *f.* concreteness. **-izzare** [A1] *tr.* to realize, to put into practice; *intr.* (*aux.* avere) to come down to brass tacks.

concrezión-e *f.* (med.) accretion, calculus; (geol.) concretion, aggregation; (chem.) concretion, congelation. **-ale** *adj.* concretional, concretionary.

concubin-a *f.* concubine. **-a·rio** *adj.* keeping a concubine. **-ato** *m.* concubinage. **†-esco** *adj.* pertaining to concubines, concubine-like. **-o** *m.* keeper of a concubine.

concu·bito *m.* sleeping together, intercourse.

†con·cula *f.* container for liquid or goods sold by cubic measure; a cubic measure.

conculc-are [A2] *tr.* to trample on; to oppress; — i diritti altrui, to suppress the rights of others. (**-a·bile** *adj.*) **-aménto** *m.* oppression, trampling down. **-ato** *part. adj.* oppressed, downtrodden. (**-atóre** *m.* **-atrice** *f.*) **-azióne** *f.* oppression, trampling underfoot.

concuo·c-ere [C15] *tr.* (med.) to digest; to assimilate; to mature (ground) for cultivation; to digest, to assimilate (in the mind). **-iménto** *m.* digestion, assimilation.

concup-ire [D2] *tr.* to covet; to lust for. **-ito** *part. adj.* coveted; desired.

concupi·sc-ere [def.] *tr.* to lust after. **-ente** *part. adj.* lustful. **-enza** *f.* lust; concupiscence; (theol.) peccato di -enza, lust. **†-e·vole** *adj.* lustful, lusting. **-i·bile** *adj.* desirable, alluring; lustful, lusting. (**-ibilménte** *adv.*) **-ibilità** *f.* allure, attraction, attractiveness; lustfulness.

†concussare *tr.* to shake; to crash, to clash.

concussión-e *f.* (leg.) extortion; †shaking; †trembling; †crashing, clashing; †clash; †bullying, overbearing behaviour. **-a·rio** *m.* (leg.) extortioner.

concuss-o *adj.* shaken. **-ivo** *adj.* shaking; concussive.

conda·lio *m.* (Rom. antiq.) *condalium*, slave's ring.

condanna *f.* condemnation; (leg.) verdict or judgement of 'guilty', or for the plaintiff; sentence; penalty; judgement against the defendant; — a morte, death sentence; (eccl.) — in globo, general condemnation, censure applied *in globo*.

condann-are [A1] *tr.* to condemn; to blame, to censure; (leg.) to condemn; to give judgement against; to sentence; — a morte, to sentence to death; — al risarcimento dei danni, to give judgement for damages against; — al pagamento di una multa, to fine heavily; (eccl.) to condemn; to fine; to impose a levy on; to bar (a door, window). **-a·bile** *adj.* deserving of condemnation. **†-agióne** *f.* condemnation; penalty. **-ato** *part. adj.* condemned, blamed; *n.m.* convict; la cella dei -ati, the condemned cell. **-atóre** *m.*, **-atrice** *f.* one who condemns, condemner. **-ato·rio** *adj.* condemning, damning. **-azióne** *f.* condemnation; deserving of condemnation; damnable.

condeb-itóre *m.* (finan.) joint debtor. (**-itrice** *f.*)

condec-ente *adj.* suitable, convenient. (**-enteménte** *adv.*) **-évole** *adj.* convenient. (**-evolménte** *adv.*)

condecor-are [A1s] *tr.* to decorate (for valour, etc.) or to knight at same time as someone else. **-ato** *part. adj.* decorated or knighted at the same time as someone else.

condégn-o *adj.* suitable; worthy, deserved; adequate; (theol.) merito —, condign merit. (**-aménte** *adv.*) **-ità** *f.* merit, deserving, worthiness.

condendo *m.* (Latin, leg.) de iure —, under law yet to be established.

†condennare *vb.* and derivs. See **condannare**.

condensa *f.* (chem.; phys.) condensate; pozzo di raccolta —, water trap.

condens-are [A1] *tr.* to condense, to cause to condense; *rfl.* to be condensed; to condense, to be condensable. **-a·bile** *adj.* condensable. **-abilità** *f.* condensability. **-aménto** *m.* condensability. **-ante** *part. adj.* condensing. **-atóre** *m.* (chem.) condenser; (electr.; radio) condenser, capacitor; -atore multiplo, gang condenser. **-azióne** *f.* condensation; (meteor.) temperatura di -azione, dew point. **-o** *adj.* dense, opaque; obscure; (poet.) overwhelmed; blinded.

†condescendere *vb.* and derivs. See **accondiscendere**.

condi·c-ere *intr.* to be fitting; to be suitable, to be appropriate. **†-évole** *adj.* convenient; suitable; appropriate; apposite.

con·dil-o *m.* (anat.) condyle. **-ino** *m.* (miner.) round crystalline fragment. **-oma** *m.* (med.) condyloma. **-ura** *f.* (zool.) star-nosed mole, *Condylura* spp.

condiménto *m.* See under **condire**.

cond-ire [D2] *tr.* to flavour, to season, to dress (a salad); (joc.) to deal with, to settle, to 'fix'; lo -iremo noi, leave him to us, we'll give him what he deserves; †to embalm. †See **candire**. **-iménto** *m.* condiment, seasoning, sauce, flavouring; (fig.) mitigation, softening. **-itóre** *m.* seasoner, one who applies flavouring.

condirett-óre *m.*, **-trice** *f.* co-director; co-editor (of a newspaper).

condiscéndere [C1] and derivs. See **accondiscéndere**.

condiscépolo *m.* fellow-disciple.

condit-o *part.* of condire, q.v.; *adj.* seasoned; dressed (of a salad); flavoured; *n.m.* seasoning, condiment. **-o·rio** *m.* (archit.) repository for burial urn or coffin. **-ura** *f.* seasoning; dressing; flavouring; †embalming.

†con·dito *adj.* created, made.

conditóre[1] *m.* See under **condire**.

condit-óre[2] *m.* founder.

condivi·dere [C3] *tr.* to divide between several persons, to share, to share out.

condizionale *adj.* conditional; (gramm.) tempo —, conditional tense; (leg.) — a condanna, a suspended sentence; conditional discharge. **-alménte** *adv.* conditionally.

condizion-are [A1c] *tr.* to condition; to pack (so as not to be broken in transit); to prepare for a special purpose; to season; to serve up with the proper dressing; to subject to a condition or proviso; ho -ato la mia offerta alla sua venuta, I made my offer on condition he came; (tan.; text.) to condition, to give the right degree of moisture content to; *rfl.* to prepare oneself; to adapt oneself; to become conditioned; to condition oneself. **-a·bile** *adj.* that may be conditioned. **-aménto** *m.* (techn.) conditioning; -amento dell'aria, air conditioning. **-ata** *f.* (horse-racing) handicap race. **-ataménte** *adv.* conditionally, provisionally. **-ato** *part. adj.* conditioned; prepared; packed; aria -ata, conditioned air, air-conditioning; conditional, subjected to a condition or proviso; accettazione -ata, conditional acceptance; †ben -ato, in good health, well set up; well conditioned. **-atóre** *m.* (industr.) conditioner; -atore d'aria, air-conditioner. **-atura** *f.* conditioning; packing; preparation; (techn.) conditioning.

condizión-e *f.* condition; circumstance; le -i economiche di un paese, the economic situation of a country; a —, on condition; (leg.) condition, proviso, stipulation; *pl.* terms; (text.) hygroscopic condition of silk; building for regulating moisture content of silk, conditioning chamber; †peril, risk; †mettere a —, to imperil. **-a·rio** *adj.* conditional; *n.m.* person enjoying a certain condition; (comm. hist.) creditor with certain conditional rights.

condogli-anza *f.* condolence; sympathy; fare le -anze a, to offer one's condolences to. **†-enza** *f.* See **condoglianza**; lament; complaint.

condol-ére [B11] *rfl.* to sorrow, to grieve; -ersi con, to offer one's sympathy to (e.g. for a bereavement). **-ente** *adj.* condolent. **†-enza** *f.* grief; regret. **-óre** *m.* condolence, fellow-feeling. **-uto** *part. adj.* grieving for another.

condolino *m.* (geol.) small round fragment of crystal.

condomi·nio *m.* (leg.) co-ownership, ownership in common (of a building or group of buildings composed of separate freehold tenements); joint government, condominium.

condo·mino *m.* (leg.) co-owner, owner in common.

condon *m. indecl.* (med.) sheath.

condon-are [A I c] *tr.* to condone, to excuse; to remit (a punishment, a debt). **-a·bile** *adj.* pardonable. (**-atore** *m.* **-atrice** *f.*) **-azione** *f.* condonation; remission. **-o** *m.* condonation; remission, grace.

condore *m.* (orn.) condor.

condott-a *f.* conduct; behaviour; good conduct; senza —, ill-mannered; arrangement of the parts of a literary composition; transport; transference; leadership; management, organization, running; command; linea di —, policy; duties and area assigned to a 'medico condotto', q.v.; the bringing of a water supply to a town; supply (of gas, etc.); (eng.) duct; convoy; escort; (hist.) status, contract of a 'condottiere', q.v. **-iero, -iere** *m.* leader of a city militia; soldier of fortune commanding troops; counsellor, guide; carter, carrier; driver.

condott-o *part.* of **condurre**, q.v.; *adj.* transported; supplied (e.g. water); stipendiary; medico —, doctor in the pay of municipality; male —, in a sorry plight; *n.m.* water main; pipe, tube, lead; canal; conduit; (metall.) channel through which molten metal is run; (mus.) conductus; †mercenary soldier; †salvo —, see **salva**. **-ura** *f.* see **conduttura**, under **conduttore**.

condrioma *f.* (biol.) chondriome, mitochondria.

condrologi·a *f.* chondrology.

†**conduca** *m.* leader; guide.

conduc-ente *part.* of **condurre**, q.v.; *adj.* leading, guiding; *n.m.* chauffeur; driver; mule driver; driver of tram or bus. **-evole** *adj.* conducive. **-i·bile** *adj.* suitable; amenable. **-ibilità** *f. indecl.* (phys.) conductivity. **-imento** *m.* leading, guiding; command; (mus.) vocal glide; †procedure; †behaviour. **-itore** *m.* leader, conductor, guide; captain; ganger, foreman; ruler. (**-itrice** *f.*)

condurre [B 2] *tr.* to conduct; to lead; to direct; to pass (time); to carry out, to execute, to prosecute; to drive (a vehicle); (comm.) to pay a salary to; to engage on a salary basis; *rfl.* to behave, to behave oneself; condursi bene, to behave well, to be well behaved.

†**condutt-a** *f.* viands, provisions, food. †**-o** see **condotto** *part.* of **condurre**.

condutt-anza *f.* (electr.) conductance. **-ibilità, -ività** *f.* (phys.) conductivity. **-ivo** *adj.* (phys.) conductive. **-i·zio** *adj.* (of soldiers) mercenary, hired.

condutt-ore *m.* leader; guide; driver of a tram, bus, or train; driver (motor and motor-cycle racing); (naut.) **-ore** di flottiglia, flotilla leader; (leg.) one who carries on a business; tenant; landlord (of an inn), publican; (phys.) conductor; *adj.* (industr.) rullo —, drawing-in roll; tube, pipe, lead; filo **-ore**, †captain. **-rice** *f.* of **conduttore**; *adj.* (watchm.) ruota **-rice**, driving wheel. **-ura** *f.* conduit, pipe; channel; piping; main; †transport, conveyance.

conduzione *f.* farming by owner; dodicimila ettari in — diretta, twelve thousand hectares of farmland farmed by the owners; bringing (e.g. of water); transporting; driving (a vehicle); (phys.) conduction; conducting.

conesta·bile *m.* high constable.

confabul-are [A I s] *intr.* (aux. avere) (joc.; iron.) to gossip, to chat; to talk together. (**-atore** *m.* **-atrice** *f.*) **-ato·rio** *adj.* chatty. **-azione** *f.* chat, gossip; conversation.

con-facente *adj.* suitable; †similar. (**-facemente** *adv.*) **-facevole** *adj.* suitable, fitting, appropriate. (**-facevolmente** *adv.*) **-facevolezza** *f.* suitability, fittingness, appropriateness; adaptability.

confalone *m.* and derivs. See **gonfalone**.

confare [B 14] *rfl.* (prep. a) to be fitting, to be suitable, to be appropriate; questi modi non si confanno ai giovani, this is not the way for young people to behave; è un'aria che non mi si confà punto, this air doesn't suit me one bit.

confarre-are [A 5] *tr.* (Rom. antiq.) to marry by confarreation. **-azione** *f.* confarreation.

confeder-are [A I s] *tr., rfl.* to federate. **-amento** *m.* see **confederazione**. **-ativo** *adj.* tending to federation; relating to federation; federative. **-ato** *part. adj.* federated; federal. **-azione** *f.* federation, confederation; la Confederazione Elvetica, Switzerland; alliance; confederacy; league, union; **-azione** del lavoro, trade union.

confer-enza *f.* conference; — stampa, press conference; lecture, paper; fare una —, tenere una —, dare una —, to give a lecture,

to read a paper; parley, colloquy; † comparison. **-enziera** *f.*, **-enziere** *m.* lecturer, speaker.

confer-ire [D 2] *tr.* to confer, to grant, to bestow; (leg.) to bring into hotchpot; (eccl.) — i sacramenti, to administer the sacraments; to bring together; to collate; *intr.* (aux. avere) to confer, to hold a conference; (prep. a) to suit, to benefit; l'aria fresca ti **-isce**, fresh air does you good. **-imento** *m.* conferring, granting; (leg.) subscribed capital of company (C.C.). (**-itore** *m.* **-itrice** *f.*)

conferma *f.* confirmation; renewal (of office, etc.).

conferm-are [A I c] *tr.* to confirm; to renew (a contract, etc.); to retain in employment; to approve; to attest; (eccl.) to confirm; (leg.) — una sentenza, to uphold a judgment; *rfl.* to become firmer (in an opinion); (in signing a letter) mi **-o**, I remain. (**-amento** *m.*) **-ato** *part. adj.* confirmed; approved; attested. (**-atore** *m.* **-atrice** *f.*) **-ativo** *adj.* confirming, corroborative. (**-ativamente** *adv.*) **-ato·rio** *adj.* confirmatory. **-azione** *f.* confirmation, corroboration; (eccl.; rhet.) confirmation.

confess-are [A I] *tr.* to admit, to own, to confess; to declare solemnly, to profess openly; (eccl.) (of priest) to confess (penitents), to hear confessions; *rfl.* (eccl.) (of penitent) to make one's confession; si **-a** dal parroco, he goes to the parish priest for confession.

confession-ale *adj.* (rel.) confessional; belonging to (sacramental) confession; belonging to a particular religious communion; sectarian; with a religious bias; *n.m.* confessional (box). **-a·rio** *m.* (rel.) confessional (box); (leg.) pawnee.

confession-e *f.* admission, acknowledgement, confession; (leg.) admission; confession; (eccl.) (sacramental) confession; quel prete non ha la —, that priest has no faculties for confession; (liturg.; archit.) *confessio*, confession; (rel.; polit.) creed, persuasion; religious body. **-ista** *m.* (eccl. hist.) Confessionist.

confesso[1] *adj.* self-convicted; reo —, accused person who has confessed himself guilty; †(rel.) shriven; — e comunicato, after confession and communion.

confesso[2] *m.* (mil. hist.) a kind of barbican or outwork of a fort.

confessor-e *m.* (eccl.) confessor (in both senses). **-ato** *m.* (eccl.) confessorship.

confett-are [A I] *tr.* to candy; †to prepare; †to concoct. **-ato** *part. adj.* candied. †**-atore** *m.* confectioner.

confetto[1] *adj.* worked, prepared; worn out; terreno —, soil baked by the sun, or hardened by frost.

confett-o[2] *n.m.* sweetmeat, sugar plum; sugared almond; — parlante, sweets with a motto inside; quando si mangeranno i **-i**?, when is the wedding going to be? (from the Italian custom of eating sugared almonds at a wedding. Note: Italian 'confetti' are not English confetti); (iron.) slap in the face, ungracious action; (joc.) **-i** di montagna, dried chestnuts; †(pharm.) electuary; †*adj.* candied. **-iera** *f.* sweet box, bonbonnière; little box in which the bride and groom send sugared almonds to their friends. **-iere** *m.* confectioner; perfumer. **-ino** *m. dim.* of **confetto**; sugared pill; (fig.) easy task, 'gift'. **-ura** *f.* confectionery; jam. **-ureri·a** *f.* confectioner's shop; sweet factory. **-uriere** *m.* confectioner.

confezion-e *f.* tailoring, dress-making; *pl.* clothing in general offered for sale; — pronta, **-i** in serie, ready-made clothing; product; preparation; manufacture; wrapping; bottling; packaging; — natalizia, Christmas wrapping; packet; — da venti, packet of twenty, packet containing twenty. **-are** [A I c] *tr.* to manufacture; to prepare; **-are** un pacco, to do up a parcel, to make up a parcel; (clothing industr.) to make; si **-ano** abiti su misura per signori, gentlemen's suits made to measure, bespoke tailoring; (comm.) to pack. **-ato** *part. adj.* made; ready-made; prepared; packed, packaged; bottled; (paperm.) carte **-ate**, papeterie, boxed stationery. **-atore** *m.* maker, manufacturer; packer. **-atrice** *f.* woman packer; packing machine.

conficc-are [A 2] *tr.* to thrust in; to hammer in; to nail up; (mil.) to spike (a gun); (fig.) to impress (into the memory), to 'knock in'. (**-amento** *m.*) **-ato** *part. adj.* thrust in; hammered in; nailed up; (fig.) fixed, driven in. **-atura** *f.* hammering in; nailing; riveting. †**-azione** *f.* nailing; la **-azione** sulla croce, the Crucifixion.

†**confi·cere** *tr.* to make; to concoct; to fabricate; — il sagramento, to consecrate at Mass.

confid-are [A I] *tr.* to entrust; to confide; — un segreto a, to impart a secret to; *intr.* (aux. avere, prep. in) to trust (in), to have faith (in); to trust (to); *rfl.* (prep. con) to confide in, to open one's

confid-are (*cont.*)
heart to; (*prep.* a) to entrust oneself (to); to rely (on). †**-anza** *f.* confidence; faith, belief; hope; trust. **-ato** *part. adj.* trusted, trustworthy; sure, confident.

confident-e *adj.* trusting; confident, sure; trustworthy, inspiring confidence; *n.m.*, *f.* confidant; close friend; confidential agent, police agent; (*theatr.*) confidant; confidante. **-emente** *adv.* trustingly; confidently.

confidenz-a *f.* confidential communication; familiarity, intimacy; confidence; trattare con —, to treat without formality; prender —, to behave with too much familiarity; prendersi una —, to take a liberty; dar —, to be too familiar; fare a —, to take advantage of a person's good nature, to take liberties with; (*provb.*) — toglie riverenza, familiarity breeds contempt. **-iale** *adj.* confidential; friendly, familiar; distribuzione -iale, restricted distribution. (**-ialmente** *adv.*) **-ia·rio** *m.* (eccl. hist.) trafficker in benefices. †**-ioso** *adj.* too familiar, free and easy.

config·g-ere [C 17] *tr.* to pierce; to nail up; to drive in; to fix. **-imento** *m.* nailing; fixing; piercing.

configur-are [A I] *tr.* to form a likeness of; to outline; (geom.) to form; (fig.) to symbolize. **-ato** *part. adj.* shaped, figured; outlined; (fig.) symbolized. **-azione** *f.* likeness; outline; structure; configuration, conformation.

confin-are [A I] *tr.* to confine, to limit, to restrict; to banish; — a, (in), un luogo, to confine to a prescribed domicile; *intr.* (*aux.* avere, *prep.* con) to border (upon); (leg.) to adjoin; il mio podere -a col Suo, my farm adjoins yours. **-ante** *adj.* bordering; (leg.) adjoining, contiguous (of land). **-ato** *part. adj.* confined, restricted; banished, deported, exiled; *n.m.* person subjected to political banishment or confinement. **-azione** *f.* frontier demarcation.

confin-e *m.* boundary, frontier, confine; border; stone, post, etc., marking a boundary; punishment of forced residence in a prescribed locality; mandare al —, to banish, to exile; a — con, bordering upon; †*adj.* bordering, adjoining; contiguous; similar; intermediate, in-between. **-a·rio** *adj.* pertaining to or belonging to a frontier, border.

†**confingere** *vb.* See **fingere**.

confino *m.* (leg.) punishment consisting of banishment to a certain place for a certain time; forced residence.

confirmare [A I] and derivs. See **confermare**.

confisca *f.* (leg.) confiscation; penalty carrying forfeiture to the public treasury of something used in the commission, or forming the subject matter of a crime; the thing confiscated.

confisc-are [A 2] *tr.* (leg.) to confiscate; to seize. **-a·bile** *adj.* (leg.) confiscable, confiscatable.

con-fite·mini *m. indecl.* Lat. psalm title; essere al —, to be at the point of death. **-fi·teor** *m. indecl.* (liturg.) confiteor; (fig.) recitare il -fiteor, to own one's fault, to cry *peccavi*.

confitto *part.* of **configgere**, q.v.; *adj.* nailed; fixed, driven in; fastened; — in croce, crucified.

conflagr-are [A I] *intr.* (*aux.* essere) to burn, to ignite; (chem.) to deflagrate. **-azione** *f.* conflagration; fire; outbreak of hostilities.

†**confl-are** *tr.* to melt (metal); to cast. †**-a·tile** *adj.* made by melting. †**-ato** *part. adj.* melted; cast; fused together; conflated. †**-azione** *f.* conflation.

†**confli·gere** *intr.* to fight, to meet in combat.

conflitt-o *m.* conflict; clash; venire a —, to conflict; in —, in conflict; in aperto — con, openly opposed to. †**-azione** *f.* combat; conflict.

conflu-ire [D 2] *intr.* (*aux.* essere, avere) to meet; to flow together; to be confluent. **-ente** *adj.* meeting, running together, confluent; (med.) confluent (e.g. of smallpox, where the vesicles all run together); *n.m.* meeting-place, confluence; affluent. **-enza** *f.* confluence.

confond-ere [C 2] *tr.* to confuse; to mix up; to confound; — qualcuno per un'altra persona, to mistake someone for somebody else; *rfl.* to be confused; to become blurred; to blend, to mix, to merge; non mi ci -o, I can't be bothered with it; non -erti!, don't bother, don't worry, don't trouble!; *intr.* (*aux.* avere) to blend; to melt; -ersi in lagrime, to melt into tears. **-i·bile** *adj.* that may be confused; likely to be confused or mistaken; facilmente -ibile, easy to mistake for another. **-imento** *m.* confounding; confusion. (**-itore** *m.* **-itrice** *f.*)

conform-are [A I c] *tr.* to conform, to accommodate; to adapt; to assimilate; *rfl.* (*prep.* a) to comply (with); to conform (to); to

become adapted. **-a·bile** *adj.* conformable. **-ativo** *adj.* conforming; conformable. **-atore** *m.* conformer; hat gauge. (**-atrice** *f.*) **-azione** *f.* conformation, form, structure; vizi di -azione, constitutional or inborn defects, congenital defects; conforming.

conform-e *adj.* (*prep.* a, con) similar, in conformity (with), according (to), in accordance (with); — la circostanza, that depends; (leg.) exactly alike; 'per copia —', 'certified true copy'; †agreed, in agreement; *adv.* conformably, accordingly; *prep.* in conformity with; *conj.* according as, as; — le frulla per il capo, just as the whim takes her. (**-emente** *adv.*) †**-e·vole** *adj.* similar, conforming; of the same nature, homogeneous. **-ismo** *m.* (rel.; pol.) conformity; outward conformity. **-ista** *n.m.*, *f.* (*pl.* -isti *m.*, -iste *f.*) (rel.) conformist (esp. Anglican); (pol.) conformist. **-i·stico** *adj.* conformist. **-ità** *f. indecl.* conformity.

confort-are [A I] *tr.* to comfort; to console; to support (with a vote); (rel.) to minister to (a dying or condemned man), to fortify with the rites of the church; — l'appetito, to stimulate the appetite; — la memoria, to revive the memory; to encourage, to urge, to exhort; to sustain; to support; to give support to; vi invitiamo a — del vostro voto, we invite you to vote for; †to strengthen; *rfl.* to take comfort; to console oneself; to find relief. **-a·bile** *adj.* capable of being comforted; *n.m.* ease, comfort. †**-agione** *f.* comforting; comfort. †**-amento** *m.* comforting; comfort; counsel, advice. **-ante** *adj.* comforting, encouraging; *n.m.* medicine to settle the stomach. †**-anza** *f.* comforting; comfort; fervent prayer. **-ativo** *adj.* comforting; *n.m.* comforter. **-ato** *part. adj.* comforted; consoled; encouraged; supported; la mia opinione è -ata dalla tua, my opinion finds support in yours. (**-atore** *m.* **-atrice** *f.*) **-ato·rio** *adj.* comforting, encouraging; *n.m.* chapel in prison where the condemned receive the last ministrations of a priest. **-atura** *f.* comfort; solace, consolation; encouragement. **-azione** *f.* comforting, consolation; renewal of strength; (med.) rally. **-evole** *adj.* comforting; encouraging; (neol.) comfortable, cosy.

confort-o *m.* comfort, consolation, solace; *pl.* (rel.) i -i della religione, the comforts of religion, esp. the last sacraments; exhortation, incitement; encouragement; (neol.) comfort, ease. **-eri·a** *f.* see **confortatorio**, *n.m.* **-ina·io** *m.* peppermint-seller, sweet-seller. **-ino** *m.* sweetmeat; peppermint for the digestion.

†**confosso** *m.* (mil. hist.) barbican; double moat.

confratello *m.* fellow-member of a brotherhood; brother-member; colleague.

confrater·nita *f.* (eccl.) confraternity, religious guild.

confratto·rio *m.* (liturg.) confractorium (in Ambrosian Rite).

confregazione *f.* See **confricazione**, under **confricare**.

confric-are [A 2] *tr.* to rub; — il petto del malato, to rub the patient's chest. (**-amento** *m.*) **-ato** *part. adj.* rubbed, massaged. **-azione** *f.* rubbing, friction.

confront-are [A I c] *tr.* to compare; to confront; *intr.* (*aux.* avere) to be an exact copy; to agree in all respects; le testimonianze non -ano, the evidence does not agree.

confront-o *m.* comparison; chiamare a —, to confront; stare a —, to be equally good; to stand up to comparison; stare a — con, to bear comparison with; in — con, compared with, in comparison with; collation; (scient.) — sperimentale, comparative test; (leg.) the confrontation, a step in criminal procedure at which witnesses or accused whose stories disagree are brought face to face to have it out among themselves, revealing the truth.

Confu·c-io *pr.n.m.* Confucius. **-ianismo** *m.* Confucianism. **-iano** *m.*, *adj.* Confucian.

†**confug·gere** *vb.* See **confuggire**.

confuggire *intr.* (*aux.* essere) to take refuge; to seek sanctuary.

confusa·neo *adj.* See under **confuso**.

confusion-e *f.* confusion; disorder; embarrassment; (leg.) merger. **-a·rio** *m.* (fam.) unsystematic person, muddler; *adj.* confused, muddled. **-ismo** *m.* great confusion, to-do, bustle; confusion of ideas, confused state of mind.

confus-o *part.* of **confondere**, q.v.; *adj.* confused; disordered, untidy; embarrassed, ashamed, mortified; in —, higgledy-piggledy. (**-amente** *adv.*) **-a·neo** *adj.* all mixed up; pane -aneo, bread made of unsifted flour.

confut-are [A I, A I S] *tr.* to confute; to disprove. **-a·bile** *adj.* confutable. **-ativo** *adj.* confuting. **-ato** *part. adj.* confuted; disproved. (**-atore** *m.* **-atrice** *f.*) **-ato·rio** *adj.* confuting, disproving. **-azione** *f.* confutation; (leg.) rebuttal.

†**conga·udere** *intr.* to rejoice together.

conged-are [A I] *tr.* to give leave to; to dismiss; to discharge; *rfl.* to take leave. **-ato** *part. adj.* dismissed; discharged; (mil.) on leave.

congedo *m.* leave of absence, furlough; in —, on leave; — assoluto, discharge; certificate given on discharge; (poetry) envoi, envoy.

congegn-are [A 5 c] *tr.* to put together; to assemble; to devise, to contrive; to plan; to concoct. **-amento** *m.* devising, contriving; the way a thing is put together. **-ato** *part. adj.* put together; devised; ben **-ato**, well contrived, cleverly thought out. **-atore** *m.* contriver; composer; (eng.) fitter. (**-atrice** *f.*) **-atura** *f.* contrivance.

congegno *m.* device, apparatus, instrument; — di sicurezza, safety device; mounting, assembling, structure.

congel-are [A I] *tr., intr.* (*aux.* essere), *rfl.* to freeze; to solidify, to congeal, to set; *rfl.* to become frostbitten. **-amento** *m.* freezing; congealing; frostbite; (phys.) punto di **-amento**, freezing-point. **-ativo** *adj.* likely to freeze or congeal. **-ato** *part. adj.* frozen; congealed; (leg.) debiti **-ati**, frozen debts. **-atore** *m.* refrigerator; deep-freeze. **-azione** *f.* freezing, setting, congealing.

†**conge-lido** *adj.* frozen; gelid.

†**conge-ne-o** *adj.* generated together. †**-ità** *f.* homogeneity.

congenerato *adj.* congenital, hereditary.

conge-nere *adj.* akin, kindred, congeneric.

conge-nero *m.* son-in-law to the same mother- or father-in-law.

congeniale *adj.* congenial; like-minded.

conge-nito *adj.* congenital, hereditary.

†**congentura** *f.* join; juncture, circumstance.

conge-rie *f. indecl.* heap, mass of miscellaneous objects, congeries.

congestion-e *f.* congestion; accumulation; traffic jam. **-are** [A I c] *tr.* to congest, to cause congestion. **-ato** *part. adj.* congested; burdened, weighed down; strada **-ata**, crowded street.

congesto *adj.* heaped; laden; crowded, congested.

congettur-a *f.* conjecture; speculation. **-a-bile** *adj.* conjecturable. **-ale** *adj.* conjectural; speculative. (**-almente** *adv.*) **-are** [A I] *tr.* to conjecture; to speculate. **-ato** *part. adj.* conjectured; surmised. **-atore** *m.* conjecturer. **-azione** *f.* conjecturing; conjecture; speculating; speculation.

†**conghiettura** *f.* and derivs. See **congettura**.

congia-rio *m.* See under **congio**.

†**congiato** *m.* congé.

con-gi-o[1] *m.* (Rom. antiq.) congius, liquid measure. **-a-rio** *m.* (Rom. antiq.) congiary.

†**congi-o**[2] *m.* congé.

congioi-re [D 2] *intr.* (*aux.* essere), *rfl.* to rejoice together; — con altri, to congratulate others.

†**congionto.** See **congiunto**.

congiu-dice *m.* co-judge.

†**congiugale** *adj.* See **coniugale**.

congiun-g-ere [C 5] *tr.* to join, to unite; — una retta, to draw a straight line; *rfl.* (*prep.* a, con) to join; to unite (with); to meet; (in criminal law) **-ersi** carnalmente con, to have carnal knowledge of, to have unlawful sexual intercourse with; *recip. rfl.* to join together. **-imento** *m.* union (sexual). (**-itore** *m.* **-itrice** *f.*)

congiunt-iva *f.* (med.) conjunctiva. **-ivite** *f.* (med.) conjunctivitis. **-ivo** *adj.* conjunctive, connective; (gram.) conjunctive; subjunctive; conjunctional.

congiunt-o *part.* of **congiungere**, q.v.; *adj.* united, joined; related; near (of a relation); (mus.) conjunct; *n.m.* relative, relation; spouse; compound; (liturg.) messa del —, nuptial mass; †(astron.) conjunction. **-amente** *adv.* in conjunction. **-is-simo** *m.* close relation. **-ura** *f.* junction; join, seam; conjuncture, set of circumstances; occasion; opportunity; (astron.) conjunction; (econ.) juncture.

congiunzione *f.* junction, joint; (gram.; astron.) conjunction; (leg.) — carnale, carnal knowledge, unlawful sexual intercourse; †affinity; †relationship; †friendship.

congiur-are [A I] *intr.* (*aux.* avere) to conspire; †to swear together, to take common oath. **-a** *f.* conspiracy, plot; **-a** del silenzio, conspiracy of silence. **-amento** *m.* swearing; oath; conspiracy; conjuration. **-ante** *part. adj.* swearing; †*n.m.* conspirator. **-ato** *part. adj.* conspired, agreed; *n.m.* conspirator. (**-atore** *m.* **-atrice** *f.*) †**-azione** *f.* conspiracy.

conglob-are [A I s] *tr.* (finan.) to lump together, to make a lump sum of; to roll into one. **-amento** *m.* (finan.) lumping together; combining; consolidation (wages, salaries, etc.); amalgamation. **-ato** *part. adj.* (finan.) lumped together, made into a lump sum; lump, total; (fig.) dense; periodo **-ato**, sentence crammed full of ideas;

(med.) conglobate; glandola **-ata**, lymphatic gland; *n.m.* (finan.) lump sum; (fig.) miscellany, collection. **-azione** *f.* (finan.) lumping together.

conglomer-are [A I s] *tr.* to conglomerate, to amass. **-amento** *m.* conglomerating, amassing. **-ato** *part. adj.* amassed, conglomerated; *n.m.* (geol.) conglomerate, pudding stone; (bldg.) concrete. **-azione** *f.* conglomeration.

conglutin-are [A I s] *tr.* to glue together; to join. **-amento** *m.* gluing together; joining. **-ativo** *adj.* adhesive. **-ato** *part. adj.* glued together; joined. **-azione** *f.* gluing together; section joined.

Cong-o *pr.n.f.* (geog.) Congo. **-olese** *adj.* of or pertaining to the Congo; (also *n.m., f.*)

congratul-are [A I s] *rfl.* to congratulate; mi **-o** con Lei, I congratulate you; †*intr.* to take mutual pleasure, to be conjubilant. **-amento** *m.* congratulating, congratulation. **-ante** *part. adj.* congratulating. (**-atore** *m.* **-atrice** *f.*) **-ato-rio** *adj.* congratulatory. **-azione** *f.* congratulation, congratulating; *pl.* congratulations.

congreg-a *f.* group, band (of people); religious guild, confraternity; (pious) congregation; (liter. hist.) — dei Rozzi, a literary society for workpeople in Siena of the sixteenth century. **-ale** *adj.* relating to a group, guild or confraternity.

congreg-are [A 2] *tr.* to call together, to assemble (esp. for religious purposes); *rfl.* to congregate, to gather together, to assemble. (**-a-bile** *adj.*) **-amento** *m.* congregating. **-ante** *part. adj.* calling, assembling. †**-anza** *f.* congregation, assembly; society. †**-ativo** *adj.* relating to an assembly or congregation. **-ato** *part. adj.* gathered together, assembled, congregated. (**-atore** *m.* **-atrice** *f.*) **-azione** *f.* assembly, gathering; (eccl.) congregation (religious order or lay guild or permanent committee of cardinals); place where such congregation meets; **-azione** di carità, charitable body. **-azionista** *m.* member of a religious order.

congress-o *m.* congress, conference; concourse, gathering; (Amer.; pol.) Congress; (leg.) congress; meeting of litigants before a judge; consultation between legal adviser and client; (med.) sexual potency; †battle; †dispute; †clash. **-ista** *m., f.* (*pl.* **-isti** *m.*, **-iste** *f.*) delegate to a congress; member of a congress. **-uale** *adj.* relating to a congress; *n.m.* member of a congress.

congro *m.* (ichth.) conger-eel.

con-gru-a *f.* (leg.) benefice; (eccl.) competency, congrua (*portio*), minimum income guaranteed to a cleric (usu. a parish priest). **-ato** *adj.* (eccl.) with guaranteed stipend.

congru-ire [D 2] *intr.* (*aux.* essere) to be congruent. **-ente** *adj.* congruent. (**-entemente** *adv.*) **-enza** *f.* congruence, suitability.

con-gru-o *adj.* congruous; suitable, appropriate, fitting, apposite; (leg.) diritto —, pre-emptive right of a vendor to re-purchase property sold to adjoining owner; (theol.) congruous (grace, merit). (**-amente** *adv.*) **-ismo** *m.* (theol.) congruism. **-ità** *f. indecl.* congruity.

conguagli-are [A 4] *tr.* to equalize, to square up, to balance (accounts). **-amento** *m.* equalizing; squaring up. **-ato** *part. adj.* adjusted, squared up. (**-atamente** *adv.*)

congua-glio *m.* balancing, squaring up; in —, to square the count.

co-nia *f.* (Tusc.) joke; reggere alla —, to take a joke well.

coni-are[1] [A I s] *tr.* to coin, to strike, to mint; to invent (news); to trick. **-ato** *part. adj.* coined; †*n.m.* coin, *pl.* money. **-atore** *m.* coiner, inventor; counterfeiter. **-atura** *f.* coining; coinage. **-azione** *f.* coining, minting.

†**coniare**[2] *tr.* to trick, to deceive.

conicina *f.* (chem.) conine, conicine.

co-n-ico *adj.* conic, conical; sezione **-ica**, conic sector; tapering; *n.f.pl.* (math.) conics, conic sections. **-icamente** *adv.* conically, taperingly. **-icità** *f.* conicity, conicalness; taper.

coniella *f.* (bot.) marjoram, *Origanum*.

coni-fer-o *m.* (bot.) conifer; *adj.* coniferous. **-e** *f.pl.* (bot.) (class of) conifers, *Coniferae*.

coni-gli-o *m.* (zool.) rabbit; (fig.) timid individual. **-a** *f.* (zool.) female rabbit, doe; foremost thwart in a galley. **-coltura** *f.* rabbit-breeding. **-era** *f.* rabbit-hutch. †**-ere** *m.* see **conigliera**. **-olo**, **-uolo** *m. dim.* young rabbit.

coni-gliolo *m.* (Tusc. pop.). See **coniglio**.

conina *f.* (chem.) conine.

co-nio[1] *m.* wedge; die for striking coins; seal, stamp; imprint; moneta senza —, empty talk; nuovo di —, newly coined; di nuovo —, newly coined, (fig.) newly invented; †da —, for hire.

†**co-nio**[2] *m.* See **cogno**.

†co·nio³ *m.* trickery, deceit; trick.

conirostri *m.pl.* (orn.) Conirostres.

conisettore *m.* conic sector.

coniugal-e *adj.* conjugal, married, pertaining to marriage. **-almente** *adv.* conjugally, matrimonially.

coniug-are [A2s] *tr.* (gramm.) to conjugate; to join in marriage; *rfl.* to get married, to marry. **-a·bile** *adj.* (gramm.) that can be conjugated. **-ato** *part. adj.* conjugated; joined in marriage; married; (math.) conjugate; *n.m.* married person. **-azione** *f.* conjugation; (anat.) pair (of nerves).

co·niuge *m.* consort, husband, partner in marriage; (leg.) abbandono del —, desertion of husband or wife (C.C.); *pl.* married couple, husband and wife; i coniugi Rossi, Mr and Mrs Rossi; (leg.) atti compiuti tra coniugi, dealings between husband and wife.

†coniu·gio *m.* matrimony.

†conlaterale *adj.* See **collaterale**.

†conlaudare *vb.* and derivs. See **collaudare**.

conlegata·rio *m.* (leg.). See **collegatario**.

†conlogare *vb.* and derivs. See **collocare**.

connato *adj.* born together, cognate; (med.) congenital; (bot.) connate (of leaves or other structures united at their base).

connatural-e *adj.* natural, coming by nature; innate; of the same nature; *n.m.* nature. **-ità** *f. indecl.* naturalness, connaturality.

connatur-are [A1] *tr.* to make (a certain quality) natural, to ingrain; *rfl.* to become natural, to become second nature, to become ingrained. **-ato** *part. adj.* developed into a second nature, ingrained.

connazionale *adj.* of the same country; *n.m., f.* fellow-countryman, fellow-countrywoman; compatriot.

†conne *m.* the MS. abbreviation C for 'cum' or 'con'; il — e il ronne, the entire story, the whole matter, the long and the short of it (see also **ronne**).

connessione *f.* (leg.) close connexion (as a ground for consolidation of actions in civil courts).

conness-o *part.* of **connettere**, q.v.; *adj.* connected; *n.m.* thing connected or belonging; annessi e -i, accessories. **-ione** *f.* connexion. **-ivo** *adj.* connecting, connective. (**-amente** *adv.*) **-ità** *f. indecl.* connexion.

connesta·bile *m.* See **conestabile**.

connet·t-ere [C19] *tr.* to connect; *abs.* non —, to be incapable of thinking or speaking to the purpose, to be inconsequential. **-imento** *m.* connecting. **-itura** *f.* connexion. **-ivo** *adj.* (biol.; tanning) sostanza -iva, collagen; tessuto -ivo, connective tissue.

connina *f.* (bot.) stinking goosefoot, *Chenopodium vulvaria*.

conniv-ente *adj.* conniving; *n.m., f.* person who connives. **-enza** *f.* connivance.

connotato *m.* characteristic feature or peculiarity by which a person can be recognized; *pl.* official description; (joc.) cambiare i connotati a uno, to knock someone about, to beat someone up, to injure a person 'so that his own mother wouldn't recognize him'.

connovi·zio *m.* (eccl.) fellow novice.

†connub·bio *m.* See **connubio**.

connu·bi-o *m.* marriage; (fig.) partnership; (pol.) deal. **-ale** *adj.* conjugal, connubial.

connumer-are [A1] *tr.* to put in numbered order, to number in series. **-a·bile** *adj.* that may be numbered in series. **-ato** *part. adj.* numbered in series. **-azione** *f.* numbering.

cono *m.* (math.) cone; tronco di —, truncated cone, frustum; cappello a —, conical hat, sugar-loaf hat; (geog.) coni di deiezione, cones of detritus; (zool.) cone-shell, *Conus mediterraneus*; (bot.) cone.

conoc·chia *f.* distaff; trarre la —, to spin; (Tusc.) bunch of flax on the distaff ready for spinning; (mil.) incendiary rocket; (naut.) thick part of a mast; (eng.) kind of toothed wheel with pegs instead of teeth.

conoc·chio *m.* (Tusc.). See **conocchia**.

con-o·ide *m.* (geom.) conoid; (geog.) — detritico, alluvial cone. **-oidale** *adj.* (geom.; geog.) conoidal. **-oi·dico** *adj.* (geom.) conoidal.

conope·o *m.* (Egypt. antiq.) mosquito-net; (liturg.) ciborium veil; tabernacle veil.

conopuleggia *f.* (eng.) cone pulley.

conoscenza *f.* consciousness; perdere la —, to lose consciousness; riacquistare la —, to regain consciousness; acquaintanceship, acquaintance; son lieto di fare la vostra —, I am very glad to make your acquaintance; desidererei fare la sua —, I should like to get to know him; fare — con, to make the acquaintance of, to be introduced to; è persona di mia —, è una mia —, he is an

acquaintance of mine; avere conoscenze in un luogo, to have influential friends; siamo di —, we know each other; la nostra è — vecchia, we have known each other a long time; knowledge; venire a — di qualche cosa, to get to know about something; è giunto alla mia —, it has come to my knowledge; prendere — di, to take cognizance of, to note, to familiarize oneself with; prendere — della situazione, to size up the situation; intimation, information, instruction; (leg.) — carnale, see **congiunzione**; aver — con una donna, to have carnal knowledge of a woman; — fraudolenta, knowledge obtained by fraudulent means (C.P.); *pl.* acquaintances, people one knows; †mark of identity, distinguishing sign.

conosc-ere [B9] *tr.* to know, to have knowledge of; — a fondo, to know thoroughly; — per filo e per segno, to know every detail of, to know from A to Z; — il mare, to be an expert sailor; — la sua materia, to have a good knowledge of one's subject; — i suoi polli, to know quite well with whom one has to deal; — il mondo, to be a man of the world, to 'know one's way about'; — mezzo mondo, to know everybody; (of a child) — le lettere, to know the letters of the alphabet; to know, to be aware, to know for a fact; -o che avrei dovuto partire, I know I ought to have left; -o di aver avuto torto, I know I was in the wrong; lo -iamo tutti come un gran matto, we all know he's quite mad; lo -evo per galantuomo, I knew him to be a man of honour; to know, to experience; to have sexual relations with; aver -iuto la miseria, to have known poverty; to know personally, to be acquainted with; non lo -o, I don't know him, I haven't met him: -i te stesso, know thyself; ci -iamo, we know each other, we have already met; — di vista, to know by sight; — di saluto, to have a nodding acquaintance with; vi farò — mio padre, I will introduce you to my father; darsi a —, to turn out, to prove to be; si diede a — per poco intelligente, he turned out to be not very intelligent; to know, to recognize, to distinguish; ti -o alla voce, I know you by your voice; ti -o mascherina!, I can recognize you (playful opening gambit used in addressing masked person in a carnival, and used fig. in other situations); il cane -e il padrone, the dog knows his master; impara a — gli amici!, you should know who your true friends are!; non — il bene dal male, to be unable to distinguish right from wrong; (leg.) to know; to consider; to hear; to take cognizance of; to try; giudice che ha -iuto il reato, judge who tried the offence (C.C.P.); — carnalmente, to have carnal knowledge of; *intr.* (*aux.* avere) to be conscious; non -e più, he has lost consciousness; to be aware, to understand; se ben -o, if I understand aright; quando sarà in età di —, when he is old enough to understand; *rfl.* to know oneself, to acknowledge oneself; -ersi vinto, to acknowledge defeat; *recip. rfl.* to know each other; cominciare a -ersi, to begin to get to know each other. **-ente** *part. adj.* knowing; recognizing; acknowledging; *n.m.,f.* person who knows; connoisseur; expert; acquaintance, person whom one knows; un mio -ente, an acquaintance of mine. **-i·bile** *adj.* recognizable; knowable; *n.m.* (philos.) cognoscible. (**-ibilmente** *adv.*) **-ibilità** *f. indecl.* recognizability. **-itivo** *adj.* (philos.) capable of knowing; cognitive; (pop.) recognizable. **-itore** *m.* one who knows; one who recognizes or acknowledges; connoisseur; art expert. (**-itrice** *f.*) **†-itura** *f.* recognition. **-iuto** *part. adj.* known; well known; è persona -iuta, he is well known. **-iutamente** *adv.* to the knowledge of all.

†conoscidore *m.* See **conoscitore**, under **conoscere**.

conquass-are [A1] *tr.* to shake violently; to shatter; to devastate. **-amento** *m.* violent shaking; shattering; devastating. (**-atore** *m.* **-atrice** *f.*) **-azione** *f.* violent shaking; shattering; devastation.

conquasso *m.* ruin; ruining; shattering; mettere in —, to ruin.

conqui·bus *m. indecl.* (joc.) wherewithal (i.e. money).

conqui·dere [C3] *tr.* to overcome; to conquer; to defeat; (Tusc.) to harass, to disturb; †*rfl.* to worry; to torment oneself.

conquisitore *m.* investigator; spy.

conquiso *part.* of **conquidere**, q.v.; *adj.* (poet.) won, conquered; won over.

conquista *f.* conquest; paese di —, conquered country occupied by the enemy; (fig.) fare una —, to make a conquest; è una mia —, she (or, he) is one of my conquests.

conquist-are [A1] *tr.* to conquer; to win; to overcome; *rfl.* to win for oneself. **-a·bile** *adj.* conquerable. **-ato** *part. adj.* conquered; won; overcome. **-atore** *m.* conqueror; maker of conquests. (**-atrice** *f.*) **-o** *m.* conquest; conquering.

conregnare [A 5c] *intr.* (*aux.* avere) to rule together, to reign together, to be joint rulers.

†**consaccevole** *adj.* See **consapevole**, under **consapente**.

consacr-are [A I] *tr.* to dedicate, hallow; to consecrate; to ordain; to anoint, to crown; to pay divine honours to, to deify; to sanction, to make respectable; to give up, to devote. ~**a·bile** *adj.* suitable for consecration. ~**ando** *adj.* about to be consecrated; *n.m.* ordinand. ~**ante** *part. adj.* consecrating; *n.m.* (eccl.) celebrant at Mass. ~**ato** *part. adj.* dedicated, hallowed; consecrated; anointed; deified; sanctioned. (~**atore** *m.* ~**atrice** *f.*) ~**azione** *f.* (rel.) consecration (esp. as part of Mass); (Rom. hist.) deification, apotheosis.

†**consagrare** *vb.* and derivs. See **consacrare**.

consangui·n-eo *adj.* related by blood; consanguineous; *n.m.* (leg.) child of the same father (but not of the same mother). ~**eità** *f. indecl.* consanguinity, blood-relationship.

consap-ente *adj.* knowing. ~**évole** *adj.* aware; conscious; far —, to inform, to let know. ~**evolmente** *adv.* knowingly; consciously. ~**evolezza** *f.* awareness. ~**uto** *part. adj.* well known, known by many people.

†**conscienza** *f.* See **coscienza**.

con·scio *adj.* conscious; aware; senza esserne —, without being conscious of it, unawares; essere — a se stesso, to know in one's own heart.

consecrare [A I] and derivs. See **consacrare**.

consecutiv-o *adj.* consecutive; successive; (med.) fenomeni ~i, after-effects. ~**amente** *adv.* consecutively; successively.

consecuzione *f.* sequence.

consegna *f.* consignment, delivery; handing-over; (comm.) pagare alla —, to pay cash on delivery; — a termine, forward delivery; (mil.) orders given to a sentry; punishment by confinement to barracks; (naut.) captain's order book, commander's daily orders; punishment by confinement to a ship; handing over of an office, transfer; verbale di —, document recording the transfer of office from one person to another.

consegn-are [A 5c] *tr.* to consign, to deliver, to hand over; to give in charge (of the police, etc.); (joc.) — un colpo, to give a blow; (mil.) — nelle caserme, to confine to barracks; (naut.) to punish by stoppage of leave. ~**amento** *m.* consigning; handing over. ~**ata·rio** *m.* (leg.; comm.) consignee; (leg.) bailee. ~**ato** *part. adj.* consigned; delivered; handed over. (~**atore** *m.* ~**atrice** *f.*) ~**azione** *f.* consigning, consignment.

conseguente *adj.* See under **conseguire**.

conseguenz-a *f.* consequence; far —, to argue; in —, di —, per —, in consequence, consequently; emendamento per —, consequential amendment; †(mus.) fugal treatment. ~**iale** *adj.* consequent; consequential. ~**ia·rio** *adj.* over-logical, too rigidly logical; *n.m.* person who makes too rigid a use of logical deduction, sometimes from false premises.

consegu-ire [D 2] *tr.* to obtain, to achieve; to win; †to pursue; *intr.* (*aux.* essere) to follow in succession, to succeed (in order), to result, to follow; to proceed, to continue. ~**ente** *adj.* consequent; logical; ~ente a se stesso, coherent, consistent; una persona ~ente, a logical, consistent person; consequential; per ~ente, consequently, later, subsequently; (geog.) consequent (of rivers, drainage, etc.); *n.m.* consequence. ~**entemente** *adv.* consequently; consequentially. ~**i·bile** *adj.* obtainable, attainable. ~**imento** *m.* obtaining, attainable; attainment. ~**ito** *part. adj.* obtained, achieved; won. (~**itore** *m.*)

conseguit-are [A I sc] *intr.* (*aux.* essere) to follow (from what has gone before); to form a sequence; †*tr.* to follow; to obtain (~**amento** *m.* ~**atore** *m.*)

consens-o *m.* consent; consensus; agreement; (leg.) consent, agreement, assent. ~**uale** *adj.* agreed to by all, consented to; separazione ~uale, separation (of a married couple) by mutual consent.

consenta·ne-o *adj.* corresponding; agreeing; consentaneous; — a, in accordance with. ~**amente** *adv.* correspondingly. ~**ità** *f. indecl.* consentaneity, fittingness, appropriateness.

consenti *m.pl.* (Rom. myth.) Consentes Di.

consent-ire [D I] *intr.* (*aux.* avere; *prep.* a) to agree (to); to consent; to yield, to give; †to be favourable; †to be suitable, to be in accordance; *tr.* to permit, to concede. ~**évole** *adj.* consenting. ~**imento** *m.* consenting; yielding; granting. ~**ito** *part. adj.* agreed, allowed, permitted, granted. ~**itamente** *adv.* in the manner allowed or agreed. (~**itore** *m.* ~**itrice** *f.*)

consenziente *part.* of **consentire**, q.v.; *adj.* consenting, willing.

conse-polto, ~**pulto** *adj.* buried with another; (theol.) buried with Christ in baptism.

consequente *adj.* and derivs. See **conseguente**, under **conseguire**.

†**conserba** *f.* place of safe-keeping; storehouse; hospice, hostel.

consert-are [A I] *tr.* to intertwine; (mus.) see **concertare**. ~**amento** *m.* intertwining. ~**ato** *part. adj.* intertwined; (of arms) folded.

conserto *apocop. part.* of **consertare**, q.v.; *adj.* intertwined; (of arms) folded; (poet.) le braccia al sen conserte, with arms folded; di —, concerted, in agreement; *n.m.* (mus.) see **concerto**.

conserva *f.* preserved food, canned food; tinned fruit; carne in —, tinned meat; — di prugne, plum jam; — di pomodoro, tomato purée; far — di, to preserve, to lay by; store; — di neve, — di ghiaccio, ice-box; reservoir, storage-tank; fish-pond, fish-tank; (naut.) fleet of ships sailing under convoy or any of the individual ships forming a fleet under convoy; (fig.) andar di —, to act together, to follow the same road.

conservag·gio *m.* See under **conservo**.

conserv-are [A I] *tr.* to preserve, to keep; — un buon ricordo di, to cherish a happy memory of; (naut.) — il vantaggio del vento, to retain the weather gauge; *rfl.* to keep; (of a person) si ~a bene, he is well preserved. ~**a·bile** *adj.* preservable, that will keep. †~**ag·gio** *m.* (naut.) going in convoy. †~**agione** *f.* see **conservazione**. ~**amento** *m.* preserving. ~**ativo** *adj.* preservative, protective; (leg.) sequestro ~ativo, precautionary seizure by the Court of the property of an insolvent debtor. ~**ato** *part. adj.* preserved; tinned, canned. ~**atore** *m.* preserver, preservative; curator, custodian; (leg.) holder; keeper; custodian; ~atore delle ipoteche, Registrar of Mortgages and Charges; (pol.) Conservative; *adj.* Conservative; il partito ~atore, the Conservative party. (~**atrice** *f.*) ~**atori·a** *f.* (leg.) office of Registrar of Mortgages and Charges, Registry of M. and C. ~**ato·rio** *adj.* (*m.pl.* ~**atori**, ~**atorii**) preserving, preservative; *n.m.* poor-house; convent school; (mus.) conservatoire, school of music. ~**azione** *f.* preservation; diritto di ~azione, right of self-preservation; keeping; (leg.) ~azione delle ipoteche; custody of mortgage deeds; (phys.) conservation.

conserv-o *m.* fellow-servant; companion in servitude. ~**ag·gio** *m.* slavery or imprisonment in common with others. ~**itù** *f. indecl.* servitude in common with others. ~**i·zio** *m.* slavery in common with others.

consesso *m.* assembly, meeting; (joc.) questo nobile —, this august gathering.

consett-aiuo·lo, ~**a·rio** *m.* fellow-sectary, fellow-member of a sect. ~**are** [A I] *rfl.* to form a sect, party or faction.

consider-are [A I s] *tr.* to consider; to judge, to deem, to estimate. ~**a·bile** *adj.* considerable. ~**abilmente** *adv.* considerably. ~**abilità** *f. indecl.* considerability. ~**ando** *m. indecl.* initial word of an official pronouncement (cf. Eng. 'whereas'); motive, underlying cause; clause. †~**anza** *f.* see **considerazione**. ~**atezza** *f.* considerateness; caution, deliberation. †~**ativo** *adj.* contemplative; considerate. ~**ato** *part. adj.* considered, deliberate; molto ~ato, highly thought-of; visto e ~ato, whereas, (joc.) this being the case; †male ~ato, imprudent, ill-advised; *conj.* ~ato che, considering that. ~**atamente** *adv.* in a considerate manner; circumspectly; deliberately. (~**atore** *m.* ~**atrice** *f.*) ~**azione** *f.* consideration; esteem, gode di molta ~azione, he is highly esteemed. ~**évole** *adj.* considerable; un numero ~evole, a goodish number, a considerable number.

consigli-are[1] [A 4] *tr.* to advise, to counsel; to recommend; le ~ò i bagni di mare, he recommended sea-bathing to her; — a qualcuno di fare qualcosa, to advise someone to do something; to exhort (to); (prep. di, foll. by *neg. infin.*) to advise against; *rfl.* to seek advice; ~arsi con, to seek advice from, to consult; to resolve. ~**a·bile** *adj.* advisable. ~**amento** *m.* advising, counselling. ~**ato** *part. adj.* advised; well-advised; recommended, counselled. ~**atamente** *adv.* advisedly. ~**atore** *m.* adviser, counsellor. (~**atrice** *f.*)

consigliare[2] *adj.* See under **consiglio**.

consiglier-e *m.* adviser, counsellor; councillor; — tecnico, technical adviser; — delegato, managing director; (comm.) — d'amministrazione, company director; (naut.) navigator's assistant, 'tankie'; (leg.) — d'Appello, — di Corte d'Appello, judge in a Court of Appeal; — dell'Ordine, Member of the Bar Council; — di Cassazione, Judge of the Court of Cassation. ~**o** *m.* adviser, counsellor. (~**a** *f.*)

consi·gli-o *m.* advice, counsel; — interessato, advice that is not disinterested; suggestion; cassetta consigli, suggestion box; (theol.) consigli evangelici, Evangelical counsels; council; board; — d'amministrazione, governing body, board of governors, board of directors; — esecutivo, executive council, executive board; — di gestione, board of trustees; — comunale, municipal council; (leg.) council; — dell'Ordine, Bar Council; — di Stato, Council of State, supreme court of administrative law; (mil.) — di guerra, council of war, court martial; (naut.) — di disciplina, disciplinary court; — sommario, summary court; Consiglio Superiore di Marina, equiv. to Board of Admiralty; *pl.* apprentice pilots; consigli dei venti, variable winds. **-are** *adj.* relating to a council; (admin.) adunanza -are, board-meeting.

†consignare *vb.* and derivs. See **consegnare**.

†consignificare *tr.* to signify when taken together.

consignore *m.* joint master, master jointly with another.

consili-are *adj.* conciliar, relating to a council. **-a·rio** *adj.* (*m.pl.* -ari) advisory.

consi·mil-e *adj.* similar. **-mente** *adv.* similarly.

†consir-o *m.* care, worry, preoccupation. **†-oso** *adj.* worried, full of care.

consi·st-ere [B I] *intr.* (*aux.* essere) to consist; to persist; — in, to consist of. **-ente** *part.* consisting; *adj.* having consistence; sizable; persistent. **-enza** *f.* consistency; un miscuglio di non troppa -enza, a mixture that is not too thick; (comm.) -enza di cassa, cash in hand; -enza di magazzino, stock on hand; patrimonio di poca -enza, fortune consisting of very little; consistence, density; resistance, toughness; substance; prende -enza la voce che, the rumour is gaining ground that.

consisto·r(i)o *m.* See **concistoro**.

†con·sito *adj.* cultivated; planted; forested.

†consobrin-o *m.* cousin. (**†-a** *f.*)

consoci-are [A 3] *tr.* to associate. (**-a·bile** *adj.*) **-ante** *part. adj.* associating, associated. **-ato** *part. adj.* associated; *n.m.* associate, companion; (comm.) co-partner. **-azione** *f.* association, society.

conso·cio *m.* colleague; fellow-member (of club, society, etc.); (comm.) co-partner.

†consodale *m.* companion.

consolare¹ *adj.* See under **console**.

consol-are² [A I c] *tr.* to console, to comfort, to solace; to restore; (euphem.) fa un freddo che -a, it's beastly cold; *rfl.* to be consoled, to derive comfort; to rejoice; -arsi con, to seek consolation in. **-a·bile** *adj.* consolable. **†-amento** *m.* consoling; consolation. **-ante** *part. adj.* consoling, comforting. **†-anza** *f.* consolation. **†-ativo** *adj.* consoling, comforting. **-ato** *part. adj.* consoled, -forted; at ease, peaceful; pleasant; acqua -ata, gentle rain. **-atamente** *adv.* with consolation; easily, restfully, gently. **-atore** *m.* consoler, comforter; (theol.) spirito -atore, Comforter, Paraclete. (**-atrice** *f.*) **-ato·ria** *f.* letter of condolence; comforting letter. **-ato·rio** *adj.* (*m.pl.* -atòri, -atorii) consoling, soothing, bringing consolation; parole -atorie, words of consolation. **-atoriamente** *adv.* consolingly; soothingly. **-azione** *f.* consolation; **†sport, recreation; †fare -azione con, to sup with, to share a meal with.

consolato¹ *part.* of **consolare²**, q.v.

consolato² *m.* See under **console**.

con·sol-e *m.* consul; (lit. hist.) principal of certain academies; (Ital. hist.) rank equivalent to Colonel in Fascist militia. **-are** *adj.* consular; l'automobile recava la targa -are, the car bore the consular badge. **-arità** *f. indecl.* consulship. **-ato** *m.* consulate; (hist.) il Consolato, the Consulate of Napoleon Bonaparte; -ato del mare, tribunal of maritime commerce; -ato magistrale, nautical code; consulship. **†-eri·a** *f.* consulate.

conso·lida *f.* (bot.) — maggiore, comfrey, *Symphytum officinale*; — tuberosa, — femmina, *S. tuberosum*; — minore, self-heal, *Prunella vulgaris*; — regale, wild larkspur, *Delphinium consolida*.

consolid-are [A I s] *tr.* to consolidate; to strengthen, to reinforce; to stiffen, to make solid; *rfl.* to become consolidated; to be stiffened; (fig.) to take root. **-amento** *m.* consolidating, consolidation; reinforcement. **-ante** *part. adj.* consolidating; *n.m.* healing medicament. **-ativo** *adj.* consolidating. **-ato** *part. adj.* consolidated; stiff, solid; (finan.) consolidated; debito -ato, public debt; *n.m.* gilt-edged stock, government stock. **-azione** *f.* consolidation; strengthening; solidification; (finan.) consolidating, funding; (med.) consolidation, healing, knitting together.

consolle *f.* console-table; (mus.) organ-console.

con·solo¹ *m.* See **console**.

conso·lo² *m.* comfort, consolation; food taken (according to S. Italian custom) to those bereaved, who are regarded as too afflicted to prepare their own.

†consomigliare *tr.* to resemble.

consonante *f.* See under **consonare**.

conson-are [A I d] *intr.* (*aux.* avere) to be consonant; to sound in agreement; to be in accord. **-ante** *part. adj.* consonant, agreeing, in accord; (mus.) consonant; *n.f.* consonant. **-anza** *f.* consonance, harmony, concord; (prosod.) rima di -anza, consonance (usu. perfect rhyme as distinct from assonance; sometimes imperfect rhyme with same consonants but different vowels); (mus.) concord; consonance; -anza perfetta, perfect concord; -anza imperfetta, imperfect concord.

con·sono *adj.* consonant, conformable; fitting, suitable; — a (con), in keeping with, in conformity with.

†consopito *adj.* overcome with sleep, stupefied; ecstatic, rapt in meditation, absorbed.

consorella *f.* (eccl.) fellow nun, sister in the same order or guild; *adj.* related; società —, sister association.

consort-e *adj.* associated, related; *n.m.* consort, husband; il Principe Consorte, the Prince Consort; blood-relation; member of a political clique; *f.* consort, wife. **-eri·a** *f.* political faction; clique; (Ital. hist.) group of families of the aristocracy which wielded power in municipalities; **†affinity; †relationship. **-ile** *adj.* referring to a clique or party. **†-o** *m.* see **consorte**.

consor·zi-o *m.* partnership, association; firm; society; union; syndicate, club; consortium; (leg.) — di bonifica, land-reclamation syndicate (C.C.). **-ale** *adj.* pertaining to a partnership, association or syndicate. **-almente** *adv.* in a manner characteristic of an association, in accordance with a partnership. **-ato** *adj.* banded together, clubbed together; forming a syndicate or association.

consostanziale *adj.* and derivs. See **consustanziale**.

consp-argere, **†-er·gere** *vb.* See **cospargere**.

†conspetto *m.* See **cospetto**.

†conspi·cere *vb. intr.* to look around, to let one's gaze wander; *tr.* to look at carefully; to fix one's gaze on; to see, to behold.

conspi·cuo *adj.* and derivs. See **cospicuo**.

†conspirare *vb.* and derivs. See **cospirare**.

†constante *adj.* and deriv. See **costante**.

†constanza *f.* See **costanza³**.

const-are [A 9?] *intr.* (*aux.* essere, *prep.* di) to consist (of); *impers.* to be evident, to be proved; to result; to be within one's knowledge; non -a che, it does not appear that; mi -a che, it has come to my knowledge that; **†to 'take', to 'set', to take on a consistency; †to coagulate.

constat-are [A I s, A I] *tr.* to establish as a fact, to verify, to authenticate; to ascertain; to observe, to note. **-ato** *part. adj.* verified; ascertained; observed, noted; evident. **-azione** *f.* confirmation, proof; establishment of a fact; observation; fare la -azione che, to establish that; faccio una semplice -azione, I am merely stating a fact.

†constellazione *f.* See **costellazione**, under **costellare**.

†constipare *vb.* and derivs. See **costipare**.

†constituire *vb.* and derivs. See **costituire**.

†constituzione *f.* See **costituzione**.

†constrin·gere *vb.* and derivs. See **costringere**.

†construire *vb.* and derivs. See **costruire**.

†construzione *f.* See **costruzione**.

consuali *m.pl.* (Rom. antiq.) the Consualia games.

†consubrin-o *m.* cousin. (**†-a** *f.*)

consud·dito *m.* fellow-subject.

consue·t-o *adj.* usual, accustomed, habitual; customary; *n.m.* usual custom; *adv. phr.* di —, per —, secondo il —, usually, customarily. **-amente** *adv.* in the usual manner, as is wont, according to habit. **†-are** *intr.* to be accustomed to, to be wont to.

consuetu·din-e *f.* custom, habit, usage; general practice; (leg.) custom; customary law; traditional usage; — del paese, local custom. **-a·rio** *adj.* habitual, customary, (leg.) diritto -ario, customary law.

consul-ente *adj.* consulting; *n.m.* consultant; — legale, legal adviser; — tecnico, assessor (C.C.P.), (eng.) consulting engineer. **-enza** *f.* position of a consultant; consultation; advice; la nostra -enza è gratuita e senza impegno, our advice is given free and without obligation.

consulta *f.* consultation; consulting room; Council of State; consultative body; Consulta Araldica, equiv. to College of Heralds; (eccl.) Sacra —, Sacred Council (papal court of justice before 1870); the name of a famous palace in Rome, built by Pope Clement XII for the Supremo Tribunale Pontificio della Consulta in 1739, which housed the Italian Foreign Office from 1870 to 1922: during this period 'Consulta' was often synonymous with 'Foreign Office'; (Ital. hist.) title of various governing bodies during the Fascist régime.

consult-are [A I] *tr.* to consult; to seek advice of; to refer to; to look up in; — un dizionario, to consult a dictionary; *rfl.* (*prep.* con) to take advice, to consult (with); *recip. rfl.* to consult together, to confer. **-ativo** *adj.* consultative. **-ato** *part. adj.* consulted; used as a reference. **-atore** *m.* consultor. (**-atrice** *f.*) **-azione** *f.* consultation; advice; previa -azione con, in consultation with, having consulted; libro di -azione, reference book.

consultivo *adj.* consultative; consultive; comitato —, advisory committee; voto —, advisory vote (of members of board, committee, etc. which does not count in deciding its resolutions).

consult-o *m.* professional consultation; (med.) consultation by two or more doctors in regard to a case; (leg.) consultation; counsel; legal advice or opinion. **-ore** *adj.* consultant, consulting; *n.m.* consultant; (Ital. hist.) Municipal Councillor (Fascist régime); *pl.* (eccl.) consultors. **-o·rio** *adj.* (*m.pl.* **-ori**) advisory, consulting; *n.m.* (doctor's) consulting room.

consuma *f.* consumption; consuming; destruction; andare alla — to ruin oneself; avere la — in corpo, to be insatiable, to be ravenous.

consum-are [A I] *tr.* to wear out, to use up, to consume; to waste, to dissipate; to consummate, to fulfil; — un delitto, to commit a crime; (liturg.) — il pane e il vino, to consume the sacred species; (theol.) — il sacrifizio, to consummate the sacrifice, to complete the sacrifice; (fig.) to complete, to perfect; *rfl.* to wear oneself out; to ruin oneself; to waste away, to perish; to consume oneself, to fret. **-a·bile** *adj.* consumable; perishable. **-amento** *m.* consuming; wearing out; using up; burning desire. **-ante** *part. adj.* consuming. †**-anza** *f.* consuming; consummation. **-ato** *part. adj.* worn out, used up; consummate, expert, skilled; *n.m.* (cul.) consommé. **-atore** *m.* waster; consumer, destroyer; patron (of café or restaurant); (econ.) consumer; †perfecter, one who completes and perfects. **-azione** *f.* consumption, waste; achievement, consummation; ruin, end; (Bibl.) -azione dei secoli, end of the world; (liturg.) -azione della messa, priest's communion at Mass; what is eaten or drunk in a restaurant, refreshments.

consumè *m. indecl.* (cul.) consommé.

consu·mere [C def.] *tr.* to consume; to wear out.

consumo *m.* consumption; use; in Italia si fa un — eccessivo di farinacei, in Italy they eat too many starchy foods; food, provisions; per —, for everyday use; — interno, home consumption; cooperative di —, co-operative store; (econ.; comm.) generi di —, consumer goods; imposta di —, excise duty or tax; (techn.) consumption; — di carburante, fuel consumption; wear; (eng.) a —, expendable, throw-away; *pl.* (naut.) stores.

consuntivo *adj.* consuming, using; (med.) absorbent; (finan.) comprising income and expenditure (of an account, etc.); bilancio —, budget for financial year or other period; rendiconto —, account of expenditure for past financial year; *n.m.* (comm.; econ.) summary, survey, balance-sheet; account; budget; final balance.

consunto *part.* of **consumere**, q.v.; *adj.* worn out, used up; wasted; (med.) suffering from consumption, tubercular; è morto —, he died of consumption; *n.m.* (med.) consumptive person, tubercular patient.

consunzione *f.* using up, destroying, wasting; waste; (med.) consumption, tuberculosis.

consuo·cer-a *f.*, **-o** *m.* terms expressing the relationship of parents to their son's or daughter's parents-in-law.

†**consur·gere** *intr.* to arise; to be born; to have origin.

consussisten-te *adj.* subsisting together. **-za** *f.* subsistence together.

consustanz-iale *adj.* (theol.) consubstantial. (**-ialmente** *adv.*) **-ialità** (theol.) consubstantiality. **-iazione** *f.* (theol.) consubstantiation.

conta *f.* The phrase 'far la —' describes a process of choosing one of a party to perform a special task, such as paying for drinks. All the party hold up their hands, each extending as many fingers as he pleases. These are counted successively, and the person

whose number added to the total of all the preceding numbers completes a previously agreed figure is the person selected. He then usually nominates a 'padrone' and a 'sottopadrone' who decide upon the drinks of the party.

conta·bil-e *m.* accountant; book-keeper; (naut.) — nocchiere, senior lower deck rating. **-ità** *f.* book-keeping; accountancy; ufficio -ità, accounts department.

contachilo·metri *m. indecl.* See under **contare**.

contadin-o *adj.* country, rustic; *n.m.* peasant; countryman; man working on the land; smallholder; farm-worker; boorish person, rustic. **-a** *f.* peasant woman; peasant girl; country dance. **-ame** *m.* countryfolk, country people, peasantry, crowd of peasants. **-anza** *f.* peasant condition. **-ata** *f.* boorish act; action or behaviour characteristic of a peasant. **-ello** *m. dim.* of **contadino**; young peasant, country boy. (**-ella** *f.*) **-esco** *adj.* (*m.pl.* **-eschi**) rustic; alla -esca, rough and ready. (**-escamente** *adv.*) **-otto** *m.* stocky peasant.

contado *m.* countryside round a city; country district; (hist.) country round a city-state; peasant population; †territory ruled by a Count.

conta-fili, **-film**, **-fotogrammi** *m. indecl.* See under **contare**.

†**contage** *f.* See **contagio**.

conta·gi-o *m.* contagion; (fig.) contact; bad influence; contamination. **-are** [A 3] *tr.* to spread by contagion; to contaminate. **-one** *m.* (med.) contagion. **-oso** *adj.* contagious; catching. **-osamente** *adv.* contagiously.

conta-giri, **-gocce** *m. indecl.* See under **contare**.

contaluzzo *m.* (ichth.) *Coryphaena hippurus*, dolphin fish, dorade.

†**contamente** *adv.* suitably, fittingly; pleasantly; elegantly; immediately; cautiously.

contamin-are [A I S] *tr.* to corrupt; to contaminate; to sully, to defile; †to dishonour; †to offend, to outrage; †to suborn; †to seduce; †to flatter, to wheedle, to coax; †to incite, †to importune. **-a·bile** *adj.* that may be contaminated; susceptible of contamination. †**-amento** *m.* contamination. **-ato** *part. adj.* contaminated; (liter. hist.) commedia -ata, (Roman) comedy blending different sources. **-atore** *m.* contaminator. (**-atrice** *f.*) **-azione** *f.* contamination; defilement, corruption; (lit. hist.) contamination, blending of sources (esp. in Plautus and Terence). **-oso** *adj.* contaminating; impure, unclean.

contante[1] *adj.* See under **contare**.

contante[2] *n.m.* (finan.) cash; in —, in cash; *pl.* ready money; per contanti, for cash; mi hanno fatto uno sconto perchè pagavo in contanti, they gave me discount because I was paying cash.

contapassi *m. indecl.* See under **contare**.

cont-are [A I C] *tr.* to count; to reckon; to esteem; — qualche cosa a colpa a qualcuno, to blame somebody for something; to recount, to tell, to narrate; -arle grosse, to tell lies; — le ragioni ai birri, to talk to the wall; to name, to indicate; *intr.* (*aux.* avere) to count, to matter; non -a, it's of no consequence; non -a perchè il gioco non era cominciato, it doesn't count because the game hadn't begun; (provb.) -ano più gli esempi che le parole, actions speak louder than words; — su, to count on, to rely on; ma non ci —, but don't count on it; — di, to intend to, to mean to; *rfl.* to number, to amount. **-achilo·metri** *m. indecl.* pedometer; distance gauge; (motor.) milage metre, mileometer, trip metre; speedometer. **-afiletti** *m. indecl.* (eng.) screw pitch gauge. **-afili** *m. indecl.* (text.) thread-counter. **-afilm** *m. indecl.* (cinem.) film counter, footage indicator. **-afotogrammi** *m. indecl.* (cinem.) frame indicator or counter. **-agiri** *m. indecl.* (mech.) revolution counter. **-agocce** *m. indecl.* glass dropper; bottiglina col -agocce, dropping bottle. †**-amento** *m.* counting; account; narration. **-ante** *part. adj.* counting, reckoning. †**-anza** *f.* knowledge, news, information; repute. **-aore** *m. indecl.* (techn.) hour metre. **-apassi** *m. indecl.* pedometer. **-asecondi** *m. indecl.* stopwatch. **-ata** *f.* count, one reckoning; rapid counting; †narration, account. **-ato** *part. adj.* counted, numbered, told; denaro -ato, exact amount; *pl.* few; i suoi giorni sono -ati, his days are numbered; †recounted, related; †aforesaid. **-atore** *m.* counter, reckoner; meter; -atore a moneta, pre-payment meter; -atore del gas, gas meter; (watchm.) stopwatch; (atom. phys.) -atore di Geiger, Geiger counter; †narrator; *adj.* used for counting. **-atrice** *f.* of **contatore**; (paperm.) teller, counter; *adj.* used for counting.

contarello *m.* See **conterello**.

†**contasta** *f.* conflict, dispute.

contatt·o *m.* contact; a — con, in contact with; prender — con, to make contact with, to contact; stare in —, to keep in touch; (electr.) — a spina, two-(three-)pin plug. **-ore** *m.* (electr.) contactor.

cont·e *m.* count; earl; (hist.) il — verde, Amedeo VI; il — rosso, Amedeo VII. **-e·a** *f.* countship; earldom; county; (hist.) property to which the title of count was attached; conte senza -ea, penniless count, lackland.

conteggiare [A 3 c] *intr.* (*aux.* avere) (finan.) to keep accounts; *tr.* to enter (an item) in accounts.

conteggio *m.* accounting, keeping of accounts; check of voting; procedere al —, to check the vote; (techn.) computation count.

†contegnen·te *adj.* continent, moderate. **†-za** *f.* environs, region.

contegn·o *m.* demeanour, bearing; behaviour, conduct; appearance; dignity, reserve; stare in —, to be reserved, to stand on one's dignity; darsi un —, to give oneself airs; †thing contained. **-oso** *adj.* staid, reserved, stiff; demure; dignified. **-osamente** *adv.* stiffly, in a constrained manner; demurely; with dignity.

contemper·are [A 1 s] *tr.* to temper, to moderate; to blend; to modify; to mitigate. **-amento** *m.* tempering; moderating; modifying. **-anza** *f.* modification; mitigation.

contempl·are [A 1] *tr.* to contemplate; to envisage; to make provision for; to foresee; (leg.) to provide for. **-a·bile** *adj.* that may be contemplated; thinkable. **-amento** *m.* contemplating; meditating. **-ante** *part. adj.* contemplating; meditating; (rel.) contemplative; *n.m.* contemplative (monk); *f.* contemplative (nun). **†-anza** *f.* contemplation. **-ativa** *f.* power of contemplation; contemplative (nun). **-ativo** *adj.* contemplative; meditative; dreamy; (rel.) contemplative; *n.m.* contemplative (monk). **-ato** *part. adj.* contemplated; foreseen; (leg.) -ato dalla legge, covered by the law. **-atore** *m.* contemplator; *adj.* contemplative. (**-atrice** *f.*) **-azione** *f.* contemplation; in -azione, in consideration.

contempo *adv. phr.* nel —, at the same time, in the meanwhile.

contempora·ne·o *adj.* contemporary; contemporaneous, simultaneous; *n.m.* contemporary. (**-a** *f.*) **-amente** *adv.* contemporaneously. **-ità** *f.* contemporaneousness.

†contemprare *vb.* and derivs. See **contemplare**.

contend·ere [C 1] *tr.* to contend; to contest; to dispute; to forbid, to prohibit; to prevent; (poet.) to deny; *intr.* (*aux.* avere) to contend, to compete; nessuno può — con lui di (in) destrezza, no one can compete with him in skill; *recip. rfl.* to contend with each other; si -evano il posto, they were rivals for the job. **-ente** *part. adj.* contending; *n.m.* rival, contestant; (leg.) contestant; opponent; i -enti, the contending parties. **†-enza** *f.* contest; strife. **-evole** *adj.* contentious, quarrelsome. **-evolmente** *adv.* contentiously. **-itore** *m.* **-itrice** *f.*)

conten·ere [B 32] *tr.* to contain; to hold; to include; to hold back, to repress; *rfl.* to contain oneself; to restrain oneself; non potè -ersi dal ridere, he couldn't help laughing; to behave; †to spread, to extend. **-ente** *part. adj.* containing; including; †continent; *n.m.* container, receptacle. **-enza** *f.* content, capacity; behaviour; reserve. **-imento** *m.* contents; †see **contegno**. (**-itore** *m.* **-itrice** *f.*)

conten·n·ere [B 1] *tr.* to despise; to contemn. **†-endo** *adj.* despicable.

content·are [A 1] *tr.* to satisfy; to gladden; to gratify, to satisfy, to delight the heart of; *rfl.* to be satisfied, to content oneself; bisogna -arsi, we musn't grumble; to allow; si -a?, may I?, will you allow me?; (iron.) chi si -a, gode, glad you're satisfied (said to or of someone who is easily pleased). **-a·bile** *adj.* capable of contentment; facilmente -abile, easy to please. **-amento** *m.* contenting; contentment. **-ato** *part. adj.* satisfied. **-atura** *f.* contentedness; di difficile -atura, difficult to please. **†-evole** *adj.* satisfying, contenting. **†-evolmente** *adv.* contentedly.

content-ezza *f.*, **-ino** *m.* See under **contento¹**.

†contenti·bile *adj.* contemptible.

†contentivo *adj.* containing, comprising; retaining; *n.m.* (surg.) old-fashioned device for keeping the edges of a broken bone, or of a wound, in apposition.

content-o¹ *adj.* content, contented; satisfied; glad, pleased, happy; — come una pasqua, as happy as can be; cuor —, stout, jolly person; doll so weighted as to return to an upright position when knocked over; mal —, dissatisfied; — lui, contenti tutti, once he's satisfied the others only too gladly refrain from criticism. **-amente** *adv.* contentedly, with contentment. **-ezza** *f.* contentment, satisfaction; joy, gladness; pleasure, delight; -ezza d'amore,

old country dance; mala -ezza, dissatisfaction, displeasure. **-ino** *m.* extra piece of indulgence; make-weight, a bit extra; sop; bonus, discount; stop-gap. **-one** *adj. augm.* more than satisfied.

contento² *m.* contentment, satisfaction; happiness, pleasure.

contento³ *adj.* taut, strained.

†contento⁴ *m.* thing contained, content.

†content-o⁵ *m.* contempt, scorn. **†-ore** *m.* despiser, contemptuous person.

contenut-o *part.* of **contenere**, q.v.; *adj.* contained; included; restrained, held back; *n.m.* contents, content; — in carbonio, carbon content; subject matter. **-i·stico** *adj.* (lit.; art) relating to subject matter; placing emphasis on subject or content more than on form.

†contenza *f.* dispute, strife.

contenzion·e *f.* contention, dispute; (leg.) contention; litigation. **-are** [A 1 c] *intr.* (*aux.* avere) to contend, to quarrel.

contenzios·o *adj.* contentious; questionable; *n.m.* (leg.) contentious business; legal department; il — diplomatico, the Foreign Office Legal Adviser. **-amente** *adv.* contentiously. **-ità** *f. indecl.* contentiousness.

conterello *m. dim.* of **conto**, q.v.; little account, little bill; small sum owing; arithmetical exercise, sum.

conteri·a *f.* ornamental glass, Venetian-type glassware; *pl.* glass beads.

conter·min·e *adj.* conterminous, conterminal; *n.m.* common ending. **-ale** *adj.* conterminal. **-are** [A 1 s] *intr.* (*aux.* avere) to end together, to be conterminous. **†-o** *adj.* see **contermin·e** or **-ale**.

conterr·a·neo, -azzano *adj.* belonging to the same village or district; *n.m.* fellow-inhabitant; fellow-countryman.

contes·a *f.* contest, opposition, disagreement; contention, strife; venire a —, venire in —, to contend, to quarrel, to disagree. **-o** *part.* of **contendere**, q.v.; *adj.* contested; disputed; hindered, prevented.

contess-a¹ *f.* countess. Note: this title is given to the wife of a count, and sometimes, as a courtesy title, to the daughter of a count. In Venetian families it is the title of a countess in her own right. **-ina** *f. dim.* courtesy title of a young daughter of a count.

Contessa² *pr.n.f.* (Tusc.) Tessa.

contes·s·ere [C 29] *tr.* to interweave; to entwine; (fig.) to compose. **-imento** *m.* interweaving; entwining; composition. **-uto** *part. adj.* interwoven; entwined (see also **contesto¹**).

contesta·bile¹ *adj.* See under **contestare¹**.

†contesta·bile² *m.* See **conestabile**.

contest-are¹ *tr.* to contest; to dispute; to oppose; to challenge; (leg.) to dispute, to contest (an allegation, claim, etc.); to give formal notice of (a violation of the law, breach of regulations, etc.). **-a·bile** *adj.* that may be contested, contestable; disputable, debatable. **-ato** *part. adj.* contested; disputed; opposed; challenged. **-azione** *f.* contestation; dispute; objection; (leg.) issue; dispute; lawsuit; objection; service of a notice; †attestation, testimony.

†contestare² [A 1] *tr.* to weave; to compose; to construct.

conteste *m.* (leg.) fellow-witness; joint deponent.

contestimon·e *m.* (leg.) fellow-witness. **-ianza** *f.* (leg.) corroborated evidence.

contest-o¹ *altern. part.* of **contessere**, q.v.; *adj.* interwoven; put together, composed. **-ura** *f.* interweaving, entwining.

contest-o² *m.* context; a text viewed as a whole; gist; (leg.) context; the whole tenor of a document. **-uale** *adj.* relating to the whole of the contents of a document; (leg.) having the same text; (hence, loosely) executed simultaneously with another deed.

contezza *f.* cognisance, knowledge, awareness; aver — di, to know about, to be aware of; dar — di, to inform about, to let know about; ne ebbi — da lui, he informed me of it.

conticino *m. dim.* of **conto**, q.v.; small account, trifling bill.

†conti·gi·a *f.* decoration, adornment; beauty; *pl.* hose and footwear combined, tights. **†-ato** *adj.* richly adorned, decked out; overdressed; wearing ornamented hose and footwear.

conti·gu·o *adj.* contiguous, next to one another; adjoining, neighbouring. **-amente** *adv.* contiguously, next to one another. **-ità** *f. indecl.* contiguity, proximity; contiguousness.

continent·e¹ *m.* (geog.) continent; (in relation to Ital. islands) mainland; l'antico —, the Old World; il nuovo —, the New World; il novissimo —, Australia. **-ale** *adj.* continental; relating to the mainland of Italy.

contin·ente² *adj.* continent, abstemious; chaste; continuous; constant; febbre —, unintermittent fever; †containing. **-entemente** *adv.* continently; chastely; modestly. **-enza** *f.* continence, abstinence, abstemiousness; moderation, temperance; chastity; (liturg.) humeral veil (at Benediction).

contingent-are [A I] *tr.* (comm.) to establish, to apportion, to fix (quotas for imports, etc.); to distribute according to a quota. **-amento** *m.* (comm.) quota system of distribution (esp. of films); apportioning, fixing of quotas; application of a quota. (**-ato** *part. adj.*)

contin·g·ere [C def.] *intr.* to happen. **-ente** *adj.* contingent; incidental; appropriate, due, expected; *n.m.* quota, share, allocation; (mil.) contingent; il — dell'anno, all the conscripts of a given year; chance, hazard, coincidental occurrence; (geom.) tangent. **-entemente** *adv.* perchance. **-enza** *f.* contingency, eventuality; occasion; emergency; (leg.) -enza di cause, overlapping of actions (C.C.P.). **-i·bile** *adj.* possible, feasible.

†**contino** *m.* dim. of **conte**, q.v.; young count.

†**continovare** *vb.* and derivs. See **continuare**.

continu-are [A 6] *tr.* to continue; to proceed with; †to frequent the company of; *intr.* (aux. essere, avere) to continue, to last; to go on; l'eruzione del volcano è -ata (ha -ato) tutta la notte, the volcano went on erupting all night; to be in process, to be unfinished; (after an instalment of an article, etc.) -a, to be continued; (aux. avere, *prep.* a, foll. by *infin.*) to continue, to go on; -ava a parlare, he went on speaking; to persevere, to keep on. **-a·bile** *adj.* continuable; unending. **-abilità** *f. indecl.* quality of being continuable. †**-amento** *m.* continuing; continuation. **-ante** *part. adj.* continuing. **-ativo** *adj.* continuative, imparting continuance. **-ato** *part. adj.* continued, continuing; continuous. **-atore** *m.* continuer. (**-atrice** *f.*) **-azione** *f.* continuation; continuing, continuance.

conti·nu·o *adj.* continual; continuous; unbroken, uninterrupted; (math.) frazione -a, recurring fraction; (electr.) corrente -a, direct current; *adv. phr.* di —, del —, continually, unceasingly, without stopping; (mus.) basso —, thorough-bass; *n.m.* continuum, continuous substance; (surg.) soluzione del —, separation of the tissue. **-amente** *adv.* continually; continuously. **-ità** *f. indecl.* continuity; (cinem.) continuity, sequence.

contitolare *adj.* (of a church) dedicated to more saints than one; (of a saint) joint patron; *n.m.* co-titular.

cont-o¹ *m.* **1.** ADDITION, calculation, reckoning; fare il —, to add up; far di —, adding up; leggere, scrivere e far di —, reading, writing and arithmetic; (boxing) count. **2.** BILL, account; fare i conti, to do one's accounts; il — torna, the bill is correct; i conti non tornano, the account doesn't balance; accertare un —, saldare un —, to settle an account; dover fare i conti con, to have to reckon with; alla resa dei conti, on the day of reckoning; fare al —, see 'fare la conta', under **conta**; fare i conti in tasca (*or* addosso) a qualcuno, to make impertinent conjectures as to a person's income, etc.; fare i conti senza l'oste, to reckon without one's host, to leave some important person or factor out of the reckoning, to count one's chickens before they are hatched; (provb.) conti chiari, amici cari (i.e. bills promptly rendered and promptly paid make for lasting friendships); in fin dei conti, al far dei conti, a conti fatti, after all, when all is said and done; (finan.; leg.) a —, in —, on account; per — di terzi, on commission; — corrente, — aperto, current account; accreditare in —, to credit on account; mettere in — a, to put to, to debit (a person's) account; — attivo, credit side of a banking account; — passivo, debit side of an account; — interessi, interest account; — scoperto, overdraft; — arretrato, account outstanding; — spento, account closed; — cassa, cash account; — di ritorno, costs (C.C.); — sociale, joint account; estratto —, statement of account; accendere un —, aprire un —, to open an account; incassare un —, to collect an account; verificare un —, to audit an account; rendere i -i, to furnish the accounts (C.C.); accettazione del —, acceptance of account (C.C.); Corte dei Conti, State Audit Court or Board (I.C.). **3.** ACCOUNT, reckoning, notice; tenere — di, to take into account, to take account of, to bear in mind, to notice; rendersi — di, to realize, to become aware of; non so rendermi — di, I can't understand; far — su (sopra), to count on, to rely on. **4.** ACCOUNT, esteem, regard, value; tenere di (da) —, to hold in esteem, to cherish; aver in buon —, to prize, to have a high regard for;

persona da (di) —, person of some account; dare ad alcuno il suo —, to give a person his due; tornare — a, to be of value to; non merita —, it's not worth while; non gli mette —, it doesn't pay him; di nessun —, of no importance, of no value, worthless; far —, to matter, to count. **5.** ACCOUNT, report; render —, to report, to render account; non dover render — a nessuno, to be accountable to no one; gli chiederò — di quel che ha detto, I'll ask him to explain what he meant by that; dare — di sè, to give an account of oneself. **6.** ACCOUNT, matter, concern, reason, consideration; è un altro —, that's another matter; sapere il suo —, to know one's business; a buon —, with good reason, all the more reason; a ogni buon —, just in case; assumere informazioni sul — di, to make inquiries concerning (e.g. a prospective employee); per — di, on behalf of; per — mio, as far as I am concerned, for my part, on my behalf; preferisco lavorare per — mio, I'd rather work on my own, I prefer to be my own master; a nessun —, on no account, for no consideration. **7.** OPINION, intention; fo — di partir subito, I intend to leave immediately; per — mio, in my opinion; fare — che, to think that, to imagine that; far — di essere, to imagine that one is.

conto² *apocop. part.* of **contare**, q.v.

conto³ *m.* narration, account.

†**conto⁴** *adj.* known, clear, manifest; ready; adorned, ornate.

contor·c-ere [C 5] *tr.* to contort, to twist; *rfl.* to writhe, to twist (as in pain). **-imento** *m.* contortion, twisting; (vet.) method of castration by torsion of the cord, bistournage.

contorn-are [A I C] *tr.* to surround; to go round; (cul.) to garnish; (paint.) to outline, to sketch in outline; to surround; to border, to edge; to trim; (archit.) to surround (esp. of ornament, like a cornice); *rfl.* (*prep.* di) to surround oneself (with), to associate (with). **-amento** *m.* surrounding; surround; edging. **-ato** *part. adj.* surrounded; bordered, edged. **-iare** [A 4] and derivs. (pop.) see **contornare**.

contorn-ire [D 2] *tr.* to cut out (wood); to carve into frets; to draft, to outline; (eng.) to blank. (**-ito** *part. adj.*) **-itrice** *f.* (eng.) routing machine. **-itura** *f.* (eng.) routing; blanking.

contorno *m.* outline, contour; ornamental border; trimming, edging; rim; (cul.) the vegetables, etc. which go with a meat or fish dish; suite, people attending a distinguished person, entourage; (paint.) outline; (textiles, embroidery) ornamental border, hem; *pl.* surroundings, environment.

contorsione *f.* contorsion, twisting; state of contorsion.

contort-o *part.* of **contorcere**, q.v.; *adj.* contorted, twisted, distorted; warped. **-amente** *adv.* contortedly, distortedly.

contra¹ *prep.* (poet.) see **contro**; (admin.) — presentazione di —, upon presentation of.

contra² *m.* factor counting against; il pro e il —, the pros and cons.

contra³ *prefix.* contra-; counter-. Note: the prefix **contra-** is usually followed by a double consonant except in the case of *x, z, gn, ps,* or impure *s*. The prefix **contro-**, on the other hand, is followed by a single consonant: e.g. **contrassegno**, but **controsenso**; **contrabbilanciare**, but **controbilanciare**.

contrab(b)andato *adj.* (herald.) bendy per bend sinister counterchanged.

contrabband-o *m.* contraband, smuggling; merce di —, smuggled goods; di —, clandestinely, surreptitiously. **-iere** *m.* smuggler; (naut.) smuggler ship. (**-iera** *f.*) **-ista** *m.* smuggler.

contrab(b)ass-o *m.* (mus.) double-bass; double diapason (organ stop). **-ista** *m., f.* double-bass player, contrabassist.

contrabastone *m.* (herald.) baston sinister; — scorciato, baston sinister couped.

contrabbat·ter-e [B I] and derivs. See **controbattere**, under **controalette**.

contrabbietta *f.* (naut.) counter-wedge.

contrabbilanciare [A 3] and derivs. See **controbilanciare**, under **controalette**.

contrabbordo *m.* See **controbordo**, under **controalette**.

contrabbracciare [A 3] and derivs. See **controbracciare**, under **controalette**.

contracatena *f.* See **controcatena**, under **controalette**.

contraccade·mia *f.* rival academy.

contrac-cambiare [A 4] *tr.* to reciprocate, to return; grazie per gli auguri di Natale, che -cambio, thank you for your Christmas wishes, which I reciprocate; — un favore, to return a favour. **-cam·bio** *m.* recompense, return; exchange; rendere -cambio, to return like for like, to give tit for tat; in -cambio di, in return for.

contracca·rico *m.* counterbalancing load.

contraccartella *f.* See **controcartella**.

contraccassa *f.* outer-casing.

contraccav-a *f.* (mil.) countermine. **-are** [A I] *tr.* (mil.) to countermine.

contracchiav-e *f.* second key for double-locking; false key; skeleton key; double turning of a key. **-are** [A I] *tr.* to double-lock.

contracchi·glia *f.* (naut.). See **controchiglia**, under **controalette**.

contracchioda·ia *f.* (techn.) riveting block.

contraccolomba *f.* (naut.). See **controcolomba**, under **controalette**.

contraccolpo *m.* counter-blow; repercussion; recoil, bounce; reaction; (motor.) backfire.

contraccoperta *f.* dust cover (of a book).

contraccorrente *f.* counter-current; cross-current; (electr.) eddy current; *adj.* running counter, flowing in the opposite direction.

contraccri·tica *f.* See **controcritica**, under **controalette**.

contraccuore *m.* terrible grief, heartbreak; *adj. indecl.* heartbreaking; *adv.* heartbreakingly; piangere a —, to cry as if one's heart would break.

contraccusa *f.* (leg.) counter-accusation.

contraci·fera *f.* counter-cipher, key to a cipher.

contracignone *m.* See **controcignone**, under **controalette**.

contracolonna *f.* See **controcolonna**, under **controalette**.

contracquist-are [A I] *tr.* to acquire in exchange. (-ato *part. adj.*)

contrad-a *f.* street; village street; district; stretch of country; veniamo dalle stesse -e, we come from the same part of the world; (Siena) neighbourhood, quarter; (poet.) country; le belle -e, Italy. Note: **contrada** is a main street; **strada** is a more general term, and several **strade** may open into one **contrada**, but not vice versa. **contrada** was, and in Siena still is, a quarter in a town, comprising main street, side-streets and alleys. The 'capitano della contrada' was originally a military official (in Siena); he now holds an influential position with certain social obligations, and is armed and mounted in the Palio procession. **-aiolo** *m.* (Siena) inhabitant of the same neighbourhood or quarter.

contrad(d)anza *f.* country dance; square dance; folk dance.

contraddetto *part.* of **contraddire**, q.v.; *adj.* contradicted; gainsaid.

contraddic-co *m.* (*pl.* **-chi**) strengthening dam.

contradd-ire [B IO] *tr.* to contradict; to gainsay; to be contradictory; *rfl.* to contradict oneself. **-icente** *part. adj.* contradicting; contradictory; objecting; rebellious. **-ittore** *m.* one who contradicts; heckler. (**-itrice** *f.*) **-itto·ria** *f.* opposite proposal. **-itto·rio** *adj.* contradictory; opposing; heckling; conflicting; (chem.) analisi -ittoria, check analysis; (leg.) contradictory; inconsistent; la sentenza può essere impugnata per -ittoria motivazione, appeal may be made against a judgement for inconsistency in the reasoning; *n.m.* confrontation of the parties to an action; cross-examination; (fig.) public discussion, debate; accettare il -ittorio, to hear the other side (in debate). **-ittoriamente** *adv.* in contradictory fashion, inconsistently. **-izione** *f.* contradiction; contradicting; denial; discrepancy; opposition; è in -izione con tutti, he has a grouse against everyone; spirito di -izione, perversity.

contrad-distin·guere [C6] *tr.* to distinguish; to mark, to label; to characterize; to counter-check. **-distinto** *part. adj.* distinguished; marked, labelled; characterized; ogni esemplare è -distinto dalla firma dell'autore, every copy bears the author's signature.

contraddote *f.* (leg.) pre-nuptial settlement, marriage settlement.

†**contradi-are** *tr.* to oppose, to counter; to challenge. †**-amento** *m.* opposition, conflict.

†**contra·di-o** *adj.* contrary, opposed; hostile; injurious; *n.m.* enemy, adversary; offence, injury. †**-oso** *adj.* contrary; hostile; injurious.

contradire [B IO] and derivs. See **contraddire**.

contradistin·guere [C6] and derivs. See **contraddistinguere**.

contraditto·rio *adj.* See **contraddittorio**, under **contraddire**.

contradivieto *m.* contraband, illicit goods.

contradizione *f.* See **contraddizione**, under **contraddire**.

†**contradota** *f.* See **contraddote**.

contraente *part.* of **contrarre**, q.v.; *adj.* contracting; *n.m.* (comm.) contractor; (leg.) contracting party (C.C.).

†**contra·ere** *vb.* and derivs. See **contrarre**.

contrae·re-o *adj.* anti-aircraft. **-a** *f.* anti-aircraft guns, ack-ack.

contrafagott-o *m.* (mus.) double-bassoon. **-ista** *m.,f.* contrafagottist.

contrafa·scia *f.* See **controfascia**, under **controalette**.

contrafasciato *adj.* (herald.) burely per pale counterchanged.

contraffac-ente *part.* of **contraffare**, q.v.; *adj.* counterfeiting; simulating, aping; †disobedient. **-imento** *m.* counterfeiting. **-itore** *m.* counterfeiter, forger. (**-itrice** *f.*)

contraff-are [B 14] *tr.* to counterfeit, to forge; to copy, to simulate; to ape; to adulterate; to disguise; *intr.* (*aux.* avere) to disobey; *rfl.* to disguise oneself. **-atto** *part. adj.* counterfeit, counterfeited, false; copied, aped; disguised, deformed; adulterated; strange, oddly assorted; apocryphal. **-attore** *m.* counterfeiter, forger; imitator; (leg.) falsifier; forger; counterfeiter. **-attura** *f.* forgery, counterfeit, imitation. **-azione** *f.* counterfeiting; forgery; copy, imitation; piracy, plagiarism.

contraf-filare [A I] *tr.* (bootm.) to trim (the welt); (text.) in doubling silk, to place a thicker or darker-coloured thread (alongside a thinner or lighter-coloured one). **-filo** *m.* (bootm.) the outer edge of the welt.

contraffisso *m.* (bldg.). See **contrafisso**.

contrafforte *m.* buttress; heavy iron bar for securing a door; (geog.) buttress, spur; (bldg.) see **contraforte**.

contrafforza *f.* reaction, countering force.

contraffosso *m.* (mil.) auxiliary trench.

contrafisso *m.* (bldg.) brace; strut.

contrafloc-co *m.* (*pl.* **-chi**). see **controfiocco**, under **controalette**.

contrafo·dera *f.* See **controfodera**, under **controalette**.

contraforte *f* (bldg.) buttress.

contragge·nio *m.* disinclination; dislike, antipathy, aversion; a — di, unwillingly, against the grain.

contragguar·dia *f.* (mil.) counterguard.

contra-go *m.* (*pl.* **-ghi**) (rlwy.) stock rail (of a switch).

contr-ierba, -ierva *f.* (bot.) name of herbs used as antidotes, especially of the bezoar root, *Dorstenia contrajerva* of S. America.

contraindicare [A 2 s]. See **controindicare**, under **controalette**.

contrainquartato *adj.* (herald.) counter-quartered.

contral·bero *m.* (eng.) countershaft, subsidiary shafting.

contralettera *f.* See **controlettera**, under **controalette**.

contralizza *f.* See **controlizza**, under **controalette**.

contralleva *f.* See **controleva**, under **controalette**.

contrallume *m.* See **controlume**, under **controalette**.

†**contralta** *f.* (mus.). See **contralto**.

contraltare *m.* 'counter-altar'; a rival project; counter-attraction; fare un — a, to damage (an enterprise) by setting up another in opposition.

contralt-o *m.* (mus.) contralto voice, contralto singer, contralto. (N.B. even when referring to a female singer the gender usually remains masc.); alto (in all senses, viz. alto part of harmony, alto instruments, alto voice), alto singer; chiave di —, alto clef. **-ino** *m.* high tenor.

contramali·a *f.* counter-charm.

contramandare [A I] and derivs. See **contromandare**, under **controalette**.

contraman·tice *m.* See **contromantice**, under **controalette**.

contramar·cia *f.* See **contromarcia**, under **controalette**.

contra-mare·a *f.* current running against the tide. **-mezzana** *f.* (naut.) mizzen topsail.

†**contramastro** *m.* (naut.) mate.

contramina *f.* See **contromina**, under **controalette**.

contrammira·glio *m.* rear-admiral.

contrammolla *f.* See **contromolla**, under **controalette**.

contrammuro *m.* supporting wall.

contraniten-te *adj.* resisting. **-za** *f.* opposing force.

contrapappafico *m.* (naut.) royal (sail).

contraparte *f.* See **controparte**, under **controalette**.

contrapertura *f.* (surg.) counter-opening.

contrapologi·a *f.* counter-apologia.

contrappal-co *m.* (*pl.* **-chi**) (bldg.) framework of a ceiling as distinct from that of the floor above.

contrappassare [A I] *intr.* (*aux.* avere) to intercommunicate; to merge; †— a, to transgress; †*tr.* to measure in steps, to walk.

contrappass-o *m.* fitting retribution, retaliation, 'an eye for an eye'; (mus.) a mutual approach in dancing; counter-part, i.e. the repetition in the cotillon by the second and fourth couples of a figure already executed by the first and third couples.

contrappello *m.* second (roll) call (e.g. in Italian Parliament).

contrappelo *m.* the wrong way of the hair; dare il —, fare il —, radere il —, to shave upwards, to shave against the hair; a —, against the hair, against the grain, 'the wrong way', (of cloth)

contrappelo (*cont.*)
against the nap; dare il — a, to criticize (a person) minutely; andare a — a, to take (a person) the wrong way, to go against the grain of.

contrappes-are [A1c] *tr.* to counterbalance; to counterpoise; to estimate the weight (of something) by trying it in the hand against something in the other hand; (*fig.*) to examine carefully, to weigh the pros and cons of. (**-amento** *m.*) **-ato** *part. adj.* counterbalanced; weighed; (*fig.*) estimated, weighed up. **-atamente** *adv.* in a considered manner; after weighing things up carefully.

contrappeso *m.* counterpoise, counterbalance; *pl.* (watchm.) counterweights.

contrappon-ibile *adj.*, **-imento** *m.* See under **contrapporre.**

contrap-porre [B21] *tr.* (*prep.* a) to contrapose, to oppose, to set against; to contrast (with); *rfl.* to be opposed (to), to oppose. **-ponibile** *adj.* capable of being opposed, susceptible of being set in opposition. **-ponimento** *m.* setting in opposition; contraposition; opposition. **-posizione** *f.* contraposition; opposition; contrast; antithesis. **-posto,** (Rom.) **-posto** *part. adj.* opposed, contrasted; reverse; (eng.) taglio -posto, conventional cut; (herald.) conjoined; *n.m.* opposite; antithesis.

contrappozzo *m.* subsidiary shaft in a mine; culvert to carry away underground water.

contrapproc·cio *m.* (mil.) counter-approach.

contrapproposta *f.* See **controproposta,** under **controalette.**

contrappunt-o *m.* (mus.) counterpoint, the art of counterpoint; a contrapuntal part; — doppio all'ottava, double counterpoint at the octave; — doppio alla duodecima, double counterpoint at the twelfth; — a quattro voci, four-part counterpoint; — alla zoppa, fourth-species counterpoint (i.e. with syncopations); — invertibile, invertible counterpoint. †**-ante** *m.* contrapuntist. **-eggiare** [A3c] *intr.* (*aux.* avere) (mus.) to make counterpoint. **-ino** *m. dim.* short contrapuntal piece. **-ismo** *m.* contrapuntalism. **-ista** *m., f.* contrapuntist. **-i·stico** *adj.* contrapuntal. †**-izzamento** *m.* making counterpoint (with). †**-izzare** *vb.* see **contrappunteggiare.**

†**contrapugnare** *tr.* to oppose.

contrarcata *f.* (mus.) false bowing (i.e. an up-bow when a down-bow would be expected, or vice versa).

contrar·gine *m.* secondary dike (in reinforcement).

contrari-are [A4] *tr.* to gainsay, to thwart, to oppose; to contradict; to vex, to upset, to distress; to disappoint. (**-amento** *m.*) **-ato** *part. adj.* opposed, thwarted; contradicted; sorry, upset, vexed; disappointed. (**-atore** *m.*)

contra·ri-o *adj.* contrary, opposed, adverse; opposite; reverse; untoward; unfavourable, hostile; *n.m.* contrary, opposite; per lo —, al —, on the contrary; in caso —, otherwise; non aver nulla in —, to have nothing against it; adversity, misfortune, tribulation; opponent; †recarsi a —, to take a dislike to, to hold in abhorrence; *adv.* contrariwise, contrarily; in the opposite direction. **-amente** *adv.* contrarily; in the opposite direction; adversely; the other way round; -amente a, contrary to; (math.) in inverse proportion. **-età** *f.* contrariness; opposition, adversity, difficulties, untoward events; disappointment; obstacle, impediment; -età del tempo, unseasonable weather. **-oso** *adj.* see **contrario.**

contrarispondere [C11]. See **controrispondere,** under **controalette.**

contrarmellino *m.* (herald.) ermines.

†**contraro** *adj.* See **contrario.**

contraronda *f.* See **controronda,** under **controalette.**

contrarre [B33] *tr.* to contract; — debiti, to incur debts; — matrimonio, to enter into matrimony; — amicizia con, to form a friendship with; — una malattia, to catch an illness, to contract a disease; — la bocca, to purse up one's lips, to make a wry mouth; †to gather, to assemble; *rfl.* to contract, to shrink; to withdraw into one's shell; *recip. rfl.* to contract, to form one, to be contracted; due vocali si contraggono in una sola, two vowels are contracted to form one.

contraruota *f.* See **controruota,** under **controalette.**

contrasaluto *m.* (naut.) answering salute.

contrasbarrato *adj.* (herald.) barry per pale countercharged.

contrascarpa *f.* See **controscarpa,** under **controalette.**

contrascena *f.* See **controscena,** under **controalette.**

contrasciamito *m.* cloth worked in fine gold.

contrascotta *f.* (naut.) brails.

contra-scritta *f.,* **-scri·vere,** **-serratura** *f.* See **controscritta,** etc., under **controalette.**

contrasforz-are [A1] *rfl.* (*prep.* a) to pit oneself (against); to oppose. †**-o** *m.* opposing force.

contrasigillo *m.* See **controsigillo,** under **controalette.**

contraspalto *m.* (mil.) second glacis.

contrasprone *m.* See **controsprone,** under **controalette.**

contrassalto *m.* (mil.) counter-attack, counter-assault.

contrassarti·a *f.* (naut.) supplementary shroud.

contrasse *f.* inner lining board of the body of a carriage or waggon.

contras-segnare [A5c] *tr.* to place a mark upon; to label; to characterize; to countersign; to indicate. **-segnato da,** characterized by, marked with. **-segno** *m.* mark, distinctive sign; password, sign; indication; token; (comm.) -segno per posta, cash on delivery.

contras-sigillo *m.,* **-soggetto** *m.,* **-stampa** *f.* See **controsigillo,** etc., under **controalette.**

contrast-are [A1] *tr.* (*prep.* con) to set (against); to contrast (with); (*prep.* a) il nemico ci -a il passo, the enemy oppose our advance; to dispute; to contend; to resist; to hold up (traffic); *intr.* (*aux.* avere; *prep.* a) to struggle (against); to vie (with), to compete (with); to be in contrast (with); *recip. rfl.* to vie with each other; i bambini si acciuffarono, -andosi il regalo, the children fought over the present. **-a·bile** *adj.* questionable, open to question, controversial. **-abilmente** *adv.* questionably. (**-amento** *m.*) **-ato** *part. adj.* opposed, resisted; disputed; questionable, doubtful; (photog.) carta -ata, hard paper; (theatr.) applausi -ati, mixed reception. (**-atore** *m.* **-atrice** *f.*)

contrast-o *m.* conflict; conflict of ideas; opposition; contrast; strife; discord; comparison; mettere in —, to contrast; to compare; (liter. hist.) contrasto, dialogue-poem (in early Italian verse); (mus.) passage from consonance to dissonance; (eng.) resistance; (fencing) 'contraste'; (art) contrast; in — con, against, opposite; venire (a) in — con, to quarrel with; essere sempre in —, to be forever at loggerheads; senza —, without doubt, without fear of contradiction; mettere in —, to question, to contradict; †avere — a, to oppose.

†**contrastra·glio** *m.* (naut.) auxiliary stay.

contrattac-co *m.* (*pl.* **-chi**) (mil.; fencing) counter-attack. **-care** [A2] *tr., intr.* (*aux.* avere) to counter-attack.

contrattamente *adv.* See under **contratto¹.**

contratt-are [A1] *tr.* to discuss the purchase or sale of; to bargain concerning, to haggle over; *intr.* (*aux.* avere) to negotiate, to carry on negotiations; to discuss a business deal, to talk business; to bargain, to haggle; to make a contract, to contract. **-a·bile** *adj.* buyable, for sale, to be bought; negotiable, ready for negotiation. (**-amento** *m.*) **-ato** *part. adj.* discussed, haggled over; fixed, settled, agreed upon. **-atore** *m.* person negotiating a sale; essere un bravo -atore, to be good at driving a bargain. (**-atrice** *f.*) **-azione** *f.* contracting, negotiation; business deal in progress; bargaining, haggling.

contrattempo *m.* delay, short interval; untoward incident, hitch; disappointment; a —, di —, at the wrong moment, inopportunely; far un —, to be disconcerting; cogliere il —, to snatch an occasion, to seize an opportunity; (of a horse) irregular movement while galloping; (mus.) syncopation; (fencing) attack in which advantage is taken of a pause.

contrat·til-e *adj.* contractile, **-ità** *f.* contractility.

contratt-o¹ *part.* of **contrarre,** q.v.; *adj.* contracted; shrunken. **-amente** *adv.* in shortened form. **-ura** *f.* contraction; shrivelling; abbreviation; (med.) contracture; permanent contraction and rigidity of the muscles.

contratt-o² *m.* contract; in —, in negotiation; (leg.) contract; covenant; agreement; fare un —, to make a contract; redigere un —, to draw up a contract; — di matrimonio, marriage contract; — di compravendita, contract of sale and purchase; — di cessione, deed of grant; — di affitto, tenancy agreement; —tacito, implied contract; — condizionale, conditional contract; — accessorio, supplementary contract; — bilaterale, bilateral contract; — unilaterale, unilateral contract; — aleatorio, hazardous or rashly speculative contract; — di lavoro, collective bargaining. **-uale** *adj.* contractual; (leg.) autonomia -uale, freedom of contract (C.C.).

contrattura *f.* See under **contratto¹.**

†**contrausanza** *f.* evil-doing, transgression.

contravaiato *adj.* (herald.) countervairy.

contraventamento *m.* (aeron.) jackstay.

contravveleno *m.* antidote.

contravven-ire [D 17] *intr.* (*aux.* avere) (leg.) to transgress, to trespass; — a, to contravene, to infringe; — ad una legge, to break a law. -**tore** *m.* (leg.) transgressor; offender; trespasser. -**zione** *f.* (leg.) breach, contravention; infringement; trespass; i reati si distinguono in delitti e contravvenzioni, offences are divided into crimes and contraventions; -zione al Codice Stradale, motoring offence; -zione all'ordine pubblico, breach of the peace; fine payable in respect of such an offence; contestare, elevare, intimare una -zione ad una persona, dichiarare una persona in -zione, to fine (under summary executive procedure enabling the police to impose 'on the spot' fines for, e.g., traffic offences, infringement of parking regulations, etc.); conciliare una -zione, to pay a fine on the spot; pagare una -zione, to pay a fine; (colloq.) ho avuto una -zione, I got fined, I 'got a ticket'.

contravviso *m.* contrary information; contradiction; countermand.

contravvite *f.* nut (of a screw-bolt).

contrazione *f.* contraction; contracting; shrinking; reduction.

contre *m. indecl.* (pron. as Fr.) (cards) double (at bridge); †(naut.) sheets.

contribol-are [A 1 s] *tr.* to afflict; to distress. -**ato** *part. adj.* afflicted, in sorrow, distressed.

contribu-ire [D 2] *tr.* (*prep.* a) to contribute (to); to help; *intr.* (*aux.* avere) to have a part (in); to contribute (to). -**ente** *part. adj.* contributing; *n.m., f.* contributor; taxpayer; ratepayer. -**ito** *part. adj.* contributed.

contribule, contri-bulo *m.* fellow-tribesman.

contribu-to *m.* contribution; — alla scienza, contribution to learning; mettere a —, to make use of, to bring into play; sum contributed; quota; share. -**tore** *m.,* -**trice** *f.* contributor; colleague, fellow-worker. -**zione** *f.* contribution; participation; quota; share; taxes, taxation; levy.

contrimboscata *f.* counter-ambush.

contrimpannata *f.* double window.

contrina *f.* one of several ropes tied to the ends of the props of nets for birds, so called because the two front ones should be opposite to those which are tied to the lower extremities, so that they may all act together.

contrindicare [A 2 s] and derivs. See **controindicare**, under **controalette**.

contrinvetriata *f.* opposite window.

†**contrire** *tr.* to crush, to reduce to powder, to pound; to mortify; *rfl.* to feel contrition.

contrist-are [A 1] *tr.* to grieve, to sadden; to afflict; to distress; *rfl.* to become sad, to grieve; to be grieved; to distress oneself. -**a·bile** *adj.* subject to sadness; liable to be grieved. -**amento** *m.* grieving. -**ato** *part. adj.* saddened, grieved; distressed. (-**atore** *m.* -**atrice** *f.*)

contrit-o *adj.* contrite, penitent; afflicted; †pounded, crushed. -**amente** *adv.* contritely, with contrition, penitently.

contrizione *f.* contrition; far atto di —, to make an act of contrition; †mortification.

contro¹ *prep.* against; over against, opposite to; (comm.) — pagamento, against payment; — assegno, cash on delivery; *adv.* against, on the opposite side; dar — a, to criticize, to oppose.

contro² *pref.* counter-, contra-. (See also note under **contra²**.)

contro³ *m.* il pro e il —, the pros and cons; (fencing) — di quarto, contre de quart; — di terza, contre de tierce; parata di —, contre parry; parare —, to parry contre.

contro-alette *f.pl.* (naut.) quarter-pieces. -**aliseo** *m.* (meteor.) counter trade wind. -**anello** *m.* keeper-ring. -**avviso** *m.* contrary information. -**ballata** *f.* antistrophe. -**barre** *f.pl.* (naut.) outriggers for giving greater spread to top-gallant backstays. -**battere** [B 1] *tr.* to counter, to answer; to refute; to bring forward as a reply; *intr.* (*aux.* avere) to rebound, to recoil; to return blow for blow; to make a rejoinder, to make a riposte. -**batteri·a** *f.* (mil.) counter-battery. -**battuta** *f.* drag of a wave off the bank of a river; (mus.) syncopation. -**belvedere** *m.* (naut.) mizzen royal sail. -**bietta** *f.* (eng.) gib. -**biglietto** *m.* ticket given in exchange for another. -**bilanciare** [A 3] *tr.* to balance, to counterbalance. -**bitta** *f.* (naut.) spur of the bitts. -**boccaporto** *m.* (naut.) hatchway cover. -**bollare** [A 1] *tr.* to counterseal. -**bollo** *m.* second seal. -**bordo** *m.* (naut.) sheathing; opposite tack or course; navigare a -bordo, to navigate in the opposite direction. -**borsa** *f.* (naut.) preventer head-earing; -borosa di terzaruolo, preventer reef-earing. -**bracci** *m.pl.*

(naut.) preventer mainbraces. -**bracciare** [A 3] *tr.* (naut.) to brace round. -**bri·glia** *f.* (naut.) preventer bobstay. -**bu·io** *m.* (cards) overblind (at poker). -**cappa** *f.* blower: flap placed to prevent a fireplace from smoking. -**carena** *f.* (naut.) sheathing. -**ca·ricaboli·ne** *f.pl.* (naut.) outer leech lines. -**cassa** *f.* see **contraccassa**. -**catena** *f.* auxiliary chain; (bldg.) straining beam. -**cava** *f.* see **contraccava**. -**cavazione** *f.* (fencing) doublée. -**chiama** *f.* second call. -**chi·glia** *f.* (naut.) false keel. -**cifra** *f.* key to a code. -**cignone** *m.* supplementary strap, safety strap. -**colomba** *f.* (naut.) false keel. -**colonna** *f.* (archit.) pillar or pier standing behind another pillar or column. -**colonnino** *m.* (paperm.) crossbars (as reinforcements for large-sized moulds). -**colpo** *m.* see **contraccolpo**. -**cono** *m.* (eng.) female cone. -**coperta** *f.* (naut.) spar deck. -**corrente** *f.* (electr.) counter-current, eddy (current); andare a -corrente, to go countercurrent, (fig.) to go contrary to the general run. -**cri·tica** *f.* counter-criticism. -**crocette** *f.pl.* (naut.) Jack cross trees, royal cross trees. -**dado** *m.* (eng.) check-nut, lock-nut, jam-nut. -**data** *f.* fresh date (e.g. date placed on a letter at the time of its despatch, it having been written and dated, but not sent, some time previously). -**decreto** *m.* counter-decree. -**diagonale** *m.* (bldg.) counterbalance. -**dichiarazione** *f.* (leg.) counter-declaration i.e. a declaration made subsequently in writing by the parties to a written agreement, modifying it. -**dote** *f.* see **contraddote**. -**fagotto** *m.* (mus.) see **contrafagotto**. -**fa·scia** *f.* extra wrapping for a heavy package; (mus.) rib (of violin). -**fasciame** *m.* (naut.) furring wood-sheathing; blisters. -**fase** *f.* counter-phase; (radio) collegamento -fase, push-pull connexion. -**ffensiva** *f.* counter-offensive. -**figura** *f.* (cinem.) stand-in, double. -**finestra** *f.* double-window, storm-window. -**fiocco** *m.* (*pl.* -**fiocchi**) (naut.) flying jib. -**firma** *f.* counter-signature. -**fo·dera** *f.* padding, material placed between the main cloth and the lining, inner lining. -**fondo** *m.* double bottom, false bottom. -**forti** *m.pl.* (naut.) risings. -**forza** *f.* opposing force. -**fosso** *m.* see **contraffosso**. -**fuga** *f.* (mus.) fugue by contrary motion. -**gab·bie** *f.pl.* (naut.) upper topsails. -**girello** *m.* (butcher.) round, topside. -**governo** *m.* (pol.) opposition (government). -**guar·dia** *f.* see **contragguardia**. -**indicare** *tr.* [A 2 s] to indicate differently from before; (med.) to contra-indicate. -**indicato** *part. adj.* (med.) contra-indicated; questo rimedio contiene dello zucchero ed è perciò -indicato per diabetici, this medicine contains sugar and so is not suitable for diabetics. -**indicazione** *f.* contra-indication; (on the label of a medicine bottle) non esiste nessuna -indicazione, suitable in all cases and for all ages. -**landa** *f.* (naut.) preventer chain-plate. -**lettera** *f.* further letter, letter modifying a former one. -**leva** *f.* (mech.) counter-lever. -**lizza** *f.* low barrier placed within the lists at a tournament. -**luce** *f.* wrong light (as when a picture is hung between two windows); *m.* (neol. photog.) picture taken against the light; *adv.* in the wrong light; against the light; with back to the light. -**lume** *m.* bad light, wrong light; light in one's eyes (referring to artificial light). -**mandare** [A 1] *tr.* to countermand. -**mano** *adv.* (motor.) on the wrong side of the road; io tenevo la destra, invece lui m'è venuto -mano e così ci siamo scontrati, I was keeping to the right, but he came towards me on the wrong side of the road and so we collided. -**mantelletto** *m.* (mining) double shelter for the protection of miners. -**man·tice** *m.* hood for covering the front part of a carriage. -**mantigli** *m.pl.* (naut.) preventer-lifts. -**marca** *f.* countermark, mark, sign; pass-out ticket. -**mar·cia** *f.* (mil.) about turn; (naut.) veer or tack in succession; per -marcia, alter course in succession; (cinem.) flashback; (eng.; motor.) reverse gear. †-**mastro** *m.* (naut.) mate. -**mezzana** *f.* (naut.) mizzen topsail. -**mina** *f.* (mil.) countermine. -**minare** [A 1] *tr.* (mil.) to countermine. (-**atore** *m.*) -**molla** *f.* extra spring. -**muro** *m.* supporting wall; double wall, extra wall to prevent loss of heat from a furnace. -**naca** *f.* (aeron.) shoulder cowl. -**naturale** *adj.* contrary to nature. -**nestà** *f.* dishonesty, dishonest action. -**nota** *f.* note in reply to, or explanatory of, another note. -**notare** [A 1] *tr.* to annotate, to write marginal notes to. -**palo** *m.* strut. -**pappafico** *m.* (naut.) royal (sail or yard) -**parte** *f.* (leg.) opponent; (theatr.) supporting part, foil; background group of characters; (mus.) counterpart, one part of a duet with respect to the other. -**partita** *f.* (comm.) counter-item. -**pat·tino** *m.* (eng.) counter-pad. -**pendenza** *f.* opposite slope. -**pensare** [A 1] *intr.* (*aux.* avere) to think over. -**perare** [A 1 s] *intr.* (*aux.* avere) to work against; to counteract. -**perazione** *f.* counter-acting. -**peri·zia** *f.* cross-check, counter-examination. -**perno** *m.*

contro-alette (*cont.*)

(watchm.) end-piece; -perno sotto, lower end-piece; (watchm.) placca di -perno, end-piece. **-pezza** *f.* (eng.) edge-strip; lap for laying on the seam between two adjoining plates; -pezza alle testate, butt-strap. **-piede** *m.* (soccer) gioco in -piede, technique whereby defensive action is quickly transformed into attack, thus catching opponents off-balance; (tennis) technique whereby opponent is led to expect the ball to be returned on wrong side; cogliere in -piede, to catch off-balance. **-piega** *f.* opposite fold. **-porta** *f.* double door; outer door, second door, screen-door. **-portello** *m.* (naut.) dead-light. **-presella** *f.* (metall.) bottom fuller. **-pressione** *f.* counter-pressure. **-prestazione** *f.* (leg.) valuable consideration. **-producente** *adj.* having reverse (and harmful) effect from the one expected. **-progetto** *m.* counter-plan; alternative scheme. **-proposta**, (Rom.) **-proposta** *f.* counter-proposal. **-protesta** *f.* counter-protest. **-prova** *f.* repetition of a test, retest; recount of a vote; (leg.) counter-proof (confirmatory evidence); counter-evidence (new evidence on a fact already proved by the other side). **-punta** *f.* (eng.) tailstock (of lathe); -punta fissa, dead centre. **-querela** *f.* (leg.) counter-charge; counter-plea; counter-claim; cross-complaint; cross-action. **-randa** *f.* (naut.) gaffsail. **-reazione** *f.* (radio) negative feedback. **-recchione** *m.* (artill.) plate covering the trunnion plates of a gun. **-relazione** *f.* minority report. **-replica** *f.* counter-reply, back-answer. **-replicare** [A 2 s] *tr., intr.* (aux. avere) to answer back. **-ricevuta** *f.* (comm.; leg.) counter-receipt. **-ricorso** *m.* (leg.) answer (pleading put in by respondent) to an appeal. **-riforma** *f.* (hist.) Counter-Reformation. **-rispondere** [C 11] *tr., intr.* (aux. avere) to counter-reply, to answer back. **-risposta**, (Rom.) **-risposta** *f.* counter-reply, back-answer. **-riva** *f.* opposite bank. **-rivoluzione** *f.* counter-revolution. **-ronda** *f.* (mil.) round made by an officer in the opposite order to the usual one. **-rota·ia** *f.* (rlwy.) guide rail, check rail, guard rail. **-ruota** *f.* (naut.) sternpost, stempost. **-scarpa** *f.* overshoe, galosh; (mil.) counterscarp. **-scena** *f.* (theatr.) business; (as reaction to dialogue) by-play; (silent) reaction. **-scotta** *f.* (naut.) see **contrascotta**. **-scritta** *f.* (leg.) counterpart; indenture. **-scrittore** *m.* person who writes in reply. **-scri·vere** [C 12] *tr., intr.* (aux. avere) to write in reply; to write against. **-senso** *m.* misconstruction, misinterpretation; misconception; wrong sense; absurdity, nonsense; action which makes no sense; a -senso, in the wrong way. **-serratura** *f.* double-lock. **-sigillo** *m.* counterseal. **-soffitto** *m.* (bldg.) double ceiling. **-soggetto** *m.* (mus.) counter-subject. **-sostegni** *m.pl.* (naut.) preventer slings of the lower yards. **-spalliera** *f.* row of fruit-trees or flowering shrubs planted as a backing to an espalier. **-spionag·gio** *m.* counter-espionage. **-sprone** *m.* extra spur of a buttress. **-sservazione** *f.* counter-observation. **-stalli·a** *f.* (comm.) demurrage. **-stampa** *f.* (typ.) counter-proof. **-stampare** [A 1] *tr.* (typ.) to counterprove. **-sti·molo** *m.* (pharm.) contrastimulant; action of a sedative. **-stimolante** *adj.* sedative; tranquillizing. **-sto·maco** *n.m.* repugnance, nausea; mi fa venire il -stomaco, it makes me want to vomit; *adv.* with repugnance; (fig.) unwillingly, reluctantly, against the grain. **-stra·glio** *m.* (naut.) preventer stay. †**-suppara** *f.* (naut.) moonsails. **-ta·glio** *m.* (art, etching) intersecting line drawn so as to deepen the shadows; lavorare di -taglio, to draw intersecting lines. **-tempo** *m.* (fencing) 'contre-temps'. **-torello** *m.* (naut.) strake of the skin of a ship next the garboard strakes. **-torpediniera** *f.* (naut.) destroyer. **-va·io** *m.* (herald.) counter-vair. **-vapore** *m.* (eng.) return steam (in a steam-engine). **-veleno** *m.* see **contravveleno**. **-ventamento** *m.* (bldg.) wind-bracing. **-ventare** [A 1] *tr.* (bldg.) to strut, to brace, to shore. **-vento** *adv.* against the wind; *n.m.* (bldg.) wind-brace. **-ver·sia** *f.* controversy; disagreement; debate; mettere in -versia, to dispute; questo non può essere messo in -versia, there can be no dispute about this; (leg.) dispute; controversy. **-versista** *m.* controversialist. **-verso** *adj.* controversial; controverted; disputed, debated. **-vertente** *part. adj.* denying. **-ver·tere** [C def.] *tr.* to controvert; to dispute. **-verti·bile** *adj.* controvertible; open to question, doubtful. **-vertibilità** *f.* capability of being controverted. **-vetrata** *f.* double window, storm window. **-vi·sita** *f.* return visit, second visit. **-voto** *m.* counter-vote.

controll-are [A 1] *tr.* to check; to examine, to inspect, to verify; to monitor; to control; *rfl.* to control oneself. **-ato** *part. adj.* checked; examined; verified; controlled; (leg.) amministrazione -ata, carrying on of business by receiver and manager (C.C.).

controll-o *m.* checking, verification, inspection; giro di —, tour of inspection, round, check-up (e.g. of a night-watchman); control; il — di sè, self-control; (sport) marking. **-ore** *m.* inspector; reviser, reader; (rlwy.) ticket collector; ticket inspector.

controra *f.* afternoon nap, siesta.

contrordin-e *m.* counter-order; countermanding. **-are** [A 1 sc] *tr.* to countermand.

†**controvare** *tr.* to invent; to simulate.

conturt-are [A 1] *tr.* to bump against. **-o** *m.* collision.

contubern-ale *adj.* occupying the same tent, contubernal. **-i·o** *m.* living together, cohabitation.

contumac-e *adj.* (leg.) contumacious; (fig.) obstinate; *n.m.,* *f.* (leg.) contumacious person, defaulter; party who fails to appear in answer to a writ, summons, etc.; †*n.f.* see **contumacia**. **-is·simo** *adj. superl.* very obstinate, persistent (esp. of an illness).

contuma·ci-a *f.* obstinacy, stubbornness; insubordination; (leg.) contumacy; default of appearance; wilful refusal to appear; (med.) quarantine; essere in —, to be in quarantine. **-ale** *adj.* (leg.) by default; giudizio -ale, judgement by default; sentenza -ale, sentence passed on a person tried in his absence; (med.) pertaining to quarantine; ospedale -ale, isolation hospital.

contume·li-a *f.* contumely; insolent reproach; insult; obloquy; disgrace; fare (dire) — a, to insult, to be offensive to. **-oso** *adj.* contumelious, despiteful, insolent. **-osamente** *adv.* insolently.

contun·d-ere [C 11] *tr.* to bruise; to blunt; -ersi la mano, to bruise one's hand. **-ente** *part. adj.* bruising; liable to bruise easily; corpo -ente, blunt instrument; ferita d'arme -ente, contusion, blow from a blunt instrument.

conturb-are [A 1] *tr.* to disturb; to trouble, to upset; to perturb. **-amento** *m.* disturbing, troubling; trouble. **-ativo** *adj.* likely to disturb; perturbing; upsetting. **-ato** *part. adj.* disturbed, put out, upset, troubled; perturbed. **-atamente** *adv.* in perturbation; in a troubled manner. **-atore** *m.* disturber. (**-atrice** *f.*) **-azione** *f.* disturbance; upset; perturbation.

contusione *f.* (med.) bruise, contusion.

contuso *part.* of **contundere**, q.v.; *adj.* contused, bruised; (chem.) pounded, triturated.

contut-ore *m.,* **-rice** *f.* (leg.) joint guardian.

contutto-chè *conj.* although, in spite of the fact that. **-ciò** *adv.* nevertheless; in any case. **-questo** *adv.* in spite of this, nevertheless. †**-siaciochè**, †**-siacosachè** *conj.* for all that, notwithstanding, despite the fact that.

convalesc-ente *adj., n.m., f.* convalescent. **-enza** *f.* convalescence. **-enza·rio** *m.* convalescent home.

conva·lida *f.* (neol.) confirmation, proof.

convalid-are [A 1 s] *tr.* (leg.) to validate; to confirm; to ratify; (fig.) to strengthen, to reinforce; to prove true. (**-amento** *m.*) **-ato** *part. adj.* (leg.) validated; confirmed; ratified; (fig.) strengthened, reinforced; proved. **-azione** *f.* (leg.) confirmation; ratification.

convall-e *f.* long wide valley; dale; meeting-place of two or more valleys; (bot.) giglio delle -i, lily-of-the-valley, *Convallaria majalis.*

convegno *m.* meeting; meeting-place; appointment; conference; (Ital. radio) — dei Cinque, Brains Trust; †agreement, pact.

conven-ente *adj.* suitable, fitting; *n.m.* happening, event, circumstances. **-entemente** *adv.* suitably. †**-enza** *f.* gathering, assembly, coming together, meeting; convenience; suitability. **-evole** *adj.* suitable; fit, fitting; seemly, decorous, decent; proper; apt, opportune; *n.m.* that which is suitable or seemly; *pl.* conventional expressions of good manners; stare sui -evoli, to stand on ceremony; fare i -evoli, to pay one's respects. **-evolmente** *adv.* suitably, fittingly; properly. **-evolezza** *f.* suitability, fittingness; what is fitting; propriety, decorum; aptness, opportuneness.

conveni-ente *adj.* fitting, appropriate; expedient; moderate; cheap; profitable, advantageous; un affare poco —, a not very profitable transaction; prezzi -enti, moderate prices; necessary, requisite. (**-entemente** *adv.*) **-enza** *f.* suitability; aptness; advantage, profit; expediency; non ho la -enza, it doesn't pay me; matrimonio di -enza, mariage de convenance; la -enza di tutte le parti fra loro e col tutto, the harmony of all the parts with each other and with the whole; conformity; la -enza di una lingua con un'altra, the similarity of structure between two languages; propriety, seemliness; mancare di -enza, to behave improperly; *pl.* polite usage, compliments, ceremony, formality; sapere le -enze, to know how to behave; (admin.) richiamare un oratore al rispetto delle -enze, to call a speaker to order.

conven-ire [D 17] *intr.* (*aux.* essere) to come together, to assemble, to meet; to concur; to converge; (*aux.* avere) to agree; ne -go, I agree; -go con lui in questo, I am in agreement with him about this; -nero di dover partire subito, they agreed they ought to leave at once; *recip. rfl.* to agree (together); to suit each other, to be appropriate one to the other; *impers.* to be right; to be suitable; to be proper; to be useful, to be advantageous; to be advisable; to be necessary; *tr.* to agree to grant; (leg.) to summon; to summons; to cite. -imento *m.* meeting, gathering, assembly.

†**conventare** *intr.* to assemble, to meet; *tr.* to grant a doctorate to, to admit to a learned body.

conventi·c-ola *f.* secret meeting; little gathering of people conspiring together. †-olo *m.* see **conventicola**.

convent-o¹ *m.* religious house; (Dominican or Franciscan) priory; convent (of friars or nuns); mettere una ragazza in —, to send a girl to a convent-school, to make a nun of a girl; stare a quel che dà il —, to take pot-luck, to accept what is offered; non si sta mica in —!, this isn't a nunnery!; †assembly, gathering, †admission to a learned body, granting of a doctor's degree; †(hist.) administrative and judicial centre of a territory.

convento² *m.* agreement; convention.

†**convento³** *m.* gap, join, chink.

†**convento⁴** *part.* of **convenire**, q.v.

conventual-e *adj.* (eccl.) conventual; minore —, Conventual (Franciscan); *n.m.* Conventual (Franciscan). -ista *m.* (eccl.) Conventual (Franciscan).

convenuto *part.* of **convenire**, q.v.; *adj.* come together, met; settled, agreed, fixed; segnale —, agreed signal; *n.m.* what has been agreed; accord, pact; (leg.) defendant.

convenzion-e *f.* convention; custom; agreement; covenant, pact; esser di —, to be in league; convention, congress; (hist.) constituent assembly (of France, 1792–5). -ale *adj.* conventional; pertaining to a convention; *n.m.pl.* (hist.) members of the constituent assembly (see **convenzione**). -alismo *m.* conventionalism, acceptance of conventional usage. -alista *m.* conventionalist. -alità *f.* conventionality. †-are *intr.* to come to an agreement.

conver·g-ere [C4] *intr.* (*aux.* essere) to converge; to tend towards a single point. -ente *adj.* converging; lente -ente, convex lens, burning glass. -enza *f.* convergence; (motor.) toe-in.

conversa¹ *f.* valley-tile for receiving the water where two slopes of a roof meet.

conversa² *f.* lay sister in a convent.

convers-are [A1] *intr.* (*aux.* avere) to converse, to talk, to hold conversation; †to dwell; †to associate; †tr. to frequent; *n.m.* conversing; conversation. †-ativo *adj.* sociable, companionable, talkative. -azione *f.* conversation; talk; -azione alla radio, talk on the wireless; custom, way of life; (paint.) conversation piece; sacra -azione, representation of the Holy Family; †evening party, 'conversazione'; †(rel.) monastic life; †friendly terms, intimacy. -evole *adj.* sociable, friendly, easy to talk to.

conversione *f.* conversion, converting, changing; turning; rotation; (rel.) conversion; (comm.; finan.) conversion; (mil.; naut.) wheeling; (astron.) circling; (liter.) dénouement, catastrophe (of tragedy).

converso¹ *part.* of **convergere**, q.v.

convers-o² *altern. part.* of **convertire**, q.v. (also **convertito**); *adj.* converted, transformed; *n.m.* converse; opposite, contrary; per —, on the other hand, on the contrary; conversely; (eccl.) lay brother. -amente *adv.* conversely. -e *adv.* the other way round. †-ivo *adj.* convertible; reversible.

†**conver·tere** *tr.* to turn; cf. **convertire**.

convert-ire [D1] *tr.* to convert; to change, to turn, to transmute; *rfl.* to be converted, to alter, to change; to become converted, to undergo conversion; to be convinced. -i·bile *adj.* convertible; exchangeable. -ibilità *f.* convertibility. -imento *m.* conversion; transformation; change. -ita *f.* (rel.) woman penitent, 'Magdalen'. -ito *part. adj.* converted; changed, transmuted; -ito ad altro uso, put to another use; †turned; *n.m.* penitent, converted person, convert. -itore *m.* (eng.; electr.) convertor; -itore di fase, phase convertor. -itrice *f.* (electr.) convertor.

convessione *f.* See **convezione**.

convess-o *adj.* convex; curva -a, convex curve; lente -a, convex lens; *n.m.* convexity. -ità *f.* convexity.

con-vettore *m.* (phys.) convector. -vezione *f.* (phys.) convection.

†**conviare** *tr.* to accompany, to escort.

†**convicin-o** *adj.* near, neighbouring; contiguous; *n.m.* neighbour. †-ità *f.* vicinity.

convin·c-ere [C5] *tr.* to convince; lo -erò del suo torto, I will convince him of his error; bisogna -erlo sulla necessità, we must convince him of the need; to persuade; to convict; to be convincing; *rfl.* to be convinced, to be won over in argument; mi convinsi della verità, I became convinced of the truth. -ente *part. adj.* convincing; forceful, telling; conclusive. -entemente *adv.* convincingly. -i·bile *adj.* convincible. -imento *m.* convincing; conviction; belief, opinion; essere di ben difficile -imento, to be very difficult to convince. -itivo *adj.* convincing.

convinto *part.* of **convincere**, q.v.; *adj.* convinced; won over, persuaded; convicted; (leg.) reo —, adjudged guilty.

convinzione *f.* conviction, persuasion, belief; convinzioni religiose, religious convictions; ho la ferma — che, I am firmly persuaded that; action of convincing, persuading.

convisitatore *m.* fellow-visitor.

convissuto *part.* of **convivere**, q.v.

convit-are¹ [A1] *tr.* to invite to dinner; to entertain; to call, to convoke; *intr.* (*aux.* avere) to give banquets. -ato *part. adj.* invited; *n.m.* guest. (-atore *m.* -atrice *f.*)

†**convit-are²** *tr.* to desire, to lust after. †-i·gia *f.* cupidity, desire, greed; lust; avarice.

convito *m.* dinner-party, banquet; †guests at a banquet or party; †invitation.

convitt-o *m.* boarding school; †cohabitation, living together. -ore *m.*, -rice *f.* pupil at a boarding school; inmate.

conviv-a *m.* table-companion. -ale *adj.* see **conviviale**, under **convivio**. †-are *intr.* (*aux.* avere) to dine together. -ante *part. adj.* banqueting.

conviv-ere [C16] *intr.* (*aux.* essere) to live together, to cohabit. -ente *part. adj.* living together, cohabiting. -enza *f.* living together, cohabitation; people living together; l'umana -enza, human society.

convi·vi-o *m.* banquet; *pr.n.m.* title of a work by Dante, consisting of four prose dissertations and three philosophical and allegorical odes. -ale *adj.* suitable for or relating to a banquet; convivial. †-are *vb.* see **convivare**.

†**convi·zi-o** *m.* insult, slander; dishonourable and malicious talk. †-are *tr.* to insult, to slander; to blacken the reputation of.

†**convizioso** *adj.* lustful, greedy, desirous.

convoc-are [A2 sc] *tr.* to convoke, to convene, to summon; to invite; — d'urgenza, to call an emergency meeting. -amento *m.* convoking, convening. -ato *part. adj.* convoked; convened; *n.m.* person summoned; guest; i -ati, those summoned to the meeting. (-atore *m.* -atrice *f.*) -azione *f.* convocation; summoning (of a committee, etc.), convening; indirizzare una -azione, to send out a letter of convocation; (football) selection of team.

convogli-are [A4] *tr.* to convoy; to escort; to sweep away, to carry away; (eng.) to convey, to transport; — a mezzo di tubazioni, to pipe. -ato *part. adj.* convoyed, escorted; swept away; (phys.; opt.) luce -ata, parallel light. -atore *m.* (techn.) conveyor; -atore a nastro, belt conveyor; -atore a coclea, worm conveyor.

convo·glio *m.* convoy, escort; (rlwy.) train; — funebre, funeral cortège.

convolare [A1] *intr.* (*aux.* essere) to fly together; to hasten together; — a giuste nozze, to marry, (joc.) to elope.

†**convol·gere** *tr.* to roll over and over; *intr.* to roll, to wallow.

con-volutivo, -voluto *adj.* (bot.) convolute.

convol·volo *m.* (bot.) bindweed, *Convolvulus*.

†**convotisa** *f.* cupidity.

convulsamente *adv.* See under **convulso**.

convuls-ione *f.* (med.) convulsion; essere preso dalle -ioni, to be seized with convulsions; *pl.* (pop.) fits; soffre di -ioni, he has fits. -ivamente *adv.* convulsively. -ivo *adj.* convulsive.

convuls-o *adj.* convulsed; in the throes of a convulsion; convulsive; shaken; (fig.) violent, jerky; *n.m.* convulsion; nervous trembling; twitch. -amente *adv.* convulsively.

conzo *m.* liquid measure, equivalent at Udine to 79·3 litres and at Treviso to 77·9 litres.

coob-are [A1] *tr.* (chem.) to cohobate. -azione *f.* (chem. hist.) cohobation.

coonest-are [A1] *tr.* to find an excuse for; to gloss over; to give a veneer of respectability to; to justify. (-amento *m.*) -ato *part. adj.* glossed over; palliated.

cooper·are [A I S] *intr.* (*aux.* avere) to co-operate; to collaborate; to work together; — a, to work towards. **-amento** *m.* co-operating; working together. **-ante** *part. adj.* co-operating; co-operative; *n.m., f.* co-operator. **-ativa** *f.* (comm.) co-operative society; co-operative stores. **-ativista** *m.* member of the Co-operative movement. **-ativo** *adj.* co-operative; (comm.) società -ativa, co-operative society. (**-atore** *m.* **-atrice** *f.*) **-azione** *f.* co-operation; co-operating.

coordin·are [A I SC] *tr.* to co-ordinate; to correlate; to set in order, to arrange. **-amento** *m.* co-ordinating; correlating. **-ate** *f.pl.* (math.) co-ordinates; -ate geografiche, latitude and longitude; -ate equatoriali, right ascension and declination. **-ato** *part. adj.* co-ordinated; (gramm.) co-ordinate. **-atore** *m.* co-ordinator. (**-atrice** *f.*) **-azione** *f.* co-ordination; co-ordinating.

†**coortare** *tr.* to exhort, to encourage.

coor·te, (Rom.) **coorte** *f.* cohort; band, troop; (Ital. hist.) a third part of a legion of the Fascist militia.

copa·ibe, copa·ive *f.* See **coppaibe**.

copale *m.* See **coppale**.

copeco *m.* (numism.) copeck.

Copena·ghen *pr.n.f.* (geog.) Copenhagen.

cope·podo *m.pl.* (zool.) copepod.

coper·chi·o *m.* lid, cover, hood; covering; (provb.) il diavolo insegna a far la pentola ma non il —, the devil shows us how to sin but not how to hide it; upper millstone; (mus.) belly (of violin). **-are** [A4] *tr.* to put the lid on, †**-ella** *f.* cover; (fig.) deception.

Coper·ni·co *pr.n.m.* Copernicus. **-cano** *adj.* Copernican, relating to Copernicus. **-chista** *m.* Copernican, follower of Copernicus.

copert·a *f.* blanket; rug; coverlet; — da viaggio, travelling rug; covering (outer cover); (naut.) upper deck; tutti in —!, all hands on deck!; — inferiore, — libera, orlop deck; — di manovra, awning deck; ponte di —, upper deck; — rasa, flush deck; sopra —, on deck; sotto —, below deck; ufficiali di —, deck officers, executive branch officers; envelope; book-cover, jacket; pretext, excuse; loin steak. **-ella** *f. dim.* coverlet; †pot-lid. **-ina** *f. dim.* small bedspread; paper-cover, jacket, wrapper; (butcher.) chuck; (bldg.) coping; (paperm.) -ine monolucide, pressings. **-ino** *m. dim.* bed coverlet. **-one** *m. augm.* tarpaulin; outer cover of a tyre; thick rug.

†**copertare** *vb.* See **coprire**.

copert·o *part.* of **coprire**, q.v.; *adj.* covered; wearing a hat; closed in; sheltered; — di, covered in, thick with; cielo —, overcast sky; il cielo è — di aeroplani, the sky is filled with aeroplanes; (naut.) decked; (of a sail) taking the wind of another; (mil.) masked (of a battery); *n.m.* cover; covered place, roof; shelter; al —, under cover, in shelter; place laid at table; una colazione di venti -i, lunch for twenty people; (in a restaurant) cover-charge. **-o·ia** *f.* (Tusc.) earthenware lid. **-o·io** *m.* lid of a large vessel; large rug; (mil. hist.) shelter for besieging operations; rough bed-cover. **-ola·io** *m.* cover-maker. **-one** *m. augm.* see under **coperta**. **-ume** *m.* roofing. **-ura** *f.* covering, cover; tyre; -ura protettiva, book-jacket; (comm.) lettera di -ura, covering letter; (finan.) cover, security; coating; lining; wrapping; (opt.) coverage; (mil., naut.) forze di -ura, covering forces; -ura aerea, air cover; (archit.) roof, roofing, covering; wall-covering (e.g. plaster); (agric.) concimazione in -ura, top dressing; †appearance, semblance.

copese *m.* (ichth.) Adriatic sturgeon, *Acipenser nacarii*.

co·pia[1] *f.* plenty, abundance; in gran —, in plenty; — di dire, fluency, eloquence; dare — di, to give forth an abundance of; fare — di, to prostitute; †crowd; †contact, proximity; †opportunity, readiness; *pl.* †troops.

co·pia[2] *f.* copy; transcription; buona —, bella —, (Tusc.) — al pulito, fair copy; ricopiare in bella —, to make a fair copy of; brutta —, rough copy, draft; — di un giornale, copy of a newspaper; — di una rivista, number of a journal; — per conoscenza a, copy for information to; (photog.) print; (leg.) per — conforme, certified true copy.

copia-fatture *f. pl.* (comm.) bill-book; invoice-book. **-let·tere** *f. indecl.* letter-book; copying press; (paperm.) carta per -lettere, copying paper, press copy.

copi·are [A4] *tr.* to copy; to imitate, to transcribe, to copy out; (photog.) to print. **-ativo** *adj.* copying; lapis -ativo, copying ink pencil; carta -ativa, copying paper; inchiostro -ativo, copying ink. **-ato** *part. adj.* copied; imitated; copied out. **-atore** *m.* copyist. (**-atrice** *f.*) **-atura** *f.* copying; transcribing.

copicco *m.* See **copeco**.

copi·gli·a *f.* cotter-pin, split-pin; (watchm.) pin; — di pila, pillar-pin; — di limitazione, banking pin; — della racchetta, curb pin. **-are** [A4] *tr.* (eng.) to fix with a split-pin.

†**copi·glio** *m.* hive.

copilota *m.* (aeron.) co-pilot, second pilot.

copione *m. augm.* of **copia**[2], q.v.; (theatr.; cinem.; radio) actor's copy, script; prompt copy.

copi·oso *adj.* copious, abundant. **-osamente** *adv.* copiously; in abundance. **-osità** *f.* copiousness, abundance, plenty.

copist·a *m., f.* copyist; copy-typist. **-eri·a** *f.* copying office; typing office, typing agency.

co·pola *f.* See **copula**.

copolimero *m.* (chem.) copolymer.

coppa *f.* goblet; (liturg.) cup, inner side of chalice; (sport) cup, trophy; la — delle Alpi (motor-racing event); pan of a pair of scales; back part of the head, cranium; (cul.) neck of pork; cooked meat containing neck of pork; beef ham; — di testa, brawn; ice-cream in a tub; (eng.) oil-bottle; (motor.) sump; †(fig.) — d'oro, person of shining probity; *pl.* the name of one of the suits in an Italian pack of cards (see note under **carta**); accennare in coppe e dare in danari, to indicate one's intention of doing one thing and then do another; (ceram.) Venetian roof tiles.

coppa·ia *f.* oil-cellar; (eng.) mandrel of a lathe.

coppa·ibe *f.* (pharm.) copaiba.

coppale *m.* copal, copal-gum.

copparosa *f.* (chem.) copperas; — verde, ferrous sulphate, green vitriol.

coppa·u *m.* (pharm.). See **coppaibe**.

coppell·a *f. dim.* of **coppa**, q.v.; cupel, crucible for refining or assaying precious metals; argento di —, oro di —, purest silver, finest gold, (fig.) person of unimpeachable character; reggere a —, to stand the test; (bot.) flower-tube, calyx-tube. **-are** [A I] *tr.* (metall.) to assay; to refine; † to test. (**-ato** *part. adj.*) **-azione** *f.* assay; assaying; cupellation.

coppett·a *f. dim.* of **coppa**, q.v.; (med.) cupping-glass. **-e** *f.pl.* (zool.) *Triops* (*Apus*) *cancriformis*.

cop·pi·a *f.* couple, married couple; pair; a —, two by two; a -e, in pairs; double roll of bread; aver tre pani per —, to be very lucky, to get an extra quantity; (joc.) una — e un paio, a fine pair (of rogues); (cards) pair (at poker); doppia —, two pairs; (naut.) voga di —, double banked boat; (eng.; mech.) torque; variatore di —, torque converter; -e di cavallo, see **coppiette**. **-etta** *f. dim.* courting couple; *pl.* pieces of dried ass or horse flesh, chewed and retained in the mouth for their piquancy.

coppi·ere, -ero *m.* cup-bearer; wine-waiter.

coppi·gli·a *f.*, **-are** [A4]. See **copigli·a, -are**.

coppino *m. dim.* of **coppo**, q.v.; back of the head; (dial. Tusc.) warming-pan; brazier; †far —, to peep.

coppiola *f.* double shot from right and left barrels, 'a right and left'; two consecutive numbers in the game of 'lotto'; (text.) accidental union of two threads in the wool making a flaw in the cloth; *pl.* the two nets of the **paretaio**, q.v.

copp·o, (Rom.) **coppo** *m.* earthenware jar; oil-jar; tile gutter; measure of approx. 3 litres; skull; socket of the eye; small fishing net fixed on a pole; (butcher.) front part of the chuck; (bot.) cupule (of acorn, etc.). **-olone** *m.* (Neap. theatr.) felt hat of Pulcinella, usu. sugar-loaf in shape. **-oluto** *adj.* rounded, domed.

copra *f.* copra, dried kernel of the coconut.

copri-bocchino *m.* (mus.) mouthpiece-cover (of clarinet). **-busto** *m.* bodice; camisole; undervest. **-capo** *m.* headgear, hat. **-catene** *m. indecl.* (eng.) chain guard. **-cricco** *m. indecl.* (watchm.) click lid. **-fuoco** *m.* curfew; lights-out. **-giunto** *m.* (eng.) butt-strap; fish-plate; cover-plate. **-mise·rie** *m. indecl.* overall, article of clothing to hide poor or dirty clothes; (fig.) person who covers up another's misdeeds. **-martello** *m. indecl.* (watchm.) hammer lid. **-morsetto** *m.* (electr.) terminal cover. **-oggetti, -oggetto** *m. indecl.* (techn.) cover-glass; slide (of a microscope). **-piatti** *m. indecl.* dish-cover; meat-cover. **-piedi** *m. indecl.* coverlet for the feet. **-pis·side** *m.* (liturg.) ciborium veil. **-posta** *f.* (paperm.) pilcher. **-rocchetto** *m.* (watchm.) ratchet-wheel cover; -rocchetto a corona, crown-wheel cover. **-ruota** *m. indecl.* wheel cover. **-ruotismo** *m. indecl.* (watchm.) gear-train lid. **-sella** *m. indecl.* saddle cover. **-targhetta** *m. indecl.* (watchm.) cover for hand-setting bolt. **-tetto** *m.* tiler; salter. **-vivande** *m. indecl.* dish cover; meat cover.

co·pridi *m.pl.* (ent.) dung-beetles.

†coprime *m.* baked tiles.

copr-ire [D I] *tr.* to cover; to obscure, to hide; (of sound) to drown, to muffle; to shield, to shelter; to occupy, to fill; — un incarico, to hold an office; — una vacanza, to fill a vacancy; — le spese, to cover expenses; — uno di benefizi, to shower benefits upon someone; (naut.) — una vela, to take the wind out of a sail; †— il corbame, to cover the frames of a ship's hull; — le artiglierie, to cover guns; *rfl.* to cover oneself; to wrap oneself up; to shield oneself; to cover one's head, to put one's hat on; non ha di che -irsi, he hasn't a stitch to put on; -irsi di gloria, to cover oneself with glory; si -ì di rossore, he blushed all over his face; (of weather) to become overcast. **-ente** *part. adj.* covering; (paint industr.) potere -ente, covering power. **-imento** *m.* coverage; cover. **-itore** *m.* coverer. **-itrice** *f.* coverer; *pl.* (orn.) wing coverts. **-itura** *f.* covering; cover; pretext; (of animals) copulation; †roof.

copro-duttori *m.pl.* (cinem.) bi- *or* multi-national film producers. **-duzione** *f.* bi- *or* multi-national film production.

copr-ofagi·a *f.* dung-eating, coprophagous habits. **-olali·a** *f.* pathological condition causing obscene talk. **-o·liti** *m.pl.* coproliths. **-osclerosi** *f.* hardness of the motions. **-ostasi** *f.*, **-ostasi·a** *f.* coprostasis, constipation.

copto *m.* See **cofto**, under **coftico**.

co·pul-a *f.* connexion; copulation; coition; (gramm.) copula. **-are** [A I S] *tr.* to join together, to couple; *intr.* (aux. avere) to copulate. **-ativo** *adj.* copulative; connective; (gramm.) congiunzione -ativa, copulative conjunction. **-ativamente** *adv.* copulatively. **-azione** *f.* copulation; union, connexion; coupling.

corac·cio *m. pejor.* of **cuore**, q.v.

cora·c-ia *f.* (orn.) chough. **-ina** *f.* (ichth.) *Sciaena cirrhosa*.

corag·gi-o *m.* courage; boldness; fearlessness, pluck; far — a, to encourage, to urge, to comfort; effrontery, impertinence, impudence, 'cheek'; ha un bel —!, he's got a nerve!; perdersi di —, to lose heart, to become discouraged; mi mancò il —, my courage failed me; — civile, public-spiritedness; *exclam.* —!, cheer up!, courage! **-oso** *adj.* courageous, brave; fearless, plucky; *n.m.* courageous man. **-osamente** *adv.* bravely, courageously, fearlessly, pluckily.

corago *m.* (Gk. antiq.) choragus.

corale¹ *adj.* (mus.) choral; libro —, choir-book (volume of plainchant large enough to be read by a group of singers); *n.m.* chorale; church-music; plain-chant, choirbook.

†corale² *adj.* cordial; affectionate.

Corallina¹ *pr.n.f.* (theatr.) a soubrette in the Commedia dell'Arte, similar to Columbine.

corallina² *f.* (bot.) *Corallina*, calcareous red alga, pink lime-encrusted seaweed; (orn.) gull with red beak, esp. — cenerina spruzzata, black-headed gull; (naut.) boat used for coral-fishing; (miner.) Sicilian jasper.

corall-o *m.* coral; (bot.) *Rochea coccinea*; rosary-pea, *Abrus precatorius*. **-a·io**, **-aro** *m.* worker in coral. **-eggiare** [A 3 C] *intr.* (aux. avere) to take on a coralline appearance. **-essa** *f.* an inferior kind of coral. **-i·fero** *adj.* coral-bearing; atollo -ifero, coral reef. **-ino** *adj.* coralline; red. **-izzazione** *f.* coral-like ramification. **-ume** *m.* quantity of coral.

coram-e *m.* hides and skins; stamped leather. **-ella** *f.* razor-strop.

corampo·p-ulo, **-olo** *adv.* in front of everybody, in public, openly.

†coramvobis *m.* dandy, fop; stare sul —, to be ostentatious; to put on airs.

Cor-ano *pr.n.m.* Koran, Quran. (**-a·nico** *adj.*)

†cor-anza *f.* care, worry; mettere — a, to worry about; to have a care for.

corat-a *f.* (anat.) pericardium; (cul.) lights; giblets; offal; (dial.) heart; †disappointment, displeasure; †stab of pain; †sorrow; †intention, secret intent. **-ella** *f. dim.* (cul.) liver and lights; giblets, offal; pluck.

corazz-a *f.* cuirass, breast-plate and back-plate; breast-plate; (hist.) cuirassier; (fencing) protective vest; (zool.) shell (of a mollusc, or scale insect); carapace; (naut.) armour-plate of a ship, armoured belt. **-a·io** *m.* cuirass maker. **-are** [A I] *tr.* to arm, to armour-plate. **-ata** *f.* ironclad warship; battleship; dreadnought. **-ato** *part. adj.* armour-plated; (electr.) cavo -ato, armoured cable. **-atura** *f.* armouring. **-iere** *m.* (mil.) cuirassier, lifeguard.

corb-a *f.* (Tusc.) large oval-shaped wicker basket; (naut.) rib of a ship's hull, frame; old Bolognese measure of approx. 79 litres; (vet.) see **curba**. **-ame** *m.* (naut.) frame.

corbacchione *m.* See under **corbo**.

†corbac·cio *m. pejor.* large ugly crow or raven; lumbering, coarse individual.

corbella·io *m.* See under **corbello**.

corbell-are [A I] *tr.* (pop.) to make fun of, to ridicule; to make a fool of; to humbug; — la fiera, to take no notice. **-ato** *part. adj.* made fun of. (**-atore** *m.* **-atrice** *f.*) **-atorio** *adj.* derisive, mocking. **-atura** *f.* derision, mockery; hoax. **-eri·a** *f.* nonsense, foolishness, rubbish.

corbell-o¹ *m.* blockhead, dolt; (colloq.) testicle; *excl.* **-i!** (expressive of surprise or contempt). **-ag·gine** *f.* stupid action. **-one** *m. augm.* great fool. **-onag·gine** *f.* folly, extreme stupidity.

corbell-o² *m.* skep, a large, round, flat-bottomed basket for vegetables or fruit; hamper; — di mele, a basketful of apples; a -i, in great quantity. **-a·io** *m.* basket-maker; basket-vendor.

corbello³ *m.* (bot.). See **corbezzolo**, under **corbezzola**.

corbezzol-a *f.* (bot.) fruit of **corbezzolo**, q.v. **-o** *m.* (bot.) strawberry tree, *Arbutus unedo*; *excl.* **-i!** (expressive of irony and of surprise).

corbina *f.* (bot.) a variety of grape, so called from its black colour, noted for its keeping quality.

corbita *f.* (naut.) old cargo vessel; corvette.

corb-o *m.* (orn.) see **corvo**; (fig.) aspettare il —, to wait in vain (as Noah for the raven). **-acchione** *m.* large raven; -acchione di campanile, one who is firm of purpose; astute individual. **-olino** *m.* (bot.) variety of black fig; variety of black cherry.

†corcare *vb.* and derivs. See **coricare**.

corcontento *m.* See 'cuor contento', under **contento¹**.

cor·coro *m.* (bot.) jute-plant, *Corchorus*.

cor·culo *m.* (bot.) embryo.

cord-a *f.*:
1. CORD, rope; hawser; rope girdle; scala di —, rope-ladder; tight-rope; danzatore di —, tight-rope walker; ballare in (sulla) —, to perform on a tight-rope; la — per impiccare, hangman's rope; parlare di — in casa dell'impiccato, to speak of rope in the house of the hanged; — da montagna, mountaineering rope; (hist.) cord, torture; tratto di —, tug, twist of the cord; (fig.) lasciare uno sulla —, to leave a person on tenterhooks; dare la — a, to extort a secret from, to wind up (a clockwork toy); mettere la — al collo a, to impose harsh conditions on; dare — a, to give some rope to, to allow some measure of freedom. **2.** STRING, wire; -e della borsa, purse-strings; — d'arco, bow-string; — di pianoforte, piano wire; — di oriuolo, wire supporting a weight in a clock; (mil.) — cotta, fuse; (bldg.) — dei muratori, string for measuring a wall; — di casa, latch-cord; (equit.) breaking rein; *adv. phr.* a —, taut, perpendicular. **3.** (GEOM.) chord; — d'una superficie, straight line which joins the extremities of an area without touching the surface; — d'un arco di curva, straight line which joins the two extremities of a curve. **4.** (GAMES) form of billiards resembling pool; stare in —, to prevent the ball from going beyond the baulk line, (fig.) to keep one's place, to toe the line, to keep to the point; palla a —, cloth-covered ball, soft ball, (hist.) *jeu de paume*, tennis, tennis court. **5.** (ZOOL.) chorda, notochord. **6.** (MUS.) (i) chord; — maggiore, major chord; — minore, minor chord; -e armoniche, harmonics; -e rotte, broken chords. (ii) note; -e di petto, chest-notes; -e di testa, head-notes; — sonora, vibrating column of air. (iii) string; strumenti a (da) —, stringed instruments; mettere in —, to string; — aperta, — vuota, open string; — di budello, — di minugio, gut string; — d'acciaio, steel string; — di metallo, metal string; — fasciata, covered string; — viva, vibrating string; una —, damping pedal; tre -e, release damping pedal; doppia —, double-stop; alla —, detached bowing; sulla quarta — (sulla IVa), on the G-string; (fig.) toccare una —, to touch upon a sensitive point. **7.** (ANAT.) any cord-like or tendon-like part of the body; sinew; -e vocali, vocal cords; le -e del collo, the two prominent muscles of the neck, the sterno-mastoids; — magna, Achilles tendon; physical tone, fitness; un po' giù di —, a bit below par, rather run down; (fig.) toccare le -e del cuore a, to touch the heartstrings of. **8.** THREAD, cloth; mostrare la —, (le -e), to be threadbare, to show signs of wear; coarse thread; †(naut.) — di bassi, reef. **9.** CORD, measure of cut wood (c. 128 cubic feet);

cord-a (*cont.*)
pile of wood. **-ag·gio** *m.* rope; cordage; -aggio nero, tarred rope. **-a·io, -ai(u)olo** *m.* rope-maker. **-ame** *m.* rope in general; cordage. **-aro** *m.* see **cordaio**. **-ata** *f.* length of rope; two or more mountaineers roped together; capo -ata, leader among two or more climbers. †**-eggiare** *intr.* to be level. **-ella** *f.* (naut.) awning roping. **-elliera** *f.* (herald.) woollen cord figured on a shield, beginning at the crown and following the line of the shield to end in a tassel. **-ellina** *f. dim.* of **corda**; braid on certain uniforms. **-ellone** *m.* ribbed silk or cloth; (naut.) boat's fender fixed to a rubbing strake. **-eri·a** *f.* rope-making; rope-factory; rope-walk. **-ẹtta, -icella** *f. dim.* fine cord; string; pack-thread; (text.) driving band. **-ifi·cio** *m.* ropery, rope works.

cordac-e *f.* (Gk. comedy) cordax, lewd dance; (prosod.) trochee; trochaic metre. **-işmo** *m.* (Gk. antiq.) lewd dancing.

cordata *f.* See under **corda**.

cordato *adj.* (bot.) cordate; †wise, sage, prudent; *n.m.pl.* (zool.) chordates.

cordella *f.* (ichth.) band fish, *Cepola rubescens*.

cordial-e *adj.* cordial; genial; expansive; heart-felt; warm, welcoming; *n.m.* broth with eggs beaten up in it and a little lemon juice; cordial; a comforting drink. **-mẹnte** *adv.* cordially; -mente antipatico, heartily disliked; (at the end of a letter) yours sincerely. **-ità** *f.* cordiality; warmth of manner; (neol.) cordial greeting. **-ọne** *m.* expansive and genial person; warm-hearted man.

cordicella *f. dim.* See under **corda**.

cordiera *f.* (mus.) tail-piece (of violin).

cordifi·cio *m.* See under **corda**.

cordifọrme *adj.* (bot.). See **cordato**.

cordigliera *f.* (geog.) mountain chain, cordillera.

cordi·gli-o *m.* (eccl.) friar's cord; priest's girdle. **-ere, -ero** *m.* (eccl.) Cordelier.

cordin-o *m. dim.* of **corda**, q.v.; (sport) floor-line in the game of 'pallone'; (mount.) small secondary climbing rope. **-iera** *f.* (naut.) brail.

cordite *f.* cordite; (med.) chorditis.

cordo·gli-o *m.* affliction; sorrow, anguish, suffering; lamentation. †**-are** *tr.* to have compassion on; *rfl.* to have regrets; to grieve. †**-enza** *f.* see **cordoglio**. **-ọso** *adj.* sorrowful, anguished; afflicted. **-osamẹnte** *adv.* sorrowfully; in anguish.

cor·dolo *m.* kerbstone; (eng.) seam.

cordon-are [A 1 c] *tr.* to gird, to girdle; to surround; to take in, to deceive. **-ata** *f.* steep paved alley with steps or ramp; palisade to prevent landslide; (archit.) ramp (with ridges of stone instead of steps); (hydraul.) camp-shot. **-ato** *part. adj.* girded, girdled; surrounded; tricked; *n.m.* see **cordonata**. **-atura** *f.* girding, girdling; deceiving, trickery, hoax, jest.

cordon-e *m.* cord, rope; priest's girdle; Franciscan's cord; kerb (of pavement); shallow step in a road; stone ridge in a ramp; row of stones across a steep road to afford foothold for animals; — del campanello, bell-pull; — sanitario, ring round a district marked off during an epidemic; (archit.) string-course, string moulding; string of stones across a ramp (cf. **cordonata**); (electr.) flex, lead; (anat.) — ombilicale, umbilical cord; (eng.) seam; the title and insignia of the head of an Order; Gran Cordone, Grand Master; (mil.) line of forts; (mus.) lowest string; (med.) cord; police-cordon; mettere un — attorno a, to throw a cordon round; edging, braid, border; simpleton. **-cino** *m. dim.* of **cordone**; silk twist; watch-guard; twist carved or moulded as an ornament on a picture frame; (electr.) flex, lead. **-eri·a** *f.* pleasantry, jest. **-iera** *f.* (naut.) boom-lift, peak halyard. **-ite** *f.* cordite.

cordovan-o *m.* morocco leather. **-iere** *m.* cordwainer.

cor(e) *m.* (poet.). See **cuore**.

Core·a[1] *pr.n.f.* (geog.) Korea; (fig.) ramshackle dwellings.

core·a[2] *f.* (med.) chorea, St Vitus's dance.

corẹggia[1] *f.* and derivs. See **correggia**[1].

corẹggia[2] *f.* See **correggia**[2].

corego *m.* See **corago**.

coregọne *m.* (ichth.) whitefish, pollan, *Coregonus* spp., edible fish found in lakes.

core·o *m.* (prosod.) choree, trochee; (ent.) various bugs of the Fam. Coreidae.

cor-eografi·a *f.* choreography. **-eogra·fico** *adj.* choreographical; (fig.) spectacular. **-eo·grafo** *m.* choreographer.

coreo·pside *f.* (bot.) tickseed, *Coreopsis* (garden plant).

corepi·scop-o *m.* (eccl. hist.) chorepiscopus. **-ato** *m.* status of chorepiscopus.

corete *m.* choretes (a mythical bird mentioned by Albertus Magnus and Pulci).

corẹtto[1] *m.* small breast-plate to protect the heart; kind of hairshirt worn near the heart.

corẹtto[2] *m. dim.* of **coro**, q.v.; (eccl. archit.) tribune (opening into church).

core·utica *f.* the art of theatrical dancing.

†**cor·gere** *vb* and derivs. See **accorgere**.

cori *m. indecl.* (bot.) *Hypericum coris*; (zool.) cowrie shell.

cori-a·ceo *adj.* leathery; tough. **-a·gine** *f.* (vet.) hidebound condition in cattle.

cori-ambo *m.* (prosod.) choriamb, choriambus. **-am·bico** *adj.* choriambic.

corian·dol-o *m.* (bot.) coriander, *Coriandrum sativum*; sweet with a coriander seed in the centre; una manciata di coriandoli, a handful of confetti (thrown at a carnival). (**-ẹsco** *adj.*)

coriandro *m.* See **coriandolo**.

Cori-bante *m.* Corybant. **-ban·tico** *adj.* Corybantian.

coric-are [A 25, Rom. A 25 c] *tr.* to lay down; to put to bed; to bed; *rfl.* to lie down; to go to bed, to retire for the night; (of the sun) to set. **-amẹnto** *m.* lying down, retiring. **-ato** *part. adj.* in bed, abed; lying down; (of the sun) set.

coricida *adj.* (joc.) heart-slaying.

coricino *m. dim.* of **cuore**, q.v.; (colloq.) darling, pet.

co·ric-o *adj.* (Gk. lit. and antiq.) choric; *n.m.* (mus.) chorist in ancient Greek drama. (**-amẹnte** *adv.*)

corifena *f.* (ichth.) dolphin fish, *Coryphaena hippurus*.

corife·o *m.* coryphaeus, leading dancer; (fig.) leader of a party; ringleader.

co·ril-o *m.* (bot.) hazel, *Corylus avellana*. **-ẹto** *m.* hazel-thicket, hazel-copse.

corimb-o *m.* (bot.) corymb; cluster. **-i·fero** *adj.* bearing corymbs.

corina *f.* (dial. Romagna) scirocco.

corindọne *m.* (miner.) corundum.

corin·tio *adj.* and derivs. See **corinzio**.

Corinto *pr.n.f.* (geog.) Corinth; uva di —, currants.

corin·z-io *adj.* Corinthian; metallo —, Corinthian brass; (archit.) Corinthian, belonging to the Corinthian order. **-i·aco** *adj.* Corinthian. **-ia·rio** *m.* worker in Corinthian brass.

co·rio *m.* (anat.) chorion; (tanning) corium, hide, hide substance; wineskin.

corista *m.* member of choir; choirboy; priest presiding in choir; *m., f.* (mus.) chorus-singer; chorister; pitch; tuning-fork; pitch-pipe; (theatr.) member of chorus; *f.* chorus-girl.

co·riz(z)a *f.* (med.) coryza, mucus in the nose, catarrh.

cormo *m.* (bot.) corm.

cormorano *m.* (orn.) cormorant.

cornac·chi-a *f.* (orn.) crow; (fig.) bird of ill omen; — bigia, — dal mantello, — palombina, hooded crow, *Corvus cornix*; — nera, carrion crow, *Corvus corone*; — azzurra, — ciarliera, roller; door handle; chatterer; croaker; prophet of evil; loose woman. **-a·ia** *f.* tiresome chatter; (vulg.) wailing for the dead. **-are** [A 4] *intr.* (*aux.* avere) to caw; to chatter. **-o** *m.* stone cannon-ball. **-ọne** *m. augm.* of **cornacchia**; (fig.) chatterbox.

cornag·gine *f.* obstinacy, pig-headedness.

cornalina *f.* (miner.) cornelian.

cornamuṣ-a *f.* (mus.) bagpipe. **-are** [A 1] *intr.* (*aux.* avere) to play on the bagpipe, to pipe, to skirl. **-ẹtto** *m.*, **-ino** *m.* small bagpipe.

corn-are [A 1] *intr.* (*aux.* avere) to sound the horn; (mus.) to play the horn; mi -ano gli orecchi, I have a singing in my ears; *tr.* to butt (with horns). **-ata** *f.* butt or blow with horns; (fig.) opposition. **-ato** *part. adj.* horned; butted; (herald.) horned, armed. †**-atore** *m.* (mus.) horn-player. **-atura** *f.* arrangement of an animal's horns; temperament, disposition; (mus.) sounding of horns.

cor·nea *f.* (anat.) cornea.

corneggi-are [A 3 c] *tr.* to butt; *intr.* (*aux.* avere) to sprout horns; (of a horse) to whistle. **-ato** *part. adj.* horned, curved, crescent-shaped.

cornẹggio *m.* (vet.) roaring, whistling sound sometimes made by horses when galloping.

cor·ne-o *adj.* horn-like; made of horn; (chem. hist.) luna -a, horn-silver, fused silver chloride; (anat.) strato —, horny layer, stratum corneum.

cornętt-a *f.* (mus.) cornet in B flat; cornet (organ stop, usually spelt **cornetto**, q.v.); †small horn; — segnale, bugle; — a chiavi, key bugle; (mil.) small flag used by cavalry; the bearer thereof or the troop under it; (naut.) pennant; powder horn; (teleph.) handset, receiver; (eccl.) cornette, the starched white coif of the Sisters of Charity; (ichth.) *Peristedion cataphractum*, a kind of gurnard; *pl. dim.* of **corna**. **-ino** *m.* (mus.) small cornet in E flat. **-ista** *m., f.* (mus.) cornet-player.

cornętt-o (*pl.m.* **-i**, or *f.* **-a**) horn (of an animal); (cul.) cornet; croissant; long thin loaf of bread; amulet, etc. shaped like a horn; (*pl.m.* **-i**) (mus.) cornett (i.e. *cornet-à-bouquin*, not to be confused with the modern brass cornet); — curvo, — torto, curved cornett; — diritto, straight cornett; — muto, mute cornett; posthorn; cornet (organ stop); — a pistoni, cornet; — acustico, ear trumpet; horn of an anvil; sheet of paper rolled to form a horn-shaped container; (typ.) bag for holding 'sorts', coffin; (agric.) shoot left on a pruned tree; (surg. hist.) cup for blood-letting; (anat.) turbinated bone of the nose; *pl.* (N. Ital.) type of bean. **-ame** *m.* (agric.) branches left on a pruned tree. **-atore** *m.* (mus.) cornett-player. **-ino** *m. dim.* of **cornetto**; (shoem.) polishing stick. **-one** *m. augm.* (mus.) large cornet (organ stop).

cor·nia *f.* agate.

†**corniale** *m.* (bot.). See **corniolo**.

cornic-e *f.* picture-frame; mettere in —, to frame; far — a, to frame; to surround becomingly, to set off; (fig.) framework; structure; setting; literary device to give unity to disparate elements; moulding; (mount.) narrow ledge on a rock, corniche; (archit.) cornice; (paperm.) deckle; (typ.) — laterale, box-rule. **-ia·io** *m.* frame-maker. **-iame** *m.* (archit.) cornicing, series of cornices. **-iare** [A 3] *tr.* to frame; to set in a frame; to build a frame for (e.g. a window). **-iato** *part. adj.* framed, in a frame; corniced; *n.m.* cornicing, cornice with its adjuncts. **-iatura** *f.* framing. **-ione** *m.* (archit.) cornice with architrave and frieze; cornice (at the top of a building); any projecting moulding over doors or windows; entablature; -ione di gronda, eaves.

corni·cine *m.* See under **corno**.

cornic-olare *adj.* (geom.) referring to the angle between a curve and its tangent or secant. **-olato** *adj.* horn-shaped.

corn-i·fero *adj.*, **-i·gero** *adj.* See under **corno**.

corniola[1] *f.* (miner.) cornelian.

corni·ol-a[2] *f.* (bot.) fruit of **corniolo**. **-o** *m.* (bot.) Cornelian cherry, *Cornus mas*; (timber) cornel-wood.

corn-o *m.* (*pl.f.* **-a**):

1. HORN; antler; -a cave, non-deciduous horns (e.g. on cattle, sheep, goats, etc.); -a piene, deciduous horns, antlers (e.g. on stags); -a della lumaca, horns of a snail; corn (on a human foot); (fig.) alzare (rizzare) le -a, to show some spirit, to recover strength; ritirare le -a, to draw in one's horns; abbassare (fiaccare) le -a a, to humiliate, to take down a peg; avere uno sulla -a, to have a grudge against someone; rompere le -a a, to beat, to abate the pride of; rompersi le -a, to be defeated; dire -a di, to speak evil of; ne dice peste e -a, he hasn't a good word to say of him (it); fare le -a, to extend the second and little finger to ward off the evil eye; fare le -a a, to cuckold; to cock a snook at; to get rid of; to leave in the lurch; portare le -a, to be a cuckold. 2. HORN (substance); un oggetto di —, something made of horn; — da calzar le scarpe, — da scarpe, shoehorn. (*pl.m.* **-i**.) 3. BUMP ON THE HEAD; horn-shaped peak of a mountain; projection; tip, point (of a flame); (electr.) — polare, pole tip; beak (of an anvil); branch of a road; reach of a river; i -i di un dilemma, the horns of a dilemma (also, le -a); i -i della luna, the horns of the moon in first or last quarter; (mil.) wing of an army or fortification; (naut.) point of gaff, peak; — da nebbia, foghorn; (liturg.) side of altar; — dell'Epistola, Epistle side; — del Vangelo, Gospel side; arm of the Cross; — dogale, Doge's cap; (astron.) Little Bear; (myth.; poet.) — dell'abbondanza, cornucopia, horn of plenty. 4. (MUS.) horn, French horn; — alto, horn-player expert in the high register; — basso, horn-player expert in the low register; — bassetto, basset-horn; — a mano, hand horn; — a macchina, — a pistoni, — cromatico, — ventile, valve horn; — da caccia, hunting horn; — da tirarsi, slide horn; — inglese, cor anglais; — segnale, flügelhorn; suonare il —, to blow the horn. 5. (VULG.) nothing; un bel —, nothing at all, (iron.) a fat lot; non me ne importa un —, I don't care a damn; non vale un —, it's not worth tuppence; un —!, nix! †**-etta** *f.* (naut.)

burgee. **-i·cine** *m.* (Rom. antiq.) *cornicen*, bugler. **-i·fero** *adj.* horned; horn-bearing; carrying a horn. **-i·gero** *adj.* horned. **-i·pedi** *m.pl.* (zool.) ungulates. **-ista** *m., f.* (mus.) horn-player, hornist. **-omọzzo** *adj.* having crumpled or broken horns. **-ọne** *m. augm.* of **corno**; (mus.) great cornett.

Cornova·gli-a *pr.n.f.* (geog.) Cornwall. **-ẹse** *adj.* Cornish; *n.m.* Cornishman; Cornish language; *f.* Cornishwoman.

cornuco·pia *f.* cornucopia, horn of plenty; (zool.) *Pollicipes cornucopia*, a kind of barnacle.

cornuta *f.* (eccl.) wooden vessel with food for cardinals in conclave; (zool.) horned viper.

cornut-o *adj.* horned; cuckold; argomento —, dilemma; (bot.) segala -a, ergot, sclerotium of *Claviceps purpurea*; *n.m.* rogue, villain; cuckold.

coro[1] *m.* (liturg.; architect.; theol.) choir; i cori degli angeli, the choirs (hierarchy) of angels; (mus.) chorus (of singers, of dancers, of instruments); chorus (composition for a large body of voices); a — pieno, in full chorus; (fig.) in —, in chorus, with one voice, of one accord; far —, to be in agreement, to chime in, to join in; (theatr.) chorus in Greek tragedy; chorus in drama or in opera.

coro[2] *m.* north-west wind; north-westerly direction.

†**cor-odi·a** *f.* (mus.) unison-singing; singing in octaves. **-odida·scalo** *m.* (Gk. antiq.) chorus trainer.

cor-ografi·a *f.* topography of a particular region; ancient nautical chart. **-ogra·fico** *adj.* topographical. **-o·grafo** *m.* topographer.

coro·id-e *f.* (anat.) choroid tunic. **-e·o** *adj.* choroid. **-ite** *f.* (med.) choroiditis.

coroll-a *f.* (bot.) corolla; porter's knot; †(naut.) fender. **-ato** (bot.) furnished with a corolla. **-i·fero** *adj.* (bot.) bearing a corolla. **-iflọre** *adj.* (bot.) furnished with a gamopetalous corolla to which the stamens are attached. **-iforme** *adj.* (bot.) shaped like a corolla.

corolla·rio *m.* corollary; addition; †garland of flowers.

corologi·a *f.* chorology.

corọn-a *f.* crown; coronet; monarch, throne; discorso della —, speech from the Throne; beni della —, private property of the monarch; aver —, to rule; portar —, to be praised; diadem, garland, wreath; deporre una —, to lay a wreath; ring, circle; far —, to form a circle; inner circle (of friends); series; — di sonetti, sonnet-sequence; — di colline, series, chain, of hills; (anat.) crown (of a tooth); (mil.) driving-band (of bullet or shell); (vet.) coronet; (techn.) rim; — dentata, rim of gearwheel; (eng.) — conica, ring bevel gear; (numis.) krone; crown; (eccl.) fringe round tonsure; (rel. art) halo; (rel.) rosary (beads or prayer); dire, recitare, la —, to say the rosary; (fig.) sfilare la —, to utter abuse, to speak one's mind; non staranno a dire la —, they're up to no good; (astron.) corona, halo (round the moon); (archit.) corona (member of a cornice); ornamental cornice at the top of a building; (hortic.) upper part of a tree; potare a —, see under **coronare**; (bot.) rosette or tuft of leaves; — imperiale, crown imperial, *Fritillaria imperialis*; — del sole, sunflower, *Helianthus annuus*; — di spine, *Lycium europaeum*; (mus.) pause-sign, ⌢; (geom.) the area enclosed between two concentric circles; rim of a wheel; a —, in a circle; (med.) — di Venere, syphilitic sores on the forehead. **-a·io** *m.* rosary-maker; rosary-vendor. **-ale** *m.* (anat.) coronal bone; coronal suture. **-cina** *f. dim.* of **corona**; (rel.) rosary; form of prayers. **-ella** *f. dim.* of **corona** (med.) onychia, sore finger; hang-nail; strengthening work to a dam or river wall.

coron-are [A I c] *tr.* to crown; to complete, to perfect, to achieve; (archit.) to adorn with a cornice; (mil.) to complete (a defence); (agric.) to prune by trimming all the branches symmetrically to the same height, preserving only the three or four principal branches. **-amento** *m.* crowning; coronation; 'crowning glory'; completing, perfecting; (bldg.) coping; -amento a schiena d'asino, saddle-backed coping; (naut.) taffrail. **-ata** *f.* (mus.) see **corona**. **-ato** *part. adj.* (*prep.* di) crowned; surrounded (by), girt (with), topped (by); le sue fatiche furono -ate da un buon successo, his labours were crowned by success; *n.m.* person of kingly mien; i Santi -ati, the Holy Crowned Ones, the Quattuor Coronati. (**-atore** *m.* **-atrice** *f.*) **-azione** *f.* crowning (cf. **incoronazione**).

corona·ria *f.* (bot.) dusty miller, *Lychnis coronaria*.

corona·rio *adj.* (anat.) coronary; for the purpose of a crown of victory; (lit. hist.) Certame —, poetic contest in Florence in 1441.

coron-cina, -ella *f. dim.* See under **corona**.

coro·nide *f.* (Gk. gramm.) coronis; per —, in conclusion; (naut.) taffrail.

coro·nio *m.* (astron.) corona, halo.

corono·ide *adj.* (anat.) coronoid.

corozo *m.* vegetable ivory, corozo.

corpacciata *f.* See **scorpacciata**.

corpacc·iolo *m.* hoop round the body of a barrel. -**iuto** *adj.* corpulent; pot-bellied, paunchy.

corp·o *m.*:

1. BODY; physique; l'educazione del —, physical training; salute del —, bodily health; (rel.) la festa del — del Signore, Corpus Christi; corpse, cadaver; trunk of the body; belly; dolori di —, stomach ache; dolori del —, bodily suffering, physical ailments; (vulg.) cavarsi il — di grinze, to fill one's guts; mettersi in —, to gulp down; (fig.) si mettono in — tanta scienza senza arrivare a digerirla, they swot up all that knowledge but they never digest it; benefizio del —, regularity of the bowels; andare di —, fare di —, to relieve oneself, to have a motion; a — pieno, on a full stomach; a — vuoto, on an empty stomach; non tenere nulla in —, not to be able to keep a thing down, (fig.) to be unable to keep a secret; aver roba in —, to hold a secret; entrare in — a uno, to come into a person's mind; ricacciare in — a uno quello che ha detto, to make a person eat his words; non aver più fiato in —, to have no breath left; (sport) clinch; a — a —, at close quarters, (boxing) in-fighting; a — morto (also 'a corpomorto'), desperately, with desperate resolution; a crepa —, headlong, flat out; dedicarsi anima e —, to devote oneself body and soul (heart and soul); era lui in anima e in —, there he was as large as life; avere il diavolo in —, to be nervy; avere l'amaro in — contro, to bear a grudge against; a male in —, grudgingly; womb; (vulg.) avere il — grosso, to be pregnant; avere un bambino in braccio e un altro in —, to have one child in arms and another on the way, 'to have one at the breast and one in the belly'; nascere a un —, to be twins; fare a un —, to bear twins; avere il — a gola (of a woman) to be near her time. 2. BODY (inorganic), material, matter; -i semplici, elements; -i composti, compounds; gli stati dei -i sono tre, solido, liquido, gassoso, matter is divided into three basic elements, solid, liquid and gaseous; (chem.) ritornare in —, to return to the metallic state; — celeste, heavenly body; — astrale, astral body; — contundente, blunt instrument; †celestial sphere. 3. SUBSTANCE, thickness, body, bulk, mass; dare — a, to give substance to; (fig.) dare — a un disegno, to put a plan into execution; vino che ha molto —, full-bodied wine; avere un bel — di voce, to have a fine strong voice; questa carta ha poco —, this paper has very little bulk; (paint.) colore di —, full-bodied paint, paint in several coats; dipingere a —, to paint in oils; (typ.) point, size of type; (comm.) l'importo totale a —, lump sum; in —, in toto. 4. MAIN PART, section, collection; nel — del discorso, in the main body of the speech; in due -i, made in five sections; back, spine of a book; corpus of writings; system of verses; (mus.) soundboard of a harp; (archit.) entasis, bulge; un — di case, a block of houses; *pl.* (anat.) parts of the brain. 5. GROUP OF PERSONS, body, corporation, corps; in —, in a body; spirito di —, esprit de corps, team spirit; — di ballo, corps de ballet; — insegnante, teaching staff; — accademico, teaching staff of a university; — diplomatico, diplomatic corps; (mil.) corps; — d'armata, army corps; — dei cavalleggieri, cavalry corps; — di guardia, guard, guard-room; (hist.) -i santi, area outside a city but within the bishop's jurisdiction, (Milanese hist.) guilds. 6. (NAUT.) hull; — morto, heavy anchor, mooring; — dell'Armata, main fleet, whole fleet, battle squadron; — dello Stato Maggiore Generale, Executive Branch; Ufficiali del Corpo Reali Equipaggi Marittimi, Naval Personnel Branch Officers; — e beni, all that a ship is carrying (crew, passengers and cargo). 7. (LEG.) — della compagnia, corporation; — del delitto, — del reato, *corpus delicti;* the material evidence of a crime. 8. OATHS: — di Bacco!, what the deuce!; — del diavolo!, what the devil!; — d'un cannone!, — di mille bombe!, what the hell! -**etto** *m. dim.* of **corpo;** undervest, vest; bodice; †man's waistcoat. -**icino** *m. dim.* of **corpo;** child's body. -**oso** *adj.* (of paper) bulking high; (paint.) suggesting a third dimension, having body to it. -**uto** *adj.* stout; dense (of a gas or liquid).

corpofranco *m.* (mil.) guerrilla band.

corpomorto *adv. phr.* a —, see under **corpo**.

†**corpora** *f.pl.* of **corpo**, q.v.

corporal-e *adj.* corporeal, bodily; corporal; esercizi -i, physical exercises; pene -i, corporal punishment; carnal; opere di misericordia -i, corporal works of mercy; *n.m.* (mil.) corporal; (liturg.) corporal. -**ità** *f.* corporality; materiality. -**mente** *adv.* corporally, in the flesh, bodily; corporeally.

corpor-are [A I S] *rfl.* to become denser, to take body. -**ativismo** *m.* (econ.) the corporative-state system. -**ativo** *adj.* corporate, corporative; (pol.) stato -ativo, corporative State. -**ato** *m.* corporate member. -**atura** *f.* figure, form, shape; †body. -**azione** *f.* corporation; (hist.) guild, association; (Fascist) corporation.

corp-o·reo *adj.* corporeal; material. -**oreamente** *adv.* corporeally; materially. -**oreità** *f.* corporeity. -**oruto** *adj.* large-bodied. -**oso** *adj.* see under **corpo**. -**ulento** *adj.* corpulent, fat, obese. -**ulenza** *f.* corpulence, adiposity; thickness (of a liquid), consistency.

cor·pus *m. indecl.* corpus, body, collection (e.g. of texts, documents).

corpu·sc·olo *m.* corpuscle; small particle, atom. (-**olare** *adj.*)

Corpus Do·mini, Corpusdo·mini *m.* (liturg.) Corpus Christi; †the Blessed Sacrament.

corputo *adj.* See under **corpo**.

Corrado *pr.n.m.* Conrad.

corre [B 7]. See **cogliere**.

corred-are [A I] *tr.* (*prep.* di) to equip, to furnish, to fit out, to rig out (with); to furnish with a trousseau; to adorn; — una lettera di un biglietto, to enclose a note in a letter. (-**amento** *m.*) -**ato** *part. adj.* equipped, supplied, furnished; accompanied, supported (by documents); una nuova edizione -ata di note, a new edition complete with notes; enclosed (of something in a letter); (hist.) cavalier -ato, newly created knight.

corredentrice *f.* (theol.) co-redemptress.

corred-o *m.* outfit, equipment; — della sposa, — nuziale, trousseau; — di un neonato, baby's layette; — di un collegiale, outfit for a boy going to boarding-school; household goods; (fig.) wealth; — di cognizione, intellectual preparation; (biol.) — cromosomico, set of chromosomes; (hist.) cavalier di —, knight who has just celebrated his inaugural feast, newly-created knight. -**ino** *m. dim.* of **corredo;** layette.

correg·g·ere [C 12] *tr.* to correct; to put right; to reprove; to amend, to rectify; to reform; to guide (animals); to revise; — le bozze, to correct proofs; — le bozze di, to proof-read; — un vino, to add spirits to a wine; to lace with spirits; to improve, to clear, to purify; (naut.) — un'altezza, to correct a sight; — una rotta, to correct a compass course; †to rule; †to punish. -**i·bile** *adj.* that may be corrected, rectifiable. (-**imento** *m.* -**itore** *m.* -**itrice** *f.*)

corregges-co *adj.* (m.pl. -**chi**) (paint.) in the manner of Correggio.

correggi-a[1] *f.* leather strap; leather girdle, belt; thong; shoelace; far corregge dell'altrui cuoio, to be generous with other people's belongings; perdere la —, to lose one's sense of shame. -**a·io** *m.* belt-maker, strap-maker. †-**ale** *m.* see **correggia**[1]. -**ame** *m.* harness of a horse; accoutrements. -**ante** *m.* (eccl. hist.) Dominican. -**ato** *m.* flail. -**ero** *m.* see **correggiaio.** -(**u**)**ola** *f. dim.* of **correggia;** small strap or belt; shoelace; †cobbler's knee-strap; (bookb.) ribbed spine; (bot.) knotgrass, *Polygonum aviculare.* -(**u**)**olo** *m.* thong; (bot.) kind of olive which turns black when ripe.

correggia[2] *f.* rumbling in the bowels; fart.

corregionale *adj.* belonging to the same region.

corregnare [A 5]. See **conregnare**.

correità *f.* See under **correo**.

correlativo *adj.* correlative; reciprocal, mutual. -**ivamente** *adv.* correlatively; reciprocally, mutually.

correlazione *f.* correlation; mutual relationship; in —, in proportion.

correligiona·rio *adj.* of the same persuasion (religion, politics, etc.); *n.m.* co-religionist; fellow-thinker, like-minded person.

†**Correngolfo** *pr.n.m.* (geog.) Gulf Stream.

corrent-e[1] *adj.* running, flowing; current; present-day; general, usual; in current use; due, payable; l'anno —, this year, the current year; del 15 — (abbrev. 'del 15 corr.'), of the 15th instant; tenere al —, to keep informed, to keep up-to-date; mettersi al —, to get up-to-date (with information); essere al —, to be well informed, to be in the swim; (comm.) conto —, current account; prezzo —, current price; la Società Pirelli — in Torino, the Pirelli Company trading in Turin; (fig.) ricevere come moneta —, to believe as true, to accept as gospel; cursive; racy (of style); fluent; swift, moving; rushing; bastimento —, pirate ship; a posta —, by return of post; easy to please, easy-going; free-and-easy;

corrent-e (*cont.*)
liquid, thin in consistency; fluid; *adv.* quickly, at once, expeditiously. **-acˑqua** *adj. indecl.* camera -acqua, bedroom with running water. **-emẹnte** *adv.* fluently; rapidly; rankly; currently. **-ẹzza** *f.* fluidity; fluency; up-to-dateness; the quality of being easy-going; (comm.) paying punctually, business-like procedure, attention to business. **-ista** *m., f.* (finan.) person who has a current account.

corrent-e[2] *f.* current, stream; — d'aria, draught; (naut.) — di flusso, flood stream; — di riflusso, ebb stream; la — del Golfo, the Gulf Stream; (fig.) general current of opinion; trend; andare contro —, to go against general opinion (or, the general trend); andare colla —, to follow the general trend; (electr.) current; — continua, direct current; (mus.) courante. **-iˑa** *f.* direction of the current; flow. **-oˑmetro** *m.* (hydraul.) current meter.

corrent-e[3] *m.* joist, beam; rafter; (fam.) contare i -i, to lie in bed idling; (archit.) triglyph; *pl.* (naut.) stringers. **-aiuolo** *m.* workman who boards floors or ceilings. **-ame** *m.* boarding, joisting. **-ino** *m. dim.* joist. **-ọne** *m. augm.* beam, main joist.

corrente[4] *adv. phr.* al —, 'au courant', up to date; essere al — di, to be well briefed concerning, to have up-to-date information about, to be well aware of.

corr-eˑo *m.* (leg.) accomplice; — in un delitto, accessory to a crime. **-eità** *f.* (leg.) complicity.

cọrr-ere [C5] *intr.* (*aux.* avere, with ref. to action; essere, with ref. to destination).
1. To RUN; ho corso due chilometri, I ran two kilometres; son corso dal medico, I ran to the doctor's; — come una lepre, to run like a hare; — come il vento, to run like the wind; — a rotta di collo, — a precipizio, to run at break-neck speed; — a spron battuto, to run full pelt; — a gambe levate, to show a clean pair of heels; fare a —, to run a race, to race; — dietro a, to run after, to hurry after, to pursue; — in aiuto di, to run to the assistance of; -o io a chiamarlo, I'll run and fetch him, let me run and get him; to run about, to be in a hurry, to rush. **2.** To TRAVEL RAPIDLY, to move swiftly, to speed, to fly; il treno -eva a tutt'andare, the train was travelling at high speed; il suo pensiero corse a lei, his thoughts flew to her; la mano mi corse alla tasca, my hand went at once to my pocket. **3.** To be CURRENT, to be valid, to run, to circulate; questo treno non -e la domenica, this train does not run on Sundays; la cambiale -e dal primo del mese alla fine dell'anno, the bill of exchange is valid from the first of the month until the end of the year; è una moneta che non -e più, it is no longer current coin; il mese che -e, the current month; -e la voce che, it is rumoured that; son voci che -ono, they're only rumours; in Italia -e l'uso della siesta, it is the custom to rest in the afternoon in Italy; -eva l'anno 1949, it was the year 1949. **4.** To FLOW, to run smoothly; l'acqua -e sotto il ponte, the water flows under the bridge; il sangue -e nelle vene, blood flows in one's veins; -e sangue, there is blood flowing, blood is being shed; lasciar —, to let things take their course, to let things slide; lasciarsi —, to let oneself go, to give way; lascia —! never mind! don't worry!; questo ragionamento -e bene, this argument is well developed; -e che, it follows that; non -e, it doesn't follow; la strade -e dritto per un chilometro, the road runs straight on for a kilometre. **5.** To BE IN A HURRY, to do things quickly; — troppo nel leggere, to read too quickly; come -e scrivendo! how quickly he writes!; nel concludere il contratto hai corso troppo, you were too quick reaching that agreement. **6.** (OF DISTANCE) to intervene, to extend; di qui alla chiesa ci -ono due chilometri, it's two kilometres from here to the church; tra le nostre idee ci -e un abisso, there is a great division of opinion between us; -e una bella differenza, there's a world of difference (between the two); ci —!, there's a lot of difference!, that's different! **7.** (OF TIME) to pass, to go by; c'è corsa un'ora, an hour went by, it's an hour since; è corso un secolo da quando, it's a hundred years since. **8.** To FALL DUE, to be payable, to become necessary, to be incurred; ogni settimana -e la pigione, every week the rent is due; mi -e l'obbligo di, I am faced with the necessity of (to); ci corsero non solo delle ingiurie ma anche dei pugni, not only insults were exchanged but blows entered into it as well. **9.** (NAUT.) to steam or sail at low speeds; — sull'ancora, to tauten the cable, to ride at anchor; — alla banda (of a cargo), to shift; — di bolina, to sail close hauled; — di bordata, to make a tack; — a fortuna, to sail in bad weather; — in fil di ruota, to run with the wind dead astern; — a palo secco, to sail under bare

poles; — a scotte mollate, to sail badly; — a terra, to approach land rapidly; — a vento largo, — di gran lusco, to run free. **10.** *tr.* To RUN; — un pericolo, to run a risk, to incur a danger; hai corso un gran pericolo, you've had a narrow escape; — la cavallina, to sow one's wild oats, to lead a dissipated life; (hist.) — una lancia, to tilt; — una cert'età, to be of a certain age; -e sessant'anni, he's sixty years old; — amore, to be in love; to sack, to raid, to plunder; — un paese, to overrun a country; (naut.) — il mare, to navigate; — lo stesso rombo, to be on parallel courses. **-imẹnto** *m.* running; flowing; swift movement.

correriˑa *f.* See scorreria.

correspettiv-o *adj.* corresponding; reciprocal; adquate, due; equivalent; (leg.) corresponding; in exchange; compensating; *n.m.* compensation; corresponding amount; equivalent; (leg.) consideration; senza —, for no consideration (C.C.). **-amẹnte** *adv.* correspondingly; reciprocally; in exchange. **-ità** *f.* proportion, relation; correspondence; (leg.) mutual obligation; mutuality.

correspons-aˑbile *adj.* (leg.) jointly responsible. **-abilità** *f.* (leg.) joint responsibility. **-iọne** *f.* (comm.) payment; (leg.) extinction of a debt by periodical payments.

corrett-o *part.* of correggere, q.v.; *adj.* corrected; correct; accurate, exact; right, true; adjusted; flavoured; caffè —, coffee laced with grappa. **-amẹnte** *adv.* correctly; accurately; in the right way. **-ẹzza** *f.* correctness; accuracy; decency, honesty, fairness. **-ivo** *adj.*, *n.m.* corrective. **-ọre** *m.* corrector; emender; (typ.) reader; (eccl.) corrector; (hist.) magistrate of the Venetian Republic; †ruler. (**-trice** *f.*) **-oriˑa** *f.* (hist.) office of 'Correttore' in the Venetian Republic. **-oˑrio** *adj.* corrective. **-ura** *f.* correction made.

correttọre[1] *m.* co-Rector, joint-Rector (e.g. of a university).

correttọre[2] *m.* See under corretto.

correzion-e *f.* correction; alteration, correcting; improvement; revision; — d'autore, author's proof, press-proof; — in piombo, correction in type; reform; (leg.) casa di —, house of correction, reformatory; istituto di —, approved school. **-ale** *adj.* (leg.) correctional; *n.m.* house of correction; approved school. **-almẹnte** *adv.* correctively.

corrida *f.* bull-fight; cycle-race.

corrid-ọio *m.* corridor; passage-way; (pol.) lobby; (naut.) main deck; (cinem.) — del film, film track. **-oino**, **-orẹtto** *m. dim.* of corridoio.

corridor-e *adj.* running; *n.m.* runner; rider; racer; racing cyclist; racing motorist; racing motor-cyclist; competitor in any race; racehorse; (mil.) forager; (naut.) runner in a deadeye; (orn.) a ratite bird; †see corridoio.

corrier-a *f.* post-woman; mail-coach; mail van; postal-bus; country bus; charabanc; (naut.) mailship. **-e**, **-o** *m.* postman; carrier; king's messenger; courier; diplomatic messenger; forwarding agent; passenger; post, mail; newspaper; daily correspondence; a volta di -e, by return of post; (fig.) viaggiar da -e, to travel without observing or learning anything; (orn.) courser; -e biondo, cream-coloured courser, *Cursorius cursor*; -e grosso, ringed plover, *Charadrius hiaticula*; -e piccolo, little ringed plover, *C. dubius*.

corrige (Lat.). See errata.

corrig-endo *m.* corrigendum; (leg.) juvenile delinquent; juvenile offender (in a reform-school). **-iˑbile** *adj.* corrigible; open to correction.

corrimano *m.* handrail; (bldg.) cap.

corrimẹnto *m.* See under correre.

corriọne *m.* (orn.) courser, stone-curlew.

†corrire *vb.* and derivs. See correre.

corrispettivo *adj.* and derivs. See correspettivo.

corrispondent-e *adj.* corresponding; relating; similar, analogous; proportionate; *n.m.* correspondent. **-emẹnte** *adv.* correspondingly; in proportion.

corrispondenza *f.* correspondence; post, mail; (journ.) despatch; — in arrivo, incoming mail; — in partenza, outgoing mail; — di oltremare, overseas mail; — per l'estero, foreign mail; mettersi in — con, to enter into correspondence with, to write to; relationship; reciprocated affection; agreement; symmetry, proportion; match; con guanti in —, with gloves to match; (mus.) consonance; (rlwy.) connexion; perdere la —, to miss one's connexion; biglietto di —, through ticket; †in —, in revenge.

corrispọnd-ere [C11] *intr.* (*aux.* avere, so *prep.* a) to correspond (to); to be in keeping, to harmonize (with); to conform (to); to have the same appearance (as); to have the same meaning (as); to respond (to), to answer; — alla fiducia di uno, to justify the

corrispond-ere (*cont.*)
confidence someone has placed in one; to give in return (for); ha corrisposto al mio affetto con l'ingratitudine, he has returned ingratitude for my affection; ho un reuma in una spalla che mi -e sul petto, I have rheumatism in one of my shoulders the pain of which I feel in my chest too; (*prep.* con) to be in correspondence, to correspond (with); to be connected (with); (*prep.* su) to look out (over), to give (on to); la finestra -e sulla piazza, the window looks on to the square; *tr.* (comm.) to pay, to remit, to make over.

corrisposto *part.* of **corrispondere**, q.v.; *adj.* corresponding; returned; repaid; reciprocal; amore —, mutual love; (comm.) paid, made over.

corriv-o *adj.* easy-going; credulous; hasty, careless; inconsiderate; obvious, banal; facile; indulgent. **-amente** *adv.* carelessly; indulgently.

corrobor-are [A I s] *tr.* to strengthen; to fortify; un bicchiere di vino -a lo stomaco, a glass of wine fortifies the stomach; to support, to corroborate. **-amento** *m.* strengthening; corroborating. **-ante** *part. adj.* strengthening; corroborating; *n.m.* (med.) tonic. **-ativo** *adj.* strengthening; confirming; corroborative. (**-atore** *m.* **-atrice** *f.*) **-azione** *f.* strengthening, fortification; support, corroboration; proof, confirmation.

corrod-ere [C I] *tr.* to corrode, to eat away; to wear away; to consume; *rfl.* to corrode, to wear away; to be consumed. **-ente** *part. adj.* corroding, corrosive. **-imento** *m.* corrosion, eating away; wearing away.

corromp-ere [C 26] *tr.* to corrupt; to deprave; to contaminate; to spoil; to bribe; to seduce; *rfl.* to become corrupted; to rot; to be spoiled; to become contaminated; to deteriorate; to decompose; to practise self-abuse; †-ersi all'acqua, (of good weather) to turn to rain. †**-evole** *adj.* corruptible. **-ibile** *adj.* see **corruttibile**. **-imento** *m.* corruption. **-itore** *m.* see **corruttore**, under **corruttibile**. †**-itore di pace**, breaker of the peace.

corros-ione *f.* corrosion, eating away. **-ivo** *adj.* corrosive; consuming, wasting; *n.m.* corrosive. **-o** *part. adj.* corroded, eaten away.

corrott-o[1] *part.* of **corrompere**, q.v.; *adj.* corrupted; corrupt; depraved; contaminated, foul; deteriorated; decomposed; *n.m.* corrupt person. **-amente** *adv.* corruptly.

†**corrotto**[2] *m.* lamentation, dirge; †mourning; †fare —, to weep, to lament; to mourn.

†**corrozione** *f.* See **corruzione**.

corrucc-iare [A 3] *tr.* to anger, to enrage; to vex; to torment, to grieve; *rfl.* to become enraged, to be roused to anger; to fly into a passion; to be vexed. **-iamento** *m.* anger; conflict. **-iato** *part. adj.* enraged, angry; vexed. **-iatamente** *adv.* angrily.

corruc·ci-o *m.* glowering rage; vexation; hostility; sorrow, mourning, regret; †conflict, feud. **-oso** *adj.* angry, enraged. (**-osamente** *adv.*)

corruda *f.* (bot.) wild asparagus, *Asparagus acutifolius*.

corrug-are [A 2 s] *tr.* to wrinkle; to corrugate; — la fronte, to knit one's brow; — le ciglia, to frown; *rfl.* to frown, to knit one's brow. **-amento** *m.* frowning, frown. **-ato** *part. adj.* wrinkled; corrugated. **-atore** *m.* wrinkler, corrugator; (anat.) muscolo -atore, corrugator. **-azione** *f.* wrinkling; corrugation.

corrus-care [A 2] *intr.* (*aux.* avere) to sparkle (of metal); coruscate; to flash, to scintillate. **-co** *adj.* (*m.pl.* **-chi**) flashing; shining, sparkling; coruscating; splendid.

corruttela *f.* corruption; wide spread of moral corruption; depravity.

corrutt-i·bile *adj.* corruptible; perishable; †in the flesh, mortal; *n.m.* corruptible (perishable) part of man; the flesh. **-ibilità** *f.* corruptibility. **-ivo** *adj.* corrupting. **-ore** *m.* corruptor. (**-rice** *f.*) **-ura** *f.* corruption.

corruzione *f.* corruption; graft; depravity; contamination; deterioration; (med.) decomposition, putrefaction; (leg.) corruption; bribery; seduction.

corsa *f.* running; a tutta —, di gran —, running, (fig.) in a great hurry, at great speed; pigliar la —, to set off at a run; fare una —, to run an errand; dare una — a un luogo, to pop over to a place; di —, running, at speed, in a rush, at once; run, trip, journey, course; perdere la —, to miss a train, (fig.) to 'miss the bus'; partire con la prima —, to leave by the first train; racing; andare alla —, to go to the races; cavallo da —, racehorse; — a piedi, running race; — con ostacoli, obstacle race; — nei sacchi, sack-race; — compensata, handicap event; — campestre, cross-country race; — di automobili, motor-race, motor-racing; — agli arma-

menti, armaments race; (naut.) course; naval raid; guerra di —, privateering; (eng.) travel, stroke (e.g. of a piston); volume della —, piston displacement.

†**corsale** *m.* thorax, chest.

corsaletto *m.* breastplate, corselet; (ent.) prothorax.

†**corsara** *f.* (naut.) pontifical customs boat.

corsar-o *adj.*, *n.m.* pirate, corsair; privateer. **-esco** *adj.* (*m.pl.* **-eschi**) pirate-like, piratical; legno -esco, pirate ship.

corsè *m. indecl.* lady's blouse; bodice; stays, corset.

corseggi-are [A 3 c] *intr.* (*aux.* avere) to be a pirate, to practise piracy; *tr.* to plunder. (**-atore** *m.*)

corsello *m.* space between a bed and a wall, or between two beds; space between the rows of seats in a hall; gangway.

corserella *f. dim.* of **corsa**, q.v.

corsesc-a *f.* (hist.) triple-bladed spear, orig. used in Corsica. **-ata** *f.* blow or thrust with a 'corsesca'.

corsetto[1] *m.* See **corsello**.

corsetto[2] *m.* see **corsè**.

cors-ia *f.* gangway; passage amongst beds, furniture or chairs in a large room or theatre, esp. the central passage down the middle of a hospital ward or of the auditorium of a theatre; hospital ward; dormitory; (athl.) lane for each runner on a running track; (motor.) lane; (in some Italian towns) the name given to a lane joining two large streets or squares; (naut.) free space on the deck for going from bow to stern, flying bridge; tie-plates outside the hatchways; bending strakes of the decks; cannone di —, bow chaser; (mining) shaft cut for draining; †current of water.

Cor·sica *pr.n.f.* (geog.) Corsica.

corsier-e, -o *m.* (poet.) steed, charger. (**-a** *f.*)

corsi·o *adj.* running, flowing; bilancia corsia, scales that are tipped too easily.

corsiv-o *adj.* flowing, running; cursive; (typ.) italic; *n.m.* article printed in italics; short leader-article; †current; †moneta -a, currency. **-amente** *adv.* flowingly. **-ista** *m.*, *f.* writer of short leader-articles.

corso[1] *part.* of **correre**, q.v.; *adj.* run; coursed; past, happened, elapsed; undergone; (mil.) sacked, plundered, raided, overrun.

corso[2] *m.* **1.** RUN, running; esercitarsi nel —, to practise running; cavallo veloce nel —, swift-running horse, fast horse. **2.** COURSE, progress, development, movement onwards; nel — di una settimana, in the course of a week; la malattia deve fare il suo —, the illness has to run its course; lavori in —, work in progress; il — della luna, the course of the moon; in — di pubblicazione, in course of publication; anno in —, current year. **3.** FLOW, stream; course; layer; il — del sangue, the blood-stream; — d'acqua, stream of water; (geol.) course; (bldg.) in corsi, coursed; (naut.) sheer-strake, run of plating or planks. **4.** STREET (orig. a street in which horse-races were run); road (wide, main road); procession or string of carriages following a fashionable route; throng of people on foot promenading up and down a 'corso'. **5.** SERIES OF LESSONS, course; un — di lingua italiana, an Italian course; un — di conferenze, a course of lectures; frequentare i corsi, to attend lectures; uno studente fuori —, a student who has not taken his degree in the appointed period; — di aggiornamento, refresher course. **6.** CIRCULATION; avere — legale, to be legal tender; in —, current, valid, (fig.) in fashion, in use; fuori —, out of circulation, (fig.) out of fashion. **7.** VOYAGE, sea-voyage; nave di lungo —, deep-sea vessel; marinaio di lungo —, blue-water sailor.

corso[3] *adj.* Corsican; *n.m.* Corsican, native of Corsica; Corsican language; Corsican wine; a large black breed of dog.

corsoio *adj.* slipping, sliding; nodo —, slip-knot; *n.m.* (eng.) slide, slider; cursor; tappet.

cortaldo *m.* horse with its tail decked and its ears cropped.

cortale *m.* See **cortaldo**.

cortamente *adj.* shortly; briefly; recently, newly.

cort-e *f.* court; uomo di —, courtier; †jester; — bandita, festivities on a great occasion in a medieval court; (fig.) tenere — bandita, to keep open house; — di Roma, Roman curia; — celeste, court of Heaven; (leg.) — d'appello, Court of Appeal; — di cassazione, Court of Cassation; — marziale, court martial; — dei conti, court which performs the duties of the Comptroller and Auditor General; andare a —, to go to court; tener —, to give an audience; — di assise, Assize Court; — internazionale delle prede, maritime prize court; — del mare, Admiralty Court; (econ. hist.) self-

cort-e (*cont.*)
sufficient villa economy (cf. **curtense**); (geog.) multiple farm; courting; far la —, to be courting; far la — a qualcuno, to court someone; courtyard; walled garden; small square.

cortecci-a *f.* bark (of trees); rind (of cheese); crust (of toast); — di mezzo, alburnum; sapwood; cortex, rind, shell, bark; (anat.) cortex; (geol.) earth's crust; clinker; slag; outer coat; surface (also fig.); (zool.) cortex, cortical layer (of an egg). **-one** *m.* (bot.) kind of fig with hard rind. **-oso** *adj.* having a thick bark of skin; bark-like. **-(u)ola** *f.* thin bark.

corteggi-are [A 3 c] *tr.* to pay court to; to pay suit to; to court, to woo; to flatter. **-amento** *m.* courting, courtship. **-ato** *part. adj.* courted, wooed; flattered. **-atore** *m.* one who pays court; suitor; flatterer. (**-atrice** *f.*)

corteggio *m.* train (of courtiers, etc.); suite, retinue, cortège; (fig.) trail, string, procession.

†**cortegiano** *m.* and derivs. See **cortigiano**.

cortello *m.* (dial. Ven., Tusc.). See **coltello**.

corte-o *m.* procession, train, cortège; group of people attending a ceremony; — nuziale, wedding procession, wedding party.

cortes-e *adj.* kind; courteous, polite; affable; gracious; essere — di consigli, to give generously of one's counsel; di modi **-i**, obliging, engaging; — ma non proprio gentile, polite but not gracious; poco —, discourteous; (of a woman) of easy virtue, accommodating; harmless; armi **-i**, arms blunted for use in tournaments; prigione —, lenient imprisonment; (joc.) short, brief; †idle. **-emente** *adv.* courteously, politely; graciously; kindly; liberally, generously; modestly; †leniently; †secretly. **-eggiare** [A 3 c] *intr.* (*aux.* avere) to spend lavishly; to be generous. **-ia** *f.* courtesy; politeness; affability; kindness; act of kindness; usare —, to be courteous, to act courteously; tip, gratuity; favour; per **-ia**, as a favour, kindly, please; mi faccia la **-ia** di, please be so kind as to…; †qualities of a courtier; †graciousness; †generosity, largesse; †menare **-ia**, to spend lavishly, to live sumptuously. **-iuola** *f. dim.* of **cortesia**; little act of kindness.

cortezza *f.* See under **corto**.

cortic-e *m.* (anat.) cortex (of the brain); bark (of trees). **-ale** *adj.* (anat.) cortical; (bot.) of or pertaining to bark. **-ina** *f.* (chem.) corticin.

cortic-ella *f.*, **-ina** *f. dim.* of **corte**, q.v.; small courtyard.

corticina[1] *f.* (chem.). See under **cortice**.

corticina[2] *f. dim.* See under **corticella**.

cortigian-o *adj.* courtly, refined; alla **-a**, in courtly fashion; *n.m.* courtier; flatterer; hanger-on. **-a** *f.* courtesan. **-accio** *m. pejor.* flatterer. **-amente** *adv.* flatteringly; insincerely. **-are** [A 1] *tr.* to flatter, to pay suit to. **-ata** *f.* action of a flatterer; low flattery. **-eria** *f.* hypocritical subservience; obsequiousness; flattery; finesse of a courtier. **-esco** *adj.* (*m.pl.* **-eschi**) like a courtier; courtly; servile, subservient; obsequious; insincere. (**-escamente** *adv.*) **-ia** *f.* harlotry; prostitution; †courtly virtues.

cortile *m.* (archit.) courtyard, court; farmyard.

cortin-a *f.* curtain (of a bed or door), hanging; (mil.) curtain; — di fumo, — di nebbia, smoke screen; (pol. fig.) — di ferro, iron curtain; *adv. phr.* oltre —, behind the iron curtain; notizie di oltre —, news from behind the iron curtain; (Gk. antiq.) tripod (of Apollo's oracle). **-aggio** *m.* (bed)-curtains, (bed)-hangings; canopy. **-are** [A 1] *tr.* to curtain; (mil.) to fortify with a curtain.

cortino *adj. dim.* See under **corto**.

†**cortiselle** *f.pl.* kind of game, possibly **cartiselle**, a game of cards.

cortisone *m.* (pharm.) cortisone.

cortivo *m.* (agric.) untilled farmland.

cort-o *adj.* **1.** SHORT, brief; calzoni **-i**, shorts, knee-breeches; (mil.) armi **-e**, short arms; avere le gambe **-e**, to be short in the leg; (provb.) le bugie hanno le gambe **-e**, truth will out; — di vista, near-sighted, short-sighted; vestire di —, to put into short clothes; (eccl.) abito —, clerical dress without cassock; tenere — un animale, to keep an animal on a short leash or halter; pigliare la più **-a**, to take the shortest route; per farla **-a**, in short, to come to the point; andare per le **-e**, to take a short cut, not to beat about the bush; alle **-e**!, no more prevarication!, quickly, get to the point!; tagliare —, to cut short; (cinem.) — metraggio, short; (electr.) — circuito, short circuit. **2.** LIMITED, in short supply; deficient; insufficient; poorly provided; a — di quattrini, short of cash; di intelligenza **-a**, of limited intelligence; tenere — a denari, to keep short of money; tenersi —, to be niggardly; non

---

la perdere per **-a**, don't spoil the ship for a ha'pworth of tar; venir —, to fail, to draw a blank, to fall short. **3.** *adv.* IN SHORT, briefly, shortly; at once, quickly; più —, sooner; di —, only recently. **-ezza** *f.* shortness, brevity; **-ezza** di mente, dull wittedness; short supply, scarcity. **-ino** *dim. adj.* rather short; rather slow-witted.

cortocircuitare [A 1] *tr.* (electr.) to short-circuit, to short.

cortola *f.* planishing hammer, with rounded head, used by kettle-makers.

cortometrag·gio *m.* (cinem.) short film, short.

Corton-a *pr.n.f.* Cortona. **-ese** *adj.* of Cortona; (joc.) short; *n.m., f.* native of Cortona.

coruc·cio[1] *m. dim.* of **cuore**, q.v.

coruc·cio[2] *m. dim.* of **coro**[1], q.v.

coruscare [A 2] and derivs. See **corruscare**.

corvatta *f.* See **cravatta**.

corvée *f. indecl.* (pron. as Fr.) (mil.) fatigue; (fig.) boring task.

corvello *m.* (ichth.). See **corvo**.

corvett-a *f.* curvet; (naut.) corvette, sloop; capitano di —, Lt.-Commander. **-are** [A 1 c] *intr.* (*aux.* avere) to curvet. (**-atore** *m.*)

corvetto *m.* See 'pesce corvo', under **corvo**.

corvina *f.* (ichth.) *Johnius umbra*, a kind of edible sea-perch.

corvino *adj.* (orn.) corvine; (naut.) becco —, caulker's knife; black, raven.

corv-o *m.* (orn.) bird of the crow family, (pop. 'crow') *sensu stricto* the rook *Corvus frugilegus*; — imperiale, — maggiore, — reale, raven, *C. corax*; — acquatico, — marino, cormorant; aspettare il —, to wait till the cows come home; (provb.) **-i** con **-i** non si cavan mai gli occhi, dog doesn't eat dog; (ichth.) pesce —, *Johnius umbra*, and also *Sciaena cirrhosa*; (joc.) priest, parson, 'crow'; calzoni a —, drainpipe trousers; (astron.) Corvus. **-etto** *m.* (orn.) jackdaw. **-olo** *m.* (ichth.). See 'pesce corvo' under **corvo**.

così *adv.* (in the phrase): così o —, one way or another; così o —?, this way or that way?

cos-a *f.* **1.** THING; object; thingummy; quella — lì, that thing over there; tra una — e l'altra, what with one thing and another; una bella —, a lovely thing, something lovely; la — non vale la fatica, the thing isn't worth the effort; qualche —, something; ogni —, everything; una — da nulla, a mere trifle; qualche — da mangiare, something to eat; non è gran —, it's nothing much; la qual —, the which, which thing; per la qual —, whereupon, wherefore; fare le **-e** una per volta, to do things one at a time; avere qualche — con, to have a grudge against, to bear resentment towards; tante **-e**!, all the best!; di' tante **-e** per me alla mamma, give mother all my fondest thoughts; tante belle **-e** a, all good wishes to, kindest greetings to; dimmi una —, chi vi ha dato il permesso?, tell me this, who gave you permission? **2.** MATTER, affair, fact; la — pubblica, the common good, (or) public affairs; la somma delle **-e**, public authority; come vanno le **-e**?, how are things?; la — era a questo punto, matters had reached this point; le **-e** d'Italia, Italian affairs, conditions in Italy; le **-e** di casa, household affairs; la — deve restare tra me e te, the matter must remain confidential between us two; è — mia, it's my affair; Giovanni è — mia, it's my business to look after John; tutt'altra —, quite another matter. **3.** EVENT, deed, happening, occurrence; di — nasce —, one thing leads to another; **-e** come **-e**, extraordinary happenings; a — fatta, after the event; (provb.) — fatta capo ha, what's done is done, (or) it's no use crying over spilt milk. **4.** USED IN INTERROG. OR NEG. EXPRESSIONS: (che) — volete?, what do you want?; (che) — hai?, what's the matter with you?, what's wrong?; —?, what?; non so — dire, I don't know what to say; guarda che — ho comprato, look what I've bought; intendo benissimo — vorreste fare, I know very well what you want to do. **5.** *pl.* PROPERTY, possessions; goods and chattels. **-accia** *f. pejor.* bad thing; piece of rubbish. **-are** [A 1] *tr.* (pop.) to 'fix', to 'cause'; to do; vedete come l'hanno **-ato**, look at the mess they've made of it. **-erella**, **-erellina**, **-etta**, **-ina** *f. dim.* of **cosa**; mere nothing, trifle; trinket.

cosac·cio *m. pejor.* of **coso**, q.v.

cosac-co *m.* (*pl.* **-chi**) Cossack. **-ca** *f.* Cossack woman or girl; Cossack national dance.

cosa·ria *f.* (bot.) dyer's greenweed, *Genista tinctoria*; yellow loosestrife, *Lysimachia vulgaris*.

coscett-a *f. dim.* of **coscia**, q.v.; leg (of a fowl). **-o** *m.* leg (of lamb); servire nel **-o**, to treat (a customer) handsomely.

co·sci·a *f.* (*pl.* **cosce**) thigh; haunch; flank; calzoni a —, tights; leg of meat; (eng.) slide bar (of lathe bed); (archit.) abutment (of an arch, or bridge); †edge; †side. **-ale** *m.* (hist.) cuisse, thigh-piece; (archit.) balustrade; (naut.) side of gaff gooseneck; (surg.) artificial thigh; pommel (of a lady's saddle).

cosciente *adj.* conscious; aware; — di sè, self-aware.

coscienz-a *f.* consciousness; awareness; conscience; direttore di —, spiritual director, confessor; uomo di —, conscientious man; caso di —, case of conscience; per sgravio di —, to satisfy one's conscience; out of a sense of duty; senza —, unscrupulous; farsi — di qualcosa, to have scruples about doing something; in —, honestly. **-iosità** *f.* conscientiousness. **-ioso** *adj.* conscientious; scrupulous; uomo -ioso, man with scruples, conscientious man; lavoro -ioso, work conscientiously carried out. **-iosamente** *adv.* conscientiously; honestly.

co·sci-o *m.* leg, joint (of meat). **-otto** *m.* leg (of lamb); -otto di selvaggina, haunch of venison. **-uto** *adj.* with large thighs, thick in the thighs.

coscritto *part.* of **coscrivere**, q.v.; *adj.*, *n.m.* conscript; recruit; (Rom. hist.) padri coscritti, members of the Roman Senate, *patres conscripti*, (joc.) members of a local council.

coscri·vere [C 12] *tr.* to conscript; to levy.

coscrizione *f.* conscription; conscripting.

cosecante *f.* (math.) cosecant, cosec.

coseno *m.* (math.) cosine, cos.

Cosen-za *pr.n.f.* (geog.) Cosenza. **-tino** *adj.*, *n.m.* native of Cosenza.

cos-erella, **-erellina**, **-etta** *f. dim.* of **cosa**, q.v.

cosf-ì *m. indecl.* (electr.) power factor (cos φ). **-i·metro** *m.* (electr.) power factor meter.

così *adv.* thus; — fan tutte, thus do all women; so; — detto, so-called; ha detto —, he said so, this is what he said; e — via, and so on; e — di seguito, and so on and so forth; per — dire, so to speak; proprio —, just so, just like this; meglio —, better so; — sia, so be it, amen; così così, so so, not too bad; likewise, similarly; — gli uni come gli altri, both the ones and the others; as; — ricco come voi, as rich as you are; come farà lui, — faremo noi, as he does, so will we do; *adj. indecl.* such, similar, of this kind; un uomo —, such a man, a man like that; *conj.* would that; — non fosse vero! would that it were not true!; — l'avesse saputo! would that he had known!; — che, so that, with the result that. (When 'così' is a prefix the following consonant is doubled, e.g. **cosiddetto**, **cosiffatto**.)

cosicchè *conj.* so that, with the result that.

cosiddetto *adj.* (so-)called, (so) styled (also 'così detto').

cosiffatto *adj.* such, similar, such-like, of this kind (also 'così fatto').

Co·sim-a *pr.n.f.* Cosima; (hortic.) an October variety of pear. **-o** *pr.n.m.* Cosimo; (joc.) stupid individual; (hortic.) pear-tree bearing an October variety of pear.

cosmesi *f.* the cosmetic art; beautifying; adornment.

cosme·tic-a *f.* cosmetics; beauty culture; beauty treatment. **-o** *adj.*, *n.m.* cosmetic; *pl.* cosmetics.

co·smia *f.* (ent.) Dun-bar moth, *Cosmia trapezina*.

co·smico *adj.* cosmic; raggi cosmici, cosmic rays, radiation.

cosm-o *m.* cosmos; universe; (fig.) order. **-ogoni·a** *f.* cosmogony. **-ogo·nico** *adj.* cosmogonal. **-ografi·a** *f.* cosmography. **-ogra·fico** *adj.* cosmographical. (**-ograficamente** *adv.*) **-o·grafo** *m.* cosmographer. **-ola·bio** *m.* (hist. science) cosmolabe. **-ologi·a** *f.* cosmology. **-olo·gico** *adj.* cosmological. **-o·logo** *m.* (*pl.* **-o·loghi**) cosmologist. **-o·poli** *f.* unknown locality; libro stampato in -opoli, book printed *sub rosa*. **-opolita** *m.* cosmopolite; cosmopolitan. **-opoli·tico** *adj.* cosmopolitic. **-opoliti·smo** *m.* cosmopolitism, world politics. **-orama** *m.* cosmorama. **-os** *m. indecl.* see **cosmo**. **-osco·pio** *m.* epidiascope.

cos-o *m.* (pop.) thingummy, thingumajig, whatsit; person, individual, 'Mr Thing'; (derog.) creature, wretch; non ci parlo, con quel — lì!, I'm not going to talk to that creature!; un — fatto e messo lì, a queer, boorish, uncouth person; an indefinite sum of money. **-ac·cio** *m. pejor.* wretch; good-for-nothing.

cospar·gere [C 4] *tr.* to sprinkle, to strew; to cover, to spread; — di fiori, to strew with flowers.

cosparso *part.* of **cospargere**, q.v.; *adj.* sprinkled, strewn, covered, spread; suolo — di fiori, ground strewn with flowers; volto — di rossore, face suffused with blushes.

†cosparto *part.* See **cosparso**.

cosper·gere [C 4] and derivs. (poet.). See **cospargere**.

cospersione *f.* sprinkling.

cosperso *part.* of **cospergere**, q.v.; *adj.* (poet.) sprinkled.

†cospessato *adj.* dense, inspissated.

cospett-o *m.* face, presence; view, sight; nel — di, al — di, in the sight of, in the eyes of, in the presence of; dinanzi al — di Dio, in the sight of God; *excl.* cospetto! (abbrev. of — di Dio!) good heavens!; (joc.) — di Bacco! Great Scott! **-ac·cio** *m. pejor.* of **cospetto**; swaggerer, blusterer, braggart. **-one** *m. augm.* of **cospetto**; (theatr.) 'mask' representing a ruffianly soldier.

†cospi·cere *tr.* to gaze at, to fix one's gaze on; to behold.

cospi·cu-o *adj.* conspicuous, eminent; outstanding; large, considerable; notable, remarkable. **-amente** *adv.* conspicuously; considerably; notably. **-ità** *f. indecl.* conspicuousness; large size; remarkability.

cospir-are [A 1] *intr.* (aux. avere) to conspire; to plot; — contro, to conspire against; (mech.) to work in the same direction. **-atore** *m.* conspirator; plotter; confederate. (**-atrice** *f.*) **-azione** *f.* conspiracy; conspiring; (mech.) direction, tendency, common effort.

coss-algi·a *f.* (med.) pain in the hip, coxalgy. **-a·rio** *adj.* coxal, pertaining to the hip.

cossen·dic-e *m.* (anat.) coxendix. **-o** *adj.* pertaining to the coxendix.

cos·sico *adj.* cossic; arte cossica, algebra.

cosso *m.* pimple; male del —, ear ache; (fig.) whim.

cost-a *f.* (anat.) rib; male di —, pleurisy; di —, sideways; beside; (butcher.) sirloin; (eng.) face (of cog); (naut.) rib, frame; (archit.) rib, ornamented rib (in vaulting); slope, hillside; salire a mezza —, to climb a slope horizontally or obliquely; una mezza —, an oblique course up or down a slope; bank; side; aiuto di —, extra payment, unexpected windfall; sea-coast, coast; back (of a knife). **-ale** *adj.* coastal; (anat.) costal, of the ribs, pertaining to the ribs. **-algi·a** *f.* (med.) pain in the ribs.

cost-à *adv.* over there; over by you. **-aggiù** *adv.* down there, down there by you. **-assù** *adv.* up there, up there by you.

costale *adj.* See under **costa**.

†costana *f.* (vet.) callosity in the lumbar region.

costantana *f.* (metall.) constantan.

costant-e *adj.* constant; faithful, unswerving; steady, firm; incessant; unremitting; enduring; unaltered; (of weather) settled; *n.f.* (math.) constant; (geog.) — solare, solar constant.

Costantino *pr.n.m.* Constantine.

Costantino·poli *pr.n.f.* (geog.) Constantinople, Stamboul.

Costanza[1] *pr.n.f.* Constance.

Costanza[2] *pr.n.f.* (geog.) Constance; il lago di —, Lake Constance.

costanza[3] *f.* constancy; firmness; persistence, perseverance; steadfastness.

costardella *f.* (ichth.) saury pike, *Scombresox saurus*.

costare [A 1] *intr.* (aux. essere) to cost; to be costly, to be expensive; quanto costa?, how much is it?; gli è costata cara, he paid dearly for it; *tr.* to cost: — un occhio della testa, — l'osso del collo, to be very expensive, to 'cost the earth'; costi quello che costi, no matter what it costs; †to consist.

Costarica *pr.n.f.* (geog.) Costarica; *m.* Costarica coffee.

costassù *adv.* See under **costà**.

costat-a *f.* chop, cutlet, entrecôte. (**-ella** *f. dim.*)

costatare [A 1] and derivs. See **constatare**.

costato *m.* (anat.) region of the ribs; thorax; (rel.) il santissimo —, the sacred side (of Christ); (naut.) framework of a ship.

costeggi-are [A 3c] *tr.* to coast, to skirt; to border; to flank, to run along the side of; (agric.) to plough along the ridges of (ploughed land); *intr.* (aux. avere) (naut.) to hug the shore, to coast. **-atura** *f.* coasting; bordering; (agric.) ploughing along the ridges.

coste·i *f.* of **costui**, q.v.; she; this woman, this person (often derog.).

costell-are [A 1] *tr.* (poet.) to strew with stars; to spangle; dei fiori -avano il prato, the meadow was spangled with flowers. **-ato** *part. adj.* strewn with stars, star-spangled; -ato di, studded with, strewn with; un libro -ato di errori, a book strewn with mistakes. **-azione** *f.* (astron.) constellation.

costerecci-a *f.* carcase. **-o** *m.* ribs of salt pork; man's ribs; side table.

costerella *f. dim.* of **costa**; gentle slope; little coast.

costern-are [A 1] *tr.* to throw into consternation, to dismay; *rfl.* to be dismayed; to suffer consternation. **-ato** *part. adj.* dismayed; in a state of consternation. **-azione** *f.* consternation.

†costetto *prn.* See **cotesto**.

cost-ì *adv.* over there, not far off; over there by you. **-ínci** *adv.* thence.

costier-a *f.* (southern) slope; (naut.) long stretch of coast; shroud. **-e** *m.* coasting pilot. **-o** *adj.* coasting, coastal, littoral; navigazione **-a**, coastal navigation; mare **-o**, waters in sight of land.

costip-are [A I S] *tr.* to constipate; to heap up, to amass; to pile together; (bldg.) to tamp; *rfl.* to catch a bad cold; to become constipated. **-aménto** *m.* cramming, stuffing; (bldg.) tamping, packing. **-ativo** *adj.* constipating, binding. **-ato** *part. adj.* crammed, stuffed; suffering from a bad cold; stuffed up, congested; constipated. **-azióne** *f.* bad head cold; -azione di ventre, constipation.

costitu-ire [D2] *tr.* to constitute, to form; to create; lo **-írono** capo, they made him head; *rfl.* to be, to come into being; si è **-íta** una società, a company has been formed; (leg.) to constitute; to settle; to elect; to establish; — una dote, to settle a dowry; *rfl.* (leg.) **-írsi** in giudizio, to enter an appearance (in civil proceedings); **-írsi** parte civile, to join in a criminal prosecution as a party claiming damages, etc., against the accused; **-írsi** ai carabinieri, to give oneself up to the police. **-endo** *adj.* to be formed; *gerund.* forming, constituting. **-ente** *part. adj.* constituting; *n.f.* constituent assembly; *m.* member of a constituent assembly; *pl.* constituents of an electoral division. **-itivo** *adj.* (leg.) atto **-itivo**, Articles of Partnership; charter; Memorandum of Association of limited company. **-ito** *part. adj.* constituted, formed; governo **-ito**, established government; composed; è **-ito** di, it consists of.

costitut-a·rio *m.* (leg.) maker of a company's statutes, foundation member. **-ivo** *adj.* constituting; (leg.) constitutive; *n.m.* essential. **-o** *adj.* constituted, formed, composed; *n.m.* (leg.) criminal proceedings before a magistrate; interrogation of the accused by the magistrate. **-óre** *m.* constituter. (**-rice** *f.*)

costituzión-e *f.* (leg.) constitution; regulations; statute (of a limited company or other incorporated body, corresponding to Memorandum and Articles of Association); act of appearing in a civil action; la — del convenuto, appearance by the defendant. **-ale** *adj.* constitutional; decreto **-ale**, constitutional decree; diritto **-ale**, constitutional law. **-a·rio** *m.* constitutionalist; person in charge of the publication and issue of constitutions.

costo *m.* cost; a prezzo di —, at cost price; l'ha pagata a caro —, he payed dearly for it; rifarsi del —, to meet expenses; — di esercizio, running expenses, maintenance; a tutti i costi, a ogni —, at all costs; a nessun —, on no account; a qualunque —, at any price; (fig.) a — della vita, at the cost of one's life; †usury; †interest; †torre danari a —, to borrow money on interest.

co·stol-a *f.* (anat.) rib; essere alle **-e**, to be close beside; avere qualcuno alle **-e**, to have someone as a dependant, to have a person as a hanger-on, to be unable to shake someone off; stare alle **-e** di, to importune; mangiare alle **-e** di uno, to feed at someone's expense; spianare le **-e** a, to beat, to cudgel; rib (of meat); (aeron.) falsa —, former; branch of a mountain chain; rib or thicker back of a sword or knife; back, spine (of a book); back (of a comb); corner (of a table, etc.); (spinning) — dell'aspa, stave of swift; (weaving) — dell'aspo, wing of warping mill. **-ame** *m.* ribs; ribbing. **-ato** *adj.* ribbed; *n.m.* loin (of beef); (naut.) ribbing, framework. **-atura** *f.* ribs, ribbing, framework. **-étta** *f.* cutlet. **-iere** *m.* one-edged sword. **-óne** *m. augm.* of **costola**; (archit.) vaulting rib; hard-hearted man; big, bulky lad; rogue. **-onato** *part. adj.* ribbed (in pattern or design). **-uto** *adj.* with thick ribs sticking out.

†costore *m.* See **cucitore**, under **cucire**.

costoro *pers. prn. pl.* of **costui** and **costei**; these people (often derog.).

costos-o *adj.* costly, expensive, dear. **-aménte** *adv.* expensively; at great cost, dearly. **-étto** *adj. dim.* rather costly, a bit on the expensive side.

costrettiv-o *adj.* coercive; restrictive; compulsive. **-aménte** *adv.* compulsorily.

costrétto *part.* of **costringere**, q.v.; *adj.* compelled, constrained, forced; confined.

†costrice *f.* See **cucitrice**, under **cucire**.

†costri·gnere *vb.* See **costringere**.

costri·ng·ere [C IO] *tr.* to compel, to constrain, to force, to oblige; lo costrinsero a dire di sì, they made him consent; to restrict, to constrict; to press, to compress. **-iménto** *m.* compelling, constraining; constricting; compressing. (**-itóre** *m.*)

costritt-ivo *adj.* constrictive; restrictive; leggi **-ive**, restrictive laws; (surg.) retentive. **-óre** *adj., n.m.* (anat.) constrictor; sphincter.

costrizióne *f.* constriction; constraint, coercion, compulsion.

costru-ire [D9] *tr.* to build, to erect; to construct; — un inganno, to plot a deception; (gramm.) to parse; to construe. **-i·bile** *adj.* constructible; construable. **-ito** *part.* See **costrutto**.

costrutt-o *part.* of **costruire**, q.v.; *adj.* constructed; built, erected; (gramm.) parsed; construed; *n.m.* (gramm.) construction; (fig.) sense, meaning, interpretation, construction; advantage, benefit, good. **-óre** *m.*, **-rice** *f.* constructor, builder; *adj.* building; società **-rice**, civil engineering company. **-ura** *f.* construction, building, structure.

costruzióne *f.* construction, building; edifice, structure; in —, in course of construction; (gramm.) construction; parsing; far la — di, mettere in —, to analyse, to parse.

costu·i *pers. prn. m. indecl.* this man (near you); this chap, this fellow; this individual (often derog.).

†costuma *f.* habit, custom, usage.

costum-are [A I] *intr.* (aux. essere) to be usual, to be customary; to be fashionable; (*prep.* di, followed by *infin.*) to be in the habit (of); *tr.* to bring up, to train, to educate. **-anza** *f.* old custom; old-fashioned social convention; (Tusc.) good manners; †darsi alla **-anza** di, to hold converse with. **-atézza** *f.* good moral behaviour; good manners. **-ato** *part. adj.* well-mannered, well-trained; good-living; well-brought-up; mal **-ato**, badly brought-up; usual, habitual, customary. **-ataménte** *adv.* in a well-mannered way; habitually. **†-azióne** *f.* training; rearing.

costum-e *m.* usage (of a people or country); habit, custom (of an individual); vita e **-i** degli animali, animal life and habits; costume; fancy dress; manners; — da bagno, bathing-suit; i **-i**, good behaviour; essere di buoni **-i**, to be good-living; mal —, bad manners; senza —, mannerless, uncouth; (leg.) custom; customary law; common usage; practice; il buon —, public morality; squadra del buon —, vice-squad. **-ista** *m.*, *f.* costume designer; wardrobe-man, wardrobe-mistress.

costur-a *f.* seam; spianar le **-e** a, to beat, to cudgel. **-ino** *m. dim.* purled stitch occupying two turns in the back of a stocking, forming a rib or seam.

†cota *f.* See **cote**.

cotale *adj.* such; *indef. prn.* such a one; †(euphem.) penis.

cotangente *f.* (geom.) cotangent.

cotanto *adv.* so much; †*adj.* such.

cote[1] *f.* hone, sharpener; whetstone.

cote[2] *f.* (pron. as Fr.) odds (in betting).

cotechino *m.* See **coteghino**.

coteghino *m.* a kind of boiling-sausage.

coténn-a *f.* hide; pigskin; mettere la —, to get fat; pigskin scalded and with the bristles removed so as to be eatable; (joc.) skin of a person's head; di grossa —, thick-skinned; crust, skin; (bot.) — erbosa, turf-forming plants; (med.) buffy coat; (fig.) miser, grasping person. **-óne** *m. augm.* of **cotenna**; skin off a pig's back with the fat attached; rough man, boor. **-óso** *adj.* thick in the hide; (med.) buffy.

cotesti[1] *adj.*, *prn. m.pl.* See **cotesto**.

†cotesti[2] *pers. prn. m.s.* this man, this person.

cotést-o *adj.* that; such; *prn.* that of yours; that one, that over there. **-i** *m.pl.* those; those ones there; those of yours. (**-e** *f.pl.*)

co·tic-a, (Rom.) **còtic-a** *f.* See **cotenna**; sward; †flesh. **-óne** *m. augm.* thick-skinned person; boor.

cotidiale *adj.* (naut.) co-tidal.

cotidian-a *f.* fever recurring daily. **-o** *adj.* see **quotidiano**.

co·til-a *m.* (anat.) socket, cotyle, acetabulum. **-o·ide** *f.* cotyloid cavity. **-oide·o** *adj.* cotyloid.

cotile·don-e *m.* (bot.) cotyledon; pennywort, navelwort, *Umbilicus rupestris*; (zool.) cotyledon (of placenta). **-are** *adj.* (bot.) of or pertaining to cotyledons. **-e·o** *adj.* (bot.) furnished with one or more cotyledons.

cotino *m.* (bot.) wig tree, *Cotinus coggygria*.

cotiss-a *f.* (herald.) bendlet. **-ato** *adj.* (herald.) bendy.

†coto *m.* thought, cogitation.

cotógn-a *f.* (bot.) quince, fruit of the **cotogno**, q.v. **-ata** *f.*, **-ato** *m.* quince jam, quince jelly; quince jelly cube. **-ella** *f.* (techn.) type of marble. **-ino** *adj.* tasting and smelling of quince; *n.m.* type of alabaster. **-o** *m.* (bot.) quince tree, *Chaenomeles sinensis*; (vet.) 'donkey foot' in a horse.

cotognola *f.* kind of pear, tasting like quince, fruit of the **cotognolo**.

cotoletta *f.* cutlet (cf. **costoletta**, under **costola**).

coton-e *m.* cotton; — idrofilo, cotton-wool; refe di —, cotton thread, sewing cotton; filato di —, cotton yarn; tessuto di —, cotton (cloth); (bot.) cotton, cotton plant, *Gossypium*; olio di —, cottonseed oil; — fulminante, — in polvere, gun cotton; olio di —, cottonseed oil; (naut.) canvas; avere tutto il — a riva, to have all sail set; (surg.) wad; pad; tampon; *pl.* cotton goods. -a·ceo *adj.* cottony. -a·ria *f.* (bot.) cotonaria. -ato *adj.* lined with cotton; *n.m.* (text.) silk-cotton mixture. -ella *f.* (bot.) dusty miller, *Lychnis cotonaria*. -eri·e *f.pl.* cotton goods. -iere *m.* cotton manufacturer; cotton operative, cotton-worker, mill-hand. -iero *adj.* relating to cotton; industria -iera, cotton industry. -ifi·cio *m.* cotton spinning mill. -ina *f.* (text.) calico; (naut.) heavy canvas. -oso *adj.* cottony, downy, fluffy; (bot.) woolly; tomentose.

cotornice *f.* (orn.). *See* **coturnice**.

cotrione *m.* (orn.). *See* **codione**.

cott-a[1] *f.* (liturg.) surplice, cotta; cloak; — d'arme, tunic worn over armour; †woman's gown. †-ardita *f.* long flowing gown.

cotta[2] *f.* cooking; baking; kilnful; amount cooked or baked; (ceram.) di tre cotte, very fine baked; (colloq.) un furbo di tre cotte, a thorough knave; (slang) infatuation, 'pash'; drunkenness; pigliare una —, to fall in love, to get drunk.

cot·tabo *m.* (Gk. antiq.) cottabus.

cotter *m. indecl.* (naut.) cutter.

cotterella *f.* flirtation.

cotticchiare [A 4] *tr.* to cook slightly, to under-cook.

cottic·ci-o *adj.* partly cooked; underdone; (fig.) slightly drunk; in love, lovesick; *n.m.* a mixture of things all cooked together.

cot·tile *adj.* brick.

cot·tim-o *m.* job, contract; lavoro a —, piece-work, jobbing; contratto a —, jobbing contract; lavorare a —, to do piece-work. -ante *m.*, -ista *m.* jobbing workman; piece-worker.

cott-o *part.* of **cuocere**, q.v.; *adj.* cooked; done; — al forno, baked; (industr.) baked, fired; nè — nè crudo, neither one thing nor the other; chi la vuol -a, chi cruda, some think one way, some another; burned, scorched; terra -a, terracotta; lavoro —, earthenware; (text.) seta -a, seta a —, boiled-off silk; (fig., slang) drunk, 'tight', 'canned'; in love, lovesick; *n.m.* cooked food; earthenware; l'industria del —, ceramics; pot; scald, scorch. -oia *f.* cooking; di buona -oia, easy to cook; di cattiva -oia, hard to cook; nature, character; poor quality land; (techn.) salt pan. -oio *adj.* easy to cook; acqua -oia, water good for cooking vegetables; (fig.) susceptible, prone to fall in love.

cottr-e, -o *m.* (naut.) cutter.

cottura *f.* cookery; cooking; baking; a —, completely cooked; venire a —, to be completely cooked; (fig.) essere di prima —, to be very susceptible, to be prone to fall in love; burn, scorch; (paperm.) digesting; (industr.) firing, baking; (text.) scalding.

co·tula *f.* (bot.) — fetida, stinking mayweed, *Anthemis cotula*.

cotunnite *f.* (miner.) cotunnite.

coturnice *f.* (orn.) rock partridge, *Alectoris graeca*; quail.

coturn-o *m.* buskin; calzare il —, to wear the buskin, to tread the boards, to go on the stage, to write for the stage. -ato *adj.* relating to drama; stile -ato, inflated, pompous style.

coulisse *m. indecl.* (pron. as Fr.) seat in rowing; — scorrevole, sliding-seat.

co·u·so *m.* (leg.) use and enjoyment of a right in common with others; user in common. -utente *m.* (leg.) one who uses and enjoys a right in common with others; joint user.

cov-a *f.* brooding, sitting (on eggs); in —, sitting; fare la — di, to hatch out; nesting-place; brood; lair; †tortoise-shell. -accino *m.* unleavened dough-cake, cooked under ashes or in boiling oil. -ac·ciolo *m.* nest (of birds or small animals); lair, den; (joc.) bed.

covacenere *m., f.* lazy person (usu. said of a servant-girl who sits by the fire instead of doing her work); (hist.) scullion.

cova·ia *f.* brood of bee grubs.

covalenza *f.* (chem.) covalence.

cov-are [A 1c] *tr.* to hatch, to hatch out; (fig.) to brood over; to sicken for; to cherish secretly; *intr.* (*aux.* avere) to be broody; to sit on eggs; to brood, to sit brooding; to smoulder; to lie hidden, to lie in wait; gatta ci -a, there's more in this than meets the eye. -ata *f.* brood; hatching; (fig.) brood of children; mettere

su una bella -ata, to have a fine brood of young ones. -atic·cio *adj.* broody. -ato *part. adj.* hatched; hatched out. -atura *f.* hatching, hatching out.

covarello *m.* (orn.) woodlark.

covariante *m.* (math.) co-variant.

†**covazzo** *m.* *See* **covacciolo**, under **cova**.

†**covelle** *adv.* somewhat, to some extent, a little; not at all, in no wise; non far —, to do nothing.

covellina *f.* (miner.) covelline, covellite, covellinite.

†**cover·chio** *m.* *See* **coperchio**.

†**co·vero** *m.* copper.

coverta *f.* *See* **coperta**.

†**covid-are** *tr.* to covet. †-i·gia *f.* cupidity, covetousness. †-oso *adj.* covetous.

coviello *m.* (theatr.) mask (see **maschera**), representing a cowardly soldier.

covile *m.* lair, den; hovel; (fig.) rude bed, pallet; *pl.* (bldg.) holes in a wall for the putlogs of the scaffolding.

cov-o *m.* lair; nest; form (of a hare); sett (of a badger); (fig.) haunt, hiding-place, den; (joc.) bed; (fig.) farsi un —, to feather one's nest; (vulg.) fare il —, to settle down, to live, to 'hang out'; (Ital. hist.) Il Covo, the office of Mussolini's journal, *Il Popolo d'Italia*; centre of Fascism. -ino *m. dim.* of **covo**; canary's nest.

†**co·volo** *m.* lair, den.

covolume *m.* (phys.) co-volume.

covon-e *m.* sheaf, shock (of corn); bundle (of hay). -cello, -cino *m. dim.* of **covone**.

†**covrire** *vb.* and derivs. *See* **coprire**.

coxalgi·a *f.* and deriv. *See* **cossalgia**.

Cozie *pr.n.f.pl.* (geog.) Cottian Alps.

cozione *f.* (scient.) cooking; digestion; decoction.

cozza *f.* (S. Ital.) (zool.) mussel, *Mytilus galloprovincialis*, and also various other edible bivalves.

cozz-are [A 1] *tr.* to butt, to butt against; to toss; to gore; to collide with; *intr.* (*aux.* avere) to clash, to contend, to be in conflict; to collide; — insieme con, to be at variance with; — col muro, to run one's head against the wall; — contro, to crash against. -ata *f.* butt; toss; goring; clash. (-ato *part. adj.* -atore *m.*) -atura *f.* butting; tossing; goring; clashing, colliding.

cozzo *m.* butt, toss; clash, shock; collision; impact; conflict; — delle opinioni, clash of opinion; dar di — in, to butt, to bump against, to clash with; (fig.) to meet, to run into, to knock up against; fare ai cozzi, to clash, to collide.

cozzolo *m.* (ichth.) star-gazer, *Uranoscopus scaber*.

cozzon-e *m.* horse-dealer; (slang) matchmaker. -eggiare [A 3 c] *intr.* (*aux.* avere) to deal in horses; (slang) to be a matchmaker.

cra cra *onomat.* caw; croak.

crabrone *m.* (ent.) hornet, *Vespa crabro*.

crac[1] *m. indecl.* (onomat.) crack; rattle, crackle; (sport) crack, ace; favourite, star horse (of racing stables).

crac[2] *m. indecl.* crash; bankruptcy; collapse, downfall.

crace *m.* (orn.) *Crax* (a genus of curassow).

Craco·via *pr.n.f.* (geog.) Cracow.

†**crai** *adv.* tomorrow; a —, on credit; 'crai, crai' was also said to be the voice of the crow (cf. **cra**), hence the proverb: di — in — si pasce la cornacchia.

cral *m. indecl.* (industr.) workers' residential estate.

crampo *m.* (med.) cramp; — di petto, angina pectoris.

crancelino *m.* (herald.) crancelin.

cra·nico *adj.* cranial.

cra·ni-o *m.* skull, cranium. -ato *adj., n.m.* vertebrate (of the craniata). -ocla·sie *m.* (surg.) cranioclast. -ologi·a *f.* craniology; phrenology. -olo·gico *adj.* craniological; phrenological. -o·logo *m.* craniologist; phrenologist. -omanzi·a *f.* phrenology. -ometri·a *f.* craniometry. -oscopi·a *f.* cranioscopy. -o·scopo *m.* cranioscopist. -otabe *f.* (med.) craniotabes. -otomi·a *f.* (surg.) craniotomy. -o·tomo *m.* (surg.) craniotome.

cranteri *m.pl.* wisdom teeth.

cra·pola *f.* *See* **crapula**.

cra·pul-a *f.* debauchery; licentiousness. -are [A 1 s] *intr.* (*aux.* avere) to be gross in one's eating and drinking, to gormandize, to guzzle. (-atore *m.*) -one *m.* immoderate eater and drinker, guzzler; debauchee.

crasi *f. indecl.* (gramm.) crasis; (med.) crasis, mixture.

crass·o *adj.* dense; crass; (anat.) intestino —, large intestine. **-am̱ento** *m.* coagulable part of blood, crassament, coagulum. **-ẹzza** *f.* denseness; coarseness.

†**cra·stino** *adj.* pertaining to tomorrow, future.

†**cratera** *f.* See **cratere**.

crat·ere *m.* crater; (archaeol.) large bowl; goblet, drinking bowl; small pot or beaker. **-e·rico** *adj.* craterous.

cratic·cio *m.* See **graticcio**.

crati·cola *f.* See **graticola**.

cra·uti *m.pl.* (cul.) sauerkraut.

cravatt·a *f.* tie, necktie, cravat; farsi la —, to tie one's tie; (fig.) far le -e, to practise usury, to get a stranglehold; (eng.) clip. **-a·io** *m.* tie-maker, tie-seller. (**-a·ia** *f.*)

cra·zi·a *f.* (numism.) ancient Tuscan coin of the value of five 'centesimi'; — imbiancata, a 'centesimo', falsified as a 'crazia', (fig.) false, untrustworthy person. †**-ante** *m.* copyist (one who copied a page for one 'crazia').

crea·bile *adj.* See under **creare**.

creanz·a *f.* good manners; breeding; non sapete la —?, where are your manners?; mala —, bad manners, ill-breeding. **-ato** *adj.* well-mannered, polite; well-bred.

cre·are [A 6] *tr.* to create; to found, to establish, to institute; to make; to appoint; to give rise to; to produce; (theatr.) to interpret, to create; — una parte, to create a role; †to bring up, to rear, to ṉurture; *rfl.* (*acc.* of *prn.* 'si') to be formed; to be founded; (*dat.* of *prn.* 'si') to gain for oneself. **-a·bile** *adj.* that may be created; potential. **-am̱ento** *m.* creating. **-ante** *part. adj.* creating; †well-mannered. **-ativo** *adj.* creative. **-ato** *part. adj.* created; brought up, bred; *n.m.* creation, all created things; †servant, dependant. **-ato·re** *m.* creator; author; il Creatore, the Creator; andare al Creatore, to go to meet one's Maker; mandare al Creatore, to kill; (eng.) hob. (**-atrice** *f.*) **-atura** *f.* creature; baby; child; favourite; *mignon*. **-azi̱one** *f.* creation; creating; foundation; instituting; thing created, creation. **-azion̲iṣmo** *m.* (theol.) creationism.

creatina *f.* (chem.) creatine.

†**crebro** *adj.* frequent, repeated, thick and fast.

credent·e *m., f.* (rel.) believer; i -i, the faithful; lui parla da —, he is speaking as a Christian, he is speaking from a religious point of view; non sono -i, they don't believe in anything.

credenz·a *f.* **1.** belief, opinion; trust; credence; lettere di —, credentials; (rel.) belief, faith, creed; (comm.) a —, on credit. **2.** sideboard, buffet, serving-table; food-cupboard; serving-room next to the kitchen; room for storing cheese, fruit and sweetmeats; piatti di —, food of this kind; (liturg.) credence table. **-iale** *adj.* credential; lettera -iale, credential; *pl.f.* le -iali, credentials. **-iera** *f.* food-cupboard; housekeeper; †confidante. **-iere** *m.* butler; steward; †confidant. **-ina** *f. dim.* of **credenza**; small cupboard; -ina a muro, service cupboard fixed in a recess; (liturg.) small credence table. **-ino** *m.* (liturg.) see **credenzina**. **-ọne** *m. augm.* of **credenza**; good-hearted, credulous person.

cred·ere [B I C] *tr.* to believe; to trust; -o tutte queste verità, I hold all these things to be true; to hold as an opinion, to think, to consider; -evo che lo sapeste, I thought you knew; lo -o capace di tutto, I believe him to be capable of anything; fate quel che -ete, do as you think best; lo -o!, I should think so!; to entrust; — la vita ai mari, to entrust one's life to the seas; (at the end of letters) -imi tuo aff. E.R.V., believe me, your affectionate E.R.V.; *abs.* (rel.) to believe, to have faith; non -o, I don't think so; chi ama, -e, he who loves, trusts; *intr.* (*aux.* avere; *prep.* in) to believe (in); — in Dio, to believe in God; — nelle streghe, to believe in witches; — nei medici, to have faith in doctors; (*prep.* a) to attach credence (to), to believe; non -o a tali notizie infondate, I don't believe such groundless rumours; — al progesso dell'umanità, to believe in progress; non ci -o, I don't believe it; — sulla parola a qualcuno, to trust someone's word; (*prep.* di) to have an opinion (about), to think (of), to consider; che -e di tali notizie? what do you think of this news?; -o di sì, I think so; -o di no, I think not, I don't think so; *rfl.* to believe oneself, to think oneself; si -e un genio, he thinks himself a genius; *n.m.* belief; a mio —, in my opinion. **-i·bile** *adj.* credible, believable; reliable, trustworthy. **-ibil̲mente** *adv.* credibly, believably. **-ibilità** *f.* credibility.

cred̲ito *m.* credit; trust; standing, repute; belief; saldo a —, credit balance; (leg.) credit; loan, standing, accommodation; — ipotecario, credit secured by mortgage; — mobiliare, credit secured by personal property; — immobiliare, credit secured by real property; lettera di —, letter of credit; dare —, to give credit; istituto di —, banking establishment. **-ọre** *m.* creditor; -ore ipotecario, mortgagee; gli son -ore di mezzo milione, he owes me half a million. **-rice** *f.* creditrix.

credo *m.* (rel.) Credo, Creed; in un —, in a moment, before you could say Jack Robinson; entrare in qualcosa come Pilato nel —, to be misplaced, to be out of one's element; (fig.) views, ideas, creed.

cre·dul·o *adj.* credulous. **-ità** *f.* credulity, credulousness. **-ọne** *m.* foolish credulous person. (**-ọna** *f.*)

crem·a *f.* (cul.) dish made of eggs, sugar and milk (cf. egg-custard); — del latte, top of the milk; — per la barba, shaving-cream; — per le scarpe, shoe-cream; — per toeletta, cold-cream; very sweet liqueur. **-ọso** *adj.* creamy.

cremagliera *f.* rack; ferrovia a —, rack railway.

crem·are [A I] *tr.* to cremate; (rubber mfr.) to cream. **-ato** *part. adj.* cremated. **-atọio** *m.* crematorium. **-ato·rio** *adj.* crematory, crematorial; forno -atorio, furnace for cremating. **-atura** *f.* (rubber mfr.) creaming. **-azione** *f.* cremation; cremating.

cre·mis·i *adj. indecl.* crimson; *n.m. indecl.* the colour crimson. **-ino** *adj.* crimson.

Cremlino *pr.n.m.* Kremlin.

cremnofobi·a *f.* (med.) cremnophobia.

cremo·metro *m.* creamometer; lactoscope.

cremon̲ese *adj.* of, from, Cremona; *n.m., f.* native of Cremona; *m.* (cul.) type of saffron cake.

cremoniano *m.* (eng.) stress diagram.

cremọre *m.* (fig.) cream, best part; — di tartaro, cream of tartar.

cremọso *adj.* See under **crema**.

cren *m. indecl.* (bot.). See **crenno**.

crenato *m.* (chem.) crenate.

cre·nico *adj.* (chem.) crenic.

crenno *m.* (bot.) horseradish, *Armoracia rusticana*.

creolina *f.* tar disinfecting fluid.

cre·ol·o *m.* Creole. (**-a** *f.*)

creoṣoto *m.* creosote.

crep·a *f.* crack, fissure, split. **-ac·cia** *f. pejor.* see **crepaccio**. **-acciata** *f.* series of crevasses; part of a glacier where crevasses occur. **-acciato** *adj.* full of cracks; split by crevasses. **-ac·cio** *m.* large crack, fissure; crevasse (in a glacier); (vet.) crack in a horse's skin. **-ac·ciolo** *m.*, **-ac·ciuola** *f.* small crevasse.

crepa-corpo *adv. phr.* a —, fit to burst. **-cuore** *m.* heartbreak. **-pan·cia** *adv. phr.* mangiare a -pancia, to eat fit to burst. **-pelle** *adv. phr.* mangiare a -pelle, to eat fit to burst; ridere a -pelle, to split one's sides with laughter, to have a good laugh.

crep·are [A I] *intr.* (*aux.* essere) to burst, to split; se mangio un altro po', -o, if I eat any more I'll burst; — di dolore, to be racked with pain; — dal ridere, to double up with laughter, to die of laughing; — d'invidia, to be eaten up with envy; — di salute, to be bursting with health; — dalla fatica, to be utterly exhausted; (fam.) to die; -a!, go to blazes! (NOTE: this is the conventional answer to 'in bocca al lupo!'). **-am̱ento** *m.* breaking, bursting; -amento di cuore, heartbreak, broken heart. **-ata** *f.* process for darkening the colour of wine. **-ato** *part. adj.* (fam.) dead; cracked, burst; †ruptured; *n.m.* crack. **-atura** *f.* crack; (on the hands) chap; †rupture, hernia.

cre·pida *f.* (Gk., Rom. antiq.) sock and buskin.

†**crepi·dine** *f.* handhold on a rock face.

crepita·colo *m.* (liturg.) rattle (used in Holy Week instead of bell); ancient bronze percussion instrument; child's rattle.

crepit·are [A I S] *intr.* (*aux.* avere) to crackle; to clang; to rustle. **-anza** *f.* crackle, crackling. **-azione** *f.* noise of crackling; crackle; (med.) crepitation. **-ìo** *m.* prolonged crackling; -ìo delle pallottole, rattle of bullets.

cre·pito *m.* crepitation; crackling.

crepol·are [A I S] *intr.* (*aux.* essere) to split; to trickle. **-atura** *f.* split, splitting; trickling. **-ìo** *m.* noise of splitting; sound of trickling.

†**crepore** *m.* dislike; hatred; essere in — a, to be hated by.

crepundi *m.pl.* (Gk. and Rom. lit.) playthings; birth-tokens (conventional clues by which a long-lost child is recognized).

crepu·scol·o *m.* twilight, dusk, gloaming; (fig.) decline. **-are** *adj.* crepuscular, twilit; of the twilight; dim, low-toned, shadowy; (lit. hist.) poesia -are, Italian 'crepuscular' poetry of the early twentieth century, subdued and 'twilit' in tone and atmosphere;

crepuscol·o (cont.)
(ent.) farfalle -ari, moths; *n.m.pl.* i -ari, the 'poets of twilight' belonging to this school (e.g. Corazzini, Gozzano, Moretti). -**ino** *adj.* twilight, twilit, crepuscular.

crepu·sculo *m.* and derivs. See **crepuscolo**.

†**crescentina** *f.* dripping toast.

cresc·ere [B9] *intr.* (*aux.* essere) to grow; to increase; to go up, to rise in price; (of tide or water level) to rise; to be left over; mi -ono mille lire, I have a thousand lire unaccounted for, there are a thousand lire left over; (mus.) to rise in pitch; to be above the pitch; (fam.) to be too big; *tr.* to grow; to increase, to augment, to put up; to rear, to bring up. -**endo** *m.* (mus.) crescendo (also fig.); *gerund.* becoming louder. -**ente** *part. adj.* growing, increasing; luna -ente, crescent moon, moon in the first quarter; *n.m.* (naut.) -ente del mare, tide; (herald.) crescent; -ente figurato, crescent with human face; croce con -enti, cross ending in four crescents; †*f.* rising tide. -**enza** *f.* growth; growing; vestito fatto a -enza, garment made with a big hem or tucks in the skirt or sleeves so as to allow for growth; febbri di -enza, the fevers which generally occur during youth; growth, excrescence; increase, rise; (cul.) a Lombard cheese; a cheese similar to 'stracchino'. -**evole** *adj.* capable of growing; allowing room for growth. -**imento** *m.* growth, growing, increase; (meteor.) -imento d'alta pressione, filling. -**itore** *m.* grower; rearer, breeder. (-**itrice** *f.*) -**iuta** *f.* growth; increase; flood-tide; see **crescita**. -**iuto** *part.* of crescere; *adj.* grown; adult; *n.m.* increasing (in knitting), casting on.

crescione *m.* (bot.) — (d'acqua), watercress, *Nasturtium officinale*.

crescita *f.* growth; period of growth; malattie della —, childhood illnesses; — dei capelli, growth of hair.

cresciuta[1] *f.* See under **crescere**.

cresciuta[2] *part. f.* of crescere, q.v.

cre·sim-a, cresim-a *f.* (liturg.) confirmation; tenere uno a —, to be someone's sponsor (godfather, godmother) at confirmation. -**are** [A1s, Rom. A1sc] *tr.* (liturg.) to confirm; †to anoint (king, emperor); *rfl.* to be confirmed. -**ando** *adj.*, *n.m.* (person) to be confirmed; confirmation candidate. (-**anda** *f.*) -**ante** *part. adj.* confirming; *n.m.* bishop who confirms. -**ato** *part. adj.* confirmed; (joc.) sticky (e.g. wineglass).

cresma *f.* See cresima.

Creso *pr.n.m.* Croesus; essere un —, to be as rich as Croesus.

†**creso** *part.* of credere, q.v.

cresolo *m.* (chem.) cresol.

cresp-a *f.* wrinkle; curl; wavelet, ripple; fold (in material), tuck; pleat; *pl.* smocking. †-**amento** *m.* curling, wrinkling. †-**are** *tr.* to curl (hair). †-**ato** *part. adj.* curled; carta -ata, crêpe paper. -**ello** *m.* dim. of crespa; wrinkle; fare -elli, to frown; crease (in gold-leaf in gilding); †fritter, waffle; -ello melato, fritter with honey. -**ezza** *f.* curliness; wrinkling.

Crespino *pr.n.m.* Crispin; patron saint of bootmakers; *excl.* Benedetto San —! (uttered when shoes do not fit); (joc.) le carceri di San —, shoes that are too tight; (bot.) barberry, *Berberis vulgaris*.

cresp-o *adj.* curly; curled; kinky; capelli -i, kinky hair, woolly hair; wrinkled; pleated; plaited; puckered; crisp; (of water) rippled; aria -a, heavy, rain-laden air; *n.m.* (text.) crêpe, crape; mourning veil; — di Cina, crêpe de chine. -**olina** *f.* dim. of crespa; (bot.) cotton-lavender, *Santolina chamaecyparissus*. -**one** *m.* (text.) crepon. -**oso**, -**uto** *adj.* wrinkled; curly.

crest-a *f.* crest, comb; crest, plume; alzare la —, to show pride; crest, ridge (of mountains); summit, peak; valore di —, peak value; crest (of a wave); (archit.) rib; (oceanog.) crest; (joc.) lady's head-dress with much ornamentation; (med.) piles; (bot.) — di gallo, yellow-rattle, *Rhinanthus crista-galli*. -**aia** *f.* (N. Ital.) milliner. -**aina** *f.* milliner's assistant. -**ato** *adj.* crested; (herald.) combed. -**ina** *f.* dim. small starched cap for waitress or parlourmaid. †-**oso** *adj.* crested; (fig.) difficult, laboured. -**uto** *adj.* crested, having a large crest.

crestomazi·a *f.* chrestomathy; anthology; collection of extracts (esp. for teaching purposes).

Cret-a[1] *pr.n.f.* (geog.) Crete. -**ense** *adj.*, *n.m.*, *f.* Cretan.

cret-a[2] *f.* chalk; clay; vessel, pot; *pl.* (geog. Tusc.) infertile clays. -**aceo** *adj.* chalky, chalk; (geol.) Cretaceous. -**oso** *adj.* chalky; (paperm.) carta -osa, coated paper, chalk overlay paper, 'make-ready' paper.

cre·tico *adj.* (prosod.) cretic; *n.m.* cretic foot.

cretin-o *m.* idiot; fool; (med.) cretin; *adj.* imbecile. -**eri·a** *f.* act of stupidity; idiotic remark; (med.) cretinism. -**ismo** *m.* (med.) cretinism; imbecility. -**o·ide** *adj.*, *n.m.*, *f.* (med.) cretinoid.

cretoso *adj.* See under **creta**[2].

crett-o *m.* crack (in a wall); flaw. -**are** [A1c] *intr.* (*aux.* avere) to crack (of a wall); to chap (of hands and lips).

cri cri *m. indecl.* (onomat.) the chirping of a grasshopper; the sound of the breaking of glass.

cri·a[1] *m.* youngest bird of a brood; the smallest and weakest of a family, cad; (of piglets) runt.

cri·a[2] *f.* (ichth.) small eel, elver.

†**cri·a**[3] *f.* (rhet.) amplification.

†**cri·a**[4] *f.* creation; (provb. Tusc.) per Santa Maria il marrone fa la —, by Our Lady's feast (Aug. 15) the chestnut begins to set (the nuts begin to form).

†**criare** *vb.* and derivs. See **creare**.

cribr-are [A1] *tr.* to sift, to sieve. (-**ato** *part. adj.*) -**azione** *f.* the separation of fluids in animal bodies.

cribr-o *m.* sieve. -**iforme** *adj.* (anat.) cribriform. -**oso** *adj.* cribrose, sieve-like.

cric *m. indecl.* (onomat.) the sound of breaking ice or glass; crack; in un —, in a jiffy; coltello a —, clasp knife; (motor.) jack.

cricca *f.* (cards) trio of three court cards or aces; clique, crew; band of suspicious characters; (typ.) piece of wood to keep the rounce in place; (metall.) crack.

cricche *m. indecl.* (onomat., Tusc.). See **cric**.

cricchiare [A4] *intr.* (*aux.* avere) to creak; to crackle.

cric·chio *m.* creak, crack.

cric-co *m.* (*pl.* -**chi**) hand-jack (for raising weights); (naut.) launching jack; (motor.) jack; coltello a —, clasp knife; (watchm.) molla del —, click spring.

criceto *m.* (zool.) hamster, *Cricetus* sp.

crich *m. indecl.* (onomat.). See **cric**.

crico·id-e *f.* (anat.) cricoid cartilage. -**e·o** *adj.* cricoid.

Crime·a *pr.n.f.* (geog.) Crimea.

crimenlese *m.* (leg.) high treason.

criminal-e *adj.* (leg.) criminal; codice —, criminal code; legge —, criminal law; causa —, criminal prosecution; action; tribunale —, criminal court; processo —, criminal trial; manicomio —, criminal lunatic asylum; *n.m.*, *f.* criminal. -**mente** *adv.* criminally. -**ista** *m.* (leg.) criminal lawyer. -**ità** *f. indecl.* criminality; la -ità è in aumento, crime is on the increase.

cri·min-e *f.* (leg.) crime, felony; *m.* crime; accusation. -**ologi·a** *f.* criminology. -**osità** *f.* guiltiness; criminality. -**oso** *adj.* criminal.

†**crimo** *m.*, †**cri·molo** *m.* parting in the hair.

†**crina** *f.* See **crine**.

crinale *adj.*, *n.m.* See under **crine**.

crin-e *m.* mane; horsehair; (poet.) hair, tresses, locks; tail of a comet; irradiation from a star; ridge (of a mountain). -**ale** *adj.* pertaining to hair; *n.m.* large comb or pin for a woman's hair; (geog.) ridge, watershed. †-**ata** *f.* name.

crinella *f.* (ent.) *Tineola biselliella*, a kind of clothes moth.

criniera *f.* mane; horsehair plume on a helmet; (hist.) armour for a horse's neck; tail of a comet; mountain ridge.

crinito *adj.* (poet.) maned; with flowing hair; stella crinita, comet; (herald.) crined.

crin-o *m.* horsehair for stuffing cushions, mattresses, etc.; a single hair from a horse's mane or tail; — vegetale, vegetable fibre (used instead of horsehair); †hair; †coat (of an animal); †ridge, mountain top. -**uto** *adj.* with flowing mane.

crino·idi *m.pl.* (zool.) crinoids; sea lilies and feather stars.

crinolina *f.* crinoline; hoop-petticoat.

criocera *f.* (ent.) — dell'asparago, asparagus beetle, *Crioceris asparagi*; — del giglio, *C. merdigera*.

cri-ofrantumazione *f.* (geog.) frost shattering. -**ogeno** *m.* (chem.) cryogen, freezing-mixture. -**olite** *f.* (miner.) cryolite. -**onivale** *adj.* (geog.) caused by freeze-thaw action, cryergetic.

cripta *f.* (eccl.; archit.) crypt.

cripto *m.* See **cripton**.

criptocomunista *m.*, *f.* cryptocommunist.

cript-o·gama *m.* see **crittogama**. -**ografi·a** *f.* see **crittografia**.

cripton *m. indecl.* (chem.) krypton.

criptopor·tico *m.* (archit.) cryptoporticus.

crisa·lide *f.* (ent.) chrysalis, pupa.

crisantemo, crisan·temo *m.* (bot.) chrysanthemum.

crisaora *f.* (zool.) *Chrysaora mediterranea*, a poisonous jelly-fish.

criselefantino *adj.* (archaeol.) chryselephantine.

crisi *f.* crisis; — ministeriale, cabinet crisis; in —, in a state of crisis; — di pianto, outburst of crying; attack, fit; — nervosa, nervous breakdown; (slang) donna —, fashionably thin woman; slump; shortage; — delle abitazioni, housing problem, shortage of houses.

crisma *m.* (liturg.) chrism; sacrament in which chrism is used, esp. confirmation; (fig.) sanction; — ufficiale, official approval; con tutti i crismi della legge, fully sanctioned by the law.

cris·oba·lano *m.* (bot.) coco plum, a West Indian fruit, *Chrysobalanus icaco*. **-oberillo** *m.* (miner.) chrysoberyl. **-ocalco** *m.* bronze; alloy in imitation of gold. **-ocolla** *f.* chrysocolla. **-o·coma** *m.* (bot.) goldilocks, *Linosyris vulgaris*. **-ografato** *adj.* (art) in chrysography. **-ografi·a** *f.* (art) chrysography. **-o·lito** *m.* (miner.) chrysolite. **-o·melo** *m.* (bot.) name of varieties of quince and peach. **-opa** *f.* (ent.) golden-eye, *Chrysopa* spp. **-opra·ş(i)o, -opra·zio** *m.* chrysoprase. **-orre·a** *f.* (ent.) *Euproctis chrysorrhoea*, gold tail moth. **-o·tile** *m.* (miner.) chrysotile.

Criso·stomo *pr.n.m.* Chrysostom.

cristall-a·io, -aro *m.* glass-worker; glass-blower; dealer in glassware. **-ame** *m.* glassware, crystal. **-eggiare** [A 3 c] *intr.* (*aux.* avere) to shine like crystal. **-eri·a** *f.* glassware factory; glassware shop; glassware; crystal ware. **-ino** *adj.* crystalline; crystal; acqua -ina, crystal-clear water; (bot.) erba -ina, ice-plant, *Cryophytum crystalinum*; *n.m.* (anat.; zool.) crystalline lens (of the eye); (glassm.) second-grade crystal.

cristallizz-are [A 1] *tr.* to crystallize, to cause to become crystallized; *intr.* (*aux.* essere), *rfl.* to become crystallized, to crystallize; (fig.) to grow old and unadaptable, to become fossilized. **-a·bile** *adj.* crystallizable. **-ato** *part. adj.* crystallized; (paperm.) carta -ata, ice paper; (fig.) fossilized, unadaptable. **-azione** *f.* crystallization; crystallizing.

cristall-o *m.* glass; pane; clock-glass, watch-glass; lens; wineglass; looking-glass; crystal; cut glass; (motor.) headlamp; — di rocca, rock crystal; — marmoreo, white cornelian; (poet.) star; crystal-clear water; pure soul. **-ografi·a** *f.* crystallography. **-o·grafo** *m.* crystallographer. **-o·ide** *f.* crystalloid or crystalline body, crystalloid; (bot.) see 'erba cristallina', under **cristallaio**; *adj.* (chem.) crystalloid.

cristiana *f.* See under **cristiano**.

cristia·nia *f.* (sport, skiing) Christiania, Christy.

cristian-o *adj.* Christian; *n.m.* Christian; far —, to be godfather to; (colloq.) human being; ogni fedel —, anyone whatsoever; ora da -i, reasonable hour, Christian hour; maniere da -i, civilized behaviour; cibo da -i, decent food; †husband. **-a** *f.* Christian woman; †wife. **-ac·cio** *m. pejor.* bad Christian; (colloq.) buon -accio, decent fellow, kind-hearted man. **-amẹnte** *adv.* in a Christian way, like a Christian; (colloq.) respectably, decently, tolerably, pretty well. **-are** [A 1] *rfl.* to become a Christian. **-eggiare** [A 3 c] *intr.* (*aux.* avere) to talk or behave very much like a Christian; to show Christian tendencies; to approach Christian standards; to be a near-Christian. **-ello** *m. dim.* poor sort of Christian; (colloq.) ignorant person; simple-minded worthy. **-ęsimo** *m.* Christianity; †Christendom. **-ificare** [A 2 s] *tr.* to convert to Christianity. **†-ismo** *m.* see **cristianesimo**. **-is·simo** *superl. adj.* (hist.) Most Christian (King of France). **-ità** *f.* Christendom; Christianity; Christian status or behaviour (of an individual). **-iẓẓare** [A 1] *tr.* to make Christian, to convert to Christianity. **(-iẓẓato** *part. adj.*) **-ọne** *m. augm.* (colloq.) big fellow.

Crist-o *pr.n.m.* Christ (seldom used of Our Lord before the Passion; thus 'the infant Christ' is 'Gesù Bambino'); avanti —, B.C.; dopo —, A.D.; segnato da —, afflicted (with some visible deformity); un — in croce, crucifix, picture of the Crucifixion, haggard or worn-out person; povero —, poor wretch; non c'è — che tenga, there's no help for it, there's no way out; †*adj.* anointed. **-ologi·a** *f.* (theol.) Christology. **-olo·gico** *adj.* (theol.) Christological. **-o·logo** *m.* Christologist.

cristobalite *f.* (miner.) cristobalite.

Cristo·foro *pr.n.m.* Christopher.

crite·rio *m.* norm; standard; yardstick; good judgement, common sense; criterion.

crite·rium *m. indecl.* (racing) race in which young horses show their form.

cri·tic-a *f.* criticism; critical judgement; critics; review; blame, censure; (philos.) critique. **-are** [A 2 s] *tr.* to criticize; to censure; to examine critically. **-ante** *part. adj.* criticizing, critical; *n.m., f.* grumbler. **-ato** *part. adj.* criticized; censured; reviewed. (**†-atore** *m.* **†-atrice** *f.* **†-azione** *f.*)

cri·ti-co *adj.* critical; crucial; ticklish, risky; censorious; età -ca della donna, menopause; *n.m.* critic; reviewer. **-castro** *m. pejor.* inferior critic. **-chẹsimo** *m.* (joc.) bevy of critics. **-cişmo** *m.* (philos.) criticism, esp. in Kantian sense; critical attitude. **-cọne** *m. augm.* of **critico**; great critic; critical person; (fam.) grumbler, discontented person. **-cọnzolo** *m. dim. pejor.* of **critico**.

critta *f.* (eccl.) (archit.) crypt; (archit.) grotto; cellar; (anat.) crypt, secretory cavity.

critt-o·gama *f.* (bot.) fungus which attacks the vine, *Uncinula necator*. **-o·gamo** *m.* (bot.) cryptogam. **-ografi·a** *f.* cryptography, cipher, code writing. **-ogra·fico** *adj.* cryptographical, in code. **-o·grafo** *m.* cryptographer. **-ogramma** *m.* cryptogram. **-onomi·a** *f.* use of a nom-de-plume. **-opor·tico** *m.* (archit.) see **criptoportico**.

crivell-are [A 1] *tr.* to sieve, to sift; to strain; to screen; to riddle with holes; — di pallottole, to riddle with bullets. **-ato** *part. adj.* sieved; sifted; riddled. (**-atore** *m.*) **-atura** *f.* sifting; what remains after sifting, residue. **-azione** *f.* screening, sifting, riddling.

crivell-o *m.* sieve; screening machine; (mus.) pipe-rack (of organ). **-a·io** *m.* sieve-maker. **-ọne** *m. augm.* of **crivello**; coarse, open cloth.

croato *adj.*, *n.m.* Croat, Croatian.

Croa·zia *pr.n.f.* (geog.) Croatia.

crocca *f.* crutch.

crocc-are [A 2] *intr.* (*aux.* avere) to crack, to give a cracked sound. **-ante** *part. adj.* crisp, crackling; *n.m.* almond cake; almond sweetmeat.

crocchẹtta *f.* (cul.) croquette.

crocchẹtto *m. dim.* See under **crocco**.

croc·chia[1] *f.* chignon, bun in the neck.

croc·chia[2] *f.* blow, stroke, hit.

†croc·chia[3] *f.* street song, crude ballad.

crocchi-are [A 4] *intr.* (*aux.* avere) to give a cracked sound on being tapped; to sound cracked; to rattle (of a loose horseshoe); non gli -a il ferro, he is by no means weak; to be in poor health, to be cracking up; to crack one's joints; to creak; to cluck; to chatter; *tr.* to 'ring', to 'sound', to tap for sound.

crocchiata *f.* See under **crocchio**[2].

croc·chio[1] *m.* cracked sound.

croc·chi-o[2] *m.* group, circle, knot of persons; andare a —, to talk in a little group; stare a (in) —, to sit chatting; tener —, to hold forth in a little group. **-ata** *f.* chatter, gossip. **-ẹtto** *m. dim.* little group. **-ọne** *m.* chatterbox; gossip.

croc·cia *f.* crutch; †(eccl. hist.) *crocea*, dress formerly worn by cardinals in conclave.

croc·co *m.* (*pl.* -chi) hook; hook for bending a crossbow; gaff used in tunny-fishing. **-chẹtto** *m. dim.* hook.

croccol-are [A 1 s] *intr.* (*aux.* avere) to cackle; to gurgle (of a liquid coming out of a bottle), to go 'glug-glug'. **-ọne** *m.* (orn.) great snipe, *Capella media*.

crọc-e *f.* cross; in —, crosswise; testa o —?, heads or tails?; (rel.) cross, rood; Invenzione della —, Finding, Invention, of the Cross (feast of 3 May); mettere in —, to crucify, (fig.) to distress; stare in —, to be crucified, (fig.) to be in pain or trouble; bandire la —, to proclaim a crusade; (fig.) gridare la — addosso a uno, to persecute someone, to rouse feeling against him; — latina, Latin cross; — greca, Greek cross; — di sant'Andrea, St Andrew's cross; — uncinata, swastika; farsi la —, to cross oneself; fare un segno di —, to make the sign of the cross; (fig.) fare una — sopra un debito, to cancel a debt; fateci una —, forget about it, think no more about it; fare, spaccare una —, to sign with a cross; trial, affliction (to be accepted willingly); quel ragazzo è la mia —, that boy is the bane of my life; portar la sua —, to bear one's cross; santa —, — santa, primer, ABC, beginning with a cross; rifarsi dalla santa —, to begin again from the beginning; La Croce Rossa, Red Cross; doppia —, symbol of the association for the prevention of tuberculosis; a occhio e —, approximately, roughly; levare uno spicchio di — ad alcuno, to offend someone; (astron.) — del Sud, Southern Cross; battere in —, to subject to cross-fire; punto in —, cross-stitch; braccia in —, arms folded; (herald.) — doppia, double cross, Lorraine cross; (naut.) — delle

croc·e (*cont.*)

catene, crossed cables; in —, squared yards; (typ.) dagger, obelus. **-ellina** *f. dim.* of **croce**; cross, small cross to wear round the neck. (See also **crocetta**.)

crocefisso *m.* See **crocifisso**.

cro·ceo *adj.* saffron-coloured.

crocera *f.* See **crociera**.

†croceri·a *f.* army of crusaders.

crocerossina *f.* Red Cross nurse (voluntary).

crocesanta *f.* See 'santa croce' or 'croce santa', under **croce**.

croce-segnato, -signato *adj.* marked with a cross; *n.m.* crusader.

crocett·a *f. dim.* of **croce**; little cross; fare -e, to have nothing to eat; (herald.) cross couped, crosslet couped; *pl.* (naut.) cross-trees which together with the trestle-trees carry the top; -e minori, simple cross-trees where there are no trestle-trees and no top; -e di velaccino, fore cross-trees; -e di gran velaccio, main cross-trees; -e di belvedere, mizzen cross-trees. **-o** *m.* locksmith's square file.

crocevi·a *m.* cross-roads; (fig.) un — della vita, a cross-roads in one's life.

crociabilità *f.* (biol.). See under **crociare**.

†crociame *m.* (naut.) the span of the yards; the whole complex of a ship's yards.

croci·are [A 3] *tr.* to mark with a cross; to give the cross to (a crusader); (biol.) to cross; *rfl.* (hist.) to take the cross, to join a crusade. **-abilità** *f.* (biol.) crossability. **-amento** *m.* crossing; (rlwy.) frog. **-ata** *f.* crusade; levy for crusade; cross-roads; (archit.) crossing (of transepts and nave in a church). **-ato** *part. adj.* in form of a cross; wearing a cross; crusading; (biol.) crossed; (herald.) surmounted with a cross; *n.m.* crusader.

crocic·chio *m.* criss-cross of little streets intersecting; cross-roads.

crocid·are [A 2 s] *intr.* (*aux.* avere) to croak, to caw. **-amento** *m.* croaking, cawing; croak, caw.

crocidolite *f.* (miner.) crocidolite, blue asbestos, cope blue.

crocier·a *f.* arrangement in the form of a cross; cross-bar; crossing place; bandeau worn over the ears held in place by straps which cross over the head; (archit.) transepts (sometimes including the choir); intersecting ridges of a vault; volta a —, vault with pointed arches; (eng.) spider, cross, cross journal; (typ.) intersection; (astron.) Southern Cross; (naut.) cruise; search; waters or cruising grounds; pleasure cruise; andare in —, to go on a cruise; (mil.) battere per —, to cross fire; (aeron.) long-distance flight; velocità di —, cruising speed; — economica, weak-mixture cruising. **-e** *m.* (orn.) crossbill, *Loxia curvirostra*; (astron.) Southern Cross. **-ista** *m., f.* passenger on a pleasure cruise.

croci·fero *m.* (eccl.) cross-bearer, crucifer; *pl.* the Camillian Attendants of the Sick; (astron.) Southern Cross.

crocifig·g·ere [C 17] *tr.* to crucify; (fig.) to torture, to harass, to vex; (joc.) to give (someone) the cross of an order, to make (him) a knight. **†-imento** *m.* crucifixion.

crocifiss·a·io *m.* maker or seller of crucifixes. **-ione** *f.* crucifixion.

crocifiss·o *part.* of **crocifiggere**, q.v.; *adj.* crucified; *n.m.* il —, the Crucified, Christ crucified; crucifix. **-ore** *m.* crucifier.

crociforme *adj.* cruciform, cross-shaped; *adv.* crosswise.

crocile *m.* standard with its cross-pieces helping to support a rope as it is being made.

crocina (bot.) *adj.* erba —, vervain, *Verbena officinalis*.

crocino *m.* (agric.) small late cabbage.

†crocitare *vb.* See **crocidare**.

cro·co *m.* (*pl.* **-chi**) (bot.) crocus; saffron. **-coite, -coisite** *f.* (miner.) crocoite, chrome yellow. **-cota** *f.* (Gk. antiq.) saffron-hued robe.

crod·a *f.* (N.E. Alps) rock face, crag. **-ai(u)olo** *m.* rock climber.

crogiolare [A 1 s] *tr.* to roast gently; to anneal; *rfl.* to make oneself very comfortable, to take one's ease; to savour to the full (a comfortable bed, or delightful situation, etc.); to wallow in blissful luxury.

cro·giolo *m.* cooking at a gentle heat; (fig.) pigliare il —, to toast oneself gently (by the fire, or in the sun); annealing; acciaio al —, crucible steel.

crogi(u)olo *m.* crucible.

†cro·io *adj.* hard, unyielding; intractable; rough, coarse; uncouth; sulky; cruel; shameful.

croll·are [A 1] *tr.* to shake; — le spalle, to shrug one's shoulders; — il capo, to toss one's head; *intr.* (*aux.* essere) to totter; to collapse; to fall in ruins, to tumble down; to crumble; to give

way. **-amento** *m.* collapse, ruin; downfall. **-ante** *part. adj.* shaky. **-ata** *f.* shake; toss; shrug.

crollo *m.* shake; collapse; heavy blow; downfall; dar il — a, to overthrow, to ruin, to upset; dare il — alla bilancia, to turn the scale.

crom·a *f.* (mus.) quaver; (opt.) chroma. **-a·metro** *m.* (mus.) apparatus for piano-tuning. **-a·tico** *m.* (bot.) kind of yellow edible fungus, chanterelle, *Cantharellus cibarius*; *adj.* (mus.) chromatic; corno -atico, valve horn; senso -atico, colour sense; non aver senso -atico, to be colour-blind. **-aticamente** *adv.* (mus.) chromatically. **-a·tidi** *m.pl.* (biol.) chromatids. **-atina** *f.* brown boot polish; (biol.) chromatin. **-atismo** *m.* (paint.) excessive coloration; exaggerated colouring; (mus.) chromaticism. **-atista** *m.* chromaticist. **-atizzare** [A 1] *tr.* to chromaticize.

crom·are [A 1] *tr.* to chrome, to chromium plate. **-ato** *part. adj.* chromium plated; (leather) chromed, chrome tanned; *n.m.* (chem.) chromate. **-atura** *f.* chroming, chromium plating.

†cro·mate *m.* (mus.) a modification of diatonic music.

cromat·o·fobo *adj.* (med.) achromatophilic. **-o·foro** *m.* (biol.) chromatophore.

cromatografi·a *f.* (chem.) chromatography, chromatographic analysis; — su carta, paper chromatography.

cro·m·ico *adj.* (chem.) chromic. **-ite** *f.* (miner.) chromite, chrome iron ore.

crom·o *m.* (chem.) chromium, chrome; carta —, chromo paper. **-ocrisolitografi·a** *f.* colour and gilt lithography. **-o·foro** *m.* (chem.) chromophore. **-ofotografi·a** *f.* colour photography. **-o·geno** *m.* chromogenic. **-ografi·a** *f.* study of colours. **-olitografi·a** *f.* colour lithography, chromolithography; chromolithograph. **-olito·gra·fico** *adj.* chromolithographic. **-omero** *m.* (biol.) chromomere. **-oplasti** *m.pl.* (biol.) chromoplast. **-osco·pio** *m.* (telev.) chromoscope, colour-picture tube. **-osfera** *f.* (astron.) chromosphere. **-osoma** *m.* (biol.) chromosome. **-otipografi·a** *f.* colour printing. **-otipogra·fico** *adj.* pertaining to colour printing.

cromorno *m.* (mus.) crumhorn; cremona (organ-stop).

cro·na·ca *f.* chronicle; current gossip; local events recorded in a newspaper; news items; society news; police reports; — nera, crime news; — sportiva, sporting news; — teatrale, theatre news; notizia di —, news item; fatti di —, events which can be reported in a news item; — scandalosa, *chronique scandaleuse*; (radio; telev.) commentary, account; (fig.) public opinion, general opinion. **-chista** *m.* chronicler; newspaper diarist.

cro·nica *f.* See **cronaca**.

cro·nic·o *adj.* chronic; incurable; *n.m.* incurable patient; ospedale per i -i, hospital for incurables. (**-a** *f.*) **-amente** *adv.* chronically. **-icismo** *m.* chronic condition. **-icità** *f.* chronic condition, chronicity.

cron-ista *m.* chronicler; diarist; reporter; (radio; telev.) commentator. **-isto·ria** *f.* history related in chronological order of events; chronicle.

crono *m.* (naut.) — indicatore meccanico, range clock.

cron-ografi·a *f.* chronography. **-ogra·fico** *adj.* chronographical. **-o·grafo** *m.* chronographer; chronicler; chronograph. **-ogramma** *m.* chronogram. **-ologi·a** *f.* chronology. **-olo·gico** *adj.* chronological. (**-amente** *adv.*) **-ologista, -o·logo** *m.* chronologist. **-ometrag·gio** *m.* (sport) time-keeping; (industr.) time and motion study. **-ometrare** [A 1 s] *tr.* to time to within a fraction of a second. **-ometri·a** *f.* chronometry, timing, time-keeping. **-ometrista** *m.* (sport) time-keeper. **-o·metro** *m.* chronometer; (mus.) metronome; (sport) stopwatch; tappa a -ometro, timed lap or stage. **-osco·pio** *m.* chronoscope.

crosciare [A 3] *intr.* (*aux.* avere) to make a continuous splashing noise; to gurgle; to rattle; to roar (of water, or applause); to splutter; to bubble; to hiss (e.g. of wet wood burning); *impers.* (*aux.* essere) to rain hard, to pelt, to pour; *tr.* to rattle on, to strike.

cro·scio *m.* gurgling; rattling; hissing; hiss; splash; — di applausi, roar of applause; — di risa, outburst of laughter.

cross *m. indecl.* (soccer) cross-pass, centre; cross-country race.

crossopo *m.* (zool.) *Crossopus fodiens*, a kind of water shrew.

crost·a *f.* crust; rind; la — terrestre, the earth's crust; (agric.) unploughed land; incrustation; scab; — lattea, milk scab; shell (of a crustacean); superficial meaning; (cul.) pie crust; (sculpt.) investment; (tanning) crust; (joc.) bad painting, daub. **-ello** *m.* (geog.) pancake ice. **-oso** *adj.* crusty; horny; scab-like, scabby. **-uto** *adj.* crusty, scabby; incrusted.

crosta·ceo *m.* (zool.) crustacean.

crost-are [A I] *tr.* (cul.) to brown, to crust. **-ata** *f.* tart; -ata di mele, apple tart, apple pie. **-atina** *f. dim.* tartlet.

crostello *m.* (geog.). See under **crosta**.

crost-ino *m.* small piece of toast; fried bread served with *hors d'œuvres* or savoury; (joc.) person who walks stiffly.

crost-oso *adj.*, **-uto** *adj.* See under **crosta**.

crota·fit-e, -o *m.* (anat.) temporal muscle.

cro·tali *m.pl.* (mus.) antique cymbals.

cro·talo *m.* (zool.) rattlesnake, *Crotalus* spp.

croton-e *m.* (bot.) *Croton*, tropical genus of plants. **-ti·glio** *m.* (bot.) croton oil plant, *Croton tiglium*; (pharm.) croton oil.

†crovatta *f.* See **cravatta**.

crovello *m.* wine from grapes which have fermented but have not been pressed; (ichth.) *Sciaena cirrhosa*, a kind of sea-perch.

cruc·cia *f.* (agric.) dibber; dibble for setting vine cuttings; crutch-shaped perch for a captive owl.

crucc-iare [A 3] *tr.* to vex, to torment; *rfl.* to be very vexed, to be annoyed; to be worried; to be distressed; to fret; to distress oneself; to torment oneself. **-iamento** *m.* annoyance, vexation. **-iato** *part. adj.* distressed; vexed, annoyed, angry. **-iatamente** *adv.* vexedly, angrily.

crucc-io *m.* mental or bodily suffering; worry, distress; vexation, anger, annoyance, resentment. **-oso** *adj.* angry, vexed. **-osamente** *adv.* angrily.

cruciale *adj.* crucial.

cruci-are [A 3] *tr.* to torment; to torture. **-amento** *m.* dire torment; torture. **-azione** *f.* torment, vexation.

cruci·fero *adj.* See **crocifero**.

crucifige (Lat. *imp.*) crucify (him)!; (fig.) gridar — contro uno, to cry out against someone, to revile someone.

crucifig·gere [C 17]. See **crocifiggere**.

cruciforme *adj.* cross-shaped, cruciform.

cruciverba *m. indecl.* crossword puzzle.

crudamente *adv.* See under **crudo**.

crudel-e *adj.* cruel; harsh; grievous; bitter, sore, painful; *n.m., f.* cruel person. **†-ezza** *f.*, **†-ità** *f.* See **crudeltà**. **-mente** *adv.* cruelly; grievously; sorely, bitterly. **-tà** *f.* cruelty; harshness; grievousness.

†crudero *adj.* See **crudele**.

crud-ezza *f.* rawness, roughness; harshness; crudity; immaturity; hardness (of water); (paint.) crudeness, roughness; †hardness, cruelty. **-ità** *f.* rawness, roughness; crudity; †(med.) indigestion.

crudi·voro *adj.* flesh-eating, eating raw meat; fierce, cruel.

crud-o *adj.* raw, uncooked; carne -a, raw meat; unbaked (of bricks, pottery, etc.); immature, unripe; harsh, cruel; crude; rough; unploughed; undigested; nudo e —, destitute; parlare nudo e —, to speak in a rough and ready way; farne di cotte e di -e, to be up to all sorts of tricks; la verità nuda e -a, the unvarnished truth; acqua -a, hard water; ferro —, pig iron; seta -a, rough silk (e.g. shantung); (paint.) crude, rough, hard. **-amente** *adv.* harshly; crudely; roughly; cruelly. **-igno** *adj.* somewhat raw; undercooked, rare. **-olezza** *f.* toughness, rawness.

cruentemente *adv.* (med.) surgically.

cruento *adj.* bloody, sanguinary; ferocious, warlike; blood-stained; fearful, dreadful.

†crullare *vb.* See **crollare**.

crumiro *m.* blackleg, strike-breaker.

cruna *f.* eye (of a needle).

cruor-e *m.* (med.) cruor; gore. **-oso** *adj.* gory.

crup *m. indecl.* (med.) croup. **-ale** *adj.* (med.) croupous.

crur-ale *adj.* (anat.) crural. **†-ifra·gio** *m.* leg-fracture.

crusc-a *f.* chaff, bran; vendere più la — che la farina, to have more lovers in old age than in youth; la farina del diavolo se ne va in —, ill-gotten gains turn to ashes in the mouth; freckles; (lit. hist.) the Accademia della Crusca, a Florentine Academy, founded in 1583, which took this name, and a bolting sieve for its emblem, to show its function of separating good linguistic usage from bad; Vocabolario della Crusca, la Crusca, the dictionary of Italian published by the Academy; parlare in —, to talk pedantically; scrivere colla — in mano, to write with affected purism. **-a·io, -ai(u)olo** *m.* bran seller; pedant. **-ante** *adj.* belonging to the Crusca Academy; pedantic; *n.m.* the language of the Crusca Academy; a member of the Crusca Academy. **-ata** *f.* a piece of writing for the Crusca Academy; meeting of the Crusca Academy.

cruscheggiare [A 3 c] *intr.* (*aux.* avere) to affect great purity of language (cf. **crusca**, Accademia della).

crus-chello *m. dim.* of **crusca**, q.v.; bran of the second sifting; pollard. **-cherella** *f.*, **-cherello** *m.* see **cruschello**; game of looking for coins in bran; lucky-dip. **-chesco** *adj.* (*m.pl.* -cheschi) pertaining to the Crusca Academy. **-chevole** *adj.* (joc.) suitable to the Crusca Academy. **-chevolmente** *adv.* in accordance with the rules of the Crusca Academy. **-chino** *m.* workman who sifts flour from bran. **-cone** *m. augm.* of **crusca**, q.v.; coarse bran; (joc.) member of the Crusca Academy. **-coso** *adj.* full of bran; freckled.

cruscotto *m.* leather apron fastened to a splash-board or mudguard; dashboard; instrument panel.

†crusero *m.* (astron.) Southern Cross.

crusta·ceo *m.* See **crostaceo**.

crust-e *f.pl.* (art) encrusted figures (decorating vases). **-a·rio** *m.* (art) modeller of 'cruste'.

cruzero *m.* (Ven.) (astron.) Southern Cross.

cteniza *f.* (zool.) trapdoor spider, *Cteniza* spp.

cuba¹ *f.* (archit.) cupola, dome; (hist.) ancient castle in Palermo; (dyeing) legno di —, fustic.

Cub-a² *pr.n.f.* (geog.) Cuba. **-ano** *adj.*, *n.m.* Cuban. (**-ana** *f.*)

cub-are¹ *intr.* (*aux.* essere) to lie, to rest. **-ato** *part. adj.* lying down; essere mal -ato, to be seriously ill.

cub-are² *tr.* (math.) to cube; to raise to the third power; to determine the cubic capacity of; to find the volume of. **-a·bile** *adj.* that may be cubed. **-ato** *part. adj.* cubed. **-atura** *f.* (mens.) measuring the cubic capacity of a solid; cubic capacity.

cub-atto, -at·tolo *m.* basket trap for taking birds in time of snow.

cubeb-e *m.* (bot.) cubeb(s), the dried unripe fruit of *Piper cubeba*, used medicinally. **-ina** *f.* (chem.) cubebin.

cubi·a *f.* (naut.) hawse-pipe.

cu·bic-a *f.* (math.; eng.) cubic curve. **-o** *adj.* (math.) cubic, cubical; radice -a, cube root; equazione -a, cubic equation; dilatazione -a, cubic expansion; pollice —, cubic inch. **-are** [A 2 s] *tr.* (math.) to cube. **-ato** *part. adj.* (math.) cubed. **-azione** *f.* (math.) cubing.

cubi·col-o *m.* (hist.) cubiculum, cubicle, bed-chamber; solitary cell. **-a·rio** *m.* (hist.) cubicular, bed-chamber servant.

cubi·culo *m.* and derivs. See **cubicolo**.

cubiforme *adj.* cube-shaped, cubic; *n.m.* (anat.) cuboid bone.

†cubile *m.* See **covile**.

cubilotto *m.* (metall.) cupola, cupola furnace.

Cub-ismo *m.* (paint.) Cubism. **-ista** *m., f.* cubist artist.

cubitale *adj.* a cubit long; lettere cubitali, letters a foot high, big block capitals; very large; (anat.) cubital.

cu·bito *m.* (poet.) elbow; forearm; (anat.) ulna; (mens.) cubit.

cub-o *m.* (math.) cube; elevare al —, to cube; (aeron.) — dell'elica, propeller boss; *adj.* cubic; metro —, cubic metre. **-icini** *m.pl.* educational building blocks.

cubo·ide *adj.* cuboid; *n.m.* (anat.) cuboid bone.

Cuccagna *pr.n.f.* (myth.) Cockaigne; Paese di —, Land of Plenty, Land of Pleasure; unexpected stroke of good fortune; merriment, high jinks; godere —, fare —, to have a good time, to be on easy street; giuoco della —, sport of climbing a greasy pole for prizes at the top of it; albero della —, greasy pole, *or* Christmas tree.

cucc-are [A 2] *tr.* (fam.) to take in, to humbug; (agric.) to prune right back; *rfl.* (*dat.* of *prn.* 'si') to enjoy; -arsi una cosa, to delight in something; (*prep.* di) to put up (with), to make the best (of).

cuccetta *f.* berth, couchette; bunk.

cucchia·i-a *f.* ladle; scoop (of a dredger). **-ata** *f.* spoonful. **-o** *m.* spoon; da raccattarsi col -o, to be dropping with fatigue; spoonful; scraper. **-olo** *m.* bricklayer's trowel. **-one** *m. augm.* of **cucchiaio** tablespoon; soup-ladle; (foundry) ladle.

cucchiaino *m. dim.* of **cucchiaio**; coffee-spoon; teaspoon; — raso, level teaspoonful; — abbondante, heaped teaspoonful.

cucchiara *f.* See **cucchiaia**; (naut.) dredger.

cuc·cia¹ *f.* resting-place, bed; dog's bed, basket; cat's basket; — per i polli, roosting-place for fowls; — di calce, bed of lime; (to a dog) a —!, to your basket!; lap-dog.

cuc·cia² *f.* (Palermo) sweet made for St Lucy's day (13 December) of wheat grains, milk, sugar and cinnamon.

cucciare [A 3] *intr.* (*aux.* avere) to curl up and lie down; (to a dog) cuccia! down!

†cuc·cio *m.* puppy; simpleton.

cuc·ciolo *m.* puppy, pup, whelp; simple-minded lad; *pr.n.m.* Italian name of the smallest of the Seven Dwarfs (Disney); a kind of motor-driven bicycle.

cucciotto *m.* baby's dummy.

cucc-o *m.* favourite, pet; il — della mamma, mother's darling; il — della veglia, the butt of the company; (fig.) stupid person; vecchio —, doddering old fool; (infant.) egg, 'chucky-egg'; cuckoo; vecchio come il —, as old as the hills. **-obeone** *m.* dressed-up bogey.

cuccù *m. indecl.* cuckoo; orologio a —, cuckoo clock; fare —, to play peek-a-boo.

cuccuino¹ *m.* (orn.). See **cuculo**.

†cuccuino² *m.* jug for coffee or hot chocolate.

cuc·cuma *f.* coffee-pot; kettle; (slang) topknot, doughnut; rompere la —, to break one's head; anger, rage; (fam.) aver la —, to be in a rage; (bot.) zedoary, the rootstock of *Curcuma zedoaria*.

cuccumeggiare [A 3 c] *intr.* (*aux.* avere) to be coquettish or flirtatious.

†cuccurucù *onomat.* cock-a-doodle-doo.

cuccutret·tola *f.* (orn.). See **cutrettola**.

cucicchiare [A 4] *tr.*, *intr.* (*aux.* avere) to sew badly or unwillingly.

cucin-a *f.* kitchen; (naut.) galley; cuisine, style of cooking; cookery; libro di —, cookery book; — casalinga, plain home cooking; — francese, French cooking; fare (di) —, to cook; cooking-stove; — a gas, gas cooker; — elettrica, electric cooker; — economica, kitchen range; soup kitchen. **-a·rio** *adj.* kitchen; culinary. **-ella**, **-ętta** *f. dim.* small kitchen, kitchenette. **-iera** *f.* cook (see note on **cuciniere**). **-iere** *m.* cook; chef (**cuciniere** is only used of the cook in a religious order or other institution; a man-cook in a private house is **cuoco**, but a woman-cook anywhere may be termed **cuciniera** as well as **cuoca**); cookery book. **†-o** *m.* cooked food, food.

cucin-are [A 1] *tr.* to cook; to prepare; (joc.) to 'cook up'; to 'fix', to 'settle', to 'deal with him'; se non fa il suo dovere, lo **-erò io**, if he doesn't do as he ought, I'll settle him. **-a·bile** *adj.* fit to be cooked. (**-atore** *m.* **-atora** *f.* **-atrice** *f.*) **-atura** *f.* cooking; cookery.

†cucino¹ *m.* See under **cucina**.

†cucino² *m.* See **cuscino**.

cuc-ire [D 1] *tr.*, *intr.* (*aux.* avere) to sew; to stitch; to tack; to join together; (surg.) to suture; — una ferita, to put stitches in a wound; (fig.) to cheat; to double-cross; — la bocca a, to stop the mouth of; macchina da —, sewing-machine; ago da —, sewing needle. **-irino** *adj.* for sewing, suitable for sewing; filato **-irino**, sewing thread; *n.m.* needle-case; *pl.* things needed for sewing, sewing materials. **-ito** *part. adj.* sewn, stitched; darned; clinker-built; (fig.) bocca **-ita**, sealed lips; stitched together; luoghi comuni **-iti** insieme, platitudes strung together; *n.m.* sewing (the action and the material); lavoro di **-ito**, sewing, needlework. **-itoio** *m.* stitching frame. **-itora** *f.* seamstress, needlewoman. **-itore** *m.* sewer, stitcher. **-itrice** *f.* seamstress, needlewoman; sewing-machine; stapler; (bookb.; shoem.) stitching machine. **-itura** *f.* sewing; stitching; seam; calze senza **-itura**, seamless stockings; (med.) suture.

cuci·tolo *m.* (bot.) common horsetail, *Equisetum arvense*.

cu·colo *m.* (orn.). See **cuculo**.

cucù *onomat.* cuckoo (the sound); *excl.* expressing disbelief; far —, to play peep-bo.

cucu·balo *m.* (bot.) berry catchfly, *Cucubalus baccifer* and other similar plants.

cuculi-are [A 4] *tr.* to laugh at, to mock. **†-e·vole** *adj.* mocking, bantering.

cuculi·o *m.* (orn.). See **cuculo**.

cucull-a *f.* (eccl.) cowl. **-ifọrme** *adj.* (bot.) cucullate, hooded. **-o** *m.* (eccl.) hood.

cucullare *m.* (anat.) trapezius muscle.

cuculo, cu·culo *m.* (orn.) cuckoo, *Cuculus canorus*; — africano, great spotted cuckoo, *Clamator glandarius*.

cucur·bit-a *f.* (bot.) name applied to various gourd-like plants; retort; cucurbit. **-a·ceo** *adj.* belonging to the gourd family. **-a·cee** *f.pl.* pumpkins, gourds, etc. **-ino** *adj.* gourd-like; *n.m.* cucurbitine tapeworm, tapeworm cysticercus (which is gourd-like in shape).

†cucuzza *f.* head, topknot.

cucuz·zolo *m.* See **cocuzzolo**.

cuf·fi-a *f.* bonnet; baby's bonnet; lady's veil; coif, woman's cap; — da bagno, bathing-cap; (radio; telegr.) headphones, earphones; (photog.) dark cloth; (eng.) cowling, casing; (bot.) calyptra; (anat.) caul; è nato con la —, he was born with a caul (a supposed sign of good luck, therefore more or less equivalent to 'he was born with a silver spoon in his mouth'); uscirne per il (dal) rotto della —, to get through by the skin of one's teeth; the villous part of tripe; gag; cowl (of a chimney or funnel); (naut.) wind cowl; far —, to turn on to its side (of a vehicle or vessel); (theatr.) — del suggeritore, prompter's box; (surg.) — d'Ippocrate, a form of head-bandage; (anat.) — aponeurotica, the fascia of the occipito-frontal muscle; †man's headgear; †wig; †(joc.) woman. **-ato** *adj.* (herald.) with hat. **-ętta** *f. dim.* of **cuffia**; baby's bonnet; cap. **-otto** *m.* man's cap, beret.

†cuffiare *tr.* to gobble, to guzzle, to eat greedily, to scoff.

cu·fico *adj.* Cufic, Cuphic, Kufik, of or pertaining to Cufa (an ancient city near Babylon); caratteri cufici, Cufic characters (a variety of Arabic writing).

cugin-o¹ *m.*, **-a** *f.* cousin; — primo, first cousin; — in secondo grado, second cousin; nipote —, first cousin once removed. **-anza** *f.* cousinship. **†-a·tico** *adj.* cousinly.

cugino² *m.* (ent.) a kind of gnat.

cu·i *prn. dat.* whom; to whom; di —, whose, of whom; l'uomo il — figliuolo, the man whose son; of, to, which; †*acc.* whom; which.

†cuit-are *intr.*, *tr.* to think. **†-anza** *f.* thought. **†-o** *m.* thought.

culaccino *m.* the end of a Bologna sausage which remains after it has been sliced up; dregs; mark on the tablecloth from a wet and dirty glass; (sculp.) small piece of wax cut away in modelling.

culac·cio *m.* (butcher.) hindquarters; un pezzo di manzo nel —, a piece of rump steak.

cul-a·ia *f.* paunch of dead fowl swollen by decomposition of intestines; (of weather) far —, to become overcast; *f. adj.* (ent.) mosca —, horse bot-fly, *Gastrophilus haemorrhoidialis*. **-a·io** *m.* (vulg.) sodomite. **-ata** *f.* shove with the rump; a fall upon the rump. **-atello** *m.* lean ham-like salame made from pig's rump.

culatta *f.* hinder part, bottom; breech (of a gun); seat of a pair of trousers; spine of a book; (butcher.) extreme top back of round of beef.

culatt-are [A 1] *tr.* to pick (a boy) up by his arms and legs and bump him on the ground; — le panche, to sit doing nothing. **-ata** *f.* a fall on the rump.

culbianco *m.* (orn.) wheatear, *Œnanthe œnanthe*; piro-piro —, green sandpiper.

cu·lice *m.* (ent.) gnat, *Culex* spp.

culina·ri-a *f.* cookery, the culinary art. **-o** *adj.* culinary; scuola **-a**, school of cookery.

†culise·o *m.* See **colosseo**.

culisse *f.pl.* runners, slides; porta a —, sliding door; (theatr.) wings; (fig.) intrigue.

cull-a *f.* cradle; cot; (fig.) hearth, origin; birthplace; dalla — alla tomba, from the cradle to the grave; (agric.) wooden box for gathering grapes; (eng.) cradle, bed. **-are** [A 1] *tr.* to rock; to soothe; to dandle; *rfl.* (*prep.* di) to delude oneself, to cherish illusions (about); **-arsi** in dolci speranze, to indulge in fond hopes. **-ata** *f.* rocking motion. **-ato** *part. adj.* rocked; dandled; cherished; lost in idle fancies.

cul·leo *m.* (Rom. antiq.) *culleus*, sack in which parricides were drowned; liquid measure.

culm *m. indecl.* (geol.) culm; orizzonte del —, culm measures.

culmi·fero *adj.* See under **culmo**.

culmin-are [A 1 s] *intr.* (*aux.* essere) (astron.) to culminate, to be on the meridian; (fig.) to culminate, to rise to the greatest height; to mount to a crisis; to be the last straw, the crowning insult; — in, to culminate in. **-ante** *part. adj.* culminating; crowning. **-azione** *f.* culmination.

cul·mine *m.* top, highest point, apex; — della gloria, height of glory; (oceanog.) height.

culm-o *m.* (bot.) culm, stalk, stem of grasses, cereals, etc. **-i·fero** *adj.* (bot.) (of plants) possessing a culm.

cul-o *m.* (vulg.) bottom, buttocks, rump, arse; backside; — di una bottiglia, bottom of a bottle; **-i** di bicchieri, false brilliants. **-orosso** *m.* (orn.) greater spotted woodpecker. **-otte**, **-ottine** *f.pl.* woman's knickers, panties.

cultellazione *f.* measurement of the area of sloping ground by projection on to a horizontal plane.

†**cultivare** *vb.* and derivs. See **coltivare**.

culto[1] *adj.* cultured, well-educated, erudite; †frequented, inhabited; †ornamented; ornate, elegant (cf. **colto**).

cult·o[2] *m.* (rel.) worship (of God), veneration (of saints, holy images, etc.), cultus (of a particular saint); form of worship, religious observances, service(s), liturgy; cult; libertà di —, freedom of worship; Ministro dei Culti, 'Minister for Religious Affairs'. **-uale** *adj.* relating to a cult.

cult·ore *m.* cultivator; erudite person; — delle lettere, man of letters; †inhabitant. (**-rice** *f.*)

cultr·o *m.* (Rom. antiq.) knife (esp. sacrificial). **-a·rio** *m.* (Rom. antiq.) *cultrarius*, slayer of sacrificial victim.

cultuale *adj.* See under **culto**[2].

cultur·a *f.* culture; higher education; learning, erudition; scholarship, scholarliness; cultivation; farming; crop; — materiale, ethnology culture. **-ale** *adj.* cultural. **-are** [A 1] *tr.* to cultivate.

cum·arato *m.* (chem.) coumarate. **-a·rico** *adj.* (chem.) coumaric. **-arina** *f.* coumarin. **-arọne** *m.* (chem.) coumarone, benzofuran. **-aruna** *f.* (bot.) tonka-bean tree, *Dipteryx odorata*.

cum·e·nico *adj.* pertaining to cumene. **-ene** *m.* (chem.) cumene, cumole. **-ilo** *m.* cumyl. **-i·nico** *adj.* cuminic, cumic. **-ino** *m.* (bot.) see **comino**. **-inolo** *m.* (chem.) cumic alcohol, cuminol.

cumis *m. indecl.* koumiss, a fermented beverage made from mare's milk (drunk by Tartars).

cumolare [A 1 S] and derivs. See **cumulare**.

cumul·are [A 1 S] *tr.* to heap up, to amass, to accumulate; — due cariche, to combine two functions; — due stipendi, to draw two salaries. **-ativo** *adj.* cumulative; inclusive; (rlwy.) biglietto -ativo, party ticket. **-ativamẹnte** *adv.* cumulatively. **-ato** *part. adj.* amassed, heaped up. **-atamẹnte** *adv.* heaped together. (**-atọre** *m.* **-atrice** *f.*) **-aziọne** *f.* accumulation, heaping up, amassing. **-ista** *m., f.* person holding several offices.

cu·mulo *m.* heap; accumulation; — di cause, consolidation of actions; — delle pene, consolidation of sentences; — di circostanze, series of circumstances; (meteor.) — tagliuzzato, fractocumulus; (meteor.) cumulus clouds, cumulus.

cuna *f.* (poet.) cradle; (archit.) volta a —, cradle vault, barrel vault.

cune·ale *adj.* wedge-shaped. **-are** [A 6] *tr.* to shape like a wedge. **-ato** *part. adj.* shaped into a wedge; provided with wedges. **-ifọrme** *adj.* cuneiform.

cunella *f.* (bot.) summer savory, *Satureia hortensis*.

cu·ne·o[1] *m.* wedge; punch, stamp; (archit.) wedge-shaped stone; voussoir; wedge-shaped block of seats in an amphitheatre; the wedge, an instrument of torture; (mil.) wedge battle formation. **-o·metro** *m.* (archit.) instrument to determine the degree of wedge-shaping required in the stones for an arch.

Cu·neo[2] *pr.n.f.* (geog.) Cuneo, a town in Piedmont which is the traditional butt of funny stories.

cunẹtta *f.* shallow pond; ditch or dike along a road; gutter, gulley; hump on a road; (mil. hist.) cunette.

cuni·c·olo[1], **-ulo** *m.* (mil.) subterranean passage in a fortress; (mining) adit.

cuni·col·o[2] *adj.* relating to rabbit-breeding. (**-ino** *adj.*)

†**cunt·a** *f.* delay. †**-abundo** *adj.* dilatory; delaying.

cun·z·ia *f.* (bot.) galingale, *Cyperus longus*. **-iera** *f.* a pot-pourri receptacle; the scent of galingale.

cuoca *f.* (woman) cook.

cuo·c·ere [C 15] *tr.* to cook; to roast; to bake; to stew; to boil; to burn, to heat; to ripen; to hurt, to vex, to torment; carta per —, cookery paper, pan liner; (ceram.) — a fuoco, to fire; *intr.* (aux. avere) to cook; lasciatelo — nel suo brodo, let him stew in his own juice; *rfl.* to scald oneself; to fall in love; to torment oneself; †to get drunk. **-itura** *f.* cooking; cookery.

cuo·co *m.* (*pl.* **-chi**) (male) cook; primo —, chef; capo —, head cook.

cuoi·o *m.* (*pl. m.* **cuo·i**) leather; skin; — di Russia, Russian leather; imitazione —, imitation leather, leatherette; — cromato, chrome leather; — scamosciato, chamois leather; — verniciato, patent leather; (anat.) — cappelluto, scalp; (paperm.) calf paper, calf board, leather board; (*pl. f.* **cuo·ia**) leg; stendere le -a, to stretch one's legs, to lie stretched out, to go to bed; tirare le -a, to die; lasciare le -a in, to leave one's bones in (to die in a place); aver le -a dure, to be strong, to resist fatigue. **-a·ceo** *adj.* leathery. **-a·io** *m.* tanner; leather-seller. **-ame** *m.* leather, leather goods.

cuoprire [C 1] and derivs. See **coprire**.

cuora *f.* swamp; combustible substance formed by the accumulation of vegetable matter, compost heap.

cuor·e *m.* heart; love; cuor mio!, my love!; mettersi il — in pace, to set one's heart at rest; feelings; generosity; di —, heartily, from the heart; uomo di —, kind-hearted man; senza —, heartless; di tutto —, with all one's heart; a —, heart-shaped; depth; height; middle, core, centre, heart; nel cuor della notte, at dead of night; stare a — a, to touch, to be of deep concern to, to be dear to one's heart; mi sta molta a —, I care a great deal about it; sentirsi allargare il —, to have a lift of the heart, to feel a surge of joy; courage; farsi —, to take courage; (cards) -i, hearts (see also under **carta**); (rlwy.) frog; punta matematica del —, theoretical point of frog; (metall.) heart, core; (timber) — del tronco, heartwood, duramen; (zool.) — di bue, heart shell, *Glossus humanus*; — edule, cockle, *Cardium edule*; — tuberculato, *Cardium tuberculatum*; (herald.) fess point. **-icino** *m. dim.* of **cuore**.

cupamẹnte *adv.* See under **cupo**.

cupè *m. indecl.* coupé; carriage.

†**cu·pere** *tr.* to covet, to long for.

†**cuperosa** (chem.). See **copparosa**.

cupẹzza *f.* See under **cupo**.

cupidamẹnte *adv.* See under **cupido**.

cupidi·gia *f.* cupidity, covetousness; greed, desire.

†**Cupi·dine**[1] *pr.n.m.* See **Cupido**[1].

†**cupi·dine**[2] *f.* cupidity.

Cupido[1] *pr.n.m.* (myth.) Cupid, Eros.

cu·pid·o[2] *adj.* covetous, desirous; greedy; — di guadagni, greedy for gain; — d'onori, covetous of glory; eager (for). **-amẹnte** *adv.* covetously; greedily; eagerly. †**-ezza** *f.* see **cupidità**. **-ità** *f.* cupidity, covetousness; greed.

†**cupilo** *m.* hive.

cuplo·metro *m.* (eng.) torque meter.

cup·o *adj.* gloomy; dejected, deeply depressed; melancholy; sullen; taciturn; deep; sepulchral; abysmal; fame senza fine -a, insatiable hunger; (mus.) con voce -a, with dark tone; *n.m.* depth, profundity; depths, hollow; hell. **-amẹnte** *adv.* gloomily; hollowly. **-ẹzza** *f.* darkness, gloom; gloominess; depth; sombre character.

cu·pol·a *f.* (archit.) dome, cupola; summer-house; the vault of heaven; a —, dome-shaped, (fig.) full to overflowing; (bot.) cupule; (eng.) dome (of a steam-engine); crown (of a hat); (oceanog.) dome. **-are** *adj.* cupular, cupulate, dome-shaped, dome-like. **-ato** *adj.* (bot.) provided with a cupule. **-ẹtta** *f. dim.* of **cupola**; (archit.) small dome, cupola; lantern-house; summer-house. **-ẹtto** *m. dim.* of **cupola**; summer-house. **-i·fero** *adj.* (bot.) cupuliferous. **-ino** *m. dim.* of **cupola**; summer-house; crown of a woman's hat; *adj.* fond of one's home town. **-o** *m.* beehive; *adj.* heaped up, very full. **-ọne** *m. augm.* of **cupola**; nato all'ombra del -one, Florentine born and bred, truly Florentine (i.e. in the shade of the dome of Santa Maria del Fiore). **-otto** *m.* (hortic.) branches trained to form a dome.

cupọne *m.* coupon; — del dividendo, dividend coupon.

cupreina *f.* (chem.) cupreine, *l*-cupreidine.

cu·pr·eo *adj.* copper-coloured; (chem.) cuprous. **-i·fero** *adj.* copper-bearing.

cu·prico *adj.* (chem.) cupric.

cuprite *f.* (miner.) cuprite.

cupr·o *m.* copper. **-uranite** *f.* (miner.) tarbernite, cupro-uranite.

cur·a *f.* care, looking after, charge; a Lei ne commetto la —, I leave it in your care; aver — di, to take care of; non se ne piglia —, he doesn't take care of it; a — di, looked after by, edited by; care, anxiety; cure, nursing, tending, treatment; aversi —, to take care of one's health; casa di —, nursing-home; avere in —, to have as a patient; fare una —, to take a cure; essere in —, to be undergoing treatment; località di —, spa, health-resort; tassa di —, tax paid at such a place; care, attention; accuracy; diligence; con —, carefully, accurately; aversi — di, to be careful to; (eccl.) cure (of souls); parish; parish church; priest's house, presbytery; bleaching establishment; public administrative office; †custody. **-ai(u)olo** *m.* (eccl.) procurator, administrator.

cura·denti *m. indecl.* toothpick. **-orẹcchi** *m. indecl.* gadget for cleaning the ears. **-porto** *m.* dredging barge.

cur·are[1] [A 1] *tr.* to take care of, to look after; to care for, to heed, to pay regard to; to edit; to revise; to bleach; (med.) to cure, to treat; to dress; (eccl.) — le anime, to have a cure of souls, to

cur·are (*cont.*)

minister spiritually to one's people; †to cleanse or heal (the soul); *rfl.* (*acc. of prn.* 'si', *prep.* di) to take care; to pay heed (to), to mind; non mi -o di lui, I don't pay any attention to him; (*dat. of prn.* 'si') -arsi la salute, to look after one's health. **-a·bile** *adj.* curable. **-abilità** *f.* curability. **-anda·io** *m.* (text.) bleacher, fuller. **-ante** *part. adj.* careful, attentive; non -ante del pericolo, heedless of the danger; medico -ante, practitioner, doctor in charge of case. **-anza** *f.* attention; tending. **-atela** *f.* (leg.) guardianship; curatorship; trusteeship in bankruptcy; (comm.) receivership. **-atello** *m.* fine bleached linen. **-ativo** *adj.* curative. **-ato** *part. adj.* cured; tended, taken care of, looked after; edited; revised; bleached; *n.m.* (eccl.) parish priest (esp. in the country); curate; andare davanti al -ato, to get married. **-atore** *m.* guardian; curator; editor; (comm.) receiver; (leg.) guardian; administrator; liquidator; Receiver; trustee; -atore di fallimento, official Receiver, trustee in bankruptcy. **-atrice** *f.* (leg.) guardian; administratrix; liquidator; Receiver; trustee. **-atuc·cio** *m.* simple country priest. **-atura** *f.* bleach, bleaching. **-azione** *f.* (med.) cure, treatment.

curar-e², **-o** *m.* curare. **-ina** *f.* (chem.) curarine.

curasnetta *f.* (vet.) hoof-rasp; hoof-pick.

curate·la *f.* See under **curare¹**.

curato *m.* See under **curare¹**.

curba *f.* (vet.) curb.

curculione *m.* (ent.) weevil.

cur·cum-a *f.* (bot.) *Curcuma*, genus of plants including *C. longa*, turmeric, and *C. zodoaria*, zedoary. **-ina** *f.* (dye) turmeric; (chem.) curcumin.

Curd-ista·n *pr.n.m.* (geog.) Kurdistan. **-o** *m.* Kurd.

cureti *m.pl.* (class. antiq.) Curetes.

cu·ri-a *f.* (Rom. antiq.) curia, a primitive division of the Roman People; its assembly-place for political or religious purposes; later, the Senate-house or Senate at Rome (and also elsewhere); (eccl.) curia (an ecclesiastical administrative centre, the Roman Curia having the official function of assisting the Pope in the task of government, and a diocesan curia that of assisting a particular bishop); (leg.) court of justice; legal profession. **-ale** *adj.* (Rom. antiq. and eccl.) relating to a 'curia'; curial; (leg.) having to do with the law courts or the legal profession; *n.m.* (Rom. antiq.) *curialis*, (fellow-)member of a curia; courtier; pettifogging lawyer. **-ato** *adj.* (Rom. antiq.) 'curiate'; comizi -ati, *comitia curiata*. **-one** *m.* (Rom. antiq.) curion; priest of a curia; herald.

curian·dolo *m.* See **coriandolo**.

curio·s-o *adj.* curious, inquisitive; curious, peculiar, strange, odd; attentive, diligent; (biblioph.) curious; *n.m.* inquisitive person; student (of a subject); *pl.* onlookers. **-ac·cio** *m.* nosey parker. **-amente** *adv.* curiously, inquisitively; curiously, oddly, strangely; diligently. **-are** [A I c] *intr.* (*aux.* avere) to wander about led by an idle curiosity. **-etto** *adj. dim.* rather strange, rather curious. **-ità** *f.* curiosity; a point of curiosity; inquisitiveness; quaintness; curio; (biblioph.) curiosity; *pl.* sights (of a city). **-one** *m.* busybody.

curri·colo *m.* curriculum; course of study; †little cart.

curr-o *m.* dolly, trolley; roller with holes to take the end of an iron bar, to place under a heavy object to be moved; movement, course; essere sul — di, to be on the point of, to be about to; †chariot; †cart. **-are** [A I] *tr.* to move along on rollers.

cursore *m.* runner, messenger; the sliding portion of a zip fastener; (mech.) slide-rule; (techn.) slide, cursor; (leg.) court runner, bailiff; (eccl.) *pl.* cursori pontifici, *cursores apostolici*, papal messengers or heralds; (math.) cursor.

cursus *m. indecl.* (rhet.) cursus (system of rhythmical cadences in post-classical Latin prose, based on stress accent and used, e.g. by Dante).

curtato *adj.* shortened; (geom.; astron.) curtate.

curtense *adj.* (econ. hist.) self-sufficient (of the economy of a villa).

†curto *adj.* See **corto**.

curucù *m.* (orn.) a species of trogon.

curule *adj.* (Rom. antiq.) curule (chair, magistrate); *n.f.* (Rom. antiq.) curule chair; (liturg.) bishop's throne.

curva *f.* bend; curve; turn; — pericolosa, dangerous bend; — a forcella, hairpin bend; — occulta, concealed turning; (math.) curve, graph; andamento di una —, shape of a curve; (naut.) — di evoluzione, turning circle; (vet.) see **curba**.

curv-are [A I] *tr.* to bend; to curve; to arch; — la fronte, to bow the head, to submit, to obey; *rfl.* to stoop, to bend; to obey. **-a·bile** *adj.* bendable. **-amento** *m.* curving; bending. **-ato** *part. adj.* curved; bent. **-atura** *f.* bending, curving; camber; sweep (of curve); (scient.) curvature; convexity; (paperm.) roll set; (archit.) tetto a forte -atura, high-arched roof. **-atrice** *f.* (eng.) bending machine.

curvili·neo *m.* curvilinear figure; curvilinear; *adj.* curvilinear.

curvità *f.* curvature.

curv-o *adj.* bent; curved; hunched; stooping; spalle -e, round shoulders; (herald.) arched; — rovesciato, arched and reversed; *n.m.* roundedness; curvature. **-amente** *adv.* in a bend; bent. **-etto** *adj.* slightly hump-backed. **-ezza** *f.* curvedness, curvature.

†cusare *vb.* and derivs. See **accusare**.

cuscin-o *m.* cushion; pillow; bolster; — pneumatico, air cushion; —appoggiaginocchia (motor-cycle), knee-grip; (pol.) stato-cuscino, buffer State. **-etto** *m. dim.* small cushion; pin-cushion; (techn.) pad, fender; (surg.) pad; (archit.) ovolo of an Ionic capital; (eng.) bearing; -etto a rulli; roller bearing; -etto a rullini; needle bearing; -etto a sfere, ball bearing; (rlwy.) chair, rail chair; chiodo per -etto, trenail; piastrina per -etto, saddle, chair-plate.

†cuscire *vb.* and derivs. See **cucire**.

cusco *m.* (zool.) *Phalanger maculatus*, spotted cuscus, tiger cat.

cuscuta *f.* (bot.) *Cuscuta*, dodder.

cu·spid-e *f.* point; apex, vertex; (archit.) spire, pinnacle; (geom.) cusp, spinode; (radar) blip, pip. **-ale** *adj.* pointed; (geom.) cuspidal; (geom.) *n.m.* see **cuspide**.

cusso *m.* (bot.) cusso, kousso, *Brayera anthelmintica*.

custod-e *m.* guardian; curator; caretaker; attendant; uniformed official on duty at public museum or monument; watchman; doorkeeper; warder; angelo —, guardian angel; (joc.) angeli -i, the police; *f.* woman caretaker or attendant; wardress.

custo·di-a *f.* custody; care; protection; safe-keeping; avere in —, to have in one's care; case; violin case; camera di —, strong-room; (eng.) housing, casing; (liturg.) pyx; monstrance; (eng.) guard, belt-guard.

custod-ire [D 2] *tr.* to take care of, to look after; to watch over; to guard, to protect; to preserve, to keep; to hold in custody; *rfl.* to look after oneself. (**-imento** *m.* **-itore** *m.* **-itrice** *f.*)

cut-e *f.* (anat.) skin (human), dermis; (Lat. provb.) in —, intimately; conoscere intus et in —, to know thoroughly, to know inside out. **-a·neo** *adj.* cutaneous, of the skin.

cuterone *m.* (ent.) *Camponotus vagus*, a kind of ant.

cuter·zola *f.* (ent.) flying ant.

cuticagna *f.* nape of the neck; hair growing on the nape of the neck; hair of the head.

cuti·col-a *f.* cuticle; epidermis; (bot.) cuticle.

†cuticugno *m.* housecoat; gown worn indoors.

cut-ina *f.* (chem.) cutin, cutose. **-ite** *f.* (med.) cutitis.

cutocellulosa *f.* (techn.) cuto-cellulose.

cutret·tola *f.* (orn.) blue-headed or yellow wagtail, *Motacilla flava*.

cutter *m. indecl.* (naut.) cutter.

cuttì *m. indecl.* (orn.). See **cutrettola**.

†cuvidi·gia *f.* See **cupidità**, under **cupido²**.

cz-. See **z-**, for certain foreign words sometimes spelt with **cz-**; e.g. for **czar**, see **zar**.

cze-co *adj.* (*m.pl.* **-chi**) Czech, Czecho-Slovakian; *n.m.* Czech; the Czech language. (**-ca** *f.*)

Czecoslovac·chia *pr.n.f.* (geog.) see **Cecoslovacchia**.

D *f.* (pron. **di**) the letter D; (mus.) — lasolre *m.* D la sol re; †the note D; †the key of D.

d' *contr.* of **di** before a vowel; *contr.* of **da** before the vowel 'a'.

da *prep.* (*contr.* with *def. art.* **dal**, **dai**, **dagli**, **dalla**, **dalle**, **dall'**; see also **d'**).

1. FROM (emanation from, distance from, extension from, origin, source, movement out of or away from): vengo — Roma, I come from Rome, I am a Roman, I live in Rome, I have just arrived from Rome; — Roma a Firenze, from Rome to Florence; dalla culla alla tomba, from the cradle to the grave; — un giorno all'altro, from one day to the next; — capo, from the beginning, all over again (see also under **capo**); Sant'Antonio — Padova,

da (*cont.*)

St Anthony of Padua; tutto il suo male viene dal fegato, all his trouble is due to his liver; uscire —, to go out of, to issue from, to leave; salvato — morte, saved from death; lo seppi — lui, I learnt it from him; — fonte attendibile, from a reliable source; il sughero si ricava dalla buccia di un albero, cork is obtained from the bark of a tree. **2.** By, by means of, through, as a result of; ucciso — briganti, killed by brigands; lodato — tutti, praised by all; morì dal dolore, he died of grief; giudicare dai fatti, to judge by events; ti riconosco dalla (usu. 'alla') voce, I know you by your voice; fare le cose — sè, to do things by oneself; lo feci — me solo, I did it all by myself. **3.** To, to the house of, near, among, towards; viene — me ogni sabato, he comes to see me (to call on me) every Saturday; — noi, at our house, in our family; — noi questo non si usa, with us there is no such custom; — parte mia, as far as I am concerned, in my opinion, for my part; vado dal sarto, I'm going to the tailor's; ti aspetto — Gatti, I'll meet you at Gatti's; dalle parti di, in the vicinity of; passò — Perugia, he travelled by way of Perugia; — questa parte, on this side, to this side; farsi — parte, to draw to one side. **4.** Fit for, suitable for, intended for, worth; una cosa — nulla, a trifle, a mere nothing; uomo — nulla, good-for-nothing; †un uomo — molto, a man of spirit; biglietto — mille lire, thousand lire note; grano — sementa, corn for sowing, seed corn; casa — vendere, house for sale; macchina — scrivere, typewriter; macchina — cucire, sewing-machine; stanza — bagno, bathroom; cuffia — bagno, bathing-cap. **5.** As, like, in the capacity of; — bambino era biondo, he was fair as a child; vivere — re, to live like a king; fare — mamma a, to be a mother to; parlo — professore, I speak in my capacity as a teacher; fare — cuoco, to do the cooking, to act as cook; — bravo, like a clever chap, cleverly, stoutly; su, — bravo!, come along, don't be afraid!; †una donna — ciò, a woman of that sort. **6.** Characterized by, recognizable by, in respect of; fanciulla dagli occhi neri, girl with dark eyes; giovanotto dalla giacca verde, young man wearing a green jacket; sordo — un orecchio, deaf in one ear; cieco — un occhio, blind in one eye. **7.** With numerals: upwards of, round about; rubarono — cento mila lire, they stole about a hundred thousand lire; guadagni — mille sterline, profits of upwards of £1000. **8.** In temporal phrases: since, for; sono qui — tre mesi, I've been here for three months; fin dall'infanzia, ever since infancy; fin — quando lo incontrai, ever since I met him. **9.** With infinitive constr.: molto — fare, much to do, a lot to be done; avere — fare, to have a lot to do; questo è — imparare a memoria e quello — scrivere, this is to be learnt by heart and that is to be written out; — completare, to be filled in; qualcosa — mangiare, something to eat; dammi — bere, give me something to drink. (In Tusc. speech a consonant following **da** is doubled: e.g. 'da capo' is pronounced 'daccapo'.)

dabbasso *adv.* below, down below; downstairs; scendo — un momento, I'm just going downstairs a moment.

dabben-e *adj. indecl.* well-behaved, decent; upright; honest; gente —, honest folk; un uomo —, a respectable man; un dabben uomo, a simple-minded man, a stupid man; è un gran dabben uomo, he's a great fool; †*n.m.* probity; goodness of heart. †**-ac·cio** *adj. augm.* (not *pejor.*) very good-natured. **-ag·gine** *f.* simple-mindedness; naïvety; credulity; foolishness; good-heartedness, good nature; probity.

†**dabbud(d)à** *m.* (mus.) steel-stringed Arab psaltery.

daccanto *adv.* near, close by, nearby; to one side (also **da canto**); aside; *prep.* beside; by the side of; *adj. indecl.* near.

daccapo *adv.* once more, over again; ricominciare —, to begin all over again; siamo —, we're back where we started; (in dictating) new paragraph (usu. **da** *or* **a capo**); at the top, on top.

dacchè *conj.* since, since the time when; since, inasmuch as, seeing that, given that.

dacri-adenite *f.* (med.) dacryadenitis. **-elcoṣi** *f.* (med.) dacryelcosis. **-oadenalgi·a** *f.* (med.) dacryadenalgia. **-ocele** *m.* (med.) dacryocele. **-ocistite** *f.* (med.) dacryocystitis.

dada-iṣmo *m.* (art) dadaism. **-ista** *m.* (art) dadaist.

dad·dol-o *m.* (fam. Tusc.) playful or affected grimace; facial contortion; *pl.* simpering manner, affectation, mincing ways. **-ino** *m. dim.* of **daddolo**; simperer (esp. child). **-one** *m.* smirker, simperer; one who makes faces; affected person. (**-ona** *f.*) **-oṣo** *adj.* simpering; affected.

†**daddovero** *adj.* See **davvero**.

dadeggiare [A 3 c] *intr.* (*aux.* avere) to play dice.

dad-o *m.* die; point in the game of dice; cube; il — è tratto, the die is cast; scambiare i -i in mano a uno, to twist someone's meaning; tessuto a -i, cloth with a check pattern; (cul.) beef-cube; soup-cube; (archit.) dado (of pedestal of a column); cube-shaped base of statue, bust or vase; square house, or similar building; metal cube used as a pivot in a grinding mill; (eng.) nut; — ad alette, wing-nut, butterfly-nut, thumb-nut; (eng.; naut.) pulley-block lining; bouching of a block sheave; pin of a block; (anat.) any small bone of the heel; (mil. hist.) lead or steel cannon shot; ferrule or rib on lower extremity of scabbard; *pl.* (naut.) stops on the shank of an anchor for holding the stock; †pagare il lume e i -i, to give satisfaction, to render account of oneself; to foot the bill; †essere pagato e del lume e dei -i, to come off badly; †pigliare i -i a, to put a spoke in the wheel of; †trarre pel —, to begin without more ado; †tirare un gran —, to escape from a great danger; non valere un —, not to be worth a fig; †in men d'un —, in a twinkling; †instrument of torture which compressed the joints of the feet. **-aiuolo** *m.* dice-player.

daffare *m.* work, business; duties; task; un gran —, a great deal to do; avrà il suo —, he's got his work cut out, he'll have his hands full; il — cotidiano, the daily grind.

Dafne[1] *pr.n.f.* Daphne.

dafn-e[2] *f.* (bot.) the genus *Daphne*. **-ina** *f.* (chem.) daphnin.

daf·nia *f.* (zool.) water-flea, *Daphnia* spp.

daga *f.* dagger, dirk.

dagherr-otipi·a *f.* daguerreotypy. **-o·tipo** *m.* daguerreotype.

da·ida·i *m. indecl.* (neol.) kind of scooter.

da·in-o *m.*, **-a** *f.* (zool.) fallow deer, *Dama dama*; doeskin; guanti di —, doeskin gloves.

†**dalfino** *m.* dolphin; Dauphin; (chess) knight.

da·lia *f.* (bot.) dahlia, *Dahlia* spp.

dallato *adv.* nearby; to one side; farsi —, to draw to one side; *prep.* — a, beside, by the side of; *adj. indecl.* near (also **da lato**).

dalma·tica *f.* (eccl.) dalmatic.

dal·mat-o *adj., n.m.* Dalmatian. (**-a** *f.*)

Dalma·zia *pr.n.f.* (geog.) Dalmatia.

dalton *m. indecl.* (atom. phys.) dalton.

dal-toniṣmo *m.* colour-blindness, Daltonism. **-to·nico** *adj.* colour-blind; Daltonic; *n.m.* colour-blind person. (**-to·nica** *f.*)

daltronde *adv.* on the other hand; in other respects; besides, moreover (also **d'altronde**).

dam-a[1] *f.* lady, noblewoman; (female) dancing-partner; — di compagnia, lady companion; — della Regina, lady-in-waiting; the woman in any couple taking part in a game or dance; (fam. Tusc.) sweetheart; fiancée; bocca di —, a kind of pastry; cosce di —, a kind of plum; draughts; draught-board; king at draughts; giuocare a —, to play draughts; andare a —, to make a king; queen (at cards, chess); †Nostra Dama, Our Lady. **-eri·a** *f.* status or airs of a great lady. **-iere** *m.*, **-iera** *f.* draught-board. **-igella** *f.* damsel; bridesmaid, -igella di compagnia, lady companion; †young lady of rank; (orn.) demoiselle crane, *Anthropoïdes virgo*; (bot.) love-in-the-mist, devil-in-a-bush, *Nigella damascena*. **-igello** *m.* (hist.) page; esquire.

†**dama**[2] *f.* See **damma**.

damare [A 1] *tr.* to crown (at draughts); to make a queen (at chess).

damaṣ-co[1] *m.pl.* (-chi) damask. **-care** [A 2] *tr.* to damask. **-cato** *part. adj.* damasked; damask; tovaglia -ata, white damask table linen. **-catura** *f.* process of damasking or damascening. **-ceno** *adj.* Damascene; (bot.) *m.* damson, bullace, *Prunus domestica*, subspecies *insititia*. **-chetto** *m.* damascin. **-china** *f.* Damascus blade. **-chinare** [A 1] *tr.* to damascene. **-chinato** *part. adj.* with dark damascened pattern. **-chino** *adj.* of Damascus; (bot.) rosa -china, damask rose, *Rosa damascena*; *n.m.* damascening; damask cloth; †kind of melon.

Damaṣco[2] *pr.n.m.* (geog.) Damascus.

dameggiare [A 3 c] *intr.* (*aux.* avere) to play the beau; *tr.* to court, to woo.

dam-erino *m.* fop, dandy; ladies' man; (vulg.) lover. †**-igello** *m.* well-born youth, page; squire.

damigella *f.* See under **dama**[1].

damigiana *f.* demijohn; (chem.) carboy; †fare una —, to fail badly.

damista *m., f.* draught-player.

†**damma** *f.* fallow deer; hind.

†**dammag·gio** *m.* damage.

dam·mar *m.* gum damar, resin obtained from the 'dammara', q.v. **-a** *f.* (bot.) *Dammara australis*.

dammeno *adv.* less; *adj. indecl.* worthless, worse; nessuno è — di lui, no one is more worthless than he is.

dam·mula *f.* fallow deer fawn.

damo (fam. Tusc.) *m.* sweetheart, 'young man'; fiancé; †gallant, beau, paramour.

Da·mocle *pr.n.m.* Damocles; la spada di —, the sword of Damocles.

damurite *m.* (geol.) damourite, hydro-mica.

dana·ide *f.* (myth.) danaid; (eng.) danaide, tub-wheel.

dana·io *m.* and derivs. See **danaro.**

danalite *f.* (miner.) danalite.

danar·o *m.* small coin (varying in value at different periods); trenta ~i, thirty pieces of silver; money; col — si può far tutto, with money you can do anything; *pl.* coins; money; name of a suit of cards (in an Italian pack; see note under **carta**). (See also **denaro**.) **-oso** *adj.* moneyed, wealthy, rich.

dancing *m. indecl.* (pron. as Eng.) dance-hall; night-club.

danda *f.* strip, string; brace-band; dividere a —, to divide by repeated subtraction; *pl.* leading-strings; 'wings' worn by seminarists; braces.

dandy *m. indecl.* an Italian dressed correctly and elegantly with a tendency towards English style and mannerisms; elegantly dressed foreigner.

danese *adj.* Danish; cane —, Great Dane; *n.m.* Dane; Danish language, Danish; *f.* Danish woman, Dane.

†**dangiero** *m.* damage, injury; danger.

Daniele *pr.n.m.* Daniel.

Danimarca *pr.n.f.* (geog.) Denmark.

da·nio *m.* (zool.). See **daino.**

dann·are [A I] *tr.* to damn; far — uno, far — l'anima a uno, to drive someone distracted; to condemn; to doom; to blame; †to damage; †to injure; †(fig.) to blight; *rfl.* (*acc.* of *prn.* 'si') to be damned; to condemn oneself; (*dat.* of *prn.* 'si') -arsi l'anima, to be worried to death, to be driven distracted. **-a·bile** *adj.* deserving condemnation; damnable. **-abilmente** *adv.* damnably. †**-ag·gio** *m.* damage, injury. †**-aggioso** *adj.* damaging, injurious; dangerous. **-ando** *adj.* (eccl.) to be condemned. **-ato** *part. adj.* damned; cursed, damnable; miserable, full of worries; appalling; paura -ata, dreadful fright; *n.m.* damned soul; i -ati, the damned; urlando come un -ato, uttering fiendish yells. **-azione** *f.* condemnation; damnation; pest, trial, curse; la -azione di Faust, the damnation of Faust. †**-e·vole** *adj.* worthy of condemnation; damaging, injurious.

danneggi-are [A 3c] *tr.* to damage; to impair; to injure, to do harm to, to harm; *rfl.* to suffer damage; to be impaired or injured. (**-amento** *m.*) **-ato** *part. adj.* damaged; injured; *n.m.* victim; injured party. (**-atore** *m.* **-atrice** *f.*)

†**dannific-are** [A 2s] *tr.* to injure; to condemn. **-ativo** *adj.* injurious.

dann-o *m.* loss; damage, harm; accertare il —, to assess the damage; è un —, it's a great pity; tuo —, so much the worse for you; far — alla salute, to impair one's health; — negl'interessi, prejudice to interests; (provb.) — fa far senno, adversity is the school of wisdom; (leg.) — emergente, consequential damage (as distinct from 'lucro cessante', q.v. under **cessare**); risarcimento dei -i, compensation for damage; damages; compensazione dei -i, compensatory damages; -i ed interessi, direct and indirect damages; -i eventuali, contingent damages; -i continui, continuing damages; -i punitivi, punitive damages; -i liquidati, liquidated damages; causa di -i, action for damages; -i di guerra, war damage; — grave, serious damage; — lieve, slight damage; — indiretto, indirect damage; — causato da negligenza, damage caused by negligence; peritare i -i, to assess damages, to estimate damages; tenere una persona responsabile per i -i, to hold a person liable for damage; — causato da forza maggiore, damage caused by act of God; — temuto, anticipated injury or damage (to real property, etc.); azione di — temuto, *quia timet* action (C.C.); rifare i -i, to make good the damage by indemnification. **-oso** *adj.* injurious; damaging. **-osamente** *adv.* injuriously. **-osità** *f.* injuriousness.

dannunzi-ano *adj.* (lit. hist.) like, or of, D'Annunzio; *n.m.* follower, or admirer, of D'Annunzio. **-eggiare** [A 3c] *intr.* (*aux.* avere) to imitate D'Annunzio, to affect the style of D'Annunzio.

dano *m.* (zool.). See **daino.**

dante[1] *m.* See **daino**; pelle di —, buckskin, deerskin, tanned skin of various deer.

dante[2] *part. adj.* of **dare**, q.v.; (leg.) *n.m.* il — causa, the person from whom one's legal title is derived; predecessor in title.

Dant-e[3] *pr.n.m.* (abbrev. of **Durante**) Dante; edition of Dante; il primo — stampato, the first printed copy of Dante's works. **-eggiare** [A 3c] *intr.* (*aux.* avere) to imitate Dante, to write in the style of Dante. **-esco** *adj.* (*m.pl.* -eschi) Dantesque; *n.m.* Dante scholar, Dantist. **-escamente** *adv.* in a Dantesque style. **-ista, -ofilo** *m.* lover of Dante, Dantophile. **-ologia** *f.* study of Dante.

Danu·bio *pr.n.m.* (geog.) Danube.

danz-a *f.* dance; — classica, classical dancing; la — dei sette veli, the dance of the seven veils; (fig.) scheming, intrigue; *pl.* dance recital. **-are** [A I] *intr.* (*aux.* avere) to dance; -are al suono di alcuno, to dance to someone's whistle; *tr.* to dance, to dance through. **-ante** *part. adj.* tè -ante, thé dansant. (**-atore** *m.* **-atrice** *f.*)

Dan·zica *pr.n.f.* (geog.) Danzig.

dap-e *f.* (poet.) feast, banquet; spiritual food. **-i·fero** *m.* dapifer; (eccl.) servant who brings food to cardinals during a conclave.

dappertutto *adv.* everywhere; on all sides (also **da per tutto**).

dappiedi, dappiede, dappiè *adv.* at the bottom, at the foot, below.

dappiù *adv.* more; *adj. indecl.* worth more, better; nessuno è — di me, I'm top dog.

dappoc-o *adj. indecl.* worthless; inefficient; *n.m.*, *f. indecl.* useless individual, good-for-nothing. **-ag·gine** *f.* worthlessness; inefficiency; ineptitude, ineptness; stupid action.

dappoi *adv.* afterwards, next, then. **-chè** *conj.* after, since; because, seeing that, since.

dappresso *adv.* near, close by, nearby; next; *adj. indecl.* near, next.

dapprima *adv.* first, at first; in the beginning; at the outset; initially; firstly.

dapprinci·pio *adv.* at the beginning; from the beginning; to start with.

Dardanelli *pr.n.m.pl.* (geog.) Dardanelles; †(mil.) fortifications.

dardanello *m.* (orn.) sand martin.

dar·dano *m.* (orn.) bee-eater.

dardeggi-are [A 3c] *tr.* to dart; to transfix, pierce; to flash; *intr.* (*aux.* avere) to shine, to flash; to quiver; (poet.) to throw darts. **-ato** *part. adj.* darted; flashed; pierced; campagna -ata dal sole, sun-drenched countryside.

dard-o *m.* dart; (poet.) missile, arrow; ardent glance; fiery ray; (herald.) ferro di —, pheon; (orn.) bee-eater; (eng.) welding flame. †**-iere,** †**-iero** *m.* dart-thrower, soldier armed with darts.

dare [A 8] *tr.*

1. TO GIVE, to donate, to give away, to hand over, to give up; to grant, to allow; — un regalo a, to give a present to; — in dono, to donate, to make a gift of; dammi da bere, give me something to drink; — in moglie, to give (one's daughter) away, to give as wife (to); — la vita per, to give (up) one's life for, to lay down one's life for; i genitori hanno dato la vita per lui, his parents have sacrificed everything for him; mi davano cento lire al giorno, they allowed me 100 lire a day; dategli del tempo, give him time; mi hanno dato una bella stanza, they've allocated me (given me/let me have) a good room; gli hanno dato il permesso di, they have given him permission to; — il congedo a, to give time off to, to dismiss; Iddio vi ha dato questa potenza, God has given you this power; non mi è dato di, it's not in my power to. **2.** TO ADMINISTER, to deliver, to give, to cause, to say; — uno schiaffo a, to give a slap to, to smack; gli diedi un calcio, I gave him a kick; — un crollo a, to shake; fungo che dà la morte, poisonous toadstool; — fuoco a, to set fire to; questo mi dà un vero piacere, this gives me real pleasure; dare il buongiorno a, to say good-day to; — una risposta, to make (give) a reply; — il benvenuto a, to welcome, to give a welcome to; — del tu a, to use the familiar form of address to (equiv. in English to using Christian names); — dello scemo a uno, to call a person a fool; — dieci anni di carcere a, to give a person ten years (in gaol); (leg.) — giuramento, to administer an oath; — sentenza, to pronounce judgement. **3.** TO CREDIT WITH, to attribute, to lay on; quanti anni mi date?, how old would you say I was?; dò la colpa a voi, I blame you, I put the blame on you; vorrebbe che tutto il merito si desse a lui, he'd like to claim all the credit; ci dò un valore di mille lire, I'd say it was worth about a thousand lire; — ragione a, to consider in the right, to believe; ti dò torto,

dare (*cont.*)

I think you're wrong; da retta a me, believe me, listen to me, do as I say, mark my words. **4.** TO YIELD, to render, to bear, to give forth; è un albero che non dà più frutto, this tree no longer bears fruit; — guadagni, to yield profit; una lampada che dà poca luce, a lamp which gives a poor light; un violino che dà un suono aspro, a violin which has a harsh tone; (provb.) la botte dà del vino che ha, by their fruits ye shall know them; — una lacrima, to shed a tear; — un sospiro, to heave a sigh; — un grido, to let out a yell. **5.** TO TAKE, to make, to undertake, to conduct, to give; — un passo, to take a step; — un gesto, to make a gesture; — una lezione, to give a lesson, to conduct a lesson; — lezioni di francese, to give French lessons, to teach French; — battaglia, to give battle; (theatr. etc.) — una commedia, to put on a comedy; che cosa danno al cinema?, what's on at the cinema? **6.** TO GIVE TO UNDERSTAND, to give out, to regard as; — una cosa per fatta, to declare something finished; — uno per spacciato, to think someone is done for; — ad intendere, to lead to believe, to give to understand; — a bere a, to make (a person) swallow (an unlikely tale); tu me la daresti buona! you expect me to believe that? **7.** (NAUT.) — abbrivo alla nave, to bear away before tacking; — alla banda, to heel over; — calumo, to veer cable; — carena a, to careen; — fondo, to cast anchor; — fuori, to turn out (boat, crane, or davit); — fuori la forza di vele, to spread sail; — indietro, to back; — in secco, to ground; — in terra, to land; — la poppa, to run; — la voga, to give the stroke; — la pratica, to give pratique; — volta, to turn up, to make fast, to secure. **8.** *Intr.* (*aux.* avere) — nell'occhio, to strike the eye, to catch the eye; — in, to bump into, (fig.) to meet unexpectedly, to run into; diede in un sasso, he tripped over a stone; — addosso a qualcuno, to fall upon, to attack someone; — ai nervi di, to get on the nerves of; — nel segno, to hit the mark, (fig.) to guess right; — a, — in, to incline towards, to tend to; — alla testa, to go to one's head; — allo stomaco, to make one sick; to lie heavy on the stomach; — in lagrime, to burst into tears; — nelle risa, to burst out laughing; in questo giardino ci dà molto sole, this garden gets a lot of sun; una casa che dà sul mare, a house facing the sea; una porta che dà sulla strada, a door opening on to the street; quel ragazzo mi dà alla spalla, that boy comes up to my shoulder; — a uno sulla testa con un bastone, to hit someone on the head with a stick; dagli! dagli!, hit him! hit him!; dacci entro!, put your back into it!; dai! dai!, come on! go it! (urging on a team or a competitor); dagli oggi, dagli domani, by sheer persistence, plodding along. **9.** *Rfl.* (*acc.* of *prn.* 'si') TO GIVE ONESELF, to devote oneself; darsi a qualcuno, to yield to someone; darsi a Dio, to give oneself to God; darsi agli studi, to devote oneself to one's studies; darsi al vizio, to give way to evil living; to take up a life of evil; darsi alla latitanza, (alla macchia), to abscond, to go into hiding; darsi per vinto, to give in, to surrender; to pass oneself off, to pretend (to be); darsi per dotto, to claim to be a learned man; darsi per ammalato, to report sick, to make out that one is ill; darsi a (*foll.* by *inf.*), to begin to; darsi a correre, to begin to run, to break into a run; si diede a fantasticare, he began to imagine, he gave himself up to daydreams; to occur, to take place; si diede il caso che, it happened that; può darsi, it may be, perhaps, possibly; (*dat.* of *prn.* 'si') to give to oneself, to take on, to assume; darsi delle arie, to put on airs; darsi da fare per, to busy oneself about; darsi un gran daffare, to take on a lot of work, to have a great deal to do, to make a great to-do about one's work; darsela a gambe, to take to one's heels; *recip. rfl.* to give to each other; darsela, to be alike; quei due ragazzi se la danno, those two boys are just of an age; se la danno, quei due, those two are six of one and half a dozen of the other, they are much of a muchness. **10.** *n.m.* DEBT; debit; liability; il — e l'avere, debit and credit.

dar·sena *f.* wet dock; dockyard; boat-house; innermost harbour.

darsonvalizzazione *f.* (electr.; med.) D'Arsonvalism.

dart-o *m.* (med.) dartos. **-o·ico** *adj.* (anat.) dartoic, dartoid.

dartr-o *m.* (med.) dartre. **-oso** *adj.* (med.) dartrous.

darviniano *adj.* and derivs. See **darwiniano**.

darwin-iano *adj.* Darwinian. **-ismo** *m.* Darwinism, theory of evolution. **-ista** *m., f.* Darwinist, evolutionist.

dascino *m.* (naut.) carpenter's boy.

dasi·a *adj.f.* (mus.) notazione —, daseian notation.

dasichira *f.* (ent.) pale tussock moth, *Dasychira pudibunda.*

das·i·metro *m.* (phys.) dasymeter. **-imetri·a** *f.* dasymetry.

dasite *f.* (med.) hypertrichosis, excessive growth of hair.

†dassa·i *adv.* enough; quite; sufficiently; as much; a great deal; *n.m.pl.* i —, the many, the majority. **†-ezza** *f.* sufficiency; readiness, willingness.

dat-a *f.* date; la vostra letter in — 12 giugno, your letter of 12th June; place in which a book is printed; d'antica —, going back a long way; di vecchia —, old; di fresca —, of recent date; (leg.) a — fissa, on a fixed date; (sport) service; (cards) deal; trick; giuoco di —, obligation to play a card of the same suit; avere la —, to lead, to play the first card; (eccl.) gift of a benefice; †tax; †nature, disposition; †character, quality, stamp; †essere in — di, to be in a position to. **-are** [A I] *tr.* to date; to put a date on; to identify the date of; *intr.* (*aux.* avere) to date, to go out of date; -are da, to date from; a -are da quel giorno, dating from that day, from that day on. **-a·rio** *m.* (eccl.) datary. **-ariato** *m.* (eccl.) office of datary. **-a·rio** *m.* see **dateria**. **-ato** *part. adj.* dated; identified as to date. **-azione** *f.* dating. **-eri·a** *f.* (eccl.) datary (branch of Papal chancery).

dativo *adj.* (gramm.) dative; (leg.) tutore —, curatore —, testamentary guardian, guardian appointed by the Court (of an infant or other person under disability).

dat-o *part.* of **dare**, q.v.; *adj.* given; addicted; inclined; fixed; — che, since, given that; — e non concesso, supposing, let us say for the sake of argument; *n.m.* datum; clue; item of evidence; -i di fatto, facts, circumstances; voglio -i, I want facts; in buon —, in large quantities; *pl.* data; (eng.) -i tecnici, specification; †gift. **-ore** *m.* giver; (econ.) -ore di lavoro, employer; producer; (finan.) -ore di una cambiale, drawer of a bill; (leg.) -ore di leggi, legislator, law-giver. **-rice** *f.* (leg.) legislatress, legislatrix.

datolite *f.* (miner.) datolite.

da·tolo *m.* (zool.). See **dattero**.

datt-ero *m.* date (fruit); date-palm, *Phoenix dactylifera*; (zool.) — di mare; — di pietra, date shell, *Lithophaga lithophaga*; — marino, piddock, *Pholas dactylus.* **-ili·fero** *adj.* date-bearing, date-producing.

dattili-o·grafo *m.* gem-engraver. **-oteca** *f.* gem-case; collection of gems.

datt-ilo *m.* (prosod.) dactyl; (bot.) *pl.* -ili di Trebisonda, date plum, *Diospyros lotus*; (zool.) see **dattero**. **-i·lico** *adj.* (prosod.) dactylic. **-ili·fero** *adj.* see under **dattero**.

dattil-ografare [A I s] *tr.* to type. **-ografato** *part. adj.* typewritten, typed; *n.m.* see **dattiloscritto**. **-ografi·a** *f.* typewriting, typing; science of communicating speech to the deaf by means of touch. **-o·grafa** *f.* (female) typist. **-ogra·fico** *adj.* typewriting, pertaining to typing; ufficio -ografico, typewriting office. **-o·grafo** *m.* typist; instrument for communicating speech to the deaf by means of touch. **-ologi·a** *f.* dactylology. **-omanzi·a** *f.* dactyliomancy. **-omegali·a** *f.* (med.) dactylomegaly. **-oscopi·a** *f.* the science of finger-prints; the taking of finger-prints. **-osco·pico** *adj.* pertaining to the science of finger-prints, rilievo -oscopico, finger-prints. **-oscritto** *adj.* typewritten; *n.m.* typescript.

dattorno *adv.* around; round about; levarsi uno —, to get rid of someone; qui —, hereabouts; le cose qui —, things around here (see also **dintorno**, **intorno**).

datur-a *f.* (bot.) thorn-apple, *Datura stramonium*, and other species. **-ina** *f.* (pharm.) daturine, atropine.

da·uco *m.* (bot.) wild carrot, *Daucus carota*; — cretico, Cretan carrot, *Athamanta cretensis.*

daumont *m., f. indecl.* carriage and four with two postillions.

davanti *adv.* before, in front; sedere —, to sit in front, to sit towards the front; levarsi —, to be off, to remove oneself; *prep.* (*foll.* by 'a') in the presence of; — a Dio, in the sight of God; mettere — a, to put in front of, to serve with; *adj. indecl.* fore, front; la parte —, the fore part; *n.m.* il —, the front; the front part; (bookb.) fore-edge.

davanzale *m.* window sill; (eng.) — del fornello, dead-plate.

†davanzo *adv.* superfluously, to excess.

Da·v·ide *pr.n.m.* David; (Bibl.) psalms of David; (art) Michelangelo's David. **-i·dico** *adj.* of David, relating to David; canti -idici, psalms of David.

davvantaggio *adv.* See 'd'avvantaggio', under **avvantaggio**.

davvero *adv.* really, seriously; indeed; dire —, to be in earnest; —?, really?; dici —?, do you really mean it?; davvero davvero, really and truly.

dazi-are [A 4] *tr.* to levy duty on. **-a·rio** *adj.* connected with toll or duty. **-ere** *m.* exciseman.

da·zio *m.* toll, excise; municipal toll; customs-duty; toll-house; — d'entrata, import duty; — d'uscita, export duty; — consumo, food-tax.

†**dazione** *f.* giving; dedication; endowing.

†**dazz-aiuolo** *m.* tax record-book. **-ino** *m.* See **daziere**, under **daziare**.

de¹ *prep.* See **di**. Note: this form, now chiefly archaic, is used before titles of works beginning with a definite article, e.g. una nuova edizione de *I Promessi Sposi*, a new edition of *I Promessi Sposi*; as part of an Italian surname, e.g. De Sanctis, De Marchi, etc., it counts as the first syllable of the name and the initial letter of such names is D, which is written as a capital. In this respect Italian usage differs from French.

†**de²** *encl.* See **ne**.

de'³ *contr.* of **dei**. See under **di**.

de-a *f.* goddess. †**-o** *m.* See **dio**.

deaerazione *f.* (phys.) de-aeration.

†**deambul-are** *intr.* to walk about in a leisurely way. **-azione** *f.* walking, ambling along.

†**debatto** *m.* See **dibattito**.

debbi-are [A 4 c] *tr.* (Tusc.) to manure (ground) by burning wood and brambles, to denshire. **-ato** *part. adj.* denshired; *n.m.* denshired ground.

dębbio *m.* burning of stumps, stubble, hedge-trimmings, etc. as manure for land; ground so treated; clearing of ground for this purpose.

debell-are [A 1] *tr.* to conquer, to subdue; to overcome; to weaken. **-amento** *m.* defeat, rout. **-ato** *part. adj.* subdued; quelled; overcome; weakened; -ato da una lunga malattia, pulled down by a long illness. (**-atore** *m.* **-atrice** *f.*) **-azione** *f.* conquest; weakening.

de·bile *adj.* and derivs. See **debole**.

†**debilire** *vb.* See **indebolire**.

debilit-are [A 1 s] *tr.* to weaken, to enfeeble; to enervate; to debilitate; to emasculate. (**-amento** *m.*) **-ante** *part. adj.* debilitating; enervating; weakening; *n.m.pl.* (med.) debilitants, debilitating remedies. **-ato** *part. adj.* weakened, enfeebled; enervated; debilitated, run down, pulled down. **-azione** *f.* enfeeblement; debilitation; mutilation, castration; infirmity.

dębit-o *adj.* due; owing; proper; in tempo — per, sufficiently early to allow; †destined; †obliged; *n.m.* duty; debt; scrivere a —, to debit; comprare a —, to buy on account; in —, in debt; contrarre -i, to get into debt; saldare un —, to settle a debt; — pubblico . national debt; (leg.) — recuperabile, — esigibile, recoverable debt; — insolvibile, — inesigibile, bad debt; — ipotecario, mortgage; — prescritto, statute-barred debt; — portato in sentenza, judgement debt; — d'onore, debt of honour; — fluttuante, floating debt. **-amente** *adv.* duly; fittingly; properly; justly, rightly. **-ore** *m.* (econ.) debtor; -ore ipotecario, mortgagor; -ore solidale, joint-debtor; -ore in mora, debtor in arrear; escutere un -ore, to levy execution on a debtor; (fig.) essere -ore a, to be indebted to. (**-ora** *f.*) **-rice** *f.* debtor (woman); (cinem.) bobina -rice, paying-out-spool.

dębol-e *adj.* weak; feeble; essere — in matematica, to be weak in mathematics; il suo lato — è, his weak point is; faint; dim; (naut.) — di fianco, crank, liable to capsize; *n.m.* weak person; weakness, weak point, weak side; avere un — per, to have a weakness or fondness for. **-mente** *adv.* weakly; feebly; faintly. **-ezza** *f.* weakness; foible; mistake.

†**debonar-ietà, -ità** *f.* goodness.

debo·sci-a *f.* debauchery. **-ato** *adj.* debauched.

debraiare [A 4] *intr.* (aux. avere) (motor.) to declutch.

debutt-o *m.* début; beginning. **-ante** *m.* débutant; *f.* débutante; beginner. **-are** [A 1] *intr.* (aux. avere) to make one's début; to make one's first appearance on the stage.

deca *f.* group of ten books (esp. of Livy's *History of Rome*).

decabrista *m.* (hist.) one who helped or took part in the liberal and reform movement which culminated in the pronunciamiento of 14 December 1825 in St Petersburg; decembrist.

dec-acordo *m.* (mus.) decachord, ten-stringed harp; †interval of tenth. **-ae·dro** *m.* decahedron. **-ae·drico** *adj.* decahedral. **-a·gono** *m.* decagon. **-agramma** *m.* decagram. **-a·litro** *m.* decalitre. **-a·logo** *m.* Decalogue, the Ten Commandments. **-a·metro** *m.*

decametre. **a·poli** *f.* Decapolis, league of ten cities. **-arca** *m.* (hist.) commander of ten men. **-archi·a** *f.* (hist.) group of ten soldiers. **-ascalmo** *m.* (Rom. antiq.) boat with ten oars. **-asil·labo** *adj.* (prosod.) decasyllabic; *n.m.* decasyllable. **-astero** *m.* decastere, ten cubic metres. **-a·stico** *m.* (prosod.) decastich. **-a·stilo** *m.* (archit.) decastyle. **-atlon** *m. indecl.* (sport) decathlon, contest of ten events.

de·cade *f.* decade; period of ten days; l'ultima — di giugno, the last third of June.

decad-ęre [B 5] *intr.* (aux. essere) to fall into decadence, to decay; (leg.) — da un diritto, to allow a right to lapse, to lose a right through disuse; — da un'azione, to allow an action (or right to take action) to lapse; to be debarred from an action. **-ente** *adj.* decadent; *n.m., f.* a decadent person. **-entismo** *m.* (art; lit.) school or style of the 'decadents'. **-enza** *f.* decadence; decline; (leg.) expiration; lapse (of a right or remedy); -enza della patria potestà, determination of paternal authority (C.C.). **-imento** *m.* decay, degeneration; (leg.) lapse; loss of right by lapse.

decaffeinizz-are [A 1] *tr.* to remove caffeine from. **-ato** *part. adj.* caffeine-reduced.

decalag·gio *m.* (aeron.) stagger (of wings), decalage.

decalc-are [A 2] *tr.* to trace (drawing, etc.); to make a transfer of. **-omani·a** *f.* transfer, decalcomania.

decalcificazione *f.* (med.) acalcerosis.

decalescenza *f.* (metall.) decalescence.

decalvare [A 1] *tr.* to shave the head of (as punishment).

Decameron(e) *pr.n.m.* Decameron, the title of a collection of 100 short stories by Giovanni Boccaccio.

decampare [A 1] *intr.* (aux. avere) to decamp; — da, to withdraw from; (fig.) to recede; to yield; — da un'opinione, to relinquish a point of view.

decan-o *m.* (Rom. antiq.) commander of ten men; doyen, senior member; il — d'età, the oldest member; (eccl.) dean; doyen (of diplomatic corps or other body); (astron.) ten degrees of the zodiac. **-ato** *m.* (eccl.) deanship.

decantare¹ [A 1] *tr.* to sing the praises of, to be constantly praising.

decant-are² *tr.* to decant. (**-ato** *part. adj.*) **-atore** *m.* (techn.) decanter. **-azione** *f.* decantation; decanting.

decap-are [A 1] *tr.* (metall.) to pickle. **-ag·gio** *m.* (metall.) pickling. (**-ato** *part. adj.*)

decapit-are [A 1 s] *tr.* to behead, to decapitate. (**-ato** *part. adj.*) **-azione** *f.* beheading, decapitation.

decap(p)otta·bile *adj.* (of a car) convertible, having a convertible hood.

decapsulazione *f.* (med.) decapsulation.

decarbossilazione *f.* (chem.) decarboxylation.

decarbur-are [A 1] *tr.* to decarbonize. (**-ato** *part. adj.*) **-azione** *f.* decarbonization.

decasil·labo *m., adj.* See under **decacordo**.

decat-issag·gio *m.* (text.) pre-shrinkage. **-iz·zare** [A 1] *tr.* (text.) to pre-shrink. **-iz·zato** *part. adj.* (text.) pre-shrunk.

dece·dere¹ [C 22 b] *intr.* (aux. essere) to decease.

†**dece·dere²** *tr.* to deceive.

deceler-are [A 1 s] *intr.* (aux. avere) to decelerate, to throttle down. **-azione** *f.* deceleration; decelerating.

decembre *m.* See **dicembre**.

decembrista *m.* (hist.). See **decabrista**.

decem·peda *f.* (Rom. antiq.) ten-foot measuring-rod.

decem·vir-o *m.* (Rom. hist.) decemvir. **-ale** *adj.* decemviral. **-ato** *m.* decemvirate.

dec-enne *adj.* ten years old; going back ten years, of ten years' standing. **-ennale** *adj.* decennial; *n.m.* tenth anniversary; (lit.) *I Decennali*, title of Machiavelli's verse Annals (of ten years). †**-enna·rio** *adj.* of ten. **-en·nio** *m.* decade, period of ten years.

decennovennale *adj.* (astron.) relating to the 'golden number' which has a periodicity of nineteen years, at the coincidence of solar and lunar years.

decen-te *adj.* seemly, decent, becoming, respectable. **-temente** *adv.* respectably; vestito -temente, neatly dressed. **-za** *f.* decency, propriety; non avere -za, to have no sense of propriety; gabinetti di -za, toilets.

decentr-are [A 1] *tr.* (admin.) to decentralize. **-amento** *m.* decentralizing; decentralization. **-ato** *part. adj.* decentralized.

decen·viro *m.* See **decemviro**.

decenza *f.* See under **decente**.

†**de·c-ere** *intr.* to be fitting, to be suited, to be appropriate. †**-e·vole** *adj.* suitable, fitting, appropriate. †**-evolezza** *f.* suitability, appropriateness.

†**decer·nere** *tr.* to establish; to distinguish, to choose.

decesso *m.* decease, death.

†**decett-ivo** *adj.* deceptive. †**-o** *adj.* deceived, duped. †**-o·rio** *adj.* deceiving, deceptive.

†**dece·vol-e** *adj.*, †**-ezza** *f.* See under **decere**.

†**decezione** *f.* deception; error; (rhet.) cavil; subtle metaphor.

†**dechinare** *vb.* and derivs. See **dichinare**.

decibe·l *m. indecl.* (acoust.) decibel.

deci·d-ere [C 3] *tr.* to decide, to settle, to resolve; to decide upon, to arrange for; (leg.) to decide; to find; to determine; †to truncate; †to lop off; †to cut away; †to separate; †to relate, to recount, to make manifest; *intr.* (*aux.* avere; *prep.* di) to decide (to); — di agire, to decide to act; to be decisive; questo non -e, this is not conclusive; questo decise della sua sorte, this determined his fate; *abs.* (leg.) to pass judgement; *rfl.* (*prep.* a) to make up one's mind, to resolve (to); -ersi a farlo, to make up one's mind to do it; (*prep.* per) to choose in favour of, to choose; mi -o per un caffè, I choose to have a coffee. **-ente** *adj.* (leg.) deciding; determining.

deci·du-o *adj.* (bot.) deciduous; (astron.) stella -a, falling star. **-a** *f.* (anat.) decidua.

deciferare [A 1 s] and derivs. See **decifrare**.

decifr-are [A 1] *tr.* to decipher, to decode; to make out, to interpret, to make something of. **-a·bile** *adj.* decipherable; legible, readable. **-amento** *m.* deciphering, decoding. **-ante** *part. adj.* codici e tabelle -anti, key to a cipher. **-ato** *part. adj.* deciphered, decoded; interpreted; understood; *n.m.* key to a cipher. (**-atore** *m.* **-atrice** *f.*) **-azione** *f.* decipherment.

dec-igrammo *m.* decigramme. **-i·litro** *m.* decilitre.

decil-e *adj.* (astron.) decile. **-ag·gio** *m.* (psych.) decile rank method.

de·cim-a *f.* tenth part; tenth thing; tenth woman; (hist.; eccl.) tithe, tenth; (mus.) tenth (interval). **-a·rio** *m.* register of tithes.

decimale *adj.* decimal; sistema metrico —, decimal system.

decimanona *f.* (mus.) nineteenth (mutation-stop of organ).

decim-are¹ [A 1 s] *tr.* to decimate; (hist.) to tithe; (mil. hist.) to kill every tenth soldier of an army (in punishment); (comm.) — una cambiale, to pay a bill a tenth at a time. **-ato** *part. adj.* decimated; having suffered heavy casualties. **-azione** *f.* decimation; decimating; (hist.) right of tithe; (comm.) payment by instalments.

decimare² [A 1] *tr.* to top, to poll (plants, trees).

decima·rio *m.* See under **decima**.

decimaterza *f.* (mus.) thirteenth (interval).

dec-i·metro *m.* decimetre, one-tenth of a metre (equiv. to 3·937 inches). **-imilli·metro** *m.* a tenth of a millimetre.

decimin-a *f.* (hist.) tax paid by a 'mezzadro', q.v. **-o** *m.* (hist.) register of tithes; (mus.) E flat piccolo.

de·cimo¹ *adj.* tenth; *n.m.* tenth part; tenth man; †idiot, half-wit.

De·cimo² *pr.n.m.* Decimus.

decimo-primo, -secondo, -terzo *adj.*, *n.m.* eleventh, twelfth, thirteenth, etc.

decina *f.* See **diecina**, under **dieci**.

De·cio *pr.n.m.* Decius.

†**deci·pula** *f.* cord binding the feet; snare, trap.

decisione *f.* settling, settlement, decision; resolution, determination; — presidenziale, ruling; chiedere al presidente di prendere una —, to ask for a ruling; (leg.) decision; resolution; finding; judgement.

decisiv-o *adj.* decisive; conclusive; positive; critical, crucial; voto —, casting vote. **-amente** *adv.* decisively; conclusively.

deciṣ-o *part.* of **decidere**, q.v.; *adj.* decided, settled; determined, resolute; bold; — a tutto, ready for anything, with a desperate courage. **-amente** *adv.* decidedly, certainly; resolutely, boldly. **-o·rio** *adj.* decisive; (leg.) giuramento -orio, interrogatory, question(s) to be answered on oath, put by one party to the other in a civil action. (**-ore** *m.* **-ora** *f.*)

decistero *m.* decistere, tenth of a cubic metre.

declam-are [A 1] *tr.*, *intr.* (*aux.* avere) to declaim; to recite; to speak (verse) with measured beat; to inveigh; to rant; — biasimi, to hurl abuse. **-ato** *part. adj.* declaimed; ranting. **-atore** *m.* ranter; vociferous speaker. (**-atrice** *f.*) **-ato·rio** *adj.* declamatory; ranting. (**-atoriamente**.) **-azione** *f.* declamation; declaiming; shouting; ranting.

declarare [A 1] and derivs. See **dichiarare**.

declarato·ri-a *f.* (leg.) declaration; declaratory judgement (C.P.). **-o** *adj.* (leg.) declaratory.

declass-are [A 1] *tr.* to transfer (railway compartment or ship) to a lower class. **-ato** *part. adj.* transferred to a lower class; (rlwy.) vettura -ata, first-class carriage used as a second-class.

declin-are [A 1] *tr.* (gramm.) to decline; (fig.) — le generalità, to give particulars about oneself (one's name, age, etc.); to decline, to refuse, to turn down; *intr.* (*aux.* avere) to sink; to decline; la febbre -a, the fever is diminishing; il giorno -a, the day is drawing to a close; la salute gli -a, his health is declining; to go down, to slope; to depart, to move away; — da, to diverge from; — dalla virtù, to deviate from virtue; — da una domanda, to decline a request. **-a·bile** *adj.* (gramm.) declinable; †mutable. **-amento** *m.* decline; sinking. **-ante** *part. adj.* declining; sloping; decreasing, diminishing. **-atore** *m.* (mens.) declinator. **-ato·ria** *f.* (leg.) plea to jurisdiction, declinatory plea. **-ato·rio** *m.* declinator; *adj.* (leg.) declinatory. **-azione** *f.* decline, sinking, waning; slope; (gramm.) declension; (astron.; scient.) declination; -azione magnetica, variation. **-o** *m.* decline, setting, decadence; (fig.) wane, waning. **-o·grafo** *m.* declinograph. **-o·metro** *m.* declinometer.

decl-ive *adj.* sloping; *n.m.* slope. **-i·vio** *m.* slope; (geog.) long profile. **-ività** *f.* slope, incline, declivity. †**-ivo** *adj.*, *n.m.* see **declive**.

decoll-are¹ [A 1] *tr.* to behead (now only of St John the Baptist, some churches and guilds having the dedication 'S. Giovanni decollato'). **-azione** *f.* (liturg.) Beheading (Decollation) of St John the Baptist.

decoll-are² [A 1] *intr.* (*aux.* avere) (aeron.) to take off. **-ag·gio** *m.*, **-o** *m.* (aeron.) take-off.

decolor-are [A 1 c] *tr.* to decolorize. **-ante** *part. adj.* decolorizing; *n.m.* decolorizing agent. **-ato** *part. adj.* decolorized. **-azione** *f.* (industr.) decolorization, fading. **-i·metro** *m.* fadeometer.

decombente *adj.* (bot.) decumbent.

decommettere [C 20] *tr.* (naut.) to untwist (a rope).

decomponi·bil-e *adj.* (scient.; math.) decomposable. **-ità** *f.* decomposability.

decomporre [B 21] *tr.* to decompose; to separate, to disintegrate; (math.) — un numero, to find the prime factors of a number; *rfl.* to become decomposed, to decompose; to putrefy.

decomposizione *f.* decomposition; decomposing; putrefaction.

decompressione *f.* (phys.; eng.) partial vacuum; decompression; artificially regulated decrease of pressure on a surfacing diver; camera di —, decompression chamber.

decontaminazione *f.* (atom. phys.) decontamination.

deconto *m.* (comm.) libretto di —, savings bank-book.

decontrostalli·e *f.pl.* (comm.) extra demurrage days.

decor-are *tr.* [A 1] to decorate; to adorn; (mil., etc.) — con medaglie, to decorate. **-amentale** *adj.* decorative. **-amento** *m.* decorating, adorning. **-ativo** *adj.* decorative. **-ato** *part. adj.* decorated; adorned; -ato al valore, decorated for valour; *n.m.* man who has been decorated; è un -ato di guerra, he has war medals. **-atore** *m.* decorator; house-decorator; interior decorator; (theatr.) scene-painter. (**-atora**, **-atrice** *f.*) **-azione** *f.* decoration, adornment; ornament; -azione al valore, decoration for valour; medal.

decor-o *m.* decorum, propriety; dignity; è il — della famiglia, he is the pride of his family; decoration; †*adj.* decorous. **-oso** *adj.* seemly, becoming, respectable, decent; having prestige value. **-osamente** *adv.* respectably, decently; in a seemly manner.

decorr-ere [C 5] *intr.* (*aux.* essere) to run downwards; (fig.) to run on; to pass, to elapse; a — dal 15 corrente, from the 15th of this month; (comm.) gli interessi -ono da, interest is chargeable from; (leg.) to elapse; to run from (e.g. a given date); to run out. **-endo** *adj.* (comm.) starting (from). **-enza** *f.* anniversary; (comm.) start (the time when interest is due); (leg.) starting point of a period of time; il giorno della -enza non è compiuto nel termine, the first day is not counted in the period; con -enza dal primo aprile, starting from 1st April.

decorso *part.* of **decorrere**, q.v.; *adj.* past, elapsed, gone by; *n.m.* course (esp. of illness); (leg.) lapse; period; per — del termine, by lapse of time.

decotto *adj.* (cul.) stewed; (leg.) bankrupt; partita decotta, frozen credit; *n.m.* (med.) decoction; (leg.) bankrupt.

decozione *f.* (med.) decoction; (pop.) brew; (leg.) bankruptcy.

decremento *m.* decrease; diminution; waning.

decre·metro *m.* (radio; electr.) decremeter.

decrepit-are [A I s] *tr.* (chem.) to decrepitate. (-ato *part. adj.*) -azione *f.* decrepitation.

decre·pit-o *adj.* decrepit; worn out; essere vecchio —, to be old and decrepit. †-à *f.* see **decrepitezza**. -ezza *f.* decrepitude.

decrẹsc-ere [B9] *intr.* (*aux.* essere) to decrease, to lessen; to abate, to wane; to diminish. -endo *m.* (mus.) decrescendo, becoming softer. -ente *part. adj.* decreasing; diminishing. -enza *f.* decrease; diminution; wane. -imento *m.* decrease. -iuto *part. adj.* decreased; diminished; lessened.

decretal-e *adj.*, *n.f.* (eccl.) decretal; *pl.* le -i, the Decretals. -ista *m.* decretalist.

decret-are [A I c] *tr.* to decree; to ordain. -ato *part. adj.* decreed; ordained. †-azione *f.* decreeing.

decreto *m.* decree; (leg.) *ex parte* order; — legge, decree of the executive power having the force of law; decree law.

decu·bito *m.* position of one lying in bed; (med.) decubitus; piaghe da —, bed-sores; *pl.* bed-sores.

de cuius *m. indecl.* (leg.) the deceased; testator, or testatrix, intestate.

decumano *adj.* decuman; *n.m.* (Rom. antiq.) road running east to west through camp or town; soldier of the tenth legion.

de·cupl-o *adj.* tenfold; ten times greater; *n.m.* ten times the amount. -icare [A 2 s] *tr.* to multiply by ten, to increase tenfold.

dec-u·ria *f.* (Rom. hist.) decury; any group of ten. -uriare [A 4] *tr.* (Rom. hist.) to group in decuries. †-u·rio *m.* see **decurione**. -urione *m.* (Rom. hist.) decurion; captain of ten. -urionale *adj.* of, relating to a decurion. -urionato *m.* decurionate.

decursione *f.* (Rom. antiq.) *decursio.*

decurt-are [A I] to curtail, to reduce; (finan.) to shorten. -azione *f.* curtailment, reduction; (finan.) shortening.

decuss-are [A I] *tr.*, *rfl.* to decussate, to cross or intersect so as to form an X. -ato *part. adj.* decussate, decussation, decussating.

decusse *f.* (Rom. antiq.) *decussis* (as figure or coin).

De·d-alo *pr.n.m.* (myth.) Daedalus; (fig.) labyrinth, maze; un — di viuzze, a labyrinth of little alleys; †*adj.* of surpassing skill, of consummate artistry. -aleggiare [A 3 c] *intr.* (*aux.* avere) to emulate Daedalus. -a·leo, -ale·o *adj.* Daedalian, pertaining, relating or similar to Daedalus or his works; formed with consummate artistry; labyrinthine, maze-like.

de·dica *f.* dedication; author's inscription (in book); esemplare con la —, copy (of a book) containing the author's inscription.

dedic-are [A 2 s] *tr.* to dedicate; to devote; to give, to offer up; to consecrate; to inscribe (a book, etc.); *rfl.* (*prep.* a) to dedicate oneself (to); to devote oneself (to); to give oneself up (to). -ante *part. adj.*, *n.m.*, *f.* dedicator. -ato *part. adj.* dedicated; devoted; given over; una vita -ata a Dio, a life dedicated to God; chiesa -ata alla Madonna, church dedicated to the Virgin. -atore *m.* see **dedicante**. -ato·ria *f.* dedicatory epistle; dedication. -ato·rio *adj.* dedicatory; lettera -atoria, dedicatory epistle, dedication. -azione *f.* dedication; dedicating; devotion.

de·dit-o *adj.* (*prep.* a) given over (to), devoted; — agli studi, engrossed in study; — agli affari, wholly taken up with business; — alla mala vita, addicted to evil ways. -amente *adv.* earnestly; devotedly; whole-heartedly. -i·zio *adj.*, *n.m.* (Rom. hist.) dedician, *dediticius.*

dedizione *f.* self-surrender; devotion, sacrifice.

dedotto *part.* of **dedurre**, q.v.; *adv.* deduced, inferred, concluded; deducted, subtracted.

†**dedu·cere** *vb.* and derivs. See **dedurre**.

deduci·bile *adj.* deducible; to be logically derived or inferred.

dedurre [B 2] *tr.* to derive, to draw; to deduce, to infer; to conclude; io ne deduco che, my conclusion is that; to deduct, to subtract; (hist.) to lead out, to found (a colony); (leg.) to deduce; to allege; to argue; to plead; †to reduce; †*rfl.* to bring oneself; to compel oneself; to condescend.

deduttiv-o *adj.* deductive; metodo —, deductive method (of reasoning); ragionamento —, deductive reasoning. -amente *adv.* by deduction; deductively.

dedut-tore *m.* one who deduces; (anat.) muscolo —, deducer muscle. (-trice *f.*)

deduzione *f.* deducing; deduction, inference, conclusion; (hist.) founding (of colony); (leg.) argument (usu. *pl.*); sentite le deduzioni della difesa, having heard the argument for the defence; statement (in writing); — della prova per testimoni, drawing-up of witnesses' proofs (C.C.P.).

†**dees·sa** *f.* See **dea**.

defalc-are [A 2] *tr.* (finan.) to deduct, to subtract, to make allowance for. (-amento *m.*) -azione *f.* deduction.

defal·co *m.* (*pl.* -chi) (finan.) deduction, allowance.

defang-are [A 2] *tr.* (mining) to deslime. -atura *f.* (mining) desliming.

defatig-are [A 2] *tr.* to weary; (leg.) to wear out. -ato *part. adj.* wearied; weary; (leg.) worn out. -ato·rio *m.* (leg.) delaying.

defec-are [A 2] *tr.* to free from impurities, to remove foreign matter from; *intr.* (*aux.* avere) to defecate, to stool. (-ato *part. adj.*) -azione *f.* defecation; clarification.

†**defen·dere** *vb.* and derivs. See **difendere**.

defenestr-are [A I] *tr.* to throw out of the window; (fig.) to throw overboard; to 'sack', to dismiss. (-ato *part. adj.*) -azione *f.* (hist.) defenestration.

defensionale *adj.* (leg.) having to do with the defence; l'arringa —, the speech for the defence.

defer-ire [D 2] *tr.* to submit (to a competent authority); (leg.) to commit; to submit; to yield; to administer; to refer; — al tribunale, to refer to court, to send for trial; †to denounce; †see **differire**; *intr.* (*aux.* avere; *prep.* a), *rfl.* to defer, to bow, to conform (to). -ente *part. adj.* deferential, submissive; (astron.; med.) deferent; *n.m.* (astron.) deferent. -enza *f.* deference, consideration. -imento *m.* deferring; submitting. -ito *part. adj.* submitted; (leg.) committed, submitted, deferred.

defervescenza *f.* (med.) defervescence, abatement of fever.

†**defesso** *adj.* weary, worn out.

defetti·bile *adj.* liable to fail or fall short.

defezion-e *f.* defection; backsliding; (mil.) desertion; †defect, failing. -are [A I c] *intr.* (*aux.* avere) to desert, to fall away, to back out.

defici-ente *adj.* deficient, insufficient; simple-minded, wanting; below examination standard; *n.m.*, *f.* mental deficient. -enza *f.* lack, insufficiency; mental deficiency; deficiency, shortage.

de·ficit *m. indecl.* (finan.) deficit; colmare un —, to make good a deficit. -a·rio *adj.* (comm.) deficient.

defilato *adj.* (neol.; mil.) defiladed, secured against enfilading fire.

defin-ire [D 2] *tr.* to define; to determine; to settle; to describe (also leg.). -i·bile *adj.* definable. -itiva *f.* in -itiva, in point of fact. -itivo *adj.* definitive; decisive; (leg.) sentenza -itiva, definitive sentence; final judgement or settlement. -itivamente *adv.* definitively. -ito *part. adj.* defined; definite. (-itamente *adv.*) -itore *m.* (eccl.) definitor; (sculpt.) chisel. (-itrice *f.*) -izione *f.* definition; settlement; description; (leg.) definition, interpretation, settlement; determination.

deflagr-are [A I] *intr.* (*aux.* avere) (chem.) to deflagrate. -atore *m.* (electr.) deflagrator. -azione *f.* (chem.) deflagration.

deflazion-e *f.* (finan.; geol.) deflation. -are [A I c] *tr.*, *intr.* (*aux.* avere) (finan.) to deflate. -a·rio *adj.* (finan.) deflationary.

deflemm-are [A I] *tr.* (chem.) to rectify (a spirit). (-ato *part. adj.*) -atore *m.* (chem.) fractionating column, dephlegmator. -azione *f.* rectification.

deflet·t-ere [C 19] *intr.* (*aux.* avere) to deflect, to alter course, to deviate; to diverge; to give way, to yield; — da un'opinione, to withdraw from a standpoint, to relinquish an opinion. -ore *m.* (phys.; aeron.) deflector; baffle.

deflor-are [A I] *tr.* to deflower; to ravish. -amento *m.* deflowering; ravishing. -ato *part. adj.* deflowered; ravished. -atore *m.* violator. -azione *f.* deflowering; ravishing; violation.

deflu-ire [D 2] *intr.* (*aux.* essere) to flow down; to flow. -ente *part. adj.* defluent.

deflusso *m.* downward flow; backwash; discharge.

†**defonto** *adj.* See **defunto**.

deform-are [A I c] *tr.* to deform; to disfigure; to distort; (eng.) to strain; *rfl.* to become distorted; to get out of shape; to warp; to buckle. -a·bile *adj.* capable of being deformed or distorted; tubetto -abile, collapsible tube. -amento *m.* disfiguring; distorting; warping. -ante *part. adj.* disfiguring; distorting. -ato *part. adj.* deformed; disfigured; distorted; misshapen; warped; buckled; *n.m.* deformed person. (-atore *m.* -atrice *f.*) -azione *f.* distortion; disfigurement; loss of shape; buckling; warping; (fig.) -azione professionale, mental characteristics and habits derived from the exercise of one's profession.

deform-e *adj.* deformed, misshapen; ill-shaped, ugly; mutilated. (-emente *adv.*) -ità *f.* deformity; disfigurement; malformation.

defosforazione *f.* (metall.) dephosphorization.

defraud-are [A I a] *tr.* to defraud; ci ha -ato di una parte del guadagno, he has defrauded us of part of the profits; to cheat

defraud-are (*cont.*)
(of), to deprive (of), to do out (of); to disappoint; non voglio — la vostra aspettazione, I do not want to disappoint your expectations. **-amẹnto** *m.* defrauding; defraudment. **-ato** *part. adj.* (*prep.* di) defrauded, cheated, done out (of). **-atọre** *m.* one who defrauds. (**-atrice** *f.*) **-aziọne** *f.* defraudation; cheating; deprivation.

†**defrescare** *tr.* to refresh.

defunto *adj., n.m.* deceased, dead, defunct; (liturg.) messa dei defunti, mass of the dead.

degalvanizẓ-are [A I] *tr.* (electroplating) to strip. **-aziọne** *f.* stripping.

degassamẹnto *m.* (phys.) outgassing, degassing, exhausting.

degaullista *m., f.* (Fr. pol.) De Gaulliste, supporter of De Gaulle.

degener-are [A I s] *intr.* (*aux.* avere, essere) to degenerate; to deteriorate; — da una famiglia, to degenerate from a family; — in, to degenerate into; l'infreddatura -ò in bronchite, the cold developed into bronchitis. **-ato** *part. adj.* degenerate; *n.m.* degenerate person. **-aziọne** *f.* degeneration, degenerating; degeneracy.

degẹ·nere *adj.* degenerate; deteriorated.

degen-te *adj., n.m., f.* patient in hospital; in-patient; — presso l'ospedale, as an in-patient at the hospital; inmate (in a prison); †inhabitant. **-za** *f.* stay in hospital; rest in bed.

dẹgli *contr.* of *prep.* di, q.v., with **gli** *def. art. m.pl.*

deglut-ire [D 2] *tr.* (med.) to swallow. **-iziọne** *f.* deglutition, swallowing.

degn-are [A 5 c] *tr.* to deem worthy, to regard as worthy; non lo -ai d'una risposta, I didn't deign to reply to him; †to make worthy; *intr.* (*aux.* avere) to be condescending, to be polite; non -a più, he has lost his affability; †to be able (to), to be capable (of); *rfl., intr.* to deign, to condescend; degnate(vi) di avvertirmi, be so kind as to let me know; †to regard oneself as worthy. **-ato** *part. adj.* deemed worthy; †made worthy; †accepted. **-aziọne** *f.* condescension, amiability. **-ẹvole** *adj.* affable; †condescending.

†**degnità** *f.* and deriv. see **dignità**; (philos., esp. Vico) axiom.

dẹgn-o *adj.* deserving, worthy, excellent; una -a persona, an honourable and good person; un vecchio signore con un'aria molto -a, an extremely dignified-looking old gentleman; — di lode, deserving of praise; è — di un monumento, he deserves a monument; esser — di esser bastonato, to deserve a beating; †suited, fit; †— a, fit for, suited to, worthy of; comparable to; †avere a —, to hold in esteem. **-amẹnte** *adv.* worthily; fittingly, suitably; in a dignified manner. †**-ificare** *tr.* to dignify; to render fitting.

degra *m.* (techn.) degras.

degrad-are [A I] *tr.* to degrade from rank or office; to degrade; to disgrace; to dishonour; (paint.) see **digradare**; *rfl.* to degrade oneself; to disgrace oneself socially; to lower one's dignity; to degenerate. **-amẹnto** *m.* degrading; disgrace; (mil.) loss of rank; lowering of security classification (e.g. from secret to restricted, etc.). **-ante** *part. adj.* degrading; lowering; sloping down in tiers. **-ato** *part. adj.* degraded; disgraced; (mil.) down-graded. **-aziọne** *f.* degradation; disgrace; degeneration; (math.) depression; (paint.) see **digradazione**, under **digradare**.

degust-are [A I] *tr.* to taste; to sample. **-ato** *part. adj.* tasted; sampled. **-atọre** *m.* taster; -atore di vino, wine-taster. **-aziọne** *f.* tasting; sampling; -azione di vino, wine-tasting.

deh *excl.* (pron. dè) (poet.) ah!; pray!; alas!

dẹi[1] *contr.* of *prep.* di, q.v., with **i**, *def. art. m.pl.*

dei[2] *m.pl.* of **dio**, q.v.

deic-ida *m.* deicide, killer of a god. **-i·dio** *m.* deicide, killing of a god.

dei·cola *m.* worshipper of God.

deidr-atọre *m.* (mining) dewaterer. **-aziọne** *f.* dewatering. **-ogenizẓa-ziọne** *f.* (chem.) dehydrogenation.

†**deiettare** *vb.* to cast down; to deject; to cast away.

deiettọre *m.* (eng.) agitator or similar device to prevent the scaling of boilers, etc.

deieziọne *f.* (med.) dejection, faecal discharge; (geol.; geog.) dejection; cono di —, talus, cone of detritus; †(fig.) dejection, depression.

deific-are [A 2 s] *tr.* to deify; to make a cult of. **-amẹnto** *m.* deifying. **-ato** *part. adj.* deified. **-aziọne** *f.* deification, apotheosis.

de-i·fico *adj.* (rel.) deific, deifying. **-ifọrme** *adj.* (rel.) deiform.

deionizẓ-are [A I] *tr.* (chem.; phys.) to de-ionize. **-atọre** *m.* de-ionizer. **-aziọne** *f.* de-ionization.

dei·para *adj.* (theol.) God-bearing; *n.f.* the Mother of God; the Deipara.

deiscen-te *adj.* (bot.) dehiscent. **-za** *f.* (bot.) dehiscence, splitting open of seed cases or other parts of a plant.

de-i·ṣmo *m.* (theol.; philos.) deism. **-ista** *m.* deist. **-ità** *f.* deity, godhead.

de iure *adv. phr.* (leg.) de jure, by right.

dẹl *contr.* of *prep.* di, q.v., with **il**, *def. art. m.sing.*

delanare [A I] *tr.* (tanning) to de-wool, to fellmonger.

†**delapidare** *vb.* and derivs. See **lapidare**.

del-atọre *m.* police informer; (leg.) delator, accuser; — di armi, person in possession of weapons without a licence; †person bearing arms. (**-atrice** *f.*) **-aziọne** *f.* laying of information; denouncing; (leg.) delation; secret accusation; -azione dell'eredità, devolution of inheritance (C.C.); -azione dell'armi, being in unauthorized possession of weapons.

delcre·dere *m.* (comm.) del credere.

dele·bile *adj.* erasable.

de·leg-a *f.* (leg.) proxy; agency; delegation of power; per —, by proxy; (colloq.) la legge delega, the (bill) law for the reform of the Italian Bureaucracy or Civil Service. **-are** [A 2 s] *tr.* (leg.) to assign; to delegate; to depute; to commit; to appoint as representative. **-ata·rio** *m.* (leg.) delegatee, creditor for a debt which is assigned to him. **-ati·zio** *adj.* (leg.) delegatory. **-ato** *part. adj.* (leg.) delegated; deputed; appointed; *n.m.* (leg.) delegate; designare in qualità di -ato, to appoint as delegate; -ato di pubblica sicurezza, police agent; (eccl.) -ato apostolico, Apostolic Delegate. **-ato·rio** *adj.* (eccl.) delegatory. **-aziọne** *f.* (leg.) delegation of powers; commission; committee; deputation; -azione di sorveglianza, committee of inspection; delegation; commission.

†**del-ere** *tr.* to delete, to cancel; to destroy. †**-endo** *adj.* deserving destruction, fit to be destroyed.

delete·rio *adj.* deleterious; having a bad effect, injurious.

†**delettare** *vb.* and derivs. See **dilettare**.

†**deletto**[1] *m.* See **diletto**[1] or **diletto**[2].

†**del-etto**[2] *m.* (mil.) levy, conscription; selection; discernment, discrimination. †**-eziọne** *f.* choice, selection.

del·fico *adj.* Delphic.

Delfinato *pr.n.m.* (geog.) Dauphiné.

delfin-o *m.* (zool.) dolphin; — comune, *Delphinus delphis*; — grigio, *Grampus griseus*; — tursio, *Tursiops tursio*; (astron.) Delphinus; (swimming) dolphin-stroke; hunchback; (hist.) Dauphin; (joc.) son and heir, successor; (Gk. antiq.) dolphin, a heavy mass of lead suspended from a yard at the bow of a war-vessel; *pl.* (naut.) cheeks of ship's head; (artill. hist.) dolphins, handles cast solid on a cannon. **-a** *f.* (hist.) Dauphiness, wife of the Dauphin. **-are** [A I] *intr.* (*aux.* avere) (of a seaplane) to porpoise; (of a submarine) to pump.

Delfo *pr.n.m.* Delphi.

deli·aco *adj.* See under **delo**.

delib-are [A I] *tr.* to taste; to sample a small quantity of. **-ato** *part. adj.* tasted; sampled. **-aziọne** *f.* tasting; (leg.) -azione delle sentenze straniere, scrutiny of foreign judgements (C.C.P.).

deli·bera *f.* (comm.) auction; adjudication; resolution; decision; (leg.) adjudication by auction.

deliber-are [A I s] *tr.* to resolve upon; to decide after mature reflection; — la guerra, to decide in favour of war; (leg.) to decide; to resolve; to adjudicate; — in camera di consiglio, to decide in chambers (or) in the Judges' Retiring Room; *intr.* (*aux.* avere) to deliberate; to ponder; to make up one's mind; -ai di andarmene, I decided to leave; (at an auction) signori! si -a, gentlemen, the bidding is open; (leg.) to deliberate; *rfl.* to decide; to resolve; mi -ai di fare così, I resolved upon this course of action. †**-amento** *m.* deliberation, decision. **-ante** *part. adj.* deliberating. **-ata·rio** *m.* highest bidder at auction sale. **-ativa** *f.* (philos.) faculty of decision. **-ativo** *adj.* (leg.) deciding, resolving; voto -ativo, deciding or effective vote; voting right; eloquenza -ativa, right to speak; (rhet.) deliberative. **-ato** *part. adj.* determined, resolute; -ato di venire, set on coming; -ato a tutto, ready for anything. (**-atọre** *m.*) **-aziọne** *f.* decision, deliberation; (comm.) -azione dei creditori, resolution of creditors; (leg.) resolution; adjudication; -azione del consiglio di amministrazione, resolution of the board of directors (C.C.); †liberation.

†**delic-amento** *m.* delight; delicacy. †**-anza** *f.* delicacy; refined and elegant beauty.

delicat-o *adj.* delicate; weak; not very strong; dainty; delicious; soft; (of food) light, digestible; fastidious, refined; sensitive; fragile; frail; squeamish; scrupulous, conscientious. (**-aṃente** *adv.*) **-ẹzza** *f.* delicacy; daintiness; softness; refinement; tact; a dainty; con **-ezza**, delicately; agitare con **-ezza**, to stir gently; †**adornment**. **-ura** *f.* luxury; daintiness; exquisiteness; dainty thing.

delignific-are [A 2 s] *tr.* (text.) to delignify. **-azione** *f.* (text.; paperm.) delignification.

†**delimare** [A 1] *tr.* to wear down, to wear away; to abrade.

delimit-are [A 1 s] *tr.* to delimit, to define; — la competenza di una commissione, to define the competence of a committee. **-azione** *f.* delimitation.

deline-are [A 6] *tr.* to delineate, to outline; to trace, to sketch. **-aṃento** *m.* delineating, outlining; sketch. **-ato** *part. adj.* delineated, outlined; traced, sketched. (**-atọre** *m.* **-atrice** *f.*) **-atura** *f.*, **-azione** *f.* delineation, sketch.

delin·qu-ere [def.] *intr.* to commit a crime or offence, to break the law. **-ente** *part. adj.* delinquent; *n.m.* delinquent; **-ente abituale**, habitual criminal. **-enza** *f.* delinquency.

†**delinqu-ire** *tr.* to consume, to wear away. †**-ito** *part. adj.* worn away.

deliquesc-ente *adj.* (chem.) deliquescent; (fig.) fulsome; languishing. **-enza** *f.* (chem.) deliquescence; (fig.) fulsomeness; languishing behaviour, languor, affected admiration.

deli·quio *m.* (med.) fainting fit, deliquium, swoon; †(chem.) deliquescence.

delir-are [A 1] *intr.* (*aux.* avere) to rave, to talk wildly, to be beside oneself; to be delirious. (**-aṃento** *n.*) **-ante** *part. adj.* raving, delirious; *n.m.*, *f.* delirious person.

deli·rio *m.* delirium, frenzy; wild desire; excessive enthusiasm.

deliro *adj.* (poet.) wild, frenzied, mad; †*n.m.* see **delirio**.

delitt-o *m.* crime; offence; felony; misdemeanour; i reati si distinguono in **-i** e contravvenzioni, offences are divided into crimes and contraventions; commettere un —, to commit a crime; accusare di un —, to charge with a crime; — colposo, crime without malice aforethought, criminal intent or premeditation; — doloso, crime with malice aforethought, criminal intent or premeditation; corpo del —, *corpus delicti*. **-uosaṃente** *adv.* criminally.

†**delivrare** *vb.* and derivs. See **deliberare**.

deli·zi-a *f.* delight; pleasure; joy; charming person, delightful creature; voluptuousness. †**-ale** *adj.* pleasurable. †**-ano** *adj.* delicious; delightful. **-are** [A 4] *tr.* to delight, to entrance; to charm; to make happy; *rfl.* (*prep.* in, di, con) to take great pleasure (in); to go into ecstasies (over). **-ọso** *adj.* delightful; charming; exquisite; delicious; voluptuous. **-osaṃente** *adv.* delightfully; charmingly; exquisitely; deliciously; voluptuously.

dell', **dẹlla**, **dẹllo** *contr.* of *prep.* di, q.v., with **l'**, **la** and **lo**, various forms of the *def. art.*

Del-o *pr.n.m.* (geog.) Delos. **-i·aco** *adj.* Delian.

delt-a *m.* (the letter) delta; (geog.) delta; (astron.) triangulum. **-azione** *f.* delta formation. **-o·ide** *m.* (anat.) deltoid muscle. **-oide·o** *adj.* deltoid. **-oto** *m.* (astron.) triangulum.

delubro *m.* (antiq.; poet.) temple, shrine.

delucidare [A 1 s] and derivs. See **dilucidare**.

delu·d-ere [C 3] *tr.* to disappoint; to delude, to deceive, to elude, to evade; †to mock; †to cheat. †**-imento** *m.* deluding; mocking.

deluṣ-iọne *f.* disappointment; delusion, deception; illusion; †mockery. **-o** *part.* of **deludere**, q.v.; *adj.* deluded; deceived; disappointed. **-ọre** *m.* deluder, deceiver, beguiler. **-o·rio** *adj.* delusive, delusory. (**-oriaṃente** *adv.*)

demagliare [A 4] *rfl.* (of a stocking) to ladder.

demagnetiẓẓ-are [A 1] *tr.* (electr.) to demagnetize. (**-ato** *part. adj.*) **-atọre** *m.* demagnetizer. **-azione** *f.* demagnetization.

demag-ogi·a *f.* demagogy; mob-rule, ochlocracy; pandering to vulgar instincts of a crowd. **-o·gico** *adj.* demagogic. (**-ogicaṃente** *adv.*) **-ogo** *m.* (*pl.* **-oghi**) demagogue.

demandare [A 1] *tr.* (leg.) to entrust; to commit. †See **domandare**.

dema·ni-o *m.* (leg.) demesne; domain; — pubblico, public property; i fiumi fanno parte del — pubblico, rivers are public property; — della corona, crown lands or property. **-ale** *adj.* (leg.) domanial.

demarc-are [A 2] *tr.* to demarcate. **-azione** *f.* demarcation.

demar-chi·a *f.* (Gk. hist.) demarchy. **-co** *m.* (*pl.* **-chi**) (Gk. hist.) demarch.

†**dement-are** *tr.* to drive out of one's mind. †**-ato** *part. adj.* demented.

demen-te *adj.* demented, insane. **-za** *f.* (med.) dementia.

†**demer·gere** *tr.* to submerge; to sink.

demerit-are [A 1 s] *tr.* to forfeit; to deserve to lose; to be unworthy of; *intr.* (*aux.* avere) to do disservice, to act unbecomingly; ha **-ato della patria**, he has deserved ill of his country. **-ẹvole** *adj.* undeserving, unworthy.

deme·rit-o *m.* demerit; shortcoming; discreditable action; bad mark (at school). **-o·rio** *adj.* demeritorious, discreditable.

demineraliẓẓaziọne *f.* (chem.) demineralizing.

demiur-go *m.* (*pl.* **-ghi**) (Gk. antiq.; philos.) demiurge; (fig.) superman, god-like human being.

demo *m.*, **demos** *m. indecl.* (Gk. hist.) demos; deme.

democra·t-ico *adj.* democratic; *n.m.* democrat. **-icaṃente** *adv.* democratically. **-iẓẓare** [A 1] *tr.*, *intr.* (*aux.* avere) to democratize.

democrazi·a *f.* democracy.

democristiano *m.*, *adj.* (abbrev. of **democratico cristiano**) Christian Democrat.

Demo·crit-o *pr.n.m.* Democritus. **-e·o** *adj.* Democritean.

demodul-atọre *m.* (radio) demodulator. **-aziọne** *f.* (radio) demodulation.

Demogọrgone, Demogorgọne, Demogorgo *pr.n.m.* Demogorgon; (joc.) boaster.

demo-grafi·a *f.* demography. **-gra·fico** *adj.* demographic; (Ital. hist.) campagna **-grafica**, national campaign for higher birth-rate during Fascist régime; pianificazione **-grafica**, planned parenthood.

demol-ire [D 2] *tr.* to demolish, to pull down; to raze to the ground; to destroy, to ruin; (naut.) to break up. **-ito** *part. adj.* demolished; destroyed; in ruins; (geog.) worn down. (**-itọre** *m.* **-itrice** *f.*) **-iziọne** *f.* demolition; destruction; bombed site.

demologi·a *f.* study of the social and cultural history of mankind; (social) anthropology.

demoltiplicaziọne *f.* (eng.) speed reduction, gearing down; (radio) demultiplication.

de·m-one *m.* demon, devil; daemon, genius; (fig.) ruling passion, violent influence. **-oni·aco** *adj.* demoniac(al); daemonic; *n.m.pl.* (rel. hist.) Demoniacs. **-o·nico** *adj.* demonic; daemonic; *n.m.* daemon, poetic inspiration, genius.

demo·n-io *m.* demon, devil; astute individual; firebrand; tireless worker; ugly person; lively or uncontrollable child; un — di donna, a virago; un — di problema, the devil of a problem. **-iẹtto** *m. dim.* little devil, imp, mischievous child. **-i·o** *m.* pandemonium. **-(i)olatri·a** *f.* demonolatry, devil-worship. **-iṣmo** *m.* daemonism, dualistic theory of good and evil spirits. **-ologi·a** *f.* demonology. **-omani·a** *f.* demonomania.

demopsicologi·a *f.* study of folk traditions and thought; folk-lore.

demoraliẓẓ-are [A 1] *tr.* to demoralize; *rfl.* to grow demoralized. **-ato** *part. adj.* demoralized. **-aziọne** *f.* demoralization; demoralizing.

demorfiniẓẓ-are [A 1] *tr.* (med.) to reduce (a person's) doses of morphine (in the case of an addict). **-aziọne** *f.* (med.) demorphinization.

†**demostrare** *vb.* and derivs. See **dimostrare**.

demo·tico *adj.* (Egyptol.) demotic.

demulc-ere [B 17] *tr.* to touch gently or soothingly, to smooth down, to soothe. **-ente** *adj.* demulcent.

demuls-ificare [A 2 s], **-iọnare** [A 1 c] *tr.* (techn.) to demulsify.

demuscaziọne *f.* fly disinfestation.

†**dena·io** *m.* and derivs. See **denaro**.

†**den-ante**, †**-anti**, †**-anzi** *adv.*, *prep.* See **dinanzi**.

denaro *m.* money; wealth; il tempo è —, time is money; coin (as opposed to paper-money); — contante, ready money; — in cassa, cash in hand; — spicciolo, small change; raccoglier —, to raise money; (text.) denier; *pl.* money; pence; name of a suit of cards in an Italian pack (see note under **carta**); (numis.) small coin; †measure of length (240 'denari' equal 1 'braccio'). See also **danaro**.

denatalità *f.* fall in birth-rate; falling birth-rate.

denatur-are [A 1] *tr.* (chem.) to denature. **-ante** *part. adj.* (chem.) denaturing; *n.m.* denaturing agent. **-ato** *part. adj.* (chem.) denatured; alcool **-ato**, methylated spirits.

denazific-are [A 2 s] *tr.* (pol.) to de-Nazify. (**-ato** *part. adj.*) **-azione** *f.* (pol.) de-Nazification.

dendr-a·gata *f.* (miner.) dendrachate. **-ite** *f.* (miner.) dendrite. **-i·tico** *adj.* (miner.) dendritic, dendritical. **-o·foro** *m.* (hist. rel.) dendrophorus (in cult of Cybele).

deneg-are [A2c, A2] *tr.* to refuse; to deny. **-ato** *part. adj.* refused; denied; (leg.) -ata giustizia, denial of justice (C.C.P.). **-azione** *f.* refusal; denial.

denga *f.* (med.) dengue, dengue-fever.

denicotinizzare [A1] *tr.* to remove nicotine from (tobacco).

denier *m.* (*pl.* deniers, pron. as Fr.) (text.) denier (1·2744 gm.).

denigr-are [A1] *tr.* to defame; to disparage; to denigrate; to belittle, to depreciate. **-ante** *part. adj.* disparaging; denigrating. **-ato** *part. adj.* denigrated; belittled. **-atore** *m.* denigrator. (**-atrice** *f.*) **-atorio** *adj.* disparaging; denigrating. **-azione** *f.* denigration; defamation; disparagement.

denitr-ificare [A2s] *tr.* (chem.) to denitrate. **-ogenizzazione** *f.* (aeron.) denitrogenation, supercharging.

denodare [A1] *tr.* to untie, to undo.

denomin-are [A1] *tr.* to denominate; to designate; to call; *rfl.* to call oneself; to be called; to be designated. **-ativo** *adj.* denominative. **-ato** *part. adj.* denominated, designated; called; (math.) concrete; *n.m.* (math.) numerator. **-atore** *m.* (math.) denominator; -atore comune, common denominator (also fig.). **-azione** *f.* denomination, title; (rhet.) metonymy; (math.) denominator.

†**denonziare** *vb.* and derivs. See **denunciare**.

denot-are [A1] *tr.* to denote, to signify, to mean; to imply, to show. **-ante** *part. adj.* denoting, signifying. **-ativo** *adj.* denotative. **-azione** *f.* denotation.

†**densare** *vb.* and derivs. See **condensare**.

desensibilizz-are [A1] *tr.* (photog.) to desensitize. (**-ato** *part. adj.*) **-atore** *m.* (photog.) desensitizer. **-azione** *f.* (photog.) desensitizing.

dens-o *adj.* dense, thick, close; libro — d'idee, book packed with ideas. **-amente** *adv.* densely; closely. **-imetro** *m.* (phys.) hydrometer, pyknometer, gravity bottle; (tanning) barkometer. **-ità** *f.* density, thickness; closeness; (phys.) density, specific gravity. **-itometria** *f.* (photog.) densitometry. **-itometro** *m.* (atom. phys.) densitometer. **-ogramma** *m.* (photog.) densogram.

dent-ale *adj.* dental; *n.f.* (phonet.) dental; *n.m.* (agr.) share-beam; *m.* (zool.) *Dentalium dentale*, elephant's tusk shell; see also **dentice**. **-ame** *m.* mouthful of teeth, array of teeth. **-are** [A1] *intr.* (*aux.* avere) to cut teeth, to teethe.

denta·ri-a *f.* (bot.) toothwort, *Lathraea squamaria*; — minore, coral-wort, *Dentaria bulbifera*; moschatel, town-hall clock, *Adoxa moscatellina*. **-o** *adj.* (med.) dentary, dental.

dentar(u)olo *m.* baby's teething ring.

dentat-a *f.* bite; tooth-mark. **-o** *adj.* toothed, cogged; serrated; (herald.) indented; (bot.) dentate. **-rice** *f.* (eng.) cog-cutter. **-ura** *f.* (med.) dentition; di buona -ura, possessed of a hearty appetite; set of teeth; dentures; teeth of a comb; serration; (eng.) toothing; (herald.) bordure indented.

dent-e *m.* tooth; — del giudizio, wisdom-tooth; — canino, eye-tooth; — molare, molar; — incisivo, incisor; — di latte, milk-tooth, first tooth; mettere i -i, to cut one's teeth; otturare un —, to stop a tooth; cavare un —, to take a tooth out; -i naturali, one's own teeth; -i artificiali, artificial teeth; spuntano i primi -i, the first teeth are coming through; tra i -i, mumblingly; fuor dei -i, plainly, frankly; armato fino ai -i, armed to the teeth; digrignare i -i, to gnash one's teeth; scricchiolare i -i, to grind one's teeth; non toccare un — a uno, not to satisfy someone's appetite in the least; rimanere a -i asciutti, to be left hungry, to go without a meal, (fig.) to be thwarted, to come away empty-handed; aver la rosa nei -i, to feel hungry; ungere il — a uno, to give someone a meal, (fig.) to grease his palm; allungare i -i, to gather strength, to increase one's claims; prima i -i e poi i parenti, charity begins at home; non è cibo per i -i tuoi, it's too difficult (or, too good) for you, it's not your cup of tea; mostrare i -i, to show one's teeth, to look threatening; perderci i -i, to be the loser thereby; reggere l'anima con i -i, to be at one's last gasp, to hold on to life by a thread; ragione tirata coi -i, far-fetched explanation; (fig.) — dell'invidia, pang of envy, gnawing envy; (provb.) la lingua batte dove il — duole, tongue ever turns to aching tooth; finché uno ha -i in bocca non sa quel che gli tocca, life is full of surprises; tusk; prong; notch; (eng.) tooth, cog; protection; fluke of an anchor; jagged peak; (fortif.) tooth-like outwork; (carpen.) tenon; (naut.) -i di cane, barnacles; (text.) wire (of carding machine); (agric.) tine; (cul.) -i di cavallo, a kind of soup; al —, firm in the cooking, underdone; (bot.) — canino, couch-grass, stroyle, *Agropyron repens*; — cavallino, *Sorghum halepense*, or white henbane, *Hyoscyamus albus*; — di

leone, dandelion, *Taraxacum officinale*. **-one** *m.*, **-ona** *f.* person with big teeth, one who is 'all teeth'. **-uto** *adj.* toothy.

dentecchiare [A4]. See **denticchiare**.

dentell-are [A1] *tr.* to notch; to indent. **-ato** *part. adj.* notched; indented; (of stamps) perforated; (bot.) denticulate. **-atrice** *f.* (tailoring) pinking machine. **-atura** *f.* notching; indentation. **-o** *m. dim.* of dente, q.v.; (archit.) dentil, dentel; lace, embroidery; notch, tooth (of some tools); kind of burnisher. †**-iere** *m.* tooth-pick.

denticchiare [A4] *tr.* to nibble at; (fig.) to carp at.

den·tice *m.* (ichth.) *Dentex dentex*, a sea bream; — praio, *Pagrus vulgaris*, a kind of sea bream.

denticolato *adj.* (herald.) denticulated.

dentiera *f.* denture; (eng.) ratchet; rack; ferrovia a —, cog railway; (naut.) — dell'argano, capstan pawl and ratchet.

dentifri·cio *m.* toothpowder, dentifrice, toothpaste; *adj.* tooth-cleansing; crema dentifricia, pasta dentifricia, toothpaste.

dentilla·ria *f.* lead-wort, *Plumbago europaea*.

dentina *f.* (anat.) dentine.

dentino *m. dim.* of dente, q.v.; milk-tooth, first tooth.

dentista *m.*, *f.* dentist; dental surgeon.

dentizione *f.* (med.) teething, dentition.

dento-alveolare *adj.* (anat.) dento-alveolar.

dentro *adv.* inside, within, in; inwardly; darci —, to fall against, to fall into; to fall to (upon food); dare — a, to attack, to fall upon; to squander (a fortune), to make inroads upon; to guess right; o — o fuori!, make up your mind!; (fam.) star —, to be 'inside', to be in jail; mettere —, to jail; dentrovi, therein, in it; *prep.* (with nouns sometimes foll. by 'di', 'a'; with *pers. prns.* always foll. by 'di') inside; — di noi, within us, in ourselves; esser — a qualcosa, to be in on something, to be in the know about something; dentr'oggi, some time today, before the day is over; — domani, by tomorrow; qui —, in here; lì —, in there; *n.m.* il —, il di —, the inside; the inner part.

denuclearizz-are [A1] *tr.* (pol.) to render nuclear-free. **-ato** *part. adj.* (pol.) nuclear-free, free of atomic weapons.

denud-are [A1] *tr.* to denude, to strip, to lay bare; (geol.) to denude. **-amento** *m.* denuding. **-ato** *part. adj.* denuded; stripped; bare; bereft. **-azione** *f.* baring, denudation; (liturg.) -azione degli altari, stripping of the altars; (geol.) denudation.

denu·ncia *f.* declaration to an official (of income, dutiable goods, etc.); (leg.) report, declaration (usu. to the authorities); denunciation of a treaty; banns of marriage.

denunci-are [A3] *tr.* to make known, to notify, to declare; to denounce, to inform against; to repudiate; (leg.) to report, to declare (usu. to the authorities). (**-amento** *m.*) **-ato** *part. adj.* notified; declared; denounced; (leg.) reported, charged. (**-atore** *m.* **-atrice** *f.*) **-azione** *f.* declaration, notification; denunciation.

denu·nzia *f.* See **denuncia**.

denunziare [A4] and derivs. (Tusc.). See **denunciare**.

denutr-ito *adj.* undernourished; *n.m.* person suffering from malnutrition. **-izione** *f.* malnutrition.

†**deo** *m.* See **dio**.

deodara *f.* (bot.) deodar, *Cedrus deodara*.

deodor-are [A1c] **-izzare** [A1] *tr.* (chem.) to deodorize. **-ante** *part. adj.*, *n.m.* deodorant.

deo gratias, deogratias *Lat. phr.*, used as *n.m.* (liturg.) Deo gratias; (fam.) thank goodness!; essere al —, to have got to the end of something.

deonestare [A1] *tr.* to dishonour, to discredit.

deonto-logi·a *f.* (philos.) deontology; (fig.) professional ethics. **-lo·gico** *adj.* (philos.) deontological.

deossid-are [A1] *tr.* (chem.) to de-oxidize, to reduce. **-ato** *part. adj.* (chem.) de-oxidized. **-azione** *f.* (chem.) reduction.

deostr-uere [def.], **-uire** [D2] *tr.* (med.) to remove an obstruction from. **-ente** *part. adj.*, *n.m.* (med.) deobstruent.

depauper-are [A1s] *tr.* (econ.; sociol.) to impoverish. **-azione** *f.* impoverishment.

†**depel·lere** *tr.* to drive away.

†**depen·dere** *vb.* and derivs. See **dipendere**.

depennare [A1] *tr.* to strike out, to strike off, to cancel.

deper-ire [D2] *intr.* (*aux.* essere) to waste away, to decay, to decline; to perish; to go bad. **-ibile** *adj.* perishable. **-imento** *m.* state of being run down in health. **-ito** *part. adj.* wasting away; run down in health; perished. **-izione** *f.* wasting, withering; perishing; decay.

depersonalizzazione f. (med.) schizophrenia.

depicklare [A 1] tr. (tanning) to depickle.

depil-are [A 1] tr. (med.) to depilate; (tanning) to unhair. **-a·to·rio** adj., n.m. (pl. **-atori**) depilatory. **-azione** f. (med.) depilation; (tanning) unhairing, depilation.

deple-tivo adj. (med.) depletive. **-zione** f. (med.) depletion.

deplor-are [A 1] tr. to bewail, to lament, to deplore; to blame, to complain of; rfl. to be mourned; non si -ano vittime, there are no casualties. **-a·bile** adj. deplorable. (**-abilménte** adv.) **-ando** adj. to be deplored. **-ato** part. adj. deplored; lamented; pur crollando la torre, nessuna vittima fu -ata, though the tower fell, the city had not a single death to mourn. (**-atore** m. **-atrice** f.) **-ato·ria** f. elegy. **-azione** f. lament, complaint. **-évole** adj. deplorable, lamentable. (**-evolménte** adv.)

depodestare [A 1] tr. to dispossess, to dethrone, to remove from power.

depolarizz-ante adj. depolarizing; n.m. depolarizer. **-azione** f. depolarization.

depolimerizzazione f. (chem.) depolymerisation.

deponente part. of **deporre**, q.v.; adj. (gramm.) deponent; (leg.) testifying; n.m. (gramm.) deponent; (leg.) deponent; (typ.) inferior figure.

deponiménto m. laying down, deposition.

depopol-are tr. to sack, to devastate, to overrun. **-ato** part. adj. sacked, devastated, overrun; n.m. area from which the population has been driven away.

deporre [B 21] tr. to lay down; to put aside; to leave off; — una carica, to relinquish an office; to abandon; to quit; to lodge in a safe place; to lay to rest; to depose; to deprive (a cleric); (chem.) to precipitate; (leg.) to testify; to declare upon oath; to depose; — una cauzione, to give security; intr. (aux. avere; prep. a) to redound to; depone a suo favore, it redounds to his credit, it speaks well for him.

deport-are [A 1] tr. to deport; to remove; to transport (convicts); to exile, to banish. **-azione** f. deportation; transportation (of convicts). **-o** m. (finan.) backwardation.

deposit-are [A 1 S] tr. to deposit; to bank; to hand in; to leave (e.g. at left-luggage office); to consign; to place, to lodge; (leg.) to file; intr. (aux. avere) (chem.) to deposit, to settle, to make a sediment. **-ante** part. adj. depositing; n.m., f. depositor; (finan.) client at a bank, depositor. **-a·rio** f. depositary; repositary; il notaio -ario del testamento, the notary with whom the will is deposited. **-ato** part. adj. deposited; consigned; lodged, placed.

depo·sit-o m. deposit, depositing; store, storehouse, depository, storeroom; object deposited; (rlwy.) cloak-room, left-luggage office; engine shed; (mil.) depot; tomb; cenotaph; (naut.) hold, storeroom; †(Ven.) sailors' families entitled to rations during the absence of husbands; (chem.) deposit, settlement, sediment; (med.) deposit; (leg.) deposit; — fiduciario, the depositing with a bailee, bailment; (comm.) deposit; in —, on deposit, on consignment; in — franco, in bond; — fruttifero, interest-bearing deposit; magazzino di —, warehouse.

deposizione f. laying down; laying of eggs; deposition; dethroning; deprivation (of a cleric); (rel.; art) Deposition; Descent from the Cross; (liturg.) deposition (of the exposed Sacrament); end of Exposition; (leg.) testimony upon oath; deposition; written answers to interrogatories; — giurata, deposition under oath; (med.) deposition; (chem.) deposition, sedimentation.

deposto, deposto part. of **deporre**, q.v.; adj. deposed; set down; laid aside; (leg.) attested; deposed; n.m. picture or sculpture of the Deposition; Descent from the Cross; (leg.) attestation; deposition.

deprav-are [A 1] tr. to deprave, to corrupt; to vitiate; to pervert; †to defame. **-ato** part. adj. depraved; corrupt; perverted. (**-atore** m. **-atrice** f.) **-azione** f. depravation, depravity; perversion.

deprec-are [A 2] tr. to deprecate; to plead against, to seek to avert by prayer; †to exorcize. **-a·bile** adj. avertible by entreaty. (**-aménto** m.) **-ativo** adj. deprecating; of entreaty. (**-ativaménte** adv.) **-ato** part. adj. deprecated; †exorcized. (**-atore** m. **-atrice** f.) **-ato·rio** adj. deprecatory. **-azione** f. deprecation.

depred-are [A 1] tr. to plunder, to devastate. **-aménto** m. plundering, devastating. **-ato** part. adj. plundered, devastated; pillaged. (**-atore** m. **-atrice** f.) **-azione** f. plunder, devastation; pillage.

†**depre·mere** vb. and derivs. See **deprimere**.

depress-ione f. depression; dejection; lowering; (scient.) depression; reduction of pressure; (phys.) partial vacuum, suction; (naut.) — dell'orizzonte, depression of the horizon. **-ivo** adj. lowering, depressive.

depress-o part. of **deprimere**, q.v.; adj. depressed; aree -e, zone -e, depressed areas; lowered; low, dispirited; (med.) (of the pulse), depressed, subnormal. (**-aménte** adv.) **-ore** m. (anat.) depressor nerve; (techn.) vacuum pump.

deprezz-are [A 1] tr. to depreciate, to lower the price of; to decry; to discredit; to undervalue. **-aménto** m. depreciating; depreciation. **-ato** part. adj. depreciated; down in price; discredited; undervalued.

depri·m-ere [C 18] tr. to depress; to press down; to crush; to lower; to dishearten; to humble. **-ente** part. adj. depressing, lowering. **-o·metro** m. (phys.) vacuum-meter.

deprofundis, de profundis m. indecl. (Bibl.; liturg.) De profundis; (fam.) cantare il — a qualcuno, to give up someone for lost.

depur-are [A 1] tr. to purify; to purge; (finan.) — debiti, to extinguish a debt; (chem.) to purify; (med.) to purge. (**-aménto** m.) **-ativo** adj. (scient.) purifying; purging; n.m. purification; purge; il medico gli consigliò un -ativo del sangue, the doctor recommended him to take something to clear his blood. **-ato** part. adj. purified; purged. **-atore** m. purifier; (techn.) strainer; (chem. eng.) scrubber, washer; -atore d'acqua, water-softener. **-ato·rio** adj. purifying; n.m. purifier; water filter. **-azione** f. purification, purge; (chem. eng.) scrubbing, washing. **-o** m. (chem.) purified material.

deput-are [A 1 S] tr. to depute; to appoint, to assign; (leg.) to appoint; to depute; †to attribute; †to judge; †to condemn. **-ato** part. adj. deputed; assigned, appointed; n.m. representative, deputy; (leg.) deputy; (pol.) -ato al Parlamento, member of the Italian Parliament; Camera dei -ati, Chamber of Deputies; †envoy; †second in a duel. **-azione** f. deputation, delegation; deputyship; committee; †deputing.

deradenite f. (med.) inflammation of the glands of the neck.

deradicare [A 2 S] tr. to uproot; to eradicate.

deragli-are [A 4] intr. (aux. avere) (rlwy.) to leave the rails, to run off the line. **-aménto** m. (rlwy.) derailing, derailment.

deramatura f. (metall.) decopperizing.

derap-are [A 1] intr. (aux. avere) (motor.; aeron.) to skid. **-ata** f. skidding; skid.

derattizz-are [A 1] tr. to clear of rats. **-azione** f. rat disinfestation, rat extermination, devermination.

derby m. indecl. (sport) the Derby; match, usually football, between two teams belonging to the same town or district, e.g. between Milan and Inter (both Milanese).

derelitto adj. abandoned, forsaken; derelict; †neglected; n.m. waif, child abandoned by its parents; ospizio dei derelitti, home for waifs and strays, foundling hospital.

derelizione f. (exist. philos.) dereliction, abandonment.

deretano m. behind, bottom; rear; adj. rear, hind; †last.

derequisire [D 2] tr. (admin.) to derequisition.

deri·d-ere [C 3] tr. to deride, to mock, to ridicule; to laugh at; †intr. to laugh. **-itore** m. derider, mocker, ridiculer. (**-itrice** f.)

deris-i·bile adj. ridiculous; laughable. **-ione** f. derision, mockery. **-ivo** adj. derisive, mocking. **-ivaménte** adv. derisively, mockingly. **-o** part. of **deridere**, q.v.; adj. derided, mocked; †n.m. derision; †avere in -o, †mettere in -o, to deride. **-ore** m. derider, mocker. **-o·rio** adj. derisive, derisory; a un prezzo -orio, absurdly cheap.

deriva f. (naut.) drift, set; andare in —, to drift; alla —, adrift; (fig.) andare alla —, to drift along helplessly or aimlessly; (aeron.) drift; fin, tail fin; base della —, fin carrier; — verticale, vertical fin; (biol.) — genetica, genetic drift.

deriv-are [A 1] tr. to divert; to draw off; to tap; (gramm.) to derive; intr. (aux. essere) to derive, to be derived; to ensue; (prep. da) to have origin (in), to be the outcome (of), to be due (to); (naut.) to go adrift, to get off one's course; to make leeway; (aeron.) to deviate. **-a·bile** adj. derivable. **-aménto** m. diverting; deriving. †**-anza** f. see **derivazione**. **-ata** f. (math.) derivative. **-ativo** adj. derivative; voce -ativa, derivative. **-ato** part. adj. derived; diverted, deflected; (mus.) accordo -ato, inversion; n.m. (gramm.) derivative; (chem.) derivative, compound. **-azione** f. derivation; deriving; diverting; deviation; (electr.) branch; shunt; (hydraul.) offtake.

†**derivieni** m. indecl. See **andirivieni**.

derivo·metro *m.* (aeron.) drift indicator.

derm-a *m.* (med.) dermis, derm; (anat.; tanning) corium. **-asche·letro** *m.* (zool.) exoskeleton. **-a·tico** *adj.* dermal, dermatic. **-atite** *f.* dermatitis. **-atologi·a** *f.* dermatology. **-ato·logo** *m.* dermatologist. **-atozo·i** *m.pl.* (zool.) ectoparasites. **-esto** *m.* (ent.) *Dermestes* spp.; (tanning) grease beetle.

der·m-ico *adj.* (anat.) dermal, pertaining to skin; (tanning) pertaining to the corium; sostanza *-ica*, hide substance. **-o·fiti** *m.pl.* dermophytes. **-ografi·a** *f.* dermatography. **-o·ide** *f.* (med.) skin-like tumour; imitation leather, leather-cloth. **-o·lisi** *f.* (med.) dermolysis. **-o·logo** *m.* (med.) dermatologist, skin specialist. **-osifilopa·tico** *adj.* pertaining to skin and venereal diseases; *n.m.* specialist in skin and venereal diseases.

derno *adv. phr.* (naut.) bandiera in —, flag shown rolled up as signal of distress.

derobare[1] [A I] *intr.* (*aux.* avere) to shy, to swerve (of a horse).

†**derobare**[2] *vb.* and derivs. See **derubare.**

de·roga *f.* (leg.) repeal; revocation (usu. partial rather than total); departure, derogation; a (in) — dei patti contrattuali, notwithstanding the terms of the contract; (loosely) postponement.

derog-are [A 2 s] *tr.* (leg.) to repeal, to revoke (a law, usu. partially rather than totally); (fig.) to derogate; *intr.* (*aux.* avere; *prep.* a) to detract (from); to depart (from), to derogate (from); to cut down or restrict the operative effect (of); — alla regola, to depart from the rule. **-a·bile** *adj.* (leg.) that may be derogated from. **-ativo** *adj.* derogative. **ato·rio** *adj.* derogatory. **-azione** *f.* (leg.) derogation.

deronza *f.* (naut. slang) drift, leeway.

derrata *f.* commodity, merchandise; victuals, foodstuff; agricultural produce; — alimentare, foodstuff; giunta alla —, make-weight; †contract, sale, buy; †income; †a buona —, cheap, cheaply; vendere la mala —, to palm off inferior wares; †action, deed, †portion, quantity; †profit; †una —, *or* †due derrate, nothing, not a whit.

derub-are [A I] *tr.* to rob; fu *-ato* dell'orologio, he was robbed of his watch. **(-amento** *m.*) *-ato part. adj.* robbed; bereft; *n.m.* victim of a theft. **(-atore** *m.* **-atrice** *f.*)

deruralizzazione *f.* depopulation of the countryside; flight to the towns.

dervi·s *m. indecl.*, **dervi·scio** *m.* (rel.; hist.) dervish.

desalific-are [A 2 s] *tr.* (chem.) to de-salt. **(-ato** *part. adj.*) **-atore** *m.* de-salting appliance. **-azione** *f.* (chem.) de-salting.

†**descen·dere** *vb.* and derivs. See **discendere.**

descenso *m.* (rel.) the Descent into Hell, the Harrowing of Hell.

deschętto *m. dim.* of **desco,** q.v.; three-legged stool; shoemaker's worktable; dressing-table, toilet-table.

desco *m.* (*pl.* **deschi**) table for meals; stare a —, to be at table; butcher's block; (art) — da parto, basin with the Nativity painted on it; †throwing the discus; †— molle, dessert, light refreshment.

descritt-o *part.* of **descrivere,** q.v.; *adj.* described; †written, composed; †registered; †*n.m.* describable. **-ivo** *adj.* descriptive. **-ore** *m.* describer; †writer. **(-rice** *f.*)

descri·v-ere [C 12] *tr.* to describe; to give an account of; to trace; (math.) to describe, to draw; †to register; †to write. **-i·bile** *adj.* describable. †**-imento** *m.* describing; description.

descrizione *f.* description; describing; †register; †census.

desensibilizz-are [A I] *tr.* (photog.) to desensitize. **(-ato** *part. adj.*) **-azione** *f.* (photog.) desensitization.

desensibilizzatore *m.* (photog.) desensitizer.

deşęrta *f.* (geog.) desert association (of plants).

†**desertare** *vb.* and derivs. See **disertare.**

deş-erto *adj.* deserted; desert; lonely, forlorn; forsaken; (leg.) causa *-erta*, abandoned case; appello —, abandoned appeal; asta *-erta*, auction sale with no bid, abortive sale; †empty; †devoid; †destitute; *n.m.* desert, wilderness; è come predicare al —, you might as well talk to the wall; †deserted person; †worthless individual. **-er·tico** *adj.* desert, of the desert.

deşiare [A 4] and derivs. (poet.). See **disiare.**

desider-are [A I s] *tr.* to desire, to long for; to wish for, to want; lasciare a —, to leave something to be desired; questo non lascia nulla a —, there's nothing the matter with this; farsi —, lasciarsi —, to appear too seldom, to appear too late, to make oneself sought after; non vi fate —, let us see you oftener, please be in good time; *rfl.* to be lacking. **-a·bile** *adj.* desirable; enticing; alluring, charming. **-abilmęnte** *adv.* desirably. **-ante** *part. adj.*

desiring, desirous; *n.m.* applicant, person desirous; i *-anti*, those desiring. **-ata** *m.pl.* desiderata. **-ativo** *adj.* desiderative. **(-ativa-męnte** *adv.*) **-ato** *part. adj.* desired; welcome; desirable, to be desired; *n.m.* desideratum. **-atamęnte** *adv.* in the way desired. **(-atore** *m.* **-atrice** *f.*) †**-azione** *f.* See **desiderio.** **-ęvole** *adj.* desirable.

deside·rio *m.* desire, longing; wish; regret; longed-for thing or person; conseguire un —, to attain one's desire; pio —, pious hope, wishful thinking; lasciò molto — di sè, he was greatly missed.

†**desidęro** *m.* See **desiderio.**

desiderǫş-o *adj.* desirous; eager, full of longing; — di venire, anxious to come. **(-amęnte** *adv.*) †desirable; †lovely; †desired.

†**desi·dia** *f.* idleness, slothfulness, sloth.

design-are [A 6] *tr.* to designate; to appoint; to nominate; to elect; to indicate, to point out; †to propose, to intend; †to design; †to denote. **-a·bile** *adj.* fit, likely, to be designated. **-amento** *m.* designating; appointing. **-ato** *part. adj.* designated; appointed; console *-ato*, consul designate. **(-atore** *m.* **-atrice** *f.*) **-azione** *f.* designation; comitato di *-azione*, nominations committee; †(rhet.) diaeresis; †space circumscribed.

deşin-are [A I s] *intr.* (*aux.* avere) (pop. Tusc.) to lunch, to have one's midday meal; *n.m.* lunch, main meal of the day; dopo —, in the afternoon. **-ata** *f.* good dinner. **(-atore** *m.* **-atrice** *f.*).

deşin-ente *adj.* (gramm.) ending. **-enza** *f.* (gramm.) ending, termination. **-enziale** *adj.* (gramm.) desinential, terminational.

deş-i·o[1] *m.* (poet.) desire; object of desire; loved one; delightful thing, joy. †**-io·re** *m.* see **desio. -iǫso** *adj.* (poet.) desirous. **(-iosamęnte** *adv.*)

De·sio[2] *pr.n.f.* (geog.) Desio (in province of Milan).

desipi-ente *adj.* silly, foolish. **-enza** *f.* silliness, witlessness.

†**desir-a** *f.*, †**-e** *m.*, †**-o** *m.* desire; longing; object of desire. †**-are** *tr.* to desire; to long for.

deşi·st-ere [C 24] *intr.* (*aux.* avere) to desist; to forbear; to cease. **-enza** *f.* desisting; cessation; (leg.) discontinuance (of an action).

deşm-o·ide *adj.* (anat.) desmoid. **-ologi·a** *f.* desmology. **-opati·a** *f.* desmopathy, disease of the ligaments. **-orressi** *f.* (med.) desmorrhexis, rupture of a ligament.

deşol-are [A I s] *tr.* to lay waste, to devastate; to distress, to make unhappy, to afflict, to dishearten; *rfl.* to become distressed; to grow disheartened. **(-amento** *m.*) **-ato** *part. adj.* desolate, forsaken; sorrowful, disconsolate; regretful; essere *-ato* di non poter accettare, to regret that one is unable to accept; la Desolata, Our Lady of Sorrows. **(-atore** *m.* **-atrice** *f.*) **-ato·rio** *adj.* devastating. **-azione** *f.* desolation.

desolforazione *f.* (chem. eng.) desulphurization.

desolino *m.* (naut.) easterly wind (in Adriatic).

desossico·lico *adj.* (chem.) deoxycholic.

†**desperare** *vb.* and derivs. See **disperare.**

†**despetto** *m.*, †**despitto** *m.* See **dispetto**[2].

†**desponsare** *vb.* and derivs. See **sposare.**

de·spot-a *m.* despot. **-ato** *m.* despotate. †**-o** *m.* see **despota.**

despo·tico *adj.* and derivs. See **dispotico.**

despum-are [A I] *tr.* to despumate, to skim. **-azione** *f.* skimming.

desquamazione *f.* desquamation; (med.) desquamation; scaling, skinning.

dessert *m. indecl.* (pron. as Fr.) (cul.) dessert; per —, come —, for dessert.

dessiografi·a *f.* writing from left to right.

dess-o *m.*, **-a** *f.*, *prn.* (used only with 'essere', 'parere' or 'sembrare', chiefly for emphasis or to avoid the hiatus of 'esso', now poet. or, in prose, affected or joc.) the very one, himself, herself; the same one; non par più *-a*, she no longer seems the same woman; son io quel —, I am that man. **-is·simo** (as rhetorical superl.) he in very deed.

dest-are [A I c] *tr.* to arouse, to awaken; to give rise to; *rfl.* to be aroused, to awaken, to wake up; to become alert. **(-amęnto** *m.*) **-ato** *part. adj.* aroused, awakened; ensuing, arising. **-atǫio** *m.* alarum; alarm of a clock; alarm-clock. **(-atore** *m.* **-atrice** *f.*)

†**desterità** *f.* dexterity; skill; adroitness.

†**destillare** *vb.* and derivs. See **distillare.**

destin-are [A I] *tr.* (*prep.* a) to destine; to intend (for); to decree; to appoint, to allot; — come giudice, to appoint as judge; ti *-iamo* sempre questa stanza, we always keep this room for you; to direct; *intr.* (*aux.* avere) to resolve; — di partire, to decide

destin-are (*cont.*)

to go. **-ata·rio** *m.* addressee; consignee. (**-ata·ria** *f.*) **-ato** *part. adj.* destined; doomed; addressed; **-ato a**, intended for. **-azione** *f.* destination; con **-azione** per, bound for; appointed residence; purpose; (*naut.*) terminal port; (in a warship) duties in the quarterbill; (*leg.*) servitù per **-azione** del padre di famiglia, servitude created by paterfamilias; avere una **-azione** unitaria, to serve a common purpose (C.C.).

destino *m.* destiny; doom; fate; destination; *pl.* high destiny; i destini d'Italia, the high destiny appointed for Italy.

destitu-ire [D 2] *tr.* (*prep.* di) to deprive (of); to dismiss, to discharge. **-ito, -to** *part. adj.* devoid; destitute; dismissed, discharged; †abandoned. **-zione** *f.* dismissal; deprivation.

desto *apocop. part.* of **destare**, q.v.; *adj.* awake; wide awake; quick-witted, alert; agile, quick.

destr-a *f.* right hand; right side; la — di un fiume, the right bank of a river; a —, to the right; (*motor.*) tenere la —, to drive on the right; tenere a —, to keep to the right; prendere a —, to bear right; cedere la —, to walk on the left; (*pol.*) right wing; (*mil. comm.*) destr'!, by the right!; †(*naut.*) guardia di —, starboard watch; (*herald.*) dexter; warp, spring. **-ale** *adj.* on the right; of the right; *n.m.* bracelet (on right hand); (*naut.*) starboard watch. †**-are** *tr.* †to escort on the right-hand side (cf. **addestrare**).

destreggi-are [A 3 c] *intr.* (*aux.* avere), *rfl.* to manœuvre cleverly, to act adroitly; to act prudently; to manage, to make do, to get along. **-amento** *m.* manœuvring. (**-atore** *m.* **-atrice** *f.*)

destrezza *f.* adroitness, dexterity, skill; (*joc.*) light-fingeredness; (*leg.*) sleight-of-hand (C.P.).

destrier-e, -o *m.* (*poet.*) steed, charger, war-horse; (*joc.*) — di Sileno, donkey. **-a** *f.* mare.

destrina *f.* (*chem.*) dextrin, dextrine.

destr-o *adj.* right; right-hand; (*herald.*) dexter; (*boxing*) right; dexterous, skilful; propitious, favourable; *n.m.* opportunity; cogliere il —, to seize one's chance; offrire il — a, to give an opportunity to; *adv.* see **destramente**. **-amente** *adv.* dexterously; skilfully; suitably. **-imano** *adj.* right-handed. **-ipiede** *adj.* (*med.*) dextropedal. **-ocardi·a** *f.* (*med.*) dexiocardia. **-ogiro** *adj.* (*phys.*) dextrogyrate, dextro-rotatory. **-oversione** *f.* (*med.*) dextroversion.

destrorso *adj.* dextrorse; (*bot.*) clockwise, dextrorse (of climbing plants); (*eng.*) right-hand, clockwise; (*zool.*) dextral (of a gastropod shell); (*joc.*) inclined to the right in politics; *adv.* to the right.

destro·sio *m.* (*chem.*) dextrose, glucose.

†**destr-u·ere, -ug·gere, -ui·re** *vb.* and derivs. See **distrug·gere**.

desuet-o *adj.* obsolete; antiquated, old-fashioned. **-u·dine** *f.* desuetude, disuse; cadere in —, to fall into disuse.

desult-ori *m.pl.* trick-riders, vaulters, acrobats. **-o·rio** *adj.* pertaining to trick-riding or acrobatics; (*fig.*) desultory; random; stile **-orio**, disjointed, disconnected style which proceeds in leaps and jerks.

des-u·mere [C 8] *tr.* to infer, to deduce, to draw (conclusion); to extract (information). **-umi·bile** *adj.* deducible. **-unto** *part. adj.* inferred, deduced; notizia **-unta** dai giornali, news learned from the Press.

deten-ere [B 32] *tr.* to hold; — un primato, to hold a championship, to hold a record; to keep in one's power; to detain; (*leg.*) to arrest; to detain; to hold in custody; †to entertain; †to give access to; †to maintain, to support. **-tore** *m.* (*leg.*) detainer; unauthorized or unlawful holder or possessor of something; possessor of an illegal thing; **-tore** di brevetto, patent-holder; (*sport*) holder of a championship; title-holder. **-uto** *part. adj.* detained; held; (*leg.*) arrested, detained, held in custody; *n.m.* prisoner; person under arrest. **-zione** *f.* detention; holding; (*leg.*) detention; confinement; imprisonment (applicable to more serious offences than 'arresto' and less than 'reclusione'); possession of an illegal thing (e.g. counterfeit coin).

detergente *adj.* detergent; *n.m.* detergent; (*med.*) abluent.

deter·gere [C 4] *tr.* to cleanse.

deterior-are [A 1 c] *tr.* to spoil, to make worse, to damage; *intr.* (*aux.* essere), *rfl.* to get worse, to deteriorate. **-amento** *m.* deterioration, worsening. **-ato** *part. adj.* deteriorated; worse. **-azione** *f.* deterioration; wear and tear.

determin-are [A 1 s] *tr.* to determine; to ascertain; to define, to specify; to decide, to settle; to bring about; questo mi **-ò** a partire, this made me decide to leave; (*leg.*) to decide, to establish, to fix; to cause; *intr.* (*aux.* avere), *rfl.* to make up one's mind, to determine; **-ò** di accettare, he decided to accept. **-a·bile** *adj.*

determinable; (*eng.*) staticamente **-abile**, statically definable. **-abilità** *f.* determinability. **-ante** *part. adj.* determining; *n.f.* decisive factor; *m.* (*math.*) determinant. **-atezza** *f.* determination. **-ativo** *adj.* decisive; (*gramm.*) articolo **-ativo**, definite article. **-ato** *part. adj.* determined; determinate; given; resolute; un **-ato** articolo, a particular article; un modo **-ato** di, a certain way of. **-atamente** *adv.* determinedly, with determination; decisively. (**-atore** *m.* **-atrice** *f.*) **-azione** *f.* determination; decision; causing; **-azione** di competenza, determination of the jurisdiction of a court; **-azione** al reato di una persona, causing of a person to commit an offence. **-ismo** *m.* (*philos.*) determinism. **-ista** *m.* (*philos.*) determinist.

deters-ione *f.* cleansing. **-ivo** *adj.*, *n.m.* detergent. **-o** *part.* of **detergere**, q.v.; *adj.* purged, cleansed, scoured. **-o·rio** *m.* (Gk., Rom. antiq.) strigil, scraper.

detest-are [A 1] *tr.* to detest, to loathe, to hate; to execrate; to express detestation of. **-a·bile** *adj.* detestable. (**-abilmente** *adv.*) **-ando** *adj.* abominable, loathsome. **-ato** *part. adj.* detested; abominated. (**-atore** *m.* **-atrice** *f.*) **-azione** *f.* detestation.

detettore *m.* (*radio*) detector.

detezione *f.* (*radio*) detection.

†**detinere** *vb.* and derivs. See **detenere**.

deton-are [A 1 c] *tr.* to detonate; to blow up; *intr.* (*aux.* avere) to blow up, to go up, to explode. **-ante** *part. adj.* detonating; sostanze **-anti**, explosives; *n.m.pl.* explosives. **-atore** *m.* detonator; *adj.* detonating. (**-atrice** *f.*) **-azione** *f.* detonation. **-o·metro** *m.* (*motor.*) detonation meter.

†**detra·ere** *vb.* See **detrarre**.

detr-arre [B 33] *tr.* to take away, to subtract, to remove; to belittle, to malign, to carp at; *intr.* (*aux.* avere, *prep.* a) to detract (from); non voglio — al suo merito, I would not detract from his merits. **-attivo** *adj.* (*gramm.*) modifying, conditional. **-atto** *part. adj.* removed; sent away; maligned. **-attore** *m.* slanderer; detractor; *adj.* slanderous. (**-attrice** *f.*) **-atto·rio** *adj.* detractive. **-azione** *f.* subtraction, deduction; detraction.

detriment-o *m.* damage, harm, detriment, prejudice. **-oso** *adj.* detrimental.

detr-ito *m.* detritus; *pl.* relic; flotsam and jetsam; (*geog.*) rubble, detritus. **-i·tico** *adj.* (*geog.*) alluvial; conoide **-itico**, alluvial cone.

detronizzare [A 1] *tr.* to dethrone, to depose.

†**detru·dere** *tr.* to hurl below, to cast down.

†**detruncare** *tr.* to truncate; to cut to bits.

†**detruso** *part.* of **detrudere**, q.v.

detrusore *m.* (*anat.*) detrusor.

detta[1] *f.* statement, assertion; a — sua, according to what he says; starsene a — di uno, to go by what someone says; †essere in — con, to be in agreement with.

†**detta**[2] *f.* debt; favour; good fortune in gambling.

detta·fono *m.* See **dittafono**.

dett-a·glio *m.* detail; retail; al —, in —, by retail; (*naut.*) watch-bill; ufficiale al —, executive officer. **-agliante** *part. adj.* detailing; retailing; *n.m.* retailer. **-agliare** [A 4] *tr.* to detail, to relate in detail; to retail, to sell by retail. **-agliato** *part. adj.* detailed; in detail; retailed, sold by retail. **-agliatamente** *adv.* in detail, with full particulars.

dettame *m.* dictate, precept; saying.

dett-are [A 1 c, Rom. A 1] *tr.* to dictate; — legge, to lay down the law; to compose; to teach (at a University); to lecture in (a subject). **-ato** *part. adj.* dictated; *n.m.* dictation; proverb, saw; style. **-atore** *m.* person who dictates. (**-atrice** *f.*) **-atura** *f.* dictation; dictating; style.

dett-o *part.* of **dire**, q.v.; *adj.* said; — fatto, no sooner said than done; named, known as, called; Simone — Pietro, Simon called Peter; aforesaid, above-named; *n.m.* the aforesaid; (*theatr.*) Fabio e **-i**, enter Fabio, other characters as before; saying; tale; narrative poem.

detum-efazione *f.* (*med.*) detumescence. **-escenza** *f.* (*med.*) detumescence, going down of swelling.

deturp-are [A 1] *tr.* to disfigure, to deface, to spoil. **-amento** *m.* disfiguring, defacing, spoiling. **-ato** *part. adj.* disfigured, defaced, spoiled. (**-atore** *m.* **-atrice** *f.*) **-azione** *f.* disfigurement, defacement.

deuter-agonista *m.* (Gk. antiq.) deuteragonist. **-ocano·nico** *adj.* (Bibl.) deuterocanonical. **-opati·a** *f.* (*med.*) secondary affection, deuteropathy. **-oscopi·a** *f.* second sight.

deute·rio *m.* (chem.) deuterium, heavy hydrogen; ossido di —, heavy water.

Deuterono·mio *pr.n.m.* (Bibl.) Deuteronomy.

devallo *m.* (comm.) devaluation.

devalutazione *f.* (finan.) devaluation.

devast-are [A I] *tr.* to devastate, to ravage, to lay waste. **-amento** *m.* devastating, ravaging. **-ato** *part. adj.* devastated; laid waste; desolate. (**-atore** *m.* **-atrice** *f.*) **-azione** *f.* devastation, ruin.

devenire [D 17] *intr.* (*aux.* essere, *prep.* a) to arrive (at); — ad una conclusione, to arrive at a conclusion.

†**devere** *m.* See dovere.

deverginare [A I s] *tr.* to deflower.

†**devesso** *adj.* sloping; *n.m.* slope, incline; concavity.

devi-are [A4] *tr.* to divert, to deflect, to send astray; *intr.* (*aux.* avere) to deviate, to turn aside; to swerve; to take the wrong direction. **-a·bile** *adj.* divertable, deflexible. **-amento** *m.* diverting, deviating; by-pass. **-atoio** *m.* (rlwy.) points. **-atore** *m.* (electr.) double switch; (rlwy.) pointsman. **-azione** *f.* deviation, deflection; derailment; by-pass; (naut.) compass deviation; (astron.) excursion; (aeron.) fishtailing. **-azionista** *m.* (Marxism) deviationist.

de·vio *adj.* off the main track, devious.

devirare [A I] *intr.* (*aux.* essere) to walk back, to veer; *tr.* (naut.) to surge or veer (a wire or cable).

devoltore *m.* (electr.) negative booster.

devol-utivo *adj.* (leg.) susceptible of, or having to do with, transfer. **-uto** *part.* of devolvere, *q.v.*; *adj.* devolved; transferred; assigned; (leg.) transferred, assigned. **-uzione** *f.* devolution; transfer; (leg.) assignment, transfer.

devol·vere [C 14] *tr.* to devolve; to transfer; to assign; (leg.) to assign, to pass, to transfer; †to roll down, to carry down; †to pour down; *rfl.* (*prep.* a) to devolve (upon); (leg.) to be assigned, passed or transferred; †to pour, to flow.

devoniano, devo·nico *adj.* (geol.) Devonian; (geog.) Devonian, of Devonshire.

†**devorare** *vb.* and derivs. See divorare.

†**devotare** *tr.* to offer up as a sacrifice; to make an ex-voto offering of.

devot-o *adj.* dedicated; freely offered; sacrificed; devoted; affectionate, attached; un amico —, a devoted friend; (rel.) devout, pious; devotional; †accursed; *n.m.* devout person, churchgoer; i -i a S. Francesco, those with a special devotion to St Francis. (**-a** *f.*) **-amente** *adv.* devotedly; devoutly. **-is·simo** *superl. adj.* (at end of letters, often *abbrev.* 'dev.mo'), suo -issimo, yours very truly, (or) yours sincerely.

devozion-e *f.* devotedness, loyalty, devotion; love; respect mingled with affection; (rel.) devoutness, piety, devotion; feste di —, days of devotion; dir le sue devozioni, to say one's (morning or night) prayers; far le sue devozioni, to go to confession and communion; (fig.) romper le devozioni a uno, to bother someone, to interrupt a person at his work; †submission; †dependence. **-ale** *adj.* devotional.

devulcanizzazione *f.* (industr.) devulcanization.

di *prep.* (*contr.* with *def. art.* del, dello, dei, degli, delli, de', della, delle, dell'; often elided to d' before a vowel).

1. OF (possession, relationship, authorship, origin, material, kind): la casa — mio padre, my father's house; la guerra dei Romani con i Cartaginesi, the war of the Romans with the Carthaginians; il ricordo — quel giorno, the memory of that day; la *Commedia* — Dante, Dante's *Comedy*; il quadro non è — Giotto, the painting is not by Giotto; è — buona famiglia, he comes of good family; Domenico — Filippo, Dominic, son of Philip; Giacomo — Giuseppe Colosi, Giacomo, the son of Giuseppe Colosi (who is still living, as distinct from 'Giacomo fu Giuseppe Colosi, Giacomo son of the late Giuseppe Colosi); la Marietta — Niccolò Machiavelli, Marietta, wife of N. Machiavelli; Lorenzo de' Medici, i.e. Lorenzo of the Medici family (Note: modern surnames which combine with di are regarded as beginning with the letter D and are catalogued accordingly; e.g. the surname of Salvatore Di Giacomo is regarded as beginning with di. In this, Italian differs from French usage; cf. note under de¹); sono — Londra, I come from London, I am a Londoner; — legno, of wood, wooden; lavorare — maglia, to knit, to do knitting; una casa — mattoni, a brick house; è — argento, it's made of silver; lagrime — gioia, tears of joy; un giorno — primavera, a spring day; tempo d'inverno, winter weather. 2. FROM, out of, away from (movement, change, distance): uscire — casa, to go out of the house, to leave the house;

gli cadde — mano, it fell from his hand; — serio diventò allegro, from grave he became gay; lontano — qui, far from here. 3. BY, with (means, instrument, extent, degree, manner); colpo — martello, blow with a hammer, hammer-blow; lavorare — cesello, to work with a chisel, to do chiselling; campare d'elemosina, to live on charity; — buona voglia, with a will, willingly; — tutto cuore, with all one's heart; — grazia, please (literally, 'by grace, of your grace'); — nascosto, secretly; — franco, frankly; — poco, by a little, to a small extent; — gran lunga, by a long way, greatly; — modo che, in such a way that. 4. AT, in; during, lasting; stare — casa, to reside, to dwell; dove stai — casa? where do you live?; — mattina, in the morning; d'autunno, in the autumn; — giorno, by day, in the daytime, during the day; — riserva, in reserve; un congresso — una settimana, a conference lasting a week. 5. AS REGARDS, in regard to, about, concerning, on; stare male — salute, to be poorly in health; pronto — lingua, glib, ready-tongued; *Del Principe e delle Lettere*, 'On Princely Government and Literature' (the title of a work by V. Alfieri); parlavo — te, I was talking about you; cambiare — colore, to change colour; completo —, complete with; aumento — peso, increase in weight. 6. BECAUSE OF, with, as a result of; morì — colera, he died of cholera; pazzo d'amore, madly in love; pazzo — rabbia, mad with rage; pazzo — musica, mad about music; tremare — paura, to shake with fright; piangere d'ira, to weep for vexation. 7. THAN (with *nouns, prns.* and *numerals*); più — me, more than me, more than I am, more than I do, etc.; meno — cinque, less than five; il migliore — tutti, the best of all; è migliore — tutti, he's better than any of them; è più astuto del demonio, he's up to more tricks than Old Nick. 8. FOLL. BY INFIN. CONSTR. (when the subj. of the main verb and the infin. are the same): riconosco — aver torto, I know I am in the wrong; disse — esser venuto, he said he had come; spero — venire, I hope to come; bramoso — sapere, eager to know. 9. WITH ADJS. OR EPITHETS: qualcosa — buono, something good; niente — male, nothing bad, no harm; dare dell'asino (— asino) a uno, to call someone an ass; dare del tu a, to use the familiar form of address to (equiv. in Eng. to the use of Christian names); quello stupido — Carlo, that idiot of a Charles. 10. AS A PARTITIVE (usu. with *art.*, sometimes without): con dei fiori, with flowers; — gran cose, great things; — queste parole, such words as these; delle penne, della carta, dell'inchiostro, some pens, paper and ink; — tali azioni a me!, to treat me like that!; fare — tutto, to do all sorts of things, to turn one's hand to anything. 11. IN ADV. OR PREP. PHRS.: verso — te, towards you; senza — lui, without him; per — qua, through here, this way; — sopra, above; — sotto, underneath; — più, more; — meno, less; — giù, down below; — su, up yonder; — là, over there, yonder; al — là —, beyond. 12. WITH 'ESSERE', OR 'STARE' AS PART OF THE PREDICATE: essere — grande aiuto, to be a great help; che n'è stato—lui?, what became of him? 13. FOR SYNTACTICAL USES IN CONSTR. WITH CERTAIN VERBS, e.g. circondare—, to surround with; riempire —, to fill with; ridere —, to laugh at; see list at end of Verb Scheme. 14. †BECAUSE OF: — ciò, because of that; — che, upon which.

dì *m. indecl.* day; a — 10 di luglio, July 10; conciare uno per il — delle feste, to give someone a thrashing; al — d'oggi, nowadays; (geog.) period during which the sun remains above the horizon; buon —!, good day!; (leg.) buon —, the right time to institute proceedings.

dia¹ *pres. subj., 1st, 2nd, 3rd sing.* of dare, *q.v.*

†**dia²** *f.* See dea.

†**dia³** *m., f.* See dì.

diabase *f.* (min.) diabase, greenstone.

diab-ete *m.* diabetes. **-e·tica** *f.* diabetics. **-e·tico** *adj.* diabetic; *n.m.* patient suffering from diabetes, diabetic. **-etina** *f.* (pharm.) diabetin. **-eto·geno** *adj.* (med.) diabetogenic.

diabo·lic-o *adj.* diabolical, devilish, fiendish; appalling. (**-amente** *adv.*)

dia·bolo *m.* (sport) diabolo.

†**diacalamento** *m.* (pharm.) mint powder.

†**diacalcite** *f.* (pharm.) a kind of plaster.

†**dia·cano** *m.* See diacono.

†**diacartamo** *m.* (pharm.) safflower electuary.

†**diacatt-o·lico**, †**-olicone** *m.* (med.) universal remedy; laxative electuary.

†**diaca·ustico** *adj.* (med.) cauterizing by means of a lens.

diaccia·ia *f.* (Tusc. pop.). See **ghiacciaia**, under **ghiaccio**.

diacciale *m.* (Tusc.) sheepfold.

diacciare [A3] and derivs. See **ghiacciare**.

diac·ci-o[1] *adj.* (Tusc. pop.) frozen, icy cold; *n.m.* ice, icy cold; (miner.) clear white spot in stone or marble. **-(u)olo** *m.* icicle; *adj.* (of a tooth) sensitive to cold; brittle, splintery; gritty; (bot.) erba -uola, ice-plant, *Cryophytum crystallinum*.

diac·cio[2] *m.* (naut.) tiller.

diacęre [B15] (Tusc. pop.). See **giacere**.

diac-etato *m.* (chem.) diacetate. **-e·tico** *adj.* (chem.) diacetic.

dia·chilon *m. indecl.* (pharm.) diachylon, lead plaster.

dia·cine *excl.* (euphem. for 'diavolo') the deuce!

†diacinto *m.* See **giacinto**[1].

dia·cio *m.* (dial. N. Ital.). See **diaccio**[2].

dia·clasi *f.* (geol.) fault, diaclase.

†diaco·dio *m.* (pharm.) poppy-head syrup.

diacon-ale *adj.* (eccl.) diaconal; of or relating to a deacon. **-ato** *m.* (eccl.) diaconate; titular church of cardinal deacon. **-ęssa** *f.* (eccl.) deaconess. **-i·a** *f.* (eccl.) status of (cardinal) deacon; titular church of cardinal deacon; diaconia.

dia·cono *m.* (eccl.) deacon.

dia·cope *f.* (gramm.) diacope; (surg.) diacope.

diacri·tico *adj.* (gramm.) diacritic, diacritical; (med.) distinctive (of a symptom).

diacu·stica *f.* diacoustics.

di·ade *f.* duad, dyad, pair (esp. of divinities).

diadem-a *m.* diadem; (rel.; art.) nimbus, aureole; tiara; *†f.* cangiar la — in un turbante, to lapse into evil ways. **-ato** *adj.* diademed.

dia·do·co *m.* (*pl.* **-chi**) (Gk. hist.) diadochos; (fig.) successor.

dia·fan-o *adj.* diaphanous, transparent. **-eità, -ità** *f.* transparency, diaphaneity. **-o·metro** *m.* (paperm.) opacimeter, opacity tester.

dia·fiṣi *f.* (anat.) diaphysis, shaft of a bone.

diaf-oni·a *f.* (mus.) diaphony, organum; dissonance; (teleph.) cross-talk. **-o·nica** *f.* diacoustics. **-o·nico** *adj.* (mus.) diaphonic; dissonant. **-ono·metro** *m.* (teleph.) cross-talk meter.

diafor-eṣi *f.* diaphoresis. **-e·tico** *adj.* diaphoretic.

diaframm-a *m.* (anat.) diaphragm; (photog.) stop; (eng.) baffle; (fig.) interval, space, gap. **-are** [A1] *tr.* (photog.) to stop down, to stop. **-a·tico** *adj.* diaphragmatic, pertaining to the diaphragm. **-atura** *f.* (photog.) diaphragm opening, 'stop'.

diage·neṣi *f.* (geol.) diagenesis.

diaglip·t-ica *f.* art of intaglio. **-o** *m.* intaglio, diaglyph.

diag·n-oṣi *f.* diagnosis. **-osticare** [A2s] *tr.* to diagnose. **-o·stico** *adj.* diagnostic; *n.m.* diagnostician. (**-osticamęnte** *adv.*)

diagon-ale *adj.* diagonal; on the cross; *n.m.* diagonal; (text.) twill. **-almęnte** *adv.* diagonally; on the cross. **-ino** *m.* diagonal stripe (in textile design, etc.).

diagramm-a *m.* diagram; (math.) graph; (mus.) †diagram (in the obs. sense of musical scale), gamut. **-a·tico** *adj.* diagrammatic.

†diagri·dio *m.* (pharm.) diagrydium.

diale *adj.* (Rom. antiq.) of Jupiter; flamine —, *flamen dialis*; apice —, *apex dialis*.

dialemma *m.* (med.) intermission of fever.

dialettale *adj.* See under **dialetto**.

dialet·tic-a *f.* dialectic, dialectics. **-o** *adj.* dialectic; *n.m.* dialectician.

dialett-o *m.* dialect; regional speech; country speech; vernacular; local accent. **-ale** *adj.* dialectal; (art) regional. **-aliṣmo, -iṣmo** *m.* dialectal form or phrase, provincialism. **-ologi·a** *f.* dialectology. **-o·logo** *m.* (*pl.* **-o·loghi**) dialectologist.

di-a·liṣi *f.* (rhet.) dialysis; (chem.) dialysis. **-a·lito** *adj.* (chem.) dialysed. **-aliẓẓare** [A1] *tr.* (chem.) to dialyse. **-aliẓẓato** *part. adj.* dialysed; *n.m.* dialysate. **-aliẓẓatore** *m.* (chem.) dialysator, dialyser.

dial·lag-e *f.* (rhet.) diallage.

dialla·gio *m.* (miner.) diallage.

diallelo *m.* (logic) diallelon, circular definition.

dialog-are [A2s] *tr.* to put into dialogue form; *intr.* (aux. avere) to converse, to discourse. **-ato** *part. adj.* put into dialogue form; *n.m.* (cinem.) dialogue.

dial-o·gico *adj.* dialogical, of dialogue. (**-ogicamęnte** *adv.*) **-ogiṣmo** *m.* use of pure dialogue form; use of dialogue inside a narrative framework. **-ogista, -oghista** *m.* writer of dialogues; dialogue-writer. **-ogi·stico** *adj.* connected with dialogue form or its users. **-ogiẓẓare, -oghiẓẓare** [A1] *tr.* to put into dialogue form; *intr.* (aux.) avere) to converse, to dialogize; to argue (idly).

dialogite *f.* (miner.) rhodochrosite.

dia·lo·go *m.* (*pl.* **-ghi**) dialogue; formal talk; (art crit.) relationship, interdependence; (pol.) conference, meeting; aprire il —, to open negotiations.

dialte·a *f.* (pharm.) marshmallow ointment.

diamagn-etiṣmo *m.* diamagnetism. **-e·tico** *adj.* diamagnetic.

diamant-e[1] *m.* diamond; a punta di —, diamond-cut, faceted; slug for a gun; (biblioph.) collezione —, Barbera series of miniature editions of Italian classics; (naut.) — dell'ancora, crown of an anchor; (mil.) V-shaped ditch or moat; †cannon shot; (geog.) Monti dei -i, Diamond Mountains. **-a·io** *m.* diamond-cutter. **-ino** *adj.* diamond-like; of a diamond; adamantine.

Diamante[2] *pr.n.m., f.* Diamond.

diamastigoṣi *f.* (Gk. antiq.) diamastigosis (in Sparta).

dia·metr-o *m.* diameter. **-ale** *adj.* diametric(al). (**-almęnte** *adv.*)

dia·mine, dia·mici *excl.*; (euph. for 'diavolo') the deuce!; what the dickens!; che — stai facendo?, what the dickens are you doing?; by Jove!; I say!; posso venire stasera? ma —!, may I come this evening? yes, of course, by all means!

diamina *f.* (chem.) diamine.

Diana *pr.n.f.* Diana; (myth.) Diana; morning star; alla bella —, in the open air, *à la belle étoile*; (euphem.) madre di —!, mother of God!; (poet.) stella —, my star, my fair one; (mil.) reveille; battere la —, to sound the reveille, (fig.; fam.) to have one's teeth chattering with cold; (naut.) morning watch (from 4 to 8 a.m.); tiro di —, morning gun.

dianella *f.* morning bell.

diano·ia *f.* (philos.) dianoia, dianoetic faculty.

dianto *m.* (bot.) dianthus, pink carnation, Sweet William.

dianzi *adv.* a short time ago, just now.

dia-palma *m.* (pharm.) diapalma. **-papa·vero** *m.* (pharm.) diacodium.

dia·pason *m. indecl.* (mus.) diapason; octave; pitch; tuning-fork; compass (of voice or instrument).

dia-pedeṣi *f.* diapedesis. **†-peni·dio** *m.* an old cough remedy resembling punch.

diapen·sia *f.* (bot.) wood-sanicle, *Sanicula europaea*.

diapente *f.* (mus.) diapente, fifth (interval).

diapositiva *f.* (photog.) lantern-slide, diapositive; transparency.

diaprato *adj.* (herald.) diapered.

diarchi·a *f.* (pol.) diarchy, dyarchy.

dia·ria *f.* day's allowance; travelling expenses (by the day).

dia·r-io *m.* diary, journal; tenere un —, to keep a diary. **-ista** *m., f.* diarist.

diarre·a *f.* diarrhoea.

diartroṣi *f.* (med.) diarthrosis.

diaschiṣma *m.* (mus.) diaschisma, diaschism (a very small interval).

dia·scol-o *m.* (euphem. for 'diavolo') devil. **-ętto** *m.* imp. **-ìo** *m.* pandemonium.

diasco·pio *m.* magic lantern, slide projector.

diaṣ-po, diaṣ-pro *m.* kind of worked silk. **-pinętto** *m.* kind of silk fabric.

dia·spora *f.* (rel. hist.) diaspora, dispersion of the Jews; (fig.) dispersion.

dia·sporo *m.* (miner.) diaspore.

diaṣpr-o *m.* (miner.) jasper; (fig.) hardheartedness; see **diaspo**. **-ino** *adj.* (of) jasper. **-ificare** [A2s] *tr.* to jasperize.

diastaṣ-i *f.* (chem.) diastase; (med.) diastasis. **-ato** *adj.* pre-digested. **-i·a** *f.* diastase.

diastem-a *m.* (mus.) diastema, diastem (interval in ancient Greek music). **-a·tico** *adj.* (mus.) diastematic.

dia·stilo *m.* (archit.) diastyle.

dia·st-ole *f.* (med.) diastole; (prosod.) diastole; (mus.) diastole, pause or comma between phrases; musical phrase or section. **-o·lica** *f.* (mus.) treatise on phrasing.

diastrof-i·a *f.* (med.) dislocation. **-iṣmo** *m.* (geol.) diastrophism.

diat-ermaṣi·a *f.* (phys.) diathermancy. **-ermi·a** *f.* (med.) diathermy. **-er·mico** *adj.* (phys.) diathermanous.

dia·t-eṣi *f.* diathesis. **-e·tico** *adj.* diathetic.

diates·saron *m. indecl.* (mus.) diatessaron, fourth (interval).

diatome·a *f.* (bot.) diatom.

diat-oni·a *f.* (mus.) diatonism. **-o·nico** *adj.* (mus.) diatonic. **-oniṣmo** *m.* (mus.) diatonicism.

diatrema *m.* (geog.) volcanic chimney, diatreme.

diatriba *f.* diatribe, bitter dispute.

dia·vol-o *m.* devil, fiend; sapere dove il — tiene la coda, to know a thing or two, to have no flies on one; il — non è brutto come si dipinge, the devil is not as black as he is painted; le donne ne sanno una più del —, women are up to more tricks than Old Nick; la farina del — va in crusca, no good can come of ill-gotten gains; fare il —, fare il — a quattro, to make a rumpus, to kick up a shindy; un casa del —, an uproar, a hubbub; essere come il — e l'acqua santa, to be incompatible; vi è entrato il — in quella famiglia, they're always quarrelling in that family; avere un — per capello, avere il — in corpo, to be very excited, to be very upset, to be beside oneself with anger; fare l'avvocato del —, to play the devil's advocate; è un buon —, he's not a bad sort; povero —!, poor devil!; clever chap, clever girl; — d'una donna, riesce a tutto, clever woman that, she makes a success of everything; quel — di Giovanni, that John's a clever chap; pezzo di —, great tall chap; ma che —!, good Lord!, good Heavens!, what the devil!; non so dove — sia, I don't know where the devil it is; va' al —!, go to the devil!; che il — lo porti!, devil take him!; c'è un caldo del —, it's as hot as the devil; è un — di problema, it's the devil of a problem; avere una fame del —, to be fiendishly hungry; il — volle che, as ill luck would have it; il — ci ha messo le corna (la coda, lo zampino), it's the devil's own luck (i.e. misfortune, ill-luck); il mio buon — mi aiutò, my good angel came to my aid; (geog.) Isola del Diavolo, Devil's Island; (bot.) albero del —, *Ficus religiosa*; (ichth.) — di notte, 'Darkie Charlie', a kind of shark, *Scymnorhinus lichia*; — di mare, devil fish, *Mobula mobula*; *adv. phr.* alla -a, carelessly, any old how; (cul.) alla -a, devilled; pollo alla -a, chicken rapidly braised and seasoned with mustard and pepper. **-a** *f.* she-devil; ugly woman; wicked woman; una buona -a, a good sort. **-ac·cio** *m.* a kind of bird-nest. **-eri·a** *f.* diabolical action, piece of wickedness; che -eria stai combinando?, what devilry are you brewing?; tangled affair; oddity, absurdity, extravagant behaviour or action. **e·rio** *m.* (N. Ital.) uproar. **-esco** *adj.* (*m.pl.* -eschi) devilish; attractive, smart. **-essa** *f.* she-devil; ugly woman. **-eto** *m.* uproar, pandemonium. **-etto** *m.* lively little imp, young rascal. **-ino** *m.* curling-pin; curl-paper; a kind of jack. **-io** *m.* noisy crew, crowd of tiresome creatures or things; uproar. **-one** *m. augm.* large devil; big tall fellow; *pl.* sweetmeats of aphrodisiac properties. **-oso** *adj.* devilish.

diaz-ina *f.* (chem.) diazine. **-otazione** *f.* (chem.) diazotization.

†**dibarbare** *tr.* to uproot; to destroy; to strip.

dibarbicare [A 2 s] *tr.* to uproot, to pull up.

dibassare [A I] and derivs. See **abbassare**.

dibat·t-ere [B I] *tr.* to beat up, to whisk; to flutter; to discuss, to debate (questions); †to torment; †to clash; †— i denti, to gnash one's teeth; *rfl.* to struggle, to make violent movements; to writhe; to be torn (as between opposing forces). **-imento** *m.* violent movement; shaking; struggling; debate, discussion; (leg.) trial; hearing of a case in court; -imento a porte chiuse, hearing *in camera*; rinviare un -imento, to adjourn a trial or hearing; †affliction; †torment; †-imento del cuore, palpitation of the heart. **-itoio** *m.* (mus.) sistrum. †**-o** *m.* dispute; conflict. **-uta** *f.* dispute; conflict; fight, battle. **-uto** *part.* of dibattere; *adj.* beaten; shaken; whipped up, whisked; †afflicted; †tormented.

dibat·tito *m.* debate, discussion, dispute; (leg.) argument; debate.

†**dibilitare** *vb.* and derivs. See **debilitare**.

†**dibonaire** *adj.* loving, fond.

dibosc-are [A 2] *tr.* to clear (of trees), to disforest. **-amento** *m.* disforestation, clearing. **-ato** *part. adj.* disforested, cleared of trees.

di·braco *m.* (prosod.) dibrach, pyrrhic.

†**dibruciare** *vb.* and derivs. See **abbruciare**.

dibruscare [A 2] *tr.* to trim (trees) of dead wood.

dibucciare [A 3] *tr.* to peel; to skin; *rfl.* to lose skin, to peel; to get angry.

diburr-are [A I] *tr.* to skim (milk). **-ato** *part. adj.* skimmed; (fig.) thin, feeble-looking.

†**dibuttare** *tr.* to shake; to beat; to toss about.

dicac-e *adj.* sarcastic, satirical; talkative; biting, mordant. **-ità** *f.* sarcasm; pungency or harshness of speech; garrulity.

†**dicadere** *vb.* and derivs. See **decadere**.

†**dicalvare** *vb.* See **decalvare**.

dicanapul-are [A I] *tr.* to decorticate (hemp). **-atrice** *f.* decorticating machine (for hemp).

†**dicapitare** *vb.* and derivs. See **decapitare**.

dica·rico *m.* (comm.) bill of lading.

dicast-ero *m.* government department or board; ministry. **-erico** *adj.* of a government department; bureaucratic.

dicatti, di catti *adv.* (Tusc.) second-best; aver — di qualcosa, to think oneself lucky to get something.

dicco *m.* (geol.) dike; (naut.) deep-water dock; dyke.

dicearchi·a *f.* the rule of law; a State embodying the rule of law.

†**dice·dere** *tr.* to deceive; to hide, to conceal.

dice·falo *adj.* dicephalous, two-headed; *n.m.* two-headed monster.

dicembre *m.* December.

dicentrare [A I, Rom. A I c] and derivs. See **decentrare**.

†**di·cere** *vb.* and derivs. See **dire**.

diceri·a *f.* long rigmarole, boring speech; hearsay; rumour; gossip; publisher's blurb; †far la — ai porri, to talk to the wall.

†**dicer·nere** *vb.* and derivs. See **discernere**.

†**dicernire** *tr.* to distinguish, to make clear; to select.

†**dicertare** *intr.* to fight, to contend.

dicervell-are [A I] *tr.* to drive (a person) wild, to send (a person) off his head; *intr.* (*aux.* essere), *rfl.* to rack one's brains; †to brain. **-ato** *part. adj.* brainless, addle-pated; †brained.

†**dices(s)ette** *card. num.* See **diciassette**.

†**dicess-are** *intr.* to cease, to leave off; to be lacking. **-o** *adv.* distant, far away.

dicevol-e[1] *adj.* seemly; becoming, fitting, suitable. **-mente** *adv.* in a seemly way; becomingly, fittingly, suitably. **-ezza** *f.* seemliness, propriety.

†**dice·vole**[2] *adj.* See **dicibile**.

dichiar-are [A I] *tr.* to declare; to state; to certify; to proclaim; to make clear, to elucidate, to explain; to specify order of (lottery number); (leg.) to declare, to certify, to state; *rfl.* to declare oneself, to reveal oneself; to make one's position clear; to come out into the open. †**-agione** *f.* see **dichiarazione**. **-amento** *m.* explanation; (Naples, underworld) challenge and duel (fought with knives or firearms). **-ante** *part. adj.* declaring, stating; *n.m., f.* person making a declaration. **-ativo** *adj.* explanatory; (leg.) declaratory. **-ato** *part. adj.* declared; stated; elucidated. **-atamente** *adv.* declaredly. (**-atore** *m.* **-atrice** *f.*) **-atorio** *adj.* declaratory. **-azione** *f.* declaration; avowal of love; proposal (of marriage); explanation; statement; (leg.) declaration; explanation; certification; adjudication; statement; -azione di fallimento, adjudication of bankruptcy; -azione falsa, false declaration, misrepresentation; -azione giurata, affidavit; sworn statement; -azione di garanzia, bond, guarantee; (pol.) -azione programmatica, policy statement. †**-ire** *vb.* and derivs. See **dichiarare**.

dichin-are [A I] *intr.* (*aux.* essere) to decline; to slope; to draw to a close; to sink; to fade; to grow dark; to diminish; to fall into disuse; to condescend, to stoop; *rfl.* to flow down; to slope; to humble oneself. †**-o** *m.* slope, decline; andare, venire al -o, to grow worse, to deteriorate; mettere a -o, to set on the downward path; mettere al -o, to ruin, to raze to the ground.

dichiocciare [A 3] *rfl.* (of a hen) to desert, to stop sitting, 'go off the sit'.

diciannov-e *card. num.* nineteen. **-ennale** *adj.* happening every nineteen years. **-enne** *adj., n.m., f.* nineteen-year-old. **-e·simo** *ord. num.* nineteenth.

diciassett-e *card. num.* seventeen. **-enne** *adj., n.m., f.* seventeen-year-old. **-e·simo** *ord. num.* seventeenth.

dici·bile *adj.* capable of being said; utterable, expressible.

diciferare [A I s]. See **decifrare**.

†**dicimare** *tr.* to lop off the top of.

diciocc-are [A 2] *tr.* (agric. Tusc. pop.) to thin out (trees, shrubs); to clear (rough ground). **-ato** *part. adj.* (agric.) thinned out; cleared; *n.m.* cleared ground. **-atura** *f.* trimmings from trees; process of thinning or trimming; clearing of rough ground.

diciott-o *card. num.* eighteen; — di vino, obstinately bent on something; tirar —, to have the greatest of luck. **-enne** *adj., n.m., f.* eighteen-year-old. **-e·simo** *ord. num.* eighteenth; (typ.) decimo ottavo.

dicit-ore *m.* speaker, reciter; elocutionist; essere un mirabile —, to possess wonderful skill at recitation; gli attori moderni sono per lo più mediocri -ori, modern actors are for the most part rather poor at elocution; — in rima, writer of verse; fino —, cabaret or music-hall reciter. †orator; †actor. (**-rice** *f.*) **-ura** *f.* diction, phrasing, wording.

†**diclinare** *vb.* and derivs. See **declinare**.

dicli·nio *adj.* (bot.) diclinous.

diclorodifeniltricloroetano *m.* (chem.) dichlorodiphenyltrichloroethane, D.D.T.

dicogami·a *f.* (bot.) dichogamy.

dicontra *f.* (naut.) skysail.

dicordo *m.* (mus.) dichord, instrument with strings tuned in pairs; ancient two-stringed instrument.

dico·reo *m.* (prosod.) ditrochee, ditrochaeus.

†**dicortare** *tr.* to shorten, to make brief.

dicotile·done *m.* (bot.) dicotyledon; *adj.* dicotyledonous.

dicotomi·a *f.* dichotomy.

†**dicreto** *m.* See **decreto**.

†**dicrinare** *vb.* and derivs. See **declinare**.

dicr-o·ico *adj.* (radar) dichroic. **-oi·șmo** *m.* dichroism. **-oi·te** *f.* (miner.) dichroite, iolite. **-oi·tico** *adj.* (photog.) dichroic. **-omișmo** *m.* dichromism; dichroism.

†**dicrollare** *vb.* and derivs. See **crollare**.

dicroma·tico *adj.* dichromatic.

dicrotișmo *m.* (med.) dicrotism, dicrotic pulse.

dicta·fono *m.* dictaphone.

didasc-ali·a *f.* instruction; information; (theatr.) stage-directions; (cinem.) title, caption; all the captions of a film (silent, or foreign); caption(s) under illustrations in a journal. **-a·lica** *f.* art of teaching; didactic poetry. **-a·lico** *adj.* didactic. **-alicamẹnte** *adv.* in a manner or style relating to instruction or captions.

didat·tic-a *f.* didactics, theory of teaching. **-o** *adj.* educational, instructive; didactic; programma **-o**, teaching programme, syllabus; direttore **-**, headmaster of an Italian elementary school. **-amẹnte** *adv.* in a didactic manner or style.

didẹntro *adv.* inside; *n.m.* il **-**, the inside.

didiacciare [A 3] and derivs. (Tusc. pop.). See **dighiacciare**.

didietro *adv.* behind; (also 'di dietro'); *n.m.* back part, back, behind.

didi·mio *m.* (chem.) didymium.

di·dimo *adj.* (bot.) twin, double, didymous.

diditizzare [A I] *tr.* to treat with D.D.T. disinfectant.

Didọne *pr.n.f.* Dido.

didramma *m.* (Gk. antiq.) didrachm.

†**didu·cere**, †**didurre** *vb.* and derivs. See **dedurre**.

†**die** *m.* See **dì**.

diec-i *card. num.* ten; (hist.) I **-**, the title of various magistracies. **-imila** *card. num.* ten thousand. **-ina** *f.* set of ten; about ten; a dozen or so. **-ino** *m.* (numis.) ten centesimi coin; (naut. hist.) **-ino del Mare**, Maritime Consuls (Tuscany).

diedro *adj.* (geom.) dihedral; *n.m.* dihedron.

†**diel** *contr.* of **dio** and **il**; **- voglia**, may God will that it be so.

dielet·trico *adj.* dielectric; rigidità dielettrica, dielectric strength; *n.m.* dielectric.

dience·falo *m.* (anat.) diencephalon.

die·reși *f.* (prosod.; gramm.) diaeresis; diaeresis sign, umlaut; (surg.) diaeresis.

diesel *m. indecl.* (pron. **dișel**) Diesel; motore **-**, Diesel engine.

dieșire, dies irae *m. indecl.* (liturg.) the sequence *Dies irae*; (fig.) day of vengeance, day of wrath; cantare il **- a** qualcosa, to give something up for lost; parere un **-**, to look extremely grim and forbidding; Judgement Day, (fig.) the day of reckoning.

die·s-is, die·și *m. indecl.* (mus.) sharp; diesis (interval in ancient Greek music); doppio **-**, double sharp. **-are** [A I] *tr.* (mus.) to sharpen, to add a sharp to.

die·t-a¹ *f.* assembly, diet; room, hall, house. **-ale** *adj.*, **-a·rio** *adj.* pertaining to a (political) diet.

die·t-a² *f.* regimen, diet; stare a **-**, to be on a diet. **-are** [A I] *tr.* to diet, to put on a diet. **-e·tica** *f.* dietetics. **-e·tico** *adj.* dietetic.

†**dieta³** *f.* space of a day.

dietera·lịși *f.* (chem.) extraction with ether.

diete·tic-a *f.*, **-o** *adj.* See under **dieta²**.

dietil-aldeide *f.* (chem.) acetal. **-amina** *f.* (chem.) diethylamine.

die·tim, die·timo *m.* (leg.) day to day interest.

†**dietreggiare** *intr.* to retreat, to withdraw.

dietro *adv.* **1.** BEHIND; at the back; lì **-**, behind there, back there; tenere a **-**, to hold back, to keep in check; lasciarsi **-** un luogo, to leave a place behind one; (naut.) aft; di **-**, behind; at the back; lui stava seduto davanti ed io di **-**, he sat in front and I behind; passare di **-**, to pass by at the back; zampe di **-**, hind legs, back paws; il di **-**, the back part, the behind. **2.** AFTER, following; andare **-**, to tag on behind, to follow after; venire **-**, to succeed, to follow on; tirarsi **-** i fischi, to draw criticism upon oneself, to make oneself unpopular; portarsi **-** qualcuno, to be accompanied by someone, to have someone tagging along behind; mi gridò **-** di fermarmi, he shouted after me to stop; tenere **- a**, to keep a close watch on, to follow closely.

   prep. **1.** BEHIND; uno **-** l'altro, one behind the other; **-** le quinte, behind the scenes; mandarsi tutto **-** le spalle, to put everything behind one, to turn one's back on everything; dire **- a** uno, to talk behind a person's back. **2.** *comp. prep.* AFTER; **- a** me, after me; andare **- a**, to follow; essere **- a** una cosa, to be engaged in something; è **- a** scrivere, he is occupied in writing (cf. Irish, 'he's after writing'); stare **- a** uno, to importune someone, to be always hanging round someone; correre **- a**, to run after, (fig.) to imitate, to be a slave to; tenere **- a** uno, to keep a close watch on someone. **3.** UPON, as a result of, in consequence of; **- richiesta**, upon request; **- pagamento di**, on payment of; **- proposta di**, on the motion of.

dietro-bottẹga *f.* back of a shop; room behind a shop. **-ca·mera** *f.* back room. **-frọnt** *m.* (mil. and fig.) about turn. **-guar·dia** *f.* rearguard. **-scena** *f.* part of a theatre behind the stage (cf. **retroscena**).

difalcare [A 2] and derivs. See **defalcare**.

†**difalta** *f.* and derivs. See **diffalta**.

di·fatti, difatto *adv.* indeed; in point of fact, as a matter of fact; camminava lentamente, e **-** aveva ottant'anni, he walked slowly for he was eighty years old.

difen-d-ere [C I] *tr.* to defend; to protect, to guard; to preserve; to prevent; (leg.) to appear for; to defend; to plead for; to represent; †to forbid; †to impede; †to shelter; *rfl.* to defend oneself; to carry on (under difficulties); to jog along; to get on pretty well. †**-e·vole** *adj.* defending, protecting; capable of being defended. **-i·bile** *adj.* defensible. **-ibilità** *f.* defensibility. **-imẹnto** *m.* defending; defence; †protection; †security. **-itivo** *adj.* defensive. **-itọre** *m.* defender. **-itrice** *f.* defender; (leg.) *f.* of difensore, q.v., under **difensiva**.

difenile *m.* (chem.) diphenyl.

†**difens-a** *f.* See **difesa**. †**-are** *vb.* and derivs. See **difendere**. †**-i·bile** *adj.* See **difendibile**, under **difendere**. †**-ione** *f.* See **difesa**.

difens-iva *f.* defensive; stare sulla **-**, to be on the defensive. **-ivo** *adj.* defensive; (med.; psych.) psiconeurosi **-iva**, defence psychoneurosis; *n.m.* means, form of defence. **-ivamẹnte** *adv.* defensively. **-ọre** *m.* defender; (leg.) counsel, solicitor, legal representative of a party in legal proceedings; **-ore d'ufficio**, counsel for the defence appointed by a criminal court; counsel with a dock-brief; gli avvocati **-ori**, counsel and/or solicitors for the parties (i.e. not only for the defence).

†**diferire** *vb.* and derivs. See **deferire**.

difes-a *f.* defence, protection; razza (canina) di **-**, watchdog, house-dog; **-e dell'elefante**, elephant tusks; (naut.) **-** costiera, coastal defence; **-** militare marittima, seaward defences of a naval base; fender; **-** d'imbarcazione, boat-fender; **- delle sartie**, 'Scotchman', timber structure used in tidal or exposed waters to prevent boats being driven under a gangway; (leg.) the defence (as opposed to the prosecution); plea; answer; legittima **-**, self-defence; linea di **-**, line of defence; la **-** personale della parte, the party's appearance in person (in civil proceedings).

difẹso *part.* of difendere, q.v.; *adj.* defended; protected; sheltered; prevented; (herald.) tusked.

difett-are [A I] *intr.* (*aux.* essere) to be lacking; **-ano** i viveri, provisions are lacking, there is a shortage of provisions; to be short of, not to have enough of; **-a** di buona volontà, he is not very well-disposed; **-ano** di viveri, they are short of provisions; †*tr.* to find wanting, to find inadequate. **-ante** *part. adj.* lacking, wanting; **-ante di**, lacking in, short of. **-ivo** *adj.* defective. **-ivamẹnte** *adv.* defectively.

difett-o *m.* defect; fault; lack, deficiency; shortcoming; weakness, bad habit, failing; blemish, flaw; drawback, snag; essere in **-**, to be at fault; lack, need; c'e **-** di, there is a lack of; in **-** di, in defect of, failing; riparare a un **-**, to make good a lack; la memoria gli fa **-**, his memory is failing, his memory is at fault; †*adj.* defective. **-(u)ọso** *adj.* defective, faulty; weak, delicate. **-(u)osamẹnte** *adv.* defectively; insufficiently, inadequately.

diffalcare [A 2] and derivs. See **defalcare**.

diffalco *m.* (naut.) dead reckoning.

diffalt-a *f.* (†but used by D'Annunzio) default; lack; deficiency; betrayal, breach of promise; fault, sin, evil deed. †**-are** *intr.* to be lacking; **-are di**, to lose, to be deprived of.

diffam-are [A I] *tr.* (leg.) to defame; to libel; to slander; (fig.) to defame; to disparage; †to spread news of. **-ativo** *adj.* slanderous. **-ato** *part. adj.* (leg.) slandered; (fig.) defamed; disparaged; (herald.) defamed, without tail. **-atore** *m.* (leg.) defamer; libeller; slanderer. **-ato·rio** *adj.* (leg.) defamatory; libellous; slanderous. **-azione** *f.* (leg.) defamation; defamatory libel; criminal libel; slander; (fig.) disparagement.

diffarreazione *f.* (Rom. antiq.) diffarreation.

different-e *adj.* different; dissimilar; various; differing; *n.m., f.* person differing, disputant. **-emente** *adv.* differently; variously; in different ways.

differenz-a *f.* difference; — **di colore**, difference in colour; **tre è la — fra cinque e otto**, the difference between five and eight is three; — **di due minuti**, difference of two minutes; discrepancy; **a — di**, unlike; disagreement; **accomodare le -e**, to settle one's differences. **-iale** *adj.* differential; (rlwy.) **tariffa -iale**, sliding scale (in railway fares); *n.m.* (math.; eng.) differential; *f.* (rlwy.) sliding scale. **-iare** [A 4] *tr.* to differentiate; to render distinct; *rfl.* to differ. **-iamento** *m.* differentiating. **-ia·metro** *m.* (naut.) draught marks. **-iazione** *f.* differentiation; (naut.) **-iazione d'immersione, -iazione di pescagione**, trim.

differ-ire [D 2] *tr.* to defer, to put off; (leg.) to defer, to adjourn, to postpone; *intr.* (*aux.* avere) to differ; **il suo stile -isce in più modi da quello dei contemporanei**, his style is in many ways different from that of his contemporaries; to disagree; to differ, to dissent; **-isco da te**, I don't agree with you. **-i·bile** *adj.* capable of deferment. **-imento** *m.* postponement; (leg.) deferment, postponement, adjournment; extension; **chiedere un -imento**, to ask for an adjournment. **-ito** *part. adj.* deferred, postponed; **radiodiffusione -ita**, recording of public performance (opera, concert, etc.); (comm.) **ordine a consegna -ita**, make and hold order. **-itore** *m.* procrastinator. (**-itrice** *f.*)

†**differmare** *tr.* to confute.

diffi·cil-e *adj.* hard, difficult; exacting, difficult, temperamental; cantankerous; unreliable; unlikely; **è — che ti venga a trovare**, he's not likely to come to see you; *n.m.* difficulty. **-mente** *adv.* with difficulty; improbably.

diffic-oltà *f.* difficulty; obstacle; **superare una —**, to master a difficulty, to overcome an obstacle; handicap; objection; **non trovo nessuna —**, I don't find any difficulty, I don't find it difficult; **non ho alcuna — a farlo**, I don't in the least mind doing it; ill-feeling, disagreement. **-oltare** [A I] *tr.* to render difficult. **-oltoso** *adj.* difficult to do; hard to please; †weak, delicate.

diffida *f.* (leg.) warning; notice; **notificare una —**, to serve a notice; †challenge; †duel.

diffid-are [A I] *intr.* (*aux.* avere) to be distrustful, to be suspicious; to be diffident, to lack confidence; (provb.) **-a di chi non ride mai**, beware of a man who never laughs; *tr.* (leg.) to warn; to give notice to; to serve a notice on (somebody); †to challenge to a duel; †to cause to lose confidence, to take hope away from. †**-anza** *f.* diffidence. **-ato** *part. adj.* discouraged; **-ato dai medici**, given up as a hopeless case by doctors; (leg.) warned; informed; given notice.

diffid-ente *adj.* diffident; mistrustful, distrustful, lacking in confidence; †held in distrust. **-entemente** *adv.* diffidently; distrustfully. **-enza** *f.* diffidence; distrustfulness, lack of confidence.

†**diffi·gnere**, †**diffin·gere** *intr.* to dissimulate; to pretend not to know, to feign ignorance.

diffil-are [A I] *tr.* (mil.) to defilade. **-amento** *m.* (mil.) art of fortifying by defilade. (**-ato** *part. adj.*)

†**diffinire** *vb.* and derivs. See **definire**.

diffluente *adj.* (med.) diffluent, softened.

diffond-ere [C 2 c] *tr.* to diffuse; to spread abroad, to give currency to; — **a mezzo radio**, to broadcast; *rfl.* to spread; to be poured out; to talk at length; to spread oneself; **-ersi su un argomento**, to dwell at some length upon a subject; †to become suffused. **-imento** *m.* diffusing; spreading. (**-itore** *m.* **-itrice** *f.*)

difform-are [A I c] *tr.* to spoil, to disfigure; *intr.* (*aux.* essere) to change, to lose one's former appearance. **-ato** *part. adj.* spoiled, disfigured; changed. (**-atamente** *adv.*)

difform-e *adj.* unlike; diverse, different; **copia — dall'originale**, copy deviating from the original; †deformed; †dissonant. **-ità** *f. indecl.* unlikeness, difference; †deformity, ugliness.

diffr-an·gere [C 5] *intr.* (*aux.* avere) to diffract, to cause diffraction. **-azione** *f.* diffraction.

†**diffreno** *adv. phr.* **in —**, full pelt, headlong.

diffus-o *part.* of **diffondere**, q.v.; *adj.* diffused; diffuse; widespread, widely circulated; (radio) broadcast; (bot.) diffuse; †*adv.* diffusely; widely. **-amente** *adv.* diffusely; widely. **-i·bile** *adj.* diffusible. **-ibilità** *f.* diffusibility. **-ione** *f.* diffusion; scattering; circulation (of newspaper, etc.); diffuseness, prolixity; (radio) broadcast; (phys.) diffusion; molecular interpenetration; (atom. phys.) scattering. **-ivo** *adj.* diffusive. **-o·metro** *m.* diffusiometer. **-ore** *m.* (motor.) choke; (electr.; opt.) diffuser.

†**dificare** *vb.* and derivs. See **edificare**.

difil-are [A I] *intr.* (*aux.* avere) to file past, to defile; (mil.) to take the shortest route, to move fast; †*rfl.* to move swiftly. **-ata** *f.* (mil.) march past, defile. **-ato** *part. adj.* direct, immediate; *adv.* forthwith, immediately, directly, straightway. **-atamente** *adv.* directly, immediately.

†**difinare** *vb.* and derivs. See **definire**.

†**diformare** *vb.* and derivs. See **difformare**.

†**difornire** *vb.* and derivs. See **fornire**.

difosgene *m.* (chem.) diphosgene.

†**difraudare** *vb.* and derivs. See **defraudare**.

difrenare [A I] *tr.* to unbridle; to unleash; to release; to undo.

di·frige *m.* copper slag.

†**difrodare** *vb.* and derivs. See **defraudare**.

dif·tera *f.* sheepskin (garment).

dift-e·rico *adj.* diphtheritic. **-eri·te** *f.* (med.) diphtheria.

difuori *adv.* See **fuori**.

diga *f.* dike, dam; sea-wall, breakwater; embankment; — **foranea**, outer defence or breakwater; (fig.) **rompere le dighe**, to burst all barriers; **opporre una —**, to set up a defence.

digamma *m.* (ling.) digamma.

di·gam-o *adj.* (leg.) digamous; *n.m.* (leg.) digamist. **-i·a** *f.* (leg.) digamy, second marriage.

diga·strico *adj.* (anat.) digastric.

†**digelare** *tr.* to thaw.

†**digenerare** *vb.* and derivs. See **degenerare**.

diger-ire [D 2] *tr.* to digest; to assimilate; to make a digest of; (fig.) to put up with, to stomach, to brook; **sono persone che non si possono —**, they're impossible people; to work off; — **la bile**, to let one's anger cool; — **un libro**, to digest a book. **-ente** *part. adj.* digesting; digestive; **apparato -ente**, digestive organs. **-i·bile** *adj.* digestible; (joc.) credible; tolerable. **-ibilità** *f.* digestibility. **-imento** *m.* digesting. **-itore** *m.* (industr.) digester.

digestione *f.* digestion; assimilation; (joc.) **visita di —**, polite call on hostess after dinner-party; (bot.) ripening of fruit in sunlight; (chem.) digestion, infusion; †(surg.) the process of maturing an ulcer.

digestivo *adj.* digestive; **apparato —**, digestive organs; **cibo —**, food which aids digestion.

digesto *m.* digest; (leg.) digest or compilation of laws or of opinions and writings of eminent lawyers. †*part.* of **digerire**, q.v.; †*adj.* digested; assimilated.

digestore *m.* (chem.) digester; autoclave.

dighiacci-are [A 3] *intr.* (*aux.* avere), *rfl.* to thaw; to melt; to unfreeze. **-ato** *part. adj.* thawed; melted.

digiambo *m.* (prosod.) iambic dipody.

digiogare [A 2] *tr.* to unyoke.

Digione *pr.n.f.* (geog.) Dijon.

digital-e *adj.* of the fingers, digital; **impronte -i**, finger-prints; *n.f.* (bot.) foxglove, *Digitalis purpurea*; (pharm.) digitalis. **-ina** *f.* (pharm.) digitalin.

digit-are [A I s] *tr.* (mus.) to finger (i.e. to indicate fingering by written numbers); *intr.* (*aux.* avere) (mus.) to finger (i.e. to use the fingers with dexterity). **-ato** *part. adj.* (mus.) fingered; (bot.) digitate. †**-atura** *f.* (mus.) see **digitazione**. **-azione** *f.* (mus.) fingering (i.e. written fingering); fingering (i.e. manner of performance); (anat.) digitation.

digita·ria *f.* (bot.) panick-grass, crab-grass, and other species of *Digitaria*.

di·gito *m.* (mens.) digit, three-quarters of an inch; (astron.; math.) digit; †finger; †ring finger.

digiun-are [A I] *intr.* (*aux.* avere) to fast; †to go without food; *tr.* to pass (a day) in fasting, to keep as a fast-day. †**-ato** *part. adj.* kept as a fast-day. **-ato·io** *adj.* fast-day, fasting-day. (**-atore** *m.*

digiun-are (*cont.*)

-**atrice** *f.*) -**è** *m. indecl.* lunch, *déjeuner.* -**o** *m.* fast, fasting; a -o, on an empty stomach; -o delle campane, silencing of bells in Holy Week; dearth, need, longing; *adj.* fasting; sono -o da tre giorni, I have been fasting for three days; lacking in, devoid of, feeling or showing the lack of; — di notizie, cut off from news; -o di matematica, quite untrained in mathematics.

digiungere [c5] *tr.* to separate, to part; †to unyoke.

digiuno *m.* See under **digiunare**.

di·glifo *m.* (archit.) diglyph.

†**dignificare** *tr.* to dignify; to render worthy.

dignit-à *f.* dignity; rank; dignitary; †venire in —, to obtain office; †a — di, worthy of; †(philos.) see **degnità**. -**a·rio** *m.* dignitary; -ari della Corte, Court dignitaries. -**oso** *adj.* dignified; grave; decorous, seemly; decent; respectable; adequate, suitable; †worthy, deserving; †valuable, precious.

†**digno** *adj.* See **degno**.

†**digozzare** *tr.* to cure of goitre; *rfl.* to remove a neckcloth, to bare the throat.

digrad-are [A1] *intr.* (*aux.* essere) to slope down; to lessen, to diminish gradually; (paint.) to be toned down, to become gradually paler, to show a gradation; †to worsen; †to be ranged in rank; *tr.* to lessen, to diminish; (paint.) to tone down, to shade off, to gradate; †to degrade. -**amento** *m.* (paint.) gradation, shading off. -**anza** *f.* (paint.) gradation (of colours). -**azione** *f.* (paint.) gradation (of colours), degradation; downward slope.

digramma *m.* (ling.) digraph.

†**digranare** *vb.* See **sgranare**.

digrappolare [A1s] *tr.* to strip (a vine) of its bunches.

digrassare [A1] *tr.* to remove fat from; to skim; — uno, to work someone's fat off; to remove grease stains from; *intr.* (*aux.* essere) to lose fat, to get thinner.

digred-ire [D2] *intr.* (*aux.* essere) to digress, to deviate. -**ito** *adj.* digressing; deviating.

digressione *f.* digression; digressing, meandering; (astron.) digression.

digress-ivo *adj.* digressive. -**ivamente** *adv.* by way of digression. †-**o** *part.* of **digredire**, q.v.; *n.m.* digression. -**ore** *m.* one who digresses, digressor. -**o·rio** *adj.* digressive.

digrezz-are [A1] *tr.* (silkb.) to scour. -**amento** *m.* (silkb.) scouring. (-**ato** *part. adj.*)

digrign-are [A5] *tr.* to grind, to gnash; —i denti, to gnash one's teeth; †*intr.* to champ the bit; to writhe. †-**ato** *part. adj.* gnashed; grimacing; writhing; angry.

digross-are [A1] *tr.* to make smaller, to trim, to whittle; to rough-hew, to rough-dress, to rough-plane; — uno, to teach someone in a rough and ready way, 'to knock the corners off someone'. -**amento** *m.* trimming; rough-hewing; (masonry) boasting. -**ato** *part. adj.* trimmed; whittled; rough-hewn. (-**atore** *m.* -**atrice** *f.*) -**atura** *f.* trimming; whittling; rough-hewing.

digrosso *adv. phr.* in —, roughly, approximately.

digrum-a *f.* voracity. -**ale** *m.* (vet.) rumen. -**are** [A1] *intr.* (*aux.* avere) to ruminate, to chew the cud; *tr.* (fig.) to ruminate upon, to meditate on, to chew over; (fam.) to eat greedily. (-**ato** *part. adj.* -**atore** *m.*)

†**diguastare** *vb.* and derivs. See **guastare**.

diguazz-are [A1] *tr.* to shake; to beat up, to whisk; *intr.* (*aux.* avere) to splash about; to wallow; †*rfl.* -arsi nel manico, to vacillate. -**ata** *f.* shaking (of liquid); beating, whisking; splashing, dabbling.

†**diguisare** *tr.* to disguise.

digusciare [A4] *tr.* to shell.

dii *m.pl.* (poet.) gods (see **dio**).

†**dilaccare** *tr.* to tear limb from limb, to rend; to lacerate; *rfl.* to rend oneself.

†**dilacciare** *tr.* to unlace, to undo, to untie, to unstrap.

dilacer-are [A1s] *tr.* to tear, to rend in pieces; to lacerate; (fig.) to torment. -**amento** *m.* tearing, rending. -**ante** *part. adj.* rending; lacerating; (fig.) tormenting. -**ato** *part. adj.* torn; lacerated; bleeding; (fig.) tormented. -**azione** *f.* (med.) dilaceration.

diladdarno *m.* (Flor.) the further side of the River Arno.

dilag-are [A2] *tr.* to flood; *intr.* (*aux.* essere), *rfl.* to overflow; to come flooding in; to spread; il vizio -a, vice spreads; *n.m.* spread; il — del Rock'n Roll, the spread of Rock'n Roll. -**ante** *part. adj.* spreading, flooding. -**ato** *part. adj.* flooded, flooded over.

dilani-are [A4] *tr.* to tear to pieces, to rend; to lacerate; il rimorso mi -a l'animo, remorse is tearing at my vitals; (fig.) to tear to bits, to denigrate; to uproot; *rfl.* to tear oneself; to rend one's garments; to tear one's hair. -**ato** *part. adj.* torn; lacerated. (-**atore** *m.* -**atrice** *f.*)

dilapid-are [A1s] *tr.* to squander, to waste; to dissipate; — la sostanza, to squander one's substance. -**amento** *m.* squandering, wasting; dissipating. -**ato** *part. adj.* squandered, wasted; dissipated. (-**atore** *m.* -**atrice** *f.*) -**azione** *f.* dissipation; waste; squandering.

dilappolare [A1s] *tr.* to pull off burrs from.

dilargare [A2] *tr.*, *rfl.* to widen; to enlarge; to dilate.

dilastrare *tr.* (naut.) to unballast.

†**dilata** *f.* negotiation.

dilat-are [A1] *tr.* to dilate; to stretch; to widen; to spread; to open; — la mente, to broaden the mind; *rfl.* to become dilated, to dilate; to expand; to spread; to swell. -**a·bile** *adj.* expandable; stretchable. -**abilità** *f.* expandability. -**amento** *m.* dilating; spreading; swelling. -**ante** *part. adj.* widening, broadening; spreading. -**ato** *part. adj.* dilated; expanded; widened; spread; swollen. -**azione** *f.* dilation; dilating; stretching, widening; spreading, spread; (phys.) expansion; -azione termica, thermal expansion. -**o·metro** *m.* (phys.; med.) dilatometer. -**ore** *m.* (scient.) dilator; (eng.) expansion joint. -**o·rio** *adj.* (leg.) dilatory, delaying; espedienti -ori, delaying practices.

dilav-are [A1] *tr.* to wash away; to wash out, to wash the colour from. -**amento** *m.* washing away; washing out; (geog.) leaching. -**ato** *part. adj.* washed away; washed out; (fig.) colourless, 'washed-out', feeble. -**azione** *f.* washing away; washing out.

dilazion-e *f.* delay; deferment, postponement; respite; (leg.) delay; extension of time (for payment, or performance of a contract); concedere —, to give time; — gratuita, grace (C.C.); †in — di tempo, in the course of time. -**are** [A1c] *tr.* (comm.) to put off, to defer, to postpone; (leg.) to delay. -**ato** *part. adj.* deferred; postponed; pagamento -ato, delayed payment.

†**dilefiare** *intr.* to perish; *excl.* che possa —!, devil take him!

dileggi-are [A3c] *tr.* to mock, to scoff at; to show contempt for. -**a·bile** *adj.* contemptible, deserving mockery. -**amento** *m.* mocking, scoffing. -**ante** *part. adj.* mocking, scoffing; *n.m.*, *f.* mocker, scoffer. -**ato** *part. adj.* mocked, scoffed. -**atore** *m.* mocker, scoffer. (-**atrice** *f.*)

dileggio *m.* mockery, derision; jeer, gibe; mettere in —, to jeer at.

†**dile·gine** *adj.* flabby; insubstantial; weak, faint.

†**dilegione** *f.* See **dileggiamento**, under **dileggiare**.

dilegu-are [A6] *tr.* to disperse, to dispel; to scatter; il sole -a la neve, the sun melts the snow; m'hai -ato ogni speranza, you have left me bereft of hope; *intr.* (*aux.* essere), *rfl.* to vanish, to fade (away), to disappear; to dissolve (e.g. of a reflection in water); la neve si -a al sole, snow melts in the sun; il suono s'andava -ando a poco a poco, the sound grew gradually fainter and fainter; il rumore -ava, the noise was dying away. -**a·bile** *adj.* that may be dispersed. -**amento** *m.* dispersing; disappearing, vanishing. -**ato** *part. adj.* dispersed; (fig.) faded, vanished; il rancore era tutto -ato, all rancour had died.

dileguo, dileguo *m.* disappearance; andare in —, to vanish; to be wasted; mandare in —, to disperse, to squander.

dilemm-a *m.* dilemma; i corni di un —, the horns of a dilemma. -**a·tico** *adj.* relating to a dilemma, dilemma-like.

†**dileticare** *vb.* and derivs. See **solleticare**.

dilett-are [A1] *tr.* to please; to entrance; to amuse; la lettura mi -a, I love reading; *intr.* (*aux.* avere) to give pleasure; (provb.) non a tutti -ano le stesse cose, tastes differ, one man's meat is another man's poison; *rfl.* (*prep.* di) to take pleasure (in), to enjoy; mi -o di leggere, I love to read; mi -o di libri, I enjoy books; to take root, to thrive; †*n.m.* delight, pleasure, will, wish. -**a·bile** *adj.* pleasurable, delightful; capable of receiving pleasure. -**abilmente** *adv.* pleasurably. -**abilità** *f.* delightfulness. †-**amento** *m.* delight. -**ante** *part. adj.* pleasing, delighting; *n.m.*, *f.* amateur; compagnia di -anti, amateur theatrical company; (sport) amateur. -**antesco** *adj.* (*m.pl.* -**anteschi**) amateurish. -**antismo** *m.* amateur sport; amateur status; amateurishness, dilettantism. †-**anza** *f.* delight; pleasure; joy. -**azione** *f.* delight, pleasure. -**evole** *adj.* pleasing, amusing; delectable. -**evolmente** *adv.* amusingly; delectably.

dilett-o[1] *m.* delight, pleasure; andare a —, to amuse oneself; prendere — a, to take delight in; a bel —, on purpose. **-oso** *adj.* delightful; pleasing, pleasurable; of delight; †loving, affectionate; †loved, dear; †interested, pleased.

diletto[2] *adj.* beloved; dear to one's heart; favourite; darling; *n.m.* beloved; il mio —, my darling.

dilezione *f.* love of God; spiritual affection; la — del prossimo, love of one's neighbour.

†**diliberare** *vb.* and derivs. See **liberare**.

†**dilibrare** *rfl.* to lose one's balance; to totter, to shake.

dilicato *adj.* See **delicato**.

diligen-te *adj.* diligent; industrious; painstaking; careful; accurate. **-temente** *adv.* diligently; carefully; accurately. **-za** *f.* diligence; industriousness; conscientiousness; (leg.) care, diligence; -za del buon padre di famiglia, ordinary, due diligence.

diligenza[1] *f.* See under **diligente**.

diligenz-a[2] *f.* stage-coach. **-a·io** *m.* stage-coachman.

†**dili·gere** *tr.* to love.

†**diligione** *f.* See **dileggiamento**, under **dileggiare**.

†**diliquidare** *rfl.* to soften; to turn to liquid; to be revealed, to be manifested.

diliscare [A2] *tr.* to dress, to comb (hemp).

†**diliticare** *vb.* and derivs. See **solleticare**.

†**diliverare** *vb.* and derivs. See **liberare**.

†**dili·zia** *f.* and derivs. See **delizia**.

†**dilocare** *tr.* to displace.

diloggiare [A3] *tr.* to dislodge, to drive out; *intr.* (*aux.* avere) to retire; to strike camp.

dilogi·a *f.* (rhet.) repetition; ambiguity; two plays in sequence.

dilollare [A1] *tr.* to winnow (corn).

dilomb-are [A1c] *rfl.* to strain one's back; si è -ato, he has ricked his back, he has slipped a disk. **-ato** *part. adj.* with strained back; (fig.) spineless, feeble; (vet.) cavallo -ato, 'shiverer'.

†**dilontanare** *tr.* to remove.

dilucid-are [A1s] *tr.* to explain, to clear up, to elucidate. **-ato** *part. adj.* elucidated; clear, lucid. **-ato·rio** *adj.* explanatory. **-azione** *f.* explanation, elucidation.

†**dilu·cido** *adj.* See **lucido**.

†**dilu·c-olo**, **-ulo** *m.* early dawn.

dilu-ire [D2] *tr.* to dilute, to water down, to let down; to break down; to weaken; to thin; *rfl.* to become diluted; to dissolve. **-ente** *adj.* diluting; *n.m.* diluent. **-i·bile** *adj.* suitable for, capable of being diluted; non è -ibile, it cannot (should not) be diluted. **-ito** *part. adj.* diluted; weak. **-izione** *f.* diluting, dilution.

dilung-are [A2] *tr.* to prolong; to lengthen; to set at a distance; to keep at a distance; *rfl.* to move away; to get ahead; to expatiate; to wander, to meander; -arsi su, to linger over, to dwell upon; -arsi a descrivere, to describe at great length; †to last, to endure. **-ato** *part. adj.* distant; separated; set apart; distinct, different.

†**dilungiare** *vb.* and derivs. See **dilungare**.

dilungo *adv.* straight on, continuously, without pause or delay; sonare a —, to ring a full peal; (typ.) comporre a —, to set up without paging, to set up in galley-proofs; †from afar; †— a, far from; †— da, away from; †for a long time; †*adj.* distant.

†**dilusione** *f.* See **delusione**.

†**diluto** *part.* of **diluire**, q.v.

diluviale *adj.* See under **diluvio**.

diluvi-are [A4] *tr.* to flood; to eat greedily, to gobble; *intr.* (*aux.* avere) to come down in torrents; to rain cats and dogs, to pour down continuously; (fig.) to flood; la corrispondenza -ava, there was a flood of correspondence; *impers.* (*aux.* essere) to pour; *rfl.* (dat. of prn. 'si') to stuff down into oneself; si è -ato tutta quella pasta, he's gobbled down all that 'pasta'. **-ato** *part. adj.* flood; flooded out; acque -ate, flood waters. **-atore**, **-one** *m.* voracious eater. (**-atrice**, **-ona** *f.*)

dilu·vi-o *m.* flood; downpour; deluge; (Bibl.) il —, the Flood; abundance; greed; a —, in great abundance; (geol.) diluvium; (orn.) large bird-net. **-ale** *adj.* torrential; pertaining to a deluge; (geog.) Pleistocene. **-ano** *adj.* pertaining to the Flood. **-oso** *adj.* torrential pouring, flood, flooding; rain-bearing, rain-producing. **-osamente** *adv.* in floods.

diluvion-a *f.*, **-e** *m.* See under **diluviare**.

diluzione *f.* dilution.

dima[1] *f.* (eng.) template.

†**dima**[2] *f.* week.

dimacchiare [A4] *tr.* to clear of trees or shrubs (from **macchia**, q.v.).

†**dimacrare**, †**dimagherare** *vb.* and derivs. See **dimagrare**.

dimagr-are [A1] *tr.* to make thin; to impoverish; *intr.* (*aux.* essere); *rfl.* to grow thin; to lose weight; to become impoverished; to lose fertility, to be emptied of population. **-amento** *m.* impoverishing. **-ante** *part. adj.* thinning, impoverishing; slimming; metodi -anti, slimming methods. **-ato** *part. adj.* thin; reduced in weight; impoverished. **-azione** *f.* loss of weight; emaciation; impoverishment.

dimagrire [D2] and derivs. See **dimagrare**.

dimanda *f.* See **domanda**.

dimandanti *m.pl.* (herald.) a enquerre.

dimandare [A1] and derivs. See **domandare**.

†**dimando** *m.* See **domanda**.

†**diman-e**, **-i** *adv.* See **domani**.

†**dimattina** *adv.* See **domattina**.

†**dimembrare** *tr.* to dismember; to separate; to dispose, to arrange; to alter, to spoil.

dimen-are [A1] *tr.* to move; to shake, to toss, to wag; — le ganasce, to keep one's jaws going, to eat greedily; — la coda, to wag its tail; *rfl.* to keep moving about; to fidget, to fuss, to be agitated; to toss about; to wave one's arms about. (**-amento** *m.*) **-ato** *part. adj.* shaken; tossed; agitated. **-io** *m.* constant movement, fidgeting, tossing.

dimension-e *f.* dimension; size; (cinem.) un film a tre -i, a 3-D film. **-ale** *adj.* dimensional. **-ato** *adj.* dimensioned.

dimentic-are [A2sc] *tr.* to forget; non — l'ombrello, don't forget your umbrella; — uno, to forget someone; ho -ato di scrivere, I've forgotten to write; to forget about; mi hai -ato?, have you forgotten about me?; *rfl.* (prep. di) to forget; si -a di tutto, quello lì, that man forgets everything (i.e. he is absent-minded); ti sei -ato del cappello, you've forgotten to get the hat, you've forgotten all about the hat, you've forgotten your hat; se ne -ò, he dismissed it from his mind; to forget oneself; †to go out of one's mind. **-ag·gine** *f.* habitual forgetfulness; absent-mindedness. **-agione** *f.* loss of memory. **-anza** *f.* piece of forgetfulness; inadvertence; oversight; mettere in -anza, to consign to oblivion. **-ato** *part. adj.* forgotten; overlooked; neglected. **-atoio** *m.* (joc.) 'forgettory'; oblivion; mettere nel -atoio, to consign to oblivion; cadere nel -atoio, to fall into oblivion. **-ato·rio** *m.* oblivion.

dimenti-co *adj.* (*m.pl.* **-chi**) forgetful, oblivious; unmindful; non — di, not unmindful of, remembering, bearing in mind; †mentally deranged. **-chevole** *adj.* forgetful. **-cone** *m.* forgetful or careless person. (**-cona** *f.*)

†**dimentire** *tr.* to give the lie to, to accuse of falsehood.

†**dimergolare** *rfl.* to totter, to walk unsteadily.

†**dimeritare** *tr.* to be unworthy of, not to merit.

dimero *m.* (chem.) dimer.

dimess-o *part.* of **dimettere**, q.v.; *adj.* laid aside; dismissed; passed over; humble, modest, unpretentious; (voice) subdued, (of dress) plain; plainly dressed; (med.) discharged (from hospital). **-amente** *adv.* plainly; humbly; modestly.

dimesticare [A2s] and derivs. See **addomesticare**.

dimestich-evole *adj.* tame; friendly, sociable. **-ezza** *f.* familiarity, intimacy; affectionate behaviour.

dime·stico *adj.* (of animals) friendly, tame (cf. **domestico**).

dimetilene *f.* (chem.) dimethylene, ethylene.

dime·trico *adj.* (miner.; cryst.) tetragonal.

di·metro *adj.*, *n.m.* (prosod.) dimeter; (a work) in two distinct metres.

dimett·ere [C20] *tr.* to dismiss; to release; to discharge; — un malato da un ospedale, to discharge a patient from a hospital; — un'offesa, to forgive an injury; — un debito, to cancel a debt; to neglect; to lay aside; †to absolve; †to condone; †*intr.* to flow out, to discharge; *rfl.* to resign; si dimise dall'impiego, he gave up his post; -ersi in favore di, to yield in favour of; †to humble oneself. (**-itore** *m.*)

dimezz-are [A1] *tr.* to halve, to divide in two. **-amento** *m.* halving. **-ato** *part. adj.* halved; diminished; defective; (herald.) party.

dimidiato *adj.* (bot.) dimidiate.

†**dimi·nio** *m.* See **dominio**.

diminuendo *m.* (mus.) diminuendo, becoming softer; (math.) the number from which the subtrahend is to be subtracted.

diminu-ire [D2] *tr.* to diminish, to lessen; to decrease; to reduce; to lower; (mus.) to soften, to diminish; *intr.* (*aux.* essere) to

diminu·ire (*cont.*)
lessen, to grow less; to decrease; to abate; to drop, to lower; (mus.) to become softer. **-i·bile** *adj.* diminishable. **-ito** *part. adj.* diminished, lessened, reduced; lowered; (mus.) settima **-ita**, diminished seventh. **-izi̯o̲ne** *f.* see **diminuzione**. **-tivo** *adj.*, *n.m.* diminutive. †**-to** *part. adj.* see **diminuito**; diminutive; short in stature; defective, deformed. **-zio̲ne** *f.* diminution; diminishing; (mus.) diminution; (radio) fading; (leg.) diminution; reduction.

dimi·ri·a *f.* (Gk. mil. antiq.) *dimoiria*, half-company. **-ta** *m.* (Gk. antiq.) leader of a *dimoiria*.

dimissi̯o̲n·e *f.* resignation; dare le **-i**, rassegnare le **-i**, to resign; dismissal. **-a·rio** *adj.* (*m.pl.* **-ari**) out-going; il ministro degli Esteri **-ario** e quello nuovo, the out-going minister for Foreign Affairs and his successor.

dimisso̲·ri·o *adj.*, **-a** *n.f.*, **-ale** *adj.*, *n.f.* (eccl.) dimissorial (letter).

dimodoch̲è *conj.* in such a way that, so that (usu. **di modo che**).

dimoi·are [A 4] *tr.* to thaw, to melt; to soften; **—i** panni, to put clothes to soak; *intr.* (*aux.* essere) to thaw, to melt. **-atic·cio** *m.* slushiness; slushy ground. **-ato** *part. adj.* melted; thawing; neve **-ata**, slush. **-o** *m.* melting, thaw.

dimo̲lto *adj.* (Tusc. fam.) much; many; dimolte cose, many things; *adv.* (also **di molto**) very, much.

dimo·nio *m.* (poet.). See **demo·nio**.

dimora, (Rom.) **dimo̲ra** *f.* stay; residence; dwelling, dwelling-place, home; (leg.) abode, dwelling (less permanent in character than either 'domicilio' or 'residenza', q.v.; **—** abituale, habitual abode (equiv. to 'residenza') (C.C.); senza fissa **—**, of no fixed address or abode; ignota **—**, address unknown; delay; senza **—**, without more ado.

dimor·are [A 1, Rom. A 1 c] *intr.* (*aux.* avere) to live, to dwell, to reside; to remain, to stay, to linger on; to persevere; †*tr.* to detain. †**-agio̲ne** *f.* delay. **-ante** *part. adj.* dwelling, residing; present, attending. †**-anza** *f.* stay; residing, residence; continuation; abode; delay; cessation; constancy. †**-ata** *f.* stay. †**-azio̲ne** *f.* stay; delay. †**-o** *m.* stay; abode, dwelling-place; delay.

dimo̲rf·o *adj.* dimorphous; *n.m.* dimorph. **-i̯smo** *m.* dimorphism.

dimorsare [A 1] *tr.* to stop biting, to let go (with one's teeth).

dimostr·are [A 1 c] *tr.* to show; to prove; to demonstrate; (geom.) come si voleva **—**, q.e.d.; to make manifest; to explain; to display; **—** più anni del vero, to look older than one is; ha già 50 anni ma non li **-a**, he is already 50 but he doesn't look it; (leg.) to prove; to establish; **—** la verità, to establish the truth; *intr.* (*aux.* avere) to appear; *rfl.* to show oneself; to prove oneself; to turn out to be; to appear. **-a·bile** *adj.* demonstrable. **-abilità** *f.* demonstrability. **-ante** *part. adj.* demonstrating; *n.m.*, *f.* political demonstrator. †**-antemente** *adj.* demonstrably. †**-anza** *f.* demonstration; manifestation; expression. **-ativa** *f.* power of demonstration. **-ativo** *adj.* demonstrative. **-ato** *part. adj.* demonstrated; made manifest. (**-ato̲re** *m.* **-atrice** *f.*) **-azio̲ne** *f.* demonstration.

dimottare [A 1] *intr.* (*aux.* essere) to slip, to slide downwards (of soil, etc.).

dimozz·are [A 1], **-icare** [A 2 s] *tr.* to trim, to lop, to pollard. (**-ame̲nto** *m.*)

din·a, **-e** *f.* (phys.; mech.) dyne.

dina·mic·a *f.* (phys.) dynamics; (mus.) dynamics, the arrangement of tone-intensities in music. **-o** *adj.* dynamic; endowed with vitality, energetic; (med.) functional. (**-ame̲nte** *adv.*)

dinam-i̯smo *m.* (philos.; scient.) dynamism; violent movement, constant activity; vitality, energy, élan, 'go'. **-ista** *m.* dynamist.

dinam-ite *f.* dynamite. **-itardo** *m.* dynamiter. **-i·tico** *adj.* of dynamite, dynamite.

di·nam·o *m.*, *f. indecl.* dynamo. **-o·do** *m.* (phys.) kilogram-metre, 100,000 ergs. **-ometamorfi̯smo** *m.* (geol.) dynamic metamorphism. **-ometri·a** *f.* (phys.) dynamometry. **-o·metro** *m.* (phys.; aeron.) dynamometer; (techn.) strength tester. **-ome·trico** *adj.* dynamometric. **-oscopi·a** *f.* (med.) dynamoscopy. **-osco·pio** *m.* dynamoscope; stethoscope for auscultation of the muscles.

†**dinant·e**, **-i** *adv.*, *prep.* See **dinanzi**.

†**dinanzare** *tr.* to get ahead of, to overtake; to forestall.

dinanzi *adv.* before, in front; in front of; in the presence of; gli misi **—** il libro, I put the book in front of him; levamiti **—!**, get out of my sight!; *comp. prep.* **—** a, before; in the presence of; in comparison with; *n.m.* il **—**, the front, the forepart.

dina·rico *adj.* (geog.; geol.) Dinaric.

dinaro *m.* (numism.) dinar; †see **denaro**.

din·asta *m.* ruler, dynast. **-asti·a** *f.* dynasty. **-as·tico** *adj.* dynastic. (**-asticame̲nte** *adv.*)

dinatron *m. indecl.* (radio) dynatron.

dinci *excl.* per **—**. See **perdinci**.

†**dinderl·o** *m.* tassel, bobble. **-ino** *m. dim.* (mus.) jingle (of a tambourine).

dindi·n (onomat.) ting-a-ling; *n.m.* tinkling, clinking (also **din din**).

din·dio *m.* (N. Ital.) turkey; (Tusc.) horse-chestnut tree.

dindo[1] *m.* (infant.) money, coin.

dindo[2] *m.* See **dindio**.

dindo·n (onomat.) ding-dong; *n.m.* sound of bells (also **din don**). **-are** [A 1 c] *intr.* (*aux.* avere) to ring, to peal, to go ding-dong.

dineg·are [A 2] *tr.* to deny; to refuse; to withhold. (**-ato** *part. adj.* **-ato̲re** *m.* **-azio̲ne** *f.*)

†**dinegrare** *vb.* and derivs. See **denigrare**.

dinerb·are, **dinerv·are** [A 1] *tr.* to unnerve; to enervate; to demoralize. **-ato** *part. adj.* unnerved; enervated; demoralized; feeble, weak; soft, flabby; lacking in tone.

dinie·go *m.* (*pl.* **-ghi**) denial, refusal.

dinnanzi *adv.*, *prep.* See **dinanzi**.

†**dinoccare** *vb.* and derivs. See **dinoccolare**.

†**dinocciolare** *vb.* and derivs. See **snocciolare**.

dinoccol·are [A 1 s] *tr.* to dislocate; to break the neck of; *rfl.* to become dislocated; to break one's neck. **-ato** *part. adj.* dislocated; lanky; loose-knit; (fig.) listless, languid, drooping.

†**dinominare** *vb.* and derivs. See **denominare**.

dinor·niti *m.* (orn.) *Dinornis*, moa.

dinosa·uro *m.*

dinotare [A 1] and derivs. See **denotare**.

dinto̲rno[1] *adv.* around, about; levarsi **—**, to clear out; *prep.* **—** a, round, around.

dinto̲rn·o[2] *m.* neighbourhood; *pl.* surroundings, environs; i **-i** di Cambridge, the Cambridge countryside; (paint.; drawing) outline. †**-are** *tr.* to outline; to surround.

dinud·are [A 1] *tr.* to undress, to bare, to strip; to reveal, to make manifest. **-ato** *part. adj.* bare; stripped.

†**dinumerare** *vb.* and derivs. See **numerare**.

†**dinun·zia** *f.* See **denunzia**.

†**dinunziare** *vb.* and derivs. See **denunziare**.

dio[1] *m.* (*pl.* **dei**, **dèi**, **dii**, *f.* **dea**) God; god; per l'amor di **—**, for God's sake, in heaven's name; per **—**, I beseech you; grazie a **—**, thank goodness; mio **—!**, my goodness, oh dear!; va' con **—!**, be off with you!; **—** lo sa, **—** sa, goodness knows; **—** sa se ho cercato di aiutarlo, God knows I tried to help him; **—** ce la mandi buona, let's hope it turns out all right; l'uomo propone e **—** dispone, man proposes, God disposes; **—** non paga il sabato, the mills of God grind slowly; (Neap.) lascia fare **—**, let things take their course; ben di **—**, grazia di **—**, abundance of good things; come **—** vuole, as God wills, (fig.) anyhow, at random; come **—** volle, alla fine se ne andarono, they went off at last, thank God; (Tusc.) a quel **—**, well, thoroughly, completely; pioveva a quel **—**, it was raining like anything; essere la mano di **—**, to be a godsend; il dito di **—**, the hand of God; quell'uomo è un'ira di **—**, that man's a holy terror; pezzo d'ira di **—**, exasperating, appalling person or thing; (colloq.) essere un **—**, to be a swell; †(naut. comm.) a **—** va!, hard up the helm! Note: after a vowel the initial **d** is doubled in speech, 'viva Dio' being pronounced 'vivaddio'. 'Gli', not 'i', is the article used before 'dei'. See also **iddio**.

†**dio**[2] *adj.* divine.

†**dio·cese** *f.* See **diocesi**.

dio·ceṣ·i *f.* (eccl.; hist.) diocese. **-ano** *adj.*, *n.m.* diocesan.

dioco *adj.* (biol.) dioecious.

diodo *m.* (electron.; radio) diode.

diodonte *m.* (ichth.) *Diodon* spp., porcupine fish.

diolo *m.* (chem.) diol.

diomedea *f.* (orn.) albatross, esp. the wandering albatross, *Diomedea exulans*.

Dion·e[1] *pr.n.f.* (myth.) Dione. **-e·a** *f.* (bot.) Venus's fly-trap, *Dionaea muscipula*.

Dio̲ne[2] *pr.n.m.* Dio, Dion.

Dionigi *pr.n.m.* Denis, Denys, Dennis.

dioni·ṣia *f.* (miner.) dionise.

Di-oni·ṣio *pr.n.m.* (myth.) Dionysius. **-oniṣi·aco** *adj.* Dionysiac. **-o·niṣo** *m.* Dionysus.

dio·pside *f.* (miner.) pyroxene.

dioptra *f.* alidade.

diorama *m.* diorama.

diorite *f.* (miner.) diorite, greenstone.

dio̧smo̧si *f.* osmosis.

diossano *m.* (chem.) dioxane.

diota[1] *f.* (archaeol.) diota, two-handled pot for wine.

†diota[2] *m.* See **idiota**.

di-ottra *f.* (opt.) dioptre, diopter; (surv.) — a traguardi, sight rule, alidade. **-ottri·a** *f.* (opt.) dioptre, diopter. **-ot·trica** *f.* dioptrics. **-ot·trico** *adj.* dioptrical.

dipan-are *tr.* [A I] to wind off; (text.) to unwind, to reel off; *abs.* to wind wool into a ball; (fig.) to disentangle, to unravel; to eat heartily; — la matassa, to disentangle a complicated mystery or problem. (**-amento** *m.* **-ato** *part. adj.*) **-ato̧io** *m.* winder. **-ato̧re** *m.* (text.) uncoiler. **-atura** *f.* winding off. **-ino** *m.* spool.

dipart-ire [D I] *intr.* (aux. essere), *rfl.* to depart, to go away; to diverge; to branch off; to differ; †*tr.* to divide; to separate; to disjoin; to remove, to carry away, to abduct; to distribute. **†-enza** *f.* departure; parting; farewell. **-imento** *m.* department; (naut.) naval coastal command. Note: the maritime administrative divisions under a Vice-Admiral (Comandante in Capo del Dipartimento militare marittimo) are: Alto Tirreno, Basso Tirreno, Ionio Adriatico, Basso Adriatico. A fifth zone (Alto Adriatico) is an independent command under the Admiral in Venice; †departure; †division; †separation. **-ita** *f.* (poet.) departure, death.

†dipelare *vb.* and derivs. See **pelare**.

†dipellare *tr.* to skin, to flay.

dipen·d-ere [C I] *intr.* (aux. essere, *prep.* da) to depend (on); questo -e da lui, this rests with him; questo errore -e solo dall'ignoranza, the mistake is due simply to ignorance; to derive; to be contingent; to be dependent. **-ente** *adj.* depending; dependent; *n.m.*, *f.* dependant; subordinate; employee; (leg.) member of staff; subordinate employee (C.C.). (**-entemente** *adv.*) **-enza** *f.* dependence; dependent condition; subordination; alle -enze di, employed by, in the service of; in -enza di, as a result of, *or* in relation to; derivation; dependency; annexe; †clientèle; †train, attendants; †downward slope; *pl.* offices; outbuildings.

†dipennare *tr.* to cancel, to strike out; to abolish; to reduce to nothing.

dipianare [A I] *tr.* to level.

†dipi·gnere *vb.* and derivs. See **dipingere**.

dipin·g-ere [C 5] *tr.* to paint; to colour; to depict, to portray, to represent; *abs.* to paint; *rfl.* to be portrayed; to depict oneself, to represent oneself; to use make-up, to use cosmetics, to put on make-up. (**-imento** *m.* **-ito̧re** *m.* **-itrice** *f.*)

dipint-o *part.* dipingere, q.v.; *adj.* painted, coloured, portrayed; made up, wearing cosmetics, painted; star —, to fit perfectly (of clothes); non lo posso vedere neanche —, I can't bear the sight of him; non ci starei neanche —, I shouldn't dream of staying in such a place; *n.m.* painting. **†-ore** *m.* **†-ora** *f.*, **†-oressa** *f.* **†-rice** *f.* painter. **†-ori·a** *f.* painting. **-ura** *f.* painting.

dipirri·chio *m.* (prosod.) proceleusmatic.

diplegi·a *f.* (med.) diplegia.

dipleidosco·pio *m.* dipleidoscope.

diplinto *m.* (archit.) wall of thickness of the length of two bricks.

diplococco *m.* (bact.) *Diplococcus*.

di·ploe *m.* (anat.) diploe, diploic tissue.

diplo·ide *f.* (Gk. antiq.) diplois, double cloak.

diplom-a *m.* diploma; charter; (academic) certificate or degree. **-a·tica** *f.* diplomatic. **-a·tico** *adj.* diplomatic; edizione -atica, edition which is a scrupulous reproduction of the original MS.; tribuna delle rappresentanze -atiche, distinguished strangers' gallery; *n.m.* diplomat, diplomatist; (cul.) a kind of cake. **-ato** *adj.* certificated; *n.m.* person possessing a diploma or degree; graduate. **-azi·a** *f.* diplomacy; diplomatic corps or service.

dipl-o·metro *m.* (med.) diplopiometer. **-opi·a** *f.* diplopia, double vision. **-osco·pio** *m.* (opt.) diploscope. **-osomi·a** *f.* diplosomia.

dipnosofista *m.* (antiq.) deipnosophist.

dipodi·a *f.* (prosod.) dipody.

dipoi *adv.* (usu. 'di poi') later; afterwards.

dipol-o *m.* (radio) dipole; antenna a —, dipole aerial. **-are** *adj.* (electr.) dipolar.

dipon·dio *m.* (Rom. antiq.) dupondius, dipondium.

†dipopolare *tr.* to depopulate; to sack.

†diporre *tr.* to depose; to set down; to abandon, to leave; to lower; to abase; to remove from office; to deposit; to pledge; to wager.

diport-are [A I] *rfl.* to behave, to conduct oneself; to disport oneself, to amuse oneself; †*tr.* to carry. **-amento** *m.* behaviour; procedure. **-ato** *part. adj.* conducted, behaved; †refreshed, restored. **†-e·vole** *adj.* playful, sportive.

diporto *m.* amusement, pastime, pleasure; place of recreation; andare a —, to go for a walk; per —, as a recreation.

†dipositare *vb.* and derivs. See **depositare**.

dipresso *adv. phr.* a un —, approximately, as near as makes no difference.

dip·saco *m.* (bot.) fullers' teasel, *Dipsacus fullonum*.

dips-e·tico *adj.* dipsetic, thirst producing. **-o·mane** *adj.* dipsomaniacal; *n.m.*, *f.* dipsomaniac. **-oman·a** *f.* dipsomania.

dip·tero *m.* (zool.). See **dittero**.

†diputare *vb.* and derivs. See **deputare**.

†dira *f.* written attack, imprecation.

dirad-are [A I] *tr.* to thin out; — le visite, to call less frequently; *intr.* (aux. essere), *rfl.* to become thinned out; to grow sparse; to be spaced out; to get thin; to be few and far between; to part, to clear (of clouds); to dissolve; to be a rare comer. **-amento** *m.* thinning out; spacing. **-ato** *part. adj.* thinned out; spaced out; few and far between. **-uva** *f.* (agric.) liquid sprayed on vines to thin out the bunches.

diradic-are [A 2 s] *tr.* to pull up; to uproot; to weed; †to scatter, to disperse. **-amento** *m.* pulling up; uprooting. **-ato** *part. adj.* uprooted; weeded.

diragnare [A 5] *tr.* to clear of cobwebs; †*rfl.* to be revealed, to be made manifest.

diram-are[1] [A I] *tr.* to clear (a tree) of boughs, to lop, to prune; to send out, to circulate; to give out, to publish; to distribute; to issue, to send out (to several recipients); *rfl.* to branch out, to divide; to ramify; to branch off; to spread. **-ata** *adv. phr.* alla -ata, full out; cantare alla -ata, to sing with all one's heart. **-ato** *part. adj.* lopped, pruned; branching. **-azio̧ne** *f.* lopping, pruning; branch (of river, railway line); branching out; branching off; ramification; sending out, circulation; (eng.) branch, T-piece.

diramare[2] [A I] *tr.* (techn.) to strip of copper.

dirappare *tr.* (bot.) to trim (a tree or bush), to lop, to disbud.

dirazzare [A I] *intr.* (aux. avere) to decline; to degenerate; to show a falling-off.

dire [B IO] *tr.*, *intr.* (aux. avere):

1. To SAY; — addio, to say farewell; — di sì, to say yes, to consent; — di no, to say no, to refuse; dillo a me, say it to me; di' un po'!, I say!; si dice, one says, people say, it is said; dicono, they say, they are saying; è un si dice e nulla più, it's gossip and nothing more; cioè a —, sarebbe a —, vale a —, viene a —, that is to say, in other words; è un ladro, e dico poco, he's a thief, to put it mildly (and that's putting it mildly); e — che l'ho conosciuto bambino, and to think I knew him when he was a child; per così —, so to speak; direi quasi, sto per —, I might almost say; quando si dice!, what an extraordinary coincidence!; come si dice 'to say' in italiano?, how do you say 'to say' in Italian?; 'to say' si dice 'dire', 'to say' is 'dire'; si diceva per —, it's only a manner of speaking; eran venti, che dico?, quaranta!, there were twenty,—what am I saying—forty! **2.** To SPEAK, to tell; — la verità, to speak the truth, to tell the truth; dimmi il vero, tell me the truth; — male di, to speak ill of; ti so — io, I can assure you; ti dirò, I'll tell you; se lo dico io!, of course it's true!, my word is good enough, isn't it?; ditemi il vostro parere, tell me your opinion; ho detto, I have spoken, I have said all I had to say; dico a te, sai?, I'm talking to you, I mean you; finirà male, te lo dico io, he'll come to a bad end, mark my words; a dirla a te, between you and me, I tell you in confidence; il cuore mi dice che ti rivedrò, I know in my heart I'll see you again; †per dirla, to tell the truth, I must admit. **3.** To TALK; lasciatelo —, let him talk; avete un bel —, non vi dà retta, it's no use your talking, he won't listen to you; dal — al fare c'è di mezzo il mare, (or) altro è —, altro è fare, easier said than done, (or) it's all very well to talk. **4.** To MEAN, to signify, to express; è quanto —, it means; quello è tutto —, that's everything; non vuol — nulla, it doesn't mean a thing; cosa vuol — questo?, what does this mean?; non vuol —, it doesn't follow; vuol — che sei buono, it means you have a kind heart; la regola

dire (*cont.*)

dice, the rule says, the rule implies; la lettera dice, the letter says, in the letter it says; — sul serio, to mean business; ora studia e dice sul serio, he's working at his studies now and really seriously; non vuol dir molto, it doesn't really matter, it doesn't signify. **5.** To RECITE, to utter; — la lezione, to recite one's lesson; — il confiteor, to repeat the 'confiteor'; — le preghiere, to say one's prayers; — la Messa, to say Mass; — Messa, to be a priest; — in chiesa, to publish the banns of; — all'asta, to bid at an auction; — ingiurie a, to insult; m'ha detto un'ingiuria, he insulted me; †— in rima, to write poetry. **6.** To CALL, to name; lo disse animoso, he called him brave; lo dicono un asino, they call him a fool; che dir si voglia, whatever you call it; come si dice quell'albero lì?, what's the name of that tree over there? **7.** To SUIT, to befall; il giuoco mi dice, my luck is in; mi dice fradicio, my luck is badly out; questo colore non ci dice con quell'altro, this colour doesn't go with the other; è un gran dire che tutto mi debba andar male, it's appalling how everything goes against me. **8.** To CRITICIZE; to speak adversely; trovarci a —, to find something to criticize; il lavoro è ben fatto, non c'è che —, the work is well done, no doubt about it; aver che — con uno, to quarrel; fra noi non c'è mai stato che —, we've never had a cross word. **9.** *rfl.* TO THINK ONESELF, to consider oneself; si dice grande uomo, he thinks he's a great man; dirsela con uno, to be on good terms with someone; *recip. rfl.* to say to each other; si dissero addio, they said goodbye, they bade each other farewell; si dissero un sacco e una sporta, they called each other all manner of names. **10.** *n.m.* SPEECH; talk; account; description; l'arte del —, rhetoric, elocution.

dire·dare, **-tare** [A 1], **-ditare** [A 1 S] and derivs. See **diseredare**.

diren·are [A 1 c] *tr.* to break the back of, to wear out; *rfl.* to break one's back; (fig.) -arsi a, to humble oneself to, to crawl before.

†diren·dere *rfl.* to yield, to give.

†direpzione *f.* depredation, sacking, plunder.

†diretano *m.* rear, posterior; *adj.* rear, hind, hindmost; younger, youngest.

†diretro *m.* back; *prep.* — a, — da, behind; led by; following; *adj.* last mentioned; *adv.* backwards; behind.

diretta·rio *m.* (leg.) owner of the freehold of land in the possession of another.

direttiv·o *adj.* directive, directing; consiglio —, managing board; comitato —, steering committee; organo —, governing body; (radio) antenna -a, directional aerial; *n.m.* steering committee. **-a** *f.* rule of conduct, directions for behaviour; directive; direction; *pl.* policy. **-ità** *f.* (radio) directivity.

dirett-o *part.* of **dirigere**, q.v.; *adj.* directed; — a, directed to, bound for, on the way to, addressed to, aimed at; educazione -a a far buoni cittadini, education designed to make good citizens; direct; (rlwy.) treno —, formerly a fast train, now less slow than an 'accelerato' and slower than a 'direttissimo'; vettura -a, through carriage; (rhet.) discorso —, direct speech; (mus.) accordo —, chord in root position; *n.m.* (boxing) a straight punch; (rlwy.) see 'treno diretto'. **-aménte** *adv.* directly; without intermediary; immediately, instantly. **-a** *f.* (radio; telev.) in -a, transmission, broadcast 'line'. **-is·simo** *adj. superl.* (leg.) giudizio -issimo, summary trial; citazione -issima, summons to appear for summary trial; la legge prescrive la citazione -issima, the law prescribes summary procedure; (alp.) via -issima, steepest route; *n.m.* (rlwy.) express. **-is·sima** *f.* (rlwy.) shortest route (e.g. between Bologna and Florence through the Apennines).

dirett·óre *m.* director; manager; editor (of paper); headmaster (of school); (theatr.) — di scena, stage-manager; (mus.) — d'orchestra, conductor; (cinem.) — di produzione, business manager; — spirituale, spiritual director, confessor; — generale delle poste, Postmaster-General; (mil.) commanding officer of technical services; officer in charge of a specific operation; (naut.) — delle armi e degli armamenti navali, naval armament officer; — delle costruzioni, director of construction; — di macchine, chief engineer of a ship; — marittimo, captain of a port or coastal command; — di mensa, president of a mess; — del tiro, gunnery officer of a ship; (leg.) — generale della società, general manager of company (C.C.); (sport) — tecnico, team-manager. **-rice** *f.* directress; manageress; headmistress; principal; matron; guiding rule, principle; road, route; (geom.) directrix; *pl.* policy. **-oriale** *adj.* (mus.) relating to conducting; l'arte -oriale, the art of con-

ducting. **-o·rio** *adj.* directorial; *n.m.* directing body; (hist.) Directory (in Revolutionary France); il -orio del partito fascisto, the Governing Council of the Italian Fascist Party; alla -oria (dress) in *Directoire* fashion; (eccl.) Ordo.

direzióne[1] *f.* guidance, management, direction, control, administration; head office; (naut.) offices of a 'direttore', q.v.; direction, course; sono avviato in quella —, I'm going that way; (traffic sign) — vietata, no entry; steering; volante di —, steering-wheel; (leg.) direction; la — dell'udienza, the conduct of the hearing or of the trial; (naut.) — del vento, direction of the wind; — della corrente, course of the current.

†direzióne[2] *f.* See **direpzione**.

diricciare [A 3] *tr.* to husk (chestnuts).

†diri·dere *vb.* and derivs. See **deridere**.

†dirieto *m.*, *prep.*, *adv.* See **dietro**.

diri·g-ere [C 13] *tr.* to manage; to control; to direct; to administer; to supervise; to send; to direct, to aim; to address; to dedicate; to recommend; to turn; (mus.) to conduct; *rfl.* (*prep.* a) to go (towards), to make (for); to apply (to). **-ente** *part. adj.* directing, guiding; classi -entì, ruling classes; *n.m.* (admin.) manager; *pl.* i -enti, those in charge. **-i·bile** *adj.* dirigible; *n.m.* airship. **-ibilista** *m.* pilot of airship. **-işmo** *m.* (econ.) planning.

diri·m-ere [B def.] *tr.* to cut short; — un ostacolo, to overcome an obstacle; — una controversia, to settle a controversy; to annul; to invalidate; †to divide, to separate, to distinguish; †to share. **-ente** *adj.* (leg.) diriment; invalidating; that absolutely bars; impedimento -ente, diriment impediment.

dirimpett-o *adv.* opposite; over there, over yonder; *prep. phr.* — a, opposite; — a me, facing me; in comparison; — a, compared with; *n.m.* opposite point, place opposite. **-a·io** *m.*, **-a·ia** *f.* (Tusc. fam.) person opposite, vis-à-vis; neighbour across the road.

†diripata *f.* precipice; gully.

†dirisione *f.* See **derisione**.

diritta *f.* right hand; place of honour; direct road, straightest way.

dirittan·golo *m.* rectangle.

diritt-o[1] *adj.* straight; erect, upright, honest, upright; right-hand, right; man -a, sword-stroke from left to right; clever, sagacious; cunning; right (side of material); good, favourable; la stagione va -a, the weather is keeping up well; (archit.) gola -a, cyma recta; *n.m.* right side; front; obverse; (knitting) un —, a plain stitch; un —, un rovescio, one plain, one purl; (archit.) footing, pedestal without moulding (cf. **piedritto**); *adv.* straight ahead; sempre —, straight on; rigar —, to keep straight, to behave properly; se seguita così, va — in prigione, if he goes on like that, he's heading straight for prison. **-aménte** *adv.* directly, straight; †exactly, just. **-ẹzza** *f.* honesty, uprightness; (Neap.) cunning, craftiness. **-óne** *m.* very crafty person.

diritt-o[2] *m.* **1.** (LEG.) LAW; — amministrativo, administrative law; — civile, civil law; — commerciale, commercial law, mercantile law; — comune, common law; — canonico, canon law; — consuetudinario, customary law; — corporativo, law relating to labour relations, corporative law (in Italian Fascist corporative state); — costituzionale, constitutional law; — ecclesiastico, ecclesiastical law; — feudale, feudal law; — delle genti, law of nations; — internazionale, international law; — interno, municipal, domestic law; — del lavoro, labour laws; — marittimo, maritime law; — naturale, natural law; — penale, criminal law; — positivo, man-made (as distinct from natural) law; (also) positive law (which requires something to be done, as opposed to that which forbids); — privato, private law; — processuale, law governing the conduct of judicial proceedings; — pubblico, public law; — romano, Roman law; — scritto, written law; contro —, against the law, contrary to law; in —, in law; oggetto del —, subject-matter of the law; formano oggetto del — di autore le opere dell'ingegno..., the subject-matter of copyright law consists of original works; soggetto del —, person who can sue and be sued under, whose rights and duties are affected by, the law; i soggetti del — di autore sono l'autore ed i suoi aventi causa, the persons who can sue and be sued under copyright law are the author and his assigns. **2.** DUE, duty, fee, perquisite, tax; — di bollo, stamp duty; -i casuali dell'Amministrazione dello Stato, civil servants' perquisites; — demaniale, royalty due to the State (the Crown); -i doganali, Customs duties; -i erariali, State taxes; — fisso, clerk's fee; -i storici degli Uffici delle Imposte Dirette, traditional perquisites of the inland revenue offices;

diritt-o (*cont.*)
~i di proroga, extension fees (patent law); (naut.) tribute, dues; diritti d'ancoraggio, harbour dues. **3.** RIGHT; a —, by right; a buon —, rightly, justifiably; di —, by rights, as one's right; membro di —, member as of right; (leg.) — acquisito, acquired right; — di asilo, right of asylum; — astratto, general right, undefined right; — d'autore, copyright; — di difesa, right of self-defence; — al lavoro, right to work; — legittimo, legal right; — personale, personal right, right *in personam*; — privilegiato, preferential right, secured right; — di proprietà, right to property, right of ownership; — reale, real right, right *in rem*; — del sangue, claim of the blood; di —, as of right; accampare un —, to assert a right, to claim a right; l'avente —, the person legally entitled, the legal (as distinct from equitable) owner; owner of the legal estate; avere —, to be entitled; beneficiario di un —, beneficiary of a right; cedere un —, to assign a right, to transfer a right; decadenza di un —, lapse of a right; esercitare un —, to exercise a right, to enforce a right; perdere un —, to lose a right; *pl.* rights; ~i di autore, royalties; ~i di brevetto, patent rights; ~i civili, civil rights, human rights; ~i fondamentali, fundamental rights; ~i politici, political rights; ~i di utilizzazione, exploitation rights (patents, etc.).

dirittur-a *f.* (Tusc.) direction; andare nella — di, to go straight on towards; straight line, straight stretch; uprightness, honesty; moral rectitude; good sense; (racing) la — d'arrivo, the finishing straight; *adv.* a —, see **addirittura**; †obsequies.

†**dirivare** *tr.* to divert; to derive; *intr.* to flow forth; to emanate; — a, to reach; *rfl.* to derive, to be derived.

dirizz-are [A I] and derivs. See **drizzare.** -atoio *m.* comb; any instrument for straightening. -atura *f.* hair-parting; redistribution. -ona·io *m.* impulsive or obstinate person. -one *m.* impulsive action or movement (usu. in wrong direction); prendere un ~one, to start off in the wrong direction, to take a sudden and ill-advised course; tiresome caprice, bad habit; thoughtless and obstinate behaviour; infatuation.

dirlindana *f.* (joc.) long fishing-line (cf. **durindana**).

diro *adj.* dire; grim; cruel.

dirobbiare [A4] *tr.* to extract madder from.

dirocc-are [A2] *tr.* to demolish, to raze; *intr.* (*aux.* essere) to crumble, to fall into ruins. -amento *m.* demolishing; crumbling. -ato *part. adj.* demolished; in ruins, falling to ruins; tumble-down. (-atore *m.*)

†**dirogare** *vb.* and derivs. See **derogare.**

diromp-ere [C26] *tr.* to break; to bruise (flax); to soften, to make pliant or supple; to break in (horses); to inure; *intr.* (*aux.* essere) to burst, to break; — in lagrime, to burst into tears; *rfl.* to be in violent motion (of water); -ersi — a qualcosa, to break oneself in to something; †-ersi a dire, to burst out with, to have one's say. -ente *part. adj.* bursting; bomba -ente, demolition bomb; esplosivo -ente, high explosive. -imento *m.* breaking; bursting.

†**dirotta** *f.* (naut.) course.

dirott-are [A I c] *tr.* (naut.) to change the course of; *intr.* (*aux.* avere) (naut.) to alter course. (-ato *part. adj.*)

dirott-o *part.* of **dirompere**, q.v.; *adj.* softened, broken; inured; pioggia ~a, violent, driving, pelting rain; pianto —, unrestrained weeping; *adv. phr.* a —, violently, in torrents; rapidly; headlong; †exhausted, all in, badly winded; †buffeted; storm-tossed; †precipitous. -amente *adv.* violently; copiously, abundantly; in torrents.

†**dirovinare** *vb.* and derivs. See **rovinare.**

dirozz-are [A I] *tr.* to rough-hew, to rough-dress, to take the roughness from; to rough out; (fig.) to polish, to educate, to 'knock the corners off'; *rfl.* to get some education, to acquire manners; to lose country boorishness. -amento *m.* rough-hewing; roughing out. -ato *part. adj.* rough-hewn; knocked into shape. (-atore *m.*) -atura *f.* (text.) wool that needs new-carding.

†**dirubare** *vb.* and derivs. See **rubare.**

dirugginare [A I s] and derivs. See **dirugginire.**

diruggin-ire [D2] *tr.* to clear of rust; — i denti, to grind one's teeth (in anger or irritation). -io *m.* rasping; grinding noise.

dirup-are [A I] *tr.* to hurl down; to fling from a precipice; *intr.* (*aux.* essere) to plunge down; (fig.) to fall, to sink; †*rfl.* to plunge down. -ato *part. adj.* precipitous, abrupt; rocky and steep.

†**dirupinare** *vb.* and derivs. See **dirupare.**

dirupo *m.* rocky precipice; crag; ruin, ruined building.

di·ruto *adj.* ruined, in ruins.

diruttore *m.* (aeron.) spoiler.

disa-, disa-. In the following compounds, the Tuscan pronunciation favours the voiced intervocalic 's' (ṣ), and Roman the unvoiced (s). In the words which follow the Tuscan pronunciation is indicated.

disabbell-ire [D2] *tr.* to disfigure; to mar; to spoil; *rfl.* to lose one's beauty, to go off in looks. -imento *m.* disfiguring; disfigurement. -ito *part. adj.* disfigured; marred; gone off in looks, faded.

disabbigliare [A4] and derivs. See **spogliare.**

disabiglié, disabillié *m. indecl.* déshabille.

†**disa·bil-e** *adj.* no longer skilled, out of practice, unpractised. -ità *f.* lack of practice, loss of skill, disability.

†**disabitare** *tr.* to depopulate, to leave unpopulated; to leave, to quit; *rfl.* to become uninhabited.

disabitato *adj.* uninhabited.

disabitu-are [A6] *tr.* to disaccustom; to break of a habit; *rfl.* to disaccustom oneself; to lose a habit. -ato *part. adj.* no longer accustomed.

disaccent-are [A I] *tr.* to remove the accent from. -ato *part. adj.* de-accented; unaccented. -uazione *f.* (telev.) de-emphasis.

disaccentr-are [A I] *tr.* (admin.) to decentralize. -ato *part. adj.* decentralized.

†**disaccerto** *m.* uncertainty; disagreement, discord.

†**disacceso** *adj.* unlit, spent.

disaccett-o *adj.* unwelcome, unacceptable. †-are *tr.* to decline, to refuse.

disacciaiare [A4] *tr.* to denaturize (steel).

disacconci-o *adj.* ill-suited, unbecoming; *n.m.* disadvantage. -amente *adv.* unbecomingly.

disaccoppi-are [A4] *tr.* to uncouple, to disjoin; (radio) to de-couple. -amento *m.* uncoupling; (radio) de-coupling.

disaccord-are [A I] *intr.* (*aux.* essere) (mus.) to be out of tune. -anza *f.* the state of being out of tune. -ato *adj.* out of tune. -o *m.* (mus.) the state of being out of tune; (leg.) disagreement; (fig.) disagreement, variance; essere, trovarsi in — con, to be in disagreement, at variance with.

disaccredit-are [A I s] *tr.* to reduce the credit of; to discredit. -amento *m.* discrediting. -ato *part. adj.* discredited.

disaccurato *adj.* careless.

disacerbare [A I] *tr.* (poet.) to sweeten; to soothe; to make less harsh; *rfl.* to be sweetened; to lose one's sting, to mellow; †*intr.* to grow less savage.

†**disacervare** *vb.* and derivs. See **disacerbare.**

disacid-are [A2s] *tr.* to de-acidify, to remove the acid from. -ato *part. adj.* de-acidified. -azione *f.* de-acidification. -ire [D2] and derivs. See **disacidare.**

disacrare [A I] and derivs. See **dissacrare.**

disadatt-o *adj.* unfit; ill-suited, inappropriate; untimely; incapable; awkward. -amente *adv.* inappropriately; awkwardly. -ag·gine *f.* awkwardness. -are [A I] *tr.* to render unfit. -ezza *f.* unfitness; inappropriateness; awkwardness.

†**disadirato** *adj.* cooled of one's anger, cooled off, no longer angry.

disadombrare [A I c] *tr.* to free from alarm or suspicion; *rfl.* to put suspicion out of one's mind.

disadornare [A I c] *tr.* to strip of ornaments, to leave bare, to make plain; to become less beautiful; to be less adorned.

disadorn-o *adj.* plain, bare, unpolished, unadorned; simple; austere; stile —, plain, unadorned style. -amente *adv.* plainly; simply; austerely.

disaffannare [A I] *tr.* to soothe, to relieve, to alleviate.

disaffezion-are [A I c] *tr.* to alienate, to estrange; *rfl.* -arsi da, to lose one's affection for. -amento *m.* alienating. -ato *part. adj.* alienated, estranged; detached; indifferent.

disaffezione *f.* alienation of affection, estrangement.

disafforcare [A2] *tr.* (naut.) to unmoor.

disagevol-e *adj.* uncomfortable, painful, distressing; hard, difficult. -mente *adv.* painfully; with difficulty. -ezza *f.* difficulty, discomfort, distress.

disag·io *m.* (finan.) loss on exchange of currency.

disaggrad-are [A I] *intr.* (*aux.* essere) to be displeasing. -evole *adj.* unpleasing, displeasing; disagreeable. -evolmente *adv.* disagreeably. -ire [D2] *tr.* to displease; to dislike.

disaggreg-are [A2] *tr.* to separate; *rfl.* to lose cohesion, to fall apart. -amento *m.* separating; falling apart. -ato *part. adj.* separated; in bits. -azione *f.* separation.

†**disagguagli-are** *tr.* to render unequal; to make uneven; *rfl.* to distinguish oneself; *recip. rfl.* to be unequal. †**-anza** *f.* inequality; difference.

disagi-are [A3] *tr.* to incommode, to trouble; *rfl.* to be in difficulties. **-ato** *part. adj.* uncomfortable, difficult; straitened; vita **-ata**, life of tribulation; †infirm; †insane. **-atamente** *adv.* uncomfortably; with difficulty.

disa·gi-o *m.* (*pl.* **disagi**) discomfort; hardship; privation; uneasiness; a —, in discomfort, uncomfortably, ill at ease; trovarsi a —, to feel uncomfortable, to be ill at ease; to be embarrassed; †pain; †lack, absence, want. **-oso** *adj.* See **disagevole**. (**-osamente** *adv.*)

†**disaiut-are** *tr.* to hinder, to impede. †**-o** *m.* hindrance, impediment.

disalber-are [A1s] *tr.* (naut.) to dismast. **-amento** *m.* (naut.) dismasting. **-ato** *part. adj.* (naut.) dismasted, unmasted. **-azione** *f.* (naut.) state of being dismasted.

disalcalizzare [A1] *tr.* to remove alkali from.

disallenato *adj.* (sport) out of training, out of practice.

†**disalloggiare** (mil.) *tr.* to turn out of quarters; to turn out of lodging; *intr.* to leave a billet; to seek other lodgings (cf. **sloggiare**).

disalveare [A6] *tr.* to change the course of, to divert (stream, river).

disam-are [A1] *tr.* to cease to love; to hate; *intr.* (*aux.* avere) to be no longer in love, to be out of love. **-abile** *adj.* unamiable, unprepossessing; disagreeable; hateful. (**-atore** *m.* **-atrice** *f.*)

disamen-o *adj.* unpleasing; displeasing; unpleasant, disagreeable; (of landscape) barren. **-ità** *f.* unpleasantness; unattractiveness; disagreeableness.

disa·min-a *f.* careful scrutiny; (leg.) close examination; dopo accurata —, after thorough examination. **-are** [A1s] *tr.* to consider carefully, to scrutinize. **-azione** *f.* careful scrutiny; (leg.) inquisition; searching inquiry; close examination.

disamor-are [A1c] *tr.* to estrange, to alienate; *rfl.* **-arsi da**, to cease to love; to become estranged from; **-arsi dello (dallo)** studio, to lose interest in one's studies. **-atezza** *f.* loss of interest; indifference. **-ato** *part. adj.* estranged, alienated; indifferent. **-evole** *adj.* unkind; unfeeling; uninterested. **-evolmente** *adv.* unkindly; unfeelingly. **-evolezza** *f.* lack of courtesy; indifference.

disamor-e *m.* indifference; dislike; estrangement. **-oso** *adj.* loveless; indifferent.

disancorare [A1s] *intr.* (*aux.* avere) (naut.) to weigh anchor.

†**disande·vole** *adj.* inaccessible.

disanellare [A1] *tr.* (naut.) to remove spectacle plates from (lower mast or bowsprit); to take thimbles out of (sails or awning); to take rings from; †to put away (one's wife), to repudiate.

disanim-are [A1s] *tr.* to dishearten, to deject, to depress; †to dispatch the soul of, to dispatch; *rfl.* to become disheartened; to lose heart; to grow dispirited. **-ante** *part. adj.* disheartening; depressing. **-ato** *part. adj.* disheartened; dispirited; low in morale.

disannoiare [A4] *tr.* to cheer, to enliven; *rfl.* to cheer up, to throw off depression, to be of good cheer.

disapostrofare [A1s] *tr.* to omit the apostrophe from.

disapparecchiato *adj.* unprepared.

disappariscente *adj.* inconspicuous.

disappassion-are [A1c] *tr.* to free from a passion; *rfl.* **-arsi da**, to lose one's love for; to become indifferent to. **-ato** *part. adj.* cured of a passion; indifferent; dispassionate. (**-atamente** *adv.*) **-atezza** *f.* indifference, detachment.

†**disappestare** *tr.* to disinfect; (fig.) to cleanse.

disappetenza *f.* lack of appetite; loss of appetite; disgust at food.

disapplic-are [A2s] *tr.* to cease to apply; (leg.) to misapply; — la legge al caso di cui si disputa, to misapply the law to the case before the Court; *rfl.* to cease to pay attention; **-arsi dagli studi**, to neglect one's studies. **-atezza** *f.* lack of attention, inattentiveness. **-ato** *part. adj.* inattentive, idle. **-azione** *f.* lack of application, half-heartedness.

disappren-dere [C1] *tr.* to unlearn.

disapprov-are [A1] *tr.* to disapprove of; to rebuke. **-ante** *part. adj.* disapproving. (**-ato** *part. adj.* **-atore** *m.*) **-azione** *f.* disapproval, disapprobation; incorrere nella **-azione di**, to incur the disapproval of.

disappunto *m.* trouble, trial, vexation; disappointment; con mio —, to my disappointment; avere un —, to suffer a disappointment; nella vita i disappunti capitano spesso, troubles and trials are frequent in life.

disargentare [A1] *tr.* to de-silver.

disargin-are [A1s] *tr.* to break down banks (of river). **-ato** *part. adj.* without banks; with broken banks.

disarm-are [A1] *tr.* to disarm; to dismantle; (naut.) to lay up, to put into reserve; to pay off for recommissioning or repairs; — i remi, to ship oars; (mil.) to dismantle; (bldg.) to take down scaffolding from; *intr.* (*aux.* avere) to disarm; (naut.) **-a!**, weigh enough! **-amento** *m.* disarming; disarmament. **-ato** *part. adj.* disarmed; unarmed; dismantled; (herald.) without claws. **-ista** *m.* (neol.) person in favour of disarmament.

disarmentare [A1] *tr.* to take cattle from.

disarm-o *m.* disarmament; dismantling; (naut.) laying up, state of a ship out of commission; (bldg.) removal of scaffolding.

disarm-oni-a *f.* (mus.) discord. **-o·nico** *adj.* discordant. **-onizzare** [A1] *tr.* to mistune. **-onizzato** *part. adj.* mistuned.

disarticol-are [A1s] *tr.* to disarticulate, to disjoint. **-azione** *f.* disarticulation.

disartificiale *adj.* unartificial, natural.

disartri·a *f.* (med.) dysarthria.

†**disascon·dere** *tr.* to reveal, to disclose; *rfl.* to be revealed; to reveal oneself.

†**disasinare** *rfl.* to turn from the form of an ass into a man.

disasprire [D2] *tr.* to mitigate; *rfl.* to be alleviated.

disass-amento *m.* (eng.) misalignment. **-ato** *adj.* (eng.) out of alignment; (aeron.) rinforzo **-ato**, offset, joggle.

disassimilazione *f.* (scient.) disassimilation.

disassociare [A3] *tr.* to dissociate; to disunite; *rfl.* to sever one's connexion.

disassuef-are [B14] *tr.* to disaccustom; *rfl.* to become disaccustomed; to lose a habit; **-arsi da**, to lose the habit of. **-azione** *f.* breaking of a habit.

disastr-are [A1] *tr.* to harm seriously, to be disastrous to. **-ato** *part. adj.* seriously harmed; *n.m.* one who has been seriously harmed or suffered grievous loss. **-evole** *adj.* disastrous, harmful.

disastr-o *m.* disaster, calamity, grievous loss; (leg.) accident, wreck, crash; — ferroviario, railway accident; — aviatorio, air-crash; (naut.) bastimento in —, ship in distress. **-oso** *adj.* disastrous; unlucky; unfavourable; prezzi **-osi**, bargain prices; †steep, rough.

disatomizzare [A1] and derivs. See **denuclearizzare**.

disatten·dere [C1] *tr.* (leg.) to disregard; — una norma, to fail to comply with a regulation.

disattent-o *adj.* inattentive; heedless, careless, negligent. **-amente** *adv.* inattentively; heedlessly, carelessly, negligently.

disattenzione *f.* inattention, lack of attention; carelessness, negligence; absent-mindedness.

disattitu·dine *f.* loss of aptitude or skill.

disattiv-are [A1] *tr.* (naut.) to disarm (a mine). **-azione** *f.* disarming (of a mine).

disattrazzare [A1] *tr.* (naut.) to remove minor equipment from.

disattrezzare [A1] *tr.* (naut.) to dismantle, to unrig; to put into fighting or bad weather trim.

†**disattristare** *tr.* to enliven, to cheer; *rfl.* to cheer up, to brighten.

disautor-are [A1?], **-izzare** [A1] *tr.* to deprive of authority, to withdraw authority from. (**-ato**, **-izzato** *part. adj.*)

disavanzare [A1] *intr.* (*aux.* avere) to have a deficit, to lose money; †to lose, to come off worst, to be a loser.

disavanzo *m.* (comm.) loss; deficit; mettere a —, to count as a loss; saldare a —, to settle an account at a loss.

disavvantaggiare [A3] *tr.* to disadvantage, to injure; *rfl.* to be at a disadvantage.

disavvantag-g-io *m.* disadvantage. **-ioso** *adj.* disadvantageous, unfavourable.

disavvedut-o *adj.* heedless, inadvertent; †unforeseen; †unaware. **-amente** *adv.* heedlessly, inadvertently. **-ezza** *f.* carelessness, heedlessness; careless action.

disavven-ente *adj.* unattractive; unprepossessing; unlovely; ungraceful; †inappropriate, unsuitable. **-ezza** *f.* unattractiveness; disagreeableness; awkwardness.

†**disavvenire** *intr.* to be inappropriate; to be unsuitable.

disavventur-a *f.* mishap, mischance, misadventure; accident. **-ato** *adj.* unfortunate, unlucky; ill-omened. **-oso** *adj.* unfortunate; dogged by misfortune, ill-fated; †unadventurous.

disavvert-enza *f.* inadvertence, inattention; lack of attention. **-ito** *adj.* inadvertent; inattentive; careless. **-itamente** *adv.* inadvertently; inattentively.

disavvezz-are [A1c] *tr.* to disaccustom; to dissuade; — da, to free from the habit of; *rfl.* to break a habit; -arsi di fumare, to break oneself of smoking. **-aménto** *m.* breaking of a habit. **-ato** *part. adj.* disaccustomed; broken (of a habit); n'è oramai -ato, he's now broken of it.

disavvèzzo *adj.* disaccustomed; unaccustomed; out of practice; — dal suonare il pianoforte, out of practice in playing the piano; †*apocop. part.* of **disavvezzare**, q.v.

disazotato *adj.* (chem.) denitrified, denitrized.

disbandare [A1] *tr.* to disband, to dispense; †(naut.) to right.

disband-eggiare [A3c] *tr.* to banish. **-ire** [D2] *tr.* to banish.

disbaragliare [A4] and derivs. See **sbaragliare**.

disbarazz-are [A1] *tr.* (*prep.* di) to clear, to disencumber (of). **-ato** *part. adj.* cleared, clear, disencumbered.

disbarc-are [A2] *tr.* to disembark, to land, to unload; *intr.* (*aux.* essere) to disembark, to land, to step ashore. **-aménto** *m.* disembarking, landing; unloading. (**-ato** *part. adj.*)

disbàr-co *m.* (*pl.* **-chi**) disembarking, landing; unloading.

disbendare [A1] *tr.* to unbind, to remove the bandage from; *rfl.* to unbind one's eyes.

disbestiare [A4] *rfl.* to recover one's temper, to become reasonable again.

disbittare [A1] *tr.* (naut.) to unbitt.

†**disboccare** *intr.* to debouch.

disborsare [A1c] *tr.* (comm.) to disburse.

disbòrso *m.* (comm.) disbursement; deposit.

disboscare [A2] and derivs. See **diboscare**.

disbraccare [A2] *tr.* (naut.) to unstrop.

disbram-are [A1] *tr.* to quench; to satisfy; to gorge; -arsi la sete, to quench one's thirst; *rfl.* to satisfy oneself; to be satisfied; -arsi di gioia, to have one's fill of joy. **-ato** *part. adj.* satisfied; quenched; gorged; sated.

disbran-are [A1] *tr.* to tear to pieces. **-ato** *part. adj.* torn, rent, in shreds.

disbrancare [A2] *tr.* to lop; to separate; to single out; *rfl.* to branch out, to leave the herd.

disbrandare [A1] *tr.* to disarm (of sword).

disbrig-are [A2] *tr.* to disentangle; to disengage; to deal quickly with, to expedite; to settle; — qualcosa, to get something done expeditiously, to rush something through; *rfl.* to disentangle oneself, to get out of a difficulty; -arsi di, to get rid of, to clear oneself of; to despatch, to settle. (**-ato** *part. adj.*)

disbrì-go *m.* (*pl.* **-ghi** *m.*) clearing-up, settlement; (leg.) despatch, disposal; il — di una pratica, the disposal of a matter or case.

disbrogli-are [A4] *tr.* to unravel, to disentangle. **-ato** *part. adj.* unravelled, disentangled; (fig.) tranquil.

†**disbrunare** *tr.* to brighten, to burnish.

discacci-are [A3] *tr.* to drive out, to drive away; to expel; to exile. **-aménto** *m.* driving away; expelling; exiling. **-ativo** *adj.* able to drive out, likely to drive out; expulsive. **-ato** *part. adj.* driven out, driven away; expelled; exiled. (**-atóre** *m.* **-atrice** *f.*)

†**discad-ere** *intr.* to diminish; to decline; to abate; to revert, to return (to a previous owner); to fall; to deviate. †**-iménto** *m.* diminution, decline, falling off. †**-uto** *part. adj.* fallen; failing in strength.

†**discagliare** *vb.* (naut.). See **disincagliare**.

discalcare [A2] *tr.* (naut.) to uncaulk.

discalz-are [A1] *tr.* to remove the shoes and stockings of; (fig.) to undermine. **-arèllo** *adj.* (eccl.) Discalced friar. (**-ato** *part. adj.*) **-o** *adj.* barefoot, barefooted; (eccl.) Discalced.

†**discamer-are** *tr.* (leg.) to restore to the rightful owner. †**-azione** *f.* (leg.) restitution.

discantare[1] [A1] *tr.* to disenchant, to break the spell of; to release from enchantment.

discant-are[2] [A1] *intr.* (*aux.* avere) (mus.) to sing a discant (or descant). **-o** *m.* (mus.) discant, descant.

discapezzare [A1c] *tr.* to lop, to prune; †to decapitate.

†**discapigliare** *vb.* and derivs. See **scapigliare**.

discapit-are [A1s] *intr.* (*aux.* avere) to suffer loss. (**-aménto** *m.*)

discà·pito *m.* loss; depreciation; detriment; loss of esteem; con — a, to the detriment of.

†**discappellare** *tr.* (naut.) to take off the rigging (at mast's head or yard's arm); — le coffe, to send down the tops; to unhood (a falcon).

discarburare [A1]. See **decarburare**.

†**discarcare** *vb.* and derivs. See **discaricare**.

discarcerare [A1s] *tr.* to release from prison; †*rfl.* to be released from this life.

†**discargare** *vb.* and derivs. See **discaricare**.

discà·rica *f.* voucher; pensioner's rent voucher; (naut.) unloading; railway dump; (mining) dump.

discar-icare [A2s] *tr.* to release from a burden, to free; to unload; †(naut.) to discharge. (**-aménto** *m.* **-ato** *part. adj.*)

discà·rico *adj.* freed, unburdened; unloaded; *n.m.* unloading; draining off; easing, alleviating; a — di coscienza, to ease one's conscience; discharging (of a responsibility); per mio —, in discharge of my duty, to clear myself; (leg.) defence; testimoni a —, witnesses for the defence; prova a —, evidence for the defence; (sport) lightening of weight.

discarn-are [A1] *tr.* to remove flesh from; *rfl.*, *intr.* (*aux.* essere) to lose flesh. **-ato** *part. adj.* lean, not plump.

discaro *adj.* disagreeable, displeasing; unacceptable; se non vi è —, if you have no objection; non vi sia — accettare, please accept.

discaten-are [A1c] *tr.* to unchain, to let loose. **-ato** *part. adj.* unchained; off the chain, loose.

discatto *m.* (comm.) loss.

discavalc-are [A2] *tr.* to unhorse; to dismount, to unlimber (a gun); *intr.* (*aux.* essere) to alight, to dismount. **-ato** *part. adj.* dismounted.

†**discavare** *vb.* and derivs. See **scavare**.

†**discazzare** *vb.* and derivs. See **discacciare**.

†**discè·dere** *intr.* to depart, to go away, to be off.

discènd-ere [C1] *intr.* (*aux.* essere, avere) to come down; to go down; to dismount, to get down; to sink; to disembark, to land; to slope; to proceed; to come to a compromise; to descend, to be a descendant; Clara Falcone -e da Pandolfo dei Falconi, Clara Falcone is a descendant of Pandolfo dei Falconi; (astron.) to set; (leg.) — in causa, to take sides in an action or dispute; *tr.* to go down, to descend; — le scale, to go down the stairs; †to cause to descend. **-ente** *part. adj.* descending; sloping; *n.m.*, *f.* descendant; *m.* (typ.) inferior figure. **-entale** *adj.* (leg.) descendant. **-enza** *f.* descent; posterity, race; -enza d'Adamo, sons of Adam, seed of Adam; (leg.) erede per -enza, heir by inheritance. **-eri·a** *f.* (mining) manway, sloping adit. **-iménto** *m.* descent.

discens-ióne *f.* descent; origin; †(astron.) descension. **-ionale** *adj.* descensional. **-ivo** *adj.* descensive. **-o** *m.* (mus.) descent; †downward motion, descent; †derivation, descent. **-óre** *m.* descender. **-o·rio** *adj.* descending, of descent.

discente *adj.* learning; *n.m.*, *f.* scholar, pupil.

discentr-are [A1, Rom. A1c] *tr.* to remove from the centre; to decentralize; *rfl.* to leave, to come away, to break away; to become detached; to be decentralized. **-aménto** *m.* decentralizing. **-ato** *part. adj.* decentralized.

discèpol-o *m.* pupil, learner; disciple; follower. (**-a** *f.*) **-ato** *m.* discipleship.

discèrn-ere [B1] *tr.* to discern, to distinguish; to judge between; to discriminate; to recognize, to descry; to choose; to distribute; †to decide; †to favour, to esteem. †**-é·vole** *adj.* see **discernibile**. **-i·bile** *adj.* discernible. **-iménto** *m.* discernment, judgement; insight; intelligence; †distinction. **-itivo** *adj.* discerning; relating to discernment. (**-itóre** *m.* **-itrice** *f.*)

discervellare [A1] and derivs. See **scervellare**.

discèsa *f.* descent; going down; in —, downhill; alighting; fall; slope; invasion, incursion; (skiing) — a Cristiania, ski descent consisting of christy turns; — libera, downhill racing; — obbligata, descent trial over fixed course, slalom; (med.) flux; (radio) — di antenna, aerial lead-in; (aeron.) traiettoria di —, glide path. **-ista** *m.*, *f.* (cycle-racing, skiing) competitor who is particularly fast on downhill stretches. **-ismo** *m.* (sport) downhill racing.

†**discett-are** *tr.* to dispute, to contend; to ravish; to scatter, to disperse. †**-azione** *f.* contest, dispute.

discever-are [A1s] *tr.* to separate; to single out. **-aménto** *m.* separating; singling out. **-anza** *f.* separation. **-ato** *part. adj.* separated; singled out (cf. **sceverare**).

dischètto *m.* *dim.* of **disco**, q.v.

†**dischiarare** *tr.* to declare; to clarify; to make clear; to cheer, to enliven; to purify (metals).

†**dischiatt-are** *intr.* to degenerate. **-ato** *part. adj.* degenerated; degenerate.

†**dischiav·acciare** *tr.* to unlatch; to unfasten; to remove nails from. †**-are** *tr.* to open; to take down from the cross; to uproot; *intr.* to burst forth, to shoot out.

dischierare [A I] *tr.* to disarrange, to throw into disorder; *rfl.* to leave the ranks.

dischiest-a *f.*, **-o** *m.* scarcity, lack, insufficiency.

dischiod-are [A I] *tr.* to break open; (mil.) to unspike (gun). (**-ato** *part. adj.*)

†**dischiomare** *tr.* to pull the hair off, to strip of hair.

dischiu·dere [C 3] *tr.* to open slightly; to disclose; to reveal; †to exclude, to except.

dischiuso *part.* of **dischiudere**, q.v.; *adj.* half-open, ajar; disclosed.

†**discieverare** *vb.* and derivs. See **sceverare**.

†**discigliare** *tr.* to remove the thread from the eyes of (a falcon).

†**disci·gnere** *vb.* and derivs. See **discingere**.

†**discin·dere** *tr.* to break; to truncate.

discin·gere [C 5] *tr.* to ungird; to undo, to loosen.

discinto *part.* of **discingere**, q.v.; *adj.* ungirt; untidy, half-undressed; slatternly.

discio·gl-iere [B 27] *tr.* to undo, to untie; to release; to dissolve, to melt; to break up; to resolve (doubt); †to absolve; †to violate, to outrage; †(naut.) to sail. **-imento** *m.* untying; dissolving (cf. **sciogliere**).

disciolt-o *part.* of **disciogliere**, q.v.; *adj.* dissolved; melted; free, untrammelled; sermone **-**, prose; agile, nimble; (agric.) light, easy to work (of soil); †dishevelled; †disbanded; †dissolute; †enervated, slowed down. **-ura** *f.* nimbleness; diarrhoea.

†**disciorre** *vb.* and derivs. See **disciogliere**.

†**discipare** *vb.* and derivs. See **dissipare**.

disciplin-a *f.* teaching, instruction; intellectual training; learning; branch of learning or study; discipline; control; tenere la **-**, to keep discipline; consiglio di **-**, disciplinary committee; punishment; (leg.) control, discipline, regulation; **-** delle attività professionali, discipline of professional activities; **-** unitaria della produzione, uniform control of production; **-** della concorrenza, regulation of competition (C.C.); (mil.) sala di **-**, guard-room; consiglio di **-**, disciplinary court; (naut.) **-** marittima, equiv. to admiralty regulations; (rel.) scourge, discipline; compagnia di **-**, penitential guild. **-are** *adj.* disciplinary.

disciplinare[1] *adj.* See under **disciplina**.

disciplin-are[2] [A I] *tr.* to discipline; to instruct; to train; to chastise; (mech.) la legge che **-a** il moto, the law governing motion; *rfl.* to discipline oneself; to train oneself. **-abile** *adj.* disciplinable; trainable. **-abilità** *f.* disciplinableness. **-amento** *m.* disciplining; instructing; training. **-ante** *m.* (rel.) disciplinant. **-ata** *f.* stroke, lash with a scourge. **-atezza** *f.* disciplined mode of behaviour; submission to discipline; habit of obedience. **-ato** *part. adj.* disciplined, trained; orderly, law-abiding; (mil.) trained; (rel.) disciplinant, flagellant. **-atamente** *adv.* in an orderly and disciplined way. **-atore** *m.* disciplinist; instructor. (**-atrice** *f.*) **-evole** *adj.* teachable; capable of being disciplined or trained.

†**disciprina** *f.* See **disciplina**.

†**disci·pulo** *m.* See **discepolo**.

discissione *f.* (med.) discission; separation.

†**disciucare** *rfl.* to turn again from the form of an ass into a man.

disc-o *m.* (*pl.* **dischi**) disk, disc; railway signal; telephone dial, (watchm.) roller; (mus.) gramophone record; **-** microsolco, **- a lunga durata**, long-playing record; (sport) discus; quoit; lancio del **-**, discus-throwing; **-** sul ghiaccio, ice-hockey; (aeron.) **-** volante, flying-saucer; (bot.) disc; (eng.) disk, wheel; plate; **-** di frizione, clutch plate; **-** per pulitrice, buffing wheel; **-** paraolio, splash guard; (radio) **-** analizzatore, scanning disk; (anat.) disk; ernia del **-**, slipped disk. **-o·filo** *m.* (mus.) collector of gramophone records. **-ografi·a** *f.* (mus.) repertoire of gramophone recordings. **-ogra·fico** *adj.* (mus.) pertaining to records; incisione **-ografica**, gramophone recording. **-oide·o** *adj.* discoid; disk-shaped.

discobla·stula *f.* (zool.) blastodisc.

disco·bolo *m.* (antiq.) discobolus.

discoccare [A 2] *tr.* to shoot (off).

discoleggiare [A 3 c]. See under **discolo**.

discol(l)ato *m.* (naut.) gunwale, sheerstrake; mettere il **-** all'acqua, gun'l under; †fregio del **-**, decorations of the gun'l.

†**discollegare** *tr.* to disconnect; to sever.

di·scol-o *adj.* idle; disorderly; undisciplined, mischievous; †hard to please; †unlettered, illiterate; *n.m.* scamp; truant; idler; gay young man; dissolute young man. **-ag·gine** *f.* prank, piece of mischief. **-ato** *m.* (Tusc. hist.) system of impressing 'vagabonds' into military service. **-eggiare** [A 3 c] *intr.* (*aux.* avere) to lead an idle, disreputable life.

discolor-are [A I c] *tr.* to take the colour from, to bleach; to discolour; *rfl.* to fade, to grow pale; to lose one's colour. **-ato** *part. adj.* discoloured; faded. **-azione** *f.* fading; bleaching; loss of colour. **-ire** [D 2] *tr.* to take the colour from; *intr.* (*aux.* essere), *rfl.* to fade; to pale.

discolpa *f.* exculpation, proof of innocence, excuse; defence; (leg.) justification; defence; a **-**, in justification; a mia **-**, in my defence.

discolp-are [A I c] *tr.* (*prep.* di) to exculpate, to justify, to prove innocent; (leg.) to clear (a person of a charge); *rfl.* to defend oneself (against), to clear oneself (of a charge).

discommet·tere [C 20] *tr.* to pull apart; (naut.) to unlay (a hawser).

†**discomodare** *tr.* to render uncomfortable, to incommode; *rfl.* to incommode oneself, to disturb oneself.

†**disco·modo** *m.* inconvenience; discomfort.

discompagn-are [A 5] *tr.* to separate; to part; to isolate; to break up (pair, set); to unmatch. **-abile** *adj.* separable. **-ato** *part. adj.* separated; isolated; broken up (of a set or pair). **-atura** *f.* separation; isolating; breaking up.

discom-porre [B 21] *tr.* to disarrange; to break up; to take to pieces. (**-posto** *part. adj.*)

discompostezza *f.* lack of dignity or composure.

disconchiu·dere [C 3]. See **disconcludere**.

†**disconciare** *vb.* and derivs. See **sconciare**.

discon·ci-o *adj.* ill-shaped; spoiled; unbecoming, unseemly; †*n.m.* unpleasant or troublesome thing; †discomfort.

disconclu·dere [C 3] *tr.* to break off (negotiations).

disconfess-are [A I] *tr.* to disown, to disavow, to refrain from owning. (**-ato** *part. adj.*) **-ione** *f.* disavowal.

†**disconfig·gere** *tr.* to destroy; to defeat; to undermine, to weaken.

disconfort-are [A I] *tr.* to grieve; to dishearten; to dissuade. †**-anza** *f.* distress, grief. **-o** *m.* affliction, trouble; discouragement.

disconosc-ere [B 9] *tr.* to refuse to recognize; to disallow; to misjudge; to disregard; to ignore; to slight; (leg.) to disown, to disclaim, to repudiate; il marito **-e** il figlio, the husband repudiates the child; il marito **-e** la paternità del figlio, the husband disclaims paternity of the child; il convenuto **-e** la sottoscrizione del contratto, the defendant disowns the signature of the contract. **-ente** *part. adj.* ungrateful. **-enza** *f.* ingratitude; lack of appreciation; lack of discernment; †erroneous information, mistake. **-imento** *m.* (leg.) disownment; repudiation; non-recognition; **-imento** della paternità, disownment of paternity (C.C.). **-iuto** *part. adj.* disallowed; misjudged; disregarded; (leg.) disowned, repudiated.

disconsen-tire [D I] *tr.* to decline, to refuse; *intr.* (*aux.* avere) to disagree. (**-tito** *part. adj.*) **-ziente** *adj.* dissentient.

†**disconsiderare** *tr.* to disregard.

disconsigli-are [A 4] *tr.* to dissuade. **-ato** *part. adj.* dissuaded; rash; counselless (cf. **sconsigliare**).

disconsol-are [A I c] *tr.* to make unhappy, to make discontented. **-ato** *part. adj.* (poet.) disconsolate, comfortless. †**-azione** *f.* disappointment; affliction.

discontent-are [A I] *tr.* to dissatisfy; to displease; to cause discontent to. **-ezza** *f.* discontent. **-o** *adj.* discontented, dissatisfied; *n.m.* discontent; annoyance.

discontinu-are [A 6] *tr.* to discontinue; to interrupt. **-azione** *f.* discontinuance; interruption.

disconti·nu-o *adj.* discontinuous; erratic; uneven. **-ità** *f.* discontinuity; unevenness.

disconven-ire [D 17] *intr.* (*aux.* essere) to be unsuitable; to be unbecoming; to be incongruous; (*aux.* avere) to disagree. **-evole** *adj.* unsuitable; unbecoming. (**-evolmente** *adv.*) **-evolezza** *f.* unsuitability. **-iente** *part. adj.* not suitable; ill-suited, clashing. **-ienza** *f.* unsuitability, unseemliness; incongruity, disparity.

discoperto *part.* of **discoprire**, q.v.; *adj.* open, unsheltered, unprotected; a **-**, in the open, under the sky.

discopr-ire [D 8] *tr.* to uncover, to lay bare; to discover; to make known, to disclose. **-imento** *m.* uncovering; discovering; disclosing. (**-itore** *m.*) (cf. **scoprire**).

discoraggi-are [A3] *tr.* to dishearten. (**-amento** *m.*)

†**discorare** *tr.* to dishearten; to discourage; to take the heart out of; *rfl.* to lose heart.

†**discorda** *f.* See **discordia**.

discord-are [A1] *intr.* (*aux.* avere; *prep.* da) to disagree, to be at variance, to clash (with); not to be in harmony with; la sua interpretazione -a dalla mia, his interpretation conflicts with mine; (mus.) to be out of tune (with); *rfl.* to forget; *tr.* to set at odds. **-a·bile** *adj.* discordant. **-ante** *part. adj.* discordant. **-anza** *f.* variance, disagreement, clash; (mus.) the state of being out of tune. **-ato** *adj.* out of tune. **-evole** *adj.* discordant.

discord-e *adj.* discordant; clashing; differing; — da, not in agreement with, different from; †*n.m.* (mus.) dissonance. **-emente** *adv.* discordantly.

discor·di-a *f.* discord; dissension, variance; disagreement; †(mus.) dissonance.

discordo *m.* (lit. hist.) descort, discordo (Provençal verse-form).

discoronare [A1c] *tr.* to uncrown, to dethrone.

discorr-ere [C5c] *intr.* (*aux.* avere) to talk, to discourse, to converse; fa per —, he's only talking, he doesn't mean what he says; non ci si -e, you can't talk to him; non se ne -e nemmeno, of course, no doubt about it, it is beyond discussion; e via -endo, and so on and so forth; (pop.) to make love; ci -e, -e con lei, he is courting her, he is walking out with her; †to run, to streak, to move swiftly, to move about, to wander; to flow; to be lax, to relax, to give way; *tr.* to discuss, to treat of; -ersela con uno, to be on good terms with someone; †to skim through, to read quickly; *n.m.* talk, conversation; c'è stato un gran —, there's been a great deal of talk. **-itore** *m.* talker. (**-itrice** *f.*)

discorsa *f.* long rambling talk, rigmarole.

discorsiv-o *adj.* fluent; talkative; sociable; relating to discourse. **-amente** *adv.* fluently; sociably; †in passing, by the way.

discors-o[1] *m.* speech; talk; conversation; gossip; commentary, treatise, oration, address; — della corona, speech from the throne; questo è un altro —, that's another story; senza tanti -i, briefly, without more ado; è un — lungo e difficile, it is a long and difficult matter to expound; cambiare il —, to change the subject; perdere il filo del —, to lose the thread of the argument; (gramm.) parti del —, parts of speech; che -i son questi?, what do you mean by that?; bei -i,! I don't think!; pochi -i!, that's enough!, hold your tongue! **-ino** *m. dim.* little talk; *pl.* prattling; twittering.

discorso[2] *part.* of **discorrere**, q.v.; *adj.* talked over, discussed, spoken of; †*n.m.* lapse; interval; flow.

discortes-e *adj.* discourteous. **-emente** *adv.* discourteously. **-ia** *f.* discourtesy (cf. **scortese**).

discoscendere [C1c] *tr.* to burst, to split; †to tear off; †to uproot; *intr.* (*aux.* essere) to rush down, to fall, to collapse.

discosceso *part.* of **discoscendere**, q.v.; *adj.* steep; precipitous; *n.m.* steep, rugged place.

discost-are [A1] *tr.* to remove, to displace; *intr.* (*aux.* essere) to be separate, to be at a distance. **-amento** *m.* removal, displacement. **-ato** *part. adj.* removed, displaced (cf. **scostare**).

discosto *adj.* separated, distant; casa poco discosta dalla mia, house not far from mine; *adv.* away; afar; far off; abitava —, he lived some distance away.

discoteca *f.* collection of gramophone records, record library.

†**discov-rire** *tr.* to disclose, to reveal; to uncover, to discover. †**-erto** *part. adj.* disclosed, revealed; uncovered; cleansed.

discrasi·a *f.* (med.) dyscrasy.

discrasi·o *m.* (metall.). See **discrasite**.

discrasite *f.* (metall.) dyscrasite.

discre-d-ere [B1] *tr.* to cease to believe; to disavow; to lose faith in; *rfl.* -ersi (di), to change one's mind (about); †-ersi con, to open one's heart to, to disburden oneself to. **-ente** *part. adj.* doubting; *n.m.,f.* unbeliever. **-enza** *f.* unbelief.

discredit-are [A1sc] *tr.* to discredit; *rfl.* to become discredited. **-amento** *m.* discrediting. **-ato** *part. adj.* discredited (cf. **screditare**).

discredito *m.* discredit; disrepute; cadere in —, to fall into disrepute; mettere in —, to throw discredit on.

discrep-are [A1] *intr.* (*aux.* essere) to be discrepant. **-ante** *adj.* discrepant; opinioni -anti, divergent views. **-anza** *f.* discrepancy; divergence.

discre·scere [B9] *intr.* (*aux.* essere) to diminish, to wane.

discrespare [A1] *tr.* to unwrinkle, to take the creases from.

discretezza *f.* See under **discreto**.

discretiv-a *f.* discernment. **-o** *adj.* of discernment, pertaining to discernment; (leg.) discretionary; potere -o, discretionary power. **-amente** *adv.* with discernment.

discret-o *adj.* discreet, discerning, tactful; modest; moderate; anni -i, years of discretion; pretty good, not bad; decent, passable; (in marking) fair; salute -a, tolerable health; prezzo —, moderate price; (math.) discrete; (med.) discrete, widely spaced; *n.m.* (eccl.) discretus. **-amente** *adv.* passably; to a considerable extent; quite well. **-ezza** *f.* discretion, prudence; moderation.

discrezion-e *f.* discretion, prudence, tact; moderation; intendere a —, to understand by the light of nature, to understand by one's own good sense; — dei contadini, food left on plate to show one is not greedy, 'manners bit'; judgement; will; disposal, choice; essere alla — d'altri, to be at someone's mercy; arrendersi a — del nemico, to surrender unconditionally; pane a —, as much bread as you please, bread *ad lib.*; tip, or stake at play, left to one's discretion. **-ale** *adj.* (leg.) discretionary; poteri -ali, discretionary powers.

†**discriminale** *m.* comb.

discrimin-are [A1s] *tr.* to distinguish; (leg.) to exonerate or relieve from criminal liability. **-ante** *part. adj.* discriminating; (math.) discriminant; (leg.) tending to relieve from criminal liability; *n.f.pl.* circumstances exonerating from criminal liability. **-ato** *part. adj.* absolved from criminal liability; (of a Jew) absolved from the anti-Jewish laws (1938–43). †**-atura** *f.* parting (of the hair). **-azione** *f.* discrimination.

†**discritt-ivo** *adj.* See **descrittivo**. †**-o** *part.* See **descritto**.

†**discri·vere** *vb.* and derivs. See **descrivere**.

†**discrizione**[1] *f.* See **discrezione**.

†**discrizione**[2] *f.* See **descrizione**.

discroismo *m.* See **dicroismo**.

discu·bit-o *m.* (antiq.) reclining position at meals. **-orio** *adj.* (antiq.) reclining at table; *n.m.* couch.

discucire [D1] *tr.* to unstitch, to undo.

†**disculminare** *tr.* to remove the top of; *rfl.* to be stripped of the top, to be left roofless.

discuoiare [A4] *tr.* to flay; †to cleanse, to strip.

†**discusare** *vb.* and derivs. See **scusare**.

discussione *f.* argument, debate; controversy; — vivace, quarrel; (leg.) oral argument, pleading (esp. in trial procedure, stage at which the pleadings are read and the oral arguments are addressed to the Court); (Rom. antiq.) auditing of public accounts.

discussivo *adj.* (med.) discutient.

discusso *part.* of **discutere**, q.v.; *adj.* discussed; talked of; in the public eye; controversial.

discuss-ore *m.* debater, disputant; **-orio** *adj.* (med.) discutient.

discu·t-ere [C19] *tr.* to discuss, to consider, to debate; (leg.) to argue; to plead orally; — una causa, to argue, to plead a case. **-ente** *part. n.m.* disputant. **-i·bile** *adj.* questionable, disputable; (leg.) arguable. **-ibilmente** *adv.* questionably.

discuziente *adj.* (med.) discutient.

disdegn-are [A5c] *tr.* to disdain; to anger; *rfl.* to become angry. †**-anza** *f.* disdain. †**-e·vole** *adj.* despicable.

disdegn-o *m.* scorn; anger; †avere a —, to hold in disdain; *adj.* scornful. **-oso** *adj.* disdainful; proud, haughty; indignant, angry. **-osamente** *adv.* scornfully; angrily.

disdetta *f.* denial; cancellation; ill-fortune; persistent bad luck; che —!, what rotten luck!; (leg.) notice to determine (a contract); dare la —, to give notice (to determine); — d'affitto di locazione, notice to quit, to determine a lease or tenancy.

disdetto[1] *part.* of **disdire**, q.v.; *adj.* forbidden; resolved; released.

†**disdetto**[2] *m.* see **disdetta**; fare —, to say no, to refuse, to deny.

disdia·pason *m. indecl.* (mus.) disdiapason, double octave, fifteenth.

disdic-ente, **-e·vole** *adj.* unseemly. (**-evolmente** *adv.*) **-evolezza** *f.* unseemliness.

disdire [B10] *tr.* to deny; to unsay; to refuse; to cancel; — la camera in albergo, to cancel one's booking in a hotel; to put off; to write off; — la casa, to give notice to quit; — la ragione, not to give a reason; (mil.) — la tregua, to give notice of termination of a period of truce; *intr.* (*aux.* avere; *prep.* a), *rfl.* to be unsuitable, to be inappropriate; queste sono maniere che disdicono a una signora, no lady should behave like that; *rfl.* to go back on one's word.

†**disditta** *f.* See **disdetta**.

disdoppi-are [A4c] *tr.* (chem.) to break down (a compound). (**-amento** *m.*)

†disdorare *tr.* to strip the gold off; (fig.) to dishonour.

disdoro *m.* disgrace, dishonour, shame, blot on reputation or prestige.

†disdotto *part.* of **†disducere**, q.v.; *adj.* amused, diverted.

†disdottorare *tr.* to strike off the register of doctors.

†disdu·cere *tr.* to divert, to amuse; to lead away.

disebbriare [A4] *intr.* (*aux.* essere) to become sober again, to sober up.

†diseccare *vb.* and derivs. See **desiccare**.

diseccit-are [A1 s] *tr.* (electr.) to de-energize. (**-ato** *part. adj.*)

diseduc-are [A2 s] *tr.* to bring up badly; to miseducate. **-ato** *part. adj.* badly brought up. **-azione** *f.* misguided upbringing; miseducation.

disegn-are [A5c] *tr.* to draw, to sketch; to outline; to describe, to indicate; to design, to plan (out), to appoint; — un luogo, to fix on a place; -a di partire, he intends to leave. **-ativo** *adj.* of drawing, of design. **-ato** *part. adj.* drawn; designed; denoted; designate. **-atoio** *m.* pencil-holder. **-atore** *m.* designer; draughtsman. (**-atrice** *f.* **-atura** *f.*)

disegno *m.* drawing, design; (archit.) plan; design, drawing; — geometrico, — regolare, scale-drawing, plan drawn to scale; — in pianta, ground-plan; — in alzata, elevation; — spaccato, sectional drawing, cross-section; arti del —, graphic and plastic arts (including architecture); (paint.) — a contorno, drawing in outline, outline drawing; — all'acquarello, water-colour drawing; *pl.* cartoons, sketches, designs; (cinem.) — animato, cartoon; (fig.) project, intention, plan; colorire un —, to carry out an idea; far — su, to rely on, to build hopes on; (leg.) draft; — di legge, draft bill (in Parliament); design; un brevetto per un nuovo —, a patent for a new design; modelli e disegni ornamentali, ornamental models and designs (in patent law).

diseguaglianza *f.* See **disuguaglianza**, under **disuguagliare**.

diseguale *adj.* See **disuguale**.

disellare [A1]. See **dissellare**.

disembriciare [A3] *tr.* to untile.

disenfi-are [A3] (Tusc.) *tr.* to reduce a swelling in; *intr.* (*aux.* essere). *rfl.* to go down (of swelling). **-amento** *m.* going down of swelling.

disennare [A1]. See **dissennare**.

disensat-o *adj.* senseless. **-amente** *adv.* senselessly.

disenteri·a *f.* and derivs. See **dissenteria**.

diseppellire [D2]. See **disseppellire**.

disequilibr-are [A1] *tr.* to unbalance, to upset the balance of. **-ato** *part. adj.* unbalanced.

disequili·brio *m.* loss of balance, unbalance.

diserb-are [A1] *tr.* to weed. **-ante** *part.*, *n.m.* weed-killer. **-atura** *f.* weeding. **-o** *m.* weeding.

disered-are [A1] *tr.* to disinherit; to deprive of an inheritance. **-amento** *m.* disinheriting. **-ato** *part. adj.* disinherited; -ato per testamento, disinherited by will (of the portion of his estate which the testator can dispose of freely); (fig.) socially 'unfortunate'; †without heirs; *n.m.* unfortunate individual, one who is down on his luck; i -ati dalla sorte, the 'have-nots'. **-azione** *f.* disinheritance.

†disered-e *m.* disinherited person; *adj.* disinherited. **†-itare** *vb.* and derivs. See **diseredare**.

diserrare [A1] and derivs. See **disserrare**.

disert-are [A1] *tr.* to lay waste, to ravage, to devastate; to destroy; to desert; (mil.) to desert from; (leg.) to desert (military law); †to defeat; †to injure; †to kill; *intr.* (*aux.* avere, essere) to desert, to be a deserter; (fam.) to miss an appointment, to fail to turn up, not to be present; †to miscarry. **†-agione** *f.* see **disertamento**. **-amento** *m.* devastation, destruction; downfall, ruin; †calamity. **-ato** *part. adj.* ravaged, devastated; destroyed; impoverished; deserted; †deformed. **-atore** *m.* ravager; destroyer; deserter. (**-atrice** *f.*) **†-azione** *f.* devastation; destruction; ruin.

diserto¹ *apocop. part.* of **disertare**, q.v.; *adj.* devastated, laid waste; despoiled; *n.m.* ruin; fare — di, to lay waste.

diserto² *adj.* eloquent.

†diserto³ *adj.* See **deserto**.

disertore *m.* deserter (military law).

†diservi·gio *m.* See **disservigio**.

diservire [D1] and derivs. See **disservire**.

diservi·zio *m.* See **disservizio**.

diserzione *f.* desertion (military law); defection; (naut.) desertion. (NOTE: in the Italian Navy, in peacetime, a leave-breaker becomes a deserter after 4 days and 5 nights.)

disestesi·a *f.* (med.) dysaesthesia.

disfac-i·bile *adj.* that can be undone; that can be taken apart; destructible. **-imento** *m.* undoing; collapse; destruction; disintegration; decomposition; †demolition. (**-itore** *m.* **-itrice** *f.*) **-itura** *f.* destruction; taking apart; decay; materials saved from building pulled down.

disfagi·a *f.* (med.) dysphagy, difficulty in swallowing.

disfalcare [A2] *intr.* (*aux.* avere) (naut.) to work up a dead reckoning.

disfaldare [A1] *tr.*, *rfl.* to flake off.

†disfallo *m.* repentance.

disfamare¹ [A1] *tr.* to feed, to satisfy the hunger of.

†disfamare² [A1] *tr.* to defame, to dishonour.

disfangare [A2] *intr.* (*aux.* essere) to climb out of mud; to rise above one's conditions.

disf-are [B14] *tr.* to undo; to untie, to untwine; to take to pieces, to pull apart; to destroy; to pull down (building); to ruin (person); to break up (home); to defeat (army); (eng.) to take down; †to kill; *rfl.* to collapse; to decay; to disintegrate; to decompose; -arsi in lagrime, to dissolve in tears; -arsi di, to get rid of.

disfasciare [A3] *tr.* (naut.) to dismantle (a ship); — una fune, to remove the serving of a rope.

disfasi·a *f.* (med.) dysphasia.

disfatt-a *f.* defeat, downfall, overthrow. **-i·bile** *adj.* that can be undone; that can be untied; defeasible. **-ic·cio** *adj.* (of land) reclaimed for crops; ploughed-up; also *n.m.* **-ismo** *m.* (leg.) defeatism; the spreading of alarm and despondency (criminal law). **-ista** *m.,f.* (leg.) defeatist; spreader of alarm and despondency (criminal law).

disfatto *part.* of **disfare**, q.v.; *adj.* undone; done away with; worn out; marred; melted; wasted; wretched, helpless; defeated; exhausted, ill-looking; volto —, haggard face; †destroyed, brought low; †devastated, ravaged; †done to death, dead.

disfavill-are [A1] *intr.* (*aux.* avere) to flash, to glitter; †to shine forth. **-ante** *part. adj.* glittering.

disfavor-e *m.* disfavour; a — di, in opposition to; misfortune. **-evole** *adj.* unfavourable. (**-evolmente** *adv.*) **-ire** [D2] *tr.* to oppose; to remove from favour.

†disfazione *f.* See **disfacimento**, under **disfacibile**.

†disfecciare *tr.* to purge.

disferenzi-are [A4] *tr.* to differentiate; to sort out into categories, to grade (e.g. according to form and colour); *rfl.*, *intr.* (*aux.* avere) to be graded or differentiated. (**-ato** *part. adj.*)

disferr-are [A1] *tr.* to free from chains; to unshoe (a horse); to draw a barb, etc. from wound; *rfl.* to draw a barb from one's own wound; (of a horse) to cast a shoe. **-ato** *part. adj.* freed from chains; (of a horse) unshod.

†disfibbiare *vb.* and derivs. See **sfibbiare**.

disfida *f.* challenge; defiance; (hist.) la Disfida di Barletta, the Challenge of Barletta.

disfid-are [A1] *tr.* to challenge; to defy; to give up for lost; †to repudiate; †— di, to banish from; *rfl.* to lack confidence, to be distrustful. **-amento** *m.* challenge; defying. **-ante** *part. adj.* challenging; defiant; †diffident; *n.m.* challenger. **†-anza** *f.* distrust; challenge to a duel. **-ato** *part. adj.* challenged; defied; given up for lost. **-atore** *m.* challenger. (**-atrice** *f.*)

disfigur-are [A1] *tr.* to disfigure, to mar. **-ato** *part. adj.* disfigured, marred. **-azione** *f.* disfigurement; grimace (cf. **sfigurare**).

†disfinire *tr.* to conclude; to resolve; to define.

disfior-are [A1c] *tr.* to deflower; to dishonour; to devastate. **-amento** *m.* deflowering. **-ato** *part. adj.* deflowered; dishonoured; devastated (cf. **sfiorare**).

disfiorentinare [A1] *tr.* to destroy the Florentine characteristics of, to de-Florentinize; *rfl.* to lose one's Florentine characteristics.

†disfogare *vb.* and derivs. See **sfogare**.

†disfogliare *vb.* and derivs. See **sfogliare**.

disfori·a *f.* (med.) dysphoria.

disform-are [A1c] *tr.* to put out of shape, to spoil; to render deformed; *rfl.* to lose one's shape; to become deformed; to change for the worse. **-ato** *part. adj.* deformed, misshapen. **-azione** *f.* loss, change, difference of shape (cf. **sformare**).

disform-e *adj.* unlike, divergent. **-ità** *f.* difference, divergence.

disfranc-are [A2] *tr.* to disfranchise; †(fig.) to unman, to dishearten. **-ato** *part. adj.* disfranchised.

disfrances-are *tr.* to remove the French characteristics of, to de-Gallicize; *rfl.* to lose one's French characteristics. **-ato** *part. adj.* de-Gallicized.

disfrasi·a f. (med.) dysphrasia.

disfrat-are [A1] tr. to unfrock; rfl. to leave one's (religious) order. **-ato** part. adj. unfrocked.

disfren-are [A1c] tr. to unbridle, to give free rein to; to unleash. **-amento** m. unleashing. **-ato** part. adj. unbridled, unrestrained, unleashed, unchecked; disorderly; impetuous (cf. **sfrenare**).

disfreno adj. unbridled, unchecked; n.m. unbridled state; a —, unrestrainedly.

disfrond-are [A1c] tr. to strip of leaves. **-ato** part. adj. stripped, bare (of leaves).

disfunzione f. (med.) irregular functioning.

disgag·gio m. (mining) barring.

†**disgambare** tr. to cut off the legs of.

†**disgangherare** tr. to unhinge.

†**disgannare** vb. and derivs. See **disingannare**.

disgarb-are [A1] intr. (aux. essere) to be displeasing. **-ato** adj. unmannerly. **-o** n.m. rudeness.

disgel-are [A1] tr., intr., impers. (aux. essere), rfl. to thaw; quest'anno **-a** tardi, the thaw is late this year; to defrost. **-ante** part. adj. thawing; (aeron.) de-icing. **-atore** m. (aeron.) de-icer.

disgelo m. thaw; thawing; thawing out.

disgiog-are [A2c] tr. to unyoke. **-ato** part. adj. unyoked, freed from the yoke.

†**disgiu·gnere** vb. and derivs. See **disgiungere**.

disgiun·g-ere [C5] tr. to separate, to part; to pull away; to unyoke. **-i·bile** adj. separable. **-imento** m. separating; pulling away; unyoking. (**-itore** m. **-itrice** f.)

disgiuntiv-o adj. disjunctive. **-amente** adv. disjunctively.

disgiunt-o part. of **disgiungere**, q.v.; adj. disjoined, separated, detached; unrelated; (mus.) disjunct; (herald.) fracted. **-amente** adv. unrelatedly. **-ore** m. (electr.) circuit-breaker.

disgiunzione f. separation; (logic; gramm.; biol.) disjunction.

†**disgomb(e)rare** vb. and derivs. See **sgombrare**.

†**disgorgare** vb. and derivs. See **sgorgare**.

disgrad-are[1] [A1] tr. to surpass, to outshine, to outclass; to put to shame; to discredit; sbagli da disgradarne quelli d'un bambino, mistakes that would put a child to shame. **-ato** part. adj. surpassed, outshone, outclassed.

†**disgradare**[2] tr. to grade.

†**disgradare**[3] intr. to be displeasing.

disgrad-ire [D2] tr. not to welcome; to disdain, to decline; intr. (aux. avere) to be displeasing. **-evole** adj. unpleasing (cf. **sgradire**).

disgrado adv. phr. a —, unwillingly, grudgingly; avere a —, not to care for, to dislike; essere in —, to be displeasing; †to be ungrateful; †n.m. dislike.

disgrafi·a f. (med.) dysgraphia, agrammatism.

†**disgramare** tr. to cheer, to cure of melancholy; intr. to take heart, to be of good cheer.

disgran-are [A1] tr. to pick grain from (an ear of corn); (naut.) see **sgranare**. **-ellare** [A1] to pick grapes from (a bunch); to pick grain from (an ear of corn).

disgratigliare [A4] tr. (naut.) to remove the bolt-ropes from.

disgrav-are [A1] tr. to disburden, to relieve, to lighten; (leg.) to discharge. **-amento** m. unburdening, lightening. **-ato** part. adj. unburdened; lightened (cf. **sgravare**).

†**disgravidare** intr. to miscarry, to have an abortion.

†**disgra·vio** m. (leg.) discharge.

disgra·zia f. accident, mishap; casualty; ill-luck, misfortune; gli sono toccate infinite disgrazie, he has had endless misfortunes; — volle che, ill-luck would have it that; per —, unluckily, by an unlucky chance; disfavour, disgrace; cadere in —, to fall out of favour, to fall into disgrace; essere in — di Dio, to have forfeited God's grace; avere in — qualcuno, to hold someone in disfavour; †unattractiveness, awkwardness, lack of grace; †displeasure.

†**disgraziare** tr. to hold a low opinion of; to feel no gratitude towards; to disdain, to have no concern for.

disgraziat-o adj. unfortunate, unlucky; evil, miserable, wretched; lacking charm, unlovely; awkward, ungraceful, lacking in grace; n.m. wretch; —!, poor thing!, poor man!; person physically or mentally unfit; (euphem.) scoundrel. (**-a** f.) **-amente** adv. unfortunately, unluckily; wretchedly; awkwardly, ungracefully.

†**disgrazioso** adj. ungracious.

disgreg-are [A2] tr. to break down, to break up; to separate; (mil.) — le forze nemiche, to scatter enemy forces; rfl. to break up; to disintegrate; to decompose. **-a·bile** adj. that may be broken

down. **-amento** m. breaking down, decomposing; (phys.) vaporization. **-anza** f. dissolution, breaking down, breakdown. **-ativo** adj. causing breakdown, disruptive. **-azione** f. breakdown, resolution; disintegration; decomposition, dispersion.

†**disgrignare** vb. and derivs. See **digrignare**.

†**disgroppare** tr. to untie, to disentangle, to undo.

disgross-are [A1] tr. to rough-hew; to rough out. **-ato** part. adj. rough-hewn; roughed out. **-atamente** adv. roughly, in a preliminary way. **-atura** f. rough-hewing; roughing out (cf. **digrossare**).

disgrupp-are [A1] tr. to untie, to undo (a knot). **-ato** part. adj. untied, undone.

†**disguagli-are** tr. to discern a difference between; rfl. **-arsi da**, to differ from.

†**disgua·glio** m. difference, distinction.

†**disguale** adj. and derivs. See **disuguale**.

†**disguardare** tr. to cease to look at.

disguido m. going astray (of letter, etc.); — postale, error in postal delivery; c'è stato un —, a letter (or parcel) has been wrongly delivered.

†**disguis-are** tr. to disguise; intr., rfl. to disguise oneself, to put on a disguise. †**-ato** part. adj. disguised; masked.

disgust-are [A1] tr. to offend; to disgust, to make sick; to vex; to shock; — uno da qualcosa, to put someone off something; rfl. to be offended; to be disgusted, to be sickened; **-arsi con**, to fall out with. **-ato** part. adj. offended; disgusted, sickened; blasé, indifferent. (**-atore** m. **-atrice** f.) **-evole** adj. offensive; distasteful. **-evolmente** adv. distastefully. **-evolezza** f. distastefulness.

disgust-o m. distaste, dislike; disgust; loathing; displeasure, vexation. **-oso** adj. disgusting. (**-osamente** adv.)

†**disi·a** f. See **disianza**.

†**disianza** f. desire; longing, yearning; love; object of desire; loved one.

disi-are [A4] (poet.) to desire, to long for, to yearn for; — di, to wish to, to be desirous of; †intr. to be pleasing; †n.m. desire, longing. **-ato** part. adj. (poet.) desired; desirèd, longed for; †desirous, desiring.

†**disiderare** vb. and derivs. See **desiderare**.

†**diside·rio, disidero** m. and derivs. See **desiderio**.

disidrat-are [A1] tr. (chem.) to dehydrate. (**-ato** part. adj.) **-atore** m. (chem.) dehydrator; (mining) dewaterer. **-azione** f. dehydration.

disidrato adj. (pop.) dehydrated.

†**disiecorare** tr. to take the heart out of (lit. the liver), to unnerve, to unman.

†**disie·vole** adj. desirous; longing, yearning.

†**disiguale** adj. See **disuguale**

disil·l-abo adj. disyllabic; n.m. disyllabic word; disyllabic foot; disyllable. **-a·bico** adj. disyllabic.

disill-u·dere [C1] tr. to undeceive, to disillusion. **-usione** f. disenchantment, disillusion.

disimball-are [A1] tr. to unpack. **-amento** m. unpacking. (**-ato** part. adj.)

disimbracare [A2] tr. to take breeching off (a horse); (naut.) to unsling; to unstrop; to unship (a propeller or wheel).

disimbraccare [A2] to unharness.

†**disimbracciare** tr. to remove from one's arm; to slip one's arm from.

disimbrigliare [A4] to unbridle (a horse).

disimbustare [A1] tr. to behead.

disimpacci-are [A3] tr. to free, to disentangle. **-ato** part. adj. easy, natural (in manner).

disimpar-are [A1] tr. to unlearn; to forget. **-ato** part. adj. unlearnt; forgotten.

disimpedi-re [D2] tr. to extricate. (**-ito** part. adj.)

disimpegn-are [A5c] tr. to release from an obligation; to redeem (pledge); (naut.) to disengage, to clear; (mil.) to relieve; to exercise (an office), to fulfil (a function); to discharge, to perform; rfl. to release oneself from an obligation; to get free; non posso **-armi** dal venire domani, I can't get out of coming tomorrow; to extricate oneself; to acquit oneself. **-ato** part. adj. free, disengaged.

disimpegno m. disengagement, release, fulfilment; far qualcosa per —, to do something out of a sense of duty, to do something because one has said one would; disuse; stanzino di —, boxroom; abito di —, dress that will just do; (watchm.) detent; rocchetto di — della molla, mainspring releasing pinion.

disimpieg-are [A2] *tr.* to discharge (from service), to throw out of work. **-ato** *part. adj.* without employment; out of service.

disimplic-are [A2] *tr.* to disentangle. (**-ato** *part. adj.*)

†**disimpri·mere** *tr.* to erase, to remove the imprint of; to remove the impression of.

†**disinare** *vb.* and derivs., *n.m.* See **desinare**.

disin-cagliare [A4] *tr.* (naut.) to refloat (a stranded ship); (fig.) — un'impresa, to get an enterprise going again; *rfl., intr.* (aux. essere) (naut.) to get afloat again; (fig.) to get going again. **-ca·glio** *m.* (naut.) refloating.

disincant-are [A1] *tr.* to disenchant. **-ato** *part. adj.* disenchanted; disillusioned, undeceived. **-o** *m.* disenchantment.

disincarn-are [A1] *tr.* to disembody. **-ato** *part. adj.* disembodied; *n.m.* disembodied spirit.

disincaten-are [A1c] *tr.* to unchain. (**-ato** *part. adj.*)

disincerare [A1] *tr.* to convince; *rfl.* to find out the truth, to make sure.

disinclinazione *f.* disinclination; dislike, antipathy.

disincrost-are [A1] *tr.* (eng.) to scale. **-ante** *m.* (eng.) scale remover (for boilers), anti-scale compound.

disinferire [D2] *tr.* (naut.). See **sferire**.

disinfest-are [A1] *tr.* to disinfest, to rid of pests or vermin. **-ante** *m.* insecticide, pest control product. **-azione** *f.* disinfestation, pest control.

disinfett-are [A1] *tr.* to disinfect. **-ante** *adj., n.m.* disinfectant. **-ato** *part. adj.* disinfected. **-azione** *f.* disinfecting. **-olo** *m.* (chem.) disinfectol. **-ore** *m.* disinfector; disinfectant.

disinfezione *f.* disinfection; disinfecting.

disinfiammare [A1] *tr.* (med.) to remove inflammation from.

disingann-are [A1] *tr.* to undeceive, to disabuse; *rfl.* to disabuse oneself. **-ativo** *adj.* revealing. **-ato** *part. adj.* undeceived; disabused (cf. **sgannare**). (**-atore** *m.* **-atrice** *f.*)

disinganno *m.* disabusing; disillusionment; disappointment; reawakening to reality, awakening.

disingranare [A1] *tr.* (eng.) to throw out of mesh, to throw out of gear.

disinnamor-are [A1c] *tr.* to estrange; — uno di, to destroy a person's love for; *rfl.* -arsi di, to lose one's affection for, to fall out of love with; to cease to like or be interested in; to lose the taste for. **-amento** *m.* estrangement; disenchantment.

disinnesc-are [A2] *tr.* (electr.) to defuse. **-o** *m.* (electr.) defusing (of bombs, etc.).

disinnestare [A1] *tr.* (eng.) to disconnect, to disengage; — la frizione, to let out the clutch; *rfl.* (motor.) to slip out of gear, to disengage.

disinnesto *m.* (eng.) disengagement, release; knock-off; — a scatto, trip; — del carrello, carriage release (of a typewriter); (motor.) doppio —, double de-clutch.

†**disino** *prep.* See **insino**.

†**disinore** *m.* See **disonore**.

†**disinpingere** *tr.* to dissimulate.

disinsegnare [A5c] *tr.* to unteach; — a se stesso, to unlearn.

disinser-ire [D2] *tr.* (mech.) to throw out; (electr.; eng.) to disconnect. **-ito** *part. adj.* disconnected; (of a switch) off. **-zione** *f.* disconnecting.

disinstalla·bile *adj.* (eng.) capable of being dismantled.

disintegr-are [A1] *tr.* to disintegrate. **-atore** *m.* disintegrator. **-azione** *f.* disintegration; -azione dell'atomo, splitting of the atom.

†**disinten·dere** *tr.* to misunderstand.

disinteress-are [A1] *tr.* to cause to lose interest; (comm.) to buy (a person) out; *rfl.* -arsi di, to lose interest in, to wash one's hands of, to cease to pursue; to neglect, to take no interest in. **-ato** *adj.* unselfish; disinterested; indifferent, no longer interested. **-atamente** *adv.* disinterestedly.

disinteresse *m.* unselfishness; disinterestedness, indifference, lack of interest.

†**disinteri·a** *f.* See **dissenteria**.

disintimazione *f.* (leg.) cancellation, withdrawal of notice; cancelled notice.

disintonizz-are [A1] *tr.* (radio) to detune. **-azione** *f.* (radio) detuning.

disintossicare [A2s] *tr.* (med.) to detoxicate, to detoxify.

disintrecciare [A3] *tr.* to untwine, to disentangle.

disintubazione *f.* (surg.) detubation, removal of a cannula.

disintugliare [A4] *tr.* (naut.) to untie, to unlash (a rope).

†**disinventore** *m.* disbeliever (Alfieri, *Sat.* 7).

disinvit-are [A1] *tr.* to cancel an invitation to (a person). **-o** *m.* cancelling of invitation(s).

disinvol·gere [C5] *tr.* to undo; to unwind; to unroll.

disinvolt-o *part.* of **disinvolgere**, q.v.; *adj.* easy, unembarrassed, unconstrained; natural; uninhibited; free and easy, offhand, jaunty, airy; cheeky, impertinent; unscrupulous; dexterous, deft. **-amente** *adv.* unconstrainedly; easily, naturally; deftly. **-ura** *f.* ease, self-possession; offhand manner, careless air; impertinence, impudence; unscrupulousness.

diṣ-i·o *m.* (poet.) yearning, longing; love, desire; object of desire; wish; †delight; †con —, with pleasure. †**-ioso** *adj.* desirous, filled with longing. †**-iosamente** *adv.* with longing; yearningly; lovingly, with desire.

†**disi·pola** *f.* (med.) erysipelas.

†**disir-are** *tr.* to desire, to long for, to aspire towards. †**-e**, †**-o** *m.* desire, love, longing; object of desire, loved object; highest good.

disistim-a *f.* lack of esteem, low estimation, disesteem; disrepute. **-are** [A1] *tr.* to despise; to have a low opinion of, to disesteem; to cease to esteem.

disistivare [A1] *tr.* (naut.). See **distivare**.

dislacci-are [A3] *tr.* to unlace; to unbuckle; to undo; to release. (**-ato** *part. adj.*)

†**dislagare** *rfl.* to rise from the waters, to emerge.

dislali·a *f.* (med.) dysphonia.

dislastrare [A1] *tr.* (naut.). See **dilastrare**.

†**dislattare** [A1] *tr.* to wean.

disleal-e *adj.* unfair; unfaithful, disloyal, false. (**-mente** *adv.*) **-tà** *f.* unfairness; dishonourable action; falsity, disloyalty.

†**disleanza** *f.* disloyalty.

disle·cito *adj.* unlawful, illicit; sinful.

disleg-are [A2] *tr.* to unbind, to untie; to release, to free; to disencumber; to make clear, to explain; *rfl.* to explain oneself, to justify oneself. **-ato** *part. adj.* unbound, untied; released, free; (of a jewel) unset; †unmarried; †celibate.

dislinguato *adj.* stammering, stuttering.

†**dislisina** *f.* (chem.) dyslysin.

dislivello *m.* difference in level, discrepancy in altitude, difference in height; (hydraul.) — in aumento, rise.

disloc-are [A2] *tr.* to displace; to remove; (mil.) to move; to station; (naut.) to displace; (naut.) to detach (a ship), to send (a ship to a station); (med.) to dislocate. **-amento** *m.* displacing, removing; (mil.) movement; move; (naut.) displacement. **-ato** *part. adj.* displaced; removed; (mil.) stationed; (naut.) detached; (med.) dislocated; (admin.; comm.) distributed. **-azione** *f.* displacement; (mil.) movement, move; position, positioning; (naut.) displacement; (geol.) see **dislogazione**, under **dislogare**.

dislodare [A1] *tr.* to deprive of praise won; to disparage, to speak against.

dislog-are [A2] *tr.* to remove, to displace; to move about; (mil.) to distribute (troops); (med.) to dislocate. (**-amento** *m.*) (**-ato** *part. adj.*) **-atura** *f.* (med.) dislocation. **-azione** *f.* removal, dislocation; distribution; (med.) dislocation; (geol.) fault.

†**disloggi-are** *tr.* to dislodge; to shift; to remove; (mil.) to unlodge; †*intr., rfl.* to strike camp. †**-amento** *m.* (mil.) means or act of striking camp.

†**dislungare** *vb.* and derivs. See **dilungare**.

†**dismag-are** *tr.* to weaken; to diminish; to dismay; to lead astray; *rfl.* to remove oneself; to depart; to become dismayed. †**-ato** *part. adj.* dismayed; disturbed in mind.

†**dismagliare** *tr.* to pierce the armoured mail of; to run through with a sword; to tear piece by piece; *rfl.* to strip off one's mail; to scratch off one's scabs.

†**dismalare** *tr.* to cure; to purify; *intr.* to be cured, to regain health.

dismaltare [A1] *tr.* to remove the paint from, to rub down; to remove enamel from.

dismantigliare [A4] *tr.* (naut.) to unsling, to remove the lifts from (a yard).

†**dismascherare** *vb.* and derivs. See **smascherare**.

dismembr-are[1] [A1] *tr.* to dismember; to divide. (**-amento** *m.*) **-ato** *part. adj.* dismembered; divided; (herald.) disjointed, dismembered.

†**dismembrare**[2] *tr.* to forget.

dismemorato *adj.* forgetful; scatter-brained; heedless, feckless.

dismenorre·a *f.* (med.) dysmenorrhoea.

†**dismentare** *tr.* to forget, to overlook.

†**dismenticare** *vb.* and derivs. See **dimenticare**.

†**dismentire** *vb.* See **mentire**.

†**dismeritare** *tr.* to have no title to, to be undeserving of.

†**disme·rito** *m.* demerit.

dis̩—mẹttere [C20] *tr.* to cease, to leave off; to cast off (clothing); — la bottega, to shut up shop, to go out of business; to take to pieces, to dismantle. **-mẹsso** *part. adj.* cast off, cast aside; no longer used, out of date; dismantled; dishevelled.

dismissiọne *f.* cessation, abandonment; (naut.) change of flag.

dismi̩s̩ur-a *f.* excess, excessiveness, lack of restraint, intemperance; a —, enormously, beyond measure, excessively; crescere a —, to grow enormously. †**-anza** *f.* excess, immoderateness.

†**dismisur-are** *tr.* to exceed; *intr.* to be excessive; to go beyond reasonable limits; to overdo it.

dismisurat-o *adj.* excessive, immoderate; unreasonable. (**-amẹnte** *adv.*)

†**dismisurità** *f.* See **dismisura**.

dismonac-are [A2s] *tr.* to remove from a monastery or convent, to unfrock. **-ato** *part. adj.* released from religious vows; detached or expelled from a religious community; unfrocked.

dismont-are [A1c] *intr.* (*aux.* essere) to dismount; to alight, to land, to come down; *tr.* to descend, to go down, to come down; — una collina, to go down a hill; to put down; to take apart, to take to pieces. **-ante** *part. adj.* descending, sinking; marea **-ante**, ebbing tide. **-ato** *part. adj.* dismounted, unhorsed, on foot; †deteriorated.

dismonticare [A2s] *tr.* to reduce; to pull down (a heap).

dismorbare [A1] *tr.* to disinfect, to purify, to sweeten the air of, to air.

†**dismuo·vere** *tr.* to remove; to change, to alter; to turn; to disturb; *intr.* to be disturbed.

†**dismurare** *tr.* to pull down the walls of, to unwall.

dismutazione *f.* (chem.) dismutation.

disnatur-are [A1] *tr.* to change the nature of. **-ato** *part. adj.* changed in nature; unnatural; cruel; denatured.

disnebbi-are [A4c] *tr.* to clear of mist; (fig.) to clarify, to free from obscurity; *rfl.* (of mist) to clear. (**-ato** *part. adj.*)

†**disnerb-are, disnerv-are** *tr.* to enervate; to weaken; to slacken; to unnerve. †**-ato** *part. adj.* enervated; weakened; slack, limp.

†**disnocciolare** *vb.* See **snocciolare**.

disnod-are [A1] *tr.* to untie, to loosen; to unfold, to explain; to make supple, to make flexible; *rfl.* to become untied; to extricate oneself, to free oneself. (**-ato** *part. adj.*)

†**disnore** *m.* See **disonore**.

disnud-are [A1] *tr.* to strip, to bare; — la spada, to draw one's sword. **-ato** *part. adj.* stripped, bare; (of a sword) drawn, unsheathed.

disobbedire [D2] and derivs. See **disubbidire**.

disobbligant-e *adj.* disobliging, rude, uncivil. (**-emẹnte** *adv.*)

disobblig-are [A2s] *tr.* to release from an obligation; *rfl.* to be released from an obligation. **-ante** *part. adj.* disobliging. **-ato** *part. adj.* freed from obligation; stanze **-ate**, self-contained rooms. **-azione** *f.* absence of obligation; release from obligation.

disob·bli-go¹ *m.* (*pl.* **-ghi**) freedom from obligation.

†**disob·bligo²** *apocop. part.* of **disobbligare**, q.v.

†**disocchi-are** *tr.* to blind, to put out the eyes of. †**-ato** *part. adj.* blinded; blind, eyeless.

disocclusiọne *f.* (med.) deoppilation.

disoccup-are [A1s] *tr.* to leave with no work, to leave with no tasks to do, to render unemployed. **-ato** *adj.* unoccupied, free, disengaged; unemployed; out of work; *n.m.* unoccupied person; unemployed; i **-ati**, the unemployed. **-azione** *f.* unoccupied state, leisure; lack of work; unemployment; sussidio di **-azione**, indennità di **-azione**, unemployment benefit.

diso·dilo *m.* (miner.) dysodyle.

disodorante *adj.* deodorizing.

disol-are¹ [A1] *tr.* (vet.) to pare or strip off the sole of the hoof (of a horse). (**-ato** *part. adj.*) **-atura** *f.* (vet.) the operation of paring or stripping the sole.

†**disol-are²** *tr.* to abandon, to forsake; to make desolate, to devastate; to destroy. †**-ato** *part. adj.* abandoned, forsaken; desolate; devastated; destroyed. †**-azione** *f.* desolation; devastation; destruction.

disolfo·rico *adj.* (chem.) disulphuric, pyrosulphuric; acido —, disulphuric acid, Nordhausen sulphuric acid, $H_2S_2O_7$.

disoliatura *f.* (text.) degreasing, backwashing.

disonestà *f.* dishonourable behaviour; trickery, fraud, dishonesty; shamelessness, indecency; *pl.* shameful, dishonourable acts.

†**disonest-are** *tr.* to dishonour; to render dishonest, to corrupt; *rfl.* to be dishonoured; to become dishonest; to be corrupted. †**-ato** *part. adj.* dishonoured; corrupt.

disonest-o *adj.* dishonest; dishonourable; shameless; immodest; corrupt; fraudulent; parti **-e**, private parts; luogo —, house of ill-fame; †dishonouring, shameful; †ill-suited, unseemly; †excessive; †ill-proportioned, gross; *n.m.* knave, trickster; †*adv.* dishonestly, shamelessly. (**-amẹnte** *adv.*)

disonnare [A1] and derivs. See **dissonnare**.

di·sono *adj.* (mus.) of two sounds.

disonor-are [A1c] *tr.* to dishonour; to spoil, to deprive of ornament; to vituperate; *rfl.* to be dishonoured; to lose one's reputation; to behave dishonourably. (**-amẹnto** *m.*) **-ante** *part. adj.* dishonouring; dishonourable; †unfair. †**-anza** *f.* dishonour; loss of esteem. **-ato** *part. adj.* dishonoured; disgraced; honourless. (**-atamẹnte** *adv.*, **-atọre** *m.*, **-atrice** *f.*) **-ẹvole** *adj.* dishonourable. (**-evolmẹnte** *adv.*)

disonọre *m.* dishonour, shame, ignominy, disgrace; essere il — della famiglia, to be the black sheep of the family; †incivility, discourtesy; †obloquy, opprobrium, vituperation.

disoppil-are [A1s] *tr.* (med.) to remove an obstruction from, to deoppilate. **-ante** *part. adj.* (med.) deoppilant. **-ativo** *adj.* (med.) deobstruent.

disọpra *adv.* above; upstairs; al — di, over, above; per —, into the bargain; *n.m.* il —, the upper part; the place above; prendere il —, to gain the upper hand (also **di sopra**).

disọrare [A1] *tr.* to ungild.

disọrbit-are [A1s] *intr.* (*aux.* avere) to go too far, to be unreasonable; to be exorbitant. **-ante** *part. adj.* excessive; exorbitant. **-anza** *f.* excess, extravagance; exorbitance.

disọrdin-are [A1sc] *tr.* to throw into disorder, to disarrange, to confuse; to upset; to derange; to cancel, to countermand; *intr.* (*aux.* avere) to be excessive, to go to excess; *rfl.* to fall into disorder; to get confused, to get into a muddle. (**-amẹnto** *m.*) †**-anza** *f.* disorder, confusion. **-ato** *part. adj.* disordered, disorderly, untidy; immoderate, intemperate, excessive; essere **-ato** nel bere, to drink to excess; ill-adapted, ill-suited. (**-atamẹnte** *adv.* **-atọre** *m.* **-atrice** *f.*) †**-azione** *f.* disorder, confusion; wretchedness, unhappy state.

†**disordina·rio** *adj.* See **straordinario**.

disọr·dine *m.* disorder, confusion; untidiness; excess; intemperate habits, disorderly life; disorder, malady, disease, illness; (naut.) in —, damaged or tangled by the weather or the enemy (of a ship or her rigging); *pl.* riot, rioting; (provb.) l'ordine è pane, il — è fame, united we stand, divided we fall.

disọressi·a *f.* (med.) dysorexia.

disọrga·nico *adj.* incoherent; wanting in order; disjunct.

disorganizz-are [A1] *tr.* to disorganize; (chem.) to render inorganic; *rfl.* to become disorganized; to disintegrate. **-ato** *part. adj.* disorganized; disintegrated; (chem.) rendered inorganic. **-azione** *f.* disorganization; disintegration.

disorient-are [A1] *tr.* to disorientate, to bewilder; to disconcert; *rfl.* to lose one's bearings; to become confused; to be at a loss. (**-amẹnto** *m.*) **-ato** *part. adj.* disorientated; bewildered, puzzled, at a loss.

disọrlare [A1] *tr.* to undo the hem of.

disọrmeggiare [A3c] *tr.* (naut.) to cast off; to weigh; *rfl.* (naut.) to weigh anchor.

†**disọrn-are** *tr.* to strip of ornament. †**-ato** *part. adj.* stripped of ornament; unadorned; stripped, bereft, devoid.

disọrpellare [A1] *tr.* to strip off the tinsel from; (fig.) to unmask.

†**disọrrare** *vb.* and derivs. See **disonorare**.

†**disọrre·vole** *adj.* dishonourable; abject; of no account, worthless.

disọsmi·a *f.* (med.) dysosphresia.

disọss-are [A1] *tr.* to bone; *rfl.* to lose one's energy, to waste away. **-ato** *part. adj.* boned; boneless; listless, bone lazy, bone idle.

disọssid-are [A1s] *tr.* (chem.) to deoxidate, to deoxidize, to remove oxygen from. **-ante** *part. adj.* deoxidating, reducing. (**-ato** *part. adj.*) **-azione** *f.* deoxidation, reduction.

disọssigen-are [A1] *tr.* (chem.) to deoxygenate. (**-ato** *part. adj.*) **-azione** *f.* deoxygenation.

disọstruente *adj.* (med.) deobstruent.

disottenebrare [A I S] *tr.* to dispel darkness from.

disotterrare [A I] and derivs. See **dissotterrare**.

disott-o *adv.* below; underneath; downstairs; *prep. phr.* al — di, below, under, lower than; *n.m.* il —, the lower part; the place below; avere il —, rimanere al —, to have the worst of it (also di sotto).

†**disovolato** *adj.* (med.) dislocated, put out.

†**dispaccare** *vb.* and derivs. See **spaccare**.

†**dispacciare** *tr.* to release from embarrassment or encumbrance; to despatch; to send.

dispac·cio *m.* despatch; telegram; (mil.) signal; order; official letter to the government from a general in the field; ambassadorial despatch; (journ.) despatch, communiqué; †academic diploma; †issue, outlet; *pl.* (mil.) despatches.

dispai-are [A4] *tr.* to separate, to break up a pair; to disproportion. **-ato** *part. adj.* not matching, disparate.

†**dispan·dere** *vb.* See **spandere**.

†**disparare**[1] *vb.* and derivs. See **disimparare**.

†**disparare**[2] *vb.* and derivs. See **dispaiare**.

disparat-o *adj.* not matching, unlike, disparate; various; (of marriage) unequal. (**-amente** *adv.*) **-ezza** *f.* dissimilarity, disparateness.

disparecchi-are [A4] *tr.* to clear (table). **-ato** *part. adj.* cleared (away); not ready, unprepared.

dispar-eggiare [A3c] *tr.* to make unequal. **-eggio** *m.* disparity, inequality.

disparente *adj.* See under **disparire**.

disparere[1] *m.* difference of opinion, disagreement.

†**disparere**[2] *vb.* and derivs. See **disparire**.

†**dispar·gere** *tr.* to pour; to scatter, to sprinkle; *rfl.* to roam, to wander, to disperse, to scatter; to spread, to be extended.

di·spar-i *adj. indecl.* uneven, odd; treno —, odd-numbered train; different; unequal; è permesso il parcheggio nei giorni —, parking on uneven dates; (naut.) guardia —, starboard watch; †inadequate; †inept; *n.f.* (ent.) gipsy moth, *Lymantria dispar*. **-imente** *adv.* unevenly; unequally.

dispar-ire [D2] *intr.* (*aux.* essere) to disappear, to vanish, to fade away; to appear at a disadvantage. (**-imento** *m.*) **-iscente** *part. adj.* fading. **-ito** *part. adj.* vanished; †sunken in visage. **-izione** *f.* disappearance.

disparità *f.* disparity; inequality; difference.

†**disparl-are** *tr.* to speak ill of; *intr.* to speak false, to speak ill. (†**-atore** *m.*)

†**di·sparo** *adj.* See **dispari**.

disparte *adv.* apart; *adv. phr.* in —, apart, to one side; mettere in —, to set aside; tirarsi in —, to draw aside; tenersi in — da, to keep aloof from, to keep out of.

†**dispartenza** *f.* See **dipartenza**.

†**dispart-ire** *tr.* to divide; to separate; to split; to disperse; *rfl.* to depart. †**-imento** *m.* division; separation; departure. †**-ito** *part. adj.* divided; separated; split into two; dispersed; departed; removed; disunited, at loggerheads, split by discord. †**-itamente** *adv.* separately.

†**disparto** *apocop. part.* of **dispartire**, q.v.

†**disparut-o** *adj.* thin, shrunken; *n.m.* object of wretched appearance. †**-ezza** *f.* paltriness; deformity; wretchedness.

†**dispaventare** *vb.* and derivs. See **spaventare**.

†**dispen·dere** *tr.* to spend; to expend; to squander.

dispen-di-o *m.* expense; expenditure; outlay; — di tempo, expenditure of time; eccessivi dispendi, wasteful spending, overspending; †money to spend. **-oso** *adj.* expensive, incurring expenditure; costly. **-osamente** *adv.* expensively.

†**dispennare** *vb.* and derivs. See **spennare**.

dispensa *f.* distribution; pantry, storeroom; sideboard; (naut.) victualling store in merchant navy; instalment, section (of book published in parts); written text of University lecture; exemption (from fees, from examination); (leg.) dispensation; exemption, relief; — dall'obbligo di conferire, relief from the duty to bring into hotch-pot (C.C.); (eccl.) dispensation; †domain; †courier; †expense.

dispens-are [A I] *tr.* to distribute, to allot; to dispense; to deal out; to exempt; — il silenzio, — dal silenzio, to allow talking (e.g. in refectory); — dal servizio, to dispense with the services of; (leg.) to relieve; (eccl.) to dispense; †to concede; †to consume, to spend; †to measure, to traverse; †to administer; †to make use of, to employ; †to ordain, to arrange; *rfl.* to be exempt; to abstain;

-arsi da, to get out of, to release oneself from the obligation of. **-a·bile** *adj.* distributable; dispensable. †**-agione** *f.* distribution; (eccl.) dispensation. †**-amento** *m.* dispensing, distributing, providing; (eccl.) dispensation. **-ante** *part. adj.* dispensing; -ante Iddio, by the ordinance of God. **-a·rio** *m.* dispensary; clinic; T.B. clinic. **-ativa** *f.* household management, domestic economy. **-ativo** *adj.* dispensative. **-ato** *part. adj.* dispensed, distributed; exempt; †ordered, ordained; †employed. †**-atamente** *adv.* by grace; with justice. **-atore** *m.*, **-atrice** *f.* dispenser; steward; bestower. **-azione** *f.* bestowal; exemption; (eccl.) dispensation; (theol.) providential ordering of events, (divine) dispensation.

dispensa·rio *m.* See under **dispensare**.

dispensier-e *m.* steward; dispenser, bestower; guardian. **-a** *f.* stewardess; dispenser, bestower; ministering power; guardian; (naut.) supply assistant.

†**dispenso** *m.* dispensation, will; dispensing, expending; expenditure.

†**dispento** *adj.* spent; quenched; destroyed, annihilated.

†**dispenza** *f.* See **dispensa**.

dis-pepsi-a *f.* (med.) dyspepsia. **-pep·tico** *adj.* (med.) dyspeptic.

dispera *f.* (Tusc.) despair.

disper-are [A I] *intr.* (*aux.* avere) to despair; (*prep.* di) to despair (of); -o della guarigione, I have given up hope of recovery; far —, to drive mad, to worry to death; quel bambino mi fa —, that child is driving me distracted; *rfl.* to be in despair; to distress oneself, to be deeply grieved. **-a·bile** *adj.* hopeless, irremediable, beyond recovery, given up. **-anza** *f.* (poet.) despair; a poem reciting the poet's despair. **-ata** *f.* desperate woman; lament; a card game. **-atezza** *f.* desperation. **-ato** *part. adj.* despaired of; given up (by doctors); un caso -ato, a hopeless case; anima -ata, lost soul; despairing, desperate; per -ato, wildly; darsi al -ato, to give oneself up to despair; alla -ata, wildly, recklessly, in frantic) haste; wretched; penniless; *n.m.* desperate man; desperado. **-atamente** *adv.* desperately. **-azione** *f.* despair, desperation, despondency; trouble, worry; tu sei la mia -azione, you drive me to despair.

disper·d-ere [C3] *tr.* to scatter, to disperse, to dispel, to destroy; to waste; *rfl.* to be scattered, to scatter, to be lost; †— il feto, to miscarry, to abort. **-ente** *part. adj.* (phys.) dispersing; *n.m.* (chem.; industr.) dispersant, dispersing agent. **-ibilità** *f.* (techn.) dispersing power. (**-imento** *m.* **-itore** *m.* **-itrice** *f.*)

disper·g-ere [C3] *tr.* to scatter; to disperse; to dissipate; to put to flight; to diffuse; *rfl.* to scatter; to disperse. (**-imento** *m.* **-itore** *m.*)

†**dispersè** *adv.* singly, separately; alone.

dispers-ione *f.* dispersion; scattering; loss; waste; (statistics) scatter. **-ivo** *adj.* dispersive.

disperso[1] *part.* of **disperdere**, q.v.; *adj.* scattered, dispersed, dispelled; destroyed; lost, missing; dato per —, reported missing; andare —, to get lost; wasted; (phys.) disperse; *n.m.* missing person (on war service). **-amente** *adv.* dispersedly. †**-ore** *m.* squanderer.

disperso[2] *part.* of **dispergere**, q.v.; *adj.* scattered, dispersed; dissipated; put to flight; diffused, diffuse.

†**dispesa** *f.* See **spesa**.

†**dispeso** *part.* of †**dispendere**, q.v.

†**dispett-are** *tr.* to despise, to scorn; to hold in angry contempt; — in parole, to speak ill of, to speak contemptuously of; *intr.* to become angry, to fall into a rage. †**-ato** *part. adj.* despised, scorned; held in contempt. (†**-atore** *m.* †**-atrice** *f.*)

†**dispetto**[1] *apocop. part.* of †**dispettare**, q.v.

dispett-o[2] *m.* annoying or spiteful action; act of mischief; per —, to annoy; fare un — a, to do an annoying thing to; far -i a, to tease; irritation, annoyance, vexation; a — di, in spite of, in defiance of; a mio marcio —, in order to spite me, totally against my wishes, in complete disregard of my feelings; volere andare in Paradiso a — dei santi, to insist on going where one is not welcome; scorn; avere in —, to despise.

dispettos-o *adj.* spiteful; mischievous, teasing; petulant; scornful; †proud, offensive; †vile, abject; †pitiful; †bleak, uncultivated; †harsh, displeasing. (**-amente** *adv.*)

†**dispezzare** *vb.* and derivs. See **spezzare**.

dispiac-ere[1] [B20] *impers.* (*aux.* essere; *prep.* a) to displease; to cause sorrow (to); gli -e di partire, he is sorry to go, he does not want to go; mi -e che sia partito, I'm sorry he has gone; se non Le -e, if you don't mind; mi -e, I'm sorry; *intr.* (*aux.* essere) to be displeasing, to give offence. **-ente** *part. adj.* displeasing, unpleasant; non -ente, not bad-looking; regretful, sorry. **-enza** *f.*

dispiac-ere (*cont.*)
displeasure; disgust; chagrin. **-ɐvole** *adj.* disagreeable, unpleasant. (**-evolmɐnte** *adv.*) **-evolɐzza** *f.* disagreeableness, unpleasantness. **-imɐnto** *m.* displeasure; sorrow. **-iuto** *part. adj.* displeasing; sorry, displeased; -iuto di, sorry about.

dispiacere² *m.* regret; sorrow, grief; displeasure; trouble; disappointment; misfortune; avere il — di, to have the misfortune to.

†**dispiannare** *tr.* to extend; to explain; *rfl.* to stretch oneself out, to lie down at full length.

dispiant-are [A I] *tr.* to uproot; to transplant; to raze. (**-ato** *part. adj.*)

†**dispiatato** *adj.* See †**dispietato**, under †**dispietà**.

†**dispiccare** *tr.* to detach; to unstick; to separate; to draw, to derive; *rfl.* to depart, to part; to branch off; to fly, to depart swiftly.

dispieg-are [A 2] *tr.* to display; to spread, to unfold; to unfurl; to explain. (**-ato** *part. adj.*)

†**dispiet-à** *f.* cruelty; mercilessness. †**-anza** *f.* lack of compassion, hard-heartedness. †**-ato** *adj.* merciless; cruel; without compassion; *n.m.* merciless person.

†**dispin·gere** *tr.* to obliterate what has been painted, to erase; (fig.) to blot out.

†**dispittare** *vb.* and derivs. See **dispettare**.

†**dispitto** *m.* See **dispetto²**.

dispiumare [A I] *tr.* to strip of feathers, to pluck; *rfl.* to moult.

†**displanato** *adj.* destroyed, razed to the ground.

†**displicenz-a, -ia** *f.* See **dispiacenza**, under **dispiacere¹**.

displu·vi-o *m.* (geog.) rainfall divide; watershed; (bldg.) hip; linea di —, ridge. (**-ale** *adj.*) **-ato** *adj.* ridged (of a roof).

dispn-e·a *f.* (med.) dyspnoea. **-o·ico** *adj.* (med.) dyspnoeic.

dispodest-are [A I] *tr.* to dispossess. (**-ato** *part. adj.*)

†**dispoe·tico** *adj.* unpoetic, prosaic.

dispogli-are [A 4] *tr.* to strip; to despoil, to plunder. **-amɐnto** *m.* despoiling; spoliating. **-ato** *part. adj.* despoiled, plundered; stripped; †unclothed; †bereft. (**-atɐre** *m.* **-atrice** *f.*)

dispolp-are [A I c] *tr.* to strip the flesh from. **-ato** *part. adj.* stripped of flesh, bare to the bone.

disponde·o *adj.* (prosod.) dispondaic; *n.m.* dispondee.

disponente *part.* of **disporre**, q.v.; *adj.* ordering, ordaining, authoritative; *n.m.* (leg.) testator; *f.* testatrix.

†**dispo·nere** *vb.* and derivs. see **disporre**; *tr.* to expose; *rfl.* to expose oneself, to take risks (cf. **esporre**).

dispon-i·bile *adj.* that can be disposed; disposable; available, free, vacant; accessible; una somma -ibile, a sum of money that is not earmarked; (leg.) disposable, transferable, alienable, available; *n.f.* (leg.) disposable portion, the part of his estate which a testator with lawful heirs can dispose of by will under (e.g.) Italian law. **-ibilità** *f.* availability; -ibilità di denaro, money available; (leg.) status of a public official at the disposal of the government; in -ibilità, on the reserve; (naut.) nave in -ibilità, ship ready for service with some notice, ship in care and maintenance. **-imɐnto** *m.* arrangement; disposal; order, decree; †deposition; †abasement, humiliation, loss of face; †exposition. **-itivo** *adj.* dispositive; *n.m.* (leg.) operative part of a sentence or judgement. **-itɐre** *m.* disposer, arranger; †expounder, interpreter. (**-itrice** *f.*)

†**dispopolare** *vb.* and derivs. See **spopolare**.

disporre [B 2 I] *tr.* to arrange; to dispose; to set in order; to display; to prepare; to induce; (leg.) to dispose; to provide; to lay down; †to use; †to depose (cf. **deporre**); †to expose (cf. **esporre**); †to compose, to set down (cf. **comporre**); *intr.* (*aux.* avere) to order things; l'uomo propone e Dio dispone, man proposes and God disposes; to decide, to resolve; — di, to have at one's disposal, to be in a position to use, to make use of; to arrange to; (leg.) to provide for; il contratto dispone di, the contract provides for; *rfl.* to get ready, to prepare; to resolve.

disposare [A I] and derivs. (poet.). See **sposare**.

dispositiva *f.* (leg.) purview.

dispositiv-o *adj.* dispositive; *n.m.* (leg.) decision; order; operative part of an act of parliament, deed or document; order of a judgement; purview; — della sentenza, operative words of judgement (C.C.P.; C.P.P.); appliance, mechanism, device, contraption, gadget. (**-amɐnte** *adv.*)

disposit-ɐre *m.* one who arranges; disposer; one who decrees. (**-rice** *f.*) **-ura** *f.* arrangement, ordering.

disposizione *f.* arrangement, disposition; distribution (of parts), composition; order, direction, instruction; avere a —, to have at one's disposal, to have available; (admin.) essere a —, to be on

reserve (of an official or civil servant); intention, plan, wish; bent, inclination, turn of mind; arrangements, preparations; dare disposizioni, to give orders; sino a nuove disposizioni, until further orders; a — di, at the disposal of; (leg.) provision; disposal; conformarsi alle disposizioni di legge, to comply with the law; — testamentaria, testamentary provision, disposition; †condition; †exposition, explanation (cf. **esposizione**); †opportuneness.

dispossess-are [A I] *tr.* to dispossess. **-ato** *part. adj.* disposed, bereft, deprived.

dispostamɐnte *adv.* See under **disposto**.

dispostɐzza *f.* symmetry, gracefulness, proportion; nimbleness, bodily skill; readiness, disposition.

dispɐst-o *part.* of **disporre**, q.v.; *adj.* arranged, ordered, regulated; inclined, willing; — a tutto, ready for anything; ben —, well-disposed; mal —, unfavourable, prejudiced; essere ben — verso, to regard favourably; healthy, fit, alert; (naut.) -i!, get ready!; (leg.) disposed; provided; come —, as provided; *n.m.* (leg.) disposition; provision; — di legge, decree, order, provision of law; secondo il — di tale articolo di legge, according to the provisions of such section of the act. **-amɐnte** *adv.* in an orderly manner; disposedly.

dispotestare [A I]. See **dispodestare**.

dispɐ·t-ico *adj.* despotic; of a despot. **-icamɐnte** *adv.* despotically. **-iʃmo** *m.* despotism.

†**di·spoto** *m.* See **despota**.

†**dispratica·bile** *adj.* unapproachable, unsociable.

†**dispregare** *tr.* to dissuade; to be indifferent towards.

dispregɐvol-e *adj.* contemptible, negligible. **-mɐnte** *adv.* contemptibly, contemptuously.

dispregi-are [A 4] *tr.* to think little of, to disregard, to despise; to undervalue, to depreciate, to belittle. **-a·bile** *adj.* negligible. **-amɐnto** *m.* belittling; despising. **-ante** *part. adj.* disparaging. †**-anza** *f.* see **dispregio**. **-ativo** *adj.* contemptuous; disparaging; *n.m.* (gramm.) word or suffix, indicating contempt or disparagement, pejorative. **-ato** *part. adj.* slighted, disregarded. (**-atamɐnte** *adv.* **-atɐre** *m.* **-atrice** *f.*)

dispre·gio *m.* disregard, disesteem, disdain; disparagement; andare in —, to go down in people's estimation, to be slighted; avere in —, to scorn; (leg.) contempt, scorn (cf. **disprezzo**); eccitamento al — delle leggi, incitement to contempt of the law; †slight, offence; †infamy, ill-fame.

disprezz-are [A I] *tr.* to despise, to scorn, to disdain; to depreciate, to undervalue, to disparage; *rfl.* not to take proper care of oneself, to be untidy, to be heedless. **-a·bile** *adj.* despicable, negligible, worthless. †**-agione** *f.* see **disprezzo**. **-amɐnto** *m.* despising; disparagement. **-ante** *part. adj.* disparaging; scornful. **-ativo** *adj.* contemptuous; (gramm.) suffisso —, suffix expressing contempt. **-ato** *part. adj.* despised, neglected; †unkempt; †natural, unaffected; †scornful, disparaging. (**-atɐre** *m.* **-atrice** *f.*) **-atura** *f.* careless ease. **-ɐvole** *adj.* despicable.

disprezzo *m.* contempt, disdain, scorn; carelessness, neglect; (leg.) contempt, scorn; far una persona segno a pubblico —, to hold a person up to public scorn; — verso le autorità, contempt for the authorities (C.P.).

†**disprigionare** *vb.* and derivs. See **sprigionare**.

†**disprofanare** [A I] *tr.* to rescue from profane uses, to reconsecrate.

†**disproporzione** *f.* and derivs. See **sproporzione**.

dispro·sio *m.* (chem.) dysprosium.

†**disprovveduto** *adj.* and derivs. See **sprovveduto**.

disprun-are [A I] *tr.* (hortic.) to clear thorns away from. (**-ato** *part. adj.*)

dispulare [A I] *tr.* (agric.) to winnow.

†**dispuro** *adj.* impure.

di·sputa *f.* dispute, debate; quarrel, altercation; (theol.; philos.) disputation.

disput-are [A I] *intr.* (*aux.* avere) to debate, to argue, to dispute; *tr.* to contest; to dispute; to discuss; — qualcosa (a uno), to contend for something (with someone); (sport) to play (a match); †(naut.) — il vento, to beat to windward; *recip. rfl.* to contend for. **-a·bile** *adj.* disputable. **-abilità** *f.* disputableness. **-amɐnto** *m.* disputing; dispute. †**-anza** *f.* see **disputa**. **-ativo** *adj.* of, connected with, disputes; disputatious. **-ato** *part. adj.* disputed; discussed, contested; (sport) un incontro -ato a Roma, a match played at Rome. (**-atɐre** *m.* **-atrice** *f.*) **-ato·rio** *adj.* of disputes. **-azione** *f.* debate, disputation.

†**disquassare** *vb.* and derivs. See **squassare**.

disquili·brio *m.* lack of balance.

disquisizione *f.* elaborate investigation, scholarly research; detailed exposition, disquisition.

diṣradic·are [A2s] *tr.* to uproot. (**-ato** *part. adj.*)

†**disragionato** *adj.* ill-reasoned, unjustified.

†**disregolato** *adj.* and derivs. See **sregolato**.

diṣruptivo *adj.* (electr.) disruptive.

dissacr·are [A1] *tr.* to unconsecrate (a sacred thing); to degrade (a sacred person). (**-ato** *part. adj.*)

dissal·are [A1] *tr.* to remove salt from, to soak (salt out of). **-ato** *part. adj.* soaked, free from salt.

dissald·are [A1] *tr.* to unsolder. (**-ato** *part. adj.*)

dissangu·are [A6, A1] *tr.* to drain of blood, to bleed to exhaustion; (fig.) to bleed (white), to ruin. **-amento** *m.* bleeding, blood-letting. **-ato** *part. adj.* drained of blood; (fig.) bled white, ruined. (**-atore** *m.* **-atrice** *f.*)

dissanguinare [A1] *tr.* to soak blood out of (hides).

†**dissapito** *adj.* insipid, tasteless.

dissapore *m.* slight disagreement, unpleasantness.

dissec·are [A2c] *tr.* to dissect, to open up. **-ato** *part. adj.* dissected, opened up. **-azione** *f.* dissection; dissecting.

dissecc·are [A2c] *tr.* to dry up, to parch; (chem.) to desiccate; *rfl.* to become parched. **-amento** *m.* drying, parching. **-ante** *part. adj.* dehydrating, parching, drying; *n.m.* **-ativo** *adj.* parching. **-ato** *part. adj.* dehydrated, dried up, parched. **-atore** *m.* (chem.) desiccator. **-azione** *f.* drying, parching.

disselci·are [A3c] *tr.* to unpave. (**-ato** *part. adj.*)

dissell·are [A1] *tr.* to unsaddle; *intr.* (*aux.* essere) to be unhorsed. (**-ato** *part. adj.*)

†**dissembrare** *intr.* to be dissimilar, to be different, to differ.

dissemin·are [A1sc] *tr.* to disseminate, to spread abroad, to sow; to strew. **-ante** *part. adj.* disseminating, diffusing. **-ato** *part. adj.* strewn, bestrown. (**-atore** *m.* **-atrice** *f.*) **-azione** *f.* (fig.) dissemination, diffusion; (bot.) dispersion, distribution.

dissenn·are [A1c] *tr.* to deprive of sense, to drive mad. **-atezza** *f.* madness, foolishness, act of folly. **-ato** *part. adj.* driven mad; wild, foolish; injudicious, unwise, ill-considered; inconsiderate, senseless. (**-atamente** *adv.*)

dissensione *f.* dissension.

dissenso *m.* dissent, disagreement; (leg.) dissent, want of agreement; — delle parti, dissent of the parties.

dissenta·neo *adj.* discordant, disagreeing, differing.

dissent·eri·a *f.* (med.) dysentery. **-e·rico** *adj.* (med.) dysenteric.

dissent·ire [D1] *intr.* (*aux.* avere; *prep.* da) to dissent (from), to disagree (with), to differ (from); to be at odds; (leg.) to disagree, to dissent. (**-imento** *m.*) **-ito** *part. adj.* denied, refuted.

dissenziente *adj.* (leg.) dissenting; il gruppo —, the minority group; *n.m.*, *f.* dissenting person; critic.

dissepar·are [A1] *tr.* to dissever, to separate. (**-azione** *f.*)

disseppell·ire [D2] *tr.* to disinter; to unearth; to bring to light again; to excavate. **-imento** *m.* disinterring; excavating. (**-ito** *part. adj.* **-itore** *m.* **-itrice** *f.*)

disserente *m.* dissertator.

disserr·are [A1] *tr.* to unlock; to open, to unfasten; †to release; †— bocca, to open one's lips; *rfl.* to be openable with a key; non si ~a, it won't unlock; †to be released, to be set free; †to fly, to race, to go at great speed; †to separate, to scatter. (**-ato** *part. adj.*)

dissert·are [A1] *intr.* (*aux.* avere) to discourse, to dissert; to expatiate; to argue, to hold forth; to be long-winded. **-ativo** *adj.*, **-ato·rio** *adj.* dissertational. (**-atore** *m.* **-atrice** *f.*) **-azione** *f.* dissertation; thesis.

disserv·ire [D1] *tr.* to serve ill, to do disservice to. **-ito** *part. adj.* ill-served; displeased.

disservi·zio *m.* disservice; bad service, faulty service (e.g. in public transport, etc.).

dissest·are [A1] *tr.* to disarrange; to put in an awkward position; to embarrass; to cause confusion in; to impair (fortune or property). **-ato** *part. adj.* disarranged, in disorder, in confusion; embarrassed, in debt, financially in a bad way.

dissesto *m.* confusion; financial ruin, (verging on) bankruptcy.

disset·are [A1c] *tr.* to quench the thirst of; to satisfy. **-ato** *part. adj.* quenched; satisfied.

disse·ttore *m.* dissector. **-zione** *f.* dissection.

dissid·ente *adj.* dissident, dissentient, dissenting; *n.m.*, *f.* dissident, dissenter; (rel.) non-Catholic Christian (e.g. Russian Orthodox, Lutheran, Methodist). **-enza** *f.* dissidence, disagreement.

dissi·dio *m.* dissension, variance, disagreement; point in dispute; quarrel.

dissigill·are [A1] *tr.* to unseal, to break the seal of; to open; *rfl.* to be unsealed; †to melt; †to vanish. (**-ato** *part. adj.*)

dissil·labo *m.* See **disillabo**.

dissimigliare [A4] and derivs. See **dissomigliare**.

dissimil·are[1] [A1s] *tr.* (ling.) to dissimilate. **-ato** *part. adj.* (ling.) dissimilated. **-azione** *f.* (ling.; chem.; med.) dissimilation; unlikeness.

dissimilar·e[2] *adj.* dissimilar. **-ità** *f.* dissimilarity, unlikeness.

dissi·mil·e *adj.* unlike, different. **-mente** *adv.* differently, variously. **-itu·dine** *f.* unlikeness.

dissimm·etri·a *f.* dissymmetry. **-e·trico** *adj.* dissymmetric.

dissimul·are [A1s] *tr.* to dissimulate, to dissemble, to hide, to disguise; egli lo sa ma ~a, he knows, but he doesn't show it; non mi ~o le difficoltà, I don't close my eyes to the difficulties; *rfl.* to be concealed, to lie hidden; si ~a, it doesn't show (as in camouflage). **-ato** *part. adj.* hidden; disguised; false, hypocritical. **-atamente** *adv.* dissemblingly. (**-atore** *m.* **-atrice** *f.*) **-azione** *f.* dissimulation, feigning, concealment; (lit.) ironical pretence.

dissip·are [A1s] *tr.* to dissipate; to squander; to dispel, to scatter; to clear away; (mil.) to disperse, to scatter; *rfl.* to become dissipated, to be scattered; (of mist, clouds) to clear, to lift; to disperse; †to bring on an abortion. **-a·bile** *adj.* that can be dispelled; dispersible. **-amento** *m.* scattering, dispelling; dissipating. **-atezza** *f.* dissipation. **-ativo** *adj.* dispersant. **-ato** *part. adj.* scattered, dispelled; squandered; dissipated, debauched; pleasure-seeking, frivolous. **-atamente** *adv.* dissipatedly, wastefully; inattentively. **-atore** *m.* dissipator; squanderer. (**-atrice** *f.*) **-ato·rio** *adj.* of, or connected with, dissipation. **-azione** *f.* dispersion; squandering, waste; dissipation; dissolute living, pleasure-seeking, wasteful idleness. **-one** *m.* spendthrift, wastrel. **-ona** *f.* extravagant woman, bad manager.

†**dissi·pido** *adj.* insipid.

†**dissipito** *adj.* insipid, tasteless; foolish, stupid, silly; feeble-minded.

dissipon·a, *f.*, **-e** *m.* See under **dissipare**.

dissoci·are [A3] *tr.* to dissociate; to separate, to sunder. **-a·bile** *adj.* dissociable; separable. **-ante** *part. adj.* disruptive. **-ato** *part. adj.* dissociated; separated; separate. (**-atore** *m.* **-atrice** *f.*) **-azione** *f.* dissociation; separation.

dissod·are [A1] *tr.* to break up (ground), to clear for tillage; (fig.) to do spadework on, to clear the ground for. **-amento** *m.* tillage. **-ato** *part. adj.* broken up (of ground); cleared.

dissolfor·are [A1] *tr.* (chem.) to desulphurize. **-azione** *f.* desulphurization.

dissolto *part.* of **dissolvere**; see **dissoluto**.

dissolu·bil·e *adj.* dissoluble, dissolvable, soluble. **-ità** *f.* dissolubility, solubility.

dissolutezza *f.* See under **dissoluto**.

dissolutivo *adj.* dissolvent.

dissolut·o *part.* of **dissolvere** q.v.; *adj.* dissolved; unrestrained; dissolute, licentious, loose; †weakened; †slackened; †defeated. **-amente** *adv.* dissolutely. **-ezza** *f.* dissoluteness, licentiousness, looseness, loose living.

dissoluzione *f.* dissolution; dissoluteness, dissolving, solution; (med.) — di corpo, diarrhoea; weakness; (leg.) dissolution; †derision, mockery.

dissol·v·ere [C14] *tr.* to dissolve; to separate, to disperse; to dispel; to break up; (leg.) to dissolve; to cancel, to abrogate, to annul; *rfl.* to be dissolved, to dissolve; to be dispersed, to scatter, to be dispelled. **-ente** *part. adj.* dissolvent; *n.m.* solvent. **-enza** *f.* (cinem.; telev.; radio) fading; apertura in **-enza**, fade in; chiusura in **-enza**, fade-out; **-enza** incrociata, fade-over, mix; in **-enza**, fading, dissolving. **-imento** *m.* dissolving; dispersing; breaking up.

dissomigli·are [A4] *intr.* (*aux.* essere), *recip. rfl.* to be unlike, to differ, to stand apart. **-ante** *part. adj.* unlike, dissimilar. (**-antemente** *adv.*) **-anza** *f.* unlikeness. **-ato** *part. adj.* unlike.

disson·are [A1d] *intr.* (*aux.* avere) to be out of tune, to sound discordantly, to jar; to be out of keeping; to disagree. **-ante** *part. adj.* dissonant, discordant, jarring; out of keeping. **-anza** *f.* dissonance; discord, discordance; divergence.

dissonn-are [A I] *tr.* to awaken, to rouse; *rfl.* to awake, to rouse oneself; to be aroused. **-ato** *part. adj.* awakened, roused; awake.

dis·sono *adj.* dissonant.

dissotterr-are [A I] *tr.* to exhume, to disinter; to bring to light again. **-amento** *m.* exhumation, disinterment. **-ato** *part. adj.* exhumed, disinterred; dug up. (**-atore** *m.*)

†**dissovenire** *impers.* to be absent from the mind; nè dissovienti dell'onor, thou art not unmindful of the honour.

dissuad-ere, dissua·d-ere [C3] *tr.* to dissuade, to deter, to discourage. **-ente** *part. adj.* discouraging. (**-itore** *m.* **-itrice** *f.*)

dissuas-ione, (Rom.) **dissuas-ione** *f.* dissuasion. **-ivo** *adj.* dissuasive. (**-ivamente** *adv.*) **-ore** *m.* dissuader. **-o·rio** *adj.* dissuading.

dissuaso *part.* of dissuadere, q.v.

dissuet-o *adj.* unaccustomed. **-u·dine** *f.* desuetude, disuse.

†**dissugare** *tr.* to dry; to drain; to exhaust.

dissuggell-are [A I] *tr.* to unseal, to open; to remove a mark from, to remove an impression from. **-ato** *part. adj.* unsealed; open, not sealed up.

dissuri·a *f.* (med.) dysuria.

distacc-are [A2] *tr.* to detach, to separate; to unstick, to ungum; to remove; — il personale, to second staff; to pull apart; to disconnect; to withdraw; to alienate; (mil.) (naut.) to detach; (art) to bring into relief, to make prominent; (cycling, athl., etc.) to leave behind, to draw away from; (motor.) — la frizione, to declutch; *intr.* (*aux.* essere) (art) to be prominent, to stand out; *rfl.* (*acc.* of *prn.* 'si') to be detached; to get separated; to come off, to come away; to part; -arsi da uno, to break with someone; -arsi dal mondo, to withdraw from the world; (*dat.* of *prn.* 'si') to leave behind one; (cycling, athl., etc.) -arsi uno, to draw away from someone (a competitor), to leave someone behind. **-a·bile** *adj.* detachable. **-amento** *m.* detachment, separation. (mil.) detachment; (naut.) detachment (small section of a fleet or squadron). **-ato** *part. adj.* detached, separate; off; (mil.) detached. **-atore** *m.* (watchm.) disconnector.

distac·co *m.* (*pl.* **-chi**) detachment, separation; disjunction; breaking off, leave-taking, parting; withdrawal; (aeron.) take-off; (sport) interval; è arrivato con un minuto di —, he got in first one minute ahead; (watchm.) ruota di —, unlocking wheel.

distaff-are [A I] *tr.* (foundry) to strip, to shake out, to knock out, to remove from mould. **-ag·gio** *m.* stripping, shake-out. **-atrice** *f.* shaken-out. **-atura** *f.* shake-out, stripping.

distale *adj.* (anat.) distal.

†**distang-are** *tr.* to unlatch, to take the latch off. †**-ato** *part. adj.* unlatched.

distant-e *adj.* distant, remote; far away, far off; è — di qui, it is a good way from here; troppo -i, too far apart; differing; diverse; alien; siamo -i d'idee, our notions have little in common; *adv.* far, far off, afar; abita molto —, he lives a long way from here; tre metri —, three metres away. **-emente** *adv.* in the distance.

distanza *f.* distance; length; range; alla — di venti metri, at a distance of 20 metres, 20 yards away; (opt.) (photog.) — focale, focal length; tenersi a —, to hold aloof, to remain aloof; tenere uno a —, to keep a person at arm's length; telefonia a grande —, long-distance telephony; comando a —, remote control; comandare a —, to remote-control; (leg.) distance; — legale, regulation distance, statutory distance (building line, etc.); (mil.) space between ranks or columns; range (measured between the muzzle and the target); (naut.) manœuvring distance between ships (N.B. In the Italian navy this is measured between the stern of the leader and the stem of next ship. In the British navy it is measured from bridge to bridge); — aperta, open order; (radar) marcatore di —, range marker.

†**distan·zia** *f.* See distanza.

distanziale *m.* (eng.) distance piece, spacer.

distanzi-are [A4] to leave behind, to outstrip; (sport) to outdistance. **-amento** *m.* outstripping; (sport) outdistancing. **-ato** *part. adj.* left behind, outstripped; (sport) outdistanced. **-atore** *m.* (eng.) distance piece, spacer; anello -atore, spacer waster; tubo -atore, distance sleeve. **-o·metro** *m.* (surv.) diastometer, distance-measuring equipment.

distare [A9s] *intr.* (*aux.* essere; *prep.* da) to be distant (from); distano 300 metri l'uno dall'altro, they are three hundred metres apart; dista otto chilometri, it's eight kilometres away; †to be at variance.

distas-are [A I] *tr.* to unstop, to free from a stoppage; †(mil.) to unplug (a mine, etc.). **-ante** *part. adj.* freeing, clearing. **-ato** *part. adj.* cleared, free, unblocked.

†**diste·gnere** *tr.* to extinguish.

disteleologi·a *f.* (philos.) dysteleology.

distemper-are [A I s] *tr.* to dilute, to let down; to water, to drench; (metall.) to soften, to anneal. **-amento** *m.* diluting; excess, immoderateness. **-ante** *part. adj.* dissolving; diluting. **-anza** *f.* alteration in natural temperature; intemperance; †drying effect of the sun. **-ato** *part. adj.* diluted; dissolved; immoderate; incontinent; †uncorded, unstrung.

distemprare [A I] and derivs. See distemperare.

disten·d-ere [C I] *tr.* to spread, to extend; to lay; to stretch out; to hammer out (metal); to roll out (pastry); — il burro sul pane, to butter one's bread; to knock down, to strike to the ground, to floor; to bring down heavily; — un colpo, to strike a heavy blow; to put down in writing, to record; to draw up; (mil.) to extend, to deploy; (naut.) to stretch (a sail); to lay out (an anchor); to run out (a hawser); to uncoil (a hawser); *rfl.* to extend, to spread, to stretch; to lie down; to expatiate, to talk at length; to descant. **-evole, -i·bile** *adj.* extensible, stretchable. **-imento** *m.* spreading, extending; stretching out; (text.) tentering. **-ino** *m.* **-io** *m.* drawing up, drafting; recording. **-itura** *f.* stretching, spreading, drawing up, drafting.

distene *m.* (min.) disthene, cyanite.

distenebr-are [A I s] *tr.* to light, to dispel the darkness from, to lessen the gloom of. (**-ato** *part. adj.*)

†**distenere** *tr.* to hold on to, to hold back; to destrain; to hold the attention of; to keep in suspense.

distens-ione *f.* tension, stretching; — di un muscolo, straining of a muscle; extension, spreading; relaxation, easing of tension, *détente*; improvement (e.g. in political relations); extension; (sport) weight-lifting, stretch. **-ivo** *adj.* tending to bring about a distension.

†**disterrare** *tr.* to banish, to exile.

distes-a *f.* expanse, sweep, extent, stretch; long line; a —, alla —, continuously, straight on, on and on, without pausing, forthwith; sonare a —, to ring a full peal; ridere alla —, to laugh boisterously; (naut.) spread or greatest width of a sail (measured along the foot).

distes-o *part.* of distendere, q.v.; *adj.* stretched, laid out; long, extended, reaching some way; lungo —, lying full length; per —, a —, in full, at length; ample, wide, spacious; extensive; capelli -i, flowing hair, straight hair; (ling.) dittongo —, diphthong with accent on first vowel (e.g. làude, cf. buòno); (mil.) extended; esercito —, army spread over a long front; (naut.) vento —, steady wind; vela —, well-set sail; (prosod.) canzone -a, extended canzone; †diligent; †set out, written; *adv.* in full, in detail; *n.m.* piece of writing; essay; report; petition; memorial; memorandum. **-amente** *adv.* in full, in detail; without interruption; straight on.

distes·sere [B I] *tr.* to unweave, to unpick.

di·stico *m.* (prosod.) couplet, distich; *adj.* (bot.) distichous.

distill-are [A I] *tr.* to distil; *intr.* (*aux.* essere) to fall drop by drop. **-amento** *m.* distilling. **-ato** *part. adj.* distilled. **-ato·io** *m.* still. **-atore** *m.* still; distillation plant. **-ato·rio** *adj.* relating to distilling. **-azione** *f.* distillation, distilling; (chem.) -azione frazionata, fractional distillation. **-eri·a** *f.* distillery.

di·stilo *adj., n.m.* (archit.) distyle.

†**distinare** *vb.* and derivs. See destinare.

distin·gu-ere [C6] *tr.* to distinguish; to draw a distinction between; — il vero dal falso, to tell truth from falsehood; to perceive, to make out, to discern; — una forma, to discern a shape; non -o senza gli occhiali, I can't see properly without my glasses; to mark off, to separate, to divide, to differentiate; to lend distinction to; to signalize; — le parole, to mark words (with accents, etc.); to make notable, to mark out; (leg.) to distinguish; to prove a case; — la fattispecie da un caso precedente, to distinguish the present case from a previous case, or precedent; *abs.* to point out an essential difference; — tra un'autorità e un'altra, to distinguish between one authority and another; *rfl.* to distinguish oneself, to come into prominence. **-i·bile** *adj.* distinguishable. **-imento** *m.* distinction; hair-splitting. (**-itore** *m.* **-itrice** *f.*)

distinta *f.* list; schedule; (comm.) price list, price catalogue; invoice; — di deposito, — di versamento, pay-in slip; — di pagamento, payment schedule; — dei pesi, list of weights; — delle pietanze, menu.

distintivo *adj.* distinctive; distinguishing; *n.m.* badge, emblem; distinguishing mark, characteristic; (mil.) regimental badge; regimental colours; shoulder or arm distinguishing mark; badge of rank; (naut.) personal flag (Admirals, etc.); squadron or unit flag; house flag (shipping companies); code distinguishing flag; racing flag (of a yacht).

distint-o *part.* of **distinguere**, q.v.; *adj.* distinct, separate, clear; distinguished; eminent; refined; gentlemanly; ladylike; i posti ~i, the average-priced (reserved) seats (in a theatre, etc.), coming after 'poltrone' and 'poltroncine'; con ~i saluti, yours faithfully; *adv.* distinctly. **~amente** *adv.* distinctly, separately; in a distinguished manner; in a refined way; vestito ~amente, dressed with taste and distinction; vi salutiamo ~amente, yours faithfully.

distinzione *f.* distinction; senza — alcuna, indiscriminately, impartially; non fare — da persona a persona, to treat everyone on an equal footing; section, division.

distirare [A I] *tr.* (naut.) to stretch (ropes).

†**distirpare** *vb.* and derivs. See **estirpare**.

distivare [A I] *tr.* (naut.) to clear (a hold) of ballast.

disto·gl·iere [B 2] *tr.* to dissuade, to deter; — uno da un'idea, to persuade someone to give up an idea, to make him give up a notion; to distract, to disturb; to divert; — lo sguardo da, to remove one's gaze from; *rfl.* ~iersi da, to turn one's attention away from, to give up the idea of, to think better of. (~imento *m.* ~itore *m.* ~itrice *f.*)

distolto *part.* of **distogliere**, q.v.

distom-a *m.* (vet.) — epatico, liver fluke. ~atosi *f.* (vet.) liver rot.

distonare [A I] (mus.). See **stonare**.

distopp-are [A I] *tr.* (naut.) to uncaulk. ~amento *m.* (naut.) uncaulking; uncaulked state (of hull, etc.). ~ato *part. adj.* (naut.) uncaulked.

distor·c·ere [C 5] *tr.* to contort, to twist; to force round, to wrench; (naut.) to unlay. ~imento *m.* contorting, twisting; wrenching.

distorn-are [A I c] *tr.* to deter; to deflect; to annul, to cancel. (~amento *m.* ~ato *part. adj.*) †~o *m.* obstacle, impediment; discouragement.

distorre [B 27]. See **distogliere**.

distorsi-o·metro *m.* (radio) distortion meter. ~one *f.* distortion; (med.) sprain; (carp.) warping.

distort-o *part.* of **distorcere**, q.v.; *adj.* crooked, twisted; curved; deformed; distorted; confused, chaotic. (~amente *adv.*)

distoscan-are [A I] *tr.* to make less Tuscan, to destroy Tuscan qualities in, to de-Tuscanize. ~ato *part. adj.* de-Tuscanized.

†**distra·ere**, †**distrag·gere** *vbs.* and derivs. See **distrarre**.

distralciare *tr.* to prune; †to decipher, to penetrate to the meaning of.

distrarre [B 33] *tr.* to pull aside, to twist; to sprain; to detach; to draw away, to withdraw; (mil.) to remove, to divert, to misroute; to distract, to divert, to amuse; — uno dagli studi, to interrupt someone's work; — la noia, to beguile one's tedium; to misappropriate, to misapply; — fondi, to misapply funds; *abs.* (leg.) to order appropriation (of costs awarded); *rfl.* to be inattentive, to let one's mind wander; to be absent-minded; to amuse oneself; to take recreation.

distrattivo *adj.* distractive, distracting.

distratt-o *part.* of **distrarre**, q.v.; *adj.* strained; turned aside; diverted; absent-minded; inattentive, careless; sguardo —, careless look; *n.m.* absent-minded person. ~amente *adv.* absentmindedly; inattentively, carelessly.

distrazione *f.* strain, wrench, twisting; removal, withdrawal; misappropriation (of funds); absent-mindedness; distraction; inattentiveness, carelessness; amusement, recreation; ha poche distrazioni, he doesn't have much fun; (leg.) appropriation; — delle spese, order for direct payment of costs (C.C.P.).

distretta *f.* necessity, need, want, straits; danger; (naut.) distress; nave in —, ship in distress; †aver —, to have need.

distrettamente *adv.* strictly; †closely; †fixedly; †severely; †urgently.

distrettezza *f.* tightening; strictness.

distrett-o[1] *m.* region, administrative district; (mil.) recruiting office; recruiting area (equiv. in U.K. to territorial district or H.Q.); (naut.) fishing district or limits. **~uale** *adj.* relating to an administrative district; †*n.m.* vassal.

†**distretto**[2] *adj.* compressed; squeezed; occupied, preoccupied, engaged, absorbed; withdrawn, distrait, remote, set apart; enamoured; anguished; rigorous; *n.m.* close relative; confidant; *adv. phr.* al —, in conclusion, to sum up.

†**distretto**[3] *m.* narrowness, tightness; essere in —, to be in prison, to be under restraint; chiudere in —, to imprison, to place under restraint.

distribu-ire [D 2] *tr.* to distribute; to hand out, to deal out; to share; to bestow; to allot, to assign; to issue; to cast (parts in play); — la posta, to deliver the post; — biglietti, to sell tickets; to arrange; (cards) to deal. ~ente *part. adj.* distributing; *n.m., f.* distributor. ~imento *m.* distributing. ~ito *part. adj.* distributed; dealt; allotted, assigned.

distributiv-o *adj.* distributive. ~amente *adv.* distributively; in distribution; in equal shares.

†**distributo** *part.* of **distribuire**, q.v.

distribu-tore *m.* distributor; (in a library) assistant who gives out books; (motor.) — di accensione, distributor; — di benzina, petrol pump; *pl.* (comm.) distributing firm, distributors. **~trice** *f.* distributor; ~trice automatica, vending machine; (eng.) palette ~trici, nozzle blades (of turbine).

distribuzione *f.* distribution; distributing; hand out, deal; issue, assignment; (theatr.) casting; arrangement; — di premi, prize giving; (eccl.) — corale, fee for choir attendance; — della posta, — delle lettere, letter-delivery; sorting office; (mil.) serving of rations, etc.

distric-are [A 2] *tr.* to disentangle; to unravel; to extricate, to release; to explain; *rfl.* to extricate oneself; ~arsi da, to get out of. (~amento *m.* ~ato *part. adj.*)

†**distridere** *vb.* See **stridere**.

distrigare [A 2] and derivs. See **districare**; *rfl.* (Ven.) see **arrangiarsi**.

†**distr-i·gnere**, ~in·gere *tr.* to constrict, to bind tightly; to hold fast, to grip; to keep prisoner; to cut off (from supplies); to hold back.

†**distritto** *adj.* sharp, cutting, stinging.

distrofi·a *f.* (bot.; med.) dystrophy.

di·strofo *adj.* (prosod.) of two strophes or stanzas.

distrug·g-ere [C 12] *tr.* to destroy, to ruin; to melt; to consume; (fig.) — il cuore, to wring the heart; †to eliminate; †to remove; †to depose; *rfl.* to be destroyed; to wear oneself out; to waste away; to pine. ~ente *part. adj.* destructive. ~i·bile *adj.* destructible. ~imento *m.* destroying; destruction. ~itivo *adj.* destructive. ~itore *m.* destroyer; enemy; victor; †waster, spendthrift. (~itrice *f.*)

distrutt-i·bile *adj.* destructible; destroying. ~ivo *adj.* destructive; tending to bring about disintegration. ~o *part.* of **distruggere**, q.v.; *adj.* destroyed; ruined; wasted; consumed; melted; †damned, lost. ~ore *m.* destroyer.

distruzione *f.* destruction; ruin, havoc; †mettere a —, to put to death.

disturb-are [A I] *tr.* to disturb; to trouble; to distress; to worry; to be a nuisance to; to vex, to annoy; to interrupt; to interfere with; vi ~o?, am I in your way?, do you mind?; (leg.) to disturb; to annoy; *rfl.* to distress oneself; to take trouble, to go to great pains; to put oneself out, to bother; non si ~i, please don't trouble, please remain seated; non ~atevi per me, don't go out of your way on my account; to worry. ~amento *m.* disturbing; interruption. ~ato *part. adj.* disturbed; troubled; worried; vexed. ~atore *m.* disturber; ~atore della pace, disturber of the peace. (~atrice *f.*)

disturbo *m.* trouble; annoyance; distress; inconvenience, disturbance; (leg.) annoyance; disturbance; recare molestia o — ad una persona, to molest or annoy a person (criminal law); (radio) disturbi atmosferici, atmospherics; (med.) mild complaint, upset, disorder; (mil.) azioni di —, harassing actions.

disturna *f.* (Flor.) exchange of quips and witticisms between towns or communities and esp. between local versifiers; i Fiorentini davano la — ai Pisani, there was an exchange of satirical verses between Florence and Pisa.

disubbid-ire [D 2] *intr.* (*aux.* avere, *prep.* a) to disobey; to disregard; to flout; (leg.) to disobey; istigazione a — alle leggi di ordine pubblico, incitement to commit a breach of the peace; *tr.* to disobey. ~iente *part. adj.* disobedient; unruly. ~ienza *f.* disobedience; (leg.) istigazione alla ~ienza delle leggi, incitement to disobey the law (C.P.). ~ito *part. adj.* disobeyed, disregarded, flouted, broken.

†**disub(b)rigare** *vb.* and derivs. See **disobbligare**.

†**disudire** *tr.* to 'unhear', to dismiss from the mind; (provb.) chi ode non disode, give a dog a bad name and hang him.

†**disuggellare** *vb.* and derivs. See **disigillare**.

disuguagli-are [A4] *tr.* to make unequal; to render uneven. **-anza** *f.* inequality; unevenness; disparity, difference. **-ato** *part. adj.* unequal; uneven.

disugual-e *adj.* unequal; uneven; irregular, up and down; disparate; †different. **-mente** *adv.* unequally; unevenly. **-ità** *f.* inequality; unevenness.

disuman-are [A1] *tr.* to dehumanize, to destroy the human qualities in; to render inhuman; †to castrate; *rfl.* to lose human attributes; to become brutish. **-ato** *part. adj.* inhuman; merciless; brutish, bestial.

disuman-o *adj.* inhuman, cruel, barbarous; bestial, subhuman. **-ità** *f.* inhumanity, cruelty, barbarity.

disum-are [A1] *tr.* to exhume, to disinter. **-azione** *f.* exhumation.

disumid-ire [D2] *tr.* to dry; to air. **-ito** *part. adj.* dried; aired; dry.

†**disunare** *tr.* see **disunire**; *rfl.* to cease to be one and the same.

disun·gere [C5] *tr.* to get the grease out of, to remove spots from.

†**disuniforme** *adj.* dissimilar, not uniform.

disunion-e *f.* disunion, separation, separateness. **-isti** *m.pl.* (U.S. hist.) Disunionists.

disun-ire [D2] *tr.* to disunite, to separate, to divide, to cause a rift between; *rfl.* to become disunited; (equit.) to break step. **-i·bile** *adj.* separable. **-ità**, **-itezza** *f.* lack of unity; unevenness; heterogeneity. **-ito** *part. adj.* disunited; uneven; not of a piece; irregular; (equit.) galoppo -ito, irregular gait. (**-itamente** *adv.*) †**-izione** *f.* See **disunione**.

disuri·a *f.* (med.). See **dissuria**.

disuṣ-are [A1] *tr.* to cease using, to give up; to disaccustom, to break of a habit; †to abuse. †**-anza** *f.* disuse; neglect; lack of custom, unfamiliarity; andare in -anza, to fall into disuse. **-ato** *part. adj.* disused, no longer in use, obsolete; unaccustomed, unwonted; -ato dalle armi, unused to arms. (**-atamente** *adv.*)

disuṣo *m.* disuse; desuetude; cadere in —, to fall into disuse.

disu·til-e *adj.* useless, worse than useless, worthless, good for nothing; harmful, injurious; *n.m.* uselessness; harm, disadvantage, loss; avere —, to suffer loss; idle or useless person, good-for-nothing. **-mente** *adv.* uselessly; to no advantage. **-ità** *f.* uselessness, harmfulness.

disvantag·gi-o *m.* disadvantage. **-oso** *adj.* disadvantageous. **-osa-mente** *adv.* disadvantageously; at a loss.

†**disvariare** *vb.* and derivs. See **variare** or **svariare**.

†**disva·rio** *adj.* See **vario**.

†**disvegliare** *vb.* and derivs. See **svegliare**.

disvel-are [A1] *tr.* to unveil; to reveal; *rfl.* to unveil oneself; to reveal oneself; to stand revealed. **-ato** *part. adj.* unveiled; revealed; manifest.

†**disvel·lere** *tr.* to uproot; to dig out; to pluck out, to tear out.

†**disvelto** *part.* of **disvellere**, q.v.

†**disvenire** *intr.* to fade away; to waste away; to pine; to faint; to become enfeebled; to be weakened; to be unsuitable, to be unfitting; (of colours) to fade.

disvest-ire [D1] *tr.* to undress; (fig.) to divest, to rid, to free; *rfl.* to undress oneself; to be stripped. **-ito** *part. adj.* undressed; stripped; divested.

disvezzare [A1c] and derivs. See **disavvezzare** or **divezzare**.

disvi-are [A4] *tr.* to lead astray, to mislead; to divert, to turn aside; to cause loss of goodwill to; — una bottega, to spoil a shop's custom; *rfl.* to turn away; to go astray; to degenerate. **-a·bile** *adj.* that can be led astray; that can be turned aside. **-amento** *m.* going astray; turning aside; †digression. **-ante** *part. adj.* straying; leaving the common path; deviating. †**-anza** *f.* inability to find the right path. **-ato** *part. adj.* misled, misguided; strayed, straying, stray; out of the way, remote.

disvigorire [D2] *tr.* to enfeeble; *intr.* (*aux.* essere) to become enfeebled.

disvilupp-are [A1] *tr.* to unwrap, to undo; to disentangle; *rfl.* to disentangle oneself; to free oneself. (**-ato** *part. adj.*)

disv-i·o *m.* (*pl.* **-i·i**) straying, wandering; deviating; miscarriage; leading astray; driving away (of customers); going astray (of post).

disviticchi-are [A4] *tr.* to untwist; to disentwine; to separate. (**-ato** *part. adj.*)

†**disvizi-are** [A4] *tr.* to cure of weakness or vices, to improve; to purge. (**-ato** *part. adj.*)

†**disvogliare** [A4] *tr.* to disincline; *rfl.* to feel disinclined.

disvogliato *adj.* unenthusiastic; disinclined; lazy, indolent; listless.

disvol·gere [C5] and derivs. See **svolgere**.

disvolere [B36] *tr.* to cease to wish, to change one's mind; volere e —, to wish and unwish; *n.m.* change of mind; contrary wish; disagreement.

ditaiuolo *m.* (surg.) whitlow.

dital-e *m.* finger of a glove; finger-stall; thimble; leather finger-shield; (mus.) plectrum; (mil. hist.) leather obturator used thimble fashion to prevent a premature or flashback in a muzzle-loading gun; (med.) — di Asdrubale, pelvimeter. **-ino** *m.* (mil.) firing tube, percussion cap, igniter.

ditata *f.* tap, with the finger; finger-mark; as much (ointment, grease, etc.) as will go on a finger; finger's dip.

Dite[1] *pr.n.m.* (class. myth.) Dis; (Dante) Satan; City of Dis, Lower Hell.

†**dite**[2] *adj.* rich.

diteggi-are [A3c] *tr.* (mus.) to finger. **-atura** *f.* (mus.) fingering.

diteggio *m.* (mus.) fingering.

diteismo *m.* (rel.) ditheism.

†**ditell-o** *m.* (*pl.f.* **-a**) arm-pit; shoulder-guard (armour).

†**diterminare** *vb.* and derivs. See **determinare**.

†**dites·sere** *tr.* to unweave, to unpick, to undo (weaving).

dition-ato *m.* (chem.) dithionate. **-ito** *m.* (chem.) hyposulphite. **-oso** *adj.* (chem.) hyposulphurous.

ditio·nico *adj.* (chem.) dithionic.

ditir-ambo *m.* (lit. hist.) dithyramb; poem in praise of wine; hymn of praise; eulogy. **-ambeggiare** [A3c] *intr.* (*aux.* avere) to compose a dithyramb; to sing praises. **-am·bico** *adj.* dithyrambic. (**-ambica-mente** *adv.*)

dito *m.* (*pl.f.* **dita**) finger; digit; — del piede, toe; — pollice, —grosso, thumb; — grosso del piede, big toe; (*pl.m.* **diti**, of specific fingers); — indice, forefinger; — medio, middle finger; — anulare, fourth finger; — mignolo, little finger; finger of a glove; mostrare a —, to hold up to ridicule, to point the finger of scorn at; non ha alzato un dito per aiutarci, he hasn't lifted a finger to help us; legarsela al —, to cherish, to hug (an injury); avere sulle punte delle dita, to have at one's finger tips; conoscere una cosa a mena —, to know a thing inside out; mordersi le dita, to repent, to be remorseful, to be enraged; tra moglie e marito non mettere il —, never interfere between husband and wife; darsi del —nell'occhio, to cut off one's nose to spite one's face; toccare il cielo col —, to be in one's seventh heaven; è stato il — di Dio, it was the will of God; finger's breadth; trifle, small quantity, tiny distance; un — di vino, a drop of wine; non ha due dita di cervello, he hasn't an ounce of sense; essere a un — di fare qualcosa, to be within an ace of doing something; (Rom. antiq.) *digitus*, digit; (astron.) digit, one-twelfth of the sun's apparent diameter.

di·tola *f.* (bot.) *Clavaria flava* (edible lichen).

ditonella *f.* (bot.). See **dittinella**.

di·tono *m.* (mus.) ditone, major third.

†**ditrarre** *tr.* to usurp, to seize; to distract; to detract; to speak ill of; to condemn.

†**ditrazione** *f.* detraction; abasement; fall from power.

ditri·glifo *m.* (archit.) ditriglyph.

ditroche·o *m.* (class. prosod.) ditrochee, ditrochaeus.

ditta[1] *f.* business firm, commercial house; company, concern; (leg.) firm name or style; Spettabile Ditta…, Messrs So-and-So.

†**ditta**[2] *f.* fortune, luck.

ditta·fono *m.* dictaphone.

dit·tamo *m.* (bot.) burning bush, *Dictamnus albus*.

†**dittare** *vb.* and derivs. See **dettare**.

dittat-ore *m.* dictator; †one who dictates or inspires. **-oriale** *adj.* (neol.) see **dittatorio**. **-o·rio** *adj.* dictatorial. (**-oriamente** *adv.*) **-ura** *f.* dictatorship.

dit·teri *m.pl.* (ent.) diptera.

†**ditte·rio** *m.* pulpit; cathedra.

ditterite *f.* (med.). See **difterite**.

dit·tero *adj.* (archit.) dipterous; *n.m.* dipteros.

dit·tico *m.* (antiq.; liturg.; art) diptych.

dittinella *f.* (bot.) *Daphne gnidium*.

†**ditto** *part.* of **dire**, q.v.; *n.m.* saying, utterance.

dit·tola *f.* (bot.). See **ditola.**

dittong-are [A 2] *tr.* (ling.) to diphthong, to diphthongize, to pronounce or write as a diphthong; to make a diaeresis of, to pronounce (a diphthong) as two distinct syllables; *intr.* (aux. avere) to form a diphthong. **-ato** *part. adj.* made into a diphthong, diphthongized. **-atamente** *adv.* pronunziare **-atamente**, to pronounce as a diphthong.

ditton·gico *adj.* (ling.) diphthongal.

ditton-go *m.* (*pl.* **-ghi**) diphthong. (NOTE: Italian grammarians classify diphthongs as either *fissi*, invariable, or *mobili*, variable, those which are replaced by simple vowels when unaccented or when followed by two consonants, e.g. 'muovo' in contrast with 'moviamo', 'mosso'.)

diur-esi *f.* (med.) diuresis. **-e·tico** *adj., n.m.* (med.) diuretic.

†diurnale *adj.* See under **diurno.**

diurna·rio *m.* See under **diurno.**

diurnista *m.* See under **diurno.**

diurn-o *adj.* diurnal, of day, belonging to daytime; (theatr.) spettacolo **—**, matinée, afternoon performance; albergo **—**, 'daytime hotel' (establishment providing 'wash and brush up', bath, shave, etc., during the day only); (poet.) la **-a** lampa, l'astro **—**, the lamp of day, the sun; (zool.) diurnal; (bot.) ephemeral; daily, everyday; *n.m.* (liturg.) diurnal. **-a** *f.* (theatr.) matinée, afternoon performance. **†-ale** *adj.* diurnal; *n.m.* journal, diary. **-a·rio** *m.* (Rom. antiq.) compiler of *acta diurna.* **-ista** *m.* (comm.; leg.) person employed by the day; day-labourer.

diuturn-ità *f.* long duration, lastingness. **-o** *adj.* lasting, long-continued. (**-amente** *adv.*)

div-a *f.* goddess, female divinity; *prima donna*; star of stage, screen or television. **-etta** *f.* second-rate star of stage, screen or television, starlet; music-hall artist; artist at a café-chantant (see also **divo[1]**).

divag-are [A 2] *intr.* (aux. avere) to ramble, to roam; (fig.) to wander from the point, to divagate; *tr.* to entertain, to divert, to distract; *rfl.* to amuse oneself. **-amento** *m.* wandering; straying. **-ante** *part. adj.* wandering; diverting. **-ato** *part. adj.* distrait. **-azione** *f.* divagation; straying, digression; amusement, recreation.

†divallare *intr., rfl.* to flow down; to descend; (of rain) to pour.

divamp-are [A 1] *intr.* (aux. essere) to flare up, to burst into flame; to spread like wildfire; (fig.) to rage; **-ava dallo sdegno**, he was blazing with rage; **†***tr.* to set fire to; to burn. **-amento** *m.* flare up, outbreak of fire. **-ante** *part. adj.* flaring, blazing; burning; fuoco **-ante**, fire that spreads rapidly; (fig.) that increases and spreads with dangerous rapidity. **-ato** *part. adj.* burning hot, blazing.

divano *m.* couch, divan, settee; (Oriental hist.) Divan.

†divari-are *intr.* to vary; to be distant; *tr.* to render varied, to vary. **†-ato** *part. adj.* varied; various; variegated; different. **†-azione** *f.* variation; discrepancy; difference.

divaric-are [A 2 s] *tr.* to open wide, to set apart, to stretch apart; (anat.) to divaricate. **-ato** *part. adj.* wide apart, opened wide (of two things usually close together, e.g. blades of a pair of scissors); a gambe **-ate**, with legs apart; (bot.) divaricate. **-atore** *m.* (surg.) retractor.

diva·rio *m.* difference; variation; discrepancy; †exception; †diversion, recreation.

†dive *adj.* rich, wealthy.

divedere [B 35] *tr.* to see clearly; dare a **—**, to show clearly, to give to understand, to claim, to pretend.

divel·l-ere [B 31] *tr.* to uproot, to pull up; to eradicate; (agric.) to break up (ground).

diveltare [A 1] *tr.* (agric.) to trench, to dig or plough deep.

divelt-o *part.* of **divellere**, q.v.; *adj.* uprooted; pulled up; (agric.) broken up, trenched; †slender; *n.m.* trenching, (piece of) deep ploughing; lavorare a **—**, to trench-plough.

diven-ire [D 17] *intr.* (aux. essere) to become; to develop into, to grow into, to make; **— rosso**, to turn red, to blush; †to come; †**— alle mani di**, to come into the power of; †**— all'estremo**, to be in sorry plight; †**— a niente**, to come to nothing; †**— in lagrime**, to dissolve into tears; †**— in povertà**, to become impoverished; †**— in tedio di**, to grow weary of; †**— meno**, to disappear; *n.m.* becoming, developing; (philos.) l'eterno **—**, the eternal becoming. **-ente** *part. adj.* becoming; developing. **-uto** *part. adj.* become; developed; †**-uto in ricchezza**, having achieved wealth (cf. **diventare**).

divent-are [A 1] *intr.* (aux. essere) (more pop. than **divenire**, and tending to suggest more sudden or violent change) to become; to change into, to turn into; **— matto**, to go crazy; **— di mille colori**, to turn all the colours of the rainbow; com'è **-ato!**, how he has altered (for the worse)!; †to come; †*tr.* to transform, to change. **-ato** *part. adj.* become; changed into.

divenuto *part.* of **divenire**, q.v.

diver·bio *m.* dispute, altercation; (Lat. comedy) *diverbium*; †(mus.) dialogue for two voices.

diver·g-ere [C def.] *intr.* to diverge; to deviate; (geom.) to be divergent. **-ente** *part. adj.* diverging; divergent; (mil.) batteria **-ente**, gun battery with all-round arc of fire. **-enza** *f.* divergence; **-enza di opinioni**, difference of opinion.

†diverre *vb.* and derivs. See **divellere.**

diversamente *adv.* See under **diverso.**

†diversare[1] *intr.* to be different, to differ.

†diversare[2] *vb.* and derivs. See **versare.**

diversific-are [A 2 s] *intr.* (aux. essere), *rfl.* to be different; to differ, to vary; **— di poco**, to differ only a little; *tr.* to make different; to make a difference to, to change the character of. **-ato** *part. adj.* distinguished, distinct. **-azione** *f.* difference, distinction.

diversione *f.* diversion; turning aside, change in direction; by-pass; deflection; diversion (of stream, traffic or road); bend, turn (in road); digression; (mil.) tactical diversion; amusement, pastime, recreation; †destruction.

diversità *f.* difference, diversity; variety; †controversy; †essere in **— di**, to possess several kinds of; †strangeness; †cruelty; †fury, vehemence; †adversity.

diversivo *adj.* distracting; diverting; *n.m.* distraction; diversion; remedy; means of escape; tactful change of subject; (hydr. eng.) diversion channel.

divers-o *adj.* (very) different; la verità è **-a** dalla menzogna, truth and falsehood are completely different things; varying, changeful; †strange; †uncouth; †extravagant; †incredible; †horrible; †cruel; †disgusting, repellent; *pl.* various, several; **-i giorni fa**, some days ago; *n.m.pl.* sundries, miscellaneous; (admin.) any other business; *adv.* differently. **-amente** *adv.* in a different way, otherwise; if not; else; venite! **-amente vi fo arrestare**, come along, or I'll have you arrested.

†diver·tere *vb.* and derivs. See **divertire.**

diverti·colo *m.* byway, bypath; subterfuge; digression; (anat.) diverticulum.

divert-ire [D 1] *tr.* to turn aside, to deflect; to divert; to distract; to amuse, to entertain; †*intr.* to go out of one's way, to take the wrong turning; *rfl.* to amuse oneself, to enjoy oneself; to be amused; to stray. **-ente** *part. adj.* entertaining, amusing; sarebbe **-ente**, it would be fun. **-evole** *adj.* see **divertente.** **-imento** *m.* amusement; pastime, recreation; per **-imento**, for fun, to amuse oneself; (theatr.) entertainment; (mus.) divertimento; episode (in a fugue); †digression; †distraction.

divetta *f.* See under **diva.**

divett-are [A 1 c] *tr.* to lop, to pollard. (**-ato** *part. adj.*)

divezz-are [A 1 c] *tr.* to disaccustom, to break of a habit; to wean. **-amento** *m.* breaking of a habit; weaning. **-ato** *part. adj.* out of the habit; grown unaccustomed; weaned. **-atura** *f.* breaking of a habit; weaning.

divezzo *apocop. part.* of **divezzare**, q.v.; *adj.* out of practice; out of training; grown unaccustomed; broken (of a habit); weaned.

†diviare *vb.* and derivs. See **deviare.**

diviat-o *adj.* quick; straight; *adv.* straightway, forthwith, at once. (**-amente** *adv.*)

dividendo *m.* (math.) dividend; (finan.) stabilire un **—**, to declare a dividend; **— provvisorio**, interim dividend; (leg.) dividend; *pro rata* share, of shareholder in distributed profits of limited company or of creditor in an insolvency.

divi·d-ere [C 3] *tr.* to divide; to distribute; to share out; to separate, to part; (math.) to divide; **— un'opinione**, to share an opinion; *rfl.* to be divided; to split; to be separated; to part. (**-itore** *m.* **-itrice** *f.*)

†divietare *vb.* and derivs. See **vietare.**

divieto[1] *m.* prohibition; **— di sosta**, no parking; **— di transito**, no thoroughfare; **— d'affissione**, stick no bills; (eccl.) laws of fasting and abstinence; (leg.) strict or absolute prohibition; il Capo dello Stato può accordare dispensa da questo **—**, the Head of the State can grant dispensation from this strict prohibition; **— al giudice**

divieto (*cont.*)
di private informazioni, absolute prohibition of private information to the judge; — di alienazione, restraint upon alienation (C.C.); †confine, boundary; †(eccl.) interdict; †essere in —, to be prohibited; †aver —, to be ineligible for election to a magistracy; †aver — da, to be barred from entering; †aver — di, to be unable to, to be incapable of; †fare —, to prohibit; †tenere in —, to refuse admittance to rival merchants.

†**divieto²** *apocop. part.* of **divietare**, q.v.

†**divimare** *tr.* to loose, to free; to disentwine; *rfl.* to get loose, to be freed, to be disentwined.

†**divinale** *adj.* See **divino**.

divin-are [A I] *tr.* to divine; to foresee; to predict. **-ato** *part. adj.* divined; foretold. **-atore** *m.* diviner, prophet. (**-atrice** *f.*) **-ato·ria** *f.* divination. **-ato·rio** *adj.* divinatory; verga ~atoria, divining-rod, dowsing-rod. **-azione** *f.* divination; prophecy; intuition.

divincol-are [A I s] *tr.* to twist; to shake; to wriggle; to wag (tail); *rfl.*, †*intr.* to writhe, to wriggle; to struggle; to shake, to tremble; to untie oneself; to get free. **-a·bile** *adj.* flexible. **-amento** *m.* wriggling, writhing; twist. **-azione** *f.* twisting, writhing. **-ìo** *m.* (*pl.* **-i·i**) continual wriggling; prolonged struggling.

divinità *f. indecl.* divinity; god; la Divinità, the Divinity, God; (hyperb.) exquisite thing or person; le —, the gods; †theology; †divination, prophecy.

divinizz-are [A I] *tr.* to deify, to divinize, to treat as divine; to sublimate; to glorify; to beatify. **-ato** *part. adj.* deified; glorified; beatified. **-azione** *f.* deification; apotheosis; glorification.

divin-o *adj.* divine; godlike; sacred; sublime; (also fig.); †divining, prophetic; †*n.m.* theologian, divine. (**-amente** *adv.*)

divis-a¹ *f.* parting (in hair); division; sharing; (herald.) bar; †division, separation; †strife; †exception; †order, arrangement; †fare — dall'amore di, to part from, to break with; †fare —, to be divided, to split, to disagree; †in —, rent, at loggerheads, split. **-a·ia** *f.* woman who makes parting in wigs.

divisa² *f.* uniform; in —, wearing uniform; (mil.; naut.) — di gala (officer's), full dress; gran —, best uniform; — ordinaria, day dress; (ratings) — estiva, summer uniform; — invernale, winter uniform; — di fatica, fatigue dress; — di professore, academic dress; livery; heraldic arms, device; family motto; slogan; (finan.; leg.) foreign exchange, foreign currency; †semblance; †manner, way; †beauty, grace, lovely movements or gestures.

†**divisa³** *f.* See **avviso**.

divis-are [A I] *intr.* (*aux.* avere) to plan, to design, to intend; to propose; ho ~ato di andare, I have planned to go; †to converse; *tr.* to conceive, to design, to plan; to ornament; to divide by colour; to design in heraldic colours; †to separate, to divide; †to order; †to distinguish; †to detail, to relate in an orderly way; †to explain, to demonstrate; †to judge, to consider, to hold; †to invent, to discover; †to imagine. **-amento** *m.* design; intention; thought; project, plan; †division; †distinction; †difference; †treatise, discourse; †pattern, emblem, distinguishing sign; †(rhetor.) analysis, subdivision; †clothing. **-ato** *part. adj.* planned; designed; †diverse, different, dissimilar; †varied; †of various colours; †striped; †clothed; †transformed, disguised; †separated; †distant. †**-atore** *m.* organizer; judge, arbiter.

divisi·bil-e *adj.* divisible; (math.) divisible. (**-mente** *adv.*) **-ità** *f.* divisibility, divisibleness.

división-e *f.* division; distinction; disagreement; chiedere di votare per —, to move that a separate vote be taken; chiedere il voto per —, to ask for a vote article by article; — delle sale, allocation of rooms; (math.) division; (eng.) indexing (on machine tool); (leg.) division; distribution; partition; severance; — del patrimonio, distribution of the estate; — della comunione, severance of the tenancy-in-common; — di terre, partition of lands; (admin.) division; department; capo —, head of a division or department; head clerk, chief clerk; (mil.) division (in Italian army peace establishment this consists of a brigade of infantry or grenadiers, and a regiment of field artillery under a mobilizing inspector whose responsibility covers a province); — blindata, armoured division; (mil. hist.) — celere, cavalry division; (naut.) naval division; ammiraglio di —, vice-admiral; generale di —, major-general; (typ.) hyphen (at end of line). **-ale** *adj.* (mil.) divisional. **-a·rio** *m.* (mil.) general officer commanding a division. **-ismo** *m.* (paint.) pointillism. **-ista** *m., f., adj.* (paint.) pointillist.

divisivo *adj.* divisive.

divismo *m.* (neol.) cult of film stars or stage celebrities; fan mentality.

divis-o *part.* of **dividere**, q.v.; *adj.* dividend; distinct; split, separated, severed; at variance; *pl.* (mus.) divided (to indicate the subdivision of a group of string-players); †contrary; *adv. phr.* †in —, privately, in camera; †per —, separately; †per non —, without division, in common, impartially; *n.m.* (paint.) drawing, design; (archit.) compartment; †thought; intention, design; †opinion; †essere —, to seem, to appear; †division. **-ore** *m.* (math.) divisor; massimo comun ~ore, greatest common factor; (naut.) factor legally established for use in calculation of tonnage from quotient of ships' dimensions; (eng.) indexing head. **-o·rio** *adj.* (*m.pl.* **-o·ri**) dividing, separating; (leg.) dividing; muro ~orio, party wall; sorte ~oria, divisory lots; *n.m.* party wall; wooden screen; glass partition in a car between the driver and passengers.

†**divi·zia** *f.* abundance, plenty; a gran —, in plenty; *pl.* wealth; possessions.

divo¹ *adj.* divine; of God; of a god; deified; superb, magnificent; exalted, illustrious; *n.m.* god, divinity; (male) celebrity of stage, screen or television; — di cinelandia, film star (cf. **diva**).

†**divo²** *adj.* rich, wealthy.

†**divolgare** *vb.* and derivs. See **divulgare**.

†**divoluto** *adj.* lapsed, no longer valid.

divor-are [A I, A I c] *tr.* to devour; to eat up; — con gli occhi, to eye greedily, to gaze intently at; — la strada, to rush along, to eat up the miles; to waste, to squander, to destroy, to consume; to read at great speed, to devour. **-ante** *part. adj.* devouring; greedy; famished; *n.m., f.* devourer. **-azione** *f.* devouring; swallowing up; consumption. **-ato** *part. adj.* devoured; swallowed; consumed; destroyed. **-atore** *m.* devourer; destroyer; glutton; consumer. (**-atrice** *f.*) ~atore di libri, avid reader.

divorzi-are [A 4] *intr.* (*aux.* avere, *prep.* da) to divorce from; — dal marito, to divorce one's husband; — dalla moglie, to divorce one's wife; *rfl.* to get a divorce; to have a divorce. **-ato** *part. adj.* divorced; *n.m.* divorced person. **-ata** *f.* divorcée, divorced wife.

divor·zio *m.* (*pl.* **divorzi**) divorce; fare — da, to divorce; Tribunale dei Divorzi, Divorce Court; causa di —, divorce suit, divorce proceedings; (fig.) detachment, separation; far — dal giuoco, to give up gambling; far — dal buon senso, to say good-bye to common sense, to leave common sense behind.

divoto¹ *adj.* and derivs. See **devoto**; †*n.m.* devotee.

†**divoto²** *adj.* empty; hollow.

†**divoto³** *m.* spiritual father.

divulg-are [A 2] *tr.* to publish; to make known; to spread; to popularize; to divulge, to disclose. (**-amento** *m.*) **-ativo** *adj.* that makes known, that spreads (information); libro ~ativo, popular manual. (**-atore** *m.* **-atrice** *f.*) **-ato** *part. adj.* published; circulated; widespread, well-known. **-azione** *f.* publication; publishing; spreading; popularization; disclosure.

divulsióne *f.* (surg.) divulsion.

†**divuoto** *adj.* See **divoto²**.

diziona·r-io *m.* dictionary; — geografico, gazetteer; (fig.) un — vivente, a walking encyclopaedia. **-ista** *m., f.* lexicographer.

dizióne¹ *f.* word, part of speech; diction, wording; enunciation, delivery; recitation.

†**dizione²** *f.* power; territory under jurisdiction.

D lasolre *m. indecl.* (mus.) D la sol re (the name of a note in the Guidonian hexachord system which remained in use till the end of the seventeenth century); †the note D; †the key of D.

do¹ *m.* (mus.) do (i.e. first degree of scale), doh; the note C; the key of C.

do² *pres. indic. 1st pers. sing.* of **dare**, q.v.

do³ *adv.* (Tusc. pop.) where; o in — tu vai?, where are you off to?

†**do⁴.** See **due**.

†**doa·gio** *m.* kind of cloth made in Douai.

†**doana** *f.* See **dogana**.

doa·rio *m.* (leg.) dower, annuity, endowment, of a widow; †dowry.

dobla *f.* (numis.) dobla, double; doubloon.

dobl-are [A I] *tr.* (text.) to plait down; †see **doppiare**. **-ag·gio** *m.* (text.) plaiting down; (naut.) tabling (strengthening cloth in awning or doubling plate in hull construction).

†**dobletto** *m.* doublet.

†**doblo** *adj.* and deriv. See **doppio**.

doblóne *m.* (numis.) doubloon; †doublet.

†**dobretto** *m.* doublet.

doccia, dǫccia *f.* (*pl.* **docce, dǫcce**) douche; shower; shower-bath; (fig.) discouragement; (bldg.) gulley, gutter, spout; jet; mill-race; — d'aria, gas-jet; — fredda, cold shower(-bath), (fig.) wet blanket, check to enthusiasm, cold douche; — scozzese, alternate hot and cold showers, (fig.) playing fast and loose, blowing alternately hot and cold; (zool.) — neurale, neural groove.

doccia·io *m.* plumber; man who repairs gutters and spouting.

docci-are [A 3 c] *tr.* to shower; to douche; to pour forth; *intr.* (*aux.* avere) to pour, to flow. **-ante** *part. adj.* flowing, flooding. **-atura** *f.* douching; douche.

†**doc·cio** *m.* See **doccia**.

doccion-e *m.* drainpipe, conduit, gargoyle, spout; gorget; †idler; †admirer, cicisbeo. **-ata** *f.* (Tusc.) drain.

doc-ente *adj.* teaching; *n.m., f.* teacher, instructor; libero —, lecturer; qualified tutor; (leg.) person qualified to teach at University level (having the title of Professore but whose lectures are usually not compulsory and are unpaid). **-enza** *f.* teaching, instruction; libera -enza, University teaching degree; competence to teach.

†**docere** *tr., intr.* to teach, to instruct, to educate.

docet-i *m.pl.* (rel. hist.) Docetae, Docetists. **-ismo** *m.* Docetism.

do·cil-e *adj.* docile; apt; manageable; tractable; biddable; amenable; materia —, workable material. **-mente** *adv.* docilely; amenably. **-ità** *f.* docility; submissiveness; tractableness.

dock *m. indecl.* (naut.) dock; (comm., usu. *pl.*) docks, warehouses.

doc·mio *m.* (class. prosod.) dochmiac; (zool.) hookworm, *Uncinaria americana*.

document-o *m.* document; certificate; proof, evidence; voucher; (leg.) document, written instrument on paper, deed; legalizzare un —, to authenticate or legalize a document; estratto di —, abstract of a document; *pl.* documents; records; papers; instructions; writings, precepts; provare con -i, to prove by documentary evidence; -i di causa, documents of, papers in, a case; esame di -i, inspection of documents; -i giustificativi, supporting documents, vouchers; -i personali, identity papers; †instruction, lesson, teaching. **-ale** *adj.* (leg.) documentary; prova -ale, documentary evidence. **-are** [A 1 c] *tr.* to document, to support with documentary evidence; *rfl.* to collect evidence; to do research. **-a·rio** *adj.* (leg.) documentary; (cinem.) pellicola -aria, film -ario, documentary film; *n.m.* documentary film. **-arista** *m.* (cinem.) director or maker of documentary films. **-ato** *part. adj.* documented; supported by written evidence. **-azione** *f.* documentation; documenting.

dodda *m. indecl.* (Tusc., fam.) self-important man (esp. youth); fa il —, he gives himself airs.

dodec-a·dico *adj.* (math.) duodecimal. **-ae·dro** *m.* (geom.) dodecahedron. **-ae·drico** *adj.* (geom.) dodecahedral. **-afoni-a** *f.* (mus.) twelve-note system. **-afo·nico** *adj.* (mus.) serie -afonica, twelve-note series, tone-row. **-a·gono** *m.* (geom.) dodecagon. **-ascalmo** *m.* (class. antiq.) twelve-oared boat. **-asil·labo** *adj.* (prosod.) dodecasyllabic; *n.m.* dodecasyllable; -asillabo francese, (French) Alexandrine. **-a·stilo** *adj.* (archit.) dodecastyle.

Dodecaneso *pr.n.m.* Dodecanese.

†**do·deci** *ord. num.* See **dodici**.

dodic-enne *adj.* twelve years old; twelve years long; *n.m., f.* twelve-year-old. **-en·nio** *m.* period of twelve years.

†**dodicentina·ia** *f.* a twelve hundred.

dodicera *f.* (Gk. antiq. naut.) polyreme, having twelve oars in each bank.

dǫdic-i *card. num. indecl.* twelve; — facce (*n.m. sing.*) dodecahedron; *n.m.* the number twelve; il —, the twelfth (in dates); (paperm.) in —, in twelvemo. **-esimale** *adj.* duodecimal. **-ęsimo**, (Rom.) **-e·simo** *ord. num.* twelfth; (bookb.) in -esimo, in duodecimo; *n.m.* twelfth, twelfth part; twelfth person; (paperm.) duodecimo, twelvemo. **-imila** *card. num. indecl.* twelve thousand. **-ino** *m.* (numis.) old Florentine coin of 12 *denari*. **-iǫna** *f.* (naut.) large twelve-oared pleasure boat.

dodone·o *adj.* (Gk. antiq.) Dodonean, of Dodona.

dodrante *m.* (Rom. antiq.) *dodrans*.

dǫga, doga *f.* stave (of cask, etc.); band, stripe; (herald.) vertical stripe on shield; *pl.* striped clothes; †cask; †stole.

†**doga·ia** *f.* depression in the earth; rut.

dogale *adj.* of a doge, dogal; *n.m.* doge's dress.

dogame *m.* collection, pile, of staves (for casks, etc.).

dogan-a *f.* customs, custom-house; (Customs) duty; bonded warehouse; in —, in bond; svincolare merci in —, to clear goods at the Customs; aver sale in —, to have one's head screwed on the right way; (naut.) — di mare, maritime customs office and buildings. **-ale** *adj.* relating to the Customs, of the Customs; visita -ale, Customs inspection; magazzino -ale, bonded warehouse. **-iera** *adj. f.* of the customs. **-iere** *m.* custom-house officer or man.

dog-are [A 2 c, A 2] *tr.* to fit staves on, to stave; to encircle, to curve across (like a stave). (**-amento** *m.*) **-ato** *part. adj.* fitted with staves; adorned with bands or stripes.

dogarẹssa *f.* doge's wife, dogesse, dogaresse.

dogato[1] *m.* See under **doge**.

dogato[2] *part.* of **dogare**, q.v.

dog-e *m.* doge (of Venice or Genoa). **-ato** *m.* dogate; a doge's office, period of office, or territory. **-ia·tico** *m.* status of a doge.

†**do·gio** *m.* See **doge**; see **duca**.

do·gli-a *f.* pain; ache; *pl.* pains in childbirth, labour pains; (vet.) — vecchia, chronic lameness (in a horse). **-anza** *f.*, †**-enza** *f.* complaint; lament; grievance; lamentation; †pain. †**-ente** *adj.* painful; suffering. **-oso** *adj.* grieved, sorrowful, sad, sorry. (**-osamęnte** *adv.*)

do·glio *m.* wooden cask; earthen jar; (zool.) tun-shell, *Dolium galea*.

dogm-a *m.* (Tusc. pron. **domma**) dogma, dogmatic belief; creed; rule, criterion. **-a·tica** *f.* dogmatic theology; dogmatics. **-a·tico** *adj.* dogmatic; opinionated. **-atiṣmo** *m.* dogmatism. **-atista** *m.* dogmatist. **-atiẓẓare** [A 1] *intr.* (*aux.* avere) to dogmatize. **-atolatri·a** *f.* worship of dogma. †**-izzare** *intr.* to dogmatize.

dogo *m.* (*pl.* **doghi**) Irish wolf-hound; (D'Annunzio) bull-dog.

dǫgre *m.* (naut.) Dutch two-masted herring boat, originally of 50–80 tons, worked on Dogger Bank (whence the name), used for coasting and even deep-sea trade.

†**doh** *excl.* alas!; oh!; oh, good!

†**doimè** *excl.* alas!; woe is me!

dolabr-a *f.*, **-o** *m.* (Rom. antiq.) mattock; (Rom. antiq.) sacrificial knife; †carpenter's plane.

†**dol-are** *tr.* to plane, to smooth. †**-ato** *part. adj.* planed, smoothed, smooth, polished.

dǫlc-e *adj.* sweet; farina —, chestnut flour; mangiare amaro e sputar —, to disguise one's resentment; tenere uno a bocca —, to keep someone dangling; acqua —, fresh (not salt) water, soft water; acque -i, soft drinks; radice —, liquorice; soft (of surface, voice, metal); smooth; gentle, easy; (of a slope) gradual; (of weather, climate) mild; delicate, tender; (of a horse) — di bocca, tender in the mouth; dear, sweet, amiable; — nido, home sweet home; la — metà, one's better half, 'the wife'; good-natured, credulous; — di sale, silly, soft; (of wood, etc.) fast burning; (lit. hist.) — stil nuovo, sweet new style of poetry (initiated by Dante in his canzone 'Donne ch'avete intelletto d'amore' but associated also more generally with his predecessors in the love lyric); †(paint.) faint, not emphasized; †violetto —, pale violet; *adv.* sweetly; softly; gently; *n.m.* sweetness; dessert, sweet; sweetmeat, cake; †consolation, joy. **-emẹnte** *adv.* sweetly; gently; tenderly; softly; quietly; imperceptibly. **-etta** *f.* (bot.) corn salad, lamb's lettuce, *Valerianella*. **-etto** *m.* a Piedmontese vine and table-wine. **-ẹzza** *f.* sweetness; softness; smoothness; gentleness; delicacy; yieldingness, good nature; tenderness.

dolcemele *m.* (bot.) spotted deadnettle, *Lamium maculatum*; (mus.) an ancient flute.

dolcestilnov-ista *m.* (lit. hist.) poet of the school of lyric writing known as the 'dolce stil nuovo', q.v. under **dolce**. **-i·stico** *adj.* relating to or characteristic of this school of lyricism.

dolcia *f.* pig's blood.

dolciamaro *adj.* bitter-sweet.

dolciano *m.* (mus.) dolcan (organ-stop).

dolci-a·rio *adj.* (comm.) relating to sweets; industria -aria, sweet-producing industry. **-ere** *m.* confectioner.

dolci-astro *adj.* unhealthily sweet; sickly, mawkish. †**-ato** *adj.* sweet; silly, soft.

dolcibene *m.* (hist.) juggler; *jongleur*.

dolcicanoro *adj.* (poet.) sweetly-singing.

dolcichino *m.* (bot.) earth-almond, rush-nut, *Cyperus esculentus*.

dolcific-are [A 2 s] *tr.* to sweeten, to make sweet; to add sweetening to, to add sugar to. **-ante** *part. adj., n.m.* sweetening. **-ato** *part. adj.* sweetened. **-azione** *f.* adding of sweetening.

dolc·igno *adj.* sweetish, slightly sweet. **-ione** *adj.* too sweet, sickly; simple-minded, gullible; *n.m.* simpleton.

dolci·loquo *adj.* mellifluous, honey-tongued.

dolcimelo *m.* (mus.). See **dolcemele**.

dolcino *m. adj. dim.* of **dolce**, q.v.; slightly sweet; *n.m.* sweet flavour of meat; (agric.) small sweet apple; (mus.) dulcion, a primitive bassoon.

†dolciore *m.* sweetness; delight; eruption of sores on a baby's mouth and skin.

†dolcire *tr.* to sweeten; *intr.* to become sweeter.

dolcisonante *adj.* sweet-sounding.

†dolcitu·dine *f.* sweetness; joy; pleasure; recreation, joyous pastime; licentiousness, wantonness; stupidity.

dolciume *m.* sweetness; excessive sweetness, sickliness; (fig.) mincing manners; *pl.* sweetmeats, sweets.

dolciura *f.* sweetness; mild weather; gentleness (of character).

dol·co *adj.* (*m.pl.* **-chi**) (Tusc.) mild; il tempo si fa **—**, the weather has turned mild; muggy, moist; †soft, malleable; †tractable; †favourable, propitious; *n.m.* mild weather. †**-corare** *tr.* to sweeten; to allay, to mitigate. †**-core** *m.* sweetness; mild weather.

dolente *adj.* See under **dolere**.

dol·ere [B 11] (*aux.* for *pers.* use, essere, avere; for *impers.*, essere only); *intr.* to cause pain, to hurt; to ache; gli duole il capo, his head hurts, he has a headache; *impers.* mi duole che sia morto, I am sorry he is dead; ci duole di non poter venire, we regret that we cannot come; *rfl.* to be sorry; to lament; to take offence; si dolgono che sia venuto, they regret his coming; mi dolgo di non sapere, I am sorry I do not know; non ho di che dolermi, I have nothing to complain about; si duol tutto, he has pains all over. **-ente** *part. adj.* sorry, sorrowful, regretful, mournful, grieved; sono **-ente** di quanto v'è successo, I am distressed at your misfortune; (poet. Dante) la città **—**, the city of Pain, Hell; miserable, unhappy; in pain, aching; †evil, wicked; †la **-ente** stagione, winter.

dolerite *f.* (miner.) dolerite.

dolfinera *f.* (Ven. naut.) harpoon; dolphin striker.

†dolfino *m.* See **delfino**.

dolicchiare [A 3], **doliccicare** [A 2 s] *intr.* (*aux.* essere, avere) (fam.) to cause slight pain; le dolicchia un dito, she has a bit of an ache in her finger.

do·lic-o *m.* (bot.) name of various runner beans, especially species of *Dolichos*.

dolicoce·falo *adj.* (ethn.) dolichocephalic, long-headed.

dolico·nice *m.* (orn.) bobolink, *Dolichonyx oryzivorus*.

dolina *f.* (geog.) sink-hole, cock-pit.

do·lio *m.* See **doglio**.

dol·laro *m.* dollar.

dolly *m. indecl.* (film; telev.) dolly-shot.

dolman *m. indecl.* woman's overcoat with cape and no sleeves (about 1870); hussar style jacket.

dolmen *m. indecl.*, **dolmenno** *m.* dolmen.

dolo¹ *m.* deceit, trickery; (leg.) criminal intent; fraud; deceit; †wrong, wrong-doing.

dolo² *m.* (Tusc. pop.). See **duolo**.

†dolomi·a *f.* (geog.) dolomite.

dolomite *f.* (miner.) dolomite; a rock consisting of dolomite.

Dolom-iti *pr.n.f.pl.* (geog.) Dolomites. **-i·tico** *adj.* relating to the Dolomites.

dol·one *m.* (naut.) bowsprit; square spritsail, jib. **-o·nico** *adj.* (naut.) pertaining to the bowsprit.

dolor-are [A 1 c] *intr.* (*aux.* avere) to be in pain; to be much distressed, to grieve; †to lament, to moan, to express grief; †*tr.* to pain, to cause sorrow to; †to lament, to mourn, to regret; †*rfl.* to grieve. **-ante** *part. adj.* sorrowing (cf. **addolorare**).

dolor-e *m.* pain, ache; letto di **—**, bed of sickness; un **—** acuto, a sharp pain; (fig.) grief, sorrow; tragic emotion; Maria dei **-i**, Our Lady of Sorrows (Dolours). **-ismo** *m.* cult of suffering; belief in pain as purificatory. **-ista** *m.* exponent of the spiritual value of pain.

doloros-o *adj.* painful, aching; sorrowful; grievous, doleful; **— a** dirsi, sad to relate; in pain, suffering; distressed, sorrowing; unfortunate, wretched; †evil; †bad, corrupt; †**— a** me!, alas!, woe is me! **-amente** *adv.* painfully; sorrowfully; grievously; dolefully. **-ità** *f.* painfulness; sorrowfulness.

dolos-o *adj.* (leg.) fraudulent; criminal; fallimento **—**, fraudulent bankruptcy; incendio **—**, arson. **-amente** *adv.* (leg.) fraudulently; with criminal intent; with malice aforethought.

†dolsuto, †dolto *part.* of **dolere**, q.v.

doluto *part.* of **dolere**, q.v.

†dolzain-a *f.*, **-o** *m.* (mus.) a kind of shawm.

†dolze *adj.* and derivs. See **dolce**.

dolzemele *m.* (mus.). See **dolcemele**.

dom *f. indecl.* (bot.) doum palm, *Hyphaene thebaica*.

doma¹ *f.* (Tusc. pop.) break (for young horses).

Doma² *pr.n.f.* shortened form of Domenica (woman's name).

doma·bile *adj.* See under **domare**.

domanda *f.* question; fare, rivolgere una **—**, to put a question; request; dare corso a una **—**, to comply with a request; accogliere, esaudire una **—**, to grant a request; ho fatto così per sua **—**, I did so at his request; application; dietro **—**, on application; **— d'impiego**, application for a job; (leg.) claim; demand; petition; far **— per**, to apply for; **— giudiziale**, claim (at law); proporre **— al giudice competente**, to put forward a claim to the competent Court; trascrizione delle domande giudiziali, registration of actions (C.C.); (econ.) **— e offerta**, supply and demand.

domand-are [A 1] *tr.* to ask; to ask for; to request; to crave; to demand; le **-ò** scusa, he begged her pardon; domandagli di venire, ask him to come; **— uno**, to ask for someone; **— di uno**, to inquire after someone; c'è qualcuno che **-a** di lei, there's someone asking for you; **— di una cosa**, to ask about a thing; non se ne **-a**, there's no question about it; ne ho **-ato** a tutti, I have asked everyone about it (or him); **-o e dico!**, well, I ask you!, well, really! (in surprise or indignation); †to name, to call, to nickname; *rfl.* to ask oneself, to wonder; **-arsi di**, to wonder about; to be called, to answer to the name of; (naut.) to sing (of hawsers overtaut).

domani *adv.* tomorrow; in the future; **— sera**, tomorrow evening; doman l'altro, the day after tomorrow; **— a otto**, tomorrow week; oggi o **—**, before long, one of these days; da oggi a **—**, all of a sudden, in a moment; (iron.) **—!**, never!, certainly not!; *n.m.* il **—**, the morrow, the next day; lo vidi il **—** della tua partenza, I saw him the day after you left; un **—**, some day.

dom-are [A 1 c] *tr.* to tame; to break in; to subdue; to master, to curb; to check, to control; to get under control; to 'break in' (new garments, etc.); to work the newness out of (shoes, linen); to wear out. **-a·bile** *adj.* tameable; workable, malleable. **-ato** *part. adj.* tamed; broken in; subdued; (of a fire) under control. **-atore** *m.* tamer; conqueror. **-atrice** *f.* conqueress; female tamer (of lions, etc.); break (cf. **doma¹**).

domattina *adv.* tomorrow morning.

domeneddi·o *m.* See **domineddio**.

domenic-a *f.* Sunday; esser battezzato in **—**, to be a fool; parlare la lingua della **—**, to talk affectedly; **— delle Palme**, †**— dell'Olivo**, †**— d'Olivo**, Palm Sunday; **— in Albis**, Low Sunday; **— di Pentecoste**, Whitsunday. **-ale** *adj.* (of) Sunday; riposo **-ale**, Sunday rest; trovarsi oziosi nella città **-ale**, to have nothing to do in town on Sunday; lettera **-ale**, Dominical letter; orazione **-ale**, the Lord's Prayer.

domenican-a *f.* (eccl.) Dominican nun. **-o** *adj.* (eccl.) Dominican; *n.m.* Dominican friar; Dominican priest; (orn.) a black and white pigeon; goldeneye; (ent.) louse, *Pediculus humanus*.

domenichino *m.* (joc.) footman or other servant hired for Sundays only; affected and tiresome person.

Domenico *pr.n.m.* Dominic.

dome·stica *f.* maid, servant.

domesticamente *adv.* See under **domestico**.

domestic-are [A 2 s] *tr.* to tame, to domesticate; to cultivate (plants). **-a·bile** *adj.* tameable, trainable. **-ato** *part. adj.* tamed, domesticated; (of plants) cultivated.

domestichezza *f.* intimacy, close association, friendly behaviour; trattare uno con **—**, to treat someone with great friendliness, to treat a person as one of the family; (zool.) domestication (of animals); (bot.) cultivation.

domesticità *f.* domesticity.

domes·tic-o *adj.* domestic; of the house; of the family or household; farsi **—** con uno, to become intimate with someone; simple, homely; alla **-a**, without ceremony; (eccl.) prelato **—**, Domestic Prelate; (industr.) operaio **—**, home worker, outworker; (zool.) domestic; (bot.; agric.) cultivated; *n.m.* intimated friend; (hist.)

domestic-o (*cont.*)
household official, domestic; Gran —, Great Domestic; servant, manservant. **-aménte** *adj.* domestically. **-ato** *m.* (Byz. hist.) office of Domestic.

†domeˑvole *adj.* docile, tameable.

domiciliare¹ *adj.* (leg.) domiciliary; perquisizione —, police search of a house; visita —, domiciliary visit.

domiciliˑare² [A 4] *tr.* (leg.) to domicile; *rfl.* to take up one's residence, to make one's home, to settle; (joc.) to be never off the doorstep. **-ataˑrio** *m.* (leg.) householder care of whom a party has chosen his residence. **-ato** *adj.* residing, living; (leg.) domiciled, resident.

domiciˑlio *m.* domicile, place of residence; (comm.) franco a —, carriage free; (leg.) domicile; address, place where a person has established the principal centre of his affairs and interests; — coatto, forced residence; d'ignoto —, of no known address; violazione di —, house-breaking; — elettivo, — detto, legal residence of choice (e.g. address for service); — politico, political domicile or residence; — commerciale, business address; — legale, legal residence; — legale di società, registered office.

domicilliaˑrio *adj.* (leg.) domiciliary.

†domila, †domilia *ord. num.* two thousand.

†domina *f.* lady; mistress; ruler.

domin-are [A I S] *intr.* (*aux.* avere) to hold sway, to be dominant; to rule; to prevail; to reign; to be domineering; *tr.* to dominate; to master; to overpower; to sway; to control completely; il monte -a il paese, the mountain towers above the town. **-aˑbile** *adj.* controllable, manageable. **-ante** *part. adj.* dominant; prevailing; fattore -ante, leading factor; outstanding; chief; città -ante, capital, ruling city; (meteor.) prevailing (of winds); (mus.) dominant; *n.f.* capital city; (mus.) dominant. **-ato** *part. adj.* dominated; ruled; overpowered; †*n.m.* domination. **-atore** *m.* ruler, commander, master; conqueror; *adj.* dominating, commanding. (**-atrice** *f.*) **-azióne** *f.* sway, rule, ascendancy, dominance; (theol.) Domination.

doˑmine (Lat. vocative *n.*, used in a few *excl.*) Lord!; — aiutaci, Heaven help us!; chi — è?, who on earth is he?; †priest, parson.

Dominéddiˑo *pr.n.m.* (colloq.) God Almighty, the good Lord.

dominicale *adj.* (leg.) dominial, belonging to the landlord; diritti dominicali, landowner's rights, landlord's rights.

dominicano *adj.* relating to San Domingo (Central Amer. Republic).

†domiˑnico *adj.* of Our Lord.

domiˑn-io *m.* (*pl.* -i) rule, sway, power, command; mastery (of a language); — di sè stesso, self-control; territory ruled or held, dominion, domain; cosa di — pubblico, public property, (fig.) not a secret, public knowledge; entrato nel — della storia, belonging to the realm of history; (leg.) dominion, rule, power; ownership; domain; — utile, usufruct, possession and enjoyment of land owned by another; — assoluto, absolute ownership, fee simple; — della corona, crown property; (of books, etc.) di — pubblico, no longer copyright; a thing in the public domain; a matter of common knowledge; — diretto, absolute ownership of the fee simple of land in the possession of another; — durante la vita, life interest, tenancy for life.

doˑmino¹ *m. indecl.* domino (garment or person at masquerade); the game of dominoes; one of the pieces; the whole set of pieces; fare al —, to play dominoes; far —, to win; †priest's hooded cape.

†doˑmino² *m.* master, lord.

†domino *m.* See **dominio**.

†doˑmito *part.* of **domare**, q.v.

domma *m.* and derivs. See **dogma**.

dommas-co *m.* (*m.pl.* -chi) and derivs. See **damasco**.

domo¹ *m.* See **duomo**.

doˑmo² *apocop. part.* of **domare**, q.v.

domo³ (Lat. ablative *n.*, used in two phrases, joc.) in — Petri, in prison; pro — sua, on his own behalf; (med.) phrase used on prescriptions made out by a doctor for his own family, and on which it is customary for the chemist to allow a discount.

†domoˑnio *m.* See **demonio**.

don¹, doˑn *m.* (title) Don; (of monks) Dom. NOTE: The title 'Don' belongs in a special way to members of princely and ducal families. It is followed by the Christian name, with or without surname. Used of the head of the family, 'Don Tommaso A.' is an alternative title, rather less formal than 'il Principe A.', 'il Duca A.'; used of a son, it is the normal title. Some noble families have the right to 'Don' but no further title. Under Spanish influence,

'Don' was once used more extensively, and it is still a common honorific in S. Italy (esp. Naples) and Sicily. 'Don' is also the normal title for secular priests. Here too it should strictly be followed by the Christian name, but is now often used with surname only. The ecclesiastical 'Don' also does duty for the monastic 'Dom' of Benedictines, Carthusians and Cistercians. In all these uses the use of a capital D is optional (cf. **donna**).

don² *onomat.* don don, ding dong.

†don³ *adv.* See **donde**.

†donagione *f.* See under **donare**.

don-are [A I C] *tr.* to present, to bestow, to give, to donate; (leg.) to donate, to bestow; to give; to confer as a gift; (fig.) to concede, to allow; anche -ando quel che si può alla sua giovinezza, making all allowances for his youth; *intr.* (*aux.* avere) to suit, to go well with, to be becoming, to improve the appearance of; il vestito nero le -a, she looks well in black; quel cappello ti -a, that hat suits you. **-aˑbile** *adj.* fit to give. **†-agione** *f.* gift; donation. **-ante** *part. adj.* giving, donating, bestowing; *n.m., f.* donor, giver, bestower; (leg.) donor. **-ataˑrio** *m.* (leg.) donee. **-ativo** *m.* (Rom. hist.) donative; bounty, largess; (hist.) 'gift' of subject to ruler (equivalent to extra tax); present, offering. **-ato** *part. adj.* given, donated, bestowed; a caval -ato non si guarda in bocca, don't look a gift horse in the mouth. **-atore** *m.* giver, bestower; -atore di sangue, blood-donor; (leg.) donor. (**-atrice** *f.*) **-azióne** *f.* donation, gift, present; (hist.) Donazione di Costantino, Donation of Constantine; (leg.) donation, gift of personal property or personalty; transfer; contratto di -azione, deed of gift.

donaˑrio *m.* (class. antiq.) temple treasury; (rel.) votive offering.

donato¹ *part.* of **donare**, q.v.

Donat-o² *pr.n.m.* Donatus; (punning provb.) San — dà in capo a San Giusto, bribery gets the better of justice; Latin grammar book. **-ello** *m. dim.* small grammar. **-iˑsmo** *m.* (rel. hist.) Donatism. **-ista** *m.* (rel. hist.) Donatist.

†donche *adv.* See **dunque**.

donchisciott-ésco *adj.* (*m.pl.* -éschi) quixotic (from the name, **Don Chisciòtte**, Don Quixote); **-iˑsmo** *m.* quixotry.

donde *interr., rel. adv.* whence, from where; of which, from which, wherewith; wherefore, why; aver ben —, to have good reason; — che, from wherever; for whatever cause, †to the place from which.

dondola *f.* rocking-chair; †rocking; †waste of time, idleness; †starsi a —, to pass one's time in idleness.

dondol-are [A I SC] *tr.* to rock, to swing, to shake backwards and forwards; to dangle; to keep waiting, to put off (e.g. a creditor); *intr.* (*aux.* avere) to swing, to sway, to rock; mi -a la testa, my head swims; *rfl.* to swing; to sway; to oscillate; to hang loosely, to droop and swing; to lounge about, to idle. **-aménto** *m.* swinging, swaying, rocking. **-ante** *part. adj.* swinging, swaying, rocking. **-ato** *part. adj.* swung, rocked; (fig.) put off. **-iˑo** *m.* (*pl.* -ii) continuous swaying, swinging, or rocking.

dondolino *m.* (bot.) *Coronilla emerus.*

dondol-o *m.* swinging object; plaything; dangling ornament; orologio a —, pendulum-clock; sedia a —, rocking-chair; cavallo a —, rocking-horse; stare a —, to dawdle about. **-óna** *f.* woman lounger; rocking-chair. **-óne** *m.* idler, loafer; *adv.* see **dondoloni**. **-óni** *adv.* swinging; dangling; lounging(ly), idly, indolently.

†dondora *f.* (mus.) ancient musical instrument (probably a corruption of **pandora**, q.v.).

dongióne *m.* (hist.) donjon.

Dongiovanni, Don Giovanni *pr.n.m.* Don Juan; fare il —, to play the lady-killer. **-iˑsmo** *m.* libertinage.

donn-a *f.* woman; si è fatta — e bellina, she has grown up into a pretty girl; — fatale, femme fatale; — crisi, thin fashionable type of woman of the 1930's; — cannone, fat woman (e.g. at a fair); (provb.) nè — nè tela al lume di candela, don't choose a wife or linen by candle-light; -e e buoi de' paesi tuoi, choose wives and cattle from your own village; (vulg.) andare a -e, to whore; — di strade, street-walker; buona —, good woman, (euphem.) loose woman; cara la mia —, my good woman; vestiti da —, women's clothes; una voce di —, a woman's voice; malattie delle -e, women's diseases; married woman; lady; — di casa, housewife, woman exclusively devoted to family life; servant; maid; — di camera, chambermaid; — a ore, daily woman; — di servizio, daily woman, charwoman; — di mezzo, woman for heavy work, maid-of-all-work; — pesce, mermaid; (fam., Tusc.) wife; — novella, bride;

donn-a (*cont.*)

le mie -e, my womenfolk; (poet.) mistress, beloved, lady; (cards) queen; (theatr.) prima —, prima donna; Nostra Donna, Our Lady; (title) Donna. NOTE: As a title, used before Christian names, with or without surname, 'Donna' has much wider application than 'Don', q.v., 'Donna Elena B.' being a correct style for any 'nobildonna', whether single or married, the wife or daughter of a prince, duke, marquis, count or baron; if married to a commoner she adds her maiden name after (or before) her husband's surname. The Italian style thus overlaps the English styles 'the Duchess of B.', 'Lady B.', 'Lady Helen B.' and 'the Hon. Helen B.'. In recent times the title has been granted to the wives of Cabinet Ministers. In the south of Italy there is a very wide courtesy use of 'Donna', much like 'Signora' elsewhere. Used of Benedictine nuns, 'Donna' corresponds to 'Dame'. In all these cases, the use of a capital D is optional (cf. **don**). **-ac·chera** *f. pejor.*, **-ac·cola** *f. pejor.* low vulgar woman. **-ac·cia** *f. pejor.* slut. **-ai(u)olo** *m.* lady-killer; flirt; *adj.* promiscuous; gallant. †**-eare** *intr.* to flirt; to play the gallant; (fig.; poet.) to be enamoured; **-eare con**, to beguile; to woo; *rfl.* to flirt. †**-eggiare** *intr.* to be the mistress, to be in command. †**-eri·e** *f.pl.* feminine behaviour. **-esco** *adj.* (*m.pl.* **-eschi**) womanly; feminine; relating to women; lavori -eschi, domestic tasks or feminine occupations such as embroidery, etc.; †lady-like, aristocratic, high-bred; †inclined to dally with women. **-escamente** *adv.* in a womanly fashion; with womanly dignity, with the authority of a woman accustomed to command; graciously. **-etta** *f. dim.* little woman; girl; farsi -etta, to be growing up, to be approaching womanhood. **-icciuola** *f. dim.* stupid woman, woman with a petty mind; woman in humble conditions; (of a man) petty-minded gossip; coward. **-ina** *f. dim.* dear little woman; sensible little girl. **-ona** *f. augm.* overgrown girl. **-one** *m. augm.* tall, big-boned woman.

†**donno** *m.* master, lord; ruler; don; man, gentleman; *adj.* commanding, ruling; in command, in control.

don·nola *f.* (zool.) weasel, *Mustela nivalis.*

dono *m.* gift; in —, as a gift; endowment; offering; i doni della terra, the fruits of the earth; il — della parola, eloquence, the gift of the gab; i doni dello Spirito Santo, the gifts of the Holy Ghost; (leg.) present; la restituzione dei doni fatti a causa della promessa di matrimonio, the return of engagement presents; †far — di, to bestow, to grant; †— di tempo, usury, money-lending.

†**do·nora** *f.pl.* of dono, q.v.

†**donqua, donque** *adv.* See **dunque**.

donzell-a *f.* (poet.) damsel, maiden, maid; (ichth.) various species of wrasse, *Crenilabrus* spp., *Julis* sp. and *Coris* sp. **-etta** *f. dim.* little maid; †fare la -etta, to play the innocent; †*pl.* (cul.) fritters. †**-ina** *f. dim.* little maid; uscir di -ina, to leave one's mother's apron-strings. **-ona** *f. augm.* old maid; (cul.) kind of pastry. †**-one** *m.* idler.

donzello *m.* (hist.) noble youth; young gentleman; page; squire (of medieval chivalry); municipal usher or messenger; (Florence) — del comune, trumpeter in public ceremony dressed in medieval costume.

†**doplare** *vb.* and derivs. See **doppiare**.

dopo, (N. Ital., Rom.) dopo *prep.* after (of time, place, order): — domani, the day after tomorrow; — tutto, after all; (with 'di' before *pers. prn.*): — di me, after me; — il palazzo, c'è la chiesa, next to the palace stands the church; — pranzo, after lunch; il — pranzo, the afternoon; — (di) aver dormito, — dormito, after sleeping; rimandare a — Pasqua, to put off until after Easter; behind; after; andare — una cosa, to pursue a thing, to go after a thing; †except; †in addition to; †— a, †— di, after; †da —, since; *adv.* afterwards, later, next, behind; il giorno —, the next day, the day after; prima mangio, — esco, I eat first, then I go out; subito —, immediately afterwards; lui camminava avanti e io —, he walked in front and I came behind. **-chè** *conj.* when, after; — (che fu) morto, after he was dead.

dopo-barba *adj. indecl.* after-shave; lozione —, after-shave lotion. **-guerra** *m. indecl.* post-war period. **-lavoro** *m. indecl.* (Fasc. hist.) a body set up under Fascism to organize recreational activities of workers; the local premises of this body, club with recreational facilities. **-lavorista** *m.* (Fasc. hist.) member of the 'dopolavoro'. **-lavori·stico** *adj.* (Fasc. hist.) pertaining to the 'dopolavoro'; una gita -lavoristica, a jaunt or spree organized by such a club; (fig.) popular, informal, unsophisticated; vulgar. **-pranzo** *m.* afternoon.

-scuola *m. indecl.* an institution where children may work after school-hours under supervision; period during which children are given supervision after school-hours.

doppi-a *f.* (numis.) doubloon, coin of varying values; lining piece at foot of skirt; (jewellery) doublet; double pay; double hinge; (naut.) doubling of a rope as in an eyesplice; (naut.) whip (having one block and two moving parts). **-etta** *f.* (motor.) double de-clutch.

doppi-are [A4c] *tr.* to double; (sport) to lap; (cinem.) to dub, to post-synchronize; (naut.) to round, to double; *intr.* (*aux.* avere) (agric.) to make two ewes suckle one lamb; *rfl.* to double; to increase; to become twice as much. **-aggio** *m.* (cinem.) dubbing, post-synchronization. **-amento** *m.* doubling. **-ato** *part. adj.* doubled; (cinem.) dubbed; *n.m.* (cinem.) see doppiaggio. **-atore** *m.* (cinem.) actor who dubs voices. (**-atrice** *f.*) **-atura** *f.* doubling.

doppieggi-are [A3c] *intr.* (*aux.* avere) (typ.) to look double (of a blurred line or letter); (naut.) to stand on and off making double turns; †(fig.) to be insincere; †(of words) to have a double meaning. **-atura** *f.* (typ.) doubling of letter or line (by blurred impression), slur.

doppier-e *m.*, †**-o** *m.* (poet.) large wax candle or torch; candlestick.

doppiett-a *f.* double-barrelled gun; a shot fired from such a gun; (numis.) Sardinian gold coin. **-o** *m.* (techn.) doublet.

doppiezza *f.* doubleness; double thickness; (fig.) duplicity, deceitfulness, insincerity, falseness; hypocrisy.

doppino *m.* (naut.) the point at which a rope is bent back upon itself to form an eye; quayside securing wire (generally doubled by splicing); (of a rope, etc.) bight.

dopp-io *adj.* double, twofold; fare il — gioco, to have a foot in both camps; esser cucito a filo —, to be hand in glove; dual; duplex; fare il — gioco a, to double-cross; two-faced, insincere; ambiguous; a — petto, double-breasted; un — petto, a double-breasted coat; (bot.) double; (comm.) scrittura -ia, duplicate copy; (aeron., etc.) — controllo, dual control; (archit.) colonna -ia, double column; colonne -ie, columns in pairs; (naut.) —fondo, double bottom; (in a submarine) double hull; (mil.) cannone —, one-hundred-pounder gun; di -ia palla, double-shotted; -ia paga, double pay; -ia sentinella, double guard; -ia spia, agent working for both sides; (mus.) — bemolle, double flat; — colpo di lingua, double-tonguing; -a corda, double-stop; — diesis, double-sharp; — movimento, twice as fast; passo —, quick march; †donna -ia, pregnant woman, woman pregnant with twins; *n.m.* double, twice the amount; al —, a due -i, twofold, twice the amount; a cento -i, a hundredfold; — di seta, cocoon made by two silkworms; (liturg.) double; (tennis) doubles; — maschile, men's doubles; — femminile, women's doubles; — misto, mixed doubles; (rowing) double sculls; (mus.) peal of bells; *adv.* twofold; in a double way; vedere —, to see double. **-iamente** *adv.* doubly. **-ione** *m.* duplicate; duplicate copy; double, identical thing; (ling.) doublet; (text.) flaw in cloth; (silkb.) twin-cocoon; (dominoes) doublet; †doubloon; †(bibliogr.) one of two copies of the same edition; †wax candle. **-ista** *m., f.* (tennis) doubles-player.

doppio-duo *m.* (metall.) dowlais mill.

Dora *pr.n.f.* Dora; (geog.) la —, the river Dora.

doradilla *f.* (bot.) rusty-back fern, *Ceterach officinarum.*

dor-are [A1] *tr.* to gild; (cul.) to glaze (with yolk of egg). (**-amento** *m.*) **-ato** *part. adj.* gilded, gilt, golden; (math.) regola -ata, golden rule; (cul.) glazed; golden brown; (ent.) mosca -ata, *Cetonia aurata*, a kind of beetle; *n.m.* gilding. **-atore** *m.* gilder. (**-atrice** *f.*) **-atura** *f.* gilding (process); gilt decoration, gold ornament; yellow part of hare's fur.

dorata *f.* (ichth.) gilt-head, *Sparus oratus.*

dorato[1] *part.* of dorare, q.v.

dorato[2] *m.* (vet.) golden chestnut or sorrel coat (of a horse).

Dordogna *pr.n.f.* (geog.) Dordogne.

dorè *adj. indecl.* golden; orange-coloured; (cul.) browned.

dorella *f.* (bot.) gold of pleasure, *Camelina sativa.*

dorema *f.* (bot.) *Dorema ammoniacum* (source of ammoniacum).

†**doreri·a** *f.* goldware, goldsmith's ware, gold vases, ornaments, etc.

dori *m.pl.* (hist.) Dorians.

dorice *f.* kind of pear from Portugal.

do·r-ico *adj.* Dorian; (mus.) modo —, Dorian mode; (ling.; archit.) Doric. **-icismo** *m.* (Gk. ling.) Doricism. **-icizzare** [A1], **-izzare** [A1] *intr.* (*aux.* avere) to Dorize. **-io**, **-iese** *adj.* Dorian.

Do·ride *pr.n.f.* (Gk. geog.; myth.) Doris; (zool.) sea slugs, sea lemon, *Doris* spp.

doridre·pano *m.* (class. antiq.) dorydrepanon; a kind of halbert.

dori·for-a *f.* (ent.) Colorado beetle, *Leptinotarsa decemliniata.* **-o** *m.* (class. antiq.) armed guard; member of bodyguard (e.g. Praetorian).

dorm(i)alfuoco *m. indecl.* sluggard, lazybones; *adj. indecl.* sluggardly, lazy.

†dorment-are *intr.* to sleep; *rfl.* to fall asleep (cf. **dormire, addormentare**). **†-ato** *part. adj.* asleep, sleeping. **†-o·r(i)o** *m.* dormitory.

dormente *part.* of dormire, q.v.

dormentone *m.* (ent.) grub of the cockchafer or maybug, *Melolontha vulgaris.*

dormi *m. indecl.* (Tusc.) sleepy person; fare il —, to be half asleep, to pretend to be asleep.

dormicchiare [A4] *intr.* (*aux.* avere) to doze, to drowse; (fig.) to nod, to be caught napping.

dormiente *part.* of dormire, see **dormente**; *adj.* sleeping; (bot.) innesto a occhio —, grafting with resting buds; *n.m.* sleeper; i sette dormienti, the Seven Sleepers; (bldg.) skewback; (naut.) standing part of a hawser; — dei bagli, longitudinal beams along the ship's side and supporting the transverse; *pl.* (bot.) kind of fungus growing beneath snow.

dormigl-iare [A4] *intr.* (*aux.* avere) to doze. **-ione** *m.* sleepyhead, late riser, lazybones, slugabed; (naut.) bedplate of a ship's machinery. (**-iona** *f.*) **-ioso** *adj.* sleepy; slumbrous; negligent, inattentive; careless, slack.

dorminterra *m. indecl.* sleeper on the ground.

dorm-ire [D1] *intr.* (*aux.* avere) to sleep; to be asleep; to slumber; sta a —, he's asleep; — della grossa, to be fast asleep; — tra due guanciali, to have nothing to worry about, to set one's mind at rest; — a occhi aperti, to be wary; — cogli occhi aperti, to be in a dazed condition; — come un ghiro, — come un tasso, — come una marmotta, to sleep like a top, to sleep like a log; — tranquillo, to sleep peacefully, (fig.) to set one's mind at rest; non c'è da —, there's nowhere to sleep, (fig.) there's no time to lose; (provb.) chi -e non piglia pesci, the early bird catches the worm; mandare a —, to send to bed, to put to sleep, (euphem.) to do in; fortuna e -i!, if you are born lucky everything goes well with you; metter qualcosa a —, to let something rest, to neglect something; to be sleepy, to be lethargic; non -e quello lì!, he's wide-awake!; to be dormant; to be in abeyance; (poet.) to be at rest, to repose; qui -ono le ossa di, here rest the bones of; *tr.* to sleep, to sleep through; — il sonno dei giusti, to sleep the sleep of the just; *rfl.* -irsela, to sleep peacefully; *n.m.* sleep; sleeping; bed, lodging; gli diede il —, he put him up for the night. **-ita** *f.* sleep; lethargy; sleep of silkworms. **-ito·rio** *m.* dormitory; **-itorio** popolare, free hostel, doss-house. **-itura** *f.* sleep (of silkworms). **-izione** *f.* (rel.) falling asleep; Dormition (of B.V.M.); †sleep, rest.

†dormitare *intr.* to doze, to slumber.

dormiveglia *m. indecl.,* *f.* drowsiness; state between sleeping and waking; stare in —, to be half asleep; nel — mi parve di vedere, just before I dropped off I thought I saw.

dormosa *f.* lounge-chair, sofa.

doro·nico *m.* (bot.) leopard's bane, *Doronicum.*

Dorote·a *pr.n.f.* Dorothy.

dorsale *adj.* of the back, dorsal; spina —, spine, vertebral column, backbone; *n.f.* (geog.) hog's back; crest of a range of mountains; (oceanog.) rise.

dorsista *m.* (sport) back-stroke swimmer.

dorso *m.* back; summit; ridge, crest; spine (of a book); (swimming) nuoto sul —, back-stroke. **-posteriore** *adj.* (obstet.) abdomino-anterior.

†dorura *f.* goldware, goldsmith's ware, gold ornaments, jewelry, etc.; cloth of gold.

dosa *f.* See dose.

dosana *f.* (naut. Ven.) low tide.

dos-are [A1] *tr.* to dose; to fix the dose of; to dole out; to meter. **-ag·gio** *m.* dosage; (chem.) proportion of constituents; metering; (naut.) the capacity of a submarine's trimming and ballast tanks. (**-ato** *part. adj.* **-atore** *m.* **-atrice** *f.*) **-atura** *f.* dosage; (of a liquid) metering; (motor.) **-atura** della miscela, mixture strength. **-i·metro** *m.* (atom. phys.) dosimeter; **-imetro** a lastrina, film badge.

dose *f.* dose; rincarare, caricare la —, to increase the dose, (fig.) to exaggerate, to lay it on thick; (fig.) in buona —, in good measure, plentifully; avere una — di maligno, to have a touch of spite in one; avere una buona — di fortuna, to have a good deal of luck; con una cospicua — di insensibilità, with an extraordinary lack of tact.

dossale *m.* cover (for precious objects); (liturg.; art) altar frontal; dossal; missal-cover (of elaborate kind).

†dossello *m.* baldachin, tester.

dossiere, dossiero *m.* back-rest.

dosso *m.* back; avere in —, portare in —, to carry on one's back; vestiti fatti al — di uno, clothes that fit one perfectly; levarsi di — qualcosa, to take something off, to get rid of something (cf. **addosso, indosso**); il — della mano, the back of the hand; (geog.) rounded hill; (oceanog.) ridge; (naut.) a — e bisdosso, goose wing; †— del piede, heel.

dossologi·a *f.* (liturg.) doxology.

dosso-mani·a *f.* passion for fame. **-sofi·a** *f.* arrogant claim to wisdom.

†dota *f.* See dote.

dotale *adj.* (leg.) dotal; beni dotali, dotal property (also *n.m.*).

dot-are [A1] *tr.* (*prep.* di) (leg.) to endow (with), to bestow; — qualcuno di qualcosa, to bestow something on someone; (fig.) to endow; to enrich; to furnish, to equip. **-ato** *part. adj.* endowed; **-ato** d'una memoria ferrea, blessed with an excellent memory. (**-atore** *m.* **-atrice** *f.*) **-azione** *f.* (leg.) endowment; dotation; dowry; settlement; **-azione** della corona, civil list; (hist.) — di Costantino, Donation of Constantine; (theatr.) properties; (comm.) in **-azione** normale, forming part of standard supply; avere in **-azione**, to be equipped with; (techn.) di **-azione** normale, standard; establishment, the arms, equipment and stores allowed to a ship; **-azione** fissa, current establishment; **-azione** di rispetto, reserve establishment; outfit, kit.

dote *f.* (leg.) dowry; endowment; (eccl.) dowry; money grant; (fig.) gift, quality, endowment; (naut.) see **dotazione**.

dotta[1] *f.* learned woman, woman scholar (cf. **dotto**).

†dotta[2] *f.* space of time, period, interval; a —, on the dot, punctually; ta' dotte, sometimes; delay; rimetter le dotte, to make up for lost time; opportunity; mala —, bad condition, bad state; a sua —, at one's convenience.

†dotta[3] *f.* fear; doubt, misgiving.

†dott-are *intr.,* *rfl.* to fear, to be afraid; to have misgivings; to be in doubt. **†-ag·gio** *m.* fear; doubt. **†-amento** *m.* doubt, suspicion. **†-ante** *part. adj.* doubting; Tommaso -ante, doubting Thomas, Thomas Didymus. **†-anza** *f.* fear; doubt; misgivings; hesitation.

dottato *adj.* fico —, kind of white fig.

dott-o *adj.* learned, scholarly; pedantic; expert; skilful, practised; alla -a, learnedly, in a scholarly manner, pedantically; (mil.) armi -e, Artillery and Engineers; *n.m.* scholar, learned man. (**-amente** *adv.*) **-i·fico** *adj.* (joc.) learned-making, pedant-producing.

dottora *f.* See under **dottore**.

dottor-are [A1c] *tr.* to make a doctor, to confer a doctor's degree upon. (**-ato** *part. adj.* ad·.)

dottor-e *m., f.* doctor (of law, letters, medicine, etc.); — in legge, doctor of law; la dottoressa Dorothy L. Sayers era dottore ad onore in lettere, Dr Dorothy L. Sayers had an honorary doctorate in letters; (pop.) learned man; medical man; Doctor of the Church; (in Italian Universities) holder of a first degree, graduate; il — angelico, the Angelic Doctor, St Thomas Aquinas; il — serafico, the Seraphic Doctor, St Bonaventure. **-a** *f.* bluestocking; pedantic woman; †wife of a man with the title of doctor; †woman holding the title of doctor (cf. **dottoressa**). **-ag·gine** *f.* (joc.) professorial status or attitude, donnishness. **-ale** *adj.* doctoral, Doctor's, professorial. (**-almente** *adv.*) **-ame** *m.* crowd of doctors, set of dons. **-ato** *m.* doctorate, doctorship; conferment or possession of a doctor's degree. **-eggiare** [A3c] *intr.* (*aux.* avere) to parade one's learning; to give oneself learned airs. **-eri·a** *f.* pedantic airs. **-esco** *adj.* (*m.pl.* -eschi) donnish; pedantic. (**-escamente** *adv.*). **-ismo** *m.* professorial manner. **-essa** *f.* woman holding a doctor's degree (cf. also under **dottore**); (derog.) blue-stocking; pedantic woman.

†dottoso *adj.* in doubt, dubious, doubtful; afraid.

dottrin-a *f.* doctrine; (eccl.) catechism; far la —, to take a catechism class; learning, scholarship; teaching, theory, school. **-ale** *adj.* doctrinal; theoretical; *n.m.* textbook, work of instruction. **-almente** *adv.* doctrinally; theoretically. **†-are** *tr.* to indoctrinate; to instruct. **-a·rio** *m.* doctrinaire; (derog.) a mere theorist;

dottrin-a (*cont.*)

(eccl.) Doctrinarian, Father of Christian Doctrine. **-eggiare** [A 3 c] *intr.* (*aux.* avere) to air one's knowledge or theories. **-ęsco** *adj.* (*m.pl.* **-ęschi**) (derog.) merely theoretical; doctrinaire. **-iṣmo** *m.* (neol.) doctrinairism.

dova·rio *m.* (leg.) dower.

dọve *interr.* where?; — mai?, where on earth?; — mai l'ho posto?, where on earth did I put it?; — vai?, where are you going?; dov'è?, where is he (she, it)?; su —?, up where?; per —?, which way?; verso —?, in which direction?, whither?; *rel. adv.* where; vado — dice lui, I am going where he tells me; se ne andarono non so —, they went off I know not where; da — abitava prima fa un chilometro, from where he lived before it is a kilometre's distance; da —, di —, whence, from where; non so di — vengano, I don't know where they come from; wherein, in which; il baule — stanno le lenzuola, the trunk in which the sheets are kept; la casa dov'è andata, the house to which he went; il terreno per — sono passati, the terrain through which they passed; *conj.* (foll. by *indic.*) where; whereas; while; — (*or* — che) ci pareva di riuscire, fallimmo, where we thought (*or* whereas, *or* while we thought) we were succeeding, we failed; — andava piano lui, lei faceva presto, whereas (*or* while) he proceeded slowly, she made haste; (foll. by *subj.*) if; — mancasse qualcosa, scrivetemi, if anything should be lacking, write to me; (poet.) dove...dove, in one place...in another, on the one hand...on the other; — che, wherever; — che sia, somewhere or other, *or* wherever it (he) may be; *n.m.* place; per ogni —, in ogni —, everywhere; so il quando ma non il —, I know when but not where. (NOTE: in Tuscan pronunciation a consonant following 'dove' is usually doubled, e.g. 'dove mai' is pronounced 'dovemmai'.)

dovè¹ 3rd *pers. sing. past. def.* of **dovere**, q.v.

dov'è² *interr.* where is it?; where is he?; where is she? (cf. **dove**).

doventare [A 1] (Tusc. pop.). See **diventare**.

dovęre [B 12] *tr.*

1. To OWE; mi deve mille lire, he owes me a thousand lire; gli devo una risposta, I owe him a reply; dovete al dottore la vostra vita, you owe the doctor your life; deve a me, se non è in carcere, he owes it to me (it's thanks to me) he's not in jail; (comm.) deve avere, due to, credit; deve dare, due from, debtor. 2. AUX. VB. FOLL. BY INFIN. (NOTE: as an *aux. vb.* 'dovere' has 'avere' as its own *aux.* if the following *infin.* is normally compounded with 'avere'; e.g. 'ha dovuto studiare'. If the *infin.* is normally compounded with 'essere', the *aux.* of 'dovere' may be either 'essere' or 'avere', e.g. 'è dovuto andare' *or* 'ha dovuto andare'. In the case of a reflexive *infin.*, 'essere' is used if the *rfl. prn.* precedes, 'avere' if it follows; e.g. 'mi sono dovuto rassegnare', or, 'ho dovuto rassegnarmi'.) To have to, to be obliged to, to be compelled to, to have a moral obligation to; devo partire, I must depart; il treno dovrebbe partire alle nove ma chi sa se sarà in orario?, the train ought to leave at nine, but will it be running to time?; avrei dovuto scrivere, I ought to have written; dovè (dovette) andare, he was obliged to go, he had to go (and he did); doveva andare, he was under an obligation to go, he often had to go, he was to have gone; deve piovere, it looks like rain; come si deve, properly, nicely; una persona come si deve, a well-behaved, respectable person; mi deve telefonare alle tre, he's due to ring me up at three; doveva cantare martedì ma poi spostarono il concerto, he was to have sung on Tuesday but they altered the day of the concert; dovrei o non dovrei?, shall I, or shan't I?; deve assolutamente, he absolutely must; dovresti fargli capire, you must make him understand; che tu debba essere sempre così sgarbato?, must you always be so rude? 3. FOLL. BY 'ESSERE': to be probable; dev'essere vero, it is very likely true, it must be true; dev'essere pazzo, he must be mad; dev'essere stato pazzo, he must have been mad. 4. *n.m.* DUTY; fare il proprio —, to do one's duty; adempimento di un —, performance of a duty; propriety, fitness; tutto sta a —, everything is as it should be; a —, in the right way; come di —, as is right and proper; tutti stanno a —, they are all behaving properly; mettere uno a —, to bring someone to see reason, to put someone in his place; the right amount, what one owes; pagare più del —, to be overcharged; what one deserves; gli sta il —, it serves him right; school task, exercise, homework; (leg.) — giuridico, legal duty, converse of legal right; *pl.* respects; i miei doveri alla signora, please pay my respects to your wife.

doverọs-o *adj.* due, dutiful, rightful, right and proper. **-amęnte** *adv.* duly; as is right; properly.

†dovi·dere *vb.* and derivs. See **dividere**.

dovi·zi-a *f.* wealth, plenty; a —, in abundance. **-ọso** *adj.* wealthy, rich; abundant. (**-osamęnte** *adv.*)

dovunque *rel. adv.* (with *subj.*) wherever; *indef. adv.* no matter where, anywhere, everywhere; all over.

dovut-o *part.* of **dovere**, q.v.; *adj.* due, proper, fitting; due, owed, outstanding; deserved; *n.m.* debt; due. (**-amęnte** *adv.*)

Doxa *pr.n.f.* Italian institution equivalent to Gallup-poll (also *adj. indecl.*).

†doze, †dozzi twelve (cf. **dodici**).

dozzin-a *f.* dozen; due **-e** di bottoni, two dozen buttons; a **-e**, in crowds; mettere uno in —, to put someone on the same level as everyone else; di —, da —, cheap, commonplace; payment for board and lodging; prendere a —, to take boarders; stare a —, to be a boarder. **-ale** *adj.* second-rate, cheap, ordinary, mediocre; vulgar. (**-almęnte** *adv.*) **-alità** *f. indecl.* mediocrity, commonplaceness; vulgarity. **-ante** *m.*, *f.* boarder.

dracarro *m.* (naut. hist.) Scandinavian boat (Drakar) having one mast, a square sail, oars, and forecastle and poop.

dracena *f.* (bot.) dragon tree, *Dracaena*.

†dracma *f.* See **dramma²**.

†draco *m.* See **drago**.

drac-ọne *m.* (Gk. hist.) Draco. **-oniano** *adj.* (Gk. hist.) Draconic, Draconian; ruthless.

drag-a *f.* (naut.) dredger; sea anchor, drogue; — a catena di secchi, bucket dredger; — a tenaglia, grab dredger; — aspirante, — pompasabbia, suction dredger. **-ag·gio** *m.* (naut.) work of dredging; minesweeping. **-amine** *m.* (naut.) minesweeper; una nave **-amine**, a minesweeper.

dragante¹ *m.* (bot.) tragacanth (gum of *Astragalus* spp.).

dragante² *m.* (naut.) transom.

drag-are [A 2] *tr.* (naut.) to dredge. **-ag·gio** *m.* dredging. **-ante** *part. adj.* pompa **-ante**, dredging pump. (**-ato** *part. adj.*)

†dragata *f.* (joc.) blow with a dragon.

dra·glia *f.* (naut.) runner, any wire to which sails or awnings are attached with moving eyes; stay; jackstay.

dra·go *m.* (*pl.* **-ghi**) (myth.) dragon; (fig.) dragon; (geog.) Porta del —, Dragon's Gate; — volante, — pallone, boy's kite; (aeron.) kite balloon; (bot.) sangue di —, dragon's blood (resin of *Dracaena draco* and *Daemonorops draco*); (geog.) Monti dei **-ghi**, Drakensberg. **-ghętto** *m.* cock of a gun.

dragomanno *m.* dragoman; interpreter.

dragọna *f.* (mil. hist.) tasselled braid ornamenting the haft of a sword.

dragon-a·rio *m.*, **-iere** *m.* (class. antiq.) dragon standard-bearer. **-ato** *adj.* (herald.) dragonesque; with dragon's tail; leone **-ato**, lion-dragon.

dragọn-e¹ *m.* dragon; (class. antiq.) dragon standard; (mil.) dragoon; (ichth.) greater weever fish, *Trachinus draco*; dragon fish, *Pegasus* spp.; (herald.) wyvern; (bot.) see **drago**. **-cello** *m. dim.* small dragon; (bot.) tarragon, *Artemisia dracunculus*; kind of fig. **-essa** *f.* dragoness, she-dragon. **-ifọrme** *adj.* dragon-like.

Dragọne² *pr.n.m.* (astron.) Draco.

dragontea *f.* (bot.) *Dracunculus vulgaris*.

†drama *m.* See **dramma¹**.

dramma¹ *m.* play, drama; — pastorale, pastoral play; — storico, historical drama; tragedy (also fig.); fare un —, to exaggerate; (mus.) — musicale, — in musica, — per musica, opera (esp. Wagnerian as opposed to Italian opera).

dramma² *f.* (numis.) drachma; (weight) drachm, dram; tiny quantity, dram, scrap; a — a —, little by little, gradually.

dramm-a·tica *f.* art of drama, art of the theatre, dramatic art, dramatics; dramatic poetry. **-a·tico** *adj.* dramatic; scrittore **-atico**, dramatist. **-aticamęnte** *adv.* dramatically. **-atiẓẓare** [A 1] *tr.* to dramatize, to render dramatic; *abs.* to exaggerate; to make a mountain out of a molehill; to be melodramatic. **-atiẓẓato** *part. adj.* dramatized. **-aturgi·a** *f.* dramatic art or composition; dramaturgy. **-aturgo** *m.* (*pl.* **-aturghi**) playwright, dramatist, dramatic author.

†drapp-are *tr.* (paint.) to drape. **†-amento** *m.* clothing. **†-ari·a** *f.* drapery.

drapp-eggiare [A 3 c] *tr.* to drape; (fig.) to clothe; *rfl.* to drape oneself, to robe oneself; to strike an attitude, to pose. (**-eggiato** *part. adj.* **-ęggio** *m.* (*pl.* **-ęggi**) drape, drapery; hanging(s).

drappella f. (mil. hist.) hook of a halberd; banderole.

†**drappellare** intr. to form into platoons.

drappello m. (mil.) squad, platoon; band, group, of people; †little piece of cloth.

drappell-onare [A I c] tr. to hang (with drapery); to festoon. **-one** m. hanging (in church); †pendant, dangling ornament.

drapp-eri·a f. drapery (esp. silk); (collection of) fine fabrics; place where such fabrics are made, kept or sold, draper's. **-ettine** f.pl. wooden wedges (as used by shoemakers).

†**drappier-e** m., **-o** m. draper; cloth merchant.

drapp-o m. cloth (esp. silk, and often worked); fine fabric; — mortuario, pall; — inglese, court sticking-plaster; clothing; †altar-cloth. **-etto** m. dim. inferior silk cloth. †**-icello** m. dim. small cloth; handkerchief.

dra·stic-o adj. drastic. (**-amente** adv.)

Dra·vidi pr.n.m.pl. Dravidians.

drenag·gio m. draining; drainage; drain; tubo di —, drain-pipe; (fig.) drain; il — sulla sterlina, the drain on sterling; (med.) draining; (radio; telev.) bleeding; resistenza di —, bleeder resistance.

†**drento** adv., prep. See dentro.

Dresda pr.n.f. (geog.) Dresden.

†**dreto** adv., prep. See dietro.

dri·ad-e f. (myth.) dryad. **-eo** m. (lit. hist.) Dryadeum (poem by Luca Pulci).

dribblare [A I] intr. (aux. avere), tr. (soccer, rugby) to dribble.

†**drieto** adv., prep. See dietro.

drillo m. (zool.) mandrill, Cynocephalus mormon.

†**dringolare** intr. to totter, to shake, to quake.

dritt-a f. right, right hand, right side, right-hand side; (naut.) starboard; di —, on the starboard side; guardia di —, starboard watch; ancora di —, elica di —, sulla —, on the starboard hand; tutto a —, hard a'starboard. **-ezza** f. upright position, uprightness; †rectitude, probity (cf. diritto, dirittezza).

dritt-o adj. straight; a —, vertical; upright; honest; favourable; proper, right; exact (of time); (archit.) gola -a, cyma recta; n.m. right side of material; upright (piece); (leg.) il —, that which the law directs; the right. (naut.) — di prora, sternpost; — del timone, rudder post; (archit.) elevation; (fig.) un —, a straight man, a sound chap, a man on the level; adv. straight on; sempre —, keep straight on, you can't miss it (cf. diritto); (naut.) — di prora, right ahead; — di poppa, right astern. †**-orove·scio** adv. upside down. **-ura** f. straight line; uprightness, rectitude (cf. drittura).

drizza f. (naut.) lift, halyard; — di penna, — di un picco, peak halyard; — di gola, throat halyard; — ad amante, standing wire coupled to the hoist of a large sail.

drizz-are [A I] tr. to direct, to turn; to put right, to straighten, to correct; to set upright, to raise; to prick up; — le orecchie, to prick up one's ears, to listen attentively; to build; (naut.) to hoist; to straighten; to turn to a new course; — prora e vela, to alter course and trim sail. **-ante** part. adj. straightening; †n.m. (naut.) seaman detailed to a hoist. **-ata** f. act of straightening; †(naut.) a pull on a hoist. **-ato** part. adj. straightened; put right; raised, erected; turned; aimed, directed. **-atura** f. straightening (cf. addirizzare[1]).

dro-ga f. article of grocery, esp. imported (e.g. pepper, coffee); spice; narcotic, drug; (crim. law) fabbricazione abusiva di -ghe, illicit manufacture of drugs. **-gare** [A 2] to spice, to flavour; to doctor, to adulterate; to drug. (**-ato** part. adj.) **-gheri·a** f. drysaltery; grocer's shop. **-ghiera** f. woman grocer; grocer's wife. **-ghiere** m. drysalter, grocer.

droma f. (naut.) masts and timber (spares).

dro·meda f., **dromeda·rio** m. (zool.) dromedary.

dro·mo m. (naut.) beacon; bollard; †(Ven.) haven.

drom-o·grafo m. (naut.) log. **-osco·pio** m. (naut.) compass correcter.

dromon-e m. (naut. hist.) three-masted ship of the Middle Ages having as many as 100 oars. **-a·rio** m. crew of a 'dromone'.

dronte m. (orn.) dodo, Didus ineptus.

drop m. indecl. (rugby) drop-kick.

†**dro·pace** m. depilatory.

droso·metro m. (meteor.) drosometer.

drud-a f. paramour, mistress; †love, lady. **-o** m. paramour; †lover, loved one; †vassal; †adj. given over to love; valorous; gracious; loyal, true; strong; well-grown; gay.

dru·id-a m., **-o** m. Druid. **-a** f., **-essa** f. Druidess.

dru-i·dico adj. Druidic, Druidical. **-idismo** m. Druidism.

drup-a f., **-o** m. (bot.) drupe, stone fruit. **-i·fero** adj. (bot.) drupe-bearing.

dru·sci-a f. caress. **-are** [A4] tr. to caress, to fondle; to brush away, to wear out.

drusiana f. slut, trollop.

Druso pr.n.m. (Rom. hist.) Drusus.

†**du[1]** ord. num. two (cf. due).

†**du[2]** adv. where (cf. dove).

†**du[3]** conj. therefore (cf. dunque).

dua ord. num. (dial. Tusc.) two (cf. due).

†**dua·gio** m. kind of cloth made in Douai, Flanders.

dual·beri m. indecl. (naut.) two-master, brig, etc.

dual-e adj. dual, twofold; n.m. (linguist.) dual. (**-mente** adv.) **-ismo** m. (philos.; theol.) dualism; (neol.) rivalry, antagonism; (pol.; neol.) dual monarchy. **-ista** m. dualist. **-i·stico** adj. dualistic. **-ità** f. duality.

dubbiamente adv. See under dubbio.

†**dubbiare** vb. and derivs. See dubitare.

†**dubbietà** f. doubt, lack of faith.

dubbiezza f. hesitation, doubtfulness.

dub·bi-o adj. doubtful, uncertain; hesitant; ambiguous, equivocal; dubious, suspect; persona di -a fama, person of dubious reputation; questionable; untrustworthy; n.m. doubt; hesitation; misgiving; uncertainty; suspicion; risk; nel — sarà meglio fare così, if there's any doubt it will be best to do this; magari non sarà contagioso ma nel — ho preferito non toccarlo, I don't suppose it's contagious, but I thought it better not to touch it just in case; mi venne il — che fosse stato lui, I thought it was he, but I wasn't sure; fare un —, to raise a difficulty, to put forward an objection; in —, in danger; mettere in —, to throw doubt on; to endanger; chiarire un —, to clear up a doubtful point; †fear. **-amente** adv. doubtfully; suspiciously.

dubbios-o adj. doubtful, doubting; irresolute; uncertain, dubious; questionable; improbable; suspect; †dim, obscure; †frightening, fearful. **-amente** adv. doubtfully, doubtingly; uncertainly; dubiously. **-ità** f. doubtfulness, uncertainty.

dubit-are [A I S] intr. (aux. avere) to doubt; c'è poco da —, there's not much room for doubt; to suspect, to fear; -o che sia tardi, I'm afraid it's late; -o che non sia vero, I rather think it may be true; -o che sia vero, I doubt whether it is true: — di, to distrust; to hesitate, to waver. **-a·bile** adj. questionable; non è -abile, it cannot be doubted. †**-amento** m. doubt. **-ante** part. adj. doubtful, hesitant; uncertain; groping; tottering. (**-antemente** adv.) †**-anza** f. doubt. **-ativo** adj. dubitative, hesitant; (ling.) expressing doubt. **-ato** part. adj. doubted; suspected; in doubt. (**-atamente** adv.) **-azione** f. doubt, hesitation; (class. rhet.) aporia, dubitatio.

dubitos-o adj. full of doubts; timid, shy; suspicious; uncertain; irresolute; †afraid, fearful; †unreliable; †dangerous; †frightening. **-osamente** adv. doubtfully; timidly; shyly; in fear.

dublè m. indecl. (jewel.) rolled gold, doublé.

Dublino pr.n.f. (geog.) Dublin.

du-ca m. (pl. -chi) duke; †leader, guide; (orn.) — cornuto, long-eared owl. **-cale** adj. ducal; (geog.) Bosco —, Bois-le-Duc, 's Hertogenbosch, Den Bosch; dogal; palazzo -cale, Doge's Palace; n.m. (hist.) supporter of the duke. (**-calmente** adv.) †**-care** tr. to create a duke. **-cato** m. duchy; dukedom; dukeship; (numis.) ducat. **-catone** m. (numis.) ducatoon.

duce m. guide; leader, captain, commander; (Fasc. hist.) the appellation assumed by Benito Mussolini; †f. female guide.

ducena·rio m. (Rom. antiq.) ducenarius.

ducento card. num. See duecento.

†**du·cere** tr. to lead; to conduct; to direct; to give shape to.

duch-esco adj. (m.pl. -eschi) ducal. **-essa** f. duchess; †leader. **-essina** f. duke's daughter; youthful duchess. **-evole** (joc.) ducal, duke-like. **-ino** m. (courtesy title of) duke's son; young duke. **-ista** m. supporter of a duke.

duda f. (mus.) Polish bagpipe; a Siberian dance.

due card. num. two; questi —, these two; a — a —, two by two; lavorare per —, to work twice as hard as anyone else (or, as usual); mangiare per —, to eat enough for two; — parole, a word or two; vo a far — passi, I'm going for a little stroll; stare fra —, to be in doubt, to be in two minds; adoperare — pesi e — misure, to be unfair (e.g. one law for the rich, another for the poor), to

due (*cont.*)

discriminate; una delle —, one of two things, you must make up your mind; *excl.* e —!, that's enough!, there you go again!; (rowing) — con, coxed pairs; — senza, coxless pairs; (mus.) a —, indication that a single line of music is played by two instruments together; divisi in — parti, players divided into two groups; — corde, release damping-pedal (pianoforte), play on two strings (violin); — piatti, clash both cymbals together; *n.m. indecl.* the figure two; cancella questo —, strike out this two; un — posti, a two-seater; un — pezzi, a two-piece (article of clothing); un — anni, a two-year-old (race-horse); tre — anni, three two-year-olds; (cards) un — di spade, a two of spades.

dueal·beri *m. indecl.* (naut.). See **dualberi**.

duecent·o *card. num., adj. indecl., n.m. indecl.* two hundred; il Duecento, the thirteenth century. **-enne** *adj.* two hundred years old. **-esco** *adj.* (*m.pl.* **-eschi**) of the thirteenth century. **-e·şimo**, **-eşimo** *ord. num.* two hundredth. **-ista** *m.* thirteenth-century man (esp. writer, artist). **-omila** *card. num., n.m.* two hundred thousand. **-omille·şimo, -omilleşimo** *ord. num.* two hundred thousandth.

duell·are [A I] *intr.* (*aux.* avere) to duel, to fight a duel. **-ante** *part. adj.* duelling; *n.m.* duellist, party to a duel; dueller. (**-atore** *m.* **-atrice** *f.*) **-ista** *m.* habitual duellist, fighter of duels.

duell·o *m.* duel; battersi in —, to fight a duel; sfida a —, challenge to a duel; (leg.) duel (criminal law); †combat. **-ista** *m.* (experienced, habitual) duellist.

duemila *card. num., adj. indecl., n.m. indecl.* two thousand.

duennale *adj.* biennial.

dueponti *m.* (naut.) two-decker.

duerno *m.* two-page printed sheet; half a quire.

duett·o *m.* (mus.) duet; (joc.) angry dialogue; pair of quarrelling, whining or ungainly people; (numis.) coin worth two 'quattrini' or 'soldi'; double deuce, double two (at backgammon or dice). **-ino** *m. dim.* (mus.) short duet. **-ista** *m., f.* (mus.) duettist.

duga·ia *f.* See **dogaia**.

dugento *card. num.* and derivs. (Tusc.). See **duecento**.

†**du·gli·a** *f.* (naut.) coil (of rope); coil (as much as one man can carry). †**-are** *tr.* (naut.) to coil.

dugo *m.* (orn.) eagle owl.

dui·no *m.* double two, double deuce (at dice, etc.); (numis.) Tuscan coin worth two centesimi.

dui·sono *adj.* (ling.) diphthongal; *n.m.* diphthong.

dulcamara *f.* (bot.) woody nightshade, bitter-sweet, *Solanum dulcamara*; *pr.n.m.* quack, charlatan.

dulciana *f.* (mus.) dulciana (organ-stop).

Dulcine·a *pr.n.f.* (joc.) Dulcinea, lady-love.

duli·a *f.* (theol.) dulia.

dum *f. indecl.* (bot.). See **dom**.

duma *f.* (Russian hist.) duma; (mus.) Dumka, folk-ballad from Little Russia.

†**dumila** *card. num.* See **duemila**.

dum·o *m.* (bot.) blackthorn, *Prunus spinosa*, and other thorny shrubs. **-eto** *m.* thicket of blackthorn or other thorny shrubs. **-oso** *adj.* thorny.

duna *f.* sand-dune; (naut.) la rada delle **-e**, The Downs.

†**dunche,** †**dunqua** *adv.* See **dunque**.

dunque *adv.* then; so; so then; well then, well now; now then; therefore, accordingly; *n.m.* venire al —, to come to the point.

duo *m. indecl.* (mus.) duet, duo; † *card. num.* See **due**.

duode·cim·a *f.* (mus.) twelfth (interval and organ-stop). **-o** *ord. num.* twelfth.

duoden·o *m.* (anat.) duodenum; †*adj.* (rel.) coro —, band of twelve, the Apostles. **-ale** *adj.* (med.; anat.) duodenal.

duodiodo *m.* (rad.) double diode.

duolo *m.* (poet.) grief, sorrow; mourning; (Tusc. pop.) bodily pain; †cry of pain; †menare —, to utter cries of grief, to lament; †mourning clothes.

duomo *m.* cathedral; other principal church in a town; (eng.) dome, steam dome or drum.

†**duo·viro** *m.* See **duum·viro**.

dupla *f.* (mus.) duple measure.

†**duplare**[1] *tr.* to multiply.

duplare[2] *m.* (Rom. antiq.) *duplicarius*.

duplex *m. indecl.* (teleph.) party-line, shared line.

du·plica *f.* (leg.) rejoinder; demurrer to a plea.

duplic·are [A 2 s] *tr.* to double; to duplicate; (mus.) — un intervallo, to add an octave to an interval, e.g. a third with an octave added becomes a tenth, or compound third; ottava **-ata**, double-octave, fifteenth. (NOTE: in English, 'double' is only used thus of an octave.) **-ato** *part. adj.* doubled; duplicated; *n.m.* duplicate; second copy, spare copy; counterpart; doubling of words or lines; (leg.) duplicate; trarre un cambiale in **-ato**, to draw a bill of exchange in duplicate. (**-atamente** *adv.*) **-atore** *m.* duplicator; (rad.) doubler. **-atura** *f.* (typ.) double. **-azione** *f.* doubling; duplication.

du·plic-e *adj.* double, twofold. (**-emente** *adv.*); *n.m.* bet in horse-racing based on picking the winner in two races, 'double'. **-ità** *f.* doubleness, duplicity.

†**duplificato** *adj.* doubled.

duplo *adj.* double; *n.m.* double quantity; (leg.) duplicate, copy, transcript.

†**duponti** *m.* (naut.). See **dueponti**.

dura[1] *f.* (bot.) great millet, *Sorghum vulgare*.

†**dura**[2] *f.* duration; delay; far —, to endure, to resist; stare alla —, to be obstinate.

dura·bile *adj.* See under **durare**.

dura·cin·e, -o *adj.* (bot.) of fruits, esp. peaches, in which the flesh is attached to the stone.

duralluminio *m.* (metall.) duralumin, dural.

durame(n) *m. indecl.* (bot.) duramen, heart-wood.

dur·are [A I] *intr.* (*aux.* essere, avere) to last, to continue, to go on; finché la **-a!**, as long as it lasts!; to keep (of perishable goods); **-ò** a lavorare, he kept on working; (with *aux.* avere) to hold out, to persevere; ha **-ato** poco in quell'ufficio, he didn't stick to that job very long; *tr.* to endure, to suffer, to put up with, to experience; **-o** fatica a credere, I find it hard to believe; **-arla**, to keep it up; chi la **-a** la vince, dogged does it; (iron.) che la **-i!**, let's hope he can keep on like that! **-a·bile** *adj.* lasting, likely to last. (**-abilmente** *adv.*) **-abilità** *f.* durability, lasting quality, lastingness. **-ante** *part. adj.* lasting; vita natural **-ante**, throughout one's life; *prep.* during; in the course of; *pr.n.m.* Durante, shortened to Dante. †**-anza** *f.* lasting, enduring; perseverance, endurance. **-ata** *f.* duration, length of time; length of currency; **-ata** normale della giornata di lavoro, normal working day; **-ata** della carica, term of office; di **-ata**, lasting, permanent, hard-wearing; colore di lunga **-ata**, fast colour; articoli di breve **-ata**, perishable goods; (eng.) life, working life; (rubber ind.) **-ata** alla flessione, flex life; prova di **-ata**, endurance test; (bot.) **-ata** della vita, duration. **-ato** *part. adj.* lasting, enduring; suffered. **-aturo** *adj.* durable, permanent, likely to remain. **-azione** *f.* duration. **-evole** *adj.* lasting, enduring, abiding. (**-evolmente** *adv.*) **-evolezza** *f.* lastingness, permanence.

Durazzo *pr.n.m.* (geog.) Durres.

durello *m.* kind of pear.

durezza *f.* hardness; (fig.) harshness, severity; insensibility; (vet.) — di bocca, hard mouth; †(mus.) dissonance.

du·rio *m.* (bot.) durian, *Durio zibethinus*.

Dur(l)indana *pr.n.f.* (lit. hist.) Durendal, the sword of Roland; (joc.) any sword.

dur·o *adj.* hard; tough; firm; difficult; bitter; harsh, rigid, severe; una vita **-a**, a hard life; patti **-i**, harsh terms; carcere —, imprisonment with hard labour; l'è **-a!**, hard lines!; pane —, stale bread; pietra **-a**, precious stone; legno —, hard wood; acqua **-a**, hard water; obstinate, slow-witted; osso —, hard nut to crack, tough customer; testa **-a**, exasperatingly dense or mulish person; — di testa, thick-headed, slow-witted; e lui —, but he wouldn't give in, but he took no notice; — di corpo, constipated; — d'orecchi, hard of hearing; avere la pelle **-a**, to have a tough constitution; *n.m.* hard part; something hard; difficulty; il — sta nel soffrire e tacere, the hardest part is to suffer and keep silence; hard boiled sweet; **-i** di menta, peppermints; (colloq.) tough guy; (numis.) duro; *adv.* tener —, to hold out, to refuse to yield, to remain firm. **-amente** *adv.* with difficulty; harshly. **-one** *m.* numskull; knot in marble; callus on hands or feet; beginnings of a corn.

duro·metro *m.* (techn.) sclerometer, hardness meter.

durra *f.* (bot.). See **dura**.

dut·til-e *adj.* ductile; (fig.) pliable, flexible, supple; (metall.) ductile. **-ità** *f.* ductility; (fig.) pliability; (metall.) ductility; limite di **-ità**, yield point.

dutto[1] *m.* (anat.) duct.

†**dutto**[2] *part.* of †**ducere**, q.v.

duum·vir-o *m.*, **duun·vir-o** *m.* (Rom. hist.) duumvir. **-ale** *adj.* duumviral. **-ato** *m.* duumvirate.

†**duvitanza** *f.* doubt; fear.

ẹ[1] *f. sing., m.pl.* the vowel E; the letter E; una E maiuscola, a capital E; una e minuscola, a small e; un'e stretta, a close e (as in 'sera'); un'e larga, an open e (as in 'bello'); ci sono troppi e accostati in quel verso, there are too many e's close together in that line.

ẹ[2] *conj.* (ed is sometimes used before another vowel, esp. before another e) and; also; and so; e...e, both...and; tutti — due, both; tutte e tre le ragazze, all three girls; bell'— fatto, readymade; se è riuscito lui — noi riusciremo, if he succeeded we shall too; and yet, but; doveva arrivare — non s'è visto, he was due to arrive but there isn't a sign of him; ha scritto così — non è un cretino, that's what he wrote, and yet he's no fool; well, well then; — che volete?, well, what do you want?; †in order that; †on condition that; †although, albeit; †very well, all right, so be it; †that is; †nevertheless; †there, where, if, when; †therefore; *n.m.* (typ.) — commerciale, ampersand.

†**e**[3] *conj., excl.* lo, behold (cf. **ecco**).

ẹ'[4] *prn.* (Tusc. pop.; poet.) he; it; they (cf. **ei, egli, eglino**); — mi disse, he said to me; — mi pare, it seems to me; domandò chi — fossero, he asked who they were.

e'[5] *conj.* (Tusc. pop.) and the (e i); i buoni e' cattivi, the good and the wicked; †the *m.pl.*

è[6] *3rd pers. sing. pres. indic.* of **essere**, q.v.

ebanist-a *m.* cabinet-maker. **-eri·a** *f.* cabinet-making; cabinetmaker's shop.

ebanite *f.* ebonite.

e·bano *m.* (bot.) ebony-tree, *Diospyros ebenus*; its heart-wood, and that of various other species; — falso, laburnum.

ebbene *conj.* well; well then.

eb·bio *m.* (bot.) danewort, dwarf elder, *Sambucus ebulus*.

e(b)br-o *adj.* intoxicated, drunk; excited, elated; — di gioia, delirious with joy; — d'amore, head over heels in love. **-ẹzza** *f.* intoxication; rapture, bliss; elation; exultation; (med.) **-ezza** Röntgen, radiotoxaemia, X-ray sickness. **-iachẹzza** *f.* drunkenness. **-iẹtà** *f.* ebriety.

ebdo·mad-a *f.* week. **-a·rio** *adj.* weekly, hebdomanal, issued every week; *n.m.* weekly journal, weekly paper.

Ebe[1] *pr.n.f.* (myth.) Hebe.

†**ebe**[2] *vb.* See under **ebere**.

†**e·beno** *m.* See under **ebere**.

†**ebere** *intr.* (def. 3rd sing. indic. only) to grow faint; to be idle; to be blunt; †ebe, grows faint; lives in idleness; is blunt, fails to cut, fails to strike.

e·bet-e *adj.* stupid, dull, obtuse; dazed; feeble-minded. **-ag·gine** *f.* stupid action; dullness, stupidity. **-işmo** *m.* dullness, stupidity; feeble-mindedness. **-u·dine** *f.* dullness, stupidity; hebetude.

E·boli *pr.n.f.* (geog.) Eboli.

†**ebollire** *intr.* to boil; to bubble; to ferment.

ebollizịọne *f.* boiling; punto di —, boiling-point; (chem.; med.) ebullition; (vet.) fomentation, poultice.

ebonite *f.* See **ebanite**.

ebora·rio *m.* worker in ivory.

ebra·ic-o *adj.* (*pl.* **ebra·ici**) Hebrew; Hebraic; Jewish; ristorante —, Kosher restaurant; *n.m.* Jew, Hebrew; Hebrew language. **-a** *f.* Jewess, Hebrew woman. **-amẹnte** *adv.* in Hebrew fashion. **-ista** *m.* Hebrew scholar.

ebra-işmo *m.* Judaism; (ling.) Hebraism. **-ista** *m.* see **ebraicista**, under **ebraico**. **-iẓzare** [A 1] *tr., intr.* (aux. avere) to hebraize. **-iẓzante** *part. adj.* hebraizing.

ebr-ẹo *m.* Jew; l'Ebreo errante, the wandering Jew; in questo posto c'è morto un —, in this seat a Jew died (said when one is having bad luck at cards); confondere Ebrei e Samaritani, to mix things or people that are incompatible; *adj.* Jewish, Hebrew; — di razza, of Jewish blood; — di fede, orthodox Jew, of the Jewish faith; il popolo —, the Jewish race, the chosen people; (pop.) miserly, avaricious. **-e·a** *f.* Jewess.

ebrẹzza *f.* See **ebbrezza**, under **ebbro**.

†**ebriaco** *adj.* See **ubbriaco**.

†**ebriare** *rfl., intr.* to become drunk.

E·bridi *pr.n.f.pl.* (geog.); le —, the Hebrides.

ebrietà *f. indecl.* intoxication, inebriety; drunkenness; (fig.) madness, blindness.

†**ebriezza** *f.* See **ebbrezza**, under **ebbro**.

†**ebrifestoso** *adj.* merry with drink; in one's cups.

ebro[1] *adj.* (poet.). See **ebbro**.

Ebro[2] *pr.n.m.* (geog.) l'—, the river Ebro.

ebulliente *adj.* ebullient, boiling; (fig.) boisterous.

ebulli-ometri·a *f.* (phys.) boiling-point determination. **-o·metro** *m.* (chem.) ebullioscope. **-oscopi·a** *f.* (chem.) ebullioscopy. **-osco·pio** *m.* (chem.) ebullioscope.

ebullizịọne *f.* See **ebollizione**.

†**e·bulo** *m.* (bot.). See **ebbio**.

eburina *f.* (chem.) eburin(e).

ebur·ne-o *adj.* of ivory; as white as ivory; ivory-like, ivory; (med.) eburneous. **-azịọne** *f.* (med.) eburnation.

ecatombe *f.* hecatomb; mass slaughter.

Ecatom·miti, Ecaton·miti *pr.n.m.m.pl. Hundred Tales*, title of a work by G. B. Giraldi, 1565.

†**ecatumbe** *f.* See **ecatombe**.

ecaudato *adj.* (zool.) tail-less.

ecbo·lico *adj.* (med.; anat.) ecbolic.

†**eccecare** *vb.* and derivs. See **acciecare**.

eccedente *part. adj.* See under **eccedere**.

eccẹd-ere [B 1] *tr.* to exceed; questo -e i miei poteri, this is beyond my powers; — la velocità permessa, to exceed the speed limit; to go beyond; to surpass; -e ogni speranza, he fulfils all that was hoped and more; (leg.) to exceed (esp. in the use of force); quando si -ono colposamente i limiti stabiliti dalla legge, when excessive force is used culpably (C.P.); *intr.* (aux. avere) to be excessive; — nel mangiare, to eat too much, to overeat; to go too far, to overstep the limit; ora voi -ete, now you are going too far; nelle punizioni -e, he's too severe with his punishments; to be immoderate, to go to extremes, to overdo things; (leg.) to use excessive force. **-ente** *part. adj.* exceeding; excessive; in excess; surplus; -ente il peso, overweight; (mus.) intervallo -ente, augmented interval; *n.m.* excess, surplus. **-entemẹnte** *adv.* exceedingly; excessively. **-enza** *f.* excess; surplus; (comm.) surplus stock; (techn.) excess.

ecce homo, eccehomo *m. indecl.* (art) painting or figure of Christ with crown of thorns; pare un —, he looks very wretched; essere ridotto un —, to be ill-treated (esp. of someone whose face has been battered).

eccellent-e *adj.* excellent; exquisite; ha un cuore —, he has a good heart; good to eat; extremely efficient. **-emẹnte** *adv.* excellently, splendidly, extremely well.

eccellenza *f.* excellence; pre-eminence; per —, par excellence, preeminently; venire in —, to attain excellence, to become excellent; (title) Excellency; Sua Eccellenza, His Excellency; Vostra Eccellenza, Your Excellency.

eccel·lere [B 1] *intr.* (aux. essere) to excel, to be pre-eminent; (prep. su, tra) to surpass; — sui contemporanei, to stand out pre-eminent among one's contemporaries.

eccels-o *adj.* lofty; high; (fig.) magnificent, best; *pr.n.m.* l'Eccelso, God, the Most High. **-amẹnte** *adv.* loftily; magnificently.

eccen·trica *f.* See under **eccentrico**.

eccen·tric-o *adj.* eccentric; odd, strange; not symmetrical; distant from the centre; luogo —, outlying spot; (geom.) eccentric; *n.m.* (eng.) eccentric; cam; (text.) scatola degli -i, cam box. **-a** *f.* (rlwy.) shunting points; guardia -a, shunter. **-amẹnte** *adv.* eccentrically; strangely, oddly. **-ità** *f.* eccentricity; oddness, strangeness; distance from the centre (of a city); (techn.) eccentricity; eccentric position; (eng.) eccentricity; throw (of a cam).

ecceomo *m. indecl.* See **ecce homo**.

eccep-ire [D 2] *tr.* to except, to object; non ho nulla da —, I have no objection; (leg.) to plead by way of exception or objection; to object to. **-i·bile** *adj.* exceptionable, reprehensible; (leg.) objectionable; which should be opposed.

eccessiv-o *adj.* excessive; immoderate; extreme; idee -e, extremist ideas (in politics). **-amẹnte** *adv.* excessively, immoderately. **-ità** *f.* excessiveness.

eccesso *m.* excess; è gentile fino all'—, he is even too kind; dare in eccessi, to fly into a passion, to make a scene, to fly into hysterics; all'—, excessively; per —, in excess; da un — all'altro, from one extreme to the other; — di peso, excess weight; (leg.) excess;

eccesso (*cont.*)
— di mandato, in excess of one's powers, *ultra vires*; — colposo, culpable excess of force (C.P.); — di potere, excess of jurisdiction (as a ground of appeal) (C.C.P.); †misdeed, misdemeanor.

ecce·tera *adv.* (abbrev. **ecc.**) etcetera, etc., and so on; *n.m.pl. indecl.* etceteras.

†**eccettare** *vb.* and derivs. See **eccettuare**.

eccetto[1] *prep.* except, excepting; save, barring, but; tutti — uno, all but one; *conj.* — che, — che non, — se, unless; †in addition to.

†**eccetto**[2] *m.* exception.

†**eccetto**[3] *m.* reception, receiving.

†**eccetto**[4] *part.* of **eccepire**, q.v.; excepted; privileged; written, noted.

eccettu·are [A 6] *tr.* to except; se ne -ano pochi, with few exceptions. -**a·bile** *adj.* that may be excepted. -**ativo** *adj.* exceptant, that excepts. -**ato** *part. adj.* excepted, not included; excluding, except. -**azione** *f.* excepting, excluding, exclusion.

eccezion-e *f.* exception; l'— prova la regola, the exception proves the rule; a — di, with the exception of; letteratura d'—, literature for the discerning few; fare -i, to make exceptions; d'—, exceptional; opporre — a, to take exception to; reproach, reproof, criticism; (leg.) plea by way of exception or objection; elevare una —, sollevare una —, to raise an objection; — declinatoria, declinatory plea, plea to the jurisdiction; — dilatoria, dilatory plea, plea put in to gain time. -**a·bile** *adj.* see **eccettuabile**. -**ale** *adj.* exceptional; extraordinary, out of the ordinary. -**almente** *adv.* exceptionally, by way of exception. -**are** [A I c] and derivs. see **eccettuare**.

ecchi·m-osi, ecchim-osi *f.* (med.) ecchymosis; bruise. -**o·tico** *adj.* (med.) ecchymotic.

ecci·dio *m.* slaughter, massacre.

eccipiente *m.* (pharm.) excipient; (chem. industr.) vehicle, medium.

†**ecciso** *adj.* excavated.

eccit-are [A I s] *tr.* to excite; to incite; to rouse; to stimulate; to fan; — il riso, to provoke laughter; — l'invidia, to arouse envy; — l'appetito, to give an appetite; — il vomito, to cause vomiting; (electr.) to excite, to produce; — il campo magnetico dal rotore, to produce the field from the rotor; (leg.) to incite; *rfl.* to get excited; to grow angry. -**a·bile** *adj.* excitable. -**abilità** *f.* excitability. -**amento** *m.* exciting, excitement; provoking, provocation; (leg.) incitement; -amento al duello, incitement to duelling; -amento al dispregio delle leggi, incitement to contempt of the law (C.P.). -**ante** *part. adj.* exciting, stimulating; *n.m.* stimulant. -**ativo** *adj.* apt to excite, stimulating. -**ato** *m.* excited; agitated; angry; (electr.) debolmente -ato, under-excited. -**atore** *m.* exciter, excitator; incitor; (electr.) discharge device. -**atrice** *f.* female incitor; (electr.) exciter. -**azione** *f.* excitation; excitement; sexual excitement; (electr.) excitation; ad -azione composta, compound-wound.

†**eccle·sia** *f.* See **chiesa**; (Gk. hist.) ecclesia, assembly.

Ecclesiaste *pr.n.m.* (Bibl.) Ecclesiastes.

ecclesia·stic-o *adj.* ecclesiastical; l'abito —, clerical dress; storia -a, Church history; *n.m.* (Bibl.) Ecclesiasticus; (eccl.) ecclesiastic, churchman, priest; (leg.) cleric; arresto di un — o di un religioso, arrest of a cleric or of a member of a religious order (C.P.P.). -**amente** *adv.* ecclesiastically.

ecclet·tico *adj.* See **eclet·tico**.

ecclissare [A I] and derivs. See **eclissare**.

ecclisse *m., f.* See **eclisse**.

ecclit·tic-a *f.*, -**o** *adj.* See **eclittic-a**, -**o**.

ecco[1] *adv.* here; there; eccomi, here I am; eccoci, here we are; eccomi arrivato, I've got here, here I am, I've come; — quello che volevo dirvi, that's what I wanted to tell you; — fatto il becco all'oca, that's the finishing touch; — servito l'amico, that's cooked his goose; — tutto, that's all, that's all I have to say, that's the lot; — com'è stato, this is what happened; quand'—spuntare la vecchina, when who should appear but the little old woman; *excl.* there!; look!; — il treno che parte!, look, the train is starting!

†**ecco**[2] *m., f.* See **eco**[1].

eccome *excl.* rather!; and how! (also **e come**).

eccondrosi *f.* (med.) chondroma.

ecde·mico *adj.* (med.) ecdemic.

ec·fora *f.* (archit.) ecphora, projection (of moulding, etc.).

echeggi-are [A 3 c] *intr.* (aux. avere, essere) to echo; to resound; *tr.* to echo, to re-echo. -**amento** *m.* echoing; resounding. -**ante** *part. adj.* echoing; resounding; resonant. -**ato** *part. adj.* echoed.

eche·o *m.* (theatr. hist.) echeion, bronze resonating vase used in ancient theatres; (mus.) resonance box of lyre.

e·chide *f.* (zool.) sand viper, *Echis arenicola*.

echidna *f.* echidna, a mythological monster; (zool.) *Echidna* spp., spiny anteater.

echidnina *f.* (chem.) echidnin, serpent venom.

echino *m.* (zool.) sea urchin, *Echinus* sp.; (archit.) ovolo moulding below the abacus on capital of a column.

e·chio *m.* (bot.) bugloss; viper's bugloss, *Echium vulgare*, and other species.

ecista *m.* (hist.) founder of a colony, colonizer.

eclampsi·a *f.* (med.) eclampsia, eclampsy; convulsions.

†**eclemma** *f.* (pharm.) medicine to be dissolved in the mouth.

eclet·tic-o *adj.* eclectic. -**amente** *adv.* eclectically. -**ismo** *m.* eclecticism.

eclettismo *m.* (pop.). See **ecletticismo**, under **eclettico**.

ecli·metro *m.* theodolite.

ecliss-are [A I] *tr.* to eclipse; (fig.) to outshine, to throw into the shade; *rfl.* to be eclipsed; (fig.) to be outshone; to withdraw silently. -**amento** *m.* eclipsing. -**ato** *part. adj.* eclipsed; (fig.) outshone, put in the shade.

ecliss-e *m., f.*, -**i** *m. indecl.* eclipse.

eclit·tic-a *f.* (astron.; geog.) ecliptic. -**o** *adj.* relating to the ecliptic; relating to eclipses.

†**ecli·zia** *f.* (bot.). See **clizia**.

e·cloga *f.* See **egloga**.

eclogite *f.* (miner.) eclogite.

ec-o[1] *m., f.* (*pl.* **echi** *m.* or *indecl.*) echo; fare — di, to repeat; farsi — di una diceria, to repeat a rumour; fare — a, to be an echo of; repercussion; echo poem, in which the final syllables echo and answer those preceding, as: Che fai tu Eco, mentre che io ti chiamo? Amo. Ami tu due, oppure un solo? Un solo. -**ochinesi·a, -ocinesi·a** *f.* imitative movement. -**o·ico** *adj.* relating to an echo.

Eco[2] *pr.n.f.* (myth.) Echo.

eco·fora *f.* (ent.) olive moth, *Oecophora olivella*.

ecogonio·metr-o *m.* echo-detection goniometer. -**ista** *m.* operator who works the echo-detection goniometer.

ecologi·a *f.* (zool.; bot.) ecology.

eco·metro *m.* echo-sounding gear, echo sounder.

econom-ale *adj.*, -**ato** *m.* See under **economo**.

economi·a *f.* economy; thrift; saving; fare —, to save, to be thrifty, to be economical; management; arrangement; economics; — domestica, domestic economy; — politica, political economy; economics; — gretta, — eccessiva, cheese-paring; (leg.) — pubblica, national economy, public weal; delitti contro l'— pubblica, offences against the national economy (C.P.); lavoro in —, job done on cost of labour and materials.

econo·mic-o *adj.* economical; economic; thrifty; cheap; (leg.) attività -a, gainful occupation (C.C.). -**amente** *adv.* economically; thriftily; cheaply.

econom-ista *m., f.* economist. -**izzare** [A I] *tr.* to save; *intr.* (aux. avere) to economize. -**izzato** *part. adj.* saved; economized. -**izzatore** *m.* economizer, saver, one who economizes; (eng.) economizer.

eco·nom-o *m.* steward; bursar; almoner; guardian, custodian, keeper; *adj.* economical; thrifty; sparing. -**ale** *adj.* relating to a steward or bursar, etc. -**ato** *m.* stewardship; bursarship; steward's office; bursar's office; assessore all'-ato e beni immobili, Town Councillor in charge of municipal budget and real estate.

ecpirosi *f.* (Stoic philos.) end of the world by conflagration.

ectasi·a *f.* (gramm.) ectasis, lengthening of a short syllable; (med.) ectasis.

ectipsi *f.* (gramm.) ecthlipsis.

ecto-dattili·a *f.* (med.) ectodactylism. -**derma** *m.* (anat.) ectoderm. -**der·mico** *adj.* ectodermal.

ectogramma *m.*, **ectolitro** *m.* See **ettogramma**, etc.

ectoplasma *m.* ectoplasm.

ectro·pio *m.* (anat.) ectropion.

Ecuador *pr.n.m.* (geog.) l'—, Ecuador.

E·cuba *pr.n.f.* (myth.) Hecuba.

ecu·leo *m.* (Rom. antiq.) wooden horse used as an instrument of torture.

ecume·nic-o *adj.* (eccl.) oecumenical; (geog.) habitable. (-**amente** *adv.*) -**ità** *f. indecl.* (eccl.) oecumenical character.

eczem-a *m.* (med.) eczema. -**atoso** *adj.* (med.) eczematous.

ed *conj.* See e².

edac-e *adj.* devouring; edacious; harmful; destructive. **-ità** *f.* voracity, edacity.

Edda *pr.n.f.* Edda.

eddo·mada *f.* and derivs. See **ebdomada**.

edelite *f.* (miner.) aedelite, prehnite.

edem-a *m.* (med.) oedema. **-atico, -atoso** *adj.* (med.) oedematous.

E·den *pr.n.m. indecl.* Eden, earthly paradise; (fig.) heaven on earth.

ęder-a *f.* (bot.) ivy, *Hedera helix*; — terrestre, ground ivy, *Glechoma hederaceum*. **-a·ceo** *adj.* (bot.) hederaceous, pertaining to ivy. **-i·fero** *adj.* (poet.) adorned with ivy, garlanded with ivy.

edi·cola *f.* (rel.) small chapel or shrine; newspaper-stall, kiosk.

edific-are [A 2 s] *tr.* to build; to erect; to raise; to edify; to enlighten; — una persona, to set a person a good example. **-amento** *m.* building, constructing; building, edifice; edifying, edification. **-ante** *part. adj.* edifying; building; †*n.m.* builder. **-antemente** *adv.* in an edifying manner. †**-ata** *f.* construction. **-ativo** *adj.* edifying. **-ato** *part. adj.* built, constructed; founded; edified. **-atore** *m.* builder. (**-atrice** *f.*) **-ato·rio** *adj.* relating to building; arte -atoria, architecture; suitable for building; suolo -atorio, building land. **-azione** *f.* (act of) building, constructing; edifying, edification.

edifi·c-io *m.* (*pl.* **-i**) building; structure; block of buildings; (leg.) abbattimento di —, pulling down of a building (C.C.); fabric; orderly composition, construction; logical construction; stratagem; l'— sociale, the social order, Society; — delle macchine, engine house; (leg.) — della difesa, the structure of the defence; del condominio negli -i, (the law) of co-ownership of buildings (C.C.).

edifi·z-io *m.* (*pl.* **-i**) (Tusc.). See **edificio**.

edil-e *adj.* (often pron. **e·dile**) building, relating to building; relating to building trade; *n.m.* (Rom. antiq.) aedile. **-i·zia** *f.* building trade, building; materiale per -izia, building material; (leg.) norme di -izia, building regulations. **-i·zio** *adj.* relating to building, building; regolamento -izio, building regulations; arte -izia, building, architecture; opere -izie, works, building; (leg.) proprietà -izia, property consisting of, in the form of, buildings; built-up property (C.C.).

†**e·dima** *f.* week.

Edimburgo *pr.n.m.* (geog.) Edinburgh.

E·dipo *pr.n.m.* (myth.) Oedipus; L'— re, *Oedipus Rex*; (psychol.) il complesso di —, the Oedipus complex.

e·dit-o *adj.* published; edited. **-ore** *m.* publisher; editor; (leg.) -ore responsabile, editor or publisher on whom civil and criminal liability rests, responsible editor (C.P.); *adj.* publishing; casa -rice, publishing firm, publishers. **-ori·a** *f.* publishing industry; publishers. **-oriale** *adj.* editorial. **-orialista** *m.* leader-writer.

Editta *pr.n.f.* Edith.

editt-o *m.* edict; (fig.) decree, law. **-ale** *adj.* relating to an edict.

†**edi·tuo** *m.* (Rom. antiq.) guardian of sacred precincts.

edizione *f.* publication; publishing; edition; l'— del libro è esaurita, the book is out of print; — a tiratura ristretta, limited edition; — tascabile, pocket edition; — economica, cheap edition; — riveduta, revised edition; (cinem.) segretaria di —, script girl; (mus.) rendering; (leg.) contratto di —, a contract of publication.

Edoardo *pr.n.m.* Edward.

edon-ișmo *m.* hedonism. **-ista** *m., f.* hedonist. **-i·stico** *adj.* hedonistic.

edotto, (Rom.) **edotto** *adj.* informed; — di, informed about, acquainted with; rendere qualcuno —, to inform someone, to put someone in the picture.

ędra *f.* See **edera**.

edredone *m.* (orn.) Eider duck, *Somateria mollissima*; eiderdown quilt.

educand-a *f.* girl pupil (in convent, or old-fashioned boarding-school, etc.); (fig.) neat and meek little girl; divisa da —, prim traditional school uniform for girls; vestita da —, primly dressed; un aspetto di —, a prim appearance. **-ato** *m.* girls' seminary; boarding-school for girls (sometimes within a convent).

educ-are [A 2 s] *tr.* to bring up; to educate, to train. **-amento** *m.* up-bringing; education. **-ativo** *adj.* educative, educational. **-ato** *part. adj.* well-bred, polite; mal -ato, rude; educated, trained. **-atamente** *adv.* politely. **-atore** *m.*, **-atrice** *f.* educator, teacher. **-ato·rio** *adj.* (*pl.* **-atòri**) girls' school; charity school or home.

educazione *f.* good-breeding, good manners; quel giovanotto è senza —, that young man is really ill-bred; education; — fisica, physical training, gymnastics; Ministero dell'— nazionale,

---

Ministry of Education; culture, rearing (of plants, silk worms, etc.); (leg.) education; mantenimento ed —, maintenance and education; le spese di mantenimento e di — non sono soggette a collazione, the expenses of maintenance and education do not have to be brought into hotchpot (C.C.).

†**edu·cere** *tr.* to lead, to conduct; to bring forth; to give rise to; to introduce.

edulcor-are [A 1 s] *tr.* to sweeten, to add sweetening to. **-ato** *part. adj.* sweetened; with sweetening added; (fig.) sickly, affected. **-azione** *f.* sweetening.

edule *adj.* edible, eatable.

†**edu·lio** *m.* food, nourishment.

†**edurre** *vb.* and derivs. See **educere**.

ef-ebo *m.* (Gk. antiq.) young man, adolescent; effeminate young man. **-e·bico** *adj.* ephebic.

e·fedr-a *f.* (bot.) sea-grape, *Ephedra distachyos*. **-ina** *f.* (chem.) ephedrine.

efe·lide *f.* freckle.

efeme·ride *f.* See **effemeride**.

efemerina *f.* (bot.) spiderwort, *Tradescantia virginiana*; *m.* (bot.) meadow saffron, autumn crocus, *Colchicum autumnale*.

efe·mero *adj.* See **effimero**.

efe·si-o *adj.* Ephesian. **-e** *f.pl.* (Gk. antiq.) festival of Artemis at Ephesus.

E·feso *pr.n.m.* (geog.) Ephesus.

†**effa·bile** *adj.* expressible; non —, ineffable.

†**effascinazione** *f.* fascination.

effato *m.* dictum, axiom.

effau·t, effaut·te *m.* (mus.) F fa ut, F below middle C.

effe *m., f. indecl.* name of the letter F; la città dell'—, Florence.

effeme·ride *f.* almanac; journal; periodical publication, usually scientific or literary; effemeridi nautiche (*or* astronomiche), nautical almanac.

effe·mero *adj.* See **effimero**.

effe(m)min-are [A 1 sc] *tr.* to make effeminate; to corrupt; *rfl.* to become effeminate. **-amento** *m.* corrupting. **-atęzza** *f.* effeminacy. **-ato** *part. adj.* effeminate; weak, soft. **-atamente** *adv.* in an effeminate manner. (**-atore** *m.* **-atrice** *f.*) **-azione** *f.* corruption; effeminacy.

efferat-o *adj.* brutal; ferocious, savage; cruel. (**-amente** *adv.*) **-ag·gine** *f.*, **-ęzza** *f.* brutality; ferocity, savagery; cruelty; atrocity.

efferente *adj.* (med.) efferent; (chem.) tubo —, cannello —, side-tube of a distillation flask, outlet.

effervesc-ente *adj.* sparkling, effervescent; (metall.) rimmed (of steel). **-enza** *f.* effervescence; excitement; agitation.

†**effeto** *adj.* feeble, effete.

effettiv-o *adj.* real; actual; costo —, actual cost; moneta -a, cash; effective; socio —, working partner; valore —, real value; entrate -e, realized revenue; (mil., etc.) in servizio permanente —, serving as a regular in the armed forces; *n.m.* total; net amount; sum total; establishment, total personnel; (mil.) l'— del battaglione, the strength of the battalion; *adv.* quite, really, just; pare — una scimmia, he looks just like a monkey. **-amente** *adv.* really, actually; effectively; quite, just so, exactly; agreed, I agree. **-ità** *f.* effectiveness; actuality, reality.

effett-o *m.* effect; consequence, result; in —, in effect, in actual fact; fare —, to have effect, to take effect, to be striking, to be effective, to make an impression; il giallo col bruno non fa —, yellow and brown are not a very striking combination; mi fece — vederlo così, it gave me quite a turn to see him like that; una corrida mi farebbe troppo —, I couldn't bear to see a bull-fight; mandare ad —, to put into effect; dare — a, to carry out, to fulfil; senz'—, inoperative, to no effect; cercare l'—, to try to make an effect; di molto —, very effective; per — di, in consequence of; purpose; all'— di, for the sake of; appearance, aspect; fare l'— di uno sciocco, to look like a fool; mi fa l'— di un uomo disgraziato, he looks to me like an unhappy man; screw, break, spin (on a ball); (eng.) action; a semplice —, single-acting; pompa a doppio —, double-action pump; (finan.) bill, note of hand, effect; — cambiario, bill of exchange; -i in portafoglio, bills in hand; (leg.) effect; per — di legge, by law; il contratto non produce — rispetto ai terzi, the contract (has no effect upon) does not affect third parties; l'— devolutivo dell'appello, the extent to which a cause or matter is handed up, upon appeal; in —, (of contracts, deeds, etc.) in proper form and manner; per ogni — di ragione

effett-o (*cont.*)
e di legge, for the purposes of law and justice; *pl.* effects, objects, articles, belongings; (leg.) gli ~i del contratto, the effects of the contract; a tutti gli ~i, for all purposes; la costituzione di parte civile una volta avvenuta produce i suoi ~i in ogni grado del procedimento, the appearance of a civil party, once made, is effective (good) throughout the proceedings; atto privo di ~i, nugatory act; matrimonio avente (*or* valido a tutti gli) ~i civili, legally valid marriage. **-ac·cio** *m. pejor.* poor effect, bad effect; superficial impression. **-ista** *m.* (art) painter who strives after effects. **-one** *m. augm.* tremendous success, great impression; fa un ~one, it's sensational, it's very spectacular.

effettua·bile *adj.* See under **effettuare**.

effettual-e *adj.* real, effectual, actual. **-mente** *adv.* really, in fact, actually **-ità** *f.* reality.

effettu-are [A6] *tr.* to effect, to execute, to carry out; to make; to bring about; *rfl.* to be accomplished, to take place. **-a·bile** *adj.* that may be effected, possible. **-abilità** *f.* possibility, potentiality. **-ato** *part. adj.* effected, carried out; (finan.) entrata ~ata, collected revenue. **-azione** *f.* execution, fulfilment.

†**effettuoso**[1] *adj.* efficacious, effective.

†**effettuoso**[2] *adj.* and derivs. See **affettuoso**, under **affetto**.

†**effezione**[1] *f.* effect, effecting.

†**effezione**[2] *f.* See **affezione**.

efficac-e *adj.* efficacious, effective, efficient; effectual; able; adequate; (theol.) efficacious (grace). **-emente** *adv.* efficaciously, effectively; efficiently.

effica·c-ia *f.* (*pl.* **-ie**) efficacy; effectiveness; potency; (mech.) efficiency; (leg.) execution, extent, operation; l'— della legge nel tempo, the temporal operation of the law (C.C.); l'— delle leggi penali, the extent of the criminal law (C.P.P.); — delle sentenze straniere, execution of foreign judgements (C.C.P.); — giuridica, validity in law; avere — giuridica, to have legal effect.

effici-ente *adj.* efficient; serviceable; causa ~, effective cause. **-entemente** *adv.* efficiently, effectively; effectually. **-enza** *f.* efficiency; in ~enza, in working order.

effigi-are [A3] *tr.* to portray; to represent; to paint; to sculpt. **-ato** *part. adj.* portrayed; represented; painted; sculptured. **-atore** *m.*, **-atrice** *f.* one who makes a picture or effigy.

effi·g-ie, effig-e *f. indecl.* effigy, image; portrait, picture; bust, statue.

effi·mera *f.* (ent.). See **efimera**.

effi·mero *adj.* ephemeral; lasting a day; transient.

†**effin·gere** *tr.* to portray, to represent.

effloresc-ente *adj.* (chem.) efflorescent. **-enza** *f.* (chem.; phys. path.) efflorescence; (techn.) bloom.

efflu-ire [D2] *intr.* (*aux.* essere) to flow out, to run out. **-ente** *adj.* effluent, outflowing; *n.m.* effluent, outflow, outfall.

efflusso *m.* effusion, efflux, discharge; outflow; — di sangue, flow of blood.

efflu·vio *m.* effluvium; exhalation; (electr.) effluvium; glow discharge; perdita per —, corona loss.

effond-ere [C2] *tr.* to pour out, to pour forth; to be generous with; to give out, to effuse; to exhale; to shed; to give vent to; to spread. **-imento** *m.* pouring forth.

effosso·rio *adj.* designed for excavating; arnesi effossori, digging tools.

effrazione *f.* (leg.) house-breaking; furto con —, larceny and house-breaking.

effren-ato *adj.* immoderate, unbridled. **-atamente** *adv.* immoderately.

effumazione *f.* exhalation.

effusio·metro *m.* (chem.) effusiometer.

effusione *f.* effusion; — di lagrime, shedding of tears.

effusivo *adj.* (geol.) effusive.

effuso *part.* of **effondere**, q.v., *adj.* poured out, shed.

efi·mera *f.* (ent.) mayfly, *Ephemera* spp.

efi·mero *adj.* See **effimero**.

e·for-o *m.* (Gk. antiq.) ephor, magistrate of ancient Sparta. **-ato** *m.* office of ephor.

ege·mon-e *m.* leader. **-ìa** *f.* hegemony.

egemo·nic-o *adj.* hegemonic. **-amente** *adv.* hegemonically.

ege·o *pr.n.m.* (geog.) Aegean; il mare —, the Aegean Sea.

Ege·ria *pr.n.f.* Egeria; (fig.) mistress and counsellor, esp. of a statesman or other public figure.

e·gida *f.* (myth.) aegis; shield; (fig.) protection; sotto l'— di, under the aegis of.

Egi·dio *pr.n.m.* Giles.

Egina *pr.n.f.* (geog.) Aegina.

egi·oco *adj.* (poet.) aegis-bearing.

e·gira *f.* (hist.) hegira, the flight of Mahomet from Mecca in A.D. 622.

†**egit·tico** *adj.* Egyptian.

Egitt-o *pr.n.m.* (geog.) Egypt; cose d'—, wonderful things; ma che libri d'—!, bother the books!; macchè moglie d'—!, quella era la sua amante, his wife?—not likely!, she was his mistress. **-ologìa** *f.* Egyptology. **-o·logo** *m.* Egyptologist.

egiz-i·aco *adj.* Egyptian; *n.m.* a kind of ointment. **-iano** *adj.* Egyptian; *n.m.* (typ.) Egyptian (type-face).

egi·zio *adj.* ancient Egyptian.

eglantina *f.* eglantine; sweet briar.

egli *m. prn. 3rd pers. sing.* (formal usage) he (cf. **lui**); (pleon.) it; che vi pare —?, what do you think of it?

eglino *m. prn. 3rd pers. pl.* (formal usage, rare) they (cf. **loro**).

e·gloga *f.* eclogue.

egocen·tric-o *adj.* self-centred, egocentric. **-ità** *f.* self-centredness.

egocentrismo *m.* See **egocentricità**.

ego-ismo *m.* selfishness; (philos.) egoism. **-ista** *m., f.* selfish person, egoist. **-i·stico** *adj.* selfish, egotistical, egoistical. **-tismo** *m.* egotism.

egre·gi-o *adj.* remarkable, distinguished; noble; excellent; worthy; — signore, Dear Sir. **-amente** *adv.* excellently; with great distinction.

egresso *m.* egress, exit; going out.

egretta *f.* (orn.) egret.

egro *adj.* (poet.) sick, weak, infirm; languishing.

egual-e *adj.* equal; even; *n.m.* equal; non ha l'—, he has no equal. **-izzatore** *m.* (text.) evener (cf. **uguale** and derivs.).

eh *excl.* (pron. è) ah! (expressing disapproval doubt, wonder, etc.); eh! (expressing surprise, impatience, etc.).

ehi *excl.* hello!; I say!; hoy!

ehm *excl.* ahem! (often used threateningly).

ei *m. prn. 3rd pers. sing.* (poet.). See **egli**.

e·ia, e·ia, alalà *excl.* (Fascist) hip, hip, hooray.

eiacul-are [A I S] *tr.* to ejaculate (fluid). **-azione** *f.* ejaculation (of fluid).

Eidelberga *pr.n.f.* (geog.) Heidelberg.

eiett-are [A I] *tr.* (phys.; hydraul.) to eject, to spout. **-ore** *m.* (eng.) ejector, educator.

ei·ra *f.* (zool.) eyra, *Felis eira*.

elabor-are [A I S] *tr.* to elaborate; to work out; to evolve; to draw up, to devise; to digest. **-atezza** *f.* elaborateness. **-ato** *part. adj.* elaborated; elaborate; evolved; drawn up, devised; digested. **-azione** *f.* elaboration; (mus.) development section.

elabro *m.* (bot.) hellebore; — bianco, white hellebore, *Veratrum album*; — nero, *Veratrum nigrum*.

elaico *adj.* (chem.) elaic.

ela·id-e *f.* (bot.) oil-nut palm-tree, *Elaeïs guineensis*. **-ina** *f.* (chem.) elaidin. **-i·nico** *adj.* (chem.) elaidic.

elamì *m.* (mus.) E la mi, E below middle C.

elarg-ire [D2] *tr.* to give liberally; to grant. **-itore** *m.*, **-itrice** *f.* generous donor. **-izione** *f.* donation, gift.

elastanza *f.* (electr.) elastance.

elasticità *f.* spring, springiness, resilience; elasticity; agility; l'— della coscienza, elasticity of conscience.

ela·stic-o *adj.* elastic; springy; resilient; buoyant; supple; coscienza ~a, accommodating conscience; intelligenza ~a, lively intelligence, nimble wits; *n.m.* elastic; spring mattress; rubber band; garter; two-way-stretch; rubber corset.

elastina *f.* (chem.) elastin.

elasto·mero *m.* (chem.) elastomer.

elatere *m.* (ent.) click beetle, *Elator* spp.

elate·rio *m.* elastic force, resilience; (bot.) squirting cucumber, *Ecballium elaterium*; its juice.

Elb-a *pr.n.f.* (geog.) Elba; l'isola d'—, the island of Elba. **-ano** *adj.* (geog.) relating to Elba; native to Elba; *n.m.* native of Elba. (**-ana** *f.*)

elc-e *f., m.* (bot.) see **leccio**. **-eto** *m.* wood or grove of holm-oaks.

eledone *m.* (zool.) a kind of octopus, *Eledone moschata*. See also **moscardino**.

elefant-e *m.* (zool.) elephant; — di mare, lobster, *Homarus vulgaris*. **-esco** *adj.* (*m.pl.* **-eschi**) elephantine. **-essa** *f.* female elephant. **-i·asi** *f.* (med.) elephantiasis; (admin. fig.) top-heaviness, clumsiness. †**-o** *m.* see **elefante**.

elegant-e *adj.* elegant; smart, stylish, fashionable; graceful; polished; distinguished; (leg.) — questione di diritto, nice point of law. **-emente** *adv.* elegantly; smartly, fashionably; gracefully. **-one** *m.* toff, dandy.

eleganza *f.* elegance; distinction; style; grace.

eleg·g-ere [C12] *tr.* to elect; to appoint; to select, to choose; — piuttosto (che), to prefer; (leg.) to choose; — domicilio speciale, to adopt a domicile of choice (C.C.P.). **-ente** *part. adj.* electing; †relating to choice; *n.m.* elector. **-i·bile** *adj.* eligible. **-ibilità** *f.* eligibility. **-itore** *m.*, **-itrice** *f.* see **elettore**.

eleg-i·a *f.* elegy. **-i·aco** *adj.* elegiac, elegiacal.

elegiambo *m.* (prosod.) elegiambus.

ele·ison, eleisonne *m. indecl.* See **chirieleison**.

elementar-e *adj.* elementary; scuola —, primary school; simple, easy; basic, rudimentary; (chem.) elementary, in element form. **-mente** *adv.* elementarily; simply, in an easy way.

element-o *m.* element; unit; member; part (of a machine), section; (biol.; electr.) cell; (chem.) element; (eng.) cartridge (of a filter); trovarsi nel suo —, to be in one's element; è un cattivo — nella scuola, he is a bad influence in the school; (leg.) element; l'— psicologico del reato, the moral element of the offence (C.P.); *pl.* elements; lottare contro gli -i, to battle with the elements; gli -i sovversivi, the subversive influences; gli -i della matematica, elementary principles of mathematics, elements of mathematics.

elemo·şin-a *f.* alms; charity; campare d'—, to live on charity; chiedere l'—, to beg; fare l'—, to bestow charity, to give alms. **-are** [A1] *intr.* (*aux.* avere) to ask alms, to beg; *tr.* to beg, to ask for. **-iere** *m.* (eccl.) almoner.

E·lena *pr.n.f.* Helen; Helena; Eleanor; (geog.) l'isola di Sant'—, the island of St Helena.

elenc-are [A2] *tr.* to make a list of, to list; to inventory; to enumerate. **-ato** *part. adj.* listed, in a list; enumerated.

elen·co *m.* (*pl.* **-chi**) list; catalogue; inventory; — degli oratori, list of speakers; — degli abbonati al telefono, — telefonico, telephone directory; (logic) elenchus, a logical refutation; (leg.) schedule; — allegato, schedule annexed.

ele·o *adj.* (poet.) Olympic (from Elis in Peloponnesus where the Olympic games were held); la palma elea, the victor's crown.

elett-a *f.* choice; élite. **-ęzza** *f.* distinction; elegance. **-ivo** *adj.* elective; having the power to elect; chosen; affinità -iva, elective affinity, elective attraction; (leg.) domicilio -ivo, domicile of choice, address for service.

elett-o *part.* of **eleggere**, q.v.; *adj.* elect; chosen; (Bibl.) il Popolo —, the Chosen People, the Chosen; elected; choice; distinguished; il suo — sapere, his outstanding knowledge; maniere -e, exquisite manners; (leg.) domicilio —, domicile of choice, address for service (C.C.P.); *n.m.* elect, chosen; successful candidate; gli -i del Cielo, God's elect. **-amente** *adv.* with distinction, with discrimination; with care.

elett-ore *m.* elector; constituent; (hist.) Elector. **-orale** *adj.* electoral; scheda -orale, ballot-paper; urna -orale, ballot-box; razza -orale ed escuriale, Saxon merino breed (of sheep). **-orato** *m.* franchise; electorship; (hist.) Electorate.

Elettra *pr.n.f.* (myth.) Electra.

elettra·uto *m.* workshop for electrical repairs to motor vehicles.

elettricista *m.* electrician.

elettricità *f.* electricity.

elet·tric-o *adj.* electric; electrical. **-amente** *adv.* electrically.

elettrific-are [A2s] *tr.* to electrify. **-ato** *part. adj.* ferrovia -ata, electric railway. **-azione** *f.* electrification.

elettrizz-are [A1] *tr.* to electricize, to charge with electricity; (fig.) to thrill, to excite; to startle; to electrify. **-ante** *part. adj.* (fig.) thrilling, exciting. **-ato** *part. adj.* charged with electricity; (fig.) thrilled, excited; startled. **-azione** *f.* charging with electricity.

elettro *m.* yellow amber; (metall.) electrum.

elettro-acu·stica *f.* electro-acoustics. **-acu·stico** *adj.* electro-acoustic. **-ana·lişi** *f. indecl.* (chem.) electroanalysis. **-biologi·a** *f.* electro-biology. **-calamita** *f.* electromagnet. **-cardio·grafo** *m.* (med.) electrocardiograph. **-cardiogramma** *m.* (med.) electrocardiogram, E.C.G. **-ca·ustica** *f.*, **-caute·rio** *m.* (med.) electrocautery, electric cauter. **-chi·mica** *f.* electrochemistry. **-chi·mico** *adj.* electrochemical; serie -chimica, electromotive series; *n.m.* electrochemist. **-choc** *m. indecl.* (prn. as in French) (med.) electric shock treatment. **-cine·tica** *f.* electrokinetics. **-cuzione** *f.* electrocution. **-deposizione** *f.* electro-plating; electro-deposition. **-dia·lisi** *f. indecl.* (phys.) electrodialysis.

-dializzatore *m.* (phys.) electrodialyzer. **-dina·mica** *f.* electro-dynamics. **-dina·mico** *adj.* electrodynamic. **-dinamo·metro** *m.* electrodynamometer. **-dome·stici** *m.pl.* household electric appliances. **-dotto** *m.* electric transmission line, electric main, power line; (leg.) -dotto coattivo, compulsory way-leave for electric power line (C.C.). **-filtro** *m.* electrostatic filter. **-fo·nico** *adj.* organo-fonico, electronic organ. **-foresi** *f. indecl.* electrophoresis. **-magnete** *m.* electromagnet. **-magne·tico** *adj.* electromagnetic. **-magnetişmo** *m.* electromagnetism. **-metallurgi·a** *f.* electrometallurgy. **-mecca·nico** *adj.* electromechanical. **-motore** *m.* electric motor; *adj.* electromotive. (**-motrice** *adj. f.*) **-motrice** *f.* (rlwy.) electric rail car. **-negativo** *adj.* electronegative. **-oşmoşi** *f. indecl.* (phys.) electro-endosmosis. **-pompa** *f.* (eng.) electric pump, motor-driven pump. **-positivo** *adj.* electropositive. **-sco·pio** *m.* electroscope; -scopio a foglie d'oro, gold leaf electroscope; -scopio condensatore, condensing electroscope. **-sta·tica** *f.* electrostatics. **-sta·tico** *adj.* electrostatic. **-tassi·a** *f.* (biol.) galvanotaxis, galvanotropism. **-tec·nica** *f.* electrical engineering. **-tec·nico** *adj.* electrical, relating to electrical engineering; *n.m.* electrical engineer. **-terape·utica** *f.* (med.) electro-therapeutics. **-terape·utico** *adj.* (med.) electro-therapeutical. **-terapi·a** *f.* (med.) electro-therapy. **-treno** *m.* (rlwy.) streamlined electric engine, express luxury train. **-tropişmo** *m.* (biol.) galvanotropism. **-valenza** *f.* (chem.) electrovalence.

elettrodo *m.* electrode.

elettr-o·fono *m.* (mus.) electronic organ. **-o·foro** *m.* (phys.) electrophorus. **-o·grafo** *m.* (electr.) electrograph. **-o·lisi** *f. indecl.* electrolysis. **-oli·tico** *adj.* electrolytic. **-o·lito** *m.* electrolyte. **-olizzatore** *m.* electrolyzer. **-o·metro** *m.* electrometer. **-one** *m.* electron. **-o·nica** *f.* electronics. **-o·nico** *adj.* electronic; moltiplicatore -onico, electron multiplier. **-otipi·a** *f.* (typ.) electrotype printing. **-o·tipo** *m.* (typ.) electrotype, electro. **-o·tono** *m.* (physiol.) electrotonus.

elettua·rio *m.* (pharm.) electuary.

Ele·uş-i *pr.n.f.* (Gk. antiq. geog.) Eleusis. **-ino** *adj.* (Gk. antiq.) Eleusinian; le feste -ine, the Eleusinia; i misteri -ini, the Eleusinian mysteries; (fig.; iron.) i misteri -ini della burocrazia, the mysterious arcana of bureaucracy.

elev-are [A1s] *tr.* to raise; to erect; to elevate; to promote; to exalt, to extol; — ai sette cieli, to laud to the skies; (math.) — al quadrato, to square; (leg.) — una contravvenzione (q.v.) ad uno, to fine someone 'on the spot'; *rfl.* to rise; to raise oneself; to get to one's feet. **-amento** *m.* raising; rise. **-ante** *part. adj.* raising. **-atezza** *f.* loftiness; nobility, dignity. **-ato** *part. adj.* raised; erected; exalted; elevated; high; noble; high-minded; a prezzo -ato, expensive. **-atamente** *adv.* nobly; in an elevated style. **-atore** *m.* (industr.) elevator, lifting device; -atore a catena, chain elevator; (mining) -atore a griglia, grizzly elevator; -atore a nastro, belt elevator; -atore a sospensione, skip hoist; -atore a tazze, bucket elevator; (eng.) -atore di pressione, -atore di tensione, booster; (electr.) -atore di tensione, step-up transformer. **-azione** *f.* elevation; raising; rise; increase; erecting, erection; height; (liturg.) elevation; (eng.) angle of elevation; (eng. drawing) elevation; (leg.) -azione di una contravvenzione (q.v.), imposition of an 'on the spot' fine.

elezione *f.* election; appointment; choice; Vaso d'—, Chosen Vessel, i.e. St Paul; (pol.) election; — parziale, by-election; — amministrativa, municipal election; (leg.) choice; — di domicilio, adoption of domicile of choice or address for service.

elfo *m.* elf, sprite.

eli·aco *adj.* (astron.) heliacal.

eliantina *f.* (chem.) helianthine, methyl orange.

e·lica *f.* helix, spiral; (naut.) propeller, screw; — destrorsa, right-handed screw; — sinistrorsa, left-handed screw; — a pale riversibili, feathering or reversible screw; mozzo dell'—, propeller boss; albero dell'—, asse dell'—, propeller shaft; †pozzo dell'—, propeller well permitting the withdrawal of the screw; (aeron.) propeller, airscrew; (zool.) snail; *pl.* (naut.) eliche gemelle, twin screw.

e·lice[1] *f.* See **elica**.

E·lice[2] *pr.n.f.* (geog.) Elice, in the province of Pescara.

elice[3] *3rd pers. sing. pres. indic.* of **elicere** q.v.; (poet.) elicits, draws out.

†eli·cere *tr.* to elicit, to draw out.

elico·id-e *f.*, *adj.* helicoid. **-ale** *adj.* helicoid, helicoidal; filo -ale, steel wire for cutting marble.

Elicọna pr.n.f. (geog.) Helicon.
elicot·tero m. helicopter.
elicrişo m. (poet.) everlasting flower.
eli·dere [C3] tr. (gramm.) to elide; to neutralize, to annul, to cancel out; to suppress; to destroy; recip. rfl. to cancel each other out.
†eligente adj. See eleggente, under eleggere.
eligi·bile adj. and deriv. See eleggibile, under eleggere.
eligibilità f. indecl. eligibility.
elimin-are [AIS] tr. to eliminate; to suppress; to dispense with; (euph.) to kill. -ato part. adj. eliminated; suppressed; weeded out; (euph.) killed. -ato·rio adj. serving to eliminate; (sport) gara -atoria, eliminating race, bout, trial (also -ato·ria f.). -azione f. elimination; expulsion.
e·li-o m. (chem.) helium. -ocen·trico adj. (astron.) heliocentric. -ofano·grafo m. heliograph. -ografi·a f. heliography; (typ.) process engraving; heliogravure. -ogra·fico adj. heliographic. -o·grafo m. heliograph. -oincisiọne f. (typ.) process engraving. -o·metro m. (astron.) heliometer. -osco·pio m. helioscope, solar prism. -ostato m. (astron.; surv.) heliostat. -oterapi·a f. heliotherapy, sun therapy. -otipi·a f. heliotypy; heliotype. -oti·pico adj. heliotypic.
eliotro·pia f. (miner.). See eliotropio.
eliotro·pio m. (bot.) heliotrope, Heliotropium europaeum; (miner.) bloodstone.
eliporto m. (aeron.) helicopter landing-ground, heliport.
Elişabętt-a pr.n.f. Elizabeth. -iano adj. (hist.) Elizabethan.
eli·şio adj. (myth.) Elysian; i campi elisi, the Elysian fields.
elişiọne f. (gramm.) elision.
elişi·r m. indecl., elişire m. elixir.
eliso[1] part. of elidere, q.v.
Eliso[2] pr.n.m. (myth.) Elysium.
elisse f. See ellisse.
e·litra f. (ent.) elytron.
elixi·r m. indecl. See elisir.
ella prn.f. (pl. esse) she; prn. m., f. you (in formal usage).
elle m., f. name of the letter L.
elle·boro m. (bot.) — nero, Christmas rose, Helleborus niger; — puzzolente, bear's foot, stinking hellebore, H. foetidus; — verde, green hellebore, H. viridis.
elle·n-ico adj. Hellenic, Greek. (-icaménte adv.) -işmo m. Hellenism. -ista m., f. Hellenist; Greek scholar, 'Grecian'. -i·stico adj. Hellenistic. -iẓẓare [AI] intr. (aux. avere) to Hellenize; to adopt Greek idioms or ideas.
el·leno[1] adj., n.m. Hellene.
†el·leno[2] prn. f.pl. they.
ęllera, (Rom.) el·lera f. (pop.). See edera.
†elli prn. m. See egli; they; them; it; there.
†ellionfante m. elephant.
elliss-e f. (geom.) ellipse. -o·grafo m. (geom.) trammel, elliptical compass. -o·ide f. (geom.) ellipsoid. -o·idico adj. (math.) ellipsoidal.
ellissi f. indecl. (gramm.) ellipsis.
ellit·tic-o[1] adj. (geom.) elliptical. (-aménte adv.)
ellit·tic-o[2] adj. (gramm.) elliptical. (-aménte adv.)
†ello prn. m. he; him; it; there.
elmętto m. dim. of elmo[1], q.v.; helmet (of simple shape without visor or throat-piece); protective headgear worn by miners; †soldier wearing helmet; (zool.) Cassis sulcosa, a marine gastropod whose shell may be engraved with cameos.
elminti m.pl. (zool.) Helminth worms.
ęlmo[1] m. helm, helmet; (herald.) helm; — graticolato, grilled helm; — posto a destra, three-quarter face to the dexter; — posto a sinistra, three-quarter face to the sinister; (zool.) Dolium galea, a marine gastropod.
†Elmo[2] pr.n.m. Elmo; fuochi di Sant'—, form of electrostatic energy producing faint light sometimes seen on the top of masts at night in bad weather, St Elmo's fire.
elocuziọne f. elocution; diction; expression, propriety of style.
elogi-are [A3] tr. to commend; to praise; to eulogize; to laud. -ato part. adj. eulogized, praised, commended; lauded. -atọre m. eulogist; adj. laudatory. (-atrice f.)
elo·g-io m. eulogy, praise. -ista m., f. eulogist.
elongaziọne f. (astron.) elongation; †separation, parting; †departure.
eloquen-te adj. eloquent; moving; significant; meaningful; possessing the gift of the gab; n.m. eloquent person; a good talker.

-teménte adv. eloquently, with eloquence. -za f. eloquence; power of expression; facility of expression; oratory; significance.
elo·quio m. speech, language; mode of expression; †utterance.
ęlsa[1] f. hilt.
Elsa[2] pr.n.f. Elsa, Ailsa.
elucid-are [AIS] tr. to elucidate, to explain. (-ato part. adj.)
elucubr-are [AIS] tr. to compose with painstaking effort, to spend 'midnight oil' upon. -ato part. adj. composed with painstaking effort. -aziọne f. painstaking cerebral effort; slow assiduous composition; painstaking and useless work.
elu·dere [C3] tr to elude, to avoid; to shirk; — la legge, to evade the law.
elu-ire [D2] tr. (chem.) to elute. -ente m. (chem.) eluent.
eluş-iọne f. evasion, eluding. -ivo adj. elusive, evasive. -ivaménte adv. elusively, evasively.
eluşo part. of eludere, q.v.
elu·vi-o m. (geol.) eluvium. -ale adj. (geog.) decomposed in heat and wet (of soil).
eluziọne f. (chem.) elution.
elve·tico adj. Swiss; la Confederazione elvetica, the Swiss Confederation, Switzerland.
Elve·zi-a pr.n.f. (hist.) Helvetia. -ano adj. (geol.) Helvetian.
Elve·zio[1] pr.n.m. (Claude) Helvetius (1715–1771).
elve·zio[2] m. (chem.; atom. phys.) helvetium, alabamium.
elẓevir-iano adj. (typ.) Elzevir, Elzevirian, from the press of the Elzevirs. -ista m., f. (journ.) writer of 'elzeviri', feature-writer. -o adj. (typ.) Elzevir; carattere -o, old style, old face; n.m. book printed by the Elzevir press; book printed in Elzevir type; (journ.) short story or literary article published on the 'terza pagina' of an Italian daily newspaper.
emaci-are [A3] tr. to emaciate, to cause emaciation of; rfl. to become emaciated. -aménto m. emaciation, growing emaciated. -ato part. adj. emaciated. -aziọne f. emaciation, state of emaciation.
eman-are [AI] intr. (aux. essere) to emanate, to issue; to derive; tr. to issue, to promulgate. -ante part. adj. emanating; deriving. -atişmo m. (philos.; theol.) doctrine of emanation, Emanationism. -ato part. adj. emanated; promulgated. -ato·rio m. (atom. phys.) emanatorium. -aziọne f. emanation; derivation; issuing, promulgation; eruption; (chem.) emanation, radon. -azionişmo m. (philos.; theol.) see emanatismo.
emancip-are [AIS] tr. (leg.) to emancipate. -ato part. adj. (leg.) emancipated; (fig.) le donne oggi sono più -ate, women nowadays are more emancipated. -atọre m. emancipator. -aziọne f. emancipation; (leg.) the act by which a paterfamilias frees his infant child from his paternal authority; the act by which an infant becomes sui juris; -azione del minore, emancipation of an infant.
Emanuela pr.n.f. Manuela.
Emanuele pr.n.m. Emmanuel.
ematina f. (physiol.) haematin; (dyeing) hematine.
ematite f. (miner.) haematite.
ematoş-i f. indecl. haematosis, aeration of the blood. -silina f. (chem.) haematoxylin.
ematu·ria f. haematuria.
ema·zia f. red blood corpuscle, erythrocyte.
embar-go m. (pl. -ghi) embargo, a suspension of commerce.
emblem-a m. emblem, symbol; badge; attribute, sign, mark; (leg.) vilipendio ad un — dello Stato, insulting behaviour towards an emblem of the State. -a·tico adj. emblematic. -aticaménte adv. emblematically.
embol-i·a f. (med.) embolism, occlusion of a blood-vessel. -işmo m. (astron.) embolism, a year coinciding with thirteen lunar months.
em·bolo m. (med.) embolus, clot or foreign body ocuclding an artery; (eng.) piston-head.
ęmbric-e m. tile, i.e. a flat tile with a raised margin. (In roofing a building, the margins of every pair of adjacent embrici are covered by a gutter-tile, tegolo, placed with its convex side upwards so as to make the roof watertight.) — a maschio e femmina, pantile with ogee curve, forming an 'embrice' and a 'tegolo' in one; — frate, tile raised up like a hood so as to ventilate the interior of the roof; (naut.) cradle lashing used when launching ships; (joc.) cotto com'un —, desperately in love, or very drunk; scoprire un —, to reveal secrets; non la guardare in un filare d'-i, do not examine the thing too minutely. -iata f. tiled roof.

embri·ologi·a *f.* embryology. **-o·logo** *m.* embryologist. **-ọne** *m.* embryo. **-onale** *adj.*, **-o·nico** *adj.* embryonal, pertaining to an embryo; still immature, not yet developed; un progetto ancora allo stato -onale, a project that is still in the early stages.

emend-are [A I] *tr.* to emend; to correct; to amend, to improve; *rfl.* to correct one's faults; se non ti -i finirai male, if you don't mend your ways, you will come to a bad end. **-a** *f.* amends, act of reparation. **-a·bile** *adj.* emendable; amendable. **-amẹnto** *m.* amendment; -amento per conseguenza, consequential amendment; fondere parecchi -amenti, to merge together several amendments. **-ativo** *adj.* emendatory. **-atọre** *m.* emendator. (**-atrice** *f.*) **-azione** *f.* emendation, correction; improvement.

emẹr·g-ere [C4] *intr.* (*aux.* essere) to emerge, to issue forth, to come into view; to achieve distinction; -erà dalla turba, he will make a name for himself. **-ente** *part. adj.* emergent; danno -ente, (leg.) direct damage, general (as distinct from special) damage; (phys.; opt.) luce -ente, emergent light. **-enza** *f.* emergence; emergency; (naut.) lightening, higher flotation of ship as it discharges; (leg.) stato di -enza, state of emergency.

emẹ·rito *adj.* emeritus, retired; professore —, Professor emeritus; (iron.) downright —, è un furfante —, he is an arrant rogue.

emeroteca *f.* stored collection of newspapers and periodicals.

emersiọne *f.* emersion; emerging; emergence, reappearance; (of a submarine) in —, on the surface of the water.

emerso *part.* of **emergere**, q.v.

em·esi *f.* (med.) emesis. **-e·tico** *adj.*, *n.m.* emetic.

emẹsso *part.* of **emettere**, q.v.

emẹtt-ere [C20] *tr.* to emit; to give out; to utter; to express; — un giudizio, to deliver a judgement; to issue; to put in circulation. **-itọre** *m.* (teleph.; radio) sender, transmitter.

emi- *pref.* hemi-, semi-, half-.

emicellulọsa *f.* (chem.) hemicellulose.

emiciclo *m.* (archit.) hemicycle; body of a hall; proibire l'accesso all'—, to forbid access to the body of the hall; semi-circular sundial.

emicra·nia *f.* (med.) migraine; hemicrania; headache.

emidat·tilo *m.* (zool.) *Tarentola mauritanica*, a kind of geck

emide *f.* (zool.) water tortoise, *Emys orbicularis*.

emidiapente *f.* (mus.) hemidiapente, diminished fifth (ancient Greek music).

emidistruziọne *f.* (atom. phys.) tempo di —, half life.

emiedri·a *f.* (chem.) hemiedry.

emigr-are [A I] *intr.* (*aux.* avere) to emigrate; to migrate; (*aux.* essere) to emigrate (to a specific place); è -ato in America, he has emigrated to America. **-ante** *part. adj.* emigrating; migrating; *n.m.*, *f.* emigrant. **-ato** *m.* emigré; refugee; political exile. **-aziọne** *f.* emigration; migration; (leg.) la frode in -azione, fraud upon emigrants (C.P.).

Emi·lia[1] *pr.n.f.* Emily, Emilia.

Emi·li-a[2] *pr.n.f.* (geog.) Emilia. (**-ano** *adj.*, *n.m.*)

emi·lio[1] *adj.* (geog.) relating to Emilia, Emilian.

Emi·lio[2] *pr.n.m.* Emil, Émile, Aemilius.

eminẹn-te *adj.* eminent; distinguished; prominent; lofty; high. **-temẹnte** *adv.* eminently; highly. **-za** *f.* eminence; distinction; prominence; high place, eminence; Eminence (title given esp. to Cardinals); Sua Eminenza (abbr. S.E.), Your (or His) Eminence; (hist.) -za grigia, Grey Eminence (i.e. François le Clerc du Tremblay, adviser and counsellor of Richelieu); (fig.) an evil counsellor, a powerful evil influence lurking in the background.

emio·lia *f.* (mus.) sesquialtera (i.e. proportion of 3:2), hemiolia, hemiola; perfect fifth (obtained by sounding two thirds of the open string on the monochord); triplet; hemiola rhythm (i.e. substitution of three lengths of two beats for two lengths of three beats, or vice versa); — maggiore, ¾ time; — minore, ⅜ time.

emio·lio *adj.* (mus.) hemiolic.

emiono *m.* (zool.) kiang, wild ass, *Equus hemionus*.

emi-ple·gia *f.* (med.) hemiplegia, paralysis of one side of the body. **-ple·gico** *adj.*, *n.m.* hemiplegic.

emir-o *m.* emir; a descendant of Mahomet; governor of a province or tribe. **-ato** *m.* emirate.

emis-fero *m.* hemisphere. **-fe·rico** *adj.* hemispherical.

emissa·rio *m.* (hydraul.) outlet, effluent; emissary, secret agent, spy; capro —, scapegoat; (vet.) stallion (esp. a stallion standing at stud).

emiss-iọne *f.* emission, issuing, issue; (finan.) banca d'—, issuing

bank; sistema dell'— libera, free bank system; (radio) broadcast. **-ività** *f.* (phys.) emissivity.

emisti·ch-io *m.* (*pl.* **-i**) (prosod.) hemistich.

emittente *adj.* emitting, issuing; *n.m.* issuer; *f.* (radio) transmitting station.

emit·teri *m.pl.* (ent.) Hemiptera.

Emmanuele *pr.n.m.* See **Emanuele**.

emme *f.*, *m.* name of the letter M.

emmetro·pico *adj.* emmetropic, normal sighted.

emo-[1] *pref.* haemo-.

emo[2] *m.* (ent.) dung beetle, *Emus hertus*.

emo·fago *adj.* (zool.) blood-sucking.

emofili·a *f.* (med.) haemophilia.

emoglob-i·metro *m.* (med.) haemoglobinometer. **-ina** *f.* haemoglobin.

emolliente *adj.* soothing; (industr.) softening, plasticizing; *n.m.* emollient.

†e·molo *m.* See **emulo**.

emolumẹnto *m.* emolument, salary; percepire gli emolumenti, to receive emoluments, to draw one's salary.

emo·pide *m.* (ent.) *Haemopis vorax*.

emorragi·a *f.* (med.) haemorrhage.

emorro·id-i *f.pl.* (med.) haemorrhoids, piles. **-ale** *adj.* haemorrhoidal.

emosta·tico *adj.* haemostatic, styptic; matita emostatica, styptic pencil; *n.m.* styptic pencil.

emoteca *f.* blood bank.

emotiv-o *adj.* emotive; easily moved; emotional, susceptible; excitable; (leg.) stato —, emotional condition (C.P.). **-ità** *f.* emotiveness; excitability.

emott-isi *f. indecl.* (med.) haemoptysis. **-o·ico** *adj.* (med.) spitting blood; *n.m.* one who spits blood.

emoziọn-e *f.* emotion; tender sentiment, compassion; emotional excitement, lively interest; excitement, thrill; fright; fare — a, to excite, to thrill; to touch, to move. **-ante** *part. adj.* thrilling, exciting; sensational; frightening. **-are** [A IC] *tr.* to excite, to thrill; to touch, to move; to upset, to frighten. **-ato** *part. adj.* thrilled, excited; upset; frightened.

Empe·docle *pr.n.m.* Empedocles.

empiastro *m.* See **impiastro**.

em·pide *m.* (ent.) robber fly, *Empis* spp.

empiema *m.* (med.) empyema.

ẹmpiere [D II]. See **empire**.

empiẹtà *f.* impiety; impiousness.

empifọndo *m.* (naut.) tide; †abnormal high water.

ẹmpi-o *adj.* (*m.pl.* **ẹmpi**, *f.pl.* **ẹmpie**) impious; irreligious; pitiless; wicked; (joc.) full up (cf. **empire**); *n.m.* wicked man; *pl.* gli empi, the wicked. **-amẹnte** *adv.* impiously; pitilessly; wickedly.

emp-ire [D II] *tr.* to fill; to fill up; to satisfy; to load; to cram, to stuff; to crowd; *rfl.* to stuff oneself; to be filled; to get crowded. **-imẹnto** *m.* act of filling; act of stuffing. **-ito** *part. adj.* filled; full; replete. **-itura** *f.* act of filling; stuffing, material used in filling.

empi·reo *adj.* relating to the Empyrean; il cielo —, the Empyrean, the highest heaven (also *n.m.*).

empire·um-a *m.* smell of burning; taste of burning. **-a·tico** *adj.* smelling of burning; tasting of burning.

empi·ric-o *adj.* (philos.) empirical; derived from experience; (fig.) rough and ready; that works by rule of thumb. **-amẹnte** *adv.* empirically.

empiriṣmo *m.* (philos.) empiricism.

†empiro *adj.*, *n.m.* See **empireo**.

empit-o *part.* of **empire**, q.v. **-ọre** *m.* (naut.) see **riempitore**, under **riempiere**.

em·pito *m.* (Tusc. pop. or poet.). See **impeto**.

empitura *f.* See under **empire**.

Em·poli *pr.n.f.* (geog.) Empoli, in the province of Florence.

empore·tico *adj.* (of paper) coarse, absorbent.

empo·rio *m.* emporium, market; trade centre; warehouse, store; (fig.) quella casa è un —, that house is as full of rubbish as a junk-shop; era un — di erudizione, he was a mine of information.

emptio rei speratae *f. indecl.* (Lat.) (leg.) purchase of a future thing (C.C.).

emptio spei *f. indecl.* (Lat.) (leg.) purchase of an expectancy or possibility (C.C.).

emul-are [A IS] *tr.* to emulate, to seek to rival. **-ante** *part. adj.* emulating; *n.m.*, *f.* emulator, rival. **-ativo** *adj.* (leg.) causing

emul·are (*cont.*)
annoyance or private nuisance. **-atore** *m.* emulator, rival. (**-atrice** *f.*) **-azione** *f.* emulation, rivalry; (leg.) atto d'-azione, annoyance, private nuisance (C.C.); *pl.* snares, tricks.

†**emul·gere** *tr.* to mulct.

e·mulo *adj.* emulous, emulating; *n.m.* emulator; imitator.

emuls·ione *f.* emulsion. **-ina** *f.* emulsin. **-iona·bile** *adj.* (chem.; phys.) emulsifiable. **-ionabilità** *f.* emulsifiability. **-ionante** *m.* (chem.; phys.) emulsifying agent. **-ionare** [A I c] *tr.* to make into an emusion, to emulsify. **-ionatore** *m.* (mot. eng.) diffuser (of a carburettor); applied to seeds (nuts, etc.) from which oil can be extracted.

emun·gere [c 5] *tr.* to mulct; to extract moisture from.

emunt·o *part.* of emungere, q.v.; *adj.* dry, dried up; emaciated. **-ore** *m.* (geog.) outlet. **-o·rio** *adj.* (med.) draining; drying; blistering.

†**en¹** *prep.* See **in**.

†**en²** *encl.* See **ne**.

enal·lage *f.* (rhet.) enallage.

enan·t·ico *adj.* (chem.) enanthic, heptanoic. **-ato** *m.* (chem.) enanthate. **-iomorfo** *adj.* (chem.; phys.) enantiomorphic, enantiomorphous. **-iotropi·a** *f.* (chem.; phys.) enantiotropy. **-iotro·pico** *adj.* (chem.; phys.) enantiotropic.

enarm·oni·a *f.* (mus.) enharmonic relationship. **-o·nico** *adj.* (mus.) enharmonic; cambiamento -onico, enharmonic change; genere -onico, enharmonic genus (ancient Greek music). **-onicamente** *adv.* enharmonically.

†**enarmo·nio** *adj.* (mus.). See enarmonico, under **enarmonia**.

encarpo *m.* (archit.) encarpus, festoons on a frieze consisting of fruit, flowers, leaves, etc.

enc·a·usto *m.* encaustic painting, an ancient method of painting with wax colours and fixing by heat. **-a·ustica** *f.* art of encaustic painting. **-a·ustico** *adj.* encaustic.

ence·f·alo *m.* (anat.) encephalon; brain. **-a·lico** *adj.* encephalic, pertaining to the brain. **-alite** *f.* encephalitis. **-o·ide** *m.* medullary cancer.

enchiri·dio *m.* manual.

enci·clic·a *f.* encyclical letter, Papal letter. **-o** *adj.* encyclical.

enciclop·edi·a *f.* encyclopaedia. **-e·dico** *adj.* encyclopaedic. **-edista** *m.* encyclopaedist; person of the cast of mind characteristic of the generation which brought about the French Revolution; *pl.* (lit. hist.) contributors to the French Encyclopaedia (eighteenth century).

encli·tic·a *f.* (gramm.) enclitic. **-o** *adj.* enclitic.

enco·bia *f.* (ichth.) *Leuciscus pigus*, a fish similar to a roach found only in Lakes Como and Lugano.

encomi·are [A 4] *tr.* to commend, to praise highly; to laud; to pay official honour to, to award official recognition to. **-a·bile** *adj.* worthy of encomium, praiseworthy. **-aste** *m.* encomiast. **-a·stico** *adj.* laudatory. (**-asticamente** *adv.*) **-ato** *part. adj.* praised, lauded. **-atore** *m.* one who sings praises. (**-atrice** *f.*)

enco·mio *m.* encomium; official honour or recognition paid in public to some outstanding personage.

endecacordo *m.* (mus.) eleven-stringed lyre; eleven-note scale; interval of the eleventh.

endecasil·labo *adj.* (prosod.) hendecasyllabic; *n.m.* hendecasyllable.

end-emi·a *f.* endemic disease. **-e·mico** *adj.* endemic.

endi·adi *f. indecl.* (gramm.) hendiadys.

†**en·dic·a** *f.* storehouse, warehouse; store, stock; fare — di, to make a corner in, to buy up, to hoard. †**-are** *tr.* to buy up, to hoard.

endice, en·dice *m.* nest-egg; china egg; decoy; †sample, remnant.

endi·via *f.* See indivia.

endo- *pref.* inner, inside. **-car·dio** *m.* (anat.) endocardium. **-cardite** *f.* (med.) endocarditis. **-carpo** *m.* inner skin of fruit. **-crino** *adj.* (med.) endocrine. **-crinologi·a** *f.* endocrinology. **-dina** *f.* (radio) self-heterodyne. **-morfismo** *m.* (geol.) endomorphism. **-rachide** *adv.* (med.) intraspinally. **-re·ico** *adj.* (geog.) draining inland. **-sco·pio** *m.* (med.) endoscope. **-smo·metro** *m.* (phys.; chem.) endosmometer. **-smosi** *f.* (phys.; chem.) endosmosis. **-sperma** *f.* (bot.) endosperm. **-teliale** *adj.* endothelial. **-te·lio** *m.* (anat.) endothelium. **-ter·mico** *adj.* (chem.) endothermic. **-tossico·si** *f.* (med.) endotoxicosis. **-tossina** *f.* (med.) endotoxin. **-vena** *adv.* (med.) intravenously. **-venoso** *adj.* (med.) intravenous, endovenous.

endo·geno *adj.* endogenous, growing from within; le forze endogene del sottosuolo, endogenous energy from the earth's interior.

Enea¹ *pr.n.m.* (myth.) Aeneas.

enea² *m.* (text.) lana di —, typha fibre.

enegra *f.* (bot.) evening primrose, *Oenothera*.

Ene·ide *pr.n.f.* Aeneid.

†**te·neo** *adj.* of bronze, brazen.

energe·tic·a *f.* (scient.) energetics. **-o** *adj.* relating to energy or power.

energi·a *f.* energy; vigour; resolution; power; — atomica, atomic energy; (mech.) energy; — cinetica, kinetic energy; — idraulica, water power; — potenziale, potential energy; (eng.) — prodotta, output; (phys.) — superficiale, surface energy; (leg.) furto dell'— elettrica, theft of electric current (C.P.); *pl.* le energie naturali, natural sources of power (C.C.).

ener·gic·o *adj.* energetic; vigorous; powerful. **-amente** *adv.* energetically; vigorously; with power.

energizz·are [A I] *tr.* (electr.) to energize. **-ato** *part. adj.* (electr.) energized.

energu·meno *adj.* possessed by a devil; obstreperous; quick-tempered; active, lively, quick-moving, always on the go; *n.m.* one possessed; termagant; è un —, there's no holding him; (of a woman) virago.

en·fasi *f. indecl.* bombast, pomposity; exaggeration; undue emphasis.

enfa·tic·o *adj.* bombastic, pompous; exaggerated; unduly emphatic. (**-amente** *adv.*)

†**enfertà** *f.* infirmity.

enfi·are [A 4 c] *tr.* (Tusc.) to swell; to inflate; to puff up; *intr.* (aux. essere), *rfl.* to swell, to become swollen. **-agione** *f.* swelling. **-amento** *m.* swelling up. **-ativo** *adj.* causing swelling. **-ato** *part. adj.* swollen, puffed up; (fig.) conceited, proud; angry; *n.m.* swelling, tumour. **-atura** *f.* swelling; part of body swollen (cf. gonfiare).

enfi·o *adj.* swollen. **-ore** *m.* swelling, tumour.

enfisema *m.* (med.) emphysema.

enfit-e·usi *f. indecl.* (leg.) emphyteusis, lease at a ground rent in perpetuity or for long term of years (C.C.). **-euta** *m.* (leg.) emphyteuta, tenant under such lease. **-eu·tico** *adj.* emphyteutal, emphyteutic.

enfizi·a *f.* (bot.) endemic blight.

enigm-a *m.* enigma; riddle; puzzle involving words. **-a·tico** *adj.* enigmatic. **-aticamente** *adv.* enigmatically. **-atizzare** [A I] *intr.* (aux. avere) to enigmatize. **-ista** *n.m.*, *f.* enigmatist, enigmatographer. **-i·stica** *f.* puzzles, puzzle-games involving words; the art of inventing or guessing riddles and word puzzles. **-i·stico** *adj.* relating to enigmas, riddles or puzzles.

enimma *m.* (Tusc.) and derivs. See **enigma**.

enn-e *f.*, *m. indecl.* the name of the letter N. **-e·simo** *adj.* (math.) nth; al -esimo grado, to the nth degree; per l'-esima volta, for the nth time, umpteen times.

ennè *m. indecl.* henna.

enneacordo *m.* (mus.) nine-stringed lyre; nine-note scale; interval of ninth.

ennera *f.* (Gk. antiq.) ship with nine oars in a bank.

en-o·fila *f.* moth whose larva is found in wine vats, etc. **-o·filo** *adj.* engaged in or concerned with the production of wine; fond of wine; circolo -ofilo, wine-growers' society; *n.m.* wine-grower; wine-bibber. **-olina** *f.* natural colouring matter in wine. **-o·lito** *m.* solution of certain substances in wine; medicinal wine. **-ologi·a** *f.* wine making. **-olo·gico** *adj.* relating to wine making; industria -ologica, wine industry. **-o·logo** *m.* œnologist. **-omele** *m.* syrup of wine and honey. **-o·metro** *m.* œnometer, instrument to measure the specific gravity of wines. **-opo·lio** *m.* wine-shop. **-otec·nico** *adj.* relating to the wine-making industry.

enorm-e, (Rom.) **enorm·e** *adj.* enormous, huge; extraordinary; monstrous, outrageous; absurd. **-emente** *adv.* enormously; outrageously. **-ità** *f.* hugeness; enormity, outrageousness; absurdity.

enotera *f.* (bot.) evening primrose, *Oenothera*.

Eno·tria *pr.n.f.* (poet.) Italy.

Eno·trio *pr.n.m.* — Romano, pseudonym of the poet, Giosue Carducci.

Enri·co *pr.n.m.* Henry. **-chetta** *pr.n.f.* Henrietta.

†**ensemora** *adv.* See insieme.

ens-i·fero *adj.* sword-bearing; *n.m.* sword-bearer; (astron.) Orion; *pl.* (hist.) Electors of Saxony. **-iforme** *adj.* (anat.; bot.) ensiform.

entalpi·a *f.* (phys.) heat content, enthalpy.

ente *m.* being; — supremo, God; society; corporation; body; object, thing; — nazionale italiano turistico (ENIT), Italian tourist information bureau; (leg.) legal entity; institution; — collettivo, corporation aggregate; — morale, corporation, incorporated body; la società si è eretta in — morale, the company has been incorporated; Ente comunale di assistenza, Public Assistance Board; Ente parastatale, quasi-governmental Board or Authority; — pubblico, public institution (C.C.).

entelechi·a *f.* (philos.) entelechy, the perfection of being; that which gives form or perfection to anything; soul; (in Leibniz) monad.

entello *m.* (zool.) langur monkey, *Semnopithecus entellus*.

enteralgi·a *f.* (med.) intestinal pain.

ente·r-ico *adj.* intestinal, enteric. **-ite** *f.* (med.) enteritis. **-ocele** *m.* (med.) enterocele. **-oclisma** *m.* enema. **-ocolite** *f.* (med.) enterocolitis. **-ostato** *m.* (surg.) intestinal clamp.

entimem-a *m.* (log.) enthymeme. **-a·tico** *adj.* (log.) enthymematic.

entità *f. indecl.* entity; importance; amount; — degli affari, extent of business; malattia di poca —, slight illness; di —, of some size; (comm.) l'— dell'ordine, the size of the order.

entofiti *m.pl.* (vet.) enterophyte (disease).

†**en·tom-o** *m.* (*pl.* †**-ata**) insect.

entom-o·fagi *adj. m.pl.* (zool.) insect-eating. **-ologi·a** *f.* entomology. **-o·logo** *m.* entomologist.

entozo·i *m.pl.* (zool.) endozooite.

†**entragn-a**, †**-o** *m.* innards; heart.

entramb-i *prn. m.pl.* (*f.* **-e**) both.

†**entram-e** *m.*, †**-enta** *f.* entrails.

entr-are [A I c] *intr.* (*aux.* essere; *prep.* in, a) to enter; to go in; to come in; to step inside; la messa è -ata ora, Mass is just beginning; alla fine t'è -ato nel cervello!, at last you understand!; è una sala che non ci s'-a in venti, there just isn't room for twenty people in this room; il soprabito non m'-a più, *or* non c'-o più nel mio soprabito, I can't get into my overcoat any longer, I have grown too big for my overcoat; -ò nella congiura, he joined the conspiracy; — in possesso di, to take possession of; — in vigore, to come into force; che c'-o io?, what is that to do with me?; che c'-a? (*or* cosa c'-a?), what's that got to do with it?; in questa pezza c'-ano venti camicie, this piece of stuff is enough to make twenty shirts; il due nell'otto c'-a quattro volte, two into eight goes four. **-amento** *m.* entrance, going in; way in. **-ante** *part. adj.* entering; in-coming; la settimana -ante, at the beginning of next week; *n.m., f.* nosey parker; gate-crasher. **-ato** *part. adj.* entered; in, inside.

entrat-a *f.* entrance, going in, entry; entrance, way in; time of entrance, or beginning; access, freedom of entry; admission, admittance; admission fee; (med.) — dell'ago, insertion of the needle (in injections); (theatr.) le -e di favore, complimentary seats; (mus.) introduction; (radio) feed; input; (comm.) entry; revenue; income; — ed uscita, income and expenditure; -e pubbliche, public revenue; (mining) adit; (naut.) gangway; — di una nave in dogana, entry of a ship in a bonded zone; †— libera, free port; †first cloth of a sail starting at the throat and tabled for strengthening where it may rub against the mast. **-atura** *f.* entrance; entry; entrance fee; diritto d'-atura, right of entry; intimacy; goodwill.

entro[1] *prep.* in; within; in the course of; *adv.* inside.

entro[2] *apocop. part.* of **entrare**, q.v.

entro-bordo *m.* in-board motorboat; *adj. indecl.* in-board. **-plano** *m.* (aeron.) gap (space between wings of biplane or multiplane). **-terra** *f.* (geog.) inland, inland region, interior, hinterland.

entropi·a *f.* (phys.) entropy.

entusiasm-o *m.* enthusiasm; rapture. **-are** [A I] *tr.* to arouse enthusiasm in (a person); to enrapture, to inflame; to enthuse; *rfl.* -arsi per, to go into raptures over. **-ato** *part. adj.* roused to enthusiasm; enraptured.

entusi-asta *m., f.* enthusiast; *adj.* enthusiastic; essere — dell'arte moderna, to be an enthusiast of modern art; sono — per le sue belle maniere, I am a great admirer of his delightful manners. **-a·stico** *adj.* enthusiastic. **-asticamente** *adv.* enthusiastically.

enucle-are [A 6 s] *tr.* to enucleate. (**-ato** *poet. adj.* **-azione** *f.*)

enumer-are [A I s] *tr.* to enumerate; to specify. **-amento** *m.* enumerating; specifying. **-ato** *part. adj.* enumerated; specified. **-azione** *f.* enumeration; specification.

enunci-are [A 3] *tr.* to express clearly; to enounce; to state; to pronounce clearly, to enunciate. **-ativa** *f.* enunciation, introductory exposition. **-ativo** *adj.* enunciative. **-ato** *part. adj.* enunciated; *n.m.* (math.) enunciation; (fig.) statement of a problem. **-azione** *f.* enunciation; pronouncement; expression.

enunziare [A 3] and derivs. See **enunciare**.

enuresi *f.* (med.) enuresis; bed wetting.

enzima *m.* (biol.; chem.) enzyme.

enzoozi·a *f.* (vet.) enzootic or endemic disease.

†**eo** *pers. prn.* See **io**.

eoc-ene *m.* (geol.) Eocene. **-e·nico** *adj.* (geol.) Eocene.

Eo·l-ia *pr.n.f.* (geog.) Aeolia. **-ismo** *m.* idiom or word belonging to the Aeolian dialects.

eo·l-ico[1] *adj.* (hist. geog.) Aeolian, relating to Aeolis; la fanciulla -ica, Sappho; (geog.) aeolian, wind-formed. **-io** *adj.* Aeolian; (mus.) arpa -ia, Aeolian harp; modo -io, Aeolian mode.

eo·lico[2] *adj.* (myth.) Aeolian, relating to Aeolus, god of the winds.

E·olo *pr.n.m.* (myth.) Aeolus.

eo·ne *m.* aeon.

eo·o *adj.* (poet.) relating to dawn; oriental, Eastern; of the morning, matutinal.

eoṣina *f.* (chem.) eosin.

epa *f.* belly.

epa·g-oge *f.* (log.) epagoge, reasoning by induction. **-o·gico** *adj.* (log.) epagogic, inductive.

epan-adiploṣi *f.* (rhet.) epanadiplosis, ending a phrase with the same word that began it. **-a·fora** *f.* (rhet.) anaphora, repetition of the same words at the beginning of successive sentences, or clauses, e.g. 'Per me si va', Dante, *Inf.* III, 1–3, etc. **-alessi** *f.* (rhet.) epanalepsis, repetition of a word after some intervening words, e.g. Dante, *Inf.* IV, 65, 66.

epar-chi·a *f.* (hist.) eparchy, province of the Byzantine Empire; an administrative division of modern Greece. **-co** *m.* (hist.) eparch, governor of an eparchy.

epat-algi·a *f.* (med.) hepatalgia, pain in the liver. **-ite** *f.* (med.) hepatitis.

†**e·pate** *m.* (anat.) liver.

epa·tic-a *f.* (bot.) hepatica, liverwort, *Anemone hepatica*. **-o** *adj.* (med.) hepatic; relating to the liver.

epatta *f.* (astron.) epact.

epen·teṣi *f.* epenthesis, insertion of a letter or sound in the middle of a word.

epeṣege·tico *adj.* (gramm.) explanatory; defining (genitive); epexegetic (infinitive).

e·pic-a *f.* epic; epic poetry. **-o** *adj.* epic; heroic.

epice·dio *m.* (mus.) epicedium, threnody, funeral ode.

†**epice·ia** *f.* (leg.). See **epicheia**.

epiceno *adj.* epicene, of either gender.

epicentro *m.* (seis.) epicentre.

†**epiche·ia** *f.* (leg.) equity; application of the spirit rather than the letter of a law; reasonableness.

epicherema *m.* (log.) epicheirema.

epicicl-o *m.* (astron.) epicycle. **-oidale** *adj.* (eng.) epicyclic; ruotismo -oidale, epicyclic train. **-o·ide** *f.* (astron.) epicycloid.

e·pic-o *adj.* epic; poema —, epic poem; poesia -a, epic poetry; poeti -i, epic poets; resistenza -a, epic resistance, heroic stand; *n.m.* epic poet. **-a** *f.* epic poetry.

epicon·dilo *m.* (anat.) epicondyle.

epicur-e·o *adj.* (philos.) Epicurean; epicurean, voluptuary; also *n.m.* **-eggiare** [A 3 c] *intr.* (*aux.* avere) to epicurize, to play the epicure. **-eiṣmo** *m.* (philos.) Epicurism, Epicureanism; pursuit of pleasure, hedonism.

epid-emi·a *f.* epidemic; (leg.) — dolosa, epidemic caused maliciously, of criminal malice (C.P.). **-e·mico** *adj.* epidemic, epidemical.

epider·m-ide *f.* (biol.) epidermis. **-oliṣi** *f.* (med.) -olisi bullosa, acantholysis bullosa. **-oṣa** *f.* epidermose.

epidiaṣco·pio *m.* (opt.) epidiascope.

epidit·tico *adj.* (rhet.) epideictic.

epifani·a *f.* (liturg.) Epiphany; la notte dell'—, Twelfth Night.

epifeno·meno *m.* (med.) epiphenomenon, secondary symptom.

epi·fiṣi *f.* (anat.) epiphysis.

epi·fita *f.* (bot.) epiphyte, a plant which grows on another.

epifonem-a *m.* epiphonema, an emphatic closing sentence. (**-a·tico** *adj.* **-aticamente** *adv.*)

epi·fora *f.* (med.) epiphora; (rhet.) epiphora, epistrophe.

epiframma *m.* (zool.; bot.) epiphragm.

epigami·a *f.* (leg.) reciprocal right of intermarriage between the citizens of two States; second marriage.

epiga·str-io, -o *m.* (anat.) epigastrium.

epige·n-eşi *f.* (biol.) epigenesis. **-e·tico** *adj.* epigenetic.

epige·o *m.* (naut.) mooring rope or cable; *adj.* (bot.) epigaeal.

epiglaciale *adj.* (geol.) post-glacial.

epiglot·t-a, -ide *f.* (anat.) epiglottis. **-ico** *adj.* epiglottic, epiglottidean. **-ite** *f.* (med.) epiglottitis.

epi·gono *m.* epigone, one of a succeeding (and less distinguished) generation; one of the sons of the 'Seven against Thebes'; imitator, successor or follower of a genius.

epi·graf-e *f.* epigraph, inscription on tomb, building, etc.; epigraph, title, quotation or motto printed at the beginning of a book. **-a·io** *m.* writer of inscriptions. **-i·a** *f.* epigraphy. **-ista** *m.* writer of inscriptions; epigraphist, student of ancient inscriptions.

epigramm-a *m.* epigram. **-a·tico** *adj.* epigrammatic. (**-aticaménte** *adv.*) **-atista, -ista** *m.* writer of epigrams.

epilar·chi·a *f.* (mil. hist.) epilarchy, troop of 128 horse. **-co** *m.* (*pl.* **-chi**) commander of an epilarchy.

epil-ato·rio *adj.* depilatory. **-azióne** *f.* depilation.

epil-essi·a *f.* epilepsy. **-et·tico** *adj.* and *n.m.* (*pl.* **-et·tici**); epileptic. **-ettifórme** *adj.* epileptiform. **-etto·ide** *m., f., adj.* epileptiform.

epilim·nio *m.* (geog.) upper layers of water in a lake.

epilo·bio *m.* (bot.) willow-herb, *Epilobium*.

epilog-are [A 2 s] *tr.* to sum up. **-aménto** *m.* summing up. (**-ato** *part. adj.*) **-atura** *f.* composition of an epilogue; summing-up. **-azióne** *f.* summing-up, epilogue.

epi·lo-go *m.* (*pl.* **-ghi**) epilogue.

epi·mone *f.* (rhet.) the dwelling upon, elaboration of, a particular point.

epini·cio *m.* hymn of victory; *adj.* celebrating a victory.

epior·nide *f.* (orn.) aepyornis.

episcop-ale *adj.* (eccl.) episcopal; Episcopalian. **-ato** *m.* episcopate.

†episco·pio¹ *m.* bishop's palace.

episco·pio² *m.* (opt.) episcope.

episinalefe *f.* synæresis, contraction of two vowels into one.

epiş-o·dio *m.* episode, incident, event; instalment of a serial; — influenzale, bout of influenza; (mus.) episode; fugal episode; section. **-o·dico** *adj.* episodic; fragmentary; not continuous.

epispa·stico *adj.* (med. hist.) epispastic; blistering.

epistassi *f.* (med.) epistaxis, nose-bleeding.

epistazióne *f.* (pharm.) pounding to a paste in a mortar.

epistemologi·a *f.* (philos.) epistemology.

episti·lio *m.* (archit.) epistyle, architrave, the lowest division of the entablature, resting upon the abacus of a column.

epi·stol-a *f.* epistle **-are** *adj.* epistolary. **-a·rio** *m.* collection of letters. **-ografi·a** *f.* composition of literary letters. **-o·grafo** *m.* writer of epistles.

episto·mio *m.* stopcock.

epi·strofe *f.* (rhet.) epistrophe.

epitaf·f-io *m.* epitaph. **-ista** *m.* composer of epitaphs.

epitagm-a *m.* (mil. hist.) formation comprising 8192 foot or 4096 horse. **-arco** *m.* commander of an 'epitagma'.

epital-a·mio *m.* epithalamium, nuptial ode. **-a·mico** *adj.* epithalamic, epithalamial.

epi·taşi *f.* (class. lit.) epitasis, part of a play where the plot thickens.

epite·li-o *m.* (anat.; bot.) epithelium. **-ma** *f.* (med.) acanthokeratodermia alveolaris.

epi·tema *m.* liniment, epithem.

epi·teşi *f.* (rhet.) paragoge; addition of a letter for sound at the end of a word.

epi·tet-o *m.* epithet. **-are** [A I s] *intr.* (*aux.* avere) to select and apply epithets.

epiti·mio, epi·timo *m.* (bot.) thyme dodder, *Cuscuta epithymum*.

epitom-e *f.* epitome, abridgement. **-are** [A I s] *tr.* to epitomize; to summarize. **-atóre** *m.* epitomizer.

epitrito *m.* (prosod.) epitrite.

epi·trope *f.* (rhet.) epitrope.

Epittéto *pr.n.m.* Epictetus.

†epit·tima *f.* ointment, medicament; foul air.

epiz-o·i *m.pl.* (zool.) epizoites, ectoparasites. **-oo·tico** *adj.* (vet.) afta -ootica, foot-and-mouth disease. **-oozi·a** *f.* (vet.) epizootic disease, cattle disease.

e·poca *f.* epoch; age; era; time, period; all'— dei Romani, in Roman times; (comm.) — della consegna, fixed delivery date; — del

pagamento, term of payment, maturity; in un'— da stabilirsi, on a date to be determined; l'— stabilita, the date fixed; (fig.) fare —, to create a new era, to be a turning-point.

ep-odo *m.* (prosod.) epode. **-o·dico** *adj.* epodic.

epo·nimo *adj.* eponymous; *n.m.* surname.

epope·a *f.* epic (also fig.); epic poem; epos; series of epic poems.

epos *m. indecl.* epic poem; epos.

eppure *adv.* nevertheless, all the same; eppur si muove, it moves all the same; grande e grosso com'è, — ha paura, big and strong as he is, he's afraid all the same; *conj.* yet; and yet.

epsil·on *m. indecl.* epsilon.

epsomite *f.* Epsom salts, sulphate of magnesia.

eptacordo (mus.) seven-stringed lyre, heptachord.

ept-ae·dro *m.* heptahedron. **-a·gono** *m.* heptagon. **-asil·labo** *m.* (prosod.) seven-syllable line. **-avalente** *adj.* (chem.) septivalent.

Eptameróne *pr.n.m.* (lit. hist.) the *Heptameron* of Marguerite de Navarre; *pl.* (D'Annunzio) gatherings for conversation.

eptano *m.* (chem.) heptane.

eptodo *m.* (electron.) heptode.

epulón-e *m.* one who lives in luxury; (Bibl.) il ricco —, Dives (Luke 16); (Rom. antiq.) *epulo*. **-ac·cio** *m. pejor.* glutton. **-işmo** *m.* gluttony.

epur-are [A I] *tr.* to purify; to refine; to purge; (fig.) to make clear; — un dubbio, to clear up a doubtful point; to disentangle; to find out for certain; (finan.) to extinguish; to pay, to settle. **-ato** *part. adj.* purified; refined; freed from impurities; cleared up; ascertained; (finan.) settled; (pol.) purged; whitewashed; (Ital. pol. 1938–43, of a Jew) relieved of persecution as having one Gentile parent. **-azióne** *f.* purge; purifying; purification; (finan.) settlement; (pol.) elimination, persecution; campagna di -azione, political purge.

equa·bil-e *adj.* (mech.) uniform (of motion), of constant velocity. (**-ménte** *adv.*) **-ità** *f. indecl.* equability.

†equale *adj.* see **eguale**; *n.m.* (mus.) elegiac piece for trombones.

equaménte *adv.* See under **equo¹**.

equare [A 6] *tr.* (math.) to equate; †(fig.) to equalize; to level; to raze.

equatór-e *m.* equator; — celeste, celestial equator, equinoctial; — terrestre, terrestrial equator; passaggio dell'—, crossing the line; — magnetico, magnetic equator, aclinic line; — termico, heat equator; la Repubblica dell'Equatore, Ecuador. **-iale** *adj.* equatorial; regione delle calme -iali, doldrums; *n.m.* equatorial (telescope).

equazióne *f.* (math.) equation; — di secondo grado, quadratic equation; equazioni a due incognite, simultaneous equations; (astron.) equation; (chem.) equation.

equestre *adj.* equestrian; relating to horse-riding; circo —, circus; knightly; ordine —, order of chivalry; (Rom. hist.) equestrian order, class of knights.

equi-an·golo *adj.* (geom.) equiangular. **-crure** *adj.* (geom.) isosceles. **-differente** *adj.* (math.) in arithmetical progression. **-differenza** *f.* (math.) arithmetical progression. **-distante** *adj.* equidistant. **-distanza** *f.* equidistance. **-la·tero, -laterale** *adj., n.m.* (geom.) equilateral.

equilibr-are [A I] *tr.* to balance; to poise; to counter-balance; (aeron.) to trim; *rfl.* to balance, to be balanced; *recip. rfl.* to balance each other, to counter-balance. **-ato** *part. adj.* balanced, in equipoise; (fig.) well-balanced. **-atóre** *m.* (electr.) equalizer; (eng.) equalizer; balancer; -atore di spinta, thrust equalizer; (aeron.) elevator. **-atrice** *f.* (eng.) balancing machine. **-atura** *f.* (eng.) balancing. **-azióne** *f.* balancing; balance.

equili·br-io *m.* equilibrium, balance, poise; (mech.) equilibrium; (naut.) — velico, balanced trim; (aeron.: meteor.) — indifferente, adiabatic lapse rate. **-işmo** *m.* (philos.) theory of free-will as presupposing an equilibrium of determinants; (pol.) political acrobatics. **-ista** *m.* equilibrist, rope-dancer, tightrope-walker.

equimolti·plice *adj., n.m.* equimultiple.

equino *adj.* equine; carne equina, horseflesh; *n.m.pl.* horses and closely related animals (mules, asses, etc.).

equino·zi-o *m.* equinox; — di primavera, vernal equinox; (joc.) prendere un —, to make a mistake. **-ale** *adj.* equinoctial; *n.m.* celestial equator, equinoctial.

equipag·gi-o *m.* (naut.) crew; ruolo d'—, muster roll, open list (Merchant Navy); (mil.) baggage train, supplies; luggage; equipage; carriage, *équipage*; (electr.) — mobile, rotor, rotating element. **-amento** *m.* equipment, outfit; -amento di prova, test equipment. **-are** [A 3] *tr.* to equip, to fit out, to furnish with stores; (naut.) see **armare**.

equipar-are [A I] *tr.* to equalize; to consider as equal. **-a·bile** *adj.* comparable; equivalent.

equipoll-ente *adj.* equipollent, equivalent, of equal force or value; (herald.) punti -enti, checky of nine pieces. **-enza** *f.* (log.) equipollence.

equisignale *adj.* (aeron.; radio) zona —, equisignal zone.

equison-anza *f.* (mus.) equisonance, the concord of octaves. **-o** *adj.* (mus.) equisonant, consonant in the octave.

equit-à *f.* (leg.) equity; natural justice; fairness; impartiality. **-ativo** *adj.* equitable.

†equit-are *intr.* to ride. **†-atore** *m.* horseman, rider.

equitazione *f.* equitation, riding; scuola d'—, riding-school.

†e·quite *m.* horseman, knight.

equival-ere [B 34] *intr.* (*aux.* avere, essere; *prep.* a) to be worth as much, to be equivalent (to); to be tantamount (to), to be the same (as). **-ente** *adj.* equivalent; tantamount; (chem.) peso -ente, equivalent weight; *n.m.* equivalent; (phys. chem.) -ente grammo, gram equivalent. **-enza** *f.* equivalence.

equivoc-are [A 2 s] *intr.* (*aux.* avere) to misunderstand; to mistake; to equivocate. **-amento** *m.* equivocation, using a word ambiguously. **-azione** *f.* equivocation; misunderstanding, mistake.

equi·voc-o *adj.* equivocal, ambiguous; dubious, doubtful, questionable; rima equivoca, 'rich' or 'identical' rhyme (as between 'porta' the noun and 'porta' the verb); *n.m.* misunderstanding, mistake; chiarire un —, to clear up a misunderstanding; a scanso di equivoci, to avoid any misunderstanding; equivocation, play on words, pun. (**-amente** *adv.*) **-ità** *f.* ambiguity.

equ-o¹ *adj.* just, equitable, fair; even; (leg.) un — componimento, a fair settlement (of a claim, etc.). **-amente** *adv.* justly, equitably, fairly; evenly.

†equo² *m.* horse.

equo·reo *adj.* (poet.) of the sea; vie equoree, ocean paths.

era *f.* epoch, era; memorable period; l'— napoleonica, the Napoleonic era; l'— Fascista, the Fascist Era.

Eraclito *pr.n.m.* Heraclitus.

†eradicare *tr.* to eradicate; to extirpate.

era·ri-o *m.* Exchequer, the Treasury; State finances. **-ale** *adj.* pertaining to public revenue or taxation; fiscal; imposte -ali, public taxation; avvocato -ale, Treasury counsel; Ufficio Tecnico Erariale, Inland Revenue Surveyor's Office.

Erasm-o *pr.n.m.* Erasmus. **-iano** *adj.* of Erasmus, Erasmian.

erb-a *f.* herb; plant; piazza delle -e, fruit and vegetable market; grass; in —, immature, (fig.) budding; un romanziere in —, a budding novelist; fare —, to cut grass for animals; far d'ogni —fascio, to live dissolutely, to think everything grist for one's mill; dar l'— trastulla, to feed on flattery, on promises; fatti — e ti mangeranno le capre, people will take you at your own valuation; — che non ha radice muore presto, a spendthrift soon comes to the end of his resources; (naut.) grassline; — filandra, seaweed which grows on a ship's hull; (bot.) — aglina, fool's parsley, *Aethusa cynapium*; — aglio, water germander, *Teucrium scordium*; — amara, costmary, *Chrysanthemum balsamita*; — amaranta, pokeweed, *Phytolacca americana*; — apiola, white horehound, *Marrubium vulgare*; — aralda, *Digitalis lutea*; — argentina, honesty, *Lunaria annua*; — astrologa, *Aristolochia rotunda*; — bacaia, *Ononis natrix*; — baccellina, *Coronilla emerus*; — bicchierina, *Convolvulus cantabrica*; — bozzolina, Yorkshire fog, *Holcus lanatus*; — brusea, sorrel, *Rumex acetosa*; — calenzuola, sun spurge, *Euphorbia helioscopia*; — cali, saltwort, *Salsola kali*; — cannella, *Apium nodiflorum, Berula erecta, Sium latifolium*; — cervina, mat grass, *Nardus stricta*; — chitarra, ragwort, *Senecio jacobaea*; — cimicina, herb Robert, *Geranium robertianum*; — cipollina, chives, *Allium schoenoprasum*; — cipressina, cypress spurge, *Euphorbia cyparissias*; — cornetta, *Coronilla emerus, Delphinium consolida, Rhagadiolus stellatus*; — corsa, *Daphne gnidium*; — costa, costmary, *Chrysanthemum balsamita, Pastinaca opopanax*; — cremesina, pokeweed, *Phytolacca americana*; — croce, crosswort, *Galium cruciata, Valantia muralis*; — crociola, herb Paris, *Paris quadrifolia*; — de' calli,

stonecrop, *Sedum maximum, S. telephium*; — de' gatti, *Teucrium marum*; — da porri, greater celandine, *Chelidonium majus*; — da sciatica, *Lepidium graminifolium*; — Doria, *Senecio doria*; — filandra, seaweed which grows on a ship's hull; — fragolina, wood sanicle, *Sanicula europaea*; — franca, sea heath, *Frankenia levis*; — fumaria, moschatel, *Adoxa moschatellina*; — galletta, meadow vetchling, *Lathyrus pratensis*; — gamberaia, water starwort, *Callitriche*; — gatta, catmint, *Nepeta cataria*; — ginestrina, *Coronilla varia*; — girarda, ground elder, *Aegopodium podagraria*; — Giulia, *Achillea ageratum*; — grassa, stonecrop, *Sedum rupestre, S. sexangulare, S. album*, etc.; water speedwell, *Veronica anagallis aquatica*; — guada, weld, *Reseda luteola*; — judaica, hemp nettle, *Galeopsis tetrahit*; — lattaria, snow in summer, *Cerastium tomentosum*; — laurina, spurge laurel, *Daphne laureola*; — lazza, *Euphorbia characias*; — leprina, black bindweed, *Polygonum convolvulus, P. dumetorum*; — limona, — limoncina, balm, *Melissa officinalis*; bastard balm, *Melittis melissophyllum*; — lunaria, moonwort, *Botrychium lunaria*; honesty, *Lunaria annua*; — maga, enchanter's nightshade, *Circaea lutetiana*; — maggenga, meadow grass, *Poa pratensis, P. trivialis*; — mazzolina, cock's foot, *Dactylis glomerata*; — media, Canterbury bells, *Campanula medium*; — medica, lucern, *Medicago sativa*; — medica di fiore giallo, sickle medick, *M. falcata*; — nocca, Christmas rose, *Helleborus niger*; — nocitola, *Laserpitium latifolium*; — paglina, *Moehringia muscosa*; — paperina, dropwort, *Filipendula vulgaris*; — pazienza, patience dock, *Rumex patientia*; — pepe, water pepper, *Polygonum hydro-piper*; — pesce, *Salvinia natans*; — Pietro, *Stachys germanica*; — pignola, — pinocchina, stonecrop, *Sedum album, S. sexangulare*, etc.; — pondia, *Euphorbia chamaesyce*; — porraia, *Heliotropium europaeum*; — quattrina, creeping Jenny, *Lysimachia nummularia*; — querciola, wall germander, *Teucrium chamaedrys*; — radioli, black spleenwort, *Asplenium adiantum-nigrum*; — rena, *Peucedanum ostruthium*; — ruchetta, *Reseda alba*; — ruota, *Achillea herba-rota*; — saetta, arrowhead, *Sagittaria sagittifolia*; — S. Giovanni, stonecrop, *Sedum maximum, S. telephium*; St. John's wort, *Hypericum perforatum*; — S. Jacopo, ragwort, *Senecio jacobaea*; — S. Pietro, samphire, *Crithmum maritimum*; sea holly, *Eryngium maritimum*; — S. Maria, costmary, *Chrysanthemum balsamita*; — serponi, *Dracunculus vulgaris*; — Spagna, lucern, *Medicago sativa*; — Spagna selvatica, sainfoin, *Onobrychis viciaefolia*; — stella, lady's mantle, *Alchemilla vulgaris*; buck's horn plantain, *Plantago coronopus*; — storna, pepperwort, *Lepidium campestre*; penny cress, *Thlaspi arvense*; — strega, snapdragon, *Antirrhinum majus*; club-moss, *Lycopodium clavatum*; — sulla, *Hedysarum coronarium*; — tinca, shining pond-weed, *Potamogeton lucens*; — topina, black twitch, *Alopecurus myosuroides*; — tortora, *Cerinthe minor*; — tremolina, quaking grass, *Briza media*; — Trinita, hepatica, *Anemone hepatica*; — veglia, *Dorycnium hirsutum*; — vellutina, hound's tongue, *Cynoglossum officinale*; — ventaglina, parsley piert, *Aphanes arvensis*; — vescica, bladderwort, *Utricularia vulgaris*; — vetriola, pellitory-of-the-wall, *Parietaria officinalis*; — zolfina; lady's bedstraw, *Galium verum*; melilot, *Melilotus officinalis*. **-ac·cia** *f. pejor.* weed. **-a·ceo** *adj.* herbaceous. **-ag·gio** *m.* pot-herbs, green vegetables, salad. **-a·io** *m.* (Tusc.) plot of grass or green corn; ground full of weeds. **-ai(u)olo** *m.* vendor or pedlar of vegetables; greengrocer. **-a·rio** *m.* herbarium, collection of dried plants; treatise on herbs, herbal; *adj.* relating to herbs or botany. **-arolo** *m.* (tanning) kip. **-a·tico** *m.* (leg.) the right of grass- or hay-cutting and pasture on public land or commons. **-ato** *adj.* grassy, grass-covered; *n.m.* grass; grassy plain. **-atura** *f.* time required for grass to grow long enough to cut; a cutting of grass. **-etta** *f. dim.* young short grass.

Erberto *pr.n.m.* Herbert.

erbicida *m.* (agric.) weed-killer.

er·bio *m.* (chem.) erbium.

erbiven·dol-o *m.* greengrocer. (**-a** *f.*)

erbi·voro *adj.* herbivorous, vegetable-feeding.

erbola·io *m.* herbalist.

erbolato *m.* pastry of herbs; herb-plaster; *adj.* covered or mixed with herbs or grass.

erbolina *f.* fine grass; young moss; andare con l'— in mano, to go carefully, to be very civil, to be anxious to make a good impression.

erbor-are [A I] *intr.* (*aux.* avere) to collect plants, to herborize. **-atore** *m.* collector of herbs or botanical specimens. (**-atrice** *f.*)

ebor·are (*cont.*)

~**azione** *f.* collecting herbs, herborization. ~**ista** *m.* collector of herbs; herbalist. ~**i·stico** *adj.* pertaining to the knowledge of herbs and plants; la medicina ~istica, herbalist remedies. ~**izzatore** *m.* see **erboratore**.

erboso *adj.* grassy; grass-grown.

ercolanense *adj.* of Herculaneum; Accademia —, Archaeological Academy, in Naples.

Ercolano *pr.n.m.* (hist. geog.) Herculaneum.

Er·col·e *pr.n.m.* (myth.) Hercules; Colonne d'—, Straits of Gibraltar, (fig.) the extreme limit attainable; un —, an exceptionally strong man; — al bivio, at the parting of the ways, at the cross-roads; (astron.) Hercules (constellation). ~**ino** *adj.* Herculean; strong; dalle gambe ~ine, slightly bow-legged.

ercotetto·nica *f.* (archit.) military architecture, art of constructing fortifications.

ercu·leo *adj.* Herculean.

E·rebo *pr.n.m.* (myth.) Erebus, the nether world; subterranean darkness; (ent.) argus and ringlet butterflies, *Erebia* spp.

ered·e *m., f.* heir; heiress; (fig.) inheritor; successor; spiritual heir; (leg.) heir; residuary legatee; — generale, heir general; — assente, absent heir; — unico, sole heir; — legittimo, lawful heir; — legittimario, statutory next-of-kin; — necessario, heir indefeasibly entitled to legitim (or a share of the estate) by operation of law; — con beneficio di (legge e) d'inventario, heir with benefit of inventory (i.e. whose acceptance of inheritance is conditional upon assets of estate exceeding liabilities); — testamentario, heir under testamentary disposition; — istituto, appointed heir (C.C.); — fiduciario, fiduciary heir; — naturale, natural heir; — universale, universal heir; sole residuary legatee; — adottivo, heir by adoption.

eredità *f.* inheritance; fare un'—, to inherit, to come into a fortune; (biol.) heredity; (leg.) inheritance; accettazione dell'—, acceptance of inheritance (C.C.); estate of a deceased person; legacy; — beneficiata, inheritance accepted conditionally upon debts being less than assets; — vacante, vacant inheritance, unclaimed estate; — giacente, inheritance in abeyance, estate under administration; diritto di —, right to an inheritance or succession; lasciare in —, to bequeath, to devise.

eredit·are [A 1 s] *tr.* to inherit, to come into; *intr.* (*aux.* avere) to be heir. ~**ato** *part. adj.* inherited. ~**arietà** *f.* heredity. ~**a·rio** *adj.* hereditary; Principe ~ario, heir to the throne, hereditary prince; (leg.) beni ~ari, massa ~aria, property constituting a deceased person's estate. ~**iera** *f.* heiress.

eredolue·tico *m.* (biol.; med.) hereditary disease.

eremacosi·a *f.* (biol.) eremacausis.

eremit·a *m.* hermit; (zool.) hermit crab. ~**ag·gio** *m.* hermitage. ~**ano** *adj., n.m.* Augustinian (hermit); belonging to a hermit of St Augustine. ~**o·rio** *m.* hermitage.

eremi·tico *adj.* pertaining to a hermit; vita eremitica, hermit's existence.

e·remo *m.* hermitage; solitary place, retreat.

e·reo *adj.* bronze, copper.

eres·i·a *f.* heresy; (pop.) blasphemous, shocking, or nonsensical language. ~**iare** [A4] *intr.* (*aux.* avere) (pop.) to use shocking language. ~**iarca** *m.* (*pl.* ~iarchi) heresiarch.

e·reso *m.* (zool.) a brightly coloured spider, *Eresa cinnabarina*.

†**eretag·gio** *m.* inheritance.

eretic·are [A 2 s] *intr.* (*aux.* avere) (theol.) to fall into heresy. ~**azione** *f.* (theol.) sharing of heretical doctrine or worship.

ere·tic·o *adj.* (theol.) heretical; *n.m.* heretic. (~**amente** *adv.*) ~**ale** *adj.* (theol.) heretical. (~**almente** *adv.*) ~**ità** *f.* (theol.) hereticalness.

eret·ismo *m.* erethism. ~**i·stico** *adj.* erethistic.

Erette·o *pr.n.m.* Erechtheum.

eret·tile *adj.* (anat.) erectile.

erett·o *part.* of **erigere**, q.v.; *adj.* erect, upright; standing; erected, founded. ~**ore** *m.* erector, founder. (~**rice** *f.*)

erezione *f.* erection; building; foundation; establishment.

erg *m. indecl.* (phys.) erg; (geol.) sand dunes.

erga·stol·o *m.* prison; dungeon; penal servitude for life; condannato all'—, sentenced to penal servitude for life. ~**ano** *m.* convict serving a life sentence.

er·gere [C4] *tr.* to raise, to erect; to elevate; to puff up with pride; *rfl.* to rise.

ergo *adv.* (joc.) therefore; *n.m.* venire all'—, to conclude, to come to the point.

erg-o·grafo *m.*, ~**o·metro** *m.* (phys.) ergometer, dynamometer.

ergo·n *m. indecl.* (phys.). See **erg**.

ergoterapi·a *f.* therapy based on work.

ergot·ina *f.* (pharm.) ergotinine. ~**ismo** *m.* (path.) ergotism.

erica, e·rica *f.* heather; rustic broom (made from heather).

Eri·dano *pr.n.m.* (anct. geog.; astron.) Eridanus; (poet.) river Po.

Eriè *pr.n.m.* (geog.) il lago di —, Lake Erie.

erig·ere [C13] *tr.* to erect; to raise; to build; to found, to institute; *rfl.* (*prep.* a) to set oneself up (as something), to assume the authority (of). ~**endo** *adj.* about to be put up; about to be founded. ~**i·bile** *adj.* erigible.

erin·gio *m.* sea-holly, *Eryngium maritimum*, and other species.

erinite *m.* (miner.) erinite.

Erinni *pr.n.f.* (myth.) Erinys, Fury.

erino *m.* (bot.) *Erinus alpinus*.

erinosi *f.* a disease in vines.

erio·foro *m.* (bot.) cotton-grass, *Eriophorum*.

erio·metro *m.* (techn.) eriometer.

eri·ş-amo, ~imo *m.* (bot.) — medicinale, hedge mustard, *Sisymbrium officinale*.

erisipel·a *f.* (med.) erysipelas. ~**atoso** *adj.* erysipelatic.

eri·stic·a *f.* (rhet.) art of disputation, love of disputation; eristics; sophistry. ~**o** *adj.* eristic, controversial, captious.

eritema *m.* (med.) erythema; rash.

Eritre·a *pr.n.f.* (geog.) Eritrea. ~**o** *adj., n.m.* Eritrean; il Mare ~o, the Red Sea.

eritrocito *m.* (med.) erythrocyte, red-blood corpuscle; — ipocromico, achromatocyte.

erm·a *f., m.* (art) herm (head or bust mounted on a pillar). ~**e·o** *m.* Temple of Hermes or Mercury.

ermafrod·ismo *m.* hermaphroditism. ~**itismo** *m.* (zool.; med.) hermaphroditism. ~**ito** *pr.n.m.* (myth.) Hermaphroditus; (zool.) hermaphrodite.

ermellin·o *m.* ermine; (zool.) stoat, ermine, *Mustela erminea*; (bot.) date plum, *Diospyrus lotus*; (herald.) ermine. ~**ato** *adj.* (herald.) ermine(d), white powdered with black tufts.

ermene·ut·ica *f.* hermeneutics, interpretation, esp. of the Scriptures. ~**ico** *adj.* hermeneutic, interpretative. ~**a** *m.* interpreter of obscure texts.

Er·mes, Ermete *pr.n.m.* (myth.) Hermes, Mercury.

erme·tic·o *adj.* hermetic; air-tight; gas-proof; (lit. hist.) poesia ~a, verse of esoteric appeal, esp. modern; *n.m.* (eng.) sealing compound. ~**amente** *adv.* hermetically; (fig.) chiudersi ~amente, to refuse to be disturbed by callers or any business. ~**ità** *f. indecl.* (eng.) tightness, airtightness.

ermetismo *m.* (philos.) hermeticism, hermetic doctrine; (fig.) obscure or esoteric character.

Ermi·nia *pr.n.f.* Herminia.

ermione[1] *m.* (ent.) *Satyrus hermione*, a butterfly similar to a grayling.

Ermione[2] *pr.n.f.* Hermione.

ermişino, erme·ş *m.* a thin silk stuff (a kind of sarsenet).

ermo, (Rom.) **ermo** *adj.* (poet.) solitary; *n.m.* (poet.) solitary place; retreat.

ermo-dat·tilo, ~dat·tero *m.* (bot.) widow iris, *Hermodactylus tuberosus*.

ermogeniano *adj.* (leg.) supplemento to or continuation of the Gregorian Codex.

er·mula *f.* (art) a small herm; a small marble column.

er·ni·a *f.* hernia, rupture. ~**a·ria** *f.* (bot.) rupture-wort, *Herniaria glabra*. ~**a·rio** *adj.* hernial; cinto ~ario, truss. ~**oso** *adj.* ruptured.

Ero *pr.n.f.* (myth.) Hero.

Erode *pr.n.m.* Herod (of Judaea); (fig.) mandare da — a Pilato, to send from pillar to post; morose, churlish individual.

erodere [C3] *tr.* to erode.

Ero·doto *pr.n.m.* Herodotus.

er-o·e *m.* hero; chief protagonist, main character, hero; (joc.) l'— della festa, birthday-child. ~**oişmo** *m.* heroism.

erog·are [A 2 s] *tr.* to supply; to devote (money) to a purpose, usually of public utility or benevolence; to distribute (e.g. water supply); (hydr.) (of a pump) to deliver. ~**a·bile** *adj.* expendable for some good purpose. (~**ato** *part. adj.*) ~**azione** *f.* supply; erogation, expenditure; bestowal; public distribution (e.g. of water supply); (techn.) production, yield, output, delivery; (electr.) circuito di ~azione, output circuit.

ero·ic-o *adj.* heroic; verso —, hexameter. **-amẹnte** *adv.* heroically. **-iẓẓare** [A I] *tr.* to hero-worship; to make heroic; to exaggerate the heroic qualities of; *intr.* (*aux.* avere) to be melodramatic, to indulge in heroics.

eroi-co·mico *adj.* (lit.) heroicomic, mock-heroic. **-cosati·rico** *adj.* (lit.) combining the heroic with the satirical.

Ero·idi *pr.n.f.pl.* the *Heroides* of Ovid; verse-letters in similar style.

eroina[1] *f.* heroine.

eroina[2] *f.* (med.; pharm.) heroin.

eroiṣmo *m.* See under **eroe**.

erọmpere [C26] *intr.* (*aux.* avere) to burst forth, to rush out.

eroṣ-iọne *f.* erosion. **-ivo** *adj.* erosive.

erọṣo *part.* of erodere, q.v.; *adj.* eroded; bronze (of coins).

Ero·strato *pr.n.m.* Herostratus.

erotema *m.* (rhet.) erotesis, assertion in the form of a question.

erọt-ico *adj.* erotic; amatory. (**-icamẹnte** *adv.*) **-omani·a** *f.* erotomania.

er·pete *m.* (med.) herpes.

erpic-are [A2s] *tr.* (agric.) to harrow. **-amẹnto** *m.* harrowing. **-ato** *part. adj.* harrowed. (**-atọre** *m.* **-atura** *f.*)

erpicatọio *m.* a net for catching quails, partridges, etc.

ẹrpice, er·pice *m.* (agric.) harrow; — a catena, chain harrow; — a denti fissi, peg-tooth harrow; — a denti flessibili, spring-tooth harrow; — a dischi, disc harrow; — a stella, rotary hoe; — a frangizolle, pulverizer harrow.

err-are [A I] *intr.* (*aux.* avere) to wander; to roam, to rove; to stray from the right way; to err. **-abọndo** *adj.* wandering, rambling. **-ante** *part. adj.* wandering; errant; le stelle -anti, the planets; (geol.) masso -ante, erratic boulder. **-ato** *part. adj.* mistaken; locuzione -ata, uso -ato, wrong usage, ungrammatical expression; andare —, to be mistaken. **-atamẹnte** *adv.* mistakenly.

errata-cor·rige *m., f.* (typ.) table of misprints or errata with corrections; corrigendum, corrigenda.

erra·tico *adj.* wandering; straying; (geol.) massi erratici, erratic boulders; (astron.) stelle erratiche, planets.

errato[1] *part.* of errare, q.v.

errato[2] *adj.* See under **erre**.

err-e *f., m. indecl.* name of the letter R; gli manca l'—, he can't pronounce R; — moscia, French R, lisped R; perder l'—, to slur one's R's, to speak as though drunk, to babble. **-ato** *adj.* spelt with R; (provb.) nei mesi -ati, non seder sopra gli erbati, don't sit on the grass when there's an R in the month.

†**erro** *m.* error.

errọn-eo *adj.* erroneous, false, mistaken; wrong; illogical; dichiarazione -ea, misrepresentation. **-eamẹnte** *adv.* erroneously; mistakenly; wrongly. **-eità** *f.* erroneousness, falsity. †**-ico** *adj.* erroneous, mistaken; vagabond, erratic.

errọre *m.* mistake; incorrere in un —, to make a mistake; fallacy; — di stampa, misprint; salvo —, if I am not mistaken; per —, accidentally, by mistake; — materiale, clerical error; — d'ortografia, spelling mistake; — di calcolo, miscalculation; (naut.) — della stima, difference from dead reckoning; (theol.) error, fault; (leg.) mistake; — di diritto, mistake of law; — di fatto, mistake of fact; la rilevanza dell'—, the effect of the mistake; †journey, wandering, peregrination.

erso *adj.* Erse; *n.m.* Erse language.

ẹrt-a, (Rom.) **ert-a** *f.* steep ascent, hill; steep path or street; all'—!, look out!; stare all'—, to be on the alert; non saper tenere un cocomero all'—, to be a useless sort of person. **-eẓza** *f.* steepness; steep place. **-o** *adj.* steep; erect. **-amẹnte** *adv.* steeply.

erubesc-ente *adj.* glowing red; flushing. **-enza** *f.* turning red, reddening; redness; flushing. **-ite** *m.* (miner.) erubescite, purple copper.

eruca *f.* (bot.) salad rocket, *Eruca sativa*; (ent.) any caterpillar with stinging hairs.

erud-ire [D2] *tr.* to teach, to instruct. **-i·bile** *adj.* teachable, amenable to instruction. **-itiṣmo** *m.* pedantry. **-ito** *part. adj.* erudite, learned; scholarly; *n.m.* learned man, scholar. **-itamẹnte** *adv.* in a learned manner. **-iziọne** *f.* erudition, copious learning, scholarship.

eru·gine *f.* verdigris.

erutt-are [A I] *intr.* (*aux.* avere) to belch; to eruct; *tr.* to erupt; to throw out, to eject. **-aziọne** *f.* belching; eruption; matter erupted. **-ivo** *adj.* eruptive.

eruziọne *f.* (med.) eruption, rash; (geol.) eruption; (mil.) breaking out, sortie.

ervalenta *f.* lentil-flour.

ervo *m.* (bot.) lentil, *Ervum lens*; *E. ervilla*.

Erzegovina *pr.n.f.* (geog.) Herzegovina.

erziano *adj.* (phys.; electr.) Hertzian.

esa- (NOTE: intervocalic S is voiced in Tuscan, unvoiced in Roman pronunciation.)

eṣabiọso *adj.* (chem.) disaccharide.

eṣacerb-are [A I] *tr.* to exacerbate, to aggravate; to embitter; to exasperate. **-amẹnto** *m.* exacerbating, aggravating; exacerbation. **-ato** *part. adj.* exacerbated, aggravated; embittered; irritated; exasperated. **-atọre** *m.* aggravator. **-aziọne** *f.* exacerbation; aggravation; irritation.

eṣacord-o *m.* (mus.) hexachord; sixth. **-ale** *adj.* (mus.) hexachordal.

eṣae·dro *m.* (math.) hexahedron.

eṣafo·nico *adj.* (mus.) la scala esafonica, the whole-tone scale.

eṣager-are [A I S] *tr.* to exaggerate; to overstate; *intr.* (*aux.* avere) to exaggerate; to exceed proper limits, to go too far; to overdo things. **-ativo** *adj.* tending to exaggerate, given to exaggeration. **-ato** *part. adj.* exaggerated; far-fetched; too lavish; not in good taste; excessive. (**-atamẹnte** *adv.*) **-atọre** *m.* exaggerator (**-atrice** *f.*). **-aziọne** *f.* exaggeration; excess. **-ọne** *m.* one who exaggerates habitually (**-ọna** *f.*).

eṣa·gio *m.* weighing of coins; sixth part of an ounce.

eṣagit-are [A I S] *tr.* to agitate greatly; to torment; to discuss again and again, to thrash out. **-ato** *part. adj.* agitated; restless, uneasy; thrashed out.

eṣa·gon-o *m.* (math.) hexagon; *adj.* hexagonal. **-ale** *adj.* hexagonal. **-ato** *adj.* hexagon-shaped.

eṣal-are [A I] *tr.* to exhale; — l'anima, to die; — l'ira, to give vent to one's wrath; *intr.* (*aux.* essere) to be exhaled; to issue; to rise; to spread. **-a·bile** *adj.* exhalable. **-amẹnto** *m.* exhaling; exhalation, breathing freely; (fig.) letting off of steam. (**-ato** *part. adj.*) **-atọio** *m.* vent. **-aziọne** *f.* exhalation; fume, vapour.

†**esaldire** *vb.* and derivs. See **esaudire**.

eṣalina *f.* (chem.) cyclohexanol.

eṣalt-are [A I] *tr.* to exalt, to raise; to extol; to enhance; — il sapore, to heighten the flavour; *rfl.* to become excited; to become elated; to get above oneself, to lose one's head; to become fanatically enthusiastic; to be high-falutin. **-amẹnto** *m.* see esaltazione. **-ato** *part. adj.* raised; excited; enraptured; fanatical; delirious, beside oneself; testa -ata, excitable person, person subject to wild imagination; *n.m.* hot-head; harmless eccentric, enthusiast; *pl.* (Ital. hist.) gli Esaltati, a faction of extreme followers of Mazzini in the Roman Republic of 1849. **-aziọne** *f.* raising; exalting; extolling; excitement, excessive fervour; enthusiasm; state of elation, exaltation; (rel.) -azione della Croce, Exaltation of the Cross; †(chem.) sublimation. (**-atọre** *m.* **-atrice** *f.*)

eṣame *m.* examination, exam; dare un —, to take an examination, to sit for an exam; bocciare (*or* essere bocciato) a un —, to fail an exam; passare un —, to pass an exam; investigation, inspection; scrutiny; (leg.) searching examination; investigation, inspection; perusal; — testimoniale, examination of witnesses; sottoporre ad un — in contraddittorio, to submit to cross-examination; — contabile, investigation of accounts (C.C.P.); — degli atti del processo, perusal of the papers in, the record of, the action (C.C.P.); — di documenti, inspection of documents; — di testimoni in udienza, examination of witnesses in open court; (comm.) inviare in —, to send on approval.

eṣamerọne *m.* space of six days, esp. the six days of the creation; *pr.n.m.* title of a collection of stories, told in six days, by Sebastiano Erizzo.

esametilentetrammina *f.* (chem.) hexamethylene tetramine, hexamine.

eṣa·mina *f.* examination; survey; appraisal of evidence.

esamin-are [A I S] *tr.* to examine; to investigate; to scrutinize; (leg.) to examine closely, to investigate, to inspect, to peruse. **-a·bile** *adj.* examinable; open to investigation. **-ando** *n.m.* candidate. **-ante** *part. adj.* examining; *n.m.* examiner. †**-anza** *f.* test, trial. **-atọre** *m.* examiner; inspector. (**-atrice** *f.*) **-aziọne** *f.* examining; †observation, careful scrutiny.

eṣangue *adj.* weak from loss of blood, pale; bloodless; dead.

eṣa·nim-e *adj.* lifeless; dead; unconscious. **-are** [A I S] *tr.* to discourage, to dishearten. **-ato** *part. adj.*; discouraged, downcast.

eṣantem-a *m.* (med.) exanthema, rash. **-a·tico** *adj.* exanthematous.

eṣa·podi *m.pl.* (zool.) hexapods, insects.

eṣar·ca m. (*pl.* **-chi**) (hist.) exarch, governor of a province of the Byzantine empire; (eccl.) exarch. **-cato** m. exarchate, dignity or office of exarch; (eccl.) exarch. **-cato** m. exarchate, dignity or office of exarch; territory subject to an exarch.

eṣarchi·a f. government by six persons or parties.

eṣar·cia f. (naut.) outfit of a ship.

eṣar·co m. (*pl.* **-chi**). See **esarca**.

eṣasper-are [A I s] *tr.* to treat harshly; to exasperate, to infuriate; *rfl.* to become exasperated. **-aménto** m. exasperating; rousing of fury. **-ante** *part. adj.* exasperating; infuriating, maddening. **-ato** *part. adj.* exasperated; (of nerves) frayed, on edge. **-atóre** m. exasperating person. (**-atrice** f.) **-azióne** f. exasperation.

eṣa·stico *adj.* (prosod.) of six lines, six-line.

eṣa·stilo *adj.* (archit.) hexastyle, having six columns.

eṣatonale *adj.* (mus.) hexatonal; la scala —, the whole-tone scale.

eṣatriọsio m. (chem.) trisaccharide.

eṣatt-o¹ *adj.* exact; precise; accurate; correct; punctual; *adv.* precisely, exactly, yes, just so, that is so. **-aménte** *adv.* exactly; precisely; accurately; correctly; punctually. **-ezza** f. exactness; exactitude; accuracy, precision; punctuality.

eṣatt-o² *part.* of **esigere**, q.v.; *adj.* exacted, demanded, insisted upon. **-óre** m. collector; -ore delle imposte, tax collector. **-ori·a** f. collector's office; collectorship. (**-oriale** *adj.*)

Eṣa·u *pr.n.m.* Esau.

eṣaud-ire [D 2] *tr.* to grant, to concede; to assent to; — un desiderio, to comply with a wish; — una preghiera, to grant a prayer. †**-e·vole** *adj.* see **esaudibile**. **-i·bile** *adj.* that may be granted or complied with. **-iménto** m. assent; fulfilment. **-ito** *part. adj.* granted, conceded; fulfilled. **-itóre** m. one who gives consent. †**-izione** f. granting, conceding.

eṣaur-ire [D 2] *tr.* to exhaust; to use up; to deplete; to wear out; to run out of, to run short of; *rfl.* to become used up; (comm.) to sell out. **-i·bile** *adj.* exhaustible; limited. **-iente** *part. adj.* exhausting; exhaustive; thorough; definitive. **-iménto** m. exhausting; depleting; exhaustion; -imento nervoso, nervous breakdown; in via di -imento, running short of stock; ad -imento del contratto, in fulfilment of the contract. **-ito** *part. adj.* exhausted; depleted; used up; spent; worn out; run down in health, on the verge of a breakdown; out of stock; out of print; sold out; all gone; off the menu; finished; considerare la pratica -ita, to regard the matter as settled (see also **esausto**).

eṣaust-o *adj.* exhausted; erario —, empty treasury; forze -e, depleted strength; sorgente -a, dried-up spring; (of a battery) run-down, flat (see also **esaurito**, under **esaurire**). **-ione** f. exhaustion.

eṣautor-are [A I] *tr.* to deprive of authority, to discredit. **-ato** *part. adj.* deprived of authority. (**-azione** f.)

eṣazione f. exaction; exacting; collection of taxes; taxes collected.

†**eṣbors-are** *tr.* to disburse. †**-azione** f. disbursement, disbursing; sum disbursed.

eṣbọrso m. payment, disbursement; outlay.

ęsc-a, (Rom.) **esc-a** f. bait; lure; (fig.) allurement; prendere all'—, to deceive with promises; tinder; fuse; †food. †**-amento** m. see **esca**.

escandesc-ente *adj.* white-hot; (fig.) hot-headed, irascible. **-enza** f. outburst of rage; dare in -enze, to flare up, to go off the deep end.

e·scar-a f. (med.) eschar. **-o·tico** *adj., n.m.* (med.) escharotic.

†**escato** m. trap, snare; deception, trickery; allurement.

escatol-ogi·a f. (theol.) eschatology. **-o·gico** *adj.* eschatological.

escav-are [A I] *tr.* excavate. **-ato** *part. adj.* excavated. **-atóre** m. excavator; digger; (eng.) excavator; -atore a cucchiaia, power shovel. **-atrice** f. (eng.) see **escavatore**. **-azione** f. excavation; dig. See also **scavare**.

e·schera f. See **escara**.

E·schil-o *pr.n.m.* Aeschylus. **-eo** *adj.* Aeschylean, of Aeschylus.

eschimese *adj., n.m., f.* Eskimo.

ęschio m. (bot.) durmast oak, sessile oak, *Quercus petraea*.

escire [D 16] and derivs. (Tusc.). See **uscire**.

esclam-are [A I] *tr., intr.* (*aux.* avere) to exclaim; to cry out; to interject; to lament. **-ativo** *adj.* exclamatory; punto -ativo, exclamation mark. **-azione** f. exclamation; (gramm.) interjection.

esclu·d-ere [C 3] *tr.* to exclude, to leave out; to shut out; to debar; not to admit; (electr.) to cut out; (leg.) to dismiss; to expel; — una parte dalla causa, to dismiss a party from the action (C.C.P.). **-ente** *part. adj.* excluding, debarring. **-itóre** m. (electr.) cut-out switch; *adj.* excluding (see also **esclusore**, under **escluso**).

esclus-ione f. exclusion; sono tutti ladri senza —, they are all thieves without exception; (leg.) expulsion; — di un socio, expulsion of a partner (C.C.); per il processo di —, by a process of elimination. **-iva** f. exclusion; (leg.) patent right; exclusive rights, sole agency; copyright; in -iva mondiale, with world copyright; right of exclusion, veto (at papal elections). **-ivista** m. patentee. **-ività** f. exclusiveness; monopoly; sole right; agente con -ività, sole agent; patent right. **-ivo** *adj.* exclusive; sole. **-ivaménte** *adv.* exclusively.

esclus-o *part.* of **escludere**, q.v.; *adj.* excluded; -i i rischi di guerra, exclusive of war-risks; deprived; *prep.* except; †ejected, emitted, expelled. **-óre** m. excluder; (electr.) cut-out switch; *adj.* excluding (see also **escluditore**, under **escludere**).

escna f. (ent.) dragonfly, *Aeschna* spp.

escogit-are [A I s] *tr.* to think out; to devise, to contrive; to excogitate. **-ativo** *adj.* cogitative; facoltà -ativa, inventive faculty. **-ato** *part. adj.* thought out; devised; excogitated. (**-atóre** m. **-atrice** f.) **-azione** f. excogitation, cogitation.

†**e·scolo** m. See **eschio**.

esco·mi-o m. (leg.) landlord's notice to agricultural tenant to quit. **-are** [A 4] *tr.* (leg.) to give notice (to agricultural tenant) to quit.

escori-are [A 4] *tr.* to flay, to excoriate; *rfl.* to flog oneself; (fig.) to drive oneself. **-ativo** *adj.* producing excoriation. **-ato** *part. adj.* flayed, excoriated. **-azione** f. flaying, excoriation; abrasion.

escreato m. (med.) phlegm and other matter expectorated.

escremént-o m. excrement; refuse; lees. **-ale**, **-i·zio**, **-ọso** *adj.* excremental.

escrẹsc-ere [B 9] *intr.* (*aux.* essere) to grow upon the surface, to be an excrescence. **-ente** *adj.* excrescent. **-enza** f. excrescence.

escretina f. (chem.) excretin.

escre-tivo *adj.* excretive, excretory. **-to·rio** *adj.* excretory. **-zione** f. excretion.

†**escu·bia** f. watch, guard, vigil.

Escula·pio *pr.n.m.* Aesculapius.

esculento *adj.* esculent, edible.

esculina f. (chem.) esculin.

escursion-e f. excursion; outing; — a piedi, walking-tour; (mil.) raid; (geog.) — annua, annual range. **-ista** m., f. excursionist; tripper.

†**escusa** f. and derivs. See **scusa**.

†**escusato·rio** *adj.* of excuse, excusing; apologetic; explanatory.

escussione f. (leg.) formal inquiry, investigation, examination of witnesses (mostly in bankruptcy and winding-up), public examination of bankrupt; — del patrimonio, formal inquiry as to assets, investigation of affairs, of partnership (C.C.).

escu·tere [C 19] *tr.* (leg.) to examine; to question; to investigate; — testimoni, to examine witnesses.

eṣecr-are [A I] *tr.* to detest, to abhor; to execrate; to curse. **-a·bile** *adj.* abhorrent, execrable. **-abilità** f. execrableness. **-ando** *adj.* execrable, detestable. **-atóre** m. execrator; *adj.* execrating. (**-atrice** f.) **-ato·rio** *adj.* (of an oath) invoking God's curse on the speaker if he be not speaking the truth.

esecutare [A I] *tr.* (leg.) to enforce; to distrain, to levy a distress upon (a debtor) (C.C.P.); — un debitore, to distrain.

eṣecutiv-o *adj.* executive; potere —, executive power; (leg.) executive; executory; enforceable; titolo —, document warranting execution (C.C.P.); administrative; official; giudizio —, Writ of Execution; sentenza -a, executory, immediately enforceable judgement; atti -i, official acts; decreto —, decree of the executive; rendere —, to make (e.g. a judgement) operative or executory; to bring (e.g. a law) into force; il provvedimento ha forza -a, the measure is binding; n.m. executive power; executive committee. **-aménte** *adv.* in an executive capacity.

eṣecut-óre m. executor; executive officer; minister; performer; (mus.) executant; (leg.) — testamentario, executor; nominare un —, to appoint an executor; — di giustizia, executioner; artisti -ori di opere musicali, performers of musical works. **-rice** f. (leg.) executrix. **-orietà** f. enforcement; -orietà della sentenza, enforcement of the judgement; -orietà del contratto, enforcement of the contract. **-o·rio** *adj.* (leg.) executory, immediately enforceable; sentenza -oria, executory, enforceable, binding judgement.

eṣecuzion-e f. execution; carrying out; performance; buono il concetto, cattiva l'esecuzione, the idea is good but badly carried out; (leg.) execution; — capitale, execution (of the death penalty); performance; enforcement; operation; dare — a, to enforce;

esecuzion-e (*cont.*)
— forzata, execution of judgement by, e.g. sheriff's officer (C.C.P.); esperire l'— di, to carry into execution; ordine di —, warrant for execution; — di un contratto, performance of a contract; andare in —, to come into operation; mettere ad —, to put into operation; sospendere l'—, to stay execution; — in forma specifica, specific performance; — di una sentenza, execution of a judgement; — provvisoria, provisional, interim execution; fascicolo dell'—, file of documents in bankruptcy; giudice dell'—, Official Receiver. †**-ale** *adj.* enforceable; executable.

esedra *f.* (antiq.) exedra; name of a covered colonnade at the top of the Via Nazionale, in Rome.

ese·g-esi *f. indecl.* exegesis, exposition of an ancient author, esp. of the Bible. **-eta** *m.* exegete, expounder. **-e·tica** *f.* (theol.) exegesis, exegetics. **-e·tico** *adj.* exegetic.

esegu-ire [D2, D1] *tr.* to execute; to perform; to carry out, to fulfil. **-i·bile** *adj.* executable, that can be performed; (leg.) enforceable. **-imento** *m.* executing; performing; fulfilment. (**-ito** *part. adj.*)

esempigra·zia *adv.* for example, for instance, e.g.

esempio, (Rom.) **esem·pio** *m.* example; per —, ad —, for instance; pattern; specimen, sample; precedent; illustration; senza —, unexampled; dare l'—, to set an example.

esemplar-e[1] *adj.* exemplary, model; *n.m.* model, example; copy, specimen; (philos.) exemplar. **-ità** *f.* exemplariness.

†**esemplare**[2] [A1] *tr.* to copy; to transcribe; to imitate.

esemplific-are [A2s] *tr.* to exemplify, to show by examples. **-ativo** *adj.* exemplicative, serving to exemplify. **-ato** *part. adj.* exemplified, illustrated, instanced. **-azione** *f.* exemplification.

†**esempligra·zia** *adv.* See **esempigrazia**.

†**esemplo** *m.* See **esempio**.

esentare [A1] *tr.* to exempt; to free, to discharge; to relieve; *rfl.* to excuse oneself (from some undertaking or expense); (cards, 'briscola') to refuse to take a trick.

esente *adj.* exempt; free; — di spese, free of charge; — d'imposte, free of tax; — da bollo, exempt from stamp duty (cf. **bollo**[1]); — dal servizio militare, exempt from military service; immune; pochi andarono esenti dal contagio, few people escaped the contagion; *n.m.* (Papal Guard) rank equivalent to that of a colonel.

esento *part.* of **esimere**, q.v.

esenzion-e *f.* exemption. **-are** [A1c] *tr.* to render exempt, to grant exemption to, to exempt. (**-ato** *part adj.*)

ese·qui-e *f.pl.* funeral; obsequies, funeral rites; a -e avvenute, after the funeral. **-are** [A4] *tr.* to render funeral honours to.

eserc-ire [D2] *tr.* to practise, to carry on; to operate, to run; to ply. **-ente** *part. adj.* practising; plying; *n.m., f.* practitioner; proprietor of hotel, restaurant, or shop; retail dealer; gli -enti, the trade.

esercit-are [A1s] *tr.* to exercise, to train by exercise; to drill; — la mano, to get one's hand in; to practise, to perform; to practise (a profession); (leg.) to practise; to exercise; to enforce; to assert; — un diritto, to assert a right, to exercise a right (C.P.); — la professione in legge, to practise law; *rfl.* (*prep.* a) to exercise oneself; to train oneself; to exert oneself; -arsi al tennis, to practise tennis; -arsi a cantare, to do one's singing practice. **-a·bile** *adj.* that may be carried out, performable, trainable. **-amento** *m.* exercising; exercise; training; exerting, exertion. **-ante** *part. adj.* exercising; training; exerting. **-azione** *f.* exercise; drill; practise; training; exert.

eser·cito *m.* army; (mil.) division; l'— dei credenti, the church militant; host; (fig.) vast collection, array; (poet.) flock.

esercito·ria *f.* (naut.) contract with charterer.

eserci·zio *m.* exercise; practice; essere fuori d'—, to be out of practice; (provb.) l'— è buon maestro, practice makes perfect; drill; -i di salvataggio, boat-drill; activity, management; essere in —, to be in working order, to be in operation, to function; (leg.) assertion; exercise; discharge; practice; carrying on, running; licenza d'—, shopkeeper's licence, licence to carry on a business, trade, profession, etc.; nell'— delle sue funzioni, in the discharge of his duties; — di giuochi di azzardo, the running of games of chance (C.P.); (finan.) capitale d'—, working capital; — finanziario, financial year; — arbitrario delle proprie ragioni, the taking of the law into one's own hands; (eccl.) -i spirituali, spiritual exercises; (neol.) business, concern, shop.

eseresi *f.* (surg.) excision.

esergo *m.* exergue, the space on the reverse of a coin, below the main device, often filled up by the date.

esib-ire [D2] *tr.* to exhibit; to display; to produce; to offer; (leg.) to produce or furnish (documents, etc.) for inspection (C.C.P.); to exhibit; *rfl.* to be exhibited; to offer one's services; to make an exhibition of oneself. **-ito** *part. adj.* exhibited; produced; evinced; displayed; on display. **-itore** *m.* (leg.) party producing (a document in) evidence; bearer.

†**esibita** *f.* (leg.) exhibit; the production of documentary evidence.

esibizion-e *f.* offer (esp. of one's services); exhibition; (leg.) production (of a document or thing) as evidence or for inspection (C.C.P.). **-ismo** *m.* (med.; psychol.) exhibitionism; self-advertisement; publicity-hunting. **-ista** *m., f.* exhibitionist.

esiccare [A2] and derivs. See **essiccare**.

esi·g-ere [D1] *tr.* to exact, to require; to demand; to call for; to necessitate; (leg.) to collect; to recover; — le imposte, to collect the taxes; — il pagamento di un debito, to recover a debt; (comm.) to collect; — un credito, to collect a debt. **-ente** *pres. part.* exacting; exigent; demanding, hard to please; particular, fastidious. **-enza** *f.* exigency, urgent need; exaction; corrispondere alle -enze di, to meet the requirements of. **-i·bile** *adj.* exigible, collectable; due; (leg.) recoverable; (comm.) receivable; debito -ibile, recoverable debt.

esi·glio *m.* and derivs. See **esilio**, etc.

esi·gu-o *adj.* (lit.) exiguous; scanty; slender; small. **-amente** *adv.* exiguously; scantily. **-ità** *f.* exiguousness; scantiness.

esilar-are [A1s] *tr.* to exhilarate, to have an exhilarating effect upon; to cheer. **-ante** *part. adj.* exhilarating; cheering; (colloq.) amusing, ridiculous; gas -ante, laughing gas. (**-ato** *part. adj.*)

e·sil-e[1] *adj.* thin, slender, slim; (of a voice) weak; faint. **-mente** *adv.* weakly; faintly.

es-ile[2] *m.* (chem.) hexyl. **-i·lico** *adj.* (chem.) hexyl.

esili-are [A4] *tr.* to banish, to exile; *rfl.* to go into exile. **-ato** *part. adj.* exiled, banished.

esi·lico *adj.* (chem.) hexyl.

esi·lio *m.* exile, banishment; place of exile; residence abroad.

esi·mere [C9] *tr.* to exempt; to free from an obligation; *rfl.* to gain exemption from; non potersi — dal, to be obliged to, to be unable to refrain from.

esi·mio *adj.* eminent, distinguished; outstanding, extraordinary; donna di esimia bellezza, extraordinarily beautiful woman; lavoro di esimia fattura, work carried out with outstanding accuracy, work executed with extraordinary skill.

esinan-ire [D2] *tr.* to annihilate; to debase; to humiliate. **-izione** *f.* annihilation; debasing.

Esi·odo *pr.n.m.* Hesiod.

esi·st-ere [C24] *intr.* (*aux.* essere) to exist; to be; to be extant. **-ente** *part. adj.* existing; in existence; il bitume -ente nell'emulsione, the bitumen present in the emulsion. **-enza** *f.* existence; life; lotta per l'-enza, struggle for existence; (comm.) stock in hand; in -enza, in stock. **-enziale** *adj.* (philos.) existential. **-enzialismo** *m.* (philos.) existentialism. **-enzialità** *f.* (philos.) existentiality.

†**esistimare** *tr.* to estimate; to esteem.

esit-are[1] [A1s] *intr.* (*aux.* avere) to hesitate; to waver; to falter. **-ante** *part. adj.* hesitating, hesitant; doubtful; irresolute. **-anza** *f.* hesitancy, hesitation. **-azione** *f.* hesitation.

esit-are[2] [A1s] *tr.* to sell; to dispose of. **-a·bile** *adj.* rateable, easy to sell.

e·sito *m.* issue; result, outcome; — dubbio, uncertain result; dénouement, catastrophe; (leg.) outcome, result; — di una contestazione, outcome of a dispute; (comm.) sale; issue; outgoings; avere —, to sell, to have a sale, to be saleable.

esi·zi-o *m.* ruin, slaughter. **-ale** *adj.* ruinous, fatal; pernicious; malattia -ale, fatal illness. **-oso** *adj.* pernicious.

eslege *adj.* extra-legal, not subject to laws.

eso- *pref.* exo-; œso-.

eso·dio *m.* (Gk. drama) exodium, end of a play; (Rom. drama) exodium, comic interlude.

e·sodo[1] *m.* exodus; going out in great number; flight; (finan.) — dei capitali, emigration of capital.

E·sodo[2] *pr.n.m.* Exodus, Book of Exodus.

eso·do[3] *m.* (radio) hexode.

eso·fa-go *m.* (*pl.* -ghi, -gi) (anat.) oesophagus, gullet. **-ge·o** *adj.* oesophageal. **-gosco·pio** *m.* (med.) oesophagoscope.

esoft-almo *m.* (med.) exophthalmus. **-al·mico** *adj.* (med.) exophthalmic; gozzo -almico, exophthalmic goitre.

esogastrulazione *f.* (zool.) exogastrulation.

eṣo·geno *adj.* (bot.; med.) exogenous.

eṣomorfiṣmo *m.* (geol.) exomorphism.

†esondare *intr.* to teem, to be overflowing; (of river) to flood its banks, to overflow.

eṣoner-are [A I S] *tr.* to exonerate; to release; to exempt; — dall'ufficio, to relieve of office, to dismiss. -**ato** *part. adj.* exonerated; released; dismissed.

eṣo·nero *m.* (leg.) release; clausola di — da responsabilità, clause providing for release from liability (C.C.).

eṣo·pico *adj.* relating to Æsop; favole esopiche, Æsop's fables.

Eṣòp-o *pr.n.m.* Æsop; (fig.) an ugly man. -**iano** *adj.* in the style of Æsop.

†esor-are *tr.* to pray, to entreat. -**a·bile** *adj.* bounteous, gracious; clement.

eṣorbit-are [A I S] *intr.* (*aux.* avere) to be exorbitant; to exceed proper bounds, to go beyond just limits; -a dalle mie funzioni, it's not my job; — dai poteri di uno, to lie outside a person's sphere or department. -**ante** *part. adj.* exorbitant; excessive. -**anza** *f.* excessiveness; (astron.) exorbitancy, deviating from its proper course or orbit.

eṣorc-iṣmo *m.* exorcism. -**ista** *m.* exorcist. -**istato** *m.* (eccl.) order of exorcists. -**i·stico** *adj.* of exorcism. -**iẓẓare** [A I] *tr.* (eccl.) to exorcize; to exhort, to urge. (-**iẓẓatore** *m.* -**iẓẓazione** *f.*)

†esor·dia *f.* long rambling discourse.

eṣordiente *m., f.* See under **esordire.**

eṣor·d-io *m.* (*pl.* -**i**) beginning, opening remarks, exordium; — d'una carriera, entrance upon a career, or into a profession, début; first appearance.

eṣord-ire [D 2] *intr.* (*aux.* avere) to begin a discourse; to enter a profession; to make one's début; to begin. -**iente** *m., f.* débutant, débutante; (sport) beginner. -**imento** *m.* beginning; making of a début.

eṣore·ico *adj.* (geog.) drained to the sea.

eṣorn-are [A I] *tr.* to embellish, to adorn. -**ativo** *adj.* ornamental.

eṣort-are [A I] *tr.* to exhort, to persuade, to encourage, to urge; — a che ricerche vengano estese, to urge that investigations be made. (-**ante** *part. adj.*) -**ativo** *adj.* exhortatory; admonishing. (-**ato** *part. adj.*) -**atore** *m.* exhortor. -**ato·rio** *adj.* (*m.pl.* -**atorii**) exhortatory. -**azione** *f.* exhortation; admonishment.

†esorto *m.* (astron.) rising.

esosche·letro *m.* (zool.) exoskeleton.

eṣo·ṣio *m.* (chem.) hexose.

eṣo·ṣmoṣi *f.* (biol.) exosmosis.

eṣoṣo *adj.* odious, hateful; unpleasant, nasty; greedy, avid; mean; ha uno zio — che non gli dà un soldo, he has a nasty, mean uncle who won't let him have a penny; (Tusc.) tiresome, annoying.

eṣote·r-ico¹ *adj.* esoteric; reserved for the initiated. -**iṣmo** *m.* esotericism.

eṣote·r-ico² *adj.* exoteric; suitable for the uninitiated. -**iṣmo** *m.* exotericism.

eṣoter·mico *adj.* exothermic.

eṣo·tic-o *adj.* exotic, strange, foreign. (-**amente** *adv.*) -**iṣmo** *m.* exoticism; tendency to adopt what is exotic; predilection for what is foreign. -**ità** *f.* the quality of being exotic.

eṣotiṣmo *m.* See **esoticismo**, under **esotico.**

espada *m. espada* (bull-fighter with sword).

espan·d-ere [C 25] *tr.* to expand, to spread, to extend; *rfl.* to expand, to increase one's business, to extend one's territory or influence; (pop.) to talk freely and confidentially, to air one's opinions or grievances, to expand. -**imento** *m.* (phys.) expansion.

espans-i·bile *adj.* expanding, spreading, capable of expansion. -**ibilità** *f.* (scient.) expansibility. -**ione** *f.* expansion, spreading; settling, colonizing; *pl.* (fig.) effusiveness; enthusiasm; exuberant expression of affection; ci accolse con grande -**ione**, he received us effusively; (scient.) expansion; (electr.) -**ione** polare, pole shoe. -**ioniṣmo** *m.* theories urging colonial, political or commercial expansion. -**ionista** *m.* expansionist.

espansiv-o *adj.* expansive; effusive, demonstrative; exuberant; talkative. -**amente** *adv.* expansively; effusively; exuberantly.

†espanto *part.* of **espandere**, q.v.

espatri-are [A 3] *intr.* (*aux.* avere, essere) to emigrate, to leave the mother-country, to settle abroad; *tr.* to expatriate, to banish. -**ato** *part. adj.* expatriated.

espa·trio *m.* (leg.) expatriation.

espediente *adj.* expedient, opportune; *n.m.* expedient, device, resource; dodge; ricorrere agli espedienti, to resort to dodges or emergency measures; gli espedienti, ways and means; (leg.) means; practices; espedienti dilatori, delaying practices.

esped-ire [D 2] *tr.* to expedite, to dispatch; *rfl.* to make haste, to execute a task quickly. -**itivo** *adj.* expedient, quick. -**ito** *part. adj.* quick; ready; unimpeded. -**itamente** *adv.* quickly, without delay or hindrance.

espedizione *f.* expedition; undertaking, enterprise; dare — a, to achieve, to execute, to expedite.

espel·lere [C 23] *tr.* to expel; to eject; to drive out; fare — di forza, to expel *manu militari*; (sport) to order off the field.

†espen·dere *tr.* to expend; to occupy, to employ; — il tempo a, to spend the time in.

Esperanto *pr.n.m.* Esperanto.

Espe·ria *pr.n.f.* (hist. geog., poet.) Hesperia, 'the Western Land'; Italy; Spain; (geog.) Esperia, in the province of Frosinone; (ent.) skipper butterflies, Fam. Hesperidae.

Espe·rid-i *pr.n.f.pl.* (myth.; geog.) Hesperides. -**e** *adj.* Hesperidean, western; orti -**i**, Garden of the Hesperides; (bot.) *f.* sweet rocket, dame's violet.

esperiente *part.* of **esperire**, q.v.

esperienz-a *f.* experiment; trial; test; experience; avere — di, to have experience of, to experience; essere di molta —, to have had a great deal of experience, to be very experienced.

esperimental-e *adj.* experimental. -**mente** *adv.* experimentally, by experiment (cf. **sperimentale** and derivs.).

esperiment-are [A I C] *tr.* to test, to make trial of; to experiment with; to experience. -**ato** *part. adj.* tried, proved; tested; experienced; expert. -**atore** *m.* tester; experimenter; *adj.* experimental; scuola -**atrice**, experimental school (cf. **sperimentare** and derivs.).

esperiment-o *m.* experiment, proof, trial, examination; test. -**ista** *m.* (techn.) tester.

espe·rio *adj.* Hesperian, western.

esper-ire [D 2] (leg.) to prove; to bring; to start; — un'azione, to bring an action; to carry out; — indagini, to carry out investigations. -**i·bile** *adj.* (leg.) demonstrable. -**iente** *part. adj.* experienced, expert; *n.m.* experimenter. -**ientemente** *adv.* with experience, expertly.

E·spero *pr.n.m., f.* Hesperus, the evening star, Venus; the west wind.

esperto *adj.* experienced; expert; skilled; — di, — in, skilled in; — a scrivere versi, expert in writing verse; *n.m.* expert; (leg.) — giudiziario, judicial expert; an expert appointed by a court of law.

†espeti·bile *adj.* desirable.

†espettare *vb.* and derivs. See **aspettare.**

espettazione *f.* (liturg.) feast of the Expectation; †see **aspettazione**, under **aspettare.**

espettor-are [A I S] *tr.* to expectorate; to spit out; *abs.* to spit. -**ante** *part. adj.* (med.) expectorant, promoting expectoration; *n.m.* expectorant. -**ativo** *adj.* (med.) expectorant. -**ato** *part. adj.* expectorated; spat out; *n.m.* mucus, phlegm, etc. expectorated. -**azione** *f.* (med.) expectoration.

espianto *m.* (biol.) explant.

espi-are [A 4] *tr.* to expiate; to make amends for; to suffer, to undergo; — la pena, to serve a sentence. -**a·bile** *adj.* expiable. -**amento** *m.* expiating, expiation. (-**atore** *m.* -**atrice** *f.*) -**ato·rio** *adj.* expiatory; capro -**atorio**, scapegoat. -**azione** *f.* expiation.

espil-are [A I] *tr.* (leg.) to defraud (a person, from a position of trust); to embezzle from (a person). -**atore** *m.* person in a position of trust who commits fraud; embezzler. -**azione** *f.* fraud committed in a position of trust; embezzlement.

espir-are [A I] *tr.* to breathe out, to exhale. (-**ato** *part. adj.*) -**atore** *m.* (anat.) expiratory muscle. -**azione** *f.* exhalation, breathing out.

†esplanare *tr.* to explain.

espletare [A I] *tr.* (admin.) to fulfil, to carry out; to despatch; to see through.

espletiv-o *adj.* expletive, redundant; *n.m.* expletive. -**amente** *adv.* expletively, pleonastically.

esplic-are [A 2 S] *tr.* to explain, to expound; to develop; — un'attività, to carry on an activity; *rfl.* to explain, to make oneself clear. -**a·bile** *adj.* explicable. -**amento** *m.* development; explanation. -**ativo** *adj.* explanatory. -**ato** *part. adj.* explained; developed. -**atore** *m.* expounder. -**azione** *f.* explanation, declaration; development.

espli·cit-o *adj.* explicit; clear; definite. **-amẹnte** *adv.* explicitly; unequivocally.

esplo·d-ere [C3] *tr.* to explode; to blow up; to fire; to burst; *intr.* (*aux.* avere) to go off, to fire (of firearms); (*aux.* essere) to explode, to go off, to blow up; (fig.) to burst, to burst out, to go up in the air, to go off the deep end; fare —, to explode, to set off; to fire. **-ente** *part. adj.*; *n.m.* explosive. **-itọre** *m.* (eng.) detonator.

esplor-are [A1] *tr.* to investigate, to explore; — una ferita, to probe a wound; to sound; (mil.) to reconnoitre; (telev.) to scan. **-a·bile** *adj.* that can be explored, explorable. **-ato** *part. adj.* investigated; sounded. **-atọre** *m.* explorer; (mil.) scout, reconnaissance patrol; giovane —, boy scout; naval patrol-boat; (horsebreeding) teaser, second-rate stallion who prepares the mare for the first-rate stallion. **-atrice** *f.* woman explorer; giovane -atrice, girl guide; nave -atrice, patrol-boat; spedizione -atrice, reconnaissance. **-ato·rio** *adj.* (*m.pl.* -atorii) exploratory; relating to exploration or investigation. **-aziọne** *f.* exploration; (mil.) reconnaissance; (telev.) scanning.

esploṣ-iọne *f.* explosion, report or noise of an explosion, outbreak of anger, outburst; (med.) sudden manifestation of pathological symptoms, outbreak. **-ivo** *adj.* explosive; (med.) vomito -ivo, projectile vomiting; *n.m.* explosive; (mil.) exploder; (phon.) explosive, plosive.

esploṣo *part.* of **esplodere**, q.v.; *adj.* exploded; fired; una teoria esplosa, a disproved theory, an exploded theory.

espon-ente *part.* of **esporre**, q.v.; *n.m.* exponent; petitioner; member of a political party; (comm.) representative; heading; (math.) exponent, index; (chem.) — di acidità, pH; (typ.) superior figure or letter. **-enziale** *adj.* (math.) exponential; serie -enziale, exponential series. **-i·bile** *adj.* that can be expounded or exhibited. **-imento** *m.* exposition, explanation (of a text).

†**espo·nere** *vb.* and derivs. See **esporre**.

espọrre [B21] *tr.* to expose; to set out, to set forth; to exhibit; to expound; *abs.* to exhibit; †to risk; *rfl.* to expose oneself; to compromise oneself; to submit oneself; (finan.) to obtain credit on the money market.

esport-are [A1] *tr., abs.* to export. **-ato** *part. adj.* exported. **-atọre** *m.* exporter. **-aziọne** *f.* exportation; export; dazio di -azione, tassa di -azione, export duty.

esposi·metro *m.* (photog.) exposure meter.

espọṣit-ivo *adj.* explanatory, expositive, expository. **-ọre** *m.* exhibitor; exposer; expounder, interpreter. (**-rice** *f.*)

espoṣiziọne *f.* exhibition; show, fair; — internazionale, world fair; exposure; aspect (of a house); display, exposition, explanation; pillory; — dei fatti, factual report; (leg.) formal statement; — dei dati, tabulated statement; (eccl.) exposition (of the Blessed Sacrament; of relics); lying in state; (mus.) exposition (of a fugue or sonata); (scient.) exposure; (photog.) exposure.

espọsto, (Rom.) **esposto** *part.* of **esporre**, q.v.; *adj.* exposed; exhibited, displayed; bambino —, foundling; — a soffrire danni, liable to break, fragile; *n.m.* foundling; ospizio degli esposti, foundling hospital; tutela degli esposti, care and protection of foundlings; (C.C.) statement, petition; (leg.) statement; contents; recital; — di sentenza, contents of a judgement; presentare un —, to file a statement; — dei fatti, recital of the facts (C.C.P.).

espressi·ọne *f.* expression; non trovo -ioni per, I have no words to express…; senza —, expressionless; phrase, saying; (leg.) expression; usare -ioni sconvenienti od offensive, to use indecent or offensive expressions; (math.) expression; (mus.) swell pedal (of organ). **-ionismo** *m.* (lit.; art) expressionism. **-ivo** *adj.* expressive; (mus.) with expression; cassa -iva, swell-box (of organ). **-ivamente** *adv.* expressively. **-ività** *f.* expressiveness.

espress-o *part.* of **esprimere**, q.v.; *adj.* pressed out; extracted; extorted; expressed; divieto —, express prohibition; caffè —, coffee made with pressure and filter machine; (colloq.) treno —, fast train; *n.m.* express letter; parcel or any item sent by express post; special messenger; special delivery; cup of black coffee made with pressure and filter machine; fast train; *adv.* lettera espresso, express letter. **-amẹnte** *adv.* expressly, explicitly; on purpose. **-ọre** *m.* squeezer.

espri·m-ere [C18] *tr.* to express; to give expression to; to voice; to declare; to explain; †to squeeze, to express; *rfl.* to express oneself; non sa -ersi bene in tedesco, he doesn't speak German well. **-i·bile** *adj.* expressible.

†**espro·bare** *tr.* to reprove, to reproach.

esprofesso *adv. ex professo*, expressly, deliberately.

espromiss-iọne *f.* (leg.) expromission, a particular kind of guarantee or suretyship (C.C.). **-ọre** *m.* (leg.) expromissor.

espropri-are [A4] *tr.* (leg.) to expropriate; to dispossess; far — i beni del debitore, to have the debtor sold up. **-atọre** *m.* compulsory acquirer; dispossessor; *adj.* compulsorily acquiring; expropriating. (**-atrice** *f.*) **-aziọne** *f.* (leg.) expropriation (C.C.); dispossession; -azione per causa di pubblico interesse, compulsory acquisition of property for public purposes; -azione forzata, seizure and forced sale (of goods, for debt) (C.C.).

espro·prio *m.* (leg.) expropriation; selling up; — forzato, eviction; causa di —, action for eviction; — per utilità pubblica, compulsory acquisition of land.

espugn-are [A5] *tr.* (mil.) to take by storm, to storm, to seize; to defeat; (joc.) to win by wooing. **-a·bile** *adj.* that can be stormed; (joc.) una donna facilmente -abile, a woman who is easily won. (**-ato** *part. adj.*) **-atọre** *m.* victor. (**-atrice** *f.*) **-aziọne** *f.* capture by siege.

espuls-iọne *f.* expulsion; (med.) expulsion; — del feto, expulsion of the foetus; (leg.) deportation; — dello straniero, deportation of alien; ordine di —, deportation order (C.P.). **-iva** *f.* (med.) expulsive power of drugs. **-ivo** *adj.* expulsive; calza -iva, elastic stocking. **-o** *part.* of **espellere**, q.v.; *adj.* expelled; ejected. **-ọre** *m.* expellent; (mil.) ejector.

espun·gere [C5] *tr.* to expunge, to cancel.

espunziọne *f.* expunging, deletion.

espurg-are [A2] *tr.* to clean out; to disinfect; to cleanse; to expurgate, to bowdlerize; †to weed. **-ato** *part. adj.* cleaned, cleansed; expurgated; †weeded. (**-atọre** *m.* **-atrice** *f.*) **-aziọne** *f.* cleansing; expurgation.

Esquilino *adj., n.m.* Esquiline, one of the seven hills of Rome; Sánta Maria Esquilina, the Church of Santa Maria Maggiore on the Esquiline.

esquimẹse *adj., n.m.* See **eschimese**.

†**esquisito** *adj.* and derivs. See **squisito**.

ẹssa *prn. f.* she; her; it.

ẹsse[1] *prn. f.pl.* they; them.

esse[2] *m., f. indecl.* name of the letter S; a —, S-shaped; (vet.) S-shaped cheek piece of a bridle.

esse, essi *f.pl.* (mus.) soundholes, *f*-holes.

es·sed-o *m.* (hist.) war-chariot. **-a·rio** *m.* (hist.) driver of a war-chariot, charioteer.

†**essem·p·io**, †**-lo** *m.* See **esempio**.

essendo *gerund.* of **essere**, q.v.

essendochè *conj.* since, seeing that, inasmuch as.

Esseni *pr.n.m.pl.* (rel. hist.) Essenes, a Jewish religious sect of the time of the Maccabees.

essenz-a *f.* essence; somma —, God; inmost character; — di rose, attar of roses; — di bergamotto, bergamot oil; petrol, motor spirit. **-iale** *adj.* essential; real; (chem.) olio -iale, essential oil, essence; *n.m.* important thing; essential; l'-iale è, the important thing is. **-ialmẹnte** *adv.* essentially.

es·s-ere [B13] *intr.* (*aux.* essere).
1. To EXIST, to be; — o non —, to be or not to be; Dio disse 'Sia fatta la luce' e la luce fu, God said 'Let there be light', and there was light; c'era una volta, once upon a time there was…; chi siete?, who are you?; sono stato ammalato, I have been ill; sei pronto? sì lo sono, are you ready? yes, I am; è stato in America, he has been in (to) America; sono italiani, they are Italian, they are Italians; (for further uses of **essere** with predicate, see separate headings, e.g. 'essere giù' see under **giù**); per —, in actual fact, to tell the truth; per — non c'è male, it's not bad in actual fact (as far as it goes); (iron.) per — m'hai aiutato benino, to be frank you've been a fat lot of use to me (see also under **per**). 2. To COME TO BE, to happen, to come to pass, to become; così sia, so be it, amen; sia pure, so be it, as you say, very well; e sia!, very well then!; sarà, it may be; tutto può —, everything is possible, anything can happen; sia…sia, whether it be…, either…or; che sarà di me?, what will become of me?; quando sarai grande, when you are grown up; quando fu giorno chiaro, as soon as it was light; cos'è stato?, what has happened?; che c'è?, what is it?, what's up? 3. To COST, to amount to, to weigh; quant'è questo libro?, how much is this book?; quant'è quel pollo?, how much does that chicken weigh?; quanto c'è da Roma a Milano?, how far is it from Rome to Milan?; c'è da

ess·ere (*cont.*)

impazzire, it's enough to drive one mad. **4.** Essere in, to be in the shoes of; s'io fossi in te, if I were you; to amount to, to number; in quanti siete?, how many are you?; siamo in tre, there are three of us. **5.** Essere di, to belong to, to be concerned with or engaged in, to come from, to be made of; di chi è?, whose is it?; è di mio fratello, it's my brother's; è di settimana, he's on duty this week; sarò di ritorno di qui a tre giorni, I shall return three days from now; sono di Roma, I come from Rome; è di legno, it's made of wood; †to confer; siatene con mio padre, you must see my father about it. **6.** Essere da, to be up to, to be capable of; — da tanto di camminare, to be strong enough to walk; non credevo che fosse da tanto, I didn't think he had it in him. **7.** Essere per, to be about to, to be on the point of; sono per partire, they're just about to leave; è per scoppiare, it's about to burst. **8.** Esserci, to understand, to follow; ci sono, I understand, I'm with you, I've found the place. **9.** In past def.: to go, to reach; ieri fui al mercato, yesterday I went to the market; quando furono al ponte, when they reached the bridge; to go at once, to go quickly; furono nella stanza, before you could say Jack Robinson they were in the room; (poet.) to be no more; ei fu, he is no more, his life is ended (cf. Vergil 'fuit Ilium', but see also under nos. 1 and 2. For the use of **fu** as *adj. indecl.* see separate heading). **10.** Che è (with repeated noun and usually with neg.) even; un soldo che è un soldo non ce l'ho, I haven't (even) a penny; il signor colonnello che è il signor colonnello non lo farebbe, the Colonel himself (in person) wouldn't dare to do it; che è che non è, in a moment, from one moment to the next, unexpectedly. **11.** In expressions of time, season, duration, etc.: che ore sono?, what time is it?; è un mese che l'aspetto, I've been waiting for it for a month; quanto c'è da oggi a Natale?, how long is it from today until Christmas?; l'ho visto tre giorni sono, I saw him three days ago; era d'autunno, it was autumn; siamo d'inverno, it is winter. **12.** *n.m.* Being, existence; dare l'— a, to bring into being; identity, status, condition; gli domandai dell'—suo, I asked him who he was; trovarsi in (buon) —, to be well, to be in good condition; being, creature, person; sono un — disgraziato, I am a poor wretch. †**-ente** *part. adj.* being. †**-uto** *part. adj.* see **stato**.

ęssi *prn. m.pl.* they; — non sono qui, they are not here; con —, with them.

essicc·are [A 2] *tr.* to dry up, to dry; (industr.) to desiccate; — al forno, to kiln-dry. **-ante** *part. adj.* drying. **-ativo** *adj.* desiccant, drying; *n.m.* (industr.) drier, siccative. **-atoio** *m.* (industr.) drier, drying-room; drying-machine, electric dryer. **-atore** *m.* (industr.) drier; (chem.) desiccator; (industr.) -atore a vuoto, vacuum drier; -atore rotativo, rotary drier. **-azione** *f.* desiccation; drying, drying process.

ęsso *prn. m.* he; it; — è partito, he has left; con —, with him (it); (leg.) chi per —, agent for, the person who acts for; †(pleon.) con — lei, with her; con — loro, with them; lungh'esso il fiume, along the river; the aforesaid, this, such.

essotę·rico *adj.* exoteric.

essud·are [A I] *tr., intr.* (*aux.* avere) to exude. **-ato** *part. adj.* exuded, discharged; *n.m.* discharge; (med.) effusion.

†**essuto** *part.* of **essere**, q.v.

est[1] *m. indecl.* east; verso —, eastwards; all'—, in the east.

est[2] *Lat.* used in telegraphese for è; (Rom.) — locanda, rooms to let; Est! Est!, name of a wine from Montefiascone.

està *f.* (poet.). See **estate**.

esta·glio *m.* (S. Ital., leg.) yearly rent roll of an estate.

†**estante** *adj.* extant; living.

e·staş·i *f. indecl.* ecstasy, rapture; mandare in —, to send into raptures; (med.) swoon, trance. **-iare** [A 4] *tr.* to send into ecstasy; *rfl.* to go into ecstasy, to go into raptures.

estate *f.* summer; in —, in the summer; vestito d'—, summer dress; — di san Martino, St Martin's summer, Indian summer.

esta·tic·o *adj.* ecstatic, enraptured, in one's seventh heaven. **-amente** *adv.* ecstatically, rapturously.

estemporal·e *adj.* extemporary. **-ità** *f.* extemporariness.

estempora·ne·o *adj.* extemporary, improvised, unprepared. **-amente** *adv.* extemporarily, extempore. **-ità** *f.* extemporaneousness, improvisation.

esten·d·ere [C I] *tr.* to extend; to spread; to enlarge; to increase; to prolong; — un documento, to draw up, to frame, to formulate

a document; *rfl.* to extend; to spread. **-i·bile** *adj.* extensible. **-imento** *m.* extending.

estense *pr.n.m.* member of the Este family; gli Estensi, the Este family; *adj.* of Este; Biblioteca —, the Este Library at Modena.

estensi·bile *adj.* extensible.

estensi·metro *m.* (eng.) extensometer, strain gauge.

estensione *f.* extension; amplification; extent, length; compass, range; in tutta l'— della parola, in every sense of the word; (mus.) compass; extension (in violin-fingering).

estensiv·o *adj.* extensive; extensible; (agric.) coltura -a, extensive cultivation; interpretazione -a della legge, the interpretation of the law in its broad sense. **-amente** *adv.* extensively; by extension; interpretare -amente la legge, to interpret the law broadly, to stretch the meaning of the law to fit the case.

estens·o *adv. phr.* per —, in full. **-ore** *m.* expander, enlarging or stretching device; chest-expander; (anat.) extensor muscle; (leg.) giudice -ore, judge appointed to draw up the judgement of a civil court (C.C.P.). **-o·rio** *adj.* (anat.) extensor.

estenu·are [A 6] *tr.* to extenuate, to enfeeble; to impoverish; to exhaust; to wear out. **-ante** *part. adj.* extenuating; caldo -ante, exhausting heat. **-ativo** *adj.* extenuating; exhausting; depressing. **-ato** *part. adj.* extenuated; thin; exhausted; emaciated. **-azione** *f.* exhaustion; (gramm.) understatement.

E·ster *pr.n.f.* Esther.

e·ster·e *m.* (chem.) ester. **-ificazione** *f.* (chem.) esterification.

esterior·e *adj.* exterior, outer, external; aspetto —, outward appearance; doti -i, physical gifts; mondo —, the world about us; *n.m.* outside, exterior; non giudicare dall'—, don't judge by appearances. **-are** [A I c] *tr.* (spiritualism) to cause to appear. **-izzare** [A I] *tr.* to make manifest. **-ità** *f.* appearances.

estermin·are [A I S] *tr.* to exterminate. (**-ato** *part. adj.*) **-atore** *m.* exterminator. (**-atrice** *f.*) **-azione** *f.* see **esterminio** (cf. **sterminare**).

estermi·nio *m.* extermination; destruction.

estern·are [A I] *tr.* to express, to manifest; to show openly; to disclose, to make no secret of; *rfl.* to open one's heart. **-ato** *part. adj.* manifested, disclosed; *n.m.* status of a day-boy at a residential school.

estern·o[1] *adj.* outside, external; pregi -i, physical qualities; atti -i, outward and visible acts; worn on top, outer; maglieria -a, knitted outer garments; posto —, outside seat; angolo —, outer angle; allievo —, day-boy (in a boarding-school); (med.) per uso —, not to be taken internally, (joc.) for the sake of appearance, for outward show; (eccl.) foro —, external forum; *n.m.* outside; exterior; all'—, on the outside; (schol.) day-boy; (sport) 'away' game; *pl.* (cinem.) externals, shots on location. **-a** *f.* day-girl (in a boarding-school). **-amente** *adv.* externally, outwardly; on the outside.

†**esterno**[2] *adj.* of yesterday.

e·stero *adj.* foreign; affari esteri, foreign affairs; commercio —, foreign trade; politica estera, foreign policy; *n.m.* countries abroad; all'—, abroad; *pl.* foreign affairs; ministero degli esteri, ministry of foreign affairs.

esterofili·a *f.* excessive love of foreign things.

esterrefatto *adj.* appalled, terrified; in a state of consternation.

estęs·o *part.* of **estendere**, q.v.; *adj.* extended; extensive; ample; large; wide; per —, in full. **-amente** *adv.* extensively; fully.

est·eta *m.* aesthete. **-e·tica** *f.* aesthetics; beauty, beautiful appearance; curare l'-etica facciale, to look after, to take care of, one's complexion and make-up; quell'edificio sciupa l'-etica della piazza, that building spoils the beauty of the square. **-e·tico** *adj.* aesthetic; *n.m.* aesthete. **-eticamente** *adv.* aesthetically. **-etişmo** *m.* aestheticism; (art) name given in Italy to the English Pre-Raphaelite School.

estim·are [A I] *tr.* to value, to esteem, to appreciate. **-a·bile** *adj.* estimable. **-ativa** *f.* judgement. **-ativo** *adj.* judging, appreciating; virtù -ativa, judgement. **-atore** *m.* valuator. **-ato·rio** *adj.* (leg.) contratto -atorio, contract of consignment on sale or return (C.C.). **-azione** *f.* estimation, judgement, esteem; appraisal; giuramento d'-azione, sworn valuation (C.C.P.).

e·stimo *m.* estimate; valuation; land valuation office or register.

estin·gu·ere [C 6] *tr.* to extinguish, to put out; to quench; — la sete, to quench one's thirst; — un debito, to pay off a debt; (chem.) to slake (lime); (finan.) to meet, to honour, to discharge; to wipe out; *rfl.* to become extinct, to fade away, to die off; (leg.) to be dissolved; la persona giuridica si -e, the corporation is dissolved

estingu·ere (*cont.*)

(C.C.). **~i·bile** *adj.* extinguishable. **~imẹnto** *m.* extinguishing; paying off.

estint-o *part.* of **estinguere**, q.v.; *adj.* extinguished; deceased; dead; debito —, debt paid or settled; calce ~a, slaked lime; extinct. **~ivo** *adj.* (leg.) extinctive; prescrizione ~iva, prescription that extinguishes the right (C.C.). **~ọre** *m.* fire-extinguisher.

estinziọne *f.* extinction; putting out; paying; (leg.) discharge; dissolution; extinction; redemption; — di ipoteca, redemption of a mortgage (C.C.); — di una cambiale, the discharge of a bill; — della persona giuridica, dissolution of corporation (C.C.); — della pena, extinction of punishment (C.P.); (chem.) slaking (of lime); (electr.) — magnetica, magnetic blow-out (of an arc).

estirp-are [A I] *tr.* to extirpate; to eradicate; to root out, to uproot; (agric.) to pull (e.g. flax). **~ato** *part. adj.* eradicated. **~atọre** *m.* extirpator; (agric.) grubber. **~aziọne** *f.* extirpation; uprooting; extraction; (surg.) removal.

estivo *adj.* summer; summery; vacanze estive, summer holidays; ora estiva, summer time; doppia ora estiva, double summer time; stazione estiva, summer resort; scuola estiva, summer school.

†esto *demons. adj.* See **questo**.

estol·lere [def.] *tr.* (poet.) to raise; to exalt; to extol; *rfl.* (poet.) to rise.

†estols-i, **†-e**, **†-ero** *past def. 1st, 3rd sing., 3rd pl.* of **estollere**, q.v.

Estọnia *pr.n.f.* (hist. geog.) Esthonia.

estor·cere [C 5] *tr.* to extort, to gain by extortion.

†estor·quere *vb.* See **estorcere**.

estorsiọne *f.* extortion; (leg.) extortion; obtaining money by force or menaces (C.P.); blackmail; condannato per —, sentenced for extortion; **†**contorsion.

estorto *part.* of **estorcere**, q.v.

estrad-are [A I] *tr.* (leg.) to extradite. **~iziọne** *f.* (leg.) extradition.

estra-dọsso *m.* (archit.) extrados. **~dotale** *adj.* (leg.) extradotal, not forming part of the dowry; paraphernal. **~giudiziale** *adj.* (leg.) extrajudicial; accordi ~giudiziali, agreements reached beyond the usual course of legal proceedings; transazione ~giudiziale, extrajudicial settlement, settlement out of court. **~legale** *adj.* (leg.) outside the law. **~polaziọne** *f.* (math.) extrapolation. **~soggettivo** *adj.* irrelevant, not relating to the subject. **~territoriale** *adj.* (leg.) extraterritorial; giurisdizione ~territoriale, extraterritorial jurisdiction.

estrai·bile *adj.* (chem.; eng.) extractable.

estra·neo *adj.* (*prep.* a) foreign, extraneous; rimanere — a, not to take part in, to have no part in, to have nothing to do with; — alla nostra attività, outside our province; *n.m.* stranger; outsider; a person who is not one of the family.

†estrano *adj.* See **estraneo**, or **strano**.

estrarre [B 33] *tr.* to extract; to take out; to draw; to draw out; to draw by lot; to win, to get; to quarry, to mine; to export; (math.) to extract.

estrattivo *adj.* extractive; industrie estrattive, mining industries (i.e. utilizing natural resources).

estratt-o *part.* of **estrarre**, q.v.; *adj.* extracted; drawn out (esp. in lottery or ballot); *n.m.* extract; summary; single number on which a stake is laid in the game of 'lotto'; excerpt; off-print; — di carne, meat extract; (leg.) — di documento, abstract; copy of a document; — dell'atto di nascita, summary of a birth certificate (a shortened form of the complete certificate); — dell'atto di morte, summary of a death certificate; — di sentenza, docket; — conto, statement of account.

estrattọre *m.* (eng.) extractor, stripper, puller; (foundry) knock-out, ejector; — per mozzi, hub puller; — a vuoto, vacuum pump.

estravagante *adj.* erratic; (lit. hist.) rime estravaganti, poems (of Petrarch) not included in the earliest collections; (eccl. hist.) *adj.* extravagant (constitution); *n.f.pl.* Extravagantes.

estraziọne *f.* extraction; drawing at lotteries; digging; quarrying; removal; (leg.) — di acqua del sottosuolo, drawing of underground water (C.C.).

†estremare *intr., tr.* to diminish; *rfl.* to burn, to be consumed.

estremità *f.* end; tip; edge; extremity.

estrem-o *adj.* extreme; utmost; last; greatest; (eccl.) ~a unzione, extreme unction; (pol.) l'~a destra, the extreme right; l'~a sinistra, the extreme left; (geog.) l'— Oriente, the Far East; *n.m.* extremity, end; tip; extreme; (logic) math.) extreme; (rugger) full-back; *pl.* (leg.) conditions, terms; — del reato, essential elements of the

crime (C.P.); essential references (e.g. an 'estratto dell'atto di nascita' gives the 'estremi' or essential references summarized from the complete 'certificato'); mancano gli ~i, the means of reference are missing (from a document); gli ~i di un contratto, the terms of a contract. **~amẹnte** *adv.* extremely, exceedingly, intensely. **~ịsmo** *m.* extremism, holding extreme or very advanced or very reactionary opinions (in politics). **~ista** *m.* extremist; die-hard reactionary.

†estricare *tr.* to extricate.

estrinsec-are [A 2 s] *tr.* to manifest; to express; to show by outward signs; to evince; *rfl.* to appear, to become visible; to express one's thoughts. **~amẹnto** *m.* manifesting; evincing. **~aziọne** *f.* manifestation; expression; (biol.) expression (of a gene in the phenotype).

estrin·sec-o *adj.* extrinsic, pertaining to an object in its external relations; beside the point, not related to the matter in hand. (**~amẹnte** *adv.*)

estr-o¹ *m.* caprice, fancy; mancare di —, to be uninspired; gli saltò l'— di partir subito, he took it into his head to go away at once; — poetico, poetic inspiration. **~ọso** *adj.* capricious, unpredictable, moody; whimsical; animated; original, talented, gifted. (**~osamẹnte** *adv.*)

estro² *m.* (ent.) horse-fly, and various other flies attacking domestic animals; — del bue, warble fly, *Hypoderma bovis*; — del cavallo, *Gastrophilus equi*, horse bot-fly; — delle pecore, *Oestrus ovis*, sheep bot-fly; (physiol.) oestrus.

estro-mẹt·tere [C 20] *tr.* (leg.) to dismiss (a party) from an action; to drive out, to expel. **~missiọne** *f.* (leg.) dismissal (of a party) from an action; (fig.) removal, expulsion, exclusion.

estru·dere [C I] *tr.* (eng.) to extrude.

estrusiọne *f.* (eng.) extrusion.

estu-are [A 6] *intr.* (*aux.* essere) (poet.) to be ardent; to boil, to seethe. **~ante** *part. adj.* (poet.) ardent; seething. **~ọso** *adj.* (poet.) ardent; tempestuous, stormy.

estua·rio *m.* estuary; firth.

estumescenza *f.* flow or rising of the tide.

†esturbare *tr.* to drive away with violence, to chase away; to disturb.

esuberan-te *adj.* exuberant; superabundant; lively; loud; (bldg.) calcestruzzo — d'acqua, wet concrete. (**~temẹnte** *adv.*) **~za** *f.* exuberance.

†esuberare *tr.* to mop up, to absorb; *intr.* to be exuberant.

esulare [A I s] *intr.* (*aux.* avere, essere) to go into (voluntary) exile; to go abroad; to emigrate; to live in exile; (*prep.* da) to be outside, to go beyond; questo esula dalla questione, this is beyond our terms of reference; this is beside the point.

esulcer-are [A I s] *tr.* to ulcerate, to cause an ulcer in; (fig.) to exasperate, to exacerbate. **~amẹnto** *m.* ulcerating; exacerbating. **~ativo** *adj.* ulcerative. **~ato** *part. adj.* ulcerated; (fig.) exasperated; col cuore ~ato, broken-hearted. **~aziọne** *f.* ulceration; small ulcer.

e·sule *m., f.* exile; *adj.* exiled.

esult-are [A I] *intr.* (*aux.* avere) to exult, to rejoice. **~ante** *part. adj.* exultant, rejoicing. **~anza** *f.* exultation. **~aziọne** *f.* exultation, rejoicing.

esum-are [A I] *tr.* to exhume, to disinter; (fig.) to unearth, to discover. (**~ato** *part. adj.*) **~aziọne** *f.* exhumation, disinterment.

†esur-ire *tr.* to hunger for. **†-iendo** *ger.* hungering for.

†esusto *adj.* burnt, parched.

et¹ *Lat.* in telegraphese used for e, and; **†***conj.* and.

†et² *m.* See **ette**.

et-a *f.* the Greek letter η, eta. **~acịsmo** *m.* (Gk. ling.) etacism.

età *f.* age; di — maggiore, of age; di minore —, under age; il decano d'—, the oldest member, the doyen; l'— dell'oro, the golden age; l'— di mezzo, the Middle Ages; di mezza —, middle-aged; — canonica, a good age, a ripe old age, a safe age; ha raggiunto l'— canonica, he is old enough not to make a fool of himself; ha una bella —, he is very old; — critica, age of menopause, change of life; novella —, adolescence; (leg.) minore di —, infant, (Scot.) minor; maggiore di —, of full age, (Scot.) major.

etacịsmo *m.* See under **eta**.

etade *f.* (poet.). See **età**.

etan-o *m.* (chem.) ethane. **~ọlo** *m.* (chem.) ethyl alcohol, ethanol.

etel-ịsmo *m.* (philos.) voluntarism. **~onte** *m.* (antiq.) a volunteer in army or navy.

etera *f.* hetaera, hetaira, courtesan.

e·t-ere *m.* ether; aether; (poet.) sky. **-e·reo** *adj.* ethereal; heavenly. **-e·rico** *adj.* etheric. **-erificare** [A2s] *tr.* (chem.) to etherify. **-erificazione** *f.* (chem.) etherification.

†eternale *adj.* and derivs. See **eterno**.

etern-are [A1] *tr.* to immortalize, to make eternal; to perpetuate; *rfl.* to win immortal fame. **-ato** *part. adj.* immortalized.

eternità *f.* eternity; eternal life; long time, an age; (colloq.) ho aspettato un'—, I waited for ages.

etern-o *adj.* eternal; everlasting; never-ending; (theol.) il Padre —, God the Father; *n.m.* l'Eterno, God Almighty; †eternal part, the soul. **-amente** *adv.* eternally.

eter-ocli·sia *f.* irregularity, being heteroclite. **-o·clito** *adj.* heteroclite, irregular, queer. **-ocroma·tico** *adj.* (phys.) heterochromatic. **-ocromosoma** *f.* (med.) accessory chromosome. **-o·crono** *adj.* (med.) heterochronic. **-odina** *f.* (radio) heterodyne; ricezione ad **-odina**, heterodyne reception, beat reception. **-odinag·gio** *m.* (radio) heterodyning. **-odino** *adj.* (radio) heterodyne, super. **-odoss·ia** *f.* heterodoxy. **-odosso** *adj.* heterodox. **-ofoni·a** *f.* (mus.) heterophony. **-ogeneità** *f.* heterogeneity. **-oge·neo** *adj.* heterogeneous; (gramm.) having different genders in *sing.* and *pl.* **-opolare** *adj.* (chem.) heteropolar. **-osessuale** *adj.* heterosexual. **-otermo** *adj.* (zool.) poikilothermic, cold-blooded. **-ozigote** *m.* (biol.) heterozygote.

ete·s-io *adj.* Etesian; *n.m.pl.* gli **-i**, north winds recurring periodically in summer in E. Mediterranean.

e·tic-a *f.* ethics; ethic. **-o** *adj.* ethical. (**-amente** *adv.*)

etichetta *f.* label; ticket; docket; tally; etiquette.

e·tico¹ *adj.* See under **etica**.

e·tico² *adj.* (med.) hectic; consumptive; *n.m.* consumptive.

etilazione *f.* (chem.) ethylation.

etil-e *m.* (chem.) ethyl. **-ato** *m.* (chem.) ethylate. **-ene** *m.* (chem.) ethylene. **-izzato** *adj.* (of petrol) leaded.

eti·lico *adj.* (chem.) ethyl; alcool —, ethyl alcohol.

etilismo *m.* (med.) alcohol poisoning.

e·tim-o *m.* (gramm.) etymon; etymological meaning; etymology. **-ologi·a** *f.* etymology. **-olo·gico** *adj.* etymological. (**-ologicamente** *adv.*) **-o·logo** *m.* etymologist; philologist.

etiol-ogi·a *f.* (med.) aetiology. **-o·gico** *adj.* (med.) aetiological. **-ogicamente** *adv.* (med.) aetiologically.

et-i·ope, -io·pico *adj., n.m.* Ethiopian.

Etio·pia *pr.n.f.* (geog.) Ethiopia.

etisi·a *f.* (med.) hectic fever, tuberculosis.

etite *f.* (myth.) aetites, eagle-stone.

Etn-a *pr.n.f.* (geog.) Etna. **-e·o** *adj.* pertaining to Mt Etna; Sicilian.

etni·a *f.* ethnic group.

et·nic-o¹ *adj.* Gentile, pagan, heathen. (**-amente** *adv.*)

et·nico² *adj.* ethnological, ethnic.

etn-ofo·nico *adj.* (mus.) pertaining to national music. **-ogeni·a** *f.* ethnogeny. **-ografi·a** *f.* ethnography. **-ogra·fico** *adj.* ethnographic. **-o·grafo** *m.* ethnographer. **-ologi·a** *f.* ethnology. **-olo·gico** *adj.* ethnological. **-o·logo** *m.* ethnologist.

eto-grafi·a *f.* ethography. **-pe·a, -pei·a** *f.* (rhet.) description of the moral character of a person. **-pedi·a** *f.* moral education.

etra *f.* (poet.) air; sky.

etriosco·pio *m.* (astron.) aethrioscope.

Etru·ria *pr.n.f.* (hist. geog.) lands of the Etruscans; Etruscan civilization; (poet.) Tuscany.

etrus-co *adj.* (*pl.* **-chi**) Etruscan. **-cologi·a** *f.* Etruscology, study of Etruscan antiquities. **-co·logo** *m.* Etruscologist.

ettacordo *m.* (mus.) seven-stringed lyre; heptachord.

ettae·dro *m.* seven-sided solid.

etta·gon-o *m.* heptagon, seven-sided figure. **-ale** *adj.* heptagonal.

et·tar-o *m.* hectare, 10,000 sq. metres, about 2½ acres. (†**-a** *f.*)

et·tasi *f.* (prosod.) ectasis.

ettasil·labo *m.* (prosod.) seven-syllable line.

ette *m.* jot, particle, tittle, iota; non ci capisco un —, I don't understand the first thing about it.

ett-o *m. abbrev.* of **ettogrammo**, q.v.; *pl.* (colloq.) **-i**.

ettogrammo *m.* hectogram, 100 grams, 3·527 oz.

etto·litro *m.* hectolitre, 100 litres, 22·01 imperial gallons.

etto·metro *m.* hectometre, 100 metres, 328·089 feet.

Et·tore *pr.n.m.* Hector.

Eube·a *pr.n.f.* (geog.) Euboea.

eucaìna *f.* (chem.) eucaine.

eucal-ipto, -itto *m.* eucalyptus.

eucaresti·a *f.* See **eucaristia**.

eucar-isti·a *f.* (theol.) Eucharist. **-i·stico** *adj.* (theol.) Eucharistic.

Euchiti *pr.n. m.pl.* (rel. hist.) Euchites.

eucla·sia *f.* (miner.) euclase.

Eucl-ide *pr.n.m.* Euclid. **-i·deo** *adj.* Euclidean; geometria non **-idea**, non-Euclidean geometry.

eudemon-i·a *f.* (philos.) happiness. **-ismo** *m.* (philos.) eudemonism. **-ista** *m.* (philos.) eudemonist.

eudi-ometri·a *f.* eudiometry. **-o·metro** *m.* eudiometer.

euf-emi·a¹ *f.* euphemism. **-e·mico** *adj.* euphemistic. **-emismo** *m.* euphemism; euphemistic expression. **-emi·stico** *adj.* euphemistic.

Eufe·mia² *pr.n.f.* Euphemia.

euf-oni·a *f.* euphony, pleasant sound (of words); (mus.) euphony (of tone-quality, or of notes combined in harmony). **-o·nico** *adj.* euphonic, euphonious. (**-onicamente** *adv.*) **-o·nio** *m.* (mus.) euphonium.

eufor·bia *f.* (bot.) euphorbia, spurge.

eufo·ria¹ *f.* (bot.) litchi, lichee, *Litchi chinensis*.

euf-ori·a² *f.* (med.) euphory, sense of well-being; (fig.) buoyant spirits; exuberance, vivacity; euphoria. **-o·rico** *adj.* (med.) in a state of euphory.

eufo·tide *f.* (miner.) euphotide, gabbro.

Eufrate *pr.n.f.* (geog.) Euphrates.

eufu-ismo *m.* (lit. hist.) euphuism. **-i·stico** *adj.* euphuistic.

euga·neo *adj.* (geog.) Euganean; i colli euganei, the Euganean hills.

eug-ene·tica, -e·nica *f.* eugenics. **-ene·tico** *adj.* eugenic.

Euge·ni·a *pr.n.f.* Eugenia. **-o** *pr.n.m.* Eugene.

eugenina *f.* (chem.) eugenin.

Eula·lia *pr.n.f.* Eulalia, Eularia.

eulogi·a *f.* (liturg.) eulogia, antidoron.

Eume·nidi *pr.n.f.pl.* (Gk. myth.) Eumenides, Furies.

eumolpo *m.* (ent.) a beetle that feeds on vine leaves, *Eumolpus vitis*.

eunu-co *m.* (*pl.* **-chi**) eunuch; *adj.* feeble, servile. **-cheri·a** *f.* moral weakness, servility.

eupateosco·pio *m.* eupatheoscope.

eupato·r-ia *f.* (bot.) hemp agrimony, *Eupatorium cannabinum*. **-ina** *f.* eupatorin. **-io** *m.* eupatorium.

Eupatridi *pr.n. m.pl.* (Gk. antiq.) Eupatrids.

Eupili *pr.n.m.* (geog.) former name of lake Pusiano (prov. of Como).

eupiteci·a *f.* (ent.) pug moth, *Eupithecia* sp.

Eura·si-a *pr.n.f.* (geog.) Eurasia, unity of Europe and Asia, as defined by H. Reusche (1858). **-a·tico** *adj., n.m.* Eurasian, Eurasiatic.

eurialino *m.* (zool.) euryhaline.

Euridice *pr.n.f.* (myth.) Eurydice.

euri·fago *adj.* (zool.) omnivorous.

Euri·pide *pr.n.m.* Euripides.

euripo¹ *m.* (geog.) narrow strait; (Rom. antiq.) *euripus*, a trench round a circus.

Euripo² *pr.n.m.* (geog.) Euripus.

euris·ti-ca *f.* (philos.) heuristic method. **-co** *adj.* heuristic.

eurite *f.* (miner.) eurite.

eur-itmi·a *f.* harmonious proportions (of architecture, style, etc.); harmonious arrangement; eurhythmy (as practised by the followers of Rudolf Steiner); eurhythmics, exercises for the harmonious development of the body (as practised by the followers of Jacques Dalcroze). **-it·mico** *adj.* eurhythmic; (med.) polso **-itmico**, regular pulse.

E·uro *pr.n.m.* (myth.) Eurus, the S.E. wind.

Europ-a *pr.n.f.* (geog.) Europe; (myth.) Europa. **-e·o** *adj., n.m.* European. **-eismo** *m.* Europeanism; (pol.) movement in favour of a united Europe. **-eizzare** [A1] *tr.* to Europeanize.

euro·p-ia *f.* (chem.) europia, europium oxide. **-io** *m.* (chem.) europium.

eusta·chio *m.* (anat.) tromba d'——, Eustachian tube.

eutana·sia *f.* euthanasia.

eut-et·tico *adj., n.m.* (phys.; metall.) eutectic. **-etto·ide** *adj.* eutectoid.

Eutichiani *pr.n. m.pl.* (rel. hist.) Eutychians.

eutimi·a *f.* euthymy, cheerfulness and patience in suffering.

†eutrapeli·a *f.* (philos.) eutrapelia.

Eva *pr.n.f.* Eva; Eve.

evacu-are [A6] *tr.* to evacuate; to void; to clear out; fare — l'aula, to order the hall to be cleared; *intr.* (*aux.* avere); to move out (from); i Francesi **-arono** il forte, the French abandoned the fort; to evacuate the bowels. **-amento** *m.* evacuation. **-ante** *part. adj.*, *n.m.* purgative, laxative. **-ato** *part. adj.* evacuated; cleared. **-azione** *f.* evacuation; motion of the bowels; (motor.; eng.) scavenging.

eva·dere [C 3] *intr.* (*aux.* essere; *prep.* a) to escape (from); *tr.* to carry out, to perform; (admin.) — una domanda, to meet a request; to deal with; — una lettera, to reply to a letter.

evanesc-ente *adj.* evanescent, fading away. **-enza** *f.* evanescence; (radio, telev.) fading.

evang-elia·rio *m.* (eccl.) *evangeliarium.* **-e·lico** *adj.* (rel.) evangelic; (eccl.) (Lutheran) Protestant; also *n.m.* (**-elicamente** *adv.*) **-elista** *m.* (eccl.) Evangelist. **-elista·rio** *m.* (eccl.) *evangeliarium.* **-elizzare** [A 1] *tr., intr.* (*aux.* avere) to evangelize.

evangelo, evange·lio *m.* See **vangelo.**

eva·nimo *m.* (bot.) — di Giappone, *Euonymus japonicus.*

evapor-are [A 1 sc, A 1 c] *intr.* (*aux.* essere) to evaporate; (*aux.* avere) to give off vapour. **-a·bile** *adj.* liable to evaporation. **-amento** *m.* evaporating. **-ativo** *adj.* evaporative, causing evaporation. **-ato** *part. adj.* evaporated; latte **-ato**, evaporated milk; legno **-ato**, artificially seasoned wood. **-atore** *m.* (techn.) evaporator. **-azione** *f.* evaporation; vaporization; exhalation, vapour.

evasione *f.* evasion; escape; — di un detenuto, escape of a prisoner; tentativo di —, attempt to escape; business reply, answer to a letter; dealing with or handling of a matter; — fiscale, tax evasion; (fig.) escapism; letteratura di —, escapist literature.

evas-ivo *adj.* evasive. **-ivamente** *adv.* evasively. **-o** *part.* of **evadere**, q.v.; *n.m.* fugitive; un -o alla giustizia, a fugitive from justice.

evel·lere [B 31] *tr.* to uproot, to eradicate. Cf. **svellere.**

Eve·mer·o *pr.n.m.* Euhemerus, a Sicilian (*c.* 316 B.C.) who maintained that the gods of Greek mythology were deified men and women. **-ismo** *m.* Euhemerism.

even-iente *adj.* occurring, liable to happen. **-ienza** *f.* occurrence, event; per ogni **-ienza**, in any eventuality; pronto ad ogni **-ienza**, ready for any eventuality. **-imento** *m.* see **avvenimento.**

event-o *m.* event; outcome; issue, result; in ogni —, in any case, at all events; (sport) fixture; calendario degli -i sportivi, fixture list. **-uale** *adj.* possible; casual. **-ualmente** *adv.* possibly; *conj.* -ualmente capitasse che, if it should happen that. **-ualità** *f.* possibility, possible event, eventuality.

evers-ione *f.* overthrow, destruction. **-o** *adj.* overthrown, destroyed; per la ragione **-a**, for the opposite reason. **-ore** *m.* destroyer.

evezione *f.* (astron.) evection (of the Moon).

e·via *f.* bacchante.

evid-ente *adj.* evident, manifest, obvious, plain; convincing; è —, obviously. **-entemente** *adv.* evidently; manifestly, obviously. **-enza** *f.* obviousness; clearness; provare all'-enza, to give incontrovertible proof; (leg.) evidence.

evin·cere [C 5] *tr.* (leg.) to recover possession of, to repossess; la cosa evitta, the thing of which one is dispossessed (C.C.).

evir-are [A 1] *tr.* to castrate, to emasculate. **-ato** *part. adj.* castrated; (herald.) emasculated; *n.m.* (vet.) castrated animal; (mus.) artificial male soprano.

evit-are [A 1 s] *tr.* to avoid; to shun; to evade; to dodge; to shirk; to dispense with. **-a·bile** *adj.* avoidable; easy to avoid. **-ando** (ger.) avoiding; †*adj.* to be avoided. **-ato** *part. adj.* avoided; shunned; evaded. **-atore** *m.* one who avoids, 'dodger'.

evitto *part.* of **evincere**, q.v.

evizione *f.* (leg.) dispossession (C.C.); recovery of possession; repossession; causa di —, action for recovery of possession; soffrire —, to be dispossessed (C.C.).

evo *m.* age, period, epoch; Medio —, Middle Ages; — antico, ancient times, antiquity; l' — moderno, modern history.

evoc-are [A 2 s] *tr.* to evoke, to conjure, to recall, to awaken. **-ato** *part. adj.* evoked; awakened. **-atore** *m.* conjurer of spirits. (**-atrice** *f.*) **-azione** *f.* evocation.

evoè *excl.* the Bacchanalian cry, 'Evoe!'.

evoluire [D 2] *intr.* (*aux.* avere) to perform evolutions, to revolve.

evolut-a *f.* (math.) evolute. **-o** *adj.* evolved, fully developed; adult; holding advanced views.

evoluzion-e *f.* evolution; development; (math.; mil.; naut.) evolution; (aeron.) momento di —, rudder moment; (mil.) — campale, field exercise; *pl.* manœuvres. **-ismo** *m.* evolutionism. **-ista** *m.* evolutionist.

evol·v-ere [C 14] *tr.* to evolve; *rfl.* to be evolved, to develop. **-ente** *part. adj.* evolving; developing; *n.f.* (math.) evolvent, involute.

evulso *part.* of **evellere**, q.v.; *adj.* uprooted, eradicated.

evviva *excl.* (abbrev. **vv**) long life!; hurrah! (iron.) — la modestia! how modest!; *n.m. indecl.* shout, cheer; gli evviva, the shouts of applause.

ex¹ *pref.* ex- (used in Italian without a hyphen): l'ex ministro, the ex-minister; l'ex combattente, the ex-serviceman.

ex² *m., f. indecl.* (colloq.) ex-husband; ex-wife.

exequatur *m. indecl.* (leg.) exequatur, credentials of a consul or commercial agent.

exoceto *m.* (ichth.) flying fish, *Exocoetus volitans.*

expo *f. indecl.* abbrev. of **esposizione**, q.v., used with reference to the Brussels International Exhibition (1958).

extra- *pref.* extra; super; extrafino, top grade; *adj. indecl.* top grade, prime quality; burro —, finest quality butter. **-coniugale** *adj.* extra-conjugal, adulterous. **-galat·tico** *adj.* (astron.) extra-galactic. **-intestinale** *adj.* (med.) abenteric. **-musicale** *adj.* (mus.) extramusical. **-parlamentare** *adj.* not due to Parliamentary action. **-temporale** *adj.* outside time. **-territorialità** *f. indecl.* extra-territoriality. **-uterino** *adj.* extra-uterine.

ex voto *m. indecl.* (rel.) votive offering, ex-voto.

Ezechi·a *pr.n.m.* Hezekiah.

Ezechiello *pr.n.m.* Ezekiel, Ezechiel.

eziandi·o *adv.* even; also.

E·zio *pr.n.m.* Ezio.

eziologi·a *f.* See **etiologia.**

f *f., m.* (pron. **effe**) the letter F; the sound F; una F maiuscola, a capital F; la città del F (dell'effe), Florence; (mus.) f. and ff., abbrev. of forte and fortissimo.

fa¹ *m.* (mus.) fa (i.e. the fourth degree of the scale); the note F; the key of F.

fa² *3rd pers. sing. pr. indic.* of **fare**, q.v.; for use in temporal phrases, e.g. due giorni fa, see under **fare** (no. 9).

fa'³ *2nd pers. sing. imper.* of **fare**, q.v.

faba·ria *f.* (bot.) orpine, livelong, *Sedum telephium; Zygophyllum fabago.*

fabbis-ogno, -ogno *m.* requisites, requirements, what is needed; (theatr.) property, prop; — di carta, paper consumption.

fab·bric-a *f.* building; new building; partly finished building; in —, in course of construction; nuovo di —, brand new; fabric (of a building); — del mondo, fabric of the world, physical universe; (fig.) una — d'inganni, a tissue of lies; factory, works; capo —, foreman of a factory; marca di —, marchio di —, trade-mark; prezzo di —, cost price, prime cost; modello di —, registered design; silversmith's furnace; (mil.) — d'armi, small arms factory, arsenal; (naut.) principal shipbuilding yard; (leg.) building, structure; distanza per fabbriche, building lines (C.C.).

fabbric-are [A 2 s] *tr.* to manufacture, to make; to construct, to build; to forge; (fig.) to fabricate, to invent; to coin; to trump up; to falsify, to 'cook'. **-a·bile** *adj.* manufacturable; that may be built; that may be built upon; area -abile, building site. **-amento** *m.* making; building; construction. **-ante** *part. adj.* constructing; *n.m.* manufacturer; maker; builder; -ante di cravatte, tie-maker, (joc.) money-lender. **-ativo** *adj.* for building upon; terreno -ativo, building land. **-ato** *part. adj.* manufactured, made, made up; built, built on; (fig.) fabricated; *n.m.* building; shell of a building; fabric of a building; (rlwy.) -ato viaggiatori, station building, public rooms. **-atore** *m.* maker; builder; constructor; (eng.) forge-hand. (**-atrice** *f.*) **-ato·rio** *adj.* (*m.pl.* -atorii) manufacturing, building. **-atura** *f.* manufacture, building. **-azione** *f.* manufacture, construction; process of making; make; -azione propria, (our) own make or brand; -azione italiana, made in Italy.

fabbric-eri·a *f.* board of those responsible for a church's fabric; their function or headquarters (cf. **opera**). **-iere** *m.* person responsible for church fabric; manufacturer, smith; builder.

fabbrile *adj.* of a blacksmith; l'arte —, blacksmith's craft.

fabbro *m.* smith; wright; — ferraio, blacksmith; (fig.) maker, creator; shaper, moulder; (poet.) craftsman, builder; carpenter.

†fabo·lico *adj.* fabulous.

fabretto *m.* (ichth.) *Heliastes chromis.*

†fa·bula *f.* and derivs. See **favola.**

Facanappa *pr.n.m.* (theatr.) a character of the marionette theatre, of Veronese origin; he has a hooked nose, is dressed in white, with green spectacles and a red tie, and speaks in Veneto dialect.

faccend-a *f.* affair; business; job; work; matter; thing; regolare una —, to settle a matter; una — seria, a serious matter, a serious thing; -e domestiche, housework, household chores; essere in -e,

faccend-a (*cont.*)
to be very busy, to be in the middle of housework; mettere in -e, to keep busy. **-ac·cia** *f. pejor.* bad business; rough chore. **-eri·a** *f.* troubles, difficulties, curiosity about other people's affairs, interference. **-iere** *m.* one who thrusts himself forward; busybody; †negotiator, intermediary. (**-iera** *f.*) †**-oso** *adj.* busy, occupied.

faccett-a *f. dim.* of faccia, q.v.; far delle -e, to assume the air of a culprit, to look guilty; facet; a -e, cut in facets. **-are** [A 1 c] *tr.* to cut (a gem). **-ato** *part. adj.* cut; facetted. **-atura** *f.* cutting (of a gem), style of cut.

facchin-o *m.* porter; stevedore; da —, rough, clumsy, crude; una vita da —, a dog's life; (zool.) granchio —, *Dromia vulgaris*, sponge crab. **-ag·gio** *m.* tip to a porter; porterage. **-ata** *f.* heavy job, lugging; vulgar language; vulgar action; ribaldry. **-eggiare** [A 3 c] *intr. (aux.* avere) to fag; to lug weights about; to act as porter. **-eri·a** *f.* porter's job; heavy task; low behaviour; 'Billingsgate language'. **-esco** *adj.* (*m.pl.* -eschi) of a porter; lavoro -esco, rough, heavy work. **-escamente** *adv.* roughly, coarsely.

fac·ci·a *f.* (*pl.* facce) face; — tosta, brazen face, 'cheek', bold face, effrontery; ma guarda che — tosta!, he's got a nerve!; viva la sua —!, good for him!; a doppia —, two-faced, insincere; perdere la —, to lose face; salvare la —, to save one's face; in — al mondo, in the eyes of the world; in — alla legge, in the eyes of the law; nella — mia, in my presence; voltar —, to change one's mind, to be a turncoat; far —, to be bold; non aver —, to be shy; senza —, shameless; non aver —, to be without shame; dir le cose in — a uno, to say things to a person's face; non guardare in — a nessuno, to be impartial; a — a —, face-to-face; di —, opposite; in (di) — a, facing; (paint.; photog.) in —, full-face, (of sails) taken aback; alla prima —, at first sight, *prima facie*; visto di —, seen from in front; aspect; faccia!, heads! (when tossing a coin); (eng.) side pane; panel; (of a book, album) page; side (of gramophone record); (naut.) forepart (of a ship); (mil.) face of a bastion or salient; front of a line or parade; †(archit.) façade, front. **-ac·cia** *f. pejor.* ugly mug; (fig.) 'cheek', sauce, nerve. **-ale** *adj.* facial, relating to the face; valore -ale, face value, nominal value. **-one** *n. augm.* large face; ham-like face; kind old face.

facciata *f.* (archit.) façade; front, frontage; elevation; page, side; mask; smoke-screen; side (of gramophone record).

†**faccidanno** *m.* See facidanno, under facibene.

†**facci·molo** *m.* black magic, satanic practices, witchcraft.

fac·cio *1st pers. sing. pres. indic.* of fare, q.v.

facci(u)ola *f. dim.* of faccia, q.v.; octavo page; *pl.* bands (as part of clerical, legal or academic dress).

fac-e[1] *f.* (poet.) torch; light; splendour; fire; heavenly orb. **-ella** *f. dim.* small light; sparkling light; (astron.) facula. **-ellina** *f.* firewood, kindling wood.

†**face**[2] *f.* See faccia.

†**face**[3] *3rd sing. pres. indic.* of fare, q.v.

facendo *ger.* of fare, q.v.; strada —, cammin —, walking along, on the way.

facente *pres. part.* of fare, q.v.; — funzione, see fungere.

†**fa·cere** *vb.* and derivs. See fare.

facet-o *adj.* facetious, waggish; jocular; humorous. **-amente** *adv.* facetiously; jocularly; humorously.

face·zia *f.* jest, witticism; humorous saying; joke.

fachiro *m.* fakir.

fachite *f.* (med.) phakitis.

faciale *adj.* See facciale, under faccia.

faci-bene *m. indecl.* welldoer. **-danno** *m.*, **-male** *m. indecl.* evildoer; despoiler; mischief-maker.

facicch-iare [A 4] *tr., intr. (aux.* avere) to do little things in a half-hearted way; to fiddle about. **-io** *m.* fiddling about, messing about.

facidanno *m.* See under facibene.

†**fa·cie** *f.* See faccia.

†**faciente** *part. adj.* of fare, q.v.

fa·cies *f. indecl.* (scient.) facies.

fa·cil-e *adj.* easy; simple; — a farsi, easily done, easy to do; di — smercio. saleable; facile; light; lavoro —, light work; donna —, light woman; di -i costumi, of easy virtue; likely, probable; è — che piova, it will probably rain; easily moved; accommodating, yielding, easy-going; ingegno —, quick mind; ragazzo — a intendere, boy who is quick on the up-take; di — contentatura, easily satisfied; inclined, prone; — all'ira, prone to anger; (poet.) smooth, flowing, supple; †*adv.* easily; †*adv. phr.* di —, easily. **-ino** *adj. dim.* rather easy; *n.m.* easy-going person; person easy to deal with; easily bribed person. **-ità** *f.* ease, easiness; aptitude; avere -ità per, to have an aptitude for; facility; fluency; †kindness, generosity; †docility, meekness. **-mente** *adv.* easily, with ease; probably. **-one** *adj.* superficial; amateurish; slick, glib; *n.m.* easy-going person; careless, lazy person; botcher. (**-ona** *f.*) **-oneri·a** *f.* laxity; easy-going behaviour; carelessness, slackness.

facilit-are [A 1 s] *tr.* to facilitate, to make easy; to simplify; — un compito, to make a task less difficult. **-amento** *m.* facilitating; simplifying. **-ato** *part. adj.* facilitated; simplified; assisted. **-azione** *f.* facilitation; pulling of strings, smoothing out of bureaucratic difficulties; note, chit, letter of introduction; concedere delle -azioni, to grant facilities.

facilone *adj.* and derivs. See under facile.

facimale *m. indecl.* See under facibene.

facimento *m.* doing (cf. fare).

†**faci·mol-a** *f.*, **-o** *m.* black magic, satanic practices, witchcraft.

facinoroso *adj.* lawless; violent; ruffianly; *n.m.* ruffian; desperado; malefactor.

facit-ore *m.* maker, creator; (leg.) official administrator; agent, steward; man of business; (derog.) — di leggi, legislator. (**-rice** *f.*) **-ura** *f.* work; constructing, building; †form, appearance.

faciucchiare [A 4] and derivs. See facicchiare.

facocero, facochero *m.* (zool.) wart hog, *Phacochoerus* spp.

fa·cola *f.* (poet.) torch; (astron.) facula.

facolite *f.* (miner.) phacolite.

facolt-à *f.* faculty, power; le — mentali, mental faculties, mental powers; in possesso delle proprie —, in full possession of one's faculties; authority; University faculty; branch (of study); (leg.) right; capacity; (admin.) sarà — di questa Amministrazione di..., the Board shall be at liberty to...; faculty; licence, authority, leave, permission; option; ciò non rientra nelle sue —, he has not the authority to do that; il signor M. ha — di parlare, I call upon Mr M. to speak; (leg.) — di astenzione dei testimoni, witnesses' right to refuse to give evidence (civil procedure); *pl.* property; wealth, riches; di molte —, wealthy. **-ativo** *adj.* optional; fermata -ativa, request stop; (leg.) permissive. **-ativamente** *adv.* optionally. **-izzare** [A 1] *tr.* to authorize; to make possible; to facilitate. **-izzato** *part. adj.* authorized; made possible; facilitated. **-oso** *adj.* wealthy; well-endowed, of means, well-off.

facond-ia *f.* readiness of speech; eloquence; fluency; loquacity; verbosity; 'gift of the gab'. **-o** *adj.* fluent; eloquent; glib, facile; talkative; garrulous. **-amente** *adv.* fluently; eloquently; glibly. †**-oso** *adj.* eloquent; gifted in intellectual powers.

fac-si·mile *m. indecl.* facsimile. **-titivo** *adj.* see fattitivo.

factotum *m. indecl.* factotum; agent.

†**facultà** *f.* and derivs. See facoltà.

†**fada** *f.* (naut.) weapon, infernal machine.

†**fadiga** *f.* See fatica.

faientin-o *adj.* of Faenza; *n.m.* native or inhabitant of Faenza; **-a** *f.* women of Faenza; faïence pottery; the Florence–Faenza railway.

Faenza *pr.n.f.* (geog.) Faenza; faïence pottery.

fa·eton *m. indecl.* phaeton (carriage).

fafaut·te *m.* (mus.) F fa ut, F below middle C.

fagget-a *f.*, **-o** *m.* See under faggio.

fag·gia *f.* (hist.) any of the six divisions formerly made of the suburban districts round Milan for a distance of six miles out, areas rather larger than the Corpi Santi; the term corresponds to the Contado or Leghe of Florence, the Masse of Siena, the Distretto delle sei miglia of Lucca, the Cortine or Camperie of Arezzo, the Camparezia of Tortona, the Saltaria of Sarzana, the Senate of Todi, the Chiusura of Brescia and Parma, the Vallera of Piacenza and the three Potesterie of Genoa.

fag·g-io *m.* beech tree, *Fagus silvatica*; beech-wood. **-eta** *f.*, **-eto** *m.* beech-wood. **-ino** *m.* beech-nut.

fagian-a *f.* (orn.) hen pheasant. **-a·ia**, **-i·a**, **-iera** *f.* pheasantry. **-are** [A 1] *tr.* (cul.) to cook as a pheasant is cooked. **-ella** *f.* (orn.) little bustard. **-o** *m.* (orn.) pheasant, esp. *Phasianus colchicus*; -o alpestre, -o nero, capercailye; -o di monte, blackcock, *Lyrurus tetrix*; (fig.) guastar la coda al -o, to spoil something at the best moment.

fagiolina *f.* (bot.) catjang, *Vigna catjang*.

fagiol-o *m.* (bot.) name of various kidney beans (*Phaseolus* spp.); *pl.* (cul.) haricot beans; broad beans; -i alla fiorentina, boiled beans served hot with olive oil and anchovies or tunny-fish; -i all'uccelletto, beans cooked in gravy or sauce; questo mi va a —, this is just what I wanted; second-year University student; blockhead; a forma di —, kidney-shaped; (vet.) corner incisor tooth of a horse; (joc.) (of a person) big tooth; (joc.) favourable vote. -a·io *m.* lover of beans; nickname for the Florentines. -ata *f.* dish of beans; stupid action, folly; trashy writing. -eri·a *f.* beans of all sorts. -ina *f.* (bot.) *Vigna cylindrica*. -ini *m.pl.* runner beans; French beans; cock's testicles. -ule *m.* haulm of the French bean, after drying for use as winter fodder.

fagiuolo *m.* and derivs. See **fagiolo**.

fa·gli-a *f.* (geol.) fault; — diretta, normal fault; — inversa, inverse fault; (text.) faille; †fault, error; †senza —, faultless. -are [A 4] *intr.* (aux. avere) to lack (a card of a given suit); -are a denari, to be short of money; *tr.* to discard (cards). -o *m.* lack (of cards of a suit); discarding of a card.

†**fagn-o** *adj.* shamming stupid but really cunning. †-one *adj.* cunning, pretending to know less than one does.

fagocit-o, fago·cit-o *m.* (biol.) phagocyte. -osi *f.* (biol.) phagocytosis.

fagopiro *m.* (bot.) buckwheat, *Fagopyrum esculentum*.

fagott-o *m.* bundle; un — di libri, a bundle of books; un — di biancheria, laundry tied in a bundle; far —, to pack up and go away, to be off, (joc.) to die; (mus.) bassoon; fagotto (organ-stop); quarto —, double curtall; †mezzo —, cor anglais. -ista *m., f.* (mus.) bassoonist.

fa·ida *f.* (hist.) feud; †(leg.) revenge; right of revenge (in medieval custom); faida, malice; deadly feud, blood feud.

fai·na *f.* (zool.) *Mustela faina*, a kind of marten; (fig.) old fogey; ugly person.

fala *f.* (mil. hist.) assault tower; †(naut.) weapon, infernal machine.

†**fa·lago** *m.* shade of black of a horse's coat.

fala-lella *f.* (mus.) song to nonsense syllables; fa-la. -nanna, -ninna *f.* ninny; worthless, effeminate man.

falang-e¹ *f.* (mil. hist.) phalanx; solid mass of people. -arca *m.* (*pl.* -archi) commander of a phalanx. -archi·a *f.* command of a phalanx. -ia·rio *m.* soldier of a phalanx. -ismo *m.* (pol.) Falangism, Spanish fascism. -ista *m., f.* (pol.) Falangist.

falang-e² *f.* (anat.) phalanx; proximate phalanx. -etta *f. dim.* (anat.) terminal phalanx. -ina *f. dim.* (anat.) middle phalanx.

falan·gio *m.* (zool.) phalangid, harvester, harvest spider, *Phalangista vulpina*; (bot.) plant said to be remedial against the bite of the harvest spider. -ite *f.* (bot.) see **falangio**.

falangista¹ *m.* (pol.). See under **falange¹**.

falangista² *m.* (zool.). See **falangio**.

falanste·r-(i)o *m.* (hist.) Phalanstery, a socialist community of the type advocated by Charles Fourier (1772–1837); (derog.) a big and ugly block of flats in a popular housing estate. -iano *adj.* Phalansterian.

†**fala·rica** *f.* (mil. hist.) firebrand, an incendiary dart on a stave.

fala·ride *f.* (bot.) canary grass, *Phalaris canariensis* and *Ph. tuberosa*.

falaropo *m.* (orn.) phalarope; — a becco largo, grey phalarope, *Phalaropus fulicarius*; — a becco sottile, red-necked phalarope, *Phalaropus lobatus*.

falasc-a *f.*, -o *m.* (bot.) name of various grasses used in straw plaiting; (naut.) grassline.

†**falavesca** *f.* spark; small particle of burning material that floats into the air.

falbalà, falpalà *m. indecl.* flounce, frill; *pl.* frills and furbelows; gewgaws; knicknacks.

falbo *adj.* tawny; (text.) fallow-coloured.

falcac·cio *m.* See under **falco**.

falc-are [A 2] *tr.* (mil. hist.) to arm (a chariot) with scythes; †to bend; †— il passo, to circle round; †to scythe; *intr.* (aux. essere) (equit.) to falcade; (fig.) to run and leap at great speed. -ata *f.* (equit.) falcade, the motion of a horse in a very rapid curvet; (sport) stride, step. -ato *part. adj.* sickle-shaped; crescent; armed with scythes. -atore *m.* man using a scythe.

falcastro *m.* (agric.) bill-hook.

falc-e *f.* sickle; scythe; — fienaia, scythe; mettere la — all'altrui messe, to interfere in other people's business; bill-hook for pruning; (eng.) leva a —, bent crank; (naut. hist.) type of cutlass; (mil. hist.) type of halberd; (vet.) hock; (anat.) corda magna, the principal tendon of the leg; falx; (poet.) crescent; — di luna,

crescent moon. -etto *m. dim.* bill-hook. -iazza *f.* rough sickle. -ino *m. dim.* small sickle; bill-hook. -ione *m. augm.* large sickle; hay-cutting knife, hay-cutter fixed in position for cutting hay against it by hand; -ione a ruota, -ione a volano trinciante, chaff-cutting machine; (mil. hist.) halberd. -i(u)olo *m.* bill-hook.

falchetta *f.* (naut.) gunwhale.

falchetto *m.* (orn.) small falcon or hawk; (equit.) see **falcata**, under **falcare**.

falci-are [A 3] *tr.* to mow (with a scythe or sickle); to scythe; (fig.) to mow down, to cut down. -ata *f.* cut with a scythe; mowing, scything. -ato *part. adj.* mown; scythed; (fig.) mown down, cut down. -atore *m.* mower, reaper; hay-cutter; (hist.) peasant rebel or defender armed with scythe. -atrice *f.* mowing machine; lawn-mower; reaping machine; woman mower or reaper; (poet.) la morte -atrice, Death with his scythe. -atura *f.* mowing, reaping; mowing season.

falciazza *f.* See under **falce**.

falci·di-a *f.* (leg.) abatement of pecuniary legacy; (fig.) large reduction; subire una vera —, to be drastically reduced; una — di candidati agli esami, a drastic number of failures in an examination. -are [A 4] *tr.* (leg.) to abate (legacy); to disallow, to reprobate (items in accounts); (comm.) to cut down (e.g. profits).

falci·fero *adj.* carrying a scythe, scythe-bearing.

falciglione *m.* (orn.) snipe.

falcinella *f.* pastry-cook's curved knife, pastry cutter.

falcinello¹ *m.* (orn.) glossy ibis.

falcinello² *m.* bill-hook.

falc-ione *m.*, -iuolo *m.* See under **falce**.

falc-o *m.* (orn.) falcon, hawk; —cappuccino, marsh harrier; —cuculo, red-footed falcon, *Falco vespertinus*; — della regina, Eleonora's falcon, *Falco eleanorae*; — di padule, marsh harrier, *Circus aeruginosus*; — giocoliere, bateleur eagle, *Terathopius ecaudatus*; — grillaio, lesser kestrel, *Falco naumanni*; — nero, black kite; — pecchiaiolo, honey buzzard, *Pernis apivorus*; — pescatore, osprey, *Pandion haliaëtus*; — pigargo, hen harrier. -ac·cio *m. pejor.* rapacious person.

†**fal·cola** *f.* candle; torch.

falconara *f.* hawk-cage; (naut.) ship's beams, scantlings; case or carriage of a block and tackle, top strake; (mil.) gun embrasure.

falconare [A 1 c] *intr.* (aux. avere) to go hawking.

falcon-e *m.* (orn.) falcon, esp. the peregrine falcon, *Falco peregrinus*, also called — pellegrino; (ichth.) devil fish, *Myliobatis aquila*; pesce —, flying gurnard, *Dactylopterus volitans*; (naut.) falcon, the smallest calibre gun carried in sailing ships; bollard, holdfast; derrick; (mil. hist.) battering ram; (eng.) derrick. -cello *m.* (orn.) small falcon, esp. the merlin. -ello *m.* (orn.) shrike; (mil. hist.) arrowslit or small gun embrasure. -eri·a *f.* falconry. -etto *m. dim.* small gun, lighter than the 'falcone'. †-iera *f.* (naut.) battery deck in a galleon; vertical pillar or deck support; see **falconara**; (mil.) arrow slit, cruciform aperture permitting the defenders to shoot at an advancing enemy. -iere *m.* falconer.

fald-a *f.* flake; layer of snow; drift of snow; a — a —, flake upon flake, (fig.) little by little; thick slice, hunk, slab; flap; pleat; loin (of meat); flounce, hem; dress coat; brim (of a hat); butt of a hare-skin for hat-making; lower slope of a mountain; (geol.) layer, stratum; — di ricoprimento, nappe; (geog.) — freatica, ground-water; (text.) lap; — alimentatrice, lap feed; (bldg.) pitch of a roof; (math.) iperboloide ad una —, hyperboloid of one sheet; *pl.* tail (of a tail-coat); skirt (of a coat); attaccarsi alle -e di, to cling to the coat-tails of; reins for a baby learning to walk; slopes of a mountain; (armour) plates protecting the small of the back and descending over the buttock and thighs; †defence, shelter; †pocket. -are [A 1] *tr.* to break with the grain; to cut along the lines of cleavage. -ato *part. adj.* flaked; pleated; (geol.) flaky, stratified, streaky. -ella *f. dim.* (surg. hist.) charpie, linen shredded down so as to form a soft material for dressing wounds; lint; (text.) quantity of wool, ten pounds in weight, beaten down before being greased for combing out; small skein of silk; †deception, trickery. -ellato *adj.* streaked with mould. -ellina *f.* lint dressing. -etta *f. dim.* snowflake.

faldi·glia *f.* (hist. costume) hooped skirt, hoop; under-skirt.

faldisto·r(i)o *m.* (liturg.) faldstool.

faldoso *adj.* streaky, striated; (of a mountain) many-sloped.

falegnam-e *m.* joiner, carpenter; nodo da —, timber hitch. -eri·a *f.* joinery; carpentry.

falen-a *f.* moth; layer of ash on red-hot charcoal; ash of burnt paper; (fig.) flighty person; thin person. **-idi** *m.pl.* (ent.) Phalaenae, an old term for a large group of moths, mainly the present Geometridae; (pop.) moths.

fa·ler-a *f.* horse brass; *pl.* string of decorations such as brasses used to decorate horses; (archaeol.) heavy necklace made of medallion-like decorations. **-ato** *adj.* decorated with horse brasses.

Falerno *pr.n.m.* (geog. hist.) Falernus; *n.m.* Falernian wine; (fig.) exquisite modern wine, 'nectar'.

fale·şia *f.* cliff, steep bank.

fale·ucio *adj., n.m.* (class. prosod.) Phaleucian (verse); hendeca-syllabic.

falimbello *m.* inconstant person.

falla *f.* leak; formazione d'una —, springing of a leak; outlet, outflow; tamponare una —, to stop a leak; (naut.) leak; — cieca, hidden leak; (mil.) break in a line, gap; (radio) — di griglia, grid leak; — di memoria, lapse of memory.

falla·bile *adj.* See under **fallare**.

fallac-e *adj.* fallacious; false; misleading; deceitful; fleeting, quickly fading (of colour); treacherous (of a horse); likely to go bad (of fruit); — ai bisogni, inadequate, unsuitable; †alla —, fallaciously. **-emente** *adv.* fallaciously; deceptively. **-ia** *f.* fallaciousness; deception; fallacy; failure (of a crop which has promised well). **-ità** *f.* fallaciousness; falseness; treachery.

†fallag·gio *m.* mistake, error; falseness; treachery.

fallagogi·a *f.* See under **fallo²**.

fall-are [A I] *intr.* (aux. avere) to err, to be mistaken; to make mistakes; (provb.) chi non fa non **-a**, he makes no mistakes who makes nothing; chi spesso parla, spesso **-a**, who talks much, errs much; (joc.) posso aver **-ato**, I may be wrong (from Renzo's saying in Manzoni's *Promessi Sposi*); (cards) to lack a suit; (naut.) to make water; †to sin; †to lack, to be lacking; †to fail; †to be necessary; †to be excepted. **-a·bile** *adj.* fallible; fallacious. **†-ante** *part. adj.* mistaken, in error; fallacious. **†-anza** *f.* error; lack; deception, fallacy; lie. **-ato** *part. adj.* mistaken, in error; failed. **†-a·zia** *f.* fallacy; error.

†fal·l-ere *intr.* to fail; to be lacking; to err. **†-ente** *part. adj.* fallible; erring; fallacious; deceiving. **†-enza** *f.* error; lacking, lack; senza **-enza**, without doubt. **†-e·vole** *adj.* fallacious; lacking; untrust-worthy.

fall·i·bile *adj.* fallible; fallacious. **-ibilità** *f.* fallibility.

fall·ico *adj.* phallic.

†falligione *f.* See under **fallire**.

falliment-o *m.* falling short, failing, failure; disappointment, let down; (leg.) bankruptcy (in trade, business or profession); — doloso, fraudulent bankruptcy; attivo del —, the bankruptcy assets; comitato dei creditori del —, Committee of Inspection; curatore del —, Trustee in Bankruptcy; dichiarazione di —, adjudication of bankruptcy; istanza di — del pubblico ministero, Public Prosecutor's bankruptcy petition; piccolo —, small bankruptcy (old procedure, superseded by 'procedimento sommario', q.v.); richiesta di — del debitore, debtor's own bankruptcy petition; ricorso di — di un creditore, creditor's bankruptcy petition; sentenza dichiarativa di —, receiving order in bankruptcy; stato passivo del —, net deficiency of the bankruptcy, final statement of affairs. **-are** *adj.* (leg.) having to do with bankruptcy; in bankruptcy; amministrazione delle attività **-ari**, administration of assets in bankruptcy; concordato **-are**, Scheme of Arrangement; concordato **-are** preventivo, composition with creditors; giudice delegato per la procedura **-are**, Official Receiver; l'istituto **-are**, the bankruptcy system; la legge **-are**, the law of bankruptcy; imprese soggette alla legge **-are**, undertakings coming within the law of bankruptcy; la procedura **-are**, bankruptcy proceedings; tribunale **-are**, Bankruptcy Court; (fig.) bankrupt; una politica **-are**, a bankrupt policy.

fall-ire [D 2] *intr.* (aux. avere) to fail; to be unsuccessful; to fall short; to be disappointing; to be inadequate, to be insufficient; to offend; to transgress; to misfire; — alle promesse, to break one's word; — al giuramento, to break one's oath; (comm.) to go bankrupt; *tr.* to miss; — il colpo, to miss one's aim; to let down, to disappoint; — il tedio, to drive away boredom, to while away the time. **†-igione** *f.* error; fault. **-ito** *part. adj.* failed; missed; unsuccessful; **-ito** il colpo, the attempt having failed; unfulfilled; **-ito** di mente, out of one's mind; andare **-ito**, to fail; non venir **-ito**, to succeed; defective; (leg.; comm.) bankrupt; dichiarato

283

-ito, adjudicated bankrupt, declared bankrupt; *n.m.* insolvent debtor; bankrupt (in trade, business or profession); creditori chirografari del **-ito**, unsecured creditors in bankruptcy; riabilitazione civile del **-ito**, discharge of bankrupt; sequestro del **-ito**, seizure of insolvent debtor's property. **†-itore** *m.* one who commits error.

fall-o¹ *m.* failing, slight fault; slip; cogliere in —, to catch out; essere in —, to be at fault; senza —, without fail; (hist.; chivalry) serious fault, sin; (geol.) fault; (sport) foul, fault; (football) — di mano, handling; (tennis) — di piede, foot-fault. **-oso** *adj.* (sport) gioco **-oso**, rough, foul, incorrect play.

fall-o² *m.* phallus. **-agogi·a** *f.*, **-ofori·a** *f.* (Gk. antiq.) procession with phallus. **-o·foro** *adj.* (Gk. antiq.) carrying the phallus. **-oidi** *m.pl.* (bot.) stink horn fungus, *Phallus impudicus*.

falloppa *f.* See **faloppa**.

falò *m. indecl.* bonfire; beacon; fare un — di, to make a bonfire of; (fig.) fare un —, to waste one's substance in riotous living; (mil.) beacon light; †(naut.) ornamental stern light.

falopp-a *f.* (silkb.) imperfect cocoon; (fig.) liar; braggart, boaster. **(-ona** *f. augm.* **-one** *m. augm.*)

falo·ti·co *adj.* queer, odd, strange. **-cheri·a** *f.* oddity.

falpalà *m. indecl.* See under **falbalà**.

falsa *f.* (mus.) discord; (dressm.) insertion.

falsa-braca *f.* (mil.) false curtain. **-gagi·a** *f.* see **gagia**. **-monete** *m. indecl.* coiner, counterfeiter. **-porta** *f.* (*pl.* **falsaporte**) sham door. **-riga** *f.* (*pl.* **falsarighe**) guide rule, ruled sheet of paper placed under a blank sheet as a guide; sulla **-riga** di, in the style of, after the pattern of, in imitation of.

fals-are [A I] *tr.* to falsify; to distort; to misrepresent; (dressm.; tailor.) to pad. **-amento** *m.* falsifying; distortion. **-ato** *part. adj.* distorted; misrepresented; falsified. **-atore** *m.* falsifier. (**-atrice** *f.*)

falsa·rio *m.* forger; falsifier; counterfeiter; liar; perjurer.

falseggiare [A 3 c] *intr.* (aux. avere) (mus.) to sing falsetto; to sing out of tune; †to lie, to speak untruths; †*tr.* to falsify, to counterfeit; to simulate.

falsetto *m.* (mus.) falsetto voice.

†falsezza *f.* See **falsità**.

†falsi·a *f.* untruth, falsehood; deception; fallacy.

falsi·dico *adj.* untruthful, lying.

falsific-are [A 2 s] *tr.* to falsify; to distort; to adulterate; (leg.) to falsify; to counterfeit; — una firma, to forge a signature; — un testamento, to forge a will. **-a·bile** *adj.* falsifiable; liable to falsification. **-amento** *m.* falsifying; falsification; forgery; counterfeiting. **-ato** *part. adj.* falsified; (leg.) forged; counterfeit; testamento **-ato**, forged will; moneta **-ata**, counterfeit money. **-atore** *m.* falsifier, counterfeiter. (**-atrice** *f.*) **-azione** *f.* falsifying, forging; falsification; (leg.) forgery; imputazione di **-azione**, charge of forgery.

falsilo·quio *m.* lie, falsehood.

falsi·loquo *m.* liar.

falsità *f.* falsity; falseness; lie, falsehood; duplicity; disloyalty; insincerity, affectation; slyness; (leg.) deceit (civil law), falsification (criminal law); — in atti, falsification of documents; — (in atti) ideologica, abstract falsification of (e.g. subject-matter, intent or purport of, or by making false statement in) a document; — (in atti) materiale, concrete falsification (e.g. of text, words, date, signature or other material part) of a document; forgery (C.P.).

fals-o *adj.* false; deceitful, untruthful, hypocritical; counterfeit, forged; not genuine, sham; dummy; (electr.) candela **-a**, dummy plug; erroneous, wrong; chiave **-a**, counterfeit key; nodo —, granny knot; virtù **-a**, simulated virtue; sorriso —, feigned smile; uomo —, deceitful man, hypocritical man; **-e** speranze, false hopes, fallacious hopes; essere sopra una **-a** strada, to be on a wrong track; mettere in una **-a** luce, to set in an unpleasant light, to defame; (leg.) false; forged; untrue; **-a** dichiarazione, false statement; — giuramento, false oath, perjury; **-a** testimonianza, false evidence; atto —, forged record or document; (bot.) pepe —, pepper tree, *Schinus molle*; (naut.) di — bordo, crank; fianco —, faulty hull construction; — ponte, half deck; — braccio, mooring line (hemp); **-a** banda, crank; **-a** chiglia, false keel; **-a** via, zigzag (to foil the enemy); †**-a** corsa, see 'falsa via'; (mus.) out of tune; discordant; **-a** consonanza, false relation of the tritone; **-a** quinta, false fifth, diminished fifth; **-a** musica, musica ficta; (sport) **-a** partenza, false start; *adv.* falsely; parole che suonano —, words

fals-o (*cont.*) which do not ring true; *n.m.* falsehood, lies; perjury, fraud, forgery; giurare il —, to forswear, to swear falsely (see also under leg.); testimoniare il —, to bear false witness; fake, fraud; impugnare di —, to challenge the truth of; mettere un piede in —, to stumble, to proceed uncertainly; (fig.) to make a false step; non mettere un piede in —, not to put a foot wrong; (leg.) giurare il —, to commit perjury; reato di —, (crime of) perjury; (criminal) fraud; proporre querela di —, to take out a summons (in civil proceedings) challenging a document put in by the other side; documento impugnato di —, challenged document; accusare di —, to bring a charge of forgery against; (fencing) feint; — della lama, part of blade nearest tip; (archit.) lack of support, void. **-amente** *adv.* falsely, untruthfully, deceitfully; insincerely.

falsobordone *m.* (mus.) faburden, fauxbourdon.

†falt-a *f.* default; lack; fault, error. **†-are** *intr.* to lack; to fail.

fam-a *f.* fame; reputation; repute, renown; notoriety; report; godere —, to be famous, to enjoy celebrity; di — mondiale, of world-wide reputation; godere — di grande chirurgo, to have a great reputation as a surgeon; avere — di essere, to be reputed to be, to be said to be; ha — di picchiare la moglie, it is rumoured that he beats his wife; di dubbia —, of doubtful reputation; di chiara —, celebrated, distinguished; venire in — di santo, to acquire a saintly reputation; essere in —, to be in vogue; è — che, it is said, it is rumoured that; conoscere per —, to know by reputation; essere notissimo per —, to be very well known by repute. **-ato** *adj.* famed; mal -ato, ill-famed (cf. **famoso**).

fam-e *f.* hunger, appetite; famine, lack of food; aver —, to be hungry; — canina, ravenous hunger; avere una — da lupo, to be as hungry as a hunter; levarsi, cavarsi la —, to satisfy one's hunger; non vederci dalla —, to be so hungry one can't see straight; cascare dalla —, to be faint with hunger; ingannare la —, to take one's mind off one's hunger; patire la —, to starve, to be starving; brutto come la —, ugly as sin; (mil.) pigliare per —, to starve out; morire di —, to die of starvation, to starve to death; morto di —, starved to death, (fig.) very poor, wretched; quel morto di —, that penniless wretch; desire, craving; — di gloria, craving for glory. **-ina** *f. dim.* quite an appetite.

fame·dio *m.* a temple of Fame (Milan, nineteenth century).

fame·lic-o *adj.* hungry; famishing; starving, ravenous; — d'onore, eager for honour, craving honour. **-amente** *adv.* ravenously.

famigerato *adj.* notorious; ill-famed; (joc.) famous.

fami·gli-a *f.* family; lineage, race, stock; l'umana —, the human race; related group, section; — di lingue, group (or family) of languages; household; (hist.) slaves, servants, retinue, escort, bodyguard; body, association; religious order; un figlio di —, a minor, a younger son, a man dependent on his parents, young man of quiet domesticated habits living at home; mettere su —, to raise a family; fare —, to take a wife and set up house, to have children; entrare a far parte della —, to become a member of the family; madre di —, mother of a family, motherly, matronly woman; padre di —, head of a family, head of the house; tutto —, devoted to one's family; di —, domestic, domesticated; festa di —, family celebration; cibo di —, homely food, home cooking; consiglio di —, family council; essere di —, to be a member of the family, to be like one of the family, to be a friend of the family; in —, in the family, at home; trattare una cosa in —, to treat a matter discreetly or confidentially; (leg.) family; legge regolatrice dei rapporti di —, law of (or governing) family relations; regime patrimoniale della —, system of the family's hereditary or quasi-settled estate or property; stato di —, vital statistics, legal state of the family; (rel.; art) Sacra Famiglia, Holy Family; (bot.) family; (silkb.) baco di —, nesting spinner. **-ona** *f. augm.* large family; large, healthy family. **-uccia** *f. dim.* small family of modest means. **-(u)ola** *f. dim.* little family; (bot.) honey fungus, *Armillaria mellea*.

famigliare *adj.* See **familiare**.

fami·glio *m.* servant; usher, page; attendant; member of a household; †hired assassin, cut-throat; †carrier pigeon.

familiar-e *adj.* family, domestic; familiar; homelike; easy-going; forward, outspoken; private, intimate; essere — con, to be on close terms with; lettere -i, private correspondence; gli è più — il francese dell'italiano, he knows French better than Italian, he is more at home in French than he is in Italian; avere — una cosa, to know a thing well, to be used to a thing; quel tono è — in lui,

that tone is natural with him; stile —, simple style, straightforward style; alla —, in private, in confidence; (leg.) assistenza —, family duty of maintenance; morale —, family morality; patrimonio —, hereditary or quasi-settled family property or estate; *n.m.* friend; servant; member of a household. **-issimo** *adj. superl.* very friendly, intimate; very familiar, common. **-mente** *adv.* with familiarity; simply; trattare -mente, to be friendly to. **-ità** *f.* familiarity; intimacy, confidence; non ci ho -ità, I don't know him (them, it, etc.) very closely; simplicity, spontaneity; prendersi troppa -ità, to take liberties, to be over-familiar; trattare con -ità, to be affable towards; -ità di stile, naturalness, lack of snobbishness, simplicity of style. **-izzare** [A I] *rfl.* (*prep.* con) to accustom oneself (to); to familiarize oneself, to make oneself familiar (with); to become the close friend (of); (of animals) to grow tame; *recip. rfl.* to get to know each other, to grow accustomed to each other.

†fami·lia *f.* See **famiglia**.

famina *f. dim.* See under **fame**.

famos-o *adj.* famous, celebrated, renowned; notorious, infamous; libellous; memorable; avvenimento —, memorable event; (leg.) libello —, defamatory libel; †notorious, of ill fame. **-amente** *adv.* famously; notoriously.

famul-ato *m.* servitude; tribute; deference, respect. **†-ato·rio** *adj.* (gramm.) auxiliary. **†-azione** *f.* family; servants, household.

†famulento *adj.* hungry, ravenous.

†fa·mulo *m.* servant, attendant.

fanal-e *m.* light, lamp, lantern; carriage lamp; lighthouse; (naut.) lantern; harbour light; ship's navigation light; — regolamentare, regulation light; — ammiraglio, admiral's top light; — di coronamento, stern light; — di fondo, anchor light; — di poppa, admiral's stern light; -i di posizione, position lights; -i di rimorchio, towing lights; — di Santa Barbara, magazine light; -i di via, -i di navigazione, navigation lights; (rlwy.) -i di treno, signal lights; (motor.) light; -i anteriori, head-lights, head-lamps; — di coda, tail-light, rear-light; (ichth.) moongazer, *Uranoscopus scaber*. **-aio** *m.* lighthouse-keeper. **-eri·a** *f.* (motor.) lighting equipment. **-etto** *m. dim.* see **fanalino**. **-ino** *m. dim.* little lamp; -ino della bicicletta, bicycle lamp; (motor.) -ino di targa, -ino di coda, tail-lamp; (joc.) -ino di coda, the last football team or cyclist to qualify in a competition. **-ista** *m.* lamplighter; (naut.) lighthouse-keeper.

fanari-ota, -otto *m.* (hist.) Greek of the Phanariot quarter of Constantinople.

fana·tic-o *adj.* fanatic, fanatical; bigoted; very keen; zelo —, fanaticism; — per la musica, mad about music; *n.m.* fanatic, enthusiast, bigot; partisan, supporter, 'fan'; fanaticism; dare nel —, to become fanatical. **-amente** *adv.* fanatically, like a fanatic.

fanat-ismo *m.* fanaticism; frenzy; bigotry. **-izzare** [A I] *tr.* to make a fanatic of, to fanaticize; *intr.* (*aux.* avere) to arouse fanaticism.

†fanc-ella, **†-illa** *f.* and derivs. See **fanciulla**.

fanciull-a *f.* girl, young girl; maid, virgin; unmarried woman; (provb.) la colpa morì —, Mr Nobody's to blame. **-accia** *f. pejor.* wicked girl; (bot.) love-in-the-mist, *Nigella damascena*. **-aggine** *f.* childishness, puerility, childish behaviour. **-aia** *f.* crowd of girls or children. **-ata** *f.* childish action. **-eggiare** [A 3 c] *intr.* (*aux.* avere) to behave childishly, to be childish. **-eria** *f.* childishness, childish behaviour. **-esco** *adj.* (*m.pl.* -eschi) childish; puerile; child-like. **-escamente** *adv.* childishly, like a child. **-ezza** *f.* childhood; early youth; boyhood; girlhood; infancy; †early stages of development (of any living thing); †childishness, childish behaviour. **-o** *m.* child, boy, simpleton, naïve person; (leg.) child of tender age; occultamento di stato di un — legittimo, concealment of the legal status of a legitimate child (criminal code); *pl.* children; libri per -i, books for children, children's books; (leg.) children under fourteen (criminal code); maltrattamento verso -i, cruelty to children; *adj.* very young, immature, youthful. **-accio** *m. pejor.* bad boy, naughty boy; man who behaves childishly. **-ino** *m. dim.* little boy; nice little boy; attractive child. **-one** *m. augm.* big child; man who behaves childishly, booby, stupid person. (**-ona** *f.*) **-otto** *m.* young boy, lad.

fandango *m.* (mus.) fandango, a Spanish dance.

fando·ni-a *f.* idle story, wild tale; lie; fib; malicious rumour; non raccontarmi -e, don't talk nonsense. **-one** *m.* (Tusc.) story-teller, exaggerator; leg-puller.

fanello *m.* (orn.) linnet, *Carduelis cannabina*; — nordico, twite, *Carduelis flavirostris*.

faner·o·gama *f.* (bot.) flowering plant, phanerogam. **-o·mero** *adj.* (geol.) phaneromerous.

fanfaluc·a *f.* ash blown about in the air; mere invention, idle story; triviality, nonsense; capricious notion; gew-gaw, bauble; †(cul.) puff pastry, mille feuilles. **-ola** *f.* ash of burnt straw, of paper or twigs.

fan·fano *m.* chatterer, chatter-box; meddler, interferer; bustling person; (ichth.) pilot fish, *Naucrates ductor*.

fanfara *f.* (mus.; mil.) fanfare; Bersaglieri band.

fanfaron·e *m.* braggart, boaster, swaggerer, blusterer; gas-bag. **-ata** *f.* fanfaronade; arrogant behaviour; boastful language.

fan·fera *adv. phr.* a —, see 'a vanvera', under **vanvera**.

fang·a *f.* deep mud. **-a·ia** *f.* muddy stretch of road. **-atura** *f.* mud-bath.

†fanghic·cio *m.* See **fanghiglia**.

fanghi·glia *f.* mire; soft mud; muddy water; (geog.) fine clay, sticky clay; (techn.) slurry, sludge.

fang·o *m.* (*pl.* **fanghi**) mud; mire; (industr.) sludge; (fig.) degradation, corruption; fare i fanghi, to have mud baths; (fig.) cadere nel —, to become morally degraded; gettare — addosso a, to slander, to fling mud at; anima di —, corrupt soul; — bianco, dregs remaining in the bottom of a barrel. **-ac·cio** *m. pejor.* mud, filth; (fig.) extreme moral degradation, utter corruption. **-oso** *adj.* muddy, filthy; low, base, corrupt. **-osello** *adj.* rather muddy. **-osità** *f.* muddiness; corruption.

†fangotto *m.* See **fagotto**.

†fannon·nolo *adj.* inept, stupid; *n.m.* booby, blockhead.

fannullon·e *m.* idle person, lazybones, idler. (**-a** *f.*)

Fanny *pr.n.f.* (pron. **fannì**) Fanny.

fano[1] *m.* temple; sanctuary.

Fan·o[2] *pr.n.f.* (geog.) Fano. **-ese** *adj.* of the city of Fano; *n.m.*, *f.* native of Fano.

fanò *m. indecl.* (Ven. naut.) light, lighthouse; coastguard; nave di —, lightship.

fanone *m.* (liturg.) fanon (papal vestment); *pl.* (zool.) whalebone.

fa·notron *m. indecl.* (electron.) phanotron.

fantaccino *m.* (mil.). See under **fante**.

fantascienza *f.* science fiction, 'scientifiction'.

fanta·scopo *m.* phenakistoscope.

fantaṣ·i·a *f.* fancy; imagination; fantasy; vision; fanciful thing; whim, fancy, inclination; thought, mind; non gli passa neppure per la —, it does not even occur to him; avere — di, to have a wish for; andare a — a, to appeal to; articoli di —, fancy goods, ornamental objects; cosa di —, freak, odd thing; stuzzicare la — a, to tickle the fancy of; (mus.) fantasia, phantasy, fancy; suonare a —, to improvise; (hist.) joust; (text.) *adj. indecl.* fancy, patterned. **-iac·cia** *f. pejor.* bizarre thing; strange idea. **-iare** [A 4] *intr.* (*aux.* avere) to daydream. **-iante** *part. adj.* fanciful; imaginative; fantastic. **-iasti** *m.pl.* (eccl. hist.) Phantasiasts. **-ioso** *adj.* strange, fanciful. **-uc·cia** *f.* childish fancy; freakish imagination.

fanta·ṣima *f.* ghost, spectre, apparition; †nightmare; †incubus.

fantaṣm·a *m.* ghost, spectre, apparition; phantasm, phantom; mental image; fantasy, fancy; illusion; — poetico, poetic fancy; **-i** di dominio, delusions of grandeur, dreams of domination; (telev.) immagine —, double image, ghost. **-acopi·a** *f.* (med.) delirium; mental derangement causing hallucinations. **-agori·a** *f.* phantasmagoria; hallucinations; — di cifre, jumble of figures; fantastic pageant, breath-taking spectacle, mammoth show; **-agoria di colori**, fantastic riot of colour; (cinem. hist.) phantasmagoria. **-ago·rico** *adj.* phantasmagoric; fantastic; spectacular. **-agoricamente** *adv.* in a weird and fantastic way. **†-are** *intr.* to have visions; to dream nightmares. **-a·tici** *m.pl.* (eccl. hist.) Phantasiasts. **-o** *m.* (ent.) leaf insect, Fam. Phasmidae; †see **fantasma**.

†fantaṣ·tica *f.* power of imagination, faculty of apprehension by means of images.

fantasticag·gine *f.* fantasy; reverie, fancy; daydream.

fantastic·are [A 2 s] *intr.* (*aux.* avere) to indulge in fancies, to dream, to daydream; to let one's imagination run on; *tr.* to dream about; to imagine, to envisage; che cosa mai vai **-ando**? whatever are you dreaming of? **-amento** *m.* imagining, dreaming; dream, fantasy. **-atore** *m.* dreamer, visionary. (**-atrice** *f.*)

fantasticheri·a *f.* reverie, daydream; fantasy, fancy.

fanta·stic·o *adj.* fantastic, fanciful; imaginary, imaginative; facoltà **-a**, power of imagination, imaginative faculty; marvellous, wonderful; (archit.) fanciful, irregular; *n.m.* whimsical person; eccentric. **-amente** *adv.* fancifully; queerly; marvellously, wonderfully. **-one** *m.* dreamer, visionary. (**-ona** *f.*) **-uc·cio**, **-uzzo** *adj.* fantastic, weird, peculiar, whimsical.

fantastron *m. indecl.* (radar) phantastron.

fant·e[1] *m.* (mil.) foot soldier; (naut.) officer's servant; (cards) knave, jack; †servant, serving-boy, page; †— di stalla, stable-boy, stable-man. **-accino** *m.* (mil.) infantry-man; †trooper (foot or mounted). **†-eggiare** *intr.* to behave in an undignified manner, to lower oneself to the level of a servant. **-eri·a** *f.* (mil.) infantry; -eria di marina, marines. **-icello** *m. dim.* servant-boy, young boy. **-icino** *m. dim.* little boy, child. **†-ile** *adj.* and derivs. see **infantile**. **†-ineri** *f.* malice, evil treachery; childish behaviour. **-inetto** *m.* (naut.) capstan, bollard lands. **-ino** *m. dim.* young boy, child; jockey; †Baby Jesus, Christ Child. **-occeri·a** *f.* childish thing, triviality; puerile action. **-oc·cia** *f.* doll; lay-figure, tailor's dummy; silly woman. **-occiag·gine** *f.* childish action; puerility. **-occia·io** *m.* maker of dolls; puppet maker. **-occiata** *f.* childish thing, foolishness; puppet-show, puppet-play. **-occino** *m.* little puppet; silly fellow. **-oc·cio** *m.* rag-doll; lay figure, tailor's dummy; scarecrow; guy; silly individual, simple-minded person; man of straw; (paint.) badly drawn figure; (theatr. and fig.) puppet; governo **-occio**, puppet government. **-occione** *m.* fat child; crude person, clumsy individual; crude statue. **-olino** *m. dim.* little boy, baby boy. **-one** *m.* idle person; dandy, fop.

†fante[2] *f.* serving-girl, maidservant, maid; woman.

fant·esca *f.* damsel; †serving-maid. **†-icella** *f.* serving-maid; young girl. **-ina** *f.* little girl, child; serving-girl; *pl.* supports for a loom. **-olina** *f. dim.* little girl, baby girl.

fantoma·tico *adj.* phantom-like, elusive, difficult to find (of a person); spooky, eerie, nightmarish.

fanto·scopo *m.* phantoscope; see **fantascopo**.

fanullone *m.* See **fannullone**.

†faonare *intr.* to bring forth young.

farabolone *m.* chatterer, prattler; swindler, cheat.

farabulone *m.* See **farabolone**.

farabutto *m.* rogue, rascal; cheat, swindler, impostor; adventurer; blackguard.

far·a·d *m. indecl.*, *f. indecl.* (electr.) farad. **-ada·ico**, **-a·dico** *adj.* (electr.) faradaic. **-adizzare** [A 1] *tr.* (med.) to faradize.

faraglione *m.* tall rock resembling a column; lighthouse; (geog.) i Faraglioni di Capri, the tall column-like rocks off Capri (cf. the Needles off the Isle of Wight).

fara·ndola *f.* (mus.) farandole, a Provençal dance.

faraona *f.* (orn.) guinea-fowl.

Faraone *pr.n.m.* (hist.) Pharaoh; (fig.) arrogant ruler; kind of wine; Faro, game of chance played with cards; kind of dance.

farao·nico *adj.* (hist.) Pharaonic, of the Pharaohs, relating to the Pharaohs.

farche·tola *f.* (orn.) a kind of duck.

farciglione *m.* (orn.) a kind of waterfowl.

farcino *m.* (vet.) farcy, a disease of horses.

farc·ire [D 2] *tr.* (cul.) to stuff; (fig.) to cram, to stuff. **-ito** *part. adj.* (cul.) stuffed. **-itura** *f.* (mus.) farsing, farcing (i.e. the interpolation of a trope into a liturgical melody); farse, farce (i.e. a trope interpolated into a liturgical melody).

fard·a *f.* filthy thing; phlegm. **-are** [A 1] *tr.* (derog.) to paint; *rfl.* to make up (one's face). **-ata** *f.* blow with a dirty rag; painting of one's face; stinging remark, vilification.

fardag·gio *m.* See under **fardo**.

†fardellare *vb.* See **affardellare**.

fardello *m.* bundle, package; (fig.) burden; fare —, to pack, to pack up and go away; — di noie, pack of trouble, weight of cares; †(naut.) — di prua, forecastle; †— di poppa, poop.

fard·o *m.* large bundle, bale; paint, rouge. **-ag·gio** *m.* (naut.) dunnage; (mil.) baggage, impedimenta.

fare [B 14]:

1. *tr.* To MAKE, to create, to produce; Dio fece il mondo, God made the world; — figli, to have children; — un bambino, to have a baby; — le uova, to lay eggs; terra magra che fa poco, poor land which produces little; — frutti, to bear fruit; — piselli, to grow peas, to sow peas; tutto fa brodo, everything comes in useful; — da mangiare, to cook a meal; — un libro, to produce,

fare (*cont.*)

compile, plan, write or publish a book; — una chiesa, to build a church; due più due fa quattro, two and two make four, (fig.) obviously, it's quite clear; la fecero sposa, they married her off; lo farete orgoglioso, you will make him conceited; (naut.) — acqua, to leak, to spring a leak, to make water, (fig. of an argument) not to hold water. **2.** To DO; una domestica a tutto —, a maid of all work; ho molto da —, I have a lot to do; che stai facendo?, what are you doing?; che —?, what's to be done?; che faremo di lui?, what shall we do with (or, about) him?; farò di tutto per aiutarlo, I will do everything to help him; — affari, to do business; — il proprio dovere, to do one's duty; — i fatti suoi, to mind one's own business, to attend to one's own affairs; ne ha fatto d'ogni sorte, he has been up to all sorts of tricks; l'hai fatta bella!, now you've done it!; quand'ebbe fatto, when he had done (concluded); farla finita, to put an end to it, to have done; non c'è nulla da —, non ci si può — nulla, there's nothing to be done about it; non farne nulla, to do nothing about it; (provb.) chi la fa l'aspetti, you must expect tit for tat; — le sette chiese, to do (visit) seven churches in one day during Holy Week; — l'Austria e la Svizzera, to tour Austria and Switzerland. **3.** To PERFORM, to conduct, to carry out, to wage, to enact, to undertake; — un duetto, to perform (play) a duet; — un sequestro, to carry out a distraint; — una (la) guerra, to make (wage) war; — una legge, to enact a law; — una scoperta, to make a discovery. **4.** To AROUSE, to excite, to inspire, to cause; — orrore, to inspire horror; — compassione a, to arouse pity in; mi fa compassione, I feel sorry for him; — paura a, to frighten; gliela farò pagare, I'll make him pay for it; — del male a, to do harm to; — del bene a, to do good to, to benefit. **5.** To SAY, to remark, to utter, to interject, to let out; fece lui, said he; non ne fate parola, don't breathe a word about it; 'ahi!' fece, 'ow!' he exclaimed; — un lamento, to utter a lament; — un urlo, to let out a yell. **6.** To GIVE, to give forth, to give off; fammi un bacio, give me a kiss; gli fece una carezza, she gave him a caress; — un gesto, to make a gesture; — un sospiro, to give a sigh; — un cenno, to give a sign; — fumo, to give forth smoke; — faville, to give off sparks; faceva il sangue dalla bocca, he was bleeding from the mouth. **7.** To EXPERIENCE, to have, to harbour, to entertain; — un sogno, to have a dream; — un sospetto, to harbour a suspicion; — un desiderio, to conceive a desire; — un pensiero, to entertain a thought. **8.** To SIGNIFY, to convey, to suggest, to give the impression of; non fa niente, it doesn't matter, it is of no significance; fa lo stesso, it is all the same; (colloq.) non mi fa nè caldo nè freddo, it doesn't matter a jot to me, I couldn't care less; questa camicia fa molto Capri, this shirt conjures up Capri (i.e. is the sort of thing worn on Capri); un vestito che fa molto distinto, a dress which makes a very elegant impression; quel salotto fa molto l'Ottocento, that drawing-room is very evocative of the nineteenth century; un ristorante che fa atmosfera, a restaurant with atmosphere. **9.** To NUMBER, to contain; to fix the price of, to sell at, to amount to; la città fa 800 mila abitanti, the city has a population of 800,000; or fan dieci anni, dieci anni fa, ten years ago; quanto fa l'olio?, what is the price of oil?; quanto fanno le uova?, what are eggs fetching?; quanto fa in tutto?, what is the total?, what does it come to altogether?; a — assai, at the most; il mio orologio fa le due, it's two o'clock by my watch. **10.** To ACQUIRE, to come by, to take, to get, to develop; — eredità, to come into a legacy; — debiti, to contract debts, to get into debt; — un bagno, to take a bath; — un passo, to take a step; — un esame, to take an examination; (of a ship or locomotive) — carbone, to take on coal; (motor.) — benzina, to fill up with petrol; (naut.) — l'acqua, — l'acquata, to embark water, to water; — quattrini, to make money; ha fatto la scarlattina, he has had scarlet fever; — scuola, to acquire a following, (of a fashion) to spread; — la bocca a, to acquire a taste for, to look forward to, to smack one's lips in anticipation of; — il callo a, to become hardened to, to get used to; — foruncoli, to develop boils; (sport) — un punto, to gain a point. **11.** To SUPPOSE, to believe; lo facemmo morto, we thought he was dead; non lo facevo così sciocco, I did not think he was so foolish. **12.** OF THE WEATHER, SEASONS, ETC. to be, to turn out; fa caldo, it is hot; fa freddo, it is cold; dopo mezzo giorno fece bel tempo, in the afternoon the weather turned fine; fa la luna, the moon is up; domani fa la luna, tomorrow there will be a new moon. **13.** To WORK AS, to exercise the trade or

profession of, to lead the life of, to be, to pretend to be, to play the part of; — l'avvocato, to practise as a lawyer, to be a lawyer; vuole — il medico, he wants to become a doctor, (iron.) he likes to pretend he knows about medicine; — l'Otello, to play Othello; — la comparsa, to play a walking-on part, to be an extra (in a film); — la vita di un principe, to lead a princely existence; — il signore, to lead a life of leisure; — le veci di, to act as, to take the place of, to represent; — il sordo, to pretend to be deaf, to turn a deaf ear; — lo gnorri (l'indiano, il nesci, l'occhio di mercante), to act the simpleton; — il furbo, to try to be clever (see also 'fare da' and 'fare del', under *intr.* uses). **14.** To DO IN, to 'fix'; — un vitello, to kill a calf; (joc.) — la pelle (*or*, la festa) a, to kill; — a (in) pezzi, to tear to pieces, to rend; — a metà, to divide into two; — la testa a, to cut off the head of; — l'ora, to kill time (until an appointment is due) (e.g. — l'ora della partenza del treno). **15.** FOLL. BY INFIN.: to make, to compel (to), to cause (to); lo feci andare, I made him go; mi fece aspettare, he kept me waiting; gli feci apportare il libro, I made him fetch the book; ci hanno fatto pagare il doppio, they made us pay double; egli la fece condannare a morte, he caused her to be condemned to death; devo farmi tagliare i capelli, I must get my hair cut. **16.** FOLL. BY SUBJUNCT.: — che, to contrive that, to see to it that, to give orders that, to arrange that; fece sì che l'altro non partisse, he saw to it that the other person did not leave. **17.** *intr.* (*aux.* avere) To DO; faccia pure!, please do!, by all means!, go ahead!; — per tre, to do the work of three; — bene, to do well, to do right, to do good; — male, to do badly, to do wrong; avere da —, to have a lot to do; farebbe meglio a partire, he would do better to leave; farne senza, farne a meno, to do without (it); — da capo, to begin again; avere da — con, to have to deal with; non avrò niente a che — con lui, I won't have anything to do with him; il saper —, know-how, technical skill, expert knowledge; non fa che piangere, he does nothing but cry; fai fai, finalmente gli è riuscita, by dint of repetition at last he managed it; come si fa ad essere così grullo?, how can anyone be so foolish? **18.** To BEHAVE, to act; fece sì che, he acted in such a way that; — a tempo, to act in time; lasciar —, to leave alone, to let things take their course; (econ.) il lasciar —, laisser-faire. **19.** To COMPETE, to fight, to play; — a pugni, to come to blows; — a chi arriva prima, to compete for first place, to race; — a gara a, to compete with; — a mosca cieca, to play hide and seek; — alla neve, to play at snowballing; — a confidenza con, to take liberties with. **20.** To GROW, to thrive, to abound, to ripen; l'ulivo non fa nelle regioni alte, the olive does not thrive at high altitudes. **21.** To BE SUITABLE, to work, to be useful or helpful; ciò non fa per me, that is no use to me; guarda se ti fa questo, see if this suits you. **22.** FARE DA, to play the part of, to act as, to undertake the role of; gli fece da mamma, she was a mother to him; — da podestà, to represent the mayor. **23.** FARE DEL, to pretend to be; — dello scemo, to pretend to be stupid. **24.** *rfl.* (*acc.* of *prn.* 'si') To BECOME; farsi prete, to become a priest; farsi sposa, to get married; farsi madre, to become a mother; farsi avanti, to get ahead, to step forward; farsi bello, to beautify oneself, to improve in looks; come s'è fatta bella quella ragazza!, how pretty that girl has grown!; farsi bello dei meriti altrui, to take the credit for other people's work; farsi nuovo di, to pretend not to know about; (*dat.* of *prn.* 'si') farsi coraggio, to take courage; farsi meraviglia, to marvel; farsi ragione, to seek to justify oneself; farsi una ragione, to resign oneself; farsi ragione di sè, to take the law into one's own hands; farsi strada, to make headway, to get ahead; farsi largo, to clear a space before one. **25.** *n.m.* DOING, making; il da —, business, things to be done; ha il suo da — anche lei, she too has her hands full. For uses of **fare** in phrases not represented above see under another item, e.g. 'fare il fieno', see under **fieno**; 'farsi la barba', see under **barba**; 'fare di cappello', see under **cappello**; 'fare all'amore', see under **amore**, etc.

†**fare·a** *f.* (myth.) kind of serpent which moves upright with its tail on the ground.

faretr-a *f.* quiver; (fig. poet.) weapons of attack; †uscir di —, to go out into the world. **-ato** *adj.* bearing a quiver, quiver-bearing, provided with a quiver.

farfall-a *f.* (ent.) butterfly; moth; (zool.) -e di mare, pteropods (pelagic molluscs); (ichth.) pesce —, butterfly blenny, *Blennius ocellaris*; (fig.) thoughtless person, a scatterbrain; bow-tie;

farfall-a (*cont.*)
(swimming) butterfly stroke; (eng.) valvola a —, throttle valve; (motor.) aprire la —, to open the throttle. **-amento** *m.* (motor.) floating (of valve); wobble (of wheels). **-ętta** *f. dim.* (ent.) small butterfly; (fig.) whim; *pl.* (ent.) *Microlepidoptera.* **-ino** *m. dim.* (ent.) small butterfly; (fig.) ornament, adornment; butterfly, scatterbrain, light-hearted person; †scrap of paper (e.g. bill or summons). **-ista** *m., f.* (sport) swimmer using butterfly stroke. **-one** *m.* (ent.) large butterfly; (fig.) flighty person, gadabout; blunder; tall story; phlegm.

farfan-ic·chio *m.* (*pl.* **-ic·chi**) fop; whipper-snapper.

far·far-a *f.*, **-o** *m.* (bot.) colt's foot, *Tussilago farfara.*

farfarac·cio *m.* (bot.) butterbur, *Petasites hybridus.*

farfarello *m.* devil; little devil, fidgety boy; fop.

far·faro *m.* (bot.). See under **farfara**.

far·fero *m.* (bot.). See **farfara**.

fargna *f.* (bot.). See **farnia**.

farin-a *f.* flour; meal; powder; fior di —, fine flour; — d'avena, oatmeal; — gialla, maize-meal; — di riso, ground rice; — lattea, dried milk powder; (fig.) — del proprio sacco, one's own work; la — del diavolo va tutta in crusca, the wicked never prosper; le chiacchiere non fan —, talking gets you nowhere. **-ac·cio** *m. pejor.* sweepings of flour (after making bread); wood made powdery by worms; (bot.) whitebeam, *Sorbus aria*; fat hen, *Chenopodium album.* **-a·ceo** *adj.* farinaceous; like flour; *n.m.* farinaceous plant; starchy food; ingrassa perchè mangia troppi **-acei**, he puts on weight because he eats too many starchy foods. **-a·io** *m.* flour-container; flour-store. **-ai(u)ola** *f.* platter of flour (on which food is covered with flour before being cooked). **-ai(u)olo** *m.* flour-merchant, miller. **-ata** *f.* pap; soup mixed with milk and flour; **-ata** d'avena, oatmeal porridge. †**-ello** *m.* rogue; evil person. **-oso** *adj.* farinaceous; floury, powdery, like flour; neve **-osa**, powdery snow.

faring-e *f.* (anat.) pharynx. **-ite** *f.* (med.) pharyngitis. **-osco·pio** *m.* (med.) pharyngoscope. **-otomi·a** *f.* (med.) pharyngotomy.

farin·geo *adj.* (anat.) pharyngeal.

fariṣ-a·ico *adj.* pharisaic, pharisaical; false, hypocritical. **-aicamente** *adv.* pharisaically; hypocritically. **-ai·ṣmo** *m.* pharisaism; religious hypocrisy. **-e·o** *m.* Pharisee; hypocrite; *adj.* pharisaic; hypocritical. **-eiṣmo** *m.* pharisaism; hypocrisy.

farmace·ut-ica *f.* pharmaceutics; pharmaceutical department. **-ico** *adj.* pharmaceutical. †**-ri·a** *f.* witch, sorceress.

farmac-i·a *f.* chemist's shop; chemist's dispensary; pharmacy; pharmaceutical preparation; vaso da —, apothecary pot. **-ista** *m.* pharmacist, chemist; prescrizione dei **-isti**, prescription of chemists' right to sue for price of medicines.

far·ma-co *m.* (*pl.* **-chi**, **-ci**) drug; medicine; remedy; poison. **-codina·mica** *f.* pharmacodynamics. **-cognoṣi·a** *f.* pharmacognosy. **-colite** *f.* (miner.) pharmacolite. **-cologi·a** *f.* pharmacology. **-cope·a** *f.* pharmacopoeia. †**-co·pola** *m.* pharmacist.

farnetic-are [A2s] *intr.* (*aux.* avere) to rave, to be delirious; to talk wildly. **-amento** *m.* raving; delirium. **-ante** *part. adj.* raving, delirious.

†**farne·tico** *m.* raving, delirium; madness; dare in —, to rave; to become delirious; madman; person in delirium.

far·nia *f.* (bot.) oak, *Quercus robur* and *Q. petraea.*

faro *m.* lighthouse, beacon; (fig.) beacon, guide; strait (of the sea); (motor.) headlight, headlamp; — antinebbia, fog-lamp; — anti-abbagliante, anti-dazzle lamp; mettere i fari antiabbaglianti, to dip one's headlights; (aeron.) — d'aeroporto, airport beacon; — di atterraggio, landing light; (naut.) light; lighthouse; light-beacon; — galleggiante, lightship, lightboat.

farra·gin-e *f.* mixed fodder; (fig.) farrago, medley, hotchpotch, jumble. †**-atore** *m.* writer of hotchpotch work. **-oso** *adj.* muddled, confused, jumbled; cumbersome; unnecessarily complicated, involved; libro **-oso**, book cluttered with unorganized material.

farro *m.* (bot.) spelt, *Triticum spelta*; — piccolo, einkorn, *T. monococcum.*

fars-a *f.* (theatr.) farce; (fig.) mockery, buffoonery; (hist. theatr.) trope; †padding, cloth filled with stuffing. †**-ata** *f.* lining of a doublet; pad; padding of a helmet. **-esco** *adj.* (m.pl. **-eschi**) farcical.

farṣętt-o *m.* doublet, peasant's short jacket; wooden component of a drum; (mil. hist.) — a maglia, quilted coat; †(fig.) trarre la

bambagia dal — a, to weaken, to debilitate. †**-a·io** *m.* doublet-maker.

fas *m. indecl.* per — o per nefas, by hook or by crook, in any way possible.

†**faṣano** *m.* See **fagiano**.

faṣatura *f.* See under **fase²**.

fascerello *m. dim.* See under **fascio**.

fascętt-a *f. dim.* of **fascia**, q.v.; small band; corset; paper band round a newly published book bearing some special blurb; (techn.) clip; hose clamp; (motor.) — della balestra, spring clip; (mil.) hoop (of a firearm barrel); see **collarino**; *pl.* hoop-staves (of a sword scabbard); (archit.) bars on a medal or decoration (stamped with the date or commemorative occasion). **-a·ia** *f.* corset-maker.

fascętto *m. dim.* of **fascio**, q.v.; small bundle; (anat.) — di nervi, fascicle.

fa·sci-a *f.* band; bandage; *pl.* swaddling clothes; (fig.) un bambino in fasce, an infant in arms; ancora in fasce, still in infancy; wrapper, wrapping paper; spedire sotto —, to send under cover; belt, order of chivalry; (eccl.) sash; (anat.) fascia; (archit.) fascia; (naut.) canvas sail-cover; (mil.) — fortificata, fortified belt or zone; reinforced ring or band on a gun; (eng.) band; (radio) — di frequenza, frequency band; (motor.) — elastica, piston ring; — elastica di tenuta, compression ring; — elastica raschiaolio, scraper ring; (herald.) fess; — ondata, fess undy, fess wavy; interzato in —, tierced fesswise; *pl.* (mus.) ribs of a violin; (geog., Liguria) terraces cut in rock; (mil.) fasce gambiere, puttees. **-acca** *f.* sash. **-ale** *m.* (anat.) sartorius muscle.

fasciacoda *f.* band used for tying up a horse's tail.

fasciame *m.* (naut.) hull plating, planks of a wooden ship; — affrontato, butt strapped plating; — accavallato, clinker built; — abbrumato, wormeaten.

fasciapiede *m.* strap fastening a horse's foot to prevent kicking.

fasci-are *tr.* [A3] to bandage; to swathe; to bind up; — una ferita, to bind up a wound; to surround, to fortify; (naut.) to serve (a rope). **-ato** *part. adj.* bound; bandaged; swathed; (herald.) barry; **-ato** di 4 pezzi, barry of 4 pieces. **-atura** *f.* bandaging; swathing; dressing (of a wound); bandage, dressing; belt; (naut.) serving on a rope.

fasci·col-o *m.* part, number, issue (of a publication); little book, booklet; folder, file; (leg.) file of documents, set of papers in a case; — d'ufficio, the record (of the Court; of an action); — dell'esecuzione, record of execution of a judgement (C.C.P.). **-ato** *adj.* (bot.) fasciated.

fascin-a *f.* bundle of sticks, faggot; bonfire; (mil.) timber or wattle buttressing, earthwork support; — incendiaria, incendiary faggot; †handkerchief. **-a·ia** *f.* wood-pile, wood-store. **-a·io** *m.* firewood merchant; man selling faggots. **-ame** *m.* firewood; faggots. **-are** [A1] *tr.* (mil.) to buttress. **-ata** *f.* (mil.) assembled quantity of strengthening materials; (naut.) quantity of fascines or bundles of rods used to support an earthwork along a river bank or dock wall. **-ato** *part. adj.* (mil.) buttressed. **-e** *f.* (naut.) see **fardaggio**, under **fardo**. **-otto** *m.* small bundle of sticks (for fire-lighting).

fascinare¹ [A1]. See under **fascina**.

fascinare² [A1s]. See under **fascino²**.

fa·scin-o¹ *m.* fascination; charm; spell; esercitare il —, to exercise charm; provare il — di, to be fascinated by; subire il — di, to be spellbound by; (archaeol.) fertility symbol used as a charm. **-are** [A1s] *tr.* to fascinate, to charm (cf. **affascinare**). **-atore** *m.* fascinator, charmer; *adj.* fascinating, charming. (**-atrice** *f.*) **-azione** *f.* fascination; charm; sorcery. **-oso** *adj.* (neol.) fascinating, charming.

†**fascino²** *m.* See **fascina**.

fascinotto *m.* See under **fascina**.

fa·sci-o *m.* bundle; burden, weight; group, grouping; jest, sport; andare in —, to go to pieces, to fall in ruins; mettere in —, to confound, to muddle, to fail to distinguish; fare d'ogni erba —, to mix good and bad, to treat everything alike, to lead a dissolute life; (phys.; opt.) — luminoso, — di luce, beam of light; (radio) beam; — catodico, cathode beam; antenna a —, beam aerial; (rlwy.) — di scambi, group of points; (eng.) — di linee di forza, tube of force; (Rom. hist.) fasces; (Ital. hist.) name of a political group of Sicilian sulphur workers (1890); labour group; i Fasci parlamentari, representatives of labour groups in the Italian government (1914–18); name of a political group organized on

fascio (*cont.*)
military lines founded by Benito Mussolini (1919); i Fasci di Combattimento, the members of the Fascist Party who took part in the Revolution of 1922; symbol, badge or heraldic device representing Italian Fascism; Casa del Fascio, Fascist Party H.Q.

Fascioda *pr.n.f.* (geog.) Fashoda.

fasc·ismo *m.* (Ital. hist.) Fascism; (pol.) Fascism or tendencies towards it in other countries; (leg.) apologia del —, defence and justification of Fascism (C.P.). **-ista** *m., f., adj.* Fascist; (leg.) repressione dell'attività -ista, suppression of Fascism (C.P.).

fasci(u)ola *f.* small band, bandage.

faṣ-e¹ *f.* phase, period; stage; cycle; (phys.) phase; — dispersa, dispersed phase; (electr.) phase; concordanza di —, phase coincidence; discordanza di —, phase difference; fuori —, out-of-phase; (watchm.) bascula delle -i, moon phase yoke; (motor.) stroke; — di aspirazione, inlet stroke, induction stroke; — di scarico, exhaust stroke; fuori —, faultily timed; mettere in —, to time; messa in —, timing; (cinem.) period; — di oscurazione, obscuring period. **-atura** *f.* (motor.) timing.

faṣe² *m.* (Jewish rel.) Passover.

faṣelo *m.* (naut.) small pleasure craft.

faṣianella *f.* (zool.) small brightly coloured marine shell, *Phasianella* spp.

faṣo·metro *m.* (phys.; electr.) phasemeter, phase indicator.

fasservizi *m. indecl.* servant-boy, errand-boy; go-between.

fassi·mile *m.* See **facsi·mile**.

fastell-o *m.* bundle; faggot; plump child; (naut.) packing; strengthening of dikes or earthworks; (text.) — di lino, strick (of flax). **-ac·cio** *m. pejor.* big, untidy bundle; big, unattractive person. **-one** *m. augm.* big man.

fasti *m.pl.* (Rom. antiq.) Fasti; records, annals, memorials.

†fastidiare *tr.* to trouble; to annoy; *rfl.* to be troubled; to be annoyed; to be put to annoyance.

fasti·di-o *m.* trouble, annoyance, worry; affliction, irritation; nausea, repugnance, disgust; dare — a, to annoy; smetti, mi dai —!, do stop, you're getting on my nerves!; pigliare uno in —, to take a dislike to someone. **-osag·gine** *f.* troublesomeness; trouble, vexation, annoyance. **-oso** *adj.* troublesome, annoying, trying; importunate; nauseating; fastidious, sensitive, difficult to satisfy. (**-osamente** *adv.*) **†-ire** *vb.* and derivs. see **infastidire**. **-ume** *m.* load of trouble; pack of worries; †filth; †ugliness.

†fastiggiare *rfl.* to be nauseated.

fasti·gio *m.* pinnacle, coping; (fig.) crowning feature; height; giungere ai più alti fastigi, to reach great heights.

fasto¹ *adj.* propitious, favourable.

fast-o² *m.* pomp, splendour; magnificence; display, ostentation. **-osità** *f.* pomp, splendour; pageantry; sumptuous clothes; luxury. **-oso** *adj.* sumptuous, splendid; gorgeous; luxurious; ostentatious. **-osamente** *adv.* sumptuously; gorgeously; luxuriously; ostentatiously.

faṣullo *adj.* fake, bogus.

fat-a *f.* fairy; paese delle -e, fairyland; racconti delle -e, fairy-tales; la — Morgana, Morgan fée, (fig.) mirage, will o' the wisp, woman who lives in close seclusion; una buona —, a good fairy, (fig.) a kind and helpful friend; (bot.) lino delle -e, esparto grass, *Stipa pinnata*; pianta delle -e, white bryony, *Bryonia alba*; †*pl.* of **fato**, q.v. **-eri·a** *f.* fairy-tale.

fatal-e *adj.* fatal; fated; destined; fateful; deadly, mortal; disastrous; colpo —, fatal blow, mortal blow; è — che, it is inevitable that; donna —, *femme fatale*; vamp; *n.m.pl.* (comm.) days of grace; lo scadere dei -i, the expiration of the time limit. **-mente** *adv.* fatally; fatefully; disastrously. **-ismo** *m.* fatalism. **-ista** *m., f.* fatalist; *adj.* fatalistic. **-ità** *f.* fatalness; disastrousness; fatality; fate, destiny; calamity, fatal event; mishap; witchery. **-ona** *f.* (Tusc., joc.) vamp. **-one** *m.* (Tusc., joc.) lady-killer.

†fatap·pio *m.* unidentified kind of bird.

fat-are [A I] *tr.* to bewitch, to enchant; to cast a spell on; to charm. **-amento** *m.* bewitching, bewitchment; destiny, fortune. **-ato** *part. adj.* bewitched; under a spell; enchanted; invulnerable; fairy. **-atura** *f.* enchantment; witchcraft, sorcery. **†-agione**, **†-azione** *f.* bewitchment; spell; sorcery.

fatebenefratelli, **fate-bene-fratelli** *m.pl.* (eccl.) Brothers of St John of God. **-bene-sorelle** *f.pl.* (eccl.) Sisters of St John of God.

fatica *f.* toil, hard work, labour, effort; vivere col frutto della —, to live by the sweat of one's brow; trouble, hardship, travail;

ingrata —, drudgery; fatigue, weariness; difficulty; camminare con —, to walk wearily, with dragging footsteps; respirare a gran —, to have laboured breathing, to breathe with difficulty; le fatiche d'Ercole, the labours of Hercules; — sprecata, waste of time, waste of breath; buttar via la —, to labour in vain; avere — a intendere, to have difficulty in understanding; dura — a pagare, he finds it difficult to pay; non reggersi, cascare dalla —, to be dropping with fatigue; uomo di —, servant for rough and heavy work; odd-job man for heavy work.

fatic-are [A 2] *intr.* (*aux.* avere) to work hard, to make an effort, to strive; to have difficulty; — ad intendere, to have difficulty in understanding; *rfl.* to work hard; to get tired; to strive; †*tr.* see **affaticare**. **-ante** *part. adj.* hard-working, active; wearying, tiring, laborious. **-ata** *f.* (Tusc.) effort; fare una -ata, to put in some hard work, to make a prolonged strenuous effort. **-ato** *part. adj.* weary, tired; troubled, annoyed.

†fatiche·vole *adj.* tiring; tiresome, wearisome; laborious; hard to bear.

faticoṣ-o *adj.* hard, difficult, laborious; troublesome, trying; tiring, wearying; tired, weary; lavoro —, hard work, tiring work. **-amente** *adv.* with difficulty; laboriously.

fati·dic-o *adj.* prophetic; destined, fateful. (**-amente** *adv.*)

fatiga *f.* (metall.) fatigue; †see **fatica**.

†fatigare *vb.* and derivs. See **faticare**.

fatiscenza *f.* disintegration.

fato *m.* fate, destiny, lot; death, doom; †parlare a —, to tell the future, to prognosticate.

fatt-a¹ *f.* sort, kind; action; gente d'ogni —, people of every sort; male -e, wicked deeds. **-amente** *adv.* sì -amente, in this way, in such wise; †actually, in effect.

fatta² *f.* droppings, spoor, trail of dung.

fattac·cio *m. pejor.* of **fatto²**, q.v.

fattapposta *adj. indecl.* purpose-made, made to customer's own design.

fatt-arello, **-erello** *m.* See under **fatto²**.

†fatte·vole *adj.* See **fattibile**.

fattezz-e *f.pl.* features; figure; appearance; charms. †-**a** *f. sing.* form, shape, figure.

†fatti·a *f.* sorcery, witchcraft.

†fattibello *m.* make-up, rouge, cosmetics.

fatti·bile *adj.* practicable; possible, feasible; realizable; *n.m.* possibility; what can be done; il —, that which can be put into effect; farò tutto il —, I'll do all that is possible.

fatticchiare [A 4] *tr.* to keep on doing; to do half-heartedly; to do incompletely.

fattic·cio *adj.* (Tusc.) thickset, robust, burly.

fatticello *m. dim.* See under **fatto²**.

fattiṣpe·cie *f. indecl.* case, instance; (leg.) the case in issue, present case.

fatt-itivo *adj.* factitive. **-ivo** *adj.* effective, efficacious; active, busy, energetic; una persona -iva, a person who gets things done, a person with drive. **-i·zio** *adj.* artificial, factitious; insincere.

fatt-o¹ *part.* of **fare**, q.v.; *adj.* done; è presto —, it is soon done; made; — a mano, handmade; — a macchina, machine made; abiti -i, ready-made clothes; bell'e —, ready-made; constructed; produced; formed; composed; ripe, mature; harvested; cooked; satiated; exhausted; drunk; suitable; nato —, made for it, born to it; è donna -a, she is a grown woman; uomo —, grown man, adult; un uomo — e messo lì, a plain man; tanto —, as big as this; a notte -a, when it is quite dark; a giorno —, in broad daylight; a conti -i, on the whole, when the account is settled; detto —, no sooner said than done; non è — per te, it doesn't suit you; se ti vien — di, if you happen to, if you manage to; (comm.) le condizioni -eci, your terms; †long past.

fatt-o² *m.* fact; action, act, deed; event, occurrence; — compiuto, *fait accompli*; alterare i -i, to distort the truth, to twist the evidence; mettere uno al corrente del —, to acquaint someone with the facts; — di cronaca, news item; affair, business; story, tale; plot; il — si svolge a, the story is laid in; raccontami il —, tell me what happened; -i, non parole, deeds, not words; i -i di casa, domestic matters; cogliere sul —, to catch in the act; — di sangue, murder, murderous assault; — d'arme, encounter, engagement; dopo il —, after the event; badare ai -i suoi, to mind one's own business; sapere il — suo, to know one's business; dire il — suo, to speak a piece of one's mind, to speak out; fare il — suo,

fatt-o (*cont.*)
to look after one's own interests; torniamo al —, let's get back to the subject; venire al —, to come to the point; in — di, in the matter of, as regards; — sta che, the fact is that, the point is that; di —, in —, in fact; non ci credo gran —, I haven't much belief in it; (leg.) act; fact; — dannoso, act causing damage; giudizio sul —, finding of fact; in — ed in diritto, in fact and law; in linea di —, in point of fact; vie di —, violent means; motivo di —, point of fact; — del terzo, act of a third party; *pl.* -i illeciti, unlawful acts (C.C.). -ac·cio *m. pejor.* evil deed, crime of violence. -arello, -erello *m. dim.* insignificant matter, minor episode; anecdote, little tale. -icello *m. dim.* small matter, trifle, little thing.

fattoi-o *m.* oil-press (for olives); place where oil is extracted. -ano *m.* oil-press worker.

fattor-e *m.* maker, creator; farm-bailiff, land-agent, steward; (Scot.) factor; farmer; (leg.) i poteri dei -i di campagna, the powers of farm-bailiffs (C.C.); (math.) factor, element; — dominante, leading factor. -essa *f.* woman employed by the owner of a 'fattoria' to do the house-keeping and cooking and look after the poultry and dairy; farmer's wife. -i·a *f.* farm, country estate; farmhouse; central farm-buildings of an estate; office of a farmer, farm-bailiff or land-agent. -iale *adj.* (math.) factorial. -ino *m.* errand-boy, office-boy; messenger, telegraph-boy; support for knitting-needle; tripod of a turnspit; cane for supporting a vine; clothes-peg, clothes-rack; handle of a stone-mason's saw; †paper weight.

fattotum *m. indecl.* See **factotum**.

fattrice *f.* brood-mare; mother cat; brood-bitch.

fattucchiara *f.* See **fattucchiera**.

fattucchier-a *f.* witch, sorceress. -e *m.* wizard, sorcerer. -i·a *f.* witchcraft, sorcery; intrigue, fraud.

fattur-a *f.* make; making; la — di questo abito m'ha portato via tre giorni, it has taken me three days to make this dress; work, workmanship, craftsmanship; creation; witchcraft, sorcery, enchantment; lavorante a —, piece-worker; (comm.) invoice; come da —, as per invoice; libro copia -e, invoice-book; (leg.) obbligo di conservazione delle -e, duty to preserve invoices (C.C.); †features, appearance. -are [A I] *tr.* to adulterate (esp. wine); to concoct (a potion); to manipulate; to bewitch, to cast a spell on; to work accurately, to form carefully; (comm.) to invoice; to charge for; me l'ha -ato mille lire, he charged me a thousand lire for it. -ato *part. adj.* (comm.) invoiced; *n.m.* (comm.) proceeds of sales; invoiced amount; turnover; (rubber indust.) substitute. -azione *f.* (comm.) invoicing. -ista *m., f.* (comm.) invoice clerk.

†fatturo *adj.* destined to make; essere —, to be destined to make, to be on the point of doing.

fattutto *m. indecl.* See **fatutto**.

fatu-amente *adv.*, **-ità** *f.* See under **fatuo**.

fa·tu-o *adj.* fatuous; vain, conceited; empty-headed; frivolous; foolish, silly; stupid; thoughtless; fuoco —, will o' the wisp; *n.m.* stupid individual. -amente *adv.* fatuously; foolishly; thoughtlessly. -ità *f.* fatuity, fatuousness; foolishness; stupidity; thoughtlessness.

fatutto *m. indecl.* busybody.

fa·uci *f.pl.* throat, gullet; mouth, opening; le — del leone, the lion's maw.

†fa·ula *f.* See **favola**.

Fa·una[1] *pr.n.f.* (Rom. myth.) the nymph Fauna.

fa·un-a[2] *f.* (zool.) fauna. -i·stica *f.* the study of the fauna of a certain region. -i·stico *adj.* relating to fauna.

fa·unico *adj.* faun-like, satyr-like.

Fa·un-o *pr.n.m.* (Rom. myth.) Faunus; faun; satyr. -esco *adj.* (*m.pl.* -eschi) faun-like, orecchi -eschi, pointed ears like a satyr's.

Fa·ust *pr.n.m.* Faust; il — di Goethe, Goethe's *Faust*. -iano *adj.* relating to Goethe's *Faust*.

Fa·ust-o[1] *pr.n.m.* (myth.) Faustus; also a Christian name. (-a *pr.n.f.*).

fa·ust-o[2] *adj.* propitious; lucky, fortunate; happy; il — evento, (periphrasis for a royal birth), the propitious event. -amente *adv.* propitiously; luckily; happily.

faut-ore *m.* favourer, supporter, follower, adherent. (-rice *f.*)

fav-a *f.* (bot.) (broad) bean, *Vicia faba*; (pharm.) — di Sant'Ignazio, ignatia; trifle, insignificant thing; prendere due piccioni ad una —, *or* pigliare due colombi ad una —, to kill two birds with one stone; -e dei morti, sweetmeats sold on All Souls' Day; (vet.)

germe di —, the 'mark' on the incisor teeth, by means of which the age of a horse can be determined; (hist.) white or black stone (formerly a bean) by means of which affirmative or negative votes were cast (e.g. in Conclave); †mettere alle -e, to put to the vote; (vulg.) penis. -ag·gine *m.* (bot.) bean caper, *Zygophyllum fabago*. -a·io *m.* bean-field. -aiolo *m.* (bot.) see **favagello**. -ata *f.* dish of beans; bean soup; braggadocio, haughtiness. -azzo *m.* (orn.) wood pigeon. -erella, -etta *f.* bean-meal, bean-pottage; wiseacre. -eto *m.* bean-field. -one *m.* braggadocio; swaggerer; wiseacre; fool, blockhead. -uc·cia *f.* (bot.) small kind of bean.

favagello *m.* (bot.) lesser celandine, pilewort, *Ranunculus ficaria*.

†favalena *f.* See **falena**.

favell-a *f.* speech; language, tongue, dialect, idiom; il dono della —, the gift of tongues; perdere la —, *or* perdere l'uso della —, to be struck dumb, to become speechless. (-amento *m.* -ante *part. adj.*) -are [A I] *tr.* to speak, to tell; *intr.* (*aux.* avere) to speak, to converse, to talk, to discourse; *n.m.* speech, discourse. (-atore *m.* -atrice *f.*) †-atura *f.* particular language, specific tongue. -io *m.* prattle, gossip; loquacity, garrulity.

†favente *adj.* propitious, favourable.

faveto *m.* and other derivs. See under **fava**.

favill-a *f.* spark; mandare, fare -e, to give off sparks; glimmer; light, gleam; glow; non c'è una — di fuoco, there isn't a glimmer of light; (prov.) poca — gran fiamma seconda (Dante, *Para.* I), cf. Eng. 'great events from trivial causes spring'. †-are *vb.* and derivs. see **sfavillare**. -ettine *f.pl.* (med.) red spots round the eyes. †-o *m.* splendour, brightness.

favisse *f.pl.* (Rom. antiq.) *favissae*, vaults under a temple.

fav-o *m.* honeycomb; (ent.) honey or brood comb of bees; (motor.) radiator; (med.) anthrax; crop of boils; malignant pustule. -oso *adj.* like a honeycomb; (med.) tigna -osa, anthrax.

fa·vol-a *f.* fable, apologue; play, drama; fiction, invention, myth; plot, story, theme; triviality, idle tale; laughing-stock; essere la — del paese, to be the laughing-stock of the village. -ac·cia *f. pejor.* lie; crude fable. -a·io *m.* fable-writer, story-teller, fabulist. †-are *adj.* fabulous, legendary.

favol-are [A I S] *intr.* (*aux.* avere) to tell stories, to relate fables; †to speak. -ata *f.* chatter, empty talk. -atore *m.* fable-writer; story-teller; chatterbox; chatterer. (-atrice *f.*) -evole *adj.* fabulous, fictitious, legendary. (-evolmente *adv.*) -one *m.* gossip, idle talker.

favolegg-iare [A 3 C] *intr.* (*aux.* avere) to tell fables or tales; to write stories, to describe fictitious things; to speak, to talk, to chat. -iamento *m.* fiction, invention; story, plot. -iatore *m.* narrator, story-teller; teller of tall stories. (-iatrice *f.*)

favolello *m.* (lit. hist.) fabliau.

favol-esco *adj.* (*m.pl.* -eschi) fantastic, improbable; like a fairy-tale.

†favo·lico *adj.* See **favolesco** or **favoloso**.

favollo *m.* (zool.) *Eriphia spinifrons*, an edible crab.

favolos-o *adj.* fabulous, mythical, mythological; fictitious, legendary; wonderful; incredible, exaggerated; prezzi -i, fabulous, exorbitant prices. -amente *adv.* fabulously. -ità *f.* fabulosity, fabulousness, fictitiousness, fictitious nature.

†favomele *m.* honeycomb.

favonio *m.* west wind, zephyr.

†favorare *vb.* and derivs. See **favorire**.

favore *m.* favour, kindness; aid, assistance; goodwill, approval; sympathy, affection; partiality, bias; chiedere un —, to ask a favour; contraccambiare un —, to return a favour; per —, please; a — di, on behalf of; lotteria a — dei ciechi, lottery in aid of the blind; condizioni di —, preferential terms; col — delle tenebre, under cover of darkness; venire in — di alcuno, to win someone's favour; biglietto di —, entrata di —, complimentary ticket; (comm.) assegno bancario a — di una persona determinata, an order cheque; assegno bancario a — del portatore, a bearer cheque; cambiale di —, accommodation bill; prezzo di —, special price; firma di —, *pro forma* signature.

favoregg-iare [A 3 C] *tr.* to aid and abet; to harbour, to protect; to support; — una congiura, to be involved in a conspiracy. -iamento *m.* favour, aid, support; (leg.) abetting, encouragement (e.g. of prostitution); -iamento personale, harbouring, giving aid or comfort to (a criminal) after the fact; -iamento reale, aiding of criminal to secure the proceeds of his crime (C.P.). -iante *part. adj.* favourable; *n.m.* favourer, supporter. -iato *part. adj.* supported; enjoying support; favoured. -iatore *m.* favourer, supporter, accomplice; (leg.) abettor; accessory; -iatore di un

favoregg-iare (*cont.*)

furto, accessory to a theft. (**-iatrice** *f.*) †**-e·vole** *adj.* favouring, supporting, in favour, favourable.

favor-ire [D 2] *tr.* to favour; to encourage, to assist, to protect, to promote; — il commercio, to promote trade; to approve, to support; — un partito, to support a political party; to give; mi ha -ito un fiore, he has given me a flower; vuoi -irmi il temperino?, would you please lend me your penknife?; vuoi —?, will you come in?, please help yourself; -ite dirgli che l'aspetto, be so good as to tell him that I am waiting for him. **-evole** *adj.* favourable; propitious. **-evolmente** *adj.* favourably; propitiously. **-ita** *f.* favourite; favourite woman; royal mistress. **-itismo** *m.* favouritism, partiality. **-ito** *part. adj.* favoured; favourite; -ito dalla fortuna, favoured by fortune; libro -ito, favourite book; *n.m.* favourite; beloved; darling; pet; (sport) favourite (in horse-racing); *pl.* favoris, side-whiskers.

favoscello *m.* (bot.). See **favagello**.

favule *m.* haulm, dried bean-stalks; bean-field; bean manure.

fa·zio *m.* simpleton, fool.

†**faziona·rio** *m.* adherent, supporter.

†**fazionato** *adj.* fashioned, made.

fazion-e *f.* faction, party, sect; (mil.) action (more than a skirmish, less than a battle); †kind, guise, sort, manner. †**-iere** *m.* adherent, supporter.

fazios-o *adj.* factious, turbulent, seditious, subversive; *n.m.* agitator, rebel, subversive element. **-amente** *adv.* turbulently; subversively.

fazzoletto *m.* handkerchief; kerchief, head-scarf; — da collo, scarf, neckerchief; (fig.) grande quanto un —, about the size of a handkerchief; possedere un — di terra, to own a little square of land; (eng.) gusset plate.

†**fazz-olo**, †**-uolo** *m.* See **fazzoletto**.

†**fazzone** *f.* faction; aspect, appearance; manner.

fè *f.* (poet.) See **fede**.

fe' abbrev. of **fece**, *3rd sing. past def.* of **fare**, q.v. (sometimes used for euphony, as in 'fe' cenno', instead of 'fece cenno').

†**Feba** *pr.n.f.* See **Febe**.

Febbra·io *pr.n.m.* February.

†**Febbraro** *pr.n.m.* See **Febbraio**.

febbr-e *f.* fever; excitement; burning desire; la — dell'oro, the passion for gold, the gold-rush; (med.) high temperature; avere la —, to have a temperature; è cessato la —, his temperature has gone down; la — gialla, yellow fever; la — del fieno, hay-fever; una — da cavalli, a violent fever, a high fever; *pl.* malaria. **-icante** *part. adj.* feverish. **-icità** *f.* feverishness. **-icitare** [A I s] *intr.* (*aux.* avere) to have a fever, to be feverish. **-icitante** *part. adj.* feverish, suffering from a fever, in a feverish state; febrile. **-icoso** *adj.* feverish; apt to cause fever. **-i·fero**, **-i·fico** *adj.* apt to cause fever, fever-bearing. **-ifu·gio** *m.* febrifuge. **-i·fugo** *adj.* (*pl.* -i·fughi) febrifuge, anti-febrile, medicine which brings down fever. **-ile** *adj.* feverish, febrile. **-ilmente** *adv.* feverishly.

Febe *pr.n.f.* Phoebe; (myth.) the Moon.

Feb-o *pr.n.m.* (myth.) Phoebus. **-e·o** *adj.* Phoebean, of Phoebus.

†**febre** *f.* See **febbre**.

fecale *adj.* See under **feci**.

fec·ci-a *f.* dregs, lees, grounds, sediment; (fig.) bere il calice sino alla —, to drink the cup to the bitter dregs; rabble, scum; la — del popolo, the scum of society; (bot.) fumitory, *Fumaria*; *pl.* faeces. **-a·ia** *f.* spigot-hole (in a cask), vent. **-a·io** *adj.* spina -aia, spigot (in a cask). **-oso** *adj.* full of dregs; dreggish, dreggy; foul, base; impure. **-ume** *m.* dregs, lees; refuse; (fig.) scum, rabble.

fec·cio *m.* deep, oblong chest used for packing sugar.

fec-i *f.pl.* faeces, excrement, stools. **-ale** *adj.* faecal.

feciale *adj.* fetial.

fe·col-a *f.* (chem.) fecula; — di patate, potato flour; (paperm.) — acetilata, feculose. **-a·ceo** *adj.* starchy.

fecond-are [A I c] *tr.* to fertilize; to make fruitful; to make productive. **-a·bile** *adj.* fertile; not sterile. **-ante** *part. adj.* fertilizing. **-ativo** *adj.* fecundative. **-ato** *part. adj.* fertilized. **-atore** *m.* fertilizer; *adj.* fertilizing. (**-atrice** *f.*) **-azione** *f.* fertilization; fertilizing; (biol.) fertilization; -azione artificiale, artificial insemination; -azione omologa, A.I.H.; -azione eterologa, A.I.D. †**-e·vole** *adj.* fertile.

†**fecon·dia** *f.* See **fecondità**.

fecondità *f.* fertility; productiveness; fecundity; fruitfulness; (fig.) richness, wealth.

fecond-o *adj.* fertile; fruitful; prolific; rich in yield; (fig.) immaginazione -a, fertile imagination; scrittore —, prolific writer. **-amente** *adv.* fruitfully; abundantly.

†**fedare** *tr.* to soil; to spoil; to contaminate.

fede *f.* faith, trust, confidence; belief, credence; creed; religion; avere — in Dio, to trust in God; la — cristiana, the Christian faith; aver — in una persona, to believe in someone, to trust someone; serbare — a, to keep faith with; prestare — a, to believe, to give credit to; in — mia, on my honour; far —, to certify, to bear witness; degno di —, trustworthy, reliable; sorprendere la buona — di, to cheat; tenere — alla parola data, to keep one's word; fidelity, honour, word of honour; safe-conduct; wedding-ring; — coniugale, marital fidelity; honesty, integrity; la — del giudice, the integrity of the judge; document, certificate; policy; — di nascita, birth-certificate; — di morte, death-certificate; (leg.) faith; witness; in buona —, bona fide, in good faith; in mala —, in bad faith; in —, in witness; in — di che, in witness thereof; — di credito, a particular form of banker's draft of limited negotiability, issued by certain Italian banks; — di deposito, warehouse receipt, weight note (C.C.); delitto contro la — pubblica, offence against public credit (C.P.); (naut.) linea di —, lubbers' line; (comm.) — di credito, deposit receipt; — di deposito, weight note; (herald.) two hands clasped.

fedecommesso *m.* See **fidecommisso**.

†**fededegno** *adj.* trustworthy; *n.m.* trustworthy person, reliable person.

fedel-e, (Rom.) **fedel-e** *adj.* faithful, constant, true; loyal; un amico —, a faithful friend; mantenersi — a, to be faithful to; — alla sua parola, true to his word; truthful, conscientious, accurate; narrazione —, truthful account; traduzione —, faithful rendering, accurate translation; copia —, true copy, exact copy; memoria —, good memory, retentive memory; authentic, genuine; devout, orthodox; un — cristiano, a devout Christian; ogni — minchione, everybody, every Tom, Dick or Harry; *n.m.* loyal subject; believer, Christian; i -i, the faithful; the parishioners, the people; preti e -i, priests and people, clergy and laity; i -i ascoltavano la predica, the congregation were listening to the sermon. **-mente** *adv.* faithfully; loyally; truthfully; accurately. **-one** *m.* excessively religious person. (**-ona** *f.*)

fedelini *m.pl.* (cul.) very thin vermicelli.

fedeltà *f.* fidelity, faithfulness, constancy; truth, accuracy; loyalty, oath of loyalty; (leg.) obbligo di —, duty of loyalty (law of master and servant); (radio) definition; alta —, high fidelity, hi-fi.

fe·der-a *f.* pillowcase; mattress cover; †cushion cover. **-etta** *f. dim.* cloth cover of a book.

feder-ale *adj.* federal; (Ital. hist.) Segretario —, provincial party secretary; la Germania —, W. Germany; (joc.) italiano —, Italian-Swiss officialese. **-almente** *adv.* federally. **-alismo** *m.* federalism. **-alista** *m.*, *f. adj.* federalist. **-ativo** *adj.* federative, confederal. **-ato** *part. adj.*, *n.m.* federate, confederate. **-azione** *f.* federation; federating; confederation (cf. **confederazione**).

Federico, Federigo *pr.n.m.* Frederick.

fedi·frago *adj.* (*pl.* -ghi) faithless; unfaithful; perfidious; treacherous; *n.m.* faithless person, one who breaks faith; one who has broken his word; treacherous person.

fedina *f.* (leg.) certificate; — penale, certificate of police record; record; *pl.* side-whiskers.

†**fed-ire** *tr.* to strike; — colpi, to strike blows; senza colpo —, without striking a blow; — torneamento, to joust; to attack; to assail. †**-ita** *f.* wound; ulcer, sore.

Fedora *pr.n.f.* Feodora.

fegatella *f.* (bot.) common liverwort, *Marchantia polymorpha*.

fegat-o *m.* (anat.) liver; mal di —, liver complaint; una colica di —, a bilious attack; olio di — di merluzzo, cod-liver oil; (fig.) courage, guts; uomo di —, courageous man, bold man, person with guts; (chem.; pharm.) — di zolfo, liver of sulphur, hepar sulphuri. **-ac·cio** *m. pejor.* unscrupulous person; dare-devil. **-ello** *m.* (cul.) slice of pig's liver; (chess) 'fried liver' variation, sacrificial attack in the Two Knights' Defence. **-ino** *m.* fowl's liver, pigeon's liver. **-oso** *adj.* suffering from a liver-complaint; liverish, bilious; peevish, resentful; viso -oso, spotty face.

felc-e *f.* (bot.) fern; — aquilina, bracken, *Pteridium aquilinum*; — dolce, common polypody, *Polypodium vulgare*; — florida, royal fern, *Osmunda regalis*; — maschia, male fern, *Dryopteris filix-mas*; — muschiata, sweet Cicely, *Myrrhis odorata*; — quer-

felc-e (*cont.*)
cina, see 'felce dolce' or 'felce maschia'. **-ęta** *f.*, **-ęto** *m.*, **-iata** *f.* bed of ferns; grove of bracken.

feldispato *m.* (miner.). See **feldspato**.

feldmaresciallo *m.* field-marshal (in non-Italian armies; a field-marshal in the Italian Army is a 'maresciallo d'Italia)'.

feldspato *m.* (miner.) feldspar.

†fele *m.* See **fiele**.

felic-e[1] *adj.* happy; contented; glad; exultant; delighted; sono — di vederti, I am delighted to see you; fortunate, lucky; successful; felicitous; matrimonio —, happy marriage, età —, childhood, golden age; vento —, favourable wind; scelta —, happy choice, good choice; memoria —, apt and quick memory; la — memoria di mio nonno, the beloved memory of my grandfather; — te!, lucky you!, how fortunate you are!; — notte a tutti!, goodnight everybody! **-emęnte** *adv.* happily; successfully; arrivare **-emente**, to arrive safely.

Felice[2] *pr.n.m.* Felix.

felicità[1] *f.* happiness; felicity; blissfulness, bliss; success; vi auguro ogni —, I wish you every happiness; felicità!, God bless you!; —! e figli maschi a volontà!, a proverbial wish addressed to a person who sneezes; — d'espressione, felicity of expression; (provb.) se l'ignoranza è —, è follia l'esser saggi, where ignorance is bliss, 'tis folly to be wise.

Felicità[2] *pr.n.f.* Felicity.

felicit-are *tr.* [A I S] to make happy, to bless; to call happy; che Dio vi **-i**!, may God bless you!; to congratulate; — una persona per il suo successo, to congratulate a person on his success; *rfl.* to congratulate; mi **-o** con Lei per il suo successo, I congratulate you on your success; †*intr.* to prosper, to thrive, to be successful. **-amęnto** *m.* prosperity; congratulating. **-ato** *part. adj.* made happy; congratulated. **-azione** *f.* felicity; congratulation.

felino[1] *adj.*, *n.m.* (zool.) feline; *n.m.pl.* cats and other Felidae.

Felino[2] *pr.n.m.* (geog.) Felino, in the prov. of Parma; a dry white wine from Felino.

fellà *m. indecl.* fellah.

fellan·drio *m.* (bot.) horseband, fine-leaved water dropwort, *Oenanthe aquatica.*

†felle *m.* See **fiele**.

fell-o *adj.* fell, sinister, evil, impious; dire; †angry; †melancholy, sad; †displeasing; †fetid. **-ǫne** *adj.* wicked; cruel; ferocious; (of a horse) vicious; (of a river) swollen and angry; *n.m.* villain; (joc.) wicked man, felon; †traitor. (**-ǫna** *f.*) **-onęsco** *adj.* (*m.pl.* **-ęschi**) villainous; wicked, bad; †cruel. **-onescamęnte** *adv.* wickedly, treacherously. **†-onęssa** *f.* wicked or treacherous woman. **-oni·a** *f.* felony; rebellion; treason, defection; wickedness; (leg. hist.) treason of vassal against feudal lord; †ferocity; martial prowess; †incestuous love. **†-onoso** *adj.* wicked; treacherous.

felp-a *f.* plush. **-ato** *adj.* plush-covered; passi **-ati**, cat-like tread, muted footfalls, sound of footsteps as on thick pile carpet.

Fel·s·ina *pr.n.f.* (hist.) Bologna (in Etruscan times); (geog.) village of Felsina in prov. of Bologna; acqua di —, a Bolognese toilet water. **-i·neo** *adj.* Bolognese.

felspato *m.* See **feldspato**.

feltrai(u)olo *m.* See under **feltro**.

feltr-are [A I] *tr.* (text.) to felt; to cover with felt; *rfl.* to become felted; to felt. **-ato** *part. adj.* felted; converted into felt, covered with felt. **-atura** *f.* felting.

feltrifi·cio *m.* See under **feltro**.

fęltr-o *m.* felt; garment of felt; under-blanket; saddle-cloth; cappello di —, felt hat; filter, sieve. **-ai(u)olo** *m.* felt worker. **-ifi·cio** *m.* felt factory. **-ino** *adj.* felt-like; *n.m.* (mil.) wad.

feluca *f.* (mil.) pointed forage cap worn by generals; cocked-hat; ceremonial hat with points back and front worn by diplomats and French Academicians; tall, lanky person.

†felucca *f.* (naut.) galley boat; (Genoa) — degli spacci, despatch boat.

fęlza *f.* (mil.) strong point; (Ven.) cabin of a gondola.

†felzata *f.* elaborately woven blanket or bed-cover.

†felze *m.* (Ven.). See **felza**.

†fema *m.*, **†fe·mena** *f.* See **femmina**.

fęmmin-a *f.* female; woman; girl; è un maschio, o una —?, is it a male or a female?, is it a boy or a girl?, is it a he or a she?; scuola di maschi e **-e**, co-educational school; — del gatto, female cat,

quean; uccello —, hen-bird; — della tigre, female tiger, tigress; — dell'elefante, cow elephant; pesce —, spawner; mala —, loose woman; vite —, female screw; chiave —, key with hollow end; (carpen.) — dell'incastro, mortise. **-ac·cia** *f. pejor.* nasty, unpleasant woman; evil woman; †large fat woman. **-ac·ciolo, -acciolo** *m.* weak, effeminate man. **†-ale** *adj.* see **femminino**; *n.m.* (Bibl.) linen breeches (as priestly vestment). **-ęlla** *f. dim.* little woman; silly woman; poor woman; (bot.) sucker; (eng.) gudgeon, brace; *pl.* (naut.) rudder gudgeons; (mil.) gudgeons of a gun-cradle. **†-eri·a** *f.* (joc.) womankind; womenfolk. **-ęsco** *adj.* (*m.pl.* **-ęschi**) feminine, womanly. **-ętta** *f. dim.* little woman; poor woman. **-ęzza** *f.* womanhood. **†-iera** *f.* (joc.) womenfolk; place where the women spend their time. **-iere, -o** *adj. n.m.* see **donnaiolo**. **-ile** *adj.* feminine, womanly; female; sesso **-ile**, female sex; *n.m.* feminine gender; al **-ile**, in the feminine; (herald.) scudo **-ile**, lozenge. **-ilmęnte** *adv.* in a feminine way, like a woman. **-ilità** *f.* femininity, womanliness. **-ino** *adj.* feminine; *n.m.* femininity, feminine charm; l'eterno **-ino**, *das Ewig-Weibliche*. **-inamęnte** *adv.* in a feminine manner; like a woman; in a womanly manner. **-iṣmo** *m.* feminism. **-ista** *m.*, *f.*, *adj.* feminist. **-iẓẓare** [A I] *intr.* (*aux.* avere) to behave in a feminine way. **-ǫna** *f. augm.* big woman, stout woman. **-uc·cia, -uzza** *f. dim.* poor little woman; humble little woman; (of a man) weakling.

femmi·neo *adj.* feminine; female; il sesso —, the female sex; femminee vesti, women's clothes; effeminate.

fe·mor-e *m.* (anat.) femur, thigh-bone. **-ale** *adj.* femoral; *n.m.pl.* (hist.) part of clothing covering the thighs.

fenacetina *f.* (chem.; pharm.) phenacetin; *p*-acetophenetide.

fenachisti·scopo *m.* (cinem. hist.) zoëtrope.

fenachite *f.* (miner.) phenacite.

fenato *m.* (chem.) phenate, phenolate.

fend-ere [B I] *tr.* to split, to break, to crack; to cut in two; to slash; to cleave; — una pietra, to split a stone; — l'aria, to cleave the air; — la folla, to squeeze through the crowd; — la terra con l'aratro, to break up the ground with the plough; (of a ship) — le onde, to cleave the waves; *rfl.* to crack, to split. **-ente** *part. adj.* splitting, cleaving; slashing; *n.m.* downward stroke with a sword; (fig.) tirare **-enti**, to speak ill of someone. **-i·bile** *adj.* which can be split; liable to split or break. **-imęnto** *m.* splitting, cracking; split, crack. **-ineb·bia** *m. indecl.* (motor.) fog lamp. **-itǫio** *m.* (agric.) blade of a pruning-hook; wedge used in splitting timber. **-itǫre** *m.* cutter, cleaver. (**-itrice** *f.*) **-itura** *f.* split, crack, cleft; slit; fissure, crevice; (timber) shake. **-uto** *part. adj.* split, cracked; cut open (cf. **fesso**).

†fener-ati·zio *adj.* pertaining to usury. **†-atore** *m.* usurer. **†-ato·rio** *adj.* relating to usury.

†fenestr-a *f.* see **finestra**; hole made in the side of a ship by a projectile. **†-ella** *f. dim.* little window; button-hole.

fengofobi·a *f.* (med.) horror of bright objects.

fenicato *adj.* See under **fenico**.

fenice *f.* phoenix; (bot.) *Phoenix*, genus of palms containing the date palm, *Ph. dactylifera*; (astron.) Phoenix; name of a famous opera house in Venice; (fig.) great rarity; volere l'araba —, to yearn for something unattainable.

†feni·ceo[1] *adj.* See **fenicio**.

†feni·ceo[2] *adj.* relating to the phoenix.

†feni·ceo[3] *adj.* dark red, purple.

Feni·c·ia *pr.n.f.* (geog. hist.) Phoenicia. **-io** *adj.* (*m.pl.* **-i**, *f.pl.* **-e**) Phoenician; *n.m.* Phoenician; i Fenici, the Phoenicians.

fenicina *f.* (chem.) sulphindigotic acid.

fe·nic-o *adj.* (chem. pop.) carbolic; acido —, carbolic acid, phenol. **-ato** *adj.* soaked in phenol; carta **-ata**, carbolic paper.

fenicot·tero *m.* (orn.) flamingo, *Phoenicopterus ruber*.

fenile[1] *m.* See **fienile**.

fenil-e[2] *m.* (chem.) phenyl. **-amina** *f.* (chem.) phenylamine, aniline.

fenissa *f.* Phoenician woman.

fenogene·tica *f.* (biol.) 'phenogenetics', the relationship between genes and the characters they produce.

fen-olo *m.* (chem.) phenol, carbolic acid. **-olftaleina** *f.* (chem.) phenolphthalein. **-o·lico** *adj.* (chem.) phenolic.

fenomenal-e *adj.* (philos.) phenomenal; (colloq.) extraordinary; amazing; fa un freddo —, it's exceedingly cold. **-męnte** *adv.* phenomenally. **-iṣmo** *m.* phenomenalism. **-ità** *f.* phenomenal nature.

fenome·nico *adj.* (philos.) phenomenal.

feno·meno *m.* phenomenon; (colloq.) quella vecchia signora è un —, that old lady is wonderful, she's a marvel.

fenomenol-ogi·a *f.* phenomenology. **-o·gico** *adj.* phenomenological.

fenoplasto *m.* (chem.) phenoplast.

fenotipo *m.* (biol.) phenotype.

†fe·nore *m.* usury; ill-gotten gains.

†fera *f.* See **fiera²**.

ferac-e *adj.* fertile, fruitful; rich, productive; i ngegno —, inventive mind, fertile imagination. **-emente** *adv.* fruitfully; productively. **-ità** *f.* fertility; productiveness.

†ferale¹ *m.* lantern; torch.

feral-e² *adj.* deathly; gloomy, distressing; fatal; sinister; notizia —, news of a fatal accident or disaster; †wild, savage. **-mente** *adv.* sadly, gloomily, fatally; †savagely, ferociously.

†ferame *m.* wild animals.

ferberite *f.* (miner.) ferberite.

fer·colo *m.* (Rom. antiq.) tray for food; course of a meal; dish; litter for carrying images or triumphal spoils; †(rel.) Eucharistic banquet.

Ferdinando *pr.n.m.* Ferdinand.

ferecr-a·tico *adj.* (prosod.) Pherecratean. **-a·zio** *m.* (prosod.) Pherecratean metre.

ferenta·rio *m.* (mil. hist.) light cavalry- or infantryman.

Fere·trio *pr.n.m.* (Rom. myth.) Feretrius (a title of Jupiter).

fe·retro *m.* bier; coffin; seguire il —, to walk in procession at a funeral.

†ferezza *f.* See **fierezza**, under **fiero**.

fe·ri-a *f.* holiday, day of rest; day off; (liturg.) feria; *pl.* holidays; (leg.) the vacation; periodo annuale di -e retribuito, annual holiday with pay (labour laws); ha diritto a 15 giorni di -e all'anno, he gets a fortnight's holiday a year; le -e natalizie, the Christmas vacation. **-ale** *adj.* ferial; ordinary, not festive; giorno -ale, working-day; business day; (liturg.) ferial. **-almente** *adv.* in an ordinary way, without ceremony. **-are** [A 4] *intr.* (aux. avere) to keep holiday, to be on holiday. **-ato** *adj.* pertaining to holiday; giorno -ato, holiday; *n.m.* holiday; (leg.) the vacation, the period when the courts are not sitting.

fericida *m.* hunter; killer of animals.

ferigno *adj.* relating to wild beasts; ferine, feral; bestial; wild; †(of bread) made with flour mixed with bran.

ferino *adj.* ferine, feral; bestial; istinti ferini, bestial instincts.

fer-ire [D 2] *tr.* to wound, to injure; — a un braccio, to wound in the arm; — l'amor proprio di qualcuno, to injure someone's self-esteem; (fig.) to strike, to touch; — la fantasia, to strike one's fancy; — uno nell'onore, to offend someone's honour; — l'occhio, — la vista, to catch the eye; senza colpo —, without striking a blow; *rfl.* to wound oneself; *intr.* (aux. avere) to strike, to fall; dove andranno a — quelle parole?, what is he driving at with those words? **-i·bile** *adj.* vulnerable. **-imento** *m.* wounding; wound; (mil.) act of wounding; crime of wounding. **-ito** *part. adj.* wounded, hit, struck; rimanere -ito, to receive a wound, to be wounded, to be hit; -ito al petto, wounded in the chest; *n.m.* wounded man; (mil.) casualty; i -iti di guerra, the war wounded. **-itoia** *f.* arrowslit-view; louvre, air hole; (archit.) crenel; (eng.) slot. **-itore** *m.* striker, wounder; †skilful swordsman; †*pl.* soldiers; i primi -itori, the front rank; *adj.* wounding. (**-itrice** *f.*)

†feristo *m.* (mil.) standard pole.

ferita¹ *f.* wound; — mortale, fatal wound; — che sanguina, bleeding wound; — rimarginata, wound that has closed up; una — al capo, a wound in the head; curare una —, to treat a wound; guarire, sanare una —, to heal a wound; — d'amore, wound of love; riaprire, rincrudire una —, to open a wound, (fig.) to cause fresh pain; injury; (leg.) see **lesione**; (mil.) distintivo delle ferite, wound-stripe.

ferita² *f.* wounded woman; cf. **ferito** *part. adj.* of **ferire**, q.v.

ferità *f.* wildness, savageness; cruelty.

ferit-o *part. adj.*, *n.m.* of **ferire**, q.v. **-oia** *f.*, **-ore** *m.* see under **ferire**.

†ferlino *m.* small coin, a quarter of a 'denaro'; counter.

ferma *f.* (mil.) period of national service or voluntary training; cane da —, pointer, setter dog; †confirmation; †agreement; †(sport, of dogs) pointing.

ferma-bu·e *m. indecl.* (bot.) rest-harrow, *Ononis*. **-carro** *m. indecl.* (rlwy.) device for stopping rolling-stock at the end of a track. **-carte** *m. indecl.* paper-weight. **-co·fano** *m. indecl.* (motor.) bonnet fastener. **-cravatta** *m. indecl.* tie-pin. **-palle** *m. indecl.* (mil.) butts. **-piastra** *m. indecl.* (watchm.) plate-fastener. **-piede** *m. indecl.* (cycl.) toe clip. **-porta** *m. indecl.* doorstop. **-scam·bio** *m. indecl.* (rlwy.) point lock; -scambio articolato, toggle-joint point lock. **-tampone**, **-tamponi** *m. indecl.* (watchm.) buffer holder.

†fermag·gio *m.* See **fermezza**, under **fermo**.

ferma·glio *m.* clasp, clip; fastening; buckle; brooch; paper-clip; (mil.) buckle (of sword belt).

fermamente *adv.* See under **fermo**.

fermanello *m. indecl.* guard-ring, keeper; (mil.) butts.

ferm-are [A I] *tr.* to stop, to halt; to detain, to arrest; — il treno, to stop the train; — qualcuno a letto, to keep someone in bed; — un individuo sospetto, to detain a suspect person; — le frutte, to arrest the growth of fruit; (cul.) — le carni, to parboil meat, to par-cook meat (to stop it from going bad); to fix, to make firm; — un bottone, to sew a button on firmly; — l'animo su, to fix one's mind on; — i momenti più belli, to catch the loveliest moments (e.g. in photography); — l'accampamento, to set up camp; — la successione, to ensure the succession; — un accordo, to conclude an agreement; — un punto, to clarify a point, to decide a matter; (mus.) — la voce, to have mastery over the voice, to sing properly; *intr.* (aux. essere) to stop; il tram non -a qui, the tram does not stop here; (of a dog) to point; *rfl.* to stop, to halt; to stay; il treno si -a, the train is stopping; la nave si -a a, the ship calls at; il mio orologio s'è -ato, my watch has stopped; -arsi con uno, to stop and talk to someone; -arsi in una città, to stay on in a city, to spend some time in a town; -arsi su un argomento, to dwell on a subject. **-amento** *m.* fixing; stopping; confirmation; establishment; stability; cessation; †fortification; †firmness; †support; †firmament. **†-anza** *f.* establishing; ratification. **-ata** *f.* stop, pause; stopping-place; il treno fa una -ata di un'ora, the train stops for one hour; -ata facoltativa, request stop; (mus.) pause; (mil.) stage. **-ato** *part. adj.* halted; detained; fixed; established; stable; †fortified; †constant, loyal, firm; †resolute, determined; †written, signed; *n.m.* (leg.) person detained. **-atura** *f.* fixing, fastening; clasp.

ferma·ria *m. indecl.* (paperm.) rulletto —, air-roll.

ferment-are [A I C] *intr.* (aux. essere) to ferment, to 'work'; *tr.* to ferment, to cause to ferment. **-a·bile** *adj.* fermentable. **-a·rio** *adj.*, *n.m.* (eccl. hist.) fermentarian. **-ato** *part. adj.* fermented; fermenting; in ferment. **-azione** *f.* fermentation; (tanning) sweating. **-esci·bile** *adj.* liable to ferment, capable of fermenting. **-ìo** *m.* rapid and audible fermenting.

fermento *m.* ferment; yeast, leaven, barm; (biol.) enzyme; (fig.) ferment, excitement, agitation.

fermione *m.* (atom. phys.) fermion.

ferm-o *adj.* firm, steady, stable; — come una roccia, as steady as a rock; salute mal -a, poor health; voce -a, steady voice; non avere terreno —, to be unsettled, to move about constantly; certain, sure, firm; tenere per —, to believe with certainty, to be convinced of; — stando che, premising that; stare — al chiodo, to stick to one's opinion, to be obstinate; offerta -a, firm offer; contratto —, cash transaction; motionless, still, stationary; terra -a, *terra firma*, dry land; acqua -a, stagnant water; star —, to stand still; — come un piolo, stock still; (mil.) — là!, halt!; fermo posta, *poste restante*, to be called for; punto —, full stop; (mus.) canto —, plainchant; *cantus firmus*; (herald.) statant; leone —, lion statant; *n.m.* arrest, detention; seizure, distraint; firmness, stability; catch, hook; dare il — a una cosa, to put a stop to something; (leg.) sequestration; seizure; arrest; detention; — di indiziati di reato, arrest of suspects; — stante, during, without prejudice to, the validity (of an act, document or instrument); mettere un — sul contrabbando, to seize contraband; mettere un — su un assegno, to stop a cheque; liberare da un —, to release; mettere il — su una persona, to issue a writ of attachment against a person; cane da —, pointer, setter; (watchm.) holder. **-amente** *adv.* firmly; steadily; unwaveringly; credere -amente, to believe absolutely. **-ezza** *f.* firmness, stability, steadiness; clasp; surety; confirmation; validity; (art) firmness (in drawing, etc.). **-ità** *f.* (leg.) validity of a document or instrument.

fernambuc-co *m.* (*pl.* **-chi**) (bot.) sappan, Brazil wood, *Caesalpinia sappan*.

fernè, **fernet** *m. indecl.* (pron. as Fr.) a medicinal liqueur.

fernetta *f.* bit (of a key).

†fero *adj.* See **fiero**.

feroc-e, (Rom.) **feroc-e** *adj.* ferocious, fierce; wild, savage, harsh; severe; bold; proud. **-eme̥nte** *adv.* fiercely; ferociously, savagely; boldly; proudly.

fero·c-ia *f.* (*pl.* **-ie**) ferocity, inhumanity, brutality; *pl.* acts of ferocity. **-ità** *f.* wildness, savageness; ferocity; boldness.

ferol-a, -ag·gine *f.* (bot.) *Ferula communis.*

Fero·nia *pr.n.f.* (myth.) Feronia (an ancient Italian deity).

ferracavallo *m. indecl.* farrier, shoeing-smith.

ferrac·ci-a *f.* (ichth.) ray; — pastinaca, *Dasybatus pastinachus,* sting ray; — violacea, *D. violaceus;* — bruco, *D. brucco.* **-o** *m.* scrap-iron, cast-iron.

ferra·glia *f.* scrap-iron; (colloq.) old and rusty machine; rumore di —, clanking of old iron; (mil.) canister, grapeshot, mixed nails and shard.

Ferragosto *pr.n.m.* August holidays; August State holiday (formerly 1 August, now coinciding with the Assumption, 15 August); extra payment or bonus paid at the time of the August State holiday.

†ferraguto *m.* outlaw; swordsman; lancer.

ferra·io, ferraro *m.* blacksmith.

ferrai(u)ol-o[1] *m.* cloak; farsi tirare per il —, to be slow in paying a debt. **-ino** *m.* (eccl.) silk band at back of priest's cloak.

ferrai(u)olo[2] *m.* (bldg.) fitter for concrete reinforcement; †see **ferraio.**

ferram-e *m.* iron, quantity of iron, iron goods; negozio di -i, ironmongery, ironmonger's shop. **-e̥nto** *m.* (*pl.* **-i** *m.*, **-a** *f.*) iron tool; *pl.* ironware, hardware; negozio di -enta, ironmonger's shop.

ferrana *f.* (agric.) forage crop.

ferrante[1] *adj.* (of a horse) having a coat the colour of corn, with black and white or bay markings; baio —, bay horse with white legs.

ferrante[2] *part. adj.* of **ferrare,** q.v.

ferr-are [A I] *tr.* to fit with iron, to bind with iron; to shoe; to shackle (convicts); — un cavallo, to shoe a horse. **-ante** *part. adj.* shoeing; maniscalco -ante, farrier. **-ato** *part. adj.* shod; fitted with iron; stivali -ati, hobnailed boots; strada -ata, railway; (colloq.) essere molto -ato in, to be very well up in; *n.m.* (chem.) ferrate. †**-ore** *m.* blacksmith. **-ura** *f.* shoeing; shoes (of a horse); hoof-print; ironwork.

Ferrar-a *pr.n.f.* (geog.) Ferrara; *adj., n.m., f.* Ferrarese.

ferrare̥ccia *f.* iron implement; *pl.* iron, iron goods, ironmongery.

ferrata *f.* iron grating; iron-mould; imprint left by a flat-iron; railway.

ferravec·chio *m.* dealer in old iron, second-hand dealer.

ferrazza *f.* (ichth.). See **ferraccia.**

fer·reo *adj.* iron; (fig.) strong, severe; harsh; adamantine; disciplina ferrea, iron discipline; salute ferrea, iron constitution, robust health; età ferrea, Iron Age; (poet.) — sonno, death.

ferreri·a *f.* iron implements, ironmongery.

ferre̥tto *m. dim.* of **ferro,** q.v.; (geog. Lomb.) clay with high iron content.

ferriata *f.* See **inferriata.**

ferri-bot *m. indecl.,* **-botto** *m.* ferry-boat; train ferry.

ferricianuro *m.* (chem.) ferricyanide.

fer·rico *adj.* (chem.) ferric.

ferriera *f.* iron-mine; iron-foundry; tool-bag; (eng.) rolling mill.

ferriero *adj.* (mil.) cannone —, gun firing iron shot as opposed to stone cannon-balls.

ferri·fero *adj.* ferriferous; iron-yielding.

ferrigno *adj.* ferruginous; like iron, as of iron; robust, firm, strong; †obstinate; †impenetrable.

ferr-o *m.* iron; l'età del —, the Iron Age; — in verghe, bar iron; minerale di —, iron ore; (pharm.) iron; (fig.) una salute di —, an iron constitution; avere uno stomaco di —, to have a hearty digestion, to be able to digest anything; braccio di —, strong man (cf. under **braccio**); avere una memoria di —, to have an excellent memory; essere in una botte di —, to be in an impregnable position; tocca —!, an Italian equivalent to Eng. 'touch wood!'; governare con mano di —, to rule with a rod of iron; battere il — mentre (finchè) è caldo, to strike while the iron is hot; battere due -i a un caldo, to kill two birds with one stone; iron implement; tool, instrument; i -i del mestiere, the tools of the trade; surgical instruments; essere sotto ai -i, to be on the operating table, to be in the dentist's chair, (joc.) to be taking an examination; -i da calza, knitting needles; — da stiro, flat-iron; — elettrico, electric iron; -i da fuoco, fire-irons; — da arricciare i capelli, curling-iron, tongs; ondulazione ai -i, Marcel waving;

chains, shackles, irons; mettere ai -i, to clap in irons, (poet.) to enchain, to make captive; mettere i -i a, to put the handcuffs on; — da cavallo, horseshoe; (cul.) ai -i, grilled; braciola ai -i, grilled steak; — di bottega, police-spy; (mil.) arm, side-arm, cold steel; (poet.) sword; a — freddo, with short arms; essere ai -i corti, to be fighting with daggers, (fig.) to have reached the climax of a dangerous situation; morire di —, to die by the sword; mettere al —, to put to the sword; mettere a — e fuoco, to sack, to give no quarter to; incrociare i -i, to cross swords; venire ai -i, to use short arms, (fig.) to reach a conclusion; (naut., of rigging) tesate a —, set up bar taut; (zool.) — di cavallo, horseshoe bat, *Rhinolophus ferrum-equinum;* — minore, *Rh. hipposideros;* (archit.) arco a — di cavallo, horseshoe arch, Moorish arch; *pl.* skates. **-obatteri** *m.pl.* (biol.) iron bacteria. **-ocianuro** *m.* (chem.) ferrocyanide. **-oguida** *f.* (naut.; mil.) catapult rails. **-olino** *m.* tool (for precision work, goldsmithery, etc.). **-o̥so** *adj.* (chem.; metall.) ferrous. **-osele·nio** *m.* (metall.) ferro-selenium. **-osili·cio** *m.* (metall.) ferrosilicon. **-otipi·a** *f.* ferrotype. **-uzzo** *m.* tool.

ferro-china *m.* a liqueur of a bitter, tonic quality.

ferrov-i·a *f.* railway, railroad; railway station; essere nelle -ie, to be a railway employee; — sotterranea, underground railway; per —, by rail; — a scartamento ridotto, narrow gauge railway; — a trazione elettrica, electrified railway; *pl.* (leg.) -ie dello Stato, State Railways; rappresentanza dell'Amministrazione delle -ie dello Stato, representation of the Management of the State Railways (civil procedure). **-ia·rio** *adj.* railway; carro -iario, railway carriage; impiegato -iario, railway employee; materiale -iario, rolling-stock; porto -iario, railway charges; movimento -iario, railway traffic. **-iere** *m.* railway employee; *pl.* (mil.) troop of military engineers, railway company.

ferrug-igno, -i·neo *adj.* ferruginous, rust-coloured. **-inosità** *f.* ferruginous quality. **-inoso** *adj.* rust-coloured; (chem.) ferruginous.

ferrumin-are [A I S] *tr.* to weld. **-ato** *part. adj.* welded. **-ato̥io, -ato̥re** *m.* welding burner. **-ato·rio** *adj.* (chem.) cannello -atorio, blowpipe.

fer·til-e *adj.* fertile, fruitful, productive, rich; prolific; terreno —, fertile land; (fig.) immaginazione —, fertile imagination. **-me̥nte** *adv.* fruitfully, copiously, abundantly. **-ità** *f.* fertility, productiveness, richness; productivity.

fertilizz-are [A I] *tr.* to fertilize, to make fertile. **-ante** *part. adj.* fertilizing; *n.m.* fertilizer. **-ato** *part. adj.* fertilized. **-azio̥ne** *f.* fertilization; (agric.) -azione a spandimento, top dressing.

†feru·col-a *f.,* **-o** *m.* small creature; insect.

fe·rul-a *f.* (bot.) see **ferola;** rod, stick, cane; lash (of critic); — di pedagogo, teacher's cane; splint; support (for a weak limb); (liturg.) ferula, kind of crosier. **-i·fero** *adj.* (poet.) thyrsus-bearing.

†ferut-a *f.* see **ferita[1].** **†-o** *part. adj.* see **ferito,** under **ferire.**

fer·v-ere [B I] *intr.* (aux. avere) to be fervent; to be active; to be ardent; to blaze; to seethe; il lavoro -e, *fervet opus,* the work is proceeding fast and furiously; -e la disputa, the dispute is at its height. **-e̥nte** *part. adj.* fervent; blazing, hot; seething; zealous; i raggi -enti del sole, the burning rays of the sun; -ente patriota, fervent patriot, zealous patriot. **-enteme̥nte** *adv.* fervently; ardently; zealously. †**-ente̥zza** *f.* heat, burning. **-e̥nza** *f.* fervency; zeal, ardour.

fervide̥zza *f.* See under **fervido.**

fer·vid-o *adj.* fervid, ardent; impassioned; heartfelt; -i auguri, warmest wishes; burning; i -i raggi del sole, the burning rays of the sun. **-ame̥nte** *adv.* fervently; fervidly; warmly. **-e̥zza** *f.* fervour; warmth, heat.

fervo̥r-e *m.* fervour; con —, fervently; heat; ardour, vehemence; excitement; nel — della battaglia, in the heat of battle; in pieno —, in full swing. **-ino** *m.* (eccl.) exhortation; (colloq.) a 'talking-to'; fare un -ino a, to scold, to upbraid. **-o̥so** *adj.* fervent; ardent; zealous, impassioned. **-osame̥nte** *adv.* fervently; ardently.

†ferz-a *f.* see **sferza.** †**-are** *vb.* and derivs. see **sferzare.**

ferzo *m.* (naut.) canvas bolt or cloth.

fescennino *adj.* (Rom. antiq.) Fescennine, scurrilous (verses).

†fesolera *f.* See **fusoliera.**

†fes·sile *adj.* breakable; friable.

fe̥ss-o *adj.* split, cracked, broken; cloven; (vulg.) foolish, silly, soft, 'cracked'; (vulg.) l'hanno fatto —, they've made a fool of him; voce -a, cracked voice, broken voice; animali dall'unghia -a, cloven-footed animals; *n.m.* crack, chink, opening; (vulg.) fool.

fess-o (*cont.*)

-**acchiotto** *m.* (vulg.; joc.) fool. -**eri·a** *f.* (vulg.) foolishness; rubbish. -**olino** *m.* chink, small crevice, small opening. -**uolo** *m.* hole, opening; (bot.) innestare a -uolo, to saddle-graft. -**ura** *f.* fissure, split; slit, slot; chink, crevice; narrow aperture, small window. -**urazione** *f.* cracking, flaw; (timber) shake; -urazione radicale, star shake.

fest-a *f.* feast, festivity, rejoicing; party; fu una gran —, it was a great feast; fête; entertainment; — da ballo, ball; feast-day, holiday; Saint's day; name-day; (eccl.) — mobile, moveable feast; — comandata, — di precetto, holiday of obligation; -e di Natale, Christmas holidays; la — di Pietro, Pietro's name-day; mezza —, half-holiday; far —, to stop work, to be on holiday; essere sotto le -e, to be nearing a holiday period (esp. Christmas and New Year); siamo sotto le-e, Easter, etc. is almost upon us; abiti da—, Sunday clothes, 'Sunday best'; dare le buone -e a uno, to wish someone a happy holiday; feast, joy, delight; rejoicing; sarà una — per me vederlo, it will be a delight (a treat) for me to see it; una — di colori, a feast of colours; welcome; fare — a uno, to welcome someone; mi fecero un monte di -e, they made a great fuss of me; (of a dog) fare le -e a, to jump up on, to greet with great joy and wagging of tail; (iron.) fare la — a uno, to kill someone; fece la — al suo patrimonio, he squandered his inheritance, he used up his inheritance; conciare qualcuno per le -e (*or*, per il dì delle -e), to give someone a drubbing; non tutti i giorni è —, Christmas comes but once a year; guastar la —, to spoil the party, to spoil the fun. -**accia** *f. pejor.* unpleasant feast; unseemly rejoicing. -**ai(u)olo** *m.* gay, party-going, sociable person; the host at a party, one who gives a party; (theatr. hist.) master of ceremonies, producer, etc. of the Florentine 'sacre rappresentazioni'. -**icci(u)ola** *f.* small party, family party.

festante *adj.* rejoicing, joyful, jubilant.

†**festare** *tr.* to celebrate; *intr.* to make merry, to hold revels.

festechino *adj.* See **fistuchino**.

festeggi-are [A 3 c] *tr.* to celebrate; to keep (as a holiday); — l'arrivo del primo figliolo, to celebrate the birth of the first child; — la Pasqua, to celebrate Easter, to keep the Easter festival; — un santo, to keep a saint's day; — l'arrivo di qualcuno, to give someone a warm welcome; to applaud, to cheer; to fête. -**amento** *m.* feasting, rejoicing; celebration; festivity, feast. -**ante** *part. adj.* feasting, rejoicing, merry; *n.m., f.* merry-maker. -**ato** *part. adj.* fêted, celebrated; *n.m.* guest of honour, person fêted. -**atore** *m.* feaster, celebrator; merry-maker. (-**atrice** *f.*)

fest-ereccio *adj.* overfond of pleasure and festivities; †rejoicing; †celebrated. †-**eria** *f.* festivities.

festevol-e *adj.* festive; merry; joyous; gay, cheerful; affectionate; modi -i, sunny, cheerful manner. -**mente** *adv.* festively; joyously; with mirth and gaiety; merrily. -**ezza** *f.* joyousness; merriment, joviality.

†**festichino** *adj.* See **fistuchino**.

†**festin-are** *intr.* to hurry, to hasten. †-**anza** *f.* hurry, haste. †-**ato** *part. adj.* in a hurry, hurrying, hastening.

festinazione *f.* (med.) festination, propulsive gait; †hurrying; hurry, haste.

festino[1] *m.* feast; ball; banquet; evening party.

†**festin-o**[2] *adj.* prompt, ready, swift; eager. †-**amente** *adv.* promptly, quickly; eagerly.

fe·stival *m. indecl.* (pron. as Eng.) (mus.; cinem.) festival. -**i·stico** *adj.* of a festival; like a festival.

festivale *m.* See **festival**.

festivamente *adv.* See under **festivo**.

†**festivare** *tr.* to fête, to celebrate.

festività *f.* festivity; (liturg.) feast; conviviality; vivacity; merriment, gaiety; (leg.) public holidays; legge della —, law of public holidays (C.P.).

festiv-o *adj.* festive, festal; giorno —, holiday, Sunday; i giorni -i, official holidays; (leg.) *dies non*; scuola -a, Sunday classes (in ordinary school subjects); abiti -i, Sunday clothes; aspetto —, cheerful appearance. -**amente** *adv.* festively; joyfully, cheerfully; vivaciously; merrily.

†**festo** *adj.* festal; *n.m.* see **festa**.

feston-e *m.* festoon, garland; embellishment; (archit.) festooned frieze, esp. over doors or windows; (naut.) sculpture or ornamentation of a ship's transom or stem; figurehead. -**ato** *adj.* festooned, in the shape of a festoon. (-**cino** *m. dim.*)

festos-o *adj.* gay; joyful, cheerful; merry, bubbling over with happiness; jovial, hearty. -**amente** *adv.* merrily; joyfully, cheerfully; jovially. -**ità** *f.* merriment, gaiety; festiveness, joyfulness; conviviality, joviality.

festu-ca *f.* piece of straw, a straw; vedere la — nell'occhio altrui e non la trave nel proprio, to see the mote in another's eye, and not the beam in one's own. -**co** *m.* (*pl.* -**chi**) piece of straw; stalk; tendril. -**cone** *m. augm.* (joc.) tall, thin man.

fetale *adj.* See under **feto**.

fetare [A I] *tr.* (N. Ital.) to hatch out; †to give birth to, to bring forth.

fet-ente *adj.* stinking, fetid; (fig.) foul, disgusting, worthless. -**enza** *f.* stench. †-**en·zia** *f.* see **fetenza**; fossa di -enzia, cesspool.

†**fe·tere** *intr.* to stink.

fet-ic·cio *m.* fetish; idol. -**ici·smo** *m.* fetishism; idolatry. -**ici·sta** *m., f.* fetishist; idolater.

fetici·dio *m.* See under **feto**.

fe·tid-o *adj.* fetid, stinking; foul, filthy, disgusting. -**amente** *adv.* fetidly; foully. -**ezza** *f.* baseness, foulness. -**ità** *f.* baseness, foulness; stench. -**oso** *adj.* filthy; foul. -**ume** *m.* stench, fetor; foulness; stinking things.

fet-o *m.* foetus; egg of insect; (joc.) card, droll individual. -**ale** *adj.* foetal. -**ici·dio** *m.* foeticide.

Fetonte *pr.n.m.* (myth.) Phaethon; (orn.) tropical bird; phaeton, light two-wheeled carriage.

fetore *m.* fetor, stench, stink, offensive smell.

fett-a *f.* slice; clod of earth; ribbon, band; (colloq.) flap of a jacket; — di vitello, fillet of veal; tagliare a -e, to cut in slices, to slice; — di casa, tall, narrow house. -**accia** *f. pejor.* thick slice, hunk. -**ina** *f. dim.* thin slice. -**one** *m. augm.* large slice; (vet.) frog (part of a horse's foot); (naut.) layer of a composite mast; reinforcement in wood or steel of a yard or mast, permanent or fixed for repair; fender, scotsman; (colloq.) tail coat. -**uccia** *f.* tape, ribbon; (surg.) wick (for drawing an abscess); (sugar industr.) -ucce esaurite, bagasse. -**uccine** *f.pl.* kind of pasta cut in strips or ribbons (Roman synonym for 'tagliatelle', q.v.). †-**uzza** *f.* tape, ribbon.

fet-ulente, -**ulento** *adj.* filthy, fetid; stinking.

fe·ud-o *m.* feud, fee, fief; feudal domain; feudal tribute. -**a·le** *adj.* feudal. -**almente** *adv.* feudally. -**ale·simo** *m.* see **feudalismo**. -**alismo** *m.* feudalism. -**alità** *f.* feudality; feudal regime; feudal obligation. -**ata·rio** *adj.*; *n.m.* feudatory; lord of manor; landed proprietor.

fez *m. indecl.* fez, Turkish cap; red cap worn by bersaglieri in undress uniform; black cap of Fascist militia.

†**fi'** *m.* See **figlio**.

†**fi** *excl.* fie! (repeated, onom. of the sound of whistling).

†**fi·a**[1] *f.* See **fiata**.

†**fi·a**[2] *3rd pers. sing. fut.* of **essere**, q.v.

fiab-a *f.* fairy-tale; idle tale, chatter, nonsense; fib, tarradiddle; -e per bambini, children's tales. -**esco** *adj.* (*m.pl.* -**eschi**) fabulous; like a fairy-tale; fairy-like.

fiac-ca *f.* listlessness; slackness; weariness, lassitude; laziness; (colloq.) batter la —, to be idle, to slack; †hullabaloo. -**cherella** *f. dim.* slight feeling of lassitude; godersi una dolce -cherella, to enjoy a few moments of relaxation.

fiaccacollo *m. indecl.* thoughtless person, scatter-brain; harum-scarum.

fiaccag·gine *f.* See **fiacchezza**, under **fiacco**[1].

fiacc-are [A 2] *tr.* to tire, to weary, to exhaust; — le forze, to exhaust one's energy; to weaken, to break down, to break; — la resistenza del nemico, to break the enemy's resistance; studi che -ano l'ingegno, work which is mentally exhausting; — lo spirito di, to break the spirit of, to dispirit; *rfl.* (acc. of prn. 'si') to grow weary, to tire; to become discouraged, to break down; *rfl.* (dat. of prn. 'si') -arsi il collo, to break one's neck; -arsi le ossa, to break one's bones. -**a·bile** *adj.* liable to weaken; breakable; liable to break; destructible. -**amento** *m.* breaking; weakening, tiring; breakage, collapse. -**ato** *part. adj.* broken; weakened; subdued, tamed; exhausted. -**atoio** *adj.* fatiguing, weakening. -**atura** *f.* breaking; collapsing; break; collapse.

fiacchera·io *m.* cab-driver.

fiac·chere *m.* (Flor.) one-horsed open cab.

fiaccherella *f. dim.* See under **fiacca**.

fiacchezza *f.* See under **fiacco**[1].

fiac·co[1] *adj.* (*pl.* -**chi**) weary, fatigued, exhausted; sluggish; weak, feeble; slack, lazy; un governo —, a feeble government; -**camente** *adv.* wearily; weakly; lazily. -**chęzza** *f.* weariness, exhaustion; lassitude; weakness; slackness, laziness.

fiacco[2] *m.* (colloq.) un — di bastonate, a shower of blows; †slaughter; destruction, ruin.

fiacco[3] *apocop. part.* of **fiaccare**, q.v.

fiac·col·a *f.* torch, flame; alla luce delle -e, by torchlight; (fig.) la — della civiltà, the torch of civilization; (eng.) blowlamp; (poet.) la — del giorno, the sun; le -e della notte, the moon and stars; portatore di —, torch-bearer, link-boy. -**are** [A I S] *intr.* (*aux.* avere) to flare. -**ata** *f.* torchlight procession.

fiacc·ọna *f.* exhaustion, languor; lazy woman. -**ọne** *m.* lazy man, idler; lazy-bones; *adj.* lazy, idle.

†**fiadone** *m.* honeycomb.

fiala *f.* phial; little bottle.

†**fial·e**, †-**one** *m.* honeycomb; cell of a honeycomb.

fiamm·a *f.* flame, flare, blaze; levar —, to blaze; dare alle -e, to burn, to throw into the fire, to consign to the flames; -e eterne, hell fire; andare in -e, to go up in flames; essere in —, to be ablaze, to be on fire; (fig.) passion, love; sweetheart; una sua vecchia —, an old flame of his; la — della libertà, the love of liberty; occhi che mandano -e, eyes that dart forth fire; mettere a fuoco e -e, to ravage with fire; (fig.) far fuoco e -e, to do one's utmost; glow, warmth of feeling; gli vennero le -e al viso, he grew (went) red in the face; (motor.) ritorno di —, backfire; (mil.) regimental or corps pennant; (naut.) ship's commissioning pennant, tricolor; captain's or officer of the guard's pennant; — di ritorno, paying-off pennant; (ichth.) red band fish, *Cepola rubescens*; (archit.) representation of flame on a tomb; (bot.) dodder, *Cuscuta*; *m. indecl.* (techn.) workman who cuts scrap-iron, etc. by means of an oxyhydrogen blowpipe. -**ella**, -**ętta** *f. dim.* little flame; love, passion; (ichth.) see **fiamma**. -**ina** *f. dim.* small flame; raw diamond. -**ista** *m.* (techn.) see **fiamma**. -**olina** *f. dim.* small flame; blush.

fiamm·are [A I] *intr.* (*aux.* avere) to flame; to flare; to blaze. -**ante** *part. adj.* flaming; blazing; glowing; flashing; rosso -ante, flaming red; nuovo -ante, brand new; *n.m.* (orn.) flamingo. -**ata** *f.* blaze, flare; flash; spurt of flame. -**eggiante** *part. adj.* flaming, blazing; shining; glowing; (herald.) wavy. -**eggiare** [A 3 c] *intr.* (*aux.* avere) to flame, to blaze; to dart forth tongues of flame; to shine, to sparkle, to flash.

fiamme·o *adj.* flaming.

fiammi·fer·o *adj.* flame-bearing; *n.m.* match; — di sicurezza, safety match; scatola di -i, box of matches; mi favorisca un —?, can I trouble you for a match?; legno da -i, matchwood; (fig.) pigliar fuoco come un —, to be very irascible, to flare up easily; essere un —, to be hot-tempered, to be a spitfire. -**a·ia** *f.*, -**a·io** *m.* seller of matches.

fiammin·go *adj.* (*m.pl.* -**ghi**) Flemish; la lingua -**ga**, the Flemish language; *n.m.* Fleming; Flemish; (orn.) flamingo.

fiammispirante *adj.* (poet.) breathing fire.

fiam·mola *f.* (bot.) *Clematis flammula*.

fia·mula *f.* (bot.). See **fiammola**.

fiancale *m.* See under **fianco**.

fianc·are [A 2] *tr.* to strengthen at the sides, to flank; to strike; -**arla** ad uno, to make a cutting remark to someone. -**ata** *f.* side flank; blow in the flank; prick with a spur; (mil.) salvo; (naut.) broad-side; (motor.) side panel; -ata del parafango, mudguard apron; *pl.* (eccl.) side-ornaments of pedestal for Exposition. -**ato** *part. adj.* flanked; (herald.) flanches, flasques, voiders.

fiancheggi·are [A 3 c] *tr.* to flank, to border; to line; una fila di soldati -ava il corteo, soldiers lined the route of the procession; to help, to support; (mil.) to cover the flank of; †to spur. -**amento** *m.* flanking; support; help; (mil.) act of covering a flank by patrols, etc.; system of mutual flank coverage. -**ato** *part. adj.* flanked; lined; supported; helped. -**atọre** *m.* supporter. (-**atrice** *f.*)

fianchętto *m. dim.* See under **fianco**.

fian·co *m.* (*pl.* -**chi**) flank, side; avere un dolore al —, to have a pain in one's side; avere una punta nel —, to have a stitch in one's side; il — di un cavallo, the flank of a horse; stare a — di qualcuno, to be at someone's side, to be a support to someone; mettersi al — di, to side with; tenersi i -chi, to hold one's sides (with laughter); prestare il — alle critiche, to behave in a way

that is open to criticism; (tanning) belly; (theatr.) parte di —, supporting role; (mil.) wing; flank; side column; girare il —, to turn a flank; pigliare nei -chi, to assault a wing; covering fortification; (naut.) ship's side; *adv. phr.* di —, sideways, obliquely. -**cale** *m.* (mil.) side armour. -**chetto** *m. dim.* of **fianco**; (archit.) exterior curve, side of an arch; (butcher.) flank. -**conata** *f.* (mil.) flank bastion; side cut in duelling or fencing. -**cuto** *adj.* broad across the hips; broad-sided.

Fiandre *pr.n.f.pl.* (geog.) Flanders.

fiandrọne *m.* braggart.

†**fi·ano** *3rd pers. pl. fut.* of **essere**, q.v.

†**fiar·e**, †-**o** *m.* See **fiale**.

fias·ca *f.* flask; jar; hip-flask; (mil.) waterbottle. -**chętta** *f. dim.* small flask; (mil. hist.) -chetta per la polvere, powder-flask.

fiaschetteri·a *f.* See under **fiasco**.

fias·co *m.* (*pl.* -**chi**) glass bottle (with straw covering); un — di vino, a bottle of wine (2–2½ litres); prendere fischi per -chi, to get hold of the wrong end of the stick; fare il —, to toss for the price of a bottle of wine; (fig.) failure, fiasco; fare —, to fail, to be unsuccessful. -**ca·io** *m.* flask-seller; maker of flask-cases. -**cheggiare** [A 3 c] *intr.* (*aux.* essere) to fail, to be unsuccessful; (theatr.) to be a flop; †to buy wine by the flask. -**cheri·a** *f.* quantity of bottles. -**chetteri·a** *f.* retail wine-shop. -**chettino** *m. dim.* small bottle; scent bottle; ink bottle. -**chettọne** *m.* (orn.) penduline tit, *Remiz pendulinus*. -**chino** *m. dim.* small flask; (mil. hist.) powder horn. -**cọne** *m. augm.* large flask; poor wine; (fig.) complete failure.

Fi·at[1] *pr.n.f.* Fiat (car).

fi·at[2] *m. indecl.* in un —, in a twinkling; con un —, with a stroke of the pen, with one word.

†**fiata** *f.* time, occasion; spesse fiate, often; una —, once; da lunga —, long since; per più fiate, many times, several times.

fiat·are [A I] *intr.* (*aux.* avere) to breathe, to whisper, to speak; non — con nessuno di quel che s'è detto, not to breathe a word to anyone about what has been said; non osa —, he doesn't dare utter a word; non si sente —, not a whisper is heard; †*tr.* to smell, to scent. -**ata** *f.* breath; foul breath; †instant.

fiat·o *m.* breath; breathing; person, animal; tirar —, to draw breath; — grosso, panting, heavy breathing; avevo il — grosso dopo la salita, I was panting after the uphill climb; gli puzza il —, his breath is bad; lo riscaldò col —, he breathed on it to make it warm; restar senza —, to lose one's breath, (fig.) to be stunned, to be taken aback, to be rendered speechless; lavoro fatto col —, fine work done with exquisite care; sprecare il —, to waste one's breath; bere in (a) un —, to drink at one draught; ripigliar —, to get one's breath back, to rest for a while; sin che c'è —, c'è speranza, while there's life, there's hope; finchè avrò — (in corpo), as long as I have breath in my body, as long as I have the strength; non avere — di, to lack the strength to; (mus.) strumenti a —, wind instruments; i -i, the wind (of an orchestra); (poet.) dare — alle trombe, to sound the trumpets; *adv. phr.* a un —, in a twinkling, without drawing breath, all in one breath; in un —, without interruption, unceasingly; †stench, stink. -**ọne** *m. augm.* heavy breathing. †-**ore** *m.* stench. †-**oso** *adj.* stinking.

fia·tola *f.* (ichth.) — dorata, blackfish, *Stromateus fiatola*.

†**fiavo** *m.* See **favo**.

fib·bi·a *f.* buckle; — da scarpe, shoe-buckle; (mus.) see **capotasto**. -**a·glio** *m.* clasp. -**a·io** *m.* buckle-maker. †-**ale** *m.* see **fibbia**. †-**are** *tr.* to buckle; to buckle up.

fibr·a *f.* fibre; (fig.) fibre, constitution; stamina; uomo di forte —, man of robust health, man of strong constitution; (anat.) fibre; *pl.* entrails. -**ato** *adj.* (anat.) densely fibred; (bot.) fibrous. †-**illa** *f.* fibril, minute fibre. -**ina** *f.* (chem.) fibrin. -**inọso** *adj.* (anat.) fibrinous. -**ocemento** *m.* (bldg.) asbestos cement. -**oi·na** *f.* (chem.; text.) fibroin. -**olite** *f.* (miner.) fibrolite, sillimanite. -**oma** *m.* (anat.) fibroma, growth. -**osità** *f.* fibrousness. -**ọso** *adj.* fibrous, fibre-like.

fi·bula *f.* (Rom. antiq.) fibula, buckle; (anat.) fibula.

fica *f.* (vulg.) female genitals; obscene gesture of defiance (made by placing the thumb between the first and middle finger); fare le fiche, to make this gesture, to 'make the figs'; (ichth.) — di mare, pesce —, *Stromateus fiatola*; †fig.

†**fica·ia** *f.* fig-tree.

fic·a·io *m.* fig-orchard; fig seller; *adj.* fig-producing; mese —, September. -**albo** *m.* kind of white fig. -**ato** *adj.* pan -ato, bread kneaded with dried figs.

ficcanas-o, -i *m. indecl.* Paul Pry; Nosey Parker; inquisitive person; meddler; intruder; interfering busybody.

ficc-are [A 2] *tr.* to thrust; to drive in, to poke; to plant; — un palo in terra, to drive a stake into the ground; — il naso negli affari altrui, to poke one's nose into other people's business; — gli occhi addosso a, to fix one's eyes on; to notice (someone); ~arla ad uno, to deceive someone; non fa nè ~a, it's of no consequence; (mil.) to strike (the target) with oblique fire (neither horizontal nor plunging); *rfl.* (*acc. of prn.* 'si') to thrust oneself; to intrude; to worm in; to hide; ~arsi dentro le lenzuola, to huddle down under the bedclothes; non so dove ~armi, I don't know where to hide myself, I don't know where to squeeze in (e.g. in a crowded room, etc.); (*dat. of prn.* 'si') ~arsi in capo una cosa, to get a thing into one's head; ~arsi le dita nel naso, to pick one's nose. **~a·bile** *adj.* which can be driven in. **~amento** *m.* thrusting, driving. **~ante** *part. adj.* thrusting; driving; (mil.) oblique; tiro ~ante, oblique shot; *adv.* (mil.) obliquely. **~ato** *part. adj.* thrust in, driven in; stuck; fixed; implanted. **~atoia** *f.*, **~atoio** *m.* quagmire. **~atura** *f.* thrusting, driving; pushing. **~o** *m.* thrusting, driving; (mil.) oblique shot; *adv. phr.* a ~o, di ~o, obliquely; †guardare a ~o, to gaze fixedly at. **~one** *m.* Nosey Parker, inquisitive person, meddlesome person.

ficher̥eto, fich̥eto *m.* fig-orchard.

fic-o *m.* (*pl.* **fichi**) **1.** (bot.) fig-tree, fig, *Ficus carica*; — banano, — d'Adamo, banana, plantain, *Musa paradisiaca*; — d'Egitto, sycamore fig, *Ficus sycamorus*; — d'India, prickly pear, *Opuntia*; — degli Ottentotti, Hottentot fig, *Carpobrotus edulis*; — dei baniani, banyan tree, *Ficus benghalensis*; — del diavolo, peepul, botree, *F. religiosa*; — del Giappone, Japanese date plum, *Diospyros lotus*; — della gomma, India rubber tree, *Ficus elastica*; — delle Isole, papaw, *Carica papaya*; — di Barberia, see 'fico d'India'; — di Faraone, see 'fico d'Egitto'; — indiano, see 'fico d'Egitto'; — infernale, *Argemone mexicana*; — per terra, *Euphorbia chamaesyce*; — sacro, see 'fico de' baniani'; — salvatico, wild fig tree, *Ficus carica* var.; **2.** fig; — secco, dried fig; far le nozze coi fichi secchi, to be mean or close-fisted on an important occasion, to try to make a great parade with inadequate means; non vale un — secco, it's not worth a fig, it's not worth a straw; non me ne importa un — secco, I don't give a damn, I couldn't care less; l'apostolo del —, Judas; serbar la pancia ai fichi, not to expose oneself to danger, to be timid; (Tusc.) affectation, smirking; (med.) tumour; (vet.) polypus, tumour in horses; (ichth.) forkbeard, *Phycis blennoides*. **~ocianina** *f.* (chem.) phycocyanin. **~oeritrina** *f.* (chem.) phycoerythrin. **~osecco** *m.* (*pl.* **~osecchi**) dried fig; see also 'fico secco'. **~oso** *adj.* mawkish; tiresome, affected.

ficodin·dia *m. indecl.* See 'fico d'India', under **fico**.

fid-a *f.* land of which the grazing rights have been acquired; (naut.) lubbers' line; †safe-conduct, security. †**~ale** *adj.* see **fedele**.

fidante *part. adj.* See under **fidare**.

fidal-go *m.* (*pl.* **~ghi**) Spanish or Portuguese nobleman.

fidanz-a *f.* confidence, trust; security, guarantee; fare a — con uno, to rely upon someone; dare — a uno di una cosa, to entrust something to someone.

fidanz-are [A 1] *tr.* to betroth; to promise in marriage; †to guarantee; *rfl.* (*prep.* con) to become engaged (to), to get engaged (to); *recip. rfl.* to become engaged to each other, to get engaged. **~amento** *m.* engagement of marriage. **~ato** *part. adj.* betrothed, engaged; about to be married; *n.m.* fiancé; (fig.) boy-friend. **~ata** *f.* fiancée; (fig.) girl-friend.

fid-are [A 1] *tr.* to entrust, to confide; — una persona a un'altra, to entrust one person to another; *intr.* (*aux.* avere; *prep.* in) to trust; to confide, to have confidence; — in Dio, to trust in God; *rfl.* (*prep.* di) to trust, to rely upon; to have confidence in; ~arsi di, to rely upon; to confide in; to have trust in; non ~arsi delle proprie forze, not to trust one's own strength, to have no confidence in one's own strength; to dare; non ~atevi a far ciò, don't dare to do that; non ti —!, beware!, don't believe him, etc. **~ante** *part. adj.* entrusting; trusting; confiding. **~antemente** *adv.* confidently, trustfully. †**~ata** *f.* oath of loyalty. **~atezza** *f.* trustworthiness. **~ato** *part. adj.* trusted; entrusted; trustworthy, reliable, faithful; trusty; amico ~ato, faithful friend, true friend; (provb.) d'amico ~ato in amico ~ato (said when a secret is divulged from one trusted friend to another until it becomes common knowledge). **~atamente** *adv.* trustingly; reliably, certainly.

fidecommiss-o *adj.* (leg.) entrusted; *n.m.* fideicommissum; disposition by will obliging heir to preserve estate for transmission intact to descendants; estate subject to such will trust (C.C.); †trust; †redigere un atto di —, to draw up a deed of trust. **~a·rio** *adj.* (leg.) entrusted; fiduciary; having to do with, subject to, a will trust; sostituzione ~aria, will trust for beneficiaries in succession (C.C.); *n.m.* beneficiary, trustee, under such a will trust; the subject-matter thereof.

fidecom-mit·tere, -mettere [C 20] *tr.* (leg.) to entrust; to leave (by will) in trust.

fide-iṣmo *m.* (theol.) fideism. **~ista** *m.* fideist. **~i·stico** *adj.* fideistic.

fideiuss-iọne *f.* (leg.) guarantee; personal security; suretyship; prestare —, to guarantee; legge della —, law of suretyship; — per obbligazioni future, guarantee of future liabilities (C.C.); — solidale, joint recognizances (for good behaviour) (C.P.). **~ọre** *m.* (leg.) fide-jussor; surety; guarantor, sponsor; rendersi ~ore, to stand surety.

†**fidele** *adj.*, *n.m.* See **fedele**.

fident-e *adj.* trusting, confident. **~emente** *adv.* trustingly, confidently.

fidenziano *adj.* (lit. hist.) pedantic, Latinizing, in the style of Fidenzio, pseudonym of Camillo Scrofa (sixteenth century) who satirized pedantry in his poems.

Fi·dia *pr.n.m.* Phidias.

fidi·aco *adj.* Phidian.

†**fidi·cin-e** *m.* (mus.) string-player. (**~a** *f.*)

Fi·dio *pr.n.m.* (Rom. myth.) Fidius.

fidi·zie *f.pl.* (Gk. antiq.) common mess at Sparta.

fido¹ *adj.* trusty, faithful; devoted; — Acate, faithful Achates, loyal companion.

fido² *m.* (comm.) credit; a —, on credit; far —, to give credit.

Fido³ *pr.n.m.* Fido (name for a dog).

fidu·ci-a *f.* confidence; trust; — in sè, self-confidence, self-assurance; ho — di riuscire bene, I am confident that I shall succeed; mancanza di —, lack of confidence; riporre — in, to place trust in; ritirare la — da, to lose trust in; voto di —, vote of confidence; porre la questione di —, to put the motion of confidence; uomo di —, specially trusted employee, right-hand man, collaborator in position of special trust; un posto di —, a position of trust; di —, confidential; di assoluta —, absolutely reliable; 'L'Impiegato di Fiducia', 'The Confidential Clerk'; abbiate — in Dio, put your trust in God; avere — nelle proprie forze, to have confidence in one's own strength or powers; la sua — lo abbandonò, his self-assurance deserted him; (leg.) trust; — testamentaria, testamentary trust. **~ale** *adj.* confident, sure. **~almente** *adv.* confidently. **~are** [A 3] *tr.* to pledge, to guarantee. **~a·rio** *adj.* (leg.) fiduciary; in, having to do with, trust; disposizioni ~arie, (testamentary) dispositions on trust; *n.m.* trustee; (Ital. hist.) Fascist official in charge of 'Gruppo Regionale Fascista'. (**~a·ria** *f.*) **~ariamente** *adv.* (leg.) fiducially. **~oso** *adj.* confident, full of confidence; trustful; trusting, hopeful. **~osamente** *adv.* confidently; trustfully; hopefully.

†**fiebole** *adj.* and derivs. See **fievole**.

†**fie·dere** *tr.* to strike, to hit; to wound; to direct towards; to project; to afflict; to divide, to split; *intr.* to issue, to emerge, to come forth.

fiele *m.* (anat.) bile; (med.) jaundice; (fig.) gall, bitterness, rancour, hatred; intingere la penna nel —, to dip one's pen in gall; avere del — contro, to hate, to bear rancour against, to have a grudge against.

†**fi·en** *3rd pers. pl. fut.* of **essere**, q.v.

fien-o *m.* hay; — serotino, late crop of hay; pagliaio di —, hayrick, haystack; febbre da (del) —, hay-fever; (bot.) — di monte, mat grass, *Nardus stricta*; — greco, fenugreek, *Trigonella foenum graecum*; — santo, sanfoin, *Onobrychis viciifolia*; — stellino, *Setaria verticillata*. **~agiọne** *f.* hay-making, hay-harvest. **~a·ia** *f.* hay-barn. **~a·io** *adj.* relating to hay, hay; forca ~aia, hay-fork. **~ai(u)ola** *f.* hay, fodder. **~ai(u)olo** *adj.* pertaining to hay, hay; *n.m.* hay-dealer. **~ale** *adj.* relating to hay, hay; forca ~ale, hay-fork. **~aroca** *f.* (zool.) *Seps chalcides*, a lizard with reduced legs, similar to a slow worm. **~greco** *m.* (bot.) see 'fieno greco'. **~ile** *m.* hay-loft; barn; dirty, untidy room. **~oso** *adj.* containing hay; like hay.

fier-a¹ *f.* fair, market; bazaar; show, exhibition; present bought at a fair; — di bestiame, cattle-market; — di beneficenza, charity-bazaar; — campionaria, industrial exhibition; — del libro, book-exhibition. **~ai(u)olo** *m.* vendor at a fair. **~ino** *m.* last day of a fair.

fier·a² *f.* wild animal, wild beast; (fig.) beast, brute. †**-ale** *adj.* savage, bestial.

fieramẹnte *adv.* See under **fiero.**

fierẹzza *f.* pride; boldness, undaunted behaviour; wildness, fierceness; violence; (paint.; sculpt.) boldness.

fi·eri *Lat. adv. phr.* (colloq.) essere in —, to exist only in the imagination, to be hardly begun, to be in the making.

fierino *m. dim.* of **fiera¹,** q.v.

†**fierità** *f.* wildness, fierceness; boldness.

fier·o *adj.* proud; bold, intrepid, undaunted; stern, harsh, severe; cruel, savage; fierce, wild; (Tusc.) vigorous, spirited; un — tiranno, a harsh tyrant; una -a malattia, a severe illness; una -a lotta, a fierce struggle; uomo — nelle armi, an intrepid fighter; essere — di, to be proud of; †burning, scorching, fierce; †remarkable, admirable, amazing; †horrible, wicked, evil; †vehement; †sonno —, heavy sleep; †colore —, bright colour. **-amẹnte** *adv.* proudly, fiercely, vehemently; boldly; haughtily.

fieru·cola *f. dim.* of **fiera²;** wild creature, small wild animal.

Fie·sole *pr.n.f.* (geog.) Fiesole (in the prov. of Florence).

fiẹvol-e *adj.* weak, feeble; low-burning (of a flame). **-ẹzza** *f.* weakness, feebleness, debility. †**-ità** *f.* see **fievolezza.** **-mẹnte** *adv.* weakly, feebly, languidly.

fifa¹ *f.* (orn.) peewit.

fif-a² *f.* (mil. slang; colloq.) fear, 'blue funk'. **-ọne** *m.* coward. **-ọso** *adj.* cowardly, timid, fearful, afraid.

fif·faro *m.* (mus.) undulating flue stop (organ).

Fi·garo *pr.n.m.* Figaro; (joc.) barber; short jacket in Spanish style.

figarola *f.* (orn.) melodious warbler.

fig·g·ere [C 12] *tr.* to fix; to drive in; to stick; — gli occhi su, to fix one's gaze on; †to run through (with a sword); *rfl.* (dat. of prn. 'si') -ersi in capo, to take into one's head.

Figi *pr.n.m.* (geog.) Fiji; le Isole di —, the Fiji Islands.

fi·gli-a *f.* daughter; girl; — mia!, my girl!; (comm.) counterfoil; bollettario a madre e —, block of tickets with counterfoils (cf. **figlio**). **-ẹtta** *f.* small daughter; little girl; *pl.* (hist.) loaded chains put on prisoners in the time of Louis XI.

figli-are [A 4] *tr.* to bring forth young, to give birth to; to produce; *abs.* to calve; to lamb; to foal. **-ata** *f.* litter. **-atic·cia** *f. adj.* able to bear young. †**-atiera** *f. adj.* heavy with young; (also *n.f.*). **-ato** *part. adj.* brought forth, littered; produced. **-atura** *f.* delivery, bringing forth young, birth, confinement. **-azione** *f.* see **filiazione.**

figliastr-a *f.* stepdaughter. **-i** *m.pl.* stepchildren. **-o** *m.* stepson.

figliẹreccio *adj.* prolific, fecund.

fi·glio *m.* son; mio —, my son; il mio — maggiore, my eldest son; *pl.* sons; children; descendants; offspring; young (of an animal); suckers (of a plant); figli di Adamo, sons and daughters of Adam, men; tal padre, tal —, like father, like son; tra maschi e femmine, ebbe sei figli, he had six children, male and female; siamo tutti figli d'una stessa patria, we are all sons of the same fatherland; il Figlio di Dio, the Son of God; il Figlio dell'Uomo, the Son of Man; essere — delle proprie azioni, to have only oneself to blame; (fig.) essere il — della serva, to be treated like dirt; (leg.) — legittimo, legitimate son; — adottivo, adopted son; — illegittimo, illegitimate son; — naturale, natural son; — d'arte, — dell'arte, actor born of a theatrical family, child of the profession, born in show-business; — di famiglia, see under **famiglia**; *excl.* — d'un cane!, well, I'll be damned!

figliọc·ci-a *f.* goddaughter. **-o** *m.* godson.

figli(u)ọl-a *f.* daughter; girl; una buona —, a good girl, a good-natured girl; una — all'antica, an old-fashioned girl, an unsophisticated girl; una bella —, a good-looking girl, a handsome girl, a fine strapping girl, a bonny lass. **-o** *m.* son; boy; young (of an animal); un buon -o, a good-natured boy; ma, -o mio, but, my dear boy; il -o prodigo, the prodigal son; (bot.) sucker. **-ame** *m.* a lot of children; brats, kids. **-anza** *f.* children, progeny; filiality; (biol.) sibship. **-ino** *m. dim.* of **figliuolo**; baby, small child.

†**figmento** *m.* il — nostro, of what we are made; fiction; imagining.

fi·gnol-o, fignol-o *m.* boil; tumour; furuncle. **-ọso** *adj.* suffering from boils; furuncular.

†**fi·golo** *m.* See **figulo.**

fi·gul-o, †**-a·io,** †**-e·io** *m.* potter. †**-ina** *f.* art of a potter, ceramics. †**-ino** *adj.* ceramic.

figur-a *f.* figure; form, shape; appearance, aspect; (neol.) figure, bodily shape; una — geometrica, a geometrical figure; libro pieno di -e, book with plenty of illustrations; engraving; plate, figure, illustration; (cards) court-card; aveva la — d'un castello, it was in the shape of a castle; un demonio in — d'angelo, a devil in the guise of an angel; symbol; fare la — di, to symbolize; in — umana, in human shape; una — simpatica, a pleasant appearance; non fare —, not to show up, not to show to advantage; far —, to have a striking appearance; to look very smart; far buona —, far bella —, to show to advantage, to cut a fine figure, to look very impressive; far cattiva —, far brutta —, to cut a bad figure; to look silly; to lose face; che —!, what a disgrace!, what a fool he made of himself!; — rettorica, figure of speech; facciamo —, let's take an example; abito da —, showy dress; fa tutto per la —, he does everything for show; apparition, spectre; una — del sogno, something seen in a dream; figure (in dancing); dancer; una — di secondo piano, a secondary character; (art) disegno di —, figure drawing, drawing from life; scuola di —, life class, life school; (sculpt.) figure, statue; (naut.) figurehead; (telev.) mezza —, medium shot, waist upwards; (leg.) manner (of procedure); †(mus.) written note. **-ac·cia** *f. pejor.* bad figure; fare una -accia, to cut a poor figure. **-ale** *adj.* figurative. **-almẹnte** *adv.* figuratively. **-alità** *f.* figurativeness. **-ẹtta, -ina** *f. dim.* small figure; figurine; picture card. **-ina·io** *m.* figurine seller.

figur-are [A 1] *tr.* to figure, to shape, to form; to represent, to symbolize; la scena -a una prigione, the scene represents a prison; la lupa -a l'avarizia, the wolf symbolizes avarice; *intr.* (aux. avere) to act, to behave; — bene, to behave decently; to appear, to figure; to show up, to be clearly visible; il suo nome -a accanto al mio nella lista, his name appears next to mine in the list; — nell'ordine del giorno, to appear on the agenda; to cut a fine figure; non pensa ad altro che a —, he things of nothing but cutting a fine figure; to pretend; -a di non conoscermi, he pretends not to know me; *rfl.* (acc. of prn. 'si') to imagine oneself, to suppose oneself; *rfl.* (dat. of prn. 'si') to imagine, to suppose, to picture to oneself; to think; me l'ero -ata così, I had pictured it like that; -arsi!, just fancy!; figùrati, of course; figùrati che non lo conoscevo!, just think that I did not recognize him!; -atevi!, just imagine! **-a·bile** *adj.* imaginable. **-amẹnto** *m.* form, figure, image. **-ante** *part. adj.* figuring, representing, depicting; *n.m., f.* figurant, figurante; ballet-dancer. **-ativo** *adj.* figurative, symbolic, metaphorical; arte -ativa, representational art. **-ativamẹnte** *adv.* figuratively, symbolically; metaphorically. **-ato** *part. adj.* figured, represented; depicted, illustrated; libro -ato, illustrated book; figurative; linguaggio -ato, figurative language; (mus.) pedale -ato, florid pedal; canto -ato, figured music (as opposed to plainsong); (comm.) vendita -ata, fictitious sale; conto -ato, pro-forma account; (herald.) with human face. **-atamẹnte** *adv.* figuratively, symbolically; metaphorically. (**-atore** *m.* **-atrice** *f.*) **-azione** *f.* representation, depiction; (mus.) figuration. **-eggiare** [A 3] *intr.* (aux. avere) to use figurative language; to depict figures.

figurina *f. and derivs.* See under **figura.**

figurin-o *m.* fashion-model; sketch of model; fashion-magazine; rascal; parere un —, to dress elegantly; *pl.* (theatr.; cinem.; telev.) costumes; sketches for costumes. **-ista** *m.* (motor.) body design stylist; *f.* (pl.f. **-iste**) dress-designer, fashion-designer.

figurista *m.* (paint.) figure painter; sculptor of human figures.

figuro *m.* scoundrel, cad.

†**fil** *m.* See **figlio.**

fila¹ *f.* row, line; una — di alberi, a line or row of trees; mettere in —, to place in a row; far —, to queue; tre giorni di —, three days running; (mil.) file; a —, per —, in file; far —, to line up; capo —, leading file (also **capofila**); — di fondo, last file; — di fronte, in line; mezza —, half file; (mil. comm.) per — destr!, right wheel!; per — sinistr!, left wheel!; rompete le file!, dismiss!; tenere in —, to keep in a straight line; perdere la —, to get out of line; fuoco di —, drum fire; serrare le -e, to close the ranks; — indiana, single file; essere in prima —, to be in the front row, to be in the van; (motor.; aeron.) motore in —, in-line engine.

fila² *f.pl.* of **filo,** q.v.

filac·ci-a *f.* ravelling, shred of cloth; rope yarn; (text.) bast; lint. **-o** *m.* (naut.) dunnage; old rope; rope yard. **-ọne** *m.* night-line for fishing. **-ọso** *adj.* of a fibrous nature; threadbare, frayed; (of meat) stringy.

filac·cic-a *f.* ravelling, thread; lint; (naut.) see **filaccio,** under **filaccia;** short length of rope; weed on a ship's bottom. **-o** *m.* (pl. -a *f.*) filament, thread. **-ọso** *adj.* filamentous; fibrous; stringy.

Filadel·fia *pr.n.f.* (geog.) Philadelphia.

filag·gio *m.* (cinem.) ghost (defect in projection); (photog.) 'travel ghost'.

filagna *f.* (agric.) line of beans; wooden barrier.

filagrana *f.* See **filigrana**.

filaloro *m. indecl.* (metall.) gold-wire drawer.

filament·o *m.* (*pl.* -i *m.*, -a *f.*) filament, thread; fibre; — di vetro, glass silk; (bot.) filament. -**oso** *adj.* filamentous, fibrous.

filand·a *f.* (silkb.) filature, reeling establishment; silk factory; spinning-mill. -**a·ia** *f.* silk-spinner. -**iere** *m.* owner of a silk factory.

filandra *f.* (zool.) thread worm; (naut.) grass weed on ship's bottom.

filantr·opi·a *f.* philanthropy. -**o·pico** *adj.* philanthropic. -**opica·mente** *adv.* philanthropically. -**opismo** *m.* philanthropism.

filan·tropo *m.* philanthropist, public benefactor.

filar·co *m.* (*pl.* -**chi**) (Gk. hist.) phylarch.

fil·are[1] *tr.* [A I] to spin; il ragno -a la tela, the spider spins the web; (text.) to spin; non è più il tempo che Berta -ava, the good old days are gone; (techn.) l'oro, to draw out gold into fine thread; to exude; to ooze; la ferita -a sangue, the wound is bleeding, the wound is oozing blood; — l'amore (*or*, il perfetto amore), to bill and coo, to make love; (naut.) to render; to walk back (a rope); to check, to veer; — in bando, to light to; — a segnaro, — per segnaro, to veer; — tenendo a collo, to veer (keeping turns for lowering); — catena, to veer cable; — per mano, to pay out, to ease away; — volontieri, to let run; — per occhio, to let slip (the cable); — acqua, to spring a leak; -i remi, to let oars trail; — dodici miglia all'ora, to steam (at) twelve knots (speed made good); (mus.) — la voce, to prolong a note while swelling and diminishing the sound; *intr.* (*aux.* avere) (colloq.) to clear out, to make a get-away, to make off; -a!, off with you!, clear off!; — all'inglese, to take French leave; fare — alcuno, to make someone behave properly, to keep someone up to the mark; to go stringy, to form thin strings; to produce a long, thin flame; to smoke; la candela -a, the candle is smoking; to purr; la macchina -ava che era un piacere, the car purred along beautifully; to become ropy (of wine, etc.); to proceed, to follow logically; to plough a straight furrow; to be courting; -a con la Rosina, he is walking out with Rosina; — con uno, to have an agreement with someone, to be in league with someone; *intr.* (*aux.* essere) (mil.) to file past; to march past in extended order. -**a·bile** *adj.* capable of being spun; (text.) fit for spinning, spinnable. -**abilità** *f.* (text.) spinning capacity (e.g. of a fibre). -**ante** *part. adj.* spinning; viscous (of melted cheese, etc.); stella -**ante**, shooting-star, paper streamer (thrown at carnivals). -**ata** *f.* long line, row. -**atera** *f.* series, succession; string; rigmarole. -**atic·cio** *m.* floss-silk. -**ato** *part. adj.* spun; drawn; extended; gone, gone off; (fig.) well arranged; due ore -**ate**, two hours on end; zucchero -**ato**, candy floss; *n.m.* (text.) yarn; goods made of cloth; — casalingo, homespun yarn; — cucirino, sewing thread. -**atamente** *adv.* continuously; in orderly fashion. -**atoio** *m.* (text.) -atoio in fino, spinning machine; -atoio continuo, water frame; -atoio continuo ad anelli, ring frame; -atoio intermittente, mule; -atoio automatico intermittente, self-acting mule. -**atore** *m.* (text.) spinner; apparato -atore, spinneret (of silkworm). -**atrice** *f.* (text.) spinner, spinster; (silkb.) cocoon reeler. -**atura** *f.* (text.) spinning; -atura in grosso, -atura preparatoria, preparation of the roving, slubbing, roving; -atura in fino, -atura definitiva, spinning (proper); spinning mill.

filar·e[2] *m.* row, line; un — d'alberi, a row of trees; vein of minerals; (colloq.) line of writing; *n.m.* (naut.) stanchion; *pl.* battens of a hatch; †column of ships; †*f.* weather boards of a galley. †-**etto** *m.* (naut.) gunwale capping.

filarmo·nic·o *adj.* (mus.) philharmonic; *n.m.* music lover; società dei filarmonici, philharmonic society. -**a** *f.* music society.

filastr·occa, -**oc·cola** *f.* long string of words; rigmarole, balderdash; long tedious story; nonsense-poetry; long nursery-rhyme or popular ballad; rhymed charm.

filat·eli·a, -**e·lica** *f.* philately. -**e·lico** *adj.* philatelic; *n.m.* philatelist.

filato *part. adj.*, *n.m.* see under **filare**.

filatte·ri·o *m.*, -**a** *f.* (Jewish rel.) phylactery; (fig.) amulet; (rel. art.) phylactery (inscribed scroll in painting, stained glass, etc.).

filat·tico *adj.* See **profilattico**.

filauti·a *f.* self-love.

fileggiare [A 3 c] *intr.* (*aux.* avere) (naut.) to flap (of sails taken aback or too close to the wind).

filell·eno *m.* philhellene, philhellenist; *adj.* philhellenic. -**e·nico** *adj.* philhellenic. -**enismo** *m.* philhellenism.

file·tico *adj.* (biol.) phyletic.

filett·are [A I c] *tr.* to decorate with fillets; to be-ribbon; to fillet; (eng.) to thread, to cut a thread in, to tap. -**ag·gio** *m.* (eng.) screw-cutting. -**ato** *part. adj.* decorated, be-ribboned; filleted; (eng.) threaded. -**atrice** *f.* (eng.) thread-cutting machine. -**atura** *f.* be-ribboning; (eng.) threading, thread.

filetto *m.* filament; fine thread; fillet, thin strip of material; fillet of meat; small preliminary stroke made when writing a letter; (equit.) snaffle bit; (naut.) downhaul of a net; (eng.) screw thread; (anat.) — della lingua, fraenum of the tongue; (mus.) purfling (of a violin); (herald.) riband.

filial·e *adj.* filial; *n.f.* (comm.) branch, branch-office; -i commissionarie, commission agents. -**mente** *adv.* in a filial manner.

filiazione *f.* filiation; derivation; (leg.) issue; offspring; legge della — illegittima, law of illegitimacy.

filibustiere *m.* adventurer; rogue; unscrupulous person; tycoon; freebooter; (hist.) pirate; (joc.) driver of a 'filobus', q.v.

filiera *f.* (eng.) die, screw-cutting die, threading die; — aperta, split-type die; — chiusa, solid die; die plate, drawplate; (text.) nozzle, spinneret (for manufacture of man-made fibres); row, line; (zool.) silk gland of a spider; (herald.) bordure.

filig·gine *f.* See **fuliggine**.

filigran·a *f.* filigree; (paperm.) watermark. -**ato** *adj.* filigreed; carta -ata, watermarked paper.

†**fi·lio** *m.* See **figlio**.

filipen·dula *f.* (bot.) dropwort, *Filipendula vulgaris*.

filippe·o *adj.* philippic; *n.m.* (numis.) gold coin.

Filipp·i *pr.n.m.pl.* (geog.) Philippi; (provb.) ci rivedremo a —, we'll meet again at Philippi (a phrase used by a temporarily defeated person who threatens to turn the tables). -**esi** *m.pl.* Philippians.

filip·pic·a *f.* Philippic, invective. -**o** *adj.* Philippic.

Filippin·e *pr.n.f.pl.* (geog.) Philippines. -**o** *adj.* pertaining to the Philippines; *n.m.* native of the Philippines. (-**a** *f.*)

filippin·o[1] *m.* (eccl.) Oratorian, Father of the Oratory. -**a** *f.* (eccl.) Philippine (nun).

filippino[2] *adj.*, *n.m.* see under **filippine**.

Filippo *pr.n.m.* Philip; (numis.) silver coin in use in certain Italian provinces under Spanish rule, of the value of five or six lire.

Filiste·o *pr.n.m.* Philistine; (colloq.) outsider (esp. in artistic matters).

Fill·i, **Fil·lide** *pr.n.f.* Phyllis.

fil·lio *m.* (ent.) leaf insect, *Phyllium siccifolium*.

fillite *f.* (miner.) phyllite.

fillos·ser·a *f.* (ent.) *Phylloxera vastatrix*, an aphid pest of vines. -**ato** *m.* infested with *Phylloxera*.

film *m. indecl.* (or *pl.* as Eng.) (cinem.) film; — muto, silent film; — sonoro, film with sound track; — parlato, talkie. -**ina** *f. dim.* film strip. -**i·stico** *adj.* pertaining to films; l'industria -istica, the film industry. -**ografi·a** *f.* list of films. -**ologi·a** *f.* study of films; history of the cinema. -**oteca** *f.* library or depository of films.

film·are [A I] *tr.* (cinem.) to film, to shoot. -**a·bile** *adj.* suitable for filming; photogenic. -**ato** *part. adj.* filmed, made into a film.

fil·o *m.* (*pl.* -i *m.*, -a *f.*) thread; twine; string; clothes line; — per cucire, sewing thread; — di cotone, cotton thread; — di Scozia, strong cotton yarn; — forte, tacking thread; — di perle, string of pearls; — (di ferro), wire; — d'argento, silver wire; — d'acciaio, steel wire; — spinato, barbed wire; — elicoidale, wire used for cutting marble, etc.; telegrafo senza -i, wireless telegraphy; — a piombo, plumb-line; — d'erba, blade of grass; thead of cobweb; thread spun by an insect; vendere sul —, to sell a crop of grass before it is cut; edge, cutting-edge; il — di un coltello, the edge of a knife; passare a — di spada, to put to the sword; a — stradale, on the edge of the road; numerosi edifici a — strada, ribbon-development; a small amount; un — d'acqua, a tiny stream of water; un — di vino, a breath of wind; non c'è — di speranza, there is not the slightest hope; rispondere con un — di voce, to reply faintly; il soprano era ridotto ad un — di voce, the soprano had hardly any voice left; the grain (of wood); the fabric (of cloth); — di trama, woof; — di ordito, warp; tagliare secondo il —, to cut according to the grain; — dell'acqua, surface of the water, direction of a stream; pimples, rash (from shaving); clue; il — d'Arianna, clue to a difficult problem; thread of an argument; avere in mano le -a di un affare, to hold the threads;

fil·o (*cont.*)
perdere il — di un discorso, to lose the thread of a speech; le ~a di una congiura, the threads of a conspiracy; le ~a di un burattino, the wires of a marionette; manovrare le ~a, to pull the strings, to be the power behind the throne; per — e per segno, exactly, accurately, in detail; dare del — da torcere a qualcuno, to give someone food for thought; di —, consecutively, without interruption; essere in —, to be getting on well; dipendere da un —, to hang by a thread; far le ~a, to be viscous (of a liquid); il — delle reni, the backbone; (bot.) fibre, stalk, haulm; (naut.) — del vento, direction of the wind; leech of a sail; in —, in irons; bracciare in —, to brace up into the wind; navigare in fil di ruota, to run with the wind dead aft. ~ello *m.* (anat.) fraenum of the tongue. ~ino, ~olino *m. dim.* of filo; fine thread. ~oso *adj.* stringy; full of threads; thread-like.

fi·lobus (Flor.), **filo·bus** (Rom.) *m. indecl.* trolley-bus.

filocali·a *f.* love of beauty.

filocarro *m.* trolley; truck.

filodosso *m.* lover of glory.

filodramma·tico *adj.* philodramatic; *n.m.* amateur actor; società dei filodrammatici, amateur dramatic society.

filoforte *m.* See 'filo forte', under **filo**.

filog-e·nesi *f.* (biol.) phylogenesis. ~ene·tico *adj.* (biol.) phylogenetic.

filogini·a *f.* love of women.

filo·gino *m.* philogynist.

filologi·a *f.* literary study; (classical) scholarship; scholarly study of literary texts; critical exegesis; philology; — comparata, comparative philology.

filolo·gic·o *adj.* scholarly; literary; concerned with literature and language; circolo —, literary club, modern language club. (~amente *adv.*)

filo·logo *m.* literary expert; (classical) scholar; linguist; authority on language and literature.

Filomela, Filomena *pr.n.f.* (myth.) Philomel; Philomela; (poet.) nightingale.

†**filomuso** *m.* lover of the Muses; student of literature; music-lover; accademico —, title of a member of a literary academy.

filo-na·uta *m.* amateur sailor, sailing enthusiast. ~na·utico *adj.* pertaining to sailing; società ~nautica, sailing-club.

filoncino *m. dim.* See under **filone**.

filondente *m.* canvas used for embroidery.

filon-e *m. augm.* of filo, q.v.; coarse thread; rogue; un — di pane, a long French loaf; un — di lava, a stream of lava; il — del fiume, the flow, direction of the river; il — della marea, the race of the tide; (miner.) intrusion, vein, lode, seam; — a gradini, lob; tendency, inclination, bent; prendere il ~one di, to develop a tendency to. ~cino *m. dim.* small vein (of minerals); small French loaf, long narrow loaf.

filoneismo *m.* love of novelty.

†**filo·safo** *m.* See filosofo.

filoso *adj.* See under **filo**.

†**filo·sofa** *f.* woman philosopher.

filosofale *adj.* See under filosofo.

filosof-are [A I S] *intr.* (*aux.* avere) to philosophize; *tr.* to treat a subject philosophically. †~ante *part. adj.* philosophizing; *n.m.* philosopher. ~ato *part. adj.* reasoned, argued. ~eggiare [A 3 c] *intr.* (*aux.* avere) to philosophize; to act the philosopher.

filosofema *m.* philosophical doctrine, philosophical statement; logical demonstration.

filosofi·a *f.* philosophy; philosophical system; philosophical treatise; dottore in —, doctor of philosophy; (fig.) resignation, philosophical state of mind; con —, philosophically, with cheerful resignation; (typ.) fount of size equivalent to French Philosophie and English Small Pica and nearly equivalent to modern Anglo-American 11 point.

filoso·fic·o *adj.* philosophical; resigned; absent-minded, careless. ~amente *adv.* philosophically; with philosophy. †~are *intr.* to philosophize.

filo·sof-o *m.* philosopher; student of philosophy; (fig.) resigned person; absent-minded person; fare il —, to hold forth ponderously; †learned person, wise man; *adj.* philosophic, philosopher; poeta —, philosopher poet. †~a·glia *f. pejor.* group or number of inferior philosophers. ~ale *adj.* philosophic; pietra ~ale, philosopher's stone. ~astro *m. pejor.* bogus philosopher; amateur philosopher. ~eri·a *f.* philosophism. ~esco *adj.* (*m.pl.*

~eschi) philosopher-like; (iron.) donnish, pedantic. (~escamente *adv.*) ~essa *f.* (joc.) woman-philosopher; woman student of philosophy; (pejor.; iron.) woman who likes to hold forth. ~ismo *m.* philosophism.

filos·sera *f.* (ent.). See fillossera.

Filo·strato *pr.n.m.* Philostratus; the title of a narrative poem by Boccaccio.

Filote·a *pr.n.f. The Introduction to a Devout Life*, by St Francis of Sales; any similar book of devotion.

filo-tecni·a *f.* love of the arts; interest in applied arts. ~tec·nico *adj.* philotechnic; istituto ~tecnico, institute of industrial arts. †~ten·nico *adj.* see filotecnico.

Filot·tete *pr.n.m.* (Gk. lit.) Philoctetes.

filov-i·a *f.* trolley-bus route (line); trolley-car route (line); aerial railway. ~ia·rio *adj.* relating to trolley-bus or car, etc.; linea ~iaria, trolley-bus line.

filtr-are [A I] *tr.* to filter; to strain, to percolate; (fig.) to analyse, to clarify; *intr.* (*aux.* essere) to leak, to ooze, to filter through. ~a·bile *adj.* filterable. ~ag·gio *m.* (techn.) filtering, filtration. ~ato *part. adj.* filtered; strained; percolated; *n.m.* filtrate. ~azione *f.* filtration; filtering; straining; percolating.

filtro *m.* filter; philtre; love-potion; cup of coffee (percolated); sigarette con —, cork-tipped cigarettes; filter, strainer; — dell'aria, air filter, air cleaner; (motor.) — a bagno d'olio, oil-bath air cleaner; (electron.) filter; (radio) — d'onda, wave filter; — passaalto, high-pass filter; — passa-banda, band-pass filter; — passabasso, low-pass filter; (photog.) filter; — di luce, colour filter, colour screen; — polarizzante, polaroid filter; (telev.) televisore con — ottico, black screen television set.

filtro-pressa *f.* (techn.) filter press.

†**filuca** *f.* (naut.). See feluca.

filugello *m.* (ent.) silk-worm.

filusello *m.* tissue made from floss-silk.

filza *f.* string; series; — di perle, string of pearls; — di bugie, string of lies; file, collection; — di documenti, file of documents; (needlew.) punto a —, running stitch.

fim-a *m.* (med.) small tumour, ulcer. ~a·tico *adj.* tumour-like. ~atosi *f.* outbreak of small tumours.

fim·bri-a *f.* fringe, border, hem; (anat.) fimbria, extremity; †fibre; †membrane. ~ato *adj.* fringed, hemmed; embroidered.

†**fime** *m.* See fimo.

fimo *m.* dung, manure.

fimosi *f.* (med.) phimosis.

fin *prep.* abbrev. of **fino²** q.v.

†**fino** *f.* See fine¹.

final-e *adj.* final; last; ultimate; conclusive; definitive; sillaba —, final syllable; (philos.) causa —, final cause; (theol.) giudizio —, Last Judgement; *n.m.* (mus.) finale; il gran —, the grand finale; final (of a mode); (typ.) tail-piece, cul-de-lampe; *f.* (sport) final; final letter or syllable of a word, final. ~mente *adv.* finally, at last; eventually; at the end; in the end. ~ismo *m.* (biol., etc.) teleology, finalism. ~ista *m.* (philos.) teleologist; (sport) finalist. ~ità *f. indecl.* finality; purpose, aim, intention.

finanche, †financo *adv.* See under **fino²**.

finanza¹ *f.* finance; *pl.* finance, financial situation; cash, money; Treasury; il Ministro delle Finanze, Chancellor of the Exchequer; guardia di —, customs officer, revenue officer.

†**finanza²** *f.* end, cessation, cease.

finanz-iare [A 4] *tr.* to finance. ~iamento *m.* financing. ~ia·rio *adj.* financial. ~iaria·mente *adv.* financially. ~iato *part. adj.* financed; backed. ~ia·tore *m.* backer, financer; sleeping partner. ~iera *f.* frock-coat, redingote; (cul.) alla ~iera, cooked with fowl's liver, sweetbreads and mushrooms. ~iere *m.* financier; customs officer, revenue officer. †~iero *adj.* see finanziario.

†**finare** *vb.* and derivs. See finire.

finattanto, finchè *conj.* See under **fino²**.

finca *f.* column in a register book for entering figures; registro ad una sola —, single-cash account book; registro a doppia —, double-cash account book.

fine¹:
   1. *f.* (sometimes *m.*) END, close, conclusion, ending; termination, completion; result; la — del libro, the end of the book; la — del giorno, the close of the day; a — mese, at the end of the month; la — del discorso, the conclusion of the speech, the end of the speech; (electr.) un — corsa, a limit switch; senza —,

fine (*cont.*)

endless, unending; alla —, in —, in the end, at last, finally; alla fin —, alla fatta —, at the very end, after all; in fin dei conti, when all is said and done, after all; dal principio alla —, from beginning to end; buona — e buon principio!, happy New Year!; condurre a —, to bring to an end, to conclude; in fin di vita, dying, the point of death; fare —, to stop; volgere alla —, to draw to a close; mettere — a, porre — a, to put an end to, to terminate; giungere a buon —, to have a good result, to turn out well; il — del soldato è l'essere ammazzato, the soldier ends up by getting killed; (mus.) da capo sino al fine, go back to the beginning and continue to the end; (comm.) salvo buon —, reserving due payment. **2.** *m.* (never *f.*) AIM, purpose, intention, end; un secondo —, an ulterior aim; a che —?, to what end?, for what reason?; a — di, in order to; a fin di bene, with honest intentions, with good intentions; il — giustifica i mezzi, the end justifies the means; al — i medici possano essere informati, so that the doctors may be informed.

fin-e² *adj.* fine, refined, pure; subtle; delicate; minute; subtle, cunning; sharp, acute; fine, thin, slender; uomo —, refined man; gusto —, delicate taste, refined taste; disegno —, fine design, delicate pattern; ingegno —, acute mind; *n.m.* thin part; delicate thing. **-emęnte** *adv.* finely; delicately; well (cf. **fino¹**).

finestr-a *f.* window; — a ghigliottina, sash-window; — ferrata, barred window, grille; porta —, French window; farsi alla —, to come to the window; affacciarsi alla —, to appear at the window; la — dà sulla piazza, the window looks on to the square; o mangiar questa minestra, o saltar questa —, you have no choice, there is no getting out of it; Dio serra un uscio e apre una —, if one way is blocked God provides another; cacciato dall'uscio rientra dalla —, there's no getting rid of him (it); (naut.) square port; — oscura, deadlight; (ceram.) medallion; (fig.) wound; opening; (poet.) entrance, entry; (anat.) fenestra; †exit, outlet, issue. **-ata** *f.* slamming of a window as a sign of disliking someone; una -ata di sole, a gleam of sunshine (through the clouds); series of windows. **-ato** *adj.* containing a window, provided with windows, glazed; (herald.) port and windows; *n.m.* row of windows. **-ella, -ętta, -ina** *f. dim.* small window. **-ino** *m. dim.* small narrow window; window (of a rlwy. compartment, tram, etc.); booking-office window. **-ọne** *m. augm.* large window; church window. **-uzza** *f. dim.* small window; small opening.

finętto *m.* See under **fino¹**.

finęzza *f.* fineness, refinement, delicacy; purity; subtlety, sharpness, shrewdness; kindness, favour, courtesy; †usare una —, to do a favour.

fing-ere [c5] *tr., intr.* (*aux.* avere) to feign, to pretend; to imagine, to invent; to suppose; to simulate, to counterfeit; — dolore, to feign grief, to pretend to be sorry; to represent, to figure; — di essere malato, to pretend to be ill, to malinger; — cose inesistenti, to invent imaginary things, to depict fictitious happenings; -iamo pure che sia così, just suppose that it is so; to be insincere, to be false; *rfl.* (*acc.* of *prn.* 'si') to feign oneself, to pretend to be; -ersi pazzo, to pretend to be mad; (*dat.* of *prn.* 'si') to imagine to oneself. **-ęnte** *part. adj.* pretending; simulating; dissimulating. **-i·bile** *adj.* which can be simulated. **-imęnto** *m.* pretending; dissimulating; pretence; fiction. **†-itivo** *adj.* fictitious, imaginary. **-itọre** *m.* pretender, deceiver. (**-itrice** *f.*)

†finice *f.* See **fenice**.

finimęnto *m.* finishing, completion; finishing touches; portare a —, to complete; (techn.) finishing; complete set; un — da tavola, a set of table-linen; un — di porcellana, a porcelain service (for the table); un — di gioielli, a 'parure', a set of jewelry all in the same stones; *pl.* harness, trappings; horse brasses.

finimọnd-o *m.* end of the world; disaster, ruin; turmoil, chaos; rumpus; show-down; †person who fears the worst, one who foretells the end of the world; †the ends of the world, the outermost rim.

fin-ire [D2] *tr.* to finish, to terminate, to end; to put an end to; to close, to conclude; — il discorso, to say one's say, to have one's say out; to kill; to satisfy; -iscila!, -itela!, stop it!; -iamo questa conversazione, let us put an end to this conversation; per -irla, to put an end to it, to have done with it; — gli studi, to complete one's studies; — il discorso, to conclude one's speech; — uno, to kill someone; questo quadro non mi -isce, this picture does not satisfy me; — il desiderio, to satisfy one's

desire; *intr.* (*aux.* avere, essere) to end, to finish, to come to an end; to die; ha -ito di penare, his sufferings are ended; — con, to end up by; ha -ito coll'ucciderlo, he ended by killing him; — con schiamazzi, to end in an uproar; -ì in mezzo ai tormenti, he died in great suffering; il bastone -isce a punta, the stick ends in a point, has a pointed end; la parola -isce in vocale, the word ends in a vowel; la Dora -isce nel Po, the Dora flows into the Po; ieri non è -ito di piovere tutto il giorno, yesterday it did not stop raining all day; la lezione è -ita, the lesson has ended, the lesson is finished; — bene, to end up well, to be successful; — male, to end badly, to be unsuccessful; la strada -isce qui, the road ends here; dove va a — questa strada?, where does this road end up?; non so dove voglia andare a — con questo discorso, I don't know what he's driving at; dove è andato a —?, what became of him? **-i·bile** *adj.* finishable; concludable. **-iente** *part. adj.* finishing, ending; tutte le parole -ienti in a, all words ending in a. **†-ita** *f.* end; finish; death; ending, termination; alla -ita, finally. **†-ità** *f.* finiteness. **-itęzza** *f.* finish, perfection. **-itivo** *adj.* final; lettera -itiva, final letter; modo -itivo, indicative mood; †definitive. **-ito** *part. adj.* finished, ended; all over; completed, terminated; closed, settled, concluded; exhausted; done for, all in; farla -ita, to have done with it, to end it; sarebbe l'ora di farla -ita, it's high time to put an end to it; perfect, accomplished, expert; finite; verbo di modo -ito, finite verb; il -ito e l'infinito, the finite and the infinite. **-itamęnte** *adv.* completely; finitely; perfectly, in a finished way. **-itọre** *m.* one who finishes; (industr.) finisher; (eng.) maschio -itore, plug tap, sizer tap. **-itura** *f.* finish, finishing; finishing touches; (text.) dressing; †end; †death. **-iziọne** *f.* end, termination; (motor. industr., etc.) fittings, trimmings.

finissag·gio *m.* (techn.) finishing.

fini·timo *adj.* neighbouring, bordering, adjacent; frontier; paesi finitimi, neighbouring countries; (leg.) adjoining; *n.m.pl.* neighbours, neighbouring inhabitants.

finiziọne *f.* See under **finire**.

Finlan·d-ia *pr.n.f.* (geog.) Finland. **-ęse** *adj.* Finnish; *n.m.* Finn, Finlander; *f.* Finnish woman.

finne *m.* (ethn.) Finn.

fin·nico *adj.* Finnish, Finnic; *n.m.* Finnish, the Finnish language.

fin-o¹ *adj.* fine, pure, noble; refined; sharp, acute, shrewd, subtle; cervello —, shrewd and subtle mind; fine, delicate, thin; oro — fine gold, pure gold; seta -a, fine silk; una mente -a, a shrewd mind; orecchio —, sharp hearing; palato —, delicate palate. (**-amęnte** *adv.*) **-ętto** *m.* (text.) fine flannel.

fin-o² *prep.* until, till; as far as, up to; — a domani, until tomorrow; — ad ora, until now; — a quando?, how long?; fin da ieri, since yesterday, ever since yesterday; viaggiare — a Roma, to travel as far as Rome; da Londra — a Parigi, from London to Paris, all the way from London to Paris; — a che, fin tanto che, until; — in chiesa, even in church. **-allora** *adv.* up to that time. **-anche, -anco** *adv.* even. **-chè** *conj.* until, till; as long as, while; aspettami -chè io (non) venga, wait for me until I come; -chè c'è fiato, c'è speranza, while there's life, there's hope. **-ọra** *adv.* until now, up to the present, so far. **-tanto, -tantochè** *conj.* until, till; while.

finoc·chio *m.* (bot.) fennel, *Foeniculum vulgare*; — acquatico, horsebane, *Oenanthe aquatica*; — arancino, — acquatica, carosella, Italian fennel, *Foeniculum vulgare* var. *piperitum*; — d'alpe, *Ligusticum mutellinoides*; — di Bologna, — di Chioggia, Florence fennel, finocchio, *Foeniculum vulgare* var. *dulce*; — marino, samphire, *Crithmum maritimum*; — porcino, *Peucedanum officinale*; (vulg.) pederast, 'pansy'; †trifle, worthless object; †dare finocchi, to deceive, to beguile.

finodicitọre *m.* compère; patter-comedian.

finọra *adv.* See under **fino²**.

fint-a *f.* feint; pretence; fare una —, to make a feint; fare — di, to pretend to; (tailoring) false pocket; flap concealing buttonholes; (football) feint. **-ina** *f. dim.*, **-ino** *m. dim.* small feint; transformation, type of wig worn on the front of the head.

fint-acchiuolo *m.*, **-ag·gine** *f.*, **-eri·a** *f.* See under **finto**.

fintan-to, -tochè *conj.* See under **fino²**.

fint-o *part.* of **fingere**, q.v.; *adj.* feigned, counterfeit, simulated; insincere; sham; false; finestra -a, false window; denti -i, false teeth; una -a battaglia, a mock battle; fiori -i, artificial flowers; (mus.) righi -i, leger lines; *n.m.* hypocrite, dissembler; — tonto, cunning man who pretends to be a fool. **-amęnte** *adv.* feignedly,

fint-o (*cont.*)
deceitfully, insincerely. **-acchi(u)olo** *m.* sharp boy, cunning boy. **-ag·gine** *f.* deceitfulness, falseness; duplicity. **-eri·a** *f.* false words; deceit; deceitfulness. **-one** *m.* hypocrite, humbug.

finzione *f.* feigning, deceiving; fiction, invention; falsehood, sham; figment; una — poetica, a poetic invention; alieno da —, sincere, candid, frank; parlare senza -i, to speak openly, to be frank; (leg.) — giuridica, — legale, legal fiction.

fio¹ *m. indecl.* penalty; pagare il — d'un delitto, to pay the penalty for a crime; ne pagherà il —, he will pay for it; †fief; †due; †homage.

†fio² *m.* See **figlio**.

†fio³ *m.* the letter Y (deriving from Greek upsilon; the last letter in some forms of alphabet); dall'A al —, from beginning to end; venire al —, to come to the end, to reach a conclusion; jot, iota; stimare men che un —, not to care a jot about, to set no store by.

†fiobono *m.* (naut. Ven.) platform of a gondola.

fiocag·gine *f.* See under **fioco**.

†fiocca *f.* snow-flake; snow; quantity, number; abundance; instep; tongue of riding-boot.

†fiocca·glio *m.* (naut.) double block secured to the upper spectacle plate and used with a mastrope.

fiocc-are [A 2] *intr.* (*aux.* essere) to fall thickly (of snow); to drift down in flakes; la neve -a, it is snowing; (fig.) to abound, to be numerous, to hail; to come thick and fast; -avano le bestemmie, there was a hail of curses; to emanate, to derive; †to flock, to crowd; †to be pressing; †*tr.* to scatter, to spread, to shower; -arle a, to insult, to abuse. **-ante** *part. adj.* falling in flakes; abounding. **-ato** *part. adj.* covered in snow, snow-clad; hoary, flecked with white.

fioc-co *m.* (*pl.* **-chi**) knot, bow; lock, flock (of wool) powder-puff; flake (of snow); tassel; tuft of hair on a horse's fetlock, 'feathers'; il — delle scarpe, shoelaces tied in a bow; il — della cravatta, the knot in a man's tie; un berretto col —, a cap with a tassel; fare il —, to do the trick; mettersi in -chi, to dress up; (mil.) — della spada, sword tassel; (fig.) coi -chi, first rate, superlative, gala; un pranzo coi -chi, a 'slap-up' dinner; (slang) fare un —, to steal; (text.) staple; (naut.) jib, foresail, headsail, staysail; (Genoa) — a pallone, balloonsail; (zool.) — di mare, *Spirographis spallanzanii*, a marine tube-dwelling worm; (herald.) cappello con -chi, ecclesiastical hat; †emblem of political faction; †theft; †booty; †vast quantity, abundance. **-chettare** [A 1 c] *tr.* to adorn with small bows. **-chettato** *part. adj.* adorned with small bows. **-chettatura** *f.* adorning with bows; adornment of bows. **-chetto** *m.* (mil.) tassel, badge, tab; aiguillettes. **-coso** *adj.* flakey, flaky; †hoary, white-haired.

fioc·colo *m.* snow-flake.

fioch-etto *adj. dim.*, **-ezza** *f.* See under **fioco**.

fio·cin-a, fiocin-a *f.* harpoon; trident; — snodata, barbed harpoon. **-are** [A 1 s, A 1] *tr.* to catch with a harpoon, to harpoon; *abs.* to fish with a harpoon; to fire a harpoon. **-ante** *m.* harpoon-fisher. **-ata** *f.* blow with a harpoon. **-etta** *f. dim.* small harpoon; carving-fork. **-iere** *m.*, **-ino** *m.* harpoon-fisher.

fio·cine *m.* pip, stone (e.g. of grapes); skin of grape; grape.

fio-co *adj.* (*m.pl.* **-chi**) weak, feeble, faint; dim; hoarse; una voce -ca, a faint voice, a hoarse voice; un — lume, a faint light, a dim light. **-camente** *adv.* hoarsely; weakly, feebly; faintly; dimly, darkly. **-cag·gine** *f.* hoarseness; weakness. **-chetto** *adj. dim.* rather hoarse; rather faint; dim. **-chezza** *f.* hoarseness; faintness; feebleness, weakness.

fionco *m.* halyard.

fiond-a *f.* sling; catapult. **†-atore** *m.* (mil. hist.) soldier armed with a sling; catapultist.

Fio·nia *pr.n.f.* (geog.) Isola —, Fünen, Fyu.

fiora·i-a *f.* flower-seller; florist. **(-o** *m.*)

fior-ale *adj.* floral; (bot.) foglie -ali, bracts. **-aliso** *m.* see **fiordaliso**. **-ame** *m.* flowering branch; ramage; flower-pattern, floral design; stoffa a -ami, material with a floral pattern.

†fiorare *intr.* to bear flowers, to flower.

fiorato *adj.* flowered.

†fiordaligi *f.* See **fiordaliso**.

fiordalis-o *m.* fleur-de-lis; (pop.) corn-flower; (herald.) — partito per mezzo, demi-fleur-de-lis couped palewise; — fiorentino, fleur-de-lis flowered. **-ato** *adj.* (herald.) croce -ata, cross fleuretty, cross flurty.

†fiordil-igi *f.*, **†-i·gio** *m.* See **fiordaliso**.

fiordo *m.* (geog.) fiord, fjord.

fior-e *m.* flower; blossom; bloom; vaso da -i, flower-pot, vase for cut flowers; -i di campo, wild flowers; -i di serra, hot-house flowers; (of a mollycoddled or closely sheltered person) essere un — di serra, to be a hot-house plant; -i d'arancio, orange-blossom; (fig.) weddings; essere in —, to be in flower, (fig.) to flourish; la città del Fiore, Florence; — a mandorla, clock (on a sock or stocking); -i retorici, flowers of speech; (poet.) il primo —, down on a young man's cheek; the flower, the best, the pick, the cream; il fior —, the choicest part; fior di latte, cream, top of the milk; fior di farina, flour; il — della gioventù italiana, the flower of Italian youth, the cream of young Italy; il — della *Divina Commedia*, the best of the *Divine Comedy*, the pick of the *Divine Comedy*; essere nel — degli anni, to be in the prime of life; un fior di galantuomo, a very fine gentleman, a very honourable and upright person; surface; a fior d'acqua, on the surface of the water; a fior di pelle, just grazing the skin; a fior di labbra, just touching the lips; (aeron.) volare a fior di terra, to hedge-hop; abundance; fior di quattrini, lots of money; small amount, grain; non ha fior di senno, he hasn't an ounce of sense; a comic, rustic dialogue in rhyme; (equit.) part of the bit where the reins are attached; small, white mark on a horse's head; (naut.) point where the ship's transverse beams meet the side plates; *pl.* (cards) clubs; il sette di -i, the seven of clubs; -i del vino, mould on wine; (chem.) -i di zolfo, flowers of sulphur; (med.) menses, courses; -i bianchi, leucorrhoea; (bot.) — campani, Canterbury bell, *Campanula medium*; — cappuccio, larkspur, *Delphinium ajacis*; — cuculo, ragged robin, *Lychnis flos-cuculi*; — d'Adone, pheasant's eye, *Adonis annuus*; — d'Aliso, corn-flower, *Centaurea cyanus*; — d'Aliso grande, *Centaurea jacea*; — d'Aliso rosso, *Xeranthemum annuum*; — d'angiolo, mock orange, syringa, *Philadelphus coronarius*; — di legna, *Limodorum abortivum*; — di morto, periwinkle, *Vinca*; — d'oro, *Chrysanthemum coronarium*; — galletto, *Lathyrus aphaca*; — maggi, poets' narcissus, *Narcissus poeticus*; — ragno, early spider orchid, *Ophrys sphegodes*; — rancio, marigold, *Calendula officinalis* and *Chrysanthemum m᾿conis*; — stella, *Anemone hortensis*; (tanning) grain; — di montone, skiver; (mus.) embellishment, grace; (archit.) acanthus leaf (on Corinthian or composite capital). **-eggiare** [A 3 c] *intr.* (*aux.* essere) to be in flower; (artill.) to be low (of shell trajectory); *tr.* (mus.) to embellish. **-eggiante** *part. adj.* in flower, flowering; just skimming the surface. **-ellino, -ello** *m. dim.* small flower, flowerlet. **-ente** *part.* of **fiorire**, q.v. **-era** *f.* flower-vase with perforated top. **-one** *m. augm.* large painted or worked flower; book decoration; (agric.) the first crop of figs (June–July); (archit.) rose window. **-ume** *m.* dust and chaff remaining under a heap of hay.

fiorentin-o *adj.* Florentine; alla -a, in the Florentine way; (cul.) bistecca alla -a, entrecote, steak with bone; *n.m.* Florentine, the Florentine tongue; a Florentine. **-amente** *adv.* in the Florentine way. **-a** *f.* Florentine woman, Florentine girl; oil-lamp; kind of dance. **-ame** *m.* the riff-raff of Florence. **-eggiare** [A 3 c] *intr.* (*aux.* avere) to imitate the Florentine accent; to behave like a Florentine. **-ello** *m.* (numis.) Florentine coin. **-eri·a** *f.* imitation of the Florentine accent. **-esco** *adj.* (*m.pl.* -eschi) Florentine-like. **(-escamente** *adv.*) **-ismo** *m.* Florentine expression. **-ità** *f.* Florentine quality. **-izzare** [A 1] *tr.* to translate into Florentine; *intr.* (*aux.* avere) see **fiorentineggiare**. **-ume** *m.* the riff-raff of Florence.

Fiorenz-a, -e *pr.n.f.* See **Firenze**.

fiorett-o *m. dim.* of **fiore**, q.v.; little flower; flowerlet; (fig.) selection; selected passage; an elegant or ornate arrangement of words or phrases; the 'cream' or highest quality, the 'flower'; il — della lana, the best quality wool; (in paper-manufacture) an inferior quality of paper; (mil.) small band of selected soldiers; — di cavalieri, picked group of horsemen; (fencing) foil; (mus.) embellishment, grace; a kind of dance-step; (electr.) insulating rod; (mining) drilling bit; (rel.) small act of sacrifice or mortification; good deed, something 'offered up'; †a kind of fine white sugar; †egg broth. **-are** [A 1 c] *intr.* (*aux.* avere) to write or compose in a flowery style; *tr.* to adorn excessively, to embellish. **-ato** *part. adj.* flowered; flowery; excessively embellished, over-ornate. **-atura** *f.* flourish; excessive use of embellishments. **-ino** *m. dim.* small flower; flower in a design.

fioricrinito *adj.* (poet.) with flowers in the hair.

fioricult·ọre *m.*, **-ura** *f.* See **floricult·ọre, -ura.**

fiori·fero *adj.* floriferous, flower-bearing.

Fiorile *pr.n.m.* (hist.) Floreal (the eighth month in the French Republican calendar).

Fiorina *pr.n.f.* a female character in the *Commedia dell'arte.*

fiorin·o *m. dim.* of **fiore**, q.v.; little flower; (numis.) Florentine coin struck in 1252; florin; †quọta, portion.

fior·ire [D 2] *intr.* (*aux.* essere) to flower, to bloom, to blossom; i gigli ~iscono, the lilies are blooming, the lilies are in flower; (fig.) to flourish, to prosper, to thrive; il commercio ~isce, trade is thriving; le arti ~iscono, the arts are flourishing; to be covered with mould; to peel (of plaster); to grow white (of hair); *tr.* to make flower, to cause to flower; to paint flowers on, to strew with flowers; to embellish; to adorn; — uno scritto, to embellish a composition; †to deck out; †(naut.) see **inferire**; †*rfl.* (hist.) to dress more ornately than was permitted by decree. **-ente** *part. adj.* flourishing, prospering, thriving; flowering, blooming; (herald.) flory. **-entemente** *adv.* flourishingly; prosperously. †**-igione** *f.* flowering, coming into bud. **-imẹnto** *m.* flowering; flourishing. †**-iscente** *adj.* flowering; blooming. **-ita** *f.* flowering; flowers strewn on ground in processions; covering; collection; una ~ita di neve, a sprinkling of snow; una ~ita di canti, a collection of songs; †scattered objects, anything strewn. †**-ità** *f.* quantity and variety of flowers; abundance; anthology, collection. **-itẹzza** *f.* floridness, ornateness. **-ito** *part. adj.* flowering; flowery; florid; excellent, elegant; flourishing; stile ~ito, florid style; conversazione ~ita, elegant conversation; vino ~ito, wine on which mould is beginning to form. **-itamẹnte** *adv.* floridly; in a flourishing style. **-itọio** *m.* (tanning) lime-pit, liming. **-itura** *f.* flowering; flourishing; time of flowering; efflorescence; embellishment; una ~itura di bollicine sul viso, an outbreak of pimples on the face; crop; (fig.) galaxy; (mus.) vocal flourish.

fiorista *m., f.* painter of flowers; artificial flower-maker; flower-lover; (N. Ital.) florist.

fiorọne *m. augm.* of **fiọre**, q.v.; (archit.) rose-window.

fiorran·c·io *m.* (bot.) marigold. **-ino** *m.* (orn.) firecrest, *Regulus ignicapillus.*

fiorume *m.* See under **fiọre.**

fiosso *m.* part of shoe between heel and sole; instep.

†**fiọ·tola** *f.* flute.

†**fiọtta** *f.* See **frotta.**

fiott·are [A 1] *intr.* (*aux.* avere) to gurgle, to gush, to murmur (of waters); to wave, to sway, to undulate; to grumble, to whimper, to whine; (of a person) to cry. **-ìo** *m.* repeated or continuous gurgling, murmuring, whimpering, etc. **-ọne** *m.* whimperer; murmurer.

fiott·o *m.* stream; wave; murmur; whimper; lamentation; surge; lapping (of water); ebb; flow; venire a ~i, to gush forth; — di luce, flood of light; †multitude; †impetus, onrush; fury; †abuse, attack; †in —, with impetus, in a rage, in fury.

Firenze *pr.n.f.* (geog.) Florence; essere di —, to be (a) Florentine; paglia di —, Leghorn straw.

†**firinguello** *m.* See **fringuello.**

firm·a *f.* signature; — collettiva, joint signature; — di favore, *pro-forma* signature; apporre una —, to affix a signature; name, well-known writer, celebrity (contributing to a journal, etc.); falsificare una —, to forge a signature; far onore alla propria —, to honour one's signature; — in bianco, signature on a blank form; (leg.) signature; — legalizzata, legalized, formally certified signature; — finale, signature at foot; — marginale, signature on previous page or pages (of deed); (admin.; comm.) andare alla —, to go up for signature; †confirmation.

firmamẹnto[1] *m.* firmament; †security, strength; †foundations.

†**firmamẹnto**[2] *m.* confirming; securing; stabilizing.

firmano *m.* firman, decree, edict; †licence to trade in the East.

firm·are [A 1] *tr.* to sign; to ratify; to subscribe; — in bianco un assegno, to sign a blank cheque; — per procura, to sign by proxy, to sign per pro; (leg.) — un atto notarile, to execute a deed; — un contratto, to sign a contract. **-ante** *m., f.* signatory. **-atạ·rio** *m.* (*pl.* **-atạ·ri**) signatory; socio ~atario, partner having the authority to sign. **-ato** *part. adj.* signed; ratified.

†**firm·o** *adj.* see **fermo.** †**-ità** *f.* see **fermezza**, under **fermo.**

firne *f.* old snow.

fisạ·lia *f.* (zool.) *Physalia* spp., Portuguese man-o'-war.

fi·ṣalo *m.* (zool.) rorqual, *Balaenoptera rostrata.*

fiṣamẹnte *adv.* See under **fiso.**

†**fisare** *vb.* and derivs. See **fissare.**

fiṣarmọ·nica *f.* (mus.) accordion; piano-accordion.

fiṣau·lico *adj.* (mus.) pneumatic (see **organo**).

fiscal·e *adj.* fiscal; relating to inland revenue; anno —, financial year; (leg.) avvocato —, Judge Advocate General; visita medica —, visit by doctor to check authenticity of a medical certificate; (fig.) rigorous; inquisitorial; *n.m.* (hist.) fiscal; (leg.) public prosecutor; inspector of public revenue. **-mẹnte** *adv.* rigorously; exigently; inquisitoriàlly. †**-ato** *m.* (hist.) office of fiscal. **-eggiare** [A 3 c] *intr.* (*aux.* avere) to make an investigation, to make inquiries; to pry. (**-eggiamẹnto** *m.* **-eggiante** *part. adj.*) **-iṣmo** *m.* fiscal system; severity, rigour; inquisitorial proceedings. **-ità** *f.* piling up of taxation; methods of tax collection; fiscality; rigorous action.

fiscella *f.* wicker-basket.

fischi·are [A 4] *intr.* (*aux.* avere) to whistle; to hiss; to boo; to hoot; ~a il vento, the wind is whistling; ~ano gli uccelli, the birds are singing; il serpente ~a, the snake hisses; mi ~ano gli orecchi, there is a buzzing in my ears, someone has been talking about me; fece — lo staffile, he cracked his whip; to be ragged, to be worn out (of clothes); †— come un biacco, to be as poor as a church-mouse, to be down and out; †— ai tordi, to waste one's breath; *tr.* to whistle; — un'aria, to whistle a tune; to hiss; — una commedia, to boo, to hiss a play; †-arla a, to deceive, to trick; to beat up, to belabour; †*rfl.* to rush, to fling oneself. **-a·bile** *adj.* which can be whistled; fit to be booed or hissed. **-amẹnto** *m.* whistling; hissing; buzzing; whistle, hiss. **-ante** *part. adj.* whistling; hissing; lettere ~anti, sibilants. **-ata** *f.* whistle, whistling; hiss, hissing; mi è costata una ~ata, I got it for a song, it cost me very little. **-ato** *part. adj.* whistled; hissed, booed. (**-atọre** *m.* **-atrice** *f.*) **-erellare** [A 1] *intr.* (*aux.* avere) to whistle softly and continuously; to whistle between one's teeth; ~erellava strada facendo, he whistled as he walked along.

fischiẹtt·o *m. dim.* of **fischio**, q.v.; little whistle; whistle; (naut.) boatswain's pipe; *pl.* (cul.) kind of macaroni. **-are** [A 1 c] *intr.* (*aux.* avere) to whistle a sharp, gay tune, to whistle continuously; *tr.* to whistle. **-ìo** *m.* whistling; continual whistling. **-ọne** *m. augm.* miserable-looking man.

fi·schi·o *m.* whistle; hiss; whistling; hissing; il — del vento, the whistling of the wind; un — d'ottone, a brass whistle; accogliere con fischi, to greet with hisses, to show one's disapproval of by hissing; non me ne importa un —, I don't care a hoot, I don't give two hoots; prendere fischi per fiaschi, to get the wrong end of the stick, to mistake one thing for another; (naut.) ship's siren; un colpo di —, one blast on the siren; — del nostromo, boatswain's pipe; (mus.) whistle, pipe; pitch-pipe. **-ọne** *m. augm.* whistle, loud whistle; (orn.) widgeon, *Anas penelope*; ~one col ciuffo, red-crested pochard, *Netta rufina.* **-otti** *m.pl.* (cul.) see **fischietti.**

†**fiscina** *f.* wicker-basket.

fisciù *m. indecl.* fichu.

fisco *m.* (*pl.* **fischi**) public treasury; Treasury; inland revenue; †fine, penalty.

fiṣema *f.* (med.). See **enfisema.**

fisetere, fisetro *m.* (zool.) sperm whale, cachalot, *Physeter macrocephalus.*

fiṣiatri·a *f.* (med.) treating an illness by allowing nature to take its course

fi·ṣic·a *f.* physics; la — atomica, atomic physics; †science; †medicine, physic; †medical science. †**-ag·gine** *f.* day-dreaming; indulgence in fantastic imaginings.

†**fisiciano** *m.* doctor, physician.

fi·ṣic·o *adj.* physical; scienze fisiche, physical sciences; forza ~a, physical force; physical strength; *pl.* †malattie ~che, diseases for which a physician, not a surgeon, is required; *n.m.* physicist; physique, physical structure, constitution; figure, appearance; †physician, as distinguished from a surgeon. **-amẹnte** *adv.* physically. **-omatema·tico** *adj.* physico-mathematical. **-omecca·nica** *f.* (phys.) mechanics. †**-oso** *adj.* over-elaborated, cerebrated, sophisticated.

fi·ṣima *f.* (usu. *pl.*) whim, caprice, fancy; strange idea, a bee in one's bonnet.

fiṣi·ochi·mica *f.* physio-chemistry. **-ochi·mico** *adj.* physio-chemical; *n.m.* physio-chemist. **-o·crate, -ocra·tico** *m.* physiocrat. **-ocrazi·a**

fisi-ochimica (*cont.*)

f. physiocracy. **-ocri·tica** *f.* (philos.) 'natural philosophy' in a seventeenth-century sense. **-ocri·tici** *m.pl.* members of a Sienese academy founded by Gabrielli in 1696. **-ognomi·a** *f.*, **-ogno·mica** *f.* physiognomy, the art of judging character and disposition from the exterior appearance of face and body. **-ogno·mico** *adj.* physiognomical (cf. **fisionomia** and derivs.). **-ognosi·a** *f.* natural science(s). **-ografi·a** *f.* physiography, natural science, descriptive geography. **-ogra·fico** *adj.* physiographical. **-o·grafo** *m.* physiographer.

fisi-ologi·a *f.* physiology. **-olo·gico** *adj.* physiological; (med.) soluzione **-ologica** salina, physiological saline. **-ologicamẹnte** *adv.* physiologically. **-o·logo** *m.* physiologist.

fisi-omante *m.* one who professes to tell destiny from the face, physiognomist. **-oman·tico** *adj.* physiognomic. **-omanzi·a** *f.* physiognomy, the art of telling destiny from the face.

fisi-onomi·a *f.* physiognomy; face, facial expression; features, countenance; external appearance, shape. **-ono·mico** *adj.* physiognomical. **-onomicamẹnte** *adv.* physiognomically. **-onomista** *m.*, *f.* physiognomist; one who is good at remembering faces. **-o·nomo** *m.* see **fisionomista** (cf. **fisiognomia** and derivs.). **-onotipo** *m.* device for making a plaster cast of a living face. **-onotrac·cia** *f.* pantograph for drawing portraits.

fisioter-api·a *f.* physiotherapy. **-a·pico** *adj.* physiotherapeutic.

fis·o *adj.* (poet.) fixed, intent; *adv.* fixedly; guardare —, to gaze fixedly at. **-amẹnte** *adv.* fixedly; †dormire **-amente**, to have a profound sleep.

fis-ocarpo *adj.* (bot.) schizocarpic. **-oce·falo** *m.* (med.) a swelling on the head. **-ocele** *m.* (med.) a tumour in the scrotum. **-ometri·a** *f.* (med.) a distension of the uterus.

†fiso·folo *m.* See **filosofo**.

fisolera *f.* See **fusoliera**.

fisonomi·a *f.* and derivs. See **fisionomia**.

fisostigmina *f.* (chem.) physostigmine, eserine.

fisotorace *m.* (med.) accumulation of gas in the pleural cavity.

fissacorde *m. indecl.* (text.) rope fitter.

fissag·gio *m.* See under **fissare**.

fiss-are [A I] *tr.* to fix; to make fast, to fasten; — gli occhi su, to fix one's gaze on; — un uscio, to make a door fast, to fasten a door; (photog.) — una negativa, to fix a negative; — un prezzo, to fix a price, to agree on a price; to establish, to set up; — delle norme, to establish rules; — il danno, to ascertain, to settle, the damage; to fix, to arrange; — l'ora di un appuntamento, to arrange the time of a meeting; to book, to engage; — una stanza, to book a room, to take a room; — un posto, to book a seat; — un impiegato, to engage, to take on, an employee; to gaze at, to stare at, to look at; — una persona negli occhi, to look a person full in the face; *rfl.* to become fixed; to become firm; **-arsi** in una città, to settle in a city, to take up residence in a city; **-arsi** in una idea, to get an *idée fixe*. **-a·bile** *adj.* fixable. **-ag·gio** *m.* clamping, fastening; clamp, fastener; (photog.) fixing; bagno di **-aggio**, fixing-bath. **-amẹnto** *m.* fixing; fastening, securing. **-ativo** *adj.*, *n.m.* fixative. **-ato** *part. adj.* fixed; fastened; engaged; intent, absorbed; obsessed; essere un po' **-ato**, to have an *idée fixe*, to have a bee in one's bonnet, to be obstinate; *n.m.* appointment; agreement. **-atore** *m.* fixer; dàgli il **-atore** a quel disegno a carbone se non vuoi che si pasticci tutto, you'd better fix that charcoal drawing if you don't want it to smudge; (anat.) preservative substance used in anatomical studies; fixative; (photog.) fixer. (**-atrice** *f.*) **-aziọne** *f.* fixation, fixing; obsession, fixation, mania, fixed idea; (anat.) preserving process.

fissẹzza *f.* fixation, application.

fis-s-ile *adj.* tending to split; (atom. phys.) fissile. **-ilin·gui** *adj. indecl.* (zool.) fork tongued (as of snakes and lizards).

fissiọn-e *f.* (atom. phys.) fission; la — dell'atomo, the splitting of the atom. **-a·bile** *adj.* (atom. phys.) fissionable.

fissịsmo *m.* (biol.) the theory of the special creation of species.

fissità *f.* fixity, fixedness; guardare con —, to stare at; la — delle specie, the immutability of species; (cinem.) steadiness (of picture).

fiss-o *adj.* fixed; fast, firm, steady; fixed, arranged; prezzo —, price on which there can be no discount; (mil.) fissi!, eyes front!, steady!; stelle **-e**, fixed stars; idea **-a**, fixed idea; una professione **-a**, a regular profession; un impiegato —, an established clerk or other employee on the regular establishment; (naut.) ufficiale —,

permanent officer; stare — in una città, to reside in a city; †transfixed, pierced; *adv.* fixedly, intently; guardare —, to gaze fixedly at; *n.m.* fixed salary. **-amẹnte** *adv.* fixedly; firmly, securely.

†fissura *f.* See **fessura**.

†fistello *m.* See **fistola**.

†fistiare *vb.* and derivs. See **fischiare**.

†fi·stio *m.* See **fischio**.

fistiọne *m.* (orn.) fischione; — turco, red-crested pochard, *Netta rufina*.

fis·tol-a *f.* (med.) fistula; (bot.) cassia —, *Cassia fistula*; (mus.) Pan-pipes, syrinx. **-are** [A I] *intr.* (*aux.* avere) (mus.) to play on the syrinx. **-atọre** *m.*, **-atrice** *f.* (mus.) syrinx player. **-eggiare** [A 3 c] *intr.* (*aux.* avere) (mus.) see **fistolare**. †**-o** *m.* see **fistola**; devil, evil spirit; avere il diavolo nel **-o**, to nose out secrets; scannare il **-o**, to be seized with rage. **-ografi·a** *f.* (med.) fistulography. **-ọso** *adj.* fistulous.

†fistuc·o *m.*, †**-o** *m.* See **festuca**.

†fistuchino *adj.* pale green, pistacchio colour.

fi·stula *f.* and derivs. (mus.). See **fistola**.

fitaurari *m. indecl.* chief of an Abyssinian village; Abyssinian military rank equivalent to colonel.

fito-biologi·a *f.* plant biology. **-chi·mica** *f.* plant chemistry. **-far·maco** *m.* agricultural chemical. **-fisiologi·a** *f.* plant physiology. **-ftora** *f.* potato disease, late blight, caused by the fungus *Phytophthora infestans*. **-ge·nico** *adj.* (geol.) phytogenetic. **-geografi·a** *f.* plant geography. **-patologi·a** *f.* plant pathology. **-terapi·a** *f.* treatment of diseased plants, plant care.

fito·fago *adj.* (ent.) phytophagous.

†fitone *m.* python; diviner, wizard.

fitta¹ *f.* sharp pain, stitch; avere una — in un fianco, to have a stitch in one's side; sentì una — al cuore, she felt a pang of jealousy (grief, etc.); crowd, mass; una — di gente, a crowd of people; una — di spropositi, a mass of blunders; soft ground; hole in the ground; spit; vangare a **-e** poco fonde, not to dig deeply, to dig a shallow spit; dent, impression; una — nel cappello, a dent in one's hat; callosity; farci la —, to become hardened to a thing; †(naut.) see **caviglia**.

fitta² *adj. f.* See **fitto²**.

fitta·bile *m.* See **fittaiuolo**.

†fitta·gnola *f.* tap root.

fitt-ai(u)olo *m.* tenant-farmer; (leg.) lessee of rural property. †**-anza** *f.* tenancy. **-a·volo** *m.* see **fittaiuolo**.

fittẹzza *f.* See under **fitto²**.

fit·tile *adj.* fictile, made of clay.

fittịo *m.* thickness; density; closeness.

fittiv-o *adj.* fictitious, imaginary. **-amẹnte** *adv.* in imagination.

fitti-zi-o *adj.* false, unreal; imaginary; fictitious. **-amẹnte** *adv.* falsely; fictitiously.

fitto¹ *m.* rent; prendere in —, to hire; price for hire of horses, etc.; periodical payment; (leg.) rent of rural property; — bloccato, restricted rent, rent blocked under rent restriction act; see also **affitto**.

fitt-o² *part.* of **figgere**, q.v.; *adj.* thrust in, stuck in; driven in; un palo — in terra, a stake driven in the ground; a capo —, head first, with head down (also **a capofitto**); fixed, firmly placed; un'idea **-a** nella mente, an idea firmly fixed in one's mind; thick, dense, frequent; la gente era **-a**, there was a dense crowd; tessuti **-i**, closely woven cloth; pettine —, dust-comb, fine tooth comb; lampeggiare —, frequent lightning; buio —, pitch dark; nel più — inverno, in the depths of winter; (naut.) nave **-a** di rame, copper-bottomed vessel; *n.m.* thick, thickest part; nel — della mischia, in the thick of the fight; nel — del bosco, in the thickest part of the wood; *adv.* thickly; frequently; nevicare —, to snow heavily. **-amẹnte** *adv.* thickly, densely, frequently. **-ẹzza** *f.* thickness, density.

†fitto³ *part.* of **fingere**, q.v.

fittone *m.* (bot.) tap-root; (eng.) keystone at the mouth of a furnace.

fittua·rio *m.* See **fittaiuolo**.

†fittura *f.* (naut.) nailing, sewing, bolting of a ship's structure.

fiumalbo *m.* (orn.) moorhen.

fium-e¹ *m.* river; stream, current; il — Tevere, the river Tiber, the Tiber; contro —, against the current; il — reale, the main river (as compared with tributaries); (fig.) stream, flood; — di parole, stream of words; — di eloquenza, flood of eloquence; romanzo —, long novel of which the action covers many generations, saga.

†**-a·ia** *f.* see **fiumana**. **-ale** *adj.* (D'Annunzio) pertaining to a river. **-ana** *f.* flood; swollen river, torrent; (fig.) flood, crowd; una **-ana** di popolo, a flood of people, a mass of people. **-ano** *adj.* river, of the river; of Fiume. **-ara** *f.* (geog. Calabria) torrent; flood; wide river. **-arolo** *m.* (Rome) keeper of a floating bathing establishment on the Tiber; boatman on the Tiber. †**-a·tico** *adj.* relating to rivers, river. †**-ato** *adj.* protected by a river. **-iciat·tolo** *m. dim.* brook, small river. **-icello** *m. dim.* small river; stream

Fiume² *pr.n.f.* (geog.) Fiume (now called Rijeka).

fiutafatti *m. indecl.* inquisitive person; eavesdropper; Nosey Parker.

fiut-are [A I] *tr.* to scent, to catch the scent of; to sniff, to smell; il bracco **-a** la selvaggina, the hound scents the game; — una rosa, to smell a rose; — tabacco, to take snuff; (fig.) to scent, to suspect, to anticipate; — il tradimento, to suspect treachery, to scent treachery; ha **-ato** un buon affare, he has got on to a good thing; †— le orme di, to be forever in the company of. **-ata** *f.* sniff; sniffing, smelling; search. **-atina** *f. dim.* little sniff; fare una **-atina**, to take a pinch of snuff. **-atore** *m.* (**-atrice** *f.*), **-one** *m.* inquisitive person; meddler, intriguer.

fiutasepolcri *m. indecl.* antiquarian, pedantic lover of things that are dead and gone.

fiuto¹ *m.* scent, smell; scenting, smelling; sense of smell; conoscere al —, to recognize by the smell; flair, instinctive perception, sixth sense; non è un erudito ma ha molto —, he's not a scholar but he has a great flair; tabacco da —, snuff.

†**fiuto²** *m.* (mus.) flute.

†**fizione** *f.* See **finzione**.

flabell-o *m.* (eccl.) *flabellum*, liturgical fan (of various materials) held by deacons over the altar (now only in Eastern rites); ceremonial fan (of ostrich and peacock feathers) held by attendants over the Pope when he is carried in state; (mil.) cowl; (aeron.) gill. **-i·fero** *m.* (eccl.) bearer of the flabellum. **-iforme** *adj.* flabelliform.

flac·cid-o *adj.* flaccid; flabby. **-ezza** *f.* flaccidity; flabbiness; a disease in silk-worms. **-ità** *f.* see **flaccidezza**.

flacon-e *m.* small bottle, flask; phial; scent-bottle with glass stopper; small medicine bottle. (**-cino** *m. dim.*)

flagell-are [A I] *tr.* to flagellate, to scourge; to lash, to beat; — i vizi, to scourge vice; *rfl.* to scourge oneself. **-amento** *m.* flagellation, scourging. **-ante** *part. adj.* flagellant; scourging; *n.m.* (eccl. hist.) Flagellant. **-ato** *part. adj.* flagellated, scourged; tormented; (biol.) flagellated. **-atore** *m.* flagellator; flagellant (**-atrice** *f.*). **-azione** *f.* flagellation; scourging; (art) la Flagellazione, the Scourging of Christ.

flagell-o *m.* scourge, whip; scourging, whipping, beating; calamity, punishment, visitation; (fig.) torment, plague, scourge, trial; è il — dei genitori, he is a great cross to his parents; il — dei principi, the scourge of princes; (fig.) abundance, plenty; un — di frutta, an abundance of fruit; *adv. phr.* a —, in abundance; studiare a —, to overwork; (biol.) flagellum. **-i·fero** *m.* man carrying a whip.

flagioletto *m.* (mus.) flageolet.

†**flagi·zi-o** *m.* wickedness, evil. †**-oso** *adj.* wicked, evil.

†**flagra** *f.* whip.

flagran-te *adj.* flagrant; in —, in the act; prendere in —, to catch red-handed; (leg.) è — il reato che si commette attualmente, an offence is 'in the very act' which is in the course of commission. **-za** *f.* flagrancy; (leg.) è in stato di **-za** chi viene colto nell'atto di commettere il reato, a person is red-handed who is caught in the very act of committing an offence.

†**flagrare** *intr.* to burn, to blaze.

flambatura *f.* (metall.) flame-hardening.

fla·m-ine *m.* (Rom. antiq.) flamen; — Diale, *flamen Dialis*, priest of Jupiter. **-inale** *adj.* ex-flamen. **-inato** *m.* flamenship, office of flamen. **-i·nica** *f.* *flaminica*, flamen's wife. **-i·nio** *adj.* of a flamen, priestly; of Flaminius, Flaminian.

flammatura *f.* (metall.) flame-hardening.

†**flam·m-eo** *adj.* burning, bright; *n.m.* (Rom. antiq.) flame-coloured bridal veil. †**-olenza** *f.* brightness, being on fire.

flan *m. indecl.* (cul.) kind of tart, pastry flan; (typ.) flong, papier mâché mould used for casting stereotype plates.

†**Flan·dria** *pr.n.f.* See **Fiandre**.

flanell-a *f.* flannel. **-ina** *f.* flannelette.

flan·gia *f.* flange.

flano *m.* (typ.). See **flan**.

flap *m. indecl.* (or *pl.* as Eng.) (aeron.) flap.

flash *m. indecl.* (photog.) flash; (pop.) electric torch.

†**flateri·a** *f.* flattery.

flat-o *m.* flatus, wind. **-ulento** *adj.* flatulent. **-ulenza** *f.* flatulence. **-uosità** *f.* flatuosity. **-uoso** *adj.* flatuous, flatulent.

fla·ut-o *m.* (mus.) flute; — a becco, — diritto, — dolce, recorder, flageolet; — in sol, bass flute in G; — piccolo, piccolo; — traverso, — traversiere, — tedesco, flute, concert-flute, transverse flute (NOTE: in early eighteenth-century scores 'flauto' without qualification often stands for 'flauto a becco'); tagliare a —, to cut obliquely, or on the cross; †(naut.) old vessel reduced to a transport. **-ando** *adv.* (mus.) producing sweet sounds on bowed instruments, either by bowing over the fingerboard or by playing harmonics. **-ato** *adj.* (mus.) flutey, sweet-toned; see also **flautando**. †**-etto** *m.* (mus.) see **flautino**. **-ino** *m.* (mus.) piccolo; any kind of small flute or recorder. **-ista** *m., f.* flautist, flute-player. †**-izzare** *intr.* to flute. **-one** *m.* bass flute.

Fla·via *pr.n.f.* Flavia.

flav-o *adj.* (poet.) fair, blonde, golden; tawny; capelli **-i**, fair hair, tawny hair. †**-i·zie** *f.* tawny hue.

fleb-ectasi·a *f.* (med.) varix. **-ite** *f.* phlebitis. **-ografi·a** *f.* treatise on veins. **-ografi·a** *f.* phlebography. **-gra·fico** *adj.* concerning the study of veins. **-o·grafo** *m.* specialist in phlebography. **-olite** *f.* phlebolite. **-ologi·a** *f.* phlebology, study of veins. **-olo·gico** *adj.* phlebological; concerning phlebology. **-omalaci·a** *f.* softening of the veins. **-opali·a** *f.* pulse in the veins. **-orragi·a** *f.* bleeding from a vein. **-orra·gico** *adj.* concerning venous bleeding. **-osclerosi** *f. indecl.* sclerosis of the veins. **-otomare** [A I S] *tr* to phlebotomize. **-otomi·a** *f.* phlebotomy. **-o·tomo** *m.* phlebotomist; blood-letter; surgeon of primitive or antiquated methods; †lancet for opening a vein.

fle·bil-e *adj.* mournful, plaintive; pitiful, weak; †(poet.) la — rugiada, a woman's tears. **-mente** *adv.* tearfully; plaintively; mournfully.

Flegeṭont-e *pr.n.m.* (myth.) the river Phlegethon. †**-a** *pr.n.m.* see **Flegetonte**. **-eo** *adj.* of or relating to the river Phlegethon.

Flegr-a *pr.n.f.* (geog.) Phlegra (in Thessaly). **-eo** *adj.* of Phlegra; (geog.) Campi **-ei**, the Phlegraean Plain, near Naples.

flemm-a *f.* phlegm; coolness, calmness; indifference, sang-froid, slowness; *pl.* brewers' grains; †perdere la —, to lose patience; †—!, have patience!; †la — gli scappa, he loses his control, he bursts into a rage. **-asi·a** *f.* (med.) phlegmasia, inflammation, swelling. **-a·tico** *adj.* phlegmatic; (fig.) cool, self-possessed; measured, calm; without passion, stolid. **-aticamente** *adv.* phlegmatically; coolly; stolidly. **-one** *m.* (med.) inflammation of the tissues; suppuration; abscess, phlegmon. **-onoso** *adj.* of the nature of an abscess.

fle·mone *m.* See **flemmone**, under **flemma**.

fless-i·bile *adj.* flexible; pliable; pliant; (bookb.) rilegatura —, limp cover; *n.m.* flexible tube; flex. **-ibilmente** *adv.* **-ibilità** *f.* flexibility; pliability; (mus.) flexibility (of voice). **-i·metro** *m.* deflectometer. **-ione** *f.* flexion; (gymn.) bend; (gramm.) inflection; (techn.) resistenza alla **-ione**, flexural strength; resistenza alla **-ione** ripetuta, flex fatigue life. **-ivo** *adj.* (gramm.) inflected. †**-o** *part. adj.* of flettere, q.v.; *n.m.* flexing; (math.) inflection, flex point, point of contrary flexure. **-ore** *m.* (anat.) flexor. **-uosità** *f.* flexuous quality. **-uoso** *adj.* graceful, supple; rippling; (fig.) yielding, pliable, accommodating. **-uosamente** *adv.* gracefully; (fig.) accommodatingly. **-ura** *f.* bending, flexing; (geol.) flexure.

fles·sile *adj.* (D'Annunzio) flexible, pliant, supple.

Flessinga *pr.n.f.* (geog.) Flushing.

†**fleto** *m.* weeping; lament; moan; grief, sorrow.

flet·t-ere [C 19] *tr.* to bend, to flex; (gramm.) to inflect, to decline; (gymn.) — il busto, to bend from the waist; *intr.* (aux. essere) to weaken (e.g. of a price). **-ente** *part. adj.* flexing, bending; (of a language) inflected; (mech.; eng.) momento **-ente**, bending moment, moment of flexure.

flicorno *m.* (mus.) flugelhorn.

†**flinguello** *m.* See **fringuello**.

flint *m. indecl.* (opt.) flint glass.

flippare [A I] *intr.* (aux. avere) (slang) to play with pin-ball machines.

flirt *m. indecl.* (pron. as Eng.) flirtation; person (man or woman) with whom someone is flirting; c'è un — tra quei due, there's a flirtation going on between those two; Maria è il — di Francesco, Francis is flirting with Mary; fare il —, to flirt, to make love; avere un —, to have a brief amorous relationship. (**-arello** *m. dim.* **-ino** *m. dim.*) **-are** [A I] *intr.* (aux. avere) to flirt.

fliscorno *m.* (mus.). See **flicorno**.

flittene *f.* (med.) blister.

†**floc·cido,** †**flo·cido** *adj.* soft, overripe; flaccid.

flogi·st·ico *adj.* (med.) inflammatory; phlogistic. †**-o** *m.* (chem.) phlogiston.

†**flogite** *f.* flame; opal.

flog-o *m.* (bot.) phlox, *Phlox*. **-opite** *f.* (miner.) phlogopite. **-oṣi** *f.* (med.) phlogosis; inflammation. **-o·stoṣi** *f.* (med.) inflammation of the bones.

Flor-a¹ *pr.n.f.* (myth.) Flora. **-ale** *adj.* relating to Flora.

flor-a² *f.* flora. **-ale** *adj.* floral.

†**flore** *m.* and derivs. See **fiore**.

Floreale *pr.n.m.* (hist.) Floreal (eighth month in the French Revolutionary calendar); *adj.* floral; (archit.; applied art) stile —, pre-Raphaelite, fin-de-siècle; (soft furnishing) flowered or 'Liberty' (of materials).

†**florentine** *adj.* See **fiorente**, under **fiorire**.

florescenza *f.* florescence.

flori-coltura *f* see **floricultura**. **-cultore** *m.* floriculturist. **-cultura** *f.* flower-growing, floriculture.

Florida, Flo·rida *pr.n.f.* (geog.) Florida.

flo·rid-o *adj.* prosperous, thriving; flourishing; florid; gli anni -i, youth; bright, vivid, colourful. **-amente** *adv.* prosperously; floridly. **-ęzza** *f.* floridness; prosperity; glow, bloom (of health or youth). **-ità** *f.* floridity.

†**flori·fero** *adj.* See **fiorifero**.

florile·gio *m.* florilegium; anthology.

Florindo *pr.n.m.* name of the young lover in many eighteenth-century Italian comedies.

†**florire** *vb.* and derivs. See **fiorire**.

†**florulento** *adj.* flourishing; florid; flowering.

flo·sc·io *adj.* soft; flabby; carne -ia, flabby flesh; limp; floppy; tessuto —, soft material; cappello —, soft hat; *n.m.* (aeron.) balloon or dirigible without frames. **-iamente** *adv.* flabbily; softly. **-ęzza** *f.* softness; flabbiness. **-ione** *m.* flabby person. **-iume** *m.* quantity of soft or flabby things.

flo·sculo *m.* (bot.) floret.

flott-a *f.* (naut.) fleet; — mercantile, merchant fleet; convoy; — in potenza, fleet in being, fleet ready for sea; — aerea, fleet-air-arm. **-ag·gio** *m.* (aeron.) taxi-ing of a flying-boat previous to taking-off; canale di -aggio, taxi channel. **-amento** *m.* (aeron.) navigation of a flying-boat at moderate speed before taking-off. **-i·glia** *f.* (naut.) flotilla, destroyers, submarines or motorboats grouped under one command; fishing fleet.

flottante *adj.* (comm.) floating; vendita di merce —, sale afloat.

flottazione *f.* (mining) flotation.

flou *m. indecl.* (pron. **flù**) (photog.) soft focus; *adj. indecl.* (dressm.) soft; un drappeggio —, a soft material.

fluente *part.* of **fluire**, q.v.

flu·id-o *adj.* fluid; fluent; stile —, fluent style; *n.m.* fluid; (fig.) personal magnetism. **-amente** *adv.* fluently; flowingly. **-ęzza** *f.* fluidity; fluency. **-iforme** *adj.* fluid, in the fluid state, gaseous. **-ità** *f.* fluidity; fluency.

flu-ire [D 2] *intr.* (*aux.* essere) to flow; to be fluent; to be fluid; to be abundant; le parole -iscono, words flow. **-ente** *part. adj.* fluent; flowing; variable; barba -ente, flowing beard; quantità -ente, variable quantity; †*n.m.* river, stream. **-itante** *part. adj.* undulating, floating; vacillating. **-itare** [A 1] *intr.* (*aux.* essere) to undulate; to vacillate. **-itato** *part. adj.* (of a stone) worn smooth by water. **-itazione** *f.* (geol.) the wearing smooth of stones by water.

fluminense *adj.* of, pertaining to, Rio de Janeiro; *n.m.*, *f.*

fluor-e *m.* (med.) discharge; (miner.) fluor; spato —, fluorspar. **-escente** *adj.* fluorescent. **-escenza** *f.* fluorescence. **-i·drico** *adj.* (chem.) hydrofluoric. **-ina** *f.*, **-ite** *f.* (miner.) fluorite, fluorspar.

fluor-o *m.* (chem.) fluorine. **-oapatite** *f.* (miner.) fluorapatite, asparagus-stone. **-ocarburo** *m.* (chem.) fluorocarbon. **-ocarbu·rico** *adj.* (chem.) fluorocarbon; resina -ocarburica, fluorocarbon resin. **-ografi·a** *f.* (X-ray) fluorography. **-oscopi·a** *f.* (med.) fluoroscopy, screening. **-osco·pio** *m.* fluoroscope. **-urazione** *f.* (chem.) fluorination. **-uro** *m.* (chem.) fluoride.

†**flussi·bil-e** *adj.* flowing; fluid; (of the bowels) loose; (fig.) transitory. †**-ità** *f.* fluidity; flexibility; looseness.

flussion-e *f.* (med.) inflammation; flux, discharge; (path.) morbid secretion. **-ac·cia** *f. pejor.* bad inflammation; bad cold; constipation.

fluss-o *m.* (med.) flux, discharge, flow; dysentery; — di sangue, flow of blood; flow, flux; — e riflusso, ebb and flow; (electr.) flux; (aeron.) — dell'elica, prop blast; (naut.) flood tide; rising tide, current resulting; flood; (cards) flush. **-o·metro** *m.* (eng.) flowmeter, (electr.) flux-meter.

flutt-o *m.* wave; billow, surge, swell; agitato dai -i, tossed by the waves, storm-tossed; — del fondo, ground swell; — corrente, drift. **-uoṣo** *adj.* surging, swelling; tempestuous, stormy; (fig.) irresolute, vacillating.

fluttu-are [A 6] *intr.* (*aux.* avere) to undulate; to toss in the waves; to fluctuate, to vacillate; to rise and fall; to float; — tra due partiti, to fluctuate between two sides. **-amento** *m.* fluctuation; fluctuating; waving, undulating. **-ante** *part. adj.* tossing in the waves, floating; fluctuating, vacillating; (finan.) debito -ante, floating debt; *n.m.* temporary resident. **-azione** *f.* (fig.) billowing, tossing; fluctuating; (poet.) -azione della nave, tossing of the ship; (mil.) ebb and flow of battle.

fluttuoṣo *adj.* See under **flutto**.

fluvi-ale *adj.* fluvial; per via —, by river; navigazione —, river navigation; †lagrime -ali, floods of tears; †*n.m.* river boat. **†-a·tico** *adj.* see **fluviale**. **†-a·tile** *adj.* pertaining to rivers.

†**flu·vido** *adj.* fluid.

†**flu·vio** *m.* river, stream.

fluvi-o·grafo *m.* river gauge. **-o·metro** *m.* fluviometer.

fobi·a *f.* (med.) phobia; dread; fear; strong aversion.

foca *f.* (zool.) seal; — monaca, *Pelagius monachus*, Mediterranean monk seal.

focac·c-ia *f.* cake, bun; (provb.) rendere pan per —, to give tit for tat, to give as good as one gets; (techn.) — di cera, wax (for making gramophone records). **-ina** *f. dim.* small sweet cake; sticky bun.

†**focace** *adj.* ardent; burning; on fire; fiery.

foca·i-a *adj. f.* flint; of flint; pietra —, flint; *n.f.* flint (for striking fire). †**-one** *m.* hard stone, of the nature of flint. **-uolo** *adj.* (of soil) flinty; warm; †*n.m.* fire-stick; fire-attendant, fireman.

focal-e *adj.* (opt.) focal; distanza —, focal length; profondità —, depth of focus. **-iẓẓazione** *f.* (phys.) focusing.

focar-a *f.* brazier; (techn.) a sort of fire-shovel used by wax refiners. **-ętta** *f. dim.* hand brazier. **-ino, -olo** *m.* fireman in an alum-works.

foca·tico *m.* hearth-tax.

foc-ato *adj.* flame-coloured; red hot. †**-at·tola** *f.* little cake baked in the shape of a snail, pastry twist.

foc-e¹ *f.* (geog.) mouth, outlet; opening, entrance; outfall, valley; mettere — in, to flow into; †origin, source. **-iata** *f.* long estuary.

†**foce²** *f.* thing; affair; sin, shame.

focena *f.* (zool.) porpoise, *Phocaena communis*.

foch-eggiatura *f.* (photog.) focusing. **-ettatura** *f.* (opt.) focusing.

foch-erello *m.* small fire. †**-et·tilo** *m.* hearth.

fochista *m.* maker or seller of fireworks; fireman; stoker.

focile *m.* steel (used with flint); (fig.) incitement; †(anat.) tibia and fibula; ulna and radius.

†**foc-ina** *f.*, †**-i·nola** *f. dim.* See **fucina**.

foco *m.* (*pl.* fochi). See **fuoco**.

focola·io *m.* see **focolare**; (med.) centre of infection; whole infection in a small area (e.g. group of boils); (fig.) place or group from which rebellion spreads; hotbed.

focol-are *m.* hearth, fireplace; fireside; il grillo del —, the cricket on the hearth; (fig.) home; combattere per il —, to fight for one's hearth and home; (metall.) furnace; (techn.) kiln; (eng.) firebox (of a boiler); — ondulato, corrugated flue; — di fucina, blacksmith's forge.

foco·mele *m.* (med.) type of foetal monstrosity.

foco·metro *m.* (opt.) focometer.

focon-e *m. augm.* large fire; touch-hole of a firearm; †(naut.) ship's galley. †**-a·io** *m.* (naut.) ship's cook for the day.

focoṣ-o *adj.* fiery; blazing, hot; (fig.) fiery, impetuous; cavallo —, mettlesome horse; indole -a, fiery temperament, excitable disposition. **-amente** *adv.* fierily, ardently; angrily. **-ętto** *adj. dim.* rather excitable.

fo·der-a *f.* lining; — di seta, silk lining; sheath, casing; — di metallo, metal casing; (naut.) sheath, protective shield; — di rame, copper bottom or lining of a ship's hull.

foder-are [A I s] *tr.* to line; — un soprabito di pelo, to line a coat with fur; to sheathe, to case, to encase; to cover; — una cassa di metallo, to put a metal casing on a box; — le parole, to repeat one's words. **-ato** *part. adj.* lined; encased. (**-atore** *m.*) **-atura** *f.* lining; sheathing; casing.

fo·der-o *m.* sheath, scabbard; (naut.) timber protection to a sea wall or dyke; (mil.) raft, provisions; †tribute of rations imposed on a conquered enemy district. **-one** *adj.* (Tusc.) see **buscherone**.

†**fodina** *f.* mine; quarry.

fog-a, **fọg-a** *f.* impetus, ardour, heat, passion; impetuosity; con —, in a rush; parlare con —, to speak heatedly; la — della passione, the warmth of passion; (mil.) light mine, countermine. †**-are** *intr.* to speed, to fly, to flee; *rfl.* to fling oneself; *tr.* to pursue. **-ata** *f.* flight, fleeing; (mil.) light surface mine.

fog·gi-a¹ *f.* fashion, style; way, manner; shape; una nuova —, a new fashion; alla — di, in the style of, after the fashion of, resembling; — di parlare, way of speaking; a — di, shaped like, like; a — di campana, bell-shaped; †a buona —, of good quality. **-are** [A 3] *tr.* to form, to shape, to give form to; to fashion, to mould; **-are** lo stile, to mould one's style. **-ato** *part. adj.* formed, shaped; **-ato** a campana, bell-shaped; †well made, good-sized.

Fog·gi-a² *pr.n.f.* (geog.) Foggia. (**-ano** *adj.*)

fo·gli-a *f.* leaf; in —, in leaf; mettere le **-e**, to put forth leaves; la pagina inferiore di una —, the underside of a leaf; la pagina superiore di una —, the right side of a leaf; (fig.) mangiare la — to understand a thing at once, to seize an allusion, to take a hint, to grasp an innuendo; to see through a thing, to perceive another person's real intentions; tremare come una —, to tremble like a leaf; (provb.) non si muove — che Dio non voglia, not a leaf falls without God's consent; (techn.) foil; lamina; — di stagno, tin-foil; — d'oro, gold leaf; (art) leaf ornament (as in Corinthian capitals); — d'acanto, acanthus-leaf (as in Vatican Museum); — di fico, fig-leaf (as in Garden of Eden). **-a·ceo** *adj.* foliaceous; leaf-like; (geol.) struttura **-acea**, foliation. **-ame** *m.* foliage; leaves; leaf pattern. **-are** *adj.* foliar. **-etta** *f. dim.* small leaf; young leaf; kind of snuff; an old Roman wine-measure equivalent to a quarter of a *boccale*, or about half a pint. **-ettato** *adj.* foliated; (geol.) formazione **-ettata**, foliation. **-olina** *f.* (bot.) leaflet. **-oso** *adj.* leafy; in leaf. **-uto** *adj.* leafy, covered with leaves; (techn.) leafy.

fogliante¹ *m.* (eccl. hist.) Feuillant (member of a Cistercian reform); (Fr. hist.) Feuillant (member of group in Legislative Assembly, 1791–2).

fogliante² *m.* (techn.) book in folio.

†**fogli-are** *intr.* to put forth leaves; *tr.* made into the shape of a leaf. †**-ato** *part. adj.* leafy; shaped like a leaf.

fogliata *f.* as much as can be wrapped up in a sheet of paper; paperful, paper (of groceries, etc.).

fogliatura *f.* foliation; leafing.

fogliazione *f.* leafing, breaking into leaf.

foglietta *f. dim.* See under **foglia**.

fogliett-o *m. dim.* of **foglio**, q.v.; small sheet of paper; slip of paper; half a folio of print, octavo; — volante, hand-bill; (anat.) the membranes of the pleura; (zool.) — embrionale, germ layer. **-ante** *m.*, **-ista** *m.* writer for second-rate newspapers, hack-journalist.

fogli·fero *adj.* (bot.) leafy.

fo·gli-o *m.* sheet, sheet of paper folded in two; un libro in —, a book in folio; quaderno a fogli sciolti, loose-leaf notebook; newspaper; pamphlet; un — domenicale, a Sunday newspaper; page; — di un libro, page of a book; — volante, loose sheet of paper, fly-sheet; note (of paper-money); un — da mille, a thousand lire note; permit; licence; receipt; — di via, travel-permit, travel-warrant; (leg.) — di via (obbligatorio), travel order, warrant for compulsory repatriation (e.g. to birth-place) (C.P.); — degli annunzi legali, journal of legal notices (provincial equivalent of Official Gazette) (C.C.P.). **-u·colo** *m.* cheap newspaper, 'rag'.

fogli-olina *f.*, **-oso** *adj.* See under **foglia**.

†**foglire** *intr.* to put forth leaves.

fogliu·colo *m.* See under **foglio**.

fogliuto *adj.* See under **foglia**.

fogn-a *f.* drain, sewer; culvert; hole in the bottom of a flower-pot; base of trench in which vines are planted; glutton. **-aiuolo** *m.* sewer-workman. **-amento** *m.* draining; elision, slurring, omitting. **-are** [A 5 c] *tr.* to provide with drains; to culvert; **-are** le misure, to give short measure; **-are** una sillaba, to slur a syllable. **-arola** *f.*

(Tusc.) drainage-channel for vines. **-ato** *part. adj.* drained; dug out; culverted; uomo **-ato**, deceitful man. **-atura** *f.* draining, sewerage; elision, slurring. †**-o** *m.* see **fogna**. **-olo** *m.* subsidiary drain; gutter. **-one** *m. augm.* main sewer.

fogo *m.* (Tusc.) choking; far —, to choke; che ti faccia —!, may it choke you!

fo·i-a *f.* lust, desire; incitement to lust; craze. **-oso** *adj.* lustful, libidinous.

fo·iba *f.* (N.E. Ital.) ditch, abyss.

foiolo *m.* (vet.) omasum.

†**foionco** *m.* (zool.) a kind of marten; marten's fur.

fola¹ *f.* fable; idle tale, nonsense; tarradiddle; old wives' tale; fole!, nonsense!

fola² *f.* (cards) pool, stack (on which players draw); †crowd; mob; fare una — addosso a, to mob.

folade *f.* (zool.) piddock, *Pholas dactylus*.

fo·laga *f.* (orn.) coot, *Fulica atra*.

fola·r *m. indecl.* foulard; scarf.

folata *f.* gust, puff; una — di vento, a gust of wind; lavorare a folate, to work by fits and starts; gush, spurt; swarm; crowd; una — di uccelli, a flight of birds; una — di gente, a swarm of people, a crowd of people; burst (of cheering, etc.).

†**fol·cere**, **folcire** (poet.) to sustain, to support.

folclore *m.* and derivs. See **folklore**.

Fọlco *pr.n.m.* Fulk.

folena *f.* See **falena**.

†**fol·gora** *f.* See **folgore¹**.

folgor-are [A I sc] *intr.* (aux. avere) to flash; to lighten; to shine; to gleam; to fulminate; *tr.* to strike with lightning; to burn. **-ante** *part. adj.* flashing, shining; gleaming; fulminating; burning; occhi **-anti**, flashing eyes; dolore **-ante**, piercing pain. **-ato** *part. adj.* struck by lightning, burnt; rapid; brilliant, showy. **-atore** *m.* hurler of thunderbolts. (**-azione** *f.*)

folgor-e¹ *f.* flash of lightning, flash; thunderbolt. **-eggiante** *part. adj.* flashing, shining. **-eggiare** [A 3 c] *intr.* (aux. avere) to flash; to shine; to speed, to rush. **-eggiato** *part. adj.* flashed; hurled; struck. **-ite** *f.* (metall.) see **fulgorite**. **-one** *m.* illuminating rocket, 'star shell'; (mil.) port fire.

†**folgore²** *m.* See **fulgore**.

†**foli·a** *f.* See **follia**, under **folle¹**.

fo·lio *m.* folio; in —, in folio.

folklor-e *m.* folk-lore, folk art, folk customs. **-ismo** *m.* study of folk-lore, etc. **-ista** *m.*, *f.* student of folk-lore, etc. **-i·stico** *adj.* connected with folk-lore, etc.; esposizione **-istica**, exhibition of folk art, peasant costumes, etc.; (mus.) un concerto di canti **-istici**, a folk-song recital.

folklo·rico *adj.* See **folkloristico**, under **folklore**.

folla¹, (Rom.) **fọlla** *f.* crowd, throng, multitude; mob; crush; una — di gente, a crowd of people; (fig.) una — di idee, a mass of ideas; far —, to throng, to crowd together; piace alla —, it appeals to the mob, it pleases the masses.

folla² *f.* (techn.) fulling liquor.

foll-are [A I c] *tr.* to press (grapes); (text.) to full, to mill; †to crowd upon, to trample. **-ata** *f.* pressing; fulling. **-ato** *part. adj.* pressed, crushed; (text.) fulled; †crowded, thronged. **-atoio** *m.* grape-press. **-atore** *m.* grape-press; fuller. **-atura** *f.* crushing (of grapes); (text.) fulling, milling. **-one** *m.* (text.) fulling machine, fuller.

foll-e¹ *adj.* crazy, foolish, mad; senseless; (eng.) idle, idling; rullino —, idler roller; posizione —, neutral position (of gears); cambio in —, gear in neutral. **-emente** *adv.* madly, foolishly, senselessly, crazily. **-eare** [A 6] *intr.* (aux. avere) to behave foolishly; to act like a madman. **-eggiamento** *m.* madness; lunacy; frolicking. **-eggiante** *part. adj.* acting foolishly, playing the fool; frolicsome. **-eggiare** [A 3 c] *intr.* (aux. avere) to act like a madman; to play the fool, to lark about; to frolic; to have a gay time, to frivol one's life away. **-eggiatore** *m.* one who habitually acts foolishly, madman; larker. (**-eggiatrice** *f.*) **-etto** *adj. dim.* rather foolish, silly; *n.m.* goblin, elf, sprite; imp; (fig.) quel ragazzo è un vero **-etto**, that boy is a real imp. **-i·a** *f.* folly; madness; lunacy; foolishness; extravagance; fare **-ie**, to act foolishly, to do foolish things, to be wildly extravagant; amare alla **-ia**, to be madly in love with; (mus.) folia, dance in triple measure composed over a conventional ground bass. †**-ire** *intr.* to go mad. †**-ore** *m.* madness, folly.

†**folle²** *m.* bellows; bag, pouch, sack.

folletto[1] *m.* (naut.) lanyard.

folletto[2] *m.* See under **folle**.

folli·col-o *m.* (bot.) follick; (med.; biol.) follicle; (naut.) leather band on an oar. **-are** *adj.* follicular. **-ato** *adj.* folliculated. **-ętto** *m. dim.* (bot.) follicle of a multiple fruit. **-ite** *f.* (med.) folliculitis. **-oso** *adj.* folliculose.

†**follire** *vb.* See under **folle**.

†**follo** *m.* See **folle**[2].

follone *m.* See under **follare**.

†**follore** *m.* See under **folle**[1].

folpo *m.* (dial. Adriatic). See **polipo**.

folt-a *f.* crush, press, throng. †**-are** *intr.* to throng; *tr.* to fling in great number.

foltezza *f.* See under **folto**.

folt-o *adj.* thick; dense; close-set; teeming; abundant; capigliatura **-a**, thick hair; bosco —, thick wood; la strada era **-a** di gente, the street was crowded with people; nebbia **-a**, thick fog; *n.m.* press; thickness; nel — della mischia, in the thick of the fight; thicket, overgrown area. **-ęzza** *f.* thickness; abundance.

Fomalhaut *pr.n.f.* (astron.) Fomalhaut, α Piscis Australis.

fomęnta *f.* See under **fomento**.

foment-are [A I C] *tr.* to foment, to incite; to cause; to excite; — la passione, to excite passion; — l'animo dei giovani, to inflame young people's minds; — le ciarle, to encourage gossip; †to encourage; †to inspire. **-ato** *part. adj.* fomented; incited; excited; promoted, urged; †encouraged; †inspired. **-atore** *m.* fomenter; instigator. (**-atrice** *f.*) **-azione** *f.* fomentation; excitement, stimulation.

fomęnt-o *m.* (med.) fomentation; (fig.) fuel; stimulus, encouragement. **-a** *f.* (med.) fomentation.

fo·mit-e *m.* tinder; (fig.) origin, cause, source; stimulus, incitement, incentive; — di male, source of evil; — del contagio, source of contagion. †**-o** *m.* see **fomite**.

fon *m. indecl.* (acoust.) phon, decibel.

fon-asco *m.* (*pl.* **-aschi**) (mus.) vocal artist; †*adj.* phonic. **-azione** *f.* (physiol.) phonation; (mus.) voice-production.

fond-a[1] *f.* holster; (naut.) anchorage; posto di —, anchor berth; stare alla —, essere alla —, (of a ship in harbour) to be anchored or moored to a buoy; †pocket; †depth; †pit; †abundance, copiousness; †bottom, sea bed. **-ina** *f.* small holster, pistol-case; (N. Ital.) soup-plate.

†**fonda**[2] *f.* sling, catapult.

†**fondaca·io** *m.* See **fondaco**.

fondac·cio *m.* See under **fondo**.

fonda-co *m.* (*pl.* **-ci**, **-chi**) draper's shop; warehouse, store; (hist.) foreigners' (esp. traders' and merchants') quarter in a town; †draper; †abundance.

fondale *adj.* of the bottom, bottom, lowest; *n.m.* depth of water; (theatr.) backcloth, rear scenery; (naut.) soundings, ocean depth.

fondamęnta *f.* (Ven.) paved street running along a canal.

fondamęnt-o *m.* (*pl.* **-i** *m.*; **-a** *f.*, of buildings) foundation; dare — a, to found; le **-a** delle mura, the foundations of the walls; porre le **-a**, to lay the foundations; (fig.) foundation, support, ground, basis; un'idea senza —, an idea without foundation; privo di —, groundless; far — sopra una persona, to place reliance upon a person; i **-i** della religione, the grounds of religious belief; (mus.) fundamental bass, root; strumenti di —, continuo instruments; †institution, foundation; †founder; †root of a tree; †fundament, arse; †means; †support. **-ale** *adj.* fundamental, foundation; regole **-ali**, fundamental rules; pietra **-ale**, foundation stone; (phys.; opt.) colore **-ale**, primary colour; (mus.) basso **-ale**, fundamental bass; nota **-ale**, root; in stato **-ale**, in root position; *n.m.* (mus.) fundamental tone. **-almęnte** *adv.* fundamentally; basically; at bottom. **-are** [A I C] *tr.* to lay the foundations of.

fondant *m. indecl.* (pron. as Fr.) fondant, sweetmeat that melts in the mouth.

fond-are [A I C] *tr.* to found; to lay the foundations of; to build; to start; to establish; — una città, to found a city; (fig.) to found, to base, to establish, to ground; — un nuovo metodo, to establish a new method; — una teoria sull'osservazione, to base a theory upon observation; to give a grounding in, to instruct; — nella matematica, to give a grounding in mathematics, to teach mathematics; †(naut.) — lo scandaglio, to cast the lead; *rfl.* (*prep.* su) to rely (upon), to base oneself (upon); to be founded upon; †to be confirmed; †to settle. **-ante** *part. adj.* founding, establishing.

-ata *f.* dregs; deposit. **-atęzza** *f.* foundation; truth. **-ato** *part. adj.* founded; built; (fig.) established, based; warranted; lagnanza **-ata**, legitimate grievance; well-founded, sure, wise; well-versed; sospetti **-ati**, well-founded suspicions; mal **-ato**, ill-founded; †cavallo **-ato**, horse that has a good stance; nel **-ato** inverno, in the depth of winter; †submerged; †*n.m.* foundation. **-atamęnte** *adv.* with foundation; justly, with good reason; †profoundly. †**-atore** *m.* founder; author; initiator. (**-atrice** *f.*) **-azione** *f.* founding, building; foundation, establishment, institution; la **-azione** di Roma, the foundation of Rome; una **-azione** ecclesiastica, an ecclesiastical foundation; bequest, foundation.

†**fondeggiare** *tr.* (naut.) to let go, to anchor.

fondello *m.* (mil.) base cover of a cartridge tube; (techn.) shank of a button; (tailor) padding (of canvas, etc., for reinforcement); *dim.* of **fondo**, q.v.

fond-ere [C 2] *tr.* to melt; to smelt; — oro, to melt gold; to cast; — una statua, to cast a statue; (fig.) to fuse, to unite, to merge, to amalgamate; — due società, to amalgamate two societies; — due colori, to blend two colours; (fig.) to dissipate; to shed; to spread abroad; to scatter; — i beni, to dissipate one's property; *intr.* (*aux.* essere) to melt, to dissolve; il ghiaccio **-e**, the ice is melting; — in lagrime, to burst into tears; *rfl.* to melt, to dissolve; **-ersi** in lagrime, to dissolve into tears; **-ersi** con, to amalgamate with; *recip. rfl.* to merge, to amalgamate. **-ente** *part. adj.* melting; dissolving; blending; merging; cioccolato **-ente**, fondant; *n.m.* fondant; (met.) flux for soldering. **-eri·a** *f.* foundry; (mil.) shell foundry, arsenal. **-i·bile** *adj.* fusible. †**-itoio** *m.* foundry. **-itore** *m.* caster, founder; †washer, dissipator; †sling bearer, catapultist. **-itrice** *f.* (typ.) caster (Monotype); casting machine. **-itura** *f.* melting, fusing.

fonderuolo *m.* (zool.) *Styela conopoides*, a kind of sea squirt.

fondęzza *f.* See under **fondo**.

fondia·rio *adj.* landed, land; connected with real property; imposta fondiaria, land-tax; proprietà fondiaria, landed property; *n.f.* la fondiaria, the land-tax.

fondi·gli-o *m.* deposit, dregs; sediment. **-uolo** *m.* lees, dregs.

fondina *f.* (N. Ital.; Ven.) soup-plate; (mil.) holster.

fond-o *m.* bottom; lowest part, base; il — del pozzo, the bottom of the well; ground-floor; basement; da cima a —, thoroughly, from beginning to end, from top to toe; andare a — di una cosa, to get to the bottom of a matter; giungere alla questione di —, to come to the substance of the matter; bed (of the sea); andare a —, to founder; (oceanog.) deep; — stradale, road surface; strato di —, undercoat, priming coat (of paint); **-i** del caffè, coffee dregs; bassi **-i**, shallow water, evil haunts, slums, disreputable neighbourhood; (fig.) i bassi **-i** della società, the dregs of society; end, remote part, back; (rlwy.) vagoni da —, rear carriages; in — alla stanza, at the far end of the room; in — alla pagina, at the foot of the page; in — al discorso, at the end of the speech; in — alla scena, at the back of the stage, upstage; dar — a, to make inroads on, to finish off; dare — alla marmellata di fragole, to polish off the strawberry-jam; stare in un — di letto, to be in bed a long time through illness; stare in un — di carcere, to be in prison a long time; a —, fully, thoroughly; in —, at bottom, in fact, fundamentally; a —, thoroughly, scrupulously; articolo di —, editorial, leading article; (fig.) depths; il — della coscienza, the depths of the conscience; character, disposition; ha il — buono, he has a good disposition; background; il — d'un quadro, the background of a picture; il — dei calzoni, the crutch of a pair of trousers; **-i** di (in) magazzino, unsold goods, goods on hand; fund; capital; section, endowment, bequest (e.g. in a library); **-i** pubblici, public funds; **-i** residui, surplus funds; — di garanzia, trust, security fund; — d'ammortamento, sinking fund; — (di) cassa, cash in hand; — capitale, stock in trade; — d'esercizio, working capital; capitale a — perduto, capital permanently locked up; collocare una somma a — perduto, to make a doubtful investment; (fig.) avere un — di buon senso, to have a fund of common sense; farm, estate; piece of ground, holding; — urbano, house; (leg.) — dominante, dominant tenement; — servente, servient tenement (C.C.); (mil.) impegnarsi a —, to go into action with all one's forces, to be fully armed; to fight until a decision has been reached; (fencing) eseguire un 'a fondo', to make a lunge; (mus.) back (of a violin) (see also *pl.*); (typ.) tail-piece, cul-de-lampe; (archit.) — di una colonna, height of a column; (paint.) background, ground; (sport) gara di —, distance trial (18 km.);

20-2

fond-o (*cont.*)
pl. (naut.) sweepings (of a hold); (mus.) foundation stops (of an organ); *adj.* deep; acqua -a, deep water; piatto —, deep plate, soup-plate. **-ac·cio** *m. pejor.* sediment, dregs, lees. **-ẹzza** *f.* depth. **-ista** *m., f.* (sport, skiing) competitor in a distance trial. **-oluto** *adj.* having a broad base. **-ovalle** *m.* valley bottom. **-ura** *f.* low ground.

fondù *m. indecl.* (cinem.) fade-out, dissolve.

fondu·a *f.* (cul.) a Piedmontese dish of hot melted cheese served with truffles.

fonduta *f.* (cul.) see **fondua**; (metall.) fusion, melting.

fonema *m.* (phon.) phoneme.

fonẹt·ica *f.* phonetics. **-ico** *adj.* phonetic **-icamẹnte** *adv.* phonetically. **-iṣmo** *m.* phoneticism.

†**fonfone** *m.* titbit.

†**fon·gia** *f.* asparagus root.

fo·nic-a *f.* phonics, acoustics; tone (of an instrument); sound-quality. **-o** *adj.* phonic; phonetic; (mus.) pertaining to sound; mezzi -i, acoustic resources; *n.m.* (cinem.; telev.) sound-recordist. **-amẹnte** *adv.* phonetically; (mus.) from the point of view of sound.

fonocamp·tica *f.* phonocamptics.

fon-ofobi·a *f.* horror of noise. **-oge·nico** *adj.* phonogenic, suited for recording. **-ografi·a** *f.* phonography. **-o·grafo** *m.* (mus.) gramophone; -ografo a tastiera, juke-box. **-gra·fico** *adj.* (mus.) disco -grafico, gramophone record. **-ogramma** *m.* (teleph.) phonogram; (cinem.) sound record. **-oinciṣore** *m.* sound recorder (on a disk). **-olite** *f.* (min.) phonolite, clink-stone. **-oli·tico** *adj.* (min.) phonolitic. **-ologi·a** *f.* phonology; phonetics. **-olo·gico** *adj.* phonologic; phonetic. **-ologicamẹnte** *adv.* phonologically; phonetically. **-o·logo** *m.* phonologist; phonetist. **-ope·ica** *f.* (mus.) tone-painting. **-o·plice** *adj.* (teleg.) phonoporic. **-opo·rio** *m.* (teleg.) phonopore. **-oregistratọre** *m.* tape-recorder and gramophone combined. **-orivelatọre** *m.* sound recorder (on a disk). **-osco·pio** *m.* phonoscope. **-osimbo·lico** *adj.* onomatopoeic. **-ospira** *f.* (mus.) instrument specially made for performance of Boito's 'Nerone'.

fontal-e *adj.* original, primal, fontal. **-mẹnte** *adv.* originally; primally.

fontan-a *f.* fountain; source, spring; fount; origin; (fig.) — di vita, fountain of life, source of life; (archit.) fountain; (naut.) signal rocket; — comune, white rocket; (cul.) heap, pile (e.g. of flour). **-acci** *m.pl.* marshy land in the plain of Pisa. †**-almente** *adv.* originally. **-ella** *f.* (anat.) entrance to windpipe; fontanelle, soft part on a baby's head; main vein in a horse's leg; cautery issue; -ella della gola, hollow in the throat. †**-e·vole** *adj.* many-fountained. **-iere** *m.* fountain-worker; one who maintains or is responsible for a fountain, or other water-supply; fountain-maker; plumber; (joc.) critico -iere, literary critic unduly concerned with research into literary sources. **-iero** *adj.* pertaining to fountains; ninfa -iera, fountain-nymph. **-ile** *m.* source of a stream; spring; (Rom.) drinking-trough. **-ino, -o** *adj.* of a fountain, of a spring. †**-oso** *adj.* many-fountained.

font-e *f.* fountain; source, spring; (fig.) source, origin; la — di ogni male, the source of all evil; le -i dell'*Orlando Furioso*, the sources of the *Orlando Furioso*; sapere da buona — (or, da — sicura), to know on good authority; (leg.) le -i del diritto, the fountains of law; *m.* font; — battesimale, baptismal font; †liquid, †(naut.) main hatch, cabin hatch. **-icella** *f. dim.*, **-icello** *m. dim.* small spring.

fontina *f.* (cul.) soft cheese from Val d'Aosta.

football *m. indecl.* (sport) soccer, Association football.

footing *m. indecl.* (gymn.) drill consisting of quick march alternated with short runs.

†**for,** †**fora** *adv., prep.* See **fuori**.

fora·bile *adj.* See under **forare**.

forabos-co (*pl.* **-chi**) (orn.) wren; †outlaw, spy.

foracchi-are [A4] *tr.* to make holes in, to riddle. **-ato** *part. adj.* holed, perforated; legno -ato, wood full of holes. **-atura** *f.* perforating, boring; perforation; holes.

†**forafic·chio** *m.* interfering person; presumptuous individual.

foraggere *m.* (mil.). See **foraggiere**, under **foraggiare**.

foraggi-are [A3] *intr.* (*aux.* avere) to forage; (mil.) to go foraging; to pillage. **-amẹnto** *m.* (mil.) foraging; procurement of forage. **-ata** *f.* foraging. **-iere** *m.* (mil.) forager, member of a troop out on forage.

forag·gio *m.* forage; fodder; (mil.) andare a —, to go foraging, to go out on forage; †andare in —, to forage.

foramac·chie *m. indecl.* (orn.) wren.

foram-e *m.* hole, aperture; slit; (anat.) foramen, opening.

foramẹnto *m.* See under **forare**.

fora·min-e *m.* hole, aperture. **-i·feri** *m.pl.* (zool.) foraminifera. **-ọso** *adj.* perforated, porous.

fora·neo *adj.* (eccl.) vicario —, vicar forane, rural dean; (naut.) seaward; vento —, wind from the offing; molo —, outer breakwater, detached mole.

fora-nẹve *f. indecl.* (bot.) see under **forare**. **-pa·glie** *m. indecl.* (orn.) see under **forare**.

for-are [A1C] *tr.* to make a hole in; to perforate, to drill, to bore; to pierce, to prick; — un biglietto, to punch a ticket; — una montagna, to drill through a mountain; — la mano, to pierce one's hand; †to penetrate into, to gain entry into, to pass through; *intr.* (*aux.* avere) to get a puncture (cycle-racing). **-a·bile** *adj.* penetrable; perforable. **-amẹnto** *m.* boring, drilling, piercing; hole, perforation. **-anẹve** *f. indecl.* (bot.) snowdrop, *Galanthus nivalis*. **-apa·glie** *m. indecl.* (orn.) sedge warbler, *Acrocephalus schoenobaenus*; — castagnolo, moustached warbler, *Lusciniola melanopogon*; — macchiettato, grasshopper warbler, *Locustella naevia*. **-apietre** *m. indecl.* (zool.) date shell, *Lithophaga lithophaga*. **-asacco** *m. indecl.* (bot.) *Anisantha sterilis*; *Bromus mollis*. **-asiepe** *m. indecl.* (orn.) name given to various small birds, esp. the wren. **-atini** *m.pl.* (cul.) a kind of 'pasta' eaten in soup. **-ato** *part. adj.* bored, drilled; pierced; punched; punctured; (herald.) round-pierced; -ato in quadrato, quarter-pierced; *n.m.* hole. **-atọio** *m.* auger; gimlet; (eng.) hollow punch. **-atọre** *m.* borer, piercer; driller. **-atrice** *f.* punch, machine for punching holes. **-atura** *f.* hole, perforation; puncture; drilling, boring; piercing, pricking; puncture.

for·bic-i *f.pl.* scissors; shears; un paio di —, a pair of scissors; — da unghie, nail-scissors; — del giardiniere, gardener's shears; claws, pincers, nippers; (fig.) slanderous person; malicious tongue; guai a chi cade sotto le sue —!, woe betide anyone he gets his claws into!; le — della censura, the censor's scissors, the cutting of the censorship; (surg.) forceps; (naut.) cleat; goosewing (sails); †frames supporting the after cabin of a galley; (mil.) — tagliafili, wirecutters; twin defences outside a fortified gate; (zool.) claws, pincers (of scorpions, lobsters, earwigs, etc.); (Rugby) 'scissors'; *sing.* scissors; shears; single blade of a pair of scissors. **-iata** *f.* scissor-cut; mark left by scissors; (fig.) cut, reduction. **-ina** *f.* (ent.) earwig. **-iọne** *m. augm.* large scissors, shears; (orn.) red kite.

forb-ire [D2] *tr.* to furbish, to polish; to wipe, to clean; (fig.) — lo stile, to polish one's style; *rfl.* (*dat.* of *prn.* 'si') -irsi la bocca, to wipe one's mouth; (*acc.* of *prn.* 'si') to cleanse oneself; to keep oneself uncontaminated. **-ita** *f.* polish, wipe; polishing, wiping. **-itẹzza** *f.* (fig.) polish, elegance, propriety, correctness; studied grace; -itezza di stile, elegance of style. **-ito** *part. adj.* polished, furbished; studied; accomplished; neat; elegant, correct, pure; oro -ito, pure gold; lingua -ita, elegant language. **-itamẹnte** *adv.* (fig.) elegantly, correctly, with polish. **-itọio** *m.* polisher, polishing machine. **-itọre** *m.*, **-itrice** *f.* polisher. **-itura** *f.* polishing, furbishing, cleaning; polish, elegance.

†**forbott-are** *tr.* to hit, to knock about, to belabour; to insult, to abuse. †**-ato** *part. adj.* beaten; abused. †**-o** *m.* blow.

fọrc-a *f.* hayfork, pitchfork; fork-shaped object; fork (in a road); pole of a bullock-wagon; gallows, gibbet; condannare alla —, to condemn to the gallows; pendaglio da —, wretch, rogue, knave, gallows-bird; far —, to play truant from school; carrello elevatore a forche, fork lift trunk; (hist.) le forche caudine, see under **caudine**; (mus.) diteggiatura a —, fork fingering (on flute). **-ac·cio** *m.* (naut.) V-shaped ribs of a ship near the stern. †**-ai(u)olo** *m.* reactionary; repressor. **-ata** *f.* forkful (of hay, etc.); stroke with a fork. **-ato** *adj.* forked, fork-shaped; (herald.) con la coda -ata, queue fourchy; croce -ata, cross moline, cross fourchy; *n.m.* framework for vines. **-atura** *f.* forkful, stroke with a fork; bifurcation.

†**force** *f.pl.* scissors; shears.

forcell-a *f.* forked stick; mountain-pass; le -e d'una bicicletta, the forks of a bicycle; una — da capelli, a large hairpin (of tortoiseshell or plastic); (anat.) pit of the stomach; (mil.) bracket, ranging ladder (artillery); (naut.) crutch rowlock. **-ọne** *m.* (Tusc. agric.) kind of two-wheeled cart. **-uto** *adj.* forked, fork-shaped.

†**forcheggiare** *intr.* to bifurcate.

forchętt-a *f.* fork, table-fork; essere una buona —, to be a hearty eater; colazione alla —, cooked breakfast, meat breakfast; fork luncheon; parlare in punta di —, to speak in an affected way, to speak mincingly; (naut.) boom crutch; (mil.) rifle support; (mil. hist.) tripod for supporting firearms; (vet.) frog of a horse's hoof. **-ata** *f.* forkful; action made with a fork, thrust with a fork. **-ato** *adj.* fork-shaped. **-iera** *f.* container for forks. **-ọne** *m. augm.* carving-fork; large table-fork; hearty eater; (joc.) politician who takes advantage of his position to improve his financial situation; **-uto** *adj.* fork-shaped, forked.

forchino *m.* a three-pronged pitchfork.

forcin-a *f.* small fork; hairpin; harpoon; (mil. hist.) gunrest, arquebus support. **-o** *m.* (naut.) punt-pole (forked).

for·cipe *m.* (surg.) obstetric forceps; parto di —, forceps delivery.

for·col-a *f.* (naut.) gondola oar crutch usually having three alternative positions. **-o** *m.* (mil.) gunrack; forked stick.

forcọn-e *m.* pitchfork. **-ale** *m.* (Tusc.) fork of a tree. **-ata** *f.* thrust with a pitchfork; as much as can be carried on a pitchfork. **-atura** *f.* fork; fork of a tree.

†**forcostumanza** *f.* evil behaviour.

forcuto *adj.* forked; split; fork-shaped.

†**fore** *adv., prep.* See **fuori**.

forense *adj.* (leg.) forensic; juridical; *n.m.pl.* i forensi, lawyers.

†**fores-e** *adj.* living outside the city, inhabiting the 'contado'; *n.m.* inhabitant of the 'contado', countryman. **-ętta**, †**-ozza** *f.* country-girl.

foresi *f.* (biol.) phoresis.

forest-a *f.* forest; — vergine, virgin forest; (fig.) una — di capelli, a mop of hair. **-ale** *adj.* forest, forestal; consisting of forest; (leg.) il demanio -ale, the public demesne consisting of forest (C.C.); leggi -ali, forest laws; guardia -ale, forester; (mil.) member of the Corps of Foresters; the Corps itself; *n.f.* la Forestale, the Corps of Foresters.

forest-eri·a *f.* guest-quarters; behaviour towards guests or foreigners; †number of foreigners; †foreignness. **-iera** *f.* hostel. **-iere**, **-iero** *m.* foreigner; stranger; visitor, guest; camera per i -ieri, guest-room; *adj.* foreign, strange; usanze -iere, foreign customs. **-ieramẹnte** *adv.* in a foreign way. **-iera·io** *m.* (eccl.) guestmaster. **-ieriṣmo** *m.* foreign habit; foreign word. **-ierume** *m.* crowd of foreigners; foreign ways; outlandish behaviour or way of speaking.

forętto *m. dim.* See under **foro**.

forfait *m. indecl.* (pron. as Fr.) contract; a —, on a lump sum basis; all in; viaggio a —, journey (or holiday) at inclusive price; pagare a —, to pay a flat rate.

†**for·fare** *intr.* to cheat; to transgress, to err; — a, to harm. †**-fatto** *part. adj.* ill-done; ill-performed; cose -fatte, misdeeds; *n.m.* evil doing; misdeed. †**-fattura** *f.* misdeed.

forfẹcch-ia *f.* (ent.) earwig, *Forficula* spp., especially small species which live in figs; kind of forked beard. **-ina** *f.* trim of a forked beard; barba a -ina, beard forked like the tail of an earwig.

forfet(t)a·ri-o *adj.* relating to a flat rate; abbonamento —, flat-rate subscription; somma forfettaria, lump sum; prezzo —, all-in price. **-amẹnte** *adv.* on a flat rate.

†**for·fici** *f.pl.* See **forbici**.

forfor-a *f.* scurf, dandruff. **-a·ceo** *adj.* (med.) pityroid. **-ọso** *adj.* scurfy; friable (of soil).

for·gi-a *f.* forge, smithy; (naut.) ship's forge. **-are** [A 3] *tr.* to forge; to shape (also fig.). **-ato** *part. adj.* forged; shaped.

forgọne *m.* van, wagon; (mil.) gun-limber; ration wagon.

†**for·gore** *f.* See **folgore**[1].

fori *adv., prep.* See **fuori**.

forier-e, **-o** *adj.* preceding, forerunning; vento — di pioggia, wind preceding rain; essere — di, to portend, to bring the first news of; *n.m.* forerunner; precursor; portent; (mil.; naut.) see **furiere**.

forlana *f.* (mus.). See **furlana**.

forlina *f.* (mil. hist.) a kind of bombard or mortar.

forma *f.* form, shape, appearance; — sferica, spherical form; un demonio in — di angelo, a devil in the form of an angel; la — del naso, the shape of the nose; una — di formaggio, a whole cheese; a — di, in the shape of; a — di V, V-shaped; fare qualchecosa pro —, to do something for appearance's sake; format; la — di un libro, the format of a book; figure; una ragazza che ha -e snelle, a girl with a slim figure; form, style; in — scritta, in writing; in — sintetica, in condensed form; la — d'uno scritto, the form of a work; nella — seguente, as follows; per la —, for form's sake, *pro forma*; form, manners; gli mancano le -e, he has no manners; manner, type, form; in — enfatica, in a rhetorical manner; una — di malattia, a type of illness; la — del governo, the form of government; formality, convention; rispettare le -e, to keep up appearances, to respect convention; è una questione di —, non di sostanza, it is a matter of form, not of substance; form, order, procedure; (leg.) fu annullato il processo per vizio di —, proceedings were quashed on procedural grounds; nelle -e stabilite dal codice, under the procedure laid down by the Code; a — di legge, in conformity with the law; titolo in — esecutiva, warrant for levying execution; esecuzione forzata in — specifica, execution of judgement by specific performance (C.C.P.); (gramm.) form; -e verbali, verbal forms; mould, shape; model, guide; calza a —, fashioned stocking; (techn.) mould; (shoem.) last; (hatm.) hat-block; (typ.) forme; (sculpt.; paint.) mould, model; (archit.) order, style; (philos.; theol.) form; (mus.) form, structure; (naut.) lines of a ship; *pl.* formers, light scantling used in ship construction; †dock, basin; (sport) form; in —, in form.

forma·bile *adj.* See under **formare**.

formag·g-io *m.* cheese; — grattugiato, grated cheese; — dolce, mild cheese. **-ia·io** *m.* cheesemonger. **-iera** *f.* cheese-dish; dish for grated cheese. **-ino** *m. dim.* small synthetic or processed cheese.

forma·io *m.* last-maker.

formaldeide *f.* (chem.) formaldehyde.

formal-e *adj.* formal; explicit, clear, exact; parole -i, precise words; (leg.) atto —, formal deed; contratto —, formal contract; interrogatorio —, examination (of party) on oath (C.C.); procedimento —, formal (as opposed to summary) procedure; (philos.; theol.) formal; *n.m.* (liturg.) morse. **-mẹnte** *adv.* formally; clearly; precisely. **-iṣmo** *m.* formalism; (philos.) (extreme) idealism. **-ista** *m.* formalist; (philos.) idealist. **-ità** *f.* formality; non so le -ità, I do not know the formalities; (leg.) formality; adempiere le -ità d'uso, to comply with the required regulations; *pl.* -ità di legge, legal formalities. **-iẓẓare** [A I] *tr.* to shock, to scandalize; to give offence to; to outrage; *rfl.* to be shocked, to be scandalized; to insist on a point of etiquette; -izzarsi per (di) nulla, to be shocked at nothing, to be easily scandalized. **-iẓẓato** *part. adj.* shocked; offended; outraged.

formalina *f.* (chem.) formalin.

form-are [A I c] *tr.* to form, to shape, to fashion, to model; to give form to; to draw; uno scultore -a una statua, a sculptor shapes a statue; to form, to constitute, to create; to establish; — un ministero, to form a ministry or a government; (teleph.) — un numero, to dial a number; — un suono, to articulate a sound; to formulate; — una proposta, to formulate a proposal; to conceive; — un'idea, to conceive an idea; to form, to educate, to train; i viaggi -ano la gioventù, travelling educates the young; to form, to constitute, to be; -a la felicità dei genitori, he is his parents' pride and joy; (mil.) — il quadrato, to form square; — la linea di fronte, to form line abreast; — la linea di fila, to form line ahead, to form single file; *rfl.* (acc. of prn. 'si') to form, to be formed; to develop, to grow; to improve; gli si è -ato un tumore sotto l'ascella, a swelling has formed in his armpit; (naut.; mil.) to form up; (dat. of prn. 'si') -arsi un'idea, to get an idea; -arsi una clientela, to build up a clientèle. **-a·bile** *adj.* formable; (techn.) mouldable. **-ante** *part. adj.* forming; shaping; constituting. **-ata** *f.* forming; *pl.* (eccl. hist.) *litterae formatae*, letters commendatory. **-ativo** *adj.* formative. **-ato** *part. adj.* formed, shaped, fashioned, designed; composed, constituted; made, created; fully formed, full-grown; donna -ata, full-grown woman; ben -ato, well-shaped, of good physique, well-built; *n.m.* shape, size, form; format; il -ato di un libro, the format of a book; (paperm.) carro del -ato, deckle frame. **-atore** *m.* maker, creator; author; teacher, educator. (**-atrice** *f.*) **-azione** *f.* formation; -azione tecnica, technical training; creation, conception; constitution; (naut.) disposition of a fleet; (sport) la -azione di una squadra, the line-up of a team; (teleph.) -azione del numero, dialling.

formell-a *f.* small form; hole in the ground for planting a tree; wooden container for making cheese; cake of vegetable matter used for fuel; (archit.) brick, tile, etc., used in patterned pavement; (archit.) coffer, caisson; panel; (vet.) ringbone, a bony growth on the leg of a horse. **-ato** *adj.* (archit.) coffered. **-ọne** *m.* (archit.) coffer or caisson in a vault.

formene *m.* (chem.) methane, marsh gas.

†**formentare** *vb.* and derivs. See **fermentare**.

†**formento** *m.* See **frumento**.

formentone *m.* (bot.) maize, corn, *Zea mays.*

For·mia *pr.n.f.* (geog.) Formia.

formiato *m.* (chem.) formate.

formi-ca¹ *f.* (ent.) ant; ha un cervello di —, he has the brains of a gnat; a passi di —, very slowly, at a snail's pace; *pl.* (naut.) low flat reefs. **-ca·io** *m.* (ent.) ants' nest, hill or heap. **-caleone** *m.* (ent.) ant lion, *Myrmeleon* spp. †**-care** *vb.* and derivs. see **formicolare.** **-chiere** *m.* (zool.) anteater. †**-cino** *adj.* ant-like; pertaining to ants.

for·mica² *f.* (industr.) Formica.

for·mico *adj.* (chem.) formic.

formi·col-a *f. dim.* (pop. Tusc.) see **formica.** **-a·io** *m.* see **formicaio,** under **formica;** (fig.) swarm, multitude; flower-pot stand with an ant-guard.

formicol-are [A I S] *intr.* (*aux.* essere, avere; *prep.* di) to swarm; to be crowded (with); i curiosi -avano, there were swarms of onlookers; quella pagina -a di spropositi, that page is full of mistakes; (of the pulse) to beat fast; to tingle, to have pins and needles in a part of the body; mi -a il piede, I have got pins and needles in my foot. **-amento** *m.* swarming; tingling. **-ante** *part. adj.* swarming, crowded with; piazza -ante di gente, square crowded with people; (med.) polso -ante, weak, rapid pulse. **-azione** *f.* tingling, pricking sensation; creepy feeling; rapid pulse. **-ìo** *m.* swarming, crowding; swarm, crowd; tingling, 'pins and needles'.

formid-a·bile *adj.* formidable; awe-inspiring; breath-taking; stupendous; of great importance; dreadful, terrible, frightful, awful, fearful; (colloq.) un esame —, a difficult examination. **-abilmente** *adv.* formidably; terribly, dreadfully, frightfully. **-abilità** *f.* formidability. †**-ato** *adj.* feared. †**-oloso** *adj.* timid, fearfully; frightening, terrible.

formile *m.* (chem.) formyl.

formina *f. dim.* of **forma,** q.v.; (cul.) patty-pan.

†**forminga** *f.* kind of zither.

for·mio *m.* (bot.; techn.) New Zealand flax, *Phormium tenax.*

†**formisura** *adv.* excessively.

formiva·rio *adj.* polymorphous.

for·mola *f.* See **formula.**

formolo *m.* (chem.) formaldehyde, formalin.

Formosa *pr.n.f.* (geog.) Island of Formosa.

formosità *f.* See under **formoso.**

formos-o *adj.* beautiful; shapely; of a full figure, rounded. **-ello** *adj.* rather beautiful. **-ità** *f.* beauty; shapeliness.

for·mul-a *f.* formula; form; formality; un uomo tutto —, a very formal man; (leg.) form; common-form; precedent; formula; sentenza munita della — esecutiva, judgement containing common-form execution clause (C.C.P.); — del giuramento, form of an oath; assoluzione con la — più ampia, acquittal without a stain on the character; (math.; chem.) formula; (mus.) explanatory table of psalm-tones. **-are** [A I S] *tr.* to formulate, to express; to draw up. **-a·rio** *m.* formulary; form; (leg.) formulary; book, collection of precedents; standard form; contratti conclusi mediante -ari, contracts made in standard form (C.C.). **-azione** *f.* formulation; formulating; (leg.) formulation; -azione del giuramento decisorio, drawing up of interrogatories (C.C.P.).

fornac-e *f.* furnace; kiln; foundry; brickyard; (fig.) quella camera è una —, that room is very hot, that room is like an oven. **-ia·io** *m.* furnace-workman, kiln-workman. **-ia·ia** *f.* wife of a furnace-workman; wife of owner of a furnace. **-iata** *f.* furnaceful; kilnful. **-ella** *f. dim.* small furnace; place beneath furnace for unwanted embers. **-ina** *f. dim.*, **-ino** *m. dim.* small furnace; part of a furnace; *adj.* relating to furnaces, of a furnace. **-ione** *m. augm.* vast factory.

forn-a·io *m.* baker; baker's shop; (naut.) ship's baker; (orn.) oven bird. †**-aro** *m.* see **fornaio.** **-a·ia** *f.* baker's wife; proprietress of a baker's shop. **-arina** *f.* baker's daughter; baker-girl. **-ata** *f.* ovenful; batch; una -ata di pane, a batch of bread.

fornell-o *m.* gas-ring; cucina a gas con quattro -i, gas cooker with four rings (or burners); — a spirito, spirit-stove; stare sempre intorno ai -i, to be always busy cooking; — a gas, gas-ring; — di una pipa, bowl of a tobacco-pipe; hot-plate; — elettrico, electric heater; — elettrico a resistenza scoperta, open type boiling-plate; furnace, stove; (mining) raise, riser; — di gettito, chute, pass;

(mil.) loaded mine chamber; small shallow mine with a single chamber; see **frenello;** *pl.* (agric.) pile of earth and rubbish burnt for use as fertilizer.

fornic-are [A 2 S] *intr.* (*aux.* avere) to fornicate. **-a·ria** *f.* prostitute. **-a·rio** *adj.* adulterous; fornicating; *n.m.* fornicator; adulterer. **-ariamente** *adv.* sinfully, adulterously. **-atore** *m.* fornicator. (**-atrice** *f.*) **-ato·rio** *adj.* adulterous; fornicating. **-azione** *f.* fornication; adultery; †simony; †apostasy.

for·nice *m.* (archit.) supporting arch, vault; (anat.) fornix.

†**forniere** *m.* See **fornaio.**

†**fornificare** *vb.* and derivs. See **fornicare.**

forn-ire¹ [D 2] *tr.* to furnish; to give, to supply, to provide, to equip; lo -ì di denaro, he supplied him with money; — notizie, to supply information; — un'impresa, to carry out an undertaking; (mil.) to furnish with arms, provisions, etc.; to lay in supplies and ammunition; †to satisfy; †to decorate; *rfl.* (*dat.* of *prn.* 'si'; *prep.* di) to provide oneself, to equip oneself; -irsi di informazioni, to get information; (*acc.* of *prn.* 'si') -irsi da, to buy from, to deal with, to obtain supplies from. **-imento** *m.* furnishing, supplying; supplies, equipment; requisites; (mil.) supplies, victuals, military furnishing; furnishings of a gun; furniture of a rifle; *pl.* (eccles.) vestments; †trousseau; †table service, table ware; †adornment. **-ito** *part. adj.* supplied, equipped, furnished; (mil.) stocked; (fig.) -ito di qualità di mente, endowed with mental gifts; (herald.; †naut.) rigged; †*n.m.* person prepared; †harness. **-itamente** *adv.* fully, completely. **-itis·simo** *adj. superl.* well-stocked. **-itore** *m.* purveyor, supplier; retailer; recognized tradesman; -itori della Real Casa, by appointment to H.M....; -itore navale, ship's chandler; *pl.* wholesalers. (**-itrice** *f.*) **-itura** *f.* supplies; shipment; equipment; supplying, furnishing; (leg.) contratti di -iture, contracts for supplies; frode in -iture, fraud in furnishing supplies (C.P.).

†**fornire²** *vb.* and derivs. See **finire.**

forno *m.* oven; bakery, baker's shop; furnace, kiln; incinerator; alto —, blast furnace; — ad arco, arc furnace; — a muffola, muffle furnace; — di ricottura, annealing furnace, (glassm.) lehr; — a riverbero, open-hearth furnace; cuocere al —, to bake; cotto al —, baked; scaldare il —, to heat the oven; (silkb.) heated chamber where cocoons used for spinning are placed to kill the chrysalises; (fig.) 'oven', hot place; questa stanza è un —, this room is like an oven; (theatr.) empty house; fare —, to play to an empty house; (fig.) large mouth; ogni tanto apre quel — e sbadiglia, every now and then he opens that great mouth of his and yawns; (mil.) field bakery, camp bakery; (naut.) ship's bakery; combustion chamber of a ship's boiler; (hist.) i Forni, a prison under a lead roof in Venice; †heat from manure.

†**fornuolo** *m.* lamp used for night snaring or fishing.

foro¹ *m.* forum; market-place; square; — boario, cattle fair; (hist.) il Foro Romano, the Roman Forum; (leg.) forum; court; bench and bar; legal profession; — competente, Court of competent jurisdiction; — facoltativo, Court of choice; (fig.) — interiore, conscience, 'still small voice'; (theatr. hist.) il — delle scene, the back cloth.

for-o² *m.* hole; aperture; tunnel; bore; — della serratura, key-hole; sistema del —, burglary carried out through boring a hole in ceiling or floor of a premises; banda del —, gang of burglars using this technique; †wound. **-etto** *m.* small hole; dimple.

forone *m.* (chem.) phorone, p-xyloquinone.

foronomi·a *f.* (mech.) phoronomy, kinematics, fluidology.

foros-ella, -etta *f.* pretty country girl; Arcadian shepherdess.

forra *f.* (geog.) ravine; †undergrowth, rough untended land.

forse *adv.* perhaps; maybe; possibly; — che sì, — che no, it may be so, it may not; forse forse finirà con l'accettare, he may just possibly end up by accepting; (in rhet. questions) 'forsooth'; non sono — il tuo amico?, am I not your friend?; *n.m.* doubt; vedo la cosa molto in —, it seems very doubtful to me; stare in — della vita, to be dangerously ill; sono in — se partire o no, I can't make up my mind whether to go or not; senza —, without doubt; mettere in —, to question, to query, to have doubts about, to doubt; lasciare in —, to leave in doubt.

forsechè *adv.* haply; — ti ho mai impedito di uscire liberamente quando volevi?, have I ever stopped you going out whenever you wanted to?

†**forsenn-are** *intr.* to rave, to be delirious, to be out of one's mind. **-atag·gine** *f.* madness, delirium.

forsennatẹzza *f.* See under **forsennato**.

forsennat-o *adj.* frantic; beside oneself; mad, insane; delirious. **-amẹnte** *adv.* madly, insanely, furiously, frantically. **-ẹzza** *f.* madness, folly; rage; insanity.

forsterite *f.* (miner.) forsterite.

fort-e *adj.* strong, powerful, robust; muscoli ⁓i, strong muscles; il sesso —, the stronger sex; è un — ingegno, he has a powerful mind; è — nella matematica, he is good at mathematics, he is strong in mathematics; una — emozione, a powerful emotion; una — cagione, a good reason; con più — ragione, all the more reason; farsi — di, to have a good reason for, to justify oneself in; è più — di me, he is stronger than I am, the thing is beyond my control, I can do nothing about it, it is more than I can bear; star —, to stand firm, to resist; dar man — a, to help, to defend; farsi — di una cosa, to buttress oneself with a thing; to rely on a thing; heavy, large, considerable; high; ⁓i spese, heavy costs; un — peso, a heavy weight; ⁓i guadagni, high profits; vento —, high wind; pioggia —, heavy rain; con — voce, in a loud voice; bad, serious, severe; un — raffreddore, a bad cold; è troppo —, it is too much, that is too bad; bold, brave; lofty; azioni ⁓i, bold deeds; vino —, strong wine; caffè —, strong coffee; sour, sharp; latte —, sour milk; sapore —, sharp taste; difficult; un — problema, a difficult problem; luoghi ⁓i, stronghold, strong point; (naut.) — alla banda, stiff, not easily listed; (mus.) loud; *n.m.* strong point, forte; la matematica è il suo —, mathematics is his strong point; strong man, brave man; tu sei un —, you are a strong man, you are a hero; (mil.) fort, fortress, strong point, pill-box, fortified position; (naut.) beam of a ship, widest point; thick, thickest part; il — della battaglia, the thick of the battle; il — di un esercito, the bulk of an army; (of wine) avere il —, to have a rather high alcoholic content, to be sour; *adv.* strongly, powerfully; steadily; a great deal; heavily; aloud, loudly; parlar —, to speak in a loud voice; lo puoi dir —!, you can say that again!; picchiar —, to strike hard; correr —, to run fast; piovere —, to rain hard, to rain heavily. **-emẹnte** *adv.* strongly, powerfully; with strength, bravely; with fortitude; sopportò ⁓emente la prigionia, he endured imprisonment with fortitude. **-erello** *adj. dim.* rather strong; rather loud; rather heavy. **-eruzzo** *adj. dim.* rather sharp (of a taste). **-is·simo** *adj. superl.*; *adv.* (mus.) very loud.

†fortepiano *m.* pianoforte.

fortẹto *m.* scrub, thicket, bush; (Maremma) rocky sea-bottom along the coast (so-called by fishermen).

fortẹzz-a *f.* fortitude, courage; mostrò gran — nelle sciagure, he showed great fortitude in his misfortunes; strength; resistance; la — d'un tessuto, the durability of a cloth; (techn.) reinforcement, stay; (mil.) fortress, stronghold, military zone; la — di Genova, Genoa command zone; (naut.) tabling (of a sail, etc.); (aeron., 1940) — volante, bomber plane, flying-fortress; (leg.) arresto in —, imprisonment (of officer) in the Tower (military law); le ⁓e fanno parte del demanio pubblico, works for the defence of the country form part of the public domain (C.C.); (theol.) fortitude (as a gift of the Holy Ghost); †difficulty; †obscurity; †sharpness of taste, sourness. **-iera** *f.* (naut.) foul bottom, rocky or bad holding ground. **-ina** *f.* padding, lining.

fortic·c-io *adj.* rather sharp (of tastes), sourish; (of game) high. **-ello** *adj. dim.* rather strong. **-ino** *adj. dim.* rather strong; rather sharp.

fortific-are [A 2 s] *tr.* (mil.) to fortify, to protect with defensive works; to strengthen, to increase the strength of (in men or weapons); (fig.) to fortify, to strengthen; — le membra, to strengthen one's limbs, to develop the limbs; *intr.* (aux. avere) to build defence works; *rfl.* (mil.) to become fortified; to become increased in strength; to build fortifications; (fig.) to be fortified; to be strengthened; to become strong, to strengthen oneself; to fortify oneself. **-a·bile** *adj.* fortifiable. **†-agione** *f.* see **fortificazione**. **-amẹnto** *m.* fortifying; fortification. **-ante** *part. adj.* fortifying, strengthening; invigorating; *n.m.* stimulant, tonic. **-ativo** *adj.* fortifying; strengthening. **-ato** *part. adj.* (mil.) fortified; strengthened; armed; (fig.) fortified, strengthened; invigorated; *n.m.* (mil.) defensive work, fort. **-atore** *m.* fortifier; *adj.* fortifying, strengthening. (**-atrice** *f.*) **-ato·rio** *adj.* fortifying, strengthening. **-azione** *f.* (mil.) fortification; defensive work or position; -azione campale, field works, trenches, etc.; redoubt; -azione offensiva, counterfortification; (fig.) strengthening; encouragement.

fortigno *adj.* rather strong; rather sour.

fortili·zio *m.* (mil.) small fortress; redoubt; stronghold.

fortino *m.* (mil.) pill-box, small fortification, strong point.

fortire [D 2] *tr.* (mil.) to strengthen, to fortify.

†fortitu·dine *f.*, **†fortitudo** *f.* fortitude; strength.

fort-ọre *m.* sourness, sharpness (of flavour or smell); avere i -ori, to suffer from acidity. **-ume** *m.* sharp flavour; sourness; sour or sharp-flavoured food.

fortu·it-o *adj.* fortuitous, accidental, casual, chance; incontro —, chance meeting; per un caso —, by chance, by a mere accident; (leg.) atto —, an act of God; casi ⁓i, accidental loss; accollo di casi ⁓i, assumption of liability for accidental loss. **-amẹnte** *adv.* fortuitously, by chance.

fortume *m.* See under **fortore**.

fortun-a *f.* fortune, luck, chance; la ruota della —, Fortune's wheel; per —, luckily; — volle che, it so happened that, as luck would have it; buona —!, good luck!; ha avuto —, he has been lucky, he was lucky; essere in —, to be in luck; un colpo di —, a stroke of luck; — che non ci sono andato, it was lucky that I didn't go; augurare — a, to wish success to; fortune, destiny; state, condition; cadere in bassa —, to fall on bad times, to be down on one's luck; un rovescio di —, a reversal of fortune; andare in cerca di —, to seek one's fortune; fortune, inheritance, patrimony; beni di —, riches, wealth; di —, makeshift, improvised, temporary; un letto di —, a shake-down for the night; fare —, to make a fortune; to be successful; il libro fece —, the book was a success; small butterfly or daddy-long-legs believed to bring good luck; (naut.) albero di —, jury mast; vela di —, stormsail; timone di —, jury-rigged rudder; prova di —, captain's declaration attesting that damage to cargo or ship was due to bad weather; †bad weather; †vento di —, gale; †— di tempo, storm; †— di mare, act of God; (aeron.) atterraggio di —, forced landing; campo di —, emergency landing ground; (poet.) storm, tempest; in —, storm-tossed. **-ac·cia** *f. pejor.* bad fortune, ill luck. **-ale** *m.* (meteor.) storm, tempest at sea; (naut.) storm which forces vessels to run or heave to for a given length of time; †*adj.* chance, fortuitous. **†-almẹnte** *adv.* fortuitously, by chance. **†-are** *intr.* to undergo misfortune; *tr.* to favour, to bless; to beset; to toss in the storm. **-ato** *adj.* fortunate, lucky; uomo ⁓ato, lucky man; successful; impresa ⁓ata, successful undertaking; happy, pleased; 'fortunatissimo', 'I am happy to make your acquaintance'; †unfortunate; †bringing good fortune; †stormy. **-atamẹnte** *adv.* fortunately, luckily; successfully. **-eggiare** [A 3 c] *intr.* (aux. avere) to be at the mercy of events; †to be exposed to a storm. **-ello** *m.* rascal, rogue. **-ọso** *adj.* eventful, chequered; stormy; storm-tossed; fraught with misfortune, full of danger; chancy, risky. **-osamẹnte** *adv.* stormily, tempestuously.

forun·col-o *m.* (med.) boil, furuncle. **-ọsi** *f. indecl.* (med.) furunculosis, crop of boils.

forvi-are [A 4] *intr.* (aux. essere) to go astray, to wander from the right path; *tr.* to lead astray, to corrupt; to send the wrong way.

†for·vici *f.pl.* See **forbici**.

forz-a *f.* force, strength, might; con tutta la sua —, with all his might; con — estrema, with all one's might; farsi —, to be brave; (iron.) bella —!, what mighty strength!; ⁓e fisiche, physical strength; le ⁓e gli vengono meno, he is losing strength; la — del vento, the force of the wind; — motrice, motive power; è superiore alle mie ⁓e, it is beyond me; la — del ragionamento, force of argument; la — dell'animo, strength of mind; la — del vino, the strength of the wine, the alcoholic content of the wine; far —, to make an effort; far — a uno, to encourage someone; su, —!, come on, try hard!, (sport) play up!, come on!; fare le ⁓e, to wrestle, to grapple in a test of strength; force, violence, physical force; contro la — la ragion non vale, reason is useless against violence; far —, to use force; far — a sè stesso, to check oneself, to restrain oneself; far — a un testo, to do violence to a text, to wrest the meaning of a text; (mil.) military power, regiment, army; bassa —, other ranks; prendere in —, to take by force; (naut.) — navale, naval force; bassa —, lower-deck ratings; in —, taut; — di vele, additional fair-weather sails, stu'n-sails, etc.; a — di remi, under oars; mezza —, half speed; tutta —, full speed; la — pubblica, the police; casa di —, prison; power, efficacy; camicia di —, straitjacket; le leggi hanno perso ogni —, the laws can no longer be enforced; le iniezioni non hanno più — su lui, injections no longer have any effect on him; (leg.) — esecutiva, legal course; operative effect; i provvedimenti dell'Autorità giudiziaria hanno

forz-a (*cont.*)

— esecutiva in tutto il territorio, the writ of the judicial authorities runs throughout the land (C.C.P.); — di gravità, the force of gravity; — d'inerzia, force of inertia; — ascensionale, buoyancy, lift, uplift; (mech.) — viva, kinetic energy; — motrice idraulica, water power; significance, function, capacity; in — di avverbio, in an adverbial capacity, with an adverbial function; questa disposizione ha — di legge, this order or provision has the force of law; — maggiore, circumstances beyond one's control, *force majeure*; eccettuati i casi di — maggiore, acts of God excepted; power, fascination; — dell'arte, power of art; le -e di Ercole, the labours of Hercules; è —, it is inevitable; è — riconoscerlo, one can't help recognizing that; per —, a —, by force, of necessity, compulsorily; volle partire a —, he insisted on leaving, he left in spite of all opposition; ci andrai? per forza!, are you going? of course! I can't help it! how can I not go?; cacciar uno a —, to force someone out; lo feci venire per —, I forced him to come; per amore o per —, willy-nilly; a — di, by dint of, by means of; riuscire a — di quattrini, to succeed thanks to money; a — di braccia, by exerting one's strength, (joc.) with elbow grease; fecero procedere il carro per — di braccia, they moved the cart forward by brute strength; a — di remi, by hard rowing; a tutta —, with all one's strength, at full speed; a mezza —, at half speed, at half strength.

forz-are [A I] *tr.* to force, to oblige, to compel; to force, to break open; to violate, to rape; — una serratura, to force a lock; — una porta, to break open a door; — la mano ad uno, to force someone's hand; — la voce, to force one's voice; to squeeze, to constrict; to press, to strain; — al pagamento, to enforce payment; — la vista, to strain the eyes; — la legge, to strain the law; (mil.) — il blocco, to run the blockade (or siege); (naut.) — l'entrata di un porto, to force a harbour; — di vele, to crowd on canvas; — di remi, to drive hard under oars. **-amento** *m.* forcing; (naut.) -amento di blocca navale, blockade running; (eng.) shrinking. **-ato** *part. adj.* forced, compelled; compulsory; prestito -ato, forced loan; strained; espropriazione -ata, compulsory expropriation; compulsory acquisition; riso -ato, forced laugh; interpretazione -ata, strained interpretation; condannato ai lavori -ati, condemned to prison with hard labour; (leg.) esecuzione -ata, execution of judgement (C.C.); (mus.) nota -ata, forced note; (mil.) marcia -ata, forced march; (naut.) nave -ata, ship out of control or unmanageable owing to bad weather; †condemned to the galleys; *n.m.* prisoner condemned to hard labour, convict. **-atamente** *adv.* by force, compulsorily; necessarily. **-atore** *m.* forcer; violator, wrestler, 'strong man' (e.g. at a fair). (**-atrice** *f.*) †**-evole** *adj.* forceful; violent. †**-evolmente** *adv.* forcefully; violently.

forzier-e, †**-o** *m.* safe, strong-box, coffer.

†**forzificamento** *m.* fortification.

forzista *m.* wrestler, participant in trials of strength; forcer.

†**forz-o** *m.* see **forza.** †**-ore** *m.* see **fortore.**

forz-oso *adj.* forced, compulsory; (finan.) corso —, forced currency; prestito —, forced loan; strong, forceful, vigorous; †(naut.) vento —, strong wind, half gale. **-osamente** *adv.* compulsorily; by force, vigorously. **-uto** *adj.* physically strong, powerful, robust; muscular.

fosch-ezza *f.,* **-i·a** *f.* See under **fosco.**

fos-co *adj.* (*m.pl.* **-chi**) dark, dull, obscure; color —, dark colour; giornata -ca, dull day; tempo —, dull weather; notte -ca, dark night; rappresentare una cosa con -chi colori, to paint something in murky colours, (fig.) to put something in a bad light; gloomy, murky; pensiero —, gloomy thought; aspetto —, gloomy appearance; (mus.) con voce -ca, with dark tone; †unknown; †secret; †occult; *n.m.* dark, darkness; gloom; sadness. **-cag·gine** *f.* darkness, dullness; dull weather. **-camente** *adv.* darkly, obscurely. **-chezza** *f.* darkness, dullness, gloominess. **-chi·a** *f.* (naut.) haze, mistiness; low visibility; fog.

foscoliano *adj.* relating to, or characteristic of, the Italian poet, Ugo Foscolo.

fosf-am·mide *m.* (chem.) phospham. **-atazione** *f.* (metall.) phosphate coating. **-a·tico** *adj.* (chem.) phosphate. **-ato** *m.* (chem.) phosphate. **-atizzare** [A I] *tr.* (chem.) to phosphatize. **-atizzazione** *f.* (chem.) phosphatizing. **-aturi·a** *f.* (med.) phosphaturia. **-eno** *m.* (opt.) phosphene; *pl.* (med.) -eni da accomodazione, accommodation phosphenes. **-azoto** *m.* (chem.) nitrophosphate. **-ina** *f.*

(chem.) phosphine. **-ito** *m.* (chem.) phosphite. **-o·nio** *m.* (chem.) phosphonium.

fosfo·rico *adj.* (chem.) phosphoric.

fo·sforo[1] *m.* (opt.) phosphor.

fo·sfor-o[2] *m.* (chem.) phosphorus; (fig.) brains, wits; gli manca il —, he hasn't any brains. **-are** [A I S] *tr.* (techn.) to tip (matches). (**-eggiamento** *m.*) **-eggiare** [A 3 c] *intr.* (*aux.* avere) to flash. **-escente** *adj.* phosphorescent. **-escenza** *f.* phosphorescence; *pl.* gleams, flashes; -escenze d'ingegno, sparkling wit, gleams of intelligence. **-ismo** *m.* (med.) phosphorus poisoning. **-ite** *f.* (miner.) phosphorite, phosphate rock. **-izzare** *tr.* [A I] (chem.) to phosphorate. **-oso** *adj.* (chem.) phosphorous.

Fo·sforo[3] *pr.n.m.* (astron.) Phosphor, the Morning Star, Lucifer.

fosfuro *m.* (chem.) phosphide.

fosgen-e *m.* (chem.) phosgene, carbonyl chloride. **-ite** *f.* (miner.) phosgenite, cromfordite.

foss-a *f.* ditch; trench; pit; long narrow hole; grave; — comune, common pit, communal grave; scavare una —, to dig a hole, to dig a grave; avere un piede nella —, to have one foot in the grave; scavarsi la — sotto i piedi, to dig away the ground under one's own feet, to cause one's own downfall; del senno di poi son piene le -e, everyone is wise after the event; cavity; -e nasali, nasal cavities; -e del viso, sunken cheeks; den; Daniele nella — dei leoni, Daniel in the lions' den; (anat.) fossa; (tanning) pit; (mil.) moat; (leg.) — di concime, compost pit; — di latrina, soil pit, latrine trench (C.C.); (bldg.) — biologica, cesspool; (ocean.) trench; (geog.) — tettonica, rift valley; (naut.) chain or cable locker; — dei leoni, boatswain's store; see **bozzo**; †ammainare in —, to strike down yards, etc. **-ac·cio** *m.* (orn.) water pipit. †**-ag·gio** *m.* (mil.) see **fossa.** **-aiuolo** *m.* ditch-digger, grave-digger. **-arello** *m.* see **fosso.** †**-ata** *f.* see **fossa.** **-etta** *f. dim.* of **fossa;** dimple, fossette.

fossat-o *m.* (mil.) long ditch, moat or entrenchment; temporary dug-out; obstacle; stream, small torrent; ditch; *adj.* dug out, excavated. **-ello** *m. dim.* small torrent; hole; furrow.

fosser-ella, -etta *f. dim.* See **fossa.**

foss-il-e *adj.* fossil; carbon —, pit coal (to distinguish it from charcoal, carbon, etc.); *n.m.* fossil; (fig.) fossil, old-fashioned person. **-i·fero** *adj.* (geol.) fossiliferous. **-izzare** [A I] *tr.* to fossilize; *rfl.* (fig.) to become old-fashioned, to become antiquated; to be unprogressive, to be hostile to innovation. **-izzato** *part. adj.* fossilized; fossil; (fig.) old-fashioned, out-of-date, fossilized, antiquated. **-izzazione** *f.* fossilization.

foss-o *m.* ditch, channel; (geog., Elba) valley of seasonal stream; — di scolo, gutter; — d'irrigazione, irrigation channel; (fig.) saltare il —, to side-track a difficulty with skill, to clear an obstacle, to take the plunge; (fig.) stare a cavallo del —, to be sitting on the fence, not to commit oneself to one side or the other; (leg.) — comune, boundary ditch (C.C.); (mil.) ditch, moat; — anticarro, tank ditch; — secco, dry ditch; — acquoso, wet ditch; secondo —, outer ditch; — doppio, dual purpose ditch (wet or dry); rimettere i -i, to clean out the ditches; scannare il —, to drain the moat. **-one** *m. augm.* (mil.) main ditch; river channel; tank trap.

fossore *m.* (eccl. hist.) fossor.

fot *m. indecl.* (phys.) phot.

fot-o *f. indecl.* photo. **-ocalcografi·a** *f.* (typ.) photocomposition. **-ocata·lisi** *f.* (chem.; phys.) photocatalysis. **-oca·todo** *m.* (electr.) photo-cathode. **-ocel·lula** *f.* (phys.; electr.) photo-electric cell. **-ochi·mica** *f.* photochemistry. **-ochi·mico** *adj.* photochemical. **-oconduttività** *f.* (phys.; electr.) photoconductivity. **-oco·pia** *f.* photocopy. **-ocromi·a** *f.* (photog.) photochromy. **-ocro·naca** *m.* pictorial, illustrated magazine. **-odisintegrazione** *f.* (phys.) photo-disintegration. **-odissociazione** *f.* (chem.) photodissociation. **-oelet·trica** *f.* searchlight, spotlight. **-oelettricità** *f.* photo-electricity. **-oelet·trico** *adj.* (phys.) photo-electric. **-oelettrone** *m.* (phys.) photo-electron. **-oemissivo** *adj.* (phys.) photo-emissive. **-oforesi** *f.* (chem.; phys.) photophoresis. **-oge·nico** *adj.* (photog.) photogenic. **-ografare** [A I S] *tr.* to photograph. **-ografato** *part. adj.* photographed. **-ografi·a** *f.* photograph; photography; successo in -ografia, photo-finish, photo-finish win. **-ogra·fico** *adj.* photographic; apparecchio -ografico, camera. **-o·grafo** *m.* photographer. **-ogramma** *m.* picture, photogram; (cinem.; telev.) frame. **-ogrammetri·a** *f.* (surv.) aerial survey, photogrammetry. **-oincisione** *f.* (photog.) photogravure; photo-engraving. **-o·lisi** *f.*

fot-o (*cont.*)
(chem.) photolysis. **-ometri·a** *f.* (phys.) photometry. **-ome·trico** *adj.* (phys.) photometric. **-ometro** *m.* exposure meter; **-ometro** a carta oliata, grease spot photometer. **-oneutrone** *m.* (atom. phys.) photoneutron. **-orecettore** *m.* (zool.) photoreceptor. **-oromanzo** *m.* (journ.) story told by means of photographs and captions. **-oscissione** *f.* (phys.) photofission. **-osensi·bile** *adj.* (photog.; phys.) photosensitive, sensitive to light. **-osensito·metro** *m.* (phys.) photosensitometer. **-osfera** *f.* (astron.) photosphere. **-osin·tesi** *f.* (bot.; biol.) photosynthesis. **-ostato** *m.* photostat. **-ostoffa** *f.* (text.) photographic fabric. **-oteca** *f.* photographic library. **-otubo** *m.* (electron.) photo-electric tube. **-oval·vola** *f.* (cinem.) light valve. **-ozincotipi·a** *f.* (typ.) photozincography.

fotone *m.* (phys.) photon.

fotta *f.* (vulg.) anger; *pl.* nonsense; (N. Ital.) fare una —, to make a mistake.

fott-ere [B I] *tr.* (vulg.) to have sexual intercourse with; to cheat; to ruin; son **-uto**, I am ruined; **-uto!**, curse! **-io** *m.* (vulg., Tusc.) large quantity, great amount; un **-ìo** di denari, bags of money. **-itoio** *m.* (vulg.) brothel.

fottivento *m.* (orn., Flor.) nightjar.

fottuttio *m.* factotum, busybody.

fox *m. indecl.* fox-terrier; foxtrot.

foziano *adj.* (eccl.) Photian; Orthodox.

fra¹ *prep.* between, among, amid; through; — Milano e Torino, between Milan and Turin; — lei e lui ci corre un abisso, there is a world of difference between them; — tutti quanti, between the lot of them; di — i sassi spicciava un ruscello, a spring gushed out between the stones; la strinse — le braccia, he hugged her in his arms; parlar — i denti, to speak through one's teeth, to mutter; — tre persone hanno una camera sola, they have only one room among the three of them; dire — sè, to say to oneself; — me e me, within myself; — una parola e l'altra si venne a discorrere di te, passing from one subject to another we came to mention you, what with one thing and another we came to talk about you; — la scuola e lo studio non ho un minuto libero, what with school and study I haven't a spare moment; within, in; — due giorni, in two days' time; — poco, shortly, soon; passerò a prenderti — una mezz'ora, I'll pick you up in half an hour from now.

fra² *m.* (eccl.) Brother (before religious name). NOTE: fra is the normal abbreviation of **frate** before consonants ('Fra Cristoforo'), and it is now often placed before vowels as well (e.g. 'Fra Antonio', instead of the once obligatory 'Frate Antonio' or 'Frat'Antonio'). It is usable as a plural: qui ci sono due Fra Paoli, there are two Brother Pauls here. It is no longer said of a priest (now always 'Padre'). Cf. **frate**.

frac *m. indecl.* dress-coat; dinner-jacket; evening-dress.

Fracassa *pr.n.m.* il capitan —, boaster, braggart; blusterer.

fracass-are [A I] *tr.* to smash, to shatter, to break; — le ossa a uno, to break someone's bones; — un vetro, to smash a pane of glass; to rout, to defeat; *intr.* (*aux.* essere) to crash, to crash down; *rfl.* to smash, to crash; to break in pieces, to break up; (fig.) to go to pieces. **-amento** *m.* breaking, smashing; smash, breakage. **†-ata** *f.* lusty blow. **-ato** *part. adj.* broken, smashed, shattered; (fig.) broken, ruined. (**-atore** *m.* **-atrice** *f.*) **-atura** *f.* breaking, smashing. **-ìo** *m.* continued smashing, crashing; din, row; uproar. **-one** *m.* clumsy person; violent person, destructive person.

fracass-o *m.* noise, crash; din, uproar; clashing, clatter, banging, crashing; destruction, damage; abundance, mass; cadere con —, to fall with a crash; il libro fece —, the book caused an uproar; un — di gente, a crowd of people; †a —, precipitately, in a rush. **†-oso** *adj.* noisy; violent.

fracco *m.* large quantity; un — di legnate, a beating.

†fraccurrado *m.* rag doll; wooden doll.

fra·cid-o *adj.* and derivs. See fradicio.

fracosta *f.* (butcher.) ribs, rib (of beef).

fra·dic-io *adj.* rotten, bad, putrid; una pera **-ia**, a sleepy pear, a rotten pear; un uovo —, a bad egg; corrupt; governo —, corrupt government; wet; bagnato —, wet through, soaking wet; ubriaco —, quite drunk, blind drunk. **-ezza** *f.* rottenness, putrefaction; wetness. **-iume** *m.* rottenness, putrefaction; corruption; wetness; mass of rotten material, mass of wet things.

†frag-a, **†-anella** *f.* See fragola.

fraga·glia *f.* (ichth.) young gurnards, etc., eaten as whitebait.

†fraganza *f.* See fragranza, under fragrante.

†fragellare *vb.* and derivs. See flagellare.

fra·gil-e *adj.* fragile, brittle; weak, frail; un bicchiere —, a fragile glass; — come il vetro, as brittle as glass; una persona —, a frail person; la natura umana è —, human nature is frail; speranze **-i**, fragile hopes, faint hopes; (on a packing case or parcel) 'fragile', 'handle with care'; (rel.) frail. **-mente** *adv.* weakly, fraily; fragilely. **†-ezza** *f.* see fragilità. **-ità** *f.* fragility; weakness; frailty.

fra·gol-a *f.* (bot.) strawberry, *Fragaria*; — secca, barren strawberry, *Potentilla sterilis*; birthmark, strawberry-mark; uva —, a very sweet kind of grape. **-ac·cia** *f.* (bot.) *P. verna*, *P. hirta*. **-a·io** *m.* strawberry-bed. **-a·io** *m.* strawberry-seller. **-ata** *f.* meal of strawberries, dish of strawberries; strawberry shortcake. **-eto** *m.* strawberry-bed. **-ina** *f. dim.* wild strawberry. **-one** *m. augm.* large cultivated strawberry.

fragolino *m.* (ichth.) *Pagellus erythrinus*, sea bream; — occhione, —occhialone, *P. centrodontus*.

fragor-e *m.* crash; din, row, roar; clang, clash; il — del tuono, the crash of the thunder; il — di un treno, the roar of a train; — delle armi, clash of arms; †fragrance; †strong odour. **-io** *m.* crashing, roaring; clashing. **-oso** *adj.* noisy, loud; resounding; applausi **-osi**, thunderous applause. **-osamente** *adv.* loudly, noisily; with a crashing noise; with great vigour.

†fragoso *adj.* sonorous; reverberating.

fragran-te *adj.* fragrant, sweet-smelling; perfumed, scented. **-za** *f.* fragrance, sweet smell, scent, perfume.

fragulino *m.* (ichth.). See fragolino.

†frail-e *adj.* frail; fragile. **†-ezza** *f.* frailty; fragility.

fraina *f.* (bot.) buckwheat, *Fagopyrum esculentum*.

frainten·d-ere [C I] *tr.* to misunderstand; to misinterpret; to get hold of the wrong end of the stick; not to hear properly. **-imento** *m.* misunderstanding; misinterpretation.

frainteso *part.* of fraintendere, q.v.; *adj.* misunderstood; misinterpreted.

†fralde *f.* and derivs. See frode.

fral-e *adj.* (poet.) frail, weak; delicate; *n.m.* the frail body; the mortal part of us. **-ezza** *f.* frailty, weakness; instance of frailty.

framatura *f.* (metall.) flame hardening.

frambe·sia *f.* (med.) yaws, framboesia.

fra·mea *f.* (hist.) Germanic lance.

framescolare [A I S] and derivs. See frammescolare.

framezzare [A I] and derivs. See frammezzare.

frammasson-e *m.* freemason, mason. **-eri·a** *f.* freemasonry.

framment-o *m.* fragment, piece; extract; i **-i** di un vaso, the fragments of a vase; **-i** di un libro, extracts from a book. **-a·rio** *adj.* fragmentary. **†-ato** *adj.* in fragments; in bits and pieces; fragmentary. **-azione** *f.* (phys.) **-azione** atomica, atomic fission. **-ismo** *m.* (lit. hist.) a fashionable trend in Italian writing current in the 1920's and associated with Soffici, Linati, Sbarbaro and others. (**-ista** *m., f.* **-i·stico** *adj.*) **-uc·cio**, **-uzzo** *m. pejor.* small, unimportant fragment; little bit.

frammescol-are [A I SC, A I S] *tr.* to mingle, to intermingle, to mix. **-ato** *part. adj.* mingled, intermingled, mixed.

frammess-o *part.* of frammettere, q.v.; *adj.* inserted; interposed; *n.m.* insertion; interpolation; (mus.) entr'acte, intermezzo; *pl.* (cul.) entremets.

frammett-ere [C 20] *tr.* to interpose, to insert, to intermingle; †— la lingua, to stutter; *rfl.* to interpose, to intervene, to interfere, to intrude. **-ente** *part. adj.* intervening; interfering. **-imento** *m.* intervention, intrusion, interference.

frammezz-are [A I] *tr.* to intermingle; to interpose. **-ato** *part. adj.* intermingled; interposed.

frammezzo *adv.* in the midst; *prep. phr.* — a, between, among.

frammischi-are [A 4] *tr.* to mix, to intermingle; to confuse; *rfl.* **-arsi** con, to intervene in, to interfere with; to mix with. **-amento** *m.* mingling, intermingling; mixture, intermixture, blend. **-ato** *part. adj.* intermingled, intermixed, blended.

fran-a *f.* landslip; landslide; (pol.) — elettorale, landslide. **-are** [A I] *intr.* (*aux.* essere) to slip, to fall (of rocks, etc.); to cave in; to crash. **-amento** *m.* slipping, falling; slip, fall; cave in. **†-ata** *f.* ruin, landslide. **-ato** *part. adj.* fallen, collapsed. **-oso** *adj.* (geog.) unstable; subject to landslides.

Franca *pr.n.f.* Franca.

francamente *adv.* See under franco³.

franc·are [A2] *tr.* to free; to liberate; to set free; to compensate for; non -a la spesa, it is not worth while; to stamp, to put a stamp on; to frank; — una lettera, to stamp a letter. (-a·bile *adj.*) †-agione *f.* liberation, freedom. †-amento *m.* act of freeing. -ato *part. adj.* freed, liberated; franked, stamped; exempt. (-atore *m.* -atrice *f.*) -atrippa *pr.n.m.* name of a coarse greedy character in the Italian 'Maschere'; (fig.) greedyguts; idler. -atura *f.* franking, stamping; stamps, postage; la -atura di una lettera, the stamps required for a letter, the postal charge for a letter. -azione *f.* franking, stamping; stamp.

francesata *f.* See under **francese**.

Francesca *pr.n.f.* Frances; Francesca; (hort.) kind of green dessert apple.

francescan-o *adj.* (eccl.) Franciscan; (fig.) evangelical; simple, humble; *n.m.* Franciscan (friar). -a *n.f.* (eccl.) Franciscan Sister.

Francesco¹ *pr.n.m.* Francis; San —, St Francis; il cavallo di San —, Shanks's pony; (orn.) — mio, sounds representing the song of the chaffinch; the chaffinch itself.

†**francesc-o²** *adj.* French. †-amente *adv.* in the French manner.

frances-e *adj.* French; andarsene alla —, to go off without saying good-bye, to take French leave; alla —, in the French style; †il mal —, syphilis; *n.m.* the French language, French; parlare —, to speak French; Frenchman; *f.* Frenchwoman; French girl; i Francesi, the French. (-emente *adv.*) -ata *f.* (derog.) typically French action. -eggiante *part. adj.* Frenchified, imitative of the French. -eggiare [A3c] *intr.* (aux. avere) to act in a French way, to imitate the French. †-eri·a *f.* passion for imitating the French, Frenchified behaviour. -ismo *m.* Gallicism. -ista *m., f.* specialist in French studies. -ume *m.* stupid French habit, unpleasant Gallicism.

francheggi-are [A3c] *tr.* to free; to assure, to encourage; †to favour, to grant benefits to; *rfl.* to feel safe. -ato *part. adj.* freed; assured; encouraged.

franch-ezza *f.* assurance, freedom; frankness, openness, sincerity; boldness; rispondere con —, to answer frankly; mentire con troppa —, to lie too freely; †liberation; †exemption; †dare a —, to set free; †lavishness.

franchi·g-ia *f.* liberty; freedom; privilege, exemption, immunity; — postale, free postage; in — postale, postage free; la — doganale, exemption from customs duty; *pl.* franchise; -e costituzionali, constitutional franchise; (naut.) shore leave; number of hours libertymen may stay ashore; marinai in —, libertymen; (mil.) exemption from duty; time off duty.

Fran·cia *pr.n.f.* (geog.) France.

Fran·cica *pr.n.f.* (geog.) Francica, prov. of Catanzaro.

fran·cico *adj.* Frank, Frankish.

†**francioso** *adj., n.m.* See **francese**.

franco¹ *adj.* (hist.) Frank, Frankish; French; guerra francogermanica, Franco-Prussian war, war between France and Germany; *n.m.* (hist.) Frank; franc (coin); — svizzero, Swiss franc; Italian lira.

Franco² *pr.n.m.* Frank.

franc-o³ *adj.* (*m.pl.* **franchi**) frank, open, sincere; con te sarò —, I will be frank with you; free, clear; ho la coscienza -a, I have a clear conscience; free, exempt; — dalle gabelle, free of tax, exempt from tax; porto —, free port; — di porto, carriage-free, post-free; dar campo — a qualcuno, to give someone a free hand; farla -a, to escape, to get away with it, to come through unscathed; — a richiesta, free on application; sure, skilled, good; essere — nel leggere, to read well, to be good at reading; franchi muratori, freemasons; — tiratore, *franc-tireur*, free shooter, sniper, Freischütz; bold, brave; difesa -a, courageous defence; (herald.) quarto —, quarter; lingua -a, a dialect formed of elements from Provençal, Italian, Spanish, Greek, Arabic, spoken during the nineteenth century in the Levant; *adv.* frankly, openly; parlare —, to speak frankly, to speak one's mind; (naut.) guardia -a, watch off duty; squadra -a, part of the watch off duty; — d'acqua, free of water, pumped out; punto —, porto —, free port, free zone; — a bordo, f.o.b.; — di porto, c.i.f.; *n.m.* free man; freedman; *pl.* (naut.) libertymen. -amente *adv.* frankly, openly; freely; boldly. -one *m.* very frank person, outspoken person. (-ona *f.*)

francobollo *m.* (*pl.* **francobolli**) stamp postage-stamp; un — da 10 lire, a ten-lire stamp; unire un — per la risposta, to enclose a stamp for the reply.

Francoforte *pr.n.f.* (geog.) Frankfurt.

francolino *m.* (orn.) francolin, esp. the black francolin, *Francolinus francolinus*; — di monte, hazel hen, *Tetrastes bonasia*.

Franco·nia *pr.n.f.* (hist.) Franconia, kingdom of the Franks.

fran·g-ere [C5] *tr.* to break; to smash; to crush; *intr.* (aux. essere) to break; *rfl.* to break, to break in pieces; il -ersi delle onde, the breaking of the waves. -ente *part. adj.* breaking; *n.m.* crisis, difficult or dangerous situation, danger; trovarsi in un brutto -ente, to be in a critical situation, to be in a 'spot'; (naut.) breaker, breaking sea, wave; reef or shoal on which waves break, usually near the surface, blinder; (motor.) cataro -ente, reflector (e.g. on a bicycle). -i·bile *adj.* breakable, frangible. -ibilità *f.* frangibility, fragility. -imento *m.* breaking; breakage; crushing; †weariness of body, aches and pains. -itura *f.* crushing, pressing (of olives).

fran·g-ia *f.* fringe; fringe of hair, bang; la — di una tenda, the fringe of a curtain; una — alta sette centimetri, a fringe seven centimetres wide; (fig.) embellishment, frill, fringe; aggiungere le -e a un racconto, to embellish a story, to exaggerate a story; senza -e, unadorned, without frills, without exaggeration. -ia·io *m.* fringe-maker; one who exaggerates a story. (-ia·ia *f.*) -iato *adj.* fringed. -iatura *f.* fringe, fringing, fringed decoration. -etta *f.* fringe (of hair). -iona *f. augm.* large fringe; woman who exaggerates.

frangi-capo *m. indecl.* kind of cudgel or truncheon; club. -cu·pola *m. indecl.* bore, importunate person. -flutti *m. indecl.* (naut.) see **frangionda**. -onda *m.* (*pl.* -onde) breakwater, detached mole. -sassi *m. indecl.* (bot.) samphire, *Crithmum maritimum*. -sedere *m. indecl.* bore, tiresome person. -tutto *m. indecl.* (agric.) hammer mill. -zolle *m. indecl.* (agric.) sod-breaker; erpice -zolle, pulverizer harrow.

fran·gola *f.* (bot.) alder buckthorn, *Frangula alnus*.

fran·golo *adj.* brittle, fragile.

franklin *m. indecl.* (hist.) kind of heating stove invented by Benjamin Franklin.

franoso *adj.* See under **frana**.

frant-o *part.* of **frangere**, q.v.; *adj.* broken, shattered; crushed, pressed. -oiano *m.* workman at an oil-press, oil-presser. -oiata *f.* as many olives as can be put into a press at once, a pressful. -oio *m.* oil-press, olive-press; place where olives are crushed; (techn.) mill; crusher; -oio a mole, edge runner; -oio a palle, ball mill.

frantum-are [A1] *tr.* to break into small pieces, to shatter, to fracture. -amento *m.* break-up, shattering. -ato *part. adj.* broken, shattered, fractured; *n.m.* (bldg.) crushed stone. -atore *m.* (eng.) crusher, breaker. -azione *f.* crushing; (geol.) detrition. -e *m.* fragment, piece, splinter.

†**fraore** *m.* See **fragore**.

frapp-a *f.* fringe; (paint.) representation of foliage; †fare -e a, to censure, to reprimand severely; †una —, nothing. -are [A1] *tr.* to decorate with a fringe, to fringe; †to cheat, to deceive; †intr. to tell cock and bull stories. (-atore *m.* -atrice *f.*) -atura *f.* fringework. -eggiare [A3c] *tr.* (paint.) to decorate with foliage; *intr.* (aux. avere) to draw or paint foliage. -eggiato *part. adj.* adorned with painted foliage; *n.m.* painting representing foliage.

frappè *m. indecl.* milk-shake; caffè —, coffee-shake..

frapponimento *m.* interposition.

frapporre [B21] *tr.* to interpose, to place in between; non — indugi, not to delay; *rfl.* to interpose, to intervene; to interfere, to intrude.

frappos-izione *f.* interposition, insertion; intrusion, interference. -to *part.* of **frapporre**, q.v.; *adj.* interposed, inserted; intruded.

frari *m.pl.* (Ven.) friars, brothers; i Frari, the famous Franciscan church in Venice (in full, S. Maria Gloriosa dei Frari).

fras-a·io, -aiuolo *m.* lover of fine phrases, phrasemonger. -a·rio *m.* collection of phrases; phraseology, language, terminology.

frasc-a *f.* bough, branch; branch or bush used to indicate an inn; bunch of twigs prepared as a nesting-place for silkworms; (fig.) thoughtless, scatter-brained person; *pl.* beansticks, peasticks; (fig.) trifles, nonsense, trivialities; idle tales; (provb.) il buon vino non ha bisogno di —, good wine needs no bush; essere mobile come una — al vento, to be as giddy as a feather in the breeze; è come un uccello sulla —, he is never still for a moment, he is always chopping and changing; aver il capo alle frasche, to have one's head full of trivialities; saltar di palo in —, to jump from one subject to another, to go off at a tangent; meglio

frasc-a (*cont.*)

fringuello in mano che tordo in —, a bird in hand is worth two in the bush. **-ame** *m.* quantity of branches; brushwood. **-arella** *f. dim.* small branch; (fig.) thoughtless woman, scatter-brain. **-arello** *m.* (cul.) quantity of sweet pancakes. **-ato** *m.* bower, arbour, pergola; booth; bushy place. **-ona·ia** *f.* thicket; place where birds are snared; trifles, trivialities; excessive ornamentation. **-one** *m.* beanstick, peastick; young person; †(naut.) main brace. **-onetto** *m.* (naut.) purchase. **-ume** *m.* quantity of branches; excessive ornamentation.

Frascat-i *pr.n.f.* (geog.) Frascati; white wine from Frascati. **-ano** *adj., n.m.* native of Frascati.

fraschegg-iare [A 3 c] *intr.* (*aux.* avere) to rustle; (fig.) to joke, to trifle. **-io** *m.* rustling.

frascher-ella *f. dim.* small leafy branch; giddy, thoughtless woman; trifle. **-i·a** *f.* trifle, triviality.

fraschetta *f. dim.* of **frasca**, q.v.; small branch, twig; decoy for birds; (fig.) thoughtless, giddy woman; flirt; (typ.) tympan.

†**fraschetto** *m.* (naut.) boatswain's pipe, type of whistle used at sea.

†**fra·schia** *f.* (naut.) constructor's graduated ruler.

fraschiere *m.* (naut. hist.) implement used for applying hot tar to the hull of a ship; (fig.) frivolous, thoughtless person.

frascone *m. augm.* See under **frasca**.

fras-e *f.* phrase; sentence; idiom, locution; style, diction; — fatta, commonplace, platitude, cliché; *pl.* empty talk, idle words; è un uomo tutto -i, he is all talk; belle -i, fine phrases; (mus.) phrase; sentence. **-eggiamento** *m.* way of forming sentences, style; (mus.) phrasing. **-eggiare** [A 3 c] *intr.* (*aux.* avere) to construct sentences, to form phrases; (mus.) *tr., intr.* to phrase. **-eggio** *m.* (mus.) phrasing. **-eologi·a** *f.* phraseology. **-etta** *f. dim.* short phrase. **-ettina** *f. dim.* affected phrase, affectation.

frassinella *f.* (bot.) dittany, burning bush, *Dictamnus albus*.

frassi·neo *adj.* made of ash-wood.

fras·sin-o *m.* (bot.) ash, *Fraxinus excelsior*; ash-pole, lance or spear of ash. **-eto** *m.* ash-wood, ash-grove.

frastagli-are [A 4] *tr.* to cut across, to slash, to cut about; — un panno, to make cuts in a piece of cloth; to intersect, to break up, to indent; to decorate with slashes or trimmings. **-amento** *m.* cutting; intersection. **-ante** *part. adj.* cutting; intersecting; bold. †**-ata** *f.* cut, slash; confusion, heap, mass. **-ato** *part. adj.* cut across; intersected; decorated with slashes or trimmings; ragged; pianura -ata da fossi, plain intersected by ditches; costa -ata, indented coast. **-atamente** *adv.* confusedly, without order. **-atura** *f.* slashes, cuts.

frasta·gli-o *m.* slash (in a garment), fringe, ornament; indentation. **-ume** *m.* lot of trimmings, quantity of superfluous and fussy trimmings.

frastorn-are [A I c] *tr.* to disturb, to distract; to bewilder; to impede, to stop, to prevent the completion of. **-amento** *m.* disturbance, diversion; stopping, hindrance; confusion. **-ato** *part. adj.* disturbed; bewildered; impeded. **-atore** *m.* disturber, hinderer. (**-atrice** *f.*) **-io** *m.* continual disturbance, prolonged disturbance. †**-o** *m.* interruption, distraction.

frastuono *m.* uproar, hubbub, din, row, clash; — di voci, hubbub; — di armi, clash of arms.

frat-e *m.* (eccl.) (strictly) friar; (loosely but frequently) monk, religious; — laico, — converso, lay brother; farsi —, to become a monk; (before religious name) Brother; (provb.) sto coi -i e zappo l'orto, I only do what I'm told, I have no say in the matter; i -i gaudenti (godenti), the Gaudenti of Our Lady at Bologna (military order, 1261–1589); i -i minori, the Franciscans; i -i predicatori, the Dominicans; (NOTE: the form 'Frate' was once used before any religious name, e.g. Frate Galdino; it is now limited to names beginning with a vowel, e.g. Frate Antonio, and even then is often replaced by **fra**, q.v.; -i e guai non van mai soli, troubles never come singly; nasce un —!, it's a Quakers' meeting! (said when conversation ceases suddenly); skylight (in the form of a hood-shaped tile); (bot.) dandelion, *Taraxacum officinale*; (Tusc.) doughnut; †brother. **-acchione** *m.* big fat friar; big fat, easy-going man. **-acchiotto** *m.* stout, sturdy friar; sturdy young man. **-a·glia** *f.* crowd of friars. **-a·io, -ai·uolo** *m.* friend of the friars, someone on close terms with monks or friars. **-ata** *f.* (derog.) monkish notion; piece of monkishness; loutish action. **-eri·a** *f.* group of friars; friary. **-esco** *adj.* (*m.pl.* **-eschi**) monkish. **-escamente** *adv.* in a monkish way, like a monk. **-icello**

m. dim. humble friar; young friar; small friar; (orn.) little tern, *Sterna minuta; pl.* (eccl. hist.) Fraticelli. †**-icida** *m.* see **fratricida**; (joc.) friar-killer. †**-ici·dio** *m.* see **fratricidio**; (joc.) monk-murder. **-icino** *m. dim.* young friar; humble friar. **-ino** *m. dim.* young friar; poor, humble friar; (orn.) Kentish plover, *Charadrius alexandrinus*; friend of the friars. *adj.* monkish. **-ismo** *m.* the religious state, monkhood; monkish leanings, liking for monks. **-oc·cio** *m.* jolly friar. **-otto** *m.* hale and hearty friar; young sturdy monk. **-uc·cio** *m.* poor friar; poor, humble friar. **-u·colo** *m. dim. pejor.* mean little friar.

fratell-o *m.* brother; Giuliano e Sandro sono -i, Julian and Alex are brothers; Adriano e Cristina sono -i, Adrian and Christine are brother and sister; Maria, Giovanna, Elisabetta e Franco sono -i, Mary, Joan and Elizabeth are sisters to Frank; — cugino, half-brother; — consanguineo, — di padre, half-brother, child of the same father but different mother, brother-consanguinean; — di madre, — uterino, half-brother, child of the same mother but different father; brother-uterine; — carnale, — germano, — vero, brother, brother through both parents, brother-german; — gemello, twin brother; — di latte, foster-brother; -i Siamesi, Siamese twins; companion, comrade, colleague; — d'esilio, companion in exile, brother exile; (eccl.) brother (used when no name follows); buon giorno, —, good morning, brother (cf. buon giorno, Fra Giovanni, good morning, Brother John); c'erano due preti e tre fratelli, there were two priests and three brothers; (naut.) -i della costa, filibusters. **-ame** *m.* the brothers or brothers and sisters in one family; a lot of brothers, a lot of brothers and sisters, a crowd of brothers and sisters; band of brothers, comrades. **-anza** *f.* brotherhood; fraternity, philanthropic association; brotherliness, affection, benevolence; (rel.) brotherhood; brotherly love or greeting (esp. as between religious or guild-members); *pl.* letters of fraternity. **-astro** *m.* half-brother, step-brother. †**-esco** *adj.* brotherly. **-evole** *adj.* brotherly, fraternal. **-evolmente** *adv.* brotherly, fraternally. **-i·a** *f.* confraternity. **-ino** *m. dim.* young brother, little brother. **-one** *m. augm.* big brother; confrere.

frateri·a *f.* See under **frate**.

fraternale *adj.* See **fraterno**.

†**fraternare** *intr.* to live as brothers.

fraternità *f.* fraternity, brotherhood; brotherliness, brotherly affection; (eccl.) fraternity, confraternity, guild.

†**frater·nita** *f.* (eccl.). see **fraternità**.

fraternizzare [A I] *intr.* (*aux.* avere) to fraternize; to behave in a friendly way together.

fratern-o *adj.* fraternal, brotherly; amor —, brotherly love. **-amente** *adv.* fraternally, in a brotherly way.

fratesco *adj.* See under **frate**.

†**fratic-ida** *m.*, **-i·dio** *m.* See under **frate** and **fratricida**.

†**fratre** *m.* brother, friar.

fratri·a, fra·tri-a *f.* (Gk. hist.) phratry. **-arca** *m.* phratriarch.

fratricida *m., f.* fratricide, one who kills his or her brother or sister; *adj.* fratricidal; guerra —, civil war.

fratrici·dio *m.* fratricide, the action of killing one's brother or sister.

fratta[1] *f.* thicket; tangled undergrowth; hedge; essere per le fratte, to be penniless, to be on the rocks.

†**fratta**[2] *f.* fracture, break.

fratta·gli-a *f.* (usu. *pl.*) entrails, internals; offal; tripe, giblets, chitterlings; liver and lights; remnants, residue, rubbish. **-a·io** *m.* seller of tripe.

frattanto *adv.* meanwhile, in the meantime.

frattazzo *m.* (bldg.) plastering trowel.

frattempo *m.* meantime, meanwhile; interval; nel —, in the meantime.

†**fratt-o** *part.* of **frangere**, q.v.; *adj.* broken. †**-oso** *adj.* (of ground) broken, uneven; full of thickets.

frattur-a *f.* (med.; miner.) fracture; break; (miner.) — concoide, conchoidal fracture. **-are** [A I] *tr.* (med.) to fracture. **-ato** *part. adj.* fractured.

fra·u *f. indecl.* poltrona —, fully upholstered armchair (from Frau, the name of the Turin manufacturing and upholstery firm, founded by a Sardinian named Frau).

†**frauda** *f.* and derivs. See **frode**.

fraud-are [A I sa] *tr.* to defraud, to cheat; to deprive. **-ante** *part. adj.* defrauding, cheating. **-ato** *part. adj.* cheated, defrauded, deprived, deceived. **-atore** *m.* impostor, cheat, swindler, deceiver. (**-atrice** *f.*) **-ato·rio** *adj.* (*m.pl.* **-atorii**) fraudulent; relating to fraud.

fra·ud-e *f.* (poet.) fraud, deceit. **-olento** *adj.* fraudulent. **-olentamente** *adv.* fraudulently. **-olenza** *f.* fraudulence.

†**fra·vol-a** *f.* see fragola. **-a·io** *m.* see fragolaio, under fragola.

fravolino *m.* (ichth.). See **fragolino**.

frazion-e *f.* breaking, rupture; (liturg.) Fraction; — di secondo, split second; (math.) fraction; — comune, vulgar fraction; — decimale, decimal fraction; — periodica, recurring decimal; — propria, proper fraction; portion, fragment; part of something separated from the rest; group of houses or village separated from the town in whose municipality it is; village, little town or community. **-amento** *m.* splitting up, breaking up; fragmenting; (chem.) fractionation. **-are** [A 1 c] *tr.* to divide, to break up, to separate; (chem.) to fractionate. **-a·rio** *adj.* fractional, fractionary. **-ato** *part. adj.* divided, broken up; in fragments; (chem.) distillazione -ata, fractional distillation. **-cella** *f. dim.* small fraction, particle.

frazzame *m.* (tanning) offal.

frea·t-ico *adj.* (geol.) water-bearing; falda -ica, ground-water; acque -iche, underground water. **-ologi·a** *f.* study of underground water.

frecc-ia *f.* arrow; scagliare una —, to shoot an arrow; — del Parto, Parthian shot; (agric.) shaft (of plough); (archit.) spire, pinnacle; dart; arrow, indicator, sign; (of a clock) hand; (motor.) traffic indicator, 'flipper', 'trafficator'; — della bussola, compass-needle; (naut.) stempiece support; (boomkin or bumpkin) over the stern of a yawl; gaffsail; wind indicator (pennant or sock); (eng.) ingranaggio a —, herringbone gear; — d'un alberetto, extreme end of top-gallant; †fore and aft beam on the poop of a galley; †pole carrying a firebomb; (fig.) request for a loan, 'touch'; (geom.; bldg. eng.) camber; (of an arch) height, rise; (of a rlwy. line) versine; (of an overhead cable) dip; (aeron.) — positiva, sweepback; a —, swept (of wings). **-ina** *f. dim.* small arrow, poor arrow; weak shot. **-one** *m. augm.* large arrow; man who asks for money, sponger. †**-ioso** *adj.* swift as an arrow.

frecci-are [A 3 c] *tr.* to shoot arrows at; (fig.) -are uno, to ask someone for money; to 'touch' someone. **-ata** *f.* arrow-shot; (fig.) cutting remark; gibe, sharp words; request for money, 'touch'. **-ato** *part. adj.* struck by an arrow, pierced; (fig.) cut to the quick, gibed at; 'touched' for money. (**-atore** *m.* **-atrice** *f.*) **-atura** *f.* arrow-shot; gibe; request for money, 'touch'.

†**fredda** *f.* northerly slope of a mountain.

freddamente *adv.* See under **freddo**.

fredd-are [A 1 c] *tr.* to chill, to cool, to allow to become cold; to lower the temperature of; — il brodo, to cool the soup; to kill; (fig.) to cool, to damp, to check, to curb; — l'entusiasmo, to curb one's enthusiasm; †to rook, to fleece, to drain of money; *intr.* (*aux.* essere), *rfl.* to cool, to become cold; lasciar -arsi la minestra, to allow the soup to become cold; vieni a mangiare: si -a tutto, —spicciati!, come to table, it's all getting cold,—hurry up!; non lasciar — una cosa, to do a thing straight away, to strike while the iron is hot. **-ato** *part. adj.* cooled, chilled; killed.

freddezza *f.* coldness, coolness; (fig.) chilliness; cold-bloodedness; frigidity; indifference; †laziness; †(of style) lack of effectiveness.

fredd-o *adj.* cold; tempo —, cold weather; piatti -i, cold dishes, food to be eaten cold; animale a sangue —, cold-blooded animal; fare una cosa a sangue —, to do a thing in cold blood; (fig.) sangue —, sang-froid, composure, coolness; (fig.) frigid, cool, chilly, apathetic, lacking warmth of feeling, lifeless; una -a accoglienza ,a cool reception; testa -a, cool head; stile —, lifeless style; ci lasciò freddi, it left us cold, it left us indifferent; toni -i, colori -i, cold tones, cold colours (grey, green, pale blue); *n.m.* cold; oggi fa —, it is cold today; fa un — cane, it's devilish cold; ho —, I am cold; i primi -i, the first cold days of the year; sento —, I feel cold; shiver (of horror, or fear); mi vien — a pensarci, it gives me the shivers to think of it, I shudder at the thought; prendere —, to catch cold; morire di —, to freeze to death; Dio manda il — secondo i panni, God tempers the wind to the shorn lamb; non mi fa nè caldo nè —, it makes no difference at all to me, I do not care at all about it; a —, cold, in a cold state, in cold blood; lavorare un metallo a —, to work a metal when it is cold; tirare una schioppettata a —, to shoot cold-bloodedly, to shoot in cold blood; (med.) operare a —, to operate between attacks; *adv.* cose che fanno sudar —, things which cause a cold sweat, frightening things. **-ac·cio** *m.* bitter cold, biting cold.

-amente *adv.* coldly, coolly, frigidly; implacably; cold-bloodedly, in cold blood. **-arello, -erello** *adj. dim.* rather cold, somewhat cold, chilly; *n.m.* coolness, moderate cold, chilliness. **-ic·cio** *adj. dim.* rather cold, slightly cold, chilly. **-ino** *adj. dim.* rather cold, cool, chilly; *n.m.* coolness, chilliness. **-olina** *f.* (bot.) meadow saffron, autumn crocus, *Colchicum autumnale*. **-olino** *adj. dim.* rather cold, cool, chilly; *n.m.* coolness, chilliness; shiver. **-oloso** *adj.* very susceptible to the cold. †**-ore** *m.* cold, coldness. **-oso** *adj.* very susceptible to the cold; sluggish. **-uc·cio, -uzzo** *adj. dim.* rather cold, cool, chilly; *n.m.* coolness, chilliness.

freddur-a *f.* cold, cold weather; laziness, idleness; (fig.) coolness; trifle, triviality; pun, play on words; witticism, 'crack'; 'damp squib', joke which does not come off; †chill, cold in the head. **-a·io** *m.*, **-ista** *m.* punster, wit, witty person; would-be wit.

frega *f.* desire, craving; whim, caprice; (of animals) andare in —, to go on heat.

fregac·ci-o *m.* rough stroke (of a pen or pencil), scrawl, scribble; rough sketch. **-olare** [A 1 s] *intr.* (*aux.* avere) to make a stroke (with pen or pencil); to scrawl, to scribble; to sketch roughly.

fregagione *f.* (med.) friction, massage; †*pl.* affectation; †formalities.

freg-are [A 2 c] *tr.* to rub; to rub up, to polish; to brush; (med.) to massage; to apply friction to; to cheat, to deceive, to dupe; to defeat, to beat, to get the better of; li ha -ati in pieno, he wiped the floor with them; in questi anni alle gare di sci gli austriaci ci hanno -ati tutti, over the last few years the Austrian skiers have beaten all comers; (vulg.) to 'swipe', to 'lift', to 'pinch'; *rfl.* (vulg.) -arsene, not to care about a thing, not to care a rap about it; me ne -o, I don't care a damn; chi se ne -a?, who cares? **-amento** *m.* rub, rubbing. **-ata** *f.* rub, rubbing; (colloq.) trick, deception; ha preso una -ata, he's got the worst of it, he has taken a beating. **-ato** *part. adj.* rubbed; cheated. **-atura** *f.* rubbing; (vulg.) cheat, fraud, deception; disappointment; è una bella -atura, it's a fine kettle of fish. **-azione** *f.* rubbing; massage.

fregarola *f.* (ichth.) minnow, *Phoxinus laevis*.

fregata[1] *f.* See under **fregare**.

fregata[2] *f.* (naut.) frigate; capitano di —, executive officer of Commander's rank; †small boat with a single lateen sail.

fregata[3] *f.* (orn.) frigate bird.

fregi-are [A 3] *tr.* to decorate, to adorn, to embellish. **-amento** *m.* decorating, adorning, embellishing; decoration, adornment, embellishment. **-ata** *f.* (naut.) the whole decorative carving and arrangement of a galley's gunwhale capping. **-ato** *part. adj.* decorated, adorned, embellished; ha il petto -ato di medaglie, he has rows of medals. **-atore** *m.* decorator, embellisher. (**-atrice** *f.*) **-atura** *f.* decoration, adornment, embellishment; (archit.) decoration, frieze, ornamentation; (zool.) slimy trail left by a slug or snail; †hem of a garment.

fre·g-io *m.* decoration, adornment, embellishment; ornament; military or other decoration, badge; (archit.; paint.) decoration, ornament, frieze; vignette, book-illustration; (naut.) ship's carving including figurehead and stern; — del discollato, gunwale decoration.

frego *m.* (*pl.* **freghi**) line, stroke, mark; tirar un —, to draw a line; dar di — a, to cancel, to cross out; scrawl, scribble; disfigurement; fine cut.

fregol-a *f.* (vulg.) desire, craving; heat, excitement; mania, longing, craze; ha la — di scrivere, he has the itch to write; (ichth.) andare in —, to spawn. **-o** *m.* (ichth.) fish eggs, spawn; †(iron.) residence of the beloved one; †minute particle.

freisa *f.* type of red Piedmontese table wine, semi-sparkling.

fremebondo *adj.* raging, frenzied, raving, quivering, trembling; passionate.

fre·m-ere [B 1] *intr.* (*aux.* avere) to quiver, to tremble; to shake, to be violently agitated; to thrill, to shudder; to rage, to rave, to fume with anger; — di sdegno, to quiver with indignation; — di paura, to shake with fear; — di orgoglio, to thrill with pride; (of horses) to fret; (of arms) to clash; *tr.* (poet.) to demand, to clamour for; *n.m.* il — delle bestie, the howling of wild beasts; il — del mare, the raging of the sea, the roaring of the sea; il — della selva, the shaking, thrashing, roar of the wind in the forest. **-ente** *part. adj.* raging, howling, roaring; quivering, trembling; impatient.

†**fremire** *vb.* and derivs. see **fremere**; *intr.* to resound, to reverberate; to sound; to whinny; to carol.

fre·m·ito *m.* roar; howl; il — della tigre, the roar of the tiger; murmur; corse un — nella sala, a murmur ran through the room; quiver, thrill, tremor; un — di gioia, a thrill of joy. †**-itare** *intr.* to tremble; to whinny, to neigh.

frena·io *m.* bit-maker, bridle-maker.

frenalgi·a *f.* (med.) diaphragmatic pain; a stitch in one's side.

fren-are [A I C] *tr.* to curb, to bridle, to check; — un cavallo, to curb a horse; to apply the brakes to; (fig.) to restrain, to moderate, to repress; — la lingua, to restrain one's tongue; — le passioni, to check the passions; — abusi, to check abuses; *intr.* (*aux.* avere) to apply the brakes, to brake, to slow down; *rfl.* to restrain oneself, to refrain; non riuscì a -arsi dal ridere, he could not refrain from laughing. **-a·bile** *adj.* restrainable. **-ata** *f.* application of the brake(s). **-ato** *part. adj.* curbed; checked, restrained; un camion -ato, a lorry with the brakes on; (aeron.) pallone -ato, barrage balloon, captive balloon. **-atore** *m.* restrainer; tamer; (rlwy.) brakesman. **-atura** *f.* (eng.) braking.

frenast-eni·a *f.* (med.) mental weakness. **-e·nico** *adj.* (med.) mentally weak.

†**fren·dere** *intr.* to tremble with rage; to roar.

†**frenella** *f.* bit (of a horse's harness); kind of soft woollen cloth; garment made from it.

frenellare [A I] (naut.). See **affrenellare**.

frenello *m.* (naut.) rudder line, tiller rope, steering rod or chain; lanyard; — d'uno scalmo, poppet lanyard; (anat.) frenulum; †muzzle; †ornament, adornment.

fren-esi·a *f.* (med.) brain fever; fury, madness; frenzy; mania, craze, rage; ha la — di viaggiare, he has a mania for travelling. **-etica-mento** *m.* frenzy, delirium; frenzied action. **-e·ticare** [A 2 S] *intr.* (*aux.* avere) to rave, to be delirious. **-e·tico** *adj.* frenzied, raving, delirious, frantic; pazzo -etico, raving mad; applausi -etici, enthusiastic applause, loud cheers, frenzied acclamation; *n.m.* frenzied person, delirious person; delirium; madman. **-eticamente** *adv.* frenziedly, deliriously, frantically. †**-etichezza** *f.* see **frenesia**. **-iatra** *m.* (med.) psychiatrist. **-iatri·a** *f.* (med.) psychiatry.

fren-o *m.* bit; bridle; (fig.) check, restraint, control; mettere un — alle spese, to curb expenditure; tenere a — la lingua, to hold one's tongue in check; mettere in — un popolo ribelle, to put a check on a rebellious people; mordere il —, rodere il —, to champ at the bit, to resent control; scuotere il —, to shake off control; to regain one's liberty; a — sciolto, freely, without restraint; brake; applicare il —, to apply the brake; — a nastro, band-brake; — sui cerchioni, rim-brake; — sulle quattro ruote, four-wheel brake; — sul mozzo, hub-brake; — a mano, hand-brake; — a pedale, foot-brake; — a depressione, vacuum-brake; — idraulico, hydraulic-brake; — ad aria, air-brake; — di sicurezza, emergency brake; — a tamburo, drum-brake; bloccare i -i, to jam the brakes; prova al —, brake test; prova dei -i, braking test; potenza al —, b.h.p.; (anat.) frenulum; (naut.) rudder line, tiller rope; — della gru, purchase of the crane; -i dei bastoni, studding sail boom lines; (artill.) — di ricupero, shock absorber.

fren-oco·mio *m.* lunatic asylum. **-ologi·a** *f.* phrenology. †**-ologista** *m.* see **frenologo**. **-o·logo** *m.* phrenologist.

fre·nulo *m.* (anat.) frenulum.

frequent-are [A I C] *tr.* to frequent, to visit often; to associate with; non -o la signora Bruni, I am not on calling terms with Mrs Brown; — i caffè, to frequent cafés; to attend; to visit regularly; — la scuola, to attend school; — i corsi, to attend lectures; -a la gente dotta, he associates with learned people; (rel.) — i sacramenti, to frequent the sacraments; (naut.) — un porto, to call at a port; †— una miniera, to work a mine; †to use frequently; †— una medicina, to take a medicine regularly; — con l'acqua, to water frequently; †— l'acqua alle piante, to water plants frequently; †to urge, to solicit; *intr.* (*aux.* avere) — in tutte le case nobili, to frequent all the houses of the aristocracy; †to be persistent; †*rfl.* to be assiduous. **-a·bile** *adj.* frequentable. **-ativo** *adj.* (gramm.) frequentative. **-ativamente** *adv.* (gramm.) frequentatively, in a frequentative form, with a frequentative meaning. **-ato** *part. adj.* frequented; populated, crowded; caffè -atissimo, very popular, much frequented café. **-atore** *m.* frequenter, frequent visitor, associate. (**-atrice** *f.*) **-azione** *f.* frequentation, frequent visiting, association; familiarity.

frequ-ente *adj.* frequent; numerous; di —, frequently; (med.) polso —, rapid pulse. **-enza** *f.* frequency; frequence; frequent visiting; la -enza dei suoi viaggi, the frequency of his travels; la -enza

della gente in una piazza, the crowd of people, the concourse of people in a square; (techn.) frequency; repetition rate; (radio) altissima -enza, V.H.F.; modulazione di -enza, F.M.; -enza portante, carrier frequency; *pl.* attendance; libretto delle -enze, attendance register.

frequenzio·metro *m.* (electr.) frequency-meter, (radio; acoust.) wavemeter.

†**frere** *m.* brother.

fre·sa *f.* (eng.) milling-cutter, mill, miller; — a bicchiere, hollow mill; milling machine.

fres-are [A I C] *tr.* (eng.) to mill; †to fringe, to ornament. **-ato** *part. adj.* milled. **-atrice** *f.* milling-machine; -atrice semplice, plano-miller; -atrice verticale, vertical spindle milling-machine; -atrice universale, universal milling-machine. **-atura** *f.* (eng.) milling; -atura a creatore, hobbing.

fresc-amente *adv.*, **-ata** *f.* See under **fresco**.

†**fresc-are** *tr.* to refresh; to restore; to comfort. †**-ante** *part. adj.* refreshing; restorative; comforting.

frescheggiare [A 3 C] *intr.* (*aux.* avere) to enjoy the coolness, to enjoy the open air (after a hot day).

freschetto *adj. dim.* of **fresco**, q.v.; rather cool, chilly; (naut.) vento —, light to fresh wind (Beaufort scale, Force 3 and 4).

freschezza *f.* coolness; freshness; la — della sera, the cool of evening; freshness, bloom, purity; — della carnagione, freshness of complexion; — dello stile, purity of style; (paint.) freshness, brightness (of colours).

freschino *adj. dim.* of **fresco**, q.v.; coolish, rather fresh; fa —, there's a nip in the air; (naut.) vento —, light breeze (Beaufort scale, Force 2 and 3).

freschis·simo *adj. superl.* of **fresco**, q.v.; (naut.) vento —, strong wind (Beaufort scale, Force 6).

fresc-o *adj.* (*pl.* freschi) cool, moderately cold; acqua -a, cold water; tempo —, cool weather; fresh, new; uova fresche, new-laid eggs; pane —, new bread; latte —, fresh milk; (naut.) vento —, fresh wind (steady) (Beaufort scale, Force 6); vento buon —, gale force wind (Force 7); vento gran —, full gale (Force 8 and 9); — di malattia, recently ill; fresh, vigorous, blooming, youthful; — come una rosa, as fresh as a daisy; erba -a, fresh grass, new green grass; un uomo ancora —, a man who is still vigorous; fiori freschi, fresh flowers; età -a, youth; fresh, untired; rested, refreshed; truppe fresche, rested troops, (or) new troops; verniciato di —, wet paint; mente -a, fresh mind, untired mind; uno stile —, a fresh style, an untainted style; (colloq.) star —, to be in a mess, to be in trouble; stai —!, you're for it!, you'll catch it!; damp, wet; pittura -a, wet paint; *adv. phr.* di —, recently, newly; *n.m.* coolness, cool, freshness; open air; prendere, godere il — della sera, to enjoy the cool of evening; fa —, it is cool; per il —, when it is cool, in the early morning, in the late evening; (colloq.) in prison, 'in the cooler'; tenere al —, to keep in jail; tenere una cosa in —, to keep a thing cool; prendere del —, to catch cold; (art) fresco, dipingere a —, to paint frescoes, to do fresco painting; †(naut.) parade of gondolas. **-amente** *adv.* freshly; recently; newly; vigorously. **-ata** *f.* chill; prendere una -ata, to catch a chill; (Tusc.) practical joke, idiotic prank. **-oc·cio** *adj.* vigorous, healthy looking; (naut.) see **freschetto**. **-olino** *adj. dim.* rather cool, pleasantly cool; *n.m.* slight coolness, pleasant coolness. **-one** *adj. augm.* (naut.) vento -one, fresh to strong wind (Beaufort scale, Force 5); *n.m.* (colloq.) silly old thing. †**-ore** *m.* see **freschezza**. †**-oso** *adj.* see **fresco**. **-otto** *adj. dim.* rather fresh, rather cool; *n.m.* slight coolness. **-ume** *m.* fresh fodder. **-ura** *f.* shady coolness, cool; cool air; cold.

fre·sia *f.* (bot.) freesia.

†**freto** *m.* strait; sea, ocean.

fretta *f.* haste, hurry; avere —, to be in a hurry; mangiare in — to eat hurriedly; in — e furia, in a great hurry; colla massima —, with all possible speed.

†**frettac·cia** *f.* (naut.). See **frettazza**.

frett-are [A I C] *tr.* (naut.) to scrub (decks). **-amento** *m.* scrubbing of decks. **-ato** *part. adj.* scrubbed; ponte -ato, scrubbed deck. **-atura** *f.* work of scrubbing hull or decks, etc. †**-eri·a** *f.* (naut.) holystoning of decks, etc.

frettazz-a *f.*, **-o** *m.* (naut.) scrubber, deck scrubber.

frettolos·o *adj.* hasty, hurried; non esser troppo —, don't be too hasty; passi -i, hurried steps. **-amente** *adv.* hastily, hurriedly.

†**frettoso** *adj.* See **frettoloso**.

freud·iano adj. (pron. **froidiano**) Freudian, relating to Freud. **-ismo** m. (psychol.) Freudianism.

†**freve** f. See **febbre**.

†**frezione** f. See **frizione**.

†**frezza** f. See **freccia**.

†**frezzoloso**, †**frezzoso** adj. See **frettoloso**.

fri·are [A 6] tr., intr. (aux. essere) to crumble. **-a·bile** adj. friable, crumbly. **-abilità** f. friability.

Friburgo pr.n.f. (geog.) Freiburg; Fribourg.

fricandò m. indecl. (cul.) fricandeau.

fricasse·a f. (cul.) fricassee; (fig.) jumble, medley.

fricativo adj., n.m. (phon.) fricative.

fric·cioli m.pl. (cul.) fine strips of pork from which the fat has been removed.

fric-ogna f., **-o·gnolo** m. kind of grape possessing a sharp flavour.

†**friere** m. brother; friar.

friga·nea f. (ent.) caddis fly, *Phryganea* spp.

frig·g-ere [C 12] tr. to fry; — la carne, to fry meat; padella per —, frying-pan; mandare qualcuno a farsi —, to send someone to the devil; va a farti —!, go to the devil!; †to torment, to plague; intr. (aux. avere) to fry, to hiss, to sputter (of hot fat); l'olio -e in padella, the oil is sputtering in the pan; (fig.) to seethe, to foam; to boil; — di rabbia, to seethe with rage; †to hiss; †to squeak, to screech; †to whine, to whimper; †to cry out in labour pains; †to be a failure, to be a flop. **-i·bile** adj. able to be fried, good for frying. **-imento** m. frying; torment, tribulation. **-io** m. continual frying; hissing; continued sputtering; (radio; acoust.) frying. **-itore** m. frier, vendor of fried food. (**-itora**, **-itrice** f.) **-itori·a** f. shop where fried food is sold.

friggi-buco m. indecl. whimpering, wailing. **-culo** m. (zool.) a kind of snail.

friggio m. See under **friggere**.

Fri·gi-a pr.n.f. (hist.) Phrygia; (geog.) Friesland. †**-ano** adj., n.m. see **frigio**. **-o** adj., n.m. Phrygian; berretto **-o**, Phrygian cap; (mus.) modo **-o**, Phrygian mode.

frigid-a·rio m. (archit. hist.) frigidarium; refrigerator. **-ezza** f., **-ità** f. frigidity, frigidness, coldness; (med.) frigidity.

fri·gid-o adj. frigid, cold; (fig.) apathetic, dull; †impotent.

fri·gio adj., n.m. See under **frigia**.

†**frigione** m. (vet.). See **frisione**, under **frisia**.

frigna f. crack, crevice; trifle, bagatelle; †female genitals.

frign-are [A 5] intr. (aux. avere) to whimper, to wail, to whine. **-io** m. (pl. **-ii**) continual wailing; constant whining. **-olare** [A 1 s] intr. (aux. avere) to wail frequently, to keep whining. **-olio** m. (pl. **-olii**) continual wailing; constant whining; whimpering. **-one** m. whiner, wailer, whimpering child.

fri·gnolo m. See **fignolo**.

frigo[1] m. (colloq.) abbrev. of **frigorifero**, q.v.; 'fridge'.

†**frigo**[2] m. See **freddo**.

frigori·a f. (phys.) frigorie, negative calorie.

frigorideserto m. (geog.) cold desert.

frigor-i·fero adj. frigorific; miscela **-ifera**, freezing mixture; n.m. refrigerator; cold storage; **-ifero elettro-domestico**, electric home refrigerator. **-i·fico** adj. frigorific.

Frima·io pr.n.m. (hist.) the third month of the French Republican calendar.

Frine pr.n.f. Phryne; courtesan.

†**frinf-ello**, †**-ino**, †**-rì**, †**-rino**, m. coxcomb, vain young man, dandy.

fringuello m. (orn.) chaffinch, *Fringilla coelebs*; — alpino, snow finch, *Montifringilla nivalis*.

frinire [D 2] intr. (aux. avere) to chirp (of cicadas); n.m. stridulation, chirping (of cicadas)

frino m. (zool.) *Phrynus* spp., poisonous arachnids related to the scorpions.

frinzello m. botch, clumsy piece of sewing or darning; ugly scar, gash, sear.

fris-are [A 1] tr. (billiards, etc.) to graze; to touch, to skim; to curl, to frizz; intr. (aux. avere) to make a grazing stroke (at billiards, etc.). **-ata** f. graze; skimming; (naut.) see **frigiata** under **frigiare**. **-ato** part. adj. grazed; barely touched, skimmed.

frisato[1] part. of **frisare**, q.v.

†**frisato**[2] m. striped cloth.

friscello m. flour-dust raised during milling.

†**frisetto** m. fine silk.

Fri·și-a pr.n.f. (geog.) Friesland; (mil.) cavallo di —, chevaux de frise, barbed-wire entanglement. **-one** m. (vet.) Frisian, type of horse with tufts of hair on its feet; (orn.) see **frosone**.

friso[1] m. (billiards, etc.) grazing stroke; (naut.) garboard strake; see **fregio**.

†**friso**[2] adj. greedy.

frisone adj.; n.m. (geog.) Frisian, Frieslander; Isole Frisoni, Frisian Islands.

fritilla·ria f. (bot.) fritillary, *Fritillaria*.

fritta f. (ceram.; glassm.) frit.

frittata f. omelette; fare una —, to make an omelette,; fried dish; una — di pesce, a dish of fried fish; (fig.) blunder; affaticarsi a rivoltar la —, to try to patch up a blunder one has made.

frittell-a f. pancake; fritter; grease-stain; rash individual, precipitate person. **-oso** adj. covered in grease-stains.

fritt-o part. of **friggere**, q.v.; adj. fried; carne **-a**, fried meat; (fig.; colloq.) sono —!, I'm done for!, I am ruined!, I've 'had it!'; cose **-e** e rifritte, things which have been said over and over again; n.m. (cul.) fried food, fry; — misto alla romana, small cutlets, liver, brains, sweetbread, cauliflower, artichokes, etc., all fried; — misto di pesce, a dish of various small fried fish. **-ume** m. unsavoury fried food. **-ura** f. frying; food, food for frying, fry; (fig.) small children, fry; †**-ura bianca**, fried sweetbread, brains, etc.

Friul-i pr.n.f. (geog.) Friuli. **-ano** adj. of Friuli; pr.n.m. native of Friuli.

fri·vol-o adj. frivolous, trifling, empty, inane, futile; ragione **-a**, trifling reason; donna **-a**, frivolous woman, shallow woman. **-amente** adv. frivolously. **-eggiare** [A 3 c] intr. (aux. avere) to behave frivolously, to speak frivolously. **-ezza** f. frivolity, trifle; frivolousness.

frizion-are [A 1 c] tr. to massage, to apply a friction to; — di, to rub into; (rubber indust.) to friction; intr. (aux. avere) (motor. slang) to work the clutch. (**-ato** part. adj.) **-atura** f. (rubber indust.) frictioning; **-atura ad un passaggio**, single-pass frictioning.

frizione f. friction; rubbing; (hairdress.) dry shampoo; (motor.) clutch; premere la — prima d'ingranare la marcia, to press down the clutch before engaging gear; disco della —, clutch plate; (watchm.) tacca di —, clam notch; †desire, craving, itch.

frizz-are [A 1] tr. to prick, to sting; intr. (aux. avere) to smart, to sting; l'aceto fa — la ferita, vinegar makes the wound smart; gli occhi mi **-ano**, my eyes smart; to sparkle, to fizz (of gassy liquids); †to have grit, to have 'guts', to be a person of spirit; †to understand, to be competent; †to be witty, to have point, to be ingenious. **-amento** m. stinging, smarting. **-ante** part. adj. stinging, smarting; pungent; aria **-ante**, bracing air; parole **-anti**, stinging words; sparkling, fizzy; vino **-ante**, semi-sparkling wine (*pétillant*); n.m. sharp flavour. **-io** m. (pl. **-ii**) continual pricking; repeated smarting. **-o** m. prick, smart, sting; witticism, pun, joke; gibe. **-one** m. minor ailment. **-ore** m. sting, smart.

†**froda** f. See **frode**.

frod-are [A 1] tr. to defraud, to cheat; to swindle; to extort, to deceive; to steal; **-ò** un amico di cento lire, he cheated a friend of a hundred lire; — la dogana, to cheat the Customs, to defraud the Customs; †to disguise; †to adulterate; †intr. to dissemble. **-a·bile** adj. easy to swindle; likely to be defrauded, to fraud. **-amento** m. deception; fraud; cheating; thieving. **-ato** part. adj. cheated, defrauded, swindled. **-atore** m. defrauder, cheat; swindler; thief. (**-atora**, **-atrice** f.)

frod-e f. fraud; deception; extortion; swindling, swindle; (leg.) fraud; contratto in — alla legge, contract in fraud of the law (C.C.); repressione delle **-i** in commercio, suppression of fraud in trade (C.C.P.); †far —, to deceive, to dissemble; †la bella —, strategy.

frod-o m. smuggling, customs-evasion, contraband; merce di —, contraband goods; pescatore di —, cacciatore di —, poacher. †**-oso** adj. fraudulent. †**-ente**, **-olento** adj. and deriv. see **fraudolente**. **-olenza** f. see **fraudolenza**.

†**fro·dulo** m. sheath, scabbard.

froebeliano adj. (pedagog.) relating to Froebel; il metodo —, the Froebel method.

froge f.pl. (sing. **frogia**) (vet.) nostrils (esp. of horses and cattle).

froll-are [A 1] tr. to make tender, to soften, to hang (meat) until it is high; intr. (aux. essere) to become tender; (of meat) to become high; rfl. to be tormented, to be consumed. **-amento** m. making

froll-are (*cont.*)
tender, process of becoming tender; tenderizing. **-ato** *part. adj.* tender, high; made tender, tenderized. **-atura** *f.* making tender, process of becoming tender; exhaustion.

frollo *adj.* tender; high; (fig.) soft, effeminate, flabby, weak; worn out, exhausted, dead beat; gioventù **-a**, tender youth, weak youth; (cul.) pasta **-a**, a very soft, sweet pastry; uomo di pasta **-a**, soft man, weak, effeminate man; è una pasta **-a**, he has no backbone, he is quite spineless; *n.m.* bank, dyke.

†**fromba** *f.* and derivs. See **frombola**.

frombol-a *f.* sling, catapult; †river stone. **-are** [A I sc] *tr.* to hurl with a sling, to fling, to catapult. **-atore** *m.*, **-iere** *m.* slinger, slingman.

†**fromentiera** *f.* frumenty, furmenty.

frond-a[1] *f.* frond, branch; leaf; foliage; *pl.* (fig.) excessive ornamentation (in writing). **-eggiante** *part. adj.* leafy, covered with leaves, verdant. **-eggiare** [A 3 c] *intr.* (*aux.* avere) to produce leaves, to be covered in leaves, to leaf. **-escenza** *f.* bursting into leaf, leafing. **-i·fero** *adj.* bearing leaves, leafy.

frond-a[2] *f.* (hist.) Fronde; (fig.) minor rebellion, opposition; (fig.) spira vento di —, there is rebellion in the air. **-ista** *m.* (hist.) member of the Fronde; (fig.) rebel; opponent; critic, objector.

frond-ire [D 2] *intr.* (*aux.* avere) to produce leaves, to leaf, to make leaves. **-ito** *part. adj.* leafy.

frond-oso *adj.* leafy, covered in leaves; (fig.) ornate. **-osità** *f.* leafiness; luxuriance; ornamentation. †**-ura** *f.* foliage. **-uto** *adj.* leafy.

frontal-e *adj.* frontal; (aeron.) resistenza —, profile drag; (mil.) frontal; attacco —, frontal attack; *n.m.* frontal, ornament worn over the forehead; (mil. hist.) frontlet, frontal; visor of a helmet; leather headpiece of a modern steel helmet; head armour of a horse; head band of a bridle; (archit.) — della casa, ornament on a house front; — del caminetto, ornamental mantelpiece. **-mente** *adv.* frontally; in the front, facing.

front-are [A I c] *tr.* (naut.) to ream (a cask or mast ring). **-atore** *m.* (naut.) reamer, reaming tool.

front-e *f.* forehead, brow; — larga, broad forehead; — corrugata, wrinkled brow; a — alta, with one's head held high, with a clear conscience, unashamedly; col sudore della —, by the sweat of one's brow; face, head; — a —, face to face; gli si legge in — la bugia, you can see from the look on his face that he is lying; abbassare la —, to hang one's head, to look down; (archit.) front, façade; *m.*, *f.* (fig.) front; il — economico, the economic front; il — popolare, the popular front; far — a, to cope with; far — a un pericolo, to face a danger; far — alla spesa, to meet expenses; (geog.) — polare, polar front; (mil.) front, forward lines of a unit; extended line; head of a number of columns; tener —, to hold a line; far —, to deploy; — di battaglia, prima —, front line; assalire di —, combattere di —, to make a frontal assault; sgombrare la —, to clear the front; (mil. commands) — indietro!, reverse front!; — a destr! (front-a-destr!), right front!; — a sinistra! (front-a-sinistr!), left front!; †face of a rampart or bastion; a —, facing, opposite, in comparison; testo greco con la traduzione a —, Greek text with translation opposite; non poter stare a — di, not to bear comparison with; nessuno gli si può mettere a —, there is no one to rival him; di —, opposite, in front; vento di —, head wind; quella casa di —, that house opposite; di — al caffè, opposite the café, facing the café; mettere qualcuno di — ai suoi accusatori, to confront someone with his accusers; (prosod.) first part of a Petrarchan canzone. **-ege·nesi** *f. indecl.* (aerodyn.) frontogenesis. **-eggiare** [A 3 c] *tr.* (mil.) to face; to resist, to oppose; to hold one's own against; (fig.) to face, to meet, to confront; **-eggiare** le spese, to meet expenses; **-eggiare** i nemici, to confront one's enemies; to be opposite, to face; la casa **-eggiava** il cimitero, the house was opposite the cemetery. **-eggiato** *part. adj.* opposed; faced; met, confronted; defended. **-icina** *f. dim.* child's forehead, little brow. **-o·lisi** *f. indecl.* (aerodyn.) frontolysis. **-ona** *f. augm.* large forehead, unusually large forehead, protruding brow.

frontespi·zi-o *m.* title-page (not 'frontispiece'); (archit.) frontispiece, cornice; (colloq.) face. **-a·io** *m.* ignorant bibliophile.

†**frontichinato** *adj.* with bowed head.

frontiera *f.* frontier, border; la — svizzera, the Swiss border; varcare la —, to cross the frontier; (mil.) piazza di —, frontier forts, fortifications; †forehead, brow; †ornament worn on the brow.

†**frontiero** *adj.* bold, audacious, brazen.

†**frontigiano** *adj.* living opposite; *n.m.* opposite partner.

frontino *m.* false hair covering the forehead, false front; fringe; part of horse's head-harness.

frontismo *m.* (pol.) coalition of left-wing parties (see also **frontista**).

frontispi·zio *m.* See **frontespizio**.

frontista *m.* owner of a house having a frontage on a street or river; riparian; (pol.) member of a political party which has the word 'fronte' as part of its name (e.g. il Fronte Popolare, a member of which is a 'frontista').

frontone *m.* (archit.) pediment, fronton.

†**fronza** *f.* first green leaves on corn.

†**fronzire** *vb.* and derivs. See **frondire**.

†**fronzo** *m.* See **fronzolo**.

fronzol-o *m.* ribbon; superfluous adornment; *pl.* finery; una donna tutta **-i**, a woman over-ornately dressed, a woman covered in trinkets and falals; (fig.) frill, embellishment; scrivere senza **-i**, to write without frills, to write plainly.

fronzuto *adj.* leafy, in leaf; very leafy, with thick foliage.

frosone *m.* (orn.) hawfinch, *Coccothraustes coccothraustes*.

frotta *f.* gathering, company, collection; band; una — di contadini, a gathering of peasants, a collection of peasants; una — di soldati, a band of soldiers; crowd, multitude, mass, flock; una — di uccelli, a flock of birds, a large number of birds; a frotte, in flocks, in crowds; †(mus.) see **frottola**.

frottatore *m.* (electr.) contact shoe.

frot·tol-a *f.* kind of popular song; invention, fib, falsehood, lie; tall story; son **-e!**, it's a pack of lies!, it's all humbug!; (mus.) song for four voices (early sixteenth century). †**-are** *intr.* to lie, to fib, to tell falsehoods, to tell cock and bull stories. **-one** *m.* liar, fibber.

†**frucare** *vb.* and derivs. See **frugare**.

frucian·dolo *m.* (Tusc.) long rod with a duster or rag on the tip used for cleaning out ovens, etc.

fru·colo *m.* (ent.) mole cricket, *Gryllotalpa gryllotalpa* (also applied to certain other insects).

fruente *part.* of **fruire**, q.v.

frufru, fru fru *m. indecl.* rustling (of a dress); shuffling (of feet); (fig.) confusion, turmoil; rush; impetuous person.

frugacchi-are [A 4] *tr.* to rummage, to search about after, to search closely. **-amento** *m.* rummaging, searching. **-ato** *part. adj.* searched. **-atore** *m.* searcher, rummager. (**-atrice** *f.*)

frugal-e *adj.* frugal, careful, sparing, economical, parsimonious; moderate, restrained; pasto —, frugal repast. **-mente** *adv.* frugally, carefully, economically. **-ità** *f.* frugality, economy, moderation.

frug-are [A 2] *intr.* (*aux.* avere) to search, to rummage; — in una valigia, to search in a suitcase, to search a suitcase; *tr.* — una persona, to search a person; — una casa, to ransack a house; to incite; to nudge; to poke. **-amento** *m.* searching, rummaging. **-ata** *f.* searching, rummaging; search, rummage. **-ato** *part. adj.* searched; ransacked; †-ato dalla coscienza, remorseful; †found, discovered. **-atoio** *m.* rod used by fishermen for frightening the fish into the net; poker, furnace rake. **-atore** *m.* searcher, rummager. (**-atrice** *f.*)

frug-i·fero *adj.* fruit-bearing, fructiferous; fertile. **-i·voro** *adj.* frugivorous.

frugnol-are [A I] *intr.* (*aux.* avere) to go night-fishing with a lantern. **-atore** *m.* night-fisherman.

fru·gnuolo *m.* lantern used in night-fishing.

frugo *m.* (comm.) uso e —, wear and tear.

frugol-are [A I s] *tr.*, *abs.* to search, to rummage; to ransack; to grub, to root, to rootle (of pigs); to urge. **-ato** *part. adj.* searched, rummaged; ransacked.

fru·gol-o *m.* lively, inquisitive boy; restless, fidgety child; smart, enterprising man; (colloq.) 'bright spark'; kind of firework, cracker. (**-a** *f.*)

frugone[1] *m.* stick used in searching and prodding; push, prod; inquisitive and importunate person (cf. **frugare**).

frugone[2] *m.* See **furgone**.

†**frugone**[3] *adv.* in a searching and urgent way.

†**frui** *m.* enjoyment.

fru-ire [D 2] *tr.* to enjoy, to have the use of, to have the advantage of, to avail oneself of; — una pensione, to have a pension, to draw a pension; *intr.* (*aux.* avere, *prep.* di) to enjoy, to get pleasure (from); — di un diritto, to enjoy a right, to have a right. **-ente** *part. adj.* enjoying, having the use of, using. **-ibile** *adj.* enjoyable, usable, available. **-itivo** *adj.* fruitive. **-izione** *f.* fruition, use, enjoyment.

frull-are [A I] *tr.* to beat, to whisk; to mill; — uova, to beat up eggs; *intr.* (*aux.* avere) to spin round, to turn round; (fig.) to whirl; chi sa che gli -a per il capo?, who knows what is whirling through his head?, who knows what he is thinking about?; to flutter, to whirr; to buzz; to hum; mi -ò una starna, a partridge whirred up in front of me; (fig.) far — una faccenda, to set an affair in motion, to start things humming. **-ato** *part. adj.* beaten up, whisked, whipped; *n.m.* milk-shake. **-atore** *m.* shredder (in electric mixer); whisk, whisking machine. **-ino** *m.* whisk, beater; trifle, triviality; (orn.) Jack snipe, *Lymnocryptes minimus*; †spinning machine. **-io** *m.* (*pl.* **-ii**) continual whisking; constant whirring, fluttering.

frull-o *m.* spinning; whirring; buzzing; tirare a —, to shoot (a bird) as it rises; whisk; a baby's rattle; snap of the fingers; trifle, bagatelle; non importa un —, it doesn't matter a snap of the fingers; (text.) twirling stick. **-one** *m.* (techn.) bolter, sifting machine; (lit. hist.) device of the Cruscan Academy; child's toy, rattle; open carriage.

frument-aceo *adj.* frumentaceous. **-are** [A I] *intr.* (*aux.* avere) (mil.) to forage.

frument-ario *adj.* grain-producing. **-azione** *f.* grain harvest. **-iere** *m.* (mil.) forager; †supply personnel, baggage train. **-ifero** *adj.* grain-producing. **-ifico** *adj.* grain-making, grain-producing.

frument-o *m.* (bot.) wheat, *Triticum*. **-one** *m.* (bot.) maize, *Zea mays*.

†frumm-ia *f.* sense of self-importance, fussiness; excitement; to-do. **†-iare** *intr.* to have much to do, to fuss. **†-ioso** *adj.* intriguing, interfering.

frusc-iare [A 3] *intr.* (*aux.* avere) to rustle. **-io** *m.* (*pl.* **-ii**) rustling (of clothes, leaves); murmuring, babbling (of water flowing); (radio; gramoph.) ground noise, needle noise.

frus-co *m.* (*pl.* **-chi**) (Calabria, Lucania) elf, sprite.

fru-scolo[1] *m.* dead twig.

fru-scolo[2] *m.* See frusco.

fruson-e *m.* (orn.) see frosone; (fig.) ladies' man, admirer of women. **-accio** *m.* tiresome, importunate individual, hanger-on, nuisance.

frusso[1] *m.* game of cards resembling **primiera**, q.v.

frusso[2] *m.* (cards) flush.

†frusso[3] *m.* noise.

frust-a *f.* whip; lash; whisk; (fig.) severe criticism; adoperare la —, to be a severe critic, to use the lash; (rel.) penitential scourge; (Tusc.) long thin loaf of bread; †see **frusto**[2]. **-aio** *m.* maker or seller of whips. **-ino** *m. dim.* cord attached to the end of a whip; stick (as used in riding); (mil.) officer's cane, swagger cane, whip; gallant, dandy, beau. **-one** *m. augm.* large whip, long whip. (See also **frusto**[2].)

frustagno *m.* See fustagno.

frusta-mattoni *m. indecl.* person who goes about shops without buying, window-shopper. **-penne** *m. indecl.* worthless writer, scribbler. **-pennelli** *m. indecl.* worthless artist, dauber.

frust-are [A I] *tr.* to whip, to lash; to scourge; to criticize severely, to castigate; to wear out; to frequent, to visit frequently; to daub; (mil.) to sweep; — con la mitraglia, to sweep with machine-gun fire. **-ata** *f.* lash, blow with a whip; cutting remark. **-ato** *part. adj.* whipped, lashed; castigated, criticized. **-atore** *m.* lasher, scourger; castigator. (**-atrice** *f.*) **-atura** *f.* whipping, lashing; castigation.

frustino *m. dim.* of frusta, q.v.

frusto[1] *adj.* worn out, exhausted; shabby, worn, outworn; †*n.m.* (naut.) wear and tear of a ship's hull and fittings.

frusto[2] *m.* piece, bit; morsel, scrap; †stick, cudgel; †club.

†frustr-a *adv.* in vain. **-aneità** *f.* uselessness, inefficacy. **-aneo** *adj.* useless, vain, ineffective.

frustr-are [A I] *tr.* to frustrate; to thwart; to make useless, to nullify. **-ato** *part. adj.* frustrated; thwarted; nullified. **-atorio** *adj.* frustrative; vain, inefficacious.

fru-tic-e *m.* shrub, bush. **-eto** *m.* undergrowth, shrubbery. **-oso** *adj.* shrub-like, shrubby.

frutt-a *f.* (*pl.* **-a**, **-e**) fruit (collectively); — matura, ripe fruit; coltello da —, fruit-knife; dessert-knife; posate da —, fruit knives and forks; *pl.* fruit; -e dolci, dessert; (colloq.) blows (cf. **frutto**). **†-aggio** *m.* fruit in general; (art) fruit ornamentation, fruit motif. **†-aglia** *f.* fruit of all kinds. **-aio** *m.* fruit-cellar, fruit-store; *adj.* fruit-bearing. **-ai(u)olo** *m.* fruiterer; fruit-vendor. **-ame** *m.* fruit, fruit of various kinds. **†-ario** *m.* see **frutteto**. **-eto** *m.* orchard. **-iera** *f.* fruit-dish.

frutt-are [A I] *intr.* (*aux.* avere) to bear fruit, to fruit; to yield, to bear; quest'albero -a bene, this tree bears well; to pay; è un commercio che -a, it's a going concern, it's a paying business; *tr.* to produce, to yield, to bring; quell'impresa gli -a il dieci per cento, that business yields him ten per cent; gli ha -ato soltanto dispiaceri, it has brought him only disappointment; †to bear young, to bring forth; †to cultivate; †to cause, to produce. **-ante** *part. adj.* yielding, bearing, producing. **-ata** *f.* open fruit tart. **†-ato** *adj.* (of land) fruit-bearing, fruit-growing; *n.m.* yield of fruit; (finan.) profit. **-evole** *adj.* fruitful, fruit-bearing; useful, profitable; fertile.

frutteto *m.* See under frutta.

frutticult-ore *m.* fruit-grower. **-ura** *f.* fruit-culture, fruit-growing.

Fruttidoro *pr.n.m.* (hist.) Fructidor, twelfth month of the calendar of the French Revolution.

fruttiera *f.* See under frutta.

frutti-fer-o *adj.* fruit-bearing, fruit-producing; (fig.) useful, profitable, fruitful; lavoro —, profitable work, work that pays well; (finan.) interest-bearing; (herald.) fructed.

fruttific-are [A 2 s] *intr.* (*aux.* avere) to bear fruit, to fructify, to fruit. **-ante** *part. adj.* fruit-bearing, fruitful. **-azione** *f.* production of fruit, fruiting; (bot.) fructification.

frutti-fico *adj.* fruit-bearing, fruitful; useful.

frutt-ivendolo *m.* fruiterer, fruit-seller. (**-ivendola** *f.*) **-ivoro** *adj.* (zool.) fructivorous.

frutt-o *m.* (*pl.* **-i**, **-a** *f.*) a fruit; one single fruit; — proibito, forbidden fruit; -i di stagione, fruit in season, (joc.) coughs and colds; alberi da —, fruit trees; essere alle -a, to be at the fruit course, to be at the end of a meal; offspring, progeny; fruit, produce; -i di mare, edible sea molluscs and sea urchins; (fig.) use, profit, advantage, gain, reward; con —, successfully; non ricavarne nessun —, to get nothing out of it; cogliere il — delle sue fatiche, to reap the harvest for his labours; senza —, fruitlessly, unsuccessfully, unprofitably; *pl.* fruit, fruits; i -i della terra, the fruits of the earth; (finan.) yield; (leg.) fruits; yield; produce; -i naturali e civili, natural and artificial produce (C.C.) (cf. **frutta**). **-ologia** *f.* treatise on fruit; carpology. **†-uare** *intr.* to fructify, to bear fruit.

fruttuos-o *adj.* fruitful; useful, profitable. **-amente** *adv.* fruitfully; usefully, profitably. **-ità** *f.* fruitfulness, fertility.

ftaleina *f.* (chem.) phthalein.

ftiri-aşi *f.* (med.) phthiriasis, vagabond's disease.

fu[1] *m. indecl.* (bot.) *Valeriana phu*.

fu[2] *adv. phr.* fare fu fu, to fuss.

fu[3] *3rd. pers. sing. past def.* of essere, q.v.

fu[4] *adj. indecl.* late, deceased; il — signor Rossi, the late Mr Rossi; la — sua sorella, his late sister; Carlo — Pietro Bruni, Charles son of the late Peter Brown; (cf. **furono**).

fucato *adj.* painted; — ad arte, artificial.

fucignone *m.* (ent.) a grub or caterpillar infesting pears.

fucil-are [A I] *tr.* to shoot (with a rifle); to execute; (mil.) to fire or shoot (with a rifle); to shoot (a deserter). **-ata** *f.* shot; (mil.) volley; single shot; fare alle -ate, to exchange shots. **-ato** *part. adj.* shot; executed. **-atore** *m.* shooter; (mil.) shooter, 'shot'; responsible authority for condemning to be shot; member of a firing squad. **-azione** *f.* shooting, execution.

fucil-e *m.* rifle; (mil.) — da posta, fixed rifle; ricaricare il —, to reload; inastare la baionetta al —, to fix bayonets; forte di 1000 -i, rifle strength of 1000; a un tiro di —, at rifle range (distance); — mitragliatore, light machine gun (L.M.G.); — pneumatico, air-gun; — subacqueo, diver's gun, spring-loaded harpoon; — da caccia, fowling-piece; (herald.) — di Borgogna, steel, fire-steel, furison; (herald.) — del tosone d'oro, flint and steel; †(anat.) the tibio-fibula; †leg of a scorpion; †collar of the order of the Golden Fleece. **-eria** *f.* quantity of rifles; sound of rifle fire; art of handling a rifle, marksmanship. **-iere** *m.* (mil.) rifleman, fusilier, infantryman, foot-soldier. **-ino** *m. dim.* toy gun.

fucin-a *f.* (metall.) forge; smithy; †(naut.) — di bordo, ship's forge; (fig.) factory; una — di menzogne, a factory of lies, a place where lies are fabricated. **-ale** *m.* (metall.) puddling furnace. **-are** [A I] *tr.* (metall.) to forge. **†-ata** *f.* great quantity, vast amount. **-ato** *part. adj.* forged; *n.m.* (metall.) forging. **-atore** *m.* (metall.) forger. **-atrice** *f.* (metall.) forging machine. **-atura** *f.* (metall.) forging; -atura a stampo, drop forging.

fuco[1] *m.* (*pl.* **fuchi**) (ent.) drone (bee).

fuco² *m.* (bot.) wrack, *Fucus* and other seaweeds; — carrageo, carragheen, Irish moss, *Chondrus crispus.*

fuc·s·ia *f.* (bot.) fuchsia, *Fuchsia.* **-ina** *f.* (chem.) fuchsine, magenta, aniline red.

Fuegini *pr.n.m.pl.* (geog.) Fuegians.

fuero *m.* (Spanish law) privilege.

fuffigno *m.* knot in a skein of wool, tangle.

fuga *f.* flight; darsi alla —, to take flight; tentativo di —, attempted escape; una — romanzesca, a romantic escape; mettere in —, to put to flight; di —, hastily, hurriedly; (Bibl.) la Fuga in Egitto, the Flight into Egypt; leak, escape; una — di gas, a gas leak; suite, succession; una — di stanze, a suite of rooms; una — di scale, a flight of stairs; (leg.) running away; evasione o — d'infermi di mente, escape or running away of mental patients (C.C.P.); (motor.) racing (of engine); (aeron.) bordo di —, trailing edge; spurt, sprint (cycling); (mus.) fugue (in both senses, namely, a method of contrapuntal imitation, and a complete composition based on such method); (med.) — epilettica, procursive epilepsy.

fugac-e *adj.* fleeting, transitory, transient, brief. **-emente** *adv.* fleetingly, briefly. **-ità** *f.* fleetingness, transitoriness; instability.

fugara *f.* (mus.) open organ-stop of wood or metal of horn or string quality.

fug-are [A 2] *tr.* to put to flight, to chase away; to disperse; il vento -a le nuvole, the wind disperses the clouds; to dispel, to drive away; — le tentazioni, to drive away temptation; (mil.) to rout; (mus.) to fugue. **-amento** *m.* putting to flight, dispersal. **-ato** *part. adj.* put to flight; (mus.) fugued, fugal; *n.m.* (mus.) fugato, fugued passage. **-atore** *m.* disperser, dispeller; (mus.) fuguist. (**-atrice** *f.*) **-azione** *f.* flight, exodus.

†**fugga** *f.* See **fuga.**

†**fug·gere** *vb.* and derivs. See **fuggire.**

fuggevole *adj.* See under **fuggire.**

fuggias-co *adj.* (*m.pl.* **-chi**) fugitive, fleeing, runaway; *n.m.* fugitive; exile; (mil.) deserter; fugitive from battle, coward; (naut.) man abandoning ship. **-camente** *adv.* like a fugitive; hastily, briefly.

fuggi-fatica *m. indecl.* one who shuns work; slacker; idler, lazy-bones, sluggard. **-fuggi** *m. indecl.* headlong flight, confusion; stampede of a crowd; il cinema s'incendiò e fra strilli e svenimenti successe un fuggi-fuggi generale, the cinema caught fire and amid shrieks and faintings a general stampede took place. **-lo·zio** *m. indecl.* pastime, occupation.

fugg-ire [D 1] *intr.* (*aux.* essere) to flee; to escape; to run away; a scappa e -i, in a great hurry, all in a rush; — dalla città, to flee from the city; — dalla prigione, to escape from prison; (fig.) mi lasciai — quella parola di bocca, I let that word escape my lips, that word slipped out; to pass rapidly, to fly; come -e il tempo!, how time flies!; (naut.) to run; — in fil di ruota, to run with the wind dead astern; *tr.* to shun, to avoid; to flee from; — un pericolo, to avoid a danger, to flee from a danger; (naut.) — il vento, to run before the wind; (art) to foreshorten. **-ente** *part. adj.* (poet.) fleeing, flying; fleeting, rapid; mento -ente, receding chin; *n.m.* fugitive. **-evole** *adj.* fleeting, brief, transitory. **-evolmente** *adv.* fleetingly, briefly. **-evolezza** *f.* fugacity, transitoriness. **-i·bile** *adj.* avoidable, fugitive. **-imento** *m.* fleeing, flight, escape; (paint.) foreshortening. **-ita** *f.* flight, escape. **-itivo** *adj.* fugitive, runaway, fleeing; fleeting, transitory; *n.m* fugitive; deserter. **-ito** *part. adj.* avoided, shunned; *n.m.* fugitive; deserter. **-itore** *m.* escaper. (**-itrice** *f.*)

fughetta *f. dim.* of **fuga,** q.v.; (mus.) a short fugue.

†**fu·ia** *f.* harlot.

†**fu·io** *adj.* thieving; dark, obscure, hidden.

fular *m. indecl.* See **folar.**

fulcro *m.* (eng.) fulcrum; pivot; (fig.) centre, heart, central point.

fulena *f.* See **falena.**

ful·g-ere [def.] *intr.* (poet.) to shine; to be resplendent; to flash, to gleam, to sparkle. **-ente** *part. adj.* shining, refulgent, resplendent; *n.m.* splendour, refulgence. †**-etro** *m.* flash; brilliance; gleam; lightning.

ful·gid-o *adj.* resplendent, shining, bright; brilliant; untarnished. **-ezza** *f.* splendour, resplendence, refulgence, brightness. **-ità** *f.* refulgence, brightness, brilliancy.

fulgor-e *m.* splendour, brightness, refulgence, radiance, brilliance. †**-ato** *adj.* illumined; brilliant, resplendent.

fulgorite *f.* (metall.) fulgurite, lightning tube.

fulig·gin-e *f.* soot; smuts; (paint.) lamp-black. **-oso** *adj.* sooty; black as soot; fuliginous.

full *m. indecl.* full-house (poker); *adv.* in —, in full.

fullon-e *m.* fuller. **-i·a** *f.* fulling.

fullo·nica *f.* See **fullonia,** under **fullone.**

fulmicotone *m.* nitrocellulose, gun-cotton.

fulmin-are [A 1 S] *tr.* to strike by lightning, to fulminate; to kill, to shoot dead; (fig.) to annihilate; to crush, to shatter the resistance of; la -ò con uno sguardo, he dumbfounded her with a look; — maledizioni contro qualcuno, to hurl curses at someone; (eccl.) — una scomunica, to launch an excommunication; *intr.* (*aux.* avere) to lighten; to emit flashes of lightning; to fulminate; to flash; to thunder (fig.). **-amento** *m.* fulmination, striking by lightning. **-ante** *part. adj.* fulminating; explosive; violent, crushing; un colpo -ante, a violent blow; una lettera -ante, a crushing letter; (med.) fulminating; cotone -ante, guncotton; *n.m.* percussion cap, primer, detonator (of cartridge, etc.); *n.m.* cheap old-fashioned match. **-ato** *part. adj.* struck by lightning; fulminated; hurled; (electr.) blown, burnt out; *n.m.* (chem.) fulminate. **-atore** *m.* fulminator, thunderer; *adj.* fulminating. (**-atrice** *f.*) **-atorio** *adj.* (*m.pl.* **-atorii**) fulminatory; thundering. **-azione** *f.* fulmination.

ful·min-e *m.* lightning, flash of lightning; thunderclap, thunderbolt; corse via come un —, he ran off like a flash of lightning; veloce come il —, as quick as lightning; i -i di Giove, Jove's thunderbolts; (eccl.) i -i della Chiesa, the thunders, the fulminations of the Church; un — a ciel sereno, a bolt from the blue; a surprise; colpito dal —, struck by lightning.

fulmi·neo *adj.* of thunder; of lightning; rapid, flashing; quick as lightning; uno sguardo —, a threatening look, a furious glance.

fulmi·nico *adj.* (chem.) fulminic; acido —, fulminic acid, carbonyl oxime.

fulmin-io *m.* (*pl.* **-ii**) frequent lightning, repeated lightning.

†**ful·vido** *adj.* See **fulgido.**

ful·vo *adj.* reddish-yellow, tawny.

fum-ac·chio *m.* piece of smoky charcoal; jet of smoke; smoke, vapour; thermal spring giving off vapour; fumigation. **-a·i·(u)olo** *m.* chimney-pot, chimney-top, chimney; (naut.) funnel; †-aiuolo della chiesola, compass binnacle lamp cowl; chimney, funnel, smoke-stack. †**-ale** *adj.* smoky. †**-ana** *f.* pall of smoke, exhalation of vapour.

fum-are [A 1] *tr.* to smoke; — la pipa, to smoke a pipe; — il sigaro, to smoke cigars; — sigarette, to smoke cigarettes; Lei -a?, do you smoke?; me la -o, I don't care; *intr.* (*aux.* avere) to smoke, to give off smoke, to give off vapour; to steam; l'incendio -a, the fire is smoking; to be blocked; to fume (in anger); *impers.* gli -a, he is angry, he is quick-tempered. **-a·bile** *adj.* smokable. **-ante** *part. adj.* smoking, steaming, fuming. **-ata** *f.* cloud of smoke, puff of smoke; smoke-signal; smoking, smoke; fare una -ata, to have a smoke, to smoke one cigarette; (mil.) see **fumo;** (eccl.) *fumata scura,* smoke-signal during conclave made with burnt ballot-papers and straw, and indicating that there is no election yet); — bianca, indication that a new Pope has been elected. **-ato** *part. adj.* smoked; (paint.) toned down, shaded. **-atore** *m.* smoker; (rlwy.) compartimento per -atori, smoking-compartment, smoker; (med.) cancro dei -atori, smoker's cancer, cancer of the lung. **-atoria** *f.* smoking-den.

fuma·ria *f.* (bot.) see **fumosterno;** (colloq.) prendere l'erba —, to go away, to make off.

fuma·rio *adj.* See under **fumo.**

fumasi·gari *m. indecl.* cigar-holder.

†**fumea** *f.* See **fumo.**

fumeggi-are [A 3 C] *intr.* (*aux.* avere) to smoke, to emit smoke; *tr.* (art) to shade off, to gradate (from one tint or tone to another). **-ato** *part. adj.* (art) shaded, gradated, toned down.

†**fu·meo** *adj.* smoky.

fumeri·a *f.* See **fumatoria,** under **fumare.**

fumett-o *m.* anisette; balloon encircling words issuing from a figure's mouth in a drawing; comic-paper, comic, comic-strip; romanzo a fumetti, story told in comic-strip. **-i·stico** *adj.* lurid, highly coloured, improbable, melodramatic.

fumicai·(u)olo *m.* chimney of a charcoal-kiln; peg, stick.

fumic-are [A 2 S] *intr.* (*aux.* avere) to smoke; to steam; to carry out fumigation; to emit vapour, to give off fumes, to fume. **-ante** *part. adj.* steaming; smoking; fuming; fumigating. **-azione** *f.* see **fumigazione,** under **fumigare.**

fumicọso *adj.* smoky; steamy.

fu·mido *adj.* smoking; steaming; smoky; steamy.

fumi·fero *adj.* smoking; steaming.

fumig·are [A2s] *intr.* (*aux.* avere) to smoke, to steam, to give off vapour; to carry out fumigation. **-ante** *part. adj.* smoking; steaming; fumigating. **-azione** *f.* fumigation; emission of smoke, steam or vapour. **-ìo** *m.* (*pl.* **-ìi**) fumigation.

fumist·a *m.* (techn.) boilerman; (fig.) practical joker. **-eri·a** *f.* form of art intended to mystify the public.

fum·o *m.* smoke; il — dell'incendio, the smoke from the fire; far —, mandar —, to smoke, to give off smoke, to steam, to give off steam; dove c'è —, c'è fuoco, where there's smoke there's fire, there's no smoke without a fire; lui per me è come il — agli occhi, non lo posso vedere, that man is a pain in the neck to me, I can't bear him; sapere di —, to taste of smoke; smoking; il — è un gran vizio, smoking is a bad habit; tabacco da —, pipe-tobacco; steam, vapour, fume, mist; il — del pantano, the steam from the fen, the mist from the fen; il — della pentola, the steam from the pot; fume; i -i del vino, the fumes from the wine; gli sono montati i -i, the wine has gone to his head; vanity, pride, haughtiness; non credete alle sue vanterie, è tutto fumo, don't believe his boasting, it's all emptiness; un uomo pieno di —, a haughty man; emptiness, nothing; vendere —, to mystify, to deceive; spacciatore di —, charlatan, swindler; andare in —, to go up in smoke, to come to nothing, to vanish; mandare in —, to destroy, to put an end to; gettare il — negli occhi a, to pull the wool over someone's eyes; (leg.) — venduto, vendita di —, the crime of pretending, fraudulently for gain, to have influence with a public servant; (mil.) smoke signal; smoke used for screening; smoke used to evict an enemy. **-a·rio** *adj.* relating to smoke; canna -aria, flue. **-o·geno** *adj.* smoke-producing; (mil.) cortina -ogena, smoke-screen; granata -ogena, smoke-shell; *n.m.* smoke-producer.

fumoir *m. indecl.* (pron. as Fr.) smoking-room.

fumọs·o *adj.* smoky; steamy; smoking; steaming; proud, arrogant. **-etto** *adj. dim.* rather smoky, rather steamy; rather scornful. **-ità** *f.* smokiness; steaminess; cloud of smoke or steam; (fig.) vanity, pride.

fumosterno *m.* (bot.) fumitory, *Fumaria.*

fun-a·io *m.* rope-maker; rope-seller. **-ai(u)olo** *m.* rope-maker. **-ale** *m.* torch made of tarred rope; †(naut.) see **frenello**. **-ambolẹsco** *adj.* (*m.pl.* **-amboleschi**) relating to tight-rope walking. **-am·bolo** *m.* tight-rope walker, rope-dancer, funambulist; (fig.) one who sits on the fence (in politics, etc.). **-ambolismo** *m.* tight-rope walking; funambulism; (fig.) vacillation, shilly-shallying. **-ame** *m.* ropes, mass of ropes. **-ata** *f.* lash with a rope; string, row, file; una -ata di prigionieri, a string of prisoners.

†fundare *vb.* and derivs. See **fondare**.

†fun·dere *vb.* and derivs. See **fondere**.

†fundità *f.* See **profondità**.

fun-e *f.* rope; — delle campane, bell-rope; attaccarsi alle -i del cielo, to try every conceivable means, to move heaven and earth; (Florence) le -i del cielo, vertical streaks of light in the sky; lash with a rope; (mus.) cord (controlling tension of side-drum membranes); (sport) tiro alla —, tug-of-war; skipping rope; **-icella** *f. dim.* thin rope, cord; (text.) driving band. **-icello** *m. dim.* cord. **-icina** *f. dim.* thin rope, cord.

fu·nebr-e *adj.* funereal, funeral; riti -i, funeral rites; servizio —, uffizio —, rito —, funeral service; spese -i, funeral expenses; impresario di pompe -i, undertaker; (mus.) marcia —, funeral march, dead march; sad, mournful; funereal, gloomy; lugubrious. **-emente** *adv.* sadly, mournfully; funereally.

funeral-e *adj.* funeral; funerary; *n.m.* funeral; obsequies; domani si farà il —, the funeral will take place tomorrow; (liturg.) funeral; (leg.) turbamento di un —, disturbance of a funeral (C.P.). **-mente** *adv.* with funeral ceremonies; funereally.

funera·rio *adj.* funerary; funeral.

fu·nere *m.* (poet.) massacre; death.

fune·reo *adj.* funereal, funeral; mournful, sad, lugubrious.

funest-are [A1] *tr.* to afflict, to ruin, to oppress; le guerre -ano il paese, wars devastate the country; to sadden, to vex, to distress; perchè -arla con quella notizia?, why should you distress her with the news?; to desolate, to desecrate, to profane; — l'altare, to desecrate the altar; *rfl.* to distress oneself; to be distressed. **-ato** *part. adj.* distressed, saddened; desolated.

funest·o *adj.* fatal; grievous, ruinous; tragic, sad, sorrowful, dis-

tressing; un colpo —, a fatal blow, un errore —, a tragic mistake. **-amente** *adv.* fatally; grievously; sadly.

fung·a *f.* mould; (bot.) the blue-green moulds, *Aspergillus herbariorum* and *Penicillum crustaceum.*

fungac·cio *m.* See under **fungo**.

funga·ia *f.* mushroom-bed; damp, mouldy place; (fig.) swarm, profusion; una — di poeti, a profusion of poets.

fung-are [A2] *intr.* (*aux.* essere) to become mouldy. **-ato** *part. adj.* anno -ato anno tribolato, a year that is good for mushrooms is a bad year.

fun·g-ere *tr.* [C5] to carry out, to fulfil; *intr.* (*aux.* avere) to act, to function; — da sindaco, to act as mayor, to represent the mayor; — da intermedio, to act as go-between. **-ente** *part.* acting, functioning. **-i·bile** *adj.* (leg.) fungible (Scots law); beni -ibili, goods of such a nature that one specimen or part may be used in place of another in satisfaction of an obligation.

fungh·eto *m.* mushroom-bed. **-etto** *m. dim.* chanterelle.

funghire [D2] *intr.* (*aux.* essere) to become mouldy.

fung-iforme *adj.* fungiform. **†-ite** *f.* (miner.) a kind of fossil coral formerly called fungite.

fung-o *m.* (*pl.* **funghi**) (bot.) fungus; — d'esca, tinder fungus, *Fomes fomentarius*; (cul.) mushroom or other edible fungus; (motor.) valve head; (rlwy.) rail head; in una notte nasce un —, things can happen very suddenly, things can crop up very suddenly; crescere come i funghi, to sprout up like mushrooms, to spring up overnight; far le nozze coi funghi, to do something stingily; a forma di —, mushroom-shaped; — velenoso, toadstool; — atomico, mushroom-shaped cloud produced by an atomic explosion. **-ac·cio** *m. pejor.* poisonous fungus, bad fungus; (bot.) see **fungo**. **-osità** *f.* (med.) fungosity; (bot.) excrescence due to disease. **-ọso** *adj.* fungous.

funic·chio *m.* See **funicolo**.

funicella *f. dim.* of **fune**, q.v.

funicolare *adj.* (rlwy.) funicular; *n.f.* funicular (railway); (naut.) chain ferry; (leg.) passaggio coattivo di via — aerea, compulsory way-leave for overhead cableway (C.C.).

funi·col-o *m.* cord; strand (of a rope or cable); (anat.) funiculus; umbilical cord; — spermatico, funiculus spermaticus, spermatic cord; (bot.) funicle; (naut.) log line, codline, mackerel line. **-ite** *f.* (med.) funiculitis, inflammation of the spermatic cord.

funi-vi·a *f.* (eng.) aerial ropeway, cableway; ski lift, téléférique. **-via·rio** *adj.* (neol.) relating to an aerial ropeway; linea -viaria, line or course of a cableway, etc.

funn·ale *m.* (naut., Naples) deep; *pl.* (naut., Sicily) deep waters. **-o** *m.* (naut., Taranto) submerged part of the hull, wetted surface.

funzion-are [A1c] *intr.* (*aux.* avere) to act, to fulfil an office; to work; to function; -are da, to act as; -are da sindaco, to act as mayor, to fill the office of mayor; il cuore non -a bene, the heart is not functioning properly; l'ascensore non -a, the lift is out of order; *intr.* (eng.) to operate, to work, to run; -are sotto carico, to run loaded; far -are, to operate, to work. **-amento** *m.* functioning, working; operation, running; tensione di -amento, working voltage; -amento a molla, clockwork action. **-ante** *part. adj.* acting, working, functioning; (leg.) acting (e.g. ad interim).

funziọn-e *f.* function; functioning; entrare in —, to become operative; (eng.) mode of operation; in —, working; (math.) function; in — di, in terms of, *or* plotted against; faculty; — intellettuale, intellectual faculty; significance, meaning, function; — di avverbio, adverbial meaning; (archit.) function (of a detail or feature in a larger member); (leg.) function, office; usurpare una — pubblica, to usurp a public office (C.P.); office, appointment, post; duties; la Funzione Pubblica, the Civil Service; la — di rettore, the office of rector; nell'esercizio delle sue -i, in the exercise of his duties; incompatibilità di -i, incompatibility of duties; far — di, to undertake the duties of, to act for; esorbita dalle mie -i, it is not my responsibility; (mil.) duty, function; — di aiutante di campo, duties of an A.D.C.; — militare, ceremonial military honours; (liturg.) service, liturgical function; le -i della settimana santa, the ceremonies of Holy Week. **-ale** *adj.* functional. **-almente** *adv.* functionally. **-a·rio** *m.* official, functionary; civil servant; officer; magistrate. **-cella, -cina** *f. dim.* (liturg.) short service.

fuochista *m.* (eng.) stoker, fireman; (rlwy.) macchinista —, footplate man.

fuoc-o *m.* (*pl.* **fuochi**) fire; accendere il —, to light the fire; legna da —, firewood; ferri da —, fire irons; al —!, fire!; prender —, pigliar —, to catch fire; dar — a una casa, to set a house on fire; cuocere a — vivo, to cook on a hot fire; a — lento, a — piccolo, on a slow fire; marcare a —, to brand; marca a —, brand; saldare a —, to weld; resistente al —, fire-proof; metterei la mano sul —, I would put my hand in the fire (in proof of a statement); non metterei la mano sul — che, I wouldn't swear that; gettarsi nel — per uno, to go through fire and water for someone; mettere il — al letto, to put the warming-pan in the bed, to warm the bed; fuochi artificiali, fuochi d'artifizio, fireworks; accendere fuochi d'artifizio, to let off fireworks; fuochi fatui, will-o'-the-wisp; fireside, hearth; sedersi accanto al —, to sit down by the fireside; (fig.) heat, passion, ardour, excitement; il — della gioventù, the fire of youth, the ardour of youth; aver il — addosso, to be very excited; quell'uomo piglia subito —, that man gets heated quickly, that man is very excitable; parole di —, soul-searing words, unforgettable words; — di paglia, fire of straw, *or* (fig.) blaze of passion; soffiar nel —, to blow on the fire, to cause trouble, to make things worse; to stir up feelings; versare olio sul —, to add fuel to the fire; to make matters worse; versare acqua sul —, to pour water on the fire, *or* (fig.) to damp down ardour; il — cova sotto la cenere, the fire is smouldering beneath the ashes, (fig.) his passion is smouldering inside him; fare — e fiamme per ottenere una cosa, to do everything possible to get a thing, to raise heaven and earth to get a thing; metter troppa carne al —, to have too many irons in the fire; trovarsi tra due fuochi, to be between two fires, to be between the devil and the deep blue sea; (mil.) shot; far —, to open fire; arma da —, firearm; ferri da —, firearms; — di artiglieria, gunfire; — di battaglione, battalion fire; bocca da —, piece of artillery, gun, cannon; — incrociato, crossfire; ore di —, hours under fire, hours in action; battesimo del —, baptism of fire; — di fila, barrage; (naut.) -hi di Sant'Elmo, St Elmo's lights (or fire), electrical discharge giving a glowing light on the masts or yards of a wooden ship; *pl.* ship's boilers; †albero di —, mizzen mast; (Rom. antiq.) — sacro, sacred fire (of the Vestals, and fig. of poets); zeal, enthusiasm, ardent faith, genius; (Rom. antiq.) interdire uno dell'acqua e del —, to forbid fire and water to someone; to banish him; (hist.) prova del —, ordeal by fire; (opt.) focus; (photog.) a —, focused, in focus; messa a —, focusing; l'immagine non è a —, the picture is not sharp. **-ato** *adj.* flame-coloured, scarlet.

†fuorabanda *f.* (naut.) outboard.

fuorchè *conj.*, *prep.* See under **fuori**.

†fuorchiu·dere *vb.* and derivs. See **forchiudere**.

†fuorgiudicato *adj.* (leg.) outside jurisdiction.

fuor-i *adv.* outside; andar —, to go outside; star di —, to be outside; fuori!, get out!; dar di —, to overflow; metter —, to put out; to publish; (colloq.) mettere — denaro, to pay out money, to 'fork out'; scappar — con una domanda, to come out with a question; sporgersi in —, to jut out, to lean out; da questo in —, apart from this; out, away; lasciar —, to leave out, to omit; tagliar —, to cut away, to detach; to cut off from; in Italia e —, inside Italy and outside, in Italy and abroad; un uomo che viene di —, a man who comes from outside; a man who comes from away; il di — di una casa, the outside of a house; *prep.* and *prep. phr.* — di, out of, outside; beyond; — della casa, outside the house; — (di) commercio, not for sale; un'edizione — (di) commercio, a private edition; — (di) mano, out of the way, remote; — (di) misura, excessively; — (di) proposito, out of place; — servizio, out of use; off duty; — (di) speranza, beyond hope; — stagione, out of season; — (di) strada, off the road, off one's route; — (di) tempo, out of time, untimely; una parola — d'uso, a word no longer in use, an obsolete word; — (di) vista, out of sight; essere — di sè, to be beside oneself, to rave; essere — della grazia di Dio, to be in a very bad temper; uscire — dei gangheri, to lose one's temper; (cinem.; telev.) — campo, off-screen; (theatr.) — scena, off-stage; (naut.) — tutto, overall (length of a vessel); † — cami(s)ciuola!, off jumper!; † — filari battaglioli!, unship weather boards!; † — rumore!, silence!; (eng.) — centro, out-of-centre; — uso, unserviceable; (sport) — classe, unbeatable, unrivalled; (football) — gioco, off-side; (boxing) — combattimento, knock-out; (admin.) — sacco, an indication (written on an envelope) that a letter is not to be placed in a mail-bag but kept for speedier sorting and delivery. **-chè** *conj.* except, unless; excepting that;

prep. except. **-ibordo** *m. indecl.* (naut.) ship's side, exterior above water; outboard motor boat (also *adj.*). **-iclasse** *adj. indecl.* unequalled, in a class on its own; *n.m.,f.* person who is unequalled; (sport) undisputed champion. **-ilegge** *m. indecl.* outlaw; bandit. **-iscalmo** *m.* (naut.) outrigger. **-ise·rie** *adj. indecl.* purpose-made, not mass-produced, model. **-ivo·glia** *adv.* against one's will, unwillingly. **-mişura** *adv.* excessively; *adj. indecl.* excessive. **-mişurare** *intr.* (*aux.* essere) to go too far. **-uscita** *f.* leakage, escape. **-uscito** *part. adj.* gone out; banished, exiled; *n.m.* political exile; outlaw; person living abroad for fear of political persecution; bandit. **-viare** [A4] and derivs. see **forviare**.

†fur-ace *adj.* thievish. **†-acuori** *adj.* indecl. charming. **†-are** *tr.* to steal. **†-ato** *part. adj.* stolen. **†-atore** *m.* thief.

†furba¹ *f.* See **furberia**.

furba² *f.*, *adj. f.* See **furbo**.

furb-eri·a *f.* cunning, slyness; astuteness; shrewdness; cleverness; malice, artfulness; cunning action. **-eriuc·cia, -eri(u)ola** *f.* low cunning. **-esco** *adj.* (*m.pl.* **-eschi**) cunning, sly; un tiro -esco, a sly thrust; linguaggio -esco, thieves' lingo. **-escamente** *adv.* slyly, artfully, cunningly. **-i·zia** *f.* cunning, malice, artfulness.

furb-o *adj.* shrewd; clever; astute, artful; roguish; sly; malicious; *n.m.* cunning man, sly person; con modi da —, cunningly; (provb.) per conoscere un — ci vuole un — e mezzo, set a thief to catch a thief. **-a** *f.* cunning woman, sly woman. **-acchione** *m.* sly old thing. **-acchiotto** *adj. dim.* rather sly, rather artful; *n.m.* cunning little fellow. **-acchiuoleri·a** *f.* piece of cunning, sly action. **-acchiuolo** *adj.* rather sly; *n.m.* artful young fellow. **-accio, -accione** *adj. pejor.* sly, unpleasantly cunning; *n.m.* nasty sly fellow. **-amente** *adv.* slyly, artfully. **-etto** *adj. dim.* rather sly, rather cunning; *n.m.* artful young fellow, sly little chap.

†furci·fero *m.* wicked; wretched.

furente *adj.* furious; raging, frenzied, mad; (rel.) (of prophet, Delphic priestess, etc.) inspired, possessed by the deity.

†fu·rere *intr.* to rage.

fureri·a *f.* (mil.) company office; †quartermaster's office (Tuscan court).

furętto *m.* (zool.) ferret.

furfant-e *adj.* rascal, rogue, scamp; scoundrel, knave. **-ag·gine** *f.* rascality. **-a·glia** *f.* collection of rogues; rabble, scum. **-are** [A1] *intr.* (*aux.* avere) to lead a rascally life; †*tr.* to rob. †**-ato** *part. adj.* stolen. **-eggiare** [A3c] *intr.* (*aux.* avere) to act knavishly, to behave dishonestly. **-ello** *m. dim.* young rogue; mischievous boy. **-eri·a** *f.* roguery, knavery; roguish action, knavish trick. **-esco** *adj.* (*m.pl.* **-eschi**) roguish, knavish, scoundrelly. **-ina** *f.* mockery, hooting, sneer; battere la -ina, to have one's teeth chattering with cold. **-ino** *adj.* roguish, scoundrelly.

†furf-are *tr.* to cheat, to steal. †**-atore** *m.* thief, robber.

furfur-a·ceo *adj.* like bran. **-i·lico** *adj.* (chem.) furfuryl. **-am·mide** *m.* furfuramide. **-ina** *f.* (chem.) furfurine. **-o·lio, -olo** *m.* furfural, furfuraldehyde.

furgon-e *m.* van; — per mobilia, pantechnicon, removal van; freight car. **-cino** *m. dim.* delivery van, small van.

fu·ri-a *f.* fury, rage; temper; in un momento di —, in a fit of rage; montare in —, to fly into a temper, to lose one's temper; montò su tutte le -e, he flew into a terrible temper, he stormed and raged; violence, force, impetus; la — del vento, the violence of the wind, the force of the wind; a — di popolo, by the violence of the mob; frenzy, passion; nella — della disperazione, in a frenzy of despair; hurry, furious hurry, haste; di —, in a hurry, quickly; aver —, to be in a hurry; in fretta e —, in a tearing hurry, in great haste; craze, lust, longing, desire; la — dell'oro, the lust for gold; la — della gloria. the desire for glory; fury, furious person; *pl.* (myth.) Furies; a — di, by dint of, by means of; a — d'insistenza, by insisting repeatedly; a — di studiare, by dint of study, by studying hard. **-ale** *adj.* (myth.) of the Furies. **-ano** *adj.* (naut.) vento -ano, Adriatic wind (between south and south-west). **-etta** *f. dim.* flash of anger; moment of impatience.

furi-are [A4] *intr.* (*aux.* avere) to rage; *rfl.* to fly into a temper. **-ante** *part. adj.* see **furente**. †**-ato** *part. adj.* furious, infuriated.

furibond-o *adj.* furious, violent, raging, wild. **-amente** *adv.* furiously, violently, wildly.

fur-iere, -iero *m.* (mil.) quartermaster (storekeeper branch); (naut.) paymaster, secretariat, stores personnel (supply branch); **-ieri** della sussistenza, victualling branch.

furiọs-o *adj.* furious, wild; violent, impetuous, vehement; hurried, hasty; era — contro di me, he was furious with me; una passione ~a, a violent passion; un mare —, a stormy sea, a tempestuous sea; violently insane; (herald.) charging, leaping. **-amẹnte** *adv.* furiously, violently, wildly, hastily. †**-ità** *f.* fury, rage, anger.

furlan-a *f.* (mus.) forlane, a folk dance from Friuli; (agric.) see **frullana.** ~**o** *adj.* of Friuli; *n.m.* native of Friuli.

†**fur-o** *m.* thief; *adj.* thieving. †**-ello** *m. dim.* young robber. †**-one** *m.* thief, robber; (ichth.) fishermen's name for any large fish.

fu·rono *adj. indecl. pl.* deceased; i — coniugi X, the late Mr and Mrs X. (Cf. **Fu⁴**.)

furọr-e *m.* fury; montò in —, he became furious; furore, rage, craze; wild enthusiasm; far —, to become very fashionable, to be all the rage; force, impetus, vehemence, violence; il — delle fiamitch the fury, the violence, of the flames; consuming desire, longing; ha il — delle ricchezze, he has a great desire for wealth. **-eggiare** [A3c] *intr.* (aux. avere) to be very successful; to arouse enthusiasm, to be a furore, to be all the rage.

†**furtare** *tr.* to steal.

furtiv-o *adj.* furtive, clandestine, surreptitious; occhiate ~e, furtive glances; (leg.) stolen; oggetti ~i, stolen goods (C.P.); (mil.) marcia ~a, a movement of troops hidden or disguised, or carried out at night. **-amẹnte** *adv.* furtively, secretly, clandestinely.

furto *m.* stealing; theft; — letterario, plagiarism; di —, secretly, furtively; (leg.) larceny, stealing (C.P.); — parziale, pilfering; — con scasso, housebreaking.

furun·colo *m.* See **foruncolo.**

fusa¹ *f.pl.* See under **fuso².**

†**fusa²** *f.* (mus.) quaver.

fusag·gine *f.* (bot.) spindle tree, *Euonymus europaeus.*

fuṣa·ia *f.* (cul.) Roman dish of salted lupins.

fuṣ-a·io, ~**aro** *m.* seller of spindles; seller of household implements. ~**ai(u)ola** *f.* (archaeol.) perforated and spindle-like object. ~**ai(u)olo** *m.* (text.) whirl, whorl; (archit.) fusarole. ~**ano** *m.* (bot.) see **fusaggine.** †~**are** *intr.* (of a cat) to purr. ~**ato** *adj.* (herald.) fusilly. ~**arola,** ~**aruola** *f.* (archit.) fusarole.

Fuṣberta *pr.n.f.* the name of Rinaldo's sword in the Italian epic romances.

fuscell-o *m.* twig, small stick; piece of straw; (fig.) very thin person; notare il — nell'occhio altrui e non veder la trave nel proprio, to see the mote in one's neighbour's eye, but not the beam in one's own; fare d'ogni — una trave, to make mountains out of mole-hills. ~**ino** *m. dim.* very small stick, small twig; *pl.* vertical strokes of letters; cominciare dai ~ini, to start from the beginning.

fusciacc-a *f.* sash (on a uniform); sash of office. ~**o** *m.* embroidered cloth; (rel.) embroidered cloth over crucifix in procession.

fusciarra *m.* (Tusc.) scamp, cheeky boy.

fuscina *f.* trident.

fuscite *f.* (miner.) fuchsite.

†**fuṣe·a** *f.* (mus.) quaver.

fuṣellat-o *adj.* (archit.) tapered, tapering. ~**ura** *f.* process of making an object spindle-shaped; tapering.

fuṣello *m. dim.* of **fuso²,** q.v.; small spindle (e.g. as used by Venetian lace-makers); (eng.) spindle, journal; stub axle.

fusẹtto *m.* spindle-shaped stiletto.

fuṣi·bil-e *adj.* (phys.) fusible, meltable; (electr.) tappo —, fuse plug; *n.m.* (electr.) fuse, cut-out. **-ità** *f.* (phys.) fusibility.

fuṣifọrme *adj.* spindle-shaped, tapering; (bot.) fusiform, spindle-shaped.

†**fu·sile** *adj.* soluble; fusible.

fuṣiọne *f.* fusion; (metall.) fusing, melting; casting; — in conchiglia, chill casting; (leg.) amalgamation; — di più società, amalgamation of several companies (C.C.); (paint.) — del colorito, blending (harmony) of colours; (fig.) fusion, assimilation.

fuṣo¹ *part.* of **fondere,** q.v.; *adj.* fused; melted; cast; assimilated; abundant; ferro —, cast iron; formaggio —, processed cheese.

fus-o² *m.* (*pl.* ~i *m.,* ~a *f.*) (text.) spindle; banco a ~i, flyer frame, speed frame; (archit.) shaft (of a column), height (of a pyramid); (naut.) shank of an anchor; capstan spindle; — orario, time zone, limits between which the same time is kept; (biol.) — cario-cinetico, — acromatico, (mitotic) spindle; (herald.) fusils; far le ~a, to purr (of a cat); far le ~a torte, to be unfaithful; dritto come un —, straight as a die, stiff as a ramrod; i miei capelli sono dritti come ~i, my hair is as straight as a yard of pump water.

fusoliera *f.* (aeron.) fuselage; allungamento della —, fineness ratio; †(naut.) light type of boat used in marshes.

fusọne *m.* (zool.) 'pricket', a two- or three-year-old stag, with unbranched antlers.

fuṣ-ọre *m.* fuser, caster. ~**o·rio** *adj.* concerning fusing, relating to casting.

fussite *f.* (miner.) fuchsite.

†**fusta** *f.* (naut.) small galley; Venetian prison hulk.

fustagno *m.* (text.) corduroy; fustian.

fusta·ia *f.* (geog.) coppice.

fustame *m.* cask, barrel.

fustanell-a *f.* skirt worn by Greek soldiers, similar to the kilt. ~**o** *m.* see **fustagno.**

fustato *adj.* (herald.) shafted.

fustell-a *f.* (eng.) hollow punch; (paperm.) knife, envelope cut out but not yet folded. ~**are** [A1] *tr.* (eng.) to punch.

fustẹtto *m.* (dyeing) fustic.

†**fusti·balo** *m.* a kind of sling.

fusticello *m.* twig.

fustig-are [A2s] *tr.* to beat, to whip, to flog; to lash, to scourge. (~**ato** *part. adj.*) ~**atọre** *m.* scourger. (~**atrice** *f.*) ~**aziọne** *f.* scourging; whipping, beating; (geog.) flagellation.

fus·tilo *m.* (dyeing) fustic.

fusto *m.* (bot.) stalk, stem, trunk, petiole; barrel, keg, cask (if made of wood); incluso il —, cost of cask included; drum (if made of metal); (timber) stock; (archit.) shaft (of a column); (leg.) stock; trunk; alberi di alto —, long-trunked trees; alberi di non alto —, short-trunked trees (C.C.); (naut.) shaft, shank, pole, axis; loom (shaft of an oar); †hull; — del letto, bedstead; plank of wood; trunk (of human body); shaft (of a key); frame; (fig.) type.

fustua·rio *m.* (Rom. antiq.) *fustuarium,* military punishment of beating to death.

futa¹ *f.* Arab robe.

†**futa²** *f.* and derivs. See **fuga.**

fu·til-e *adj.* trifling, paltry; worthless, frivolous; futile, vain, useless. **-mẹnte** *adv.* idly, vainly; frivolously; uselessly. **-ità** *f.* futility; trifling matter; uselessness.

futur-o *adj.* future; coming; la vita ~a, the future life, the life to come; il tempo —, the future; (gramm.) the future tense; la mia ~a sposa, my future wife; (leg.) future; esame a ~a memoria, examination (of witnesses) for future record; *n.m.* future; il — è in mano di Dio, the future is in God's hands; in —, in future; (gramm.) il —, the future tense; il — anteriore, the future-perfect; *pl.* i ~i, posterity, future generations. **-amẹnte** *adv.* in the future, in future. **-iṣmo** *m.* futurism. **-ista** *m., f.* futurist.

fuz·zic-o *m.* (Tusc.) stick. ~**are** [A2s] *tr.* to search.

fylgien *m. indecl.* See **filgien.**

g *f., m.* the letter G; the consonant G; una G maiuscola, a capital G; una g minuscola, a small g; G raddoppiato, double G.

gabanella *f.* See **gabbanella.**

gabardina *f.* (text.) gabardine.

gabarr-a *f.* (naut.) barge; †small punt; †transport, armed merchant-man. ~**iere** *m.* bargee.

gabazza *f.* (mil.) truck for working in trenches.

†**gabba** *f.* See **gabbo.**

gabba-compagni *m. indecl.* cheat, humbug. **-cristiani** *m. indecl.* cheat, rogue, impostor. †**-de·i** *m.* see **gabbadeo.** **-de·o** *m. indecl.* hypocrite, humbug. **-minchiọni** *m. indecl.* cheat; one who takes advantage of credulous fools. **-mọndo** *m. indecl.* (or *pl.* **-mọndi**) impostor, charlatan; rogue. **-pensieri** *m. indecl.* distraction, diversion. **-santi** *m. indecl.* hypocrite.

gabbana *f.* (Romagna) see **gabbano;** voltar —, to change sides, to be a turncoat.

gabbanella *f.* hospital-gown, white coat, or tunic, worn by doctors, attendants or convalescent patients; overall; essere di —, to be on duty (of a surgeon, etc.).

gabban-o *m.* loose, sleeveless cloak; man's house-coat; posare il —, to become civilized; stare in —, to lead a rural life. ~**ẹtto** *m. dim.* of **gabbano;** riding habit.

gabbapensieri *m. indecl.* See under **gabbacompagni.**

gabb-are [A1] *tr.* to cheat, to delude; to deceive; to impose upon; to deride, to scorn; to mock; — San Pietro, to give up an eccle-

gabb·are (*cont.*) siastical career; (provb.) avuta la grazia, ‑ato lo santo, when the favour's granted, the promise goes by the board; *rfl.* to amuse oneself; ‑arsi di, to make fun of. **‑amento** *m.* cheating; deceit; deluding; scorn, derision, mockery; practical joke, leg-pull. **‑ato** *part. adj.* cheated; derided; mocked, scorned. **‑atore** *m.* impostor; mocker, derider; practical joker, leg-puller. (**‑atrice** *f.*) **†‑evole** *adj.* comic, laughable.

gabbasanti *m. indecl.* See under **gabbacompagni**.

gabbe·o *m.* drainage board in salt works where the salt is set to dry.

gab·bi·a *f.* cage; pen; bird-cage; hen-coop; — ritrosa, cage trap; una — di matti, a crowd of noisy people, an unconventional, extroverted family; è una — di matti ma sono simpatici, they're all as mad as hatters but I like them; entrare in —, to take on a liability or obligation; (fam.) prison; essere da —, to deserve to be in gaol; (comm.) crate; wicker basket or strainer for olive oil; wicker muzzle for oxen; — dell'ascensore, lift-cage; (eng.) cage (of bearing); (electr.) — di scoiattolo, squirrel cage; (leg.) — degli accusati, dock; (naut.) topsail; top; crow's nest; †look-out stage on a ship; (eng.) recess for a valve. **‑a·io** *m.* cage-maker. **‑ata** *f.* cageful. **‑ere** *m.* (naut.) upper yardman, picked seaman. **‑etta** *f. dim.* crate. **‑onata** *f.* (mil.) gabionade. **‑one** *m. augm.* (pop.) dock (in a court of law); (hydraul.) wicker basket filled with concrete for building a dam or underwater foundations; (mil.) gabion; ‑ione di filo spinato, Dannert wire. **‑uc·cia, ‑uzza** *f. dim.* of **gabbia**; bird-trap. **‑(u)ola** *f. dim.* (naut.) small topsail.

gabbian·o *m.* (orn.) gull, esp. black-headed gull, *Larus ridibundus*; — capinero, cenerino, corallino, Adriatic gull, *L. melanocephalus*; — corso, Audouin's gull, *L. audouini*; — nero, pomatorhine skua, *Stercorarius pomatorhinus*; — reale, herring gull, *Larus argentatus*; — terragnolo, — tridattilo, kittiwake, *Rissa tridactyla*; — roseo, slender-billed gull, *Larus gelastes*; (fig.) fool. **‑ello** *m.* (orn.) little gull, *L. minutus*.

gabbiere *m.* See under **gabbia**.

gabbion·e *m. augm.*, **‑ata** *f.* See under **gabbia**.

gabb·o *m.* joke, game; jest, mockery, derision; pigliare, prendere a —, farsi — di, to make a joke of, to make light of, to make fun of.

gabbr·o *m.* (geol.) gabbro, euphotite. **‑eto** *m.* earth containing gabbro. **‑onite** *f.* (geol.) gabbro rock.

gabell·a *f.* (comm.) excise; tax on moveables; duty; toll; gabel; toll-house. **‑are** *adj.* excisable, subject to tax, dutiable. **‑etta** *f. dim.* small duty or excise.

gabellare¹ *adj.* See under **gabella**.

gabell·are² [A I] *tr.* to excise; to levy excise duty on; to tax; to rate for taxation; to impose local toll on; (fig.) — per, to pass off as; lo ‑ano un grand'uomo, they make him out to be a great man; la ‑ano un'opera d'arte, they pass it off as a work of art. **‑a·bile** *adj.* excisable; liable to excise duty. **‑ato** *part. adj.* levied; taxed; rated. **‑atura** *f.* cost of administration of excise collection.

gabell·iere *m.* excise officer; gabeller; a collector of excise duty or gabelle; toll-collector. **‑ino** *m.* excise officer; office of the excise collector; toll-house. **‑otto** *m.* excise office; (derog.) toll-collector.

gabina *f.* See **cabina**.

gabinetto *m.* study, private room; consulting room; laboratory; water-closet, lavatory; (leg.) cabinet; private secretariat (of, e.g., Minister, Prefect); capo del —, head or president of the cabinet; private secretary (to, e.g., Minister, Prefect); consiglio di —, cabinet council.

Gabriele *pr.n.m.* Gabriel; (fig.) a meek and mild looking person.

Gabriella¹ *pr.n.f.* Gabrielle.

†gabriella² *f.* somersault, handspring.

Gabriello *pr.n.m.* See **Gabriele**.

gado *m.* (ichth.) *Gadus* spp., various edible fishes related to the haddock and whiting.

gadol·i·nio *m.* (chem.) gadolinium. **‑inite** *f.* (miner.) gadolinite.

gae·lico *adj.* Gaelic; *n.m.* Gael.

†gae·tola *f.* crow-like bird.

gaffa *f.* (naut.) boat-hook.

gaffe *f.* (pron. as Fr.) blunder, gaffe; prendere, fare, commettere una —, to make a 'faux pas', to drop a brick, to commit a gaffe.

gaffi *m.pl.* (Rome) the two sections of a head of beef.

gaffin·are [A I] *tr.* (techn.) to refine. **‑ato** *part. adj.* (techn.) refined; argento ‑ato, refined silver.

gagà *m. indecl.* (colloq.) dandy, toff, young man-about-town of exaggerated elegance.

ga·gate *m.* (miner.) jet.

†gag·gia¹ *f.* See **gabbia**.

gagg·i·a² *f.* (bot.) acacia flowers; mimosa flowers; blossom of the following trees. **‑i·o** *m.* (bot.) false acacia, American locust tree, *Robinia pseudoacacia*; ‑io di Costantinopoli, silk-tree of Constantinople, *Albizzia julibrissin*; ‑io odoroso, popinac, *Acacia farnesiana*.

†gag·gio¹ *m.* pledge; gage; engagement; dare il — della battaglia, to declare war; prestare a —, to put out on loan; hostage; stipend, wages; recompense; joy, happiness.

gaggi·o² *m.* (bot.). See under **gaggia²**.

gagliarda *f.* (mus.) galliard; (typ.) minion.

gagliard·o *adj.* strong, hardy, robust; vigorous; powerful; vento —, strong wind; vino —, full-bodied wine; (Tusc.) peso —, good weight; hale and hearty; brave, bold; alla ‑a, bravely, stoutly, robustly, vigorously; *n.m.* strong man; brave man; (naut. hist.) picked sailor on Venetian ships; †ensign. **‑amente** *adv.* robustly; vigorously. **‑etto** *adj. dim.* quite vigorous; rather brave; *n.m.* (naut.) burgee; ‑etto dei principi reali, standard of the royal princes; pennant. **‑ezza** *f.* boldness; strength, hardiness, robustness. **‑i·a** *f.* boldness, bravery; strength, vigour.

ga·glio¹ *m.* (bot.) Lady's bedstraw, *Galium*.

†ga·glio² *m.* rennet.

gaglioff·o *m.* lout; lazy person, †good-for-nothing; scoundrel; *adj.* loutish; clumsy; lazy. **‑ag·gine** *f.* loutishness; laziness. **‑eri·a** *f.* loutish act; dirty, useless thing; group of lazy louts. **‑ezza** *f.* loutishness; laziness.

gagno *m.* hiding place, lair; intrigue; (joc.) belly.

gagnol·are [A 5 s] *intr.* (*aux.* avere) to whine, to howl, to yelp (used properly of foxes, but also of dogs) **‑amento** *m.* whine, howl, yelp. **‑i·o** *m.* (*pl.* ‑ii) continual whining, howling, yelping.

gaiezza *f.* See under **gaio**.

ga·i·o *adj.* gay, joyful, joyous; vivacious; sprightly; vivid; bright; gaudy; — a promesse, free with promises which are not kept; (Prov. lit.) il — sapere, the *gai saber*, the art of the troubadour; borsa ‑a, well-lined purse; †lovely, charming, delightful; *n.m.* gaiety. **‑amente** *adv.* gaily; joyously; vivaciously; vividly, brightly. **‑etto** *adj. dim.* gaily-coloured; variegated, speckled, stippled; gay, happy. **‑ezza** *f.* gaiety; happiness, joy; vivacity; sprightliness; brightness, vividness.

gaiserite *f.* (miner.) geyserite.

gal *m. indecl.* (seism.) gal.

gala¹ *f.* piece of finery; frill; (naut.) gran —, ship dressed overall with flags; piccola —, ship dressed masthead flags only (used at sea or in certain circumstances in harbour).

gala² *f.* festivity, gala; pomp, luxury, show; serata di —, gala evening; mettersi in —, to dress as for a gala occasion; †andare a —, to be organized on a sumptuous scale; †cantare di —, to sing for joy.

galacto·fago *m.* See **galattofago**, under **galattico**.

galagone *m.* (zool.) *Galago* spp., various kinds of lemur.

galalite *f.* casein-formaldehyde resin; casein-plastic.

†galana *f.* (zool.) a kind of turtle.

†galano¹ *m.* See **galana**.

galano² *m.* tassel, bow; furbelow, piece of finery or ornamentation on a woman's dress; (Ven.) a kind of home-made biscuit.

galant·e *adj.* polite; courteous; complimentary; attentive; gallant; luxurious; donna —, woman of easy virtue; elegant; showy; un vestito —, a strikingly smart dress; *n.m.* gallant, lover; fare il —, to play the gallant. **‑emente** *adv.* with gallantry, gallantly. **‑eggiare** [A 3 c] *intr.* (*aux.* avere) to play the gallant. **†‑e·o** *m.* gallantry, courtship. **‑eri·a** *f.* politeness; courtesy; gallantry; foppishness in dress; delicacy, dainty, appetizing food; knick-knack; pleasing or delightful object.

galantina *f.* (cul.) galantine.

galanto *m.* snowdrop, *Galanthus nivalis*.

galantom·ismo *m.* honourable or gentlemanly behaviour. **‑is·simo** *adj. superl.* extremely honourable. **‑one** *m. augm.* of **galantuomo**, q.v.

galant-uomo *m.* (*pl.* ‑uo·mini) man of integrity and honour; good man; ve lo dico da —, I tell you on my honour; è un fior di —, he is the soul of honour; (provb.) il tempo è —, injustice will be remedied by time; (hist.) il re —, Vittorio Emanuele II; (S. Ital.) man of good social standing; †ehi —!, my good man!

†galap·pio *m.* trap, snare.

galas·sia *f.* (astron.) galaxy, Milky Way.

Galate·a[1] *pr.n.f.* (myth.) Galatea.

galate·a[2] *f.* (zool.) squat lobster, *Galathea* spp.

galate·o *m.* book of rules of politeness and etiquette (from the title of the work, *Il Galateo*, compiled by Monsignor Giovanni della Casa, 1503–56); etiquette, code of manners; good breeding; non sa il —, he has no manners; è contro il —, it is not good manners, it is contrary to good breeding.

Gal-ati *pr.n.m.pl.* (Bibl.) Galatians. **-a·zia** *pr.n.f.* (geog.) Galatia.

galattagogo *adj.* (med.) galactagogue.

galat·t-ico *adj.* (astron.) galactic. **-ite** *f.* (miner.) milk-stone, a sort of clay used in degreasing wool. **-ocele** *m.* (med.) breast tumour. **-o·fago** *adj.* galactophagist, milk-fed (also *n.m.*). **-oforite** *f.* (med.) galactophoritis. **-o·foro** *adj.* (anat.) galactophorous, lactiferous. **-ometri·a** *f.* lactometry, milk testing. **-o·metro** *m.* lactometer. **-opoie·si** *f. indecl.* (med.) lactation. **-opoie·tico** *adj.* galactopoietic. **-o·sio** *m.* (chem.) galactose. **-uri·a** *f.* (med.) the secretion of milky urine.

galavern-a *f.*, **-o** *m.* hoar-frost, rime; (N. Ital.) sleet; (Pistoia) icicles.

gal·bano *m.* (bot.) galbanum plant, *Ferula galbaniflua*; (techn.) resinous gum, galbanum.

galbe *m.* ((pron. as Fr.) charm.

gal·beo *m.* (Rom. antiq.) *galbeus*, bracelet as badge of military valour.

gal·bula *f.* (orn.) jacamar.

ga·le-a[1] *f.* helmet. **-ato** *adj.* helmeted, galeated (esp. of Minerva).

gal-e·a[2] *f.* (naut. hist.) galley. **-eazza** *f.* galleass, large galley.

†gale-are *tr.* to deceive, to trick. **†-ato** *part. adj.* deceived, tricked. **†-atore** *m.* deceiver, trickster. **†-one** *m.* good-for-nothing, scoundrel.

galeato[1] *adj.* See under **galea**[1].

†galeato[2] *part.* of **galeare**, q.v.

galeazza *f.* (naut. hist.) galleass.

†galeffare *tr.* to mock; to trick.

galena *f.* (miner.) galena, native lead sulphide, lead glance; — falsa, black jack; (radio) apparecchio a —, crystal set.

gale·nico[1] *m.* (phys.) radioactive substance which emits negative electrons.

gale·nico[2] *adj.* See under **Galeno**.

Gal-eno *pr.n.m.* Galen; (fig.) a physician. **-e·nico** *adj.* Galenic, relating to Galen; arte -enica, medicine, medical science. **-enismo** *m.* Galenism. **-enista** *m.* Galenist.

galeone[1] *m.* (naut. hist.) galleon.

†galeone[2] *m.* See under **galeare**.

galeop·si(de) *f.* (bot.) hemp nettle, *Galeopsis*.

†galeoto *m.* See **galeotto**, under **galeotta**.

galeott-a *f.* (naut.) galliot, small galley. **-o** *m.* galley-slave, rower; da -o a marinaio, as between two evenly matched rogues; convict, jailbird; scoundrel; †pilot.

Galeotto[1] *pr.n.m.* Galahad; Galleot, Galehalt; (fig.) pander, go-between, pimp.

galeotto[2] *m.* See under **galeotta**.

galera *f.* galley; convict prison; andare in —, to go to prison, (fig.) to end up badly; avanzo da — pezzo da —, scoundrel; si comincia così, si finisce in —!, this sort of thing will land you in prison; (fig.) vita di —, life of drudgery.

galer-o *m.* (Rom. antiq.) *galerus*, head-dress of *flamen dialis*; (Rom. antiq.) women's false hair; (myth.) Mercury's cap; (eccl.) bishop's or cardinal's hat; sailor's or countryman's round cap, beret. **-i·culo** *m. dim.* (Rom. antiq.) small leather cap.

galeropi·a *f.* (med.) optical defect which makes it easier to see in dim light.

galeruca *f.* (ent.) various species of chrysomelid beetle, pests of crops.

galestr-o *m.* (geol.) marl; (geog. Emilia) unstable flaky clay. **-ino** *adj.* containing marl. **-oso** *adj.* containing marl.

ga·letra *f.* (orn.) kittiwake, *Rissa tridactyla*.

galettam-e *m.* (silkb.) spoiled cocoon, galetta. **-ino** *m.* (silkb.) husks.

galiga·io *m.* leather dresser.

†galigare *intr.* to grow misty, to become obscured.

Galil-e·a *pr.n.f.* (geog.) Galilee; il lago di —, the Sea of Galilee. **-e·o** *adj.*, *n.m.* Galilean.

galileo[1] *adj.*, *n.m.* See under **Galilea**.

Galile-o[2] *pr.n.m.* Galileo. **-iano** *adj.* Galilean, pertaining to Galileo. **-ismo** *m.* the doctrines of Galileo.

†galione *m.* See **galeone**.

†galiosso *m.* ninepin; skittle; giuoco dei galiossi, game of ninepins; skittles.

galiotto *m.* (ichth.) *Fierasfer acus*, a parasitic fish.

Gali·zi-a *pr.n.f.* (geog.) Galicia. **-ano** *adj.*, *n.m.* Galician.

galla[1] *pr.n.m.* Galla, a tribe in Abyssinia.

gall-a[2] *f.* (bot.) gall, — della quercia, oak-apple, oak-gall; — del cipresso, cone of cypress tree; — moscata, nutmeg; gall in the skin, esp. of horses; air-bubble, in glass, etc.; blister; any very light object; frivolous person, inconstant person; a —, floating on the surface, afloat; venire a —, to come to the surface, to come to the forefront, (of a diver) to surface; stare a —, to keep one's head above water (also fig.); pill. **-are** [A I] *intr.* (*aux.* avere) to float.

gallare[1] [A I]. See under **galla**[2].

gall-are[2] [A I] *tr.* to fertilize (an egg); *intr.* (*aux.* essere) to become fertilized (of an egg). **-ato** *part. adj.* fertilized, fertile. **-atura** *f.* fertilization, fertilizing (of an egg).

gallastrone *m.* big cockerel, or one imperfectly caponized.

gallato[1] *part.* of **gallare**[2], q.v.

gallato[2] *m.* (chem.) gallate.

galleggi-are [A3c] *intr.* (*aux.* avere) to float; to keep afloat; to remain on the surface; to hover; to lie lightly on the top; (of the stomach) to rise, to heave. **-a·bile** *adj.* buoyant. **-abilità** *f.* buoyancy; (naut.) riserva di -abilità, reserve of buoyancy. **-amento** *m.* floating; buoyancy; flotage; flotation; (naut.) linea di -amento, waterline; -amento di stomaco, sickness, nausea. **-ante** *part. adj.* floating; ghiaccio -ante, iceberg; (leg.) gli edifici -anti reputati immobili, floating buildings deemed real property (C.C.); *n.m.* float (e.g. of seaplane, a ball-cock, etc.); large raft, pontoon; marker buoy; trattato dei -anti, hydrostatics; (aeron.) -ante luminoso, float light.

galleri·a *f.* gallery; arcade; art gallery; (railway) tunnel; subway; — del vento, — aerodinamica, wind tunnel.

gallerone *m.* large cockerel, or cockerel imperfectly caponized.

gallesco *adj.* See under **gallo**[1].

Gal·les *pr.n.m.* (geog.) Wales; il paese di —, Wales; il principe di —, the Prince of Wales; tessuto principe di —, worsted of Glenurquhart pattern.

gallese *adj.* Welsh; *n.m.* Welshman; the Welsh language, Welsh; *f.* Welshwoman, Welsh girl.

galletta[1] *f.* a kind of gold-work in little balls; a variety of grape, as called from its shape resembling that of a fowl's kidneys; cocoon; *pl.* tumours in a horse.

gallett-a[2] *f.*, **-ista** *m.* (naut.) hard tack, ship's biscuit; water biscuit, cracker; — dietetica, starch-reduced, slimming biscuit.

galletta·io *m.* See under **galletto**.

gallettane *m.* (text) shoddy.

galletto[1] *m. dim.* See under **gallo**[2].

gallett-o[2] *m.* (agric.) uva —, a kind of grape with long pointed pips; fagioli —, a large-sized variety of kidney bean; (cul.) a kind of fried 'pasta'; (eng.) thumb-nut; wing-nut; cock of a tap. **-a·io** *m.* seller of fried 'pasta'.

Gal·lia *pr.n.f.* (hist. geog.) Gaul.

galliambo *adj.*, *n.m.* (prosod.) galliambic.

gal·lica *f.* (techn.) drill driven by a piece of string.

gallican-o *adj.*, *n.m.* (eccl.) Gallican. **-ismo** *m.* (eccl. hist.) Gallicanism.

†gallici·nio *m.* dawn, cock-crow.

gal·lic-o[1] *adj.* Gallic, French; (zool.) cane —, a kind of setter (dog); lue -a, morbo —, virulenza -a, venereal disease, syphilis; †trivella -a, see **gallica**; *n.m.* Gaul. **-amente** *adv.* in the French manner. **-ismo** *m.* Gallicism. **-izzare** [A I] *intr.* (*aux.* avere) to adopt Gallicisms; to follow French habits; *tr.* to Gallicize. **-ume** *m.* Frenchified manners.

gal·lico[2] *adj.* (chem.) gallic.

galligiambo *adj.*, *n.m.* (prosod.). See **galliambo**.

gallin-a *f.* (orn.) domestic fowl, hen; (cul.) carne di —, chicken; latte di —, egg-flip, (fig.) unobtainable delicacy; pelle di —, goose-flesh; giuoco delle -e, illicit lottery; andare a -e, to be ruined, to die; raspatura di —, illegible handwriting, scrawl; (provb.) — vecchia fa buon brodo, (an old saw quoted in praising the charms of an elderly woman); la — che canta ha fatto l'uovo, qui s'excuse, s'accuse; meglio l'uovo oggi che la — domani, a bird in the hand is worth two in the bush; (Tusc.) — mugellese,

gallin-a (*cont.*)
campa tre anni e mostra un mese (said of a woman who looks young but isn't); — della Madonna, swallow; — faraona, guinea-fowl; — prataiola, little bustard, *Otis tetrax*; (bot.) morso di —, chickweed. -**ac·cio** *adj.* (orn.) gallinaceous; *n.m.* (orn.) turkey; (bot.) chanterelle (fungus or mushroom), *Cantharellus cibarius*; goosefoot, *Chenopodium*. -**a·cei** *m.pl.* (orn.) galliformes. -**a·ia** *f.*, -**a·io** *m.* poultry keeper; †poultry thief. -**ame** *m.* poultry. -**ella** *f.* (pop.) young hen, pullet; (orn.) waterhen, esp. water rail, *Rallus aquaticus*; woodcock; — d'acqua, moorhen; — palustre piccola, little crake; — terrestre, corncrake; (bot.) lesser snapdragon, *Antirrhinum orontium*; chickweed, *Stellaria media*; (ichth.) — di mare, gurnard, *Trigla* spp.; *pl.* (astron., pop.) le sette Gallinelle, the Pleiades. -**etta** *f. dim.* of **gallina**; (ent.) -etta della Vergine, ladybird, *Coccinella* spp.

gal·lio *m.* (chem.) gallium.

gallione *m.* imperfectly caponized fowl; (fig.) clumsy lout.

gallismo *m.* characteristic behaviour of S. Italian and Sicilian males consisting of being preoccupied with the opposite sex and boasting of sexual success and prowess (cf. **gallo²**).

gallispano *m.* See gall(o)ispano, under **gallo¹**.

gallizz-ante *adj.* Frenchified. -**ato** *adj.* Gallicized.

gall-o¹ *adj.* Gallic; *n.m.* Gaul; Frenchman; (hist. rel.) priest of Cybele. -**oba·varo** *adj.*, *n.m.* Franco-Bavarian. -**ocor·sico** *adj.*, *n.m.* Franco-Corsican. -**esco** *adj.* (*m.pl.* -**eschi**) Frenchified. -**ofili·a** *f.* Gallophilism, Gallomania. -**o·filo** *m.* Francophile, lover of the French. -**ofobi·a** *f.* Francophobia. -**o·fobo** *m.* Francophobe, hater of the French. -**ogreco** *m.* Galatian. -(**o**)**ispano** *m.* Celt-iberian. -**oli·gure** *m.* Gallo-Ligurian. -**omani·a** *f.* Francomania. -**o·mane** *m.* Francomaniac. -**oromano** *adj.* Gallo-Roman. -**osardo** *adj.*, *n.m.* Franco-Sardinian. -**ume** *m.* objectionable French customs.

gall-o² *m.* (orn.) cock; weathercock; il canto del —, cockcrow; fare il —, to be cocksure (esp. in relation to women); camminare a —, to strut; un passo di —, a short distance; il — di Monna Flora, il — della Checca, the only man among a crowd of women, lady-killer; — banchiva, jungle fowl, *Gallus bankiva*; — cedrone, capercaillie; — d'India, turkey; — di monte, black grouse; (boxing) peso —, bantam-weight. -**etto** *m. dim.* cockerel, young cock, bantam; fare il -etto, to be cocky, *or* to play the gallant; (orn.) -etto di bosco, waxwing; -etto di maggio, -etto di marzo, -etto di montagna, hoopoe.

galloc·cia *f.* (naut.) belaying cleat.

gallon-e¹ *m.* (text.) galloon, lace, braid; chevron; *pl.* (mil.) stripes; guadagnarsi i -i, to obtain promotion, to be promoted. -**a·io** *m.* lace-seller, lace-maker. -**are** [A I C] *tr.* to trim with lace or braid; to decorate (with stripes). -**ata** *f.* (ent.) lappet moth, *Gastropacha neustria*. -**ato** *part. adj.* braided; decorated; striped. -**cino** *m. dim.* narrow braid, piping.

gallone² *m.* gallon.

gallone³ *m. augm.* of **gallo²**, q.v., or of **galla²**, q.v.

†**gallone⁴** *m.* side; hip-bone; sheath for a sword; avere molti anni in sul —, to be getting on in years.

†**gallop·p(ol)a** *f.* croup (part of a horse).

gallori-a *f.* mirth; revelry, noisy merrymaking, merriment. -**are** [A 4] *intr.* (*aux.* avere) to indulge in noisy merriment, to revel, to make merry; (if a baby) to crow with delight.

gallozza *f.* See **galozzola**.

galloz·zol-a *f.* oak-apple; bubble; blister; pimple. -**oso** *adj.* blistered; pimply. -**uto** *adj.* bubble-shaped.

Gal·lule *pr.n.f.pl.* (astron.) the Pleiades.

gallume *m.* See under **gallo¹**.

galluto *adj.* (naut.) with lofty stem and stern.

†**gallu·zia** *f.* affected smirking woman.

†**galluzza** *f.* See **gallozzola**.

galluzzare [A I] *intr.* (*aux.* avere) to be merry; to make merry, to revel.

galopp-are [A I] *intr.* (*aux.* avere) (equit.) to canter; — a tutta forza, to gallop; — sul tappeto, to gallop flat out; (fig., and imprecisely) to gallop; il cavaliere partì galoppa galoppa e arrivò al castello, the knight went on his way, and rode on and on till he came to the castle. -**ante** *part. adj.* galloping; tisi -ante, galloping consumption; (mil. hist.) al —!, at the gallop!, charge! -**ata** *f.* (equit.) canter; (fig., and imprecisely) gallop. -**atoio** *m.* ride; riding-track. -**atore** *m.* galloper. (-**atora** *f.* -**atrice** *f.*) -**ino** *m.* errand boy;

messenger; (Tusc.) priest who goes round in search of masses to say; canvasser; (eng.) guide pulley; jockey pulley.

galoppo *m.* (equit.) canter; gran —, gallop; al —, at the gallop, very fast; (mus.) galop.

galo·scia *f.* galosh, rubber over-shoe.

galtella *f.* (naut.) cheek of a mast.

†**galuppo** *m.* (mil. hist.) soldier, baggage-bearer; low, abject individual.

galva·n·ico *adj.* galvanic. -**icamente** *adv.* galvanically. -**ismo** *m.* galvanism. -**izzamento** *m.* galvanizing, electrifying; galvanization. -**izzare** [A I] *tr.* to galvanize; (fig.) to electrify, to excite; to stimulate, to rouse. -**izzato** *part. adj.* galvanized; (fig.) electrified, excited; stimulated. -**izzatore** *m.* galvanizer. (-**izzatrice** *f.*) -**izzazione** *f.* galvanization.

galvan-o *m.* (typ.) galvanograph; electrotype. -**oca·ustica** *f.* galvano-cautery. (-**oca·ustico** *adj.*) -**ocaute·rio** *m.* apparatus for galvano-cautery. -**ocera·mica** *f.* pottery electrically coated with a layer of copper. -**ocromi·a** *f.* the colouring of metals by electric process, oxidation. -**odoratura** *f.* gold-plating. -**oglifi·a** *f.* (typ.) a block-making process. -**ografi·a** *f.* (typ.) galvanography. -**ogra·fico** *adj.* galvanographic. -**omagnetismo** *m.* electro-magnetism. -**ome·trico** *adj.* galvanometric. -**o·metro** *m.* galvanometer; (electr.) -ometro a filo teso, string galvanometer. -**opla·stica** *f.* electro-plating, galvanoplasty. -**opla·stico** *adj.* electro-plated, galvano-plastic. -**opuntura** *f.* (med.) galvano-puncture. -**osco·pio** *m.* (electr.) galvanoscope, rheoscope. -**ostegi·a** *f.* electro-plating. -**otec·nica** *f.* the technical application of electricity. -**oterapi·a** *f.* galvano-therapeutics, electro-therapy. -**otipi·a** *f.* electric block-making process. -**oti·pico** *adj.* pertaining to electric block-making. -**otropismo** *m.* galvanotropism.

gamarra *f.* See **camarra**.

ga·maso *m.* (zool.) a parasitic acarine mite, *Gamasus* spp.

gamb-a *f.* leg; shank; (butcher.) leg; (di) sotto —, lightly without due reflection; prendere una cosa (di) sotto —, to take a thing lightly, to attach no importance to a thing; prendere qualcuno di sotto —, to ride rough-shod over someone; fare il passo secondo la —, to cut one's coat according to one's cloth; fare il passo più lungo della —, to bite off more than one can chew (esp. as regards expense); mettere i bastoni tra le -e, to put a spoke in the wheel; mettersi la via tra le -e, to go away; a -e, on foot; a -e larghe, with legs apart; sgranchirsi le -e, to stretch one's legs; la bugia ha le -e corte, be sure the truth will find you out; mettersi tra le -e di alcuno, to get in someone's way, to get under someone's feet; a —, di buone -e, quickly, running; correre con dieci -e, to hasten eagerly; cavarci le -e, to get out of a difficulty; (provb.) chi non ha testa abbia -e, if you don't think in advance you will have to work all the harder; dare alle -e a, to hinder, to oppose; levare le -e da una cosa, to get over something; pigliar le -e, to take to one's heels; darsela a -e, to bolt, to run away; mettere le -e in spalla, scappare a -e levate, to run away as fast as possible; mandare uno a -e levate, to trip someone up, (fig.) to upset someone; mandare a -e all'aria, to ruin (esp. a plan); sentirsi bene in —, to feel on top of the world; una persona in —, a competent person, a smart, clever individual; essere in —, to be quick off the mark, to be bright, to be able, to be good (at something), to be active, to be in good health, (of an elderly person) to have all one's faculties, to have one's wits about one, to be young for one's age, to be active for one's age; in — il vecchio!, remarkable old boy!, the old boy is very spry!; essere una buona —, to be a good walker; rimettersi in -e, to pick up (e.g. after an illness); a -e levate, a -e in aria, ruined; (slang) distendere le -e, stirare le -e, 'to turn up one's toes', to die; sentirsi male in -e, to feel that one is in danger; raddrizzare le -e ai cani, to attempt the impossible, to be quixotic, to be a busybody, to be a misguided idealist; non aver -e, to be tired; aver -a, to be good at, to be clever at; fare le -e a, to support; a mezza —, knee-length, calf-length; pantaloni a mezza —, knee-breeches; il fango gli arrivava a mezza —, the mud came up to his calves; vinestock; stem of a letter, number or note; (mus.) stem (of a note); — doppia, unison (indicated by a two-stemmed note); viola da —, bass viol; (organ) viola da gamba. -**acorta** *m. indecl.* lame person; (provb.) l'ultimo a comparir fu -acorta, better late than never. -**ale** *m.* leg of a boot; legging; (mil. hist.) greave; boot tree; splint; (bot.) stem of a plant. -**aletto** *m.* half-stocking, stocking coming to the knee, half-hose. -**armato** *adj.* (poet.)

gamb-a (*cont.*)

greaved. †**-aruolo** *m.* see **gamberuolo**. **-ata** *f.* kick with the leg; dar la **-ata**, to marry someone engaged to someone else. **-ato** *adj.* (mus., organ) registri **-ati**, string-toned stops. †**-atura** *f.* (naut.) dog leg of a cable. **-erǫne** *m.* leg with varicose veins; long-legged person, long-shanks. **-eruolo** *m.* (mil. hist.) greave. **-ǫne** *m. augm.* of **gamba**; large leg; large stem; †pride, arrogance, licence; †stare al **-ǫne** di, to rival.

gam·baro *m.* (zool.). See **gambero**.

gambęc-chio *m.* (*pl.* **-chi**) (orn.) little stint, *Calidris minuta*; — frullino, broad-billed sandpiper, *Limicola falcinellus*; — nano, Temminck's stint, *Calidris temminckii*.

gam·ber-o *m.* (pop.) lobster; (zool.) — fluviale, — di fiume, crayfish, *Potamobius pallipes*, *P. astacus* and *P. torientium*; — marino, lobster, *Homarus vulgaris*; — delle rocce, prawn, *Leander serratus*; — imperiale, *Penaeus kerathurus*, a large species of prawn; — sega, prawn, *Leander serratus* and *L. squilla*; (fig.) far il viaggio del —, to go backwards. **-ella** *f. dim.* (zool.) **-ella** notturna, *Nika edulis*. **-ello** *m. dim.* small shrimp. **-ettino** *m. dim.* (pop.) shrimp. **-ętto** *m. dim.* (zool.) **-etto** grigio, common shrimp, *Crangon vulgaris*; **-etto** d'acqua dolce, *Palaemonetes varians*. **-ǫne** *m. augm.* (zool.) large shrimp, lobster, etc.

gambętt-a *f. dim.* of **gamba**, q.v.; (joc.) giocar di —, to dance, to kick; (orn.) ruff, reeve, *Philomachus pugnax*; — americana, upland sandpiper, *Bartramia longicauda*; — fosca, dusky redshank, *Tringa erythropus*; — reale, greenshank. **-are** [A I C] *intr.* (*aux.* avere) to wave one's legs about; to prance, to skip and leap; to gambol, to frolic.

gambier-a *f.* (mil. hist.) greave, leg-guard; †channel or conduit, shaped like a greave. **-ato** *adj.* greaved, wearing a leg-guard. **-o** *m.* see **gambiera**.

gambir *m. indecl.* (tanning) gambier.

gambitto *m.* (chess) gambit.

gamb-o *m.* stalk, stem; shaft, haft; shank; stroke of a letter; tail of a letter. **-ętto** *m. dim.*; little stem, slender stalk; dare il **-etto** a, to trip up; (chess) gambit; (zool.) **-etto** di sabbia, common shrimp, *Crangon vulgaris*.

gambriniṣmo *m.* excessive indulgence in beer; the pathological consequences of excessive beer-drinking (from Gambrinus, the legendary Germanic king, said to have invented beer).

gambuto *adj.* long-legged, spindle-shanked.

game·lio *adj.* bridal, nuptial.

gamell-a *f.* mess-tin; mangiare alla —, to be soldiering; venire dalla —, to rise from the ranks. **-ino** *m.* billy-can.

gamet-e *m.* (biol.) gamete, sex cells. **-ocito** *m.* (biol.) gametocyte. **-ogeneṣi** *f. indecl.* (biol.) gametogenesis.

gamma *m.* the Greek letter Γ; *m.*, *f.* (photog.) gamma, Γ; (mus.) gamma, Γ ut, gamut (i.e. G, the lowest note of the lowest hexachord); scale; (paint.) grades of colour, range of tints (of a particular colour); (radio) — di sintonia, tuning band; (fig.) gamut, range; — di sentimenti, range of emotions; (comm.) — di prodotti, range of products.

gam·maro *m.* (zool.) *Gammarus* spp., a genus of small crustaceans.

gammato *adj.* shaped like a gamma; croce gammata, swastika.

gammau·t(te) *m. indecl.* (surg.) bistoury; (mus.) gamut, scale.

gamo-logi·a *f.* the study of marriage. **-mani·a** *f.* gamomania.

gamurra *f.* a form of gown formerly worn by women; a kind of cloth.

Gana[1] *pr.n.f.* (geog.) Ghana.

†**gana**[2] *f.* desire; di —, willingly, eagerly; di mala —, unwillingly, reluctantly.

gana·sc-ia *f.* jaw; jowl; dente o —, no matter what the cost; carico di —, heavy-jowled; mangiare a doppie **-e**, to eat heartily, (fig.) to make large profits; (eng.) shoe; (rlwy.) fish-plate, splice bar. **-ino** *m. dim.* cheek; chin; pigliare pel **-ino**, to take the chin (e.g. of a child or young girl) between finger and thumb (a gesture of affection or familiar gallantry). **-iǫne** *m. augm.* large heavy jowl; slap.

gan·c-io *m.* hook; (eng.) chiave a —, hook wrench; al —, on the hook; mettere un — alla gola, to force, to hold a pistol to the head of; scribble, badly-formed letter; †booty; †thief. **-èr** *m. indecl.* (Ven.) man who secures a gondola by means of a long hook and helps the passenger out on to a landing-stage. **-iata** *f.* hook, act of hooking; load on a hook.

Gand *pr.n.f.* (geog.) Ghent.

ganga[1] *f.* (miner.) gangue, the matrix in which an ore is found.

ganga[2] *f.* (orn.) pin-tailed sandgrouse, *Pterocles alchata*.

ganga[3] *f.* (slang) gang, mob.

gan·ga-ma *f.*, **-mo**, **-no** *m.* type of small net for fishing.

gan·gava *f.* net for catching sponges.

Gange *pr.n.f.* (geog.) River Ganges.

gangheggiare [A 3 C] *intr.* (*aux.* avere) to chafe at the bit.

gangher-are [A I S] *tr.* to set on hinges; to provide with hinges; to provide with hooks; to hinge; to hook. **-ato** *part. adj.* on hinges; hooked. **-atura** *f.* place where a hook is fastened.

gan·gher-o *m.* hook for an eye; — e gangherella, hook and eye; hinge; essere fuori dei **-i**, to be beside oneself with rage; uscir dei **-i**, to go off the deep end; fatto a **-i**, hard to please; the sudden twist made by a hare to get away from a hound that catches up with it; (fig.) elusive movement, dodge, backward turn; dare —, fare un —, to turn about. **-ella** *f.* eye for a hook. **-ello** *m. dim.* of **ganghero**; the quick swerve of a hunted hare.

ganghire [D 2] *intr.* (*aux.* avere) to fret; to be in a state of longing.

gan·gl-io *m.* (anat.) ganglion; (fig.) nerve-centre. **-iforme** *adj.* (anat.) gangliform. **-iocito** *m.* (biol.) gangliocyte. **-ioma** *f.* (med.) tumour on the lymphatic glands. **-ionare**, **-onico** *adj.* ganglionic. **-onite** *f.* (med.) adenitis.

gan·gol-a *f.* (pop.) swollen gland in the neck; swollen tonsil; scar on the neck; spot of disease in the liver of an animal; ulcer under the tongue; canker; (fig.) far **-e**, to show spite. **-ǫso** *adj.* having swollen glands; cankerous.

gangrena *f.* See **cancrena**.

Ganimede *pr.n.m.* (myth.) Ganymede; handsome and vain young man; fop; dandy, beau; (joc.) waiter; (alchem.) white sulphur or sublimed mercurous chloride.

ganisto *m.* (miner.) ganister.

gannire [D 2] *intr.* (*aux.* avere) to whimper, to whine.

ganẓ-a *f.* (vulg.) mistress, paramour; (naut.) loop of rope; †three-cornered hat. **-are** [A I] *intr.* (*aux.* avere) to indulge in an illicit love affair; †to treat, to pay for, to treat to. **-ata** *f.* (Tusc.) clever action, smart trick. **-erino** *m.* dandy. **-o** *m.* lover, paramour; (Tusc.) a smart one, a sly individual; *adj.* extraordinary, amazing; ingenious.

gappista *m.* (Ital. hist.) member of the Gruppo Azione Patriottica, a small clandestine anti-Fascist, anti-Nazi formation specializing in sabotage (1943–5).

gara *f.* rivalry; match, competition, race; a —, for a wager; fare a —, andare a —, to compete, to race, to vie; (sport) race; contest; — libera, open event; — a vantaggi, handicap event; — eliminatoria, heat; (techn.; comm.) tender; †pigliare —, to compete; †pigliare in — una cosa, to attack a thing obstinately.

garabat·tole *f.pl.* See **carabattole**.

†**garabullare** *tr.* to deceive, to trick.

garag-e *m.* (pron. as Fr.) garage. **-ista** *m.* garage proprietor; garage hand.

†**garagoll-are** *vb.* and derivs. see **caracollare**. †**-o** *m.* see **caracollo**.

garamǫn-e *m.* (typ.) bourgeois type of 10 points. **-cino** *m. dim.* (typ.) bourgeois type of 9 points.

garante *m.* (leg.) guarantor; — in solido, surety jointly and severally liable; rendersi —, to act as guarantor; me ne rendo —, I'll answer for it; essere — verso qualcuno per qualche cosa, to pledge oneself to someone for something; (econ.; finan.) guarantor; *adj.* vouching, guaranteeing, warranting.

garant-ire [D 2] *tr.* (leg.) to guarantee; to stand as surety on behalf of; to warrant; — da, to be a sure defence against. (**-ito** *part. adj.*)

garanz-a *f.* (bot.) madder, *Rubia tinctorum*; (chem.) garancin, madder. **-are** [A I] *tr.* to dye with madder. **-ato** *part. adj.* dyed with madder. **-ina** *f.* (chem.) garancin. **-ǫso** *m.* extract of madder.

garanzi·a *f.* (econ.; finan.; leg.) guarantee; security; — reale, security on property; dare — a, to guarantee; atto di —, security bond; chiamata in —, call on, notice to, guarantor to pay; — ipotecaria, mortgage security; security by way of mortgage (C.C.).

garavina *f.* (orn.) gull.

garavog·giolo *m.* piece of wood or rag or paper round which a ball of wool is wound; spool, reel.

garba *f.* flour sieve.

garbac·cio *m. pejor.* See under **garbo**.

garb-are [A I] *intr.* (*aux.* essere, avere; *prep.* a) to suit, to be becoming to, to please; *tr.* to give form to, to shape. **-atęzza** *f.* politeness,

garb-are (*cont.*)
agreeableness; geniality; urbanity (of style); polish. **-ato** *part. adj.* formed, shaped; agreeable; well-mannered, polite, civil; graceful; (of work) in good taste, elegant, fine; congenial. **-atamente** *adv.* politely. **-atone** *adj.* (iron.) pleasing (applied to a person who is quite otherwise). **-eggiare** [A 3 c] *intr.* (*aux.* avere; *prep.* a) to please; *tr.* to beautify; (paint.) -eggiare un colore, to graduate a colour.

garbino *m.* south-west wind.

garb-o¹ *m.* good manners, courtesy; charm; con —, politely, graciously, gracefully; a —, well-mannered, pleasing, agreeable; di —, good, honest, loyal; grace, harmony of line or form; good cut of clothes (esp. sufficient fullness); qui mi pare un po' stretto, gli darei un po' più di — intorno ai fianchi, it seems rather tight here, I'd make it a bit fuller over the hip-line; legname di —, wood which already in the rough state has the required curve for the work in question; prendere il —, to take shape; gesture, sign, movement; (naut.) line, model; lines of a ship; drawing office; template, mock-up; sala dei -i, exhibition of all the models of ships of times past; medium-sized Levantine sailing vessel; pleasing taste; suitability. **-ac·cio** *m. pejor.* incivility, rudeness; bad manners.

garbo² *adj.* sour; harsh; bitter.

†Garbo³ *pr.n.m.* (hist. geog.) Garb (Algarve), a region of N. Africa; lana di —, wool from Garb; panni di —, cloth from Garb; tessuto di —, woven material of wool and linen; (Ven.) tempo al —, temperature tending to fall; †(naut.) Sicilian and N. African craft.

garbu·gli-o *m.* tangle, confusion; mix-up, disorder; turmoil; agitation. **-one** *m.* muddler.

garde-enfant *m. indecl.* (pron. as Fr.) a quilted silk sleeping bag for an infant. (The expression does not exist in French but was coined by Milanese or sub-Alpine speakers.)

garde·nia *f.* (bot.) gardenia, Cape jasmine, *Gardenia jasminoides.*

gareggi-are [A 3 c] *intr.* (*aux.* avere) to vie, to compete, to race, to contend; †*tr.* to compete with, to rival; †*rfl.* to compete with one another. **-amento** *m.* race; competition; vying, contending, rivalry. **-ante** *part. adj.* competing, contending; *n.m.* rival, competitor.

gareggio *m.* long drawn-out competition, constant vying.

garenna *f.* rabbit-warren.

garetta *f.* See **garitta**.

garetto *m.* See **garretto**.

†gargali-are *intr.* to rumble, to mumble, to mutter. **†-ata** *f.* rumbling, mumbling, muttering.

garganell-a *f.* gurgling sound; bere a —, to drink straight out of the bottle, to gulp down, to guzzle; (orn.) — marmorizzata, marbled duck, *Anas angustirostris.* **-o** *m.* (orn.) goosander, teal, garganey.

†gargant-e *m.* (mus.) throat; cantare di —, to trill, to shake. **†-i·glia** *f.* necklace.

gargantues·co *adj.* (*m.pl.* **-chi**) gargantuan; voracious.

gargar-ismo *m.* gargle; gargling; (mus.) trilling, shaking, warbling (always in pejor. sense). **-izzare** [A 1] *tr., intr.* (*aux.* avere) to gargle; (mus.) to trill, to shake, to warble (always in pejor. sense).

gargarozzo *m.* (vulg.) throat, gullet.

gar·gia *f.* (zool.) gill.

†gargo *adj.* crafty.

garg-olla *f.* **-u·glia** *f.* gargoyle.

gargotta *f.* cook-shop, eating-house, third-rate restaurant, chop-house.

garibaldiano *m.* See **garibaldino**.

garibald-ino *adj.* (hist.) pertaining to Garibaldi; worthy of Garibaldi; (fig.) audacious, gallant; alla -ina, gallantly, dashingly, impetuously, without proper preparation; *n.m.* follower of Garibaldi. **-ismo** *m.* impetuous dashing gallantry, enthusiasm, undisciplined and improvised daring (the Italian characteristics which Garibaldi put to use). **-ista** *m.* supporter of Garibaldi; *adj.* in favour of Garibaldi.

gari·glio *m.* See **gheriglio**.

gariglione *m.* See **cariglione**.

Garisenda *pr.n.f.* name of a famous tower at Bologna.

garitta *f.* look-out tower or post; sentry-box; workman's hut (esp. on the railway); (naut.) oak or elm strips protecting a bulwark or strengthening a crow's nest.

garnierite *f.* (miner.) garnierite.

garo·fana *f.* (agric.) an October variety of pear.

garofanata *f.* (bot.) herb bennet, avens, *Geum urbanum.*

garo·fan-o *m.* (bot.) clove, i.e. dried flower-bud of clove tree, *Sysygium aromaticum*; (cul.) chiodi di —, cloves; (pharm.) essenza di —, oil of cloves; (bot.) clove pink, carnation, *Dianthus caryophyllus* and other species of *Dianthus*; — indiano, so-called African marigold, *Tagetes erecta*; (zool.) — di mare, sea anemone. **-are** [A 1 s] *tr.* (cul.) to flavour with cloves. **-ato** *part. adj.* clove-scented; (cul.) flavoured with cloves; (bot.) viola -ata, clove-pink, *Dianthus caryophyllus.* **-ini** *m.pl.* (bot., pop.) pinks.

Garonna *pr.n.f.* (geog.) River Garonne.

garontol-o *m.* (vulg.) punch, clout, biff. **-are** [A 1 sc] *tr.* (vulg.) to clout, to biff.

garo·pera *f.* (naut.) Brazilian fishing vessel.

garosello *m.* See **carosello**.

†garoso *adj.* contentious.

†garrare *vb.* and derivs. See **garrire**.

garrese *m.* withers.

garretto *m.* back of the heel; (of a horse) pastern, hock, fetlock; (fig., of an athlete) calf, strength of leg.

garr-ire [D 2] *intr.* (*aux.* avere) to utter shrill cries; to shriek; to squabble; to cackle; to chirp; to screech; (poet.) to flutter, to flap (of the noise of a banner in the wind); *tr.* to speak in harsh tones to, to chide, to scold, to reproach. **-imento** *m.* twittering; cackling; chirping; screeching; chiding, scolding; squabbling. **†-issa** *f.* garrulity. **†-issa·io**, **†-issa·rio** *adj.* garrulous; chiding, scolding. **-itivo** *adj.* twittering; chiding; scolding. **-ito** *part. adj.* chidden, chided; *n.m.* twittering; scolding, chiding; screeching, squabbling. **-itore** *m.* twitterer; screecher. **-itrice** *f.* scold.

garrotta *f.* garrotte.

garrul-ante *adj.* talkative; garrulous; chattering. **-ità** *f.* garrulousness; talkative, loquacity.

gar·rulo *adj.* garrulous; talkative; *n.m.* (orn.) laughing thrush, *Garrulax*; — di Boemia, waxwing.

garz-a¹ *f.* jaw-bone of a horse. **-iero** *adj.* (of a horse) holding its head too high; andare -iero, to hold its head too high and stretched forward.

garz-a² *f.* gauze; (naut.) eye splice, rope loop, bight. **-are** [A 1] *tr.* (text.) to card, to tease out; to raise. **-ato** *part. adj.* (text.) carded, teased; raised. **-atore** *m.* carder. **-atrice** *f.* female carder; carding machine. **-atura** *f.* (text.) carding; (text.) raising. **-ella** *f.* (text.) comb for carding wool. **-eri·a** *f.* carding shop. **-etta** *f.* (naut.) reef becket. **-o** *m.* (bot.) thistle-head; teasel-head; (text.) dare il -o a, to card.

garz-a³ *f.* (orn.) heron. **-a·ia** *f.* heronry. **-etta** *f.* (orn.) egret.

garziero *adj.* See under **garza¹**.

garzi(a)gnuola *f.* (agric.) a kind of pear grown in the region of Padua.

garzo *m.* (bot.). See under **garza²**.

garzolo *m.* See **garzuolo**.

garzon-a *f.* female worker, female hand (usu. in a farmhouse). **†-etta** *f.* young girl.

garzon-e *m.* boy, boy in service; farm-boy; shop-boy; errand-boy; — del fornaio, baker's boy; — del macellaio, butcher's boy; apprentice; †young man; †young bachelor. **-astro** *m. pejor.* unpleasant boy. **-ato** *m.* apprenticeship. **-cello** *m. dim.* youth; shop-boy. **-cino** *m. dim.* youngster. **-eggiare** [A 3 c] *intr.* (*aux.* avere) to be adolescent, to become adolescent. **†-ezza** *f.* young manhood.

garzuolo *m.* carded hemp fibre of the best quality; irregular piece of wax produced during refining in hot water; heart of a cabbage, lettuce, etc.

gas *m. indecl.* gas; becco del —, gas-burner; contatore del —, gas-meter; fornello a —, gas-cooker, gas-stove, gas-oven; motore a —, gas-engine; radiatore a —, gas-fire; tubo del —, gas-pipe; turbina a —, gas-turbine; officina del —, gas-works; luce del —, gas-light; illuminazione a —, gas-lighting; maschera contro i — asfissianti, gas-mask; Società del —, Gas Company; — esilarante, laughing gas; camera a —, gas-chamber; — asfissiante, poison gas; (motor.) petrol; pedale del —, accelerator; a tutto —, with open throttle, at full speed; fare —, to fill up the tank.

gas-are [A 1] *tr.* to aerate, to charge with gas; (text.) to singe. **-atura** *f.* (text.) singeing.

gasbeton *m. indecl.* (bldg.) gas concrete, porous concrete.

gaschetto *m.* gasket.

gasdotto m. gas-pipe.

gasindo m. (hist.) free servant of a prince in the Middle Ages, esp. in Lombardy.

gasista m. See **gassista**.

†**gaso** m. a stitch in needlework; (Ven.) backstitch.

gas·olina f. gasoline, petrol. -**o·lio** m. gasoil.

gaso·metro m. See **gassometro**, under **gassaiuolo**.

gasoso adj. See **gassoso**, under **gassaiuolo**.

gassa f. (naut.) eye (round loop); — impiombata, eye splice; — d'amante semplice, bowline; — d'amante, bowline upon the bight; — con mezzo parlato, bowline hitch; — a serraglio e mezzo collo, timber hitch.

gass-ai(u)olo m. see **gassista**. -**are** [A I] tr. to gas. -**ato** part. adj. gassed. -**ista** m. gas-worker, gas-man, gas-fitter; man who comes to read the gas-meter; †lamp-lighter. -**ochi·mica** f. gas chemistry. -**o·geno** m. gas-producer; gas-generator; gazogene. -**ometri·a** f. gasometry. -**o·metro** m. gas-holder, gas-container; gasometer. -**osa** f. soda-water; carbonated drink, fizzy drink. -**oso** adj. gassy, gaseous, fizzy, aerated.

gastaldo m. See **castaldo**.

gastaurello m. (ichth.) saury pike, *Scomberesox saurus*.

gastero·podo m. (zool.) gastropod.

gasterotomi·a f. (surg.) gastrotomy.

gastigare [A 2] and derivs. See **castigare**.

Gastone pr.n.m. Gaston.

gastr-algi·a f. (med.) gastralgia, pain in the stomach. -**al·gico** adj. gastralgic. -**ectasi·a** f. see **gastroectasia**. -**ectomi·a** f. (surg.) gastrectomy, gastric resection. -**elci·a** f. (med.) ulceration of stomach. -**ente·rico** adj. (anat.) gastro-intestinal, gastro-enteric. -**enterite** f. (med.) gastro-enteritis. -**i·loquo** m. gastroloquist, ventriloquist. -**imargi·a** f. gluttony, intemperate eating. -**ite** f. gastritis. -**ocele** m. gastrocoele, hernia of the stomach. -**ochena** f. (zool.) *Gastrochaena* sp., a marine mollusc found boring in rocks. -**ocne·mio** m. (anat.) gastrocnemius, calf-muscle. -**oectasi·a** f. dilatation of the stomach. -**oente·rico** adj. gastro-enteric. -**oenterite** f. gastro-enteritis. -**oenterocolite** f. gastro-enteritic colitis. -**oenterostomi·a** f. (surg.) gastro-enterostomy, making a link between the stomach and the intestine when the pylorus is obstructed. -**epa·tico** adj. gastro-hepatic. -**epatite** f. gastric hepatitis, gastric inflammation of the liver. -**ointestinale** adj. gastro-enteric. -**ologi·a** f. gastrology, cookery, good eating, gastronomy. -**omalaci·a** f. (med.) gastromalacia, softening of the lining of the stomach. -**onomi·a** f. gastronomy. -**ono·mico** adj. gastronomic(al). -**o·nomo** m. gastronome, gourmet. -**opaca** f. (ent.) lappet moth, *Gastropaca* sp. -**o·podo** m. (zool.) see **gasteropodo**. -**optosi** f. indecl. (med.) fallen stomach. -**orragi·a** f. haemorrhage of the stomach. -**orre·a** f. (med.) morning sickness. -**oscopi·a** f. (med.) gastroscopy. -**osco·pio** m. (med.) gastroscope. -**osi** f. (med.) stomach trouble. -**ospasmo** m. stomach cramp. -**otomi·a** f. (surg.) gastrotomy.

ga·stric-a f. (med.) gastric fever. -**ismo** m. stomach trouble. -**ità** f. indecl. stomach disturbance. -**o** adj. gastric.

ga·strula f. (zool.) gastrula.

gatta f. (zool.) female cat, quean, she-cat; puss, pussy; tabby cat; (provb.) quando la — non c'è, i topi ballano, when the cat's away, the mice do play; — di Masino, sly, wily person (cf. **gattamorta**); — ci cova!, there's more in this than meets the eye, there's something in the wind; una — da pelare, an awkward job, *or* 'other fish to fry'; tanto va la — al lardo che vi lascia lo zampino, sooner or later one always gets caught; comprare la — nel sacco, to buy a pig in a poke; non portar — in sacco, to speak frankly; non bisogna dire quattro finchè la — non è nel sacco, don't count your chickens before they are hatched; — cieca, blind man's buff; (miner.; motor.) occhio di —, see under **gatto**; (bot.) erba —, cat-mint, *Nepeta cataria*.

gatta-bu·ia f. (joc.) prison, 'clink'. †-**fora**, †-**fura** f. tart, pastry. -**morta** f. indecl. (fam.) sly, wily person; fare la -morta, to feign sleep, death or indifference, to lie low; uscire di -morta, to come out into the open, to throw aside all pretence.

gatta·ia f. (bot.) See **gattaria**.

gattai(u)ola f. hole in a door for the cat; †(fig.) way out of a difficulty, remedy, device.

gattamorta f. See under **gattabuia**.

gatta·ria f. (bot.) cat-mint, *Nepeta cataria*.

gatteggi-are [A 3 c] intr. (aux. avere) to have a play of colours, like

a cat's eyes, to glisten, to glint. -**amento** m. glistening, glinting, as of a cat's eyes. -**ante** part. adj. glistening, glinting. -**esco** adj. (m.pl. -**eschi**) iridescent.

gatt-ello m. dim. of **gatto**, q.v.; kitty; (archit.) corbel. -**esco** adj. (m.pl. -**eschi**) feline, cat-like; (vulg.) andare in -esco, to go out on the tiles.

gat·tero m. (bot.). See **gattice**.

gat·tice m. (bot.) white poplar, abele, *Populus alba*.

gattic-ida m. (joc.) cat-killer. -**i·dio** m. (joc.) cat-killing.

gattigliare [A 4] intr. (aux. avere) to fight like cats.

Gattinara pr.n.f. (geog.) Gattinara, in the prov. of Novara; m. a noted red wine from that region.

gattino m. dim. See under **gatto**.

†**gattivo** adj. and derivs. See **cattivo**.

gatt-o m. cat; — maschio, male cat, tom-cat; — castrato, neuter cat; — d'Angora, Persian cat; — soriano, tabby cat; — rosso, marmalade cat; — siamese, Siamese cat; Gatto cogli Stivali, Puss-in-Boots; — selvatico, wild cat, *Felis catus*; — sardo, Sardinian wild cat, *F. ocreata*; essere come cani e -i, to fight like cat and dog; andarsene come un — frustato, to go away with one's tail between one's legs; due -i, quattro -i, very few people, 'one man and a dog'; mal —, cunning, crafty, thieving; (Bologna) c'è il — nel fuoco, a poor welcome, scant hospitality; la sera tutti i -i sono grigi (i.e. never choose women or linen by candlelight); (bot.) erba da -i, *Teucrium marum*; catkin, amentum; (zool.) — zibetto, civet cat, *Viverra civetta*; (naut.) merchant vessel used on the Baltic; hull scrubber; buco del —, lubber's hole, a hatch in the platform on a mast; †armed barge; (mil. hist.) type of battering ram on wheels, having a protecting roof (the bronze head was decorated to look like a cat); bore gauge; pile-driver; (geog.) Montagne dei -i, Kota Gora; (miner.) occhio di —, cat's-eye; (motor.) occhi di —, cat's-eye reflectors. -**ino** m. dim. of **gatto**; pussy, kitty; kitten; far -ini, to have kittens, (fig., colloq.) to be sick, to vomit; (bot.) catkin, amentum. †-**ofo·dero** m. lining of cat's fur. -**omammone** m. imaginary animal of fairy-tale or folk-lore, monstrous, terrifying cat; witch's cat; a demon in the form of a cat. -**onare** [A I c] intr. (aux. avere) to stalk; to creep stealthily. -**one** m. augm. of **gatto**; large cat; (fig.) sly, cunning person; hypocrite. -**oni** m.pl. mumps; adv. gatton -oni, crawling quietly on all fours, stealthily, stalking. -**opardo** m. (Tusc., S. Italy) see **leopardo**; (ichth.) nursehound, *Scyliorhinus stellaris*. -**uc·cio** m. (ichth.) dogfish, *S. canicula*; -uccio boccanero, black-mouthed dogfish, *Galeus melanostomus*; (carpen.) keyhole saw; compass saw.

†**gaude** m. See **gaudio**.

gaudeam-us, -**o** m. indecl. (liturg.) *Gaudeamus* (opening of festal introit); (fam.) rejoicings, jollity; stare in —, to enjoy oneself, to make merry.

gaudent-e adj. self-indulgent, pleasure-loving; Epicurean; jolly, cheerful, merry; (eccl. hist.) Frati -i, *Frati Gaudenti*, Knights of Our Lady (quasi-military order, 1262–1589); n.m. person who lives well, pleasure-loving person; epicurean. -**emente** adv. joyfully, merrily.

†**gaudere** vb. and derivs. See **godere**.

†**gaudiare** intr. to feel joy, to experience bliss (esp. spiritual).

ga·udi-o m. bliss; happiness, joy (esp. spiritual); (provb.) mal comune, mezzo —, misfortune shared is misfortune halved. -**oso** adj. joyful, joyous; (rel.) Misteri -osi (del Rosario), Joyful Mysteries (of the Rosary). -**osamente** adv. blissfully, joyfully, joyously.

ga·ulo m. a kind of drinking-bowl; (naut. hist.) merchant-ship; (orn.) bee-eater.

gaulthe·ria f. (bot.) wintergreen, *Gaultheria procumbens*.

†**gavagno** m. See **cavagno**.

gavai·na f. blacksmith's tongs.

†**gavardina** f. house-frock, indoor robe.

gavazz-a f. revelling, merry-making; revelry. -**are** [A I] intr. (aux. avere) to revel unrestrainedly, to have a riotous time. -**amento** m. merry-making, making merry. -**atore** m. merry-maker. (-**atrice** f.) -**iere** m. reveller, merry-maker.

†**gaveggiare** vb. and derivs. See **vagheggiare**.

gavello m. felloe, the exterior rim or a part of the rim of a wheel.

gavett-a[1] f. mess-tin; mess-bowl; venir dalla —, to rise from the ranks; mess, group of men (usu. 7) who mess together; square of men (usu. 7 in number), esp. of the papal guards.

gavetta² *f.* skein of cat-gut for musical instruments; gold wire as first drawn from the machine.

gaviale *m.* (zool.) gavial, a kind of Indian crocodile.

†gavign-a *f.* nape of the neck; armpit. **†-are** *tr.* to clasp round the neck; to seize, to hold fast.

†gavillare *vb.* and derivs. See **cavillare.**

gavin-a¹ *f.* (orn.) common gull, *Larus canus.* **-ello** *m.* boorish, rough person.

gavin-a² *f.* (med.) scrofulous glands in the neck, or the scars after their excision. **-oso** *adj.* suffering from scrofula.

†ga·vio *m.* See **gavolo** or **gavello.**

gavitell-o *m.* buoy, esp. that attached to the buoy-rope of an anchor; il — veglia, the buoy watching. **-one** *m. augm.* large buoy.

gavo *m.* See **gavitello.**

gavoc·ciolo *m.* lump under the skin, esp. the bubo of bubonic plague.

ga·volo *m.* felloe, exterior rim or part of the rim of a wheel; sector of any circular structure; *pl.* (Romagna) bricks set in a circle (e.g. as in a well).

gavon·chio *m.* (ichth.) a kind of marine eel.

gavone *m.* (naut.) — di prua, the narrow after or fore part of a vessel's hold, near the stem or stern; — di poppa, boatswain's store, or captain's cabin.

gavotta¹ *f.* (ichth.) a kind of gurnard, *Trigla obscura.*

gavotta² *f.* (mus.) gavotte.

gavozza *f.* dosser, a wooden scuttle of determinate capacity for feeding mineral and flux into a furnace.

gaz *m. indecl.* See **gas.**

gazofila·cio *m.* treasure-house.

gazolina *f.* gasoline.

gaz-o·metro *m.*, **-oso** *adj.* See **gassometro, gassoso,** under **gassaiuolo.**

†gazuolo *adj.* (of a horse) wall-eyed.

gazza¹ *f.* (orn.) magpie, *Pica pica;* — ghiandaia, jay; — marina, razorbill, *Alca torda,* roller; color — marina, bluish colour; — sparviera, great grey shrike; — marina minore, little auk, *Plautus alle;* (pop.) — ladra, magpie; (provb.) nido fatto, — morta, said of a man dying just as he has made his fortune; (fig.) chattering woman.

gazza² *f.* (naut.) reef-becket; see **gassa. -etta** *f. dim.* (naut.) reef-point; (fig.) battere le -ette, to be shivering with cold.

gazzarra¹ *f.* uproar, din; rejoicing; noise of quarrelling; †noise of artillery or fireworks; †hubbub of war.

gazzarra² *f.* (naut. hist.) river boat on the Po.

gazzella *f.* (zool.) gazelle.

gaz·zer-a *f.* (orn.) magpie. **-are** [A I s] *tr.* to trick, to deceive, to hoodwink. **-ino** *adj.* bluish (usu. of eyes), magpie-coloured; (bot.) pruno -ino, fire-thorn, *Pyracantha coccinea.* **-otto** *m.* chatterbox.

†gazzeri·a *f.* river boat.

gazzetta¹ *f. dim.* of **gazza²,** q.v.

gazzett-a² *f.* gazette, newspaper; journal; andare per le -e, to get talked about; cose da -e, newspaper talk; gossip; (leg.) Gazzetta Ufficiale, Official Gazette (in which new legislative acts, decrees, etc., are published). **-ante** *m.* writer to the newspapers; great reader of newspapers; spreader of news. **-iere** *m. pejor.* journalist. **-ino** *m. dim.* of **gazzetta;** news-sheet; announcements columns of a newspaper; gossip, news-bearer.

gazzetta³ *f.* (numis.) a small Venetian coin (seventeenth century); †money.

gazz-o *adj.* bluish green; *n.m.* (hist.) hat worn by the Doge of Genoa. **-ino** *adj.* bluish green. **-olino, -uolo** *adj.* (vet.) wall eye.

gazzoso *adj.* See **gassoso,** under **gassaiuolo.**

†gazzurro *m.* revelry; trick, joke; understanding, agreement.

gè *m. indecl.* (miner.) jet.

gecar·cino *m.* (zool.) land-crab.

†gecch-ire *intr.* to be humbled; to feel reverence. **†-imento** *m.* humility; reverence. **†-ito** *part. adj.* humbled; humiliated. **-itamente** *adv.* humbly; with reverence.

geco *m.* (zool.) gecko lizard.

gedanite *f.* (miner.) a variety of amber.

Geen·na *pr.n.f.* (Bibl.) Gehenna; hell.

gei·stica *f.* (geog.) the description of the continents.

gel *m. indecl.* (phys.) gel.

gelad *m. indecl.* (zool.) gelada baboon, *Theropithecus gelada.*

†gelarchi·a *f.* See **gerarchia,** under **gerarca.**

gel-are [A I] *tr.* to freeze; to chill; *rfl., intr.* (aux. essere) to freeze; (of a plant) to catch the frost; oggi si -a, it's freezing cold today;

gli si -ò il sangue nelle vene, his blood ran cold; (aux. avere) to make ice-cream; si -a!, ice-cream made here! **-amento** *m.* freezing; chilling. **-ata** *f.* frost, cold; hard frost; stanotte ci sarà una -ata, there will be a frost tonight. **-ateri·a** *f.* ice-cream shop, ice-cream parlour. **-atiera** *f.* freezer, ice-cream machine; (mil.) gelignite container. **-atiere** *m.* ice-cream merchant, ice-cream vendor. **-atificazione** *f.* gelatinization. **-atina** *f. dim.* of gelata; gelatine; jelly; isinglass; freezing mixture; (chem.) gelatin; -atina esplosiva, dynamite; (photog.) emulsion. **-atiniforme** *adj.* like gelatine. **-atinoso** *adj.* gelatinous. **-ato** *part. adj.* frozen, chilled; iced; acqua -ata, iced water; cold, frigid; (fig.) dead; congealed; *n.m.* ice-cream, ice; -ato alle fragole, strawberry ice; -ato alla vainiglia, vanilla ice; (fig., joc.) -ato da passeggio, ice-cream lolly, person who bears himself stiffly. (**-atamente** *adv.* fig.)

†geldra *f.* multitude, mob, herd, crowd.

†geleri·a *f.* jelly; gelatine.

gelici·dio *m.* (geog.) glazed frost.

ge·lid-o *adj.* cold, chilly; icy; frigid; le -e stelle, the polar constellations. **-amente** *adv.* coldly; icily; frigidly. **-ezza** *f.* coldness, frigidity.

†gelifalco *m.* firearm.

gelivo *adj.* freezable; non —, frost-proof.

gelo¹ *m.* (phys.; chem.) gel; — di silice, silica gel.

gel-o² *m.* frost; cold; freezing-point; corroso dal —, frost-bitten; (provb.) Dio manda il — secondo i panni, God tempers the wind to the shorn lamb; iced drink; (poet.) numbness, lack of feeling; †winter, winter cold; †dew; †freshness, coolness; †candied sugar. **-one** *m.* chilblain. **†-ore** *m.* frost; cold.

gelosi·a *f.* jealousy; an outside shutter to a window opening outwards and consisting of overlapping slats which filter the light; peep-hole; trellis; (naut.) tendency to capsize; †taffrail.

gelos-o *adj.* jealous; envious; zealous; touchy; delicate, easily put out of order; (of a vessel) easily capsized, tender; delicate, sensitive (of an instrument); negozio —, ticklish business. **-amente** *adv.* jealously; enviously; zealously. **†-eggiare** *intr.* to be jealous; to show jealousy; *tr.* to envy.

gels-o *m.* (bot.) mulberry-tree, *Morus;* mulberry; (ent.) farfalla del —, bombice del —, mulberry silk moth. **-ato** *adj.* planted with mulberry trees. **-eta** *f.,* **-eto** *m.* mulberry plantation.

gelsomino *m.* (bot.) jasmine, jessamine; — comune bianco, common white jasmine, *Jasminum officinale;* — giallo, (native) Italian yellow jasmine, *J. fruticans;* — d'Arabia, *J. sambac;* — di notte, marvel of Peru, *Mirabilis jalapa;* — della Virginia, trumpet-vine, bigonia, *Campsis radicans.*

Geltrude *pr.n.f.* See **Gertrude.**

†gelura *f.* cold season.

gemebondo *adj.* mournful, moaning; piteous; groaning; lamenting.

gemella *f.* female twin; twin sister; anima —, twin soul, soul-mate; (eng.) maglia —, studded link; (herald.) bar gemel.

gemelli·para *f.* mother of twins.

gemell-o *adj.* twin; one of a pair; muscoli -i, biceps, a pair of muscles; (eng.) macchina a cilindro —, twin-cylinder engine; (naut.) bucket dredger; nave -a, sister ship; *n.m.* twin; twin brother; double; *pl.* cuff-links; twin barges for dredging; *pr.n.m.pl.* (astron.) i Gemelli, Gemini. **-ologi·a** *f.* the scientific study of twins.

ge·m-ere [B I] *intr.* (aux. avere) to moan; to groan; to weep; (of a vessel) to leak; (of doves) to coo; (aux. essere) to leak, to drip; to ooze; to trickle. **-ente** *part. adj.* groaning; weeping; leaking; oozing. **†-icare** *vb.* and derivs. see **gemere.**

gemin-are [A I s] *tr.* to double; to couple, to duplicate; to repeat; *intr.* (aux. avere) to damascene, to engrave a plate and pour an alloy of silver and lead into the incised lines; (bot.) to geminate. **-ato** *part. adj.* doubled; twin; arranged in pairs; coupled; duplicated, repeated; run together (e.g. letters in an abbreviated form of written words, as 'VSS' for 'Vostre Signorie', etc.); (scient.) geminate. **-atura** *f.* doubling. **-azione** *f.* doubling, duplication; repetition; coupling.

Ge·mini *pr.n.m.pl.* (myth.; astron.) Gemini; (biol.) homologous chromosome pairs.

ge·mino *adj.* (poet.). See **gemello.**

gem-ire [D 2] *intr.* (aux. avere) to moan; to coo (of a dove). **-itio** *m.* (*pl.* -itii) continuous groaning; constant dripping; sweating (of walls); (naut.) weep, slow leak; *adj.* see **gemitivo. -itivo** *adj.* sweating (of a wall).

ge·mito *m.* moan; groan; lamentation; cooing.

gemm-a[1] *f.* gem; jewel; sal —, see **salgemma**; (bot.) bud, of branch or flower; mettere le -e, to put forth buds; *pl.* spots on the face. †**-a·io** *m.* collection of gems, gemmary, jewel-house.

Gemma[2] *pr.n.f.* a woman's name; (astron.) name of a star in the constellation of Ariadne's crown.

gemm-are [A I] *intr.* (*aux.* avere) to produce buds, to bud; *rfl.* to deck oneself with jewels, to put on gems. **-amento** *m.* the production of buds. **-ato** *part. adj.* laden with buds; bejewelled; la coda -ata, the peacock's tail. **-azione** *f.* (bot.) act of producing buds; (biol.) vegetal reproduction by budding.

gemm-a·rio *adj.* pertaining to jewelry; l'arte -aria, the jeweller's art. †**-iera** *f.* see **gemma**. †**-iero** *m.* jeweller. **-i·fero** *adj.* producing buds. **-oso** *adj.* rich in buds.

gemme·o *adj.* gem-like.

gemmini *m.pl.* (bot.) garden nasturtium, Indian cress, *Tropaeolum majus.*

gemmiparità *f.* (biol.) tendency to have twins.

Gemo·nie *pr.n.f.pl.* (Rom. hist.) Gemoniae, steps on the Aventine Hill leading to the Tiber, to which the bodies of criminals were dragged to be thrown into the river.

gena[1] *f.* (biol.). See **gene**.

gena[2] *f.* (Piedm.) gêne.

†**gena**[3] *f.* cheek.

†**genarca** *m.* See **genearca**.

gendarm-e *m.* policeman; (eccl.) -i pontifici, papal gendarmes; (joc.) tall, mannish and formidable woman. **-eri·a** *f.* police, gendarmerie. **-esco** *adj.* (*m.pl.* -eschi) police-like.

gene *m.* (biol.) gene.

geneal-ogi·a *f.* genealogy; pedigree. **-o·gico** *adj.* genealogical; albero -ogico, family tree. (**-ogicamente** *adv.*) **-ogista** *m.* genealogist. **-ogizzare** [A I] *intr.* (*aux.* avere) to genealogize.

genearca *m.* (leg.) genearch, head of a family; (fig.) founder of a race.

†**genea·tico** *m.* astrologer.

†**gene·bro** *m.* See **ginepro**.

geneffa *f.* (Milan) pelmet (cf. **mantovana**).

†**geneologi·a** *f.* See **genealogia**.

genepì *m. indecl.* (bot.) Alpine mugwort, wormwood, *Artemisia glacialis.*

genera·bile *adj.* and derivs. See under **generare**.

general-e[1] *adj.* general; proposizione —, general proposition; con parole -i, in general terms; significato —, general meaning; in —, generally speaking, as a rule; usual, commonly accepted; common; widespread; (comm.) spese -i, overhead expenses; (eccl.) capitolo —, general chapter; ministro —, minister-general; capitano —, captain general; stato —, estate general; *n.m.* general point of view; *f.pl.* le -i, general statements and ideas; star sulle -i, to keep to generalities; *f. sing.* fall-in; sonar la —, to sound the fall-in, to beat to quarters; (naut. comm.) —!, general quarters!, action stations! **-mente** *adv.* generally; -mente parlando, generally speaking; usually; commonly. †**-eggiare** *intr.* to speak generally, to speak in generalities.

general-e[2] *m.* general; (leg.) avvocato —, advocate-general; (mil.) — di brigata, brigadier; — di divisione, tenente —, (artillery and engineers) major-general; — di corpo d'armata, lieutenant-general; — d'armata, general; †(naut.) — di mare, admiral; (eccl.) general, superior-general. **-a** *f.* (joc.) general's wife; (eccl.) superior(ess)-general. **-ato** *m.* generalship; (eccl.) generalate. **-eggiare** [A 3 c] *intr.* (*aux.* avere) to command, to act as general. **-essa** *f.* (joc.) general's wife; imperious, commanding woman. **-is·simo** *m.* (mil.) commander-in-chief, generalissimo. **-i·zio** *adj.* pertaining to a general; (eccl.) pertaining to a superior-general.

generalità *f.* generality; the general run of things; majority; *pl.* general remarks; (leg.) personal particulars; name and address, etc.; rifiuto di —, refusal to give name, address and other personal particulars required by Italian law (C.P.); †(mil.) all the generals in an army.

generali·zio *adj.* See under **generale**[2].

generalizz-are [A I] *tr.* to make general, to publish abroad, to broadcast, to spread; *intr.* (*aux.* avere) to generalize. **-a·bile** *adj.* that may be generalized about; that may be spread; publishable. **-ato** *part. adj.* generalized; made known. (**-atore** *m.* **-atrice** *f.*) **-azione** *f.* generalization; generalizing; spreading abroad.

gener-are [A I s] *tr.* to generate; to create, to produce; to breed, to beget; to compose. **-a·bile** *adj.* generable, that may be generated or produced. **-amento** *m.* generating; creating; producing. †**-ati·o** *adj.* generative. **-ativo** *adj.* generative; productive. **-ato** *part. adj.* generated; created; produced; begotten; caused; originated. **-atore** *m.* producer; creator; (eng.; electr.) generator. **-atrice** *f.* creatrix; genitrix; (geom.) generatrix; (electr.) generator. **-azione** *f.* generation, begetting; race; descendants; genus; type; sort, quality; (theol.) generation; †kind, quality, †manner; †gender.

gener-e *m.* kind, sort, type; genus; species; il — umano, mankind, the human race; in —, generally; (art, lit., etc.) genre; quadro di —, painting representing a scene from everyday life (not a religious or historical subject); (gramm.) gender; type of verb (e.g. transitive, intransitive, deponent, etc.); (comm.) — d'affari, line of business; *pl.* (comm.) goods; commodities; articles; -i d'importazione, imports; -i d'esportazione, exports; -i coloniali, colonial goods, imported groceries (e.g. coffee, cocoa); -i di lusso, luxury goods; -i alimentari, foodstuffs (often used as the name of a general grocer's shop); (biol.) genus; (ancient Greek music) genus. **-icità** *f.* see under **generico**.

gene·ric-o *adj.* generic; general; in termini -i, in generic terms; vague, indeterminate; (theatr.) attore —, an actor able to play any type of part; *n.m.* such an actor, sometimes equivalent to 'character actor'. **-amente** *adv.* generically. **-ità** *f.* the quality of being generic.

ge·nero *m.* son-in-law; (leg.) divieto al — di testimoniare, son-in-law's incompetence as witness.

generone *m.* (Rome) a section of the new bourgeoisie which set up at the end of the nineteenth century to rival the aristocracy.

generos-o *adj.* generous; bountiful, lavish; unstinting; vino —, full-bodied wine; of noble bearing. **-amente** *adv.* generously; bountifully; lavishly; unstintingly. **-ità** *f.* generosity; greatness of spirit, liberality; productivity, fertility, strength.

Ge·nesi[1] *pr.n.f.* (Bibl.) Genesis, Book of Genesis.

ge·nes-i[2] *f. indecl.* genesis; origin; formation. **-i·aco** *adj.* pertaining to genesis, relating to origin. **-iologi·a** *f.* genesiology.

gene·tic-a *f.* genetics. **-o** *adj.* genetic; relating to the origin of a thing. **-amente** *adv.* genetically.

genetista *m., f.* geneticist.

gen-etli·aco *adj.* relating to a birthday; relating to the casting of a horoscope; genethliacal; *n.m.* birthday (e.g. of Royalty, etc.). **-e·tlio** *adj.* pertaining to a birthday, invoked on a birthday. **-etlio·grafo** *m.* genethliologist. **-etliologi·a** *f.* genethliology. **-etlio·logo** *m.* genethliologist; astrologer.

genetta *f.* (zool.) genet, a kind of wild cat.

genga *f.* slut; (miner.) argillaceous tufa.

†**gen·gero** *m.*, †**gengevo** *m.* ginger.

†**gengiovo** *m.* ginger.

gengiv-a *f.* (anat.) gum. **-ale** *adj.* pertaining to the gums, gingival. **-a·rio** *m.* preparation for preserving or strengthening the gums. **-ite** *f.* (med.) gingivitis.

geni·a *f.* evil brood, disreputable crowd, low set.

genial-e *adj.* clever; ingenious; original, talented, inventive, gifted; brilliant; congenial; letto —, bridal bed; genial; likeable. **-mente** *adv.* genially; congenially; cleverly; brilliantly. **-ità** *f.* cleverness; touch of genius, brilliance; geniality; likeableness. **-o·ide** *adj.* gifted, talented; un uomo di genio è spesso figlio di padre -oide, a genius is often the son of a man of talent; *n.m., f.* gifted, talented person who is untrained; scatterbrain.

genici·dio *m.* See **genocidio**.

genicolato *m.* (anat.) geniculate.

ge·ni-o *m.* genius; a person of genius; (joc.) un — incompreso, a misunderstood genius; guardian spirit; talent; inclination, taste; dare nel — a, to be to the liking of, to please; è un genere di lavoro che non gli va a —, he is not really cut out for that kind of work; character; instinct; (mil.) engineers, corps of engineers; compagnia del —, sappers; (naut.) — navale, corps of naval constructors; — civile, corps of civil engineers in state employment. **-ere** *m.* (mil.) soldier in the engineers, sapper. **-etto** *m.* (art) cupid, small statuette; genius, prodigy. **-evole** *adj.* genial, good-natured.

genioioide·o *m.* (anat.) genio-hyoid (muscle).

genitale *adj.* genital; *n.m.pl.* genital organs.

genitivo *adj.* (gramm.) genitive; al caso —, in the genitive case; †generative; *n.m.* (gramm.) genitive; questo sostantivo è al —, *or* è un —, this noun is in the genitive.

ge·nito *adj.* born; begotten; *n.m.* offspring; primo —, first-born; ultimo —, youngest son.

genitofemorale *adj.* (anat.) genitofemoral, genitocrural.

genit·ore *m.* parent; father; i miei -ori, my parents; firma del — o di chi ne fa le veci, signature of parent or guardian; creator; (leg.) legge regolatrice dei rapporti fra -ori e figli, law of parent and child (C.C.). **-rice** *f.* mother; genetrix. **-ura** *f.* engendering, production, bringing forth, birth.

genn-aio *m.* January; pulcini di —, children of one's old age; sudar di —, to be in great difficulties, to have great anxieties; lontano quanto — dalle rose, poles apart; (joc.) person who likes to sit near the fire, 'cold mortal'.

†**gennaro** *m.* See **gennaio**.

†**geno** *m.* womb.

Ge·noa *pr.n.m.* name of the Genoa football club, originally started (in 1893) by British residents.

genoci·dio *m.* killing off of a race or social group, genocide.

geno·ide *f.* (biol.) plasmagene, genoid.

geno-tipo *m.* (biol.) genotype. **-ti·pico** *adj.* (biol.) genotypical, hereditary.

Ge·nov-a *pr.n.f.* (geog.) Genoa; pasta di —, quince jam; (bot.) bellezze di —, Jerusalem cherry, *Solanum pseudo-capsicum.* **-ęse** *adj.* Genoese; (cul.) pesto -ese, a Genoese green sauce compounded with basil and garlic; *n.m.* inhabitant of Genoa, native of Genoa; the Genoese dialect, Genoese; *f.* Genoese woman. **-esemęnte** *adv.* after the Genoese manner, in Genoese style. **-esiṣmo** *m.* Genoese idiom; Genoese custom. **-ina** *f.* (numis.) golden Genoese coin of the value of 100 lire (eighteenth century). **-ino** *m.* (numis.) golden Genoese coin of 24 carats (thirteenth century); ducato -ino, the same coin slightly increased in weight (fifteenth century).

gent-e¹ *f.* clan, tribe, *gens*; people, nation; diritto delle -i, law of nations; people, persons; folk; people in general; cosa dirà la —?, what will people say?; crowd; company; callers, visitors; far —, to draw a crowd; — di tavolino, writers, students, etc.; (naut.) seamen, crew, company, ship's company; — franca, libertymen; — di guardia, duty watch; — di mare, seafaring folk, registered seamen; — del mare, seamen's union; †— di spada, infantry carried in a ship; (leg.) rischio di mare e di —, the risk of storms and pirates (in mercantile law); diritto delle -i, *jus gentium*, law of nations. **-ac·cia** *f. pejor.* unpleasant people; wicked people; †wretched people. **-a·glia** *f.* mob, rabble. **-ame** *m.* crowd. **-arella** *f.*, **-erella** *f. dim. pejor.* worthless set of people. **-ina** *f. dim.* lowly people. †**-uca** *f.* rabble. **-uc·cia** *f.* people of little standing.

†**gent-e²**, **-o** *adj.* gentle; noble; *adv.* gently; nobly. †**-ezza** *f.* gentleness; nobility.

gentildonna *f.* gentlewoman, noblewoman.

gentil-e¹ *adj.* noble, gentle; Gentile Signore, Dear Sir (NOTE: this form of address is common at the beginning of formal, personal letters and sometimes on the envelope; the slightly more formal 'Gentilissimo Signore' is also used and may be abbreviated Gentilmo. Sig.); il — sesso, il sesso —, the gentle sex; kind, kindly; Lei è molto —, you are very kind, how kind of you; courteous, polite; (lit.; poet.) il gentil cuore, the gentle heart (i.e. a conception prevalent in the love poetry of the 'Stilnovisti', q.v.); tender, delicate, soft; carne —, tender meat; terra —, ground that is easily worked; fine; pianta —, cultivated (i.e. not a wild) plant; colla —, glue made of parchment pieces. **-mente** *adv.* in a kind manner; courteously; politely; gently. **-ęsco** *adj.* (*m.pl.* **-ęschi**) gentlemanly; ladylike; pertaining to gentlefolk; noble; well-appointed. **-ęzza** *f.* gentleness; nobility; courtesy, politeness; favour, kind action; fammi una -ezza, do me a favour; kindness; delicacy, softness, tenderness; luxury gift article. †**-i·a** *f.* see **gentilezza**. **-i·gia** *f.* nobility. **-i·zio** *adj.* noble, ancestral; (herald.) stemma -izio, heraldic bearings; *n.m.* (med.) nulla nel -izio, nothing in the family history (relating to disease). **-omo** *m.* (*pl.* **-o·mini**, pop. Tusc.) see **gentiluomo**.

gentil-e² *adj.* Gentile; non-Jewish; pagan; non-Christian; *n.m.*, *f.* Gentile. **-ęsco** *adj.* (*m.pl.* **-ęschi**) heathen, pagan. (**-escamęnte** *adv.*) **-ęsimo** *m.*, **-ità** *f. indecl.* heathenism, paganism; heathendom, the pagan world.

gentil-uomo *m.* (*pl.* **-u·omini**) gentleman; nobleman; *pl.* †(naut. Ven.) midshipmen; -uomini di poppa, senior officers.

†**gento** *adj.* See under **gente²**.

genu-cubitale *adj.* (med.) genucubital; posizione —, knee/elbow position. **-pettorale** *adj.* (med.) genupectoral; posizione -pettorale, knee/chest position.

genufless-ione *f.* genuflection, bending the knee; — profonda, kneeling on both knees. **-ioncella** *f. dim.* bow with a slight bend of the knee. **-o** *part.* of **genuflettere**, q.v.; *adj.* kneeling, on one's knees. **-o·rio** *m.* prie-Dieu.

genuflet·tere [C 19] *rfl.* to genuflect, to bend the knee; to kneel, to kneel down.

genuin-o *adj.* genuine; authentic; real. **-amęnte** *adv.* genuinely. **-ità** *f.* genuineness.

genziana *f.* (bot.) gentian.

ge-o *m.* (fam. Tusc.) lover; person pulling faces; grimace. **-a** *f.* mistress.

geocen·trico *adj.* geocentric.

geod-e *m.* (geol.) geode; (med.) caseous tubercular cavity in the lung. **-eṣi·a** *f.* geodesy; topography. **-eṣi·metro** *m.* protractor. **-eta** *m.*, *f.* geodesist. **-e·tico** *adj.* geodetic. **-ina·mica** *f.* geodynamics; study of the forces acting in the earth's crust. **-ina·mico** *adj.* geodynamic.

ge-ofagi·a *f.* geophagy, the habit of eating earth, etc. **-o·fago** *m.* one who eats earth, etc., geophagist.

geo-fi·ṣica *f.* geophysics. **-fi·ṣico** *adj.* geophysical. **-geni·a** *f.* see **geogonica**. **-ge·nico** *adj.* see **geogonico**. **-gnoṣi·a** *f.* geognosy. **-gnosta** *m.* geognost. **-goni·a** *f.* geogony. **-go·nico** *adj.* geogonic(al).

geogr-afi·a *f.* geography; †map. **-a·fico** *adj.* geographical; (med.) lingua -afica, pityriasis linguae. **-aficamęnte** *adv.* geographically.

geo·grafo *m.* geographer; ingegnere —, cartographer.

geo·ide *m.* geoid.

geol-ogi·a *f.* geology. **-o·gico** *adj.* geological. **-ogicamęnte** *adv.* geologically.

geo·lo-go *m.* (*pl.* **-ghi**, **-gi**) geologist.

geom-ante *m.* geomancer. **-an·tico** *adj.* geomantic. **-anzi·a** *f.* geomancy.

geo·metr-a *m.* geometer; geometrician; land-surveyor. **-i** *m.pl.* geometers, etc.; (ent.) geometrid moths. **-i·a** *f.* geometry. †**-izzare** *intr.* to geometrize.

geome·tric-o *adj.* geometric(al); (fig.) exact, real. **-amęnte** *adv.* geometrically.

geometrini *m.pl.* (ent.) looper caterpillars, the caterpillars of geometrid moths (cf. **geometri**, under **geometra**).

geo·mide *m.* (zool.) mole rat, *Geomys bursarius.*

geo-montografi·a *f.* the printing of coloured relief maps. **-morfologi·a** *f.* study of the form of the earth's surface. **-nomi·a** *f.* mathematical geography. **-pla·stica** *f.* relief model or relief map of the earth's surface. **-poli·tica** *f.* political geography. **-po·nico** *adj.* geoponic, relating to husbandry; *n.m.* writer on agriculture. **-rama** *m.* georama. **-sinclinale** *adj.* (geol.) geosyncline. **-sta·tica** *f.* statics of a rigid body, geostatics. **-ter·mica** *f.* (geol.) geothermics. **-ter·mico** *adj.* (geol.) geothermic; geothermal.

Georgia *pr.n.f.* (geog.) Georgia; — Australe, South Georgia.

geor·gic-a *f.*, *pr.n.f.* georgic; le *Georgiche*, the *Georgics*. **-o** *adj.* agricultural; poema -o, georgic.

georgo·filo *m.* patron of agriculture.

geo·trupe *m.* (ent.) dor beetle, *Geotrupes stercorarius.*

Ge·ova *pr.n.m.* (Bibl.) Jehovah.

Geppętto *pr.n.m.* abbrev. of **Giuseppe**, q.v.; the name of the father of Pinocchio in the story of Collodi; (fig.) a patient and long-suffering father of a mischievous urchin; (haidressing) taglio, pettinatura, messa in piega alla —, long bob.

gera·nio *m.* (bot.) geranium, applied, as in English, to various species of *Geranium* and *Pelargonium.*

ge·rano *m.* ancient Greek dance.

gerar-ca *m.* (*pl.* **-chi**) (rel.) hierarch; il supremo —, il sommo —, the Pope; high official, politically important person; (Ital. hist.) — fascista, Fascist party official. **-cato** *m.* a hierarch's term of office; office of hierarch. **-chi·a** (theol.; eccl.) hierarchy; (pol.) structure of a service (e.g. Navy, bureaucracy) according to rank; (Ital. hist.) -chia fascista, organization of the Fascist party rulers.

gerar·chic-o *adj.* hierarchic(al); trasmettere una domanda per via ~a, to forward a request through the proper channels. **-amente** *adv.* hierarchically.

gerardina *f.* (bot.) goat-weed, ground elder, *Aegopodium podagraria*.

Gerardo *pr.n.m.* Gerard.

gerb-a *f.* (bot.) kinds of sedge (*Carex*), reed-mace (*Typha*), and bur-reed (*Sparganium*). **-aio** *m.* place overgrown with such plants. **-one** *m.* (bot.) crimson clover, *Trifolium incarnatum*.

gerbeggiare [A 3 c] *intr.* (*aux.* avere) to pull faces.

ger·bido *m.* (geog. Piedm.) infertile bleached soil.

Gerem-i·a *pr.n.m.* (Bibl.) Jeremiah; Jeremias; Jeremy; (fig.) dismal person, a Jeremiah. **-i·aco** *adj.* doleful. **-i·ade** *f.*, **-iata** *f.* Jeremiad; (fig.) tale of woe, lamentation.

ger-ente *m.* (leg.) director; manager; socio —, managing partner; (comm.) manager; agent; (journ.) editor. **-enza** *f.* management; agency. **-ire** [D 2] *tr.* (admin.) to manage; *intr.* (*aux.* avere) to be a director or manager.

gerfal-co *m.* (*pl.* **-chi**) (orn.). See **girfalco**.

gerg-o *m.* (*pl.* **gerghi**) slang; cant; jargon. **-ale** *adj.* slangy; pertaining to jargon or slang. **-alismo** *m.* word of slang origin; word of jargon. **-alista** *m.*, *f.* specialist in slang or jargon. **-onare** [A 1 c] *intr.* (*aux.* avere) to speak slang; to use jargon. **-one** *m.* jargon.

geri-atri·a *f.*, **-a·trica** *f.* geriatrics.

Ge·rico *pr.n.f.* (geog.) Jericho.

Gerione *pr.n.m.* (myth.) Geryon.

gerire [D 2]. See under **gerente**.

gerl-a *f.* (N. Ital.) basket in shape of a cornucopia to be carried on the back, used esp. for carrying loaves of bread; a ~e, in basketsful, (fig.) in abundance; una — di ragazzi, a crowd of boys. **-inaro** *m.* man who measures and loads ores, charcoal, etc., into a furnace. **-inata** *f.* the amount of charcoal, etc., which is held by a 'gerlino'. **-ino** *m. dim.* basket for measuring corn, ores, charcoal, etc.

gerl-o *m.* (naut.) sail gasket. **-iare** [A 4] *intr.* (*aux.* avere) to tie the gaskets when making up sail.

Germa·nia *pr.n.f.* (geog.) Germany.

germa·nio *m.* (chem.) germanium.

germ-ano[1] *m.* Teuton. **-a·nico** *adj.* Germanic, Teutonic. **-anesimo**, **-anismo** *m.* Germanism. **-anista** *m.*, *f.* Germanist, specialist in Germanic studies. **-anizzare** [A 1] *tr.*, *intr.* (*aux.* avere) to Germanize. **-anizzato** *part. adj.* Germanized. **-ano·filo** *m.* Germanophile, one who is pro-German. **-ano·fobo** *m.* Germanophobe, one who dislikes Germany.

german-o[2] *adj.* natural, blood, full (of brother or sister); fratello —, brother-german; sorella ~a, full-sister, sister-german; *n.m.* own brother, real brother, blood brother. **-ità** *f.* blood-relationship of true brothers.

germano[3] *m.* (orn.) mallard, *Anas platyrhynca*; — di mare, black scoter; — forestiero, ruddy sheld-duck; — turco, red-crested pochard, *Netta rufina*.

germ-e *m.* germ, seed, embryo; (fig.) first cause; (vet.) the mark on a horse's incisors showing its age. **-icida** *adj.*, *n.m.* germicide. **-ile** *pr.n.m.* (hist.) see **germinale**. **-inale** *adj.* germinal; (med.) non ~inale, ablastemic; *pr.n.m.* (hist.) Germinal, the seventh month of the French Revolutionary Calendar. **-inello** *m. dim.* seedling.

Germina·ia *pr.n.f.* (geog.) Germinaia, in the prov. of Pistoia; the name of a wine from that region.

germin-are [A 1 s] *intr.* (*aux.* essere, avere) to germinate, to shoot; *tr.* to produce. **-a·bile** *adj.* capable of germinating. **-abilità** *f.* capacity to germinate. **-amento** *m.* germinating; shooting. **-ante** *part. adj.* germinant. **-ativo** *adj.* germinative. **-ato** *part. adj.* germinated; produced. (**-atore** *m.* **-atrice** *f.*) **-azione** *f.* germination.

†germ-ine *m.* germ; seed; *pl.* kind of card game.

germinello *m. dim.* See under **germe**.

germogli-are [A 4 c, Rom. A 4] *intr.* (*aux.* essere, avere) to shoot, to sprout; to bud; (silkb.) to be ready to hatch; *tr.* to produce, to bring forth, to bear, to yield. **-a·bile** *adj.* capable of shooting or sprouting. **-amento** *m.* shooting, sprouting; budding. **-ato** *part. adj.* shooting, sprouting; in shoots, showing sprouts; produced. (**-atore** *m.* **-atrice** *f.*) **-azione** *f.* shooting, sprouting.

germoglio *m.* shoot, sprout, bud; offshoot, offspring, origin.

gerocomi·a *f.* care of the old, gerocomy.

geroderma *m.* (med.) senile condition of the skin.

gerof-ante *m.* hierophant, high-priest. **-anti·a**, **-anzi·a** *f.* hierophancy, high-priesthood. **-an·tico** *adj.* hierophantic. **-an·tide** *f.* high-priestess.

gerogl-i·fico *adj.*, *n.m.* hieroglyphic; hieroglyph. **-ificamente** *adj.* by means of hieroglyphics. **-ificare** [A 2 s] *tr.* to symbolize by means of hieroglyphics, to mark in hieroglyphs. **-ifichiere** *m.* (joc.) dabbler in hieroglyphs. **-i·ptico** *m.* hieroglyphist.

gerogr-afi·a *f.* hierography. **-a·fico** *adj.* hierographic. **-amma** *m.* hierogram. **-am·mate** *m.* hierogrammate.

Gero·lam-o *pr.n.m.* see **Girolamo**. **-ino** *m.* (eccl.) Oratorian; Hieronymite.

gerolimiano *adj.*, *n.m.* old Cyrillic (characters); Glagolitic (alphabet).

geromanzi·a *f.* See **ieromanzia**.

Gero·nim-o *pr.n.m.* see **Girolamo**. **-ita** *m.* (eccl.) Hieronymite.

ger-onte *m.*, *pr.n.m.* (Gk. antiq.) *geron*, elder in Spartan council; (eccl. hist.) monk or presbyter; (lit. hist.) Géronte (in French comedy). **-ia·trica** *f.* (med.) geriatrics. **-on·tico** *m.* (Eastern eccl.) geronticon. **-ontismo** *m.* (med.) annular opacity in the cornea in the aged. **-oco·mio** *m.* home for the aged. **-ocrazi·a** *f.* gerontocracy. **-ontoiatri·a** *f.* (med.) see **geriatria**. **-ontologi·a** *f.* (med.) science of the care of the aged.

Geroso·lim-a *pr.n.f.* (poet.) Jerusalem. **-itano** *m.* (hist.) Knight of Jerusalem.

gerotro·fio *m.* home for the aged.

†gerrettier-a *f.* Order of the Garter. **†-o** *m.* Knight of the Garter.

†gersa *f.* a kind of make-up for the face, cosmetic.

Gertrude *pr.n.f.* Gertrude.

gerun·d-io *m.* (gramm.) gerund; (joc.) long route; dare nei ~i, to go mad. **-ivo** *adj.* (gramm.) gerundive.

Gerusalemme *pr.n.f.* (geog.) Jerusalem.

Gerusi·a *pr.n.f.* (Gk. antiq.) Gerusia.

gesmino *m.* (poet.). See **gelsomino**.

geso *m.* ancient Gallic javelin.

gessa-i·a *f.* gypsum quarry; chalk-pit. **-o** *m.* plaster-cast maker or seller. **-(u)olo** *m.* gypsum quarryman; plasterer; plaster-cast maker.

gess-are [A 1 c] *tr.* to add gypsum to wine to clarify it; to plaster (cf. **ingessare**). **-ato** *part. adj.* treated with gypsum; impregnated with chalk; plastered. **-atura** *f.* treatment with gypsum or chalk.

gess-o *m.* (miner.) gypsum; chalk, piece of chalk (for writing); plaster, plaster of Paris; — da presa, plaster of Paris; — da murare, wall plaster; — da legno, putty for filling holes in wood; pipa di —, clay pipe; (sculp.) plaster-cast; crumbling cheese; (slang) wine. **-etto** *m. dim.* piece of chalk (for writing); chalk-pencil; (sculp.) small plaster cast; (art) chalk drawing. **-ina·io** *m.* chalk seller; statuette seller or maker; plasterer; plaster-cast maker. **-ino** *m. dim.* small plaster statuette. **-one** *m.* name of an alabaster quarry near Volterra. **-oso** *adj.* rich in gypsum; chalky.

gest-a *f.* (*indecl.* or *pl.* **-e**) enterprise, feat, deed; exploit; race, family; (lit. hist.) Canzoni di —, *Chansons de geste*, the Carolingian cycle of epic poems; †race, stock, people; †army, host.

gestante *adj.*, *n.f.* See under **gestare**.

Gestapo *pr.n.m.* (pron. with hard G) (hist.) Gestapo.

gest-are [A 1 c] *tr.* to gestate; *intr.* (*aux.* avere) to be gestating; to be pregnant. **-ante** *adj.* pregnant, expectant; *n.f.* expectant mother; corredi per ~anti, maternity wear. **-ato** *part. adj.* gestated. **-ato·rio** *adj.* (eccl.) gestatorial; sedia ~atoria, *sedia gestatoria*, gestatorial chair, ceremonial chair in which the Pope is carried in state. **-azione** *f.* (med.) gestation; (fig.) time of preparation; time during which something is thought out or planned.

gesteggi-are [A 3 c] *intr.* (*aux.* avere) to make gestures, to gesticulate. **-ante** *part. adj.* gesticulating; *n.m.*, *f.* person making gestures.

gesticol-are [A 1 s] *intr.* (*aux.* avere) to gesticulate. **-amento** *m.* gesticulating. **-ante** *part. adj.* gesticulating, making gesticulations; *n.m.*, *f.* person gesticulating. **-atore** *m.* gesticulator (**-atrice** *f.*). **-azione** *f.* gesticulation.

gestione *f.* administration; conduct of affairs; tenure of office; the running of a concern; spese di —, overheads; management; capo —, chief manager; — di azienda, management of a firm; relazione di —, report on the management; (leg.) chi assume la — di un affare altrui, a person undertaking the management of somebody else's affairs (C.C.).

gestire[1] [D 2] *intr.* (*aux.* avere) to accompany speech with appropriate actions; to make gestures; to gesticulate.

gest·ire² [D 2] *tr.* to administer, to conduct, to direct, to manage, to run. **-ito** *part. adj.* administered, managed, run.

gesto¹ *m.* gesture; movement; gesticulation; act, action.

gesto² *m.* action, deed, undertaking; geste, exploit.

gestore *m.* administrator, director; supervisor, manager (esp. of goods traffic at a railway station); — della piccola (velocità), superintendent of goods traffic by freight train; — della grande (velocità), superintendent of goods traffic by passenger train; — alle merci, head clerk of goods depot; (leg.) manager, esp. of another person's affairs (C.C.).

gestr·o *m.* grimace; person making grimaces. **-one** *m.* person who grimaces. (**-ona** *f.*) **-oso** *adj.* prone to make faces, given to making grimaces, grimacing.

Geṣ·ù *pr.n.m.* Jesus; — Cristo, Jesus Christ; — bambino, the Christ child; fare —, to join one's hands (of a child saying his prayers, or of anyone expressing thanks or emotion); fare — con cento mani, to be overwhelmed with gratitude; esser tutto — e madonne, to be a pious hypocrite; picture or figure of Christ; (eccl.) Compagnia di —, Society of Jesus; il —, Jesuit church, esp. the famous building in Rome; (Tusc.) — pietoso, pawnbroker's shop; carta —, (equiv. to) super-royal paper.

Geṣuat·o *m.* (eccl. hist.) Jesuate. **-ata** *f.* Jesuatess.

geṣu-ita *m.* Jesuit; *f.* (cul. Pistoia) a kind of pastry. **-itante** *m.* pro-Jesuit. **-iteri·a** *f.* Jesuitry. **-itesco** *adj.* (*m.pl.* **-iteschi**) Jesuitical. **-itessa** *f.* Jesuitess. **-i·tico** *adj.* of the Jesuits, pertaining to Jesuits, Jesuit. **-itismo** *m.* Jesuitry.

Geṣum-mari·a *excl.* gracious heavens; *pr.n.m.* the Jesus and Mary hospital at Naples. **-mi·o** *excl.* good heavens!

geto *m.* jess; (fig.) beccarsi i -i, to kick against the pricks.

gettaione *m.* (bot.) corncockle, *Agrostemma githago*.

gett-are [A 1] *tr.* to throw, to fling, to hurl, to cast; — via, to throw away, to waste, to squander; — a mare, to throw overboard, (fig.) to drop; — la colpa su, to throw the blame on; — bombe, to drop bombs; radici, to put out roots; — l'ancora, to cast anchor; — le basi di, to lay the foundations of (also fig.); (metall.) to cast; *intr.* (*aux.* avere) to throw; to give off; scrivere come la penna -a, to write as the pen flows; (of a fountain) to play; (bot.) to sprout, to shoot; (econ.) to yield (of a tax); *rfl.* to throw oneself; -arsi su, to fling oneself upon; to jump, to fall; to rush, to be precipitate. **-amento** *m.* throwing; abjection; †cast-off, object cast aside. **-ata** *f.* throw, cast; (bot.) shoot; range (of a gun); missile; (naut.) jetty; dike. **-atello** *m.* foundling; cast-away. **-ato** *part. adj.* thrown; thrown away, wasted; -ato lì, stated without special care, flung out (of words); merci -ate, jettisoned goods; (metall.) cast. **-atoio** *m.* rubbish tip; chute. **-atore** *m.* one who throws; iron-founder; 'Jonah', one who brings bad luck, one possessed of the evil eye; †waster, squanderer. (**-atrice** *f.*)

get·tito *m.* throw, cast; (naut.) jettison, jetsam; (comm.) output, yield; †vomit; †sputum.

getto *m.* throw, cast; (naut.) jettison, jetsam; (leg.) the act of throwing or tipping; — pericoloso di cose, throwing of articles to the public danger (C.P.); far — di, to jettison, to throw overboard, (fig.) to fling aside; (techn.) stick of wax used in making castings; (metall.) casting; (med.) vomit; flux, issue (of blood); jet, spurt; gush; chute; (bot.) shoot; (fig.) draft; output; a — continuo, non-stop, in a continuous stream; un'opera nata di —, a work produced in a single outburst of creative energy; di primo —, in the first version (e.g. of a work of art); (sport) — del peso, putting the weight; †chute for house refuse and sewage; †protuberance, bulge; †al —, immediately, without more ado, straightway.

getton-e¹ *m.* counter, token; — di presenza, disc or medallion given to persons attending committee meetings, identity disc, (industr.) attendance-check; type of wrapped sweet thrown on festive occasions; (gambling) chip, *fiche*; disc used instead of a coin in public telephones, etc.; macchina a -i, slot machine; macchina a -i per biglietti d'ingresso, platform-ticket slot-machine; a —, coin-freed. **-are** [A 1 C] *tr.* (slang) to ring up, to give (someone) a tinkle on the telephone.

gettone² *m.* (bot.). See **gettaione**.

geys-er *m. indecl.* (geol.) geyser, hot spring. **-erite** *f.* (miner.) geyserite.

†gheffo *m.* overhang, projection on a building beyond the outer wall.

ghe·iscia *f.* geisha.

ghemme *pr.n.m.* (geog.) Ghemme, in the prov. of Novara; red wine from Ghemme.

ghenga *f.* (slang), see **ganga**².

ghepardo *m.* (zool.) cheetah.

Ghepeù *pr.n.m.* Soviet Secret Police.

gheppio *m.* (orn.) kestrel, *Falco tinnunculus*.

†ghera *f.* See **ghiera**.

gherardinismo *m.* system of spelling in Italian based on etymology (e.g. 'academia', 'catedra', etc.), from the name of the Milanese philologist, G. Gherardini (1778–1861).

Gherardo *pr.n.m.* Gerard.

†gherbellire *tr.* to seize, to snatch.

†gherbino *m.* See **garbino**.

gheri·glio *m.* kernel.

gherl(in)o *m.* (naut.) line, hemp or manilla hawser.

gherminella *f.* trick; sleight of hand; escapade; peccadillo; mischievous trick.

gherm-ire [D 2] *tr.* to seize; to snatch; to clutch; to claw; to carry off. **-ito** *part. adj.* snatched, clutched; tener -ito, to hold in one's grip, to carry off in one's talons. (**-itore** *m.* **-itrice** *f.*)

gheron-e *m.* gusset, gore; quel che non va nelle maniche va nei -i, what you lose on the swings you make up on the roundabouts; piece of cloth; (herald.) gyron; **-ato** *adj.* (herald.) gyronny; -ato di 8 pezzi, gyronny of 8.

Ghestapo *pr.n.m.* (hist.) Gestapo.

ghett-a¹ *f.* the semivitreous oxide of lead, litharge, produced in the cupellation of silver. **-are** [A 1 C] *tr.* to refine silver.

ghett-a² *f.* gaiter. **-ina** *f.* spat. **-one** *m.* legging.

ghett-o *m.* ghetto, Jewish quarter; the Jews of a locality; slum district; any sharply defined or cut-off community; confusion, chaos, fare un —, to make a commotion. **-ume** *m.* uproar.

ghezzo *adj.* dark-skinned (applied to the colour of the Moors of Barbary who are not quite black); beginning to darken in colour (of grapes); †some kind of crow or indeterminate bird of dark plumage.

ghi *m. indecl.* ghee, Indian clarified butter.

ghi·a *f.* (naut.) whip, gantline; — doppia, double-whip, whip upon whip; — di coffa, tail jigger; — delle aste, boom tricing-line; — del bozzello del capone, cat-rope, — di testa, bull-rope; — del ventrino, bunt-whip; — doppia del ventrino, bunt-jigger.

†ghiaccesco *adj.* icy.

†ghiac·cia *f.* See **ghiaccio**.

ghiacci-a·ia *f.*, **-a·io** *m.* See under **ghiaccio**.

ghiacci-are [A 3] *rfl.*, *intr.* (*aux.* essere) to freeze, to ice; to turn to ice; (aeron.) to ice up. **-ata** *f.* ice chips with fruit syrup or other flavouring poured on top. **-ato** *part. adj.* frozen, iced; cooled; ice-cold; icy, ice-covered; frosted; vetro -ato, frosted glass; *n.m.* flaw in a jewel. **-atura** *f.* frosty weather; ice-cream making.

ghiac·ci-o *m.* ice; — secco, — asciutto, dry ice; — galleggiante, iceberg; nave trattenuta dai ghiacci, ice-bound ship; flaw in a precious stone; (of weather) frost; *adj.* icy. **-a·ia** *f.* ice-house, ice-safe. **-a·io** *m.* glacier. †-oso *adj.* icy, frozen; frosty. **-uo·la** *f.* a variety of pear. **-uo·lo** *m.* icicle; ice-bucket; ice crystal in the upper atmosphere; hailstone; lump of ice; ice-lolly; flaw in a precious stone; (zool.) slow-worm, *Anguis fragilis*; *adj.* that breaks like ice; dente -uolo, a tooth which is sensitive to cold. **-uoletto** *m. dim.* small flaw in a precious stone.

†ghiacinto *m.* jacinth (cf. **giacinto**).

†ghiada *f.* See **ghiado**².

†ghiado¹ *m.* excessive cold; chill.

†ghiado² *m.* knife; sword; morto a —, stabbed; put to the sword.

ghia·i-a *f.* gravel; shingle. **-ata** *f.* fine gravel; strewing of gravel; load of gravel; gravel path; a blow from gravel that has been thrown; a graze from gravel. **-etto** *m.* (bldg.) gravel. **-one** *m.* gravel, gravelly soil; loose sweep of stones, scree. **-oso** *adj.* gravelly; shingly. **-ot·tolo** *m.* bit of gravel, tiny pebble. **-uzza** *f.* very fine gravel.

ghiand-a *f.* acorn; caffè di —, a beverage prepared from roasted acorns in the manner of coffee; acorn-shaped button fastened to the fringes of curtains, etc.; (mil. hist.) acorn-shaped missile, shot from a sling; oval ball used for holding a number of tickets to be drawn by lot; lump, swelling; (med. hist.) bubo of the plague; ti venga la —!, a pox on you!; (with neg.) nothing at all; (anat.) glans. †**-ellino** *m.* little bit; tiny distance. **-i·fero** *adj.* acorn-bearing; (herald.) acorned. **-one** *m. augm.* of **ghianda**; big, worth-

ghiand-a (*cont.*)
less individual. **-oso** *adj.* producing acorns; (med.) producing tumours or swellings (as the plague). **-uc·cia**, **-uzza** *f.* small tumour, boil.

ghianda·i-a *f.* (orn.) jay, *Garrulus glandarius*; — marina, roller, *Coracias garrulus*; — nocciolaia, nutcracker, *Nucifraga caryocatactes*. **-one** *m.* chatterbox. **-otto** *m.* young jay.

ghiandale *m.* (zool.) barnacle.

ghian·dol-a *f.* gland. **-ato** *m.* (vet.) strangles. **-oso** *adj.* glandular.

†ghiara *f.* and derivs. see **ghiaia**; (geog.; hist.) la Ghiara d'Adda, the territory between the River Mincio and the River Adda where the Venetians were defeated in 1509.

ghiareto *m.* bank of shingle; gravelly river-bed.

†ghiargione *m.* chatterbox; gossip.

ghiattire [D 2] *intr.* (*aux.* avere) (of hounds) to bay; to yelp.

†ghia·volo *m.* and derivs. See **diavolo**.

†ghiazzerino *m.* coat of mail.

ghibellin-o *adj.*, *pr.n.m.* (hist.) Ghibelline, the name of the Imperial party in medieval Italy as opposed to the Guelphs. (NOTE: these names are derived from 'Waiblingen' and 'Welf', the names of two families who in the twelfth century were at the head of rival parties in the Holy Roman Empire.) **-amente** *adv.* after the manner of Ghibellines. **-esco** *adj.* (*m.pl.* -eschi) Ghibelline-like. (**-escamente** *adv.*) **-ismo** *m.* Ghibellinism.

ghibli *m. indecl.* hot desert wind (in Tripolitania).

†ghie·colo *m.* baby's cradle.

ghier-a *f.* ferrule (of a walking-stick, etc.); metal ring or cap; (mil.) locking-ring of a bayonet; *pl.* (mil.) cheek pieces of a gun; (naut.) end bands, driving bands, spectacle plates on masts, etc.; iron hoop round the head of a pile; (eng.) bush; ring nut; mould for making cheese; †(pharm.) electuary containing bitter aloes. **-abaldana** *f.*, **-abaldano** *m.* (Tusc.) tittle-tattle, trifle. **-ato** *adj.* fitted with a ferrule or ring.

†ghieva *f.* glebe.

ghigle *f.pl.* braid; †cunning, trickery.

ghigliottin-a *f.* (hist.) guillotine; finestra a —, sash window; guillotine (for cutting paper). **-are** [A 1] *tr.* to guillotine. **-ato** *part. adj.* guillotined.

ghign-a *f.* sinister, grotesque or leering face; grimace, cheeky look; impudence; run of bad luck. **-are** [A 5] *intr.* (*aux.* avere) to sneer; to grin impudently; to smile sarcastically. **-ata** *f.* sneer; sarcastic smile; derisive laugh. **-atore** *m.* sneerer; grimacer. (**-atrice** *f.*) **-azzare** [A 1] *intr.* (*aux.* avere) to sneer; to laugh derisively. **-o** *m.* leer; sneer; grin; derisive laugh, scornful smile; malicious look or gesture. **-oso** *adj.* leering; sneering; sinister or unpleasant-looking.

ghind-a *f.* (naut.) a lift or any rope used for hoisting; hoist or height to be lifted; (mil. hist.) portable shield; *pl.* (mil.) vertical stays on a bridge; (naut.) mast rope. **-ag·gio** *m.* hoisting. **-ale** *m.* hoisting rope. **-ame** *m.* rigging; set of ropes for hoisting. **-ante** *part. adj.* hoisting; *n.m.* (naut.) the mast end of a flag or the head of a sail where it is laced to a yard. **-are** [A 1] *tr.* to hoist; (mil.) to place (the lifts) on a bridge; (naut.) to sway away, to hoist. **-aressa** *f.* (naut.) mast rope. **-ata** *f.* hoisting. **-atoio** *m.* hoisting winch. **-atura** *f.* hoisting; means of hoisting. **-azzo** *m.* windlass.

ghin-e·a *f.* guinea; (text.) a coarse cotton fabric. **-eone** *m.* (text.) see **ghinea**.

ghin·gheri *m.pl.* gewgaws; in —, dressed up, in festive attire.

†ghiomo *m.* ball of thread.

†ghiosa *f.* and derivs. See **chiosa**.

ghiotta *f.* pan for catching dripping.

ghiott-o *adj.* greedy; gluttonous; eager; — di gloria, thirsting for glory; fond of; sono — di gelati, I simply love ice-cream; delicious, appetizing; boccone —, *bonne bouche*, (fig.) easy-going attractive woman, 'nice bit'; †self-indulgent; †wicked; *n.m.* greedy man; glutton; (provb.) una ne pensa il — e un'altra il tavernaio, (said of two people hoping to make profit out of each other). **-amente** *adv.* greedily; gluttonously; eagerly. **-erello**, *adj. dim.* rather greedy. **-eri·a** *f.* gluttony; greed. **-orni·a** *f.* gluttony; greed; greediness; avidity, covetousness; tasty food. **-ume** *m.* tasty morsel, *bonne bouche*. **-uzzo** *adj. dim.* See **ghiotterello**.

ghiotton-e *m.* greedy person; glutton; gourmand; (provb.) nella chiesa coi santi ed in taverna coi -i (Dante, *Inf.* XXII, 14–15), cf. adversity doth make strange bedfellows of us all, *or* when in Rome do as the Romans do; (zool.) glutton, *Gulo luscus*;

adj. greedy, è — di gelati, he's a pig for ices. **-eggiare** [A 3 c] *intr.* (*aux.* avere) to indulge in gluttony. **-eria** *f.*, **-i·a** *f.* greediness; avidity; covetousness; delicious food; tit-bit; dainty morsel.

ghiott-orni·a *f.*, **-ume** *m.* See under **ghiotto**.

ghiova *f.* sod, clod.

ghiozzo[1] *m.* (ichth.) goby, *Gobius* spp.; — fluviale, *Gobius fluviatilis*; — nero, — comune, *Gobius niger*; (fig.) simpleton, booby.

ghiozzo[2] *m.* drop; drip; tiny bit.

ghirba *f.* leather water bucket; (mil. slang) portare a casa la —, to return home safe and sound; salvare la —, to save one's skin.

ghiribizz-o *m.* whim, caprice, fancy; gli è saltato il — di, he has suddenly taken it into his head to; fantasy; baroque conceit. **-amento** *m.* fantasy; whim, caprice, fancy. **-ante** *part. adj.* fanciful; whimsical; capricious. **-are** [A 1] *intr.* (*aux.* avere) to indulge in fantasy; to have caprices; to be whimsical; to have one's fancies; to romance. **-oso** *adj.* capricious; fantastic; whimsical; freakish; full of fantasy; bizarre. **-osamente** *adv.* fantastically; whimsically; freakishly.

ghirigoro *m.* scroll; flourish (in writing); rigmarole; doodle, squiggle; scribble; camminare a —, to walk zigzag; (mus.) see **girigogolo**.

ghirland-a *f.* garland, wreath; (provb.) un fiore non fa —, one swallow doesn't make a summer; far — d'ogni fiore, to be indiscriminate, to think all one's geese are swans; morir con la —, to die an old maid; tiara, coronet; (naut.) fender, fendering; breast-hook; (lit.) garland, anthology, miscellany (of poems); — di sonetti, sonnet-sequence; (astron.) the constellation Corona; (geog.) — d'isole, island arc. **-a·io** *m.* maker or seller of wreaths. **-are** [A 1] *tr.* to garland, to wreathe. **-ato** *part. adj.* garlanded, wreathed. **-etta** *f. dim.* little garland. **-ina** *f. dim.* little garland; *pr.n.* (archit.) bell-tower of the cathedral of Modena.

ghir-o *m.* (zool.) edible dormouse, *Glis glis*; dormire come un —, to sleep like a top. **-a·ia** *f.* establishment for fattening edible dormice for the table.

ghironda *f.* (mus.) hurdy-gurdy, barrel-organ.

ghisa *f.* cast-iron; — di prima fusione, pig-iron; — bianca cavernosa, porous pig-iron; — a fiori, white pig-iron with semi-granular texture; — marezzata, — picchiettata, — tigrata, mottled pig-iron; — grigia, ordinary cast-iron.

†ghizz-are *intr.* to long, to suffer longing; to be in a state of ardent desire. **†-o** *m.* excessively devout person.

già *adv.* already; abiti — fatti, ready-made clothes; formerly; once; yes, yes of course, naturally, assuredly; indeed; non —, not at all, certainly not; non — che, not that.

giacamaro *m.* (orn.) jacamar.

giacca *f.* jacket; short coat; jacket of a man's suit or a woman's coat and skirt; cardigan; — a vento, windcheater.

giacchè *conj.* since, inasmuch as, as, now that.

Giaccheri·a *pr.n.f.* (hist.) Jacquerie, a rising such as that of the French peasantry in 1358.

giacchett-a *f.* jacket; (naut.) best jumper (No. 1); (mil.) fatigue tunic. **-ino** *m. dim.* little jacket; lady's jacket; bolero.

giacchi-are [A 4] *tr.*, *intr.* (*aux.* avere) to fish with a casting-net. **-ata** *f.* cast with a casting-net.

giac·chio *m.* casting-net; gettare il — tondo, to be no respecter of persons; gettare il — sulla siepe, to engage in a fruitless task.

giac·ci-o *m.* (naut.) tiller. **-are** [A 3] *tr.* (naut.) to steer; *intr.* (*aux.* avere) to work the tiller. **-ata** *f.* movement of the tiller. **-ato** *adj.* fitted with a tiller.

giac-ere [B 1] *intr.* (*aux.* essere) to lie; to be situated; to lie idle; to be inert, to stagnate; (of goods) to be stopped or detained; to be in abeyance; to be pending; to be in the dead-letter office; to lie low; (provb.) non toccare il can che -e, let sleeping dogs lie; come sta e -e, as it is written, as it stands (in the text); qui -e, *hic jacet*, here lies; (fam.) qui -e Nocco, there is a snag here; (provb.) il morto -e e il vivo si dà pace, dead men tell no tales; †senza —, on one's feet; †porre a —, to kill, to lay low. **-ente** *part. adj.* lying; situated, (of a letter) poste restante; out of course; pending; in abeyance; (finan.) capitale -ente, idle capital; (of goods) unsold; immobile, inert, stagnant; (leg.) vacant; in abeyance; eredità -ente, unclaimed inheritance; (deceased's) estate under administration (C.C.); *n.m.* (sculpt.) recumbent figure. **-enza** *f.* lying; stay; (comm.) demurrage; avviso di -enza, notice of detention; stock, stock unsold; (finan.) capital lying idle; (chem.) standing. **-i·glio** *m.* bed; couch, pallet; resting place; lair; hammock, bunk. **-imento** *m.* lying; lying together, coitus;

giac·ere (*cont.*)
layer; (geol.) stratum, seam, deposit; -imento di carbone, coal-bed; (fig.) inertia, oblivion. **-itoio** *m.* a place to lie down; bed, couch; lair. **-itura** *f.* way of lying, position; posture; coitus; (naut.) bearings of objects taken with the compass.

giacint-o[1] *m.* (bot.) hyacinth, *Hyacinthus orientalis* and other species; (text.) purple-dyed wool; (miner.) hyacinth, jacinth. **-ino** *adj.* hyacinth-blue.

Giacinto[2] *pr.n.m.* Hyacinth.

giaco *m.* (*pl.* **giachi**) (mil. hist.) coat of mail; (herald.) papelonne.

Giacob·be, Giaco-b *pr.n.m.* Jacob; la scala di —, Jacob's ladder.

Giacob-ino *pr.n.m.* (hist.) Jacobin, extreme revolutionary, one of the Jacobin club; revolutionary, violent Liberal, unscrupulous demagogue; unbeliever. **-inata** *f.* act of a Jacobin. **-ineri·a** *f.*, **-inismo** *m.* Jacobinism. **-ita** *m., adj.* (eccl.) Jacobite; (Eng. hist.) Jacobite.

Gia·com-o *pr.n.m.* James; dolt, simpleton; avere le gambe che fanno Giacomo Giacomo, to be wobbly on one's legs (e.g. after an illness). **-etta** *pr.n.f.* (theatr.) a character in Piedmontese comedy, the wife of Gianduia, q.v.

giaconetta *f.* (text.) jaconet.

giaculato·ri-a *f.* short prayer; short impassioned appeal; (joc.) curse, oath. **-o** *adj.* impassioned, ejaculatory.

giad-a *f.*, **-o** *m.* (miner.) jade, nephrite. **-eite** *f.* (miner.) jadeite.

Giafe·t *pr.n.m.* See **Iafet**.

Giaffa *pr.n.f.* (geog.) Jaffa.

†giafossecosachè, †giafossechè *conj.* although.

giaggi(u)olo *m.* (bot.) gladiolus; iris, *Iris florentina*.

giaguaro *m.* (zool.) jaguar, *Felis onca*.

giaietto *m.* (miner.) jet.

gialappa *f.* (bot.) jalap, *Ipomoea* spp.

†giald-a *f.* (mil. hist.) lance, pike. **†-oniere** *m.* soldier of fortune; lancer.

gialdone *m.* (silkb.) silkworm affected by disease.

giallamina *f.* (miner.) calamine.

giall-o *adj.* yellow; farina -a, maize flour; libro —, yellow book (govt. publication); romanzo —, thriller, murder story; film —, film based on a murder story or with a strong element of suspense; — di terra, — ocra, terra -a, yellow ochre; (dyeing) legno —, fustic; diventar —, to bruise; pale, pallid, haggard; (of red wine) avere i piedi -i, to begin to turn sour; (med.) suffering from jaundice; (geog.) Mare —, Yellow Sea; Fiume —, Hwang Ho; *n.m.* yellow, yellow colour, colour of yellow; — di cromo, chrome yellow; — di rosa, yellow pollen in the middle of a rose; yolk; (joc.) money, 'dough'; murder story, thriller; un giallo-rosa, a detective story with love-interest. **-astro** *adj.* yellowish. **-eggiare** [A3C] *intr.* (*aux.* essere) to turn yellowish; to be on the yellow side. **-etto** *adj., n.m. dim.* pale yellow, delicate yellow. **-ezza** *f.* yellowness. **-ic·cio** *adj.* slightly yellow, turning yellow. **-igno** *adj.* nearly yellow, yellowish. **-ino** *adj. dim.* light yellow, pale yellow, straw-coloured. **-o·gnolo** *adj.* dirty yellow; yellowish. **-olino** *m.* (paint.) Naples yellow, golden yellow paint used as priming and in ceramics. **-one** *adj.* deep yellow; *n.m.* deep yellow shade; person with yellow complexion. **-ore** *m.* yellow coloration, yellow complexion; yellowness; jaundice. **-orlino, -osanto** *m.* yellow paint prepared from buckthorn berries. **-oso** *adj.* dirty yellow; *n.m.* (slang) gold coin. **-uc·cio** *adj. pejor.* sickly yellow. **-ume** *adj.* sickly yellow, disgusting yellow; *n.m.* sickly yellow hue; yellow stain; yellow spot on the skin; disease of silkworms. **-ura** *f.* yellowness; (med.) jaundice.

Giama·ica *pr.n.f.* (geog.) Jamaica (also **Giammaica**).

†giamb·are, †-eggiare *tr.* to mock.

giambe·lego *f., m.* (prosod.) iambelegus.

giam·bice *m.* (mus.) sambuca, sambuke, sambuque, an ancient triangular harp.

giam·bico *adj.* (prosod.) iambic.

giambo *m.* (prosod.) iambus; iambic foot or verse; satirical verse, invective, mockery; dare il (del) — a, to mock, to satirize.

giambone *m.* (Milan) ham.

Giambracone *pr.n.m.* 'John with the wide breeches', an easygoing person; che la duri, —!, let's hope your luck holds!, I hope you can keep it up!

giamma·i *adv.* once already; ever; (with neg., or neg. implied) never, not ever.

Giamma·ica *pr.n.f.* (geog.) Jamaica (also **Giamaica**).

giammengola *f.* trifle, bagatelle.

Giandu·i-a *pr.n.m.* (theatr.) a mask of the popular Piedmontese theatre, symbol of Piedmontese characteristics (cf. Eng. 'John Bull'); i figli di —, the Piedmontese; a kind of chocolate cream. **-otti** *m. pl.* chocolates (of very soft, sweet milk chocolate, made in Turin).

gianfrull-o, -one *m.* simpleton.

Giani·colo *pr.n.m.* (Rome) Janiculum.

gianna[1] *f.* (orn.) lesser heron.

Gianna[2] *pr.n.f.* (abbrev. of **Giovanna**) Joan.

giannett-a *f.* (mil. hist.) throwing spear; officer's cane, swagger-stick; (naut.) bearing off spar; (text.) jenny; †walking-stick. **-a·rio** *m.* (mil. hist.) trooper of Spanish light cavalry. **-ata** *f.* blow with a walking-stick. **-iere** *m.* (mil. hist.) see **giannettario**. **-one** *m. augm.* (mil. hist.) heavy lance.

giannetto *m.* jennet; black lambskin.

Gianni *pr.n.m.* (abbrev. of **Giovanni**) Johnnie, Jack, Ian; dolt, simpleton; Prete —, Prester John.

gianniz·zero *m.* janissary.

†giannizzo *m.* foot soldier of the Turkish militia founded by Osman.

Gian-o *pr.n.m.* (myth.) Janus; — bifronte, two-faced Janus (used fig. of a two-faced or hypocritical person); il mese di —, January; (hist.) part of the Roman Forum used as a meeting-place for merchants. **-ua·rio** *adj.* pertaining to Janus; pertaining to January.

giansen-iano *adj.* (eccl. hist.) Jansenist, Jansenistic. **-ismo** *m.* Jansenism. **-ista** *m., adj.* Jansenist. **-i·stico** *adj.* Jansenist, Jansenistic. **(-isticamente** *adv.*)

Giapeto *pr.n.m.* (myth.) Iapetus; il figlio di —, Prometheus; (Bibl.) Japeth.

Giappon-e *pr.n.m.* (geog.) Japan. **-esco** *adj.* (*m.pl.* **-eschi**) (joc.) Japanese-like. **-ese** *adj.* Japanese; (sport) la lotta -ese, jujitsu; *n.m.* a Japanese; the Japanese language; *f.* a Japanese woman.

giappo·nico *adj.* (tanning) terra giapponica, cutch.

giara[1] *f.* earthenware jar; oil-jar; drinking-cup with two handles and no foot; (naut. hist.) powder bowl on board ship; †the eighth part of a 'cantaro' (measure of oil).

giara[2] *f.* (geog. Sard.) basaltic hill; †gravel, shingle.

giard-a *f.*, **-o** *m.* (vet.) spavin (in horses); ring bones and/or side bones; (fig.) mockery; lie. **-oni** *m.pl.* (vet.) spavin.

giardin-ag·gio *m.* (the art of) gardening. **-a·io** *adj.* pertaining to gardens; (provb.) maggio -aio non fa fiorire il granaio, gardening in May doesn't fill the barn; †*n.m.* gardener. **†-ato** *adj.* abounding in gardens. **-eri·a** *f.* gardening. **-iera** *f.* woman gardener; gardener's wife; flower-holder (esp. with several arms); -iera a ventaglio, fan-shaped flower-holder; basket-carriage; large coach with seats along the sides; wicker basket for gathering olives; cart with wicker-work round it; (cul.) Jardinière soup; (pedagog.) maestra -iera, kindergarten mistress, nursery school teacher; (motor.) see **giardinetta**, under **giardino**; †necklace. **-iere** *m.* gardener; nurseryman; †garden.

giardin-o *m.* garden, flower-garden; (Sicily) lemon and orange groves; — inglese, landscape garden, romantic style of gardening; — pensile, hanging garden, roof garden; — d'inverno, conservatory, winter-garden; — zoologico, zoo; — d'infanzia, kindergarten, nursery school; -i pubblici, public park; fiori da —, garden flowers; (leg.) private pleasure garden; -i esenti della servitù di passaggio coattivo, gardens not subject to rights of way of necessity (C.C.); (poet.) — delle delizie, Earthly Paradise; il — dell'Impero, Italy; (naut.) sternwalk (cf. **giardinetto**); †latrine, closet. **-etta** *f.* (motor.) station wagon, utility car, shooting brake, estate car. **-etto** *m. dim.* small garden; (at a restaurant) dish of fruit after dinner, dessert; dish of assorted salami; game of billiards; Neapolitan ice-cream made in layers of different colours; (naut.) quarters of a ship; vento al -etto, wind on the quarters; sternwalk; poop cabin; roundhouse, heads; †stern gangway.

giargone[1] *m.* (miner.) jargon.

giargone[2] *m.* See **gergone**, under **gergo**.

gia·rolo, giaroncello *m.* (orn.) sandpiper, dunlin.

giarra *f.* see **giara**[1]; (Sicily) watertower.

giarrettiera *f.* garter; Ordine della —, Order of the Garter.

Giasone *pr.n.m.* (myth.) Jason.

†gia·spide *m.* jasper.

†**giatt-anza**, †**-azione** *f.* vanity, conceit, pride, self-aggrandizement. †**-ura** *f.* grave loss; serious damage.

giaur·ro *m.* giaour, infidel (in Mahometan sense).

Giav-a[1] *pr.n.f.* (geog.) Java. **-anese** *adj.* Javanese; *n.m.* a Javanese; the Javanese language; *f.* a Javanese woman.

†**giava**[2] *f.* (naut.) magazine, ship's store, captain's store.

giavà *excl.* (naut.) sailor's reply to a command, equivalent to 'aye aye!' (also 'già va!'); used in cheering, equivalent to 'hurrah!'

Giavarino *pr.n.m.* (geog.) Györ (Raab).

giavazzo *m.* (miner.) jet.

giavellott-o *m.* javelin; (sport) lancio del —, throwing the javelin. **-ista** *m.* (sport) javelin-thrower.

giavone *m.* (bot.) green bristle-grass, *Setaria viridis.*

gibbo *m.* (anat.) gibbus, hump curvature; †rise, mound; hill.

gibbone *m.* (zool.) gibbon, *Hylobates* spp.

gibb-oso *adj.* humped; curved; hunchbacked; gibbous; convex. **-osità** *f.* hump; curvature; gibbosity; convexity. **-uto** *adj.* humped, arched.

giberna *f.* (mil.) cartridge-case; cartridge-pouch.

gibetto *m.* gibbet, gallows.

gibigiana *f.* reflected ray of sunlight.

Gibilterra *pr.n.f.* (geog.) Gibraltar.

gibus *m. indecl.* opera hat, crush-hat; gibus.

gi·chero *m.* (bot.). See **gigaro.**

giell-ismo *m.* (Ital. hist., pol. 1946, etc.) the politics of the anti-Fascist group known as 'Giustizia e Libertà', originally associated during Fascism with the Rosselli brothers and their Parisian adherents. **-ista** *m., f.* a supporter of 'Giellismo'.

†**gienit** *m.* See **zenit.**

†**gieno** *m.* See **genere.**

†**gie·sia** *f.* See **chiesa.**

giesiola *f.* (naut.) binnacle.

giga *f.* (mus.) jig, gigue; rebec.

gigant-e *m.* giant; (geog.) Monti dei –i, Giant Mountains; fare passi da —, to progress by leaps and bounds, to make prodigious progress; *adj. indecl.* (colloq.) colossal, huge, gigantic. †**-a** *f.* see **gigantessa.** **-eggiare** [A3c] *intr.* (*aux.* avere) to tower, to stand out, to loom up; to rise like a giant. **-e·o** *adj.* giant, giant-sized; giant-like. **-esco** *adj.* (*m.pl.* **-eschi**) gigantic; pertaining to a giant. **-essa** *f.* giantess. †**-ino** *adj.* see **gigantesco.** **-ismo** *m.* (med.) gigantism; (art) larger-than-life style of representation; il –ismo michelangelesco fu la prima forma del barocco, the Michelangelesque super-sized figure was the first expression of the baroque. **-omachi·a** *f.* (myth.) gigantomachy, battle of the giants against the gods.

gi·garo *m.* (bot.) Lords-and-Ladies, cuckoo pint, *Arum maculatum* and other species.

gigion-e *m.* (theatr. slang) actor or singer who plays to the gallery. **-eggiare** [A3c] *intr.* (*aux.* avere) to play to the gallery; to ham.

giglia·ceo *adj.* See under **giglio.**

gigli-are [A4] *rfl.* to take the form of a lily. **-ato** *part. adj.* stamped with a lily; danari –ati, safe money, gilt-edged security; *n.m.* coin bearing the impression of a lily.

giglieto *m.* See under **giglio.**

gi·gli-o *m.* (bot.) lily, plant belonging to the genus *Lilium* or with more or less lily-like flowers; — azzurro, *Iris germanica*; — d'acqua giallo, yellow water-lily, brandy-bottle, *Nuphar lutea*; — degli stagni, white water-lily, *Nymphaea alba*; — tigrato, tiger-lily; — di Sant'Antonio, Madonna lily, *Lilium candidum*; — delle convalli, lily-of-the-valley, *Convallaria majalis*; (zool.) — di mare, sea lily, crinoid, feather star, *Antedon rosacea*; (herald.) lily, fleur-de-lis; — partito per mezzo, demi-fleur-de-lis couped palewise; la città del —, Florence; lily on a coin; giocare a –i e santi, to play heads and tails; hand, arrow-head of a needle or similar indicator. **-a·ceo** *adj.* liliaceous. **-astro** *m.* (bot.) wild lily, esp. martagon lily, *Lilium martagon.* **-eto** *m.* bed of lilies. **-etto** *m. dim.* of **giglio**; a kind of lace; (herald.) small frieze of lilies. **-one** *m. augm.* of **giglio**; (naut.) handle, strictly a spindle-shaped piece, like a lily-leaf, finishing the handle of the sweep of a galley.

†**gignore** *m.* apprentice to a craft.

gigotto *m.* leg of mutton or kid.

gilda *f.* guild.

gilè *m. indecl.* waistcoat.

giletta·ia *f.* woman seamstress who finishes waistcoats for a tailor.

gi·lia *adj. f.* terra —, clay.

gi·lico *m.* (bot.) *Arisarum vulgare.*

†**gimè** *m.* (bot.). See **gelsomino.**

gimnoto *m.* (ichth.). See **ginnoto.**

gin *m. indecl.* gin (the liquor).

Gina *pr.n.f.* (abbrev. of **Giovannina**, *dim.* of **Giovanna**) Jennie, Jean.

ginandr-i·a *f.* (med.) gynandria. **-omorfismo** *m.* (biol.) gynandromorphism.

ginan·tropo *m.* hermaphrodite.

gincana *f.* gymkhana.

ginec-e·o *m.* (Gk. and Rom. antiq.) gynaeceum, women's apartments; harem; (fig.) a crowd of women; (bot.) gynoecium, gynaeceum. **-ea·rio** *m.* (Gk. and Rom. antiq.) attendant in a gynaeceum.

ginec-ocrazi·a *f.* gynaecocracy. **-ofobi·a** *f.* fear in the presence of women. **-ologi·a** *f.* gynaecology. **-o·logo** *m.* gynaecologist. **-omani·a** *f.* gynaecomania. **-omasti·a** *f.* (med.) gynaecomastia. **-o·mio** *m.* hospital for women. **-oni·tide** *f.* gynaeceum.

ginepr-a *f.* (bot.) juniper berry. **-a·io** *m.* juniper thicket; (fig.) intricate and thorny situation; labyrinth. **-ella** *f.* gin, a liquor made from juniper berries. **-eto** *m.* juniper thicket. **-o** *m.* (bot.) juniper, *Juniperus.* **-one** *m.* (bot.) *Juniperus macrocarpa.*

gine·reo *m.*, **gine·sio** *m.* (bot.) pampas grass, *Cortaderia sellowiana.*

ginestr-a *f.* (bot.) broom, Spanish broom, *Spartium junceum*; (naut.) grassline. **-ag·gine** *f.* (bot.) dyer's greenweed, *Genista tinctoria.* **-ella** *f.* (bot.) *Osyris alba.* **-eta** *f.*, **-eto** *m.* thorny place; (fig.) difficult and thorny situation. †**-e·vole** *adj.* thorny, overgrown with broom, wild. **-i·fero** *adj.* broom-producing. **-ifi·cio** *m.* factory for manufacturing products from broom. **-ina** *f.* (bot.) birdsfoot trefoil, *Lotus corniculatus.* **-one** *m.* (bot.) furze, gorse, whin, *Ulex europaeus.*

Ginevr-a[1] *pr.n.f.* (geog.) Geneva. **-ino** *adj.* of Geneva; *n.m.* inhabitant or native of Geneva. (**-ina** *f.*)

Ginevra[2] *pr.n.f.* Guinevere.

†**ginevro** *m.* See **ginepro**, under **ginepra.**

†**gin·ghia** *f.* See **cinghia.**

†**gingi·a** *f.* See **gengiva.**

gingill-o *m.* toy; nick-nack; bauble; trifle; ornament on a watch-chain; small lock-picker's tool; handy little implement for any purpose; any small fragile object; a petite person; waste of time; waster of time. **-a** *f.* idler, loiterer; woman who fritters away her time. **-are** [A1] *intr.* (*aux.* avere), *rfl.* to fritter time away, to idle; to fiddle, to play idly; to linger; to loiter. **-ino** *m.*, **-one** *m.* idler, loiterer, person who fritters time away; waster.

gingiolieri·a *f.* red strings tied round the heads of cattle as a charm against witchcraft.

gingiva *f.* See **gengiva.**

gin·glimo *m.* (anat.) ginglymus.

ginnarco *m.* (ichth.) *Gymnarchus.*

ginna·si-o *m.* grammar school (attended by children, aged 11–15, hoping to go on to a University); il — patavino, the faculty of literature at Padua (cf. Note under **liceo**). **-ale** *adj.* pertaining to a gymnasium; pertaining to grammar school education; licenza -ale, school-leaving diploma. **-arca** *m.* (*pl.* **-archi**) gymnasiarch.

ginn-are [A1] *tr.* (text.) to gin. **-atrice** *f.* (text.) gin. **-atura** *f.* (text.) ginning.

ginn-asta *m.* gymnast; athlete. **-aste·rio** *m.* gymnasium. **-a·stica** *f.* gymnastics, physical training; gymnastic display; -astica svedese, Swedish drill. **-a·stico** *adj.* gymnastic.

ginnetto *m.* jennet (small horse).

gin·nic-a *f.* gymnastics. **-o** *adj.* gymnic, gymnastic; saggio -o, gym display.

ginno-pedi·a *f.* (Gk. antiq.) dance of naked Spartan boys, gymnopaedic dance. **-sofisti** *m.pl.* gymnosophists; the name of an academy in Padua concerned with the chivalrous, liberal and mathematical arts in the seventeenth century. **-somi** *m.pl.* (zool.) gymnosomatous pteropods (Mollusca). **-sperme** *f.* (bot.) gymnosperm.

ginnoto *m.* (ichth.) electric eel, *Gymnotus electricus*; underwater mine which is detonated by an electric current.

Gino *pr.n.m.* Jimmy; Johnnie.

ginoc·chi-o *m.* (*pl.* **-a** *f.*) knee; rotella del —, knee-cap, knee-pan; a — kneeling, on one's knees; le -a della mente, humble thoughts; far venire il latte alle -a, to be very tiresome; — valgo, knock-knee; — varo, bandy-leg, bow-leg; (math.) — inferiore, toe (of a curve); — superiore, shoulder (of a curve); (*pl.* **ginocchi** *m.*) movable joint; a —, jointed; (eng.) pressa a —, toggle lever press;

ginocchi-o (*cont.*)

(naut.) middle part of an oar. †**-are** *tr.* to embrace round the knees; *intr.*, *rfl.* see **inginocchiare**. **-ata** *f.* blow with the knee; blow on the knee. **-ello** *m. dim.* (butcher.) pig's leg below the knee, trotter; knee-cap for a horse; injury to the knee; bulge in the knee of trousers; (zool.) *Murex trunculus*, a mollusc; (mil. hist.) knee cover of mail armour; (mil.) gun shield (below the barrel). **-era** *f.* (eng.) toggle; pressa **-era**, toggle press; giunto a **-era**, toggle joint; (med.) knee-bandage; (sport) knee-pad; **-era** elastica, elastic knee-band. **-ętto** *m. dim.* of **ginocchio**; (bot.) burning bush, *Dictamnus albus*. **-ǫni**, **-ǫne** *adv.* on one's knees, kneeling; on one's hands and knees. **-uto** *adj.* (bot.) geniculate.

†**giò**[1] *excl.* gee-up!; andare —— —, to go slowly.

†**gio**[2] *f.* See **gioia**[1].

Gioacchino *pr.n.m.* Joachim.

Gioachimiti *pr.n.m.pl.* (eccl. hist.) Joachimists, Joachists.

Gioanniti *pr.n.m.pl.* See **Giovanniti**, under **Giovanni**.

Giob·be *pr.n.m.* (Bibl.) Job, the patriarch; amici di —, Job's comforters; avere la pazienza di —, to have the patience of Job.

giobertiano *adj.* (hist.) Giobertian, connected with, or in accordance with, the religious, philosophical or political ideas of Vincenzo Gioberti (1801–52); *n.m.* follower of Gioberti.

gioc-are [A 2 d] *intr.* (*aux.* avere) to play; un bambino che **-a** con gli amici, a child playing with his friends; — di un bastone, to play with a stick; — di uno, to make fun of someone; — a (alle) carte, to play cards; — a scacchi, to play chess; — a (al) bigliardo, to play billiards; — a dadi, to play dice; — a palla, to play ball; — alle bocce, to play bowls; to joke; to be playful; not to be serious, to be frivolous; ma Lei **-a** o dice sul serio?, but are you joking or do you mean it seriously?; (finan.) to speculate; — in borsa, to play the market; — al rialzo, to buy when prices are rising; — al ribasso, to buy when prices are falling; *tr.* to play; to stake, to gamble; to bet; quanto **-a**?, how much are you putting on?; *rfl.* (*dat.* of *prn.* 'si') to lose in gambling; **-arsi** l'anima, to gamble away one's soul; **-arsi** una persona, to lead a person by the nose. **-ata** *f.* game; play; stake, bet; coming into play; turn to play; è la mia **-ata**, it's my go; length of a game; (cards) deal. **-ato** *part. adj.* played; (colloq.) tricked, fooled, 'had'. **-atore** *m.* player; gambler; **-atore** di bussolotti, conjurer; trickster. **-atǫra** *f.* woman gambler. **-atrice** *f.* woman player.

giocat·tol-o *m.* toy, plaything. **-aio** *m.* toy-manufacturer.

giocherell-are [A 1] *intr.* (*aux.* avere) to play idly; to fiddle, to toy; to waste time. **-o** *m. dim.* little game; toy, plaything; pastime.

†**giochessa** *f.* joke, jest; trick.

giochętt-o *m. dim.* of **gioco**; little game; joke; clever trick; — di parole, play upon words, pun. **-ino** *m. dim.* party game; conjuring trick.

giochęvol-e *adj.* playful; facetious. **-mẹnte** *adv.* playfully; facetiously.

gio-co *m.* (*pl.* **-chi**) game; play; — di destrezza, game of skill; — solitario, game of patience; — di sala, parlour game; — di parole, play upon words, pun; — duro, rough play, horse play; aver bel (buon) —, to stand a good chance of winning; lavorare a buon —, to work well, to work with success; levarsi da —, to abandon an undertaking, to throw in one's hand; alla fine del —, when all is said and done; a —, at will, freely, in fun; stare al —, to co-operate, to 'play ball'; ma a che — giochiamo?, what's your game?, what do you think you're up to?; fare al — di, to play into the hands of; (econ.) — di borsa, stock-exchange activity, speculation, playing the markets; joke, jest; sport; mettere in —, to make fun of; (provb.) un bel — dura poco, brevity is the soul of wit; dare — di sè, to make a laughing stock of oneself; trick, deceit; un brutto —, a dirty trick; chi sa il — non l'insegni, if you are on to a good thing keep it under your hat; (sport) game; ground where the game is played; (tennis) 'game'; i **-chi**, athletic sports; — navale, naval display, mock naval battle; (theatr.) plot, action; (eng.) action, movement; amount of play, clearance; lasciare un po' di —, to leave a little play (e.g. between two metal sections for expansion); — assiale, end play; eliminare il —, to take up the slack; (mus.) — dell'arco, art of bowing; (naut.) set of the sails; (leg.) — d'azzardo, game of chance (C.P.); casa di —, illicit gaming house; sala da —, licensed gaming rooms (C.P.); debito di —, gambling debt; l'esito di un — o di una scommessa, the result of a game or wager (C.C.); **-chi** pubblici, public games; **-chi** proibiti, forbidden games (C.C.).

giocoforza *f.* necessity; è —, it is inevitable; mi fu —, I was compelled, my hand was forced, I had to, willy-nilly.

giocol-are [A 1 s] *intr.* (*aux.* avere) to juggle; to perform; to perform on the tight rope; to play. **-atore** *m.* juggler; tumbler, acrobat.

gio·col-o *m.* joke, trick. †**-eri·a** *f.* juggling; conjuring. **-iere** *m.* (sport) outstanding playing, 'wizard', 'artist'; **-iere** di football, football wizard; †juggler; †conjurer. **-ino** *m. dim.* toy, game; joke.

giocǫnd-o *adj.* joyful, joyous; cheerful; blithe; jocund. **-amẹnte** *adv.* joyfully, joyously; cheerfully; blithely; jocundly. **-are** [A 1 c] *tr.* to cheer up; *intr.* (*aux.* avere) to be cheerful. **-ẹvole** *adj.* see **giocondo**. **-ẹzza** *f.* (poet.) see **giocondità**. **-ità** *f.* joyfulness, joyousness; a happy and cheerful demeanour; delight.

giocǫs-o *adj.* jocose, merry, playful; jocular; blithe. **-amẹnte** *adv.* jocosely; jocularly; in fun, playfully.

giocucchiare [A 4] *intr.* (*aux.* avere) to play or gamble a little, to have a flutter.

gioddu *m.* (Sardinia) a kind of yoghourt.

gioga·ia *f.* dewlap (of cattle); (geog.) mountain range, chain of mountains; watershed; succession of ridges along the skyline.

giogale *adj.* See under **giogo**.

†**giog-are** *tr.* to put under the yoke, to yoke. †**-ata** *f.* a measure of land area. †**-a·tico** *m.* payment made either in money or in kind for the use of a team of oxen; dare i buoi al **-atico**, to let out one's oxen for payment. †**-ato** *part. adj.* yoked, looped together in a yoke (of vine stems). †**-atura** *f.* cost of ploughing or other work with a team of oxen.

gioglio *m.* (bot.). See **loglio**.

giog-o *m.* (*pl.* **giǫghi**) yoke; (fig.) oppression; sotto il — del tiranno, beneath the tyrant's yoke; condition of interdependence; (euphem.) il — maritale, il dolce —, marriage; pair of oxen or other beasts of burden; trellis for training vines; (naut. hist.) thwartship beams in a galley; (electr.) yoke; (geog.) mountain ridge; high continuous zone of mountain peaks and cols; beam of a balance; (mus.) yoke (of the lyre); (bot.) jugum. **-ale** *adj.* relating to a yoke or mountain ridge. **-olare** *adj.* see **giugulare**. †**-oso** *adj.* girt round with mountain peaks.

gio·i-a[1] *f.* joy, happiness; pleasure; delight; fuochi di —, fireworks, bonfires; sweetheart, treasure; — mia!, my treasure!; (comm.) consideration for good will; †menare —, to be joyful; †(iron.) bella —, good-for-nothing. **-ale** *adj.* jovial, festive. **-alità** *f.* joviality, geniality. **-alǫne** *m.* good-natured fellow. †**-are** *vb.* and derivs. see **gioire**.

gio·i-a[2] *f.* precious stone; jewel; (mil.) strengthening band at the breech or counterpoise weight at the muzzle of a gun; †(naut.) ship's compass; slave who used to be given to a captain who had taken an enemy ship (cf. Note under **gioiello**).

gioiell-o *m.* jewel, piece of jewelry; (fig.) beloved, treasure. (NOTE: 'gioia' is a precious stone, whether rough or worked. 'gioiello' is an ornament worked by a jeweller in gold, silver or precious stones.) **-are** [A 1] *tr.* to adorn with jewels, to set with gems. **-eri·a** *f.* jeweller's craft; jeweller's shop. **-iera** *f.* jeweller's wife; woman jeweller. **-iere** *m.* jeweller.

gioiǫs-o *adj.* joyous, joyful; cheerful; cheering; merry; (lit. hist.) La Gioiosa, La Joyeuse, the name of Charlemagne's sword. **-amẹnte** *adv.* joyously, joyfully; cheerfully; merrily.

gio-ire [D 2] *intr.* (*aux.* avere) to rejoice; — di, to rejoice in, to be glad of; †*tr.* to enjoy. **-ito** *part. adj.* cheery, happy.

†**gioladro** *m.* See **giullare**.

†**gio·lito** *m.* quiet enjoyment, serenity; rest; stare in —, to be tranquil; andare in —, to become very pleased with oneself; (naut.) in —, under weigh, (or) at anchor and rolling.

†**giollaro** *m.* See **giullare**.

†**giomella** *f.* See **giumella**.

Giona *pr.n.m.* (Bibl.) Jonah.

Gio·nata *pr.n.m.* Jonathan.

†**gio·nico** *adj.* See **ionico**.

Gioppino *pr.n.m.* (abbrev. of **Giuseppino**) (theatr.) character of comedy and puppetry of Bergamo representing a peasant with triple goitre.

Giord-a·nia *pr.n.f.* (geog.) Jordan. **-ano** *adj.* pertaining to Jordan.

Giordano[1] *pr.n.m.* (geog.) river Jordan.

Giordano[2] *pr.n.m.* Jordan.

giordano[3] *adj.* See under **giordania**.

Giorgina[1] *pr.n.f.* Georgina.

giorgina² *f.* (bot.) dahlia.

Giọr·g·io *pr.n.m.* George; San —, statue of St George, (fig.) the Republic of Genoa; il gabinetto di San —, the British Government; mostrar la strada di San —, (said of a horse which has one of its front legs more bent or stretching further forward than the other), to be on guard; †fare il —, to be brave, to feign ignorance. **-eri·a** *f.* finery.

giorgionẹs-co *adj.* (*m.pl.* **-chi**) (paint.) in the manner of Giorgione, Giorgionesque.

giornal-e *adj.* daily, everyday; (leg.) libro —, journal, day-book (C.C.); †relating to the daytime; *n.m.* diary, journal; (comm.) journal; day-book; (naut.) — di bordo, journal; diary; — di chiesuola, deck log; daily newspaper; — della Domenica, Sunday paper; — murale, wall newspaper; — parlato (1929–35), — radio, news on the wireless; (colloq.) magazine; stile da —, journalese; l'ho letto sul —, I read it in the paper; (leg.) sequestro dei -i, impounding of newspapers. **-a·io** *m.* newsagent, newsvendor; newspaper-boy. **-ẹtto** *m.* dim. of **giornale** (leg.) gazette. **-iere** *adj.* see **giornaliero**. **-iero** *adj.* daily; everyday; lasting twenty-four hours; orario -iero, twenty-four hours' time-table; la vita -iera, everyday life; fickle, capricious; *n.m.* day-labourer. **-ino** *m.* dim. children's newspaper. **-iṣmo** *m.* journalism. **-ista** *m., f.* (*pl.* **-isti** *m.*, **-iste** *f.*) journalist. **-i·stico** *adj.* journalistic. **-isticamẹnte** *adv.* in a journalistic way; in journalese. **-mẹnte** *adv.* daily; everyday; day-by-day. **-ume** *m.* the press, all the newspapers viewed collectively and disparagingly.

giornante *m.* (rel.) brother on duty in the Florentine *Misericordia*; *f.* daily help, charwoman.

giornarello *m.* dim. **giorno**; red-letter day; sorrowful day.

giornat-a *f.* day, as a period of time or as a specimen of good or bad weather; day's work; day's pay; day's journey; day's march; che bella —!, what a lovely day!; in —, before the day is over, during the day, in the course of the day; a -e, by the day, (fig.) at intervals, by fits and starts, spasmodically; vivere alla —, to live from hand to mouth; (hist.) battle; Le Cinque -e di Milano, the five days fighting against the Austrians at Milan in 1848; le quattro -e di Napoli, the popular rising in Naples against the Germans (1944); a -e, a grandi -e, rapidly; lavorare a —, far la —, to work by the day; journey; durata normale della — di lavoro, normal working day. **-a·ia** *f.* (Sicily) girl farm-labourer who works by the day.

giorne·a *f.* mantle, cloak; (fig.) mettersi in —, affibbiarsi la —, cingersi la —, to speak with an air of affected authority; †military cloak; †(naut.) working rig or overall; †royal apparel; †day; †day's work; †interval of twenty-four hours; †(mil.) andare in —, to be on fatigue duty.

†giorne-are *intr.* to waste the day in gossip. **†-one** *m.* idler.

giornello *m.* bricklayer's hod.

giornina·ia *f.* professional hem-stitcher (cf. 'orlo a giorno', under **giorno**).

giọrn-o *m.* day, daytime; in pieno —, in broad daylight; di — o di notte, by day or night; a —, at daybreak; far del — notte, to sleep during the daytime and work at night; far di notte —, to work at night as well as in the day; legare a —, (of a jewel) to set without any backing, so that the light shines through when it is held up; (needle-w.) punto a —, openwork; orlo a —, hemstitch; buon —!, good morning!; — artificiale, artificial light; fra otto -i, in a week's time; fra quindici -i, in a fortnight's time; di meno -i, younger; (poet.) pieno di -i, full of days, old; — estremo, dying day, day of death; non aver tutti i suoi -i, not to have profited from experience, to be stupid; vedere la luce del —, to see the light of day, to be born; mai dei miei -i, never in my life; verrà —, verrà il —, the day will come; verrà il — 13, he will be coming on the 13th; tutto —, always; a -i, in fits and starts; verrà a -i, he will be here any day now; — per —, regularly every day; di — in —, from one day to another, day after day; da un — all'altro, overnight, all of a sudden; un —, one day, once upon a time; ordine del —, agenda, (mil.) order of the day; (leg.) — utile, the time limit by which an act can be performed; del —, current; giorno giorno, al — di oggi, nowadays; nei primi -i della settimana ventura, early next week; negli ultimi -i del mese, late in the month; tenere uno a —, to keep someone posted, to keep someone up to date; mettere a —, to bring up to date; essere a -i, essere in -i, (of a woman) to be on the point of labour, to be near her time; il — dopo, next day, the day after; il suo —

di ricevimento, her at-home day; il — delle Ceneri, Ash Wednesday; il — dei morti, All Souls' Day; — feriale, working day; — festivo, holiday, non-working day, (leg.) *dies non*; — di magro, abstinence day; ultimi -i di carnevale, Shrovetide; (leg.) -i di rispetto, days of grace (C.C.).

Giọṣa-fa·t, Giọṣafà, Giọṣafatte *pr.n.m.* (Bibl.) Jehoshaphat, Josaphat; la valle di —, the valley of Jehoshaphat, traditionally regarded as the scene of the Last Judgement.

Giosi·a *pr.n.m.* (Bibl.) Josiah.

†giosta *f.* See **giostra**.

giostr-a *f.* joust; merry-go-round, roundabout; (eng.) capstan, trunnion; (theatr. hist.) a theatrical exhibition held in the Tuscan mountains, the actors being dressed up as knights and singing their parts and fighting with wooden swords; tournament-poem; joke, jest, trick; †jousting arena. **-are** [A 1] *intr.* (*aux.* avere) to joust; to tilt; to jostle; to wrestle; (theatr. hist.) to represent a play in the Tuscan mountains; to argue; -are col diavolo in agonia, to die unshriven; to loiter about; *tr.* to trick, to make believe; †to joust with; †to propel violently, to knock, to send flying. **-ante** *part. adj.* jousting; jostling; *n.m.* jouster. **-atọre** *m.* jouster; (theatr. hist.) actor taking part in tournament performances in the Tuscan mountains. **-one** *m.* loiterer. **-oni** *adv.* (Tusc.) andar -oni, to idle about.

Giọ·ṣue *pr.n.m.* Joshua.

giọttẹs-co *adj.* (*pl.* **-chi**) (paint.) Giottesque, in the manner of Giotto; of or pertaining to Giotto.

giovamẹnto *m.* See under **giovare**.

giọvan-e, giọvin-e *adj.* young; il — tempo, springtime; il re —, (a) Henry, son of Henry II of England; (b) one of the Three Wise Men (Balthazar); younger, junior; Plinio il —, the younger Pliny; immature; new, unpractised; *n.m., f.* youth, young man, young woman; da —, as a young man; -i carissimi!, my young friends!; learner, apprentice; shop assistant; — di camera, room steward. **-ac·cio** *m. pejor.* young scamp; callow young man. **-a·glia** *f. pejor.* gang of youths. **(in)-astro** *m.* boy in his teens, lad; young man. **(in)-cello** *m.* dim. (joc.) young lad; *adj.* youngish. **-eggiare** [A 3 C] *intr.* (*aux.* avere) to behave like a youth. **†-esco** *adj.* youthful; youth-like. **-ẹtto** *m.* dim. boy, young boy; *adj.* youthful; early; †gallina -etta, pullet. **-evec·chio** *m.* elderly bachelor. **-ẹzza** *f.* youth; youthful action; tornare in -ezza, to enter one's second childhood. **(an)-ile** *adj.* juvenile; youthful; suitable for a young person; young in style. **(an)-ilmẹnte** *adv.* youthfully. **-ino** *adj.* dim. very young, of tender years; rather young. **†-itudine** *f.* see **gioventù**. **-ọna** *f.*, **-ọne** *m.* prospering young person. **-otto** *m.* young man, youth; strong lad, robust young man; bachelor; ship's 'boy'. **-ottata** *f.* act of youthful boldness or thoughtlessness. **-ottẹllo, -ottẹtto** *m.* youth, adolescent.

Giovanna *pr.n.f.* Joan, Jane, Jayne.

Giovann-i *pr.n.m.* John; compare di San —, godfather (at baptism); San — Battista, St John the Baptist; fratelli di San —, Brothers Hospitallers of St John of God; (bot.) erba di San —, orpine, livelong, *Sedum telephium*; Don —, Don Juan; (poet.) il bel San —, the Baptistery at Florence. **-iti** *m.pl.* (eccles. hist.) Johannines, Johannites.

giovanotto *m.* See under **giovane**.

giovara *f.* (butcher.) front part of the chuck of beef.

giov-are [A 1 C] *tr., intr.* (*aux.* avere, essere) to be useful, to help; fare a giova giova, to help one another; *impers.* non -a, it's no use; (prep.) a) to matter, to be of import, to be opportune; mi -a credere, I can well believe; †to give pleasure, to delight; †non — a, to disgust, to be revolting to; *rfl.* (prep.) di to profit (from); to utilize, to make use (of); to avail oneself (of). **-amẹnto** *m.* advantage, value; benefit; avail; relief, improvement (as a result of treatment in illness). **-ẹvole** *adj.* useful, serviceable. **(-evolmẹnte** *adv.*) **†-evolezza** *f.* usefulness.

Giọv-e *pr.n.m.* Jove, Jupiter; — statore, Jupiter Stator; — pluvio, Jupiter the rain-bringer (jokingly blamed for inopportune rain); monte di —, St Gotthard; il giorno di —, Thursday; (orn.) uccel di —, eagle; (astron.) Jupiter; il cielo di —, the Heaven of Jupiter.

giovedì *n.m.* Thursday; — santo, Holy Thursday, Maundy Thursday; — grasso, last Thursday of Carnival; (colloq.) gli manca un —, he has a screw loose, he's not quite all there.

Giovenal-e *pr.n.m.* Juvenal. **-ẹsco** *adj.* (*m.pl.* **-ẹschi**) in the manner of Juvenal.

gioven-ca *f.* (zool.) heifer. **-co** *m.* (*pl.* **-chi**) (zool.) yearling bull; *pl.* young of all bovine cattle.

gioventù *f. indecl.* youth, youthfulness, prime of life; youth, young people; la — bruciata, people who grew up during World War II, the 'young outsiders', young existentialists, young delinquents, the 'beat generation'; stock of young plants; (Ital. hist.) la Gioventù Italiana del Littorio (1937–43), a Fascist youth organization in charge of army drill, sport and other recreational activities.

gioverẹccio *adj.* (Tusc. fam.) bright and healthy-looking, beautifully clean; helpful, useful; pleasant, agreeable.

giovẹvole *adj.* See under **giovare**.

giovial-e *adj.* cordial, jovial; jolly; affable. **-mẹnte** *adv.* cordially, jovially; affably. **-ità** *f.* cordiality, joviality; jolliness; affability. **-oc·cio** *adj.* jolly. **-ọne** *m.* cordial, jovial, jolly person. (**-ọna** *f.*)

giọvine *adj., n.m., f.* and derivs. (Tusc.). See **giovane**.

giovinẹzza *f.* (Tusc.) youth, youthfulness; young people, youth; *pr.n.f.* title of the Fascist anthem.

†giovo *m.* See **giogo**.

gipẹto *m.* (orn.) lammergeyer, bearded vulture, *Gypaëtus barbatus.*

gippọne *m.* (slang) a large jeep or car, esp. as used by Italian police.

gipsoteca *f.* gallery of plaster casts.

†gira *f.* (comm.). See **girata**, under **girare**.

gira-barchino *m. indecl.* (eng.; carp.) brace. **-capo** *m.* dizziness; attack of giddiness; nuisance; (bot.) campernelle jonquil, *Narcissus odorus.* **-dischi** *m. indecl.* (mus.) turntable (of gramophone, radio, etc.); disk jockey; record-player (attached to wireless). **-dito** *m. indecl.* (med.) whitlow. **-filiera** *f.* (eng.) diestock. **-maschi** *m. indecl.* (eng.) tap wrench.

gira·bile *adj.* See under **girare**.

giraffa *f.* (zool.) giraffe; (cinem.) movable platform supporting the camera and cameraman; (radio) — del microfono, microphone boom, movable microphone arm.

giramẹnto *m.* See under **girare**.

giramọndo *m.* vagrant; globe-trotter; adventurer.

giran·dol-a *f.* Catherine wheel; (fig.) dar fuoco alla —, to speak out regardless of consequences, to put into effect secret preparations; la — ha preso fuoco, 'the balloon has gone up'; toy windmill; artifice; whim; voluble person; †(naut.) wind vane. **-are** [A I S] *intr.* (*aux.* avere) to roam; to stroll, to ramble; (fig.) to romance. **-ẹtta, -ina** *f. dim.* small Catherine wheel. **-ino** *m. dim.* voluble person; weathercock; boy fond of wandering; †whirligig. **-ọne** *m.* wanderer, globe-trotter. **-ọni** *adv.* wandering; andar **-oni**, to roam about.

gira·nio *m.* (bot., pop.). See **geranio**.

girardina *f.* See **gerardina**.

gir-are [A I] *tr.* to turn round, to swing round, to make to revolve; to turn; to rotate; to spin; — la frase, to turn a phrase; — il periodo, to round off a sentence; — il discorso, to change the subject; -a e rigira, whichever way you look at it, after considerable efforts; -a e rigira, alfine l'ho trovato, after looking here, there and everywhere, at last I found it; (billiards) — la palla, to put on screw; (comm.) to endorse; — una polizza di carica, to endorse a bill of lading; — una cambiale, to back a bill of exchange; — i denari, to assign money; (archit.) — un arco, to construct an arch; to go round, to travel through; to surround; to go round, to get round; (mil.) — la posizione, to outflank, to turn, to avoid direct frontal attạck (also fig.); (cinem.) to shoot, to film; *intr.* (*aux.* avere) to revolve; to go round; to rotate; che ti -a?, what have you got in your head now?; se mi -a, if the fancy takes me, if I feel in the mood; — largo, to keep one's distance, to be cautious; to swing; (naut.) — sull'ancora, to swing at anchor, to turn short on one's anchor; to turn (about); to wander round, to go around; è tutt'oggi che -o senza trovarlo, I've been trying to find him all day; to circulate; si vedono — delle brutte facce, there are some sinister-looking types about; to be in circulation; to turn, to go off, to go bad; (naut.; aeron.) to yaw. **-a·bile** *adj.* that may be turned round; (comm.; leg.) assignable by endorsement. **-amẹnto** *m.* turning round, revolution, rotation; -amento di capo, dizziness; strange notion; volubility; tediousness. **-ante** *part. adj.* turning; returning; *n.m.* (leg.; comm.) endorser; -ante di una cambiale, backer, endorser of a bill of exchange; il -ante precedente, the prior endorser; il -ante successivo, the subsequent endorser; (eng.) impeller; rotor; turbine wheel. **-ata** *f.* turn, twist, revolution; ride, tour; (leg.; finan.) endorsement; endorsement over; transference by endorsement; -ata condizionata,

qualified endorsement; munire di -ata, to endorse; privo di -ata, unendorsed; -ata in bianco, endorsement in blank; deal (at cards); (naut.) alteration of course. **-ata·rio** *m.* (comm.) endorsee; assignee by endorsement; *adj.* (naut.) punto -atario, turning point of a vessel; periodo -atario, turning time. **-atina** *f. dim.* little trip, ride, 'spin'; small turn. **-ato** *part. adj.* turned; (leg.) endorsed; backed; endorsed over; *n.m.* roast; (cinem.) shot; location. **-atore** *m.* (techn.) turner, wheel-turner. **-ato·rio** *adj.* (motor.; techn.) coppa -atoria, roundabout. **-aziọne** *f.* see **giramento**. **-ẹvole** *adj.* revolving; twisting; whirling; that operates by twisting or turning; swivelling; rotating; gru -evole, slewing crane; (motor cycle) manopola -evole, twist-grip control; (fig.) inconsistent; fickle. **-evolmẹnte** *adv.* in a whirling movement; inconsistently.

girarrọsto *m.* roasting-jack, turnspit; dog trained to turn a roasting spit.

girasọle *m.* (bot.) sunflower, *Helianthus annuus*; — del Canadà, Jerusalem artichoke, *H. tuberosus*; *Chrozophora tinctoria*; (miner.) girasol.

giravolt-a *f.* turn round, right-about face; twist and turn; change of front; shift; †journey. **-are** [A I] *intr.* (*aux.* avere) to turn about; to twist and turn; to shift; to change one's tone.

gire¹ [def.] *intr.* (*aux.* essere) (poet.) to go; girsene, to go away, to depart; †to die. †— di più, to go further, to progress.

†gire² *m.* procedure, activity; goings on.

gir-ella *f.* a wooden disc as a toy, made like a little cartwheel with a groove in its rim on which string may be wound, so that when the string is pulled off, it spins the disc round so that it will roll away some distance; yo-yo; (eng.) pulley; rowel (e.g. of a spur); (draughts, backgammon) piece, man; round cheese; †(naut.) astrolabe; (fig.) tricks, wiles; foibles; (Tusc.) dare nelle -e, to go off one's head; (ichth.) rainbow wrasse, *Coris julis*; *m. indecl.* turncoat, political weathercock. **-ella·io** *m.* maker or seller of 'girelle'; inconstant person. **-ellare** [A I] *intr.* (*aux.* avere) to wander about; to stroll; andare -ellando, to stroll about; fare -ellare, to twirl. **-elliọ** *m.* (*pl.* -ellii) constant wandering about, ceaseless meandering. **-ello** *m.* little circle, little ring; ring inserted between the nave of a wheel and the axle-tree to make them fit more closely; little wooden circular frame, mounted on castors, used to support a child in its first attempts to walk; washer; heart or bottom of an artichoke; flattened portion of axis at the base of an onion; (butcher.) round (English butchers use the terms 'round', 'topside' and 'silverside' for what in Italian is termed 'culatta' or 'pezza', 'girello' and 'controgirello'; the cuts do not exactly correspond); †armilla, bracelet; †sleeve opening. **-ellonare** [A I C] *intr.* (*aux.* avere) to saunter; to wander; to loaf. **-ellọne** *m.* saunterer; wanderer; loafer; a person who is always out and about. **-ellotto** *m.* spinning disc; washer.

girẹtto *m. dim.* See under **giro**.

girẹvole *adj.* See under **girare**.

gir(i)fal-co *m.* (*pl.* **-chi**) (orn.) gyrfalcon, *Falco rusticolus*; (mil.) piece of artillery, falconet.

girigo·gol-o *m.* scrawl; spiral; meaningless curves and flourishes added to writing; (mus.) whirligig tune. **-are** [A I S] *intr.* (*aux.* avere) to scrawl, to draw flourishes; to 'doodle' spiral-shaped designs.

†girime·o *m.* street entertainment; whim, caprice; fantasy.

girino *m.* (zool.) tadpole.

girlo¹ *m.* (bot.) bitter vetch, *Vicia ervilia.*

girlo² *m.* die.

gir-o *m.* circle, ring; circuit; circumference; rim (of a jar, etc.); — della manica, arm-hole; tour; stroll; drive; run; andar in —, to go around, to go about; dopo una breve malattia è di nuovo in —, after a brief illness he is up and about once more; fare un —, to do a tour, to take a trip, to go for a drive; (theatr.) tour; compagnia di —, touring company; -i in provincia, provincial touring; prendere in —, to make fun of, to tease, to pull (a person's) leg; — di parole, circumlocution; revolution; turn; rotation; (eng.) -i al 1′, r.p.m.; numero di -i, rotation speed; — di vite, turn of the screw; (fig.) dare un — di vite a, to put pressure on; a — di posta, by return of post; un — di sole, a year; far mezzo —, (of a person) to turn round, to face about; turn (of a phrase); turn (e.g. in a rota); nel — di qualche minuto, in a matter of a few minutes; nel — di pochi mesi, in the course of a few months; round (e.g. of visits, calls); circulation (e.g. of

gir-o (*cont.*)

money, news); period; sphere, compass; — d'orizzonte, wide-ranging survey; arrangement of the rooms in a house; lay-out; (econ.) — d'affari, turnover; (comm.) — di capitali, turnover; — di fondi, cash transfer; (naut.) space required by a ship at single anchor; non vi è il —, it is a berth with insufficient swinging room, a foul berth; — di barre, punishment or exercise which consists of sending men aloft, over the yard and down on the opposite side of the ship; — di bussola, compass correction swing at a buoy; — di orizzonte, astronomical swing at sea; (slang) — di bitta, 'curl' on an executive officer's uniform gold lace (nineteenth century, now worn by all officers of the R.N. and Marina Militare); (naut.; aeron.) yaw; momento di —, yawing moment; (agric.) rotation (of crops); (sport) lap. **-ẹtto** *m. dim.* little tour; walk, stroll; trip; jaunt, spin; curl; (shoem.) welt. **-olo** *m.* slip on writing-paper to facilitate sealing.

girò *m. indecl.* a Sardinian wine.

girobus·sol-a *f.* gyroscopic compass. **-isti** *m.pl.* (naut.) compass maintenance personnel.

girocọnto *m.* (finan.) clearance account.

girodano *m.* (text.) willow.

giroguidato *adj.* steered by a gyroscope.

Giro·lamo *pr.n.m.* Jerome.

giro·metro *m.* gyrometer.

Girometta *pr.n.f.* a popular song in praise of the various parts of a woman's dress, etc.; it begins: 'Chi t'ha fatto sì belle scarpette Che ti stan sì ben? Che ti stan sì ben, Girometta, che ti stan sì ben?'; La bella —, nickname given to a woman who is affected in her dress and speech.

gironda[1] *f.* (mus.). See **ghironda**.

Girond-a[2] *pr.n.f.* (geog.) Gironde. **-ino** *adj.* coming from the French department of Gironde; *n.m.* native of Gironde; (hist.) Girondist.

girondolare [A I s] and derivs. See **girandolare**, under **girandola**.

girone *m. augm.* of giro, q.v.; (mil.) encircling wall; †whirlwind; †whirlpool; (poet.) one of the divisions of the seventh circle of Dante's Hell and of the lower spheres of Heaven; (football) division of a league; — di andata, first half of the season; — di ritorno, second half of the season; (sport) series, round, heat; — finale, cup final; — all'italiana, tournament in which each team plays all the others; major turn in a river or road; (naut.) bulbous loom of an oar, between the handle and the rowlock; *adv.* see **gironi**. **-oni** *adv.* loafing about, wandering, loitering; andare **-oni**, to loiter, to loaf.

gironẓ-are [A I c], **-olare** [A I sc] *intr.* (*aux.* avere) to saunter; to ramble about; to snoop.

giro-pilota *m.* (naut.; aeron.) automatic pilot, 'George'; gyropilot. **-plano** *m.* (aeron.) gyroplane. **-rota** *m. indecl.* (naut.) stabilizer wheel.

girosc·o·pio *m.* gyroscope. **-o·pico** *adj.* gyroscopic.

girostabiliẓatore *m.* (naut.; aeron.) gyroscopic stabilizer.

giro·stato *m.* gyrostat, gyrostatic stabilizer.

girotondo *m.* round, dance; child's dance or game, somewhat similar to Ring a ring o' roses (the words differ according to region, one version being:

'Giro girotondo,
Il pan come un pan tondo,
Un mazzo di viole,
Per darle a chi le vuole,
Le vuol la più piccina'…etc.'

girotta *f.* streamer; rudder-yoke.

girovag-are [A 2 s] *intr.* (*aux.* avere) to roam about. **-ante** *part. adj.* roaming, vagrant; mercante **-ante**, hawker.

giro·va-go *adj.* (*m.pl.* **-ghi**) wandering, strolling; rambling; attore **-**, strolling player; *n.m.* wanderer; strolling pedlar, hawker; tramp.

Girumẹtta *pr.n.f.* See **Girometta**.

gisolreut[te] *m.* (mus.) G sol re ut, G below middle C.

†gisso *adj.* beautiful; good.

git-a *f.* excursion; trip; tour; jaunt; ramble; tradesman's round; †(chess) move; †(other games) play, turn, 'go'. **-erella** *f. dim.* little jaunt; walk; trip; spin.

gitan-a *f.* Spanish gipsy woman; Spanish gipsy girl; (mus.) *seguidilla gitana*, slow seguidilla in gipsy style. **-o** *m.* Spanish gipsy; *adj.* gipsy-like, gipsy-style; l'amore **-o**, gipsy love; nozze **-e**, gipsy wedding.

gitante *m., f.* tripper; — a piedi, hiker; delivery-boy; cercansi gitanti per recapito giornali a domicilio, newspaper boys wanted for delivery rounds.

gittaiọne *m.* See **gettaione**.

gittare [A I] and derivs. See **gettare**.

gittata *f.* see gettata, under **gettare**; range of a gun; a lunga —, long range; (agric.) seminare a —, to sow broadcast.

gitterọne *m.* See **gettaione**.

giù *adv.* down; below; downstairs; in —, down below; guardare uno in — in su, to look a person up and down; (to a dog) —!, down!; e —!, and down came…!; e — applausi!, there was thunderous applause; — —, way down, a long way down; — di qua, down here, along this way; porre —, to put down, to set down, to set aside, (fig.) to put out of one's mind; mandare —, to gulp down; mandar — una brutta notizia, to receive bad news; non lo posso mandare —, I can't (and won't) put up with it; andare —, to go down, to fall, (fig.) to go down in the world or in health; è molto —, he's very down in the mouth, he is run down in health, he's depressed; su e —, up and down; su per —, — di lì, more or less, roughly speaking, by and large; buttare —, to fling down, to toss off, to jot down, (fig.) to depress; (cul.) to put on to cook; buttar — la pasta, to put the 'pasta' into the boiling pot; buttarsi —, to fling oneself down, to become depressed; dare —, to fall, to collapse, (of sediment) to be deposited, (fig.) to be defeated, to calm down; (mus.) arcata in —, down-bow; tirare —, to swear, to do slap-dash work; †mandare —, to kill; †torsi —, to desist; †trarsi —, to desert.

giubb-a[1] *f.* mane. **-ato** *adj.* maned, having a mane.

giubb-a[2] *f.* swallow-tail coat; evening tail coat; dress-coat; man's coat or jacket; farsi tirar la —, to run up bills, to be always in arrears with one's debts; rivoltar —, to change sides; —, rivoltata, turncoat; (naut.) — di gala, best jumper (No. 1); †skirt of a woman's dress. **†-erello** *m.* jacket; jerkin. **-ẹtto** *m. dim.* loose jacket. **-oncello** *m. dim.* of giubbone, q.v. **-ọne** *m. augm.* rough greatcoat; spolverare il **-one** a, to give a beating to; piegare il **-one**, to go to work with a good will, to put one's shoulder to the wheel. **-otto** *m.* jerkin. **-otto** di salvataggio, life jacket.

giubbẹtto[1] *m. dim.* of giubba[2], q.v.

†giubbẹtto[2] *m.* gibbet.

giubil-are [A I s] *intr.* (*aux.* avere) to rejoice; to be jubilant; to exult; *tr.* to pension off; to put out to grass. **-ante** *part. adj.* rejoicing; jubilant; exultant. **-ato** *part. adj.* retired, pensioned off; (joc.) marito **-ato**, grass-widower. **-atọre** *m.* rejoicer. (**-atrice** *f.*) **-aziọne** *f.* jubilation, rejoicing; pensioning off, superannuation, retirement. **†-i·o** *m.* see giubilo.

giubile·o *m.* (Bibl.) Jubilee, (fiftieth) year of remission; (eccl.) Jubilee (year), Holy year (when special indulgences may be gained); (fig.) jubilee anniversary (strictly 50th but now often 25th), esp. of a priest's ordination or a professor's appointment to his chair; †see **giubilo**.

giu·bil-o *m.* joy, jubilation. **†-oso** *adv.* jubilant.

giuc-co *adj.* (*m.pl.* **-chi**) foolish; — per vino, drunk; *n.m.* silly ass. **-cag·gine** *f.* foolishness. **-cata** *f.* foolish action. **-cheri·a** *f.* stupidity, foolishness; asinine behaviour.

Giud-a[1] *pr.n.m.* Judah; (bot.) orecchio di —, Jew's ear fungus, *Hirneola auricula-judae.* **-aẹsmo** *m.* see giudaismo. **-a·ico** *adj.* Jewish, Judaic; bitume **-aico**, asphalt; (bot.) erba **-aica**, golden rod, *Solidago virgaurea.* **-aicamẹnte** *adv.* in Jewish fashion; ruthlessly. **-aiṣmo** *m.* Judaism. **-aiẓẓare** [A I] *intr.* (*aux.* avere) to follow Jewish customs.

Giuda[2] *pr.n.m.* Judas; albero di —, Judas tree, *Cercis siliquastrum*; il buon —, Judas Maccabaeus; (fig.) traitor (from Judas Iscariot); bacio di —, traitor's kiss.

Giud-ẹa *pr.n.f.* (geog.) Judaea; noto in —, notorious; (bot.) vite di —, bitter-sweet, woody nightshade, *Solanum dulcamara.* **-e·o** *adj. pejor.* Jewish; *n.m.* Jew; Israelite.

Giudecca *pr.n.f.* island in the Venetian lagoon; (poet.) the circle of the traitors in Dante's *Inferno*.

Giudi·a *adv. phr.* (cul.) carciofi alla —, artichokes dipped in boiling oil.

giudic-are [A 2 s] *tr.* to judge; to think, to deem, to consider; (leg.) to sentence, to pass sentence on; to adjudicate, to decide, to determine (an action, cause or matter); to judge; to adjudge in accordance with the provisions of a will; to bequeath; *intr.* (*aux.* avere) to judge; (naut., of a rope) -a bene, it has a clear lead;

giudic-are (*cont.*)

-a male, it has a foul lead; (leg.) to give judgement, to pronounce sentence, to adjudicate. **-a·bile** *adj.* that may be judged, assessable; *n.m.*, *f.* (leg.) defendant; accused; person who is being judged. †**-amento** *m.* judgement; Last Judgement; law; opinion; discretion; discernment; sense, judgement; franco -amento, free will. **-ante** *part. adj.* (leg.) judging; judicial; il tribunale -ante, the Court trying the case; *n.m.* judge; the person who acts as a judge; judicator. **-ativo** *adj.* that helps in judging; (leg.) judicative. **-ato** *part. adj.* judged; sacco legato fu mal -ato, it is unwise to make untimely judgements (esp. as regards sex before birth); (leg.) causa -ata, decided case; cosa -ata formale, *res giudicata* (C.C.P.); passare in cosa -ata, to become final; decisive (of a battle); *n.m.* judgement; (leg.) -ato penale, judgement of criminal Court; sentenza passata in-ato, judgement, order that has become final (C.C.P.); -ati passati, precedents; (hist.) one of the four self-governing districts of Sardinia (eleventh to thirteenth centuries). **-atore** *m.* judge, critic, one who judges. (**-atora** *f.*) **-ato·rio** *adj.* (*m.pl.* **-atorii**) judiciary. **-atrice** *adj. f.* giving judgement. **-atura** *f.* judicature. **-azione** *f.* judgement.

giu·dice *m.* judge; una donna —, a woman judge; the Bench; justice; magistrate; erigersi a —, to be raised to the Bench; ricorrere al —, to go to court; citare innanzi al —, to have up; Giudice Supremo, Supreme Judge, God; (leg.) judge of any of several grades of court, civil and criminal, in Italian judicial system (narrower term than 'magistrato', q.v.); — degli incidenti, judge superintending the execution of sentence, judgement or order (C.C.P.); — di prima istanza, judge of first instance; — d'appello, judge of an appeal court; — collegiale, member of the Court; — competente, judge of competent jurisdiction; — conciliatore, justice of the peace; magistrate (C.C.P.); — delegato, official receiver; — istruttore, examining magistrate; coroner (C.P.P.); examining judge of 'Tribunale' (member of the Court also performing certain functions of master, registrar, etc.) (C.C.P.); — naturale, judge whom the law assigns to every man according to the nature of the cause or matter and the natural and legal condition of the parties thereto (cf. — competente); essere distolto del — naturale precostituto, to be denied the right to be judged by one's natural and preordained judge (I.C.); — popolare, lay assessor (in Court of Assize) (C.P.P.); juryman; — tutelare, tutelary judge (of person under disability), Master in Lunacy; — di sorveglianza, superintending judge (C.P.P.); — unico, judge sitting alone; ausiliari del —, expert assistants of the Court (C.C.P.); ricusare un giudice, to challenge a judgement; (sport) — di partenza, starter; — di arrivo, judge at the finish (athletics, skiing, etc.); (fig.) lasciar — alcuno, to leave the decision to someone else; farsi —, erigersi a —, to set oneself up as a judge; essere buon — in cose di musica, to be a good judge of music; (Bibl.) il Libro dei Giudici, the Book of Judges.

giudich̤essa *f.* (joc.) woman sitting as it were in judgement; judge's wife.

giudicial-e *adj.* judicial. **-mente** *adv.* judicially.

giudici-a·rio, -oso *adj.* judicious.

Giuditta *pr.n.f.* Judith; — e Oloferne, Judith and Holofernes.

giudizial-e *adj.* judicial; (leg.) judicial; vendita —, sale by order of court; domanda —, claim; procedere per via —, to take legal proceedings; †il dì —, the Day of Judgement. **-mente** *adv.* judicially.

giudizia·r·io *adj.* judiciary; (leg.) judicial; amministratore —, receiver and manager (appointed by the court); riforma -ia, judicial reform; atti -i, judicial acts; procedimento —, judicial proceedings; ufficiale —, bailiff; usher; cauzione -ia, security for costs; potere —, judicial power; †(med.) giorni -i, critical days; *n.m.* astrologer. **-iamente** *adv.* judicially.

giudi·z·io *m.* (leg.) judgement; opinion; reason; decision; action; proceedings; trial; suit; iniziare —, to start proceedings; essere chiamato in —, to be sued, to be summonsed; sospendere in —, to stay judgement; assistenza in —, legal aid; rinnovazione di —, retrial; forma del —, procedure; sotto —, sub judice; citare in —, to cite; to summons; to sue; integrare un —, to complete a suit; rappresentare in —, to represent legally; comparire in —, to appear in court; comparizione in —, appearance before a court; spese di —, legal costs; — imparziale, impartial judgement; riassunzione di —, resumption of proceedings or trial; deporre in —, to give evidence; rinviare a —, to commit for trial; — decisivo, final judgement; — direttissimo, summary trial

without preliminary investigation (C.P.P.); parte estratta da un —, extract from a judgement; rinviare un —, to adjourn a suit or action; recedere un —, to desist from an action; — esecutivo, executive judgement, executory judgement; — contumaciale, judgement by default; — possessorio, action of possession, possessory action; — dei giurati, verdict; — di primo grado, trial at first instance; — d'appello, trial at appeal; — di prima istanza, judgement of first instance; — di ultima istanza, judgement of last resort; — sommario, summary proceedings; (fig.) hasty, ill-considered judgement; — nullo, mistrial; — civile, civil action; — criminale, criminal trial; — per decreto, trial and judgement by decree (C.P.P.); — sulle impugnazioni, trial at appeal (generically) (C.P.P.); (fig.) età del —, age of reason; denti del —, wisdom teeth; avere —, to be sensible, to be prudent; abbi —!, take care!, don't be hasty!; a suo —, in his opinion; stare al — di, to abide by the judgement of; stando al — del critico della *Stampa*, according to the opinion of the *Stampa* critic; il Giudizio Universale, il giorno del —, Judgement Day; — finale, Last Judgement; — di Dio, judgement of God; fare —, to act fairly, to be fair. **-oso** *adj.* judicious, prudent, circumspect. **-iosamente** *adv.* judiciously; prudently; with circumspection.

†**giue** *adv.* See **giù**.

†**giuggiare** *vb.* and derivs. See **giudicare**.

giug·giol-a *f.* (bot.) fruit of the jujube (see **giuggiolo**); jujube sweet; andare in brodo di -e, to show the greatest delight, to go into ecstasies, to gush; trifle, bagatelle. **-a·io** *m.* jujube seller. **-ena** *f.* (bot.) sesame, *Sesamum indicum*. **-etta** *f.* trifle. **-ino** *adj.* reddish yellow; made of jujubes. **-o** *m.* (bot.) jujube, *Zizyphus jujuba*; (provb.) quando il -o si veste, e tu ti spogli, quando il -o si spoglia, e tu ti vesti, when the jujube tree gets dressed, you undress, when the jujube tree gets undressed, you get dressed: this is based on the observation that the jujube tree is the last to leaf and the first to lose its leaves (cf. Eng. provb. 'cast ne'er a clout till May be out', which can be interpreted to refer to the may-tree; but cf. also under **giugno**). **-ona** *f.*, **-one** *m. augm.* large jujube; stupid person; gushing individual.

giu·gnere [C5] and derivs. See **giungere**.

giugn-o *m.* June; (provb.) giugno, getta il cuticugno, cast ne'er a clout till May be out. **-olino** *adj.* pertaining to June; (agric.) mela -olina, a type of apple which is ripe in June.

giu·gnolo *adj.* pertaining to June; (agric.) pera giugnola, a variety of pear which is ripe in June.

giugolare, giugulare[1] *adj.* (anat.) jugular; *n.m.* jugular vein.

giugolare, giugulare[2] [A I s] *tr.* to cut the throat of; to throttle, to strangle.

giugurtino *adj.* Jugurthine.

†**giul-adro,** †**-atro** *m.* See **giullare**.

giulebb-e *m.* aromatic syrup, julep; (fig.) too sweet a thing; sweet content, sweet illusion. **-are** [A I] *tr.* to coat with sugar; to sweeten; to candy; (fig.) to keep (a person) in cotton wool; to keep and take care of (a person) whether willingly or not (e.g. a daughter for whom no husband can be found); *rfl.* (*dat.* of *prn.* 'si') to cherish. **-ato** *part. adj.* candied; (fig.) cherished.

†**giulecc-a** *f.*, †**-o** *m.* dress worn by slaves.

giuleone *m.* three cards of the same denomination in the game of 'bazzica'.

†**giuleppo** *m.* See **giulebbe**.

Giu·lia *pr.n.f.* Julia; (bot.) erba —, *Achillea ageratum*.

Giuliana *pr.n.f.* Juliana; (cul.) Julienne soup.

Giuliano *pr.n.m.* Julian; (hist.) Julian, pertaining to Julius Caesar; il calendario —, the Julian calendar.

Giuli̤etta *pr.n.f.* Juliet; name of a car made by Alfa Romeo.

giuli̤ette *f.pl.* (bot.) Canterbury bells, *Campanula Medium*.

giu·li·o[1] *adj.* (hist.) Julian; astro —, the comet which is said to have appeared at the time of the death of Julius Caesar; (geog.) Foro —, Friuli; *n.m.* (numism.) coin first minted by Pope Julius II, 1503–13; (phys.) joule; †July. **-ense** *adj.* pertaining to Julius Caesar; inhabitant of Friuli.

Giu·lio[2] *pr.n.m.* Julius; — Cesare, Julius Caesar.

†**giuli·o**[3] *m.* joy; bliss; *adj.* blissful; rejoicing.

giuliv-o *adj.* merry, festive, joyous. (**-amente** *adv.*) **-ività** *f.* joyfulness, festivity.

giull-are *m.* strolling player; minstrel; jester; buffoon. **-aresco** *adj.* (*m.pl.* **-areschi**) pertaining to a strolling player, troubadour. **-eri·a** *f.* trade of a strolling player; bands of strolling players.

giumella *f.* double-handful; a giumelle, in great quantity; (herald.) two similar bands, waves, etc.; (naut.) doubling plates; strengthening spars; capstan whelps.

giument-a *f.* female donkey, mule, or horse, used as a pack animal; (fig.) attaccar la —, to fall into a deep sleep. **-o** *m.* donkey, mule, or horse, used as pack animal. **-ose** *f.pl.* turbid or cloudy urine.

Giumna *pr.n.f.* (geog.) Jumna.

†**giunare** *vb.* and derivs. See **digiunare**

giunca *f.* (naut.) junk.

giun-chi·glia *f.*, **-chi·glio** *m.* (bot.) jonquil, *Narcissus jonquilla.* **-cone** *m.* (bot.) campernelle jonquil, *N. odorus.*

giunchina *f.* junket.

giun-co[1] *m.* (*pl.* **-chi**) (bot.) rush, *Juncus;* (naut.) grassline; cercare il nodo nel —, to keep making difficulties where there are none; costa più il — che la carne, i.e. the accessory is worth more than the article (referring to an old mode of carrying meat upon rushes); (naut.) halyard, lift, cable-laid rope. **-ca·cee** *f.pl.* (bot.) rush-like plants; (pop.) rushes. **-ca·ceo** *adj.* overgrown with rushes. **-ca·ia** *f.* bed of rushes. **-care** [A2] *tr.* to strew or cover with rushes; †to beat. **-castrello** *m.* (bot.) arrow-grass, *Triglochin.* **-cata** *f.* pressed unsalted curds which used to be served up on a mat of little rushes; junket. **-cheto** *m.* bed of rushes. **-coso** *adj.* overgrown with rushes.

†**giunco**[2] *m.* See **giunca**.

giun·g-ere [B5] *intr.* (*aux.* essere) to arrive; — nuovo, to be new information; mi -e nuovo, it's new to me, that's news to me; — a, to succeed in, to reach the point of, to manage to; to reach; †to happen; *tr.* to join, to unite, to put together; to combine; — le mani, to clasp hands, to join hands; to hit, to reach; †— i buoi, to yoke oxen; †to add. **-imento** *m.* joining, joint; arrival, reaching.

giungla *f.* jungle; (fig.) la legge della —, the law of the jungle.

Giuno *pr.n.f.* (poet.). See **Giunone**.

Giun-one *pr.n.f.* (myth.) Juno; il messo di —, Iris, the rainbow; uccello di —, peacock; (fig.) tall, handsome woman of Junoesque build. **-o·nico** *adj.* pertaining to Juno; bellezza -onica, Junoesque, opulent, majestic beauty. **-o·nio** *adj.* of or pertaining to Juno.

giunta[1] *f.* addition, extra piece, appendix; increase; surplus; è più la — che la derrata, the trimmings are more than the article; make-weight; per —, in addition, extra, into the bargain, moreover; di prima —, a —, at once, at first sight; (sport) handicap, start; (naut.) butt; *pl.* addenda; †arrival; †(anat.) joint.

giunta[2] *f.* board of management; Spanish *junta;* examination board; (local govt.) municipal council; (admin.) executive committee.

giunt-are [A1] *tr.* to trick, to cheat; to join together; to sew together; to piece together. **-ag·gio** *m.* (techn.) jointing, splicing. **-ato** *part. adj.* tricked, cheated; swindled; joined, united; sewn together; pieced together; jointed. **-atore** *m.* cheat, fraud, impostor; swindler. **-atrice** *f.* cheat; (text.) piecing machine; (cinem.) splicer (for film). **-eri·a** *f.* cheating, trickery; swindle; swindling.

giuntina[1] *f. dim.* of **giunta**[1], q.v.

giuntina[2] *f.* edition published by the Giunta, celebrated printers of the fifteenth century, who had presses in several cities of Italy, France and Spain.

giunt-o *part.* of **giungere**, q.v.; *adj.* arrived; joined; caught, taken by surprise; tricked; clasped; added; reached; †enjoined; †understood; *n.m.* (eng.) coupling; joint; — a briglia, — a labbro, flange, flanged coupling; — a cannocchiale, telescope joint; — a compensazione, expansion joint; — ad anelli, double ring-joint; — a frizione, clutch coupling; — a ginocchiera, ball and socket joint; — ad innesto, engaging and disengaging gear; †fraud, trickery. **-amente** *adv.* jointly. **-oie** *f.pl.* two short ropes which secure the yoke on the necks of a pair of oxen. **-ura** *f.* connexion, joint; -ura a caldo, welding; (anat.) joint, articulation; (of the skull) suture; †(gramm.) conjunction.

giunzione *f.* (techn.) junction, jointing, connexion; linea di —, seam; senza —, seamless.

giuocare [A2] and derivs. See **giocare**.

giuo-co *m.* (*pl.* **-chi**). See **gioco**.

†**giupp-a** *f.* and derivs. See **giubba**.

Giura[1] *pr.n.m.* (geog.) Jura.

†**giura**[2] *f.* See **giuramento**, under **giurare**.

†**giur-abbacco** *excl.* Deuce! (Bacchus). †**-addiana** *excl.* Deuce! †**-addi·o** *excl.* Good heavens!; *n.m.* (*pl.* **-addi·i**) exclamation of surprise.

giuracchi-are [A4] *intr.* (*aux.* avere) to swear a little. **-amento** *m.* a mild oath.

giur-are [A1] *tr.*, *intr.* (*aux.* avere) (leg.) to swear; to declare under oath; to take an oath; — in falso, to commit perjury; (colloq.) **-arci**, to be sure; ci -o che sono scappati, I bet they have done a bunk; puoi -arlo!, you can be sure of that!; l'avevo -ato!, I was right! **-a·bile** *adj.* to be sworn to. **-amento** *m.* oath; swearing; prendere (prestare) -amento, to take an oath; dichiarare sotto -amento, to state on oath; dichiarazione sotto -amento, affidavit; violare il -amento, to break the oath; deferire al convenuto un -amento, to administer an oath to the defendant; -amento promissorio, promissory oath; -amento solenne, solemn oath; -amento falso, perjury; -amento decisorio, interrogatories; -amento di fedeltà, oath of allegiance; -amento d'ufficio, oath of office; -amento affermativo, assessory oath; -amento assertorio, confirmatory oath; -amento suppletorio, suppletory oath; -amento politico, official oath, oath of office; -amento volontario, voluntary oath; -amento legale, judicial oath; -amento condizionale, limited oath. **-ativo** *adj.* swearing. **-ato** *part. adj.* sworn; *n.m.* (leg.) juror; juryman; perito -ato, sworn expert (C.P.P.); ricusazione di -ato, challenge of a juror; il verdetto dei -ati, the verdict. **-atamente** *adv.* by swearing. **-atore** *m.* person who takes an oath; swearer. (**-atrice** *f.*) **-ato·rio** *adj.* (*m.pl.* **-atorii**) pertaining to the oath; juratory. **-azione** *f.* juration.

giuras·sico *adj.* (geol.) Jurassic.

giur-e *m.* (leg.) jurisprudence; law. **-econsulto** *m.* jurisconsult; master of jurisprudence. **-econsultissimo** *m.* jury. †**-ì** *m.* expert lawyer; see **giure**. **-i·a** *f.* jury; selection committee. **-idiciale** *adj.* juridical; jurisprudential. **-idicità** *f.* quality of being juridical. **-i·dico** *adj.* juridical; persona -idica, body corporate, corporation, legal 'person' (C.C.). NOTE: the following are the general concepts of academic terms, full definition of which is beyond the scope of this work: fatto -idico, act or omission, or event, whereof the law takes cognizance which creates, extinguishes or varies a right; atto -idico, act or omission causing effect of which the law takes cognizance; negozio -idico, manifestation of will with intent lawfully to vary, replace or extinguish a right; negozio -idico bilaterale, the like manifestation of will, as to a right in contract; negozio -idico unilaterale, the like manifestation of will, under a power; atto -idico illecito, unlawful act or omission giving rise to liability in tort. **-idicamente** *adv.* juridically. **-idizione** *f.* jurisdiction. **-isconsulto** *m.* jurisconsult; jurisprudent. **-isdizionale** *adj.* jurisdictional; attività -isdizionale, exercise of jurisdiction (C.C.). **-isdizione** *f.* jurisdiction; -isdizione contenziosa, contentious jurisdiction, jurisdiction in contentious business; -isdizione civile, civil jurisdiction; -isdizione criminale, -isdizione penale, criminal jurisdiction; -isdizione territoriale, territorial jurisdiction; conflitto di -isdizione, conflict of jurisdiction; mancanza di -isdizione, want of jurisdiction. **-isperito** *adj.* jurisprudent; jurist. **-isprudente** *m.* jurisprudent; jurist. **-isprudenza** *f.* jurisprudence. **-ista** *m.* jurist. **-i·stico** *adj.* juristic. †**-izione** *f.* jurisdiction.

giuro *m.* (poet.) oath.

gius *m. indecl.* (leg.) just; law; authority; equity; rule; right.

giusarma *f.* (hist.) a kind of battle-axe; scimitar.

giusdicente *m.* (leg.) judge; justice.

Giusep·p-e *pr.n.m.* Joseph; (fig. joc.) il casto —, (with ref. to Potiphar's wife) man run after by an older woman, or any man fleeing from a temptress; (bot.) mazza di San —, oleander, *Nerium oleander.* **-ino** *adj.* (hist.) supporting Joseph Buonaparte (in Spain). **-ista** *m.* supporter of Joseph Buonaparte in Spain.

Giuseppina *pr.n.f.* Josephine.

†**giuso** *adv.* See **giù**.

giuspatronato *m.* (eccl.) patronage.

giusqui·amo *m.* (bot.) common henbane, *Hyoscyamus niger;* — bianco, white henbane, *H. albus;* (pharm.) estratto di —, tincture of henbane.

giust-a[1] *prep.* according to, in accordance with; in conformity with. **-ac(u)ore** *m.* close-fitting jacket; doublet, jerkin; justaucorps. **-apporre** [B21] *tr.* to juxtapose. **-apposizione** *f.* juxtaposition. **-appunto** *adv.* precisely; exactly, just.

Giusta[2] *pr.n.f.* Justina.

giustamente *adv.* See under **giusto**.

giustezza *f.* exactness, accuracy, precision; correctness, rectitude; nicety; (typ.) justification.

giustific-are [A 2 s] *tr.* to justify; to vindicate; to make good; (typ.) to justify; (theol.) to justify; *rfl.* to justify oneself, to excuse oneself. **-a·bile** *adj.* justifiable. **-abilménte** *adv.* justifiably. **-ante** *part. adj.* justifying; (theol.) grazia -ante, justifying grace. †**-anza** *f.* proof that justifies; justifiable judgement; judgement. **-ativo** *adj.* justifying, giving justification; (leg.) documento -ativo, supporting document; *n.m.* (comm.) voucher. **-ato** *part. adj.* justified; put right, made right; pardoned, forgiven, absolved; right; (leg.) justified; held to be right; justifiable; reclamo -ato, justifiable claim; denari -ati, money well spent. **-atamÉnte** *adv.* justifiably, with good reason. **-ato·rio** *adj.* justifying, rendering justifiable. **-azione** *f.* justification; explanation; vindication; excuse; (leg.) justification; presentare le sue -azioni, to show sufficient reasons; correction; (typ.) justifying.

giustina[1] *f.* (numis.) Venetian coin of 160 or 124 soldi.

Giustina[2] *pr.n.f.* Justina.

giustinia·neo *adj.* of or pertaining to Justinian; codice —, diritto —, Codex Justinianeus, Justinian's Code.

Giustiniano *pr.n.m.* Justinian.

giusti·zi-a *f.* justice; (leg.) amministrazione della —, administration of justice; rendere — a qualcuno, to give someone his due; (theol.) — originale, original justice (righteousness); (Ital. hist.) Giustizia e Libertà, an anti-Fascist movement founded by the Rosselli brothers in 1929; partisan formations (1943–5). **-are** [A4] *tr.* to execute, to put to death; (joc.) to illtreat, to misuse, to 'murder'; *rfl.* to torment oneself. **-ato** *part. adj.* executed; †condemned to death; *n.m.* man executed; †condemned man. **-erato** *adj.* justiciary. **-ere** *m.* justician; †executioner. **-o** *m.* (Rom. hist.) justitium, suspension of legal business. †**-oso** *adj.* just.

giust-o[1] *adj.* just, fair; righteous; strict; deserved, merited; legitimate; la -a causa, just cause; una pugna -a, a fair match; prezzo —, fair price; quel che è — è —, fair's fair; non è —!, it's not fair!; è più che —, it's only fair (or, how right you are); siamo -i!, let's be fair!, let's face it, let us admit; fare le cose -e, to share things equally, to be fair; suitable, reasonable; una famiglia -a, a family of reasonable size; a passo —, at an ordinary walking pace; naso —, nose of an average size; — di sale, with just the right amount of salt; il momento —, the right moment; peso —, correct weight; il — mezzo, the happy mean; correct for size; troppo —, too tight a fit; darle -e, to give back a good one (answer); exact; alle dieci -e, exactly at ten o'clock; (mus.) intervallo —, just interval; quarto —, perfect fourth; a tempo —, at a moderate speed, in strict time; proper, right; il — erede, the rightful heir; *n.m.* upright man, righteous man; rights, what is fair, justice, fairness; fair price; *adv.* just; — te volevo vedere!, you're the very man I wanted to see!; — te! venivo in cerca di te, oh there you are! I was looking for you; — ora, just now; —! ti ricordi mica quando disse che sarebbe tornato?, by the way, (or) à propos, you don't remember, do you, when he said he'd be back?; il treno delle dieci l'ho preso — —, I caught the ten o'clock train, but it was a near thing; ti sta — —, it only just fits you; (iron.) not at all; io andar da lui? —!, I go and see him? I don't think! (no fear!). **-aménte** *adv.* justly; rightly; with righteousness.

Giusto[2] *pr.n.m.* Justus.

†**giuvenca** *f.* See **giovenca**.

glaba *f.* (bot.) cutting of a tree.

glabella *f.* (anat.) glabella, space between the eyebrows.

glabro *adj.* glabrous, smooth, hairless.

glacial-e *adj.* icy, frigid; glacial. **-ménte** *adv.* icily, frigidly.

glaciazione *f.* (geol.) Ice Age; glaciation.

gladi-atore *m.* gladiator. **-ato** *adj.* (poet.) bearing a sword. **-ato·rio** *adj.* gladiatorial. **-atrice** *f.* female gladiator. **-atura** *f.* duel, fight; gladiatorship.

gla·dio *m.* (Rom. antiq.) gladius, short, two-edged sword.

gladi·olo *m.* (bot.). See **giaggiolo**.

glagoli·tico *adj.* Glagolitic; messale —, Glagolitic missal.

glande *m.* (anat.) glans penis.

glan·dol-a *f.* (anat.) gland; — tiroide, thyroid gland. **-are** *adj.* glandular. **-iforme** *adj.* glandiform. **-oso** *adj.* glandulous.

glan·dula *f.* and derivs. See **glandola**.

glare·ola *f.* (orn.) pratincole.

glasine *f.pl.* (bot.) — delle Alpi, bilberry, blaeberry, whortleberry, *Vaccinium myrtillus.*

glassare [A 1] *tr.* (cul.) to glaze, to make *glacé.*

---

glast(r)o *m.* (bot.) woad, *Isatis tinctoria.*

glauberite *f.* (miner.) glauberite.

gla·uc-o[1] *adj.* (m.pl. **gla·uchi**) sea-green, blue-green; (bot.) glaucous; *n.m. Glyphis glaucus,* a species of shark whose skin is made into shagreen. **-e·dine** *f.* glaucoma. **-ina** *f.* (chem.) fumaric acid. **-ità** *f. indecl.* glaucous quality. **-oma** *m.* (med.) glaucoma. **-o·nia** *f.* (miner.) glauconite. **-o·pide** *f.* (Gk. lit.) Homeric epithet of Pallas, prob. 'the gleaming-eyed'.

Gla·uco[2] *pr.n.m.* (myth.) Glaucus.

gleb-a *f.* clod; glebe; servo della —, serf. **-oso** *adj.* glebous.

gled-ic·cia *f.* (bot.) honey locust, *Gleditschia triacanthos.*

glen-e *f.* (anat.) glene. **-o·ide** *adj.* glenoid; *n.f.* glenoid cavity. **-oidale** *adj.* glenoidal.

gli[1] *def. art. m.pl.* (before vowel, impure s, z or gn) the.

gli[2] *pers. prn. m. sing. dat.* to him; to it; *f. sing. dat.* (combined with **lo, la, ne: gliele, gliela, gliene**) to her; (colloq.) *m.pl.* to them.

gli[3] *prn.* (Tusc. pop.) it; — è che, the fact is that.

gli·a *f.* (anat.) glia, neuroglia.

glicemi·a *f.* (med.) glycaemia.

glicer-ato *m.* (chem.) glycerate; (pharm.) glycerate; glyceric. **-ina** *f.* glycerine; (chem.) glycerin, glycerol. **-ofosfato** *m.* glycerophosphate. **-ofosfo·rico** *adj.* glycerophosphoric. **-o·leo** *m.* (pharm.) glycerole. **-olo** *m.* (chem.) glycerol, glycerin.

glice·rico *adj.* glyceric.

gli·cine *m.* (bot.) wistaria.

glicirrizina *f.* (chem.) glycyrrhizin.

glic-ocolla *f.* (chem.) glycocoll. **-o·geno** *m.* glycogen. **-ogene·si** *f. indecl.* (med.) glycogenesis. **-oge·nico** *adj.* glycogenic. **-olato** *m.* glycollate. **-ole** *m.* glycol; (chem.) -ole etilenico, ethylene glycol. **-o·lico** *adj.* glycollic. **-o·lide** *m.* glycollide. **-o·side** *m.* glycoside. **-o·sio** *m.* see **glucosio**. **-osu·ria** *f.* (med.) glycosuria.

glicone·o *adj., n.m.* See **gliconio**.

glico·nico *adj., n.m.* See **gliconio**.

glico·nio *adj., n.m.* (prosod.) glyconic (verse).

gliÉl-a, -o, etc. See under **gli**[2].

glifo *m.* (archit.) glyph; (eng.) link block (of steam engine); — oscillante, crank and slotted link; distribuzione a —, link motion.

glif-ografi·a *f.* glyphography. **-o·grafo** *m.* glyphograph.

glioma *m.* (med.) glomus, glioma, gelatinous tumour.

gliom·mero *m.* (lit. hist.) poem for recitation, in hendecasyllabics and with internal rhyme.

glios·s-alo *m.* (chem.) glyoxal. **-ima** *f.* (chem.) glyoxime.

glissando *gerund.* (mus.) glissando; *n.m. indecl.* glissando passage; dei — virtuosistici d'ottave, some brilliant octave glissandoes. NOTE: this word has been formed from a non-existent verb, 'glissare' (to glide), and is used by composers to denote any kind of gliding movement, whether across the keys of a keyboard instrument or the strings of the harp, or along a single string of a violin, or from harmonic to harmonic on stringed or wind instruments, or from note to note on a slide instrument such as the trombone, or on the human voice. Although not an Italian word it appears in the scores of some Italian composers, e.g. Casella and Busoni. The correct Italian words are **strisciando** and **portato**, q.v. Other incorrect formations are **glissato, glissicando** and **glissicato.**

glit·t-ica *f.* glyptic; the art of cutting or engraving upon gems. **-ico** *adj.* glyptic; lavoro -ico, cameo or similar work. **-ografi·a** *f.* glyptography. **-o·grafo** *m.* glyptographer. **-ote·ca** *f.* collection of engraved gems or sculptures.

glo (onomat.) glug (the noise of a liquid coming out of a bottle); gobble (of a turkey).

glob-o *m.* globe; ball; sphere; orb; roundshot; in —, all together, all over; — dell'occhio, eyeball; troop, squad, detachment; †circle formed by troops to protect themselves from all directions (equiv. to 'forming a square'). **-ale** *adj.* inclusive, over-all, total; aggregate; universal; somma -ale, grand total, lump sum, global sum. **-alménte** *adv.* in the lump, in gross. **-ali·smo** *m.* (pedag.) theory according to which a child learning to read should be taught to grasp the word as a whole instead of analysing it into letters and syllables. **-Étto** *m. dim.* of **globo**; (anat.) corpuscle. **-ice·falo** *m.* (zool.) ca'ing whale, *Globocephalus melas.* **-icino** *m. dim.* of **globo**. **-ina** *f.* (chem.) globin. **-o·ide** *m.* globoid. **-osità** *f.* globosity, roundness. **-oso** *adj.* globose, spherical, spheroidal. **-ulare** *adj.* globular. †**-ulento** *adj.* globular, spherical. **-ulenza** *f.* globularity, globosity. **-ulina** *f.* (biol.) globulin.

glo·bulo *m.* globule; (anat.) corpuscle; aver molti globuli rossi, to have plenty of red corpuscles, (fig.) to be strong and vigorous; (metall.) air bubble; (biol.) — polare, polar body.

gloglò (onomat.) glug glug (the noise of a liquid coming out of a bottle); gobble gobble (of a turkey).

gloglott-are [A I] *intr.* (*aux.* avere) (onomat.) to go glug glug; to gurgle; (of a turkey) to gobble. -**ìo** *m.* (*pl.* -**ìi**) gurgling; gobbling.

glom-ere, -e·ride *f.* (zool.) *Glomeris* spp., a kind of millipede. -**e·rulo** *m.* (anat.) corpuscle, glomerule; -erulo di Malpighi, Malpighian corpuscle. -**erulite** *f.* (path.) glomerulitis.

glo·ri-a *f.* glory; fame; honour; splendour; pride; (iron.) lavorare per la —, to be paid little or nothing for one's work; (theol.) glory; bliss; Dio l'abbia in —, God rest him (of someone dead), God bless him (of someone living), (iron.) bother him, curse him; che Dio ti abbia in —!, God bless you! (expr. of affectionate exasperation or impatience); sonare a —, to ring a full peal; sonar la —, to ring the bell for a festival; a —, with festivities; andare in —, to be in ecstasy, to be delighted; farsi — di, to exult in, to glory in; (joc.) essere in —, to be drunk; (paint.) una — di angeli, a company of exulting angels; *m.* (liturg.) Gloria (greater or lesser doxology); tutti i salmi finiscono in —, it's always the same story; (provb.) alla fine del salmo si canta il —, 'judge not the play before the play is done'; (mus.) Gloria, a musical setting of either the *Gloria in excelsis* or the *Gloria Patri.* -**etta** *f. dim.* of gloria; small honour, some little honour; boast; summer-house, arbour. -**o·la** *f.* see **glorietta**.

glori-are [A4] *intr.* (*aux.* avere), *rfl.* (*prep.* di) to be proud (of), to show off; to glory (in), to exult (in); *tr.* to exalt. -**amento** *m.* exaltation, praise. -**ante** *adj.* fêted, honoured. -**ato** *part. adj.* glorified; held in high esteem; exalted. †**azione** *f.* glorifying; exalting.

glorific-are [A2s] *tr.* to glorify. -**amento** *m.* glorifying. -**ante** *part. adj.* glorifying; enjoying fame. -**ativo** *adj.* imparting glory. -**ato** *part. adj.* glorified, esteemed, honoured. -**azione** *f.* glorification.

glorio·s-o *adj.* glorious, illustrious; nome —, proud name; (theol.) glorified (body); Glorious (Mysteries of the Rosary); (saint) in glory; — e trionfante, glorious and triumphant (of Christ returning to Heaven); (iron.) unabashed; matto —, raving madman; testa -a, a dreamer; *n.m.* braggart. -**amente** *adv.* gloriously.

†**glos-a** *f.*, †**-are** *vb.* and derivs. See **glossa, glossare**.

gloss-a[1] *f.* explanatory note, gloss, footnote; annotation; — marginale, marginal note; (fig.) far la — a, to criticize adversely. -**are** [A I] *tr.* to annotate; to gloss; to comment; to interpret. -**a·rio** *m.* glossary. -**ato** *part. adj.* annotated; glossed; commented; interpreted. -**atore** *m.* annotator, writer of glosses; commentator; interpreter. -**ema** *m.* gloss, abstruse word. -**ema·tico** *adj.* pertaining to a gloss or abstruse word. -**ografi·a** *f.* lexicology. -**ogra·fico** *adj.* lexicographical. -**o·grafo** *m.* lexicographer, glossarian, glossarist. -**ologi·a** *f.* lexicology; philology, science of language, linguistics.

gloss-a[2] *f.* (anat.) tongue. -**algi·a** *f.* (med.) glossalgia. -**ite** *f.* (med.) glossitis. -**oca·toco** *m.* (med.) tongue-depressor. -**ocele** *f.* (med.) glossocele. -**oepiglot·tico** *adj.* glossoepiglottidean. -**ofarin·geo** *adj.* (med.) glossopharyngeal. -**oplegi·a** *f.* (med.) glossoplegia. -**otomi·a** *f.* (surg.) glossotomy.

glos·sico *adj.* (anat.) glossal.

glossina *f.* (ent.) tsetse fly, *Glossina* spp.

glott-a *f.* tongue; glottis. -**ogoni·a** *f.* (neol.) speculation as to the origin of language. -**ologi·a** *f.* comparative philology, linguistics. -**olo·gico** *adj.* philological. -**o·logo** *m.* philologist. -**otec·nica** *f.* study of technical aspects of linguistics.

glot·tide *f.* (anat.) glottis.

glu glu *m.* (onomat.) glug glug, gurgling, gurgle (of a liquid coming out of a bottle); (of a turkey) gobble gobble, gobbling.

gluc-ina *f.* (chem.) glucina. -**i·nio** *m.* (chem.) glucin(i)um, beryllium. -**o·metro** *m.* glucometer. -**o·side** *m.* (chem.) glucoside. -**o·sio** *m.* (chem.) glucose, dextrose. -**osuri·a** *f.* see **glicosuria**.

gluma *f.* (bot.) glume, lemma.

glu·teo *m.* (anat.) gluteus, gluteal.

glu·tin-e *m.* (chem.) gluten; glue; glutin; (miner.) cement, in agglutinated rock; †(anat.) synovial fluid. -**are** [A I s] *tr.* to glue. -**ato** *part. adj.* glued; gluten; pane -ato, gluten-bread. †**-o** *m.* see **glutine**. -**osità** *f.* glutinosity; stickiness. -**oso** *adj.* glutinous; sticky, viscous.

'gna *f.* (S. Ital.). See **signora**.

gnac·cher-a *f.* (colloq.) see **nacchera**. -**one** *m.* awkward, clumsy person.

gnafa·lio *m.* (bot.) cudweed, *Gnaphalium*; edelweiss, *Leontopodium alpinum.*

gnaff-a *f.* despicable person. †**-e** *excl. vulg.* faith!

gnaffo *m.* flattened nose, ugly snout.

gnafione *m.* Turkish opium.

gna·gnera *f.* (vulg.) itching; desire; caprice; lassitude.

gna-o, -u *m.* (onomat.) miaow, mew, mewing. -**ulare** [A I s] *intr.* (*aux.* avere) to mew (of a cat); to cry, to whine (of a child). -**ulata** *f.* mew, mewing; whine. -**ule·vole** *adj.* whining. -**ulìo** *m.* (*pl.* -**ulìi**) continued mewing or whining. -**one** *m.* one who whines a lot; moaner. (-**ona** *f.*)

gne·gnera *f.* monotonous whining, sing-song voice.

gne·gnero *m.* (fam.) brain, ideas, wisdom, nous.

gneiss *m.* (pron. as German) (miner.) gneiss.

gni·dio *m.* (bot.) *Daphne gnidium.*

'gno *m.* (S. Ital.). See **signore**.

gnocc-o *m.* (*pl.* **gnocchi**) (cul.) a sort of dumpling made from polenta of maize, semolina or potato, with butter and seasoning; (provb.) ciascuno fa della sua pasta gnocchi, everyone can do as he likes with his own things; Baccanale dello —, Carnival at Verona; dollop, lump the size of a mouthful; gnocchi di fango, lumps of mud; (joc.) blockhead; *pl.* (cul.) gnocchi. -**ata** *f.* country celebration with abundant consumption of 'gnocchi', esp. as held at Guastalla. -**olaro** *adj.* Venerdì -olar(o), Friday before Lent (at the Carnival of Verona).

gnoccoluto *adj.* (text.) neppy; lumpy.

gnom-e *f.* dictum; inscrutable or enigmatic maxim; aphorism, gnome. -**ologi·a** *f.* gnomology. -**olo·gico** *adj.* gnomological. -**ologista** *m.* gnomologist, writer of aphorisms.

gno·mico *adj.* gnomic; didactic; *n.m. pl.* (Gk. lit.) Greek gnomic poets such as Theognis.

gnom-o *m.* elf, sprite, gnome, goblin. (-**a** *f.*)

gnom-one *m.* gnomon, pointer of a sundial; (geom.) gnomon; (vet.) tooth by which a horse's age is known. -**o·nica** *f.* gnomonics, the art of sundial making. -**o·nico** *adj.* gnomonic.

gnornò *excl.* (army style) No, Sir.

†**gnoro** *adj.* ignorant.

gnorri *m. indecl.* fare lo —, to pretend to be stupid or unaware, to feign ignorance.

gnorsì *excl.* (army style) Yes, Sir.

gnosi *f. indecl.* (philos.) gnosis.

gno·stic-o *adj.* gnostic. -**ismo** *m.* gnosticism.

gnu *m. indecl.* (zool.) gnu.

gnucca *f.* (vulg.) neck, nape; brains, wisdom, sense, nous.

†**gnudo** *adj.* See **nudo**.

†**gnuno** *prn.* no one.

Go·a[1] *pr.n.f.* (geog.) Goa.

†**go·a**[2] *f.* (naut. Rome and Genoa) measure of length (27 inches).

gobb-a *f.* hump; la — del cammello, the camel's hump; far la —, to bend one's back at work; spianar la — a, to beat; curve, curvature; humpbacked woman. -**are** [A I] *tr.* (naut.) to bend. -**amento** *m.* (naut.) bend of a mast. -**ino** *adj., n.m. dim.* of gobbo; moneta -ina, clipped coin, light-weight coin. -**o** *adj.* hunchbacked, humpbacked; humped; crooked; bent; curved; *n.m.* hump; bump; bulge; heap; (orn.) — rugginoso, white-headed duck, *Oxyura leucocephala*; (naut.) skiff; *pl.* (Ven.) scantlings (convex); hunchback; le camice dei -i tagliate male tornano bene, hunchbacks' shirts, when cut badly, fit well (said of ill-disposed people when they do the right thing out of perversity); dimmi —, blow me (oath uttered when making an assertion); (Tusc. joc.) a thing pawned; *pl.* (bot.) blanched phyllaries of cardoon, *Cynara cardunculus*; *m.pl.* (slang) students of dramatic academies. -**oni** *adv.* like a hunchback; andar -oni, to walk with a stoop. †**-uto** *adj.* hunched, humped; hunchbacked.

†**gob·bia** *f.* See **sgorbia**.

gobbo[1] *adj., n.m.* See under **gobba**.

gobbo[2] *m.* light- and sound-proof screen used in film studios.

†**gob·bola** *f.* See **cobbola**.

gobione *m.* (ichth.) gudgeon, *Gobio fluviatilis.*

gocc-ia *f.* drop; drip; rassomigliarsi come due -e d'acqua, to be as like as two peas; — a —, drop by drop; (provb.) la — che fa traboccare il vaso, the last straw that breaks the camel's back; la — scava la pietra, constant dripping wears away a stone;

gocc·ia (*cont.*)

(med.) — militare, gleet, apoplexy; orecchino a —, drop-earring; *pl.* drizzle of rain; (miner.) pinpoints of gold in ore; (archit.) drops, guttae (in the Doric order). **-iare** [A 3 c] *intr.* (*aux.* avere) to drip; — di sudore, to drip with sweat. **-iato** *adj.* (herald.) gutty. **-etta** *f. dim.* of **goccia**; droplet; (med.) gleet. **-io** *m.* (Rome) drop to drink.

gocciol·a *f.* (Tusc.) drop; rassomigliarsi come due -e, to be as like as two peas; fico con la —, very ripe fig; drop-earring; glass pendant; fit of apoplexy; la — al naso, dewdrop (on the end of one's nose); *pl.* lead shot; (archit.) drops, guttae (in the Doric order; see also **goccia**). **-ame** *m.* fringe of tassels or similar ornaments. **-are** [A I sc] *intr.* (*aux.* avere) *tr.* to drip, to drop; to leak, to ooze. **-amento** *m.* leak; dripping; drops. **-ato** *part. adj.* leaked, dripped; spotted. **-atoio** *m.* (archit.) dripstone; (chem.) side tube (of a distillation flask), adaptor; (naut.) grating used for drying tarred hemp; -atoio da portellino, scuttle drip pan. **-atura** *f.* dripping, leaking, leakage; stain from drips. **-etta** *f. dim.*, **-ina** *f. dim.* drop, very small dose or portion. **-ino** *m. dim.* droplet. **-io** *m.* (*pl.* **-ii**) constant dripping, leaking. **-o** *m.* (*pl.* **-e** *f.*) drop, very small dose or portion. **-one** *m. augm.* person with a running nose; simpleton. **-oni** *m.pl.* large shot. **-oso** *adj.* dripping, guttering, running. **-otti** *m.pl.* buckshot; icicles; lines of wax dripped down a guttering candle.

†**godendardo** *m.* (mil. hist.) Flemish pike.

god·ere [B I] *intr.* (*aux.* avere) to rejoice; to be glad; mi -e l'animo, my soul rejoices; to thrive; to benefit; (provb.) tra i due litiganti il terzo -e, in a quarrel between two, a third party benefits; chi si contenta -e, it is easy to be happy if one is easily pleased; (*prep.* a, di) to rejoice (in); to be glad (of); — a vedere, to rejoice to see; — della felicità altrui, to rejoice in the happiness of others; to rejoice in, to possess, to enjoy; — di una buona salute, to enjoy good health; -e del nome di Eusebio, he rejoices in the name of Eusebius; to make fun (of); *tr.* to enjoy; to have pleasure in; to possess; to profit from; (finan.) — gli interessi, to draw interest; *rfl.* (*acc.* of *prn.* 'si', *prep.* di) to enjoy oneself; to content oneself (with); (*dat.* of *prn.* 'si') -ersi il papato, to enjoy a life without upsets; -ersela, to enjoy oneself, to enjoy life. **-ente** *part. adj.* rejoicing, enjoying; (rel.) Frati -enti, see **gaudenti**. **-ereccio** *adj.* merry, inclined to merriment; delightful, enjoyable; *n.m.* draught weight. **-eri·a** *f.* enjoyment. **-evole** *adj.* enjoyable. **-evolmente** *adv.* happily; enjoyably. **-i·bile** *adj.* enjoyable; that may be had, to be had. **-imento** *m.* pleasure, delight; enjoyment; exploitation, use; avere il libero -imento di, to enjoy full possession of; (comm.) date from which interest is payable. (**-itore** *m.* **-itrice** *f.*) **-uta** *f.* enjoyment. **-uto** *part. adj.* enjoyed; rejoiced in; possessed.

godron·are [A I c] *tr.* (eng.) to knurl. **-ato** *part. adj.* knurled, milled. **-atura** *f.* knurl, knurling.

goff·o *adj.* clumsy, awkward; stupid; embarrassed; †astonished, astounded, dumbfounded; *adv. phr.* alla -a, awkwardly; *n.m.* awkward, clumsy person, dolt; combination of four cards of the same suit in the game of 'primiera', q.v. **-amente** *adv.* clumsily; awkwardly; stupidly. **-ag·gine** *f.* awkwardness, clumsiness; stupidity; stupid action; blunder. **-eri·a** *f.* (N. Ital.) awkwardness; stupidity. **-etto** *adj. dim.* rather clumsy; *n.m.* a game of chance. **-ezza** *f.* awkwardness; clumsiness; stupidity. **-otto** *adj.* somewhat awkward; rather clumsy.

goffr·are [A I] *tr.* (paperm.) to emboss; to corrugate. **-ato** *part. adj.* (paperm.) embossed. **-atura** *f.* (paperm.) embossing.

Goffredo *pr.n.m.* Godfrey; Geoffrey; il pio —, Geoffrey of Bouillon, the leader of the First Crusade and hero of Tasso's *Gerusalemme Liberata*.

Goga e Magoga *pr.n.m.* Gog and Magog.

gogn·a *f.* the part of the pillory which enclosed the neck; mettere alla —, to pillory, (fig.) to expose to ridicule; (in casting a gun) the hoop used to retain the core of the mould in proper position; †shame; †disgrace. **-ato** *adj.* shaped like a pillory or casting ring.

goi *m. indecl.* Jewish term for Gentiles, goy.

Go·ito *pr.n.f.* (geog.) Goito, in the province of Mantua.

gol *m. indecl.* (sport) a goal scored (cf. **porta**).

gol·a *f.* throat; gullet; gorge; mal di —, sore throat; aver il cibo alla —, to have one's food 'lying on one's chest' (i.e. undigested); mettersi ogni cosa giù per la —, to spend all one's money on food and eating; un osso in —, a bone in one's throat; (fig.) a great obstacle; aver l'acqua alla —, to be in water up to one's neck,

(fig.) to be in dire straits; a —, up to the neck, up to the hilt, up to the very top; aver debiti a —, to be up to one's eyes in debt; faccende a —, a great deal to do, (joc.) the business of eating; a piena —, hungrily, greedily; col boccone in —, only just having eaten; atto della —, breathing, breath; a piena —, vociferously; a — aperta, full-throated; cantare a — aperta, to sing with plenty of volume; gridare con quanto fiato si ha in —, to shout at the top of one's voice; nodo alla —, lump in one's throat; stringere la — a uno, to stop someone from speaking; ricacciare in — a uno, to make someone eat his words; mentire in —, to tell a barefaced lie; parlare in —, to speak indistinctly; voce di —, throaty voice; porgere la —, to volunteer to die, to offer one's life; avere il corpo in — (of a woman) to be near her time (i.e. of childbirth); appetite, desire, hunger; mortificare la —, to fast; fare — a, to be a temptation to, to tempt; far venir la —, to excite the appetite; greed, gluttony; (theol.) il peccato della —, gula; prendere per la —, to force (a person) by playing on his gluttony or vice; glutton; recess (similar to that between the head and the chest); la — di tiraggio, vent draught of a chimney; (archit.) — diritta, cyma recta; — rovescia, cyma reversa, ogee; (bookb.) fore-edge; (eng.) groove of a sheave; belt groove (of a pulley); narrow opening; orifice; inlet, outlet; (geog.) narrow valley, gorge; strait(s); neck (of a vase or cup); (mus.) upper part of the stem of a note; il re fuori delle righe in chiave di violino ha due tagli in —, D above the stave in the treble clef has two leger-lines; (naut.) — della puleggia, throat of a block; — del picco, gooseneck; — della ronda, throat of a sail, knock; — della rabazza, mastrope sheave; — della scalmiera, throat of a crutch; (mil.) muzzle (of a gun); — del baluardo, postern; — d'una cannoniera, covered gate into a fort. **-ac·cia** *f. pejor.* of **gola**; glutton. **-ag·gine** *f.* gluttony. †**-are** *tr.* to long for, to covet, to desire. †**-ato** *part. adj.* much desired, longed for; coveted. **-eri·a** *f.* titbit; gluttony. **-etta** *f. dim.* of **gola**; lady's embroidered collar; shirt collar; (geog.) narrow gorge; †(eccl.) priest's collar; (mil. hist.) part of the helmet fitted on to the visor; (naut.) schooner; -etta a gabbiola, topsail schooner; nave -etta, barquentine; -etta a palo, barque; narrow entry to a harbour. **-etto** *m.* shirt-collar; a wide collar stiffened with whalebone; lady's plain white collar (not embroidered). **-ettone** *m.* person wearing a large collar. †**-iare** *tr.* to long for, to desire, to covet. **-oseri·a** *f.* titbit; greediness. **-osità** *f.* greediness, gluttony; covetousness, longing; titbit. **-oso** *adj.* greedy; gluttonous; appetizing, tempting. **-osamente** *adv.* greedily, gluttonously.

goldone *m.* (med.) condom, sheath.

goldoniano *adj.* of, relating to, or characteristic of Goldoni, the playwright.

golena *f.* (Po Valley) high-water bed.

golf *m. indecl.* golf; giuocare a —, to play golf; una partita a —, a game of golf; giuocatore di —, golfer; pullover, sweater; cardigan. **-ino** *m. dim.* light sweater, cardigan.

golfare *m.* (naut.) eye-bolt, ring-bolt; (eng.) lifting lug.

Golfiera *pr.n.f.* (geog.) the Gulf Stream.

golfist·a *m., f.* (*pl.m.* -i, *pl.f.* -e) golfer.

golfo[1] *m.* See **golf**.

golfo[2], (Rom.) golfo *m.* gulf; a — lanciato, on the high seas; il Corrente del Golfo, the Gulf Stream; †abundance.

†**golfo**[3] *adj.* narrow; restricted; enclosed; swollen; puffed up, proud.

Gol·gota *pr.n.m.* Golgotha.

Goli·a *pr.n.m.* Goliath; giant.

goli·ar·dico *adj.* goliardic; cappello —, hat worn on festive occasions by Italian University students; canti -ardici, medieval student songs, student songs in general; relating to students or undergraduates; attività -ardiche, student activities. **-ardo** *m.* goliard; wandering scholar; *pl.* students engaged in extra-curriculum activities.

gollista *m., f.* (Fr. pol.) member or supporter of de Gaulle; *adj.* of or relating to de Gaulle.

goloso *adj.* and derivs. See under **gola**.

golp·e[1] *f.* (bot.) smut (of cereals), *Ustilago carbo*; blight; mildew. **-ato** *adj.* (bot.) affected with smut (of cereals); blighted, blasted; mildewed.

†**golpe**[2] *f.* See **volpe**.

†**golpone** *m.* See **volpone**.

†**gomberuto** *adj.* hunchbacked.

gombina *f.* (techn.) thong of a flail; †(agric.) space between furrows.

†**gombito** *m.* cubit.

gomen-a *f.* cable; anchor cable; hemp hawser; cable's length (200 metres or 112 fathoms); — da rimorchio, tow rope. **-etta** *f. dim.* hawser of hemp or manila, used for kedge anchor, warping and towing.

gomita·ria *f.* (bot.) caper spurge, *Euphorbia lathyris.*

gomit-o *m.* elbow; dolore di —, pain in the funny-bone, (fig.) momentary twinge; andar avanti coi -i, to elbow one's way ahead; riuscire a forza di -i, to be ruthless; alzare il —, to drink too much, to 'raise the elbow'; olio di —, sugo di —, elbow-grease; bend; sharp bend, hairpin bend; crank; bent piece of tubing; (plumbing) U-bend; (eng.) throw (of a crankshaft); albero a —, crankshaft; cubit. †**-ale** *m.* cubit. **-ata** *f.* blow or shove with the elbow; fare alle -ate, to elbow one's way. †**-ello** *dim.* of gomito; dormire a -ello, to sleep on one's arm. **-iera** *f.* (fencing) protection for elbow (used by sabreurs). **-one, -oni** *adv.* leaning on one's elbows.

gomi·tol-o *m.* ball or skein of wool, or other fibre; clew; swarm, knot; †globe; †circle. **-a·io** *m.* (text.) baller, ball winder. (**-a·ia** *f.*)

gomm-a *f.* gum; resin; rubber; — da masticare, chewing-gum; — arabica, gum arabic; (bot.) albero di —, rubber tree; (paint.) colori a —, gouache; — adragante, gum dragon; — gutta, gamboge; — elastica, indiarubber; lapis di —, ink eraser; — getania, guttapercha; — lacca, shellac; — resina, gum resin; tyre; — piena, solid tyre; — gomma, gumma. **-agutta** *f.* gamboge. **-ammoni·aco** *m.* (pharm.) gum ammoniac, ammonia gum. **-apiuma** *f.* foam rubber. **-ara·bica** *f.* gum arabic. **-are** [A I C] *tr.* to rubberize. **-ato** *adj.* gummed; containing gum; rubberized; (motor.) with rubber tyre, complete with tyre; *n.m.* (chem.) arabate. **-au·t** *f. indecl.* gamboge. **-i·fero** *adj.* gum-producing, rubber-bearing. **-osi** *f.* (bot.) a kind of canker in olive trees. **-osità** *f.* gumminess. **-oso** *adj.* gummy, resinous, rubbery; (colloq.) foppish, dandified.

gom·mico *adj.* (chem.) arabic.

gomona *f.* See gomena.

Gomorra *pr.n.f.* Gomorrah.

go·nade *m.* (zool.) gonad.

gon-agra *f.* gout of the knee. **-algi·a** *f.* pain in the knee. **-artrite** *f.* arthritis of the knee-joint.

†**gonda** *f.* boat.

gondol-a *f.* gondola; ship's boat; (fig.) andar in —, to enjoy oneself. **-are** [A I SC] *intr.* (*aux.* avere) to go in a gondola; to scull; *adj.* pertaining to a gondola. **-iera** *f.* (mus.) Venetian song. **-iere, -iero** *m.* gondolier.

gonfalon-e *m.* banner, standard, gonfalon; portare il —, to be leader; standard-bearer; colour-party; (herald.) gonfanon. **-ierato** *m.* office and dignity of standard-bearer, gonfaloniership; period of gonfaloniership. **-iere** *m.* standard-bearer; gonfalonier; (Tusc., until 1859) Podestà; (eccl.) -iere della chiesa, Gonfalonier of the Holy Roman Church.

gonfia *m.* (*pl.* gonfi) glass-blower.

gonfi-are [A 4 C] *tr.* to inflate, to blow up, to fill with air; to pump up; — il pallone, to blow up the balloon, (fig.) to flatter; — l'otre, to eat heavily, to have a blow-out; to puff up, to swell up; — le gote, to blow out one's cheeks; (techn.) to blow (glass); to fuse; (fig.) to exaggerate, to magnify; to overstate; to overrate; to puff up, to flatter; (vulg.) to make pregnant; to bore, to annoy; to produce swelling in; *intr.* (*aux.* essere) to swell; to grow; to increase; to rise (of water, of bread); to swell with pride. **-ag·gine** *f.* feeling of repletion; fulness; pretentious, inflated literary style; swollen-headedness; swaggering. **-ag·gio** *m.* inflation. **-agione** *f.* inflation, swelling. **-agote** *m., f. indecl.* swaggerer, boaster. **-amento** *m.* inflation, swelling; exaltation, flattery; pride, overbearing, arrogance. **-nu·goli, -nu·vole** *m., f. indecl.* swaggerer, boaster. **-ato** *part. adj.* swollen, dilated, inflated; risen; pumped up; enraged; fused, cast; exaggerated; puffed up, conceited; pallone -ato, conceited individual, one whose reputation has been artificially inflated. (**-atamente** *adv.*) **-atoio** *m.* blower; valve for inflation; inflator; tyre-pump. (**-atore** *m.* **-atrice** *f.*) **-atura** *f.* inflation; swelling; flattery; exaggeration; è stata tutta una -atura a scopo pubblicitario, it was all a publicity stunt; boasting; puffing up, puff. **-avesciche** *m., f. indecl.* gas-bag; flatterer.

gonfi-o *m.* swelling, lump, bulge; *adj.* swollen, dilated, distended; filled out; bombastic, padded (of style); (naut.) a -e vele, with a favourable wind, plain sailing, (fig.) smoothly, successfully, easily;

proud, overbearing, vainglorious, swollen-headed; (vulg.) pregnant. **-ettare** [A I C] *intr.* (*aux.* avere), *tr.* to inflate a little, to swell somewhat. **-etto** *adj. dim.* somewhat swollen, inflated a little; *n.m.* swelling; (Tusc.) inflation valve, pump. **-ezza** *f.* swelling; inflation; distension, fulness; (fig.) pride. **-one** *m.* fat, corpulent person; person swollen with rage; person puffed up with conceit. **-ore** *m.* swelling, lump.

gonfosi *f.* (anat.) gomphosis.

gong *f. indecl.* gong.

†**gonga** *f.* swollen gland; scrofula; scrofulous person.

†**gon·ghia** *f.* See gogna.

gon·gola *f.* (zool.) shell (of a mollusc); trough shell, *Mactra corallina.*

gongol-are [A I SC] *intr.* (*aux.* avere) to chuckle, to be delighted; *rfl.* to hug oneself for joy; to preen oneself. **-acchiare** [A 4] *intr.* (*aux.* avere) to keep chuckling. **-amento** *m.* chuckling, chuckle.

†**gongolo** *m.* merriment; gaiety; amusement.

gongoloso *adj.* suffering from swollen neck glands.

gongor-ismo *m.* (lit. hist.) Gongorism. **-ista** *m.* Gongorist.

gongro *m.* (ichth.) conger eel.

goni·dio *m.* (bot.) gonidium.

goni·glia *f.* Spanish frilled collar, *gonilla.*

gonilite *f.* (med.) inflammation of the knee-joint.

goni-ometri·a *f.* goniometry. **-ome·trico** *adj.* goniometric(al). **-o·metro** *m.* goniometer; protractor.

gonn-a *f.*, (Rom.) **gonna**, skirt; petticoat; gown; — calzoni, divided skirt; †long gown worn by men; †— papale, papal *mantum*; †skin of an animal; †(anat.) tunic (esp. of the eyeball); †(fig.) human frame. **-ella** *f. dim.* skirt; slip, petticoat; star attaccato alla -ella, to be tied to someone's apron strings; stare in -ella, to be dead; (fig.) woman; (fig.) priest; †(priest's) cassock; (monk's, friar's) habit; *pr.n.m.* name of a buffoon in the court of Ferrara (Sacchetti). **-ellina** *f. dim.* of gonnella. **-ellino** *m.* child's skirt. **-ello** *m.* petticoat for a child or for a doll; (eccl.) dress for a statue. **-ellona** *f. augm.* of gonnella; woman who is always gadding about, giddy woman, gadabout. **-ellone** *m. augm.* of **gonnello**, large tunic or skirt; cassock; man who runs after women.

gonoco·rico *adj.* (biol.) dioecious, having separate sexes.

gonorr-e·a *f.* (med.) gonorrhœa. **-eato** *m.* sufferer from gonorrhœa.

gonzo *m.* simpleton; blockhead, dolt; *adj.* stupid.

gor-a *f.* conduit, irrigation canal; channel; millpond; compensating basin; leat; gulf; trench; stream (e.g. of blood or sweat); stain left by a trickle; trickle of perspiration; tear-stain; damp stain on a book; marsh, stagnant water; (poet.) la morta —, the Stygian marsh (of Dante's *Inferno*); whirlpool in the sea; (joc.) pool of water. **-a·io** *m.* deep pond or conduit. **-ata** *f.* the water in a millpond, mill-race; water of a conduit. **-ella** *f. dim.* secondary conduit. **-ello** *m. dim.* gulley, conduit, drain.

gorbia *f.* gouge, hollow chisel; groove; spike at the end of a walking-stick or flagstaff; (vet.) turnover in the thigh; metal tube for grinding a substance to a powder.

gordiano *adj.* (hist.) Gordian; tagliare (sciogliere) il nodo —, to cut the Gordian knot.

†**gorga**[1] *f.* gullet, throat.

†**gorga**[2] *f.* See gorgo.

gorgata *f.* draught, gulp.

gorgheggi-are [A 3 C] *intr.* (*aux.* avere) (mus.) to trill, to shake, to warble; to sing. **-amento** *m.* (mus.) trilling, warbling. **-atore** *m.* (mus.) warbler. (**-atrice** *f.*)

gorgheg·gio *m.* singing exercise; trilling; trill.

gorghegg-io *m.* (*pl.* **-ii**) continual warbling, trills and shakes.

gor·gi-a *f.* strong guttural pronunciation of 'r'; burr; la — toscana, the Tuscan habit of aspirating 'c' before 'a', 'o' or 'u'; (mus.) trill, shake; vocal ornament; (naut.) throat of sail or yard; (carpen.) joggle. **-are** [A 4] *intr.* (*aux.* avere) to speak with a guttural accent.

gorgiera *f.* frilled collar; ruff; gorget; choker; chain of office; neck-band; throat protector in armour; †throat.

†**gorgione** *adj.* gorging; gluttonous; *n.m.* glutton, one who gorges himself.

gor-go *m.* (*pl.* **-ghi**) whirlpool; whirling stream; abyss; †(anat.) — del cuore, ventricle of the heart.

gorgogli-are [A 4 C] *intr.* (*aux.* avere) to gurgle; to bubble; to be crawling with maggots; to be infested with greenfly; *tr.* to gurgle, to babble. **-atore** *m.* (chem. eng.) scrubber, washing tower.

gorgoglio *m.* gurgle; gurgling; bubbling.

gorgogl-io *m.* (*pl.* *-ii*) continuous gurgling or bubbling.

gorgoglione *m.* (ent.) aphis, greenfly; — della rosa, *Siphonophora rosae*, rose aphis.

Gorgon-e, Gorgone *pr.n.m.* (myth.) gorgon; *f.* La Gorgone, Medusa; (fig.) gorgon. **-eggiante** *adj.* Gorgon-like; making a fearsome noise. **-eo** *m.* Gorgoneion. **-eo** *adj.* Gorgonian.

gorgonia *f.* (zool.) sea fan, *Gorgonia* spp.

Gorgonzola *pr.n.f.* (geog.) Gorgonzola (in prov. of Milan); *m.*, *f.* gorgonzola (cheese).

gorgozz-o *m.* gurgling sound made by molten metal when running into the mould. **-ule** *m.* (joc.) gullet; rinfrescare il -ule, to drink, to wet one's whistle.

gorilla *f.* (zool.) gorilla.

Gori·zia *pr.n.f.* (geog.) Gorizia.

†gorna *f.* rain pipe; canal; conduit.

gorra *f.* peasant's hat; withy, wicker.

†gorzar-etto, †-ino *m.* gorget.

†Gostanza *pr.n.f.* See **Costanza.**

got-a *f.* cheek; bagnar le -e, to weep; cheek-piece of a helmet; (of an animal) jowl; (naut.) *pl.* curve of the bows of a vessel (cf. **guancia**). **-ata** *f.* slap, blow on the cheek; light blow on the cheek, buffet, *alapa*, given (liturg.) at confirmation, (hist.) in conferring knighthood.

Gotha *pr.n.f.* (geog.) Gotha; l'almanacco di —, the Continental European equiv. of Debrett.

Goti *pr.n.m.pl.* (hist.) Goths.

go·tic-o *adj.* Gothic; scrittura -a, Gothic script; caratteri -i, Gothic lettering; (hist.) linea -a, Gothic line (along the Apennines, north of Florence, 1944–5). **-ume** *m.* a collection of Gothic or pseudo-Gothic objects.

gotlandiano *adj.* (geol.) Upper Silurian.

Goto *m.* See **Goti.**

gott-a, gotta *f.* gout; aver la —, to suffer from gout; (fig., iron.) avere la — alle mani, to be slow in paying; — artritica, pain in the joints; — serena, amaurosis; (bot.) — del lino, dodder, *Cuscuta epilinum*; †see **goccia.** **-oso** *adj.* gouty; (fig.) slow, lame.

gottardo *m.* (geog.) tunnel; il San Gottardo, the St Gothard tunnel.

Gottinga *pr.n.f.* (geog.) Göttingen.

gott-o *m.* goblet, large glass; (N. Ital.) sip, mouthful (cf. **goccia**); (eng.) lower pump box. **-are** [A1] and derivs. See **aggottare.** **-azza** *f.* (naut.) skeet, scoop: a kind of shovel for throwing water on the side of a ship; bailer.

govern-are [A1] *tr.* to steer; to guide, to direct; to regulate; to govern, to rule; to command; to tend, to mind, to look after (e.g. cattle or children); to provide for (a family); to sit on (eggs); — un cavallo, to groom a horse; to treat, to dress; to manure; to treat (wine, to improve colour, strength, etc.); (naut.) — i forni, to stoke up the boilers; *intr.* (*aux.* avere) to steer; -a?, is the ship answering (to her rudder)?; -a così!, steady as you go!; come -a?, how much rudder are you carrying?; — a mano, to steer by hand; — con le macchine, to steer by main engines; — di bolina, to steer close-hauled; — al maroso, to head the seas; *rfl.* to control oneself; to act, to behave; to look after oneself. **-a·bile** *adj.* controllable, easy to govern. **-amento** *m.* governing; regulation, control; steering; upbringing; †rudder. **-ante** *adj.* ruling, regulating, steering; *n.m.* ruler; governor; steersman, helmsman; *f.* housekeeper; manageress of a residential club, etc.; governess. **-ativo** *adj.* official, state, government, governmental; impiegato -ativo, civil servant, government official; palazzo -ativo, government house; scuola -ativa, State school; †capable of ruling. **-atora** *f.* governor's wife; governess; woman who takes charge. **-atorato** *m.* governorship. **-atore** *m.* governor; administrator; tutor; (eccl.) head of religious guild; (Fascist hist.) the mayor of Rome; (Ven. hist.) -atore del golfo, Venetian admiral in command of the Adriatic. **-atrice** *f.* governor's wife; governess; *adj. f.* ruling, in charge, most important. **-atura** *f.* manuring, dressing; husbandry; care of crops or stock. **†-azione** *f.* governing; rule. **-ime** *m.* see under **governo.**

govern-o *m.* steering; helm; management; care, guidance; administration; maintenance; upbringing, rearing; government; rule; il partito al —, the party in power; State; mangiare il pane del —, to be employed by the government, to be in government service; regulation, control; per vostro —, for your guidance; care; donna di —, housekeeper; manuring, dressing; treatment and colouring

of wine; (Tusc.) process of second fermentation to produce sparkling effect; uva da —, grapes used in conditioning wine. **†-ale** *m.* rudder, helm; tail stave of a rocket; governor. **-ime** *m.* fodder. **-u·colo** *m. pejor.* poor government.

govinda *f.* (orn.) pariah kite, *Milvus migrans govinda.*

†go·vito *m.* See **gomito.**

gozz-o *m.* crop (of a bird); bleb; goitre; double chin; a kind of water-bottle with a long, narrow neck; (naut.) a kind of small fishing-smack employed in tunny fishing, etc.; type of net used in lake fishing; ship's jolly boat; (vulg.) throat, stomach, belly (as a place for food and drink). **-a·ia** *f.* contents of the crop; abscess; large crop. **-ata** *f.* cropful; gulp; old score, rancour. **-ante** *m.* (naut.) seaman in charge of a 'gozzo'. **-one** *m. augm.* of gozzo; (naut.) camber of a deck. **-uto** *adj.* suffering from goitre, affected with goitre.

gozzovi·gli-a *f.* revelling, riotous living; orgy. **-are** [A4] *intr.* (*aux.* avere) to revel, to indulge in revelry; to banquet; to guzzle, to swill, to eat and drink heartily. **-ata** *f.* revel, revelry.

Graal *m. indecl.* Grail; il sacro —, the Holy Grail.

†graba(t)to *m.* wretched bed, palliasse.

Gracchi *pr.n.m.pl.* (Rom. hist.) Gracchi; Cornelia, madre dei —, Cornelia, the mother of the Gracchi.

grac·chi-a *f.* (orn.) see **gracchio**; chatterbox. **-amento** *m.* croaking; croak; chirping; chirp; chattering, chatter. **-are** [A4] *intr.* (*aux.* avere) to croak (of a raven or frog); to chirp (of a grasshopper); to jabber continuously in a harsh voice. **-ata** *f.* croak. (**-atore** *m.* **-atrice** *f.*)

grac·chi-o *m.* (orn.) chough, *Pyrrhocorax pyrrhocorax*; — corallino; Alpine chough, *P. graculus*. **-one** *m.* grumbler, moaner; person who goes jawing on.

gracco¹ *m.* (orn.). See **gracchio.**

Gracco² *pr.n.m.* Gracchus.

gracid-are [A1S] *intr.* (*aux.* avere) to prate (of hens); to cackle (of geese); to croak (of frogs); to moan. **-ante** *part. adj.* cackling; croaking; moaning. (**-atore** *m.* **-atrice** *f.*) **-azione** *f.* cackle, cackling; croaking. **-io** *m.* (*pl.* *-ii*) continued cackling, croaking or moaning. **†-oso** *adj.* cackling, croaking.

gra·cil-e *adj.* delicate; graceful; slender, slim; puny, thin; underdeveloped, undernourished, having small, brittle bones; complessione —, delicate constitution. **-mente** *adv.* gracefully; slenderly. **-ente** *adj.* sickly, delicate, weakly. **-ità** *f.* slenderness, gracefulness, grace; weakness, puniness; delicacy of bone structure.

graci·mol-o *m.* bunch of grapes left on vine after harvest; small portion. **-are** [A1S] *tr.* to glean (grapes).

gra·cola *f.* (orn.) mynah.

†grada *f.* See **grado¹.**

†gradag·gio *m.* pleasure; pleasing thing.

grad-are [A1] *tr.* to gradate; *intr.* (*aux.* essere) to be divided into compartments or steps; to progress, to advance. **-ato** *part. adj.* made in steps; (herald.) grady, indented. **-atamente** *adv.* step by step, gradually; by degrees. **-azione** *f.* gradation; grading; degree; (paint.) gradation (esp. of colours); (mus.) tone-gradation, shading, nuance.

Gradass-o *pr.n.m.* name of a Saracen king, a character in the romantic epics of Boiardo and Ariosto; (fig.) boaster, braggart; blusterer; far il —, to boast, to brag; to bluster. **-ata** *f.* blustering; blustering or boastful action.

gradazione *f.* See under **gradare.**

gradell-a *f.* wicker enclosures in a swampy ground for enclosing fish. **-ato** *adj.* fenced off with wickerwork.

gradetto *m. dim.* of **grado²**, q.v.

gradevole *adj.* See under **gradire.**

gradiente *m.* gradient, slope.

gradimento *m.* See under **gradire.**

gradin-a *f.* (sculp.) claw-tool. **-are** [A1] *tr.* (sculp.) to work (marble, etc.) with a claw-tool. **-ato** *part. adj.* (sculp.) worked with a claw-tool; *n.m.* (paint.) picture showing brush-strokes like a sculptor's claw-marks. **-atura** *f.* (sculp.) claw-marks; use of a claw-tool.

gradinat-a *f.*, **-ura** *f.* See under **gradino.**

gradin-o *m.* step (of a flight of steps); rung of a ladder; (liturg.) gradine; (archit.) stone platform, pedestal; (geol.) shelf; †(sculp.) see **gradina.** **-ata** *f.* (archit.) steps, flight of steps; (Gk. and Rom. antiq.) tier of broad steps used as seats in an arena; (geog.) -ata di faglie, step-faults. **-atura** *f.* (mining) benching.

grad-ire [D 2] *tr.* to receive with favour; to be pleased to accept; to oblige by accepting; to appreciate; to like to have; to find agreeable; *intr.* (*aux.* essere) to be agreeable, to please. **-ęvole** *adj.* agreeable, pleasing; acceptable; gratifying. **-evolmęnte** *adv.* agreeably, pleasingly; acceptably; gratifyingly. **-evolęzza** *f.* agreeableness. **-imęnto** *m.* enjoyment, pleasure; gratification, satisfaction, liking, approval; formal acceptance by foreign government of proposed ambassador, reception of an ambassador by Head of State; (leg.) vendita con riserva di -imento, sale on approval. **-ito** *part. adj.* pleasing; approved; appreciated; welcome, agreeable; esteemed; mal -ito, not appreciated, unwelcome.

Gradivo¹ *pr.n.m.* (Rom. myth.; poet.) Gradivus (a title of Mars).

†**gradivo²** *adj.* willing; spontaneous; pleasing.

grado¹ *m.* goodwill, benevolence, pleasure; a —, to taste, as desired; andare a —, essere a —, to be agreeable; avere a —, to find agreeable, to enjoy; di buon —, willingly; mal —, displeasure; *adv. phr.* mal —, a mal —, unwillingly; a suo mal —, a mal suo —, against his will (see also **malgrado**); contro suo —, contrary to his wishes; gratefulness, gratitude; saper — di, to thank for, to be grateful for; render —, to give thanks; †love; †il — divino, divine Love.

grad-o² *m.* step; i -i del teatro, stone benches (in an open-air theatre); (liturg.) gradine; †(liturg.) foot-pace, predella; degree; a — a —, by degrees, gradually, step by step; al sommo —, al massimo —, to the highest degree; inclinato di 45 -i, heeling over at an angle of 45 degrees; rank, grade, standing; di alto —, high-ranking; tenere al suo —, to stand on one's dignity; (leg.) degree; — di parentela, degree of relationship, consanguinity (C.C.); — di pena, degree of punishment (C.P.); usurpazione di un — accademico, unwarranted assumption of an academic degree (C.P.); grade; instance, degree of jurisdiction; giudice di primo —, judge of first instance; competenza di secondo —, appellate jurisdiction (C.P.P.); priority, ranking; l'ipoteca prende — dalla sua iscrizione, mortgage ranks, takes priority, from its registration (C.C.); point; — d'infiammabilità, flash-point; carat (i.e. fineness in gold, weight in jewels); shade (of a colour); (mus.) degree (of scale); position in the stave (whether line or space); (phys.) degree, measure or scale of heat; il — centigrado è diverso da quello Fahrenheit, Centigrade is a different measurement of heat from Fahrenheit; inferiore di un — a zero, one degree below zero; state, condition; in — di, in a position to; mettere in — di, to enable to. †**-ag·gio** pleasure; pleasing thing. **-ale** *m.* il santo -ale, the Holy Grail.

Grado³ *pr.n.f.* (geog.) Grado (seaside resort near Trieste).

gradual-e *adj.* gradual; erta —, gentle slope; (finan.) estinzione — di un debito, ammortisation of a debt; *n.m.* (liturg.) gradual antiphon; *graduale*, gradual book. **-męnte** *adv.* gradually, by degrees; gently. **-ismo** *m.* (pol.) policy of gradual reform, gradualism. **-ista** *m., f.* (pol.) gradualist. **-i·stico** *adj.* (pol.) gradualistic. **-ità** *f.* gradualness.

gradu-are [A 6] *tr.* to graduate; to grade; to mark out in degrees; to confer a degree, rank or title upon; (comm.) to rank for dividend in bankruptcy; to apportion; (mil.) to time (a fuse); (naut.) to set (a torpedo). **-a·bile** *adj.* that may be graduated; (leg.; comm.) ranking for dividend; apportionable. **-abilità** *f.* possibility of being graduated. **-ato** *part. adj.* graduated, calibrated; graded; marked out in degrees; ordered; listed; apportioned; conferred a title; holding rank; *n.m.* (mil.) non-commissioned officer, i.e. soldier with a rank (corporal to sergeant). **-atamęnte** *adv.* by degrees; according to grading; gradually. **-ato·ria** *f.* (sport) classification, position in table; (leg.) list of admitted creditors or proofs of debt. **-ato·rio** *adj.* pertaining to the listing or ranking of creditors and debtors or assets and liabilities. **-azione** *f.* graduation; advancement, preferment, promotion; division into degrees; apportionment; (leg.) ranking of creditors according to time, quality and amount of the debt due; lo stato di -azione, list of creditors in order of preference (C.C.); (geog.) the latitude and longitude of a place. †**-ire** *tr.* to raise in rank, to ennoble.

graff-a *f.* clip, fastener; clamp; double bracket or parenthesis; boat-hook. **-atrice** *f.* (eng.) clinching machine. **-atura** *f.* (eng.) clinching.

graffi-are [A 4] *tr.* to scratch; to claw at; to botch; to wound with words; *rfl.* to scratch oneself; to hurt oneself by scratching; *recip. rfl.* to scratch each other; (fig.) to scratch each other's eyes out.

-amęnto *m.* scratching; scratch. **-asanti** *m., f. indecl.* religious humbug. **-ata** *f.* scratch; scratching. **-ato** *part. adj.* scratched; badly carved. **-atore** *m.* scratcher; bad carver; unfavourable critic. (**-atrice** *f.*) **-atura** *f.* scratch; wound or sear from a scratch.

graf-fi-o *m.* scratch; nail extractor (on a hammer); pitchfork; (artill.; eng.) lug; *pl.* grappling irons for fishing up objects which have fallen down a well. **-etto** *m. dim.*; (techn.) marking gauge, mortise gauge; scribe.

graffito *m.* (art) graffito, scratched or incised drawing; technique for decorating walls.

†**graffo·fono** *m.* (mus.). See **grammofono**.

grafi·a *f.* spelling; handwriting.

gra·fic-a *f.* graphic art, drawing; book-illustrating; book-production. **-o** *adj.* graphic; arti grafiche, graphic art, illustration; stabilimento -o, printing house; typographical; orthographical; *n.m.* graph; diagram; chart; (miner.) graphite; i -i, people employed in book-production. **-amęnte** *adv.* graphically; typographically; orthographically.

grafiosi *f. indecl.* (bot.) Dutch elm-disease.

grafit-e *f.* (miner.) graphite, plumbago. **-are** [A 1] *tr.* (techn.) to graphitize. **-izzazione** *f.* (techn.) graphitizing.

†**grafo·fono** *m.* See **grammofono**.

graf-ologi-a *f.* graphology, study of handwriting. **-olo·gico** *adj.* graphological. **-o·logo** *m.* graphologist. **-o·mane** *m.* person affected with a craze for unnecessary writing. **-omani·a** *f.* craze for writing. **-o·metro** *m.* graphometer. **-ospaṣmo** *m.* writer's cramp.

gragnol-are [A 1 s] *impers.* to hail; *tr.* to hail down upon. **-ata** *f.* hail-storm.

gragn(u)ola *f.* fine hail; una — di bastonate, a shower of blows; la — sulla stoppa, much ado about nothing, a storm in a teacup; (cul.) fine 'pasta' for soup; (mil.) grapeshot, canister.

gralle *f.pl.* (orn.) wading birds.

grama·glia *f.* (usu. *pl.*) mourning (clothes); black hangings in church.

†**gramanzi·a** *f.* necromancy.

†**gramare** *tr.* to sadden; to make wretched.

gramęzza *f.* See under **gramo**.

gramign-a *f.* (bot.) grass; weed; (fig.) attaccarsi come la —, to cling like a limpet. **-are** [A 6] *tr.* (tanning) to grass-dry (hides), to spread out to dry. **-ato** *part. adj.* fed with dog-grass; (tanning) grass-dried. **-oso** *adj.* weedy, full of weeds.

gramina·c-eo *adj.* (bot.) graminaceous, of grasses. **-ee** *f.pl.* grasses, graminaceous family of plants.

†**gramma** *f., m.* See **grammo**.

gramma·estr-o *m.* Grand Master. **-ato** *m.* office of Grand Master.

gramm-a·tica *f.* grammar; — comparata, comparative grammar; (fig.) something abstruse; †Latin. **-aticag·gine** *f.* pedantic detail. **-aticale** *adj.* grammatical; relating to grammar; †Latin. **-atical-męnte** *adv.* grammatically. **-aticamęnte** *adv.* grammatically; according to the grammarians; like a grammarian. †**-aticare** *intr.* to write grammatically. **-aticastro** *m.* poor grammarian; pedant. **-aticheri·a** *f.* pedantic grammatical accuracy. **-atichętta** *f.* small grammar-book; first-year Latin class in a 'ginnasio'. **-atichęvole** *adj.* (joc.) grammatical. **-atichista** *m., f.* teacher of grammar. **-a·tico** *m.* grammarian; philologist; *n.m.* †man of letters; †*adj.* see **grammaticale**.

grammat-iṣi·a *f.* book-learning, clerkship. **-ista** *m.* teacher of grammar; writer; grammatist. **-i·stica** *f.* art of reading and writing; letters. **-i·stico** *adj.* grammatistical. **-ite** *f.* graphite. **-ologi·a** *f.* alphabetics. **-olo·gico** *adj.* pertaining to alphabetics.

grammatura *f.* (paperm.) substance, basis weight.

gramm-o *m.* gram, gramme (= 15·432 grains). **-omole·cola** *f.* (chem.) gram molecule, mole.

grammo·f-ono *m.* gramophone. **-o·nico** *adj.* of or pertaining to a gramophone.

gram-o *adj.* wretched, sad, miserable; poor; melancholy; undernourished; scanty, meagre; inadequate. **-ęzza** *f.* wretchedness, misery; scantiness, inadequateness. †**-ore** *m.* sadness; rancour; anger.

gra·mol-a *f.* (text.) flax-brake, hand brake; kneading apparatus. **-are** [A 1 s] *tr.* (text.) to break (flax or hemp); to knead. **-ata** *f.* ice-pudding. **-atrice** *f.* (text.) flax-breaking machine, brake for flax. **-atura** *f.* (text.) breaking of flax or hemp; kneading.

gram·p-ia *f.* (naut.) cramp-iron. **-ino** *m.* (naut.) boarding-grapnel.

Grampiani *pr.n.m.pl.* (geog.) Grampians.

gran[1] *adj.* abbrev. of **grande**, q.v.

gran[2] *m.* abbrev. of **grano**, q.v.

gran·a *f.* cochineal; grain (of leather, of a fracture, etc.); grain in wood; grain, particle; dry cheese, crumbly cheese; Parmesan cheese; (photog.) grain; di — fine, fine-grained; di — grossa, coarse-grained; (vet.) infestation of pigs with tapeworm cysticerci resulting in 'measly pork'; (slang) trouble, bore, tedious task; money; quello ha tanta —, that man is rolling in money.

granadi·glia *f.* (bot.) passion flower, *Passiflora quadrangularis.*

†**granagione** *f.* See under **granare**.

gran-a·glie *f.pl.* cereal, cereals; corn, grain; granulated gold or silver. **-agliare** [A4] *tr.* to granulate (gold or silver). **-a·io** *adj.* cereal; pertaining to corn; *n.m.* barn, granary; loft for storing grain; box-room, junk-room. **-ai(u)olo** *adj.* grain-eating, granivorous; (orn.) oca -aiuola, bean goose, *Anser fabalis; n.m.* corn-chandler. †**-aro** *m.* see **granaio**.

gran-are [A1] *tr.* to granulate; to grain; *intr.* (*aux.* essere) to seed, to run to seed. **-ato** *part. adj.* granulated; grained; ripe, formed (of corn). †**-agione** *f.* grain; gathering of grain.

Granata[1] *pr.n.f.* (geog.) Granada.

granat-a[2] *f.* broom, brush; dipingere con la —, to paint clumsily; pigliar la —, to give everyone the sack; puntellar l'uscio con la —, to leave the house-door insecurely fastened; benedir col manico della —, to thrash, to drub; (provb.) — nuova spazza ben tre giorni, a new broom sweeps clean; (mil.) grenade; — a pallottole, shrapnel; shell; — ad alto esplosivo, high-explosive shell (H.E.); — fumogena, smoke shell; — incendiaria, incendiary shell; — perforante, armour-piercing shell; schegge di —, shell splinters. **-a·io** *m.* broom-maker. **-ata** *f.* a sweep with a broom. **-iere** *m.* (mil.) grenadier. NOTE: in Italy the first two regiments of the line are grenadiers; (fig.) tall, strong man; (joc.) very tall, strong, woman. **-ina** *f.* hand-brush; lavatory brush.

granatina[1] *f. dim.* See under **granata**[1].

granatina[2] *f.* See under **granato**[2].

granat-o[1] *part.* of **granare**, q.v.

granat-o[2] *m.* (bot.) pomegranate, *Punica granatum.* **-ina** *f.* pomegranate syrup, grenadine.

granat-o[3] *m.* (miner.) garnet. **-i·fero** *adj.* garnetiferous. **-ite** *f.* (miner.) eclogite.

gran-be·stia *f.* (zool.) elk, *Alces machlis;* unghia (or, ugna) della —, elk's hooves or shavings of elk's horn (orig. regarded as a panacea for all ills); long nails; vulgar, repellent person; the mob, the many-headed. **-brettagna** *f.* (bot.) garden hyacinth, *Hyacinthus orientalis.* **-cancelleri·a** *f.* chancellery. **-cancelliere** *m.* High Chancellor. **-cane** *m.* (hist.) Great Khan. **-cassa** *f.* big-drum, bass-drum.

Gran Bretagna *pr.n.f.* (geog.) La —, Great Britain.

granc-ella *f.* (zool.) *dim.* of **granchio**, q.v.; — pieghettata, swimming crab, *Portunus* spp. **-eola**, **-evola** *f.* (zool.) spider crab, *Maia squinado.*

gran·chi-o *m.* (zool.) crab (various species); also, in some dialects, (ichth.) electric ray, *Torpedo ocellata;* crabs of various species: — ammaccato, *Doripe lanata;* — facchino, *Dromia vulgaris;* — favollo, — fellone, *Eriphia spinifrons;* — fluviale, *Potamon edule* and or *Thelphusa fluviatilis;* — piatto, *Pachygrapsus marmoratus;* — ripario, — marino comune, shore crab, *Carcinus moenas;* (fig.) stitch, muscular cramp; pigliare un — a secco, to pinch oneself, to get a stitch, to get a cramp, to make a blunder; (at bowls) avere il —, to play one against two; avarice; avere il — alle mani, to be tight-fisted; (astron.) Cancer; (med.) cancer; clamp, cramp, vice; bench-hook; planing-stop; nail extractor, claw (on a hammer); (agric.) type of harrow; (naut.) gudgeon plate on a rudder (so-called because the two strips of metal form a claw gripping the timber). **-a·io** *m.* crab-fisherman; crab-seller. **-erella** *f.* (bot.) dodder, *Cuscuta epilinum.* **-esco** *adj.* (*m.pl.* -eschi) crab-like. **-escamente** *adv.* crab-fashion, crab-wise. **-olino** *m. dim.* little crab; curl-paper. **-one** *m. augm.* (zool.) large crab.

gran·ci-a[1] *f.* (hist.) 'grange', farm belonging to a religious house or feudal lord; shepherd's cottage with outbuildings. **-ere** *m.* (hist.) 'granger', farm-bailiff.

†**granci-a**[2] *f.* (med.) ulcer.

gran·ci-o *m.* grappling-iron, claw; (zool.) see **granchio**. **-porretto** *m.* (zool.) *Pilumnus hirtellus*, a species of crab. **-porro** *m.* (zool.) *Xanthus floridus* and *X. rivulosus*, species of crab; edible crab, *Cancer pagurus;* (fig.) blunder, gaffe, *faux pas;* pigliare un — porro, to 'catch crab', to make a *faux pas*, to drop a brick.

granc·ire [D2] *tr.* to seize, to grab. **-itello** *m.* (orn.) ulcer in a bird's mouth. **-ito** *part. adj.* grabbed, snatched.

gran-collare *m.* the highest dignity in the Order of the Annunziata; one who has been awarded this dignity. **-consi·glio** *m.* Council of State. **-cordone** *m.* head of an Order. **-croce** *m.* the title of the head of certain Orders of Knighthood.

grandangolare *adj.* (opt.; photog.; telev.) wide-angle; obiettivo —, wide-angle lens.

grand-e *adj.* (before a noun beginning with a consonant other than **z** or impure **s**, **gran**, unless emphasis is desired) big, large; broad, wide; great; il gran dì, the Judgement Day; il gran padre, Jupiter; la gran madre, Mother Earth; non è un gran che, it's not up to much, it's nothing great; tall; high; un gran monte, a high hill; loud; heavy; chief; il gran pubblico, the general public; grand; alla —, in the grand manner; il gran mondo, high society; Grand'Ammiraglio, supreme title of the Italian Navy; numerous, many; (di) gran debiti, many debts; grandi debiti, large debts; thick (of hair); (liturg.) messa —, High Mass; (leg.) — invalido di guerra, disabled ex-service man; (pop.) war hero; *adv.* greatly, much; un gran bel bambino, a very fine baby; una gran bella donna, a really beautiful woman; una gran brutta cosa, a really horrible thing; *n.m.* grown-up, adult; a great man; greatness; fare le cose in —, to do things on a grand scale; un — di Spagna, a Spanish grandee. **-ac·cio** *m. pejor.* big and clumsy. **-ato** *m.* grandeeship. **-eggiare** [A3c] *intr.* (*aux.* avere) to loom up; to stand out, to excel; to soar; to be ostentatious, to put on airs of grandeur, to show off. **-emente** *adv.* greatly, strongly, much; grandly; deeply; highly. **-ezza** *f.* bigness, largeness; size; greatness; grandness; Sua Grandezza, His Highness; grandeur, display; (astron.) intensity, magnitude; stella della prima -ezza, star of the first magnitude; (phys.) quantity. **-ezzata** *f.* ostentation. **-ezzoso** *adj.* ostentatious. **-iccione**, **-icciuolo** *adj.* rather tall. **-icello** *adj.* big, older, getting quite big (of a child); s'è fatto -icello, he has grown quite a big boy. **-i·gia** *f.* ostentation; pride, arrogance. **i·glia** *f.* Spanish style collar. **-iglione** *adj.* big, overgrown; *n.m.* boy who has outgrown his strength. **-iglionac·cio** *adj. pejor.* hulking and rather backward (of a child). **-iloquente** *adj.* grandiloquent. **-iloquenza** *f.* grandiloquence. **-i·loquo** *adj.* grandiloquent. **-iosità** *f.* grandeur, magnificence; grandiosity. **-ioso** *adj.* grand, stately, imposing, impressive; sumptuous; prodigal; majestic; grand, noble; grandiose. **-iosamente** *adv.* grandly; sumptuously; grandiosely. **-ire** [D2] *intr.* (*aux.* avere) to grow bigger. **-isonante**, **-i·sono** *adj.* high-sounding. †**-i·zia** *f.* greatness, grandness. **-one** *adj. augm.* of **grande**; pompous. †**-ore** *m.* grandeur. **-otto** *adj.* hefty.

gran-din-e *f.* hail; chicco di —, hailstone; (cul.) thin strips of 'pasta' for soup; stye on the eyelid. **-are** [A1s] *impers.* (*aux.* essere) to hail; *tr.* to hail down upon. **-ata** *f.* hail-storm. **-ato** *part. adj.* struck by a hail-storm; damaged by hail. **-oso** *adj.* mixed with hail.

granduc-a *m.* (*pl.* **granduchi**) Grand Duke; (orn.) eagle owl, *Bubo bubo.* **-ale** *adj.* Grand-ducal. **-ato** *m.* Grand Duchy.

granduchessa *f.* Grand Duchess.

grandufficiale *m.* Grand Officer.

grandule *f.* (orn.) sand-grouse, esp. the pin-tailed sand-grouse, *Pterocles alchata.*

granella *f.pl.* cereals.

granell-o *m.* (*pl.* **-i** *m.*, **-a** *f.*) grain (e.g. of corn, or sand); stone, pip (of fruit); seed; kernel; minute particle; *pl.* testicles of fowls and various animals, for cooking; le -a, cereals. **-are** [A1] *tr.* to granulate. **-ato** *part. adj.* granulated. **-eri·a** *f.* folly, nonsense. **-osità** *f.* ruggedness; lumpiness; granulation. **-oso** *adj.* rough, lumpy; granular; (of soil) sandy.

granfarro *m.* See **farro**.

granfatto *adv.* much; very; a great deal, a lot; non è —, it is not long ago.

gran·fi-a *f.* (zool.) claw; talon; *pl.* (fig.) clutches. **-are** [A4] *tr.* to seize, to grab, to claw, to clutch. **-ata** *f.* grabbing; fistful. **-ato** *part. adj.* grabbed; clawed; seized.

gran·gia[1] *f.* (hist.). See **grancia**.

gran·gia[2] *f.* (geog., Piedm.) land used for grain-growing.

granguar·dia *f.* (mil.) main-guard.

grani·fero *adj.* grain-producing; corn-carrying.

grani·gli-a *f.* (techn.) grit. **-atrice** *f.* (eng.) grit-blasting machine, sand-blasting machine. **-atura** *f.* grit blasting. **-etta** *f.* (bldg.) crushed stone.

gran-ire [D 2] *intr.* (*aux.* essere) (bot.) to form grains, to seed, to run to seed; *tr.* to develop the fruit or kernel of; (tanning) to grain, to board; to granulate; (of babies) — i denti, to cut teeth, to teethe; (mus.) to articulate. **-igione** *f.* (bot.) formation of grain in corn, ripening of seed; seeding, running to seed. (**-imento** *m.*) **-ita** *f.* granular ice (for eating); a cold drink poured over smashed ice (e.g. una -ita di caffè, una -ita di limone). **-itella** *f.*, **-itello** *m.* (miner.) diorite. **-i·tico** *adj.* granitic; unbreakable; (fig.) hard as nails. **-itiforme** *adj.* granitiform. **-ito** *part. adj.* (bot.) gone to seed; granulated; (mus.) articulated; massive, solid; firm, robust; *n.m.* (cul.) special quality of flour for making 'pasta'. **-ito·ide** *adj.* granitoid. **-itoio** *m.* graining chisel; leather sieve for granulating gunpowder. **-itura** *f.* seeding; milling, milled edge (of a coin); (photog.) graininess; (tanning) graining.

granito[1] *part.* of **granire**, q.v.

granit-o[2] *m.* granite. **-one** *m.* (miner.) euphotide. **-oso** *adj.* granite-like, hard as granite.

grani·voro *adj.* graminivorous, grain-eating, grain-feeding.

gran-lama *m.* Grand Lama (of Tibet). **-ma·estro** *m.* Grand Master (Masonry, Knights of St John); (mil.) master gunner (NOTE: this term is still used in an honorific sense in the British Army, but has been discontinued in Italy where the gunners are formed into regiments). **†-mercè** *excl.* grammercy. **-mogo·l** *m. indecl.* (hist.) Mogul Emperor. **-visire** *m.* Grand Vizier.

†granne *adj.* See **grande**.

gran-o *m.* (bot.) grain; wheat, *Triticum*; — canino, mouse barley, *Hordeum murinum*; — da uccelli, canary grass, *Phalaris canariensis*; — di vacca, cow-wheat, *Melampyrum*; — di Turchia, maize, Indian corn, *Zea mays*; — nero, —saraceno, buckwheat, *Fagopyrum*; (naut.) — d'orzo, wedge, fillet; (provb.) non ogni uccello conosce il suo —, it's a wise child that knows his own father; pip; speck, minute particle; bead of a rosary; plug (for filling, in metalwork); piece of copper through which the touch-hole is made for a gun; (eng.) dowel, centring pin; *pl.* **-a** *f.* grain (weight); (numism.) Neapolitan and Sicilian coin in use from the fourteenth to the nineteenth century. **-one** *m.* a kind of bead made of gold or silver wire; (bot.) Indian corn, maize, *Zea mays*. **-oso** *adj.* of corn; grained. **-osprone** *m.* (bot.) ergot of rye, sclerotium of *Claviceps purpurea*, formerly called *Secale cornuta*.

granoc·chi-a *f.* (zool.) frog. **-a·ia** *f.* (orn.) heron, egret. **-a·io** *m.* swampy ground. **-ella** *f.* (zool.) tree frog.

granturco *m.* (bot.) Indian corn, maize, *Zea mays* (cf. **granone**, under **grano**).

ggrantur·col-o, -e *m.* (bot.) stem of Indian corn; its flowering shoots dried and used as fodder; place where Indian corn is collected.

granulare[1] *adj.* granular.

granul-are[2] [A I S] *tr., intr.* (*aux.* essere) to granulate. **-ato** *part. adj.* granulated; rough. **-atoio** *m.* powder mill; sieve, riddle. **-azione** *f.* granulation; (med.) granulation (prior to cicatricization).

gra·nul-o *m.* granule; (bot.) granule, plastid, chloroplast; (pharm.) pellet; (med.) granulation. **-are** *adj.* granular. **-ite** *f.* (geol.) granulite. **-oma** *m.* (med.) granuloma. **-ometri·a** *f.* (techn.) particle size; screen analysis. **-oso** *adj.* granular. **-osità** *f.* (photog.) graininess.

granvisire *m.* See under **granlama**.

grapp-a[1] *f.* clamp, cramp-iron; (eng.) belt fastener; (typ.) brace, bracket; (mus.) brace; (vet.) grapes, a mangy tumour in a horse's hoof; brandy, spirits, strong eau-de-vie made in Northern Italy. **-are** [A I] *tr.* to seize. **-i·glia** *f.* skirmish; raid. **-ino** *m.* hook; grappling-iron; (mil. hist.) -ino mascellare, tongs for loading red-hot shot; (naut.) -ino di arrembaggio, boarding-iron; (naut.) grapnel; drop of 'grappa'; lo prendi un -ino?, will you have a little drop of 'grappa'?; small glass in which 'grappa' is served.

Grappa[2] *pr.n.m.* (geog.) mountain between the Brenta and the Piave, near Asolo, where the Italians held the invaders in 1917; il difensore del monte —, General Giardino; (mus.) la canzone del Monte —, a popular patriotic song of unknown origin, commemorating the successful resistance of the Italian army to the Austrian advance in 1917 and beginning with the words, 'Monte Grappa, tu sei la mia patria'.

†grappo *m.* See **grappolo**.

grap·pol-o *m.* (bot.) raceme; un — d'uva, a bunch of grapes; a grappoli, in bunches, in large groups, thickly, in large quantities;

— umano, cluster of people hanging on to an overloaded vehicle. **-ino** *m. dim.* small bunch (e.g. of grapes, etc.).

graptoliti *f.pl.* (geol.) graptolites.

grascella *f.* (vet.). See **grassella**, under **grasso**.

†grasceta *f.* rich pasture.

gra·sc·ia *f.pl.* victuals; (hist.) board set up by the Florentine Republic which inspected the quality and regulated the price of provisions; payments in kind due from country tenants to their landlords; **†**profit, **†**earnings; **†**money; **†**wealth; **†**andare alla —, to go up in smoke; **†**non c'è —, it's no laughing matter. **-iere** *m.* municipal food inspector. **-ino** *m.* food inspector; weights inspector.

graspa *f.* See **grappa**.

graspo[1] *m.* (fam.) grape-stalk; spirito di —, brandy.

graspo[2] *m.* (pop.). See **raspo**.

grass-atore *m.* (leg.) highway robber; footpad; bully, violent and tyrannical person in power. **-azione** *f.* (leg.) highway robbery.

grass-o *adj.* fat, stout; (of food) fat, greasy, rich, oil; giovedì —, the last Thursday before Lent, in Carnival; martedì —, Shrove Tuesday; (eccl.) giorni -i, meat days, non-abstinence days; cucina -a, rich food; mangiare di —, not to fast; (provb.) -a cucina povero testamento, (or) a -a cucina povertà è vicina, luxurious living leads to poverty; fertile, productive, abundant; plentiful; terreno —, manured land; rich, expensive; (Flor. hist.) il popolo —, members of the Arti maggiori; (chem.) fatty; corpi -i, fats; acidi -i, fatty acids; olii -i, fixed oils; (of grapes) not completely pressed; heavy; oppressive; tempo —, cloudy, overcast weather; (typ.) carratteri -i, heavy type; gross, coarse; loud, lewd, licentious; -e risate, lewd laughter; è andata -a, it went off well; a farla -a, at the most, at the best; *n.m.* fat; grease; productivity, fertility (of the soil); — vegetale, vegetable fat; — pinato, solid fat, firm flesh; — di balena, blubber; — per le cuoia, dubbin. **-ac·cio** *adj. pejor.* excessively fat. **-amente** *adv.* greasily; grossly; richly; copiously, abundantly, unstintingly. **-ella** *f.* (vet.) patella (of a horse). **-ellino** *adj. dim.* rather fat; *n.m. dim.* see **grassello**. **-ello** *m. dim.* piece of fat (removed from meat); suet; slaked lime. **†-eri·a** *f.* animal fat. **-etto** *adj. dim.* rather fat; *n.m.* (typ.) heavy type; sentire del -etto, to estimate the weight (of an animal). **-ezza** *f.* fatness, greasiness; stoutness; richness, fertility, abundance; pulp from which olive oil is extracted. **-ime** *m.* manure, dung, soil food. **-ina** *f.* manure, dung. **-ino** *adj. dim.* rather fat; *n.m.* piece of fat meat. **-occino** *adj. dim.* chubby. **-oc·cio** *adj.* plump; indecent, lewd. **-occione** *adj. augm.* too fat, overweight. **-oli** *m.pl.* lard residues. **-one** *m.* very fat man. (**ona** *f.*) **-otto** *adj.* plump, podgy; fat; *n.m.* leaf of lard. **-uc·cio** *adj.* corpulent. **-ume** *m.* fatty matter; grease; manure, dung. **†-ura** *f.* fat, fattiness.

grat-a *f.* grating; **-ella** *f.* grating; grid-iron, grill; (cul.) cotto sulla -ella, grilled; carne alla -ella, grilled meat, grill; grid on a map; (mil. hist.) grid for heating cannon balls. **-elletta, -ellina** *f. dim.* of **gratella**; grating, esp. over a drain. **-ina** *f.* grating; mesh.

gratamente *adv.* See under **grato**[1].

gratic·ci-o *m.* wickerwork shelf (for fruit or rearing silkworms); hurdle (for steeplechases, or for retaining loose earth); lathing for plaster; duckboard; trellis-work; trellis on which mattress-makers beat up wool; — di rete del lettino, wire netting supporting a mattress; **†**wattle hurdle or other form of earth support used in trenches, etc. **-are** [A 3] and derivs. see **ingraticciare**. **-ata** *f.* fence or screen made of wickerwork; trellis, trellis-work. **-ato** *m.* set of wickerwork shelves for drying fruit, etc.; lathing (for a ceiling).

grati·col-a *f.* small grating; grate, basket of a fireplace; gridiron, grill; (eccl., Tusc.) grille of confessional; (art) graticule. **-are** [A I S] *tr.* to draw lines across; to divide by a grid; to close with a grating. **-ato** *part. adj.* like a grating; shut with a grating; *n.m.* railing; grating; trellis; espalier for fruit trees; wall made in the ancient Roman way with square bricks placed diagonally on edge; grid for careening ships.

grati·fica *f.* (admin.; comm.) gratuity, bonus.

gratific-are [A 2 S] *tr.* to give a gratuity to; to give a bonus to; to reward; to remunerate; **†**to accept gratefully; *intr.* (*aux.* avere; *prep.* a) to give pleasure (to), to be gratifying (to); *rfl.* (*prep.* a) to win the favour (of); to ingratiate oneself (with). **-ante** *adj.* rewarding; (theol.) grazia -ante, ingratiating grace, *gratia gratum faciens*. **-azione** *f.* gratuity; bonus; fee for a special service; gratification.

†grati·glia *f.* grating.

gratile *m.* (naut.) leech, bolt-rope; — d'inferitura, head-rope; — di caduta, leech-rope; — di scotta, — di lunata, foot-rope; — centrale, — di mezzo (di una tenda), ridge rope (of an awning).

gratis *adv.* free of charge, gratis; (iron.) lo feci — et amore Dei, I did it for love, not a penny did I get out of it. **-dato** *adj.* (theol.) charismatic; grazie -date, *gratiae gratis datae*.

gratitu·dine *f.* gratitude, thankfulness; †pleasing things; †quality of being pleasing.

grat·o¹ *adj.* pleasing; agreeable, pleasant; acceptable; kind; grateful, welcome; ci è — informarvi, we are pleased to inform you; vi sarò — se, I shall be much obliged to you if; *n.m.* satisfaction, pleasure; a mio —, to my satisfaction; di buon —, gladly; †gratitude. **-amente** *adv.* agreeably; pleasantly; thankfully, gratefully; †gratuitously. **†-ivo** *adj.* gratuitous.

†grato². See **grado**.

gratta-ca·cio *m. indecl.* cheese-grater. **-capo** *m.* worry, anxiety; preoccupation, disturbing thought; problem, poser, 'headache'; prendersi dei -capi, to take on worrying responsibilities; non volere -capi, to steer clear of bother and complications. **-cielo** *m.* skyscraper. **-culo** *m. indecl.* (bot.) cabbage rose, *Rosa centifolia*. **-mento** *m.* see under **grattare**. **†-na·tiche** *m. indecl.* (anat.) broad muscle of the back, latissimus dorsi. **-nu·vole** *m. indecl.* skyscraper. **-pu·gia** *f. indecl.* goldsmith's wire brush; brush for cleaning printers' type. **-pugiare** [A 3] *tr.* to clean with a wire brush.

gratt-are [A I] *tr.* to scratch; to make someone talk; — i piedi alle dipinture, to affect piety; — gli orecchi, to flatter; to grate; to scrape; — il violino, to scrape on the violin (i.e. to play badly); to scratch out, to rub out, to erase; (vulg.) to steal, to 'pinch'; *rfl.* (acc. of prn. 'si') to scratch oneself; (dat. of prn. 'si') -arsi la pancia, to scratch one's stomach, (fig.) to be idle, to be angry. **-amento** *m.* scratching; scraping, scratching out, erasing. **-ata** *f.* scratch; scrape. **-atic·cio** *m.* mark of erasion, erasure. **-ato** *part. adj.* scratched; scraped; grated; pane -ato, bread-crumbs, or bread pap beaten up with egg for soup. **-atore** *m.* scratcher; scraper; end-scraper. (**-atrice** *f.*) **-atura** *f.* scratch, scratching; scrape, scraping, scratch. **-ino** *m.* ink-erasing knife; scraper used in dry-point engraving for removing the burr left by the edge of the burin as the shaving comes away from the plate.

grattugi-a *f.* grater; viso di —, pock-marked face; vedere per un buco di —, to get a mere glimpse of; essere un cacio tra due -e, to be between the devil and the deep blue sea; (joc.) razor; (joc.) grille of confessional; andare alla —, to go to confession. **-are** [A 4] *tr.* to grate. **-ato** *part. adj.* grated; formaggio -ato, grated cheese. (**-atore** *m.* **-atrice** *f.*)

gratu·it-o *adj.* gratuitous, free of charge; unearned, unmerited; unasked for, unnecessary, gratuitous; affermazione -a, unnecessary remark; free of interest; unprovoked; (theol.) gratuitous; atto a titolo —, an act without valuable consideration; prestito —, interest-free loan; — patrocinio, legal aid; difensore d'ufficio in — patrocinio, counsel assigned *in forma pauperis* (i.e. without paying any fees or costs); *adv.* gratuitously, free. **-à** *f.* gratuitousness. **-amente** *adv.* gratuitously, free; without charge; unnecessarily, for no reason; unwarrantably.

†gratulare *vb.* and derivs. See **congratulare**.

gratulato·rio *adj.* congratulatory.

grava·bile *adj.* See under **gravare**.

gravafogli *m. indecl.* See under **gravare**.

grav-ame, -a·mine *m.* gravamen; accusation; burden; grievance; complaint; duty, tax; (leg.) charge; encumbrance; libero di ogni vincolo o —, free from encumbrances; statement of grounds of appeal (C.C.P.).

gravamento *m.* See under **gravare**.

grav-are [A I] *intr.* (aux. avere) to weigh heavy; to be displeasing; *tr.* to load, to weigh upon; to weigh down; to lie heavy on; to afflict, to oppress, to grieve; (leg.) to mortgage; to serve an order of sequestration of; to burden; to encumber; to assign; to charge; to seize; to levy; †to mark with a 'grave' accent; *rfl.* to be offended; to complain; -arsi di vino, to get drunk, 'to take a load'. **-a·bile** *adj.* taxable, dutiable; liable; (leg.) assignable; that may be mortgaged; chargeable by way of mortgage; †heavy; †grievous. **-afogli** *m. indecl.* letter-weight. **-amento** *m.* weighing; burden; (leg.) charge; mortgage; burden; seizure; sequester. **-ante** *part. adj.* heavy, grievous; weighing, bearing, lying. **†-anza** *f.* heaviness; †sorrow, affliction. **-ato** *part. adj.* weighed down; afflicted, oppressed; offended; (leg.) burdened; encumbered;

(comm.) -ato d'assegno, cost and charges to be paid on delivery. **-ato·ria** *f.* (eccl.) papal interdict. **†-azione** *f.* burdening; weight.

grav-e *adj.* heavy; vesti -i, heavy clothes, winter clothes; — d'anni, weighed down in years; weighty; grave, serious; painful, grievous; difficult; displeasing, irksome; non ti sia —, let it not irk you; dangerous; stern; (phys.) specificamente più —, of higher specific gravity; (gramm.) 'grave' (of an accent); suono —, deep sound; (mus.) deep, low (in pitch); †pregnant; *n.m.* serious attitude, seriousness; (phys.) heavy body; weight; *adv.* seriously, gravely; (mus.) slowly and seriously. **-acciuolo** *adj.* heavy, slow-moving, ponderous. **-e·dine** *f.* heaviness, cold in the head. **-emente** *adv.* gravely, seriously; grievously; heavily; deeply; †with difficulty. **†-enza** *f.* sorrow, grief; suffering; torment. **-eolente** *adj.* noisome, foul-smelling, evil-smelling. **-ezza** *f.* heaviness, weightiness; gravity; seriousness; sadness, weariness, heaviness of spirit; hardship; affliction; imposition; headache; heaviness in the stomach; (leg.) damages; costs; burden of duty or tax; †difficulty; †ponderousness. **-icciuolo** *adj.* rather ponderous and slow-moving.

gravicembalo *m.* (mus.) harpsichord.

grav-ifremente *adj.* (poet.) trembling violently. **-isonante, -i·sono** *adj.* (poet.) deep-sounding. **-itonante** *adj.* (poet.) thundering loudly.

gra·vid-o *adj.* pregnant, expectant, with child; with young; gravid; (fig.) loaded, fraught; stuffed; (Tusc.) panini -i, see 'panini imbottiti', under **imbottire**. **-anza** *f.* pregnancy. **†-are** *intr.* to become pregnant; *tr.* to make pregnant.

gravi·m-etro *m.* specific gravity meter. **-e·trico** *adj.* gravimetric.

gravina *f.* mattock; pickaxe; mason's pick.

gravit-à *f.* gravity; seriousness; importance; dignity; pain, affliction; (phys.) gravity; density; (paint.) gravity, intensity, importance; (leg.) — del reato, gravity of the offence (C.P.). **-are** [A I S] *intr.* (aux. avere) to weigh down; (phys.) to gravitate. **-azione** *f.* (phys.) gravitation.

gravos-o *adj.* grievous, sad; rather serious; onerous, burdensome; oppressive (esp. of taxes); vexatious, troublesome; †foul smelling. (**-amente** *adv.*) **-ità** *f.* grievousness, seriousness.

gra·zi-a¹ *f.* grace, favour; boon; essere in — di, essere nelle -e di, to be in the good graces of; aver — presso alcuno, to find favour with someone; avere in —, to be fond of; faccia —?, will you do me the favour?; con vostra buona —, by your leave, with your kind permission; di —!, pray!; in — di, on account of, in consideration of, with the help of, thanks to; per — d'esempio, by way of example; di —, graciously; con mala —, with a bad grace; è — se..., (or) — se..., it is a lucky thing that (things are no worse), you may consider yourself fortunate (at getting off so lightly); (theol.) grace (actual, habitual, sanctifying, sufficient); esser nella — di Dio, to be in a state of grace; esser fuori della — di Dio, to be in a bad temper; anno di —, year of grace; (rel.) favour, special grace, boon (from God or a saint); Madonna delle -e, Our Lady of Graces; avuta la — gabbato lo santo, ask a boon for the vow you make, and diddle the saint with the vow you break; troppa —, sant'Antonio, this is too much of a good thing; aspettare la — di Dio, to expect Providence to do one's work for one, to expect things to drop into one's lap; Re per — di Dio, by the grace of God, King; oggi, per — di Dio, son libero, I'm free to-day, thank goodness; tutta quella — di Dio, all that profusion of delightful things (esp. of food and drink); non si sciupa la — di Dio, you mustn't waste good food (esp. bread); par che non abbia mai veduto — di Dio, he eats as if he'd never seen decent food before; grace, comeliness, elegance; mala —, uncomeliness; (mus.) tenore di —, light tenor; excl. la —!, uttered when something turns out to be larger than one was led to believe; la — di un bambino!, what a big child!; la — di quella mano!, what a large hand!; alla —!, goodness gracious!; Le Grazie, The Graces; sacrificare alle Grazie, (in writing) to be concerned only with elegance of style; grace, pardon; mercy; colpo di—, *coup de grâce*; (typ.) serif; (leg.) pardon; mercy; grace; la — della Regina, the Queen's pardon; Ministero per — e giustizia, Ministry of Mercy and Justice; domanda di —, ricorso di —, petition for mercy or pardon; — condizionata, conditional pardon (C.P.P.); giorni di —, days of grace; *pl.* thanks; thank you; -e mille, (or) mille -e, thank you very much; -e tante, (or) tante -e, many thanks; -e infinite, a thousand thanks; -e sì o -e no?, do you mean yes or no? (asked of a person who has simply answered 'grazie' to an offer); -e a, thanks to; -e al cielo, thank Heavens, luckily; (rel.) rendimento (azioni) di -e, thanksgiving;

grazi·a (*cont.*)

n.m. indecl. un grazie, a 'thank-you', an expression of thanks. **-adei** *f.* (bot.) see **graziola**. †**-ano** *adj.* ingratiating. **~ola** *f.* (bot.) herb of grace, *Gratiola officinalis*.

Gra·zi·a², **-ella** *pr.n.f.* Grace.

grazi·are [A4] *tr.* to pardon; to grant a favour to. **-a·bile** *adj.* pardonable. **-ato** *part. adj.* pardoned; favoured; welcomed, shown favour; †grateful. †**-e·vole** *f.* pleasing; agreeable; welcome.

graziola *f.* (bot.). See under **grazia¹**.

grazios·o *adj.* gracious; graceful, charming; pretty; neat, apt; witty; gratuitous; dainty, elegant; un — imprestito, a loan on easy terms, a loan with nominal interest; (mus.) andante —, with a graceful, easy motion. (**-amente** *adv.*) **-ità** *f.* graciousness; graces; prettiness.

†**grazire** *tr.* to thank; *intr.* to be ingratiating.

gre·bani (Ven.) *m.pl.* large stones and rocks on the seashore.

greca *f.* See under **greco**.

grecchia *f.* (bot.) heather, ling, *C alluna vulgaris*.

grech-eggiare [A3c] *intr.* (*aux.* avere) to imitate Greek ways; (naut.) to back or veer (of a wind) to the north-east of a compass. **-eri·a** *f.* pejor. Graecism. **-esco** *adj.* (*m.pl.* **-eschi**) Greek, Greekish. **-etto** *m. dim.* of **greco**; little Greek boy.

Gre·cia *pr.n.f.* (geog.) Greece; Magna —, the ancient Greek settlements in southern Italy.

grec-ismo *m.* Graecism, Hellenism. **-ista** *m., f.* Hellenist, Greekist, Greek scholar. **-ità** *f.* Greece; all that is Greek. †**-iuolo** *m. pejor.* Greek. **-izzare** [A1] *tr.* to Graecize; to adopt Greek fashions.

grec-o *adj.* Greek; Grecian; pece **-a**, resin, colophony; fede **-a**, treachery, duplicity; *n.m.* Greek; Greek language; — romaico, modern Greek; north-east wind; — levante, east-north-east wind; — tramontana, north-north-east wind; wine made from Greek grapes; (miner.) a kind of green stone. **-a** *f.* Greek woman; Greek girl; woman's garment open down the front with short wide sleeves and edged with gold embroidery; (art) Greek key-pattern; vine from which 'greco' wine is made. **-alata** *f.* north-east gale. **-ale** *adj.* Grecian; *n.m.* north-east wind. **-alaggiare** [A3c] *intr.* (*aux.* avere) (naut.) see **grecheggiare**. **-amente** *adv.* after the Greek fashion; in Greek; elegantly. **-a·nico** *adj.* half-Greek; aping Greek. **-ante** *adj.* showing a knowledge of Greek. **-astro** *adj., n.m.* impure Greek; born in Greece (usu. referring to a Jew).

gre·colo *m. pejor.* Graeculus esuriens; philosopher; wiseacre.

greg-ale *adj.* belonging to a herd; gregarious; lacking in individuality; mass-produced. **-a·rio** *adj.* ordinary; gregarious; sheep-like, following the crowd; (Rom. antiq.) soldato **-ario**, private soldier; (Fascist hist.) militiaman; *n.m.* follower (of a doctrine, a leader, etc.); (naut.) see **grecale**, under **greco**; (sport) minor member of cycling team; *pl.* gregarious animals; members of a gang or sect; lower orders of an organization.

gregg-e *m.* (*pl.* **greggi** *f.*, **gregge** *f.*) flock; herd, drove; cane da —, sheep-dog; razza da —, sheep-dog breed; (rel.) flock. **-iuola** *f. dim.* little flock.

greggia *f.* (poet.). See **gregge**.

greggiare [A3c] *tr.* to hang out (hides) to dry; see **aggreggiare**.

greg·gio *adj.* raw, crude (of a material); unbleached (of cloth); rough; unrefined; unprocessed; undressed; materia greggia, raw material; zucchero —, brown sugar; *n.m.* (eng.) blank.

greggiuola *f. dim.* of **gregge**, q.v.

gregna *f.* (agric.) stook.

gregoriano *adj.* Gregorian (Sacramentary, University, calendar); (mus.) canto —, Gregorian chant, plainchant, plainsong; cavaliere —, Knight of St Gregory; (leg.) codice —, Gregorian code; *n.m.pl.* (hist.) members of the commission for calendary reform.

Grego·rio *pr.n.m.* Gregory.

grembial-e *m.* apron; (liturg.) *gremiale*; (mil.) leather apron worn by sappers and pioneers. **-ata** *f.* apron-full. **-ino** *m. dim.* of **grembiale**; pretty little apron or pinafore; apron of a coach to cover the knees of the passengers; covering to protect rider of a scooter, apron; *pl.* (liturg.) ends of humeral veil.

grembiato *adj.* (herald.) gyronny.

grem·bi·o *m.* (Tusc. pop.) see **grembo**. **-ata** *f.* lapful. **-ulata** *f.* apron-full. **-ule** *m.* apron (NOTE: the three sections of the Confraternità della Misericordia in Florence are: i nobili, i grembiuli, il clero); (mil.) **-ule** del tamburino, leather apron fastened to the belt and left knee to protect that side of a drummer's leg. **-ulone** *m. augm.* of **grembiule**; large apron; overall; apron of a carriage.

grembo *m.* lap; (fig.) bosom; womb; centre; pale; in — alla famiglia, in the bosom of one's family; essa teneva il bambino in —, she held the child in her arms (*or*, on her lap); in — alle acque, on the bosom of the waters; womb; bulge; far —, (of water) to widen; (of mountains) to form a valley.

†**gre·mio** *m.* See **grembo**.

grem-ire [D2] *tr.* to stuff, to cram, to fill; to crowd, to load. **-ito** *part. adj.* (*prep.* di) stuffed, crammed (with); filled; crowded, loaded.

gremo *adj.* (Tusc.) full, crammed full; stuffed; — di, full of, stuffed with.

greppa *f.* See **greppo**.

greppia *f.* manger; crib; rack; *excl.* alla —!; by way of calling a person an ass; (joc.) la — dello Stato, the civil service; mangiare alla — dello Stato, to be a civil servant; alzare la —, to raise the rack so that the animals cannot eat so much, (fig.) to reduce salaries.

greppina *f.* lounge-chair.

grepp-o *m.* steep, rocky bank; cliff, crag; embankment bounding a country road where there is no hedge; side of a ditch extending from the rim to the water; †ditch; †valley; †hut; †far —, to pout, to screw up the face as though about to cry. **-arello** *m. dim.* of **greppo**.

†**grep·pola** *f.* tartar (in wine casks).

grès *m. indecl.* (pron. grè) (miner.) grit stone; stoneware.

gressi·bile *adj.* (zool.) capable of moving by steps.

gret-o *m.* bed of gravel left bare in a river bed; pebbly shore of the sea or river; †river bed. **-oso** *adj.* gritty, gravelly; pebbly.

gretola *f.* bar of a bird-cage; short piece of cane to keep apart the adjacent ribs of a distaff; pretext, loophole; person full of excuses; †splinter.

grett-o *adj.* stingy, shabby, mean; niggardly; petty; narrow; limited; narrow-minded; *n.m.* meanness; niggardliness; narrowness. **-amente** *adv.* meanly; narrowly. **-eri·a** *f.* meanness; shabby trick. **-ezza** *f.* meanness, stinginess; shabbiness.

grev-e *adj.* heavy; grievous. **-emente** *adv.* heavily; grievously.

grezzo *adj.* See **greggio**.

†**griare** *vb.* and derivs. See **gridare**.

griban(n)a *f.* (naut.) Flemish barge.

†**gric·chio** *adj.* curly.

gric·ciolo *m.* shudder, shiver; whim.

†**griccione** *m.* unknown aquatic bird.

grid-a *f.* proclamation; edict, ban; le **-e** dei governatori spagnuoli di Milano, laws and decrees unheeded (an expression derived from Manzoni's *Promessi Sposi*); †fame, reputation; †scolding. **-acchiare** [A4] *intr.* (*aux.* avere) to keep crying a little, to grizzle, to whine.

grid-are [A1] *intr.* (*aux.* avere) to shout; to cry out; to clamour; to yell; to scream; to call; to bawl; — a più non posso, to yell at the top of one's voice; *tr.* to shout for; to call for; to call the name of; to proclaim; — vendetta, to cry out for vengeance, to be atrociously bad. **-amento** *m.* crying, shouting; proclamation. **-a·rio** *m.* (leg.) collection of edicts, proclamations or decrees. **-ata** *f.* shouting, shout; bawling; scolding, reproof. **-ato** *part. adj.* scolded, reproved; *n.m.* shout, cry. **-atore** *m.* one who shouts; crier, town-crier. **-io** *m.* (*pl.* **-ii**) incessant shouting or bawling; clamour. **-one** *m.* clamorous person.

gridellino *adj., n.m.* lilac colour.

grid-o *m.* (*pl.* **-a** *f.*) cry; shout; scream; outcry, tumult; — di guerra, war-cry; fame, repute; rumour; general opinion; di —, famous, well-known, popular, distinguished, celebrated; alzare —, levar —, to become famous; a — di popolo, by popular acclamation; *pl.* **-i** *m.* small quiet utterances; i **-i** della coscienza, the still, small voice of conscience. **-one** *m.* see under **gridare**. †**-ore** *m.* clamour, shouting.

†**grieve** *adj.* See **grave**.

grifagno *adj.* rapacious, ravenous; fierce, frightening; hawk-like; (of eyes) piercing, far-seeing.

grif-are [A1] *tr.* to devour, to eat greedily. **-ata** *f.* see under **grifo**.

griffa *f.* (eng.) claw; trasporto a —, claw movement.

grif-o *m.* snout (properly of a pig); muzzle, nose; ungersi il —, to eat the bread of idleness; torcere il —, to turn up one's nose; puzzle, riddle; see **grifone**. **-accio** *m. pejor.* fare un **-accio**, to pull an ugly face. **-oide** *adj.* snout-like. **-olare** [A1s] and derivs. see **grufolare**.

grifóne *m.* griffin; (rel.) gryphon as symbol of Christ; (orn.) griffon vulture, *Gyps fulvus*; griffon (breed of dog); — belga, miniature griffon; †snout; †punch on the nose.

gri·g·io *adj.* grey, gray; — perla, pearl grey; — verde, grey-green; il — verde, the colour of the Italian Army uniform (1914–43); the stuff itself (cf. khaki); — perla, pearl grey; ora -ia, hour of sadness; *n.m.* grey colour; (leg.) le leggi del —, laws forbidding youthful offences. **-ero·gnolo** *adj.* greyish. **-iastro** *adj.* greyish, dirty-grey. **-iolato** *adj.* speckled, black and white; greyish. **-ióne** *m.* (zool.) grison, *Grisonia vittata*; canton of Grisons. **-ióre** *m.*, **-iume** *m.* greyness.

Grigióni *pr.n.m.pl.* (geog.) Grisons.

gri·gli·a *f.* iron grating, grille (e.g. in fron tof a window); grille, grill; kitchen grate; furnace firebars; (cul.) alla —, grilled; (radio) grid. **-ato** *m.* fire-surface; (naut.) wire door or hatch cover.

grignolino *m.* a Piedmontese table wine.

grilla·ia *f.* See under **grillo**.

grilla·io *m.* (orn.) lesser kestrel, *Falco naumanni*.

†grillanda *f.* See **ghirlanda**.

grill-are [A I] *intr.* (*aux.* avere) to sizzle (as oil in a frying-pan); to simmer; to bubble, to seethe; to hiss; (of wine) to ferment, to work; to dart (of a fish); (of a cricket) to chirp; (of the heart) to rejoice; (of the eyes) to sparkle; (of the brain) to take a fancy, to have a whim, to have a brainwave. **†-eggiare** *intr.* to rejoice, to exult. **-ettare** [A I c] *tr.* and *intr.* (*aux.* avere) to sizzle (in frying).

grillétt-o *m.* *dim.* of **grillo**, q.v.; (watchm.) pawl; trigger; (mus.) tongue of a Jew's harp. **-are** [A I c] see under **grillare**.

grill-o *m.* (ent.) cricket; — campestre, field cricket, *Liogryllus campestris*; — domestico, — focolare, hearth cricket, *Gryllus domesticus*; — d'Italia, *Oecanthus pellucens*; — di mare, lobster, *Homarus vulgaris* (in certain dialects); (also, sometimes) the sea crawfish, *Palinurus vulgaris*; (pop.) grasshopper· †locust; (fig.) cuore di un —, chicken-heart; il — di Pinocchio, il — parlante, the still small voice of conscience; (vulg.) andare a sentir cantare i -i, to die, to push up the daisies; non cavare un — da un buco, not to achieve anything; andare alla caccia dei -i, to go on a wild goose chase; *excl.* indovinala —!, uttered when one cannot explain or foresee something; fancy, whim, caprice; gli saltò il — he took a fancy, he took it into his head; avere qualche — per la testa, to have a bee in one's bonnet; avere il capo ai -i, to be always talking nonsense; (at bowls) the jack; (at Italian billiards) the small ball; (in cleaning or repairing a dome) flying-bridge, platform or cradle hung from the top; (naut.) boatswain's chair, cradle; joining shackle; special type of assault craft used against boom defences; (mil.) type of fuse; (mil. hist.) assault tower. **-a·ia** *f.* barren spot, where only crickets abound. **-astro** *m.* (ent.) a kind of small grasshopper. **-óne** *m.* (mus.) Jew's harp, Jew's trump.

grillotalpa *f.* (ent.) mole cricket, *Gryllotalpa gryllotalpa*.

grimaldello *m.* picklock; jemmy (leg.) possesso ingiustificato di grimaldelli, unjustified possession of picklocks (C.P.).

grimaldi *pr.n.m.* type of cigar (named after an Italian minister).

grimo *adj.* miserable, wretched; wrinkled; rugged.

grin·fia *f.* claw, talon; (fig.) nelle grinfie di, in the clutches of.

grin-go *m.* (*pl.* -ghi) (slang) Spanish-American name for foreigner (esp. non-Latin white).

grinta *f.* villainous, sinister-looking face; sulky expression; insolence; a — dura, severely.

grinz-a *f.* wrinkle; crease; fold; (fig.) non fa una —, it is going on smoothly, there's no getting away from that (i.e. the argument is irrefutable), (dressm.) it is a perfect fit; cavar il corpo di -e, to stuff oneself with food. **-a, -o** *adj.* wrinkled, creased. **-olina** *f. dim.* small crease, little wrinkle. **-osino** *adj.* wrinkled (of a baby). **-oso** *adj.* wrinkled; creased. **-ume** *m.* mass of wrinkles. **-uto** *adj.* old and wrinkled.

griotta *f.* (bot.) sour cherry, *Prunus cerasus*.

gripo *m.* type of fishing net.

gripp-ag·gio *m.* (eng.) seizing up (of an internal combustion engine). **-are** [A I] *rfl.* (eng.) to seize (up).

grip·pe *m.* (pron. as Fr.) influenza, 'flu.

grip·pi-a *f.* (naut.) buoy-rope, attached to the anchor and to a buoy marking its position. **-ale** *m.* anchor-buoy; *adj.* pertaining to a buoy-rope. **-are** [A 4] *tr.* to tug, to handle (a buoy-rope).

grippo *m.* pirate-ship; hospital-ship.

grisatóio *m.* riesel-iron, a kind of nipper used by glaziers for removing irregularities from the edges of glass.

grisèll-e *f.pl.* (naut.) ratlines. **-are** [A I] *tr.* (naut.) to fit ratlines to.

grisèllino *adj.* lilac-coloured.

grisètt-a *f.* (N. Ital.) working girl, esp. dressmaker or milliner; grisette; working girl of easy virtue. **-o** *m.* grey fur.

grisò·lito *m.* See **crisolito**.

Grisò·stomo *pr.n.m.* See **Crisostomo**.

grisòu *m. indecl.* (pron. grisù). See **grisù**.

grispi·gnolo *m.* (bot.). See **cicerbita**.

grissino *m.* (cul. Piedm.) a kind of crisp bread made in long, thin rods.

grisù *m. indecl.* (mining) firedamp.

grò *m. indecl.* (text.) heavy silk fabric: gros de Naples.

groana *f.* (geog. Lomb.) infertiie, uncultivated land.

Groenlan·d-ia *pr.n.f.* (geog.) Greenland. **-ése** *adj.* of Greenland; *n.m., f.* Greenlander.

grofo *m.* incrustation on a salt-pan.

grog *m. indecl.* hot grog.

grogo *m.* (bot.) crocus; — gruogo, safflower, *Carthamus tinctorius*.

†gro·lia *f.* See **gloria**.

†grollare *vb.* and derivs. See **crollare**.

gromm-a *f.* soggy or damp incrustation; crust; tartar (in a wine-cask); fur (in a water-pipe); †tartar on teeth. **-are** [A I c] *intr.* (*aux.* essere) to fur up. **-ato** *part. adj.* crusted; encrusted; furred. **†-o** *m.* clot. **-oso** *adj.* furred up, incrusted.

grònchio *adj.* numbed with the cold; *n.m.* slow-witted person.

gronco *m.* (ichth.). See **grongo**.

grónd-a *f.* eaves; part of a roof overhanging the walls; correnti da —, rafters supporting the eaves; cappello a —, sou'wester (hat); slope; box pleats in a skirt; gutter tile; *pl.* the ends of branches which extend over one's neighbour's land; — della barca del grano, row of sheaves to let the water run off a corn-stack; catchment area; gutter under a porthole. **-a·ia** *f.* gutter (on a roof); rain-pipe; drip of water from a roof; (provb.) fuggir l'acqua sotto le -aie, to get out of the frying-pan into the fire. **-aiola** *f.* long, flat tile used in forming the eaves, eaves-tile. **†-e·a** *f.* see **gronda**. **-óne** *m.* gutter.

grond-are [A I c] *intr.* (*aux.* avere) to run off, to pour away; to trickle; to gush; to stream; to ooze; il sudore gli -ava di dosso, the sweat poured off him; *tr.* to shed, to drip with. **-ante** *part. adj.* dripping; trickling; streaming; oozing. **-atóio** *m.* (archit.) larmier, drip (at the top of a Doric cornice); dripstone. **-atura** *f.* drip, dripping. **-óne** *m.* see under **gronda**. **-óni** *adv.* very slowly; crawling along, head bent; grondon -oni, creeping along.

grón-go *m.* (*pl.* -ghi) (ichth.) conger eel, *Conger conger*.

groom *m. indecl.* (pron. as Eng.) lift-boy; messenger-boy; page-boy in a hotel, etc.; groom.

gropp-a *f.* crupper, the back of a beast of burden from the saddle to the tail; croup; back; rump; in —, pillion, behind the saddle; aver 80 anni sulla —, to be all of 80 years; (Tusc.) in —, free, gratis, 'thrown in'; (butcher.) rump; back, backside (of a person); shoulder of a hill; mountain ridge. **-ata** *f.* (equit.) croupade, high curvet, buck-jump. **-iera** *f.* crupper-strap, from the saddle to the loop for the tail; caparison.

gropp-o, (Rom.) **gropp-o** *m.* knot; tangle; small group; — nella gola, lump in the throat; (naut.) squall; (meteor.) nastro di -i, line squall. **-oso** *adj.* knotty.

Gròppoli *m., pr.n.m.* (geog.) Groppoli, in the prov. of Pistoia, a fine wine from that region.

groppón-e *m. augm.* of **groppa**; back; piegare il —, to put one's back into it; avere tant'anni in sul —, to be weighed down in years; crupper, croup; (leatherm.) butt; mezzo —, bend. **-ag·gio** *m.* (tanning) rounding, cropping. **-are** [A I c] *tr.* (tanning) to round, to crop. **-ata** *f.* blow on the back; thrust with the rump.

†gro·ria *f.* See **gloria**.

grosgrain *m. indecl.* (pron. as Fr.) (text.) grosgrain.

grossa *f.* See under **grosso**.

Grosset-o *pr.n.f.* (geog.) Grosseto. **-ano** *adj.* of or relating to Grosseto; *n.m.* man from Grosseto; country round Grosseto.

gross-o *adj.* big; grande e —, big and strong; caccia -a, big-game; dito —, thumb, big toe; cane —, pesce —, important person, 'bigger fish'; — dirigente d'azienda, big business man; pezzo —, important person, 'big bug', V.I.P.; dirle -e, to lie, to exaggerate, to tell tall stories; (of a river) swollen; (of the sea) heavy, rough; aver il sangue —, to feel one's blood boil; thick; rough, coarse; vino —, wine with a lot of body; parola -a, offensive word; avere

gross-o (*cont.*)

il fiato —, to pant, to be out of breath; harsh, loud; scarpe -e e cervello fino, a phrase applied to a sharp-witted yokel; wholesale; —d'orecchio, hard of hearing; (fam.) quest'è -a!, that's a good'un!, this is too much!; l'hai fatta -a!, that's torn it!, now you've done it!; *f.* (vulg.) pregnant; *n.m.* big part, thick part; greater part, main part, bulk, majority; il — del lavoro l'ho fatto, I have broken the back of the work; rough person, lout; tumour, lump; weight of about one-eighth of an ounce; (Milan) a weight of 10 grammes (used by tobacconists); heavy silk; (numism.) silver coin (varying according to place, but usu. of 5 soldi); *adv.* roughly; clumsily; (of a pen) scrivere —, to write thick; *adv. phr.* di —, in great number; in —, roughly speaking; — modo, roughly; a un di —, more or less; (paint.) tirato di —, painted with large brush-strokes. **-a** *f.* gross, twelve dozen; the third and longest sleep of a silkworm; dormir della —, to sleep deeply, to be sound asleep; rough life, vivere alla —, to rough it. **-ag·gine** *f.* grossness, coarseness; stupidity, ignorance; bluntness, roughness. **-agrana** *f.* (text.) grogram, grosgrain. **-amẹnte** *adv.* grossly; coarsely; roughly. **-erello** *adj.* rather thick, rather coarse, rather stupid. **-eri·a** *f.* goldsmith's work of some size; stupidity, folly. †**-ero** *adj.* rough, coarse. **-ẹtto** *adj. dim.* rather gross, rather coarse; *n.m.* (numism.) medieval bronze or silver coin. **-ẹzza** *f.* fatness, thickness; size; bigness; swelling; density, volume; -ezza di animo, rancour; roughness, coarseness; crudeness; deafness; height, depth; †pregnancy. **-iere** *adj.* rough, coarse, rude; wholesale; *n.m.* manufacturer of gold plate. **-ista** *m.* wholesaler, wholesale dealing; *adj.* casa -ista, wholesale firm. **-oc·cio** *adj.* rather coarse; fattish. **-ọne** *adj. augm.* of **grosso**; enormously fat; *n.m.* (numism.) old Tuscan silver coin (equiv. to 21 quattrini). **-otto** *adj.* rather coarse; rather fat, stout. **-ume** *m.* sediment; †fat, coarse objects. **-ura** *f.* coarseness, rudeness; roughness, ignorance.

grossolan-o *adj.* coarse; rough; crude; gross; awkward; alla -a, coarsely, roughly. **-amẹnte** *adv.* coarsely; grossly; crudely. **-ità** *f.* coarseness, roughness.

grossula·ria *f.* (bot.) gooseberry, *Ribes uva-crispa*; (miner.) grossular, gooseberry garnet.

grott-a *f.* cave, grotto, cavern; cellar; sloping bank; dar — alla palla, (in playing bowls), to send one's bowl against the sloping side of the pitch as a means of bowling it where desired. **-aione** *m.* (orn.) see **gruccione. -eggiare** [A3c] *intr.* (*aux.* avere) see 'dar grotta alla palla'. **-ẹto** *m.* locality full of caves. **-o** *m.* grotto; steep, rocky place. **-ọso** *adj.* full of caves; cavernous.

†**grot·tola** *f.* little grotto.

grottẹs-co *adj.* (*m.pl.* **-chi**), grotesque; *n.m.* (paint.; sculp.) grotesque; (theatr.) medley, fantasy; *pl.* grotesques. **-camẹnto** *m.* grotesque ornament. **-care** [A2c] *tr.* to adorn with grotesques. (**-camẹnte** *adv.* **-cheri·a** *f.*)

grott-o *m.* see under **grotta. -olino** *m.*, **-olina** *f.* (naut.) shooting punt (Venice).

Grọt·tole *pr.n.f.* (geog.) Grottole, in the province of Matera.

grovịera *m.*, *f.* (pop.) Gruyère cheese (cf. **gruera**).

grov-i·glio *m.* kink in a twisted string; tangle; (fig.) entanglement, confusion. **-i·gliola** *f.* kink. **-i·gliolo** *m.* knot in a fabric.

gru *f. indecl.* (orn.) crane, esp. the common crane, *Megalornis grus*; (eng.) crane; — a carroponte, — a carro, overhead travelling crane; (naut.) davit; — di capone, cat-head; — a vapore, steam crane; — di caricamento, loading crane; — mobile, travelling crane; — galleggiante, floating crane, crane barge; spese di —, diritto di —, cranage. **-ista** *m.* (eng.) crane driver.

gru gru (onomat.) coo (of doves).

gru-a *f.* (pop.) see **gru** (eng.; naut.). **-ẹtta** *f.* (naut.) bumkin; a kind of belaying bitt; small davit.

gruc·c-ia *f.* (N. Ital.) crutch; crutch-shaped perch for a captive owl; tenere alcuno sulla —, to keep someone on tenterhooks; T-shaped door-handle; Y-shaped or any clothes hanger; dibble for planting vine cuttings; (agric.) dibble; (tanning) drying frame. **-are** [A3c] *tr.* (tanning) to hang up to dry. **-iata** *f.* blow with a crutch.

grucciọne *m.* (orn.) bee-eater, *Merops apiaster*; — egiziano, blue-cheeked bee-eater, *M. persicus*.

grue *f.* See **gru**.

grue·ra *m.* gruyère cheese.

†**grufare** *vb.* and derivs. See **grufolare**.

grufol-are [A1s] *intr.* (*aux.* avere) to root, to rootle, to grub; to poke about; to nose; to eat with one's head almost in the plate; *rfl.* to wallow. **-ọne** *m.* one who noses and pokes about.

†**gruga** *f.* See **gru**.

grugare [A2] *intr.* (*aux.* avere) to coo.

grugn-ire [D2] *intr.* (*aux.* avere) to grunt; to snort. **-ito** *m.* grunt; grunting; snort. **-itọre** *m.* grunter; snorter. (**-itrice** *f.*)

grugn-o *m.* snout; (herald.) snout; (colloq.) face, mug; far il —, to pout, to sulk, to pull a long face. **-ọne** *m.* person with a sulky expression; empty husk of a chestnut; †blow in the face.

gruiera *f.* See **gruera**.

gruista *m.* See under **gru**.

grull-o *adj.* (Tusc.) foolish, silly, stupid; impassive; *n.m.* fool; bravo —!, you silly chump! **-ag·gine** *f.* foolishness; stupidity. **-erello** *m. dim.* fool. **-eri·a** *f.* stupidity. **-ina** *f. dim.* silly little thing (of a woman). **-ọne** *m.* fathead.

grum *m. indecl.* See **groom**.

grum-a *f.* incrustation, esp. the tartar of a wine cask; sediment in a pipe (smoker's); clot. **-ata** *f.* solution of tartar. **-ọso** *adj.* clogged, encrusted, furred; stickily coated.

grumello[1] *m.* fine wine from Valtellina.

grumello[2] *m.* (text.) nep.

grumerẹccio *m.* aftermath, second crop of hay.

grum-o *m.* clot; lump in a liquid; grume; flower bud. **-ọso** *adj.* clotted; lumpy; grumous.

gru·mol-o *m.* heart of a cabbage, lettuce, etc.; inside of a water-melon, after removal of the seeds; core. **-ọso** *adj.* hearted, having a heart (like a cabbage or lettuce, etc.).

grungo *m.* (bot.) dodder, *Cuscuta*.

gruppe *m.* (med.) croup.

gruppito *adj.* (of a diamond) cut with eight facets, and therefore too high in proportion to its base.

grupp-o *m.* group; batch; cluster; knot; nodo —, bend; company; party; set; — di lavoro, working party; — di studi, study group; package of valuables entrusted to the guard of a train; squall; (mus.) division; turn; double relish; lump (in the throat); (rel. art) pedestal for monstrance (with silvered or gilded clouds); (radio) — di lunghezze d'onda, wave-band; (techn.) group; set, unit; (eng.) assembly. **-ẹtto** *m. dim.* of **gruppo**; (mus.) turn.

†**gruzzo** *m.* collection.

gruz·zol-o *m.* savings collected little by little; hoard, nest-egg. **-ẹtto** *m. dim.* un buon -oletto, a tidy sum.

gua' *excl.* (Tusc., abbrev. of **guarda**) exclamation of surprise, impatience or irony: what the...!

guacco *m.* (orn.) little bittern, *Ixobrychus minutus*.

guaciaro *m.* (orn.) guacharo, *Steatornis*.

guaco *m.* (*pl.* **guachi**) (bot.) *Mikania*.

guada *f.* square fishing-net; (bot.) dyer's rocket, weld, *Reseda luteola*.

guada·bile *adj.* See under **guadare**.

guadagn-are [A5] *tr.* to earn; -arsi la vita, to earn one's living; to gain; non c'è nulla da — a, there's nothing to be gained by; to win; — tempo, to gain time; to win; — qualcuno a una causa, to win someone over to a cause; to get; to acquire; to make up for; to recover; to catch; — terreno, to gain ground; *intr.* (*aux.* avere) to improve, to gain; vestita di nero ci -a, she looks better in black. **-amẹnto** *m.* earning; winning; earnings; gain. **-ata** *f.* winnings, earnings, profit; (in the game of 'pallone') the boundary of the ground; (fig.) passare la -ata, to go too far, to exceed the decencies of conversation. **-ato** *part. adj.* gained; earned; won; è tanto di -ato, so much to the good. **-atọre** *m.* winner; earner. (**-atrice** *f.*) **-ẹvole** *adj.* able to earn; in a position to win. **-ucchiare** [A4] *intr.* (*aux.* avere) to manage to earn a little.

guadagn-o *m.* gain, profit; — lordo, gross profit; — netto, net profit; produrre un —, to yield a profit; lauti -i, handsome profit; wages, earnings; winnings; advantage; cavallo di —, stallion at stud; (radio) — di antenna, aerial gain. **-erello** *m.* gain, profit. **-eri·a** *f.* profit; ill-gotten gains. †**-ọso** *adj.* lucrative, profitable.

guad-are [A1] *tr.* to ford; to wade across; to cross by fording. **-a·bile** *adj.* fordable, passable by fording.

guaderella *f.* (bot.) dyer's rocket, weld, *Reseda luteola*.

guad-o[1] *m.* ford; passare a —, to ford, to wade across. **-ọso** *adj.* shallow in parts, having fords; fordable.

guado[2] *m.* (bot.) woad, *Isatis tinctoria*; dyer's greenweed, *Genista tinctoria*.

†**guaffo** *adj.* rough, uncultured, coarse.

†**guaglianza** *f.* See **eguaglianza**.

gu·glia *f.* (oceanography) pinnacle; (archit.) see **aguglia**.

guaglio·ne *m.* (Neap.) boy, youth.

†**guagnel-e** *f.pl.* gospels; *excl.* alle —!, by the Gospels! †-**ista** *m.* Evangelist. †-**o** *m.* Gospel.

guai *excl.* woe!; — a!, woe betide!; allora t'impresto la macchina e — a te se me la rompi, all right, I'll lend you the machine, but mind you don't break it; — se non ci si dovesse mai distrarre, it would be the end if we could never take our minds off our troubles (cf. **guaio**).

guaiac-o *m.* (bot.) lignum vitae, *Guaiacum.* -**olo** *m.* (chem.) guaiacene.

guai·me *m.* (agric.) aftermath, growth after haymaking.

guain-a *f.* (zool.) tube of a tubicolous animal; sheath, scabbard; (dressm.) corset or dress fitting tightly round the body; slot (for ribbon or cord). -**ella** *f.* (bot.) carob tree, locust tree, *Ceratonia siliqua.*

gua·io *m.* mishap; predicament; misfortune; calamity; accident; difficulty; failure; trouble, sorrow, woe; trovarsi in un mare di guai, to be beset with trouble on all sides; un sacco di guai, a host of troubles; è un —, it's a pity; è un bel —, it's a fine kettle of fish; il — è che, the trouble is that; passare per un brutto —, to be in trouble; cercare i guai, to look for trouble; allora furono guai, then the fat was in the fire, then there was trouble.

gua-i·re [D 2] *intr.* (*aux.* avere) to squeal; to howl; to yelp; to whine; *rfl.* to complain. -**iolare** *intr.* (*aux.* avere) to whine continuously.

†**guaitare** *vb.* and derivs. See **guatare**.

guai·to *m.* yelp; yelping; whining; moan; howl; lament.

gualc-a *f.* fulling mill. -**are** [A 2] *tr.* to full. -**amento** *m.* fulling.

gualch-eratore *m.* fuller. -**iera** *f.* fulling mill.

gualc-ire [D 2] *tr.* to crease, to crumple, to rumple; to crush; to wrinkle. -**ito** *part. adj.* crumpled, rumpled; creased; wrinkled (cf. **sgualcire**).

†**gualdana** *f.* troop of armed men despatched to lay waste enemy territory.

†**gualdo** *m.* defect; fault.

gualdrapp-a *f.* saddle-cloth. -**ato** *adj.* (herald.) with trappers.

†**guale** *adj.* See **eguale**.

Gualtiero *pr.n.m.* Walter.

guan·ci-a *f.* cheek; porgere l'altra —, to turn the other cheek. -**ata** *f.* slap in the face. -**one** *m. augm.* hard slap.

guancial-e *m.* pillow; cushion; dormire tra due -i, to be in clover, to have no qualms, to set one's mind at rest; (liturg.) cushion for missal; faceguard of a helmet; (eng.) cushion; (Rom.) bacon. -**a·io** *m.* man who hires out pillows, e.g. at a railway station. -**ata** *f.* biff with a pillow; pillow-fight. -**etto** *m. dim.* of **guanciale**; padding on an owl's perch; padding in clothing to improve the figure; ink-pad; (archit.) bozze a -etto, ornamentation in the shape of rounded knobs. -**ino** *m. dim.* of **guanciale**; -ino da cucire, pin-cushion; (surg.) pad, tampon; a child's game in which he hides his head in a person's lap and guesses who touches his back; a seat made for a third person by two persons clasping hands; fare a -ino, to carry someone in this way. -**one** *m. augm.* of **guanciale**; large pillow; cushion; large cushion for a baby to kick on.

guanci-ata *f.,* -**one** *m.* See under **guancia**.

guan-o *m.* guano; — artificiale, fish manure. -**idina** *f.* (chem.) guanidine. -**ina** *f.* (chem.) guanin.

guant-o *m.* glove; mezzi -i, -i monchini, mittens; in -i gialli, all dressed up; gauntlet; mandare il —, to challenge; gettare il —, to throw down a challenge; raccogliere il —, to accept the challenge; l'amore passa il —, there is no need for friends to stand on ceremony (i.e. they may shake hands with their gloves on); fare un —, to beg; (slang) — di Parigi, French letter, contraceptive sheath; arm-shield used in the game of 'pallone'; (fig.) balzar la palla sul —, to take a favourable opportunity; (swimming) -i palmati, flippers. -**a·io** *m.* glover, glove manufacturer; glove-maker; glove-seller. -**eri·a** *f.* glove-factory; glove-shop. -**iera** *f.* glove-box; silver sweet-dish. -**one** *m.* gauntlet; boxing-glove.

guapp-o *m.* (Neap.) blusterer; swaggerer; hired assassin. -**eri·a** *f.* (Neap.) low life, underworld; bullying or swaggering behaviour or act.

†**guaraguato** *m.* guard; sentinel.

guarana *f.* (pharm.) guarana paste.

†**guarda¹** *f.* See **guardia**.

†**guarda²** *f.* See **guardaroba**, under **guardabarriere**.

guarda-barriere *m., f. indecl.* (rlwy.) level-crossing keeper. -**boschi** *m. indecl.* woodman; forester; forest-keeper, gamekeeper. -**buoi** *m. indecl.* (orn.) cattle egret, *Ardeola ibis.* -**cac·cia** *m. indecl.* gamekeeper. -**ca·mera** *f.* see **anticamera**, under **anti²**. -**ca·napo** *m. indecl.* running ring (for a rope). -**cappe** *m. indecl.* cloakstand. -**capre** *m.* goatherd. -**cartocci** *m. indecl.* (mil. hist.) limber box. -**casa** *m., f. indecl.* caretaker; (bot.) house-leek, *Sempervivum.* -**cavo** *m. indecl.* iron rope ring. -**cenere** *m. indecl.* ash-preventer. -**ciurma** *m. indecl.* warder, guard. -**corda**, -**corde** *m. indecl.* stoppiece in a watch to prevent overwinding. †-**core** *m.* jerkin; justaucorps. -**corpo** *m. indecl.* (naut.) lifeline, man-rope. -**coste** *m. indecl.* coastguard; nave -coste, coastal defence vessel. -**cucina** *f.* scullery. †-**donna** *f.* midwife. †-**feste** *m. indecl.* regular church-goer. -**fili** *m. indecl.* (telegr.) linesman. -**forzati** *m. indecl.* warder, guard. -**freni** *m. indecl.* (rlwy.) brakesman. -**fuoco** *m. indecl.* (naut.) fire shield used when breaming. †-**gio·ie** *m. indecl.* jewel-casket. -**lato** *m. indecl.* (naut.) rope or cork fender. -**li·nee** *m. indecl.* (sport) linesman. -**mac·chie** *m. indecl.* trigger-guard, safety-catch. -**magazzino** *m. indecl.* storekeeper, quartermaster. -**malati** *m. indecl.* male nurse; sick-berth attendant. -**man·drie** *m. indecl.* herdsman. -**mano** *m. indecl.* leather gauntlet; basket-hilt of a sword; trigger-guard of a gun; handrail; ladder-rope. -**mento** *m.* see under **guardare**. -**merci** *m. indecl.* warehouse watchman. -**ni·d(i)o** *m. indecl.* nest-egg, pot-egg. -**palma** *m. indecl.* sail-maker's palm guard. -**petto** *m.* breast-guard (for working with an auger); breast-plate. -**piedi** *m. indecl.* foot-muff. -**pinna** *f.* (zool.) pea crab, *Pinnotheres pisum.* -**porta** *m. indecl.* (Naples) doorkeeper. -**porto** *m. indecl.* port superintendent; police vessel; coastguard cutter; guardship. -**portone** *m. indecl.* (or, *pl.* -**portoni**) liveried porter, commissionaire, doorkeeper. -**reni** *m. indecl.* body-belt; cummerbund. -**roba** *f. indecl.* linen-room; linen-cupboard; wardrobe; cloakroom; *m.* clothing; contents of wardrobe; rinnovare il -roba, to replenish one's wardrobe; †*m., f.* cloakroom attendant. -**robiera** *f.,* -**robiere** *m.* (neol.) cloak-room attendant; †housekeeper in charge of linen-room. -**sala** *m. indecl.* ticket collector at a station entrance. -**scartocci** *m. indecl.* (mil. hist.) see **guardacartocci**. -**sigilli** *m. indecl.* (leg.) keeper of the seals; (Eng.) Lord Privy Seal; Lord Chancellor. -**spalle** *m. indecl.* bodyguard. †-**stelle** *m.* astronomical glass. -**stinco** *m. indecl.* shinguard. -**stiva** *m. indecl.* (naut.) captain of the hold. -**testa** *m. indecl.* (naut.) mast net protecting the upper deck, splinter net. -**via** *m. indecl.* (rlwy.) permanent-way inspector. -**vivande** *m. indecl.* meat-guard.

guard-are [A 1] *intr.* (*aux.* avere) to look; — a, to pay attention to, to see to, to take care of; — di (foll. by *neg. infin.*) to take care not to; -a di non perderlo, be sure not to lose it; -a di non far tardi, mind you're not late; — a casa, to stay at home; *tr.* to look at; to observe; -a chi si vede!, look who's here!; — a vista, to keep in sight, to look into; to examine; to keep an eye on; to look after, to attend to; to keep; to watch; to guard, to defend, to protect; — uno in faccia, to look a person in the face; Dio (ne) -i, God forbid!; *rfl.* to look at oneself; -arsi allo specchio, to look at oneself in the looking-glass; to keep oneself; -arsi da, to be on one's guard against; *recip. rfl.* to look at one another. -**amento** *m.* looking; regarding. -**ante** *part. adj.* looking; (herald.) rear-regardant. -**ata** *f.* look; glance. -**atac·cia** *f. pejor.* evil look; spiteful glance. -**atina** *f. dim.* peep, glimpse; a little look round. -**ato** *part. adj.* looked at; regarded. (-**atore** *m.* -**atrice** *f.*) -**atura** *f.* look, way of looking; observation; care.

guar·di-a *f.* guard; di —, on duty; stare in —, to be on guard, to be on one's guard; mettere qualcuno in —, to put someone on his guard; cane da —, watch-dog; fare la — a, to watch over, to guard; posto di —, guard-post; (naut.) watch; — di dritta, — impari, — dispari, starboard watch; — di sinistra, — pari, port watch; — prima, first watch (8 p.m. to midnight); seconda —, middle watch (midnight to 4 a.m.); — della diana, morning watch (4 a.m. to 8 a.m.); — del mattino, forenoon watch (8 a.m. to noon); — del pomeriggio, afternoon watch (noon to 4 p.m.); — franca, watch below; — di servizio, watch on deck; (boxing) — destra, right-hand guard, 'South-paw'; guard (*f.* even if it refers to a male person); (pop.) traffic-policeman; — notturna, night-watchman; — forestale, Italian State forester; — finanziaria, preventive officer, coastguard; — morta, scarecrow; (equit.) the

guardi-a (*cont.*)
part of a bit which does not go inside the horse's mouth; basket hilt, guard of sword; flood-mark on river-bank; (bookb.) fly-sheet; *m*. (Tusc.) gamekeeper. **-acac·cia** *m. indecl.* gamekeeper. **-amarina** *m. indecl.* (naut.) midshipman; acting sub-lieutenant.

guardianato *m.* See under **guardiano**.

guardian-o *m.* guardian; custodian; curator; warden; (eccl.) (Franciscan) guardian; (rel.) head of a confraternity; sacristan; (sport) goalkeeper; herdsman; caretaker; (orn.) — del coccodrillo, crocodile plover, *Pluvianus aegyptius*; warder; port superintendent; (agric.) young vine-shoot cut short so as to leave only two buds; (naut.) anchor used to indicate if a ship drags; mole, breakwater; ship-keeper; †sheet or stream anchor. **-a·tico** *m.* herdsman's wage. **-ato** *m.* guardianship; (eccl.) Franciscan guardianship.

guardina *f.* (leg.) temporary place of custody; guardroom.

guardinfante *m.* crinoline.

guardin-go *adj.* (m.pl. **-ghi**) cautious; wary; circumspect; careful; †attentive, watchful. **-gamente** *adv.* cautiously; warily; with circumspection.

guar·di-o *m.* (naut.) guard chain, preventer, guard rail, guard. **-(u)ola** *f.* guard-house; room for the police at a theatre. **-(u)olo** *m.* night-watchman. †**-one** *m.* (shoem.) seat (of a heel).

guardo *m.* (poet.) glance, look.

guardolo *m.* (shoem.) welt.

guarent-i·gia *f.* (leg.) mortgage; guarantee; security; bond; carta di —, guarantee bond; mortgage deed; (hist.) Legge delle **-igie**, Law of Guarantees. **-igiare** [A4] *tr.* (leg.) to guarantee; *intr.* (aux. avere) to act as security. **-i·gio** *m.* (leg.) guarantee; security.

guarentire [D2] *tr.* (leg.) to vouch for; to guarantee; to protect (cf. **garantire**).

gua·r-ento *m.* (leg.) guarantor. **-enza** *f.* (leg.) guarantee; guarantor.

guari *adv.* (used only with neg.) much; very; a long time; non ha —, it is not long, not long ago; non aveva —, not long before.

guar-i·bile *adj.*, **-igione** *f.* See under **guarire**.

guarignone *m.* aged stallion used to see whether a mare is in season.

guar-ire [D2] *tr.* to cure, to heal; *intr.* (aux. essere) to be cured, to recover, to get better; to heal, to be healed. **-i·bile** *adj.* curable; lesione, malattia **-ibile** in dieci giorni, injury, illness from which one recovers in ten days. **-igione** *f.* cure; recovery. **-imento** *m.* cure; curing. **-itore** *m.* healer; faith-healer. (**-itrice** *f.*)

†**guarnacca** *f.* long cloak; robe; a kind of smock or overall formerly worn by peasants.

†**guarnello** *m.* stuff made of flax and cotton; gown made of this material.

guarn-igione *f.*, **-imento** *m.* See under **guarnire**.

guarn-ire [D2] *tr.* to fit out, to provide; to equip; to rig out; to furnish; to garnish; to trim, to adorn; (eng.) to pack (a joint); (naut.) to rig up. **-igione** *f.* (mil.) garrison; garrison headquarters; †fortress; †flank archers of a pike regiment; (naut.) crew; (joc.) all the inhabitants of a place. **-imento** *m.* supplies, provisions; (naut.) rigging; outfit; †(mil.) armed company. **-ito** *part. adj.* (prep. di) furnished; equipped; rigged out; garnished; decorated, ornamented, trimmed; (herald.) hilted. **-itore** *m.* supplier. (**-itrice** *f.*) **-itura** *f.* provision, supply; fitting out; trimming; garnishing; (naut.) stores; rigging. **-izione** *f.* supply, provision; rigging; trimming; (cul.) dressing (of a dish); (eng.) packing; gasket; lining; washer; c'è uno sgocciolio dal rubinetto dell'acqua calda, bisogna cambiar la **-izione**, the hot-water tap keeps dripping, the washer needs to be changed; †(mil.) establishment of archers.

guarti *excl.* (*abbrev.* of 'guardati!') beware!; mind!; look out!

†**guascherino** *adj.*, *n.m.* fledgling.

guas-co *adj.* (m.pl. **-chi**) (geog.) Gascon. **-cone** *m.* Gascon. **-conata** *f.* Gasconade; act of bravado.

Guascogna *pr.n.f.* (geog.) Gascony; il Golfo di —, the Bay of Biscay.

guascone *m.* and deriv. See under **guasco**.

guasta-ca·voli *m. indecl.* bore. **-città** *m. indecl.* sacker of cities. **-feste** *m. indecl.* kill-joy, spoil-sport, wet blanket. **-mestieri** *m. indecl.* bungler, bad workman; (comm.) cut-price trader, scab. **-sto·machi** *m. indecl.*, **-sto·maco** *m.*, bad food, indigestible dish. †**-ville** *m.* destroyer of cities.

guastada *f.* glass or china bottle with narrow foot and neck.

guast-are [A1] *tr.* to spoil, to ruin; to mar; to spoil, to lay waste, to devastate; *impers.* **-a**, that is annoying; non **-a**, it does not

matter, it does no harm; il che non **-a**, which is a further asset; (mil.) to lay waste, to demolish, to blow up, to wreck; — la creatura, to have a miscarriage; *rfl.* to spoil, to go bad; to hurt oneself; **-arsi con**, to fall out with, to quarrel with; soggetto a **-arsi**, perishable; (of weather) to cloud over, to change for the worse; *recip. rfl.* to slay one another; to hurt one another. **-amento** *m.* spoiling; marring; disfigurement; destruction, havoc; devastation. **-atic·cio** *adj.* partly destroyed; knocked about, damaged. **-ato** *part. adj.* spoiled, wasted, ruined, gone wrong; damaged; **-ato** dal successo, spoilt by success. **-atore** *m.* spoiler, ruiner; one who lays waste; (mil.) pioneer; sapper; reparto **-atori**, wrecking squad. (**-atrice** *f.*) **-atura** *f.* spoiling, laying waste. **-ime** *m.* work badly done; something spoiled; rubbish.

guasto *apocop. part.* of **guastare**, q.v.; *adj.* spoiled, spoilt; laid waste, devastated; desolate; broken; out of order; tainted; decayed, bad (e.g. a tooth, fruit); latte —, milk that has turned; avere il sangue — con qualcuno, to be angry with someone; corrupt; vicious, depraved; *n.m.* devastation, laying waste, sacking; ruin; damage, something needing repairs; c'è un — al motore, there is something wrong with the engine; (leg.) wilful damage (C.P.); *pl.* ravages.

guat-are [A1] *tr.* to gaze at (usu. with some feeling implied of fear or suspicion); to stare at; to eye; to pry into; to look askance at. **-amento** *m.* eyeing; looking at in suspicion. (**-ato** *part. adj.*)

guatemalteco *adj.* of Guatemala; (also *n.m.*)

guat·ter-a *f.*, **-o** *m.* See **sguatter-a**, **-o**.

guattire [D2] *intr.* (aux. avere) to give tongue (of hounds); to yelp.

guazza *f.* morning mist, heavy dew; (Tusc.) money; mi è venuta la —, I've won a packet.

guazzabu·gli-o *m.* muddle; medley; mass of contradictions; mixture of foods, concoction; slush. **-are** [A4] *tr.* to muddle, to confuse. **-one** *m.* muddler.

guazz-are [A1] *tr.* to ford, to wade across; to let (cattle or horses) cool themselves in a stream or pond; to shake (a liquid) in a container; †to dissipate, to squander; *intr.* (aux. avere) to splash when shaken (e.g. of a bad egg); — in, to have plenty of, to be rolling in; to splash about; to wallow. **-amento** *m.* splashing; watering; wallowing. **-ata** *f.* watering of cattle or horses; †fall of dew. **-atoio** *m.* watering-place for horses and cattle; horse-pond; place for washing wool.

guazz-o *m.* pool, puddle; water splashed about; flood; ford; passare a —, to ford, to wade across; passare a —, to omit to talk of, to skip, to pass over; liquor in which cherries, peaches, etc. are preserved; (paint.) gouache; calamaio a —, inkwell liable to spill (without a stopper); slush; liquid; *adj.* rotten, gone bad. **-erone** *m.* loose smock, widened below the waist, worn by peasants in the Marche; scrap of material. **-etto** *m.* (cul.) a kind of stock in which meat is stewed; (fig.) andare in **-etto**, to go into ecstasies. **-ino** *m.* (Tusc.) ruffian. **-oso** *adj.* wet; soft; rotten; slushy. **-ume** *m.* dirty puddle.

gub·bia *f.* pair of horses or mules abreast; (Tusc.) long cart pulled by three or more horses or mules.

†**guberna·colo** *m.* rudder.

†**guc·chia** *f.* See **agucchia**.

†**gueffa**¹ *f.* cape.

†**gueffa**² *f.* skein.

†**gueffa**³ *f.* wall, bastion.

guelf-o *adj.*, *n.m.* (hist.) Guelph (see note under **ghibellino**); (archit.) merlatura **-a**, battlements with square tops; (numism.) an old Florentine coin; (joc.) non mi pare il caso di fare i **-i** e i Ghibellini, there's no need to keep up this old strife and antagonism. **-amente** *adv.* in the manner of a Guelph. **-eggiare** [A3c] *intr.* (aux. avere) to have Guelph leanings. **-ismo** *m.* (hist.) Guelph policy, Guelphism; (pol.) Demochristian or alleged clerical influence in Italian politics; alleged tendency towards theocracy.

guenc-ire [D2], **-iare** [A3] *intr.* (aux. essere) to slip away.

guer·c-io *adj.* squinting, squint-eyed, cross-eyed; è — dall'occhio destro, he has a squint in his right eye. **-ezza** *f.* squinting, squint; being cross-eyed.

guereza *m.* (zool.) *Colobus guereza*, a kind of monkey.

Guerin *pr.n.m.* — meschino, burlesque of a crusading knight (named from the hero of a poem of that name); (fig.) unwarlike or puny warrior.

†**guerire** *vb.* and derivs. See **guarire**.

guernire [D2] and derivs. See **guarnire**.

guernito *adj.* (herald.) garnished.

†**guero** *adv.* See **guari**.

guerr-a *f.* war; warfare; strife; feud; dichiarare —, to declare war; muovere la — contro, to go to war with; consiglio di —, council of war; teatro di —, theatre-of-war; — di logoramento, war of attrition; — lampo, blitzkrieg; — fredda, cold war; — chimica, chemical warfare; — manovrata, open warfare; — di posizione, — di trincea, trench warfare; †Ministero della —, War Office; (leg.) stato di —, state of war; bottino di —, war booty; danni di —, war damage; leggi di —, wartime legislation; grido di —, war-cry; nave da —, man-of-war; uomo di —, professional soldier, 'regular'. **-ai(u)olo** *m.* warmonger. **-icciuola** *f. dim.* little war. **-i·glia** *f.* guerrilla warfare. **-igliero** *m.* guerrilla. **-iuola** *f. dim.* war over very little.

guerregg-iare [A3c] *intr.* (*aux.* avere) to make war, to wage war; *tr.* to make war on. **-amento** *m.* waging war. (**-iatore** *m.* **-iatrice** *f.*) **-evole** *adj.* warlike. **-evolmente** *adv.* in a warlike manner.

guerr-esco *adj.* (*m.pl.* **-eschi**) warlike, bellicose; martial; in tempi -eschi, in wartime. **-escamente** *adv.* in a warlike manner. †**-ero** *m.* warrior. †**-era** *f.* enemy. **-iere**, **-iero** *n.m.* warrior; †enemy; *adj.* warlike; wartime. **-ista** *m.* warrior; warmonger.

guf-o *m.* (orn.) owl; — comune, long-eared owl, *Asio otus*; — di padule, short-eared owl, *A. flammeus*; — reale, eagle owl, *Bubo bubo*; — selvatico, tawny owl, *Strix aluco*; (fig.) person who makes a blowing noise when eating; unsociable person; (eccl.) kind of almuce. **-aggine** *f.* unsociableness, habits of a recluse. **-are** [A1] *intr.* (*aux.* avere) to hoot; *tr.* to mock.

gu·gli-a *f.* spire, pinnacle, obelisk, guglio. **-ata** *f.* needleful, length of thread; threaded needle. **-etta** *f.* pinnacle.

Guglielm-o *pr.n.m.* William. **-ino** *adj.* (hist.) pertaining to the reign or period of Kaiser Wilhelm II. **-one** *pr.n.m.* (1918) Kaiser Bill.

gugnolino *m.* (bot.) cup, cupule (of acorn).

Guia·na *pr.n.f.* (geog.) Guiana.

guida *f.* guide (*f.* also when referring to a male person); leader; guidance; direction; driving; steering; guide-book; directory; manual; instruction book; rail; rut; runner carpet or rug; — rossa, red carpet; wheel-track; volante di —, steering-wheel; scuola —, school of motoring; (eng.) guide; guide-rail; guide-rein; (mus.) leading-voice, dux or antecedent in fugue or canon; direct, i.e. sign to indicate places of entry in canon, or (in plain-chant) sign at the end of a line to indicate the next note in the following line; (mil.) leading file, sergeant or flank guide; — generale, battalion guide; — particolare, left-wing subordinate officer; general's escort company; leader, marker; Le Guide, title of 19th regiment of cavalry (cf., in U.K., The Guides); (naut.) runner, wire stays to which square sails or foresails are bent; jackstay on a yard; guide pennant; (typ.) jigger.

guida-filo *m. indecl.* (text.) filament guide. **-giuoco** *m. indecl.* games leader. **-mano** *m. indecl.* (mus.) guide-main, hand-guide, a mechanical device invented by Kalkbrenner to fix the position of the wrist in piano-playing. **-nastro** *m. indecl.* (text.) sliver guide.

†**guidai(u)olo** *m.* bell-wether.

guidales-co *m.* (*pl.* **-chi**) sore, gall (on a draught animal); (fig.) trouble, sore point; †withers. **-cato**, †**-coso** *adj.* full of sores.

†**guidardone** *m.* and derivs. See **guiderdone**.

guid-are [A1] *tr.* to guide; to steer; to lead, to conduct; — un'automobile, to drive a car; — un cavallo, to drive a horse; — una motocicletta, to ride a motor-cycle; (mus.) il tempo, to fix or establish the tempo. **-abile** *adj.* guidable; teachable; steerable. **-amento** *m.* guiding; steering; leading; driving. **-ato** *part. adj.* guided; steered; led; driven. **-atore** *m.* driver. (**-atrice** *f.*)

guiderdon-e *m.* recompense; reward; incentive; merit; esteem; guerdon. **-are** [A1c] *tr.* to recompense; to reward. **-ato** *part. adj.* rewarded. (**-atore** *m.* **-atrice** *f.*)

Guid-o *pr.n.m.* Guy. (**-arello**, **-erello** *pr.n.m.*)

guidon-e *m.* (naut.) triangular flag, letter code or numeral; squadron or flotilla flag; — regolatore, senior officer's flag; (mil.) battalion colours, markers; colour guard; †corps or company colours; †soldiers attached to a guide; †rogue, cad. **-eria** *f.* roguery.

guidoslitta *f.* bob-sleigh.

guidrigildo *m.* (leg. hist.) forfeit due to victim of crime under Longobardic law.

guig·gia *f.* sandal-strap, shoe-strap; arm-strap of a shield.

†**guigliardone** *m.* See **guiderdone**.

guilandina *f.* (bot.) Kentucky coffee tree, *Gymnocladus dioica*.

guin·dolo *m.* (silkb.) reel for winding silk as it comes off the cocoon; (naut.) log-reel.

guinz-aglio *m.* dog's lead; leash; cani al —, dogs must be led, dogs must be on the lead; signore eleganti con cani al —, fashionable women with dogs on leads; (fig.) restraint. **-agliare** [A4] *tr.* to put on the lead, to tie on a leash.

†**guirenza** *f.* cure; recovery.

guisa *f.* wise, mode, manner; guise; a — di, after the manner of; si mise la coperta sulle spalle a — di mantello, he put the rug round his shoulders like a cloak; di — che, so that.

guitt-o *m.* strolling player; bad professional actor, bit-part actor; †*adj.* poor, low, sordid. **-eri·a** *f.* sordidness; bit-part actors and actresses who scrape a precarious living, the dregs in show-business.

Guizzante[1] *pr.n.f.* (geog.) Wissant, between Calais and Gris Nez.

guizzante[2] *part.* of guizzare, q.v.

guizz-are [A1] *intr.* (*aux.* avere) to dart (esp. of fish); to quiver; to squirm; to flicker; to flash; — via, to flash past (e.g. of time); to vibrate (of strings) (naut.; aeron.) to yaw; to scull; *tr.* to brandish, to wave. **-ante** *part. adj.* darting; quivering; squirming; flickering; flashing; vibrating. **-ata** *f.* flick, flip, dart; (naut.) yaw. **-o** *m.* flick; flip; dart; leap; (radar) blip, pip; (naut.) surfacing of a torpedo during its run or at the end of its course when fired for practice.

guntero *m.* (math.) slide-rule.

†**gurge** *m.* (poet.) river of light.

gurgugliare [A4] *intr.* (*aux.* avere) to gobble (of a turkey).

gu·sci-o *m.* (bot.) shell, husk; pod; (zool.) shell (of a tortoise, mollusc, etc.); shell of an egg; avere il — in capo, to be young and foolish; scale-pan; gusci della bilancia, scales; (archit.) horizontal hollow-moulding; punt; hull; cover; — di guanciale, ticking which contains the filling of a pillow or cushion; questa federa è un po' trasparente, si vede il rigato del — del guanciale, this pillow-case is rather transparent, you can see the stripes of the ticking through it; †scale-pan; †dead part of a horse's hoof. **-ata** *f.* powdered cuttle-fish shells (as a cosmetic). **-one** *m. augm.* of guscio; empty chestnut husk, of which the fruit has failed to develop.

gusla *f.* (Pascoli) a kind of single-string viol played in Jugoslavia.

gust-are [A1] *tr.* to taste; to try; to have a taste of; — il morso, (of a horse) to foam at the bit; to enjoy; to relish; to like. *impers.* (*aux.* avere) to be pleasing; (S. Ital.) non mi -a questo vino, this wine is not to my taste; *rfl.* (*prep.* di) to enjoy. **-abile** *adj.* enjoyable; agreeable; pleasant; pleasing to the taste. **-amento** *m.* tasting; relishing. **-ativo** *adj.* (anat.) gustatory; calice -ativo, gustatory bud. **-ato** *part. adj.* tasted; tried; relished. **-azione** *f.* tasting; gustation. **-evole** *adj.* pleasing; tasty, palatable, appetizing. (**-evolmente** *adv.*)

Gustav-o *pr.n.m.* Gustave; (techn.) marmo —, cocoa marble.

gust-o *m.* taste; flavour; relish; gusto, zest; con —, with relish; pleasure; liking; prendere — a, to acquire a taste for, to become engrossed in; avere —, prendere —, provare —, to be very glad; cavarsi il — di, to give oneself the satisfaction of, to satisfy a long felt wish to; un giorno mi caverò il — di dirgli esattamente quello che ne penso, one day I'll give myself the pleasure of telling him just what I think of him; avere — a, to be glad of (often vindictively); ben gli sta! ci ho —!, serve him right! I'm glad!; avere un — matto a, to be delighted with, to adore; ma che — c'è a...?, what's the point of...?; bel —, rovinarsi un'amicizia per il piacere di dire pane al pane, there's no point in spoiling a friendship for the sake of calling a spade a spade; (provb.) sui -i non ci si disputa, (or) tutti i -i sono -i, there's no accounting for tastes; (fig.) a —, heartily. **-ac·cio** *m. pejor.* nasty taste. **-osità** *f.* tastiness; delicacy of flavour. **-oso** *adj.* tasty, savoury; amusing; pleasant, enjoyable. (**-osamente** *adv.*)

gutta[1] *f.* See **goccia**.

gutt-a[2] *f.* gamboge. **-alina** *f.* synthetic rubber. **-aperca**, **-aperga** *f.* gutta-percha. **-arama** *f.* (orn.) gaturamo, *Euphonia* (a South American bird). **-azione** *f.* (bot.) guttation.

guttural-e *adj.* guttural; *n.m.* guttural. **-ismo** *m.* guttural pronunciation.

guzla *f.* See **gusla**.

h *f.* (pron. 'acca'; always mute at the beginning of a word; **c** and **g** followed by **h** are hard); un'— minuscola, a small h; un'— maiuscola, a capital H; for fig. uses, see **acca**.

ha¹ *excl.* ha!

ha² *pres. indic. 3rd sing.* of **avere**, q.v.

habanera *f.* (mus.). See **avanera**.

habitat *m. indecl.* (biol.) habitat.

habitus *m. indecl.* (med.) general appearance of a patient.

hac *excl.* ahem (cough).

ha·i *pres. indic. 2nd sing.* of **avere**, q.v.

halfa *f.* (bot.) esparto grass, *Stipa tenacissima*.

halite *m.* rock salt.

hallalì *excl.* hunting call at death of a stag; (mus.) tally-ho!

†hal-o, **†-one** *m.* See **alone**.

hama·c *m. indecl.* See **amaca**.

hamster *m. indecl.* (zool.) hamster, *Cricetus cricetus*.

handicap *m. indecl.* (pron. as Eng.) handicap; **-pato** *adj.* (sport and fig.) handicapped.

hangar(d) *m. indecl.* (aeron.) hangar.

hanno *pres. indic. 3rd pl.* of **avere**, q.v.

hara *f.* pigsty.

harakiri *m. indecl.* hara-kiri.

hare·m *m. indecl.* harem.

harmoniphon *m. indecl.* (mus.). See **armonifono**.

harmo·nium *m. indecl.* (mus.). See **armonio**.

hasci·sc *m. indecl.* hashish.

haute *f.* (pron. as Fr.) high society, beau monde.

heckelpho·n *m. indecl.* (mus.) heckelphone.

hegelian-o *adj.* (philos.) Hegelian; (fig.) abstruse, obscure. **-ismo** *m.* (philos.) Hegelianism.

helium *m. indecl.* See **elio**.

henné *m. indecl.* (pron. as Fr.) henna; henna dye.

hen·rio, henry *m. indecl.* (electr.) henry (unit of inductance).

herbosa *f.* (geog.) grassland association (of plants).

hertziano *adj.* See **erziano**.

hia·co *m.* (bot.). See **guaiaco**.

Higiaz *pr.n.m.* (geog.) Hejaz.

hiho·n *excl.* (onomat.) hee-haw (a donkey's bray).

Himala·ia *pr.n.f.* (geog.) Himalaya.

ho *pres. indic. 1st sing.* of **avere**, q.v.

hobby *m. indecl.* (pron. as Fr.) hobby.

hock-ey *m. indecl.* (pron. as Fr.) — su ghiaccio, ice-hockey; — su prato, hockey; — a rotelle, hockey on roller-skates. **-eista** *m., f.* hockey-player.

honorem (Lat.) laurea ad —, degree *honoris causa*.

Hoorn *pr.n.m.* (geog.) Capo —, Cape Horn.

hoplà *excl.* ups-a-daisy!

hornpipe *m. indecl.* (mus.) hornpipe.

hostess *f. indecl.* (pron. as Eng.) air-hostess, stewardess.

huco *m.* (ichth.) Danube salmon, *Salmo hucho*.

hu·i *excl.* (of surprise) well!; whew!

humite *f.* (miner.) humite.

humu·s *f. indecl.* humus; (fig.) ground suitable for the growth of a certain feeling or opinion.

huro·nico *adj.* (geog.) huronian.

hurrà *excl.* hurrah!

hussita *m.* follower of Huss, Hussite.

i¹ *m., f.* the letter i; the vowel i; (prosod.) i lunga, long i; i breve, short i; (pop.) i lungo, the letter j; i corto, the letter i; l'i greco, the letter y; l'i consonantica si scriveva j, i as a semi-consonant was formerly written j; un punto sull'i, a dot on the i; (fig.) mettere i punti sugli i, to speak plainly, to speak out; mettere i puntini sugli i, to be scrupulously exact.

i² *def. art. m.pl.* (used before all consonants except impure s, z, x, and usually gn, ps, otherwise **gli**) the. NOTE: **i** combines with *preps.* to form **ai, coi, dei, nei, pei**.

i³ *def. art. m. sing.* (Tusc. pop.). See **il**.

i⁴ *excl.* See **ih**.

†i⁵ *pers. prn. 3rd sing. m., f. dat.* to him; to her.

†i⁶ *pers. prn. 3rd pl. m. acc.* them; *dat.* to them.

†i⁷ *adv.* there.

†i' *prn.* See **io**

jaborandi *m. indecl.* (bot.) jaborandi, *Pilocarpus microphyllus* and other species. The alkaloid pilocarpine is obtained from the leaves.

†iacere *vb.* and derivs. See **giacere**.

iacint-e·o, -ino *adj.* hyacinthine.

†ia·colo *m.* dart; arrow.

Ia·copo *pr.n.m.* James (see also **Jacopo**).

†ia·culo *m.* (zool.) dart-like snake (perh. *Eryx jaculus*).

i·adi *prn. f.pl.* (myth.; astron.) Hyades.

Iafet *pr.n.m.* Japhet.

ialappa *f.* (bot.). See **gialappa**.

ia·lea *f.* (zool.) sea butterfly, *Hyalea* spp.

ial-ino *adj.* transparent, translucent, hyaline; (miner.) quarzo —, vitreous quartz; (anat.) strato —, hyaline layer (of the skin). **-ite** *f.* (miner.) hyalite. **-odiabase** *f.* (miner.) vitreous diorite. **-ografi·a** *f.* hyalography, art of writing on glass. **-o·ide** *m.* (anat.) hyaloid membrane. **-oplasma** *f.* (biol.) hyaloplasm. **-urgi·a** *f.* glass manufacture.

†iambo *m.* and derivs. See **giambo**.

iantina *f.* (zool.) *Janthina* spp., purple sea snail.

iarda *f.* yard (0·914399 metre).

†iaspe, **†ia·spide** *m.* jasper.

ia·stio *adj.* (mus.) modo —, Iastian mode.

iatagan(o) *m.* scimitar.

iato *m.* (gramm.; prosod.) hiatus, break between two vowels coming together without an intervening consonant in successive words or syllables; gap in a series; break in a chain of events; (geol.) the Mesolithic Age, a period between the Palaeolithic and the Neolithic.

iatrali·tico *adj.* (med.) iatraliptic.

ia·trico *adj.* (med.) iatric, medical.

iatt-anza *f.* arrogance, boastfulness, boasting, bragging. **-ura** *f.* misfortune, ruin, wreck; per nostra somma -ura, to crown our misfortunes, to our undoing; continued misfortune, run of bad luck.

†iatt-are *tr.* to toss; to dash, to hurl; to boast, to brag.

Ibe·ria¹ *pr.n.f.* (hist. geog.) Iberia.

ibe·ria² *f.* (bot.) — bianca, wild candytuft, *Iberis amara*; — rossa, globe candytuft, *I. umbellata*.

ibe·r-ico *adj.* Iberian. **-ide** *f.* (bot.) see **iberia²**.

ibern-ante *adj.* hibernating. **-azione** *f.* hibernation.

iber·nia *f.* (ent.) winter moth, *Chaematobia brumata*.

†iberno *adj.* relating to winter; wintry.

ibi *f. indecl.* (orn.). See **ibis**.

†i·bice *m.* (zool.) ibex, *Capra ibex* (see **stambecco**).

ibis *f. indecl.* (orn.) ibis.

ibisco *m.* (bot.) hibiscus.

ibis redibis *m. indecl.* a Sybilline reply, an ambiguous answer (from the Latin 'ibis redibis non morieris in bello', the reply of an oracle to a soldier who asked if he would return from the war. The reply has two meanings according to whether a pause is made before or after 'non').

ibleo *adj.* (poet.) Hyblean (from Hybla in Sicily, noted for its honey); miele —, Hyblean honey.

i·brid-o *adj.* (biol.) hybrid; cross-bred, half-bred, mongrel; (fig.) hybrid, spurious; composed of incongruous elements; *n.m.* hybrid. **-are** [AIS] *tr.* to hybridize; to cross or interbreed. **-azione** *f.* hybridization, the formation of hybrids, cross-breeding. **-ismo** *m.* hybridism, the fact or condition of being hybrid; the production of hybrids, cross-breeding.

Ica·ri-a *pr.n.f.* name of a Utopia invented by the French Communist Etienne Cabet (1788–1856), author of *Voyage en Icarie* (1842). **-ano** *adj.* relating to the ideals of Cabet.

I·c-aro *pr.n.m.* (myth.) Icarus. **-ariano** *adj.* giochi -ariani, trapeze acrobatics (in a circus, etc.). **-a·rio** *adj.* (myth.) Icarian, of, pertaining to, characteristic of, Icarus.

ica·stic-a *f.* the art of representation by images; (fig.) lively portrayal; visible expression. **-o** *adj.* relating to the art of representation by images; (fig.) expressive, representative; pictorial; vivid; graphic.

ic·cas(s)e *m., f.* See **icchese**.

ic·chese *m., f.* (Tusc., pop.) name of the letter X; gambe a —, knock-knees; seggiola a —, camp-stool (cf. **ics**).

iceberg *m. indecl.* (pron. as Eng.) iceberg (cf. under **ghiaccio**).

icneumo·ne, icne·umone *m.* (zool.) mongoose, *Herpestes ichneumon*; (ent.) ichneumon fly.

icnogr-afi-a *f.* ichnography, ground plan; horizontal section of a building or part of it. **-a-fico** *adj.* ichnographic; pertaining or relating to ichnography. **-aficamente** *adv.* ichnographically.

icno-grafo *m.* draughtsman skilled in ichnography.

ic-one, -ona *f.* (eccl.) icon. **-o-nico** *adj.* iconic, of or pertaining to an icon; (hist. art) relating to or characteristic of ancient portrait-statues of victorious athletes. **-onismo** *m.* representation of an image or figure; imagery; metaphor. **-onoclasta** *m.* (rel. hist.) iconoclast; (fig.) one who assails cherished beliefs or venerated institutions. **-onoclasti-a** *f.* iconoclasm, the breaking or destroying of images (also fig.). **-onocla-stico** *adj.* iconoclastic, pertaining to iconoclasts or iconoclasm. **-onografi-a** treatise on or study of representative art; description of a subject by means of figures, drawings, etc. **-onogra-fico** *adj.* graphic. **-ono-grafo** *m.* iconographer. **-onolatra** *m.* (rel.) iconolater. **-onologi-a** *f.* iconology. **-ono-maco** *m.* (*pl.* **-ono-machi**) (rel. hist.) iconoclast. **-onomani-a** *f.* passion for pictures. **-onosco-pio** *m.* (telev.) iconoscope. **-ono-stasi** *f.* (liturg.; archit.) iconostasis, the screen separating the sanctuary from the main body of the church and on which the icons are placed.

icor-e, i-cor-e *m.* (myth.) ichor; (med.) pus, ichor. **-oso** *adj.* (med.) ichorous, pus-like. **-e-a** *f.* (med.) sanies, sanious matter; discharge of pus. **-e-mia** *f.* (med.) ichoraemia.

icorre-a *f.* (med.) ichorrhoea.

icos-ae-dro *m.* (geom.) icosahedron, a solid contained by twenty plane faces; *adj.* (geom.) icosahedral, having twenty faces. **-ae-drico** *adj.* icosahedral. **-a-gono** *m.* (geom.) polygon with twenty faces and twenty angles. **-an-dria** *f.* (bot.) icosandria, a Linnaean class containing plants with twenty or more stamens inserted on the calyx. **-andro** *adj.* (bot.) icosandrian, icosandrous.

ics *f.* name of the letter X; i raggi —, X-rays (cf. **icchese**).

ictiocolla *f.* See **ittiocolla**.

ictus *m. indecl.* (prosod.) ictus; (mus.) ictus, stress; (med.) ictus, attack, fit.

Ida *pr.n.f.* Ida.

iddea *f.* (poet.) goddess.

idd-i-o *m.* God; god (*pl.* **-i-i**). †**-iastro** *m.* false god, pagan divinity.

ide-a *f.* **1.** IDEA; — chiara, clear idea; — confusa, confused idea; (philos.) idea; l'— platonica, the eternally existing pattern of any class of things of which the individual things are imperfect copies and from which they derive their existence; esprime bene le sue idee, he expresses his ideas well; manca il legame delle idee, there is no connecting link between the ideas. **2.** THOUGHT; la parola è espressione dell'—, words are an expression of thought; gli si confusero le idee, his thoughts became confused; seguire l'ordine delle idee, to follow the development of the thought (or ideas). **3.** CONCEPTION, notion, impression, idea; non aver neppur l'— di, to have no conception of; Lei non ha — come sia difficile, you have no idea how difficult it is; da non averne —, inconceivably; andarsene per un'—, to have a faint idea of; non lo so bene, ne ho appena un'—, I don't know, I'm quite vague about it; dare l'— di, to give the impression of; farsi un'— di, to get a rough idea of; nemmeno per —, by no means, not in one's wildest dreams. **4.** OPINION, supposition, belief; essere della stessa —, to agree, to see eye to eye to; cambiare —, to change one's mind; all'— sua, in his view; è mia — che, I believe that, it is my opinion that. **5.** PLAN, intention, idea; questa sarebbe la mia —, here is what I suggest; mi pare una saggia —, I think that is a wise plan; l'— sua è di fare l'avvocato, his plan is to go in for law; fu un'— luminosa, it was a brilliant idea; ho una mezza — di, I am half inclined to, I was thinking perhaps I might; mutare d'—, to change one's plans; un'— gentile, a kind thought. **6.** CAPRICE, fancy, whim, something merely imagined; avere delle idee, to have whims and fancies; (med.) — fissa, *idée fixe*, (fig.) bee in one's bonnet; son idee!, it's all imagination!; (iron.) bella — quella tua!, that was a bright thought of yours!; disegnare a —, to draw out of one's head; l'ho fatto di mia —, it was all my own idea. **7.** IDEAL, central idea, aim, purpose; l'— cristiana, the Christian ideal; questa fu l'— di tutta la sua vita, this was the aim of his whole life; l'— del suo discorso è questo, the central idea of his speech is as follows. **8.** LIKENESS, style; Pietro ha una musica lontana — dello zio, Peter looks rather like his uncle; una musica sull'— dell'ungherese, Hungarian-style music; in quella chiesa c'è già qualche — del barocco, in that church there is already a hint of baroque; Gianni a me non dà l'— dello scemo,

Ian doesn't look like a fool to me; appena un'— di, the merest hint of, the slightest touch of.

idea-bile *adj.* See under **ideare**.

ideal-e *adj.* ideal; perfect, flawless; una pace —, perfect peace; imaginary; unreal; fictitious; relating to ideas; (art) imaginative, painted or modelled from imagination; (telev.) bianco —, equal-energy white; *n.m.* ideal; non avere —, to have no ideals; person held to be an ideal; non ha altro — che mangiare e dormire, his ideals don't go beyond eating and sleeping. **-mente** *adv.* ideally; in imagination. **-eggiare** [A 3 c] *intr.* (*aux.* avere) to disregard reallty, to pursue the ideal. **-ismo** *m.* idealism; unrealistic habits of thought. **-ista** *m., f.* idealist; dreamer, unpractical and unrealistic person. **-i-stico** *adj.* idealistic. **-isticamente** *adv.* relating to idealism, idealist, characteristic of an idealist, idealistically; according to certain ideals. **-ità** *f.* idealism; ideality, quality of being ideal; ideals, elevated sentiments, aspiration. **-izzare** [A 1] *tr.* to idealize. **-izzato** *part. adj.* idealized.

ide-are [A 6] *tr.* to conceive; to imagine; to visualize; to devise, to design, to plan; to form the idea of; to think of. **-a-bile** *adj.* imaginable, thinkable, conceivable. **-ato** *part. adj.* imagined, conceived; visualized; devised, designed; thought out. **-atore** *m.* person who conceives of or thinks out something; inventor, author. (**-atrice** *f.*) **-azione** *f.* conceiving; visualizing; devising.

idem *Lat.* ditto; the same; likewise; la madre è una linguaccia infame, la figliuola —, the mother is a spiteful gossip and the same goes for her daughter.

iden-tic-o *adj.* identical; (in diplomacy) identic. **-amente** *adv.* identically. **-ità** *f.* see **identità**.

identific-are [A 2 s] *tr.* to identify; to make identical; *rfl.* to identify oneself; -arsi con una causa, to embrace a cause; -arsi con qualcuno, to adopt the outlook of someone; *recip. rfl.* to be identical one with another; to be seen to be identical. **-ato** *part. adj.* identified; lo sconosciuto fu -ato per tale Bianchi Gino, the unknown man was identified as a certain Gino Bianchi; recognized as identical. **-azione** *f.* identification; identifying; (leg.) previa -azione, upon identification.

identità *f.* identity; individuality; carta d'—, identity card; documento d'—, certificate of identity; state of being identical, sameness, oneness; (philos.) identity.

ide-o *adj.* (poet.) relating to Mount Ida; il pastore —, Paris.

ideo-geni-a *f.* (science of the) genesis of ideas. **-grafi-a** *f.* ideography. **-gra-fico** *adj.* ideographic(al). (**-graficamente** *adv.*) **-gramma** *m.* ideogram. **-logi-a** *f.* ideology. **-lo-gico** *adj.* ideological; (leg.) abstract; falsità -logica, see under **falsità**. **-logismo** *m.* (philos.) ideology.

ideo-logo *m.* ideologist; (fig.) visionary, mere theorist.

Idi *pr.n.m., f.pl.* Ides (in the Roman calendar).

idil-lic-o *adj.* idyllic; romantic. **-amente** *adv.* idyllically; in a romantic way.

idil-l-io *m.* idyll; filare l'—, to have a romantic love affair, to be happily in love. **-i-aco** *adj.* idyllic, relating to an idyll.

idio-croma-tico *adj.* (miner.) idiochromatic. **-elet-trico** *adj.* containing static electricity. **-morfo** *adj.* (miner.) idiomorphic. **-pati-a** *f.* (med.) idiopathy. **-sincrasi-a** *f.* (med.) idiosyncrasy. **-sincra-tico** *adj.* (med.) idiosyncratic.

idiom-a *m.* idiom; turn of phrase, manner of speech; language, tongue; l'— materno, one's native tongue; l'— gentile, pure Italian, Tuscan; dialect. **-a-tico** *adj.* idiomatic; characteristic of a particular tongue or idiom. **-aticamente** *adv.* idiomatically.

idiop-ati-a *f.* (med.) idiopathy. **-a-tico** *adj.* (med.) idiopathic.

idiosincrasi-a *f.* and deriv. See under **idiocromatico**.

idi-ota *m., f.* idiot; stupid person; half-witted person; illiterate person; (med.) imbecile; †one who is uninstructed; *adj.* idiotic, stupid. **-otag-gine** *f.* ignorance, stupidity; stupid action. **-o-tico** *adj.* idiotic, stupid and uneducated. **-otismo** *m.* idiom, turn of phrase peculiar to one language; (med.) idiocy, imbecility. **-otizzare** [A 1] *intr.* (*aux.* avere) to use idioms; *tr.* to idiotize.

idiozi-a *f.* (med.) idiocy.

idnee *f.pl.* (bot.) *Hydnum imbricatum*, an edible fungus.

idocrasia *f.* (miner.) vesuvian.

†**idolare** *tr.* to idolize, to worship.

idolatr-a *m., f.* idolater; *adj.* idolatrous. **-are** [A 1] *tr.* to worship as an idol; to idolize. **-amento** *m.* idolatry; idolizing. **-i-a** *f.* idolatry.

idola-trico *adj.* idolatrous.

idole-o *m.* (rel. hist.) idol's temple.

i·dol-o *m.* idol; (fig.) cherished ideal or person; visual or mental image. **-eggiare** [A 3 c] *tr.* to represent in the form of an idol; (fig.) to idolize, to cherish; to represent in concrete form, to give outward expression to. (**-eggiamento** *m.* **-eggiato** *part. adj.*)

ido·ne-o *adj.* fit; fitting; proper; suitable; — a, fit for; serviceable; able; (of a schoolchild who has passed a certain exam) eligible to be moved up into a higher class. **-ità** *f.* fitness, suitability; (leg.) fitness, ability; (techn.) -ità all'assorbimento, absorbing power.

idra *f.* (myth.) hydra; (fig.) hydra, an evil which is widespread and difficult to eradicate; (astron.) Hydra, an ancient southern constellation represented as a water-snake or sea-serpent; (zool.) hydra.

idra·cido *m.* (chem.) hydracid.

idragogi·a *f.* water engineering.

idragogo *m.* (med.) hydragogue, drastic purge.

idram·nia *m.* (med.) excessive abundance of amniotic fluid.

idran·gea *f.* (bot.) hydrangea.

idrant-e *m.* (hydraul.) hydrant; (aeron.) hydrofoil, hydrovane; hose; — da incendio, fire-hose; watercart. **-argiri·a** *f.*, **-argirismo** *m.* mercurial poisoning. **-argi·rico** *adj.* mercurial. **-argi·rio**, **-ar·giro** *m.* (pharm.) mercury, quicksilver. **-argirosi** *f.* mercurial poisoning. **-argiruro** *m.* amalgam. **-artro** *m.* (med.) dropsy of the joints.

idraste *f.* (bot.) golden seal, orange root, *Hydrastis canadensis*.

idrat-o *adj.* hydrated; *n.m.* (chem.) hydrate, hydroxide; — di carbonio, carbohydrate. **-are** [A I] *tr.* to hydrate. **-ato** *part. adj.* hydrated. **-azione** *f.* (chem.) hydration.

idra·ulic-a *f.* hydraulics. **-o** *adj.* hydraulic; energia -a, water power; (mus.) organo -o, hydraulicon, hydraulis, hydraulus, water-organ; *n.m.* hydraulic engineer; plumber.

idra·ulo *m.* (mus.) water-organ (see also 'organo idraulico', under **idraulica**).

idrazide *f.* (chem.) hydrazide.

idrazina *f.* (chem.) hydrazine.

idremi·a *f.* (med.) polyplasmia, hydraemia.

idrence·falo *m.* (med.) hydrocephalus.

i·dria *f.* (Gk. antiq.) hydria, jar, pitcher; (archit.) hydria represented in statuary; funeral urn.

i·drico *adj.* watery, for water; dieta idrica, non-alcoholic diet; approvvigionamento —, water supply; impianto —, waterworks; cura idrica, taking the waters.

idro[1] *m.* water-snake.

Idro[2] *pr.n.m.* (astron.) Hydrus; (geog.) a lake in prov. Brescia.

idro[3] *m. indecl.* (abbrev. of idrovolante) seaplane.

idr-oaeroplano *m.* seaplane. **-obro·mico** *adj.* (chem.) hydrobromic. **-ocarbonato** *m.* carbohydrate; hydrocarbon. **-ocarburo** *m.* (chem.) hydrocarbon. **-ocaucciù** *m. indecl.* (techn.) hydro-rubber. **-ocefali·a** *f.* (med.) hydrocephalus. **-oce·falo** *m.* person suffering from hydrocephalus. **-ocefa·lico** *adj.* hydrocephalic. **-o·cele** *f.* (zool.) hydrocoele, water vascular system (of an echinoderm). **-ocellulosa** *f.* hydrocellulose. **-ochinone** *m.* (chem.) hydroquinone. **-ocia·nico** *adj.* hydrocyanic. **-ocine·tico** *adj.* (mech.) hydrokinetic. **-oclorato** *m.* (chem.) hydrochloride. **-oclo·rico** *adj.* see **cloridrico**. **-oco·tile** *f.* (bot.) pennywort, white-rot, *Hydrocotyle vulgaris*. **-odina·metro** *m.* hydrodynamometer. **-odina·mica** *f.* hydrodynamics; hydrokinetics and hydrostatics. **-odina·mico** *adj.* hydrodynamic. **-oelet·trico** *adj.* hydro-electric. **-oemi·a** *f.* see **idremia**. **-oestrattore** *m.* (techn.) hydro-extractor; spin-dryer. **-o·fano** *adj.* (miner.) hydrophanous. **-oferrocianato** *m.* (chem.) ferrocyanide. **-o·fide** *f.* (zool.) *Hydrophis sublaevis*, a poisonous snake. **-o·filo** *adj.* absorbent; cotone -ofilo, absorbent cotton, cotton wool; *n.m.* (ent.) *Hydrophilus piceus*, a water beetle. **-ofobi·a** *f.* (med.) hydrophobia, rabies. **-o·fobo** *adj.* (med.) hydrophobous; (fig.) furious, raving; *n.m.* hydrophobe. **-o·fono** *m.* hydrophone, submarine detector. **-o·foro** *adj.* bearing water; capable of draining or sucking (e.g. a pump); (sculp.) statua -ofora, statue with a hydria. **-oftalmo** *m.* (med.) hydrophthalmy: increase of the aqueous humour in the eye. **-ofugina** *f.* alum compound for impregnating textiles. **-o·fugo** *adj.* (*m.pl.* -o·fughi) waterproof, impermeable. **-ogala** *f.* sweetened milk and water. **-ogelo** *m.* (phys.) hydrogel. **-ogenare** *tr.* [A I] (chem.) to hydrogenate (oil techn.) to hydrogenate, to harden. **-ogenazione** *f.* hydrogenation. **-o·gene** see **idrogeno**. **-o·geno** *m.* hydrogen. **-ografi·a** *f.* hydrography, chart-making. **-ogra·fico** *adj.* hydrographic. **-o·grafo** *m.*

expert in hydrography. **-oiatri·a** *f.* hydrotherapeutics. **-o·idi** *m.pl.* (zool.) hydroids. **-o·lisi** *f.* (chem.) hydrolysis. **-oli·tico** *adj.* hydrolytic. **-o·lito** *m.* hydrolyte. **-olizzare** [A I] *tr.* (chem.) to hydrolyse. **-ologi·a** *f.* hydrology. **-olo·gico** *adj.* hydrologic. **-olo·gio** *m.* (archaeol.) clepsydra. **-o·logo** *m.* hydrologue. **-oma** *m.* (med.) watery tumour. **-omante** *m.* hydromantic. **-oman·tico** *adj.* hydromantic. **-oman·zia** *f.* hydromancy, divination by means of water. **-omecca·nica** *f.* (scient.) hydromechanics. **-omele** *m.* hydromel, mead. **-ometeora** *f.* (meteor.) hydrometeor. **-ometra** *m.* hydraulic engineer; *f.* (med.) uterine dropsy; (ent.) pond skater, *Hydrometra* spp. **-ometri·a** *f.* hydrodynamics. **-ome·trico** *adj.* hydrodynamic. **-o·metro** *m.* hydrodynamometer; rain-gauge; hydrometer; water-level indicator, depth-scale. **-om·falo** *m.* umbilical hernia. **-omotore** *m.* (eng.) turbine. **-on·falo** *m.* see **idromfalo**. **-onefrosi** *f. indecl.* hydrotherapeutics. **-opati·a** *f.* (med.) hydropathy. **-opericar·dio** *m.* (med.) dropsy of the pericardium. **-o·pico** *adj.* suffering from dropsy; *n.m.* dropsy (see also **idrope**). **-opinna** *f.* hydrofoil. **-opisi·a** *f.* dropsy. **-oplano** *m.* hydroplane, seaplane; hydrofoil. **-opneuma·tico** *adj.* hydropneumatic. **-opo·nica** *f.* method of growing vegetables in saline solutions. **-opo·nico** *adj.* relating to such method. **-oporto** *m.* seaplane base. **-orepellente** *adj.* water-repellent. **-orre·a** *f.* (med.) discharge of fluid. **-osalpingite** *f.* (med.) dropsy of the Fallopian tubes. **-osarca** *m.* (med.) watery tumour. **-oscafo** *m.* (naut.) vessel using propulsion by reaction on the water (as in kitchin rudder). **-oscalo** *m.* seaplane base. **-oscivolamento** *m.* hydroplaning. **-oscivolante** *m.* (naut.) hydrofoil; hydroplane. **-osco·pio** *m.* hydroscope, under-water telescope. **-o·scopo** *m.* water-diviner, water-clock, clepsydra; hydroscope. **-osfera** *f.* (geog.) hydrosphere. **-osilurante** *m.* motor torpedo-boat. **-oso·le** *m.* (chem.) hydrosol. **-os·sido** *m.* (chem.) hydroxide. **-ossile** *m.* (chem.) hydroxyl. **-ossi·lico** *adj.* (chem.) hydroxyl. **-ossilammina** *f.* (chem.) hydroxylamine. **-osta·tica** *f.* hydrostatics. **-osta·tico** *adj.* hydrostatic. **-o·stato** *m.* (hydraul.) hydrostat; level indicator; depth gauge. **-oteca** *f.* water-tank (esp. in ships). **-oterape·utico** *adj.* hydrotherapeutic. **-oterapi·a** *f.* hydrotherapeutics. **-otera·pico** *adj.* hydrotherapeutic. **-o·tico** *adj.* (med.) hydrotic, pertaining to perspiration. **-oti·metro** *m.* water hardness gauge. **-otorace** *m.* (med.) hydrothorax, dropsy of the chest. **-ovolante** *m.* seaplane; -ovolante a scafo, flying-boat. **-o·vora** *f.* water-scooping machine. **-o·voro** *adj.* (eng.) removing (waste) water rapidly; exhaust. **-ozo·o** *m.* (zool.) hydrozoan. **-uro** *m.* (chem.) hydride.

i·drope *m.* See **idropisia**, under **idro-**.

idume·o *adj.* (Bibl.) Idumaean; l'arpa idumea, the harp of David, (fig.) biblical poetry.

Iefte *pr.n.m.* Jephtha.

Ie·hov-a *pr.n.m.* (Bibl.) Jehovah. **-ista** *m.* (Bibl. crit.) Jehovist, Jahvist.

iella *f.* bad luck, misfortune; evil eye.

iemal-e *adj.* (poet.) wintry. **-izzare** [A I] *tr.* (agric.) to treat (plants and seeds) so that they react as though they had passed a winter.

Iemen *pr.n.m.* (geog.) Yemen.

iena *f.* (zool.) hyaena; (fig.) cruel person; low, despicable individual.

iera·tic-o *adj.* hieratic, hieratical, pertaining to or used by the priestly class; (Egypt.) hieratic; (fig.) solemn; stylized; enigmatic. **-amente** *adv.* hieratically.

ieri *adv.* (the initial semi-consonant is never elided after i, but in Tuscan elision after other vowels occurs) yesterday; l'altro —, the day before yesterday; (Tusc.) l'altr'—, the other day; (Tusc.) ier(i) l'altro, the day before yesterday; — mattina, yesterday morning; — notte, last night, — sera, yesterday evening; son cose di —, those things occurred recently; il giorno di —, yesterday; non è nato —, he wasn't born yesterday, he's not a fool, — dicevamo, we were saying yesterday (an expression used to mark the return of free speech, first by Luis de León after the Inquisition and later by Einaudi after Fascism); *n.m.* yesterday; tutto —, the whole of yesterday.

ier-obotane *m.* (bot.) vervain (used in magic), *Verbena officinalis*. **-omirto** *m.* (bot.) butcher's broom, *Ruscus aculeatus*.

ierof-ante *m.* (rel. hist.) hierophant, an official expounder of sacred mysteries or ceremonies, esp. in ancient Greece; (fig.) minister of any 'revelation', interpreter of any esoteric principle. **-an·tico** *adj.* hierophantic. **-anzi·a** *f.* hierophancy.

†**ieroglifico** *adj.* and derivs. See **geroglifico**.

†**ietometro** *m.* rain-gauge.

jett·are [A I] *tr.* to bewitch, to cast an evil spell on. **-atore** *m.* one who has the evil eye; jinks, Jonah, one who brings bad luck. **-atura** *f.* the evil eye; bad luck; the power of bringing ill fortune to others.

Ifigeni·a *pr.n.f.* (myth.) Iphigenia.

igaṣu·rico *adj.* (chem.) igasuric.

Ige·a *pr.n.f.* (myth.) Hygieia, daughter of Æsculapius; (astron.) Hygieia, the tenth asteroid. **-ologi·a** *f.* hygiene.

igi·ene *f.* hygiene; hygienics; health; sanitation; public health; Ministero dell'Igiene Pubblica, Ministry of Health; ufficio d'—, sanitary inspector's office, or local public-health office. **-e·nico** *adj.* hygienic; healthful, salubrious; cibi -enici, health-giving food; carta -enica, toilet paper; assorbenti -enici, sanitary towels. **-enicamente** *adv.* hygienically; healthily. **-enista** *m., f.* hygienist, expert in public health.

igloo, iglù, iglò *m. indecl.* igloo.

igname *m.* (bot.) Chinese yam, *Dioscorea opposita*.

ignaro *adj.* unaware; — di, unaware of, ignorant of, unacquainted with; unsuspecting.

†ignatone *m.* parasite; guzzler; good-for-nothing.

ign·a·via *f.* laziness; sloth; cowardice. **-avo** *adj.* slothful; pusillanimous; cowardly.

ignaziano *adj.* (eccl.) Ignatian.

Igna·zio *pr.n.m.* Ignatius.

†igne *m.* fire.

i·gn·eo *adj.* fiery; flaming; (geol.) igneous. **†-i·colo** *m.* principle or element causing warmth and heat. **-i·fero** *adj.* igniferous. **-i·fugo** *adj.* (*m.pl.* -i·fughi) fire-proof, fire-resistant; *n.m.* antifire paint. **-ipuntura** *f.* (med.) ignipuncture. **-ispi·cio** *m.* (antiq.) divination by fire. **-ito** *adj.* ardent, flaming. **-i·vomo** *adj.* ignivomous; monte -ivomo, volcano. **-izione** *f.* ignition; igniting.

igno·bil·e *adj.* vulgar; ignoble, dishonourable; despicable, shameful; metalli -i, base metals; plebeian. **-mente** *adv.* ignobly; dishonourably; despicably, shamefully. **†-(i)tà** *f.* baseness; ignobility; vulgarity.

†ignocco *m.* see **gnocco**; simpleton, dolt.

ignomi·ni·a *f.* ignominy; infamy; dishonour; shameful action; shame, disgrace; quel ragazzo è l'— della famiglia, that boy is the black sheep of the family; (joc.) un quadro che è un'—, a painting that is disgracefully bad; †venire in —, to fall into ignominy, to be disgraced. **-oso** *adj.* ignominious; infamous; disgraceful, shameful. **-osamente** *adv.* ignominiously; infamously; disgracefully, shamefully.

ignoran·te *adj.* ignorant; uneducated; illiterate; rude, ill-mannered, boorish; *n.m., f.* ignoramus, ignorant person; illiterate person; rude, ill-mannered, boorish person. **-temente** *adv.* ignorantly. **-telli** *m.pl.* (eccl.) Ignorantelli, Ignorantines. **-za** *f.* ignorance; (provb.) la meraviglia è figlia dell'-za, marvel is the daughter of ignorance; (leg.) -za della legge, ignorance of the law.

ignor·are [A 5] *tr.* to be ignorant of, to be unaware of, -ava che fosti qui, he did not know you were here; not to know; -avo d'essere malato, I did not know I was ill. **-a·bile** *adj.* of which ignorance may be excused, not well known. **-ato** *part. adj.* unknown; neglected; è un grand'uomo -ato, his greatness is not appreciated.

†igno·scere *tr.* to condone; to pardon.

ignot·o *adj.* unknown; il Milite —, the Unknown Soldier; poesia di scrittore —, anonymous poem, (in an index or title) anon.; destinazione -a, destination unknown; *n.m.* unknown person; quadro di —, painting by an unknown artist; -i, persons unknown; figlio d'-i, foundling. **†-amente** *adv.* secretly, privately.

ignud·o *adj.* (Tusc.) naked, bare; in the nude; spogliarsi —, to strip naked; gettarsi nell'acqua — nato, to plunge naked into the water; mezzo —, half naked; (poet.) destitute; *n.m.* nude; vestire gl'-i, to clothe the naked. **-are** [A I] *vb.* and derivs. see **nudare**. **†-ità** *f.* see **nudità**.

†ignuno *adj.* See **niuno**.

igr·o·grafo *m.* (meteor.) hygrograph. **-oma** *m.* (med.) collection of fluid, esp. housemaid's knee. **-ometri·a** *f.* hygrometry. **-ome·trico** *adj.* hygrometric. **-o·metro** *m.* hygrometer. **-oscopi·a** *f.* hygroscopy. **-oscopicità** *f.* (scient.) hygroscopicity. **-osco·pico** (scient., bot., etc.) *adj.* hygroscopic. **-osco·pio** *m.* hygroscope. **-o·stato** *m.* (phys.; bldg.) humidostat, hygrostat. **-otermo·grafo** *m.* (meteor.) hygrothermograph. **-otropiṣmo** *m.* (scient.) hygrotropism.

†iguale *adj.* and derivs. See **uguale**.

iguana *f.* (zool.) iguana lizard.

iguanodonte *m.* iguanodon.

igu·meno *m.* (eccl.) hegumen.

iguvino *adj.* (geog.; archaeol.) relating to Gubbio; tavole iguvine, Etruscan inscriptions found at Gubbio (sixteenth century).

ih *excl.* (expression of disgust or to inculcate terror); —! che schifo! un cappello nella minestra, ugh! how disgusting! a hair in the soup; la strega rise ih! ih!, hah! hah! laughed the witch.

il² *def. art. m. sing.* (used before all consonants except s impure, z, x and usually gn, ps; otherwise lo) the; — che, which, a thing which; cento lire — mese, a hundred lire a month. NOTE: 'Il' combines with *preps.* to form: al, col, del, nel, pel (cf. i²).

il¹ *prn. m. sing. acc.* (poet.) him; it.

ila *f.* (zool.) tree frog, *Hyla arborea*.

i·lar·e *adj.* cheerful, merry; hilarious. **-ità** *f.* hilarity, good humour, cheerfulness. **-otrage·dia** *f.* (lit. hist.) burlesque tragedy.

Ila·r·ia *pr.n.f.* Hilary. **-io** *pr.n.m.* Hilary.

ilatro *m.* (bot.) *Phillyrea*.

Ildebrando *pr.n.m.* Hildebrand.

Ildegarda *pr.n.f.* Hildegarde.

i·le·o *m.* (anat.) ileum. **-ectomi·a** *f.* (surg.) ileectomy. **-ite** *f.* (med.) ileitis. **-occecale** *adj.* (anat.) ileocaecal. **-oco·lico** *adj.* (anat.) ileocolic; plica -ocolica, ileocolic fold. **-otifo** *m.* (med.) typhoid fever.

ilesino *m.* (ent.) *Myelophilus* (= *Hylesinus*) *testaceus*, a beetle pest of fir trees.

ili·aco¹ *adj.* (med.). See under **ilio¹**.

ili·aco² *adj.* See under **ilio²**.

Ili·ade *pr.n.f.* Iliad.

i·lic·e *f.* (bot.) holm-oak, evergreen oak, ilex, *Quercus ilex*. **-ina** *f.* (chem.) ilicin.

i·l·io¹ *m.* (anat.) ilium. **-i·aco** *adj.* (med.) iliac.

I·l·io², **-ion** *pr.n.m.* Ilium, Ilion, Troy. **-i·aco** *adj.* Trojan.

illacrim·a·bile *adj.* (poet.) not worthy of tears, unworthy of regret; that cannot move to tears. **-ato** *adj.* (poet.) unwept; unmourned, unregretted.

illagazione *f.* inundation.

illaid·ire [D 2] *tr.* to disfigure, to make ugly, to deform. **-ito** *part. adj.* disfigured; made ugly; deformed.

illanguid·ire [D 2] *tr.* to make languid; to weaken; to enfeeble; *intr.* (*aux.* essere), *rfl.* to become languid; to languish; to grow feeble; to droop. **-imento** *m.* enfeebling effect; becoming languid. **-ito** *part. adj.* rendered languid; languishing; weakened; drooping.

illaqueare [A 6] *tr.* (fig.) to ensnare.

illasciv·ire [D 2] *intr.* (*aux.* essere) to become lascivious, to act lasciviously. **-ito** *part. adj.* lascivious.

illat·ivo *adj.* introducing or stating an inference; of the nature of an illation; inferential; (gramm.) illative; (leg.) inferential; consequential. **†-ore** *m.* (leg.) one who implies or infers.

illaud·a·bile *adj.* not laudable, not deserving of praise. **-ato** *adj.* unpraised, unsung. **†-e·vole** *adj.* see **illaudabile**.

illazione *f.* illation, the act of drawing a conclusion from premisses; deduction; (leg.) inference; conclusion; consequence.

†ille·cebr·a *f.* allurement; enticement; pleasure. **†-oso** *adj.* alluring, enticing.

illeceità *f.* illicitness.

ille·cit·o *adj.* illicit; not sanctioned by law; forbidden; unlawful; (leg.) fatto —, breach of duty; wrongful act; (broadly) tort (C.C.). **-amente** *adv.* illicitly; unlawfully.

illegal·e *adj.* (leg.) contrary to, or forbidden by, law; illegal; unlawful; procedimento —, illegal proceedings; proceedings not in proper form. **-mente** *adv.* illegally; unlawfully. **-ità** *f.* illegality.

illeggiadr·ire [D 2] *tr.* to embellish; to make pretty; to make more attractive, to enhance; *intr.* (*aux.* essere) to become beautiful; to be enhanced. **-ito** *part. adj.* embellished; made pretty; enhanced.

illeggi·bil·e *adj.* illegible; unreadable. **-mente** *adj.* illegibly. **-ità** *f.* illegibility.

illegit·tim·o *adj.* (leg.) bastard, illegitimate; not in accordance with natural law; unfounded; figlio —, illegitimate child; pretesa -a, unfounded claim. **-amente** *adv.* illegitimately; unlawfully. **-ità** *f.* illegitimacy.

illeonito *adj.* (herald.) leopardo —, leopard rampant, lion rampant guardant.

illeopardito *adj.* (herald.) leone —, lion passant.

ille·pid-o *adj.* dull, stupid; clumsy, awkward. (**-amente** *adv.*)

illeṣ-o, illeṣ·o *adj.* unhurt; unharmed; safe and sound; undamaged; intact. **-amente** *adv.* safely; suffering no harm.

illetterato *adj.* illiterate; unlettered.

illibat-o *adj.* unsullied; pure; spotless; chaste; above reproach; above suspicion. **-amente** *adv.* vivere **-amente**, to live a pure life. **-ezza** *f.* purity; integrity; **-ezza dei costumi**, blameless life.

illiberal-e *adj.* illiberal; le arti **-i**, the mechanical arts, handicrafts, technology; ungenerous. **-mente** *adv.* illiberally. **-ità** *f.* illiberality, illiberalness; lack of culture; meanness.

illiceità *f.* See **illeceità**.

il·lico *adv.* (Lat.) — et immediate, then and there, at once, *instanter*.

illimitat-o *adj.* unlimited; indefinite; endless; boundless; (leg.) unlimited; competenza **-a**, unlimited jurisdiction; (mil.) congedo —, indefinite leave. **-amente** *adv.* without limit; indefinitely; endlessly. **-azione** *f.* boundlessness.

illiquid-ire [D2] *intr.* (*aux.* essere) to liquefy, to melt, to become liquid; to soften; (fig.) to fail under stress of emotion. **-ito** *part. adj.* liquefied; melted; softened.

Illi·r-ia *pr.n.f.* Illyria. **-ico** *adj.* Illyrian; Dalmatian. **-iṣmo** *m.* (pol. hist.) cultural and political movement of Croats (1835–48).

illi·rio *adj.* See **illirico**, under **Illiria**.

illivid-ire [D2] *intr.* (*aux.* essere) to turn livid; to turn pale; *tr.* to make livid; to make pale. **-imento** *m.* turning livid; turning pale, paling; pallor. **-ito** *part. adj.* livid; pale.

illo·gic-o *adj.* illogical, contrary to logic. **-amente** *adv.* illogically.

†**illucente** *adj.* resplendent, lucent.

illu·d-ere [C3] *tr.* to delude; to deceive; *intr.* (*aux.* essere), *rfl.* to delude oneself; to flatter oneself; to hope; to believe. **-ente** *part. adj.* deluding; deceptive. **-itore** *m.* see **illusore**, under **illuso**. **-itrice** *f.* deceiver.

†**illuiare** *rfl.* (Dante) to enter into him.

illumin-are [A1s] *tr.* to light, to light up, to illuminate; to give light to; (fig.) to enlighten; — la giustizia, to give information to the police; *rfl.* to light up, to grow bright; (fig.) to become illumined; to become radiant; s'-ò tutta perchè il giovane le aveva sorriso, she became radiant at the young man's smile; to educate oneself, to acquire knowledge. **-a·bile** *adj.* illuminable. **-amento** *m.* manner of illuminating or lighting up; light; (theol.) illumination. **-ante** *part. adj.* illuminating, illuminative; gas **-ante**, coal gas; (theol.) grazia **-ante**, illuminating grace. **-ativa** *f.* illuminative power. **-ativo** *adj.* illuminative; (theol.) illuminative (way); illuminating (grace). **-ato** *part. adj.* illuminated, lit up, lighted; **-ato a cera**, illuminated by candles; **-ato a giorno**, very brightly lit; (fig.) informed, enlightened; *n.m.pl.* (rel. hist.) Illuminati. **-atore** *m.* illuminator; one who illuminates or enlightens; (electr.) apparecchio **-atore**, traction-engine generator. (**-atrice** *f.*) **-azione** *f.* lighting, illumination(s); **-azione a fluorescenza**, fluorescent lighting; (fig.) restoration of sight; spiritual enlightenment; (art) illumination (of MSS.); (naut.) circolo d'**-azione**, range (of a lighthouse light); **-azione sottomarina**, submarine lighting (carried by a diver). **-ismo** *m.* (hist.) enlightenment; a movement of ideas which culminated in the doctrines of the French philosophers of the eighteenth century. **-isti** *m.pl.* writers who contributed to the movement of enlightenment. **-o·metro** *m.* (opt.) illuminometer. **-otec·nica** *f.* lighting technique.

illun-e, -ato *adj.* (poet.) moonless.

†**illusinga·bile** *adj.* not susceptible to flattery.

illuṣion-e *f.* illusion; — ottica, optical illusion; phantasm; dream; fond hope; una pia —, a pious illusion; si pasce di **-i**, he cherishes false hopes, he lives in a dream-world. **-iṣmo** *m.* conjuring. **-ista** *m.* conjurer.

illuṣ-o *part.* of **illudere**, q.v.; *adj.* deluded, deceived; *n.m.* deluded person, one who cherishes false hopes. **-ore** *m.* deluder, deceiver. **-o·rio** *adj.* illusory; deceptive. **-oriamente** *adj.* deceptively.

illustr-are [A1] *tr.* to illuminate, to light up; (fig.) to illustrate, to make clear, to clarify, to explain; to expound; to annotate; to render illustrious; to reflect glory upon; *rfl.* to achieve fame, to become illustrious. **-amento** *m.* illustrating; exposition, annotation. **-ativo** *adj.* illustrative, explanatory. **-ato** *adj.* ennobled, made illustrious; illustrated, annotated; collezione d'autori **-ati**, collection of annotated texts; edizione **-ata**, illustrated edition; cartolina **-ata**, picture postcard. **-atore** *m.* illustrator; annotator. (**-atrice** *f.*) **-azione** *f.* illustration; plate, picture; (aesthet.) painting

which illustrates a story but is deficient in artistic qualities; celebrity, shining light; explanation, annotation, note(s).

illustr-e *adj.* illustrious; famous, celebrated, renowned; distinguished; (joc.) — sconosciuto, self-styled celebrity. **-amente** *adv.* illustriously.

illustris·simo *adj. superl.* a courtesy title once very widely used (abbrev. in writing to 'Ill.mo'), now becoming rare; V.S.I., Vostra Signoria Illustrissima, Your Lordship.

†**illu·vie** *f.* filth; flood of filthy persons or objects.

illuvione *f.* inundation; flood; (fig.) invasion, incursion.

ilmenite *f.* (miner.) ilmenite.

ilo *m.* (bot.; anat.) hilum.

ilobate *m.* (zool.) gibbon, *Hylobates* spp.

ilo·bio *m.* (ent.) *Hylobius* spp., a kind of weevil.

ilone *m.* (med.) callus in the eye.

ilota *m.* (Gk. antiq.) Spartan helot; (fig.) slave, person oppressed, or in servile conditions.

iloẓoiṣmo *m.* (philos.) hylozoism.

ilvaï·te *f.* (miner.) lievrite, ilvaite.

†**image**, †**imago** *f.* (poet.) image, concept.

imaginare [A2s] and derivs. See **immaginare**.

ima·gine *f.* and derivs. See **immagine**.

imagini·fico *m.* (lit., with ref. to D'Annunzio) creator of images.

imag-iṣmo *m.* (lit. hist.) imagism, American school of lyric poetry associated with Ezra Pound. (**-ista** *m.*)

imam-o, iman-o *m.* Imam, title of certain religious and secular officials in Mahommedan countries. **-ato** *m.* office, jurisdiction, etc. of Imam.

imantosi *f. indecl.* (med.) a disease causing hardening and lengthening of the uvula.

imbac-are [A2] *tr.* to cause to become maggoty, to fill with maggots; *intr.* (*aux.* essere) to go maggoty, to become filled with maggots. **-ato** *adj.* maggoty. **-atura** *f.* becoming maggoty; impedire l'**-atura** della carne, to prevent meat from going maggoty.

†**imbaccare** *tr.*, *rfl.* (joc.) to get drunk (cf. **bacco**).

imbacchetton-ire [D2] *intr.* (*aux.* essere) to become a religious humbug; *tr.* to fill with pious prejudices. **-ito** *part. adj.* gone unhealthily pious; turned 'churchy'.

imbach-ire [D2] *intr.* (*aux.* essere) (of fruit, nuts) to go off, to wither. **-ito** *part. adj.* (of fruit, nuts) gone bad, withered.

imbacucc-are [A2] *tr.* to muffle up, to wrap up (esp. the head); (mil.) to cocoon, to protect (a gun, etc.) by an airtight cover; *rfl.* to muffle oneself up, to wrap oneself up, to swathe one's head in a hood. **-ato** *part. adj.* muffled up; wrapped up; hooded.

imbagasci-are [A3] *tr.* to prostitute; to debauch, to corrupt. **-ato** *part. adj.* prostituted; debauched; corrupt.

†**imbagnare** *vb.* and derivs. See **bagnare**.

imbalconato *adj.* (of roses) pink.

imbaldanz-ire [D2] *intr.* (*aux.* essere), *rfl.* to grow bold, to become bold, to be emboldened; *tr.* to embolden, to make bold. **-ito** *part. adj.* emboldened; perky, cocky.

imball-are [A1] *tr.* to wrap up; to embale; to pack into crates; (motor.) — il motore, to race the engine; *rfl.* (motor.) to race (of an engine). **-ag·gio** *m.* packing; wrapping; carta d'**-aggio**, wrapping paper, brown paper; (comm.) distinta **-aggio**, packing list. **-ato** *part. adj.* packed; wrapped up; embaled; (motor.) racing (of an engine); (fam.) drunk, tight. **-atore** *m.* professional packer. **-atrice** *f.* professional woman packer; baling machine. **-atura** *f.* see **imballaggio**. **-o** *m.* packing.

imbalord-ire [D2] *intr.* (*aux.* essere) to become dizzy; to grow bewildered; *tr.* to bewilder; to make dizzy. **-imento** *m.* bewilderment; dizziness. **-ito** *part. adj.* bewildered; dizzy.

imbals-amare [A1s] *tr.* to embalm; to stuff. **-amato** *adj.* embalmed; aria **-ata**, balmy air; uccello **-ato**, stuffed bird. **-amatore** *m.* embalmer; taxidermist. (**-atrice** *f.*) **-atura** *f.*, **-azione** *f.* embalming; taxidermy.

imbambag-iare [A4] *tr.* to line with cotton-wool; to wrap in cotton-wool. **-iato** *part. adj.* lined with cotton-wool; wrapped in cotton-wool; padded, quilted.

imbambinire [D2] and derivs. See **rimbambinire**.

imbambol-are [A1s] *intr.* (*aux.* essere) (of the eyes) to be tearful; to grow heavy. **-ato** *part. adj.* (of eyes) half-closed, heavy with sleep or illness; aria **-ata**, drowsy, stupefied appearance. **-ire** [D2] *intr.* (*aux.* essere) to grow childish. **-ito** *part. adj.* childish in one's old age.

imbanc-are [A2] *tr.* (naut.) to furnish with benches, or thwarts; *intr.* (*aux.* essere) to run aground. **-amento** *m.* (naut.) grounding, running aground. (**-ato** *part. adj.*)

imbandier-are [A1] *tr.* to deck with flags; (naut.) to dress; *rfl.* to put out bunting. **-amento** *m.* decking; (naut.) dressing. **-ato** *part. adj.* decked with flags; **-ato** a festa, hung with bunting; (naut.) dressed.

imband-ire [D2] *tr.* to lay (a table) for a banquet; to prepare, to cook, for a banquet; (fig.) to prepare. **-igione** *f.* preparation for a banquet; dishes for a banquet; una ricca **-igione**, a rich banquet, a magnificent feast. **-ito** *part. adj.* laid for a feast; prepared for a banquet. **-itore** *m.* one who prepares a banquet; one who offers a banquet, host.

imbando *m.* (naut.) slack; ricuperare l'—, to haul in the slack.

imbarazz-are [A1] *tr.* to embarrass; to cause embarrassment to, to place in an embarrassing position; to obstruct, to impede; to block; to perplex; — lo stomaco, to lie heavy on the stomach, to spoil the digestion; (naut.) to foul (the rigging of another ship); to misload (a hold); to become embarrassed; *rfl.* to become entangled; (naut.) to foul the anchor. **-amento** *m.* embarrassing; embarrassment; impeding, obstructing; obstacle. **-ante** *part. adj.* embarrassing; perplexing; impeding; obstructing, blocking. **-ato** *part. adj.* embarrassed; obstructed, blocked; perplexed.

imbarazzo *m.* embarrassment; essere in —, nell'—, to be embarrassed; trarre d'—, to help out of an embarrassment; obstacle; perplexity, quandary; — di stomaco, indigestion; essere in imbarazzi finanziari, to be in financial difficulties; metter in —, dar — a, esser d'— a, to cause embarrassment to, to give trouble to; encumbrance.

imbarbarescare [A2] and derivs. See **imbarbarire**.

imbarbar-ire [D2] *intr.* (*aux.* essere), *rfl.* to become barbarous; (of language) to become contaminated with barbarisms; *tr.* to reduce to barbarism, to barbarize; to contaminate with barbarisms. **-imento** *m.* barbarizing. **-ito** *part. adj.* barbarized; contaminated with barbarisms.

imbarbog-ire [D2] *intr.* (*aux.* essere) to enter one's dotage, to enter one's second childhood; to grow old. **-ito** *adj.* in one's dotage, in one's second childhood; suffering from senile decay.

†**imbarbottato** *adj.* (naut. hist.) equipped like a 'barbotta', q.v., under **barba**.

imbarc-are [A2] *tr.* (naut.) to put on board, to embark; — un colpo di mare, to ship water; *rfl.* to embark, to go on board; (fig.) **-arsi** in un'impresa, to embark on an undertaking; to fall in love; (joc.) **-arsi** per Civitavecchia, to fall in love with an elderly woman; *intr.* (*aux.* essere) (mil.) le truppe **-arono**, the troops embarked. **-adero** *m.* see **-atoio**. **-amento** *m.* embarking. **-ato** *part. adj.* embarked, shipped; (fig.) embarked (on a course), engaged (in an affair); legno **-ato**, warped wood; persona **-ata**, round-shouldered person. **-atoio** *m.* landing-stage; wharf, pier. **-atura** *f.* (of wood) warping. **-azione** *f.* embarkation; taking on board; boat; ship; small boat, dinghy.

imbar-co *m.* (*pl.* **-chi**) *m.* embarkation; passage; loading, shipping; landing-stage; boat; ship.

imbard-are[1] [A1] *tr.* to arm (a horse with armour); to caparison; to harness; †to seduce, to allure; †*rfl.* to fall in love. **-ato** *part. adj.* caparisoned; harnessed.

imbard-are[2] [A1] *intr.* (*aux.* avere) (aeron.) to yaw. **-ata** *f.* (aeron.) yaw; momento d'**-ata**, yawing moment.

imbaril-are [A1] *tr.* to put in barrels; to store in barrels; to cask. **-ato** *part. adj.* in barrels; casked.

†**imbarrare** *tr.* to bar, to obstruct.

imbas-are [A1] *tr.* (archit.) to base; *rfl.* to rest on a base. **-amento** *m.* basing; base, footing; groundwork; basis. **-ato** *part. adj.* based. **-atura** *f.* base, basing, footing, foundation (cf. **basare**).

imbasciata *f.* See **ambasciata**.

imbastard-ire [D2] *intr.* (*aux.* essere), *rfl.* to degenerate; to become debased; *tr.* to debase, to corrupt. **-imento** *m.* degenerating; debasing; l'**-imento** di una lingua, the corruption of a language. **-ito** *part. adj.* degenerated; debased; corrupted; corrupt.

imbast-are [A1] *tr.* to put a pack-saddle on. **-ato** *part. adj.* saddled with a pack-saddle, bearing a pack-saddle.

imbast-ire [D2] *tr.* (sewing) to baste, to tack; (fig.) to plan out, to sketch, to outline, to rough out; †to prepare (food, etc.) for a banquet; *intr.* (*aux.* avere) to truss together the staves of a cask before hooping it; (hat-making) to carry out the first operation in felt-making. **-imento** *m.* basting; tacking. **-ito** *part. adj.* tacked;

(fig.) sketched, outlined, roughed out; put together extempore; †(of a table) laid for a banquet. **-itoio** *m.* cooper's truss-hoop. **-itura** *f.* tacking, tacking thread; cramp, stitch (e.g. in athletes); (eng.) saldatura di **-itura**, tack welding; (fig.) sketch, rough outline, plan.

imbatt-ere [B1] *rfl.* to happen; (*prep.* in) to meet by chance, to fall in with; to 'strike', to run into, to come across; s'-è in un giudice molto severo, he happened to come before a very severe judge; *n.m.* merest chance; è un **-ersi**, it's all a matter of luck. **-o** *m.* chance meeting; obstacle; vento d'-o, sea-breeze, wind off the sea; (mil.) punto d'-o, point of impact.

imbatti·bile *adj.* unbeatable, invincible, unconquerable; indefatigable.

imbatto[1] *m.* See under **imbattere**.

imbatto[2] *m.* See **impatto**.

imbaul-are [A1] *tr.* to pack in a trunk; to pack. **-ato** *part. adj.* packed in a trunk; packed.

imbavagli-are [A4] *tr.* to gag; (fig.) to muzzle, to silence. **-ato** *part. adj.* gagged; (fig.) muzzled, silenced.

imbav-are [A1] *tr.* to smear with spittle, foam or slime; to slaver over, to slobber over; *intr.* (*aux.* avere) to drivel. **-ato** *part. adj.* flecked with foam or slime; slobbered over, covered with slaver.

imbecc-are [A2c] *tr.* (of birds) to feed; to put food into the beak of; (fig.) — uno, to put words into a person's mouth, to prompt someone; to cram. **-ata** *f.* beakful (of a bird); (fig.) words put into a person's mouth, suggestion, prompting; bribe; (Tusc.) slight cold in the head. **-ato** *part. adj.* fed; (fig.) prompted; crammed; (herald.) beaked. **-atoio** *m.* seed-box or food-tray for birds or poultry.

imbeccatellare [A1] *tr.* (archit.) to build corbels on to.

imbecher-are [A1] *tr.* to wheedle; to suborn; lasciarsi —, to give way to persuasion; to allow oneself to be suborned. **-ato** *part. adj.* won over, suborned.

imbecill-e *adj.* imbecile; silly, foolish; *n.m.*, *f.* imbecile; (colloq.) fool. **-aggine** *f.* foolishness, folly, stupidity; foolish action; imbecility. **-ire** [D2]·*intr.* (*aux.* essere) to become imbecile; (colloq.) to become stupid. **-ità** *f.* imbecility. **-ito** *part. adj.* imbecile; suffering from softening of the brain.

imbelle *adj.* unwarlike; timid, cowardly.

imbellett-are [A1c] *tr.* to make up (the face); (fig.) to adorn with artifice; to embellish; *rfl.* to make oneself up, to apply cosmetics to one's face. **-amento** *m.* making-up; embellishment. **-ato** *part. adj.* made up, wearing make-up, with make-up on, painted. **-atura** *f.* making up, use of cosmetics; make-up, cosmetics; ornament, embellishment.

imbell-ire [D2] *intr.* (*aux.* essere) to grow beautiful, to become prettier, to improve in looks; *tr.* to adorn, to embellish. **-ito** *part. adj.* adorned, embellished; more beautiful, prettier, improved in looks, better-looking.

†**imbend-are** *tr.* to bandage; to bind round with wrappings; to disguise by means of a woman's bandeau or fillet. †**-ato** *part. adj.* wearing a bandeau or fillet.

imberbe *adj.* beardless; young; shaven.

imberci-are [A3c] *tr.* (Tusc., pop.) to hit (mark, target); (fig.) to guess, to 'get'; *intr.* (*aux.* avere) to get a bull's eye. **-atore** *m.* good marksman.

imbercio *m.* target.

imberrett-are [A1c] *tr.* to put a cap on. **-ato** *part. adj.* wearing a cap.

imbertesc-are [A2c] *tr.* (archit.) to fortify with bartisans. **-ato** *part. adj.* fortified, battlemented.

†**imberton-are**, **-ire** *rfl.* to fall in love; *tr.* to enamour.

imbestial-ire [D2] *intr.* (*aux.* essere), *rfl.* to become like a wild animal; to fly into a rage, to become wild with rage; to be very obstinate; *tr.* to brutalize; to infuriate. (**-ito** *part. adj.*)

imbesti-are [A4c] *intr.* (*aux.* essere), *rfl.* to become brutish; to act in a brutish way. **-ato** *part. adj.* brutish, animal-like.

imbev-ere [B4] *tr.* to absorb; to soak up; to assimilate; to imbibe; *rfl.* (*prep.* di) to be impregnated (with); to be soaked (in, with); (fig.) to become imbued (with). **-imento** *m.* absorbing; imbibing. **-uto** *part. adj.* soaked, drenched, saturated; uno straccio **-uto** di benzina, a rag soaked in petrol; (fig.) imbued (with).

imbiacc-are [A2] *tr.* to paint with ceruse or white lead; to apply make-up to. **-ato** *part. adj.* covered with white lead; painted made-up; (fig.) sham. **-atura** *f.* coating of white lead; painting, making up (of face).

imbiad-are [A 1] *tr.* to sow with wheat. **-ato** *part. adj.* sown with wheat.

imbianc-are [A 2] *tr.* to whiten; to whitewash; to wash white; — una persona, to turn a person down (in application for a post); (text.) to bleach; *rfl.*, *intr.* (*aux.* essere) to grow white, to turn white; (of the sky) to grow pale with the first light of dawn. **-amento** *m.* whitening; bleaching; turning white. **-ato** *part. adj.* whitened; (text.) bleached; sepolcri -ati, whited sepulchres, hypocrites. **-atoio** *m.* laundry, wash-house. **-atora** *f.* laundress, washerwoman. **-atore** *m.* laundryman; (text.) bleacher; see **imbianchino**. **-atura** *f.* whitewashing; washing.

imbianchino *m.* house-painter; whitewasher; (iron.; derog.) painter of inferior pictures.

imbianch-ire [D 2] *tr.* to bleach; to whiten; *intr.* (*aux.* essere) to be bleached; to grow white; to turn pale. **-imento** *m.* bleaching, growing white; (text.) bleaching; (paint indust.) blushing. **-ito** *part. adj.* bleached; whitened. See **imbevere**.

†imbi·bere *vb.* and derivs. See **imbevere**.

imbib-ire [D 2] *tr.* (techn.) to absorb, to soak up, to imbibe. **-izione** *f.* (scient.) imbibition; adsorption; (phys.) adsorption; (bot.) meccanismi d'-izione, imbibition.

imbietol-ire [D 2] *intr.* (*aux.* essere) to become foolish; to grow soft; to go into ecstasies over a trifle; to be easily moved. **-ito** *part. adj.* silly, soft.

imbiett-are [A 1 c] *tr.* to wedge in; to fix firmly; (eng.) to key. **-ato** *part. adj.* wedged; firmly fixed; (eng.) keyed. **-atura** *f.* wedging; (eng.) keying.

imbigiare [A 4] *rfl.* to become grey.

imbigottare [A 1] *intr.* (*aux.* avere) (naut.) to fix the dead-eyes to the shrouds and the chain-plates; to rig the dead-eyes.

imbiond-are [A 1 c] *tr.* to dye yellow, to cause to turn yellow, blonde or fair. **-ire** [D 2] *tr.* to dye yellow; *intr.* (*aux.* essere) to become blonde or fair; *rfl.* to dye one's hair blonde, fair, or golden; (of wheat) to ripen. **-ito** *part. adj.* dyed blonde; (of wheat) ripe, golden.

imbirbon-ire [D 2] *intr.* (*aux.* essere) to become a rascal; to go to the bad; *tr.* to corrupt, to be a bad influence upon. **-ito** *part. adj.* corrupted.

imbisacciare [A 3] *tr.* to put in a bag.

†imbisognato *adj.* occupied, busy.

imbittare [A 1] (naut.). See **abbittare**.

imbitum(in)-are [A 1] *tr.* to asphalt, to pave with asphalt; to tar. (**-(in)ato** *part. adj.*)

imbiut-are [A 1] *tr.* to plaster down (esp. a threshing-floor) with powdered marble, cow-dung, etc.; to tar; to cover with asphalt. (**-ato** *part. adj.*)

imbizzarr-ire [D 2] *tr.* to excite, to make fresh (esp. a horse); *intr.* (*aux.* essere), *rfl.* to become frisky; to get excited or angry; (of a horse) to get out of control. **-imento** *m.* excitement; passion, rage; friskiness. **-ito** *part. adj.* fresh, restless; angered.

imbizz-ire [D 2] *intr.* (*aux.* essere), *rfl.* to fly into a rage, to get upset; to become angry or unmanageable. **-ito** *part. adj.* in a rage; angry; unmanageable.

imbizzocchire [D 2] *intr.* (*aux.* essere) to become very devout; to become hypocritical.

imboccaccito *adj.* (lit.) Boccaccesque, imitative of Boccaccio.

imbocc-are [A 2 c] *tr.* to feed, to put food into the mouth of, to spoon-feed; to spoon-feed in teaching, to teach thoroughly, to cram; to put (a wind-instrument) to one's mouth; to prompt; to enter; — una via, to turn into a street, to enter a street; — la scala, to go upstairs; to fit, to insert; (mil.) to enfilade; (mech.) to engage; to plaster up, to fill (cracks) with mortar or plaster; — un cavallo, to bridle a horse, to fit bit and bridle; *intr.* (*aux.* essere; *prep.* in) to fit (into); to flow (into); to open (into); il tappo -a nella bottiglia, the stopper fits into the bottle; il Ticino -a nel Po, the Ticino flows into the Po; dal Po la barca -ò nel Ticino, from the Po the boat turned from the Ticino; *recip.*, *rfl.* to fit together. **-ato** *part. adj.* fed, spoon-fed; prompted; taken into the mouth; (mil.) enfiladed. **-atura** *f.* feeding; (fig.) opening, mouth, entrance; bit (of a horse), bit head-stall; (mus.) mouthpiece; embouchure; (mus.) avere una bella -atura, to have a good lip.

imbocci-are [A 3] *intr.* (*aux.* essere) to bud, to come into bud. **-ato** *part. adj.* in bud, budding.

†imbocciolare *tr.* to put into a socket.

imboc-co *m.* (*pl.* **-chi**) entrance (of a tunnel, etc.); opening, beginning; (of a river); mouthpiece; inlet, intake.

imboccolare [A 1 sc] *tr.* (eng.) to bush, to sleeve.

†imbolare *tr.* to steal; to steal away; to obtain, to procure; to seize, to surprise; essere preso ad —, to be caught in the act of stealing; *rfl.* to disappear, to vanish.

†imbolo *adv.* furtively.

imbols-ire [D 2 c] *intr.* (*aux.* essere) to become short-winded, to grow fat and lazy; (of a horse) to become broken-winded. **-imento** *m.* becoming short-winded; growing fat and lazy. **-ito** *part. adj.* short-winded; fat and lazy; broken-winded.

imbon-are [A 1 d] *tr.* (naut.) to make good, to repair (putting in new material). (**-ato** *part. adj.*) **-o** *m.* (naut.) making-good; repair.

imbon-ire [D 2] *tr.* to pacify; to solicit; to cajole; to allure; *rfl.* to grow calm, to die down (of wind or waves). **-imento** *m.* cajolery, solicitation; advertisement. **-ito** *part. adj.* pacified; cajoled. **-itore** *m.* cheapjack.

imbono *m.* See under **imbonare**.

†imborbottato *adj.* (naut. hist.). See **imbarbottato**.

imborditura *f.* groove (in upper surface of horseshoe).

†imborgare *rfl.* to become filled with townships.

imborghes-ire [D 2] *intr.* (*aux.* essere), *rfl.* to adopt bourgeois habits; to become bourgeois; to settle down into a conventional way of life; to become stodgy. **-imento** *m.* trend towards bourgeois ways and outlook. **-ito** *part. adj.* bourgeois, tending towards bourgeois habits; grown conventional and stodgy.

imborrare *tr.* to stuff with flock or hair.

imbors-are [A 1 c] *tr.* to pocket; to put in one's purse; to imburse; to put in a hat or box (for drawing lots); to put in a ballot-box; — uno, to vote for someone; †to place, to repose; †— fidanza in, to trust in; †to judge, to consider; †to include. **-amento** *m.* pocketing. **-ato** *part. adj.* pocketed. **-atura** *f.*, **-azione** *f.* pocketing; placing of lots; voting.

imbosc-are [A 2] *tr.* to hide in a wood; to place in ambush; to hide in order to avoid requisition; to place (silkworms) on trees, or leaves; (naut.) to erect the frames of (a ship); *intr.* (*aux.* essere) to go into the bush; to lie in ambush; to lie low; *rfl.* to hide in a wood; to lie in ambush; (fig.) to shirk, to dodge the risks of war (esp. 1915–18). **-ata** *f.* (mil.) ambush. **-ato** *part. adj.* thickly wooded; lying in ambush; hidden; ciclamino -ato, evader of military service in war; *n.m.* shirker.

imbosch-ire [D 2] *tr.* to afforest; *intr.* (*aux.* essere) to become covered with trees; to run wild; to turn into forest. **-imento** *m.* afforestation. **-ito** *part. adj.* afforested; wooded; overgrown, run wild.

imbossolare [A 1 s] *tr.* See **imbussolare**.

imbott-are [A 1 c] *tr.* to put (wine) into casks; — nebbia, to make a fuss but do nothing; — buio, to commit blunders; *intr.* (*aux.* avere) to drink to excess; † — al pozzo, to drink water. **-ato** *part. adj.* put into a cask or barrel, casked, barrelled; bound with iron hoops, like a cask; *n.m.* wine in the cask; tax on wine-making. **-atoia** *f.*, **-atoio** *m.*, **-avino** *m. indecl.* funnel (for casking wine). **-atore** *m.* man who casks wine. **-atura** *f.* filling casks with wine, casking.

imbotte *f.* (archit.) intrados, the under surface of an arch, esp. of door or window.

imbottigli-are [A 4] *tr.* to bottle; (naut.) to bottle-up, to blockade. **-amento** *m.* bottling. **-ato** *part. adj.* bottled; in bottles; (naut.) blockaded. **-atrice** *f.* bottling-machine.

imbottinare [A 1] *tr.* to manure (esp. with liquid from a cesspool).

imbott-ire [D 2] *tr.* to stuff; to pad; to upholster. **-ita** *f.* quilt. **-ito** *part. adj.* stuffed, padded, filled; (cul.) stuffed; panini -iti, rolls with ham or other filling; ha il portafogli bene -ito, he has a well-lined pocket-book, he carries wads of notes; (metall.) lamiera -ita, pressed sheet; *n.m.* quilted jacket (armour). **-itura** *f.* stuffing, padding, quilting; punto d'-itura, back-stitching, Italian quilting stitch.

imbovinare [A 1] *tr.* to plaster with cow-dung (esp. the threshing-floor).

imbozzacch-ire [D 2] *intr.* (*aux.* essere) to be stunted, to shrivel (esp. of fruit); to wither away. **-ito** *part. adj.* stunted, shrivelled; withered.

imbozzare [A 1] (naut.). See **abbozzare**.

imbozzim-are [A 1 s] *tr.* (weaving) to size; to smear with size or any sticky liquid; *rfl.* (joc.) to make up one's face. **-ato** *part. adj.* sized. (**-atore** *m.* **-atura** *f.*) **-atrice** *f.* (text.) sizing machine.

imbozzolare [A 1 s] *rfl.* (silkb.) to spin in.

imbrac-a *f.* (harness) breeching; (fig.) buttarsi sull'—, to hang back, to go slow, to avoid work or risk; sling for supporting a workman or a load; (naut.) sling, boatswain's chair. **-are** [A2] *tr.* to sling, to tie up in a sling; to secure (a load) for hoisting; to put a napkin on (a baby); to tie the feet of (a decoy-bird). **-ata** *f.* load hoisted with a sling. **-atore** *m.* (industr.) slinger. **-atura** *f.* sling; strapping; napkin; harness (of parachute).

imbracci-are [A3] *tr.* to put (shield, gun, cloak, etc.) on the arm. **-atoie** *f.pl.* goldsmith's tongs. **-atura** *f.* loop (of a shield); sling (of a rifle).

imbrachett-are [A1c] *tr.* (bookb.) to mend (a torn page) by gumming on a slip. (**-ato** *part. adj.*) **-atura** *f.* gummed slip (for mending torn paper).

imbraga *f.* and derivs. See **imbraca**.

†**imbrago** *m.* (naut.) freight, hire of a vessel, charter.

†**imbramare** *rfl.* to long, to desire.

imbranc-are [A2] *tr.* to put among the herd, to herd together; (fig.) to gather together, to assemble; *rfl.* to keep the wrong kind of company (usu. said of going to the bad, but sometimes of snobs attaching themselves to social superiors); to push in, to gate-crash; vide entrare gli altri, e s'-ò anche lui, he saw the others go in, and he joined the crowd.

imbrandare [A1] *tr.* (naut.) to sling (a hammock).

imbrand-ire [D2] *tr.* to seize, to grasp the handle of; to brandish. **-ito** *part. adj.* seized; brandished.

†**imbrasciare** *rfl.* to burn; to burn to embers.

imbratt-are [A1] *tr.* to dirty, to soil, to stain; — un muro, to scribble on a wall. **-acarte**, **-afogli** *m. indecl.* scribbler, inferior writer, hack. **-amondo** *m. indecl.* trouble-maker. **-amuri** *m. indecl.* dauber, inferior painter. **-ascene** *m. indecl.* incompetent actor. **-amento** *m.* soiling, dirtying; spots, stains, filth. **-atele**, **-atela** *m. indecl.* dauber. **-ato** *part. adj.* dirty, stained, filthy (also fig.). **-atore** *m.* dauber; è un -atore di tele famoso, he's well known as an incompetent painter. (**-atrice** *f.*) **-o** *m.* pig-swill; badly-cooked food; daub; scribble; bad piece of writing; (archit.) rough-cast plaster. **-atura** *f.* dirtying; daubing; daub; scribbling; scribble.

imbrecci-are [A3c] *tr.* to cover with chipped rock, or gravel; to ballast. **-ata** *f.* layer of chipped rock, or gravel; foundation of a road. **-ato** *part. adj.* gravelled; ballasted. **-atura** *f.* gravelling; ballasting.

imbren·t-ane, **-ina**, **-ine** *f.* (bot.). See **brentine**.

†**imbreviare** *vb.* and derivs. See **abbreviare**.

imbriac-are [A2] *tr.* (vulg.) to make drunk; (provb.) vino di casa non -a, you don't get into bad habits at home; (fig.) — uno, to turn a person's head; *rfl.* to get drunk; (fig., joc.) to become infatuated. **-ato** *part. adj.* drunk, intoxicated.

imbric-ato *adj.* imbricated. **-azione** *f.* imbrication.

†**im·brice** *m.* See **embrice**.

imbri·fero *adj.* (drainage, irrigation) catchment; bacino —, catchment area.

†**imbrigare** [A2] *tr.* to involve in trouble; to involve in intrigue; to provoke; *rfl.* to intrigue; to become involved in intrigue; to be contaminated. †**-ato** *part. adj.* involved; implicated.

imbrigli-are [A4] *tr.* to bridle, to harness; to curb, to restrain; to prevent erosion of, to consolidate (land); (med.) to compress with a plate. **-amento** *m.* bridling; curbing; restraining; (fig.) restraint. **-ato** *part. adj.* bridled; harnessed; curbed, restrained; (of land) consolidated; (herald.) bridled. **-atura** *f.* manner of bridling; method of preventing erosion.

imbrocc-are [A2] *tr.* to hit (the mark), to get plumb centre; (fig.) to guess correctly; non ne -a una, he never gets anything right; to meet (by good luck); to find; (shoem.) to peg or fasten together (parts of a shoe on the last); (mech.) to engage (e.g. the cogs of a wheel or the teeth of a ratchet); †*intr.* to come out in bud; (provb.) quando -a d'aprile, vacci col barile, buds in April mean a good olive crop. **-ata** *f.* (fencing) prime, a downward thrust, guard with point downwards; (mech.) engaging (of cogs). **-atore** *m.* (shoem.) workman who pegs or fastens shoes on the last. **-atura** *f.* engaging (of cogs).

imbrod-are [A1] *tr.* to soil; to slop soup on; *rfl.* to slop soup on oneself. (provb.) chi si loda, s'-a, self-praise is no recommendation. **-olare** [A1s] *tr.* to stain, to spot; *rfl.* to splash oneself in eating; s'è tutto -olato di sugo, he has dropped gravy down his front; (fig.) to get a bad reputation, to be involved in shady business. **-olìo** *m.* soiling; slovenly eating. **-olone** *m.* dirty eater.

imbrogli-are [A4] *tr.* to tangle, to shuffle, to mix up, to confuse; to interrupt; to cheat, to deceive; to swindle; to get in the way of; — una scrittura, to misinterpret a document; (naut.) to clew up (a sail); *rfl.* to get confused, to get into a muddle; to meddle (with), to get mixed up (in something); le cose s'-ano, the plot thickens, (or) things are going from bad to worse; il tempo s'-a, the weather is breaking up. **-ante** *part. adj.* entangling; *n.m.* swindler. **-ato** *part. adj.* tangled, confused; cheated; embroiled; (naut.) clewed up, brailed, furled. **-atamente** *adv.* in a confused way. **-atore** *m.* one who confuses, or mystifies; cheat, swindler, deceiver; (naut.) clew-line, brail. (**-atrice** *f.*) **-one** *m.* mystifier; cheat, swindler, deceiver. (**-ona** *f.*)

imbro·glio *m.* confusion, tangle, mess; obstacle; misunderstanding; fraud; scrape; non fate imbrogli, do not cheat, (or) do not try to hide the truth; (naut.) brail, clew-line.

†**imbromiare** *rfl.* to become like Bacchus, to become intoxicated.

imbroncare [A2] *intr.* (*aux.* avere) (naut.) to top a yard; to lower a yard; to scandalize the yards (usu. a sign of mourning).

imbronci-are [A3c] *intr.* (*aux.* essere) to be sulky; to pout; to take offence; to be huffy, to be touchy; (of the sky) to grow dark. **-ato** *part. adj.* sulky; pouting; surly; (of the sky) dark.

imbroncire [D2] and derivs. See **imbronciare**.

imbronzare [A1c] *tr.* (eng.) to bush.

imbrumare [A1] *intr.* (*aux.* essere) (naut.) to run into fog, to be held up in fog.

imbrunali *m.pl.* (naut.) scuppers.

imbrun-are [A1] *intr.* (*aux.* essere) (poet.) to grow dark; to darken; *tr.* see abbrunare. **-ire** [D2] *intr.* (*aux.* essere) to grow dark; *tr.* to make dark, to blacken; to tan; *n.m.* sull'-ire, at dusk, at night fall.

imbrutire [D2] and derivs. See **abbrutire**.

imbrutt-are [A1] *tr.* to soil, to stain; to dirty; to defile. **-ato** *part. adj.* soiled; dirtied; dirty; defiled.

imbrutt-ire [D2] *tr.* to make ugly; to deform; to disfigure; to mar; to show to disadvantage; quel cappello la -isce, that hat is very unbecoming to her; *intr.* (*aux.* essere) to grow ugly; to go off in looks. **-ito** *part. adj.* made ugly; deformed; disfigured; marred; grown plain, gone off in looks.

imbubbolare [A1s] *tr.* to stuff with nonsense; to deceive with idle tales; *rfl.* (*prep.* di) to disregard, not to care (about).

imbuc-are [A2] *tr.* to put in a hole; to put in a letter-box, to post; *rfl.* to creep into a hole; (fig.) to hide, to keep out of the way. **-ato** *part. adj.* hidden in a hole; posted (of a letter).

imbucatare [A1] *tr.* to put into the wash-tub, to wash.

imbudellare [A1] *tr.* to put into sausage-skins; *intr.* (*aux.* avere) to make sausages, salame, etc.

imbuggerare [A1s] *rfl.* (vulg., Flor.) not to care, not to give a damn.

†**imbugliare** [A4] *tr.* (naut.) to clew up; to parcel (ropes).

†**imbu·glio** *m.* (naut.) parcelling.

imbu-inare [A1] and derivs. see **imboinare**. **-ire** [D2] *intr.* (*aux.* essere) to become stupid or bovine. **-ito** *part. adj.* slow-witted; stupid.

imbullett-are [A1c] *tr.* to furnish with hobnails. **-ato** *part. adj.* hobnailed; coi piedi -ati, wearing hobnailed boots; avere il viso -ato, to be pockmarked, or spotty.

imburchi-are [A4] *tr.* to prompt, to plagiarize, to copy, to crib; (naut.) to put in a lighter; to tow. **-ato** *part. adj.* prompted; cribbed, copied; (naut.) in tow.

†**imburiass-are** *tr.* to teach, to prime; to prompt. **-ato** *part. adj.* primed; prompted; puffed up with confidence.

imburr-are [A1] *tr.* to butter; (fig.) to flatter, to soft-soap. **-ato** *part. adj.* buttered; una fetta di pane -ato, a slice of bread and butter; (fig.) flattered.

†**imburraschito** *adj.* squally, stormy.

imbuscherare [A1s] *rfl.* (vulg., Flor.) to be indifferent, not to care; ha un'aria di me ne imbuschero, he puts on an air of indifference.

imbusecchiare [A4] *tr.* to make sausages, to stuff (meat) into sausage-skins; (vulg.) to stuff (a person) with food; to stuff with knowledge.

imbussol-are [A1s] *tr.* to put into a ballot-box; to put into an urn for drawing lots; (eng.) to bush. (**-amento** *m.* **-ato** *part. adj.*)

imbusto *m.* bust; thorax; upper part of the body; †body; †bodice; †bell—, see **bellimbusto**.

imbut-o *m.* funnel; mangiare coll'—, to gobble (one's food); to devour. (chem.) — a chiave, tap funnel; — separatore, separating funnel. **-iforme** *adj.* funnel-shaped. **-ini** *m.pl.* (bot.) bats-in-the-belfry, Campanula trachelium. **-ire** [D2] *tr.* (eng.) to dish; to spin

imbut-o (*cont.*)
(sheet metal on a lathe); to draw. **-ita** *f.* metal plate hollowed out into the shape of a basin or funnel. **-itura** *f.* (eng.) drawing; **-itura profonda**, deep-drawing.

imbuzz-are [A 1] *tr.* (vulg.) to stuff with food, to cram, to overfeed. **-ato** *part. adj.* stuffed with food, overfull, bursting, overfed.

imbuzz-ire [D 2] *intr.* (*aux.* essere), *rfl.* to sulk, to pout; to grow surly. **-ito** *part. adj.* sulking, pouting, sulky; surly.

Imen-e *pr.n.m.* (myth.) Hymen; (fig.) marriage, wedding; wedding hymn, hymeneal, epithalamium; (anat.) hymen. **-e·o** *adj.* nuptial; *pr.n.m.* (myth.) Hymen; *n.m.pl.* nuptials, wedding. **-ot·teri** *m.pl.* (ent.) Hymenoptera.

ime·nio *m.* (bot.) hymenium (of fungi).

imide *f.* (chem.) imide.

imit-are [A 1 s, A 1] *tr.* to imitate; to mimic; to copy; to follow the example of; to be similar to, to look like. **-a·bile** *adj.* imitable. **-amento** *m.* imitating, copying; imitation. **-ante** *part. adj.* imitating; imitative of. **-ativo** *adj.* imitative, given to imitating. **-ativamente** *adv.* in imitation, imitatively. **-ato** *part. adj.* imitated; copied. **-atore** *m.* imitator; copy-cat. (**-atrice** *f.*) **-azione** *f.* imitating; imitation; mimicry; (mus.) imitation, **-azione alla seconda**, **-azione alla terza**, etc., imitation at the second, at the third, etc.

immacchi-are [A 4] *rfl.* to take to the woods, to hide in the 'macchia', q.v.; to live as an outlaw. **-ato** *part. adj.* in hiding; in the 'macchia'.

immacchiato[1] *part.* See under **immacchiare**.

†immacchiato[2] *adj.* immaculate.

immacinante *adj.* (of a mill) not working.

immacolat-o *adj.* immaculate. **-a** *n.f.* L'Immacolata, the Blessed Virgin; Mary Immaculate; church or feast of the Immaculate Conception.

immagazzin-are [A 1] *tr.* to store, to put in store; (fig.) to store up (in the mind), to accumulate; (mech.) to store, to reserve. **-aggio** *m.* storage, storing; **piazzale per -aggio**, storage yard. **-ato** *part. adj.* stored, put into store.

†immage *f.* See **immagine**.

immagina·bile *adj.* See under **immaginare**.

immagin-are [A 1 s] *tr.* to imagine; to conceive; to suppose; to conjecture; to picture; to fancy; to make up, to invent; to think up; *rfl.* (*dat.* of *prn.* 'si') to imagine to oneself, to imagine; **s'-i!**, please don't mention it!, (or) just imagine!; **-atevi**, just imagine, picture to yourselves; **va bene?**, **-atevi!**, is it all right?, rather!; **me l'-o**, I can just imagine it. **-a·bile** *adj.* imaginable; credible; conceivable. **-amento** *m.* imagining; fancy. **-ato** *part. adj.* imagined; conceived of; pictured; supposed, conjectured. **-azione** *f.* fancy, fantasy; imagination; concept; supposition, conjecture.

immagina·ri-o *adj.* imaginary; imagined; fanciful; unreal; ideal; **ammalato —**, 'malade imaginaire', hypochondriac; (math.) imaginary. **-amente** *adv.* in imagination.

immaginativ-a *f.* faculty of imagination; fancy. **-o** *adj.* imaginative; **potenza -a**, power of imagination.

imma·gin-e *f.* image; living image, likeness; **quella bambina è tutta l'— della madre**, that little girl is the image of her mother; figure, picture, portrait; **è l'— della salute**, he is the picture of health; **— sacra**, sacred image; (opt.) image; **— virtuale**, virtual image; (opt.) **persistenza dell'—**, persistence of vision; **-i poetiche**, poetic imagery; **†symbol**. **-i·fero** *adj.* bearing a standard; *n.m.* standard-bearer. **-i·fico** *adj.* given to imagery; abounding in images. **-oso** *adj.* imaginative, using many images; fantastic, fanciful; **stile -oso**, style rich in images.

immagr-ire [D 2] *intr.* (*aux.* essere) to grow thin, to lose weight. **-ito** *part. adj.* grown thin; thin; gone down in weight.

immalincon-ire [D 2] *intr.* (*aux.* essere), *rfl.* to grow melancholy. **-ito** *part. adj.* grown melancholy.

immalizz-ire [D 2] *tr.* to teach mischief to, to make mischievous. **-ito** *part. adj.* made mischievous.

†immaltare *vb.* and derivs. See **ammaltare**.

immalvag-ire [D 2] *tr.* to corrupt, to lead into evil ways. **-ito** *part. adj.* corrupted; corrupt; led astray.

†immamolare *rfl.* (of eyes) to fill with tears.

immanca·bil-e *adj.* certain; unfailing. **-mente** *adv.* unfailingly; without fail.

imman-e *adj.* monstrous; huge, enormous; horrible, frightful; cruel; **— sciagura**, immeasurable catastrophe. **-ità** *f.* bestiality; savagery, cruelty; ferocity.

immaneggia·bile *adj.* intractable, unmanageable.

immanen-te *adj.* inherent; (schol. philos.; theol.) immanent. **-tismo** *m.* immanentism. **-tista** *m.* immanentist. **-za** *f.* immanence.

immangia·bile *adj.* uneatable.

immanic-are [A 2 s] *tr.* to furnish with a handle; to put sleeves on (a garment). **-ato** *part. adj.* with a handle; with sleeves; (mil.) **schioppo -ato**, gun furnished with its stock.

immanifesto *adj.* immanifest, not evident, obscure.

immanità *f.* See under **immane**.

immansueto *adj.* untamed, fierce; intractable.

†immansuire *tr.* to tame; *intr.* to become tame; to soften.

immantinente *adv.* immediately, without delay, at once.

immarcesci·bil-e *adj.* everlasting, not subject to decay; unfading; incorruptible; immarcescible. **-mente** *adv.* everlastingly.

†immarcire *vb.* and derivs. See **marcire**.

immargin-are [A 1 s] *tr.* to join at the edges; *rfl.* to heal up, to close (of a wound); to cicatrize. **-ato** *part. adj.* joined together at the edges; healed up; cicatrized.

immarzapanato *adj.* mixed with marzipan.

immascher-are [A 1 s] *tr.* to mask, to disguise by means of a mask; *rfl.* to put on a mask; to mask oneself. **†-ata** *f.* see **mascherata**. **-ato** *part. adj.* masked, wearing a mask.

immastic-are [A 2 s] *tr.* to putty. **-ato** *part. adj.* puttied; sealed.

immaterial-e *adj.* non-material; incorporeal; spiritual. **-mente** *adv.* spiritually. **-ità** *f.* immateriality, immaterialness.

immatricol-are [A 1 s] *rfl.* to matriculate, to register as student in a University; *tr.* to admit to a University, to matriculate; **— un'autovettura**, to register a motor vehicle (with the licensing authority); (naut.) **— una nave**, to register a ship. **-ato** *part. adj.* matriculated; admitted to a University; registered. **-azione** *f.* matriculation; registration.

†immatrimoniare *tr.* to join in matrimony; *rfl.* to marry, to get married.

immattire [D 2] and derivs. See **ammattire**.

immatur-o *adj.* immature; unripe; insufficiently prepared; premature, precocious; **morte -a**, early death, untimely demise. **-amente** *adv.* prematurely. **-ità** *f.* immaturity.

immecca·nico *adj.* non-mechanical, not mechanically propelled.

immedagli-are [A 4] *tr.* to portray on a medal, or medallion. **-ato** *part. adj.* portrayed on a medal or medallion.

immedesim-are [A 1 sc] *tr.* to combine, to unite, to make into one; *rfl.* (*prep.* con) to identify oneself (with); to sympathize (with); **il bambino s'-ava nel gioco**, the child was completely absorbed in the game; (theatr., of an actor) **-arsi in una parte**, to live a part. **-ato** *part. adj.* combined, united; identified. **-azione** *f.* combining, uniting; identifying; identification.

immediat-o *adj.* immediate; direct; first-hand; *adv.* immediately. **-amente** *adv.* immediately, at once; directly; at first hand. **-ezza** *f.* immediacy.

immedic·a·bile *adj.* incurable; irremediable. **-abilmente** *adv.* irremediably. **-ato** *adj.* (poet.) cureless; uncured; incurable.

immeditat-o *adj.* unpremeditated. **-amente** *adv.* without premeditation.

†immegliare *tr.* to improve, to better; *rfl.* to become better, to improve.

immelanconire [D 2] and derivs. See **immalinconire**.

†immel-are *tr.* to sprinkle with honey; to make honeyed. **†-ato** *part. adj.* honeyed.

immelens-ire [D 2] *tr.* to make dull, or stupid; to stupefy; to stun; *intr.* (*aux.* essere) to become dull, or stupid. **-ito** *part. adj.* dull, stupid; stupefied.

immellett-are [A 1] *tr.* to muddy, to begrime, to besmear with grime; *rfl.* to become smeared, to become filthy. **-ato** *part. adj.* begrimed; muddied; muddy; smeared.

immelm-are [A 1] *rfl.* to sink in mud, to sink in the mire; (fig.) to become corrupt, to touch pitch. **-ato** *part. adj.* sunk in the mud; (fig.) steeped in corruption.

immemora·bil-e *adj.* immemorial; **da tempo —**, from time immemorial; **uso —**, immemorial usage or custom; (leg.) immemorial. **-mente** *adv.* immemorially.

imme·more *adj.* (*prep.* di) unmindful, forgetful (of); forgetting; **non — di**, not unmindful of, not ungrateful for; (poet.) bringing forgetfulness; lifeless, senseless.

immens-o *adj.* immense; enormous; infinite; le ~e solitudini dello spazio, the infinite solitude of space; un — piacere, an immense pleasure; ~e difficoltà, enormous difficulties. **-amente** *adv.* immensely; enormously; infinitely. **-ità** *f.* immensity; infiniteness.

immensur-abile *adj.* immeasurable; measureless. **-abilmente** *adv.* immeasurably; infinitely. **-abilità** *f.* immeasurableness; measurelessness; immensity. **-ato** *adj.* infinite, immense.

immercantire [D2] *rfl.* to become a merchant, to turn merchant, to go into trade.

immer·g-ere [C4] *tr.* to dip, to plunge into a liquid, to immerse; to steep, to soak; *rfl.* to immerse oneself; aspetta che sia cessato il sudore, prima d'~erti nel mare, wait till you have finished perspiring before you plunge into the sea; ~ersi nelle tenebre, to merge into the shadows; (fig.) ~ersi nello studio, to become absorbed in one's studies; ~ersi nel vizio, to plunge into vice; ~ersi nell'ambiente, to merge with one's surroundings. **-i·bile** *adj.* immersible. **-imento** *m.* immersing; plunge.

immerit-ato *adj.* unmerited, undeserved. **-atamente** *adv.* undeservedly, unjustly. **-evole** *adj.* undeserving, unworthy. **-evolmente** *adv.* undeservingly.

imme·rit-o *adj.* undeserving; undeserved. **-amente** *adv.* undeservingly; undeservedly; unjustly.

immerl-are [A1] *tr.* (archit.) to embattle. **-ato** *part. adj.* (archit.) embattled.

immersione *f.* immersion; plunge; fare un'—, to dive, to go under water; (underwater sport) submersion; in —, underwater, submerged; steeping; dipping; (astron.) immersion; (naut.) linea d'—, Plimsoll line; (of submarines) submerging; draught; (eccl.) battesimo per —, baptism by immersion.

immerso *part.* of **immergere**, q.v.; *adj.* immersed, absorbed; submerged; deep in; (naut., of submarines) submerged.

imme·ttere [C20] *tr.* to send in; to put in; to infuse; to let in; to introduce; to induct; — acqua in un tubo, to cause water to flow into a tube; (leg.) — in possesso di, to put in possession of; — fumo, to infiltrate smoke (C.C.); (naut.) — una nave in un bacino, to put a ship in dock.

†**immezz-are**, †**-ire** *vbs.* and derivs. See **ammezzire**.

†**immiare** *rfl.* (Dante) to become one with me, to enter into me, to enter into my thoughts.

immigr-are [A1s] *intr.* (aux. essere) to immigrate. **-ante** *part. adj.* immigrating; *n.m., f.* immigrant. **-ato** *part. adj.* immigrated; *n.m.* immigrant. **-azione** *f.* immigration; immigrating; immigrants.

immilanare [A1] *rfl.* (joc.) to go to live in Milan; to become Milanese; to adopt Milanese ways.

†**immillare** *rfl.* to increase by thousands, to be multiplied by thousands (from the story of the chessboard and the grains of wheat; see Dante, *Para.* XXVIII, 93).

imminchionire [D2] and derivs. See **rimminchionire**.

imminen-te *adj.* imminent, about to happen, impending; un libro d'— pubblicazione, forthcoming publication; due any moment; overhanging, hanging overhead; l'— sole, the sun overhead. **-za** *f.* imminence.

†**imminuire** *vb.* and derivs. See **diminuire**.

immischi-are [A4] *tr.* (*prep.* in) to thrust (upon); to thrust (into); *rfl.* (*prep.* a, con) to thrust oneself (upon); to meddle (with); to interfere (with, in). **-ato** *part. adj.* thrust, forced (upon).

immiser-ire [D2] *tr.* to impoverish; to make miserable, to make wretched; to wither; il gelo ~isce le piante, frost damages the plants; *intr.* (aux. essere) to become poor; to grow wretched; to wither; to become weak; to sicken; to become narrow-minded and provincial. **-imento** *m.* impoverishment; becoming wretched; withering; shrinkage; decline in health. **-ito** *part. adj.* impoverished; made wretched; withered; grown narrow-minded; ill and weak.

immissa·rio *m.* affluent; tributary; intake, sluice.

immiss-ione *f.* induction; letting in; breaking in, forcing; (techn.) inlet; (leg.) conferment; — in possesso, act of putting in possession; infiltration, insertion; — di fumo, infiltration of smoke; — di travi, insertion of beams (in party wall) (C.C.). **-ivo** *adj.* (leg.) giving possession.

immistione *f.* mixing, mingling; (leg.) — in possesso, the act of meddling with a deceased's estate whereby heir forfeits right to renounce inheritance.

immisto *adj.* unmixed; pure; unadulterated; †mixed.

immisura·bile *adj.* unmeasurable, that cannot be measured.

immite *adj.* harsh, cruel, pitiless.

immitiga·bile *adj.* immitigable, that cannot be mitigated, softened or appeased.

†**immitri-are** *tr.* to mitre. †**-ato** *part. adj.* mitred.

immo·bil-e *adj.* motionless; immovable; still; immobile; stationary; fixed; bene —, immovable property; beni ~i, real property, real estate, immovables, landed property; cessione di beni ~i, transfer of real property; investimento in beni ~i, investment in real property. **-mente** *adv.* without moving. **-iare** *adj.* (leg.) real; having to do with real property; proprietà ~iare, immovables; vendita ~iare, sale of real property; (comm.) immovable property; credito ~iare, loan on security of real property (C.C.). **-ismo** *m.* (pol.) ultra-conservatism, policy of wait-and-see or masterly inactivity. **-ità** *f.* immobility, motionlessness. **-itare** [A1] see **immobilizzare**. **-izzare** [A1] *tr.* to immobilize; to put out of action; to render immovable. **-izzato** *part. adj.* immobilized; (finan.) capitale ~izzato, locked up capital; (techn.) accumulatore a liquido ~izzato, accumulator with unspillable electrolyte. **-izzazione** *f.* immobilization; freezing (of capital); (techn.) locking.

immoderat-o *adj.* immoderate; excessive; intemperate; unrestrained. **-amente** *adv.* immoderately; to excess. **-ezza** *f.* immoderation; excess (cf. **smoderato**).

immode·st-ia *f.* immodesty; brazenness. **-o** *adj.* immodest; brazen. **-amente** *adv.* immodestly; brazenly.

immol-are [A1] *tr.* (rel.) to immolate, to sacrifice; *rfl.* (fig.) to sacrifice oneself; to immolate oneself. **-ato** *part. adj.* immolated, sacrificed; offered up. **-atore** *m.* immolator; sacrificer. (**-atrice** *f.*) **-azione** (rel.) immolation, sacrifice.

immoll-are [A1] *tr.* to wet; to soak, to steep; to drench; ogni acqua lo ~a, his health is affected by the slightest thing. **-amento** *m.* wetting; drenching; soaking. **-ato** *part. adj.* soaked; drenched.

immond-o *adj.* unclean; dirty, filthy; foul; evil-living; (rel.) unclean (of animals, spirits); sullied (of conscience). **-amente** *adv.* dirtily, filthily; foully, uncleanly. **-ezza** *f.* uncleanliness; filth; foulness; impurity. **-ezza·io** *m.* rubbish dump, garbage dump. **-i·zia** *f.* filth; dirt; (fig.) filthiness, obscenity; (rel.) uncleanness (esp. in ceremonial sense); *pl.* garbage, refuse; sweepings; trash, rubbish; cassetta delle ~izie, dustpan with long handle.

immoral-e *adj.* immoral. **-mente** *adv.* immorally. **-ità** *f.* immorality.

immorbidire [D2] and derivs. See **ammorbidire**.

immorire [D2] and derivs. See **ammorire**.

immors-are [A1] *tr.* to notch, to dovetail, to join (wood); †to fit the bit (to a horse). **-ato** *part. adj.* jointed; bitted, bridled. **-atura** *f.* mortise-and-tenon joint.

immortal-e *adj.* immortal; eternal; perpetual, enduring, lasting for ever; *n.m.* immortal, immortal being; *pl.* gl'~i, the immortals, the gods. **-mente** *adv.* immortally; for eternity, for all time. **-are** [A1] *tr.* to immortalize. **-ato** *adj.* immortalized. **-ità** *f.* immortality; enduring fame; immortal life. **-izzare** [A1] *tr.* to immortalize; *rfl.* to be immortalized, to achieve immortality. **-izzato** *part. adj.* immortalized.

immortific-ato *adj.* not mortified; unbridled. **-atamente** *adv.* without moderation, unrestrainedly. **-azione** *f.* (theol.) unmortified state, immortification.

immot-are [A1] *tr.* to splash with mud. **-ato** *part. adj.* splashed with mud; muddy.

immoto *adj.* motionless; still; unmoved.

immucidire [D2] and derivs. See **ammucidire**.

immun-e *adj.* immune, not liable, exempt; — da, free from; uninjured. **-ità** *f.* immunity, exemption; (eccl.) immunity; (leg.) immunity; exemption. **-izzare** [A1] *tr.* to immunize. **-izzato** *part. adj.* immunized. **-ologi·a** *f.* (med.) immunology.

immus-ire [D2] *intr.* (aux. essere) to be cross, to pout, to become sulky. **-ito** *part. adj.* cross, sulky.

immuta·bil-e *adj.* immutable; unchanging, constant. **-mente** *adv.* immutably. **-ità** *f.* immutability.

immut-are [A1] *tr.* to modify, to change; (leg.) to alter (i.e. 'to tamper with') (C.P.). **-ato** *part. adj.* modified, changed; (leg.) altered. (**-atore** *m.* **-atrice** *f.*) **-azione** *f.* (leg.) dishonest or improper alteration (C.P.); †modification, change.

immutato¹ *part.* See under **immutare**.

immutato² *adj.* unchanged.

im-o *adj.* lowest, low; *n.m.* deepest part; bottom; humblest, lowest person; (Lat. phr.) ab —, from the depths. **-oscapo** *m.* (archit.) imoscapo., end of column resting on base.

I·mola *pr.n.f.* (geog.) Imola.

impac·care [A2] *tr.* to pack; to wrap up. **-cato** *part. adj.* packed, wrapped. **-catore** *m.*, **-catrice** *f.* packer; (text.) bundler. **-catura** *f.* packing; cost of packing. **-chettare** [A1c] *tr.* to pack, to package. **-chettato** *part. adj.* packed, packaged, packeted. **-chettatrice** *f.* (indust.) packaging machine; baler. **-co** *m.* (*pl.* **-chi**) bath in a wet sheet; cold compress, hot fomentation, poultice.

impacci·are [A3] *tr.* to hinder; to impede; to embarrass; to inconvenience; to trouble; *rfl.* (*prep.* con) to interfere (with), to meddle (in); to busy oneself (with). **-ato** *part. adj.* impeded; inconvenienced; hindered; embarrassed; hesitating, hesitant; awkward, clumsy; uncomfortable. (**-atamente** *adv.*) **-o** *m.* hindrance; encumbrance; dare -o a, to encumber, to get in the way of; embarrassment; obstacle; trouble; cavarsi d'—, to get out of an awkward situation. **-one** *m.* meddler, trouble-maker. (**-ona** *f.*) **-oso** *adj.* meddling; tiresome; *n.m.* meddler.

impacco *m.* See under **impaccare**.

impaciare [A3] *tr.*, *rfl.* (at games) to call a truce; to cry quits, to draw.

impadronire [D2] *tr.* to make master; *rfl.* (*prep.* di) to master; impadronirsi di una lingua, to master a language; to appropriate; (mil.) to gain possession (of), to seize.

impadulare [A1] and derivs. See **impaludare**.

impaga·bile *adj.* priceless, invaluable.

impagin·are [A1s] *tr.* (typ.) to page, to make up into pages; to do the lay-out of. **-ato** *part. adj.* paged; *n.m.* page-proof. **-atura** *f.* (typ.) make-up, making-up; impagination; lay-out.

impagli·are [A4] *tr.* to pack in straw; to stuff with straw; to cover with straw; to plait with straw. **-ato** *part. adj.* covered with straw; packed in straw, stuffed with straw; mixed with straw; straw-plaited. **-atore** *m.* straw-operative; straw-plaiter; chair-mender; taxidermist. (**-atrice** *f.*) **-atura** *f.* straw-plaiting; straw-bottoming; chair-mending; packing in straw. **-ettatura** *f.* barricade.

impalancato *m.* palisade, fence of boards.

†**impalandranato** *adj.* gowned, robed, wearing a gown.

impal·are [A1] *tr.* to thrust a pointed stake through the body of, to impale; to stake (plants or trees); *rfl.* to stand stiff like a stake; (of a horse, mule, etc.) to stiffen the forelegs and refuse to move. (**-amento** *m.*) **-ato** *part. adj.* impaled; (fig., joc.) stare -ato, to stand stock still and stiff as a ramrod. **-atura** *f.* impaling, impalement.

†**impalazzato** *adj.* built in the style of a palace.

impalc·are [A2] *tr.* (bldg.) to floor, to make the floor of (a room). (**-amento** *m.*) **-ato** *part. adj.* (bldg.) floored; *n.m.* frame (beams or joists) of floor or ceiling. **-atura** *f.* flooring; framework, scaffolding; (fig.) framework; ramification, branching out.

impal·co *m.* (*pl.* **-chi**) scaffolding; trellis.

impalizz·are [A1] *tr.* to palisade. †**-ata** *f.* palisade. **-ato** *part. adj.* palisaded.

impall·are [A1] *tr.* (billiards) to baulk. **-ato** *part. adj.* baulked. **-atura** *f.* baulking.

impallid·ire [D2] *intr.* (*aux.* essere) to turn pale; to grow dim, to fade; cosa da far — le stelle, a thing to make the stars turn pale. **-ito** *part. adj.* pale; dim, faded.

impallin·are [A1] *tr.* to hit with small shot; to riddle with shot. **-ato** *part. adj.* hit, riddled with small shot. **-atura** *f.* shooting, riddling with small shot.

impalm·are [A1] *tr.* to gain the hand of, to win as a bride; (naut.) to whip (rope-ends), to seize (a rope-end) with twine; to palm; †to seize; †*intr.* to open wide the hand revealing the palm; *rfl.* (*prep.* a) to betroth oneself (to); to marry. **-ato** *part. adj.* married, espoused; †clasped. **-atura** *f.* splice, splicing.

impalpa·bil·e *adj.* impalpable. **-mente** *adv.* impalpably. **-ità** *f.* impalpability.

impalp·are [A1] *tr.* (rope making) to twist (fibre) into a strand. (**-ato** *part. adj.* **-atura** *f.*)

impalud·are [A1] *tr.* to make swampy, to flood; *rfl.* to turn into a swamp; to become swampy. (**-amento** *m.* **-ato** *part. adj.*)

†**impampinare** *rfl.* to adorn oneself with vine-leaves.

impan·are¹ [A1] *tr.* (eng.) to glaze, to wear smooth; *rfl.* to wear smooth (e.g. of a grinding wheel); to screw up. (**-ato** *part. adj.*) **-atrice** *f.* (eng.) thread-cutting machine. **-atura** *f.* (eng.) thread; -atura destrorsa, right-handed thread.

impanare² [A1] and derivs. See **panare**.

impanc·are [A2] *tr.* to furnish with benches; *rfl.* (fig.) to assume authority (unwarrantably), to lay down the law; -arsi a giudice, to set oneself up as judge; to sit down on a bench, to sit down to table; -arsi coi signori, to get in with people who are one's social superiors. **-ato** *part. adj.* furnished with benches; seated.

impani·are [A5] *tr.* to smear with bird-lime; *rfl.* (of birds) to be caught with bird-lime; (fig.) to be caught or deluded by flattery, to swallow the bait. **-ato** *part. adj.* smeared with bird-lime; caught, trapped; deluded. (**-atore** *m.* **-atrice** *f.*) **-atura** *f.* snaring with bird-lime.

impanicci·are [A3] *tr.* to paste; to plaster with paste; (fig.) to embarrass, to confuse.

impann·are [A1] *tr.* to cover with cloth. **-ata** *f.* cloth stuffed into a window frame instead of glass. **-ato** *part.adj.* covered with cloth; cloth-covered; canvas-backed. **-atore** *m.* small-scale textile manufacturer. **-ellare** [A1] *tr.* to cover (dough) with a cloth when it is left to rise.

impantan·are [A1] *tr.* to make swampy, to turn into a swamp; to bemire; *rfl.* to become swampy; to plunge into a swamp; to stick in the mud; to get plastered with mud; (fig.) to sink into a morass; to get bogged down (e.g. in difficulties), to get stuck; -arsi in affari loschi, to become deeply involved in shady business. **-ato** *part. adj.* swampy; become swampy; bemired; sunk in a morass.

impaperare [A1s] *rfl.* to blunder, to slip up, to make a mistake (in speaking).

impappafic·are [A2] *rfl.* (naut.) to hoist a skysail; †**-ato** *part. adj.* hooded.

impappin·are [A1] *tr.* to confuse, to muddle; *rfl.* to be confused; to get muddled or flustered; to lose the thread of one's discourse. **-ato** *part. adj.* confused, muddled; flustered.

impappol·are [A1s] *tr.* to dirty; (fig.) to deceive with lies. **-ato** *part. adj.* dirtied; (fig.) deceived.

imparacchi·are [A4] *tr.* to learn badly, to half-learn. **-ato** *part. adj.* badly learnt, half-learnt.

imparadiṣ·are [A1] *tr.* (poet.) to imparadise; to transport, to ravish; una voce che -a, a ravishing voice. **-ato** *part. adj.* ecstatic, in ecstasy, transported; imparadised.

imparagona·bile *adj.* incomparable.

impar·are [A1] *tr.* to learn; — a mente, — a memoria, to learn by heart; errando s'-a, we learn by our mistakes; così -i!, that'll teach you!; non si finisce mai d'—, you can always learn something; desideroso d'—, eager to learn; — bene, to be a quick learner; — a ballare, to learn to dance; — il ballo, to learn dancing; ho -ato ad amarlo, I have come to love him; -a a vivere!, learn some manners!; to hear of, to get to hear; l'ho -ato da Giorgio, I heard it from George; to teach; la matematica gliel'ho -ata io, I taught him mathematics myself. **-ante** *part. adj.* learning; *n.m.*, *f.* learner. **-atic·cio** *m.* thing badly learnt; beginner's work. **-ato** *part. adj.* learnt; -ato a memoria, -ato a mente, got by memory, conned by rote, learnt by heart. **-atore** *m.* learner. (**-atrice** *f.*)

impareggia·bil·e *adj.* incomparable; unrivalled. **-mente** *adv.* incomparably.

imparent·are [A1] *tr.* to ally by marriage; *rfl.* (*prep.* a) to become related (to); (*prep.* con) to marry (into). **-ato** *part. adj.* related by marriage.

im·par·i *adj. indecl.* unequal; — al compito, unequal to the task; uneven; odd; (naut.) of the starboard watch; *n.m.* starboard watch. **-idigitato** *adj.* (anat.) imparidigitate. †**-imente** *adv.* unequally. **-isil·labo** *adj.* imparisyllabic; versi -isillabi, lines (of poetry) having an odd number of syllables. **-ità** *f.* imparity, disparity; essere in condizioni d'-ità, to be on an unequal footing, to be handicapped.

†**imparolato** *adj.* verbose.

imparrucc·are [A2] *tr.*, *rfl.* to put on a wig. **-ato** *part. adj.* bewigged, wearing a wig.

imparti·bile *adj.* indivisible.

impart·ire [D2] *tr.* to impart; to communicate; to dispense; — un ordine, to issue an order; to assign, to grant; (eccl.) to give (blessing, Holy Communion). **-ito** *part. adj.* imparted; communicated; given; granted, assigned; (eccl.) given (of blessing, Holy Communion).

imparucchiare [A4] and derivs. See **imparacchiare**.

imparzial·e *adj.* impartial; (leg.) impartial; equitable. **-mente** *adv.* impartially; equitably. **-ità** *f.* impartiality; impartial action.

impasse *f. indecl.* (cards, bridge) finesse; (fig.) deadlock, impasse; difficult situation.

†**impasseggia·bile** *adj.* impassable.

impassi·bil-e *adj.* impassive, insensible, impassible; unemotional, phlegmatic. **-mente** *adv.* impassively, imperturbably. **-ità** *f.* impassibility, imperturbability.

†**impassionare** *tr.* to cause to experience, to cause to feel; to fill with feeling.

†**impassire** *vb.* and derivs. See **appassire**.

impast-are [A I] *tr.* to knead; to make into paste; to stick on with paste; to spread with paste; (fig., joc.) t'hanno -ato male, they've (i.e. your parents) made a poor job of you; (industr.) to knead, to pug; (mus.) to blend; *intr.* (aux. avere) (paint.) to mix colours; to impaste, to lay on colour thickly; *rfl.* (eng.) to clog, to become gummed up; (techn.) to become sticky. **-a·bile** *adj.* capable of being kneaded, malleable. **-atrice** *f.* (industr.) kneading machine, pug mill, mixer. †**-ata** *f.* intrigue; entanglement. **-amento** *m.* kneading; pasting. **-ato** *part. adj.* kneaded; made into paste; mixed; formed; (fig.) -ato di miele, sweet-tempered; -ato di sonno, always drowsy. **-atore** *m.* kneader; paster. **-atrice** *f.* kneading trough; (mech.) mixer. **-atura** *f.* dough-making, kneading; mixture. **-o** *m.* kneading; mixture; paste; (fig.) medley; -o di menzogne, tissue of lies; (paint.) impasto; (mus.) blend (of tone-colours or of voices).

impasticci-are [A 3] *tr.* to mix, to make a mixture of; to bungle, to botch; to muddle; to daub; *rfl.* to get into a mess. **-ato** *part. adj.* mixed, made up into a mixture; bungled, botched; muddled; daubed. **-one** *m.* slovenly worker, one who makes a mess, or creates confusion.

impasto¹ *m.* See under **impastare**.

†**impasto²** *adj.* fasting; hungry.

impastocchiare [A 4] *tr.* (fam.) to blurt out (lies or excuses); — scuse, to make up excuses on the spur of the moment; to gull, to delude, to deceive with lies.

impastoi-are [A 4 c] *tr.* to fetter; to tether; (fig.) to cramp, to impede. **-ato** *part. adj.* fettered; tethered; impeded, cramped; awkward.

impastran-are [A I] *tr.* to wrap up in a greatcoat; *rfl.* to wrap oneself up well. **-ato** *part. adj.* wrapped up; -ato fino agli occhi, muffled up to the tip of one's nose.

impatacc-are [A 2] *tr.* (colloq.) to splash, to stain, to dirty. **-ato** *part. adj.* splashed, stained, dirty.

†**impatriare** *vb.* and derivs. See **rimpatriare**.

impattare¹ [A I] *intr.* (aux. avere) (of a game) to draw, to be even, to be quits; *tr.* to draw; non si può nè vincerla nè impattarla, he wants it all his own way, it is impossible to come to any agreement with him.

impattare² *tr.* to bed down (animals). **-ato** *part. adj.* bedded down.

impatto¹ *m.* litter, bedding for animals.

impatto² *m.* impact; (ballistics) punto d'—, point of impact; angolo d'—, angle of impact.

impaurare [A I] (poet.). See **impaurire**.

impaur-ire [D 2] *tr.* to frighten; to intimidate; to terrify; *intr.* (aux. essere), *rfl.* to become afraid; to be terrified; -irsi di tutto, to take fright at everything. **-ito** *part. adj.* frightened; terrified; afraid.

†**impausa·bile** *adj.* restless, unresting.

impavesata *f.* (naut.). See **pavesata**.

impa·vid-o *adj.* fearless, undaunted; impavid. **-amente** *adv.* fearlessly.

impazi-ente *adj.* impatient, eager; — di, intolerant of, unable to bear; *n.m.* (bot.) touch-me-not, *Impatiens noli-tangere* and other spp. **-entemente** *adv.* impatiently. **-entare** [A I] and derivs. see **impazientire**. **-entire** [D 2] *rfl.*, *intr.* (aux. essere) to become impatient; to lose patience; *tr.* to try the patience of, to make impatient. **-enza** *f.* impatience; intolerance; anxiety.

impazz-are [A I] *intr.* (aux. essere) (Tusc.) to go mad, to become insane (cf. **impazzire**); to rage, to run wild, to riot; il Carnevale -ava per le vie, the Carnival was thronging the streets with its mad rioting; (cul., of cream, custard, or mayonnaise) to fail to set (cf. **impazzire**). **-ata** *adv. phr.* all'-ata, recklessly, madly, wildly, foolishly.

impazz-ire [D 2] *intr.* (aux. essere) to go mad, to become insane; to lose one's head; far —, to drive mad; — per, — dietro, to be mad about, to be crazy about. **-imento** *m.* going mad; madness, insanity; trouble; long trying task. **-ito** *part. adj.* mad; gone mad, insane; crazy; devoted; (of a compass) out of order (cf. **impazzare**).

impecca·bil-e *adj.* impeccable, faultless; (theol.) impeccable. **-ità** *f.* (theol.) impeccability; faultlessness.

impecett-are [A I c] *tr.* to plaster; to put a plaster on; to soil or stain with sticky matter, to make sticky; *rfl.* to become sticky. **-ato** *part. adj.* plastered; sticky.

impeci-are [A 3 c] *tr.* to pitch, to coat with pitch or tar; to make sticky or greasy; *rfl.* to become coated with pitch or tar; (fig.) to touch pitch; -arsi le orecchie, to pretend not to hear, to turn a deaf ear. **-ato** *part. adj.* tarred; covered with pitch; baffi -ati, waxed moustache. **-atura** *f.* coating with tar; coat of tar; layer of pitch; waxing.

impecor-ire [D 2] *intr.* (aux. essere) to become timid (like a sheep); to become like a lamb. **-ito** *part. adj.* sheep-like; mild as a lamb; tamed.

impedant-ire [D 2] *intr.* (aux. essere), *rfl.* to become pedantic; *tr.* to make pedantic. **-ito** *part. adj.* turned pedant; pedantic.

impedenza *f.* See under **impedire**.

†**impedicare** *tr.* to fetter; to tether; to hobble; to impede; to distract; *intr.* to err; to fail.

†**impe·dico** *m.* obstacle; impediment.

imped-ire [D 2] *tr.* to prevent, to hinder; to impede; to be a hindrance to; — a qualcuno di fare qualcosa, to prevent someone from doing something, -ì a tutti d'entrare, he stopped everyone going in, he would let nobody in; -irono che scoppiasse la mina, they prevented the mine from blowing up; — un delitto, to prevent a crime; ve lo -isce la legge, the law forbids you to do it; un macigno -iva il passo, a boulder blocked the way; quel muro -isce la vista del mare, that wall cuts off the view of the sea; (mus.) to cover, to drown (other instruments or voices). **-enza** *f.* (electr.; radio) impedance. **-i·bile** *adj.* preventible. **-iente** *adj.* obstructive, hindering, impeding; *n.m.pl.* (eccl.) impediments. **-imento** *m.* hindrance; obstacle, impediment; (leg.) impediment; -imento legittimo, lawful impediment; -imento procedurale, bar to an action; -imento dirimente, diriment impediment (to marriage); *m.pl.* (mil.) impedimenta, baggage-train, transport. **-itivo** *adj.* obstructive, impeditive. **-ito** *part. adj.* impeded, obstructed, hindered; (euphem.) paralysed; ha il braccio -ito, he has lost the use of his arm; non vi può ricevere, è -ito, he is unable to see you, he is engaged. **-itore** *m.* hinderer, obstructor. (**-itrice** *f.*)

impegn-are [A 5 c] *tr.* to pledge; to pawn; to engage; — la parola, to pledge one's word; — un ballo, to make an engagement for a dance, to promise a dance; — una ragazza, to become engaged to a girl; — una discussione, to engage in a discussion; to book, to reserve; — una camera, to book a room; to attract; to win over; (leg.) to bind; to pledge; — merce, to pledge goods; (mil.) to send into action, to join battle, to attack; — il nemico, to engage the enemy; (naut.) — l'ancora, to hold, to bite, to engage; *rfl.* to pledge oneself; s'-ò a non parlare, he pledged himself to secrecy; -arsi di ottenere, to promise to obtain; -arsi in una lite, to become involved in a quarrel; -arsi a fondo, to become deeply committed; -arsi in un cattivo affare, to be involved in an unsuccessful speculation; (comm.) -arsi a consegnare per la fine del mese, to undertake to deliver by the end of the month; to make a social or business engagement; (leg.) to bind oneself. **-ativo** *adj.* (leg.) binding; offerta -ativa, firm offer; (fig.) exacting; engaging, attractive; *n.f.* -ativa di vendita, contract of sale. **-ato** *part. adj.* pawned; pledged; engaged; bound; committed, involved; sono già -ato, I have a previous engagement.

impegn-o *m.* pledge; obligation; promise; commitment; social or business engagement; appointment; diligence, zeal; è un affare d'—, it is a matter that requires great care and attention; ci vedremo probabilmente domani, ma senza —, we'll probably meet tomorrow, but let's keep it open; (comm.) senza —, without obligation, (fig.) half-heartedly; mettere ogni — a, to give one's best care and attention to; (leg.) liability; — scritto, written undertaking; assumersi un —, to undertake a responsibility; (finan.) liability. **-oso** *adj.* troublesome, requiring considerable care; provocative, quarrelsome.

impegol-are [A I sc] *tr.* to coat with pitch; *rfl.* to become coated with pitch; (fig.) -arsi con, to become involved in, to get mixed up with; non t'— con quella gente, don't get mixed up with those people. **-ato** *part. adj.* coated with pitch; (fig.) involved, implicated; essere -ato nei guai fino al collo, to be up to one's neck in trouble.

impelag-are [A2s] *rfl.* to plunge into a sea of troubles, to run into difficulties, to undertake difficult and troublesome tasks. **-ato** *part. adj.* submerged, flooded, made into a lake; (fig.) involved, beset with difficulties.

impelare [A1c] *tr.* to cover with hairs, to cover with fluff.

†impellegrinare [A1] *rfl.* to become a pilgrim, to go on pilgrimage.

impel·l-ere [C23] *tr.* to impel; to thrust; to push; to force. **-ente** *part. adj.* impelling, compelling; of the greatest urgency, inescapable.

impellicci-are [A3] *tr.* to cover with fur, to wrap in furs, to put a fur on; to line with fur. **-ato** *part. adj.* wrapped in furs; lined with fur.

†impen·dere *vb.* and derivs. See **impiccare**.

impenetra·bil-e *adj.* impenetrable; impervious; — all'acqua, watertight; — all'aria, airtight; (mech.) impenetrable; (fig.) inscrutable. **-ità** *f.* impenetrability.

impeniten-te *adj.* (theol.) impenitent, unrepentant; (fig.) incorrigible. **-za** *f.* (theol.) impenitence; (fig.) obduracy.

impenna·bile *adj.* (aeron.). See under **impennare**.

impennacchi-are [A4] *tr.* to deck with plumes. **-ato** *part. adj.* decked with plumes; plumed.

impennag·gio *m.* (aeron.). See under **impennare**.

impenn-are [A1c] *tr.* to put feathers on; to feather; to cover with feathers; (poet.) — il piede, to set wings to one's feet; — il cuore, to lift up one's heart; to give wings to, to wing; (mus.) — un cembalo, to quill a harpsichord; *intr.* (aux. avere) to take up one's pen, to write vigorously; (naut.) to hoist a yard, sail or pennant; (aeron.) to feather; to climb; *rfl.* to become fledged; (of a horse) to rear; (of a bird) to ruffle up its feathers; (fig.) to become ruffled. **-a·bile** *adj.* (aeron.) capable of feathering; elica -abile, (of a bomb) fins. **-ag·gio** *m.* (aeron.) feathering; mozzo d'-aggio, feathering hub. **-ata** *f.* (of a horse) action of rearing; fare un'-ata, to rear; †penful of ink. **-ato** *part. adj.* feathered; winged; quilled; (of a horse) on its hind legs, rearing; (herald.) feathered. **-atura** *f.* (mus.) quilling, voicing (of a harpsichord); †fine, penalty.

impennellare [A1] *tr.* to paint; *intr.* (aux. avere) to make brushstrokes; (naut.) to back (an anchor, by shackling a smaller one to it); to lay out (a kedge); †to give blows.

impennonare [A1c] *intr.* (aux. avere) (naut.) to rig yards or spars; to bend a sail to a spar.

impens-a·bile *adj.* unthinkable. **-ata** *adv. phr.* all'-ata, suddenly, unexpectedly; cogliere all'-ata, to take unawares. **-ato** *adj.* unforeseen, unexpected. **-atam·ente** *adv.* unexpectedly.

impensier-ire [D2] *tr.* to make anxious, to worry; *rfl.* to become anxious, to be troubled, to be worried. **-ito** *part. adj.* anxious, worried.

impep-are [A1c] *tr.* to pepper, to season with pepper; (fig.) to make piquant. **-ato** *part. adj.* peppered, seasoned with pepper; (fig.) spicy, piquant.

†imperadore *m.* See **imperatore**.

†imperadrice *f.* See **imperatrice**.

imper-are [A1] *intr.* (aux. avere) to rule; to be emperor; to reign; to be in authority; to prevail. **-ante** *part. adj.* ruling, reigning; -ante Adriano, under Hadrian's rule; dominant; cagione -ante, imperative reason. **-ativo** *adj.* imperative; commanding; (leg.) compulsory; *n.m.* (gramm.) imperative; (philos.) -ativo categorico, categorical imperative (Kant). **-ativam·ente** *adv.* imperatively; commandingly. **†-ato** *part. adj.* ruled over; commanded; *n.m.* period of an Emperor's rule.

imperat-ore *m.* emperor; (paint.) tela d'—, enormous canvas. **-o·rio** *adj.* (m.pl. **-o·rii**) imperial.

imperatrice *f.* empress.

impercepi·bile *adj.* See **impercettibile**.

impercetti·bil-e *adj.* imperceptible. **-mente** *adv.* imperceptibly. **-ità** *f.* imperceptibility.

†impercetto *adj.* unperceived.

†imperchè *conj.* because; *n.m.* the reason why.

†imperciò *conj.* because; inasmuch as.

imperciocchè *conj.* since; inasmuch as; whereas; because.

†imperocchè *conj.* See **imperciocchè**.

imperdi·bile *adj.* that cannot be lost; that cannot fail, certain.

imperdona·bil-e *adj.* unforgivable, unpardonable. **-mente** *adv.* unforgivably, unpardonably. **-ità** *f.* unforgivableness, unpardonableness.

imperfett-o *adj.* imperfect; faulty; defective; unfinished; (gramm.) imperfect; (mus.) consonanza -a, imperfect consonance; tempo —, imperfect time (i.e. division of the long into two breves in medieval music); *n.m.* (gramm.) imperfect tense, imperfect; all'—, in the imperfect.

imperfezi·one *f.* imperfection; fault, defect; flaw; nessuno è senza imperfezioni, nobody is perfect, everyone has his faults; (mus.) imperfection (in medieval mensural notation).

imperfor-ato *adj.* imperforate, not perforated. **-azi·one** *f.* imperforation.

impergol-are [A1s] *tr.* to make into a pergola, or arbour. **-ata** *f.* pergola, arbour. **-ato** *part. adj.* trained into a pergola or arbour.

imperial-e *adj.* imperial; carta —, imperial paper (for printing 22 × 32 in., for writing 22 × 30 in.); (ichth.) luccio —, spet, a kind of barracuda, *Sphyraena vulgaris*; (pharm.) acqua —, a purgative drink (also called 'limonata inglese'); *n.m., f.* top (of coach, omnibus or tram-car); *m.pl.* gl'-i, the imperial troops, soldiers of the Emperor. **-mente** *adv.* imperially. **-esco** *adj.* (m.pl. **-eschi**) imperial. **-ismo** *m.* imperialism. **-ista** *m., f.* imperialist. **-i·stico** *adj.* imperialistic. (**-isticamente** *adv.*) **-ità** *f.* imperiality.

†imperiare *vb.* and derivs. See **imperare**.

†imperi-a·tico *m.*, **-ato** *m.* empire.

†impericolosire *intr.* to be in danger; *tr.* to endanger.

impe·rio *m.* (poet.) dominion, command, empire.

imperios-o *adj.* imperious, peremptory; piglio —, imperious manner; voce -a, peremptory voice; imperative; ragioni -e, pressing reasons. **-amente** *adv.* imperiously; peremptorily. **-ità** *f.* imperiousness.

imper-ito *adj.* unskilled, inexperienced; awkward. **-itam·ente** *adv.* in an unskilled manner; awkwardly. **-i·zia** *f.* inexperience; lack of skill; awkwardness; (leg.) want of skill; unskilfulness (C.P.).

imperituro *adj.* imperishable, immortal.

†imperlaqualcosa *conj.* for which reason.

imperl-are [A1] *tr.* to adorn with pearls; (fig.) la rugiada -a le foglie, the leaves are pearly with dew-drops; il sudore gl'-ava la fronte. beads of sweat stood on his brow. **-ato** *part. adj.* pearled; pearly,

impermal-ire [D2] *tr.* to annoy, to make angry; to offend; to vex; *rfl., intr.* (aux. essere) to be annoyed, to be offended, to take umbrage; to be touchy; s'-ì delle tue parole, he took offence at what you said; s'-ì che non l'avessimo visitato, he was offended because we didn't visit him; -irsi con una persona, to be angry with a person. **-imento** *m.* anger; vexation. **-ito** *part. adj.* angry, vexed; offended.

impermea·bil-e *adj.* watertight, waterproof; airtight; impermeable, impervious; *n.m.* mackintosh, waterproof, raincoat; — foderato, trenchcoat. (**-mente** *adv.*) **-ità** *f.* impermeability, waterproofness; (naut.) being watertight. **-izzare** [A1] *tr.* (techn.) to waterproof, to proof. **-izzante** *part. adj.* waterproofing; *n.m.* waterproofing material. **-izzazi·one** *f.* (techn.) proofing; waterproofing.

impermisto *adj.* unmixed.

impermuta·bil-e *adj.* unchangeable, immutable. **-mente** *adv.* immutably. **-ità** *f.* immutability; unchangeableness.

impernare [A1] and derivs. See **imperniare**.

imperni-are [A4] *tr.* to pivot; to hinge; *rfl.* to pivot; to be pivoted; (prep. su) (fig.) to be founded (upon), to depend (upon). **-ato** *part. adj.* pivoted; hinged; (bot.) versatile. **-atura** *f.* pivoting; manner of pivoting; things that pivot (upon something).

impero *m.* empire; imperial rule; stile —, Empire style (of the time of Napoleon I); dominion, rule, command; overriding influence; (fig.) l'— della legge, the authority of the law.

imperò *conj.* for the reason that, inasmuch as; nevertheless; however.

†imperocchè *conj.* See **imperò**.

imperscruta·bil-e *adj.* inscrutable. **-mente** *adv.* inscrutably. **ità** *f.* inscrutability.

imperseveran-te *adj.* not persevering, fickle. **-za** *f.* fickleness.

impersonal-e *adj.* impersonal; unbiased (by personal considerations), impartial; (gramm.) impersonal. **-mente** *adv.* impersonally. **-ità** *f.* impartiality; absence of personal bias.

imperson-are [A1c] *tr.* to personify; to impersonate; to act the part of; *rfl.* to be personified; in lei s'-ano la grazia e la bontà, she is the personification of grace and goodness. **-ato** *part. adj.* personified; impersonated. **-ificazi·one** *f.* (leg.) personation.

impersuadi·bile *adj.* impossible to persuade, immovable, adamant.

†impertanto *adv.* nevertheless; on that account; therefore; meanwhile; *conj.* for the reason that.

imperter·rito *adj.* intrepid, undaunted; unperturbed.

impertinen-te *adj.* not pertinent, irrelevant; unseemly; impertinent, insolent; (leg.) immaterial; irrelevant. **-temẹnte** *adv.* impertinently; insolently. **-za** *f.* impertinence; dire delle -ze, to make insolent remarks; scusi l'-za, excuse me (when taking a liberty, or asking a personal question); (leg.) irrelevance.

imperturba·bil-e *adj.* imperturbable, unruffled, calm. **-mẹnte** *adv.* imperturbably. **-ità** *f.* imperturbability, tranquillity.

imperturbat-o *adv.* unperturbed. **-amẹnte** *adv.* unperturbedly.

impervers-are [A I] *intr.* (aux. avere) to rage, to storm; to be furious; — contro qualcuno, to rage against someone; to be perverse. **-amẹnto** *m.* raging, storming; fury. **-ato** *part. adj.* raging; cruel; possessed.

†**impervertire** *vb.* and derivs. See **pervertire**.

imper·vi-o *adj.* inaccessible; impervious; (med.) imperforated, stenotic. **-età** *f.* inaccessibility; imperviousness; (med.) stenosis, stricture of a passage, duct or canal.

†**impeschiata** *f.* opening barred by grating.

impest-are [A I] *tr.* to impest; to infect with foul air; (vulg.) to infect (esp. with venereal disease). **-ato** *part. adj.* impested; (vulg.) infected with venereal disease (cf. **appestare**).

impetecchito *adj.* spotty, blotchy; (fig.) miserly.

impeti·gin-e *f.* (med.) impetigo. **-ọso** *adj.* (med.) impetiginous.

im·peto *m.* impetus; impetuosity; violence; vehemence; attack; outburst; onset; rush; in un — di gioia, in a transport of joy; esser di primo —, to be easily moved, to be irascible, to be impetuous; di primo —, at first, at the first onset.

impetr-are¹ [A I] *tr.* to obtain (by asking); to seek, to ask for; noi -iamo da te questa grazia, we pray thee to bestow this grace upon us. **-a·bile** *adj.* that may be granted. **-ante** *part. adj.* beseeching; *n.m., f.* suppliant. **-ato** *part. adj.* asked for; sought; granted, bestowed. **-atọre** *m.* suppliant; bestower. **-atrice** *f.* (theol.) Maria -atrice di grazie, Mary Mediatrix of graces. **-ato·rio** *adj.* beseeching. **-aziọne** *f.* asking; request.

impetrare² *intr.* (aux. essere) to turn to stone, to become like stone.

impettito *adj.* upright with chest thrown out; (fig.) conceited; camminare —, to strut.

impetuọs-o *adj.* violent; impetuous; irascible. **-amẹnte** *adv.* impetuously. **-ità** *f.* impetuosity.

impiacevol-ire [D 2] *tr.* to sweeten; to make agreeable; to make pleasant; *rfl.* (fig.) to become pleasant; to be agreeable; to give way. **-ito** *part. adj.* sweetened; agreeable.

impiag-are [A 2] *tr.* to wound; to cover with wounds; *rfl.* to become covered with wounds; *intr.* (aux. essere) to turn into a wound. **-amẹnto** *m.* wounding. **-ato** *part. adj.* wounded. (**-atọre** *m.* **-atrice** *f.*) **-atura** *f.* wounding.

impiallacci-are [A 3] *tr.* to veneer; to inlay; to encrust; (charcoal-burning) to cover with turves. **-ato** *part. adj.* veneered; inlaid; encrusted; turfed over. **-atọre** *m.* workman in veneering or inlaying. **-atura** *f.* veneering; veneer; inlaying; inlay.

impianell-are [A I] *tr.* to tile; to pave (with flat tiles). **-ato** *part. adj.* tiled; paved (with flat tiles); *n.m.* tiling; paving.

impiant-are [A I] *tr.* to fix together, to fit up, to fit; to install; to found, to establish; to open (an account), to open (a set of account books). **-amẹnto** *m.* fitting, fixing; installing; founding. **-ato** *part. adj.* fixed, fitted; installed; founded.

impiant-ire [D 2] *tr.* to floor; to pave. **-ito** *part. adj.* floored; paved; *n.m.* (Tusc.) floor; -ito di mattoni, tiled floor; (bldg.) flooring.

impianto *m.* establishment, founding, foundation; (naut.) mounting (of a big gun); plant (usu. in *pl.* gl'impianti); system; installation; — idrico, waterworks; — di riscaldamento, heating-plant, heating-system; — del timone, steering-gear; spese d'—, installation charges.

impiastr-are [A I] *tr.* to plaster; to smear, to soil; to daub, to paint badly; to scribble; *rfl.* to plaster, smear or soil oneself; to paint one's face. **-acarte**, **-afogli** *m., f. indecl.* scribbler. **-amẹnto** *m.* plastering; daubing; scribbling. **-ato** *part. adj.* plastered; smeared; daubed; scribbled. **-atọre** *m.* plasterer; dauber; scribbler.

impiastro *m.* plaster, poultice; — su una gamba di legno, useless remedy; sono guai che non si curano con impiastri, it takes more than a poultice to cure these ills; (fig.) bad work; tiresome person, bore.

†**impiattare** *tr.* to hide; *rfl.* to crouch; to hide in a hole.

impicc-are [A 2] *tr.* to hang, to execute by hanging; — per la gola, to hang by the neck; to string up; — alla forca, to hang on the

---

gallows; — a un albero, to string up on a tree; — nella croce, to hang on the cross; neanche a -arlo!, nothing would make him do it; Maestro Impicca, the hangman; *rfl.* to hang oneself; (fig.) to get oneself into difficulties, to put one's head in a noose, to 'stick one's neck out'. **-agiọne** *f.* hanging, execution. (**-amẹnto** *m.*) **-ato** *part. adj.* hanged; (joc.) stare -ato, to have a long thin neck; *n.m.* gallows-bird. **-atura** *f.* hanging.

impicci-are [A 3] *tr.* to encumber; to hinder; to trouble; *intr.* (aux. avere) to be a nuisance, to be inconvenient; to be in the way; Maestro Impiccia, troublesome person; bore; *rfl.* -arsi con uno, to get tied up with someone; -arsi in una cosa, to become encumbered or involved in a (tiresome) matter; -arsi di uno, to interfere with someone; -arsi dei fatti altrui, to intrude into other people's affairs. **-ato** *part. adj.* encumbered; hindered; avere tutta la giornata -ata, to have one's whole day occupied with tiresome matters. **-ọne** *m.* troublesome person; meddler (cf. **impiccio**). (**-ọna** *f.*)

impiccinire [D 2] and derivs. See **rimpiccinire**.

impic·c-io *m.* obstacle, hindrance, encumbrance; nuisance; troublesome affair or task; oggi ho molti -i da sbrigare, I have a lot of tiresome jobs to get through today; intrigue; debt, mortgage. **-iọso** *adj.* troublesome; inconvenient; cumbersome; annoying (cf. **impicciare**).

impicciolire [D 2] and derivs. See **impiccolire**.

impiccol-ire [D 2] *tr.* to reduce in size, to diminish; to lessen; to make smaller; *rfl.* to grow smaller; to humble oneself. **-imẹnto** *m.* reducing, diminishing; reduction. **-ito** *part. adj.* reduced in size; diminished.

impidocch-iare [A 4] *tr.* (vulg.) to fill with lice, to make lousy; *rfl.* to become lousy. (**-ato** *part. adj.*) **-ire** [D 2] *intr.* (aux. essere), *rfl.* to become lousy; (of plants) to become infested with greenfly. (**-ito** *part. adj.*)

impieg-are [A 2] *tr.* to employ; to use; to make use of; to bring into play; to spend; to invest; questo treno -a tre ore ad andare a Venezia, this train takes three hours to get to Venice; -ai tre ore per arrivare a casa, it took me three hours to get home; *rfl.* to be employed; to employ oneself; to obtain employment, to accept a post, to get a job. **-a·bile** *adj.* employable; (finan.) available for investment. **-ati·zio** *adj.* clerical. **-ato** *part. adj.* employed; used; spent; invested; *n.m.* clerk; 'white-collar worker'; -ato governativo, -ato di Stato, Civil Servant. **-atume** *m.* clerks, (clerical) staff, personnel.

impie-go *m.* (*pl.* **-ghi**) employment; job; commitment; post; (in advertisements) offerte d'—, situations vacant; investment (of capital); (theatr.) parte d'—, character part.

†**im·piere** *vb.* and derivs. See **empire**.

†**impietà** *f.* See **empietà**.

impietos-ire [D 2] *tr.* to move to pity, to touch; to fill with compassion; *rfl.* to be moved to pity, to be touched; -irsi di, to pity. **-ito** *part. adj.* moved to pity, touched.

†**impietoso** *adj.* pitiless.

†**impietrare** *vb.* and derivs. See **impietrire**.

impietr-ire [D 2] *tr.* to petrify, to turn to stone; to make stony; to harden the heart of; *rfl.* to be turned to stone; to harden one's heart, to become insensible. **-ito** *part. adj.* petrified; turned to stone; hard-hearted, stony-hearted; insensible.

†**impiezza** *f.* See **empiezza**.

impigli-are [A 4] *tr.* to entangle; to catch, to entrap; *rfl.* to be entangled; to get caught; to be confused; (of plants) to take root. **-ato** *part. adj.* entangled; trapped, caught; confused.

impi·glio *m.* entanglement, obstacle, hindrance.

impignora·bil-e *adj.* (leg.) exempt from distress, undistrainable (C.C.). **-ità** *f.* (leg.) exemption from distress (C.C.P.).

impigr-ire [D 2] *tr.* to make lazy; *intr.* (aux. essere), *rfl.* to grow lazy, to become lazy. **-ito** *part. adj.* grown lazy; lazy.

†**impigro** *adj.* diligent; industrious; active; hard-working.

impilamẹnto *m.* (industr.) stacking.

impillaccher-are [A I s] *tr.* (Tusc.) to splash with mud; (fig.) to stain, to soil. **-ato** *part. adj.* splashed with mud; muddy; (fig.) stained, soiled.

†**impin·gere** *vb.* and derivs. See **spingere**.

impingu-are [A 6] *tr.* to fatten; (fig.) to enrich; to pad, to fill out, to fill up; — la borsa, to line one's purse, to feather one's nest; (agric.) to manure; *rfl.* to grow fat; (fig.) to get rich. **-amẹnto** *m.* fattening. **-ato** *part. adj.* fattened; enriched; (agric.) manured.

impinguire [D2] and derivs. See **impinguare**.

†**impinta** f. push, shove.

impinzare [A1] and derivs. See **rimpinzare**.

†**im·pio** adj. and derivs. See **empio**.

impiomb-are [A1c] tr. to seal with lead; to line with lead; — un dente, to fill a tooth, to stop a tooth; (naut.) to splice; ferro da —, marline-spike. **-ato** part. adj. sealed with lead; lined with lead; (of a tooth) filled, stopped; vetri -ati, leaded lights; †vetro -ato, mirror; (naut.) spliced. **-atura** f. covering with lead; sealing; stopping, filling (of a tooth); lead covering; (naut.) splice, splicing.

impipare [A1] rfl. (vulg.) not to care, to be indifferent; me ne impipo, I couldn't care less; un'aria di me ne impipo, an air of (insolent) indifference.

impippiare [A4] tr. to feed forcibly, to cram (fowls, etc.), to fatten; (fig.) to prompt, to prime.

impium-are [A1] tr. to adorn with plumes or feathers; — un nido, to feather a nest; to wing, to give wings to; rfl. to grow feathers, to become fledged; to begin to grow a beard. **-ato** part. adj. plumed, feathered. (**-atura** f.)

implaca·bil-e adj. implacable, unrelenting. **-mente** adv. implacably. **-ità** f. implacableness.

implacat-o adj. unrelenting; inveterate. **-amente** adv. unrelentingly.

†**implacid-ire** tr. to appease, to pacify; to soothe, to quieten. **-ito** part. adj. appeased; soothed; quietened.

implausi·bile adj. not meriting applause; not plausible.

implic-are [A2] tr. to implicate; to involve; to entangle; to imply. **-ato** part. adj. implicated; entangled; -ato in un reato, implicated in a crime. **-azione** f. implication.

impli·cit-o adj. implied, implicit; (leg.) implied; rinuncia -a, implied waiver. **-amente** adv. implicitly. **-ezza** f. implicitness.

implo·dere [C3] tr. (phys.) to implode.

implor-are [A1] tr. to implore; to entreat, to beg for; to pray for; — da uno il perdono, to entreat someone's forgiveness. **-a·bile** adj. that can be entreated, subject to supplication. **-ante** part. adj. imploring; n.m., f. suppliant. **-ato** part. adj. implored; besought; asked for, prayed for. **-atore** m. implorer, beseecher. (**-atrice** f.) **-azione** f. imploring; supplication.

implume adj. unfledged, without feathers; beardless; (joc.) bipede —, featherless biped, man.

implu·vio m. (Rom. antiq.) impluvium, basin in atrium of a Roman house; (geog.) linea d'—, watershed; bacino d'—, catchment area.

impoe·tico adj. unpoetical.

impoggiare [A3] intr. (aux. avere) (naut.) to bear away.

†**impolare** rfl. to be fixed between poles, to exist in space.

impoli·tic-o adj. impolitic; imprudent; inexpedient; unwise, inopportune. **-amente** adv. imprudently.

impollinazione f. (bot.) pollination.

impolluto adj. unpolluted, inviolate.

†**impolminato** adj. yellow-skinned, sallow.

impolp-are [A1] tr. to fatten; to stuff; (fig.) to pad; intr. (aux. essere), rfl. to grow fat; to become plump, to put on weight. **-ato** part. adj. fattened; stuffed; (fig.) -ato di citazioni, padded with quotations.

impoltron-ire [D2] tr. to make lazy; to make cowardly; intr. (aux. essere), rfl. to grow lazy; to become cowardly. **-ito** part. adj. grown lazy; made cowardly, cowed.

impolver-are [A1sc] tr. to cover with dust; to sprinkle with sand; rfl. to get dusty; (joc.) to powder one's nose; †to powder one's hair. **-ato** part. adj. covered with dust, dusty; sanded.

impom-are [A1] rfl. (of trees) to bear fruit. **-ato** part. adj. (of trees or gardens) bearing fruit, full of fruit.

impomat-are [A1] tr. to pomade. **-ato** part. adj. pomaded; (derog.) tutto bello e -ato, dandified.

impomiciare [A3] tr. and derivs. See **pomiciare**.

imponder-a·bile adj. imponderable; that cannot be weighed. **-abilità** f. (phys.) imponderability.

imponen-te part. of **imporre**, q.v.; adj. imposing; grand, majestic; solemn. **-za** f. grandeur, majesty; solemnity.

†**impo·nere** vb. and derivs. See **imporre**.

imponi·bil-e adj. (finan.) taxable; dutiable; rateable; reddito —, taxable income; valore —, rateable value; n.m. taxable amount or value. **-ità** f. (finan.) taxability.

impopolar-e adj. unpopular. **-mente** adv. unpopularly. **-ità** f. unpopularity.

impopp-are [A1c] tr. (naut.) to poop; intr. (aux. essere), rfl. (naut.) to be down by the stern, to poop. **-ata** f. pooping. **-ato** part. adj. down by the stern.

†**impopulare** tr. to plant with poplars; rfl. to become covered with poplars.

imporcare¹ [A2] tr. (agric.) to furrow, to harrow.

imporcare² [A2] tr. to soil, to dirty; rfl. to dirty oneself; to become piggish.

imporpor-are [A1sc] tr. to empurple; to dye purple; to crimson; to redden; rfl. to grow purple; to redden; to blush, to turn crimson. **-ato** part. adj. stained purple; dyed purple; dyed crimson; reddened.

imporr-are [A1], **-ire** [D2] intr. (aux. essere) (techn.) to rot (mainly of wood). **-ito** part. adj. legno -ito, rotten wood.

imporre [B21] tr. to impose; — una tassa, to impose a tax; — certe condizioni, to impose certain conditions; — un castigo, to inflict a punishment; — una cosa a, to inflict a thing on; — una colpa a, to lay blame on; — un nome a, to give a name to; — la propria volontà a, to impose one's will on, to coerce; il bisogno impone ch'io accetti, necessity obliges me to accept; to lay (upon); to command; to enjoin (on); (eccl.) to impose (hands); (mus.) — un canto, to intone a chant; intr. (aux. avere; prep. a); gl'impose di tacere, he imposed silence upon him; — a, to arouse admiration in, to inspire respect or fear in; (of corn) to grow well; to take root; (of fruit) to set; rfl. to assume authority, to take command, to gain the upper hand; to be imposing; to impose oneself.

importa·bile adj. See under **importare**.

importante¹ part. See under **importare**.

importan-te² adj. important; significant; of importance; — per, important to, for; n.m. l'—, the main thing, the essential thing; per me l'— è, in my view the important thing is; the main point. **-za** f. importance; dare -za a, to attribute importance to; darsi aria d'-za, to give oneself airs; d'-za, important; avere grande -za, to be very important; senza -za, privo d'-za, unimportant, without importance; †main point, essential thing; †care, concern, affair, undertaking.

import-are [A1] tr. to import; — carbone, to import coal; to involve, to signify, to mean; to imply; to amount to; il viaggio -a mille lire, the journey costs a thousand lire; un'impresa che -a gravi spese, an undertaking which involves heavy expense; — danni, to involve, to bring about damage; intr. (aux. avere) to signify, to matter, to be important; to be of interest; impers. (aux. essere) non -a, it does not matter; che -a?, what does it matter?; a te che ne -a?, what do you care about it?; non -a che vi disturbiate, please don't trouble; non m'-a nulla di tali chiacchiere, such gossip is of no interest to me; m'-a che mio figlio sia contento, I want my son to be happy; n.m. amount. **-a·bile** adj. importable; †intolerable; †intolerant. **-ante** part. importing; signifying (see also **importante²** adj.). **-ato** part. adj. imported; involved; signified. **-atore** m. importer; adj. importing; †signifier, bearer of meaning. **-atrice** f. l'Italia è grande -atrice di carbone, Italy imports a great deal of coal; also adj. **-azione** f. importation; importing; import; commercio d'-azione, import business; dazio d'-azione, import duty, customs duty; pl. imports, goods imported. †**-e·vole** adj. unbearable, intolerable. **-o** m. (comm.) value; amount, total cost.

importun-are [A1] tr. to pester, to worry, to importune. **-ante** part. adj. importunating, pestering; importunate. **-ato** part. adj. pestered, importunated.

importun-o¹ adj. troublesome, tiresome; importunate; pestering; n.m. person who is a nuisance, pest. **-amente** adv. importunately. **-ità** f. importunity; tiresome persistence.

importuno² adj. (pop.). See **inopportuno**.

†**importuoso** adj. lacking harbours.

impositore m. (typ.) imposer.

imposizione f. imposition; overbearing demand; impost, duty, tax; (typ.) imposing; — delle mani, imposition of hands, laying on of hands.

impossente adj. powerless.

impossess-are [A1] rfl. (prep. di) to take possession (of), to take, to appropriate; to master; ha capito la lezione, ma ancora non se n'è -ato, he understands the lesson but has not yet mastered it.

impossi·bil-e adj. impossible; a Dio nulla è —, with God all things are possible; most unlikely, improbable; intractable; unbearable; unacceptable; useless; pare —!, it can't be true!; pare — che non

impossibil-e (*cont.*)
si possa trovare, surely we can find it, you'd think it was possible to find it; *n.m.* what is impossible; farò l'—, I will do all I can and more. **-mente** *adv.* impossibly; improbably. **-is·simo** *adj. superl.* absolutely impossible; out of the question. **-ità** *f.* impossibility; mi trovo nell'-ità di farlo, I am quite unable to do it. **-itare** [A I] *tr.* to render impossible; to render incapable. **-itato** *part. adj.* made impossible; unable; è -itato a pagare, he is unable to pay.

imposta[1] *f.* imposition, tax, impost, duty; (leg.) — di (sulla) successione, death duty (C.C.); — progressiva, graduated tax; Ufficio delle Imposte Dirette, Inland Revenue Office; — sul reddito, — di ricchezza mobile, income-tax.

imposta[2] *f.* shutter; leaf of a folding door; window-shutter; (archit.) impost; (agric.) row of grains in an ear.

†imposta[3] *f.* expressed wish, command; mi fu gradito d'ubbidire l'— vostra, I obeyed your command with pleasure.

impost-are[1] [A I c] *tr.* (archit.) to lay, to put in position, to erect (e.g. a dome or arch); — un problema, to state a problem; to make a plan of, to lay down the lines of, to do the preliminary work for; (naut.) — una nave, to lay down the keel of a ship on the stocks; (comm.) — un conto, to open an account; to enter (in a ledger), to post; (mus.) — la voce, to place the voice. **-amento** *m.* (naut.) laying a ship on the stocks. **-ato** *part. adj.* set in position; (mil.) (of a sentry) posted; (naut.) laid on the stocks, laid up, moored; †vascello -ato, well-found ship; †*n.m.* berthing. **-atura** *f.* (archit.) laying down, setting in position, erecting; walls, piers or columns upon which an arch or vault rests; seating, bearing (of an arch or vault); (fig.) pose, attitude; (mus.) placing (of the voice); (naut.) keel (as the first part of a ship to be laid down in shipbuilding). **-azione** *f.* laying down, setting in position; (cinem.) location.

impost-are[2] [A I c] *tr.* to post (letters, etc.). **-ato** *part. adj.* posted. **-azione** *f.* posting (of letters, etc.); postage.

impostem-ire [D 2] *intr.* (*aux.* essere) (med.) to fester, to gather, to impostumate. **-ito** *part. adj.* festered, gathered.

impostim-e *m.* sediment, deposit, ooze. **-are** [A I] *intr.* (*aux.* avere) to deposit mud, to form mud-banks.

imposto *part.* of **imporre**, q.v., *adj.* imposed; enjoined; laid on; *n.m.* the first wax-coating of the wick of a candle.

impost-ore *m.* impostor; deceiver; fraud. (**-ora** *f.*) **-ura** *f.* imposture; fraud, deception; fake. **†-are** *tr.* to deceive; to defraud.

impota·bile *adj.* undrinkable, unfit for drinking.

impoten-te[1] *adj.* weak; impotent; incapable; powerless; essere — al lavoro, to be unable to work; *n.m.* weakling; man who is sexually impotent. **-temente** *adv.* impotently; incapably; feebly; ineffectively. **-za** *f.* feebleness; powerlessness; ridurre all'-za, to render powerless; (med.) impotence; (leg.) impotence, impotency; incapacity; -za di generare, impotence (of male), incapacity (of female) to procreate (C.C.); -za perpetua, permanent impotence or incapacity (C.C.); -za relativa, impotence or incapacity with particular marriage partner; -za strumentale, organic impotence or incapacity (as contrasted with '-za funzionale', functional ditto).

†impotente[2] *adj.* very powerful.

impover-ire [D 2] *tr.* to impoverish; *intr.* (*aux.* essere), *rfl.* to become poor, to be reduced to poverty. **-imento** *m.* impoverishing; impoverishment. **-ito** *part. adj.* impoverished; reduced to poverty.

impratica·bil-e *adj.* impracticable; impractical; impassable. **-ità** *f.* impracticability; l'-ità delle strade, the bad state of the roads.

impraticato *adj.* See **impraticabile**.

impratich-ire [D 2] *tr.* to train; to drill; to exercise; to familiarize; to make expert; *rfl.* (*prep.* di, a) to practise; to exercise oneself (in); to become expert. **-ito** *part. adj.* trained; drilled; exercised; in practice; practised; expert.

imprec-are [A 2] *tr.* to curse; to call down curses upon; — la morte a uno, to curse someone (wishing he may die); *intr.* (*aux.* avere; *prep.* a, contro) to curse, to wish ill (to). **-ativo** *adj.* imprecatory. **-ato** *part. adj.* wished, called down; cursed. **-atore** *m.* curser; ill-wisher. **-ato·rio** *adj.* (*m.pl.* -atorii) imprecatory; giuramento -atorio, curse. **-azione** *f.* imprecation, curse; cursing; uscire in -azioni, to utter curses.

imprecis-ione *f.* inexactness, want of precision; inaccuracy. **-o** *adj.* inaccurate, incorrect; inexact, not precise; vague, imprecise. **-amente** *adv.* inaccurately, incorrectly; inexactly; vaguely.

†impregionare *vb.* and derivs. See **imprigionare**.

impregiudic-a·bile *adj.* incapable of being prejudiced; (leg.) to be deemed 'without prejudice'. **-ato** *adj.* unprejudiced; without prejudice; -ata ogni azione, every action reserved; -ato ogni altro diritto, without prejudice to any other right; *n.m.* one who has no previous conviction (C.P.).

impregn-are [A 5 c] *tr.* to fertilize, to impregnate, to fecundate; to render pregnant; (fig.) to imbue; (techn.) to impregnate (e.g. timber). **-amento** *m.* impregnating; impregnation. **-ante** *part. adj.* fertilizing, impregnating; *n.m.* (paint) filler, primer. **-ato** *part. adj.* impregnated, fertilized; (fig.) imbued. **-azione** *f.* fecundation; (techn.) impregnation, adsorption.

impremedit-ato *adj.* unpremeditated, spontaneous; (leg.) unintentional; unpremeditated; *adv.* extempore. **-atamente** *adv.* unintentionally; involuntarily. **-azione** *f.* unpremeditatedness.

impren·d-ere [C I] *tr.* to undertake; to initiate, to begin; †to learn; †to include. **-i·bile** *adj.* well-defended, impregnable. **-imento** *m.* undertaking; initiating. **-itore** *m.* contractor; one who undertakes or initiates an enterprise; (econ.) entrepreneur; (leg.) person carrying on trade, business or profession (C.C.); head of commercial or industrial enterprise employing labour (C.C.). (**-itrice** *f.*) **-itoriale** *adj.* relating to a contractor; (econ.) associazione -itoriale, association of entrepreneurs.

†imprensione *f.* conception, opinion; fare —, to believe, to hold as an opinion.

†imprenta *f.* See **impronta**.

†imprentare *vb.* and derivs. See **improntare**.

imprepar-ato *adj.* unprepared. **-azione** *f.* unpreparedness.

impres-a *f.* undertaking, enterprise; exploit; deed; feat; è un'—, it's quite an undertaking; contract; firm of contractors; business firm; management; managerial staff, management; emblem, coat of arms with motto, heraldic achievement; (leg.) commercial or industrial enterprise or undertaking (C.C.); interessato in una —, having an interest in such an enterprise; †(agric.) cultivation; †*adv. phr.* a tutte -e, on all occasions; †per —, expressly, on purpose. **-are** [A I c] *tr.* (agric.) to divide or allot (plots of land) for cultivation. **-a·rio** *m.*, **-a·ria** *f.* (*m.pl.* -ari, *f.pl.* -a·rie) (theatr.; mus.) manager, impresario; -ario di pompe funebri, undertaker; (leg.) contractor.

imprescienza *f.* lack of prescience.

imprescindi·bil-e *adj.* necessary, indispensable; that cannot be prescinded, done away with, set aside, or delayed. **-mente** *adv.* necessarily, indispensably.

imprescritti·bil-e *adj.* indefeasible; (leg.) imprescriptable; diritto —, imprescriptable right. **-mente** *adv.* indefeasibly; imprescriptably. **-ità** *f.* imprescriptableness.

imprescritto *adj.* not prescribed; unforfeited.

impreso *part.* of **imprendere**, q.v.; *adj.* undertaken; begun, started; beginning; †infected, tainted.

†impressa[1] *f.* imprint, impression.

†impressa[2] *adv. phr.* all'—, hurriedly.

†impressare *tr.* to impress, to imprint; to write; to press upon; to importune; to worry, to torment.

impression-a·bile *adj.*, **-ante** *adj.* See under **impressionare**.

impression-are [A I c] *tr.* to impress; to affect, to strike, to make a deep impression upon; to shock; (mech.) to pass on (pressure, motion, heat, etc.); (photog.) to expose; *rfl.* to be deeply moved; to be shocked; to become discouraged; -arsi facilmente, to be impressionable. **-a·bile** *adj.* impressionable, easily moved; (mech.) malleable. **-abilità** *f.* impressionability, susceptibility to impressions. **-ante** *part. adj.* impressive; striking; shocking. **-ato** *part. adj.* impressed; affected; shocked; male -ato, unfavourably impressed; (photog.) exposed.

impression-e *f.* impression; fare buona —, to make a good impression; fare — a, to strike, to affect deeply, to surprise; fa —!, how astonishing!, how disagreeable!; mi ha fatto —, it made a deep impression on me, (or) I was quite startled; sensation; per assuefarsi ai bagni freddi bisogna vincere la prima —, once you get over the first shock you soon get used to cold baths; printing; imprint, imprinting, impression; issue; (mil.) pressure; tactical success in attack. **-ismo** *m.* (art) impressionism. **-ista** *m.*, *f.* (art) impressionist. **-i·stico** *adj.* (art) impressionistic.

†impressiva *f.* faculty of receiving impressions from external objects.

impress-o *part.* of **imprimere**, q.v.; *adj.* impressed; printed, imprinted, stamped. **-ore** *m.* printer; (typ.) pressman.

imprest-are [A I] *tr.* (pop.) to lend. †**-anza** *f.* loan. **-ato** *part. adj.* lent (cf. **prestare**).

impres·tito *m.* (pop.). See **prestito**.

†**impresto** *m.* See **imprestito**.

†**impretare** *rfl.* to take Holy Orders, to become a priest.

impreteri·bil-e *adj.* indispensable; that cannot be disregarded; inescapable. **-mente** *adv.* unavoidably, inescapably.

imprevedi·bil-e *adj.* unforeseeable; unforeseen. **-mente** *adv.* unforeseeably.

imprevedut-o *adj.* unforeseen. **-amente** *adv.* unexpectedly.

impreviden-te *adj.* without foresight; improvident; heedless, thoughtless. **-mente** *adv.* improvidently. **-za** *f.* lack of foresight; improvidence; heedlessness, thoughtlessness.

imprevisto *adj.* unforeseen; unexpected; *n.m.* unexpected occurrence, unforeseen eventuality; non ho potuto venire a causa di un —, I was prevented from coming by an unexpected occurrence.

†**imprezia·bile** *adj.* priceless; inestimable.

imprezios-ire [D 2] *tr.* to make precious, to increase the value of; *intr.* (*aux.* essere), *rfl.* to become precious; to become fastidious or affected. **-ito** *part. adj.* rendered precious.

imprezza·bile *adj.* inestimable, invaluable; (leg.) impretiabilis.

impri·a *adv.* See **imprima**.

imprigion-are [A I c] *tr.* to imprison; to take prisoner; to confine; to lock in, to shut in; (microscopy) to embed (a specimen). **-amento** *m.* imprisonment. **-ato** *part. adj.* imprisoned; taken prisoner; confined; locked in, shut in; (naut.) nave **-ata**, icebound ship. (**-atore** *m.* **-atrice** *f.*)

imprim-a *adv.* in the first place, first; all'—, at once, immediately; †*conj.* — che, before; †*prep.* — di, before, in front of. †**-amente** *adv.* see **imprima**. †**-ante** *adj., adv. phr.* l'-ante cosa, in the first place.

imprimatur *m. indecl.* (leg.) imprimatur; (typ.) passed for printing.

imprimé *adj. indecl.* (text.) printed.

impri·m-ere [C 18] *tr.* to impress; to imprint; to print; to stamp; — il carattere, to give a particular trait to a character; (fig.) to engrave; — il moto a, to set in motion; *rfl.* to be imprinted; **-ersi** nella mente, to be impressed upon the mind. **-i·bile** *adj.* printable; impressible. **-itura** *f.* (paint.) priming, undercoat, preparatory coat.

improba·bil-e *adj.* improbable. **-mente** *adv.* improbably. **-ità** *f.* improbability, unlikelihood.

†**improbare** *tr.* to disapprove of; to prove.

†**improbativo** *adj. n.m.* (gramm.) pejorative.

im·prob-o *adj.* wicked; dishonest; continual; unendurable; lavoro —, long, laborious and difficult work; fatica **-a**, unrewarding, laborious toil. **-ità** *f.* wickedness; dishonesty; depravity.

†**improcciare** *tr.* to reproach.

improcedi·bil-e *adj.* (leg.) lapsed; that cannot be proceeded with; l'appello è dichiarato —, the appeal is declared lapsed (C.C.P.). **-ità** *f.* (leg.) lapse (for want of prosecution of appeal) (C.C.P.).

improduttivo *adj.* unproductive; terreno —, barren soil, impresa improduttiva, profitless undertaking.

†**improm-essa** *f.* see **promessa**. †**-essione** *f.* see **promissione**.

impromettere [C 20] and derivs. (pop.). See **promettere**.

†**impromissione** *f.* See **promessa**.

impromptu *m. indecl.* (pron. as Fr.) (mus.) impromptu.

impronta *f.* imprint, impress; impression; mark; — del piede, footprint; impronte (digitali), fingerprints; — del vaiuolo, pockmark; — del genio, mark of genius; l'— della miseria, the signs of poverty; gli si legge in faccia l'— del bugiardo, you can see from his face he's a liar, he has liar written all over him; (mus.) lettura all'—, sight-reading; fare una cosa all'—, to do something without previous rehearsal.

improntamente *adv.* See under **impronto¹**.

impront-are¹ [A I c] *tr.* to imprint, to impress; to mark; — qualcuno di (con) qualche cosa, to impress something on someone; (mus.) to sing or play at sight. **-ato** *part. adj.* imprinted, impressed; marked; col viso **-ato** a mestizia, with a sorrowful expression on one's face; parole **-ate** di sincerità, words that have the hall-mark of sincerity. **-atore** *m.* die-engravers; (mus.) good sight-reader.

impront-are² [A I c] *tr.* to lend; to borrow; (comm.) to advance (a loan). **-amento** *m.* request for an advance or a loan. **-ato** *part. adj.* lent; borrowed; (comm.) advanced.

†**improntare³** *tr.* to prepare, to make ready; to contrive; *intr.* to insist, to be importunate.

improntitu·dine *f.* See under **impronto¹**.

impront-o¹ *adj.* importunate; insistent; impudent. **-amente** *adv.* importunately; impudently; with effrontery. **-itu·dine** *f.* importunity; insistence; impudence; effrontery; impatience; rashness.

impronto² *adv. phr.* all'—, at sight, at first sight; without rehearsal; (mus.) lettura all'—, sight-reading; †see **impronta**.

impronunzia·bile *adj.* unpronounceable; not to be uttered.

†**improperare** *tr.* to reprove; to reproach; to abuse, to insult.

impropep·r-io *m.* abuse; insult; injury; reproach; caricare d'-i, to heap insults upon; votare il sacco degli -i, to empty the vials of one's wrath; *pl.* (liturg.; mus.) Improperia, Reproaches (sung on Good Friday). **-iare** [A 4] *tr.* to abuse; to insult. †**-ioso** *adj.* ignominious; abject.

†**impro·pio** *adj.* and derivs. See **improprio**.

improporzion-ale *adj.* out of proportion; badly proportioned. **-almente** *adv.* to a disproportionate extent. **-alità** *f.* lack of proportion. **-ato** *adj.* disproportionate; unsuitable.

impro·pr-io *adj.* improper; inappropriate; lacking in propriety; unbecoming, unsuitable, unfit; (math.) improper. **-iamente** *adv.* improperly; unbecomingly, unsuitably. **-ietà** *f.* impropriety.

improroga·bile *adj.* (leg.) that cannot be prorogued or adjourned; (fig.) pressing.

improsciuttire [D 2] *intr.* (*aux.* essere) (fam., of a person) to become thin and shrivelled.

†**improvare** *tr.* to disapprove of.

improverare [A I s] and derivs. See **rimproverare**.

improvvedut-o *adj.* unprovided. **-amente** *adv.* unawares, unexpectedly.

improv·vid-o *adj.* imprudent, ill-considered; improvident. **-amente** *adv.* imprudently; improvidently. **-enza** *f.* imprudence; improvidence.

improvvisamente *adv.* See under **improvviso**.

improvvis-are [A I] *tr., intr.* (*aux.* avere) to improvise; to make up, to put together without preparation; to speak extempore, to speak impromptu; (mus.) to improvise, to extemporize. **-amento** *m.* improvising; improvisation. **-ante** *part. adj.* improvising; *n.m., f.* improviser; improvisator. **-ata** *f.* surprise, pleasant surprise; fare un'-ata a uno, to give someone an unexpected treat. **-ato** *part. adj.* improvised; extempore; unprepared; professore **-ato**, unqualified teacher. **-atore** *m.* improviser; improvisator, one who composes (poetry, music) extempore; (lit. hist.) Italian 'improvvisatore' or improvisator of the Italian type. (**-atrice** *f.*) **-azione** *f.* improvisation.

improvvis-o *adj.* sudden; unforeseen, unexpected; improvised; *n.m.* improvisation (i.e. poem or other composition improvised); (mus.) improvisation, extemporization; gli Improvvisi di Schubert, Schubert's Impromptus; *adv.* unexpectedly; extempore; *adv. phr.* d'—, all'—, unexpectedly, suddenly, without preparation; comporre all'—, to improvise. **-amente** *adv.* suddenly, unexpectedly, without warning.

improvvist-o *adj.* unprovided; *adv. phr.* all'-a, suddenly, unexpectedly. †**-amente** *adv.* improvidently; heedlessly.

impru-are [A 6] *tr.* (naut.) to put (a vessel) down by the head; *intr.* (*aux.* essere), *rfl.* to be down by the head. **-ato** *adj.* (naut.) down by the head.

impruden-te *adj.* imprudent; indiscreet; incautious; rash, bold. (**-temente** *adv.*) **-za** *f.* imprudence; indiscretion, heedlessness; fare, commettere un' **-za**, to commit an indiscretion; rashness, boldness; (leg.) careless act.

imprun-are [A I] *tr.* to obstruct (a passage), with a thorn hedge or thorn bushes; *intr.* (*aux.* avere) to close a gap in a hedge; †to seek shelter. **-ato** *part. adj.* obstructed; closed, barred.

impube *adj.* (leg.) under the age of puberty.

impu·bere *adj.* under the age of puberty; *n.m.* (leg.) a male under the age of fourteen; *n.f.* (leg.) a female under the age of twelve.

impuden-te *adj.* impudent; shameless; immodest; un'— menzogna, a barefaced lie. **-temente** *adv.* impudently; shamelessly; immodestly. **-za** *f.* impudence; shamelessness; immodesty; impudent action; shameless or immodest act.

impudi-co *adj.* (*m.pl.* **-chi**) immodest; indecent; obscene; wanton; lewd. †**-cità** *f.* see **impudicizia**. **-ci·zia** *f.* immodesty; indecency; obscenity; wantonness, lewdness; *pl.* acts of indecency, lewd behaviour.

†**impugna** *f.* battle; fight.

impugna·bile *adj.* See under **impugnare²**.

impugn-are¹ [A 5] *tr.* to grasp, to grip, to seize, to hold; (mil.) to attack; *intr.* (*aux.* avere) to clench one's fist. **-ato** *part. adj.* grasped, gripped; clenched. **-atura** *f.* hilt (of sword); handle (of knife, etc.); grip; (naut.) loom of an oar; (mus.) stopping (of strings).

impugn-are² [A 5] *tr.* to contest; (leg.) to impugn; to question; to attack by words or arguments; to appeal against (C.C.; C.C.P.; C.P.P.); †(mil.) to attack; to attempt (an assault). **-a·bile** *adj.* contestable; (leg.) impugnable; objectionable; sentenza -abile, judgement open to appeal. **-ativa** *f.* (leg.) notice, petition of appeal. **-ativo** *adj.* contesting, contradictory, tending to impugn. **-ato** *part. adj.* contested; (leg.) impugned; appealed against. **-atore** *m.* contestant, opponent, impugner. (**-atrice** *f.*) **-azione** *f.* contradiction, opposition, attack; (leg.) appeal; attack; opposition; mezzo di -azione, remedy (C.C.P.).

impulciare [A 3] *tr.* to infest with fleas.

impulcin-are [A 1] *tr.* to fertilize (eggs); (vulg., joc.) to render pregnant, to put in the family way. **-ato** *part. adj.* (of an egg) fertilized.

impulit-o *adj.* rough; unpolished; rude, crude. (**-amente** *adv.*) **-ezza** *f.* roughness; boorishness; crudity.

impuls-atore *m.* propeller, propellant. **-ione** *f.* impulsion, propelling, propulsion; (mech.) impulsion, impulsive force. **-ore** *m.* instigator.

impuls-o *m.* impulse, impetus; push; (fig.) motive; impulse; — naturale, natural impulse; urge; secondare un —, to give way to an impulse; dare — a, to encourage, to stimulate. **-ivo** *adj.* impelling; propulsive; impulsive; lacking in self-control or restraint; temperamento -ivo, impulsive temperament. **-ività** *f.* impulsiveness, impulsive temperament; (med.) irresistible tendency.

impun-e *adj.* unpunished; not liable to punishment; unpunishable; scatheless. **-emente** *adv.* with impunity. **-i·bile** *adj.* unpunishable. **-ità** *f.* impunity. **-ito** *adj.* unpunished; without punishment; restare -ito, to go unpunished. **-itamente** *adv.* with impunity.

impunt-are [A 1] *intr.* (*aux.* avere) to stumble; (*prep.* in) to strike one's foot (against); (fig.) to falter; to hesitate, to stammer (in reading or reciting); to stop, to stick, to be unable to go on; *rfl.* to jib, to stop dead; to refuse to budge, to be obstinate; to dig one's toes in; -arsi in, to stick to, to hold to, to be obstinate about; -arsi a dir di no, to refuse obstinately. **-amento** *m.* stumbling; (electr.) crawling (of electric motor). **-ato** *part. adj.* at a deadlock; obstinate. **-atura** *f.* stopping, sticking (esp. of a watch or clock).

impuntigliare [A 4] *rfl.* to be obstinate; to be pernickety; impuntigliarsi a fare una cosa, to take it into one's head to do something.

impunt-ire [D 2] *tr.* to sew, to stitch; to quilt, to point. **-ito** *part. adj.* sewn, stitched; quilted; (of shoe sole) hand-sewn. **-itura** *f.* quilting. **-ura** *f.* back-stitching, close stitching.

impuntual-e *adj.* unpunctual. **-ità** *f.* unpunctuality, lack of punctuality.

impuntura *f.* See under **impuntire**.

impur-o *adj.* impure; adulterated; unchaste; immoral. **-amente** *adv.* immorally. **-ità** *f.* impurity; immorality.

imput-are [A 1 s, A 1] *tr.* to impute; to attribute; to ascribe; to assign; -arono a lui la perdita, they blamed the loss on him; questo non mi si può — a colpa, this can't be blamed on me; (leg.) to charge; to apply; to impute; — una persona di furto, to charge a person with theft. **-a·bile** *adj.* (leg.) imputable; chargeable; (fig.) -abile di, responsible for. **-abilità** *f.* (leg.) imputability; liability (C.C.). **-aggio** *m.* (text.) tying up. **-ante** *part. adj.* imputing; *n.m., adj.* accuser. **-ato** *part. adj.* imputed; (leg.) charged; accused; prosecuted; -ato di un reato, charged with a crime; *n.m.* accused, defendant; assolvere l'-ato, to acquit the accused. (**-ata** *f.*) **-atore** *m.* accuser. (**-atrice** *f.*) **-azione** *f.* imputation; imputing; (leg.) charge; accusation; prosecution (C.P.P.); -azione di assassinio, murder charge; atto d'-azione, indictment; capo d'-azione, count of indictment; prosciogliere da una -azione, to acquit (C.P.P.); charging in account; marshalling (C.C.); -azione dei debiti, the charging in account of advances, in hotchpot; collazione per -azione, the charging in account of the value (of specific property) in hotchpot; -azione di pagamenti, marshalling of payments (C.C.).

imputr-efatto *adj.* not putrefied, not rotten, sound. **-esci·bile** *adj.* not subject to putrefaction, imputrescible. **-escibilità** *f.* imputrescibility. **-i·bile** *adj.* not subject to putrefaction.

imputrid-ire [D 2] *intr.* (*aux.* essere) to putrefy, to go bad, to go rotten, to rot, to decompose, to decay; *tr.* to cause to putrefy, to make rotten, to rot. **-imento** *m.* putrefaction, decomposition. **-ito** *part. adj.* putrefied; gone bad; rotten; decomposed; decayed; coscienza -ita, guilty conscience.

impuzzare [A 1] *intr.* (*aux.* essere) to stink, to be stinking; to become stinking.

impuzz-ire [D 2] *tr.* to cause to stink; questa frutta fradicia -isce la stanza, this decayed fruit is making the room stink; se tocchi quell'erba, t'-isci le mani, if you touch that weed you'll make your hands stink; *intr.* (*aux.* essere) to stink, to be stinking; to become stinking. **-ito** *part. adj.* made foul or stinking.

†impuzzol-ire *vb.* see **impuzzare**, **impuzzire**. **†-ito** *adj.* stinking.

in¹ *prep.* (*contr.* with *def. art.*: **nel, nello, nell', nei, negli, nella, nelle**; a word beginning with an impure s preceded by **in** sometimes acquires an initial **i** for euphony, e.g. 'in iscuola', but this usage is less frequent than formerly. See also 'Syntactical Uses', under no. 18.) **1.** IN, at, inside, within (of place); — Italia, in Italy; — Isvizzera, in Switzerland; — chiesa, in church; — iscuola, in school; — istrada, in the street; — casa, at home, in the house; — prigione, in prison; tenere — braccio, to hold in one's arms; con le mani — tasca, with one's hands in one's pockets; — mano, in one's hand; — mente, in mind; nel cuore, in one's heart; — cuore a, in the heart of; — grembo a, in the lap of, in the bosom of; sentire — sè, to feel within oneself; nel bel mezzo, right in the very middle; — fondo a, at the bottom of; avere un bambino — collo, to hold a child in one's arms; il bambino era — collo alla madre, the child was in its mother's arms; (sport) giocatori — nazionale, footballers playing for Italy. **2.** IN (of condition, state, feeling); — moto, in movement; — esame, under examination; — miseria, in poverty; — buona salute, in good health; un'anima — pena, a soul in torment; avere — odio, to hate; essere — forse, to be in doubt; stare — speranza, to live in hopes; — guerra, at war; vivere — pace, to live at peace, to live in peace; essere — pena per, to be anxious about (someone). **3.** IN, by, on, by means of (transport); andare — macchina, to go by car, to go out in a car; andare — carrozza, to ride in a carriage; — barca, in a boat, by boat, on the boat; — bicicletta, on a bicycle, by bicycle; — motocicletta, on a motor-cycle, by motor-cycle; — aeroplano, by plane, on the plane; viaggiare — treno, to travel by train; nel treno c'era molta gente, there was a crowd on the train; — viaggio, on the journey, during the journey; — isbaglio, by mistake. **4.** INTO; cadere nel pozzo, to fall into the well; dare — un laccio, to fall into a trap; intoppare — un muro, to bump into a wall; dividere — due, to divide into two; tagliare — quattro pezzi, to cut into four pieces; cambiare — mostro, to change into a monster; l'ingresso di Napoleone — Milano, Napoleon's entry into Milan; andare — Svizzera, to cross over into Switzerland; andare — collera, to get angry, to fly into a temper; mettere — moto, to start up (engine, etc.); mettersi — viaggio, to set out on one's journey; tradurre dall'italiano — inglese, to translate from Italian into English. **5.** To (motion towards, sequence); andare — America, to go to America; portare — tavola, to bring to the table; andare — perdizione, to go to perdition; andare — Paradiso, to go to Heaven; andare — malora, to fall into ruin, to go to the dogs; venire — mente a, to come to (one's) mind; di volta — volta, from one time to the next, progressively each time; di giorno — giorno, from day to day; di male — peggio, from bad to worse; di grado — grado, by degrees; d'ora — avanti, from now on, henceforward. **6.** ON, on to, on top of; — capo, — testa, on one's head; — tavola, on the table; — croce, on the cross; porre — croce, to crucify, (fig.) to torment; — piedi, on one's feet, standing; — capo a, on the top of; — vetta a, on the summit of; — punta di, on the tip of; — punta di piedi, on tiptoe; — terra, on the ground; cadere — terra, to fall to the ground; sputare — terra, to spit on the ground; è — tavola, dinner is on the table, dinner is served. **7.** IN, within, at, during (of time); — un'ora, within an hour, in the space of an hour; si spicciò — poco tempo, he got through his work in a short time; nel frattempo, in the meantime; nell'Ottocento, in the nineteenth century; — punto di morte, at the point of death; — viaggio, on the journey; verremo — settimana, we'll come during (in the course of) the week; — quella, — quel mentre, in the meantime; — men che non si dica, in less than no time; — capo a un anno, at the end

in (*cont.*)

of a year; — ogni ora della giornata, at any time of day; †cominciò a regnare — 35 anni, he entered on his reign at the age of 35; †— dì 13 giugno, on 13 June. **8.** IN, wearing; vestito — seta. dressed in silk; — guanti, wearing gloves; — fasce, nelle fasce, in swaddling clothes; — ciabatte, in slippers; — gala, in one's best clothes; — maniche di camicia, in one's shirt-sleeves; — cappello, wearing a hat; — abito da sera, wearing evening-dress. **9.** IN, of, concerning, regarding; versato — teologia, versed in theology; dottore — medicina, doctor of medicine; laureato — lettere, graduate in arts, arts graduate; laurearsi — scienze, to take a degree in science; bravo — latino, good at Latin; ricco — poderi, rich in farm lands; mercante — legname, timber merchant, dealer in wood; crescere — bellezza, to increase in beauty; fratello negli anni, contemporary, of an age, of the same age; fratello — Cristo, brother in Christ; (sport) esordiente — maglia azzurra, player awarded Italian national colours for the first time, capped for the first time; (leg.) considerazioni — fatto, findings of fact. **10.** IN, with, by means of (of form, material); — ottave, in octaves; — prosa, in prose; — inglese, in English; lavorare — marmo, to work in marble; scultore — bronzo, sculptor in bronze; lampadario — legno dorato, lamp-stand in gilt wood; scrittura — corsivo, cursive script; libro — quarto, quarto book; statua — gesso, clay model; fatto — velluto, made of velvet; tagliato — croce, cut on the cross, crosswise, crossed. **11.** IN THE PLACE OF; se fossi — voi, if I were in your place, if I were you; vorrei essere — lui, I'd like to be in his shoes; †dare piombo — oro, to give lead in exchange for gold. **12.** As, in the form of; avere — dono, to receive as a gift; chiedere — grazia, chiedere — cortesia, to ask as a favour; dire — iscusa, to say in excuse, to offer as an excuse; — prova di, as proof of; fatto — cerchio, made in the shape of a circle; — lode di, in praise of; — tutto, in all; fare mille lire — tutto, to total 1000 lire. **13.** AMONG, between; — noi è perfetto accordo, there is complete agreement between us; †benedetta nelle figlie di Eva, blessed among women. **14.** TOWARDS, to, for, against; con gli occhi — terra, with eyes cast down; usare crudeltà —, to be cruel towards; avere pietà —, to feel compassion for; avere riverenza —, to feel reverence for; volto — altra parte, facing the other way, turned in the other direction; peccare — Dio, to sin against God; farla — barba a uno, to defy someone, to do a thing under a person's very nose. **15.** WITH: accogliere — lieta fronte, to greet with cheerful countenance; sorrise — una dolce espressione di pace, she smiled with a gentle peaceful expression; disse — un inchino, he said with a bow; dire — un sorriso, to say with a smile. **16.** CULINARY USES: pesce — bianco, boiled fish; pollo — fricassea, fricasseed chicken; carne — umido, meat in casserole; pasta — bianco, pasta served with oil and cheese without tomato sauce. **17.** As PART OF FORMULA FOR LEGAL NAME OF MARRIED WOMAN: Ruby Johnson — Roatta, Ruby Roatta *née* Johnson. **18.** SYNTACTICAL USES. **(i)** Followed by possessive adjectives: when the def. art. of the poss. adj. is used, it combines with **in** to form **nel, nella**, etc., e.g.: nel mio paese, in my country; nella vostra automobile, in your car; nei suoi libri, in his books. In some phrases the def. art. is omitted, e.g.: — mia assenza, in my absence; — vece vostra, — tuo luogo, in your place; scritto — suo omaggio, written in his honour; — casa mia (cf. nella mia casa), in my house; — cuore a (cf. nel cuore di), in the heart of. When the noun is followed by the prep. **di**, the def. art. of the poss. adj. is used, e.g.: nella mia qualità di direttore, in my capacity as director; nel treno di Milano, on the Milan train (cf. andare a Milano — treno, to go to Milan by train). **(ii)** With infinitives: nell'andare, going along; nell'udire ciò, on hearing this; nel partire, at the time of departure, on leaving. **(iii)** With prepositions or adverbs: — su, up above; — basso, — giù, down below; — fuori, outside, turned out; — avanti, ahead; — là, further on. **(iv)** With adjectives or nouns to form adv. phr.: — apparenza, apparently; — astratto, in the abstract; — lieta fronte, with a joyous countenance; — breve, briefly; — fretta, hastily, hurriedly; — fondo, at bottom, basically, after all. **(v)** With numerals: siamo — quattro, there are four of us; si riunirono — cento, a hundred of them met together; di 12 — 13, about 12 or 13.

in-² *pref.* in-, un-, signifying negation or privation, e.g. **indicibile, inappetente**; or contrariness, e.g. **infelice**.

in-³ *pref.* en-, signifying combination with, transformation into, entrance into, etc., e.g. **inabissare, inamidare**.

†**inabbondante** *adj.* unfertile.

ina·bil-e *adj.* unable, unfit; disabled; unqualified, ineligible; — al servizio militare, unfit for military service; (leg.) not having the requisite qualifications; insufficient; — a testare, not competent as witness; (mech.) ineffective; †(med.) incapacitated. **-ità** *f.* unfitness, disablement; inability; (leg.) incapacity; insufficiency; disability; -ità permanente, permanent disability. **-itando** *m.* (leg.) respondent in incapacitation proceedings (C.C.P.). **-itare** [A I S] *tr.* to render unfit, to disable; (leg.) to deprive of legal capacity; to incapacitate (C.C.P.); (naut.) to render (a ship) unseaworthy; (mil.) to incapacitate; *rfl.* (mil.) to self-incapacitate. **-itato** *part. adj.* rendered unfit; (leg.) under disability; disqualified; legally incapacitated (C.C.); (naut.) rendered unseaworthy; (mil.) incapacitated. **-itazione** *f.* disablement; incapacity; (leg.) disqualification; disability; legal incapacitation (C.C.); -itazione giudiziaria, judicial incapacitation.

inabiss-are [A I] *tr.* to plunge into an abyss, to engulf; *rfl.* to be plunged into an abyss; to sink; vorrei piuttosto -armi!, I'd rather die. **-amento** *m.* sinking; plunging; †state of being engulfed. **-ato** *part. adj.* sunk; engulfed; †deep; †depressed; dejected.

inabita·bil-e *adj.* uninhabitable, unfit for habitation. **-ità** *f.* uninhabitableness.

†**inabitare** *vb.* and derivs. See **abitare**.

inabitato *adj.* uninhabited.

inaboli·bile *adj.* that cannot be abolished, abrogated or done away with; indefeasible.

inaccessi·bil-e *adj.* inaccessible; beyond reach; impenetrable; (mil.) breccia —, impracticable breach; †impossible; not feasible. **-mente** *adv.* inaccessibly; -mente elevato, so high up as to be beyond reach. **-ità** *f.* inaccessibility, inaccessibleness; impenetrability.

inaccesso *adj.* inaccessible, beyond reach; segreto —, impenetrable secret.

inaccetta·bil-e *adj.* unacceptable, not acceptable; dichiarare — un emendamento, to declare an amendment out of order. **-ità** *f.* unacceptableness.

inaccorda·bile *adj.* irreconcilable; impossible to tune, untunable; that cannot be granted, unallowable.

inaccorto *adj.* unwary, improvident; uninformed; unskilful.

inaccusa·bile *adj.* that cannot rightly be accused.

inacerb-ire [D 2] *tr.* to embitter; to exacerbate; †— la voce, to render the voice strident; *rfl.* to become embittered; to become exacerbated. **-ito** *part. adj.* embittered; exacerbated.

inacet-ire [D 2] *intr.* (*aux.* essere) to turn sour, to turn to vinegar; *tr.* to turn sour, to make sour. **-ito** *part. adj.* gone sour; turned to vinegar; soured.

inacid-ire [D 2] *tr.* to turn sour, to cause to taste sour; to acidify; *intr.* (*aux.* essere) to turn sour; *rfl.* to acidify, to become acid. **-ito** *part. adj.* gone sour; acidified.

inacquare [A 6] and derivs. See **inacquare**.

†**inacquoso** *adj.* dry, dried up, gone dry.

†**inacuire** *vb.* and derivs. See **inacutire**.

inacut-ire [D 2] *tr.* to sharpen; to whet; to make pointed; to render more acute; (mus.) to raise the pitch of, to sharpen; *rfl.* to become more acute; (mus.) raised in pitch, sharpened.

inadatta·bil-e *adj.* unadaptable. **-ità** *f.* unadaptability; unsuitableness; insufficiency; incapacity.

inadatto *adj.* unsuited; unsuitable; unfit; unqualified.

inadeguat-o *adj.* inadequate, insufficient; unsuitable. **-amente** *adv.* inadequately, insufficiently. **-ezza** *f.* inadequacy, insufficiency; unsuitableness.

inademp-i·bile *adj.* that cannot be fulfilled; difficult to fulfil. **-iente** *part. adj.* defaulting (C.C.P.); *n.m.* defaulting party (C.C.). **-ienza** *f.* (leg.) default; non-fulfilment; -ienza di promessa, breach of promise; -ienza dell'aggiudicatario, default of purchaser at auction (C.C.P.). **-imento** *m.* non-performance; -imento del contratto, non-performance of contract (C.C.). **-ito, -iuto** *adj.* unfilled; promessa -ita, broken promise; obbligo -iuto, unfulfilled obligation.

inadombra·bile *adj.* that cannot be adumbrated.

inadop(e)ra·bile *adj.* unserviceable, not usable.

inadula·bile *adj.* not susceptible to flattery.

inafferra·bile *adj.* that cannot be grasped; incomprehensible; elusive; difficult to catch.

inaffettato *adj.* unaffected, without affectation, natural.

inaffiare [A 4] and derivs. See **innaffiare**.

inaggrega·bile *adj.* not capable of being assimilated.

inagitato *adj.* unruffled, unmoved, untroubled.

†**inagrare** *vb.* and derivs. See **inagrire**.

inagrestire [D 2] *intr.* (*aux.* essere) to taste sour (like unripe grapes); to become sour.

inagr-ire [D 2] *tr.* to turn sour; to make sourer; *intr.* (*aux.* essere) to become sour, or sourer. (**-ito** *part. adj.*)

inaiare [A 4] *tr.* to spread on the threshing-floor.

inal-are [A 1] *tr.* to inhale. **-ante** *part. adj.*, *n.m.*, *f.* inhalant. **-ato** *part. adj.* inhaled. **-atore** *m.* (med.) inhaler. **-ato·rio** *m.* (*pl.* **-atorii**) (med.) inhaling chamber. **-azione** *f.* (med.) inhalation.

inalb-are [A 1] *tr.* to make white; *intr.* (*aux.* essere), *rfl.* to turn white, to grow white, to dawn. **-amento** *m.* whitening. **-ato** *part. adj.* whitened

inalber-are [A 1 S] *tr.* (naut.) to hoist, to fly, to run up (a flag, or flags, for any purpose); to raise (oars, in salute); to brandish (a spear); (fig.) to stir up (trouble, agitation); to raise, to proclaim, to put forward (a doctrine); to plant with trees; *rfl.* (of a horse) to rear; (of a person) to get angry, to lose one's temper; to grow proud; to climb up a tree. **-amento** *m.* hoisting; rearing. **-ato** *part. adj.* hoisted, hoist, brandished; treed; (fig.) proclaimed; planted with trees; (herald.) forcene, rearing. **-atore** *m.* (naut.) ship's carpenter (in charge of the masts). (**-atura** *f.*)

†**inalborato** *adj.* planted with trees.

†**inale** *m.* (zool.) viper.

inalidire [D 2] *intr.* (*aux.* essere), *rfl.* to become dry and withered.

inaliena·bil-e *adj.* (leg.) inalienable; not transferable. **-mente** *adv.* (leg.) inalienably. **-ità** *f.* (leg.) inalienability.

†**inalpare** *rfl.* to seek refuge in the mountains.

†**inaltare** *tr.* to raise.

inalter-a·bile *adj.* unalterable; colori **-abili**, permanent colours; fast colours; affetto **—**, constancy, undying affection; cielo **—**, set fair, sky always cloudless; uomo **—**, even-tempered man; (mus.) nota **—**, natural note. **-abilmente** *adv.* unalterably. **-abilità** *f.* unalterability, permanence; (of colours) fastness, fadelessness; (of persons) evenness of temper, calmness, phlegm. **-ato** *adj.* unaltered; unvarying; constant.

†**inalturare** *tr.* to raise aloft; to extol.

inalve-are [A 6] *tr.* to canalize, to lead (waters) into a river-bed; *rfl.* to flow into a channel (or river-bed). (**-ato** *part. adj.* **-azione** *f.*)

inalzare [A 1] and derivs. See **innalzare**.

inama·bil-e *adj.* unamiable; disagreeable; †hateful. **-mente** *adv.* unamiably; disagreeably. **-ità** *f.* unamiability; disagreeableness.

†**inamare**[1] *tr.* to catch on a hook, to hook.

†**inamare**[2] *vb.* and derivs. See **innamorare**.

inamar-ire [D 2] *tr.* to embitter, to make bitter; to afflict; *intr.* (*aux.* essere) to become embittered; to be troubled. **-ito** *part. adj.* embittered; afflicted.

†**inambrare** *rfl.* to be coloured or perfumed like amber.

inambu *m. indecl.* (orn.) tinamou.

inamen-o *adj.* displeasing, unpleasant, disagreeable; desolate; campagna **-a**, desolate countryside of displeasing aspect. **-ità** *f.* displeasing aspect, unattractiveness.

inamid-are [A 1 S] *tr.* to starch; (joc.) to plaster with cosmetics; *intr.* (*aux.* avere) (chem.) to add starch as an indicator. **-ato** *part. adj.* starched; (fig.) (of a person) stiff, starchy, standing on his dignity. **-atura** *f.* starching; starchiness.

inammenda·bile *adj.* incorrigible; that cannot be amended or improved.

inammissi·bil-e *adj.* inadmissible; unacceptable; (leg.) inadmissible; prova **—**, evidence that should not be accepted; ricorso dichiarato **—**, appeal dismissed (C.C.P.). **-ità** *f.* inadmissibility, unacceptableness; (leg.) dismissal (of appeal) (C.C.P.).

inamovi·bil-e *adj.* irremovable, not subject to dismissal or transfer; (leg.) that cannot be removed by arbitrary power. **-ità** *f.* irremovability, irremovableness; (surg.) plaster-cast for a fracture.

inan-e *adj.* empty, vain, useless; inane; tutti i suoi sforzi furono **-i**, all his efforts were in vain; vanto **—**, empty boast. **-ità** *f.* emptiness; uselessness.

inanell-are [A 1] *tr.* to curl, to form into ringlets; to form into rings; to thread into rings; †to place the wedding ring on the finger of,

to wed as wife; *rfl.* to curl, to go into curls; to be linked. **-ato** *part. adj.* in ringlets; in curls; in rings; threaded through rings; †wedded.

inanim-are [A 1 S] see **inanimire**. **-ato** *adj.* inanimate, lifeless; unconscious, in a faint; lacking animation; cold, indifferent. **-atore** *m.* encouraging, heartening, animating person. (**-atrice** *f.*)

ina·nime *adj.* See **esanime**.

inanim-ire [D 2] *tr.* to encourage, to inspire courage in; to exhort; to instigate; †*intr.* to grow brave, to become filled with courage; *rfl.* to grow bold; to get angry; (of chestnuts) to fill out, to grow. **-ito** *part. adj.* encouraged; heartened; (of a chestnut) filled out.

†**inanire** *tr.* to render vain *or* void; to confound.

inanità *f.* See under **inane**.

inanizione *f.* (med.) inanition; (theol.) self-abasement (of Christ); †vanity, uselessness, futility.

inappag-a·bile *adj.* insatiable, that cannot be satisfied, unquenchable. **-ato** *adj.* unsatisfied.

inappanna·bile *adj.* that cannot be dimmed; unsmirchable.

inappella·bil-e *adj.* (leg.) not open to appeal, inappellable; final; la sentenza è **—**, no appeal lies from the judgement (C.C.P.); (fig.) unappealable, admitting of no appeal. **-mente** *adv.* unappealable, finally, irrevocably. **-ità** *f.* irrevocableness; (leg.) inappellability; **-ità della sentenza**, absence of right of appeal from judgement (C.C.P.).

inappeten-te *adj.* lacking appetite. **-za** *f.* loss of appetite; lack of appetite; sofferente di **-za**, off one's food, suffering from lack of appetite.

inapplica·bil-e *adj.* inapplicable, not applicable. **-mente** *adv.* in a manner that is not applicable. **-ità** *f.* inapplicability; unsuitability.

inapplicazione *f.* lack of application, lack of diligence.

inapprendi·bile *adj.* See **inapprensibile**.

inapprensi·bil-e *adj.* that cannot be learnt; difficult to learn; difficult to grasp, incomprehensible. (**-mente** *adv.* **-ità** *f. indecl.*)

inapprezza·bile *adj.* inestimable, priceless, invaluable; †valueless.

inapproda·bile *adj.* (naut.) not suitable for landing.

inappunta·bil-e *adj.* irreproachable, blameless, faultless. **-mente** *adv.* faultlessly.

inappura·bile *adj.* unverifiable; that cannot be cleared up.

inara·bile *adj.* (agric.) unsuitable for ploughing.

inarato *adj.* (poet.) unploughed.

†**inarborare** *vb.* and derivs. See **inalberare**.

inarc-are [A 2] *tr.* to arch, to curve; **—** la schiena, to bend one's back; **—** le ciglia, to raise one's eyebrows (in surprise); to knit one's brows (in thought). **-amento** *m.* arching, bending, bowing; curving; (naut.) hogging. **-ato** *part. adj.* arched; curved; bowed. (**-atore** *m.* **-atrice** *f.* **-atura** *f.*)

†**inarcocchiare** *vb.* and derivs. See **inarcare**.

†**inardire** *tr.* to embolden.

inaren-are [A 1 C] *tr.* to strew with sand, to sand; to fill with sand. **-ato** *part. adj.* sanded.

inargent-are [A 1] *tr.* to coat with silver; **—** a bagno, to plate with silver; (fig.) to silver, to make to shine like silver, to turn silver. **-ato** *part. adj.* silvered; silver-plated; capelli **-ati**, silvery (grey) hair. (**-atore** *m.* **-atrice** *f.*) **-atura** *f.* see **argentatura**, under **argentare**.

inarguto *adj.* not witty, lacking in subtlety, or sharpness; non **—**, lacking in wit, not without subtlety.

†**inaridare** *vb.* and derivs. See **inaridire**

inarid-ire [D 2] *tr.* to dry up, to make arid; *intr.* (*aux.* essere), *rfl.* to dry up, to wither. **-ito** *part. adj.* dried up; arid; withered.

†**inarmato** *adj.* unarmed; disarmed.

inarmo·nic-o *adj.* (mus.) inharmonious; lacking in euphony. **-amente** *adv.* inharmoniously.

inarmonioso *adj.* (mus.) inharmonious.

†**inarpicare** *vb.* and derivs. See **inerpicare**.

inarrare [A 1] *tr.* (poet.) to give an earnest of; to pledge.

inarrendevol-e *adj.* unyielding, inflexible, unbending. **-ezza** *f.* inflexibility.

inarresta·bile *adj.* that cannot be stopped or arrested; fonte **—**, perennial waters; un moto **—**, a movement (or series of events) that cannot be checked.

inarriva·bil-e *adj.* unattainable, unreachable; (fig.) incomparable; inimitable. **-mente** *adv.* unattainably; (fig.) incomparably; inimitably.

inarsicci-are [A3] *tr.* to roast; to toast; to scorch. **-ato** *part. adj.* roasted; toasted; scorched; *n.m.* scorch; scorching; slight burn.

inarticolat-o *adj.* not articulated; suoni -i, slurred sounds; un-jointed, without articulations. **-amente** *adv.* inarticulately.

inartificios-o *adj.* without artifice; without artificial aids. **-amente** *adv.* unartfully, unartificially.

inascoltato *adj.* unheard; unheeded.

inasin-ire [D2] *tr.* to make an ass of; to make stupid; *intr.* (*aux.* essere), *rfl.* to become an ass, to become asinine, to grow stupid. **-ito** *part. adj.* rendered asinine.

inaspetta·bil-e *adj.* unforeseeable. **-mente** *adv.* unexpectedly, unforeseeably.

†inaspettativato *adj.* expectant, having expectancies.

inaspett-ato *adj.* unexpected, unforeseen; all'-ata, unexpectedly. **-atamente** *adv.* unexpectedly. **†-azione** *f.* sense of surprise; unexpectedness.

†inasprare *vb.* and derivs. See **inasprire**.

inaspr-ire [D2] *tr.* to exacerbate; to embitter; to make harsher; to make more painful; to aggravate; to irritate; to make rough; (of plants) to stunt, to wither; *intr.* (*aux.* essere), *rfl.* to become rough; to become inclement; (of plants) to wither. **-imento** *m.* exacerbation; embittering; aggravation. **-ito** *part. adj.* exacerbated; embittered; harsh; roughened; aggravated; (of plants) stunted, withered.

inast-are [A1] *tr.* (naut.) to hoist on a mast; — la bandiera, to fly the flag; (mil.) — la baionetta, to fix bayonets. **-ato** *part. adj.* hoisted; flying; con le baionette -ate, with fixed bayonets.

inattacca·bil-e *adj.* unassailable; — dalle tarme, moth-proof; (mil.) unassailable, impregnable; (fig.) unimpeachable; irreproachable. **-ità** *f.* (mil.) unassailableness, impregnability.

inattendi·bil-e *adj.* unacceptable, inadmissible; unfounded; unreliable. **-ità** *f.* unreliableness.

inatten-to *adj.* not attentive, inattentive. **-zione** *f.* lack of attention, inattention.

inattes-o *adj.* unexpected. **-amente** *adv.* unexpectedly.

inattingi·bile *adj.* out of reach, unreachable.

inattiv-o *adj.* inactive; inert; sluggish. **-amente** *adv.* inertly; sluggishly. **-ità** *f.* inactivity; inertness; sluggishness; (leg.) inaction; -ità delle parti, want of prosecution (C.C.P.).

inatt-o *adj.* inapt, ill-adapted; unfitted; unskilful. **-amente** *adv.* inaptly. **-itu·dine** *f.* inaptitude, lack of aptitude; lack of skill.

inattua·bil-e *adj.* incapable of realization, impracticable; that cannot be put into effect. **-ità** *f.* impracticability.

inaud-i·bile *adj.* inaudible. **-ito** *adj.* unheard of; incredible; extraordinary; unprecedented; (leg.) unheard; decreto emanato — a altera parte, *ex parte* order (C.C.P.).

†inaugmenta·bile *adj.* that cannot be added to.

inaugurale *adj.* inaugural; orazione —, inaugural address; dissertazione —, thesis for a degree; (hist.) diploma —, charter given by a ruler at the beginning of his reign; giuramento —, inaugural oath taken by a ruler.

inaugur-are [A1a] *tr.* to inaugurate; to dedicate; — una statua, to unveil a statue; — un nuovo edifizio, to open (officially) a new building; (joc.) — un cappello, to wear a new hat for the first time. **-ativo** *adj.* inaugural. **-ato** *part. adj.* inaugurated; dedicated; unveiled; opened (to the public). **-atore** *m.* opener, inaugurator, one who performs an inaugural ceremony. (**-atrice** *f.*) **-azione** *f.* ceremonial opening; dedication; unveiling; inauguration.

inaur-are [A1a] *tr.* (poet.) to gild. **-ato** *part. adj.* gilded. (**-atore** *m.*)

inauspicat-o *adj.* inauspicious, unlucky, ill-omened, unpropitious. **-amente** *adv.* inauspiciously, unpropitiously.

†inavarare *vb.* and derivs. See **inaverare**.

†inavarire *intr.* to become miserly.

†inaverare *tr.* to wound; to strike; to run through with the sword.

inavvedut-o *adj.* inadvertent; careless; thoughtless; imprudent, unwise; **†unnoticed.** **-amente** *adv.* inadvertently; carelessly; thoughtlessly; imprudently, unwisely. **-ezza** *f.* inadvertence; carelessness; inattention; thoughtlessness; imprudence; unwisdom; naïvety.

†inavventura *f.* misfortune; disaster.

†inavvertente *adj.* See **inavveduto**.

inavvertentemente *adv.* inadvertently; heedlessly.

inavvertenza *f.* inadvertence, inadvertency; inattention; heedlessness; carelessness; oversight; per —, inadvertently.

inavvertit-o *adj.* overlooked, unnoticed, unobserved; uninformed; careless; inattentive; heedless. **-amente** *adv.* unthinkingly; inad-

vertently; without noticing; without consideration; without being noticed.

inazione *f.* inaction; idleness; inactivity; (med.) retarding of the vital processes.

inazzurr-are [A1] *tr.* to dye blue, to colour blue; *rfl.* (poet.) to become blue, to take on a blue tint, to turn blue. **-ato** *part. adj.* dyed blue; coloured blue.

inca[1] *f.* (orn.) inca tern, *Naenia inca*.

inc-a[2] *m.* Inca. **-a·ico** *adj.* relating to Inca civilization.

†incacare *tr.* to foul, to dirty (with excrement).

†incacciare *tr.* to pursue, to hunt, to give chase to; (fig.) to excite, to stimulate.

incaci-are [A3] *tr.* to sprinkle with grated cheese. **-ato** *part. adj.* flavoured with cheese, containing cheese; schiacciata -ata, cheese cake. **-ata** *f.* sprinkling of grated cheese.

incadaver-ire [D2] *intr.* (*aux.* essere) to become cadaverous; to become a corpse; to decay. **-imento** *m.* becoming cadaverous; putrefaction, decay. **-ito** *part. adj.* grown cadaverous; decayed, rotten.

†incadere *intr.* to lapse; — in peccato, to fall into sin.

†incagionare *tr.* to give as a reason for; to blame; to cause, to occasion.

incagion-ire [D2] *intr.* (*aux.* essere) to become infirm, to become sickly, to fall into poor health. **-ito** *part. adj.* infirm, sickly, weak.

incagli-are[1] [A4] *intr.* (*aux.* essere) (naut.) to be stranded, to run aground; (fig.) to come to a standstill; to come to a full-stop; *rfl.* to be stranded, to run aground; to encounter obstacles; (joc.) to come to a sudden stop; *tr.* to hinder, to hold up. **-amento** *m.* (naut.) running aground; check, impediment. **-ato** *part. adj.* stranded; brought to a standstill.

incagli-are[2] [A4] *intr.* (*aux.* essere) to coagulate, to clot; to curdle; *tr.* to cause to coagulate; to cause to curdle. **-ato** *part. adj.* coagulated; clotted; curdled.

inca·glio *m.* (naut.) grounding, running aground; obstacle, hindrance, check, impediment; c'è un —, there's something in the way.

†incagnare *vb.* and derivs. See **incagnire**.

incagn-ire [D2] *intr.* (*aux.* essere) to go mad like a dog, to rage. **-ito** *part. adj.* raging mad, rabid.

inca·ico *adj.* See under **inca**[2].

incalappiare [A4] and derivs. See **accalappiare**.

incalavernare [A1] *tr.* (naut.) to parcel with leather (oars, spars, etc.).

†incalcare *tr.* to tread; to pound; to press; to fill to overflowing, to cram.

incalciatura *f.* shape of the stock of a gun.

incalcin-are [A1] *tr.* to plaster; (agric.) — il grano, to mix seed-grain with lime; — le viti, to limewash the vines; *rfl.* to splash oneself with whitewash, or with lime. **-ato** *part. adj.* plastered; mixed with lime; splashed with whitewash, dusted with lime. **-atura** *f.* plastering, limewashing.

incalcola·bil-e *adj.* incalculable; that cannot be calculated. **-mente** *adv.* incalculably, immeasurably.

†incalere *intr.* to be of moment, to be important, to be of concern.

incalescenza *f.* feverishness.

incaligin-are [A1s] *tr.* to obscure with fog or mist; to cloud (the vision). **-ato** *part. adj.* obscured; misty; clouded. **-ire** [D2] *intr.* (*aux.* essere) to become obscured; to grow misty, to cloud over.

incall-ire [D2] *intr.* (*aux.* essere), *rfl.* to form corns, to harden, to become hardened; (fig.) to grow callous; — nel vizio, to become a hardened sinner; *tr.* to harden; lo zappare gli ha -ito le mani, digging has made him horny-handed. **-imento** *m.* hardening; formation of callouses. **-ito** *part. adj.* hardened; horny; dalle mani -ite, horny-handed; callous; avere il cuore -ito, to be hard-hearted.

†incalm-are *tr.* to graft; *rfl.* to become grafted; (fig.) to be joined; to be mingled; to dwell, to be found. **†-ato** *part. adj.* grafted; inserted; joined; placed, established, dwelling.

incalor-ire [D2] *tr.* to warm; (med.) to heat; to inflame; cibi che -iscono, overheating food; *rfl.* to grow warm; to become hot. **-imento** *m.* warming; (med.) heating, inflaming. **-ito** *part. adj.* warmed; overheated; (med.) heated; inflamed.

†incalvare *vb.* and derivs. See **incalvire**.

incalv-ire [D2] *intr.* (*aux.* essere) to go bald; †(of hill-tops) to become covered with snow. **-inire** [D2] *intr.* (*aux.* essere) (joc.) to become a Calvinist; to go bald.

incalz-are [A I] *tr.* to pursue closely, to follow on the heels of; il tempo ~a, time presses; il pericolo ~a, the danger is imminent; (mil.) to hunt or pursue relentlessly; (naut.) legare ~ando, to secure firmly, to wedge; (mus.) to increase the speed of, to hurry. ~amento *m.* chase, close pursuit. ~ando *ger.* (mus.) increasing the speed. ~ante *adj.* pressing, urgent. ~ato *part. adj.* chased, urged, hard-pressed; (herald.) enchaussé. (~atore *m.* ~atrice *f.*) ~ellare [A I] *tr.* (naut.) to make fast (esp. with wedges or the like, to increase the tension). ~o *m.* chase, pursuit, urging (on), pressing; support; stiffening; reinforcement.

†incamare *tr.* to bridle, to check, to restrain.

incamer-are [A I s] *tr.* (leg.) to acquire compulsorily; to forfeit to the public treasury (C.C.); (eng.) to counterbore; †(mil.) to chamber. ~a·bile *adj.*(leg.) liable to forfeiture to the public treasury. ~amento *m.* (leg.) forfeiture to the public treasury. ~ato *part. adj.* (leg.) la cauzione è ~ata, the deposit is forfeited to the public treasury (C.C.); †(mil.) chambered; †imprisoned. †~atura *f.* (mil.) chambering.

incamerellato *adj.* honeycombed, divided into cells; pareti incamerellate, walls full of niches (e.g. in ancient cemeteries).

incamici-are [A 3] *tr.* (techn.) to treat with a coat of whitewash or other material; to line with plaster, to coat; (eng.) to line; (mil.) to earth (a wall); †(naut.) — le vele, to put covers on the sails; *rfl.* (joc.) to put on a shirt, robe or gown. ~ata *f.* (mil.) night sortie (in white shirts for concealment in snow or recognition in the dark). ~ato *part. adj.* whitewashed, coated with whitewash or plaster; faced with masonry, revetted; wearing a shirt, robe or gown; (eng.) lined. ~atura *f.* coat (of lime, plaster, etc.), facing, revetment; (eng.) lining; (mil.) facing, lining (of an earthwork).

incammin-are [A I] *tr.* to put on the road; to put in the way; to initiate, to show the way to; to start (a person) off; *rfl.* (*prep.* per) to set out (for); to make a start; ~iamoci, let's get going; to embark on a career; ~arsi per ingegnere, to be going in for engineering, to study to become an engineer. ~amento *m.* putting on the road; setting off; initiating; starting off; early stages. ~ato *part. adj.* started off; initiated, 'bound for'.

†incampan-are *tr.* (mil.) to bell. †~ato *part. adj.* (mil.) bellmouthed (of a weapon).

incamuffare [A I] and derivs. See **camuffare**.

incanagl-iare [A 4] *tr.* to count among the rabble, to confuse with the rabble; *rfl.* to mix with the rabble, to associate with bad characters. (~iato *part. adj.*) ~ire [D 2] and derivs. see **incanagliare**.

incanal-are [A I] *tr.* to lead (waters) into a channel, to canalize; to direct, to guide (to a certain destination), to put on the road, to send; — un affare, to initiate a transaction, to put an affair in hand; †(mil.) — una colonna, to set a column in motion; †(naut.) to route (ships). ~amento *m.* canalizing; slotting; guiding, directing. ~ato *part. adj.* canalized; directed. ~atura *f.* canalizing; channel; groove; directing; (archit.) fluting (of a column); †(mil.) column (of prisoners).

incancella·bil-e *adj.* indelible; irremovable. ~mente *adv.* indelibly.

†incancellare *tr.* to enclose in gates, to close with a gate.

incancellato¹ *adj.* uncancelled; (fig.) still remembered.

†incancellato² *part.* of **†incancellare**, q.v.

†incancherare *vb.* and derivs. See **incancherire**.

incancher-ire [D 2] *intr.* (*aux.* essere) to become cancerous; (fig.) to become a bore; *tr.* to render cancerous; to irritate; — le ire a, to exasperate, to arouse the ill-feeling or hatred of. (~ito *part. adj.*)

incancrenire [D 2] *intr.* (*aux.* essere), *rfl.* to become gangrenous.

incandescen-te *adj.* incandescent, white-hot. ~za *f.* incandescence; lampada a ~za, electric-light bulb.

incandidire *tr.* to make white; *intr.* to become white; to become incandescent.

†incand-ire [D 2] *tr.* to make luminous; il sole ~isce la luna, the sun gives light to the moon. ~ito *part. adj.* luminous, white.

†incanire¹ *vb.* and derivs. See **accanire**.

†incanire² *vb.* and derivs. See **incanutire**.

incann-are¹ *tr.* (text.) to spool; to wind (warp). ~aggio *m.* (text.) spooling; winding. ~ata *f.* reel-full; net (with canes) for catching mullet; fence of canes. ~ato *part. adj.* (text.) spooled; wound. ~atoio *m.*, ~atore *m.*, ~atrice *f.* (text.) winder. ~atura *f.* (text.) winding.

†incannare² *tr.* to swallow, to gulp down.

†incannare³ *tr.* to tie, to fasten to a stake.

†incannare⁴ *vb.* and derivs. See **ingannare**.

incann-icciata *f.* basket-work; trellis, trellis-work. ~ucciare [A 3] *tr.* to fence with reeds, to trellis; to support (plants) with canes, to stake. ~ucciata *f.* trellis work. ~ucciato *part. adj.* supported by canes, fenced with canes. ~ucciatura *f.* fencing; staking.

†incanovare [A I] *tr.* to put in a wine-shop, to put in store.

incanta·bile *adj.* (mus.) unvocal, unsingable.

incant-are¹ [A I] *tr.* to bewitch, to cast a spell upon, to enchant; (fig.) to enchant, to delight; *rfl.* to stand stock still; to stand as if spellbound; to be charmed, to be enchanted; ~arsi a guardare, to gaze spellbound; (mech.) to break down, to jam. ~ademoni *m. indecl.*, ~adia·voli *m. indecl.* wizard, sorcerer. ~agione *f.* magic, sorcery, enchantment. ~amento *m.* enchantment; magic. ~ato *part. adj.* under a spell, bewitched, enchanted; in a daze; stare lì ~ato, to stand staring; anello ~ato, magic ring; castello ~ato, enchanted castle; armi ~ate, magic weapons; (fig.) charmed, delighted, enchanted; spellbound. ~atore *m.* sorcerer, wizard; enchanter; charmer; *adj. m.* enchanting, fascinating. ~atrice *f.* sorceress; enchantress; charmer; *adj. f.* enchanting, fascinating. †~azione *f.* see **incantesimo**. ~esimo *m.* magic art, sorcery, witchcraft; rompere l'~esimo, to break the spell. ~evole *adj.* bewitching, (fig.) enchanting, charming, delightful. ~evolmente *adv.* delightfully, charmingly.

incant-are² [A I] *tr.* (comm.) to auction; to sell by auction. ~ato *part. adj.* auctioned; sold by auction.

incanto¹ *m.* spell, charm, enchantment, magic; (fig.) charm; delight; d'~, charmingly; marvellously well.

incanto² *m.* auction; public sale; vendere all'—, to sell by auction; mettere all'—, to put up for auction.

incantucciare [A 3] and derivs. See **rincantucciare**.

incanut-ire [D 2] *intr.* (*aux.* essere) to become white-haired; to turn white; to go grey; *tr.* to cause to turn grey or white. ~imento *m.* going white-haired; greying. ~ito *part. adj.* white-haired; grey-haired, turned grey.

incapac-e *adj.* (*prep.* di) unable (to); incapable (of); unfit (for); unable to contain; (leg.) incapable; disabled; — di provvedere ai propri interessi, incapable of managing his own affairs (C.C.); *n.m.* disabled or incapacitated person; *pl.* (leg.) persons under disability (widest Italian term, which includes infants, emancipated infants, the legally incapacitated, persons of unsound mind, etc.) (C.C.); circonvenzione d'—, the procuring, for gain, by undue influence or fraud, of a person under a disability to do a harmful act (C.P.); affidamento di ~i, handing over of persons of disability (C.P.). ~ità *f.* incapacity, inability, lack of ability; unsuitability; (leg.) incapacity; inability; disability; (naut.) lack of space; ~ità della stiva, smallness of the hold.

incapann-are [A I] *tr.* (agric.) to put into a barn, to stack under cover. ~ato *part. adj.* stacked under cover.

incaparb-ire [D 2] *intr.* (*aux.* essere), *rfl.* to become obstinate; to persist obstinately. ~ito *part. adj.* obstinately determined; stubborn.

incap-are [A I] *rfl.* (fam., Tusc.) to take it into one's head; to get it fixed in one's head; *intr.* to take it into one's head; *tr.* to fix on, to decide on. ~ato *part. adj.* having a fixed idea; determined.

incaparrare [A I] and derivs. See **accaparrare**.

incapato¹ (naut.) between two capes; that has doubled a cape.

incapato² *part.* See under **incapare**.

incapestr-are [A I] *tr.* to put a halter on; — i piedi a, to tether, to hobble; *rfl.* (of a horse) to get its legs entangled in the tether; (of persons, fig.) to get into trouble, to become entangled. ~ato *part. adj.* with a halter on; tethered. ~atura *f.* (vet.) pastern gall, gall at or above the pastern caused by chafing of the tether.

incapocch-ire [D 2] *intr.* (*aux.* essere) (of plants) to grow a large head; *rfl.* (fig.) to become obstinate; to grow mulish; to be stupid. ~ito *part. adj.* (of plants) large headed; (fig.) mulish; stupid.

incapon-ire [D 2] *intr.* (*aux.* essere), *rfl.* to be obstinate, to persist unreasonably; (naut.) not to answer the helm when in a dangerous position. ~imento *m.* obstinate persisting. ~ito *part. adj.* obstinate; unreasonably persistent.

incapp-are¹ [A I] *tr.*, *rfl.* to put a cape on; to put on a cloak or gown. ~ato *part. adj.* wearing a cape; cloaked; gowned; (herald.) chapé; *n.m.* (eccl.) gli ~ati, members of a religious guild in their cloaks.

incapp-are² [A I] *intr.* (*aux.* essere; *prep.* in) to fall in (with); to encounter; to meet (with), to run (into); to get (into); — col piede, to stumble; *recip. rfl.* to bump into one another.

incappell-are [A I] *tr.* to put a hat on; (naut.) to cap, to serve; — le sartie, to slip on shrouds and stays over the masthead by means of an eyesplice or cutsplice; †— il vino, to top wine with some more of the same quality; *rfl.* to put on one's hat; (eccl.) to become cardinal; (joc.) to take offence. **-ag·gio** *m.*, **-amento** *m.* (naut.) point of attachment or the whole system of securing shrouds at the upper end. **-ato** *part. adj.* wearing a hat; (joc.) offended. **-atura** *f.* (naut.) shroud plate, hemp collar; action of putting shrouds on a mast; wave coming over the side of the ship and breaking on deck.

†**incapperucciare** *vb.* and derivs. See **incappucciare**.

incappiare [A 4] and derivs. See **accappiare**.

incapponare [A I] and derivs. (naut.). See **accapponare**.

incappott-are [A I] *tr.* to put an overcoat on, to wrap up in an overcoat; *rfl.* to put on an overcoat. **-ato** *part. adj.* wearing an overcoat; wrapped up well against the cold.

incappucci-are [A 3] *tr.* to put a hood on; to muffle up; *rfl.* to put on a hood; to hood oneself; to muffle oneself up; (eccl.) to put one's hood on or up; to take the habit, to enter religion (esp. as friar); (of a horse) to bow the head between the forelegs. **-ato** *part. adj.* hooded; muffled up; (herald., of a falcon) jessed, hooded.

†**incapricciare** *vb.* and derivs. See **incapriccire**.

incapricc-ire [D 2] *rfl.* (prep. di) to take a fancy (to); to get a thing into one's head, to get a bee in one's bonnet; to fall in love (with), to become infatuated (with). **-ito** *part. adj.* infatuated; having a fixed idea.

†**incarare** *vb.* and derivs. See **rincarare**.

incarbonchire [D 2] *intr.*, *rfl.* (agric.) to become mildewed, to be blighted, to have the blight.

incarbon-ire [D 2] *tr.* to carbonize, to char. (**-imento** *m.*) **-ito** *part. adj.* carbonized, charred.

†**incarcare** *vb.* and derivs. See **incaricare**.

incarcer-are [A I s] *tr.* to imprison, to put in prison, to incarcerate. **-amento** *m.* imprisonment; putting in prison; (med.) strangulation (of hernia). **-ato** *part. adj.* imprisoned, incarcerated. **-azione** *f.* imprisonment, confinement, incarceration.

incarco *m.* (poet.) See **incarico**.

incardin-are [A I s] *tr.* to found upon a principle, to make dependent on a principle; *rfl.* to depend upon a principle; to hinge (upon), to turn (upon). **-ato** *part. adj.* hinged.

†**inca·rica** *f.* See **incarico**.

incaric-are [A 2 s] *tr.* (prep. di) to charge (with); to entrust (to); to charge, to instruct; t'-o di vigilarlo, I trust you to watch over him; vorrei -arvi di un favore, I should like to ask you a favour; (leg.) to entrust, to direct; to instruct; — un avvocato, to instruct a lawyer; *rfl.* to take upon oneself (to); to assume responsibility (for); me ne -o io, I will see to it; non me n'-o, I won't bother about it. **-ato** *part. adj.* (prep. di) entrusted (with), responsible (for); holding office; -ato di rappresentare, instructed to represent; professore -ato, university teacher appointed on a temporary basis, the appointment being renewable annually; *n.m.* official, officer, employee; -ato d'affari, chargé d'affaires; -ato di un ufficio, holder of an office; (comm.) business agent; (leg.) -ato di un pubblico servizio, public servant (C.P.).

inca·ri·co *m.* (pl. **-chi**) responsibility, task, charge; office, mission; commission; (leg.) undertaking, charge, appointment, order; per l'— di, by order of; assumere l'— di, to undertake; †obligation, debt; †affront, insult; †blame, dishonour; †annoyance; †(mil.) onslaught.

incarit-atevole, †**-e·vole** *adj.* uncharitable.

†**incarnagione¹** *f.* See **carnagione**.

†**incarnagione²** *f.* See **incarnazione**, under **incarnare**.

incarn-are [A I] *tr.* (theol.) to incarnate; to flesh, to plunge into the flesh of; (fig.) to express in corporeal form, to represent in a person, to express in action; to embody, to incarnate, to be the incarnation of; (paint.) to paint in flesh-colour; †to apprehend, to seize, to grasp (with the mind); †— falconi, to train falcons to seize prey; *rfl.* (theol.) to be incarnate, to become incarnate; (fig.) to be incarnated, to be expressed (in a person or character); to be realized; to be joined, to be united, to be grafted. **-amento** *m.* penetrating of the flesh; joining, grafting. **-ante** *part. adj.* incarnating. **-atino** *adj.* rosy, the colour of a rosy cheek; *n.m.* flesh pink, rosy colour. **-ato** *part. adj.* (theol.) incarnate; (fig.) embodied; realized; incorporated; fused; *n.m.* flesh-colour, rosy,

flesh pink; †blood relation. **-azione** *f.* (theol.) incarnation; (hist.) anni dell'-azione, style of the Incarnation (reckoning years from 25 March); (Ind. rel.) -azioni di Visnu, avatars of Vishnu; (fig.) incarnation, realization; embodiment; corporeal representation; (paint.) flesh-pink, rosy flesh-colour.

incarn-ire [D 2] *intr.* (aux. essere) to grow in (esp. of toenails). **-ito** *part. adj.* ingrowing; unghia -ita, ingrowing toenails; (fig.) un vizio -ito nelle ossa, an incorrigible bad habit.

†**incarognare** *intr.* to putrefy; *rfl.* to become enamoured.

incarogn-ire [D 2] *intr.* (aux. essere), *rfl.* to rot, to putrefy, to become carrion; (of illness) to become chronic, to be deeply rooted; (fig.) to grow lazy, to become good for nothing. **-ito** *part. adj.* rotten; putrefied; -ito nell'ozio, sunk in sloth.

incarrare [A I] *tr.* (mil.) to mount (artillery) on carriages; to mount (tanks) on transporters.

†**incarrozzare** *tr.* to put into a carriage; *rfl.* to take a carriage, to get into a carriage.

incarrucolare [A I s] *tr.* (eng.) to reeve, to fit (a rope round a pulley).

incartapecor-ire [D 2] *intr.* (aux. essere) to become dry and wrinkled like parchment; (fig.) to become dry-as-dust, to become an old fossil. **-ito** *part. adj.* dried up, wrinkled; (fig.) dry-as-dust.

incart-are [A I] *tr.* to wrap up, to wrap in paper; (eng.) to planish; †to put in writing, to describe; †to strike, to hit; *intr.* (aux. avere) to become hard and stiff; la biancheria ha -ato, the laundry has turned out stiff (owing to too much starch or the use of too hot an iron); (silkb.) i bozzoli hanno -ato bene, the cocoons have hardened well; *rfl.* (agric., of grass, etc.) to become tangled or matted. **-amento** *m.* wrapping up; papers; documentation; (leg.) file of documents, dossier. **-ata** *f.* wrapping up; wrapping; paper bag. **-ato** *part. adj.* wrapped in paper, packaged; hard and stiff. †**-eggiare** *tr.* to record, to note down.

incarto *m.* (comm.) carton (sometimes including a coupon to be cut out); (silkb.) hardening of cocoons; (laundry) undesired stiffening of laundry.

incartocci-are [A 3] *tr.* to put into a paper bag; to wrap in paper. **-ato** *part. adj.* wrapped, wrapped in paper.

incartonare [A I c] *tr.* to put between pieces of cardboard; to pack with layers of cardboard; (bookb.) to put (a book) between pasteboards.

incaschito *adj.* old and weak; weakened by illness and old age.

incasell-are [A I] *tr.* to pigeon-hole; (fig.) to shelve, to put on one side; (fig.) to classify rigidly; sono questioni che non si possono — in una sola definizione, such questions cannot be classified under a single heading. **-ato** *part. adj.* pigeon-holed; (fig.) shelved, put on one side.

incass-are [A I] *tr.* to pack in a case (or cases); — un cadavere, to put a corpse in a coffin; — una gemma, to set, to mount a jewel; to put (the movement of a watch) into the case; to fit (the barrels of a gun) to the stock; (comm.) to collect; to cash; (boxing) — colpi, to receive blows, to take punishment; *intr.* (aux. avere) to fit (into a slot, case, cavity, etc.); to tally. **-amento** *m.* packing; fitting; mounting, setting; encasing. **-ato** *part. adj.* packed; fitted; cased; (techn.) flush, fitted, built-in; (archit.) porta -ata, flush-door; fiume -ato, river confined (between high banks, walls or cliffs); strada -ata, sunken road; occhi -ati, sunken eyes, deep-set eyes; (comm.) collected; cashed. **-atore** *m.* (techn.) packer; (boxing) è un buon -atore, he can take a lot of punishment. **-atura** *f.* packing; fitting, setting, encasing; socket, slot, case. **-o** *m.* amount collected; collection; takings; l'-o di un giorno, the daily takings or turnover; i diritti d'-o, collection charges; (eng.) embedding, fitting in, flush mounting; (watchm.) molla d'-o, case spring.

†**incastagnare** *tr.* to reinforce with chestnut wood; *rfl.* to become entangled, to get muddled or confused.

incastell-are [A I] *tr.* to fortify with castles; to fortify like a castle; to mount the castle on (the elephant); †(naut.) to fortify a (ship) fore and aft; †to shut up in a castle; †*rfl.* to encamp; to set up residence. **-amento** *m.* fortifying; fortification; group of forts; (mil. hist.) wooden towers and other constructions raised for fortifying a town. **-ato** *part. adj.* fortified with castles, having many castles or forts; fieno -ato, stacked hay, hay in the rick; (vet.) piede -ato, contracted hoof. **-atura** *f.* (vet.) abnormal contraction (of a horse's hoof); (eng.) frame; support; crankcase; carriage support (of a typewriter); -azione di fondazione, soleplate; (bldg.) scaffolding.

†**incast-o** *adj.* unchaste; impure. †**-ità** *f.* unchasteness; unchaste living; impurity.

incaston-are [A I c] *tr.* to set (jewelry), to mount; to insert; *intr.* (*aux.* avere) (fig.) to introduce fine phrases, to speak with affectation, to indulge in purple passages. **-ato** *part. adj.* (of jewels) set; mounted; inserted. **-atura** *f.* (of jewels) setting; mount.

incastr-are [A I] *tr.* to fit in, to fix in; (techn.) to engage; to enmesh; (bldg.) to restrain; (carp.) — a linguette, to tongue; (naut.) — un albero, to step a mast, (or) to fish a broken mast; (fig.) to insert; *intr.* (*aux.* essere) to fit, to fit in; *rfl.* to become jammed; *recip. rfl.* to fit together. **-amento** *m.* fitting, fit; (med.) impaction. **-ato** *part. adj.* fitted in, fixed in; fitted together; (med.) impacted; (techn.) built-in, restrained; (fig.) inserted, introduced. **-atura** *f.* fitting; fit; (mech., welding) -atura a V, fishmouth splice.

incastro *m.* fitting; fit; (carp.) mortise joint; (naut.) — dell'argano, pigeon-holes of the capstan; stepping of a mast; point where a broken spar is joined; (mil.) gun pivot; cradle bearing; gun-carriage bearing; word-puzzle the solution of which involves fitting one word into another and forming a third (e.g. atto, testa, attestato); frase —, a variation of the puzzle involving a phrase (e.g. morte, strada, mostra d'arte); (billiards) tirar l'—, to aim between the cushion and a ball close to it.

†**incastronire** *intr.* to become stupid.

incatarr-are [A I] *intr.* (*aux.* essere), *rfl.* to catch a cold; to develop catarrh; *tr.* to foul with mucus. **-ato** *part. adj.* suffering from a cold; suffering from catarrh. **-atura** *f.* catching cold; catarrhal condition.

incatarrire [D 2] and derivs. See **incatarrare**.

incatenacciare [A 3] *tr.* to put the chain on (a door, etc.).

incaten-are [A I] *tr.* to chain, to secure with chains; to fetter; to bar with chains; to support with chains; to chain together; to fasten, to secure; (fig.) to captivate, to enthral; to keep in subjection; (naut.) — l'armata, to keep close order, to sail in close formation; (of a convoy) to keep closed up; *rfl.* to be chained, to be bound, to be fastened, to be enchained; *recip. rfl.* to be chained together; (fig.) to be connected, to be closely associated. **-amento** *m.* chaining, securing, strengthening with chains (esp. of defences). **-ato** *part. adj.* chained, fettered; in chains; chained together; on a chain; linked; sciarada -ata, see under **sciarada**; (prosod.) rima -ata, terza rima; (fig.) captivated, enthralled; in subjection. **-atura** *f.* chaining; fastening; securing.

†**incatorbiare** *tr.* to put in prison (cf. **catorbia**).

incatorciare [A 3] *tr.* to bolt (cf. **catorcio**).

incatorzol-ire [D 2] *intr.* (*aux.* essere) (of fruit) to shrivel and remain hard, instead of ripening. **-ito** *part. adj.* shrivelled; (fig.) wizened.

incatram-are [A I] *tr.* to tar. **-ato** *part. adj.* tarred.

†**incatricchi-are** *tr.* to ruffle, to rumple; to dishevel; *rfl.* to become ruffled or rumpled; to become dishevelled. †**-ato** *part. adj.* ruffled, rumpled; dishevelled.

†**incattivare** *tr.* to take prisoner; to hold captive; see **incattivire**.

incattiv-ire [D 2] *tr.* to make bad; to make ill-tempered; to spoil the temper of; (naut.) to foul (a rope); *intr.* (*aux.* essere) to become ill-tempered; (of fruit, etc.) to go bad; to become depraved, to go to the bad; *rfl.* to lose one's temper; to turn ugly. **-ito** *part. adj.* spoilt in temper, made ill-tempered; (naut.) fouled; (of fruit) gone bad; depraved.

†**incaugliare** *rfl.* to become entangled, to be knotted (cf. **incavigliare**).

inca·ut-o *adj.* imprudent, heedless, rash; (leg.) incautious; — acquisto, incautious purchase or acquisition. **-amente** *adv.* rashly, unwisely; imprudently; incautiously.

incavalc-are [A 2] *tr.* to put on horseback, to set astride; — gli occhiali sul naso, to put one's spectacles on; to superimpose; to stagger, to space; (mil.) — le artiglierie sull'affusto, to ship guns on their mountings, cradle or bearings; (knitting) — la maglia, to slip a stitch, (or) to slip one and knit one; *rfl.* to be superimposed; *recip. rfl.* to fall upon one another. **-ato** *part. adj.* superimposed; set astride; astride. **-atura** *f.* bestriding, being astride; superimposing.

incavall-are [A I] *tr.* to superimpose; †*rfl.* to mount on horseback; to provide oneself with a horse (or horses). †**-ato** *part. adj.* (joc.) horsed. **-atura** *f.* (bldg.) truss.

incav-are [A I] *tr.* to hollow out, to make a groove in; to carve deeply; to bore, to pierce, to perforate. **-ato** *part. adj.* hollow, hollowed out; medaglie -ate, ancient coins having a design in relief on one side and corresponding hollows on the other; occhi -ati, deep-set eyes, sunken eyes; (herald.) scudo -ato, targe à bouche. **-atura** *f.* hollowing out; hollow, groove; depression; hollowness; bell'-atura di vita, well-formed waist; l'-atura dei fianchi, rounded hips. **-o** *m.* cavity, depression; lavoro d'-o, intaglio, incised work, incised carving; (carpen.) mortise; (eng.) notch; -o per chiavetta, keyway; (techn.) grooving; (naut.) moulded depth, height of a ship from the keel to the upper deck; belly of a sail.

incavern-are [A I] *tr.* to excavate, to make a cavern (in); *rfl.* (of water) to hollow out a cavern, to flow underground. **-ato** *part. adj.* hollowed out; occhi -ati, very deep-set eyes. **-atura** *f.* subterranean excavation due to water; (mil.) chambering of a gun.

†**incavestrare** *vb.* and derivs. See **incapestrare**.

incavezzare [A I] *tr.* to put a halter on (cf. **cavezza**).

incavicchi-are [A 4] *tr.* to peg, to fasten with a peg. **-ato** *part. adj.* pegged; (of a horse) tied in at the knees, spalla -ata, stiff shoulder (cf. **cavicchio**).

incavigliare [A 4] and derivs. see **accavigliare**; (techn.) to peg, to pin.

incavo *m.* See under **incavare**.

†**incavonare** *vb.* (naut.). See **incaponire**.

incazz-are [A I] *rfl.* (vulg.) to become angry, to fly off the handle, to 'blow up'. **-ato** *part. adj.* angry; irritated.

incazzottare [A I] *tr.* (naut.) — una bandiera, to make up a flag for breaking at the masthead.

ince·dere [B I] *intr.* (*aux.* avere) to walk (with dignity); to pace; to advance; to proceed; to walk in procession; *n.m.* procession.

incelare [A I] and derivs. See **incielare**.

†**ince·lebre** *adj.* obscure, unknown.

incen·d-ere [B I] *tr.* to burn; (surg.) to cauterize; †to fix (a dye); †to incite; †to stimulate; †to vex, to torment; †*intr.* to be displeasing; *rfl.* to catch fire; †to burn with anger. †**-e·vole** *adj.* inflammable; burning, ardent. **-imento** *m.* burning; fire, conflagration; sting, stinging, burning pain.

incendi-are [A 4] *tr.* to set on fire, to set fire to; to set light to; to burn; to burn down; *rfl.* to catch fire, to burn. †**-amento** *m.* conflagration; incentive; incitement. **-ante** *part. adj.* incendiary; burning hot. **-a·rio** *adj.* incendiary; (mil.) bomba -aria, incendiary bomb; (fig.) inflammatory; seditious; occhi -ari, blazing eyes; *n.m.* incendiary, one who commits arson. **-ato** *part. adj.* set on fire; burnt down. (**-atore** *m.* **-atrice** *f.*)

incen·di-o *m.* fire; house on fire; bocca d'—, fire hydrant; pompa d'—, fire-engine, fire-pump; (fig.) ardour, flame (of love); fire (of passion); (leg.) — doloso, arson. †**-oso** *adj.* incendiary; inflammatory; burning.

incendivo *m.* (techn.) percussion composition.

incener-are [A I sc] *tr.* to strew with ashes, to soil with ashes; to cover with cinders; †see **incenerire**; *rfl.* to put ashes on one's head, to humiliate oneself. **-ato** *part. adj.* strewn with ashes. **-azione** *f.* strewing of ashes; (chem.) ashing, calcination.

incener-ire [D 2] *tr.* to reduce to ashes; to cremate; to burn up, to incinerate; (chem.) to calcine, to ash; (hyperb.) con un'occhiata lo -ì, he annihilated him with a blazing glance; *rfl.* to be reduced to ashes; to be cremated; to be incinerated; to be annihilated. **-imento** *m.* incineration; cremation; reducing to ashes; (chem.) ashing. **-ito** *part. adj.* reduced to ashes; cremated; incinerated.

incens-are [A I] *tr.* (rel.) to cense, to incense; (fig., joc.) to flatter, to eulogize. **-amento** *m.* (rel.) censing; (fig.) adulation, flattery, exaggerated praise; società di mutuo -amento, mutual admiration society. **-a·ria** *f.* (bot.) fleabane, *Pulicaria* sp. **-ata** *f.* (rel.) incensation; swing of censer. (**-ato** *part. adj.*) **-atore** *m.* flatterer, adulator. **-atura** *f.* flattery, adulation, fulsome praise. **-azione** *f.* (rel.) censing, incensing. **-iere** *m.* thurible, censer; dare l'-iere sul naso, to praise fulsomely. **-o** *m.* incense; bruciare l'— ai morti, to waste one's pains; (bot.) name given to various incense-yielding plants. **-omanna** *f.* frankincense.

incensur-a·bile *adj.* irreproachable, free from blame, faultless; not meriting censure. **-ato** *adj.* free from blame; (leg.) having no police or criminal record; *n.m.* first offender.

incentivo *m.* incentive; stimulus; incitement; occasion.

incentr-are [A I, A I c] *tr.* to place in the centre, to make central; to concentrate; *rfl.* (*prep.* in) to centre (in); (fig.) to be comprised (in). **-amento** *m.* **-ato** *part. adj.* centred.

incepp-are [A I c] *tr.* to shackle; to hinder, to hamper; (naut.) to stock (the anchor); *rfl.* (eng.) to jam, to stick. **-amento** *m.* impedi-

incepp-are (*cont.*)
ment; obstacle; (eng.) jamming. **-ato** *part. adj.* shackled; impeded; stile -ato, halting style; (naut.) ancora -ata, anchor-chain fouled with the stock. **-atura** *f.* (naut.) fouling (of anchor-chain with the stock).

incer-are [A I] *tr.* to wax, to put wax polish on; *intr.* †to go waxen in colour. **-ata** *f.* application of wax; waterproof material; oil-cloth; oilskin; mackintosh sheet; tarpaulin. **-ato** *part. adj.* waxed, wax-polished; tela -ata, see **incerata**; strong, tough, resistant; †waxen in colour; *n.m.* waterproof material. **-atino** *m. dim.* strip of oilcloth; waterproof sheet; band-lining of a man's hat. **-atoio** *m.* waxed stick for waxing cloth. **-atura** *f.* waxing, polishing; proofing.

†**incercare** *tr.* to search for; to investigate; to examine.

incerchiare [A 4] *tr.* to curve into a circle; to hoop (a cask); †to surround; *rfl.* to become a circle, to take the form of a circle.

†**incer·chio** *adv.* around; in a circle.

incercon-ire [D 2] *intr.* (*aux.* essere), *rfl.* (of wine) to turn sour; (fig.) to go bad. **-ito** *part. adj.* turned sour; vino -ito, wine that is past its prime (cf. **cercone**).

incert-o *adj.* uncertain; variable; hesitating, hesitant, irresolute; doubtful, dubious; luce -a, twilight, poor light; wavering, faltering; tempo —, unsettled weather; (leg.) causa -a, doubtful action or suit; (poet.) -a sabbia, shifting sand; *n.m.* uncertainty; *pl.* occasional earnings, tips, perquisites; gl'-i del mestiere, occupational hazards; (eccl.) -i di stola, stole fees. **-amente** *adv.* uncertainly; with no certainty; doubtfully; hesitatingly. †**-ano** *adj.* see **incerto**. **-arello** *m.*, **-erello** *m.* casual earnings, tip, perquisite. **-ezza** *f.* uncertainty; unreliability; hesitation; irresoluteness; irresolution; -ezza del tempo, unsettled state of the weather. †**-itu·dine** *f.* see **incertezza**.

inceso *part.* of **incendere**, q.v.

†**incespare** *tr.* to cover with shrubs or bushes; *rfl.* to spread like a shrub; *intr.* to take cover in shrubbery.

incespicare [A 2 sc] *intr.* (*aux.* avere) to stumble, to trip; — in una pietra, to trip over a stone; — nel parlare, to hesitate in one's speech, to stammer.

†**incespitare** *vb.* and derivs. See **incespicare**.

incessa·bil-e *adj.* unceasing, incessant, continuous. **-mente** *adv.* unceasingly, incessantly, continuously. †**-ezza** *f.* persistence; perpetualness.

incessan-te *adj.* incessant, continuous, never-ending, perpetual. **-temente** *adv.* incessantly, continuously, perpetually. †**-za** *f.* continuation; con -za, unceasingly.

incesso *m.* solemn pace, dignified progress (cf. **incedere**).

incest-are [A I] *tr.* to pack in a basket. **-ato** *part. adj.* basketed, in baskets.

incest-o *m.* incest; incestuousness; (leg.) incest; (rel.) — spirituale, spiritual incest; †*adj.* unchaste, impure; foul. †**-atore** *m.* one who commits incest. **-uoso** *adj.* incestuous; figlio -uoso, child of incestuous union (C.C.). **-uosamente** *adv.* incestuously.

incett-a *f.* buying, buying up; cornering; forestalling; collecting. **-are** [A I] *tr.* to buy up; to corner; to clear the market of; to monopolize. **-ante** *part. adj.* buying up, cornering; *n.m.* cornerer. **-ato** *part. adj.* bought up, cornered. **-atore** *m.* one who corners the market. (**-atrice** *f.*)

†**inchiavacciare** *tr.* to lock, to bolt.

inchiavard-are [A I] *tr.* to bolt, to fasten with screw-bolts. **-ato** *part. adj.* bolted.

†**inchiavare** *tr.* to lock; to lock out; to lock in; to keep under lock and key.

inchiavato (herald.) *adj.* indented.

†**inchiavellare** *tr.* to nail.

inchiavett-are [A I c] *tr.* (eng.) to key. (**-ato** *part. adj.*) **-atura** *f.* (eng.) keying.

inchiavistellare [A I] *tr.* to bolt (a door); to put the chain on (a door).

inchiedere [B 6] *tr.* to investigate minutely; (leg.) to inquire into, to investigate; †to request.

†**inchie·r-ere** *tr.* to ask about, to inquire. †**-imento** *m.* see **inchiesta**.

inchiesta *f.* inquiry, investigation; organo d'—, fact-finding organ; commissione d'—, committee of inquiry; survey (opinion polls, market research, etc.); (leg.) inquest; investigation, inquiry; fare un'—, to conduct an investigation.

inchin-are [A I] *tr.* to incline, to bow down — la fronte, to bow one's head (in reverence, fear or shame); — l'animo alle preghiere

di, to yield to the entreaty of; — uno, to bow down before someone; *rfl.* to bow; -arsi a uno, to bow to someone; *intr.* (*aux.* essere); *prep.* a) to be inclined (to, towards); †(astron.) see **inclinare**. **-amento** *m.* inclining; bowing; bow; tendency, inclination, propensity. **-ante** *part. adj.* inclining; declining; inclined, tending. †**-ata** *f.* bow, bowing; reverence; obeisance. **-ato** *part. adj.* inclined; bowed down; †humbled. †**-atura** *f.* bend, curve. †**-azione** *f.* bow; reverence, obeisance; inclination, aptitude, disposition. **-evole** *adj.* yielding; inclined; (fig.) prone, having a propensity; †sloping; †descending; †bowed down. (**-evolmente** *adv.*)

inchino[1] *m.* bow; curtsey; accennare un —, to make a bow, to drop a curtsey; nod (when falling asleep).

inchino[2] *apocop. part.* of **inchinare**, q.v.; (poet.) inclined, bowed, bent. **-o·metro** *m.* clinometer.

inchiodacristi *m. indecl.* (bot.) *Lycium europaeum*.

inchiod-are [A I] *tr.* to nail, to nail up, to nail down; — alla croce, to crucify; (joc.) — a letto, to confine to bed; (mil.) to spike (a gun); *rfl.* (naut.) to become locked in the grip of ice or stuck on a reef. **-amento** *m.* nailing. **-ato** *part. adj.* nailed down, nailed; (joc.) è -ata in cucina tutto il giorno, she is stuck in the kitchen all day; (herald.) nailed. **-atrice** *f.* (industr.) box-nailing machine. **-atura** *f.* nailing; (of horses) puncture of the quick of the hoof.

inchiostr-are[1] [A I] *tr.* to ink; to blot, to smudge with ink; to write in ink; *rfl.* to get covered in ink. **-ato** *part. adj.* inked; blotted; smudged with ink; written in ink. **-atore** *m.* (typ.) inker.

†**inchiostrare**[2] *tr.* to shut up in a cloister; to enclose.

inchiostr-o *m.* ink; — di Cina, Indian ink; — copiativo, copying ink; — simpatico, invisible ink; — da stampa, — tipografico, printer's ink; nero come l'—, black as ink, black as pitch, pitch-dark; (fig.) black as thunder, in a bad temper.

inchiu·dere [C 3]. See **includere**.

†**inchiusa** *f.* See **inclusa**.

inchiuso *part.* of **inchiudere**, q.v.

†**inchiusura** *f.* imprisonment.

†**inci** *adv.* See **ivi**.

inciamp-are [A I] *intr.* (*aux.* avere, essere) to stumble, to trip; — in uno, to run into someone, to bump into someone; — nel codice (penale), to fall foul of the law. **-amento** *m.* stumbling, tripping. **-ata** *f.* stumble. **-o** *m.* obstacle, hindrance; pietra d'-o stumbling-block; difficulty; tu sei d'-o, you are in the way, you are a hindrance.

inciden-te *part.* of **incidere**[1], q.v.; *adj.* coming to pass; incident, incidental; (gramm.) proposizione —, parenthesis; (phys.; opt.) luce —, incident light; *n.m.* incident; episode; digression; accident; — mortale, fatal accident; — aviatorio, air crash; (leg.) interlocutory matter; — processuale, interlocutory proceeding (C.C.P.). **-tale** *adj.* incidental, secondary; (leg.) incidental; interlocutory; domanda, eccezione, sentenza -tale, interlocutory application, objection, order (C.C.P.). **-talmente** *adv.* incidentally. **-za** *f.* incidence; fare -za, to digress, to make a digression; articoli d'-za, incidental matters, accessories; per -za, incidentally, accidentally; (opt.) incidence; angolo di -za, angle of incidence; (eng.) -za radiale, radial clearance.

inci·dere[1] [B I] *intr.* (*aux.* avere) to come to pass, to fall out; — sulla spesa, to add to expense; †*tr.* to make a digression concerning.

inci·d-ere[2] [C 3] *tr.* to cut into, to cut, to incise; (art) to engrave, to carve (in wood, stone or metal); to do intaglio work; — ad acqua forte, to etch; (mus.; radio; cinem., etc.) to record, to make a recording of; (industr.) to tap (a rubber tree); *intr.* (*aux.* avere) to record, to make a recording.

incielare *tr.* (poet.) to place in paradise; to place in heaven; to imparadise.

†**incigliare** *tr.* (agric.) to plough over the ridge between two furrows; (fig.) to lay into, to devastate.

incignare [A 5] *tr.* (Tusc.; Neap.) to broach; to initiate; to inaugurate; to handsel; to use for the first time; — un vestito, to wear a new garment for the first time.

incile *m.* intake (to a water-channel or canal).

incimic-ire [D 2] *intr.* (*aux.* essere) to become infested with bugs. **-ito** *part. adj.* bug-ridden.

incimurr-ire [D 2] *intr.* (*aux.* essere) (of dogs) to get distemper; (of horses) to get glanders; (joc., of persons) to catch cold. **-ito** *part. adj.* suffering from distemper; suffering from glanders; suffering from a bad cold.

incincignare [A5] *tr.* (Flor.) to crumple, to crush, to fold (material) inexpertly so that it becomes wrinkled.

incincischiare [A4] and derivs. See **cincischiare**.

†**incinerare** *vb.* and derivs. See **incenerire**.

incinera-tore *m.* incinerator. **-zione** *f.* (agric.) dressing of land with ashes; cremation.

†**incinfrignare** *tr.* to botch, to patch up, to cobble.

incin·gere [c5] *tr.* to gird, to surround, to fence in; *intr.* (*aux.* essere), *rfl.* to conceive, to become pregnant.

†**incinghiare** *vb.* and derivs. See **cinghiare**.

†**incinquare** *rfl.* to be increased fivefold, to return five times.

incinta *part. adj. f.* pregnant, with child, enceinte; — di, pregnant with; *n.f.* expectant mother.

†**incioccare** *tr.* to knock together; to rattle; to chatter (one's teeth).

incipiente *adj.* incipient; in its early stages; *n.m.pl.* (ascetic theol.) beginners.

incipoll-are [A1], **-ire** [D2] *intr.* (*aux.* essere) (of a trunk or branch that has been truncated) to widen and split on exposure to damp. (**-ato** *part. adj.*) **-atura** *f.* mark in wood where it has begun to widen and split (cf. **cipolla**).

incipri-are [A4] *tr.* to powder (the face, hair, etc.); *rfl.* to powder one's face; to powder one's hair; imbellettarsi ed -arsi, to put on powder and make-up. **-ato** *part. adj.* powdered.

inciprign-ire [D2] *intr.* (*aux.* essere), *rfl.* to fester; (fig.) to become enraged; *tr.* to cause to fester. **-ito** *part. adj.* festering, festered; (fig.) evil-tempered; angry; grudge-bearing, unforgiving.

incirca *adv.* about, approximately; round about; nearby; all'—, a un —, nearly (also **in circa**).

incirconciso *adj.*, *n.m.* uncircumcized.

incircoscr-itti·bile *adj.* illimitable; (theol.) uncircumscribable. **-itto** *adj.* uncircumscribed, unlimited, infinite; (theol.) uncircumscribed.

incircoscrizione *f.* freedom from limitations; incircumscription.

†**incischiare** *tr.* to pierce; to cut into small pieces.

incis-ione *f.* incision; cut; notch; (art) engraving; etching; cutting wood-blocks for printing; carving of letters on stone or metal; (surg.) incision; (mus.) gramophone record; recording; (rubber industry) tapping. **-ivo** *adj.* incisive, cutting, penetrating; dente -ivo, incisor; (fig.) stile -ivo, incisive style; *n.m.pl.* incisors. **-o** *part. adj.* incised, engraved; (mus.) riproduttore di musica -a, record-player; *n.m.* (gramm.) parenthesis; sia detto per -o, let it be said in parenthesis. **-ore** *m.* engraver; recorder, recording machine; -ore su disco, disc-recorder. **-orio** *adj.* incising; (med.) sala -oria, dissection room. **-ura** *f.* (anat.) notch; -ura mastoidea, mastoid notch; †incision.

incit-are [A1s, pop. A1] *tr.* to incite; to urge; to stimulate; to instigate; to exhort. **-a·bile** *adj.* readily stimulated; open to incitement. **-amento** *m.* incitement; stimulus; stimulation; insti-gating; (leg.) incitement; instigation; -amento a delinquere, incitement to crime. **-ativo** *adj.* inciting. **-ato** *part. adj.* incited; instigated; stimulated; urged on. **-atore** *m.* inciter; instigator. (**-atrice** *f.*) **-azione** *f.* inciting; instigation.

incitrullire [D2] (Tusc.) *intr.* (*aux.* essere) to become silly, to become stupid; *tr.* to make silly, to cause to become stupid.

†**incittadare** *rfl.* to take up one's abode in a city; to move from the country to the city.

†**incittadinare** *rfl.* to become a citizen; to take on citified ways.

inciuccare [A2] *tr.* (pop.) to make drunk; *rfl.* to get drunk.

inciuch-ire [D2] *intr.* (*aux.* essere) to grow stupid; to continue in ignorance. **-ito** *part. adj.* stupid; ignorant.

incivett-ire [D2] *intr.* (*aux.* essere) to become a coquette, to become a flirt; †to grow saucy; †to be impudent; †to prove to be empty and futile. †**-ito** *part. adj.* bold, saucy; impudent; vain, futile.

incivil-e *adj.* uncivil, rude, discourteous, impolite; ungentlemanly; unladylike; uncivilized, barbarous. **-mente** *adv.* rudely, discourteously, impolitely, uncivilly; barbarously. **-tà** *f.* rudeness, rude behaviour, discourtesy, impoliteness, incivility, want of manners, expression or act of impertinence or discourtesy.

incivil-ire [D2] *tr.* to civilize; *rfl.* to become civilized. **-imento** *m.* becoming civilized; civilizing; state of being civilized. **-ito** *part. adj.* made civilized.

inciviltà *f.* See under **incivile**.

inclem-ente *adj.* severe, merciless; unyielding; inclement, intem-perate; stagione —, inclement season. **-enza** *f.* severity, inclemency.

inclina·bile *adj.* See under **inclinare**.

inclin-are [A1] *tr.* to incline, to lower; to bow; to bend down; to tilt; (fig.) to dispose, to influence; *intr.* (*aux.* avere) to incline, to be inclined; -o a credere, I am inclined to think; to lean; to slope, to slant; (naut.) to list; (during a vessel's construction) to heel (on a sloping slipway); to droop (of a mast); (astron.) to decline; *rfl.* to bow down, to show servility, to abase oneself; to slope, to tilt; (of a building) to lean over; (aeron.) -arsi in curva, to bank. **-a·bile** *adj.* capable of being bent down or lowered. **-amento** *m.* inclining; (astron.) declination; inclination. **-ante** *part. adj.* inclining; tending; †declining, drawing to a close. **-ativo** *adj.* (gramm.) particelle -ative, enclitic particles. **-ato** *part. adj.* bowed down, bent down, lowered, inclined; slanting; sloping; tilted, tilting; lop-sided; disposed, tending, inclined, prone. (**-atore** *m.*) **-atorio** *m.* (*pl.* -atorii) (electr.) dipping needle, in-clinatorium. **-atura** *f.* bend, place where a body bends. **-azione** *f.* inclining; bending, leaning; bend; tilt; inclination; slope; slant; avere -azione per il disegno, to have a bent for drawing; avere una certa -azione per uno, to have a certain liking for someone; fare una cosa per -azione, to do a thing of one's own inclination; (naut.) -azione degli alberi, rake of the masts; (aeron.) -azione in curva, bank; (magnetism) dip; (astron.) inclination, angle between orbital plane and ecliptic; (leg.) -azione al delitto, propensity to crime (C.P.).

inclin-e *adj.* inclined, disposed; bent; bowed. **-evole** *adj.* see **incline**.

inclino·metro *m.* (electr.) dip circle; (surv.; aeron.) inclinometer; (naut.) clinometer; (aeron.) — longitudinale, pitch indicator; — trasversale, bank indicator.

in·clito *adj.* glorious, illustrious, famous; *n.m.* (joc.) il colto e l'—, a phrase signifying a theatre audience (from an antiquated style of addressing the public as 'rispettabile or colto pubblico e inclita guarnigione').

includ-ere [c3] *tr.* to enclose; to include, to comprise; to imply. **-ente** *part. adj.* enclosing; including, comprising; implying.

inclusa *f.* letter enclosed, enclosure.

inclus-ione *f.* including; inclusion; con —, without excluding; (miner.; geol.) inclusion, xenolith; (techn.) — d'aria, air lock. **-iva** *f.* including; inclusion; (eccl.) reception into conclave of cardinal arriving late. **-ive** *Lat. adv.* inclusive of; inclusively. **-ivo** *adj.* inclusive; to be included; implied. **-ivamente** *f.* inclusively. **-o** *part.* of **includere**, q.v.; *adj.* enclosed; included.

inco-are [A def.] *tr.* (leg.) to inchoate. **-ativo** *adj.* (gramm.) inchoative, inceptive. **-ato** *part. adj.* (leg.) inchoate.

incocc-are [A2] *tr.* to notch, to fit (an arrow) to the bowstring; to fasten (the thread) to the spindle; (naut.) to reeve, to slip over the funnel or mast stop (the eyeplate for shrouds, etc.). **-ato** *part. adj.* notched; fitted to the bowstring; (herald.) notched. **-atoio** *m.* (naut.) instrument for putting on the funnel stop or shroud ring. **-atura** *f.* point of notching, fitting or fastening arrow, thread, etc.

incocci-are [A3] *intr.* (*aux.* essere), *rfl.* to persist obstinately; *tr.* (naut.) to secure, to belay, to bring to. **-ato** *part. adj.* obstinate; (naut.) secured, belayed. **-atura** *f.* obstinate persistence; ob-stinacy.

incodard-ire [D2] *intr.* (*aux.* essere), *rfl.* to become a coward, to grow cowardly. **-ito** *part. adj.* grown cowardly.

incoerci·bil-e *adj.* incoercible; unrestrained; not subject to restraint; that cannot be held back; (phys.) incoercible, incompressible. **-ità** *f.* incoercibility.

incoer-ente *adj.* incoherent; disjointed; disconnected; inconsistent. (**-entemente** *adv.*) **-enza** *f.* incoherence; inconnexion; incon-sistency; inconsistent conduct; incongruity.

†**incogita·bile** *adj.* incredible; unthinkable.

inco·gliere [B7] *intr.* (*aux.* essere) to befall, to happen unexpectedly; c'incolse una disgrazia, we had a misfortune; mal gliene incolse, it was unlucky for him, it was a misfortune for him; *tr.* to catch.

inco·gnit-o *adj.* unknown; *adv. phr.* viaggiare in —, to travel incog-nito; nel più stretto —, in strict incognito; *n.m.* unknown quan-tity, unknown factor; unknown person. **-a** *f.* (math.) unknown quantity, unknown; unknown woman; (fig.) egli è un'-a, he's an unknown quantity, he's a dark horse.

incoiare [A4] and derivs. See **incuoiare**.

†**in·col-a** *m.* inhabitant. †**-ato** *m.* habitat. †**-o** *adj.* indigenous.

incoll-are¹ [A1] *tr.* to gum; to glue; to paste; to stick; — manifesti, to stick bills; to size; (jewellery) to cement; (paint.) to coat with gum; *abs.* to put one or more coats of gum on canvas or wood to

incoll·are (*cont.*)
prepare the surface for painting; *rfl.* to get stuck; (eng.) to jam, to stick. **-aménto** *m.* gumming; gluing; pasting; sticking; (eng.) jamming, sticking. **-ato** *part. adj.* gummed; gummy; glued; pasted; stuck; (fig.) frase -ata, phrase stuck in, phrase inserted awkwardly. **-atrice** *f.* (text.) sizing machine; (cinem.) splicer (for film).

incoll·are² [A I] *tr.* to put (a load) on the shoulders of; *rfl.* to sling over one's shoulder. **-ato** *part. adj.* slung over the shoulder. **-atura** *f.* the set of the head (on the shoulders); (of a horse) the head and neck; (racing) vincere di un'-atura, to win by a neck; (naut.) scantlings, thickness of beams at the middle and where they meet the keel.

incoller·ire [D 2] *intr.* (*aux.* essere), *rfl.* to get angry, to become enraged, to lose one's temper, to fly into a passion. **-ito** *part. adj.* furious, enraged.

incolma·bile *adj.* that cannot be filled up; un abisso —, a bottomless abyss; un vuoto —, a gap that cannot be filled.

incolonn·are [A I c] *tr.* (archit.) to set up as a column; to place upon a column; (typ.) to tabulate, to set out in columns; (mil.) to draw up (troops) in columns. **-aménto** *m.* setting up as a column; drawing up in columns; (motor.) -amento predirezionale, instruction to drivers to enter the appropriate lane before turning left or right. (**-ato** *part. adj.*) **-atore** *m.* tabulator (of a typewriter).

†incolorare *intr.* to be tinged, to assume a colour, to become coloured.

incolóre *adj.* See incoloro.

incolóro *adj.* colourless; (fig.) insipid, faded.

incolp·are [A I c] *tr.* to blame, to lay the blame on; ne -o me stesso, I blame myself for it, I am to blame; to inculpate; (leg.) to accuse, to charge; — di un reato, to accuse of a crime; †*intr.* to be guilty, to be to blame. **-a·bile** *adj.* blameworthy, blameable; culpable; †blameless, not blameworthy, guiltless. **-abilménte** *adv.* blamelessly. **†-agione** *f.* see incolpamento or incolpazione. **-aménto** *m.* blaming, censuring, imputation of blame. **-ato** *part. adj.* blamed, accused; (leg.) accused; -ato di falso, accused of forgery; -ato a torto, wrongfully accused. **-atore** *m.* accuser; one who blames. (**-atrice** *f.*) **-azione** *f.* blame, inculpation, incrimination, censure.

incolpévol·e *adj.* blameless, guiltless, innocent. **-ménte** *adv.* blamelessly, innocently.

incólt·o¹ *adj.* uncultivated, wild, waste; (fig.) unkempt, untidy, straggling, neglected; uncultured, uncultivated; *n.m.* waste piece of ground. (**-aménte** *adv.*) **-ézza** *f.* boorishness; lack of culture, ignorance; want of cultivation.

incolto² *part.* of incogliere.

incólum·e *adj.* safe and sound, intact, unhurt, uninjured; tutti sono rimasti -i, there were no casualties. **-ità** *f.* safety; -ità della vita, conservation of life; la pubblica -ità, public safety; (leg.) delitti contro l'-ità pubblica, crimes to the public danger; delitti contro l'-ità individuale, crimes to the danger of the person (C.P.).

†incomandato *adj.* unbidden, not ordered.

incombatti·bile *adj.* unassailable.

incómb·ere [B I def.] *intr.* (not used in compound tenses; *prep.* a) to weigh (upon), to be incumbent (on); non -e a me il dirglielo, it is not my place to tell him. **-ente** *part. adj.* incumbent; impending; *n.m.pl.* duties. **-ènza** *f.* job, errand, task, commission. **-enzare** [A I] *tr.* to entrust; to put upon, to charge.

incombriccol·are [A I s] *rfl.* to join a gang, to join a subversive or criminal society; -arsi con, to join up with. **-ato** *part. adj.* involved in subversive activity, committed to a gang.

incombusti·bile *adj.* incombustible, not combustible, fire-proof. **-ità** *f.* incombustibility, resistance to fire.

incombusto *adj.* (techn.; poet.) unburnt, not burnt.

†incomenzare *vb.* and derivs. See incominciare.

†incomiatare *vb.* and derivs. See accomiatare.

incominci·are [A 3] *tr.* (Tusc., pop.) to begin, to commence, to start; *intr.* (*aux.* essere) to begin; (of an illness) to set in; (*prep.* da) to extend (from); to set out (from). **-aménto** *m.* commencing, commencement, beginning. **-ante** *part. adj.* beginning; il giorno -ante, the early part of the day. **†-ata** *f.* beginning. **-ato** *part. adj.* begun, commenced, started. **†-atore** *m.* initiator; beginner (cf. cominciare).

†incomitato *adj.* unaccompanied.

incommensura·bil·e *adj.* incommensurable, immeasurable; immense. **-ménte** *adv.* immeasurably. **-ità** *f.* incommensurability.

incommercia·bil·e *adj.* unsaleable; not having a price; that cannot be bought and sold. **-ità** *f.* (leg.) unmerchantability.

incommissi·bile *adj.* incapable of being joined or fitted together.

incommisti·bile *adj.* that cannot be mixed.

incommodare [A I s] and derivs. See incomodare.

incom·modo *m.* See incomodo.

incommuta·bil·e *adj.* not changeable; not commutable, unexchangeable; (leg.) incommutable; final. **-ménte** *adv.* incommutably. **-ità** *f.* incommutability.

incomod·are [A I s] *tr.* to cause inconvenience to, to put to inconvenience; to incommode, to inconvenience, to disturb; to trouble; non s'-i, do not get up, don't let me disturb you; scusi se l'-o, forgive my intrusion, forgive me for troubling you. **-ato** *part. adj.* indisposed, slightly unwell.

incò·mod·o *adj.* uncomfortable; inconvenient; annoying, unwelcome; *n.m.* inconvenience, trouble, annoyance; il terzo —, a 'gooseberry' (cf. 'two's company, three's a crowd'); ti levo l'—, I'll make myself scarce; mi levò l'—, he left me in peace, I got rid of him; posso farlo senz'—, it will be no trouble, I can quite easily do that; quant'è il vostro —?, how much do you want for your trouble?; indisposition, infirmity, ailment. **-aménte** *adv.* uncomfortably, inconveniently. **-ità** *f.* inconvenience; indisposition; (naut.) minor damage.

incompara·bil·e *adj.* incomparable, matchless, peerless; beyond compare. **-ménte** *adv.* incomparably. **-ità** *f.* matchlessness, peerlessness.

†incomparare [A I] *rfl.* (joc.) to be thick (as thieves), to chum up to become close friends.

incomparti·bile *adj.* indivisible; indistributable.

incompati·bil·e *adj.* incompatible, contradictory; irreconcilable; intolerable, that cannot be tolerated; (leg.) incompatible; inconsistent. **-ità** *f.* incompatibility; -ità di carattere, incompatibility of temperament; (leg.) -ità del giudice, disqualification of judge (C.C.P.).

incompatto *adj.* not compact.

incompensa·bile *adj.* that cannot be compensated or made good, not liable to compensation.

incompeten·te *adj.* incompetent, without competence, unqualified; (leg.) incompetent; giudice —, judge without jurisdiction; *n.m.* incompetent person, an incompetent; *pl.* incompetent persons, those who have no qualifications. **-teménte** *adv.* incompetently. **-za** *f.* incompetence; lack of qualifications; sollevare l'obiezione di -za di, to challenge the competence of; (leg.) incompetence, want of jurisdiction.

incompianto *adj.* unlamented, unregretted, unwept.

incompiut·o *adj.* incomplete, uncompleted, unfinished; *n.f.* (mus.) l'Incompiuta, the Unfinished (Symphony of Schubert). **-aménte** *adv.* incompletely, not fully. **-ézza** *f.* incompleteness; unfinished state.

incomplessito *adj.* (of persons) well-grown, fully grown, sturdy, of good physique.

incomplesso *adj.* not complex, simple; (gramm.) verbo —, simple verb (not compound).

incomplet·o *adj.* incomplete, imperfect, defective; una serie -a, broken set (e.g. of a journal, etc.); (bot.) incomplete. **-aménte** *adv.* incompletely.

incomport-a·bile, -évole *adj.* intolerable, unbearable, insufferable; inadmissible. **-abilménte** *adv.* intolerably. **-abilità** *f.* intolerableness.

incompòst·o *adj.* disordered; ill-arranged; (mus.) intervallo —, indivisible interval, diastema (in ancient Greek music); movimento per intervalli -i, movement by leaps; †simple, not complex, not compound. **-aménte** *adv.* untidily, in disorder (cf. scomposto).

incomprendi·bile *adj.* not in the same class; unsuitable for inclusion, that cannot be included.

incomprensi·bil·e *adj.* incomprehensible; difficult to understand; un uomo —, an eccentric, a mysterious man, a taciturn and morose man. **-ménte** *adv.* incomprehensibly. **-ità** *f.* incomprehensibility.

incompreso *adj.* not included; not understood, misunderstood, not appreciated; (iron.) un genio —, an unrecognized genius.

incompressi·bil·e *adj.* incompressible. **-ità** *f.* incompressibility.

incomprimi·bil·e *adj.* (phys.) incompressible. **-ità** *f.* (phys.) incompressibility.

incomputa·bil-e *adj.* that cannot be counted, incalculable, incomputable; insignificant, not worth counting. **-mente** *adv.* incalculably.

incomunica·bil-e *adj.* incommunicable; †untransportable. (**-mente** *adv.*) **-ità** *f.* incommunicability.

inconc-are [A 2 c] *tr.* (laundry) to put in soak, to put to soak; to put in the wash-tub; (text.) to steep. **-atoio** *m.* (text.) steeping bowl. **-atura** *f.* (laundry) soaking, soaking in.

inconcepi·bil-e *adj.* inconceivable; incredible. **-mente** *adv.* inconceivably; incredibly. **-ità** *f.* inconceivability, inconceivableness; incredibility, incredibleness.

inconcesso *adj.* not allowed, not granted; forbidden.

inconcilia·bil-e *adj.* irreconcilable; incompatible. (**-mente** *adv.*) **-ità** *f.* irreconcilability; incompatibility.

inconciliato *adj.* unreconciled.

inconcludente *adj.* inconclusive, indecisive; undecided, irresolute.

inconcluso *adj.* unconcluded; undecided.

inconcusso *adj.* unshaken, unmoved; uninjured; †uncorrupted.

†**incon·dito** *adj.* confused, disordered, in disorder, ill-composed.

incondizionat-o *adj.* (leg.) unconditional; (philos.) unconditioned; absolute. **-amente** *adv.* unconditionally; absolutely.

inconfessa·bile *adj.* unspeakable, shameful; unavowable.

inconfesso *adj.* not owning to a charge; (rel.) unconfessed; unshriven.

inconfiden-te *adj.* diffident, lacking in confidence. **-za** *f.* diffidence, lack of confidence.

inconfondi·bile *adj.* unmistakable, not to be confused with anything else.

inconforta·bile *adj.* inconsolable, not to be comforted.

inconfut-a·bile *adj.* irrefutable, inconfutable. **-abilmente** *adv.* irrefutably. **-ato** *adj.* not refuted, not confuted.

incongela·bile *adj.* frost-resisting; olio —, cold test oil.

incongiungi·bile *adj.* that cannot be joined or united.

incongiunto *adj.* not joined.

incongruamente *adv.* See under **incongruo**.

incongruen-te *adj.* inconsistent; not in conformity. **-temente** *adv.* inconsistently. **-za** *f.* inconsistency; inconsistent statements; things not in conformity.

incon·gru-o *adj.* incongruous. **-amente** *adv.* incongruously. **-ità** *f.* incongruity; incongruousness.

inconocchiare [A 4] *tr.* to lay upon the distaff.

inconosci·bil-e *adj.* unknowable, unfathomable. **-mente** *adv.* in a way that man cannot know. **-ità** *f.* unfathomableness.

†**inconosciuto** *adj.* not known; unknown, unheard of, strange (cf. **sconosciuto**).

†**inconquassa·bile** *adj.* unshakable; unbreakable.

inconsapevol-e *adj.* unaware; ignorant; uninformed; unconscious. **-mente** *adv.* without being aware, unawares; unwittingly; unconsciously. **-ezza** *f.* ignorance; want of information; unconsciousness; unawareness.

incon·sci-o *adj.* unconscious; *n.m.* (psych.) the unconscious. **-amente** *adv.* in one's unconsciousness (cf. **inconsapevole**).

inconseguen-te *adj.* inconsequent; falsely inferred; inconsistent. **-za** *f.* inconsequence; inconsistency.

inconsidera·bile *adj.* inconsiderable, insignificant; †imperceptible; †unimaginable.

inconsiderat-o *adj.* unconsidered; inconsiderate, thoughtless; rash, foolish; impetuous. **-amente** *adv.* without consideration; inconsiderately, thoughtlessly; rashly, foolishly, impetuously. **-ezza** *f.* inconsiderateness; lack of consideration; thoughtlessness.

inconsiderazione *f.* see **inconsideratezza**, under **inconsiderato**.

inconsisten-te *adj.* unsubstantial; lacking in consistency; unreal; ill-founded, unfounded, without foundation; inconsistent. **-za** *f.* lack of foundation; lack of consistency; inconsistency.

inconsola·bil-e *adj.* inconsolable. **-mente** *adv.* inconsolably.

inconsolato *adj.* (poet.) disconsolate.

inconsonante *adj.* (mus.) discordant.

†**inconspi·cuo** *adj.* not visible, invisible.

inconsueto *adj.* unusual, strange, extraordinary, unaccustomed.

inconsult-o *adj.* ill-advised, injudicious; thoughtless, unthinking, imprudent, rash. **-amente** *adj.* injudiciously; thoughtlessly, unthinkingly.

inconsum-a·bile *adj.* inconsumable, unconsumable, not consumable; †unending, never-ending. **-ato** *adj.* unconsumed, not exhausted; everlasting, enduring.

inconsunto *adj.* unconsumed, not exhausted, enduring; never emptied, ever full.

inconsu·tile *adj.* seamless; (rel.) tunica —, seamless robe (of Christ).

incontadin-are [A I] *tr.* to make countrified; *rfl.* to become a countryman, to go in for country life; to become boorish. **-ato** *part. adj.* countrified; turned rustic or boorish.

incontamina·bile *adj.* incorruptible, not liable to contamination.

incontaminat-o *adj.* uncontaminated, undefiled, pure; incontaminate. (**-amente** *adv.*) **-ezza** *f.* purity.

†**incontanente** *adv.* See **incontinente**[2].

†**incontasta·bile** *adj.* See **incontrastabile**.

incontempla·bile *adj.* that cannot be contemplated.

†**incontenente** *adv.* See **incontinente**[2].

incontenta·bil-e *adj.* insatiable; exacting, hard to please. **-mente** *adv.* insatiably. **-ità** *f.* insatiability; exacting standards.

incontesta·bil-e *adj.* unquestionable; incontrovertible; (leg.) incontestable; undisputed. **-mente** *adv.* incontestably, undisputably, incontrovertibly. **-ità** *f.* incontrovertibility.

incontinen-te[1] *adj.* incontinent, intemperate, unrestrained; *n.m.* incontinent person. **-temente** *adv.* incontinently, intemperately, without restraint. **-za** *f.* incontinence, lack of restraint, intemperance; (theol.) incontinence; (med.) incontinence; -za d'urina, enuresis, bed-wetting.

incontinente[2] *adv.* immediately, straightway, forthwith; †— che, as soon as.

†**inconto** *adj.* rough, unpolished, uncultivated, inelegant.

†**incontra** *prep., adv.* See **incontro**[2].

incontradici·bile *adj.* incontrovertible, not open to contradiction.

incontraf-facente *adj.* counterfeiting, forging, simulating. **-fatti·bile** *adj.* inimitable, that cannot be counterfeited.

incontr-are [A I c] *tr.* to meet, to come across, to run into, to fall in with, to encounter; — il favore di, to be well received by, to please, to be pleasing to, to find favour with; to face, to meet, to stand up to; †to come towards with hostile intent; †to go to do honour to; †to go towards, to come towards, to approach; †— le mani intorno a, to clasp one's hands round; *intr.* (*aux.* essere) to occur, to happen; to be pleasing, to be liked, to be a success; (archit.) to correspond, to balance, to be in balance; *recip. rfl.* to meet each other; to agree, to correspond, to fit; i geni s'-ano, great minds think alike; to clash, to come into conflict. **-ato** *part. adj.* met, encountered. **-atura** *f.* meeting, encounter; conjuncture; predicament.

incontrasta·bil-e *adj.* indisputable, incontestable; unavoidable; irresistible; invincible. **-mente** *adv.* indisputably; irresistibly.

incontrastato *adj.* undisputed; uncontested.

incontro[1] *m.* meeting, encounter; oh, cara, che bell'—!, my dear, how lovely to see you!; favour, favourable reception; la sua proposta ebbe buon —, his proposal was well received; joint, joining; conjuncture, occasion; duel; (sport) match; — triangolare, three-cornered fight; (archit.) fittings; matching, harmony, balance; (paint.) soggetto di —, favourite subject, subject frequently treated.

incontro[2] *adv.* opposite, over there, across the way; †in opposition, unfavourably; *adv. phr.* all'—, on the other hand, on the contrary, otherwise; †in exchange; *prep.* (foll. by 'a') towards; opposite; against; andare — a, to go to the help of, *or* to meet, to face; (comm.) venire — a, to meet; †to move towards with hostile intent.

incontrover-so *adj.* undisputed, not controverted, not in dispute, unquestioned; (leg.) not disputed, not contested. **-ti·bile** *adj.* incontrovertible, unquestionable, indisputable. **-tibilmente** *adv.* incontrovertibly; unquestionably.

inconturb-a·bile *adj.* imperturbable. **-ato** *adj.* not perturbed, imperturbed, unmoved.

inconvenevol-e *adj.* unsuitable; unbecoming; inconvenient. **-mente** *adv.* unsuitably; unbecomingly; inconveniently. **-ezza** *f.* unsuitableness; impropriety.

inconvenien-te *adj.* unsuitable; unbecoming; improper, not right; inconvenient; *n.m.* disadvantage, drawback; snag, catch; defect; trouble, annoyance, obstacle, inconvenience. **-temente** *adv.* unsuitably; unbecomingly; improperly; inconveniently. **-za** *f.* unsuitableness; impropriety; inconvenience.

inconversa·bile *adj.* unsociable.

inconverti·bil-e *adj.* inconvertible; immutable; not interchangeable, not exchangeable; not amenable to conversion; (comm.) inconvertible. **-mente** *adv.* immutably. **-ità** *f.* inconvertibility; immutability.

inconvertito *adj.* unconverted, not converted; not exchanged.

inconvinci·bile *adj.* difficult to convince; impossible to convince.

incoppigliare [A4] *tr.* (eng.) to split pin.

incoraggi-are [A3] *tr.* to encourage; to promote; to incite; *rfl.* to take courage, to take heart. **-amento** *m.* encouraging; encouragement; promoting, inciting. **-ante** *part. adj.* encouraging; heartening. **-ato** *part. adj.* encouraged; heartened. (**-atore** *m.* **-atrice** *f.*)

incoraggire [D2] and derivs. (Tusc.). See **incoraggiare**.

incorare [A1 d] and derivs. See **incuorare**.

incord-are [A1] *tr.* to cord, to rope, to string, to tie up; — l'arco, to string one's bow; (mus.) to string, to furnish with strings; — l'orologio, to wind up a pendulum clock; *rfl.* to become stiff (e.g. of muscles, joints, etc.). **-amento** *m.* (mus.) tension (of strings); (med.) rigidity of muscles or joints owing to prolonged work or exercise. **-ato** *part. adj.* cording, roping, stringing; (med.) muscoli -ati, muscles made stiff or knotted. **-atura** *f.* (mus.) stringing (act of); stringing (i.e. arrangement and tuning of a set of strings); (med.) stiffening of muscles or joints.

incorn-are [A1] *tr.* to butt with the horns; to gore; to be unfaithful to (one's husband); to seduce the wife of, to cuckold; *rfl.* (vulg.) to persist obstinately, to be obstinate. **-ato** *part. adj.* gored; cuckold. **-atura** *f.* disposition, nature; obstinate behaviour, obstinacy, mulishness; (naut.) deadeye, sheave at the masthead.

incornici-are [A3] *tr.* to frame, to set in a frame; to serve as a frame for. **-ato** *part. adj.* framed, set in a frame. **-atura** *f.* framing; frame.

incoron-are [A1 c] *tr.* to crown; to award a prize to; — le tazze di vino, to fill the wine-cups to the brim; (joc.) — il marito, to be unfaithful to one's husband; (mus.) to put a pause-sign over (a note). **-amento** *m.* crowning. **-ata** *f.* (rel.) the B.V.M. crowned, the Incoronata; her feast or church; (mus.) pause-sign. **-ato** *part. adj.* crowned; una valletta -ata di poggi, a valley set in a frame of hills. **-azione** *f.* coronation; (rel.) -azione di Maria Vergine, Coronation of the B.V.M. (in heaven); -azione d'una Madonna, crowning of a (statue of the) Madonna (in church); (paint.) -azione della B. Vergine, Coronation of the Blessed Virgin (the subject of several famous pictures).

†incorporal-e *adj.* not pertaining to the body; spiritual; non-corporeal. **†-mente** *adv.* non-corporeally.

incorpor-are [A1 s] *tr.* to incorporate; to assimilate; to embody; (mil.) to enlist (recruits in a regiment); to assimilate (troops); to incorporate or embody (units) into a large formation; (leg.) to incorporate; *rfl.* (acc. of prn. si) to be incorporated, to be united, to unite, to mix; (dat. of prn. si) to annex; -arsi una provincia, to annex a province. **-a·bile** *adj.* that can be incorporated. **-amento** *m.* incorporation, uniting, unification, annexation; (theol.) -amento mistico, incorporation into the Mystical Body (of the Church). **-ato** *part. adj.* incorporated; assimilated; annexed; -ato a, incorporated in, annexed to; (eng.) motore -ato, built-in motor. **-azione** *f.* incorporation; union; unification, annexation; confiscation; assimilation.

incorpo·re-o *adj.* incorporeal, immaterial, having no body; disembodied; incorporate. **-amente** *adv.* incorporeally. **-ità** *f.* incorporeality, incorporeity.

†incorre *vb.* and derivs. See **incogliere**.

incorreggi·bil-e *adj.* incorrigible; incurable. **-mente** *adv.* incorrigibly. **-ità** *f.* incorrigibleness.

incorrent-are [A1] *tr.* (archit.) to fix battens on. **-ire** [D2] *rfl., intr.* (aux. essere) to become stiff as a board; to stiffen. **-ito** *part. adj.* gone stiff; stiffened.

incorr-ere [C5] *intr.* (aux. essere; prep. in) to run (into); — nel pericolo, to run into danger; — in una multa, to incur a fine; — in difficoltà, to come up against difficulties; to make an onrush, to make an attack; †to occur, to come to pass, to fall out; *tr.* (leg.) to incur; — spese legali, to incur legal costs; — l'ira di, to incur the wrath of. **-imento** *m.* incurring; occurrence; encounter.

incorrett-o *adj.* not corrected; incorrect; improper. **-amente** *adv.* incorrectly; improperly. **-ezza** *f.* incorrectness; impropriety; dishonesty.

incorrezione *f.* lack of correction; incorrectness, faultiness.

incorrott-o *adj.* uncorrupted; not decayed, not decomposed. **-amente** *adv.* with integrity; virtuously.

incorrutti·bil-e *adj.* not liable to decay; incorruptible; eternal; everlasting. **-mente** *adv.* without being liable to decay or corruption. **-ità** *f.* incorruptibleness.

incorruzione *f.* spotlessness, purity; incorruption.

†incorsamento *m.* incursion.

incorsatoio *m.* (carp.) moulding-plane.

incorso *part.* of **incorrere**, q.v.; **†***n.m.* incursion.

incortin-are [A1] *tr.* to fit with curtains, to curtain off. **-ato** *part. adj.* curtained, curtained off.

incoscien-te *adj.* unconscious, without consciousness; unaware; unconscientious, without conscientiousness; irresponsible; *n.m.* unconscientious person; irresponsible person; se non pensi ai tuoi, si vede che sei un —, if you show no consideration for your family, you are behaving like an irresponsible person. **-za** *f.* unconscientiousness, lack of conscientiousness; unconsciousness.

incospi·cuo *adj.* inconspicuous.

incostan-te *adj.* changeable, fickle, inconstant; variable; unsettled. (**-temente** *adv.*) **-za** *f.* fickleness, inconstancy, changeableness, mutability.

incostituzional-e *adj.* unconstitutional. **-mente** *adv.* unconstitutionally. **-ità** *f.* unconstitutionality; unconstitutional act.

†incotto *adj.* scorched; *n.m.* scorch-mark.

†incoturnito *adj.* wearing the buskin.

†incover-chiare, †-tare *vbs.* and derivs. See **coverchiare**.

increanza *f.* bad manners; impoliteness, incivility; impolite action.

increato *adj.* (theol.; philos.) uncreated, uncreate.

incredi·bil-e *adj.* unbelievable, incredible. **-mente** *adv.* unbelievably, incredibly. **-ità** *f.* incredibility.

incre·d·ulo *adj.* incredulous, unbelieving, sceptical; (rel.) unbelieving; *n.m.* unbeliever. (**-ula** *f.*) **-ulità** *f.* incredulity, scepticism.

increment-o *m.* increase, increment; (gramm.) word-building (by adding terminations, suffixes, etc.); (math.) increment; dare — a, to increase, (comm.) to favour, to push the sales of. **-are** [A1 c] *tr.* to increase, to add an increment to, to increment; *intr.* (aux. avere) to grant an increment. **-ato** *part. adj.* increased, incremented. **-atore** *m.* (radio) booster.

†increp-are *tr.* to scold, to rebuke. **†-azione** *f.* scolding, rebuke. **†-ore** *m.* anger; avere -ore, to be angry.

incresc-ere [B9 c] *impers.* (aux. essere; prep. a) to be displeasing (to), to occasion displeasure or regret; to be wearisome; m'-e, I regret, I'm sorry; **†***rfl.* to feel compassion. **†-enza** *f.* regret; annoyance. **-evole** *adj.* see **increscioso**. **-imento** *m.* displeasure, regret. **-ioso** *adj.* troublesome, annoying; unpleasant; regrettable (cf. **rincrescere**).

incresp-are [A1 c] *tr.* to wrinkle; to curl; to pleat; — la bocca, to curl one's lip; *rfl.* to grow wrinkled; to become creased; to cockle up. **-amento** *m.* creasing, wrinkling; rippling; curling; (mus.) trilling, warbling. **-ato** *part. adj.* wrinkled; cockled; curled; pleated; ribbed; (of water) rippled, ruffled; (herald.) dancy; dancetty. **-atura** *f.* wrinkle; ripple; curl; pleat; (text.) curliness; -atura di ritorno, curling back.

incretare [A1] *tr.* to cover or smear with clay; *rfl.* to become like clay.

incretin-ire [D2] *tr.* to make stupid; (fig.) è un lavoro che -isce, it is a job that drives you dotty; *intr.* (aux. essere) to become an idiot; to grow stupid. (**-imento** *m.*) **-ito** *part. adj.* made stupid; driven silly.

incret-o *m.* (med.) incretion. **-o·rio** *adj.* (med.) incretory, endocrine.

incrimin-are [A1 s] (leg.) to incriminate; to bring a criminal charge against. **-a·bile** *adj.* incriminatory. **-ato** *part. adj.* incriminated; criminally charged. **-azione** *f.* incrimination; bringing of criminal charge.

incrin-are[1] [A1] *tr., intr.* (aux. avere), *rfl.* to crack. **-ato** *part. adj.* cracked; flawed. **-atura** *f.* crack; flaw.

†incrinare[2] *vb.* and derivs. See **inclinare**.

incrisalid-are [A1 s] *intr.* (aux. essere) (ent.) to pupate. **-azione** *f.* pupation.

†incristallare *tr.* to turn to ice.

incritica·bile *adj.* not open to criticism; beyond criticism.

incroci-are [A3 c] *tr.* to cross; — le braccia, to fold one's arms, (fig.) to stand idle; (naut.) to cross (a track); — la rotta a un bastimento, to cross the bows of a ship; — i pennoni, to square the yards; — le gomene, to cross the cables; to overlap; — le tavole, to lap the planking clinker fashion; (mil.) — le armi, to cross swords, (fig.) to go into action; †to form a pike palisade; — le baionette, to thrust forward bayonets as in the position of standing at ease; — i tiri a, to subject to cross-fire; *recip. rfl.* to cross (of persons, letters, etc. travelling in opposite directions);

incroci-are (*cont.*)
to intersect; *intr.* (*aux.* avere) (naut.) to stand on and off maintaining a station at sea; to cruise; to patrol. **-aménto** *m.* crossing;
criss-cross; cross-breeding. **-ata** *f.* (archit.) intersection of cross-
springers in a groined roof; †cross-roads. **-ato** *part. adj.* crossed;
punto -ato, cross-stitch; parole -ate, crossword puzzle; (finan.)
assegno -ato, crossed cheque; (mil.; fig.) fuochi -ati, cross-fire;
(agric.) lavori -ati, cross-ploughing; (opt.) fili -ati, hair lines,
cross lines. **-atore** *m.* (naut.) cruiser. NOTE: In the Italian Navy
distinctions persist, such as light or heavy cruiser. In the British
Navy no such distinction is now used and even the term 'battle-
cruiser' is only applicable to that obsolete class. **-atura** *f.*
crossing; cross; point of intersection; (naut.) crossing of two
cables.

incrocicchi-are [A4] *tr.* to interlace; *rfl.* to form a network. **-aménto**
m. interlacing; network. **-ato** *part. adj.* interlaced; criss-crossed.

incrocio *m.* crossing, intersection; cross-roads; hybrid, cross; cross-
fertilization; crossing (of letters in the post); passing (e.g. of
trains).

incrodare [A1] *rfl.* (rock-climbing) to get stuck (i.e. to be unable to
go up or down).

incrolla·bile *adj.* unshakable; firm; steadfast; unwavering.

†**incronicare** *tr.* to chronicle; *rfl.* to waste one's time, to become
involved in long and useless activity.

incrost-are [A1] *tr.* to make a crust on, to cover with crust; to cover
with a thin layer; (archit.) to encrust, to overlay. **-aménto** *m.*
encrusting. **-ato** *part. adj.* (*prep.* di) encrusted (with); (archit.)
overlaid. **-atura** *f.* incrustation; (archit.) facing, inlay; -atura di
caldaia, boiler scale; tartar (deposited on teeth); plaster. **-azione**
f. incrustation, deposit, fouling, scale, fur; (motor.) -azione
carboniosa, carbon deposit.

†**incrosticato** *adj.* encrusted; crusted over, crusty.

†**incrucciato** *adj.* angry.

incrudel-ire [D2] *tr.* to make cruel; *intr.* (*aux.* essere) to become
cruel; to be pitiless; to rage furiously, to be inflamed; (*aux.*
avere) to perform acts of cruelty, to behave mercilessly; — contro,
to treat cruelly; *rfl.* to be exasperated; to become furious; to
become pitiless or cruel. **-iménto** *m.* cruel or ferocious behaviour.
-ito *part. adj.* cruel; pitiless, merciless; †painful.

incrud-ire [D2] *intr.* (*aux.* essere) (of weather or climate) to become
inclement, to deteriorate, to worsen, to become more severe;
(of persons) to become harsh or cruel; (metall.) to work-harden;
tr. to make harsh; to make worse, to aggravate; to embitter.
-iménto *m.* (metall.) work-hardening. **-ito** *part. adj.* worsened,
more severe, harsher.

incruento *adj.* bloodless; vittoria incruenta, victory without bloodshed; (theol.) il sacrificio — della Messa, the unbloody sacrifice
(of the Mass, in contrast with the bloody sacrifice of the
Cross).

incrunare [A1] *tr.* to put through the eye of a needle; to fill or thread
(a needle); (fig.) — l'ago, to put a piece of work in hand.

incrusc-are [A2] *tr.* to cover with bran; to fill with bran; *rfl.* (joc.)
to become a member of the Crusca Academy; to use stilted
language; to waste one's time with pedantic and useless details.
-ato *part. adj.* containing too much bran.

incub-atrice *f.* incubator. **-azione** *f.* incubation; hatching; (anct.
rel.) incubation (practice of sleeping in a temple, esp. of Aesculapius,
to receive help or healing from the god).

in·cubo *m.* nightmare, incubus; weight on one's mind; burden.

incude *f.* (poet.). See **incudine**.

incu·dine *f.* anvil; esser fra l'— e il martello, to be between the
devil and the deep sea; dura più l'— che il martello, the oppressed
will outlast the oppressor; (anat.) incus; (meteor.) anvil cloud;
piano dell'—, anvil surface; corni dell'—, anvil horns; coda dell'—,
anvil point.

inculc-are [A2] *tr.* to inculcate; — buone abitudini a, to inculcate
good habits upon; to impress upon; bisogna -argli che smetta,
it must be impressed upon him that he has to stop. **-ato** *part. adj.*
inculcated. (**-atore** *m.* **-atrice** *f.*) **-azione** *f.* inculcation; incul-
cating; reiteration, frequently repeated lesson.

incult-o *adj.* rough; untutored, uncultivated, uncultured. **-aménte**
adv. roughly; in ill-tutored fashion. **-ura** *f.* lack of culture.

incumbenza *f.* See **incombenza**.

incuna·bolo *m.* incunabulum, incunable.

incuna·bulo *m.* See **incunabolo**.

incune-are [A6] *tr.* to wedge; to drive in, to fix in; *rfl.* to be wedged;
to penetrate like a wedge; (fig.) to penetrate. **-aménto** *m.* wedging;
driving in; (med.) impaction. **-ato** *part. adj.* wedged; driven in;
(med.) impacted.

incuocere [C15] *tr.* to scorch; of frost, to nip (plants).

incuoi-are [A4] *intr.* (*aux.* essere), *rfl.* to become leathery; *tr.* to
back with leather. **-ato** *part. adj.* leathery; leather-backed.

incuor-are [A1d] *tr.* to encourage, to exhort; to console; *rfl.* to take
courage. **-aménto** *m.* encouragement. **-ante** *part. adj.* encouraging, heartening. **-ato** *part. adj.* encouraged, heartened.

incup-ire [D2] *tr.* to hollow out, to deepen; (dyeing) — una tinta,
to sadden a colour; *intr.* (*aux.* essere), *rfl.* to become hollowed out,
to deepen; to grow ill-humoured, to become surly, gloomy or
melancholy; a quelle parole si è -ito, at these words he began to
scowl.

incura·bil-e *adj.* incurable; incorrigible; *n.m., f.* chronic invalid,
incurable. **-mente** *adv.* incurably. **-ità** *f.* incurableness.

incur-ante *adj.* careless, unheeding; indifferent; — del pericolo,
heedless of danger; — del dovere, neglectful of one's duty.
-anza *f.* carelessness, heedlessness; indifference; negligence.

incu·ria *f.* negligence, carelessness, indifference; (leg.) neglect; carelessness; — volontaria, wilful neglect.

incurios-ire [D2] *tr.* to make curious, to excite (the) curiosity of;
to arouse the interest of; *rfl., intr.* (*aux.* essere) to become curious.

incursióne *f.* (mil.; naut.) raid; — aerea, air-raid; incursion; inroad;
†inundation.

incurv-are [A1] *tr.* to bend, to curve; *rfl.* to bend, to become bent;
to bulge. **-a·bile** *adj.* unbendable; bendable, capable of being
bent or curved. **-aménto** *m.* bending; bend, curve. **-ato** *part. adj.*
curved; bowed, bent. **-atura** *f.* bending; bend, curve; curvature.
-azione *f.* bend, curve; curvature. †**-e·vole** *adj.* bowed, bent.
-ire [D2] *intr.* (*aux.* essere) to grow bent, to become bowed.
-ito *part. adj.* bent, bowed. **-o** *adj.* bent, curved, bowed.

†**incusare** *tr.* to accuse.

incuso *adj.; n.m.* (antiq.) incused (coin), esp. early Italic.

incusso *part.* of **incutere**, q.v.; *adj.* inspired, instilled; †impelled.

incustodito *adj.* unguarded, untended, without a keeper.

incu·tere [B1 def.] *tr.* to arouse, to excite; — rispetto, to command
respect; — timore a, to strike terror into; — coraggio, to instil
courage.

indacanuri·a *f.* (med.) urocyanosis, indicanuria.

in·daco *m.* indigo; color —, blue indigo; (bot.) indigo, *Indigofera
tinctoria*.

indag-are [A2] *tr.* to investigate, to inquire into; to conduct research
into; *intr.* (*aux.* avere) to make inquiries; la Questura -a, the
police are making inquiries. **-a·bile** *adj.* capable of being investigated. **-aménto** *m.* investigating; inquiry. **-ato** *part. adj.* investigated; inquired into. **-atore** *m.* inquirer, searcher, investigator,
researcher; *adj.* uno sguardo -atore, an inquiring glance, a
searching glance. **-atrice** *f.* inquirer; *adj.* mente -atrice, an
inquiring mind. **-azione** *f.* investigation; inquiry; research.

inda·gine *f.* inquiry, investigation; search; research; far delle indagini
su, to conduct research into, to inquire into.

†**indanaato**[1] *adj.* enamoured of Danae.

†**indanaato**[2] *adj.* changed into money.

†**indanaiare** *tr.* to chequer; to spot.

indantrene *m.* (chem.; industr.) indanthrene.

indarno *adv.* (poet.) in vain, uselessly; esser —, to be useless.

†**inde** *adv.* thence.

†**indebil-ire, -itare** *vbs.* and derivs. See **indebolire**.

indebitaménte *adv.* See under **indebito**.

indebit-are [A1 sc] *tr.* to burden with debts, to cause to run into
debt; *rfl.* to run into debt, to get into debt, to contract liabilities;
-arsi con, verso, to get into debt with. **-aménto** *m.* getting into
debt; running up bills; indebtedness; liabilities. **-ato** *part. adj.*
in debt; burdened with debts; -ato fin agli occhi, up to the eyes
in debt; indebted; beni -ati, mortgaged property.

indebit-o *adj.* not due, not owing; undeserved; undue, improper;
(leg.) undue; appropriazione -a, misappropriation (C.P.), embezzlement; — arricchimento, unjust enrichment; *n.m.* that which
is undeserved; (leg.) pagamento dell'—, payment of that which is
not owing (C.C.). **-aménte** *adv.* unduly; wrongfully; undeservedly.

indebol-ire [D2] *tr.* to weaken, to enfeeble; — la disciplina, to relax
discipline; (photog.) to reduce; (leg.) to impair (C.P.); *rfl.* to grow
weak, to grow feeble; (of sound) to become faint; (of colour)

indebol·ire (*cont.*)
to grow faded. **-imento** *m.* weakening, enfeeblement; (leg.) impairment; **-imento** di un senso, impairment of a sense (C.P.). **-ito** *part. adj.* weakened, enfeebled; faint; faded, toned down, softened (of colour); (leg.) impaired.

indec-ente *adj.* indecent, obscene, improper; untidy, in one's working clothes; vestito —, shabby, dirty garment. **-entemente** *adv.* indecently; vestito **-entemente**, untidily dressed, wearing one's working clothes. **-enza** *f.* indecency, obscenity; act of indecency; untidiness, untidy appearance.

indecifr-a·bile *adj.* indecipherable; illegible; enigmatic. **-ato** *adj.* undeciphered.

indeciṣ-ioṇe *f.* indecision, irresolution, uncertainty, hesitation. **-o** *adj.* undecided, irresolute, doubtful, hesitant.

indeclina·bile *adj.* (gramm.) indeclinable; invariable; (fig.) inevitable, inescapable, unavoidable; †inflexible, unyielding.

indecomponi·bile *adj.* (scient.) indecomposable, indivisible.

indecompọsto *adj.* undecayed, not decomposed.

†**inde·core** *adj.* dishonoured.

†**indecoro** *adj.* indecorous, improper; *n.m.* indecorum, impropriety.

indecorọṣ-o *adj.* unworthy, unbecoming, undignified, indecorous, unseemly; indecent. **-amente** *adv.* unworthily; indecorously; indecently.

†**indefensi·bil-e** *adj.* indefensible. †**-mente** *adv.* indefensibly; overpoweringly.

indefesṣ-o *adj.* untiring, unwearying, indefatigable; unrelenting; unceasing. **-amente** *adv.* untiringly; unceasingly.

indefetti·bil-e *adj.* unfailing; faultless. **-mente** *adv.* unfailingly; faultlessly. **-ità** *f.* faultlessness.

indeficien-te *adj.* never-failing, inexhaustible. **-temente** *adv.* inexhaustibly. **-za** *f.* inexhaustibleness.

indefini·bil-e *adj.* indefinable; enigmatic; (joc.) nondescript. **-mente** *adv.* indefinably; enigmatically.

indefinit-o *adj.* indefinite, not defined, vague; persona **-ita**, unspecified person, anyone; (gramm.) indefinite. **-amente** *adv.* indefinitely; vaguely, imprecisely.

indeforma·bile *adj.* indeformable.

indegnare [A 5] and derivs. See **indignare**.

indẹgn-o *adj.* unworthy; base, worthless; (leg.) unfit; unworthy. **-amente** *adv.* unworthily; undeservingly. **-ità** *f.* unworthiness; baseness; worthlessness; indignity; è un'**-ità**!, it's a scandal!; (leg.) unfitness; **-ità** dell'adottante, unfitness of adoptive parent; **-ità** dell'adottato, unworthiness of adopted child (C.C.).

indeiscen-te *adj.* (bot.) indehiscent. **-za** *f.* (bot.) indehiscence.

indele·bil-e *adj.* indelible; ineffaceable; enduring, eternal. **-mente** *adv.* indelibly; enduringly.

indeliber-ato *adj.* unpremeditated. **-atamente** *adv.* without forethought, on the spur of the moment. **-azioṇe** *f.* lack of forethought, hastiness.

indelicat-o *adj.* wanting in delicacy, indiscreet; unscrupulous. **-amente** *adv.* indelicately; indiscreetly. **-ẹzza** *f.* want of discretion; lack of scruple; act of indiscretion; unscrupulous action.

indemaglia·bile *adj.* (of a knitted garment) interlock; (of a stocking) non-laddering.

indemani-are [A 4] *tr.* (leg.) to incorporate in an estate. **-amento** *m.* (leg.) incorporation in an estate. **-ato** *part. adj.* (leg.) incorporated in an estate.

indemoni-are [A 4] *tr.* to cause to be possessed by a devil, to make mad; to make furious; *rfl.* to become possessed by a devil; to behave like one possessed; to become furious. **-ato** *part. adj.* possessed; tempo **-ato**, wretched weather, devilish weather.

†**indenaiato** *adj.* well-off; moneyed.

indene *m.* (chem.) indene.

indenn-e *adj.* unhurt, uninjured, undamaged, unharmed; (leg.) harmless; not to be held liable. **-ità** *f.* compensation, damages, indemnity; expenses allowance, expenses (reimbursed); **-ità** di soggiorno, subsistence allowance; **-ità** carovita, cost of living allowance or bonus; **-ità** di alloggio, accommodation allowance; (mil.) allowance, for rations, etc.; (leg.) compensation; conduct-money; fee; indemnity; **-ità** di carovita, cost-of-living allowance; **-ità** di sosta, demurrage; fissare un'**-ità**, to assess compensation or indemnity; richiedere un'**-ità**, to demand compensation; **-ità** al testimone, witness' conduct-money; **-ità** all'esperto, expert's fee (C.C.P.). **-iẓẓare** [A 1] *tr.* to compensate, to make good, to

reimburse, (leg.) to indemnify. (**-iẓẓato** *part. adj.*) **-iẓẓazione** *f.* action of compensating; indemnifying. **-iẓẓo** *m.* compensation, payment for damages, indemnity.

indent-are [A 1] *intr.* (aux. avere) to cut teeth, to teethe; *tr.* (naut.) — la catena, to bring the cable to the capstan, to bring to; (mil.) to fortify, to endow with dragon's teeth or other anti-tank obstructions. (**-ato** *part. adj.*) **-atura** *f.* teething.

indentrare [A 1 c] *rfl.* (*prep.* a) to penetrate (into).

indẹntro *adv.* inside, within; sta troppo —, it is too far in; tagliare più —, to cut more deeply; all'—, inwards; si apre all'—, it opens inwards.

indepreca·bile *adj.* inexorable, inevitable, unavoidable.

inderoga·bil-e *adj.* (leg.) that cannot be derogated from; that cannot be cut down (C.C.P.). **-ità** *f.* (leg.) unsusceptibility to be cut down; **-ità** convenzionale della giurisdizione, impossibility of derogating from jurisdiction by agreement (C.C.P.).

indescrivi·bil-e *adj.* indescribable. **-mente** *adv.* indescribably.

indeṣidera·bil-e *adj.* undesirable; ospite —, unwelcome guest. **-ità** *f.* undesirability.

†**indeṣinente** *adj.* unending, endless.

†**indestinare** *vb.* and derivs. See **destinare**.

indetermin-a·bile *adj.* indeterminable. **-atẹzza** *f.* indefiniteness, indeterminateness. **-ativo** *adj.* (gramm.) indefinite. **-ato** *adj.* indeterminate, indefinite, undecided, uncertain; imprecise, vague, undetermined; (leg.) indeterminate; unspecified; indefinite; domanda **-ata**, unspecified claim; a tempo **-ato**, for indefinite period. **-atamente** *adv.* indeterminately. **-azioṇe** *f.* indefiniteness, irresolution, uncertainty.

indeterminiṣmo *m.* theory of free-will, indeterminism.

indett-are [A 1 c] *tr.* to coach, to prime; lo hanno **-ato**, they put him up to it; *recip. rfl.* to have an understanding, to agree beforehand (what to say or do). **-ato** *part. adj.* primed; prepared beforehand. **-atura** *f.* priming; coaching; put-up job.

indẹtto *part.* of **indire**, q.v.

indevo-to *adj.* not devout, undevout. (**-tamente** *adv.*) **-zioṇe** *f.* lack of religious devotion, scanty zeal.

indi *adv.* (poet.) thence; then, thereafter, afterwards; — a poco, after a little while; †— che, as soon as; †— appresso, afterwards.

In·dia *pr.n.f.* (geog.) India; le Indie Orientali, the East Indies; le Indie Occidentali, the West Indies; (bot.) canna d'—, canna, Indian shot, *Canna indica*; castagno d'—, horse-chestnut, *Aesculus hippocastanum*; fico d'—, fruit of the cactus, *Opuntia ficus-indica*; also the plant; noce d'—, coconut, *Cocos nucifera*; zafferano delle Indie, turmeric, *Curcuma longa*; pollo d'—, turkey; porcellino d'—, guinea-pig; uomo d'—, very short man; una specie d'—, a mine of wealth.

indiadem-are [A 1] *tr.* to crown with a diadem. **-ato** *part. adj.* crowned, wearing a diadem.

indiamant-are [A 1] *tr.* to cause to shine like diamonds; to change into diamonds. (**-ato** *part. adj.*)

Indiana[1] *pr.n.f.* (geog.) Indiana. -

indiana[2] *f.* See under **indiano**.

indian-o *adj.* Indian; Red Indian; *n.m.* Indian; Red Indian, redskin; far l'—, to feign ignorance. **-a** *f.* Indian woman; Indian girl; Red Indian squaw. **-iṣmo** *m.* Indian studies. **-ista** *m.* Indianist.

indĩ-are [A 6] *tr.* (rel.; poet.) to deify, to make a god; to make godlike; to cause to share in the divine nature; *rfl.* (rel.; poet.) to be deified; to become like God or a god; to be made one with God; to be lost in God. **-ato** *part. adj.* deified. **-azioṇe** *f.* apotheosis, deification.

indiavol-are [A 1 s] *tr.* to make devilish; to cause to be possessed by a devil; to bedevil; *rfl.* to become furious, to fly into a rage. **-amento** *m.* bedevilling. **-ato** *part. adj.* possessed by a devil; devilish; very naughty; extremely lively; tempo **-ato**, very stormy weather; lavoro **-ato**, devilish hard work. **-ìo** *m.* row, hubbub, pandemonium.

indic-are [A 2 s] *tr.* to point out; to point to, to point at; to indicate, to show; to suggest, to advise. **-a·bile** *adj.* that might be indicated or suggested; advisable. **-ativo** *adj.* (gramm.) indicative; *n.m.* (gramm.) indicative mood. **-ato** *part. adj.* pointed out; pointed at; indicated; obvious; recommended, suitable, fit, proper; è l'uomo **-ato**, he is the right man; *n.m.* the obvious thing; the person indicated; (leg.) assignee (C.C.). **-atore** *m.* indicator, gauge; directory; **-atore** telefonico, telephone directory; **-atore** delle strade ferrate, railway guide; **-atore** stradale, sign-post;

indic·are (*cont.*)
cartello -atore, road sign; -atore del voto, vote indicator; (naut.) -atore delle correzioni, fire-control table; (chem.) indicator; (orn.) honey-guide; *adj.* indicating, indicative; serving as an indicator; (naut.) fuoco -atore, flare on a lifebuoy or torpedo. **-atrice** *f.* indicator; (math.) indicatrix; *adj. f.* indicative. **-azione** *f.* indication, information, direction; (med.; pharm.) indication; (leg.) assignment (C.C.); -azione di pagamento attiva, assignment of debt by creditor; -azione di pagamento passivo, assignment by debtor to creditor of debt due to debtor.

in·dice *adj.* (*prep.* di) indicative (of); il dito —, the forefinger, the index-finger; *n.m.* forefinger, index-finger; (of a book) index *or* contents; sign; (eccl.) Index; mettere all'Indice, to put on the Index; essere all'Indice, (joc.) to be banned, (joc.) to be ostracized, to be sent to Coventry; (eng.) pointer, indicator, hand, needle; (math.) index; (scient.) index, value; — di rifrazione, refractive index; (mus.) indici acustici, vibration numbers.

†**indi·cere** *vb.* and derivs. See **indire**.

indici·bil-e *adj.* unspeakable, unutterable, inexpressible, indescribable. (**-mente** *adv.*)

†**indi·cio** *m.* See **indizio**.

in·dico *m.* See **indaco**.

indicolite *f.* (miner.) indicolite.

indietr·o *adv.* behind; back; backwards; voltarsi —, to turn round; andare avanti e —, to go to and fro; essere —, to be behind the times, not up to date; (of a clock or watch) to be slow; (motor.) dare macchina —, to reverse, (fig.) to hold back, to withdraw; punto —, back stitch; (naut.) dare —, to go astern; (naut. command) macchina — a mezza forza!, half speed astern!; (motor.) marcia —, reversing, backing; *excl.* stand back!, make way!. **-eggiare** [A 3 c] *intr.* (*aux.* avere, essere) to (draw) back; to give way.

indifendi·bil-e *adj.* indefensible. **-mente** *adv.* indefensibly.

indifeso *adj.* undefended; unprotected; unarmed.

indifferen-te *adj.* indifferent; mi è —, it's all the same to me; immaterial, unimportant; unconcerned, uninterested, not interested; indifferent; impartial; per me è persona —, I neither like nor dislike him; not different; (chem.) inert; una somma non —, a considerable sum of money; (meteor.) equilibrio — dell'aria, adiabatic lapse rate; (theol.; philos.) indifferent. **-temente** *adv.* indifferently; indiscriminately. **-tismo** *m.* indifferentism, adiaphorism. **-za** *f.* indifference, lack of interest, unconcern, apathy; (theol.; philos.) indifference.

indifferi·bil-e *adj.* that cannot be deferred, that cannot be delayed. **-mente** *adv.* urgently.

indi·geno *adj.* native, indigenous; home-grown; *n.m.* native.

indigen-te *adj.* extremely poor, indigent, destitute; *n.m.* pauper, a poor man; *pl.* gli -ti, the poor. **-za** *f.* poverty, indigence, penury, destitution.

†**indi·gere** *intr.* (*prep.* di) to be in need of, to lack, to want.

indigeri·bil-e *adj.* indigestible; insupportable, unendurable; that cannot be stomached; una persona —, an insufferable person. **-ità** *f.* indigestibility; intolerableness.

indigest-i·bile *adj.* indigestible. **-ione** *f.* indigestion; prendere un'-ione, to get indigestion; (fig.) more than enough, plethora, surfeit. **-o** *adj.* indigestible; undigested; (of the stomach) out of order; (joc.) sickening, boring; (fig.) confused, uncoordinated.

indi·gete *m.* (Rom. rel.) native and patronal (deity); deified local hero; *adj.* relating to such. NOTE: this is the usual (nineteenth century) Italian interpretation of Lat. *indiges, pl. indigetes*, which is used of a special class of Roman gods but whose exact meaning is still in dispute.

indign-are [A 5] *tr.* to excite the indignation of, to make indignant; *rfl.* to be indignant; to be angry, to feel indignation; to be roused to anger; to rage. **-ato** *part. adj.* indignant; angry; shocked, disgusted. **-azione** *f.* indignation, wrath.

†**indigno** *adj.* and derivs. See **indegno**.

indigo·fera *f.* (bot.) indigo, *Indigofera indica*.

indigotina *f.* (chem.) indigotin.

indigrosso *adv.* See **digrosso**.

indilata·bile *adj.* unexpansive, not dilatable.

indilegua·bile *adj.* impossible to disperse.

indiligen-te *adj.* not diligent, lacking in diligence, not industrious. **-za** *f.* lack of diligence, idleness.

indimentica·bil-e *adj.* unforgettable, never-to-be-forgotten, memorable. **-mente** *adv.* unforgettably; memorably.

indimostr·a·bile *adj.* indemonstrable, not susceptible of proof. **-abilità** *f.* indemonstrability. **-ato** *adj.* unproved.

in·dio *m.* (chem.) indium.

indipenden-te *adj.* independent; — da, independent of, free from; underivative; self-reliant; unrelated; (gramm.) proposizione —, main clause. **-temente** *adv.* independently; in an independent manner; -temente dalla cagione suddetta, quite apart from the above-mentioned cause; vivere -temente, to lead an independent existence. **-za** *f.* independence.

indire [B 10] to announce, to declare, to fix, to arrange; to appoint; to establish; to summon; — un'adunanza, to call a meeting.

indirett-o *adj.* indirect; oblique; (mil.) tiro —, indirect fire; (leg.) indirect; prova -a, indirect evidence; circumstantial or presumptive evidence; danni -i, consequential damages; *adv. phr.* per —, indirectly. **-amente** *adv.* indirectly; obliquely.

†**indiri·gere** *vb.* and derivs. See **indirizzare**.

indirizz-are [A 1] *tr.* to direct; — il pensiero a Dio, to turn one's thoughts to God; to dedicate; to send, to refer; — una convocazione, to address, to send out, a letter of convocation; *rfl.* (*prep.* a) to direct one's steps (towards), to make one's way (towards); to set out (for); to apply (to); to go to see; to refer. **-amento** *m.* directing; addressing; ordering. **-ato** *part. adj.* directed; addressed; referred; headed, heading, tending. (**-atore** *m.*) **-atrice** *f.* addressing machine.

indirizzo *m.* direction, course, turn; gl'indirizzi seguiti, the lines followed (e.g. in research, in an article, etc.); guiding rule; address; domicile; qual'è il suo —?, what is your address?; discourse, speech, address; petition; dedication.

indiscerni·bil-e *adj.* imperceptible; impalpable; indiscernible. **-mente** *adv.* imperceptibly; impalpably. (**-ità** *f.*)

indisciplin-a *f.* lack of discipline, indiscipline. **-a·bile** *adj.* intractable, unruly, indisciplinable, not amenable to discipline. **-atezza** *f.* unruliness, disorderly conduct. **-ato** *adj.* undisciplined, ill-trained; disorderly.

indiscolpa·bile *adj.* that cannot be exculpated, disculpated or cleared from blame.

indiscret-o *adj.* indiscreet; inquisitive; imperceptible, indistinct. (**-amente** *adv.*) **-ezza** *f.* indiscretion.

indiscrezione *f.* indiscretion; commettere un'—, to commit, to be guilty of, an indiscretion; si seppe per —, it leaked out owing to an indiscretion; rashness.

indiscusso *adj.* undiscussed; indisputable, beyond dispute; self-evident.

indiscuti·bil-e *adj.* unquestionable, indisputable; beyond dispute. **-mente** *adv.* unquestionably; indisputably.

†**indi·sia** *f.* kind of silk cloth used for lining.

†**indisiare** *tr.* to fill with longing, to cause to desire.

indispensa·bil-e *adj.* indispensable; basic; unavoidable; (leg.) indispensable; condizione —, indispensable condition; *n.m.* what is necessary; l'— per l'accampamento, basic camping equipment. **-mente** *adv.* indispensably. **-ità** *f.* indispensableness.

indispett·ire [D 2] *tr.* to make angry, to vex, to annoy; *rfl.*, *intr.* (*aux.* essere) to become angry, to be vexed. **-ito** *part. adj.* angry; vexed, annoyed; piqued.

indisporre [B 21] *tr.* to annoy, to impress unfavourably, to disgust; to trouble; to cause to become indisposed.

indisposizione *f.* indisposition, slight malaise.

indisposto *part.* of **indisporre**, q.v.; *adj.* indisposed; unwell, poorly; troubled; annoyed; (finan.) denaro —, idle money; †not suitable, inapt.

indisputa·bil-e *adj.* unquestionable; indisputable. **-mente** *adv.* unquestionably; indisputably.

indisputato *adj.* undisputed.

indissipa·bile *adj.* that cannot be dissipated, scattered or dispersed.

indissolu·bil-e *adj.* indissoluble. **-mente** *adv.* indissolubly. **-ità** *f.* indissolubleness.

indissoluto *adj.* united, unseparated.

indistacca·bil-e *adj.* undetachable; inseparable. **-mente** *adv.* inseparably.

indistingui·bil-e *adj.* indistinguishable; imperceptible. **-mente** *adv.* indistinguishably; imperceptibly. **-ità** *f.* imperceptibleness.

indistint-o *adj.* indistinct; confused, blurred; vague, indeterminate; faint. **-amente** *adv.* indistinctly; confusedly; vaguely; tutti -amente, every single one without exception, all to a man.

indistinzione *f.* indistinctness; confusion; †lack of discernment.

indistrutti·bil-e *adj.* indestructible. **-mẹnte** *adv.* indestructible. **-ità** *f.* indestructibleness.

indisturbato *adj.* undisturbed.

†**indisusato** *adj.* unusual; unaccustomed.

†**inditto** *part.* of **indire**, q.v.

indiumizzato *adj.* (eng.; metall.) indium-plated.

indi·via *f.* (bot.) endive, *Cichorium endivia.*

individual-e *adj.* individual; particular, personal; libertà —, personal freedom. **-mẹnte** *adv.* individually. **-işmo** *m.* individualism; egoism, selfishness. **-ista** *m.* individualist; egoist. **-ità** *f.* individuality; important person, personality. **-izzare** [A 1] *tr.* to specify, to individualize. (**-izzato** *part. adj.* **-izzazione** *f.*)

individu-are [A 6] *tr.* to characterize; to individualize; to specify exactly; to locate; to single out; to pin-point. **-a·bile** *adj.* easily identifiable, recognizable. **-ato** *part. adj.* characterized; individualized; specified; located; singled out. **-azione** *f.* individualization; individualizing; location, locating; (leg.) identification; effect of sorting out; particular designation (C.C.); sigla di -azione, identification mark.

indivi·du-o *adj.* individual; single and indivisible; *n.m.* individual; person, fellow. †**-ità** *f.* individualness.

†**indivinare** *vb.* and derivs. See **indovinare**.

indivisamẹnte *adv.* See under **indiviso**.

†**indivisare** *tr.* to describe, to relate.

†**indivisato** *adj.* dressed in uniform, in livery.

indivişi·bil-e *adj.* indivisible, inseparable; joint; (leg.) immobile —, real property that cannot be partitioned (C.C.); (rel.) tunica —, seamless robe (of Christ); *n.m.* (math.) prime number. **-mẹnte** *adv.* inseparably. **-ità** *f.* indivisibility; (leg.) -ità delle obbligazioni, indivisibility of liabilities (C.C.).

indiviş-o *adj.* undivided; (leg.) capitale —, joint capital; proprietà -a, owned in common; per —, pro —, in common; †per —, for all one is worth, with all one's might and main; (bot.) foglia -a, simple leaf; (mus.) intervallo —, interval not filled in with intermediate notes; (theol.) la -a Trinità, the undivided Trinity. **-amẹnte** *adv.* without distinction; jointly.

indivoto *adj.* and derivs. See **indevoto**.

indi·zi-o *m.* sign; indication; symptom; clue; (leg.) sign; indication; — di prova, a piece of circumstantial evidence. **-are** [A 3] *tr.* to point to; to render suspect; to throw suspicion on; (leg.) to suspect. **-a·rio** *adj.* (leg.) presumptive; prova -aria, circumstantial evidence. **-ato** *part. adj.* suspect; (leg.) suspected on circumstantial evidence.

indizione *f.* (hist.) indiction, fiscal period of fifteen years (fixed A.D. 312); †intimation, notice.

Indo *pr.n.m.* (geog.) the Indus river.

indo·cil-e *adj.* unruly, undisciplined, recalcitrant; not amenable. **-mẹnte** *adv.* in an unruly or undisciplined manner. **-ità** *f.* unruliness, lack of discipline.

indocil-ire [D 2] *tr.* to discipline; to train; to render docile; (of materials) to soften, to make fit for working. **-ito** *part. adj.* disciplined; trained; docile.

Indocin-a *pr.n.f.* (geog.) Indo-China. **-ẹse** *adj.* Indo-Chinese; *n.m.,f.* native of Indo-China.

indolc-ire [D 2] *tr.* to sweeten; (agric.) — le olive, to make olives more palatable (by applying a special fertilizer to the trees); (fig.) to mitigate, to sweeten, to soften; to make tractable; *intr.* (aux. essere) to become sweeter, to sweeten; to grow milder.

in·dole *f.* character; disposition, nature; l'— umana, human nature; temperament; lo fa per —, it is his nature to do it; cavallo d'—focosa, spirited horse; l'— di una lingua, the genius of a language; l'— di una malattia, the nature of an illness.

indol-ente *adj.* indolent, negligent, apathetic; inert; listless; insensible; (med.) painless. **-entemẹnte** *adv.* indolently; listlessly. **-enza** *f.* indolence; apathy; indifference; listlessness, laziness. **-enzire** [D 2] *tr.* to benumb, to make numb; *intr.* (aux. essere) to be benumbed; to become numb or torpid. **-enzimẹnto** *m.* numbness; stiffness; soreness; **-enzito** *part. adj.* numb, benumbed; mi è -enzito il collo, I have got a stiff neck; ho il piede -enzito, my foot has gone to sleep.

indol-ire [D 2] *tr.* to cause to ache, to give pain; *rfl.* (aux. essere) to ache; to feel pain or discomfort. **-imẹnto** *m.* aching, stiffness, soreness. **-ito** *part. adj.* aching, stiff, sore.

indolore *adj.* painless; (med.) parto —, natural childbirth, painless childbirth.

indoma·bil-e *adj.* untamable, indomitable, invincible; (techn.) pietra —, intractable stone. (**-mẹnte** *adv.*)

indomandato *adj.* unasked.

indomani *m.* l'—, the next day, the day after, the morrow; *adv. phr.* l'—, on the morrow.

indomato *adj.* untamed, refractory.

indo·mit-o *adj.* untamed, unsubdued; indomitable; (techn.) pietra -a, intractable stone. **-amẹnte** *adv.* indomitably.

indonn-are [A 1] *rfl.* to become mistress; -arsi di, to dominate, to master; †to become a woman, to become womanly, to increase in womanly virtues; †to turn into a woman. **-ire** [D 2] *rfl. intr.* (aux. essere) (of a girl) to grow up, to become a woman.

indor-are [A 1] *tr.* to gild; (fig.) — la pillola, to sugar the pill; (cul.) to brush yolk of egg over before cooking. **-amẹnto** *m.* gilding. **-ato** *part. adj.* gilded; (cul.) brushed with yolk of egg. (**-atore** *m.* **-atrice** *f.*) **-atura** *f.* gilt; gilt applied, gilding.

indormentire [D 2] and derivs. See **intormentire**.

indoss-are [A 1] *tr.* to put on (clothes, etc.); to wear; to have on, to be wearing, to be dressed in. **-ata** *f.* trying on; fitting. **-ato** *part. adj.* tried on; on, worn. **-atore** *m.* male mannequin. **-atrice** *f.* mannequin, model girl. **-o** *adv.* on, avere -o, to wear, to be wearing (also 'in dosso').

indossile *m.* (chem.) indoxyl.

Indost-an *pr.n.m.* (geog.) Hindustan. **-a·nico**, **-ano** *adj.*, *n.m.* Hindustani.

†**indotta** *f.* inducement; incitement; example.

indott-o¹ *adj.* unlearned, not learned; †ignorant, unaware, uninformed. **-amẹnte** *adv.* in an unlearned way.

indotto² *part.* of **indurre**, q.v., *adj.* induced, persuaded, led; (electr.) induced; *n.m.* (electr.) rotor, armature.

†**indovare** *rfl.* to find one's place; to be placed, to be located.

indove *adv.* (pop.) See **dove**.

indovin-are [A 1] *tr.* to guess; to divine; to surmise; -ate chi ho visto?, guess who I saw?; ve la do a — in tre, I give you three guesses; -arla, to guess right, to hit it; non ne -a una, he is never right, he never does anything right; *intr.* (aux. avere) to hit the mark, to succeed; (colloq.) to be on to a good thing. **-a·bile** *adj.* guessable, open to conjecture. **-a·glia** *f.* matter for conjecture, riddle (see **-ello**). **-amẹnto** *m.* guessing, guess, conjecture. **-ante** *part. adj.* guessing, divining. **-ativo** *adj.* conjecturable, that may be surmised. **-ato** *part. adj.* successful, well-chosen; una speculazione -ata, a lucky speculation. **-atore** *m.* guesser, diviner, soothsayer. (**-atrice** *f.*) **-ato·rio** *adj.* (m.pl. **-ato·rii**) divining, divinatory. **-azione** *f.* divination, soothsaying. **-ello** *m.* riddle; enigma; puzzle, guessing-game; — veronese, a conundrum in Veronese dialect (end of eighth or beginning of ninth century), the earliest literary composition that has come down in any Italian dialect or Romance language. **-o** *m.* soothsayer, fortune-teller; *adj.* †prescient. (**-a** *f.*)

indovut-o *adj.* undue; improper. **-amẹnte** *adv.* unduly; improperly.

†**indozz-a** *f.* pain, suffering. †**-are** *intr.* to suffer, to be in pain.

indrag-are [A 2] *intr.* (aux. essere), *rfl.* to become fierce like a dragon; (aux. avere), to be cruel, to act cruelly; *tr.* to make wild, to make ferocious. **-ato** *part. adj.* ferocious, wild.

†**indrento** *adv.* See **indentro**.

†**indreto**, †**indrieto** *adv.* See **indietro**.

†**indrizzare** *vb.* and derivs. See **indirizzare**.

†**induare** *tr.* to make into two; *rfl.* to be doubled; *recip. rfl.* to join with one other, to be accompanied by one another.

indubbiamẹnte *adv.* See under **indubbio**.

†**indubbiare** [A 4] *intr.* to begin to doubt, to become doubtful.

indub·bi-o *adj.* undoubted, unquestioned. **-amẹnte** *adv.* undoubtedly, unquestionably.

indubita·bil-e *adj.* indubitable, beyond doubt, certain. **-mẹnte** *adv.* indubitably. (**-ità** *f.*)

indubitamẹnte *adv.* undoubtedly, without doubt; doubtless.

†**indubitare** *vb.* and derivs. See **dubitare**.

indubitat-o *adj.* not doubted. **-amẹnte** *adv.* undoubtedly.

inducente *part.* of **indurre**, q.v., *adj.* conducive, inducing; impelling.

†**indu·cere** *vb.* and derivs. See **indurre**.

induc-imẹnto *m.* instigation; temptation; inducement. **-itore** *m.* instigator; inducer. (**-itrice** *f.*)

†**indu·gia** *f.* See **indugio**.

indugi-are [A 3] *tr.* to delay, to put off, to postpone; †— uno, to make a person wait, to keep a person waiting, to delay someone; †to

indugi-are (*cont.*)
wait for; *intr.* (*aux.* avere), *rfl.* to delay; to linger, to loiter, to stay; — su un argomento, to dwell upon a subject. **-amento** *m.* delay; delaying; waiting; lingering. **-ato** *part. adj.* delayed, deferred. **-atore** *m.* delayer; lingerer. (**-atrice** *f.*)

indu·gio *m.* delay; senz'—, without delay, straightway; period of waiting or delay; rompere, troncare gl'indugi, to cut down delay.

indul·g-ere [C5] *tr.* to grant, to allow; to indulge; — a, to be indulgent towards; *intr.* (*aux.* avere) to be indulgent, to give way. **-ente** *part. adj.* indulgent; lenient. **-entemente** *adv.* indulgently; leniently. **-enza** *f.* indulgence, clemency, benevolence, lenience; (eccl.) indulgence.

indulto *m.* (leg.) pardon; reduction of sentence; — e grazia, remission of punishment and pardon (C.P.); (eccl.) indult.

indumento *m.* garment, article of clothing; (eccl.) sacri indumenti, vestments.

indur-are [A1] *tr.* to harden; (paint.) to fix, to confirm (a style or manner, in drawing or painting); *intr.* (*aux.* essere) to harden, to set. **-a·bile** *adj.* susceptible to hardening, liable to harden. **-amento** *m.* hardening, developing resistance; resistance, persistence. **-ato** *part. adj.* hardened, resistant; (colloq.) tough; -ato alla fatica, inured to fatigue.

indur-ire [D2] *tr.* to harden; to make resistant; to make less sensitive; to toughen up; (metall.) to case-harden; *intr.* (*aux.* essere; *prep.* a), *rfl.* to harden, to become hard, to set; to become inured (to). **-imento** *m.* hardening; toughening, setting, fixing; (photog.) hardening; (med.) hardening, sclerosis. **-ito** *part. adj.* hardened, hard, set; tough; inured (to fatigue); pane -ito, stale bread.

indurre [B2] *tr.* to induce; to lead; to impel, to actuate; to deduce, to infer; — in errore, to mislead; non c'— in tentazione, lead us not into temptation; *rfl.* to resolve, to decide, to make up one's mind; non sapeva indursi a crederlo, he could not bring himself to believe it.

indu·sio *m.* (Rom. antiq.) *indusium*, shift; (bot.) indusium.

industr-e *adj.* busy, industrious; diligent; clever. **-emente** *adv.* industriously; diligently.

indu·stri-a *f.* industry, diligence, skill; industry, manufacture, factory; (pop.) cavaliere d'—, swindler. **-ale** *adj.* industrial; *n.m.* industrialist; manufacturer. **-alismo** *m.* industrialism. **-alizzare** [A1] *tr.* to industrialize. (**-alizzato** *part. adj.*) **-alizzazione** *f.* industrialization. **-ante** *m.* manufacturer; one who lives by his wits. **-are** [A4] *rfl.* to try, to endeavour, to do one's best; s'-a e tira avanti alla meglio, he scrapes a living by taking any job he can find. **-evole** *adj.* industrious, clever. **-uola** *f.* ingenuity. **-oso** *adj.* clever, ingenious; diligent, hardworking; †mannered, affected; †laboured.

indutt-anza *f.* (electr.) inductance. **-ivo** *adj.* inductive; (electr.) inductive. **-ivamente** *adv.* inductively; according to the inductive method of reasoning. **-ività** *f.* (electr.) inductivity, inductance. **-ore** *m.* inductor, inducer; (biol.) -ore embrionale, (embryonic) inductor; (electr.) inductor, inductance.

†**indutto** *part.* of **indurre**, q.v.

induzione *f.* inducement, induction; conjecture; (electr.) induction; rocchetto d'—, induction coil; (leg.) inducement (C.P.).

ine(b)bri-are [A4] *tr.* to make drunk; (fig.) to intoxicate; *rfl.* to get drunk, to become intoxicated; (fig.) to go into raptures. **-ante** *part. adj.* intoxicating. †**-anza** *f.* intoxication; joy, rapture. **-ato** *part. adj.* intoxicated, drunk; filled with rapture; †(naut.) bussola -ata, compass wander.

inebet-ire [D2] *tr.* to make stupid. **-ito** *part. adj.* made stupid; stupefied; stupid, dull.

ineccepi·bile *adj.* (leg.) not irregular; not objectionable, unobjectionable; informazione —, reliable information.

ine·dia *f.* abstention from food; lack of food, inanition, starvation; tedium, boredom; è un'—, it bores me to death, how tiresome!

ine·dito *adj.* unpublished; unknown in any printed work; inedited; *n.m.* unpublished work, unpublished document.

ineduc-a·bile *adj.* that cannot be educated. **-ato** *adj.* uneducated; undisciplined; untrained; rude, impolite. **-atamente** *adv.* rudely, impolitely.

ineffa·bil-e *adj.* ineffable, inexpressible, unspeakable, unutterable; (theol.) ineffable. **-mente** *adv.* ineffably, inexpressibly. **-ità** *f.* ineffableness; unspeakableness.

ineffettua·bil-e *adj.* inexecutable, that cannot be executed, unrealizable; unfeasible. (**-ità** *f.*)

ineffic-ace *adj.* inefficacious, ineffectual, ineffective. **-acemente** *adv.* ineffectually, ineffectively. **-a·cia** *f.* inefficacy; ineffectualness.

inefficien-te *adj.* not effective; inefficient. **-za** *f.* inefficiency.

ineguaglia·bile *adj.* unbeatable.

ineguaglianza *f.* inequality, unevenness; irregularity; roughness, dissimilarity.

ineguagliato *adj.* unequalled, unparalleled.

inegual-e *adj.* unequal; uneven; irregular; rough; lacking uniformity; changeable. **-mente** *adv.* unequally. **-ità** *f.* inequality; unevenness.

inelegan-te *adj.* inelegant; ungraceful; unpolished. (**-temente** *adv.*) **-za** *f.* inelegance, lack of elegance.

ineleggi·bil-e *adj.* ineligible, not eligible. **-ità** *f.* ineligibility.

ineloquent-e *adj.* ineloquent, void of eloquence. **-emente** *adv.* ineloquently.

inelutta·bil-e *adj.* unavoidable, inevitable, inescapable, ineluctable. **-mente** *adv.* unavoidably, inescapably. **-ità** *f.* unavoidability, inevitability.

inemenda·bil-e *adj.* that cannot be emended. (**-mente** *adv.*)

inemendato *adj.* not emended.

inenarra·bil-e *adj.* unspeakable, unutterable, indescribable. (**-mente** *adv.*)

†**inentro** *adv.* inwards.

†**inequa·bil-e** *adj.* (scient.) inequable. **-ità** *f.* lack of equability.

inequila·tero *adj.* (math.) inequilateral.

inequivalente *adj.* not equivalent.

inequivoca·bile *adj.* unequivocal, free from ambiguity.

inerente *adj.* See under **inerire**.

iner-ire [D2 def.] *intr.* (*inf., ger., pres. part.* only; *prep.* a); to inhere; to be inherent (in). **-ente** *part. adj.* (*prep.* a) inherent (in), attached (to); concerning; (leg.) inherent (in); attending; spesa -ente all'incasso, cost of collecting (debt); infrazione -ente alla viabilità, road-traffic offence. **-enza** *f.* inherence.

inerme *adj.* unarmed, without defence; disarmed.

inerpic-are [A2sc] *rfl., intr.* (*aux.* essere; *prep.* su) to climb, to clamber (up). **-ante** *part. adj.* climbing; clambering; rosa -ante, climbing rose.

†**inerr-a·bile**, †**-ante** *adj.* (astron.) that does not move, fixed; that does not err.

inert-e *adj.* inert, idle, lazy, motionless, sluggish; acqua —, stagnant water; (chem.; phys.; mech.) inert; non-reactive; (econ.; comm.) capitale —, unproductive capital, idle capital. **-anza** *f.* (phys.) inertance.

inerud-ito *adj.* inerudite, not erudite, unlearned. **-itamente** *adv.* in an inerudite way. **-izione** *f.* lack of culture; ignorance.

iner·zia *f.* idleness, slothfulness, laziness, inertness; (scient.; techn.) inertia; inertness; momento d'—, moment of inertia.

inesatt-o *adj.* inaccurate; incorrect, inexact; unpunctual; (of debts) uncollected, unpaid, outstanding. **-amente** *adv.* inaccurately; incorrectly. **-ezza** *f.* inaccuracy; error, mistake.

inesaud-i·bile *adj.* that cannot be granted. **-ito** *adj.* ungranted, not complied with.

inesauri·bil-e *adj.* inexhaustible. **-imente** *adv.* inexhaustibly.

inesausto *adj.* unexhausted; inexhaustible; sorgente —, perennial spring, fountain that never runs dry.

inesc-are [A2c] *tr.* to bait (a hook); (fig.) to decoy, to entice, to seduce; (mil.) see **innescare**. †**-amento** *m.* enticement. **-ato** *part. adj.* baited; (fig.) decoyed, allured, enticed.

ines-co *m.* (*pl.* **-chi**) (explos.) primer; fuse; (electr.) striking (of a vapour lamp).

inescogita·bile *adj.* inconceivable, unimaginable.

inescusa·bil-e *adj.* inexcusable. **-mente** *adv.* inexcusably. **-ità** *f.* inexcusability, inexcusableness.

inesegui·bile *adj.* inexecutable, impossible to carry out (or perform).

inesercit-a·bile *adj.* that cannot be practised, that cannot be exercised, impracticable. **-ato** *adj.* unpractised, untrained.

inesigi·bil-e *adj.* (finan.) irrecoverable; credito, debito —, bad debt. **-ità** *f.* irrecoverableness; unrecoverability.

inesi·st-ere [C24] *intr.* (*aux.* essere) (philos.) to inexist, to exist in (something else). **-ente** *part. adj.* inexistent, non-existent. **-enza** *f.* inexistence, non-existence.

inesora·bil-e *adj.* inexorable, unrelenting; implacable. **-mente** *adv.* inexorably. **-ità** *f.* inexorability; inexorableness.

inesorato *adj.* (poet.). See **inesorabile**.

inespedito *adj.* not expedited, not performed or completed.

inesperienza *f.* inexperience, lack of experience; per —, from, owing to, inexperience.

inesperimentato *adj.* not proved by experiment.

inespert-o *adj.* inexperienced; inexpert, unskilled; essere — della vita, to have had no experience of life, to be inexperienced. **-amente** *adv.* inexpertly; unskilfully.

inespi-a·bile *adj.* inexpiable. **-ato** *adj.* inexpiate, unexpiated.

†**inesple·bile** *adj.* that cannot be filled up, insatiable.

inesplica·bil-e *adj.* inexplicable, unaccountable. **-mente** *adv.* inexplicably, unaccountably. **-ità** *f.* inexplicability, inexplicableness.

inesplicato *adj.* unexplained.

inesplor-a·bile *adj.* that cannot be explored. **-ato** *adj.* unexplored; archivio -ato, archives that have not been searched.

inesploso *adj.* unexploded.

inesprimi·bil-e *adj.* inexpressible, ineffable, unspeakable, unutterable. **-mente** *adv.* inexpressibly, ineffably, unspeakably, unutterably.

inespugna·bil-e *adj.* impregnable, inexpugnable; (mil.) impregnable; (fig.) incorruptible, inflexible. (**-mente** *adv.* **-ità** *f.*)

inespugnato *adj.* See **inespugnabile**.

inespurgato *adj.* unexpurgated.

inessicca·bile *adj.* incapable of drying up, inexhaustible.

inestensi·bile *adj.* inextensible, non-extending.

inestensione *f.* (philos.) inextension.

inesteso *adj.* unextended, inextended.

inestima·bil-e *adj.* inestimable, invaluable. **-mente** *adv.* inestimably, invaluably.

inestimato *adj.* not esteemed; †unforeseen, unforeseeable.

inestingui·bil-e *adj.* inextinguishable; unquenchable. **-mente** *adv.* inextinguishably; unquenchably.

inestinto *adj.* inextinguished, unextinguished; unquenched.

inestirpa·bile *adj.* ineradicable, inextirpable.

inestrica·bil-e *adj.* inextricable; dubbio —, insoluble doubt. **-mente** *adv.* inextricably.

inestricato *adj.* entangled, confused, unsolved.

inett-o *adj.* inept, without aptitude; unfit, unsuitable; senseless, foolish; osservazione -a, inept remark. **-amente** *adv.* ineptly. **-ezza** *f.* ineptness, ineptitude. **-itu·dine** *f.* ineptitude.

inevaso *adj.* unanswered; inexhausted; unfulfilled; unattended to; lettera inevasa, unanswered letter; pratiche inevase, matters in arrears.

ineviden-te *adj.* not evident; lacking evidence; obscure. **-za** *f.* lack of evidence, inevidence.

inevita·bil-e *adj.* inevitable, unavoidable, inescapable; (leg.) inevitable, unavoidable; danno —, unavoidable damage. **-mente** *adv.* inevitably; unavoidably.

ine·zia *f.* trifle, bagatelle; foolish remark; è un'—, it's not worth bothering about.

†**infaccendato** *adj.* See **affaccendato**, under **affaccendare**.

infacet-o *adj.* dull, stupid; non —, rather witty. **-amente** *adv.* in a dull manner; stupidly.

infacond-ia *f.* lack of eloquence, ineloquence, laconism. **-o** *adj.* ineloquent, lacking in eloquence. (**-amente** *adv.*)

infagott-are [A 1] *tr.* to wrap up, to pack up, to make into a bundle; *rfl.* to wrap (oneself) up, to put on an overcoat; to bundle oneself up, to make a bundle of oneself. **-ato** *part. adj.* wrapped up; bundled up, done up in a bundle.

infalli·bil-e *adj.* infallible, unfailing; (theol.) infallible. **-mente** *adv.* infallibly; unfailingly. **-ista** *m.* (eccl. hist.) infallibilist. **-ità** *f.* (theol.) infallibility.

infam-are [A 1] *tr.* to defame, to slander; to disgrace, to dishonour; to render infamous; *rfl.* to bring shame upon oneself; to be disgraced, to be dishonoured. **-ante** *part. adj.* slanderous; libellous; (leg.) infamous; pena -ante, punishment bringing disgrace. **-ato** *part. adj.* disgraced; defamed, dishonoured; (herald.) membered. †**-atore** *m.* defamer, slanderer. (†**-atrice** *f.*) **-ato·rio** *adj.* slanderous, defamatory; disgraceful. †**-azione** *f.* disgrace, dishonour.

infam-e *adj.* infamous; scandalous; casa —, house of ill fame; (leg.) calunnia —, infamous calumny, accusation or slander; (colloq.) horrible; fa un caffè —, he makes revolting coffee; (joc.) ero — ed ora sono empio, I was hungry and now I am full; *n.m.* infamous person, scoundrel. **-ità** *f.* infamous deed; infamousness.

infa·mi-a *f.* (leg.) infamy; slander; defamation; (fig.) infamous behaviour; insult. †**-are** *tr.* to defame, to slander.

†**infamire** *intr.* to hunger.

infanatich-ire [D 2] *tr.* to make fanatical; to make enthusiastic, to fill with enthusiasm; *rfl.* to become fanatical; to grow enthusiastic; s'era -ito di quella ragazza, the girl had turned his head; *intr.* (aux. avere) to be fanatical, to behave like a fanatic; (aux. essere; *prep.* di) to become enthusiastic (about), to conceive a passion (for), to become infatuated (with); to become fanatical. (**-ito** *part. adj.*)

†**infando** *adj.* unspeakable, unmentionable.

infang-are [A 2] *tr.* to bespatter with mud, to cover with mud, to muddy; (fig.) to smirch; — la memoria di qualcuno, to smirch the memory of someone; *rfl.* to get spattered with mud; to become degraded. **-ato** *part. adj.* muddied, spattered with mud; smirched; dragged in the mud.

infanta *f.* Spanish Infanta; razza —, Negretti merino breed (of sheep).

†**infantare** *tr.* to bring forth, to give birth to.

†**infantasi·a** *f.* vision, fantastic apparition.

infant-e *m.*, *f.* infant, baby, babe, young child; Spanish Infante. †**-eri·a** *f.*, †**-esca** *f.* infantry. **-icida** *m.*, *f.* (*pl.* **-icidi** *m.*, *f.*) infanticide (person). **-ici·dio** *m.* (*pl.* **-ici·dii**) infanticide (deed). **-igliole** *f.pl.* (med.) eclampsia. **-ile** *adj.* infantile, childish; asilo -ile, children's home, nursery, kindergarten; scuola -ile, infant school. **-ilmente** *adv.* childishly. **-ilismo** *m.* (med.) infantilism. **-ilità** *f.* puerility, childishness.

infan·zia *f.* infancy, babyhood; infants, babies, young children; asilo d'—, nursery school, kindergarten.

infarc-ire [D 2] *tr.* to stuff; to cram; (fig.) to fill out, to pad; *rfl.* (med.) to infarct, to develop infarction. **-imento** *m.* stuffing; padding; work that is padded. **-ito** *part. adj.* stuffed; crammed; padded; (cul.) stuffed.

infard-are [A 1] *tr.* to make up (the face), to paint (the face); *rfl.* to make up, to put on make-up, to make up one's face; †to mingle, to intermix, to become intermingled.

†**infardellare** *vb.* and derivs. See **affardellare**.

†**infaretrato** *adj.* See **faretrato**.

†**infarfall-are, -ire** *rfl.* to change into a butterfly. †**-ato** *adj.* changed into a butterfly.

infarin-are [A 1] *tr.* (cul.) to dip in flour, to cover with flour, to dust with flour; (fig.) — alcuno d'una scienza, to teach someone a smattering of a science; †to grind into flour; *rfl.* to get covered with flour; (joc.) to powder one's face or hair; (provb.) chi va al mulino s'-a, he that toucheth pitch shall be defiled therewith. **-ato** *part. adj.* covered with flour; (joc.) heavily powdered; (fig.) having a smattering (of some subject, science, etc.); †ground into flour. **-atura** *f.* dusting with flour; powdering (with flour or face-powder); (fig.) smattering.

infarto *m.* (med.) infarct.

†**infasciare** *vb.* and derivs. See **fasciare**.

†**infastidi-are** *tr.* to hold in distaste; to be annoyed with; *intr.* to be annoying. †**-ato** *part. adj.* annoyed; offensive.

infastid-ire [D 2] *tr.* to annoy, to trouble, to disturb; to molest; to bore; to disgust; *rfl.* to feel annoyed, to become annoyed; to be impatient; to be bored; to become disgusted. **-imento** *m.* annoyance; disturbance; disgust. **-ito** *part. adj.* annoyed; disturbed; molested; disgusted; bored.

infatica·bil-e *adj.* indefatigable, tireless, unwearying. **-mente** *adv.* indefatigably. **-ità** *f.* tirelessness.

infaticato *adj.* unwearied, unwearying.

infatti *adv.* in fact; indeed; really; actually, as a matter of fact.

infatti·bile *adj.* impracticable, not feasible; impossible to do.

infatu-are [A 6] *tr.* to make foolish; to infatuate, to turn the head of; *rfl.* (*prep.* di) to become silly; to be infatuated; to be carried away (by); to have one's head turned (by). **-ato** *part. adj.* fond, foolish; infatuated; †tasteless, that has lost its savour. **-azione** *f.* infatuation.

infa·ust-o *adj.* unlucky; ill-omened, inauspicious; unfortunate; hapless. **-amente** *adv.* unluckily; inauspiciously.

†**infazzardare** *tr.* to sprinkle.

infecond-o *adj.* sterile, unfruitful; barren; infecund; (fig.) fruitless. **-amente** *adv.* unfruitfully; (fig.) fruitlessly. **-ità** *f.* sterility; barrenness; unfruitfulness.

infedel-e *adj.* unfaithful, faithless; citazione —, inexact quotation; memoria —, faulty memory; inaccurate; dishonest; false; (rel., chiefly hist.) unbelieving, misbelieving; (leg.) dishonest; disloyal (C.P.); *n.m.* infidel, unbeliever, heathen; nelle parti degl'-eli,

infedel-e (*cont.*)
in partibus infidelium. **-mente** *adv.* unfaithfully; inaccurately; dishonestly. **-tà** *f.* infidelity, unfaithfulness; (rel., chiefly hist.) misbelief, infidelity; (leg.) **-tà in affari di Stato**, disloyalty in affairs of State (C.P.).

infelic-e *adj.* unhappy; unfortunate, unlucky; unsuccessful; unpropitious; wretched; **in una condizione —**, in an awkward situation; mad, imbecile; *n.m., f.* wretch; unfortunate person; handicapped person; unhappy person; imbecile, fool. **-emente** *adv.* unhappily, unfortunately, unsuccessfully. **-ità** *f.* unhappiness; misfortune; wretchedness; affliction, calamity. **-itare** [A 1 s] *tr.* to make unhappy, to make wretched.

infellon-ire [D 2] *intr.* (*aux.* avere) to become cruel, to persist in wickedness. (**-ito** *part. adj.*)

infelpato *adj.* See **felpato**.

infeltr-are [A 1] *tr.* to felt, to cover with felt; *rfl.* to become felted. **-ire** [D 2] *tr.* to make like felt, to make into felt; to cause (e.g. woollen knitwear) to felt; *intr.* (*aux.* essere), *rfl.* to become matted like felt. **-ito** *part. adj.* felted; become like felt; (of woollen knitwear) felted and shrunk after washing; (fig.) ingrained, inveterate.

infemmin-ire [D 2] *tr.* to make effeminate; *intr.* (*aux.* essere), *rfl.* to become effeminate. **-ito** *part. adj.* made effeminate; become effeminate.

inferenza *f.* See under **inferire**.

infe·ria *f.* (Rom. rel.) sacrifice (in honour of the dead).

inferigno *adj.* (of bread) brown; *pr.n.m.* nickname of Bastiano dei Rossi as a founder of the Accademia della Crusca.

inferior-e *adj.* lower; less tall; inferior; (geog.) southern; **Italia —**, southern Italy; nether; under, bottom; **la pagina — di una foglia**, the under side of a leaf; less; (mil.) **ufficiale —**, subaltern; **— di forze**, weaker in forces; *n.m.* inferior, underling, subordinate. **-mente** *adv.* in an inferior manner. **-ità** *f.* inferiority; **complesso di -ità**, inferiority complex.

infer-ire [D 2] *tr.* to cause, to occasion; (leg.) to inflict; to infer, to deduce; (naut.) to reeve or clip (sails) on to their stays; to reeve (running rigging) through blocks or sheaves. **-enza** *f.* inference, deduction. **-ito** *part. adj.* caused, occasioned; (leg.) inflicted; inferred, deduced; (naut.) tied, lashed. **-itoio** *m.* (naut.) tied or lashed rope or runner rope used as runner for lashing the peak of a sail. **-itura** *f.* (naut.) lashing; method of lashing.

inferm-are [A 1] *tr.* to weaken; to invalidate; to make ill; *rfl.*, †*intr.* to fall ill, to become ill. **-ato** *part. adj.* ill, sick, infirm. **-azione** *f.* (leg.) invalidation.

infermeri·a *f.*, **infermier-a** *f.*, **-e** *m.* See under **infermo**

inferm-o *adj.* ill, sick, ailing, infirm; weak, cowardly; (leg.) **— di mente**, of unsound mind; †**luogo —**, unhealthy spot, insalubrious place; †**acqua -a**, water unfit for drinking; *n.m.* sick person, patient; (rel.) **visitare gl'-i**, to visit the sick; (leg.) **curatore di un — di mente**, Receiver in lunacy (C.C.). **-eri·a** *f.* sick-room; infirmary; sick-bay, sanatorium; †general sickness, widespread illness; †illness. **-ic·cio** *adj.* sickly, ailing, in poor health. **-iera** *f.* nurse; hospital nurse, sick-nurse. **-iere** *m.* hospital orderly, stretcher-bearer; male nurse. **-ità** *f.* sickness, infirmity, illness; weakness; (leg.) **-ità mentale**, insanity (C.P.).

Infern-o *m.* Hell, Inferno, Hades, the Underworld; (provb.) **l'Inferno è lastricato di buone intenzioni**, the way to Hell is paved with good intentions; (fig., with small initial) **una vita d'inferno**, a hell of a life; **quella casa è un —**, that house is hell; **pareva che si fosse scatenato l'—**, it seemed like hell let loose; **un tizzone d'—**, a firebrand; **mandare uno all'—**, to tell someone to go to hell, to get rid of someone, (euphem.) to 'bump off' someone; **all'—!**, go to hell!; (industr.) reservoir, depository; †*adj.* infernal, relating to Hell. **-ale** *adj.* infernal, hellish; (chem.; pharm.) **pietra -ale**, lunar caustic; *n.m.pl.* gods of the Underworld; demons. **-almente** *adv.* infernally, hellishly, diabolically. †**-alità** *f.* hellishness.

in·fero *adj.* lower; (geog.) **mare —**, Tyrrhenian Sea; (naut.) **posizione infera**, leeward side or position; *n.m.pl.* Lower Regions, Hell; gods, shades, of the Lower Regions; (joc.) **mandare agl'inferi**, to send to hell.

inferoc-ire [D 2] *tr.* to make fierce; to make ferocious, to make cruel; *intr.* (*aux.* essere), *rfl.* to become fierce, to turn ferocious; to become cruel; (*aux.* avere) to act ferociously, to commit atrocities. **-ito** *part. adj.* fierce; ferocious; cruel.

inferraiol-are [A 1] *rfl.* to wrap oneself in a cloak; to wrap up. **-ato** *part. adj.* wrapped up, cloaked.

inferr-are [A 1] *rfl.* (fencing) to be pricked, to get wounded by one's opponent's sword; †*tr.* to chain, to fetter. **-iata** *f.* iron bars, grating, grille; **-iata inginocchiata**, grating curved outwards in its lower part. **-iato** *adj.* barred; (herald.) trellised, fretty nailed. †**-iucciare** *tr.* to chain, to fetter; to bind in chains.

†**infertà** *f.* See **infermità**, under **infermo**.

infer·til-e *adj.* sterile, unfruitful, barren; unfertile. **-ità** *f.* infertility; sterility; barrenness.

infertil-ire [D 2] *tr.* to fertilize. **-ito** *part. adj.* fertilized.

infervor-are [A 1 c] *tr.* to excite, to fill with fervour; *rfl.* to be filled with fervour, to become excited. **-amento** *m.* exciting, filling with fervour; increase in fervour. **-ato** *part. adj.* ardent, filled with fervour, enthusiastic; excited.

inferzare [A 1] *intr.* (*aux.* avere) (naut.) to make sail-cloth strips.

infestamente *adv.* See under **infesto**.

infest-are [A 1] *tr.* to ravage, to lay waste; to infest; to importune; (mil.) **— il nemico**, to harass the enemy. †**-agione** *f.* ravaging; ravages; overbearing behaviour. **-amento** *m.* ravaging; infestation; harassing. **-ato** *part. adj.* ravaged; infested; importuned. (**-atore** *m.* **-atrice** *f.*) **-azione** *f.* ravaging; infestation; harassing.

infest-o *adj.* (lit.) harmful, hurtful, dangerous; detrimental; obnoxious. **-amente** *adv.* harmfully; detrimentally.

infett-are [A 1] *tr.* (med.) to infect; (fig.) to taint, to corrupt, to infect; *rfl.* (med.) to become infected; (fig.) to become tainted; *recip. rfl.* to infect each other. **-amento** *m.* (med.) infecting. **-ato** *part. adj.* infected. **-atore** *m.* infectious person or thing. (**-atrice** *f.*) **-ivo** *adj.* (med.) infectious, catching; contagious. **-o** *adj.* (med.) infected; septic; (fig.) contaminated, corrupt.

infeud-are [A 1] *tr.* (leg.) to enfeoff. **-amento** *m.* enfeoffment. **-ato** *part. adj.* invested with possession in fee. **-azione** *f.* enfeoffment.

infezione *f.* (med.) infection; contagion.

infiacch-ire [D 2] *tr.* to enfeeble, to weaken, to enervate; *intr.* (*aux.* essere), *rfl.* to become enfeebled, to be weakened, to grow weak, to lose one's vigour; (of the wind) to die down, to drop. **-imento** *m.* enfeebling; enfeeblement. **-ito** *part. adj.* weakened, enfeebled.

infiamm-are [A 1] *tr.* to set fire to, to light, to set alight, to set ablaze, to kindle; (fig.) to inflame, to excite; (med.) to inflame, to cause inflammation of; *rfl.* to catch fire, to light, to burn; (fig.) to get excited; to be inflamed (with passion); **-arsi subito**, to be very fiery; (med.) to become inflamed. **-a·bile** *adj.* inflammable; (fig.) excitable; passionate. **-abilità** *f.* inflammability; (techn.) **punto di -abilità**, flash-point. **-ativo** *adj.* (med.) inflammatory. **-ato** *part. adj.* alight, kindled, aflame, burning; (fig.) inflamed, ardent; excited; **uno sguardo -ato d'odio**, a look of blazing hatred; **avere il viso -ato**, to blush fiery red; (med.) inflamed. **-ati** *n.m.pl.* (lit. hist.) name of an Academy founded in 1540 at Padua by Bishop Leone Orsini. **-atore** *m.* inflamer; instigator. (**-atrice** *f.*) **-ato·rio** *adj.* (*m.pl.* **-ato·rii**) (med.) inflammatory. **-azione** *f.* inflaming; excitement, irritation; instigation; (med.) inflammation. †**-eggiare** *rfl.* to shine, to be resplendent.

†**infiancare** *tr.* to spur; to sting; *intr.* to exaggerate.

infiasc-are [A 2] *tr.* to bottle; to put in flasks. **-ato** *part. adj.* bottled; in flasks. **-atura** *f.* bottling; cost of bottling.

†**infi·cere** *tr.* to infect; to render abominable.

inficiare [A 3] *tr.* (leg.) to question the validity of, to challenge.

†**infidele** *adj.* and derivs. See **infedele**.

infid-o *adj.* faithless, unfaithful; untrustworthy, false. **-amente** *adv.* faithlessly, unfaithfully; untrustworthily, falsely.

infier-ire [D 2] *intr.* (*aux.* avere) to behave with ferocity; to act cruelly; (*aux.* essere) to rage; to be raging; to become more severe (e.g. of epidemics). **-ito** *part. adj.* ferocious; cruel; increased in severity.

infievol-ire [D 2] *tr.* to enfeeble; to weaken; *rfl.* to become feeble. **-ito** *part. adj.* enfeebled, weakened (cf. **affievolire**).

infig·gere [C 17] *tr.* to drive in; to fix in; to nail; to drive into; (leg.) to affix (C.C.); *rfl.* to penetrate; to be driven in; to go deep; **infiggersi nella memoria**, to be deeply impressed on the memory.

infigur-a·bile *adj.* unimaginable. **-ato** *adj.* unimagined.

infil-are [A 1] *tr.* to thread (a needle, beads, etc.); to insert; **— gli aghi al buio**, to talk nonsense; to file; to run through; to transfix; **— uno con la spada**, to run someone through; **— una strada**, to go down a street, to turn into a street; **— la chiave**, to put the key in the keyhole; **— il soprabito**, to slip on one's overcoat; **non ne -a mai una**, he never succeeds in anything; **— tutte le chiacchiere**, to listen to every bit of gossip; (naut.) to reeve; to

infil-are (*cont.*)

rake (of a ship swept fore and aft by seas); (mil.) to enfilade; *intr.* (*aux.* essere) to follow on, to come in succession; — per una via, to go down a street, to turn into a street; *rfl.* to be threaded; to slip (in), to slip (into), to squeeze (through); *recip. rfl.* to follow each other, to come one after the other. **-acappi** *m. indecl.* bodkin. **-ata** *f.* series, suite; row, file; (mil.) enfilade. **-ato** *part. adj.* threaded, strung together; (naut.) pooped by seas. **-atura** *f.* threading; stringing; slipping on.

infiltr-are [A 1] *rfl.* (*prep.* in) to filter (into, through), to seep; to penetrate (into); to seep; (fig.) to penetrate stealthily, to insinuate oneself (into), to infiltrate, to creep (into); *tr.* to insinuate, to introduce stealthily. (**-ato** *part. adj.*) **-azione** *f.* infiltration; penetration; seepage.

infilz-are [A 1] *tr.* to run through, to transfix, to pierce; to spike; to skewer; to string together; — esempi, to give a long series of examples; — concetti, to write an exaggerated quantity of conceits; *rfl.* to run oneself through; s'-ò sulla sua spada, he fell on his sword; to be put on a spike and preserved (e.g. documents on a skewer). **-a** *f.* (sewing) tacking. **-amento** *m.* stringing together; piercing; transfixing; skewering. **-ata** *f.* string (e.g. of pearls); series, long series; long story, yarn; (sewing) tacking. **-ato** *part. adj.* strung together; pierced, transfixed; skewered; pare una Madonnina -ata, she has a very demure expression, she looks as if butter wouldn't melt in her mouth; †*adv.* straightway. **-atura** *f.* stringing together; piercing, impaling; string, succession, series; unclassified documents (skewered, instead of filed).

in·fim-o *adj.* (*superl.* of **inferiore**, q.v.) lowest; extremely low; last; base; l'-a plebe, the dregs of society; vino d'-a qualità, wine of the poorest quality; *n.m.* lowest place; worst person or thing; è l'— dei professori, he is the worst possible teacher. **-amente** *adv.* in the lowest degree; most basely.

infine *adv.* at last, after all, finally; in short (also 'in fine').

infinestr-are [A 1] *tr.* to mend or patch up (a torn page) with transparent gummed paper. (**-ato** *part. adj.*) **-atura** *f.* transparent gummed strip of paper mending a torn page.

infingard-o *adj.* lazy, slothful, slack, lax; †slow to respond; †simulated, feigned. **-ag·gine** *f.* laziness, slackness; sloth; cowardice. **-amente** *adv.* lazily, slothfully. **-ire** [D 2] *tr.* to make lazy or slothful; *intr.* (*aux.* essere), *rfl.* to become lazy or slothful. **-ito** *part. adj.* lazy, slothful, slack.

infin·g·ere [C 5] *rfl.*, *intr.* (*aux.* avere) to feign, to pretend; †*tr.* to ape, to feign, to simulate. †**-e·vole** *adj.* insincere, feigning. **-imento** *m.* feigning; simulating; deceit. **-itore** *m.* simulator, deceiver; hypocrite. (**-itrice** *f.*)

infinità *f.* infinity; infinitude, vast number, great quantity; un'— di gente, a great concourse of people.

infinit-o *adj.* infinite; boundless, limitless; endless, unending; innumerable, countless; immense; (gramm.) modo —, infinitive mood; *n.m.* infinite; (gramm.) infinitive; (math.) infinity; all'—, without end, endlessly, times without number; la sua fama crescerà in —, his fame will last for ever; lavorando così lentamente si va nell'—, it will take you till doomsday if you work so slowly. **-amente** *adv.* infinitely; endlessly. **-esimale** *adj.* infinitesimal, infinitely small; (math.) infinitesimal; calcolo -esimale, infinitesimal calculus. **-e·simo** *adj.* infinitesimal; *n.m.* infinitesimal part, tiny bit. **-ezza** *f.* infiniteness; vastness. **-ivo** *adj.* (gramm.) infinitive; also *n.m.* **-u·dine** *f.* infinitude, infinity, vast number, great quantity.

infino *prep.* (*foll.* by *prep.* 'a') till, until; up to; as far as.

infinocchi-are [A 4] *tr.* (colloq.) to bamboozle, to hoax, to make a fool of, to lead up the garden path. (**-ato** *part. adj.*) **-atura** *f.* bamboozling, bamboozle, hoax.

†**infinta** *f.* feint, pretence.

infint-o *part.* of **infingere**, q.v.; *adj.* feigned, simulated, pretended; *adv. phr.* alla -a, on false pretences, by deception. **-amente** *adv.* deceitfully; insincerely. †**-ura** *f.* deception.

infiocc-are [A 2] *tr.* to deck with tassels, to adorn with tassels. **-ato** *part. adj.* tasselled, with tassels on; decked out; (joc.) tutto -ato, all got up.

infiochire [D 2] and derivs. See **affiochire**.

infior-are [A 1 c] *tr.* to deck with flowers, to strew with flowers; -a il suo stile con ardite metafore, he adorns his style with bold metaphors; *rfl.* to deck oneself with flowers; to blossom; le api s'-ano, the bees visit the flowers. **-amento** *m.* decorating with

flowers; strewing with flowers. **-ata** *f.* flower arrangement; scattering of flowers. **-ato** *part. adj.* decked with flowers; flowery, in bloom.

infiorentin-ire [D 2] *tr.* to make Florentine; to Florentinize; *rfl.* to become Florentine; to assume Florentine ways; to acquire a Florentine accent. **-ito** *part. adj.* Florentinized.

infiorescenza *f.* (bot.) inflorescence.

infirm-are [A 1] *tr.* (leg.) to invalidate; †to weaken, to enfeeble. **-ato** *part. adj.* invalidated. **-atore** *m. adj.* invalidating. **-azione** *f.* invalidation.

†**infirmità** *f.* See **infermità**, under **infermo**.

†**infiscare** *vb.* and derivs. See **confiscare**.

infischiare [A 4] *rfl.* (*prep.* di) (colloq.) not to care (for, about), not to mind; to laugh (at); me ne infischio, I don't give a hoot.

infissione *f.* (leg.) servitù di — chiusa, easement of right to affix sluice (C.C.).

infisso *part.* of **infiggere**, q.v., *adj.* fixed; *n.m.* (gramm.) epenthesis; (bldg.) fixture, frame, casing; *pl.* (leg.) fixtures.

infistol-ire [D 2] *intr.* (*aux.* essere) to fistulate; (fig.) to get into a bad way, to decline (e.g. of a business); to be incorrigible (of a vice); *tr.* to cause to fistulate.

infitt-ire [D 2] *intr.* (*aux.* essere) to grow thicker, to become more dense; (of darkness) to deepen; *tr.* to thicken, to make denser. **-ito** *part. adj.* thickened; thicker.

†**infizzare** *vb.* and derivs. See **infilzare**.

inflammato·rio *adj.* (med.) inflammatory.

inflazion-e *f.* (econ.) inflation. **-ista** *m.* (econ.) inflationist.

inflessi·bil-e *adj.* inflexible; unbending; inexorable; unyielding. **-mente** *adv.* inflexibly; inexorably. **-ità** *f.* inflexibility, inflexibleness; inexorableness.

inflession-e *f.* flexion, bending; deflexion; (gramm.) inflexion, inflection; (mus.) — di voce, vocal inflexion. **-ale** *adj.* (gramm.) inflexional, inflectional.

inflesso *part.* of **inflettere**, q.v.; *adj.* bent, flexed; (gramm.) inflected; conjugated; declined.

inflet·tere [C 19] *tr.* to bend, to flex; (gramm.) to inflect; to decline; to conjugate; *rfl.* to bend; (archit.) to curve (of volutes of a capital).

inflig·g·ere [C 12] *tr.* to inflict; gl'inflisse una grande punizione, he inflicted a serious punishment on him; to impose; le inflissero una multa, they imposed a fine on her. **-imento** *m.* inflicting, infliction; imposing, imposition. **-itore** *m.* inflictor. (**-itrice** *f.*)

inflitto *part.* of **infliggere**, q.v.

inflizione *f.* inflicting, imposition; infliction.

influenz-a *f.* influence; power; avere molta —, to be very influential; (med.) influenza; †flowing. **-are** [A 1] *tr.* to influence; to affect; to sway, to bias; to have an effect on; *intr.* (*aux.* avere; *prep.* su) to have an influence (upon); (*aux.* essere) to have an attack of influenza. **-ale** *adj.* pertaining to influenza; un attacco -ale, an attack of influenza. **-ato** *part. adj.* influenced, swayed; biased; suffering from influenza.

influ-ire [D 2] *intr.* (*aux.* avere; *prep.* su); to have an influence (upon); (*prep.* a) to contribute (to); le difficoltà -iscono a farlo tennennare, the difficulties tend to make him hesitate; (*prep.* in) l'inalfabetismo -isce nel rendere gli uomini infelici, illiteracy contributes to human unhappiness; (of rivers) — in, to flow into; *tr.* to influence; non -isce niente, he has no influence. **-ente** *part. adj.* influential; -ente in, flowing into; *n.m.* influential person; tributary.

influss-o *m.* planetary influence; (fig.) — benefico, good influence; — malefico, evil influence; effect, after-effects; influx. †**-are** *tr.* to influence.

†**influ·vio** *m.* planetary influence.

infoc-are [A 2 d] *tr.* to make red-hot, to heat; (fig.) to influence, to excite; — contro, to incite against; *rfl.* to become red-hot; (fig.) to get overexcited, to be inflamed. **-amento** *m.* heating, inflaming, excitement, heat. **-ato** *part. adj.* red-hot, burning; aflame, inflamed; viso -ato, burning cheeks; (mil.) palle -ate, heated incendiary shot; *n.m.pl.* (lit. hist.) Gli Infuocati, members of a sixteenth-century Florentine academy. **-atamente** *adv.* ardently, fervently, in a very excited manner.

infoder-are [A 1 s] *tr.* to sheathe; to line; *rfl.* -arsi nel mantello, to slip one's cloak on; -arsi tra le lenzuola, to slip into bed.

†**infogliare** *rfl.* to put forth leaves, to become leafy.

infognare [A 5 c] *rfl.* to sink, to plunge deeply (into the mire, etc.); infognarsi nei debiti, to get deeper and deeper in debt.

in-fo·lio *m. indecl.* un in-folio, a folio book (also 'un in folio').

†**infoll·ire** *tr.* to drive insane, to make mad; *intr.* to go out of one's mind. †**-ito** *part. adj.* out of one's mind; *n.m.* madman.

infolt·ire [D 2] *intr.* (*aux.* essere) to thicken, to grow thick. **-ito** *part. adj.* thickened; grown thick.

infondacare [A 2 s] *tr.* to store, to put into store.

infondat·o *adj.* unfounded, baseless, false; (leg.) groundless; pretesa -a, groundless claim. **-amente** *adv.* baselessly. **-ezza** *f.* baselessness, falseness.

infond·ere [C 2 c] *tr.* to pour in; to infuse, to instil; le sue parole m'infusero un po' di speranza, his words instilled a little hope in me; — nuovo vigore in, to give new strength to. **-imento** *m.* infusing. (**-itore** *m.* **-itrice** *f.*)

†**infondi·bolo** *m.* funnel.

infora·bile *adj.* impenetrable, unpierceable.

inforc·are [A 2 c] *tr.* to take up on a pitchfork; to bestride; — gli occhiali, to put one's spectacles on; (chess) — due pezzi, to fork two pieces; — la scuola, to play truant from school; †to hang from the gallows; *intr.* (*aux.* avere) to play truant; *rfl.* to fork, to bifurcate; (naut.) see **afforcare**. **-ata** *f.* quantity of hay, etc., taken up on a pitchfork, forkful; forking, bifurcation; (anat.) forks. **-atura** *f.* forking.

inforestierare [A 1] and derivs. See **inforestierire**.

inforestier·ire [D 2] *tr.* (linguist.) to introduce foreign elements into; *intr.* (*aux.* avere) to adopt foreign customs; to become foreign. (**-ito** *part. adj.*)

inform·are [A 1 c] *tr.* to shape, to give shape to, to form; — l'animo dei giovani a nobili ideali, to mould the mind of youth to noble ideals; -ò tutta la sua opera a queste idee, all his work was informed with these ideas; to spread through, to permeate; il sole -a il mondo di luce, the sun permeates the world with light; to inform, to instruct, to notify; — di, to notify concerning, to acquaint with; ti prego d'-armi delle ultime notizie, please keep me informed of the latest developments; (leg.) to inform, to furnish with information; to instruct; to inquire; *rfl.* to make inquiries, to inquire; to collect information; to take shape. **-ativa** *f.* instruction, letter of information. **-ativo** *adj.* formative; informative; (leg.) processo -ativo, inquiry. **-ato** *part. adj.* shaped, formed, informed, instructed; inquest; judicial inquiry; (leg.) essere -ato a criteri di, to conform with the principles of (I.C.). **-atore** *m.* informer, spy; (mil.) scout, spy; †(leg.) coroner. **-azione** *f.* informing; information, piece of information; assumere -azioni, to make inquiries; ufficio -azioni, inquiry office; (leg.) information; inquiry; instruction; (mil.) intelligence.

inform·e *adj.* shapeless; formless; massa —, formless mass, chaos; †deformed. (**-mente** *adv.*) †**-ità** *f.* lack of form, formlessness.

informicolare [A 1 s] and derivs. See **informicolire**.

informicol·ire [D 2] *tr.* to cause to tingle; *rfl.*, *intr.* (*aux.* avere) to have pins and needles, to tingle. **-imento** *m.* tingling; pins and needles. **-ito** *part. adj.* tingling; irritated.

infornaci·are [A 3] *tr.* to put into a furnace, to put into a kiln. **-ata** *f.* firing (bricks, china, etc.). **-ato** *part. adj.* fired.

inforn·are [A 1 c] *tr.* to put in the oven; (joc.) to eat greedily. **-apane** *m. indecl.* baker's peel, baker's shovel. **-ata** *f.* batch; putting (bread) in the oven; (joc.) large assembly of persons. **-ato** *part. adj.* in the oven. **-atore** *m.* baker's man.

inforsare [A 1 c] *tr.* (poet.) to put in doubt; to endanger; *rfl.* to be hesitant, to appear uncertain.

†**infortare** *intr.* to grow strong.

infortifica·bile *adj.* (mil.) not fortifiable, unfortifiable.

infort·ire [D 2] *intr.* (*aux.* essere) (of milk) to turn sour; (of wine or vinegar) to taste more acid, to become stronger; *tr.* to fortify, to make stronger; to make more acid. **-imento** *m.* turning sour; making acid, fortifying. **-ito** *part. adj.* gone sour; made acid; fortified.

†**infortore** *m.* strength.

†**infortun·a** *f.* ill-fortune. †**-are** *tr.* to bring ill-fortune to.

infortunabilità *f.* (industr.) accident-proneness.

infortunat·o *adj.* injured in an accident; †unfortunate, hapless; *n.m.* person injured in an accident, casualty; †unlucky, unfortunate person, victim of misfortune. **-amente** *adv.* unluckily, unfortunately. †**-o** *adj.* unlucky; bringing ill-luck.

infortu·n·io *m.* accident; misfortune; (leg.) accident; danni per —, damages for accident; (naut.) shipwreck, collision; — marittimo, disaster on the seas. **-i·stica** *f.* study of accidents (for statistics, legislation on insurance). **-i·stico** *adj.* relating to accidents.

inforz·are [A 1 c] *tr.* to strengthen, to fortify; *intr.* (*aux.* essere) to become more potent; (of wine) to turn sour. **-ato** *part. adj.* strengthened, reinforced; *n.m.* (leg.) Infortiatus, Infortiate (in *Pandectae* or *Digesta*).

infosc·are [A 2 c] *tr.* to darken; *intr.* (*aux.* essere), *rfl.* to grow dark; to grow sad; il cielo s'-a, the sky is clouding over; (fig.) to become confused. **-amento** *m.* darkening, obfuscation. (**-ato** *part. adj.*)

infoss·are [A 1] *tr.* (agric.) to bury (grain) in storing; to bury, to inter; *rfl.* to sink; to become emaciated; le gote gli s'-ano sempre più, he is becoming more and more hollow-cheeked. **-amento** *m.* sinking; hollow, cavity. **-ato** *part. adj.* hollow; occhi -ati, sunken eyes.

infra *prep.* among, between; within; †below.

infracidare [A 1 s] and derivs. See **infradiciare**.

†**infracidire** *vb.* and derivs. See **infradiciare**.

infradici·are [A 3 s] *tr.* to drench, to soak; to harass, to worry; *rfl.* to get drenched; to go bad, to go rotten, to decay. **-ata** *f.* a drenching, a wetting; prendere una bella -ata, to get soaked, to get drenched. **-ato** *part. adj.* drenched, soaking wet. **-atura** *f.* see **infradiciata.**

infral·ire [D 2] *intr.* (*aux.* essere) to become frail, to grow weak; *tr.* to enfeeble. **-imento** *m.* growing weak; frailty, feebleness. **-ito** *part. adj.* weakened, enfeebled; frail.

infra(m)mett·ere *tr.* to interpose; *rfl.* (*prep.* in, a) to intrude (in), to meddle, to interfere (with, in). **-ente** *part. adj.* meddlesome, intrusive, intruding. †**-enza** *f.* meddlesomeness, intrusiveness.

infra(m)mezzare [A 1] and derivs. See **intramezzare**.

inframmischiare [A 4] and derivs. See **frammischiare**.

infranc·esare [A 1] *tr.* to Frenchify; to Gallicize; (joc.) to infect with the 'French disease' (i.e. syphilis); *rfl.* to become Frenchified. (**-esato** *part. adj.*) †**-escare** *vb.* and derivs. see **infrancesare**. **-iosare** [A 1] and derivs. see **infrancesare**.

infranero *adj.* (telev.) blacker-than-black.

infran·g·ere [C 5] *tr.* to crush, to shatter; (fig.) to violate; to break; *rfl.* to be crushed, to be broken, to be shattered. **-i·bile** *adj.* unbreakable; (fig.) irrefrangible, inviolable, irrefragable. (**-ibilmente** *adv.*) **-imento** *m.* breaking. (**-itore** *m.* **-itrice** *f.*)

infrant·o *part.* of **infrangere**, q.v.; *adj.* crushed, broken; (fig.) exhausted; idolo —, fallen idol; (phon.) suoni -i, liquid sounds. **-oiata** *f.* an oil-press-full (of olives). **-oio** *m.* oil-press; millstone for crushing woad. †**-ume** *m.* see **frantume**. **-ura** *f.* fracture, breaking, crushing.

infrapporre [B 21] and derivs. See **frapporre**.

infra(r)rosso *adj.* infra-red; *n.m.* infra-red ray.

infrascapolare *adj.* (anat.) infrascapular.

infrasc·are [A 2] *tr.* to cover with branches; to support (climbing plants) with branches; to tie to branches; to put (silkworms) to mulberry leaves or branches; *intr.* (*aux.* avere) to use a florid or overornamented style in writing or speaking; *rfl.* to hide among branches; (fig.) to be overelaborate (in speech or writing). **-amento** *m.* covering or supporting with branches. **-ato** *part. adj.* covered with branches. **-atura** *f.* action or manner of covering or supporting with branches; branches thus used, branches entwined or woven together.

infras·co *m.* (*pl.* **-chi**) branch used to stake or otherwise support a climbing plant. **-conare** [A 1 c] *tr.* to cover with branches; to layer (a vine or similar plant); (fig.) to overload with ornament. (**-conamento** *m.* **-conato** *part. adj.*)

infrascritto *adj.* following, undermentioned.

infraso·nico *adj.* (phys.) infrasonic, subsonic.

infrastruttura *f.* infrastructure, substructure; (aeron.) ground organization.

infrat·ire [D 2] *intr.* (*aux.* essere) (silkb., of cocoons which are not put to mulberry leaves) to become a 'frate' (the technical term for such cocoons); †to become a monk.

infrattanto *adv.* See **frattanto**.

infrazione *f.* infringement; — delle regole, breaking of rules; (leg.) breach; violation; infraction; — di un contratto, breach of contract.

infredd·are [A 1 c] *tr.* to chill; to cool; *intr.* (*aux.* essere), *rfl.* to catch a cold, to get a chill. **-amento** *m.* chilling; catching cold; cold. **-ato** *part. adj.* suffering from a cold; essere molto -ato, to have a bad cold. **-atura** *f.* cold, chill; -atura di testa, cold in the head; -atura di petto, cold on the chest. **-olire** [D 2] *intr.* (*aux.* essere), *rfl.* to feel very cold, to shiver with cold. **-olito** *part. adj.* chilled to the bone.

infren-are [A I c] *tr.* to check, to restrain, to moderate. **-a·bile** *adj.* unrestrainable. **-ato** *part. adj.* checked, restrained; unrestrained, unbridled, unchecked. (**-atore** *m.* **-atrice** *f.*) **-ellare** [A I] and derivs. (naut.) see **affrenellare**.

infreneṣ-ire [D 2] *tr.* to render frantic; *intr.* (*aux.* essere), *rfl.* to become frantic; to rave; to fly into a rage. **-ito** *part. adj.* frantic, raving, raging.

infrenetic-are [A 2 s] *tr.* to render frantic; *intr.* (*aux.* essere) to become frantic. **-ato** *part. adj.* frantic; †mad; †*n.m.* madman.

infrequen-te *adj.* infrequent, rare; non —, not infrequent, quite frequent; †unfrequented. **-temente** *adv.* infrequently, rarely. **-za** *f.* rarity.

†**infrescare** *vb.* and derivs. See **rinfrescare**.

†**infrigidare** *tr.* to make frigid; (poet.) to make deathly cold; *intr.* to become frigid; to turn cold.

infrigid-ire [D 2] *tr.* to render frigid; (agric.) to waterlog; *intr.* (*aux.* essere), *rfl.* to be chilled; (agric.) to become waterlogged. **-ito** *part. adj.* rendered frigid; chilled; (agric.) waterlogged.

infrigno *adj.* wrinkled, lined, creased; (Tusc.) sickly.

infroll-ire [D 2] *tr.* to enfeeble; *intr.* (*aux.* essere), *rfl.* to become feeble; to grow soft; (of meat) to become high, to become tender. **-imento** *m.* enfeebling; softening; tenderizing. **-ito** *part. adj.* enfeebled; (of meat) tenderized.

†**infrondare** *tr.* to cover with leaves; *intr., rfl.* to put forth leaves, to become leafy; (poet.) to become adorned with leaves, to be embowered with leaves.

infrondire [D 2] *intr.* (*aux.* essere), *rfl.* to become leafy, to put forth leaves, to grow green with leaves; *tr.* to cover with leaves.

infronẓolare [A I sc] *tr.* to deck with finery, to trim; *rfl.* to deck oneself out in furbelows.

†**infruenza** *f.* See **influenza**.

†**infruire** *vb.* and derivs. See **inferire**.

†**infrunito** *adj.* mad, insane; animo —, mind unhinged.

infrusc-are [A 2] *tr.* to tangle; to confuse; to bewilder; *rfl.* to become confused. **-ato** *part. adj.* tangled; confused; bewildered.

infrutt-escenza *f.* (bot.) infructescence. **-i·fero** *adj.* barren, unfruitful; (econ.) idle; without profit; capitale **-ifero**, idle capital; conto **-ifero**, account bearing no interest. **-uoso** *adj.* fruitless, vain, useless. **-uosamente** *adv.* fruitlessly.

in·ful-a *f.* (Rom. antiq.) infula; (eccl.) lappet of mitre; (complete) mitre; (hist.) imperial crown. **-ato** *adj.* wearing infula or mitre.

infun-are [A I] *tr.* to fasten with ropes, to rope together; to fit a rope to (any gear). **-ata** *f.* a group of persons roped together. **-ato** *part. adj.* roped. **-atura** *f.* roping together; fastening with ropes.

infundi·b-olo, -ulo *m.* (Rom. antiq.) funnel; (anat.) infundibulum; (bot.) funnel-shaped portion of flower.

†**infunestare** *vb.* and derivs. See **funestare**.

infungh-ire [D 2] *intr.* (*aux.* essere) to grow mouldy; (fig.) to get stale; to stick in a rut; †to be irritated, to be vexed. **-ito** *part. adj.* mouldy; (fig.) stale; †irritated, vexed.

infuocare [A 2 d] and derivs. See **infocare**.

infuori *adv.* outwards; out; all'— di, with the exception of, except (also 'in fuori').

infurb-ire [D 2] *intr.* (*aux.* essere), *rfl.* to grow cunning; to become shrewd. **-ito** *part. adj.* cunning; shrewd.

infurfant-ire [D 2] *intr.* (*aux.* essere) to become a scoundrel. (**-ito** *part. adj.*)

infuri-are [A 4] *intr.* (*aux.* essere), *rfl.* to rage, to become furious; to fly into a temper, to get angry; (*aux.* avere) to act furiously, to rage; una burrasca **-ava**, a storm was raging; *tr.* to enrage; lo hanno **-ato** contro di me, they have turned him against me. †**-ativo** *adj.* likely to excite rage; infuriating; likely to arouse enthusiasm; enrapturing. **-ato** *part. adj.* infuriated, enraged; in a rage; †in a tearing hurry.

infuṣi·bil-e *adj.* infusible, not fusible. **-ità** *f.* infusibility.

infuṣiọne *f.* infusion; liquid resulting from infusion; (theol.) infusion.

infuṣo *part.* of **infondere**, q.v.; *adj.* infused; supernatural (of knowledge, virtue); (joc.) non ho mica la scienza infusa, I haven't a private revelation on the subject; †suffused; *n.m.* infusion, liquid resulting from infusion.

infuṣito *adj.* straight as a poker.

infuṣo·rio *m.* (biol.) infusorian.

infust-ire [D 2] *intr.* (*aux.* essere) to grow stiff, to stiffen; *tr.* to make stiff, to stiffen. **-ito** *part. adj.* stiff as a poker; *n.m.* (vet.) rheumatism; cramp, neuralgia (in horses).

infutur-are [A I] *tr.* (poet.) to prolong into the future; *rfl.* to extend into the future. †**-o** *adj.* see **futuro**.

ingabban-are [A I] *rfl.* to wrap oneself in a cloak. **-ato** *part. adj.* wrapped in a cloak.

ingabbi-are [A 4] *tr.* to cage, to encage, to confine in a cage; (joc.) to put in prison; (naut.) to lay down (the keel of a ship). **-ata** *f.* caging; cageful; apparatus for catching birds. **-ato** *part. adj.* caged; (joc.) in prison.

ingaggi-are [A 3] *tr.* to engage; to join (battle); (naut.) to enlist; to foul (a rope, etc.); †to pawn; †(mil.) to engage (volunteers). **-ato** *part. adj.* engaged; †pawned; †enlisted. †**-atore** *m.* (mil.) recruiting agent.

ingag·gio *m.* pledge; engagement; (sport) premio di —, transfer fee; (mil.) engagement; (slang) 'taking the shilling', acceptance of military service and pay.

ingagliard-ire [D 2] *tr.* to strengthen, to invigorate, to harden; *intr.* (*aux.* essere), *rfl.* to grow stronger, to become robust; to take courage. **-imento** *m.* strengthening; growth; increase in robustness. **-ito** *part. adj.* strengthened; grown strong.

ingall-are[1] *tr.* to steep (cloth) in a solution of galls. (**-ato** *part. adj.* **-atore** *m.* **-atura** *f.*)

ingallare[2] *tr.* to fertilize (eggs).

†**ingallonare** *intr., rfl.* (naut.) to list.

ingalluzzire [D 2] *rfl.* to become elated; to bob up like a cork on the water; to show off, to strut.

ingambalare [A I] *tr.* to put (boots) on trees.

†**ingamb-are** *intr.* to take to one's heels; to run into danger; to be defective. †**-atura** *f.* impediment, obstruction. †**-o** *m.* danger; impediment.

ingangher-are [A I s] *tr.* to hinge, to fix on hinges. **-ato** *part. adj.* fixed on hinges.

ingann-are [A I] *tr.* to deceive, to cheat, to swindle; — il tempo, to kill time, to pass the time; — la moglie, to be unfaithful to one's wife; (leg.) to defraud; to deceive; to abuse; *rfl.* to be mistaken; Lei s'-a, you are mistaken, you are wrong; se non m'-o, if I am not mistaken; -arsi di grosso, to be greatly mistaken. **-a·bile** *adj.* credulous, gullible. **-acontadini** *m. indecl.* (paint.) a flashy artist, one who does showy work of little artistic merit. **-amento** *m.* deceiving, deception. **-ativo** *adj.* deceptive. **-ato** *part. adj.* deceived, cheated; mistaken; wronged by conjugal infidelity; seduced. **-atore** *m.* deceiver; cheat; swindler. (**-atrice** *f.*) **-evole** *adj.* deceptive, false, misleading, delusive, deceitful. **-evolmente** *adv.* deceitfully.

inganno *m.* deceit; deception; trick; fraud; stratagem; (mus.) cadenza d'—, deceptive cadence, interrupted cadence; (leg.) fraud; deceit; con —, by fraud; errore determinato dall'altrui —, mistake caused by another's deceit (C.P.).

†**ingarbare** *tr.* to make charming, to make graceful; to arrange gracefully; to adapt, to adjust; to introduce gracefully; *rfl.* to ingratiate oneself.

ingarbugli-are [A 4] *tr.* to entangle, to tangle, to muddle, to confuse, to embroil; to perplex. **-amento** *m.* entangling; confusing. **-ato** *part. adj.* entangled; confused; embroiled. (**-atore** *m.* **-atrice** *f.*) **-one** *m.* muddler.

†**ingastada** *f.* container with narrow foot and neck used for wine at table.

ingastig-ato *adj.* unpunished. †**-azione** *f.* remission of a punishment, pardon.

ingavonare [A I c] *rfl.* (naut.) to lay over and hang; †to capsize.

†**ingegna** *f.* See **ingegno**.

ingegn-are [A 5 c] *rfl.* to strive, to endeavour, to try to do one's best; to resort to expedients; -arsi di (a) acquistare, to strive to obtain; -arsi alla meglio, to do the best one can; *tr.* to contrive, to arrange; †to deceive, to trick. **-amento** *m.* striving; endeavour; †ingenuity; †see **ingegno**. **-ato** *part. adj.* contrived, arranged.

ingegner-e *m.* engineer; architect; title of a graduate in engineering; technologist; (naut.) — navale, naval constructor; — meccanico, engineer officer; — del porto, harbour engineer; †— di marina, naval constructor; †— idrografico, surveyor; (mil.) engineer. **-i·a** *f.* engineering; profession of engineering.

ingegno *m.* **1.** TALENT, intelligence, liveliness of mind; uomo d' —, gifted man; avere —, to be talented; to have a certain flair; avere troppo —, to have more natural aptitude or intuitive ability than real intelligence; un — vivace, a lively, quick-witted mind. **2.** INGENUITY; ci mise —, he used his ingenuity; a forza d'—

ingegno (*cont.*)
by using one's ingenuity. **3.** MIND, intellect; avere sommo —, to have a magnificent mind; opere d'—, works of the mind (as distinguished from 'opere di mano', etc.); alzata d'—, brain-wave, brilliant idea; a person with a good intellect; è un —, he has a good brain. **4.** EXPEDIENT, contrivance, mechanism; — della chiave, business end of a key; *pl.* wards of a lock. **5.** GENIUS, special talent; l'— italiano, the Italian genius; ha — per la musica, he has a genius (*or* talent) for music; l'— poetico, poetic genius; l'— inventivo, inventive genius.

ingegnọs-o *adj.* ingenious; witty; resourceful; il bisogno fa l'uomo —, necessity is the mother of invention. **-amẹnte** *adv.* ingeniously; wittily, resourcefully. **-ità** *f.* ingenuity; industry; ingenious contrivance or mechanism.

ingelos-ire [D2] *tr.* to make jealous; *rfl.*, *intr.* (*aux.* essere; *prep.*) di to become jealous (of); to be jealous. **-ito** *part. adj.* made jealous.

ingeminare [A1s] *tr.* (gramm.) to tautologize, to use tautology.

ingemm-are [A1] *tr.* to adorn with jewels; to embellish; *intr.* (*aux.* avere) (bot.) to bud; *rfl.* to bedeck oneself with jewels. **-amẹnto** *m.* embellishing; adornment. **-ato** *part. adj.* bejewelled, jewelled; (bot.) in bud, budding.

ingenera·bile[1] *adj.* generable, that can be generated or produced.

†**ingenera·bile**[2] *adj.* See under **ingenerare.**

ingener-are [A1s] *tr.* to generate, to produce, to give rise to, to engender, to cause; *rfl.* (*prep.*) da) to originate, to arise (from). †**-a·bile** *adj.* †not generable, that cannot be generated or produced. **-amẹnto** *m.* generation, begetting, engendering. **-ato** *part. adj.* engendered; innate; †not generated, unengendered. †**-azione** *f.* see **generazione.**

ingenerọs-o *adj.* ungenerous; grudging; not magnanimous. **-amẹnte** *adv.* ungenerously; grudgingly. **-ità** *f.* lack of generosity; meanness.

†**inge·nio** *m.* See **ingegno.**

inge·nit-o *adj.* innate, congenital, inborn; cattive inclinazioni -e all'uomo, evil tendencies which are innate in man; virtù -e in certe piante, properties inherent in certain plants; †per —, innately; by inheritance. **-amẹnte** *adv.* innately.

ingente *adj.* huge, enormous, vast; outsize.

ingentil-ire [D2] *tr.* to refine, to civilize, to cultivate; *rfl.*, *intr.* (*aux.* essere) to become civilized; to acquire polish; to become more courteous, to learn manners. **-imẹnto** *m.* refining, civilizing, polishing of manners. **-ito** *part. adj.* refined, civilized; polished; improved in manners.

inge·nu-o *adj.* natural, simple, ingenuous, simple-minded; (Rom. hist.) free-born; (leg.) feudo —, complete ownership; †liberal, humane; *n.m.* ingenuous person. **-a** *f.* (theatr.) ingénue. **-amẹnte** *adv.* ingenuously. **-ità** *f.* ingenuousness, simple-mindedness, innocence, sincerity; ingenuous action; ingenuous remark; (Rom. hist.) free status, gentle birth.

†**ingergo** *m.* mystery; puzzle.

inger-ire [D2] *tr.* to ingest, to absorb, to take in; †— un sospetto, to arouse suspicion; *rfl.* to interfere, to meddle. **-enza** *f.* interference; participation; non ho nessuna -enza nei suoi affari, I am not concerned with his affairs, I never interfere in his affairs; *pl.* duties, official business. **-imẹnto** *m.* ingestion, absorption; †arousing. **-ito** *part. adj.* ingested, absorbed, taken in; †aroused.

ingerlare [A1] *tr.* (naut.) to reef (a sail).

ingess-are [A1] *tr.* to plaster; to whitewash; (agric.) to lime, to dress with lime; (billiards) to chalk (a cue) (paint.) to dress with chalk; to limewash; to plaster. (amẹnto *m.*) **-ato** *part. adj.* plastered; whitewashed; (agric.) limed; chalked. **-atura** *f.* plastering, plaster; whitewashing, limewashing, dressing with lime; (surg.) setting in plaster; plaster casing.

ingessire [D2] *intr.* (*aux.* essere) to become chalky (of silkworms).

ingestiọne *f.* ingestion, absorption (cf. **ingerire**).

†**ingesto** *adj.* assimilated; drawn in; put in, placed in.

ingesuato *adj.* (myst. theol.) one with Christ, lost in Christ; *n.m.* (eccl. hist.) Gesuato, Jesuate.

†**inghestada** *f.* See **ingastada.**

inghiai-are [A4] *tr.* to gravel, to cover with gravel; (rlwy.; civ. eng.) to ballast; (naut.) to ballast with shingle; *intr.* (*aux.* avere) (naut.) to place some other material under the ballast; to beach a vessel. **-ata** *f.* ballast; load of gravel. **-ato** *part. adj.* gravelled; *n.m.* gravelling, strewing gravel; ballasting, ballast. **-atura** *f.* gravelling; ballasting; gravel; ballast.

Inghilterra *pr.n.f.* (geog.) England; (often, erroneously) the United Kingdom, Great Britain.

inghindare [A1] and derivs. (naut.). See **ghindare.**

†**inghiomellare** *tr.* to wind into a ball, to coil.

inghiott-ire [D2] *tr.* to swallow, to swallow up, to engulf. **-imẹnto** *m.* swallowing (up), engulfing; gulf, abyss. **-ito** *part. adj.* swallowed up, engulfed; *n.m.* (geog.) swallow-holes. **-itọio** *m.* drain, sewer; intake; (geog.) swallow-hole; †(anat.) oesophagus, gullet. (**-itọre** *m.* **-itrice** *f.*)

inghiottonire [D2] *tr.* to make greedy, to make gluttonous; *intr.* (*aux.* essere), *rfl.* to become greedy; to become a glutton; †(fig.) to fall in love.

†**inghiozzare** *vb.* and derivs. See **ingozzare.**

inghirland-are [A1] *tr.* to garland, to wreathe; to adorn with wreaths or garlands; (fig.) to encircle, to form a wreath round; to fill to the brim; (naut.) to reinforce the stem and stern of (a vessel); to serve (a rope) to prevent it from chafing. **-amẹnto** *m.* engarlanding, wreathing; encircling; (naut.) serving; (fig.) excessive ornamentation. **-ato** *part. adj.* garlanded, wreathed; encircled; (naut.) reinforced in stem and stern; served.

†**inghistara** *f.* See **ingastada.**

ingiallare [A1] *tr.* (poet.) to cause to turn yellow; *rfl.*, *intr.* (*aux.* essere) to turn yellow (cf. **ingiallire**).

ingiall-ire [D2] *tr.* to cause to turn yellow, to yellow, to make yellow; *rfl.*, *intr.* (*aux.* essere) to turn yellow. **-imẹnto** *m.* turning yellow, yellowing. **-ito** *part. adj.* yellowed; turned yellow.

ingiardinare [A1] *tr.* to adorn with gardens; to make into a garden; *rfl.* to become like a garden.

ingiaro *m.* (naut.) brail.

ingigant-ire [D2] *tr.* to magnify; to exaggerate; to represent as gigantic; *rfl.*, *intr.* (*aux.* essere) to appear gigantic; to be magnified; to be exaggerated. **-ito** *part. adj.* magnified; exaggerated; made to appear gigantic.

ingigliare [A4] *tr.* to adorn with lilies; *rfl.* to take on the form of a lily; to become like a lily; to become adorned with lilies, to adopt lilies (on coat of arms).

inginocchi-are [A4] *tr.* to cause to curve outwards; *rfl.* to kneel down, to kneel; to fall on one's knees; to make a genuflexion; (of a horse) to stumble. **-amẹnto** *m.* kneeling down, falling on one's knees; genuflexion; show of humility or subservience. **-ata** *f.* genuflexion; (archit.) a window protected by iron bars bulging outwards; a window with two curved supports. **-atọio** *m.* faldstool. **-atura** *f.* curve like that of a knee, knee-curve. †**-azione** *f.* kneeling; bowing of the knee. **-ọni** *adv.* kneeling, on one's knees.

ingiocọndo *adj.* unpleasant; tiresome; non —, not unpleasant.

ingioiare[1] [A4] and derivs. See **ingioiellare.**

†**ingioiare**[2] *tr.* to give joy to, to fill with joy.

ingioiell-are [A1] *tr.* to adorn with jewels; *rfl.* to put on jewelry, to wear jewels; to adorn oneself with jewelry. **-ato** *part. adj.* wearing jewels; (archit.) adorned with crystals or glass resembling precious stones.

†**ingioire** *vb.* and derivs. See **gioire.**

ingiornalare [A1] *tr.* (comm.) to journalize, to enter in the day-book.

ingiovanire [D2] *intr.* (*aux.* essere), *rfl.* to be rejuvenated, to renew one's youth, to feel young again.

ingiù *adv.* down, downwards; i ragazzi dai dieci anni —, boys of ten years old and under; (of running water) downstream; all'—, down below *or* downwards; (fig.) lasciar correre l'acqua all'—, to let things slide, to let things take their course (cf. **giù**).

ingiudicato *adj.* (leg., etc.) undecided, *sub judice.*

†**ingiu·lia** *f.* See **ingiuria.**

†**ingiumai** *adv.* See **oggimai.**

ingiunc-are [A2] *tr.* to strew with rushes; to tie with rushes; (naut.) to put a hemp stopper on (a sail). **-ato** *part. adj.* rush-strewn, rush-covered. **-atura** *f.* (naut.) stoppering, method, action or position of stopper.

ingiun·gere [C5] *tr.* to enjoin; to prescribe, to command, to order; (leg.) to enjoin, to order; il Tribunale ha ingiunto, the Court has ordered (summarily); †to include; †to unite, to join; †to ascribe to, to impute to; †to catch out; to catch red-handed.

ingiunto *part.* of **ingiungere**, q.v., *adj.* enjoined, prescribed, ordered; (leg.) enjoined; ordered; †annexed, added; †caught, surprised.

ingiunziọne *f.* injunction, order, command; (leg.) summary order; — di consegna, summary order to deliver; — di pagamento, summary order to pay (C.C.P.).

†**ingiura** *f*. See **ingiuria**.

ingiu·ri·a *f*. insult; injury, wrong; outrage; offensive remark; *pl.* abuse; damage; le -e del tempo, the ravages of time; le -e del vento, damage due to the buffeting of the wind; (leg.) offence to a person's dignity, honour, self-respect or susceptibilities (C.P.); il fatto costituisce un'— grave, it amounts to an insult (C.C.). -**are** [A4] *tr*. to insult, to abuse, to revile; to wrong. -**ante** *part. adj.* (leg.) offending; offensive; *n.m., f.* offender. -**ato** *part. adj.* insulted; abused; offended; reviled; *n.m.* offended party. -**atore** *m*. reviler; *adj.* abusive. (-**atrice** *f*.) -**oso** *adj.* insulting, offensive; abusive; wrongful. -**osamente** *adv.* insultingly, offensively; abusively; wrongfully.

ingiustific·a·bile *adj.* unjustifiable; unwarrantable. -**abilmente** *adv.* unjustifiably, without justification. -**ato** *adj.* unjustified, unwarranted.

ingiusti·zia *f*. injustice; unfairness; wrong, injury; che —!, how unfair!; †unrighteousness, sin.

ingiust·o *adj.* unjust; unfair; essere — con, to be unjust towards, to be unfair to; (leg.) unlawful, wrongful; *n.m.* unjust (man); patisce il giusto per l'—, the innocent suffer for the guilty; unfair thing; pretendi l'— da me, you expect too much of me. -**amente** *adv.* unjustly; unfairly; (leg.) accusato -amente, wrongfully accused.

inglese *adj.* English; (often, erroneously) British; partirsene all'—, to take French leave; (cul.) zuppa —, trifle; letti inglesi, twin beds; (mus.) corno —, *cor anglais*, English horn; *n.m.* English (language); Englishman; far l'—, to feign ignorance; gli Inglesi, the English; *f*. la Inglese, the English woman, the English girl.

†**inglo·rio** *adj.* inglorious, devoid of glory; obscure, retired.

inglorios·o *adj.* inglorious, without glory; obscure. -**amente** *adv.* ingloriously; obscurely.

†**inglu·via** *f*. voracity, greed.

inglu·vie *f*. crop (of a bird).

ingluvina *f*. (chem.) ingluvin.

ingobbiare [A4] *tr*. to fill the crop of, to cram (poultry); *intr.* (*aux.* avere) to gobble.

ingobb·ire [D2] *intr* (*aux.* essere) to become hunchbacked; — sul lavoro, to sit hunched over one's work, to swot. -**ito** *part. adj.* hunchbacked; hunched.

†**ingoffare** *tr*. to punch, to hit, to belabour, to trounce.

ingoff·ire [D2] *tr*. to make look clumsy; quel vestito t'-isce, that dress makes you look ungainly; *intr.* (*aux.* essere), *rfl.* to become ungainly; to behave clumsily.

ingoi·are [A4c] *tr*. to swallow, to gulp down; — un boccone amaro, to swallow a bitter pill; to read through, to wade through (a large quantity of reading matter); to swallow greedily, to devour. -**amento** *m*. gulping; swallowing. -**ato** *part. adj.* gulped down; swallowed up. (-**atore** *m.* -**atrice** *f.*)

ingolf·are [A1c] *rfl.* (of the sea) to form a gulf; (naut.) to become embayed; (fig.) -arsi in, to become engulfed in, to plunge into, to become immersed in, to become engrossed in; -arsi nei debiti, to plunge heavily into debt; *tr*. to engulf, to implicate, to involve (esp. in debts). -**amento** *m*. engulfing. -**ato** *part. adj.* (fig.) engulfed; absorbed; -ato nei debiti, deeply in debt; (motor.) flooded (e.g. of carburettor).

ingolla *f*. (agric.) basket fixed to a pole for picking fruit.

ingoll·are [A1] *tr*. (pop.) to gulp down; to guzzle. -**ato** *part. adv.* gulped down; (herald.) swallowing.

ingolos·ire [D2] *tr*. to whet the appetite of; to excite the greed of; *rfl., intr.* (*aux.* essere) to become greedy. -**ito** *part. adj.* made greedy, tempted.

ingolpare [A1] and derivs. (agric.). See **involpare**.

ingombr·are [A1c] *tr.* to encumber; to obstruct; to crowd; to block up; questo baule m'-a, this trunk is in my way; to load; dense nuvole -avano il cielo, heavy clouds obscured the sky; troppi dettagli -ano la mente, too many details confuse the mind; (naut.) to encumber (a hold or deck-space occupied by larger objects). -**amento** *m*. encumbering; blocking. -**ante** *part. adj.* encumbering; cumbersome. -**ato** *part. adj.* encumbered; blocked; obstructed; -ato di, encumbered with, weighed down by, loaded with, piled with.

ingombro[1] *m*. encumbrance; obstruction, obstacle; impediment; fare —, essere d'—, to be an obstruction, to get in the way; (naut.) machinery space and volume occupied by other equipment or cargo; dimensioni di —, overall dimensions.

ingombro[2] *apocop. part.* of **ingombrare**, q.v.; *adj.* encumbered; — di, encumbered with, impeded by, laden with.

ingomm·are [A1c] *tr*. to gum (i.e. to stick with gum or to cover with gum). -**ato** *part. adj.* gummed; carta -ata, sticky paper.

ingorbi·are [A4] *tr*. to put a ferrule on (e.g. a stick). -**ato** *part. adj.* having a ferrule. -**atura** *f*. ferrule; chuck (of a brace).

ingordamente *adv.* See under **ingordo**.

†**ingordare** *rfl.* to become greedy, to grow voracious.

ingord·o *adj.* voracious, greedy; gluttonous; covetous; excessive; exorbitant; interesse —, exorbitant interest, usury; macina -a, rough millstone that grinds too quickly; *n.m.* glutton; greedy man. -**amente** *adv.* voraciously, greedily; covetously; exorbitantly. †-**ezza** *f*. greed; exorbitance, excessiveness. -**i·gia** *f*. voracity, greediness; covetousness, avidity; exorbitance. -**ina** *f*. rasp or file that scrapes too much away at one rasp.

ingorg·are [A2c] *tr*. to block, to choke; to check; *rfl.* to become choked; to be blocked; to accumulate (of water, etc. on account of obstruction); to get stopped up; (of traffic) to be held up, to form a traffic-block. -**amento** *m*. blocking, choking. -**ato** *part. adj.* blocked; choked; obstructed; forming a bottleneck; (med.) suffering from a stoppage.

†**ingorgiare** *tr*. to swallow; to gulp down.

ingor·go *m*. (*pl.* -**ghi**) blocking, choking; obstruction, blockage; — stradale, traffic jam; (med.) stoppage.

ingoverna·bile *adj.* ungovernable, difficult to govern; unruly.

ingozz·are [A1] *tr*. to gulp down; to swallow greedily; to swallow quickly with repugnance; (fig.) non posso -arla, it sticks in my throat; — un'ingiuria, to swallow an insult; to stuff, to cram; — le oche, to cram geese forcibly; (fig.) — dieci pagine di grammatica, to cram ten pages of grammar into one's head. -**atura** *f*. cramming of a hat down over a person's eyes; (vet.) choking, obstruction in throat.

ingracil·ire [D2] *intr.* (*aux.* essere), *rfl.* to become thin; to grow slim; *tr*. to make thin. -**ito** *part. adj.* grown thin; slim, fined down in physique.

†**ingradare** *rfl.* to be graded, to extend in gradation; to increase step by step; to be multiplied.

ingradua·bile *adj.* that cannot be graded; not susceptible of differentiation by degree.

†**ingramignare** *rfl.* to grow well (of graminaceous plants).

ingranag·gio *m*. (eng.) gears, spur or sprocket wheels; cogging, cogwheels; gear system; engaging; (fig.) wheels within wheels (cf. **ingranare**[2]); — conico, bevel gear.

ingranare[1] [A1] *tr*. to dye (hides) with sumach.

ingran·are[2] [A1] *tr*. (eng.) to engage, to throw into mesh, to put into gear; (motor.) — la marcia, to engage the gears, (colloq., abs.) to put her into gear; to interlock; to pitch; *intr.* (*aux.* essere) to engage, to mesh; *recip. rfl.* to engage; to seize, to seize up; (colloq.) to understand each other, to get on together, to suit each other. -**amento** *m*. (eng.) mesh, engagement; (eng.) seizing. (-**ato** *part. adj.*) -**o·fono** *m*. (eng.) gear sound tester.

†**ingranato** *m*. garnet.

ingranch·ire [D2] *tr*. to make numb, to benumb; *intr.* (*aux.* essere) to grow numb. -**ito** *part. adj.* numbed, numb.

ingrandimento *m*. See under **ingrandire**.

ingrand·ire [D2] *tr*. to enlarge; to magnify; to extend; to increase; to augment; (mus.) to swell upon (a prolonged note); *intr.* (*aux.* essere), *rfl.* to grow taller; to increase in size; (fig.) to become grand; to become more important. -**imento** *m*. enlargement, magnification, growth, increase; lente d'-imento, magnifying glass, magnifying lens. -**ito** *part. adj.* enlarged; magnified; augmented; grown bigger; become more important, grander. -**itore** *m*. enlarger; magnifier; (watchm.) cerchio -itore di piastra, plate enlargement ring; *adj.* enlarging; magnifying. (-**itrice** *f*.)

ingrano·fono *m*. See under **ingranare**[2].

ingrass·ag·gio *m.,* -**amento** *m*. See under **ingrassare**.

ingrass·are [A1] *tr*. to fatten; to enrich; to manure; to grease; *abs.* to be fattening; il burro -a, butter is fattening, butter causes one to put on weight; (tanning) to stuff; — a tampone, to handstuff; *intr.* (*aux.* essere), *rfl.* to grow fat, to get stout; — a, to grow fat on, to thrive on, to take pleasure in. -**abue** *m. indecl.,* -**amanzo** *m. indecl.* (bot.) names of various fodder plants. -**aporci** *m. indecl.* (bot.) dandelion, *Taraxacum officinale*, and allied plants. -**ag·gio** *m*. greasing; oiling, lubricating. -**amento** *m*. process of fattening. -**ante** *part. adj.* fattening; *n.m.* fattening substance,

ingrass-are (*cont.*)
fattening food. †**-ativo** *adj.* fattening, rich (of food). **-ato** *part. adj.* fattened; enriched; manured. **-atore** *m.* (eng.) lubricator, grease nipple. **-atura** *f.* (eng.) greasing, lubrication. **-o** *m.* fattening; enricher; manure, fertilizer; dubbin. **-ucchiare** [A4] *intr.* (*aux.* avere) to put on a little weight.

ingratamente *adv.* See under **ingrato**.

ingraticci-are [A3] *tr.* to fit with lattice-work, to trellis; to close behind a lattice; to fence with hurdles; *rfl.* to be ruffled; to become tangled (of hair). **-ata** *f.* trellis; trellis-work; lattice-work. **-ato** *part. adj.* trellised; hurdled; tangled (of hair). **-atura** *f.* trellising, latticing.

ingraticol-are [A1s] *tr.* to close with a grating. **-amento** *m.* putting up of grating; grating; grille. **-ata** *f.* grating, grille; series of squares (printed on squared paper), grid. **-ato** *part. adj.* barred with a grating; *n.m.* grating, grille. **-atura** *f.* putting up of grating; grating, grille.

ingratigliare [A4] *tr.* (naut.) to put roping on (a sail or net).

ingratitu·dine *f.* ingratitude, ungratefulness, thanklessness; ungrateful action; atti d'—, ungrateful behaviour; pagare d'— i benefizi, to be ungrateful for benefits.

ingrat-o *adj.* unpleasant; displeasing; unrewarding; ungrateful, thankless; non vi sarò —, I shall not forget your kindness; terreno —, soil that yields very little; *n.m.* ungrateful person, ingrate. (**-a** *f.*) **-amente** *adv.* ungratefully; unpleasantly.

ingravid-are [A1s] *tr.* (vulg.) to render pregnant; *intr.* (*aux.* essere), *rfl.* to become pregnant, to conceive. **-amento** *m.* pregnancy; conception. **-ata** *part. adj. f.* pregnant.

†**ingravire** *tr.* to make heavier; to put weight upon; (mus.) to flatten; *rfl.* to become grave.

ingrazi-are [A4] *rfl.* (*acc.* of *prn.* si, *prep.* con) to ingratiate oneself, to curry favour (with); riuscì a -arsi col Ministro, he managed to win the Minister's favour; (*dat.* of *prn.* si) -arsi uno, to ingratiate oneself with someone, to gain someone's favour; †*tr.* to thank. **-ato** *part. adj.* favoured, looked on with favour.

†**ingraziato** *adj.* full of grace.

†**ingrazionire** [D2] (Tusc.). See **ingraziare**.

†**ingrec-are** *intr.* to become angry, to be roused to fury. †**-ato** *part. adj.* angered, infuriated, roused to fury.

ingrediente *m.* ingredient; (fig.) element, component part; †*adj.* component.

†**ingremire** *vb.* and derivs. See **ghermire**.

ingresso *m.* entrance, way in, entry; admittance; price of admission; quanto è l'—?, how much does one pay to go in?; vietato l'—, no admittance; — vietato agli estranei, no admittance except on business; entering; (astron.) ingress; (leg.) — abusivo, unlawful entry (C.P.).

†**ingrillandare** *vb.* and derivs. See **inghirlandare**.

ingrinzire [D2] and derivs. See **aggrinzire**.

ingrippare [A1] *rfl.* (eng.) to bind, to seize.

ingrognare [A5c] and derivs. See **ingrugnare**.

ingromm-are [A1c] *tr.* to cause (wine) to form a crust; to deposit tartar on (teeth); *intr.* (*aux.* avere) to form a crust (of wine); to become covered with tartar (of teeth). **-ato** *part. adj.* crusted (of wine); covered with tartar (of teeth).

ingroppare[1] [A1] and derivs. See **aggroppare**[1].

ingroppare[2] [A1] *tr.* to take up as a pillion rider; (mil.) to mount (infantry); †to force (a horse) on to its haunches.

ingross-are [A1] *tr.* to enlarge; to swell; to increase; to thicken; to cause to appear bigger; to blunt, to dull; to coarsen; to cause to swell, to cause a swelling in; (mil.) to strengthen, to reinforce; *intr.* (*aux.* essere), *rfl.* to grow bigger, to increase; to swell; to rise; to grow stout; (of the sea) to get rough; (fig.) to become blunted; to grow insensitive; to grow dull; to become gross. **-amento** *m.* growing bigger, swelling; increase; (med.) -amento della milza, enlargement of the spleen, splenomegaly; (archit.) thickness. **-ato** *part. adj.* enlarged; swollen; increased; thickened; blunted, dulled. (**-atore** *m.* **-atrice** *f.*) **-atura** *f.* increasing; swelling; thickening; thickness.

ingrosso *adv. phr.* all'—, wholesale; vendere all'—, to sell wholesale, to be a wholesaler; comprare all'—, to buy wholesale.

†**ingrottare** *tr.* to hide in a grotto; to conceal; *rfl.* to enter a grotto.

ingrugn-are [A5] *intr.* (*aux.* essere), *rfl.* (fam.) to sulk, to pout; to look sulky. **-atura** *f.* sulking, pouting; sulkiness.

ingrugn-ire [D2] *intr.* (*aux.* essere), *rfl.* see **ingrugnare**. **-ito** *part. adj.* sulky; pouting. **-itura** *f.* see **ingrugnatura**.

ingrull-ire [D2] *intr.* (*aux.* essere) (Tusc.) to grow stupid; *tr.* to render stupid. **-ito** *part. adj.* made stupid, dulled.

ingruppare [A1] and derivs. See **aggruppare**.

inguada·bile *adj.* unfordable.

inguadare [A1] *tr.* to dye with woad.

inguain-are [A1] *tr.* to sheathe; to insert a draw-string in. **-amento** *m.* sheathing, encasing. **-ato** *part. adj.* sheathed; having a sheath.

†**inguala** (hist. naut. command) oars forward!

ingualci·bil-e *adj.* uncreasable, crease-proof, uncrushable, wrinkle-proof. **-ità** *f.* crease-resistance.

inguant-are [A1] *rfl.* to put on one's gloves. **-ato** *part. adj.* wearing gloves; gloved; mano -ata, gloved hand.

inguari·bil-e *adj.* incurable; malattia —, incurable illness; malato —, incurable patient; *n.m.*, *f.* incurable. **-mente** *adv.* incurably; irremediably.

†**ingubbiare** *tr.* to guzzle, to gobble.

inguidalesc-are [A2] *tr.* to gall (a horse); *rfl.* to become galled. **-ato** *part. adj.* galled.

†**inguiderdonato** *adj.* unrewarded.

in·guin-e *m.* (anat.) groin. **-ale** *adj.* in the groin, of the groin, inguinal.

†**inguistara** *f.* carafe.

ingurgit-are [A1s] *tr.* to devour, to swallow greedily, to gobble, to guzzle. †**-atore** *m.* guzzler.

†**ingusciare** *intr.* to enter a shell, pod or cover; to slip in.

ingusta·bile *adj.* tasteless; insipid.

inib-ire [D2] *tr.* (leg.) to prohibit; to restrain; to forbid; (med.; psych.; scient.) to inhibit. †**-ita** *f.* see **inibitoria**. **-ito** *part. adj.* (leg.) prohibited; restrained. **-itore** *m.* (scient.) inhibitor. **-ito·ria** *f.* (leg.) order staying execution; interim injunction. **-ito·rio** *adj.* (leg.) restraining; staying; (scient.) inhibiting. **-izione** *f.* (leg.) stay of execution; restraining order; prohibition; restraint; (med.; psych.; scient.) inhibition; check, stoppage.

†**inico** *adj.* See **iniquo**.

inido·ne-o *adj.* unfitted, unfit, unsuitable. **-ità** *f.* unfitness, unsuitability.

iniett-are [A1] *tr.* to inject; to inject into, to inject with; la vipera -a il veleno, the viper injects poison; (med.) to inject; *abs.* to give an injection; (eng.) to inject; — con, to impregnate with. **-ato** *part. adj.* injected; occhi -ati di sangue, bloodshot eyes. **-ore** *m.* injector, syringe; (eng.) injector; (Diesel engine) injector, injection valve, vaporizer.

iniezione *f.* injection; (scient.; eng.) injection; (motor.) — diretta, solid fuel injection.

inimic-are [A2] *tr.* to alienate; to estrange; to make hostile; to set at variance; to treat as an enemy; *rfl.* (*acc.* of *prn.* si, *prep.* con) to fall out (with), to get on the wrong side (of), to fall foul (of); s'-ò con il preside, he fell out with the principal; (*dat.* of *prn.* si) to inspire the hostility of; to make an enemy of; s'-ò il preside, he turned the principal against him; *recip. rfl.* to become enemies; to fall out (with one another); si sono -ati, they have quarrelled, they are no longer friends. **-ato** *part. adj.* estranged, alienated; hostile; †hated.

†**inimiche·vol-e** *adj.* unfriendly; hostile, inimical. (†**-mente** *adv.*)

inimici·zia *f.* hostility; enmity; aversion, dislike; hatred; aver — con, to be hostile towards.

inimico *adj., n.m.* See **nemico**.

inimita·bil-e *adj.* inimitable; unequalled; unrivalled. **-mente** *adv.* inimitably.

inimitato *adj.* not imitated.

inimmagina·bil-e *adj.* unimaginable; inconceivable. **-mente** *adv.* unimaginably. **-ità** *f.* unimaginableness.

infiamma·bil-e *adj.* (techn.) uninflammable. **-ità** *f.* (techn.) non-inflammability.

inintelligente *adj.* unintelligent.

inintelligi·bil-e *adj.* unintelligible; illegible; inaudible. (**-mente** *adv.*) **-ità** *f.* unintelligibility; illegibility; inaudibility.

ininterrotto *adj.* uninterrupted; continuous; unceasing.

ininvestiga·bile *adj.* not fit for investigation.

iniquit-à *f.* injustice, inequality; iniquity; iniquitous action; disse un'—, he uttered an iniquitous remark; — della stagione, inclemency of the weather, unseasonable weather; (theol.) iniquity. †**-anza** *f.* see **iniquità**. †**-ire** *intr.* to grow iniquitous, to become wicked. †**-oso** *adj.* see **nequitoso**, or **iniquo**.

ini·qu·o *adj.* wicked, iniquitous; unjust; unequal; (joc.) shockingly bad, wicked, frightful; (leg.) inequitable (C.C.). **-amẹnte** *adv.* iniquitously; unjustly; wickedly.

†**inirasci·bile** *adj.* not easily moved to anger.

in-ire [D def.] *tr.* (leg.) to start, to commence; to initiate; to originate. **-ito** *part. adj.* initiatory; originating.

†**inispagnolire** *tr.* to influence with Spanish customs or characteristics; *rfl.* to assume Spanish ways, to become like the Spanish; to show signs of the influence of Spain or Spanish.

†**inistima·bile** *adj.* See **inestimabile.**

inizial-e *adj.* initial, first, original; opening, beginning; stipendio —, commencing salary; (mus.) corda —, mese, or keynote of a scale in ancient Greek music; *n.f.* initial letter, initial; quali sono le sue -i?, what are your initials? **-mẹnte** *adv.* initially, first, firstly, to begin with.

inizi-are [A4] *tr.* to initiate; to originate; to begin; to instruct in the elements of; (rel.) to admit to the mysteries; to initiate (rarely with ref. to Christian sacraments or the religious life); *rfl.* to have its beginning, to originate, to be initiated. **-a·bile** *adj.* fit for initiation; suitable to be begun. **-amẹnto** *m.* see **inizio.** **-a·tico** *adj.* (rel.) relating to initiation, initiatic. **-ativa** *f.* initiative; enterprise; libera **-ativa,** free enterprise; undertaking; prendere l'-ativa, to take the initiative; pieno d'-ativa, full of initiative; mancare d'-ativa, to be lacking in initiative; a -ativa di, on the initiative of. **-ativo** *adj.* commencing; originating. **-atore** *m.* initiator. (**-atrice** *f.*) **-ato** *part. adj.* initiated; begun, started. **-azione** *f.* beginning; initiation.

ini·zio *m.* beginning, commencement, start; fin dall'—, right from the start, from the very beginning; avere — da, to originate in, to begin with; (sport) calcio d'—, kick-off; *pl.* elements, rudiments; first steps; prendere i primi inizi, to have one's earliest beginnings; initiation.

†**inizzare** *vb.* and derivs. See **aizzare.**

†**inlacciare** *tr.* to share, to trap, to net; to deceive, to trick; *intr., rfl.* to fall into a trap.

†**inlagare** *rfl.* to spread out into a lake, to become a lake.

†**inlato** *m.* inlay.

†**inleare** *rfl.* to draw near, to become assimilated to the 'ultima salute' (formed from the *prep.* 'in' and the *f. prn.* 'lei'; Dante, *Para.* XXII).

†**inleggiadrire** *tr.* to embellish, to beautify; to make empty; to lighten.

†**inlibrare** *tr.* to hold balanced, to hold as in a balance.

†**inlitterato** *adj.* See **illetterato.**

†**inlividire** *tr.* to render livid.

†**inlocale** *adj.* not in space, without spatial definition.

†**inlucidare** *rfl.* to become illustrious.

†**inluiare** *vb.* See **illuiare.**

†**inluminare** *vb.* and derivs. See **illuminare.**

†**inlusione** *f.* See **illusione.**

†**inmalincon-icare, -ire** *vb.* and derivs. See **immalinconire.**

†**inmiare** *rfl.* See **immiare.**

innacquare [A6] *tr.* to water, to add water to, to dilute; †to water (plants); †to wet, to sprinkle; †to flood (cf. **annacquare**).

innaffi-are [A4] *tr.* to water, to sprinkle with water, to wet; — un pranzo con vini generosi, to wash down a dinner with excellent wines. **-amẹnto** *m.* watering; sprinkling. **-ato** *part. adj.* watered, sprinkled. **-atọio** *m.* watering-can. **-atrice** *f.* sprinkler.

innalz-are [A1] *tr.* to raise; to set up; to erect; to promote; to ennoble; to exalt; to heighten; to elevate; — uno al settimo cielo, to laud someone to the skies; †(naut.) to luff; *rfl.* to rise; -arsi a Dio, to lift up one's heart to God; -arsi sugli altri, to climb to the top of the tree; †(naut.) -arsi al vento, to come head to wind. **-amẹnto** *m.* raising; erecting, elevating; exalting; heightening; promoting; erection; elevation. **-ato** *part. adj.* raised, erected; set up; elevated; exalted, heightened; promoted. (**-atore** *m.* **-atrice** *f.*) **-atura** *f.* see **innalzamento.**

innamor-are [A1c] *tr.* (*prep.* di) to inspire with love; — uno di, to fill a person with love for; to enchant, to fascinate, to delight; *abs.* to be delightful; un visino che -a, a delightful little face; *rfl.* (*prep.* di) to fall in love (with); to conceive a passion (for); -arsi di una persona a vederla, to fall in love with someone at first sight; *recip. rfl.* to fall in love with each other. †**-acchiare** *rfl.* to flirt, to philander. **-amẹnto** *m.* enamourment; falling in love; courtship. †**-anza** *f.* love. **-ata** *f.* mistress; sweetheart, girl

friend. **-ato** *adj.* (*prep.* di) in love (with); very fond (of), enamoured (of); (rel.) spiriti -ati, fervent souls; *n.m.* sweetheart; boy friend; lover.

†**innamoro** *m.* love, falling in love.

†**innanim-are, -ire** *vb.* and derivs. See **inanimare.**

†**innant-e, -i** *adv., prep.* See **innanzi.**

innanz-i *prep.* before; — tempo, before the proper time, aforetime; (foll. by 'a') in front of, before, in the presence of; — a Dio, in the sight of God; before, in preference to; mettere una cosa — ad un'altra, to prefer one thing to another; — ad ogni altro, above everything else, in preference to everything else; (foll. by 'di') — di fare così, before doing so; *adv.* before, in the past; in front, ahead, first; tirare —, to go ahead, to proceed, to keep on; tirarsi — per una professione, to study for a profession; da quel giorno —, since that day; d'ora —, henceforth; forward; farsi —, to come forward; further; sapere più —, to be more expert (than others); procedere troppo —, to go too far; *n.m.* future; per l'—, henceforth; example, model, fair copy; (fig.) model, inspiration; coll'— del padre, with the example of his father to inspire him. †**-imet·tere** *tr.* to put before, to place in front; *rfl.* to put (or thrust) oneself forward. †**-inome** *m.* forename, Christian name. †**-ipenul·timo** *adj.* antepenultimate. †**-iporre** *tr.* to put before, to place in front; to prefer.

inna·rio *m.* hymn book, hymnal; (mus.; liturg.) hymnary, hymnarium.

†**innarra·bile** *adj.* See **inenarrabile.**

†**innarrare** *vb.* and derivs. See **narrare.**

†**innascondere** *vb.* and derivs. See **nascondere.**

innasp-are [A1] *tr.* (text.) to reel. **-amẹnto** *m.,* **-atura** *f.* (text.) winding; amount of thread wound.

innat-o *adj.* innate, inborn; congenital. **-ịsmo** *m.* (philos.) doctrine of innate ideas.

innaturale *adj.* unnatural.

†**innaturare** *vb.* and derivs. See **connaturare.**

innaviga·bil-e *adj.* unnavigable; (naut.) nave —, ship that is unseaworthy; not navigable owing to damage, or shortage of equipment or of crew; (of a sea, lake or river) impassable to navigation. (**-ità** *f.*)

innega·bil-e *adj.* undeniable, unquestionable, incontrovertible. **-mẹnte** *adv.* undeniably, unquestionably; without question.

inneggi-are [A3] *tr.* (mus.) to hymn; (fig.) to celebrate, to praise, to laud; *intr.* (*aux.* avere; *prep.* a) to sing hymns (to); (fig.) to sing the praises (of); (iron.) -ano a chi li paga, they sing the praises of those who pay them. **-amẹnto** *m.* (mus.) hymning; (fig.) adulation. **-ante** *part. adj.* hymning; praising. **-ato** *part. adj.* hymned; praised; lauded, celebrated. (**-atore** *m.* **-atrice** *f.*)

†**inne onne** *adv. phr.* carelessly; heedlessly; inne onne, (a phrase conveying uncertainty, cf. Eng. 'um, er'), hums and haws.

†**innerare** *intr.* to grow dark.

†**innervare** *intr.* to grow strong, to become robust.

innesc-are [A2c] *tr.* (mil.) to fuse; (naut.) to arm (the lead); (eng.) to prime (a pump, etc.); (electr.) to strike (a discharged lamp, etc.); — l'arco, to strike an arc. **-ato** *part. adj.* (mil.) fused; (naut., of the lead) armed; primed (of a pump). **-atura** *f.* (mil.) fuse, primer, igniter.

innẹs-co *m.* (*pl.* **-chi**) priming; (mil.) fuse.

†**inness-ione** *f.* setting (e.g. of precious stones); interconnexion. †**-o** *adj.* set (of precious stones).

innest-are [A1] *tr.* (agric.; hort.) to graft; — a occhio, to bud; (med.) to vaccinate, to inoculate; — il vaiuolo, to give an inoculation against smallpox; to cross-breed; to insert; (fig.) to graft; (eng.) to engage; to couple; (motor.) — la frizione, to engage the clutch, to let in the clutch; (leg.) — un muro in un altro, to bond one wall with another (C.C.); (mil.) — la baionetta, to fix bayonets; (naut.) — un albero, to step a mast; †(arith.) — i rotti, to multiply fractions. **-a·bile** *adj.* suitable for grafting; capable of being grafted. **-amẹnto** *m.* (agric.; hort.) grafting; inoculating, vaccinating; inoculation; cross-breeding; †(arith.) -amento dei rotti, multiplication of fractions. **-atọio** *m.* (agric.; hort.) grafting knife. (**-atore** *m.* **-atrice** *f.*) **-atura** *f.* (agric.; hort.) act of grafting; place where graft is inserted; time of grafting.

innesto *m.* (agric.) graft, scion, grafting; — a corona, rind graft; — a occhio, — a marza, — a croce, bud graft; — per approssimazione, approach grafting, inarching; (med.) — del vaiolo,

innesto (*cont.*)
inoculation against smallpox; (leg.) the act of bonding (walls) (C.C.); (eng.) clutch, coupling; (motor.) — per l'avviamento, starting dogs.

in·nico *adj.* (mus.) relating to hymns, hymnic.

†**innito** *m.* whinny; whinnying.

inn-o *m.* hymn, song of praise; anthem; (rel.) hymn (usu. liturgical); — ambrosiano, Te Deum; — angelico, Gloria in Excelsis; — della Trinità, Sanctus Deus, Sanctus Fortis, Sanctus Immortalis; — nazionale, national anthem; (poet.) -i sacri, poems on sacred themes; (hyperbol.) panegyric, encomium, eulogy. **-odi·a** *f.* (mus.) hymnody, hymn-singing; hymn-collection; hymnal. **-odo** *m.* (mus.) hymn-singer, hymnodist. **-ografia** *f.* (mus.) hymnography, hymn-collection, hymnal. **-ogra·fico** *adj.* (mus.) relating to hymns. **-o·graf-o** *m.* (mus.) hymnographer, hymn-writer. **-ologi·a** *f.* (mus.) hymnology, treatise on hymns. **-o·logo** *m.* (mus.) hymnologist, hymn-writer.

†**inno·bile** *adj.* and derivs. See **ignobile**.

innoc·ente *adj.* innocent; ignorant of evil; innocuous, harmless; (leg.) innocent; ritenuto —, found not guilty; dichiararsi —, to plead not guilty; *n.m.* (liturg.) festa degli Innocenti, Holy Innocents' Day; (art) la strage degli Innocenti, the slaughter of the Innocents; Spedale degli Innocenti, Foundling Hospital. **-ente·mente** *adv.* innocently, in innocence; harmlessly. **-enza** *f.* innocence; età dell'-enza, age of innocence, childhood.

Innocenzo *pr.n.m.* Innocence.

†**innoc·evole**, †**-iente**, †**-ivo** *adj.* innocent; innocuous.

inno·cu-o *adj.* innocuous; without venom; (fig.) harmless. **-amente** *adv.* innocuously; harmlessly. **-ità** *f.* innocuousness; harmlessness.

†**innoioso** *adj.* See **noioso**, under **noia**.

innomina·bile *adj.* nameless; unspeakable, unmentionable; (theol.) unnameable, ineffable.

†**innominare** *vb.* and derivs. See **nominare**.

innominat-o *adj.* unnamed; nameless; of unknown name; (anat.) osso —, innominate bone; *pr.n.m.* l'Innominato, the Unnamed (a character in Manzoni's *Promessi Sposi*). †**-amente** *adv.* anonymously, without mentioning names.

†**innondare** *vb.* and derivs. See **inondare**.

†**innorare**[1] *vb.* and derivs. See **onorare**.

†**innorare**[2] *vb.* and derivs. See **indorare**.

†**innorare**[3] *tr.* to pray, to supplicate, to entreat.

innormal-e *adj.* abnormal. **-mente** *adv.* abnormally. **-ità** *f.* abnormality.

†**innos·sio** *adj.* innocent.

innov-are [A I] *tr.* to innovate; to change; (paint.) to restore; to touch up; to do up; *rfl.* to change, to alter, to acquire a new look. **-amento** *m.* innovation, change. **-ato** *part. adj.* altered; (paint.) restored. **-atore** *m.* innovator. (**-atrice** *f.*) **-azione** *f.* innovation, change; renovation, reform.

†**innovellare** *vb.* and derivs. See **rinnovellare**.

innovera·bile *adj.* (poet.) innumerable, countless.

innumera·bil-e *adj.* innumerable, numberless, unnumbered, countless. **-mente** *adv.* without number, innumerably. **-ità** *f.* countlessness, unendingness.

†**innumerare** *vb.* See **numerare** and derivs.

innu·mer-e, **-o** *adj.* countless.

innumerevole *adj.* and derivs. See **innumerabile**.

ino *dim. suff.* (fam., used adjectivally, repeating a suffix) teeny-weeny; mi basta un pezzettino, ma proprio —, I only want the tiniest bit, really only a teeny-weeny bit.

inobbediente *adj.* and derivs. See **disubbidiente**, under **disubbidire**.

inoblia·bile *adj.* unforgettable.

inocchiare [A4] *tr.* (agric.; hort.) to bud.

inocculta·bile *adj.* unconcealable.

inoccup-ato *adj.* unoccupied, vacant, empty; untenanted, uninhabited; not yet employed; *n.m.* person who has not yet found employment, person not previously employed. **-azione** *f.* state of unemployment of persons who have not yet been employed (cf. **disoccupazione**).

inocondrite *f.* (med.) inochondritis.

inocul-are [A I s] *tr.* (agric.; hort.) to graft by budding; to bud, to inoculate; (fig.) — di, to inculcate, to inspire with; (med.) to inoculate. **-ato** *part. adj.* (agric.; hort.) grafted, budded; (fig.) inculcated; (med.) inoculated. **-azione** *f.* (agric.; hort.) grafting; (med.) inoculation.

†**inodiare** *vb.* and derivs. See **odiare**.

†**inodorare** *tr.* to scent, to perfume, to make fragrant.

inodore *adj.* see **inodoro**, under **inodorifero**.

inod-ori·fero *adj.*, **-oro**, **-oro** *adj.* odourless.

inoffens-i·bile *adj.* invulnerable. **-ivo** *adj.* inoffensive, harmless; non-dangerous.

inoffeso *adj.* unhurt, uninjured; unoffended.

inofficios-o *adj.* inconsiderate, discourteous, casual; (leg.) inofficious; testamento —, irregular will; donazione -a, inofficious donation. **-amente** *adv.* inofficiously. **-ità** *f.* inofficiousness.

inoli-are [A4] *tr.* to oil; to season with oil; †(rel.) to anoint. **-ato** *part. adj.* oiled; mixed with oil; per S. Liberata l'oliva è -ata, on 8 October the olives are ripe; †(rel.) anointed.

†**inolmare** *rfl.* to become grown with elm trees.

inoltr-are [A I c] *rfl.* to go further, to go on; to advance, to proceed; l'inverno s'-a, the winter is far advanced; *tr.* (admin.) to forward, to send forward; to transmit; (leg.) to file, to lodge; — un ricorso, to lodge a petition. **-amento** *m.* (admin.) forwarding; transmitting. **-ato** *part. adj.* advanced; a notte -ata, late at night; -ato negli anni, well on in years.

inoltre *adv.* besides, in addition, moreover, furthermore.

inoltro *m.* (admin.) forwarding; transmitting, passing on.

inombr-are [A I c] *tr.* to shade, to darken; *rfl.* to become covered with shade; to be shady; to be in the shade. **-ato** *part. adj.* shady, shaded, in the shade.

inond-are [A I c] *tr.* to flood, to inundate; (fig.) i forestieri -ano l'Italia, foreigners flock into Italy; (poet.) la gioia m'-a il petto, joy fills my heart; (mil.) to flood, to open (dykes, etc.). **-ante** *part. adj.* overflowing. **-ato** *part. adj.* inundated, flooded. **-atore** *m.*, *adj.* (poet.) flooding, flood. (**-atrice** *f.*, *adj.*) **-azione** *f.* flood, flooding, inundation; (fig.) wave, flood.

inonest-à *f.* lack of honesty, dishonesty; dishonour. **-o** *adj.* not strictly honest, somewhat dishonest. **-amente** *adv.* dishonestly.

inonorato *adj.* unhonoured, without fame or honours.

i·n-ope *adj.* poor, indigent; impoverished. **-o·pia** *f.* poverty, indigence; lack.

inopera·bile *adj.* (med.) inoperable.

inoperos-o *adj.* idle, inactive; disused, unused; inert; unemployed, idle. **-amente** *adv.* idly. **-ità** *f.* inactivity; idleness; inertness.

inopessi·a *f.* (med.) inopexia.

inopina·bil-e *adj.* unthinkable, inconceivable, incredible; unforeseeable. **-mente** *adv.* unthinkably; incredibly.

inopinat-o *adj.* unthought of; unforeseen. **-amente** *adv.* suddenly, unexpectedly.

inopponi·bil-e *adj.* (leg.) — al terzo, that cannot be set up against a third party. **-ità** *f.* (leg.) disqualification for being so set up.

inopportun-o *adj.* untimely, inopportune; inadvisable; inconvenient; unfitting, not suitable, awkward. **-amente** *adv.* inopportunely. **-ità** *f.* untimeliness; inconvenience; unsuitability.

inoppugna·bil-e *adj.* incontestable, unimpeachable, incontrovertible; (leg.) indisputable; argomento —, irrefutable argument. **-mente** *adv.* incontestably; incontrovertibly. **-ità** *f.* incontestability; (leg.) indisputability (C.P.P.).

inor-are[1] *tr.* to gild. **-ato** *part. adj.* gilded; gilt.

†**inorare**[2] *vb.* and derivs. See **onorare**.

inordin-anza *f.* lack of order, disorder. **-atezza** *f.* disorder, irregularity. **-ato** *adj.* disordered, confused, disorderly; inordinate. **-atamente** *adv.* inordinately. †**-azione** *f.* disorder, lack of order, disorderliness.

inorecchito *adj.* attentive, listening, with ears pricked, all ears.

inorga·nic-o *adj.* (scient.) inorganic; (fig.) disordered, without organic unity. **-amente** *adv.* inorganically.

inorgogl-ire [D 2] *tr.* to make proud; to elate; to turn (a person's) head; *intr.* (*aux.* essere), *rfl.* to grow proud; to be elated; to have one's head turned. **-ito** *part. adj.* proud; elated; cocksure.

†**inorme** *adj.* and derivs. See **enorme**.

inornat-o *adj.* unadorned, plain. **-amente** *adv.* unadornedly, plainly.

inorpell-are [A I] *tr.* to tinsel, to decorate with tinsel; to make showy. **-amento** *m.* tinselling, decorating with tinsel. **-ato** *part. adj.* tinselled; showy. (**-atore** *m.* **-atrice** *f.*) **-atura** *f.* tinselling; tinselling decoration.

†**inorrato** *adj.* See **onorato**, under **onorare**.

inorrid-ire [D 2] *tr.* to terrify, to strike with horror; quella vista m'-ì, that sight struck terror into me; *intr.* (*aux.* essere) to be

norrid-ire (*cont.*)
terrified, to be struck with horror; -ii a vederlo, I was horrified to see him. -**ito** *part. adj.* horrified; terrified; fuggirono -iti, they fled in terror.

inortodoss-o *adj.* (rel.) unorthodox. -**i·a** *f.* (rel.) unorthodoxy.

inoṣa·bile *adj.* that should not be dared; *n.m.* that which cannot be dared, the ever-challenging; osarono l'—, they dared the impossible.

inoscul-are [A I s] *recip. rfl.* to fit together, to join; to flow into each other; *tr.* (surg.) to anastomose. -**amento** *m.* fitting together, joining; flowing together. -**azione** *f.* fitting together; joining; place of joining; (biol.; anat.; surg.) anastomosis.

in-o·ṣico *adj.* (chem.) inosinic. -**oṣite** *f.* (chem.) inositol, meat sugar.

inospital-e *adj.* inhospitable, unfriendly, unwelcoming. -**mente** *adv.* inhospitably. -**ità** *f.* inhospitality, inhospitableness; unfriendliness; wildness (of country).

ino·ṣpit-e, -o *adj.* (of territory) inhospitable; wild, uninhabitable.

inoss-are [A I] *intr.* (aux. essere) to grow bone; to cut teeth; to ossify; (paint.) to prepare (a surface) with bone-ash. -**ato** *part. adj.* ossified; (of teeth) formed; (paint.) treated with bone-ash.

inosserv-a·bile *adj.* unobservable, imperceptible; regola —, rule that cannot be observed. -**anza** *f.* breaking (of agreements); flouting (of regulations); failure to carry out (duties). -**ato** *adj.* unobserved, unnoticed, unseen; not respected.

inossida·bile *adj.* (metall.) stainless; acciaio —, stainless steel; (chem.) inoxidizable.

inossire [D 2] and derivs. See **inossare**.

inostr-are [A I] *tr.* (poet.) to adorn with red; to adorn with purple. (-**ato** *part. adj.*)

inottuṣ-ire [D 2] *intr.* (aux. essere) to become obtuse, blunt or dull; *tr.* to make obtuse. -**ito** *part. adj.* obtuse; made dull, blunted.

inox *adj. indecl.* acciaio —, stainless steel.

inquadr-are [A I] *tr.* to frame; to pigeon-hole, to arrange in proper order; to set (in a frame or background); — in un sistema, to incorporate in a system; to divide into squares; to enclose in a square; (mil.) to straddle (artillery), to enrol; *intr.* (aux. avere) (mil.) to make out a quarter bill; *rfl.* to fit (into), to take its place (in); questa iniziativa s'-a nella politica del governo, this undertaking forms part of government policy; to divide into squares; to be divided into squares. -**amento** *m.* framing; dividing into squares. -**ato** *part. adj.* framed; pigeon-holed; arrayed in proper order; made part of a system; set in a frame; divided into squares. -**atura** *f.* setting in a frame; pigeon-holing; (photog.) framing; (cinem.; telev.) shot.

inqualifica·bile *adj.* indescribable; indecent, most improper.

inquanto *adv.* See 'in quanto', under **quanto**.

inquart-are [A I] *tr.* (herald.) to quarter; †(naut.) to moor with two anchors and two stern hawsers. -**ata** *f.* (naut.) mooring with four hawsers for'ard. -**ato** *part. adj.* (herald.) quarterly, quartered; -ato in croce di Sant'Andrea, quartered per saltire; -ato in isquadra, quarterly en equerre. -**azione** *f.* (metall.) inquartation, quartation; (agric.) ploughing for the fourth time.

inquiet-are [A I] *tr.* to make uneasy, to worry; *rfl.* to become worried; to be uneasy, to worry; *intr.* (*infin.* after 'fare') fare — uno, to cause someone to worry. -**ante** *adj.* disquieting; worrying, disturbing, alarming. -**ato** *part. adj.* worried, uneasy, disturbed. (-**atore** *m.* -**atrice** *f.*) †-**azione** *f.* unrest, disquietude; -azioni di guerre, turbulence of wars.

†**inquiete** *f.* disquietude; disturbance; unrest.

inquiet-o *adj.* restless; uneasy; sei — con me?, are you annoyed with me?; sonno —, disturbed sleep; notte -a, restless night. -**ezza** *f.* restlessness; uneasiness. -**u·dine** *f.* uneasiness, anxiety, uncertainty; worry, cause for anxiety.

inquilin-o *m.* lodger, paying guest; (leg.) tenant; (zool.) inquiline; †inhabitant; †temporary inhabitant; †*adj.* -i sotto i longobardi, subject to the Longobards. -**ato** *m.* status of lodger, status of tenancy.

inquin-are [A I] *tr.* to make filthy; to corrupt; to pollute; to contaminate; to infect; to foul; to falsify, to adulterate. -**amento** *m.* corrupting; infecting; fouling; polluting; pollution; (geog.) dust haze; contaminating, contamination; -amento atomico, atomic pollution; -amento radioattivo, radioactive pollution. -**ato** *part. adj.* filthy; infected; corrupt; fouled; polluted; adulterated.

inqui·r-ere [def.] *tr.* (leg.) to inquire; to investigate. -**ente** *adj.* inquiring; of inquiry; *n.m., f.* inquirer; investigator. †-**ire** *vb.* see **inquirere**. -**ito** *part. adj.* investigated; inquired into.

inquiṣ-ire [D 2] *tr.* (leg.) to inquisition; to inquire into judicially; to investigate; (eccl.) to examine (for heresy); (fig.) to pry into, to be inquisitive about; †to search. -**i·bile** *adj.* liable to investigation. -**ito** *part. adj.* inquired into, examined; (leg.) investigated. -**itore** *m.* investigator, questioner, snooper; (leg.) inquisitor; investigator, an official inquirer; (eccl.) inquisitor. (-**itrice** *f.*) -**itoriale, -ito·rio** *adj.* (eccl.) inquisitorial; (fig.) harsh, threatening. -**itoriato** *m.* (eccl.) examination by the Inquisition. -**izione** *f.* investigation; research; (hist.) Inquisition; (leg.) inquiry; inquest.

inracconta·bile *adj.* See **irraccontabile**.

†**inricompera·bil-e** *adj.* unredeemable. -**mente** *adv.* beyond redemption.

†**inriservato** *adj.* not protected.

inritare [A I] *tr.* (leg.) to annul.

†**inromitare** *rfl.* to become a hermit, to retire to a hermitage.

†**inrossare** *vb.* and derivs. See **arrossare**.

insabbi-are [A 4] *tr.* to fill up with sand, to silt up; (fig.) — una pratica, to shelve a negotiation; *rfl.* to get filled up with sand, to get silted up. -**amento** *m.* silting up. -**ato** *part. adj.* silted up; (fig.) shelved.

insacc-are [A 2] *tr.* to bag, to put into sacks; to put in a sack; to stuff into (some receptacle); (naut.) to take aback; *abs.* to put meat into sausage skins; *rfl., intr.* (aux. essere) to squeeze, to pack, to crowd (into a small space); -arsi nel soprabito, to put on one's coat; (of the sun) to set in a bank of heavy clouds; (pop.) to stuff oneself, to fill one's guts. -**ata** *f.* (mil.) loss; (naut.) blow or damage suffered by masts and rigging due to sails taken aback. -**ato** *part. adj.* in sacks; carne -ata, sausages, salami; dressed in loose-fitting clothes; (naut.) vela -ata, sail taken aback; *n.m.* competitor in a sack race. -**atrice** *f.* (industr.) bagging machine. -**atura** *f.* stuffing into sacks; filling of sacks.

insal-are [A I] *tr.* to salt, to pickle, to preserve in salt; to season with salt; †to deal out with skill and judgement; †to weigh with discernment and prudence; *rfl., intr.* (aux. essere) to become salt (esp. of rivers flowing into the sea). -**ata** *f.* salad; condire l'-ata, to dress the salad; -ata verde, lettuce, etc.; -ata di campo, -ata campagnuola, -ata contadina, salad of wild plants; -ata russa, Russian salad; (fig., fam.) fare un'-ata, to create confusion, to make a mess or muddle of things; esser all'-ata, to have reached the end (of a job); (cinem.) jamming (of film). -**ata·io** *m.* market-gardener. (-**ata·ia** *f.*)-**atiera** *f.* salad-bowl. -**ato** *part. adj.* salted; salt; seasoned with salt. -**atura** *f.* salting, pickling, preserving; time for preserving, pickling season.

insalato[1] *part.* of **insalare**, q.v.

†**insalato**[2] *adj.* unsalted, without salt.

insalda·bile[1] *adj.* See under **insaldare**[1].

†**insalda·bile**[2] *adj.* that cannot be healed or made sound; incurable.

insald-are[1] [A I] *tr.* to starch; (fig.) to stiffen. -**a·bile** *adj.* that can be stiffened or starched. -**ato** *part. adj.* starched; stiffened. -**atora** *f.* laundress (who starches and irons). -**atura** *f.* starching.

†**insald-are**[2] *tr.* to make sound; to heal. †-**ato** *part. adj.* made sound; healed.

insaliv-are [A I] *tr.* to insalivate, to moisten with saliva. -**azione** *f.* insalivation, mixing with saliva.

†**insalsare** *rfl.* (of rivers) to flow into the sea.

insalu·br-e *adj.* unhealthy, insalubrious. -**ità** *f.* unhealthiness, insalubriousness.

insalutato *adj.* unsaluted, ungreeted; andarsene — ospite, to take French leave.

insalva·bile *adj.* that cannot be saved, beyond hope.

insalvatich-ire [D 2] *tr.* to make wild; to enrage; *intr.* (aux. essere) to become wild, rough, to become overgrown. -**ito** *part. adj.* wild; rough; overgrown.

insana·bil-e *adj.* incurable; irremediable. -**mente** *adv.* incurably; irremediably. -**ità** *f.* incurableness.

†**insanesito** *adj.* Sienese by adoption.

insanguin-are [A I] *tr.* to bespatter with blood, to make bloody, to stain with blood; †*intr.* to bleed; *rfl.* to become spattered with blood; to become blood-stained. -**amento** *m.* making bloody; staining with blood. -**ato** *part. adj.* bloody; blood-stained; drenched with blood.

insa·nia *f.* insanity, madness; folly.

†**insani-are** *tr.* to cause to go insane, to drive mad. †**-ante** *part. adj.* raving; raging. †**-ato** *part. adj.* driven mad; insane.

insan-ire [D 2] *intr.* (*aux.* essere) to become insane, to go mad; *tr.* to cause to go insane, to drive mad. **-ito** *part. adj.* driven mad; insane.

insan-o *adj.* insane, demented; mad; crazy, foolish; †— di, mad about, in love with; †l'onda -a, the raging sea; †ill, unhealthy. **-amente** *adv.* insanely, madly; crazily.

†**insapien-te** *adj.* unwise; foolish; ignorant. **-za** *f.* lack of wisdom; foolishness, ignorance.

insapon-are [A I c] *tr.* to soap, to lather; (fig.) to flatter, to 'soft-soap'. †— le parole, to speak unctuously. **-ato** *part. adj.* soaped; soapy. **-atura** *f.* soaping; lathering; lather; flattery. **-ifica·bile** *adj.*, *n.m.* (chem.) unsaponifiable.

†**insaporare** *vb.* and derivs. See **insaporire**.

insapor-ire [D 2] *tr.* to flavour; to make tasty; to make appetizing; *intr.* (*aux.* essere) to take on a flavour; to become tasty; to become appetizing. **-ito** *part. adj.* flavoured; tasty; appetizing.

insaporo *m.* tasteless, insipid.

insaputa *adv. phr.* a mia —, unbeknown to me; all'— di, without the knowledge of, unbeknown to, behind the back of.

†**insassare** *tr.* to turn to stone; to make as hard as stone; *rfl.* to turn into stone, to become a stone; to become as hard as stone; to become insensate.

insatanass-are [A I] *tr.* to make a devil of; to enrage. **-ato** *part. adj.* furious, enraged; possessed by a demon.

insatirito *adj.* become lascivious like a satyr.

insatolla·bile *adj.* insatiable, greedy.

insazia·bil-e *adj.* insatiable. **-mente** *adv.* insatiably. **-ità** *f.* insatiability, insatiableness.

insaziato *adj.* unsatiated.

insazi-età *f.* insatiableness. **-evole** *adj.* insatiable.

†**inscampa·bile** *adj.* inescapable; inevitable.

inscatol-are [A I] *tr.* to tin, to can. **-ato** *part. adj.* tinned, canned; in tins. **-atrice** *f.* canning machine.

inscen-are [A I] *tr.* (theatr.) to produce, to put on, to stage; — manifestazioni, to organize manifestations. **-ato** *part. adj.* (theatr.) produced, put on, staged; adapted for the stage. (**-atore** *m.*).

†**inschiavire** *tr.* to enslave.

†**inschidionare** *tr.* to put on the spit.

inscien-te *adj.* unaware; ignorant. **-temente** *adv.* ignorantly; in ignorance; unawares. **-za** *f.* ignorance.

inscindi·bile *adj.* inseparable; necessarily involved.

insc-i·o *adj.* ignorant, ingenuous; unaware. **-iamente** *adv.* unwittingly, unknowingly.

†**inscogliare** *tr.* (naut.) to run (a ship) on to rocks.

inscritt-o *part.* of **inscrivere**, q.v.; *adj.* inscribed, registered, matriculated; entered (in accounts); (geom.) inscribed; †dedicated; *n.m.* inscribed member, member; gli -i al partito, party members. **-i·bile** *adj.* (geom.) that may be inscribed.

inscri·vere [C 12] *tr.* (leg.) to enter; to record; to register; (geom.) to inscribe (cf. **iscrivere**).

inscrizione *f.* (leg.) entry; record; tassa d'—, registration fee; (geom.) inscribing, inscription (cf. **iscrizione**).

inscruta·bil-e *adj.* inscrutable. **-mente** *adv.* inscrutably. **-ità** *f.* inscrutability, inscrutableness.

†**inscul·pere** *tr.* to carve; to inscribe.

†**insculse** *past def. 3rd pers. sing.* of †**insculpere**, q.v.

inscurire [D 2] *tr.* to darken; *intr.* (*aux.* essere) to grow darker.

inscusa·bile *adj.* and derivs. See **inescusabile**.

inseca·bile *adj.* indivisible; (geom.) that cannot be bisected.

insecch-ire [D 2] *intr.* (*aux.* essere) to dry up, to become dry; to get thin; to wither; *tr.* to dry up, to desiccate, to wither. **-ito** *part. adj.* dried up; withered; desiccated.

insecu-tore *m.* persecutor, pursuer. (**-trice** *f.*)

insedi-are [A 4] *tr.* to install; to induct; *rfl.* to take office, to enter upon office, to be installed; to establish oneself; to settle. **-amento** *m.* installing; installation; induction; entering upon office. **-ato** *part. adj.* installed; inducted; settled.

inseduci·bile *adj.* incorruptible, unyielding.

inseg-are [A 2 c] *tr.* to smear with tallow; to grease; *rfl.* to become greasy. **-ato** *part. adj.* smeared with tallow, greased.

insegna *f.* insignia; badge; decoration; coat of arms; distinctive dress; robes; cap and gown; signboard; insegne regali, regalia; insegne episcopali, bishop's insignia; (mil.) insignia; flag; sotto

le insegne, under the colours; spiegare le insegne, to fly the colours; abbandonare le insegne, to surrender; ripiegare le insegne, to haul down the colours, (fig.) to give in; (naut.) standard, ensign (appropriate to royalty, chief of naval staff, etc.); — di comando, admiral's flag, squadron commander's flag; (fig.) attribute, sign; (derog.) man of straw.

†**insegnale** *m.* See **segnale**.

insegn-are [A 5 c] *tr.* to teach, to be a teacher of; to be an instructor of; — il francese, to teach French; — la scherma, to be a fencing instructor; gli ho -ato l'aria di quella canzone, I've taught him the tune of that song; to indicate, to point out, to show; la storia c'-a che, history shows that; gli -ai la buona strada, I told him the right way to go; m'-ò la persona adatta, he put me on to the right person; *abs.* to be a teacher; to teach; -a al Ginnasio, he teaches at the grammar school; che cosa fa, Lei, di professione? Io? -o, what is your profession? I'm a teacher; *intr.* (*aux.* avere) — a leggere, to teach reading; -ò a leggere al bambino, he taught the child to read; -ò al pappagallo a dire 'buon giorno', he taught the parrot to say 'good morning'. **-a·bile** *adj.* suitable for teaching; fit to be taught; teachable. **-amento** *m.* teaching; education; tuition; lesson, precept; quadri per l'-amento oggettivo, visual aids; abilitazione all'-amento di primo grado, Teaching Certificate; abilitazione all'-amento di secondo grado, Diploma in Education, Teacher's Diploma. **-ante** *pres. part.* teaching; *n.m.*, *f.* teacher, schoolmaster, schoolmistress; instructor; -ante universitario, university lecturer. **-ativo** *adj.* didactic; metodo -ativo, teaching method. **-ato** *part. adj.* taught; imparted; instructed; educated, well-educated; expert. **-atore** *m.* teacher, instructor; inculcator. (**-atrice** *f.*) †**-e·vole** *adj.* teachable, docile. **-ucchiare** [A 4] *tr.* to teach a little of; -ucchiare un po' di disegno, to give a few drawing lessons.

insegu-ire [D I] *tr.* to follow, to pursue, to chase; (fig.) pursue, to go in pursuit of. **-ente** *part. adj.* pursuing; *n.m.* pursuer. **-imento** *m.* pursuit, chase; (sport) gara a -imento, pursuit race (cycling). **-ito** *part. adj.* pursued; chased. **-itore** *m.* pursuer; (sport) runner-up. (**-itrice** *f.*)

†**inseguitare** *vb.* and derivs. See **seguitare**.

†**inseliciare** *tr.* to pave, to lay with paving stones.

insell-are [A I] *tr.* to saddle; (naut.) — una nave, to build a vessel with a lift at the extremities and sag in the middle; *rfl.* to mount (on horseback), to get into the saddle; to sag (in the middle). **-amento** *m.* saddling; (naut.) sag of a ship due to straining or fault in her construction. **-ato** *part. adj.* saddled; mounted; hollow-backed, curved like a saddle; (naut.) sagging. **-atura** *f.* hollow of the back, curve like that of a saddle; (naut.) camber of a deck.

inselv-are [A I c] *rfl.* to take to the woods; to grow into a wood; to become wooded. †**-ato** *part. adj.* lost in the woods; swallowed up by the woods.

inselvatich-ire [D 2] *intr.* (*aux.* essere) to go out of cultivation; to run wild, to grow wild. **-ito** *part. adj.* wild, overgrown.

†**insembr-a**, †**-e** *adv.* together.

inseminato *adj.* unsown, uncultivated, wild.

†**insemitare** *rfl.* to set out on one's path.

†**insemprare** *rfl.* to last for ever, to be eternal.

insen-are [A I c] *rfl.* to form an inlet, small bay or harbour. †**-ata** *f.* bay, gulf. **-atura** *f.* inlet, creek; (geog.) re-entrant (among mountains); †(naut.) permanent lashing breeching.

insensat-o *adj.* senseless, foolish; bemused; stupid; insensible, without senses, lifeless; intractable; meaningless; *n.m.* stupid, lifeless individual; *pl.* (lit. hist.) Gli Insensati, name of Academies at Perugia and at Pistoia in the sixteenth century. **-amente** *adv.* stupidly, foolishly. **-ag·gine** *f.*, **-ezza** *f.* senselessness, foolishness, stupidity; folly; foolish action; foolish words.

insensi·bil-e *adj.* imperceptible, very slight; pendio —, very gentle slope; insensible, insensitive; apathetic, indifferent; unconcerned; unfeeling, hard-hearted. **-mente** *adv.* imperceptibly; insensibly; insensitively. **-ità** *f.* insensibility; insensitiveness.

insensitiv-o *adj.* insensitive, unfeeling. **-amente** *adv.* insensitively, unfeelingly. **-ità** *f.* insensitivity, lack of feeling.

†**insensivo** *adj.* lifeless.

†**insensualità** *f.* coldness, insensibility, impassiveness, impassibility.

insepara·bil-e *adj.* inseparable; indivisible. **-mente** *adv.* inseparably. **-ità** *f.* indivisibility.

inseparato *adj.* unseparated, not separate; conjoined, united.

insepolt-o *adj.* unburied. **-ura** *f.* lack of burial; state of being unburied.

insequestra·bil-e *adj.* not liable to sequestration. (**-ità** *f.*)

inser-ire [D2] *tr.* to insert; to fit in; to add; to interpolate; — nell'ordine del giorno, to include in the agenda; (electr.) to connect, to plug in; (agric.; hort.) to graft; *rfl.* to be inserted; to be included; to become part of. **-imento** *m.* insertion; adding; including; grafting. **-ito** *part. adj.* inserted; added; included; grafted; (electr.) plugged in; switched on, 'on'.

†**inserpent-are** *rfl.* to wrap oneself in serpents, to let snakes coil round one's body. †**-ire** *intr.* to become snake-like in venomousness.

†**inserrare** *vb.* and derivs. See **serrare**.

inserta *f.* enclosure; enclosed document.

insert-are [A1] *tr.* to entwine, to weave together; *rfl.* to become entwined; to be interwoven. **-ato** *part. adj.* entwined, interwoven.

inserto *adj.* inserted; added, included; enclosed; *n.m.* enclosure; dossier; (telev.) film insert; †(agric.; hort.) graft.

inservi·bile *adj.* useless; unserviceable; rendere —, to put out of action.

inserviente *m.* man employed in a large building (e.g. a hospital, block of offices) for rough work; cleaner, odd-job man.

inserzion-e *f.* insertion; advertisement in a newspaper; announcement; (leg.) — per sentenza del tribunale, legal notice; (bot.) insertion (of the ovary, etc.; e.g. hypogonous, etc.); (electr.) connecting up, switching on. **-ista** *m., f.* one who inserts an advertisement or announcement in a newspaper; advertiser.

†**inset-are**, †**-ire** *vb.* and derivs. See **innestare**.

insett-o *m.* (ent.) insect. **-icida** *m.* insecticide. **-i·voro** *adj.* insectivorous. **-ologi·a** *f.* entomology. **-olo·gico** *adj.* entomological. **-o·logo** *m.* (*pl.* **-o·loghi**) entomologist.

insever-ire [D1] *tr.* to make stricter; *intr.* (*aux.* essere) to become stricter. **-ito** *part. adj.* made stricter; tightened up.

insi·di-a *f.* snare, trap; (mil.) ambush; — anticarro, anti-tank trap or obstacle; (fig.) deception, deceit; danger; le -e del mare, the perils of the sea. **-are** [A4] *tr.* to lay a trap for; to ensnare, to lie in wait for; to attack treacherously; to try to seduce; *intr.* (*aux.* avere; *prep.* a) to behave treacherously; -are alla vita di una persona, to make an attempt on a person's life. **-amento** *m.* ensnaring; lying in wait. **-ante** *part. adj.* ensnaring. **-ato** *part. adj.* threatened; liable to treacherous attack; plotted against. **-atore** *m.* snarer; treacherous attacker; l'-atore fu preso nella sua stessa insidia, the enemy was caught in his own trap, the enemy was hoist with his own petard. **-oso** *adj.* insidious; treacherous; underhand. **-osamente** *adv.* insidiously; treacherously.

insiem-e *adv.* together; at the same time; d'accordo —, in agreement with one another; mettere —, to put together, to assemble, to fit together; mettere — una fortuna, to make a fortune; mettere — uomini, to gather men together; (leg.) jointly; tutto —, altogether, the whole, taken as a whole; tutto — non vale cento lire, the whole lot is hardly worth a shilling; mandò giù un grammo di chinino tutto —, he swallowed a gramme of quinine at a draught; piangere e ridere —, to laugh and cry at the same time; — a, in addition to; — con, with, in company with; levare d'—, to separate; *n.m.* whole; nell'—, on the whole; tutto l'— dell'edificio, the building as a whole; movimento d'—, concerted movement; combined movement; (mus.) un pezzo d'—, a concerted piece. †**-emente** *adv.* see **insieme**.

†**insiepare** *rfl.* to hide in (or behind) a hedge.

insign-e *adj.* notable; remarkable; signal; famous; illustrious; (iron.) arrant, infamous; (of a church) enjoying precedence. **-emente** *adv.* notably, remarkably; (iron.) -emente sfacciato, remarkably impudent.

insignific-a·bile *adj.* indistinguishable; insignificant, negligible. **-ante** *adj.* meaningless; insignificant, trivial.

insign-ire [D2] *tr.* to honour, to decorate; to bestow an honour, or mark of distinction on. **-ito** *part. adj.* decorated, honoured; (eccl.) chiesa -ita, privileged church, church with title *insignis*.

insignor-ire [D2] *tr.* to appoint as ruler or feudal lord; *rfl.* (*prep.* di) to make oneself master (of); (fig.) to become a gentleman; to become rich or powerful. **-ito** *part. adj.* appointed lord; (fig.) risen in the world.

insil-are [A1] *tr.* (agric.) to store (grain, fodder, etc.) in a silo. (**-amento** *m.*) **-ato** *part. adj.* stored in a silo.

insimpatichire [D2] *rfl.* (*prep.* di) to become friendly (with).

insincer-o *adj.* insincere, false. **-amente** *adv.* insincerely, falsely. **-ità** *f.* lack of sincerity; duplicity.

insinchè *conj.* See under **insino**.

insindaca·bile *adj.* that cannot be censured; la decisione della Commissione è —, the Commission's decision is not open to question.

insin-o *prep.* till; until, to, as far as; — a, even, including; — a tanto, until. **-chè** *conj.* until. **-ora** *adv.* until then.

insinu-are [A6] *tr.* to insinuate, to insert gradually, to introduce stealthily; (fig.) to insinuate, to suggest; (leg.) — un credito, to prove a debt; to lodge a proof in bankruptcy (C.C.); *rfl.* (*prep.* in) to find one's way (into), to get (into); to penetrate, to creep (into); (fig.) to curry favour (with); to achieve recognition. **-a·bile** *adj.* that can be introduced; acqua -abile, water liable to seep through. **-abilità** *f.* power of penetration; ability to penetrate. **-ante** *part. adj.* persuasive, ingratiating; insinuating. **-ativo** *adj.* see **insinuante**. **-ato** *part. adj.* introduced, put in; insinuated, suggested. **-atore** *m.* insinuating person. (**-atrice** *f.*) **-azione** *f.* insinuation, insinuating suggestion; (leg.) -azione di credito, creditor's proof in bankruptcy.

insi·pid-o *adj.* without taste, tasteless; lacking in taste; diventare —, to lose its flavour; (fig.) insipid; dull, uninteresting; nonsensical; *n.m.* insipid person, colourless individual; insipidity; tastelessness. **-amente** *adv.* insipidly; nonsensically. **-ezza** *f.* tastelessness; insipidity; dullness; foolish action, silly chatter. **-ire** [D2] *intr.* (*aux.* essere) to lose flavour, to become tasteless, to grow insipid; *tr.* to make tasteless; to cause to become insipid or dull. **-ità** *f.* see **insipidezza**.

insipien-te *adj.* stupid; ignorant; foolish, silly. **-temente** *adv.* stupidly; ignorantly; foolishly. **-za** *f.* stupidity; ignorance; foolishness.

insi·st-ere [C24] *intr.* (*aux.* avere; *prep.* in, sopra, su; before an *infin.* a) to persist, to persevere; — nelle indagini, to make persistent inquiries; -eva a consigliare, he insisted on giving advice; to persist (in); to insist (on); -erò col maestro perchè acconsenta, I shall keep (on) urging the teacher to give his consent; (geom.) — su, to be subtended by; l'angolo A -e sull'arco BCD, angle A is subtended by the arc BCD. **-ente** *part. adj.* insistent; persistent; persevering; incessant; pressing; obstinate; †resting; leaning. **-entemente** *adv.* insistently; persistently; perseveringly; incessantly. **-enza** *f.* insistence; persistence, perseverance; pressure; cedere alle -enze di tutti, to yield to pressure.

†**insitare** *vb.* and derivs. See **innestare**.

in·sito *adj.* innate, congenital, natural, inherent; la natura del rischio professionale — nelle diverse lavorazioni, the nature of the professional hazard inherent in the various forms of employment.

†**insmorza·bile** *adj.* unquenchable; inextinguishable.

insoav-e *adj.* unpleasant; disagreeable; displeasing; insipid. **-emente** *adv.* unpleasantly; insipidly.

†**insoccorso** *adj.* without succour, unhelped.

insocia·bil-e *adj.* solitary, unsociable; incompatible. **-mente** *adv.* unsociably; incompatibly. **-ità** *f.* incompatibility.

insoci-ale *adj.* unsocial, anti-social. **-almente** *adv.* in an anti-social manner. **-e·vole** *adj.* unsociable. **-evolmente** *adv.* **-evolezza** *f.* unsociability; misanthropy.

inso(d)disf-atto *adj.* unsatisfied; (leg.) unpaid. **-azione** *f.* discontent.

insofferen-te *adj.* intolerant; impatient, irritable; — di, unable to bear; era — di ogni indugio, he would brook no delay. **-za** *f.* intolerance; impatience.

†**insoffiare** *tr.* to blow into; to breathe into.

†**insofficiente** *adj.* and derivs. See **insufficiente**.

insoffri·bil-e *adj.* unbearable; intolerable; insufferable. **-mente** *adv.* unbearably; insufferably. **-ità** *f.* unbearableness; insufferableness.

insoggett-ire [D2] *tr.* to make afraid; to inspire fear in; *rfl.* to become afraid. **-ito** *part. adj.* intimidated.

†**insogn-are** *tr., rfl.* to dream, to imagine. †**-o** *m.* see **sogno**.

†**insol-are** *tr.* to expose to sunshine. **-ato** *part. adj.* exposed, sunny.

insolazione *f.* exposure to sunshine; (med.) sunstroke; (meteor.) insolation.

insolca·bile *adj.* that cannot be ploughed.

insolc-are [A2c] *tr.* to furrow, to mark with furrows; to mark boundaries in (a piece of land) with the plough. **-ato** *part. adj.* unfurrowed; unploughed; (of the sea) unnavigated; uncharted. **-atura** *f.* furrowing.

†**insoldatare** *rfl.* to become a soldier; to behave like a soldier.

insolent-e *adj.* insolent; impudent; arrogant; rude, cheeky, saucy; *n.m.* insolent individual; sei un —, you're being insolent. **-emente** *adv.* insolently; arrogantly; impudently. **-ire** [D 2] *intr.* (*aux.* essere) to become insolent, to be insolent; (*aux.* avere; *prep.* contro) to be insolent (to); *tr.* to be insolent to; to be rude to; to treat insolently.

insolenza *f.* insolence; arrogance; impudence; rudeness; insolent behaviour; insolent remark; mi disse un'—, he made an insolent remark to me.

insolfare [A I C] and derivs. See **inzolfare**.

insolfitato *adj.* (chem.; techn.) unsulphited.

inso·lit-o *adj.* unusual; unwonted; unaccustomed; extraordinary. **-amente** *adv.* unusually; in an unaccustomed manner.

†**insollare** *tr.* to soften; to weaken; to slow down.

†**insoll-ire** *intr.* to rise in tumult, to revolt. **-ito** *part. adj.* in a state of insurrection; up in arms.

insolu·bil-e *adj.* indissoluble, that cannot be loosed; insoluble, unsolvable, insolvable; (chem.) insoluble; (leg.) that cannot be met or carried out; debito —, a debt that cannot be paid, bad debt; *n.m.pl.* (chem.) insolubles. **-mente** *adv.* indissolubly; insolubly. **-ità** *f.* indissolubility; (chem.) insolubility.

insoluto *adj.* undissolved; unsolved; (leg.) unpaid; debito —, unpaid debt, bad debt; una cambiale insoluta, dishonoured bill.

insolv-ente *adj.* (leg.; finan.) insolvent; bankrupt. **-enza** *f.* insolvency; bankruptcy. **-i·bile** *adj.* that cannot be paid; (leg.) who cannot pay (C.P.). **-ibilità** *f.* insolvency; (leg.) inability to pay (C.P.).

insomma *adv.* in conclusion; finally; in short; in a word; in other words; on the whole; after all; in fact; —, finiscila!, that'll do! that's enough of that!; *excl.* well!

insommergi·bil-e *adj.* unsinkable; not submersible. **-ità** *f.* unsinkability.

†**insonnare** *tr.* to make sleepy; to cause to droop.

insonne *adj.* sleepless; wakeful; notte —, a sleepless night; alert, wakeful; vigilant.

inson·nia *f.* insomnia; sleeplessness; patire d'—, to suffer from insomnia.

inson·nio *m.* See **insonnia**.

insonnolito *adj.* sleepy, drowsy, somnolent.

insonoriẓẓ-are [A I] *tr.* (acoust.) to sound-proof. (**-ato** *part. adj.*) **-azione** *f.* (techn.) sound-proofing.

†**insonte** *adj.* harmless, innocuous.

insopporta·bil-e *adj.* unbearable; unendurable; intolerable; insufferable. **-mente** *adv.* unbearably; intolerably; insufferably. **-ità** *f.* unbearableness; insufferableness.

insorbettito *adj.* (joc.) frozen (cf. **sorbetto**).

insord-ire [D 2] *intr.* (*aux.* essere) to grow deaf. **-ito** *part. adj.* grown deaf, deaf.

insorg-ere, insor·g-ere [C 5] *intr.* (*aux.* essere; *prep.* contro) to rise in revolt; to rebel; to revolt; to be up in arms (against); insorse una tempesta, a storm arose; -e qui una nuova difficoltà, a further difficulty arises here. **-ente** *part. adj.* insurgent; arising. **-imento** *m.* rising; †insurrection.

insormonta·bile *adj.* insuperable, unsurmountable.

insorto, insorto *part.* of **insorgere**, q.v.; *adj.* risen, in revolt; arisen; le difficoltà insorte, the difficulties which have arisen; la provincia insorta, the rebel province; *n.m.* insurgent, rebel; rioter.

insospett-a·bile *adj.* not under suspicion; unsuspected, unlikely. **-ato** *adj.* not suspected.

insospett-ire [D 2] *tr.* to make suspicious; to arouse suspicion in; *rfl., intr.* (*aux.* essere) to feel suspicious; to become suspicious; to smell a rat; s'-ì della cosa, he got wind of the matter. **-imento** *m.* arousing suspicion; growing suspicion. **-ito** *part. adj.* suspicious.

insostanziale *adj.* unsubstantial.

insosteni·bile *adj.* untenable, unsustainable; unendurable; *n.m.* that which is untenable; volere sostenere l'—, to try to prove the impossible.

insostitui·bile *adj.* unrivalled, unbeatable.

†**insozia·bile** *adj.* and derivs. See **insociabile**.

insoẓẓ-are, insozz-are [A I C] *tr.* to soil, to dirty, to stain; (fig.) to sully; to corrupt; *intr.* (*aux.* essere) to become soiled. **-ato** *part. adj.* soiled, dirtied; sullied. †**-ire** *intr.* to become soiled.

†**inspar·gere** *tr.* to sprinkle with, to shower upon.

inspera·bile *adj.* not to be hoped for; beyond hope; fortuna —, unlooked-for good fortune; benefizio —, kindness beyond all expectation.

†**insperanz-ire** *tr.* to inspire with hope, to comfort with hope. **-ito** *adj.* filled with hope, made hopeful.

†**insperare** *intr.* to despair.

insperat-o *adj.* unhoped for; unlooked for; unexpected. **-amente** *adv.* unexpectedly.

†**inspessare** *vb.* and derivs. See **inspessire**.

inspess-ire [D 2] *tr.* to thicken; to condense; *rfl.* to thicken, to become thicker; to become condensed, to condense. **-imento** *m.* thickening; condensing; -imento delle arterie, hardening of the arteries. **-ito** *part. adj.* thickened; condensed.

inspieg-a·bile *adj.* inexplicable. **-abilmente** *adv.* inexplicably. **-ato** *adj.* unexplained.

inspir-are [A I] *tr.* to breathe in; to inhale; to breathe into. **-a·bile** *adj.* breathable; inhalable. **-amento** *m.* inhaling; breathing in; breathing into. **-ato** *part. adj.* inhaled. **-atore** *m.* one who inhales; *adj.* (anat.) muscoli -atori, inspiratory muscles. (**-atrice** *f.*) **-azione** *f.* inhaling, breathing in (cf. **ispirare**).

insta·bil-e *adj.* unstable; uncertain; insecure; variable; unsettled; inconstant; unsteady. **-mente** *adv.* insecurely; unsteadily. **-ità** *f.* instability; inconstancy.

install-are [A I] *tr.* to install; *rfl.* to take a seat; to become installed; to settle in. **-ato** *part. adj.* installed; seated; settled. **-atura** *f.* (naut.) positioning; -atura di un albero, stepping of a mast. **-azione** *f.* installation; installing.

instanca·bil-e *adj.* tireless; indefatigable; unwearying. **-mente** *adv.* tirelessly; indefatigably. **-ità** *f.* indefatigability.

instanta·nea *f.* (photog.). See **istantanea**, under **istantaneo**.

inst-are [A 9] *intr.* (*aux.* avere) to be insistent; to persist; to be urgent; to be menacing; (leg.) to apply. **-ante** *part. adj.* insistent; pressing; urgent; threatening; menacing; *n.m.* importunate person. **-ante-mente** *adv.* insistently.

instaur-are [A I a] *tr.* to restore; to establish; to make good; to institute; to set up. **-ato** *part. adj.* restored; established. (**-atore** *m.* **-atrice** *f.*) **-azione** *f.* restoring; restoration; establishing; instituting.

†**instellare** *rfl.* to become adorned with stars.

instill-are [A I] *tr.* (*prep.* in) to instil (into); to infuse; (fig.) to inspire; to inculcate; — buoni principii nell'animo di uno, to instil good principles into someone; *rfl.* to become instilled; to penetrate; to permeate. **-ato** *part. adj.* instilled; infused. **-azione** *f.* instilling; infusing; inculcation; (med.) instillation.

†**instingui·bile** *adj.* See **inestinguibile**.

†**instinto** *m.* See **istinto**.

instit-ore *m.*, (leg.) agent; institor. **-o·rio** *adj.* (*m.pl.* **-o·rii**) (leg.) institorial.

instituire [D 2] and derivs. See **istituire**.

†**instituta** *f.pl.* institutions.

†**instolidire** *intr.* to grow stupid.

instradare [A I] and derivs. See **istradare**.

insù *adv.* upwards; up; gli uomini dai venti anni —, men of twenty and over; col naso all'—, with one's nose in the air; dal naso all'—, having a tip-tilted nose.

insubordinat-o *adj.* insubordinate; refractory; undisciplined. (**-amente** *adv.*) **-eẓẓa** *f.* insubordination; rebelliousness.

insubordinazione *f.* act of insubordination; disrespectful remark.

in·subre *adj.* (anct. hist.) Insubrian (approx. Lombard); *n.m.pl.* Insubres; Insubrians.

insuccesso *m.* failure; (theatr.) flop, frost.

insudici-are [A 3 s] *tr.* to dirty; to soil; (fig.) — i ginocchi, to eat humble pie, to crawl; — la carta, to draw badly; — la tela, to daub; *rfl.* to get dirty; to become soiled; (fig.) to touch pitch.

insueto *adj.* and derivs. See **inconsueto**.

insufficien-te *adj.* insufficient; inadequate; unsuitable; unsuited; below examination standard; deficient; defective; unfit (for). **-temente** *adv.* insufficiently; inadequately. **-za** *f.* insufficiency; deficiency; defect; incapacity; lack of ability; (med.) insufficiency; (leg.) insufficiency; -za di prove, want or lack of evidence.

insuffl-are [A I] *tr.* to blow into; to breathe into; (fig.) to suggest; to inspire; — il male a, to incite to evil. (**-ato** *part. adj.*) **-azione** *f.* (rel.) insufflation (in exorcism); (med.) insufflation.

insular-e *adj.* relating to an island; characteristic of an island; insular. **-ità** *f.* insularity.

insulina *f.* (med.) insulin.

Insulin·di-a *pr.n.f.* (geog.) the islands of the Indian Archipelago. (**-ano** *adj.*)

insuls-o *adj.* tasteless, insipid; (fig.) silly; witless; insipid; dull. **-aménte** *adv.* stupidly; insipidly. **-ag·gine** *f.* stupidity; silliness; foolish remark; boring conversation. †**-ità** *f.* see **insulsaggine**.

insult-are [A I] *tr.* to insult; to abuse; (mil.) to attack; to assault; to assault repeatedly; to make a sudden frontal attack upon; *intr.* (*aux.* avere; *prep.* a) to speak ill of. **-a·bile** *adj.* liable to abuse, open to insult; (mil.) open to sudden attack; subject to sudden assault. **-ante** *part. adj.* insulting; insolent; offensive. **-ato** *part. adj.* insulted; abused. (**-atore** *m.* **-atrice** *f.*) †**-azione** *f.* see **insulto**.

insult-o *m.* insult; un — alla, contro, la memoria di, an insult to the memory of; (mil.) attack, assault; esposto agl'-i del nemico, exposed to assault; (med.) attack; fit, access, paroxysm; — di tosse, fit of coughing; — apoplettico, apoplectic fit. **-arello, -erello** *m. dim.* of **insulto**.

insupera·bil-e *adj.* insuperable; unsurmountable. **-ménte** *adv.* insuperably; unsurmountably. **-ità** *f.* insuperableness.

insuperato *adj.* unsurpassed; matchless.

†**insuperb-are, -iare** *vb.* and derivs. See **insuperbire**.

insuperb-ire [D 2] *tr.* to make proud; to turn the head of; *intr.* (*aux.* essere), *rfl.* to be proud; to give oneself airs; **-irsi di**, to take pride in. **-iménto** *m.* puffing up, swelling with pride. **-ito** *part. adj.* proud; swollen with pride; puffed up; fiume **-ito**, river in flood, swollen river.

†**insur·gere** *vb.* and derivs. See **insorgere**.

insurrezión-e *f.* insurrection; rising; revolt; rebellion. **-ale** *adj.* insurrectionary; insurrectional.

†**insusare** *rfl.* to be raised; to rise; to ascend.

insuscetti·bile *adj.* See **insuscettivo**.

insuscettivo *adj.* not susceptible to modification.

insussisten-te *adj.* baseless; without foundation; non-existent; unreal. **-za** *f.* baselessness; unreality.

†**insusurrare** *vb.* and derivs. See **susurrare**.

intabacc-are¹ [A 2] *tr.* to soil with snuff; to stain with tobacco; *rfl.* to soil oneself with snuff; to become tobacco-stained. (**-ato** *part. adj.*)

†**intabaccare²** *tr.* to enamour; *rfl.* to become enamoured.

intabarr-are [A I] *tr.* to wrap in a cloak; *rfl.* to wrap oneself in a cloak. **-ato** *part. adj.* cloaked; ben **-ato**, well wrapped up.

†**intacca** *f.* See **tacca**.

intacc-are [A 2] *tr.* to notch; to cut into; to damage; (provb.) chi non sa scorticare **-a** la pelle, a cobbler should stick to his last; to corrode; to etch; l'acquaforte **-a** il rame, acid bites into copper; to dip into (capital); ha **-ato** il capitale, he has spent some of his capital; to attack; — la riputazione di qualcuno, to injure someone's reputation; to impugn; (naut.) (of the wind) to rise; (of a ship) to begin to feel the wind; *intr.* (*aux.* avere) to stammer; to hesitate in speech. (**-a·bile** *adj.*) **-aménto** *m.* see **intaccatura**. **-ato** *part. adj.* notched; corroded; damaged; partly used up; attacked. **-atura** *f.* notch; notching; indentation; damage; injury; score (registered by notches); (archit.) fascia; fillet; band; impediment in speech; (naut.) sailing close hauled; ruffling; catspaw.

intac-co *m.* (*pl.* **-chi**) see **intaccatura**, under **intaccare**; (fig.) defect; slur.

†**inta·glia** *f.* costume; uniform; fashion of dress.

intagli-are [A 4] *tr.* to carve (wood or stone, for ornament); — all'acquaforte, to etch; to cut; to engrave; to incise; to cut out (embroidery). **-aménto** *m.* carving; engraving; incising; (vet.) 'speedy cutting' (in horses). **-ato** *part. adj.* carved; engraved; incised. **-atore** *m.* carver; engraver. (**-atrice** *f.*) **-atura** *f.* carving; engraving; incising; (shoem.) slashing.

inta·glio *m.* carving; engraving; lavoro d'—, carving; work engraved; intaglio engraving.

†**intalentare** *tr.* to fill with longing; to arouse desire in; *rfl.* to feel longing; to be desirous.

†**intam-are** *tr.* to spoil, to contaminate. (†**-ato** *part. adj.*)

†**intamato** *adj.* uncontaminated.

†**intamburare** *vb.* and derivs. See **tamburare**.

intaminato *adj.* (poet.) uncontaminated.

†**intamolare** *tr.* to penetrate; to enter.

†**intanagliare** *vb.* and derivs. See **attanagliare**.

intan-are [A I] *rfl.* to hide; to conceal oneself; to go to earth. **-ato** *part. adj.* hidden; gone to earth.

intanfire [D 2] *intr.* (*aux.* essere) to moulder; to grow musty; (fig.) to become old and snuffy.

intangi·bil-e *adj.* intangible; untouchable; not to be touched; inviolable; inviolate. **-ità** *f.* intangibleness; inviolability.

intanto *adv.* meanwhile; in the meantime; (fam.) but, yet; dice sì e sì, e — non fa nulla; he says yes, yes, but he does nothing; puoi gridare quanto vuoi, — non mi muovo, you can shout as much as you like, but I'm not going; *conj.* — che, while.

†**intardato** *adj.* slow; slow-moving; leisurely.

intarl-are [A I] *intr.* (*aux.* essere) to become worm-eaten. **-aménto** *m.* becoming worm-eaten. **-ato** *part. adj.* worm-eaten; dente **-ato**, decayed tooth; (joc.) moth-eaten. **-atura** *f.* worm-eaten condition; being reduced to a worm-eaten state.

intarm-are [A I] *intr.* (*aux.* essere) to become moth-eaten. (**-ato** *part. adj.* **-atura** *f.*)

intarsi-are [A 4] *tr.* to inlay; to mix (colours) in embroidery; (fig.) **-a** i suoi scritti di pensieri altrui, he embellishes his writings with ideas from other people's works. (**-aménto** *m.*) **-ato** *part. adj.* inlaid; adorned with inlay. (**-atore** *m.* **-atrice** *f.*) **-atura** *f.* inlaying.

intar·sio *m.* inlay; lavoro d'—, inlaid work.

intartar-ire [D 2] *rfl.* to become encrusted with tartar. **-ito** *adj.* encrusted with tartar.

intaş-are [A I] *tr.* to stop up, to choke; to obstruct; to clog; *intr.* (*aux.* essere), *rfl.* to be stopped up; l'acquaio si è **-ato**, the kitchen sink has got stopped up; (of the nose) to become stuffed up. (**-aménto** *m.*) **-ato** *part. adj.* stopped up; blocked; stuffed up; clogged; essere un po' **-ato**, to have a cold in one's nose. **-atura** *f.* obstruction; stoppage; blockage; stuffing up.

intasc-are [A 2] *tr.* to pocket; to put into one's pocket; to receive (payment); — mille lire, to be 1000 lire in pocket; (naut.) to furl or house (flag, sail or awning). **-ato** *part. adj.* pocketed; received; (naut.) furled.

intassell-are [A I] *tr.* to peg; to plug; to bolt; to fix with peg or bolt, etc. **-ato** *part. adj.* pegged; bolted. (**-atura** *f.*)

intatt-o *adj.* intact; untouched; unbroken; uninjured; unimpaired; puro e —, unsullied; (fig.) la questione rimane **-a**, the problem is still unsolved. (**-aménte** *adv.*)

intavol-are [A I s] *tr.* to put on the table; (of bread) to put on a board (to carry to the oven); to surround with planks; to board up; (chess) to arrange the pieces on the board; (mus.) to score; — la discussione, to open the discussion; — delle trattative, to open negotiations; to table; (fig.) to embark on (an enterprise, a transaction). **-ato** *part. adj.* put on the table; set on a board; surrounded by planks; inlaid; decorated with inlay; (fig.) broached, begun; opened; (paint.) painted on wood; *n.m.* wooden partition; wood floor (planks); roof-boarding; (archit.) cyma reversa, ogee moulding. **-atura** *f.* putting on a table or board; boarding; negotiation; (mus.) tablature.

intedesc-are [A 2] *tr.* to Germanize; *rfl.* to become Germanized; to be susceptible to German influence. **-ato** *part. adj.* Germanized; under the influence of Germany or a German.

†**integamare** *tr.* to put in a pan.

integer·rimo *adj.* (*superl.* of **integro**, q.v.) strictly honest; of the utmost integrity.

integral-e *adj.* entire; complete; full; unexpurgated; pane —, wholemeal bread, brown bread; parte —, integral part; necessary component; (math.) calcolo —, integral calculus; (math.) integral; in full; pagamento —, payment in full; *n.m.* (math.) integral. **-ménte** *adv.* fully; completely; (leg.) pagato **-ménte**, paid in full.

integr-are [A I s] *tr.* to complete; to make up into a whole; to put right; (math.) to integrate; (leg.) to integrate; to complete; *rfl.* to be completed; to join into one body, or whole; to become integrated; **-a·bile** *adj.* that may be completed or made up into a whole. (**-abilità** *f.*) **-aménto** *m.* completing; making whole. **-ante** *part. adj.* integrating; completing; (leg.) integral; parte **-ante** del contratto, integral part of the contract. **-ativo** *adj.* tending to integrate; integrating; integrative; esame **-ativo**, entrance examination; norme **-ative**, Statutory Rules. **-ato** *part. adj.* integrated; completed. (**-atore** *m.* **-atrice** *f.*) **-azióne** *f.* integrating; integration; supplement; corsi d'**-azione**, supplementary classes; (leg.) integration; completion (C.C.P.).

†**integri·zia** *f.* See **integrità**, under **integro**.

in·tegr-o *adj.* entire; complete; honest; upright; showing integrity. **-aménte** *adv.* completely; honestly; with integrity. **-ità** *f.* completeness; wholeness; (fig.) uprightness; honesty; integrity; (leg.) tutelare l'**-ità** fisica, to safeguard the physical well-being (C.C.).

inte·gro *adj.* See **in·tegro.**

integumẹnt-o *m.* (scient.) integument. **-ale** *adj.* (scient.) integumental; integumentary.

intelai·are [A4] *tr.* to put on a loom; to frame; to set up; to assemble (a machine). **-ata** *f.* (techn.) assembling. **-ato** *part. adj.* put on a loom; set up; assembled. **-atura** *f.* setting up; framing; framework; frame; trestle; (motor.) chassis; (naut.) -atura dei remi, framework of a galley; thwarts; -atura di sostegno, cradle (of a ship).

†**intelletti·bile** *adj.* possessing the faculty of intelligence; capable of understanding; intelligible.

intellettiv·o *adj.* (philos.) intellective. (**-amẹnte** *adv.*)

intellett-o[1] *m.* intellect; understanding; intelligence; uomo d'—, man of understanding; person of intelligence; privo d'—, unintelligent; brain; mind; era uno dei migliori -i, he was one of the best brains; (schol. philos.) — attivo, active intellect; — possibile, possible intellect; †concept; †opinion; †meaning; †intention. †**-ore** *m.* one who understands. (†**-rice** *f.*) **-uale** *adj.* intellectual; lavoro -uale, intellectual work, brain work; (schol. philos.) virtù -uale, intellectual virtue; sostanza -uale, intellectual substance; *n.m.* intellectual; brainy individual; brain worker; scholar. **-ualmẹnte** *adv.* intellectually. **-ualịsmo** *m.* (philos.) intellectualism. **-ualista** *m., f.* (philos.) intellectualist. **-uali·stico** *adj.* (philos.) intellectualist, intellectualistic. **-ualità** *f.* intellectuality. **-ualịzzare** [A1] *tr.* (philos.) see **intellettuare. -ualo·ide** *adj.* (contempt.) brainy. **-uare** [A6] *tr.* (philos.) to intellectualize.

†**intelletto**[2] *adj.* understood.

intellezione *f.* (philos.) intellection, act of knowing; †thing understood.

intelligen-te *adj.* intelligent; clever; bright; quick; understanding; è molto — della botanica, he knows a lot about botany. **-temẹnte** *adv.* intelligently. **-za** *f.* intelligence; understanding; ability; ha grande -za della musica antica, he is a connoisseur of ancient music; restarono d'-za che, they were agreed that; a maggiore -za dei lettori, for the better understanding of the reader; questa parola è necessaria per l'-za del testo, this word is vital for the understanding of the text; mind, intellect; è una bella -za, he has a fine mind; (philos.) intelligence; understanding; (theol.) intelligence, angel; (mil.) affirmative flag (five black crosslets on a white background, i.e. British negative flag); (naut.) answering pendant; alza -za!, hoist!; -za a metà!, at the dip!; -za a segno!, close up!; (leg.) -ze col nemico, intelligence with the enemy (C.P.).

intelligi·bil-e *adj.* intelligible, comprehensible; facilmente — da tutti, easily understood by all; (philos.) intelligible; *n.m.* intelligible; object of intellect. **-mẹnte** *adv.* intelligibly; comprehensibly. **-bilità** *f.* intelligibility.

intelucciare [A3] *tr.* to stiffen with canvas; to pad.

intemerat-o *adj.* unblemished; stainless, spotless; irreproachable. **-a** *f.* (from a long Latin prayer to the B.V.M.) (colloq.) a serious scolding; fare un'-a ad alcuno, to give someone a serious talking to, to scold, to threaten. **-amẹnte** *adv.* spotlessly; irreproachably.

intemper-ante *adj.* intemperate; excessive; *n.m., f.* intemperate individual. **-antemẹnte** *adv.* intemperately; excessively. **-anza** *f.* intemperance; excess; violence; †see **intemperie. -ato** *adj.* intemperate; immoderate; unrestrained. **-atamẹnte** *adv.* intemperately; immoderately; unrestrainedly.

†**intemperare** *vb.* and derivs. See **temperare.**

intempe·rie *f. indecl.* bad weather; inclemency of the weather; *pl.* storms; resistente alle —, weatherproof.

intempestiv-o *adj.* untimely; unseasonable; inopportune; unexpected; (leg.) not in good time; lapsed; azione -a, lapsed action; domanda -a, application out of time. **-amẹnte** *adv.* unseasonably, inopportunely. **-ità** *f.* untimeliness; unseasonableness.

†**intempesto** *m.* time of night towards midnight.

intendente[1] *part.* of **intendere,** q.v.

intenden-te[2] *m.* superintendent; bailiff; steward; manager; administrator; inspector; (mil.) chief paymaster; head of pay office; †(naut.) intendant; marine superintendent; harbourmaster; *f.* †(eccl.) Mother Superior. **-za** *f.* intendancy; superintendence; bailiffship; stewardship; administration; managership; manager's office; (mil.) paymaster's office; administrative branch (4th Bureau); 'Q' Branch; †meaning; †love; †love of woman; †loved person.

inten·d-ere [C1]   **1.** *tr.* To INTEND; to have the intention of; to mean; -evo il contrario, I meant the opposite; quale dei due -e?, which of the two do you mean?; -eva dire, he meant to say; -o che mi ubbidisca, I intend him to obey me; così -o e voglio, those are my instructions. **2.** To UNDERSTAND; -o benissimo, I understand perfectly; — il significato di, to understand the meaning of; chi l'-e è bravo, I doubt if anyone understands it; dare ad — a uno, to mislead someone, (Tusc.) to make a person understand; me l'ha data ad —, he quite took me in; dare ad — lucciole per lanterne, to trick; to grasp (mentally), to take in (with one's mind); la volete —?, have you got that into your head?; gli fu fatto — che, he was made to understand that; lasciare — che, to infer that, to give to understand that. **3.** To HEAR; -o che ci lasciate, I hear you are leaving us; l'ho inteso dire che, I have heard it said that; non intese sonare, he did not hear the bell; non — a sordo, to require no second intimation; to listen to, to pay heed to; non -e ragione, he won't listen to reason. **4.** To SEE, to conceive, to regard; non la -o così, I do not see it like that, I look on it differently. **5.** (poet.) To TURN; to direct; — lo sguardo a, to turn one's gaze towards; — l'animo a, to think on. **6.** *intr.* (*aux.* avere; *prep.* a) To BE INTENT (on); — al lavoro, to be occupied with one's work; to pay heed (to); -evano ad altra cosa, they were busy with something else; (foll. by *infin., prep.* 'a') to be intent (on), to be occupied (in); -evamo a studiare la carta geografica, we were busy poring over the map; (*prep.* di) to intend (to), to mean (to); non -evo d'offenderla, I didn't mean to offend her; che cosa -ete di fare?, what do you intend to do?; -e di non pagare, he doesn't intend to pay; -o d'essere ubbedito, I mean to be obeyed. **7.** *rfl.* (*prep.* di) To HAVE A GOOD KNOWLEDGE (of), to be a good judge (of), to be a connoisseur (in, of); non m'-o di pittura, I know nothing about painting; -ersi con, to be on good terms with; -ersela con, to have an understanding with; *recip. rfl.* to be in agreement; to come to terms; vediamo d'-erci, let us come to some agreement; vediamo d'-erci bene, let us get the matter quite clear; to be in love with each other; -ersela, to have an understanding; se la -ono da un pezzo, there has been an understanding between them for some time; se l'-evano, i briccioni, those scoundrels had it all fixed up between them. **8.** IMPERSONAL PHRASES: s'-e che, it is understood that; s'-e!, of course!, naturally!, to be sure! **-ente** *part. adj.* understanding; intelligent; well-informed; competent; essere -ente di, to be a connoisseur of, to know a lot about; *n.m., f.* connoisseur; expert; †fare -ente, to inform; to give a false information to; †essere -ente di, to intend to; †intelligible; easy to understand. †**-e·vole** *adj.* understandable; comprehensible; intelligible; expectant; anticipatory; understanding; intelligent. **-imẹnto** *m.* understanding; intelligence; meaning; purpose; intention; idea; opinion; †news; information; intelligence; †dare -imento a, to give to understand; †inclination; †love; loved person. **-itọre** *m.* an intelligent person; person quick to understand; connoisseur; judge; †lover. (**-itrice** *f.*)

intendicchiare [A3] *tr.* to know a smattering of; to have a glimmering of an idea of.

intenebr-are [A1s] *tr.* to darken; to obscure; *intr.* (*aux.* essere) to be filled with shadow; to grow dark; to grow blind. (**-amẹnto** *m.*) **-ato** *part. adj.* filled with shadows; darkened; obscure; confused. †**-ire** *vb.* and derivs. see **intenebrare.**

intener-ire [D2] *tr.* to soften; to make tender; (fig.) to move; to move to pity; to touch the heart of; *rfl.* to grow soft; to become tender; to be moved; s'-ì e pianse, he was moved to tears. **-imẹnto** *m.* softening; tenderness; pity; feeling; compassion. **-ito** *part. adj.* softened; made tender; touched; moved; filled with compassion.

intens-o *adj.* intense; vehement; violent; colore —, vivid colour. **-amẹnte** *adv.* intensely; vehemently; violently. **-ificare** [A2s] *tr.* to intensify; to make more frequent; to increase. **-iọne** *f.* urgency; strength; intensity; †(mus.) tension; intensity. **-ità** *f.* intensity; strength; severity; vehemence; violence; (scient.) intensity; -ità luminosa, luminous intensity, candle power; (atom. phys.) counting rate; (meteor.) force (of wind); (mus.) intensity. **-ivo** *adj.* intensive; intensifying; (gramm.) intensive. **-ivamẹnte** *adv.* intensively.

intenta·bile[1] *adj.* that cannot be attempted; *n.m.* tentare l'—, to attempt the impossible.

intenta·bile[2] *adj.* See under **intentare.**

intent-are [A 1] *tr.* (leg.) to start; to bring; to institute; — causa a, to bring an action against; — procedimento legale contro, to start legal proceedings against. **-a·bile** *adj.* that may be proceeded against. **-ato** *part. adj.* begun, instituted. **-azione** *f.* (leg.) commencement (of action); institution (of proceedings, etc.).

intentato¹ *part.* See under **intentare**.

intentato² *adj.* untried; unattempted; unexplored; per non lasciar cosa alcuna intentata (*or* nulla d'—), to leave no stone unturned.

intentazione¹ *f.* See under **intentare**.

†intentazione² *f.* temptation; diabolical instigation.

†intentivo *adj.* and derivs. See **intento¹**.

intent-o¹ *adj.* intent; tense; bent (on); attentive; — al lavoro, intent upon one's work; essere — ad ascoltare una persona, to be listening to a person attentively. **-amente** *adv.* intently; attentively.

intento² *m.* intent; intention; aim; purpose; object; giungere all'—, to reach one's goal; con l'— di, with a view to; (leg.) purpose; aim; intent.

†intenz-a *f.* intelligence; understanding; concept; intention; intent; love; loved one. **†-are** *tr.* to put in mind of; to cause to be enamoured of; to cause pain to; *rfl.* to intend.

intenzion-e *f.* intention; purpose; ho — di fare una gita, I am minded to take a trip; è mia — che questo si faccia, I intend this to be done; con —, on purpose; intentionally; con piena —, quite deliberately; senza —, unintentionally, without design; oltre l'—, further than was (*or* is) intended; era una semplice —, it was only an idea; di buone -i è lastricato l'inferno, the road to Hell is paved with good intentions; wish; contro la mia ferma (*or* espressa) —, against my express wish; meaning; (leg.) intention; la comune —, mutual intent (C.C.); (schol. philos.) concept, 'intention'; **†attention**, intentness, concentration of the mind; **†tendency**; **†intelligence**; **†affirmation**; **†opinion**; **†meaning**; **†per —**, purposely; expressly; **†intense** gaze; **†object** of an intention. **-ale** *adj.* intentional; premeditated; questioni -ali, leading questions; (leg.) intentional; wilful; (schol. philos.) mental, of the mind, conceptual, 'intentional'; specie -ale, intentional species. **-almente** *adv.* intentionally; wilfully. **-ato** *adj.* intentioned; inclined; disposed; willing; bene -ato, well-intentioned; well-disposed; **†temo** che sia male -ato, I fear he means mischief.

intepidire [D 2] and derivs. See **intiepidire**.

inter- *prep.* inter-; between.

interalleato *adj.* (hist.) inter-allied.

†interame *m.* entrails of an animal.

interamente *adv.* See under **intero**.

†interare *tr.* to make whole; to complete.

interarticolare *adj.* (anat.) interarticular.

interasse *m. indecl.* (eng.) distance between centres; (motor.) wheelbase.

interbina·rio *m.* (rlwy.) six-foot.

intercal-are¹ *adj.* inserted; interpolated; intercalary; giorno —, 29 February, Leap-year day; (class. antiq.) intercalary; *n.m.* (poet.) refrain; burden; (colloq.) stock phrase; (mus.) vocal refrain.

intercal-are² [A 1] *tr.* to insert; to interpolate; to intercalate; *intr.* (*aux.* avere) (naut.) to add or skip a day when crossing the Date Line. **-ato** *part. adj.* inserted; interpolated; intercalated.

intercambi-are [A 4] *tr.* to interchange. **-a·bile** *adj.* interchangeable. **-abilità** *f.* interchangeability.

intercape·dine *f.* (archit.) cavity; space; gap; (bldg.) parete con —, cavity wall; (naut.) double bottom; space between inner and outer hull; space in saddle tanks of a submarine.

intercardinale *adj.* intercardinal (of points of the compass).

interce·d-ere [B 1] *intr.* (*aux.* avere) to intercede; -è per lui presso il Ministro, he interceded for him with the Minister; (of time) to be; to exist; to lie between; la distanza che -e fra i due villaggi, the distance between the two villages; to occur (between two stated events); *tr.* to obtain by intercession; gli potè — la grazia del Re, he succeeded in obtaining the king's pardon for him by intercession. **-ente** *part.* interceding; intervening; *n.m., f.* person interceding. **-itore** *m.* see **intercessore**, under **intercessione**. **-itrice** *f.* intercessor (esp. of the B.V.M.).

intercellulare *adj.* (biol.) intercellular.

intercervicale *adj.* (anat.) intercervical.

intercess-ione *f.* intercession; intervention. **-ore** *m.* intercessor. **-o** *part.* of **intercedere**, q.v.; *adj.* interceded; interposed; elapsed; intervened.

intercett-are [A 1] *tr.* to intercept; to seize; to carry off; to cut off; to interrupt; (geom.; mech.) to intercept; (radio; telev.) to monitor. **-amento** *m.* interception; intercepting; (radio; telev.) monitoring. **-ato** *part. adj.* intercepted. **-azione** *f.* interception; interruption. **-ivo** *adj.* see under **intercetto**. **-ore** *m.* interceptor.

intercett-o *apocop.-part.* of **intercettare**, q.v.; *adj.* intercepted; stopped; cut. **-ivo** *adj.* interceptive; apt to intercept.

intercezione *f.* interception; intercepting.

interchiu·d-ere [C 3] *tr.* to block the way of; to stop; to impede; to shut out; to shut in; to enclose; to half-close; (leg.) — un fondo, to enclose a piece of land (C.C.).

interchiusione *f.* (leg.) enclosure (C.C.).

interci·d-ere [C 3] *tr.* to cut in two; to separate; to divide; †— le dimore, to put aside delay. **†-imento** *m.* dividing; division.

intercine·tico *adj.* (biol.) nucleo —, interphase nucleus; *n.m.pl.* interphase chromosomes.

intercisione *f.* dividing; cutting; cut; division by cutting.

intercis-o *part.* of **intercidere**, q.v.; *adj.* cut in two; divided; separated; S. Giacomo —, St James Intercisus (martyred by being cut to pieces); (bot.) foglie -e, divided leaves; (med.) polso —, intermittent pulse; (Rom. antiq.) giorni -i, *dies intercisi* (when legal business was lawful for a short period only). **-amente** *adv.* intermittently; with interruptions.

†interclu-dere *vb.* and derivs. See **interchiudere**.

intercolleg-are [A 2] *tr.* (eng.) to interconnect. (**-ato** *part. adj.*)

intercolun·nio *m.* (archit.) intercolumniation.

intercorr-ere [C 5] *intr.* (*aux.* essere) to elapse; to intervene; to come to pass. **-ente** *part. adj.* intervening.

intercorso *part.* of **intercorrere**, q.v.; *adj.* elapsed; intervened; intervening; occurred.

intercostal-e *adj.* (anat.) intercostal; dolore —, pain between the ribs. **-mente** *adv.* (anat.) intercostally.

intercuta·neo *adj.* (med.) intercutaneous.

interdentale *adj.* (phon.) linguo-dental.

interdetto *part.* of **interdire**, q.v.; *adj.* prohibited; forbidden; speechless, amazed, bereft of speech; (leg.) forbidden; restrained; prohibited; deprived; (eccl.) interdicted; under an interdict; *n.m.* (Rom. hist., eccl.) interdict; (leg.) person deprived of civil rights; 'patient', person of unsound mind (C.C.).

interdicendo *m.* (leg.) person the subject of proceedings in Lunacy (C.C.).

interdipenden-te *adj.* interdependent; (eng.) interlocked. **-za** *f.* interdependence.

interdire [B 10] *tr.* to forbid; to prohibit; (leg.) to interdict; to restrain; to forbid; to prohibit; to ban; — uno per alienazione mentale, to place a person of unsound mind under judicial disability (C.C.); (Rom. hist.) to interdict; — dall'acqua e dal fuoco, to debar from fire and water; to banish; (eccl.) to interdict.

†interditto *part.* of **interdire**, q.v.

interdizione *f.* prohibition; forbidding; (leg.) interdiction (Scot.); deprivation of civil rights; receiving order in Lunacy (C.C.); (eccl.) interdiction, interdict; (mil.) tiro d'—, barrage fire, shots preventing supplies or reinforcements.

†interdotto *m.* mediation; intervention.

interess-are [A 1] *tr.* to interest; to concern; to touch; to affect; to influence; to apply to; ho -ato in vostro favore il Ministro, I have applied to the Minister on your behalf; — uno negli utili di un'azienda, to give someone a share in the profits of a business; (scient.; med.) to affect; *abs.* to be interesting, to be of interest; ciò non -a, that does not matter; *intr.* (*aux.* avere; *prep.* a) to be of interest (to), to be of importance or relevance (to); -a a tutti, it is everybody's business, it is important to everyone; *rfl.* (*prep.* a) to take an interest (in); vedevo che s'-ava al racconto, I could see he was interested in the story; (*prep.* di, per) to interest oneself on behalf of; m'-ai di (per) lui (*or* a, in, suo favore), I interested myself, I intervened, on his behalf; (*prep.* di) to care (about), to care (for). **-amento** *m.* interest; concern; (comm.) an interest in; vi assicuriamo del nostro -amento, we assure you we will do all we can. **-ante** *part. adj.* interesting; exciting; in uno stato -ante, in an interesting condition (pregnant). **-atezza** *f.* lack of disinterestedness, selfishness, self-interest. **-ato** *part. adj.* interested; concerned; having an interest in; le parti -ate, the interested parties; selfish; calculating; taking an interest; interested; amused; diverted; pleased; (leg.) having an interest in; interested; concerned; -ato in un'azienda, having a share in a business;

interess-are (*cont.*)

n.m. interested party; i ringraziamenti di tutti gli -ati, the thanks of all concerned. (-**ata** *f.*) -**atamente** *adv.* from interested motives; with interest. -**enza** *f.* (finan.) share; profit-sharing.

interess-e *m.* interest; advantage; lo faccio nel vostro —, I do it in your (own) interest; nell'— della verità, for truth's sake; affair, concern; badare ai propri -i, to look to one's own affairs, to mind one's own business; con molto —, with deep concern; ciò non ha — per me, that does not interest me; prendere — a, to take an interest in; (finan.) interest; — semplice, simple interest; — composto, compound interest; (leg.) avere — in un contratto, to have an interest in a contract (C.C.); — ad agire, *locus standi* (C.C.P.); danni e -i, damages; conflitto d'-i, conflict of interests; -i convenzionali, agreed rate of interest; -i legali, legal rate of interest; -i moratori, interest payable after default (C.C.); -i civili, interests under civil law (C.C.P.); -i sugli -i, compound interest; anatocism (C.C.). -**enza** *f.* see under **interessare**. -**oso** *adj.* having an eye to the main chance. (-**osamente** *adv.*)

interezza *f.* wholeness; entirety; integrity.

interfacoltà *adj. indecl.* concerning or common to two or more university faculties; *n.f.* committee of students representing all university faculties, Students' Union Committee.

interfer-ire [D 2] *intr.* (*aux.* avere; *prep.* a) to interfere (in, with); (phys.) to produce interference. -**enza** *f.* (eng.) interference; negative allowance; (radio) interference; chatter; (fig.) interference; overlapping or duplicating of functions.

interfero·metro *m.* (phys.) interferometer.

†**interfett-o** *adj.* (leg.) murdered. †-**ore** *m.* (leg.) murderer.

†**interfezione** *f.* (leg.) murder.

interfoglia·ceo *adj.* (bot.) interfoliar.

interfogli-are [A 4] *tr.* to interleave (in a book); to interfoliate. -**ato** *part. adj.* interleaved (usually with blank sheets between printed ones). -**atura** *f.* interleaving.

interfo·glio *m.* interleaf.

inter-fono *m.* internal address system. (-**fo·nico** *adj.*)

intergranulare *adj.* (eng.) intergranular.

interiettiv-o *adj.* (gramm.) interjectional; parenthetical. (-**amente** *adv.*)

interiezione *f.* (gramm.) interjection.

interim *adv.* (Lat.) in the meantime; (leg.) interim; *n.m.* assumere l'— d'un Ministero, to take over a Ministry temporarily; (eccl. hist.) Interim (in 1541 and 1548).

interinale *adj.* See under **interino**.

interin-are [A I] *tr.* (leg.) to ratify. -**ato** *part. adj.* ratified. -**azione** *f.* ratification.

interin-o *adj.* temporary; *n.m.* locum (tenens). -**ale** *adj.* temporary. (-**almente** *adv.*) -**ato** *m.* temporary office.

interior-e *adj.* interior; inner; inside; mental; spiritual; (rel.) vita —, life of the soul, life of prayer, spiritual life; *n.m.* interior (part), inside; the inner man; mind; heart; *f.pl.* -a (*or* gl'-i), innards, internal organs, entrails. -**mente** *adv.* inwardly. -**ità** *f.* inmost being; spiritual life.

interito¹ *adj.* (Tuscan) bolt-upright; stiff.

†**inte·rito²** *m.* death.

†**interizzato¹** *adj.* See **intirizzito**.

†**interizzato²** *adj.* See **interito²**.

†**interlasciare** *vb.* and derivs. See **intralasciare**.

interli·ne-a *f.* space between lines; (typ.) lead; spacing (of a typewriter, or in typing). -**are** *adj.* between the lines; interlinear.

interline-are¹ [A 6] *tr.* to interline; to separate lines by a space; to space; (typ.) to lead. -**ato** *part. adj.* interlined; lined; (typ.) leaded. -**atura** *f.*, -**azione** *f.* (typ.) leading.

interlineare² *adj.* See under **interlinea**.

interli·neo *m.* space between lines.

interlocut-ore *m.* interlocutor; speaker (in a dialogue or drama). (-**rice** *f.*)

interlocut-o·rio *adj.* (*m.pl.* -**o·rii**) (leg.) interlocutory; intermediate; not finally determinate; preliminary. -**o·ria** *f.* (leg.) interlocutory order.

interloquire [D 2] *intr.* (*aux.* avere) to put in a word; to join in a conversation; (colloq.) to butt in; (leg.) to make an interlocutory order; to give preliminary judgement.

interlu·dio *m.* interlude, entr'acte; (mus.) interlude; an organ-verset played between the verses of a psalm; the episodic portion of a fugue.

interl-unare *adj.* (astron.) interlunar. -**u·nio** *m.* (astron.) interlunar period.

interme·di-o *adj.* intermediate, middle; misura -a, middle course; tempo —, interval; persona -a, go-between, intermediary; (eng.) fondo —, false bottom; *n.m.* (mus., theatr. hist.) see **intermezzo**; (eng.) intermediate shaft; (chem.) intermediate. -**a·rio** *adj.* intermediary, intermediate; *n.m.* go-between, middleman; intermediary, mediator.

intermesso *part.* of **intermettere**, q.v.; *adj.* interrupted; abandoned, omitted.

intermet-tere [C 20 c] *tr.* to interrupt, to intermit; to omit; *intr.* (*aux.* essere) (med.) to be intermittent, to become irregular; *rfl.* to intervene; to interfere; †to elapse; †to act as mediator; †to take part, to participate.

intermezzo *m.* interval; interlude; (mus.) intermezzo; (theatr. hist.) an instrumental piece or a ballet performed between the acts of an opera or play; (in sixteenth and seventeenth centuries) a quasi-dramatic musical piece performed at court festivities; (in eighteenth century) a comic scene interpolated into an *opera seria* (chem.; techn.) medium, vehicle; mutual solvent; †*adj.* intermediate.

intermin-a·bile *adj.* endless, interminable. -**abilmente** *adv.* endlessly, interminably. -**ato** *adj.* endless, infinite; †indeterminate. -**atamente** *adv.* endlessly; to infinity.

intermissione *f.* cessation, intermission, respite; (theatr.) interval; senza —, without respite, incessantly, continuously.

intermitten-te *adj.* intermittent, fitful; (med.) polso —, intermittent pulse; febbre —, intermittent fever. -**za** *f.* fitfulness; intermittence; discontinuance, pause, interruption.

intermodulazione *f.* (radio) intermodulation.

intermond-io *m.* (*pl.* -**ii**) space (between worlds), interplanetary space. -**iale** *adj.* interplanetary; relating to outer space.

intermuscolare *adj.* (anat.) intermuscular.

internamente *adv.* See under **interno**.

intern-are¹ [A 4] *tr.* to thrust in; -ò la lama nelle carni, he plunged the blade into flesh; — la radice di, to plant; to bury; to shut up; to imprison; to place under restraint; to intern; *rfl.* (*prep.* in) to penetrate, to enter; to dive; s'-ò nel bosco, he plunged into the wood; la palla s'è -ata tra i muscoli della coscia, the bullet has lodged in his thigh muscles; (fig.) to become absorbed, to bury oneself, to lose oneself; -arsi con un personaggio, to identify oneself with a character. -**amento** *m.* internment; imprisonment; campo d'-amento, internment camp; penetration; burying. -**ato** *part. adj.* thrust; plunged; buried; penetrated; examined thoroughly; *n.m.* internee; inmate.

†**internare²** *rfl.* to be threefold.

internato¹ *part.* of **internare¹**, q.v.; also *n.m*

internato² *m.* See under **interno**.

internazional-e *adj.* international; Corte Internazionale di Giustizia, International Court of Justice; diritto —, international law; *pr.n.f.* International (socialist or communist); International (socialist hymn). -**ismo** *m.* internationalism. -**ista** *m.*, *f.* internationalist. (-**i·stico** *adj.*) -**ità** *f.* internationality, international character or validity. -**izzare** [A I] *tr.* to make international. -**izzato** *part. adj.* internationalized. (-**izzazione** *f.*)

intern-o *adj.* internal; interior; indoor; antenna -a, indoor aerial; inside, inner; inland; foro —, conscience; (archit.) interior, inside, inner; sicurezza -a, police (responsible for public order); nemici -i, fifth column; alunno —, boarder; medico —, house surgeon, house physician, house man; (Rom. hist.) mare —, the Mediterranean; (geom.) angolo —, interior angle; *n.m.* inside; nell'—, inland; soul, mind; Ministro dell'Interno, Minister for Home Affairs, Minister for the Interior, Home Secretary; medical student working in hospital; (paint.; photog.) interior; (sport) inside-forward; — destro, inside-right; — sinistro, inside-left. -**amente** *adv.* internally. -**ato** *m.* boarding-school system, boarding; period spent by a doctor in hospital when qualifying. -**ista** *m.* (art) painter of interiors; (med.) specialist in internal diseases.

intern-o·dio, -**odo** *m.* (bot.) internode.

internun-zi-o *m.* (eccl.) internuncio. -**atura** *f.* (eccl.) status of internuncio.

inter-o, **intér-o** *adj.* whole, entire; una giornata tutt'-a, an entire day, a whole day; intact, unabridged; undamaged; unadulterated; oro —, pure gold; cavallo —, stallion; avere -a fiducia, to have complete faith, to trust utterly; può fare a suo — arbitrio, he can

inter-o (*cont.*)
do exactly as he chooses; -a rovina, utter ruin; (archit.) arco —, semicircular arch, round-headed arch; full, complete, perfect; uomo —, man of complete integrity; (bot.) foglie -e, entire leaves; (math.) numero —, whole number, integer; *n.m.* whole; total; (math.) gl'-i e le frazioni, whole numbers and fractions; *adv.* per —, in —, completely, entirely. **-amente** *adv.* entirely, wholly, completely. **-ezza** *f.* wholeness; entirety; integrity.

interocea·nico *adj.* between continents, interoceanic.

interos·seo *adj.* (anat.) interosseous.

interparietale *adj.* (anat.) interparietal.

interpell-are [A I] *tr.* to interrupt; to question; to call in, to consult; to refer to; (leg.) to question; *intr.* (*aux.* avere) to put a question (e.g. in Parliament). **-amento** *m.* putting a question; interruption. **-ante** *part. adj.* putting a question; *n.m., f.* questioner. **-anza** *f.* question (in Parliament); motion of 'no confidence', interpellation; (leg.) interpellation; question; citation. **-ato** *part. adj.* interrupted; questioned; consulted. (**-atore** *m.* **-atrice** *f.*) **-azione** *f.* (leg.) an application declaring a debtor in arrears. **-o** *m.* (leg.) questioning (C.C.P.).

†**interpetrare** *vb.* and derivs. See **interpretare**.

interplaneta·rio *adj.* (astron.) interplanetary.

interpol-are [A I s] *tr.* to interpolate, to insert, to incorporate; to vary, to alternate; — lo studio col divertimento, to alternate work with amusement; (leg.) to interpolate; to insert (words) in a complete document; (maths) to interpolate. **-amento** *m.* interpolating; inserting. **-ato** *part. adj.* interpolated; inserted; added; (med.) febbre -ata, intermittent fever. **-atamente** *adv.* alternately; intermittently. (**-atore** *m.* **-atrice** *f.*) **-azione** *f.* interpolation; insertion; incorporation of marginal notes in the text; per -azione di tempo, from time to time; (leg.) interpolation.

interpolo *m.* (electr.) interpole, commutating pole.

interponimento *m.* interposing; interposition; intervention (cf. **interporre**).

interponte *m.* (naut.) space between decks, 'tween decks.

interporre [B 21] *tr.* to interpose, to insert; (leg.) — appello, to appeal; — appello contro una sentenza, to appeal against a judgement; — una persona, to make use of a nominee (C.C.); *rfl.* (*prep.* tra) to intervene (in); to mediate, to intercede; to raise an objection, to create an obstacle; to cause delay.

interpo·ṣ-ito *part.* of **interporre**; see **interposto**. **-itore** *m.* mediator, intermediary. (**-itrice** *f.*) **-izione** *f.* interposition, insertion; intervention, intercession; mediation; (of time) delay; interruption, suspension; (gramm.) parenthesis; (leg.) -izione di persona, use of nominee (C.C.); -izione gestoria, dealing for undisclosed principal.

inter-posto, -posto *part.* of **interporre**, q.v.; *adj.* interposed; inserted; interrupted; persona -posta, intermediary, nominee; (leg.) atti per -posta persona, acts done through intermediary or nominee; †*n.m.* (gramm.) interjection.

interpret-are [A I] *tr.* to interpret; to construe; to explain; to translate; (theatr.) to interpret; to play; to present, to perform; (cinem., of actors) to make (a film). **-a·bile** *adj.* susceptible of interpretation. **-amento** *m.* interpreting; explaining; (rhet.) synonymy. (**-ante** *part. adj.*) **-ativo** *adj.* interpretative. (**-ativamente** *adv.*) **-ato** *part. adj.* interpreted; explained; understood. **-azione** *f.* interpretation, exposition, explanation, exegesis; (theatr.) performance; (rhet.) synonymy; -azione erronea, misinterpretation; (leg.) interpretation, construction.

inter·prete *m., f.* interpreter; translator; commentator; exponent; mouthpiece, spokesman; (mus.) performer, artist, vocalist; (theatr.) actor, player; un grande —, a great actor.

interpun·gere [C 5] *tr.* (gramm.) to punctuate.

interpunzione *f.* punctuation; segni d'—, punctuation marks; (mus.) phrasing.

interr-are [A I] *tr.* to bury; to inter; to cover or plaster with earth; (civ. eng.) to backfill, to fill with earth; to lay underground (e.g. a cable); (mil.) — una batteria, to dig in a battery; *rfl.* to bury oneself, to cover oneself with earth; (hydr.; naut.) to silt up; (mil.) to go to earth. **-amento** *m.* burial, burying, interment; filling or covering with earth. **-ato** *part. adj.* dirty; covered with earth, buried; underground; silted up; (mil.) supplied with earthworks; entrenched, dug in; batteria -ata, protected or covered battery.

interrè *m.* (Rom. hist.) interrex.

interrefrigerazione *f.* (eng.) intercooling.

interregno *m.* interregnum.

interriflessione *f.* (opt.) inter-reflection, flare.

interr-ire [D 2] *tr.* to fill with earth; *intr.* (*aux.* essere) to become silted up. **-imento** *m.* silting up. **-ito** *part. adj.* filled with earth; silted up.

interriscaldamento *m.* (eng.) re-heating.

interrog-are [A 2 s] *tr.* to question, to ask questions of, to interrogate; to inquire of; to consult (documents, authorities); (leg.) to examine, to question; — i testimoni, to examine the witnesses. **-ante** *part. adj.* questioning, examining. **-ativa** *f.* question, interrogation. **-ativo** *adj.* interrogative, punto -ativo, question mark; *n.m.* interrogative; all'-ativo, in the interrogative. **-ativamente** *adv.* interrogatively. **-ato** *part. adj.* interrogated, questioned, examined; subjected to questioning; asked, consulted; *n.m.* person interrogated; †interrogation. **-atore** *m.* interrogator. (**-atrice** *f.*) **-ato·rio** *adj.* (*m.pl.* -ato·rii) questioning, interrogatory; *n.m.* (leg.) examination; subire l'-atorio, to undergo an examination; l'-atorio della parte avversaria, cross-examination; -atorio delle parti, questioning of parties (C.C.P.). **-azione** *f.* questioning, interrogation; question; presentare un'-azione a un ministro, to demand an explanation from a Minister.

interromp-ere [C 26] *tr.* to interrupt; to discontinue, to suspend; to break off; — le comunicazioni, to cut communications; — la scala, to break up the staircase (into several flights of steps); (leg.) to interrupt; — la prescrizione, to stop prescription running (C.C.); *rfl.* to cease; to stop; s'interruppe improvvisamente, he stopped suddenly. (**-ente** *part. adj.*) **-imento** *m.* interrupting. (**-itore** *m.* **-itrice** *f.*)

interrott-o *part.* of **interrompere**, q.v.; *adj.* interrupted; broken off; discontinued; cut; sonno —, broken sleep; (bot.) interrupted. **-amente** *adv.* interruptedly, with interruptions.

interruttivo *adj.* (leg.) interruptive, having the effect of interrupting.

interrut-tore *m.* interrupter; (electr.) switch; cut-out; circuit-breaker; — a coltelli, single-throw knife switch; — a levetta, tumbler switch. (**-trice** *f.*)

interruzione *f.* interruption; breaking off, break; cut (in communications, current, etc.); senza —, without a break, uninterruptedly; (photog.) bagno di —, stop bath; (leg.) — della prescrizione, interruption of period of prescription (C.C.); — del processo, abatement, discontinuance of action (C.C.P.); — dei termini, suspension of time-limit.

interscal·mio *m.* (naut.) scantling, distance between frames.

interscapolare *adj.* (anat.) interscapular.

intersec-are [A 2 s] *tr.* to intersect; to cut across; (geom.) to intersect; *rfl.* to intersect, to cross, to cut each other. **-amento** *m.* intersecting, intersection. **-ante** *part. adj.* intersecting; crossing. **-ato** *part. adj.* intersected; crossing; crossed. **-azione** *f.* intersection, cutting (each other); crossing; (geom.) intersection; point of intersection.

†**intersegare** *vb.* and derivs. See **intersecare**.

intersess-o *m.* (biol.) intersex. **-ualità** *f.* (biol.) intersexuality.

intersezione *f.* (geom.) intersection; point of intersection.

intersociale *adj.* social, sociological.

interspaziale *adj.* (astron.) interspatial, 'space'; viaggi interspaziali, space travel.

interspinale *adj.* (anat.) interspinal.

interstellare *adj.* (astron.) interstellar.

intersti·zi-o *m.* interstice; momentary pause or delay; †(astron.) — solare, solstice. **-ale** *adj.* interstitial.

interstrato *m.* (techn.) inside layer, interlay.

intersuola *f.* (shoem.) mid-sole.

†**intertenere** *vb.* and derivs. See **intrattenere**.

†**intertesto** *adj.* intertissued.

intertri·gine *f.* (med.) intertrigo.

intertropicale *adj.* (geog.; meteor.) intertropical.

interurban-o *adj.* between or linking two cities; telefonata -a, trunk call.

interuso·rio *m.* (leg.) discounted value.

intervallato *adj.* spaced out; with intervals.

intervallo *m.* interval; space; gap; dopo un lungo — di tempo, a long time after; ad intervalli, at intervals, from time to time; riunirsi ad intervalli regolari, to meet at regular intervals; lucido —, lucid interval; (mus.) interval; (mil.) spacing, interval between ranks, companies, regiments, columns, etc.; (typ.) space.

intervalvolare *adj.* (radio) intervalve.

interven-ire [D 17] *intr.* (*aux.* essere) to happen, to come about, to come to pass; (*prep.* a) to be present (at), to make a public appearance (at), to attend; to interpose; to interfere; (*prep.* in) to take part (in); (leg.) to intervene; (surg.) to intervene, to operate. **-ente, -iente** *part. adj.* intervening. †**-imento** *m.* intervention; occurrence, happening, event; intervening; presence; help; means. **-tore** *m.* (leg.) intervener. **-uto** *part. adj.* happened, occurred; present, attending; *n.m.pl.* gl'-uti, the audience, those present. **-zione** *f.* intervening, intervention; (leg.) intervention; (surg.) intervention, operation.

intervent-o *m.* presence, attendance; intervention, interference; assistance, help; chiedere l'— di, to call in; non —, non-intervention; (leg.) intervention; — di terzo, intervention by a third party or person; security; pledge; (surg.) intervention, operation. **-ista** *m., f.* interventionist.

intervenzione *f.* See under **intervenire**.

interversione *f.* (leg.) change of possessor's title from lawful to adverse (C.C.).

intervertebrale *adj.* (anat.) intervertebral.

intervist-a *f.* interview. **-are** [A 1] *tr.* to interview. **-ato** *part. adj.* interviewed; *n.m.* person being interviewed, interviewer. **-atore** *m.* interviewer. (**-atrice** *f.*)

intervivo *adv.* (leg.) *inter vivos*, during the lifetime.

interz-are [A 1] *tr.* to put one between two, to insert; to alternate; (archit.) to alternate (different courses of masonry, ornament, etc.); (naut. hist.) to put on a third rower; (mil.) to reform (a group) with troops from different units, to regroup; *rfl.* to come in third, to be the third to enter. **-ato** *part. adj.* alternating, inserted (between two others); entered third; reinforced, strengthened (with additional nails or bolts); (herald.) tierced; -ato in banda, tierced bendwise; -ato in fascia, tierced fesswise; -ato in palo, tierced palewise; -ato in pergola, tierced palewise; -ato in sbarra, tierced per bend sinister.

intes-a *f.* understanding, agreement; siamo d'—, we are agreed, it is understood; agire d'— con, to act with the connivance of; eravamo d'— che gliene avrei parlato, we had agreed that I should speak to him about it; nell'— che, on the understanding that; star sull'—, to be on one's guard; darsi l'—, to come to an agreement, to make an arrangement; (pol.) l'— cordiale, the Entente Cordiale; †attention. **-ista** *m., f.* (pol.) supporter of the 'Entente'.

intes-o *part.* of **intendere**, q.v.; *adj.* intended; understood; heard; agreed; mal —, misunderstood; siamo -i!, agreed!; ben —, (of a piece of work) properly made, satisfactory; ben —!, of course!; ben — che, provided that; (colloq.) non darsene per —, to disagree (with), *or* not to care about; fare — a, rendere — a, to inform, to give to understand, to warn; intent, engrossed; (leg.) valuta -a, the agreed consideration; †*n.m.* see **intesa**. **-amente** *adv.* in agreement.

intes·s-ere [B 1] *tr.* to weave, to interweave; to entwine; — lodi, to compose a panegyric; — intrigo, to hatch a plot. **-itura** *f.* wickerwork; weaving, entwining. **-uto** *part. adj.* woven, interwoven; composed. **-uto di bugie**, a tissue of lies.

intest-are [A 1] *tr.* to head; — una pagina, to head a page; to write the heading of; (comm.) to supply with a heading or top; to inscribe; to assign; ha -ato la casa a sua moglie, he has taken the house in his wife's name; *rfl.* to take (an idea) into one's head; to be obstinate, to persist (in an idea or project). **-a·bile** *adj.* inscribable, subject to registration; -abile a noi, chargeable to our account; (leg.) not of testamentary capacity. **-ato** *part. adj.* headed, entitled; carta -ata, headed paper; inscribed, registered; obstinate, pig-headed; rendita -ata, settled income; libretto -ato, register of inscribed stock; (leg.) intestate. **-atura** *f.* heading (of page or pages), repetition of title(s); (techn.) butt. **-azione** *f.* heading; title; registration, inscribing.

intestin-o *adj.* intestine, internal; guerre -e, civil wars; *n.m.* (anat.) intestine, gut. **-ale** *adj.* (anat.) intestinal.

intesto *adj.* (poet.). See **intessuto**, under **intessere**.

†**intiepidare** *vb.* and derivs. See **intiepidire**.

intiepid-ire [D 2] *tr.* to cool, to make tepid; to warm; to take the chill off; (fig.) to cool, to make less ardent; to abate, to mitigate; *intr.* (*aux.* essere), *rfl.* to cool; to lose heat; to grow lukewarm; **-ito** *part. adj.* cooled; cooled down, cooled off; warmed; reduced; mitigated.

intiero *adj.* and derivs. See **intero**.

intigliare [A 4] *intr.* (*aux.* essere) to grow fibrous (esp. of hemp).

intign-are [A 5] *intr.* (*aux.* essere), *rfl.* to become moth-eaten; to lose the hair; to grow bald; †to become dull or tarnished. **-ato** *part. adj.* moth-eaten. **-atura** *f.* damage by moths; moth-holes.

intignosire [D 2] *tr.* to infect with ringworm; to make scabby; *intr.* (*aux.* essere) to become scabby; to rot.

intim-are [A 1] *tr.* to order; to enjoin; v'-o di uscire!, I order you to leave!; -ò che si presentasse subito, he ordered him to come at once; to notify, to intimate; — la guerra, to declare war; (leg.) to notify; to serve a notice on; to give formal notice to; to summon; — l'arresto, to serve warrant of arrest; — il pagamento, to request payment; (mil.) to convey by signal, to signal, to command by trumpet, bugle or drum; — la resa, to acknowledge surrender, to haul down the colours; (eccl.) to summon (a council); to order (e.g. a fast); †to make intimate. **-ante** *part. adj.* intimating. **-ato** *part. adj.* intimated; conveyed; indicated; summoned. **-azione** *f.* order; injunction, summons; notification, intimation; le -azioni della forza pubblica, warning by trumpets to a mob to disperse (cf. Eng. 'reading the Riot Act'); (leg.) summons; legal notice; notificare un'-azione, to serve a notice; (naut.) tiro d'-azione, warning shot.

†**intimidare** *vb.* and derivs. See **intimidire**.

intimidazione *f.* (leg.) intimidation (C.P.).

intimid-ire [D 2] *tr.* to intimidate, to make shy; to frighten, to scare; *intr.* (*aux.* essere), *rfl.* to become timid; to grow shy; to be frightened. **-imento** *m.* intimidating; growing shy. **-ito** *part. adj.* intimidated; scared.

in·tim-o *adj.* innermost; deepest; intimate; very friendly; pranzo —, a small dinner-party among friends; avere un'-a persuasione, to have a feeling in one's bones; vita -a, inner life; worn underneath or next the skin; maglieria -a, underclothes; *n.m., f.* close friend; divenire -i, to become bosom friends; nel suo —, in his heart; dall'— del suo cuore, from the very bottom of his heart; nell'— della coscienza, deep down in his conscience. **-amente** *adv.* intimately, closely; conoscere -amente, to have a thorough knowledge of, to know very well. **-ismo** *m.* (lit. crit.) expression of intimate feelings and experiences. (**-ista** *m.*) **-ità** *f.* intimacy; avere -ità con qualcuno, to be intimate with someone.

intimor-ire [D 2] *tr.* to frighten, to make afraid; *intr.* (*aux.* essere), *rfl.* to be frightened; to become afraid. **-imento** *m.* frightening, making afraid; growing afraid. **-ito** *part. adj.* frightened.

intimpanire [D 2] *intr.* (*aux.* essere), *rfl.* (Tusc. pop.) to grow as tight as a drum; *tr.* to cause to grow as tight as a drum (e.g. abdomen, etc., with illness or overeating).

intin·g-ere [C 5] *tr.* to dip (into a liquid); to moisten; to soak; (fig.) — la penna nel fiele, to dip one's pen in gall; *intr.* (*aux.* avere) — nel piatto, to help oneself (to food); -erci, to have one's share; — in un affare, to take a share, to have a hand in a business. **-imento** *m.* dipping; moistening.

intin·golo *m.* (cul.) gravy, sauce; ragout; highly spiced dish; — di lepre, jugged hare.

intint-o *part.* of **intingere**, q.v.; *adj.* soaked, wet; moistened; tainted; — fradicio, wet through; *n.m.* gravy, sauce. **-ura** *f.* soaking; moistening; tainting.

intirann-ire [D 2] *intr.* (*aux.* avere), *rfl.* to tyrannize; to become a tyrant. **-ito** *part. adj.* tyrannical.

†**intirizzare** *vb.* and derivs. See **intirizzire**.

intirizz-ire [D 2] *tr.* to numb, to benumb; to stiffen; *intr.* (*aux.* essere), *rfl.* to become numb (esp. with cold); to be numb, to be benumbed. **-imento** *m.* numbness, stiffness (from cold). **-ito** *part. adj.* numbed; numb, stiff; frozen stiff.

intisich-ire [D 2] *tr.* to make consumptive; to weaken; to make pale; to impoverish; *intr.* (*aux.* essere), *rfl.* to become consumptive; to go into consumption; to grow weak and thin; to go into a decline; to pine away; to languish; (of plants) to do badly, to be stunted. **-ito** *part. adj.* consumptive; weak; impoverished; languishing; stunted.

intitol-are [A 1 S] *tr.* to entitle; to name, to call; — con il nome di, to call by the name of; -a sempre i suoi libri con i nomi più strani, he always gives his books the strangest titles; to confer a title (an honour) upon; (eccl.) to dedicate (church) under a given title; — al nome di, to dedicate to; -arono la piazza al nome di Cavour, they named the square after Cavour; *rfl.* to call oneself; to be called, to bear the title of; to entitle oneself; to derive one's title.

intitol-are (*cont.*)
-amento *m.* entitling, entitlement. **-ato** *part. adj.* entitled; called. **-azione** *f.* entitling; title; dedication.

†**intitulare** *vb.* and derivs. See **intitolare**.

†**into** *prep.* See **entro**.

intogliare [A4] and derivs. See **intugliare**.

intoller-a·bile *adj.* unbearable; intolerable; insufferable. (**-abilmente** *adv.*) **-bilità** *f.* unbearableness, intolerableness. **-ando** *adj.* not to be borne, insufferable. **-ante** *adj.* intolerant; prejudiced; impatient; uno stomaco -ante di certi cibi, a stomach that cannot digest certain foods; impatient; -ante del freddo, unable to bear cold. **-anza** *f.* intolerance; lack of tolerance; impatience.

†**intombare** *tr.* to entomb.

†**into·mito** *m.* bulge.

intona·bile *adj.* See under **intonare**.

intonac-are [A2s] *tr.* to plaster; to smooth, to prepare a smooth surface on; to whitewash; (bldg.) to plaster, to render; *rfl.* to plaster oneself, to get spattered (e.g. with mud); to make up one's face. **-ato** *part. adj.* plastered; whitewashed; *n.m.* plaster; (fig.) attaccarsi all'-ato, to catch at a straw. **-atore** *m.* plasterer. **-atura** *f.* plastering; plaster; (bldg.) plastering, rendering, grouting; -atura grezza, pargeting.

into·na·co *m.* (*pl.* **-chi**) plaster; rifare l'—, to whitewash; (paint.) plaster surface prepared for fresco or tempera painting; (iron.) make-up, cosmetics. **-chino** *m.* (bldg.) plaster finish; putty.

inton-are [A1d] *tr.* to start to sing; to strike up; to intone; to tune; (paint.) to match (colours); to tone; to tone down; (telegr.; radio) to tune in; (mus.) to tune; to sing; to sing in tune; to intone; to set to music; *rfl.* (*prep.* con) to be in tune (with), to be in harmony (with); questa mobilia non s'-a con la tappezzeria, this furniture does not tone with the wallpaper. **-a·bile** *adj.* tuneable. **-arumori** *m. indecl.* (theatr. hist.) cuebar, name given to various noise-making instruments devised for the futuristic theatre (1913). **-ato** *part. adj.* sung; played; tuned; sung in tune; struck up (of a song, air, etc.); voce -ata, voice (singing) in tune; tinta ben -ata, tint (or colour) that tones with its surroundings; (fig.) star sull'-ato, to speak in solemn tones. (**-atore** *m.* **-atrice** *f.*) **-atura** *f.* (mus.) intonation. **-azione** *f.* intoning; singing; intonation; tuning; tuning up; prelude, beginning (of a speech); (mus.) intonation (i.e. tuning); intonation (i.e. first few notes of a psalm-tone, credo, etc.); organ-prelude (sixteenth century); (paint.) toning, harmony of colours.

intonso *adj.* unshaven, uncut; (of pages) uncut; (paperm.) bordo —, deckle-edge; (poet.) unshorn (esp. as classical epithet of Apollo).

intont-ire [D2] *tr.* to stun; to amaze; *rfl.*, *intr.* (*aux.* essere) to be stunned; to be astonished; to become stupid. **-ito** *part. adj.* stunned, amazed.

intopp-are [A1] *tr.* to bump into; to stumble upon; *intr.* (*aux.* essere, avere), *rfl.* (*prep.* in) to bump (into, against); to stumble; (fig.) to stumble (over a word). (**-amento** *m.*) †**-icare** *vb.* and derivs. see **intoppare**.

intoppo *m.* obstacle, stumbling-block; difficulty, hindrance; stumbling, stumble.

†**intorbare** *vb.* and derivs. See **intorbidare**.

intorbid-are [A1s] *tr.* to trouble; to make turbid, to make muddy; (fig.) to trouble; to confuse; to confound; *intr.* (*aux.* essere), *rfl.* to become turbid, to become muddy; to become dirty, or dark; to become clouded, to cloud over; gli si è -ata la vista, his sight has grown dim. **-amento** *m.* clouding. **-ato** *part. adj.* troubled, muddy, dirty, cloudy; clouded; darkened; confused; acque -ate, troubled waters. (**-atore** *m.* **-atrice** *f.* **-azione** *f.*)

intorment-ire [D2] *tr.* to benumb; to send to sleep; *intr.* (*aux.* essere), *rfl.* to grow numb. **-imento** *m.* growing numb, benumbing; numbness; torpor. **-ito** *part. adj.* benumbed; numb; asleep (of a limb).

intorni-are [A4c] *tr.* to surround; to walk or travel round. **-amento** *m.* a turn; a going round. **-ato** *part. adj.* surrounded; (art) figura -ata, figure drawn in outline.

intorno *adv.* around; on every side, on every hand; avere uno sempre —, to be always accompanied by someone; molte persone gli stavano —, he was the centre of a group of people; erano — a cinquemila persone, there were about five thousand people; *prep.* (*usu. foll. by* 'a') around; round; — alla città, around the city; — a cento, about a hundred; on the subject of, about, concerning; dobbiamo discutere — a una grave questione, we

have a serious matter to discuss; lavorava — al suo libro, he was working on his book; (poet.) — di, — da, near, round (of place); *adv. phr.* d'ogn'—, on every hand.

intorpid-ire [D2] *tr.* to benumb, to make numb; — il cervello a uno, to make a person's brain inert; to make languish, to enervate; *intr.* (*aux.* essere), *rfl.* to become numb, to be benumbed; l'ingegno -isce nell'ozio, talents rust for want of use, ability withers away in idleness. **-imento** *m.* numbness, torpor. **-ito** *part. adj.* numbed; numb.

†**intorriare** *tr.* to fortify with towers.

intorsione *f.* (bot.) intorsion, contorsion.

intortigli-are [A4] *tr.* to twist; to twine, to entwine. **-ato** *part. adj.* twisted; entwined; (bot.) twining.

intorto *adj.* twisted, twisting, winding; wound; (fig., of person) reserved.

intoscan-ire [D2] *tr.* to make conform to Tuscan usage, to Tuscanize (esp. of language); *intr.* (*aux.* essere), *rfl.* to conform to Tuscan usage. **-ito** *part. adj.* Tuscanized.

intossic-are [A2s] *tr.* to poison. **-ato** *part. adj.* poisoned; *n.m.* (leg.) person under influence of drink or drug (C.P.). **-azione** *f.* (med.) intoxication; food poisoning; (leg.) poisoning; cronica -azione da alcool, chronic alcoholic intoxication (C.P.).

intostito *adj.* hardened, hard.

intozz-are [A1], **-ire** [D2] *intr.* (*aux.* essere), *rfl.* to grow fat and dumpy. **-ato**, **-ito** *part. adj.* grown fat and dumpy; squat.

intra[1] *prep.* (poet.) among; between; — tanto, meanwhile.

intra-[2] *pref.* among; inside; intra-.

†**intrabescare** *rfl.* to become enamoured.

intrabiccol-are [A1s] *rfl.* to clamber, to climb precariously. **-amento** *m.* risky climbing; (machine) contraption.

intracci·glio *m.* space between eyebrows.

†**intrachiu·dere** *tr.* to enclose, to close round; to impede, to prevent, to hinder.

†**intracor·rere** *intr.* to run between.

†**intraddire** *vb.* and derivs. See **interdire**.

intradosso *m.* (archit.) intrados, the interior curve of an arch or its stones.

intraduci·bil-e *adj.* untranslatable. **-ità** *f.* untranslatability.

intraeffetto *m.* (radio) inverse amplification factor.

†**intra-fatto**, **-finefatto** *adv.* immediately.

intraferro *m.* (electr.) air gap.

intralasci-are [A4] *tr.* to leave off; to cease; to leave undone; to leave out, to omit, to neglect; to abandon. **-amento** *m.* leaving off; respite; omitting, hindrance, obstacle. **-ato** *part. adj.* interrupted; neglected; abandoned; left undone.

intralci-are [A4] *tr.* to entangle; to impede; to hamper; (fig.) to make involved; to complicate; *rfl.* to become entangled; to grow involved. **-amento** *m.* hindering; hindrance, obstacle. **-ato** *part. adj.* entangled; hampered, hindered; embarrassed; involved, confused.

intral·cio *m.* entanglement, hindrance, impediment; obstacle.

intralicciatura *f.* (bldg.) bracing, latticework.

intrallazz-o *m.* illegal business, racket, black-marketeering; political compromise; ambiguous, shady relationship. **-are** [A1] *intr.* (*aux.* avere) to have illegal dealings; to deal in the black market. **-ista** *m.* racketeer; black-marketeer.

†**intramb-e**, †**-o**, †**-odu·e** *prn.* both.

†**intramendu·e** *prn.* both.

intramess-a *f.* digression, interpolation. **-o** *part. adj.* interposed, interpolated; *n.m.* entremets, side-dish; (naut.) deck beams.

intramett-ere [C20c] *tr.* to interpose; to interrupt; *rfl.* to intervene; to interfere. **-imento** *m.* interposing; intervening.

intramezz-are [A1] *tr.* to interpose; to alternate. **-ato** *part. adj.* interposed; alternated, alternating.

intramezzo *m.* (N. Ital.) partition; insertion.

†**intramissione** *f.* intermission.

intramolecolare *adj.* intramolecular; (bot.) respirazione —, intramolecular respiration.

intramonta·bile *adj.* indomitable; è —!, he's still going strong!

intransigen-te *adj.* intransigent; obstinate; intolerant; strict; severe; uncompromising; bigoted; *n.m.*, *pl.* (pol.) extremists. **-za** *f.* intransigence; strictness; severity.

intransitiv-o *adj.* (gramm.) intransitive; *n.m.* intransitive verb. **-amente** *adv.* intransitively.

†**intransito** *adj.* never passed over, never traversed, never crossed.

intra(p)porre [B21] and derivs. See **interporre**.

intrappol·are [A1s] *tr.* to entrap, to ensnare. *-ato part. adj.* ensnared; caught in a trap.

intrapren·d-ere [C1] *tr.* to undertake; to enter upon (a career, or course of action); to embark upon; — una lotta, to engage in a struggle; to venture upon, to set out on; †to intercept; †to comprehend; †to choose (of two things); †*rfl.* to be contained (within). *-ente part. adj.* enterprising; amorous, gallant; risky. *-enza f.* spirit of enterprise; enterprise; boldness; initiative. *-imento m.* undertaking, enterprise. *-itore m.* contractor; impresario; undertaker. (*-itrice f.*)

intraprẹsa *f.* undertaking, enterprise (cf. **impresa**).

intraprẹso *part.* of **intraprendere**, q.v.; *adj.* undertaken; entered upon; set out upon; begun; †contained, comprised.

†**intrare** *vb.* and derivs. See **entrare**.

†**intrarom·pere** *vb.* and derivs. See **interrompere**.

†**intrasegare** *vb.* and derivs. See **intersecare**.

intrasẹgna *f.* ensign; mark, badge; management.

intrasettimanale *adj.* mid-week.

intrasgredi·bile *adj.* inviolable.

intrasmuta·bile *adj.* untransformable, not transmutable.

†**intrata** *f.* See **entrata**.

intratora·cico *adj.* (anat.) intrathoracic.

intratta·bil-e *adj.* unreasonable; rude; intractable. *-ità f.* unreasonableness; rudeness; intractability.

intratten-ẹre [B32] *tr.* to entertain; to amuse; to hold in conversation; to detain; — una corrispondenza, to carry on a correspondence; — grandi speranze, to cherish great hopes; (mil.) to retain (forces) under one's command (contrary to instructions); †see **trattenere**; *rfl.* to stay (talking), to linger, to dwell, to talk at length; *-ersi a parlare di*, to talk a little longer about; *-ersi con*, to have a talk with; *recip. rfl.* to hold a conversation; s'erano *-uti a conversare*, they had lingered to converse with each other. *-imento m.* entertainment; diversion. *-uto part. adj.* entertained; diverted; held in converse; detained.

intrauterino *adj.* (anat.) intra-uterine.

†**intravagliare** *tr.* to weary, to tire.

intravat-a *f.* stockade, barrier made of beams. *-o adj.* barred with beams.

intraved-ẹre [B35] *tr.* to catch a glimpse of; to see indistinctly; to have an inkling of; to foresee; non s'-eva la fine, the end was not in sight. *-uto part. adj.* glimpsed; seen indistinctly; foreseen.

intravenọso *adj.* (med.) intravenous.

intravers-are [A1] *tr.* to cross; to work across; to cross-plough; to cut on the cross; †to transfix; to run through; *intr.* (*aux.* avere), *recip. rfl.* to cross. *-amento m.* crossing, intersecting. *-ato part. adj.* placed crosswise, crossed; hindered.

intravvedẹre [B35] and derivs. See **intravedere**.

intravvenire [D17] *intr.* (*aux.* essere) to be present; to take part; to happen.

†**intreare** *rfl.* to become three, to unite into three.

intrecci-are [A3c] *tr.* to plait, to braid; to twist; to weave; to entwine; to interlace; — danze, to dance, to perform (figure) dances; — le mani, to clasp one's hands; — le gambe, to cross one's legs; — fiori, — una ghirlanda, to weave a garland; (naut.) — i remi, to slide the oars across a boat from the shipped position so that the loom rests on the gunwale; *rfl.* to be twisted (plaited) together; to become entwined, to intertwine, to interlace; to intermingle. *-amento m.* plaiting; twisting, twining. *-ato part. adj.* plaited; twisted; *n.m.* plait; tiara. †*-atoio m.* tiara. (*-atore m. -atrice f.*) *-atura f.* plait, braid; things entwined or twisted together; tangle; tiara; (text.) grafting.

intrẹccio *m.* plait; knot; interlacing; (archit.) mouldings; (fig.) plot (of a novel, *ɸ*lay); commedia d'—, comedy of intrigue; (text.) plaited work; (mus.) interweaving (of parts in counterpoint).

intrefol-are [A1] *tr.* (naut.) to twist (the strands); †*rfl.* to become confused, to get muddled.

intrẹgnatura *f.* (naut.) worming.

†**intreguare** *rfl.* to make a truce, to make peace.

intre·pid-o *adj.* intrepid, fearless, undaunted; brave; ascoltò — la sentenza di morte, he heard the death sentence without flinching; bold, brazen, barefaced; l'avevano visto rubare, e lui negava —, they saw him steal, but he brazenly denied it; *pr.n.m.pl.* (lit. hist.) members of an Academy founded at Ferrara in 1600. *-amente*

adv. intrepidly; fearlessly; boldly, brazenly. *-ẹzza f.* fearlessness, intrepidity, bravery. *-ità f.* fearlessness; brazenness, impudence.

†**intrescare** *tr.* to involve, to confuse; *rfl.* to become confused.

intric-are [A2] *tr.* to entangle; *rfl.* to get entangled, to become involved. *-amento m.* entangling; entanglement, intrigue. *-ato part. adj.* entangled; tangled; intricate, involved. *-atamẹnte adv.* intricately.

†**intrico** *m.* tangle, knot; thicket.

intri·dere [C3] *tr.* to soak; to make into a paste; to knead; to moisten; to stain; to imbue; *rfl.* to dirty oneself, to befoul oneself.

intrig-are [A2] *tr.* to entangle, to tangle; *intr.* (*aux.* avere) to intrigue, to scheme, to exert influence secretly; *rfl.* to interfere, to meddle; non s'-a della politica, he does not concern himself with politics; non me ne voglio —, I don't want to get mixed up in it. *-amento m.* intrigue, entanglement; tangle, obstacle. *-ante part. adj.* intriguing, interfering, meddling; *n.m.* intriguer; meddler. *-ato part. adj.* entangled, tangled, confused, complicated; *n.m.* entanglement, tangle. *-atamẹnte adv.* intricately. (*-atore m. -atrice f.*)

intri-go *m.* (*pl.* **-ghi**) intrigue, plot; plotting; entanglement; trick; difficult position, fix; complexity. *-gọne m.* intriguer. (*-ọna f.*)

intrinsec-are [A2s] *tr.* to make intimate; to render intrinsic; *intr.* (*aux.* essere), *rfl.* (*prep.* in) to plunge deeply (into); — in una scienza, to become a master of some branch of learning; *-arsi con uno*, to become intimate with someone. (*-amẹnto m.*) *-ato part. adj.* rendered essential, intrinsic; inherent.

intrin·se-co *adj.* (*m.pl.* **-chi, -ci**) intrinsic, internal; intimate; essential; valore —, intrinsic value; amico —, intimate friend; causa *-ca*, necessary cause; principio —, essential principle; *n.m.* intimate friend, intimate; intrinsic value; essential qualities; heart, soul; nel suo — pensava diversamente, his private opinion was quite different; amount of intrinsic value; d'— c'è poco, there is little of real value. *-camẹnte adv.* intrinsically; intimately. *-chẹzza f.* intimacy; *pl.* acts of intimacy.

†**intrin·sico** *adj.* and derivs. See **intrinseco**.

intripp-are [A1] *tr.* (vulg.) to stuff food into; *rfl.* to stuff oneself. *-ato part. adj.* stuffed, gross with food. *-atura f.* stuffing, overeating.

intrisọ *part.* of **intridere**, q.v.; *adj.* soaked, moistened, mixed; farina *-a con acqua*, flour mixed to a paste with water; — di sangue, drenched with blood, blood-stained; — di polvere, covered with dust; calce *-a*, lime paste; †involved; implicated; *n.m.* paste, mixture, mash; mortar; (wet) plaster.

intrist-ire [D2] *intr.* (*aux.* essere) to languish; to pine away; to grow melancholy; to droop; to worsen; to deteriorate; to decay; (of plants) not to thrive; to be stunted; to droop; (of food) to go bad. *-imento m.* deterioration; degeneration; decay; falling off; pining away; drooping; being stunted. *-ito part. adj.* languishing; pining; drooping; decayed; stunted.

†**intro** *prep.* See **entro**.

†**introcque** *adv.* meanwhile.

introdọtto *part.* of **introdurre**, q.v.; *adj.* introduced; brought in; imported; ben —, having good references, well recommended; — di contrabbando, smuggled (in); †*n.m.* introduction; insinuation.

introdurre [B2] *tr.* to introduce; to put in, to insert; to slip in; to usher in, to show in; to let in; l'introdusse in casa di soppiatto, he let him into the house secretly; (leg.) — animali nel fondo, to bring animals on to the land (C.P.); — una lite, to take or start proceedings; *rfl.* (*prep.* in) to get (into); to penetrate (into); to creep in, to break in; i ladri s'introdussero nella casa per la finestra, the thieves broke into the house through the window.

introdutt-ivo *adj.* introductory; (mus.) coro —, opening chorus; (leg.) atto —, notice to appear; summons. *-ọre m.* introducer; (eng.) feed; intake; (text.) taker in (of carding machine); fiocchi dell'-ore, ciuffetti dell'-ore, taker-in droppings; polvere dell'-ore, taker-in fly. (*-rice f.*) *-o·rio adj.* (*m.pl.* **-orii**) introductory, preliminary.

introduziọne *f.* introduction; commencement; preamble; dazio d'—, customs (import) duty; — illecita (di contrabbando), smuggling; (naut.) loading; (mus.) introduction, overture; (leg.) — della causa, commencement of action (C.C.P.); — clandestina in luoghi militari, entry by stealth into military places (C.P.).

introflesso *adj.* (bot.) inflexed.

introgol·are [A 1 s] *tr.* to make a mess upon; to wet; *rfl.* to get in a mess; to wet oneself. (**-amento** *m.* **-ato** *part. adj.* **-atura** *f.*)

introiare [A 4] *tr.* (vulg.) to dirty, to foul; *rfl.* to dirty oneself.

introi·bo *m. indecl.* (liturg.) the beginning, the preparatory prayers (at Mass).

introit-are [A 10] *tr.* (comm.) to receive; to encash; to enter. (**-ato** *part. adj.*)

intro·ito *m.* entrance; (liturg.) introit; (mus.) introit; (leg.) the start of proceedings; (comm.) cash received; entry; takings; gate-money.

intromessa *f.* see **intermissione**; †intermezzo.

intromesso *part.* of **intromettere**, q.v.; *adj.* introduced; inserted; intrusive; *n.m.* entremets.

intromett-ere [C 20 c] *tr.* to insert; to introduce; *rfl.* (*prep.* in) to intervene; to interfere (in); to enter; to penetrate. (**-itore** *m.* **-itrice** *f.*)

intromissione *f.* intervention; interference; intercession; intrusion; intromission.

intron-are [A 1] *tr.* to stun (with noise); to daze; rimbombi che **-ano** l'aria, reverberations which fill the air with deafening roar; to deafen; *rfl.*, *intr.* (*aux.* essere) to be stunned (with noise); to be deafened; to be shaken; to crack. **-amento** *m.* deafening; rattling; thundering; (fig.) thunderous noise; shaking, trembling. **-ante** *part. adj.* thundering, deafening. **-ata** *f.* deafening noise; exorbitant demand. **-ato** *part. adj.* deafened; stunned; stupefied; stupid; shaken (up); *m.pl.* (lit. hist.) members of a Sienese Academy founded in 1525. (**-atore** *m.* **-atrice** *f.*) **-atura** *f.* see **-amento**; deafness induced by noise.

intronfi-are [A 4 c] *intr.* (*aux.* essere) to swell with pride; to be puffed up; to put on airs. **-amento** *m.* swelling with pride. **-ato** *part. adj.* swollen with pride; swollen-headed. **-atura** *f.* being swollen with pride; airs and graces; haughtiness.

intronizz-are [A 1] *tr.* to enthrone; to crown; (eccl.) to enthrone. **-ato** *part. adj.* enthroned; crowned. **-atura** *f.* enthronement; (joc.) majestic air (as of one enthroned). **-azione** *f.* enthronement; coronation.

introrso *adj.* (archit.) turned inwards; (bot.) introrse.

introspezione *f.* introspection; (med.) internal examination.

introva·bil-e *adj.* not to be found. (**-ità** *f.*)

intru·dere [C 3] *tr.* to insert; (canon law) to intrude; *rfl.* to intrude; to thrust oneself.

intrufolare [A 1 s] *tr.* to thrust; *intr.* (*aux.* avere) to rummage; *rfl.* to intrude, to poke one's nose in.

intrugli-are [A 4] *tr.* to mix (wine) with other liquor; to mix into a liquid; (fig.) to confuse; — un discorso, to muddle a speech; to make a mess of a speech; — lo stomaco, to load one's stomach with unsuitable food, or with harmful medicines; *intr.* (*aux.* avere) to mess about; *rfl.* to dirty oneself; (fig.) to get mixed up in shady business; non mi voglio — con loro, I don't want to get mixed up with them. **-ato** *part. adj.* soiled, dirtied; messed up; adulterated. **-one** *m.* muddler, messer; (fig.) intriguer. (**-ona** *f.*)

intru·glio *m.* nasty mixture (liquid); distasteful or harmful medicine; (fig.) medley; muddle; mess, hotch-potch; shady business; intrigue.

intrupp-are [A 1] *rfl.* (*prep.* con) to join company (with); to join the crowd; *recip. rfl.* to flock together. **-amento** *m.* flocking together; crowd; gathering. **-ato** *part. adj.* banded together; in a troop.

intrus·ione *f.* insertion; interpolation; intrusion. **-ivo** *adj.* (geol.) intrusive.

intruso *part.* of **intrudere**, q.v.; *adj.* inserted; intruded; intrusive; *n.m.* intruder; interloper.

†**intuare** *rfl.* to enter into thee, to become one with thee.

intuf-are [A 1] *intr.* (*aux.* essere) to become stuffy or foul (of air in a confined space); *rfl.* to bury oneself (in basement, dungeon). **-ato** *part. adj.* stale, stuffy, foul (of air); buried; in the dark, cut off from air.

intuff-are [A 1] *tr.* to dip; to steep; to soak. (**-amento** *m.* **-ato** *part. adj.*)

intugli-are [A 4] *tr.* (naut.) to bend (one rope to another). **-atura** *f.* (naut.) bend, a method of joining two hawsers; the point where they are so joined; carrick bend (used when ropes are required to pass round a capstan).

intu-ire [D 2] *tr.* to perceive by intuition; to understand immediately; to guess. (**-ente** *part. adj.*) **-itivo** *adj.* intuitive; virtù, facoltà, **-itiva**, intuitive faculty, intuition; evident; (scient.) self-evident;

(philos.) intuitive; (theol.) visione **-itiva**, Beatific Vision; contemplazione **-itiva**, intuitive contemplation (mystical union). **-ito** *part. adj.* perceived (by intuition); guessed; understood. (**-itore** *m.* **-itrice** *f.*) **-izione** *f.* intuition; perception; (philos.) intuition; (theol.) direct vision of God; (art) inspiration; stroke of genius. **-iz·ionismo** *m.* (philos.) intuitionism.

intu·ito¹ *m.* intuition; l'— femminile, female intuition; intendere per —, to know intuitively; fu un —, it was pure guesswork.

intuito² *part.* See under **intuire**.

intuizione *f.* See under **intuire**.

intumescen-te *adj.* (med.) intumescent. **-za** *f.* (med.) intumescence.

intumid-ire [D 2] *intr.* (*aux.* essere) to swell. **-ito** *part. adj.* swollen.

intumor-ire [D 2] *intr.* (*aux.* essere) to swell up; to form a tumour. **-ito** *part. adj.* swollen; puffed up.

intuonare [A 1 d] and derivs. See **intonare**.

inturchinire [D 2] *tr.* to colour blue; *intr.* (*aux.* essere) to become blue.

inturgid-ire [D 2 s] *intr.* (*aux.* essere) to swell up; to become turgid. (**-imento** *m.*) **-ito** *part. adj.* swollen; turgid; stile **-ito**, turgid style.

intuzzare [A 1] and derivs. See **rintuzzare**.

inubbidiente *adj.* and derivs. See **inobbediente**.

inubbriacare [A 2] and derivs. See **ubbriacare**.

inudito *adj.* See **inaudito**.

inuguale *adj.* and derivs. See **ineguale**.

inul-a *f.* (bot.) *Inula.* **-ina** *f.* (chem.) inulin, alantin, alant starch.

inulto *adj.* (poet.) unavenged, unpunished.

inumanazione *f.* (theol.) incarnation, assumption (by Christ) of human nature.

inuman-o *adj.* inhuman, brutal; inhumane; barbarous; uncivilized, rude; (joc.) outrageous. **-amente** *adv.* inhumanly, without humanity; inhumanely. **-ità** *f.* inhumanity, brutality.

inum-are [A 1] *tr.* to inter, to bury. **-ato** *part. adj.* interred. **-azione** *f.* interment.

inumid-ire [D 2] *tr.* to damp, to damp down (linen); to moisten; to wet; *rfl.* to become damp. **-imento** *m.* damping; moistening. **-ito** *part. adj.* damped; moistened.

inurban-o *adj.* rude, discourteous, impolite. **-amente** *adv.* rudely, impolitely, discourteously. **-ità** *f.* rudeness, discourtesy, incivility.

†**inurbare** *rfl.* to enter into a city.

inus·ato *adj.* not used, disused; unaccustomed; unusual, extraordinary. **-atamente** *adv.* unusually. **-itato** *adj.* not used, unusual, unwonted. (**-itamente** *adv.*)

inu·til-e *adj.* useless, of no use; of no effect; idle; unnecessary; è —!, it's no good!, it's no use!; (Bibl.) servo —, unprofitable servant. **-mente** *adv.* in vain, to no purpose, uselessly, unnecessarily. **-ità** *f.* uselessness. **-izzare** [A 1] *tr.* to render useless, to put out of action.

inuzzol-ire [D 2] *tr.* to excite, to arouse desire in; *rfl.* to become roused, to become excited. **-ito** *part. adj.* excited, expectant.

invacchire [D 2] *intr.* (*aux.* avere) (of a silkworm) to swell up and die after feeding, as a result of a disease.

inva·d-ere [C 3] *tr.* to invade; la folla invase il palazzo, the crowd broke into the palace; — i diritti di un altro, to encroach upon another's rights; il colera invase l'Europa, cholera spread into Europe. **-ente** *part. adj.* intrusive, encroaching; è un uomo **-ente**, he is a busybody; *n.m.* busybody. (**-itore** *m.* **-itrice** *f.*)

†**invagare** *vb.* and derivs. See **invaghire**.

invagh-ire [D 2] *tr.* to charm, to attract; — uno di, to make someone fond of; to arouse a desire in; *rfl.* (*prep.* di) to become fond (of); to fall in love (with); to be charmed (by), to take a fancy (to); **-irsi** del potere, to conceive a lust for power. (**-imento** *m.*) **-ito** *part. adj.* charmed, attracted, fond; *pr.n.m.pl.* (lit. hist.) members of an Academy founded at Mantua in 1562.

invagin-are [A 1] *tr.* to sheathe. (**-amento** *m.* **-ato** *part. adj.*) **-azione** *f.* (surg.; biol.) invagination.

invai-are [A 4], **-olare** [A 1] *intr.* (*aux.* essere) to turn dark-coloured (of grapes and olives). (**-(ol)ato** *part. adj.*)

invalere [B 34] *intr.* (*aux.* essere) to be established; to come into force.

invalica·bile *adj.* impassable.

invalid-are [A 1 s] *tr.* (leg.) to invalidate. **-a·bile** *adj.* (leg.) that can be invalidated. (**-abilità** *f.*) **-amento** *m.* invalidation. **-ante** *part. adj.* invalidating. **-ato** *part. adj.* invalidated. **-azione** *f.* invalidation.

inva·lid-o *adj.* infirm, invalid, disabled, incapable (of work), incapacitated; (leg.) invalid; *n.m.* (mil.; naut.) disabled pensioner. (**-amente** *adv.*) **-ità** *f.* disablement, incapacity, infirmity; (leg.) **-ità** del contratto, invalidity of contract (C.C.); **-ità** permanente, permanent disablement.

invaligi·are [A 3] *tr.* to pack (in a bag, suitcase). (-am**ẹ**nto *m.*) -ato *part. adj.* packed in suitcases.

invall-are [A I] *intr.* (*aux.* essere) to flow into a valley. (-am**ẹ**nto *m.* -ato *part. adj.*)

†**invalorire** *vb.* and derivs. See **avvalorare**.

invalso *part.* of **invalere**, q.v.; *adj.* established, prevailing, in fashion.

invan-ire [D 2] *tr.* to make vain, proud, conceited; to turn the head of; to render useless; to make null and void; *intr.* (*aux.* essere), *rfl.* to become vain, to grow conceited; to disappear, to dissolve, to melt away. -im**ẹ**nto *m.* vanity, conceit, pride. -ito *part. adj.* made vain, conceited, spoilt.

invano *adv.* in vain, vainly, to no purpose; uselessly; (archit.) posare —, to rest on an arch (or similar opening).

invaria·bil-e *adj.* invariable, constant; (gramm.) uninflected, indeclinable, invariable; quel vocabolo è — al plurale, that word does not change in the plural. -m**ẹ**nte *adv.* invariably. -ità *f.* invariableness.

invarian-te *adj.* (math.) invariant. -za *f.* (math.) invariance.

invariat-o *adj.* unchanged, constant. -am**ẹ**nte *adv.* unchangingly.

invaṣ-are[1] [A I] *tr.* to obsess; (of a devil) to possess; *rfl.* to be obsessed, to be infatuated; to be possessed (by a devil). (-am**ẹ**nto *m.*) -ato *part. adj.* possessed (by a devil), obsessed, infatuated; furious. (-at**ọ**re *m.* -atrice *f.* -azi**ọ**ne *f.*)

invaṣ-are[2] [A I] *tr.* to pot, to put into pots or jars; *tr.* (naut.) to cradle; to flood (by closing lock-gates or other water exit). -ato *part. adj.* (naut.) cradled, shipped. -atura *f.* (naut.) cradling.

invaṣ-iọne *f.* invasion; (of water) flooding; (mil.) invasion and occupation of territory or fortress; (leg.) arbitraria —, unauthorized entry (C.P.). -ivo *adj.* (mil.) offensive; armi -ive, offensive weapons, bombers, etc. -o *part.* of **invadere**, q.v.; *adj.* invaded, encroached upon; invaded; (mil.) occupied. -**ọ**re *m.* (mil.) invader; *adj. m.* invading; occupying; (of water) flooding, overflowing, torrente -ore, a stream in flood, a torrent (of water) rushing in; -ore dei diritti altrui, encroaching on another's rights.

invecchi-are [A 4] *intr.* (*aux.* essere) to grow old; to age; — nel vizio, to become hardened in vice; to fall out of use; to become dated or antiquated; certi libri non -ano mai, some books never date; *tr.* to make old, to age; to make (one) look old; questo cappello t'-a, this hat makes you look older than you are; to cause to mature; *rfl.* to make oneself look old; to give oneself out as older than one is. -am**ẹ**nto *m.* growing old, ageing; (of wines) maturing; (eng.; metall.) ageing. -ante *part. adj.* making one old; making one look old; decaying, in decay. -ato *part. adj.* grown old (or older), aged; un libro -ato, a book out of date; obsolete; un male -ato, a chronic disease.

invẹce *adv.* on the other hand; on the contrary; but; e —, and instead; *prep. phr.* — di, instead of, in the place of (cf. **vece**).

†**inveceri·a** *f.* vanity.

inveire [D 2] *intr.* (*aux.* avere; *prep.* contro) to inveigh (against), to rail (at).

invel-are [A I] *tr.* (naut.) to supply with sail; *intr.* (*aux.* avere) to make sail; to spread sail and let draw; to spread additional sail. -ato *part. adj.* (naut.) under sail.

invelen-ire [D 2] *tr.* to poison, to envenom, to embitter; *intr.* (*aux.* avere), *rfl.* to become embittered; to be enraged, to be irritated. (-im**ẹ**nto *m.*) -ito *part. adj.* envenomed; bitter; enraged.

invellutare [A I] *tr.* to cover with velvet.

invendi·bil-e *adj.* unsaleable. -ità *f.* unsaleability.

invendica·bile *adj.* that cannot be avenged; unpunishable.

invendicato *adj.* unavenged; unpunished.

invenduto *adj.* unsold; (comm.) roba invenduta, remainders, remnants.

inve·nia *f.* (usu. *pl.*) devout action; gesture of humility; plea for pardon; (fig., *pl.*) affected airs, mincing ways.

†**invenire** *tr.* to invent; to find; to come upon; to recognize; to prove.

invent-are [A I] *tr.* to invent; to find out; to devise; to imagine; to fabricate; to make up, to tell a lie about; to forge; (iron.) non ha -ato la polvere, he is not very bright, (or) that is nothing new; l'Ariosto ha -ato assai meno che non si creda, Ariosto was much less original than has been thought. (-am**ẹ**nto *m.*) -ato *part. adj.* invented; imagined; fabricated, made up; è -ato di sana pianta, it is a pure fabrication; personaggio -ato, fictitious character. (-atam**ẹ**nte *adv.*) -at**ọ**re *m.*, -**ọ**ne *m.* story-teller, romancer, liar. (-atrice *f.* -**ọ**na *f.*)

inventari-are [A 4] *tr.* to inventory, to catalogue, to make an inventory of; to put on the inventory. -ato *part. adj.* inventoried; put on inventory.

inventa·r-io *m.* inventory; catalogue; fare l'— della merce in magazzino, to take stock; (leg.) to inventory; compilare l'— di, to draw up an inventory of; (leg.) accettazione con beneficio d'—, acceptance of inheritance (of dubious solvency) with benefit of inventory, i.e. with reservations (C.C.); (fig.) si può credergli, ma con beneficio d'—, you can believe him, with reservations. -iale *adj.* (leg.) inventorial.

inventatore *m.* See under **inventare**.

inventiva *f.* inventiveness, imagination, originality.

inventiv-o *adj.* inventive; facoltà -a, virtù -a, inventive power, creative faculty, imagination, fancy; la parte -a (e.g. of a historical novel), the fictitious part. -am**ẹ**nte *adv.* fictitiously; inventively.

inventọne *m.* See under **inventare**.

invent-ọre *m.* inventor; discoverer; liar, story-teller; (leg.) finder (C.C.); inventor (C.C.); *adj.* genio —, inventive genius. (-rice *f.*)

†**inventrare** *rfl.* to become pierced (with) through and through.

†**invẹnturato** *adj.* fortunate.

invenust-à *f. indecl.* gracelessness, lack of charm. -o *adj.* graceless, awkward; without charm; plain. (-am**ẹ**nte *adv.*)

invenziọn-e *f.* invention; thing invented; fare un'—, to invent something; contrivance, device; fabrication, lie; tutto d'—, entirely fictitious; discovery, finding; fiction; (leg.) proprietà acquistata per —, property acquired by finding (C.C.); brevetto per un'—, patent for an invention (C.C.); (liturg.) — della Croce, Invention, Finding, of the Cross; (rhet.) invention (selection of topics or arguments); (mus.) invention (referring to the 2- and 3-part inventions of J. S. Bach); (dressmaking and crafts) model; novelty, creation. -are [A I c] *intr.* (*aux.* avere) (paint.) to paint an imaginative composition.

†**inver** *prep.* See **verso**.

†**inverare** *rfl.* to enter into the true nature (of), to participate in the truth (of), to be informed with the truth (of).

†**inverberire** *rfl.* to become angry.

inverd-ire [D 2] *intr.* (*aux.* essere) to turn green, to become green; *tr.* to make green, to colour green. -ito *part. adj.* turned green, coloured green.

inverecond-ia *f.* immodesty; impudence. -o *adj.* immodest, bold, saucy; impudent; brazen. -am**ẹ**nte *adv.* immodestly; brazenly.

inverg-are [A 2] *intr.* (*aux.* avere) (text.) to cross the ties, to make the lease; *tr.* (naut.) to bend on (sail or flag); to mark, to write upon (cf. **vergare**). -at**ọ**re *m.*, -atrice *f.* (text.) leaser. -atura *f.* (text.) lease; crossing.

inveri-simiglianza *f.*, -si·mile *adj.* and derivs. See **inverosimiglianza** and **inverosimile**.

invermigliare [A 4] *tr.* (poet.) to dye vermilion, to redden, to incarnadine; *rfl.* to blush.

invermin-are [A I] *intr.* (*aux.* essere) to have worms; to become maggoty. (-am**ẹ**nto *m.*) -ato *part. adj.* having worms; ciliegia -ata, maggoty cherry. -ire [D 2] *intr.* (*aux.* essere), *rfl.* to verminate, to have worms; to be maggoty. -ito *part. adj.* wormy, maggoty.

inverna *f.* (naut.) S.W. wind (on Lake Maggiore).

invern-ale *adj.*, †-are *vb.*, -ata *f.* See under **inverno**.

invernici-are [A 3] *tr.* to varnish; to paint; to polish; *rfl.* (joc.) to make up one's face. -am**ẹ**nto *m.* varnishing; polishing. -ata *f.* coat of varnish; polishing. -atina *f. dim.*; dare un' -atina a, to brush up, to shine, to give a quick polish to. -ato *part. adj.* varnished; painted; polished. -at**ọ**re *m.* painter; french polisher. -atura *f.* varnishing; coat of varnish; polishing; painting; tinsel; -atura di dottrina, veneer of learning.

invern-o *m.* winter; d'—, in the winter; giardino d'—, winter garden; (mil.) quartieri d'—, winter quarters. -ale *adj.* wintry; relating to winter; occurring in the winter; suitable for winter; la stagione -ale, the season of winter; vestiti -ali, winter clothes. †-are *intr.*, *rfl.* to pass the winter; to turn to spring (cf. **svernare**). -ata *f.* winter (with ref. to duration or weather); una brutta -ata, a bad winter; fare l'-ata, to winter.

invero *adv.* indeed, in fact (also **in vero**).

inverosimiglianza *f.* unlikelihood, improbability.

inverosi·mil-e *adj.* unlikely, improbable; unconvincing. -m**ẹ**nte *adv.* improbably; unconvincingly.

inversamẹ**nte** *adv.* See under **inverso**[1].

invers·ione *f.* inversion; — sessuale, sexual inversion; (gramm.; rhet.) metathesis; anagram; (leg.) — dell'onere della prova, shifting of burden of proof; (mil.) reverse order (of marching, etc.); (eng.) reversal; ad — di marcia, reversible; (opt.) reversal. **-ivo** *adj.* showing inversion; serving to invert.

invers·o[1] *adj.* inverse; contrary; in senso —, in the opposite direction; (bot.) seme —, pendulous seed; (mech.; math.) inverse; (mil.) ordine —, reverse order, manœuvre reversing the order; *adv. phr.* all'-a, badly, wrong; tutto va all'-a, everything is going wrong; *prep.* towards; (before *prn.*, *foll.* by 'di') — di lui, with regard to him. **-amente** *adv.* inversely; -amente proporzionale, in inverse ratio.

inverso[2] *prep.* (poet.). See **verso**.

invertebrato *adj.* (zool.) invertebrate.

†**inver·tere** *vb.* and derivs. See **invertire**.

invertina *f.* (bot.) invertine.

invert·ire [D I] *tr.* to invert; to reverse; to transpose; to reverse the direction of; (leg.) — l'onere della prova, to shift the burden of proof; (mil.) to reverse order, to exchange wing. **-i·bile** *adj.* invertible; reversible. (**-ibilità** *f.* **-imento** *m.*) **-ito** *part. adj.* inverted; reversed; transposed; inverse; upside-down; (chem.) invert; zucchero -ito, invert sugar; (aeron.) avvitamento -ito, outside roll; (motor.) carburatore -ito, downdraft carburettor; *n.m.* invert (also *adj.*). **-itore** *m.* (watchm.) reverser; (eng.) reversing gear, reverse; (electr.) reverser; -itore di polarità, pole reverser; (radio) inverter. (**-itrice** *f.*)

inverzicare [A 2 s] *tr.* to turn green; *rfl.* to grow green.

invesc·are [A 2 c] *tr.* to lime (with bird-lime); (fig.) to entice; *rfl.* to become ensnared, to fall in love; to yield to a lure. (**-amento** *m.*) **-ato** *part. adj.* caught (as by bird-lime); ensnared. (**-atore** *m.* **-atrice** *f.*)

investi·bile *adj.* and derivs. See under **investire**.

investig·are [A 2 s] *tr.* to investigate; to inquire into, to look into; to ask about; to sound, to test. **-a·bile** *adj.* suitable for investigation; †ineffable, incomprehensible, not to be explored by human intellect. (**-abilità** *f.*) †**-agione** *f.* see **investigazione**. (**-amento** *m.* **-ante** *part. adj.*) **-ativo** *adj.* investigating, trained to investigate; agente -ativo, detective. **-ato** *part. adj.* investigated; examined. **-atore** *m.* investigator, inquirer; detective; one engaged in research; *adj.* inquiring, investigating, searching. (**-atrice** *f.*) **-azione** *f.* investigation, inquiry; research.

invest·ire [D I] *tr.* to collide with, to come into collision with; to run down, to knock down; il direttissimo -ì un treno merci, the express ran into a goods train; (finan.) to invest; — danari, capitali. in un'impresa, to invest money, capital, in a concern; — di pieni poteri, to invest with full powers; to attack, to accost, to beset; m'-ì di domande, he beset me with questions; to inform, to give full information about, to brief; to strike, to fall upon; luce che -e la superficie, light falling upon the surface; (leg.) to invest, to give possession to; (mil.) to assault; to surround, to invest; to lay siege to; to hit, to wound; (naut.) to collide with, to ground, to ram; — la corrente, to go against the current; *intr.* (*aux.* essere) (naut.) — in un banco, to ground on a shoal; *rfl.* to be fully conscious (of one's rank or power); to behave with proper dignity; (of an actor) to enter into one's part, to live the part; *recip. rfl.* to collide, to come into collision. **-i·bile** *adj.* available for investment. (**-ibilità** *f.*) †**-igione** *f.* see **investitura**. **-imento** *m.* collision, accident; (finan.) investment, placing (of capital); (mil.) investing; sudden attack; besieging; (naut.) collision; grounding. †**-ità** *f.* see **investitura**. **-ito** *part. adj.* (*prep.* di) covered (with), decorated (with); run down, knocked down; suited, suitable, proper; invested, employed; (admin.) membro -ito di tutti i poteri, fully-fledged member; il comitato è -ito dell'esame di una relazione, the committee has a report before it. **-itura** *f.* investiture; (hist.) lotta delle -iture, conflict of investitures, investiture contest; (leg.) investiture; (naut.) grounding.

†**inveterare** *intr.* to grow old.

inveterato *adj.* inveterate; ingrained; odio —, inveterate hatred; long established, of long standing.

invetr·iare [A 4] *tr.* to glaze, to make like glass; (techn.) to glaze, to fit with glass; to glaze (bricks, pottery, etc.). **-iamento** *m.* hardening, glazing. **-iata** *f.* (glazed) window; window-pane(s); glass-partition; glass-door; glazed frame; (joc.) spectacles, glasses; (naut.) scuttle, glass light over a porthole or in a deck. **-iato** *part. adj.* glazed (i.e. having glass in windows, doors,

partitions); serra -iata, greenhouse, glasshouse; occhi -iati, glassy eyes; shiny; faccia -iata, impudent face; (cul.) glazed, brushed with white of egg; *n.m.* something glazed. **-iatura** *f.* glazing.

invetr·ire [D 2] *intr.* (*aux.* essere) to turn to glass. (**-ito** *part. adj.*)

invettiv·a *f.* invective; scagliare una —, to give vent to invective. **-o** *adj.* invective, abusive. **-amente** *adv.* abusively.

†**invezzare** *vb.* and derivs. See **avvezzare**.

invi·are [A 4] *tr.* to send, to dispatch; to convey; vi -o i miei migliori saluti, I send you my best wishes; to set in motion; to put on the right road. (**-a·bile** *adj.* **-amento** *m.*) **-ato** *part. adj.* sent; *n.m.* envoy; delegate; (journ.) correspondent, representative; -ato speciale, special correspondent. (**-atore** *m.* **-atrice** *f.*)

†**invidendo** *ger.* envying; *adj.* — a, envious of.

invi·dia[1] *f.* envy; avere, portare, sentire — contro, a, to be envious (of), to envy; — nobile, emulation; essere superiore alle invidie, to be above envy; fare — a tutti, to make everybody envious; crepare d'—, to be dying, bursting, with envy; essere l'— di tutti, to be the envy of all, to be envied by all; (theol.) envy (as deadly sin); †hate, hatred; †righteous anger; †— amorosa, jealousy.

†**invi·dia**[2] *f.* See **indivia**.

invidi·are [A 4] *tr.* to envy; — una cosa a sè stesso, to deny oneself something; to forego something; t'-o questi bei libri, I envy you your fine books; (fig.) questo vino non ha nulla da — allo sciampagna, this wine is just as good as champagne; †to hate. **-a·bile** *adj.* enviable, desirable; ricchezza non -abile, ill-gotten wealth. **-ante** *part. adj.* envying, envious; *n.m.*, *f.* an envious person. **-ato** *part. adj.* envied. **-atore** *m.* envious person; one who is envious; è un -atore del vostro successo, he is envious of your success; *adj.* envious; fortuna -atrice delle gioie altrui, fortune envious of men's happiness. (**-atrice** *f.*)

invidios·o *adj.* envious; invidious; occhiate -e, envious glances; raccolta -a, invidious harvest (i.e. unfairly distributed); *n.m.* envious person, malicious person. **-amente** *adv.* enviously, with envy; invidiously.

in·vid·o *adj.* (poet.) envious; *n.m.* envious person. **-amente** *adv.* enviously, maliciously; resentfully.

invigil·are [A I s] *intr.* (*aux.* avere; *prep.* a) to watch (over); to be attentive (to), to see (to); — che nulla manchi, to see that nothing is lacking; *tr.* to look after, to supervise, to invigilate; to watch over. **-ante** *part. adj.* invigilating; watchful; *n.m.*, *f.* invigilator; superintendent. (**-atore** *m.* **-atrice** *f.*)

invigliacch·ire [D 2] *intr.* (*aux.* essere), *rfl.* to grow cowardly, to become faint-hearted. (**-imento** *m.* **-ito** *part. adj.*)

invigorare *vb.* and derivs. See **invigorire**.

invigor·ire [D 2] *tr.* to strengthen, to invigorate; to encourage; *intr.* (*aux.* essere), *rfl.* to become invigorated; to gain strength; to be encouraged, to take heart. (**-imento** *m.*) **-ito** *part. adj.* invigorated, strengthened; heartened, encouraged.

invil·ire [D 2] *tr.* to debase; to degrade; to lower (value, price, morale); to make cowardly; to depress, to dishearten; *intr.* (*aux.* essere), *rfl.* to be debased, to grow cowardly, to become contemptible; to become of no account; to lose value, to become cheap; to be frightened. **-ito** *part. adj.* debased; degraded; depressed; disheartened.

invillan·ire [D 2] *intr.* (*aux.* essere), *rfl.* to adopt country ways, to live like a countryman; to become boorish. **-ito** *part. adj.* become countrified.

†**invillare** *rfl.* to become the owner of a villa.

invilupp·are [A I] *tr.* to wrap up; to envelop, to surround; to hide, to conceal; *rfl.* to wrap oneself up; to become involved. (**-amento** *m.*) **-ante** *part. adj.* enveloping; (bot.) foglie -anti, sleeping leaves. **-ato** *part. adj.* wrapped up, enveloped; involved. **-o** *m.* tangle; confusion; envelope; packet.

invinci·bil·e *adj.* invincible, unconquerable; evidenza —, irrefutable evidence. **-mente** *adv.* invincibly; irrefutably. **-ità** *f.* invincibility.

invincid·ire [D 2] *tr.* (Tusc.) to soften; *intr.* (*aux.* essere) to go soft. (**-ito** *part. adj.*)

inv·i·o *m.* (*pl.* -i·i) dispatch, forwarding; shipment; sending; posting; (of money) remittance; sono sospesi tutti gl'-ii di armi e munizioni, all consignments of arms and ammunition have been held up; (poet.) envoi.

inviola·bil·e *adj.* that cannot be violated; (leg.) inviolable. **-mente** *adv.* inviolably. **-ità** *f.* inviolability.

inviolat·o *adj.* inviolate, intact; unbroken; unprofaned. (**-amente** *adv.*)

inviper-ire [D 2] *intr.* (*aux.* essere), *rfl.* to become spiteful or viperish; to get angry, to be enraged; -irsi contro, to become viperish towards. (-im̧ento *m.* -ito *part. adj.*)

†**invironare** *tr.* to surround.

inviscer-are [A 1 s] *tr.* to swallow, to consume; to cause to penetrate; *rfl.* (*acc.* of *prn.* si, *prep.* in) to penetrate (into); to go to the heart (of); -arsi in una cosa, to be wholly taken up with a matter; (*dat.* of *prn.* 'si') to appropriate; to assimilate, to digest; (fig., joc.) s'è -ato tutto quel libro, he has swallowed the whole book. (-ato *part. adj.*)

invischi-are [A 4] *tr.* to snare with bird-lime; to entangle, to entice; *rfl.* to be caught with bird-lime; to be ensnared, entangled; to be beguiled. (-am̧ento *m.* -ante *part. adj.* -ato *part. adj.*)

invisc-idire [D 2] *intr.* (*aux.* essere) to become sticky or viscid. (-idim̧ento *m.* -idito *part. adj.*) -osire [D 2] *intr.* (*aux.* essere) to become viscous or viscid. (-osito *part. adj.*)

invisi·bil-e *adj.* invisible; unseen; imperceptible; (colloq.) vi siete fatto —?, where have you been hiding? -m̧ente *adv.* invisibly. -ità *f.* invisibility.

inviso *adj.* disliked; hated; distasteful, unpleasant; essere — a tutti, to be hated by all.

invisp-ire [D 2] *intr.* (*aux.* essere), *rfl.* to become lively. -ito *part. adj.* become active, brisk, lively.

invit-are[1] [A 1] *tr.* to invite; -alo ad entrare,. ask him to come in; lo -eremo a pagare, we shall ask him to pay; — a farsi rappresentare, to invite to be represented; accetta senza farti troppo —, accept without having to be asked over and over again; vi -o a dire le vostre ragioni, please tell me your reasons; una scena che -a gli occhi, an inviting scene; questo pensiero m'-ava a tacere, this thought induced me to keep silent; un vino che -a a bere, a delectable wine; to call, to convoke; to provoke, to challenge; to call on; -o il dottor Gabrieli a parlare, I call on Dr Gabrieli to speak; (in games) to call the stakes, to call a suit, to call for a card; (poet.) to urge, to incite; *rfl.* to introduce oneself; *recip. rfl.* to invite one another; †to toast one another. -ante *part. adj.* inviting, attractive; *n.m.* host; *f.* hostess. †-anza, †-ata *f.* see invito. -ativo *adj.* inviting, serving as an invitation. -ato *part. adj.* invited; called (together), convoked; *n.m.* guest; beneficiary (under a will). (-ata *f.* -atore *m.* -atrice *f.*) -atorio *adj.* (*m.pl.* -ato·rii) relating to an invitation; (eccl.) lettere -atorie, papal letters summoning bishops to a council; *n.m.* (liturg.) Invitatorium. †-atura *f.*, †-azione *f.* see invito. †-e·vole *adj.* inviting, enticing.

invit-are[2] [A 1] *tr.* to screw in; to screw up; to screw on. -ato *part. adj.* screwed; screwed in; screwed up; screwed on. -atura *f.* screwing.

invitire [D 2] *tr.* to plant with vines.

invito[1] *m.* invitation; letter of invitation; invitation card; exhortation, request; hint, intimation; non seppe resistere all'— della bella giornata, ed uscì, he couldn't resist the call of the fine day, so went out; (at cards) call; — sacro, notice outside church (advertising special services, etc.); (archit.) a short flight of two or three steps leading to a staircase; (leg.) — ad offrire, invitation to tender or bid.

†**invito**[2] *m.* unwilling, reluctant.

invitt-o *adj.* unconquered; unconquerable, invincible, indomitable; l'amianto sta — al fuoco, asbestos is not affected by fire. -am̧ente *adv.* invincibly; indomitably.

inviz-iare [A 4] *tr.* to spoil; to vitiate; *intr.* (*aux.* essere) to get into bad habits, to become vicious. (-iato *part. adj.*)

invizz-ire [D 2] *intr.* (*aux.* essere) to wither, to fade. (-im̧ento *m.* -ito *part. adj.*)

invoc-are [A 2] *tr.* to invoke, to call upon; — un diritto, to invoke a right; to call to witness; to appeal to; to call for; — aiuto, to call for help; — la benedizione su, to call down a blessing on; la terra inaridita -a la pioggia, the parched earth needs rain. -ante *part. adj.* invoking; calling (upon *or* for); -ante aiuto, calling for help. -ativo *adj.* invocatory. -ato *part. adj.* invoked. (-atore *m.* -atrice *f.*) -azione *f.* invocation; (rel.) invocation; dedication, title (of church); (liturg.) epiclesis.

†**invo·glia** *f.* wrapping, covering; sack.

invogli-are[1] [A 4] *tr.* to induce; to lure; to arouse a wish or desire in; *rfl.* (*prep.* di) to become desirous (of); to desire; to fall in love (with). (-am̧ento *m.*) -ato *part. adj.* (*prep.* di) desirous (of).

†**invogliare**[2] *tr.* to wrap, to cover; to put in sacking.

invo·glio *m.* package, parcel; bundle; wrapping, packing-sheet; (bot.) involucre, perianth.

invol-are[1] [A 1] *tr.* (*prep.* a) to steal, to ravish; — all'oblìo, to bring to light, to restore to fashion; to carry off; to hide; *rfl.* to steal away, to disappear; to fly away, to flee; s'-a ai nostri occhi, it disappears from our view. (-am̧ento *m.*) -ato *part. adj.* stolen away; hidden; -ato agli occhi del mondo, concealed from the world. †-atore *m.* thief.

involare[2] [A 1 c] *intr.* (*aux.* essere) to take off (of aircraft).

invol·g-ere [C 5] *tr.* to wrap up (up); to pack (up); to envelop; to be wrapped round; to coil (rope); carta da —, wrapping paper; (fig.) to involve, to implicate. (-ente *part. adj.*) †-ime *m.* bundle. -im̧ento *m.* envelopment; involvement, entanglement; †wrapping.

invo·lo *m.* (of aircraft) take-off.

involonta·r-io *adj.* unintentional, involuntary; unwitting; unwilling; (leg.) unintentional. -am̧ente *adv.* unintentionally; involuntarily; unwittingly; unwillingly.

involpare [A 1] *intr.* (*aux.* essere) (of wheat) to grow smutty, to become blighted.

involp-ire [D 2] *intr.* (*aux.* essere) to grow cunning (like the fox). (-ito *part. adj.*)

involt-are [A 1] *tr.* to wrap up, to pack up; (archit.) to vault; to roof or span with arches; to build with arches; *rfl.* (*prep.* di) to wrap oneself up; to become involved (in), to meddle (with). -ata *f.* wrapping up; dare un'-ata a, to wrap lightly round, to wrap up loosely, with one wrapping. -ato *part. adj.* wrapped up.

involt-o *part.* of involgere, q.v.; *adj.* wrapped up, enveloped; involved; rami -i, interlacing branches; (bot.) foglie -e, involute leaves; *n.m.* package, parcel; bundle; cover, carton, wrapping-paper (or any wrapping material); sheath; (bot.) see invoglio. -ino *m.* case (for medals, etc.), locket; envelope. -ura *f.* wrapping; tying up; (colloq.) hedging, beating about the bush.

invo·lucro *m.* envelope, cover, covering; pod; sheath; casing; (bot.) involucre; (aeron.) envelope, gas-bag, gas-container (of balloon or airship); (eng.) shell, envelope, casing.

†**involutare** *rfl.* to become transformed.

involut-o *adj.* involved, complex, complicated; (bot.) involute. -o·rio *adj.* (math.) involutory.

involuzione *f.* complication; involution; decay; (med.) involution, regression.

invol·v-ere [C 14] *tr.* to envelop; to overwhelm; to involve. -ente *part. adj.* enveloping; (bot.) involucrating.

invulnera·bil-e *adj.* invulnerable; beyond reproach. -ità *f.* invulnerability.

invulnerato *adj.* unwounded, unhurt, safe, intact.

inzacçher-are [A 1 s] *tr.* to splash with mud; to bespatter; *rfl.* to get splashed with mud; (fig.) to get into trouble. -ato *part. adj.* muddied.

inzafard-are [A 1] *tr.* to smear with grease; to make sticky. -ato *part. adj.* greasy; sticky.

inzaff-are [A 1] *tr.* to plug; to stuff in; to stuff up. (-ato *part. adj.*)

inzafferan-are [A 1] *tr.* to sprinkle with saffron; to colour with (or like) saffron. (-ato *part. adj.*)

inzaffir-are [A 1] *rfl.* to become adorned with sapphires. -ato *part. adj.* ensapphirined.

†**inzampagliato** *adj.* implicated, involved, caught up.

inzampogn-are [A 5 c] *tr.* to enchant; to delude; to ridicule; to impose upon. (-ato *part. adj.*)

inzavardare [A 1] and derivs. See inzafardare.

inzavorr-are [A 1] *tr.* to load with ballast; *rfl.* to meddle, to become entangled. (-ato *part. adj.*)

inzepp-are [A 1] *tr.* to fix with a wedge (or wedges); to stuff, to fill very full; to pack tight, to cram; to stuff with food; to attack; — dei colpi, to deal blows; (mil.) to spike (a gun). (-ato *part. adj.* -atura *f.*)

inzibettato *adj.* scented with civet.

†**inzigare** *tr.* to instigate; to incite; to stir up.

†**inzimino** *m.* See zimino.

inzipiliare [A 1] *tr.* to incite, to instigate, to urge on.

inzoccolato *adj.* wearing clogs, in clogs.

inzolf-are [A 1 c] *tr.* to spray with sulphur; to fumigate with sulphur. (-am̧ento *m.*) -ato *part. adj.* sprayed with sulphur; fumigated with sulphur. -atoio *m.* sulphur bellows (for spraying sulphur on to vines). -atura *f.* sulphuring. (-azione *f.*)

inzotich-ire [D2] *tr.* to make boorish; *intr.* (*aux.* essere), *rfl.* to become boorish; to become clumsy; to grow unmannerly. (-im**e**nto *m.* -ito *part. adj.*)

inzozz-are [A1] *tr.* (joc.) to ply with drink (grog); *rfl.* to drink spirits (in quantity); to get sozzled. -ato *part. adj.* sozzled.

inzucc-are [A2] *tr.* (of wine) to go to the head of, to make tipsy; *rfl.* to get tipsy; to fall in love; to be obstinate. (-ato *part. adj.*)

inzucch-are [A1s] *tr.* to sugar, to put sugar in, to add sugar to; (fig.) to be sweet to (someone), to flatter. -am**e**nto *m.* sweetening, sugaring. -ato *part. adj.* sweetened, sugared; sweet; parole -ate, honeyed words.

inzufol-are [A1s] *tr.* to instigate, to urge, to prompt; to delude, to deceive. (-ato *part. adj.* -at**o**re *m.* -atrice *f.*)

inzupp-are [A1] *tr.* to soak; to drench; to dip; to immerse; *rfl.* to get wet, soaked, drenched; to be dipped. -am**e**nto *m.* immersing. -ato *part. adj.* soaked, drenched, wet through; dipped; immersed. -atura *f.* immersion.

i·o *pers. prn. 1st sing. nom.* (frequently omitted where the prn. would be expressed in English; when expressed it often marks special emphasis): I; sono —, it is I; —, no!, not me!; — sottoscritto, I, the undersigned; non fui — che dissi questo, it was not I who said so; 'chi è?' 'Io.' 'Io chi?' 'Io, Baldini', 'who is it?' 'It's me.' 'Me?, who's me?' 'Me, Baldini'; — stesso andrò, I will go myself; ve lo dico —!, I can assure you!; — per me, —come —, for my part; da quel giorno non sono stato più —, since that day I have not been myself; o me la paga, o non son più —, you shall pay me, as sure as my name is...; (with the verb understood) ed — a lui, and I said to him; contento — contenti tutti, if I am satisfied then we all are; *n.m.* ego; the self.

io·ide *adj.* (anat.) hyoid.

io·d·io *m.* iodine; tintura di —, tincture of iodine. -ato *m.* (chem.) iodate. -ico *adj.* (chem.) indice -ico, iodine value. -idrato *m.* (chem.) hydroiodide. -ofo·rmio *m.* (chem.) iodoform. -uro *m.* (chem.) iodide.

ioglosso *m.* (anat.) hyoglossus.

iole *f.* (naut.) jolly boat; (pop.) rowing-boat.

iolito *m.* (min.) cordierite, iolite.

iolla *f.* (naut.) yawl.

ionadat·tico *adj.* (lit. hist.) describing a kind of slang based on alliteration or initial rhyme which flourished in the sixteenth century; lingua ionadattica, any type of rhyming slang.

ion-e *m.* (phys.; chem.) ion. -izzante *part. adj.* (chem.) ionogenic. -izzare [A1] *tr.* (phys.; chem.) to ionize. -izzazi**o**ne *f.* (phys.) ionization. -o·metro *m.* (phys.) ionometer. -osfera *f.* (meteor.) ionosphere. -osfe·rico *adj.* (meteor.) ionospheric.

Io·n-ia *pr.n.f.* Ionia. -ico *adj.* Ionic (dialect, foot, metre); (mus.) modo -ico, Ionian mode; (archit.) ordine -ico, Ionic order; (Gk. philos.) scuola -ica, Ionian, Ionic, School. -io *adj.*, *n.m.* Ionian.

io·nico[1] *adj.* (phys.; chem.) ionic (cf. **ione**).

io·nico[2] *adj.* See under **ionia**.

io·nio[1] *m.* (chem.) ionium.

io·nio[2] *adj.*, *n.m.* See under **Ionia**.

ion-izzare [A1] and derivs., -o·metro *m.*, -osfera *f.* See under **ione**.

iosa *adv. phr.* (Tusc.) a —, in plenty, abundantly, galore.

iosciamina *f.* (chem.) hyoscyamine.

iot *m. indecl.* (naut.) yacht.

iot-a *m. indecl.* iota, jot; non sa un —, he knows nothing. -acismo *m.* (linguist.) iotacism. -acista *m.* iotacist. -acizzare [A1] *tr.* to iotacize.

ipal·lage *f.* (rhet.) hypallage.

i·pat-e *m.* (mus.) hypate (lyre-string which, except for proslambano-menos, is highest in position and lowest in pitch); thumb. -o *m.* dignitary at Byzantine court; consul. -o·ide *adj.* (mus.) in the region of the hypate.

ipecacuana *f.* (bot.) Ipecacuanha.

iper- *prefix.* hyper-, signifying excess.

iperanto *m.* (ent.) ringlet butterfly, *Aphantopus hyperanthus.*

iper·bato *m.* (rhet.) hyperbaton.

iper·bero *m.* (numism.) silver coin of the Republic of Ragusa in the eighteenth century.

iper·bol-e *f.* (rhet.) hyperbole; exaggeration; (maths.) hyperbola. -eggiare [A3c] *intr.* (*aux.* avere) to use hyperbole, to indulge in hyperbole. -e·o *adj.* (mus.) tetracordo -eo, the tetrachord *hyperbolaion* (in ancient Greek music).

iperbo·lic-o *adj.* hyperbolical, hyperbolic; exaggerated, excessive; (math.) curva -a, hyperbolic curve. (-am**e**nte *adv.*)

iperbolifo**rme** *adj.* (geom.) hyperbolic.

iperbolo·ide *adj.*, *n.f.* (math.) hyperboloid; — ad una falda, hyperboloid of one sheet, unparted hyperboloid; — a due falde, hyperboloid of two sheets, parted hyperboloid.

iperbo·reo *adj.* hyperborean; of the far north; (fig.) barbarous; (astron.) l'orsa iperborea, the Great Bear; *n.m.pl.* Hyperboreans, people living within the Arctic Circle.

iperbuli·a *f.* (philos.) excessive will-power, self-assertiveness.

ipercalissi *f.* 'super-revelation', short title commonly used in reference to the satirical work in Latin by Ugo Foscolo, *Didimi Clerici prophetae minimi Hypercalypseos liber singularis.*

ipercatalet·tico *adj.* (prosod.) hypercatalectic.

ipercheratosi *f.* (med.) acanthokeratodermia, hyperkeratosis.

ipercl-orato *m.* (chem.) perchlorate. -o·rico *adj.* (chem.) perchloric.

ipercloridri·a *f.* (med.) hyperchlorhydria.

ipercorrettismo *m.* (ling.) phenomenon whereby a form, considered wrong, is corrected, the result being actually wrong.

ipercrisi *f. indecl.* (med.) very violent crisis.

ipercri·tic-o *adj.* hypercritical; *n.m.* hypercritic, an overcritical person. -a *f.* hypercriticism. -ismo *m.* tendency towards, or habit of, unduly severe criticism.

iperdattili·a *f.* hyperdactyly, growth of supernumerary fingers.

iperdo·ri-co, -o *adj.* (mus.) modo —, Hyperdorian mode.

iperduli·a *f.* (theol.) hyperdulia, special veneration paid to the B.V.M. (in contrast with the worship of God and also with the ordinary veneration of saints).

iper-emi·a *f.* (med.) hyperaemia. -e·mico *adj.* hyperaemic.

iperestesi·a *f.* (med.) hyperaesthesia.

ipereutecto·ide *adj.* (metall.) hypereutectoid.

iperfocale *adj.* (opt.; photog.) hyperfocal.

iperfri·gio *adj.* (mus.) modo —, Hyperphrygian mode.

iperglobuli·a *f.* (med.) polycytosis.

iperidrosi *f.* (med.) hyperhidrosis, excessive perspiration.

ipe·rigo *m.* (bot.) St John's Wort, *Hypericum.*

iperli·dio *adj.* (mus.) modo —, Hyperlydian mode.

iper·m-etro *adj.* (pros.) hypermetric, hypercatalectic. -e·trope *adj.* (med.) hypermetropic. -etropi·a *f.* (med.) hypermetropia.

ipermnesi·a *f.* hypermnesia, exceptional power of memory.

ipernutrizio**ne** *f.* (med.) hypernutrition.

iperos·sido *m.* (chem.) peroxide.

iperplasi·a *f.* (med.) hyperplasia.

ipersensi·bil-e *adj.* hypersensitive. -ità *f.* hypersensitivity.

ipersensibilizza-to**re** *m.* (photog.) oversensitizer. -zi**o**ne *f.* (photog.) oversensitizing.

iperso·nico *adj.* hypersonic, supersonic.

ipersostentato**re** *m.* (aeron.) wing flap.

iperspa·zio *m.* (math.; phys.) hyperspace.

ipersta·tico *adj.* (eng.) statically indeterminable.

iper·sten-e *m.* (miner.) hypersthene. -i·a *f.* (med.) hypersthenia.

iperteli·a *f.* (zool.) hypertely.

ipertensio**ne** *f.* (med.) hypertension, high blood pressure.

ipertermi·a *f.* (med.) hyperthermia, hyperthermy.

iper·ton-o *adj.* (mus.) tuned to a high pitch. -i·a *f.* (mus.) an excessively high tuning; (med.) hypertonia.

ipertricosi *f.* (med.) hypertrichosis.

ipertrofi·a *f.* (biol.) hypertrophy, overgrowth.

iperventilazio**ne** *f.* (aeron.; med.) hyperventilation.

ipetro *adj.* (archit.) hypoethral.

ipn-o *m.* (bot.) wood moss, *Hypnum.* -o·geno *adj.* somniferous, sleep-inducing; hypnogenic, hypnogenous. -ologi·a *f.* hypnology. (-olo·gico *adj.*) -o·logo *m.* hypnologist. -one *m.* (chem.) acetophenone, hypnone.

ipn-osi *f. indecl.* hypnosis. -o·tico *adj.* somniferous; hypnotic; *n.m.* (med.; pharm.) sedative; tranquillizer. -otismo *m.* hypnosis; hypnotism. -otista *m.* hypnotist. -otizzante *part. adj.* hypnotizing; hypnotic. -otizzare [A1] *tr.* to hypnotize. -otizzato *part. adj.* hypnotized. -otizzat**o**re *m.* hypnotist. (-otizzatrice *f.*)

ipo- *pref.* hypo-, signifying lack of.

ipoalgesi·a *f.* (med.) hypo-algesia.

ipobuli·a *f.* submission of the will, unassertiveness.

ipoca·usto *m.* (Rom. antiq.) hypocaust.

ipocentro *m.* (geol.) focus (of earthquake); (geog.) hypocentre.

ipociclo·ide *adj.* (geom.) hypocycloid.

ipoclor·idri·a f. (med.) hypochlorhydria. **-ito** m. (chem.) hypochlorite; **-ito di calcio**, chloride of lime. **-oso** adj. (chem.) hypochlorous.

ipocondr·i·a f. (med.) hypochondria. **-i·aco** adj. (med.) hypochondriac, hypochondriacal; n.m. hypochondriac; pr.n.m.pl. (lit. hist.) Hypochondriacs, members of an Academy at Modena in the eighteenth century. **-iare** [A4] intr. (aux. essere) to become a hypochondriac; to become depressed.

ipocon·dr-ico adj., n.m. see **ipocondriaco**, under **ipocondria**. **-io** m. (anat.) hypochondrium.

ipoco·tile m. (bot.) hypocotyl.

ipocrisi·a f. hypocrisy; insincerity; hypocritical action or word.

ipo·crit-a m., f. hypocrite; fare l'—, to be hypocritical. **-o** adj. hypocritical; †n.m. hypocrite. **-amente** adv. hypocritically.

†ipocri·tico adj. hypocritical; simulated.

ipocro·mico adj. (med.) eritrocito —, achromatocyte.

ipoderma m. (bot.) hypodermis; (ent.) warble fly, Hypoderma bovis.

ipoder·m-ico adj. hypodermic, subcutaneous. **-oclisi** f. (med.) hypodermoclysis.

ipodo·r-ico, -io adj. (mus.) modo —, Hypodorian mode.

ipoeo·li-co, -o adj. (mus.) modo —, Hypoaeolian mode.

ipoeutecto·ide adj. (metall.) hypo-eutectoid.

ipo·fis-i f. (anat.) pituitary gland, hypophysis. **-ina** f. (chem.) hypophysin, posterior pituitary extract.

ipofosf·ito m. (chem.) hypophosphite. **-oroso** adj. (chem.) hypophosphorous.

ipofri·gio adj. (mus.) modo —, hypophrygian mode.

ipoga·str-ico adj. (anat.) hypogastric. **-io** m. hypogastrium.

ipoge·o adj. (archit.) hypogean, subterranean; (bot.) hypogeal; (geog.) underground; n.m. hypogeum, underground chamber; pl. catacombs; (astron.) place on the earth's surface vertically beneath a celestial object.

ipo·gino adj. n.m. (bot.) hypogynous.

ipoglosso adj. (anat.) hypoglossal, sublingual; n.m. (anat.) hypoglossal nerve, hypoglossus.

ipogramma m. (Gk. antiq.) inscription on base of monument.

ipo·ide adj. (eng.) hypoid.

ipoio·ni-co, -o adj. (mus.) modo —, hypoionian mode.

ipoli·dio adj. (mus.) modo —, hypolydian mode.

ipoli·mnio m. (geog.) lower layers of water in a lake.

ipome·a f. (bot.) morning glory, Ipomoea.

ipome·trop-e adj. (med.) hypometropic. **-i·a** f. hypometropia.

ipomisoli·dio, ipomessoli·dio adj. (mus.) modo —, Hypomixolydian mode.

†ipomo·clio m. fulcrum.

†ipone·a f. allegory.

iponitroso adj. (chem.) hyponitrous.

iponomeuta f. (ent.) ermine moth, Hyponomeuta.

ipoplasi·a f. (med.) hypoplasia, atrophy.

iporchem-a m. (Gk. antiq.) hyporchema (song with dance and mime). **-a·tico** adj. (Gk. antiq.) of, for, the hyporchema.

iposantina f. (chem.) hypoxanthine, sarcine.

iposce·nio m. (Gk. antiq.; theatr.) hyposcenium.

iposideremi·a f. (med.) achalybaemia.

iposolf·ito m. (chem.) hyposulphite, thiosulphate; (photog.) hypo. **-oroso** adj. hyposulphurous.

ipo·st-asi, -a·si f. (philos.; theol.) hypostasis; (med.) hypostasis. **-a·tico** adj. (philos.; theol.) hypostatic; (med.) hypostatic. (**-aticamente** adv.)

ipo·stilo m. (archit.) hypostyle.

iposviluppato adj. (biol.) underdeveloped.

†ipotalas·sica f. (naut.) submarine navigation.

ipotallo m. (bot.) hypothallus.

ipot-assi f. (gramm.) subordination of clauses. (**-at·tico** adj.)

ipotec-a f. mortgage; mettere in —, to pawn; (joc.) avere il cervello in —, to have no brains; (leg.) pledge; mortgage; vincolo d'—, mortgage; soggetto a —, subject to a mortgage; gravato d'—, encumbered by a mortgage; garantito da prima —, secured by first mortgage; estinguere un'—, to discharge a mortgage; purgazione d'—, redemption of a mortgage; conservatore delle ipoteche, Registrar of Mortgages and Charges; — legale, lien; — legale dell'alienante, vendor's lien (C.C.); — mobiliare, mortgage of registered personal property, Bill of Sale. **-a·bile** adj. mortgageable. **-are** [A2] tr. to mortgage; to charge by way of mortgage; (fig.) to take possession of, to commandeer; (fig.) -are

il futuro, to make plans for the future as if it could be determined by one's will. **-a·rio** adj. relating to a mortgage; on mortgage; debitore -ario, mortgagor; creditore -ario, mortgagee; iscrizione -aria, registered charge (C.C.P.); n.m. mortgagee; money-lender, pawnbroker. (**-ariamente** adv.)

ipotenare m. (anat.) hypothenar.

ipotensione f. (med.) hypotension, low blood pressure.

ipotenusa f. (geom.) hypotenuse.

ipotermi·a f. (med.) hypothermy, hypothermia.

ipo·tesi f. hypothesis; supposition; quest'è una semplice —, this is only a supposition; nella peggiore —, if the worst comes to the worst; facciamo un'—, let us suppose, let us put an imaginary case; dire per —, to say for argument's sake; campo delle —, field of hypothesis.

ipote·tic-o adj. hypothetical; conditional; giudizio —, hypothetical judgement. **-amente** adv. hypothetically; conditionally.

ipotiposi f. (rhet.) hypotyposis.

ipo-trofi·a f. (med.) dystrophy. **-tro·fico** adj. (med.) dystrophied.

†ipozom-a f. (naut.) rudder-slings. †**-ato** adj. (naut.) ready for sea.

†ippagogo m. (naut. hist.) horseboat (early form of landing craft with embarcation ports at water level).

ippagro m. (zool.) wild horse.

ippar-chi·a f. (Gk. hist.) cavalry squadron. **-co** m. (pl. -chi) (Gk. hist.) hipparch, cavalry commander.

ipp-iatri·a f. (vet.) horse doctoring, the veterinary care of horses. **-ia·trico** adj. veterinary (of horse, donkeys and mules only). **-iatro** m. veterinary surgeon specializing in horse practice.

ip·pic-a f. horsemastership, horse-training; horse-racing. **-o** adj. of or concerning horses; concorso -o, horse-show.

ippobosco f. (ent.) forest fly (a kind of horse fly), Hippobosca equina.

ippocampo m. (ichth.) sea-horse, Hippocampus spp.; (myth.) hippocamp.

ippocastano m. (bot.) horse-chestnut, Aesculus Hippocastanum.

ippocenta·uro m. (myth.) hippocentaur.

ippocolla f. chinese gelatine.

Ippo·cr-ate pr.n.m. Hippocrates; seguace d'—, physician, doctor. **-a·tico** adj. Hippocratic; scienza -atica, vino -atico, Hippocras medicine, hippocras, a kind of spiced wine; (med.) faccia -atica, Hippocratic facies. **-atismo** m. Hippocratism, Hippocratic doctrine. **-atista** m. disciple of Hippocrates.

Ippocr-ene pr.n.f. (myth.) Hippocrene. **-ene·o, -enio** adj. (myth.) of Hippocrene. **-enidi** f.pl. (myth.) Muses.

ippocricco m. (joc.) donkey.

ippo·dromo m. hippodrome; race-course, horse-racing stadium

ipp-ofagi·a f. hippophagy, eating horse-flesh. **-o·fago** m. hippophagist, eater of horse-flesh.

ippoglosso m. (ichth.) halibut, Hippoglossus vulgaris.

ippogrifo m. (poet., myth.) hippogriff, winged horse.

ippolasso m. (vet.) brace to restrain a horse during a surgical operation.

ippologi·a f. the study of horses.

ippo·man-e f. (vet.) hippomanes; foetal membrane, or caul, on the head of a new-born foal (reputed to be an aphrodisiac); (bot.) manchineal, Hippomane Mancinella, W. Indian poisonous tree. **-zi·a** f. hippomancy, prognostications founded on the behaviour of horses.

ippo·metro m. (vet.) measuring stand, for horses.

Ippona pr.n.f. (geog.) Hippo, Bône.

ipponatte·o adj. (prosod.) Hipponactic (iambic with a final spondee).

ippopodologi·a f. (vet.) the study of the diseases, etc. of the horse's foot; farriery.

ippopo·tamo m. (zool.) hippopotamus; (fig.) fat, clumsy person.

ipposan·dali m.pl. (vet.) nail-less horse-shoes.

ippotigre m. (zool.) zebra.

ippotrainato adj. horse-drawn.

ip-purato m. (chem.) hippurate. **-pu·rico** adj. (chem.) hippuric.

ippuro m. (ichth.) sea-horse, Hippocampus.

iprite f. (chem.) yperite, mustard gas, dichloroethyl sulphide.

ip·silon m. indecl. the letter y.

ipso·fon-o adj. (mus.) high-voiced. **-i·a** f. (mus.) high-pitched quality (of voice).

ipsogr-afi·a f. (geog.) hypsography. **-a·fico** adj. (geog.) hypsographic.

ips-ometri·a f. (phys.) hypsometry. **-ome·trico** adj. hypsometric. **-o·metro** m. hypsometer.

ira *f.* anger, wrath, rage, fury; pieno d'—, angry, wrathful; frenare l'—, to restrain one's anger; avvampare d'—, montare in —, to fly into a passion; fremere d'—, to shake with rage; sfogare l'—, to give vent to one's anger; accecato dall'—, blinded with fury; essere in — ad alcuno, to be the subject of someone's anger; avere in —, to hate; prendere — contro, to be furious with; in — a tutti, hated by all; — di Dio, scourge, malicious person; dire — di Dio di, to speak maliciously of; è successa un'— di Dio, there was a terrible row; (rel.) giorno dell'—, day of wrath, *dies irae*; violence; l'— dei venti, the fury of the wind; l'— del mare, the violence of the waves; discord, strife; le -e degli invidiosi, envious wrath, the anger of envious people.

Ira·c, Ira·q *pr.n.f.* (geog.) Iraq.

irace *f.* (zool.) *Hyrax* spp. (the 'coney' of the Bible).

iracheno *adj.* pertaining to Iraq; (also *n.m.*)

iracond-ia *f.* wrath, anger, wrathfulness; wrathful deed or word. **-o** *adj.* wrathful, choleric, hot-tempered. (-amȩnte *adv.*)

iradè *m.* Sultan's decree; (joc.) despotic command.

iradiddi·o *m. indecl.* see 'ira di Dio', under **ira**.

ira·n-ico *adj.* from Iran, Persian. **-ista** *m., f.* specialist in affairs of Iran, or in Persian studies.

†**irare** *rfl.* to become angry, to be moved to anger.

†**ira·scere** *intr., rfl.* to be moved to anger.

irasci·bil-e *adj.* irascible, irritable, hot-tempered; appetito —, irascibility, instinctive inclination to anger. **-ità** *f.* irascibility; irritability.

irat-o *adj.* angry, enraged, irate, in a rage; — a, angry with; mare —, angry sea, rough sea; †sad, sorrowful. **-amȩnte** *adv.* angrily, irately.

irbis *f. indecl.* (zool.) snow leopard, *Felis uncia*.

ircano *adj.* (anct. geog.) Hyrcanian; mare —, Caspian Sea.

ir-co *m.* (*pl.* **-chi**) (zool.) male wild goat, buck. **-cino** *adj.* relating to the wild goat.

ircocer·v-ico *adj.* of the hircocervus. **-o** *m.* hircocervus, a fabulous creature, half-goat, half-stag.

ire [def.] *intr.* (*aux.* essere) (poet.) to go; (joc.) è ito, he's dead; è bell'e ito, he's done for; è ita, it's all over, that's how it was; *rfl.* to go away; to go bad.

Iren-e *pr.n.f.* (Gk. antiq.) Eirene, Irene (Peace personified; later a woman's name). **-arca** *m.* (Gk. hist.) eirenarch. **-archi·a** *f.* (Gk. hist.) magistracy of an eirenarch. **-e·o** *m.* (archit.) temple of peace.

ireos *m. indecl.* (bot.) orris root, powdered rootstock of *Iris florentina*.

i·rid-e¹ *f.* (anat.) iris; rainbow; (phys.) iris; (miner.) iris, rainbow quartz; (ent.) purple emperor butterfly, *Apatura iris*. **-are** [A I] *tr.* to colour with the colours of the rainbow. **-ato** *adj.* iridescent; coloured like the rainbow; *n.m.* (chem.) iridate. **-azione** *f.* iridation. **-escente** *adj.* iridescent. **-escenza** *f.* iridescence.

I·ride² *pr.n.f.* Iris.

iri·d-ico *adj.* (chem.) iridic. **-io** *m.* (chem.) iridium. **-osmina** *f.* (miner.) iridosmine, osmiridium. **-otomi·a** *f.* (surg.) iridotomy.

i·r-is *f.* (anat.) iris. **-ite** *f.* (med.) iritis.

Irland-a *pr.n.f.* (geog.) Ireland; Stato Libero d'—, Irish Free State, Eire. **-ȩse** *adj.* Irish; (bot.) muschio -ese, Carrageen moss, *Chondrus crispus*; *n.m.* Irishman; Irish language, Irish; *f.* Irish woman; Irish girl.

†**iron·dine** *f.* see **rondine**.

ironeggiare [A 3 c] *intr.* (*aux.* avere) to be ironical, to speak (or write) ironically.

ir-oni·a *f.* irony; — del destino, irony of fate; dire per —, to say in irony; fare -onie, to speak ironically, to be ironical; un discorso che è tutto un'—, a speech that is entirely ironical; sorriso d'—, ironical smile; ironical remark; è un'—!, it is a downright insult! **-o·nico** *adj.* ironical, ironic. **-onicamȩnte** *adv.* ironically. **-onista** *m., f.* ironist. **-onizzare** [A I] *tr.* to treat ironically, to express ironically.

irọs-o *adj.* wrathful, prone to anger. **-amȩnte** *adv.* wrathfully.

irracconta·bile *adj.* not worth the telling; not repeatable.

irradi-are [A 4] *tr.* to light (up), to shed light upon, to irradiate; to illumine; *intr.* (*aux.* avere) to radiate (light), to shine out; *rfl.* to spread out, to radiate. **-amȩnto** *m.* irradiation, radiation. **-ante** *part. adj.* radiating, diffusing light. **-ato** *part. adj.* irradiated, illuminated, lit up; shining; radiated. (-atore *m.* -atrice *f.*) **-azione** *f.* irradiation, radiation; (med.) irradiation.

irraffrena·bile *adj.* See **irrefrenabile**.

irraggi-are [A 3] *tr.* (fig.) to irradiate, to illumine, to shine upon. **-amȩnto** *m.* radiating, shining; (phys.) radiation. **-ato** *part. adj.* illuminated, lit up; radiating, formed into rays.

irraggiungi·bil-e *adj.* unattainable, out of reach. **-ità** *f.* unattainability.

irragionȩvol-e *adj.* irrational; unreasonable; absurd; unfair. **-mȩnte** *adv.* irrationally; unreasonably; absurdly. **-ȩzza** *f.* irrationality; absurdity; unreasonableness.

irrancid-ire [D 2] *intr.* (*aux.* essere) to turn rancid. **-imȩnto** *m.* going rancid. **-ito** *part. adj.* gone rancid; (fig.) soured.

irrappresenta·bile *adj.* unimaginable; not suitable for representation (esp. in the theatre), unactable.

irraziona·bil-e *adj.* irrational; absurd. **-mȩnte** *adv.* irrationally. **-ità** *f.* irrationality; absence of reason.

irrazional-e *adj.* irrational, without reason; illogical; absurd; (maths.) numero —, irrational number, surd. **-mȩnte** *adv.* irrationally. **-iṣmo** *m.* irrationalism. **-ità** *f.* irrationality.

irreal-e *adj.* unreal. **-tà** *f.* unreality.

irreclama·bil-e *adj.* unobjectionable; not admitting complaints; unclaimable. **-ità** *f.* unobjectionableness.

irreconcilia·bil-e *adj.* irreconcilable; implacable. **-mȩnte** *adv.* irreconcilably. **-ità** *f.* irreconcilability.

irrecupera·bil-e *adj.* irrecoverable; irretrievable; lost. **-mȩnte** *adv.* irretrievably. **-ità** *f.* irretrievability.

irrecuṣa·bil-e *adj.* undeniable; irrefutable. **-mȩnte** *adv.* irrefutably. **-ità** *f.* undeniability; irrefutability.

irredent-o *adj.* unredeemed; not liberated; (hist.) l'Italia Irredenta, the Trentino and Istria. **-iṣmo** *m.* (pol.) Irredentism, the political doctrine and action of those who, before 1918, wished to see the Trentino and Istria united with Italy. **-ista** *m., f.* (pol.) Irredentist.

irredimi·bil-e *adj.* irredeemable, unredeemable; (leg.) irredeemable; capitale —, irredeemable capital; obbligazione —, irredeemable bond or debenture. (-ità *f.*)

irreduci·bile *adj.* and derivs. See **irriducibile**.

irrefraga·bil-e *adj.* irrefutable, indisputable, irrefragable. **-mȩnte** *adv.* irrefutably, indisputably. (-ità *f.*)

irrefrangi·bil-e *adj.* irrefrangible, inviolable; unbreakable. (-ità *f.*)

irrefrena·bil-e *adj.* unrestrainable; corsa —, wild, madcap course; riso —, irrepressible laughter. **-mȩnte** *adv.* without restraint, unrestrainedly; wildly, madly. (-ità *f.*)

irrefrenato *adj.* unbridled, unrestrained.

irrefuta·bil-e *adj.* irrefutable, incontrovertible, incontestable. **-mȩnte** *adv.* irrefutably. (-ità *f.*)

irreggiment-are [A I] *tr.* to regiment, to discipline; to draft; to re-form, to regroup (scattered units); (fig.) to regiment, to discipline. **-ato** *part. adj.* disciplined, regimented, organized.

irregolar-e *adj.* irregular; unusual; against the rule; contrary to the norm; abnormal; stagione —, abnormally warm or cold season, *or* season with irregular changes of temperature; (bot.) irregular; (geom.) irregular; (mil.) fortificazione —, irregular fortification; milizie -ari, irregulars, fencibles, volunteers; auxiliaries; (med.) irregular, abnormal; (gramm.) verbi -i, irregular verbs; (eng.) moto —, uneven motion, irregular motion; (leg.) irregular, not in order; (eccl.) irregular (excluded from priestly functions). **-mȩnte** *adv.* irregularly; unevenly; improperly. **-ità** *f.* irregularity; something irregular; case of irregularity; abnormality; (euphem.) misappropriation (of public funds); (eccl.) irregularity (bar to receiving or exercising holy orders).

irregolato *adj.* undisciplined; appetito —, unbridled appetite, capricious appetite.

irreligi-ọne *f.* irreligion. **-osità** *f.* irreligiousness. **-ọso** *adj.* irreligious; impious. **-osamȩnte** *adv.*)

†**irremea·bile** *adj.* of no return, without return; impassable.

†**irremed-ia·bile**, †**-ie·vole** *adj.* See **irrimediabile**.

irremissi·bil-e *adj.* unpardonable, irremissible. **-mȩnte** *adv.* without remission; irremediably; unpardonably. (-ità *f.*)

irremovi·bil-e *adj.* irremovable; immovable; unshakable, inflexible, firm; unyielding. **-mȩnte** *adv.* irremovably; immovably; unshakably, inflexibly. (-ità *f.*)

irremunera·bil-e *adj.* irremunerable, that cannot be suitably rewarded or repaid. (-ità *f.*)

irremunerato *adj.* unremunerated; unpaid; unremitted.

irrepara·bil-e *adj.* irreparable; without remedy. **-mȩnte** *adv.* irreparably. **-ità** *f.* irreparableness.

irreperi·bil-e *adj.* not to be found; rendersi —, to conceal oneself; (leg.) imputato —, defendant, accused, who cannot be found (C.C.P.). **-mente** *adv.* so that (it) cannot be found. **-ità** *f.* (leg.) impossibility of finding (C.P.P.).

irrepeti·bile *adj.* (leg.) disallowed.

irreprensi·bil-e *adj.* irreproachable, blameless. **-mente** *adv.* irreproachably. (**-ità** *f.*)

irrepugna·bil-e *adj.* irrefutable, unobjectionable, incontestable. **-mente** *adv.* irrefutably, incontrovertibly. **-ità** *f.* irrefutability; (leg.) -ità delle prove, irrefutability of the evidence.

irrequiet-o *adj.* restless; passeggiava —, he paced restlessly up and down; lacking repose; sguardo —, wandering glance. **-amente** *adv.* restlessly. **-ezza** *f.* restlessness. **-u·dine** *f.* see irrequietezza.

irresipol-ire [D2] *intr.* (*aux.* essere), *rfl.* (med.) to become erysipelatous. **-ito** *part. adj.* (med.) erysipelatous.

irresisti·bil-e *adj.* irresistible; (phys.) forza —, irresistible force. **-mente** *adv.* irresistibly. (**-ità** *f.*)

irresolu·bil-e *adj.* irresoluble; indissoluble; legame —, bond that cannot be loosed. **-mente** *adv.* indissolubly. **-ità** *f.* irresolubleness; indissolubleness.

irresolu-to *adj.* irresolute, undecided, uncertain; unsolved. **-tamente** *adv.* irresolutely; uncertainly. **-tezza** *f.* uncertainty, indecision; perplexity. **-zione** *f.* state of being unsolved; undecision, indecision; perplexity.

irrespira·bil-e *adj.* unbreathable; (fig.) intolerable, unbearable. (**-ità** *f.*)

irresponsa·bil-e *adj.* irresponsible; not responsible; imbecile. **-mente** *adv.* irresponsibly. **-ità** *f.* (leg.) -ità del Presidente della Repubblica, immunity of the President of the Republic (C.P.).

†irrestora·bile *adj.* that cannot be restored.

irrestringi·bil-e *adj.* unshrinkable. **-ità** *f.* unshrinkableness.

irret-ire [D2] *tr.* to net, to catch in a net; (fig.) to take with guile, to trap, to entangle; to seduce; to bemuse. (**-imento** *m.* **-ito** *part. adj.*)

irretratta·bile *adj.* See irritrattabile.

irretroattiv-o *adj.* non-retroactive; (leg.) not retrospective. **-amente** *adv.* non-retroactively. **-ità** *f.* non-retroactivity; (leg.) -ità della legge, rule against law having retrospective effect (I.C.).

irreverberato *adj.* unreflected.

irreverente *adj.* See irriverente.

irreversi·bil-e *adj.* irreversible. **-ità** *f.* irreversibility.

irrevoca·bil-e *adj.* irrevocable; (leg.) irrevocable; la querela è —, the prosecution is incapable of being withdrawn (C.P.). **-mente** *adv.* irrevocably. **-ità** *f.* (leg.) -ità del contratto, irrevocability of contract (C.C.); -ità della confessione, impossibility of withdrawal of formal admission (C.C.).

irrevocato *adj.* (poet.) not recalled but involuntarily remembered.

irricevi·bil-e *adj.* (leg.) non-receivable. **-ità** *f.* (leg.) non-receivability.

irriconcilia·bile *adj.* and derivs. See irreconciliabile.

irriconosci·bil-e *adj.* unrecognizable. **-mente** *adv.* unrecognizably. (**-ità** *f.*)

irricordevole *adj.* unremembered, immemorial.

irricupera·bile *adj.* and derivs. See irrecuperabile.

irricusa·bile *adj.* and derivs. See irrecusabile.

irri·dere [C3] and derivs. See deridere.

irriduci·bil-e *adj.* irreducible; volontà —, unshakable will (determination); (surg.; math.) irreducible. **-mente** *adv.* irreducibly. **-ità** *f.* irreducibility, irreducibleness.

irrifless-ione *f.* thoughtlessness. **-ivo** *adj.* thoughtless, inconsiderate. **-ivamente** *adv.* thoughtlessly, without reflection, without reflecting.

irriforma·bil-e *adj.* irreformable, incapable of reformation. (**-ità** *f.*)

irrig-are [A2] *tr.* to irrigate; to water; (fig.) to flood, to bathe. (**-a·bile** *adj.* **-abilità** *f.*) **-amento** *m.* irrigation. (**-ante** *part. adj.*) **-ato** *part. adj.* irrigated, watered; ruled with lines; furrowed; (fig.) il terreno era -ato di sangue, the field was steeped in blood, the field ran with blood. **-atore** *m.* irrigation apparatus; (med.) irrigator; *adj.* canale -atore, irrigation canal; latrina -atrice, water-closet. **-ato·rio** *adj.* (*m.pl.* -ato·rii) relating to irrigation. **-azione** *f.* irrigation; canale d'-azione, irrigation canal; (med.) irrigation.

irrigid-ire [D2] *intr.* (*aux.* essere) to grow stiff, numb, or rigid; to stiffen; to become hard-hearted; *tr.* to stiffen, to harden; *rfl.* to grow stiff, to be benumbed; to grow hard-hearted; -irsi sull'attenti, to stand stiffly to attention. **-imento** *m.* stiffening, hardening;

numbing; stiffness, hardness. **-ito** *part. adj.* stiff, hardened; benumbed, numb; hard-hearted.

irriguardoso *adj.* disrespectful, lacking in respect; irreverent.

irri·guo *adj.* well-watered, abounding in irrigation.

irrilevant-e *adj.* unimportant, of little importance; (leg.) of little or no importance; having little or no effect; nugatory. **-mente** *adv.* in an irrelevant manner, irrelevantly.

irrimedia·bil-e *adj.* irremediable, irreparable; beyond repair; malattia —, incurable disease. **-mente** *adv.* irremediably. **-ità** *f. indecl.* irremediableness.

irrimediato *adj.* unremedied.

†irrimedie·vole *adj.* See irrimediabile.

irrimessi·bile *adj.* and derivs. See irremessibile.

irrimunera·bile *adj.* and derivs. See irremunerabile.

†irrimuta·bile *adj.* immutable.

irripara·bile *adj.* and deriv. See irreparabile.

irripeti·bile *adj.* unrepeatable; (of bad language) unprintable.

irriprensi·bile *adj.* and derivs. See irreprensibile.

irriproduci·bile *adj.* that cannot be reproduced.

irriprovevole *adj.* irreproachable.

irrisarci·bile *adj.* (leg.) irreparable.

irris-ione *f.* derision, mockery. **-ivo** *adj.* derisive. **-o** *part.* of irridere, q.v.; *adj.* derided, laughed at, scoffed, mocked. **-ore** *m.* mocker, scoffer, derider. (**-ora** *f.*) **-o·rio** *adj.* (*m.pl.* -o·rii) derisory; paltry, laughable. (**-oriamente** *adv.*)

irrisipolire [D2] and derivs. See irresipolire.

irrisoluto *adj.* and derivs. See irresoluto.

irrispettoso *adj.* disrespectful.

irrit-are [A1] *tr.* to irritate; to provoke, to inflame, to enrage; to excite; to stir up; to be irritating, to be an irritation; (med.) to irritate; *rfl.* to be irritated; to get angry; to become inflamed. **-a·bile** *adj.* irritable, touchy; excitable; (med.) irritable, erethismic. **-abilità** *f.* irritableness; touchiness; (med.) irritability, excitability. **-amento** *m.* irritation; irritating; *pl.* irritating substances. **-ante** *part. adj.* irritating; stimulating. **-ativo** *adj.* irritating, provoking. **-ato** *part. adj.* irritated, angry, provoked; inflamed. **-atore** *m.* irritant; one who irritates or provokes. (**-atrice** *f.*) **-azione** *f.* irritation; provocation; anger; (med.) irritation; inflammation.

ir·rito *adj.* (leg.) void; †(fig.) ineffectual.

irritratta·bil-e *adj.* irrevocable, not retractable. **-mente** *adv.* irrevocably. **-ità** *f.* (leg.) -ità dell'azione penale, impossibility of withdrawing criminal prosecution (C.C.P.).

irritros-ire [D2] *intr.* (*aux.* essere), *rfl.* to become shy, awkward, or reluctant; to jib; *tr.* to make shy. (**-ito** *part. adj.*)

†irriusci·bile *adj.* unlikely to succeed; incapable of succeeding.

irrivela·bil-e *adj.* not to be revealed. (**-ità** *f.*)

irriveren-te *adj.* irreverent; insolent; disrespectful. **-temente** *adv.* irreverently; insolently; disrespectfully. **-za** *f.* irreverence; insolence; disrespect; word or action lacking in reverence or respect; dire un'-za, to make an insolent remark.

irrobust-ire [D2] *tr.* to strengthen, to make robust; *rfl.* to grow stronger. (**-ito** *part. adj.*)

irrog-are [A2] *tr.* (leg.) to inflict; to pass; to award; — condanna, to pass sentence. **-ato** *part. adj.* inflicted; passed; awarded. **-atore** *m.* the person who inflicts a fine, a punishment, etc. (**-atrice** *f.*) **-azione** *f.* the action of inflicting or passing sentence.

irromp-ere [C26] *intr.* (*aux.* essere; *prep.* in) to break (into); to rush (into); to flood (into, over); *abs.* to break all bounds; to flood, to surge; la folla -eva furente, the raging mob surged in. **-ente** *part. adj.* invading, breaking in. (**-itore** *m.* **-itrice** *f.*)

irror-are [A1] *tr.* to bedew, to bathe with dew; to sprinkle; (agric.) to spray. **-amento** *m.* see irrorazione. (**-ante** *part. adj.*) **-ato** *part. adj.* bedewed; sprinkled, sprayed; -ato di sudore, bathed with sweat. (**-atore** *m.*) **-atrice** *f.* (agric.) sprayer, spray. **-azione** *f.* bedewing, sprinkling; (agric.) spraying.

irrotazionale *adj.* (electr. eng.) irrotational.

irruen-te *adj.* impetuous; rash; violent; surging. **-za** *f.* impetuosity, violence.

†irrugiadare *tr.* to sprinkle with dew.

irruggin-ire [D2] *intr.* (*aux.* essere), *rfl.* to rust, to go rusty; (fig.) to get rusty; *tr.* to rust, to make rusty. **-ito** *part. adj.* rustied; rusty.

irruvid-ire [D2] *tr.* to roughen, to make rough; *intr.* (*aux.* essere), *rfl.* to become rough. (**-imento** *m.*) **-ito** *part. adj.* roughened.

irruzione *f.* breaking in, irruption; invasion; fare — in, to break into; (mil.) irruption, incursion, foray.

irsuto *adj.* shaggy, hairy, hirsute; rough; (poet.) twinkling (e.g. of a planet which appears to have many rays or a corona).

irto *adj.* bristling; erect; capelli irti, bristling hair; shaggy; thorny; mare — di scogli, sea strewn with rocks; (fig.) — di difficoltà, bristling with difficulties; impresa irta di ostacoli, enterprise beset with obstacles; discorso — di citazioni, speech liberally sprinkled with quotations; rugged, rough.

irunda·ria *f.* (bot.) greater celandine, *Chelidonium majus.*

isa *excl.* heave!

Isabella *pr.n.f.* Isabel; Isabella; greyish yellow, light buff (said to refer to the vow taken by the Archduchess Isabella, daughter of Philip II, at the siege of Ostend, 1601-4, that she would not change her linen till her husband had taken the town).

Isacco *pr.n.m.* Isaac.

isadelfi *m.pl.* Siamese twins.

isag-o·ge *f.* (lit.) introduction. (-o·gico *adj.*)

isa·gono *m.* (geom.) similar figure.

Isa·ia *pr.n.m.* Isaiah.

isallobara *f.* (meteor.) isallobar.

Isara *pr.n.f.* (geog.) Isère (river).

is-a·tide *f.* (bot.) woad, *Isatis tinctoria*. **-atato** *m.* (chem.) isatate. **-a·tico** *adj.* (chem.) isatic.

isba·glio, ischerzare, etc., see **sbaglio**, etc. NOTE: many Italian words beginning with impure s, when preceded by a word ending in a consonant (*esp.* non, in, per), are found written with an i prefixed for euphony. (Such words are here listed under the letter s.) This usage is now becoming antiquated, but cf. specialized meanings of **istoriare** and **istrumento**.

Iscariota *pr.n.m.* l'—, *or* Giuda —, Judas Iscariot; (fig.) traitor; *adj.* treacherous.

ischeletr-ire [D 2] *tr.* to reduce to a skeleton; *rfl.* to be reduced to a skeleton, to fade away. **-ito** *part. adj.* reduced to a skeleton.

isch-emi·a *f.* (med.) ischaemia. **-e·mico** *adj.* (med.) ischaemic.

i·schia *f.* See **ischio²**.

ischialgi·a *f.* sciatica; see **ischio¹**.

i·sch-io¹ *m.* (anat.) ischium. **-i·ade** *f.* (med.) sciatica. **-ia·dico, -ia·tico** *adj.* (anat.) sciatic, ischiatic. **-iagra** *f.* (med.) sciatica. **-ialgi·a** *f.* (med.) ischialgia, sciatica. **-ial·gico** *adj.* (med.) ischialgic. **-ia·tica** *f.* (med.) sciatica. **-ioce·le** *m.* (med.) ischiocele, ischiatic hernia.

i·schio² *m.* (bot.) durmast oak, *Quercus petraea.*

†isciente *adv. prn.* a nostro —, unknown to us, without our knowing.

iscorsione *f.* (vet.) flux.

iscorto *adj.* (paint.) foreshortened.

iscri·vere [C 12] *tr.* to register; to inscribe; to enrol, to record; la storia lo iscriverà fra i più grandi uomini del paese, history will record him as one of the greatest men of his country; (leg.) to enter; to record; to register; — al processo verbale, to place on record in the minutes, to minute; — la causa nel ruolo, to set the action down in the list (C.C.P.); (geom.) to inscribe; *rfl.* to register, to enter, to put one's name down; iscriversi a un partito, to join a party; iscriversi al congresso, to register at the congress.

iscritto *part.* of **iscrivere**, q.v.; *adj.* inscribed; registered; recorded; *n.m.* member; registered member; un nuovo —, a new pupil.

iscrizione *f.* inscription; (of schools, examinations, competitions, etc.) entry; si ebbero dieci iscrizioni, there were ten entries; tassa d'—, entrance fee; modulo per la domanda d'—, application form; chiedere l'—, to apply for membership (or admission); (leg.) record; entry; registration; — della causa a ruolo, setting down of action (C.C.P.).

iscuri·a *f.* (med.) ischuria.

isen-tal·pico *adj.* (thermodyn.) isoenthalpic. **-tro·pico** *adj.* (thermodyn.) isentropic.

iserina *f.* (miner.) iserine.

isetio·nico *adj.* (chem.) isethionic.

Is-i, I·s-ide *pr.n.f.* Isis, Egyptian goddess. **-i·aco** *adj.* Isiac, of Isis; tavola -iaca, Isiac table (at Turin). **-e·o** *m.* temple of Isis, Isideum.

i·sio *adj.* pertaining or relating to Isis.

Isl-a·m *pr.n.m.* Islam, Mohammedanism. **-a·mico** *adj.* Mohammedan. **-amismo** *m.* Mohammedanism. **-amita** *adj. n.m.* Mohammedan. **-ami·tico** *adj.* Mohammedan, Islamitic, Moslem; arte -amitica, Islamic art.

Isl-anda *pr.n.f.* (geog.) Iceland. **-andese** *adj.* Icelandic; *n.m.* Icelander, inhabitant of Iceland; Icelandic language; *f.* woman from, of, Iceland. **-an·dico** *adj.* Icelandic.

Ismae·l-e *pr.n.m.* Ishmael. **-ismo** *m.* Judaism (or Jewish religious elements) in Arabia before Mahomet. **-ita** *adj. n.m.* Ishmaelite; Arabian, Arab.

ismo *m.* See **istmo**.

†isnec·chia *f.* Viking ship.

iso- prefix, used in many scientific terms, signifying 'equality'. For derivatives in which the tonic accent falls on the second syllable, see separate head-words.

iso-bara *f.* (meteor.; geog.) isobar. **-ba·rico** *adj.* (meteor.) isobaric. **-baro** *adj.* isobaric; *n.m.* (chem.) isobar. **-cli·nico** *adj.* isoclinic. **-colesterina** *f.* (chem.) isocholesterin, isocholesterol. **-croma·tico** *adj.* (phys.) isochromatic. **-crono** *adj.* (telev.) isochronous. **-foto** *m.* (opt.) isophote. **-fo·tico** *adj.* isophotic. **-gami·a** *f.* (bot.) isogamy. **-geotermo** *adj.* (geog.) isogeothermal. **-go·nico** *adj.* (geog.) isogonic. **-ieto** *adj.* (geog.) isohyetal; linea -ieta, isohyet. **-ipsa** *f.* (geog.) contour line. **-luxa** *f.* (phys.) equilux curve. **-meri·a** *f.* (chem.) isomerism. **-me·rico** *adj.* (chem.) isomeric. (**-mericamente** *adv.*) **-merizzazione** *f.* (chem.) isomerization. **-meromorfismo** *m.* isomeromorphism. **-metri·a** *f.* (geom.) the quality of being isometric. **-me·trico** *adj.* (geom.) isometric. **-morfismo** *m.* (scient.) isomorphism. **-morfo** *adj.* (chem.; miner.) isomorphous; (math.) isomorphic. **-nomi·a** *f.* (leg.) isonomy. **-pati·a** *f.* (med.) isopathy. **-peri·metro** *adj.* (geom.) isoperimetrical. **-polita** *adj.* having equal political rights. (**-poli·tico** *adj.*) **-prene** *m.* (chem.) isoprene. **-po(r)ra·chio** *m.* (naut.) cotidal, isotidal. **-terma** *f.*, **-termo** *m.* (geog.; meteor.) isotherm. **-ter·mico** *adj.* (geog.; phys.) isothermal. **-tero** *m.* (geog.) isothere. **-timi·a** *f.* (leg.) equal rights; legal equality.

iso·bata *f.* (phys.) isobath, depth contour.

iso·gon-o *adj.* (geog.) isogonic; (geom.) isogonal, equiangular, similar; *n.m.* (geom.) equiangular figure, isogonal. **-a** *f.* (phys.; geog.) isogonal line. **-ale** *see* **isogono**.

i·sol-a *f.* island, isle; le -e britanniche, the British Isles; (fig.) island: district isolated by ethnographic, linguistic or political features, 'pocket'; (archit.) detached dwelling-house (or block of flats); buildings on an island site; — spartitraffico, traffic island. **-ano** *adj.* inhabiting an island; insular; *n.m.* islander. **-a·rio** *m.* collection of maps of islands. **-etta** *f. dim.*, **-otto** *m. dim.* islet, ait.

isol-are [A I s] *tr.* to isolate; to separate; to cut off; (electr.; phys.) to insulate; — acusticamente, to soundproof; (chem.) to isolate; *rfl.* to live apart, to shun society. **-amento** *m.* isolation; insulation; (leg.) -amento diurno, notturno, solitary confinement by day, by night (C.P.). **-ante** *part. adj.* isolating; insulating; lingue -anti, isolating languages (e.g. Chinese); (electr.; phys.) insulating, non-conducting; *n.m.* insulating material, insulator, non-conductor. **-ato** *part. adj.* isolated; separated; (silkb.) baco -ato, individual spinner; (techn.) insulated; -ato acusticamente, soundproofed; *n.m.* (bldg.) block (of houses); block (of buildings); (archit.) buildings on an island site; separate group of houses. **-atore** *m.* isolator; (electr.) insulator; -atore serrafilo, cleat insulator; (watchm.) disconnector; *adj.* isolating. (**-atrice** *f.*)

isolazion-ismo *m.* isolationism. **-ista** *m., f.* isolationist. **-i·stico** *adj.* isolationist.

isoletta *f. dim.* See under **isola**.

isolina *f.* (chem.) isoline.

isolotto *m. dim.* See under **isola**.

iso·mero *m.* (chem.) isomer.

isonne *adv. phr.* a —, plentifully, galore.

iso·pico *adj.* (geol.) isopic.

isopo *m.* (bot.). See **issopo**.

isoprene *m.* (chem.) isoprene.

iso·scele *adj.* (geom.) isosceles.

isosi·smico *adj.* (geol.) isoseismal.

isosta·tico *adj.* (phys.) isostatic.

iso·tel-e *m* (Gk. antiq.) metic paying the same taxes as a citizen. **-i·a** *f.* (Gk. antiq.) equality (with citizens) in tax and tribute.

iso·tera *f.* (meteor.) isothere.

isot-erma *f.* (phys.; meteor.) isotherm. **-e·rmico** *adj.* isothermal.

iso·tono *adj.* (phys.; mus.) isotonic.

iso·t-opo *m.* (phys.; chem.; atom. phys.) isotope. **-opi·a** *f.* (chem.) isotopy. **-o·pico** *adj.* (phys.) isotopic.

isotrone *m.* (atom. phys.) isotron.

iṣo·tr-opo *m.* (miner.) isotrope. **-opi·a** *f.* (phys.) isotropy. **-o·pico** *adj.* (phys.) isotropic; (atom. phys.) diffusione -opica, isotropic scattering.

Ispagna *pr.n.f.* (geog.). See **Spagna**.

isp-a·nico *adj.* Spanish; of Spain. **-aniṣmo** *m.* Hispanicism, Spanish idiom. **-ano** *adj.* Hispanic; -ano americano, Spanish-American; -ano gotico, Spanish Visigoth; *n.m.,pl.* Hispanic people(s), ancient inhabitants of Spain.

ispess-ire [D 2] *tr.* to thicken; *rfl.* to become thicker; to become more frequent. **-imento** *m.* thickening. (**-ito** *part. adj.*)

ispettivo *adj.* inspecting, inspectoral.

ispet-tore *m.* inspector; — di circolo, district inspector; — scolastico, inspector of schools; (mil.) inspector (of small arms, artillery, etc.). **-trice** *f.* inspectress, lady inspector; *adj.* commissione -trice, commission of inspection; giunta -trice, board of inspectors, inspecting board. **-torato** *m.* inspectorship, inspectorate; staff of inspectors; inspector's office.

ispeziọn-e *f.* inspection; examination; non è di mia —, I am not competent to deal with it, it is no concern of mine; (comm.) — contabile, audit; (leg.) perquisizione o — personale, search or inspection of the person (C.P.). **-a·bile** *adj.* available for inspection. **-are** [A 1 c] *tr.* to inspect, to hold an inspection of.

i·spida *f.* (orn.) kingfisher.

i·spid-o *adj.* bristling; hairy; shaggy; (fig.) rude, ill-mannered. (**-amente** *adv.*) **-ezza** *f.* shagginess; roughness; rudeness.

ispir-are [A 1] *tr.* (*prep.* a) to inspire (with); to breathe into; — fiducia, to inspire confidence; (fig.) to inspire, to arouse, to instil; to suggest; to dictate; *rfl.* (*prep.* a) to be inspired (by), to draw inspiration (from); per -arsi, in order to seek inspiration; (joc.) beve per -arsi, he drinks to get inspiration; -arsi a sentimenti di perdono, to allow oneself to follow the promptings of forgiveness (cf. **inspirare**). **-a·bile** *adj.* that can be inspired, instilled, inculcated, suggested, or aroused. (**-abilità** *f.* **-amento** *m.*) **-ante** *part. adj.* inspiring. **-ato** *part. adj.* inspired; non bene -ato, ill-advised; *n.m.* far l'-ato, to pretend to be a genius. **-atamente** *adv.* like one inspired; in an inspired manner. **-atore** *m.* inspirer; prompter; suggester; *adj.* inspiring; (anat.) muscoli -atori, inspiratory muscles. **-atrice** *f.* inspirer; muse; *adj.* poesia -atrice, inspiring poetry. **-azione** *f.* inspiration; breathing; inspired idea or suggestion; avere una buona -azione, to have a brain-wave; versi senza -azione, uninspired verses; advice; ideas suggested (to a writer or speaker); (theol.) inspiration.

ispi·rito *m.* (used after a consonant, esp. after 'in'). See **spirito**.

†isporre *vb.* and derivs. See **esporre**.

†Isprucco *pr.n.m.* (geog.) Innsbruck.

Israel-e *pr.n.m.* Israel, Jacob (son of Isaac); Israelites, Children of Israel, Hebrews; Jewish religion; tribù d'—, tribe of Israel; *f.* (geog.) Israel, Palestine. **-iano** *adj.* of Israel. **-ita** *adj.* Israelite, Hebrew, Jewish; *n.m.* Israelite, Jew; tempio degl'-iti, synagogue. **-i·tico** *adj.* Jewish.

†issa *adv.* now; immediately.

iss-are [A 1] *tr.* to hoist; (naut.) -a!, hoist! **-amento** *m.* action of hoisting; means of hoisting. **-ato** *part. adj.* hoisted, hoist.

issop-o *m.* (bot.) hyssop, *Hyssopus officinalis.* **-ina** *f.* (chem.) hyssopin.

istamina *f.* (physiol.) histamine.

Istanbùl *pr.n.f.* (geog.) Istanbul.

istanta·ne-o *adj.* instantaneous; luce -a, flash (as of lightning); la sua morte fu -a, his death was instantaneous; fotografia -a, snapshot. **-amente** *adv.* instantaneously. **-a** *f.* snapshot, snap; lightning sketch. **-ità** *f.* instantaneousness.

istant-e *adj.* imminent; pressing; urgent; insistent; *n.m.* instant, moment; si fa in un —, it's done in an instant; in un —, in a moment, presently; sull'—, all'—, immediately, instantly; solo pochi -i, only a few moments. **-emente** *adv.* pressingly; urgently; insistently; pregare -emente, to urge, to insist.

istanza *f.* importunity; entreaty; application, petition, request; fare — a, presso, to make application to, to apply to; far viva — a, to entreat earnestly; accogliere un'—, to grant a request; respingere un'—, to reject an application or petition; con —, urgently, earnestly; deliberare in ultima —, to give a final ruling; (leg.) application (to magistrate or judge); summons (esp. interlocutory); instance; in prima —, in the first instance; giudizio di seconda —, judgement on appeal; tribunale di prima, ultima —, Court of primary, final jurisdiction; rigetto di —, rejection of application.

†istate *f.* See **estate**.

istaurare [A 1 a] and derivs. See **instaurare**.

iste·reṣi *f.* (phys.) hysteresis; (electr.) ciclo di —, hysteresis loop.

istereṣi·metro *m.* (electr.) hysteresis meter.

ist-eri·a *f.* (med.) hysteria. **-e·rico** *adj.* hysterical. (**-ericamente** *adv.*)

isteril-ire [D 2] *tr.* to make barren, to render sterile; to quench, to dry up, to check. **-imento** *m.* making barren, impoverishment. **-ito** *part. adj.* sterilized; rendered barren; quenched, checked.

ister-iṣmo *m.* (med.) hysteria; essere preso d'un accesso d'—, to go into hysterics, to become hysterical. **-ocele** *m.* (med.) hysterocele. **-o·foro** *m.* (med.) pessary. **-o·metro** *m.* (med.) hysterometer, uterine sound. **-otomi·a** *f.* (surg.) hysterotomy. **-oepilessi·a** *f.* (med.) hysteroepilepsy.

isterologi·a *f.* (gramm.) hysteron proteron.

isteṣso *prn.* see **stesso**; *adj.* same; (mus.) l'— tempo, at the same speed. NOTE: although current Italian prefers 'lo stesso tempo', this traditional phrase is still employed by composers.

istig-are [A 2] *tr.* to incite; to instigate; — uno a mentire, to influence a person to lie; c'è qualcuno che lo -a, there is someone who puts him up to it; — le passioni, to arouse the passions. (**-amento** *m.*) **-ato** *part. adj.* instigated; egged on; incited. (**-atore** *m.* **-atrice** *f.*) **-azione** *f.* incitement, instigation; per -azione di una donna, driven to it by a woman; (leg.) instigation; incitement; per -azione di, at the instigation of; -azione a delinquere, incitement to crime (C.P.).

istillare [A 1] and derivs. See **instillare**.

istint-o *m.* instinct; per —, instinctively, by instinct; l'— della propria conservazione, the instinct of self-preservation; inspiration, genius. **-ivo** *adj.* instinctive; spontaneous. **-ivamente** *adv.* instinctively, without reflection.

†istiocope *f.* (naut.) navigation by sail or oars.

†istiodromi·a *f.* (naut.) sailing, the art of sailing.

istio-foro *m.* (ichth.) sail fish, *Histiophorus* spp.

istitu-ire [D 2] *tr.* to institute, to found, to establish; to initiate; to nominate; (leg.) to institute; to start; to appoint; to nominate; — un giudizio, to start an action; — alcuno erede, to appoint someone heir; — qualcuno successore, to appoint someone successor. **-ito** *part. adj.* instituted, founded; initiated; nominated, appointed; (leg.) l'erede -ito, the appointed heir (C.C.).

istitut-o *m.* institute; — di magistero superiore, teachers' training college; — tecnico, technical school; — tipografico, printing establishment — di bellezza, beauty parlour; — di credito, bank (C.C.); institutions, constitution; terms of reference (of a special commission); appointed task; teaching, education. **-ivo** *adj.* instituting, serving to establish; institutive; establishing; enabling; legge -iva, enabling act. **-ore** *m.* founder, author, institutor; schoolmaster; tutor; instructor. **-rice** *f.* schoolmistress; governess.

istituziọn-e *f.* founding; establishment, institution; teaching, education; (canon law) institution; *pl.* elementary or fundamental principles; (leg.) — di erede, appointment of heir (C.C.); le istituzioni costituzionali, the institutions of the Constitution (C.P.). **-ale** *adj.* institutional.

i·stm-ico *adj.* Isthmian; (Gk. antiq.) Isthmian (games, Odes). **-io** *adj.* see **istmico**. **-o** *m.* (geog.; anat.) isthmus; (meteor.) ridge.

ist-ogeni·a *f.* (biol.; anat.) histogenesis, histogeny. **-ologi·a** *f.* histology. **-olo·gico** *adj.* histological. (**-ologicamente** *adv.*) **-o·logo** *m.* histologist. **-onomi·a** *f.* histological laws, histology.

isto·ri-a *f.* history; (paint.; sculp.) historical work (i.e. with a historical or legendary subject). **-a·io** *m.* historian. **-ale** *adj.* historical, relating to history; Specchio -ale, *Speculum historiale*, title of a thirteenth-century work by Vincent de Beauvais. (Cf. **storia**.)

istori-are [A 4] *tr.* (paint.; sculp.) to adorn with representations of historical or legendary scenes, to history; to illuminate (manuscript). **-ato** *part. adj.* adorned, historied, storied; illuminated; vetrate -ate, stained-glass windows.

isto·rico *adj., n.m.* see **storico**.

istor-iografi·a *f.* historiography. **-io·grafo** *m.* historiographer, biographer. **-iṣmo** *m.* view which considers the story of the human race as more important than the natural sciences.

istrad-are [A 1] *tr.* to put on the road, to put in the way; to direct; to route. **-amento** *m.* putting on the road; (teleph.) routing. **-ato** *part. adj.* routed.

I·stri-a *pr.n.f.* (geog.) Istria. **-ano** *adj.* Istrian, of Istria; *n.m.* man from Istria. (**-ana** *f.*)

i·strice *m., f.* (zool.) porcupine, *Hystrix* spp.; (ichth.) pesce —, porcupine fish, *Diodon* spp.; (fig.) difficult, prickly, churlish person; (of woman) shrew; (mil.) hedgehog-wired enclosure, defensive stockade, 'box'; (mil. hist.) strong-point, quadrilateral or other formation protected by pikes, etc.; ordinanza — di picche, pike lines.

istrion-e *m.* (derog.) actor; clown, buffoon. **-esco** *adj.* (*m.pl.* **-eschi**) histrionic; stagey.

istrio·nic-a *f.* acting, histrionism. **-o** *adj.* histrionic. **-amente** *adv.* histrionically.

†**istrologi·a** *f.* See **astrologia**.

†**istromento** *m.* See **istrumento** and **strumento**.

istru-ire [D 2] *tr.* to teach, to instruct; to educate; to give instruction to; to advise; lo feci — a mie spese, I had him taught at my expense; chi t'ha -ito in latino?, who taught you Latin?; s'è -ito da sè, he is self-taught, he taught himself; (iron.) l'hanno -ito bene!, how well he has been brought up!; to convey information to; to direct; — un cane, to train a dog; — un cavallo, to break in a horse; (leg.) — una causa, to assemble the evidence in an action (C.C.P.). **-ito** *part. adj.* well educated; well informed; instructed; learned; trained; broken in.

istrument-o *m.* instrument; tool; (leg.) deed; instrument; legal writing; — notarile, deed authenticated or drawn up by a notary (cf. **strumento**). **-ale** *adj.* (mus.) instrumental; *n.m.* (mus.) orchestration. **-almente** *adv.* (mus.) instrumentally. **-are** [A 1 c] *tr.* (mus.) to orchestrate; (leg.) to enter into a deed or contract. **-a·rio** *adj.* instrumental; *n.m.* (mus.) musical instrument maker; (surg.) instrumentarium, set of instruments. **-ato** *part. adj.* instrumented; (mus.) messa -ata, mass with orchestral accompaniment. **-atore** *m.* (mus.) orchestrator; composer. (**-atrice** *f.*) **-atura** *f.* (mus.) orchestration. **-azione** *f.* (mus.) instrumentation.

istrutt-o *adj.* well-informed; (mil.) ordered; instructed; schiere -e, ordered ranks; (Tusc. pop.) see **istruito**. **-ivo** *adj.* instructive. **-ivamente** *adv.* instructively. **-ore** *m.* teacher, instructor; drill-sergeant; (mil.) military instructor; (leg.) giudice -ore, investigating judge (who functions like Master of Supreme Court but is member of bench trying action) (C.C.P.); examining justice or magistrate (C.P.P.); coroner. **-rice** *f.* teacher, instructress. **-o·ria** *f.* (leg.) investigation (stage in procedure of Italian civil and criminal Courts in which facts of case are investigated by Court and evidence is assembled, C.C.P. and C.P.P.); depositions (C.P.P.); findings; aprire un'-oria, to open a judicial inquiry or inquest. **-o·rio** *adj.* (*m.pl.* **-orii**) (leg.) investigating.

istruzione *f.* education; teaching, instruction; Ministero della Pubblica, —, former title of the Italian Ministry of Education; learning; (mil.) instruction (theoretical and practical); exercises, syllabus, rules, orders, notices; executive, information; tenersi alla —, to await commands; foglio d'—, directive; (leg.) preliminary investigation (interlocutory stage in procedure of Italian Courts preparatory to setting case down for trial; cf. **istruttoria**, under **istrutto**); *pl.* instructions; attenere alle istruzioni, to follow the instructions; detailed orders; (leg.) directions, instructions, investigations; findings; (naut.) sailing orders; (admin.) riunione preliminare per le istruzioni, meeting for briefing.

istupid-ire [D 2] *tr.* to make stupid; to stupefy; to stun; *intr.* (*aux.* essere), *rfl.* to grow stupid, to become dull. (**-imento** *m.*) **-ito** *part adj.*

†**isvivare** *vb.* and derivs. See **svivare**.

Isviz·zera *pr.n.f.* See **Svizzera**.

it-a *f.* name of the Greek letter η (with modern Greek pronunciation). **-acismo** *m.* itacism (pronunciation of Gk. η like Ital. i). **-acista** *m.* itacist.

ita-conato *m.* (chem.) itaconate. **-co·nico** *adj.* itaconic.

Ita·lia *pr.n.f.* (geog.) Italy; — settentrionale, Northern Italy; — meridionale, Southern Italy.

italian-o *adj.* Italian; *adv. phr.* all'-ana, in the Italian manner, in the Italian style; *n.m.* un Italiano, an Italian; gl'Italiani, the Italians, Italians; Italian language; parlare —, to speak Italian; (fig.) questo si chiama parlare —, that's plain speaking; in buon —, 'in plain English'; non sa l'—, he does not know Italian; parla poco l'—, he speaks only a little Italian. **-a** *f.* Italian girl; Italian woman. (**-amente** *adv.*) **-eggiare** [A 3 c] *intr.* (*aux.* avere) to ape the Italians, to imitate Italians. **-ismo** *m.* Italianism, Italian idiom. **-is·simo** *superl. adj.* extremely Italian; very Italian in use of

language, fashion, or in mode of thought. **-issimamente** *adv.* in a thoroughly Italian manner. **-ista** *m., f.* student or specialist (usu. a foreigner) of Italian language and literature. **-ità** *f.* Italian character; Italian sentiments; Italian nationality. **-izzare** [A 1] *tr.* to Italianize, to put into Italian (form, or language). (**-izzato** *part. adj.*)

ita·lic-o *adj.* Italic, Italian (chiefly relating to ancient Italy, but commonly used in certain other expressions); (hist.) Regno-Italico, Kingdom of Italy (founded by Napoleon in 1805); Penisola Italica, Italian Peninsula; dialetti gallo-italici, Gallo-Italic dialects. (**-amente** *adv.*)

italiota *adj. n.m.* (anct. hist.) Italiot.

i·talo *adj.* (poet.) Italian; l'Itala gente, the Italian race; l'— canto, Italian poetry; italo-greco, Graeco-Italian, e.g. of Magna Graecia; (eccl.) Italo-greci, Italo-Greeks (Catholics with Byzantine rite chiefly in Calabria and Sicily).

iter-are [A 1 s] *tr.* to repeat. **-ativo** *adj.* repetitive, iterative; frequentative. **-ato** *part. adj.* repeated. **-atamente** *adv.* repeatedly, several times. (**-atore** *m.* **-atrice** *f.*) **-azione** *f.* iteration, reiteration, repetition.

itif-allo *m.* (Gk. antiq.) phallus; ithyphallic ode; lewd dancer at Bacchic festival. **-al·lico** *adj.* ithyphallic (metre); lewd.

itinera·rio *m.* itinerary, route; (hist.) — di Antonino, Antonine Itinerary; (rel.) itinerarium (form of prayer before travel); *adj.* misura itineraria, (corresponding roughly to) milestone; colonna itineraria, signpost.

ito *part.* See under **ire**.

ittar·golo *m.* (pharm.) ichthargol.

itter·bio *m.* (chem.) ytterbium.

it·t-ero[1] *m.* (med.) icterus, jaundice, biliousness. **-e·rico** *adj.* (med.) icteric, suffering from jaundice (also fig.). **-eri·zia** *f.* (med.) icterus, jaundice. **-o·ide** *adj.* (med.) icteroid.

it·tero[2] *m.* (orn.) icterine warbler, *Hippolais icterina*.

it·tico *adj.* relating to or concerning fish; l'industria ittica, the fishing industry.

†**it·tide** *f.* (zool.) polecat.

itti-ocolla *f.* (ichth.) sound, swim bladder; fish-glue, isinglass; (pharm.) ichthyocolla. **-ofagi·a** *f.* ichthyophagy, fish-eating. **-o·fago** *m.* fish-eater; *pl.* ichthyophagi. **-olo** *m.* (pharm.) ichthyol. **-ologi·a** *f.* ichthyology. **-olo·gico** *adj.* ichthyological. **-o·logo** *m.* ichthyologist. **-osa·uro** *m.* (paleont.) ichthyosaur. **-osi** *f. indecl.* (med.) ichthyosis; -osi istrice, ichthyosis hystrix. **-o·sico** *adj.* (med.) ichthyotic.

it·trio *m.* (chem.) yttrium.

iu·gero *m.* (Rom. meas.) juger, *iugerum*.

Iugosla·v-ia *pr.n.f.* (geog.) Jugoslavia. **-o** *adj.* Jugoslav, of Jugoslavia; *n.m.* Jugoslav, Southern Slav. (**-a** *f.*)

iu·gul-o *m.* (anat.) root of the neck. **-are** *adj.* (anat.) jugular; *vb.tr.* to cut the throat of; to throttle; to kill; (fig.) to impose upon.

iulo *m.* (zool.) millipede, *Julus* spp.

†**iungla** *f.* See **giungla**.

†**Iuno** *pr.n.f.* See **Giunone**.

†**iussione** *f.* (leg.) command.

iut-a *f.* jute. **-ifi·cio** *m.* jute-factory.

Iva·noe *pr.n.m.* Ivanhoe.

iv-i *adv.* there; — entro, in there; (of time) then; — a poco tempo, shortly afterwards; ibid., op. cit. †**-iritta** *adv.* just there.

†**izz-a** *f.* wrath, anger; irritation. †**-oso** *adj.* wrathful, angry; irritated.

j *m., f.* (called 'I lungo'). As an initial consonant J is now used in Italian less frequently than in previous times, having been replaced by Gi or I. In terminations it used to signify a double I, but this usage is now antiquated. To distinguish 'tempi' (*pl.* of 'tempo') from 'tempi' (*pl.* of 'tempio'), the latter is now written 'tempii' 'or tempî', and no longer 'tempj'.

Ja·copo *pr.n.m.* James; Jacob (cf. **Giacomo**). NOTE: this form of the name was used by Ugo Foscolo for the protagonist of his epistolary novel, *Le Ultime Lettere di Jacopo Ortis*.

Jacuti *pr.n.m.pl.* (geog.) Yakuts.

Jago *pr.n.m.* Iago, Jago.

jarda *f.* See **iarda**.

jazz *m. indecl.* jazz. **-i·stico** *adj.* jazz; orchestra -istica, jazz band.

Jokiakarta *pr.n.f.* (geog.) Jogjakarta.

jole *f.* See **iole**.

jolly *m. indecl.* (cards) joker.

Jonkers *pr.n.m.pl.* (geog.) Yonkers.

†**Josaphat** *pr.n.f.* (Bibl.). See **Giosafat**.

†**Joseppo** *pr.n.m.* See **Giuseppe**.

jota *f.* (mus.) jota, Spanish dance from Aragon.

†**Jove** *pr.n.m.* See **Giove**.

†**joventude** *f.* See **gioventù**.

†**juba** *f.* See **giubba**.

†**jubbilare** *vb.* and derivs. See **giubilare**.

†**ju·bere** *tr., intr.* to command.

†**juda·ico** *adj.* See **giudaico**.

†**jude·o** *adj.* See **giudeo**.

†**judicare** *vb.* and derivs. See **giudicare**.

†**ju·dice** *m.* See **giudice**.

judò *m. indecl.* jujitsu, juijitsu; judo.

†**Juliano** *pr.n.m.* See **Giuliano**.

†**Juno** *pr.n.f.* See **Giunone**.

†**jurare** *vb.* and derivs. See **giurare**.

†**juridizione**, †**jurisdizione** *f.* See **giurisdizione**.

†**jurisconsulto** *m.* See **giureconsulto**.

†**jurista** *m.* See **giurista**.

†**jusdicenza** *f.* place of a judge's jurisdiction.

†**justa** *prep.* near.

†**justificare** *vb.* and derivs. See **giustificare**.

†**just·ità**, †**-i·zia** *f.* See **giustizia**.

juta *f.* (text.). See **iuta**.

†**juven·colo** *m.* young man.

†**juvenile** *adj.* See **giovanile**.

Juven·t-us *pr.n.f.* name of a Turin football club. **-ino** *m.* member of that team.

k *m., f.* (pron. ' cappa ') the letter K.

kainite *f.* (miner.) kainite.

kaki *m., adj. indecl.* See **cachi**.

kalinite *f.* (miner.) kalinite, alum.

kanguro *m.* (zool.). See **canguro**.

kant-iano *adj.* (philos.) Kantian. **-ismo** *m.* (philos.) the philosophy of Kant, Kantianism. **-ista** *m.* (philos.) Kantian.

kapok *m. indecl.* See **capoc**.

karakiri *m. indecl.* (pop.). See **harakiri**.

kediv-e *m.* Khedive. **-ale** *adj.* Khediv(i)al.

kepì *m. indecl.* See **chepì**.

kepleriano *adj.* (astron.) relating to Kepler.

keratina *f.* (chem.) keratin.

kermes *m. indecl.* (techn.) kermes, a dyestuff; (ent.) *Kermes ilicis* the insect that produces it.

kermesse *f.* See **chermessa**.

kieserite *f.* (miner.) kieserite.

kilo *m.* See **chilo**.

kimono *m.* See **chimono**.

kinesiterapi·a *f.* and derivs. See **chinesiterapia**.

kino *m.* (bot.) kino.

kircheriano *adj.* pertaining to A. Kircher (d. 1680), founder of the museum of prehistory, Rome; pertaining to the Museo Romano.

ki·rie *m.* See **chirie**.

kla·xon *m. indecl.* (motor.) horn.

knut *m. indecl.* knout; governo dello —, government by the knout.

koine *f.* the 'lingua franca' used by non-Tuscan Italian writers.

kopeck *m. indecl.* (numism.) copeck, a Russian coin.

krapfen *m. indecl.* doughnut.

kreuzer *m. indecl.* (numism.) kreutzer, an Austrian coin.

krumiro *m.* See **crumiro**.

Kuku Nor *pr.n.f.* (geog.) Koko Nor.

kummel *m. indecl.* See **cumino**.

kuraro *m.* See **curaro**.

ky·rie *m.* See **chirie**.

L *m., f.* (pron. ' elle ') the letter L.

la[1] *def. art. f. sing.* (*pl.* **le**) the; *contr.* with *preps.* **di, a, da, in, su** to form **della, alla, dalla, nella, sulla**; with *prep.* **con** it does not usually form a compound in modern Italian; used untranslatably with proper nouns, e.g. la Maria, Mary; la Bianchi, Mrs Bianchi, Miss Bianchi (cf. **il**).

la[2] *pers. prn. f. 3rd sing. acc.* her; — conosco, I know her; it; ho qui la lettera, — leggerò, I have the letter here, I'll read it.

La[3] *pers. prn. acc.* (polite form of address) you; La riverisco, I send you my kindest regards; La prego di salutarmi il fratello, please give my greetings to your brother.

La[4] *pers. prn. nom.* (polite form of address) you; La m'intende!, you understand me!

la[5] *impers. prn.* it; things in general; — va male, things are bad.

la[6] *impers. conj. prn.* it; smettila!, stop it!; darsela a gambe, to take to one's heels; prendersela, to take offence, to take it to heart.

la[7] *m.* (mus.) Lah, the note A; the key of A; dare il —, to give the A; (fig.) to set the tone (of the conversation).

là *adv.* there; chi va —?, who goes there?; guarda —, look over there; eccolo —, there he is, there; qua e —, here and there; è sempre —, he's still there, (fig.) he's jogging along, he's still in the same old job; siamo —, there we go again, we're back where we started from; about, round about; — sulle cinque, round about five o'clock; di —, over there; di — delle Alpi, beyond the Alps; al di — del fiume, across the river; il di —, the surplus; il di — di, the yonder side of, the far side of; (euphem.) l'al di —, il mondo di —, the next world; essere più di — che di qua, to be more dead than alive; in —, on, onwards; più in —, further on; da quel giorno in —, from that day onwards; da qui in —, between now and then; mandare in —, to defer; in — cogli anni, well on in years; tirarsi in —, to move out of the way; andare troppo in —, to overstep the bounds of discretion, to go too far; — —, slowly; veniva avanti — —, he came slowly along, taking his time about it; poorly, indifferently; è una cosina fatta — —, it's a miserable little thing, poorly made; †più — che, more than; *excl.* alto —!, halt!; va —!, get on with you!; zitto —!, quiet there!; eh —!, here!, I say!; —! —!, now, now!; *n.m.* (euphem.) diceva che ero un qui, un —, he called me a so-and-so.

†**labandina** *f.* semi-precious stone resembling a garnet.

†**labarda** *f.* and derivs. See **alabarda**.

labardone *m.* stockfish, dried unsalted cod.

laba·ria *f.* (zool.) fer-de-lance snake, *Bothrops lanceolatus*.

la·baro *m.* standard; banner; labarum, banner of the Cross; masonic sign; (fig.) raccogliersi sotto lo stesso —, to band together.

†**lab·bia** *f.* face; upper part of the body; human figure.

labbiale *adj.* See **labiale**.

labbiato *adj.* See **labiato**.

labbo *m.* (orn.) Arctic skua, *Stercorarius parasiticus*; — coda lunga, long-tailed skua, *S. longicaudus*.

labbr-o *m.* (*pl.f.* **-a**) lip; — superiore, upper lip; — inferiore, lower lip; leccarsi le -a, to lick one's lips; mordersi le -a, to bite one's lips (in rage, or in an effort to restrain one's laughter); avere sulle -a, to have on the tip of one's tongue; rimanere a -a asciutte, to have nothing to eat; (fig.) a fior di -a, from the teeth out; fare il —, to pout, to sulk; mouth; dal suo — non uscì mai un lamento, he never uttered a word of complaint; morì col tuo nome sul —, he died with your name on his lips; la parola le morì sul —, *or* sulle -a, the word died on her lips; (mus.) lip (of a wind player); (med.) — leporino, hare-lip; (geol.) — sollevato, upthrow side (of a fault); — abbassato, downthrow side (of a fault); (*pl.m.* **-i**) rim; brim; border; edge; i -i d'una ferita, the edges of a wound; (mus.) lip (of organ flue-pipe); basin; shell; (naut.) a —, clinker built; † — molle, drinker, tippler. **-ata** *f.* (Tusc., vulg.) blow on the mouth with the back of the hand. †**-eggiare** *intr.* to move the lips, to mouth; *tr.* to mutter, to murmur. (**-ino** *m. dim., pl.* Tusc. **-ina** *f.*) **-one** *m. augm.* large lip; man with large, thick lips. **-ona** *f.* woman with large, thick lips; (Tusc.) *f.pl.* large lips.

labdacismo *m.* (philol.) lambdacism, labdacism.

†**labe** *f.* stain.

†**labefattare** *tr.* to knock down, to bring to the ground; to shake down.

labello[1] *m.* (bot.) labellum, lip.

†**labello**[2] *m.* basin; small vase.

†**la·b·ere** *tr.* to wash against, to brush against; *intr.* to slide along, to slip along. (†**-endo** *ger.* †**-ente** *part. adj.*)

laberinto *m.* See **labirinto**.

labiale *adj.* labial; (mus.) canna —, flue-pipe (of organ).

labiato *adj.* (bot.) labiate, lipped.

la·bil-e *adj.* fleeting, ephemeral; transient; unsteady, collapsing; memoria —, enfeebled memory; (scient.) labile, unstable. **-ità** *f.* transience; feebleness, weakness; unsteadiness.

labina *f.* (geol.). See **lavina**.

†**la·bio** *m.* See **labbro**.

labio-dentale *adj., n.m., f.* (philol.) labiodental. **-velare** *adj.* (philol.) labiovelar.

labirint-o *m.* labyrinth; maze; — d'acque, meandering streams; (fig.) confusion, tangle; (anat.) — membranoso, labyrinthine membrane; (eng.) tenuta a —, labyrinth seal. **-ite** *f.* (med.) labyrinthitis.

†**la·bole** *adj.* See **labile**

†**laborare** *vb.* and derivs. See **lavorare**.

laborato·rio *m.* laboratory; workshop; workroom.

†**labore** *m.* work; effort, toil; fatigue (cf. **lavoro**).

laborios-o *adj.* laborious; hardworking; industrious; arduous; difficult; discussione -a, earnest and toilsome discussion; le classi -e, the working classes; una giornata -a, a busy day, a full day; (of bee or ant) industrious; pasto —, heavy, indigestible meal; (med.) digestione -a, poor digestion; respiro -a, laboured breathing; (naut.) traversata -a, rough crossing. **-amente** *adv.* laboriously; labouredly; industriously. **-ità** *f.* industriousness; arduousness; difficulty.

laborismo *m.* and deriv. See **laburismo**.

labrace *m.* (ichth.) bass, *Morone labrax*.

labradorite *f.* (miner.) labradorite, Labrador feldspar.

labro[1] *m.* (ichth.) wrasse; — pappagallo, *Labrus viridis*; — merlo, *L. merula*; — pavone, *L. mistus*, cuckoo wrasse.

†**labro**[2] *m.* See **labbro**.

labro·nico *adj.* (geog.) of or relating to Leghorn.

labro·stino *m.* See **abrostine**.

labrusca *f.* See **lambrusca**.

labur-ismo *m.* (Eng. pol.) Labour, Labour politics; Labour policy. **-ista** *adj.* (Eng. pol.) Labour; il partito -ista, the Labour Party; *n.m., f.* member of the Labour Party.

laburno *m.* (bot.) laburnum, golden rain, *Laburnum*; — fetido, *Anagyris foetida*.

lacc-a[1] *f.* lacquer; lac; shellac; — nera, black japan; — giapponese, japan; — in bacchette, stick lac. **-are** [A2] *tr.* to lacquer; to japan. **-ato** *part. adj.* lacquered; japanned. **-atore** *m.* lacquerer. **-atura** *f.* lacquering; japanning.

lacca[2] *f.* cavity; ditch; slope.

lacca[3] *f.* buttock of a quadruped; (anat.) popliteal space; (vet.) growth on the gaskin of a horse.

lacca[4] *f.* (Tusc.) large portion of anything; entrance fee; gain, profit, earnings.

lacca[5] *f.* (Tusc.) blow, hit, buffet; loss; damage.

laccamuffa *f.* (chem.) litmus.

laccare [A2] and derivs. See under **lacca**[1].

laccetto *m.* (vet.) thymus gland (in cattle); (cul.) sweetbread; whey.

lacchè *m. indecl.* lackey; footman; manservant; flunkey; (fig., derog.) subservient or servile individual.

lacchezzo *m.* (Tusc. colloq.) juicy morsel; spicy bit; titbit; intrigue; gossip; flattery.

lac·cia *f.* (ichth.) shad, *Alosa alosa*.

laccia·ia *f.* See under **laccio**.

lac·c-io *m.* noose; slip knot; thong, lace; snare, gin, trap; ambush; stratagem; prendere, cogliere, al —, to snare; cadere, dare, nel —, to fall into the trap; la pena del —, hanging, the gallows; mettere un — al collo a uno, to coerce a person; -i delle scarpe, shoelaces; (herald.) — di amore, wake and ormond knot; (paint.) — painting with gold background; *pl.* (naut.) tiller ropes. **-ia·ia** *f.* lassoo. **-iola·io** *m.* trapper. **-i(u)olo** *m. dim.* of **laccio**; trap for snaring birds; -iuolo di setole, trap for catching moles; (fig.) deception, trickery.

†**lacco**[1] *m.* See **lacca**[1].

lacco[2] *m.* a kind of tub or bucket; subterranean cavity in which religious sacrifices were made; (dial., S. Ital.) land subsidence.

lacco[3] *adj.* (Tusc.) weak, feeble; limp (cf. **bislacco**).

laccolite *f.* (geol.) laccolith.

laccone *m.* (Tusc., naut.) small one-masted vessel with large lateen sail and one foresail; (Rome) large boat for transport of materials.

lacer-are [A1 S] *tr.* to tear; to rend; to tear up, to tear to shreds; to lacerate, to wound; to wear out; to consume; to waste, to squander, to run through; to slander, to tear to pieces; *rfl.* to

lacerate oneself; (naut.) to split (of a sail blown out by a squall); *recip. rfl.* to tear each other to pieces; to fight tooth and nail. (**-a·bile** *adj.* **-abilità** *f.*) **-amento** *m.* tearing; rending; lacerating. **-ante** *part. adj.* tearing; rending; lacerating; strumento -ante, sharp instrument; wounding, heart-breaking. **-ativo** *adj.* sharp, cutting. **-atore** *m.* lacerator; *adj.* wounding; (of sound) piercing. (**-atrice** *f.*) **-atura** *f.* see **lacerazione**. **-azione** *f.* rending, tearing; (fig.) distress, hurt; (med.) lacerating; laceration.

lacerna *f.* (Rom. antiq.) mantle (for cold weather), *lacerna*.

la·cero *adj.* torn; rent; in rags and tatters; (med.) lacerated; una ferita lacero-contusa, a lacerated-contused wound; (bot.) laciniate.

†**lac-erta** *f.*, †**-ertola** *f.* See **lucertola**.

lacerto *m.* (anat.) lacertus fibrosus, bicipita fascia; sinew, muscular part of the arm, biceps; (ichth.) mackerel, *Scomber scomber*; †see **lucertola**.

La·chesi *pr.n.f.* (myth.) Lachesis.

†**laci** *adv.* there; in —, yonder.

lacini-a *f.* (Rom. antiq.) lappet of garment; *pl.* (zool.) doddles of a goat. **-ato** *adj.* (bot.) laciniate.

lacmo *m.* (chem.) litmus.

lacno *m.* (ent.) *Lachnus* spp., a genus of aphids.

†**laco** *m.* (poet.). See **lago**.

lac-one *adj., n.m., f.* Spartan. **-oneggiare** [A3c] see **laconizzare**. **-o·nico** *adj.* laconic; (hist.) Spartan. **-onicamente** *adv.* laconically. **-onicismo** *m.*, **-onicità** *f.*, **-onismo** *m.* quality of being laconic; brevity, terseness; conciseness. **-onizzare** [A1] *intr.* (aux. avere) to be laconic; to speak tersely; to write concisely; *tr.* to make terse or concise.

la·crim-a *f.* tear; versare -e, to weep tears; non fece, diede, una —, he didn't shed a single tear; -e di gioia, tears of joy; prorompere in -e, to burst into tears; struggersi, sciogliersi, in -e, to dissolve into tears; ingoiare le -e, bere le -e, to stop oneself from crying, to gulp down one's tears; con le -e agli occhi, with tears in one's eyes; -e di coccodrillo, crocodile tears; asciugare le -e, to dry one's tears; piangere a calde -e, to weep passionately; piangere a -e di sangue, to cry one's heart out; avere le -e in tasca, to weep easily; asciugarsi le -e, to dry one's tears; (fig.) asciugare le -e a, to console, to comfort; avere le -e nella voce, to have a sob in one's voice, to speak in tearful tones; — Christi, Lacrima Christi, a Neapolitan and Sicilian wine; drop, drip; -e del formaggio, liquid part of ripe cheese (e.g. of Camembert); (rel.) dono delle -e, gift of tears; valle di -e, vale of tears; (bot.) fir resin; -e di Giobbe, Job's tears, *Coix lacrima*; bladder-nut, *Staphylea pinnata*. **-a·bile** *adj.* pitiful, pathetic. **-abilmente** *adv.* pitifully. **-ale** *adj.* lachrymose, tearful; (anat.) lachrymal; (archaeol.) vaso -ale, lachrymal vase, vase to hold tears; *n.m.* (anat.) lachrymal duct. **-ante** *part. adj.* weeping; *n.m., f.* weeping person. **-are** [A1 S] *intr.* (aux. avere) to shed tears, to weep; (of the eyes) to water; to ooze liquid, to run with moisture; *tr.* (poet.) to weep for, to mourn. **-ato** *part. adj.* wept, mourned. **-ato·rio** *adj.* (archaeol.) vaso -atorio, lachrymal vase; (anat.) lachrymal. **-azione** *f.* weeping; (med.) lacrimation. **-evole** *adj.* pitiful, pathetic; tearful; voce -evole, tearful voice, whining voice. **-evolmente** *adv.* pitifully; tearfully. **-o·geno** *adj.* lachrymatory; gas -ogeno, tear gas; (joc.) tear-producing; oratore -ogeno, orator skilled at bringing tears to the eyes of his audience. **-oso** *adj.* tearful; lachrymose; weeping; pitiful, sorrowful, moving; oozing, dripping; fumo -oso, smoke that makes the eyes water. **-osamente** *adv.* tearfully; pitifully; movingly.

lacuale *adj.* pertaining to a lake, similar to a lake.

lacun-a[1] *f.* gap; hiatus; blank; lacuna; empty space; colmare una —, to fill a gap, to make good a lack; -e della memoria, lapses of memory, gaps in one's memory; -e nella propria dottrina, gaps in one's learning; (anat.) lacuna, cavity; *pl.* (bot.) -e aerifere, aerenchyma. **-are** *m.* (archit.) lacunar; ceiling with coffers and/or painted panels. **-oso** *adj.* full of gaps; (bot.) tessuto -oso, spongy parenchyma.

†**lacuna**[2] *f.* and derivs. See **laguna**.

lacustre *adj.* lake-side; lake-dwelling; *adj.* (geol.) lacustrine.

Ladachi *pr.n.m.* (geog.) Ladakh.

la·dano[1] *m.* (ichth.) *Huso huso*, a kind of sturgeon.

la·dano[2] *m.* (bot.) ladanum (fragrant exudate of *Cistus* spp.).

laddov-e *conj.* while; whilst; whereas; *adv.* (fig.) there where, in circumstances in which; mostrare clemenza — conviene usare severità, to be clement in circumstances which call for severity; †there where, where. †**-unque** *adv.* anywhere there; *conj.* wherever.

†**la·dico** *adj.* and derivs. See **laico.**

ladino[1] *adj.* (philol.) Ladin; *n.m.* Ladin, Romance language spoken in the Engadine, the Grisons and the Alto Adige.

ladino[2] *adj.* fluent; easy; ready; †(mil. hist.) palla ladina, a ball that is easily loaded; *n.m.* (naut.) slack rope; ill-made seizing.

†**lado** *adj.* and deriv. See **laido.**

ladr-o *m.* thief; robber; — di strada, pickpocket, bag-snatcher; — di casa, burglar; — in guanti gialli, gentleman burglar; al —!, thief!; (joc.) — di cuori, 'heart-throb', lady-killer; -i di Pisa, thieves who fall out in the daytime but combine to rob at night; (provb.) l'occasione fa l'uomo —, opportunity makes a thief; in casa di -i non ci si ruba, there is honour amongst thieves; non ride sempre la moglie del —, everyone has their troubles; (colloq.) vestito come un —, poorly dressed, *or* dressed in a slovenly way; tempo da -i, foul weather; (naut.) — d'arsenale, dockyard pilferer; — di fiume, river thief; — di mare, pirate; — d'arena, — di sabbia, hour-glass shaker; glass or metal funnel for drawing wine from a cask; piece of wick which falls on to a lighted candle and partly extinguishes it; *adj.* thieving, thievish; dishonest; il gatto è — per natura, the cat is thievish by nature; (joc.) occhi -i, eyes that kill; (colloq.) frightful, horrible, bad; un — sonetto, a shockingly bad sonnet. **-a** *f.* woman thief; (Tusc.) inside pocket of a coat or overcoat; stick for knocking down fruit; fragment of burning wick which causes the candle to melt in a down-flowing stream. **-eri·a** *f.* theft; thieving action; evil deed; (colloq.) ugly and inferior work of art. **-esco** *adj.* (*m.pl.* **-eschi**) thieving; typical of a thief; pertaining to thieves. **-oci·nio** *m.* see **latrocinio.** **-ona·ia** *f.* hide-out for thieves; band of thieves; band of brigands. **-onata** *f.* theft. **-oncello** *m.* boy thief. **-one** *m.* thief; assassin; highwayman; (naut.) -one di mare, pirate. **-oneccio** *m.* theft. **-oneggiare** [A 3 c] *intr.* (aux. avere) to thieve, to steal. **-oneri·a** *f.* theft. **-onesco** *adj.* (*m.pl.* **-oneschi**) thieving, thievish. **-onescamente** *adv.* thievishly.

†**lagare**, †**laggare** *vb.* and derivs. See **lasciare.**

lagena *f.* (archaeol.) narrow-necked flask; measure of liquid.

laggiù *adv.* down there; there below; down yonder; yonder.

†**laggiue**, †**laggiuso** *adv.* See **laggiù.**

laghetto *m.*, **laghista** *m.* See under **lago.**

†**lagi** *m.* essere il —, to have a finger in every pie (from the name of a broker in Florence who financed most of the commercial activities in the town).

la·gia *adj. f.* (orn.) passera —, rock sparrow, *Petronia petronia.*

†**lagna** *f.* affliction; grief, sorrow.

lagn-are [A 5] *rfl.* to complain; to grumble; ha sempre qualcosa da -arsi, he's always complaining about something; non mi -o, I'm not grumbling; non posso -armi, I can't complain. **-anza** *f.* complaint; lament; suscitare -anze, to arouse complaints; sporgere delle -anze, fare le proprie -anze, to lodge complaints. **-io** *m.* (*pl.* **-ii**) continual complaint; unending grumble. **-o** *m.* lament, plaint. **-oso** *adj.* complaining; discontented.

lagno[1] *m.* See under **lagnare.**

lagno[2] *m.* (geog., S. Italy) channel of water flowing from the mountains after heavy rains.

lagnoso[1] *adj.* See under **lagnare.**

lagnoso[2] *adj.* (dial., Sicil., S. Ital.) dirty.

la-go[1] *m.* (*pl.* **-ghi**) lake; mere; flood; un — di parole, a flood of words; un — di miserie, a sea of troubles; in un — di sudore, in a bath of perspiration; (anat.) — del cuore, ventricle. **-ghetto**, **-ghettino** *m. dim.* of lago; small lake; pond; artificial lake. **-ghigiano** *m.* lake-dweller. **-ghista** *m.* boatman on the Lombard lakes; (paint) lake (landscape) painter; (lit. hist.) lake poet; inhabitant of the region of the English or Scottish Lakes. **-gone** *m. augm.* of lago; lagoon. **-goso** *adj.* (geog.) abounding in lakes. †**-gume** *m.* marsh; lagoon.

lago[2] *m.* (dial. Tusc.) See **ago.**

lag-oftalmo *m.* (med.) lagophthalmus. **-o·podo** *m.* (orn.) ptarmigan.

lagorare *vb.* and derivs. See **lavorare.**

lagrimotomo *m.* (surg.) dacryocystotome.

†**lagume** *m.* See under **lago**[1].

lagun-a[1] *f.* lagoon; — morta, non-tidal lagoon; — viva, tidal lagoon. **-are** *adj.* pertaining to a lagoon.

†**laguna**[2] *f.* and derivs. See **lacuna.**

la·i *m. indecl.* (prosod.) lay; *pl.* (poet.) lamentations; trar —, to lament, to utter lamentations.

la·ic-o *adj.* lay, non-clerical; frate —, lay-brother (as distinct from priest or choir-monk); secular, non-religious (state, school); secularist, anti-clerical, anti-religious; †unlettered; *n.m.* lay-brother, layman. **-amente** *adv.* secularly. **-ale** *adj.* lay, non-clerical. (-**almente** *adv.*) **-ato** *m.* laity; lay status. **-ismo** *m.* (neol.) secularism. **-ità** *f.* lay status. **-izzare** [A 1] *tr.* (neol.) to secularize (a state, education, etc.). (-**izzato** *part. adj.*) **-izzazione** *f.* (neol.) secularization (esp. of schools).

la·id-o *adj.* foul; dirty; loathsome, repugnant; filthy; obscene. **-amente** *adv.* foully; loathsomely; obscenely. †**-are**, †**-ire** *tr.* to make ugly; to foul; to spoil; *rfl.* to foul oneself; to become ugly or foul. **-ezza** *f.* foulness; filth; loathsomeness; obscenity; indecency; ugliness. **-ume** *m.* collection of filth; dirt; foulness. †**-ura** *f.* ugliness; abusive and foul language.

†**lald-a** *f.* see **lauda.** †**-are** *vb.* and derivs. see **laudare.**

lallazione *f.* (philol.) labdacism in children.

lal·lera (Tusc. pop.). See **lilleri.**

lalofobi·a *f.* (med.) lalophobia.

lam-a[1] *f.* (Tusc., N. Ital.) flooded ground; marshland; (geog.) sheet erosion; (naut.) — d'acqua, sheet of water, †wave; (naut. eng.) — d'acqua, water-jacket; — d'acqua di raffreddamento, cooling water-space; — di fondo, ground swell. **-ata** *f.* expanse of flooded ground.

lama[2] *f.* blade; steel; cutting-edge; thin metal sheet; safety-razor blade; (fig.) swordsman, 'blade'; — a denti, saw; (fig.) prendere il coltello per la —, to cook one's goose; † ornamental lamen.

lama[3] *m.* (zool.) llama.

lam-a[4] *m.* Lama, Tibetan priest; il Dalai —, the Dalai Lama. **-ismo** *m.* (rel.) 'Lamaism', a (mostly hostile) term for the Buddhism of Tibet and Mongolia.

lamantino *m.* (zool.) manatee, *Manatus* spp.

lam-are [A 1] *tr.* (eng.) to spot-face. **-atura** *f.* spot-facing.

lambd-a *f.* (gramm.) lambda; (anat.) lambda. **-acismo** *m.* (philol.) lambdacism, labdacism. **-o·ide** *m.* (anat.) lambdoid.

lambella *f.* (herald.) troncato in —, dovetailed.

lambello *m.* (herald.) label.

lambente *adj.* See under **lambire.**

lambicc-are [A 2] *tr.* to distil; *rfl.* (dat. of prn. 'si') -arsi il cervello, to rack one's brains. **-amento** *m.* distilling. **-ato** *part. adj.* distilled; (fig.) strained, far-fetched; affected; artificial. **-atore** *m.* one who racks his brains; †distiller. **-atura** *f.* distilling; racking of one's brains; straining for effect.

lambic-co *m.* (*pl.* **-chi**) (chem.) retort; alembic.

lamb-ire [D 2] *tr.* to lap; to lap up; il gattino -isce il latte, the kitten laps milk; to lick, to graze lightly; to skim over; to glide over; (of a flame) to play upon; (of water) to wash, to flow by; *intr.* (aux. avere) (naut.) to graze, to touch lightly; to 'smell the bottom'. **-ente** *part. adj.* lapping; superficial, grazing, glancing; fuoco -ente, lambent fire, will o' the wisp. **-imento** *m.* licking; lapping. **-ito** *part. adj.* licked; lapped; grazed, touched lightly; skimmed.

lambrecchina *m.pl.* (herald.) mantling, ambrequins; (archit.) lambrequin(s), esp. as ornament at the edge of a roof.

lambrino *m.* See **lambris.**

lambris *m. indecl.* (pron. **lambri**) (bldg.) panelling, wainscoting.

lambrusc-a *f.* (bot.) see **abrostine.** **-are** [A 2] *tr.* to allow (a vine) to grow wild. **-o** *m.* grape of the wild vine; red sparkling wine of Modena.

lamell-a *f.* lamina; little blade. **-are** *adj.* (geol.; miner.) foliated, lamellar, spathose. **-ato** *adj.* laminated; in layers. **-ibranchi** *m.pl.* (zool.) lamellibranchs. **-icorni** *m.pl.* lamellicorn beetles. **-oso** *adj.* laminated.

lament-are [A 1 c] *rfl.* to lament, to complain; to utter laments; to moan; -arsi di, to complain about, of; -arsi con, to reproach; -arsi da uno, to complain to someone; *tr.* to lament, to bewail, to mourn; to deplore; to regret; to complain of; da un pezzo non si -ano più furti, no thefts have been reported for some time. †**-a·bile** *adj.* and deriv. see **lamentevole.** †**-amento** *m.* lamenting; lament, lamentation. **-ante** *part. adj.* lamenting. **-anza** *f.* lament; complaint; plaint. †**-ata** *f.* see **lamentanza.** **-ativo** *adj.* complaining, lamenting. **-ato** *part. adj.* lamented; mourned; greatly missed; late lamented. **-atore** *m.* **-atrice** *f.*) **-ato·rio** *adj.* (*m.pl.* **-ato·rii**) lamenting. **-azione** *f.* lamentation; reproach; **-ela** *f.* long lament, complaint. **-evole** *adj.* lamenting; plaintive; complaining; lamentable. **-evolmente** *adv.* plaintively; lamentably. **-io** *m.* (*pl.* **-ii**) constant, repeated lamenting.

lament-o *m.* lament; complaint; plaint; cry of pain; cry of grief; reproof, reproach, remonstrance; (poet.) distant rumbling of thunder. **-oso** *adj.* lamenting, complaining, full of complaints; voce -osa, doleful voice; invocazione -osa, mournful invocation. **-osamente** *adv.* lamentingly; complainingly, plaintively; mournfully, dolefully.

La·mia[1] *pr.n.f.* (myth.) Lamia; witch; she-demon; (ichth.) shark, *Carcharodon rondeletii*; tope, *Galeorhinus galeus*; (ent.) a genus of beetles, *Lamia* spp.

†la·mia[2] *f.* (archit.) vault, natural vaulted roof of cave or grotto.

†lami·a[3] *f.* See **lumia**.

†lamicare *impers.* to drizzle with rain.

lamiera *f.* (metall.; eng.) sheet metal, sheeting; plate; — cilindrata, rolled plate; — stagnata, tinplate; — ondulata, corrugated sheet-iron; — zincata, galvanized sheet-iron; (naut.) ship's plating.

la·min-a *f.* thin plate; lamina; thin sheet,| thin layer; (bot.) lamina. **-are** *adj.* laminar, laminal, laminary. **-oso** *adj.* laminose, laminous.

laminare[1] *adj.* See under **lamina**.

lamin-are[2] [A I S] *tr.* to roll (metal); to laminate; (metall.) to roll; — a caldo, to hot roll. **-ato** *part. adj.* laminated; laminate; oro -ato, rolled gold. **-atoio** *m.* (metall.) rolling-mill.

lamina·ria *f.* (bot.) tang, tangles, kelp, oar weed, *Laminaria*.

lamiola *f.* (ichth.). See **lamia**[1].

lampa *f.* (poet.). See **lampada**.

lam·pad-a *f.* lamp; oil-lamp; (fig.) light; — di Aladino, Aladdin's lamp; — a spirito, spirit-lamp; — ad arco, arc-lamp; — di sicurezza, safety-lamp; — chiusa, hurricane lamp. **-ario** *m.* chandelier; lamp-stand. **-ina** *f. dim.* of **lampada**; small lamp; electric-light bulb; pilot-light; -ina elettrica tascabile, pocket torch. **-odromi·a** *f.* (Gk. antiq.) (sacred) torch-race. **-ofori·a** *f.* (Gk. antiq.) carrying of torches, torch-race.

†lam·pade *f.* See **lampada**.

lampan-a *f.* (Tusc.) lamp; oil-lamp. **-aio** *m.* lamp-maker, lamp-man; lamp bracket. **-eggio** *m.* lamplight; moonlight; †firelight, glow; †flash of lightning.

lampante[1] *adj.* shining, brilliant; clear; evident; lucid; obvious; transparent; *adv.* chiaro —, brilliantly clear; *n.m.* new coin.

lampante[2] *adj.* (of oil) limpid, clear.

lampara *f.* net with lights for night fishing.

†lampare *vb.* and derivs. See **lampeggiare**.

lampasco *m.* (vet.) lampas (in horses).

lampassato *adj.* (herald.) langued, with tongue.

lampa·zio *m.* (vet.) see **lampasco**.

lampeggi-are [A 3 c] *intr.* (aux. avere) to flash; to gleam; to glisten; to be resplendent; to shine; *impers.* to flash lightning, to lighten; -a, it is lightening; *tr.* (poet.) — un riso, to flash a smile; *n.m.* flashing; flash; gleam. **-amento** *m.* flashing; gleaming; flashing of lightning. **-ante** *part. adj.* flashing, gleaming; occhi -anti, shining eyes. **-ato** *part. adj.* flashed. **-atore** *m.* (motor.) winking light, winker-flashing indicator; (photog.) electronic flash.

lampeggio *m.* lightning; sheet lightning; flash of lightning.

lampegg·io *m.* (*pl.* -ii) continual flashing; flashes; coruscation.

lampion-e *m.* street-lamp; lamp-post; carriage-lamp; — alla veneziana, paper lantern lit with a candle; (mil.) — di ronda, night round's lamp, dark lantern (capable of being screened); †(naut.) see **fanale**. **-aio** *m.* lamplighter. **-cino** *m. dim.* fairy lamp; paper lantern; little lamp.

lampi·ridi *m.pl.* (ent.) fireflies, *Lampyris* spp.

lampist-a *m.* official or workman in charge of lamps; (rlwy.) lamp-man. **-eri·a** *f.* (rlwy.) lamp room.

lampo *m.* flash; lightning; gleam; — di poesia, poetic inspiration; un — di genio, a stroke of genius, a flash of genius; passare come un —, to pass by in a flash, to be over in a flash; in un —, in a flash; chiusura —, zip-fastener; cerniera —, zip-fastener round a handbag or case; (aeron.) faro a -i, flashing light; telegramma —, express telegram; guerra —, Blitzkrieg; (naut.) fast picket boat armed with a bow gun; motor gunboat.

lampone *m.* (bot.) raspberry, *Rubus idaeus*.

lamposco·pio *m.* magic lantern.

lampred-a *f.* (ichth.) lamprey, *Petromyzon* spp. **-otto** *m.* young lamprey; (cul., Tusc.) offal.

lampride *m.* (ichth.) king fish, *Lampris luna*.

lampuga *f.* (ichth.) *Stromateus fiatola*, also *Coryphaena hippurus* and *Brama rayi*, marine fishes.

lan-a *f.* wool; — pettinata, worsted; mezza —, union cloth, wool and cotton; una matassa di —, a skein of wool; manto di —, fleece; vestito di —, woollen dress *or* jersey, jumper; (also *abs.*) porta la —, he is wearing his jersey; fluff; woolly hair; — penna, silky textile fabric made from the byssus threads of *Pinna nobilis*, a large mussel (also 'lanapenna'); — seta, silk and wool mixture; (fig.) della stessa —, of that ilk; vendere — per capecchio a, to deceive, to trick, to 'do'; questioni di — caprina, fruitless discussions; (hist.) Arte della Lana, the Wool Guild in medieval Florence; (joc.) rascal, scamp; quella buona — di Giuseppe, that rascal Joe; i suoi amici sono certe — e!, his friends are a fine lot of rogues!. **†-ara** *f.* (naut.) see **lanata**. **-ario** *m.* (orn.) lanner falcon, *Falco biarmicus*. **-ata** *f.* (mil.) pullthrough, ramrod cloth; (naut.) long Tom (for painting); ramrod head, 'woolly headed bastard'. **†-ato** *adj.* woolly.

lanca *f.* flooded ground; river bed.

lance[1] *f.* (poet.) pan of a balance; balance; porre in —, to compare, to weigh.

lance[2] *pl.* of **lancia**, q.v.

lancett-a *f.* small lance; (med.) lancet; hand (of a clock); pointer (of a metronome); needle (of a compass); (bot.) lady tulip, *Tulipa clusiana*. **-ina** *f. dim.* of **lancetta**; (watchm.) second hand. **-are** [A I C] (med.) to lance. **-atura** *f.* (med.) lancing. **-ato** *part. adj.* (med.) lanced. **-one** *m.* (vet.) lancet.

lan·ci-a[1] *f.* lance; spear; javelin; dart; nozzle of a hose-pipe; harpoon; — d'arrembaggio, grappling hook; (fig.) spezzare una —, to come to the defence; (mil.) lancer; (hist.) knight with shield-bearer and squire; (hist.) — spezzata, tried and trusty knight. **-aio** *m.* lance-maker. **-ata** *f.* spear's throw; thrust with a lance. **-ere** *m.* (mil.) lancer; lance-maker; (mus.) i Lancieri, the Lancers. **-otto** *m.* lance; dart; (mil.) lancer.

lan·ci-a[2] *f.* (naut.) ship's boat; launch (sail or oars); — a vapore, steam pinnace; — a motore, motorboat; — cannoniere, gunboat (M.G.B.); — del porto, harbour launch; — della ronda, night round's boat; — armata in guerra, armed boat; — di salvataggio, lifeboat. **-ere** *m.* (naut.) lighterman. **-one** *m. augm.* (naut.) lighter; †coast defence bomb ketch.

lanci-are [A 3] *tr.* to throw; to fling; to hurl; to shy; to toss; to pitch; to shoot; to fire; to drop (bombs); to launch; to initiate; to promote; — un grido, to utter a shout; to give a cry; (joc.) — campanili, to tell cock-and-bull stories; to strike with a lance, to pierce; (fig.) to torment; to grieve; *rfl.* to hurl oneself; to fling oneself; -arsi col paracadute, to do a parachute jump, to bale out. (**-abile** *adj.*) **-abombe** *m. indecl.* (mil.) bomb-thrower; (naut.) depth-charge thrower; seaman detailed for depth-charge throwing. **-afiamme** *m. indecl.* (mil.) flame-thrower. **-amento** *m.* flinging, hurling; grief; pain, torment. **-anavetta** *m. indecl.* (text.) picker. **-ante** *part. adj.* flinging; thrusting; (naut.) firing of torpedoes. **-asabbia** *m. indecl.* (rlwy.) sander. **-asiluri** *m. indecl.* (naut.) torpedo tube. **-ato** *part. adj.* flung; hurled; tossed; wounded by a lance; made in the shape of a lance; a volo -ato, as the crow flies; (herald.) at speed; (sport) chilometro -ato, flying kilometre (in motor-, motor-cycle-, or cycle-racing). **-atoia** *f.* bat-fowling net. **-atore** *m.* flinger, thrower; launcher; -atore di fandonie, spreader of nonsense; (naut.) harpoon thrower; harpoon gunner. **†-necco** *m.* see **lanzichenecco**, under **lanzi**.

lancinante *adj.* (of pain) stabbing, piercing, shooting; lancinating.

lan·cio *m.* fling; throw; (sport) — del disco, throwing the discus; (naut.) firing of torpedoes; — angolato, angled running; — in guerra, firing with warheads; — da esercizio, practice running; — simulato, water shot, dummy attack; campo di —, torpedo practice area; pontile di —, fixed firing point; stazione di —, torpedo control tower; centrale di —, torpedo transmitting and calculating station; launching; rampa di —, missile launching base.

lanci(u)ola *f. dim.* of **lancia**[1], q.v.; (bot.) ribwort, *Plantago lanceolata*.

landa *f.* sandy waste; heath, moor; prairie.

lande *f.pl.* (naut.) sheer pole shroud bolts; boats lifting bolts.

landgra·vio *m.* See **langravio**.

†landra *f.* prostitute.

landre *f.pl.* (naut.) chain-plates; — dei paterazzi, back-stay plates; — delle sartie di gabbia, — delle bigotte di coffa, futtock plates.

landrone *m.* See **androne**.

la·n-eo *adj.* woollen. **-eri·a** *f.* woollen goods, woollens. **-etta** *f.* (text.) inferior wool, wool mixed with cotton, 'mixed'; fluff; (fig.) -etta fina, blackguard.

lanfa *f.* orange flower water.

lan·gio *m.* (vet.) ulcer in the tail of cattle.

langite *f.* (miner.) langite.

langra·vi·o *m.* (hist.) landgrave. **-ato** *m.* (hist.) landgraviate.

†**langueggiare** *vb.* and derivs. See **languire**.

lan·guid-o *adj.* languid; languishing; weak, drooping. **-amẹnte** *adv.* languidly. **-ẹtto** *adj. dim.* rather weak, weakly; limp. **-ẹzza** *f.* languor; weakness. †**-ore** *m.* languor.

langu-ire [D2] *intr.* (*aux.* avere) to languish. **-ente** *part. adj.* languishing; weak, faint; (of business) slow, quiet. **-imẹnto** *m.* languishing; languor.

languọre *m.* languor; droopiness; sluggishness; listlessness; weakness, faintness.

†**langura** *f.* See **languore**.

†**laniare** *tr.* to tear; to lacerate.

lanic·cio *m.* fluff, the woolly flock that comes off bedding.

laniere *m.* (orn.) shrike; †*adj.* rough, wild, uncouth.

lan-iero *adj.* pertaining to wool; *n.m.* woollen manufacturer. **-i·fero** *adj.* wool-bearing; wool-producing. **-ifi·cio** *m.* wool mill; wool manufacture. **-i·fico** *adj.* wool manufacturing. **-i·gero** *adj.* wool-bearing. **-ina** *f.* mixed cloth. **-ino** *m.* wool-worker; carder.

lanista *m.* (Rom. antiq.) trainer of gladiators.

lanital *m. indecl.* (text.) lanital.

lan-o *adj.* woollen. **-olina** *f.* lanolin(e), wool-grease.

lanọs-o *adj.* woolly; similar to wool, wool-like. **-ità** *f.* woolliness.

lantana *f.* (bot.) wayfaring tree, *Viburnum lantana*; also *Lantana camara*, a cultivated American plant.

lant-ano, -a·nio *m.* (chem.) lanthanum. **-anite** *f.* (miner.) lanthanite.

lantern-a *f.* lantern, lamp; hurricane lamp; cercare i mali colla —, to go out looking for trouble; mostrare lucciole per -e, to cheat, to hoodwink; — magica, magic lantern; (zool.) — di mare, *Pyrosoma elegans*, a pelagic tunicate; (archit.) lantern, skylight; (naut.) foot of a mast or topmast; principal lighthouse at a port or on the extremity of a mole; white object (stone, bone, rag) used to bring tunny fish to surface in order to count them; — cieca, lamp fitted with a shutter, 'dark lantern'; †(mil.) firebrand; *pl.* (fam.) eyes; spectacles; squadernar le -e, to open one's eyes wide. **-ag·gio** *m.* (naut.) lighting; diritto di -aggio, lighting dues. **-a·io** *m.* lamp-trimmer; lamp-maker; lamp-seller; lighthouse keeper. †**-are** *tr.* to illuminate. **-a·tico** *m.* see **lanternaggio**. **-ino** *m. dim.* of **lanterna**; (naut.) lighted buoy; lantern-buoy; small beacon light. **-ọne** *m. augm.* of **lanterna**; outside lamp; (naut.) gondola lamp; *pl.* lanterns on poles for carrying in processions; guide for the blind; (joc.) tall, thin man. **-u·cola** *f. pejor.* of **lanterna**. †**-uto** *adj.* tall and thin.

lantopina *f.* (chem.) lanthopine.

lan-u(g)·gine *f.* down, downy beard; downy covering; (bot.) tomentum. **-uginọso** *adj.* downy. **-uto** *adj.* woolly, covered with wool; wool-like; *n.m.* woolly animal. **-uzza** *f.* rogue, scoundrel.

†**lanza** *f.* See **lancia**[1].

lanzardo *m.* (ichth.) Spanish mackerel, *Scomber colias*.

lanz-i *m. indecl.* abbrev. of **lanzichenecco**. **-ichenẹcco, -ighinẹtto, -inẹcco** *m.* (hist.) Landsknecht, German armed soldier (of the mercenaries who served in Italy). **-o** *m.* abbrev. of **lanzichenecco**, mercenary soldier, esp. of those who were in the service of the Medici. The Loggia de' Lanzi in Florence took its name from the sentinels posted there; ubbriaco come un -o, drunk as a lord.

Laocoon·te *pr.n.m.* (myth.) Laocoon.

laọnde *adv.* therefore; wherefore; there, thence; where, whence.

lapalissiano *adj.* self-evident, obvious; absurdly ingenuous (from the name of La Palisse, a French soldier of the sixteenth century, concerning whom it was said: 'Un quart d'heure avant sa mort il était encore en vie').

lapar-atomi·a *f.* (surg.) laparotomy. **-ato·mico** *adj.* laparotomical. **-atomista** *m.* laparotomist. **-oscopi·a** *f.* laparoscopy. **-osco·pico** *adj.* laparoscopical. **-otomi·a** *f.* see **laparatomia**.

lapa·zio *m.* (bot.) patience dock, *Rumex patientia*.

lapicida *m.* sculptor; stone-mason.

la·pida *f.* stone cover (e.g. for a cesspool).

lapid-are [A1s] *tr.* to stone. **-ato** *part. adj.* stoned, done to death by stoning; (joc.) honoured with a stone inscription. **-aziọne** *f.* stoning.

la·pid-e *f.* headstone, memorial stone, memorial tablet; (hist.) milestone; †precious stone. **-a·ria** *f.* science and art of inscriptions; epigraphy. **-a·rio** *adj.* lapidary; stile -ario, lapidary style. **-escẹnte** *adj.* petrifying. **-ificare** [A2s] *tr.* to petrify. **-ificaziọne** *f.* petrification. **-i·fico** *adj.* petrifying. **-ifọrme** *adj.* stony, resembling stone. **-ọso** *adj.* stony.

lapi·deo *adj.* stone, made of stone; arca lapidea, stone sarcophagus.

lapill-o *m.* small stone; crystal; particle; albo —, with a white stone (indicating either a lucky day or an acquittal in court); *pl.* small fragments of solidified lava. **-are** [A1] *tr.* to reduce to particles; *rfl.* to solidify, to crystallize. (**-amẹnto** *m.*) **-ato** *part. adj.* reduced to particles; crystallized. **-aziọne** *f.* making into fragments; crystallization. **-ọso** *adj.* lumpy.

la·pis *m. indecl.* pencil; — copiativo, copying ink pencil; — di gomma, ink eraser; (art) pencil (originally of a kind of stone which made red marks on paper; now any kind of drawing pencil).

lapis-armẹno *m.* (miner.) Armenian stone, lapis armenus. **-laẓ·ẓoli, -laẓ·ẓolo, -laẓ·ẓuli** *m. indecl.* lapis lazuli.

lappa *f.* See **lappola**.

lapp-are [A1] *tr.* to lap, to lap up. **-atọre** *m.* (eng.) lap. **-atrice** *f.* (eng.) lapping machine.

lappe *onom.* sound of water lapping; la gola gli fa — —, his mouth is watering; †fare — —, to be in a blue funk.

lappeggiare [A3c]. See **lappare**.

lap·pol-a *f.* (bot.) bur-bearing plant; bur; (fig.) tiresome bore, hanger-on. **-ato** *adj.* (text.) burry.

lap·pol-e *f.pl.* eye-lashes. **-eggiare** [A3c] *intr.* (*aux.* avere) to blink for the purpose of getting rid of a speck in the eye.

Lapp-oni·a *pr.n.f.* (geog.) Lapland. **-ọne** *adj., n.m.* Lapp.

lapsus *m. indecl.* (Lat.) lapse; — linguae, slip of the tongue.

laqueare *m.* (archit.) laquear.

laque-a·rio *m.,* **-atọre** *m.* (Rom. antiq.) laqueator (gladiator).

larà *onom.* tra-la-la.

lara·rio *m.* (Rom. antiq.) lararium.

lard-o *m.* bacon; lard; pork dripping; nuotare nel —, to live on the fat of the land; (provb.) tanto va la gatta al — che ci lascia lo zampino, be sure your sins will find you out. **-a·ceo** *adj.* lard-like; bacon-like. **-ai(u)olo** *adj.* tasting or smelling like bacon; *n.m.* pork butcher. **-are** [A1] *tr.* to lard, to grease; (naut.) to lard, to sew thrums on to (canvas, etc.). **-atọio** *m.* (naut.) larding needle. **-atura** *f.* larding; greasing. **-ellare** [A1] *tr.* to lard, to stuff with bacon; to interlard. **-ellatura** *f.* larding, interlarding. **-ite** *f.* soap-stone, used by tailors to mark clothes when fitting them. **-ọne** *m.* salt pork. **-ọso** *adj.* fat; greasy.

lare *m.* See **lari**.

larẹn-zia *f.* (ent.) *Larentia* spp., geometrid moths.

†**larg-are** [A2] *tr.* to spread; to set free; *rfl.* to go out to sea. †**-atira** *f.* (naut.) long, slow stroke in rowing.

larheggi-are [A3c] *intr.* (*aux.* avere) to be profuse; to be generous, to be liberal; to be open-handed; to abound; — di parole, to make a lot of promises. **-amẹnto** *m.* pouring forth, profusion. **-atọre** *m.* generous or liberal person. (**-atrice** *f.*)

larghẹtto *adj. dim., n.m.* See under **largo**.

larghẹzza *f.* width, breadth; diameter; largeness; size; (fig.) open-handedness, generosity, liberality; usare —, to be generous, to give generously; abundance; amplitude; †permission; †— poetica, poetic licence.

larg-ire [D2] *tr.* to grant, to bestow; to free. **-imẹnto** *m.* granting; freeing. †**-ità** *f.* width, breadth; liberality, munificence. **-ito** *part. adj.* granted, bestowed; freed. **-itọre** *m.* bestower. (**-itrice** *f.*) **-iziọne** *f.* bestowal, granting; donation, gift.

lar-go *adj.* (*pl.* **-ghi**) wide, broad, large, vast, extensive; — venti metri, twenty metres wide; ample; gonna -ga, full skirt; — di spalle, broad-shouldered; su -ga scala, on a large scale; il mondo è —, there is room in the world for everybody, (or) go somewhere else; di manica -ga, easy-going; (art) dipingere a -ghi tratti, fare —, to paint in broad outline, to give a general impression; (mus.) broad, sustained, slow; (naut.) out at sea, offshore, far from the shore; vento —, wind on the quarter; liberal, generous; abundant, plentiful, copious; *n.m.* width, breadth; wide space; widening in a street; open space, square; prendere il —, to clear off; far —, to make way, to make room; farsi —, to make headway; in lungo e in —, in all directions, on all sides, far and wide; open sea; (naut.) vento dal —, wind off the sea; al — di, off...; tredici miglia al —, thirteen miles out to sea; (mus.) Largo, a broad sustained slow movement; *adv.* widely, broadly; cavalcar —, to

lar·go (*cont.*)
straddle; generously, amply; (mus.) broadly, in a sustained manner, slowly; *excl.* make way!, mind your backs!; *adv. phr.* alla -ga, at a distance, far apart, at arm's length; alla -ga da...!, keep away from...!; parlare alla -ga, to talk in a roundabout way. -ga·mente *adv.* widely, broadly, extensively, amply; liberally, generously, profusely; copiously, plentifully; (agric.) potare —, to prune lightly. -ghetto *adj. dim.* of **largo**; rather wide, etc.; *n.m.* (mus.) Larghetto, a movement which is not quite so sustained as a Largo; widening of a street, small square. -goc·cio *adj.* rather wide, rather large, roomy. †-gume *m.* broad space. -gura *f.* open space; wide extent.

lari *m.pl.* lares, household gods of ancient Rome; (fig., *usu. sing.*) home.

la·rice *m.* (bot.) larch, *Larix decidua*.

lari·cio *m.* (bot.) Corsican pine, *Pinus nigra*, sp. *laricio*.

laring-e *f.* (anat.) larynx. -ite *f.* laryngitis. -ismo *m.* (med.) laryngismus. -ologi·a *f.* laryngology. -olo·gico *adj.* laryngological. -o·logo *m.* laryngologist. -oscopi·a *f.* laryngoscopy. -osco·pico *adj.* laryngoscopical. -osco·pio *m.* laryngoscope. -otomi·a *f.* laryngotomy. -o·tomo *m.* laryngotome.

larin·geo *adj.* (anat.) laryngeal, relating to the larynx.

larv-a *f.* spectre, shade; (theatr.) mask; (zool.) larva. -ale *adj.* (zool.) larval. -are [A 1] *tr.* to mask; to disguise. -ato *adj.* masked; disguised; in modo -ato, disguisedly. (-ata·mente *adv.*) -i·cola *f.* (ent.) parasitoid.

lasagn-a *f.* (usu. *pl.*) broad strips of macaroni; nuotar nelle -e, to be rolling in money; aspettare a bocca aperta le -e, to expect good fortune to drop into one's mouth. -a·io *m.* maker or seller of 'lasagne'. -ino *adj.* (agric.) broad-leaved (of a type of cabbage). -one *m. augm.* of **lasagna**; (joc.) large, clumsy and stupid individual.

lasca *f.* (ichth.) *Chondrostoma genei*, beaked carp; (fig.) sano come una —, fit as a fiddle; *pr.n.m.* (lit. hist.) pseudonym of A. F. Grazzini, founder of the Accademia degli Umidi (1540), out of which the Accademia della Crusca was developed.

lascare [A 2] *tr.* to slacken (a rope, etc.).

lasciapassare *m. indecl.* pass, permit.

lasci-are [A 3] *tr.* **1.** To LEAVE, to quit, to go away from; — il paese, to leave the country; — casa, — la sua casa, to leave home; — il suo posto, to leave one's job. **2.** To ABANDON, to desert, to forsake, to leave; — la moglie, to desert one's wife; — in asso, to leave in the lurch; to jilt; — la famiglia sul lastrico, to abandon one's family in the gutter; -ò la moglie e tre bambini, he left a wife and three children (on dying); il buon umore non lo -a mai, he is unfailingly good-tempered; questa tosse non mi vuole —, I can't get rid of this cough. **3.** To LEAVE UNTOUCHED, to leave on one side, to save, to keep; -ami una fetta del dolce, leave me a piece of cake; hai -ato molte immondizie in cucina, you've left a lot of things to be cleared away in the kitchen. **4.** To LEAVE BEHIND, to forget; ho -ato l'ombrello, I've left my umbrella behind; — l'impronta, to leave a mark; — l'odore, to leave a smell; — parecchi dettagli, to leave out several details; — con, to leave in the care of; — in casa, to leave at home. **5.** To LEAVE OFF, to give up, to interrupt, to stop; — la carriera, to give up one's career; — le speranze, to give up hope; — gli scrupoli, to abandon scruples; — in tronco, to cut short. **6.** To LEAVE, to bequeath; ha -ato un bel patrimonio, he left a tidy fortune; — per testamento, to leave in one's will; ha -ato tutto ai poveri, he left everything to the poor. **7.** To LEAVE ALONE, to let be; -alo stare, leave him alone; — in pace, to leave in peace. **8.** To ENTRUST, to leave, to give; mi hanno -ato troppo da fare, they have left too much for me to do; ha -ato una lettera per te, he has left a letter for you; — detto che, to leave word that; -a fare a me, leave it to me. **9.** WITH ADVERBIAL PHRASES: — in dubbio, to leave in doubt; — in sospeso, to leave in suspense; — in dono, to leave as a present; — in libertà, to set free; — fuori, to leave out, to omit, to exclude. **10** To LOSE; -arci la vita, to lose one's life; ci -ò una gamba, he lost a leg (in the war, by so doing, etc.); to drop; -ò il capo della fune, he dropped the end of the rope; to slacken, to let droop. **11.** To PERMIT, to allow; vivere e — vivere, live and let live; -alo parlare, let him speak; -ami indovinare, let me guess; -ate che se ne vada, let him go away; — posare il liquido due ore, let the liquid stand for two hours; — passare la luce, to show light, to be transparent; — cadere, to drop, to let fall (cf. under No. 10); — andare, to let things

slide; — andar di bocca una parola, to let a word slip out; — fare, to let things alone; — molto a desiderare, to leave much to be desired. **12.** To CEASE, to stop; -a di molestarmi!, stop annoying me!; -ò di frequentare le taverne, he gave up hanging around pubs. **13.** *rfl.* To PERMIT ONESELF, to allow oneself; -arsi persuadere, to be persuaded; -arsi andare, to neglect one's health and appearance, to let oneself go; -arsi vedere, to put in an appearance, to be seen out and about; *recip. rfl.* to separate, to part, to leave each other. †-amento *m.* see **lascito**. -ato *part. adj.* left; deserted; untouched.

†**lasci·bile** *adj.* see **lascivo**.

†**la·scio¹** *m.* bequest; legacy; will, testament.

†**la·sc·io²** *m.* lead, leading-string, leash. †-ità *f.* weakness, laxity.

la·scito *m.* (leg.) legacy; bequest (of personal property); devise (of real property) (C.C.).

†**lascivanza** *f.* See **lascivia**.

lasci·v-ia *f.* lasciviousness, sensuousness, licentiousness; *pl.* caresses. -iente *adj.* lascivious, lecherous. -ire [D 2] *intr.* (*aux.* avere) to be lascivious.

lasciv-o *adj.* lascivious; dissolute; wanton; lustful; †frivolous, light, gay; †pleasing, delightful, ornamental. -a·mente *adv.* lasciviously; lustfully. -ità *f.* lasciviousness, wantonness.

las-co *adj.* (*m.pl.* -chi) slack, lax, loose-fitting; (of a wind) slight; terreno —, light, broken soil that is soon covered with grass and weeds; (naut.) ricuperare i -chi, to take in the slack; di gran —, wind abaft the beam; (eng.) clearance.

la·ser-o *m.* (bot.) — odoroso, *Laserpitium gallicum*. -pi·zio *m.* (bot.) *Laserpitium* (genus).

lassa *f.* (Romance prosod.) *laisse*; †leash, lead.

†**lassare¹** *tr.* to weary, to fatigue, to tire.

†**lassare²** *vb.* and derivs. See **lasciare**.

lassativo *adj.*, *n.m.* laxative.

lass-o¹ *adj.* tired, weary; slack; (mus.) corda -a, slack string; unhappy, wretched, 'down'; *excl.* ahi, —!, alas! alack! -ezza *f.* weariness, tiredness. -ismo *m.* (eccl. hist.) laxism. -ista *m.* (eccl. hist.) laxist. -itu·dine *f.* lassitude, weariness; languor; (med.) exhaustion.

lasso² *m.* lapse; — di tempo, interval, period, lapse of time.

lass-ù *adv.* up there, above; there above; (poet.) il furor di —, the northern (Teuton) fury. †-uso *adv.* see **lassù**.

lastr-a *f.* slab, sheet, plate; paving-stone, flagstone; una — di ghiaccio, a slab of ice; glass pane; (photog.) plate, glass negative; (eng.) — di fondamento, sole plate. -ai(u)olo *m.* pavior. -are [A 1] *tr.* to stow (a ship's cargo); to load with ballast of stone slabs; to rub down (e.g. paintwork, etc.). -ato *part. adj.* -atore *f.*) -atura *f.* stowing; rubbing down; (motor eng.) body-metal working. -one *m. augm.* of **lastra**; slab; sheer face of rock; stone for closing the opening of an oven; (Flor., vulg.) dare il deretano sul -one, to be stony broke.

lastric-are [A 2s] *tr.* to pave; to pave with stones, to flag, to slate, to tile; (fig.) — la via a uno, to pave the way for someone. -amento *m.* paving; tiling (i.e. the process). -ato *part. adj.* paved; flagged; tiled; aver la gola -ata, 'to have a cast-iron gullet' (i.e. to be able to drink things very hot); la via dell'inferno è -ata di buone intenzioni, the way to Hell is paved with good intentions; *n.m.* paving; tiling (i.e. the surface). (-atore *m.*) -atura *f.* paving; tiling (i.e. the surface, process or cost).

la·stri-co *m.* (*pl.* -chi, -ci) pavement, paving; (fig.) sul —, in the gutter, on one's beam ends; — solare, sun-terrace, solarium.

lastrone *m.* See under **lastra**.

lata *f.* (naut.). See **latta**.

latamente *adv.* See under **lato²**.

late·br-a, **la·tebr-a** *f.* (poet.) hiding-place; recess; hidden depths. -oso *adj.* full of hiding-places.

latente *adj.* latent; dormant; potential; hidden, obscure. -ente·mente *adv.* latently; dormantly; obscurely.

lateral-e *adj.* side; lateral; carrozzino —, side-car; (rugby) rimessa —, line-out; (football, rugby) throw-in from touch; *n.m.* (football) — destro, right-half; — sinistro, left-half. -mente *adv.* laterally, at the side.

Lateran-o *pr.n.m.*, *adj.* Lateran. -ense *adj.* (Basilica, Canon) of the Lateran; concilio -ense, Lateran council.

later·colo *m.* (geom.) infinitely small side of imaginary polygon representing a circle; small brick.

†**la·tere¹** *intr.* to lie hidden, to be concealed.

la·tere[2] *adv. phr.* (Lat.) (hist.; eccl.) *a latere*; (fig.) essere a — di uno, to be always at someone's side; *n.m.* inseparable companion.

laterite *f.* (geol.) laterite.

lateri·zio *adj.* made of terracotta, earthenware, brick; *n.m.pl.* earthenware, bricks, tiles; fabbrica di laterizi, brick-kiln.

†latezza *f.* See **latitudine**.

lati·bolo *m.* hiding-place; lair, den.

†la·tica *f.* (med.) slight recurrent daily fever.

la·tic-e *m.* latex. **-i·fero** *adj.* containing latex.

lati-cla·vio *m.* (Rom. antiq.) broad purple band on the tunic worn by Roman senators; concedere il — a, to appoint senator; *adj.* having a purple band. **-fo·lio** *adj.* (bot.) broad-leaved. **-fondo** *m.* (leg.) latifundium; extensive landed estate (essentially undercultivated). **-fondista** *m.* large landowner (of such an estate).

latin-o *adj.* Latin; Roman; (naut.) lateen; clear, plain, intelligible; †easy; †— di bocca, foul-mouthed; †skilled, expert; †broad, of easy access; *n.m.* Latin; saper di —, to know a little Latin; to have some Latin; il — volgare, vulgar Latin; il — ecclesiastico, church Latin; il basso —, low Latin; — di sagrestia, dog Latin; — maccheronico, macaronic Latin; language; lingua franca; (fig.) capire il —, to take a hint; incomprehensible jargon; †discourse; †doctrine; †Roman, inhabitant of Latium, Latin. **-ag·gine** *f.* (joc.) Latin. **-amente** *adv.* in Latin, after the Latin fashion; clearly; easily. **-amento** *m.* fellmongering; liming of sheepskins. **-ante** *adj.* studying or speaking Latin. **-are** [A I] *tr.* to line (sheepskins); to fellmonger; †*intr.* to talk in Latin; to study Latin. **-eggiare** [A 3 c] *intr.* (aux. avere) to use Latin constructions in writing a modern language. **-eri·a** *f.* (joc.; iron.) the Latin world (usu. of the Roman Church). **-i·geno** *adj.* derived from Latin. **-ismo** *m.* Latinism. **-ista** *m., f.* Latinist, Latin scholar; humanist. **-ità** *f.* Latinity; Latin writers; the Latin language; bassa -ità, popular Latin, low Latin. **-izzamento** *m.* Latinizing. **-izzare** [A I] *tr.* to translate into Latin; to Latinize; *intr.* (aux. avere) to use Latinisms; *rfl.* to become Latinized; to adopt Roman civilization or Latin culture. **-izzato** *part. adj.* Latinized. (**-izzatore** *m.* **-izzatrice** *f.*) **-obar·baro** *m.* barbarous Latin. **-oitaliano** *m.* Italianized Latin. **-orum** *m.* (joc.) Latin, 'Latinorum'. **-uc·cio** *m.* simple Latin, elementary Latin; exercise in Latin composition; essere ai -ucci, to be at the beginning of the study of grammar.

la·tir-o *m.* (bot.) — silvestre, narrow-leaved everlasting pea, *Lathyrus sylvestris*. **-ismo** *m.* (med.) lathyrism.

latit-are [A I] *intr.* (aux. avere) (leg.) to abscond; to hide from justice. **-ante** *part. adj.* latitant; absconding; hiding from justice; rendersi -ante, to abscond; *n.m.* fugitive from justice. **-anza** *f.* (leg.) absence to avoid arrest, latitancy (C.P.). **-azione** *f.* (leg.) latitation.

latitu·din-e *f.* width; latitude; breadth; extension; comprehensiveness; tolerance; (provb.) l'uomo vive sotto tutte le -i, man lives in all climates and conditions. **-ale** *adj.* latitudinal, of latitude. **-a·rio** *adj., n.m.* (rel.) latitudinarian.

lato[1] *m.* side; part; faction; flank; dai due lati, on both sides; da un —, dall'altro —, on the one hand, on the other; in ogni —, everywhere; dal — mio, for my part; al — di, beside; dormire sul — destro, to sleep on one's right side.

lat-o[2] *adj.* broad, wide; extensive; in senso —, in a broad sense, broadly speaking. **-amente** *adv.* broadly, in a wide sense. **-ezza** *f.* breadth, width, broadness.

latoflessione *f.* (med.) lateral flexion (usu. of the uterus).

lat-omi·a, -o·mia *f.* the stone or marble quarries at Syracuse used in ancient times as prisons.

latore *m.* bearer (of a letter).

latr-are [A I] *intr.* (aux. avere) to bark; to howl. **-amento** *m.* barking; howling. **-ato** *m.* bark; howl. **-atore** *m.* barker; howler; grumbler; maligner. (**-atrice** *f.*)

latre·a *f.* (bot.) toothwort, *Lathraea squamaria*.

latr-e·utico *adj.* (theol.) latreutic. **-i·a** *f.* (theol.) latria (worship given to God alone; cf. **dulia, iperdulia**).

latrin-a *f.* public lavatory, latrine; cesspool, sewer. **-a·io** *m.* lavatory attendant.

latroci·nio *m.* theft, larceny.

†latrocino *adj.* abominable.

latt-a[1] *f.* tinplate, tinned sheet iron; tin can; in -e, tinned; (naut.) deck plating beam. **-iera** *f.* tinplate factory. **-one** *m.* reflector for use with a spit; sheet brass. **-oniere** *m.* tinsmith; brass worker.

latt-a[2] *f.*, **-one** *m.*, **-onata** *f.* (Tusc.) a blow, crushing a person's hat in.

latta·gogo *m.* See **galattagogo**.

latt-a·io *adj.* milk-producing; *n.m.* milkman, dairyman; tinsmith. **-ai(u)ola** *f.* (bot.) milk cap, saffron milk cap, *Lactarius deliciosus*, an edible fungus; also various plants with milky juice. **-ai(u)olo** *adj.* dente -aiuolo, milk tooth; *n.m.* milk tooth; sort of saffron cake; (bot.) see **lattaiuola**. **-a·mide** *m.* (chem.) lactam.

latt-are [A I] *tr.* to suckle, to breast feed; *intr.* (aux. avere), *tr.* to suck. **-ante** *adj., n.m., f.* suckling. **-aşi** *f.* (chem.) lactase. **-ato** *part. adj.* suckled, breast-fed; beaten up in milk; milk-white; (bot.) fiore -ato, orange blossom; *n.m.* (chem.) lactate. **-atrice** *f.* nursing mother; wet nurse. **-azione** *f.* lactation; breast-feeding.

latt-a·ria *f.*, **-a·rio** *m.* (bot.) see **lattaiuola**, under **lattaio**. **-aro** *m.* (zool.) *Solenocurtus strigilatus*, an edible bivalve mollusc. **-aruolo** *m.* see **lattaiolo**, under **lattaio**.

latt-e *m.* milk; — acido, sour milk; — sciolto, watery milk; febbre del —, milk fever; dare il — a, to breast feed; levare il — a, to wean; figliuolo di —, foster-child; fratello di —, foster-brother; denti di —, milk teeth; vitello di —, sucking-calf; avere il — alla bocca, to be still very young; — concentrato, — condensato, condensed milk; — in polvere, powdered milk; — umanizzato, humanized milk; mosca nel —, the nigger in the wood-pile, the fly in the ointment; (cul.) fiore di —, a kind of 'mozzarella', q.v.; fiore del —, cream; — scremato, — spannato, skimmed milk, separated milk; (of meat) è un —, it is tender, it is very white; (of a person) essere — e sangue, to have a very pink and white complexion; far venire il — alle ginocchia a, to bore, to be a nuisance to; essere tutto — e miele, to be full of honeyed words; — di gallina, yoke of eggs beaten up with milk and flavoured with cognac or rum; (joc.) il — dei vecchi, wine; (bot.) — di gallina, Star of Bethlehem, *Ornithogalum umbellatum*; (ichth.) — di pesce, milt, fish semen, soft roe; aringhe di —, male herrings; (astron.) Via di —, Milky Way; (miner.) pietra di —, galactite; — di luna, agaric mineral; succhiare col —, to drink in with one's mother's milk, to be brought up to believe; money given in charity to a poor mother without milk for her baby to pay for a wet nurse; mezzo —, half the wages of a wet nurse; (bot.) latex, milky juice. **-eggiante** *adj.* milky. **-eggiare** [A 3 c] *intr.* (aux. avere) to be milky; *tr.* (paint.) to lighten (a colour) by going over it with a dry brush. **-emiele** *m.* (Lomb.) whipped cream; (fig.) honeyed words. **-eri·a** *f.* dairy, milk-shop. **-erino** *m.* (ichth.) atherine, sand smelt; -erino sardaro, *Atherina hepsetus*; -erino comune, *A. boyeri*. **-er(u)ola** *f.* (bot.) see **lattaiuola**, under **lattaio**. **-escente** *adj.* lactescent. **-escenza** *f.* lactescence. **-ic·cio** *m.* (pop.) see **latice**. **-ici·fero** *adj.* see **laticifero**. **-ici·nio** *m.* dairy product. **-icino** *m.* (pop.) see **latticinio**. **-icinoşo** *adj.* see **lattiginoso**. **-icre·polo** *m.* (bot.) *Picridium vulgare*. **-ide** *f.* (chem.) lactide, lactic anhydride. **-iera** *f.* milk-jug; dairy, buttery. **-i·fero** *adj.* lactiferous; milk-producing; (bot.) lactiferous. **-ifi·cio** *m.* (bot.) latex. **-i·fugo** *adj.* (*pl.* -i·fughi) (med.) lactifuge. **-i·geno** *adj.* milk-producing. **-iginoşo** *adj.* milky; lactiferous; (bot.) see **lattifero**. **-ime** *m.* (med.) milk-scab. **-imoşo** *adj.* suffering from milk-scab. **-işmo** *m.* (med.) quickening, felt movement of foetus. **-ista** *m.* (agric.) believer in the use of milk of lime for combating mildew. **-ite** *f.* casein plastic. **-ivendolo** *m.* milkman. **†-i·zio** *m.* see **lattizzo**. **-izzo** *m.* skin of a sucking animal. **-odensi·metro, -o·metro** *m.* milk hydrometer, lactometer, lactoscope. **-onzo(lo)** *m.* suckling; sucking-pig; sucking-calf. **-osco·pio** *m.* lactoscope. **-o·şio** *m.* (chem.) lactose, milk sugar. **-oşo** *adj.* abounding in milk. **†-ume** *m.* see **lattime**.

lat·te-o *adj.* milky; dieta -a, milk diet; (med.) crosta -a, milk-scab; febbre -a, milk fever; (astron.) Via -a, Milky Way.

lat·tico *adj.* (chem.) lactic; fermenti lattici, lactic ferments (remedy for stomach upsets).

lattiera[1] *f.* See under **latte**.

lattiera[2] *f.* See inder **latta**[1].

latton-e[1] *m., f.*, **-iere** *m.* See under **latta**[1].

latton-e[2] *m., f.*, **-ata** *f.* See under **latta**[2].

lattone[3] *m.* (chem.) lactone; *pl.* milk left over in a dairy; *adj.* sucking.

latt-onzo *m.*, **-onzolo** *m.*, **-osco·pio** *m.*, **-o·şio** *m.*, **-oşo** *adj.* See under **latte**.

†lattovaro *m.* (pharm.) electuary.

lattuc-a *f.* (pharm.) lactucarium, inspissated latex of *Lactuca virosc*. **-a·rio** *m.* (pharm.) lactucarium, lettuce opium, i.e. the dried latex of *L. virosa*.

lattug-a *f.* (bot.) lettuce, *Lactuca sativa* and other species; — montana, *Prenanthes purpurea*; — ranina, curled pondweed, *Potamogeton crispus*; — velenosa, — virosa, *Lactuca virosa*; acqua di —, lettuce water; (hist. costume) ruff. **-ac·cio** *m.* (bot.) *Chondrilla juncea* and *Urospermum dalechampii*. **-ọne** *m.* (bot.) teasel, *Dipsacus fullonum*.

la·ud-a (*pl.* -e), **la·ud-e** (*pl.* -i) *f.* (lit. hist.) lauda, spiritual poem (in ballad-like form); *pl.* (liturg.) le -i, lauds; (mus.) -e, -i spirituali, hymns of praise, non-liturgical religious hymns in ballad metre sung by the Umbrian flagellants of the thirteenth century; polyphonic hymns sung at spiritual conferences at the Oratory of St Philip Neri; -e, lauds; (pedag.) dieci con -e, full marks and commended. **-a·bile** *adj.* (poet.) praiseworthy. **-are** [A I a] *tr.* (poet.) see **lodare**. **-a·rio** *m.* collection of sacred 'laude'; (mus.) collection of 'laude spirituali'. **-ativo, -ato·rio** *adj.* (poet.) laudatory. **-ẹse** *m.* member of confraternity for singing 'laude'; writer of 'laude'; (mus.) singer of 'laude spirituali'. **-ista** *m.* (mus.) singer or composer of 'laude spirituali'.

la·udano *m.* (pharm.) laudanum.

laude·mio *m.* (leg.) premium, fine or consideration paid to renew or acquire a lease or possession (C.C.).

laud-ẹse *adj.*, **-ista** *m.* See under **lauda**.

†**la·udo** *m.* award; arbitrament.

laumontite *f.* (miner.) laumontite.

La·ura¹ *pr.n.f.* Laura.

la·ura² *f.* (Christian archaeol.) laura.

laurato *m.* (chem.) laurate.

la·ure-a *f.* University degree; diploma; doctorate; prendere la —, to take a degree; laurel wreath. **-ando** *m.* candidate for the 'laurea'. **-are** [A 6] *tr.* to crown with laurels; to confer a degree upon; *rfl.* to graduate, to take a University degree; -arsi in lettere, to take an arts degree. **-ato** *part. adj.* possessing a University degree; wearing a laurel crown; laureate; *n.m.* graduate; -ato in legge, bachelor of law. **-azione** *f.* degree ceremony; graduation; crowning with laurel.

lauren·tico *adj.* (geol.) Lawrentian.

laurenzian-o *adj.* (basilica, canons) of St Laurence (Florence); of Lorenzo (de' Medici); Biblioteca -a, Laurentian Library (Florence); (geol.) Lawrentian. **-a** *pr.n.f.* the Laurentian Library (Florence); (bot.) *Inula Britannica* (not a British plant in spite of its name).

la·ureo *adj.* laurel; relating to the bay-tree.

laure·ola¹ *f.* (bot.) — alpina, *Daphne alpina*; — nana, *Daphne Cneorum*.

†**laure·ola²** *f.* See **aureola**.

lauretano *adj.* (geog.) of Loreto; *n.m.* native of Loreto.

la·ur-ico *adj.* (chem.) lauric. **-i·como** *adj.* (poet.) wearing a laurel crown, crowned with bay. **-i·fero** *adj.* abounding in laurel. **-i·gero** *adj.* garlanded with laurel. **-ina** *f.* (chem.) laurin. **-ino** *adj.* (of) laurel. **-ipotente** *adj.*, *pr.n.m.* 'lord of laurel' (epithet of Apollo). **-oce·raso** *m.* (bot.) cherry laurel, *Prunus laurocerasus*. **-ospinọsa** *f.* (bot.) holly, *Ilex aquifolium*. **-otino** *m.* (bot.) laurustinus, *Viburnum tinus*.

la·ur-o *m.* (bot.) laurel, bay tree, *Laurus nobilis*. **-ẹto** *m.* laurel copse, laurel grove.

la·ut-o *adj.* sumptuous, splendid; lavish; bountiful; handsome; una -a mancia, a generous tip. **-amẹnte** *adv.* sumptuously; lavishly; generously, handsomely. **-ẹzza** *f.* sumptuousness; lavishness; abundance; generosity.

lava *f.* lava; paving-stone made of lava.

lavabiancheri·a *m. indecl.* See under **lavare**.

lava·bil-e *adj.*, **-ità** *f.* See under **lavare**.

lavabo *m. indecl.* (liturg.) lavabo (versicle or part of Mass; basin in sacristy); (liturg.) altar-card (with words of lavabo); wash-hand basin; washing-place.

lavacapo *m. indecl.* See under **lavare**.

lavacro *m.* bath; water for irrigation; (colloq.) drink, swill; wash; washing; (theol.) laver (of baptism); cleansing; washing (away, of guilt); (poet.) fount.

lavag·gio *m.* washing (earth for gold, etc.); washing (a ship's decks); (text.) washing; washing of clothes; cleansing; — a secco, dry cleaning.

lavagn-a *f.* (miner.) slate; blackboard; school slate. **-ino, -ọso** *adj.* slaty, scaly, shaly.

lav·anda¹, -an·dula *f.* (bot.) lavender, *Lavandula*.

lavanda² *f.* See under **lavare**.

lavandino *m.* washbasin.

lav-are [A I] *tr.* to wash; to clean; to wash down; (provb.) una mano -a l'altra e tutt'e due -ano il viso, many hands make light work; — i piatti, to wash up; — il capo a, to reprove; to 'tell off'; — la testa all'asino, to do something for someone who will not appreciate it; — la bocca d'uno, see under **bocca**; (theol.) to cleanse, to wash (the soul); to wash away (sin); *intr.* (aux. avere) to do the washing; to be a washerwoman, to take in washing; *rfl.* (acc. of prn. 'si') to wash (oneself); to be watered (of land, by a river); (dat. of prn. 'si') -arsi le mani, to wash one's hands. **-abiancheri·a** *m. indecl.* washing-machine. **-a·bile** *adj.* washable; *n.m.* (slang) dirty dog, scoundrel. **-abilità** *f.* washability. **-abotti·glie** *m. indecl.* bottle-washer. **-acapo** *m. indecl.* scolding, 'telling off'. **-amano, -amani** *m. indecl.* washstand. **-anda** *f.* thorough wash; (med.) wash-out; (liturg.) maundy, *mandatum*, washing of the feet on Maundy Thursday. **-anda·ia** *f.* washerwoman, laundress; (med.) ginocchio della -andaia, sinovitis, housemaid's knee. **-anda·io** *m.* laundryman. **-andaro** *m.* see **lavandaio**. **-anderi·a** *f.* laundry; washhouse. **-apiatti** *m. indecl.* dish-washer, washing-up machine. **-arello** *m.* (naut.) breakwater dwarf bulkhead. **-ascodelle** *m. indecl.* (Tusc.) scullery-hand, dishwasher. **-ata** *f.* wash; wash down; -ata di capo, shampoo, hairwash, (colloq.) scolding. **-ativo** *m.* enema; injection; good-for-nothing person; badly made or badly worn utensil. **-ato** *part. adj.* washed; (Tusc.) pane -ato, bread soaked in water and served with oil and vinegar. **-atọio** *m.* public washhouse; wash-tub; washing-board; place for dipping sheep, sheep-dip. **-atrice** *f.* washing-machine. **-atura** *f.* washing; dishwater; -atura di ceci, bad coffee; -atura di piatti, weak, watery soup.

laveggio *m.* saucepan, casserole.

lavello *m.* blacksmith's tempering bath.

lavẹtta *f.* (mil. hist.) limber box.

la·vico *adj.* (of) lava, resembling lava.

lavin-a *f.* landslide; avalanche. **-ale** *adj.* relating to, or formed by, a landslide.

lavor-are [A I c] *tr.*, *intr.* (aux. avere) to work; — a giornata, to work by the day; — a cottimo, to do piece-work; fare —, to employ, to give work to; — di falegname, to be a carpenter; — d'intaglio, to do intaglio work; — di fine, to do fine work; to labour; to toil; to drudge; to be employed; to be active; to apply oneself; to study; to operate; — la terra, to till the soil; — di ganasce, to eat greedily; — di mani e piedi, to fidget; — sott'acqua, to work secretly, to be underhand; — di mano, to steal; — a mano, to do manual work; — di schiena, to do back-breaking work, to put one's back into one's work; — uno, -arsi uno, to win someone over; — addosso a uno, to speak ill of someone; (naut.) to work (of a ship or rope); to drag (of an anchor); to work, to function; (eng.) to come into play; to work on, to manipulate; to make; to repair; — intorno a, — a, to work on, to work at. **-a·bile** *adj.* that may be worked or worked on; operable; workable. **-abilità** *f.* workability. **-acchiare** [A 4] *intr.* (aux. avere) to work roughly, to work in a slapdash fashion, to botch. **-ante** *part. adj.* working; bovi -anti, plough-oxen, draught-oxen; *n.m.* worker, workman, hand; (joc.) -ante a spasso, unemployed person. **-ata** *f.* job of work, batch of work, process. **-ati·o, -ativo** *adj.* arable; (techn.) ciclo -ativo, operational cycle; workable; giornate -ative, working days. **-ato** *part. adj.* worked; fine; treated, processed, purified; adorned; finished; cultivated; arranged, 'worked'; un affare -ato, a put-up job; *n.m.* finished work; cultivated land. **-atọre** *m.* worker; labourer; (leg.) -atore autonomo, independent worker; -atore subordinato, employed worker (C.C.). (-atọra, -atrice *f.*) **-atọ·rio** *m.* workshop. **-atura** *f.* processing, working. **-azione** *f.* processing, treatment, working, manufacture; in -azione, in work, in the course of manufacture; di facile -azione, easy to work; (eng.; metall.) rame di facile -azione, high-speed brass. **-icchiare** [A 4] *intr.* (aux. avere) to do light work, to work a little. **-io** *m.* (*pl.* -ii) constant work; intense toil; (geol.) constant action (e.g. of water); intrigue. **-ucchiare** [A 4] *intr.* (aux. avere) to do very little work.

lavọr-o *m.* work; mettersi al —, to set to work; abile al —, good at one's work; — di braccio, labour, labouring; — di mano, manual work; — straordinario, overtime; eccesso di —, overwork; legname da —, wood for joining or carpentry; stanza da —, study; bestia da —, draught animal; task, job in hand, work

lavor-o (*cont.*)
 undertaken; workmanship; che bel —!, what beautiful work!; finished work; autore di parecchi -i, author of several works; — in legno, woodwork; — d'ago, needlework; — fantasia, fancy work; labour, toil; (geog.) Terra di Lavoro, Campania; (phys.) work; (bricklaying) bond; gruppo di —, working party; relazione sullo stato dei -i, progress report; documento di —, working paper; lingue di —, working languages (e.g. at a Congress); (leg.) — domestico, domestic service; — ad economia, job done on cost of labour and materials at owner's risk; i rapporti di —, labour relations (C.C.); (naut.) purchase, tackle, block, system of blocks; work, affair, operation, business; (leg.) -i forzati, hard labour; -i preparativi, preparatory work (of Act of Parliament, Treaty, etc.). **-eccio** *m.* (agric.) light tilling. **-ieri** *m.pl.* permanent eel-fishing installations at the mouths of rivers and canals.

La·zi-o *pr.n.m.* (hist.; geog.) Latium; province of Rome. **-ale** *adj.* of Latium, Latin; *pr.n.f.* a Rome football team.

lazz-a *f.* landslide; see **lazzo**. **-are** [A I] see under **lazzo**.

Laz·zar-o *pr.n.m.* (Bibl.) Lazarus, the beggar; Lazarus, the brother of Mary and Martha; (fig.) leper; beggar. **-etto** *m.* fever hospital; quarantine station. **-ista** *m.* (eccl.) Lazarist; *sing.* rascal, wretch, good-for-nothing, lazy and slovenly individual. **-onata** *f.* action characteristic of a 'lazzarone', q.v. **-oni** *m.pl.* (hist.) name given by the Spaniards to the lower classes in Naples.

lazzaruolo *m.* (bot.). See **lazzeruolo**.

lazzeron-e *m.* (rel., Tusc.) funeral responsory. **-are** [A I c] *intr.* (*aux.* avere) (rel., Tusc.) to sing the funeral responsory.

lazzer(u)ol-o *m.* (bot.) Neapolitan medlar, *Crataegus azarolus*. **-a** *f.* fruit of same.

lazz-o[1] *m.* quip, jest, gibe; drollery; tenere il —, reggere al —, to take a joke, *or* to give as good as one gets; *pl.* (theatr.) buffoonery and jokes improvised in the Commedia dell'Arte and also in interludes of regular comedies, chiefly associated with 'Zanni' and 'Pantaloon'. **-are** [A I] *intr.* (*aux.* avere) to quip. **†-eggiare** *vb.* and derivs. see **lazzare**.

lazz-o[2] *adj.* sour, tart, sharp, harsh in taste; bitter. **-ezza** *f.* sourness, tartness, sharpness of taste.

†lazzo[3] *m.* See **laccio**.

lazzulite *f.* (miner.) lazurite.

le[1] *def. art. f.pl.* the.

le[2] *pers. prn. f. pl. conj. acc.* them.

le[3] *pers. prn. f. sing. conj. dat.* to her, her; to you.

†le[4] *prn. m. sing. dat.* See **gli** or **loro**.

lea[1] *f.* (geog.) mud, mire.

lea[2] *f.* (Pavia) avenue of trees.

†lea[3] *f.* lioness.

leagno *m.* (bot.) *Elaeagnus angustifolia*.

leal-e *adj.* true, sincere, honest, trustworthy; †legal. **-mente** *adv.* loyally; faithfully; truly. **-ismo** *m.* loyalty to the crown. **-tà** *f.* loyalty, faithfulness, trustworthiness; (leg.) fidelity (C.C.).

Leandro[1] *pr.n.m.* (myth.) Leander.

leandro[2] *m.* (bot.) oleander, *Nerium oleander*.

†leanza *f.* loyalty; fidelity.

leardo *adj.* dapple grey.

lea·tico (bot.) *m.* See **labbio**.

leb·bio *m.* (bot.) dwarf elder, danewort, *Sambucus ebulus*.

lebbr-a, lebbr-a *f.* leprosy; (fig.) scourge, plague, evil; (vet.) farcy. **-olina** *f.* skin eruption, eczema. **-osa·rio** *m.* leper hospital. **-osi·a** *f.* leprosy. **-oso** *adj.* leprous, suffering from leprosy; *n.m.* leper.

lebe *m.* (Pascoli). See **lebete**.

lebete *m.* (archaeol.) metal urn.

†lebra *f.* See **lebbra**.

lebrica *f.* shrimping net, crab net.

leca·nico *adj.* (chem.) lecanoric.

lecan-omante *m.* lecanomant. **-omanzi·a** *f.* lecanomancy. **-o·metro** *m.* pelvimeter.

lecc-are [A 2 c] *tr.* to lick; to lap; il cane -ava la mano al padrone, the dog licked its master's hand; to skim; (fig.) to flatter, to 'butter up'; to finish off carefully, to overpolish; to graze; (paint) to brush lightly, to paint with very light brush-strokes; *rfl.* (*acc.* of *prn.* 'si') to lick oneself; to lick one's wounds; (fig.) to spruce oneself up, to titivate oneself; (*dat.* of *prn.* 'si') -arsi le labbra, to lick one's lips. **-amento** *m.* licking; flattery. **-a** *m.* slight slap, brush, flip; (fam.) fop. **-apiatt(in)i** *m., f. indecl.* glutton; guzzler; parasite; mean servant. **-apiedi** *m. indecl.*

cringing flatterer. **-arda** *f.* drip pan, basting pan; (eng.) oil pan, drip pan. **-asanti** *m. indecl.* overpious or mock-pious person. **-ascodelle** *m. indecl.* parasite; sponger, scrounger. **-asporte** *m. indecl.* glutton. **-ata** *f.* lick; skimming. **-atina** *f. dim.* graze, brush, flick; small profit, 'tear-off', 'rake-off'. **-ato** *part. adj.* licked; grazed; flicked; affected; stilted; stile -ato, laboured style; (paint.) painted overcarefully, or in too minute detail. **-amente** *adv.* affectedly; labouredly. **-atore** *m.* licker; parasite; glutton; servile flatterer; (leg.) leccator, a debauched person. (**-atrice** *f.*) **-atura** *f.* licking; lick; graze, brush, flick; flattery; affectation; stiltedness; (paint.) light touch (of the brush). **-azampe** *m., f. indecl.* cringing flatterer, toady, lick-spittle.

Lecc-e *pr.n.f.* (geog.) Lecce. **-ese** *n., f., adj.* native of Lecce.

leccia *f.* (ichth.) fish resembling mackerels, *Lichia amia*, also *Seriola dumerilii*; — bastarda, *Lichia glauca*; also 'darkie Charlie', *Scymnorhinus lichia*; also *Seriola dumerilii*; (bot.) acorn of holm oak, *Quercus ilex*.

lecc-io *m.* (bot.) ilex oak, holm oak, *Quercus ilex*; — spinoso, a species of Mediterranean oak with prickly, holly-like leaves, *Q. coccifera*. **-eto** *m.* grove of ilex.

lec-co *m.* (*pl.* **-chi**) titbit; bait, inducement, incentive; profit, 'tear-off', 'rake-off'; centre, mark (in a game). **-cone** *m.* glutton; parasite, sponger; lecher; flatterer. (**-ona** *f.*) **-oneri·a** *f.* titbit; gluttony. **-orni·a, -or·nia** *f.* gluttony; titbit; 'tear-off', 'rake-off'. **-ucchiare** [A 4] *tr.* to lick continually, to keep licking. **-ume** *m.* titbit; incitement, inducement.

†lece *m.* placet, 'it is allowed', 'agreed'; *adj.* permitted, allowed.

†le·cere *impers.* to be permissible; to be fitting, to be suitable; to be allowed; to be possible.

†leceri·a *f.* lechery.

lecitin-a, -e *f.* (chem.) lecithin.

lecit-o *adj.* permissible; permitted; farsi — di, to take the liberty of; mi sia —, if I may be allowed; (leg.) lawful; licit; not forbidden by law; sanctioned by law. **-amente** *adv.* with permission; lawfully. **-ezza** *f.* permissibility; lawfulness.

Leda *pr.n.f.* (myth.; astron.) Leda.

le·d-ere [def.] *tr.* to injure, to harm; (leg.) to damage; to injure; to prejudice; — la legge, to violate the law. **-ente** *part. adj.* injurious, harmful, damaging.

†leena *f.* lioness.

leg-a[1] *f.* league, alliance; confederation; society; union; alloy; the base metal part of an alloy; quality, class; moneta di bassa —, base coin; di buona —, of good quality or character, sterling; strap or band of metal for joining two things together; hardening, setting (of cement, etc.); small dam to collect water to drive a mill.

le·ga[2] *f.* league (measure of distance); (naut.) league. NOTE: two units were formerly in use in the Italian Navy: (1) lega da 25 al grado (=4·445 km.); (2) lega da 20 al grado (=5·556 km.).

legac·cia *f.* (naut.) reef point.

leg-ac·cio *m.* band, fastening; garter; bootlace; ribbon; (surg.) ligature; *pl.* (naut.) strands, seizings. **-accetto** *m. dim.* of legaccio; wrapper; package. **-ac·ciolo** *m.* shoelace, bootlace; thong; band, garter. **-ag·gio** *m.* postage and packing.

legal-e *adj.* legal; lawful; according to law; armi -i, lawful weapons; corso —, legal tender; interessi -i, legal interests; norme -i, legal rules; ora —, summer time; poteri -i, legal powers; termini -i, prescribed times; annunzi -i, legal notices; (leg.) legal (with special regard to forms and observances prescribed by law with sanction for default); atti -i, legal acts; procedere per vie -i, to institute legal proceedings; effetti -i, legal effects; questione —, legal question; massime -i, legal maxims or principles or truths; prova —, legal evidence; scienza —, legal science; consulente —, counsel; facoltà —, faculty of law; libro —, law book; materie -i, legal matters; medicina —, forensic medicine; assistenza —, legal aid; spese -i, legal costs; *n.m.* lawyer, legal adviser. **-mente** *adv.* legally; lawfully. **-ità** *f.* legality; lawfulness; nella -ità, within the law; uscire della -ità, to go outside the law; nella stretta -ità, within the strict meaning of the law. **-izzare** [A I] *tr.* to certify; to authenticate; (leg.) to legalize (C.C.). **-izzato** *part. adj.* certified; authenticated. **-izzatore** (*m.*) legalizer; *adj.* legalizing, certifying. (**-izzatrice** *f.*) **-izzazione** *f.* legalization; authentication; ratification.

legame *m.* bond, connexion, tie, link; union; (canon law) *ligamen*; *pl.* (naut.) ties.

legamẹnto *m.* See under **legare**[1].

leg·are[1] [A2c] *tr.* to tie, to bind, to tie up; — strettamente, to bind fast; è matto da —, he is raving mad; — la lingua a uno, to silence someone; (naut.) to join, to tie together (of ropes); to tie in; (archit.) to bind (with dressed stone, metal ties or beams); (theol.) to bind; facoltà di sciogliere e di —, power to bind and loose; (eccl.) — le campane, to silence the bells (between Maundy Thursday and Holy Saturday); to alloy; to amalgamate; (text.) to reel; — la matassa, to skein; to connect, to link together; to set, to mount (jewels, etc.); — un libro, see **rilegare**; (fencing) to move (opponent's blade) from its line by resting one's blade over it; *intr.* (aux. avere, *prep.* con) to mix (with), to go well (with); (agric.) to set (of fruit); to take (of a grafting); *rfl.* to be bound, to be linked; (fig.) -arsela al dito, to bear in mind (an injury or wrong); (naut.) to meet, to abut, to run together; (mus.) to be slurred; to be tied. **-amẹnto** *m.* bond, link; connexion; tying; joint, fastening; (archit.) binding (in masonry), bond; (naut.) scantling (in frame); (anat.) ligament; sinew; (phon.) liaison; (fencing) the action of moving opponent's blade from its line by resting one's blade over it. **-amentọso** *adj.* pertaining to a bond, etc. **-ante** *part.*; *n.m.* (techn.) binder. **-ata** *f.* act of tying or binding. **-ato** *part. adj.* tied up, bound up; tied together, bound together, united; smooth, easy; (of script) cursive; (mus.) legato, played (or sung) smoothly; tied; -ato puntato, half staccato, half detached; contrappunto -ato, fourth species counterpoint; awkward, reticent; dense, thick, viscous; (paint.) maniera -ata, cramped style; (herald.) stringed; (of falcon) jessed, hooded. **-atọre** *m.* one who ties; bookbinder; jewel-setter. (**-atrice** *f.*) **-atori·a** *f.* bookbinder's workshop. **-atura** *f.* tying, binding; connecting stroke, ligature; (surg.) ligature; jewel-setting; (archit.) tie, binding; bookbinding; (text.) skeining; (mus.) ligature; tie; suspension; -ature doppie, double suspensions; (naut.) lashing or knot at the end of a mooring hawser to prevent it from rendering; -atura piana, plain seizing; -atura in croce, cross lashing (working); -atura portoghese, double (plain and cross) lashing; -atura volante, temporary seizing.

leg·are[2] [A2c] *tr.* (leg.) to bequeath; to leave by will; to devise; †to send as legate. **-ante** *m.* testator; legator; devisor. **-ata·rio** *m.* legatee; devisee (C.C.). **-ativo** *adj.* devising; bequeathing. **-ati·zio** *adj.* (eccl.) legatine. **-ato** *part. adj.* (leg.) bequeathed; devised; *n.m.* bequest; devise; legacy; -ato modale, legacy to one beneficiary charged with something for benefit of another; -ato di alimenti, bequest of maintenance and (where appropriate) educational expenses; -ato di vitalizio, bequest of life annuity; -ato in sostituzione di legittima, specific devise or bequest in substitution for legitimate portion; riduzione di -ato, abatement of legacy (C.C.).

legato[1] *part.* of **legare**[1], q.v.

legato[2] *part.* of **legare**[2], q.v.

legato[3] *m.* ambassador; representative; (eccl.) legate (whether as ambassador or, hist., as ruler of a Legation).

legaziọne *f.* legation; (eccl.) legateship, legation; (hist.) legation, province of Papal States.

legg·e *f.* (leg.) law; act; rule; il potere della —, the power of the law; protezione della —, protection of the law; sono più i casi che le -i, there are more lawsuits than laws; offendere la —, to break the law; ledere la —, to violate the law; trasgredire la —, to transgress the law; la lettera della —, the letter of the law; lo spirito della —, the spirit of the law; — agraria, agrarian law; — salica, Salic law; consuetudine passata in —, custom which became law; — suntuaria, sumptuary law, law in restraint of luxury; respingere la —, to reject the law; modificare la —, to modify the law; mutare la —, to change the law; convertire il decreto in —, to convert the decree into law; sancire la —, to lay down the law; promulgare la —, to promulgate or proclaim the law; abolire la —, to abolish the law; — liberale, liberal law; — equa, equity, just law; — iniqua, unjust law; — draconiana, Draconian law, extremely severe law; — scritta, written law; — consuetudinaria, customary law; far —, to enact; to have the force of law; la necessità non ha —, necessity has no law; ricorrere alla —, to go to law; braccio della —, the arm of the law; in nome della —, in the name of the law; facoltà di —, school or faculty of law; laurea in —, degree in law; dottore in —, doctor of laws; uomo di —, legal man; scienza delle leggi, science of law, jurisprudence; colla — della mano, with the law of his arms; por mano alla —, to enforce the law, to lay down the law; — delle 12 tavole, law of the Twelve Tables, Leges Decemvirales; -i giustiniane, Justinian code; le tavole della —, the tables of the law, Mosaic law; benefici di —, benefits of the law; in fatto di —, in point of law; — del taglione, the law of 'an eye for an eye'; — giudaica, Judaic law; — cristiana, Christian law; — maomettana, Mohammedan law; vivere sotto una stessa —, to live under or to abide by one and the same law; — umana, human law; — di natura, law of nature; — cosmica, cosmic law; -i del moto, laws of motion; -i di Keplero, Kepler's laws; -i fonetiche, phonetic laws; -i di continuità, laws of continuity or sequence; — della domanda e dell'offerta, law of supply and demand; farsi —, to undertake an obligation; per —, by law; dar — ai vinti, to dictate terms of surrender; per effetto di —, by law; fatta la —, scoperto l'inganno, no sooner is a law made than people find a way round it; dar — ai cappelli, to tidy or comb the hair; dettar —, to lay down the law; — morale, moral law; Parigi dà — alla moda, Paris sets the fashion; un fuori —, an outlaw; (leg.) law (in all senses, but especially in that of legislative act or measure; one of the sources of 'diritto', q.v.); Act (of Parliament); una — civile, a civil law; una — comunale, municipal by-law; una — con forza retroattiva, a retrospective law; la — costituzionale, constitutional law; una — costituzionale, a Constitutional Act, C. statute (I.C.); una — criminale, a criminal law; una — delega, una — delegata, law made under delegated power; la — fallimentare, Bankruptcy Act, law of bankruptcy; una — finanziaria, Finance Act; la — marittima, maritime law, the law merchant; il valore di — ordinaria, the force of an ordinary law (I.C.); una — provinciale, County or Provincial by-law; la — Vanoni, Vanoni's Act, the Vanoni law (on tax returns); la — vigente, the existing law; la — sul bollo, Stamp Act; un decreto —, Decree Law; un decreto convertito in —, Decree converted into Law (I.C.); un disposto della —, a provision of the Act, of law; le disposizioni di —, the provisions of law; un disegno, un progetto di —, a (parliamentary) Bill; una proposta di —, a draft (parliamentary) Bill; la proposta di un progetto di —, the presentation, tabling of a (parliamentary) Bill (I.C.); un provvedimento con forza di —, a provision having the force of law (I.C.); un trattato di —, law-book, legal text-book; contrario alla —, contrary to the law; a termine di —, as required by law; a norma di —, according to law; under the law; in base alla, in conformità alla —, in accordance, in compliance with the law; per effetto della —, by virtue of the Act; by operation of the law; per effetto di —, by law; conforme alla —, according to the law; fuori della —, contrary to, outside the law; le -i costituzionali, Constitutional statutes; le -i vigenti, the law of the land; la formazione delle -i, law-making; l'iniziativa delle -i, the power to introduce legislation (I.C.); abrogare una —, to repeal an Act; approvare una —, to pass an Act; eludere la —, to evade the Act; infrangere, violare la —, to violate the law; modificare la —, to amend the Act, law; acquistare forza di —, to acquire the force of law, to become law, to become legally operative; mettere fuori —, to outlaw; conformarsi alla —, to comply with the law; contravvenire alla —, to contravene, to infringe the law.

leggend·a *f.* legend; story; fable; superstition; idle tale, old wives' tale; (typ.) caption; reference note; explanatory note; superscription; (on a map) conventional signs; symbols. **-a·rio** *adj.* legendary; *n.m.* collection of legends.

leg·g·ere [C12] *tr.* to read; to peruse; — ad alta voce, to read aloud; — fra le righe, to read between the lines; non saper — altro che nel suo libro, to be unwilling to hear what anyone else has to say; — la musica, to read music; — a prima vista, to play at sight, to sight-read; — sul giornale, to read in the paper; nell'attesa di -ervi, hoping to hear from you; — la vita a uno, to speak ill of someone; to interpret, to read, to understand; — le carte, to tell fortunes by cards; †to elect, to choose; †to prefer; *abs., intr.* (aux. avere) to read, to be a reader; saper —, to know how to read, to be able to read; io non lo -o, I can't make head or tail of it. **-i·bile** *adj.* legible; readable. **-ibilmẹnte** *adv.* legibly; readably. **-i(u)cchiare** [A4] *tr.* to read a little of, to skim through. **-itọre** *m.* (techn.) reader. (**-itrice** *f.*)

legge·r-o *adj.* see **leggiero**. **-a** *f.* (slang) poverty, state of being penniless. **-ẹzza** *f.* lightness, agility; buoyancy. **-mẹnte** *adv.* slightly, lightly; frivolously; thoughtlessly.

leggiadr-o *adj.* pretty, graceful; comely; charming. **-i·a** *f.* prettiness, elegance; pretty thing; (paint.) grace and lightness (of figures).

leggiai(u)olo *adj.* hard, unyielding (of a person); *n.m.* (iron.) lawyer.

legg-i·bile *adj.*, **-ibilità** *f.* See under **leggere**.

†leggidatore *m.* lawgiver.

leggier-o *adj.* light; — come una piuma, light as a feather; agile, nimble; avere la mano -a, to have a light touch, to possess manual skill; tinte -e, light, pale colours; slight; barely perceptible; frivolous, giddy; a cuor —, light-heartedly; alla -a, lightly; *adv.* camminare —, to walk with light steps (cf. **leggermente**, under **leggero**).

leggi·o *m.* (*pl.* **-ìi**) reading-desk; (eccl.) lectern; stare a —, to be a cantor; missal-stand; pulpit; (mus.) music-stand, desk; rimettere sul —, to start playing again at the beginning; (paint.) easel.

leg·gio² *adj.* (naut.) light (cf. **alleggio**).

legifer-are [A I S] *intr.* (*aux.* avere) to make laws, to legislate; (joc.) to lay down the law. **-azione** *f.* laying down of the law.

legion-e *f.* legion; great multitude; (mil.) regiment (of Carabinieri). **-a·rio** *adj.*, *n.m.* legionary.

legisl-ativo *adj.* (leg.) legislative; potere —, legislative power; consiglio —, legislative council; corpo —, legislative body. **-atore** *m.* legislator. (**-atora** *f.* **-atrice** *f.*) **-ato·rio** *adj.* (*m.pl.* **-atorii**) legislatorial. **-atura** *f.* legislature. **-azione** *f.* legislation; -azione comparata, comparative legislation.

leg-ismo *m.* (leg.) observance of the letter of the law. **-ista** *m.* legist; lawyer.

legisperito *m.* legal expert, legist.

legit·tim-o *adj.* (leg.) legitimate (with special regard to what is essentially just, conforming with natural law); figlio —, legitimate son; erede —, legitimate heir, person with legal right to inherit; matrimonio —, lawful marriage; età -a, legal, full age; impedimento —, lawful or just impediment; interesse —, legitimate interest; -a difesa, self defence; prova -a, legitimate evidence; moneta -a, legal coin; misura -a, legal measure; — portatore, holder in due course (C.C.). **-a** *f.* legitime. **-amente** *adv.* legitimately; lawfully; legally. **-ante** *adj.* legalizing; lawful. **-are** [A I S] *tr.* to legitimate; to legitimize. **-a·rio** *m.* legitimer; person with legal right to inherit. **-ismo** *m.* legitimism. **-ista** *m.* legitimist. **-ità** *f.* legitimacy. **-azione** *f.* legitimation; -azione per susseguente matrimonio, legitimation by subsequent marriage; (naut.) certificato di -azione, boat's licence.

legn-a *f.* firewood; fuel; (fig.) mettere -e al fuoco, to add fuel to the fire, to fan the flames; portar — alla selva, to carry coals to Newcastle; tagliar le -e addosso a, to malign. **-a·ceo** *adj.* see under **legno**. **-ag·gio** *m.* right of cutting firewood, 'wooding'; **†see lignaggio. -a·ia** *f.* wood-store; andare a -aia, to be beaten; mandare a -aia, to give a hiding to (these two phrases are based on a play of words with Legnaia, the name of a suburb of Florence; cf. Eng. 'up the stairs to Bedfordshire'). **-ai(u)olo** *m.* cabinet-maker; (naut. slang) carpenter. **-amaro** *m.* cabinet-maker. **-ame** *m.* timber; woodwork; maestro di -ame, carpenter; (naut.) timbers; spars; (bot.) woody tissue. **-are** [A 5 c] *intr.* (*aux.* avere) to gather firewood; *tr.* to beat. **-ata** *f.* blow; beating. **-a·tico** *m.* right of cutting firewood. **-atura** *f.* gathering firewood; beating. **-eggiare** [A 3 c] *intr.* (*aux.* avere) to cut wood. **-etta** *f. dim.* small firewood.

legnaperda *f.* (ent.) goat moth (especially its caterpillar), *Cossus cossus*.

legnificare [A 2 s] *rfl.* (agric.) to lignify.

legn-o *m.* (*pl.* **legni** *m.* or **legna**, **legne** *f.*, the latter two forms now being used to mean 'firewood'; cf. **legna**) wood; (bot.) — duro, lignum vitae, *Guiacum officinale*, *G. sanctum*; — dolce, — tenero, softwood; — giovane, alburnum; (bot.) — santo, date-plum, *Diospyros lotus*; pane di — e vin di nuvole, chestnuts to eat and water to drink; il — verde non sta mai fermo, young people can never keep still; testa di —, blockhead; (mus.) col — , with the stick of the bow; i -i, the woodwind; stick; log; club; morir su tre -i, to be hanged; (naut.) vessel (generic name for craft of considerable size); — quadro, square rigger; carriage, coach; tree (Dante, *Par.* XXVI, 115); pole (of a chariot) (Dante, *Purg.* XXXII, 24). **-a·ceo** *adj.* woody. **-erello** *m.* chip of wood. **-etto** *m. dim.* (naut.) small craft. **-i·pede** *adj. indecl.* (joc.) on stilts; having a wooden leg, 'peg-leg'. **-(u)olo** *m.* (naut.) 'part' or strand of a rope or hawser. **-osità** *f.* woodiness. **-oso** *adj.* woody; (text.) fibra -osa, woody fibre; (bot.) woody, ligneous. **-otto** *m.* tough wood. **-ot·tolo** *m.* chip of wood.

lego-grafologi·a *f.* the art of teaching to read and write. **-logi·a** *f.* the art of teaching to read.

legul-e·io *m.* (derog.) an argumentative and domineering lawyer.

legum-e *m.* pulse; pod. NOTE: not 'vegetable'; only 'fagioli', 'fave', 'ceci', 'pisalli', 'lenticchie' are 'legumi' (cf. **verdura**). **-ina** *f.* (chem.) legumin, vegetable casein.

leh *excl.* whoa!

lehm *m. indecl.* (geol.) loam.

lei¹ *pers. prn. 3rd sing. f. disj.* she; her.

Lei² *pers. prn. 3rd sing. m., f. disj.* you (the formal mode of address); dare del Lei, to use the formal mode of address.

†lei³ *f.* See **legge**.

†leiale *adj.* loyal; legal.

leibniziano *adj.* (philos.) pertaining to Leibniz.

Leida *pr.n.f.* (geog.) Leiden; (electr.) boccia di —, bottiglia di —, Leyden jar.

leio-coma *f.* gum, paste. **-gomma** *f.* see **leicoma**.

leitmotiv *m. indecl.* (mus.) leitmotiv, leading motif.

Le·lio *pr.n.m.* a character in one of Goldoni's comedies, now proverbial for a liar.

†lellare *intr.* to go slow; to hesitate; to vacillate.

Lemano *pr.n.m.* (geog.) Lago —, Lake of Geneva, Lake Leman.

lembo *m.* border, edge; margin; side; strip; hem; flap; (eng.) flange; limb, graduated edge of the dial of an instrument; (astron.) limb, edge of a heavenly body; (bot.) limb; †(naut.) type of sloop or river craft.

lemm-a *f.* (logic) assumption; (math.) lemma; †argument, summary. **-a·tico** *adj.* (math.) pertaining to a lemma.

lemme *adv. phr.* lemme lemme, slowly, deliberately; bit by bit, by degrees; gently, peacefully.

lemnis-co *m.* (*pl.* **-chi**) (hist.) lemniscus. **-cata** *f.* (math.) lemniscate. **-cato** *adj.* adorned with lemnisci, beribboned.

†Lemosì *pr.n.f.* (geog.) Limoges.

lemo·sina *f.* and derivs. See **elemosina**.

le·mur-e *m.* (Rom. antiq.) ghost; spirit of the departed; (zool.) lemur. **-ale** *adj.* lemurine. **-i·o** *m.* (Rom. antiq.) feast in honour of the lemures, from 9 to 13 May.

len-a¹ *f.* courage, spirit to exert oneself, will to carry on; vigour, effort, staying-power; breath; wind; di —, with zest; lavoro di lunga —, work requiring sustained effort; perdere la —, to lose one's nerve. **†-anza** *f.* see **lena**. **†-are** *vb.* and derivs. see **allenare**.

lena² *f.* (Rom. antiq.) *laena*, cloak.

Lena³ *pr.n.f.* abbrev. of **maddalena**.

len·din-e *m.* nit, louse's egg. **†-ella** *f.* a kind of coarse cloth. **-ino** *m. dim.* of **lendine**; scurf, dandruff. **-oso** *adj.* nit-infested, lousy; scurfy.

len-e *adj.* (poet.) light, delicate, soft, gentle; mellow, sweet; (gramm.) spirito —, soft breathing (of a Greek initial vowel). **-emente** *adv.* softly, gently, lightly, delicately. **-ità** *f.* gentleness, delicateness, lightness, softness; †slowness. **-o** *adj.* soft, gentle, bland; weak, feeble, yielding; (pop.) see **lene**.

lene·o *adj.* Bacchic.

leni-ente *adj.* (med.) soothing, calming. **†-ficare** *tr.* (med.) to soothe, to calm; cf. **lenire**. **†-ficativo** *adj.* see **lenitivo**.

lenimento *m.* See under **lenire**.

Leningrado *pr.n.f.* (geog.) Leningrad.

leninismo *m.* (pol.) Leninism.

len-ire [D 2] *tr.* to soothe, to mitigate, to placate. **-imento** *m.* soothing, mitigating, placating. **-itivo** *adj.* calming, soothing; *n.m.* lenitive, demulcent. **-ito** *part. adj.* soothed; placated; mitigated. (**-itore** *m.* **-itrice** *f.*)

lenità *f. indecl.* See under **lene**.

Lenno¹ *pr.n.m.* (geog.) Lemnos.

†lenno² *m.* (naut.) hawser, preventer.

leno *adj.* See under **lene**.

len-oci·nio *m.* (leg.) panderism; (fig.) blandishment; spurious attraction. **-one** *m.* (leg.) pander, a procurer of means to gratify base passions; pimp. **-ona** *f.* procuress. **-oni·a** *f.* (leg.) panderism.

lentag·gine¹ *f.* (bot.) wayfaring tree, *Viburnum lantana*; laurustinus, *Viburnum tinus*.

lentag·gine² *f.* slowness.

lentamente *adv.* See under **lento**.

lent-are [A I] *tr.* to loosen, to untighten, to slacken; cf. **allentare**. **-ando** *ger.* (mus.) becoming slower.

lente¹ *f.* (bot.) lentil, *Lens culinaris*; — di palude, great duckweed, *Lemna polyrhiza* and other species.

lente² *f.* lens; (anat.) lens of the eye; bob (of a pendulum); *pl.* pince-nez.

†**lente³** *adj.* See **lento**.

lenteggiare [A3c] *intr.* (*aux.* essere) to be loose, to work loose; (joc.) to be slow, to proceed slowly.

lentẹzza *f.* slowness; laziness; looseness, slackness; le sue solite lentezze, his usual slow procedure; †— d'animo, loss of courage, failing spirits, faintheartedness.

lent-i·a *f.* (naut.) parbuckle; method of hoisting by parbuckling. **-iare** [A4] *tr.* (naut.) to parbuckle.

lent-ic·chia *f.* (bot.) see **lente¹**; un piatto di -icchie, a mess of pottage; *pl.* lentil-shaped 'pasta' for soup; (numism.) Spanish gold coin. **-icella** *f.* (bot.) lenticel. **-icolare** *adj.* (bot.) resembling a lentil; (miner.; surg.; anat.) lenticular; riflettore -icolare, spotlight. **-icola·ria** *f.* (geol.) nummulite fossil. **-icolato** *adj.* see **lenticolare**. **-icula·ria** *f.* (geol.) see **lenticolaria**. **-iforme** *adj.* lenticular. **-ig·gine** *f.* freckle. **-igginọso** *adj.* freckled, having freckles. †**-i·glia** *f.* see **lentiggine**.

lenti·grado *adj.* (zool.) slow-stepping.

lenti·schio, lentisco *m.* (bot.) mastic, *Pistacia lentiscus*.

lent-o *adj.* slow; tardy; long drawn out; cuocere a fuoco —, to cook on a low fire; to simmer; lazy, inert; loose, slack, not taut; calm (of the sea); febbre -a, low, persistent fever; *n.m.* (mus.) a Lento movement; *adv.* slowly; ponderously; parlare —, to speak slowly; avanzarsi — —, to approach with slow steps; (mus.) slowly, slower than 'adagio', q.v. **-amẹnte** *adv.* slowly; lazily; loosely; (mus.) slowly. **-ọre** *m.* slowness; (of liquids) thickness, viscosity, stickiness, 'body'.

lenza¹ *f.* fishing-line; pescare a —, *or* con la —, to fish with rod and line; measuring cord; a — dritta, perpendicular.

†**lenz-a²** *f.* linen bandage; bond, league. †**-are** *tr.* to bind, to bandage; to league.

lenzuol-o *m.* (*pl.* -a *f.*, -i *m.*) sheet (of a bed); le -a, the pair of sheets on a bed; i -i, sheets (in general); (joc.) sugo di —, bed (as a remedy for colds); consumare le -a, to stay in bed a great deal; — funebre, — mortuario, shroud, winding-sheet; (occasionally) i -i, bedclothes.

leo-corno *m.* unicorn. †**-fante** *m.* elephant.

leonardẹs-co *adj.* (*m.pl.* **-chi**) in the manner of Leonardo da Vinci; *n.m.* disciple of Leonardo da Vinci.

leọn-e *m.* (zool.) lion, *Panthera leo*; cuor di —, lion-heart; fare le volte del —, to pace up and down; (astron.) Grande —, Leo; Sol —, dog days, when the sun is in Leo; †(naut.) bow decoration of a galley (Venice); †fossa dei -i, boatswain's store; (numism.) Venetian silver coin; (bot.) coda di —, Jerusalem sage, *Phlomis fruticosa*. **-ato** *adj.* tawny; *n.m.* tawny colour. **-cello** *m. dim.* of **leone**; small lion; lion cub; (archit.) capital, bracket. **-cino** *m.* (zool.) lion cub; breed of dog. †**-efante** *m.* elephant. †**-epardo** *m.* see **leopardo**. **-ẹsco** *adj.* (*m.pl.* **-ẹschi**) lion-like. **-ẹssa** *f.* lioness. **-ina** *f.* (numism.) gold coin minted by Pope Leo XII (1823–29). **-ino** *adj.* lion-like, leonine; società -ina, a society where all the advantages go to the strongest (cf. Eng. 'lion's share'); patto -ino, leonine contract (C.C.); (hist.) città -ina, Leonine city; (prosod.) Leonine. **-ti·aṣi** *f.* (med.) leontiasis. **-topo·dio** *m.* (bot.) edelweiss, *Leontopodium alpinum*. †**-za** *f.* lioness.

Leo·nidi *pr.n.f.pl.* (astron.) the Leonids.

leopard-eggiare [A3c] *intr.* (*aux.* avere) (lit. hist.) to write in a sorrowful and pessimistic style in imitation of the Italian poet, Giacomo Leopardi (1798–1837). **-iano** *adj.* pertaining to Leopardi; similar to the style of Leopardi; *n.m.* poet who imitates the style of Leopardi; one who is influenced by Leopardi.

leopard-o *m.* (zool.) leopard; (herald.) lion passant gardant, leopard; — illeonito, leopard rampant, lion rampant gardant. **-ato** *adj.* (herald.) having a lion passant and gardant.

leopold-iano *adj.*, *n.m.* (hist.) partisan of Leopold I against the Roman Curia. **-ino** *adj.* pertaining to Leopold I, Grand Duke of Tuscany; leggi -ine, laws passed under Leopold I in relation to the Roman Curia; scuole -ine, designation of certain schools for girls in Florence.

Leopoldo *pr.n.m.* Leopold.

Leo·poli *pr.n.f.* (geog.) Lwów.

le·pade *f.* (zool.) goose barnacle, *Lepas* spp.

lepid-amẹnte *adv.*, **-ẹzza** *f.* See under **lepido**.

lepi·d-io *m.* (bot.) — di calcinacci, narrow-leaved pepperwort, *Lepidium ruderale*. **-ina** *f.* (chem.) lepidine.

le·pid-o *adj.* sprightly; smart, facetious; jaunty, jocular, perky. **-amẹnte** *adv.* in a sprightly manner; facetiously, jauntily, jocularly. **-ẹzza** *f.* sprightliness; facetiousness; witticism.

lepid-olite *f.* (miner.) lepidolite, lithia mica. **-omelano** *m.* (miner.) lepidomelane. **-ot·teri** *m.pl.* (ent.) butterflies and moths, lepidoptera.

lepora·rio *m.* game preserve.

lepọre¹ *m.* sprightliness, gaiety; facetiousness.

†**le·pore²** *m.* See **lepre**.

leporeamb-i *m.pl.* (lit. hist.) burlesque poems by, or in the style of, Lodovico Leporeo. **-iṣmo** *m.* (lit. hist.) baroque style resembling that of Leporeo.

leporino *adj.* relating to a hare; labbro —, hare-lip.

leppo¹ *m.* (ichth.) *Labrus viridis*, green wrasse.

†**leppo²** *m.* stench.

†**lepra** *f.* See **lebbra**.

lepr-e *f.*, *m.* (zool.) hare; — comune, *Lepus timidus*; — alpina, *L. variabilis*; — di mare, sea hare, *Aplysia punctata*; dormire come la —, to sleep with one's eyes open; vedere dove sta la —, to find out the truth of the matter; pigliar la — col carro, to accomplish one's purpose by patience and cunning; avere la voglia della —, to have a hare-lip; piede di —, hare's foot (used as a duster); (vet., of a horse) testa di —, a prominent convex forehead. **-a·io** *m.* (*pl.* **-a·ia** *f.*) game preserve; gamekeeper. **-aiuolo** *m.* (orn.) black vulture. **-atto** *m.* (zool.) leveret, baby hare. **-otto** *m.* older leveret that can be eaten. **-ino** *m. dim.* of **lepre**; *adj.* see **leporino**.

†**leproso** *adj.* See **lebbroso**, under **lebbra**.

lept-inite *f.* (miner.) granulite. **-ocordi** *m.pl.* (zool.) Cephalochordata, *Amphioxus* spp. **-omeri·a** *f.* (med. hist.) leptomere.

†**lerciare** *tr.* to soil; to contaminate; to infect; to corrupt; *rfl.* to soil oneself.

lerc-io *adj.* filthy; foul. **-iọso** *adj.* dirty. **-ume** *m.* filth.

ler·fia *f.* (Tusc.) thick, protruding lip.

lern-eonina *f.* (zool.) *Lernaea* spp. a crustacean parasite of fish. **-e·o** *adj.* Lernaean.

†**ler·nia** *adj. f.* dainty (of a mouth), finicky.

lero *m.* (bot.) bitter vetch, *Vicia ervilia*.

lẹṣa *f.* (mil. hist.) mantlet.

Lẹ·ṣbia¹ *pr.n.f.* Lesbia.

†**les·bia²** *f.* (bldg.) Lesbian rule.

les·b-io, -ico *adj.* Lesbian; amore —, Lesbianism. **-iṣmo** *m.* Lesbianism.

Lẹṣbo *pr.n.m.* (geog.) Mytilene, formerly Lesbos.

leṣẹna *f.* (archit.) fascia, fillet; pilaster (engaged in a wall).

leṣin-a, le·ṣina *f.* awl; (fig.) stinginess; miserliness; che —!, how mean!; carefulness, thrift. **-a·io** *m.* miser, curmudgeon. **-are** [A1sc] *intr.* (*aux.* avere) to economize, to be thrifty; to be stingy, to haggle, to scrape, to pinch and screw; *tr.* to grudge. **-eri·a** *f.* economy; stinginess, meanness. **-ino** *m. dim.* small awl; person who economizes; stingy, miserly person.

leṣ-iọne *f.* (med.) lesion; break, interruption; (archit.) crack; (leg.) damage to property or rights; lesion; injury; rescissione per —, rescission of contract for lesion (C.C.); — personale, personal injury (C.P.). **-ionare** [A1c] *tr.* to cause cracking in, to crack. **-ionato** *part. adj.* suffering lesion. **-ivo** *adj.* wounding, injuring, offending; ferita -iva, lesion; (leg.) injurious; detrimental; vendita -iva, rescindable sale; -ivo di interessi, detrimental to interests.

lẹṣo *part.* of **ledere**, q.v.; *adj.* wounded, injured, offended; (leg.) injured; parte lesa, injured party; lesa prerogativa, offence against the prerogative (C.P.).

less-are [A1c] *tr.* to boil, to stew; to cook in water. (**-amẹnto** *m.*) **-ata** *f.* act of boiling or stewing; dare una -ata a, to boil. **-ato** *part. adj.* boiled; stewed. **-atura** *f.* process of boiling or stewing.

lẹssic-o *m.* lexicon, dictionary; vocabulary; choice of words. **-ale** *adj.* lexic, pertaining to vocabulary. **-ista** *m.* lexicographer. **-ografi·a** *f.* lexicography, the technique and art of dictionary compilation. **-ogra·fico** *adj.* lexicographical. **-o·grafo** *m.* lexicographer, compiler of a dictionary. **-ologi·a** *f.* lexicology, the technique and art of compiling a dictionary. **-olo·gico** *adj.* lexicological.

lẹss-o *adj.* boiled; stewed; (provb.) chi la vuol -a, chi la vuole arrosto, there's no accounting for tastes, tastes differ; tasteless, insipid; (colloq.) fico —, fool; *n.m.* boiled beef; — di vitello, stewed veal; — di pollo, boiled chicken; boiling; a —, boiled.

lest·o *adj.* agile, nimble; quick, swift, rapid; early, speedy; brisk; alla -a, quickly, briskly; — di mano, neat-handed, *or* light-fingered; — di gambe, nimble on one's pins; — di mente, quick-witted; quickly over, of short duration; (Tusc.) ready, finished; un'altra pagina e sono —, one more page and I've finished; (of two or more people) quits; sono -i, they've settled their accounts between them; — fante, see **lestofante**; (naut.) ready, with work completed; -i a virar di bordo!, ready about!; *adv.* quickly, speedily; —, via!, quick, be off! **-aménte** *adv.* nimbly; rapidly; swiftly; agilely; briskly. **-ẹzza** *f.* nimbleness, agility; briskness; swiftness. **-ofante** *m.* (*pl.* -ofanti) rogue, twister, swindler; cheap-jack.

lestri·gone *m.* Laestrygonian; (fig.) cruel person.

leṣura *f.* lesion; damage; offence.

letal-e *adj.* deadly, lethal, mortal, vital, fatal. **-mẹnte** *adv.* fatally, lethally, mortally. **-ità** *f.* deadliness.

letam-e *m.* stable manure, dung. **-a·io** *m.* dung-heap. **-are** [A 1] *tr.* to manure. **-ato** *part. adj.* manured. **-azione** *f.* manuring, muck-spreading. †**-inare** *vb.* see **letamare**.

†**letan-a** *f.*, †**-i·a** *f.* See **litania**.

letargi·a *f.* lethargy.

letar·gico *adj.* lethargic; (silkb.) periodo —, sleeping period.

letargo *m.* lethargy; torpor; inertia; oblivion; hibernation; (silkb.) sleeping sickness.

Lẹt-e *pr.n.m.* (myth.) Lethe; (fig.) oblivion. **-e·o** *adj.* pertaining to Lethe.

leticare [A 2 s] and derivs. (Tusc.). See **litigare**.

letichino *m.* wrangler, quarrelsome person.

leti·fero *adj.* (poet.) fatal, death-dealing.

letific-are [A 2 s] *tr.* to gladden. **-ante** *part. adj.* gladdening; (med.) tonic.

Leti·zia[1] *pr.n.f.* Letitia.

leti·zi-a[2] *f.* joy; gladness; gaiety; happiness; object of delight. **-are** [A 4] *rfl.* to rejoice; to experience joy; †*tr.* to give joy to, to gladden; *n.m.* rejoicing, joy, gladness. †**-oso** *adj.* joyful.

†**leto** *m.* death.

letta[1] *f.* hasty reading; skipping through; dare una — ad un libro, to skim a book through.

†**letta**[2] *f.pl.* of **letto**[2], q.v.

let·ter-a *f.* 1. LETTER, epistle; note; — per via aerea, airmail letter; — raccomandata, registered letter; — espresso, express letter; — aperta, open letter; — morta, dead letter, (fig.) useless, ineffectual thing; — amorosa, love-letter; — di presentazione, — di raccomandazione, — commendatizia, letter of introduction, *or* testimonial; — anonima, anonymous letter; carta da —, writing-paper, note-paper; amicizia per -e, pen friendship; (comm.) — di credito, letter of credit; — di cambio, bill of exchange; (leg.) — minatoria, threatening letter; — di vettura, way-bill (C.C.); -e patenti, letters-patent. 2. LETTER, character; type; una — maiuscola, a capital letter; una — minuscola, a small letter, a lower-case letter; -e di scatola, -e cubitali, block capitals; scrivere in tutte -e, to write out in full; alla —, literally, word for word; handwriting; *adj., adv. phr.* avanti —, *avant-lettre* (of engravings made as first specimens before the engraving of the inscription); (fig.) before the proper time; *pl.* letters, literature; knowledge; uomo di -e, man of letters; senza -e, unlettered; repubblica delle -e, the world of literature; laureato, dottore in -e, graduate with a degree in literature; belle -e, *belles-lettres*, literature; calcolo di -e, algebra; sacre -e, (sacred) scripture; -e pontificie, papal letters; †canon law; *pl.* tails (when tossing a coin); †Latin; †per —, in Latin, †sapere —, to understand Latin; †parlare per —, to talk Latin. **-a·io** *m.* (derog.) pedantic teacher of grammar. **-ina** *f.*, **-ino** *m. dim.* of **lettera**. †**-ista** *m.* letter-writer. **-ọna** *f.*, **-ọne** *m. augm.* of **lettera**; long letter. **-uzza** *f. dim.* of **lettera**; *pl.* the first rudiments. **-uto** *adj.* (derog.) learned, lettered; *n.m.* man of letters, learned man.

letteral-e *adj.* literal; calcolo —, algebra; written; arabo —, written Arabic; †Latin: †sermone —, sermon in Latin. **-mẹnte** *adv.* literally; in the literal sense; word for word.

lettera·ri-o *adj.* literary; relating to literature; (leg.) proprietà -a, literary property, copyright. **-amẹnte** *adv.* from a literary point of view; in a literary sense.

letterat-o *m.* well-read man, *littérateur*, man of letters; educated man; author; scholar; †Latinist; †person able to read; *adj.* literary; †incised, bearing an inscription, lettered. (-a *f.*) **-amẹnte**

adv. in a literary manner; in a learned manner. **-ello** *m.* (derog.) superficially well-read man. **-essa** *f.* (derog.) learned woman. **-ọne** *m.* (joc.) learned or well-read person. **-uc·cio** *m. pejor.* inferior scholar, pedant. **-ume** *m. pejor.* crowd of literary people.

letteratura *f.* literature; monumenti della —, classical works of literature; writing, literary culture; darsi alla —, to take up writing as a profession, *or* to become a student of literature; — scientifica, works of science, learned works; — musicale, books on music; — narrativa, narrative fiction; — d'intrattenimento, literature of entertainment; — musicale, books on music; — amena, *belles lettres*; bibliography; su questo argomento esiste abbondante —, there is a vast bibliography on this subject; (derog., of a writer) fare della —, to pay more heed to form than to content; †character, letter; †script, writing; †knowledge of the technique of writing.

lett-erello, -icciuolo, -ello, -ino *m. dim.* of **letto**[2], q.v.

let·tico *adj.* Lettish, Latvian.

lettiera[1] *f.* bedstead; head-board between the bed and the wall; bedding for animals; †see **lettiga**.

lettiera[2] *f.* See **lettera**.

letti·ga *f.* litter; stretcher on wheels. **-ghiere**, †**-ghiero** *m.* litter-bearer.

lettime *m.* bedding for animals.

lettister·nio *m.* (Rom. antiq.) Lectisternium, religious feast in which the gods (represented either by statues or by bundles of herbs) had couches prepared for them as human banqueters.

letto[1] *part.* of **leggere**, q.v., *adj.* read; perused; dare per —, to take as read; (leg.), confermato e sottoscritto, read, confirmed and signed; — ed approvato, read and approved.

lett-o[2] *m.* bed; bedstead; camera da —, bedroom; — a una piazza, — a uno, single bed; — a una piazza e mezzo, large single bed; — a due, — a due piazze, — matrimoniale, double bed; -i gemelli, -i inglesi, twin beds; — bastardo, three-quarter bed; — da campo, camp bed; — a canapè, divan bed; — a vento, — a libriccino, — pieghevole, folding bed; — di ammalato, — di dolore, sick-bed; — di morte, death-bed; — di fortuna, shake-down; acconciare il —, rifare il —, to make the bed; rincalzare il —, to tuck in the bed; andare a —, to go to bed; ma va' a —!, don't bother me!; mettersi a —, to take to one's bed; essere costretto al —, to keep to one's bed, to be confined to bed; stare fra — e lettuccio, to be an invalid; inchiodato a —, bed-ridden; cacciarsi in —, to get under the bedclothes; (joc.) — di tre colonne, gallows; marriage tie, marriage; marriage bed; dello stesso —, of the same marriage; figli del primo —, children of the first marriage; couch; bedding for animals; (geog.) bed; — di fiume, river bed; — del fiume, river bed; — del mare, sea bed; (eng.) bed; (tanning) first scudded skin left on the beam to form a base for further skins; (paint.) couch (of paint); (naut.) launching cradle; — del vento, direction of the wind; (mil.) cradle; (silkb.) litter (for silkworms); (agric.) far —, (of corn) to be laid by the rain; sediment, foots; far —, (of a liquid) to deposit a sediment. **-erello, -icciuolo** *m. dim.* of **letto**; little bed, wretched little bed. **-icello** *m. dim.* little bed. **-icino** *m. dim.* cot; doll's bed. **-uc·cio** *m. dim. pejor.* of **letto**; litter; couch; tra letto e —, not very well, convalescent; †portable bed, matting.

Let·ton-e[1] *m.* Lett, Latvian. **-i·a** *pr.n.f.* (geog.) Latvia.

lettọne[2] *m. augm.* of **letto**[2], q.v.

lettọr-e *m.* reader; (at an Italian University) lector; (eccl.) lector; †elector. **-ato** *m.* readership; (at an Italian University) lectorship; (eccl.) lectorate. †**-i·a** *f.* readership.

†**lettra** *f.* See **lettera**.

lettrice *f.* of **lettore**, q.v.

lettur-a *f.* reading; perusal; sala di —, reading-room; uomo di molta —, very well-read man; reading (of a bill in parliament); esaminare in seconda —, to proceed to a second reading; reading, interpretation; reading matter, material for reading; text; exercise in reading; -e giovanili, children's reader; libro di —, reading book, reader, primer; lecture; (typ.) pica; †instruction; †doctrine.

leuc-angite *f.* (med.) lymphangitis. †**-ato** *adj.* white. **-emi·a** *f.* (med.) leukaemia. **-ina** *f.* (chem.) leucine. **-isco** *m.* (*pl.* -ischi) (ichth.) *Leuciscus* spp., chub, dace, etc. **-ite** *f.* (miner.) leucite. **-ociti** *m.pl.* (anat.) leucocyte, white blood corpuscle. **-ocitọsi** *f. indecl.* (med.) leucocytosis. **-oder·mia** *f.* (med.) achromodermia. †**-oflemmasia** *f.* dropsy. **-o·dio** *m.* (bot.) wallflower, *Cheiranthus cheiri*. †**-oflemma·tico** *adj.* pertaining to dropsy, dropsical. **-olo** *m.* leucoline, quinoline. **-oma** *m.* (med.) leucoma. **-oplaci·a** *f.* (med.)

leuc-angite (*cont.*)

leucoplakia. **-oplasto** *m.* zinc oxide plaster. **-orre·a** *f.* (med.) leucorrhoea, whites. **-orro·ico** *adj.* **-otrichi·a** *f.* (med.) achromotrichia.

Leuc-o·tea, **-ote·a** *pr.n.f.* (Gk. myth.) Leucothea.

†**leuto** *m.* (mus.). See **liuto**.

Leut·tra *pr.n.f.* (geog.) Leuctra (Greece).

leva *f.* lever; fulcrum; fare — a, to lever up; (naut.) launching jack; rudder lift; a —, walk away (with a rope); swell (of the sea); onda di —, ground swell; tiro di —, executive signal (gun or rocket); — di mare, National Service (with the Navy); (naut.) — forzata, press gang; (mil.) conscription, levy, call-up; — in massa, general call-up; essere di —, to be liable to call-up.

levabobine *m., f. indecl.* (text.) bobbin doffer.

levaldina *f.* (slang) shop-lifting.

†**lavame** *m.* yeast.

levante *m.* See under **levare**.

lev-are [A 1] *tr.* to raise, to lift; — di peso, to lift bodily; — le mani da un lavoro, to finish a task; to bring up; to elevate; — il bollore, to simmer, to be on the boil; — rumore, to make a fuss; — al cielo, to laud to the skies, to overpraise; — l'assedio, to raise the siege; — grido, to become well known; (sport) — una lepre, to raise a hare; to take off, to take away, to remove; to take out; — le tende, to strike camp, (joc.) to depart; — una sete, to quench a thirst; — la seduta, to adjourn the sitting; — la pelle a, to skin; to deduct, to subtract; — il fiato a, to make breathless; — di mezzo, to get rid of; (provb.) chiodo -a chiodo, set a thief to catch a thief; — di bocca un segreto a uno, to worm a secret out of someone; — le carte, to cut the cards; (eccl.) — la messa, — la confessione (a un prete), to withdraw (a priest's) faculties for saying mass or hearing confessions; to put up (a bird or animal in hunting); (naut.) — l'ancora, to weigh anchor; — barra, to ease the helm; — la caccia, to abandon the chase; — l'orza, to let fly the sheets; — per poppa, to tow; — una vela, to take in a sail; — volta, to take off turns; — le volte alle catene, to take turns out of the cable; — le volte a un cavo, to take turns and kinks out of a hawser; (naut. command) leva!, hoist!, hoist away!; — a remi!, oars!;†to conscript; †to elect; *rfl.* (acc. of prn. 'si') to rise, to get up; -arsi in piedi, to stand up, to rise to one's feet; si -a il vento, the wind is getting up; al -arsi del sole, at sunrise; -arsi a volo, to take off, to take wing; -arsi in superbia, to swell with pride; to remove oneself, to get out of the way; lèvati di torno, get out of my way; (naut.) -arsi in latitudine, to increase one's latitude; -arsi al vento, to make to windward; (of the wind) to freshen; †-arsi dalla posta, to sail; (dat. of prn. 'si') to remove from oneself; lèvati la giacca, take off your coat; -arsi una curiosità, to satisfy one's curiosity about a thing. **-amento** *m.* removal, subtraction; rising, rise, lifting. **-ante** *part. adj.* rising; *n.m.* East; Levant; East wind; (joc.) occhi a -ante e a ponente, cross-eyed; gambe a -ante e a ponente, bow-legs; venuto da -ante, stolen. **-antera** *f.* (naut.) E.S.E. wind in Adriatic. **-antina** *f.* twilled silk. **-antino** *adj., n.m.* Levantine. **-ata** *f.* raising; removal, taking away; -ata di sangue, blood-letting; collection (of letters from a posting box); rising, getting up (from bed); di prima -ata, only just out of bed; -ata del sole, sunrise; (naut.) porto di -ata, rada di -ata, convenient harbour for departure (owing to favourable wind, etc.); †weighing of anchor; †osservazione di -ata, morning observations; di -ata, first thing in the morning; (mil.) lifting of a siege; -ata di scudi, rebellion; †levy (cf. **leva**); (comm.) -ata di merci, purchase of goods wholesale; import of goods; rebuff, reproach; importance, elevation; relief map; brain wave, inspiration, happy thought, repartee. **-atac·cia** *f. pejor.* getting up too early; getting out of bed the wrong side; sharp reply. **-ato** *part. adj.* lifted, raised; andare a gambe -ate, to fall head over heels; fuggire a gambe -ate, to run away as fast as one's legs will take one; a bandiere -ate, with flying colours; got up, up, awake, out of bed; risen (also of bread); ben -ato!, good morning!; removed; excepted. **-atoio** *adj.* ponte -atoio, drawbridge. **-atore** *m.* lifter, raiser; riser; buon -atore, early-riser; †drawbridge. **-atrice** *f.* midwife, -atrice autorizzata, certified midwife; fare la -atrice, to be a midwife; fare da -atrice, to act as midwife; riser. **-atura** *f.* lifting, raising, rise; removal; standard, level; understanding; talent; degree of intelligence; di alta -atura, of lofty intellect, possessed of high I.Q.; di poca -atura, di piccola -atura, of low intelligence; stimulus; excitability; di piccola -atura, di poca -atura, responsive to a slight stimulus, excitable, emotional, (or, of things) readily movable; moment, importance; di poca -atura, of little importance. †**-azione** *f.* raising, elevating; spiritual elevation. **-enti** *m.pl.* pirates, buccaneers.

leve *adj.* and derivs. See **lieve**.

Leviatano *pr.n.m.* (Bibl.) Leviathan; (fig.) anything monstrous or enormous; (text.) wool-bleaching machine.

levig-are [A 2 s] *tr.* to polish; to smooth; to gloss; †to pulverize. **-atezza** *f.* polish, polished surface. **-ato** *part. adj.* polished; smooth **-atrice** *f.* (eng.) lapping machine. **-azione** *f.* polishing; (chem.) levigation.

levirato *m.* levirate.

levi·stico *m.* (bot.) lovage, *Livisticum officinale*.

levita *m.* (Bibl.) Levite; (eccl.) deacon (esp. of St Stephen or St Laurence); cleric, priest.

levit-à *f. indecl.* lightness. **-are** [A 1 sd] and derivs. see **lievitare**; to ferment. **-azione** *f.* levitation.

†**levi·tica** *f.* long gown or tunic worn by men or women (eighteenth century).

Levi·tico *pr.n.m.* Leviticus; *adj.* levitical.

levogiro *adj.* (chem.; phys.) laevo-rotatory.

†**le·vore**[1] *m.* See **lepre**.

†**levo·re**[2] *m.* softness; gentleness.

†**levra** *f.* See **lebbra**.

levrier-e, **-o** *m.* greyhound. **-a** *f.* greyhound bitch.

†**le·zia** *f.* See **lezio**.

le·zio *m.* (usu. *pl.*) affectation, smirking; mincing ways (cf. **lezioso**).

lezion-e[1] *f.* lesson; class; lecture; rebuke, reprimand; reading; variant; interpretation; uomo di molta —, well-read person; (mus.) lesson, exercise. **-cella** *f. dim.* mild rebuke.

†**lezion-e**[2] *f.* see **elezione**. **-ale** *m.,* **-a·rio** *m.* (eccl.) lectionary.

lezios-o *adj.* affected; mincing; mawkish. **-amente** *adv.* affectedly; mincingly; mawkishly. **-ag·gine** *f.* affected habit. **-ità** *f.* affectedness (cf. **lezio**).

†**lezzare** *intr.* to stink.

lezzino *m.* (naut.) sennet.

lęzz-o *m.* stink, stench; filth; *adj.* stinking, filthy. **-one** *m.* (pop. Tusc.) filthy man. (**-ona** *f.*) **-oneri·a** *f.* (pop. Tusc.) filthiness. **-ume** *m.* (pop. Tusc.) filth; filthy habits.

lherzolite *f.* (miner.) lherzolite.

li[1] *pers. prn. 3rd pl.m. conj.* them.

li[2] *def. art. m.pl.* the (in certain uses only, otherwise **i** or **gli**); — 17 dicembre, the 17th of December; (poet., dial.) — scogli, — scopi, etc. (instead of 'gli scogli', 'gli scopi', etc.).

†**li**[3] *pers. prn.* See **gli, le, loro**.

lì *adv.* there; over there; eccolo —, there it is, there; quello —, that man over there; zitto —!, quiet there!; state —!, stay where you are!; per —, in that neighbourhood; sempre —, still in the same place; sta sempre —, he has made no progress; giù di —, thereabouts, *or*, down from there; di — a un mese, in a month from then; finire —, to be over and done with; ha lo stipendio e finisce —, he has his salary and nothing else; fatto e messo —, rough, uncivilized (of a person); ora qui e ora —, now here, now there; — per —, there and then, instantly, on the spur of the moment, point blank; essere lì lì per, to be on the verge of; *excl.* here!; e —, col solito discorso!, there you go again with the same old story!

†**liale** *adj.* and derivs. See **leale**.

†**liama** *f.* link; bond.

liana *f.* (bot.) liana, liane.

lianos *m. indecl.* (geog.) llanos, the steppes of South America.

li-as *m. indecl.* (geol.) lias. **-as·sico** *adj.* liassic; calcare -assico, lias limestone.

lib-agione *f.,* **-ame** *m.,* **-a·mina** *f.* See under **libare**[1].

liban-o[1] *m.* (naut.) rope (various sizes and uses). **-ella** *f. dim.* (naut.) small rope (usually of esparto grass).

Li·ban-o[2] *pr.n.m.* (geog.) Lebanon; (bot.) cedro di —, cedar of Lebanon. **-e·o,** **-ęse** *adj., n.m., f.* Lebanese.

libanomanzi·a *f.* divination by incense.

lib-are[1] [A 1] *tr.* to make libations to; to touch lightly with the lips; to sip, to taste. **-agione** *f.* libation. **-ame** *m.* libation, offering. **-amento** *m.* libation; first taste. **-ato** *part. adj.* given as an offering. **-ato·rio** *m.* (archaeol.) vessel used for pouring libations. **-azione** *f.* libation; drinking to someone's health; taste.

lib·are² [A I] *tr.* (naut.) to lighten (a ship). **-ato** *part. adj.* (naut.) 'in ballast'.

libarol *m. indecl.* (naut.) lighterman; (Venice) owner.

libbr·a *f.* pound weight; — sottile, a 'light pound' (in Milan it was 326 grammes, while the 'libbra grossa' was almost double that); a kind of tax. **-étta** *f. dim.* a bare pound. **-óna** *f. augm.* a good pound.

libècci·o *m.* south-west wind. **-ata** *f.* south-westerly gale. **-óso** *adj.* south-westerly. **-uolo** *m.* fresh south-westerly wind.

†libella *f.* See **livella**.

libell·o *m.* small book; (leg.) written pleading instituting proceedings; — (famoso), defamatory libel; (eccl. hist.) *libellus*, certificate (of sacrifice); †copy, transcript. **-ac·cio** *m. pejor.* (leg.) gross libel. **-a·tici** *m.pl.* (eccl. hist.) *libellatici*. **-ista** *m.* pamphleteer; (leg.) libeller; defamer.

libel·lula *f.* (ent.) dragon fly.

libente *adj.* willing; pronto e —, ready and willing.

liberal·e *adj.* liberal; openhanded; le arti -i, the liberal arts; (pol.) liberal; †in honour of Bacchus; *n.m., f.* (pol.) liberal. **-astro** *m.* (pol.) pseudo-liberal. **-ésco** *adj.* (*m.pl.* **-éschi**) (pol.) inclined towards liberalism. **-éssa** *f.* (joc., pol.) woman liberal. **-ismo** *m.* (pol.) liberalism. **-ità** *f.* liberality; generosity; munificence; (leg.) gratuity (C.C.); †liberty. **-ménte** *adv.* liberally; generously; freely. **-o·ide** *adj., n.m.* (pol.) near-liberal. **-óne** *m. augm.* enthusiastic liberal; alla **-óna**, freely.

liber·are [A I s] *tr.* to liberate, to free, to relieve; to set free, to release; to let out; to deliver; Dio ci -i!, Heaven forbid!; (leg.) to discharge (from mortgage) (C.C.); (finan.) — un'azione, to pay a share fully; (cards, bridge) to unblock, to establish; *rfl.* to free oneself; **-arsi di**, to get rid of, to be released from, to shake off. **-aménto** *m.* freeing, setting free; releasing. **†-anza** *f.* freeing; (mil.) paying-off paper. **-ata·rio** *m.* successful competitor, to whom the prize is awarded or the work allotted. **-ato** *part. adj.* freed, set free; released; delivered. **-atóre** *m.* liberator; deliverer. (**-atrice** *f.*) **-ato·rio** *adj.* (*m.pl.* **-ato·rii**) releasing (from an obligation). **-azióne** *f.* liberation; freeing; release; redemption; exemption; (leg.) release, discharge (C.C.).

liber·colo *m. pejor.* inferior book, 'rag'.

Libe·ri·a *pr.n.f.* (geog.) Liberia. **-ano** *adj., n.m.* (geog.) Liberian.

liber·ismo *m.* theory of free market, free economy. **-ista** *m.* champion or supporter of free economy; free-trader. **-i·stico** *adj.* relating to free economy, laisser-faire, or free trade.

li·ber·o *adj.* free; independent; freed; released; fare —, to free; untrammelled; frank, open, uninhibited; unoccupied, not busy; lasciare —, to give free time to; — di sè, with free time on one's hands; aria -a, open air; — arbitrio, free will; — scambio, free trade; — pensatore, free thinker; (leg.) a piede —, at liberty, on bail; without detention pending trial; certificato di stato —, certificate of civil status (showing freedom to marry) (C.C.); — di ogni vincolo o gravame, free from incumbrances; carta -a, unstamped paper; occhio —, naked eye; (paint.) pennello —, masterly painter, a master; disegno a mano -a, freehand drawing; traduzione -a, free translation; strofe -e, blank verse; donna -a, woman of easy virtue; discorsi -i, loose, coarse talk; free, vacant empty; available; clear, open; *adv. phr.* (Tusc.) alla -a, freely; *n.m.* freed man; i -i, the free peoples; *adv.* freely; loosely; parlare —, to speak freely, to speak loosely or coarsely. (**-aménte** *adv.*) **-oscambista** *m.* free-trader. **-otto** *adj. dim.* rather licentious.

libert·à *f.* liberty, freedom; free time; mi prendo la — di, I take the liberty of; era in mia — accettare o no, I was free to accept or refuse; essere in —, to be free; mettersi in —, to take off one's formal attire, to be in one's shirt-sleeves; stare in —, to 'make oneself at home'; (leg.) — provvisoria, provisional liberty; release on bail (C.P.P.); — personale, personal liberty; — politica, political liberty or freedom; — vigilata, liberty under supervision (C.P.); — di volere, freedom of will; mettere in —, to set free; — di stampa, freedom of the press; — di parola, freedom of speech; limitazione della —, restriction of freedom; †liberality. **†-are** *tr.* to set free. **-a·rio** *m.* anarchist; *adj.* libertarian. **-icida** *adj.* liberty-destroying; *n.m.* destroyer of liberty, liberticide.

libert·ino *m.* libertine, profligate; (hist.) son of a freedman; *adj.* rakish, libertine. **-ina** *f.* (numis.) silver coin of Ragusa. **-inag·gio** *m.* libertinism, libertinage; licentiousness. **-inità** *f.* libertinism, libertinage. **-o** *m.* (hist.) freedman; *adj.* freed. (**-a** *f.*)

Li·bia *pr.n.f.* (geog.) Libya.

li·bico *adj., n.m.* (geog.) Libyan.

libi·din·e *f.* lust; lechery; la — del potere, lust for power. **†-are** *intr.* to satisfy lust. **-óso** *adj.* lustful, lecherous, lascivious, libidinous. **-osaménte** *adv.* libidinously.

libi·stico *m.* (bot.). See **levistico**.

Libitin·a *pr.n.f.* (myth.) goddess of funerals. **†-a·rio** *m.* undertaker.

li·bito *m.* will, desire; caprice; a —, at will, at pleasure, *ad lib.*; che — fe' licito in sua legge (Dante, *Inf.* v, 56), who gave free rein to inclination (a phrase become proverbial).

libo¹ *m.* (bot.) yew, *Taxus baccata*.

libo² *m.* (naut.) lighter.

†lib·o³ *m.* wind blowing from Libya (cf. **libeccio**). **†-onoto** *m.* wind from the south-south-west.

libr·a *f.* balance, scales; tenere in equa —, to keep in equilibrium; (astron.) Libra; (comm.) duty; tax.

libra·io *m.* See under **libro**.

libr·are [A I] *tr.* to balance, to poise; (mil.) to set up (a gun) on its platform or mounting, to line up (a gun); to lay; *rfl.* to balance, to keep one's balance; (aeron., etc.) to hover. **-aménto** *m.* balance, poise; pondering; weighing; (phys.) libration. **-ataménte** *adv.* in a well-balanced manner. **-a·tile** *adj.* apt or liable to balance. **-ato** *part. adj.* balanced; poised, in equilibrium; levelled, equalled; deliberated, pondered; (aeron.) volo -ato, hovering. **-atóre** *m.* (mil. hist.) captain of a catapult. **-azióne** *f.* swaying, balancing; (astron.) libration.

libr·o *m.* book; volume; — di lettura, reading book, reader; — illustrato, picture book, book with illustrations; — di preghiere, prayer-book; — di consultazione, reference book; — esaurito, book out of print; — usato, second-hand book; — di testo, text-book; i -i sacri, the Bible; — d'oro, a book in which noble families are registered; portar dietro i -i a uno, to fetch and carry for a person; leggere nel — di alcuno, to speak ill of someone; non è nel mio —, I don't like him, he is not in my good books; a —, hinged, with a flap, opening like a book; porta a —, folding door; — giallo, thriller, 'whodunnit'; (mus.) suonare a — aperto, to play at sight; (techn.) bast; (leg.) — nero, a black book of offences; (comm.) book of accounts; — mastro, — maestro, ledger; — giornale, journal; — di cassa, cash book; — delle commissioni, commission account book; mettere a —, to enter (a transaction); — bollato, book with revenue stamp affixed on each page of the book; presentare i -i in tribunale, to submit books of accounts to Court; — di protocollo, register, record book; — dei soci, register of shareholders; — verde, the book which contains Italian diplomatic papers during a certain period; (naut.) — dei segnali, signal manual; — di disciplina, punishment register; (naut., aeron.) — di bordo, log; †— di evoluzioni, see 'libro dei segnali'; (bot.) inner bark, liber. **-a·io** *m.* bookseller; bookshop. **-a·rio** *adj.* pertaining to books; mercatura -aria, book trade; fiera -aria, book fair; libertà -aria, freedom to publish without submission to censorship. **-eri·a** *f.* bookshop; bookcase. **†-et·tine** *f.pl.* beginner's arithmetic book; A.B.C.; primer; sketch-book. **-ettino** *m. dim.* of **libro**; packet of cigarette papers. **-ettista** *m.* (mus.) librettist. **-étto** *m. dim.* of **libro**; note-book, memorandum; booklet; -etto di assegni, cheque book; current account or savings book; -etto della banca, pass-book; scala a -etto, pair of steps; (naut.) -etto di costruzione, ship's book; -etto personale, rating's pay and identity card; (mus.) libretto, opera-book; book of tickets, etc.; season ticket. **-iccino** *m. dim.* of **libro**: tiny book (printed); (liturg.) -iccino della Madonna, Little Office. **-icciuolo** *m. dim.* of **libro**. **-iciat·tolo** *m.* cheap and nasty little book. **-icino** *m. dim.* of **libro**.

†liburna *f.* (naut.) lake or river shooting-punt; fast rowing-boat (like a gig); Dalmatian pirate vessel.

libur·n·ico, -o *adj.* (geog.) relating to Liburnia (Croatia).

lic·ambe·o *adj.* in the nature of a bitter satire, such as that with which Archilochus assailed Lycambes. **-antropi·a** *f.* (med.) lycanthropy. **-an·tropo** *m.* werewolf.

Licaóne *pr.n.m.* (myth.) Lycaon; †(zool.) wild hunting dog.

lic·cia¹ *f.* (ichth.). See **leccia**.

†lic·cia² *f.* See **lizza**.

lic·ci·o *m.* (text.) heddle, warp-cord, as used by weavers to raise or to spread out the threads of the warp. **-ai(u)ola** *f.* saw-wrest, for setting the teeth of a saw. **-are** [A 3] *tr.* to set (a saw); (text.) to fix the warp-cords; *intr.* (aux. avere) (Tusc.) to bolt, to run off. **-atura** *f.* setting (of a saw); (text.) fixing the warp-cords.

liceal-e *adj.*, **-ista** *m.* See under **liceo**.

liceità *f.* (leg.) lawfulness.

licena *f.* (ent.) 'blue' butterflies, *Lycaena* spp.

licenz-a *f.* licence, leave, permission, permit; diploma at the end of a course of study; school-leaving certificate; notice, dismissal; epilogue of a play; *envoi* of an author to his reader at the end of a book; licence, liberty; (leg.) licence; authority; power; permit; — di porto d'armi, licence to carry arms, gun licence. **-iata·rio** *m.* licensee. **-ino** *m.* first year's test for engineers.

licenzi-are [A 4] *tr.* to give leave to, to release; to discharge, to fire, to sack; to dismiss; to send away; to allow; to give permission to; to license; (typ.) to pass (a proof); †to exempt; *rfl.* to take one's leave, to take leave, to go away. (**-amento** *m.*) **-ando** *m.* a person who has completed a course of study and is about to take the final examination. **-ata·rio** *m.* (leg.) -atario di brevetto, licensee of patent. **-ato** *part. adj.* fired, dismissed, sent away; freed, exonerated; allowed, permitted; licensed; (typ.) corrected, seen (of a proof); holding a 'diploma di licenza'; *n.m.* licentiate. (**-atore** *m.* **-atrice** *f.*) **-atura** *f.* qualification of the 'licenza'. **-osità** *f.* licentiousness; capriciousness. **-oso** *adj.* licentious, dissolute; †unconventional, irregular; †inciting to licentiousness; †uncontrollable, wild, furious. **-osamente** *adv.* licentiously, irregularly; arbitrarily; recklessly.

lic-e·o *m.* Lyceum; high school, grammar school; (geog.) Mount Arcady; (mus.) — musicale, college or academy of music; conservatoire (cf. Note under **scuola**). **-eale** *adj.* pertaining to a 'liceo'; *n.m.,f.* pupil at a 'liceo'. **-ealista**, **-eista** *m., f.* see **liceale**.

†li·cere *impers.* See **lecere**.

licet *m. indecl.* (euphem.) lavatory, toilet.

lichen-e *m.* (bot.) lichen; (pop. med.) rash, eruption. **-ina** *f.* (chem.) lichenin; (pharm.) mucilaginous cough mixture.

†lici *adv.* there.

li·cio[1] *adj.* (hist. geog.) Lycian, relating to Lycia.

li·cio[2] *m.* (bot.) thorn of Christ, species of cedar in Palestine.

licit-are [A 1 s] *intr.* (aux. avere) to bid (at an auction); (cards, bridge) to bid. **-azione** *f.* bid; mettere in -azione, to put up for auction.

†li·cito *adj.* See **lecito**.

lico-per·sico *m.* (bot.) tomato, *Lycopersicum esculentum*. **-po·dio** *m.* (bot.) club moss, *Lycopodium clavatum* and other species; (pharm.) polvere di -podio, vegetable brimstone, lycopodium.

†licore *m.* See **liquore**.

licoressi·a *f.* (med.) lycorexia, bulimia.

licorna *f.* (herald.) unicorn.

liddite *f.* (chem.) lyddite.

li·d-io *adj.* (geog.) Lydian; (mus.) modo —, Lydian mode; pietra -ia, Lydian stone, touchstone. **-ite** *f.* lydite, touchstone.

lido *m.* shore; lido; bathing-beach; (geog.) sand-bar; (fig., poet.) native shores, native land.

†lie *adv.* See **lì**.

lied *m.* (pl. **-er**) (mus.) Lied. **-eri·stico** *adj.* (mus.) in the style of a Lied, in Lieder style.

Liegi *pr.n.f.* (geog.) Liège.

lient-eri·a *f.* (med.) lientery. **-e·rico** *adj.* lienteric.

lie·o *adj.* (class. myth.) Lyaean, Bacchic; (fig.) jovial; *n.m.* (poet.) Bacchus; wine.

†lieta *f.* clear smokeless flame.

liet-o *adj.* glad; joyous, joyful; (euphem.) il — evento, the happy event (birth of a baby); (poet.) fertile; thriving. **-amente** *adv.* gladly, joyously, joyfully, happily. **-ezza** *f.* gladness, happiness, joyfulness, joyousness. **†-itu·dine** *f.* see **lietezza**.

†lieva[1] *f.* See **leva**.

†lieva[2] *f.* importance; matter, affair, concern.

†lievare *tr.* to remove; — la pace, to break the peace; *rfl.* to rise (cf. **levare**).

liev-e *adj.* light, slight; easy; trifling; soft; — come una piuma, light as a feather; un — sorriso, a slight smile; una — brezza, a gentle breeze; †swift; †nimble; †easy; †gentle, gradual; †unimportant; †poor, humble, low; †— di cervello, simple-minded; †acqua —, clear, pure water; *adv.* lightly; †di —, easily; *n.m.* lightness. **-emente** *adv.* lightly. **-ezza** *f.* lightness; frivolity, inconstancy, levity. **†-ificato** *adj.* made light, lightened. **-ità** *f.* lightness; inconstancy, levity, frivolousness; frailness, smallness, weakness.

lievit-are [A 1] *intr.* (aux. essere) to ferment; to be leavened; to rise; to be slaked (of lime); *tr.* to leaven; to slake (lime). **-ato** *part.*
adj. fermented; leavened; risen; pane -ato, leavened bread; slaked. **-atura** *f.* leavening; slaking.

lie·vito *m.* yeast; ferment; pane senza —, unleavened bread; (fig.) stimulus, incitement.

†lievre *f.* See **lepre**.

li·fore *m.* (dial. S. Ital.). See **fiffaro**.

†ligame *m.* See **legame**.

ligamento *m.* See **legamento**, under **legare**.

li·geo *m.* (ent.) *Lygaeus equestris*, a hemipterous pest of oak trees.

†ligiare *vb.* and derivs. See **lisciare**.

li·gio *m.* sworn vassal; liege; *adj.* subject; loyal, faithful, true; servile, submissive.

lignag·gio *m.* lineage, pedigree.

li·gn-eo *adj.* woody, ligneous. **-ificare** [A 2 s] *intr.* (aux. essere) (bot.) to lignify, to become woody. **-ificato** *part. adj.* lignified. **-ificazione** *f.* lignification. **-ina** *f.* (chem.) lignin. **-ite** *f.* lignite, brown coal. **-ocellulosa** *f.* (chem.) lignocellulose. **-osa** *f.* (geog.) forest association (of plants).

†ligostra *f.* (zool.). See **aragosta**.

li·gula *f.* (bot.) ligule.

liguor-iano, **-ista** *adj.*, *n.m.* (eccl.) Redemptorist.

li·gur-e *adj.*, *n.m.,f.* (geog.) Ligurian.

Ligu·ria *pr.n.f.* (geog.) Liguria.

†ligu·rio *m.* a semi-precious stone such as agate.

liguro *m.* (zool.) green lizard, *Lacerta viridis*.

†ligusta *f.* (ent.). See **locusta**.

ligu·stico *adj.* (geog.) Ligurian.

ligustro *m.* (bot.) privet, *Ligustrum vulgare*.

lili-a·ceo *adj.* (bot.) liliaceous. **-ale** *adj.* lily-white, pure as a lily. **†-ato** *adj.* adorned with lilies.

lilion *m. indecl.* (text.) trade name of a synthetic fibre.

Lilla[1] *pr.n.f.* (geog.) Lille.

lill-a[2] *m.* (bot.) Persian lilac, West Indian bead tree, *Melia azedarach*. **-ato** *adj.* decorated with lilacs. **-atro** *m.* (bot.) *Phillyrea angustifolia*.

lil·leri *m.pl.* (Tusc. pop.) senza — non si lallera, no credit given (a phrase sometimes seen written up in country inns, equiv. to 'senza lire non si mangia').

lillipuziano *adj.*, *n.m.* Lilliputian.

lillo *m.* (Tusc.) foppish adornment, dangling ornament; glass stopper.

lim-a *f.* file, rasp; — sorda, silent file, (fig.) someone who works quietly and underhand; (fig.) nagging thought; (poet.) the file, repolishing; far — —, to rub one finger on another, as if filing, by way of mocking a person whose efforts have failed; — —, mockingly; (agric.) loose soil; (zool.) *Lima inflata*, file shell; (bot.) see **limetta**.

limac·cia[1] *f. pejor.* of **lima**, q.v.

†limac·cia[2] *f.* (zool.) slug.

limac·ci-o *m. pejor.* of **limo**, q.v.; mud, slime. **-oso** *adj.* muddy.

limacologi·a *f.* (zool.) malacology.

liman *m. indecl.*, **limano** *m.* (geog.) natural saline on a sea-shore; evaporated salt deposit on the coast of the Black Sea.

limarcuola *f.* (vet.). See **limassuola**.

lim-are [A 1] *tr.* to file; to sharpen; (fig.) to clean, to purge; to polish. **-atamente** *adv.* in a refined manner. **-atezza** *f.* refinement. **-ato** *part. adj.* filed; sharpened; purified; elegant; polished; refined. **-atore** *m.* (techn.) polisher. **-atura** *f.* filing; filings; viver di -atura, to live on a shoe-string, to live from hand to mouth.

limassuola *f.* (vet.) 'foot rot' in cattle, a boil between the toes.

limbello *m.* snippet for leather or cloth; wooden tongue for a joint; (herald.) see **lambello**; (joc.) tongue; ficcare il — in qualche cosa, to put one's spoke in.

†limbicco *m.* See **lambicco**.

limbo *m.* (theol.) Limbo; — dei bambini, *limbus infantium*; (joc.) va al —!, go to blazes!; essere come le anime del —, to be in anxious suspense; (astron.) limb; outer circle of an astrolabe.

Limburgo *pr.n.f.* (geog.) Limburg.

Limena *pr.n.f.* (geog.) Limena, near Padua; *m.* a light red wine from the district.

limenite *f.* (ent.) — del pioppo, *Limenitis populi*, a species of butterfly related to the White Admiral.

limetta[1] *f. dim.* of **lima**, q.v.

limetta[2] *f.* (bot.) sweet lemon, *Citrus limonium* var. *dulcis*.

limi·coli *m.pl.* (orn.) Limicolae.

limiere *m.* pointer (breed of dog).

li·min-e *m.* threshold; border, limit; *pl.* (eccl.) visita ai limini, visit *ad limina*; †(naut.) harbour or entrance to a harbour. †**-are** *adj.* relating to the threshold.

limitare¹ *m.* threshold; (fig.) beginning, outset.

limit-are² [A I S] *tr.* to limit; to restrict; to restrain; to curtail; *rfl.* to be limited, to be bounded, to restrict oneself; -arsi a una cosa, to be content with a thing. **-a·bile** *adj.* limitable. **-abilità** *f.* limitability. (**-amento** *m.*) **-atezza** *f.* restrictedness, paucity, exiguousness. **-ativo** *adj.* restrictive; (leg.) limiting, restricting. (**-ativamente** *adv.*) **-ato** *part. adj.* limited; modest; -ato di mezzi, of limited means; bounded; confined; restricted; (finan.) società -ata, limited company. **-amente** *adv.* in a limited way. (**-atore** *m.* **-atrice** *f.*) **-azione** *f.* limitation; limit; restraint; fare -azione alla regola, to make an exception to the rule; (watchm.) copiglia di -azione, banking pin; (leg.) -azione della responsabilità, limitation of liability (C.C.).

li·mit-e *m.* limit; boundary; check; restraint; extent; — di velocità, speed limit; — delle nevi, snow-line; in casi —, in extreme cases; *pl.* limitations; (leg.) limits; agire nei -i del mandato, to act within the limits of the power. †**-a·neo** *adj.* (Rom. hist.) relating to frontier guards.

limi·trofo *adj.* bordering, border; marginal.

limma *m.* (mus.) limma.

limn-i·metro *m.* graduated hydrometric scale. **-ite** *f.* (miner.) limonite.

limo *m.* mud, slime; mire; (poet.) — umano, human clay.

limon-e *m.* (bot.) name of various kinds of *Citrus*, e.g. lemon, *Citrus limon*, and citron, *C. medica*; buccia di —, lemon peel, (fig.) small thing which causes something to slip or fall; spremuta di —, lemon squash; succo di —, lemon juice; — spremuto, squeezed lemon, (fig.) a person one abandons after having got out of him all one can; più agro del —, very mean; strizzare i -i, to wring one's hands; (zool.) di mare, *Cinthia papillosa*, a tunicate. **-a·io** *m.* lemon-seller; shed for keeping lemon plants in the winter. **-ata** *f.* lemonade; lemon squash. **-ato** *adj.* lemon-coloured. **-cello** *m. dim.* (bot.) small kind of lemon with very acid pulp and smooth peel. **-e·a** *f.* lemonade. **-ella** *f.* (bot.) burning bush, *Dictamnus albus*. **-ina** *f.* (chem.) limonin. **-i·o** *m.* (bot.) large wintergreen, *Pirola rotundifolia*; sea lavender, *Limonium vulgare*. **-ite** *f.* (miner.) limonite; -ite delle torbiere, bog iron-ore, limonite.

limo·sin-a *f.* and derivs. See **elemosina**.

limosino *adj.* (geog.) of Limoges, Limousine; *n.m.* Limousine.

limos-o *adj.* muddy, slimy. **-ità** *f.* muddiness, sliminess.

lim·pid-o *adj.* clear, limpid. (**-amente** *adv.*) **-ezza** *f.*, **-ità** *f.* bright; transparent; pure; clearness, clarity; limpidity; purity; transparency.

†**linag·gio** *m.* See **legnaggio**.

lin-aiola *f.* (bot.) toadflax, *Linaria vulgaris*. **-aiuolo** *m.* worker or dealer in flax.

lince *m.* (zool.) lynx, *Lynx lynx*.

lince·o¹ *adj.* lynx-like; occhi -ei, lynx eyes.

Lince·o² *pr.n.m.* (myth.) Lynceus; Accademia dei Lincei, a Roman scientific society founded in 1603 by Federico Cesi; Nuovi Lincei, Academy of the Lincei as revived by Pius IX.

†**linci** *adv.* thence.

linci-are [A 3] *tr.* to lynch. **-ag·gio** *m.* lynching, lynch-law. **-ato** *part. adj.* lynched. **-atore** *m.* lyncher. (**-atrice** *f.*)

linda *f.* index arm of an astrolabe, vernier; curled border of a wig.

lindano *m.* (chem.; agric.) lindane.

lind-o *adj.* neat, trim, spruce, smart; tidy. (**-amente** *adv.*) **-ezza** *f.* neatness, trimness, spruceness, smartness. **-ura** *f.* neatness, elegance; affectation in dress.

li·ne-a *f.* line; in — d'aria, as the crow flies; trattare a grandi -e, to deal with in outline; line, cable; -e telegrafiche, telegraph wires; in — di amicizia, by way of friendship; mettersi in — con, to keep up with; shape, profile; conservare la —, to keep its shape; — di condotta, behaviour; (mens.) line, twelfth of an inch; non cedere di una —, not to give in an inch; (med.) tenth part of a degree centigrade; (geog.) — di displuvio, watershed, rainfall divide; (zool.) — primitiva, primitive streak (of an embryo); (sport) — di fondo campo, base-line (tennis); — di uscita laterale, touch-line (rugby); — di metà campo, half-way

line; — di meta, goal line (rugby); — di pallone morto, dead-ball line; — di vantaggio, advantage line; prima — di mischia, front row; seconda —, second row; terza —, back row; terza — centro, lock; terza — ala, wing-forward; — di porta, base-line (football); (leg.) line; relationship; — collaterale, collateral line or relationship; — diretta, direct line; — discendente, lineal descent (C.C.); (naut.) route, line; servizio di —, passenger service; — d'acqua, waterplane plan; — d'acqua naturale, waterline in ballast; — d'asse, thrust line of a shaft; — di bolina, a ship or line of ships close hauled; — di fila, line ahead; — di fronte, line abreast; — di fede, lubber's line; — di rispetto, limit of territorial waters; — di manovra, line (direction) of pull of a hawser; — di posizione, position line (navigational); — di bordo libero, di massimo carico, — di massima immersione, Plimsoll line; — di rilevamento, line of bearing (stationing of ships); — di scandaglio, — batometrica, fathom lines (given in metres); mettersi in —, to take up station; serrare la —, to take up close order; tagliare la —, to cut the enemy line or cross his T; uscire di —, to quit the line; (mil.) line, front; alignment; — d'approccio, approach line, support line; — del tiro, trajectory; essere di prima —, to be in the van; reggimento di —, infantry, regiment of the line. **-ale** *adj.* linear; in a straight line. **-almente** *adv.* in a straight line; in a direct line; lineally. **-amento** *m.* outline; feature; (art) outline; -amento con carbone, outline drawing in charcoal; (mil.) alignment. **-are** [A 6] *tr.* to delineate, to outline; to line, to rule with lines; *adj.* linear; in outline; (fig.) clear, straightforward; lucid; disegno -are, line drawing, mechanical drawing; (chem.) catena -are, straight chain; (bot.) foglie -ari, linear leaves. †**-a·rio** *adj.* see **lineare**. **-arità** *f.* (telev.) linearity; -arità del quadro, frame linearity. **-armente** *adv.* by lines; in a linear manner. **-ato** *part. adj.* outlined, in outline; delineated; lined, ruled; underlined; mattoni -ati, reticular masonry. **-atrice** *f.* ruling machine. †**-atura** *f.* features; line; line of descent, line of succession. **-azione** *f.* outline. **-etta** *f. dim.* of **linea**; hyphen; dash; (math.) minus sign; due -ette, equals sign.

lin-eri·a *f.*, **-eto** *m.* See under **lino**.

linf-a *f.* (anat.) lymph; (bot.) sap; †water. **-adenite** *f.* (med.) lymphadenitis. **-adenoma** *m.* (med.) lymphadenoma. **-angioite** *f.* lymphangiitis. **-angioma** *m.* lymphangioma. **-atici·smo** *m.* lymphatic temperament; languidness; (med.) lymphatism. **-a·tico** *adj.* (med.) lymphatic; weak, languid, anaemic; *n.m.* anaemic person. (**-aticamente** *adv.*) **-ati·smo** *m.* (med.) lymphatism. **-ociti** *m.pl.* (med.) lymphocytes. **-ocitosi** *f.* (med.) lymphocytosis; achroacytosis. **-oma** *m.* (med.) lymphoma, lymphadenoma. **-omatosi** *f.* (med.) lymphomatosis, multiple lymphoma. **-omatoso** *adj.* (med.) lymphomatous. **-orragi·a** *f.* (med.) lymphorrhoea. **-orre·a** *f.* (med.) lymphorrhoea. **-osarcoma** *m.* (med.) Hodgkin's disease, lymphosarcoma. **-osi** *f.* (med.) lymphosis, lymphatic leucaemia.

lingeri·a *f.* lingerie.

lingott-o *m.* ingot, nugget; *pl.* (typ.) furniture (metal or wood).

lingu-a *f.* **1.** (ANAT.) TONGUE; con tanto di — fuori, with one's tongue hanging out, panting, out of breath; seccarsi la —, to die; aver la — in bocca, to be able to speak for oneself, to have a tongue in one's head; — brutta, — sporca, coated tongue; avere la — legata, to be tongue-tied; tenere la — a freno, to hold one's tongue; a —, orally, avere il cuore sulla —, to be sincere; avere la — lunga, to be slanderous; mala —, evil tongue; (fig.) tongue, strip, of land; (cul.) — di passeri, 'sparrow's tongues', a sort of 'pasta'; (mus.) tongue (of organ-reed pipe); colpo di —, tongue-stroke, colpi di —, flutter-tonguing; (ichth.) sole, *Solea* spp.; (bot.) — cervina, dei pozzi, hart's tongue fern, *Phyllitis scolopendrium*; — da esca, edible fungus; — di cane, ribwort, *Plantago lanceolata*; — di bue, — di manzo, alkanet, *Anchusa*; — di serpe, adder's tongue, *Ophioglossum vulgatum*; -e d'acqua, broad-leaved pond weed, *Potamogeton natans*; †(mil.) — di fuoco, rocket. **2.** LANGUAGE, tongue, idiom, speech; in — povera, in plain words; — materna, mother tongue; aver —, to be informed, to hear; prender —, to find out; parlare in —, to speak the standard language (as against the local dialect); — d'acquisto, linguistic borrowings; (provb.) — toscana in bocca romana, description of the 'best' Italian, i.e. the Tuscan language pronounced in the Roman fashion. **-ac·cia** *f. pejor.* of **lingua**; evil tongue; coated tongue. **-acciuto** *adj.* foul-mouthed; slanderous. †**-adro** *adj.* evil-tongued, spiteful, malicious. **-ag·gio** *m.*

lingu-a (*cont.*)
language; style; parlance; diction; il ~aggio dei fiori, the language of flowers; ~aggio scientifico, scientific language; means of expression or communication; †nation. **-a·io** *m.* pedant in language. **-ai(u)olo** *m.* pedant (esp. in linguistic matters). **-ale** *adj.* lingual, of the tongue. †**-ardo** *adj.* evil-tongued, spiteful, malicious. **-ata** *f.* (ichth.) sole, *Solea* spp. **-at·tola** *f.* (ichth.) *Citharus linguatula*, a kind of sole; (vet.) fluke. **-a·tula** *f.* (vet.) fluke. †**-eggiare** *intr.* to chatter. **-ella** *f. dim.* of **lingua**; wick: strip of felt for filtering a liquid by transferring it from one vessel to another by capillary action; ploughshare. **-etta** *f. dim.* of **lingua**; wagging tongue; wick; tongue (of a shoe); (watchm.) brace; (bot.) *Ruscus hypophyllum*; flap of the lock of a trunk; catch; cam; the sharp end of a strap or leather belt; (mus.) reed; ~etta battente, beating reed, tangent (of a clavichord); (techn.) flame of an oxyacetylene plant. **-ettare** [A1c] *tr.* to stutter. **-ett(u)ola** *f.* gossip; wagging tongue. **-iforme** *adj.* tongued, tongue-shaped. **-ina** *f. dim.* of **lingua**. **-ino** *m.* tip of the tongue; fare il ~ino, to put out the tip of the tongue. **-ista** *m., f.* philologist. **-i·stica** *f.* philology; linguistics. **-i·stico** *adj.* philological; linguistic; sezione ~istica, divisione ~istica, language department. †**-ola** *f.* pointer of a balance. †**-oso**, **-uto** *adj.* evil-tongued.

Linguadoca *pr.n.f.* (geog.) Languedoc.
linifi·cio *m.* linen mill; flax mill.
linimento *m.* liniment.
†**lin-ire** *tr.* (med.) to rub, to massage. †**-ito** *part. adj.* (med.) rubbed, massaged; (pharm.) medicated.
lin-o *m.* (bot.) flax, *Linum usitatissimum* and other species; — delle fate, feather grass, *Stipa pennata*; — d'acqua, brookweed, *Samolus valerandi*; flax fibre; linen; (text.) flax; — tessile, harl flax, bast flax; seme di —, linseed; olio di —, linseed oil; tela di —, linen; *adj.* linen. **-eri·a** *f.* linen goods. **-ina** *f.* (biol.) linin. **-o·leum** *m. indecl.* linoleum; oil-cloth. **-one** *m.* (text.) fine linen, lawn. **-osa** *f.* linseed pulp. **-oso** *adj.* of linen; linen-like.
lino-tipi·a *f.* linotype. **-ti·pico** *adj.* linotype. **-tipista** *m.* linotype operator.
linseme *m.* linseed.
lin·teo *adj.* of linen; *n.m.* linen (cloth) (esp. of the shroud of Christ).
linter·colo *m.* (mus.) kit-fiddle, kit-violin.
linterno *m.* (bot.) *Rhamnus alaternus*.
†**lintinoso** *adj.* freckled.
lio-corno *m.* (zool.) *Pandalus pristis*, a kind of shrimp; †unicorn. †**-fante** *m.* elephant. †**-pardo** *m.* leopard.
lio·n *m. indecl.* dandy, fop (nineteenth century).
Lione[1] *pr.n.f.* (geog.) Lyons.
†**lion-e**[2] *m.* see **leone**. †**-fante** *m.* elephant.
lipacidemi·a *f.* (med.) lipacidaemia.
Li·par-i *pr.n.m.pl.* (geog.) Aeolian Islands. **-ite** *f.* (miner.) liparite.
lipa·ride *f.* (ichth.) sea snail, *Liparis* spp.; (bot.) a kind of orchid, *Liparidae*; *pl.* (ent.) tussock moths.
lipasi *f. indecl.* (chem.) lipase.
lip-emi·a *f.* (med.) lipaemia. **-erolito** *m.* pomade.
li·pico *adj.* (chem.) lipic.
lip-o·ide *adj.* lipoid. **-oma** *m.* lipoma. **-omatosi** *f.* lipomatosis. **-omatoso** *adj.* lipomatoid. **-otimi·a** *f.* lipothymia, syncope.
lippa *f.* cat in the game of tip-cat; (vet.) rheum in a horse's eye.
lipp-itu·dine *f.* (med.) lippitude, blear-eye. †**-o** *adj.* blear-eyed; short-sighted. †**-oso** *adj.* blear-eyed.
Li·psia *pr.n.f.* (geog.) Leipzig.
†**liquare** *rfl.* to liquefy; to melt, to dissolve; to be manifested, to appear.
liqu-ativo *adj.* see **liquefattivo**. **-azione** *f.* melting an alloy of different metals for the purpose of cooling out the components separately. **-efaci·bile** *adj.* liquefiable. **-efacimento** *m.* liquefaction. **-efare** [B1A] *tr.* to liquefy. **-efatti·bile** *adj.* liquefiable. **-efattivo** *adj.* liquefying. **-efatto** *part. adj.* liquefied; condensed; fused, molten. **-efazione** *f.* liquefaction. **-escenza** *f.* liquid state or condition.
liquidamb-ar *m. indecl.*, **-ara** *f.* (bot.) *Liquidamber orientalis*.
liquid-are [A1s] *tr.* (comm.; leg.) to wind up; to liquidate; to settle; — un'azienda, to wind up a business; — un conto, to settle an account; — una domanda, to ascertain the amount of a claim; (euphem.) to 'liquidate', to 'eliminate' (i.e. to kill). **-a·bile** *adj.* which can be wound up. **-abilità** *f.* liquidity. **-amento** *m.* liquidating; settling. **-ato** *part. adj.* wound up; settled; liquidated;

(leg.) danni ~ati, liquidated damages (C.C.); spese ~ate, taxed costs (C.C.P.). **-atore** *m.* (leg.) liquidator; ~atore d'avaria, average adjuster. **-atrice** *f. adj.* commissione ~atrice, official liquidator or receiver. **-azione** *f.* liquidation; winding-up; (leg.) ~azione coatta amministrativa, compulsory winding-up (of company); ~azione convenzionale del danno, agreement on liquidated damages; ~azione giudiziale del danno, ascertainment by Court of amount of damages; ~azione giudiziaria, winding-up by Court; ~azione dell'eredità, winding-up of deceased's estate (C.C.).
li·quid-o *adj.* liquid; fluid; (finan.) denari ~i, liquid money; conto —, settled bill on account; sentenza ~a, final judgement; *n.m.* liquid, fluid; (techn.) liquor. **-amente** *adv.* fluently, easily; in a fluid way. **-astro** *adj.* bordering on the liquid state. **-etto** *adj. dim.* rather fluid. **-ezza** *f.* fluidity. †**-ire** *intr.* to become liquid; to melt. **-ità** *f.* fluidity; the liquid state. **-o·metro** *m.* (aeron.) liquidometer.
liquiri·zia *f.* (bot.) liquorice, *Glycyrrhiza glabra*.
li·quor *m.* (physiol.) liquor, spinal fluid.
liquor-e *m.* liquor; liqueur; (leg.) — alcoolico, spirituous liquor (C.P.). **-i·zia** *f.* see **liquirizia**. **-oso** *adj.* very alcoholic (of wine).
lir-a[1] *f.* (finan.) lira, the monetary unit in Italy; un biglietto da cinque cento ~e, a five hundred lire note; — toscana, Tuscan lira; — greca, drachma; — turca, Turkish pound; — austriaca, crown; — inglese, — sterlina, English £; mancare 19 soldi per fare una —, to be broke; avere 25 soldi per —, to have more than one's due. **-azza** *f.* (numism.) low denomination silver coin of the Venetian Republic. **-etta** *f. dim.* of **lira**; a mere lira; barely a lira; (numism.) Venetian silver coin.
lir-a[2] *f.* (mus.) lyre; lyra, rebeck; — arciviolata, bass lyra; — barberina, (or) della Barberia, kind of lyre invented by G. B. Doni, 1636; — chitarra, French lyre-shaped guitar (nineteenth century); — da braccio, treble lyra; — da gamba, bass lyra; — moderna, lyra (as distinct from the ancient Greek lyre); — tedesca, hurdy-gurdy; †poetry; †harmony; essere come l'asino al suon della —, to be tone-deaf; (astron.) Lyra; (orn.) lyre bird. **-ato** *adj.* lyre-shaped. †**-essa** *f. pejor.* (mus.) wretched lyra. †**-oldo** *m.* (mus.) lyra-player. **-one** *m.* (mus.) bass lyra; (Emilia) violoncello. **-uro** *m.* (orn.) lyre bird.
†**lira**[3] *f.* straight line, furrow.
li·ric-o *adj.* lyric, lyrical; (mus.) artista —, opera singer; dramma —, opera; commedia ~a, lyric comedy (sub-title of Verdi's *Falstaff*); teatro —, opera theatre, opera (as art-form); opera ~a, opera; stagione ~a, opera season; *n.m.* lyric poet. **-a** *f.* lyric. **-amente** *adv.* lyrically.
lir·io *m.* (bot.) madonna lily, *Lilium candidum*. **-odendro** *m.* (bot.) tulip tree, *Liriodendron tulipiferum*.
lir-ismo *m.* lyricism; lyrical form. †**-ista** *m.* (mus.) lyre-player.
liroconite *f.* (miner.) liroconite.
lir-oldo *m.*, **-one** *m.*, **-uro** *m.* See under **lira**[2].
Lisbona *pr.n.f.* (geog.) Lisbon.
lis-ca *f.* scaling, gratings of hemp, removed in preparing the fibre; morsel; una — di —, a very thin slice; non saper —, not to know anything at all; small fish-bone; il pesce senza le ~che, rose without a thorn; (liturg.) piece of blessed palm (locally placed on altar crucifix); large pocket knife; (text.) awn, shove, boon (of flax); lisp. **-ca·io** *m.* a quantity of hemp scalings or of fish bones. †**-cardo** *m.* sal ammoniac. **-chino** *m.* the tiniest quantity. **-coso** *adj.* full of bones; thin.
liscezza *f.* smoothness.
li·sci-a[1] *f.* flat-iron, smoothing iron; polishing stone. **-ai(u)ola** *f.* weaver of plain linen.
†**lisci·a**[2] *f.* See **lisciva**.
lisci-are [A3] *tr.* to smooth, to stroke; to caress, to pat; to preen; to flatter; to coax; to blandish; to lick (of animals); to adorn, to embellish; to gloss, to polish; *rfl.* to preen oneself; to adorn oneself; to dress one's hair; to dress oneself with care. **-amento** *m.* stroking; preening; cosmetic; flattery. **-ata** *f.* preening, tidying up; caress; piece of flattery. **-ato** *part. adj.* smoothed, preened, tidy, spick and span; caressed; titivated. **-atoio** *m.* (foundry) sleeker. **-atura** *f.* smoothing, tidying; titivation; affectation.
li·sc-io *adj.* smooth, soft; plain, simple; alla ~ia, easily, the easiest way; per le ~e, quickly, smoothly; (of a drink) neat; straight; straightforward; *n.m.* cosmetic; *pl.* (vet.) white or yellow spots on a horse. †**-iura** *f.* see **liscezza**.
lisciva *f.* lye, soda-water for washing; (techn.) liquor.

lisci·v-ia *f.* (chem.). See **lisciva**. **-iare** [A4] *tr.* to lixiviate. **-iatoio** *m.* (paperm.) acid plant. **-iatori** *m.pl.* lixiviators. **-iazione** *f.* lixiviation.

liscoso *adj.* See under **lisca**.

liş-i *f. indecl.* (med.) lysis; gradual abatement. **-imachi·a** *f.* (bot.) yellow loosestrife, *Lysimachia vulgaris.* **-olo** *m.* lysol.

†lisire *m.* See **elisire**.

†lisma *m.* bundle of sheets of paper (about 500).

liso *adj.* worn, worn out, worn smooth; threadbare.

liss-a *f.* (vet.) lyssa; rabies; (med.) hydrophobia; (naut.) ship's plate. **-ofobi·a** *f.* (med.) terror of contracting hydrophobia.

list-a *f.* strip; line; streak (of hair); stripe, band; (archit.) list, fillet; (herald.) riband; list; schedule; — delle vivande, menu; mangiare a prezzo di —, (in a restaurant) to choose a meal of a fixed price; scrutinio della —, *scrutin-de-liste*, voting for a list of candidates; — elettorale, electoral roll, register of voters; una — di candidati, a panel of nominees; — civile, civil list; (naut.) — nera, — di punizioni, punishment list. **-are** [A1] *tr.* to border, to edge; to list. **-arella** *f. dim.* of **lista**; small strip. **-ato** *part. adj.* edged; **-ato** a bruno, edged with black (in mourning); (joc.) unghie **-ate** a bruno, finger-nails 'in mourning' (i.e. dirty). **-ella** *f. dim.* (archit.) see **listello**; (herald.) riband. **-ello** *m.* (archit.) listel, fillet; (mil.) chasing or ornamentation of a gun. **-erella** *f. dim.* of **lista**; small strip. **-etta** *f. dim.* of **lista**; (typ.) -etta di piombo, lead. **-ino** *m. dim.* of **lista**; list; -ino di borsa, stock exchange price-list; price-list; time-table; quotation, specification. **-one** *m. augm.* of **lista**; paved place in a market-square reserved for vegetable stalls; (naut.) rubbing strake (sometimes decorated gunwale capping).

†litame *m.* See **letame**.

litan-i·a *f.* (usu. *pl.*) (liturg.) litany; litanie della Madonna, Litany of our Lady; (fig., joc., usu. *sing.*) rigmarole, list (of names), string (of curses). **-iare** [A4] *tr.* to sing the praises of.

litantrace *m.* anthracite.

litargi·rio *m.* (chem.) litharge.

lite *f.* brawl; quarrel; row; contest; controversy; dispute; lawsuit; (leg.) case; litigation; suit; intentare, muovere una — a, to bring an action against; vincere una —, to win a case; — civile, civil action; — criminale, criminal prosecution; — perdere una —, to lose a case; — pendente, pending action; — giudiziaria, lawsuit; prevenire una —, to prevent litigation (C.C.); procuratore alle liti, solicitor.

lites·sere *m.* (surg.) lithoclast.

liti·aşi *f. indecl.* (med.) lithiasis.

liticare [A2s] and derivs. See **litigare**.

li·tico *adj.* (chem.) lithic; of stone.

litig-are [A2s] *intr.* (*aux.* avere) to quarrel; to fall out; (leg.) to litigate; *tr.* (leg.) to contest; to sue. **-amento** *m.* litigating; contesting; suing. **-ante** *part. adj.* litigating; quarrelling; (leg.) litigant; la parte **-ante**, the contending party; *n.m.* contending party; litigant; (provb.) di (fra) due **-anti** il terzo gode, while two dogs strive for a bone, the third takes it.

litigh-ino *m.* mischief-maker, quarrel-seeker. **-io** *m.* constant strife; continual quarrelling.

liti·gi-o *m.* altercation; dispute; quarrel; (leg.) dispute; la ragione del —, the cause of the dispute. **-one** *m.* quarrelsome person; mischief-maker. **(-ona** *f.*) **-osità** *f.* (leg.) -osità di un credito, contentious nature of a debt; its being the subject-matter of litigation (C.C.). **-oso** *adj.* quarrelsome; (leg.) contentious; disputed, credito **-oso**, disputed debt. **(-osamente** *adv.*)

li·t-io *m.* (chem.) lithium. **-ina** *f.* (chem.) lithia.

litisconsorto *m.* (leg.) co-party in litigation (C.C.).

litispendenza *f.* (leg.) pending action, *lis pendens* (C.C.).

†lito *m.* see **lido**; sea; region, country.

lit-o·bio *m.* (zool.) a kind of centipede, *Lithobius* sp. **-oclaşi** *f. indecl.* (geol.) fault. **-oclasti·a** *f.* (med.) lithotripsy. **-oclasto** *m.* (surg.) lithoclast. **-ocolla** *f.* cement for sticking marble. **-ocromi·a** *f.* chromo-lithography, chromo-lithograph. **-o·domo** *m.* (zool.) *Lithodomus* sp., a boring bivalve. **-o·fiti** *m.pl.* coral polyps. **-ofotografi·a** *f.* lithophotograph(y). **-ofotogra·fico** *adj.* lithophotographic. **-ografare** [A1] *tr.* to lithograph. **-ografi·a** *f.* lithography. **-o·grafo** *m.* lithographer. **-o·ide** *adj.* stone-like. **-olatra** *m.* stone worshipper. **-olatri·a** *f.* stone worship. **-ola·trico** *adj.* pertaining to stone worship. **-ologi·a** *f.* (miner.) lithology; (surg.) study of calculi. **-olo·gico** *adj.* lithological. **-o·logo** *m.* (*pl.* **-o·loghi**) litho-

logist. **-omante** *m.* person practising lithomancy. **-omanzi·a** *f.* lithomancy, divination from stones. **-omarga** *f.* (miner.) lithomarge. **-ontrit·tico** *adj.*, *n.m.* lithontriptic, lithonthryptic. **-opone** *m.* lithopone. **-osfera** *f.* (geog.; geol.; meteor.) lithosphere. **-ospermo** *m.* (bot.) gromwell, grummel, *Lithospermum officinale.* **-o·strato** *m.* (class. antiq.; Bibl.) stone pavement, tessellated pavement. **-otomi·a** *f.* lithotomy. **-oto·mico** *adj.* lithotomical. **-otomista** *m.* lithotomist. **-o·tomo** *m.* lithotome. **-otripsi·a** *f.* lithotrity. **-otritore** *m.* lithotritist. **-otrizi·a** *f.* lithotrity.

litor-ale, -a·neo *adj.* See **littor-ale, -aneo**.

litorina *f.* (zool.) winkle, *Littorina* spp.

litote *f.* (rhet.) litotes.

litr-o *m.* litre (about 1¾ pints).

†litta *f.* fine sand.

littor-ale *adj.* on the shore, littoral, coastal. **-a·neo** *adj.* relating to a shore. **†-ano** *m.* inhabitant of coastal area; *adj.* coastal. **-aria** *f.* (naut.) small coaster.

littor-e *m.* (Rom. hist.) lictor; (Ital. hist.) winner of annual University athletic (or other) sports during Fascism. **-iale** *adj.* relating to the Roman lictors; *n.m.pl.* University annual sporting events under Fascism.

Litto·ria *pr.n.f.* (geog.) Italian town and province, formed during Fascist era by the draining of the Pontine Marshes; nowadays Latina.

littorina *f.* diesel-powered rail-car (now called 'automatrice').

litto·rio *adj.* relating to the Roman lictors; (Ital. hist.) relating to Fascism; fascio —, Fascist emblem; casa littoria, local branch of the Fascist party; *n.m.* (Ital. hist.) emblem of Fascism.

Litu-a·ni-a *pr.n.f.* (geog.) Lithuania. **-ano** *adj.* Lithuanian; *n.m.* Lithuanian; Lithuanian language. **(-ana** *f.*) **-şlavo** *adj.* Balto-Slavic.

li·tuo *m.* (Rom. antiq.) augur's crook; (mus.) lituus, ancient Roman cavalry trumpet.

†litura *f.* cancellation; mark, stain.

lit-urgi·a *f.* (eccl.; Gk. antiq.) liturgy. **-ur·gico** *adj.* liturgical. **-urgicamente** *adv.* liturgically. **-urgista** *m.* liturgist.

liut-o *m.* (mus.) lute; **†**porla sul —, to beat about the bush, to be a long time in saying or doing anything; **†**il diavolo può sonare il —, there is no danger of temptation; **†**(naut.) coastal vessel (two-masted or dumb); **†**(chem.) porcelain boat. **-a·io** *m.* lutemaker; stringed-instrument maker. **-eri·a** *f.* art of making stringed instruments. **†-essa** *f. pejor.* (mus.) wretched lute. **-ista** *m.* (mus.) lutanist.

livarda *f.* (naut.) sprit; parcelling.

livella *f.* mason's level; plummet; — a bolla d'aria, spirit-level; — a cannocchiale, surveyor's level.

livellare¹ *adj.* level, on the level.

livell-are² [A1] *tr.* to level; to level down; to level up; to take the levels of (in surveying); (mil.) to lay (a gun); *intr.* (*aux.* essere; *prep.* con) to be on a level (with); *rfl.* to find one's level; to level out; *recip. rfl.* to become level with each other. **-amento** *m.* levelling. **-ato** *part. adj.* levelled; made level. **-atore** *m.* leveller; surveyor. **(-atrice** *f.*) **-atura** *f.* level; surveying. **-azione** *f.* levelling; surveying.

livell-are³ *tr.* (leg.) to lease for a term of years; to grant a long lease of. **-a·rio** *m.* (leg.) see under **livello²**. **-ato** *part. adj.* (leg.) leased. **-azione** *f.* (leg.) deed of lease.

livello¹ *m.* level; a —, on a level; passaggio a —, level crossing; (naut.) — del mare, sea level; — medio, mean sea level; — medio delle alte maree, mean high water springs; — di riduzione degli scandagli, chart datum; — di scarico, unladen immersion line; mason's level; — a bolla d'aria, spirit level; — d'acqua, water level.

livell-o² *m.* (leg.) property held on long lease; deed of lease; the annual rent received thereunder. **-a·rio** *m.* (leg.) long leaseholder; *adj.* (leg.) leasable; leasehold.

†liverare¹ *tr.* to finish; to consume; to wear out; to condemn; *rfl.* to be on the point of death.

†liver-are² *tr.* to deliver. **†-agione** *f.* deliverance.

†livi *adv.* there.

Li·via *pr.n.f.* Livia.

li·vid-o *adj.* livid; grey (of sky); ashen; bruised; discoloured; spiteful; envious; *n.m.* lividity; bruise. **-amente** *adv.* spitefully, maliciously; enviously, with envy. **-astro** *adj.* bluish, greyish. **-ezza** *f.* greyness, lividness; bruised state, bruising; **†**envy, spite, rancour.

livid-o (*cont.*)
 -ic·cio *adj. dim.* rather livid; somewhat bruised. **-ọre** *m.* livid colour; bruise; lividity; †envy. **-ume** *m.* mass of bruises; bruised patch. **-ura** *f.* bruise; mark of a bruise, discoloration.
Li·vi-o *pr.n.m.* Livy. **-ano** *adj.* Livian, in the style of Livy.
†**liviritta** *adv.* there, in that very place.
livọre *m.* bruise; lividness; envy.
†**livornina** *f.* a safe conduct.
Livọrn-o *pr.n.f.* (geog.) Leghorn. **-ẹse** *adj.* of Leghorn; *n.m., f.* inhabitant or native of Leghorn.
†**livra** *f.* unit of money (cf. **libbra, lira**).
livr-e·a *f.* livery; uniform; uomo di due **-ee**, servant of two masters; non portare la — di nessuno, to be one's own master; a —, in livery, †in the same style; †dress, disguise; †quarter; †abode, dwelling, palace. **-eato** *adj.* liveried; *n.m.* liveried servant.
†**livriere** *m.* greyhound.
lizza[1] *f.* lists, arena, field of combat; contest; scendere in —, to enter the lists.
lizza[2] *f.* (ichth.). See **leccia**.
lizzare [A I] *intr.* (*aux.* avere) (geog.) to slide, to skid.
lo[1] *def. art. m. sing.* (*pl.* **gli**; used before impure **s, z, gn, ps, x, bd, cn**) the.
lo[2] *pers. prn. m. sing. acc.* him; it; — so, I know; — dicevo io, I told you so; — credo, I believe you; non — credo, I don't think so; Maria è molto intelligente, Lucia — è assai meno, Mary is very intelligent, Lucy is much less so.
Loanda *pr.n., f.* (geog.) Luanda.
lobato *adj.* See under **lobo**.
lobe·l-ia *f.* (bot.) lobelia. **-ina** *f.* (chem.) lobeline.
lob-o *m.* (anat.) lobe; (bot.) lobe. **-ato** *adj.* lobed.
lo·bul-o *m.* lobule. **-olato** *adj.* lobulated, having lobules.
local-e *adj.* local; colore —, local colour, atmosphere; usi **-i**, local customs; *n.m.* room; place; house; accommodation; headquarters; pianta dei **-i**, plan of the premises. **-mẹnte** *adv.* locally. **-ità** *f.* locality; place; position; whereabouts. **-iżżare** [A I] *tr.* to localize; to circumscribe; to prevent from spreading. (**-iżżato** *part. adj.*) **-iżżazione** *f.* localization; localizing; circumscribing.
locand-a *f.* inn; *adj. f.* to be let; (Rome, Lucca) est —, to let; a lettere di camera —, in big block letters. **-iere** *m.* inn-keeper, landlord, host. **-iera** *f.* inn-keeper's wife, landlord's wife; landlady; hostess of an inn.
loc-are [A 2] *tr.* (leg.) to let on hire; to let on lease; to rent; † to place; **-ante** *part. adj.* letting out. **-ata·rio** *m.* (leg.) lessee; tenant; hirer. **-ativo** *adj.* locative; pertaining to location; (gram.) locative; (leg.) for letting; valore **-ativo**, letting value; buono stato **-ativo**, good tenantable repair (C.C.). **-ato** *part. adj.* leased; hired. **-atọre** *m.* landlord; lessor; letter-on-hire. **-atrice** *f.* landlady. **-azione** *f.* location; (leg.) lease: letting on hire (especially of personal property); letting on lease (especially of urban property); letting (especially of furnished premises); letting at a rent (see also under **Pigione**); tenancy; dare in **-azione**, to lease, to hire out; contratto di **-azione**, lease; tenancy agreement; disdetta di **-azione**, notice to quit; **-azione** di nave, time-charter of ship; sub **-azione**, sublease; sublet (C.C.).
locca *f.* (ichth.) *Johnius umbra*, a kind of sea perch.
†**locchè** *prn.* the which, which.
lochi *m.pl.* (med.) lochia.
lochiano *adj.* (philos.) of, or relating to, John Locke; *n.m.* follower of Locke.
loco *m.* (poet.) see **luogo**; (provb.) acqua e foco, fagli —, always give way to water and fire; (mil. hist.) detachment of soldiers, infantry company; *adv.* (mus.) at written pitch, to countermand a preceding instruction such as 'all'ottava alta' or 'all'ottava bassa'.
loco-mo·bile *f.* traction-engine. †**-motilità** *f.* locomotive power. **-motiva** *f.* locomotive, engine. **-motivo** *adj.* locomotive. **-motọre** *adj.* (med.; phys.) locomotor; *n.m.* electric locomotive. **-motrice** *f.* (electric) locomotive. **-mozione** *f.* locomotion.
lọcrio *adj.* (mus.) modo —, Locrian mode.
lo·culo *m.* tomb; place reserved in a cemetery; (scient.) loculus.
†**locuplet-are** *tr.* to enrich. †**-azione** *f.* profit, makings. †**-is·simo** *adj. superl.* very wealthy.
locust-a[1] *f.* (ent.) locust; †crawfish, *Palinurus vulgaris*; (bot.) lamb's lettuce, corn salad, *Valerianella locusta*, and other spp. **-ella** *f.* (orn.) grasshopper warbler, *Locustella naevia*.
Locusta[2] *pr.n.f.* (Rom. hist.) Locusta, the famous woman poisoner.

†**locuto·rio** *m.* (eccl.) parlour.
locuzione *f.* locution; expression; phrase; idiom; saying.
loda *f.* (pop. Tusc.). See **lode**.
lod-are [A I] *tr.* to praise; to laud; to extol; to commend; to celebrate; — sino alle stelle, to laud to the skies; (leg.) to award (at arbitration); *rfl.* to praise oneself; (provb.) chi si **-a** s'imbroda, self-praise is no praise; (*prep.* di) to be satisfied (with), to be fond (of). **-a·bile** *adj.* and deriv. see **lodevole**. **-ativo** *adj.* praising, complimentary, laudative. **-ato** *part. adj.* praised, honoured; Dio sia **-ato**, God be praised; il su **-ato**, the above-mentioned. **-atọre** *m.* praiser; commender. (**-atrice** *f.*) **-ẹvole** *adj.* praiseworthy, laudable; commendable. **-evolmẹnte** *adv.* laudably; commendably. **-evolẹzza** *f.* praiseworthiness, laudability; commendableness.
lode *f.* praise; (in an examination) mark of distinction, honourable mention.
lodẹvole *adj.* and derivs. See under **lodare**.
lodigian-o *adj.* (geog.) of, relating to Lodi; *n.m.* native or inhabitant of Lodi. (**-a** *f.*)
lodo *m.* award; approval of work done; (leg.) — arbitrale, arbitrator's award (C.C.); †see **lode**.
lo·dol-a *f.* (orn.) lark, esp. the skylark, *Alauda arvensis*; — gola gialla, shorelark, *Eremophila alpestris*; la carne della — piace, flattery (or praise) is pleasing. **-a·io** *m.* (orn.) hobby, *Falco subbuteo*.
Lodovico *pr.n.m.* Louis, Ludwig, Lewis.
†**lodretto** *m.* preserved food.
loess *m. indecl.* (geol.) loess.
lo·f-io *m.* (ichth.) angler fish, *Lophius piscatorius*. **-iodonte** *adj.*, *n.m.* (anat.) lophodont.
Lofoti *pr.n.f.pl.* (geog.) Lofoten Islands.
logae·dico *adj.* (Gk. prosod.) logaoedic.
logaiuolo *m.* (Tusc.) peasant who cultivates a farm for which he pays rent in kind, share-cropper.
†**logaone** *m.* (anat.) rectum.
loga-ritmo *m.* logarithm. **-ri·tmico** *adj.* logarithmic.
loggẹtta *f. dim.* of **loggia**, q.v.
loggher *m. indecl.* (naut.) lugger.
log·g-ia *f.* balcony; (archit.) loggia, gallery; masonic lodge; (bot.) loculus; †lodging, accommodation; †shelter; †far —, to hold a reunion or congress; †tenere a —, to keep under restraint; †tener — di, to proclaim publicly; †comparire a —, to become publicized; †a —, in abundance; †famiglie di **-e**, noble families. **-iato** *m.* (archit.) long portico, gallery. **-iọne** *m. augm.* of **loggia**; (theatr.) gallery.
logh-ẹtto, -icciuolo, -iciat·tolo *m. dim.* of **luogo**, q.v.
lo·gic-a *f.* logic. †**-ale** *adj.* see **logico**. **-almẹnte** *adv.* according to, in accordance with logic. **-are** [A 2 s] *intr.* (*aux.* avere) to reason. **-astro** *m.* bad logician; false or petty reasoner. **-iṣmo** *m.* 'logicism', belief that logic is the most fundamental part, or truest form, of philosophy.
lo·gic-o *adj.* logical; rational; reasoned; reasonable, what one would expect; è — che, it is only natural that; *n.m.* logician, reasoner. **-amẹnte** *adv.* logically; reasonably. **-ità** *f.* reasonableness, logicalness. **-uzzo** *m.* pseudo-philosopher.
lo·gio *m.* (Gk. antiq.) logeion, front part of stage.
log-iṣmografi·a *f.* a method of book-keeping invented by Cerboni. **-iṣmogra·fico** *adj.* pertaining to 'logismografia'. **-iṣmografo** *m.* a person versed in 'logismografia'. **-ista** *m.* accounting officer; accountant. **-i·stica** *f.* accountancy; logistics; (math.) logistic curve, logarithmic curve; (mil.; naut.) logistics, the comprehensive planning and management of every form of supply for maintaining an army in the field or a fleet at sea. **-i·stico** *adj.* logistic, logistical; (math.) logistic, logarithmic; (mil.; naut.) catena **-istica**, chain of supply; comando **-istico**, command of the baggage train or fleet train.
lo·gli-o *m.* (bot.) darnel, *Lolium temulentum*; — palustre, *Carex muricata* agg.; (fig.) tare; distinguere il grano dal —, to sort the wheat from the tares. **-ato** *adj.* full of tares. **-erella** *f.* (bot.) rye grass, ray grass, *Lolium perenne*. **-ọso** *adj.* full of tares; useless, valueless.
Logodoro *pr.n.m.* (hist.) the name of the largest of the four Giudicati or Judicial divisions of Sardinia in Dante's time, when the island was held by the Pisans; it comprised the north-west portion. (*Inf.* XXII, 89.)

log-ografi·a *f.* rapid writing system. **-ogra·fico** *adj.* written in short-hand. **-o·grafo** *m.* chronicler. **-o·grifo** *m.* logogriph, game of making up words from the letters of another; confused remarks. **-olatri·a** *f.* word worship. **-omachi·a** *f.* logomachy, wordy strife. **-o·metro** *m.* (math.) slide-rule.

logor-are [A I sc] *tr.* to wear out; to waste; to use up, to consume; *rfl.* to wear oneself out; to worry; to become worn out; to be used up; si -a la vita, he is wearing himself out. **-amento** *m.* wearing out; wear; wear and tear. **-ato** *part. adj.* worn out; exhausted; used up. **-atura** *f.* wearing out; (eng.) wear (and tear). **-ìo** *m.* constant wear.

logoro[1] *adj.* worn, worn out; consumed; threadbare; outworn; in tatters; abused; †giorno —, evening; †luna logora, moon on the wane; *n.m.* wear.

logoro[2] *m.* falconer's lure; sportsman's whistle; decoy; †attraction.

log-orre·a *f.* stream of talk, flood of words, logorrhoea. **-oteta** *m.* (hist.) logothete.

†**lograre** *vb.* and derivs. See **logorare**.

†**logro** *adj.* See **logoro**[1].

lo·ia *f.* dirt, layer of grease and dirt (on skin or clothes).

†**lo·ica** *f.* See **logica**.

†**lo·ico** *adj.*, *n.m.* and derivs. See **logico**.

†**lolica** *f.* rusty iron nail or tool.

lolla *f.* husk; essere di —, to be decrepit.

lolli·gine *f.* (zool.) squid, *Loligo* spp.

lombag·gine *f.* (med.) lumbago.

Lombard-i·a *pr.n.f.* (geog.) Lombardy. **-o** *adj.* Lombard; (archit.) Lombardic, Lombard Romanesque. **-a** *f.* Lombard woman; a Lombard folk-dance; (leg.) the systematic interpretation of the Lombardic law in the twelfth century. **-ag·gine** *f.* Lombardism (in language). **-amente** *adv.* in the Lombard fashion. **-ata** *f.* a line of workmen to make a chain of buckets or to pass bricks, etc. **-ella** *f.* (orn.) oca -ella, white-fronted goose, *Anser albifrons*. **-esco** *adj.* (*m.pl.* -eschi) Lombardesque. **-esimo**, **-ismo** *m.* Lombardism (in language).

lomb-o *m.* (anat.) loin; regione dei -i, lumbar region; aver buoni -i, to be strong; fare i -i, to grow strong; (butcher.) rump; -e filetto, rump fillet. **-ale**, **-are** *adj.* (anat.) lumbar. **-ata** *f.* loin (of meat).

lombr-ico *m.* (*pl.* -ichi) (zool.) earthworm, *Lumbricus* spp.; — della sabbia, lugworm, *Arenicola* spp. **-a·io** *m.* place full of worms. **-ale** *adj.* (anat.) lumbrical.

†**lome** *m.* light.

lonchite *f.* (bot.) holly fern, *Polystichum lonchitis*.

lond-inese *adj.* of London, from London, London; *n.m.*, *f.* Londoner. †**-onese** *adj.* see **londinese**.

Londra[1] *pr.n.f.* (geog.) London.

†**londra**[2] *f.* (naut.) small craft about half the size of a galley (from Turkish 'lundra', a boat).

longa *f.* (mus.) long (a note longer than a breve).

longa·nim-e *adj.* patient, persevering; forbearing; long-suffering; indulgent. **-ità** *f.* patience, perseverance; tolerance; forbearance; long-suffering.

†**longare** *vb.* and derivs. See **allungare**.

longarina *f.* (naut.) building chocks; (bldg.) see **longherina**.

longev-o *adj.* long-lived. **-ità** *f.* longevity.

longher-ina *f.* (bldg.) girder; I-beam; (naut.) see **longarina**. **-one** *m.* (aeron.) spar; strut.

†**longi-amente** *adv.* for a long time. †**-are** *tr.* to keep distant.

long-imetri·a *f.* measuring of heights and distances. **-ime·trico** *adj.* pertaining to the measurement of heights and distances. **-i·metro** *m.* measuring tape. **-ipenne** *adj.* (orn.) having long (wing) feathers.

Longino *pr.n.m.* Longinus (traditional name of the soldier with the spear at the Crucifixion); viso da —, brutal face.

†**long-inquo** *adj.* remote, distant. †**-ità** *f.* length; distance. †**-itano** *adj.* remote, distant.

longitu·din-e *f.* longitude. **-ale** *adj.* longitudinal. **-almente** *adv.* longitudinally; lengthwise.

longobar·dico *adj.* See **longobardo**.

longobard-o *adj.* Longobard; dente —, Lombard avarice; *n.m.* Longobard. **-amente** *adv.* in the Longobard fashion.

lontan-o *adj.* distant, far, far-off, remote; absent; è mio — parente, he is a distant relative of mine; son ben — dal crederlo, I am far from believing it; tenersi —, to stand aloof, to keep away; con gli occhi -i, with a far-away look in one's eyes; †lasting, long-lived, enduring; †alien, different, strange; *adv.* far, far away, afar, a long way; lo vidi da —, I saw him in the distance; vedere —, to be far-sighted; *n.m.* distance, far place; i -i, descendants. **-amente** *adv.* in the distance; vaguely. **-anza** *f.* distance; in -anza, in the distance; guardare in -anza, to gaze into the distance; †to foresee the future; quadro di -anza, picture designed to be viewed from a distance; separation; absence from home. †**-ezza** *f.* see **lontananza**.

lontra *f.* (zool.) otter, *Lutra lutra*.

lonza[1] *f.* (zool.) jaguar, *Felis onca*; †name applied to various leopards and panthers.

lonz-a[2] *f.* loin (of meat); (tanning) spetch; side, flank; (bot.) kind of grape borne in long racemes. **-o** *adj.* flabby; (provb.) cavolo -o e ciccia pigiata, vegetables should be cooked with plenty of water, meat with little.

†**lo·pia** *f.* (naut.) after cabin of a felucca.

†**lopi·zia** *f.* baldness, alopecia.

lopp-a *f.* chaff; non è —, it is not rubbish; iron slag. **-i** *m.pl.* dross of iron. **-oso** *adj.* full of husks.

lop·p-io, **-o** *m.* (bot.) field maple, *Acer campestre*; *A. opalus*; — falso, *A. monspessulanum*.

†**lop·polo** *m.* (med.) heat spot.

lopposo *adj.* See under **loppa**.

loquac-e *adj.* talkative, loquacious; fluent; eloquent; expressive. **-emente** *adv.* loquaciously; fluently. **-ità** *f.* talkativeness; loquacity; fluency; eloquence.

loquela *f.* talking, power of speech; way of talking; dono della —, gift of the gab; language, tongue.

†**loquen-te** *adj.* see **eloquente**. **-za** *f.* see **eloquenza**.

†**lora** *adv.* See **allora**.

†**lorchè** *conj.* See **allorchè**.

loranto *m.* (bot.) *Loranthus europaeus*.

lora·rio *m.* (Rom. antiq.) *lorarius*, man who flogged slaves.

lord-are [A I C] *tr.* to soil; to sully, to make filthy; *intr.* (*aux.* avere) to commit a nuisance; *rfl.* to dirty oneself; to get dirty. **-ag·gine** *f.* filth, filthy act. **-ato** *part. adj.* soiled, dirtied; sullied. **-ezza** *f.* filth, ordure; filthiness.

lord-o *adj.* dirty, filthy; vicious; (comm.) gross; stipendio —, gross salary; beneficio —, gross profit; (of a metal) crude; (naut.) gross; tonnellaggio — di registro, gross register tonnage; stazza -a, gross tonnage (measured as the internal volume of a vessel); ancora -a, foul anchor. **-amente** *adv.* filthily, dirtily. **-ume** *m.* filth, filthy mess. **-ura** *f.* filth; filthiness; excrement; evil and corrupt behaviour; evil people; scum.

lordosi *f. indecl.* (med.) lordosis, anterior curvature of the spine.

Loren-a *pr.n.f.* (geog.) Lorraine. **-ese** *adj.* of Lorraine; *n.m.*, *f.* native or inhabitant of Lorraine.

Lorenzo *pr.n.m.* Laurence, Lawrence.

loretano *adj.* of Loreto; (liturg.) litanie loretane, Litany of Loreto; *n.m.* native or inhabitant of Loreto (cf. **lauretano**).

loric-a *f.* cuirass; (bot.) pod, involucre. **-ato** *adj.* cuirassed; (zool.) armoured.

lorichetto *m.* (orn.) lorikeet.

loro[1] *pers. prn. 3rd pl.m.*, *f. disj.* they; them; *poss. adj.*, *prn. indecl.* their; theirs; (with a capital L) *pl.* of **Lei**, q.v.

loro[2] *m.* (orn.) lory.

losanga *f.* (geom.) rhombus; (herald.) lozenge; — forata, lozenge round-pierced, rustre; — vuota, lozenge voided. **-ato** *adj.* (herald.) lozengy.

Losanna *pr.n.f.* (geog.) Lausanne.

losca *f.* (naut.) rudder lifting hole; rudder or bowsprit shaft; †propeller well.

los-co *adj.* (*m.pl.* -chi) short-sighted; squint-eyed; one-eyed; furtive, underhand, suspect; dubious; dishonest; una figura -ca, a sinister figure; affari -chi, shady business, sharp practice. **-chetto** *adj. dim.* of **losco**; rather short-sighted; peering. **-chezza** *f.* short-sightedness.

losso-dromi·a *f.* (naut.) rhumb line. **-dro·mico** *adj.* (naut.) loxodromic, pertaining to rhumb line; distanza -dromica, rhumb line distance; navigazione -dromica, rhumb line sailing; rotta -dromica, rhumb line course.

lot-o[1] *m.* mud, filth; lute, tenacious clay or cement. **-atura** *f.* sullying; application of mud; luting; layer of lute or cement. †**-olento** *adj.* muddy; filthy; dense, thick. **-oso** *adj.* muddy, filthy. **-ume** *m.* slime, filth.

lot-o² *m.* (bot.) lotus; — falso, — d'Egitto, date plum, *Diospyros lotus*; — sottile, slender birdsfoot trefoil, *Lotus tenuis*. **-o·fago** *adj.* lotus-eating; *n.m.* lotus-eater.

lott-a *f.* wrestling; — libera, free-style wrestling; — giapponese, jujitsu; — americana, all-in-wrestling; — grecoromana, Graeco-Roman wrestling; struggle, fight; contest; strife; l'istinto della —, the fighting instinct; la — contro le malattie, the campaign against disease; — di classe, class-warfare; (mil.) combat, battle. **-are** [A 1] *intr.* (*aux.* avere) to wrestle; to struggle, to fight, to campaign; -are contro, to fight with, to struggle against. **-ante** *part. adj.* wrestling; fighting, struggling. **-atore** *m.* wrestler; fighter; one who struggles, contends or strives. (**-atrice** *f.*) **†-eggiare** *intr.* see **lottare**.

lott-o *m.* game of lotto; lot; allotment; *pl.* lots; vendere a -i, to sell by lots; dividere in -i, to divide into lots. **-eri·a** *f.* lottery. **-iẓẓare** [A 1] *tr.* to divide by lots. (**-iẓẓaẓione** *f.*)

lotume *m.* See under **loto¹**.

loure *f.* (mus.) Loure (old French dance).

Lova·nio *pr.n.f.* (geog.) Louvain.

loẓione *f.* (med.) ablution; lotion.

†lubbione *m.* (theatr.) gallery (cf. **loggione** and **piccionaia**).

Lubecca *pr.n.f.* (geog.) Lübeck.

lubẹcchio *m.* cog wheel of water-mill.

Lubiana *pr.n.f.* (geog.) Laibach, Ljubljana (in Jugoslavia).

lu·bric-o *adj.* slippery; (med.) laxative; wanton, lewd, indecent, coarse, lubricious; scurrilous; †vain, fallacious; *n.m.* slippery place. **-ante** *adj.* lubricant, making slippery; *n.m.* (med.) laxative. **-are** [A 2 s] *tr.* to make slippery; (med.) to loosen (the bowels); (eng.) to oil, to lubricate. **-ativo** *adj.* laxative. **-atọio** *m.* (eng.) oil-can. **-atore** *m.* lubricator; loosener; oil-can; oiler, greaser. (**-atrice** *f.*) **-ità** *f.* slipperiness; (med.) laxative quality; indecency, vulgarity, lubricity, coarseness.

lubrific-are [A 2 s] *tr.* to lubricate, to oil, to grease. **-ante** *adj., n.m.* lubricant. **-ato** *part. adj.* lubricated, oiled, greased. **-atore** *m.* lubricator, oiler, greaser. **-aẓione** *f.* lubrication, oiling, greasing.

Luca *pr.n.m.* Luke; — fa presto, one who is quick in his work (an allusion to the painter, Luca Giordano, 1632–1705).

Luca·nia *pr.n.f.* (geog.) Lucania.

Lucan-o *pr.n.m.* Lucan. **-ẹsco** *adj.* (*m.pl.* **-ẹschi**) (Lat. lit.) Lucanesque, in the style of Lucan (epic poet, A.D. 39–65). **-iṣmo** *m.* (Lat. lit.) the epic style, the 'baroque' manner, of Lucan.

luca·nica *f.* a kind of sausage.

lucardino *m.* Lucardo cheese.

lucarino *m.* (orn.) siskin, *Carduelis spinus*.

Luc-ca *pr.n.f.* (geog.) Lucca; figurine di —, plaster figures; Madonnina di —, a beautiful but cold-hearted woman; (Tusc.) ti farò veder —, I'll make you see Lucca (said when one holds up a little child). **-chẹse** *adj.* of Lucca; *n.m., f.* native or inhabitant of Lucca; little boy selling plaster figures; dialect of Lucca; *f.* woman of Lucca. **-chesi·a** *f.* region around Lucca. **-chesina** *f.* sort of heavy cotton and wool blanket. **-chesino** *adj.* of a rich red colour.

lucchẹtto *m.* padlock; — a cifra, combination lock.

luc·cia *f.* (bot.) adder's tongue, *Ophioglossum vulgatum*.

lucci-care [A 2 s] *intr.* (*aux.* avere) to sparkle, to shine; (of the eyes) to glisten with tears; (of the day) to dawn. (**-camẹnto** *m.*) **-cante** *part. adj.* shining, sparkling, glistening. **-chente** *adj.* glistening, glittering. **-chìo** *m.* sparkle, glistening, glitter. **-cọne** *m.* big, fat tear (usu. of a person starting to weep). **-cọre** *m.* sparkle, splendour, shine, brightness.

luc·cico *m.* first light of day.

luc·ci-o *m.* (ichth.) pike, *Esox lucius*. **-sa·uro** *m.* (ichth.) saury pike, *Scomberesox saurus*. **-operca** *f.* (ichth.) pike-perch, sander, *Lucioperca sandra*.

luc·ciol-a *f.* (ent.) firefly, *Lampyris splendidula*; far vedere le -e a uno, to make a person see stars; prendere -e per lanterne, to get something quite wrong, to get hold of the wrong end of the stick; (vulg.) ulcer. **-a·io** *m.* a quantity of fireflies; (provb. Tusc.) bel -aio, bel granaio, a lot of fireflies means a good harvest. **-ato** *m.*, **-o** *m.* (ent.) glow-worm, *Lampyris noctiluca*. **-ọne** *m.* big, glistening tear.

lucco *m.* magistrate's robe in medieval Florence, fastened close round the waist; vestire il —, to stand on ceremony.

luc-e *f.* light; accendere la —, to put on the light; spegnere la —, to put out the light; alla prima —, at daybreak; mettere alla —, dare alla —, to give birth to *or* to publish; uscire in —, uscire alla —, to be published; mettere in cattiva —, to put in a bad light;

rimettere in —, to re-establish; alla — del sole, in broad daylight; venire in —, to come to light; brightness; splendour; (astron.) anno —, light-year; opening; aperture; (archit.) light (i.e. window); port-hole; archway (of a bridge, or elsewhere); ponte a tre -i, three-span bridge; pozzo di —, skylight, opening giving light from above; (leg.) light (one kind of 'finestra': opening in wall admitting light and air; distinguished from 'veduta': opening giving view over neighbour's property) (C.C.); (eng.) — della valvola, valve aperture; (photog.) alta —, highlight; (paint.) light (in a picture); (motor.) -i di città, *or* — città, parking lights; (naut.) -i di posizione, navigation lights.

luc-ẹre [C def.] *intr.* (*3rd pers. sing. pl. pres. indic.* only); to shine, to glitter. **-ente** *adj.* shining, bright; *n.m.* brightness. **-entemẹnte** *adv.* brightly. **-entẹzza** *f.* brightness, brilliance; gloss, lustre.

Lucerna¹ *pr.n.f.* (geog.) Lucerne.

lucern-a² *f.* oil-lamp (of the ancient shape); la fida —, light of a student burning the midnight oil; saper di —, to give an impression of book-learning, to be fusty, to lack freshness, to smell of the lamp; mettere la — sotto il moggio, to hide one's light under a bushel; three-cornered hat; the type of hat worn by the 'carabinieri', q.v.; (poet.) la — del mondo, the glorious lamp of heaven; (cul.) type of 'pasta', for soup; receiver for the oil from an oil press. **-a·io** *m.* lamp-seller; lamp-stand. **-a·rio** *m.* see **lucernaio**; (archit.) skylight. **-ata** *f.* as much oil as will fill a lamp; (Tusc.) the amount of oil obtained from a single pressing. **-iere** *m.* lamp-stand; (fig.) a tall, lanky woman. **-ino** *m. dim.* of **lucerna**; small lamp; policeman (from his hat). **-ọne** *m. augm.* of **lucerna**; hat of a 'carabiniere'; (joc.) 'carabiniere', q.v.

lucerna³ *f.* (ichth.) moongazer, *Uranoscopus scaber*.

lucernic·chia *f.* (bot.) rue-leaved saxifrage, *Saxifraga tridactylites*.

†lucerta *f.* (zool.). See **lucertola**.

lucer·tol-a *f.* (zool.) lizard; (joc.) aver mangiato le -e, to be skinny. **-o** *m.* silverside (of beef). **-ọne** *m.* (zool.) green lizard, *Lacerta viridis* and any other large species of lizard.

†luchera *f.* expression of the face, look.

lucherino *m.* (orn.). See **lucarino**.

Luc-i·a *pr.n.f.* Lucy; Lucia; Santa —, St Lucy (patroness of eye-sight); *excl.* Santa —!, where are your eyes?; Santa — m'acciechi!, strike me blind if I didn't see it!; (zool.) skink (lizard with reduced limbs); †a kind of dance with contorted movements, esp. of the arms.

lucian-o *m.* inhabitant of the popular quarter of S. Lucia in Naples. (**-a** *f.*)

luciare [A 3] *tr.* to stare at; *intr.* (*aux.* avere) to stare fixedly.

lucid-are [A 1 s] *tr.* to polish; (tanning) to glaze; (art) to trace (with tracing paper). **-amẹnto** *m.* polishing; (tanning) glazing; (art) tracing. **-ato** *part. adj.* polished; (tanning) glazed; (art) traced. **-atọio** *m.* (art) tracing frame. **-atore** *m.* polisher; glazer (of leather); tracer; *adj.* polishing; cleaning. **-atrice** *f.* polishing machine, burnishing machine; floor-polisher; macchina -atrice frutta, fruit-cleaning machine; *adj.* polishing; cleaning. **-atura** *f.* polishing; polish; cleaning. **-aẓione** *f.* polishing; cleaning; (tanning) glazing; (art) tracing.

lu·cid-o *adj.* shining; bright; clear, lucid; — intervallo, lucid interval; (art) carta -a, tracing-paper; *n.m.* brightness, shine, polish; boot polish; furniture polish, furniture cream; starch for linen; (art) sheet of tracing paper; tracing; (eng. drawing) tracing cloth. **-amẹnte** *adv.* brightly; lucidly. **-ẹzza** *f.* brightness, shine. **-ità** *f.* brightness, brilliance; lucidity.

luci·fero¹ *adj.* light-bringing; (miner.) pietra lucifera, lucifer stone.

Luci·fero² *pr.n.m.* Lucifer; (fig.) diabolical creature; (proud or raging) devil; morning star, Venus.

†lucificare *tr.* to illumine.

luci·fugo *adj.* lucifugous, shunning daylight.

lucignola *f.* (zool.). See **luscignola**.

luci·gnol-o *m.* wick; guardare al — e non all'olio, to be penny wise and pound foolish; barba a -i, wispy beard; (fig.) very thin, emaciated person; (text.) slubbing, roving; attaccare un —, appiccare un —, to start a long conversation. **-are** [A 1 s] *tr.* to twist like a wick. **-ẹtto** *m. dim.* of **lucignolo**; lock of hair.

luciliano *adj.* (Lat. lit.) resembling Lucilius, satirical.

lucilina *f.* kerosene.

luci·metro *m.* photometer.

lu·cio¹ *m.* (orn.) turkey.

lu·cio² *m.* (ichth.). See **luccio**.

luciola *f.* (ent.). See **lucciola**.

luci·operca *f.* (ichth.). See **luccioperca**, under **luccio**.

†**luco** *m.* wood, forest.

lucore *m.* (poet.) light, splendour.

lucr-are [A I] *tr.* to earn, to win, to make; (rel.) — un'indulgenza, to gain an indulgence. **-abile** *adj.* purchasable; obtainable; (rel.) to be gained (of an indulgence). **-ativo** *adj.* lucrative. **-ativamente** *adv.* lucratively.

Lucre·z-ia *pr.n.f.* Lucretia, Lucrece. **-iano** *adj.* Lucretian. **-io** *pr.n.m.* Lucretius.

lucr-o *m.* lucre, revenue; (leg.) gain; profit; — emergente, consequential gain; — cessante, loss of profit (C.C.). **-oso** *adj.* lucrative, profitable. **-osamente** *adv.* lucratively, profitably.

lucubrare [A I S] and derivs. See **elucubrare**.

†**luculento** *adj.* splendid, resplendent, luminous.

luculliano *adj.* Lucullan, worthy of Lucullus, sumptuous, succulent.

lucumon-e *m.* (anct. hist.) *lucumo*, Etruscan chief; (official title of) the President of the Etruscan Academy at Cortona; (joc.) mayor, alderman, member of town council. **-i·a** *f.* (anct. hist.) status of a *lucumo* or district controlled by one.

luda *f.* (geog.) large valley formed by a landslide.

†**lu·dere** *intr.* to play; to dance and sing.

ludi·brio *m.* ridicule, scorn; mockery; (fig.) plaything.

†**ludificare** *tr.* to mock; to deceive; to trick.

†**ludimagistro** *m.* schoolmaster, pedant.

ludione *m.* Cartesian imp, a scientific toy named after Descartes illustrating the principle of specific gravity.

ludo *m.* public games; spectacle; game; recreation.

lu-e *f.* pestilence, plague, contagious disease; — (gallica), — (celtica), venereal disease; (fig.) scourge. **-etico** *adj.* pestilence; tabe -etica, venereal disease.

luf(f)a *f.* (bot.) loofah, fibrous reticulum of *Luffa cylindrica*.

†**luffo** *m.* pad.

†**luffomastro** *m.* grand seneschal.

luga·niga *f.* See **lucanica**.

lu·gar-o *m.*, **-ino** *m.* (orn.). See **lucarino**.

lu·gli-o *m.* July; un sole di —, burning sun; una giornata di —, a July day, a blazing hot day; vendere il sol di —, to sell something that everyone already has; farsi onore col sole di —, to make unwarranted boasts. **-atico** *adj.* ripening in July. **-enga** *f.* grapes which ripen in July. **-ese** *adj.* ripening in July.

lu·gliolo *adj.* (Tusc., agric.) ripening in July.

lugre *m.* (naut.) lugger.

lu·gubr-e, **lugubr-e** *adj.* lugubrious, dismal. **-emente** *adv.* lugubriously, dismally.

lu·i *pers. prn. m. sing. disj.* him; he.

luì *m. indecl.* (orn.) *Phylloscopus*; — bianco, Bonelli's warbler, *P. bonelli*; — forestiero, yellow-browed warbler, *P. inomatus*; — grosso, willow warbler, *P. trochilus*; — piccolo, chiffchaff, *P. collybita*; — verde, wood warbler, *P. sibilatrix*; (fig.) tiny person.

Lui·g-i *pr.n.m.* Louis, Lewis; Louis (gold coin); San —, St Louis or (more usu.) St Aloysius; parere un San —, to look very meek and mild. **-ino** *m.* (numism.) gold Genoese coin (1665).

Luigiana *pr.n.f.* (geog.) Louisiana.

Luitpoldo *pr.n.m.* (geog.) Terra —, Leopold Coast.

lulla *f.* cant, the half-moon-shaped segment forming a side-piece in the head of a cask.

lull-iano *adj.* (eccl.) pertaining to Raymond Lull; *n.m.* Lullist, disciple of Raymond Lull. **-isti** *m.pl.* (mus.) followers of G. B. Lully (seventeenth-century French composer of Florentine origin).

luma-ca *f.* (zool.) slug; snail; spiral; scala a —, winding staircase; (eng.) worm; coil; (text.; eng.) scroll; (fig.) slowcoach; a passo di —, at a snail's pace. **-cag·lia** *f.* drizzle. **-cato** *adj.* spiral-shaped. **-catura** *f.* see **allumacatura**, under **allumacare**. **-chella** *f.* (zool.) small slug. **-chetta** *f. dim.* small winding staircase. **-chino** *m.* (zool.) small slug. **-cone** *m. augm.* (zool.) large slug; -cone ignudo, *Agriolimax agrestis*; -cone dei boschi, *Arion empiricorum*; -cone maggiore, *Limax maximus*; worm of a screw; (fig.) insinuating rogue; sluggard; tell-tale; tiresome person, bore. **-cato** *adj.* (archit.) spiral. **-coso** *adj.* streaked like the trail left by a snail; (fig.) secretive; morose.

lumac·cia *f.* (zool.). See **lumaca**.

luma·io *m.* See under **lume**.

†**lumbo** *m.* See **lombo**.

lumbricale *adj.* See **lombricale**, under **lombrico**.

lum-e *m.* light (NOTE: 'lume' is usually something which gives light, while 'luce' is the light emitted); portable light, lantern; accendere i -i ad alcuno, to honour a person; (theatr.) batteria di -i, footlights; (paint.) source of light (in a picture); intelligence, wisdom; al — del senno di poi, in the light of events; — della ragione, natural intelligence; enlightenment; — degli occhi, light of one's eyes; (leg.) foglio di -i, the evidence furnished to a coroner; (naut.) dimension of mesh of a fishing net, calculated in knots in every 9½ inches; (anat.) lumen, aperture; †eye; †*pl.* sight, eyesight. **-a·io** *m.* lamplighter; lamp-seller. †**-are** *tr.* to illumine. **-eggiamento** *m.* lighting up. **-eggiare** [A 3 C] *tr.* to light up; (paint.) to paint light (opposed to shade); to lighten; to explain, to throw light on. **-eggiato** *part. adj.* illumined; lightened; lit up. **-eggiatura** *f.* lighting, illuminating, illustrating; painting light (in a picture), lightening. **-ella** *f.* air vent in a glass furnace. **-en** *m. indecl.* (phys.) lumen. **-en(o·)metro** *m.* (phys.) lumenmeter, integrating photometer. †**-era** *f.*, †**-ero** *m.* see **lumiera**. **-etto**, **-icino** *m. dim.* of **lume** (NOTE: 'lumetto' usu. refers to a lamp in a house, while 'lumicino' usu. refers to a light shining in the distance); essere al -etto, to be in a very bad way, to be at the last gasp. **-inale** *m.* (naut.) glass light. **-ino** *m. dim.* small light; night-light.

lumen christi, **lumencristi** *m. indecl.* (liturg.) the versicle *Lumen Christi*; (liturg.) Paschal Candle (in church); (rel.) blessed candle (kept in house).

lumi·a *f.* (S. Ital., Sicily) lime, *Citrus limonia*.

lumicino *m. dim.* of **lume**, q.v.

lumiera *f.* chandelier; torch; touch-hole of a gun; †(naut.) see **mastre**; †alum works; †(mil.) torch, brazier.

lumin-a·io *m.* rough wooden candlestick. **-a·r(i)a** *f.* public illumination. **-are** *m.* luminary; †*vb.* and derivs. see **illuminare**.

†**lu·mine** *m.* See **lume**.

lumin-ella *f.* pupil (of the eye). **-ello** *m.* socket of a candlestick; float for a night-light; wick-holder; touch-hole of a match-lock, *or* nipple of a muzzle-loading fowling piece. **-escenza** *f.* luminescence. †**-iera** *f.* see **lumiera**. **-i·stica** *f.* lighting technique. **-oso** *adj.* luminous; bright, shining; (photog.) obiettivo -oso, fast lens; of light; (phys. opt.) fascio -oso, beam of light. **-osamente** *adv.* luminously; brightly. **-osità** *f.* luminousness, luminosity.

lun-a *f.* moon; satellite; fa la —, there is a new moon; — crescente, crescent moon; — calante, waning moon; — piena, full moon; chiaro di —, moonlight; le -e medicee, the satellites of Jupiter; far vedere la — nel pozzo a, to trick, to deceive, to lead up the garden path; più su sta Monna —, you have not guessed right, *or* we have not come to the end yet; essere nel mondo della —, to have one's head in the clouds; essere nato sotto la —, to be born lucky; abbaiare alla —, to exert oneself for nothing; mezza —, half-moon, crescent, semi-circular kitchen-knife, vegetable chopper; (mil.) schieramento a mezza —, convex front; (miner.) pietra —, moonstone; month, moon; — di miele, honeymoon; temper, humour, whim; aver la —, to be moody, to be bad tempered; essere in buona —, to be in a good mood; mal della —, epilepsy; (vet.) see **lunatico**. **-ale** *f.* half-moon (of a finger-nail). †**-amento** *m.* (astron.) phase of the moon. **-are** *adj.* lunar, of the moon; (miner.) pietra -are, moonstone; *n.m.* month. **-a·ria** *f.* (bot.) honesty, *Lunaria annua*; (miner.) moonstone. **-arino** *m.* small calendar, almanac. **-arista** *m.* (geog.) bay washed out in a river bank by the action of the current; (naut.) camber (of a deck); foot (of a sail). **-aticheri·a** *f.* mad action, capricious act. **-a·tico** *adj.* moody; mal -atico, epilepsy; essere più -atico dei granchi, to be finicky; *n.m.* moody person, person who changes with the phases of the moon; †(vet.) a disease of the eyes in horses, probably cataract. **-ato** *adj.* crescent-shaped. **-azione** *f.* lunar month; (naut.) lunation.

luned-ì *m. indecl.* Monday; fare il —, to take Monday off. †**-iana** free Monday; †fare la -iana, to have Monday off, to do no work. **-iata** *f.* a Monday off, a free Monday.

†**lunella** *f.* pupil (of the eye).

lunello *m.* (herald.) four crescents joined millsailwise.

lunetta *f.* semi-circular shape; (techn.) moon-knife; (archit.; paint.) lunette; (mil.) lunette, fortification open on one side; (liturg.) lunette.

lunga *f.* lungeing rein for training a horse; jess for the feet of a hawk; (mus.) note equivalent to two breves (canto fermo); *adj. f.* see **lungo**.

lung·ac·cio *adj. pejor.* tediously long; endless; boring, slow. **-ag·gine** *f.* slow, tedious procedure; dallying, dawdling; long-drawn-out, tedious business. **-agnata** *f.* long, tedious speech; rigmarole; tirade; boring concert or solo; drawling pronunciation. **-a·gnola** *f.* long net for catching land animals; (fig.) crafty device, trap; boring discourse. **-amẹnte** *adv.* see under **lungo.** †**-are** *tr.* see **allungare;** to delay; to defer.

Lungarn·o *pr.n.m.* street along the bank of the river Arno. **-ata** *f.* walk along the 'Lungarno'; street along the bank of the Arno.

†**lunge** *adv.* See **lungi.**

lungher·i·a *f.* delays, dallying, dawdling; long-windedness. **-ọne** *m.* (aeron.) -one della fusoliera, longeron.

†**lunghesso** *prep.* along.

lunghẹzza *f.* length; extent, extension; duration; height, tallness; (horse-racing, rowing, etc.) length; vincere per due lunghezze, to win by two lengths; (naut.) shackle (25 metres); (radio) — d'onda, wave-length; †longitude; †delay.

lung·i *adv.* far away; a long way off; — da, far from; — da me!, get thee gone! **-imirante** *adj.* far-seeing. **-imiranza** *f.* far-sightedness.

lun·go¹ *adj.* (*m.pl.* **-ghi**) **1.** Long; calzoni -ghi, long trousers; abito —, cassock; una -ga strada, a long road; un — viaggio, a long journey; prendere un passo più — della gamba, to bite off more than one can chew; avere il viso —, to have a long face; (fig.) fare il muso —, to pull a long face; avere le mani -ghe, to have long hands, (fig.) to be light-fingered, to steal; avere la lingua -ga, to gossip, to be spiteful; avere -ga vista, to be long-sighted; (prosod., etc.) una sillaba -ga, a long syllable; una vocale -ga, a long vowel; (naut.) -ga la voga!, lengthen the stroke! **2.** Tall; elongated; un omone —, a great tall man (usu. tall and thin); — come una pertica, — come un palo, as tall as a pikestaff; non guardare uno quant'è —, not to look at a person (out of anger, or feigning indifference); — disteso, stretched out; cadere — disteso, to fall headlong. **3.** Thin, diluted, weak; brodo —, thin, watery soup; caffè —, weak coffee; vino —, wine with little body. **4.** Of long duration, lasting a long time, long; una -ga vita, a long life; due -ghi giorni, two long days; di -ga memoria, of lasting memory; a — andare, in the long run; di -ga mano, a long way off (in time), a long way ahead. **5.** Slow, tedious, long-drawn-out; — come una quaresima, endless. **6.** †Distant. **7.** Adverbial Phrases: a —, at length, extensively, for a long time; al più —, at the most; tirare di —, to go on one's way, to proceed unperturbed; tirare in —, to draw out, to go on and on, to come to no conclusion; tirare troppo per le -ghe, to be long-winded, to ramble on; (mil.) tirare —, to overshoot, to 'over'; alla -ga, in the long run, eventually; di gran -ga, by far, infinitely, by a long chalk; di gran -ga superiore, by far superior; sbagliare di gran -ga, to be utterly mistaken; alla più -ga, at the latest, at the most; saperla -ga, to be shrewd, to be long-headed. **8.** *n.m.* Length; distance; tre metri di —, three metres long, three metres in length; misurare in — e in largo, to measure the length and breadth of; per il —, per —, lengthwise; tagliare per il —, to cut along the length. **-gamẹnte** *adv.* for a long time; at great length. **-gomet·rag·gio** *m.* (cinem.) full-length film. **-gọne** *m. augm.* very tall person; person who delays or rambles on. (**-gọna** *f.*)

lun·go² *prep.* along, by the side of, beside, by. **-gobanco** *m.* (mining) drive. **-golago** *m.* lakeside promenade. **-gomare** *m.* seaside promenade. **-gopò** *m.* street running along the bank of the river Po. **-gotẹvere** *m.* street running along the bank of the river Tiber.

Lunigiana *pr.n.f.* (geog.) territory round Luni; (hist.) capital of Etruria.

lun·isolare *adj.* (astron.) luni-solar; precessione —, precession of the equinoxes. **-isti·zio** *m.* (astron.) lunistice. **-ọna** *f. augm.* of **luna;** big moon, full moon. **-ọne** *m. augm.* of **luna;** big moon, full moon, harvest moon; (fig.) round-faced person.

lu·nula *f.* meniscus; crescent; moon (of the fingernail).

luoghicciuolo *m. dim.* of **luogo;** little village; little farm.

luog·o (*pl.* **luoghi**) place; spot; site; region; a — a —, here and there; extract, passage (in a text); in — di, instead of; occasion, cause; (leg.) non farsi — a procedere, to have no case; (comm.) — di consegna, place of delivery; — del domicilio, domicile; fuor di —, out of place, inappropriate; aver —, to occur, to take place, to happen; sul —, on the spot; (geom.) locus. **-otenente** *m.* replacement, stand-in; (mil.) lieutenant; †divisional commander. **-otenenza** *f.* lieutenancy. **-otenenziale** *adj.* of a lieutenant; (leg.) acting by vicarious authority.

lup·a *f.* (zool.) she-wolf; (med.) mal della —, inordinate appetite, bulimia; (agric.) mildew, rot; dry-rot; (naut.) sudden stormy and breaking sea; wolfishness, greed; †black sail (for camouflage or mourning); †prostitute. **-ara** *f.* (ichth.) Gadus poutassou, a kind of whiting; sawn-off shotgun. **-a·ria** *f.* (bot.) globe flower, *Trollius europaeus.*

lupin·o *m.* (bot.) lupin, Lupinus; — giallo, L. luteus; — rosso, French honeysuckle, Hedysarum coronarium; (zool.) Donisia lupinina, a bivalve mollusc; non valere un —, to be worthless; corn between the toes; (vet.) disease of the eyes in fowls; *adj.* pertaining to a wolf; mantello -ino, dun coat, wolf-coloured coat (of a horse). **-inamẹnte** *adv.* wolfishly, maliciously. **-ọsi** *f.* (vet.) lupin poisoning.

lup·o *m.* (zool.) wolf, Canis lupus; in bocca al —, (usu. wish expressing ill-luck but signifying the reverse) 'all the best', 'good luck'; gridare al —, to cry 'wolf, wolf!'; (provb.) il — perde il pelo ma non il vizio, old habits die hard; (text.) willow; battere la lana con -i, to willow wool; (ichth.) — di mare, catfish, Anarrhichas lupus; (naut.) — di mare, old sea dog, (fig.) brave and downright man; -i mai, Maytime mist; (mil. hist.) grappling hook; (hist. chem.) native antimony sulphide; (med.) lupus. **-acchino** *m.* (zool.) new-born wolf cub. **-acchiotto** *m.* (zool.) young wolf. **-ac·cio** *m. pejor.* glutton. **-a·ia** *f.* wolf's den; (bot.) Aconitum lycoctonum. **-a·io** *m.* wolf-hunter. **-atto** *m.* (zool.) young wolf; (Boy Scouts) wolf cub. **-ercale** *adj.* (Rom. antiq.) Lupercalian; *n.m.* Lupercal. **-ercali** *m., f.pl.* (Rom. antiq.) Lupercalia. **-erc(h)i** *m.pl.* (Rom. antiq.) Luperci. **-erco** *m.* (Rom. myth.) Lupercus. **-ẹsco** *adj.* (*m.pl.* **-ẹschi**) wolfish, wolf-like. **-ẹtto** *m. dim.* (zool.) small wolf; (fig., joc.) child with a big appetite. **-i·a** *f.* (med.) cystic tumour. **-icante** *m.* (zool.) lobster, Homarus vulgaris. **-icino** *m.* wolf-like. **-obattitore** *m.* (text.) shaker.

lup·pol·o *m.* (bot.) hop, Humulus lupulus. **-iera** *f.* hop-field. **-ino** *m.* (chem.; brewing) lupulin.

lupus *m. indecl.* (med.) lupus.

lur·co *adj.* (*m.pl.* **-chi**) gluttonous; *n.m.* glutton. **-cọne** *m. augm.* of **lurco;** greedy-guts.

lu·rid·o *adj.* lurid; foul, filthy, squalid; loathsome. **-ẹzza** *f.* filthiness; squalor.

Lusa·zia *pr.n.f.* (geog.) Lusatia.

luscẹngola *f.* (zool.) Seps chalcides, a legless lizard similar to a slow-worm.

lu·schero *adj.* half-drunk, tipsy.

lus·co *adj.* (*m.pl.* **-chi**) see **losco;** fra il — e il brusco, in the twilight, at twilight; **-chẹtto** *adj. dim.* rather short-sighted. **-chẹzza** *f.* short-sightedness.

luṣi·ade *adj., n.m., f.* Lusitanian, Portuguese.

luṣing·a *f.* flattery; hope, promise; *pl.* adulation; false declarations of love. **-amẹnto** *m.* flattery, praise. **-are** [A2] *tr.* to flatter; to delight; *rfl.* to flatter oneself; to kid oneself, to delude oneself. **-ato** *part. adj.* flattered; deluded.

luṣingh·eri·a *f.* flattery. **-ẹvole** *adj.* flattering; tempting, alluring. (**-ẹvolmẹnte** *adv.*) **-iero** *adj.* flattering, pleasing, caressing; alluring; promising; kind, sympathetic; favourable.

luṣino *m.* (naut.) serving, seizing, whipping.

†**luṣione** *f.* see **illusione;** insult, abuse; mockery, scorn.

lusitaniano *adj.* Lusitanian.

luṣo·ria *f.* (naut.) tramp shipping.

lussare *tr.* (med.) to dislocate.

Lussemburgo *pr.n.f.* (geog.) Luxemburg.

luss·o *m.* luxury; pomp; display; magnificence; extravagance, lavishness; fare del —, to show off, to make a vulgar display; di —, luxury, de luxe. **-uọso** *adj.* luxurious, luxuriant, sumptuous, magnificent.

lussureggi·are [A3c] *intr.* (aux. avere) to luxuriate; to grow luxuriantly; to live luxuriously. (**-amẹnto** *m.*) **-ante** *part. adj.* luxuriant; thriving, flourishing; growing luxuriantly.

lussur·i·a *f.* wantonness, lasciviousness; (theol.) lust; luxuriance; (leg.) excess and extravagance; †luxury. **-ante** *adj.* given to luxury; luxuriant. **-are** [A4] *intr.* (aux. avere) to live in luxury; to luxuriate; to be lustful; to commit acts of lewdness. **-eggiare** [A3c] and derivs. see **lussureggiare. -ọso** *adj.* luxurious; lascivious, dissolute. **-osamẹnte** *adv.* lasciviously; †luxuriously.

lustra¹ *f.* den, lair.

lustra² *f.* pretence, simulation, deception.

lus·trico *adj.* (Rom. antiq.) lustral; giorno —, (child's) naming-day.

lustr-o[1] *adj.* shiny, polished; lustrous; glossy; glittering; *n.m.* lustre, shine, sheen, gloss, polish; polishing; dare il — a, to polish; brilliance, splendour. **-ante** *part. adj.* shining, polished, resplendent. **-are** [A I] *tr.* to polish, to shine; to burnish, to furbish, to impart a gloss to; to flatter. **-ascarpe** *m. indecl.*, **-astivali** *m. indecl.* boot-black. **-ata** *f.* quick polish, quick brush-up. **-ato** *part. adv.* polished; burnished; shining. **-atore** *m.* polisher; †(mil.) inspector, superintendent. (**-atrice** *f.*) **-atura** *f.* polishing. **-ente** *adj.* shiny. **-ino** *m.* boot-black, 'boots'; shine, brightness; avere i -ini negli occhi, to have bright eyes; bead or spangle for decorating embroidery, etc.; false ornament, tinsel; affectation; *pl.* a disease of silkworms causing them to swell up and become shiny; silkworms having this disease.

lustr-o[2] *m.* lustre, period of five years.; (Rom. antiq.) lustrum, lustration; **-ale** *adj.* lustral; acqua -ale, lustral water; holy water. **-are** [A I] *tr.* (Rom. antiq.) to lustrate. **-azione** *f.* (Rom. antiq.) lustration.

†**lustro**[3] *m.* See **lustra**[1].

lut-are [A I] *tr.* (techn.) to lute, to grout, to cement. (**-ato** *part. adj.*) **-atura** *f.* (techn.) luting, grouting, cementing.

lutei·nico *adj.* (med.) unità luteinica, progesterone unit.

lu·t-eo *adj.* saffron; (physiol.) corpo —, corpus luteum. **-eolina** *f.* (chem.) luteol.

lu·ter-e, -o *m.* bath, tub.

luterina *f.* (chem.). See **luteolina**, under **luteo**.

Luter-o *pr.n.m.* Luther. **-ano** *adj., n.m.* (rel.) Lutheran; (loosely) heretical. **-aneggiare** [A 3 c] *intr.* (aux. avere) (rel.) to have Lutheran tendencies. **-anesimo, -anismo** *m.* (rel.) Lutheranism.

luteziano *adj.* (geol.) Lutetian, Middle Eocene.

lute·zio *m.* (chem.) lutecium, cassiopeium.

lutidina *f.* (chem.) lutidine, dimethyl pyridine.

lut-o *m.* mud; clay; lute, sealing cement. **-ifi·golo** *m.* potter. †**-oso** *adj.* muddy.

lutre·ola *f. Putorius lutreola*, an aquatic stoat with webbed feet, like a small otter.

lutrina *f.* (ichth.) *Pagellus acarne*, a kind of sea bream.

†**lutta** *f.* See **lotta**.

†**luttare** *intr.* to lament; to complain; to mourn; to grieve.

lutt-o *m.* mourning; grief; abito di —, mourning (clothes); — pesante, deep mourning; carta da —, black-edged writing-paper; vestire di —, to dress in mourning, to wear mourning; (leg.) — vedovile, legal period of mourning of widow (C.C.); †mourning clothes; †grief, sorrow; †weeping; †punishment. **-uoso** *adj.* mournful, doleful. **-uosamente** *adv.* mournfully, dolefully.

lutulento *adj.* dirty, muddy, sluggish, filthy; turbid.

lu·varo *m.* (ichth.) *Luvarus imperialis*, an edible marine fish.

luvetto *m.* (vet.) phlegmon, inflammation.

lux *m. indecl.* (phys.; opt.) lux (unit of surface illumination).

luxmetro *m.* (phys.) luxmeter.

luzerna *f.* (ichth.) gurnard, *Trigla* spp.

luzzo *m.* (ichth.) *Sphyraena spet*, an edible marine fish.

m *f., m.* (pron. **emme**) the letter M; the consonant M.

ma[1] *conj.* but; vuole — non può, he wants to but he cannot; non per me — per lui, not for me but for him; notwithstanding, yet, still; pare, — non è, it seems so but it isn't; incredibile, — vero, incredible, yet true; non l'amo, — l'adoro, I don't only love her, I just worship her; (resuming an argument or introducing a new subject) — torniamo donde partimmo (Machiavelli), but let us return to what we were saying; (in a logical syllogism, introducing the second premise) ogni uomo è bugiardo; — tu sei uomo; dunque tu sei bugiardo, all men are liars; you are a man; therefore you are a liar; †and; †or rather, nay; †(before a vowel) **mad**; *excl.* heaven knows! well!; — che errore hai fatto!, why, what a mistake you've made!; —finiscila!, for heaven's sake stop it!; — è possibile?, did you ever hear the like?, would you believe it?; — sì!, yes, of course!; — che!, not at all!, please don't mention it!, of course not!, what nonsense! (*or* affirm.) yes, rather!, yes, indeed! (*or* iron.) really!, you don't say!; *n.m. indecl.* but, objection; dimmi sì o no, senza tanti —, answer yes or no and let's not have so many buts; a forza di — e di se non si risolve nulla, all these ifs and buts will get us nowhere; deve fare il suo dovere, non c'è — che tenga, he must do his duty and no buts about it.

†**ma**[2] *poss. adj. procl.* (also dial., Central and S. Ital.) my; madrema, my mother; figliuolma, my daughter; mogliema, my wife.

†**ma·**[1] *adv.* see **mai**; se — mai, if ever by any chance.

†**ma·**[2] *adv.* more; — che, more than, apart from, except.

†**ma·**[3] *f.* (Tusc.) abbrev. of **mamma, madre**.

†**ma·**[4] *adj. m.pl.* evil, wicked; (provb.) adagio a' — passi, look before you leap (cf. **malo**).

ma·cabro, maca·bro *adj.* macabre; danza macabra, *danse macabre*, dance of death; grim, horrid, gruesome; ghastly; un — spettacolo, a ghastly sight.

maca·co *m.*, †**macacco** (*pl.* **-chi**) (zool.) Macaque monkey; (fig.) short, ugly or stupid individual; brutto —, ugly beast.

macada·m *m. indecl.* (civ. eng.) macadam. **-izzare** [A I] *tr.* to macadamize.

maca·o[1] *m.* macao, a card game resembling 'vingt-et-un'.

maca·o[2] *m.* (orn.) macaw.

macaone *m.* (ent.) swallow-tail butterfly, *Papilio machaon*.

macca *f.* (Tusc. pop.) plenty; a —, plentifully, in abundance, †gratuitously; (Florent.) free pass, free entrance ticket; †avere una —, to have got a bargain.

maccabe·o *adj.* (Bibl.) Maccabean; Giuda —, Judas Maccabeus; i Maccabei, (the family of) the Maccabees; (Bibl.) (the Books of) Maccabees.

†**macca·glia** *f.* slaughter.

†**maccare** *vb.* and derivs. See **ammaccare**.

maccarello *m.* (ichth.) mackerel, *Scomber scomber*.

maccaro·nico *adj.* and derivs. See **maccheronico**.

†**maccatell-a** *f.* meat-ball; (fig.) muddle, mistake; defect, fault; deception; giocare di -e, to practise deception. †**-eri·a** *f.* barratry; fraud.

maccheri·a *f.* (naut.) calm sea.

maccheron-i *m.pl.* (cul.) macaroni; pasticcio di —, macaroni cheese; — fatti in casa, home-made (i.e. not machine-made) macaroni; questo è cacio sui —, this is most opportune; (iron.) innocente come la broda dei —, i.e. anything but. **-e** *m. sing.* a single piece of macaroni; (fig.) dolt, simpleton; (theatr.) il babbo dei -i, a Venetian 'mask'; †*adj.* (of wine) thick, muddy. **-ata** *f.* feast of macaroni.

maccheron-e·a *f.* macaronic poem, a composition in a doggerel of Italian words with Latin endings. **-esco, -on·ico** *adj.* macaronic.

mac·chi-a[1] *f.* spot; blot, stain, blemish; speck; blotch; smudge; — d'inchiostro, blot, spot of ink; — solare, sunspot; shame, disgrace; avere -e sulla coscienza, to have an uneasy conscience; senza — nella sua vita, of unsullied reputation; cavaliere senza — e senza paura, *chevalier sans peur et sans reproche*; (telev.) spot; (paint.) sketch, sketch in outline; caricature; impressionistic painting or sketch; fare alla —, to paint or sketch impressionistically (see also under **macchia**[2]); †abbozzato alla —, roughly sketched or painted; †cavarne la —, to come off victorious, *or* to get out of a difficulty. **-ai(u)olo** *m.* (paint.) landscape painter (sketching from nature), impressionist; pointillist; *pl.* a school of Florentine painters (late nineteenth century). **-are** [A 4] *tr.* to spot; to blot, to stain; to mark, to leave a spot or stain; l'acqua non -a, water doesn't stain; (fig.) to tarnish; ha -ato la famiglia, he has spoilt the family's good name; (paint.) to paint or sketch impressionistically; *rfl.* (acc. of prn. 'si') to get dirty; to soil oneself; così ti macchi tutto!, you'll get all dirty doing that!; -arsi di molti delitti, to be guilty of many crimes; (dat. of prn. 'si') -arsi gli abiti, to get one's clothes soiled. (**-amento** *m.*) **-ato** *part. adj.* spotted; dappled; dirtied, soiled; stained, sullied; blemished; latte -ato, milk with a spot of coffee in it. (**-olina** *f. dim.* **-uc·cia** *f. dim.*)

mac·chi-a[2] *f.* copse, thicket; thick hedge; scrub, maquis; darsi alla —, to take to the bush, to become a bushranger; stampare alla —, to print clandestinely; *pl.* (paint.) foliage or flowers (see also under **macchia**[1]). **-ai(u)olo** *m.* secret sinner; piratical printer; forger; *adj.* relating to the scrub or bush; porco -aiuolo, wild boar. **-a·tico** *m.* right of cutting underwood; price of purchasing this right. **-eto** *m.* place full of thickets. **-one** *m. augm.* jungle, dense scrub; stare al -one, to lie in ambush, to be on the watch; star sodo al -one, not to stir from a place, *or* to stand firm.

macchiett-a[1] *f. dim.* of **macchia**[1]; little spot, speck; spruzzato di -e, speckled; (paint.) sketch, portrait sketch; caricature; (fig.) odd, eccentric person, an 'original'; (theatr.) character-part, vividly realized minor part. **-are** [A I c] *tr.* to spot, to speckle. **-ato** *part.*

macchiett-a (*cont.*)
adj. spotted, speckled; grigio ~ato, dapple-grey. **-ista** *m.*, *f.* caricaturist; character actor or actress.

macchiętta² *f. dim.* of **macchia²**; little group of trees or shrubs.

mac·chin-a *f.* machine; engine; mettere in moto la —, to start the engine; dare, far — indietro, to reverse the engine; machinery; — a vapore, steam-driven machine; — da cucire, sewing-machine; — pneumatica, air pump; — tipografica, — da stampare, printing-machine; foglio di —, final proof; mentre andiamo in —, as we go to press; — da scrivere, typewriter; — fotografica, camera; cigarette lighter; fatto a —, machine-made; (eccl.) frame for carrying statue; processione delle ~e, procession with statue; motor-car; andare in —, to go by car; aeroplane; — di rinforzo, assistant engine; machination, plot; essere persona di —, to be astute; big man; big building; — umana, body, stomach; (paint.) picture with very complex subject; (theatr.) mechanical contrivance; (lit.) intervention of supernatural powers in the dénouement. **-ale** *adj.* mechanical; automatic. **-almẹnte** *adv.* mechanically; automatically. **-amẹnto** *m.* machination, intriguing. **-ante** *part. adj.* machinating, given to intrigue. **-are** [A I] *tr.* to plot, to contrive, to machinate; ~are di tradire qualcuno, to plot to betray someone. **-a·rio** *m.* (industr.) machinery. **-atọre** *m.* plotter, contriver. (**-atrice** *f.*) **-aziọne** *f.* machination, plot, plan; †(mil.) war-engine. **-ẹtta** *f. dim.* of **macchina**; (derog., fig.) instrument, tool; ~etta da caffè, percolator. **-ista** *m.* machinist; (rlwy.) engine driver; (naut.) ship's engineer; (typ.) pressman, machine-man; composer of poem or fable. **-ọso** *adj.* complex; involved; full of machinery; dramma ~oso, overcomplicated play; †mechanical. (**-osamẹnte** *adv.*)

macchiọne *m. augm.* See under **macchia²**.

†**maccian·ghero** *adj.* (Florent.) stocky, heavily built; (fig.) gross, slow, stupid.

†**macco¹** *m.* mash of boiled beans; thickened ink; slush of snow; dar del — a uomini grossi, to give pudding to pudding-heads.

†**macco²** *m.* great slaughter.

mace *f.* (cul.) mace.

mace·a *f.* See **macia**.

mace·done *adj.* Macedonian; (fig.) irresistible (plea); *n.m.* Macedonian.

Maced-o·nia *pr.n.f.* (geog.) Macedonia; (Italian) cigarette; (cul.) macédoine; — di frutti, fruit-salad; — di legumi, vegetable hotch-potch. **-o·nico** *adj.* (bot.) prezzemolo ~onico, Macedonian parsley, *Athamanta macedonica*; alexanders, *Smyrnium olusatrum*; †(hist.) of Macedon; †Alessandro ~onico, Alexander of Macedon.

Macedoniani *pr.n.m.pl.* (eccl. hist.) Macedonians (fourth-century heretics).

macell-are [A I] *tr.* to slaughter, to butcher; (fig.) to kill; †to spoil, to corrupt. **-a·bile** *adj.* fit for slaughter. **-a·io** *m.* butcher. **-amẹnto** *m.* slaughtering. **-ara** *f.* butcher's wife; woman who keeps a butcher's shop. **-arino** *m.* butcher-boy. **-aro** *m.* (Tusc.) see **macellaio**. **-ato** *part. adj.* slaughtered, butchered; carne ~ata, butcher's meat. **-atọre** *m.* slaughterer; (fig.) butcher. **-aziọne** *f.* slaughter; butchery. **-eri·a** *f.* butcher's shop; †slaughtering.

macell-o *m.* slaughter-house; (fig.) a great slaughter; fare — di, mettere al —, to slaughter; mandare al —, to send to certain death; se ci sarà una guerra coi mezzi che ci sono di distruzione vorrà essere un gran —, if there comes a war with the present means of destruction there will be great slaughter; (tanning) pelle da —, domestic hide. **-ẹsco** *adj.* (m.pl. **-ẹschi**) pertaining to slaughter, butcherly; murderous, cruel. †**-ino** *m.* slaughtering-tax.

ma·cera *f.* See **maceria**.

macer-are [A I] *tr.* to macerate, to steep; (text.) to ret; (techn.) — la calcina, to slake lime; (fig.) to mortify; to abuse, to vilify; *rfl.* (fig.) to do penance; to be afflicted, to be consumed; to waste away; ~arsi della gelosia, to be consumed with jealousy. (**-a·bile** *adj.* **-amẹnto** *m.*) **-ante** *part. adj.* macerating, steeping; *n.m.* (tanning) bate. **-ato** *part. adj.* macerated; retted; (fig.) consumed; wasted away; †weakened; †lacerated. **-atọio** *m.* (text.) retting box, retting crate. (**-atọre** *m.* **-atrice** *f.*) **-aziọne** *f.* (text.) retting (e.g. of flax); ~azione al fango, hole retting; ~azione sul prato, dew retting, grassing; (fig.) mortification of the flesh.

macerẹto *m.* heap of stones.

mace·ria *f.* dry wall (built without mortar); *pl.* ruins; il terremoto ha ridotto la città a un mucchio di macerie, the earthquake has reduced the city to a heap of débris; (bldg.) rubble.

ma·cero¹ *m.* macerating-vat; tank for slaking lime; (paperm.) giornali nuovi da —, returns; mandare al —, to sell as waste-paper.

ma·cero² *apocop. part.* of **macerare**; *adj.* macerated, steeped; (fig.) exhausted, worn out; wasted by fasting, mortified; senza lasciarle osso addosso che non fosse —, not leaving a sound bone in her body.

ma·cero³ *m.* See **macerazione**, under **macerare**.

macerọne *m.* (bot.) Alexanders, *Smyrnium olusatrum*.

mach *m. indecl.* (aeron.) numero di —, Mach number; indicatore del numero di —, Machmeter.

ma·chi-a *f.* cunning; aver molta —, to be very astute. NOTE: Machiavelli was dubbed 'il Machia' by his contemporaries. **-ọne** *m.* crafty individual. **-onac·cio** *m. pejor.* base trickster.

machiavellẹs-co *adj.* (m.pl. **-chi**). See **machiavellico**.

machiavẹl·l-ico *adj.* Machiavellian, crafty, cunning. (**-icamẹnte** *adv.*) **-iṣmo** *m.* Machiavellism (properly, the doctrines of Machiavelli, but more generally used for cunning and dissimulation). **-ista** *m.* follower of Machiavelli.

machi-ọne *m.* (colloq., Tusc.) one who dissimulates. (**-ọna** *f.*)

machmetro *m.* (aeron.) machmeter.

maci·a *f.* (pop. Tusc.) heap of stones (cf. **maceria**).

ma·cie *f.* emaciation.

†**macigna** *f.* See **macigno**.

macign-o *m.* hard, blue-grey sandstone; stone; large stone; (fig.) cuore di —, heart of flint; obstinate fool, blockhead; (geog., Emilia) large bank of compacted sand; (N.W. Apennines) layered sandstone. **-ọso** *adj.* bluish, blue-grey.

macilen-te **-to** *adj.* emaciated. **-za** *f.* emaciation.

ma·cin-a *f.* millstone; †milling; †grain milled; †load; large quantity. **-are** [A I] *tr.* to grind; to mill; to crush; to pound; (fig.) to eat; ~are a due palmenti, to have a good tuck-in; to punish; to consume; ~are fino, to grind small; (provb.) chi è primo al mulino, prima ~a, first come, first served; acqua passata non ~a più, let bygones be bygones, *or* an opportunity missed never returns; ~are il patrimonio, to consume one's inheritance; *intr.* (*aux.* avere) to feel extreme regret; a veder quel ragazzo così svogliato ci si ~a, it makes one perfectly wretched to see that boy so idle. **-amẹnto** *m.* grinding; pulverizing. **-ante** *part. adj.* grinding, milling; having to do with a mill; fosso ~ante, mill-stream. **-ata** *f.* grinding, milling; quantity ground at one time. **-ato** *part. adj.* ground, milled; *n.m.* meal, flour; tassa di ~ato, grist-tax. **-atọio** *m.* press, mill; (mining) edge mill. **-atọre** *m.* grinder. **-atura** *f.* grinding; grist, charge for grinding. **-aziọne** *f.* grinding. **-ẹllo** *m.* miller. **-ẹlla**, **-ẹtta** *f. dim.*, **-ino** *m. dim.* of **macina**; ~ino da caffè, coffee-grinder; ~ino da pepe, pepper-mill. **-ìo** *m.* (*pl.* **-ìi**) continuous or frequent grinding; (fig.) ~ìo di quattrini, continuous spending. **-ọne** *m. augm.* of **macina**; (fig.) spendthrift.

macis *m. indecl.* (bot.). See **mace**.

maciull-a *f.* (text.) brake (for flax), scutch; — a mano, hand brake; — a cilindri, roller braking machine. **-are** [A I] *tr.* (text.) to break (flax), to scutch; to masticate; to grind between one's teeth; †to eat. **-atrice** *f.* (text.) brake (for flax). **-atura** *f.* (text.) breaking (of flax).

maclura *f.* (bot.) Osage orange, *Maclura pomifera*.

macol-are [A I] *tr.* (agric.) to bruise (fruit); to leave a mark on (by beating). **-ato** *part. adj.* (of fruit) bruised (cf. **maculare**).

ma·colo *apocop. part.* of **macolare**; *adj.* (agric., of fruit) bruised.

†**Macomẹtto** *pr.n.m.* Mahomet.

macọne¹ *m.* (Tusc.). See **magone¹**.

†**Macone²** *pr.n.m.* Mahomet.

†**macontento** *adj.* See **malcontento**.

†**macramà** *f.* table-cloth.

†**macramè** *m.* (needlw.) a kind of fringe of knotted thread used on hand-towels, etc.

†**macr-o¹** *adj.* see **magro**. †**-ẹdine** *f.* see **magrezza**.

macro-² *pref.* (scient.) long. **-cefali·a** *f.* (med.; anat.; biol.) macrocephaly. **-ce·falo** *adj.* macrocephalic. **-coṣmo** *m.* macrocosm. **-dat·tilo** *adj.* (med.; anat.; biol.) macrodactylic, macrodactylous. **-grafi·a** *f.* (metall.) macrography. **-gra·fico** *adj.* macrographic. **-logi·a** *f.* macrology, long-windedness. **-sciano** *adj.* casting a long shadow; *n.m.*, *f.* inhabitant of Arctic or Antarctic zone. **-sco·pico** *adj.* macroscopic, visible to the naked eye. **-spora** *f.* macrospore, as in clubmosses. **-struttura** *f.* (metall.) macrostructure.

macro·metro *m.* macrometer, instrument for measuring distant objects.

macrosa *f.* (orn.) scoter.

macub-a *f.* Macuba snuff. **-ino** *m.* coarse snuff.

ma·cul-a *f.* spot, blemish, stain; damage, injury. **-are** [A I s] *tr.* to spot, to stain, to blemish; to corrupt. (**-ato** *part. adj.* **-azione** *f.*)

†**mad** *conj.* See **ma**.

madam-a *f.* Madame, madam; (used iron. or derog., as in Eng.) mistress; manageress of a brothel. **-ina** *f.* affected woman.

Maddalena *pr.n.f.* Magdalene; Maria —, Mary Magdalene; fare da Marta e —, to do all the work; fare la —, to show oneself very good and pious; name of a bell on the tower of the Bargello at Florence which was tolled at an execution; ti dia la —!, may you be hanged!; (geog.) name of an island off Sardinia.

maddaleone *m.* (pharm.) roll of sticking plaster or the medicated salve for making it.

made-fatto *adj.*, **-fazione** *f.* See under **madido**.

†**madenò** *excl.* No, never!

Madera *pr.n.f.* (geog.) Madeira; *n.m.* Madeira wine.

†**maderno** *adj.* and derivs. See **materno**.

†**madesì** *excl.* Yes, certainly!

ma·di-a *f.* bread-bin; kneading-trough; bin (of which the upper part opens to serve as a kneading-trough, whilst the lower consists of a cupboard); other pieces of furniture of similar construction; goldsmith's bench; fatto e spianato nella stessa —, made in the same mould; (zool.) *Mactra corallina*, an edible bivalve. **-ata** *f.* contents of kneading-trough; †(naut.) raft, beams tied together for towing. **-ella** *f.* shop or stall in the thickness of a wall or under an archway; the cupboard part of a 'madia', q.v. **-one** *m.* stall-holder.

ma·d·ido *adj.* moist, damp; — di sudore, bathed in sweat; wet, wet through. **-efatto** *adj.* moistened, wetted. **-efazione** *f.* wetting. **-ore** *m.* dampness, moisture; slight sweat.

madiella *f.* shop or stall, in the thickness of a wall or under an archway; the cupboard part of a 'madia', q.v.

madiere *m.* (naut.) strengthened central portion of the ribs in wooden vessels.

madione *m.* stall-holder.

Madonn-a *pr.n.f.* the Virgin Mary; Madonna; la — della Seggiola di Raffaello, Raphael's Madonna of the Chair; statue of the Madonna; lady; essere donna e —, to be absolute mistress. **-aro** *m.* painter of Madonnas. **-etta** *f. dim.* a little madonna. **-ina** *f. dim.* a little madonna, small picture of the Madonna, a small shrine or chapel to the Madonna; una -ina infilzata, an affectedly modest girl, one who is insincerely coy. **-ino** *m.* a little madonna; a small coin bearing the image of the Madonna. **-one** *m. augm.* a large picture, statue or shrine of the Madonna. **-uc·cia** *f. dim. pejor.* small, poorly painted Madonna.

madore *m.* See under **madido**.

madornal-e *adj.* (Tusc.) enormous, huge; maternal; born in lawful wedlock; zio —, uncle on one's mother's side; (of branches) growing from the trunk; errore —, gross error. **-ità** *f.* enormity, hugeness; maternality.

madre *f.* mother; female parent; dam; —artificiale, brooder, apparatus for rearing chickens; — di famiglia, mother of a family; — di latte, foster mother; fare da — a, to be a mother to; — spirituale, godmother; la gran —, the Earth (as mother of all things); — patria, mother country; — lingua, lingua —, mother tongue; idea —, main idea; Madre Superiore, Mother Superior; casa —, mother house; mould; womb; counterfoil; libro a — e figlia, counterfoiled book; (anat.) dura —, pia —, dura mater, pia mater; female screw; socket; mother, cause, source; — dell'aceto, mother, dregs, sediment of vinegar; — del vino, dregs, lees of wine; — dell'olio, dregs of oil; (geog.) Isola —, name of an island on Lake Maggiore; (comm.) ufficio —, head office. **-branca** *f.* (agric.) runner or layer for propagating a plant. **-cicala** *f.* (ent.) cast skin of a cicada. **-curva** *f.* (naut.) lift of keel line. **-fami·glia** *f.* mother of a family. **-pa·tria** *f.* motherland, mother-country. **-perla** *f.* (zool.) pearl oyster; mother of pearl. **-perla·ceo** *adj.* nacreous, pearly, mother-of-pearl. **-selva** *f.* (bot.) honeysuckle. **-vite** *f.* (eng.) female screw, nut thread; -vite per tubi, pipe die.

madreggiare [A 3 c] *intr.* (*aux.* avere) to take after one's mother; to be motherly, to behave in a motherly way.

†**ma·drema** *f.* my mother (cf. **ma²**).

madre·p-ora *f.* (zool.) madrepore; (pop.) corals. **-o·rico** *adj.* (zool.) madreporic. **-orite** *f.* (zool.) madreporite.

†**madriale** *m.* (mus.). See **madrigale**.

madrigal-e *m.* (mus.) madrigal. **-eggiare** [A 3 c] *intr.* (*aux.* avere) (mus.) to compose madrigals; (fig.) to make flattering remarks. **-esco** *adj.* (*m.pl.* **-eschi**) (mus.) madrigalian. **-essa** *f.* (joc.) madrigal. **-etto** *m. dim.* (mus.) short madrigal. **-ismo** *m.* (mus.) madrigal writing. **-ista** *m.* (mus.) madrigalist, madrigal composer. **-izzato** *adj.* (mus.) composed in madrigal style. **-one** *m. augm.* long madrigal. **-uc·cio** *m. pejor.* inferior madrigal.

madrign-a *f.* see **matrigna**. **-ale** *adj.* see **matrignesco**.

madrilen-o *adj.* Madrilenian, of Madrid; *n.m.* native of Madrid, inhabitant of Madrid. (**-a** *f.*)

madrina *f.* godmother; midwife; — d'una nave, one who breaks the bottle during launching-ceremony of a ship; fare da — al varo, to perform the launching-ceremony.

madrone *m.* stitch, pain in the side.

madros-o *adj.* (miner.) porous. (**-ità** *f.*)

maestà *f.* majesty; Sua —, His, Her Majesty; Sua — imperiale, His, Her Imperial Majesty; (art) God or the B.V.M. in majesty; wayside shrine; grandeur, majestic aspect, noble proportions; (leg.) delitto di —, delitto di lesa —, lèse majesté.

†**maest-erio** *m.*, †**-ero** *m.* See **magist-erio, -ero**.

maestevol-e *adj.* majestic. **-mente** *adv.* majestically.

maestos-o *adj.* majestic; stately; grand, imposing; (mus.) majestic, dignified. **-amente** *adv.* majestically; in a stately or imposing manner. **-ità** *f.* stateliness, majesty; imposing and dignified bearing.

mae·stra, maestra *f.* schoolmistress; teacher; forewoman in a workshop; (ent.) queen-bee; (naut.) net-line; cork float buoying the head-line of a fishing-net; albero di —, mainmast; pennone di —, mainyard; fusto di —, main lowermast; vela di —, mainsail; †agent, medium; *adj.* see **maestro**.

maestral-e *adj.* north-west; *n.m.* north-west wind. **-ata** *f.* north-westerly gale. **-eggiare** [A 3 c] *intr.* (*aux.* avere) to blow from the north-west.

maestramento *m.* conferring of a doctor's degree; teaching, instruction.

maestranza *f.* the masters of a trade; mastery of a trade; mastery, skill; freedom of a company, right to membership of a guild; the workmen collectively engaged on a job, staff, hands; *pl.* guilds, representatives of various trades; c'interverranno legnaiuoli, muratori, fabbri e tutte le altre maestranze, carpenters, masons, smiths and representatives of all other trades will take part.

†**maestrare** *vb.* See **ammaestrare**.

†**maestrato** *m.* See **magistrato**.

maestrella *f.* (text. industr.) upper part of the frame of a loom, which carries the pulley or pulleys controlled by the weaver.

maestrevol-e *adj.* masterly, skilful. **-mente** *adv.* skilfully; in masterly fashion.

maestri·a *f.* mastery, skill; proficiency; control; con grande —, very skilfully; trick, stratagem; se la cavò con —, he got away with it by means of a trick; mastership, dignity or office of master.

†**maestricello** *m.* (mus.). See **maestrino**.

maestrina *f.* young schoolmistress; nursery governess; forewoman's assistant in silk spinnery.

maestrino *m.* (mus.) pupil teacher in a conservatoire.

mae·stro, maestro *m.* master, teacher; tutor, instructor; — di scuola, schoolmaster; — di musica, music master; — di scherma, fencing master; — di campo, field-marshal; foreman; — di legname, carpenter; — d'equipaggio, boatswain; — di campo generale, quarter-master general; — di casa, house-steward; Gran Maestro, Grand Master; — di stalla, Master of Horse; — eterno, God; — di giustizia, executioner; un colpo da —, master-stroke; (mus.) conductor, teacher of music, composer; master (i.e. great composer); a title (abbreviated Mo.) applied to one who has obtained a diploma in composition and, more loosely, to any musician holding a position of responsibility; pitch-pipe; — di cappella, choir-master; — al cembalo, orchestral conductor (seated at the harpsichord in eighteenth century); — concertatore, conductor; — dei putti, Master of the Children at St Peter's; — di concerto, leader (of orchestra); (geog.) north-west wind; (naut.) head or chief; — d'ascia, chief carpenter; †constructor; †owner; †captain of a gun, etc.; † — di casa, messman; *adj.* chief; main; acqua -a, lye; albero —, mainmast; barba -a, tap-root; colpo —, master-stroke; libro —, ledger;

maestr-o (*cont.*)

mal —, epilepsy; mano -a, master-hand; muro —, main wall; penna -a, quill; porta -a, main gate; trave -a, king-post in roof; strada -a, high road. **-ale** *adj.* (mus.) stretto -ale, masterly stretto, i.e. passage in which all the voices of a fugue are engaged in canon; (naut.) main; albero -ale, mainmast. **-ọna** *f. augm.* excellent teacher; teacher who is physically big. **-ọne** *m. augm.* excellent teacher; great composer. **-uc·cio** *m. dim. pejor.* inferior teacher. **-u·colo** *m. dim. pejor.* ignorant schoolmaster. (**-u·cola** *f.*)

maf·fia *f.* See **mafia**.

Ma·fi·a *pr.n.f.* (Sicily) the Mafia, a secret society (esp. prevalent in Sicily) notoriously contemptuous of the law; (journ.) association of members of criminal underworld; far —, to affect elegance. **-ọso** *adj.* belonging to the Mafia; affecting elegance; *n.m.* member, associate of the Mafia.

maga *f.* sorceress, enchantress, witch; (fig.) hag; domineering woman (cf. **mago**).

magadi·s *m. indecl.* (mus.) magadis, ancient Greek dulcimer with strings arranged in octaves.

magadiẓẓare [A I] *intr.* (*aux.* avere) (mus.) to magadize, to sing or play in octaves.

magagn-a *f.* rottenness (esp. of fruit); flaw, defect; fault; vice; corruption; ci dev'essere sotto qualche —, there's some dirty work going on; *pl.* troubles, afflictions. **-are** [A 5] *tr.* to spoil, to damage (fruit); to weaken; to impair; to corrupt. **-amẹnto** *m.* blemish; vice; rottenness (e.g. of fruit). **-ato** *part. adj.* spoiled, damaged; queste mele sono tutte -ate, these apples are all bad; feigned, insincere. **-atura** *f.* act of spoiling; effect of spoiling.

†**magalda** *f.* prostitute.

†**magaluffo** *m.* auctioneer's fee.

maganzẹse *adj.* of the house of Maganza, a family hostile to Charlemagne of which Ganelon was believed to be a member; *n.m.* one of the Maganza.

†**magare** *tr.* to bewitch.

magari *excl.* would it were so!; I wish it were so; — mi dicesse di sì, I wish he would agree; even, even if; — dovessi andarci dieci volte, lo vedrò, even if I have to go there ten times, I shall see him; maybe, perhaps; lei dirà, —, di non volerne sentire, she may say, perhaps (*or* even), that she doesn't want to hear anything about it; — Dio!, would to God!, would to Heaven!

magaẓẓin-o *m.* warehouse; storehouse; — di deposito, place for storing furniture or luggage; store, shop; — di mode, store selling women's clothes, etc.; — a catena, chain stores; merci in —, goods on hand; (comm.) -i generali, bonded warehouse (C.C.); (rlwy.) — merci, goods shed; (naut.) engineers' store; — di bordo, ship's store; — d'acqua, fresh-water compartment; — della marina, naval store. **-ag·gio** *m.* storage; warehousing; — refrigerato, cold storage; (spese di) —, storage charges. **-iere** *m.* warehouseman; (naut.) engineers' storekeeper.

magdaleọne *m.* See **maddaleọne**.

Magdeburgo *pr.n.f.* (geog.) Magdeburg; emisferi di —, Magdeburg hemispheres (a contrivance invented by Otto von Guericke of Magdeburg to demonstrate the pressure of air).

Magellano *pr.n.m.* (geog.) Magellan.

magenta *m.* magenta, a colour which became fashionable after the Battle of Magenta (1859).

maggengo *adj.* (agric.) ripening in May; fieno —, May hay; *n.m.* (geog.) intermediate pasture; alpine hut (cf. **maggio**).

maggẹs-are [A I c] *tr.* to lay fallow. **-ato** *part. adj.* left fallow. **-atura** *f.* fallowing.

maggẹs-e *m.* (agric.) fallow; fallow land; fallow field; — completo e intero, twelve months' fallow; — incompleto, — semestrale, mezzo —, six months' fallow; in —, fallow, lying fallow; *adj.* see **maggengo** (cf. **maggio**).

mag·gi-o *m.* (the month of) May; primo (giorno) di —, calen di —, May-day; branch of fresh green or spring blossom placed before the door of a sweetheart; maying; May weather; the flowers of spring; (fig.) parere una rosa di —, to be young and blooming; (joc.) il cantore di —, donkey, braying ass; (iron.) aspettar che venga —, to wait forever; (provb.) — adagio, cast ne'er a clout...; (bot.) Spanish broom, *Spartium junceum*; may, may-tree; (mus.) May song formerly sung at the 'calendimaggio', q.v., spring song (also called canto di —); il Maggio musicale fiorentino, music festival held at Florence during May and June.

maggiociọndol-o, -ino *m.* (bot.) laburnum.

maggiolata *f.* (mus.) May song, spring song.

maggiolino[1] *m.* (ent.) cockchafer, may bug, *Melolontha vulgaris*.

maggiolino[2] *m.* kind of furniture with inlaid decoration shaded by a special firing process made by G. Maggiolini (1738–1814).

maggiorana *f.* (bot.) marjoram, *Majorana hortensis*.

maggioranza *f.* majority; pre-eminence; — assoluta, absolute majority; la — degl'Italiani, most Italians; a grande —, by a great majority; con debole —, con scarsa —, with a slender majority; essere in —, aver la —, to have a majority; la — è acquisita, the majority is obtained; — ripartita per gruppi, distributed majority; a — relativa, by a relative majority; a — assoluta, by an absolute majority, by a simple majority; eleggere a — qualificata, to elect by a qualified majority; la — richiesta, the requisite majority; deliberazione a —, majority resolution; — di voti, majority vote.

maggior-are [A I C] *tr.* (comm.) to increase; — i prezzi, to raise prices. **-ato** *part. adj.* (comm.) increased; (of prices) raised, up; (eng.) oversize. **-azione** *f.* (comm.) increase; rise (in prices).

maggiorasco *m.* (leg.) majorat.

maggiordomo *m.* major-domo; house-steward, butler.

maggiọr-e *adj.* (*comp.* of **grande**, q.v.):

1. LARGER, bigger; il salotto è — della camera, the sitting-room is larger than the bedroom; mi occorre un cappello —, I need a bigger hat; greater; il tutto è — della parte, the whole is greater than the part; forza —, *force majeure*; la sua autorità è — della mia, his authority is greater than mine; il maggior numero, the greater number; la maggior parte, the greater part, the major part, the majority; con voce —, in a louder voice; essere — di se stesso, to excel oneself; un uomo — di ogni eccezione, a man of undisputed authority. **2.** MORE IMPORTANT; major; longer established; high, higher; (hist.) Arti Maggiori, the major guilds in medieval Florence; l'età —, full age, majority; divenire — di età, raggiungere l'età —, to come of age, to attain one's majority; la premessa —, the major premise (in a syllogism); (eccl.) Ordini -i, the three higher Orders (sub-deacon, deacon, priest, as opposed to 'Ordini minori'); basilica —, major basilica; S. Maria Maggiore, Great St Mary; (poet.) il maggior Piero, the Pope; l'altar —, the high altar; messa —, high mass; fare — a tutti, to place in a position of authority over all others. **3.** ELDER, older; Scipione —, Scipio the elder; Plinio —, the elder Pliny; mio fratello —, my elder brother; è — di me di tre anni, he is three years older than I am; c'era anche la signora Bruni con la figliuola —, Mrs Brown was also there with her elder (*or* eldest) daughter (cf. under No. 4). **4.** USED AS SUPERLATIVE (usu. with *def. art.*): il Po è il maggior fiume d'Italia, the Po is the largest river in Italy; Dante è il maggior poeta italiano, Dante is the greatest Italian poet; gli astri -i, the largest stars; con la maggior cura, with the greatest, utmost, care; vi auguro ogni maggior bene, I wish you all the best; il maggior offerente, the highest bidder; il figlio —, the eldest son. **5.** (Mus.) major (attribute of mode or interval). **6.** (Mil.) Stato —, staff, general staff; ufficiale di Stato —, staff-officer; major; — generale, major-general; sergente —, sergeant-major; tamburo —, drum-major; (naut.) Lieutenant-Commander's rank in all non-executive branches. **7.** *pl.* ANCESTORS, forefathers; elders; i -i della città, the authorities, notable personalities, dignitaries, etc. of the city. *f.* la —, the greater part; the foremost people; un artista che va per la —, an artist who is among the best known; (mus.) maggiore, a section or variation in the major mode contrasting with a preceding passage in the minor; (logic) major premise. **-mẹnte** *adv.* more; to a greater extent, more fully.

maggiorẹnne *m.* major, person of full age; *adj.* of age, of full age.

maggior-ẹnte *m.*, †**-ingo** *m.* one of the most influential men in a community; notable man; bigwig; *pl.* those in charge; the management.

†**maggiorẹzza** *f.* (mus.) major modality.

maggiorin-o *m.* eldest of family. (**-a** *f.*)

maggiorità *f.* (mil.) majority.

maggiorita·rio *m.* (pol.) member of the party in power.

maggiormẹnte *adv.* See under **maggiore**.

†**maggiornato** *m.* eldest of a family.

†**maggiostrina** *f.* man's straw hat.

ma·ghero *adj.* (pop. Tusc.). See **magro**.

maghẹtto *m.* gizzard; *pl.* giblets; (dial. Lomb.) grief.

Magi *pr.n.m.pl.* of **magio**, q.v.; the Magi.

magi·a *f.* magic.

ma·giaro *m.*, *adj.* Magyar.

ma·gic-o *adj.* magic; magical; enchanting; bacchetta ‑a, magic wand; lanterna ‑a, magic lantern, slide projector. **-amẹnte** *adv.* magically; enchantingly.

ma·gio *m.* one of the Magi; (fig., Tusc.) wise man, philosopher; ritto, fermo come un —, perfectly still; (pop.) conjurer.

magiọn-e *f.* house, habitation, mansion; (poet.) — di Dio, church. **-cella** *f. dim.*, **-ẹtta** *f. dim.* small house or habitation.

magiostra *f.* (bot.) large kind of strawberry which ripens in May.

magiscoro *m.* choir-master.

magiṣmo *m.* (rel.) Magianism.

magistero *m.* mastery, skill, power; education, discipline; teaching; profession of teacher; patente di —, teacher's certificate; Facoltà di Magistero, University Faculty to which only those students are eligible who hold a teaching diploma; Gran Magistero, the highest office in certain Italian orders of chivalry; (pharm.) magistery; precipitate; — di bismuto, magistery of bismuth; — di zolfo, magistery of sulphur.

magistral-e *adj.* magistral; magisterial; relating to the profession of teacher; cattedra —, professorial chair; congresso —, congress of teachers; Istituto —, Training College; masterly; skilful; haughty; authoritative, commanding; chief; cinta —, outer line of circumvallation; rimedio —, sovereign remedy. **-mẹnte** *adv.* in a masterly manner; in masterly fashion. **-ità** *f.* manner and demeanour characteristic of a teacher; magisterial tone and air.

magistrat-o *m.* magistracy; magistrate (official with administrative or judicial functions); il primo — della città, the mayor; chief magistrate; the governor; — d'accusa, Public Prosecutor's office. **-ura** *f.* the Bench; judiciary; judicature (I.C.); magistracy; magistrature; cittadini estranei alla -ura, citizens not members of the judiciary (I.C.).

ma·gli-a *f.* knot, link; stitch in knitting; lavorare a —, to knit; lavorazione a —, knitting; lavoro di —, knitting, knitted work, net work; a —, knitted; t'è cascata una —, you've dropped a stitch; armatura di —, chain armour; ring, link in coat of mail; mesh of net; mail, coat of mail; ring (e.g. for hanging up a clock); tessere a —, to knit hosiery; tessitura a —, hosiery knitting; (text.) stitch, loop; knitted garment; tights; light pullover; long-sleeved vest; (sport) — rosa, pink jersey worn by racing cyclist who has won the previous completed stage in a race; essere una — rosa, to be a cyclist wearing such a garment; (anat.) spot on the cornea; (eng.) mesh; link (of a chain); — a molinello, swivel link; — per cingolo, track link; (naut.) space between frames; eyesplice at the end of a rope; sail cringle; — cieca, sprat net; — di avvistamento, linked watch tower or warning posts. **-are** [A 4] *tr.* to mail; to net. **-ato** *part. adj.* mailed, mail; netted.

Magliabechiana *pr.n.f.* Library named after Antonio Magliabechi (1633–1714), whom the Grand-Duke Cosimo III of Florence appointed librarian of the Biblioteca Palatina.

maglieri·a *f.* hosiery; hosier's shop; (text.) hosiery mill; macchina per —, knitting machine.

magliẹtt-a *f. dim.* of **maglia**, q.v.; ring, small ring; eye of 'hook and eye'; — del quadro, the half-ring on a picture-frame used for hanging it; sleeveless pullover; any light-knitted garment; football shirt; ring for hinging a small door on to a pivot. **-are** [A I c] *tr.* (naut.) to floor (the hold of a ship) with broad triangular nails. **-atura** *f.* (naut.) work done as above or on the outside of a ship, the planks being covered with bigheaded triangular nails, to prevent the ravages of ship-worms.

magliẹtto *m. dim.* See under **maglio**[1].

maglifi·cio *m.* hosiery; hosiery-factory.

ma·gli-o[1] *m.* hammer; mallet; head of steam hammer; 'monkey' in pile driving; pall-mall hammer; pall-mall, game resembling croquet; mallet used in playing croquet; bat; rammer; (eng.) power hammer; — a caduta libera, drop hammer; — a leva, helve hammer; stampaggio al —, drop forging; (naut.) mandare una nave al —, to condemn a ship. **-ẹtto** *m. dim.* small hammer.

ma·glio[2] *m.* (anat.) malleus (one of the ossicles or small bones of the ear).

magliolina *f. dim.* of **maglia**, q.v., esp. in sense of small spot on corner of the eye.

magliuc·cia *f.* (naut.) hemp rope.

magli(u)olo *m.* (agric.) cutting; shoot; sucker.

magliọne *m. augm.* of **maglia**, q.v.; thick pullover, sweater; (rlwy.) coupling link.

magma *m.* (geol.) magma.

magnac·cio *m.* one who lives on the earnings of a prostitute, bully.

magna·lio *m.* (metall.) magnalium, aluminium-magnesium alloy.

magn-a·nimo *adj.* magnanimous; generous. **-animamẹnte** *adv.* magnanimously; generously. **-animità** *f.* magnanimity; generosity.

magnanina *f.* (orn.) Dartford warbler, *Sylvia undata*; — sarda, La Marmora's warbler, *Sylvia sarda*.

magnano *m.* locksmith; coppersmith; nero come un —, black as soot, as black as a chimney-sweep.

magnare [A 5] *tr.* (dial. Milan) see **mangiare**.

magnarọne *m.* (ichth.) miller's thumb, sea scorpion, etc., *Cottus* spp.

magnat-e *m.* a noble; important citizen; magnate; — dell'acciaio, steel magnate. **-i·zio** *adj.* noble; rich; pertaining to a magnate.

magne·ṣ-ia *f.* (chem.) magnesia, magnesium oxide. **-i·aco** *adj.* magnesian. **-ite** *f.* (min.) magnesite. **-io** *m.* (chem.; metall.) magnesium.

magnet-e *m.* magnet; magneto. **-iṣmo** *m.* (phys.) magnetism; -iṣmo animale, animal magnetism; -iṣmo residuo, residual magnetism, remanence. **-ite** *f.* (miner.) magnetite, lodestone. **-iẓẓare** [A I] *tr.* (phys.) to magnetize. **-iẓẓaziọne** *f.* (phys.) magnetization; (electr.) -iẓẓazione residua, residual magnetism. **-oelettricità** *f.* (electr.; phys.) magneto-electricity. **-oelet·trico** *adj.* (electr.; phys.) magneto-electric. **-o·fono** *m.* tape-recorder. **-o·grafo** *m.* magneto-graph. **-o·metro** *m.* (electr.) magnetometer. **-osco·pio** *m.* (electr.) magnetoscope. **-ostriziọne** *f.* (electr.) magnetostriction. **-rọne** *m.* (radio) magnetron; -rone ad anodo spaccato, split-anode magnetron.

magne·tico *adj.* magnetic.

magnific-are [A 2 s] *tr.* to magnify, to exalt; to exaggerate. **-amẹnto** *m.* magnifying, exalting. **-at** *m. indecl.* (rel.; mus.) Magnificat. **-ato** *part. adj.* magnified; exalted; exaggerated. **-atamẹnte** *adv.* magnificently; exaggeratedly. **-atore** *m.* one who magnifies or exalts; extoller; magnifier. (**-atrice** *f.*)

magnificen-te *adj.* (of a personage) magnificent. (**-temẹnte** *adv.*) **-za** *f.* magnificence; grandeur; Vostra Magnificenza, a title formerly given to nobles or persons of importance, now used ceremonially in addressing a dignitary such as the Rector of a University.

magni·fic-o *adj.* magnificent; splendid; grand, fine; munificent; il — Rettore, title of the Rector of an Italian University; *n.m.* (hist.) title bestowed esp. on Venetian magnates, Grandee; (Tusc. hist.) il Magnifico, (Lorenzo) the magnificent. **-amẹnte** *adv.* magnificently; munificently.

magn-iloquente *adj.* grandiloquent; highfalutin. **-iloquenza** *f.* grandiloquence; exalted speech, lofty eloquence. **-ilo·quio** *m.* grandiloquence. **-i·loquo** *adj.* grandiloquent.

magnitudine *f.* magnitude, great size.

magn-o *adj.* great; Carlo —, Charlemagne; Gregorio —, Gregory the Great; aula -a, main hall; la -a Carta inglese, the Magna Carta; *magna pars*, a person who plays an important part in any affair; (iron.) great; vedremo finalmente questo tuo — lavoro, at last we shall see this great work of yours.

magno·lia *f.* (bot.) magnolia.

magnos-a *f.* (zool.) *Scyllarides latus*, **-ella** *f.* (zool.) *Scyllarus arctus*, two related species of edible lobster-like crustaceans.

mago *m.* (*pl.* **maghi**) wizard, sorcerer; (Rome) — sabino, man dressed as a wizard and selling lottery tickets, (Milan) necromancer, (fig.) strange bearded figure; *adj.* magic; parole maghe, magic words.

Magog-a *pr.n.f.* Oga —, an expression for any far distant countries, the ends of the earth. **-o** *pr.n.m.* Magog; (fig.) outlandish person.

mago·gano *m.* See **mogano**.

ma·gol-o[1] *m.* (agric.) ridge of a furrow. **-ato** *m.* (agric.) space between two furrows; ground ploughed in narrow furrows.

†ma·gol-o[2] *m.*, **†-azzo** *m.* See **mago**.

magọn-a *f.* iron foundry; ironworks; ironmonger's shop; any place of abundance. **-cina** *f. dim.* forge; ironmonger's shop. **-iere** *m.* iron founder.

magọne[1] *m. augm.* of **mago**, q.v.; great wizard, sorcerer.

†magọne[2] *m.* See **maghetto**.

Magọn-za *pr.n.f.* (geog.) Mainz. **-tino** *adj.* of Mainz; *n.m.* inhabitant or native of Mainz. (**-tina** *f.*)

magra *f.* thin woman; (geog.) low water (cf. **magro**).

†magrana *f.* (med.). See **emicrania**.

magredo *m.* (geog., Friuli) poor, uncultivated land.

magr·o *adj.* thin, meagre, lean; poor; annate -e, lean years; cibi -i, food allowed on abstinence-days, Lenten fare; giorno —, abstinence-day; carne -a, the lean of a joint of meat; zuppa -a, thin soup, vegetable soup; luce -a, feeble light; maniera -a, dry manner; un omino —, a wizened little man; ricompensa -a, meagre reward; suolo, terreno —, poor soil; *n.m.* the lean of meat; tagliare nel —, to cut from the lean; Lenten fare; mangiare di —, far di —, to abstain from meat; pasto di —, a meal of fish. **-amẹnte** *adv.* poorly; meagrely. **-ettino**, **-ẹtto** *adj. dim.* rather thin. **-ẹzza** *f.* thinness, leanness. **-o·gnolo** *adj. dim.* thin. **-otto** *adj. dim.* not very fat. **-uc·cio** *adj. pejor.* wretchedly thin.

magrọne *m.* pig meant for fattening.

†**magu·glio** *m.* (naut.) pointed hook for drawing out oakum from the seams.

mahar·a·gia *m.* Maharaja. **-ani** *f.* Maharani.

mahd-i *m.* Mahdi. **-iṣmo** *m.* Mahdism. **-ista** *m.* Mahdist.

mahogọni *m.* See **mogano**.

mai[1] *adv.* **1.** EVER; più che —, more than ever; peggio che —, worse than ever; la finirete —?, will you ever finish it? *or* will you ever have done?; se —, if ever; se — —, if by any chance; se —, lo direi temerario, if anything I'd call him rash; quanto —, very much indeed; quanto — ?, how much?, how long?; tante — cose, ever so many things; come — ?, why?, how do you make that out?, how on earth?; caso —, if anything, if by any chance; gli voglio un bene che —, I love him like anything. **2.** NEVER (with neg. expressed or implied); non lo vidi —, I never saw him; — e poi —!, never, never!; — più, never more, never again; †never before; — dei miei giorni, never in my life; ora o —, now or never; meglio tardi che —, better late than never; non si sa —, you never can tell.

mai[2] *m.* See **maggio**.

mai[3] *contr.* of **mali**, *pl.* of **male**, q.v.

maial-a *f.* sow; dirty woman; lewd woman. **-ata** *f.* piggish action; foul trick. **-atura** *f.* preparation and dressing of a pig's carcase; season for such preparation.

maial-e *m.* pig, swine; (properly, castrated boar kept for fattening, but the word is now used more generally); pork; (fig.) filthy man; che fai, brutto — ?, what are you doing, you dirty pig?; carne di —, pork. **-ẹsco** *adj.* (*m.pl.* **-ẹschi**) filthy, dirty. **-ino** *m. dim.* little pig, piglet. **-ọne** *m. augm.* large pig; (fig.) filthy pig.

†**maice** *m.* See **mais**.

ma·iden *adj. indecl.* (of a horse) that has never won a race.

mai·d·ico *adj.* relating to maize; (med.) relating to pellagra. **-iṣmo** *m.* (med.) pellagra.

maiella *f.* (bot.) *Cytisus sessilifolius.*

maiest-à *f.* majesty. **-a·tico** *adj.* pertaining to majesty; il 'Noi' -atico, the royal 'We'.

maieu·tica *f.* maieutics, midwifery.

maimọne *m.* (zool.) Macacques, and other monkeys.

†**mainare** *vb.* and derivs. See **ammainare**.

†**mainò** *adv.* certainly not, not at all.

†**ma·io** *m.* may; mayflower; branch placed before the door of a sweetheart; appiccare il — ad ogni uscio, to make love to anything in petticoats (cf. **maggio**).

maio·lica *f.* majolica; majolica ware; †(geog.) see **maiorca**.

maionẹse *f.* (cul.) mayonnaise.

†**maioranza** *f.* See **maggioranza**.

†**maiorasco** *m.* See **maggiorasco**.

Maiorca *pr.n.f.* (geog.) Majorca.

†**maiordomo** *m.* See **maggiordomo**.

†**maior·i·a** *f.*, **-ità** *f.* See **maggioranza**.

mais *m. indecl.* (bot.) maize.

†**maisì** *adv.* most certainly.

maitacaca *m.* (orn.) a species of South American parrot, *Pionias menstruus.*

maiu·scol·o *adj.* capital (of letter); lettere -e, capital letters; (fig.) big, gross; un errore —, a gross error. **-i** *m.pl.* (typ.) caps. NOTE: in printing this word is masculine, since the word understood is 'caratteri'; -i corsivi, italic capitals. **-ẹtti** *m.pl.* (typ.) small caps.

†**maiz** *m.* See **mais**.

maki *m. indecl.* (zool.) lemur.

makò *m. indecl.* (text.) variety of very fine Egyptian cotton.

mal- *pref.* evil-, ill-. †**-abbiato** *adj.* evil, wicked. **-accẹtto** *adj.* unacceptable. **-accọlto** *adj.* coldly welcomed; ill-received; undesired, unwelcome. **-accọncio** *adj.* unfit, unsuitable. **-accorto**

adj. incautious; unwise, imprudent; rash; awkward. (**-accortamẹnte** *adv.*) **-adọrno** *adj.* ill-adorned. **-affare** *m.* base life; evil living; donna di -affare, prostitute. **-affẹtto** *adj.* ill-disposed. **-agẹvole** *adj.* difficult, hard; inconvenient, awkward; tedious; uncomfortable; irksome; awkward; intricate. (**-agevolmẹnte** *adv.*) **-agevolẹzza** *f.* difficulty; tediousness; irksomeness. **-agiato** *adj.* badly off; in difficult circumstances; hard-up. †**-agu·ria** *f.* see **malaugurio**. †**-andanza** *f.* misfortune. **-andare** [A 7] *intr.* (*aux.* essere) to go to ruin; to go bad; to take a bad turn; to fall into a poor condition. **-andato** *part. adj.* ruined; dilapidated, in poor repair; -ato in salute, run down in health. **-andrinac·cio** *m.* rascal. **-andrinag·gio** *m.* highway robbery. **-andrinẹsco** *adj.* (*m.pl.* **-andrinẹschi**) pertaining to a robber or highwayman. **-andrino** *m.* highwayman; robber; ruffian; *adj.* evil; rascally. **-a·nimo** *m.* ill-will; malice, spite, malevolence. †**-annag·gio** *excl.* confound it!, a plague on...! **-anno** *m.* grave misfortune, calamity; illness, disease; infirmity; il male, il -anno e l'uscio addosso, every kind of misfortune; il -anno e la mala pasqua, very rough reception; con questa guerra avremo il male, il -anno e l'uscio addosso, this war will bring us to utter ruin; che ti colga il -anno, blast you!; (fig.) blackguard. **-appropo·ṣito** *adj.* inopportune. **-a·ria** *f.* bad air; malaria. **-a·rico** *adj.* malarial; malarious; *n.m.* person suffering from malaria. **-arnẹse** *m.* rogue, scoundrel. **-arrivato** *adj.* in a bad way; wretched, unfortunate; unwelcome; *n.m.* unfortunate person. **-assetato** *adj.* disordered. **-augurato** *adj.* unlucky, unfortunate; inauspicious; un affare -augurato, a bad business; un incidente -augurato, a regrettable incident. (**-auguratamẹnte** *adv.*) **-augu·rio** *m.* bad omen; uccello di -augurio, bird of ill omen. **-augurọso** *adj.* of ill omen, inauspicious. (**-augurosamẹnte** *adv.*) **-avveduto** *adj.* imprudent, unwise. (**-avvedutamẹnte** *adv.*) **-avventura** *f.* mischance; misfortune. **-avventurato** *adj.* unlucky, unfortunate. (**-avventuratamẹnte** *adv.*) **-avvẹzzo** *adj.* ill-mannered, ill-bred, unmannerly, uncouth. **-avviato** *adj.* unruly; straggling. **-avviṣato** *adj.* ill-advised; unwise. **-azzato** *adj.* poorly, unwell. **-caduco** *m.* (*pl.* **-caduchi**) epilepsy. †**-biga(t)to** *adj.* ill-intentioned; *n.m.* evilly-disposed person. **-capitato** *adj.* unfortunate, unlucky. **-ca·uto** *adj.* incautious, imprudent. (**-ca·utamẹnte** *adv.*) **-certo** *adj.* uncertain, doubtful; dubious; irresolute. **-collocato** *adj.* ill-placed. **-cominciato** *adj.* badly begun. **-composto** *adj.* awkward; disorderly. (**-compostamẹnte** *adv.*) **-concepito** *adj.* ill-conceived. **-concertato** *adj.* ill-contrived. **-cọncio** *adj.* damaged; in a sorry state; knocked about; beaten up. **-condiscendente** *adj.* disobligingly; uncouth, rough. **-confacẹvole** *adj.* ill-agreeing, ill-suited. **-considerato** *adj.* ill-considered. **-consigliato** *adj.* ill-advised; incautious; thoughtless. **-contento** *adj.* discontented, dissatisfied; *n.m.* discontent; dissatisfaction; prima il -contento poi addirittura la ribellione, first discontent, then open rebellion; dissatisfied person, malcontent. **-coperto** *adj.* half-naked; casa -coperta, house with damaged roof. **-corrisposto** *adj.* ill-requited. **-costumato** *adj.* immoral; immodest; vicious; ill-mannered. **-costume** *m.* debauchery; immorality. **-creatello** *adj. dim.* rascally; spoilt; un po' -creatello è quel bambino, that child is a little rascal. **-creato** *adj.* ill-bred; wicked; churlish. **-cubato** *adj.* sickly, rather ill. **-curante** *adj.* careless, negligent. **-curato** *adj.* badly cared for. **-dentato** *adj.* having few teeth; having bad teeth; *n.m.* (zool.) edentate. **-destro** *adj.* awkward, clumsy. **-dẹtto** *adj.* not well said (of words and phrases incorrectly or badly used). **-dicente** *adj.* slanderous; evil-speaking; *n.m.* slanderer; slanderous person. **-dicenza** *f.* slander; scandal; backbiting; 'La Scuola della Maldicenza', 'The School for Scandal'. **-difẹso** *adj.* ill-defended. **-disposto** *adj.* ill-disposed. **-distẹso** *adj.* ill-extended; badly laid out; ill-arranged. **-doc·chio** *m.* see **malocchio**. **-durẹvole** *adj.* of short duration. **-educato** *adj.* ill-bred; ill-mannered; *n.m.* ill-bred person. **-e·fico** *adj.* evil; mischievous; pernicious; baleful; malignant. (**-eficamẹnte** *adv.*) **-erba** *f.* weed; noxious weed; essere conosciuto come la -erba, to be known everywhere. **-es·sere** *m.* indisposition; malaise; discomfort; uneasiness; bad financial condition. **-estro** *m.* mischief. **-famato** *adj.* of bad reputation; una casa -famata, a house of ill fame. **-fare** [B 14] *intr.* (*aux.* avere) to do evil; *n.m.* evil-doing. **-fatto** *part.* of **malfare**; *adj.* ill-done; deformed, ill-shaped; *n.m.* misdeed. **-fattọre** *m.* evil-doer; malefactor; (leg.) criminal, malefactor; offender against the law. **-fẹrmo** *adj.* unsafe, insecure, shaky, feeble; di salute -ferma, in poor health. **-ferrato** *adj.* (of a horse) badly shod. **-fidato** *adj.* distrustful; diffident. **-fidente** *adj.* dis-

mal- (cont.)

trustful. **-fido** adj. unreliable, untrustworthy. **-fiorito** adj. with few blossoms. **-fondato** adj. ill-founded; (of an argument) weak, feeble. **-formato** adj. ill-formed. **-formazione** f. malformation. **-forte** adj. weak. †**-fusso** adj. villainous; n.m. villain, cad. **-garbo** m. clumsiness; boorishness; clumsy behaviour; con -garbo, with a bad grace; dire con -garbo, to be brusque. **-giudicare** [A 2 s] tr. to misjudge. **-governo** m. misgovernment, maladministration, mismanagement; maltreatment; (leg.) -governo di animali, failure to control animals (C.P.). **-gradito** adj. unwelcome. **-grado** prep. in spite of; a -grado dell'evidente innocenza, notwithstanding the fact that his action was clearly blameless; adv. willy-nilly; suo -grado, against his will; nostro -grado, much to our regret. **-grazioso** adj. ungracious; unattractive; uncouth. **-guardato** adj. badly looked after; without defence. **-gusto** m. bad taste. **-intenzionato** adj. with evil intentions; evil-minded; n.m. evil-minded person. **-inteso** adj. misconceived, wrong; onore -inteso, mistaken sense of honour; n.m. misunderstanding; a scanso di -intesi, to avoid misunderstandings. **-inventurato** adj. unlucky. **-luogo** m. (pl. **-luoghi**) evil place; brothel. **-maritata** adj. f. ill-married. **-menare** [A 1] tr. to ill-treat, to treat roughly; -menare una lingua, to 'murder' a language. **-menato** part. adj. ill-treated, ill-used. **-menìo** m. ill-usage. **-meritare** [A 1 s] intr. (aux. avere) to deserve ill. **-messo** adj. poorly dressed; in a poor condition; badly off. **-mettere** [C 20] tr. to dissipate, to waste. **-nato** adj. ill-born; ill-bred; deplorable; unfortunate, unlucky; accursed; n.m. unfortunate individual; (tanning) stillborn calf-skin. **-noto** adj. little known. **-occhio** m. the 'evil eye'; vedere di -occhio, to dislike, to regard with dislike. **-occlusione** f. (med.) abocclusion. **-ora** f. ruin, perdition; andare in (a) -ora, to go to the devil; mandare in (a) -ora, to send to the devil; ha mandato alla -ora un intero patrimonio, he has wasted an entire inheritance. **-ore** m. illness; fu colto da un improvviso —, he was suddenly taken ill. **-otico** adj. spiteful, malignant. †**-otta** f. see **malora**. †**-parato** adj. in a sorry plight. †**-pari** adj. unequal. **-parlante** adj. speaking badly, or incorrectly; n.m. one who speaks badly, or incorrectly. **-pelo** adj. red-haired. **-pensante** adj. unsound, wrong-thinking. **-pensato** adj. badly thought out; ill-contrived; ill-devised. **-persuaso** adj. unpersuaded; not fully persuaded. **-piglio** m. act of disdain or anger; disdain, scorn; frown. **-pratico** adj. inexperienced; unskilful. **-preparato** adj. ill-prepared. **-prò** m. indecl. hurt, harm, damage. **-procedere** m. misbehaviour, misconduct; discourteousness. **-proprio**¹ adj. improper. **-proprio**² adj. unclean. **-provveduto, -provvisto** adj. ill-provided. **-puzzo** m. stench. **-sanìa** f. ill-health; insalubrity. **-sano** adj. unhealthy; unwholesome; unsound; cibo -sano, unwholesome food; dottrine -sane, unsound doctrines; cervello -sano, unsound mind. **-servito** adj. ill-served. **-sicuro** adj. uncertain, unsafe; unsteady. **-sincero** adj. insincere, feigned. **-soddisfatto** adj. dissatisfied. **-sofferente** adj. (prep. di) intolerant (of); putting up (with) unwillingly; impatient (of); -sofferente del giogo straniero, intolerant of foreign domination. **-sussistente** adj. insubstantial; non-existent. **-tagliati** m.pl. (cul.) pieces of 'pasta' of irregular shape eaten in soup. **-talento** m. evil disposition; bad frame of mind; ill-will. **-tempo** m. bad weather. **-tenuto** adj. badly kept. **-tinto** adj. badly coloured; la mattina usciva dal letto col viso verdegiallo -tinto, he got up in the morning with a blotchy greenish yellow face. **-tollerabile** adj. intolerable, insupportable. **-tollerante** adj. intolerant. **-tolto** adj. ill-gotten; unjustly exacted; n.m. ill-gotten gain; exaction. **-trattamento** m. ill-treatment, maltreatment; (leg.) -trattamento in famiglia, verso fanciulli, di animali, cruelty in the home, to children under 14, to animals (C.P.). **-trattare** [A 1] tr. to ill-treat; to ill-use. (**-trattato** part. adj.) **-umore** m. bad humour; bad temper; spleen. **-vagio** adj. wicked. **-vagità** f. wickedness; (leg.) -vagità del colpevole, wicked character of the offender (C.P.). **-vedere** [B 5] tr. to regard with ill-will; to hate. **-veduto** part. adj. disliked, hated. **-versazione** f. (leg.) embezzlement; fraudulent conversion; malversation; misappropriation. **-vestito** adj. badly dressed. **-vissuto** adj. having lived an evil life. **-visto** part. adj. disliked, hated. **-vivente** adj. dissolute, ill-living; n.m. rogue, scamp; criminal. **-vivenza** f. dissoluteness. **-vivo** adj. half-dead. **-volente** part. adj. malevolent; n.m., f. malevolent person. **-volentieri** adv. unwillingly. **-volere** [B 36] tr. to dislike, to hate; era -voluto da tutti, he was universally disliked; n.m. ill-will, wickedness. **-volto** adj. ill-disposed.

mala¹ adj. f. of **malo**, q.v.

mala-² pref. evil; inferior. **-bestia** f. monster, ogre; (naut.) caulking-hammer. **-carnaio** m. offal store. **-carne** f. inferior meat; unwholesome meat; offal; (fig.) undesirable person. **-creanza** f. (pl. **malecreanze**) bad manners; ill-breeding; impoliteness, rudeness. †**-dicere**, †**-dire** vb. and derivs. see **maledire**, under **male**. **-fatta** f. fault, slip; pl. (**malefatte**) evil deeds. **-fede** f. (pl. **malefedi**) bad faith; (leg.) act of bad faith (C.C.). **-fitta** f. quagmire, bog. **-giunta** f. unfortunate occurrence, mishap. **-grazia** f. uncouthness; rudeness; bad grace; ungraciousness; con -grazia, ungraciously. **-guida** f. bad guide. **-lingua** f. (pl. **malelingue**) slanderer, backbiter. †**-paga** f. (hist., Florence) debtors' prison. **-pena** adv. phr. a -pena, scarcely, hardly; with difficulty. †**-tasca** pr.n.m. the Devil. **-tolta** f. extortion. **-vita** f. low life; life of gangsters, prostitutes, etc.; gangsters; rogues, ruffians; il gergo della -vita, gangsters' slang. **-voglia** f. ill-will; reluctance; unwillingness; sloth; di -voglia, unwillingly, reluctantly.

mala·batro m. (bot.) malabathrum, the malabar leaf; (of Cinnamomum Tamala and other species); ointment prepared from it.

Malacca pr.n.f. (geog.) Malacca; penisola di —, Malay Peninsula; Malaya; stretto di —, Malay Straits, the Straits of Malacca.

malac·cio m. pejor. See under **male**.

Malachi·a pr.n.m. (Bibl.) Malachi.

malachite f. (miner.) malachite.

malaci·a f. morbid softening of any part of the body; morbid or fanciful appetite.

malac-ologi·a f. malacology. **-ozoi** m.pl. (zool.) Mollusca.

Ma·laga pr.n.f. (geog.) Malaga; m. Malaga wine; Malaga grape.

malaga·sci·o adj. (geog.) relating to Madagascar; n.m. native or inhabitant of Madagascar. (**-a** f.)

malagma m. poultice.

mal-andra, -andria f. (vet.) malanders, chronic dry eczema behind knee (of horses).

malassare [A 1] tr. to malaxate, to soften by kneading.

malat-o adj. ill; sick; sore: un bambino —, a sick child; un dito —, a sore finger; n.m. sick person, patient. (**-a** f.) **-ic·cio**, **-ino**, **-uc·cio** adj. dim. rather ill; sickly, delicate, ailing.

malatti·a f. illness; disease, malady; ailment, complaint; malattie di raffreddamento, colds and chills; — cardiaca, heart disease; — cronica, chronic ailment; una lunga —, a long illness; (leg.) — di mente, mental infirmity (C.C.); (fig.) evil; trouble; ill; le malattie della società, the evils of society.

mal-augurato adj., **-avveduto** adj., etc. See under **mal-**.

mala-vita f., **-voglia** f. See under **mala**².

malazzato adj. sickly; rather ill; in bad health; ailing.

mal-e I. m. (usu. abbrev. to **mal** before prep. 'di') **1.** EVIL; la scienza del bene e del —, knowledge of good and evil; genio del —, evil genius; i -i della vita, the evils (ills) of life; il — e il bene ci viene da Dio, good and ill (fortune) come to us from God. **2.** PAIN, ache, illness; mal di capo, di testa, headache; mal di cuore, heart disease; mal di denti, toothache; mal di gola, sore throat; mal di ventre, colic; mal caduco, epilepsy; mal francese, syphilis; mal sottile, consumption; mal di petto, chest disease; male al petto, a pain in the chest; è un male pericoloso, it is a dangerous illness; a -i estremi, estremi rimedi, desperate ills need desperate remedies; mal di mare, sea-sickness; — del paese, homesickness; dare il — del paese a, to make homesick; aver —, to be ill, to have pain; dare in —, to fall ill; far — a, to hurt, to cause pain to; andare a —, to fail in health (see also under No. 5); non c'è —, pretty well, not bad; farsi venir —, to (feign a) swoon. **3.** SORROW; la notizia mi fece molto —, the news gave me much sorrow. **4.** HARM; il vino ti fa —, wine does not suit you; voler — a qualcuno, to bear someone a grudge, to hate someone; non c'è niente di —, there's no harm in it. **5.** BAD (state, condition, lit. or fig.); andare a —, to go bad (see also under No. 2); di — in peggio, from bad to worse; mandare a —, to spoil, to dissipate (e.g. a fortune); mandare a — un figliuolo, to have a miscarriage through lack of proper care. **6.** MISUNDERSTANDING, trouble, discord; aversi a —, aversela per —, to take it amiss, to be offended; metter — fra due persone, to make trouble between two people, to set two persons against one another.

II. adv. **1.** BADLY, ill, imperfectly; quel ragazzo scrive molto —, that boy writes very badly; dice — la zeta, he pronounces his z's wrongly; sa — la lezione, he does not know his lesson properly; ha inteso — he has not heard properly, or you did not understand.

mal-e (*cont.*)

2. ILL, unwell, uncomfortable; sentirsi —, to feel ill; trovarsi —, to feel unwell or uneasy; rimanere —, to be vexed, to feel hurt or disappointed; star —, to feel unwell, to be unwell (see also under No. 3); sto — in piedi, I can't stand very well; sto — a quattrini, I am short of money. **3.** UNSUITABLY, unfitting, ill-mannered; star —, to be unsuitable, unbecoming, not to fit; questo cappello vi sta —, this hat doesn't suit you; risponder —, to answer badly, to answer insolently; parlare —, to speak badly, *or* evilly. **4.** BADLY, to one's disadvantage, in bad condition; cavarsela —, to come off badly; finire —, to end badly, to turn out badly, *or* to end in a fight; riuscir —, to turn out badly; per — che vadano le cose, however badly things go; mi sa — che…, I am sorry that…; — gliene incolga!, woe to him! **5.** ILL, with malice, harmfully; parla — di voi, he speaks ill of you. **6.** As OPPOSITE OF 'BENE': manco —!, fortunately!, very good!, I'm glad of it; meno — che sei venuto, it's a good job you've come, I'm very glad you've come. **-ac·cio** *m.* serious evil; dangerous illness; come stai? Non c'è -accio, how are you? Not at all bad, pretty well. **-ebolge** *pr.n.f.pl.* name given by Dante to the eighth circle of Hell (*Inf.* XVIII); (fig.) a hellish place. **-ebranche** *pr.n.f.pl.* the demons of Malebolge, q.v. (*Inf.* XXVI). **-edetta** *f.* bad luck; alla -edetta, desperately; piove alla -edetta, it's raining cats and dogs; correva alla -edetta, he was running like the devil; *adv.* not at all. **-amente** *adv.* horribly, wretchedly; desperately; studia -amente, he works like the devil. **-edetto** *part.* of maledire, q.v., *adj.* cursed; abominable; sia -edetto, cursed be; *excl.* curse!, curse it! **-e·dico** *adj.* slanderous. **-edicamente** *adv.* slanderously. **-edire** [B 10] *tr.* to curse; -edico il giorno che lo conobbi, I curse the day I met him. **-edizione** *f.* curse, malediction. **-efatta** *f.* fault, slip (originally in weaving); error, blunder. **-e·fica** *f.* witch. **-eficiato** *adj.* bewitched, charmed. **-efi·cio**, **-efi·zio** *m.* wicked action, crime, misdeed; witchcraft; qui ci deve essere qualche -eficio, this place must be bewitched. **-eficioso** *adj.* wicked; bewitching; fungo -eficioso, toadstool. **-e·fico** *adj.* harmful; pernicious; sorcerer's curse. **-eme·rito** *adj.* ill-deserving. **-eolente** *adj.* stinking. **-estante** *adj.* poor, indigent, needy. **-uccino** *adv.* not very well. **-uc·cio** *m.* slight ailment; *adv.* rather badly.

male·o¹ *m.* (orn.) maleo, *Megalocephalon* spp.

†male·o² *adj.* sickly, ailing.

male·scio *adj.* sickly, ailing; noce —, a variety of walnut tree of which the nuts ('noci malesce') are difficult to remove from the shells.

Mal-e·sia *pr.n.f.* (geog.) Malaya. **-ese** *adj.* Malay; *n.m.* Malay; the Malay language.

malestr-o *m.* damage, mischief; quando i ragazzi stan cheti, hanno fatto qualche —, when boys are quiet, they've been up to something. **-ino** *m. dim.* mischievous child. **-oso** *adj.* mischief-making; damaging; blundering.

males·truo *m.* wretch; contriver of evil.

male·vol-o *adj.* malevolent; malignant. **-enza** *f.* malevolence.

malga *f.* (geog.) Alpine hut, summer dwelling; Alpine pasture.

malgarbo *m.* See under **mal-**.

mal-i·a *f.* charm, enchantment. **-iardo** *m.* sorcerer, wizard; charmer; *adj.* enchanting; bewitching. **-iarda** *f.* witch, sorceress; fascinating woman. **-ioso** *adj.* casting a spell upon; enchanting; charming.

Malibran *pr.n.f.* Malibran, the famous opera singer; *f. indecl.* a kind of open carriage (named after her).

malign-are [A 5] *intr.* (*aux.* avere) to think or speak malignantly; *tr.* to malign; to put a bad meaning upon. **-ato** *part. adj.* maligned. **-azione** *f.* maligning; slander. **-ità** *f.* malignancy; wickedness. **-o** *adj.* malignant, evil; malicious; mischievous; spirito -o, evil spirit; febbre -a, malignant fever; *n.m.* evil person; il Maligno, the Evil One. **-amente** *adv.* maliciously, spitefully; evilly.

malina¹ *f.* (naut.) high tide.

†malina² *f.* illness.

malin-coni·a *f.* melancholy; *pl.* sad things, melancholy matters. **-co·nico** *adj.* melancholy; gloomy; sad. **-conicamente** *adv.* sadly, in a melancholy manner. **-conioso** *adj.* melancholy.

malincorpo *adv. phr.* a —, unwillingly; against one's will; resentfully.

malincuore *adv. phr.* a —, unwillingly; reluctantly.

maliscalco *m.* one who tends horses; farrier; commander; marshal; one of the chief functionaries of a household or court.

maliscen-te *adj.* not quite recovered from illness, convalescent. (**-za** *f.*)

†malistalla *f.* stable.

mal-i·zia *f.* malice; knowledge of evil; cunning; artfulness; fatto a —, done on purpose; roguishness; mettere uno in —, to put someone on his guard; (leg.) malice; actual malice. **-izina** *f. dim.* mischievousness; la -izina dei bambini, children's mischievous ways. **-izietta** *f. dim.* artful trick. **-iziare** [A 3] *intr.* (*aux.* avere) to think ill; to speak ill.

malizios-o *adj.* malicious, cunning; mischievous, roguish. **-amente** *adv.* maliciously; cunningly; mischievously, roguishly. **-ità** *f.* maliciousness.

mallea·bil-e *adj.* malleable; (fig.) adaptable; ghisa —, malleable cast iron. **-ità** *f.* malleability. **-izzare** [A 1] *tr.* (metall.) to malleablize. **-izzazione** *f.* (metall.) malleablizing.

mallegato *m.* black pudding.

malle·ol-o *m.* (onat.) malleolus, ankle-bone. **-are** *adj.* malleolar.

mallev-adore, **-atore** *m.* guarantor; (leg.) surety (originally one who puts hand up); stare, entrare, essere —, to go bail, to stand surety. (**-adrice**, **-atrice** *f.*) **-adori·a** *f.* (leg.) recognizance(s); prestare cauzione o -adoria, to put up bail or find recognizances (C.P.P.). **†-are** *intr.* to be guarantor; *tr.* to be surety for. **-eri·a** *f.* guarantee; suretyship.

mallo¹ *m.* husk, outer shell, skin.

mallo² *m.* (hist.) public judgement, mallum.

malloppo *m.* parcel; (Roman slang) stolen goods; (aeron.) trail rope.

mal-o *adj.* (often contracted to **mal** in *masc.*; the plural is contracted to **ma'** in the proverb 'adagio a' ma' passi') bad, wicked; -a copia, rough copy; — luogo, brothel; in — modo, badly, rudely; -a lingua, spiteful tongue; -a ventura, ill-luck; prendere qualchecosa in -a parte, to take something in bad part, to be offended; — mondo, Hell; di -a voglia, unwillingly; essere — in gambe, to be weak; morire di -a morte, to die miserably, to die by violence; il — punto, the wrong moment; in — punto, inopportunely. **-amente** *adv.* badly; awkwardly; scarcely; è morto -amente, he died a miserable death, he met a violent end.

malsussistente *adj.* See under **mal-**.

malt-a¹ *f.* mortar; maltha; mud, mire; (bldg.) mortar; riempimento con —, grouting; — fresca, green mortar; — liquida, grout. **-are** [A 1] *intr.* (*aux.* avere) to mix mortar.

Malt-a² *pr.n.f.* (geog.) Malta; Croce di —, Maltese cross; (eng.) cross wheel, star wheel; (cinem.) trascinamento a —, Geneva movement, star and cam movement. **-ese** *adj.* Maltese; (med.) febbre -ese, Malta fever; *n.m.* Maltese man or boy; a kind of white poodle; Maltese, the Maltese language; *f.* Maltese woman.

Malta³ *pr.n.f.* a papal prison on Lake Bolsena (Dante, *Par.* IX, 54).

malt-e, **-ea** *m.* (ichth.) bat fish, *Malthe vespertilio*.

malt-o *m.* malt. **-eri·a** *f.* malthouse.

malto·sio *m.* (chem.) maltose.

maltuşian-o *adj.* Malthusian. **-eşimo** *m.* Malthusianism.

Maluine *pr.n.f.pl.* (geog.) Archipelago —, Falkland Islands.

malv-a *f.* (bot.) mallow, *Malva*; — arborea, tree mallow, *Lavatera arborea*; — canapina, *Lavatera cannabina*; color fiore di —, mauve; (derog.) person of narrow, backward ideas.

malva·gia *f.* See **malvasia**.

malvaşi·a *f.* Malmsey (wine).

malvavi·schio *m.* (bot.) *Althaea cannabina*, marsh mallow.

mal-vedere, **-versare**, etc. See under **mal-**.

malvizzo *m.* (orn.) redwing, *Turdus musicus*.

malv-one *m.* (bot.) hollyhock, *Althaea rosea*; tree mallow, *Lavatera arborea*.

mamestra *f.* (ent.) cabbage moth, *Mamestra brassicae*.

mamm-a *f.* mother; mamma; — mia!, goodness gracious!; figliuolo che è tutto —, mother's boy, child that sticks close to its mother's petticoats; esser sempre attaccato alla gonnella della —, to be tied to one's mother's apron strings; casa mia — mia, my home is my all; nudo come lo fece la —, as naked as the day he was born; female breast; dregs (of wine). **-ac·cia** *f. pejor.* unnatural mother, cruel mother. **-ina** *f. dim.* dear mother; mummy; mammy. **-uc·cia** *f. dim.* (affectionate) mummy, mother; fare alle -ucce, (of children) to play at being mothers.

mammale *m.* See **mammifero**.

mammalucc-o *m.* bully, mameluke; simpleton; foolish man. **-a** *f.* stupid woman.

mammami·a *m. indecl.* timid person; inexperienced person; hypocrite; fare il —, to pretend to be ingenuous or inexperienced.

†**mammana** *f.* midwife; governess.

mamma·rio *adj.* (anat.) mammary; ghiandole mammarie, mammary glands.

mammatocu·mulo *m.* (meteor.) mammatocumulus.

mammell-a *f.* breast; udder; teat. **-are** *adj.* mammillary.

mammellone *m.* (geog.) hummock, rounded peak.

mammi·fero *adj.* (zool.) mammalian; *n.m.* (zool.) mammals.

mammillare *adj.* (anat.) mamillary.

mam·mol-a *f.* (bot.) violet; (fig.) child; (iron.) a modest person. **-o** *m.*, **-etta** *f. dim.*, **-ino** *m. dim.* little child.

mammon-a *m., f.,* **-e**[1] *m.* Mammon; riches. **-ismo** *m.* cult of Mammon.

mammone[2] *m.* monkey; gatto —, mythical animal resembling a monkey.

mammoso *adj.* mammiform; big-breasted.

mammù *m. indecl.* See **mammut**.

mammu·t, mammou·th *m. indecl.* (zool.) mammoth.

mamozzo *m.*, **mamo·zio** *m.* rough sketch or cast of a human figure; doll.

†**mamzero** *m.* mamzer, son of a harlot.

mana·ide *f.* (naut.) Mediterranean sardine boat with six to eight oars.

manai(u)ola *f.* a small chopper.

manale *m.* half-glove or palm made of leather worn by shoemakers or saddlers to protect the hands when pulling cord.

manarese *m.* (agric.) double-edged.

manata *f.* handful; a manate, in handfuls, by the handful; blow with the hand, cuff; slap; tap, pat.

manato *m.* (zool.) manatee.

manca *f.* left, left-hand side; a dritta e a —, on all sides, right and left.

manc-are [A 2] *intr.* (*aux.* avere, essere) to be lacking; mi -ano due denti, I have two teeth missing; ciò che gli -a è il coraggio, what he lacks is courage; -a una pagina di questo libro, a page of this book is missing; to fail, to give way; le -arono le ginocchia, her knees gave way; venuta a — quella famiglia ne prese il casato quell'altra, that family having died out, its name was taken by this one; badi alla scadenza, non manchi di pagare, mind you don't fail to pay at the due date; confesso che qui ho -ato, I admit I was wrong here; — (ai vivi), to pass over, to die; sentirsi —, to turn faint; se venisse a —, if he were to die; -a un quarto alle sette, it's a quarter to seven; non mancherò di farlo, I shall not fail to do it; poco -ò che non cadessi, I very nearly fell; -ò poco non ballasse dalla gioia, she almost danced for joy; gli -ò il terreno sotto i piedi, the ground gave way under his feet; — di parola, to break one's word; — a un voto, to fail to keep a vow; dopo che era -ato da casa due giorni, when he had been away from home two days; quanti alunni -ano?, how many pupils are absent?; vien -ando di giorno in giorno, he gets weaker every day; non -ava che questo!, this is the last straw!; ci mancherebbe altro!, what next!; ci mancherebbe altro se, …it would be a nice state of affairs if…; (naut., of wind) to fail; — d'acqua, to have insufficient water to float; *tr.* (naut.) — la virata, to miss stays. **-amento** *m.* defect; want, lack; deficiency; failing, failure; absence; omission; fainting-fit. **-ante** *adj.* lacking; wanting; missing; -ante di, in need of; -ante di coraggio, lacking courage; -ante di peso, deficient in weight; -ante di una mano, one-handed; (herald.) disjointed. **-anza** *f.* want, lack; absence; sentirò la sua -anza, I shall miss you; breach; defect; default; in -anza di meglio, for want of better, *faute de mieux*; supplire la -anza di, to make good the lack of; (leg.) -anza di giurisdizione, want of jurisdiction (C.C.P.); -anza di parola, breaking of word; -anza del protesto, failure to protest; -anza di promessa, breach of promise; -anza di prove, lack of evidence; in -anza di prova contraria, in the absence of evidence to the contrary; (comm.) -anza di fiducia, lack of confidence; per -anza d'accettazione, for non-acceptance; in -anza di, in default of. **-ato** *part. adj.* unsuccessful; omicidio -ato, attempted murder; (leg.) -ata accettazione, non-acceptance; -ata consegna, non-delivery, non-performance; -ato pagamento, non-payment (C.C.). **-atore** *m.* one who fails; -atore di parole, -atore di fede, -atore di promessa, one who breaks his promise, one who does not keep faith.

mancego *adj.* of Mancha; l'idalgo —, Il cavalier —, Don Quixote.

†**manceppare** *tr.* **1.** To ENSLAVE, to mancipate, to turn into a chattel; to subject. **2.** To EMANCIPATE.

mancese *adj., n.m.* Manchurian.

mancesteriano *m.* (econ.) one of the Manchester school, free-trader.

manchevol-e *adj.* lacking; wanting; defective, deficient; faulty. (**-mente** *adv.*) **-ezza** *f.* defect, deficiency, imperfection.

man·cia *f.* tip, gratuity, gift; — competente, suitable reward (for return of lost property, etc.); una lauta —, a lavish tip; dare una — a, to tip; dare cento lire di —, to give 100 lire as a tip.

manciata *f.* handful; a good handful.

mancina *f.* left; left hand; (naut.) heavy crane, sheers; — galleggiante, floating crane; (comm.) diritto di —, cranage.

mancinello *m.* (bot.) manchineal, *Hippomane mancinella*.

mancino *adj.* left (hand); left-handed; — manritto, ambidextrous; treacherous, underhand; un colpo —, a dirty trick; *n.m.* left-handed man.

mancione *m.* (motor.) patch on inside of outer cover of tyre.

†**man-cipare** *vb.* see **manceppare**. **-ci·pio** *m.* (poet.) slave.

Manciù *pr.n.m.* (geog.) Manchu; *adj. indecl.* Manchu.

Manciu·ria *pr.n.f.* (geog.) Manchuria.

manco *m.* want, lack; defect, fault; verrò senza —, I'll come without fail; *adj.* defective, weak; left; a mano manca, to the left; a botta dritta e a manca, to right and left; *adv.* less; not even; nè —, not even; — male, all the better; al —, at least; — per sogno, by no means.

mancorrente *m.* handrail.

mandament-o *m.* command; commission; area of jurisdiction of local authority; borough; district. **-ale** *adj.* of the borough, of the district; consiglio -ale, district council.

mandante *m.* (leg.) principal; (Scot.) mandator; il potere di agire in nome del —, power to act in name of principal (C.C.); *pl.* constituents.

mand-are [A I] *tr.* to send; to forward; to put into circulation; to drive (a machine); — in prigione, to send to prison; la -ò a vedere chi fosse, he sent her to see who was there; — a dire a qualcuno, to send word to someone; — a chiamare uno, to send for someone; — via, send away, to dismiss; piove come Dio la -a, it is raining cats and dogs; — in lungo, — per le lunghe, to delay; — giù, to swallow; — ad effetto, to carry out, to put into practice; — in pezzi, to smash; — a male, — a monte, to spoil, to ruin; Dio te la -i buona, may God cause it to turn out well for you, may God favour you; — da Erode a Pilato, to send from pillar to post; — a spasso, to dismiss; Dio -a il freddo secondo i panni, God tempers the wind to the shorn lamb; — dietro le spalle, to disregard, to neglect; (leg.) to discharge; to release; (naut.) — a fondo, — a picco, to sink. (**-atore** *m.* **-atrice** *f.*)

mandarin-ato *m.* mandarinate. **-esco** *adj.* (*m.pl.* **-eschi**) pertaining to a mandarin. **-o** *m.* mandarin; mandarine (orange).

mandata *f.* quantity sent; batch, lot; series; turn of the key; chiudere con due mandate, chiudere a doppia —, to double lock the door; (eng.) delivery (of a pump); altezza di —, delivery head; (of a fan or heater) throw.

mandata·rio *m.* (leg.) agent (of 'mandante', q.v.); (Scot.) mandatory (C.C.); (comm.) — commerciale, mercantile agent; — generale, general agent; nominare un —, to appoint an agent.

mandato *m.* order, command; mandate; warrant; — di pagamento, order for payment, money order; — di riscossione, order for collection; terms of reference; eccesso di —, *ultra vires*; term of office; prorogare il —, to extend the term of office; rinnovare il —, to renew the term of office; (leg.) — civile, contract by one person to act for another (concerning affairs of principal, which does not affect third-parties as does 'procura', q.v.); warrant; — con, senza, rappresentanza, contract of agency with disclosed, with undisclosed, principal (C.C.); — generale, speciale, general, special power; General, Special Power of Attorney (more properly rendered by 'procura'); — a donare, power of appointment (C.C.); — di credito, warrant to grant credit (C.C.); — alle liti, warrant of attorney; litigant's formal instructions to solicitor or counsel (C.C.P.); — di accompagnamento, warrant to escort accused before magistrate; — di arresto, provisional warrant of arrest; — di cattura, warrant of arrest; — di comparizione, summons (in criminal proceedings); — di perquisizione, search-warrant (C.P.P.).

mandi·bol-a *f.* (zool.) mandible; jaw. **-ato** *adj.* mandibulate.

mando·la *f.* (mus.) mandore, a kind of small lute.

mandolino *m.* (mus.) mandoline.

†**mandora** *f.* (mus.). See **mandola**.

man·dorl-a *f.* almond; kernel of any stone fruit; fatto a —, almond-shaped; Porta della —, one of the entrances to the Cathedral at Florence, so named from its shape; pasta di -e, almond-paste; fiore a —, clock (on a stocking); *pl.* (herald.) bottoms, spindles. -**ato** *m.* almond-cake; nougat; lattice-work; *adj.* almond-shaped. -**o** *m.* (bot.) almond tree, *Prunus amygdalus*.

mandra *f.* herd; flock; cattle-shed; (fig.) herd; (leg.) l'usufrutto stabilito sopra una — o un gregge, usufruct of herd or flock (C.C.).

†**mandrac·chia** *f.* prostitute.

mandrac·chio *m.* inner harbour of a port.

man-dra·gola, -dra·gora *f.* mandrake; mandragora; †mostrar —, to deceive.

man·dria *f.* See **mandra**.

mandriale[1] *m.* shepherd, herdsman; iron hook used in letting molten iron out of a furnace.

†**mandriale**[2] (mus.). See **madrigale**.

mandrian-o *m.* herdsman, shepherd. -**a** *f.* shepherdess, herdswoman.

mandrillo *m.* (zool.) mandrill; debauched man.

mandrin-o *m.* (eng.) mandrel, chuck, arbor. -**are** [A I] *tr.* (eng.) to expand (a tube). -**atura** *f.* (eng.) expanding (tubes).

mandritta *f.* right hand; voltare a —, to turn to the right.

manduc-are [A 2] *tr.* (joc.) to eat. -**a·bile** *adj.* (joc.) eatable. -**ato·rio** *adj.* manducatory. -**azio·ne** *f.* manducation.

mane *f.* (poet.) morning; da — a sera, from morn till night.

†**manecare** *tr.* to eat.

manęcchia *f.* plough-handle.

maneggęvol-e *adj.* manageable, easily handled, handy; (eng.) suitable for a handlathe; manœuvrable; vento —, good working wind; semicerchio —, less dangerous semicircle of a revolving storm. -**ęzza** *f.* (eng.; motor.) manœuvrability, controllability.

manęggia *f.* (agric.) strip of ground two furrows in width in a ploughed field.

maneggia·bile *adj.* See **maneggevole**.

maneggi-are [A 3 c] *tr.* to handle; to finger; to manage; to use; — un trattato, to negotiate a treaty; sa — la penna, he knows how to handle the pen (i.e. he writes well, often in the sense of writing with polemical fervour); *rfl.* to manage, to manage skilfully; to behave with cunning; (techn.) to knead, to pug. -** amęnto** *m.* handling, management. -**atore** *m.* manager. (-**atrice** *f.*)

manęggio *m.* handling; management; cunning; plot; — d'armi, drill; riding-school; riding-ground; horsemanship, *manège*.

maneggiọne *m.* meddler, intriguer; wine-shop manager.

manell-a *f.*, -**o** *m.* See **mannella**.

†**manente** *adj.* stable, enduring; rich, wealthy; *n.m.* tenant farmer.

manescalco *m.* See **maniscalco**.

manęs-co *adj.* (*pl.* -**chi**) ready with one's hands, ready to strike a blow; truculent; aggressive; linguacciuto e —, quick with one's tongue and hands; †ready to hand; manageable. -**camęnte** *adv.* with one's hands.

manętta *f.* handcuff; grip, gripping-place, handle; assicurare con manette, to handcuff; (eng.) hand lever; (motor.) — del gas, throttle lever; dare —, to open the throttle.

manęvole *adj.* supple; yielding, pliant; soft to the touch.

manfanile *m.* (Tusc.). See **manfano**.

man·fano *m.* handle of flail; (fig.) rogue.

manforte *f. indecl.* help, assistance.

manfrina *f.* a rustic dance; the music for it.

manga *f.* (bot.) mango (fruit).

mangan-are [A I] *tr.* to mangle; to throw from a mangonel. -**are** *m.* mangler. -**ato** *part. adj.* (text.) mangled, calendered. -**atura** *f.* mangling.

manganato[1] *part.* of **manganare**, q.v.

manganato[2] *m.* (chem.) manganate.

manganella *f.* mangonel; lever, prop; tirar di manganelle, to beat; flap (to be raised or let down, esp. of misericord seats in a choir).

manganello *m.* small calendar; lever; cudgel, club.

mang-anęse *m.* (chem.) manganese. -**a·nico** *adj.* (chem.) manganic. -**anite** *f.* (min.) manganite, grey manganese ore. -**anọso** *adj.* (chem.) manganous.

man·gano *m.* mangle; dare il — a, to mangle; (fig.) oppression; big-boned person.

†**mange·a** *f.* banquet.

mangeręccio *adj.* edible; nice to eat, tasty.

mangeri·a *f.* illegitimate gains; swindle.

man·gia *f.* eating; season for eating; right way of eating; la — del popone è nell'agosto, the season for eating melons is in August; *n.m.* the name (abbrev. of Mangiaguadagni) given to a large bronze figure which used to strike the hours on the clock of the Palazzo Municipale at Siena; also the clock itself; (fig., Tusc.) ogre.

mangi-are [A 3] *tr.* to eat; to eat up, to devour; — troppo, to over-eat; in questo ristorante si -a male, the food is poor in this restaurant; ci si -a bene, the food is good there; to corrode; la ruggine -a il ferro, rust eats away iron; (fig.) to understand; di greco ne -a poco, he understands only a little Greek; to cheat; mi -ò cento lire, non me ne -a più, he cheated me of a hundred lire, he won't cheat me again; (at cards) il tre -a il due, the three beats the two; (at chess, draughts) to take a piece; -o di torre, I take with the rook; chi non -a ha del -ato, if a person does not eat, it is because he has food inside him; chi più -a, meno -a, he who eats most will eat least (i.e. because his life will be shortened); — del suo, to be independent; to elide (a vowel); i meridionali si -ano la finale, Southern Italians clip the final vowel; far da —, to cook, to prepare a meal; aspirare non è —, breathing is not eating (said of one who does not pronounce well); — vivo uno, to jump down a person's throat; — bestie e cristiani, to pronounce furious threats; — la sporta a Brandano, to have a great appetite; — la peppa (minestra, torta) in capo a uno, to be much taller than someone; — la zuppa co' ciechi, to have to do with very simple-minded people; to take bribes; -a tu che -o io, -amo tutti col nome di Dio (provb. jingle describing dishonest administrators and agents); — il porro dalla coda, to deal with the least important thing first; non gli manca che — il fuoco, he's done everything except eat fire, i.e. he's exhausted every other kind of folly; pare d'aver -ato una minestra di fusi, he seems to have swallowed the poker (i.e. he carries himself stiffly); — il grano in erba, to count one's chickens before they are hatched; — con due guance, to rob two parties at once, to take bribes from both sides; — a due palmenti, to chew greedily; — il pane a tradimento, to eat unearned bread; — il patrimonio, to squander one's inheritance; -a da sano e bevi da malato, eat plenty and drink sparingly; — la strada, to devour the road (i.e. to go fast); — pane e veleno, to lead a very uncomfortable life; — del pan pentito, del pan disperato, to be repentant, to be in despair; -arsi il cuore, to eat one's heart out; -arsi l'erba e la paglia sotto, to consume rashly what one has; -arsi le lastre, to take to the road, to be a highway robber; -arsi le unghie, to bite one's nails; -arsi il fegato, to chafe and fume; *n.m.* eating; food, victuals. -**abambini** *m. indecl.* imaginary monster, bogey-man; a man who looks an ogre, but is really good-natured. -**a·bile** *adj.* edible, eatable. -**abotte** *m.* (zool.) grass snake, *Tropidonotus natrix*. -**acaparre** *m. indecl.* one who receives earnest money but does not set to work; cheat, swindler. -**acarte** *m. indecl.* pettifogging lawyer. -**aca·voli** *m. indecl.* Crambophagus, 'Cabbage-eater', name of a frog in the Greek *Battle of Frogs and Mice*. -**achiac·chiera** *m. indecl.* great talker. -**acristiani** *m. indecl.* man who threatens and blusters. -**afagiuoli** *m. indecl.* bean-eater (nickname for Florentines). -**afango** *m. indecl.* mud-eater; the N.E. wind. -**aformiche** *m. indecl.* (zool.) anteater. -**aguadagni** *m. indecl.* casual labourer. -**amęnto** *m.* eating, great eating; swindling, cheating. -**amoc·coli** *m. indecl.* pious humbug. -**apagnotte** *m. indecl.* lazy official. -**apane** *m. indecl.* idler. -**apattọna** *m. indecl.* worthless fellow. -**apelli** *m. indecl.* (ent.) biting lice, Mallophaga. -**apellice** *m. indecl.* (ent.) see **mangiapelli**. -**apęre** *m. indecl.* green grasshopper. -**apolenta** *m. indecl.* good-for-nothing. -**apo·poli** *m. indecl.* hater of the people; oppressor, bloodsucker. -**apreti** *m. indecl.* priest-hater, anti-clerical. -**arino** *m.* light meal; dainty dish. -**arospi** *m. indecl.* (zool.) see **mangiabotte**. -**ata** *f.* meal; una buona -ata, a hearty meal. -**ativo** *adj.* for eating; edible. -**atọia** *f.* crib; trough; dining-table; (fig.) place providing food. -**atọio** *m.* (naut.) spurnwater; dwarf bulkhead; space enclosed by a cableroom breakwater. -**atọre** *m.* eater; great eater, hearty eater. (-**atrice** *f.*) -**ato·ria** *f.* eating; (fig.) swindling. -**atura** *f.* eating; bite, sting. -**atutti** *m. indecl.* overbearing individual. -**atutto** *m.* spendthrift. -**aufo** *m.* parasite, sponger. -**avento** *m. indecl.* (naut.) running jib.

mangime *m.* food for animals or birds; fodder; (agric.) — fresco, green fodder.

mangione *m.* great eater, glutton.

mangiucchi-are [A4] *tr.* to eat slowly, to eat without appetite; to nibble; non ha appetito a tavola perchè -a tutto il santo giorno, he has no appetite for his meals because he's nibbling something or other all day long. **-ato** *part. adj.* nibbled.

mangusta *f.* (zool.) mongoose.

mani[1] *m.pl.* Manes, shades of the departed.

mani[2] *f.pl.* of **mano**, q.v.

man-i·a *f.* mania; madness; (fig.) craze; ha la — dei cavalli, he's mad about horses; fad; hobby. **-i·aco** *m.* maniac; *adj.* maniacal; (fig.) eccentric, odd.

ma·ni·ca[1] *f.* sleeve; senza -che, sleeveless; essere in -che di camicia, to be in one's shirt-sleeves; tirarsi su le -che, to roll up one's sleeves; esser di — larga, to be easy-going, tolerant, indulgent; esser di — stretta, to be strict; quello è un altro paio di -che, that's another kettle of fish; aver roba in —, to have something up one's sleeve; quel che non va nelle -che va ne' gheroni, what you lose on the swings you gain on the roundabouts; — d'Ippocrate, piece of filter-paper twisted up into a funnel; chemical furnace; wing (of a house); armlet; handle; hilt; troop of soldiers; una — di birbanti, a gang of scoundrels; — di caricamento, inflation valve; hose-pipe; — d'aspirazione, suction hose; (meteor.; aeron.) — a vento, wind sleeve, wind-sock; (aeron.) — rimorchiata, sleeve target; (naut.) tube, sheath, scotsman serving on a hawser; wind-direction indicator; anti-aircraft practice drogue; — degli oblò, scuttle cowl; — degli ombrinali, scupper lip; — del timone, water excluder fitted to a rudder; rinfrescare la —, to freshen the nip.

ma·nica[2] *f.* (geog.) inlet; the English Channel; la — di Tartaria, the Gulf of Tartary.

manica·io *m.* (zool.) razor shell; — fodero, *Solen vagina*; — baccello, *Solen siliqua*.

manic-are [A2s] *tr.* to eat; *recip. rfl.* -arsi l'un l'altro col sale, to hate each other. **-ato** *art. adj.* eaten. **-aretto** *m.* tit-bit; dainty dish.

manicato[1] *part.* of **manicare**, q.v.

manicato[2] *adj.* with a handle, having a handle.

manicce *f.pl.* (naut. hist.) grips on the oars of a galley.

mani·cchia *f.* shaft (of a fowling net).

manich-eismo *m.* Manichaeism. **-eo** *m.* Manichee; *adj.* Manichaean.

manichetta *f. dim.* of **manica**, q.v.; covering for the forearm used by writers; ruffle; cuff; hosepipe; — antincendi, fire hose; — di tela, canvas hose.

manichetto *m. dim.* of **manico**, q.v.; small handle; cuff; gesture of contempt made with one hand on the other arm; alzarsi i manichetti, to roll up one's sleeves, (fig.) to do one's utmost, to set to work in earnest.

manichino *m.* manikin; mannequin; cuff; handcuff; ruffle; gesture of contempt; scrivere in —, to write with affectation.

ma·nico *m.* (*pl.* **ma·nichi**, **ma·nici**) handle; — di scopa, broomstick; benedire col — della scopa, to beat; aveva promesso aiuto ma ha girato nel —, he had promised help but failed to keep his word; trovar il — a uno, to find a handle against someone; uscir del —, to break loose, to become violent, to fly off the handle; ciurlare nel —, to waver; ce n'è per la mestola e per il —, there's plenty of it; handle, helve; (mus.) neck (of any stringed instrument); (slang) skilled driver.

manico·mio *m.* lunatic asylum; (leg.) mental hospital (C.C.); — giudiziario, criminal lunatic asylum (C.P.).

manicone[1] *m. augm.* of **manica**, q.v.

manicone[2] *m. augm.* of **manico**, q.v.

mani-cordo *m.*, **-cor·dio** *m.* (mus.) manichord, clavichord.

manic-otto *m.* muff; (provb.) a Ognissanti -otti e guanti, when All Saints' Day comes put on winter clothing; (eng.) clutch; socket; pipe lining; — d'accoppiamento, coupling-box; (naut.) -otti degli occhi d'ormeggio, hawse-pipes. **-ottino** *m.* child's muff; — ottino di raggio, spoke nipple (of a bicycle). **-ot·tolo** *m.* long loose sleeve.

manicure *f.* (pron. as Fr.) manicurist.

manier-a *f.* manner, way, style; alla solita —, in the usual way; la — di Giotto, Giotto's style; non mi piace la sua — di parlare, I don't like his way of speaking; in ogni —, in qualunque —, anyhow; in nessuna —, not at all; di — che, so that; in — che, in such a way as; modo e —, ways and means; buone -e, good manners; brutte -e, bad manners; scrittore di —, affected writer,

mannered writer; avere la — di, to have a weakness for. **-ato** *adj.* affected, unnatural, mannered; pittore -ato, mannerist. **-atamente** *adv.* affectedly; in a mannered way. **-ina** *f. dim.* pleasing manner; *pl.* mincing ways. **-ismo** *m.* mannerism. **-ista** *m., f.* mannerist. **-ona** *f. pejor.* clumsy manner. **-oso** *adj.* well-mannered; polite. (**-osamente** *adv.*) **-uc·cia** *f. pejor.* silly manner, stupidly or exaggeratedly affected manner; gushing manner.

maniere[1] *adj.* convenient; well-mannered; well-trained; affable; valiant, bold.

manier-e[2], **-o** *m.* manor house.

manifat-tore *m.* workman; manufacturer; *adj.* manufacturing. (**-trice** *f.*)

manifattur-a *f.* manufacture; — inglese, English make; manufactory, works; cost of manufacture. **-iere**, **-iero** *adj.* manufacturing, industrial.

manifest-are [A1] *tr.* to manifest; to show; to declare; to reveal; to exhibit; *rfl.* to show oneself; to reveal oneself; to show what one can do; to appear. **-amento** *m.* manifesting. **-ato** *part. adj.* manifested; shown; declared, revealed. **-atore** *m.* person taking part in manifestation, manifestor. (**-atrice** *f.*) **-azione** *f.* manifestation; event; (leg.) -azioni sediziose, seditious demonstrations (C.P.).

manifest-o *m.* public announcement, poster; manifesto; — elettorale, electoral manifesto; (comm.) manifest; — di bordo, — di carico, manifest, freight list; (naut.) harbour regulation. **-ino** *m.* leaflet.

mani·gli-a *f.* handle; — della porta, door-handle; shackle; bracelet; *pl.* handcuffs; strap (in a bus, tram, etc.). **-are** [A4] *tr.* to shackle; to handcuff. **-ato** *part. adj.* shackled; handcuffed. **-one** *m.* (naut.) anchor shackle.

manigold-o *m.* rascal, ruffian; scoundrel; †executioner. **-a** *f.* hussy.

†**manila** *f.* cord.

†**manile** *m.* bracelet.

Manilla *pr.n.f.* (geog.) Manilla; (techn.) manilla hemp.

maniluvio *m.* (med.) medicated bath for the hands.

†**manimessa** *f.* beginning; broaching of a cask of wine.

manimettere [C20] *tr.* to begin using; to broach; — una botte di vino, to broach a cask of wine; — un foglio di mille lire, to break into a thousand lire note.

†**manimorcia** *adj. f.* slovenly, sluttish.

manimorte *f.pl.* (leg.). See **manomorta**.

manina *f. dim.* of **mano**, q.v.; little hand; (typ.) fist, sketch of hand as a pointer; (bot.) name of several fungi; manine della Madonna, honeysuckle flowers; — di Gesù, wild carnation.

†**manincо·nia** *f.* See **malinconia**.

manino *m. dim.* of **mano**, q.v.; child's hand; baciar —, kiss hands as a mark of reverence.

manioca *f.* (bot.) manioc.

manipolare[1] *m.* soldier; *adj.* pertaining to a maniple or band of soldiers.

manipol-are[2] [A1s] *tr.* to manipulate, to work; to handle; to treat, to deal with; (instruction on merchandise) — con cura, handle with care; to adulterate; to falsify. (**-ato** *part. adj.*) **-atore** *m.* manipulator; plotter; (teleg.) sending key, morse key. **-azione** *f.* manipulation; handling; adulteration; falsification; (teleg.) keying.

mani·polo *m.* handful, bundle; un — di spighe, a sheaf of corn; (liturg.) maniple (vestment); (Rom. hist.) maniple (subdivision of legion); handle; baciar il —, to kiss the rod; (text.) strick; — di lino, strick of flax; (herald.) maniple.

maniscal-co *m.* (*pl.* **-chi**) farrier; smith.

manizza[1] *f.* See **manubrio**.

†**manizza**[2] *f.* muff.

manlev-a *f.* (leg.) liability of surety. **-are** [A1] *tr.* to stand surety for.

manna[1] *f.* manna; blessing; è stata una —, it's been a godsend; — celeste, the Eucharist; the inspissated juice of the flowering ash or other tree used as a purgative; delicacy.

manna[2] *f.* sheaf, bundle.

mannag·gia *excl.* damn!; devil take it!

Mannaggia la Rocca *pr.n.f.* (theatr.) a mask, of Romagna.

manna·i-a *f.* axe, chopper; heavy knife; la — del boia, the executioner's axe; la — della ghigliottina, the blade of the guillotine; (fig.) tyranny, despotism; essere sotto la —, to be in mortal danger. **-ola** *f.* axe; bill-hook. **-uolo** *m. dim.* hatchet.

mannaro *adj.* bogey; lupo —, werewolf; (pop.) epileptic.

mannell·a *f.*, **-o** *m.* sheaf, bundle; — di spago, skein of pack-thread wound upon the fingers.

mannerino *m.* fat wether; castrated singer; lackey; spy; judge.

mannite *f.* (chem.) mannite; mannite-sugar.

manno *m.* sheaf, bundle.

mannocchi·o *m.*, **-a** *f.* faggot, fascine.

manno·sio *m.* (chem.) mannose, seminose.

man·o *f.* (*pl.* **-i**; abbrev. to **man** in some phrases) **1.** HAND; stringere la — a, to shake hands with; una stretta di —, a handshake; tenere uno per (la) —, to hold someone by the hand; a -i giunte, with hands clasped (e.g. in prayer or entreaty); -i in fede, design of two clasped hands; s'intrecciarono le -i, they clasped each other's hands; tenere le -i a sè, to keep one's hands to oneself; le -i a voi!, hands off!; battere le -i, to clap, to applaud; menare le -i, to fight; venire alle -i, to come to blows; a — avanti, hand over hand; stare con le -i in —, stare con le -i alla cintola, to twiddle one's thumbs; fatto a —, hand-made; manifestino distribuito a —, hand-bill; valigetta a —, suitcase, weekend case; giuoco di —, sleight of hand, trick, artifice; (fig.) allargare, aprire la —, to be generous; a larga —, lavishly, abundantly; una persona alla —, an affable person; avere le -i bucate, to spend money like water; cavare di — a, to get from, to receive from, to provoke from; la sua insolenza caverebbe di — un ceffone anche a un santo, his insolence would try the patience of a saint; parlare col cuore in —, to speak with the utmost sincerity; portare uno in palma di —, to be much attached to, to think highly of, someone; portare una cosa in palma di —, to boast of a thing, to tell everyone about a thing; avere alle -i, alla —, tra —, fra le -i, un lavoro, to have a piece of work on hand; mettere — a, to put one's hand to, to have a hand in, to begin work on; mettere — a, mettere di —, una botte, to broach a cask; fare la — (a), to get one's hand in (on), to acquire skill (in); perdere la — (a), to lose one's skill (in), to get out of practice; mettere le -i innanzi per non cadere, to make excuses beforehand; metterei la — sul fuoco, I'd stake my life on it; lavorare di —, work by hand, (iron.) to steal; tornare a -i vuote, to come away empty-handed; avere le -i di lolla, avere le -i di burro, to be butter-fingered; con le -i e coi piedi, with every means at one's disposal; me l'ha fatto toccare con —, he gave me tangible, incontrovertible, proof of it; prendere con due -i, to seize eagerly; lavarsi le -i di, to wash one's hands of; (on letters) sue -i, sue proprie -i (abbrev. S.M., S.P.M.), personal, personal for addressee. **2.** POWER; possession; influence, control; agency; custody; l'isola cadde in — agli, nelle -i degl'Inglesi, the island fell into English hands; riconosco la tua — in questo, I can see you have had a hand in this; è nelle -i di Dio, it is in God's hands; è stato la — di Dio, it was providential; essere in -i buone, to be in good hands; essere in — sicura, to be in safe hands; vincere la —, to be victorious, to come top; vincere, guadagnare, la — a, to get out of the control of, to gain the upper hand of; avere le -i lunghe, to be very influential, to have a finger in every pie (*or* to be light-fingered, to steal); fare — bassa a, to plunder, to lay waste; avere buono in —, to be sure of one's position; a — regia, in the name of, by the authority of, the government; governare con — ferrea, to rule with a rod of iron. **3.** HELP, assistance, a helping hand; dateci una —!, give us a hand!; prestare — a, to lend a hand to; tenere (di) — a uno, to be in league with; — d'opera, labour, workmen, hands; costa molto la — d'opera, labour is very expensive; (leg.) scambio di — d'opera, interchange of man-power. **4.** HANDFUL; small quantity; una — d'uova, six eggs (i.e. as many as can be held in two hands); (paperm.) quire; una — di prodi, a handful of brave men; prendere tutta la —, to take more than is offered, to grab the lot; a dargli un dito prende tutta la —, give him an inch and he'll take an ell; buona —, tip, gratuity. **5.** HANDWRITING; scrive una bella —, he writes a good hand, he has a good handwriting; una lettera di sua —, a letter in his handwriting; †— di scritto, hand o' write; touch, style; avere la — pesante, to be heavy-handed; avere la — leggiera, to have a light touch; lavoro di — maestra, work by a skilled hand; (cards) deal; hand; (the) lead; sei di —, hai la — tu, it's your lead; ora la — tocca a lui, now it's his lead. **6.** RANGE, reach; a —, sotto —, at hand, handy; a portata di —, within reach; a un trar di —, within a stone's throw; fuori di —, out of the way; una stazioncella fuori di —, a little wayside station; di lunga —, by a long chalk, *or* for a long time. **7.** SIDE, direction; source; a man destra, to the right, on the right; di prima —, (at) first hand; di seconda —, (at) second hand; da ogni —, on all sides; da una —, on one side; contro —, against the stream, in the opposite direction, going the other way. **8.** COAT, covering; due -i di vernice, two coats of varnish; dare una — di bianco a, to whitewash; — del fondo, undercoat; seconda —, second coat; ultima —, top coat, (fig.) finishing touch (e.g. to a work of art). **9.** ADVERBIAL PHRASES: man —, a — a —, gradually; man — che, as soon as, just as; man — che la luna spuntava, as the moon gradually rose above the horizon; scrissi le cifre a — a — che mi vennero dettate, I wrote down the numbers as they were dictated; di — in — che si vedevano, as they appeared in turn, one after the other. **10.** (LEG.) — morta, see manomorta; a — salva, without hindrance, with impunity. **11.** (ZOOL.) — di morto, dead men's fingers, *Alcyonium palmatum.* **12.** (HERALD.) — d'aquila, eagle's claw winged.

manobalista *m.* crossbow.

manodo·pera *f.* the work of manufacturing an article; manual labour; cost of labour; hands employed in (manual) labour.

†**manoletto** *m.* valet.

†**manomessa** *f.* wine from newly tapped cask.

man-o·metro *m.* (eng.) pressure gauge, manometer; (motor.) — per pneumatici, tyre gauge. **-ome·trico** *adj.* (phys.) manometric.

manomęttere [C20] *tr.* to begin the use of; to open; to lay hands upon; to tamper with; to handle roughly; to ill-treat; to impair, to damage; to violate; to plunder, to lay waste; to search illegally; to open (letters, etc.) illegally; (Rom. hist.) to manumit, to set (a slave) free.

manomissione *f.* violation; segni di —, signs of having been tampered with; (Rom. hist.) manumission.

manomorta *f.* (leg.) mortmain, dead hand (i.e. land that is inalienable).

mano·pola *f.* gauntlet; iron glove; fencing-glove; the part of a glove that extends above the wrist; sling for the wrist (in a carriage, car, etc.); elbow-rest; handle, hand grip; (radio, etc.) knob.

†**manosco·pio** *m.* See **manometro.**

manoscritto *m.* manuscript; *adj.* handwritten; in manuscript.

manoso *adj.* soft, yielding.

manovaldo *m.* guardian, tutor.

manovale *m.* labourer, unskilled worker; day-labourer; (bldg.) — di muratore, bricklayer's labourer.

manovell·a *f.* handle, lever; hand-spike; (eng.) crank; (motor.) throw (of a crankshaft); — d'avviamento, starting handle, cranking handle; albero a —, crankshaft; albero a gomiti a quattro -e, four-throw crankshaft; — alza-cristalli, window winder. **-ismo** *m.* (eng.) crank mechanism, crank gear.

†**mano·vile** *adj.* handy; manageable.

manovr·a *f.* move; manœuvre; — falsa, false move, tactical error; — aggirante, outflanking manœuvre; (eng.) manœuvre, move; (rlwy.) shunting; — a spinta, pushing off; (naut.) manœuvre, rigging; — alta, upper rigging (above the crow's nest or control top); — fissa, — stante, — stabile, — dormiente, standing rigging; — corrente, running rigging; — bassa, lower rigging; — di fortuna, — di battaglia, — di rispetto, preventer or reserve rigging; — di cautela, preventer rigging; — chiara, rigging free to run; — di combattimento, battle rigging; — indipendente, separate rigging; — di rovescio, slack rigging; — alla festa, coiled rigging (on deck); coperta di —, bridge; camera di —, control room (submarine) or control cabinet (turret); rassetta e cogli —! para la —!, ready about! stand by! **-abilità** *f.* (eng.) manœuvrability, controllability. **-are** [A I] *tr.* to manœuvre. (**-ato** *part. adj.*) **-atore** *m.* (eng.) driver; (rlwy.) -atore di scambi, shunter, pointsman.

manritt·a (Tusc.) right hand. **-o** *adj.* right; right-handed.

manrove·scio *m.* blow given with the back of the hand; back-handed blow, back-stroke; (tennis) back-hand.

mansalva *adv. phr.* a —, with impunity.

mansarda *f.* (archit.) mansard.

mansion-a·rio *m.* (eccl.) 'mansionary', beneficed priest with duties in choir but no vote in chapter. **-ariato** *m.*, **-eri·a** *f.* (eccl.) status of 'mansionary'.

mansiona·tico *m.* maintenance, provision by a vassal for the lodging of his lord's retinue when passing through his property.

mansione *f.* stay, sojourn; halt; abode; address; office, duty, function; permanent post; (theatr. hist.) mansion.

mansioneri·a *f.* See under **mansionario**.

manso *adj.* (poet.) gentle, tame; mild; †blunt, not prickly.

mansuefare [B14] *tr.* to tame; to subdue; to domesticate; to calm, to pacify, to soothe, to appease, to quiet.

†mansue·scere *intr.* to grow gentle, to become tame.

mansuet·o *adj.* gentle; docile; tame; meek, mild. **-amẹnte** *adv.* gently; meekly; mildly. **-u·dine** *f.* gentleness; docility; tameness; mildness, meekness.

†man·taco *m.* see **mantice**; (poet.) lungs.

†mantadura *f.* cloak.

†mantanente *adv.* See **immantinente**.

†mantarro *m.* shepherd's cloak.

mante *m.* (naut., Taranto). See **amante²**.

mantec·a *f.* pomade; salt butter. **-are** [A2] *tr.* to mix (fats) to form a pomade. **-ato** *part. adj.* pomaded; *n.m.* a rather soft ice-cream.

mantella *f.* woman's long cloak or mantle.

mantell·o *m.* cloak, cape, mantle; (fig.) aver — a ogni acqua, to be ready for anything; mutare il —, to turn one's coat, to be a turn-coat; (zool.) mantle (of a mollusc); (of animals, esp. horses) coat; (eng.) — dello stantuffo, piston skirt; (metall.) — del forno, cupola shell. **-are** [A1] *tr.* to cloak, to cover with a mantle. **-ate** *pr.n.f.pl.* (eccl.) Mantellates, Servite or Dominican women tertiaries. **-ato** *part. adj.* mantled, cloaked; (herald.) mantled. **-ẹtta** *f. dim.* (hist. costume) mantlet, short cape of kind worn by important dignitaries. **-ẹtto** *m. dim.* mantle, cape; (mil.) mantlet, mantelet; (mining) roof-support; †(naut.) top-lining; hood. **-ina** *f.* short mantle, cape; cloak for soldiers, policemen, etc.; covering for statues in churches; coat of lime round the inside of the upper part of a well.

†mantenente *adv.* See **immantinente**.

manten·ere [B32] *tr.* to keep; to maintain; to hold; to support; — i vecchi genitori, to keep one's aged parents; — l'onore della famiglia, to keep up the good name of the family; — la promessa, to keep one's promise; — l'equilibrio, to keep one's balance; — il segreto, to keep the secret; *rfl.* to keep oneself, to support oneself; **-ersi** in buona salute, to keep in good health. **-i·bile** *adj.* maintainable; tenable. **-imẹnto** *m.* maintenance, keeping; preservation; (leg.) maintenance; the keeping in repair; i mezzi di -imento, (means of) maintenance; le spese per il -imento del condannato, (cost of) maintenance of convicted person (C.P.); -imento in buono stato locativo, the keeping in good and tenantable repair (C.C.). **-uta** *f.* mistress, kept woman. **-uto** *part. adj.* maintained, supported; kept up; sustained; kept in good order.

†man·tica *f.* art of divining the future.

man·tic·e *m.* bellows; hood of a carriage; (motor.) hood; (photog.) bellows; (rlwy.) vestibule (corridor connecting two coaches); (mus.) organ-bellows; organo senza —, mechanically blown organ. **-eri·a** *f.* (mus.) blowing-system (of organ). **-ia·io** *m.* bellows-maker.

manticora *f.* (myth.) four-footed beast with three rows of teeth and human face.

man·tide *f.* (ent.) praying mantis.

manti·glia *f.* mantilla.

†mantile *m.* coarse table-cloth; kitchen cloth, drying-cloth.

†mantinente *adv.* See **immantinente**.

mantissa *f.* (math.) mantissa.

manto *m.* cloak, mantle, esp. regal mantle; il gran —, the mantle of the Pope; il — ducale, the mantle of the Venetian Doge; coat; covering; (fig.) protection, defence; sotto il — delle religione, under the cloak of religion; (poet.) mantle, covering; un — di neve, a mantle of snow; (civ. eng.) surfacing, carpet; — asfaltico, asphalt surface; — stradale, featheredge; (bldg.) mantle (of a wall); dummy boards; †(poet.) body; †skin of a snake; †garment.

mantò *m. indecl.* cloak, mantle.

Man·tov·a *pr.n.f.* (geog.) Mantua. **-ana** *f.* (bldg.) gableboard; pelmet; woman from Mantua. **-ano** *adj.* (geog.) Mantuan; il poeta -ano, Virgil; la musa -ana, Virgil, Virgil's poetry; *n.m.* Mantuan; Mantuan dialect.

mantrugiare [A3] *tr.* to finger; to feel; to maul.

manual·e¹ *adj.* manual; lavoro —, manual labour; †*n.m.* see **manovale**. **-mẹnte** *adv.* manually, by hand. **-ità** *f.* (techn.) operation, procedure.

manual·e² *m.* handbook, manual. **-ista** *m.* writer of a handbook. **-i·stico** *adj.* characteristic of a handbook, manual-like.

manuale³ *m.* (mus.) manual (of organ or harpsichord); manuali accoppiati, coupled manuals.

†manubal-estro, †-ista *m.* crossbow.

manu·brio *m.* haft; handle, grip; dumb-bell; (of cycle) handlebar; (of gun) bolt handle; (of organ) stop-handle.

†manucare *vb.* and derivs. See **mangiare**.

manucodiata *f.* (orn.) bird of paradise.

Manuell·e, -o *pr.n.m.* Manuel (abbrev. of **Emanuele**, Emmanuel).

manufatto *adj.* manufactured; prodotti manufatti, manufactured goods; †hand-made; *n.m.* manufactured article.

manumissiọne *f.* (Rom. hist.) manumission.

manuten·golo *m.* receiver of stolen goods; accomplice.

manutenziọne *f.* maintenance, upkeep; (eng.) maintenance, servicing; (leg.) azione di —, action to maintain possession (of land, etc.); — ordinaria (nella locazione), ordinary repairs (under lease); le riparazioni di piccola —, tenant's repairs (C.C.).

manẓa *f.* heifer.

manẓo *m.* steer; bullock; beef; — lesso, boiled beef; (fig.) fat man, clumsy person; (ichth.) pesce —, Mediterranean shark, *Hexanchus griseus*.

manẓonian·o *adj.* Manzonian; *n.m.* follower or imitator of Manzoni; specialist in studies relating to Manzoni. (**-a** *f.*) **-iṣmo** *m.* literary fashion or tendency deriving from Manzoni. **-ista** *m., f.* specialist in studies relating to Manzoni.

mao *onom.* miaow.

Maomẹtt·o *pr.n.m.* Mahomet, Mohammed. **-ano** *m. adj.* Mohammedan. **-aniṣmo** *m.* Mohammedanism.

maọna *f.* punt, barge, lighter (Levantine).

mapp·a¹ *f.* map; plan; — celeste, map of the heavens. **-atọre** *m.* cartographer.

mappa² *f.* tablecloth; napkin.

mappamọndo *m.* map of the world; map shown in hemispheres; globe; (fam.) the buttocks, the behind.

mara *f.* (zool.) Patagonian cavy, *Dolichotis patachonica*.

marabatto *m.* (naut.) storm-sail.

marabottino *m.* (numism.) Saracen coin of Arabic Spain.

marabù *m. indecl.*, **marabutto¹** *m.* (orn.) marabou stork, *Leptoptilos crumeniferus*.

marabutto² *m.* (naut.) lowest of a galley's sails.

marabutto³ *m.* Moslem hermit; guardian of a mosque; marabout.

marachella *f.* trick; fraud; illicit act; far la —, to spy.

Maragià, Mara·gia, Mahara·gia *m. indecl.* Maharajah.

marama·glia *f.* See **marmaglia**.

maramald·o *m.* one who is cruel to the defenceless (from the name of Fabrizio Maramaldo, who stabbed and killed Francesco Ferrucci, his unarmed prisoner, 1530). **-eggiare** [A3c] *intr.* (aux. avere) to be cruel to the defenceless, to behave treacherously.

marama·o *excl.* not on your life!, not likely!; *onom.* miaow.

marame *m.* rubbish; refuse; †abundance.

marame·o *excl.* See **maramao**.

marangọne¹ *m.* (orn.) cormorant, *Phalacrocorax carbo*; — col ciuffo, shag, *P. aristotelis*; — minore, pygmy cormorant, *P. pygmaeus*.

marangọne² *m.* (Tusc.) carpenter, joiner.

maras·ca *f.* (bot.) a variety of morello cherry, *Prunus cerasus*, used in making maraschino. **-chino** *m.* maraschino liqueur.

marascal·co *m.* (*pl.* **-chi**) farrier.

maraṣm·a *f.*, †**-o** *m.* (med.) marasmus, wasting disease; (fig.) decay, atrophy.

marasso *m.* (zool.) *Vipera berus*, an Italian species of poisonous viper.

marata *f.* tidal wave; action of the sea; force of the tide.

Maratọn·a *pr.n.f.* (geog.) Marathon; *m.* Marathon race. **-ẹta** *m.* Marathon runner.

mara·vedi, -vedino *m.* (numism.) Arabic coin current in Spain in the fifteenth century; coin of low value, copper coin.

maravi·glia *f.* and derivs. See **meraviglia**.

marazz·o *m.* swamp, marsh. **-ọso** *adj.* swampy, marshy.

marca *f.* mark; token; counter; brand (of goods, etc.); — di fabbrica, maker's mark, trade mark; — depositata, registered trade mark; — da bollo, revenue stamp; contraffazione di — di fabbrica, infringement of trade mark; — a fuoco, brand; border; district, region; (geog.) le Marche, the Marches; (naut.) mark on a rope or cable (cables are marked with a wire seizing on the first studded link either side of the joining shackle for the first shackle,

marca (*cont.*)
on the second link for the second shackle, etc.); (leg.) — da bollo, revenue stamp; la contraffazione delle marche, counterfeiting of revenue stamps (C.P.).

marcanto·nia *f.* (pop.) plump woman; che pezzo di —!, what a weight she is!

Marcanto·nio *pr.n.m.* Mark Antony; (pop.) fat man; (ichth.) rabbit fish, *Chimera monstrosa*.

marc-are [A 2] *tr.* to mark, to place a mark upon; — la biancheria, to mark one's linen; to note, to make a note of; — i punti, to keep the score; — dei punti, to score, to score points; (soccer, rugby) to mark; — a fuoco, to brand; *intr.* (aux. avere) to mark, to be bordering. **-amento** *m.* (sport) marking. **-apiano** *m. indecl.* (bldg.) water table, string course. **-ato** *part. adj.* marked; scored; (mus.) emphasized, accentuated. **-atore** *m.* marker; scorer.

marcassite *f.* (miner.) marcasite, white iron pyrites.

Marc'aure·lio *pr.n.m.* Marcus Aurelius.

Marcello *pr.n.m.* Marcellus; (provb.) e un Marcel diventa ogni villan che parteggiando viene (Dante, *Purg.* VI, 125–6), said of a man who receives unmerited honours for partisanship; (numis.) Venetian coin current in the time of the doge Niccolò Marcello (1473–4).

marcesc-ente *adj.* marcescent. **-i·bile** *adj.* perishable; corruptible.

Marche *pr.n.f.pl.* (geog.). See under **marca**.

march-e̜sa *f.* marchioness. **-e̜sina** *f. dim.* daughter of an Italian marquis. **-e̜sana** *f.* marchioness. **-e̜sato** *m.* marquisate. **-e̜se** *m.* marquis, marquess; (hist.) Margrave. **-e̜sino** *m. dim.* son of an Italian marquis.

Marche̜si *pr.n.f.pl.* (geog.) Marquesas Islands.

marche̜tto *m.* (eng.) cushion; — pneumatico, pneumatic cushion.

marchiano *adj.* huge, enormous; gross; un errore —, a gross error; spropositi marchiani, gross blunders.

marchiare [A 4] and derivs. See **marcare**.

marchigiana[1] *adj. f., n.f.* of **marchigiano**, q.v.

†**marchigiana**[2] *f.* See **marchesa**.

marchigiano *adj.* (geog.) of the Marches; *n.m.* native or inhabitant of the Marches.

mar·chio *m.* (*pl.* **marchii**) (leg.; comm.) brand, mark; stencil; — di fabbrica, — di impresa, trade-mark; l'azione in materia di brevetti per — d'impresa, trade-mark action (C.C.); — collettivo, combined trade-mark (C.C.); — contraffatto, false mark (C.P.); — registrato, registered trade-mark (C.C.); l'esclusività del —, exclusive right to trade-mark; il preuso del —, prior use of trade-mark; la soppressione del —, erasure of maker's mark; il trasferimento del —, assignment of trade-mark (C.C.).

marchionale *adj.* marquisial, relating to a marquis.

mar·cia[1] *f.* (*pl.* **mar·cie**) march; a marcie forzate, by forced marches; in —, on the march; mettersi in —, to march off; (motor., etc.) gear; (eng.) mettere in —, (eng.) to start up; messa in —, starting up; cambiare —, to change gear; a tre marcie, three-speed; (mus.) march; alla —, with the style and rhythm of a march; — funebre, funeral march, dead march; — nuziale, wedding march; (naut.) way; (fig.) progress, advance.

mar·cia[2] *f.* pus, festering matter. **-a·ia** *f.* (vet.) rot (in cattle, sheep, etc.).

marciano *adj.* of St Mark; relating to St Mark; la Biblioteca Marciana (*or* la Marciana), St Mark's Library in Venice.

marciapiede *m.* pavement; footpath; (rlwy.) platform; (naut.) footropes under a yard for the sailor to stand on while furling a sail; (of a prostitute) battere i marciapiedi, to walk the streets.

marci-are [A 3] *intr.* (aux. avere) to march; to go; — in carrozza, to drive in a carriage, (fig.) to be well off; to proceed; to advance, to progress; to travel; to work, to function; le cose non -ano bene, things are not going too well. **-ante** *part. adj.* marching; going; (of engine) running. **-ata** *f.* march; marching. **-avanti** *m. indecl.* (mining) forepoling, spiling.

marcida·glia *f.* the soft membrane that holds the pips of a melon.

mar·cido *adj.* rotting, half-rotten, going bad; withered; tainted; (colloq.) drunk, tight; (bot.) marcescent (of a corolla that withers without falling).

marcime *m.* (agric.) litter thrown out of stall to make manure, stable manure.

marcino *m.* wine made from sweet grapes that have started to go rotten (speciality of Carmignano).

mar·c-io *adj.* rotten, bad; spoiled; tainted; uova -e, rotten eggs; carne -ia, bad meat; (of a wall) crumbling; tisico —, far gone in (with) consumption; briaco —, blind drunk; avere torto —, to be totally in the wrong; perderla -ia, to lose a game without scoring a point; lo dovette sposare a — dispetto, she had to marry him entirely against her will; *n.m.* rottenness, rotten part; double loss in any game; rompere il —, to stop the rot; c'è del — in Danimarca, something is rotten in the State of Denmark. **-iolino** *m.* smell of something beginning to go bad; smell of Marcino wine. **-ioso** *adj.* purulent, festering; (fig.) filthy.

marc-ire [D 2] *intr.* (aux. essere) to decay, to go bad, to fester, to rot; (of a wall) to crumble; mi -isce questo dito, this finger of mine is festering; to waste away; — in prigione, to rot in prison; to become morally corrupt. **-imento** *m.* rotting; decaying. **-ita** *f.* (geog.) (Lomb.) irrigated meadow. **-io̜tio** *m*; macerating-vat. **-itura** *f.* rotting; maceration. **-iume** *m.* rottenness, rot; festering sore; pus; (fig.) corruption.

Marco[1] *pr.n.m.* Marcus; Mark; San —, St Mark, the patron saint of Venice; le navi di San —, the ships of Venice.

mar-co[2] *m.* (*pl.* **-chi**) (numism.) mark; (rugby) mark.

marcolf-o, -a *f.* See **margolfa**.

marcon-igrafi·a *f.* wireless telegraphy. **-igramma** *m.* radiogram. **-ista** *m.* wireless operator. **-iterapi·a** *f.* (med.) diathermy.

marcorella *f.* (bot.) mercury, *Mercurialis*.

mare *m.* sea; in alto —, on the high sea, (fig.) at sea; la questione è ancora in alto —, the matter is still undecided; — grosso, rough sea, heavy sea; braccio di —, inlet; — libero, open water; — territoriale, territorial waters; sul livello del —, above sea-level; uomo in —, man overboard; mal di —, sea-sickness; gettare in —, to throw overboard, to jettison; portare acqua al —, to carry coals to Newcastle; prometter mari e monti, to make great promises, to promise the earth; verde —, sea green; — artico, Arctic Ocean; (leg.) il lido del —, foreshore (up to high-water mark); le rive del —, seashore; le cose gettate in —, flotsam; le cose rigettate dal —, jetsam (C.C.); (comm.) trasporto per —, carriage by sea; (fig.) crowd, vast quantity; un — di gente, a vast crowd of people.

mare·a *f.* tide; ebb and flow; alta —, high tide; bassa —, low tide; — stanca, slack tide; — quadraturale, neap tide; — sigiziale, spring tide.

mareggi-are [A 3 c] *intr.* (aux. avere) to rise and fall in waves; to undulate; to surge, to swell; to float; to rise and fall with the waves; to be seasick; *n.m.* swell, surge, surging; undulating. **-amento** *m.* seasickness. **-ata** *f.* heavy sea; surge, surging, swell.

mare̜ggio *m.* undulation; surge, swell.

mare̜mm-a *f.* (geog.) maremma; fen, marsh, swampy coast; la Maremma, usu. the Tuscan Maremma. **-ano** *adj.* relating to a marsh or to fenland; relating to the Tuscan Maremma; fieno -ano, sainfoin; febbre -ana, swamp-fever; *n.m.* inhabitant of the Maremma; peasant who goes down from the hills in winter to work in the Maremma; parer un -ano, to be boorish.

maremoto *m.* sea-quake, submarine earthquake; onda di —, tidal wave.

marena[1] *f.* morello cherry; sweet drink made from morello cherries.

marena[2] *f.* (ichth.) white-fish, *Coregonus marena*.

marenga *f.* (cul.) meringue.

Marengo *pr.n.m.* (geog.) Marengo; (cul.) Marengo sauce; (numism.) Napoleon (French gold twenty-franc coin of Napoleon I).

mareo·grafo *m.* tide-gauge.

marescal-co *m.* (*pl.* **-chi**). See **maniscalco**.

maresciallo *m.* (mil.) marshal; highest grade of non-commissioned officer (equiv. to R.S.M.); — maggiore (dei Carabinieri), Warrant Officer in the Carabinieri; — d'Italia, field-marshal; police inspector; (naut.) Chief Petty Officer.

†**marese** *m.* swamp, marsh.

mare̜tta *f.* choppy sea; slight swell.

marezz-are [A 1 c] *tr.* to water (silk); to give a veining to (wood); to marble. **-ato** *part. adj.* watered (of silk); wavy; moiré; marbled; veined (e.g. of wood); (paperm.) carta -ata, marbled paper. **-atura** *f.* watering (of silk), moiré effect; marbling; veining.

mare̜zzo *m.* artificial marble; marbling; veining.

Marfo·rio *pr.n.m.* mutilated statue at Rome to which, as to that of Pasquino, popular satires ('pasquinades') were affixed.

marga *f.* (agric.) marl, loam.

margarina *f.* margarine.

margassita *f.* pyrites.

margherit-a[1] *f.* pearl; (naut.) nodo —, sheepshank knot; (bot.) ox-eye daisy, *Chrysanthemum Leucanthemum.* **-ina** *f. dim.* (bot.) small daisy, *Bellis perennis*; glass bead.

Margherita[2] *pr.n.f.* Margaret; Marguerite.

margin-ale *adj.* marginal. **-a·lia** *m.pl.* marginalia. **-are** [A I s] *tr.* (typ.) to margin; (fig.) to border; *intr.* (*aux.* avere) to leave a margin. **-ato** *part. adj.* marginated. **-atura** *f.* (typ.) margining; (fig.) edging, border. **-oso** *adj.* having a wide margin.

mar·gine *m.* border, margin, edge; il — di un burrone, the edge of a precipice; non c'è — per far questa spesa, we have no margin from which to meet this expense; scar; (econ.) buon —, fair margin; — di guadagno, margin of profit; in — a, apropos of, on the subject of, talking of; (typ.) — di taglio, fore-edge.

†**margo** *m.* border; bank (of river); shore.

margolf-a *f.* clumsily built woman (from the name of the mother of Bertoldino in the popular tale of Bertoldo and Bertoldino). **-o** *m.* clumsy person, figure of fun.

†**margolla** *f.* she-devil.

margone[1] *m.* See **marga.**

margone[2] *m.* gulley or ditch through which water from a mill flows away.

margott-a *f.* (agric.) layer. **-are** [A I] *tr.* (agric.) to layer, to propagate by layering.

margra·vi-o *m.* (hist.) margrave. **-ato** *m.* (hist.) margraviate.

†**margutto** *adj.* ugly and evil (from the name of Margutte in Pulci's *Morgante*).

Mar-i·a *pr.n.f.* Mary; Maria; the Virgin Mary; essere tutto Gesù e —, to be a sanctimonious hypocrite; cercare — per Ravenna, to search for a thing where it will not be found, (or) to look for trouble; parere le tre -ie, (of women) to weep bitterly; far le -ie, to feign simplicity and piety; far viva —, to rob in the name of religion; il mese di —, the month of May. **-ętta, -uc·cia** *pr.n.f. dim.* Marykins, May. **-iano** *adj.* of Mary; (rel.) of or dedicated to the B.V.M.; mese -iano, the month of May; usciva il mese -iano, the May devotions were just over.

†**maricello** *m.* bitterness.

†**maricino** *m. dim.* of **mare**; choppy sea.

marigiana *f.* (orn.). See **morigiana.**

marimba *f.* (mus.) marimba.

marimonda *f.* (zool.) spider monkey, *Ateles* spp.

marina *f.* sea, ocean; sea-coast; seaside resort; esplanade; navy, marine; la regia —, the Royal Navy; — mercantile, mercantile marine, merchant shipping; fanteria di —, soldati di —, marines; Ministro della —, Navy Minister; (fig.) vedere la — to see dangers ahead; (paint.) sea-piece; (fig.) batter —, to pretend to be wretched in order to be pitied; unità di appoggio della —, naval support to land forces.

marina·io *m.* sailor; mastro —, captain of a ship; da galeotto a —, from galley-slave to sailor (i.e. diamond cut diamond); — di coperta, deck hand, deck rating; — scelto, able seaman; *adj.* maritime.

marin-are [A I] *tr.* (cul.) to marinate; (fig.) to keep laid by; ma quelle ragazze le tieni in casa a —?, do you keep those girls of yours at home for pickling (i.e. don't you ever let them go out?); — una lezione, to cut a lesson; — la scuola, to play truant. **-ato** *adj.* (cul.) marinated; (herald.) leone -ato, sea-lion; *n.m.* salted fish.

marinar-o *m.* (pop) see **marinaio**; *adj.* sea-faring; seaman-like; nazione marinara, sea-faring nation; *adv. phr.* alla marinara, in the manner of sailors, in sailor fashion; colletto alla -a, middy collar. **-a** *f.* child's sailor suit; sailor's hat; sou'wester. **-ęsco** *adj.* (*m.pl.* -ęschi) nautical.

marineri·a *f.* navy, marine; — mercantile, merchant navy; seaman-ship.

marin-işmo *m.* (lit. hist.) Marinism, the style of G. B. Marino (1565–1627) and his followers, a literary affectation comparable to euphuism. **-ista** *m.* Marinist, follower or imitator of Marino.

marino *adj.* of the sea, marine; acqua marina, sea-water, salt water; (zool.) vitello —, seal; (motor.) motore —, marine engine; (mus.) tromba marina, marine trumpet (obsolete bowed instrument from whose single string only the harmonics were produced), (naut.) waterspout.

mariolatri·a *f.* (rel.) Mariolatry.

mariol-eri·a *f.* trick, cheat, fraud, swindling; roguery; prank. **-ęsco** *adj.* (*m.pl.* -ęschi) fraudulent, swindling. **-o** *m.* rogue, cheat, swindler.

marionętt-a *f.* marionette; puppet; spettacolo di -e, marionette show; puppet show. **-ista** *m.* marionettist; puppet-master, puppet-showman. **-i·stico** *adj.* pertaining to marionettes or puppets.

marit-a·bile *adj.* marriageable, nubile. **-ag·gio** *m.* marriage, matrimony. **-ale** *adj.* marital. **-almęnte** *adv.* maritally; vivere -almente, to live as husband and wife. **-amęnto** *m.* marrying, marriage. **-are** [A I] *tr.* to marry, to give in marriage; Antonio ha -ato la figlia, Antonio has given his daughter in marriage; *rfl.* to marry, to get married. **-ata** *f. adj.* married; *n.f.* married woman.

marito *m.* husband; prender —, to take a husband, to get married; perdere il —, to lose one's husband, to become a widow; riprender —, to remarry; una figlia in età da —, a daughter of marriageable age; (provb.) fra moglie e — non mettere il dito, don't interfere between husband and wife.

marit·timo *adj.* marine, maritime; guerra marittima, sea war; stazione marittima, harbour station; (leg.) diritto —, maritime law; *n.m.pl.* seafaring folk.

mariuolo *m.* See **mariolo**, under **marioleria.**

marma·gli-a *f.* rabble. **-ume** *m. pejor.* filthy rabble, scum of the earth.

marmeg·gia *f.* (ent.) bird louse (Mallophaga).

marmellata *f.* jam; marmalade; preserve.

marm-iera *f.* marble-quarry. **-i·fero** *adj.* containing marble; marble-bearing; abounding in marble; società -ifera, company trading in marble.

marmitt-a *f.* kettle, pot; saucepan; (motor.) silencer; (mil. slang) grenade. **-one** *m.* (mil. slang) soldier who takes no interest in his duty, slacker.

marm-o *m.* marble; marble bust; marble statue; cava di —, marble-quarry; pallina di —, marble (child's toy); *pl.* kinds of marble; statues; steps of the Cathedral in Florence. **-ino** *m. dim.* marble stop for a door. **-ista** *m.* worker in marble. **-o·reo** *adj.* of marble, in marble; worked in marble; marmoreal; marble-like.

marmoc·ch-io *m.* (*pl.* -i) brat; urchin.

marmorare [A I] and derivs. See **marmorizzare**, under **marmorario.**

marmor-a·rio *m.* marble-cutter, worker in marble. **-eggiare** [A 3 c] and derivs. see **marmorizzare**. **-izzare** [A I] *tr.* to marble. **-izzato** *part. adj.* marbled. **-izzazione** *f.* marbling.

marmott-a *f.* (zool.) marmot, *M. marmota*; (fig.) sleepy individual; idler, lazy-bones; recluse; dormire come una —, to sleep like a dormouse. **-ina** *f. dim.* (slang) sample-case of a commercial traveller. **-ino** *m.* little boy; cobbler's last. **-o** *adj.* dumb; *n.m.* deaf-mute.

marn-a[1] *f.* (geol.) marl. **-are** [A I] *tr.* to dress with marl. **-iera** *f.* (mining) marl pit. **-oso** *adj.* rich in marl; calcare -oso, lias limestone.

Marna[2] *pr.n.f.* (geog.) the river Marne.

marnętta *f.* (rubber industr.) batch pan.

marò *m. indecl.* (abbrev. of 'marinaio ordinario') able-seaman.

maro *m.* (bot.) *Teucrium marum.*

Maroc-co *pr.n.m.* (geog.) Morocco. **-chino** *m.* native of Morocco, Moroccan; morocco (leather); *adj.* Moroccan. **-ca·io** *m.* one who dresses morocco leather; morocco-dresser. **-care** [A 2] *tr.* to dress (morocco leather).

maronita *m.* (rel. hist.) Maronite.

†**maroso** *m.* billow, breaker.

marr-a *f.* hoe, mattock; instrument like hoe used in mixing mortar; (naut.) fluke. **-aiuolo** *m.* sapper; delver, pioneer. **-ata** *f.* blow with a hoe. **-eggiare** [A 3 c] *tr., intr.* (*aux.* avere) to hoe.

marran-cio *m.* butcher's carving-knife.

marran-o *m.* term of opprobrium for newly baptized Moors and Jews in Spain; lout, brute; traitor, miscreant. (**-ac·cio** *m. pejor.*)

marrata *f.* See under **marra.**

marreggiare [A 3 c]. See under **marra.**

marrimęnto *m.* See **smarrimento**, under **smarrire.**

marritta *f.* See **manritta.**

marrob·bio *m.* (bot.) white horehound, *Marrubium vulgare*; — fetido, black horehound, *Ballota nigra.*

marrochino *m., adj.* See **marocchino**, under **marocco.**

marron-e *m.* (bot.) fine variety of Spanish chestnut; — candito, marron glacé, candied chestnut; Alpine guide; gross error, blunder; *adj.* chestnut-coloured; brown. **-ęto** *m.* chestnut plantation.

marrub·bio *m.* (bot.). See **marrobbio.**

marruc-a *f.* (bot.) Christ-thorn, *Paliurus Spina-Christi.* **-a·io** *m.* thicket.

Marsala *pr.n.f.* (geog.) Marsala; *f., m.* Marsala wine.

Marsi·gli-a *pr.n.f.* (geog.) Marseilles. **-ęse** *adj.* (geog.) of Marseilles; *n.m., f.* native or inhabitant of Marseilles; *f.* (mus.) Marseillaise, French national anthem.

marsina *f.* evening dress (men's), tails; dress jacket; tail-coat.

marsovino *m.* (zool.) porpoise, *Phocaena communis.*

marsu·pi-o *m.* (zool.) pouch. **-ale** *adj.* (zool.) marsupial. **-ali** *m.pl.* (zool.) marsupials.

Marta *pr.n.f.* Martha; far da — e da Maddalena, to do all the work, to be rushed off one's feet.

martagọne *m.* (bot.) martagon lily, *Lilium martagon.*

Marte *pr.n.m.* Mars, the god of war; figli di —, popolo di —, the ancient Romans; campo di —, parade-ground; (astron.) the planet Mars; (in alchemy) iron.

martedì *pr.n.m.* Tuesday; — grasso, Shrove Tuesday.

martell-are [A I] *tr.* to hammer; to torture; (fig.) dagli, picchia e -a, try and try again; *intr.* (aux. avere) to throb, to pulsate. **-amẹnto** *m.* hammering; beating, pulsing, throbbing. **-ata** *f.* hammer-blow. **-ato** *part. adj.* hammered; (mus.) hammered (either of staccato bow-strokes or of a percussive style of piano-playing). **-atọre** *m.* hammerer; (mus.) percussive. (**-atrice** *f.*) **-atura** *f.* hammering; result of hammering. **-ìo** *m.* (*pl.* **-ii**) constant hammering; throbbing; pounding.

martelliano *m.* (prosod.) verse of fourteen syllables, named after Pier Jacopo Martelli (1665–1727), who reintroduced it; *adj.* relating to such verse.

martellina *f.* steel hammer used by masons in building; steel hammer used in dressing hard stones; the steel of a flint-lock gun.

martellio *m.* See under **martellare**.

martellista *m.* See under **martello**.

martell-o *m.* hammer; — da fabbro, sledge hammer; — da muratore, bricklayer's hammer; — a due punti, mandrel, miners' pick; taglio di —, the flat end of a hammer; bocca di —, the round end of a hammer; fra l'incudine e il —, between the anvil and the hammer, i.e. between the devil and the deep blue sea; questo metallo regge al —, this metal can stand hammering; campana —, alarm-bell; sonare a —, to ring the alarm; piano-tuner's key; piano hammer; door-knocker; gavel, auctioneer's hammer; (anat.) malleus; (fig.) torment; (ichth.) pesce —, hammer-headed shark, *Sphyrna zygaena*; (sport) lancio del —, hammer-throwing. **-ẹtto** *m.* (electr.) distributor arm. **-ista** *m.* (sport) hammer-thrower.

martensite *f.* (metall.) martensite.

†martì, †martidì *pr.n.m.* See **martedì**.

†mart-idiare [A4] *tr.* to martyr. **†-idiato** *part. adj.* martyred. **†-i·dio** *m.* martyrdom.

martinac·cio *m.* (zool.) a kind of edible land-snail.

Martinella *pr.n.f.* (hist.) the name of a bell in Florence which was rung a month before the army set out from the city and was then taken with the army (carried on the 'Carroccio').

martinẹllo *m.* (mech.) lifting-jack; (orn.) plover.

martinẹtto *m.* (eng.) trip hammer, stamping mill; jack; alzare mediante —, to jack up; outrigger (e.g. to give stability to a mobile crane).

martingala *f.* (hist. costume) martingale, a flap (sixteenth century) which was hung from a girdle round the waist and covered the seat of the breeches.

Martinica *pr.n.f.* (geog.) Martinique.

martinicca *f.* wheel-drag.

Martino *pr.n.m.* Martin; (provb.) per un punto — perse la cappa, Martin lost his priorship for a comma (cf. 'to spoil a ship for a ha'porth of tar'); San —, Martinmas, the 11th of November, often referred to as the beginning of winter; estate di San —, St Martin's summer; (colloq.) fare il San —, to move house (from the custom of avoiding the payment of rent which fell due at this period); (ichth.) *Lophius budegassa*, smaller angler fish; (orn.) martin pescatore, kingfisher, *Alcedo atthis.*

martirare [A I] and derivs. See **martirizzare**.

mar·tire *m., f.* martyr; Re dei -i, Christ; Regina dei -i, the Madonna; atteggiarsi a —, to make a martyr of oneself.

marti·r-io *m.* (*pl.* **-ii**) martyrdom; torment; torture.

martir-izzare [A I] *tr.* to martyr; to martyrize. **-izzato** *part. adj.* martyred; martyrized; *n.m.* martyr. **-olo·gio** *m.* martyrology; book of martyrs.

mar·tor-a *f.*, **-o** *m.* (zool.) marten, *Mustela martes.*

martori-are [A4] *tr.* to torture; to torment. **-amẹnto** *m.* torturing; tormenting. **-ato** *part. adj.* tortured; tormented; *n.m.* martyr. **-atọre** *m.* torturer; tormentor.

†mart-o·rio, -oro *m.* torture; torment.

martuffo *adj.* stupid, worthless; *n.m.* fool.

Marucellian-a *pr.n.f.* the library at Florence founded by Marucelli (d. 1703). **-o** *adj.* pertaining to this library.

maruzza *f.* (zool.) — bianca, *Natica josephinia*; — monaca, *N. millepunctata* and *N. hebraea*, marine gastropods.

marvizzella *f.* (ichth.) *Crenilabrus ocellatus*, a kind of wrasse.

marx-ișmo *m.* (pol.) Marxism. **-ista** *m., f.* Marxist; *adj.* Marxist. **-i·stico** *adj.* Marxist.

marza¹ *f.* (bot.) graft, scion.

†marza² *f.* (geog.) port, harbour.

marzai(u)ola *f.* (orn.) garganey, *Anas querquedula.*

marzai(u)olo *adj.* of the month of March.

marzamina *f.* (bot.) kind of sweet black grape with thick skin.

marzapane *m.* (cul.) marchpane, marzipan; (fig.) fatto di —, delicate, tender.

marzeggiare [A3C] *intr.* (aux. avere), *impers.* to be March weather; to be uncertain.

marzial-e¹ *adj.* martial, bellicose; warlike; soldierly; aspetto —, warlike appearance; corte —, court-martial; legge —, martial law; acque -i, ferruginous waters. **-ità** *f.* soldierliness.

Marziale² *pr.n.m.* Martial (the Roman poet).

marziano *m.* (myth.) Martian, inhabitant of Mars.

mar·zio¹ *adj.* relating to Mars; martial; campo —, military exercise ground, drill ground, parade ground.

Mar·zio² *pr.n.m.* Martius; (provb.) il regalo che fece — alla nuora, a worthless gift; Don — Maldicente, a character in a comedy by Goldoni.

marz-o *pr.n.m.* March; gl'idi di —, the Ides of March. **-olino** *adj.* of March; vento -olino, March wind; cacio -olino, Marzolino cheese (a cheese made in March from sheep's milk). **-uolo** *adj.* of March; grano -uolo, corn sown in March; galletto -uolo, a spring chicken; parere un galletto -uolo, to be sprightly.

Marz-oc·co *pr.n.m.* name of the heraldic device (lion) of Florence. **-chẹsco** *adj.* (*m.pl.* **-chẹschi**) Florentine.

MAS *m. indecl.* (abbrev. of 'motoscafo antisommergibile') (naut.) M.T.B., motor torpedo-boat (as in other navies, the name was retained even when they became motor gun-boats).

masaneta *f.* (zool.) a 'berried' crab, carrying eggs.

Masaniello *pr.n.m.* (Ital. hist.) name of the hero of a Neapolitan rising (against the Spaniards, 1647); fare il —, to be bold; to start a revolution.

mascagni *adv. phr.* pettinatura alla —, hair brushed back without a parting (as the composer, Pietro Mascagni, wore his).

†mascagno *adj.* cunning; astute.

mascalci·a *f.* farriery; horse-shoeing; †see **guidalesco**.

†mascalciato *adj.* ill; in poor health.

mascalzọn-e *m.* rascal, rogue; scoundrel, blackguard. **-ag·gine** *f.* rascality. **-ata** *f.* piece of roguery, dishonest action.

Mascarene *pr.n.f.pl.* (geog.) Mascarenhas (Islands).

mascarpọne *m.* (cul.) a kind of fresh cheese.

Mascate *pr.n.f.* (geog.) Muscat.

mascavato *m.* muscovado, raw or unrefined sugar obtained from the juice of the sugar-cane by evaporation and draining of the molasses.

mascẹll-a *f.* (anat.) jaw; jaw-bone; — inferiore, lower jaw; — superiore, upper jaw. **-are** *adj.* maxillary; osso -are, jaw-bone; dente -are, back-tooth, molar.

ma·scher-a *f.* mask; disguise; portare la —, to wear a mask; to be masked; gettare la —, to drop one's disguise, to come out into the open; face, expression, features; una — interessante, an interesting head; era la — stessa della disperazione, his face conveyed utter desperation; ballo in —, masked ball, fancy-dress ball; masque; masqued figure, masker; (theatr.) uniformed attendant, usherette, programme girl; (hist. theatr.) originally an actor wearing a mask; later, a conventional character (e.g. Harlequin, Pantaloon) of the 'Commedia dell'arte'; make-up; person heavily made-up; (fencing) face-guard; (archit.) gargoyle; protective mask; — antigas, gas-mask; (animal) mask; il mio gatto è nero, con — bianca, my cat is black with a white face; (orn.) — corallina, Mediterranean gull, *Larus melanocephalus*; death-mask;

mascher-a (*cont.*)
(med.) facies, symptomatic expression due to some condition or disease; — gravidica, facial aspect due to pregnancy; (eng.) jig, die, template; (motor.) louvre. **-ina** *f.* masked person, mummer; (colloq.) -ina, ti conosco!, you can't fool me!, I see what you're up to!; medallion, face engraved on small metallic shield used for ornament (e.g. on harness); toe-cap; (photog.) mask; (eng.) template. **-ino** *m. dim.* see **mascherina**; (cinem.) matte, vignette.

mascher-are [A I s] *tr.* to mask; to disguise; to camouflage; to screen; *rfl.* to put on a mask; to masquerade; to be screened or camouflaged. **-aménto** *m.* masking; disguise; concealment; (mil.) camouflage. **-ata** *f.* (mus.) sixteenth-century *villanella* sung at masqued balls; masque; masquerade. **-atura** *f.* masking; disguise; (mil.) camouflage.

†**mascherizzo** *m.* livid mark, spot.

mascherpóne *m.* See **mascarpone**.

maschétte *f.pl.* (naut.) cheek pieces of a block; fore and aft supports of a crow's nest or control top secured on either side of a mast; stringers of a ladder; deadeyes on mizzen sheets.

maschiac·c-io *m. pejor.* of **maschio**, q.v.; *adj.* rough, uncouth man; mannish woman; hoyden; virago.

maschi-aménte *adv.*, **-étta** *f.*, **-ézza** *f.* See under **maschio**.

maschil-e *adj.* male; virile, manly; scuola —, boys' school; (gramm.) masculine; nome —, masculine noun. **-ménte** *adv.* in a manly way; virilely.

ma·sch-io *adj.* male; un figlio —, a son; manly, masculine; una voce -ia, a masculine voice; vigorous, manful, virile; viso —, manly face; (techn.) vite -ia, male screw; *n.m.* male, boy, son; ha tre -i ed una femmina, he has three sons and a daughter; keep (of a castle), fortress; (eng.) tap, screw tap; (carp.) — dell'incastro, tenon. (**-aménte** *adv.*) **-iare** [A 4] *tr.* (eng.) to tap. **-iétta** *f.* boyish girl; overgrown girl; tomboy; hoyden; capelli alla —, bobbed hair, hair in a bob, bob. **-iétto** *m. dim.* little boy; nice little chap. **-iézza** *f.* masculinity; virility; manliness. **-otta** *f.* tomboy; hoyden. **-otto** *m.* a fine baby boy; sturdy little boy; strong lad.

†**mascicano** *adj.* See **massiccio**.

mascolin-o *adj.* masculine; manly. **-ità** *f.* masculinity; manliness. **-izzare** [A I] *tr.* to make masculine, to render manly; to make a man of; *rfl.* to become manly; to assume masculine ways. **-izzato** *part. adj.* rendered manly.

†**mas·colo** *adj.* see **maschio**, or **mascolino**; *n.m.* a sort of iron cartridge-case for the gunpowder of an old breech-loading mortar; (eng.) piston; plunger.

Maşino *pr.n.m.* (abbrev. of Tommasino) Tommy; far la gatta di — che chiudeva gli occhi per non vedere i topi, to play the game of Masino's cat which shut its eyes in order not to see the mice (said of someone who shams blind and later pounces).

maşnad-a *f.* set, gang; una — di ladri, a gang of thieves, armed band; †group, company; †family. **-iére** *m.* highway robber; brigand; bandit; †feudal retainer; †trooper.

Maşo¹ *pr.n.m.* (abbrev. for Tommaso) Tom; — delle ragionacce, one who invents all kinds of bad excuses for his faults.

maşo² *m.* (geog., Trentino) — chiuso, family holding.

maşoch-işmo *m.* masochism. **-ista** *m., f.* masochist.

mass-a *f.* mass, bulk; heap, pile; lump; in —, in a mass, in a body, in bulk; una — di gente, a large crowd of people; una — di lavoro, a pile of work; una — di persone, a host of people; adunata in —, mass-meeting; fare —, to crowd; fare — su, to charge in a body on; (agric. econ.) large farm or several farms collectively; agricultural administrative district; (mil.) leva in —, mass levy; majority; le -e, the masses; la — della gente, the majority of people; (phys.) mass; — critica, critical mass; (electr.) mass, earth; (comm.) assets; — fallimentare, bankruptcy assets; (leg.) — dei creditori, assets; — ereditaria, deceased's estate; (comm.) bulk; vendere in —, to sell by bulk; fund.

massacr-are [A I] *tr.* to massacre; to slaughter; to butcher; to slay. **-ante** *part. adj.* (colloq.) exhausting. **-ato** *part. adj.* massacred; slaughtered; butchered; *n.m.pl.* i -ati, the slain. **-atóre** *m.* slaughterer.

massacro *m.* massacre; slaughter; butchery; (herald.) stag's massacre.

massag·gi-o *m.* massage; massaging; massage treatment. **-are** [A 3] *tr.* to massage. **-ato** *part. adj.* massaged. **-atóre** *m.* masseur. **-atrice** *f.* masseuse.

mass-a·ia *f.* housewife; manager of household affairs; buona —

good housewife, thrifty woman. **-a·io** *m.* householder; steward, manager superintendant of a 'massa' or group of farms; husbandman.

massaiola *f.* (orn.) wheatear, *Oenanthe oenanthe*.

†**massari·a** *f.* See **masseria**.

massell-are [A I] *tr.* to hammer, to beat out, to strike (hot iron). **-ato** *part. adj.* hammered, beaten out. **-atura** *f.* hammering; hot iron beaten out. **-o** *m.* lump of red-hot or beaten iron; lump, block, mass; oro in -o, gold ingot.

masseri·a *f.* large farm, large holding; collection of farms under one management; tenancy of farms; farm-house; herds of cattle, stock.

masseri·zi-a *f.* furniture; household goods or effects; thrift; good husbandry; far —, to save, to economize; *pl.* utensils, implements; fittings. **-óso** *adj.* thrifty.

massetere *m.* (anat.) masseter, muscle of the jaw.

masséto *m.* place strewn with boulders, rough country, rocky territory.

massicézza *f.* See under **massiccio**¹.

massicci-are [A 3] *tr.* to lay down foundation or substratum for (a road); to ballast. **-ata** *f.* foundation; ballast; (civ. eng.) road-bed; (rlwy.) ballast. **-ato** *part. adj.* (of a road) laid; ballasted; *n.m.* see **massicciata**.

massic·c-io¹ *adj.* massive, bulky; solid; stout; braccia -e, brawny arms; oro —, solid gold; errore —, enormous blunder, gross error; pubblicità -ia, vast publicity; *n.m.* bulk; main body. **-ézza** *f.* massiveness, bulkiness.

massic·cio² *m.* massif, group of mountain peaks; Massiccio Centrale, Central Massif; (naut.) chock.

†**massillare** *adj.* See **mascellare**, under **mascella**.

mas·sima¹ *f.* maxim, principle; rule; in —, as a rule, as a matter of principle; in linea di —, generally speaking; schizzo di —, general sketch; progetto di —, preliminary project; un accordo di —, an informal arrangement, an understanding; aver per —, to make it a rule, to make a principle of.

mas·sima² *f.* (mus.) large, duplex longa.

massimale *m.* (math.) maximum of a series.

massimal-işmo *m.* (pol.) Maximalism, extreme socialism, Bolshevism. **-ista** *m.* (pol.) maximalist, extreme socialist, Bolshevik, 'Bolshy'.

massimaménte, mas·sime *adv.* especially, chiefly, above all; particularly; most (cf. **massimo**¹).

massimizzare [A I] *tr.* (neol.) to magnify.

mas·simo¹ *adj.* greatest; most; maximum; al — grado, in the highest degree; prezzo —, maximum price, top price; (naut.) circolo —, great circle; *n.m.* maximum; utmost; highest; al —, at the most; il — che posso dirvi, all I can tell you; lo condannarono al — della pena, he was given the maximum penalty.

Mas·simo² *pr.n.m.* Maximus.

massinelli *pr.n.m.* (joc.) young blockhead, stupid boy at school (from the name of a character in a comedy by the Milanese playwright, Ferravilla).

massista *m.* (naut.) one of the crew of a 'mas', q.v.

mass-o *m.* boulder; block (of stone); rock; (geol.) -i erratici, erratic boulders. **-olétta** *f. dim.* of **masso**. **-óso** *adj.* rocky; stony.

mass-óne *m.* freemason; mason. **-oneri·a** *f.* freemasonry. **-o·nico** *adj.* masonic; loggia -onica, masonic lodge.

massor-a *f.* (Jewish rel.) Mas(s)orah, Masoreth. **-éti** *m.pl.* Mas(s)o-retes; *adj. pl.* Mas(s)oretic. **-e·tico** *adj.* Mas(s)oretic.

massoterapi·a *f.* (med.) massotherapy.

mastacc-o *adj.* sturdy; stocky, burly. **-óne** *m.* sturdy person; stocky, burly figure. (**-óna** *f.*)

mast-algi·a *f.* (med.) mastalgia, mastodynia. **-al·gico** *adj.* (med.) mastalgic. **-atrofi·a** *f.* (med.) mastatrophy. **-elcóşi** *f.* (med.) masthelcosis.

mastell-o *m.* (agric.) tub, bucket; — per bucato, wash-tub. †**-a** *f.* see **mastello**. **-are** [A I] *tr.* to put (grapes, olives, etc.) into vats or tubs.

mastic-are [A 2] *tr.* to chew, to masticate; to mutter; to chew over; to ponder, to cogitate; — le parole, to bring one's words out slowly and indistinctly; — una lingua, to know a few words of a language; gomma da —, chewing-gum. **-a·bile** *adj.* capable of being masticated; non -abile, too tough to chew. **-aménto** *m.* masticating; chewing. **-atóre** *m.* masticator. (**-atrice** *f.*) **-ato·rio** *adj.* masticatory. **-atura** *f.* what is chewed; chewing. **-azióne** *f.* mastication.

ma·stic-e *m.* gum mastic; cement; — di vetraio, putty. **-iare** [A 3] *tr.* to putty.

†**mastiette** *f.pl.* (naut.). See **maschette**.

mastiętto *m.* (zool.) *Tapes aureus*, an edible bivalve.

mastino *m.* mastiff; †*adj.* relating to a mastiff; mastiff-like; rough, crude.

†**ma·stio** *m.* See **maschio**.

mastite *f.* (med.) mastitis.

mastod-onte *m.* (zool.) mastodon; (fig.) enormous person, heavily-built, hulking individual. **-on·tico** *adj.* mastodontic, relating to a mastodon; enormous, huge; hulking; bulky.

mast-o·ide *f.* (anat.) mastoid. **-oide·o** *adj.* mastoid; incisura -oidea, mastoid notch. **-oidite** *f.* (med.) mastoid disease, mastoiditis, (pop.) mastoids.

mastra *f.* baker's kneading-trough; (naut.) mast hole or step; space in deck to take a mast or capstan shaft; — di boccaporto, hatch; †mainsail.

†**mastrimpicca** *m.* hangman.

mastro¹ *m.* (comm.) ledger; riportare a —, registrare a —, to post (in a ledger), — a fogli sciolti, loose-leaf ledger; *adj.* libro—, ledger.

†**mastro²** *m.* see **maestro**; this form is still used in certain compound designations, e.g. — d'ascia, master carpenter; — marinaio, master mariner; — di casa, major-domo; Mastro-Impicca, Master-hangman.

†**mastr-uca, -ucca** *f.* sheepskin garment worn by shepherds in Sardinia, Sicily, and Africa.

masturb-are [A I] *rfl.* to masturbate. **-atore** *m.* masturbator. (**-atrice** *f.*) **-azione** *f.* masturbation.

mataco *m.* (zool.). See **macaco**.

matadòr *m. indecl.* matador.

mataf(f)ione *m.* (naut.) sail or awning lacing; gasket; — di terzaruolo, reef point.

matass-a *f.* (text.) hank; skein; (fig.) tangle; arruffare la —, avviluppare la —, to create confusion, to get things muddled; trovare il bandolo della —, to disentangle a complicated matter, to get the clue. **-atore** *m.*, **-atrice** *f.* (text.) hank winder, skeiner. **-ina** *f.* (text.) skein, lea; matassa legata in -ine, skeined hank.

match *m. indecl.* (pron. as Eng.) (sport) match; — nullo, draw.

mate, matè *m.* (bot.) maté, Paraguay tea, *Ilex paraguensis.*

matema·tic-a *f.* mathematics; †astrology. **-o** *m.* mathematician; *adj.* mathematical, mathematic. **-amente** *adv.* mathematically.

mateologi·a *f.* mataeology, vain or unprofitable discourse, discussion or study of useless subjects.

matera¹ *f.* (naut.) rib of a ship, ship's beam.

†**matera²** *f.* See **materia**.

materass-a *f.* mattress; — a molle, spring mattress. **-a·io** *m.* mattress-maker, mattress-manufacturer. **-o** *m.* see **materassa**.

mate·ri-a *f.* matter; substance, material; subject; indice delle -e, table of contents; si vede che è padrone della sua —, one can see that he is master of his subject; approvato in tutte le -e, passed in all subjects; (med.) (philos.) — prima, primary (primordial) matter; (leg.) matter; — per un processo, grounds to take proceedings; in — di, in the matter of…, re…; in — di legge, in point of law; le azioni in — di invenzioni industriali, Patent actions (C.C.); in — d'amministrazione, where administration is concerned, as far as administration goes; non hanno competenza in —, they have no competence here, they have no authority on such a point; (econ.) — prima, raw material. **-ato** *adj.* composed; -ato di, consisting of, composed of.

material-e *adj.* material; physical; bodily; manual; gross, coarse; sensual; clumsy; prosaic, unimaginative, matter-of-fact; actual, effectual; possesso —, vacant possession; un errore —, a clerical error; (leg.) falsità —, concrete (as distinguished from 'abstract') falsification (C.P.); *n.m.* material; — bellico, war material; (leg.) le opere fatte con -i propri, works carried out with one's own materials (C.C.); (comm.) consumo del —, wear and tear. **-mente** *adv.* materially; physically; bodily; coarsely; unimaginatively. **-ismo** *m.* materialism. **-ista** *m.* materialist. **-i·stico** *adj.* materialistic. **-ità** *f.* materiality, the character of being material. **-izzare** [A I] *tr.* to render material; to represent as material; (spiritualism) -izzare spettri, to materialize spirits by means of ectoplasm; *rfl.* (spiritualism) to materialize, to be materialized. **-izzazione** *f.*, (spiritualism) materialization. **-one** *m.* (colloq.) coarse, clumsy, uncouth man; unimaginative, matter-of-fact individual.

materiato *adj.* See under **materia**.

matern-o *adj.* maternal; motherly; l'amor —, maternal love, mother-love; lingua -a, native language, mother tongue; terra -a, motherland, mother country; avo —, ancestor on one's mother's side, maternal ancestor; (leg.) diritto —, maternal right. **-amente** *adv.* maternally; in a motherly way. **-ità** *f.* maternity; motherhood; casa di -ità, maternity home; ospedale di -ità, maternity hospital; (leg.) la domanda per la dichiarazione di -ità naturale, application for declaration of maternal descent (C.C.).

ma·tero *m.* (bot.) shoot from a pollarded tree.

materoz·zolo *m.* small wooden tab to which keys are attached.

matit-a *f.* black lead, graphite; pencil, lead-pencil; crayon, chalk; disegni a tre -e, drawings made in black, white and red chalk; — sfera, ball-pointed pen. **-atoio** *m.* pencil-box, pencil-case.

†**ma·tre** *f.* see **madre**. **-ma** *f.* my mother. **-ta** *f.* thy mother. **-selva** *f.* see **madreselva**, under **madre**.

†**ma·tria** *f.* motherland.

matriarc-ale *adj.* matriarchal. **-ato** *m.* matriarchy; (leg.) matriarchate.

matriciana *adv. phr.* (cul. Rome) spaghetti alla —, sphaghetti with pieces of tomato, bacon, etc., seasoned with peppers.

matric-e *f.* (anat.) matrix; (fig.) mould; (comm.) counterfoil; (eng.) die; (typ.) matrix; (poet.) mother; *adj.* chiesa —, principal church. **-ale** *adj.* (anat.) pertaining to the womb, uterine. **-ina** *f.* (zool.) pecora -ina, ewe. **-ino** *m.* (bot.) joining shoots left to grow as brushwood; (zool.) a ram or other male animal kept for breeding.

matric-ida *m., f.* (*pl.m.*, *f.* **-idi**) (leg.) (person guilty of) matricide. **-i·dio** *m.* (*pl.* **-i·dii**) crime of matricide; case of matricide.

matricin-a *f.*, **-o** *m.* See under **matrice**.

matri·col-a *f.* register, roll; register fee or number; (Univ.) matriculation; matriculation fee or number; freshman, first-year man (or woman) student; festa delle -e, freshers' rag; (hist.) qualifications entitling a person to practise an art or profession; tax charged for the practice of same; place or register where practitioners were enrolled. **-are** [A I S] *tr.* to register; (Univ.) to enter on the matriculation roll; *rfl.* to matriculate; to enter a University. **-ato** *part. adj.* registered; matriculated; (fig.) thorough, out-and-out; un birbante -ato, an arrant knave; un furbo -ato, a thorough-paced cunning rascal. **-azione** *f.* registration; (Univ.) matriculation. **-ino** *m.* (Univ.) freshman, first-year man.

matrign-a *f.* stepmother; (fig.) unloving mother; cruel mother. **-esco** *adj.* (*m.pl.* **-eschi**) like a stepmother; unloving; cruel. **-escamente** *adv.* unfeelingly; cruelly.

matrimo·ni-o *m.* wedlock; matrimony; chiedere in —, to ask in marriage; marriage, wedding; match; — d'amore, — d'inclinazione, love-match; — di convenienza, *mariage de convenance*; (leg.) marriage, matrimony; — concordatario, marriage conforming to Concordat with Holy See; — civile, civil marriage; — in imminente pericolo di vita, marriage *in extremis*; — legittimo, legal marriage, lawful wedlock; — morganatico, morganatic marriage; — davanti all'ufficiale di stato civile, marriage before Registrar; l'atto di celebrazione di —, registration of marriage; marriage certificate; marriage lines; la celebrazione di —, celebration of (religious) marriage, performance of (civil) wedding ceremony; il contratto di —, ante-nuptial contract, marriage contract, marriage settlement; l'inadempienza di promessa di —, breach of promise of marriage; la pubblicazione di —, publication of notice of marriage (C.C.); ratto a fine di —, abduction with object of marriage (C.P.). **-ale** *adj.* matrimonial; conjugal; nuptial; letto -ale, double-bed; (leg.) causa -ale, matrimonial cause; i capitoli, le convenzioni -ali, marriage articles, marriage settlement (C.C.). **-almente** *adv.* matrimonially; conjugally. **-one** *m. augm.* splendid marriage, wealthy marriage, fine match.

†**matrina** *f.* godmother.

matrizzare [A I] *intr.* (*aux.* avere) to take after one's mother, to resemble, to favour, one's mother.

matr-ona *f.* matron, married woman. **-onale** *adj.* matronly. **-onalmente** *adv.* in a matronly way. **-o·neo** *m.* (eccl.) gynaeceum, part of church reserved for women (esp. in churches of Byzantine pattern).

matroni·mico *adj.* matronymic.

matta *f.* mad woman, insane woman; (colloq.) crazy woman; (cards) joker, 'wild' card which can be made to vary in value according to the convenience of the player (at poker, canasta, etc.); *adj. f.* of **matto**, q.v.

mattacchione *m.* jolly individual, a good sport; wag, 'nut'; scatterbrain; an eccentric.

mattacin·o *m.* acrobat, strolling dancer; jester; mimic; (colloq.) slightly crazy but lively person; (lit. hist.) *I Mattacini*, title of a series of sonnets written by Caro against Castelvetro. **-ata** *f.* a trick characteristic of a 'mattacino'.

mattadore *m.* matador.

mattafione *m.* (naut.). See **matafione**.

mattaion·e *m.* (geol.) a barren kind of clay soil. (**-oso** *adj.*)

mattana *f.* fit of bad humour, depression, bad temper; spleen; lasciategli passare la —, wait till his evil mood passes; whim, mad freak.

matt·are [A I] *tr.* (chess) to checkmate; to kill, to slaughter; (fig.) to conquer; †to torture; †to punish. **-anza** *f.* capture and slaughter of tunny fish. **-atoio** *m.* slaughter-house. **-atore** *m.* slaughterer; conqueror. **-azione** *f.* slaughter (of animals).

mattarella *f.* long club used by cattle-drovers.

matt-ata *f.*, **-eggiare** [A 3 C]. See under **matto**.

†mattema·tica *f.* see **matematica**; (joc.) studiar la —, to be mad.

Matte·o *pr.n.m.* Matthew; (joc.) madman; secondo —, as the whim takes him; (dial., joc.) husband.

matterello[1] *m.* rolling-pin; roller (for a towel).

matterello[2] *adj.* See under **matto**.

†matteri·a *f.* See under **matto**.

†mat·tero *m.* cudgel, club; rolling-pin (cf. **matterello**[1]).

matt-ezza *f.*, **-i·a** *f.*, **-ic·cio** *adj.* See under **matto**.

mattin-a *f.* morning; dawn; forenoon; domani —, tomorrow morning; ier —, yesterday morning. **-ale** *adj.* matutinal; of the morning, occurring in the morning; lezioni -ali, morning lessons. **-ata** *f.* duration of the morning; morning time; forenoon; -ata nebbiosa, misty morning; ha perduto tutta la -ata allo specchio, she has spent the whole morning in front of her mirror; (mus.) aubade, dawn-song; -ata musicale, morning concert; (theatr.) matinée, afternoon performance. **-iero** *adj.* early morning; good at getting up in the morning. **-o** *m.* early morning; dawn; di buon -o, early in the morning; (N. Ital.) morning; name of an Italian newspaper (cf. Fr. 'Matin'); (fig., poet.) beginning, dawn; il -o della vita, youth, the morning of life; esposto al -o, facing east, that gets the morning sun.

matt-o *adj.* mad, insane, deranged; diventar —, to go mad, to go off one's head, to go out of one's mind; — da legare, — da catena, stark staring mad, raving, crazy, eccentric, foolish; extreme; ho una voglia -a di, I'm longing to; gusto —, frantic delight; testa -a, hot-headed fool; cavallo —, horse that is difficult to manage; pecore -e, sheep that have the staggers; fila -e, short threads in a tangled skein; (chess) scacco —, checkmate; dare scacco — a, to checkmate, (fig.) to defeat; (of colour) mat, dull, lustreless; oro —, dull gold; penna -a, down, downy feathers on a bird; — di, crazy about, wild about; va — per la musica, he's crazy about music; — dalla gioia, wild with joy; †weak, under-developed; *n.m.* madman, lunatic; crazy fool; (cards) joker; (in the game of Tarocchi) a card which can neither take nor be taken; (fig.) esser come il — ne' tarocchi, to be welcome everywhere; (at roulette) the partition occupied by the zero. **-a** *f.* mad woman, insane woman; crazy, foolish woman. **-ata** *f.* mad action; foolish behaviour; foolery. **-eggiare** [A 3 C] *intr.* (*aux.* avere) to play the fool. **-erello** *adj.* foolish, crazy, silly. †**-eri·a** *f.* madness; mad action; mad words, extravagance, freak of madness. **-ezza** *f.*, **-i·a** *f.* madness; whim; freak; craze; foolish action, piece of foolishness. **-ic·cio** *adj.* light-headed, frivolous; thoughtless, feckless. **-o·ide** *adj.* half-mad, half-crazy; partly deranged; *n.m.* madcap; half-crazy person.

mattolina *f.* (orn.) woodlark.

matton·e *m.* brick; tile; — refrattario, fire-brick; -i crudi, unbaked bricks; -i cotti, baked bricks; -i arrotati, rubbed bricks; -i lustri, glazed bricks; -i verniciati, highly glazed bricks; — leggiero, — galleggiante, a light porous brick that floats in water; — pianello, — pianella, a flat roofing-tile; muro di mezzo —, a wall as thick as a brick is broad; muro di un —, wall as thick as a brick is long; — per coltello, — per ritto, — per taglio, a brick laid edgeways on its side; muro a -i per ritto, a thin wall built of bricks on edge; avere que' tre -i, to have a little house; — sopra —, two simpletons together; far tre passi in un —, to move very slowly; (cards) diamonds; è un —, he (it) is very heavy, very boring (of person, book, etc.); avere un — sullo stomaco, to have a weight on one's stomach (i.e. indigestion). **-a·ia** *f.* brick-yard, brick-field. **-a·io** *m.* brick-maker, brick-manufacturer. **-ame** *m.*

quantity of bricks (usu. rubble); brick-work. **-are** [A I C] *tr.* to pave with bricks; to cover (floor) with tiles. **-ato** *part. adj.* paved with bricks; *n.m.* tiled floor. **-ella** *f. dim.* small brick; floor-tile; paving-tile; cushion of billiard-table; di -ella, on the rebound; (fig.) indirectly; ice to eat in shape of a brick; briquette of coal; a boys' game (see **muriella**).

mattu·gio *adj.* (orn.) passera mattugia, tree sparrow, *Passer montanus*; (fig.) feeble-minded.

mattutin-o *adj.* of the morning; matutinal; early; stella -a, the morning star; *n.m.* (liturg.) Matins. †**-ale** *adj.* matutinal, early.

†matu·polo *m.* confused heap.

matur-are [A I] *intr.* (*aux.* essere) to ripen, to mature, to come to maturity; to become due; far —, to maturate; i tempi -ano, the time is nearly ripe; (provb.) col tempo e con la paglia -ano le sorbe, time and patience bring all things to maturity; (comm.) to mature, to fall due, to become payable; (med.) to come to a head, to suppurate; *tr.* to cause to mature, to maturate, to mature, to ripen; — un pensiero, to mature a thought, to ponder upon an idea; *rfl.* to become ripe, to ripen, to mature. **-amento** *m.* ripening, maturing; maturating; falling due. **-ante** *part. adj.* ripening, maturing; (med.) suppurating. **-anza** *f.* see **maturazione**. **-ativo** *adj.* having the power or function of maturing; of or pertaining to maturation; (med.) maturative. **-ato** *part. adj.* ripened, matured; (comm.) due, matured; pagare i frutti prima che siano -ati, to pay the interest before it falls due. **-azione** *f.* ripening, maturing; maturation; precoce -azione, early ripening; tarda -azione, late ripening; venire a -azione, to come to maturity, (fig.) to come to a head; (comm.) maturity; (med.) suppuration.

matur-o *adj.* ripe, mature, fully developed; età -a, anni -i, prime, mature age; giudizio —, mature judgement; sound, reflective, experienced; i tempi non sono -i, the time is not ripe; dopo -a discussione, on mature consideration; — a un ufficio, sufficiently experienced for a function or office; (med.) parto —, confinement at full time; tumore —, suppurating tumour; tosse -a, cough with phlegm, loose cough. **-amente** *adv.* maturely. **-ità** *f.* ripeness; venire a piena -ità, to become perfectly ripe; maturity; completion; esame di -ità, school-leaving examination, entrance examination to a University.

Matusalemme *pr.n.m.* Methuselah; avrà oramai gli anni di —, he must be as old as Methuselah.

ma·u *excl., onom.* miaow.

maurino *adj., n.m.* (eccl.) Maurist.

Mauri·zi·o *pr.n.m.* Maurice; (geog.) Mauritius; l'isola — Mauritius. **-ano** *adj.* of Mauritius; of the Knightly Order of St Maurice and St Lazarus.

ma·uro *adj.* of Mauretania; Moorish; *n.m.* inhabitant of Mauretania; Moor.

mauro·lico *m.* (ichth.) a small marine fish.

mausole·o *m.* (anct. hist.) the tomb of Mausolus, satrap of Caria, at Halicarnassus (one of the seven wonders of the world); mausoleum.

†mavi *m.* light blue.

mavor·zio *adj.* (poet.) of Mars, martial.

ma·ximum *m. indecl.* maximum.

mazaneta *f.* (zool.). See **masaneta**.

mazurca *f.* (mus.) Mazurka.

mazz-a *f.* cudgel, club; walking-stick; hammer, sledge-hammer; pole-axe; stamper; (typ.) rounce; staff; handle; bar between the legs of a chair; mallet; menare alla —, to lead (an animal) to slaughter; (fig.) to lure to destruction; girar la — attorno, to deal blows all round; (fig.) to speak ill of everything and everyone; (sport) bat; (mus.) drumstick; — di grancassa, bass drumstick; (eccl.) mace; (text.) bruising mail (for flax); (paint.) maulstick, mahlstick; (bot.) — d'oro, yellow loosestrife, *Lysimachia vulgaris*; — di San Giuseppe, oleander, *Nerium oleander*; — sorda, reed-mace, *Typha*. **-ata** *f.* blow with a cudgel, stunning blow; (fig.) blow. **-etta** *f. dim.* cane; mallet; hammer; (of paper) quire.

†mazzacastello *m.* monkey for pile-driving.

mazzacavallo *m.* long lever working on a pivot for raising water from a well; pile driver.

mazzac·chera *f.* eel-pot.

mazzacorto *m.* coil of cod-line; string for winding a child's top.

†mazzacul-are *intr.* to fall head over heels. **-o** *m.* fall, tumble.

mazzafrusto *m.* cat-o'-nine-tails; a sling.

mazzagatti *m. indecl.* pocket pistol.

†**mazzamarrone** *m.* booby; simpleton; large, gross individual.

†**mazzamurro** *m.* crumbs made up into cattle-food.

mazzancollo *m.* (bot.) corn cockle, *Agrostemma githago*.

mazza-picchiare [A4] *tr.* to beetle, to ram, to strike with a mallet. **-pic·chio** *m.* beetle, mallet.

mazzata *f.* See under **mazza**.

maz·zer-a *f.* bag of stones for weighting down the net used in tunny fishing. **-are** [A I s] *tr.* to drown by throwing into the water inside a sack with a heavy weight attached.

mazzerang-a *f.* beetle, rammer for turf. **-are** [A2] *tr.* to level; to tread (ground).

mazziere *m.* mace-bearer; dealer (at cards).

mazziniano *adj.* (hist.) Mazzinian; pertaining to Giuseppe Mazzini; *n.m.* follower of Mazzini; admirer of Mazzini.

mazz-o *m.* a bunch (of flowers, keys, etc.); group (of persons); bundle; ball (of wool); coil (of rope); club; stick; rammer; mettere a —, to gather together; metter tutti in un —, to lump everyone together; tutti insieme fanno un bel —!, all together they make a fine set of people!; (cards) the pack; fare il —, to deal; mischiare il —, to shuffle. **-ętto** *m. dim.* little bundle; small bunch; nosegay; bouquet; cantare le litanie a -etti, to group the invocations of the Litany in threes; (bot.) fiori a -etto, corymb. **-ettino** *m. dim.* small bunch; fare il -ettino, to shuffle cards unfairly. **-olino** *m. dim.* little bunch; (of flowers) nosegay; il giuoco del -olino, game of the names of flowers. **-one** *m. augm.* large bunch. **-otto** *m.* mallet.

mazzoc·chio *m.* ducal cap; an ornament for a cap; part of the headgear formerly worn by higher magistrates at Florence; aggiustare il — a uno, to bring a person to his senses; (archit.) torus of a column.

mazz(u)ol-a *f.* stone-breaker's hammer; mallet; execution of criminals by clubbing; †little stick. **-are** [A I] *tr.* to kill by clubbing; to hammer; to thresh. **-ata** *f.* blow with a hammer or mallet. **-o** *m.* stone-breaker's hammer; mallet; *pl.* strips of arable land in the Maremma of Tuscany raised above the swamp level and separated from each other by ditches.

mazzone[1] *m. augm.* See under **mazzo**.

mazzone[2] *m.* (ichth.) grey mullet, *Mugil cephalus*.

†**mazzoneri·a** *f.* masonry; drawing or painting of architectural background in a painting.

†**mazzucolare** *intr.* to fall headlong.

me[1] *1st pers. prn. disjunct.* me; secondo —, in my opinion; tra — e —, in my own mind, in my heart of hearts; dissi tra —, I said to myself; l'ho fatto da —, I did it by myself; che m'importa a —?, what does it matter to *me*?; non saper nè di te nè di —, to be empty or insipid; o — disgraziata!, o poor me!; nel mio —, as far as I am concerned, in my situation; il mio Signor —, I myself; fate come —, do as I do; ne sai quanto —, you know as much as I do about it; tu non sei —, you're not in my shoes, you are not me.

me[2] *1st pers. prn. conjunct.* See under **mi**.

me'[1] abbrev. of **meglio**, q.v.

me'[2] abbrev. of **mezzo**[1], q.v.

Mea *pr.n.f.* abbrev. of **Bartolomea**; a game played with figures and pointer.

mea culpa, meaculpa (Lat. phrase from the *Confiteor*) 'through my own fault'; *n.m.* dire, recitare, il —, to confess one's guilt, to cry *peccavi*.

meandro *m.* meandering, winding, maze.

†**meare** *intr.* to flow, to trickle; to pass along a canal; to derive; to be transferred.

meato *m.* (anat.) meatus, channel, passage; canal.

Mecca[1] *pr.n.f.* (geog.) Mecca; (fig.) an ideal place; arrivare a —, to reach one's Mecca; va alla —!, go to the devil!; a distant place; pare che venga dalla —, he looks as though he's come from Timbuctoo; vieni dalla —?, where have you been all this time?, how is it you haven't heard?

mecca[2] *f.* varnish for gilding silver.

mecc-a·nica *f.* mechanics; (phys.) — degli aeriformi, pneumatics. **-anicamente** *adv.* mechanically. **-a·nico** *adv.* mechanical; machine-like; automatic; (text.) lana -anica, shoddy; remanufactured wool; †of the working-class; *n.m.* mechanic; mechanician; engineer; operator; driver; †member of the working-class. **-anismo** *m.* mechanism; gear; works; machinery; il -anismo di un orologio, the works of a watch; il -anismo amministrativo, the

administrative set-up. **-anizzare** [A I] *tr.* to mechanize. (**-anizzato** *part. adj.*) **-anizzazione** *f.* mechanization.

†**mecco** *m.* adulterer.

Mecenat-e *pr.n.m.* Maecenas; (fig.) patron. **-ismo** *m.* system of patronage. **-eri·a** *f.* protection, patronage.

mechitarrista *m.* (rel. hist.) Mekhitarist; one of the Armenian Benedictines whose mother house is in S. Lazzaro, Venice.

męco *pers. prn.* and *prep.* (poet.) with me.

meco·n-io *m.* (med.) meconium, first faeces of new-born infant; †juice of a poppy. **-ico** *adj.* (med.) meconic.

meda *f.* (naut.) beacon (at sea).

meda·gl-ia *f.* medal; ancient coin; horse brass; il rovescio della —, the reverse of the medal; il diritto della —, the obverse of the medal; (fig.) ogni — ha il suo rovescio, there are two sides to every question; (comm.) — di presenza, attendance fee. **-iere** *m.* collection of coins or medals; cabinet of coins. **-ione** *m.* medallion; (fig.) portrait (written); (joc.) dignified but heavy personage. **-ista** *m.* coin-collector, numismatist; maker of medals, engraver.

†**medela** *f.* medicine.

medęsim-o, †**medesmo**, †**medemo** *adj.* same, selfsame; al — tempo, at the same time; *prn.* self: lo vidi io —, I saw it myself; egli —, he himself; l'uomo —, the very man. **-amente** *adv.* likewise, in the same way. **-are** [A I] *rfl.* (*prep.* con) to identify oneself (with); to merge (into). †**ezza** *f.* identity; sameness.

me·dia *f.* average, mean; in —, on an average; (comm.) average (in appos.) prezzo —, average price, *or* middle price; (geog.) — annua, annual mean; — annua normale, normal annual mean; — diurna, daily mean; — mensile, monthly mean; (soccer) — inglese, system of scoring which, in assessing results, takes into account whether a given match (won, drawn or lost) was played at home or away.

mediana *f.* centre line; (soccer) half-back line; (watchm.) grande —, large driving wheel.

medi-a·nico *adj.* mediumistic; by means of a spiritualist medium; pertaining to phenomena produced by a spiritualistic medium. **-anismo** *m.* mediumism.

median-o *adj.* middle, medium; (archit.) arco —, middle arch; (watchm.) ruota -a, third wheel and pinion; (naut.) albero —, mizzen mast; remo —, stroke oar; scuttle strongback; (med.) median; *n.m.* (soccer) half-back; centro —, centre-half; — destro, right-half; — sinistro, left-half; -i laterali, wing-halves; (rugger) *pl.* backs; — di apertura, fly-half or stand-off; — di mischia, scrum-half.

mediante *prep.* by means of; through; si può entrare — questo biglietto, you can get in by using this ticket; — l'aiuto di, with the help of.

†**mediare** *intr.* to be interposed, to come between.

media·stin-o *m.* (anat.) mediastinum; *adj.* mediastinal. **-a** *f.* mediastinal vein. **-e·o** *adj.* mediastinal. **-ite** *f.* (med.) mediastinitis.

medi-ato *adj.* indirect; interposed; intermediate. **-atamente** *adv.* indirectly; through an intermediary. **-atore** *m.* mediator; intermediary, middle-man, broker; agent; -atore di borsa, stockbroker; (cards) the same game as Quadrigliati or Quadresella; (leg.) broker; commission-agent; go-between; -atore professionale, commercial broker; la pluralità di -atori, duplication, multiplicity of go-betweens; la provvigione del -atore, broker's, go-between's, commission (C.C.). **-atrice** *f.* mediatrix. **-azione** *f.* mediation; brokerage, commission; (leg.) agency as go-between; brokerage; commission-agency (C.C.).

me·dic-a *f.* woman doctor. **-ona** *f.* female quack doctor; faith healer (cf. **medico**).

medic-are [A 2 s] *tr.* to doctor, to treat; to heal, to medicate; — una ferita, to dress a wound; *rfl.* to doctor oneself; to dose oneself, to take medicine. **-a·bile** *adj.* curable. **-amento** *m.* medicament, remedy; treatment. **-amentoso** *adj.* medicinal. **-atore** *m.* medicator; healer; *adj.* healing, curative. (**-atrice** *f.*) **-atura** *f.* (med.) medication, treatment. **-azione** *f.* medication, treatment; posto di -azione, first-aid post.

medi·ceo *adj.* (Ital. hist.) Medicean, relating to the Medici.

medicheri·a *f.* out-patient department.

medichęssa *f.* woman doctor, lady doctor.

medicin-a *f.* medicine; facoltà di —, faculty of medicine; studente in —, medical student, medical; esercitare la —, to practise medicine; — legale, forensic medicine; physic, medicine; remedy; (fig.) cure. **-ale** *adj.* medicinal; *n.m.* drug, medicine, potion, draught of medicine; remedy. **-almente** *adv.* medicinally.

me·dic-o *m.* doctor; physician; medical man; medical officer; (fig.) healer; — condotto, panel doctor, municipal doctor; — curante, doctor in charge of a case; — specialista, specialist; — chirurgo, surgeon; donna-medico, woman doctor; *adj.* medicinal; medical; cura -a, medical treatment; certificato —, medical certificate; (bot.) erba -a, lucerne, *Medicago sativa*; erba -a di fiore giallo, sickle medick, *M. falcato*. **-astro** *m.* quack doctor, charlatan.

medievale *adj.* and derivs. See **medioevale**.

me·di-o *adj.* intermediate; middle; middling; average; mean, medium; il — Evo, the Middle Ages; età -a, middle-age; di età -a, di -a età, middle-aged; (boxing) di peso —, middle-weight; velocità -a, average speed; scuole -e, secondary schools (in Italy); *n.m.* mean; mean term; middle-finger.

mediocr-e *adj.* mediocre; middling; common-place, ordinary; indifferent, poor, second-rate. (**-emente** *adv.*) **-ità** *f.* mediocrity; narrowness, narrow-mindedness; l'aurea -ità, the golden mean; la felice -ità, the happy mean.

medioev-ale *adj.* medieval. **-alista** *m.* medievalist. **-o** *m.* Middle Ages.

medit-are [A I s] *tr.* to meditate upon, to reflect on, to ponder; to plan, to design, to think out; to plot; *intr.* (*aux.* avere) to meditate, to muse, to browse. **-a·bile** *adj.* worthy of meditation; worth thinking over; needing consideration. **-abondo** *m.* meditative, thoughtful, reflective; sunk in meditation, pensive; *n.m.* meditative, reflective type of person. **-amento** *m.* meditating; thought. **-ativo** *adj.* meditative. **-ato** *part. adj.* meditated, thought over; thought out. **-atamente** *adv.* designedly; deliberately; advisedly; after due consideration. **-azione** *f.* meditation; thoughtfulness; pensiveness; musing.

mediterra·neo *adj.* (geog.) Mediterranean; *pr.n.m.* (geog.) the Mediterranean.

me·dium *m. indecl.* spiritualistic medium.

Medusa *pr.n.f.* Medusa; (zool.) medusa.

Mefisto·f-ele *pr.n.m.* Mephistopheles. **-e·lico** *adj.* Mephistophelean; sardonic.

mef-ite *f.* mephitis; fetid air; (zool.) skunk, *Mephitis* spp. **-i·tico** *adj.* fetid, pestilential; mephitic.

mega·cero *m.* (zool.) extinct 'Irish elk', *Megaceros*.

megaciclo *m.* (phys.; radio) megacycle.

mega·fono *m.* megaphone; loudspeaker.

mega·l-ito *m.* megalith. **-i·tico** *adj.* megalithic.

megalo-cardi·a *f.* (med.) megalocardia, cardiac hypertrophy. **-cefali·a** *f.* megalocephaly. **-ce·falo** *adj.* megalocephalic.

megal-o·mane *m.* megalomaniac. **-omani·a** *f.* megalomania.

mega·scopo *m.* megascope.

mega-ohm *m. indecl.* (electr.) megohm.

Megera *pr.n.f.* (myth.) Megaera (one of the Furies); (fig.) witch, hag; (ent.) *Pararge megera*, a kind of butterfly.

†meg·gia *f.* dung.

meggion-e *m.* phlegmatic person; simpleton. (**-a** *f.*)

me·glio *compar. adv.* better; mi sento — oggi, I feel better today; tanto —!, so much the better!; amerei — andare domani, I should prefer to go tomorrow; per — dire, to put it in a better way (in speaking and writing); (Note: it is often used instead of the adjective 'migliore': non potreste trovarne delle —, could you not find any better ones?); fare alla —, to do the best one can in the circumstances.

megliorare [A I] and derivs. See **migliorare**.

meiosi *f.* (biol.) meiosis.

mel-a *f.* apple; — cotogna, quince; — renetta, rennet; — del duomo, ball on top of a cathedral dome; rose of a watering-pot; buttock. **-a·ia** *f.* apple-woman. **-a·io** *m.* apple-vendor. **-are** [A I c] *tr.* (colloq.) to pelt with apples; to jeer at; farsi -are, to draw ridicule on oneself. **-ata** *f.* blow or pelting with apples; jibe.

†melacchino *adj.* tasting of honey.

melagran-a *f.* (zool.) *Calappa granulata*, a kind of crab; (bot.) pomegranate. **-o** *m.* pomegranate tree (cf. **melograno**).

melampo *m.* (zool.) Impala antelope, *Aepyceros melampus*.

melanc-oli·a *f.*, **-oni·a** *f.* See **malinconia**.

melan·gola *f.* (bot.) Seville or bitter orange, *Citrus aurantium*.

melan-ismo *m.* (biol.) melanism. **-ite** *f.* (miner.) a dark variety of garnet.

melanzana *f.* (bot.) aubergine, egg-plant, brinjal (in India), *Solanum melongena*.

melap·pio *m.* rennet apple syrup.

melaran·ci-a *f.* orange. **-o** *m.* orange-tree.

melare [A I c] and derivs. See under **mela**.

†mela·rio *m.* bee-hive.

melassa *f.* molasses.

melata¹ *f.* See under **mela**.

melata² *f.* honey-dew.

melato *adj.* sweet, honeyed.

†mele *m.* See **miele**.

†melea *f.* hand-to-hand fight, mêlée.

melega·rio *m.* (bot.) stalk of great millet, *Sorghum vulgare*.

melena *f.* (med.) melaena.

†melengiana *f.* See **melanzana**.

melens-o *adj.* dull, stupid, silly. **-ag·gine** *f.* stupidity; silliness.

meleto *m.* apple orchard; (joc.) the buttocks.

†meletrice *f.* See **meretrice**.

me·l-ia *f.* (bot.) Persian lilac, bead tree, *Melia azecarach*. **-i·aca** *f.* apricot. **-i·aco** *m.* (bot.) apricot tree, *Prunus armeniaca*.

melica *f.* (bot.) great millet, *Sorghum vulgare*.

†melichino *m.* mead.

me·lico *adj.* melic; poesia melica, melic poetry.

melifaga *f.* (orn.). See **mellisuga**.

melilite *f.* (miner.) melilite.

meliloto *m.* (bot.) — odoroso, melilot, *Melilotus*.

melinite *f.* (chem.) melinite.

melism-a *m.* (mus.) melisma. **-a·tico** *adj.* (mus.) melismatic; *n.m.* (mus.) melismatic chant.

melissa¹ *f.* (bot.) balm, *Melissa officinalis*.

Melissa² *pr.n.f.* Melissa.

mellett-a *f.* mud, slime. **-one** *m. augm.* thick mud.

melli·fero *adj.* honey-bearing; honey-producing.

mellific-are [A 2 s] *intr.* (*aux.* avere) to make honey. **-azione** *f.* honey-making.

melli·flu-o *adj.* mellifluous; parole -e, honeyed words. **-amente** *adv.* mellifluously. **-ità** *f.* mellifluence; mellifluousness.

†melli·foro *adj.* See **mellifero**.

melliloto *m.* See **meliloto**.

†mellina *f.* (text.) Malines cloth.

mellisuga *f.* (orn.) honey-sucker, honey-eater, family Meliphagidae; name also given to various humming-birds.

mell-itato *m.* (chem.) mellitate. **-i·tico** *adj.* (chem.) mellitic. **-itoso** *m.* (chem.) raffinose, mellitose. **-ite** *f.* (miner.) mellite.

mellon-e *m.* see **melone**. **-ag·gine** *f.* stupidity. **-a·io** *m.* melon-bed.

melm-a, melma *f.* mire, mud (esp. that deposited by floods); slime; †coating in the mouth due to indigestion. **-oso** *adj.* muddy.

melo¹ *m.* (bot.) apple-tree, *Malus silvestris*.

†mel-o² *m.*, **†-oda**, **†-ode** *f.* (mus.) melody.

mel-odi·a *f.* (mus.) melody; — popolare, folk-song. **-odiare** [A 4] *intr.* (*aux.* avere) (mus.) to melodize. **-odiante** *part. adj.* (mus.) melodizing. **-o·dica** *f.* (mus.) a kind of keyed instrument with a flute-stop; melody. **-o·dico** *adj.* (mus.) melodic. **-odicamente** *adv.* (mus.) melodically. **-o·dicon** *m. indecl.* (mus.) melodicon, a kind of keyboard instrument in which the sound is produced by the friction of metal pins against a steel cylinder. **-o·dion** *m. indecl.* (mus.) melodion, in both senses, viz. a keyboard instrument invented by Dietz, and a kind of harmonium. **-odioso** *adj.* (mus.) melodious. **-odista** *m., f.* (mus.) melodist. **-odramma** *m.* (mus.) serious opera. Note: this word must never be translated by the English 'melodrama', for which the Italian equivalent is **melologo**, q.v. **-odramac·cio** *m.* (mus.) bad opera. **-odramma·tico** *adj.* (mus.) operatic. **-odrammatista** *m., f.* (mus.) opera composer. **-ofa·ro** *m.* (mus.) music-lantern with paper transparencies on which music for serenades is printed. **-o·fono** *m.* (mus.) melophone, a free-reed instrument in the shape of a guitar. **-o·logo** *m.* (mus.) melodrama, i.e. speech accompanied by orchestral music whether in a play or not. **-o·mane** *adj.* music-mad; *n.m., f.* person who is mad about music. **-omani·a** *f.* (mus.) melomania. **-omani·aco** *adj., n.m.* see **melomane**. (**-omani·aca** *f.*) **-ope·a** *f.* (mus.) melopoeïa, art of melodizing; counterpoint. **†-ope·o** *m.* (mus.) contrapuntist. **-opiano** *m.* (mus.) melopiano, pianoforte with device for producing sustained sounds. **-oplasto** *m.* (mus.) meloplast, device for teaching the elements of music by visual means. **-os** *m. indecl.* (mus.) melos, melody (with particular reference to Wagner). **-otrage·dia** *f.* (mus.) tragic opera.

melocatto *m.* (bot.) melon thistle, Turk's head cactus, *Melocactus communis*.

melo·faga *f.* (ent.) sheep tick, ked, *Melophagus ovinus.*

melo·gono *m.* (bot.) kind of black grape, very sweet.

melo·logo *m.* See under **melodia.**

melolonta *f.* (ent.). See **maggiolino**[1].

melone *m.* (bot.) — a pane, melon, *Cucumis melo*; — d'acqua, water melon, *Citrullus vulgaris.*

melopopone *m.* (bot.) squash, pumpkin, *Cucurbita pepo,* var *melo-pepo.*

melopsit·taco *m.* (orn.) budgerigar, *Melopsittacus undulatus.*

membran-a *f.* (anat.; bot.) membrane; (eng.) diaphragm; (fig.) thin tissue, film; — mucosa, mucous membrane.

membrato *adj.* (herald.) membered.

membratura *f.* frame, structure; framework; (archit.) arrangement (of the several parts of a building).

membr-o (*pl.* **-a** *f.*) limb, member; racquistò l'uso delle -a, he regained the use of his limbs; (fig.) part, section; (*pl.* **-i** *m.*) member; i -i di una famiglia, the members of a family; i -i di una società, the members of a society; quanti sono i -i?, how many members are there?, how extensive is the membership?; — onorario, honorary member; — di diritto, member as of right; — investito di tutti i poteri, fully-fledged member; — a vita, life-member; qualità di —, membership; (gramm.; math.) term; (archit.) member, feature. **-etto** *m. dim.* (archit.) subordinate feature; moulding, ornament. **-ettare** [A I c] *tr.* (archit.) to ornament (with mouldings, bosses, etc.). **†-ificare** *tr.* (paint.) to design, to arrange the several parts of a picture. **-olino** *m. dim.* of **membro. -uto** *adj.* stout-limbed, well-built.

memento *m.* memento.

Memfi *pr.n.f.* (geog.) Memphis.

meminna *f.* (zool.) chevrotain, *Tragulus meminna.*

†memma *f.* See **melma.**

memor-a·bile *adj.* memorable; worthy of commemoration; *n.m.pl. memorabilia.* **-abilmente** *adv.* memorably; unforgettably. **-abilità,** memorableness. **-ando** *adj.* memorable; not to be forgotten. **-andum** *m. indecl.* memorandum; reminder; engagement-book, memorandum-book; diary. **-are** [A I] *tr.* to remember, to recollect; to commemorate. **-ativo** *adj.* pertaining to the memory.

me·mor-e *adj.* mindful; sarò sempre — dei loro benefizi, I shall always be grateful for their kindnesses; rich in memories, full of memories. **-evole** *adj.* see **memorabile.**

memo·ri-a *f.* memory; — forte, tenace, fedele, strong, tenacious, trustworthy memory; di buona —, of blessed memory; riabilitare la — di, to re-establish the reputation of; imparare, mandare a —, to commit to memory, to learn by heart; recitare a —, to recite from memory; non s'era mai sentita una cosa simile a — d'uomo, such a thing had not been heard of within living memory; note of reminder; remembrance; in — di, in memory of; un monumento in — dei caduti, a monument commemorating those killed in the war; short dissertation; memorial; record; souvenir; back of the head (as the seat of memory); *pl.* memoirs; libro di -e, note-book; -e dell'Accademia, transactions of the Academy; (of a dead person remembered in more or less religious fashion) la felice — di tuo padre, your father, of happy memory; mia madre, buona —, my mother, God rest her; (liturg.) tomb-altar and structure over this, *memoria,* memorial chapel or church; commemoration (at Mass or office); (leg.) a written pleading; rinunciare alle -e di replica, to agree to close the pleadings (C.C.P.).

memorial-e *m.* book of memorials; memoir; memorial of grievances; catalogue; memorandum; (leg.) memorial; (hist.) a register of deeds drawn up by a notary; (eccl. hist.) segretario dei -i, Secretary of Memorials. **-ista** *m.* memorialist.

mena[1] *f.* underhand dealing; intrigue.

†mena[2] *f.* state, condition.

menabò *m. indecl.* (typ.) rough layout, showing contents of each page of a book.

menaccanite *f.* (miner.) ilmenite, menaccanite, titanic iron ore.

me·nade *f.* Maenad, Bacchante.

menadito *adv. phr.* a —, perfectly, with complete accuracy; sapere a —, to know inside out, to have at one's finger-tips; (joc.) far andare un orologio a —, to make a watch keep the right time by moving the hands with one's fingers.

menageri·a *f.* menagerie.

menagione *f.* motion; looseness of the bowels; purging.

mena·ide *f.* (naut.). See **manaide.**

†menale *m.* (naut.). See **vetta** or **tirante.**

menandara *f.* procuress.

menante[1] *part.* of **menare,** q.v.

†menant-e[2] *m.* copyist, scribe. **-eri·a** *f.* office of copyist.

men-are [A I] *tr.* to lead, to conduct; to take, to pull, to carry along; — i bambini alla scuola, to take the children to school; — una vita molto tribolata, to live a life full of tribulation; — per il naso, to lead by the nose; — a fine (capo) un lavoro, to finish a work; — le mani, to fight, to lay about one; — un colpo, to deliver a blow; — calci, to kick; — delle calcagne, to take to one's heels; — carole, to dance; — la lingua a danno di qualcuno, to speak ill of someone; — il mantice, to blow the bellows; — per le lunghe, to drag out; — in lungo, to drag out; — uno in lungo, to put a person off with specious talk; — per parole, to drag out; — il can per l'aia, to beat about the bush; — moglie, to marry, to take a wife; — buono, — buona, to admit, to allow, to forgive; — a tondo, to treat (all) alike; — gioia, — allegrezza, to be joyful, to be happy; — l'orso a Modena, to carry coals to Newcastle; — di punta, to strike with the point; — di piatto, to strike with the flat (of a blade); to wield; — la frusta, — la sferza, to crack or wield the whip, (fig.) to be severe; (of a dog, etc.) — la coda, to wag its tail; — il capo, to shake one's head; (of medicine) to act; (of soil or water) to produce (e.g. plants); to be a sign of, to bring; to beget; aria rossa da sera buon tempo -a, red sky at night is shepherd's delight. **-amento** *m.* leading; -amento di vita, way of life. (**-ante** *part. adj.*) **-arrosto** *m.* turnspit. **-ata** *f.* blow; shake, toss; handful. (**-ato** *part. adj.*) **-atoio** *m.* stirrer, pump-handle. **-atore** *m.* leader; person or thing conducting or wielding. **-atura** *f.* tossing, turning; joint.

menarola *f.* (carp.) brace

menci-o *adj.* flabby, soft. (**-one** *adj. augm.*)

mend-a *f.* fault, defect; sin; compensation; uno scritto pieno di -e, a work full of errors. **-oso** *adj.* faulty; inaccurate, full of mistakes.

mend-ace *adj.* mendacious, lying; false. (**-acemente** *adv.*) **-a·cia** *f.* mendacity. **-a·cio** *m.* lie, falsehood.

†mendare *vb.* and derivs. See **emendare.**

mendic-are [A 2 s] *tr.* to beg; to beg for; *intr.* (*aux.* avere) to go begging, to be a beggar. **-ante** *adj.* begging; *n.m.* beggar; mendicant; *pl.* (eccl.) Mendicants, mendicant friars. **-ato·rio** *adj.* mendicant. **-azione** *f.* mendicity. **-ità** *f.* beggary; mendicity; beggars, (leg.) mendicancy; street begging (C.P.); ospizio, ricovero di -ità, casual ward, *or* workhouse.

mendichevole *adj.* begging.

men·dico *adj.* begging, mendicant; *n.m.* beggar; *m.pl.* (hist.) Sea-Beggars, *Gueux de mer.*

mendola *f.* (ichth.). See **menola.**

menefreghismo *m.* (vulg.) indifference; couldn't-care-less attitude (from 'me ne frego'; cf. **fregare**).

meneghino *m.* the Milanese dialect; inhabitant or native of Milan; (theatr.) a Milanese mask; *adj.* relating to Milanese dialect or local customs.

menestrello *m.* minstrel.

Menfi *pr.n.f.* (geog.). See **memfi.**

mengoi *m.pl.* (pop. Tusc.) money.

menilina *f.* aniline yellow.

†me·nimo *adj.* See **menomo.**

menimpipo *m.* (slang, vulg.) indifference (from 'me ne impipo', I fill my pipe with it); con un'aria di —, with an air of indifference.

mening-e *f.* (anat.) meninx; usu. *pl.* i -i, the meninges. **-e·o** *adj.* (anat.) meningeal. **-ite** *f.* (med.) meningitis.

menipp-e·o *adj.* Menippean. **-e·a** *f.* satire.

menisco *m.* (phys.) meniscus; (opt.) — convergente, converging concavo-convex lens; — divergente diverging concavo-convex lens.

menno *adj.* sexually impotent; with little or no beard; (also *n.m.*).

mennonita *m.* (rel.) Mennonite.

Meno[1] *pr.n.m.* (geog.) Main (river).

meno[2] *adj. indecl.,* *adv.* (often abbrev. to **men**) less; dite—spropositi, don't talk so much nonsense; questo mi piace —, I like this one less; ho fatto — di quel che avrei dovuto, I've done less than I should have; in men che non si dice, in less time than it takes to mention it, in the twinkling of an eye; la necessità o —, the necessity or otherwise; venir —, to faint, to fail; venne — al proprio dovere, he failed in his duty; a — che, unless; fare a — di, to abstain from; non poteva fare a — di ridere, he couldn't help

meno (*cont.*)

laughing; fare di —, di, to abstain from, to do without; — male!, that's lucky!; nè più nè —, neither more nor less; ciò non di —, nevertheless; a —, per —, at a lower price; essere da — di qualcuno, to be inferior to someone; — che —, even less, all the less; a — che (non), unless; senza —, certainly, doubtless; (math.) minus; sette — cinque fa due, five from seven leaves two; — due o tre sono tutti qui, they are all here, apart from two or three; *n.m. indecl.* the less; the lesser; ragionare del più e del —, to talk of this and that; dal più al —, from the highest to the lowest; the least; per lo —, al —, at least; *pl.* i —, the minority.

menola *f.* (ichth.) small edible marine fish; *Merolepis vulgaris* is usually 'menola' or 'menola bianca' but it may also be called 'mendola' or 'mendola comune'; *Spicara alcedo* is 'menola schiava'; and *S. vulgaris* is 'menola', or 'menola comune'; there are regional differences in the application of these names and other spelling variants may be found.

menolo·gio *m.* menology.

menom-are [A I sc, A I s] *tr.* to diminish, to lessen. (**-a·bile** *adj.*) **-amẹnto** *m.* lessening, diminishing; (rhet.) litotes. **-anza** *f.* privation. **-aziọne** *f.* diminution.

mẹnom-o, me·nọm-o *adj.* least; smallest. **-amẹnte** *adv.* by no means; not in the least. †**-ezza** *f.* smallness.

men-opa·usa *f.* (med.) menopause, climacteric. **-orragi·a** *f.* (med.) menorrhagia. **-orre·a** *f.* (med.) menstrual bleeding; menorrhagia. **-ostaṣi** *f.* (med.) amenorrhoea.

†**meno-sdire** *tr.* to speak ill of. †**-vale** *adj.* of little worth. †**-vare** *tr.* to diminish.

mens-a *f.* table; (fig.) meal; preparare, apparecchiare, la —, to lay the table; levare, togliere, la —, levar le -e, to rise from the table; (mil.) mess; — degli ufficiali, officers' mess; (industr.) canteen; (canon law) mensa, mensal property (appropriated to a bishop a chapter, etc.); (liturg.) *mensa*, altar slab; la sacra —, the sacred feast, Holy Communion; †church treasury; (leg.) separato di —, separated from table; separazione di — e di toro, a judicial separation 'a mensa et thoro'. **-ale** *adj.* convivial; compagno -ale, boon companion; *n.m.* (geom.) figure with four regular sides. †**-eggiare** *intr.* to sit at table.

mensil-e *adj.* monthly; *n.m.* monthly pay or salary. **-mẹnte** *adv.* once a month; by the month; monthly. **-ità** *f.* quality of being monthly; monthly payment.

me·nsol-a *f.* (archit.) corbel, bracket, console; shelf; (masonry) corbel. **-ino** *m. dim.* (archit.) truss.

mensuale *adj. and derivs.* See **mensile**.

mensuraliṣmo *m.* (mus.) measured music.

mẹnt-a *f.* (bot.) mint, *Mentha*; — peperina, — piperata, peppermint, *Mentha piperita*; — romana, penny-royal. **-astro** *m.* (bot.) flea-bane, *Pulicaria dysenterica*; various wild species of mint. **-ina** *f.* peppermint lozenge.

mentale[1] *adj.* pertaining to the chin (cf. **mento**).

mental-e[2] *adj.* mental (cf. **mente**); restriziọne, riserva —, mental reservation; facoltà -i, mental faculties; (leg.) malattia —, insanity, lunacy; alienazione —, mental alienation, insanity. **-mẹnte** *adv.* mentally; in relation to mentality; with the mind. **-ità** *f.* mentality; intelligence.

mentastro *m.* See under **menta**.

mẹnte *f.* mind; intellect; intelligence, understanding; le forze della —, mental powers; imparare a —, to learn by heart; avere in — di, to intend to; avere a —, ritenere in —, to keep in one's mind; tenere a —, to bear in mind; porre — a, to pay attention to; non mi viene in —, I can't recall; gli venne in — di, he took it into his head to; m'è uscito di —, it slipped my memory, I forgot; essere fuori di —, to have one's head in the clouds, to be absent-minded; a — calma, with calm of mind; (admin.) a — del paragrafo tale della legge, according to such and such a paragraph of the code; (leg.) infermo di —, of unsound mind; curatore di un infermo di —, a receiver in lunacy; sano di —, of sound mind.

mentecatt-o *adj.* imbecile, half-witted; *n.m.* idiot. **-ag·gine** *f.* idiocy.

ment-ire [D 2] *intr.* (*aux.* avere) to be misleading; to lie; to give one the lie; to be a liar; †*tr.* to deny; to contradict. **-ita** *f.* lie; dare la -ita a, to accuse of lying, to give the lie to. **-ito** *adj.* false; insincere; lying; sotto -ite spoglie, in disguise. **-itamẹnte** *adv.* falsely; dishonestly. **-itọre** *m.* liar. (**-itrice** *f.*)

mẹnt-o *m.* chin; — sporgente, — innanzi, — in fuori, protruding

chin; — bucato, dimpled chin; (joc.) far ballare il —, to eat; l'onor del —, the beard. **-iera** *f.* bandage round the chin.

mentolo *m.* (chem.) menthol.

mentoniera *f.* (mus.) chin-rest (of violin).

Me·ntore *pr.n.m.* (Gk. lit.) Mentor, the friend and adviser of Odysseus; (fig.) mentor, adviser.

mentov-are [A I s] *tr.* to mention, to name; to record. (**-ato** *part. adj.*)

mẹntre *conj.* while, whilst; stava leggendo — ch'io scrivevo, he was reading while I wrote (in temporal clauses 'mentre che' is preferred); — egli parlava, ecco lei che rideva, while he was talking, there she was laughing; whereas; egli se ne andò, — noi restammo, he went away, whereas (*or* while) we remained; in questo —, in quel —, fra questo —, in the meantime, *or* just at that moment.

†**men·tula** *f.* (zool.) a marine fish, possibly *Uranoscopus scabes*.

menziọn-e *f.* mention; record; degno di —, worthy of mention; fare — di, to mention; onorevole —, — d'onore, honourable mention; (leg.) ordinare la non — della condanna, to order no mention of conviction (C.P.). **-are** [A I c] *tr.* to mention. (**-ato** *part. adj.*)

menzọgn-a *f.* lie, untruth; falsehood; un tessuto di -e, a tissue of lies. **-ero** *adj.* lying, false; deceitful; illusory. (**-eramẹnte** *adv.*)

Meo[1] *pr.n.m.* (abbrev. of **Bartolomeo**); (fig., derog.) simpleton; è la camicia di —, (to describe something spun out, of inordinate length).

meo[2] *poss. adj.* (dial.). See **mio**.

meo[3] *m.* (bot.) bearwort.

Meo·nidi *pr.n.f.pl.* the Muses.

meo·nio *adj.* of Maeonia, in Asia Minor; il — cantore, Homer.

meravi·gli-a *f.* marvel, wonder; amazement, astonishment; che —!, how marvellous!; che — di fragole!, what marvellous strawberries!; la — è figlia dell'ignoranza, astonishment arises from ignorance; far — a, to surprise, to amaze; mi fa —, I'm amazed at it; farsi — di, to be surprised at; mi fo — di Lei!, I'm surprised at you!; le sette -e del mondo, the seven wonders of the world; *adv. phr.* a —, marvellously; (bot.) kind of grape; an ornamental plant from the E. Indies, *Amaranthus tricolor*. **-are** [A 4] *tr.* to surprise, to astonish; *rfl.* to marvel, to be amazed; non c'è da -arsi, there's nothing to be surprised at; non me ne -o, I don't wonder at it; mi -o molto che tu sia qui, I am astonished that you are here. **-ọso** *adj.* wonderful, marvellous; wondrous. **-osamẹnte** *adv.* marvellously, wonderfully; wondrously.

†**mercadante** *m.* See **mercante**.

mercant-e *m.* merchant; dealer; — all'ingrosso, wholesale dealer; far l'orecchio di (da) —, to pretend not to hear, to turn a deaf ear, not to mind what people say. †**-are** *intr.* to do business, to deal. **-eggiare** [A 3 c] *intr.* (*aux.* avere) to transact business, to deal; -eggiare di, in, sul grano, to deal in corn; (derog.) -eggiare sull'onore, to sell one's honour; to haggle; *tr.* to sell; to prostitute; to speculate on; -eggiare l'onore, to sell one's honour. **-esco** *adj.* (*m.pl.* -eschi) mercantile. **-essa** *f.* (derog.) resembling, relating to, a merchant; tradeswoman; merchant's wife. **-ile** *adj.* mercantile; Marina Mercantile, Merchant Navy. (**-ilmẹnte** *adv.*)

mercanzi·a *f.* merchandise, goods; ogni mercante loda la sua —, no one cries stinking fish, every merchant praises his own wares; — di fallo, goods liable to be spoilt; (hist.) the name of a principal guild in medieval Florence; (iron.) una certa —!, some rubbish!; — reale, real property, (fig.) 'the goods', thing or person of value.

mercare [A 2] *and derivs.* (poet.). See **mercanteggiare**, under **mercante**.

mercat-o *m.* market; mart, money-market; corso del —, market price; ragguaglio del —, market-report; giorno di —, market-day; termini del —, market terms; valore del —, market value; — fermo, steady market; prezzo del —, market rate; — nero, black market; sopra —, into the bargain; a buon —, cheaply; deal; cattivo —, disadvantageous deal; (fig.) fare — di, to sell, to prostitute. †**-ante** *m.* see **mercante**. †**-an·zia** *f.* see **mercanzia**. †**-are** *intr.* to trade. **-ọre** *m.* trader, tradesman. **-o·rio** *adj.* relating to trade. (**-rice** *f.*) **-ura** *f.* trade, trading.

merc-e *f.* goods, wares, merchandise; (rlwy.) un treno -i (*or* un -i), a goods train; stazione -i, goods station; scalo -i, luggage section of station; la — deve essere pagata alla consegna, goods must be paid for on delivery; (comm.) -i di contrabbando, smuggled goods; -i in deposito, on consignment; deposito di -i, warehouse; -i a condizione, goods on approval; -i in deposito franco, bonded goods; -i in magazzino, goods on hand.

†**mercè** *f.* (abbrev. of **mercede**, q.v.) recompense, reward; grace, help, pity, mercy; la Dio —, thanks be to God; — il dottore, thanks to the doctor; — che, since, as; alla — di, at the mercy of; essere all'altrui —, to be at the mercy of others.

mercede *f.* reward, recompense; wages, payment; grace, pity; vivere alla — di uno, to be at the mercy of someone's whims; (comm.) salary, wage; (eccl.) S. Maria della —, Our Lady of Ransom; religiosi della —, Mercedarians.

mercena·r-io *adj.* mercenary; grasping, mercenary-minded; giudice —, corrupt judge; (hist.) soldati -i, milizie, armi -ie, mercenary troops; *n.m.* mercenary soldier; una truppa di -i, a troop of mercenaries. (-**iamente** *adv.*) -**ietà** *f.* mercenariness.

merceol-ogi·a *f.* study of the quality of commercial articles. -**o·gico** *adj.* pertaining to the study of the quality of commercial articles.

merceri·a *f.* haberdasher's shop; *pl.* haberdashery; †small, luxury goods, knick-knacks, ornaments.

mercerizz-are [A I] *tr.* (text.) to mercerize. -**aggio** *m.* (text.) mercerizing. -**ato** *part. adj.* (text.) mercerized; cotone -**ato**, mercerized cotton. -**azione** *f.* (text.) mercerizing.

merci-a·io, -**aiolo** *m.* haberdasher; pedlar. -**a·ia**, -**aiola** *f.* woman selling haberdashery; woman pedlar.

†**merciè** *excl.* gramercy, thank you.

mercimo·nio *m.* illegitimate trade; (fig.) prostituting; fare — dell'onore, to sell one's honour.

merco *m.* mark; bruise; branded mark on cattle; (bot.) *Urospermum dalechampii*.

mercoledì *pr.n.m.* Wednesday.

mercorella *f.* (bot.) annual mercury, *Mercurialis annua*; — bastarda, dog's mercury, *M. perennis*.

Merc-u·rio *pr.n.m.* (myth.) Mercury; (chem.; metall.) mercury, quicksilver. -**uriale** *adj.* (pharm.) mercurial; *pr.n.f.* (leg.) market-report (C.C.). -**u·rico** *adj.* (chem.) mercuric. -**uri·fero** *adj.* (miner.) mercuriferous. -**uroso** *adj.* (chem.) mercurous.

merd-a *f.* excrement, dung; (vulg.) arrogance, conceit; *excl.* —!, shit! -**a·io** *m.* dunghill; cess-pool; (fig.) place of filth or evil. †-**aiolo** *m.* road-sweeper, crossing-sweeper. -**oso** *adj.* filthy with excrement.

merdac·chio *m.* dregs of alum lye.

merdocco *m.* depilatory ointment; depilative.

merend-a *f.* light meal; afternoon tea; snack; morning luncheon; picnic; c'entra come il cavolo a —, it is completely irrelevant *or* out of place.

meretr-ice *f.* prostitute; whore; harlot; (fig.) faccia di —, brazen-faced hussy. -**i·cio** *adj.* meretricious; pertaining to a prostitute; *n.m.* life, behaviour, of a prostitute; prostitution; (leg.) un locale di -**icio**, place of prostitution (C.P.). †-**icioso** *adj.* lascivious. †-**i·cola** *f.* see **meretrice**.

†**me·rgere** *tr.* to plunge, to immerse.

merg-o *m.* (orn.) see **smergo**; (agric.) layer. -**one** *m.* (orn.) goosander.

mer-i·a, **me·r-ia** *f.* (poet.) shady place in the country; le pecore stanno a —, the sheep have sought the shade. -**are** [A4] *intr.* (aux. avere) to pass the hottest hours of the day in the shade. -**iò** *m.* place in which flocks and herds seek shelter from the sun.

meridian-a *f.* sun-dial; (astron.) meridian line. -**o** *m.* (astron.) meridian line; primo -**o**, prime meridian, zero meridian (Greenwich); *adj.* meridian, midday; l'ora -**a**, the hour of noon; (fig.) a luce -**a**, as clear as noonday.

†**meri·die** *f.* See **meriggio**.

meridional-e *adj.* southern, south, southerly; meridional; l'Italia —, Southern Italy; *n.m.,f.* person from the South of Italy; Southerner. -**mente** *adv.* in the Southern manner; in the style or manner of Italians from the South of Italy.

merigg-e *m.* (poet.) midday. -**iare** [A4] *intr.* (aux. avere) to lie in the shade during the heat of the day; to take a siesta; *tr.* to bring sheep to the shade.

merig·gi-o *m.* noon, midday; fare —, to take a midday rest; (Tusc.) cool, shady place in which to rest; (astron.) cerchio di —, meridian circle; (geog.) south; south wind; †*adj.* see **meridionale**. -**one** *m.* lazy man, idler; †*adv.* andare -**one**, to idle.

meringa *f.* (cul.) meringue.

merino *m.* (zool.) merino breed of sheep.

meriò *m.* See under **meria**.

merit-are [A I S] *tr.* to deserve; to earn; to merit; to earn the reward (of); -ò di essere coronato, he earned the tribute of a crown; ben — di, to deserve well of; -a aiuto, he deserves help; trattare uno come -a, to treat someone according to his deserts; non -a che se ne parli, it's not worth talking about; — la pena, to be worth while; to reward; to obtain, to win; la sua opera gli -ò la medaglia, his work won him the medal; *intr.* (aux. avere) to be worth while; non -a, it's not worth the trouble; *rfl.* (dat. of prn. 'si') to earn; to be entitled to; se l'è -ato, he has earned it, *or* serve him right. -**ato** *part. adj.* deserved, merited; earned. -**atamente** *adv.* deservedly.

meritevole *adj.* See under **merito**.

me·rit-o *m.* merit; persona di —, deserving person; il suo miglior — è l'aver dato sempre buon esempio, his great merit is that he has always set a good example; in ordine di —, in order of merit; punti di —, merit marks; reward; Dio ve ne renda —, may God reward you; entrare nel — di una questione, to examine a subject fully; in — a, as to, about; parlare in — a, to speak concerning; per — vostro, thanks to you; io non ne ho colpa nè —, it has nothing to do with me; interest paid at a pawnshop. -**evole** *adj.* deserving, meritorious; worthy. (-**evolmente** *adv.*) -**o·rio** *adj.* meritorious, deserving, worthy. (-**oriamente** *adv.*)

merla *f.* (orn.). See **merlo¹**; i tre giorni della —, Jan. 29–31.

merlango *m.* (ichth.) hake, *Merluccius merluccius*.

merlano *m.* (ichth.) poor cod, *Gadus minutus*.

merl-are [A I] *tr.* (archit.) to embattle, to furnish with battlements. -**ato** *part. adj.* embattled, battlemented; (herald.) embattled; -**ato** rovesciato, embattled in base; doppio -**ato**, bretessed; contra -**ato**, embattled-counter-embattled. -**atura** *f.* (archit.) battlements, line of battlements.

merlett-o¹ *m.* (usu. *pl.*) lace; — all'ago, point-lace; — a fuselli, pillow-lace. -**a·ia** *f.* woman who sells or makes lace. -**are** [A I c] *tr.* to trim with lace. -**ato** *part. adj.* lace-edged, lace-trimmed, edged with lace, trimmed with lace.

merletto² *m.* See under **merlo²**.

†**merletto³** *m.* (ichth.) See **merluzzo**.

merlin-are [A I] *tr.* (naut.) to sew or lace (canvas) to its roping. -**o** *m.* (naut.) lacing.

merl-o¹ *m.* (orn.) blackbird, *Turdus merula*; — acquaiolo, dipper, *Cinclus cinclus*; — dal collare, ring ouzel, *Turdus torquatus*; — nero, blackbird; (fig.) cunning person, sly person; quello lì è un certo —, that chap is a real rogue; simpleton, fool. -**otto** *m.* young blackbird; (fig.) simpleton.

merl-o² *m.* (usu. *pl.*) (archit.) battlements. -**etto** *m.* (archit.) embrasure, loop-hole; (herald.) merlette, martlet.

merl-uzzo, -**uc·cio** *m.* (ichth.) cod, *Gadus morrhua*; hake, *Merluccius merluccius*.

mermide *f.* (zool.) earthworm.

mer-o *adj.* pure, mere; per — caso, by pure chance; per -**a** curiosità, out of sheer curiosity; per — sbaglio, purely by mistake; simple; undiluted; †brilliant; resplendent; †frank, sincere. -**amente** *adv.* purely, merely, simply.

Me·rope *pr.n.f.* (myth.) Merope.

†**merore** *m.* sadness.

†**mertare** *vb.* See **meritare**.

†**merto** *m.* See **merito**.

†**merz-è**, †-**ede** *f.* See **mercè**, **mercede**.

†**mesa·gio** *m.* discomfort, hardship (cf. **disagio**).

mes-aiolo *m.*, -**ano** *m.* servant hired by the month. (-**aiola** *f.*) -**ata** *f.* a month; a month's pay, monthly wages; una -**ata** anticipata, a month's pay in advance.

mesc-ere, **mesc-ere** [B I] *tr.* to pour out; to pour forth; to shed; to mingle, to mix; (fig.) — quattrini, to pour out money; (joc.) — pugni, to hand out blows. -**iacqua** *f. indecl.* (Tusc.) water-jug. -**i·bile** *adj.* that can be poured. -**iruba** *m. indecl.* ewer, esp. for use in churches.

†**mes·chi-a** *f.* mixture; honey and wine. †-**are** *vb.* and derivs. see **mescolare**. †-**o** *adj.* see **misto**, **mischiato**.

meschin-o *adj.* poor, miserable, wretched; mean; shabby; petty; paltry; *n.m.* poor individual, wretched person; stingy man; †servant. †-**a** *f.* handmaiden. -**amente** *adv.* meanly, poorly.

meschita *f.* (poet.) mosque.

mesciac·qua *f. indecl.* See under **mescere**.

mesci·bile *adj.* See under **mescere**.

mesciroba *m. indecl.* See under **mescere**.

mescit-a *f.* pouring; tap-room; wine-shop; ragazza della —, bar-maid. -**ore** *m.* pourer; bar-tender; barman. (-**rice** *f.*)

mescola *f.* (techn.) mix.

mescol-are [A I sc] *tr.* to mix; to mingle; to blend; to confound, to confuse; — le carte, to shuffle the cards; -ate prima dell'uso, (of medicine) to be shaken before use; (cul.) to stir; to whip; *rfl.* to mix with; l'olio non si -a con l'acqua, oil does not mix with water; non ti — con quella gente, don't get mixed up with those people. **-a·bile** *adj.* that can be mixed. **-amento** *m.* mixing; mingling; confounding. **-anza** *f.* blending; combination; blend; (Tusc.) mixed salad. **-ata** *f.* mixing; shuffling. **-ato** *part. adj.* mixed; blended. **-atamente** *adv.* mixedly; confusedly. **-atore** *m.* mixer; cocktail-shaker. **-io** *m.* continual mixing; thorough mixing; mix-up; confusion, muddle.

mescolo *m.* (Tusc.) mixture; *adj.* mixed.

†**mesconoscere** *vb.* and derivs. See **misconoscere**.

mescu·glio *m.* (pop. Tusc.). See **miscuglio**.

†**mescurare** *tr.* to neglect.

mes-e *m.* month; il — corrente, il — volgente, the present month; il — scorso, il — prossimo passato, last month; il — prossimo, il — prossimo futuro, next month; ai primi del —, at the beginning of the month; agli ultimi del —, at the end of the month; month's salary; quanti ne abbiamo del —?, what day of the month is it?; non mi ha pagato il —, he has not paid me my salary for the month; (of an expectant mother) esser nel —, to be in the month when she expects her baby; non aver tutti i suoi -i, to be weak in the head; *pl.* menses, menstruation. **-etto** *m. dim.* a little less than a full month. **-one** *m. augm.* a little over a full month.

mesent-erio *m.* (anat.) mesentery. **-erico** *adj.* (anat.) mesenteric. **-erite** *f.* (med.) mesenteritis.

mesera·ico *adj.* (anat.) mesaraic.

me·ser-e, -o *m.* a shawl covering the head and the shoulders.

†**mesfatto** *adj.* See **misfatto**.

mesit-ilene *m.* (chem.) mesitylene. **-ina** *f.* (miner.) messitite, breunnerite.

mesm-e·rico *adj.* mesmeric. **-eri̇smo** *m.* mesmerism.

mesocefa·lico *adj.* mesocephalic.

meso·coro *m.* (Gk. antiq.) leader of musical performers.

mesolite *f.* (miner.) mesolite.

mesom-eri̇a *f.* (chem.) mesomerism. **-e·rico** *adj.* (chem.) mesomeric.

mesomorfo *adj.* (phys.) mesomorphic.

mesone *m.* (atom. phys.) meson.

mesoro *m.* (ichth.) stargazer, *Uranoscopus scaber*.

mesoto·rio *m.* (chem.) mesothorium.

mesotrone *m.* (atom. phys.) mesotron.

mesozo·ico *adj.* (geol.) Mesozoic, Secondary.

mess-a[1] *f.* (liturg., mus.) mass; — letta, — piana, — bassa, low mass; — grande, — solenne, high mass; — cantata, sung mass, *missa cantata*; — novella, first mass (of newly ordained priest); — buona, mass that 'counts' (i.e. for which one has not come in too late to satisfy the obligation of hearing mass); sentire, ascoltare, (la) —, to hear mass; andare a, alla —, to go to mass, to be a practising Catholic; (joc.) va' alla —!, get away with you!; assistere alla —, to be (present) at mass; dir —, to say one's first mass; dir la —, to say mass in the ordinary way; servir (la) —, to serve mass, (fig.) to report someone's misbehaviour; levar la — a un prete, to inhibit a priest from saying mass; elemosina della —, mass offering; libro da —, missal; (mus.) Mass, musical setting of Kyrie, Gloria, Credo, Sanctus, Benedictus and Agnus; — da requiem, di requie, da morto, funebre, per i defunti, requiem mass.

mess-a[2] *f.* putting; putting-up; setting-up; laying; placing; — in scena, *mise-en-scène*; — in azione, putting into action, starting; shampoo e — in piega, shampoo and set; — in vigore, enforcement, putting into force; (leg.) — in istato d'accusa, putting on charge, indictment; — in piega, set, wave (of hair); (agric.) young shoot, sprout; putting forth of buds; (cards) stake; (cul.) course; (motor.) — in marcia, starting; (comm.) — a bordo, shipping; — a magazzino, warehousing; (watchm.) — all'ora, setting, hand-setting; (leg.) — al punto, settling (of draft document); (mus.) — di voce, the art of singing a sustained note while gradually swelling from pianissimo to fortissimo and back to pianissimo again.

messaggeri·a *f.* goods department, parcels office; forwarding agency; book-distributing agency; mail-service; boat or coach service; coach office.

messagger-o, †-e *m.* messenger; harbinger; envoy; (admin.) — postale, grade in the Italian postal service held by those responsible for conveying mail on and off trains and boats. (**-a** *f.*)

messag·gio *m.* message; communication, word, note; news.

messale *m.* missal; (fig.) non saper leggere che nel suo —, to be unable to venture beyond a limited range of interests; (joc.) large, heavy book.

Messalina *pr.n.f.* (Rom. hist.) Messalina; title of a play by Pietro Cossa; (fig.) debauched woman.

mess-e *f.* harvest; crop; falciare la —, to reap the harvest; raccogliere la —, to gather the harvest in; le bionde -i, the golden corn; (fig.) harvest; mettere la falce nella — altrui, to interfere in other people's business.

messer-e *m.* (now joc.) Sir; Mr; Master; gentleman; †— il Re, our Lord the King. **†-a·tico** *m.* title of 'messere'.

Mess-i̇a *pr.n.m.* Messiah. **-ia·nico** *adj.* Messianic. **-iani̇smo** *m.* Messianism. **-iato** *m.* Messiahship.

Mes·sic-o *pr.n.m.* (geog.) Mexico. **-ano** *adj.* Mexican; *n.m.* native of Mexico, Mexican; a kind of cocktail. (**-ana** *f.*)

Messidoro *pr.n.m.* Messidor, the tenth month of the French revolutionary calendar.

Messin-a *pr.n.f.* (geog.) Messina. **-ese** *adj.* of, relating to, Messina; *n.m., f.* person, native of, or resident in, Messina.

messinscena *f.* (theatr.) production, *mise-en-scène*.

messitic·cio *m.* shoot, offset planted out.

mess-o *part.* of **mettere**, q.v.; *adj.* put; situated; placed; set; — d'oro, wrought in gold; — insieme, put together; mal —, badly arranged, badly dressed; — in forse, questioned, doubted, in doubt; *n.m.* messenger; public officer; public crier; message, sign; — di Giuno, the rainbow, Iris.

†**messona** *f.* dish of food.

mest-are [A I c] *tr.* to stir; — la minestra, to stir the soup; *abs.* to interfere, to stir up trouble. **-amento** *m.* stirring. **-atoio** *m.* stirrer; ladle. **-atore** *m.* stirrer; (fig.) one who interferes or stirs up trouble. (**-atora, -atrice** *f.*)

†**mest-e·rio, †-ero** *m.* See **mestiere**.

†**mestiare** *vb.* and derivs. See **mescolare**.

mes·ti-ca *f.* (paint.) priming; mixed colours; paints on a palette. **†-canza** *f.* see **mestica**. **-care** [A 2 s] *tr.* to mix, to prepare (paints, colours); to prime. **-catore** *m.* colour merchant, one who prepares or sells painters' colours. **-cheri·a** *f.* oil and paint shop, colour stores. **-chino** *m.* palette knife.

mesticc-iare [A 3] *tr.* to stir up; to agitate; to meddle with; to interfere in. **-ione** *m.* one who agitates; interferer.

mestierante *m.* jobber; (derog.) one who works solely for what he can get out of a job; clock-watcher; opportunist.

mestier-e, †-o *m.* trade, occupation; che — fai?, what is your trade?; fare tutti i -i, to turn one's hand to any trade; sono falegname di —, I am a carpenter by trade; i libri per noi sono i ferri del —, books are for us the tools of our trade; essere del —, to be in the same business; (leg.) — girovago, itinerant calling; una professione o un — rumoroso, a noisy profession or calling (C.P.); †need, necessity; †non c'è —, there is no need; non c'è mestier lusinghe, there is no need for flattery (Dante, *Purg.* I); †è -i fare così, it is necessary to do this.

†**mestieri** *m.* See under **mestiere**.

†**mestizzo** *m.* half-breed.

mest-o *adj.* sad, sorrowful, mournful; dejected. **-amente** *adv.* sadly, mournfully. **-i·zia** *f.* sadness.

mestol-a *f.* ladle; trowel; washerwoman's bat; (joc.) long chin; *pl.* hands; adoperar le -e, to fight; (bot.) water plantain, *Alisma plantago-aquatica*. **-o** *m.* small wooden ladle; skimmer; wooden spoon for cooking; avere il -o in mano, to rule the roost, to be master, to have the whip-hand. **-a·io** *m.* maker, vendor of ladles. (**-a·ia** *f.*) **-ata** *f.* a ladleful; a blow with a ladle, trowel or bat. **-iera** *f.* ladle-holder. **-one** *m. augm.* large ladle; (fig.) lout, boor; (orn.) shoveler, *Spatula clypeata*.

meston-e *m.* (Tusc.) wooden stick for stirring; (fig.) agitator. **-a** *f.* female agitator (cf. **mestare**).

mes·tru-o *m.* (med.) menstruum. **-ale** *adj.* menstrual. **-are** [A 6] *intr.* (*aux.* avere) to menstruate. **-azione** *f.* menstruation. **†-osa** *adj. f.* menstruant.

mestura *f.* (Tusc.). See **mistura**.

†**mesventura** *f.* See **sventura**.

meta[1] *f.* (Rom. antiq.) group of three conical posts marking the turning-point in the ancient Roman circus for chariot races; goal, aim, end, object; proporsi una —, to set oneself a target; conical mass, heap; haycock; boundary; (hist.) maximum price, tariff

meta (*cont.*)

price for bread, etc.; (archit.) spire; pinnacle, small ornamental pyramid; (rugby) try; — trasformata, converted try.

mẹta² *f.* patch of dung; droppings, turd.

metà *f.* half; moiety; tagliare a (in) —, to cut in half; dividere per —, to divide equally in half; fare a —, to go halves, to go fifty-fifty; lasciare una cosa a —, to leave a thing unfinished; essere a —, to be half-way; essere a — del mese, to be half-way through the month; fermarsi a —, to stop half-way; fare le cose a —, to do things by halves; a — luglio, in the middle of July; a — strada fra Novara e Torino, half-way between Novara and Turin; stare a — degli utili, to go half-shares; — della —, a quarter; (provb.) quattrini e santità, — della —, in reckoning a man's real fortune or virtue, take a quarter of what they are priced at; (colloq.) la mia —, my better half, 'the wife'.

meta-bisolfito *m.* (chem.) metabisulphite. **-bolịsmo** *m.* (biol.) metabolism. **-carpo** *m.* (anat.) metacarpus. **-centro** *m.* (eng.) metacentre. **-cịsmo** *m.* metacism. **-cronịsmo** *m.* metachronism, putting an event posterior to its real date.

metafị·sic-a *f.* metaphysics. **-o** *adj.* metaphysical; *m.* metaphysician. (**-amẹnte** *adv.*) **-are** [A 25] *intr.* (*aux.* avere) to pursue metaphysical speculation; *tr.* (fig.) to indulge in quibbling arguments about; che stai -ando?, what are you quibbling about?

meta·f-ora *f.* metaphor; figurative speech; ditelo senza tante -ore, say what you mean in so many words. **-o·rico** *adj.* metaphorical. **-oricamẹnte** *adv.* metaphorically. **-oreggiare** [A 3 c] *intr.* (*aux.* avere) to use metaphors; to make frequent use of metaphors. **-orịsmo** *m.* frequent use of metaphors. **-orista** *m.*, *f.* one who uses metaphors; *pl.* (rel. hist.) Metaphorists (followers of the French Calvinist Daniel Chamier).

metaframma *m.* (ent.) metaphragma.

meta·fr-asi *f.* metaphrase. **-a·stico** *adj.* metaphrastic.

metage·nẹsi *f.* metagenesis.

meta-lẹpsi, -lẹssi *f.* (rhet.) metalepsis.

metal·lico *adj.* metallic; metal, made of metal; spazzola metallica, wire brush; (finan.) valuta metallica, coin, metallic currency.

metall-o *m.* metal; spotted metal (alloy of tin and lead for organpipes); tone, timbre (of voice). **-ị·fero** *adj.* metalliferous. **-iẓẓaziọne** *f.* metallizing, metallization. **-o·ide** *m.* metalloid. **-urgị·a** *f.* metallurgy. **-ur·gico** *adj.* metallurgical. **-urgo** *m.* (*pl.* **-urghi**) metallurgist.

meta-mor·fico *adj.* metamorphic. **-morfịsmo** *m.* (geol.) metamorphism; -morfismo di carico, static metamorphism. **-morfisti** *m.pl.* (rel. hist.) Metamorphists (sixteenth-century sect). **-mor·fosi** *f.* metamorphosis; le *Metamorfosi* di Ovidio, the *Metamorphoses* of Ovid; (zool.) metamorphosis.

metan-o *m.* (chem.) methane, marsh gas. **-iẓẓatọre** *m.* (chem.; industr.) methanator. **-iẓẓaziọne** *f.* methanation. **-odọtto** *m.* methane pipeline. **-olo** *m.* (chem.) methanol, methyl alcohol.

meta-plạsmo *m.* metaplasm. **-silicato** *m.* (chem.) metasilicate. **-somatọsi** *f.* (geol.) metasomatosis. **-sta·bile** *adj.* (phys.; chem.) metastable.

meta·st-asi *f.* metastasis. **-a·tico** *adj.* metastatic.

metastasiano *adj.* (lit. hist.) in the manner of Metastasio (Pietro Trapassi, 1698–1782).

metatarso *m.* (anat.) metatarsus.

meta·tẹsi *f.* (ling.) metathesis, transposition.

metato *m.* (agric.) oast-house for chestnuts, a room with a latticework platform where the chestnuts are spread out to be dried by a fire below.

metatọre *m.* (Rom. antiq.) *metator*, official who chose the site of an encampment.

meteco *m.* (Gk. hist.) metic (resident alien with certain privileges).

metempsicọsi *f.* (philos.) metempsychosis, transmigration of souls.

met-e·ora *f.* any atmospheric phenomenon; la — fallace dei deserti, mirage; meteor. **-eo·rico** *adj.* meteoric. **-eorịsmo** *m.* (med.) meteorism. **-eorite** *f.* meteorite. **-eografị·a** *f.* meteorography. **-eogra·fico** *adj.* meteorographic. **-eoro·grafo** *m.* meteorograph. **-eorologị·a** *f.* meteorology. **-eorolo·gico** *adj.* meteorological; previsioni -eorologiche, bollettino -eorologico, weather forecast. **-eorologista, -eoro·logo** *m.* meteorologist. **-eorosco·pio** *m.* meteoroscope.

metic·cio *adj.*, *n.m.* half-breed, half-caste; white-Amerind cross-breed.

meticolọs-o *adj.* meticulous; fastidious. (**-amẹnte** *adv.*) **-ità** *f.* meticulousness; fastidiousness.

†**meti·dio** *m.* See **mitidio**.

†**metigione** *f.* See **mietitura**, under **mietere**.

met-ile *m.* (chem.) methyl. **-ilẹnolo** *m.* (chem.) caesol. **-ị·lico** *adj.* methyl; alcool -ilico, methyl alcohol, methanol. **-ilo** *m.* see **metile**.

me·t-odo *m.* method, system, way; rule; order; custom; — scientifico, scientific method; (sport) soccer technique in which the centre-half plays an attacking game in line with wing-halves. **-o·dica** *f.* method of teaching; study of method; methodology. **-odicità** *f.* orderliness; methodical procedure. **-o·dico** *adj.* methodical; orderly. **-odicamẹnte** *adv.* methodically; in an orderly way. **-odicọne** *m.* overmethodical, punctilious man. **-odịsmo** *m.* (rel.) Methodism. **-odista** *m.*, *f.* (rel.) Methodist. **-odiẓẓare** [A I] *tr.* to make methodical; to reduce to order; to regularize. **-odologị·a** *f.* methodology. **-odolo·gico** *adj.* methodological.

meton-i·mia *f.* metonymy. **-i·mico** *adj.* metonymical. (**-imicamẹnte** *adv.*)

metonomạ·ṣia *f.* changing one's name, by translating it into another language (e.g. Metastasio, a Greek version of Trapassi).

me·topa, me·tope *f.* (archit.) metope.

metop-oscopị·a *f.* metoposcopy, the art of judging character or of telling a fortune by the forehead or face. **-osco·pico** *adj.* metoposcopic. **-o·scopo** *m.* metoposcopist.

†**metra** *f.* See **mitra¹**.

metr-ag·gio *m.* measurement (in metres); length (in metres); (cinem.) footage. **-atura** *f.* measurement, length.

metr-algị·a *f.* (med.) metralgia, uterine pain. **-ite** *f.* (med.) metritis. **-optọṣi** *f.* (med.) uterine prolapse. **-orragị·a** *f.* (med.) metrorrhagia, uterine bleeding. **-orrẹssi** *f.* (med.) metrorrhexis.

metreta *f.* (class. antiq.) 'metrete', liquid measure of some 9 gallons; cask.

me·trica *f.* prosody, metrics; metre; versification.

me·tric-o *adj.* metric; metrical; sistema — decimale, metric system, decimal system.

metr-o *m.* metre (equiv. to 39·3701 in.) — quadrato, square metre (equiv. to 10·7639 sq. ft.); — cubo, cubic metre (equiv. to 35·3148 cu. ft.); (prosod.) metre. **-ocordo** *m.* (mus.) string-gauge. **-ologị·a** *f.* (phys.) metrology. **-olo·gico** *adj.* metrological. **-ologista** *m.* metrologist. **-o·mane** *m.* metromaniac. **-omanị·a** *f.* metromania. **-o·metro** *m.* metrometer. **-o·nomo** *m.* (mus.) metronome.

metr-o·poli *f.* metropolis. **-opolita** *m.* metropolitan, inhabitant of a metropolis; metropolitan bishop. **-opolitano** *adj.* metropolitan; *n.m.* (eccl.) metropolitan; policeman (in large town). **-opolitana** *f.* underground railway, tube; metropolitan church; la -opolitana di Westminster, Westminster Cathedral.

mẹtt-ere [C 20] **1.** *tr.* To PUT; to place; — il sale nella minestra, to put salt in the soup; — le merci in magazzino, to put goods in store; — a letto i bambini, to put the children to bed; — al caldo, to put in a warm place; — insieme, to put together, to save; — in atto, to effect; — in ordine, to put in order; — a posto, to put in order; — a segno, to put in the proper place; — in bucato, to put to the wash, to send to the laundry, to launder; — in italiano, to put into Italian, to translate into Italian; — al pulito, to make a fair copy of; — all'asta, to put up for auction; — in vendita, to put on sale, to put up for sale; — in scena, to put on the stage, to stage; — in capo, to put on one's head; (comm.) — a libro, to enter; (leg.) — al punto, to settle (a draft document); — in mora, to fix a time limit for performance or payment. **2.** To SET; — in libertà, to set free; — in moto, to set in motion; — piede in, to set foot in; — il cuore in pace, to set one's heart at rest; — il cuore a, to set one's heart on; — in carta, to set down on paper; — in musica, to set to music; — in punto l'orologio, to set one's watch (*or* clock); — da parte, to set aside, to save. **3.** To PUT ON, to apply, to attach; — un vestito nuovo, to put on a new dress; — una pezza, una toppa, to put on a patch; — i quadri alla parete, to put the pictures on the wall; — uno spillo a, to stick a pin in; — un chiodo a, to knock a nail in; — il paletto, to shoot the bolt (into its fastenings); — la minestra, to put the soup on; — gli occhi addosso a, to look upon, *or* to desire; — amore a, to feel love for. **4.** To PUT, to add, to say, to write, to give, to include; -ete anche questa citazione, put this quotation in also; ora -i il nome e la data, now put your name and the date; — una cosa per paragone, to put (mention) a thing by way of comparison; l'autore lo -e come vero, the author gives it as authentic; ora -a cinque, now add five; (provb.) chi più ne ha, più ne -e, the more

mett-ere (*cont.*)

one has the more one wants. **5.** To ADMIT, to grant, to suppose; -iamo che, let us suppose that; -iamo caso (*or* il caso) che, let us put the case that; -endo che sia come dici, granting that it is as you say. **6.** To CONTRIBUTE, to invest, to put, to stake, to risk; ci ho messo molto lavoro, I have put a lot of work into it; ci ha messo tutto il suo capitale, he has put all his capital into it; — in terre, to invest one's money in land; — il denaro a frutto, to put money out at interest; — al lotto, to gamble on the lottery; — denaro sui cavalli, to bet money on horses; — su, to put up, to stake; — impegno a, to devote care and attention to; — diligenza a, to perform diligently; — studio a, to look into carefully, to investigate; — tempo in mezzo, to waste no time; — in valore, to utilize, to turn to account. **7.** To GIVE RISE TO, to cause, to inspire; — la febbre, to cause fever; — discordia fra, to cause disharmony between; — soggezione a, to make nervous, to inspire apprehension in; un racconto che -e i brividi, a story that makes one shudder; questo brutto tempo mi -e addosso un'uggia!, this awful weather makes me so depressed!; — orrore a, to horrify; — male tra due persone, to cause ill feeling between two people; il vino rosso -e forza, red wine gives strength; — conto, to be worth while. **8.** To INSTALL, to lay on, to lay in; — la luce elettrica, to install electric light; — il gas, to put in gas. **9.** To LAY DOWN, to put (down), to lay; to set up, to institute; — le basi, le fondamenta, to lay the foundations; — la tavola, to lay the table; — le mani addosso a, to lay hand on; — al di sotto, to put down, to set down; (fig.) — sotto, to put down, to subject, to gain the upper hand of; — sotto una bestia, to put an animal to work; — bottega, *or* — su bottega, to open a shop; — casa, *or* — su casa, to set up house. **10.** To RATE, to put at, to ask for (in price), to require; quanto -e queste pere?, how much are you asking for these pears?; le -o venti lire, I'm asking twenty lire for them; — in cielo, to rate highly, to praise to the skies; — in terra, to rate low, *or* to plant; quanto -e il treno di qui a Firenze?, how long does the train take between here and Florence?; quanto ci -e a finire questo lavoro!, what a long time it takes to finish this work! **11.** To PUT FORTH, to emit; to show forth, to exhibit; l'albero -e le foglie, the tree is putting forth leaves; il bambino -e i denti, the baby is cutting its teeth; l'uccellino -e le ali, the little bird's wings are sprouting; — radice, to strike root; — guai, to lament, to utter lamentations; — fuori, to put forth, to put outside, *or* to vomit; (poet.) le saette che -e fuor dell'arco, the arrows he shoots from his bow; (fig.) — cervello, to acquire sense, to grow sensible; — giudizio, to become prudent, to exercise caution; — superbia, to put on airs. **12.** To RENDER, to submit (to); — a sacco, to sack, to plunder; — a ferro e fuoco, to put to fire and sword; — a soqquadro, to turn topsy-turvy; — a nudo, to strip, to denude; — in burla, to make fun of; — a nuovo, to renew; — uno a dovere, *or* a segno, to put a person in his place, to make a person submit (cf. also under No. 1); — uno sul lastrico, to reduce a person to poverty. **13.** To THRUST, to stick, to intrude; — le mani nei capelli, to thrust one's hands into one's hair (in desperation); — il naso in, to stick one's nose in; — le mani in, to intrude in, to interfere in. **14.** *intr.* (*aux.* avere) To FLOW, to discharge; la Sieve -e in Arno, the river Sieve flows into the Arno; l'uscio -e in salotto, the door leads to the sitting-room; to proceed; la cosa -e bene, the affair is going on well. **15.** *rfl.* (*acc.* of *prn.* 'si') To PUT ONESELF, to place oneself, to set oneself; -iti là, stand over there; -ersi in ginocchio, to kneel; -ersi al lavoro, to set to work; -ersi con uno, to come to an understanding with someone; si mise a correre, he broke into a run; -ersi in letto, to go to bed, to take to one's bed; -ersi in guardia, sulle difese, to be on one's guard; -ersi in cammino, to set out; -ersi per una via, to set out upon a path, course; to dress; si -e bene, he is well turned out; -ersi a meno buono, to change into one's everyday clothes; -ersi in gala, to put on festive clothes, to dress for a gala occasion; (*dat.* of *prn.* 'si') si mise il cappello ed uscì, he put on his hat and went out; -ersi in animo di, to determine to, to resolve to; le guardie se lo misero in mezzo e via, the guards set him in their midst and off they went; *recip. rfl.* -ersi d'accordo, to come to an agreement; -ersi in due, in dieci, to form a party of two, of ten; -ersi in società, to form a society; *impers.* (of weather) -ersi al bello, to turn out fine; s'è messo a piovere, it has begun to rain. **-i·bile** *adj.* wearable. **-itore** *m.* setter, placer; gamester. **-itrice** *f.* (tanning) -itrice a

vento, setting-out machine. **-itura** *f.* putting; laying; l a -itura dei tappeti, laying the carpets.

metti-bocca *m.*, *f. indecl.* interferer, meddler. **-fo·glio** *m. indecl.* (typ.) feeder. **-loro** *m. indecl.* gilder. **-male** *m.*, *f. indecl.* mischief-maker. **-scan·dali** *m.*, *f. indecl.* trouble-maker, scandal-monger; one who is subject of scandal. **-stoppa** *f. indecl.* (naut.) caulking tool.

Me·vio *pr.n.m.* (Lat. lit.) Maevius (proverbial name for a poetaster and spiteful critic).

mezz-a *f.* half portion; half share; one half; half-hour; è sonata la —, it has struck the half hour; è la —, it is half past (used esp. for half-hour after midday, after midnight or after an appointed hour); †three and a half hours after sunset; (billiards) short cue; (tanning) side. **-abarba** *m. indecl.* young man with downy beard. **-abotte** *f. indecl.* (archit.) barrel vault. **-acalzetta** *adj. f.* (colloq.) suburban (of people); gente -acalzetta, suburban people. **-afesta** *f. indecl.* (eccl.) feast when one must go to Mass but need not refrain from work; half-holiday. **-alana** *f. indecl.* (text.) linsey-woolsey; (fig.) suspicious character. **-aluna** *f. indecl.* half-moon, crescent; la -aluna, l'impero della -aluna, the Ottoman empire; (fortification) lunette; (tanning) staking knife; two-handled knife, with semi-circular blade, which is rolled from side to side; side-plate. **-amac·chia** *f.* (paint.) coloured sketch; painting, drawing or engraving in which the shadows are not fully rendered. **-amosca** *f.* (orn.) common gull, (Amer.) mew gull or short-billed gull. **-anave** *f.* (naut.) beam wind; *adv.* athwartship. **-anotte** *f.* midnight; a -anotte, at midnight; †the North. †**-apoppa** *f.* (naut.) poop in line with the keel. **-aruota** *f.* (naut.) stem or stern post. **-ateia** *f.* (text.) cloth partly cotton partly linen. **-atesta** *f.* iron skull-cap. **-atinta** *f.* (paint.) half-tone, medium tint; shading.

mezz-adri·a *f.* (leg.) métayage; métayer system; a form of agricultural holding under which landlord and tenant go shares (originally half-and-half) in produce (C.C.), (Amer.) cropping, sharecropping. **-adro** *m.* métayer, (Amer.) cropper, sharecropper. **-aiuolo, -aiolo** *m.* see mezzadro.

mezzale *m.* cross-bar.

mezzan-a *f.* go-between, procuress; flooring-brick; side of bacon salted like a ham; milliner's assistant; (mus.) great mean, greater mean (lute-string); middle string (of any instrument); (zool.) trough shell, *Mactra corallina*; (naut.) mainsail; spanker; albero di —, mizzen mast. **-ella** *f. dim.* of mezzana; (mus.) see mezzana. **-ello** *m.* (text.) linsey-woolsey. **-i·a** *f.* (naut.) fore and aft line of the upperdeck, longitudinal axis, midship section. †**-iere** *m.* (naut.) rower or sailor working amidships or assigned to the mizzen mast. **-ina** *f.* (mus.) see mezzana. **-ino** *m.* (archit.) entresol, mezzanine; (naut.) ridgerope or centre stay of an awning; spiller or brail; †centre frame of a ship; go-between; procurer; broker, middle-man; *pl.* pupils of an intermediate age.

mezzan-o *adj.* mean, middle, medium; middle-sized; uomo di statura -a, man of medium height; il fratello —, the brother in the middle of the family; un uomo di -a età, a middle-aged man; intermediate; middle-class. (**-amente** *adv.*) **-ità** *f.* mean; average quality.

mezzanotte *f.*, **mezzatinto** *f.* See under **mezza**.

†**mezzari·a** *f.* See mezzadria.

†**mezzatore** *m.* mediator.

†**mezze·dima** *f.* mid-week, Wednesday.

mezzeri·a *f.* métayage; (geom.) centre line; (naut.) see **mezzania**, under **mezzana**.

mezzett-a *f.* a measure equivalent to about half a litre. **-ino** *m.* (bot.) *Vaccaria pyramidata*. **-o** *m.* (typ.) imperfect sheet of paper.

mezzina *f.* copper or earthenware jug.

mezzo[1] *adj.* (of fruit) overripe; (of pears) sleepy; (of persons) sickly; flabby; bagnato —, wet through; briaco —, dead drunk; — di vino, saturated with drink; *n.m.* the soft part of a fruit.

mezz-o[2] *adj.* **1.** HALF; part; semi-; incomplete; una mezz'ora, half an hour; un — litro, half a litre (cf. imprecise uses under No. 5); le -e misure, half-measures; una -a verità, a half-truth; due -i fogli, two half-sheets; donna a — servizio, part-time domestic help; -i guanti, mittens; — lutto, half mourning; -a gala, court dress of half mourning; bandiera a mezz'asta, flag at half-mast; (bookb.) in -a pelle, in half calf; (mus.) un — soprano, a mezzo-soprano (voice or singer); -a voce, singing at half power (cf. under No. 2); — tono, semi-tone, half-tone; -a battuta, half a beat; -a cadenza, half-close; (Tusc.) — il libro, half the book; — il suo

mezz·o (*cont.*)

patrimonio, half his inheritance. **2.** Medium, intermediate, average, middle; un — canapo, a cable of medium strength; una persona di -a età, a middle-aged person; a -a voce, in a medium, average voice, neither soft nor loud (cf. under no. 1); (colloq.) mezz'e —, half and half, betwixt and between, neither one thing nor the other, middling, so-so; è una musica mezz'e -a, it is music that is neither light nor serious; mi sento mezz'e —, I'm not feeling up to much; come stai? Mezz'e —, grazie, how are you? Middling, thanks. **3.** Mid; i vestiti di -a stagione, mid-season clothing; a — novembre, in mid-November; a -a gamba, midway up one's leg; a -a via, midway; -a quaresima, mid-Lent. **4.** Slight, little, faint; una -a speranza, a faint hope; non dirne -a parola, not to breathe a word about it; ancora un — passo, one more little step; un — dito di cognac, just a spot of brandy; non perde — minuto, he doesn't waste a second; a -a bocca, grudgingly. **5.** Close, near, approximate; un — trionfo, almost a victory, a near miss; lo sa -a Roma, nearly all Rome knows it; dirlo a — mondo, to tell about half the world; mi pare — secolo, it seems an endless time to me; sarà forse un — chilometro, it is about a kilometre; un — migliaio, about a thousand; mettiamo una -a dozzina, let's say about a dozen; una mezz'oretta, just a little while (cf. precise uses under No. 1).

adv. Half; partly; almost, nearly; — morto, half-dead, nearly dead; — matto, crazy, mad, half-witted; — nudo, half-naked, nearly naked; — aperto, ajar; gliel'ho — detto, I have as good as told him.

n.m. **1.** Half; due -i fanno un intero, two halves make a whole; portare a — un lavoro, to do half a piece of work; a —, by halves; facciamo a —, let's go halves; le spese sono a —, the expenses are equally shared; per —, in half, in two. **2.** Centre, middle; middle part; mid position; nel bel —, right in the middle; colpire nel bel —, to score a bull's eye; darla nel —, to hit on the right solution; in — a, in the middle of, surrounded by; mettersi, entrare di — a, to come between, to intervene in; togliere di —, to get rid of; lèvati di —, get out of the way; non metter tempo in —, to lose no time; stare di —, to be neutral; in quel —, in questo —, in the meantime; (naut.) timone in —!, midships! **3.** Means, expedient; per — di, by means of, through the intermediary or agency of; -i di trasporto, transport; questo è l'unico —, this is the only way; (provb.) il fine giustifica i -i, the end justifies the means; non ha -i per farlo, he hasn't the means to do it; non avere -i, to have no means, to be destitute; uomo di molti -i, a man of considerable means, a wealthy man; †uomo di —, intermediary; (leg.) -i di mantenimento, means of support, maintenance; — di conservazione di, measures for protection of (C.C.); — di correzione, correctional measures (C.P.); i -i per impugnare le sentenze sono…, judgements can be contested by means of…; (mil.) -i di assalto, attacking craft; (naut.) liberty-boat; — d'orario, routine boat. **4.** Medium, mean; il giusto —, the happy mean, the happy medium; il — respirabile, the atmosphere. **-uc·cio** *m. pejor.* underhand means, subterfuge; make-shift.

mezzo-³ *pref.* semi-, half-. **-busto** *m.* (sculp.) bust (without arms); (paint.) portrait (head and shoulders), portrait bust. **-cannone** *m.* (mus.) see **cannone.** **-cer·chio** *m.* semicircle. **-collo** *m.* (naut.) half turn (of a rope on a bollard, etc.). **-colore** *m.* undecided colour, intermediate colour. **-dì** *m. indecl.* noon, midday; a -dì, at noon; il -dì, the south. **-di·o** *m.* demi-god; hero. **-dotto** *m.* (*pl.* **mezzi-dotti**) half-educated person. **-fiera** *m.* monster, half-beast, half-man. **-fino** *adj.* (techn.) medium fine. **-fondo** *m.* middle-distance; corsa di -fondo, middle-distance race; atleta di -fondo, middle-distance runner. **-giorno** *m.* midday, noon; south; il Mezzogiorno d'Italia, Southern Italy. **†-lana** *f.* mediocrity. **-marinaro** *m.* boathook. **†-minerale** *m.* semi-metal. **-nodo** *m.* half-hitch. **-pazzo** *m.* half-mad person. **†-punto** *m.* a stop formerly used where a colon is now employed, a stop not followed by a capital letter. **-rilievo** *m.* (sculp.) high-relief, i.e. with some figures almost in the round (the English term is more comprehensive). **-ter·mine** *m.* expedient; subterfuge. **-tondo** *adj.* (sculp.) see **mezzorilievo.** **-vino** *m.* wine and water; weak wine.

mezz'ombra *f.* (paint.) shading, shadow, half-shadow.

mezzone *m.* inferior wine made from crushed grapes, from which most of the juice has been pressed; (archit.) main beam.

mezz'volo *m.* (arch.) ovolo (moulding), quarter-round.

mezzuc·cio *m. pejor.* See under **mezzo².**

mezzule *m.* head of a cask, moveable stave of a barrel.

mi¹ *pers. prn. conjunct. 1st sing.* me; to me; — vedono, they see me; — hanno scritto, they've written to me; dimmi, tell me; — piace, I like it; — dispiace, I don't like it, I am sorry; *rfl. prn.* — diverto, I am having an amusing time; — lavo le mani, I am washing my hands; statemi bene, keep well (for my sake); io — son un, I am one (who); (dial. N. Italy.) I; l'Italia del —, N. Italy.

mi² *m. indecl.* (mus.) mi (i.e. the third degree of the scale); the note E; the key of E.

mia *poss. adj., f.* See **mio**; †*m.pl.*

miagol·are [A I S] *intr.* (*aux. avere*) to mew, to miaow; (of bullets) to whine. **-amento** *m.* mewing, miaowing. **-ata** *f.* long mewing, a miaow. **(-atore** *m.* **-atrice** *f.*) **-io** *m.* (*pl.* **-ii**) continued mewing; caterwauling. **-one** *m.* cat that mews a great deal. (**-ona** *f.*)

mia·golo *m.* mew, miaow.

miagro *m.* (bot.) gold of pleasure, *Camelina sativa*.

mi-algi·a *f.* (med.) myalgia, muscle pain. **-al·gico** *adj.* myalgic. **-asteni·a** *f.* (med.) myasthenia. **-aste·nico** *adj.* myasthenic.

mia·o, mia·u *onom.* miaow (cf. **miagolare** and derivs.).

mi-as·ma *m.* (med.) miasma. **-asma·tico** *adj.* (med.) miasmal, miasmatic.

miaulare [A I] and derivs. See **miagolare.**

mica¹ *f.* crumb; *adv.* not at all, not in the least; non voglio — offendervi, I don't in the least want to offend you; a noi non piaceva —, we didn't like it at all; non costa — tanto, it isn't really expensive.

mic-a² *f.* (miner.) mica. **-a·ceo** *adj.* (miner.) micaceous. **-aschisto, -ascisto** *m.* (miner.) mica-schist.

Micado *pr.n.m.* Mikado.

micalato *m.* (numism.) a Byzantine gold coin.

mic·cia *f.* fuse (for firing an explosive), slow-match; powder train; (naut.) foot of a mast; stepping of a capstan; squared end of a tiller; hemp heart of a steel wire rope.

micc-ino *m.* tiny crumb; scrap; *adv. phr.* a —, stingily, meanly; in dribs and drabs; sparingly. (**-ichino** *m. dim.*)

micco *m.* (zool.) marmoset monkey *Hapale* sp.; (fig.) debauched individual; roué.

mice·lio *m.* (bot.) mycelium.

Mic-ene *pr.n.f.* (geog.) Mycenae. **-e·neo** *adj.* Mycenaean.

micète *m.* (zool.) howler monkey, *Alouatta* (*Mycetes*) spp.

micet-ologi·a *f.* (bot.) mycetology. **-ozoi** *m.pl.* slime fungi, Myxomycetes, Mycetozoa.

Michel-e *pr.n.m.* Michael; (rel.) San —, St Michael; giorno di San —, Michaelmas; far San —, to move house, to clear out, to pack up (as on Michaelmas Quarter-day). **-ac·cio** *pr.n.m. pejor.* of **Michele**; far la vita di Michelaccio, to eat, drink and be idle (in the manner, it is said, of the Florentine Michele Panichi).

michelangiolèsco *adj.* in the manner of, pertaining to, Michelangelo Buonarroti, Michelangelesque.

michelètto *m.* (hist.) a Spanish soldier of the seventeenth century, a *miquelete*.

mi·cia *f.* See under **micio.**

micidial-e *adj.* deadly; killing; murderous; homicidal; mortal. **-mente** *adv.* murderously.

mi·c-io *m.* (zool.) cat; (pop.) puss, pussy, pussy-cat; stare, farla in barba di —, to be a cat doing its whiskers, (fig.) to be very comfortable; (techn.) tailor's chalk. **-ia** *f.* female pussy. **-ino** *m. dim.* kitten.

micolin-a *f.*, **-o** *m.* little crumb; scrap (cf. **mica¹**).

mic-ologi·a *f.* mycology. **-o·logo** *m.* mycologist.

micragn-a *f.* (colloq.) penury, pennilessness. **-oso** *adj.* (colloq.) penniless, broke, down-and-out.

microbaro·grafo *m.* microbarograph.

micr-o·bio *m.* (biol.) microbe. **-obicida** *adj.* bacteriocidal. **-obiologi·a** *f.* microbiology. **-ocefali·a** *f.* (med.) microcephaly. **-oce·falo** *adj.* (med.) microcephalous; (fig.) stupid, imbecile. **-ochi·mica** *f.* microchemistry. **-ococco** *m.* (biol.) micrococcus. **-ocosmo** *m.* microcosm. **-oco·smico** *adj.* relating to a microcosm. **-ofarad** *m. indecl.* (electr.) microfarad, μF. **-ofoni·a** *f.* (radio) microphony. **-o·fono** *m.* microphone; parlare al -ofono, to broadcast; mouthpiece (of a telephone). **-fotografi·a** *f.* microphotography; microphotograph. **-foto·metro** *m.* (phys., opt.) microphotometer. **-ografi·a** *f.* micrography. **-ogra·fico** *adj.* micrographic. **-o·grafo** *m.* micrographer. **-ologi·a** *f.* micrography. **-o·logo** *m.* (mus.) micrologus, epitome, compendium, esp. referring to the *Micro-*

micr·obio (*cont.*)

logus of Guido d'Arezzo, c. 1025, or to *Musice active micrologus* of Ornithoparcus, 1517. **-omani·a** *f.* pusillanimity, micromania. **-ometri·a** *f.* micrometry. **-ome·trico** *adj.* micrometric; vite -ometrica, micrometer screw. **-o·metro** *m.* micrometer, micrometer gauge. **-omilli·metro** *m.* micron, *μ*. **-omotore** *m.* moped, a bicycle driven by a small engine. **-oonda** *f.* (radio) micro-wave. **-o·pilo** *m.* (biol.) micropyle. **-organismo** *m.* micro-organism. **-oscopi·a** *f.* microscopy. **-osco·pico** *adj.* microscopic; (fig.) minute. **-osco·pio** *m.* microscope; -oscopio elettronico, electron microscope; -oscopio spettroscopico, spectromicroscope. **-oscopista** *m.* microscopist. **-osismo·grafo** *m.* microseismograph. **-osolco** *adj. indecl.* (gramoph.) long-playing; dischi -osolco (dischi a -osolco), micro-groove records, long-playing records; *n.m.* (*pl.* **-chi**) long-playing record; portami qui i miei -osolchi, bring my long-playing records over here. **-osporangi** *m.pl.* (bot.) microsporangium. **-ospo·re** *f.pl.* microspore. **-otele·fono** *m.* (teleph.) receiver. **-o·tomo** *m.* (biol.) microtome.

micro·n *m. indecl.* micron, *μ*, 0·001 millimetre.

Mida[1] *pr.n.m.* Midas; gli orecchi di —, i.e. ass's ears (said of a man who is rich, but a fool).

mida[2] *f.* (zool.) tamarin monkey, *Midas* spp.

mida[3] *f.* (zool.) green turtle, *Chelone mydas*.

midoll·a *f.* pulp of orange or other fruit; crumb (of a loaf, as opposed to crust); bagnato fino alla —, soaked to the skin. **-are** *adj.* (anat.) medullar, medullary. **-o** *m.* marrow, pith; (anat.) medulla; (zool.) -o spinale, spinal cord; bagnato fradicio al -o, soaked to the skin; un freddo che arriva al -o delle ossa, a cold that chills one to the marrow. **-ona** *f. augm.* large piece of bread without crust. **-one** *m. augm.* (fig.) flabby person. **-oso** *adj.* full of marrow; pithy.

midri·asi *f.* (med.) mydriasis.

miei *poss. adj., prn. m.pl.* mine, my; i —, my family, my people (see also **mio**).

miele *m.* honey; parole di —, honied words; luna di —, honeymoon; (pharm.) — rosato, honey and rosewater.

miel·ite *f.* (med.) myelitis. **-oma** *m.* (med.) myeloma.

miemite *f.* (geol.) miemite, a kind of dolomite.

mie·t-ere [B I] *tr.* to reap, to mow; — a terra, to mow short, close; — a collo, to mow the heads of the crop, leaving a long stubble; (fig.) to reap, to gather; non era bella ma con il suo fascino slavo -eva molte vittime, she was not beautiful but with her Slav fascination she made many conquests; — allori, to win laurels. **-itore** *m.* reaper, harvester; mower. **-itrice** *f.* woman reaper, woman harvester; harvesting-machine. **-itura** *f.* reaping, harvesting; mowing; harvest; tempo della -itura, harvest-time. **-uto** *part. adj.* reaped, harvested; mown.

†**miga** *f.* See **mica**[1].

migade *m.* movable bridge of a violin.

migliac·ci-o *m.* black pudding; chestnut-flour cake; mass of dough; (iron smelting) fare un —, to fail in the casting, (joc.) to bleed from the nose. **-ola** *f.* a kind of fritter made of flour and water fried with oil.

miglia·i-o *m.* (*pl.* **-a** *f.*) thousand; -a di uomini, thousands of men; un — di lire, about 1000 lire; a -a, in thousands, by the thousand; parecchie -a, several thousand.

migliare *adj.* See **miliare**.

migliarina *f.* (bot.) four-leaved all-seed, *Polycarpon tetraphyllum*.

migliarini *m.pl.* See **migliarola**.

migliarino *m.* (orn.) — di padule, reed bunting, *Emberiza schoeniclus*; (bot.) gromwell, grummel, *Lithospermum officinale*.

†**migliaro** *m.* See **migliaio**.

migliarola *f.* small shot.

mi·gli-o[1] *m.* (*pl.* **-a** *f.*) mile; — inglese, English mile (1·524 km.); — terrestre, statute mile; — marino, — nautico, nautical mile (NOTE: a nautical mile varies slightly in different latitudes; in U.K. 2000 yards is generally accepted (1853·18 m. corresponding to a latitude of 48°); in France 1852 m. and in Italy 1851·85 m. are assumed for a latitude of about 44°); un tre -a, a distance of three miles; si sentiva il rumore a un — di distanza, one could hear the noise a mile away; milestone (cf. **miliare**); il mille miglia, the 1000-mile motor race; (fig.) mille -a, any immense distance; essere lontano mille -a dal, never to dream of, never to imagine; noi siamo lontani mille -a, our views are miles apart; farla lunga un —, to grumble ceaselessly; cavallo da —, corridore da —,

miler; — romano (antico), Roman mile or milestone; — d'oro, golden milestone (in Forum).

mi·glio[2] *m.* (bot.) millet, *Panicum miliaceum*; bird-seed.

migliora·bile *adj.* See under **migliorare**.

miglioramento[1] *m.* (ichth.) a very large specimen of the common eel, *Anguilla anguilla*.

miglioramento[2] *m.* See under **migliorare**.

miglior-are [A I c] *tr.* to improve, to make better, to ameliorate; *intr.* (*aux.* essere) to improve, to get better; to recover, to mend; la situazione è -ata, the situation has improved; -a di giorno in giorno, he is getting better every day; *rfl.* to improve, to mend one's ways; to improve oneself. **-a·bile** *adj.* improvable; capable of improvement. **-amento** *m.* improvement, amelioration, betterment; recovery (of health); la casa ha bisogno di qualche -amento, the house needs to be done up; (leg.) le opere di -amento fondiario, land-improvement works; -amenti apportati alla cosa locata, improvements to the thing hired (C.C.). **-ativo** *adj.* ameliorative. **-ato** *part. adj.* improved, ameliorated.

miglior-e *adj.* better; finer; superior; *n.m., f.* il (la) —, the best; the finest; i -i, the best ones, the best people. **-mente** *adv.* see **meglio**. **-i·a** *f.* improvement, amelioration.

mignano *m.* (archit.) external gallery (esp. in Rome).

mignatt-a *f.* (zool.) leech; (fig.) usurer, blood-sucker; importunate person, fearful bore. **-aio** *m.* one who collects or sells leeches, leech-gatherer; (orn.) glossy ibis, *Plegadis falcinellus*.

mi·gnol-o[1] *m.* olive-blossom. **-are** [A I S] *intr.* (*aux.* avere) (of olives) to blossom; (provb.) quando -a d'aprile ammannisci un buon barile, quando -a di maggio n'avrai tanto per assaggio, quando -a di giugno t'ungerai appena il grugno, when the olive blossoms in April provide a barrel for the oil, when in May there will be enough for a sample, when in June hardly enough to oil your face. (**-atura** *f.*)

mi·gnolo *m.* little finger; little toe; olive bud; *adj.* little; il dito —, the little finger.

mignone *m.* favourite; (hist.) piece of armour for the forearm; (typ.) minion type.

mignotta *f.* harlot, whore.

migr-are [A I] *intr.* (*aux.* avere, essere) to migrate. **-abondo** *adj.* migrant. **-atore** *adj., n.m.* migrant; uccelli -atori, migrant birds. **-ato·rio** *adj.* migratory. **-azione** *f.* migration.

Mikado *pr.n.m.* See **Micado**.

mila *pl.* of **mille**, q.v., when conjoined with another numeral; diecimila, ten thousand.

Milan-o[1] *pr.n.f.* (geog.) Milan. **-ese** *adj.* Milanese; *n.m.* native of Milan, Milanese; Milanese dialect; *f.* Milanese woman, Milanese girl.

milano[2] *m.* (orn.) buzzard.

miliard-o *m.* milliard, a thousand million. **-a·rio** *m.* man who is worth a milliard lire, multi-millionaire.

miliare *adj.* marking miles; pietra —, milestone; *n.m.* milestone; (fig.) landmark.

milio·bate *m.* (ichth.) devil fish, *Myliobatis aquila*.

milion-e *m.* million. **-a·rio** *m.* millionaire; (fig.) wealthy man. **-cino** *m. dim.* (colloq.) a cool million. **-esimo**, **-e·simo** *adj.* millionth; la -esima parte, the millionth part.

militante *adj.* militant; combative, fighting; la Chiesa —, the Church Militant.

militare[1] [A I S] *intr.* (*aux.* avere) to serve; aveva militato con Garibaldi, he had fought under Garibaldi; to militate; a mio favore militano cento ragioni, a hundred reasons militate in my favour.

militare[2] *adj., n.m.* and derivs. See under **milite**.

mi·lit-e *m.* soldier, militiaman; (hist.) Roman soldier, legionary; il — Ignoto, the Unknown Soldier; — di Cristo, soldier of Christ. **-are** *m.* soldier, military man; (leg.) member of armed forces (C.C.; C.P.); *adj.* military; tribunale -are, military tribunal. **-armente** *adv.* militarily. **-aresco** *adj.* (*m.pl.* **-areschi**) soldierly. **-arismo** *m.* militarism. **-arista** *m.* militarist. **-ari·stico** *adj.* militaristic. **-ariẓẓare** [A I] *tr.* to militarize. **-ariẓẓazione** *f.* militarizing; militarization. **-eṣente** *adj.* exempt from, not liable to, military service.

mili·zia *f.* the profession of arms; warfare; soldiering; darsi alla —, to take up soldiering; a body of soldiers, militia, army; — territoriale, Territorial Army; (Ital. hist.) la — Fascista, the Fascist Militia; (rel.) la — di Cristo, the faithful soldiers of Christ; — celeste, host of heaven, heavenly warriors, angels.

millanta *f.* (colloq., joc.) a thousand; a great number.

millant-are [A I] *tr.* to boast of; to exaggerate; -ava le sue ricchezze, he boasted of his wealth; *rfl.* to boast, to brag. -a·mento *m.* boasting. -ato *part. adj.* (leg.) -ato credito, crime of pretending, fraudulently for gain, to have influence with a public servant (defined in C.P., 1930, Art.. 346); -ato credito del patrocinatore, the like false pretence, by counsel representing, or solicitor acting for, lay client (*ibid.* Art 382); (fig.) false pretences. -atore *m.* boaster, braggart. (-atrice *f.*) -eri·a *f.* boasting, bragging; brag, boast; queste sono ridicole -erie, these are ridiculous boasts.

mill-e *card. num.* (*pl.* **mila**) a thousand; one thousand; il —, the eleventh century; — novecento cinquanta sette, 1957; (hist.) I Mille, the Thousand, the volunteers who accompanied Garibaldi on his Sicilian expedition in 1860; uno su —, one in a thousand; — grazie, very many thanks; mi pare — anni di, I long to; *Le Mille e una Notte, The Arabian Nights*; (geog.) Mille Isole, Thousand Isles. -e·cuplo *adj.* thousandfold. -efiori *m.* scented toilet water of the fragrance of many flowers. -efo·glie *m.* (bot.) yarrow, milfoil, *Achillea millefolium*; (cul.) mille-feuille. -egrani *m.pl.* (bot.) *Hippocrepis multisiliquosa*. -emor·bia *f.* (bot.) figwort, *Scrophularia nodosa*.

millena·r·io *adj.* millenary; Millenarian; *n.m.* Millenarian. -ismo *m.* Millenarianism.

mill-enne *adj.* millenary. -en·nio *m.* millennium.

millepiedi *m. indecl.* (zool.) millipede.

millerite *f.* (miner.) millerite, nickel monosulphide.

mill-esimo *ord. num.* thousandth; la -esima volta, the thousandth time; *n.m.* thousandth part; millennium; in a date, the figure marking the thousands; the date itself; manca il —, the date's missing.

mill-iampero·metro *m.* (electr.) microammeter. -igrammo *m.* milligram, milligramme. -i·litro, -ilitro *m.* millilitre. -i·metro *m.* millimetre. -imetrato *adj.* calibrated in millimetres; carta -imetrata, graph paper. -ivolt *m. indecl.* (electr.) millivolt. -ivolt·metro *m.* (electr.) millivoltmeter.

milor·d, milord-e, -o *m.* a grand gentleman; elegant gentleman. -ino *m.* elegant young man. -ina *f.* grand young woman.

†**miluogo** *m.* half-way house; half-way spot, mark.

mil·vulo *m.* (orn.) scissor-tailed flycatcher, *Muscivora* spp.

milza *f.* (anat.) spleen; (butcher.) milt; (fig.) avere male alla —, to have a stitch in one's side.

milzadella *f.* (bot.) spotted dead nettle, *Lamium maculatum*.

†**milzo** *adj.* thin; poor (cf. **smilzo**).

mim-a *f.* mime; dancer in mime. -are [A I] (*aux.* avere) to mime. -esco *adj.* (*m.pl.* -eschi) pertaining to mime. -esi *f. indecl.* mimesis, imitation. -e·tico *adj.* mimetic, mimetical. (-eticamente *adv.*) -etismo *m.* mimicry. -o *m.* mime; actor; clown; mimic.

mimetite *f.* (miner.) mimetite, memetesite.

mimetizz-are [A I] *tr.* to camouflage. -ato *part. adj.* camouflaged. -azione *f.* camouflage.

mi·mic-a *f.* mimicry; gesticulation; faceva la — di un vero duello, he went through the actions of a real duel. -o *adj.* relating to mime; l'arte -a, mime; (class. antiq.) mime; dramatic form used, e.g., by Sophron and Herodas; actor in such drama; (orn.) mockingbird, *Mimus polyglottus*. -o·grafo *m.* (class. antiq.) writer of mimes. -o·logo *m.* (class. antiq.) actor, speaker, in mime.

mimm-o *m.* (colloq.) baby, babykins; †*adj.* babyish. (-a *f.*)

mimo *m.* See under **mima**.

mimosa *f.* (bot.) sensitive plant, *Mimosa pudica*; erba —, mimosa (name, as in English, of several ornamental species of *Acacia*); (tanning) corteccia di —, wattle bark.

min-a *f.* mine (to be exploded); — subacquea, underwater mine; — magnetica, magnetic mine; — galleggiante, floating mine; (Gk. antiq.) mina (unit of weight or money); a Tuscan measure (about half a bushel); †threat; †mien, appearance. -are [A I] *tr.* to mine, undermine. -a·bile *adj.* that can be mined. -atore *m.* miner.

mina·bile *adj.* See under **minare**.

minac·c-ia *f.* threat, menace; una — alla pace d'Europa, a threat to the peace of Europe; vane -e, empty threats; proferire -e, to threaten, to utter threats. -evole *adj.* menacing, threatening. -evolmente *adv.* menacingly; in a threatening manner. -ia·bile *adj.* capable of being frightened by threats. -iamento *m.* heavy threatening. -iante *part. adj.* threatening, menacing. -iare [A 3] *tr.* to threaten; lo -iò con un'occhiata, he gave him a threatening glance; lo -iò di morte, he threatened to kill him; -iava di dimettersi, he threatened to resign; il tempo oggi -ia, the weather is threatening today. (-iato *part. adj.*) -iatore *m.* threatener; menacer. (-iatrice *f.*) -iato·rio *adj.* threatening. -ioso *adj.* threatening; menacing; tempo -ioso, unpromising weather. (-iosamente *adv.*)

†**minace** *adj.* menacing.

min-are [A I] *tr.* to mine (with an explosive mine); to undermine; to injure; to sap; — l'ingresso, to mine the approaches; la malattia gli -ava le forze, illness was sapping his strength. -a·bile *adj.* capable of being mined. -ato *part. adj.* mined; campo -ato, zona -ata, minefield. -atore *m.* sapper; miner, pitman, collier.

minareto *m.* minaret.

minato·rio *adj.* minatory; menacing, threatening; una lettera minatoria, a threatening letter.

†**minchiate** *f.pl.* a form of the card-game 'tarocchi', played with 97 cards.

minchion-e *m.* fool, simpleton, ninny, dunce; fare il —, to pretend not to understand; *adj.* silly, stupid. -a *f.* stupid woman. -ag·gine *f.* foolishness, silliness. -are [A I c] *tr.* to mock, to ridicule, to make fun of; to make a fool of; pigliava quelle lodi per vere e non s'accorgeva che lo -avano, he took the praise as genuine and did not realize that they were ragging him; farsi -are, to make a fool of oneself; *intr.* (*aux.* avere) to fool, to jest; non -are, to be very much in earnest; ieri pioveva e oggi non -a, it rained yesterday, and there's certainly no letting-up today. -atore *m.* mocker. (-atrice *f.*) -ato·rio *adj.* mocking, jeering; un risolino -atorio, a mocking smile. -atura *f.* mocking, jeering; foolery; leg-pull. -eri·a *f.* foolish deed or word; *pl.* nonsense. †-evolezza *f.* silliness.

minchiotto *m.* (naut.) extremity of a mast.

†**minera** *f.* See **miniera**.

mineral-e *adj.* mineral; *n.m.* mineral, ore; — di ferro, iron ore; olio —, mineral oil. -ista *m.* mineralogist. -iz·zare [A I] *tr.* (geol.) to mineralize, to petrify. (-iz·zato *part. adj.*) -iz·zazione *f.* petrification. -ogi·a *f.* mineralogy. -ogista *m.* mineralogist.

minera·rio *adj.* (pertaining to) mining; industria mineraria, mining industry.

Minerv-a *pr.n.f.* (myth.) Minerva; (Rome) Palazzo —, the seat of the Ministry of Education. -ale *adj.* pertaining to Minerva; feste -ali, Minerva's festival; *n.m.* fee paid to tutors in Ancient Rome.

minestr-a *f.* vegetables, 'pasta', etc. in a thick soup; — di grasso, di magro, this soup made with or without meat; — asciutta, dry 'pasta' with sauce, etc.; food; (fig.) pension, wages; ho paura di perder la —, I'm afraid of losing my livelihood; (hist.) i principi delle sessanta -e, the republican government of Lucca which lasted for sixty days. -a·io *m.* great eater of minestra. -one *m. augm.* large bowl of soup; a different kind of dish from 'minestra', the most characteristic being: -one alla genovese (with pesto, a flavouring of basil, pecorino cheese, garlic and pine kernels soaked in oil); -one alla milanese (vegetables with bacon and rice, served hot or cold); -one alla fiorentina (with 'soffritto', a flavouring made of pork, red chillies, giblets of chicken and tomato sauce).

mingere [C 5] *intr.* (*aux.* avere) to urinate.

mingherlino *adj.* slim, lean; slender.

minghetti *m. indecl.* a kind of cigar, named after the statesman Minghetti (1818–86).

minghiale *m.* (ichth.) — di scoglio, — di pietra, *Phycis phycis*, an edible marine fish.

mini-are [A 4] *tr.* (paint.) to miniate, to paint with red-lead; to illuminate, to illustrate with miniatures; (fig.) to describe in detail; to embellish; *intr.* (*aux.* avere) to paint miniatures (in the later sense of small portraits on ivory, etc.). (-ato *part. adj.*) -atore *m.* illuminator of MSS. -atura *f.* miniature (action of miniating, or result); illumination; miniature (i.e. small-scale portrait with minute finish); pare una -atura, it is finely and delicately painted. -aturista *m., f.* miniaturist.

miniera *f.* mine; quarry; una — di carbone, a coal-mine; — a cielo aperto, open-cast mine; — d'oro, gold-mine; (fig.) una — di notizie, a mine of information.

mi·nima *f.* (mus.) minim.

minima-mente *adv.*, **-lista** *m.* See under **minimo**.

mini·metro *m.* (techn.) dial gauge.

mi·nim-o *adj.* least; smallest; lowest; slightest; very small; senza il — sforzo, without the least effort; senza la -a difficoltà, without the slightest difficulty; non ho la -a idea, I haven't the slightest idea; la differenza è -a, the difference is very slight; ogni errore benchè —, even the least error; ridotto ai -i termini, reduced to the simplest terms, (fig.) destitute; il prezzo —, the lowest price; (math.) il — comune multiplo, the lowest common multiple; (leg.) -a unità colturale, smallest farm acreage that can support a family (C.C.); *n.m.* il —, the least; the least important; minimum; the least little thing; (eccl.) Minim (Friar); (eng.) idling speed. **-amẹnte** *adv.* in the least; not in the least; not at all. **-alista** *m.* (pol.) minimalist.

mi·nio *m.* (chem.) red-lead; pittura al —, red-lead paint.

miniot·tero *m.* (zool.) *Miniopterus schreibersi*, long-winged bat.

†miniposs-anza *f.* feebleness. **-ente** *adj.* feeble.

†minisfatto *m.* See **misfatto**.

minist-ero, **†-e·rio** *m.* office, function, ministry; board, department; — degli Affari Esteri, Foreign Office; — delle Finanze, Ministry of Finance; government; la formazione del nuovo —, the forming of a new government; — di coalizione, coalition government; (eccl.) sacred ministry; (leg.) Pubblico —, Public Prosecutor. NOTE: this important Office in the 'ordinamento giudiziario' performs many of the functions of Attorney-General, Director of Public Prosecutions, Official Receiver, Official Solicitor, etc. **-eriale** *adj.* ministerial; crisi -eriale, cabinet crisis. **-erialmẹnte** *adv.* ministerially.

ministr-are [A I] *tr.* to administer, to minister, to govern; (eccl.) to administer (the sacraments); to assist (the celebrant at mass); *intr.* (*aux.* avere; *prep.* a) to minister (to). **-ante** *part. adj.* ministering; assisting; administering; *n.m.* (eccl.) assistant (cleric); minister (at mass). (**-atore** *m.* **-atrice** *f.*) **†-azione** *f.* office, function, ministry.

ministr-o *m.* minister; Primo —, Prime Minister; — degli Affari Esteri, Foreign Secretary; — di Stato, cabinet minister; carta —, foolscap paper; (eccl.) (of Catholic clergy in a few contexts) -i di Dio, dell'altare, ministers of God, of the altar; -i sacri, sacred ministers (assisting the celebrant at High Mass); (Franciscan) — generale, minister-general; -i degl'infermi, Attendants of the sick, Camillians; (of Protestant clergy generally) minister, pastor, clergyman; (admin.) — del culto, minister of religion (C.C.).

mino *m.* (orn.) mynah.

mino·ico *adj.* Minoan.

†mi·nomo *adj.*. See **menomo**, or **minimo**.

minor-e *adj.* less, minor, lesser; younger; con minor lode, with less praise; di — importanza, of less importance; Asia Minore, Asia Minor; (eccl.) ordini -i, minor orders; (mus.) minor (attribute of mode or interval); (leg.) essere di età —, to be an infant, to be under age; *n.m.* il —, the lesser, the smaller; person under age, minor; (leg.) infant; un — degli anni 14, a child under 14; un — degli anni 18, young person under 18; impiego di -i nell'accattonaggio, employment of children in begging (C.P.); (mus.) minore, a section or variation in the minor mode contrasting with a previous passage in the major. **-anza** *f.* minority; essere in -anza, to be in a minority; rispettare i diritti della -anza, to respect minority rights; in -anza di cento voti, by a minority vote of a hundred. **-are** [A I C] *tr.* to lessen, to diminish; to disable, to weaken, to impair. **-asco** *m.* (*pl.* **-aschi**) (leg.) trust estate held for younger brother. **-ativo** *adj.* serving to lessen; attenuating. **-ato** *part. adj.* diminished, lessened; disabled; weakened, impaired; (eng.) undersize. **-azione** *f.* lessening, diminution; disablement; impairing, weakening; (comm.) -azione del valore, depreciation of value. **-enne** *adj.* under age; *n.m.,f.* infant; person under age; i -enni, children and young persons; Tribunale per i -enni, Juvenile Court. **-ennità** *f.* minority. **-ile** *adj.* minor. **-ita** *m.* (eccl.) Minorite, Friar Minor. **-ità** *f.* state of being under age; essere fuori di -ità, to be no longer under age. **-i·tico** *adj.* (eccl.) Minorite.

Min-osse, **-òs** *pr.n.m.* (class. myth.) Minos; (fig.) grim judge. **-os·sico** *adj.* (archaeol.) Minoan (culture). **-ota·uro** *m.* (class. myth.), Minotaur.

†minuale¹ *adj.* of humble condition.

†minuale² *m.* See **manovale**.

†minuare *vb.* and derivs. See **minuire**.

minuẹndo *m.* (math.) minuend.

minuẹtto *m.* (mus.) minuet. NOTE: the incorrect form **menuetto** (by confusion with the French *menuet*) is not used by Italian composers.

minu·gia *f.* (**†minu·gio** *m.*) (mus.) gut, catgut; string (even when made of metal).

minuire [D 2] *tr.* to diminish; to minish; to reduce (cf. **diminuire**).

minu·scol-o *adj.* small; little, tiny; una lettera -a, a small letter (i.e. not a capital); (fig.) paltry; trifling, trivial; small. **-a** *f.* small letter; (palaeog.) minuscule hand, minuscule. **-i** *m.pl.* (typ.) lower-case letters (see Note under **maiuscoli**).

minuta *f.* See under **minuto¹**.

minut-o¹ *adj.* minute, tiny, very small; fine; tagliar —, to chop up fine; lineamenti -i, fine, delicate features; pioggia -a, fine rain; detailed; disegno —, drawing or figure showing fine detail; precise; overscrupulous about every little detail; petty-minded; troppo per —, too detailed; (comm.) spese -e, petty charges; commercio —, retail trade; al —, retail; gente -a, popolo —, common people, ordinary, lower-class people; unimportant; pescheria -a, small fry (also fig.); bestiame —, smaller livestock (e.g. pigs, sheep, goats, as opposed to cattle). **-amẹnte** *adv.* minutely; in detail; on a small scale; finely; scrupulously. **-a** *f.* draft, rough copy; bill of fare, menu; (leg.) draft; heads of agreement. **-a·glia** *f.* small things; petty details, minutiae; unimportant, insignificant people, small fry. **-ame** *m.* see **minutaglia**. **-ante** *m.,f.* one who draws up documents; taker of minutes at a meeting; secretary. **-are** [A I] *tr.* to draw up; to draft; -are una lettera, to draft a letter; to minute; (agric.) -are un campo, to plough a field in narrow furrows. (**-ato** *part. adj.*) **-eri·a** *f.* small article, trinket; (watchm.) ruota della -eria, minute wheel; ruotismo di -eria, minute work. **-ẹzza** *f.* minuteness; fine detail; smallness, pettiness; *pl.* trifles; minutiae. **-iere** *m.* worker in small jewellery; dealer in small jewellery or other small articles.

minuto² *m.* minute (of time); instant; — primo, minute; — secondo, second; dieci -i e cinque secondi, ten minutes and five seconds; un mezzo —!, half a minute!; è affare di due -i, it won't take a minute; (watchm.) lancetta dei minuti, minute-hand; ruota, rocchetto, dei minuti, cannon pinion.

minu·zi-a *f.* small detail; non occupartene, sono -e, don't bother about them, they're of trifling importance; perdersi in -e, to be finicking, to be particular about trifling details. **-osag·gine** *f.* fastidiousness. **-osità** *f.* minuteness; accuracy; scrupulousness; fastidiousness. **-oso** *adj.* paying attention to details; paying attention to trifles; pedantic; careful; fastidious; scrupulous; minute, detailed. (**-osamẹnte** *adv.*) **-u·cola** *f. dim.* merest trifle. **-uola** *f. dim.* tiny thing.

minuzz·a·glia *f.*, **-ame** *m.* See **minutaglia**, under **minuto¹**.

minuzzare [A I] *tr.* to break into small pieces.

minuz·z-olo *m.* bit; shred; morsel, crumb, scrap; little shrimp (of a child). **-are** [A I] *tr.* to break into little pieces, to crumble; to shred. **-atore** *m.* shredder. (**-atrice** *f.*) **†-o** *m.*, **†-ola** *f.* shred.

minzionẹ *f.* urination.

mi·o *poss. adj.* (*m.pl.* **miei**) my; mine; la mia casa, my house; — padre, my father; un — cugino, a cousin of mine; voglio la roba mia, I want my property; questo è —, this is mine; amico —, my dear friend; *poss. prn.* il —, mine; vivo del —, I have independent means; voglio il —, I want what is mine; i miei, my relatives, my people; questo —, this of mine; ti scrivo questa mia da Torino, I am writing you this letter from Turin.

mio-car·dio *m.* (anat.) myocardium, heart muscle. **-cardite** *f.* (med.) myocarditis.

mioc-ene *m.* (geol.) Miocene. **-e·nico** *adj.* (geol.) Miocene.

miogale *f.* (zool.) desman, *Desmana* spp.

mi·op-e *adj.* short-sighted, myopic; (fig.) myopic; *n.m.,f.* short-sighted person. **-i·a** *f.* myopia, short-sightedness.

mi-opla·stico *adj.* (med.) myoplastic. **-oressi·a** *f.* (med.) myorrhexis. **-osclerosi** *f.* (med.) mysclerosis. **-osi** *f.* (med.) myosis. **-o·sico** *adj.* (med.) myotic. **-osina** *f.* (chem.; biol.) myosin. **-osite** *f.* (med.) myositis. **-o·tico** *adj.* (med.) myotic.

mioso·tide *f.* (bot.) forget-me-not, *Myosotis*.

miotomi·a *f.* (med.) myotomy.

miot·tero *m.* (zool.) bat.

mira *f.* aim; mettere a — il fucile, to aim one's gun; prendere, pigliare la —, to take aim; avere buona —, to be a good shot; direction; purpose, object; (fig.) prendere, pigliare di — una cosa, to make a thing a target, to attack it; avere delle -e sopra, to

mira (*cont.*)

have designs on; avere in — di, to intend to; avere in — una cosa, to aim at a thing, to have a thing in view; la sua — è questa, his purpose is this; mettere la — in fallo, to misfire; (fig.) to be disappointed in one's hopes; (fig.) avere la — troppo alta, collocare la propria — troppo in alto, to aim too high; cogliere la —, to achieve one's aim.

mir·a·bile *adj.* admirable; wonderful, marvellous. **-abilmente** *adv.* admirably; wonderfully, marvellously. **-abi·lia** *f.pl.* wonderful things; wonderful deeds; fece -abilia, he worked wonders; dire -abilia di, to speak wonders of. **-abolante** *adj.* (usu. iron.) stunning, amazing, astounding. †**-a·bole** *adj.* see **mirabile**.

mirabilite *f.* (miner.) mirabilite, Glauber salt.

mira·col·o *m.* miracle; wonder; prodigy; marvel; un — di dottore, a wonderful doctor; operare, fare -i, to work wonders, to perform miracles; (iron.) far -i, to make a great to-do; per —, by a miracle; che —!, how marvellous!, what a miracle!; —, che non t'abbiano ammazzato, it's a wonder they didn't kill you. **-a·io** *m.* person quick to see miracles in everything; one who believes all sorts of incredible things. **-ato** *part. adj.* miraculously cured; *n.m.* miraculously cured person. **-ino** *m. dim.* minor miracle; infant prodigy. **-ismo** *m.* credulous belief in wonders and miracles. **-osità** *f.* miraculousness. **-oso** *adj.* miraculous; marvellous, wonderful; prodigious. **-osamente** *adv.* miraculously, by a miracle; marvellously, wonderfully; prodigiously.

†**miradore** *m.* mirror; admirer; looker.

mirag·gio *m.* mirage; — superiore, looming; (fig.) illusion, mirage.

†**mira·gli·a** *m.* admiral. †**-ato** *m.* Admiralty.

mira·glio *m.* (naut.) top mark on a buoy; †mirror.

miraguano *m.* (text.) kapok.

†**mirallegro** *m.* congratulation; fare, dare il — a, to congratulate.

Miranda *pr.n.f.* Miranda.

†**mirando** *adj.* wondrous (cf. **mirare**).

mir·are [A I] *tr.* to look at, to stare at, to gaze on; to admire; to aim at, to direct at; to tend towards; (fig.) to consider; -ate il danno!, consider the harm!; †to see; *rfl.* to look at oneself; -arsi allo specchio, to look at oneself in the mirror, to study one's reflection in the glass; *intr.* (*aux.* avere; *prep.* a) to take aim; to aim (at); — intorno, to look around, (fig.) to be on one's guard. (**-ato** *part. adj.*) **-atore** *m.* one who looks or stares; good marksman, good shot. (**-atrice** *f.*)

mirbana *f.* (chem.) essenza di —, oil of mirbane, nitrobenzene.

mir·i·ade *f.* myriad. **-iagrammo**, **-iagramma** *m.* ten kilogrammes. **-ia·litro** *m.* ten hectolitres, 1000 litres. **-ia·metro** *m.* (geog.) 10,000 metres, 10 kilometres. **-ia·podi** *m.pl.* (zool.) myriapods.

miriarca *m.* (mil. hist.) commander of 10,000 men.

miric·a, **-e** *f.* (bot.) tamarisk, tamarisk-tree.

miricina *f.* (chem.) myricin, myricyl palmitate.

mirichi *m. indecl.* (zool.) spider monkey, *Ateles* sp.

miri·fico *adj.* (poet.; joc.) magnificent, marvellous, wonderful.

mirino *m.* sight (of gun); (photog.) viewfinder; (opt.) — ottico, direct vision finder.

†**miriofillo** *m.* See **millefoglie**.

miristato *m.* (chem.) myristate.

miri·st·ica *f.* (bot.) nutmeg, *Myristica fragrans*. **-ico** *adj.* (chem.) myristic; acido -ico, myristic acid, tetradecanoic acid. **-ina** *f.* (chem.) myristin.

mirm·eco·bio *m.* (zool.) Australian ant-eater, *Myrmecobius fasciatus*. **-eco·file** *f.* (bot.) myrmecophile. **-i·cide** *m.* (ent.) Myrmicine ant. **-ico·fago** *m.* (zool.) ant-eater. **-icoleone** *m.* (ent.) ant-lion, *Myrmicoleone* spp. **-i·doni** *m.pl.* (Gk. lit. and myth.) Myrmidons.

mir·mica *f.* red-ant.

mirmillone *m.* (Rom. antiq.) Mirmillo, (kind of) gladiator.

miro *adj.* (poet.) wondrous, marvellous.

mirobalano *m.* (tanning) myrobalan.

†**miroll·a** *f.* see **midolla**. †**-o** *m.* see **midollo**, under **midolla**.

mirosina *f.* (chem.) myrosin.

mirr·a *f.* (bot.) myrrh (resin of *Commiphora molmol*). **-are** [A I] *tr.* to impregnate with myrrh; (fig.) to render incorruptible, immortalize. **-olo** *m.* myrrh oil, oil of myrrh.

mir·ride *f.* (bot.) name of umbelliferous plants, as: *Anthriscus silvestris*, *Chaerophyllum aromaticum*, *Myrrhis odorata*, etc.

mirrino *m.* murrhine, extract of myrrh.

†**mirro** *m.* measure for oil (about 10 kilogrammes).

mirrolo *m.* See under **mirra**.

mirsinite *f.* (bot.) *Salix myrsinites*.

mirtillo *m.* (bot.) bilberry, blaeberry, whortleberry, *Vaccinium myrtillus*.

mirt·o *m.* (bot.) myrtle, *Myrtus communis*. **-e·o** *adj.* of, relating to myrtle. **-eto** *m.* myrtle thicket, myrtle grove. **-ino** *adj.* of, relating to myrtle.

†**misa·gi·o** *m.* discomfort; need. **-ato** *adj.* in discomfort, needy.

†**misalta** *f.* fresh salted pork; plump person; (fig.) uscir di —, to be past one's (its) best.

mis·an·tropo *m.* misanthropist. **-antropi·a** *f.* misanthropy. **-antro·pico** *adj.* misanthropic. **-antropicamente** *adv.* misanthropically.

†**misavveduto** *adj.* heedless; ill-considered.

†**mis·avvenimento** *m.* misfortune. †**-avvenire** *intr.* to fail.

misavventura *f.* misadventure; misfortune.

†**miscadere** *intr.* to turn out badly.

misc·e *m.* mixture; *imp.* mix (formerly used in recipes). **-e·a** *f.* trifle, worthless thing, bagatelle. **-ela** *f.* mixture; medley; blend; (motor.) mixture; -ela del minimo, idling mixture; -ela grassa, rich mixture; -ela povera, weak mixture. **-ela·bile** *adj.* miscible.

miscella·ne·a *f.* (lit.) miscellany; anthology. **-o** *adj.* (lit.) miscellaneous.

mi·schi·a *f.* fight; scuffle, hand-to-hand fight; fray, affray; nel fitto, nel folto, della—, in the thick of the fight; (rugby) scrum, scrummage; the forwards as a whole; — aperta, loose scrum; — chiusa, tight scrum, set scrum; — girata, wheel; †mixture. **-ag·gio** *m.* (radio) mixing. **-are** [A4] *tr.* to mix; to mingle; to blend; to jumble; (cards) to shuffle; *recip. rfl.* to mix, to intermingle; to become jumbled. **-ato** *part. adj.* mixed, mingled; blended; jumbled. **-atamente** *adv.* confusedly, in a jumbled or chaotic manner. **-atura** *f.* mixture; jumble.

†**mischino** *adj.* See **meschino**.

mi·schio *m.* mixture; medley; jumble; *apocop. part. adj.* mixed.

†**miscianza** *f.* mixture.

misci·bile *adj.* miscible, which can be mixed; i colori sono miscibili fra loro, the paints can be mixed with each other.

†**misciolfo** *adj.* stupid; *n.m.* stupid person.

†**misco** *adj.* (of grain) adherent to the husk.

misconosc·ere [B9] *tr.* to refuse to recognize; not to acknowledge; to repudiate, to disown; to disregard. **-ente** *adj.* ungrateful. **-enza** *f.* ingratitude. **-imento** *m.* repudiation; disregard. **-iuto** *part. adj.* disowned, repudiated; disregarded; not appreciated; slighted.

miscre·d·ere [B I] *intr.* (*aux.* avere) to disbelieve (usually with reference to religious truth); to hold a false belief. **-ente** *part. adj.* unbelieving; *n.m.* unbeliever. **-enza** *f.* unbelief.

miscu·glio *m.* mixture; sorry mixture; medley; (techn.) mixture, blend.

†**misdire** *tr.* to speak ill of; to contradict, to gainsay.

†**misello** *adj.* wretched; leprous.

miser·a·bile *adj.* wretched; mean; indigent, needy, poor; unhappy, miserable; guadagno —, meagre pittance; *n.m.* wretch; pauper. (**-abilmente** *adv.*). **-abilità** *f.* wretchedness, meanness; destitution, indigence, poverty; †(leg.) fede di -abilità, a certificate issued when a person was admitted to sue *in forma pauperis*; benefizio di -abilità, benefit of the poor. **-ando** *adj.* pitiable, pitiful; uno spettacolo -ando, a wretched sight. **-azione** *f.* compassion; commiseration. **-ello** *m.* wretch. **-ere** *m.* miserere; ridotto al -ere, at the last extremity; *excl.* mercy!; faccia da -ere, face looking like death; (med.) il mal del -ere, volvulus. **-evole** *adj.* miserable; lamentable; piteous; pitiable. (**-evolmente** *adv.*)

mise·ri·a *f.* poverty; essere in —, to be destitute; morì nella —, he died in great poverty; scarcity; want; lack; quest'anno c'è gran — di vino, wine is very scarce this year; distress, wretchedness, misfortune, misery; pianger —, to plead poverty, to complain of, and exaggerate, one's misfortunes; fare della —, to be in low water financially; wretchedly bad piece of work; porca —!, hell!; trifle, wretched little thing of no importance; little failing or weakness; meanness; fare delle -e, to be niggardly; (bot.) spiderwort, *Tradescantia*.

mise·ricorde *adj.* merciful; kind.

mise·rico·rd·ia *f.* mercy; Dio, nella sua infinita —, God, in His infinite mercy; aver, sentir — di, to feel pity for; gridare —, to call for mercy; far, usar — a, to be merciful to; (theol.) opere di — (corporali, spirituali) (corporal, spiritual) works of mercy; (eccl.) compagnia della —, Misericordia guild (esp. in Tuscany);

misericord-ia (*cont.*)
(hist.) 'misericord', dagger for giving the 'coup de grâce'; *excl.* bless us!, good gracious!; -ie celesti!, merciful heavens! **-iante** *m.* member of the Misericordia. †**-ianza** *f.* act of mercy, charity. †**-iare** *intr.* to be merciful. **-ioso** *adj.* merciful; kind. (**-iosamente** *adj.*)

mi·ṣer-o *adj.* poor, indigent; pitiable; wretched, unhappy; paltry; vile, mean; miserly, stingy, niggardly; shabby; una -a fine, a wretched end; un compenso —, a paltry reward; un abito —, a wretched old coat. **-amente** *adv.* wretchedly; meanly.

miṣer·rimo *adj. superl.* of misero, q.v.

misfatto *m.* misdeed; crime; wrong-doing; *pl.* misbehaviour.

†**misfidare** *tr.* to distrust.

Mi·ṣi-a *pr.n.f.* (geog.) Mysia, in Asia Minor. **-o** *adj.* (geog.) of Mysia.

misidi·a *pr.n.m.* (mi si dia) name of a card game, a kind of Tresette for three players.

†**misirico·rdia** *f.* See misericordia.

misirizzi *m. indecl.* (mi si rizzi) a toy, usu. in the shape of a clown, having a weight at its base so that it stands upright again whenever it is pushed over, 'wobbly man'.

†**misle·a** *f.* mêlée.

†**misle-ale** *adj.* disloyal. (**-almente** *adv.*) **-altà** *f.* disloyalty. **-anza** *f.* perfidy.

†**miso** *part.* of mettere, q.v.

miṣogallo *m.* hater of the French and all French ways (the title of an anti-French work by Vittorio Alfieri).

miṣogami·a *f.* misogamy.

miṣo·gin-o *m.* misogynist. **-i·a** *f.*, **-iṣmo** *m.* misogynism.

miṣoli·dio *adj.* (mus.) modo —, mixolydian mode.

miṣone-ista *m.* misoneist, hater of novelty. **-iṣmo** *m.* misoneism, hatred of anything new.

†**misper-o** *m.* despair. †**-are** *intr.* to despair.

†**mispregiare** *tr.* to despise.

†**mis-pren·dere** *intr.* to make a mistake, to fail; *tr.* to despair of; to deceive. †**-preso** *f.*, †**-priso** *m.* mistake.

missag·gio *m.* (cinem.) mixing; tecnico del —, mixer.

mis·sil-e *adj.* capable of being thrown; *n.m.* missile. **-i·stico** *adj.* relating to missiles, missile.

missino *m.* (pol.) member of the Movimento Sociale Italiano (M.S.I.), the neo-Fascist party.

mission-e *f.* mission; expedition; discharge from service; (theol.; eccl.) mission; Congregazione della —, Congregation of (Priests of) the Mission; (leg.) mission. **-a·rio** *m.* (eccl.; fig.) missionary; *pl.* esp. the Lazarists, the Vincentians.

missiva *f.* missive, message; (leg.) a letter sent.

missomiceto *m.* (bot.) myxomycete.

Missuri *pr.n.f.* (geog.) Missouri.

†**mist-à**, †**-anza** *f.* See amistà.

mista-gogi·a *f.* mystagogy. **-go·gico** *adj.* mystagogic. **-gogo** *m.* (*pl.* -goghi) mystagogue.

mistamente *adv.* See under misto.

mist-ero, †**-e·rio** *m.* mystery; *pl.* (antiq.) mysteries, secret rites such as those of Isis, Demeter, Mithras; (theol.) mystery; -eri dolorosi, -eri gloriosi (del rosario), Joyful, Sorrowful, Glorious, Mysteries (of the rosary); (in some parts of Italy) procession with emblems of the Passion; mystery-play; (fig.) mystery; problem; secret; unexplainable thing; fare — di, to make a mystery of. **-e·rico** *adj.* pertaining to a mystery; iniziazione -erica, initiation into a religious mystery. **-eriosità** *f.* mysteriousness. **-erioṣo** *adj.* mysterious. (**-eriosamente** *adv.*) **-i** *m.pl.* mystae, candidates for admission into the mysteries.

mi·stia *f.* and derivs. (Tusc., pop.). See mischia.

mi·stica *f.* See under mistico.

†**misticare** *vb.* and derivs. See mescolare.

mi·sti-co *adj.* (rel.) mystical, mystic; Rosa -ca, Mystic Rose, the B.V.M.; spiritual, symbolical, allegorical; occult, esoteric; (joc.) golfo —, invisible orchestra in theatre, *n.m.*, *f.* mystic. **-camente** *adv.* mystically. **-ca** *f.* mystical theology, mysticism; (fig.) *mystique*, (idealizing) theory, (romantic) propaganda (e.g. of bullfighting or politics). **-cheri·a** *f.* (derog.) vague uplift, religiosity; dreamy notion. **-ciṣmo** *m.* mysticism; theory and practice of spiritual union with God. **-cità** *f.* mysticity, mysticalness. **-cume** *m.* (derog.) mystical nonsense.

†**mistier-e**, †**-i**, †**-o** *m.* See mestiere.

mistific-are [A 2 s] *tr.* to mystify; to hoax; to deceive; to mix; to adulterate. (**-ato** *part. adj.*) **-atore** *m.* mystifier; hoaxer. (**-atrice** *f.*) **-azione** *f.* mystification; hoax, deception; adulteration.

†**mistigare** *tr.* to mix.

mistione *f.* mixture.

mist-o *adj.* mixed; combined; compounded; variegated; lana -a di cotone, wool and cotton mixture; matrimonio —, mixed marriage; scuola -a, co-educational school, mixed school; commissione -a, joint committee; comitato —, mixed committee; (finan.) circolazione -a, mixed currency; assicurazione -a, comprehensive insurance policy; (cul.) fritto —, mixed grill; (rlwy.) treno —, train carrying goods and passengers; (mus.) stile —, writing for solo voices and chorus with orchestra; coro —, mixed chorus; a voci -e, for mixed voices; (leg.) tribunale —, a tribunal of judges of mixed nationalities; *n.m.* mixture; combination; un — di tragedia e di farsa, a mixture of tragedy and farce; (miner.) variegated marble. **-amente** *adv.* promiscuously.

mistrà *f. indecl.* aniseed; aniseed cordial.

Mistral *pr.n.m.* Mistral (the wind or the poet).

mistur-a *f.* mixture; blend; medley; combination; compound; senza —, pure, unadulterated; (mus.) mixture stop (organ). †**-ag·gine** *f.* ingredient, mixture. **-are** [A 1] *tr.* to mix; to mingle; to blend. **-ato** *part. adj.* mixed; mingled; vino -ato, blended wine.

miṣur-a *f.* measure; — giusta, fair measure; — abbondante, very good measure; pesi e -e, weights and measures; prender la — di, to measure (for clothes, etc.); abiti fatti su —, clothes made to measure; — a nastro, tape-measure; measurement, size; di che — è?, what size is it?; in diverse -e, in different sizes; che — volete?, what size do you want?; extent, dimensions; in una certa —, to a certain extent; con —, moderately; fuori —, senza —, excessively; oltre —, beyond measure; colmare la —, to pass all bounds; passare la —, to go too far; a — che, in measure as; (prosod.) metre, scansion; questo verso manca di —, this line doesn't scan; (mus.) time, measure, bar; senza —, without time, unbarred; — binaria, duple time; — ternaria, triple time; — composta, compound time; — di quattro quarti, four-four time, common time; (fencing) the distance between the combatants when both are on guard; (sport) vincere di —, to win by a narrow margin; measure, expedient; precaution; mezze -e, half-measures; prendere -e, to take steps; (admin.) -e amministrative, regulations; -e amministrative di sicurezza, precautionary measures by police; -e restrittive, restrictive measures; -e legislative, legislative measures; -e di sicurezza personali, patrimoniali, precautionary measures affecting the person, affecting property (C.P.).

miṣur-are [A 1] *tr.* to measure, to gauge; to pace; — la profondità di, to measure the depth of; — gli altri da sè stesso, to measure others by oneself; ogni lato -a dieci metri, each side is ten metres long; to survey (land); *rfl.* to take one's measure, to try one's strength; -arsi con qualcuno, to contend, to compete, with someone. **-a·bile** *adj.* measurable. (**-abilità** *f.*) **-aca·napi**, **-acavi** *m. indecl.* (naut.) cablemaker's gauge. †**-aflusso** *m. indecl.* (naut.) see mareografo. **-amento** *m.* measuring. **-apiog·gia** *m.* rain-gauge. **-atezza** *f.* moderation. **-ato** *part. adj.* measured; moderate; cautious; scanty. **-atamente** *adv.* in moderation. **-atore** *m.* instrument for measuring; measurer; meter; -atore del gas, gas-meter. **-atrice** *f.* woman measurer; (techn.) measuring machine; (ent.) looper caterpillar (of a geometrid moth). †**-avento** *m.* (naut.) wind-gauge. **-azione** *f.* measuring; gauging; surveying.

miṣurino *m. dim.* of misura, q.v.; small measure; small milk-can.

miṣuṣ-o *m.* misuse, abuse. †**-are** *tr.* to misuse; to abuse.

†**misven-ire** *intr.* to fail; to faint; to suffer misfortune. †**-tura** *f.* misfortune.

mitaciṣmo *m.* See metacismo.

mit-e *adj.* mild, gentle; meek; docile; clima —, mild climate; moderate; prezzi -i, moderate prices. (**-emente** *adv.*) **-ezza** *f.* mildness; meekness; gentleness; moderateness; -ezza di prezzi, lowness of prices.

mitene *f.pl.* mittens.

mit-era *f.* (pop.) see mitra; †the fool's cap that was placed on the head of a person condemned to the pillory or to being tied on an ass and led round in scorn; lasciarsi metter una —, to be induced to do an undignified act. †**-are** *tr.* to crown with a fool's cap. (†**-azione** *f.*) †**-ino** *adj.* worthy of the fool's cap, fit for the pillory.

mitezza *f.* See under **mite**.

mi·tic-o *adj.* mythical. **-amęnte** *adv.* mythically.

miticolǫso *adj.* See **meticoloso**.

†miti·dio *m.* (Tusc. joc.) gumption, sense.

mitific-are [A 2 s] to mythicize. (**-ato** *part. adj.* **-azione** *f.*)

mitig-are [A 2 s] *tr.* to mitigate; to alleviate, to allay, to assuage; to appease, to placate; *rfl.* to grow slacker; to become less severe; to mellow. (**-a·bile** *adj.*) **-amęnto** *m.* mitigating. **-ativo** *adj.* mitigatory, mitigating; alleviating. **-ato** *part. adj.* mitigated; alleviated; allayed, assuaged; appeased. (**-atore** *m.* **-atrice** *f.*) **-azione** *f.* mitigating; alleviating, alleviation; (leg.) mitigation.

Mitile·ne *pr.n.f.* Mytilene.

mi·tilo *m.* (zool.) mussel, *Mytilus* spp.

mit-o¹ *m.* myth; legend; parable. **-ografi·a** *f.* mythography. **-o·grafo** *m.* mythographer. **-ogra·fico** *adj.* mythographic. **-ologi·a** *f.* mythology. **-olo·gico** *adj.* mythological. **-ologicamęnte** *adv.* mythologically. **-o·logo** *m.*, **-ologista** *m.* mythologist. **-osto·rico** *adj.* part myth, part history; 'mythistorical'.

†mito² *adj.* See **mite**.

mit-osi *f.* (biol.) mitosis. **-o·tico** *adj.* mitotic.

mitr-a¹ *f.* (eccl.) mitre ('precious', 'cloth-of-gold', or 'simple'); turban; woman's coif. **-ale** *adj.* mitre-shaped; (anat.) mitral; valvola -ale, mitral valve, bicuspid valve. **-are** [A 1] *tr.* to mitre. **-ato** *part. adj.* (eccl.) mitred; i -ati, prelates.

mitra² *m., f. indecl.* small automatic weapon; sub-machine gun; Tommy gun (used in close combat, house-to-house fighting and by gangsters, bootleggers, etc. followed by customs and other preventive officers).

mitra·gli-a *f.* (mil.) canister, grapeshot, pelletshot. **-are** [A 4] *tr.* (mil.) to fire small shot at; to sweep with machine-gun fire. **-ato** *part. adj.* (mil.) fitted with small shot; armed with machine guns; riddled with small shot. **-atore** *m.*, **-ere** *m.* (mil.) machine gunner. **-atrice** *f.*, **-era** *f.* (mil.) machine gun; nastro di -atrice, machine-gun belt; annaffiare con le -atrici, to spray.

mitre·o *m.* shrine of Mithras, Mithraeum.

mi·tria *f.* and derivs. (pop.). See **mitra²**.

Mitrid-ate *pr.n.m.* Mithridates. **†-ato** *m.* antidote against poisons, from the legend that Mithridates rendered himself proof against poisons. (**-a·tico** *adj.*) **-atiṣmo** *m.* (med.) Mithridatism. **-atiẓẓare** [A 1] *tr.* to immunize against poisons. **-atiẓẓazione** *f.* (med., fig.) immunization.

mitteleurope·o *adj.* Central European.

mittente *m.* sender; da rispedire al —, to be returned to the sender; (leg.) consignor (C.C.); principal; (Scot.) mandator; *adj.* forwarding, sending.

†miva *f.* medicament compounded of quince juice and honey.

mixag·gio *m.* (radio, telev., cinem.) mixing; sala di —, 'mixer'.

mix-edema *m.* (med.) myxoedema. **-oma** *m.* (med.) myxoma.

mixomiceti *m.pl.* See **missomiceto**.

mixoteiṣmo *m.* (neol.) medley of inconsistent religious beliefs.

miẓẓonite *f.* (miner.) mizzonite.

mnemo·nic-a *f.* mnemonic. **-o** *adj. n.m.* mnemonic.

Mnemo·ṣine *pr.n.f.* (myth.) Mnemosyne.

mnemotec·nic-a *f.* mnemotechny. **-o** *adj.* mnemotechnic.

mo, mo' *adv.* (archaic, but still very widely used in dialects) now; pur —, just now; *n.m.* abbrev. of 'modo', and usually written with an apostrophe (e.g. a mo' d'esempio, by way of example); is widely used in the sense of give!, show! (possibly derived from 'mostra'); fare a mo' e to', to buy or sell for cash (i.e. one gives while the other takes).

moa *f.* (orn.) moa.

Moabiti *pr.n.m.pl.* (Bibl.) Moabites.

moarè *m.* (text.) watered silk, moiré.

mo·bil-e *adj.* movable; festa —, movable feast; mobile; (fig.) fickle, capricious, inconstant; la donna è —, woman is fickle; libro a fogli -i, loose-leaf book; (leg.) beni -i, chattels; personal estate; personal property; personalty; (Scot.) moveable property; (admin.) imposta di ricchezza —, income-tax in respect of personal property and earnings; la scala —, sliding scale; sabbie -i, quicksands; *n.m.* piece of furniture; i -i, the furniture; bel —!, a fine type!; (watchm.) runner; — riduttore, reduction gear; (mil.) pezzo —, mobile gun; cucina —, mobile kitchen. (**-męnte** *adv.*)

mobi·l-ia *f.*, **-io** *m.* furniture; suite of furniture; (fig.) fare da -ia, to be present without contributing to the proceedings. **-iare** [A 4] *tr.* to furnish; *adj.* having to do with personal property; Istituto

-iare Italiano, bank which makes advances on security of personal property; proprietà -iare, personal property, personalty. **-iatura** *f.* furnishing. **-iere** *m.* furnisher. **-ità** *f.* mobility; fickleness, changeableness; (phys.) mobility. **-itare** [A 1 s] *tr.* (mil.) to mobilize; (naut.) to render seaworthy or seagoing. **-itato** *part. adj.* (mil.) motorized, rendered mobile; (naut.) rendered seaworthy; seagoing. **-itazione** *f.* (mil.) act of mobilizing; (naut.) process of rendering seaworthy. **-iẓẓare** [A 1] *tr.* (mil.) to render mobile.

†mo·bol-e *m.* wealth, property. **†-ato** *adj.* wealthy, possessing property.

moca *m.* Mocha, Mocha coffee.

†mocaiardo, †mocaiarro *m.* hair-cloth.

mocassini *m.pl.* slippers; moccasins.

mocc-a *f.* (Tusc. pop.) money; (naut.) — isolante, porcelain rigging insulator; **†deadeye** on a forestay. **†-adore** *m.* handkerchief. **†-are** *tr.* to earn, to pick up; *rfl.* to blow one's nose.

mocchętt-a *f.*, **-o** *m.* (text.) moquette.

mocc-io *m.* mucus from the nose; snot, snivel; catarrh; (vet.) glanders. **†-eca** *m.* person with dirty nose; sniveller; (fig.) worthless fellow; mere child. **-ica·glia**, **-ica·ia** *f.* mucus from the nose; slime of snail. **-icare** [A 2 s] *intr.* (aux. avere) (of nose) to run; (of people) to cry, to snivel. **-ico** *m.* mucus, snot. **-ichino** *m.* baby with running nose; **†handkerchief**. **-icone** *m.* person with dirty nose; person of little importance; mere child; old dodderer. **-icǫna** *f.* 'baby', silly. **-iconeri·a** *f.* stupid act, foolishness. **-icǫso** *adj.* slimy, snivelling; snotty; vecchio -icoso, old man in second childhood. **-ione** *m.* see **moccicone**. **-iǫso** *adj.* snivelling.

moc·col-o *m.* wax taper; candle, candle-end; (fam.) non aver altri -i, to have no other means; se non hai altri -i, if there is no other way; oath, curse; tirare, mandare, accendere, attaccare -i, to curse; excessive mucus from the nose; **†tip** of the nose; **†candle-**wick. **-a·ia** *f.* candle-snuff, the end of the wick when not properly burned away. **-ętto** *m. dim.* small taper; festa dei -etti, feast of the tapers; mild oath. **-ino** *m. dim.* small taper; spegnersi come un -ino, to die of consumption; curse. **-ǫne** *m.* sniveller.

moccǫsa *f.* (anat.) mucosa.

moco *m.* (bot.) bitter vetch, *Vicia ervillia*; a mere nothing, a trifle.

mococo *m.* (zool.) *Lemur catta*.

mod-a *f.* fashion; essere di —, to be in fashion; venire di —, to come into fashion; passare di —, to go out of fashion; essere fuori di —, to be out of fashion; secondo la —, alla —, after the fashion, of the sort in fashion; il male di —, the fashionable ailment; vestirsi all'ultima —, to dress in the latest style; negozio di -e, milliner's shop.

modal-e *adj.* modal; (mus.) modal. **-ità** *f.* modality; particular, detail; way; mode of procedure; (techn.) instructions (for use); (leg.) formality; *pl.* terms; le condizioni e le -ità per la concessione del brevetto, terms and conditions for grant of patent (C.C.).

mo·dan-o *m.* measure, mould, model for workmen employed to execute a design of any kind; a kind of crochet work, made with round holes and square holes; crochet-needle, netting-needle; scale of brightness of stars; (archit.) module. **-are** [A 1 s] *tr.* to mould. (**-ato** *part. adj.*) **-atura** *f.* (archit.; carp.) moulding.

modell-o *m.* model, pattern; servire da —, to serve as a model; tutti fatti sullo stesso —, all made to the same pattern; un — di virtù, a model of virtue; madre —, a model mother; (paint.) model; lay-figure; (archit.) — dimostrativo, show model; — in scala, scale model; (leg.) la registrazione di -i industriali, registration of industrial models, patterns and designs; — d'utilità, utility model; improvement process; -i e disegni ornamentali, ornamental patterns and designs (C.C.). **-a** *f.* artist's (female) model; fare da — a, to act as a model; model-girl, mannequin. **-a·bile** *adj.* that can be modelled, or shaped. **-amęnto** *m.* modelling. **-are** [A 1] *tr.* to model; to mould, shape, fashion; -ò il suo stile su quello dell'Ariosto, he modelled his style on Ariosto's; (sculp.) to model; *rfl.* to model oneself; -arsi sul Manzoni, to take Manzoni as a model. **-ato** *part. adj.* modelled; shaped, formed; moulded; shapely. **-atore** *m.* modeller. (**-atrice** *f.*) **-atura** *f.* modelling. **-ista** *m., f.* pattern-cutter; designer.

Mo·den-a, **†Modona** *pr.n.f.* (geog.) Modena. **-ęse** *adj.* of Modena; pozzo -ese, artesian well; *n.m., f.* native of Modena.

†mo·deno *m.* See **modano**.

moder-are [A 1 s] *tr.* to moderate; to check, to curb; to slacken; to mitigate; to restrain; *rfl.* to check oneself; to restrain oneself;

moder·are (*cont.*)

to control oneself; ~arsi nelle spese, to cut down one's spending, to be moderate in expenditure; to be moderated, to become moderate. ~a·bile *adj.* that can be moderated. ~atẹzza *f.* moderateness; restraint; temperance; discretion. ~ativo *adj.* moderating. ~ato *part. adj.* moderated; moderate; restrained, temperate, sober; (mus.) allegro ~ato, fairly quick; *n.m.* (pol.) man of moderate views; i ~ati, the moderates, progressive Conservatives. ~atamẹnte *adv.* moderately; in moderation. ~atọre *m.* moderator; (atom. phys.) moderator; *adj.* moderating. ~atrice *f.* moderatrix. ~ato·rio *adj.* making for moderation. ~atume *m.* (pol.) the moderate party. ~azione *f.* moderation, restraint; discretion; temperance; †government.

modern·o *adj.* modern; recent; new; up-to-date; (Gk. lit.) Commedia ~a, New Comedy; *n.m.* modern. ~amẹnte *adv.* recently; after the latest fashion; in a modern way. ~iṣmo *m.* (theol.) modernism (the movement condemned by Pius X in 1907). ~ista *m.* (theol.) modernist. ~is·tico *adj.* (theol.) modernist(ic). ~ità *f.* modernity. ~iẓẓare [A I] *tr.* to modernize; to bring up to date; to renovate. ~iẓẓato *part. adj.* modernized; up-to-date; renovated. ~iẓẓazione *f.* modernization; modernizing; renovating; renovation.

mode·stia *f.* modesty; humility; meekness; simplicity; chastity.

modest·o *adj.* modest; humble; simple; moderate; prezzo ~, moderate price. ~amẹnte *adv.* modestly; humbly; moderately.

mo·dic·o *adj.* moderate; modest; cheap; prezzi ~i, moderate prices; a ~ interesse, at a low rate of interest. (~amẹnte *adv.*) ~ità *f.* moderation; cheapness.

modi·fica *f.* modification, alteration, change.

modific·are [A 2] *tr.* to modify, to alter, to change; se non ~a la sua condotta finirà male, if he doesn't change his ways he'll come to a bad end; (leg.) — l'atto costitutivo, to alter Articles of Association (C.C.); — le condizioni di un contratto, to alter or modify the terms of a contract. ~a·bile *adj.* modifiable, alterable. ~amento *m.* modifying; modification. ~ante *part. adj.* modifying. ~ativo *adj.* modificatory. ~atọre *m.* modifier; *adj.* modifying. (~atrice *f.*) ~azione *f.* modification, change; non approvò queste ~azioni, he did not approve of these changes; (leg.) ~azione della competenza, extension of jurisdiction (C.C.P.).

modigliọn·e *m.* (archit.) modillion, bracket. ~cino *m. dim.* small bracket.

mo·dio *m.* (Rom. antiq.) *modius*, corn-measure containing sixteen *sextarii* (i.e. nearly one peck).

modist·a *f.* milliner; dressmaker, modiste. ~eri·a *f.* milliner's shop; dressmaker's shop.

mod·o *m.* **1.** MODE, way, manner; — di pensare, way of thinking; questo è il mio — di vedere, this is how I see it; in certo —, in a way; in certo qual —, almost, nearly, more or less, possibly; in ogni —, in any case; ad ogni —, at any rate; in che —?, how?; in — giusto, justly; in qualsiasi —, anyhow; d'un —, equally; di — che, di tal —, †per — che, in such a way that, so that; in — da..., so as to...; fare in — che..., to see that...; per — di dire, so to speak (inferring untruth); a — mio, in my own way; è un ragazzo che vuol fare a — suo, he's a boy who goes his own way; il suo solito —, his usual manner; con bel —, civilly; *pl.* manners; avere bei (brutti) ~i, to have good (bad) manners. **2.** STYLE, shape; vestito a — del Trecento, dressed in fourteenth-century style; a — degli Inglesi, in the English style, as the English do it; una coda a — di ventaglio, a fan-shaped tail; sono tutti fatti a un —, they're all cast in the same mould. **3.** MODERATION; sopra, oltre, †fuor di —, extremely, excessively; fare le cose a —, to do things carefully, gently. **4.** MEANS; non ho — di scrivere, I have no means of writing; trovar —, to find means; dar — di, to make it possible to; uomo di ~i, man of means. **5.** CONDITION; stare sempre di un —, to be always in the same state. **6.** (GRAMM.) avverbio di —, adverb of manner; — avverbiale, adverbial phrase; mood; — congiuntivo, subjunctive mood; (mus.) mode (whether scale or rhythmic species). For the names of the modes see **dorico, eolico, eolio, frigio, iastio, ionico, ionio, iper-dorico, ~dorio, ~frigio, ~lidio, ipo-dorico, ~dorio, ~eolico, ~eolio, ~frigio, ~ionico, ~ionio, ~lidio, ~misolidio, ~messolidio, lidio, locrio, misolidio**; (leg.) modus; manner; way; i ~i di acquisto, ways of acquiring property (C.C.).

†mo·dula *f.* See **modulo**.

modul·are [A I S] *tr.* to modulate; l'oratore deve saper — la voce,

a speaker should know how to vary his tone of voice; (radio) to modulate; (mus.) to modulate, to change key; †to set to music. ~a·bile *adj.* singable. ~ante *part. adj.* modulating. ~ato *part. adj.* modulated; †set to music. ~atamẹnte *adv.* harmoniously. ~atọre *m.* (radio) modulator; ~atore di fase, phase modulator; ~atore di frequenza, frequency modulator; †(mus.) composer. ~azione *f.* (radio) modulation; ~azione di ampiezza, amplitude modulation, A.M.; ~azione di frequenza, frequency modulation, F.M.; (mus.) modulation; †musical setting, composition. ~o·metro *m.* (radio) modulation meter.

mo·dul·o *m.* form; riempire un —, to fill in a form; un — stampato, a printed form; — bianco, blank form; skeleton form, draft; model; (archit.) module; (leg.) — d'acqua, unit of measurement of water; contratti conclusi mediante ~i, contracts made on printed forms (C.C.); (phys., eng.) modulus; — di elasticità, modulus of elasticity; — di Young, Young's modulus; — di elasticità tangenziale, shear modulus; (bldg.; eng.) — di resistenza, section modulus; — inglese, diametrical pitch; — metrico, module (of gears); (numism.) diameter of a coin or medal.

moedo *m.* moidore.

moerr·e, ~o *m.* See **amoerre**.

mof·eta *f.* (geol.) mephitis, mofette. ~e·tico *adj.* mephitic.

moffẹtta *f.* (zool.) skunk, *Mephitis mephitis*.

mo·gano *m.* (bot.) mahogany, wood of *Swetenia mahogani*.

mogarino *m.* See **mugherino**.

mog·g·io *m.* (*pl.* ~ia *f.*) measure of capacity varying in different places, but generally equal to eight bushels; — fiorentino, 585 litres; — di Milano, 146·23 litres; bushel (esp. in sense of vessel); mettere la lucerna (*or* fiaccola) sotto il —, to hide one's light under a bushel. ~iata *f.* as much land as would take a 'moggio' of seed (also 'moggio di terreno').

mogigrafi·a *f.* writer's cramp.

†mogilali·a *f.* stammer; stammering.

mo·gio *adj.* crestfallen, low-spirited, dejected; quiet; cane — e cavallo desto, a quiet dog and a spirited horse (are the right thing).

mọ·gli·e *f.* (*pl.* mọgli) wife; è mia —, she's my wife; prender, pigliare, torre, menar —, to take a wife; ebbe per —, he took as wife; dar in —, to give in marriage; dar — al figlio, to find a wife for one's son, to marry off one's son; esser da —, to be of marriageable age; far passar per —, to pass off as one's wife; (leg.) alimenti alla —, wife's maintenance. †~azzo *m.* wedding.

†mogliera *f.* See **moglie**.

mogo·gano, mogo·gon *m.* See **mogano**.

mo·gol, (pop.) **mogolle** *m.* Mogul; Gran —, Grand Mogul.

mo·i·a *f.* (geol.) salt-spring, salt-marsh. ~atọre *m.* worker at salt-springs (esp. Volterra).

moicano *m. adj.* Mohican; *L'Ultimo dei Moicani, The Last of the Mohicans*.

moiẹtta *f.* (metall.) strip, band.

moïn·a *f.* simper, smirk; *pl.* blandishments, caresses, cajolery; mincing ways. ~eri·a *f.* affected blandishments.

Moka *pr.n.m.* Mocha, Mocha coffee.

mol·a *f.* grindstone, millstone; (ichth.) pesce —, sunfish, *Mola mola*. ~are *adj.* relating to a millstone or grindstone; pietra ~are, millstone; (anat.) dente ~are, molar, molar tooth.

mol·are[1] *adj.* (chem.) molar. ~arità *f.* (chem.) molarity, molar concentration.

mol·are[2] [A I] *tr.* (techn.) to grind; — ad umido, to wet-grind. ~ato *part. adj.* (techn.) ground; vetro ~ato, ground glass.

molare[3] *adj.* See under **mola**.

molassa *f.* (geol.) molasse.

molazz·a *f.* (techn.) muller; mill; — mescolatrice, pug mill; (eng.) edge-runner. ~atura *f.* (found.) mulling.

mọl·cere [B def.] *tr.* to soothe, to calm; to caress.

mole *f.* mass, pile; massive building; size, bulk; di piccola —, small in bulk; un lavoro di gran —, a very heavy job; (Rom. antiq.) *moles*, mausoleum such as that of Hadrian (Castel Sant'Angelo).

moleca *f.* (zool.) a crab that has recently moulted, soft-shelled crab.

mole·col·a *f.* (chem.) molecule. ~are *adj.* molecular. ~ina *f. dim.* teeny-weeny thing.

molend·a *f.* multure. ~are [A I] *tr.* to exact multure; to grind.

molest·are [A I] *tr.* to molest; to annoy, to trouble, to disturb; to vex; to tease. †~amento *m.* molesting; annoyance. ~ante *part. adj.* molesting. ~atọre *m.* molester. (~atrice *f.*)

mole·stia *f.* molestation; trouble; nuisance; cause of worry; *pl.* (leg.) molestation; nuisance; disturbance; (mil.) nuisance raid; nuisance value.

molest-o *adj.* troublesome; annoying; vexatious; grievous. (**-aménte** *adv.*)

molett-are [A I c] *tr.* (eng.) to knurl. **-atura** *f.* (eng.) knurling, milling.

†**mol·gere** *tr.* to milk; to suck.

moli *m.* (class. myth.) (the magic plant) moly; (bot.) *Allium nigrum.*

mol-ibdato *m.* (chem.) molybdate. **-ibdeno** *m.* (chem.) molybdenum. **-ibdenite** *f.* (miner.) molybdenite, molybdenum glance. **-i·bdico** *adj.* (chem.) molybdic. **-ibdite** *f.* see **-ibdenite.** **-ibdoso** *adj.* (chem.) molybdous.

molin-a·io, †**-aro** *m.* miller.

molin-are [A I] *tr.* (in weaving) to turn rapidly, to whirl. **-ello** *m.* whirl; winch; (naut.) swivel; **-ello d'afforco,** mooring-swivel.

molin-iṣmo *m.* (eccl. hist.) Molinism. **-ista** *m.* (eccl. hist.) Molinist.

molino *m.* See **mulino.**

molito·rio *adj.* industria **-a,** milling trade.

moll-a *f.* spring; serratura a **—,** spring lock; **-e di una poltrona,** springs of a chair; **-e d'una carrozza,** carriage springs; motore a **—,** clockwork; motorino a **—,** clockwork motor; funzionamento a **—,** clockwork action, 'clockwork driven'; (watchm.) **—** del bariletto, mainspring; **—** del cricco, click spring; †(naut.) splice; †bell stroke; *pl.* tongs; un paio di **-e** per il fuoco, a pair of fire-tongs; sproposito da prendersi con le **-e,** dreadful blunder, 'clanger'. **-ette** *f.pl. dim.* **-ette** per lo zucchero, sugar-tongs. **-etto** *m.* kirby grip, hair grip.

molla-ia *f.* marsh.

†**mollame** *m.* soft stuff; †soft parts of the body.

moll-are [A I] *tr.* (naut.) to let go, to ease, to check; to walk back; to slacken; **—** in bando, to let fly, (fig.) to abandon (a ship, job, person); **—** l'ancora, to cast anchor; **—** la barra, to ease the helm; **—** a mano, to walk back hand over hand; **—** gli ormeggi, to cast off mooring wires; **—** in poppa, to run; **-a!,** let go!; †to immerse, to dip; †*intr.* to cease, to desist. **-aménto** *m.* (naut.) act of easing or casting off. **-ata** *f.* (naut.) short surge.

moll-e *adj.* soft; pietra **—,** soft stone; **—** come la cera, soft as wax; wet; occhi **-i** di pianto, eyes wet with tears; (fig.) soft; effeminate; luxurious; flabby; un uomo **—,** a milksop; amori **-i,** lascivious love-affairs; **-i** costumi, lax way of life; acqua **—,** soft water; le sue **-i** paroline, her sweet words; *n.m.* wet; liquid; mettere in **—,** to put to soak; mettere il becco in **—,** to drink; (mil.) dare nel **—,** to attack the weak point, to go for the soft underbelly; *pl.* (naut.) soft pads threaded every half hour to keep count of time; †half hours. **-eménte** *adv.* softly; languidly. **-ac·cio** *adj. pejor.* (of wine) weak. **-ẹzza** *f.* delicacy, effeminacy; softness; pliability. **-ic·chio** *m.* small stretch of wet land. **-ic·cico** *adj.* wet, soft. **-ic·cio** *adj.* wet, damp, soft; *n.m.* wet patch, muddy patch. **-icello** *adj. dim.* tender, delicate.

†**molleca** *f.* (zool.). See **moleca.**

molleggi-are [A 3 c] *intr.* (*aux.* avere) to be elastic, to be springy; questa poltrona **-a** bene, this chair is very springy; *tr.* (naut.) to test the tension of a hawser or cable (usually with the foot); to surge and check; **—** le dita, to keep the fingers flexible; (eng.) to spring. **-aménto** *m.* elasticity, springiness; flexing. **-ata** *f.* action of flexing.

molleggio *m.* (eng.; motor.) springing, suspension.

mollettiera *f.* puttee.

mollettóne *m.* (text.) swanskin.

mollic-a *f.* crumb, soft part of bread; †gross blunder. **-ola** *f. dim.* crumb. **-ume** *m.* soft stuff; mud.

mollific-are [A 2 s] *tr.* to mollify; to soften. **-aménto** *m.* mollifying; softening. **-ativo** *adj.* (med.) emollient. **-ato** *part. adj.* mollified; softened. **-azióne** *f.* mollification.

†**molli·zi-a** *f.* softness, effeminacy; luxurious living; carnal abuse. **-e** *pl.* softness; luxury.

†**mollo** *adj.* See **molle.**

moll-óre *m.* wet; humidity; wet patch of ground. **-ume** *m.* wet; ground wet from rain.

mollus-co *m.* (*pl.* **-chi**) (zool.) mollusc; (pop.) shellfish; (bot.) gnarled branch, woody excrescence, burr.

mol-o *m.* breakwater, mole; pier; quay, wharf; (comm.) diritti di **—,** wharfage; (ichth.) pesce **—,** poutassou, *Gadus poutassou.* **-óne** *m.* (mil. hist.) battlement, merlin.

Mo·loc, mo·loch *pr.n.m.* Moloch.

molos·s-o *adj.* (Gk. antiq.) Molossian; *n.m.* Molossian hound (kind of mastiff); (prosod.) molossus. **-ico** *adj.* (Gk. antiq.) Molossian.

molotro *m.* (orn.) cowbird, *Molothrus ater.*

molteplic-e *adj.* manifold; having many parts; numerous; complex. **-eménte** *adv.* in many ways. **-ità** *f.* multiplicity.

molti-capsulare *adj.* and other formations see under **multi-.**

†**moltic·cio** *m.* (tanning) layaways, tan liquor.

molti·plica *f.* (eng.) multiplication, gearing up; gear ratio; pedal wheel (of a cycle); †(math.) multiplication.

moltiplic-are [A I s] *tr.* to multiply; to increase; (math.) to multiply; *rfl., intr.* (*aux.* essere) to multiply; (fig.) to increase; to be everywhere, see to everything at once. **-a·bile** *adj.* multipliable. (**-abilità** *f.*) †**-aménto** *m.* multiplying; increase; (math.) multiplying, multiplication. **-ando** *m.* (math.) multiplicand. **-ativo** *adj.* multiplying. **-ato** *part. adj.* multiplied; increased; (eng.) geared up. **-atóre** *m.* (math.) multiplier; (techn.) multiplier, amplifier; (eng.) overgear; (motor.) **-atore di velocità,** overdrive; (electron.) **-atore elettronico,** electron multiplier. **-atrice** *f.* multiplier, multiplying machine. **-azióne** *f.* multiplicaton; increase; (math.) multicatipliion.

†**molti·plice** *adj.* and derivs. See **molteplice.**

†**mol·tiplo** *adj.* See **multiplo.**

moltitu·dine *f.* multitude; una **—** di gente, a crowd of people; la **—** dei presenti, a majority of those present.

mọlt-o *adj.* much; *pl.* many; avete **-a** paẓienza, you have great patience; ho **-i** amici, I have many friends; *prn.* a dir **—,** at most; è **—** che non lo vedo, I haven't seen him for a long time; fra non **—,** in a short time, before long; da Roma a Frascati non c'è **—,** it is not far from Rome to Frascati; ci corre **—,** there is a vast difference; uomo da **—,** important man; **—** di male, a lot of evil, a lot that is wrong; **-i** dicono, many (people) say...; *adv.* very; very much, a great deal; **—** bene, very well; **—** conosciuto, very well known; ride **—,** he laughs a great deal; di **—,** very. **-un·goli, -ungolati** *m.pl.* (zool.) subungulates.

molva *f.* (ichth.) **—** allungata, ling, *Molva elongata.*

momẹnt-o *m.* moment; in quel **—,** at that moment; a **-i** arriverà, he will be here any moment now; a **-i,** sometimes; non vedere il **—** di, to be most impatient to; dal **—** che, since, inasmuch as, given that; per il **—,** for the time being; importance, moment; di gran **—,** of great importance; (mech.) moment; **—** d'inerzia, moment of inertia; (eng.) **—** di rovesciamento, tilting moment, overturning moment; (eng.) **—** di rotazione, **—** torcente, torque. **-ac·cio** *m. pejor.* è stato un **-accio,** it was a really bad moment, it was a 'mauvais quart d'heure'. **-ino** *m. dim.* a little moment; just a moment. **-a·neo** *adj.* momentary. **-aneaménte** *adv.* momentarily.

mọmmo *m.* (Tusc. fam.) something to drink.

Mom-o *pr.n.m.* (class. myth.) Momus; (fig.) scoffer, fault-finder. **-ẹtto** *m. dim.* wretched little critic.

momoro *m.* (ichth.) poor cod, *Gadus capelanus.*

mọn *m.* abbrev. form of **monte,** q.v.

†**mona** *f.* abbrev. of **madonna,** q.v.

mo·na-co[1] *m.* (*pl.* **-ci,** †**-chi**) (eccl.) monk; (provb.) l'abito non fa il **—,** see under **abito**; (bldg.) post; **—** unico, king-post; doppio **—,** capriata a due **-ci,** queen truss; (ent.) black arches moth, *Lymantria monacha.* **-ca** *f.* (eccl.) nun (of the older kind of religious community, esp. Benedictine); farsi **-ca,** to take the veil; poesia per **-ca,** poem on a girl's entering a convent (fashionable lit. form in seventeenth and eighteenth centuries); †pagan priestess or Vestal; (ent.) see **monaco**; (orn.) **-ca bianca,** smew. **-cale** *adj.* monastic, of a monk or nun; monkish, nun-like. (**-calménte** *adv.*) **-canda** *adj. n.f.* (girl, woman) about to become a nun, future nun. **-care** [A 2 s] *tr.* to make a nun (monk) of someone, to give someone the religious habit; *rfl.* to become a nun (rarely, a monk). **-cato** *m.* status of monk or nun; monastic or convent life; monasticism; monks and nuns collectively. **-cazióne** *f.* entry into the religious life; taking of the veil or the habit. **-cello, -chello** *m. dim.* of **monaco;** (zool.) an edible snail, usually *Helix aperta.* **-chella** *f. dim.* of **monaca;** (orn.) black-eared or black-throated wheatear, *Œnanthe hispanica;* **-chella nera,** black wheatear, *Œnanthe leucura.* **-chẹtto** *m.* keeper for latch; (naut.) bollard or stagshorn used for sewing wires or hemp ropes on deck. †**-chile** *adj.* monastic. **-china** *f. dim.* young nun, little nun; (fig.) demure or coy woman; *pl.* sparks, the last sparks from burnt paper. **-chino** *m. dim.* of **monaco;** (orn.) bullfinch; **-chino di palude,** reed bunting; †bruise; *adj.* dark red. **-chiṣmo** *m.* monachism, monasticism.

Mo·na·co² *pr.n.m.* (geog.) Munich (usually written 'Monaco di Baviera' to distinguish it from **Monaco³**, q.v.). -**chęse** *adj.*, *n.m.f.*

Mo·naco³ *pr.n.m.* (geog.) Monaco.

†**monacordo** *m.* (mus.). See **monocordo**.

mo·n-ade *f.* monad. -**a·dico** *adj.* monadic. -**adişmo** *m.* monadism. -**adologi·a** *f.* monadology. -**ammina** *f.* (chem.) monamine.

monar·ca *m.* (*pl.* -**chi**) monarch. †-**cale** *adj.* monarchical. -**cato** *m.* monarchy; sovereignty. -**chęsco** *adj.* (derog.) monarchic. -**chęssa** *f.* (joc.) queen. -**chi·a** *f.* monarchy; -**chia costituzionale**, constitutional monarchy; sovereignty, rule; (hist.) uomini della quinta -chia, Fifth-monarchy men. -**chişmo** *m.* monarchism.

monar·chic·o *adj.* monarchic; *n.m.* monarchist, royalist. (-**amęnte** *adv.*)

†**monacordo** *m.* (mus.). See **monocordo**, under **monoassiale**.

†**monarmo·nio** *adj.* (mus.) monodic, homophonic, monophonic (of an instrument sounding only one note at a time).

monast-ero, †-**e·rio** *m.* (eccl.) monastery; convent, nunnery. -**eriani** *m.pl.* (eccl. hist.) the Münster Anabaptists.

mona·stic·o *adj.* monastic; of a monastery or convent. (-**amęnte** *adv.*)

monatto *m.* monatto (person employed to bury the dead in time of plague).

mona·ulo *m.* (mus.) monaulos.

monazite *f.* (miner.) monazite, cryptolite, mengite, turnerite.

moncello *m.* hillock; mound, heap.

Monceni·sio *pr.n.m.* (geog.) Mont Cenis.

mon·co *adj.* (*pl.* -**chi**) maimed (applied almost solely to arm, or to person lacking a hand); — di ambo le mani, lacking both hands; braccio —, see **moncherino**; (fig.) deficient, incomplete, stunted; istruzione -ca, incomplete education; *n.m.* person who has lost one, or both, of his hands; cripple; cavar di mano a un — le bastonate, to behave with such insolence as to provoke a thrashing even from a cripple; (joc.) banca dei -chi, bank where no payment is made. -**ca** *f.* woman with one or no arm; †an arm in an olive press to collect the pulp under the millstone. -**cherino** *m.* handless arm; stump. -**chęzza** *f.* lack of one or both hands. -**chino** *m.* stump; person maimed of a hand; *pl.* mittens. -**cone** *m.* stump; stump of leg.

monda *f.* weeding of the rice fields.

mondan-o *adj.* of this world, terrestrial; worldly; gli piace la vita -a, he likes the pleasures of society; fare vita -a, to be prominent in society; femmina -a, dissolute woman; *n.m.pl.* people who pursue worldly pleasures. -**a** *f.* dissolute woman; prostitute. -**amęnte** *adv.* in a worldly or dissolute way. -**ętto** *adj. dim.* rather fond of the pleasures of the world. -**ità** *f.* worldliness; frivolous thing, *pl.* vanities; correre dietro alle -ità, to pursue the things of this world.

mond-are [A I C] *tr.* to peel; — le patate, to peel the potatoes; to clean, to clear, to weed; — il grano, to winnow the corn; — le uova sode, to shell hard-boiled eggs; (fig.) to cleanse (from sin); non — nespole, not to be peeling medlars (i.e. not to be wasting one's time). -**a·bile** *adj.* which can be peeled or cleaned. -**amęnto** *m.* peeling; cleaning; cleansing from sin. -**arella** *f.* weeding; second weeding. -**ariso** *m.*, *f. indecl.* worker who weeds the rice fields. -**ato** *part. adj.* weeded; cleaned. -**atore** *m.*, -**atrice** *f.*) -**atura** *f.* peeling; winnowing; weeding; peel taken off in peeling; chaff; dirt; siftings. -**azione** *f.* peeling; cleaning, winnowing. -**ina** *f.* girl who weeds the rice fields; peeled chestnut boiled or (rarely) roasted.

mond-ęzza *f.*, -**ęzza·io** *m.*, -**i·a** *f.* See under **mondo¹**.

mondiale *adj.* See under **mondo²**.

mond-o¹ *adj.* clean, spotless, pure; acqua -a, clear water; (rel.) coscienza -a, clear conscience; anima -a, pure, undefiled soul; animali -i, clean beasts (in ritual sense); peeled; pere -e, peeled pears; winnowed; (joc.) zucca -a, bald head. -**amęnte** *adv.* cleanly. -**ęzza** *f.* cleanliness, purity. -**ęzza·io** *m.* heap of dirt; rubbish-heap; dust-bin; dung-heap. †-**i·a** *f.* purity; siftings. †-**ificamęnto** *m.* cleaning. †-**ificante** *adj.* cleansing. -**i·gia** *f.* cleanliness, purity. -**i·glia** *f.* siftings; chaff; refuse; dross; rubbish; alloy. -**i·zia** *f.* cleanliness, purity; neatness in dress; †sweepings, dirt. †-**ume** *m.* dirt, filth.

mond-o² *m.* world; la creazione del —, the creation of the world; il — vecchio, the Old World; il — nuovo, the New World; fece il giro del —, he travelled round the world; mettere al — un bambino, to bring a child into the world; andare all'altro —, to die; mandare all'altro —, to kill; cose dell'altro —, strange,

incredible things; come va il —?, how goes the world with you?; non c'è giustizia a questo —, there's no justice in this world; (provb.) tutto il — è paese, it's the same the whole world over; pigliare il — come viene, to take things as they come; da che — è —, from the time of the creation; uomo di —, man of the world; donna di —, woman of bad reputation; non sa stare al —, he cannot fit into society; rinunziare al —, to give up the world, to renounce the pleasures of the world; il bel —, high society; il — musicale, the musical world; tutto il — lo sa, the whole world, everyone, knows it; mezzo —, an immense number of people; lontano un —, miles away; a great deal, an infinite amount; gli usò un — di cortesie, he was infinitely courteous to him. -**ac·cio** *pejor.* a dreadful world. -**iale** *adj.* world-like; universal; lingua -iale, world language; uomo di fama -iale, a man famous the whole world over.

†**monduald-o** *m.* (leg. hist.) guardianship order; guardian to represent a woman to enter into a contract or dispose of her dowry. -**are** [A I] *tr.* to dispose of (a dowry) by such order.

monegas-co *adj.* (*m.pl.* -**chi**) of Monaco; *n.m.* inhabitant of Monaco, Monégasque. -**ca** *f.* woman or girl of Monaco (cf. **Monaco³**).

monell-o *m.* urchin; rascal, rogue. -**a** *f.* tomboy. -**ata** *f.* deed of an urchin; rascally action. -**eri·a** *f.* trick, prank. -**ęsco** *adj.* (*m.pl.* -**ęschi**) roguish. -**ino** *m. dim.* little urchin; *pl.* children at an orphanage once situated in Florence.

monera *m.pl.* (zool.) protozoa.

monęt-a *f.* coin: una — di rame, a copper coin; una — del valore di una corona, a crown piece; change; non ho — spicciola, I have no small change; — di acconto, money of account; (leg.) — alterata, fraudulently altered coin; — contraffatta, counterfeit coin; — falsificata, falsified coin (comprising both previous descriptions); — avente corso legale, coin that is legal tender (C.P.); il tempo è —, time is money; battere —, to strike, to mint, to utter coins, (colloq.) to lay hands on some ready money; (Rom. antiq.) Giunone —, Juno Moneta (whose temple came to be used as a mint); — cartacea, carta —, paper money; pagar di mala —, to repay with ingratitude; (hist.) piece worth ten paoli (in Tuscany). -**a·bile** *adj.* that can be coined. -**ag·gio** *m.* mintage. -**ale** *adj.* (Roman antiq.) (official) belonging to the mint. -**are** [A I C] *tr.* to mint, to coin. -**a·rio** *adj.* monetary. -**ato** *part. adj.* minted; carta -ata, paper money. -**azione** *f.* minting, coining. -**iere** *m.* coiner. -**ina** *f. dim.* little coin. -**izzare** [A I] *tr.* to monetize. -**izzazione** *f.* monetization.

monferrina *f.* manfrina, country dance.

mongana *f.*, *adj.* vitella —, sucking calf.

Mongibello *pr.n.m.* (geog., poet.) Mount Etna.

mongio·ia *f.* medieval French war-cry (Montjoie et Saint-Denis); soldier's pay; (joc.) money.

mongolfiera *f.* montgolfier, fire-balloon (invented by the Montgolfier brothers in 1783).

Mong-o·lia *pr.n.f.* (geog.) Mongolia. -**o·lico** *adj.*, *n.m.* Mongolian; Mongol.

Mon·gol-o *m.* Mongol. (-**işmo** *m.*) (-**o·ido** *adj.*)

Mo·nica¹ *pr.n.f.* Monica; (fig.) warming-pan.

mo·nica² *m.* white wine made in the region of Cagliari.

monile *m.* necklace (pop.) trinket.

†**monimento** *m.* See **monumento**.

†**monipo·lio** *m.* See **monopolio**.

mon-işmo *m.* monism. -**ista** *m.* monist. -**is·tico** *adj.* monistic.

†**monistero** *m.* See **monastero**.

mo·nit-o *m.* warning, admonition. -**ore** *m.* admonisher; adviser; monitor; gazette; (radio) monitor; -ore di uscita, actual monitor; (naut.) monitor. -**o·rio** *adj.* (eccl.) monitory; *n.m.* monitory letter; (leg.) decreto -orio, summary judgement.

†**monizione** *f.* See **ammonizione**, under **ammonire**.

monna¹ *f.* abbreviation of Madonna; (form of address) lady; — onesta, hypocrite.

monn-a² *f.* ape, monkey; (Tusc., colloq.) dar la —, to ape, to mock, to make fun of; pigliar la —, to get drunk; cotto come una —, to be rolling drunk, drunk as an owl.

mon-oassiale *adj.* (opt.) uniaxial. -**oato·mico** *adj.* (chem.) monoatomic. -**oba·sico** *adj.* (chem.) monobasic. -**oblessi·a** *f.* (med.; opt.) monoblepsia. -**oblocco** *m.* (*pl.* -**oblocchi**) (motor.) cylinder block. †-**oc·chio** *m.* see **monocolo**. -**oce·falo** *m.* monster consisting of two bodies with only one head. -**o·cero** *m.* (zool.) rhinoceros; (myth.) unicorn. -**ociclo** *m.* monocycle. -**ocilin·drico** *adj.* (motor.)

mon-oassiale (*cont.*)
single-cylinder. **-ocine·tico** *adj.* (atom. phys.) monokinetic. **-oclinale** *adj.* (geol.) monoclinal. **-oclino** *adj.* (bot.) monoclinous; *adj.* monoclinic. **-ocloruro** *m.* (chem.) monochloride. **-o·colo** *adj.* one-eyed; *m.* monocle. **-ocolore** *adj.* (pol.) one-party (used of governments based on a single party); *n.m.* one-party government. **-ocomando** *adj. indecl.* (eng.; aeron.) single-control. **-ocordo** *m.* monochord; *adj.* (fig.) monotonous, single-toned. **-ocotile·done** *adj.* (bot.) monocotyledonous. **-ocroma** *f.* (paint.) monochrome. **-ocroma·tico** *adj.* (paint.; opt.) monochromatic. **-ocuspidale** *adj.* (archit.) having one spire. **-odat·tilo** *adj.* monodactylous. **-odi·a** (mus.) monody. **-o·dico** *adj.* (mus.) monodic, homophonic. **-odramma** *m.* monodrama. **-o·dromo** *adj.* (math.) monodromic. **-oe·cio** *adj.* (bot.) monoecious. **-oenerge·tico** *adj.* (atom. phys.) monoenergetic. **-o·fago** *adj.* (zool.) monophagous. **-ofase** *adj.* (electr.) single-phase. **-ofisişmo** *m.* (eccl. hist.) Monophysitism. **-ofişita** *m.* (eccl. hist.) Monophysite. **-ogami·a** *f.* monogamy. **-o·gamo** *adj.* monogamous; *m.n.* monogamist. **-oge·neşi** *f.* monogenesis. **-oge·nico** *adj.* monogenic. **-ogenişmo** *m.* monogenism. **-ogenista** *m.* monogenist. **-ografi·a** *f.* monograph. **-ogra·fico** *adj.* monographic. **-ografista** *m.* monographist. **-ogramma** *m.* monogram. **-ogramma·tico** *adj.* monogrammatic. **-o·ico** *adj.* (bot.) see **monoecio.** **-oidrato** *m.* (chem.) monohydrate. **-oli·tico** *adj.* monolithic. **-olito** *m.* monolith. **-o·logo** *m.* (*pl.* **-o·loghi**) monologue. **-o·mane** *adj.* monomaniac. **-omani·a** *f.* (med.; leg.) monomania, **-omani·aco** *adj.* monomaniacal. **-o·mero** *adj.* (chem.) monomeric; *n.m.* (chem.) monomer. **-ometallişmo** *m.* monometallism. **-o·metro** *adj.* (prosod.) monometric, in one metre. **-o·mio** *m.* (math.) monomial. **-omolecolare** *adj.* (chem.) monomolecular; (phys., chem.) strato -omolecolare, monomolecular layer. **-opat·tino** *m.* scooter. **-ope·talo** *adj.* (bot.) sympetalous, gamopetalous. **-oplano** *m.* monoplane. **-oplegi·a** *f.* (med.) monoplegia, paralysis of one limb. **-opo·lio** *m.* monopoly. **-opolista** *m.* monopolist. **-opolis·tico** *adj.* monopolistic. **-opolizzare** [A 1] *tr.* to monopolize. **-oposto** *adj.* (motor.; aeron.) single-seater. **-op·tero** *adj.* (archit.) monopteral. **-orimo** *adj.* (prosod.) having the same rhyme throughout. **-oritmo** *adj.* (prosod.) with the same number of feet or syllables throughout. **-orota·ia** *f.* monorail. **-osco·pio** *m.* (telev.) monoscope, monotron. **-osilicato** *m.* (chem.) monosilicate. **-osilla·bico** *adj.* monosyllabic. **-osil·labo** *m.* monosyllable. **-osizi·a** *f.* habit of eating once a day only. **-os·sido** *m.* (chem.) monoxide. **-osti·chio** *m.* composition consisting of but one line. **-os·tilo** *adj.* (archit.) of one column. **-ostro·fico, -ostrofo** *adj.* (prosod.) consisting of only one strophe or stanza. **-oteişmo** *m.* monotheism. **-oteista** *m.* monotheist. **-oteis·tico** *adj.* monotheistic. **-otelişmo** *m.* (eccl. hist.) Monothelitism. **-otelita** *m.* (eccl. hist.) Monothelite. **-otipi·a** *f.* monotype. **-o·tipo** *m.* monotype; (naut.) class, standard; design boat. **-o·tono** *adj.* monotonous; (mus.) always in the same key. **-otonamęnte** *adv.* monotonously. **-otoni·a** *f.* monotony. **-otrave** *f.* (aeron.) single span. **-otremi** *m.pl.* (zool.) monotremes. **-otri·glifo** *m.* (archit.) monotriglyph. **-otropi·a** *f.* (phys.; chem.) monotropy. **-ottongo** *m.* monophthong. **-ovalente** *adj.* (chem.) monovalent, univalent.

Monreale¹ *pr.n.m.* (geog.) Montreal.
Monreale² *pr.n.m.* (geog.) Monreale, nr. Palermo.
Monsanęşe, Monseniso *pr.n.m.* (geog.). See **Moncenisio.**
monsignor-e *m.* (eccl.) monsignore. **-ato** *m.* status of monsignore. NOTE: 'Monsignore' is now the characteristic title of a secular prelate who is neither a cardinal ('Eminenza') nor a bishop ('Eccellenza'); older usage survives in the third-person title 'Monsignor Vescovo', 'his lordship the Bishop'. The 'e' of 'Monsignore' is regularly dropped before a proper name or another title: 'Monsignor Perosi', 'Monsignor Sacrista'. Otherwise it must be kept: 'un monsignore alto e dignitoso'; 'sì, Monsignore'.
monsiù *m.* (joc.; iron.) Signore, Mr.
monsone *m.* monsoon.
†**monstro** *m.* monster; *adj.* monstrous, enormous, prodigious.
monsù *m.* Monsieur, a form of address often used to cooks.
mont-a *f.* covering (of the female by the male); stagione di —, covering season; menare una cavalla alla —, to take a mare to stud; jockey; (equit.) seat, way of riding. **-aca·richi** *m. indecl.* hoist; goods-lift. **-ace·neri** *m. indecl.* ash hoist. **-achiara** *f.* whisk. **-ali·quidi** *m. indecl.* (eng.) feed pump, force pump; **-avivande,** service-lift. **-asec·chia** *f. indecl.* bucket hoist, skip hoist.

montag·gio *m.* mounting; (eng.) assembly; (cinem.) editing; (radio) montage.
montagn-a *f.* mountain; hill; catena di -e, a mountain chain; mal di —, mountain sickness; grande come una —, as big as a mountain; (prov.) le -e stanno ferme e gli uomini camminano, mountains remain, but men move (used on meeting someone thought to be far away); (hist. ⊛ French Rev.) la —, the Mountain; (mil.) artiglieria di —, mountain artillery, pack battery; (Bibl.) il sermone della —, the Sermon on the Mount. **-ardo** *m.* (hist, of French Rev.) one of the group of deputies known as the Mountain, Montagnard; †see **montanaro.** **-oşo** *adj.* mountainous. **-(u)olo** *m.* mountaineer; *adj.* of the mountains.
montambanco *m.* mountebank.
montan-aro *m. adj.* mountaineer; highlander; of the mountains; il — di Biella, Quintino Sella. **-ello** *m.* (orn.) linnet, *Carduelis cannabina*; -ello forestiero, twite, *C. flavirostris*. **-ino** *adj.* of the mountains; aria -ina, mountain air. **-ina** *f.* women from the mountains; the great bell of Pistoia; †pelle -ina, chamois leather; (orn.) passera -ina, rock sparrow. **-o** *adj.* of or on the mountains; strada -a, mountain road; villaggio -o, mountain village. **-işmo** *m.* montanism. **-ista** *m.* (eccl. hist.) Montanist; mining engineer. **-i·stico** *adj.* Montanistic.
montante *part.* of **montare,** q.v.; *adj.* ascending; *n.m.* amount; stand, support; (aeron.) — portante, lift strut; (boxing) uppercut; (soccer) upright of goal mouth.
mont-are [A 1 c] *intr.* (*aux.* essere) to mount, to climb; to rise up, to rise; to increase; — a cavallo, to mount a horse, to ride; — in carrozza, to get into a carriage; (naut.) — a riva, to go aloft; — su, to go up, to climb; il sangue gli -ò alla testa, the blood rose to his head; il vino gli -ò alla testa, the wine went to his head; — in collera, to become angry; to amount; to be of consequence; non -a, it does not matter; -a poco, it is of little consequence; *tr.* to mount, to set up, to set; — un cavallo, to ride a horse; *abs.* -a benino, he rides very well; (of the male) to mount, to cover; to organize; — una casa, to set up house; — un orologio, to wind a watch; (cul.) to whip; — la panna, to whip the cream; — una gemma in oro, to set a gem in gold; — una macchina, to assemble a machine; (mil.) — la guardia, to mount guard; (naut.) — i cannoni, to mount a battery; (fig.) to stir, to rouse, to excite; — la testa a, to excite; *rfl.* (*dat.* of *prn.* 'si') -arsi la testa, to get excited, to get a swollen head. **-ata** *f.* ascent; rise, hill. **-atoio** *m.* step; footboard; mounting-block. **-atore** *m.* fitter; assembler; (cinem.) editor. (**-atrice** *f.*) **-atura** *f.* assembling; puffing, boosting; a got-up affair, stunt; (opt.) mount (of a lens); -atura rientrante, sunk mount; -atura sporgente, flange mount.
mont-e *m.* mount, hill; mountain; il — Everest, Mt Everest; una catena di -i, a chain of mountains; a —, upstream; heap, mass, pile; in —, in bulk; tutt'in un —, all together; un — di stracci, a heap of rags; (geog.) — Pulciano (or Montepulciano) a place in Tuscany noted for its wine; — citorio (or Montecitorio) the Lower House or Chamber of Deputies in Rome; — della Bussola, Compass Berg; — Cervino, Matterhorn; -i Metalliferi, Ore mountains; (Rom. hist.) — Tarpeo, Tarpeian Rock; (Bibl.) — Carmelo, Mount Carmel; — Oliveto, Mount Olivet, the Mount of Olives; salire sul —, to climb the mountain (hill); promettere mari e -i, to promise heaven and earth; — di credito (C.C.), — di pietà, pawnshop; portare l'orologio al —, to pawn one's watch; andare a —, to come to nothing; il matrimonio andò a —, the marriage didn't come off; far —, mandare a —, to stop the game (and have, possibly, a fresh deal); (prov.) i -i stanno fermi e gli uomini camminano, mountains remain, but men move (said on meeting someone in an unexpected place); (anat.) — di Venere, mons Veneris, mons pubis. **-ic·chio** *m. dim.* hillock; name of mountain in the province of Avellino, celebrated for mineral waters. **-icello** *m. dim.* hillock, mound. **-icellite** *f.* (miner.) monticellite. **-icino** *m. dim.* little heap; little hillock. **-ista** *m.* person who has invested in the public loan or public debt; pawnbroker.
montgo·mery *m. indecl.* duffle coat.
montone¹ *m. augm.* of **monte,** q.v.
monton-e² *m.* ram; sheepskin; carne di —, mutton; salto del —, buck-jump (of a horse); (astron.) the constellation Aries; (numism.) an old French coin; breaker; *pl.* white horses; (mil.) battering ram; (fig.) ram, doggy individual, randy fellow; trovare il quinto piede al —, to cavil. **-ata** *f.* buck-jump (of a horse);

monton-e (*cont.*)
(geol.) roche moutonnée. **-ato** *adj.* (geol.) rounded. **-cello, -cino** *m. dim.* ram; sheepskin.
montuọs-o *adj.* mountainous. **-ità** *f.* mountainousness.
montur-a *f.* harness; (mil.) cavalry equipment; uniform, military dress complete with appropriate distinguishing badges. **-ato** *adj.* uniformed.
monumẹnt-o *m.* monument; erigere, alzare un —, to raise a monument; tomb; un — di dottrina, a monument of learning; important building, statue, etc.; i -i della città, the sights of the city; (leg.) un comitato promotore di un —, committee for putting up a monument (C.C.); — nazionale, national monument (classified historic building). **-a·bile** *adj.* worthy to be honoured with a monument. **-ale** *adj.* monumental; huge; città -ale, town with many important buildings. **-alità** *f.* momumentality.
monzọne *m.* See **monsone.**
mops *m. indecl.* a small breed of pet dog, short-haired and pug-nosed.
mor-a[1] *f.* delay, interval; il pericolo in —, the danger of delay; (leg.) default; delay; period of grace; — del creditore, — del debitore, default by creditor, by debtor; la costituzione in —, formal placing of debtor in default (C.C.); concedere la —, to grant a period of grace; cadere in —, to fall into arrear(s); essere in —, to be in default, in arrear(s); essere considerato in —, to be deemed in default; purgare la —, to allow a respite; il giorno della —, the day of default (C.C.). **†-ag·gine** *f.* tardiness.
mora[2] *f.* (bot.) mulberry, fruit of the **moro**[2], q.v.; — (selvatica), blackberry.
mora[3] *f.* (zool.) morula stage of embryo.
mora[4] *f.* negress; *adj. f.* of **moro**[1], q.v.
mora[5] *f.* mora, morra, a game in which one player guesses the number of fingers held up by another; giocare, fare alla —, to play morra; (joc. of horses, mules, etc.) giocare alla —, to kick.
†mora[6] *f.* stone pillar; cairn; stone wall or pier.
mora·glia *f.* (vet.) bit; twitch.
moral-e *adj.* moral; senso —, moral sense; filosofia —, scienza —, moral philosophy, ethics; significato —, moral sense, moral meaning; virtual; (leg.) ente —, corporation, incorporated body; la capitale — d'Italia, the virtual capital of Italy (Milan); *n.f.* morals, morality; *La — cattolica*, title of a work by Alessandro Manzoni on Catholic morality; moral; la — della favola, the moral of the fable; trarre la —, to draw the moral; (leg.) delitto contro la — familiare, crime against family morals (C.P.); *n.m.* morale, moral condition; il — dell'esercito è altissimo, the morale of the army is very high; (bldg.) plank. **-mẹnte** *adv.* morally; virtually. **-eggiare** [A 3 c] *intr.* (*aux.* avere) to moralize. **-ista** *m.* moralist. **-ità** *f.* morality; uomo di dubbia -ità man of doubtful morals; moral; la -ità che se ne ricava, the moral that can be drawn from it; (leg.) delitto contro la -ità pubblica, crime against public morality (C.P.). **-izẓare** [A 1] *tr.* to moralize; to expound in a moral sense. **-izẓaziọne** *f.* moralizing; moralization.
moran·dola *f.* (bot.) bugle, *Ajuga reptans.*
†morato *adj.* black; nero —, jet black.
morato·ri-o *adj.* delaying, reprieving; (leg.) interessi moratori, interest payable after default (C.C.). **-a** *f.* (leg.) moratorium; deferment; postponement; chiedere la -a, to ask for a postponement (of payment).
Mora·v-ia *pr.n.f.* (geog.) Moravia. **-o** *adj.* Moravian; (rel.) Fratelli -i, Moravian Brethren, Moravians; *n.m.* Moravian.
mo·rbida *f.* See under **morbido.**
mo·rbid-o, †mo·rbi-o *adj.* soft; guanciale —, soft pillow; cappello —, Trilby hat, felt hat; mani -e, soft hands; tender (of meat); easily worked (of ground); stile —, delicate style; (of a horse) soft-mouthed; (of fruit) mellow; effeminate; delicate; lascivious; morbid; (paint.) soft, mellow; (geog.) colline -e, rounded hills. **-amẹnte** *adv.* softly, tenderly; weakly; delicately; morbidly. **-a** *f.* low level of water in a river. **†-are** *tr.* to soften; to weaken. **-ello** *m.* (bot.) lamb's lettuce, corn salad, *Valerianella.* **-ẹzza** *f.* softness; (of fruit) mellowness; lasciviousness; morbidity (in horses) the quality of being soft-mouthed, easily restrained; (paint.) softness, mellowness. **-ic·cio** *dim. adj.* softish, *n.m. dim.* soft patch; something soft. (**-ino, -ẹtto** *dim. adj.*) **†-ire** *intr.* to grow soft. (**-ọne** *augm.*) **-ume** *m.* soft part; soft stuff; thick mud.
morb-o *m.* disease; — asiatico, Asiatic cholera; — gallico, syphilis; — caduco, epileptic fit; plague; illness; vice, evil passion; stink; †— regio, King's evil; †— arido, phthisis in animals. **-i·fero** *adj.* disease-carrying. **-i·fico** *adj.* morbific. **†-iglione** *m.* (med.) see **morviglione.** **-illo** *m.* (med.) German measles. **†-ino** *m.* playfulness, sprightliness. **-inọso** *adj.* (Ven. dial.) playful, sprightly. **-osità** *f.* morbidity, unhealthiness. **-ọso** *adj.* morbid; stato -oso, morbid condition; gelosia -osa, pathological jealousy.
morchella *f.* (bot.) — esculenta, morel, *Morchella esculenta*; — conica, *M. conica.*
mọrchia *f.* dregs of pressed olives.
mordac·chia *f.* twitch (for restraining a horse); muzzle; gag.
mordac-e *adj.* biting; pungent, stinging; sarcastic; lingua —, sharp tongue; cane —, beware of the dog; *n.m.* (eng.) vice cap. (**-emẹnte** *adv.*) **-ità** *f.* pungency; mordacity.
mor·d-ere [B I] *tr.* to bite, to gnaw, to sting; — la mano che soccorre, to bite the hand that feeds one; -ersi le labbra, to bite one's lips; (fig.) to profit; leccare non —, to lick, not to bite (i.e. to be satisfied with reasonable gains); (fig.) — il freno, to champ at the bit. **-ente** *part. adj.* biting, pungent; caustic; *n.m.* (chem.; dyeing) mordant, striker; passare al -ente, to mordant; passaggio al -ente, mordanting; (mus.) mordent. **-enzatura** *f.* (dyeing) mordanting. **†-icare** [A 2 s] *tr.* to dry up, to corrode. **-icante** *part. adj.* corrosive; drying. **-icchiare** [A 3] *tr.* to nibble; to bite. **-igallina** *f.* (bot.) scarlet pimpernel, poor man's weather glass, *Anagallis arvensis.* **-imẹnto** *m.* biting; backbiting. **-itọre** *m.* biter; backbiter. (**-itrice** *f.*) **-itura** *f.* bite; sting; reproof.
more[1] *f.* (bot.) — di rovo, blackberry, *Rubus fruticosus.*
more[2] (Lat.) *adv.* according to the custom of.
morẹccio *m.* (bot.) *Boletus* (genus of edible fungi).
morella *f.* (bot.) black nightshade, *Solanum nigrum.*
morello *adj.* nearly black; *n.m.* horse of that colour; (provb.) — senza segno non te ne fidar col pegno, i.e. a spotlessly black horse is sure to be vicious; the name of a select Chianti wine.
mor-ena[1] *f.* (geol.) moraine; — centrale, medial moraine; — frontale, terminal moraine; — profonda, ground moraine. **-e·nico** *adj.* (geol.) morainal, morainic.
morena[2] *f.* (ichth.). See **murena.**
morente *part.* See under **morire.**
morẹs-co[1] *adj.* (*m.pl.* **-chi**) Moorish. **-ca** *f.* (mus.) Morisca, Morris dance. **†-care** *intr.* to dance a Moorish dance.
†moresco[2] *adj.* pertaining to **mora**[5], q.v.
morẹto *m.* See under **moro**[2].
morẹtt-o *m. dim.* of **moro**[1]; Moorish boy; negro boy; dark boy; (eccl.) i -i del padre Ludovico da Casoria, the African children at the school founded by Father Ludovico; black servant; (pol., iron.) faithful follower; *pr.n.m.* (paint.) il Moretto, name given to Alessandro Bonvicino of Brescia, a pupil of Titian (1498–1554). **-a** *f.* Moorish girl; negro girl; brunette; black mask, esp. of a harlequin; (orn.) tufted duck, *Aythya fuligula*; -a arlecchino, harlequin duck, *Histrionicus histrionicus*; -a codona, long-tailed duck, (Amer.) old squaw, *Clangula hyemalis*; -a grigia, scaup, *Aythya marila*; -a tabaccata, ferruginous duck, *A. nyroca.*
morfe·a *f.* (med.) a leprous or scurfy eruption.
Morfe·o *pr.n.m.* (class. myth.) Morpheus; (fig.) andare in braccio a —, essere in braccio a —, to go to sleep, to be asleep, to be in the arms of Morpheus.
mor·fico *adj.* (pharm.) with a morphine base.
morfin-a *f.* (chem.; pharm.) morphine.
-izẓare [A 1] *tr.* (med.) to inject with morphine. **-omani·a** *f.* (med.) morphinism, morphine addiction. **-o·mane** *m., f.* (med.) morphine addict.
morfol-ogi·a *f.* morphology. **-o·gico** *adj.* morphological. **-ogicamẹnte** *adv.* morphologically. **-ogista** *m.* morphologist.
†mor-fonduto, -fuso *m.* (vet.) rheumatic condition.
Morgana *pr.n.f.* Fata —, Morgan le Fay; mirage.
morgana·tic-o *adj.* morganatic; matrimonio —, morganatic marriage. (**-amẹnte** *adv.*)
†morganato *m.* lord; *adj.* lordly, noble; beautiful, comely.
mor-i·a *f.* high mortality; pestilence. **-ibọndo** *adj.* moribund; at the point of death.
moric·ci-a *f.* ruin; heap of rubble; dry-stone wall. (**-uolo** *m. dim.*)
moriger-are [A 1 s] *tr.* to instruct, to give guidance to (in good morals, honest behaviour). **-atẹzza** *f.* good morals; honest behaviour; temperance. **-ato** *adj.* temperate; of simple life; of good morals; well-conducted; of good manners.
morigiana *f.* (orn.) widgeon.

moriglione m. (orn.) pochard, *Aythya ferina*.

morind-a f. (bot.) *Morinda citrifolia*. **-ina** f. (chem.) morindin.

mori·ngico adj. (chem.) moringatannic; acido —, moringatannic acid, maclurin.

morintan·nico adj. (chem.) moringatannic, moritannic; acido —, moringatannic acid, maclurin.

morione[1] m. (mil. hist.) morion.

morione[2] m. (miner.) morion, black smoky quartz.

mor-ire [D 3] intr. (aux. essere) to die; — di colera, to die of cholera; — impiccato, to be hanged; — di morte naturale, to die a natural death; — di crepacuore, to die of a broken heart; — sul suo letto, to die in one's own bed; — sul patibolo, to die on the scaffold; — sul rogo, to be burnt at the stake; vide — tutti i suoi, he outlived all the rest of the family; gli è morta la mamma, he has lost his mother; — dalla voglia di, to be dying to (do something); credevo di —, I thought I should have died; — dal ridere, — dalle risa, to die of laughter; — di fame, to starve; sentirsi — di fame, to feel absolutely dying of hunger, to be starving; un caldo da —, terribly hot; fare —, to kill; lo fece — soffocato, he strangled him; duro da —, die-hard; vorrei — se non dico il vero, may I drop down dead if I'm not telling the truth; se seguiti così, mi fai —, if you keep on in this way, you'll be the death of me; (fig.) to go out, to die away; la voce andò -endo, the voice died away; lasciar — un discorso, to let a subject drop; lasciar — il fuoco, to let the fire go out; (of running water) to end in a marsh; tutti i treni muoiono a Roma, all trains come to a stop at Rome; *rfl.* to die a natural death, to die slowly; tornò in patria e poco dopo se ne -ì, he returned to his native land and died soon afterwards; *tr.* (colloq.) to kill; non ha morto che due, he's only killed two; n.m. death; non mi spaventa il —, death has no terrors for me. **-endo** ger. (mus.) dying away, becoming softer. **-ente** part. adj. dying; moribund; fading away; faint. **-iente** part. adj. (poet.) see **morente**. **-ituro** adj. about to die; doomed to die; dying.

morlac-co adj. (m.pl. **-chi**) Moldo-Wallachian; (fig.) simple, rustic.

†**mormillo, mormiro** m. (ichth.) *Mormyrus oxyrhincus*.

morm-one m. Mormon. **-o·nico** adj. Mormonite. **-onismo** m. Mormonism.

mo·rmora f. (ichth.) *Pagellus mormyrus*, a kind of sea bream.

mormor-are [A I sc] intr. (aux. avere) to murmur; to mutter; to speak in whispers; to speak in an undertone; — di, contro, alcuno to complain of someone, to speak ill of, to mutter against someone; *tr.* to murmur; to mutter; si -a che, it is rumoured that; †to slander, to speak ill of. **-acchiare** [A 4] intr. (aux. avere) to mutter; to grumble a little. **-amento** m. murmuring; whispering; grumbling. **-ante** part. adj. murmuring; complaining. **-atore** m. (**-atrice**, pop. **-atora** f.) murmurer; grumbler; mutterer. **-ato·rio** m. (joc.) a grumbling-place. **-azione** f. murmuring; complaining; slander. **-eggiamento** m. murmuring; whispering. **-eggiare** [A 3 c] intr. (aux. avere) to murmur; to whisper. **-io** m. (pl. **-ii**) murmuring; il -io della folla, the murmur of the crowd; il -io delle foglie, the rustling of the leaves; grumbling, slander.

mor-o[1] m. Moor, negro; Il — di Venezia, the Moor of Venice, Othello; adj. black, dark-complexioned; tabacco —, negro-head.

mor-o[2] m. (bot.) mulberry-tree, *Morus*. **-eto** m. mulberry grove.

†**moroco·mio** m. madhouse.

†**moropetino** m. See **marabottino**.

moros-o[1] adj. tardy; (leg.) being behindhand, in arrear(s); contribuenti -i, abbonati -i, tax-payers, subscribers, in arrears; debitore —, defaulting debtor. **-amente** adv. tardily; late. **-ità** f. tardiness; (leg.) state of being in arrear; lo sfratto per -ità, eviction for non-payment of rent (C.C.P.).

†**moros-o**[2] adj. amorous; n.m. lover, sweetheart. †**-a** f. sweetheart.

morra[1] f. See **mora**[5] and **mora**[6].

morsa[1] f. See under **morso**.

morsa[2] f. (herald.) horse-brays, horse-barnacles; (naut.) boats' crutches (deck storage).

morsettiera f. (electr.) terminal board; — chiusa, junction box.

mors-o part. of **mordere**, q.v.; adj. bitten; n.m. bite; il — della morte, death's sting; morsel, bit; un — di pane, a morsel, mouthful, of bread; mangiare a -i, to eat greedily; bit (for horse); cavallo delicato di —, a soft-mouthed horse; mettere, allentare, stringere il —, to use, loosen, tighten the bit; (vet.) secondo —, permanent dentition (as opposed to milk teeth); (geog.) erosion,

weathering; (bot.) — del diavolo, devil's-bit scabious, *Succisa pratensis*; — di rana, frog-bit, *Hydrocharis morsus-ranae*. **-a** f. vice; lo stringe con le mani come in una —, he grips it in his hands as if it were in a vice; twitch (for horse); nose-ring; (eng.; carpen.) vice; — da banco, bench vice; — da tubi, pipe vice; (of a machine tool) chuck; (naut.) boat's crutches, cradle. **-a·io**, **-aro** m. bit-maker. **-ata** f. weedy patch abounding in fish; †(naut.) scantling. **-atura** f. (naut.) seating or jointing of ship's plates. **-ecchiare** [A3] tr. to nibble. **-eggiare** [A3c] intr. (aux. avere) tr. to nibble; to harrow. **-ellare** [A I] tr., intr. (aux. avere) to nibble. **-ellato** part. adj. nibbled; n.m. minced meat. **-ello** m. morsel; (naut.) sennet used for seizing or for tholepin strops; †cat-o'-nine-tails. **-etto** m. dim. morsel; m. (electr.) terminal; -etto di carica, charging clip; (eng.) clamp; clip; holdfast; -etto a vite, screw clamp, hard vice; -etto da falegname, carpenter's cramp, glue press; (naut.) -etto di ottone, brass bit or spanner used with mines or torpedos. **-ettina** f. dim. clothes-peg. **-icare** [A 2 s] tr. to bite; to sting; to nibble. **-icchiare** [A 3] tr. to nibble. **-ino** m. dim. little bite. **-ura** f. bite; -ura di stomaco, violent pains in the stomach.

morta f. dried-up river-bed.

mortadell-a f., †**-o** m. (cul.) mortadella, spiced pork sausage; Bologna sausage.

morta·io m. mortar; pestar l'acqua nel —, to do a vain thing, to beat the air; (agric.) bed made round foot of tree for manure; (mil.) mortar, heavy calibre, high-trajectory gun.

mortal-e adj. mortal; colpo —, fatal blow; deadly; peccato —, mortal sin, deadly sin; salto —, somersault; n.m. mortal; agli occhi dei -i, in the sight of mortals; mortal part of man, body. **-mente** adv. mortally. **-ità** f. mortality; loss of life; death-rate.

morta-letto, **-retto** m. small mortar; cracker.

mort-e f. death; — naturale, natural death; — immatura, untimely death; è sul letto di —, he is on his death-bed; essere in punto di —, to be at death's door; darsi la —, to commit suicide; (eccl.) la buona —, Bona Mors (devotion or confraternity); (leg.) l'atto di —, registration of death; certificato di —, death certificate; — presunta, presumed death; la pena di —, the death penalty (C.P.); — civile, loss of civil rights; (fig.) cause of death; quel figliolaccio sarà la sua —, that wicked son will be the death of him; end, cessation; destruction.

mortella f. (bot.) myrtle, *Myrtus communis*.

morticino m., adj. See under **morto**.

morti·fer-o adj. mortiferous, death-dealing; veleno —, deadly poison. (**-amente** adv.)

mortific-are [A 2 s] tr. to mortify; to grieve, to vex; to humiliate; to repress; (med.) to cauterize; rfl. to mortify oneself; to be humiliated. **-amento** m. mortifying; mortification. **-ante** part. adj. mortifying; humiliating; vexing. **-ativo** adj, mortifying; humiliating. **-ato** part. adj. mortified; humiliated; grieved; ashamed; (paint.) toned down. (**-atamente** adv.) **-atore** m. mortifier; adj. mortifying. (**-atrice** f.) **-azione** f. mortification; humiliation; grave rebuke; shame; (rel.) mortification.

mortina f. (bot.) lesser and greater periwinkle, *Vinca minor* and *V. major*; †myrtle.

mort-o part. of **morire**, q.v.; adj. dead: — e seppellito, dead and buried; acqua -a, stagnant water; palla -a, dead ball; peso —, dead weight; binario —, siding; stagione -a, dead season; terreno —, barren land; giungere a un punto —, to come to a dead end; taglio —, a dull edge; nato —, still-born; (paint.) toned down, deadened; (comm.) capitale —, unemployed capital; (chem.) corpo —, inert body, (naut.) mooring buoy; opera -a, hull of a vessel above the waterline; spent, extinguished; lost; ruined; fruitless, sterile; essere lettera -a (of a law, etc.), to be a dead letter; n.m. dead man, deceased; i -i non parlano, dead men tell no tales; un — di fame, a down-and-out; il giorno dei -i, All Souls' Day; rammentare i -i a tavola, to recall the dead at table, i.e. to make untimely remarks; fare il —, to feign death, to lie doggo, *or* to float on one's back; (at cards) dummy; hoard of money, treasure; (naut.) mooring bollard. **-a** f. dead woman; **-a** di fiume, old river-bed. **-amente** adv. as if dead; limply, weakly. **-ic·cio** adj. spoilt; withered; decomposed. **-ici·nio** m. a duty which the prince exacted from the heirs after the death of one of his vassals. **-icino** m. dead child; pale, sickly child; (tanning) murrain hide, fallen skin; adj. (text.) lana morticina, dead wool, morling wool; dead wood. **-o·rio**, †**-oro** m. funeral, burial; un -orio

mort-o (*cont.*)
continuo, a depressing person, *or* occasion; il ricevimento riuscì un -orio, the reception bored us to death; a heap of dead. **-oriante** *m.* see **mortuario. -ua·rio** *adj.* mortuary; pertaining to a funeral; carro -uario, hearse; letto -uario, bier; registro -uario, register of deaths; fede -uaria, death certificate; *n.m.pl.* (eccl.) members of a burial guild.

morula *f.* (zool.). See **mora**[3].

morva *f.* (vet.) glanders.

mor·vido *adj.* (Tusc., pop.). See **morbido.**

†morviglione *m.* (med.) measles.

Moṣa *pr.n.f.* (geog.) the river Meuse.

moṣa·i·co[1] *adj.* Mosaic, of Moses; la legge -ca, Mosaic Law. **-ṣmo** *m.* Mosaism.

moṣa·ic-o[2] *m.* (art) mosaic; un paviment a —, a mosaic pavement; (fig.) patchwork. **-ista** *m.* mosaicist.

moṣc-a[1] *f.* (ent.) fly; house fly; — carnaria, carrion fly, *Sarcophaga carnaria*; — cavallina, forest fly, *Hippobosca equina*; — tze-tze, — ze-ze, tsetse fly, *Glossina* spp.; — dell'olivo, olearia, *Dacus oleae*, a pest of olives, causing the oil to be foul smelling; non farebbe male a una —, he wouldn't harm a fly; non si sentiva (volare) una —, you could have heard a pin drop; fare d'una — un elefante, to make a mountain of a mole-hill; morivano come le mosche, they died like flies; restare, tornare, trovarsi, con un pugno di mosche, to be left empty-handed at the end (after expecting gain); se mi salta la — al naso, if I lose my temper; non si lascia posare le mosche sul naso, he doesn't put up with bullying; — cieca, blind man's buff; — bianca, a rarity, a rare kind of person; — di Milano, a vesicating ointment; black spot on a horse's coat; beauty spot (patch of taffeta worn by women on the cheek); imperial (beard), goatee; —!, hush!; (bot.) sea club-rush, *Scirpus maritimus.* **-ado** *m.* muscatel; muscat; *adj.* muscat; spotted, with dark patches. **-a·io** *m.* swarm of flies; place full of flies. **-ai(u)ola** *f.* fly-net; meat-cover; fly-catcher, fly-trap. **-aragno** *m.* (ent.) forest fly, *Hippobosca equina.*

Mosca[2] *pr.n.f.* (geog.) Moscow.

moscardina *f.* muscardine.

moscardino *m.* (zool.) dormouse, see **moscarolo**; also *Eledone moscato*, a kind of octopus; dandy; fop.

moscardo *m.* (orn.) a name given loosely to the spotted flycatcher, sparrow-hawk and red-footed falcon.

†moscarino *m.* See **moscerino.**

moscarolo *m.* (zool.) topo —, dormouse, *Muscardinus avellanarius.*

moscat-o *m.* muscat (wine or grape), muscatel; *adj.* marked with dark spots; having a flavour of musk; muscat; vino —, muscat wine, noce -a, nutmeg. **-ello** *m.* muscadine; muscatel. **-ellato** *adj.* with muscatel flavour.

moscatura *f.* (herald.) spot.

moscello *m.* (naut.). See under **moscio.**

moscerino *m.* (ent.) any small fly, especially *Drosophila* spp.; — del mosto, *Drosophila ampelophila*, a small fly found on fermenting grapes; — del formaggio, *Piophila casei*; acchiappare i moscerini, to catch midges, i.e. to waste one's time on trifles; fare montare i moscerini al naso di, to anger.

mosche·a[1] *f.* mosque.

Mosch-e·a[2] *f.* title of a macaronic poem by Folengo. **-e·ide** *f.* title of a comic poem by G. B. Lalli. **-ereccio** *adj.* (joc.) of flies; pertaining to flies.

moscherino *m.* (ent.). See **moscerino.**

moschett-o[1] *m.* (orn.) musket (the male sparrow-hawk in falconry). **-ato** *adj.* speckled. **-atura** *f.* speckling, spots. **-one** *m.* (orn.) black-tailed godwit; (techn.) spring catch.

moschett-o[2] *m.* musket; †arquebus. **-are** [A I c] *tr.* to kill with a musket; to shoot with a musket. **-ata** *f.* musket-shot. **-ato** *part. adj.* shot. **-eri·a** *f.* (mil.) musketry. **-iere, †-iero** *m.* (mil.) musketeer. **-one** *m. augm.* large musket; blunderbuss; more commonly, clasp, fastener, swivel; clip (to attach sword to belt).

mosch-icida *adj.* fly-killing. **-ile** *m.* nest of flies; carta -ile, flypaper; *n.m.* fly-killer.

moschino *m. dim.* little fly; bumptious person; black spotted dog.

mosci-ame, -à *m.* tunny-fish pressed and salted.

moscino *m.* (ent.) see **moscherino**; (bot.) red clover, *Trifolium pratense* and *Dorycnium pentaphyllum.*

moṣc-io[1] *adj.* flabby, soft; muffled; cappello —, soft hat; carne -ia, flabby flesh; (of a person) dull; (of pockets) empty. **-ello** *m.* (naut.

strand, seizing. **-ezza** *f.* flabbiness; softness. **-icone** *adj.* soft; flabby. **-ione** *adj. augm.* flabby, inert; *n.m.* heavy drinker.

mo·ṣc-io[2] *m.*, **-ione** (ent.) small fly, esp. flies, mainly *Drosophila* spp., found round fermenting grapes, etc.

mos-co *m.* (*pl.* **-chi**) (zool.) musk deer, *Moshcus moschiferus.*

moṣcolo *m.* (mil. hist.) siege shield used to approach the walls; (naut. hist.) fishing craft (Chioggia); †(zool.) trunk of an elephant.

moscon-e *m.* (ent.) large fly; — azzurro, bluebottle, *Calliphora* spp.; (fig.) suitor, wooer; ha uno sciame di -i, she has a crowd of admirers; raft of two long floats with seats for rowers (resembling a catamaran).

moscongreco (bot.) *m.* musk.

Mos-co·via *pr.n.f.* Muscovy; (joc.) kingdom of the flies in the *Moscheide*, q.v. **-covita** *adj., n.m.* Muscovite.

Moṣè *pr.n.m.* Moses.

Moṣella *pr.n.f.* (geog.) Moselle; *m.* moselle (wine).

mosquito *m.* (ent.) mosquito.

moss-a *f.* movement, move; (chess) fare una —, to make a move (also fig.); una — sbagliata, a false move; una — falsa, a false start; basterebbe la — di un dito, one would only have to raise a finger; fece una — improvvisa, he moved suddenly; lo buttò in terra con una —, with one movement he threw him to the ground; sudden change; temo che il tempo voglia far qualche —, I fear that there's going to be a change in the weather; (of wine, milk, etc.) far —, to turn sour; shoot; far la —, to grow new shoots; gesture; ha certe -e graziose, he moves gracefully, he has pleasing ways; (mil.) strategic move, movement of troops; (med.) — di corpo, motion of the bowels; (archit.) spring (of an arch or vault); (vet.) avere, fare, la prima, la seconda —, (of a horse) to have its first, second teeth; *pl.* start, starting-place; dar le -e, to give the signal to start, (fig.) to incite; lasciare, pigliare le -e, to start, to be off the mark; rubar le -e, to leave before the signal is given; essere sulle -e, to be on the move, to be about to start; non poter più stare sulle -e, to be unable to wait any longer. **-ac·cia** *f. pejor.* discourteous act, or gesture; bad move. **-iere** *m.* starter. **-o** *part.* of **muovere**, q.v.; *adj.* moved, agitated; -o a compassione, moved to pity; capelli -i, wavy hair; mare -o, rough sea; (mus.) più -o, faster; meno -o, slower.

†mossolina *f.* See **mussolina.**

mostac·c-hio *m.* (usu. *pl.*) moustache. **-io** *m.* face; glielo dirò sul -io, I'll tell him to his face. **-iac·cio** *m. pejor.* ugly mug. **-iata** *f.* slap in the face.

mostac·cione *m.* See **mostacciata.**

mostacciuolo *m.* spiced cake.

mostard-a *f.* mustard; — di Cremona, a kind of chutney; far venire la — al naso a, to make angry, to vex. **-iera** *f.* mustard-pot.

mostardina *f.* (bot.) dittander, broad-leaved pepperwort, *Lepidium latifolium.*

most-o *m.* must; wort. **-a·io** *adj.* juicy; vitigno -aio, vine yielding an abundance of juice. **-i·metro** *m.* saccharimeter. **-oso** *adj.* full of must, juicy.

mostoṣa *f.* (slang) breast, nipple, teat.

moṣtr-a *f.* show, display, exhibition: — di macchine agrarie, agricultural machinery exhibition; — campionaria, sample fair; sala di —, show-room; vetrina di —, show-window; — di panno, sample of cloth; (naut.) regatta; naval review; (mil.) tattoo; military review, display, march past; dial of watch; frame of doorway; show, ostentation; mette in — le gambe, she shows her legs; far — di, to pretend to; lo fa per —, he does it for the sake of appearances; mettersi in —, to make oneself conspicuous. **-ina** *f.* (mil.) badge. **-ino** *m. dim.* small dial on watch face for a second hand; small plate that shows the position of the regulator.

mostr-are [A I c] *tr.* to show, to point out, to exhibit, to display; mi -ò la sua biblioteca, he showed me his library; — a dito, to point to; — gran coraggio, to display great courage; (fig.) — i denti, to show one's teeth; to point out, to demonstrate, to prove; ve lo -erò con un esempio, I'll prove it to you with an example; non -a la propria età, he doesn't look his age; to seem, to look; non -a di capire, he doesn't seem to understand; -a di ignorare tutto, he pretends to know nothing about it; *rfl.* to show oneself, to be seen, to come out; non vuol -arsi in pubblico, he doesn't wish to appear in public; si -ò molto coraggioso, he showed great courage. **-a·bile** *adj.* that can be shown; presentable. **-amento** *m.* showing; demonstration. **†-arombi** *m. indecl.* (naut.) compass course table, used by the helmsman to indicate distances run on

mostr-are (*cont.*)

each course in order to work up the dead reckoning. †**-atempesta** *m. indecl.* (naut.) storm gauge. **-ativo** *adj.* showing. **-ato** *part. adj.* shown. (**-atore** *m.* **-atrice** *f.*) **-avento** *m. indecl.* (naut.) wind-vane, pennant; (aeron.) windsock. **-eggiato** *part. adj.* furnished with facings (of coat). **-eggiatura** *f.* facings (of a coat); coat-sleeve.

mostr-o¹ *m.* monster; monstrous person; prodigy; (paint.) grotesque. **-icciat·tolo** *m.* little monster. **-icino** *m.* little monster; deformed child; ugly creature. **-uosità** . monstrosity, monstrousness; *f.* (biol.) monstrosity. **-uoso** *adj.* monstrous; enormous. **-uosa-mente** *adv.* monstrously.

mostro² *apocop. part.* of **mostrare**, q.v.

mot-a *f.* mud, mire; (Tusc., fig.) pezzo di —, worthless or insensitive person. **-ic·chio**, **-i·glio** *m. dim.* a little mud here and there. **-oso** *adj.* muddy. **-ri·glia** *f.*, **-ri·glio** *m.* mud.

motacilla *f.* (orn.) wagtail.

motella *f.* (ichth.) rockling, *Onos tricirratus*.

motellina *f.* (bot.) *Meum mutellina*.

moterello, see under **moto**.

motetto *m.* (mus.). See **mottetto**.

motiv-are [A 1] *tr.* to state the reasons for; to justify; to motivate, to cause; (leg.) to allege or state reason of or for; to motivate. **-ato** *part. adj.* justified; based on; motivated; (leg.) la sentenza -ata, reasoned judgement (C.C.P.). **-azione** *f.* statement of the motives, of the reasons (for); -azione considerando, recital of reasons; citation (in award of military decoration); (leg.) -azione della sentenza, statement of reasons for decision, in judgement (C.C.P.).

motiv-o *adj.* motive; *n.m.* motive; reason, cause; non ho — di crederlo disonesto, I have no reason to believe that he is dishonest; (leg.) motive; ground; — abietto, base motive (C.P.); giusto —, just motive; senza —, without motive; senza giustificato —, without justification; — di appello, — di impugnazione, ground of appeal (C.C.P.); — di fatto, point of fact; — di diritto, point of law; i -i in fatto e in diritto, considerations of fact and law (C.C.P.); -i per l'arresto, grounds for arrest; (mus., etc.) motif; (paint.) subject.

motivo-guida *m.* (mus.) leitmotiv, leading motif.

mot-o *m.* motion; — perpetuo, perpetual motion; leggi di —, laws of motion; mettere in —, to set in motion, (eng.) to start up; mettersi in —, to set out, to start; sarà meglio mettersi in —, we'd better get going; di — proprio, of one's own accord; emotion, commotion; — dell'animo, agitation; movement, exercise, exertion; far —, to take exercise; (fig.) — rivoluzionario, revolutionary movement; un — popolare, a rising among the people; (mus.) motion; — contrario, contrary motion; — obliquo, oblique motion; — perpetuo, continuous succession of quick notes; — retto, similar motion; (gramm.) verbi di —, verbs of motion; †*part. adj.* moved. **-erello** *m. dim.* slight movement; (med.) irregularity of the pulse. **-ilità** *f.* motility.

moto-aratrice *f.* tractor plough. **-aratura** *f.* ploughing with a tractor. **-barca** *f.* motor-boat. **-battello** *m.* motor-boat. **-ca·mera** *f.* (cinem.) motor-driven camera. **-carrozzetta** *f.*, **-carrozzino** *m.* side-car; combination. **-cicletta** *f.*, **-ciclo** *m.* motor-cycle. **-ciclismo** *m.* motor-cycling. **-ciclista** *m.* motor-cyclist. **-cicli·stico** *adj.* relating to motor-cycling; campionato -ciclistico, motor-cycling championship. **-coltura** *f.* mechanical ploughing. **-lan·cia** *f.* (naut.) motor-boat. **-leggera** *f.* light motor-cycle with small engine. **-livellatore** *m.* bulldozer. **-mac·china** *f.* (cinem.) motor-driven camera. **-na·uta** *m.* pilot of motor-boat. **-na·utica** *f.* speed-boat racing. **-na·utico** *adj.* pertaining to motor-boats. **-nave** *f.* motor-ship. **-pattino** *m.* see **motoscooter**. **-peschereccio** *m.* (naut.) motor-trawler. **-scafo** *m.* (naut.) motor-boat; -scafo contro i sommergibili, motor torpedo-boat, anti-submarine craft (i.e. fitted with depth charges). **-scooter** *m. indecl.* motor-scooter. **-veliero** *m.* (naut.) sailing craft with auxiliary motor.

moto·dromo *m.* racing-track.

motopro·prio *adv. phr.* (leg.) motu proprio, of his own accord.

mot-ore *m.* motor; mover; il primo —, the Prime Mover, God; (mech.; eng.) engine, motor; — a benzina, petrol engine; — Diesel, Diesel engine; avviare il —, to start the engine; spegnere il —, to shut off the engine; (aeron.) approssimazione con —, power approach; (naut.) — fuoribordo, outboard motor; *adj.* driving, impelling; forza -rice, motive power; (anat.) nervi

-ori, motor nerves; (watchm.) ruota -rice, power wheel. **-oretta** *f. dim.* light motor-cycle, motor-scooter. **-orino** *m. dim.* small engine, small motor. **-o·rio** *adj.* (m.pl. **-orii**), **-ori·stico** *adj.* motor; gare -oristiche, motor races. **-orista** *m.* (eng.) mechanic (N.B. not 'motorist'). **-orizzato** *adj.* motorized; travelling by road; siate cortesi con il vostro prossimo, -orizzato o non, be courteous to others whether they are travelling by car or not. **-rice** *f.* driving-car; driving tram-car; *adj.* see under **motore**.

mott-o *m.* saying, word; pleasantry, witticism; — popolare, popular saying, proverbial expression; — di spirito, witticism, joke; non fece —, he said not a word; senza far —, without a word; (herald.) motto; (mus.) motto; riddle (concealing solution of an enigmatic canon); †see **mottetto**; (mil.) word of command; †— d'ordine, password. **-eggevole** *adj.* jesting, bantering; facetious. **-eggevolmente** *adv.* jokingly, jestingly; facetiously. **-eggiamento** *m.* jesting; joking; bantering. **-eggiante** *part. adj.* bantering, joking. **-eggiare** [A 3 c] *intr.* (*aux.* avere) jest, joke; *tr.* to mock, make fun of. **-eggiatore** *m.* jester, joker; mocker. (**-eggiatrice** *f.*) **-eggio** *m.* jest, joke; dire, fare -eggi, to make jests. **-eggio** *m.* frequent jesting, banter. **-etto** *m.* †short poetic composition of epigrammatic nature; (mus.) motet.

moustela *f.* (ichth.) *Phycis phycis*, an edible marine fish.

†**moveca** *f.* See **mormeca**.

mo·v-ere [C 15] see **muovere**. **-ente** *part. adj.* moving; (med.) rimedio -ente, purgative; *n.m.* motive, cause; qual fu il -ente?, what caused it?; i segreti -enti del cuore, the secret impulses of the heart; (leg.) cause; -ente del delitto, motive of crime. **-enza** *f.* movement, gesture, bearing; con gentili -enze, with gentle gait; (paint.; sculp.) movement, suggestion of movement. **-i·bile** *adj.* movable. **-imentare** [A 1] *tr.* to make busy, to fill with movement. **-imentato** *part. adj.* busy; una strada -imentata, a busy street; eventful; agitated; lively. **-imentista** *m.* traffic superintendent. **-imento** *m.* movement; stir; change; non ho libero il -imento del collo, I cannot move my neck freely; -imento letterario, literary movement; gesture; slight emotion; ebbe un -imento di compassione, he was stirred with pity; motion; mettere in -imento, to set in motion; (comm.) -imento d'affari, turnover; -imento dei prezzi, price movement; (naut.) -imenti navali, warship movements; (mus.) movement; indication of tempo; beat; (naut.) -imenti navali, means of propulsion (steam, sail, etc.), or movements of ships; (mil.) tactical manœuvre, movement of troops. **-itoso** *adj.* full of movement.

Mozambico *pr.n.m.* (geog.) Mozambique.

moz-a·rabo *m.* Mozarab. **-ara·bico** *adj.* Mozarabic; (liturg.) rito -arabico, Mozarabic Rite.

mozione *f.* motion; — degli affetti, exciting of the emotions; oratore efficace nella — degli affetti, orator who knows how to move his audience; (admin.) motion; resolution; la — è respinta, the motion is rejected; la — è approvata con 12 voti contro 9, the resolution is adopted (carried) by 12 votes to 9; presentare una — d'ordine, to raise a point of order; — sul fondo della questione, substantive motion; †*pl.* monsoons; †tumult.

mozz-are [A 1] *tr.* to cut off, to lop off; faceva — il piede o la mano ai prigionieri, he used to have a hand or a foot cut off each of his prisoners; — la coda a un cane, un cavallo, to dock a dog, a horse; — la parola, to cut short a speech; — il fiato, to take one's breath away. **-amento** *m.* cutting away; docking; mutilation. **-ato** *part. adj.* lopped off. (**-atore** *m.* **-atrice** *f.*) **-atura** *f.* cutting off; docking. **-icare** [A 2 s] *tr.* to lop off; to tear; -icare le parole, to clip one's words. **-icoda** *adj.* docked. **-icone** *m.* stump; -icone di sigaretta, cigarette-end, stub.

mozzarella *f.* (cul.) cheese made from buffalo's milk.

mozz-o¹ *m.* hub, wheel-hub; stout piece of wood in belfry to which bell is attached; part of bellows to which nozzle is fitted; (naut.) — dell'elica, propeller boss.

mozz-o² *adj.* cut off; docked; ebbe la testa -a, he was beheaded; guanto —, glove with the fingers cut off, mitten; *n.m.* boy, stable-boy; — di stalla, groom; (naut.) boy, 1st or 2nd class; scuola dei -i, boys' training establishment; (in charcoal-burning) short bricket of wood thrown in to keep fire alight. **-amente** *adv.* with clipped words; incompletely. **-etta** *f.* (eccl.) mozzetta. †**-etto** *m.* ankle boot. **-ino** *m. dim.* (typ.) page with only a few lines printed on it. **-one** *m.* lash; whip; piece, end, stump; (dial.) cigarette-end. **-orecchi** *m.* rascal; pettifogger. **-orecchio** *m.* cropped horse or dog.

†**mucaiardo** *m.* See **mocaiardo**.

mucato *m.* See **muco**.

mucc-a *f.* milch cow; (provb.) anche le mucche nere danno il latte bianco, even black cows give white milk, i.e. do not judge solely by appearance; now frequently used euphemistically for **vacca**, q.v. **-aio** *m.* cow-herd.

mucchignero *m.* (bot.) *Cytinus hypocistis*.

muc·chi-o *m.* heap; pile; crowd; flock; a mucchi, in plenty; (ichth.) ray, *Raia clavata*; *pl.* branch stripped of leaves (in bird-snaring). **-erello, -etto, -ettino** *m. dim.* small heap. **-one** *m. augm.* large heap.

mucci-are [A 3] *intr.* (*aux.* essere) to hide, to conceal oneself, to sneak off; *tr.* to shun, to avoid; to mock, to make fun of; -a!, surely not!, you don't say!

mucela·gine *f.* See **mucillagine**.

muc-i (word for calling cat) puss! puss!; (slang) hush! **-ia**, †**-mu·scia** *f.* pussy; fox-tail used for dusting. **-iatto** *adj.* (orn.) zigolo -iatto, rock bunting, *Emberiza cia.* **-ina** *f.*, **-ino** *m.* kitten. (**-inuzzo** *m. dim.*)

mu·cico *adj.* (chem.) mucic.

mu·cido *adj.* musty; rotten; mouldy; bad; carne mucida, bad meat; *n.m.* mould; dampness.

mucil(l)a·g(g)in-e *f.* mucilage.

mucillaginizzare [A 1] *rfl.* (bot.) to become mucilaginous.

muc-o *m.* (physiol.) mucus. **-ato** *m.* (chem.) mucate. **-ina** *f.* (chem.) mucin; see under **muci**. **-osa** *f.* (anat.) mucosa, mucous membrane. **-osità** *f.* mucosity. **-oso** *adj.* mucous.

mucron-e *m.* (anat.) mucro, of the heart; (bot.) mucro. **-ato** *adj.* (bot.) mucronate.

†**mud-are** [A 1] *intr.* (*aux.* avere) (orn.) to moult. **-a** *f.* moult, mews; small prison; change: a -a, in turn; (mil. hist.) sentry or duty watchman. †**-agione** *f.* (orn.) moult.

muezzino *m.* muezzin.

muff-a *f.* (bot.) mould; — comune, *Mucor mucedo*; — della patata, *Peronospora infestans*; — glauca, *Aspergillus glaucus*; mould; must; far la —, to become mouldy; sentir di —, to smell mouldy; trarre il cervel di —, to return to one's studies, to read; anger; prender la —, to grow angry; (paint.) effect of mould on paint of frescoes. **-are** [A 1] *intr.* (*aux.* essere) to grow mouldy. **-atella, -atellina** *f. dim.* light mould. **-atic·cio** *adj.* rather mouldy; (fig.) in rather poor health. **-ato** *adj.* mouldy, musty. **-etta** *f.* vine fungus. **-igno** *adj.* mouldy, musty. **-ire** [D 2] *intr.* (*aux.* essere) to grow musty; to fall into desuetude. **-ito** *adj.* musty, mouldy. **-o** *apocop. part.* mouldy. **-osità** *f.* mustiness; (fig.) pride; disdain. **-oso** *adj.* disdainful; haughty.

muf·fola *f.* mitten (with bag-like covering for the fingers); †muff; (eng.; metall.) muffle; forno a —, muffle furnace; (electr.) box; — di giunzione, junction box; — di derivazione, dividing box.

muflone, muffione, mufione *m.* (zool.) mouflon, wild sheep, *Ovis musimon*.

mu·fola *f.* See **muffola**.

muftì *m. indecl.* Mufti.

Mugell-o *pr.n.m.* (geog.) valley of the river Sieve (Tuscany). **-ese** *adj.* relating to that region; (provb.) gallina -ese, campa tre anni e mostra un mese (said of a woman who looks young but isn't).

mugghetto *m.* (zool.) *Eledone moscata*, a kind of octopus.

mugghi-are [A 4] *intr.* (*aux.* avere) to bellow; to low; (of sea) to roar; (of wind) to howl. **-amento** *m.* lowing; bellowing. **-ante** *part. adj.* bellowing; roaring; howling.

mug·ghio¹ *m.* lowing; bellow; roar; howling.

mug·ghio² *m.* (ichth.) sting ray, *Dasybatus pastinachus*.

mug·gine *m.* (ichth.) grey mullet; — comune, *Mugil cephalus*; — calamita, *M. capito*; — dorato, — orifrangio, *M. auratus*; — musino, *M. saliens*; — pietra, chelone, *M. chelo*. **-ara**, **-iera** *f.* fishing nets for catching grey mullets.

mugg-ire [D 1] *intr.* (*aux.* avere) to bellow; to low; (of sea) to roar. **-ente** *part. adj.* bellowing; lowing. **-ito** *m.* bellowing; lowing; roar.

mugherino *m.* (bot.) Arabian jasmine, *Jasminum sambrac*.

mughetto *m.* (bot.) lily of the valley, *Convallaria majalis*.

mugic *m. indecl.* moujik, Russian peasant.

mu·glio *m.* and derivs. See **mugghio, mugghiare**, etc.

mugn-aio, †-aro *m.* miller; pesare con la stadera del —, to weigh with the miller's steelyard, i.e. to judge very roughly; affogare il —, to drown the miller, to put too much water, to make the dough too thin (in bread-making); parere un —, to look like a miller (said of someone white with dust, or dressed completely in white); (orn.) gull (name used loosely for several species).

-a·ia *f.* miller's wife; (orn.) gull. **-iac·cio** *m.* (orn.) great black-backed gull, *Larus marinus*.

mu·gnere and derivs. See **mungere**.

mugo *m.* (bot.) Swiss mountain pine, *Pinus mugo*.

mugol-are [A 1 S] *intr.* (*aux.* avere) to yelp; to whine; to howl; to moan; to mumble. **-amento** *m.* whining; moaning; howling; mumbling. **-io** *m.* yelping; moaning; mumbling.

mu·golo *m.* moaning; whining. **-one** *m.* yelping, whining dog; moaner.

†**muina** *f.* See **moina**.

mula *f.* See **mulo**.

mulac·chia *f.* (orn.) hooded crow, jackdaw. †**-aia** *f.* a flock of crows.

mulatto *m.* negro-white cross-breed.

mul·cere, -ire. See **molcere**.

mul·esco, -etto. See under **mulo**.

†**mul·gere** *vb.* and derivs. See **mungere**.

†**muli·aca** *f.* See **meliaca**.

†**mulica** *f.* See **mollica**.

mul-i·ebre, -iebre *adj.* feminine, womanly; womanish; dolcezza —, feminine sweetness. **-iebrità** *f.* femininity, womanliness.

†**muliere** *f.* See **mogliera**.

mulin-o¹ *m.* (*pl.* †**-a**) mill; — ad acqua, water-mill; — a vento, windmill; — a vapore, steam-mill; — da olio, olive press; tirar l'acqua al suo —, to bring grist to one's own mill; chi va al —, s'infarina, you can't touch pitch and not be defiled; prendersela coi -i a vento, to tilt against windmills; essere un — a vento, (fig.) to be a weathercock; (herald.) ferro di —, millrind, fer de moline. **-a·ia** snow-blizzard. **-aio, -aro** *m.* miller. **-are** [A 1] *intr.* (*aux.* avere), *tr.* to indulge in idle fancies; to muse; to plot, to scheme; to whirl around. **-ato** *adj.* (herald.) croce -ata, cross moline. **-ello** *m. dim.* (*pl.* †**-a** *f.*) whirl; swivel; windlass; reel; silk-mule; fan driven by wind; whirlwind; whirlpool; lì ci sono dei -elli pericolosi ai nuotatori, there are some whirlpools there which are very dangerous to swimmers; whirling round (a stick or sword); (fig.) intrigue; (meteor.) eddy. **-etto** *m. dim.* small mill; coffee-mill, coffee-grinder. **-io** *m.* whirling; milling (of ideas).

mulino². See under **mulo**.

mulla·ghera *f.* (bot.) yellow-vetchling, *Lathyrus aphaca*; birdsfoot-trefoil, *Lotus corniculatus*.

mullo¹ *m.* (ichth.) gurnard, *Trigla* spp.

†**mullo²** *m.* See **mulo**.

mul-o *m.* (zool.) mule; ostinato, caparbio come un —, as stubborn as a mule; (fig.) bastard; wretch; †mullet. **-a** *f.* she-mule; la -a si rivolta al medico, the mule rebels against the doctor, i.e. a person may resent a warning; reggere la -a, to act as go-between in a love-affair; o pelle o -a, happen what will, e.g. non mi ritiro, o pelle o -a, I shall not withdraw, no matter what may happen. **-ag·gine** *m.* obstinacy, mulishness. †**-are** *adj.* mulish. **-attiera** *f.* mule-track, mule-road. **-attiere** *adj.* pertaining to mules; sentiero -attiere, mule-path; *n.m.* muleteer. **-atto, †-azzo** *adj. m.* see **mulatto**, above. **-esco** *adj.* (*m.pl.* **-eschi**) mulish. **-etto** *m. dim.* young mule. †**-ino** *adj.* of a mule; mulish. †**-omedicina** *f.* veterinary science. **-ona** *f. augm.* large mule. **-otto** *m.* medium-sized mule.

mulsa *f.* hydromel, mead.

mult-a *f.* (leg.) fine; pecuniary penalty; mulct (imposed for 'delitto', crime, as distinct from 'ammenda', imposed for 'contravvenzione', misdemeanour, C.P.); cadere in —, to be liable to a fine; condannare a una —, to sentence to a fine; liquidare una —, to pay a fine; mettere in —, to fine or to penalize; pagare una —, to pay a penalty. **-are** [A 1] *tr.* (leg.) to fine; to make (a person) pay a penalty; to mulct; to surcharge.

mult-ibande *adj. indecl.* (radio) multiband. **-icolore** *adj. indecl.* many-coloured. **-ifilare** *adj.* (radio) multiple wire. **-ifloro** *adj.* multiflorous. **-iforme** *adj.* multiform. **-ifronte** *adj.* having many aspects. **-ilaterale, -ila·tero** *adj.* multilateral. **-ilin·gue** *adj.* multilingual. **-iloquacità** *f.* loquacity. **-iloquenza** *f.* fluency; eloquence. **-ilo·quio** *m.* loquacity; †*adj.* loquacious. **-ilo·quo** *adj.* loquacious. **-ilustre** *adj.* old. **-imiliona·rio** *adj.n.m.* multi-millionaire. †**-inomato** *adj.* very famous. **-ino·mio** *adj.* polynomial. **-i·paro** *adj.* multiparous. **-iplano** *m.* multiplane. **-isenso** *adj.* having several meanings. **-isil·labo** *adj.* polysyllabic. **-isonante** *adj.* noisy. **-itu·dine** *f.* see **moltitudine**. **-ivalvo** *adj.* multivalve. **-ivibratore** *m.* (radio) multivibrator.

mul·tiplo *adj.* multiple; (watchm.) ponte —, combined bridge; *n.m.* (math.) multiple.

mummarella *f.* earthenware pot used as a trap for octopus.

mum·mi-a *f.* mummy; — egiziana, Egyptian mummy; (paint.) mummy (colour), a rich brown colour. **-ficare** [A 2 s] *tr.* to mummify; *intr.* (*aux.* essere) to become mummified. **-ficato** *adj. part.* mummified. (**-ficatore** *m.* **-ficatrice** *f.*) **-ficazione** *f.* mummification.

†**munaste·rio** *m.* See **monastero**.

†**mundare** *vb.* and derivs. See **mondare**.

mun·d-io *m.* (leg.) guardian whose consent is required to make or enter into a valid contract. **-ualdo** *m.* see **mondualdo**.

mun·g-ere [C 5] *tr.* to milk; — una mucca, to milk a cow; (fig.) to milk, to exploit; to sponge on. **-ereccio** *adj.* that can be milked. **-itoio** *m.* milking-pail, milking-can. (**-itore** *m.*) **-itrice** *f.*, milking-machine; milkmaid. **-itura** *f.* milking; (fig.) exploitation.

municipal-e *adj.* municipal; palazzo —, town-hall; impiegati -i, local government officers. **-mente** *adv.* municipally. **-ismo** *m.* municipalism. **-ità** *f.* municipality; residence of municipal authorities; *pl.* the municipal authorities. **-izzare** [A 1] *tr.* to municipalize.

munici·pio *m.* (Rom. hist.) municipium; municipality; town-hall.

muni·fic-o *adj.* munificent; bountiful; generous. **-amente** *adv.* munificently, generously. **-ente** *adj.* munificent. (**-entemente** *adv.*) **-enza** *f.* munificence; generosity.

mun-ire [D 2] *tr.* to fortify; to furnish, to provide, to supply; -ì la città di vettovaglie, he supplied the city with victuals; (comm.) — di girata, to endorse. **-ito** *part. adj.* (*prep.* di) supplied (with), furnished (with); ben -ito, well provided, secure, fortified; (rel.) -ito dei sacramenti, fortified with the sacraments of the Church. **-izionare** [A 1 C] *tr.* (*prep.* di) (mil.) to furnish (with), to store (with); to stock up (with); -izionare la batteria, to replenish a battery, to load guns. **-izione** *f.* munition; stores; equipment. **-izionere** *m.* (mil.) ammunition carrier; ration carrier; supply personnel; quartermaster's troop; †(naut.) ship's chandler.

mun-o *m.* (*pl.* -i, -era) gift.

munto *part.* of **mungere**, *q.v.*; *adj.* milked; (fig.) exploited; exhausted; pale.

muo·v-ere [C 15] *tr.* to move; non -e un dito per aiutarti, he's not lifting a finger to help you; (chess) — una pedina, to move a pawn, (fig.) to make a move, to act; to work, to drive; l'elettricità -e molte macchine, electricity drives many machines; — un cavallo, to walk a horse; lo -e l'invidia, he is moved by envy; — il passo, to move a step, to walk; to stir; (fig.) — i primi passi, to take the first steps; — le gambe, to 'stretch one's legs'; — il fuoco, to poke the fire; — uno al riso, to move someone to laughter; — l'appetito, to stimulate the appetite; — il corpo, to purge the bowels, to bring about a motion; — guerra, to wage war; — il campo, to break up camp; (of young animal) — i denti, to cut teeth; — un dubbio, to raise a doubt; — una domanda, to put a question; (leg.) — causa, to start proceedings; *intr.* (*aux.* essere) to go; to come; to begin; to start (from); il treno -e da Napoli, the train begins its journey at Naples; i fiumi che -ono dalle Alpi, the rivers that have their sources in the Alps; to advance; — incontro a qualcuno, to meet someone; — in guerra contro, to go to war against; — alla volta di, to start for; (archit.) to run (of frieze or band of decoration); (eng.) la macchina è mossa da un motore, the machine is driven by a motor; *rfl.* to move, to stir; ogni animale può -ersi, all animals are capable of movement; to bestir oneself; to set off; -ersi da un luogo, to move from a place; ditegli che oggi non può -ersi, tell him that today he cannot leave this place; non si -e mai da casa, he never stirs from the house; nessuno si -a, keep still everyone; eppur si -e, and yet it *does* move (a saying attributed to Galileo).

mura[1] *f.* (naut.) tack; chain hawser or tackle at the foot of a sail holding it forward; cambiare le mure, to change tack, i.e. to go about.

mura[2] *f.pl.* of **muro**, *q.v.*

muracchiare [A 3] *intr.* (*aux.* avere) to build (esp. as a hobby).

mura·gli-a *f.* wall; high wall; long wall; la Gran — della Cina, the Great Wall of China; rampart, (fig.) barrier; (vet.) 'wall' of a horse's hoof. **-one** *m. augm.* barrier; great wall; dike.

murai(u)ol-a *f.* (bot.) pellitory-of-the-wall, *Parietaria diffusa*; (numism.) Roman coin worth four baiocchi made in time of Pius IV. **-o** *m.* (orn.) wall creeper, *Tichodroma muraria*; *adj.* climbing, living or growing on walls.

murale *adj.* mural; (Rom. antiq.) corona —, mural crown; macchina —, siege-engine, battering-ram, etc.; (paint.) mural (esp. of ancient Roman wall paintings); carta —, wall map; (bot.) pianta -ale, see **murai(u)ola**.

mur-are [A 1] *tr.*, *intr.* (*aux.* avere) to wall; to build; — una casa, to build a house; — a secco, to build a dry wall, (fig.) to eat without drinking, to construct something which is unlikely to last; — sulla rena, to build on sand; to wall up; — una porta, una finestra, to wall up (brick up) a door, a window; to build in; — un armadio, to build a cupboard into the wall; — un arpione, to fix a hook in the wall; to immure; vorrebbe — le figliole in casa, he never lets his daughters stir from the house; to build a wall around; — una città, to build a wall round a city; to seal with mortar or some other substance; — i tini, to seal the vats; (naut.) to haul taut the tack; murarsi la bocca, to preserve absolute silence; *rfl.* to immure oneself. **-amento** *m.* building. **-a·rio** *adj.* of a mason, of building; arte -aria, the art of building. **-ata** *f.* wall, city wall; (naut.) ship's side; a -ata, at or near the side (contrary of 'inboard', i.e. near the centreline); dormire a -ata, to sleep alongside the guns; *pl.* prison; formerly convent in Florence; mettere alle -ate, to lock up. **-ato** *part. adj.* built; walled; città -ata, walled city; finestra -ata, bricked-up window; immured; (eccl. hist.) monache -ate, nuns who lived in rigidly sealed cells like those, e.g., of English medieval anchoresses; (herald.) masoned. **-atore** *m.* bricklayer; mason; franco -atore, freemason; stoker expert in brickwork for furnaces; (orn.) picchio -atore, nuthatch, *Sitta caesia*; picchio -atore corso, Corsican nuthatch, (Amer.) red-breasted nuthatch, *S. canadensis*; picchio -atore dalmatino, rock nuthatch, *S. neumayeri*. **-atura** *f.* construction; masonry; brickwork; lavoro in -atura, brickwork; ponte in -atura, stone bridge.

mura·rio. See under **murare**.

†**murell-a** *f.* low wall; pile of a bridge. **-o** *m.* low wall.

murena *f.* (ichth.) moray, murry-eel, *Muraena helena*.

mur-ettino, -etto *m. dim.* See under **muro**.

murgulen *m. indecl.* (bot.) *Stachys glutinosa*.

mu·ri-a *f.* brine. **-a·tico** *adj.* (chem.) muriatic; acido -atico, muriatic acid, spirits of salt, commercial hydrochloric acid. **-ato** *m.* muriate, chloride.

mur-iccia *f.*, **-icciolo** *m.* See under **muro**.

mu·rice *m.* (zool.) *Murex* spp., marine gastropods; — comune, *M. brandaris*; — troncato, *M. trunculus*; — riccio, *Ocenebra erinaceus*.

mur-icello, -icino *m. dim.* See under **muro**.

muriella *f.* disk, esp. of kind used in playing hopscotch; the game of hopscotch.

mur·mure *m.* (poet.) murmur.

mur-o *m.* wall; (*pl.* -i *m.*, -a *f.*, the latter in the sense of peripheral walls, e.g. le -a della città, the city walls; le -a domestiche, the home; (archit.; leg.) — comune, party-wall (C.C.); — divisorio, dividing wall (C.C.); — tramezzo, interior wall; — maestro, — principale, main wall, supporting wall; — di cinta, surrounding wall (C.C.); — di facciata, front wall, façade; — di fondazione, foundation wall; footings; — d'appoggio, — di sostegno, supporting wall; — sul confine, boundary wall (C.C.); — di cotto, brick wall; — di pietra lavorata, (hewn) stone wall; — di sassi, rubble wall; — a secco, ashlar or rubble wall, without mortar; — soprammattone, one-brick wall; — a coltello, wall with bricks laid as 'stretchers'; — a cortina, wall in Flemish bond, i.e. with alternate headers and stretchers; — a bozze, wall with regular projections (of brickwork or stone); — a scarpa, wall with an escarp; — a tenuta, wall with watertight plaster; — che fa pancia, bulging wall; puntellare un —, to prop a wall; rimpellare un —, to repair a wall; †(naut.) stemplating on either side of the stem-post; (geol.; mining) lower side of the lode; (aeron.) — del suono, sound barrier; (herald.) ferro di —, millrind, fer de moline; — del pianto, Wailing Wall (in Jerusalem); (fig.) parlare al —, to talk to the wall; battere il capo nel —, dar la testa nel —, dar del capo nel —, to bang one's head against the wall; aver le spalle al —, to have one's back to the wall; stare, abitare, aver la casa a — a — con uno, to be a next-door neighbour to someone; trovarsi tra l'uscio e il —, to be in a fix; (provb.) i -i hanno orecchi, walls have ears; duro con duro non fa buon —, two obstinate persons cannot be expected to agree. **-a·ccio** *m. pejor.* old wall, ruined wall. **-a·rio** *adj.* see under **murare**. **-azzo** *m.* dike, sea-wall. **-ello**

mur-o (*cont.*)
m. dim. small wall. **-icciola·io** *m.* second-hand bookseller. **-icci(u)olo** *m. dim.* low wall; parapet wall; wall forming bench; andare a finire sui -icciuoli, (of books) to find their way to the second-hand bookstalls.

murr-a *f.* (Rom. antiq.) *murra*, a precious mineral substance from Parthia, perhaps fluorspar or jade. **-ina** *f.* piece of murrine ware. **-ino** *adj.* murrine, (ware) made of 'murra' or imitating its texture in glass.

muṣ-a¹ *f.* (class.) Muse; muse; art of poetry; lady who is a poet's 'inspiration'; la — del Petrarca, Laura. **-agete** *adj., n.m.* (Gk. myth.) Leader of the Muses (epithet of Apollo; 'Musegetes' in Attic Gk., 'Musagetas' in Doric).

muṣa² *f.* (bot.) banana, *Musa*.

†musa·ico *m.* See **mosaico**.

muṣaragno *m.* (zool.) shrew, *Sorex* spp.

muṣ-are [A I] *intr.* (*aux.* avere) to stand staring, to stand agape; to look for; to sniff after. **-ante** *part. adj.*; *n.m.* dandy. **-ata** *f.* blow with the snout; il cavallo gli diede una -ata, the horse struck him with its nose; blow on the nose; grimace; sniff.

muscarin-a *f.* (bot.) muscarin. **-iṣmo** *m.* (med.) muscarinism, fungus poisoning.

muscello *m.* See **moscello**.

muschiarolo *m.* (zool.). See **moscardino**.

mu·schi-o¹ *m.* musk, moss; †musk-deer. **-ato** *adj.* musky; (bot.) rosa -ata, musk rose, *Rosa moschata*.

mu·schio² *m.* (bot.). See **musco**.

musci·capa *f.* (orn.) flycatcher (a general term covering many species).

muscina *f.* See **micino, mucino**.

mus-co *m.* (bot.) moss; — terrestre, stag's horn moss, common clubmoss, *Lycopodium clavatum*. **-chini** *m.pl.* grape hyacinth, *Muscari*. **-oṣo** *adj.* mossy.

mu·scol-o¹ *m.* muscle; sinew; (butcher.) shin of beef; †(mil.) siege-machine. **-are** *adj.* muscular; sinewy. **-atura** *f.* musculature. **-ina** *f.* (chem.) myosin, muscular fibrin. **-oṣità** *f.* muscularity. **-oṣo** *adj.* muscular, brawny; sinewy. **-uto** *adj.* muscled, strongly muscled.

muscolo² *m.* (zool.) edible mussel, *Mytilus* spp.; — peloso, horse mussel, *Modiolus barbatus*.

muscoṣo *adj.* See under **musco**.

muscovite *f.* (miner.) muscovite, white mica, muscovy glass.

muṣ-e·o *m.* museum; il — britannico, the British Museum; il — del Louvre, the Louvre; — etrusco, museum of Etruscan antiquities; roba da —, stuff that ought to be in a museum, (fig.) rubbish; (class. antiq.) temple or haunt of the Muses; home of poetry or learning; academy, esp. the Museum of Alexandria; *pr.n.m.* (Gk. myth. and lit.) Musaeus. **-ętta** *f.* (mus.) musette, French bagpipe; Musette (dance composed over a drone bass). **-ętte** *f.* (mus.) Musette.

muṣeragno *m.*, **muṣeragn·olo** *m.* See **musaragno**.

muṣeruola *f.*, (pop.) **muserola** *f.* muzzle; nose-band; mettere la — a uno, to muzzle a person; togliere la — a, to unmuzzle.

mu·ṣi-ca *f.* music; musical work; military band; *Le nuove musiche*, 'the new music', a book of airs published by Caccini in 1602 whose title has been used to describe the new style of monodic composition; far —, to make music, to practise music together; mettere, porre in —, to set to music; carta da —, music paper; — concreta, concrete music; — falsa, *musica ficta*; — da camera, chamber music; — di organo, organ-music; — di violino, violin-music; — di flauto, music for the flute; orchestra, band; la — in piazza, the orchestra in the public square; — del reggimento, regimental band; — dei carabinieri, the band of the carabinieri; cambiare la —, to change the tune; (fig.) è un'altra —, that's another matter; facevano una certa —, they were making a terrible noise; metterla in —, to waste time in chatter or in pointless compliments, to make a song and dance about it. **-ca·bile** *adj.* suitable for music-setting. **-cac·cio** *m.* wretched music, strumming. **-cale** *adj.* (mus.) musical; fondo -ale, background music. **-calmente** *adv.* (mus.) musically. **-calità** *f.* (mus.) musicianship. **-cante** *m.* (mus.) musician; itinerant musician (nowadays used of a less dignified musician than a 'musicista'). **-care** [A 2 S] *tr.* to set to music; *intr.* to play or sing. **-chessa** *f.* female musical practitioner (joc.). **-chetta** *f.* musical trifle. **-chetto** *m.* little musician. †**-che·vole** *adj.* (mus.) musical. **-chiere**, †**-chiero** *m.* (mus.) musical performer (joc.), musicioner. **-china** *f.* (mus.) graceful piece of music. **-cista** *m., f.* (mus.) musician. **-co** *m.* musician; eunuch (castrated for the

sake of his voice); *adj.* musical. **-co·filo** *m.* music-lover. **-co·fobo** *m.* music-hater. **-co·grafo** *m.* (mus.) mechanical device for noting down music played on the pianoforte; musicographer. **-cologi·a** *f.* (mus.) musicology. **-colo·gico** *adj.* musicological. **-co·logo** *m.* musicologist. **-cone** *m.* solemn music; loud or pompous music. **-cuccia** *f.* (pop.) grand music. **-cuc·cio** *m.* bad musician, musicaster. **-comani·a** *f.* musicomania. **-coterapi·a** *f.* musicotherapy.

musiera, muṣino *m.* See under **muso**.

muṣiv-o *adj.* mosaic, in mosaic, tessellated; (techn.) oro —, tin sulphide used in gilding.

muṣme *f.* young Japanese woman; geisha.

muṣ-o *m.* snout, muzzle (of animal); il — del porco, the pig's snout; (derog.) face (of man); che brutto —!, what an ugly mug!; son capace di dirglielo sul —, I don't mind telling him so to his face; torcere il — a, to turn up one's nose at; allungare il —, to make a long face; rompere il — a uno, to smash a person's face, to 'punch his mug in'; fare il —, metter su il —, to pout, to sulk; è un — duro, he is a brazen person, *or* he is fearless; a — duro, without losing composure; far — duro, to persist; person; non è — lui da farmi paura, I wouldn't be afraid of *him*; (butcher.) snout. **-ac·cio** *m. pejor.* ugly face, face of person in ugly mood. **-ello** *m.* lower lip of horse. **-etto** *m. dim.* little face; cheeky little face. **-iera** *f.* nose-bag. **-ino** *m. dim.* nice little face; (ichth.) a small eel; muggine -ino, *Mugil saliens*, a kind of grey mullet. **-oliera** *f.* see **museruola**. **-ona** *f.* sullen woman; pouting girl. **-one** *m. augm.* large face; pouter, sulky fellow; slap, blow; (mil.) lug. **-oneri·a** *f.* pouting, sulkiness, sullenness; haughty behaviour. †**-orno** *adj.* sulky; (of the sky) lowering.

muṣo·faga *f.* (orn.) violet plantain-eater, *Musophaga* spp.

Muṣogoni·a *pr.n.f.* (Ital. lit.) the 'Musogony', poem by V. Monti (1793) on the origin of the Muses.

muss-are [A I] *intr.* (*aux.* avere) to foam, to froth, to hiss; far —, to draw attention to, to boast about, to make the most of.

mussulmano *m.* See **musulmano**.

mustac·chi *m.pl.* (joc.) moustache(s); (naut.) bowsprit stays.

mustacchino *m.* (orn.) bearded tit, *Panurus biarmicus*.

mustan-go *m.* (*pl.* -ghi) (zool.) mustang, feral horses of America.

mustel-a *f.* (zool.) *Mustela* spp., stoats, weasels, etc. **-ino** *m. dim.* of **mustela**; (ichth.) *Mustelus* spp., dogfish, *Onos tricirratus*, rockling.

mustiolo *m.* (zool.) lesser white-toothed shrew, *Crocidura suaveolus*.

musulmano *m. adj.* Mussulman; Mohammedan.

muta¹ *f.* pack of hounds; team of horses.

muta² *f.* (silkb.) moulting (of silkworm) (cf. **muda**).

muta³ *f.* See under **mutare**.

muta⁴ *f.* See under **muto**.

mutaciṣmo *m.* (path.) metacism.

muta·geno *adj.* (biol.) mutagenic.

mut-are [A I] *tr.* to change, to alter; — padrone, to change masters; — nome, to change one's name; — casa, to move to a different house; — idea, — proposito, to change one's mind; — i panni, to change one's clothes; — l'ammalato, to change the patient's bedclothes; — tono, to change one's tune; (of animals) — la pelle, to shed the skin; (of birds) — le penne, to moult; — da greco in latino, to translate from Greek into Latin; — da, to dissuade; (of wine) to decant; *intr.* (*aux.* essere) to change; to alter; le cose non -arono, things did not alter; to move; (iron.) tanto per —!, it's a change anyway!; — di colore, to change colour; *rfl.* to change, to alter; s'è -ato in un altro uomo!, he's become a different man!; to change one's clothes; -arsi di scarpe, to change one's shoes; to move; (of a boy's voice) to break. **-a** *f.* change; una -a di cavalli, a fresh team of horses; (mil.) -a di sentinelle, -a di custodi, relief (of sentries), changing of the guard; (naut.) complete suit of sail; (motor.) una — di segmenti, a change of piston rings. **-a·bile** *adj.* mutable, changeable, inconstant. **-abilmente** *adv.* mutably; inconstantly. **-abilità** *f.* mutability, inconstancy, fickleness; †transiency. **-amento** *m.* change, alteration; un -amento nel tempo, a change in the weather. **-ande** *f.pl.* drawers; un paio di -ande, a pair of drawers, shorts, knickers; -ande da bagno, bathing-trunks. **-andine** *f.pl.* shorts; knickers; -andine da bagno, bathing-trunks. **-ante** *part. adj.* changing. **-ativo** *adj.* mutative. **-ato** *part. adj.* altered, changed. **-atore** *m. adj.* changing, transforming. (**-atrice** *f.*) **-atura** *f.* changing; una -atura nuova, a change of clothing, a new outfit. **-azione** *f.* change, alteration, mutation; -azione della voce, breaking of voice at puberty; (mus.) mutation, i.e. the change from one

mut-are (*cont.*)

hexachord to another involving the change of the syllable applied to a given note; registri di -azione, mutation-stops (organ); (biol.) mutation; (prosod.) name of first two sections of the stanza of a ballata or canzone, each section consisting of two or three lines rhyming with those of the other. **-azionismo** *m.* (biol.) mutation theory of evolution. **-ęvole** *adj.* mutable; variable; changeable; inconstant, fickle. **-evolęzza** *f.* changeableness, inconstancy. **-evolmęnte** *adv.* mutably; inconstantly.

mutessarif *m.* (Turkish) prefect.

mutęzza *f.* See under **muto**.

mu·tico *adj.* (bot.) muticous.

mutil-are [A I S] *tr.* to mutilate, to maim; lo -ò dei pollici, he cut his thumbs off; — il testo, to mutilate the text. **-amęnto** *m.* mutilation. **-ato** *part. adj.* mutilated, maimed, crippled; incomplete; *n.m.* disabled man; i -ati di guerra, the war-disabled. **-atore** *m.* mutilator. (**-atrice** *f.*) **-azione** *f.* mutilation; (leg.) -azione della propria persona, self-mutilation, self-wounding (C.P.).

mu·tilo *adj.* mutilated; incomplete; libro —, book of which a part is missing; *n.m.* †(archit.) modillion, bracket.

mut-o *adj.* mute, dumb, speechless; — dalla nascita, dumb from birth; — per il dolore, struck dumb by grief; consonante -a, mute consonant; (mus.) suoni -i, weak or feeble sounds; (cinem.) film —, silent film; silent, deserted; casa -a, deserted house; carta -a, skeleton map; (theatr.) scena -a, dumb show; *n.m.* deaf man; sordo —, deaf mute; fingersi —, to pretend to be dumb. **-a** *f.* dumb woman; dumb girl. **-amęnte** *adv.* speechlessly; noiselessly. **-ęzza** *f.* dumbness; muteness. **-ismo** *m.* mutism, muteness; obstinate silence, taciturnity; dumbness.

mu·tolo *adj.* dumb; taciturn; lettere mutole, mute letters; game played without speaking; †*n.m.* (archit.) modillion, bracket. (**-olęzza** *f.*)

mu·tri-a *f.* haughtiness; haughty expression; pouting, sulkiness; pout. **-one** *m.* sulky person, pouter; haughty person. (**-ona** *f.*)

mu·tua *f.* mutual benefit society (cf. **mutuo**).

mutual-e *adj.* mutual. **-ista** *m.* mutualist. **-ità** *f.* mutuality; **-alità** scolastica, society for the assistance of needy schoolchildren.

mutualismo *m.* (biol.) symbiosis in which each partner is dependent upon the other.

mutualità *f.* See under **mutuo**.

mutu-are [A 6] *tr.* to lend; to borrow; to mortgage. **-ante** *part. adj.* lending; *n.m., f.* lender (C.C.). **-atario** *m.* borrower (C.C.). **-ato** *part. adj.* borrowed; mortgaged. **-azione** *f.* mutual exchange.

mu·tu-o *adj.* mutual, reciprocal; — affetto, mutual affection; per — consenso, by mutual consent; società di — soccorso, (mutual) benefit society, friendly society; (joc.) società di — incensamento, mutual admiration society; *n.m.* loan; dare a —, to give as a loan, to lend; capitale a —, borrowed capital; contratto di —, loan agreement; estinguere un —, to discharge a loan; concedere un —, to grant a loan; — ipotecario, mortgage loan; — garantito, secured loan. **-amęnte** *adv.* mutually, reciprocally.

---

n *f., m.* (pron. enne) the letter N; the consonant N.

n' abbreviated form of Non, in the phrase: n'è vero?, isn't that true?

nab-ab, -abbo *m.* nabob; (fig.) person of ostentatious wealth and luxury; — visir, British Viceroy of India.

†**nabissare** *tr.* and derivs. see **inabissare**; *intr.* to rage, to storm.

†**nabisso** *m.* imp, little devil; restless little boy; abyss, hell.

nabla *f.* (mus.) psaltery.

Nabucodo·nosor *pr.n.m.* Nebuchadnezzar.

naca *f.* (S. Italy, Sicil.) cradle; dragnet; (naut.) Flemish craft (eighteenth century); *pl.* overhanging branches.

†**naccaiuolo** *m.* (Tusc.) maker of castanets.

nac·car-a¹ *f., -o m.* (zool.). See **naccherone**.

†**nac·cara²** *f.* See **nacchera**.

nac·cher-a *f.* (mus.) kettledrum, naker; *pl.* castanets; (zool.) see **naccherone**; †mother-of-pearl. **†-are** *intr.* to play upon a naker; to daydream, to muse. **-ino** *m.* pretty little child; †player upon castanets or kettledrums; †*dim.* of **nacchera**. **†-o** *m.* see **nacchera**.

naccherone *m.* (zool.) *Pinna nobilis*, a large bivalve; pelo di —, a kind of silk made from the byssus of *P. nobilis*.

na·chero *m.* dwarf; *adj.* dwarfish; crooked, stunted.

nacqui. nacque, nac·quero, *1st, 3rd pers. sing., 3rd pers. pl. past def.* of **nascere**, q.v.

nacrite *f.* (miner.) nacrite.

†**nada** *adv.* nothing, nil.

†**nadaro** *m.* (Sicil.) official in control of weights and measures.

nadi·r *m. indecl.* nadir.

†**naffè** *excl.* corrupn. of **mia fè**, i' faith (cf. **gnaffe**).

naft-a *f.* naphtha, white spirit; Diesel oil; fuel oil; a —, oil fired. **-a·lico** *adj.* (chem.) naphthalic. **-alina** *f.* (chem.) naphthalene. **-ilammina** *f.* (chem.) naphthylamine. **-olo** *m.* (chem.) naphthol.

na·ia¹ *f.* (zool.) cobra, *Naja*.

na·ia² *f.* (slang) army discipline; call-up, National Service; essere sotto la —, to be called up, to be doing one's National Service.

na·iade *f.* (myth.) Naiad, water-nymph; (bot.) water lily.

naib *m. indecl.* Abyssinian chieftain.

na·ibi *f.pl.* (dial. Lucca) playing cards.

na·ilon *m. indecl.* (text.) nylon (also **nylon**).

†**nalbescente** *adj.* at dawn.

†**nalda** *adj. phr.* alla —, in the style of Hainault (cf. **analda**).

†**namorare** *vb.* and derivs. See **innamorare**.

Namunas *pr.n.f.* (geol.) Niemen.

nana *f.* female dwarf; goose; 'nane nane', call used to summon geese.

Nanchin-o *pr.n.f.* (geog.) Nanking; *n.m.* nankeen. **-ata** *f.* nankeen cotton stuff.

nandu *m. indecl.* (orn.) rhea, *Rhea americana*.

†**na·neo** *adj.* dwarfish; pertaining to a dwarf.

†**nanfa** *f.* acqua —, rose water (cf. 'acqua lanfa', under **lanfa**).

nanghinata *f.* long-handled Japanese sword.

nanismo *m.* See under **nano**.

nann-a¹ *f.* (fam.) bye-byes; fare la —, andare a —, to go to bye-byes; mettere a —, to put to bye-byes; hush-a-bye (cf. **ninna-nanna** under **ninna**). **-odi·a** *f.* lullaby.

Nanna² *pr.n.f.* abbrev. of Giovanna, Marianna, or affectionate familiar form of Anna (cf. Nan).

Nanni *pr.n.m.* abbrev. of Giovanni.

nanno *excl.* (fam.) ta.

nan·nolo *m.* See **ninnolo**.

nannu·f-aro, -ero *m.* See **nenufara**.

nan-o¹ *m.* dwarf; *adj.* dwarfish, stunted; piante -e, dwarf plants; (orn.) gallina -a, bantam; (archit.) low; flattened. (**-etto, -ino** *m. dim.* **-erello, -erot·tolo, -uc·cio** *m. dim. pejor.*) **-ismo** *m.* nanism.

nano² *prep.* small (in scientific compounds, e.g. **nanocefali·a** *f.* (med.) underdevelopment of the head).

Nante¹ *pr.n.f.* (geog.) Nantes.

†**nan-te², †-ti, †-zi** *adv.* see **innanzi**. †**-tidetto** *adj.* see **anzidetto**, under **anzi**. †**-tiporre** *vb.* and derivs. see **anteporre**.

nape·a *f.* (myth.) dryad, nymph of the dells or woodland.

napello *m.* (bot.). See **nappello**.

Napole-one *pr.n.m.* Napoleon; (numism., 1809) napoleon, gold coin of twenty francs; gold coin of twenty lire (see also **marengo**); — d'argento, five-franc piece, five-lira piece; (hist. finan.) Monte —, institution of public credit established by Napoleon I at the period of the Kingdom of Italy and continuing under Austrian rule until 1860. **-oncino** *m.* a little Napoleon, little man aspiring to be a great leader. **-o·nico** *adj.* Napoleonic, relating to Napoleon I; il codice -onico, the Napoleonic Code. **-o·nide** *m., f.* one of the Napoleon family. **-onista** *m., f.* (hist.) Napoleonist, supporter of Napoleon, Bonapartist; specialist in the history of Napoleon I or the Napoleonic era.

Na·pol-i *pr.n.f.* (geog.) Naples; vedi — e poi muori, see Naples and die. **-etano** *adj.* Neapolitan; letteratura -etana, literature written in the Neapolitan dialect; alla -etana, in the Neapolitan manner, (cul.) cooked in the Neapolitan fashion (e.g. of 'pasta' served with tomatoes); *n.m.* Neapolitan, native or inhabitant of Naples; Neapolitan dialect; kind of strong cigar; *pl.* a kind of stuffed macaroni. **-etana** *f.* Neapolitan woman or girl; (cards) trick taken in the game of 'tressette' with the ace and the two and three of the same suit. **-etanamęnte** *adv.* in the Neapolitan manner; in the Neapolitan dialect. **-etaneri·a** *f.* local custom of Naples. **-etanismo** *m.* word, meaning or phrase peculiar to Neapolitans or Neapolitan dialect.

napp-a *f.* tassel; un berretto con —, a cap with a tassel; tuft; sprinkler, rose; (colloq., joc.) large nose; (zool.) 'feather' on a horse's leg; (liturg.) altar-cloth; communion-cloth; (bot.) cockscomb, *Celosia cristata*; †goatee beard. **-ina** *f. dim.,* **-ino** *m. dim.* tuft; pom-pom; top-knot; (colloq.) le -ine azzurre, the police.

nappello *m.* (bot.) monkshood, *Aconitum napellus.*

nappo *m.* (poet.) cup, goblet, drinking vessel; silver jug; ewer; (Tusc.) tin jug used for holding small amount of oil; †candle-socket; †bowl, basin, dish.

†**napuriello** *adj., n.m.* (derog.) Neapolitan.

†**naran·ci-a** *f.*, †**-o** *m.* See **aranci-a, -o.**

†**narato** *adj.* gilded.

Narbona *pr.n.f.* (geog.) Narbonne.

narceina *f.* (chem.) narceine.

Narciş-o *pr.n.m.* (myth.) Narcissus; a man who indulges in self-love; (bot.) daffodil, *Narcissus pseudo-narcissus* and other species; — marino, *Pancratium maritimum.* **-işişmo** *m.*, **-işmo** *m.* (psychol.) narcissism. (**-ista** *m.* **-i·stico** *adj.*)

narc-olessi·a *f.* (med.) narcolepsy. **-oşi** *f.* (med.) narcosis; (leg.) in stato di **-oşi**, in a state of insensibility or stupefaction (C.P.). **-o·tico** *adj., n.m.* narcotic; soporific; (leg.) portare indosso **-otici**, to carry narcotics upon the person (C.P.). **-oticamente** *adv.* by narcosis. **-otizzare** [A I] *tr.* to narcotize, to drug or render insensible by means of a narcotic. **-otizzazione** *f.* narcotization.

nard-o *m.* (bot.) lavender, *Lavandula officinalis*; mat grass, *Nardus stricta*; *Valeriana celtica*; (hist.) nard, spikenard, an aromatic plant, esp. that yielding the ointment used by the ancients (supposed to be *Nardostachys jatamansi*).

†**nar-e, -i** *f., m.pl.* See **narice.**

narghilè *m.* narghile, an Oriental tobacco-pipe in which the smoke passes through scented water before reaching the mouth.

narice *f.* (anat.) nostril.

narr-are [A I] *tr.* to narrate; to recount; to tell the story of; to relate; — sè stesso, to relate one's life-story; †to manifest, to show forth. **-a·bile** *adj.* narratable, recountable. †**-amento** *m.* narration. **-ante** *part. adj.* narrating; recounting; telling; relating; †*n.m.* narrator. **-ativa** *f.* narrative; fiction; narrating; narration; (leg.) count; report; narrative; **-ativa dell'atto d'accusa**, bill of indictment; †manner of narrating. **-ativo** *adj.* narrative; poesia **-ativa**, narrative poetry. **-ativamente** *adv.* in narrative form. **-ato** *part. adj.* narrated; recounted; told; related. **-atore** *m.* narrator. (**-atrice** *f.*) †**-ato·rio** *adj.* narrative. **-azione** *f.* narration; narrative; tale; story; recital; account; exposition; **-azione precisa**, precise account; **-azione dei fatti**, recital of the facts; (leg.) **-azione oratoria**, plea, address.

nartece *m.* (liturg.; archit.) narthex, a vestibule or portico stretching across the western end of some early Christian churches set apart for catechumens, etc.; (Gk. antiq.) casket, esp. that in which Alexander the Great carried his edition of Homer.

narvalo *m.* (zool.) narwhal, *Monodon monoceros.*

nas-ag·gine *f.*, **-ale** *adj.*, **-ata** *f.* See under **naso.**

naşardo *m.* (mus.) nasard, nazard (organ-stop).

na·sc-ere [B 18] *intr.* (*aux.* essere) to be born; to come into the world; son nato prima di te, I am older than you; l'ho visto —, I was alive before he was born; — di sabato, to be born on a Saturday; nacqui a Firenze, I was born in Florence; — di buona famiglia, to be of good family; non sono nato ieri!, I wasn't born yesterday!; non sono nato per questo!, I'm not fit for this!; un altr'uomo così ha da —, there has yet to be born another man like this; — bene, to be born of good family, to be well born; — cieco, to be blind from birth, to be born blind; (fig.) — vestito, to be born with a silver spoon in one's mouth; — sotto cattiva stella, to be born under an unlucky star; — senza la camicia, to be born unlucky; è nato all'arte, he is a born artist; c'era nato, he was born to it; **-e** un frate! (said when sudden silence occurs in conversation); to sprout; to come through; to appear; to come up; to grow; — come i funghi, to spread like mushrooms; to hatch out; non si sa se sia nato prima l'uovo o la gallina, which came first, the hen or the egg?; to begin; to arise; to come into being; (of publications, organizations, etc.) to be launched; da cosa **-e** cosa, one thing leads to another; da un male **-e** un bene, it's an ill wind that blows nobody any good; **-a** quel che vuole, come what may; to originate; to have one's beginning; la cetra nacque in Grecia, the cithara originated in Greece; (of the sun, stars, etc.) to rise; to dawn; (of a train) to start; **-e** qui, it starts from here; (of a building) to be built; (of a river) to rise; to proceed; to issue; to emanate; far —, to give rise to, to originate, to occasion; *n.m.* birth; beginning; outset. **-ente** *part. adj.* beginning; rising; dawning; nascent; l'ordine del Sol Nascente, the order of the Rising Sun; la generazione **-ente**, the rising generation; l'erba **-ente**, the growing grass; istituzione **-ente**, newly formed institu-

tion; (herald.) Leone **-ente**, demi lion naissant; (chem.) nascent. **-enza** *f.* birth; growth; excrescence; mould; mildew; rust. **-imento** *m.* birth; beginning; rise.

na·sc-ita *f.* birth; certificato di **-ita**, fede di **-ita**, birth certificate; di buona **-ita**, of good birth; essere inglese di **-ita**, to be English by birth; di bassa **-ita**, of humble, lowly, origin; bambino di **-ita**, new-born child; giorno di **-ita**, day of a person's birth; cieco dalla **-ita**, blind from birth; controllo, limitazione, delle **-ite**, birth-control; (leg.) atto di —, record of birth (in official register); †horoscope. †**-ito** *m.* birth; horoscope. **-ituro** *adj.* that is to be born; about to be born; yet to be born; future; (leg.) unborn; *n.m.* child about to be born, unborn child.

nascond-ere [C II] *tr.* to hide; giuocare a —, or a **-ersi**, to play (at) hide-and-seek; to conceal; mio figlio non mi **-e** nulla, my son has no secrets from me; to dissemble; to keep secret; to conceal; to mask; to dissimulate (feelings); to disguise; quelle parole **-ono** un'insidia, there is a trap behind those words; to stand in the way of; to block the view of; *rfl.* to hide, to be hidden; to be concealed from view; to hide oneself; to keep out of sight; to go into hiding; vatti a —!, you ought to be ashamed of yourself!; †to speak obscurely; †to dissimulate. †**-ello** *m.* see **nascondiglio.** **-ente** *part. adj.* hiding; concealing; in hiding. **-erella** *f.* giuocare a **-erella**, to play hide-and-seek. †**-e·vole** *adj.* sheltering; concealing. **-i·glio** *m.* hiding-place; lair; den. **-imento** *m.* hiding; concealment; †hiding-place; †lair; †allegorical fiction. **-ino** *m.* see **nasconderella.** **-itore** *m.* concealer; dissembler. (**-itrice** *f.*)

†**nascosa·glia** *f.* See **nascondiglio**, under **nascondere.**

nascos-o *part.* (poet.) of **nascondere**; see **nascosto.** **-amente** *adv.* (poet.) see **nascostamente**, under **nascosto.**

nascost-o, nascosto *part.* of **nascondere**, q.v.; *adj.* hidden; concealed; dissembled; disguised; covered; senso —, hidden meaning; secret; underhand; giuoco —, underhand game; *adv. phr.* di —, secretly, in secret; stealthily; on the sly; di — ai genitori, unbeknown to one's parents. **-amente** *adv.* secretly; in secret; stealthily.

naseggiare [A 3 c]. See under **naso.**

nasello[1] *m. dim.* See under **naso.**

nasello[2] *m.* (ichth.) hake, *Merluccius merluccius.*

nasiera *f.* See under **naso.**

nas-o *m.* nose; da —, for the nose; tabacco da —, snuff; fazzoletto da —, pocket handkerchief; arricciare il —, to turn up one's nose; soffiarsi il —, to blow one's nose; parlare nel —, parlare col —, to speak through one's nose; — a punta, pointed nose; — a peperone, big nose; — all'insù, turned-up nose, tip-tilted nose; — rincagnato, snub-nose; (fig.) dar di — in, mettere, ficcare il — in, to stick, to poke one's nose into; affilare il —, to grow thin; non veder più in là del proprio —, to see no further than the end of one's nose; menar per il —, to lead by the nose; si toccherebbe il — a dirgli che l'ha perso, he would believe anything; non rammentarsi dal — alla bocca, to have a very bad memory; gli montò la mosca al —, gli salì la mostarda al —, he lost patience; allungare il —, to crane one's neck; rimanere con un palmo di —, rimanere con tanto di —, to be left empty-handed, to be disappointed; fare un palmo di — a uno, to cock a snook at someone; fare due palmi di —, to cock a two-handed snook; dar nel — a, to arouse suspicion in, to arouse disgust in; questo affare mi dà nel —, this business smells fishy to me, this business makes me sick; sense of smell; avere buon —, to have a keen sense of smell, (fig.) to have keen judgement; aver buon — per, to have a flair for; non aver —, to have no sense of smell; giudicare a lume di —, to judge instinctively; face; — a —, face to face; chiudere la porta sul — ad uno, to shut the door in someone's face; non aveva il coraggio di mostrare la punta del —, he didn't dare to show his face; la bugia ti corre su per il —, it is written all over your face that you are lying; chi lo sa dove ha ficcato il —?, wherever can he have got to?; spout; nozzle; — dell'ombrello, umbrella handle; — della sella, saddle-bow; (anat.) setto di —, nasal septum; (mus.) nut (of violin-bow); (naut. slang) bows, stempiece, 'eyes of the ship'; nose of an animal, muzzle, snout; (zool.) — dell'elefante, elephant's trunk; (vet.) 'snip', part of the muzzle of a horse (between the nostrils); (bot.) — mozzo, bladdernut, *Staphylea pinnata.* **-ag·gine** *f.* nasal pronunciation; speaking through the nose. **-ale** *adj.* (anat.) nasal; pronunzia **-ale**, nasal pronunciation; *n.f.* nasal consonant; *n.m.* (mil. hist.) noseguard of a helmet. **-almente** *adv.* nasally. **-ata** *f.*

nas-o (*cont.*)

blow on the nose; smack in the face; repulse. †-**eca** *f.* ignoble nose. -**eggiare** [A3C] *intr.* (*aux.* avere) to speak with a nasal intonation; (*mus.*) to have a nasal tone-quality. -**ello** *m. dim.* small nose; man with a small nose; catch for a door-latch; cam on a wheel-rim; (*archit.*) drainpipe protruding from a wall; (*mus.*) nut (of violin-bow); *pl.* (*vet.*) bull-holders; bull-dogs. -**etto** *m. dim.* little nose; man with little nose; catch on a door-latch. -**evole** *adj.* (*joc.*) of the nose, pertaining to the nose. -**ica** *m.* (*zool.*) *Nasalis larvatus*, proboscis monkey; (*joc.*) big-nosed person. -**icorne** *m.* (*ent.*) rhinoceros beetle. -**iera** *f.* nose-ring for oxen, pigs, etc.; nose-band; (*herald.*) horse-brays; horse-barnacles. †-**iter·gio** *m.* handkerchief. -**obianco** *m.* (*zool.*) *Lasiopyga fantientis,* white-nosed monkey. -**ologi·a** *f.* (*joc.*) science of noses. -**one** *m. augm.* big nose; man with large nose. -**uto** *adj.* large-nosed, having a large nose; (*fig.*) perceptive; perspicacious; wise; judicious; †scornful, contemptuous, mocking.

naspo *m.* fire hose; (silkb.) reel.

nass-a *f.* basket-work trap used for catching octopus, similar to a lobster pot; (*chem.*) narrow-necked phial.

nasso[1] *m.* (*bot.*) yew, *Taxus baccata.*

Nasso[2] *pr.n.m.* (*geog.*) Naxos.

nastr-o *m.* ribbon; band; tape; strip; border; (*cul.*) 'pasta' in ribbon shape; — al cappello, hat-band; decoration; medal-ribbon; il — azzurro, the Blue Riband; — metrico, metro a —, tape-measure; tape (of sound recording, etc.); registrare su —, to record on tape; registratore a —, tape-recorder; registrazione a —, tape-recording; (*teleg.*) ticker tape; (*electr.*) — isolante, insulating tape; (*text.*) sliver; — della macchina da scrivere, typewriter ribbon; — trasportatore, conveyor belt; sega a —, bandsaw, endless saw; — di ferro, band iron, scrap iron; pulitrice a —, belt grinder; (mining) elevatore a — belt elevator; (mil.) — della mitragliatrice, machine-gun belt; (meteor.) — di groppi, line squall; (ichth.) pesce —, ribbon fish, *Trachypterus iris.* -**a·io** *m.* ribbon-seller; (*text.*) trimming manufacturer. (-**a·ia** *f.*) -**ino** *m. dim.* fine ribbon; narrow ribbon; narrow tape; ribbon book-marker; medal-ribbon; (*teleg.*) ticker tape; (shooting) fillet; (mil.) wire-winding of a gun-barrel; (*mil. hist.*) fuse; *pl.* (*cul.*) thin strips of 'pasta' served in soup.

nastur·z-io *m.* (*bot.*) watercress, *Nasturtium officinale*; (garden) nasturtium, *Tropaeolum.*

natal-e *adj.* native; città —, native city; natal; giorno —, birthday; *n.m.* birth; birthday; birthplace; il — di Roma, the anniversary of the foundation of Rome (21 April); (*eccl.*) feast of a saint, esp. of a martyr (as the anniversary of his birth into heaven); *pl.* birth; Dante ebbe a Firenze i suoi -i, Dante was born in Florence; essere di illustri -i, to be of noble birth; (*fig.*) beginnings; origin; *pr.n.m.* Christmas; il giorno di —, Christmas Day; buon —!, happy Christmas!; Nativity; la Vigilia di —, Christmas Eve; albero di —, Christmas tree; auguri di —, Christmas Greetings; (*mus.*) cantico di —, Christmas carol; †il -e del calice, Maundy Thursday; †i quattro -i, Christmas, Easter, Whitsunday and All Saints; (geog.) Isola del —, Christmas Island. -**ità** *f.* birth-rate. -**i·zio** *adj.* natal; giorno -izio, birthday; relating to Christmas; vacanze -izie, Christmas holidays; *n.m.* birthday; birthday celebrations.

nat-ante *part. adj.* floating; swimming; *n.m.* craft; boat. -**atoia** *f.* (*zool.*) fin, and any other structure used for swimming, such as a webbed foot; swimming-bladder. -**ato·ria** *f.* (*Rom. antiq.*) bathing-pool; swimming; nose-bladder. -**ato·rio** *adj.* natatorial, natatory, swimming; of swimming, for swimming; piscina -atoria, swimming-bath, swimming-pool; (ichth.) vescica -atoria, swim-bladder. †-**atura** *f.* place for swimming.

†**natare** *vb.* See nuotare.

na·tic-a *f.* (*anat.*) buttock. -**uto** *adj.* having big buttocks, big-bottomed.

nat-io *adj.* (*m.pl.* -**ii**) native; essere — di, to be a native of; tetto —, home; popolazione -ìa, native population; (of plant) indigenous; innate, inborn, natural. -**ismo** *m.* see nativismo. -**ivismo** *m.* (*philos.*) nativism, doctrine of innate ideas. -**ività** *f.* birth, nativity; (of a city) foundation; (*eccl.*) la -ività di Gesù, the Nativity, the Birth of Christ, Christmas; -ività di Maria Vergine, Nativity of Our Lady (8 Sept.); -ività di San Giovanni Battista, Nativity of St John Baptist (24 June); †descent, genealogy. -**ivo** *adj.* native; terra -iva, native land; local; il dialetto -ivo, the

native dialect; indigenous; innate, inborn, natural; sincere, plain, open, frank, straightforward; la -iva fierezza di questa gente, the simple pride of these people; (*miner.*) native; *n.m.* native.

nat-o *part.* of nascere, q.v.; *adj.* born; hatched out; sprouted, grown; risen, sprung; launched, begun; written, published; built; derived; Maria Gigli -a Bosi, Maria Gigli *née* Bosi; essere cieco —, to be blind from birth; non c'è anima -a, there is not a soul to be seen; — morto, stillborn (also fig.); (*herald.*) leone — morto, lion without tail, tongue and claws, lion normé; nudo —, stark naked; (*joc.*, of a baby) non essere ancora —, essere — ieri, to be very tiny; — ieri, born yesterday, inexperienced; essere — fatto per la musica, to be a born musician; pare suo padre — e sputato, he is the very spit of his father; *n.m.* son, child; little one; *pl.* young (of animals); †nestlings.

na·tola *f.* (*naut.*) rowlock.

natrice *f.* (*zool.*) grass snake, *Tropidonotus natrix,* also *T. tessellatus.*

natr-on *m. indecl.* (*miner.*) natron, native sodium carbonate. -**olite** *f.* (*miner.*) natrolite, needle zeolite.

natta *f.* (*med.*) wen, cyst; (*vet.*) 'sit fast' and other galls and sores produced by harness in a horse; †(*naut.*) rushmat or similar lining used in storerooms; (Genoese) cork; †joke, trick.

natur-a *f.* nature; natural world; sentimento della —, love of nature; — madre, Mother Nature; le scienze della —, the natural sciences; landscape, countryside, scenery; quivi la — si fa selvaggia, here the landscape becomes wild; force of nature; lasciar fare la —, to leave it to nature; ubbidire alla —, to obey nature; cedere alla —, to yield to nature, to die; (*philos.*) — naturante, *Natura naturans* (God, or Nature as the creative principle); — naturata, *Natura naturata* (visible creation, or Nature as created); natural order; secondare la —, to aid nature; stato di —, state of nature; in —, natural; di cervello, la — gliene ha dato poco, nature has not blessed him with much brain; nature, essence; definire la — di, to define the nature of; property, natural characteristic; la — del coniglio vuol che fugga, the rabbit's natural instinct is to flee; per —, da —, by nature, naturally; seconda —, second nature; character, temper, temperament; constitution; è una — ardente, he has a fiery character; timido per —, shy by nature; la — umana, human nature (also, the human race, see below); kind, sort, class; esempi di varia —, various kinds of examples; pagare in —, to pay in kind; natural species, form of life; ogni — ha il suo istinto, every form of life has its own instinct; la — umana, the human race; (paint.) — morta, still life; — viva, life; (anat.) female genital organs; †male genital organ; †nobile per —, of noble birth. -**ale** *adj.* natural; of the natural world; storia -ale, Natural History; bellezze -ali, beauties of nature; in a natural state; olio -ale, raw oil; based on an innate moral sense; diritto -ale, natural law; normal; calore -ale dell'uomo, man's normal temperature; morte -ale, natural death; vita -ale durante, during one's life, for the whole of one's natural life; non è cosa -ale, it isn't natural; innate, inborn; incapacità -ale, congenital incapacity; (of person) simple, uncouth, unlettered, crude, raw; unsuited; soda -ale, pure soda; easy, unselfconscious; essere -ale nel muoversi, to move naturally; illegitimate; figlio -ale, natural son; (leg.) maternità, paternità -ale, illegitimate maternity, paternity (C.C.); produced by nature (not artificial); una grotta -ale, a natural cave; capelli -ali, real hair; magia -ale, natural magic; vita -ale, rustic life; (leg.) frutti -ali, natural produce (C.C.); real, genuine; ritratto di grandezza -ale, life-sized portrait; rightful; (*mus.*) natural; (leg.) giudice -ale, competent or rightful judge; il giudice -ale precostituito, one's natural and preordained judge (I.C.); erede -ale, natural heir; ordinary, obvious, to be expected; è -ale!, ben -ale!, naturally!, of course!; †membro —, *membrum virile; n.m.* state of nature; al -ale, naturally, (of food) served raw; (of pictures, etc.) life-size; (art) life, living model; disegnare dal -ale, to draw from life; constitution, physical make-up; nature, disposition, temperament; native; i -ali di un luogo, the native inhabitants of a place. -**almente** *adv.* naturally; certainly, of course; by nature. -**alezza** *f.* naturalness, simplicity of manner, unselfconsciousness; un-affectedness; con -alezza, unaffectedly; simply, plainly; †natural inclination, propensity; †nature, natural instincts. -**alismo** *m.* (*philos.*) naturalism; (rel.) primitive nature-worship; (in art, literature, etc.) realism. -**alista** *m.* naturalist, student of natural sciences; one who believes in naturalism; (in art, literature, etc.) realist; naturopath. -**ali·stico** *adj.* naturalistic; of naturalism; of

natur-a (*cont.*)

the natural sciences. **-alità** *f.* political status; citizenship; ottenere la -alità italiana, to become a naturalized Italian; grande -alità, status carrying with it full political rights; †see **naturalezza**. **-alizzare** [A I] *tr.* (leg.) to naturalize; *rfl.* to become naturalized; to obtain the rights of citizenship; to assume nationality or citizenship; (fig.) to become accustomed or inured, to come to feel at home. **-alizzato** *part. adj.* (leg.) naturalized; cittadino -alizzato, naturalized citizen. **-alizzazione** *f.* (leg.) naturalization. **-are** [A I] *tr.* to create, to form, to constitute; †to generate; †*rfl.* -arsi in, to allow (something, e.g. a habit) to become second nature. **-ante** *part. adj.* (philos.) *naturans* (cf. under **natura**). **-ato** *part. adj.* naturally disposed, constituted; innate; naturalized; grown natural; vocaboli -ati in una lingua, words (of foreign origin) that have come to belong to a language. **-ismo** *m.* 'back-to-nature' movement; (rel.) nature-worship (cf. **naturalismo**); (med.) nature cure. **-ista** *m.* naturopath.

nauclero *m.* (orn.) kite.

naufrag-are [A 2 s] *intr.* (*aux.* essere, avere) to shipwreck, to wreck, to be wrecked; (fig.) to come to grief, to come to nothing, to founder; to fall through, to miscarry, to fail. **-ante** *part. adj.* shipwrecked; foundering; †andare -ante, to be wrecked, to founder; *n.m., f.* shipwrecked person. **-ato** *part. adj.* wrecked; shipwrecked; foundered; (fig.) come to nothing, fallen through.

naufra·gio *m.* shipwreck; fare —, to be shipwrecked; (fig.) wreck, ruin, failure; miscarriage; destruction; il — delle speranze, the wreck of one's hopes.

na·ufra-go *m.* (*pl.* -ghi) shipwrecked person; wreck; drowning man; castaway; (fig.) failure in life, a down-and-out; †andare —, to shipwreck.

na·ulo *m.* (comm.) naulage, the freight of passengers in a ship.

naumachi·a *f.* (Gk. hist.) sea battle; (Rom. antiq.) sham sea fight as theatrical spectacle; a flooded arena.

na·use-a *f.* nausea; queasiness; (fig.) nausea, loathing, disgust, repulsion; fino alla —, ad nauseam; far — a, to nauseate, to disgust, to sicken. **-abondo** *adj.* nauseous, nauseating; loathsome, repellent, disgusting; sickening. **-ante** *part. adj.* nauseating. **-are** [A I] *tr.* to nauseate; to disgust, to make sick; †to abhor. **-ato** *part. adj.* nauseated; disgusted; si sentì -ato di tutto, he felt sick of everything. **-oso** *adj.* nauseous, nauseating; sickening; disgusting; offensive; loathsome. **-osamente** *adv.* nauseously; sickeningly.

†**na·uta** *m.* pilot; boatswain.

na·utica *f.* navigation, art of navigation, ship handling.

na·utic-o *adj.* nautical; architettura -a, ship designing; sala -a, charthouse.

na·utilo *m.* (zool.) nautilus, *Nautilus* spp.

nav *f. indecl.* (naut., Pavia) boat used on the Ticino.

navale *adj.* and derivs. See under **nave**.

nav-arca *m.*, **-arco** *m.* and derivs. See under **nave**.

Navarr-a *pr.n.f.* (geog.) Navarre. **-ino** *adj.* of Navarre, Navarrese; (zool.) razza -ina, Navarrese breed of horses; *n.m.* inhabitant of Navarre, Navarrese; Navarre pony; (hist.) i -ini, epithet given in contempt to the French in Italy during the reign of the French King Henry IV (Henry of Navarre); (agric.) a kind of dark red grape grown in Tuscany.

navata[1] (archit.) nave; — laterale, aisle.

navata[2] *f.* See under **nave**.

nav-e *f.* ship; full-rigged ship; vessel; boat; craft; liner; — appoggio, depot ship; — di basso bordo, — bassa di bordo, low freeboard; — di battaglia, — di linea, — corazzata, ship of the line, battleship; — capofila, leading ship, guide; — cisterna, tanker; — civetta, decoy, Q ship; — corsara, — corsaro, corsair, pirate ship; — deposito, hulk; — da diporto, yacht; — dragamine, minesweeper; — fanale, — faro, lightship; — goletta, barquentine; — da guerra, warship; — idrografica, surveying ship; — perno, turning ship, guide; — al più presso, ship close hauled; — portaerei, aircraft carrier; — portareti, — posareti, net carrier, net layer; — posacavi, cable ship; — posamine, minelayer; — regolatrice, guide; — rompighiaccio, ice-breaker; — rimorchio bersaglio, target-towing ship; — a ruote, paddle ship; — salvataggio, salvage ship; — da scorta, di scorta, escort ship, escorting vessel; — serrafila, end ship, last in line; — trasporto, naval auxiliary (N.B. not troop carrier); — travagliata, ship labouring; — vedetta, scout; — a vela, sailing ship; — alla vela, — invelata, ship under

sail; (leg.) testamento a bordo di —, will made aboard ship (C.C.); capitano di —, master; urto di -i, collision; (fig.) la — dello stato, the ship of State; (aeron.) — aerea, airship; (archit.) nave. **-ale** *adj.* naval; pertaining to the navy; relating to the sea; Accademia -ale, Naval College; (Rom. antiq.) corona -ale, naval crown; †*n.m.* shipyard. **-alestro** *m.* punt; ferry; ferryman. **-alismo** *m.* seafaring (used esp. of Gt. Britain). **-arca, -arco** *m.* (*pl.* -archi) (naut.) captain-general of a squadron; captain of a private ship; master; (Gk. antiq.) captain of a ship. †**-arolo** *m.* pilot. **-ata** *f.* cargo, shipload. †**-eggiare** *intr.* see **navigare**. **-etta** *f.* shuttle; (fig.) far la -etta, to go to and fro, to go backwards and forwards, to ply a shuttle-service. **-icella** *f.* (naut.) small craft; (fig.) la -icella di (San) Pietro, the barque of Peter, the Catholic Church; (liturg.) incense-boat; (chem.) porcelain boat; (aeron.) car, nacelle, gondola; basket (of balloon); -icella motore, nacelle; fish-strainer, perforated tray of fish-kettle; (archit.) side aisle. **-icella·io** *m.* boatman. †**-icellata** *f.* (naut.) capacity of a small boat. **-icello** *m.* two-masted craft (Tuscany); (joc.) large and sloppy shoe; †voluble and insincere individual; †sly, knowing individual. **-icellone** *m.* (naut., Tusc.) large two-masted craft. †**-ichiere, -ichiero** *m.* boatman, pilot. †**-i·cola** *f. dim.* small craft, little boat; cradle. **-icolare** *adj.* (vet.) osso -icolare, navicular bone. **-icolite** *f.* navicular disease (inflammation of the bone).

navig-are [A 2 s] *intr.* (*aux.* avere) to cruise, sail or row; to be at sea; — in armata, (of a fleet) to sail; — di bolina, to sail close hauled; — sui bordi, to tack; — a gonfie vele, to sail sails full; — in linea di rilevamento, to sail quarterline; — nella scia di, to keep in the wake of (also fig.); — a secco, to sail under bare poles; †— col terreno in mano, to sail keeping land in sight; (fig.) — in cattive acque, to sail into difficult waters; sapere —, to manage one's affairs cleverly; — a ogni vento, to adapt oneself to circumstances; *tr.* — i mari, to sail the seas; to convey by sea, to transport. **-a·bile** *adj.* navigable; seaworthy; vino -abile, wine that will travel by sea without detriment to its condition. **-abilità** *f.* navigability; seaworthiness; (aeron.) -abilità aerea, airworthiness. **-amento** *m.* navigating; navigation. **-ante** *part. adj.* navigating; *n.m.* navigator; sailor. **-ato** *part. adj.* navigated; sailed; carried by sea; (fig.) clever, acute, wise, crafty; much travelled (also fig.); acque -ate, frequented waters. **-atore** *m.* navigator; sea explorer; *adj.* seafaring; una nazione -atrice, a seafaring nation. †**-ato·rio** *adj.* nautical. **-azione** *f.* navigation; navigating; art of navigating; -azione aerea, aerial navigation; -azione di piccolo cabotaggio, coastal navigation in Mediterranean and adjacent waters as far as Casablanca and Lisbon in the Atlantic and Kosseir in the Red Sea; -azione di gran cabotaggio, navigation in above waters and also as far as Baltic and Senegal in the Atlantic, the Persian Gulf and Bombay in the Indian Ocean; -azione alturiera, -azione di altura, navigation on the high seas, out of sight of land; società di -azione, equivalent of steamship company; -azione generale italiana, N.G.I., United Steamship Companies (Cosulich, Lloyd Triestino and others).

†**navi·gio** *m.* craft, ship, boat; fleet; navigation.

navi·glio *m.* (naut.) fleet; squadron; flotilla; craft; convoy; — da traffico, — mercantile, merchant fleet; — da diporto, yacht squadron; — portaerei, carrier force; — sottile, — leggero, light craft (cruisers and destroyers); †ship; †per —, by ship; †fare —, to set sail; canal; (N. Italy) navigable canal.

†**navi·lio** *m.* (naut.) shipping fare; charter (cf. **naviglio**).

navisfera *f.* (naut.) celestial globe.

na·volo *m.* See **naulo**.

navon-e *m.* (bot.) rape, colza, cole-seed, *Brassica napus* var. *arvensis*; swede, Swedish turnip, *Brassica napus* var. *napobrassica*. **-cella** *f.*, **-ella** *f.* (ent.) green-veined white butterfly, *Pieris napi*.

naz-ardo *m.* (mus.). See **nasardo**.

naz-areno *adj.* see **nazzareno**. **-areato** *m.* (bibl.) Naziriteship, Nazarite vow. **-are·o** *adj.*, *n.m.* (Bibl.) Nazarite, Nazarene.

Nazare·t *pr.n.f.* (geog.) Nazareth.

nazion-e *f.* nation; people, country; dignità di —, national status; nationality; gente di ogni —, people of every nationality; †group of nationals living in a foreign country; †generation; †native country, place of origin; †birth; †race, stock, family. **-ale** *adj.* national; festa -ale, national holiday; sentimento -ale, national feeling, nationalism; home (not foreign); prodotti -ali, home products; mercato -ale, home market; *n.m.* (sport) player who has represented Italy in international matches; *f.* la -ale, 'national'

nazion-e (*cont.*)

road, trunk road. **-alménte** *adv.* nationally; as a nation. **-alismo** *m.* nationalism. **-alista** *m.,f., adj.* nationalist. **-alità** *f.* nationality; nation; appartenevano a -alità diverse, they were of various nationalities, they belonged to various nations; acquisto di -alità, acquisition of nationality; prendere la -alità inglese, to take British nationality. **-alizzare** [A I] *tr.* to nationalize. **-alizzato** *part. adj.* nationalized. **-alizzazione** *f.* nationalization. **-alsocialismo** *m.* (hist.) Nazism, German National Socialism. **-alsocialista** *m.* (hist.) Nazi, German National Socialist. **-alsociali·stico** *adj.* (hist.) relating to German National Socialism.

nazir-eato *m.,* **-e·o** *adj.* See **nazareato, nazareo,** under **nazareno.**

naz-ismo *m.* (hist.) Nazism, Naziism. **-ista** *m.* (hist.) Nazi. **-is·tico** *adj.* (hist.) Nazi.

nazzaren-o *adj.* Nazarene; *n.m.* il Nazzareno, the Nazarene, Christ; capelli alla -a, shoulder-length hair on a man; barba alla -a, beard such as Christ is depicted as having; (eccl. hist.) *m.pl.* Nazarenes (whether early Jewish-Christian or nineteenth-century Hungarian); (eccl.) frati -i, friars of the Order of Penance; the Scalzetti.

ne¹ *prn. conj.* of him; of her; of it; of them; — ho sentito parlare, I have heard of him (of her, of it, of them); se — pentì, he repented of it; di sciocchi — conosco tanti, I know so many fools; his; her; its; their; — sentii i passi, I heard his (her, its, their) footsteps; with it; che — fai?, what do you do with it?; about it; non me ne parlare, don't talk about it; non me — importa nulla, it doesn't matter to me at all; thence, from thence; — veniamo proprio adesso, we've just this minute come from there; starsene lontano, to keep a long way away from there; andarsene, to go away; starsene da parte, starsene con le mani in mano, to do nothing about it, to keep out of it; aversene a male, to take offence at (referring to stories, tales, mistakes, insults, etc., understood); — so delle belle sul tuo conto, I have heard some fine tales about you; — fa sempre delle belle, he is always putting his foot in it, *or* he is always up to something or other; gliene disse un sacco, he showered him with insults; *partitive* some of it, any; dammene, give me some; non — ho, I haven't any.

ne² *prep.* (poet.) in; ne la profondità, in the depth (instead of 'nella profondità'; Giosue Carducci and other poets have affected this style, and it is not uncommon in inscriptions, dedications, etc.).

†ne³ *prn. conj.* us, to us.

ne' *contr.* of in and i usu. written nei (see under **in**); in the; se fossi ne' tuoi panni, if I were in your shoes; if I were you; Marianna Rinuccini — Trivulzi, Marianna Trivulzi, *née* Rinuccini.

nè¹ *conj.* neither; nor; ha voluto far così, — io lo condanno, he wanted to do it and I don't blame him; nè...nè, neither...nor; †not even.

†nè² *conj.* lest, in order that...not.

nean·che *conj.* not even; — per sogno, not at all, by no means; not on your life; non l'ha detto — a me, he did not even tell me; neither, nor; se tu non vai, non ci andrò — io, if you don't go, neither shall I; 'A teatro non ci vado. E tu?' 'Neanche'; 'I'm not going to the theatre? How about you?' 'I'm not either.'

†neanco *conj.* See **neanche.**

neartrosi *f.* (med.) nearthrosis.

neato *adj.* having a small mark, patch, stain or slight defect; †marked with a mole (cf. **neo¹**).

nebbi-a *f.* fog; — spessa, dense fog; — da tagliar col coltello, fog you could cut with a knife; mist; haze; arcobaleno della —, fog bow; (mil.) cortina di —, smoke screen, smoke curtain; (fig.) una — di sospetto, a shadow of suspicion; le -e dell'ignoranza, the mists of ignorance; dimness, indistinctness, obscurity; addensare le -e, to cloud the issue; le -e del settentrione, abstruseness attributed by Italians to writers and philosophers of Northern countries; aver in tasca la —, to pay heed to nobody; il primo anno che non è —, the first year without mist, i.e. never; stringer —, to grasp thin air; (med.) aerosol, mist spray; (phys.) camera a —, Wilson's cloud chamber; (bot.) *Aira capillaris; Erysiphe.* **-ac·cia** *f. pejor.* thick mist; dense fog; smog. **-a·io** *m.* foggy weather; misty weather. **-o·geno** *m.* (mil.) smoke-making apparatus or canister. **-olina** *f. dim.* thin, drifting mist. **-one** *m. augm.* dense fog; smog. **-ore** *m.* mistiness. **-osità** *f.* mistiness, fogginess; haziness. **-oso** *adj.* misty; foggy; hazy; (fig.) nebulous; obscure, confused, abstruse.

nebbiolo *m.* (bot.) Piedmontese black vine from which choice red wine is obtained (e.g. 'barolo', 'barbaresco'); also used as a name of red wine.

ne·bride *f.* (Gk. antiq.) (Bacchic) fawnskin.

ne·bul-a *f.* obscurity, darkness; mist; (vet.) conical opacity, cataract, moon blindness in horses; †cloud. **-are** *adj.* (astron.) nebular. **†-ento** *adj.* misty; clouding, obfuscating. **-izzare** [A I] *tr.* to spray with aerosol, to atomize (cf. **nebbia**). **-izzatore** *m.* sprayer (of aerosol), spray, atomizer. **†-one** *m.* rogue, good-for-nothing; blockhead; wretch. **-osa** *f.* (astron.) nebula; star-cluster; (fig.) nebulous object, obscure happening. **-osità** *f.* nebulosity; mistiness; cloudiness, haze, haziness; vagueness, uncertainty, obscurity, indistinctness; indistinct object, nebulous object. **-oso** *adj.* nebulous, misty, cloudy, hazy; foggy; vague, indeterminate, uncertain; obscure; (of style) abstruse, obscure; (herald.) nebuly.

†nec-are *tr.* to kill; **†***f.* the act of killing.

†Nec·care *pr.n.m.* (geog.) the river Neckar.

nec·chia *f.* Viking ship.

neccio *m.* chestnut-meal cake; — cieco, chestnut-meal cake sandwiched with ham, etc.

nécessaire *m. indecl.* (pron. as Fr.) dressing-case, toilet-case; work-box, work-basket.

necessa·ri-o *adj.* necessary; indispensable; needful; requisite; essential; evident, obvious; conseguenza -a, inevitable consequence; bisogno —, urgent need, (euphem.) call of nature; luogo —, lavatory; nessuno è — al mondo, no one is indispensable; ritenere —, to deem necessary, to consider essential; (leg.) erede —, heir of right (entitled to legitime by operation of law); *n.m.* necessity; the necessary; il puro —, the bare necessities, il — per scrivere, the wherewithal to write, writing materials; il — per il campeggio, camping outfit. **-amente** *adv.* necessarily; indispensably; inevitably; evidently, obviously; se ne conchiude -amente, we must necessarily conclude.

necess-e *Lat. neuter adj.* (philos.) necessary (as opposed to contingent); *n.m.* the necessary; necessity. **†-e·vole** *adj.* necessary, essential.

necessit-à *f.* necessity, far di — virtù, to make a virtue of necessity; di assoluta —, indispensable; di —, necessarily, of necessity; per —, from necessity; need; che — c'è di gridare?, why do you have to shout?; non vedo la — di, I see no need to; le — della vita, the necessities of life; soddisfare alle — di uno, to satisfy someone's needs; want, hardship, indigence, penury; trovarsi in —, to find oneself in dire straits; la — non ha legge, necessity knows no law; una grande — di uomini, a great need of men; (leg.) lo stato di —, jeopardy (C.C.); necessity, destiny; la — cieca, blind Fate; conoscere le proprie —, to know one's own interests; †natural law, natural property; inherent nature; †tie of kinship or relationship. **-are** [A I S] *tr.* to compel, to constrain; la sfortuna mi -a a chiedere, misfortune compels me to ask; *intr.* (aux. avere; *prep.* di) to be in want (of); *impers.* to be necessary; -a di provvedere a questo, it is necessary to see to this. **-ante** *part.* necessitating; *adj.* compelling; constraining. **-a·rio** *adj., n.m.* (philos.) necessitarian, necessarian. **-ato** *part.* constrained, compelled; made necessary. **-oso** *adj.* needful, needy. **†-u·dine** *f.* tie of kinship.

necr-obiosi *f.* (med.) necrobiosis. **-o·fago** *m.* (zool.) necrophagous. **-ofili·a** *f.* necrophilism, obsession with dead bodies. **-ofobi·a** *f.* necrophobia, horror of dead bodies. **-o·foro** *m.* undertaker's assistant; sexton; (ent.) burying beetle, *Necrophorus vespillo.* **-ologi·a** *f.* obituary, necrology; obituary notice; funeral oration. **-olo·gico** *adj.* necrological. **-olo·gio** *m.* register of deaths; obituary notice; obit. **-ologista** *m.* writer of obituary notices. **-omanzi·a** *f.* necromancy; see also **negromanzia.** **-o·poli** *f.* cemetery; necropolis. **-opsi·a** *f.* (med.) necropsy, autopsy, post mortem examination. **-oscopi·a** *f.* necropsy. **-osco·pico** *adj.* pertaining to autopsy. **-o·scopo** *m.* pathologist engaged in autopsy; municipal physician whose duty it is to ascertain cause of death. **-osi** *f.* (med.) necrosis. **-osato** *adj.* (med.) necrosed, mortified. **-ospermi·a** *f.* (med.) necrospermia. **-o·tico** *adj.* necrotic. **-otizzare** [A I] *tr.* necrotize; to mortify. **-otomi·a** *f.* dissection of a cadaver.

nec·tria *f.* (bot.) *Nectria ditissima,* a kind of fungus.

Neerlan·d-ia *pr.n.f.* (geog.) Netherlands. **-ese** *adj.* of the Netherlands, Dutch; *n.m.* Dutchman, Netherlander; *f.* Dutch woman.

nef-ando *adj.* infamous, execrable, iniquitous, abominable; unspeakable; foul, obscene, unrepeatable. **-andamente** *adv.* infamously, abominably, unspeakably; obscenely. **-andezza** *f.*

nef-ando (*cont.*)
infamy, iniquity, abominableness, baseness; foulness, filthiness, obscenity. **-andità** *f.* infamy, iniquity, abominableness, baseness, foulness, filthiness, obscenity; infamous deed, abomination; infamous word; filthy word; obscene deed or language. **-a·rio** *adj.* nefarious, iniquitous, wicked; evil, abominable. **-ariaménte** *adv.* nefariously, wickedly; evilly. **-asto** *adj.* fateful, ill-omened, inauspicious, unpropitious; unlucky; uomo -asto, man who brings ill fortune; in quel giorno -asto, on that fateful day; †infamous.

nefe·lide *f.* (zool.) a kind of leech, *Nephelis vulgaris.*

nefel-ina *f.* (miner.) nephelite. **-osco·pio** *m.* see **nefoscopio.**

nefosco·pio *m.* (meteor.) nephoscope.

nefr-algi·a *f.* (med.) nephralgia. **-ectomi·a** *f.* (surg.) nephrectomy. **-ite** *f.* (med.) nephrites; (miner.) nephrite; jade. **-i·tico** *adj.* (med.) nephritic; *n.m.* nephritic, sufferer from nephritis. **-i·tide** *f.* (med.) nephritis. **-ocele** *f.*, *m.* (med.) nephrocele. **-olito** *m.* (med.) renal calculus, nephrolith.

nefrope *m.* (zool.) *Nephrops norvegicus*, 'Dublin Bay prawn' (cf. **scampo**).

neg-are [A 2] *tr.* to deny; -ò d'essere italiano, he denied that he was Italian; — l'esistenza di Dio, to deny the existence of God; (leg.) to deny; to disavow; — la verità, to deny the truth; to refuse, to withhold permission from; me lo -ò, he refused to let me have it; — l'accesso, to refuse admittance; — fede a, to disbelieve; to disown, to repudiate; to contradict; non —, to admit; non lo -o, I don't deny it; *rfl.* to deny oneself; -arsi di intervenire, to refuse to interfere; †— sè stesso, to deny oneself, to practise self-denial. **-a·bile** *adj.* deniable; that can be refused or withheld. (**-abilità** *f.*) **-ante** *part. adj.* denying; refusing; withholding; repudiating. **-ativa** *f.* denial, stare sulla -ativa, to persist in denying; negative, negative reply; dare una -ativa, to refuse; nella -ativa, in caso di -ativa, in the negative; negative statement; (leg.) una formale —, a formal denial; *n.f.* (photog.) negative. **-ativo** *adj.* negative; l'esito delle indagini fu -ativo, the result of research was negative, the inquiries produced no result; comando —, prohibition; (phys.; electr.; math.) negative; (leg.) l'imputato si mantiene -ativo, the defendant persists in denying; giudizio -ativo, unfavourable judgement; voto -ativo, adverse vote; risposta -ativa, denial; fu dato parere -ativo, it was decided in the negative; (fig.) passive, inactive, negative. **-ativaménte** *adv.* negatively; in the negative. **-ato** *part. adj.* denied; refused, withheld; not granted; ore -ate al riposo, hours of lost sleep; unsuited, unfit; esser -ato per, to have no aptitude for. **-atore** *m.* denier; refuser. (**-atrice** *f.*) **-ato·rio** *adj.* (*m.pl.* **-atorii**) negatory; (leg.) l'azione -atoria, action of quiet enjoyment (C.C.). **-azione** *f.* negation; denial; una debole -azione, a feeble denial; una -azione della giustizia, a negation of justice; refusal; disavowal; -azione di sè medesimo, abnegation, self-sacrifice, renunciation; negative; la -azione, the negative particle 'non'; non sempre due -azioni affermano, two negatives do not always make an affirmative.

negarit *m. indecl.* Abyssinian drum.

†**negghienza** *f.* laziness, sloth; avere in —, mettere a —, not to care about, to be indifferent concerning.

neghitt-oso *adj.* slothful, lazy, indolent; listless; careless; indifferent, inert; †uncertain, vague. **-osaménte** *adv.* slothfully, lazily; listlessly; carelessly; indifferently.

neglett-o *part.* of **negligere**, q.v.; *adj.* uncared for, untidy, unkempt, dishevelled; unaffected; (of style) unadorned, unaffected; careless, negligent; inaccurate. **-aménte** *adv.* neglectedly; untidily; carelessly; inaccurately; unaffectedly. †**-are** *tr.* to despise, to scorn; not to care for, to neglect; non -are, to appreciate.

†**neglezione** *f.* neglect; indifference.

negli *prep.* and *def. art. m.pl.* See under **in** (*prep.*).

negli·g-ere [C 13] *tr.* to neglect; to slight; to disregard; to leave untidy or uncared for; to leave out; to omit; — a fare il suo dovere, to neglect to do one's duty.

neglig-ente *part. adj.* negligent, neglectful; inattentive, careless; lazy, slothful; †scornful. **-enteménte** *adv.* negligently, neglectfully; carelessly, inattentively, untidily; lazily, slothfully. †**-entare** *vb.* and derivs. see **negligere**. **-enza** *f.* negligence; carelessness, heedlessness, inattention; fu una -enza colpevole, it was a piece of culpable negligence; (leg.) negligence; default; un danno attribuito a -enza, damage due to negligence; -enza grave, gross negligence. †**-en·zia** *f.* see **negligenza**.

---

†**nego** *m.* See **niego**.

negoss-a *f.* (naut.) fishing net used with a pole like a large landing net. †**-o** *m.* see **negossa.**

nego·zia *f.* (joc., of a woman) baggage, piece of goods.

negozi-are [A 4] *intr.* (*aux.* avere) to negotiate, to enter into negotiations; (comm.) to trade, to carry on a trade; to transact business; to bargain; to do a deal; *tr.* to negotiate; — la pace, to negotiate peace; (comm.) to sell, to deal in, to traffic in; — una cambiale, to negotiate a bill; — titoli, to sell stocks and shares. **-a·bile** *adj.* negotiable; marketable; (finan.) negotiable. **-abilità** *f.* negotiability. **-aménto** *m.* negotiating, negotiation. **-ante** *part. adj.* negotiating; *n.m.* tradesman; dealer; -ante di granaglie, cornchandler; il ceto dei -anti, tradespeople; un ricco -ante, a prosperous shopkeeper. **-ato** *part. adj.* traded; transacted; negotiated; *n.m.* deal; agreement; business deal; negotiation; transaction; *pl.* negotiations; iniziare i -ati, to open negotiations; (leg.) see **trattative**. **-atore** *m.* negotiator; transactor. (**-atrice** *f.*) **-azione** *f.* negotiation; transaction; business, dealing; (comm.) -azione di una cambiale, negotiation of a bill of exchange; (leg.) negotiation, treaty of a business matter.

nego·zio *m.* business; fare — in gioielli, to do business in jewellery; bargain; transaction; fare un buon —, to make a good bargain, to pull off a deal; (fig.) business, matter, concern, affair; un — difficile, a difficult business; un — amoroso, an affair of the heart; (joc.) thing, affair, contraption; che è questo —?, what's this contraption?; work, business, occupation; shop, store, business; commesso di —, giovine di —, shop-assistant; aprire un —, to set up shop, to open a shop; (leg.) — giuridico, see under **giuridico**.

negra *f.* negress, negro-girl, negro-woman; (ichth.) darkie Charlie, *Scymnorhinus lichia.*

negr-o *adj.* negro, black; *n.m.* negro; blackamoor; black; la tratta dei -i, the slave-trade; un piccolo —, a little nigger-boy. **-eggiare** [A 3 c] *intr.* (*aux.* essere) to appear black; to be blackish, to be almost black; i monti -eggiano di foreste, the mountains are black with forests. **-etto** *m. dim.* small negro; nigger-boy, piccaninny. †**-ezza** *f.* blackness, black; obscurity. **-iere, -iero** *m.* slave-trader, slave-dealer; (fig.) slave-driver; †(naut.) slaver, slave-ship; member of crew of slave-ship; *adj.* of slaves; nave -iera, slave-ship. †**-ita** *m.* negro, moor. **-ofumo** *m.* see **nerofumo**. **-o·ide** *adj.*, *n.m.* negroid.

negro-mante *m.* necromancer; sorceress *f.* **-mantésco** *adj.* like a necromancer, after the fashion of necromancers. **-man·tico** *adj.* necromantic; *n.m.* necromancer. **-manzi·a** *f.* necromancy. †**-man·zio** *adj.* see **negromantico**.

†**negrore** *m.* blackness, black; darkness.

negundo *m.* (bot.) box elder, *Acer negundo.*

Negus *pr.n.m.* Negus, ruler of Abyssinia.

neh *excl.* eh; ti piacerebbe, —?, you'd like that, wouldn't you?; è bello, —?, it's lovely, isn't it?; look here!; indeed!; I say!

nei *prep.* and *def. art. m.pl.* See under **in** (*prep.*).

†**neiente** *prn. indef.* See **niente**.

nel, nella, nelle, nello *prep.* and *def. art.* See under **in** (*prep.*).

nelum·bio *m.* (bot.) lotus lily, *Nelumbo nucifera.*

nemb-o *m.* cloud; rain-cloud, nimbus; cloud-burst, squall; — di polvere, cloud of dust; un — di fiori, a shower of flowers; dense mass, large cluster. **-i·fero** *adj.* stormy; cloudy. **-oso** *adj.* stormy, tempestuous; cloudy; cime -ose, cloud-capped peaks.

Nembrot, Nembrotte, Nembrotto *pr.n.m.* Nimrod; (poet.) seguace di —, huntsman.

neme·o *adj.* (Gk. antiq.) Nemean (lion, games, odes).

Ne·mesi *pr.n.f.* (Gk. myth.) Nemesis; (fig.) fate, nemesis; retributive justice, vengeance.

†**nemiche·vole** *adj.* cruel; hostile; alien; stormy, rough, storm-tossed; hard, difficult.

†**nemici·zia** *f.* enmity, hostility.

nemic-o *adj.* hostile, inimical; assalto —, enemy attack; contrary, adverse; la sorte gli è -a, fate is against him; opposed, averse; essere — dei libri, to hate books; è — all'acqua, he never goes near water; farsi — il mondo, to make oneself generally hated; essere — di sè stesso, to be one's own worst enemy; giornale — del governo, opposition newspaper; harmful; il gelo è — alle piante, frost is bad for plants; *n.m.* enemy; opponent; adversary; antagonist; rival; farsi un —, to make an enemy; il Nemico, the Adversary, Satan; (collective) enemy; passare al —, to desert to the enemy; (fig.) menace, danger, peril; il tabacco è un vero —

nemic·o (*cont.*)
per la salute, tobacco is a real menace to health. **-amente** *adv.* inimically, with enmity. †**-are** *tr.* to hate; to persecute; to treat as an enemy; to estrange, to alienate, to make an enemy of.

nemmeno, nemmanco *conj.* not even; neither; (colloq.) non lo farei — per sogno, I shouldn't dream of it.

nemorense *adj.* (geog.) of Nemi, in the Alban hills.

Nen·c·ia *pr.n.f.* Nancy; bellezza della —, dimple in the chin. **-etta** *pr.n.f. dim.* little Nancy; (colloq.) il corredo di -etta, two of everything.

ne·nia[1] *f.* (Rom. antiq.) *nenia*; (fig.) dirge; children's song; rigmarole; lamentation; wail; monotonous song; tedious speech.

Ne·nia[2] *pr.n.f.* (myth.) Nenia, goddess of the dying.

nenu·f·ara, -aro, -ero *m.* (bot.) yellow water-lily, brandy-bottle, *Nuphar lutea.*

neo[1] *m.* mole (on the skin); small defect, slight imperfection; patch, beauty-spot.

neo[2], **neon** *m.* (chem.) neon.

neo[3] *pref.* neo-; new, recent, modern, later; latter, latter-day. (For derivatives in which the stress falls on the o of neo, see separate headings.)

neo-catto·lico *m.* (recent) Catholic convert; *adj.* belonging or pertaining to such a convert. **-classicismo** *m.* neo-classicism, revival of classicism. **-classicista** *m., f.* neo-classicist. **-clas·sico** *adj.* neoclassical; *n.m.* neo-classicist. **-comiano** *adj.* (geol.) Neocomian. **-criticismo** *m.* (philos.) Kantian criticism, Kantianism. **-fili·a** *f.* love of what is new, love of innovations. **-formazione** *f.* (bot.) regeneration. **-greco** *adj., n.m.* modern Greek. **-guelfo** *adj., n.m.* (hist.) neo-Guelf, modern Guelf; one who (in the period of the Risorgimento) recommended an Italian confederation under the Pope's presidency. **-latino** *adj.* of Latin extraction; le lingue -latine, the romance languages; i popoli -latini, the Latin races; *n.m.* Latin writer of the Renaissance. **-li·tico** *adj.* (archaeol.) neolithic. **-logi·a** *f.* (ling.; theol.) neology, use of (suspect) novelties. **-lo·gico** *adj.* neological. **-logismo** *m.* neologism (in language or religion). **-meni·a** *f.* neomenia, the new moon (esp. as kept by the ancient Greeks or Hebrews). **-nato** *adj.* new-born, newly born; *n.m.* new-born child. **-pitagorismo** *m.* (philos.) Neopythagoreanism. **-pitago·rico** *adj., n.m.* Neopythagorean. **-plasi·a** *f.* (med.; biol.) neoplasia. **-plasma** *m.* (med.; biol.) neoplasm. **-plastico** *adj.* (med.; biol.) neoplastic. **-platonismo** *m.* (philos.) Neoplatonism (in antiquity or at the Renaissance). **-plato·nico** *adj.* Neoplatonic; *n.m.* Neoplatonist; Renaissance Platonist (esp. Florentine). **-rama** *m.* (archit.; paint.) interior view of a building. **-realista** *m.* (cinem.) neo-realist. **-realismo** *m.* (cinem.) neo-realism. **-scola·stica** *f.* (philos.) Neo-scholasticism. **-scola·stico** *adj., n.m.* Neo-scholastic. **-te·rico** *adj.* neoteric, modern, newfangled. **-tomismo** *m.* (philos.) Neo-thomism; the Thomist revival. **-tomista** *m.* Neo-thomist; modern Thomist. **-zo·ico** *adj.* (geol.) Neozoic, post-Palaeozoic; Quaternary.

neo·fita *m.* (pop.). See **neofito**.

neo·fito *m.* (rel.; fig.) neophyte; new convert; novice; newcomer.

neo·gene *m.* (geol.) Upper Tertiary (geological series).

neossina *f.* (orn.) neossine.

neotto·lemo *m.* (ent.) *Morpho neoptolemus*, a tropical butterfly whose brilliant blue wings are used in jewellery, etc.

nepa *f.* (zool.) water-scorpion; (astron.) Scorpio.

nepente *m.* (bot.) pitcher-plant, *Nepenthes*; anodyne.

nepitella *f.* (bot.) calamint, *Calamintha satureia.*

nepitello *m.* (anat.) palpebral fringe.

nepot·ismo *m.* nepotism; favouritism. **-ista** *m.* nepotist.

neppure *conj.* not even; non lo vidi —, I did not even see him.

†**ne·puta** *f.* (bot.). See **nepitella**.

†**nequ-iore** *comp. adj.* more evil, worse. †**-is·simo** *superl. adj.* extremely evil, of extreme wickedness. **-ità** *f.* evil, iniquity. **-itoso** *adj.* wicked, iniquitous. **-i·zia** *f.* wickedness, iniquity; evil deed, wicked deed, crime, sin.

nera *f.* cup of coffee and chocolate mixed; woman with black hair and dark eyes.

nerb·o *m.* scourge, lash, thong (whip made from plaited dried ligaments taken from the necks of horses or bulls); sinew, muscle; stamina, vigour, strength, force; essere di buon —, to be strong, to be a man of muscle; stile senza —, style lacking in vigour; best part, core; (mil.) see nervo; †nerve. **-are** [A I] *tr.* to scourge, to whip, to beat. **-ata** *f.* stroke of the whip, blow; flogging;

beating; un sacco di -ate, a sound flogging. **-atore** *m.* scourger. **-atura** *f.* scourging, whipping, flogging. **-olino** *m.* little whip, switch, small branch, rod. **-oruto** *adj.*, **-uto** *adj.* muscular, sinewy, strong; sturdy, robust; vigorous.

nereggiare [A 3 c] and derivs. See under **nero**.

nere·ide *f.* (myth.) nereid, sea-nymph; *pl.* (zool.) rag-worms, nereids.

Nerina *pr.n.f.* Nerina.

ner·o *adj.* black; — come il carbone, coal-black; — fumo, greyish black (cf. **nerofumo**); fumo —, black (dark) smoke; abito —, (men's) evening dress; Foresta Nera, Black Forest; il Mar Nero, the Black Sea; lettera -a, letter written on black-bordered writing-paper; l'aristocrazia -a, the Papal aristocracy; (art) terra -a, dark ochre (cf. **verdaccio**); poncino —, punch with coffee; (joc.) bocca -a, firearm, pistol; (bot.) pioppo —, black poplar, *Populus nigra*; (eccl.) giorni -i, fasting days; (eccl. hist.) giorni tutti -i, days of 'black fast'; (herald.) sable; (fig.) sad, gloomy, sombre, mournful; giornate -e, dark days; nuvole -e, dark clouds; umor —, sombre mood; veder tutto —, to have a gloomy outlook; aver pensieri -i, to have sombre thoughts, to be in the dumps; dark; le razze -e, the coloured races; pane —, brown bread; vino —, red wine; dirty; acqua -a, muddy water; mani -e, dirty hands; pozzo —, cesspool; wicked, evil, atrocious; black-hearted; sangue —, evil disposition; una calunnia -a, a dark calumny; -a ingratitudine, black ingratitude; envious, livid with envy; (slang) essere — dal ridere, to laugh one's head off; punto —, black mark, stain, spot (on reputation), drawback, danger, weak spot; angelo —, devil, demon; (provb.) non bisogna fare il diavolo più — che non è, the devil is not as black as he is painted; cronaca -a, crime column in a newspaper; farne delle -e, to do all kinds of wicked things; borsa -a, mercato —, black market; bestia -a, *bête noire*, pet abomination; *n.m.* black, the colour black; vestirsi di —, to dress in black, to wear mourning; chiesa parata a —, church draped in black; mostrare il — pel bianco, to make black equal white; metter il — sul bianco, to write, to sign, to put down in black and white; chiamare — il — e bianco il bianco, to call a spade a spade; (paint.) — di seppia, sepia; — d'avorio, ivory-black; disegnare a bianco e —, to be a black-and-white artist; (chem.) — animale, potash. **-acchiuolo** *adj.* (of complexion) dark. **-astro** *adj.* blackish. **-eggiante** *part. adj.* blackish, almost black; dark. **-eggiare** [A 3 c] *intr.* (*aux.* avere) to be blackish, to be almost black; to appear black, to appear dark; i monti -eggiavano di foreste, the mountains were black with forests; un punto -eggiava sull'orizzonte, a black dot was visible on the horizon; *tr.* to shade, to tint with black. **-ellino** *adj.* blackish; *n.m.* black spot, black mark. **-etto** *adj. dim.* dark, blackish; *n.m.* (typ.) bold type. **-ezza** *f.* blackness; darkness. **-icante** *part. adj.* blackish; almost black; dark. **-icare** [A 2 sc] *intr.* (*aux.* avere) to be blackish, to be almost black; to appear black. **-ic·cio** *adj.* blackish, fairly black. **-i·dola** *f.* (zool.) painted top shell, *Calliostoma zizyphinum*. **-igno** *adj.* blackish; on the dark side. **-ino** *adj.* dark, almost black. **-ofumo** *m.* carbon black, lamp black, gas black. **-ognolo** *adj.* blackish, almost black; dark. **-one** *adj. augm.* very black, pitch black; *n.m.* very dark person; *pr.n.m.* see **Nerone** as separate heading. **-ume** *m.* black, blackness; smut; soot; black things, black stuff; black stains, black spots.

ne·roli *m.pl.* neroli oil.

Neron·e *pr.n.m.* (Rom. hist.) Nero; (fig.) tyrant. †**-eggiare** *intr.* to be a tyrant, to tyrannize. †**-eri·a** *f.* tyranny. **-iano** *adj.* Neronian; cruel, licentious, tyrannical.

nerv·o *m.* (anat.) sinew; muscle; taglio che è tutto —, gristly piece of meat; nerve; *pl.* nerves; avere i -i, to be nervy, to be full of nerves, to be highly strung; tensione dei -i, nervous tension; avere i -i scoperti, to be in a highly nervous state; dare ai -i a, to get on the nerves of; il caffè dà ai -i, coffee stimulates the nervous system; attacco di -i, fit of nerves; urtare i -i, to cause a nervous shock; courage, strength, vigour; troncare i -i a, to take away the strength from, to sap the courage of; uomo tutto -i, strong, vigorous man; (mil.) core of a unit; support; (mus.) string (of musical instrument); (bot.) vein; (archit.) rib (of vault); (aeron.) secondary structure in air-frame; (vet.) *Dracunculus medinensis*, and other subcutaneous parasitic worms. **-ale** *adj.* (anat., med.) neural; nervine. **-atura** *f.* (med.) constitution; (ent.) vein (of a wing); (bot.) nervation; (archit.) ribbing (of a vault); (aeron.) rinforzo a -atura radiale, finger patch. **-eo** *adj.* (anat.) nervous, relating to the nerves. **-igno** *adj.* muscular, strong, robust,

nerv-o (*cont.*)

vigorous. **-ino** *m.* (med.) nervine, nerve-tonic; *adj.* nervine. **-olino** *m.* (anat.) nerve filament. **-osiṣmo** *m.* nervousness, excitability; nervous disorder; nervous disability. **-osità** *f.* nervous excitability, restlessness; (of style) vigour, tenseness; (techn.) snap (property of rubber, etc.). **-oso** *adj.* (anat.) sinewy; muscular; nervous; tensione -osa, nervous tension; excitable, temperamental; strong; vigorous, muscular, robust; *n.m.* (colloq.) nervousness; patire il -oso, to suffer from nerves; fit of nerves, fit of nervous irritation; mi fai venire il -oso, you get on my nerves. **-osaménte** *adv.* excitably; in a nervy manner; temperamentally; vigorously, strongly. †**-uto** *adj.* sinewy, muscular, robust, sturdy.

nesc-i *m.* fare da —, fare il —, to feign ignorance; to turn a deaf ear. **-iénte** *adj.* unknowing, unaware; ignorant. **-ienteménte** *adv.* unknowingly, unawares. **-iénza** *f.* ignorance (of a given fact). †**-io** *adj.* unknowing, ignorant.

†**ne·spilo** *m.* See nespolo, under nespola.

nes·pol-a *f.* (bot.) medlar, fruit of the medlar tree (cf. **nespolo**); (provb.) col tempo e con la paglia si maturano le -e, Rome was not built in a day; contraffare le -e, to sleep on straw; non mondar -e, to waste no time, to get on with the job; *excl.* -e!, good heavens!, good gracious!; blow; gli diede certe -e, he gave him a good buffeting. **-o** *m.* (bot.) medlar tree, *Medlar, Mespilus germanica*; — del Giappone, loquat, *Eriobotrya japonica*.

Nesso[1] *pr.n.m.* (Gk. myth.) Nessus; (myth. and fig.) la camicia di —, the shirt of Nessus.

nesso[2] *m.* connexion, link; — logico, logical connexion; nexus; (mus.) tie, ligature; (in handwriting) contraction, abbreviation; (leg.) — di causalità, relation of cause and effect (C.P.).

ness-uno *adj.* (terminates as *indef. art.* **uno**, q.v.) no; a nessun patto, by no means; in nessun luogo, nowhere; la -una utilità di, the uselessness of; none; ha qualche giornale? Nessuno, have you any papers? None; any; senza -una provocazione, without any provocation; *prn.* no one, nobody; — viene, non viene —, nobody is coming; — di voi, not one of you; non guardare in faccia a —, to be impartial; roba di —, common property; i figli di —, unwanted children; non esser —, to be a nobody; non c'è proprio —, there is really no one at all; anybody; c'è stato —?, has anybody been?; c'è un incomodo? —, is there any drawback? none. **-is·simo** *prn., adj. superl.* none whatever; not the slightest; no one at all.

nest-o *m.* (bot.) graft, scion (cf. **innesto**). **-a·ia** *f.*, **-a·io** *m.*, **-aiuola** *f.* nursery of young trees; (ichth.) fish-pond.

Ne·store *pr.n.m.* (Gk. lit.) Nestor; (fig.) 'grand old man'; wise old man; senior; doyen; il — dei medici italiani, the doyen of Italian physicians; (orn.) kea parrot, kaka parrot, *Nestor* spp.

nestorian-o *adj., n.m.* (eccl. hist.) Nestorian. **-iṣmo**, **-eṣimo** *m.* Nestorianism.

nete *f.* (mus.) nete (shortest string of Greek lyre).

neto *m.* (bot.). See aneto.

nett-are[1] [A I c] *tr.* to clean; — i denti, to clean one's teeth; to wash; to cleanse; to clear; — la campagna, to sweep the countryside clear (of enemy forces); — il campo, to clear off, to abscond, to decamp; (fig.) — la propria coscienza, to relieve one's conscience; (mil.) to mop up (a battlefield, town, etc.); to sponge out (a gun); *intr.* (*aux.* avere) to decamp, to escape; †(naut.) see scopare; *rfl.* (*dat. of prn.* 'si') -arsi le mani, to wash one's hands; -arsi la bocca, to rinse one's mouth, (fig.) to be disappointed. **-adenti** *m. indecl.* metal toothpick; †tooth brush. **-aménto** *m.* cleaning; washing; cleansing; clearing. **-apénne** *m. indecl.* pen-wiper. **-apipa** *m. indecl.* pipe-cleaner. †**-ativo** *adj.* cleansing. **-ato** *part. adj.* cleaned; washed; cleansed; cleared, swept clear. **-atoia** *f.* (bldg.) mortar-board. **-atoio** *m.* cleaner, instrument for cleaning; cleaning material; detergent. **-atore** *m.* cleaner, person who cleans. (**-atrice** *f.*) **-atura** *f.* cleaning; washing; cleansing; clearing.

nett·are[2] *m.* nectar; sweet drink. **-a·reo** *adj.* nectarean; nectareous. **-a·rio** *m.* (bot.) nectary. **-aro·vie** *f.pl.* nectar guides.

nett-o *adj.* clean; foglio —, clean sheet; neat, whole; farla -a, levarla -a, to bring it off nicely, to succeed; (fig.) troncare una cosa con un colpo —, to make a clean break with something, to break something off finally; uscirne —, to come out unscathed; aver -a la vittoria, to win a complete victory; clear, distinct, profilo —, clear-cut profile; contorni -i, clear-cut edges, clean outline; exact, precise; un anno —, exactly a year; significato —, exact significance; (of space, ground, etc.) free, unencumbered; (naut.) mare —, clear waters; porto —, clear harbour (i.e. free from navigational dangers or from pirates, etc.); — di colpa, guiltless, blameless; good, honest, upright; menare una vita -a, to lead an honest life; pure, unadulterated; farina -a, pure flour; (leg.) fede -a, good conduct; (naut.) patente —, clean bill of health (also fig.); (comm.) net; — di spese, free of charge; peso —, net weight; rendita -a, net income; importo —, net amount; guadagno —, utile —, net profit; — di dazio, free of duty, duty-free; *adv.* suddenly, at once; dire chiaro e —, to make it quite clear and plain; giocare —, to play fair; di —, completely, clearly, cleanly; la macchina gli portò via un dito di —, the machine cut his finger clean off; *n.m.* clear part; clean or distinct section; mettere al —, to make a fair copy of; cavare il — di un discorso, to grasp the essential argument of a speech; (comm.) al —, after deducting tax, charges and discount; (archit.) height of a column (without base or capital); *apocop. part.* of nettare[1], q.v.; *adj.* cleaned; cleansed, cleared. **-aménte** *adv.* cleanly; neatly; clearly, distinctly; honestly, openly; precisely, exactly, freely. **-ézza** *f.* cleanness, cleanliness; la -ezza urbana, municipal department concerned with the removal of rubbish, sweeping of streets, etc.; niceness, precision, exactness; clarity; neatness; purity, brightness.

Nett-uno *pr.n.m.* (Rom. myth.) Neptune; (fig.) the sea; statue of Neptune; (astron.) Neptune. **-uniano** *adj.* of Neptune; relating to Neptune; Neptune-like; (geol.) Neptunian. **-u·nico** *adj.* (geol.) Neptunian. **-u·nio** *adj.* (myth.) Neptunian. **-uniṣmo** *m.* (geol.) Neptunism.

ne·um-a *f.* (mus.) neum, neume. **-a·tico** *adj.* (mus.) neumatic.

neur-algi-a *f.* (med.) neuralgia. **-al·gico** *adj.* neuralgic. **-asse** *m.* (anat.) neuraxis; (zool.) central nervous system. **-asteni·a** *f.* (med.) neurasthenia. **-aste·nico** *adj.* (med.) neurasthenic; *n.m.* neurasthenic subject. **-ectomi·a** *f.* (surg.) neurectomy. **-ina** *f.* (anat.) neurine. **-ite** *f.* (med.) neuritis. **-o·liṣi** *f.* neurolysis. **-ologi·a** *f.* neurology. **-oma** *m.* neuroma. **-one** *m.* neuron, nerve cell. **-o·nia** *f.* (ent.) *Neuronia popularis*, a caterpillar infesting poplar trees. **-opati·a** *f.* neuropathy, nervous disease. **-opatologi·a** *f.* neuropathology. **-oṣi** *f.* (med.; psych.) neurosis. †**-ospasto** *m.* marionette. **-o·tico** *adj.* neurotic. **-otomi·a** *f.* (surg.) neurotomy. **-ot·teri** *m.pl.* (ent.) Neuroptera.

neustri·a *f.* (ent.) lappet moth, *Gastropacha neustria*.

neutonianiṣmo *m.* See niutonianismo.

ne·utr-o *adj.* neuter; (gramm.) nome —, neuter noun; verbi -i, intransitive verbs, verbs neither active nor passive; (bot.) fiore —, sterile flower; (of territory, state, etc.) neutral; zona -a, neutral zone; indefinite, vague, indeterminate; tinta -a, neutral tint; in busta -a, in a plain envelope, under plain cover; *n.m.* (gramm.) il —, the neuter gender; (biol.) neuter; (ent.) sterile worker (of ants, bees, etc.); *m.pl.* subjects of neutral state, neutrals. **-ale** *adj.* neutral; restar -ale, to remain neutral; (chem.) neutral; *n.m.* neutral State; neutral person. **-alménte** *adv.* neutrally; (gramm.) in the neuter; (of a verb) intransitively. **-aliṣmo** *m.* policy of non-intervention. **-alista** *m., f.* partisan of neutrality. **-alità** *f.* neutrality; -alità armata, armed neutrality; -alità assoluta, complete, strict or impartial neutrality; -alità condizionale, conditional neutrality; (chem.) neutrality. **-aliẓẓare** [A I] *tr.* to neutralize, to exclude from sphere of hostilities; to counter-balance, to render ineffective; (chem.) to neutralize. **-aliẓẓazione** *f.* neutralization. **-one** *m.* (phys.) neutron.

nev-e *f.* snow; campo di —, snowfield; stivali da —, snow-boots; fare alla —, to play at snowballing; spalare la —, to shovel away the snow; palla di —, snowball; sott'acqua fame, e sotto — pane, rain spoils the crops but snow will be followed by a good harvest; coperto di —, snow-capped (of a mountain); -i persistenti, -i perpetue, perpetual snows; valanga di —, avalanche of snow; fiocco di —, snowflake; bufera di —, snowstorm; (geog.) limite delle -i, snow-line; Montagne della Neve, Sneeuw Geberge, Nassau Mts; (bot.) -rossa, red snow (coloured by the alga, *Sphaerella nivalis*); (eccl.) la Madonna della —, Our Lady of the Snow; (fig.) bitter cold; snowy whiteness; collo di —, snow-white neck; la — dei capelli, snow-white hair. **-a·ia** *f.*, **-a·io** *m.* heavy snowfall; snow-drift; snowfield, glacier. †**-ale** *adj.* snowy. †**-are** *vb.* and derivs. see nevicare. **-ata** *f.* fall of snow, snowfall. **-ato** *adj.* snow-white; snow-covered; (of water, drinks, etc.) iced; *n.m.* snowdrift;

nev·e (*cont.*)

glacier; (geog.) nevé. **-icare** [A2sc] *impers.* (*aux.* essere, avere) to snow; (fig.) mi è -icato sui capelli, my hair is turning white; (provb.) non -ica tutto l'inverno, bad luck cannot last forever; *tr.* (fig.) to shower, to pour; — lettere sopra uno, to shower someone with letters. **-icamento** *m.* snowing; (fig.) showering, pouring. **-icata** *f.* snowstorm; fall of snow, snowfall. **-icato** *adj.* snowy, snow-covered. **†-icoso** *adj.* snowy. **-i·schio** *m.* sleet; very fine wind-driven snow. **-osità** *f. indecl.* snowiness; snowy whiteness, shining whiteness. **-oso** *adj.* snowy; snow-capped; snow-covered; snow-white; *pr.n.m.* Nivose, fourth month of French Revolutionary year.

†nevo *m.* slight defect; little fault; peccadillo.

nevr-algi·a *f.* (med.) neuralgia. **-al·gico** *adj.* neuralgic. **-asteni·a** *f.* neurasthenia. **-aste·nico** *adj.* neurasthenic; *n.m.* (fig. of excitable or ill-tempered person) hopeless case; lascialo stare, è un —, leave him alone, he needs a psychologist. **-ite** *f.* neuritis. **-oṣi** *f. indecl.* neurosis. **-o·tico** *adj.* neurotic. **-otomi·a** *f.* neurotomy. **-ot·tero** *m.* (ent.) see **neurottero**.

nevvero *excl.* isn't that so?; isn't it?

newtonianiṣmo *m.* See **niutonianismo**.

†nezza *f.* niece.

Niassa *pr.n.f.* (geog.) Nyasa (Lake); Terra di —, Nyasaland.

nib·bio *m.* (orn.) kite; — bruno, black kite, *Milvus migrans*; — maggiore, red kite, *M. milvus*; — nero, black kite; — reale, red kite; **†**dir come il —, to cry 'mio'; **†**nuovo —, fool.

Nibelunghi *pr.n.m.pl.* Nibelungs.

nicchese *adv.* (mil. slang, 1915–18) nix!

nic·chi·a *f.* (zool.) shell; (archit.) niche; corner, hole, recess; nascosto in qualche —, hidden away; (biol.) niche; (fig.) niche, occupation, job, place; trovare una — adatta, to find a suitable niche, to find the right groove; (geog.) recess, hollow; — di nivazione, frost hollow, nivation hollow; **†**(naut.) see **cuccetta**; (mil. hist.) look-out post on the walls of a fort. **-are** [A4] *intr.* (*aux.* avere) to hesitate, to waver; to grumble, to complain; to moan; to groan, to creak; *rfl.* to withdraw oneself, to hide oneself away, to retire into one's shell. **-eri·a** *f.* collection of shells.

nic·chio *m.* (zool.) shell of a snail; farsi un —, to crouch, to curl up, to huddle; non valere un —, to be worth nothing; (eccl.) priest's three-cornered hat; (archaeol.) three-cornered earthenware lamp.

nic·cio *m.* See **neccio**.

niccolite *f.* (miner.) niccolite, nickelin, arsenic nickel.

Niccolò[1] *pr.n.m.* Nicholas; o Cesare o — (corruption of 'aut Caesar aut nihil'), all or nothing.

†nic·colo[2]. See **nichel**.

Nic-e·a *pr.n.f.* (geog.) Nicæa. **-eno** *adj.* Nicene, Nicæan.

nich·el, **-e·lio** *m.* (chem.; metall.) nickel. **-el(l)are** [A1, A1s] *tr.* to nickel, to coat with nickel, to nickel-plate. **-el(l)atura** *f.* nickel-plating. **-eli·fero** *adj.* (miner.) nickeliferous. **-elina**, **-elite** *f.* (miner.) niccolite.

nicheri *m.pl.* (bot.) nicar bean, *Caesalpinia bonducella*.

nichil-iṣmo *m.* (philos.) nihilism; (rel.) Buddhist Nirvana; (fig.) negative outlook, rejection of current beliefs; (hist.) Russian nineteenth-century nihilism. **-ista** *m.* nihilist.

†nichilo *m.* nothing, nihil.

Nicodemo *pr.n.m.* Nicodemus; the Wandering Jew; ci vorrebbe le tanaglie di — per spremerne un soldo, it would take an extortioner to get a penny from him.

Nicope·ia *pr.n.f.* Nicopoia ('Victory-Giver'), Greek title of the B.V.M., used esp. of the Byzantine icon in St Mark's, Venice.

nicotin-a *f.* nicotine. **-iṣmo** *m.* (med.) nicotinism, nicotine poisoning.

nicoziana *f.* (bot.) Nicotiana, the tobacco plant (so-called from Jacques Nicot who introduced tobacco into France in 1560); a genus of plants (chiefly American) to which the tobacco-plant belongs.

nict-alopi·a *f.* (med.) nyctalopia, day blindness. **-a·lope**, **-a·lopo** *adj.* (med.) nyctalopic; *n.m.* nyctalops. **-itro·pico** *adj.* (bot.) nyctitropic. **-ofobi·a** *f.* nyctophobia, dread of the dark.

†nida *f.pl.* of **nido**, q.v.

nid-o *m.* nest; roost; (provb.) ad ogni uccello il suo —è bello, there's no place like home; uccello di —, nestling; — di vespe, wasps' nest; — aerio, eyrie; — di rondine, swallow's nest, (cul.) chocolate bird's nest; far —, to nest, to settle; brood; swarm; den, lair; — di briganti, robbers' den; (fig.) home, shelter, lodging; abbandonare il —, to leave the nest; farsi il proprio —, to make one's

home; esser di cattivo —, to be cunning, to be crafty; country, native land; bed; wartime school or nursery for the children of those on active service; — di polvere, dust-trap; (needle-w.) punto a — d'ape, honeycomb stitch; (bot.) — di uccello, bird's nest orchid, *Neottia nidus-avis*; (astron.) — di Leda, Gemini, the Twins. **-iace** *adj.* unfledged; (of baby hawk or falcon) taken from the nest to be trained; *n.m.* fledgling, nestling. **-ian·dolo** *m.* nest-egg. **-iata** *f.* brood of nestlings, hatch; -iata di topolini, litter of baby mice; -iata di bambini, brood of children; swarm, crew, set; una -iata di scrittorelli, a collection of scribblers. **-ificare** [A2s] *intr.* (*aux.* avere) to build a nest; to nidificate, to nidify; (fig.) to make oneself at home. **-ificazione** *f.* nest-building, nidification.

†nidore *m.* rotten smell, smell of bad eggs.

nie·go *m.* (*pl.* **-ghi**) denial; mettersi al —, stare sul —, to persist in denying; refusal.

niell-o *m.* (art) niello, a black composition consisting of metallic alloys for filling in engraved designs on silver or other metals; ornamental work in niello; lavorare di —, to work in niello. **-are** [A1] *tr.* to inlay with niello, to niello; *intr.* (*aux.* avere) to work in niello. **-ato** *part. adj.* nielloed, inlaid with niello; *n.m.* piece of niello work. **-atura** *f.* niello work.

nient-e *prn. indef.* nothing; non fa —, he doesn't do anything, *or* it does not matter; — di grave, nothing serious; tornare a —, finire in —, to come to nothing; il far —, leisure, idleness; il dolce far —, sweet idleness; avere una cosa per —, to get something for nothing; tenere a —, to think nothing of; chi — osa — ottiene, nothing venture nothing have; un bel —, — affatto, — di —, nothing at all, absolutely nothing; — meno, — di meno, **†**none the less, **†**nevertheless; ha finito poi con lo sposare — meno che la cuoca, he ended up by marrying his cook, believe it or not; — meno!, you don't say so!; non ho — in contrario, I have nothing against it; fare finta di —, to pretend not to know (not to mind, not to see, etc.), to pretend nothing is up; — di male!, there is no harm done!; un —, a trifle, a mere nothing; nothingness, nullity; dopo questo c'è il —, after this life will come the void; littleness, unimportance; riconosco il mio —, I recognize my own nothingness; poverty; venire su dal —, to rise from nothing; (in interrog., conditional or quasi-neg. phrases) anything; se ti occorre —, if you want anything; come —, as easy as anything; se nient'è, if there is any occasion; è successo —?, has anything happened; non per —, not at all; non sono per — persuaso, I am by no means persuaded; non ci andrei per —, I would not go there for anything; *adv.* in no way, certainly not, by no means; non ci credo —, I don't believe a word of it; — —, at all, the least bit; se ci pensa — —, capirà, if he gives it the slightest thought he will understand; *adj. indecl.* no; — scuse, no apologies; — paura!, never fear!; non avere — utilità, to be quite useless; da —, unimportant; un uomo da —, a nonentity, a nobody. **-edimanco**, **-edimeno** *adv.* none the less, nevertheless, notwithstanding; no less; neither more nor less; in fact, really; *excl.* no!; really?

Nietzscheniṣmo *pr.n.m.* (philos.) Nietzscheanism.

†nieve *f.* See **neve**.

†nievo *m.* See **nipote**.

niffo, **nif·folo** *m.* snout of a pig.

nigella *f.* (bot.) love-in-the-mist, *Nigella damascena*.

†nigrigen-te *adj.*, **†-za** *f.* See **negligen-te**, **-za**.

†nigro *adj.* See **nero**.

†nigromante *adj.* and derivs. See **negromante**.

nigr-o·metro *m.* (techn.) nigrometer. **-ome·trico** *adj.* nigrometric; valore -ometrico, nigrometer reading.

†nigrore *m.* darkness, obscurity.

nigrosina *f.* (dyeing) nigrosine.

Nil-o *pr.n.m.* (geog.) Nile; il — azzurro, the Blue Nile; il — bianco, the White Nile. **-o·metro** *m.* Nilometer, graduated pillar showing height to which the Nile rises. **-o·tico** *adj.* Nilotic; *n.m.pl.* (anthropol.) Nilotics.

nimb-o *m.* flash of light; bright light; halo, aureole; (archaeol.) gold band on forehead worn by women; (herald.) nimbus, halo; (meteor.) see **nembo**. **-ato** *adj.* haloed, nimbused. **-oso** *adj.* stormy, tempestuous; cloudy; cloud-covered. **-ostrato** *m.* (meteor.) nimbostratus.

Nimega *pr.n.f.* (geog.) Nijmegen.

nimic-i·zia *f.* see **inimicizia**. **-o** *m.* see **nemico**.

†**ni·mi·o** *adj.* excessive; too great; superabundant. †**-età** *f.* excess; superabundance.

†**nimist-à**, †**-ade**, †**-anza** *f.* enmity, hostility.

†**nimo** *m.* no one, nobody; *adj.* in — loco, nowhere.

Nina *pr.n.f.* Nina (abbrev. of **Giovannina**, or of **Carina**).

ninf-a *f.* nymph; (fig.) young girl; sweetheart, beloved lady; (ent.) nymph, chrysalis, *pl.* (anat.) nymphae, labia minora. **-ale** *adj.* of nymphs, of a nymph; alla -ale, in the manner of nymphs; nymphean, nymphish, nymph-like; *n.m.* (mus.) portative organ, regal; poem or story about nymphs. **-e·a** *f.* (bot.) white water lily, *Nymphaea alba.* **-eggiare** [A 3 c] *intr.* (*aux.* avere) to behave in an affected manner, to adopt a mincing manner. **-e·o** *m.* (class. antiq.) nymphaeum; sanctuary of the nymphs with fountain, etc.; bathing-pool; (fig.) pleasant watering-place, swimming baths. **-omani·a** *f.* (med.) nymphomania.

nin·folo *m.* (vet.) slaughterhouse; term for the hard palate and lower part of the muzzle of an ox; †mug, ugly face; †proboscis.

ninn-a *f.* baby girl; (fam.) bye-byes. **-a·ia** *f.* affected woman. **-ananna** *f.* lullaby; fare la -ananna a, to sing a lullaby to, to sing to sleep. **-are** [A I] *tr.* to sing to sleep; to lull; to rock to sleep; (fig., iron.) to placate, to humour; -arla, -arsela, stare a -are, to be undecided, to vacillate. **-o** *m.* baby boy; toy, trifle, trinket; †coin; *pl.* baby boys; trinkets; †money. **-olare** [A I s] *tr.* to amuse, to play with; *intr.* (*aux.* avere), *rfl.* to amuse oneself, to play about.

nin·nol-o *m.* toy, plaything; trifle; trinket; knick-knack; abbigliarsi con -i, to dress oneself up in frippery; skinny person, slight person; -i e nannoli, odds and ends, bits and pieces. **-one** *m.* playboy, trifler. **(-ona** *f.*)

Nin-o *pr.n.m.* Nino; term of affection, especially for babies; — mio, my pet, my little one, my love.

Ni·ob-e *pr.n.f.* (myth.) Niobe; (art) la sala della —, the Niobe room in the Uffizi Gallery.

nio·bico *adj.* (chem.) columbic.

nio·bidi *m.pl.* (myth.) children of Niobe.

nio·b-io *m.* (chem.) columbium; niobium. **-ato** *m.* (chem.) columbate. **-ite** *f.* (miner.) niobite, columbite. **-o** *m.* see **niobio**.

nipitella *f.* (bot.). See **nepitella**.

nip-ote *m.*, *f.* nephew; niece; grandson; granddaughter; grandchild; — cugino, cousin's child, first cousin once removed; *pl.* descendants; i -oti d'Adamo. the sons of Adam, the human race; progeny; issue; (leg.) nephews and nieces (C.P.); †tendril. **-otame** *m.*, **-oteri·a** *f.* crowd of nephews and nieces; crowd of grandchildren. **-otismo** *m.*, **-otista** *m.* see **nepot-ismo**, **-ista**.

†**nipotente** *adj.* See **onnipotente**.

nipp-o·filo *adj.* pro-Japanese. **-o·nico** *adj.* Japanese.

†**niquit-à**, †**-oso** *adj.* See **iniquit-à**, **-oso**.

Nirvana *pr.n.m.* Nirvana; beatitude in the Buddhist tradition; (fig.) tranquil state of a mind untouched by worldly desires.

†**Nisa** *pr.n.f.* (geog.) river Neisse.

nisba *excl.*, *adv.* (slang, Rome) nix!

†**niscon·dere** *vb.* and derivs. See **nascondere**.

nisi[1] *f.* (bot.) tupelo gum, *Nyssa aquatica.*

nisi[2] *conj.* (Lat.) nisi, unless.

†**niso** *m.* (poet.) falcon; bird of prey.

Nissa *pr.n.f.* (geog.) Nis, Nisch.

nistagmo *m.* (med.) nystagmus.

†**nitente** *adj.* resplendent; shining, bright.

ni·tid-o *adj.* bright, shining; clear, translucent; lucid; distinct, orderly, neat, precise; (photog., etc.) sharp. **-amente** *adv.* brightly; clearly, translucently; lucidly; distinctly. **-ezza** *f.* brightness; clearness, translucence; lucidity; distinctness, clarity, orderliness, precision; (photog.) definition; sharpness.

niton *m. indecl.* (chem.) radon, niton.

nitore *m.* (poet.) brightness, luminosity; translucence.

nitr-are [A I] *tr.* (chem.) to nitrate. **-ato** *part. adj.* (chem.) nitrated; *n.m.* (chem.) nitrate. **-azione** *f.* (chem.) nitration.

ni·trico *adj.* (chem.) nitric.

nitr-ire [D 2] *intr.* (*aux.* avere) to neigh; to whinny. **-ente** *part. adj.* neighing; whinnying. **-ito** *m.* neigh; neighing; whinny; whinnying.

nitr-o *m.* (miner.) nitre, saltpetre. **-a·gine** *f.* (agric.) addition of *Bacillus radicicola* to chemical manures. **-a·ia** *f.* (geol.) nitre bed. **-atina** *f.* (miner.) saltpetre. **-ato** *m.* (chem.) nitrate. **-ile** *m.* (chem.) nitrile, organic cyanide. **-ito** *m.* (chem.) nitrite. **-oa·mido** *m.* (chem.) nitrostarch. **-obatteri** *m.pl.* nitrobacteria. **-obenzene** *m.*, **-obenzina** *f.*, **-obenzolo** *m.* (chem.) nitrobenzene, oil of mirbane.

-ocellulosa *f.* nitrocellulose. **-ocotone** *m.* gun-cotton. **-oglicerina** *f.* (chem.) nitroglycerine. **-o·metro** *m.* (chem.; techn.) nitrometer. **-oprussiato** *m.* nitroprusside, nitroferricyanide. **-oprus·sico** *adj.* nitroprussic. **-oso** *adj.* (chem.) nitrous. **-uro** *m.* (chem.) nitride. **-urare** [A I] *tr.* (metall.) to nitride, to ammonia harden. **-urato** *part. adj.* acciaio -urato, nitrided steel. **-urazione** *f.* (metall.) nitriding, ammonia hardening.

nitt-a·lope, **-a·lopo** *adj.*, *n.m.* See **nictalop-e**, **-o**, under **nictalopia**.

nitticora *m.* (orn.) night heron, *Nycticorax nycticorax.*

nittitante *adj.* (orn.) membrana —, nictitating membrane; (med.) spasmo —, spasmus nictitans.

niuno *adj.*, *n.m.* See **nessuno**.

niutonian-ismo *m.* Newtonianism, the Newtonian system. **-o** *adj.* Newtonian.

niv-ale *adj.* (poet.) snowy. **-e·o** *adj.* snow-white; snowy.

Nizz-a[1] *pr.n.f.* (geog.) Nice (France); Nizza Monferrato (Piedmont). **-ardo** *adj.* of Nice; dialetto -ardo, Provençal; *n.m.* inhabitant or native of Nice. **-arda** *f.* woman of Nice; lady's straw hat with wide brim; kind of country dance.

†**nizza**[2] *f.* low cart with large wheels used for conveying marble from quarries.

†**nizza**[3] *f.* press, crowd, congestion.

†**nizza**[4] *f.* a little tongue-shaped slip of paper tucked into a flap to seal a letter.

nizz-olo, **-urro** *m.* (zool.). See **nocciolino**.

no *neg. particle* no; — certo!, certainly not!; — e poi —, a thousand times no; come —?, of course, most certainly; rispondere di —, to reply in the negative, to say 'no'; gli chiesi se mi avesse riconosciuto, e disse di —, I asked him if he had recognized me, and he said he hadn't; credo di —, I don't think so, I think not; non dico di —, I shan't say no; verrete, —?, you'll come, won't you?; pare di —, it seems otherwise; fare di —, accennare di —, fare cenno di —, to shake one's head (in disagreement or refusal), to make a gesture meaning 'no' (pointing the index finger of the right hand upwards and moving it horizontally from left to right and from right to left); lo vuoi sì o —?, do you want it, yes or no?; or sì or —, intermittently; più sì che —, more or less, rather, pretty well; ci credeva più sì che —, he just about believed it; era felice sì e —, happy? well, he was and he wasn't; ma questo —, non si capisce, but this, this is quite incomprehensible; not; perchè —?, come —?, why not?; —, perchè —, why not, because I say not; chi lo loda, chi —, some praise him, some do not; se —, if not, otherwise; e se —?, and what if I don't, and what if it isn't, etc.; se mi piace lo compro e se —, —, if I like it I'll buy it and if not I shan't; bello o —, mi piace, pretty or not, I like it; forse sì, forse —, perhaps so, perhaps not; anzi che —, rather; mi pare strano anzi che —, it seems rather strange to me; *n.m. indecl.* the answer no; denial; refusal; un — chiaro e tondo, a flat refusal; essere tra il sì e il —, to be undecided one way or the other; *pl.* i —, the noes; i — sono in maggioranza, the noes have it; †see **non**.

no' *prn.* See **noi**.

†**noarese** *adj.*, *n.m.*, *f.* See **novarese**.

no·bil-e *adj.* (sometimes abbrev. to **nobil** before a noun) noble; elevated; illustrious; magnanimous, generous; fine, admirable, excellent; worthy, dignified; vivere nella povertà —, to live in virtuous poverty; si diede a più -i studi, he applied himself to loftier studies; of noble birth; nobil Donna, for the use of this title see under **Donna**; (theatr.) padre —, heavy father; nobil uomo, gentleman; (eccl.) guardia —, Noble Guard; il nobil animale, the horse; splendid, magnificent, stately, imposing; (archit.) piano —, first floor (often over an entresol, and esp. in seventeenth- and eighteenth-century palaces, where it is most magnificent); precious, rare; metalli -i, precious metals; (chem.) gas, noble gas, rare inert gas; *n.m.* nobleman; il ceto dei -i, the nobility; — spiantato, distressed nobleman; †(naut.) — di poppa, apprentice; †— di artiglieria, gunnery officer of a galley; †— di galera, officer or captain of a Venetian galley; (poet.) il —, the lion (in medieval narrative verse about animals); a kind of snuff; (numism.) Bolognese coin. **-ac·cio** *m. pejor.* wicked baron. **-e·a** *f.* (derog.) the aristocracy, the nobility; pretensions to noble status. **-esco** *adj.* (*m.pl.* **-eschi**) (derog.) of the nobility. †**-ezza** *f.* see **nobiltà**. **-iare** *adj.* nobiliary, of the nobility; almanacco -iare, peerage, book containing list of nobles. **-ità** *f.* see **nobiltà**. **-itare** [A I s] *tr.* to ennoble, to confer nobility upon; (fig.) to ennoble; il lavoro -ita l'uomo, man is ennobled by work; *rfl.* to be

nobil-e (*cont.*)
ennobled; to make oneself illustrious, to distinguish oneself. (**-itaménto** *m.*) **-itato** *part. adj.* ennobled; raised to the rank of a noble; †notorious. **-itatore** *m.* ennobler; *adj.* ennobling (**-itatrice** *f.*) **-itazione** *f.* ennoblement. **-ménte** *adv.* nobly, illustriously; magnanimously, generously; admirably; worthily, virtuously; loftily; magnificently, splendidly; richly, in lordly style. **-tà** *f.* nobility; excellence, illustriousness, distinction; magnanimity, generosity; magnificence, splendour, lordliness; noble rank; la -tà, the nobility, the aristocracy. **-ume** *m.* (derog.) crowd of nobles.

noc·ca *f.* (*pl.* **-che**, **-ca**) (anat.) joint connecting fingers to the hand, and toes to the foot; knuckle; dar delle -che a, to punch; (bot.) spike-rush, *Eleocharis palustris*; (vet.) see **nodello**. **-chino** *m.* blow with knuckles. **-coluto** *adj.* having large knuckles.

noc·chia *f.* (bot.) hazel nut still green.

nocchier-e *m.* (poet.) boatman, pilot; oarsman; †(naut.) master. **-o** *m.* (naut.) coxswain; see **nostromo**.

nocchino *m.* See under **nocca**.

noc·chi-o *m.* (timber) heartwood; (bot.) knot (in wood); (anat.) vertebra. **-eroso** *adj.* (of wood) knotty, full of knots. **-eruto** *adj.* knotted. **-oluto** *adj.* knotted. **-oroso** *adj.* knotty, full of knots. **-oruto**, **-uto** *adj.* knotted. **-oso** *adj.* strong, muscular; (of muscles) knotty.

nocciol-a *f.* (bot.) hazel nut, cob nut, fruit of the hazel tree, **nocciolo**[1], *q.v.*; color —, hazel-coloured. **-a·ia** *f.* (orn.) nutcracker, *Nucifraga caryocatactes*. **-a·io** *m.* nut-seller, nut-vendor. **-ine** *f.pl.* (cul.) 'pasta' for soup made into pieces shaped like half nutshells; -ine americane, peanuts, monkey nuts, *Arachis hypogaea*.

nocciolino[1] *m.* (zool.) dormouse, *Muscardinus avellanarius*.

nocciolino[2] *m. dim.* See under **nocciolo**[3].

nocciolo[1] *m.* (bot.) hazel, *Corylus Avellana*.

nocciolo[2] *m.* (ichth.) smooth hound, *Mustelus canis*.

noc·ciol-o[3] *m.* (bot.) stone (of fruit); (fig., of two intimate friends) due anime in un —, twin souls; non valere un —, to be worth nothing; non vale un —, it is not worth a fig; il — della questione, the kernel of the question; la pesca avrà il —, the matter will come to an end; del bariletto, barrel core; *pl.* children's game with peach-stones; giuocare a -i, (fig.) to play without staking money; nucleus. **-ino** *m.* children's game with peach-stones.

nocciuola *f.* and derivs. See **nocciola**.

nocciuolo *m.* See **nocciolo**[1].

Nocco *pr.n.m.* (provb.) qui giace Nocco, here is the point, there's the rub.

noc·cola *f.* See **nocca**.

noc-e *m.* (bot.) walnut tree, *Juglans regia*; — d'India, coconut, *Cocos nucifera*; — vomica, nux vomica, *Strychnos nux-vomica*; — del Perù, Brazil nut, *Bertholtetia excelsa*; — di Betel, Betel nut, *Areca catechu*; — del cocco, coconut, *Cocos nucifera*; — moscado, — moscata, — mosca, nutmeg tree, *Myristica fragrans*; — di cola, cola, *Cola acuminata*; — puzza, — spinosa, thorn-apple, *Datura stramonium*; *f.* walnut; nut; walnut wood; tingere a —, to stain (wood) giving it the appearance of walnut wood; (cul.) una — di burro, a knob of butter; grande come un guscio di —, the size of a walnut; una — in un sacco non fa rumore, one person alone is not much use; sono quattro -i in un sacco, they are too few to be of any use; schiacciare le -i, to plant one's feet awkwardly; lasciarsi schiacciar le -i in capo, to let oneself be put upon, to submit to ill-treatment; chi ha le voci e chi le -i, those who talk most often do least; gente che non ci piglierei una — con sette gusci, people I wouldn't touch with a barge-pole; barattar le -i in coccole, to make a bad bargain; mangiare le -i col mallo, to ask for trouble; nut-shaped object; (text.) wharve; (mil.) hammer head of a scattergun; (mil. hist.) — della balestra, button holding the string of a balister or crossbow. **-ella** *f.* (anat.) lower head of the ulna; *pl.* children's game with peach-stones. **-eto** *m.* plantation of walnuts, walnut orchard, walnut grove. **-iaiuolo** *m.* walnut-seller. **-i·fero** *adj.* walnut-bearing. **-ino** *m.* a children's game in which they try to knock down little heaps of walnuts by throwing another walnut from a distance.

noc-ente *adj.* noxious, harmful; guilty; † see **innocente**. †**-enza** *f.* guilt. **-ere** [B 20] *tr.* see **nuocere**. **-évole** *adj.* harmful, hurtful; noxious, unwholesome. **-evolménte** *adv.* harmfully, hurtfully; noxiously. **-evolezza** *f.* harmfulness, hurtfulness; noxiousness, unwholesomeness. **-iuto** *part.* from **nuocere**, q.v. **-ivo** *adj.* harm-

ful, hurtful, injurious; noxious, unwholesome; (leg.) una sostanza velenosa o -iva, a poisonous or noxious substance (C.P.); *n.m.* harmful, unwholesome thing. **-ivaménte** *adv.* harmfully, hurtfully, injuriously, noxiously. **-uménto** *m.* injury, harm, damage; (fig.) detriment; senza -uménto a, without damage to, without detriment to. †**-u·o** *adj.* harmful.

nod-o *m.* knot; fare un — al naso, fare un — al fazzoletto, to tie a knot in one's handkerchief; cravatta a — da farsi, unmade-up tie; noose; farsi il — al collo, to put one's head into a noose; (naut., etc.) — di ancorotto, fisherman's bend; — d'anguille, running eyesplice; — di bolina, bowline; — di bozza, stopper; — dell'asino, — di ciuccio, — falso, slippery hitch, 'granny' knot; — comune, overhand knot; — di gancio, — di gancio semplice, hook knot, blackwall hitch; — di gancio con volta, double blackwall hitch; — di gancio a gruppo di scotta, midshipman's hitch; — di gancio a bocca di lupo, bale sling knot; — parlato semplice, clove hitch; — parlato doppio, rolling hitch; — piano, — marino, reef knot; — di garza, — della margherita, sheepshank; — di scotta, sheet bend; — doppio di scotta, double sheet bend; — vaccaio, see **intagliatura**; — volante, see **legatura**; — di Savoia, figure-of-eight knot (worn on the lapel of cadets at Nautical College or on cuff by volunteer reservists); — di gassa di amante semplice, bowline; — di gassa di amante doppio, double bowline; — di gassa di amante scorsoio, running bowline; — di mezzo collo, half hitch; — gassa a serraglio, timber hitch; knot (measure of speed); — di Salomone, cabalistic medieval design showing a knot without any ends to the cords being visible; tutti i -i vengono al pettine, sooner or later your sins will find you out; avere un — alla gola, to have a lump in one's throat; far — alla gola a uno, to stick in someone's throat; — di tosse, fit of coughing; (med.) — isterico, globus hystericus; problem, difficulty, puzzle; knotty situation; il — della questione, the crux of the matter; — da falegname, timber hitch; (theatr.) scioglimento del —, dénouement; bond, embrace, tie; — coniugale, marriage bond; — gordiano, Gordian knot; i -i della vita, the ties of the soul to the body; point of intersection; — ferroviario, railway junction; (geog.) — di monti, point where mountain ranges conjoin; (astron.) node, nodal point; — di vento, hurricane, whirlwind; -i di S. Giuseppe, -i di S. Marco, strong winds prevalent at the season of these festivals; — del cuculo, strong wind prevalent during the season when the cuckoo is heard; — d'acqua, whirlpool; (bot.) node; knot in wood; cercare il — nel giunco, to look for difficulties where there are none; (anat.) — del collo, nuchal crest, vertebra; bunion; excrescence; (archit.) — delle torri, projecting bands of stone, etc. encircling towers; (mil.) cadre; hardness of stone or metal; (theatr.) plot. **-ale** *adj.* (scient.) nodal. **-atura** *f.* (anat.) joint. **-ello** *m.* (anat.) articulation; (ent.) body segment of insects; (vet.) fetlock; (archit.) ring round the shaft of a column; (bot.) joint in a cane. **-eroso** *adj.* knotty, full of knots (also of wood); (herald.) raguly, ragged. **-eruto** *adj.* knotted; (of wood) covered with large knots. **-oruto** *adj.* see **noderuto**.

nodos-o *adj.* nodose; knotty, knotted; gnarled; (of wood) knotted, full of knots; †difficult; †harsh. (**-aménte** *adv.*) **-ità** *f.* knottiness, knottedness, nodosity; hardness of wood round a knot.

†**nodrire** *vb.* and derivs. See **nutrire**.

no·dulo *m.* nodule.

No-è *pr.n.m.* (Bibl.) Noah, Noë; vecchio quanto —, as old as the hills, as old as Methuselah; l'arca di —, Noah's ark. **-a·chide** *m.* descendant of Noah. **-e·tico** *adj.* of Noah; il diluvio -etico, the Flood.

noi *pers. prn.* we; — altri, we, we for our part (also **noialtri**); — altri Italiani facciamo così, we Italians do this; siamo —, it is we, it's us; tutto considerato, siamo —, after all, remember who we are; — si crede, we believe; — si felici, we are happy; also corresponding to English royal and editorial 'we'; us; emphatically, as direct object after the verb; volevano proprio —, it really was us they wanted; as indirect object after a *prep.*: a — lo disse, he said it to us; da —, among our people, in our country, at home; ora veniamo a —, now to come to our point; ourselves; non sembriamo più —, we no longer seem ourselves; — stessi, ourselves; *impers.* one; quando — siamo in punto di morte, when we are at the point of death; *excl.* (of encouragement) a —!, come on!, come along!; also *excl.* of crowd, corresponding to English: we want so-and-so!

no·ia *f.* tedium; ripetere sino alla —, to repeat *ad nauseam*; venire a —, to pall, to grow tedious; avere a —, recarsi a —, to find tedious, to be sick and tired of; boredom; ennui, mental weariness; dislike, aversion; avere a —, to dislike; prendere a —, to take a dislike to; venir a — a sè medesimo, to come to loathe oneself; trouble, annoyance; worry; dar — a, to annoy, to vex, to tease, to irritate on purpose; to get in the way of, to be a nuisance to; i grandi cappelli mi danno —, I find large hats a nuisance; (of thing or person) nuisance, trouble, bore; †sorrow, grief; †affliction.

noialtr-i, -e *prn.* See under **noi**.

noi-are [A4] *tr.* to trouble; to tease; to annoy; to bore; to weary; *rfl.* to be annoyed; to be bored; to get weary. **-aménto** *m.* boredom, tedium; annoyance, irritation. **-ato** *part. adj.* bored; annoyed; wearied; fed-up. (**-atóre** *m.* **-atrice** *f.*) †**-e·vole** *adj.* see **noioso**. **-osità** *f.* boringness, tedium; annoyingness. **-óso** *adj.* boring, tedious; annoying, irritating; troublesome. **-osa-ménte** *adv.* boringly; annoyingly.

noisette *adj. indecl.* (pron. as Fr.) hazel, hazel-coloured.

nol *contr.* of 'non lo'.

noleggiare [A3c] and derivs. See under **nolo**.

nolente *adv. phr.* volente o —, willy-nilly.

noli me tangere *m. indecl.* (art) picture of risen Christ with Mary Magdalene; (bot.) touch-me-not, *Impatiens noli-tangere*; sensitive plant, *Mimosa pudica*; (fig.) person or thing which must not be touched.

nol-o *m.* hire; prendere a —, to hire; dare a —, to let, to hire out; da —, for hire; price of hire, cost of hire; (naut.) charter, freight or fare; pigliare a —, to take on charter; — assegnato, freight unpaid. **-eggiare** [A3c] *tr.* to hire; to hire out, to let on hire; (naut.) to charter, to hire. **-eggiaménto** *m.* hiring. **-eggiante** *m.* (naut.) owner, lessor. **-eggiato** *part. adj.* hired; let; chartered. **-eggiatóre** *m.* hirer; (naut.) charterer. (**-eggiatrice** *f.*) **-éggio** *m.* hire; price of hire; shop which hires out cars, bicycles, etc.; freightage; **-éggio a tempo**, time charter; **-éggio a viaggio**, voyage charter; (naut.) charter; contratto di **-éggio**, charter party.

no·mad-e *adj.* nomad, nomadic; *n.m.* nomad, wanderer. **-ísmo** *m.* nomadism.

nomarca *m.* (hist.) nomarch, governor of one of the 36 regions of ancient Egypt; prefect of a province of modern Greece.

nóm-e *m.* name; di —, per —, by name; fare il —, to reveal one's name; prendere, avere — da, to be called after; chiamar le cose coi loro -i, to call a spade a spade; è un — venerato, it is a name held in great honour; nemici del — italiano, enemies of the name of Italy; cose senza —, indefinable things, unspeakable horrors; first name, Christian name; rifare un —, to hand down a Christian name; — e cognome, name and surname; surname, family name; si sposò per dare il — al figlio, she married to give the child a name; nickname; word, term; con — greco si dice democrazia, democracy is a Greek term; title; principe solo di —, a prince only in name; la virtù per lui era un — vano, virtue meant nothing to him; (comm.) mettere una partita a — di, to open an account in the name of; a — di dote, as dowry; — di ragazza, maiden name; sotto falso —, under an alias; godere buon —, to enjoy credit; reputation; avere cattivo —, to have a bad name; passare con — di erudito, to have a name for scholarship; farsi un —, acquistar —, to make a name for oneself; meaning; gli è ignoto il — di fede, he doesn't know the meaning of the word faith; noun; substantive; name-day; signature; dare il — a, to subscribe to, to support, to join; scrivere il — in tutte lettere, to subscribe fully; stampare un' opera senza —, to print a work anonymously; — di battaglia, *nom de guerre*, *nom de plume*, pseudonym; (mil.) password; dare il —, to give the password; prendere il —, to accept or take over the password; a — di, on behalf of, in the name of; in — di, for the sake of; (eccl.) — di religione, religious name, name in religion; (liturg.) — di Gesù, Feast of the Holy Name. †**-anza** *f.* reputation. †**-are** *tr.* to name; to call; to choose; to mention; to relate; *rfl.* to be named, to be called; to be renowned. †**-ato** *part. adj.* named; mentioned; determined, fixed; renowned; *n.m.* celebrated person. †**-atamente** *adv.* by name; individually. **-e·a** *f.* renown, reputation; notoriety. **-i·gnolo** *m.* nickname; pet-name. †**-o** *m.* (†*pl.f.* **-ora**) see **nome**.

nomenclat-óre *m.* (Rom. antiq.) nomenclator; (fig.) giver or inventor of names; †catalogue, glossary. **-ura** *f.* nomenclature, terminology; naming, art of naming.

no·min-a *f.* appointment, nomination; right of nominating for appointment; termini e condizioni di —, terms and conditions of appointment; †entrance ticket. **-a·bile** *adj.* eligible; mentionable. **-ale** *adj.* nominal; pertaining to a noun; definizione -ale, nominal definition; autorità puramente -ale, purely nominal authority; appello -ale, roll-call; votazione per appello -ale, (in Italian Parliament) voting in answer to a roll-call of members in alphabetical order; (comm.) valore -ale, nominal value; face value; (philos.) filosofi -ali, nominalists. **-alménte** *adv.* nominally. **-alísmo** *m.* (philos.) nominalism. **-alista** *m.* nominalist. **-ali·stico** *adj.* nominalist(ic). **-anza** *f.* renown, fame, reputation; glory; rea -anza, ill fame; †rumour, story; †account. **-are** [AIS] *tr.* to name; lo -arono Paolo, they named him Paul; to mention by name; mi son sentito -are, I heard my name mentioned; certe cose non si -ano tra le persone educate, certain things are not mentioned by nice people; to appoint; fu -ato presidente, he was elected president; -are una commissione, to appoint a committee; -are un esecutore, to appoint an executor; to propose for election, to nominate; to call; to term; non è da -are gentiluomo, he can't be called a gentleman; *rfl.* to be called; to be named; to appoint oneself. (**-ante** *part. adj.*) †**-ata** *f.* see **nominanza**. **-ato** *part. adj.* named; mentioned by name; sopra -ato, above mentioned; renowned, famous; elected, appointed; nominated, proposed for election; persona -ata, nominee. **-atamente** *adv.* by name; singly; particularly, individually. (**-atóre** *m.* **-atrice** *f.*) **-azióne** *f.* nomination; naming; mention; election, appointment; fame, renown, reputation.

nominativ-o *adj.* nominative; (gramm.) caso —, nominative case; nominating, able to nominate; relating to or consisting of names; stato —, list of names; ruolo — dei contribuenti, roll of contributors' names; titoli -i, registered securities; nota -a, nominal roll; *n.m.* (gramm.) nominative case; — assoluto, nominative absolute; (colloq.) name; mi ha dato un — sbagliato, he gave me the wrong name; (naut.) ship's pennants (numbers on code flags corresponding to ship's name); alzare il —, to hoist ship's pennants; fare il —, to make ship's pennants by morse or other signal. **-aménte** *adv.* by name, individually. **-ità** *f.* (leg.) -ità obbligatoria delle azioni, compulsory registration of shares (C.C.).

no·mine *m.* in — Patris, the Lat. liturg. formula, 'in the name of the Father'; (joc.) patire nel — Patris, to be weak in the head (in making the sign of the Cross, the forehead is touched as these words are said).

nomi·sma *m.* See **numisma**.

nomo-fílli *m.pl.* (bot.) ordinary green assimilating leaves. **-g·enèsi** *f.* (biol.) nomogenesis, orthogenesis. **-gramma** *m.* alignment chart.

nompari·glia *f.* (typ.). See **nonpariglia**, under **non**.

non *adv.* not. **1.** PRECEDING MAIN VERB: — so, I do not know; — posso, I cannot; — te lo direbbe, he would not tell you. **2.** PRECEDING NOUN, PRONOUN, ADJECTIVE OR ADVERB (with verb understood): tuo figlio lo fece, — io, your son did it, not I. **3.** FOLLOWED BY AN INFINITIVE: — sporgersi, do not lean out; — lo credere, do not believe it; cose da — credersi, unbelievable things; il — vedere, lack of sight, failure to see. **4.** FOLLOWED BY A NOUN OR ADJECTIVE (equivalent to English non-): il — intervento, non-intervention; è un — senso, it is nonsense; una — riuscita, a failure, a negative result; oggetti — visibili, invisible objects; — corrispondenza, lack of correspondence; (colloq.) dottore o — dottore, è un asino, doctor or no doctor, he's an ass; (philos.) l'io e il — io, I and not-I, ego and non-ego, self and non-self; il — essere, non-being; (leg.) il — luogo a procedere, nonsuit; ordinare la — menzione della condanna, to order no mention of conviction (C.P.). **5.** EMPHATIC IN THE FOLLOWING CONSTRUCTIONS: che — può un'alma ardita?, what can a fearless spirit not accomplish?; — hanno armi, — danari, — buon governo, they have no arms, no money, no good government; — per contraddirti, not that I wish to contradict you; può essere e può — essere, it may be and it may not be. **6.** PLEONASTIC IN THE FOLLOWING CONSTRUCTIONS: — appena lo vidi, as soon as I saw him; prima che — venne, before he came; finchè — venne, until he came; le gentilezze che — gli ho fatte!, the kindnesses I have done him!; poco mancò che — cadessi, I nearly fell; — più che — con altri, no more than with others; in men che — si dica, in a split second. **7.** PRECEDING NESSUNO, NIENTE, NULLA, MAI, ETC.: — ho visto nessuno, I have seen no one; — ci

non (*cont.*)

sono mai stato, I have never been there. **8.** AFTER VERBS EXPRESSING DOUBT, FEAR AND SUSPICION: dubito che — venga, I doubt whether he will come. **9.** IDIOMATIC USES: — pochi, not a few; — senza, not without; — altrimenti che, in the same way as; pregava — fossero uccisi, he prayed that they might not be killed; se —, except, apart from; — è se — un bugiardo, he's nothing but a liar; se — che, but, moreover; except; suona molto male se — che mai non si deve dirlo, he plays very badly only one must not say so; — ce n'era se — che d'acciaio, there were only steel ones there; — che, not only, not just; — che far fresco, fa freddo, it's not just cool, it's cold; — che, and, also; c'era lui, — che sua moglie, he was there and his wife as well; è proibito parlarne, — che scriverne, it is forbidden to speak of it, let alone write about it; — che, not that; — che me l'avessero detto, not that they had told me; — che altro, at least; — altro, that is all, no more; un — so che, a 'je ne sais quoi', a certain something; un — so che di bianco, an indefinable white object; — punto, — affatto, not at all; — mi piace affatto, I do not like it at all; — più, — meno, no more and no less; — ancora, not yet; — cale, it does not matter; porre in — cale, to neglect, to lay on one side; elides with lo to form nol: nol sa, he does not know it; †— solo, — tanto che..., not only, not so far from. **-curante** *adj.* careless, heedless; indifferent, unmoved, nonchalant; disdainful. **-curanza** *f.* carelessness, heedlessness; indifference, nonchalance; disdain. **-dimanco** *adv.* see **nondimeno**. **-dimeno** *adv.* nevertheless, however, all the same. **-dormire** *m.* sleeplessness. **-linearità** *f.* (telev.) non-linearity. **-nulla** *m.* a nothing, a mere nothing, trifle; un -nulla lo indispone, the least thing puts him out. **-ostante** *prep.* notwithstanding, in spite of; ciò -ostante, in spite of this; *adv.* nevertheless, however; -ostante che, although, in spite of the fact that. **-pari·glia** *m.* (typ.) nonpareil; †very narrow ribbon. **-pertanto** *adv.* nevertheless, all the same, notwithstanding. †**-possa** *f.* impotence. **-ti-scordar-di-me** *m. indecl.* (bot.) forget-me-not, *Myosotis palustris* and *M. pyrenaica*. **-usanza** *f.* non-usage. **-uso** *m.* non-use. **-volente** *adj.* unwilling, unconsenting.

non-a *f.* ninth (woman or thing); (liturg.) none; (mus.) ninth (interval); (med.) malattia della —, epidemic encephalitis; †fare le -e, sonare le -e, to refuse. **-agena·rio** *m.* nonagenarian. **-age·simo** *adj.* ninetieth. **-a·gono** *m.* (geom.) nonagon, enneagon. †**-a·rio** *adj.* ninefold. **-e** *f.pl.* (Rom. antiq.) Nones.

nonetto *m.* See under **nono**.

no·nio *m.* (math.) nonius, vernier, vernier scale.

nonn-o *m.* grandfather; grandpapa, grandpa; esser fatto —, to become a grandfather; i miei -i, my (four) grandparents; i nostri -i, our grandfathers, our ancestors; vivere con le idee del —, to have old-fashioned ideas, to be out of date. **-a** *f.* grandmother; grandma, granny; anche la mia -a, se non fosse morta sarebbe viva, if wishes were horses beggars would ride; (orn.) heron. **-otto** *m.* (orn.) little bittern, *Ixobrychus minutus*.

non-o *ord. num.* ninth; ninth span; ninth part. **-etto** *m.* (mus.) nonet. **-ode·cimo** *ord. num.* nineteenth.

nontiscordardime *m.* (bot.). See under **non-**.

no·nupl-o *adj.* ninefold; *n.m.* figure multiplied by nine.

nopal *m. indecl.* (bot.) cochineal cactus, *Nopalea coccinellifera*.

norcin-o *m.* native of Norcia, in Umbria; pork-butcher; swine-gelder; (fig.) clumsy surgeon; dirty person; clumsy writer. **-eri·a** *f.* pork-butcher's shop.

nord *m. indecl.* north; nord-est, north-east; nord-nord-est, north-north-east; il mare del —, the North Sea; il —, the North; proveniente dal —, coming from the North; il polo —, the North Pole.

nor·di-co *adj.* northern; gli stati -ci dell'America, the Northern States; Nordic; mitologia -ca, mythology of Nordic races; letteratura -ca antica, ancient Icelandic literature; (prosod.) ritmica -ca, 'Germanic' versification (based, as in *Piers Plowman*, on alliteration and a fixed number of stresses); *n.m.* northerner; Scandinavian, Northman.

no·rico *adj.* (geol.) Upper Trias; (geog.) inhabiting the east central regions of the Alps (from the ancient Roman province of Noricum).

Norimber-ga *pr.n.f.* (geog.) Nuremberg. **-ghese** *adj.* of Nuremberg; *n.m., f.* native or inhabitant of Nuremberg.

norm-a *f.* guide, standard, measure, norm; prendere — da, to take one's standard from; prendere a —, to take as a guiding principle, to take as a pattern, model, or example; tanto per vostra —, just for your information; questo vi serva di —, let this be an example to you; rule, regulation; (admin.; leg.) -e integrative, Statutory Rules; secondo le -e ora vigenti, according to the present regulations; — di vita, rule of life; attenersi a una —, to stick to a rule; fare tutto a — e a corda, to do everything exactly according to rule; di —, as a rule, normally; a —, according to, in conformity with; a — degli ordini da noi ricevuti, in accordance with the orders we received; a — di legge, according to law; derogare alla —, to depart from the rule; precept, principle; le -e generali dell'educazione, the general principles of education; le -e del comporre, the principles of composition; teaching method. **-ale** *adj.* normal, conforming to standard, regular, usual; condizioni -ali, normal conditions; guiding, setting the standard; (mus.) corista -ale, French diapason normal pitch; †scuola —, teachers' training college; (math.; phys.; chem.) normal; (techn.) standard; *n.f.* (math.) normal, perpendicular; abbassare la -ale, to drop a perpendicular; *m.* normality; standard pattern; normal state; al di sopra del -ale, above normal, higher than normal. (**-almente** *adv.*) **-alista** *m.* student at or of the Scuola Normale at Pisa; †student at a teachers' training college. **-alità** *f.* normality. **-aliz̧zare** [A I] *tr.* to normalize, to make normal; to standardize. (**-aliz̧zato** *part. adj.*) **-aliz̧zaz̧ione** *f.* restoring to normal. **-ativo** *adj.* normative, setting up a norm or standard.

Norman-di·a *pr.n.f.* (geog.) Normandy. **-no** *adj.* Norman; architettura -na, Norman architecture; *n.m.* Norman.

normo·grafo *m.* perforated stencil or set of stencils for lettering, etc.

Norve·g-ia *pr.n.f.* (geog.) Norway. **-ęse** *adj.* Norwegian; *n.m.* Norwegian, native of Norway; Norwegian (language); *f.* Norwegian woman or girl.

†**nosco** *prn.* with us, together with us.

noş-oco·mio *m.* (med.) hospital; infirmary. **-oge·neşi** *f.* pathogenesis. **-ografi·a** *f.* nosography, description of diseases. **-ogra·fico** *adj.* nosographical. **-ologi·a** *f.* nosology, classification and arrangement of diseases. **-olo·gico** *adj.* nosological.

†**nossa** *f.* altercation.

nossignora *excl.* no, Madam!; certainly not!

nossignore *excl.* no, Sir!; certainly not!

nost-algi·a *f.* nostalgia; — della casa, homesickness; aver — di, to long for. **-a·lgico** *adj.* nostalgic; homesick; *n.m.* (neol.) one who regrets the passing of the Fascist régime. (**-algicamente** *adv.*)

nostoc *m. indecl.* (bot.) witches' butter, *Nostoc commune*.

nostras *adj. indecl.* (med.) endemic.

nostr-o *poss. adj.* our; la -a Maestà, a formula used by a king when speaking of himself; (joc.) la — signoria, facetious formula used by a speaker referring to himself; (fig.) i -i fratelli, our fellow-countrymen; i -i tempi, the times we live in; *poss. prn.* our belongings, our possessions; non vogliamo rimetterci del —, we do not want to lose what is ours; il —, our author; *pl.* our men, our soldiers; those on our side; our party; our relatives; oggi sarai dei -i, today you will be one of us; vuole esser dei -i?, will you join us?; ours; la tua camera è vicina alla -a, your bedroom is near ours; (with reciprocal value) our mutual; il — amore, our love for each other. **-ale** *adj.* home-grown, home-produced, national, domestic; prodotti -ali, home products; i vini -ali, the wines of our country; la musica -ale, our own music; *adv. phr.* alla -ale, according to the custom of our country. **-almente** *adv.* in our own way; in a homely manner. **-ano** *adj.* see **nostrale**. **-(u)omo** *m.* (naut.) coxswain; boatswain; cala del -(u)omo, boatswain's store; fischio, fischietto del -(u)omo, boatswain's pipe; †master.

not-a *f.* **1.** SIGN, mark, distinguishing feature, token; -e caratteristiche, identification details (e.g. on a passport); characteristic; le -e d'un vero patriota, the marks of a true patriot; (sculp.) sculptor's mark, signature; (philos.) note, distinguishing mark; -e lasciate dal tempo, marks left by time; (fig.) mark of censure, stigma; — di biasimo, reprimand. **2.** NOTE; prendere — di, to make a note of; prendere -e, to take notes; note, comment; — a piè di pagina, footnote; corredare di -e, to annotate; — diplomatica, diplomatic note; (leg.) -e d'udienza, counsel's written observations on argument of other side (C.C.P.). **3.** (MUSIC) note (whether sound or written symbol of sound); *pl.* music, melody, harmony; fare le -e a, to set to music; mettere in -e, to set to music; muoversi a —, to dance in time to the music; -e alte, -e acute, high notes; -e basse, -e gravi, low notes; — chiusa, adjacent note; — falsa, wrong note; — fondamentale,

not-a (*cont.*)

tonic; le -e musicali, the notes of the scale; — di passaggio, passing note; — puntata, dotted note; — cambiata, changing note; — di recitazione, reciting note; trovare la — giusta, to hit the right note; la — obbligata, the correct conventional phrase; accent, sound; una — di tristezza, a note of sadness; (poet.) dolenti -e, lamentation. **4.** EMINENCE, distinction; notice, attention; degno di —, worthy of note; far — di, to note, to notice. **5.** LIST; — del bucato, laundry list; — delle vivande, bill of fare; (comm.) delivery note; invoice; bill; (leg.) — delle spese, bill of costs (C.C.P.); account; report; -e informative, full conduct report drawn up for a specific reason; — di pegno, warehouse warrant (C.C.); — ipotecaria di trascrizione, demand for registration of mortgage (C.C.); (finan.) — di banca, banknote; — di accreditamento, credit-note. **6.** CHARACTER, letter of the alphabet; number; -e latine, Roman numerals; (Rom. antiq.) -e tironiane, *notae Tironianae*, Tironian shorthand; scrivere nel cuore con -e indelebili, to write indelibly upon the heart; word; dire a chiare -e, to say distinctly. **-ina** *f.* (mus.) small-headed note, grace-note. †**-oso** *adj.* stained, spotted.

not-a·io *m.* notary, a public official who attests and authenticates deeds or writings (formerly all public officials were notaries); atto rogato da —, a deed attested by a notary; studio di —, notary's office; pubblico —, notary public.

notalgi·a *f.* (med.) back-ache.

not-are [A 1] *tr.* to mark, to indicate; — i passi più belli d'un libro, to mark the best passages in a book; to note down, to make a note of; to enter, to register, to record, to keep a note of; to denote, to mean, to signify; to observe; to notice, to note, to consider; -a bene, N.B., *nota bene*; farsi —, to call attention to oneself, to distinguish oneself; (comm.) to quote. **-abene** *m. indecl.* note, footnote. **-a·bile** *adj.* notable, remarkable; eminent; considerable; memorable; *n.m.* important personage, notability. **-abilmente** *adv.* notably; considerably, very much. **-abilità** *f.* notability, worthiness of notice; important personage, celebrity. **-amento** *m.* note; record; list. †**-ando** *adj.* noteworthy. †**-antemente** *adv.* notably. **-ato** *part. adj.* marked, indicated; entered, recorded, noted; observed, noticed; described; (fig.) branded, stigmatized. †**-atamente** *adv.* notably. (**-atore** *m.* **-atrice** *f.*) **-azione** *f.* marking; annotation; pagine imbrattate di -azioni indecifrabili, pages black with indecipherable notes; manca la -azione delle pagine, the pages are not numbered; observation; delle fini -azioni psicologiche, some acute psychological observations; (mus.) notation; -azione boeziana, Boëthian notation; -azione dasia, daseian notation; -azione diastematica, diastematic notation; -azione gregoriana, plainsong notation; -azione neumatica, neumatic notation; -azione quadrata, square notation; †etymology, origin. **-evole** *adj.* notable, eminent; remarkable; considerable; a -evole distanza, at a considerable distance. **-evolmente** *adv.* notably; considerably, very much; remarkably.

notar-o *m.* see **nota·io**. **-iale** *adj.* see **notarile**. **-iato** *m.* (leg.) office and profession of a notary. **-ile** *adj.* notarial; having to do with a notary; attested, done or made by a notary; archivi -ili, notarial records; atto -ile, notarial deed; certificato -ile, declaration by a notary; consiglio -ile, Council of Notaries; diritti -ili, notarial fees; procura -ile, Power of Attorney; scrittura -ile, document under the hand and seal of a Notary Public; tariffa -ile, scale of notary's fees.

notes *m. indecl.* note-book.

notidano *m.* (zool.) see **nocciolino**[1]; (ichth.) Mediterranean shark, *Hexanchus griseus*.

noti·fic-a *f.* notice, notification; communication; (leg.) notice; service; — di comparsa, summons to appear; — di citazione, service of summons, of process; — di decreto, service of decree. **-are** [A 2 s] *tr.* to notify; -are una deliberazione al popolo, to notify the people of a decision; to announce, to make known, to inform, to report; vi -o che, I hereby give notice that; to denounce, to reveal; (leg.) to notify; to serve; -are un atto, to serve paper (C.P.P.); -are una citazione, to serve a summons (C.C.P.); †to explain; *rfl.* to reveal oneself; to reveal one's identity or whereabouts. **-a·bile** *adj.* notifiable. **-amento** *m.* notification, announcement, report, manifesto, declaration, statement. **-ato** *part. adj.* announced, reported, made known, declared. (**-atore** *m.* **-atrice** *f.*) **-azione** *f.* notification; announcement, manifesto, declaration; (leg.) formal notice; service (C.C.P.; C.P.P.).

notio·metro *m.* hygrometer.

noti·zi-a *f.* knowledge, notice; portare a — di qualcuno, to bring to someone's notice; degno di —, worthy of notice, noteworthy; dar — di, to inform of, to communicate; per vostra —, for your information; notion, concept; (philos.) prime -e, first principles; la -a di Dio, knowledge of God; le -e di un'arte, the rudiments of an art; item of news, piece of news; nessuna —, no news; *pl.* news; quali -e?, che -e sono?, what's the news?; ricevere -e da qualcuno, to hear from someone; chiedere -e di uno, to ask about someone; ultime -e, latest news; mi mandi Sue -e, let me hear news of you; rumour, report; circola la — che, there is a rumour going about that; (leg.) la propagazione di -e false, spreading of false news (C.P.); information; libro ricco di -e storiche, book abounding in historical information; cercare -e intorno alla vita di un poeta, to seek out material concerning the life of a poet; (leg.) indebita pubblicazione di —, unlawful publication of information (C.P.); account; report; -e storiche (as part of a title), a historical account. **-a·rio** *m.* (radio) news, news bulletin; (journ.) news column.

not-o[1] *adj.* known; persona a me -a, person known to me; rendere —, to make known; il mondo — agli antichi, the world as the ancients knew it; è — che, it is known that; well-known; noted, famous; mal —, little known; †knowledgeable, informed; *n.m.* the known; procedere dal — all'ignoto, to proceed from the known to the unknown.

noto[2] *m.* (poet.) south wind; wind.

†**noto**[3] *m.* natural son, bastard.

not-ocorda *f.* (zool.) notochord. **-ocordati** *m.pl.* (zool.) chordates. **-onetta** *f.* (ent.) water boatman, *Notonecta* spp.

†**notomi·a** *f.* and derivs. See **anatomia**.

noto·ri-o *adj.* well-known, commonly known; notorious; fatto —, well-known fact, matter of common knowledge. **-amente** *adv.* notoriously. **-età** *f.* notoriety, fame; (leg.) atto di -età, declaration attested by several witnesses before notary or magistrate, stating that a certain fact is known to them.

†**notoso** *adj.* spotted, stained.

nott-e *f.* night; di —, by night; di giorno e di —, giorno e —, night and day, continually; a —, at night; a — avanzata, a — fatta, ad alta —, late at night, in the deep of the night; da —, for the night; camicia da —, night-gown, night-shirt; vaso da —, chamber pot; la — di sabato, la — sul sabato, Friday night; sabato —, Saturday night; si faceva —, night was falling; questa —, tonight, *or* last night; buona —, good-night; buona — al secchio!, l'ho cacciato via e buona —!, that's the end of that!; far di — giorno, to stay up all night; — bianca, sleepless night; ci corre quanto dal giorno alla —, they are as different as chalk from cheese; (fig.) darkness, obscurity; la — dei tempi, the mists of time; (fig.) blindness; †un'ora di —, one hour past the Angelus; †a gran —, far into the night. **-ambulismo** *m.* night-wandering, noctambulism, walking by night. **-am·bulo** *adj.* noctambulant, walking by night; *n.m.* person who enjoys night life; †sleep-walker. **-ante** *m.,* *f.* night-nurse. †**-are** *intr.* to grow dark, to come on for night. **-ata** *f.* night; passare una buona -ata, to have a good night; fare -ata, to stay up all night, to watch all night; perdere la -ata, to spend a sleepless night; un paio di -ate, a couple of nights up. **-etempo** *adv.* by night, at night time. **-i·vago** *adj.* (m.pl. **-i·vaghi**) noctivagant, noctivagous, night-wandering. †**-olata** *f.* see **nottata**.

not·tol-a *f.* (zool.) noctule bat, *Nyctalus noctula*; (ichth.) *Pteromylaeus bovina*, a kind of devil fish; portar -e ad Atene, to take coals to Newcastle; large wooden latch; — di sicurezza, safety catch. **-ina** *f.* (eng.) pawl, pallet, ratchet; (joc.) Adam's apple. **-ino** *m.* small door-latch; far d'una trave un -ino, to use much material to very little effect. **-one** *m.* night-walker, night-wanderer; big clumsy person, good-for-nothing lout; (orn.) nightjar, esp. *Caprimulgus europaeus*.

†**not·tolo** *m.* (zool.) bat.

not·tua *f.* (ent.) nocturnal moth.

notturn-o *adj.* nocturnal; nightly, of the night; night; campanello —, night-bell; guardiano —, night-watchman; la quiete -a, the quiet of night; *n.m.* (liturg.) Nocturn; (mus.) nocturne, serenade.

notus in Judaea *m.* (Lat. phrase from Vulgate Ps. 75, 'known in Judaea'; used iron.) someone known all too well; notorious person, esp. moneylender.

nou·meno *m.* (pron. **nu·meno**) (philos.) noumenon.

nou·s *m. indecl.* (pron. **nus**) (philos.) intellect, nous.

novale *m.* (agric.) fallow (land); (leg.) novale, land newly ploughed and converted into tillage.

novant-a *card. num.* ninety; (fig.) — volte, heaps of times, dozens of times; il — per cento, nearly double; *n.m.* il —, the number ninety; nel —, in the year '90. **-acinque** *card. num.* ninety-five. **-adue** *card. num.* ninety-two. **-anove** *card. num.* ninety-nine; -anove su cento, ninety-nine times out of a hundred. **-aquattro** *card. num.* ninety-four. **-asei** *card. num.* ninety-six. **-asette** *card. num.* ninety-seven. **-atrè** *card. num.* ninety-three. **-enne** *adj.* ninety-year-old, ninety years old; *n.m.* nonagenarian. **-ennio** *m.* space of ninety years. **-esimo** *ord. num.* ninetieth; -esimo primo, ninety-first (more commonly -ina *f.* about ninety; una -ina di lire, about ninety lire; la -ina, the nineties; vicino alla, -ina getting on for ninety. **-otto** *card. num.* ninety-eight. **-unesimo, -aduesimo,** etc.); *n.m.* ninetieth, ninetieth part. **-uno** *card. num.* ninety-one.

Novar-a *pr.n.f.* (geog.) Novara. **-ese** *adj.* relating to Novara; *n.m.* region round Novara; *m., f.* native or inhabitant of Novara.

†**novare** *vb.* and derivs. See **rinnovare**.

nov-atore *m.* innovator. (**-atrice** *f.*) **-azione** *f.* innovation; (leg.) novation (C.C.).

nov-e *card. num.* nine; — volte su dieci, nine times out of ten; (typ.) corpo —, nine point. **-ecento** *card. num.* nine hundred; *n.m.* il -ecento, the twentieth century; *adj. indecl.* relating to or characteristic of the twentieth century; stile -ecento, modernistic, contemporary style. **-ecentesimo** *ord. num.* nine-hundredth; -ecentesimo primo, nine hundred and first (more commonly -ecentunesimo, -ecentoduesimo, etc.). **-ecentismo** *m.* twentieth-century school of thought or artistic fashion. **-ecentista** *m., f.* person living in the twentieth century; follower of a twentieth-century school of thought or artistic fashion. **-ecentouno, -ecentuno** *card. num.* nine hundred and one (-ecentodue, -ecentotrè, etc.). **-ecentomila** *card. num.* nine hundred thousand. **-ecentonovantanove mila** *card. num.* nine hundred and ninety-nine thousand. (**-ecentonovantanovemillesimo** *ord. num.*) **-emila** *card. num.* nine thousand. **-esimo** *adj.* ninth.

novell-a[1] *f.* story, short story, tale, fable; -e da contare a veglia, tall stories; (Ital. lit., nineteenth century) — in versi, short narrative poem; news; (rel.) la Buona Novella, the Gospel, the 'Good News'; chatter, gossip; *pl.* tales, rumours, gossip; *pl.* (Rom. law) the *Novellae* (of Justinian); (leg.) *Novellae*, or *Novellae Constitutiones*. **-aio** *m.* short-story writer; story-teller. **-ame** *m.* see under **novello**. **-are** [A I] *intr.* (*aux.* avere) to tell stories; to chatter, to talk; †to be renewed, to come forth anew. **-ante** *part. adj.* story-telling; *n.m.* story-teller. †**-ato** *part. adj.* recounted, related. **-atore** *m.* story-teller; short-story writer; chatterer, talker. (**-atrice** *f.*) **-iere** *m.* story-teller; short-story writer; collection of short stories; †gossip-monger; †ambassador. (**-iera** *f.*) **-ina** *f.* fable, little tale; (agric.) see under **novello**. **-ino** *m.* (lit. hist.) title of a collection of short stories; *adj. dim.* see under **novello**. †**-io** *m.* telling of tales; gossip, chattering. **-ista** *m., f.* short-story writer; story-teller; †journalist; †news-bearer; †gossip. **-istica** *f.* writing of short stories; art of short-story writing; story-telling; tales, short stories; la -istica italiana, Italian short stories. †**-izia** *f.* first fruits; first tidings; harbinger.

novella[2] *f.* (naut.) preventer.

novell-o *adj.* new; fresh; (of fruit, flowers, etc.) early; patate -e, new potatoes; le rose -e, the first roses; (poet.) l'età -a, youth; (liturg.) messa -a, a first mass (of newly ordained priest); recent, recently made; sposa -a, bride; inexpert, untrained; (naut.) orza -a, preventer stay; new, second; un — Michelangelo, a second Michelangelo; Guido Novello, Guy the Younger; di —, again, †for the first time; †per —, recently; *n.m.pl.* i -i, the new shoots of a plant. **-amente** *adv.* again, afresh; newly; in a new way; †recently; †latterly. **-ino** *adj. dim.* new; young; tender; (of fruit, etc.) early; (of person) inexperienced, new, raw, green; *n.m.* essere un -ino, to be new to one's job, to be a novice. **-ina** *f.* fresh salad.

novembr-e *m.* November. **-ino** *adj.* November, of November.

novemila *card. num.* See under **nove**.

noven-a *f.* (rel.) novena. **-ario** *adj.* of nine syllables; *n.m.* (prosod.) nine-syllable line. **-diale** *adj.* lasting for nine days; (Rom. antiq.) novendial; nine-day or ninth-day (ceremony); *n.m.* (Rom. antiq.) novendial; (eccl.) 'the Pope's Novena'; nine-day ceremonies after a pope's death. **-nale** *adj.* recurring every nine years; of nine years' duration. **-ne** *adj.* nine-year-old, lasting nine years.

noven-nio *m.* space of nine years.

†**noveno** *adj.* See **nono**.

nover-are [A I S] *tr.* to number, to enumerate, to count, to reckon. **-ato** *part. adj.* (**-atore** *m.* **-atrice** *f.*)

†**noverca** *f.* stepmother.

novero *m.* number; amici senza —, friends without number; class, category; mettere uno nel — dei suoi amici, to number someone among one's friends.

novicordo *m.* (mus.) nine-stringed lyre; nine-note scale; interval of ninth.

novilunio *m.* (astron.) time of new moon.

novireme *f.* (naut. hist.) nine-oared galley.

novis-sim-o *adj. superl.* newest, very new; last; (rel.) il — bando, the summons to the Last Judgement, the Last Trump; i -i, the Four Last Things (Death, Judgement, Hell, Heaven).

novità *f.* newness, originality, novelty; innovation; new book, new play, etc.; — librarie, new books; questo è una —, this book is just out; novelty; articoli di —, novelties, fancy goods; new fashion; ultima —, latest fashion; correre dietro alle —, to follow all the latest trends; news; le — del giorno, the day's news; che —?, what news?; revolt, sedition; innovation, reform.

noviz-io *m.* novice, beginner; insegnante ancora —, novice in the art of teaching; (eccl.) novice; †(naut.) conscript; †apprentice. **-ia** *f.* (eccl.) (girl, woman) novice; †bride; †fiancée. **-iale** *adj.* (eccl.) relating to a novice or novitiate. **-iato** *m.* novitiate; training; apprenticeship; pagare il -iato, to suffer for one's inexperience; (eccl.) novitiate.

novo *adj.* and derivs. (Tusc.). See **nuovo**.

nozion-e *f.* notion, idea; knowledge; hai qualche — di francese?, have you any knowledge of French?; element, rudiment; le prime -i del latino, the first rudiments of Latin; meaning, sense; la — di giusto, the meaning of the word 'just'; (philos.) notion, idea, concept; (leg.) le -i di fatto, factual knowledge (C.C.).

nozz-e *f.pl.* marriage, wedding; nuptials; marriage, wedlock; il giorno delle —, the wedding day; partecipazione di —, invitation to a wedding; viaggio di —, honeymoon; — d'argento, silver wedding; — d'oro, golden wedding; passare a seconde —, to marry a second time; andare a —, to get married, to go to a wedding, to have a good time; per lui dare un esame è come andare a —, for him taking an exam is just a piece of cake; invitare a —, to invite someone to a wedding, to invite someone to come and have a good time; fare le — coi fichi secchi, fare le — coi funghi, to attempt a large undertaking with insufficient means, or in a miserly fashion; finire come le — di Pulcinella, to finish by coming to blows; le — del maiale, rustic festivities on killing a pig; (eccl.) le — (con Gesù), a nun's profession; (bot.) a — palesi, phanerogamous; a — segrete, cryptogamous.

nub-e *f.* cloud; haze, mist; (fig.) cloud, shadow; felicità senza -i, unclouded happiness. **-ecula** *f.* little cloud; (med.) nubecula, cloudiness of the cornea. **-iaddensatore** *m.*, **-iaduna** *m.* (poet.) cloud-gatherer (epithet of Zeus in Homer). **-icalpestatore** *adj., m.* (poet.) cloud-trampling (epithet of Pegasus). **-ifendente** *adj.* (poet.) cloud-cleaving. **-ifero** *adj.* cloudy, overclouded, heavy with clouds. **-ifragio** *m.* cloudburst; downpour, heavy shower; storm.

†**nu-bil-a** *f.* cloud. †**-are** *tr.* to obfuscate, to overcloud.

nu-bil-e *adj.* (of a woman) unmarried; morì —, she died unwed; marriageable, nubile; figlia di età —, daughter of marriageable age; *n.f.* unmarried woman; -i e maritate, married and unmarried women; (leg.) feme sole, single woman, spinster.

nu-bil-o *adj.* cloudy, overclouded. †**-ità** *f.* darkness, obscurity. †**-oso** *adj.* dark, overclouded, overcast; †troubled, distressed.

†**nubiola** *f.* See **nebbiolo**.

nuca *f.* (anat.) nape of the neck, nucha; spine; (vet.; zool.) nuchal crest.

nucella *f.* (bot.) nucellus, the essential part of an ovule containing the embryo-sac.

nu-cl-eo *m.* (biol.) nucleus; (scient.) core; (fig., of persons in a society, political movement, etc.) nucleus, central group; — celere, flying squad; il — della questione, the gist of the matter. **-eare** *adj.* nuclear; energia -eare, nuclear energy, atomic power. **-eina** *f.* (bot.) nuclein. **-eolo** *m.* (biol.) nucleolus. **-eone** *m.* (atom. phys.) nucleon. **-ide** *f.* (atom. phys.) nuclide.

†**nucrea** *f.* See **nuca**.

nud-are [A I] *tr.* to denude, to lay bare; to uncover; to deprive; *rfl.* to uncover oneself, to undress oneself; -arsi il petto, to bare one's breast. **-ato** *part. adj.* laid bare; denuded; undressed, uncovered, bared.

nud-o *adj.* naked; spogliarsi —, to strip naked; — nato, stark naked; undressed; poorly dressed; simple, plain, unadorned; ridursi —, to be reduced to semi-nakedness, to fall into extreme poverty; uncovered, bare; a piedi -i, barefoot; a testa -a, bare-headed, hatless; cavalcare a dorso —, to ride bare-back; (naut.) bare; naviglio —, hull only; scafo —, bare hull (without engines or equipment); albero —, pennone —, bare poles; (of ground) barren, waste; dormire sulla -a terra, to sleep on the bare earth; casa -a, unfurnished house; — di, empty of, uncovered by, stripped of; a occhio —, with the naked eye; clear, open, visible; mettere a —, to lay bare, to reveal; confessione -a, clear confession; dirò la verità -a e cruda, I will tell the plain, unvarnished truth; (leg.) -a proprietà, remainder, residuary right of ownership, reversion, reversionary interest (C.C.); — proprietario, estate owner expectant on death of tenant-for-life, remainderman, reversioner; (ichth.) pesce —, poor cod, *Gadus minutus*; *n.m.* naked person; (paint.; sculpt.) nude model; nude. (-a *f.*) **-amente** *adv.* nakedly; barely, explicitly, plainly, simply. **-ezza** *f.* nakedness; bareness, plainness. **-ibranchi** *m.pl.* (zool.) nudibranchs, sea slugs. **-ismo** *m.* nudism; campo di -ismo, nudist camp. **-ista** *m., f.* nudist. **-ità** *f.* nakedness; lack of clothing; expanse of bare flesh; le -ità della moda, the exposure of various parts of the body as decreed by fashion; bareness, plainness, clarity, explicitness. **-onato** *adj.* stark naked.

nudrire [D 2] *tr.* (poet.). See **nutrire**.

†**nug-a** *f.* trifle, bagatelle. †**-ace** *adj.* occupied in trifles or bagatelles; idle-minded; gossiping. †**-atorio** *adj.* nugatory. †**-azione** *f.* trifle, bagatelle; joke, jest; superfluous, long drawn-out discourse. †**-ella** *f.* trifle.

†**nugola** *f.* and derivs. See **nuvola**.

†**nui** *prn.* See **noi**.

null-a *neg. particle, n.m. indecl.* nothing; creare dal —, to create from nothing; buono a —, good for nothing; un bel —, nothing at all; non c'è proprio il bel —, there is absolutely nothing; — di grave, nothing serious; avere a —, avere per —, to scorn, to hold as nothing; per —, in no way, by no means, not at all; for no price, for any price, free, for nothing; non per — influenzato, not affected in the slightest; nulla nulla, practically nothing, the merest nothing; lo vendè per —, he sold it for a song; non per —, not for nothing, for a very good reason; in modo che — più, superlatively, inimitably; questo e — è lo stesso, it amounts to nothing; già, lui, o grosse o —!, trust him to put his foot in it!, trust him to tell a pack of lies!; — di —, absolutely nothing; poco assai per non dir —, little enough, if anything at all; andare in —, finire in —, to vanish, to disappear; to come to nothing; (leg.) concedere il — osta, to grant a permit; è un —!, it is nothing!; nothing, (not) anything; — ti piace, non ti piace —, you don't like anything; non lo farei per —, I wouldn't do it for anything; non fa —, fa —, it doesn't matter, it doesn't make any difference; non farne —, to make nothing of it; non me ne fo —, I couldn't care less; non mancar di —, to lack nothing; ha la voce così forte che il Caruso non c'è per —!, he has such a strong voice, Caruso just isn't in it!; nonentity; chi è lui? —!, who is he? Nobody!; venire dal —, to come from the gutter, to be an upstart; emptiness, worthlessness, vanity, nullity; il — delle umane cose, the nothingness of things human; ritornare al —, to return to nothingness; (in interrog., conditional or quasi-neg. phrases) anything; c'è — per me?, is there anything for me?; vediamo se c'è —, let's see if there's anything; senza —, without anything; se ti occorre —, domandalo pure, if you want anything do ask for it; *adv.* not at all, by no means; non contar —, to be of no account; nulla nulla, in the slightest degree; un uomo — educato non farebbe così, anyone with the slightest tinge of good manners would not behave like that. **-adimanco**, **-adimeno** *adv.* see **nondimeno**, **nientedimeno**. **-aggine** *f.* emptiness, vanity; nothingness; insignificance; worthlessness. †**-amanco**, †**-ameno** *adv.* see **nondimeno**, **nientedimeno**. **-amente** *adv.* (leg.) in a voidable way. **-aosta** *m. indecl.* (leg.) permit, permission. **-atenente** *m.* one who owns nothing; *adj.* owning nothing; essere -atenente, to own nothing. **-atenenza** *f.* lack of property; certificato di -atenenza, paper certifying that holder owns no property. **-ipore**

f.pl. (bot.) nullipores (group of red seaweeds with tissues impregnated with lime). **-ismo** *m.* (philos.) nihilism. **-ità** *f.* nullity, worthlessness; worthless thing; worthless person, nonentity; (leg.) nullity, -ità di contratto, nullity of a contract; -ità assoluta, absolute nullity; -ità relativa, voidability; -ità del testamento, invalidity of will (C.C.); sanare la -ità, to make good the invalidity (C.C.P.). **-o** *adj.* null, invalid; (of person) worthless, useless; (leg.) null; void; un contratto -o, a void contract; considerare una proposta come -a e non avvenuta, to consider a proposal as null and void; punto -o, zero mark; -a nuova, buona nuova, no news is good news; †see **nessuno**.

num-e *m.* (rel.) divine power, divine will; divinity, god (esp. of anct. Rome); †saint; (colloq.) santi -i!, o -i!, ye Gods!; si crede un —, he thinks he's God Almighty.

nu·meno *m.* See **noumeno**.

numerale *adj.* See under **numero**.

numer-are [A I s] *tr.* to count; — sino a cento, to count up to a hundred; to count out, to pay; -ò centomila lire, he counted out a hundred thousand lire; to number; — un libro, to number the pages of a book; le case sono -ate, the houses are numbered. **-a·bile** *adj.* numerable, capable of being counted. (**-abilità** *f.*) †**-ando** *adj.* to be numbered. **-a·rio** *adj.* see under **numero**. **-ativo** *adj.* enumerative. **-ato** *part. adj.* counted; (comm.) denaro -ato, ready cash; numbered, of limited number; numbered, marked by number; pagine -ate, numbered pages; (mus.) figured; basso -ato, figured bass. **-atamente** *adv.* by number, one by one. **-atore** *m.* one who counts, one who numbers; (math.) numerator. (**-atrice** *f.*) **-azione** *f.* numbering; -azione delle pagine, numbering of pages; system of numbering; -azione romana, Roman numbering system; (naut.) fleet numbers; (arith.) numbering, notation; -azione arabica, Arabic numbers; (comm.) -azione del denaro, payment of cash.

†**nume·rica** *f.* (mus.) figured bass.

nu·mer-o *m.* number, figure; cipher; — della pagina, page-number; — del telefono, telephone number, owner of telephone so numbered; il — 5392 non risponde, there is no answer from 5392; formazione del —, dialling; (in a hotel) il — 30, the occupant of room 30; il — 100, the lavatory; numeral; — cardinale, cardinal numeral; — ordinale, †ordinativo, ordinal numeral; -i romani, Roman numerals; -i arabici, — d'abbaco, Arabic numerals; non conosce i -i, he doesn't know his numbers; number, quantity; in gran —, in great numbers; di —, precisely, in number; tre di —, three in number; il loro — fu di trecento, they were three hundred in number; ci furono in —, there were numbers of them there, *or* the required number were there; —, legale, quorum; essere in —, to form a quorum; verificare il — legale, to ascertain that there is a quorum; con la forza del —, by force of numbers; se tu sapessi il numero dei candidati, if you knew how many candidates there are; far —, to be present, to make up the numbers; verrò per far —, I will come just to make up the party; sopra —, supernumerary; group, class, category; tu non entri nel — di quelli, you don't count as one of those; passare nel — dei più, to join the great majority, to die; (of a weekly magazine or other periodical) number; — unico, single number (of an occasional publication in magazine or pamphlet form); — uno, first-rate, first-class, A1, excellent; ci offrì un vinetto — uno, he offered us a first-rate little wine; quality, gift; avere tutti i -i, to have all the good points; (comm.) size or grade; vendere a —, to sell for cash; (theatr.) number, item (in revue or variety); (gramm.) number (singular, dual or plural); (astron.) — aureo, golden number; (mil.) regimental number; division corps; call-up number for military service; (naut.) ship's number or pennants; numbered flag; — di bordo, individual's ship's number; *pl.* (Bibl.) Numbers; (rhet.) rhythm (esp. of classical verse or prose); musical speech. **-ale** *adj.* numeral, denoting a number; nome -ale, number; aggettivo -ale, ordinal number. **-almente** *adv.* numerically. **-a·rio** *adj.* belonging to the normal number (of staff, etc.), not employed as supernumerary; (comm.) -ario di cassa, cash; pagare in -ario, to pay in hard cash; †see **numerale**. **-osità** *f.* numerousness; rhythm; harmony. **-oso** *adj.* numerous; abundant, plentiful; rhythmical, harmonious; prosa -osa, rhythmical prose (with carefully chosen cadences, as in Dante's Latin letters). **-osamente** *adv.* numerously; in large numbers; harmoniously, rhythmically.

nume·ric-o *adj.* numerical; maggioranza -a, numerical majority. **-amente** *adv.* numerically.

nu·mid-a, -o *m. adj.* Numidian; *f.* (orn.) guineafowl.

numinọso *adj.* (rel.; anthropol.) numinous; (fig.) holy.

numiṣm-a *m.* coin, medallion, medal. **-ale** *adj.* coin-shaped. **-a·tica** *f.* numismatics, numismatology. **-a·tico** *adj.* numismatic; *n.m.* numismatist.

numm-o *m.* (Rom. antiq.) *nummus* (coin). **-a·rio** *adj.* nummary. **-o·grafo** *m.* numismatist. **-ola·ria** *f.* (bot.) creeping Jenny, *Lysimachia nummularia*. **-ola·rio** *m.* (Rom. antiq.) money-changer.

numm-olito *m.*, **-ulito** *m.* (geol.) nummulite. **-uli·tico** *adj.* (geol.) nummulitic.

nun·cio *m.* See **nunzio**.

nun·cius *m. indecl.* (leg.) agent who exceeds his powers (C.C.).

nuncup-ativo *adj.* (leg.) nuncupative; testamento —, nuncupative will. **-ativamẹnte** *adv.* (leg.) nuncupatively. **-azione** *f.* (leg.) nuncupation.

nun·din-e *f. pl.* (Rom. antiq.) *nundinae* (market held every eighth day). **-ale** *adj.* nundinal.

†nunziare *vb.* and derivs. See **annunziare**.

nunzi-ata[1] *f.* (eccl.) Annunciation (feast, church, picture, statue). **-atura** *f.* (eccl.; pol.) nunciature.

Nunziata[2] *pr.n.f.* Nunziata.

nun·zio *m.* (theol.) — celeste, heavenly messenger, angel; (eccl.; leg.) nuncio; (ent.) — della morte, churchyard beetle, *Blaps mortisaga*; †announcement; †tidings; †herald; †harbinger, indication.

nuo·c-ere [B15] *intr.* (aux. avere; *prep.* a) to be harmful, to be injurious, to be hurtful; tentare non -e, there is no harm in trying; tutto il male non viene per —, it's an ill wind that blows nobody any good; to injure, to hurt, to harm; il troppo bere -e alla salute, too much drink is harmful to one's health; ciò nocque al suo prestigio, that was detrimental to his prestige; la pioggia ha nociuto al raccolto, the rain has damaged the harvest; *recip. rfl.* to hurt each other, to do each other harm.

nuora *f.* daughter-in-law; stare come suocera e —, to fight like cat and dog; dire a — perchè suocera intenda, to address one person with the purpose of being overheard by another; suocera e —, two-in-one jar for oil and vinegar with bottle-necks pointing in opposite directions; (bot., pop.) pansy.

nuot-are [A1d], [Tusc. A1] *intr.* (aux. avere) to swim; sapete —?, can you swim?; — come una gatta di piombo, to be unable to swim; (cul.) — nel vino, to be soaked in wine; — nel miele, to be in clover, to live on the fat of the land; to float; to wallow; — nel sangue, to revel in bloodshed; — nel sudore, to be bathed in sweat; — nel denaro, to be rolling in money. **-ata** *f.* swim; swimming; swimming-stroke; fare una -ata, to take a dip. **-atọio** *m.* swimming-bath. **-atọre** *m.* swimmer. (**-atrice** *f.*) **-o** *m.* swimming; passare un fiume a -o, to swim across a river; essere amante del -o, to love swimming; gara di -o, swimming race; gettarsi a -o, to dive in for a swim; †fish's swim-bladder.

nuov-o *adj.* new; gli sposi -i, the newly married couple(s); il medico —, the new doctor; il — medico, the newly qualified doctor; i -i arricchiti, the newly rich; — venuto, newcomer; gente -a, newly arrived people (in a town, in public life, etc.); (geog.) Nuova Amsterdam, New Amsterdam; Nuova Bretagna, New Britain; Nuova Galles, New South Wales; Nuova Inghilterra, New England; Nuovo Meclemburgo, New Mecklenburg; Nuovo Messico, New Mexico; Nuova Scozia, Nova Scotia; Archipelago della Nuova Siberia, Novosibirsk; Nuova Zelanda, New Zealand; (Rom. hist.) uomini -i, *novi homines*; essere un uomo —, to be an upstart; essere — alla politica, to have had no political experience; essere — di un luogo, to be new to a place; mostrarsi, farsi — di una cosa, to show oneself ignorant of something; to show surprise at something; fare il —, to feign ignorance; new, recent; la -a eruzione, the latest eruption, this last eruption; modern; metodi -i, modern methods; new, unused; — di trinca, — di pezza, — fiammante, brand-new; — di zecca, brand-new, newly issued, newly minted; di —, (of words) newly coined; terra -a, uncultivated land, virgin soil; sembra —, it looks like new; (provb.) granata -a spazza ben tre giorni, a new broom sweeps clean; — di pianta, (of buildings) newly erected; (leg.) la denunzia di -a opera, objection to new works (C.C.); rimettere a —, to renew, to renovate, to make as good as new; addobbare a —, to redecorate; new, second; è un — Raffaello, he is a second Raphael; di —, again; di bel —, over again; fare di —, to renovate, to remake, to renew; young, early; patatine -e, new potatoes; il tempo —, the spring-time; other, further; cavò fuori un — sigaro,

he took out another cigar; una -a difficoltà, a further difficulty; strange, unaccustomed; questo non mi riesce —, this is not new to me; provare un sentimento —, to experience a new feeling; (mus.) le -e musiche, see under **musica**; farne delle -e, to do odd things, to behave strangely; ne fa sempre delle -e, he is always up to some new trick; unheard of, extraordinary; marvellous, unexampled, rare; sono -i modi di trattare la gente, this is a strange way of treating people; *n.m.* newness, originality, novelty; amare il —, to love novelty; non vedo il — di quest'idea, I don't see what's new in this idea; vestirsi di —, to wear new clothes; che c'è di —?, what's the news? **-a** *f.* news; nessuna -a buona -a, no news is good news; una buona -a, a piece of good news; le -e della guerra, the war news. **-amẹnte** *adv.* again, once more; newly, freshly, recently, lately.

nura-ghe *m.* (*pl.* **-ghi**) (geog., Sard.) prehistoric drystone round tower.

†nuro *f.* See **nuora**.

†nusca *f.* necklace.

nut-ante *adj.* (med.) spasmo —, spasmus nutans, nodding spasm. **†-are** *intr.* to move about, to shake, to wave, to waver, to flutter. **-azione** *f.* (astron.) nutation, a slight oscillation of the earth's axis; the oscillation of a top in spinning; the action of nodding the head; (bot.) nutation, curvature in the stem of a growing plant.

nutric-are [A2] *tr.* to nourish, to foster; to suckle; to feed; to bring up; to care for, to cultivate. **-amẹnto** *m.* nourishing, feeding; nutriment, food, sustenance. **†-ativo** *adj.* nourishing, nutritive. **-ato** *part. adj.* nourished, fed.

nutr-ice *f.* nurse, wet-nurse; nursing mother; foster-mother; (fig.) la terra che gli fu —, the land where he was born; patria — delle arti, land where the arts are fostered. **†-iche·vole** *adj.* nourishing. **†-i·cia** *f.* see **nutrice**. **†-i·cio** *m.* nourisher; educator; tutor.

nutr-ire [D1, D2] *tr.* to nourish; il pane -e molto, bread is very nourishing; to feed; to sustain; to nurture; to foster; to cherish; to suckle; to keep; l'ho -ito a mie spese, I kept him at my expense; — la mente di, to feed the mind on; to harbour, to entertain (feelings); — dubbi, to have doubts; — odio, to harbour hatred; — gratitudine, to bear gratitude; — le memorie, to foster memories; — le arti, to cultivate the arts; †to raise up, to bring up; *rfl.* -irsi di, to feed on; to delight in; si -e di studi, study is meat and drink to him. **-i·bile** *adj.* capable of being nourished; †nutritive. **-iente** *adj.* nutritious; nourishing; nutrient; †*n.m.* nurturer. **†-imentale** *adj.* nutritive. **-imẹnto** *m.* nourishment; nutriment; food; feeding; (fig.) -imento dello spirito, spiritual refreshment. **-itivo** *adj.* nutritious, nutritive, nourishing. **-ito** *part. adj.* nourished; fed; nurtured; ben -ito, well-nourished, healthy, strong, well-developed, substantial, solid; -ito negli studi, studiously brought up; -ito di storia, soaked in history; *n.m.* well-fed child; pupil, disciple. **-itino** *m.* fat baby. **-itọre** *m.* nourisher, fosterer; foster-parent; *adj.* nourishing. (**-itrice** *f.*) **†-itura** *f.* nourishment; nurture; nourishing, nurturing. **-izione** *f.* nourishment; nutrition; food, source of nourishment.

†nuve *f.* See **nube**.

nu·vol-a *f.* cloud; cielo senza -e, cloudless sky; aver il capo nelle -e, to have one's head in the clouds; cascare dalle -e, to be astonished, to be dumbfounded; andare per le -e, perdersi nelle -e, to talk up in the air; cloudiness, mistiness (in a jewel or piece of glass, etc.); (fig.) cloud, mist, fog; una — di sospetto, a cloud of suspicion; — passeggiera, passing cloud. **-a·glia** *f.* mass of clouds. **-ame** *m.* cloudiness (in liquids). **-ata** *f.* cloud-burst, sharp shower; mass of clouds. **-ato** *m.* cloudiness, bank of clouds; *adj.* overcast; cloudy; (paint.) cloud-coloured (a bluish grey).

nu·vol-o *m.* large threatening cloud; cloudy weather; non verrò se è —, I shan't come if it is overcast; (fig.) mass, swarm; un — di polvere, a cloud of dust; un — di mosche, swarm of flies; *adj.* cloudy. **-ac·cio** *m. pejor.* storm cloud; black cloud. **-osità** *f.* cloudiness. **-oso** *adj.* cloudy, clouded; overclouded, overcast; (of liquid) turbid, cloudy, muddy.

nuzial-e *adj.* nuptial; bridal; veste —, wedding dress; il corteo —, the wedding party; il corredo —, the trousseau; bridal; (mus.) marcia —, wedding march. **-mẹnte** *adv.* as befits a wedding; †vestito -mente, wearing a wedding garment. **-ità** *f.* marrying; marriages; anno di elevata -ità, year with a high marriage rate; premi di -ità, marriage bonuses.

nylon *m. indecl.* See **nailon**.

o¹ *f.* the letter O; the vowel O; the sound O; un'— maiuscola, a capital O; un'— minuscola, a small O; un'— stretta, chiusa, a close O (as in **forse**); un'— aperta, an open O (as in **forte**); *m.* the shape of an O; non saprebbe fare un — con un bicchiere, he can't do the simplest thing, he's quite helpless; tondo come l'O di Giotto, simple-minded, childish, stupid.

o² *excl.* **o**; (introducing vocative: in this sense never **oh**; often lit. or formal, but not necessarily archaic): — Dio, O Lord; tu non sai, — Carlo..., you do not know, (my dear) Charles...; (emphatic; in this sense often **oh**, q.v.) Oh; — sì!, Oh yes!; (fam. in calling attention) — di casa!, hi there!, is there anyone about?; (Tusc., esp. before questions; not always to be translated) — che fai?, (I say) what are you doing?

o³ (before a vowel, strictly, **od**) *conj.* or; o...o, either...or; o che...che, (with subj.), whether...or; sia o non sia, whether it is so or not.

†o⁴ *adv.* where.

oà *m.* (ichth.). See **orata**.

o·asi *f. indecl.* (geog.) oasis; (fig.) un'— nel deserto, an oasis in the desert, a place of consolation amid desolation.

obbedien-te *part.* of **obbedire**, q.v.; *adj.* obedient, docile; dutiful; submissive; (naut.) — al timone, answering to the helm. **-temente** *adv.* obediently; docilely; dutifully; submissively. **-za** *f.* obedience; stare all'-za del medico, to do as the doctor says; (rel.) obedience; task or penance imposed by superior; fare l'-za, to do something under obedience; casa di -za, house of one's profession; (med.) regularity of the bowels; (naut.) chiamare una nave in -za, to call or take a ship under one's orders, to interrogate a ship on the high seas; (leg.) obedience; rifiuto di -za commesso da un agente della forza pubblica, disobedience on the part of a police officer (C.P.).

obbed-ire [D2] *intr.* (*aux.* avere; *prep.* a) to be obedient (to); to obey, to submit (to); to comply (with); to be subject (to); to respond (to); (naut.) to respond to the trim of sails and rudder; *tr.* to obey (see also **ubbidire**). **-itore** *m.* one who obeys. **(-itrice** *f.*)

obbiada *f.* (ichth.) *Oblada melanura*, a kind of sea bream.

obbiettare [A1c] and derivs. See **obiettare**.

obbiettivo *adj.* and derivs. See **obiettivo**.

obbietto *m.* and derivs. See **obietto**.

obbiezione *f.* See **obiezione**.

†obbioso *adj.* See **ubbioso**, under **ubbia**.

obblatore *m.* See **obl-atore**, under **oblata**.

obblazione *f.* See **oblazione**, under **oblazionario**.

obbl-iare [A4], io *m.* See **obliare, oblìo**.

obblig-are [A2s] *tr.* to compel, to oblige; l'-arono a chiedere scusa, they made him apologize; mi sento -ato a farlo, I feel bound to do so; to be kind or helpful to, to oblige; (leg.) to bind legally; to constrain; to make or render liable; — in solido, to bind jointly and severally; — la parola, to promise, to enter into a voluntary engagement by parole; *rfl.* to enter into an obligation; to bind oneself; -arsi a, to undertake to, to engage to; to be surety for. **-ante** *part. adj.* polite, obliging; obligatory, binding. **-ato** *part. adj.* obliged, grateful; vi sono molto -ato, I am much obliged to you; *excl.* (sometimes iron.) -ato!, thank you (for nothing)!; forced, constrained; -ato al letto, confined to bed; fui -ato ad andare, I was obliged to go; (leg.) legally bound; liable; (mil.) -ato alle armi, conscripted; (lit.) rime -ate, set rhymes (for *bouts-rimés*); (mus.) obbligato, obligato; *n.m.* (leg.) debtor; person liable; -ato principale, principal debtor (C.C.P.). **-atamente** *adv.* with constraint, in a forced manner. **-atorietà** *f.* obligatoriness. **-ato·rio** *adj.* obligatory, compulsory; fermata -atoria, (bus, etc.) stop (as opposed to 'fermata facoltativa', request stop); (leg.) binding; contratto -atorio, binding contract; scrittura -atoria, bond. **-atoriamente** *adv.* compulsorily; of necessity. **-azione** *f.* obligation; bond; debt; (leg.) bond; debenture; duty; liability; mortgage security; obligation; -azione ammortizabile, redeemable debenture; -azione ipotecaria, mortgage debenture; -azione irredimibile, debenture stock; -azione morale, moral obligation (C.C.); -azione negativa, duty to abstain; -azione nominativa, registered debenture; -azione pagabile dopo la morte, *post obit* bond; -azione pagabile in oro, gold bond; -azione sorteggiata, called bond; -azione al portatore, bearer bond; -azione di avaria, average bond; -azione di società, debenture; ammortamento di -azione, ammortization of debenture. **-azionista** *m.* (comm.) bond-holder, debenture-holder; debenture stockholder.

ob·bli-go *m.* (*pl.* **-ghi**) obligation; compulsion; duty; fare l'— suo, to do one's duty; sono in — di farlo, it is my duty to do so; non ho — di andare, I am not obliged to go; d'—, obligatory, *de rigueur*; gli -ghi di madre, motherly duties; questo non è —, this is not obligatory; (rel.) feste d'—, holidays of obligation; te lo do con l'— di restituirlo, I let you have it on condition you return it; (leg.) burden; duty; obligation; — alimentare, duty of maintenance (C.C.); — di fornire le prove, burden of proof; (mil.) — di leva, military service; †biglietto d'—, note of hand.

obblio *m.* See **oblìo**, under **obliare**.

obbro·bri-o *m.* disgrace, infamy, opprobrium; che — della famiglia!, what a disgrace to the family!; *pl.* insulting language, abuse. **-osità** *f.* infamousness. **-oso** *adj.* shameful; infamous; disgraceful. **-osamente** *adv.* shamefully; infamously; disgracefully.

†obdormire *intr.* to sleep; — nel Signore, to fall asleep in Christ.

†obdur-are *tr., intr.* to harden. **†-ato** *part. adj.* hardened; obdurate. **†-azione** *f.* constancy, firmness; imperturbableness.

obelis-co *m.* (*pl.* **-chi**) obelisk.

o·belo *m.* obelus.

ober-are [A1s] *tr.* (fig.) to overwhelm, to overload; — di gentilezze, to overwhelm with kindness. **-ato** *adj.* overwhelmed; burdened with debt, debt-ridden (esp. class. antiq., of those enslaved for debt); loaded, laden; -ato di lavoro, overworked.

obes-o *adj.* corpulent; (med.) obese. **-ità** *f.* corpulence; (med.) obesity, adiposity.

o·bice¹ *m.* (mil.) mortar; shell.

†o·bice² *m.* obstacle, impediment.

obiett-are [A1c] *tr.* to adduce, to bring forward (argument, difficulty); to object; to allege; to object to, to object against; *intr.* (*aux.* avere; *prep.* su) to raise objections (concerning). **(-ato** *part. adj.*)

obiettiv-o *adj.* objective; detached, impartial; (philos.) objective; *n.m.* objective, purpose, aim, goal; (mil.) objective; (photog.; opt.) objective, object glass, lens; (photog.) — a fuoco fisso, fixed-focus lens. **-amente** *adv.* objectively. **-are** [A1] *rfl.* to take an objective attitude. **-ività** *f.* objectivity.

obietto *m.* object; aim, purpose; (see also **oggetto**); †*adj.* contrasting, opposite, opposed.

obiezione *f.* objection; fare, muovere, sollevare un'—, to raise an objection; sollevare un'— di principio, to object on principle; non tenere conto di una —, to overrule an objection.

o·bit-o *m.* death; †(eccl.) obit. **-o·rio** *m.* mortuary. **-ua·rio** *m.* register of deaths; †(eccl.) obituarius.

†obiurg-are *tr.* to reprove, to rebuke. **†-azione** *f.* reproof, rebuke.

oblat-a¹ *f.* (eccl.) (woman) oblate; suore -e, oblate sisters; (hist. liturg.) oblations. **-o** *m.* (eccl.) oblate. **-ore** *m.* giver, donor (to pious or charitable cause); (comm.) bidder; (leg.) tenderer of money in lieu of fine (C.P.). **(-rice** *f.*)

oblata² *f.* (ichth.). See **obbiada**.

†oblatratore *m.* barker; howler; slanderer, malicious gossiping individual.

oblazi-ona·rio *m.* (hist. liturg.) oblationarius. **-one** *f.* offering, gift; (liturg.; theol.) oblation, offertory; (comm.) bid; bidding; (leg.) offer; -one nella contravvenzione, tender, before trial, or conviction, of money in settlement of alleged contravention (C.P.).

†oblettazione *f.* See **dilettazione**.

obl-iare [A4i] *tr.* (poet.) to forget; †*rfl.* -iarsi in, to become absorbed in, to be lost in. **-ia·bile** *adj.* (poet.) forgettable. **†-ianza** *f.* oblivion; forgetfulness. **-ìo** *m.* (poet.) oblivion; forgetfulness; morire in —, (nell'—), to die forgotten; coperto d'—, forgotten, neglected; sottrarre all'—, to rescue from oblivion. **-ioso** *adj.* oblivious, forgetful; bringing forgetfulness.

obliqu-o *adj.* oblique; slanting; sideways, indirect; tiro —, glancing blow; sguardo —, sidelong glance; skew, raking; (anat.) muscolo —, obliquus muscle; (gramm.) caso —, oblique case (i.e. not nominative or vocative); (naut.) corso —, course made good owing to drift; vento —, oblique wind; †(mil.) figura -a, not square; (morally) devious, crooked, underhand; suspect; andare in —, to sin; per —, obliquely; †*n.m.* unrighteousness. **-amente** *adv.* obliquely, sideways; crookedly, dishonestly, unfairly; guardare -amente, to look askance at; (mil.) marciare -amente, to march inclined. **-an·golo** *adj.* (geom.) non-right-angled. **-are** [A1] *tr.* to cut across; to bend sideways; (mil.) to strike with glancing blows; *intr.* (*aux.* essere) to move sideways; to edge; (naut.) to beat; (mil.) to progress diagonally. **-ità** *f.* obliquity, obliqueness; (slang) crookedness.

obliter-are [A I s] *tr.* to obliterate; to efface; to cancel, to stamp out. **-ato** *part. adj.* obliterated; effaced; cancelled. **-azione** *f.* obliteration; effacement; cancelling; (surg.) obliteration.

obliv-ione *f.* (poet.) oblivion, forgetfulness; (med.) stupor; †(leg.) amnesty. †**-ioso** *adj.* oblivious.

oblò *m. indecl.* (naut.) scuttle; porthole.

oblun-go *adj., n.m.* (*pl.* **-ghi**) oblong.

†**obnubilare** *tr.* to cloud, to obscure, to obfuscate.

obnubilazione *f.* (med.) obnubilation.

o·boe, oboè *m. indecl.* (mus.) oboe, hautboy; — d'amore, oboe d'amore; — da caccia, oboe da caccia, cor anglais.

oboista *m., f.* (mus.) oboist.

o·bol-o *m.* (Gk. antiq.; numism.) obol, obolus; small coin (esp. for alms), mite; (eccl.) l'— di S. Pietro, Peter's pence.

obombr-are [A I C] *tr.* to obumbrate, to overshadow (sometimes theol., as in Luke I, 35). (**-amento** *m.*) **-ato** *part. adj.* obumbrated, overshadowed. †**-azione** *f.* overshadowing, clouding; obumbrating.

obovato *adj.* (bot.) obovate.

obretti·zio *adj.* (leg.) obreptitious.

†**obrizzo** *m.* pure gold.

†**obsediare** *tr.* to besiege.

†**obsequente** *adj.* obedient, submissive; obsequious.

†**obsesso** *adj.* besieged.

obsolescenza *f.* obsolescence.

obsoleto *adj.* obsolete, outworn, antiquated.

†**obtento** *m.* intention, intent.

†**obtrett-atore** *m.* detractor. †**-azione** *f.* calumny, disparagement.

oc *m.* (linguist.) Oc; lingua d'—, *langue d'Oc*, (Old) Provençal; il paese dell'—, Languedoc.

oca¹ *f.* (orn.) goose; — collo rosso, red-breasted goose, *Branta ruficollis*; — colombaccio, Brent goose, *B. bernicla*; — faccia bianca, barnacle goose, *B. leucopsis*; — granaiola, bean goose, *Anser fabalis*; — lombardella, white-fronted goose, *A. albifrons*; — selvatica, grey-lag goose, *A. anser*; ecco fatto il becco all'—, there, that's finished, that's the finishing touch; pelle d'—, gooseflesh; mi fai venir la pelle d'—, you give me the creeps; collo d'—, goose-neck; giuoco dell'—, a game somewhat like 'snakes and ladders'; fool; parere un'—, to look a fool; *in appos.* foolish; stupid; popolo —, stupid nation; scolari oche, stupid pupils.

oca² *f.* (weight) oka, oke.

ocarina *f.* (mus.) ocarina.

occa *f.* (ichth.) — nera, black umber, *Johnius umbra*.

occasa *f.* (naut.) setting azimuth.

occasion-e *f.* occasion, juncture; poesia d'—, occasional verse; (theol.) — prossima di peccare, proximate occasion of sin; impiego d'—, occasional employment; opportunity, chance; dare — a uno di, to give an opportunity to someone of (to); mettere uno nell'— di, to enable someone to; pigliare l'— di (a, per), to seize the occasion to; (provb.) l'— fa l'uomo ladro, opportunity makes the thief; *adv. phr.* all'—, as opportunity offers, on occasion; bargain; d'—, second-hand; comprare d'—, to buy at sale-price, *or* to buy second-hand; è un'—, it's a bargain. **-ale** *adj.* fortuitous, chance, arising from a particular occasion; (philos.) causa -ale, occasional cause, immediate cause; (med.) febbre -ale, specific fever. **-almente** *adv.* casually, accidentally, as it happened; occasionally. **-alismo** *m.* (philos.) occasionalism. **-are** [A I C] *tr.* to occasion, to cause. **-ato** *part. adj.* caused; accidental.

occaso *m.* (poet.) setting, decline; setting-place; west.

oc·chia *f.* See oca².

occhi-a·ia *f.* eye-socket; *pl.* dark rings under the eyes; (naut.) — delle gomene, the point where eyes or splices have been let into hawsers. **-ala·io** *m.* spectacle-maker, optician. **-aletto, -alino** *m.* lorgnette; eyeglass, monocle. **-ali** *m.pl.* glasses, spectacles; goggles; è miope, dovrebbe portare gli -ali, he's short-sighted, he ought to wear glasses; -ali a stringinaso, pince-nez; -ali da sole, sun-glasses; -ali acustici, spectacle-hearing-aid; (industr.) -ali di protezione, protective goggles; (draughts) fare gli -ali, to move a draught between two enemy pieces so that both are challenged. **-alone** *m.* (ichth.) sea bream, *Pagellus centrodontus*; †spyglass, telescope. **-aluto** *adj.* bespectacled. **-are** [A 4] *tr.* to eye; to set eyes on, to espy, to discover; †(naut.) to put eyelets in (canvas, sails, etc.).

occhiata¹ look, glance; scambiarsi un'—, to exchange looks; glimpse; dare un'— a, to glance at; †view.

occhiata² *f.* (ichth.) a kind of sea bream, *Oblada melanura*.

occhiatella *f.* (ichth.). See occhiata².

occhiatina *f.* (ichth.) electric ray, *Torpedo ocellata*.

occhi-ato *adj.* full of eyes, ocellated, marked with eye-shaped design; le penne -e del pavone, the peacock's feathers patterned with eyes. †**-atura** *f.* glance, look.

occhi-azzurro *adj.* (poet.) blue-eyed. **-bendato** *adj.* (poet.) blindfold. **-ceru·leo** *adj.* (poet.) blue-eyed. **-eggiare** [A 3 C] *tr.* to ogle, to cast glances at; *intr.* (*aux.* avere) to gleam, to glint. **-ella·ia** *f.* buttonholer. **-ellatura** *f.* buttonholing; line of buttonholes. **-ello** *m.* small hole; buttonhole; (joc.) sword-wound; (agric.) shallow furrow; (naut.) eyelet; metal thimble in an eyelet; (text.) eye; (typ.) page almost blank, *or* the small group of words on it (e.g. printed half-title, or separate chapter-title, or MS. address at bottom corner of document). **-etto** *m. dim.* little eye; far l'-etto, to wink; round hole; ring; †(naut.) see occhiello; (typ.) small group of words, or page bearing them; cf. occhiello. **-nero** *adj.* (joc.) dark-eyed, black-eyed.

occhino *m.* See under occhio.

occh-io *m.* **1.** EYE; cieco da (d') un —, blind in one eye; globo, bulbo, (pop.) palla dell'—, eye-ball; orbita, (pop.) cavo, incassatura dell'—, eye-socket; la sclerotica, (pop.) il bianco, dell'—, the white of the eye; -i sporgenti, protruding eyes; -i incavati, infossati, incassati, sunken eyes; -i di pesce lesso, cod-fish eyes; -i a mandorla, slanting, almond eyes; avere gli -i bellissimi, to have beautiful eyes; battere gli -i, to blink; in un batter d'—, in the twinkling of an eye; strizzare l'—, to wink; — per —, dente per dente, an eye for an eye, a tooth for a tooth; uovo all'— di bue, fried egg; costare un — della testa, to be exorbitantly dear; aprire gli -i alla luce, to be born; chiudere gli -i, to close one's eyes, (euphem.) to die; non ho chiuso —, I didn't sleep a wink; piangere ad -i caldi, to weep bitterly; perdere il lume degli -i, to fly into a rage; ne ho fino agli -i, I'm sick of it; avere gli -i tra i peli, to be sleepy; a quattr'-i, privately, *tête à tête*. **2.** EYE-SIGHT, vision; glance, look; a — nudo, with the naked eye, to the naked eye; a vista d'—, within sight; a perdita d'—, as far as the eye can reach; essere tutt'-i, to be all eyes, to gaze fixedly and eagerly; — pio, tender glance; far l'— di triglia, to cast sheep's eyes; mettere gli -i su, addosso a, to have one's eye on; avere lasciato gli -i sopra, to long for, to desire, to covet; rifare l'—, to look at pleasant things (for a change, after ugly or sordid sights); bisogna fare l'— a, one gets used to the sight of; a —, as far as one can judge; a — e croce, roughly speaking. **3.** NOTICE, attention, observation; tenere d'—, tenere gli -i addosso a, to keep an eye on; mi cadde sott'-i, it came to my notice, I happened to catch sight of; dare nell'— a, to attract the notice of; quel colore da nell'—, that colour is too startling; ci vuole l'—, you need to have your wits about you; una cosa che salta agli -i, something that leaps to the eye; chiudere un —, to turn a blind eye; aprire gli -i a uno, to open someone's eyes for him; avere la benda agli -i, to be unaware of what is going on; dormire ad -i aperti, to be wary, to be on the alert; l'— del padrone ingrassa il cavallo, i.e. a business thrives when the proprietor is able to keep an eye on it personally; gettare il fumo, la polvere negli -i a, to throw dust in the eyes of; — alle mani!, look out for pickpockets!; lontano dagli -i, lontano dal cuore, out of sight, out of mind; (provb.) se l'— non mira, cuor non sospira, what the eye doesn't see the heart doesn't grieve over. **4.** REGARD, way of looking upon, view; vedere di buon —, to have a high regard for, to look favourably upon; guardare di mal —, to look on with disfavour; il mal d'—, the evil-eye; agli -i miei, in my view; nulla è piu caro agli -i suoi, he holds nothing dearer; agli -i del mondo, in the eyes of the world. **5.** ROUND HOLE, eye-hole; — di bue, bull's eye window; (radio) — magico, magic eye, tuning indicator; (bot.) — bud; eye of potato; — dormiente, resting bud; — d'asino, arrow-head, *Sagittaria sagittifolia*; — di bue, *Chrysanthemum myconis*; — di civetta, primrose, *Primula vulgaris*, oxlip, *P. elatior*; (geog.) — di fontana, centre of a spring; (naut.) hawsepipe or any aperture in ship's side; per —, through the hawsepipe; andare per —, colare a fondo per —, to sink; filare per —, lasciare per —, to slip the cable; — alla penna!, watch the wind!; — del vento, eye of the wind; — della nave, porthole (NOTE: in English the 'eyes of the ship' is the foremost part on the upper deck); eyelet in awning or sail; impiombatura a —, eye-splice; †curl on an executive officer's sleeve (before 1910 in Ital. Navy); (mil.)

occh·io (*cont.*)

orifice in any bomb or torpedo for detonators, primers, etc.; (meteor.) — di un ciclone, central zone of a cyclone; (biol.) ocellus, an eye-shaped mark on a bird's feather, as in the peacock's tail; (miner.) — di gatta, cat's eye; — di pernice, kind of muscat (grape or wine), kind of soup; (radio) — magico, tuning indicator; (typ.) face; few words on page, or page with few words (cf. **occhiello**). **-iac·cio** *m. pejor.* ugly look; mi guardava con certi -iacci, he gave me a dirty look. **-ino** *m.* eye-bath. **-iocotto** *m.* (orn.) Sardinian warbler, *Sylvia melanocephala.* **-iolino** *m. dim.* little eye; far l'-iolino a, to make eyes at. **-ione** *m. augm.* large or wide eye; (ichth.) see **occhialone**, under **occhiaia**; (orn.) stone curlew, *Burrhinus œdicnemus.* **-iorossa** *m.* (orn.) see **occhiocotto.** **-isanguigno** *adj.* with bloodshot eyes. **-iuto** *adj.* sharp-eyed; shrewd; cautious; (bot.) well furnished with buds.

occident·e *m.* west; occident; (hist.) Impero d'—, Western Empire. **-ale** *adj.* western, west, occidental; westerly; this side of the Iron Curtain

†**occi·dere** *vb.* and derivs. See **uccidere.**

occi·du·o *adj.* (poet.) western; sole —, setting sun; luce -a, waning light. **-a** *f.* (naut.) setting azimuth.

occi·p·ite *m.* (anat.) occiput; (of sheep) scrag. **-itale** *adj.* occipital. †**-i·zio** *m.* occiput.

†**occisione** *f.* See **uccisione.**

occita·nico *adj.* Provençal (literature, culture).

occlu·dere [C3] *tr.* to occlude; to close; to obstruct; to stop up.

occlusione *f.* occlusion; (med.) stoppage.

†**occoltare** *vb.* and derivs. See **occultare.**

†**occolto** *adj.* See **occulto.**

occorr·ere [C5c] *intr.* (*aux.* essere) to be necessary; to be required; to be lacking; mi -ono cento lire, I need a hundred lire; ti -e altro?, do you need anything else?; *impers.* -e farlo, it must (needs to) be done; non -e farlo, there is no need to do it; non -e che lui venga, there is no need for him to come; †to happen, to occur. **-ente** *part. adj.* necessary, needful; *n.m.* what is needed; tutto l'-ente, all the requisites, everything necessary. **-enza** *f.* circumstance, occasion; need; all'-enza, if need be, when required; far le sue -enze, to relieve oneself.

occorso *part.* of **occorrere**, q.v.; †*adj.* come to pass.

occult·are [A1] *tr.* to conceal, to hide; to keep secret; (leg.) — un cadavere, to conceal a corpse; — un impedimento al matrimonio, to conceal an impediment to marriage (C.P.). **-a·bile** *adj.* concealable. **-amento** *m.* concealing; (leg.) -amento di un evaso, concealment of an escapee (C.P.). **-ato** *part. adj.* hidden, concealed; kept secret. **-azione** *f.* concealment; (astron.) occultation; (cinem.) fase di -azione, dark interval.

occult·o *adj.* hidden, secret; in —, secretly; occult; (astron.) occulted; (comm.) socio —, secret partner; (med.) sangue —, occult blood, concealed blood; †*n.m.* the occult; secret; hidden truth. **-amente** *adv.* secretly. **-i·smo** *m.* occultism.

occup·are [A1s] *tr.* to occupy (space, territory, attention); to employ; to take up, to use; to spend (time); to give employment to; l'ho -ato a pulire le stanze, I've given him the job of cleaning the rooms; l'hanno -ato in una banca, they have found him a job in a bank; (leg.) to occupy; to take possession of; — una cosa mobile, to take possession of, to appropriate to oneself, a chattel; — un fondo altrui, to occupy another's land (C.C.); †to cover; †to block, to impede; †to hide; † — a, to wrest from, to divest of; *rfl.* (*prep.* di) to busy oneself (with, in); to be interested (in), to be concerned (with); mi -avo di trovarlo, I was intent on finding it; òccupati degli affari tuoi, mind your own business; to find work. **-a·bile** *adj.* that may be occupied. **-ante** *part. adj.* occupying; *n.m.f.* occupier; (leg.) occupant; possessor; holder; primo -ante, first occupant (of real property), first to reduce (chattel) into possession. **-ato** *part. adj.* occupied; working, busy, engaged; -ato a, busy with; engaged in; taken up; full; un posto non -ato, a free place, a seat not occupied. **-azione** *f.* occupation, work, business; pursuit; employment; -azione totale, piena -azione, full employment; (leg.) act of taking possession; appropriation to oneself; reduction into possession (C.C.); occupation (C.P.); (econ.) investimento per l'-azione, investment to promote employment.

Ocea·nia *pr.n.f.* (geog.) Oceania.

oce·a·nico *adj.* oceanic; ocean-going; deep-sea. **-anino** *adj.* of the ocean; *n.f.pl.* (class. myth.) le -anine, the Oceanids, sea nymphs. **-anografi·a** *f.* oceanography. **-anogra·fico** *adj.* oceanographical.

oce·an·o[1], †**oceano** *m.* ocean, esp. the Atlantic; — Australe, Southern Ocean; (fig.) — di guai, sea of troubles; vast amount, unending quantity; una goccia nell'—, a drop in the ocean; *adj.* oceanic, of the ocean.

Oce·ano[2] *pr.n.m.* (class. myth.) Oceanus.

ocello *m.* (zool.) ocellus.

oche·ista *m., f.* hockey-player. **-i·stico** *adj.* relating to hockey (cf. **hockey**).

o·cipo *m.* (ent.) *Ocypus olens*, a large staphylinid beetle.

oclocr·a·tico *adj.* ochlocratic. **-azi·a** *f.* ochlocracy.

oclofobi·a *f.* (psych.) ochlophobia.

ocr·a *f.* (miner.) ochre. **-a·ceo** *adj.* ochraceous. †**-ia** *f.* see **ocra.**

o·crea *f.* (Rom. antiq.) greave; (bot.) ochrea.

ocro·dermi·a *f.* (med.) ochrodermia, ochrodermatosis. **-no·si** *f.* (med.) ochronosis.

oct·ano *m.*, **-ilammina** *f.* See **ottano, ottilammina**, under **ottacordo.**

oc·tile *m.* (chem.) octyl.

octo·stilo *adj.* (archit.) having eight columns; *n.m.* (archit.) a series of eight equal columns; a façade with eight columns.

ocul·are *adj.* ocular, optical; nervo —, optic nerve; testimonio —, eyewitness; lente —, eyepiece; *n.m.* eyepiece. **-armente** *adv.* ocularly, optically. **-a·rio** *m.* (Rom. antiq.) oculist. **-arista** *m.* ocularist. **-ate·zza** *f.* cautiousness, wariness, shrewdness. **-ato** *adj.* sharp-sighted, heedful, circumspect, sagacious; wary; †furnished with eyes; possessing eyes; †con -ata fede, with one's own eyes, verily, without doubt. **-atamente** *adv.* shrewdly; sagaciously; warily. **-ista** *m.* oculist, eye specialist, ophthalmologist. **-i·stica** *f.* ophthalmology. **-i·stico** *adj.* ophthalmological. **-ocardiaco** *adj.* (med.) oculocardiac. **-omotore** *adj.* (anat.) oculomotor, oculogyric.

od *conj.* See **o**[3].

oda *f.* See **ode.**

odalisca *f.* odalisque.

odassi·smo *m.* (med.) odaxismus, odaxesmus.

od·e *f.* ode; (fig.) panegyric. **-e·o** *m.*, **-e·on** *m. indecl.* (Gk. antiq.) odeum.

†**odepo·rico** *m.* description of a journey; *adj.* relating to a journey or travelling.

odi·are [A3] *tr.* to hate, to detest, to loathe, to dislike; to shun; farsi — a morte, to get oneself hated; — a morte, to hold in deadly hatred. **-a·bile** *adj.* hateful, loathsome; detestable. **-ante** *part. adj.* hating; *n.m., f.* hater. **-ato** *part. adj.* hated, detested, loathed; disliked. (**-atore** *m.* **-atrice** *f.*)

†**odi·bile** *adj.* hateful; annoying, displeasing.

odiern·o *adj.* of today; contemporary, modern; condizioni -e, conditions nowadays; (comm.) la vostra lettera -a, your letter of today. **-amente** *adv.*)

Od·ino *pr.n.m.* (rel.) Odin. **-i·nico** *adj.* of Odin, Odinic.

o·di·o *m.* hatred, hate, loathing; avere in —, to abhor; portare — a, to bear hatred towards; per — contro, out of hatred of; in — alla legge, despite, in defiance of, the law; odium; essere in — a uno, to be detested by someone; venire in — a, to be hated by; (leg.) — fra le classi sociali, hatred between classes of society (C.P.); in — a, against. †**-osamato** *adj.* (Alfieri) loved and hated at the same time. **-osità** *f.* natural aversion; enmity; hatefulness; odious behaviour; odium. **-oso** *adj.* hateful; odious. **-osamente** *adv.* hatefully, odiously.

Odisse·a *pr.n.f.* Odyssey; (fig.) storm-tossed life; adventure.

Odisse·o *pr.n.m.* Odysseus.

odo *1st pers. sing. pres. indic* of **udire**, q.v.

odo·metro *m.* odometer, hodometer, mileage meter, mileometer; †(naut.) see **solcometro.**

odont·agra *f.* (med.) odontagra. **-algi·a** *f.* odontalgia, toothache. **-al·gico** *adj.* odontalgic. **-iatri·a** *f.* (med.) dentistry. **-ia·trico** *adj.* (med.) dental, pertaining to dentistry; complesso -iatrico, dental unit. **-odini·a** *f.* (med.) odontodynia, toothache. **-o·foro** *adj.* (med.) dentigerous. **-ogeni·a** *f.* (med.) odontogeny. **-o·grafo** *m.* (eng.) odontograph. **-oiatra** *m.* dentist. **-oiatri·a** *f.* dentistry. **oia·trico** *adj.* relating to dentistry. **-o·ide** *adj.* (anat.) odontoid. **-olite** *f.* (miner.) bone turquoise, odontolite. **-olito** *m.* (med.) odontolith, tartar deposit. **-ologi·a** *f.* dentistry, odontology. **-oma** *m.* (med.) odontoma. **-opati·a** *f.* odontopathy, dental disease. **-orragi·a** *f.* haemorrhage following extraction. **-o·si** *f.* (med.) odontosis, odontogenesis. **-otec·nica** *f.* dental mechanics. **-otec·nico** *adj.* dental mechanic.

odont-o·metro, -osco·pio *m.* (philat.) perforation gauge.

odonto·rniti *m.pl.* (orn.) Odontornithes.

odor-are [A I C] *tr.* to smell; — un buon affare, to scent a bargain; to perfume, to scent; *intr.* (*aux.* avere) to have a smell; — di buono, to smell nice, to smell good; — di, to smell of, to smack of, to savour of; *n.m.* (sense of) smell. **-a·bile** *adj.* that can be smelt; that has a smell; †fragrant. **-acchiare** [A 3] *intr.* (*aux.* avere) to have a slight smell (esp. unpleasant). **-amento** *m.* giving forth smell; †smell, odour; †fragrance. **-ante** *part. adj.* smelling. †**-anza** *f.* odour. **-ativo** *adj.* olfactory. **-ato** *part. adj.* fragrant; scented, perfumed; *n.m.* sense of smell; scent (of hound).

odor-e *m.* smell, odour, fragrance; stench; perfume, scent; flavour, flavouring; *pl.* sweet herbs; sense of smell; inkling, token, indication; dar buon — di sè, to be in good repute; morire in — di santità, to die in the odour of sanctity. **-i·fero** *adj.* odoriferous, fragrant. †**-ificante,** †**-i·fico** *adj.* odoriferous. **-ista** *m.* lover of scents, connoisseur of perfumes. **-oso** *adj.* sweet-smelling, fragrant; odorous. **-osamente** *adv.* fragrantly; odorously.

Odra *pr.n.f.* (geog.) Oder (which is the more usual form of the name in Italian).

oè *excl.* See **ohè.**

oersted *m. indecl.* (electr.) oersted.

ofanità *f.* conceit, arrogance, pretentiousness.

Ofe·lia *pr.n.f.* Ophelia.

off-a *f.* cake; gettar l'— a uno, to throw a sop to someone; bribe. †**-ella** *f.* little cake, sweetmeat. **-elleri·a** *f.* confectioner's shop.

offen·d-ere [C 3] *tr.* to harm physically, to hurt, to damage; (mil.) to attack, to bombard; to insult, to outrage; to offend, to be offensive to; to distress; non per ~ervi, ma…, excuse my saying so, but…; †to impede, to obstruct; (leg.) to offend; to injure; to insult; to commit an offence against (C.P.); *intr.* (*aux.* avere) to be offensive, to give offence; *rfl.* (*prep.* di, per) to take offence, to take umbrage (at). **-i·bile** *adj.* vulnerable. †**-i·colo** *m.* obstruction, impediment, obstacle. **-imento** *m.* offending; offence. **-itore** *m.* offender; *adj.* offending; offensive. (**-itrice** *f.*)

†**offens-a** *f.,* †**-anza** *f.,* †**-ione** *f.* See **offesa.**

offens-iva *f.* (mil.) offensive, attack; prendere l'—, to take the offensive; iniziare l'—, to start an offensive, to launch an attack. **-ivo** *adj.* offensive. †**-o** *part.* of **offendere,** q.v. **-ore** *m.* offender; attacker. (**-ora** *f.*)

offer-ire [D I] and derivs. see **offrire.** †**-enda** *f.* (theol.) offering, oblation. **-ente** *m., f.* offerer; bidder; tenderer.

offert-a *f.* offer, offering, proposal; proffer; si ricevono ~e, donations are invited; (theol.) oblation, offering; †offertory; (econ.) supply; (comm.) bid, tender; — affermativa, firm offer; prima —, upset price; (econ.) — e domanda, supply and demand; (leg.) offer; tender; — di adempimento, tender of performance; — reale, tender of payment (C.C.). †**-o** *m.* (eccl.) oblate. **-o·rio** *m.* (liturg.) offertory; (mus.) offertorium; offertory piece.

offes-a *f.* harm, damage, injury; offence; affront; insult, outrage; recare — a, to give offence to, to offend; (mil.) assault, offensive; stare sull'—, to be on the offensive; portare l'— nel territorio nemico, to carry the offensive into enemy territory; esporsi alle ~e, to court attack; (leg.) offence; injury, insult; — al pudore, offence against decency; *pl.* — in scritti, offending matter in writings (C.P.). †**-anza** *f.* see **offesa.**

officiale *adj.* and derivs. See **ufficiale.**

offici-are [A 3] *intr.* (*aux.* avere) to officiate; *tr.* to serve (a church). **-ante** *part. adj.* officiating; *n.m.* (eccl.) officiant. (**-atore** *m.*)

officin-a *f.* workshop; works; working place; workroom; factory; — del gas, gasworks; l'— scrittoria, scriptorium; capo —, foreman; (fig.) manufactory; masonic lodge; (med., joc.) — orinaria, 'waterworks'. **-ale** *adj.* (pharm.) medicinal, officinal.

offi·ci-o *m.* (good) office, service, task. **-osità** *f.* obligingness, readiness to help. **-oso** *adj.* courteous, helpful. **-osamente** *adv.* courteously, helpfully.

offrire [D 8] *tr.* to offer; to give; — in dono, to present as a gift, to give as a present; to present; to afford; non offre interesse, it affords no interest; offre molte difficoltà, it presents many difficulties; ti offro di venire con me, I invite you to come with me; (rel.) to dedicate, to offer up (sacrifice, sufferings); (leg.) to offer; to tender (C.C.); (comm.) to bid; — all'asta, to bid at an auction; to offer, to put on the market; to ask for tenders; *rfl.* to offer oneself; to present oneself; to stand forth, to come forward;

to volunteer; s'offrì a (di) andare, he volunteered to go; un'idea mi s'offre alla mente, an idea occurs to me; quando si offre l'occasione, when the opportunity arises.

offusc-are [A 2] *tr.* to darken, to cloud; to dim, to bedim; to obscure, to blur; to obfuscate; *rfl.* to grow dark; to grow dim; to become clouded. **-amento** *m.* darkening; dimming; dimness; (med.) obfuscation. **-ante** *part. adj.* dimming; clouding. **-ato** *part. adj.* darkened; dimmed; dim; clouded. (**-atore** *m.* **-atrice** *f.*) **-azione** *f.* clouding; (astron.) obfuscation, occultation.

†**ofiasi** *f.* (med.) ophiasis, alopecia.

of-icalcite *f.* (miner.) ophicalcite. forsterite marble. **-icle·ide** *m.* (mus.) ophicleide. **-i·dio** *m.* (ichth.) *Ophidium* spp.; *pl.* (zool.) snakes, *Ophidia.* **-idismo** *m.* (med.) snake-bite poisoning. **-iolite** *f.* (miner.) serpentine. **-iologi·a** *f.* (zool.) scientific study of snakes. **-iotossina** *f.* (med.; chem.) ophiotoxin. **-ite** *f.* (miner.) ophite. **-iti** *m.pl.* (rel. hist.) Ophites. **-iuco** *m.* (astron.) Serpentarius, Ophiuchus. **-iura** *f.* (zool.) brittle star, *Ophiura* spp.

ofrio·n *m. indecl.* (anat.) ophryon.

oftalm-ectomi·a *f.* (surg.) ophthalmectomy, removal of the eyeball. **-i·a** *f.* (med.) ophthalmia. **-ico (-a·lmico)** *adj.* (med.) ophthalmic; affected with ophthalmia; (pharm.) used for ophthalmia; *n.m.* person suffering from ophthalmia. **-(o)iatri·a** *f.* ophthalmology. **-(o)iatro** *m.* ophthalmologist, oculist. **-ologi·a** *f.* ophthalmology. **-olo·gico** *adj.* ophthalmological. **-o·logo** *m.* ophthalmologist. **-ometri·a** *f.* (med.) ophthalmometry. **-ome·trico** *adj.* ophthalmometric. **-o·metro** *m.* (med.) ophthalmometer. **-oplegi·a** *f.* (med.) ophthalmoplegia. **-oscopi·a** *f.* ophthalmoscopy. **-osco·pico** *adj.* ophthalmoscopical. **-osco·pio** *m.* (med.) ophthalmoscope. **-oterapi·a** *f.* ophthalmology, ophthalmic treatment. **-o·tropo** *m.* (med.) ophthalmotrope.

Oga Magoga *pr.n.m.* proverbial name for distant, fabulous, or dangerous place: 'the end of the world'; 'wonderland'.

oggett-o *m.* object; subject; theme; thing, article; aim, purpose; (leg.) — osceno, obscene object (C.P.); — del contratto, subject-matter of contract (C.C.); in risposta alla Vs. pregiata del 13 u.s. in —, in reply to yours of the 13th ult. in re.; (comm.) per quale —?, a che —?, for what purpose?; (gramm.) object. **-ivare** [A I] *tr.* (philos.) to objectivize. **-ivismo** *m.* (philos.) objectivism. **-ivista** *m.* (philos.) objectivist. **-ività** *f.* (philos.) objectivity. **-ivo** *adj.* (philos.; gramm.) objective; proposizione ~iva, object clause; insegnamento ~ivo, object-teaching; *n.m.* goal, objective. **-ivamente** *adv.* objectively.

oggi *adv.* today; quest'—, today as ever is; da — in poi, from today on; — a otto, today week; — sette giorni fa, a week ago today; — anno, a year ago today; — come —, (just) at present; tutt'—, the whole of today, all today; a tutt'—, (right) up till now, till today; — o domani, one day or other; da — a domani, from one day to the next; rimandare d'— in domani, to put things off from day to day; nowadays; la moda d'—, present-day fashions; non esser più d'—, to be no longer young; (S. Italy) this afternoon; *n.m.* l'—, the day; the present time; dall'— al domani, from day to day.

oggi-dì *adv.* (pop.) nowadays; today. **-diano** *m.* one who thinks the old days were much better and that everything nowadays is going to the dogs. **-giorno** *adv.* (pop.) in these days, now. †**-ma·i** *adv.* see **oramai.**

ogiv-a *f.* (archit.) ogive, diagonal groin crossing another at the centre of a vault; pointed arch; (mil.) curvature of the nose of a projectile; cone of a missile; (aeron.) spinner; (statistics) ogive. **-ale** *adj.* (archit.) ogival; architettura ~ale, Gothic architecture, pointed architecture; cigar-shaped. **-o** *adj.* (mil.) curved (of the nose of a projectile).

ogliastra *m.* Sardinian red wine.

†**ogliente** *adj.* See **olente.**

†**ogna** *f.* See **ugna.**

†**ognaccordo** *m.* (mus.) stringed instrument (cf. **dabbudà**).

ogn-i *adj.* every, each; — due giorni, every two days, every other day; — tanto, every so often; — poco, every so often; — qual volta, whenever; — dove, d'ogn'intorno, everywhere; — sempre, for ever; — lettor più longanime, even the most patient reader; in — ora della giornata, at any hour of the day; in — caso, in any case, at any rate; †*pl.* all. **-itempo** *adj. indecl.* all-weather; (mil.; aeron.) caccia —, all-weather fighter. **-issanti** *m.* (eccl. Tusc.) All Saints' (Day, Church). **-ora** *adv.* always; ~ora che, whenever, every time that. **-uno** *prn.* (*sing.* only) everyone, each (one).

ọh, (Tusc.) **oh,** *excl.* oh!; (naut.) —! tira!, haul now!; — issa!, hoist now!

ọhe, ohẹ *excl.* hi! I say!

ohi, ọhi *excl.* oh!, ah! (esp. of pain).

ohibò *excl.* oh, come! for shame!

ohimè *excl.* alas!; oh dear!

ohm *m. indecl.* (electr.) ohm.

ohm·metro *m.* (electr.) ohmmeter.

oh·mico *adj.* (electr.) ohmic.

Oia Scio *pr.n.m.* (geog.) Oyashio.

oil *adv., n.m.* (linguist.) *oïl*; lingua d'—, *langue d'öil*, Old French.

oilta·nico *adj.* (linguist.) of, relating to, Old French.

oka *f.* See oca².

olà *excl.* hallo!; hi there! (commandingly or threateningly, but often joc.); look!

Oland-a *pr.n.f.* (geog.) Holland; (text.) Holland cloth. **-ẹse** *adj.* Dutch, *n.m.* Dutchman; Dutch language; *f.* Dutch woman; (paperm.) hollander, beater. **-ẹtta** *f.* (text.) Holland cloth.

ole-a·ceo *adj.* oily. **-agi̧noso** *adj.* oleaginous. **-andrina** *f.* (chem.) oleandrin. **-andro** *m.* (bot.) oleander, *Nerium oleander.* **-a·rio** *adj.* relating to, oil; for oil; containing oil; (ent.) mosca -aria, see under **mosca**. **-astro** *m.* (bot.) wild olive, *Olea europaea,* var. *oleaster.* **-ato** *m.* (chem.) oleate.

ole·cr-ano *m.* (anat.) olecranon, olecranon process. **-a·nico** *adj.* (anat.) olecranal.

ol- (chem. hist.) hydrocarbon obtained from dry distillation of fatty acids. **-e·ico** *adj.* (chem.) oleic. **-ei·colo** *adj.* pertaining to olive-tree growing. **-eicoltọre** *m.,* **-eicoltura** *f.* see **olivicultore, olivicultura,** under **oliva.** **-ei·fero** *adj.* oleiferous. **-eifi·cio** *m.* oilworks; oil-making. **-eifiọre** *m.* (bot.) oil-bearing plant. **-eina** *f.* (chem.) olein.

olefina *f.* (chem.) olefin.

olente *adj.* (poet.) fragrant.

o·le-o *m.* (chem.) oleum, fuming sulphuric acid. **-odotto** *m.* (oil) pipeline. **-ografi·a** *f.* oleography; oleograph. **-ogra·fico** *adj.* oleographic. **-o·metro** *m.* (techn.; phys.) oleometer; (motor.) oil gauge. **-osità** *f.* oiliness; greasiness. **-ọso** *adj.* oily; greasy; containing oil; (agric.) oleiferous.

oleum *m. indecl.* (chem.) oleum, fuming sulphuric acid.

olezz̧-are [A 1] *intr.* (*aux.* avere) to smell sweet. **-ante** *part. adj.* sweet-smelling, fragrant. **-o** *m.* fragrance, scent.

†**olfare** *intr.* to give forth scent.

†**olfato** *m.* See olfatto.

olfatt-i·a *f.* minimum quantity of substance capable of stimulating the sense of smell, olfacty. **-ivo** *adj.* relating to the sense of smell, olfactory. **-o** *m.* sense of smell, olfaction; grato all'-o, fragrant, sweet-smelling. **-o·rio** *adj.* olfactory. **-o·metro** olfactometer.

olia·ndolo *m.* See under **olio.**

oli-are [A 4] *tr.* (text.) to oil, to batch. **-ag·gio** *m.* (text.) oiling, batching. **-ata** *f.* yield of oil (for one year). **-ato** *adj.* dressed with oil, oiled; carta -ata, grease-paper; (agric., of olives) full of oil, ripe; (phys.; opt.) fotometro a carta -ata, grease-spot photometer. **-atọre** *m.* oil-can. **-atura** *f.* (text.) oiling.

oliastro *m.* (bot.). See oleastro, under **oleaceo.**

oli·bano *m.* (bot.) olibanum, incense (resin of *Boswellia*).

Oliena *pr.n.f.* Oliena, in prov. of Sassari, Sardinia; a red wine from Oliena.

oliera *f.* cruet-stand.

olifante *m.* olifant, oliphant, ivory horn.

olig-arca *m.* oligarch. **-archi·a** *f.* oligarchy. **-ar·chico** *adj.* oligarchic. (**-archicamẹnte** *adv.*)

oligisto *m.* (min.) oligiste-iron, specular iron ore (also **ferro oligisto**).

oligo-cene *m.* (geol.) Oligocene. **-chili·a** *f.* (med.) oligochylia. **-chimi·a** *f.* (med.) oligochymia. **-citemi·a** *f.* (med.) oligocythaemia. **-cla·sio** *m.* (min.) oligoclase, lime-soda feldspar. **-dattili·a** *f.* (med.) oligodactylia. **-emi·a** *f.* (med.) oligaemia, anaemia. **-e·mico** *adj.* (med.) anaemic. **-po·lio** *m.* (econ.) combine, cartel. **-siderite** *f.* (miner.) oligosiderite. **-spermi·a** *f.* (med.) oligospermia.

oliguri·a *f.* (med.) oliguria.

†**olimento** *m.* fragrance, perfume.

Olim·pia *pr.n.f.* (geog.) Olympia.

olimp-i·aco *adj.* Olympic; periodo —, Olympiad. **-i·ade** *f.* Olympiad; *pl.* modern 'Olympic games'; *adj.* Olympian; muse -iadi, Olympian muses.

ol-im·pico *adj.* Olympic; Olympian. **-impio·nico, -impioni·co** *m.* victor at the Olympic games (ancient or modern); (neol.) competitor at modern Olympic games; *adj.* Olympic.

Olimpo *pr.n.m.* (geog.; myth.) Olympus; (fig.) heaven.

o·li-o *m.* olive-oil; oil; — minerale, mineral oil; — di sasso, rock-oil; — essenziale, essential oil; — fisso, fixed oil; — combustibile, fuel oil; — lubrificante, lubricating oil; — di paraffina, paraffin oil; — da ardere, lamp oil; lampada ad —, oil-lamp; — da tavola, salad oil; — di ricino, castor oil; — di merluzzo, cod-liver oil; (cul.) sott'—, in oil; il mare è un —, the sea is like a millpond; non metterci nè sale nè —, not to alter (a tale, an anecdote) for good or evil; dipingere a —, to paint in oils; (rel., fig.) — santo, holy oil, esp. oil of the sick; portar, dar, l'— santo, to give extreme unction; essere all'— santo, to be at the last gasp. **-a·ndolo** *m.* oilmonger; oil-pedlar.

oliọs-o *adj.,* **-ità** *f.* See oleoso, -ità, under **oleo.**

†**olire** *intr.* to send forth fragrance, to be perfumed, to smell sweet.

oliv-a *f.* olive, fruit of **olivo,** q.v.; color —, olive colour; vestito —, olive (-green) dress; verde —, olive-green; (anat.) olive. **-agno** *m.* (bot.) *Elaeagnus angustifolia.* **-are** *adj.* (anat.) olivary. **-astro** *m.* (bot.) *Phillyrea angustifolia; adj.* olive (-coloured, -hued). **-ato** *adj.* planted with olives; (pop. for **oliato**) ripe. **-ella** *f.* fruit of **olivello,** q.v.; bit, (locking part) of pear-shaped key; iron wedge for hoisting stones. **-ello** *m.* (bot.) common privet, *Ligustrum vulgare.* **-enite** *f.* (miner.) olivenite. **-etano** *adj.* (eccl.) Olivetan; *n.m.* Olivetan monk. **-ẹto** *m.,* †**-eta** *f.* olive grove; Monte Oliveto, Mount Olivet, Mount of Olives. **-ẹtta** *f.* (cul. Lomb.) kind of croquette; silk button; frog (on frogged coat); imitation pearl, olivette. **-icultọre** *m.* olive-grower. **-icoltura, -icultura** *f.* olive-growing. **-igno** *adj.* olive (-coloured); †*n.m.* olive wood. **-illa** *f.* (chem.) olivil. **-ina** *f.* (miner.) olivine, chrysolite, peridot. **-o** *m.* (bot.) olive tree, *Olea europaea* var. *sativa;* (rel.) -o benedetto, blessed 'palm' (olive replacing palm).

Oli·via *pr.n.f.* Olivia.

Oli·vio *pr.n.m.* Oliver.

oll-a *f.* earthenware pot; (archaeol.) — cineraria, cinerary urn; — podrida, *olla podrida,* pot-pourri.

†**ollaba** *excl.* expression of anger.

o·lmio *m.* (chem.) holmium.

ọlm-o *m.* (bot.) elm, *Ulmus.* **-a·ia** *f.,* **-ẹto** *m.* elm wood, plantation of elms.

ol-oca·usto *m.* (rel.; fig.) (burnt-)offering; sacrifice; offrire in —, to sacrifice; (fig.) slaughter, holocaust; *adj.* sacrificed, sacrificial. **-ocene** *m.* (geog.) Holocene. **-ocentro** *m.* (ichth.) *Holocentrum* spp., a marine fish. **-oe·drico** *adj.* (cryst.) holohedral. **-ofra·stico** *adj.* (linguist.) holophrastic. **-o·grafo** *m.* (leg.) holograph; document written wholly by person in whose name it appears; will entirely in testator's handwriting (C.C.); *adj.* holographic; testamento -ografo, holograph will (C.C.).

Oloferne *pr.n.m.* Holofernes.

Olọna *pr.n.f.* (geog.) Olona; tela d'—, sail-cloth, canvas.

†**olor** *m.* odour; fragrance; allurement, attraction; greed. †**-i·fero, †-i·fico** *adj.* odorous. †**-ire** *intr.* to be fragrant.

olo-se·rico *adj.* all silk. **-siderite** *f.* (miner.) holosiderite. **-ste·rico** *adj.* (phys.) holosteric. **-tu·ria** *f.* (zool.) sea cucumber, *Holothuria* spp.

†**Olste·nio** *pr.n.m.* (geog.) Holstein.

oltano *m.* a kind of fishing-net.

†**oltra** *prep.; adv.* See oltre.

oltracciò *adv.* moreover, furthermore.

oltracotan-te *adj.* arrogant; overbearing; overweening. **-za** *f.* arrogance; overbearing manner; insolence.

oltraggi-are [A 3] *tr.* to outrage, to insult, to offend. **-a·bile** *adj.* exposed to outrage. **-ato** *part. adj.* outraged, insulted, offended. (**-atọre** *m.* **-atrice** *f.*)

oltrag·gi-o *m.* outrage, insult; offence; gli oltraggi del tempo, the ravages of time; (leg.) — alla Corte, contempt of Court; — al pubblico impiegato, insult to public servant; — al pudore, gross indecency, *or* grossly indecent conduct (C.P.); †excess; †a —, †d'—, excessively. **-ọso** *adj.* outrageous; offensive, insulting; abusive; †disorderly; †excessive; †superfluous. **-osamẹnte** *adv.* outrageously; offensively, insultingly.

oltr-alpe *adv.* beyond the Alps; costumi d'—, Transalpine (esp. French) customs. **-amontano** *adj., n.m.* ultramontane. **-amontanişmo** *m.* (rel. hist.) Ultramontanism. **-anza** *adv. phr.* a -anza,

oltr-alpe (*cont.*)

to the bitter end, to the death, *à outrance*; †*n.f.* see **oltraggio**. †**-apagare** *tr.* to pay too dear. †**-arioso** *adj.* insulting, abusive.

Oltrarno *pr.n.m.* district of Florence across the river Arno.

†**oltrare** *intr.* to advance, to go forward.

oltre *prep.* beyond; — il colle, the other side of the hill; — ogni credere, beyond belief, past belief; — cento persone, over a hundred people; per — un mese, for more than a month; besides; — a ciò, as well as this, not to mention this; — che (oltrechè) perdonargli, apart from, besides, forgiving him; — che spregevole, è inutile, it is not only despicable but useless; — misura (oltremisura), beyond measure; *adv.* beyond, further; andar troppo —, to go too far; vedremo più —, we shall see later on; (after another *adv.*) near; qui —, hereabouts, somewhere here, in this neighbourhood; (admin.) passare — a, to overrule. **-liberale** *adj.* ultra-liberal. **-maraviglioso** *adj.* most wonderful. **-mare** *adv.* overseas (in medieval references, esp. of Palestine); paesi d'-mare, countries beyond the seas; *n.m.* lapis lazuli; ultramarine blue. **-marino** *adj.* overseas, from beyond the seas; ultramarine. **-mira·bile** *adj.* most wondrous. **-misura** *adv.* extremely, immeasurably. **-modo** *adv.* exceedingly. **-mondano** *adj.* beyond this world, of the other world. **-montano** *adj.* see **oltramontano**. **-monti** *adv.* beyond, the other side of, the mountains (esp. to or in France). **-nu·mero** *adv.* beyond number. **-pagato** *adj.* overpaid. **-passa·bile** *adj.* that can be passed or exceeded. **-passare** [A I] *tr.* to pass; to surpass; to go beyond; to exceed; to outstrip; to overstep; (naut.) to round (a headland, etc.). **-rosso** *adj.* see **ultrarosso**. **-tomba** *adv.* beyond the grave; *n.m.* the life beyond, the next world.

omac·cio *m. pejor.* of **uomo**, q.v.; unpleasant man; ill-bred man.

omag·gio *m.* homage; rendere — a, to do homage to; fare — di un libro, to send a presentation copy of a book; copia in —, presentation copy; in —, in token of one's respect; in — alla verità, out of regard for truth; -i dell'autore, with the author's compliments; (comm.) ricevere in —, to receive free of charge; *pl.* i miei -i, my (respectful) compliments; gift, thing given; (comm.) free sample, gift.

omagra *f.* (med.) omagra, gout of the shoulder-joint.

omai *adv.* (poet.) now; henceforth, from now on; at last.

omarino *m. dim.* (Central Italy) of **uomo**, q.v.

o·maro *m.* (zool.) lobster, *Homarus vulgaris.*

omaso *m.* (vet.; zool.) omasum.

ombellico *m.* (anat.) see **umbellico**; (bot.) — maggiore, *Umbilicus horizontalis*; — di Venere, pennywort, navelwort, *Umbilicus rupestris.*

ombilicato *adj.* (biol.) umbilicate (as of certain snails' shells).

ombilico *m.* (geog.) small hollow; (herald.) nombril point.

ombr-a *f.* shadow; fare —, to cast a shadow; *pl.* shadows, darkness; essere nato all'— della cupola di San Pietro, i.e. to be a Roman born and bred; è diventato un'—, he has worn away to a shadow; l'— di se stesso, the shadow of one's former self; dare corpo alle -e, to imagine things; seguire uno come l'— il corpo, to shadow somebody; pareva, era, la sua —, he was always trailing after her; ha paura dell'— sua, he is afraid of his own shadow; (paint.) shadow, shade; in —, in shadow; terra d'—, umber; (astron.) umbra, complete shadow; (radar) zona d'—, blind area, risk area; shade; stare all'—, to be in the shade; senza un palmo d'—, without a spot of shade; (fig.) un'— di sospetto, a shade of suspicion; senz'— di malizia, without the slightest trace of spitefulness; latte con un'— di caffè, milk with a dash of coffee; nemmeno per —!, by no means!; non c'è — di dubbio, there is not a shadow of doubt; non ha l'— di un quattrino, he hasn't a penny to his name; veil, suggestion; un'— di tristezza, a touch of sadness; spectre, phantom, ghost, shade; -e dei morti, apparitions; (Rom. antiq.) uninvited guest, *umbra*; umbrage; prender —, to take umbrage, (of a horse) to shy; dar — a, to give offence to, to arouse suspicion in; tutto gli dà —, he takes offence at the slightest thing; pretence, guise; sotto l'— dell'amicizia, under the guise of friendship; nell'—, secretly, furtively; protection, covering; all'— della legge, under shelter of the law; (cards) 'ombre'; (ichth.) black umber, *Johnius umbra*; (herald.) in —, 'ombre de. †**-a·colo** *m.* shady branch; defence, protection. **-are** [A I c] *tr.* to shade, to overshadow; (paint.) to shade; *rfl.* to darken, to become dark, to be overcast; *intr.* (aux. essere) (of a horse) to shy; (fig.) to take offence, to be suspicious. **-a·tico** *adj.* (of a horse) nervous, inclined to shy; †apparent, feigned. **-a·tile** *adj.*

see **umbra·tile**. **-ato** *part. adj.* (paint.) full of light and shade; *n.m.* (paint.) light and shade, chiaroscuro, play of shadow. **-atura** *f.* (paint.) shade, shading. **-azione** *f.* shadowing, dimming. **-eggiamento** *m.* shading; (mus.) light and shade. **-eggiante** *part. adj.* shady. **-eggiare** [A 3 c] *tr.* to shade; (paint.) to make stand out by marking shadows; to sketch, to adumbrate; (fig.) to touch lightly on; †to cover up, to obscure. **-eggiato** *part. adj.* shaded, shady. **-eggiatura** *f.* shading. **-eggio** *m.* shading, shade. **-ella** *f.* (leafy) shade, umbrage; (bot.) umbel; (aeron.) -ella del paracadute, parachute canopy; (dial. N. Ital.) umbrella; parasol, sunshade. **-ella·io** *m.* umbrella-maker, -seller or -mender. **-ellino** *m. dim.* parasol, sunshade; (liturg.) (small) canopy, *ombrellino.* **-ellini** *m.pl.* (bot.) -ellini delle steccie, *Tordylium maximum.* **-ello** *m.* umbrella; -ello da sole, parasol. **-evole** *adj.* (poet.) shady, umbrageous. **-i·a** *f.* (poet.) shade. **-i·fero** *adj.* umbrageous. **-ina** *f.* (ichth.) black umber, *Johnius umbra*; -ina leccia, *J. hololepidotus.* **-inale** *m.* (naut.) scupper; cuoi, maniche, degli -inali, scupper lips. **-inotto** *m.* (ichth.) male black umber, *J. umber* (not such good eating as the female). **-oso** *adj.* shadowy; shady; suspicious, touchy (of a person); nervous, skittish (of an animal). †**-osi·a** *f.* ignorance; doubt. **-osità** *f.* shadiness, suspiciousness, touchiness, nervousness.

ombr-o·filo *adj.* (bot.) piante -ofile, ombrophils **-o·fobo** *adj.* (bot.) piante -ofobe, ombrophobes. †**-o·metro** *m.* ombrometer.

†**Omburgo** *pr.n.m.* (geog.) Homburg.

omega, o·mega *m.* (Gk. lang.) omega; (fig.) alpha ed —, alpha and omega, the beginning and the end.

†**omei** *m.pl.* lamentations, cries of woe; sorrows; *excl.* alas!

omeli·a *f.* homily (esp. a bishop's).

oment-o *m.* (anat.) omentum. **-ale** *adj.* (anat.) omental. **-opessi** *f.* (surg.) omentofixation, omentopexy.

omeo-grafi·a *f.* lithographic reproduction. **-meri·a** *f.* (Gk. philos.) homoeomery. **-pati·a** *f.* (med.) homoeopathy. **-pa·tico** *adj.* homoeopathic. **-patista** *m., f.* homoeopathist; homoeopath. **-tele·uto** *adj.* (class. rhet.) homoeoteleutic. **-termo** *adj.* (zool.) homoiothermic, warm-blooded.

o·mer-o¹ *m.* shoulder; (anat.) humerus. **-ale** *adj.* (anat.) humeral; (liturg.) velo -ale, humeral veil.

Om-ero² *pr.n.m.* Homer. **-e·rico** *adj.* Homeric. (**-ericamente** *adv.*) **-erista** *m., f.* Homeric scholar; imitator of Homer. **-erizzare** [A I] *intr.* (*aux.* avere) to imitate Homer.

omertà *f.* (S. Italy) conspiracy of silence (in criminal underworld).

omettere [C 20] *tr.* to omit, to leave out; — di dire, to fail to say, non — di dirgli, be sure to tell him.

om-etto, **-icciuolo**, **-iciat·tolo** *m. dim.* of **uomo**, q.v.; (bldg.) king post; capriata a due -etti, queen truss.

Om·fale *pr.n.f.* (myth.) Omphale, queen of Lydia, whom Hercules served as a slave.

omicid-a *m., f.* murderer, slayer; *adj.* murderous, homicidal, destructive. †**-iale** *adj.* homicidal; *n.m.* murderer, homicide.

omici·dio *m.* (leg.) homicide; felonious, unlawful or wilful killing; murder (N.B. Italian criminal law knows different degrees of homicide from English law); — colposo, homicide without malice aforethought, killing by culpable negligence, manslaughter; — preterintenzionale, killing by criminal act not intended to cause death, felonious homicide without malice aforethought, manslaughter; — del consenziente, unlawful killing of consenting party (C.P.); — volontario, — doloso, wilful murder; — circostanziato, — aggravato, wilful murder attended by an aggravating circumstance; — premeditato, wilful murder attended by the aggravating circumstance of premeditation; †slaughter.

o·micron *m.* (Gk. lang.) omicron.

omil-e·tico *adj.* homiletic. **-i·a** *f.* see **omelia**. **-ia·rio** *m.* (eccl.) homiliary.

ominazione *f.* (scient.) origin of Man.

o·mini *m.pl.* of **uomo**, q.v. (cf. **uomini**).

omino *m. dim.* of **uomo**, q.v.; clothes-hanger.

omissione *f.* omission, leaving out; oversight; neglect; (theol.) peccato d'—, sin of omission; (leg.) default; failure; neglect; omission; l'azione od —, act or omission; (comm.) salvo errore od —, errors and omissions excepted.

omissis *m. indecl.* (leg.) omission; words, etc. left out, 'omissis'.

ommati·dio *m.* (zool.) ommatidium.

om·nibus *m. indecl.* horse-bus, omnibus (cf. **autobus**); slow train, stopping train; (finan.) — finanziario, omnibus fiscal regulations; *adj. indecl.* quaderno —, general notebook; treno —, slow train.

om·nium *m. indecl.* (sport) race open to all comers, open race; cycling trial consisting of four events: flying kilometre, speed test, pursuit and 'australiana', q.v., under **australia**; (finan.) omnium, aggregate value of different stock.

omo[1] *m.* See **uomo**.

omo-[2] *pref.* meaning similarity or identity (cf. Eng. homo-).

om-ocroma·tico *adj.* (phys.; opt.) homochromatic. **-ocromi·a** *f.* (zool.) cryptic coloration, mimicking the environment. **-odini·a** *f.* (med.) omodynia, pain in the shoulder. **-ofoni·a** *f.* (mus.) homophony; unison; (ling.) homophony. **-ofo·nico** *adj.* (mus.) homophonic; unisonous. **-o·fono** *adj.* (mus.) homophonous; voci -ofone, voices in unison; (ling.) homophonous, voci -ofone, homophones. **-ofo·rio** *m.* (Eastern liturg.) omophorion. **-ogeneità** *f.* homogeneousness; homogeneity. **-oge·neo** *adj.* homogeneous. **-ografi·a** *f.* (geom.) homography. **-oioide·o** *adj.* (anat.) omohyoid.

omolog-are [A 2 s] *tr.* (leg.) to agree; to approve, to confirm; to initial; to ratify; (Scot.) to homologate; fare — un testamento, to obtain probate of a will; — un concordato fallimentare, to approve a Scheme of Arrangement (C.C.). (**-ato** *part. adj.*) **-azione** *f.* (leg.) approval; confirmation; ratification; (Scot.) homologation; -azione di testamento, Probate of Will; -azione da parte del Tribunale, approval of Court (C.C.).

omol-ogi·a *f.* (med.; biol., math., etc.) homology. **-o·gico** *adj.* homological.

om-o·logo *adj.* (*m.pl.* **-o·loghi**) (scient.) homologous; (mus.) in enharmonic unison. (**-ologamente** *adv.*) **-omorfi·a** *f.* (anat.) homomorphism, homomorphy. **-onimi·a** *f.* homonymy. **-o·nimo** *adj.* homonymous; *n.m.* homonym; namesake. **-oplata** *f.* (anat.) omoplate, scapula. **-osessuale** *adj., n.m., f.* homosexual. **-osessualità** *f* homosexuality. **-oteti·a** *f.* (geom.) homothety. **-otoni·a** *f.* (mus.) homotony, uniform tone. **-o·tono** *m.* hum, vibration, singing (as of rigging or telegraph wires). **-ot·teri** *m.pl.* (ent.) *Hemiptera-Homoptera*, greenfly, cicadas, etc. **-ozigote** *m.* (biol.) homozygote.

om-uc·cio, -un·colo *m. dim.* of **uomo**, q.v.

onagr-a *f.,* **-o** *m.* (zool.) wild ass, onager, *Equus onager*; †(mil.) catapult.

onagrot·tolo *m.* See **onocrotalo**.

onan-iṣmo *m.* (med.) onanism, self-abuse. **-ista** *m.* onanist.

ọncia *f.* (hist.) ounce (of varying weight); small quantity; a — a —, gradually; (numis.) coin (a twelfth part of a whole of varying value); (hist.) inch.

onciale *adj.* (palaeog.) uncial.

†oncino *m. and derivs.* See **uncino**.

onc-o *m.* (med.) oncoma, tumour. **-o·liṣi** *f.* (med.) oncolysis. **-oli·tico** *adj.* (med.) oncolytic. **-olito** *m.* (med.) cancerous cell. **-ologi·a** *f.* (med.) oncology. **-o·metro** *m.* (med.) oncometer. **-otomi·a** *f.* (surg.) oncotomy, incision of an abscess.

ọnd-a *f.* wave, billow; (poet.) sea, main, water; wave-like shape or movement; dar l'— ai capelli, to wave hair; andare a -e, to zigzag, to reel; surge; l'— di ribellione, the tide of rebellion; (herald.) a -e, undee; (naut.) wave; — di mare morto, swell; — di sotto vento, wave proper (as opposed to 'onda di calma'); (archit.) ogee (moulding); (phys.) wave; — d'urto, shock wave; — luminosa, light wave; — sonora, sound wave; (radio) wave; lunghezza d'—, wave-length; — corta, short wave; — diretta, ground wave; — media, medium wave; — persistente, continuous wave; — portante, carrier wave. **-a·metro** *m.* (radio) wavemeter; -ametro di assorbimento, absorption wavemeter, grid-dip meter. **-ante** *adj.* waving, wavy; overflowing, brimming; surging. **†-are** *intr.* to wave; *tr.* to inundate. **-ata** *f.* wave, undulating movement, surge; breaker; -ata di caldo, heat-wave; (econ.) -ata di ribasso, a wave of falling prices. **-ato** *adj.* wavy, waved; (herald.) undy, wavy. **-azione** *f.* undulation; billowy motion; (phys.) wave motion; oscillation. **-ẹtta** *f. dim.* of **onda**; (archit.) ogee (moulding).

ondatra *f.* (zool.) beaver, *Castor zibethicus*.

ọnd-e *interr. adv.* whence?, from where?; *rel. adv.* whence, from where, from which, with which, wherewith; *final conj.* (with *subj.*) — egli impari, so that he may learn; in order to; — imparare, so as to learn. **†-echè** *conj.* whencesoever; wherefore.

ondeggi-are [A 3 c] *intr.* (*aux.* avere) to wave, to undulate; to rise and fall; to toss; to rock, to flutter; to waver, to fluctuate, to be undecided. **-amento** *m.* waving, wavering, wavy surface, veining, watering (of silk); (aeron.) surging (of fuel in tank); (mus.)

undulating tremolo (in violin-playing); vibrato. **-ato** *adj.* wave-covered; waving, wavy; (mus.) tremulous, undulating.

ond-i·fero *adj.* (poet.) shower-laden. **-ifremente** *adj.* (poet.) surging or undulating like waves. **-ina** *f.* undine, nixie; woman swimmer; (med.) basin, kidney bowl; *adj. indecl.* (text.) wavy (of colour and pattern); wavy (in texture, producing a crepe effect); nailon —, seersucker nylon. **-inatante** *adj.* (poet.) wave-breasting, swimming through the water. **-isonante** *adj.* (poet.) billowy-echoing. **-i·vago** *adj.* (poet.) ocean-roving. **-o·grafo** *m.* (electr.) ondograph. **-ogramma** *m.* (electr.) ondogram. **-osità** *f.* undulation. **-ọso** *adj.* billowy; surging; undulating. **-ulare** [A I s] *tr.* to wave (hair), to make wavy; *intr.* (*aux.* avere) to undulate, to oscillate. **†-ulativo** *adj.* (mus.) pulsating, vibrant. **-ulato** *part. adj.* wavy, undulating; veined (surface); watered (silk); cartone -ulato, corrugated cardboard. **-ulatore** *m.* (electr.) inverter, inverted rectifier. **-ulato·rio** *adj.* (phys.) undulatory. **-ulazione** *f.* undulation, waving; le -ulazioni del terreno, the rolling nature of the ground; hair-waving; -ulazione permanente, permanent wave; waviness; (radio) tensione di -ulazione, ripple voltage.

o·ner-e *m.* burden, task, load; (leg.) burden; charge; onus; invertire l'— della prova, to shift the burden of proof (C.C.); capitolato d'-i, specifications, articles and conditions (e.g. for a tender). **-are** [A I s] *tr.* to burden, to load. **†-a·rio** *adj.* †nave -aria, cargo boat. **-osità** *f.* (leg.) burdensomeness; l'eccessiva -osità del mutuo, oppressive terms of loan (C.C.). **-ọso** *adj.* burdensome, onerous, oppressive; (leg.) un legato -oso, onerous legacy (C.C.). (**-osamente** *adv.*)

onest-à *f.* probity, uprightness; honourable dealing; integrity; honour; honesty, chastity, virtue (in a woman); seemliness, propriety, decency. **-are** [A I] *tr.* to justify, to gloss over; †to adorn. **-ato** *part. adj.* justified, glossed over; †adorned; †honourable.

onest-o *adj.* honourable, upright, fair, honest; giuoco —, fair play; chaste, virtuous (of a woman); decent, respectable; courteous, polite; reasonable, just; prezzo —, fair price; worthy, edifying; †honoured; *n.m.* honesty; honour; honourableness; duty; that which is honest or just; †*adv.* honestly; honourably; modestly. **-amente** *adv.* honestly; honourably; respectably. **†-ura** *f.* see **onestà**.

on·fal-o *m.* (anat.) umbilicus. **-ectomi·a** *f.* (surg.) omphalectomy, excision of the umbilicus. **-ite** *f.* (med.) omphalitis. **-ocele** *m.* (med.) umbilical hernia, omphalcoele. **-omesẹn·trico** *adj.* (anat.) omphalomesenteric. **-orragi·a** *f.* (med.) umbilical haemorrhage. **-otomi·a** *f.* (med.) cutting the umbilical cord. **-otrissi** *f.* (med.) omphalotripsy.

†ongarese *adj.* see **ungherese**; (mus.) all'—, in gipsy style.

†onic·cio *m.* See **ontano**.

o·nice *f.* onyx.

onichi·a *f.* (med.) onychia, inflammation of the matrix of the nail.

onic-ofagi·a *f.* (med.) nail biting, onychophagy. **-oṣi** *f.* (med.) onychosis, onychopathy.

†onire *tr.* to put to shame, to dishonour.

oni·r-ico *adj.* (med.) oneiric. **-iṣmo** *m.* (med.) oneirism. **-ologi·a** *f.* oneirology, science of dreams. **-omanzi·a** *f.* oneiromancy.

onisco *m.* (zool.) woodlouse, *Oniscus* spp.

onn-inamẹnte *adv.* altogether, wholly. **-ipotente** *adj.* omnipotent, almighty, all-powerful; *n.m.* l'-ipotente, the Almighty. **-ipotentemẹnte** *adv.* omnipotently. **-ipotenza** *f.* omnipotence; the Almighty. **-ipresente** *adj.* omnipresent, ubiquitous. **-ipresenza** *f.* omnipresence, ubiquity. **-isciente** *adj.* omniscient, all-knowing. **-iscienza** *f.* omniscience. **-iveggente** *adj.* all-seeing. **-iveggenza** *f.* all-seeingness. **-i·voro** *adj.* omnivorous.

onocenta·uro *m.* (myth.) onocentaur, a centaur with the body of an ass.

onocro·talo *m.* (orn.) pelican.

onom-anzi·a *f.* onomancy. **-a·stica** *f.* onomatology. **-a·stico** *adj.* onomastic, of a name or names; giorno -astico, name-day; *n.m.* name-day, feast of one's patron saint; dictionary (esp. of proper names); †lexicographer. **-atomani·a** *f.* (psych.) onomatomania. **-atope·a, -atope·ia** *f.* onomatopoeia. **-atope·ico** *adj.* onomatopoeic.

onor-are [A I c] *tr.* to honour; to do honour to; to adorn; (comm.) — una cambiale, to take up a bill; *rfl.* to be honoured; to be adorned; to consider it an honour; mi -o d'essergli stato maestro, I am proud to have been his master. **-a·bile** *adj.* honourable; respected. **-abilmẹnte** *adv.* honourably. **-abilità** *f.* honourableness; good name. **-ando** *adj.* honoured, honourable, revered,

onor-are (*cont.*)
venerable. **-ante** *part. adj.* honouring; *n.m., f.* one who does honour, one who honours. †**-antemente** *adv.* honourably; with honour. **-anza** *f.* mark of honour; sign of esteem; *pl.* public tribute to a great man; academic celebration; *Festschrift*, volume in someone's honour; estreme **-anze**, last funeral honours. **-atezza** *f.* honoured status, esteem. **-ato** *part. adj.* honoured, revered, honourable, venerable. **-atamente** *adv.* with honour; in honour. (**-atore** *m.* **-atrice** *f.*) **-evole** *adj.* honourable, respectable; estimable; dignified; (as title of member of Italian Parliament) Honourable; *n.m.* l'Onorevole, the M.P., the Honourable Member. **-evolmente** *adv.* honourably; respectably; in a dignified way. **-evolezza** *f.* honourable position; dignity.

onor-e *m.* (usu. abbrev. to **onor** when followed by a consonant in a phrase) honour; distinction; rank; glory; fare — a, to honour, to do ample justice to; partita d'—, duel; a onor del vero, to tell the truth, truth to tell; parola d'—, word of honour; farsi —, to distinguish oneself; farsi onor di qualcosa, to give something away; chastity; comitato d'—, patrons, Committee of Honour; dama d'—, lady-in-waiting; (joc.) l'onor del mento, beard; (leg.) causa di —, motive of honour; delitto contro l'—, crime against honour; (comm.) fare — alla firma, to honour a signature; pagamento per onor di firma, payment for honour supra protest; *pl.* 'honours' (at bridge); (naut.) **-i** navali, naval honours (NOTE: as in other Navies these consist of manning ships, 'parate'; gun salutes, 'salve di artiglieria'; dressing ship, 'gala di bandiere'; cheering ship, 'saluto alla voce'; bugles or pipes, 'segnali di tromba o di fischietto'); ala di —, guard of honour; (herald.) posto d'—, honour point; †ornament, adornment. **-ario** *adj.* honorific, betokening honour; honorary; *n.m.* honorarium, professional fee; (leg.) **-ari** di avvocato, counsel's, solicitor's fees; spese ed **-ari**, disbursements and fees; costs (C.C.). †**-ificare** *vb.* and derivs. see **onorare.** **-ificenza** *f.* (mark of) honour (usu. of titles, decorations, etc.). **-ifico** *adj.* (**-ificentissimo** *adj. superl.*) honourable, of honour, distinguished; honorary.

Ono-rio *pr.n.m.* Honorius.

ont-a *f.* shame, disgrace; insult; affront; ad — di, in — a, in defiance of, in spite of. †**-oso** *adj.* shameful; disgraceful; ashamed.

ontan-o *m.* (bot.) alder, *Alnus.* **-eta** *f.*, **-eto** *m.* (bot.) alder wood, alder carr.

onto-genesi *f.*, **-genia** *f.* (biol.) ontogenesis, ontogeny, embryology. **-genetico** *adj.* ontogenetic.

ont-ologia *f.* (philos.) ontology. **-ologico** *adj.* (philos.) ontological. **-ologismo** *m.* (philos.) ontologism. **-ologista** *m.* ontologist, supporter of ontologism. **-ologo** *m.* ontologist, metaphysician.

†**ontoso** *adj.* See under **onta.**

onusto *adj.* (poet.) laden, loaded.

onza *f.* (zool.) jaguar, *Felis onca.*

oo-blasto *m.* (biol.) oöblast. **-forite** *f.* (med.) oöphoritis, ovaritis. **-gamia** *f.* (bot.) oögamy. **-gemma** *f.* (bot.) archegonium. **-gone** *m.* (bot.) oögonium. **-lite** *f.* (miner.) oölite. **-litico** *adj.* (miner.) oölitic. **-logia** *f.* (orn.) oölogy. **-manzia** *f.* oöscopy. **-sfera** *f.* (bot.) oösphere. **-spora** *f.* (bot.) oöspore. **-teca** *f.* (ent.) oötheca.

ooh *excl.* o-oh!

opa-co *adj.* (*pl.* **-chi**) opaque; shady, shaded; dull, lustreless; (of a voice) thick, husky; (of sound) dull; (paint.) matt; vetro —, ground glass; (chem.) soluzione **-a**, cloudy solution. **-cimetro** *m.* (paperm.) opacimeter. **-cità** *f.* opacity; dullness; shadiness, dimness. **-cizzante** *m.* (techn.) opacifying agent.

opal-e *m.* opal. **-escente** *adj.* opalescent. **-escenza** *f.* opalescence. **-ino** *adj.* opaline. **-izzare** [A1] *intr.* (*aux.* essere) to opalesce. **-izzato** *part. adj.* iridescent.

o-per-a *f.* work; mettere in —, to use, to make ready for use, to set going; (iron.) per compir l'—, into the bargain, to make things worse; (eccl.) **-e** servili, servile work; — del Duomo, works department of the cathedral; mano d'—, labour, man-power; workmanship; raso a —, worked (patterned) satin; capo d'—, masterpiece; action; l'— e le parole, deeds and words; vorrei vederti all'—, I should like to see you at it; peccato d'—, sin of commission; — santa, virtuous action; per — di, through the action of, thanks to; day's work, period of work; ho prestato la mia —, I gave a hand; lavorare a —, to work by the day; workman, 'hand'; — pia, charitable institution; — Nazionale Maternità e Infanzia, National Institute for Mother and Child Welfare; (leg.) — d'arte o di scienza, artistic or scientific work (C.P.);

contratto d'—, contract for work; prestazione di — intellettuale, rendering of professional services; **-e** pubbliche, public works; **-e** di bonifica, land reclamation works; **-e** dell'ingegno, original works; **-e** di miglioramento, land-improvement works (C.C.); (archit.) building; architectural order, style of buildings; (joc.) — del Duomo, a work that never reaches completion (with ref. to Milan Cathedral); (naut.) floating structure; — morta, superstructure and hull above the waterline; — viva, hull below the waterline; altezze dell'— viva, depth of submerged hull; **-e** portuarie, docks, lighthouses, etc.; **-e** di marea, work carried out between tides (such as careening); (mus.) opera; work, composition; — buffa, an Italian form of comic opera; — lirica, opera; — semiseria, seriocomic opera; — seria, serious opera, heroic opera; teatro dell'—, opera house, opera theatre. **-a-ballo** *m.* (mus.) opera-ballet. **-aia** *f.* workwoman, work-girl, worker, female hand; (text.) tenter. **-aio** *m.* workman; worker, hand; head of works department of a cathedral; official in charge of the fabric; *pl.* (eccl.) **-ai** pii, (congregation of) Pious Workers; (text.) tenter, minder; ora di **-aio**, man-hour; (ent.) worker ant, bee or termite; (naut.) dockyard labourer; *adj.* working, working-class, workingmen's; società **-aia**, trade union. **-etta** *f.* (mus.) operetta, light opera. **-ettista** *m.* (mus.) composer of light opera. †**-iere** *m.* see **operaio.** **-ina** *f.* (mus.) one-act opera. **-ista** *m.* (mus.) opera-composer. **-istico** *adj.* (mus.) operatic.

oper-are [A1s] *intr.* (*aux.* avere) to act, to operate; to behave; to work, to function; to take effect; (med.) to operate; *tr.* to do, to work (good, miracles); to work (silk, etc.) with a design; (med.) — di, to operate on for. **-abile** *adj.* practicable, feasible; (med.) operable; (techn.) workable. **-abilità** *f.* (med.) operability; (techn.) workability, workableness. **-ante** *part. adj.* operating, working, functioning; *n.m., f.* operator. **-ativo** *adj.* operative; active; effective; (med.) operative. **-ativamente** *adv.* operatively; actively. **-ato** *part. adj.* operated; worked on; operated on; è stato **-ato** di appendicite, he was operated on for appendicitis; *n.m.* action, deed; handiwork. **-atore** *m.* operating surgeon; (techn.) operator; (cinem.) camera-man; projectionist; (finan.) **-atore** di borsa, stockbroker. (**-atrice** *f.*) **-azione** *f.* operation; functioning; working; (med.; scient.) operation; subire un'**-azione**, to undergo an operation; (math.) le quattro **-azioni**, the four rules; (leg.) transaction; **-azione** di borsa, stock-exchange transaction; (mil.) operation.

oper-c-olo, **-ulo** *m.* (biol.) operculum. **-olare** *adj.* (anat.) opercular.

operos-o *adj.* industrious, active, busy. **-ità** *f.* industry, activity.

†**opi-fice** *m.* creator; craftsman; artisan.

opifi-cio *m.* factory, works; (text.) — di maglierie, knitting factory.

opimo *adj.* rich, fertile, abundant; (Rom. hist.) spoglie opime, *spolia opima.*

opin-are [A1] *intr.* (*aux.* avere) to opine, to deem, to hold, to decide; (leg.) il tribunale **-ò** in modo contrario, the court was of the opposite opinion. **-abile** *adj.* thinkable, conceivable, tenable, opinable. **-abilità** *f.* conceivability. **-ativo** *adj.* opining, concerned with opinion. **-ato** *part. adj.* deemed, held as an opinion. (**-atore** *m.* **-atrice** *f.*)

opinione *f.* opinion; matter of opinion; judgement; conviction; belief, view; essere d'— che, to be of the opinion that; l'aritmetica non è un'—, facts are facts; esprimere un'— dissidente, to cast a dissenting vote; sentire l'— di un'avvocato, to consult a solicitor.

opistio-n *m. indecl.* (anat.) opisthion.

opist-o-como *m.* (orn.) hoatzin, *Opisthocomus hoazin.* **-o-domo** *m.* (Gk. antiq.) opisthodomos. **-o-tono** *m.* (med.) opisthotonos.

oplà, o-pla, oppe là *excl.* (sport; joc.) come on, jump!

oplit-e, -a *m.* (Gk. antiq.) hoplite.

opo-bal-samo *m.* (bot.) Mecca balsam (resin of *Commiphora Opobalsamum*). **-deldòc(h)** *m. indecl.* (pharm.) opodeldoc. **-pa-naco** *m.* (bot.) opoponax (resin of *Opoponax* spp.).

opoterapi-a *f.* (med.) opotherapy, organotherapy.

oppi-a-nico *adj.*, **-anina** *f.*, **-are** [A4]. See under **oppio.**

†**op-pido** *m.* castle.

oppignor-are [A1] *tr.* (leg.) to distrain; to seize. **-azione** *f.* (leg.) distraint.

oppil-are [A1] *tr.* (med.) to constipate. **-ativo** *adj.* (med.) constipating. **-azione** *f.* (med.) constipation.

op-pi-o¹ *m.* opium. **-aceo** *adj. n.m.* opiate, narcotic. **-are** [A14] *tr.* to mix with opium; to drug with opium; (colloq.) to drug. **-ato** *part. adj.* mixed with opium; drugged with opium; (colloq.)

oppi·o (*cont.*)

drugged; *n.m.* opiate, narcotic. **-ofagi·a** *f.* (med.) opium-eating, opiophagism. **-o·mane** *m., f.* opium-addict; drug-fiend. **-omani·a** *f.* (med.) opiomania, opium addiction.

op·pio[2] *m.* (bot.) field maple, *Acer campestre*; — riccio, Norway maple, *A. platanoides*.

oppon-ente *part.* of **opporre**, q.v.; *adj.* opposing; *n.m., f.* opponent, adversary. **-i·bile** *adj.* opposable. **-imento** *m.* opposing; objection, opposition; (astron.; astrol.) opposition.

†**oppo·nere** *vb.* and derivs. See **opporre**.

opporre [B 21] to oppose, to set against, to set over against; to contrast; to refute; — ragioni a, to bring arguments against; — resistenza, to offer resistance; — ostacoli a, to put obstacles in the way of; — un rifiuto, to give a refusal; non ho nulla da —, I have no objection to make; *intr.* (*aux.* essere; *prep.* a) (leg.) — a una sentenza, to appeal against a judgment; *rfl.* (*prep.* a) to oppose, to be opposed (to), to object (to), to thwart; to set oneself (against); opporsi al nemico, to face the enemy.

opportun-o *adj.* opportune, seasonable, timely; advisable, expedient; well-chosen, suitable; welcome; needful. **-amente** *adv.* opportunely; suitably, appropriately; fortunately. **-ismo** *m.* opportunism. **-ista** *m., f.* opportunist. **-i·stico** *adj.* opportunistic. **-ità** *f.* opportuneness, expediency, appositeness, appropriateness; opportunity, favourable occasion; †need, †necessity.

oppos-itore *m.* opponent; opposer. (**-itrice** *f.*)

opposizione *f.* opposition, objection, argument; (leg.) opposition, objection; (astron.) opposition; (electr.) — di fase, phase opposition, antiphase; (radio) in — di fase, push-pull.

oppost-o, oppost-o *part.* of **opporre**, q.v.; *adj.* opposite; opposing, contrary; (bot.) opposite; *n.m.* opposite, reverse; all'—, on the contrary; tutto l'—, quite the reverse. **-amente** *adv.* in an opposite sense; in reverse.

oppress-o *part.* of **opprimere**, q.v.; *adj.* oppressed, weighed down, downtrodden; respiro —, laboured breathing. †**-are** *tr.* to oppress; to tyrannize over; to torment, to afflict; to compress. †**-atore** *m.* oppressor. **-ione** *f.* oppression, affliction; tiresome thing, annoyance; (med.) oppression, heavy feeling. **-ivo** *adj.* oppressive; wearing. **-ore** *m.* oppressor; tyrant. **-ura** *f.* oppressiveness, oppression.

oppri·m-ere [C 18] to oppress, to weigh down, to burden; to overwhelm; to lie heavy on. **-ente** *part. adj.* oppressive, exhausting, burdensome; cruel, crushing; povertà -ente, grinding poverty; tempo -ente, sultry, suffocating weather.

oppugn-are [A 5] *tr.* to oppose, to assail, to attack; to impugn, to refute, to confute; †(mil.) see **impugnare**. **-a·bile** *adj.* assailable, impugnable; to be attacked. **-abilità** *f.* vulnerability. **-ato** *part. adj.* ascribed; impugned, refuted. **-atore** *m.* assailant. (**-atrice** *f.*) **-azione** *f.* (fig.) attack, assault.

oppure *conj., adv.* or; else; or else.

opr-a *f.* (poet.) see **opera**. **-are** [A 1] and derivs. (poet.) see **operare**, under **opera**.

†**oprire** *vb.* and derivs. See **aprire**.

opso·nico *adj.* (biol.) opsonic. **-ina** *f.* (biol.) opsonin.

optare [A 1] *intr.* (*aux.* avere; *prep.* per) (leg.) to choose, to opt (for); to decide (in favour of); diritto, facoltà di — per la cittadinanza italiana, right to opt for Italian citizenship.

optimum *m. indecl.* (scient.) optimum.

opt-ogramma *m.* (med.) optogram. **-ometri·a** *f.* (opt.) optometry. **-o·metro** *m.* (opt.) optometer. **-ostriato** *adj.* (anat.) optostriate.

opulen-to *adj.* opulent, rich; fertile. **-za** *f.* opulence, wealth; fertility; buxomness.

opu·scolo *m.* pamphlet; brochure; short study, monograph.

opzione *f.* (leg.) option, choice of an alternative; diritto, facoltà di —, right of option (cf. under **optare**); (comm.) option; — di compra, option to purchase; (finan.) — per la vendita, put, put option; — doppia, spread, put and call straddle; — per la vendita del doppio, put of more.

or[1] abbrev. of **ora**[2], q.v.

or[2] *m.* abbrev. of **oro**, q.v.

or[3] *m.* abbrev. of **orto**, q.v., as in 'Or San Michele'.

or·a[1] *f.* hour; -e comuni, equal hours reckoned A.M. and P.M.; -e francesi, equal hours on the modern 24-hour system; -e italiane, unequal hours on the old 24-hour system ending at sunset instead of midnight; -e canoniche, canonical hours, (joc.) — canonica, meal-time; un'— di notte, an hour after sunset; essere alle ven-

titrè -e, to have one foot in the grave; le -e una, 1 o'clock; -e piccole, -e piccine, small hours; (industr.) -e straordinarie, overtime; (liturg.) le quarant'-e, the Forty Hours; time; che — fate voi?, what time do you make it?; — estiva, — legale, summer time; — ufficiale, standard time; — bruciata, hot time of day, bad time (for doing something); -e rubate, odd moments (of leisure); sarebbe — di andare, it is really time to go; alla buon'—!, good!, at last!; di buon'—, early; non veder l'— di partire, to long to go, to look forward to going; far l'— della cena, to while away the time till supper; a quest'—, by this time; in ogni — della giornata, at any hour of the day, at any time of day; l'— d'accendere le luci, lighting-up time; — di chiusura, closing-time; l'— di andare a letto, bedtime; (radio) l'— per i piccoli, children's hour; l'— di mangiare, l'— dei pasti, meal-time; -e d'ufficio, office hours; -e di punta, -e di affluenza, -e di maggior traffico, rush hour, peak hour; (naut.) hour time (NOTE: as in the British Navy, time is kept from midnight in four-hour watches, one stroke of the ship's bell for every 30 minutes up to 8 bells at the end of each watch); — dell'alta marea, time of high water; — della bassa marea, time of low water; — di bordo, ship's time; — locale, local time; — media, mean time; — siderea, sidereal time; — vera del primo meridiano, right ascension of the meridian; — comune, local mean time; l'— media di Greenwich, Greenwich mean time; (aeron.; naut.) aereo nemico a -e tre, i.e. enemy craft approaching from the right (position charted as on the dial of a clock); (provb.) le -e del mattino hanno l'oro in bocca, morning hours are golden; (watchm.) meccanismo di messa all'—, setting mechanism; (mech.) cavallo —, horse-power hour. **-etta** *f. dim.* about an hour, under an hour; una mezz'-etta, under half an hour, a little while.

ora[2] *adv.* now; or ora, just now, a moment ago; at any moment now, in a moment; — come —, as things are now, just now; d'— in poi, henceforward; — è un anno, a year ago; or bene (orbene), well now; — avvenne che..., now it happened that...; — per sempre, once for all.

†**ora**[3] *f.* See **aura**.

ora·col-o *m.* oracle; †chapel, oratory. **-eggiare** [A 3 c] *intr.* (*aux.* avere) (iron.) to speak like an oracle.

orada *f.* (ichth.). See **orata**.

o·rafo *m. adj.* relating to a goldsmith; arte orafa, goldsmith's art; †*n.m.* goldsmith; — d'ottone, worker in brass.

oral-e *adj.* oral; *n.m.* oral (examination), 'viva'; (liturg.) fanon, orale. **-mente** *adv.* orally; verbally, by word of mouth. **-ità** *f.* oral character.

orama·i *adv.* now, by now, henceforward.

orango *m.*, **orangutan** *m.* (zool.) orang-utan, *Pongo satyrus*.

orangutango *m.* See **orango**.

or-are [A 1] *intr.* (*aux.* avere) to pray; †*tr.* to pray to; to utter (prayers); to adore, to worship; to harangue, to orate. **-ante** *f.* (Chr. archaeol.) orante, orans.

ora·rio *adj.* of hours, by the hour; velocità oraria, speed per hour; tavola oraria, time-table; in senso —, in a clockwise direction; (radio) segnale —, time signal; (eccl.) preghiere orarie, breviary prayers; *n.m.* time-table; office hours; horarium; (set) hours; in —, punctual; partire in —, to leave on time.

orata *f.* (ichth.) kind of Mediterranean sea bream, *Chrysophrys aurata*; gilthead, daurade, *Sparus auratus*.

†**orato** *adj.* gilded; gilt; golden, of gold; golden in colour.

orat-ore *m.* orator; speaker; — sacro, preacher; (leg.) — della legge, a lawyer; a petitioner or plaintiff; †(rel.) one who prays or worships. **-o·ria** *f.* the art of speaking, oratory, rhetoric. **-oriano** *m.* (eccl.) Oratorian; *adj.* of the Oratory. **-o·rio** *adj.* oratorical, rhetorical; *n.m.* (eccl.) oratory, chapel, (the) Oratory (of St Philip Neri); *n.m.* (mus.) oratorio; sacred opera; †prayer; †oracle. (**-rice** *f.*)

Ora·zi-o *pr.n.m.* Horace; Horatius; Horatio. **-ano** *adj.* Horatian.

orazione *f.* oration, speech; (gramm.) le parti dell'—, the parts of speech; (rel.) prayer; — domenicale, the Lord's Prayer, the Our Father.

orbace *m.* Sardinian woollen cloth.

orb-are [A 1] *tr.* to bereave; to deprive. **-ato** *part. adj.* bereft; blind.

orb-e *m.* orb, sphere, globe; l'— cattolico, the Catholic world; †— dell'occhio, eye-ball. **-ello** *m.* slicker, smoothing-iron (for leather). **-ettino** *m.* (zool.) slow-worm, *Anguis fragilis*. **-icolare** *adj.* orbed, circular, spherical; (anat.) orbicular; *n.m.* (anat.) orbicular muscle. **-icolato** *adj.* orbicular, spherical, globular.

orbene *adv.* well; well now; well then.

†**or·bido** *adj.* blind.

orbi·glio *m.* (bot.) garden pea, field pea, *Pisum sativum*.

Orbi·lio *pr.n.m.* Orbilius.

o·rbit-a *f.* orbit; limit; (anat.) orbit, eye-socket. **-ale** *adj.* (anat.) orbital.

orb-o *adj.* bereft; widowed, orphaned; blind; purblind; squinting; *n.m.* blind man; botte da **-i**, blows of blind fury, violent knocks; (mus.) viola da **—**, hurdy-gurdy. **-ętto** *m. dim.* small blind person; (theatr. slang) l'**-etto**, the public. **-ęzza** *f.* deprivation, loss.

orca[1], **ǫrca** *f.* (zool.) killer whale, *Orca gladiator*; (myth.) sea monster, grampus; orc.

ǫrca[2] *f.* (naut.) Dutch barge, flat-bottomed and bluff-bowed (construction adapted for use in the Mediterranean); *adj. f.* (naut.) unmanageable, unseaworthy, cranky.

Or·cadi *pr.n.f.pl.* (geog.) Orkneys; **—** Australi, South Orkneys.

orceina *f.* (chem.) orcein.

orceolato *adj.* (bot.) urceolate.

orcheşiografi·a *f.* choreography.

orchessa *f.* ogress (cf. **orco**[1]).

orch-e·stica *f.* orchestics. **-e·stico** *adj.* orchestic, of dancing.

orchestr-a *f.* (Gk. and Rom. antiq.) orchestra; (mus.) orchestra; sinfonia a piena **—**, symphony for full orchestra. **-ale** *adj.* (mus.) orchestral; *n.m.* player in an orchestra or band. **-are** [A I] *tr.* (mus.) to orchestrate, to score; (fig.) to stage. **-ato** *part. adj.* orchestrated, scored; (fig.) staged, 'rigged'; lo sciopero fu ben **-ato** dai comunisti, the strike was well rigged by the communists. **-azione** *f.* (mus.) orchestration, scoring. **-ina** *f. dim.* (mus.) light orchestra, dance-orchestra, hotel-orchestra.

orche·strion *m. indecl.* (mus.) orchestrion.

orchętto *m.* (orn.) **—** marino, common scoter, *Melanitta nigra*.

orch-ide·a *f.* (bot.) orchid. **-idectomi·a** *f.* (surg.) orchidectomy. **-iocele** *m.* (med.) orchiocele. **-iotomi·a** (surg.) orchiotomy. **-ite** *f.*, †**-i·tide** *f.* (med.) orchitis, didymitis, testitis.

†**or·cia**[1] *f.* (naut.). See **orza**.

†**or·cia**[2] *f.* pitcher, jug.

orcia·ia *f.* (Tusc.) cellar for oil-jars.

orcifǫrme *adj.* (scient.) urceiform.

orc-i·glia *f.* (bot.) orchil, *Roccella tinctoria*. **-ina** *f.* (chem.) orcin, orcinol.

or·c-io *m.* jar (esp. for oil); earthenware vessel, pitcher; jug; (hist.) liquid measure (a third of a barrel). **-ia·io**, **-iola·io** *m.* jar-maker, jar-seller. **-i(u)olo** *m.* jug.

†**orcipog·gia** *f.* (naut.). See **orzapoza**.

Or-co[1], **Or-co** *pr.n.m.* (*pl.* **-chi**) (Rom. myth.) Orcus; the underworld *or* the god of it; ogre, bogey; (joc.) frightening or ugly person.

or-co[2] *m.* (*pl.* **-chi**) (orn.) **—** marino, velvet scoter, (Amer.) white-winged scoter, *Melanitta fusca*.

orda *f.* (hist. and fig.) horde; **—** d'oro, Golden Horde.

orda·lia *f.* (hist.) ordeal.

ordea·ceo *adj.* of, made with, barley.

ordigno *m.* implement; gear, tackle; contrivance, device; (fig.) tool, instrument; (pop.) hand grenade, bomb; †ingenious idea or plan.

ordimęnto *m.* See under **ordire**.

ordina·bile *adj.* See under **ordinare**.

ordinal-e *adj.* (math.) ordinal; †ordinary; †usual; †ordered, in order, orderly; prepared; *n.m.* (eccl.) ordinal. †**-mente** *adv.* in order, in an orderly way.

ordin-amento *m.*, **-anza** *f.* See under **ordinare**.

ordin-are [A I sc] *tr.* to put in order, to arrange; to regulate; to tidy (up); to marshal (ideas); to decree, to ordain, to dispose; to command, to order; gli **-ò** di partire, he bade him go; to prescribe, to order; **—** il pranzo, to order dinner; (eccl.) to ordain; (mil.) to array, to deploy; †to destine, to intend; †*intr.* **—** in sè, to decide; **—** di una cosa con uno, to consult with someone about something; *rfl.* to get ready; (eccl.) to be ordained. **-a·bile** *adj.* capable of being ordered or arranged. **-amento** *m.* ordering, setting in order; arranging; order; ordinance; (leg.) **-amento** giudiziario, establishment of the judicature (I.C.); †precept, law. **-ando** *adj.* (eccl.) to be ordained; *n.m.* ordinand. **-ante** *m.* (eccl.) ordaining bishop, ordinant. **-anza** *f.* order, arrangement; (mil.) file of men in battle order; spiegare le **-anze**, to deploy troops; (naut.) line of ships in battle order; **-anza** sotto vela, order of sailing; **-anza** di marina, naval regulation; personal servant attached to an officer; ufficiale d'**-anza**, personal staff, e.g. flag-

lieutenant to an admiral, equerry to a member of the Royal Household; †order of the fleet or squadron; (leg.) interlocutory order, provision, or ordinance; law, rule, precept. **-ata** *f.* tidying up; (math.) ordinate; (aeron.) frame, former; (naut.) section of a ship, ship's frames; **-ata** maestra, midship cross-section. **-ata·rio** *m.* (comm.) payee. **-ativo** *adj.* directive (of principles); ordinal (of numerals); *n.m.* (comm.) order; note. **-ato** *part. adj.* ordered, ordained, destined; orderly, organized, neat, tidy; (herald.) mal **-ato**, set 1 and 2. **-atamęnte** *adv.* in an ordered way. (**-atore** *m.* **-atrice** *f.*) **-ato·rio** *adj.* (leg.) abbreviazione del termine **-atorio**, shortening of time fixed by order (C.C.P.). **-azione** *f.* order, ordering; (eccl.) ordination; (comm.) order; indent; (med.) prescription.

ordina·ri-o *adj.* ordinary, usual, accustomed; normal; common, vulgar, cheap, rough, coarse; (leg.) ordinary, general; giurisdizione **-a**, ordinary jurisdiction; (comm.) valori **-i**, ordinary stocks or shares; *n.m.* custom, usual way; fuori dell'**—**, out of the ordinary; d'**—**, per l'**—**, secondo l'**—**, usually, normally; (univ.) professor; (eccl.) ordinary; ordinary confessor (to a convent); set meal, usual meal, ordinary; †regular courier; †day on which post was regularly delivered. **-a** *f.* (leg.) Chair of Roman Law. **-amęnte** *adv.* ordinarily; usually, normally. **-ato** *m.* (univ.) position on regular staff; (eccl.) status of ordinary. **-ǫne** *adj. augm.* vulgar; *n.m.* vulgarian.

or·dine *m.* **1.** ORDER, position in a series; in **—** di merito, in order of merit; in **—** di precedenza, in order of precedence, according to priority or seniority; in **—** alfabetico, in alphabetical order; parola d'**—**, headword; numero d'**—**, serial number; (leg.) **—** delle ipoteche, priority of mortgages (C.C.). **2.** RANK; class, category; di prim'**—**, first-rate, first-class; order; **—** cavalleresco, order of knighthood; ecclesiastical order; (mil.) array, alignment; (leg.) **—** degli Avvocati, Bar Association, Law Society; (naut.) row of oars (in tiers); (hist.) order. **3.** ORDER, orderliness, control; disposition, arrangements; **—** pubblico, public order; mettere in **—**, to set in order; mantenere l'**—**, to maintain order; (admin.) richiamare all'**—**, to call to order; incorrere in un richiamo all'**—**, to be called to order; **—** del giorno, agenda; **—** del giorno provvisorio, provisional agenda; **—** del giorno definitivo, approved agenda; attenersi all'**—** del giorno, to stick to the agenda; passare all'**—** del giorno, to proceed to the next business. **4.** ORDER, command; regulation; (comm.) **—** di consegna, delivery order; ordini d'imbarco, broker's orders, shipping orders; (comm.) polizza all'**—**, bill of lading to order; assegno all'**—**, cheque to order; (leg.) injunction; order, writ; **—** di non luogo a procedere, nonsuit. **5.** (REL.) religious order; *pl.* (sacred) orders. **6.** (ARCHIT.) order. **7.** †(MUS.) scale.

†**ordingo** *m.* See **ordigno**.

ord-ire [D 2] *tr.* (text.) to lay the warp for, to warp; to mount on the loom; (naut.) to reeve; **—** una cima, **—** un cavo, to pass or reeve a hawser; (fig.) to weave (plots), to scheme; to work at, to compose. (**-imęnto** *m.*) **-ito** *part. adj.* (text.) warped; (fig.) woven; devised; schemed; composed; *n.m.* (text.) warp; network; plotting (of maps, etc.); (fig.) web; plot; un **-ito** di bugie, a tissue of lies. **-itoio** *m.* (text.) warp-beam. **-itore** *m.* (text.) warping-mill. **-itura** *f.* (text.) warping (see also **catanella**); (bldg.) **-itura** del tetto, roof frame; (fig.) shape, structure; pattern; plot; scheming.

†**ord-o** *adj.* deformed, hideous; monstrous; foul, filthy; *n.m.* foulness. †**-ura** *f.* ordure.

ordoviciano *adj.* (geol.) Ordovician.

ore·ade *f.* (Gk. myth.) oread; mountain-nymph.

oręcchi-a *f.* ear, hearing (cf. **orecchio**); fare le **-e** ad un libro, to dog-ear the pages of a book; (fig.) con le **-e** basse, crestfallen; ear-shaped thing (e.g. handle of pitcher); (bldg.) crossette; (naut.) palm of an anchor; **—** della cicala, anchor head pierced to take the anchor shackle; fare le **-e** di lepre, fare le **-e** dell'asino, to goosewing; **—** del bompresso, see **orecchione**; (zool.) **—** marina, **—** di San Pietro, ormer, ear shell, *Haliotis tuberculata*. **-ętta** *f.* (anat.) auricle of the heart; (naut.) fluke of an anchor.

orecchi-are [A 4 c] *intr.* (*aux.* avere) to listen, to eavesdrop; to pick up by ear. **-a·bile** *adj.* (fam.) easily remembered; (of a tune) catchy; superficial; amateurish; imitative. **-ante** *m.* one who sings or plays by ear; amateur or dabbler of any kind; eavesdropper. **-ata** *f.* box on the ear; tweaking of the ear.

orecchino *m.* ear-ring; clip-on style ear-ring; (vet.) twitch for horse; †(naut.) block hanging from mast; tackle used 'luff upon luff'.

orecchi-o m. ear; a portata d'—, within ear-shot; prestar — a, to listen to, to pay heed to; stare ad orecchi tesi, to prick up one's ears, to listen intently; dolore all'—, ear-ache; esser tutt'orecchi, to be all ears; da quest'— non (ci) sente, he's deaf in that ear, (fig.) he won't listen; fare l'— di mercante, to pretend not to hear; tirar l'— a uno, to scold someone; mettere una pulce nell'— a uno, to suggest a suspicion to someone; sturare gli orecchi a uno, to tell someone home truths; per un — entra e per l'altro esce, in one ear and out the other; a —, by ear; aver — per la musica, to have an ear for music; hearing; duro d'—, hard of hearing; ear-shaped object (e.g. handle of pitcher); (agric.) mouldboard (of plough); (naut.) fluke (of anchor); (bot.) — d'orso, *Primula* spp., esp. — auricula, *P. auricula*; — di topo, mouse-ear, hawkweed, *Hieracium pilosella*; (skating) the figure three. **-one** m. augm. big ear; (eng.) lug; (mil.) trunnion of a gun; (naut.) cathead; (zool.) long-eared bat, *Plecotus auritus*; pl. (med.) mumps, epidemic parotitis. **-oniera** f. (mil.) trunnion bearing. **-uolo** m. shoe-flap, ear-flap of cap; †ear-ring (cf. **orecchino**). **-uto** adj. long-eared; (fig.) donkey-like, asinine.

orefic-e m. goldsmith; jeweller; vendor of gold and silver plate, etc.; vendor of jewellery. **-eri-a** f. goldsmith's or jeweller's workshop; jeweller's shop; gold, silver, platinum ware; jewellery.

†**oreggiare** intr. to glow with golden light, to glisten like gold.

†**oreg-gio** m. See **orezzo**.

†**ore-gli-a** f., †**-o** m. See **orecchia** and **orecchio**.

oremus m. indecl. (the liturg. invitation) *Oremus*; a prayer.

oreo-trago m. (zool.) *Oreotragus saltatrix*, a species of Abyssinian antelope.

oreri-a f. goldsmith's work; gold things; gold plate.

Orest-e pr.n.m. Orestes; — e Pilade, Orestes and Pylades (provb. for two inseparable friends); (fig., usu. joc.) le furie d'—, implacable destiny. **-i-ade** f. (Gk. lit.) *Oresteia*.

oretta f. dim. See under **ora¹**.

orezz-o m. (poet.) light breeze, breath of air; cool shade, coolness (cf. **rezzo**). †**-are** intr. to blow gently (of a breeze), to breathe softly; to enjoy the cool shade. †**-amento** m. breeze; cool shade.

orfan-o m. orphan, orphan boy, male orphan; adj. orphan, orphaned; è — del padre, his father is dead. **-a** f. orphan girl, female orphan. **-ello** m. dim. orphan boy; orphaned baby. (**-ella** f. dim.) **-ezza** f., **-ità** f. indecl. orphanhood. **-otro-fio** m. orphanage, home for orphans, children's home.

orfe-a f. (orn.) Orphean warbler, *Sylvia hortensis*.

Orfe-o pr.n.m. (Gk. myth.) Orpheus; (lit. hist.) play or opera so entitled; (fig.) great musician; l'— pesarese, Rossini.

o-rfico adj. (Gk. rel. and lit.) Orphic.

organ-di(s), organdis-se m. indecl. (text.) organdie.

orga-nica f. (mil., etc.) organization of armed forces; (mus.) instrumental music.

orga-nic-o adj. (scient.) organic; regno —, animal kingdom; structural; (fig.) fundamental; inherent; well composed and constructed, having its parts well related, organic; (mus.) pertaining to organs; l'arte -a, organ-building; n.m. (mus.) combination, ensemble; (admin.) body, staff, personnel; aumentare l'—, to take on more staff; (mil.) cadre. **-amente** adv. organically.

organizino m. (text.) organizine.

organizz-are [A I] tr. to organize; to arrange; to set up. **-amento** m. organizing; arranging. **-ato** part. adj. organized; arranged. **-atore** m. organizer; (biol.) (embryonic) organizer; -atore chimico, evocator. (**-atrice** f.) **-azione** f. organization, method, arrangement; structure; body, organization, organizing body; -azione apparentata, related organization.

organ-o m. organ, physical organ; gli -i vocali, the vocal organs; (eng.) mechanism, unit, gear; (admin.) body, organ; — permanente, standing body; — responsabile delle direttive, policy-making body; — direttivo, governing body; — d'inchiesta, fact-finding organ or committee; (leg.) -i costituzionali, organs of the Constitution (C.P.); -i giudiziari, Courts of Justice; (mus.) organ; organum; †musical instrument; — a bocca, mouth-organ; — di Barberia, street-organ, barrel-organ; — da concerto, concert-organ; — eco, echo-organ; — espressivo, swell-organ; — fisaulico, pneumatic-organ; — idraulico, water-organ, hydraulicon; — liturgico, church-organ; — a manovella, street-organ; — ninfale, portative organ; — pneumatico, pneumatic organ; portabile, portative organ; — portatile, portative organ; harmonium; — positivo, choir-organ; — reale, regal; — recitativo, swell-

organ; — rigabello, portative organ; — solo, solo-organ; — torsello, portative organ; concerto d'—, organ recital; grand'—, great organ; (lit.; philos.) organon; Organum; spokesman, mouthpiece, newspaper, organ (of party or opinion); (mech.) organ; (aeron.) — d'atterraggio, landing gear; radiofaro tipo —, fan marker; (mil.) portcullis; multiple-barrelled gun; (naut.) — di direzione, steering gear; (ichth.) cappone —, gurnard, *Triglia lyra*; †means, intermediary; †instrument. **-ac-cio** m. pejor. (mus.) wretched organ. **-ai-o, -aro** m. (mus.) organ-builder. †**-ale** adj. (anat.) vene -ali, veins of the neck. **-are** [A I S] tr. see **organizzare**; †(mus.) to organize (i.e. to add a *vox organalis* to the *vox principalis*). **-etto** m. dim., **-etta** f. dim. (mus.) small organ; portative organ; harmonium; mouth-organ; -etto a manovella, -etto di Barberia, barrel-organ, street-organ; (neol. iron.) second-rate party paper, 'rag'; (orn.) redpoll, *Carduelis flammea*. **-ino** m. dim. (mus.) portative organ; street-organ. **-ismo** m. organism; living structure; system. **-ista** m., f. (pl. m., f. -isti) organist; †organ-builder; (mus.) organist; *Euphonia* spp. **-istro** m., **-istrum** m. indecl. (mus.) organistrum, hurdy-gurdy. **-ogeni-a** f., **-oge-nesi** f. (biol.) organogeny, organogenesis. **-oge-nico** adj. organogenic, organogenetic. **-ografi-a** f. (biol.) organography; (mus.) writing about organs. **-o-ide** adj. (med.) organoid. **-olet-tico** adj. (med.; scient.) organoleptic. **-ologi-a** f. (anat.) organology. **-ope-ia** f. making of musical instruments. **-opessi** f. (surg.) organopexy. **-oplasti-a** f. (med.) organoplasty. **-opla-stico** adj. (med.) organoplastic. **-oscopi-a** f. (med.) organoscopy. **-oterapi-a** f. (med.) organotherapy. **-o-tropo** m. (med.) organotrope. **-uc-cio** m. pejor. (mus.) organ of indifferent quality. **-um** m. indecl. (mus.) organum †**-uto** adj. articulated (of sound proceeding from vocal organs).

orga-nulo m. dim. (anat.) small organ.

orga-smo m. great agitation; violent excitement; anxiety; essere in —, to be anxious, worried, agitated or upset; orgasm; turgescence.

or-g-ia¹ f. (pl. -e, -ie) (Gk. antiq.) orgy; (fig.) orgy, orgiastic indulgence; riot. **-iasta** m. Bacchant, licentious reveller. **-ia-stico** adj. orgiastic.

†**or-gia²** f. fathom length.

orgogli-o m. pride; haughtiness; vainglory; ostentation; boasting; montare in —, to get a swollen head; something to take pride in; essere l'— della mamma, to be a mother's pride and joy. †**-amento** m. pride, proud behaviour. †**-anza** f. see **orgoglio**. †**-are** rfl., intr. to become proud; to behave haughtily. **-ato** part. adj. proud, conceited. **-oso** adj. proud, haughty, boastful, conceited; elated; essere -oso di, to be proud of, to take pride in; (of an animal) lively, spirited; (of wine) vigorous, generous. **-osamente** adv. proudly; with due pride; boastfully; conceitedly.

orical-co m. (pl. -chi) (antiq.) orichalc; (poet.) brass; brass vessel; trumpet.

†**oricanno** m. small vase with narrow aperture for containing scented water.

o-rice m. (zool.). See **orige**.

oricello m. (bot.) orchil, *Roccella tinctoria*; (dyeing) orchil, cudbear.

orichicco m. (bot.) gum of plum-trees, cherry-trees, etc.

†**ori-chiomato**, †**-crinito** adj. golden-haired.

orient-are [A I] tr. to orient, to orientate; to direct; to point, to set; (naut.) to trim (sails) to the direction of the wind; — di bolina, to trim close hauled; — la bussola, to adjust the lubbers' line; †— i pennoni, to square the yards; rfl. to get one's bearings, to orientate oneself; †(naut.) to fix the ship; to ascertain the ship's position by recognition of a coast. **-a-bile** adj. capable of being oriented; (text.) moving, adjustable, revolving, swivelling. **-amento** m. orientating; orientation; senso d'-amento, sense of direction; -amento professionale, vocational guidance; (naut.) relative bearing of guns, trim of sails, etc.; (aeron.) bearing. **-ato** part. adj. orientated; directed; guided; turned, pointed, set. **-azione** f. orientation, direction; bearings.

orient-e¹ m. (geog.) east, orient; l'estremo —, the Far East, il vicino —, the Near East; il medio —, the Middle East; (hist.) Impero d'—, Eastern Empire; (freemasonry) Grande —, Grand Lodge; la Chiesa d'—, the Eastern Church, the Orthodox Church; (astron.) east; †sunrise; †birthplace. **-ale** adj. oriental, eastern; Indie -ali, East Indies; n.m., f. Oriental. **-almente** adv. (astron.) in the East. **-alista** m., f. Orientalist.

oriente² adj. rising (of the sun).

orifiamma *f.* (hist.; herald.) oriflamme; (fig.) banner.

†**orificeri·a** *f.* See oreficeria, under orefice.

orifi·cio *m.* See orifizio.

orifi·zi·o *m.* orifice; hole, aperture; (fig.) mouth, opening. **-ale** *adj.* (med.) orificial.

ori·gano *m.* (bot.) essence of marjoram (*Origanum*).

o·rige *m.* (zool.) *Oryx leucoryx*, a kind of antelope.

Origen-e, Ori·gen-e *pr.n.m.* Origen. **-ista** *m.* (eccl. hist.) Origenist.

origin-ale *adj.*, **-are** [A 15]. See under origine.

ori·gin-e *f.* origin, beginning; source, starting-point; cause; periodo delle -i, first, earliest, period (e.g. of a literature); avere —, to originate, to take rise; italiano d'—, d'— italiana, of Italian descent, of Italian extraction; di alta —, of noble birth; (theol.) peccato d'—, original sin; (comm.) certificato d'—, certificate of origin. **-ale** *adj.* original; first; primary; new, fresh, novel; inventive, creative; eccentric, queer, odd; (comm.) cambiale -ale, original bill; *n.m.* original; original copy, manuscript; prima copia che serve di -ale, blue-print; master-copy; queer person, odd individual, an 'original'; (leg.) original; una copia conforme all'-ale, a true copy. **-almente** *adv.* originally; in origin; in an original way. **-alità** *f.* originality; novelty; freshness; inventiveness, eccentricity, queer behaviour; outlandishness. **-amento** *m.* originating; deriving; proceeding. **-are** [A 1 s] *tr.* to originate, to give rise to; to set in train, to set going; †to state the origin of, to trace the beginnings of; *intr.* (*aux.* essere. *prep.* da) to originate; to spring (from); to derive (from); to take rise, to proceed, to begin, to start. **-a·rio** *adj.* original, first, pristine; originating; famiglia -aria di Francia, family that came originally from France; native; il gelso è -ario della Cina, the mulberry was brought, introduced, from China. **-ariamente** *adv.* originally, formerly, in earlier times; in the beginning. **-ato** *part. adj.* originated; derived; begun. **-atore** *m.* originator, inventor. (**-atrice** *f.*) **-azione** *f.* origin, derivation; etymology.

origliare [A 4] *intr.* (*aux.* avere) to eavesdrop; to pry, to spy; †*tr.* to investigate, to look into closely.

origliere *m.* pillow; †cushion.

orignale *m.* (zool.) elk, *Alces palmatus*.

†**origo** *f.* See origine.

orin-a *f.* urine; fare l'—, to urinate, to make water. **-ale** *m.* chamberpot; urinal. **-are** [A 1] *intr.* (*aux.* avere) to urinate, to make water. **-a·rio** *adj.* (anat.) urinary. **-atoio** *m.* public urinal, gentlemen's lavatory, convenience. **-ato·rio** *adj.* urinary. **-azione** *f.* urinating, urination.

oriola *f.* (bot.) bird's-foot trefoil, *Lotus corniculatus*.

oriolo[1] *m.* (orn.) oriole, esp. the golden oriole, *Oriolus oriolus*.

†**oriolo**[2] *m.* See orologio.

Orione *pr.n.m.* (myth.; astron.) Orion.

oripe *m.* (zool.) vinegar eel worm, *Anguillula aceti*.

†**oriscello** *m.* crust, little bit; un — di pane, a crust of bread.

oritt-e·ropo *m.* (zool.) anteater, *Orycteropus capensis*. **-ogeni·a** *f.* (geol.) the origin of fossils. **-ognosi·a** *f.*, **-ologi·a** *f.* palaeontology, study of fossils.

oriundo *adj.* native (of); — di Napoli, born at Naples, of Neapolitan origin or descent; *n.m.* (sport) a foreign footballer whose Italian extraction makes him eligible for any Italian League club.

†**oriuolo** *m.* See orologio.

orizzont-e *m.* horizon; fare un giro d'—, to scan the horizon, (fig.) to have general talks (e.g. in international politics); (astron.) — visibile, apparent horizon; (aeron.) — artificiale elettrico, altitude gyroscopic indicator. **-ale** *adj.* pertaining to the horizon; horizontal; level, flat, place; *n.m.pl.* (in crossword puzzles) 'across'. **-almente** *adv.* horizontally. **-alità** *f.* flatness; quality or state of being horizontal; horizontal position. **-are** [A 1] *tr.* to place in a horizontal position; *rfl.* to take one's bearings.

Orland-o *pr.n.m.* Roland; Orlando; (joc.) mettersi sul caval d'—, to be very sure of oneself, to talk big. †**-eri·a** *f.* (joc.) doughtiness, prowess.

orl-are [A 1 c] *tr.* to hem, to edge, to border; to reinforce the edge of; — a giorno, to hem-stitch; (naut.) to put roping on (canvas); †— il cappello a, to insult, to humiliate; †— il cappello a, — sotto il mantello a, to plot against. **-ato** *part. adj.* edged, bordered; hemmed; -ato a giorno, hem-stitched. **-atore** *m.* hemmer (man or thing). **-atrice** *f.* hemming machine. **-atura** *f.* bordering, edging, hemming; -atura a giorno, hem-stitching.

orleanista *m.* (hist.) Orleanist.

Or·leans (or **Orléans**, pron. as French) *pr.n.f.* (geog.) Orléans; (text.) Orleans.

†**orliqu(i)a** *f.* See reliquia.

orl-o *m.* border, edge; — vivo, sharp edge; — arrotondato, rounded edge; hem; — sfilato, — a giorno, openwork hem, hem-stitching; — a impuntura, stitched hem; rim, brim; brink; sull'— della rovina, on the verge of ruin; (naut.) — della vela, roping of the sail; †top strake (see soglia); †end, termination; †toccare l'—, to get to the end, to finish, to conclude. **-etto** *m. dim.* rim of train-wheel. **-ic·cio** *m.* extreme outer edge; extreme outside crust of bread; edge of any broken surface; (bot.) excrescence at the margins of a scar on the trunk of a tree.

orm-a *f.* footmark, footprint; seguire le -e di, to follow in the steps of; trace, track, imprint; mark, sign; slot; (of a tyre) tread; (geol.) trail, spoor; ritrovare le proprie -e, to retrace one's steps; †chiappare l'—, (of hounds) to pick up the scent; †foot. **-are** [A 1 c] *tr.* to track, to follow the track of, to pursue. **-ato** *part. adj.* tracked; pursued; †shaped. **-eggiare** [A 3 c] *tr.* to track; to follow in the footsteps of.

orma·i *adv.* See oramai.

ormeggiare[1] [A 3 c]. See under orma.

ormeggi-are[2] [A 3 c]. See under ormeggio.

ormeggi-o *m.* (naut.) the manœuvre of securing a ship or making fast; anchorage or ships' berths; method of securing a ship; — a ruota, — su un'ancora, swinging berth; — afforcato, — su due ancore, moored; — di fianco, alongside; — col pennello, anchorage with a second anchor backing up the first; banchina d'—, quay; boa (cassa) d'—, mooring buoy; piloni d'—, (colonne, cannoni) d'—, dolphins, bollards, mooring posts; linea d'—, line of the cable; posto d'—, berth. **-amento** *m.* (naut.) action of securing a vessel, mooring. **-are** [A 3 c] *tr.* (naut.) to secure, to moor. **-ato** *part. adj.* (naut.) secured with hawsers, moored. **-atore** *m.* (naut.) form of towing bollard in the bows of Mediterranean boats (cf. Samson post in a British small decked boat or yacht); member of a mooring party employed securing ships. **-atura** *f.* (naut.) lashing or knot at the end of a mooring hawser to prevent it from rendering.

†**ormesino** *m.* a kind of thin silk, sarcenet, so called from the island of Ormuz in the Persian Gulf whence it was imported.

ormino *m.* (bot.) *Salvia horminum* and *S. pratensis*.

ormon-e *m.* (biol.) hormone. **-iterapi·a** *f.* (med.) hormone therapy. **-ogenesi** *f.* (physiol.) hormonogenesis. **-opoiesi** *f.* (physiol.) hormonopoiesis. **-opoie·tico** *adj.* hormonopoietic.

ormo·nico *adj.* (physiol.) hormonic.

ornament-o *m.* ornament; decoration; embellishment, adornment; grace; *pl.* (mus.) ornaments, graces; (herald.) attributes. **-ale** *adj.* ornamental. **-azione** *f.* decoration; adorning; (mus.) ornamentation.

orn-are [A 1 c] *tr.* (*prep.* di) to adorn, to ornament, to deck, to embellish, to decorate, to beautify; *rfl.* to adorn oneself; to deck oneself (in). **-atezza** *f.* elegance, grace; ornateness, richness. **-atista** *m.*, *f.* ornamenter, ornamentist, ornamentalist. **-ativo** *adj.* decorative. **-ato** *part. adj.* adorned; elegant; ornate; rich; flowery (of style); *n.m.* ornamental design; decoration; (art) design; frieze; moulding (of various kinds); (leg.) le norme di -ato pubblico, public ornamentation regulations (C.C.). **-atura** *f.* ornament; ornamenting. **-azione** *f.* ornamentation.

orneblenda *f.* (miner.) hornblende, amphibole.

orn(i)ello *m.* (bot.) manna ash, *Fraxinus ornus*.

ornit-ologi·a *f.* ornithology. **-olo·gico** *adj.* ornithological. **-o·logo** *m.* (*pl.* -o·loghi, -o·logi) ornithologist. **-omanzi·a** *f.* ornithomancy, divination by watching the flight of birds. **-orinco** *m.* (zool.) duck-billed platypus, *Ornithorhynchus anatinus*.

orno *m.* (bot.). See orniello.

oro *m.* gold; — di coppella, 24-carat gold; — di zecchino, fine gold; — di Genova, gold-leaf; — di Napoli, a base gold much alloyed; — laminato, rolled gold; placcato in —, gold-plated, rolled gold; miniera d'—, gold mine; (finan.) — di lega, pure gold; moneta d'—, gold coin; punto d'—, gold or specie point; riserva d'—, gold reserve; — in verghe, bullion; (herald.) or; nuotano nell'—, they are rolling in money; vale tant'— quanto pesa, he is worth his weight in gold; affare d'—, wonderful bargain; persona d'—, sterling person; capelli d'—, golden hair; bue d'—, wealthy boor, *nouveau riche*; vello d'—, Golden Fleece; età dell'—, golden age, age of gold; pesce d'—, goldfish; *pl.* gli ori, things made of gold,

oro (*cont.*)

gold plate; *pl.* (cards, 'scopa') point scored when a player or a team of two players secure more than five cards of the diamond suit.

oro-chinaṣi *f.* (physiol.) orokinase. **-faringe** *f.* (anat.) oropharynx. **-naṣale** *adj.* (med.) oronasal.

orogene·tico *adj.* (geol.) orogenic.

orogr-afi·a *f.* orography, description of mountains. **-a·fico** *adj.* (meteor.) orographic.

orolinguale *adj.* (anat.) orolingual.

orolo·g-io *m.* watch; clock; time-piece; — a peso, grandfather clock; — a ripetizione, repeater; — da torre, tower clock; — a suoneria, chiming clock; — solare, sun-dial; — da polso, wrist-watch; avere l'— in testa, to have a good sense of time; è un —, he is as regular as clockwork; stare con l'— in mano, to be a stickler for punctuality; caricare l'—, to wind up the clock (or, one's watch); (ent.) — dei morti, death watch beetle, *Xestobium rufovillosum*. **-eri·a** *f.* watchmaking, clockmaking; clockmaker's, watchmaker's (shop); clockmaking, watchmaking; clockwork; bomba ad -eria, time-bomb. **-ia·io**, **-iere** *m.* clockmaker, watchmaker.

Oronte *pr.n.m.* (geog.) Orontes.

oroptere *m.* (opt.) horopter.

oro·sc-opo *m.* horoscope. **-opi·a** *f.* horoscopy, casting of horoscopes. **-o·pico** *adj.* horoscopic.

orottere *m.* See **oroptere**.

orpell-o *m.* tinsel; (fig.) glitter; (metall.) tombac. **-are** [A I] *tr.* to tinsel, to cover with tinsel; (fig.) to disguise, to mask, to gild over; †to deceive; †*rfl.* to pretend to prestige or nobility. **-amento** *m.* tinselling. **-ato** *part. adj.* tinselled, covered in tinsel; disguised, glossed over, gilded. **-atura** *f.* tinselling; tinsel-work; pretence, disguise.

orpimento *m.* (chem.) orpiment.

†**orr-are** *vb.* and derivs. see **onorare**. †**-anza** *f.* see **onoranza**.

orr-endo *adj.* horrible, terrifying; hideous; dreadful, frightful, fearful, awful; repellent. (**-endamente** *adv.*) †**-ere** *tr.* to abhor, to loathe; *rfl.* to be terrified.

†**orre·vole** *adj.* See **onorevole**, under **onorare**.

orri·bil-e *adj.* horrible, frightful, awful, dreadful; fearful, atrocious. **-mente** *adv.* horribly, dreadfully; atrociously. **-ità** *f.* dreadfulness, awfulness, atrociousness.

or·rid-o *adj.* fearful; horrid, frightful, dreary; grim, awesome, wild; luogo d'una bellezza -a, scene of rugged beauty; (lit.) bristling, shaggy; *n.m.* piece of wild scenery (e.g. ravine, gully, mountain waterfall). **-amente** *adv.* horridly; dreadfully; awesomely. **-ęzza** *f.*, **-ità** *f.* frightfulness; awesomeness; shagginess.

orr-ipilante *adj.* hair-raising, terrifying; film —, horror film. **-ipilazione** *f.* shuddering, terror. **-isonante** *adj.* (poet.) grim-sounding, awesome.

orrore *m.* horror, terror; awe; dread; sacro —, sacred awe; loathing; avere in —, to abominate; costa un —, it's a hideous price; awfulness, awesomeness, grimness, ruggedness; (poet.) shagginess.

orrorre·a *f.* (med.) orrhorrhœa.

orṣ-o *m.* (zool.) bear; — bruno, brown bear; — bianco, — polare, polar bear; — grigio, grizzly bear; (fig.) bear-like, uncouth person; (stone) rubber; (geog.) Isola degli Orsi, Bear Island; Lago degli Orsi, Great Bear Lake. **-a** *f.* (zool.) she-bear; (astron.) l'— Maggiore, Ursa Major, the Great Bear, King Charles's Wain, the Plough; — minore, Ursa Minor, the Little Bear. **-ac·chio** *m.*, **-acchino** *m.* (zool.) bear cub. **-acchiotto** *m.* (zool.) young male bear; Teddy-bear. **-atto** *m.* bear cub. †**-ata** *f.* grumbling and growling as of a bear. **-iero** *m.* bear keeper, owner of performing bears, bear-leader. **-ino** *adj.* of a bear, ursine; bear-like.

orso·i-o *m.* (text.) organzine, twisted silk. **-are** [A4] *tr.* (text.) to organzine.

Orṣol-a *pr.n.f.* Ursula. **-ina** *f.* (eccl.) Ursuline (nun).

orsù *excl.* come now!; forward!; on!

ort-aggi *m.pl.* vegetables; greens; pot-herbs; market-garden produce; market garden. **-a·glia** *f.* kitchen garden, vegetable garden; market garden; *pl.* garden produce.

ortagorisco *m.* (ichth.) sun fish, *Orthagoriscus mola*.

ortali·a *f.* (zool.) python.

†**orte·fica** *f.* (med.) nettle rash.

ortense *adj.* (bot.) cultivated in gardens, garden; pertaining to gardens.

orten·sia *f.* (bot.) hydrangea, *Hydrangea macrophylla*.

ortic-a *f.* (bot.) stinging nettle, *Urtica*; (fig.) stimulus; gettare l'abito (la tonaca) alle ortiche, to quit the monastic life; (vet.) rowel (for draining). **-aia** *f.* see **orticaria**. **-aio** *m.* nettle-bed. **-ante** *adj.* (med.) urticarial. **-are** [A2] *tr.* to sting; *rfl.* to be stung; to become nettled. **-a·ria** *f.* (med.) urticaria, nettle-rash. **-azione** *f.* (med.) urtication.

orticello *m. dim.* See under **orto**.

ortich-eggiare [A3c] *tr.* to sting with nettles. **-eto** *m.* place overgrown with nettles.

orti-coltore, **-cultore** *m.* horticulturist. **-coltura**, **-cultura** *f.* horticulture; gardening; market-gardening.

orticonosco·pio *m.* (telev.) orthicon.

ortighetta *f.* (vet.) rowel (for draining).

ortite *f.* (miner.) orthite, allanite.

ort-o[1] *m.* garden; — botanico, botanical garden; — secco, herbarium, *hortus siccus*; (Bibl.) l'— di Getsemani, the Garden of Gethsemane. **-icello** *m. dim.* miniature garden. **-icino** *m. dim.* flower-border; box for seedlings. **-ivo** *adj.* relating to a garden; terreno -ivo, garden land. **-olano** *m.*, *adj.* (bot.) gardener; director of a garden; greengrocer; (orn.) ortolan, *Emberiza hortulana*; — grigio, Cretzschmar's bunting, *Emberiza caesia*; name also given loosely to other buntings.

ort-o[2] *m.* (astron.) ascension, rising; (poet.) East, Levant; (fig.) beginning, dawn, rise. **-ivo** *adj.* (astron.) ortive, ascensional.

orto[3] *adj. indecl.* (chem.) ortho; la posizione —, the ortho position.

ort-ociṭoṣi *f.* (med.) orthoytosis. **-ocla·ṣio** *m.* (miner.) orthoclase. **-ocroma·tico** *adj.* orthochromatic. **-odonti·a** *f.* (med.) orthodontia. **-odoṣṣi·a** *f.* orthodoxy; (eccl.) Orthodoxy, the Orthodox Church. **-odosso** *adj.* orthodox, Orthodox. **-oepi·a** *f.* (gramm.) orthoepy, correct pronunciation. **-oe·pico** *adj.* (gramm.) orthoepic. **-oevoluzione** *f.* (biol.) orthogenesis. **-ofoni·a** *f.* (gramm.) correct pronunciation. **-ofo·nico** *adj.* (gramm.) orthoepic. **-ognato** *adj.* (anat.) orthognathous. **-ogonale** *adj.* (geom.) at right angles, orthogonal; proiezione -ogonale, orthographic projection. **-ogonalmente** *adv.* at right angles. **-ogonalità** *f.* squareness. **-ogo·nio** *adj.* right-angled; triangolo -ogonio, right-angled triangle. **-ogrado** *adj.* (anthrop.) orthograde, walking erect. **-ografi·a** *f.* orthography, spelling; (archit.) elevation (drawing). **-ogra·fico** *adj.* orthographic; errori -ografici, spelling mistakes. **-ografica·mente** *adv.* orthographically. **-o·grafo** *m.* orthographer. **-ologi·a** *f.* orthoepy. **-opedi·a** *f.* (med.) orthopaedics. **-ope·dico** *adj.* orthopaedic. **-opne·a** *f.* (med.) orthopnoea. **-oradioscopi·a** *f.* (med.) orthoradioscopy. **-oscopi·a** *f.* orthoscopy. **-osco·pico** *adj.* (opt.) orthoscopic. **-osco·pio** *m.* (med.; opt.) orthoscope. **-o·ṣio** *m.* (miner.) orthoclase. **-osta·tico** *adj.* (scient.) orthostatic. **-o·stica** *f.* (bot.) orthostichy. **-o·tomo** *m.* (orn.) tailor-bird, *Orthotomus* spp. **-otono** *m.* (med.) orthotonus. **-o·tropo** *m.* (bot.) orthotropous. **-ot·teri** *m.pl.* (ent.) Orthoptera.

Orviet-o *pr.n.m.* (geog.) Orvieto; Orvieto wine. **-ano** *adj.* of Orvieto; *n.m.* inhabitant of Orvieto. (**-ana** *f.*)

orza *f.* (naut.) windward or weather side; andare ad —, to sail close to the wind; mettersi ad —, to haul to windward; orza!, luff!; a —!, keep her close to the wind; weather halyard; luff tackle; bowline; una caviglia all'—, a spoke of weather helm.

orẓai(u)olo[1] *m.* (med.) sty.

orẓai(u)olo[2] *m.* seller of barley, etc.

orzapoza *f.* (naut.) tackle amidships capable of being used either side.

orẓ-are [A I] *intr.* (*aux.* avere) (naut.) to luff. **-ata** *f.* (naut.) luff. **-eggiare** [A3c] *intr.* (*aux.* avere) (naut.) to bear to windward.

orẓ-o *m.* (bot.) barley; — selvatico, mouse barley, *Hordeum murinum*. **-arolo** *m.* see **orzai(u)olo**[2]. **-ata** *f.* barley-water; almond syrup; scolding, dressing-down. **-ato** *adj.* made with barley.

oṣann-a *excl.*, *n.m. indecl.* (rel.) hosanna; (fig.) shout of praise, acclamation; cantare (gli) —, to be loud in one's praises; (mus.) hosanna, musical setting of *Hosanna in excelsis*. **-are** [A I] *intr.* (*aux.* avere) to sing hosanna, to cry hosanna; to sing hymns of praise.

oṣ-are [A I] *intr.* (*aux.* avere) to dare; to be bold enough; -o sperare che..., I venture to hope that...; non -avo, I didn't dare; *tr.* to risk, to venture. **-ato** *part. adj.* dared, ventured, risked; daring, bold.

osazone *m.* (chem.) osazone.

†**osbergo** *m.* See **usbergo**.

oscen-o *adj.* obscene, lewd, indecent; disgusting, hideous, ill-omened. **-amente** *adv.* obscenely, lewdly; hideously. **-ità** *f.* obscenity; lewd action; indecency; disgusting behaviour.

osche-ite *f.* (med.) oscheitis. **-ocele** *m.* (med.) oscheocele, scrotal hernia.

oscill-are [A I] *intr.* (*aux.* avere) to oscillate, to swing; to vibrate; to vary, to fluctuate, to go up and down; to waver, to hesitate. **-ante** *part. adj.* oscillating; swinging; varying; wavering; (mus.) registro -ante, pulsating stop (of organ). **-atore** *m.* (electr.; radio; eng.) oscillator. **-atorio** *adj.* oscillatory, oscillating. **-azione** *f.* oscillation; (eng.) -azione pendolare, hunting; (cinem.) -azione dell'immagine, unsteady picture; (cinem.) -azione del suono, flutter; (comm.) fluctuation; swing. **-ografo** *m.* oscillograph; -ografo catodico, cathode-ray oscillograph. **-ogramma** *m.* (electron.; med.) oscillogram. **-ometro** *m.* (med.) oscillometer. **-oscopio** *m.* (electr.) oscilloscope.

oscitan-te *adj.* heedless, negligent; hesitating, uncertain of purpose. †**-za** *f.* heedlessness, indolence.

oscul-atore *adj.* (geom.) osculatory. **-atorio** *m.* (liturg.) osculatory, pax. **-azione** *f.* (math.) osculation, higher order contact; osculation; kissing.

o·sculo *m.* (anat.) osculum, small orifice.

oscur-are [A I] *tr.* to obscure, to darken; to dim, to cloud; to eclipse; to tarnish; to besmirch; *rfl.* to grow dark; to become tarnished or dim; (of the sky) to become overcast. **-abile** *adj.* that may be dimmed or tarnished. **-amento** *m.* darkening, dimming; black-out (during Second World War). **-antismo** *m.* obscurantism. **-antista** *m.* obscurantist. **-azione** *f.* obscuration; (astron.) obscuration; occultation, eclipse; (cinem.) fase di -azione, dark interval.

oscur-o *adj.* dark; overcast; clouded; darkened; dim; murky; il suo volto si fece —, his face darkened; obscure, far from clear; mysterious; doubtful; little known, humble; (fig.) *n.m.* darkness; all'—, in the dark; essere all'— di tutto, to be in the dark about everything; (photog.) camera -a, dark room, (hist. photog.) camera obscura. **-amente** *adv.* obscurely; darkly; dimly; mysteriously. **-ità** *f.* obscurity, dimness, darkness; humbleness (of birth).

osella *f.* (numis.) Venetian coin worth four sequins (sixteenth century).

osf-ialgi·a *f.* (med.) osphyalgia, sciatica. **-ite** *f.* (med.) osphyitis.

Osi·ride *pr.n.m.* (myth.) Osiris.

osmano *adj.* Turkish.

osmegma *m.* See smegma.

o·smico *adj.* (chem.) osmic.

o·smi-o *m.* (chem.) osmium. **-ato** *m.* (chem.) osmiate. **-diosi** *f.* body odour, 'b.o.' **-uro** *m.* alloy containing osmium.

o·sm-osi *f.* (scient.) osmosis. **-o·tico** *adj.* osmotic.

oso *apocop. part.* of osare, q.v.; *adj.* (poet.) bold, daring.

†**ospe** *m.* See ospite.

ospedal-e *m.* hospital; infirmary; finire all'—, to end up in the workhouse; (mil.) — da campo, field dressing-station; nave —, hospital ship; entrare all'—, to go into hospital. **-iero, -iere** *adj.* of a hospital; cavalieri -ieri, Knights Hospitallers; frati -ieri, Brothers Hospitallers.

ospital-e *adj.* hospitable; welcoming; (Rom. antiq.) tessera —, *tessera hospitalis* (token of guest-friendship between the two parties concerned and kept by them and their descendants as a means of recognition); †*n.m.* hospital. **-mente** *adv.* hospitably. **-iere** *adj.* relating to hospital; cura -iera, hospital treatment; see also ospedaliero, under ospedale. (**-iera** *f.*) **-ità** *f.* hospitality; comitato per l'-ità, reception committee; (leg.) l'abuso di -ità, abuse of hospitality (C.P.).

o·spit-e *m., f.* host, hostess; guest; †*adj.* unfamiliar (with), ignorant (of). **-are** [A I S] *tr.* to offer hospitality to; to entertain; to shelter, to put up for the night; il paese che -a, the host country; to house, to contain; (eng.) to house.

ospi·zio *m.* asylum, almshouse, hospice; home (for the aged, orphans, etc.); shelter; dwelling, abode; hostel; — marino, seaside holiday home for children; — di mendicità, workhouse.

ospodar-o *m.* (hist.) hospodar. **-ato** *m.* status, or term of office, of hospodar.

†**ossa·io** *m.* See under osso.

oss-alato *m.* (chem.) oxalate. **-a·lico** *adj.* (chem.) oxalic. **-a·lide** *f.* (bot.) wood-sorrel, *Oxalis*. **-aluri·a** *f.* (med.) oxaluria. **-am·mico** *adj.* (chem.) oxamic. **-am·mide** *f.* (chem.) oxamide.

ossame *m.* bones, heap of bones; (archit.) skeleton, ossature.

oss-a·mmico *adj.* (chem.) oxamic. **-am·mide** *m.* (chem.) oxamide, oxalamide.

ossa·rio *m.* charnel-house, ossuary; (archit.) ossuary.

ossatura *f.* frame, framework; firm foundation; skeleton, bony structure; (naut.) rib-work; hull.

ossecr-are [A I] *tr.* (poet.) to obsecrate; to entreat. **-azione** *f.* (rel.) entreaty, fervent prayer; (rhet.) obsecration.

osseina *f.* (chem.) ossein.

os·seo *adj.* (med.; anat.) osseous, bony.

ossequ-ente *adj.* deferential, respectful; submissive; figlio —, dutiful son; — alle leggi, law-abiding. **-iare** [A4] *tr.* to pay one's respects to, to honour, to do homage to, to wait upon.

osse·qui-o *m.* homage; respect, deference; obedience; in — a (di), in obedience to, out of respect for; i migliori ossequi, kindest regards; †obsequies. **-osità** *f.* respectfulness; deferential action; obsequiousness. **-oso** *adj.* respectful, polite; obsequious. (**-osamente** *adv.*)

osserv-are [A I] *tr.* to observe; to notice; to watch; to look at; to scan; to keep, to respect, to comply with; to remark, to point out; to object, far — una cosa a uno, to draw the attention of someone to something; — la domenica, to observe, to keep, Sunday. **-a·bile** *adj.* observable, noticeable; notable; perceptible, visible; to be observed or complied with. **-abilmente** *adv.* observably; noticeably; perceptibly. **-ante** *part.* observing, noticing; *adj.* observant; careful, scrupulous; strict (e.g. in church-going); -ante delle leggi, law-abiding; *n.m.* (eccl.) Observant, Friar Minor of the Regular Observance. **-antemente** *adv.* observantly. **-anza** *f.* observance, regard (of law or religious rule); compliance (with custom or agreement); (in official letters) con perfetta -anza, yours obediently; (eccl.) religious rule of life (esp. with Franciscans), Regular Observance; fulfilment, performance; *pr.n.f.* (eccl.) l'Osservanza, church and convent of the Osservanti near Siena, founded by San Bernardino in 1423; †reverence; †observation. **-ativo** *adj.* relating to observation; scienze -ative, scientific subjects of which principles are derived from observation rather than from experiment or inductive reasoning; †worthy of being observed. **-ato** *part. adj.* observed; complied with; kept; fulfilled, performed; (mus.) stile -ato, traditional style (applied to the polyphonic church music of the sixteenth century); contrappunto -ato, strict counterpoint; (mil.) tiro -ato, observed fall of shot; †cautious, wary; †observant. **-atore** *m.* onlooker, spectator; observer; *pr.n.m.* l'*Osservatore*, (title of periodical) *Observer* (e.g. of Gozzi's paper or in the title of Vatican daily); (mil.; aeron.) observer. (**-atrice** *f.*) **-ato·rio** *m.* (*pl.* -atorii) observatory; (mil.) observation post. **-azione** *f.* observation; reflection; remark, comment; critical note; criticism, fare un'-azione, to make a remark; fare -azioni, to raise objections; observance, fulfilment; spirito d'-azione, power of observation; (naut.) observation, astronomical or land fix; nave in -azione, reporting ship; squadra in -azione, patrolling squadron.

ossession-e *f.* obsession; (psych.) obsession; fixation. **-ante** *part.* of ossessionare; *adj.* haunting; worrying. **-are** [A I C] *tr.* to obsess, to haunt, to worry. **-ato** *part. adj.* obsessed; *n.m.* person obsessed, or in an exalted condition.

ossess-o *adj.* (rel.) possessed; (fig.) maniacal, obsessed; *n.m.* one possessed; person suffering from obsessions. (**-a** *f.*)

ossetto *m. dim.* of osso, q.v.

ossi·a *conj.* or; that is, in other words, or rather; (mus.) to indicate an alternative passage which is usually a simplification.

ossiacetilene *m.* (eng.) oxy-acetylene.

ossi-anesco *adj.* Ossianic, Ossian-like. **-a·nico** *adj.* Ossianic, of Ossian.

oss-i·bele *m.* (zool.) *Oxybelis fulgidus*, a kind of snake. **-icrato** *m.* (pharm.) kind of dilute vinegar.

ossicino *m. dim.* See under osso.

ossicloruro *m.* (chem.) oxychloride.

ossid-are [A I S] *tr.* (chem.) to oxidize; *rfl.* (chem.) to oxidize. **-a·bile** *adj.* oxidizable. **-abilità** *f.* oxidizability. **-ante** *adj.* oxidizing; *n.m.* oxidizing agent. **-ato** *part. adj.* oxidized. **-azione** *f.* oxidation, oxidizing.

ossidiana *f.* (miner.) obsidian.

†**ossidione** *f.* siege.

ossidionale *adj.* (Rom. antiq.) obsidional.

os·s-ido *m.* (chem.) oxide. **-i·drico** *adj.* oxy-hydrogen; cannello -idrico, blow-pipe, blow-lamp; fiamma -idrica, oxy-hydrogen flame; (eng.) saldatura -idrica, oxy-hydrogen welding.

ossidr·ile *m.* (chem.) hydroxyl, hydroxyl group. **-i·lico** *adj.* hydroxylic.

ossiemoglobina *f.* (biochem.) oxy-haemoglobin.

ossi·f-ero *adj.* ossiferous; containing fossilized bones; caverne **-ere**, caves containing bones (of prehistoric times). **-icare** [A 2 s] *tr.* to ossify; *rfl.* to become ossified. **-icato** *part. adj.* ossified. **-icazione** *f.* ossification.

ossifluenza *f.* (med.) osteolysis.

ossiforme *adj.* (anat.) ossiform.

ossi·fraga *f.* (orn.), ossifrage (a Biblical bird, probably the bearded vulture, see Leviticus xi. 13); giant petrel, *Macronectes giganteus.*

ossi·gen-o *m.* (chem.) oxygen. **-are** [A I s] *tr.* to oxygenate. **-ato** *part. adj.* oxygenated; acqua **-ata**, hydrogen peroxide. **-azione** *f.* oxygenation; oxygenating.

ossiriduzione *f.* (chem.) redox, oxidation-reduction.

ossirin-a *f.,* **-o** *m.* (ichth.) long-nosed skate, *Raia oxyrhynchus.*

ossi·tono *adj.* (linguist.) oxytone.

ossiuro *m.* (zool.) *Oxyuris* spp., intestinal nematode worm.

oss-o *m.* (*pl.* **-a** *f.* and, esp. of killed animals, **-i** *m.*) bone; in carne e **-a**, in the flesh, in person; essere di carne e d' **-a**, to be human; far l'— a, to get used to; siamo all'—, there's nothing more to be got out of this; rompersi l'— del collo, to break one's neck, (fig.) to ruin oneself; — duro, hard nut to crack; fino all'—, to the bone; bagnato fino alle **-a**, wet through; buttare un — a, to throw a sop to; — della seppia, cuttle bone; — della tartaruga, tortoise-shell; — di balena, whalebone; fruit-stone; framework; (paperm.) overs, spoilage. **†-a·io** *m.* worker, carver in bone. **-icino** *m. dim.* (anat.) ossicle, ossiculum. **-obuco** *m.* (*pl.* **ossibuchi**) (cul.) marrow-bone. **-oso** *adj.* osseous, bony. **-ua·rio** *m.* ossuary; charnel-house; bone urn. **-uto** *adj.* bony; big-boned.

†osta *f.* (naut.) backstay, vang.

osta·col-o *m.* obstacle; obstruction; hindrance, impediment; handicap; hurdle (athletics); fence; corse a **-i**, obstacle race, *or* steeple-chase. **-are** [A I s] *tr.* to hinder, to impede; to handicap; to obstruct; to interfere with; **-are il passaggio**, to obstruct the passage. **-ista** *m.* (sport) hurdler.

†osta·dico *m.* See **ostaggio**.

ostag·gio *m.* hostage; tenere in —, to hold as a hostage.

ost-are [A I] *intr.* (*aux.* avere) to be opposed; to be a hindrance; to be in the way, to form an obstacle; nulla **-a**, there is no objection, *nihil obstat*; *n.m. indecl.* (leg.) permit, pass, consent. **-ante** *part. adj.* opposing; non **-ante**, see **nonostante**.

†osta·tico *m.* See **ostaggio**.

oste¹ *m.* innkeeper, host; landlord; fare i conti senza l'—, see under **conto**; (leg.) publican; la responsabilità degli albergatori e degli osti, innkeepers' and publicans' liability (C.C.); **†guest**; **†land-owner.**

oste² *f.* (poet.) army, host; l'— nemica, the enemy.

osteal-e *adj.* (anat.; med.) osteal, osseous, bony. **-gi·a** *f.* (med.) ostealgia.

osteggi-are [A 3 c] *tr.* to oppose, to show hostility to; to obstruct. **†-amento** *m.* encampment; attack, assault. (**-ato** *part. adj.*) **-atore** *m.* adversary, enemy, foe; *adj.* hostile, ironical. (**-atrice** *f.*)

osteina *f.* See **osseina**.

oste-ite *f.* (med.) osteitis; — deformante, osteitis deformans. **-i·tico** *adj.* (med.) osteitic.

ostell-o *m.* (poet.) home, abode, dwelling; refuge; (Carducci) l'ostel di città, the town hall. **-ag·gio** *m.* youth hostel; **†lodging**; cost of lodging; storing, housing. **†-ano** *m.* landlord, innkeeper, host. **†-iere** *m.* inn; landlord, innkeeper.

†osten·dere *tr.* to show.

ostens-i·bile *adj.* ostensible; professed. **-ibilmente** *adv.* ostensibly; professedly. **-ione** *f.* display; (eccl.) exposition (of relics). **-ivo** *adj.* ostensive; demonstrable; palpable. (**-ivamente** *adv.*) **-ore** *m.* exhibitor. **-o·rio** *m.* (eccl.) monstrance.

ostent-are [A I, A I c] *tr.* to display, to show off; to parade, to make a show of, to affect, to feign; to boast. **-amento** *m.* showing off; (fig.) display, show, parade. (**-ato** *part. adj.*) **-atore** *m.* boaster, ostentatious person; exhibitionist; *adj.* ostentatious; boastful; inclined to show off. (**-atrice** *f.*) **-azione** *f.* ostentation, show, pomp, affectation; pretence. **†-o** *m.* display. **†-oso** *adj.* ostentatious.

oste-oartrite *f.* (med.) osteo-arthritis. **-oartropati·a** *f.* (med.) osteo-arthropathy, disease of the joints. **-oartrotomi·a** *f.* (med.) osteo-arthrotomy. **-oblasta** *m.* (biol.) osteoblast. **-ocele** *f.* (med.) osteocele. **-oclasi·a** *f.* (med.) osteoclasis. **-oclaste, -oclasto** *m.*

(surg.) osteoclast. **-ocondrite** *f.* (med.) osteochondritis. **-ocon-droma** *m.* (med.) osteochondroma. **-ocopo** *adj.* (med.) osteocopic; dolore **-ocopo**, osteocope. **-odini·a** *f.* (med.) osteodynia. **-odi·nico** *adj.* osteocopic. **-o·ide** *adj.* (med.) osteoid. **-o·lisi** *f.* (med.) osteolysis. **-olite** *f.* (miner.) osteolite. **-oli·tico** *adj.* (med.) ossi-fluent. **-ologi·a** *f.* (anat.) osteology. **-oma** *m.* (med.) osteoma. **-omalaci·a** *f.* (med.) osteomalacia. **-omielite** *f.* (med.) osteo-myelitis. **-opati·a** *f.* (med.) osteopathy, bone disease. **-operiostite** *f.* (med.) osteoperiostitis. **-opla·stica** *f.* (surg.) osteoplasty. **-opla·stico** *adj.* osteoplastic. **-oporosi** *f.* (med.) osteoporosis. **-osclerosi** *f.* (med.) osteosclerosis. **-osi·mile** *adj.* (anat.) ossiform. **-otomi·a** *f.* (surg.) osteotomy. **-o·tomo** *m.* (surg.) osteotome.

osteri·a *f.* inn, tavern; wine-shop; eating-house.

osterig·gio *m.* (naut.) skylight.

ostessa *f.* hostess (of inn), innkeeper's wife.

os-te·trica *f.* midwife; woman obstetrician. **†-tetrice** *f.* midwife. **-tetri·cia** *f.* obstetrics. **-te·trico** *adj.* obstetric; *n.m.* obstetrician. **-tetricamente** *adv.* in relation to obstetrics.

o·stia¹ *f.* (rel.) sacrificial victim; (rel.) offering, sacrifice; (liturg.) (Eucharistic) host; altar-bread; wafer for seal or for administering powder; *excl.* (vulg.) equiv. to 'crikey!'.

†o·stia² *f.* mouth of a river.

O·stia³ *pr.n.f.* (geog.) Ostia.

Osti·achi *pr.n.m.pl.* (geog.) Ostyaks.

ostia·ri-o *m.* (eccl.) ostiary; 'doorkeeper'. **-ato** *m.* (eccl.) office of ostiary.

o·sti-co *adj.* hard, harsh; unpleasant, nasty; unpalatable; repulsive; irksome; difficult; **†hostile**, inimical. **-chezza** *f.* unpleasantness, disagreeableness; irksomeness; difficulty; harshness.

†ostier-e¹, -o *m.* inn; lodging, dwelling; host, landlord.

†ostiere² *m.* enemy camp.

ostil-e *adj.* hostile, inimical, unfriendly; sullen; adverse. **-mente** *adv.* hostilely; sullenly; adversely. **-ità** *f.* hostility; hostile or unfriendly action; opposition; aversion; *pl.* (mil.) hostilities.

ostin-are [A I] *rfl.* to show obstinacy; to grow obstinate; **-arsi nell'errore**, to persist obstinately in error; to dig one's toes in, to hang on, to be determined; si **-a** a negare, he persists in denying. **-atezza** *f.* obstinacy, stubbornness; pig-headedness; persistence. **-ato** *adj.* obstinate, stubborn; pig-headed, insistent; dogged, per-sistent; (mus.) basso **-ato**, ground bass; *n.m.* (mus.) ostinato, ground. **-atamente** *adv.* obstinately; persistently, doggedly. **-azione** *f.* obstinacy, stubbornness; doggedness, persistence; (mus.) delayed resolution.

ostino *m.* (naut.) brace, running rigging on a yard.

ostolare [A I s]. See **ustolare**.

ostrac-ismo *m.* (Gk. hist. and fig.) ostracism; dar l'— a, to ostracize, to boycott, to taboo. **-izzare** [A I] *tr.* to ostracize; to exclude; to taboo.

ostra·lega *f.* (orn.) oystercatcher, *Haematopus ostralegus.*

o·streca *f.* (zool.). See **ostrica**.

o·stria *f.* (bot.) hop-hornbeam, *Ostrya carpinifolia.*

o·stric-a *f.* (zool.) oyster; — comune, *Ostrea edulis*; — alata, *Avicula tarentina.* **-oltura, -ultura** *f.* artificial culture of oysters. **-a·io, -aro** *m.* oyster-seller; oyster-bed, oyster-farm. **-oso** *adj.* oystery; rich in oysters.

ostro¹ *m.* purple (crimson, red) dye; purple garment.

ostro² *m.* (poet.) south; south wind.

ostrog-oto *adj.* (hist.) Ostrogothic; barbarous, uncouth; *n.m.* Ostro-goth; (fig.) vandal. **-o·tico** *adj.* Ostrogothic; (fig.) barbarous.

ostru-ire [D 2] *tr.* to obstruct, to hinder, to bar; to stop up, to block. **-ente** *part. adj.* (med.) obstruent, obstructive; *n.m.* obstruent, obstructive.

ostrutt-ivo *adj.* obstructive. **†-o** *part.* of **ostruire**, q.v.

ostruzion-e *f.* obstruction; hindrance; impediment; stoppage; ob-structing; hindering; impeding. **-ismo** *m.* (pol.) obstructionism; **-ismo parlamentare**, filibustering. **-ista** *adj., n.m.* (pol.) ob-structionist. **-i·stico** *adj.* relating to obstructionist behaviour.

†ostupefare *tr.* to render stupid; to stupefy; *intr.* to be stupefied.

ot-algi-a *f.* (med.) otalgia, ear-ache. **-al·gico** *adj.* otalgic.

otarda *f.* (orn.) great bustard, *Otis tarda.*

Otello *pr.n.m.* Othello; (joc., fig.) excessively jealous husband.

o·tico *adj.* (anat.) otic.

ot-ite *f.* (med.) otitis, inflammation of the ear; — media, otitis media, middle ear inflammation. **-oce·falo** *m.* (med.) otocephalus. **-ofaringe·o** *adj.* (med.; anat.) otopharyngeal. **-oiatro** *m.* ear

ot-ite (*cont.*)

specialist, otologist. **-olite** *f.* (med.; zool.) otolith. **-ologi-a** *f.* (med.) otology. **-olo-gico** *adj.* otological. **-o-logo** *m.* (med.) otologist, ear specialist. **-omeningite** *f.* (med.) otomeningitis. **-omicoṣi** *f.* (med.) otomycosis. **-opla-stica** *f.* (surg.) otoplasty. **-orinolaringo-logi-a** *f.* (med.) otorhinolaryngology, ear, nose and throat medicine. **-orragi-a** *f.* (med.) otorrhagia, bleeding from the ear. **-orre-a** *f.* (med.) otorrhoea. **-oscopi-a** *f.* otoscopy. **-oscò-pio** *m.* (med.) auriscope, otoscope.

otr-e *m.* leather bottle (esp. for wine or oil); goatskin (bottle); pieno come un —, stuffed with food; — di vento, absurdly conceited person; (myth.) l'— dei venti, the bag in which Aeolus bottled up the winds; bottleful; belly; drunkard; (naut.) inflated skins for flotation. †**-icciuolo**, **-icello** *m.* (mus.) bagpipe. **-icida** *m.* utricide, 'skin-slayer' (as in Apuleius). **-icolare** *adj.* utricular.

†**otta** *f.* See **ora**[1].

ott-acordo *adj.* (mus.) octachord, octochord, eight-stringed; *n.m.* (mus.) octachord (scale of eight notes); octachord (eight-stringed lyre). **-ae-drico** *adj.* (math.) octahedral. **-aedrite** *f.* (miner.) anatase, native titanium dioxide. **-aedro** *m.* (math.) octahedron. **-agonale** *adj.* (math.) octagonal. **-a-gono** *m.* octagon. **-a-metro** *m.* (prosod.) octameter. **-ana-rio** *adj.* (med.) octan, recurring every eight days. **-angolare** *adj.* (geom.) octagonal. †**-angolato** *adj.* octagonal. **-an-golo** *adj.* (geom.) octagonal; *n.m.* octagon. **-ano** *m.* (chem.) octane; (motor.; aeron.) numero di **-ano**, octane number, octane rating. **-ante** *m.* (naut.; aeron.) octant. **-a-stilo** *adj.* (archit.) octastyle. **-atti-nie** *f.pl.* (zool.) see **ottopode**.

ottant-a *card. num.* eighty. **-enne** *adj.* eighty years old; *n.m.*, *f.* octogenarian. **-eṣimo** *adj.* eightieth. **-ina** *f.* (group, set, of) eighty; four score; aver passato l'**-ina**, to be over eighty.

†**ott-are** *tr.* to desire; to ask for; to choose, to opt for. †**-ato** *part. adj.* longed for, wished for, desired.

ottativo *adj.* (gramm.) optative; proposizione ottativa, clause of wish.

ottav-a *f.* (eccl.) octave; octave day; (prosod.) octave, *ottava rima*; (mus.) octave; principal (organ-stop); — aumentata, augmented octave; — battuta, accented octave (when in strict counterpoint two voices approach the octave stepwise in contrary motion); — corta, short octave; — diminuita, diminished octave; — eccedente, augmented octave; — giusta, — perfetta, perfect octave; — ripiegata, — in sesta, short octave; all'— at the octave; abbrev. 8va, e.g. all'8va bassa, an octave below; (hist.) 'octave', ancient measure of weight or capacity. **-a-rio** *m.* (eccl.) octave; octave-day; services during an octave; eighth day after. **-iante** *adj.* (mus.) (of a wind-instrument) overblowing at the octave; flauto **-iante**, harmonic flute, †flûte harmonique (organ-stop). **-ina** *f.* (mus.) higher octave. **-ino** *m.* (mus.) piccolo; octave clarinet; small virginal at 4 ft. pitch; eighth of a litre.

Otta-via *pr.n.f.* Octavia.

Otta-vio *pr.n.m.* Octavius.

ottavo *ord. num.* eighth; volume in —, octavo volume; (comm.) octavo.

ottemper-are [A I s] *intr.* (*aux.* avere) to be obedient to; — alle leggi, to comply with the laws. **-ante** *part. adj.* obedient. (**-anteménte** *adv.*)

ottenebr-are [A I s] *tr.* to cloud, to darken; to obscure. **-aménto** *m.* clouding, darkening; obscuring. **-ato** *part. adj.* clouded over, dark; obscured, obscure. **-azióne** *f.* darkening; obscuring.

otten-ére [B 32] *tr.* to get, to win; to reach; to achieve; to obtain; — il proprio scopo, to attain one's aim; *abs.* chi vuole, ottiene, where there's a will, there's a way; *rfl.* to be obtained; to be obtainable. **-i-bile** *adj.* gettable, obtainable, available. **-iménto** *m.* getting; acquiring. (**-itóre** *m.* **-itrice** *f.*)

ott-enne *adj.*, **-en-nio** *m.* See under **otto**.

Ottentotto *pr.n.m.* Hottentot; (fig.) barbarian.

ot-tic-a *f.* optics; lens. **-o** *adj.* optical; optic; (photog.) complesso **-o**, optical train; *n.m.* optician.

ottigra-vida *f.* (med.) octigravida.

ottilammina *f.* (chem.) octylamine.

ot-tim-o *adj.* excellent, admirable, very good; capital, first-rate; *n.m.* l'—, the best; l'Ottimo, the *Ottimo Commento* on Dante's *Commedia*. **-aménte** *adv.* excellently, admirably. **-ate** *m.* optimate, patrician, member of ruling class (esp. in anct. Rome), usu. *pl.* gli **-ati**, the optimates. **-iṣmo** *m.* (philos.) optimism; (fig.) optimistic state of mind, optimism. **-ista** *m.*, *f.* optimist. **-istico** *adj.* optimistic. **-isticaménte** *adv.* optimistically.

otti-para *f.* (med.) octipara.

ott-o *card. num.* eight; oggi a —, today week; domani a —, to-morrow week; — giorni, a week; in quattro e quattr'otto, at once; (hist.) gli — (di Balìa), the Council of Eight at Florence; (typ.) corpo —, eight-point body; *n.m.* (figure) eight; (in school) good mark, eight out of ten; — volante, switchback; (skating; aeron.) figure-of-eight; (naut.) battere —!, make it noon!, eight bells! **-enne** *adj.* eight years old. **-en-nio** *m.* period of eight years. **-ẹtto** *m.* (mus.) octet, octette. **-ilustre** *adj.* (lit.) two-score years old. **-i-pode**, **-i-pede** *m.* (zool.) see **ottopode**. **-ocentẹṣimo** *ord. num.* eight-hundredths. **-ocento** *card. num.* eight hundred; *pr.n.m.* l'Ottocento, the nineteenth century. **-ocentẹsco**, **-ocenti-stico** *adj.* (of the) nineteenth century. **-ocentista** *m.*, *f.* nineteenth-century personage (esp. writer or painter); specialist on nineteenth-century history, etc. **-ocordo** *m.* (mus.) see **ottacordo**. **-oe-co** *m.* (mus.) octoechos, Byzantine hymnary arranged according to the eight modes. **-omila** *card. num.* eight thousand. **-omillẹṣimo** *ord. num.* eight-thousandth. **-osil-labo** *adj.* (prosod.) octosyllabic; *n.m.* octosyllabic line.

ottọbr-e *m.* October. **-ata** *f.* picnic, excursion, in October. **-ino** *adj.* (of) October; ripening in October.

†**ottò-brio** *m.* See **ottobre**.

ottodo *m.* (electron.) octode.

ottoman-o *m.*, Ottoman; Turk; *adj.* Turkish. **-a** *f.* Turkish woman; ottoman, settee.

ottona-rio *adj.* (prosod.) octosyllabic; *n.m.* octosyllabic line.

Ottọne[1] *pr.n.m.* Otho.

otton-e[2] *m.* brass; (metall.; eng.) saldatura ad —, brazing; *pl.* (mus.) gli **-i**, the brass (instruments). **-a-io** *m.* brass-worker, brazier. **-ame** *m.* brass ware, brass goods. **-are** [A I c] *tr.* to coat with brass, to brass. (**-ato** *part. adj.*) **-atura** *f.* coating with brass. **-ino** *adj.* like brass; of brass.

otto-pode *m.* (zool.) octopod.

†**ottriare** *tr.* to grant; to authorize.

ottuagen-ario *adj.*, *n.m.* octogenarian.

ottun-dere [C I] *tr.* to blunt, to take the edge off; to deaden; to weaken, to soften, to enfeeble; to dull, to stupefy, to make obtuse.

ot-tupl-o *adj.* eightfold. **-are** [A I s], **-icare** [A 2 s] *tr.* to multiply by eight.

ottur-are [A I] *tr.* to block up, to stop up; to bung, to plug; to obstruct; to choke; to stop (a tooth). **-aménto** *m.* blocking up; stoppage. (**-ato** *part. adj.*) **-atóre** *m.* (photog.) shutter; (hydraul.) valve; (naut.) bolt, breech, lock; **-atore** a vite interrotta, interrupted screw block; testa dell'**-atore**, mushroom head. **-azióne** *f.* plugging; stopping; (cinem.) fase di **-azione**, dark interval; (mil.) culatta di **-azione**, breech block.

ottuṣ-o *part. adj.* blunt, dull; obtuse; feeble; suono —, muffled sound; colore —, faint colour; dim; obscure; stanza **-a**, small stuffy room; (bot.) obtuse; (math.) obtuse. **-an-golo**, **-ian-golo** *adj.* obtuse-angled. **-ióne** *f.* dullness, dazed condition. **-ità** *f.* obtuseness, thickness; dullness, stupidity; dazed feeling.

oubara *f.* (orn.) Houbara bustard, *Chlamydotis undulata*.

outsider *m. indecl.* (pron. as Eng.) (horse-racing) outsider.

ouverture *f.* (pron. as Fr.) (mus.) overture.

ouwarowite *f.* (miner.) uvarovite.

ov-a-ia *f.* (anat.) ovary. **-a-io** *m.* egg-seller; *adj.* gennaio **-aio**, January, the best month for laying. **-ai(u)olo** *m.* egg-seller; egg-cup.

oval-e *adj.* oval; palla —, Rugby ball, game of Rugby; *n.m.* oval. **-ità** *f.* (math.; eng.) ovality, out-of-roundness. **-iẓẓare** [A I] *tr.* (eng.) to ovalize. **-iẓẓazióne** *f.* ovalization; ovality.

†**ov-ante** *adj.* triumphant. †**-are** *intr.* to give or receive an ovation.

ov-a-rio *m.* (biol.) ovary; (anat.) see **ovaia**. **-arialgi-a** *f.* (med.) ovarialgia, ovarian pain. **-ariocele** *f.* (med.) ovariocele. **-ario-tomi-a** *f.* (surg.) ovariotomy. **-arite** *f.* (med.) ovaritis.

ov-ato *adj.* (bot.) ovate; oval; *n.m.* (archit.) oval, ovate; formal garden with statues, etc. **-atrice** *f.* incubator.

ovatt-a *f.* cotton or silk wadding; cotton wool; (text.) lap. **-are** [A I] *tr.* to line with wadding; (fig.) to soften down, to tone down.

ovazióne *f.* (Rom. hist.) ovation; (fig.) festive welcome, applause, ovation.

ọv-e *conj.* where; ov'è?, where is it?; — che (with subj.), wherever; — che sia, anywhere, everywhere; when; (with subj.) if, provided that; whereas (cf. **dove**). **-unque** *conj.* wherever; *adv.* anywhere, everywhere.

†**ove·glia** *f.* sheep.

†**o·vera** *f.* See **opera**.

o·vest *m. indecl.* west; ad —, to the west, in the west.

Ovi·d·io *pr.n.m.* Ovid. **-iano** *adj.* Ovidian.

ovi·dutto, -dotto *m.* (zool.; anat.) oviduct. **-forme** *adj.* egg-shaped, oviform.

ov·ile *m.* sheepfold; (fig.) ritornare all'—, to return to the fold; (poet.) l'ovil di San Giovanni, Florence (*Par.* XVI, 25). **-ino** *adj.* ovine, of sheep; *n.m.* sheep.

ov·i·paro *adj.* (zool.) oviparous. **-isacco** *m.* (biol.) ovisac.

ov·o *m.* (*pl.* **-a** *f.*) see **uovo**; (zool.) — di mare, *Microcosmus vulgaris*, an edible tunicate. **-ocita** *m.* (zool.) oöcyte. **-oge·nesi** *f.* (biol.) oögenesis. **-olato** *adj.* (archit.) adorned with ovolo mouldings. **-olazione** *f.* see **ovulazione**. **-oposi̱tore** *m.* (zool.) ovipositor. **-ovivi·paro** *adj.* (zool.) ovoviviparous. **-ulazione** *f.* (biol.) ovulation.

o·vol·o *m.* (bot.; anat.) see **ovulo**; (archit.) ovolo (moulding); (bot.) *Amanita caesarea*, edible fungus. **-ac·cio** *m.* (bot., pop.) *A. muscaria*, edible fungus.

o·vul·o *m.* (bot.; anat.; biol.) ovule. **-are** *adj.* ovular.

†**ovr·a** *f.* see **opera**. †**-ag·gio** *m.* work, manual work. †**-are** *intr.* to work; *n.m.* working, doing.

ovunque *conj., adj.* see under **ove**.

ovvero *conj.* or, or else.

ovvi·a[1] *excl.* oh, come!, nonsense!

ov·via[2] *f.* of **ovvio**, q.v.

ovvi·are [A4] *tr.* to obviate, to avoid; *intr.* (*aux.* avere) to provide a remedy; — al male, to obviate, to prevent, trouble. **-azione** *f.* avoidance, remedy, prevention.

ov·vi·o *adj.* obvious, plain, ordinary, everyday. **-amente** *adv.* obviously.

Oxford *pr.n.m.* (geog.) Oxford; (geol.) Oxford clay; (text.) Oxford mixture; carta —, India paper.

ozena *f.* (med.) ozaena.

†**ozi·aco** *adj.* inauspicious, unlucky.

ozi·are [A4], **-eggiare** [A3c] *intr.* (*aux.* avere) to idle, to lounge, to waste one's time, to loaf.

o·zio *m.* idleness, laziness; sloth; leisure (hours), spare time, freedom (from toil); quiet, holiday; in —, free; per —, idly.

ozi·oso *adj.* idle; leisurely; fruitless, otiose; sluggish; (comm.) capitale —, uninvested capital; (leg.) noto come — o vagabondo, known as idle or vagabond (C.P.P.); *n.m.* idler; (leg.) l'arresto degli -osi e dei mendicanti, arrest of loafers and beggars (C.P.P.). **-osamente** *adv.* idly; sluggishly. **-osag·gine** *f.* sloth, slothfulness. **-osità** *f.* sloth, idleness; idle talk.

ozocerite *f.* (miner.) ozokerite.

ozon·o *m.* ozone. **-iz̧zare** [A1] *tr.* (chem.) to ozonize. **-iz̧zatore** *m.* ozonizer. **-iz̧zazione** *f.* ozonizing. **-o·metro** *m.* ozonometer.

p *m., f.* the letter P; the consonant P.

†**pa·**[1] *m.* abbrev. of **padre**, q.v.

†**pa·**[2] *m.* abbrev. of **paio**, q.v.

pabarile *m.* (geog., Sardinia) small plot of land.

pa·bol·o *m.* pasture; (fig.) pabulum; †(rel.) spiritual nourishment.

†**pa·bul·o** *m.* see **pabolo**. †**-oso** *adj.* abundant; fertile.

pac·are [A2] *tr.* to quieten, to placate, to pacify. **-ato** *part. adj.* quietened, placated, pacified; quiet, calm; tranquil; placid; rendere -ato, to sober. **-atamente** *adv.* calmly; tranquilly. **-atezza** *f.* calm; tranquillity.

pacca *f.* slap, smack; whack; flick with a whip; aver le pacche, to get the worst of it.

pacche·o *m.* (Tusc.) fathead, fool.

pacchetto *m. dim.* See under **pacco**.

pac·chi·a *f.* life of eating, drinking and being merry; per lui è una —, he is living on the fat of the land; che —!, what a wonderful life! †**-amento** *m.* revelling. **-anata** *f.* greedy or gross behaviour; (slang) stupid mistake, 'gaffe'. **-ano** *adj.* riotous; *n.m.* waster, idler; guzzler. **-are** [A4] *intr.* (*aux.* avere) to eat greedily, to guzzle. **-arone** *m.* well-fed person. (**-arona** *f.*) **-arotto, -erotto** *m.* plump young man. †**-o** *m.* guzzling; food; a bite to eat. †**-one** *m.* glutton.

pacchin·a *f. dim.* of **pacca**, q.v.; light tap or slap; rap on the back of the head. **-are** [A1] *tr.* to slap, to smack; to hit; to cuff on the back of the head.

†**pac·chio** *m.* See under **pacchia**.

†**pacchiuc·o** *m.* mud, mire; mess; disorderly work. †**-one** *m.* pastrycook; meddler, mischief-maker.

pacci·ame, -ume *m.* litter of dead leaves, sticks, twigs, etc.; decaying vegetable matter; rotten fruit.

pac·co *m.* (*pl.* **-chi**) parcel; packet, package; bundle. **-chettino** *m. dim.* small packet; -chettino di sigarette, packet of cigarettes. **-chetto** *m. dim.* small parcel; small packet; (typ.) lines of type set solid (i.e. with no lead between the lines); (naut.) packet, steam-packet, packet-boat, mail-boat; ammainare in -chetto, to strike down (yards, etc.). **-cotti·glia** *f.* parcel of goods worth little or nothing; trumpery goods, trash, shoddy; goods carried by a private passenger; untidy parcel, badly made parcel; (comm.) job-lot; slop goods.

pac·e *f.* peace; — bianca, — patta, peace without reparations or cession of territory; far —, mettere —, to make peace; essere in —, to be at peace; non voler nè — nè tregua, to be in a state of continual strife; con tutta —, without dispute; tranquillity; lasciar in —, to leave in peace, to leave alone; andare in —, to pass away, to go away; (iron.) dare — a uno, to kill someone, to put someone out of his misery; darsi —, to resign oneself; non darsi —, to give oneself no rest, to worry continually; porre in —, to satisfy, to placate; con vostra buona —, by your leave, with your permission, if you'll excuse me (usually as an introduction to a contradiction); fate la vostra —, do as you please; siamo —, we are quits, we drew (the match); dare il buon per la —, to put up with something for the sake of peace and quietness; tranquillity, repose; in —, tranquil; non mi dà un momento di —, he doesn't give me a moment's peace; il mare era in —, the sea was calm; (leg.) giudice di —, justice of the peace (non-existent in Italian 'ordinamento giudiziario'); (rel.) Dio l'abbia in —, God rest him; (on tombstones) riposare in —, R.I.P., 'requiescat in pace'; (liturg.) kiss of peace (at High Mass); (liturg.) pax; (hist.) — di Dio, truce of God; (Rom. myth.) Pax, Peace personified; (geog.) Fiume della —, Peace River.

pac(h)fong *m. indecl.* (metall.) pachtong, paktong, alloy of copper, nickel and zinc.

pachi·derma, -dermo *m.* (zool.) pachyderm; (fig.) thick-skinned person. **-meningite** *f.* (med.) pachymeningitis.

†**pac·iale** *adj.* bringing peace; peaceable; *n.m.* peacemaker. †**-iare** *tr.* to pacify. †**-iaro** *m.* peacemaker, negotiation for peace. †**-ibilmente** *adv.* peaceably. †**-iente** *adj.* see **paziente**. †**-ienza** *f.* see **pazienza**. **-iere** *m.*, **-iero** *m.* peacemaker; fare da -iere, to act as a peacemaker. (**-iera** *f.*) †**-i·fero** *adj.* peace-bearing. **-ifica·bile** *adj.* appeasable. **-ificamente** *adv.* peacefully. **-ificamento** *m.* reconciliation, pacification. **-ificare** [A2s] *tr.* to pacify, to appease, to placate; to reconcile; to soothe; *rfl.* to become reconciled, to reconcile oneself; *recip. rfl.* to become reconciled to one another. **-ificativo** *adj.* pacificatory. **-ificato** *part. adj.* reconciled. **-ificatore** *m.* peacemaker. (**-ificatrice** *f.*) **-ificazione** *f.* pacification, reconciliation. **-i·fico** *adj.* peaceful, pacific, placid, peaceable, peace-loving; obvious, indubitable, not in dispute, undisputed; questo è ormai -ifico, this is by now an undisputed fact; (geog.) Pacific; *n.m.* il Pacifico, the Pacific (Ocean). **-ificone** *m.* affable, placid person. **-ifismo** *m.* pacifism, pacificism. **-ifista** *m., f.* pacifist, pacificist. **-ifi·stico** *adj.* pacifist, pacificist. **-ioccone** *m.* plump, affable person. (**-ioccona** *f.*) **-ione** *m.* easy-going person. (**-iona** *f.*) **-ioso** *adj.* meek, mild, easy-going. **-iozza** *f.* reconciliation (e.g. as when two children 'make it up').

paco *m.* (zool.) alpaca, *Auchenia pacos*.

padano *adj.* (geog.) pertaining to the Po valley; la pianura padana, the Lombard (or Po) plain.

padda *f.* (orn.) Java sparrow, *Padda oryzivora*.

padell·a *f.* frying-pan; cascar dalla — nella brace, to jump out of the frying-pan into the fire; la — dice al paiuolo, 'fatti in là che tu mi tingi', the pot calls the kettle black; aver un occhio alla gatta e uno alla —, to have eyes in the back of one's head, to keep one's eye on two things at once; warming-pan; bed-pan; (techn.) crucible; (cinem.; telev.) floodlight; (Tusc., slang) miss (when shooting); far —, to miss, to fall wide of the mark; (anat.) patella, kneecap; †flat-bottomed boat. **-a·io, -aro** *m.* pan maker, pan seller; miss, flop. **-ata** *f.* panful. **-etta** *f. dim.* little pan. **-ina** *f. dim.* little pan; candle-ring, drip-glass; (zool.) keyhole limpet, *Fissurella* spp.; (eng.) footstep bearing; pan for a small candle at public illuminations. **-ino** *m. dim.* little pan; spittoon. **-ista** *m.*

padell-a (*cont.*)

(Tusc., slang) bad shot, poor shot. **-one** *f.*, **-ona** *m.*, **-otto** *m. augm.* large pan; (cinem.; telev., etc.) floodlighting, bank (of lights).

padiglion-e *m.* pavilion, tent; — maestro, general's tent; canopy; letto a —, canopied litter; (eccl.) festal hangings; ward (of a hospital); pavilion; summer house; the part of a brilliant-cut diamond between the girdle and the collet; (mus.) bell (of trumpet or French horn); -i in aria, with bells up; (numism.) pavilion, French gold coin struck by Philip VI of Valois in 1329; (anat.) pavilion of the ear, pinna, auricle; (anat.) pavilion or fimbriated extremity of the Fallopian tube; (eng.) turret top; (teleph.) earpiece; (bldg.) tetto a —, hip roof.

padino *m.* (bot.) bird cherry, *Prunus padus*.

padiscià *m. indecl.* Padishah, Shah of Persia; Sultan of Turkey.

padoana *f.* (mus.) see **padovana**, under **Padova**.

Pa·dov-a *pr.n.f.* (geog.) Padua. **†-anella** *f.* two-wheeled carriage with one seat; fare le -anelle, to beat about the bush. **-ano** *adj.*, *n.m.* Paduan. **-ana** *f.* woman of Padua; (mus.) Pavan, Pavane.

padr-e *m.* father; sua moglie lo fece — d'una bambina, his wife bore him a daughter; trasmesso di — in figlio, handed down from father to son; i nostri -i, our ancestors; (fig.) mentor, guide; begetter; l'ozio è — dei vizi, idleness begets bad habits; (theol.) Dio —, God the Father; (eccl.) father (priest who is also a religious); il Santo —, the Holy Father, the Pope; (eccl. hist.) i -i, the early fathers of the Church; (leg.) buon — di famiglia, good paterfamilias; diligenza del buon — di famiglia, ordinary diligence (C.C.); i -i, elders, parents, seniors; (hist.) i -i coscritti, Senators (of Rome), (pop.) members of a municipal council; (techn.) master negative (e.g. of gramophone record); (animal breeding) sire. **†-ecciuolo** *m. dim.* of **padre**. **-efami·glia** *m.* paterfamilias. **-eggiare** [A 3 c] *intr.* (*aux.* avere) to take after one's father. **-eterno** *m.* (theol.) God the Father; (colloq.) non fare il -eterno, don't try to behave like God Almighty; (eng.) stud driver. **†-icciuolo** *m. dim.* of **padre**. **-igno** *m.* see **patrigno**. **-ino** *m.* godfather; (leg.) i -ini o secondi del duellante, duellist's supporters or seconds (C.P.).

†pa·dria *f.* See **patria**.

†padroci·nio *m.* See **patrocinio**.

padrona *f.* See under **padrone**.

padron-e *m.* master; (provb.) legare l'asino dove vuole il —, the man who pays the piper picks the tune; essere a —, to be employed; esser senza —, to be unemployed; esser — in casa propria, to be master in one's own home; non essere più — di sè, to lose control of oneself; — della materia, master of the subject; owner, proprietor, head of a firm, 'boss'; far il — in casa altrui, to behave as though one owns the place; (naut. hist., thirteenth to fifteenth centuries) owner and commissioner of a ship; (sixteenth-century Venice) master; boatswain; skipper of a small vessel, coxswain of a boat; (Merchant Navy) master, skipper, captain; (Navy) coxswain of a ship's boat; (techn.) pattern, model; patron; (eccl.) patron (saint); (leg.) — e domestico, master and servant (C.C.); landlord; (as courtesy title) padron mio (riverito), honoured sir (now joc. or iron.); padrone!, granted! (in reply to a request); (iron.) padrone!, All right then!; non mi vuol pagare? padrone! lo citerò!, won't he pay me? all right then! I'll sue him!; essere — di far qualcosa, to be at liberty, to have a right, to do something; **†**— di causa, advocate, lawyer. **-a** *f.* master's wife, mistress, landlady, proprietress. **-ac·cio** *m. pejor.* disagreeable master. **†-ag·gio** *m.* ownership; control, authority. **-ale** *adj.* of or relating to an owner or master; l'autorità -ale, the master's or owner's authority. **-anza** *f.* ownership, proprietorship; mastery (of a subject); domineering bearing or manner. **†-a·tico** *m.* see **padronato**. **-ato** *m.* ownership, proprietorship; estate; country property; (can. law) patronage; **†**owners; **†**authority, over-rule, ascendancy; **†**protection; **†**protectorate. **-cina** *f. dim.* of **padrona**. **-cino** *m. dim.* of **padrone**; owner-driver (particularly of taxi). **-cione** *m. augm. joc.* of **padrone** **-eggiare** [A 3 c] *tr.* to master, to be master of, to control, to rule; *rfl.* to control oneself, to keep a rein on oneself, to retain one's self-control. **-ello** *m. dim.* (derog.) little master, high and mighty person. **†-eri·a** *f.* estate, property. **-esco** *adj.* (*m.pl.* -eschi) acting like an owner; lordly. **†-essa** *f.* woman owner. **-is·simo** *m.* absolute master, lord of all; Lei è -issimo di restare, you are quite entitled, perfectly at liberty, to stay; (also iron., cf. **padrone**).

padul-e *m.* swamp, marsh; bog; (bot.) giunco di —, (pop.) biottolo di —, bulrush, *Schoenoplectus lacustris*. **†-a** *f.*, **†-o** *m.* see **padule**. **-ano** *m.* marsh-dweller; *adj.* pale-faced. **†-esco**, **†-igno** *adj.* see **paduloso**. **-ina** *f.* (bot.) species of sedge, *Cyperus rotundus*. **-oso** *adj.* swampy, marshy.

paes-e *m.* country; land; il bel —, Italy; Bel Paese, name of a kind of soft cheese; i Paesi Bassi, the Low Countries, (joc., euphem.) the nether regions (of the body); mandar a quel —, to tell a person to go to hell; district, region, locality; (provb.) — che vai, usanze che trovi, cf. *autres pays autres mœurs*, it takes all sorts to make a world; donna e buoi de' -i tuoi, get your wife and cattle from your own neighbourhood; tutto il mondo è —, people are the same the world over; del —, local, of the locality; — natio, native town, native village (when used in this and similar senses, 'paese' is also used to denote cities and their surrounding districts, e.g. 'Napoli è un bel —, Naples is a lovely place'); village, country, rural area (as opposed to city); gente di —, country people, provincials; landscape, countryside. **-ac·cio** *m. pejor.* ugly country; wretched village. **-ag·gio** *m.* landscape, countryside; view; da questa finestra si vede un bel -aggio, there is a wonderful view from this window; (art) landscape(-painting); (geog.) -aggio antroponomo, -aggio umanizzato, cultured landscape. **-ano** *adj.* native, indigenous, local; prodotto -ano, home product; peasant; alla -ana, in the local manner; *n.m.* native, local inhabitant; fellow-countryman; peasant, country person. **-ante** *adj.* (art) landscape painting; *n.m.* landscape painter. **†-are** *intr.* to go into the country, to stay in the country. **-ello** *m. dim.* of **paese**; little village; little place. (**-etto**, **-ettino** *m. dim.*) **-ino** *m. dim.* little place; little village; (art) small landscape painting; (sculp.) Florentine mottled marble. **-ista** *m.*, *f.* (art) landscape painter. **-i·stico** *adj.* (art) relating to landscape painting. **-one** *m. augm. pejor.* large ugly place. **-otto** *m.* fairly big village. **-uc·cio** *m. dim. pejor.* of **paese**; wretched little village; 'one-horse town'. **-u·colo** *m. pejor.* of **paese**; poverty-stricken place.

paf (onom.) bang, slap, wallop; bang of a gunshot.

paff-a *f.* food; good living, luxury; ease, comfort. **-utezza** *f.* plumpness. **-uto** *adj.* plump; fat; stuffed full, blown out; menzogna -uta, gross lie, whopper. **-utello** *adj. dim.* of **paffuto**; plump (of a child).

paf·fete (onom.) bang, crash, wallop.

Pafo *pr.n.f.* (geog.) Paphos.

paga *f.* payment, instalment; pay; wages; salary; per —, in payment, in return; — intera, full pay; mezza —, half pay; — morta, pay received for doing nothing; giorno di —, pay-day; busta —, pay-packet; libro —, pay-roll; riscuotere, tirar la —, to draw one's pay; tabella base delle paghe, wage scale; (joc.) assicurarsi la —, to go to gaol; rubar la —, not to earn one's pay; reward; mala —, punishment; payer (usu. in bad sense); è una mala —, he is a bad payer.

paga·bile *adj.* See under **pagare**.

paga·i-a *f.* paddle (of canoe). **-are** [A 4] *intr.* (*aux.* avere) to paddle. **-atore** *m.* canoeist.

pagamento *m.* payment; condizioni di —, terms of payment; giorno di —, pay-day; — in natura, payment in kind; — per intervento, — per onore di firma, payment for honour, payment supra protest; — in numerario, payment in specie; — in contanti, cash payment; — alla consegna, contro assegno, cash on delivery, C.O.D.; — in anticipo, payment in advance, prepayment; — differito, deferred payment; dietro —, against payment, for payment; resta a —, (it has) to be paid for; — completo, payment in full; — rateale, payment by instalments; *pl.* pay, pay-roll; recompense, reward; punishment, deserts.

pagan-o *adj.*, *n.m.* pagan; heathen; 'paynim', Saracen. **-amente** *adv.* in a pagan manner, in an unchristian way. **-eggiare** [A 3 c] *intr.* (*aux.* avere) to act or think in a heathen way, to flaunt one's paganism; *tr.* to paganize. **-ello** *m.* (ichth.) rock goby, *Gobius paganellus*. **-esco** *adj.* (*m.pl.* -eschi) heathenish. **-esimo**, **†-esmo** *m.* paganism; heathendom. **†-i·a** *f.* 'paynimry'. **-izzare** [A 1] *tr.* to paganize.

pag·are [A 2] *tr.* to pay; to settle; to pay for; non ho ancora -ato l'abito, I haven't yet paid for the coat; (comm.) — alla consegna, contro assegno, to pay cash on delivery; — il riporto, to pay contango; (fig.) — uno della stessa moneta, to repay someone in his own coin; — caro, to pay dearly for; — male, to make but a shabby return for; pagherei un occhio, I would give the world;

pag-are (*cont.*)

— il debito della natura, to die, to go the way of all flesh; — di mala moneta, to show ingratitude; — il fio, to pay the consequences; quanto pagherei, non so che pagherei...!, what wouldn't I give...!; (provb.) Dio non -a il sabato, i.e. the judgements of Heaven are slow but sure; *rfl.* to insist on one's due, to enforce payment. **-a·bile** *adj.* (comm.) payable; -abile alla consegna, payable on delivery; -abile a domanda, payable on demand; -abile al portatore, payable to bearer; -abile a vista, payable at sight; obbligazione -abile dopo la morte, post obit bond. **-ante** *part. adj.* paying, soci -anti, paying members (as opposed to honorary members); carica -ante, payload; *n.m., f.* payer, person paying. **-ato** *part. adj.* paid, rewarded, recompensed; (comm.) -ato anticipatamente, prepaid; risposta -ata, reply paid. **-atore** *m.* payer; ufficiale -atore, paymaster; (leg.) payer. (**-atora** *f.* **-atrice** *f.*) **-atura** *f.* payment, paying.

pagella *f.* account for a professional fee; school report or certificate.

pagell-o *m.* (ichth.) various species of sea bream; — acarne, — abastardo *Pagellus acarne*; — mormora, *P. mormyrus*; — fragolino, *P. erythrinus*; — bocaravello, *P. bogaraveo*.

paggino[1] *m. dim.* of paggio, q.v.

paggino[2] *adj.* facing south, on a southerly exposure.

pag·g-io *m.* page; page-boy; †young boy; †uscire di —, to reach manhood. **-eri·a** *f.* group of pages; training establishment for pages; the rank of page. **-etto**, **-ino** *m. dim.* of paggio.

†pagheri·a *f.* guarantee, surety.

pagherò *m. indecl.* (comm.) I.O.U. (I owe you...); — cambiario, promissory note.

pa·gin-a *f.* page; a —, page by page; — pari, left-hand page, verso; — dispari, right-hand page, recto; voltar —, to turn over the page, (fig.) to change the subject; le sacre -e, Holy Scripture; side of a leaf; la — inferiore, superiore, di una foglia, the underside, right side, of a leaf. **-atura** *f.* paging, numbering of pages.

pa·gli-a *f.* straw; mettere nella —, to lay out (fruit, etc.) to ripen; segare a mezza —, to reap leaving a high stubble; arte della —, straw-weaving; filter tip (of a cigarette); straw colour; filo di —, single straw; inciampare in un filo di —, to be deterred by the slightest obstacle; fuoco di —, flash in the pan, short-lived enthusiasm; uomo di —, man of straw, dummy; signore colla — nelle scarpe, apparently well-off man who is penniless; aver — in becco, to know something but keep quiet about it; avere la coda di —, to be always suspecting something; battere la —, to speak very discursively; (metall.) seam (surface defect); (naut.) bitt pin, battledore. **-accesco** *adj.* clownish; nonsensical. **-accetto** *m. dim.* of pagliaccio, q.v. **-ac·cia** *f. pejor.* inferior straw; filthy straw. **-acciata** *f.* clownish act; (theatr.) clowning, buffoonery. **-ac·cio** *m.* straw chopped fine; mattress; clown; buffoon; *I Pagliacci*, title of an opera by Leoncavallo concerning a company of players; (colloq.) bruciar -accio, to fail to keep an appointment. **-accione** *m. augm.* big fat clown, buffoon; tu -accione!, you great clown! **-a·io**, **-aro** *m.* straw stack; can da -aro, useless watch-dog. **†-aiuolo** *m.* stable-boy; stable, stall; vendor of straw; peasant. **†-ardo** *m.* libertine. **-arolo** *m.* (orn.) aquatic warbler, *Acrocephalus paludicola*. **-ata** *f.* chopped straw. **-ato** *adj.* straw-coloured. **-ereccio** *m.* straw hut, hut with thatched roof. **-eresco** *adj.* (*m.pl.* -ereschi) made of straw. **-eric·cio** *m.* palliasse; chopped straw. **-erino** *adj.* straw-coloured, pale yellow. **†-etana** *f.* eel. **-etta** *f. dim.* peasant's straw hat; (derog.) astute lawyer (after the black straw hats formerly worn by Neapolitan lawyers); (bot.) palea, pale; (geol.) flake (of mica, etc.); grain of gold dust (in stream); spangle, paillette. **-ettare** [A I C] *tr.* to spangle; to fleck. (**-ettato** *part. adj.*) **-etto** *m.* straw mat; chair seat made of plaited straw; (naut.) swordmat, paunchmat; netting, hammock-netting; -etto parascheggie, splintermat; -etto a tralice, chafing mat, fender; -etto a trama, gripe (securing a seaboat), -etto turafalle, collision mat; -etto lardato, protecting mat made like a collision mat (i.e. canvas on one side, rope matting on the other and having canvas strips inserted in its weave; these strips or thrums make the mat watertight when pressed against the matting under water). **-ola·ia** *f.* straw-stuffed cushion put under the yoke on draught oxen; †dewlap; †wattles. **-(u)olo** *m.* (naut.) bottom boards, grating, etc.; the bottom of a boat, the hold, the walls (interior); movable grating; floor of a boiler room; shelves for stores; breadroom of a galley; †-uolo dei cerusici, sick berth;

di poppa -uolo di prua, sterncabin, forecastle, locker. **-olato** *m.* (naut.) bottom gratings, bottom boards; plating forming the deck of a hold. **†-oliere** *m.*, **†-oliero** *m.* (naut.) storekeeper. **-one** *m.* coarsely chopped straw; bruciar il -one, to fail to keep an appointment; palliasse. **-oso** *adj.* (agric.) with too much straw (of a crop); faulty, vicious. **-uca** *f.* blade of straw; speck, mote. **-uc·cia** *f. dim. pejor.* bit of straw. **-u·cola** *f. dim.* tiny blade of straw; giocare alla -ucola, a game of drawing long and short straws held in the hand. **-ume** *m.* chaff, chopped straw. **-uola** *f.* tiny bit of straw; small, shiny particle visible in a large mass. **-uolo** *m.* chaff; (comm.) dunnage. **-uzza** *f.* small piece of straw; tiny particle of silver or gold visible in a mass of earth, etc.; speck in wool.

pagl-ic·cio *m.* finely chopped straw. **-ino** *m.* seat of rush-bottomed chair; *adj.* straw-coloured.

pagnott-a *f.* loaf; (fig., derog.) wages, earnings, living. **-ista** *m.* hireling; (fig.) time-server.

pa-go[1] *adj.* (*m.pl.* -ghi) contented, satisfied; darsi per —, to express oneself satisfied; †*n.m.* contentment.

pago[2] *m.* payment; just recompense, due reward; non aver —, to be priceless; †non aver — con qualcuno, to be unable to recompense someone.

†pago[3] *m.* country district.

pagod-a *f.* Eastern temple; pagoda. **†-e** *m.* see **pagoda**. **-o** *m.* sacred statue venerated in a pagoda; Indian coin.

pagro *m.* (ichth.) *Pagrus pagrus*, a kind of sea bream.

†pagur-a *f.* see **paura**. **†-oso** *adj.* see **pauroso**, under **paura**.

paguro *m.* (zool.) hermit crab, especially *Eupagurus bernhardus*.

pah *excl.* pah!; nonsense!; pooh!

paidofili·a *f.* (med.) paedophilia.

†paiese *m.* See **paese**.

pa·ino *m.* (dial. Rome, C. Italy) fop, dandy.

pa·i-o *m.* (*pl.* -a *f.*) pair, couple; brace; un — di scarpe, a pair of shoes; un — d'uova, a couple of eggs, two eggs; un — di settimane, a couple of weeks, a few weeks; un — di forbici, a pair of scissors; un — di occhiali, a pair of spectacles; un — di carte, a pack of cards; essere un altro — di maniche, to be quite another matter (another pair of shoes); formano un bel —, they are well matched; (iron.) sono una coppia e un —!, they are a fine pair!; non saper quante -a fan tre buoi, not to know how many beans make five.

paiuol-o *m.* metal pot, cauldron; kettle; nero come un —, black as a cooking-pot; (mil.) boiler, camp kettle, soyer boiler; negare il — in capo, to deny that two and two make four. **-ata** *f.* potful. **-etto** *m. dim.* small pot; kettle. **-ina** *f. dim.* gluepot. (**-one** *m. augm.*)

pal-a[1] *f.* shovel; (fig.) con la —, in abundance, by the bucketful; — dei fuochisti, coal-shovel, stoker's shovel; — da fornaio, baker's peel; ruota a -e, paddle-wheel, water-wheel; (eng.) blade; vane; scoop, bucket; (aeron.) blade (of propeller); (mil.) — di zappatori, entrenching tool; — di pontonieri, bridge builder's shovel; (naut.) blade of an oar or propeller; paddle of a turbine or wheel; after part of a balanced rudder; (paint.) — d'altare, altar-piece, reredos; (liturg.) altar-frontal; — d'oro, the great golden and jewelled ornament of St Mark's altar at Venice, originally a frontal, now a reredos; †(liturg.; variant for **palla**) pall; (geol.) pinnacle. **-ac·cio** *m.* (techn.) iron stirrer used to stir molten glass in glass-blowing. **-ata** *f.* see under **palare**. **-ino** *m. dim.* a baker's shovel or peel.

†pala[2] *f.* fare — di, to make manifest, to display; fare — che, to show that.

paladin-o *m.* paladin (of Charlemagne); knight-errant; champion, defender; (joc.) 'knight of the shovel', i.e. road sweeper, dustman (using a 'pala'); *adj.* cuore —, noble heart. **-a** *f.* (hist.) fur tippet (also **palatina**). **-esco** *adj.* (*m.pl.* -eschi) (joc.) like or of a paladin.

palafitt-a *f.* (archit.; bldg.) pile; prehistoric lake village built on piles. **-are** [A I] *tr., intr.* (*aux.* avere) to pile, to drive or fix piles (into). **-ata** *f.* building on piles. **-i·colo** *m.* (archaeol.) inhabitant of a pile-dwelling.

palafren-o *m.* palfrey; saddle-horse. **-iere**, **-iero** *m.* groom; footman.

†pala·gio *m.* and derivs. See **palazzo**.

pala·i-a *f.* wood grown for poles and stakes; heap of poles; (ent.) a kind of cicada; (ichth.) this, and variants, is a common dialect name for several species of sole. **†-uolo** *m.* (mil.) pioneer, member of a digging party; member of a wrecking party; member of a demolition party.

Palamed-e *pr.n.m.* (Gk. myth.) Palamedes. **-e·e** *f.pl.* (orn.) screamers, *Palamedeiformes.*

palamẹnto *m.* See under **palare**.

palamida *f.* (ichth.). See **palamita**.

palamidọne *m.* lanky man; stupid person, ass; frock-coat; long overcoat.

pala·mit-a, palami·t-a *f.* (ichth.) bonito, a kind of small tunny or large mackerel, *Sarda sarda.* **-ara** *f.* long fishing-net. **-a·rio** *m.* bonito-fisher. **-e, -o** *m.* fishing-line with multiple hooks.

palan-ca *f.* pole, large stake; beam; plank-bridge; gangway; (mil.) stockade; (slang) penny, halfpenny; non ho una —, I haven't got a bean; *pl.* money. **-care** [A2] *tr.* to move (heavy objects) by means of planks or posts and rollers. **-castro** *m.* (Apulia) deep sea line. **-ca·tico** *adj.* relating to a stockade. **-cato** *m.* stockade, palisade; enclosure. **-chinẹtto** *m.* see **palanco**. **-chino** *m.* palanquin; crowbar. **-co** *m.* (*pl.* **-chi**) tackle; roller for moving heavy weights. **-cọne** *m. augm.* 2 soldi copper coin.

pala·ncola *f.* plank-bridge; gangway; (bldg.) sheet-piling.

pala·ncrişe *m.* (naut.) deep sea line fishing boat.

palandr-a *f.* (naut. hist.) waiship, longboat (eighth century); Turkish houseboat (twelfth century); Venetian craft (fourteenth century); gun vessel monitor (sixteenth century); see **palandrana**. **-ana** *f.*, **-ano** *m.* frock-coat; overcoat. **-e·a** *f.* (naut. hist.) see **palandra**. **-ẹtta** *f. dim.*, **-ina** *f. dim.* frock-coat. **-ọne** *m. augm.* large overcoat; man wearing a frock-coat (or overcoat).

palan-garo, -grẹşo *m.* (naut.) line, long fishing-line. **-grẹşare** *adj.* peschereccio **-gresare**, line fishing vessel. **-grişara** *f.* customs vessel.

†palante *adj.* wandering.

pal-are [A1] *tr.* to prop, to support with posts, poles, etc.; to shovel; to row (pushing with the blade of the oar; cf. **pala**). **-amẹnto** *m.* posts, stakes, etc. to support vines; (joc.) set of teeth, 'pegs'; (naut.) complement or outfit of oars. **-ata** *f.* shovelful; a -ate, in abundance; blow with a shovel; (naut.) a stroke of an oar; a stroke in swimming; nuotavo come un pesce e in quattro -ate gli fui addosso, I could swim like a fish and in four strokes I had caught up with him; -ata a secco, a stroke, (for demonstration purposes) in the air, (or, if by accident) 'catching a crab'. **-ato** *part. adj.* supported on (by, with) posts, poles or piles; (herald.) paly. **-atura** *f.* (agric.) work of supporting vines (or sim.) with poles.

palatale *adj.* See under **palato¹**.

palatin-o¹ *adj.* (hist.) Palatine; Conte —, Count Palatine; elettore —, Elector Palatine; guardie **-e**, papal guards, palace guards; fondo —, collection of books in the Vatican Library coming from the Elector Palatine of Bavaria; biblioteca **-a**, formerly library of the Grand Dukes of Tuscany, now the National Library, in Florence; (eccl.) chiese **-e**, 'Palatine churches', four basilicas in Apulia founded by the Hohenstaufen; *n.m.* (hist.) (Elector) Palatine; (topog.) Palatine (hill, in Rome). **-a** *f.* fur tippet. **-ato** *pr.n.m.* (geog.) Palatine, Palatinate.

palatino² *adj.* See under **palato¹**.

palat-o¹ *m.* (anat.) palate; — molle, soft palate; gradevole al —, palatable; (fig.) palate, taste. **-ina** *f.* (phon.) palatal. **-ale** *adj.* (phon.) palatal. **-ino** *adj.* (vet.) inflammation of the palate (in horses). **-ino** *adj.* (anat.) palatine, palatal. **-opla·stica** *f.* (surg.) palatoplasty, uranoplasty.

palato² *part.* of **palare**, q.v.

palatura *f.* See under **palare**.

palazz-o¹ *m.* palace; mansion; palatial house; mansions, block of flats; — reale, Royal palace; — municipale, City Hall, Town Hall; il — del sindaco di Londra, the Mansion House; il — della borsa, the Stock Exchange; (hist.) conti di —, Counts Palatine; donna di —, courtesan. **-ina** *f. dim.* small palace (usu. with garden); small country mansion, country house, villa. **-ino** *m. dim.* little palace, villa; †*adj.* relating to a palace; palatial. **-otto** *m.* mansion, manor-house, country house.

palazzo² *m.* (bot.) — di capre, *Asparagus acutifolius.*

pal-co *m.* (*pl.* **-chi**) platform; flooring; stand; scaffold; scaffolding; (archit.) — morto, — a tetto, structure of joists, etc. supporting a flat roof; ceiling; top-floor, attic, lumber-room; — di mattoni, tiled floor; giardino in —, roof-garden, hanging garden; (for spectators) stand, grandstand; (theatr.) box; — in faccia, front box or tier; — di proscenio, stage-box; stall; — di platea, pit-stall; una fila di -chi, a tier of boxes, *or* a row of stalls; — scenico, stage, 'the boards'; — della banda musicale, bandstand; — di

giustizia, scaffold; alzare, rizzare un —, to raise (construct) a scaffold; tier, layer; (of stag's horn) palm; dispose le frutta a -chi sulle stuoie, he laid the fruit in layers on the matting; (naut.) — di comando, navigating bridge, bridge; †thwart, rowing position in a galley; †nave a tre -chi, three-decker. **-cato** *adj.* constructed, built (e.g. of a stage, stand, scaffold). **-chettista** *m., f.* (theatr.) box-holder. **-chẹtto** *m. dim.* (theatr.) box; (in cupboard, bookcase, etc.) shelf; wood-floor; (mining) stull; (naut., Merchant Navy) foresheets of a boat; crow's nest. **-chettọne** *m.* (theatr.) stage-box. †**-uto** *adj.* furnished with antlers.

palear·tica *f.* (geog.) palearctic.

paleggi-are [A3c] *tr.* to shovel; to toss with a shovel; to stake, to support with poles. **-amẹnto** *m.* shovelling; supporting with stakes. **-ato** *part. adj.* shovelled; cleared away by shovels; supported by stakes.

palell-a *f.* (techn.) mortise; (naut.) lapping; method of joining ship's timbers; paddle or small oar; caulking tool. **-are** [A1] *tr.* (naut.) to paddle; to row gently; to caulk. (**-atura** *f.*)

Pale·mone *pr.n.m.* (Gk. myth.; Rom. hist.) Palaemon; (zool.) *Palaemon* spp., and related shrimps and prawns.

pale·o¹ *m.* spinning-top, peg-top.

pale·o² *m.* (bot.) sweet vernal grass, *Anthoxanthum odoratum;* — argentino gentile, *Koeleria cristata;* — delicato, *Festuca heterophylla;* — duretto, *F. rubra;* — ovino, sheep's fescue, *F. ovina;* — de' prati, *F. arundinacea.*

pale-obota·nica *f.* palaeobotany. **-o·gene** *adj.* (geol.) palaeocene, Lower Tertiary. **-ografi·a** *f.* palaeography. **-ogra·fico** *adj.* palaeographic. **-o·grafo** *m.* palaeographer. **-oli·tico** *adj.* palaeolithic. **-onisco** *adj.* (*m.pl.* **-onischi**) (geol.) relating to palaeontography. **-ontografi·a** *f.* (geol.) palaeontography, distribution of fossils. **-ontologi·a** *f.* (geol.) palaeontology, study of fossils. **-ozo·ico** *adj.* (geol.) Palaeozoic, Primary.

Palerm-o *pr.n.f.* (geog.) Palermo. **-itano** *adj.* of Palermo; *n.m.* native of Palermo. **-itana** *f.*)

palẹş-e *adj.* clear, manifest; well-known; obvious, evident; voglio far — questo, I want to make this clear; la sua ignoranza è —, his ignorance is obvious, *or* well-known; in —, publicly, manifestly; mostrare in —, to show openly, to reveal. (**-emẹnte** *adv.*) **-amẹnto** *m.* disclosure, revealing; revelation. **-are** [A1c] *tr.* to disclose, to reveal, to make known, to divulge; -are un segreto, to reveal a secret; *rfl.* to show oneself, to reveal oneself, to prove (to be), to turn out (to be); to make oneself known; si -ò un uomo intelligente, he proved to be an intelligent man. **-ato** *part. adj.* revealed, manifested . **-atọre** *m.* revealer; *adj.*(**-atrice** *f.*)

Palestina¹ *pr.n.f.* (geog.) Palestine.

palestina² *f.* (typ.) two-line pica.

palestr-a *f.* (Gk. antiq.) palaestra, palestra, wrestling-school (usu. private) (sport) gymnasium; (fig.) training-ground; exercise, competition; la — della vita, the battle of life. †**-ale**, †**-are** *adj.* relating to a palaestra. **-ita** *m.* gymnast.

paletot *m. indecl.* See **paltò**.

pal-ẹtta *f. dim.* of **pala**, q.v.; small shovel; — del focolare, fireside shovel; ladle; blade (of oar, mill-wheel, etc.); (paint.) palette; *f.* (watchm.) pallet; — d'entrata, entry pallet jewel, receiving pallet; — d'uscita, exit pallet jewel, discharging pallet; (eng.) blade; paddle; (anat.) knee-cap, patella; — della spalla, shoulder-blade; (typ.) galley-slice; (slang) good luck. **-ettare** [A1c] *tr.* (agric.) to stake (plants). **-ettata** *f.* (small) shovelful, (blow with a) shovel. **-ettato** *part. adj.* (agric.) staked; (eng.) bladed. **-ettatura** *f.* (agric.) staking; (eng.) blading. **-ettino** *m.* small bolt (on a door). **-ẹtto** *m.* bolt; chiudere la porta col -etto, to bolt the door; wedge; stake, pole; (surv.) stadia; (techn.) crow-bar; (watchm.) -etto del bariletto, barrel bolt. **-ettọne** *m.* (orn.) shoveller. †**-icciata** *f.* see **palizzata**.

pali *m. indecl.* Pali (Indian language).

pa·lico *adj.* Pali; testi palici, Pali texts; *n.m.* Pali (language).

palificaziọne *f.* (bldg.) piling.

Pali·lie *pr.n.f.pl.* (Rom. antiq.) Parilia (Palilia), feast of Pales.

palilogi·a *f.* (rhet.) palilogy, repetition of a word or phrase.

palina *f.* and derivs. See under **palo**.

palindromi·a *f.* (med.) relapse.

palin·dromo *m.* (liter.) palindrome.

palinge·neş-i *f.* palingenesis, palingenesy; renewal, restoration; (rel.; philos.) rebirth in various senses; metempsychosis, transmigration of the spirit; cosmic renewal (e.g. in Stoic thought); restoration

palingenes-i (*cont.*)
of the world after Noah's flood; spiritual regeneration, esp. in baptism. **-i·aco** *adj.* palingenetic.

palino *m. dim.* See under **pala**.

palinodi·a *f.* palinode, recantation, retraction.

palinsesto *m.* palimpsest.

Palinuro *pr.n.m.* (Lat. lit.) Palinurus; (zool.) sea crawfish, *Palinurus vulgaris*.

pa·li-o *m.* cloak; canopy; cloth of velvet, silk, etc. given as prize for a race; la festa del —, the famous horse-race held every July and August in the city of Siena; also used to denote similar races in othe. Italian towns; — da altare, see **paliotto**; mettere in —, to offer as a prize. **-otto** *m.* (liturg.) altar-frontal, antependium.

†paliscalmo *m.* (naut.). See **palischermo**.

palischermo *m.* (naut.) boat, ship's boat, launch.

palissandro *m.* (bot.) name of various tropical timbers used for furniture, e.g. rosewood.

palisson-are [A I C] *tr.* (tanning) to stake. **-atrice** *f.* staking machine.

palizzat-a *f.* fence, paling, palisade; stockade; railing; (bldg.) starling; — di sostegno, sheet piling; (bot.) palisade parenchyma. **†-o** *m.* see **palizzata**.

pall-a¹ *f.* **1.** BALL; giuocare alla —, to play ball; — di gomma, rubber ball; — da biliardo, billiard-ball; — da tennis, tennis-ball; shot; — smorzata, drop-shot; — tagliata, sliced shot; — ovale, rugby ball, the game itself; — di neve, snowball, (bot.) see 'pallone di neve', under **pallone**; fare alle -e, to play at snow-balling; — di cavolfiore, head of cauliflower; — dell'occhio, eyeball; globe; — celeste, celestial globe; aver la — in mano, to have the ball in one's hand, to be in favourable circumstances; aspettare la — al balzo, to watch an opportunity; cogliere la — al balzo, to catch the ball on the rebound, (fig.) to seize an opportunity; porre la — in mano a uno, to give someone an opening; portare la — al piede, to be successful; dare — bianca a, to vote in favour of; dare — nera a, to black-ball; a -e ferme, in the end, when all is said and done; *pl.* (vulg.) balls, testicles; dire -e, to tell tall stories; (herald.) balls; giocare a -e e santi, to play (toss for) heads or tails (from the Medicean arms on Florentine coins); (archit.) ball ornament, on cupola, pinnacle, etc. **2.** (MIL.) SHELL; shot; bullet; ball shot, ball cartridge; — di schioppo, lead pellet; — carica, filled shell; — fumifera, smoke shot, 'tracer'; — incendiaria, incendiary shell; boregauge; — rovente, — infocata, red-hot shell; — luminosa, starshell; — incatenata, — ramata, chain shot (used against rigging); — stracca, — spenta, — morta, spent shot; sparare a —, to fire live shot, to use ball. **-acanestro** *f. indecl.* (sport) netball; basket-ball. **†-acorda** *f.* lawn-tennis; tennis-court. **-a·io** *m.* ball-boy; maker or seller of balls; billiard marker; bowling-alley, bowling-green. **†-ama·glio** *m.* game of pall-mall or mall croquet. **-anuoto** *m.* (sport) water-polo. **-ata** *f.* blow from a ball; fare a -ate di neve, to play at snowballing; snowball. **-ato** *adj.* (vet.) of a horse's coat with scattered round spots. **-avolo** *f. indecl.* (sport) volley-ball. **-eggiamento** *m.* tossing to and fro; bandying. **-eggiare** [A 3 C] *intr.* (*aux.* avere) to play ball; (football) to dribble, to pass; *tr.* to toss; to toss about; to bandy, to bemuse; (fig.) to shift; *recip. rfl.* -eggiarsi la responsibilità, to shift the responsibility on to one another. **-eggiatore** *m.* (soccer) dribbler. **-eggio** *m.* (sport) knock-up, practice play; (soccer) dribbling. **†-erino** *m.* ball-player. **†-esco** *adj.* relating to a ball or ball-game; *n.m.* (hist.) adherent of the Medici, at the time of Savonarola. **-etta** *f. dim.* little ball; (mil.) grape-shot. **-iera** *f.* (mil.) shell rack, ready-use locker. **-ina** *f. dim.* little ball (esp. of glass); marble; giocare con le -ine, to play marbles; *pl.* small shot (for sporting guns); (mil.) anti-personnel shot; †canister grapeshot, etc.; lead pellets in a cartridge of a scatter gun. **-inac·cio** *m.* small bullet; pellet. **-inatura** *f.* (eng.) shot-peening. **-ino** *m.* little ball; (bowls) jack; small shot, pellet; knob; pommel (of saddle); † usual name for a hunting dog; †sciogliere -ino, to unleash the hounds. **-ona** *f. augm.* large ball; balloon (cf. **pallone**).

palla² *f.* (Rom. antiq.) *palla*, the outdoor cloak of Roman women.

palla³ *f.* (liturg.) pall (square of stiff linen covering chalice); †(liturg., variant for **pala**) altar frontal.

Pal·lade *pr.n.f.* (myth.) Pallas Athene; (astron.) Pallas.

Palla·di-o¹ *pr.n.m.* Andrea Palladio, Italian architect (1518–80). **-ano** *adj.* (archit.) Palladian.

Palla·d-io² *pr.n.m.* (myth.) Palladium; (fig.) palladium, talisman which protects an idea or institution; (fig.) safeguard, shield, protection; defender; *adj.* Palladian, of, relating to, Pallas; la -ia fronda, the Palladian branch (olive branch).

pall-a·dio³ *m.* (chem.; metall.) palladium (named after the minor planet, Pallas). **-a·dico** *adj.* (chem.; metall.) palladic, of palladium.

pallente *adj.* (poet.) pallid, pale, wan.

pallettizzare [A I] *tr.* (industr.) to palletize.

palli-are [A4] *tr.* (fig.) to cloak, to cover up; to palliate; to disguise; (paint.) to veil, to drape; *rfl.* to make excuses; to dissimulate. **-amento** *m.* palliating; excusing, dissimulating. **-ativo** *adj., n.m.* (med.) palliative. **-ato** *part. adj.* covered up; excused; disguised; (Lat. lit.) commedia -ata, favola -ata, palliata, Latin play adapted from Greek New Comedy. **-atamente** *adv.* covertly, secretly. **-azione** *f.* palliation; dissimulation.

pa(l)licaro *m.* (hist.) fighter for Greek independence (1820–7).

pal·lid-o *adj.* pale, pallid; (of light) faint, feeble; verde —, pale green; una -a idea, a faint idea, a glimmering of an idea; un'immagine -a, a feeble image; un — ricordo, a dim memory. **-amente** *adv.* faintly, palely, feebly; dimly. **-astro** *adj.* wan, sallow, deathly pale. **-etto, -ic·cio, -ino, -uc·cio** *adj. dim.* rather pale; wan. **-ezza** *f.* paleness, pallor; (fig.) faintness; -ezza di morte, deathly pallor; (paint.) dead tone, dull colour. **-ità** *f.* paleness, pallor. **-one** *adj. augm.* very pale; always pale; *n.m.* pale-faced person. **†-ore** *m.* see **pallidezza**. **-ume** *m.* leaden pallor.

pallinatura *f.* See under **palla¹**.

pal·lio *m.* (class. antiq.) pallium; man's cloak, esp. in Greece (often associated with philosophers); (eccl.) pallium, band of wool over neck and shoulders, worn by the pope himself and by archbishops (seldom by bishops) as sharing in the pastoral office of the pope).

pallon-e *m. augm.* of **palla¹**, q.v.; football; an Italian game played with a large ball struck with a wooden guard worn over the hand and wrist; — (volante), balloon; — dirigibile, dirigible balloon, dirigible (airship); — frenato, — drago, captive balloon; (fig.) è un — gonfiato, he is puffed up with conceit; (slang) essere nel —, to be drowsy, to be as though drugged; (mus.) button, pin (of violin); (chem.) flask; — tarato, measuring flask; (bot.) — di neve, snowball tree, *Viburnum lantana* var. *sterile*. **-a·io** *m.* balloon-maker (or seller); (dial. Neap.) one who tells tall stories. **-are** [A I C] *intr.* (*aux.* avere) to play pallone; *tr.* to jeer at. **-ata** *f.* blow with a football; (fig.) boasting; bravado; bluff; exaggeration. **-cino** *m.* chinese lantern; toy balloon; whisk for whipping cream or eggs. **-cini** *m.pl.* (bot.) winter cherry, *Physalis alkekengi*. **-esco** *adj.* (*m.pl.* -eschi) vainglorious. **-etto** *m.* (tennis) lob; (techn.) gasbag.

pallore *m.* pallor; paleness.

pallott-a *f.* little ball; (mil. hist.) shot, roundshot. **-iera** *f.* (mil. hist.) notch holder on a bowstring.

pallottizzazione *f.* (industr.) sintering.

pallot·tol-a *f.* little ball; pellet; bullet; naso a —, snub nose; (mil.) ball shot, musket shot; (slang) — che non uccide, the shot that missed; — tracciante, tracer bullet; bowl (for playing bowls); small ball (for lottery, etc.); small ball for voting; pill. **-a·ia** *f.* bowling-green, bowling-alley. **-a·io** *m.* bowling-green; seller of bowls. **-iera¹** *f.* (mil. hist.) see **pallottiera**, under **pallotta**. **-iera²** *f.*, **-iere** *m.* abacus. **-olina** *f.* (rel.) (small) rosary bead.

palm-a¹ *f.* (bot.) palm; — Christi, castor-oil plant, *Ricinus communis*; — da datteri, date palm, *Phoenix dactylifera*; — nano, — di S. Pier martire, dwarf palm, *Chamaerops humilis*; (rel.) 'palm' for liturgical use, which may be literally of palm or else of some recognized substitute (in Italy often olive, in England often box or willow); — benedetta, blessed palm (usu. kept over one's bed, passed through crucifix, from Palm Sunday one year till the beginning of Lent the next, when it is burnt and may furnish ashes for Ash Wednesday); Domenica delle -e, Palm Sunday; olio di —, palm-oil; (fig.) victory, victor's crown; la — del martirio, the palm (crown) of martyrdom; portare la —, to bear the palm; cedere la —, to yield the palm (to acknowledge superiority). **-are** *adj.* relating to the palm-tree; palmy, flourishing. **-ato** *adj.* having a palm-leaf design or pattern; (Rom. antiq., of a robe) worked with palm-branches (worn in triumphal processions); (fig.) triumphal. **-ato·ria** *f.* (eccl.) (prelate's) hand-candlestick, *bugia*. **-eto** *m.* palm-grove. **-iere** *m.* palmer. **-i·fero** *adj.* palm-bearing. **-iforme** *adj.* palmiform, palm-shaped. **-ina** *f.*

palm-a (*cont.*)

(chem.) palmitin. **-itato** *m.* (chem.) palmitate. **-i·tico** *adj.* (chem.) palmitic. **-itina** *f.* (chem.) palmitin, glycerol tripalmitate. **-izia·io** *m.* maker or seller of palms for Palm Sunday. **-i·zio** *m.* (bot.) date palm, *Phoenix dactylifera*; (liturg.) (plaited) palm blessed on Palm Sunday.

palm-a² *f.* (anat.) palm; battere le -e, to clap one's hands; giungere le -e, to clasp one's hands (in prayer); nella — di mano, in the palm of one's hand; (fig.) portare in — di mano, to esteem highly; mostrare in — di mano, to show openly, to make no secret of; (orn.) webbed foot (of geese, etc.); (naut.) palm of an anchor; blade of an oar. **-are** *adj.* (anat.) palmar; arcata -are, palmar arch; large; pera -are, pear large enough to fill the hand, 'as big as your fist'; (fig.) evident, clear, prova -are, clear proof; contraddizione -are, evident contradiction. **-a·rio** *m.* lawyer's fee; gift in return for service rendered, remuneration; hush-money. **-ata** *f.* clap; blow with, or on, the palm of the hand; bribe, tip, greasing someone's palm; †(naut.) handshake sealing a seaman's engagement when signing on. **-ato** *adj.* (bot.) palmate; (zool.) web-footed. **-e·a** *f.* agreement, bargain, sale. †**-eggiare** *tr.* to betroth; to marry; to smooth with the hand, to caress, to pat. †**-ella** *f.* short wool.

Palma³ *pr.n.f.* (geog.) Palma.

palmento *m.* millstone (of a water mill); hopper that receives the ground flour; macinare a due palmenti, to eat greedily, to make money in various ways; wine-press.

palmer *m. indecl.* (eng.) micrometer gauge; light tyre for a racing bicycle.

palm-eto *m.*, **-iere** *m.*, **-i·fero** *adj.*, etc. See under **palma¹**.

palmi·pede *m.* (zool.) palmipede; *adj.* web-footed.

pa·lmite *m.* vine-shoot, shoot; (fig.) offshoot (of a family stock).

palmo *m.* span; hand's breadth; hand (unit of height for measuring horses); ancient linear measure varying in several regions; foot, inch, etc. as a vague expression of length or area; possiede pochi palmi di terra, he owns a few feet of land; il terreno fu conquistato a — a —, ground was won inch by inch (yard by yard); battere a — a — una campagna, to beat a covert; conoscere un luogo a — a —, to know every inch of the ground; è alto un — e già vuol comandare, he is only a wee thing and he's already ordering people about; ha la barba lunga un —, he has a week's growth of beard; (of news) avere un — di barba, to be stale, to 'have whiskers on it'; un muso lungo un —, a face as long as a fiddle; restare con un — di naso, to be disappointed, to be taken in; pulito come il — della mano, quite bald, bald as an egg; (Rom. antiq.) palm of nine inches, *dodrans*; †see **palma¹**; †(naut.) palm, one-third of a cubit, measure used in boat construction; (N. Italy) measure used when counting the meshes of a net.

pa·lmol-a *f.* pitchfork, hayfork; (eng.) cam, lifter; (watchm.) — di bloccaggio, blocking cam. **-ino** *m. dim.* pitchfork.

†**palmone** *m.* bird-limed tree; bough smeared with bird-lime.

†**palmoso** *adj.* full of palm-trees.

pal-o *m.* pole, post; stake; pile; — telegrafico, — di telegrafo, telegraph pole; dritto come un —, straight as a die; ritto come un —, straight as a post; essere — in pelliccia, to be nothing but skin and bone; avere un — in corpo, to be as stiff as a ramrod; saltare di — in frasca, to jump from one subject to another, to ramble on; conficcare -i, to drive in piles; (bldg.) — di fondazione, foundation pile; il ponte è sostenuto da -i, the bridge is supported on piles; (sport) — di partenza, starting-post; — d'arrivo, winning-post; — della porta, goal-post; — indicatore, signpost; — a traliccio, pylon; mettere al —, to impale, to tie to a post; pena del —, impalement; (slang) a 'tout', one who keeps watch while a robbery, etc. is in progress; (naut.) — d'ormeggio, mooring post; mast pole, polemast, mast without topmasts; mizzen not carrying square sails; nave a —, fourmaster with fore and aft sails on the mizzen; goletta a —, fore and aft schooner; brigantino a —, barque; (herald.) pale; — ritratto, pale retracted, demi-pale in chief; interzato in —, tierced palewise. †**-ificare** *intr.* to erect a palisade. †**-ificata** *f.* palisade. **-ificato** *part. adj.* palisaded; (herald.) urdy, palisado. **-ina** *f.* (agric.) wood, usu. chestnut, grown for making poles and stakes; a number of posts, poles or stakes, palings; (surv.) ranging rod, stadia. **-inare** [A 1] *tr.* (surv.) to stake (out). **-inata** *f.* paling(s), fence, palisade. **-uc·cio** *m. dim.* small, rough stake. **-uzzo** *m. dim.* thin stake.

paloma *f.* (naut.). See **paroma**.

palomb-a *f.* (orn.) see **palombo**; †(naut.) strop, bollard strop. **-a·ia** *f.* pigeon- or dove-cot. **-aro** *m.* diver; campana da -aro, diving-bell. **-ella** *f.* (orn.) stock dove. **-ina** *f.* (agric.) kind of white grape.

palomb-o *m.* (orn.) pigeon, esp. the wood pigeon; (pop.) dove; (ichth.) dogfish of various species; — liscio, smooth hound, *Mustelus mustelus*; — nocciolo, *M. canis*. **-ino** *adj.* dove-like; dove-colour.

palo·scio *m.* hunting-knife.

palp-are [A 1] *tr.* to pat; to feel, to touch; to handle; to finger; — gli usci, to try the doors, i.e. to beg from door to door; (med.) to palpate; *intr.* (*aux.* avere) (naut.) to inspect a rope, to underrun a hawser; to hold water; (naut. command) -a!, -a remo!, hold water! (i.e. to stop a boat by holding the oars with the blades vertical in the water); (Ven.) to tickle eels and fish in shallow water; †to palpitate. **-a·bile** *adj.* palpable, that can be felt; tangible, evident, manifest. **-abilmente** *adv.* palpably, evidently. **-abilità** *f.* palpability. **-amento** *m.* feeling, touching, patting; handling; fingering. **-ata** *f.* pat, touch. **-atina** *f. dim.* little pat, light touch; timid little touch. **-atore** *m.* one who pats, feels, touches, etc.; (fig.) cajoler, wheedler; (eng.) feeler; tracer point. (**-atrice** *f.*) **-azione** *f.* feeling, handling; (med.) palpation. †**-e·vole** *adj.* see **palpabile**. †**-one** *adv.* gropingly; a -one, groping.

pa·lp-ebra, -e·bra *f.* eyelid; battere le -ebre, to blink. **-ebrale** *adj.* palpebral. **-ebrare** [A 2 s] *intr.* (*aux.* avere) to blink. **-ebrazione** *f.* frequent blinking. †**-ebro** *m.* see **palpebra**.

palpeggi-are [A 3 c] *tr.* to keep on feeling, handling, touching; to finger; (fig.) to flatter. **-amento** *m.* feeling, handling, fingering. **-ata** *f.* touch; action of feeling. **-atina** *f. dim.* little pat, light touch.

†**pa·lpiro** *m.* See **palpebra**.

palpit-are [A 1 c] *intr.* (*aux.* avere) to throb, to pulsate; to palpitate; to be in a flutter; to tremble, to quiver; mi -a il cuore, my heart is beating fast; — di paura, to be trembling with fear; — per uno, to be enamoured of someone. **-amento** *m.* throbbing, pulsating; palpitation. **-ante** *part. adj.* throbbing, thrilling, pulsating; palpitating; quivering; un argomento di -ante attualità, an extremely topical subject. **-ativo** *adj.* relating to palpitation; throbbing. **-azione** *f.* (med.) palpitation.

pa·lpito *m.* throb, beat; flutter, fluttering; i palpiti del cuore, heart-throbs, beating of the heart; i palpiti dell'amore, the pangs of love; — di gioia, thrill of pleasure.

palpo *m.* (zool.) palp.

palt-ò, -òn *m. indecl.* overcoat. **-oncino** *m.* child's overcoat.

†**paltone** *m.* See **paltoniere**.

paltonier-e, -o *m.* rascal, scoundrel, hooligan; beggar; vagrant; *adj.* rascally; scurrilous.

paludale *adj.* See under **palude**.

palud-amento *m.* (Rom. antiq.) *paludamentum*; general's cloak; (later) imperial cloak. **-ato** *adj.* (Rom. antiq.) wearing a military cloak.

palud-e *f.* marsh, fen; le -i Pontine, the Pontine Marshes; dissecare, bonificare la —, to drain (reclaim) the marsh; (chem.) gas delle -i, marsh gas, methane. **-ale** *adj.* relating to marsh; terreno -ale, marsh land. **-ismo** *m.* (med.) paludism, malaria, marsh fever. **-oso** *adj.* marshy.

palustre *adj.* marshy; of the marshes, marsh; terreno —, marshy ground, marsh land; febbre —, marsh fever, malaria.

palves-e *m.* (mil. hist.) body-shield. **-a·io, -aro** *m.* (mil. hist.) shield-bearer. **-ata** *f.* (mil. hist.) array of shielded troops; shielded advance guard of an assault; covered battering ram.

†**pambollito** *m.* See **panbollito**.

Pamela *pr.n.f.* Pamela; woman's broad-brimmed straw-hat.

pamell-a *f.* (tanning) graining board. **-are** [A 1] *tr.* (tanning) to grain.

pampa *f.* (*pl.* **pampas**) (geog.) pampa.

pa·mpano *m.* (ichth.) pilot fish, *Naucrates ductor*; and derivs. see **pampino**.

pa·mp-ino *m.* vine-leaf, vine-tendril, vine-branch; andare in -ini, (of a vine) to make growth without bearing grapes; (herald.) vine-slip; *pl.* (poet.) vine; (fig.) unnecessary things. †**-ina·io** *adj.* see **pampinario**. **-ina·rio** *adj.* (of a vine branch) producing vine-leaves. **-i·neo** *adj.* leafy, covered with vine-leaves. **-ini·fero** *adj.* bearing vines. **-iniforme** *adj.* shaped like vine-leaves. **-inoso** *adj.* covered with vine-leaves; colli -inosi, vine-clad hills.

pamporcino *m.* (bot.) *Cyclamen europaeum*.

pampsichismo *m.* (philos.) 'panpsychism', either the belief that everything that exists has in some sense a soul or spirit, or else an extreme idealism affirming matter to be non-existent and spirit the only reality.

†**pana** *f.* See **pania**.

panabase *f.* (geol.) panabase.

panace·a *f.* panacea; universal remedy; (bot.) hogweed, billers, *Heracleum sphondylium*.

†**pan-ag·gio** *m.*, †**-a·io** *adj.* See under **pane**.

pana·gia *f.* (rel.) the Panagia ('All-Holy'), a favourite Eastern title of the Blessed Virgin.

Pa·nam-a *pr.n.m.* (geog.) Panama. *m. indecl.* panama (straw-hat). **-ense** *adj., n.m., f.* (geog.) Panamanian.

panare [A I] and derivs. See under **pane**.

panaric·cio *m.* See **patericcio**.

panarm-oni·a *f.* (mus.) panharmony, harmony of all the concords (ancient Greek music). **-o·nico** *adj.* (mus.) panharmonic, adapted to all musical modes (ancient Greek music).

panartrite *f.* (med.) panarthritis.

panaten-e·a *f.* (Gk. antiq.) Panathenaea. **-e·o** *adj.* Panathenaic.

panatti·nico *adj.* (photog.; opt.) panactinic.

pan-ca *f.* bench, form; praying-stool; le -che della chiesa, church pews; far ridere le -che, to make feeble jokes; andare a scuola a scaldare le -che, to waste one's time at school; non poter levarsi a —, to be very ill; (provb.) esser — da tenebre, to be assailed by everyone, to be buffeted by foes or fortune (like seats in church struck to produce a noise at the end of Tenebrae); (aeron.) — del motore, engine mount. **-cac·cia** *f. pejor.* rough bench; public bench; stare alle -acce, to hang about taverns, bars, etc.; †(naut.) captain's berth in a galley; quartermaster's stool. **-cac·cio** *m. pejor.* rough bench; plank-bed; camp-bed. **-caccione** *m.* bench with a back. **-ca·io** *m.* man who lets out benches on hire. **-cale** *m.* ornamental cloth, bench-cover. **-cata** *f.* benchful; (agric.) connected rows of vines. **-chetta** *f. dim.* footstool; small bench; -chette del letto, bed planks, on which the mattress is laid; plank-bridge (crossing a stream or sim.); †(archit.) platform (e.g. in a railway station). **-chettina** *f. dim.* small bench. **-chettino** *m.* footstool. **-chetto** *m.* stool; footstool; -chetto piegatore, camp-stool, folding stool. **-china** *f.* garden seat, stone bench; railway station platform; (geol.) shelly limestone. **-concellatura** *f.* planking. **-concello** *m.* narrow plank, lath. **-cone** *m.* bench, workbench; -cone da falegname, carpenter's bench; (mus.) wind-chest (of organ); -cone a tiro, slider wind-chest; wrest-plank (of pianoforte); (archit.) ground prepared for the foundations of a building; sub-soil of hard clay; -cone di sabbia, -cone di rena, sandbank. **-conoso** *adj.* full of hard earth, clayey. **-cuc·cia** *f. dim.* little bench.

pancacci(u)ol-a *f.* (bot.) *Gladiolus segetum.* **-o** *m.* (bot.) *Bunium bulbocastanum.*

pancetta *f.* See under **pancia**.

panch-etta *f.*, **-etto** *m.*, **-ina** *f.* See under **panca**.

pan·c-ia *f.* belly, paunch; un individuo con una gran —, a big-bellied person, a paunchy man; stare con la — all'aria, to lie on one's back; (fam.) mettere su —, to develop a paunch, to grow corpulent; che — che ha fatto!, how stout he has got!; tenersi la — per le risa, to hold one's sides with laughing; tutto per la —, everything is spent on food; mangiare a crepa -pancia, to eat one's bellyful, to eat 'fit to burst'; grattarsi la —, to do nothing, to stand idle; serbare la — ai fichi, to save one's skin, to 'dodge the column'; to pass the buck; bulge (of a barrel, wall, etc.); il muro fa —, the wall is bulging; la — di un fiasco, the belly of a flask. **-iata** *f.* bellyful; blow on the belly. **-iera** *f.* (mil. hist.) breast-plate. **-ietta** *f. dim.* rather corpulent person; (butcher.) brisket; (N. Ital.) -etta di maiale, bacon; (zool.) stomach, especially of a tunny fish; (hist.) cuirass. **-ino** *m. dim.* rather fat tummy. **-iolle** *adv. phr.* in -iolle, lounging on a chair or sofa, sitting at ease with waistcoat unbuttoned. **-ione** *m. augm.* very stout person; big belly; (zool.) rumen, paunch. (**-iona** *f.*) **-iotta·ia** *f* waistcoat maker. **-iotto** *m.* waistcoat; -iotto di maglia, pullover. **-iuto** *adj.* paunchy, corpulent; (of things) bulging, vaso -iuto, rounded pot or vase.

pancon-e *m. augm.*, **-oso** *adj.* See under **panca**.

pancotto *m.* See under **pane**.

pancr-atista *m.* (Gk. antiq.) pancratiast. †**-azi·a** *f.* see **pancrazio**. **-aziaste** *m.* (Gk. antiq.) pancratiast. **-a·zio** *m.* (Gk. antiq.) pancratium, an athletic contest combining wrestling and boxing;

(bot.) sea-squill, *Urginea marittima*; **-azio** marino, *Pancratium maritimum*.

†**pancrea** *m.* See **pancreas**.

pa·ncre-as *m. indecl.* (anat.) pancreas. **-a·tico** *adj.* pancreatic. **-atina** *f.* (chem.) pancreatin. **-atite** *f.* (med.) pancreatitis.

pancresto *m.* (med.) panacea.

pancristiano *adj.* oecumenical, concerned with the unity of Christendom.

pancroma·tico *adj.* (photog.) panchromatic.

pandano *m.* (text.) fibra di —, pandanus fibre.

pan-de·mia *f.* (med.) pandemic. **-de·mico** *adj.* (med.) pandemic; (fig.) common to all, public. **-de·mio** *adj.* see **pandemico**; Venere -demia, whore.

pandemo·nio *m.* pandemonium; confusion, uproar.

†**pa·ndere** *tr.* to show, to manifest, to reveal.

Pandette *pr.n.f.pl.* (leg. hist.) the Pandects (of Justinian).

pandiculazione *f.* (med.) pandiculation.

Pandione *pr.n.m.* (myth.) Pandion.

Pandora¹ *pr.n.f.* (myth.) Pandora; vaso di —, Pandora's box, (fig.) all sorts of trouble.

pandora² *f.* (mus.) cithern, bandore, pandora.

pando·rio *m.* (mus.) Pan-pipes, syrinx.

pandura *f.* (mus.). See **pandora²**.

panduri *m.pl.* (mil. hist.) originally personal troops attached to Magyar nobles; later, bandits; eventually, an Austrian infantry regiment.

pandurina *f.* (mus.) a small lute or mandoline.

pandu·rio *m.* (mus.) ancient stringed instrument.

Pane¹, Pan *pr.n.m.* (myth.) Pan.

pan-e² *m.* (often **pan** before a consonant). **1.** BREAD; una fetta di —, a slice of bread; cestino del —, bread-basket, bread-bin; stare a — ed acqua, to live on bread and water; non si vive di solo —, man does not live by bread alone; — bianco, white bread; — bigio, — scuro, brown bread; — casereccio, — casalingo, home-made bread; — integrale, wholemeal bread; — arrostito, — abbrustolito, toast; — giallo, maize bread, (Rome) a kind of sugared bun made with eggs; — pepato, gingerbread; — fresco, new bread; — raffermo, stale bread; — ramerino, rosemary bread (made in Florence, during Lent, of fine flour mixed with oil, containing raisins and rosemary); — stantio, very stale. mouldy bread; — secco, dry bread, i.e. bread alone; — azzimo, unleavened bread; — di munizione, army bread; — trito, grated bread; — grattato, bread-crumbs; (rel.) il — degli angeli, the bread of angels, the Blessed Sacrament; — benedetto, blessed (but not consecrated) bread, *pain bénit* (at some times and places distributed after High Mass, esp. in France and Canada, but occasionally in Italy); (Bibl.) frazione del —, breaking of bread, the Eucharist; †(naut.) — di poppa, soft bread (i.e. ordinary bread, as opposed to ship's biscuit or hard tack). **2.** LOAF; filone di —, very long loaf; fila di —, three loaves joined; un'infornata di —, a batch of loaves; cappello a — di zucchero, sugar-loaf hat, conical hat; lump; — di burro, pat of butter; (metall.) pig, ingot; (agric.) lump of earth clinging to the roots of a plant. **3.** BREAD, living, livelihood; guadagnarsi il —, to earn one's bread; mangiare il — a tradimento, to eat unearned bread, not to be worth one's keep; — sudato, bread earned by the sweat of one's brow, hard-earned living; perdere il —, to lose one's situation (livelihood); cercare miglior — che di grano, to try to get more than honest gains; uscire di — duro, to be less poverty-stricken, to achieve somewhat easier living; (fig.) mangiar — pentito, to eat the bread of repentance, to be truly sorry for wrong done; dire — al —, to call a spade a spade; distinguere il — dai sassi, to know what's what; ha comprato un podere per un pezzo di —, he bought a farm for a song; esser come — e cacio, to be hand in glove, to be on the best of terms; rendere — per focaccia, to give tit for tat; esser meglio del —, esser buono come il —, to be good and kind; trovar — per i propri denti, to find one's match, to find work suitable to one's capacity; spezzare il — della scienza, to break the bread of knowledge, i.e. to give instruction in the rudiments of knowledge; se non è zuppa è pan bagnato, it's all one, it comes to the same thing. **4.** (BOT.) — di cuculo, wood-sorrel, *Oxalis acetosella* and other species; (bot., pop.) pan porcino, cyclamen. **-ac·cio** *m. pejor.* nasty, inferior, bread. †**-ag·gio** *m.* provision of bread. †**-a·io** *adj.* relating to bread; *n.m.* apple with spongy pulp. **-are** [A I] *tr.* to cover with

pan-e (*cont.*)

bread-crumbs. -**ata** *f.* bread-soup; pap. -**a·tica** *f.* (naut., mil. hist.) bread supplies in a galley, or for troops; victuals, crew's ration in a merchant ship or equivalent financial allowance. -**ato** *part. adj.* covered with bread-crumbs; acqua -**ata**, water with pieces of toasted bread; (S. Ital.) fetta -**ata**, slice of bread. †-**atello** *m. dim.* small loaf. †-**atteri·a** *f.* see panetteria. -**attiera** *f.* bread platter. †-**attiere** *m.* baker; place where bread is stored. -**cotto** *m.* bread-soup; pap. -**doro** *m.* a Veronese cake. -**ella** *f.* (S. Ital.) round home-made loaf. -**ellino** *m. dim.* roll, bun, little cake, small piece, cake, lump (e.g. of beeswax); (rel.) -**ellino** benedetto, piece of small loaf of blessed bread (cf. 'pane benedetto'). -**ello** *m. dim.* cake, loaf (of substances compressed together); oilcake. -**eperso** *m.* good-for-nothing, ne'er-do-well. -**etteri·a** *f.* bakery; baker's shop. -**ettiere** *m.* baker; (mil.; naut.) baker, regimental baker, ship's baker. -**etto** *m. dim.* small loaf (of bread); lump, cake (of various substances). -**ettone** *m.* a kind of Milanese cake. -**forte** *m.* a kind of Sienese cake, flavoured with almonds and eaten mainly at Christmas. -**frutto** *m.* plum cake. -**grattato** *m.* bread-crumbs; soup with grated bread in it. -**ic·cia** *f.* paste made with flour; (fig.) farne -**iccia**, to pound into a jelly. -**ic·cio** *m.* dough, paste, mash. -**icuo·colo** *m.* (dial. S. Ital.) baker (for private customers). -**ino** *m. dim.* roll (of fine bread); bun; -**ino** ripieno, -**ino** imbottito, (Tusc.) -**ino** gravido, sandwich (a roll with salame, cheese, meat or ham inside); -**ino** di zucchero, lump of sugar. -**unto** *m.* bread and dripping; aver studiato i libri del -**unto**, to think only of eating; (joc.) Maestro -**unto**, cook, chef.

panegi·r-ico *adj.* panegyric(al); *n.m.* panegyric, eulogy; (rel.) special sermon for feast, usu. in praise of a saint or a deceased person. -**ista** *m.* panegyrist.

panelle·nico *adj.* panhellenic.

pa·nera *f.* (cul.) frozen milk and coffee.

panereccio *adj.* See patereccio.

Panero·poli *pr.n.f.* a name for Milan.

panett-eri·a *f.*, -**iere** *m.*, -**one** *m.* See under **pane**.

panfago *m.* (ent.) *Pamphagus marmoratus*, a large wingless grasshopper.

pan-fano, -**fi·lio**, -**filo** *m.* (naut. hist.) ninth-century warship, galley; thirteenth and fourteenth-century two-masted galley. -**filo** *m.* yacht.

panfrutto *m.* See under **pane²**.

pangerman-esimo *m.* Pan-Germanism. -**ista** *m.,f.* Pan-Germanist.

pa·ni-a *f.* bird-lime; pitch, or any other sticky substance; (fig.) trap, snare, entanglement; cadere nella —, to fall into the trap; — amorosa, the toils of love. -**ac·cio** *m.*, -**acciolo** *m.* leather bag for limed twigs; bonds of love; dare nel -**accio**, to fall in love; (joc.) rough umbrella of oilskin, etc. -**one** *m.* limed twig. -**oso** *adj.* sticky. -**uzza** *f.*, -**uzzo** *m.* limed twig (for catching birds).

panic-ale *adj.*, -**astrella** *f.*, -**ato** *adj.* See under **panico¹**.

panicaṣeiti *m.pl.* (eccl. hist.) Artotyrites.

panic·ci-a *f.*, -**o** *m.* See under **pane**.

panic-o¹ *m.* millet, *Setaria italica*; — falso, *S. viridis*; — selvatico, *Echinochloa crus-galli*. -**ale** *m.* dried panic-grass. -**astrella** *f.* (bot.) name of various grasses; *Setaria glauca*, *S. viridis*, *S. verticillata*, *Echinochloa crus-galli*. -**ato** *m.* (vet.) 'measly', of pork or beef infected with tapeworm cysticerci. -**atura** *f.* (vet.) disease in pork or beef caused by tapeworm cysticerci.

pa·ni-co² *adj.* (*m.pl.* -**chi**) panic; timor —, panic terror; *n.m.* panic; preso dal —, panic-stricken.

pani·col-a *f.* maize cob. †-**a·io** *m.* jumble, confused composition.

†**panicona** *f.* dressing-gown.

panicuo·colo *m.* See under **pane**.

panier-a *f.* large open basket, pannier; — da caminetto, log-basket (for firewood). -**a·io** *m.* basket-maker, basket-seller; hawker (of foodstuffs carried in a basket). -**ata** *f.* basketful. -**e** *m.* basket; (needle-w.) punto -**e**, basket stitch; guastare le uova nel -**e** ad uno, to upset someone's plans; far la zuppa nel -**e**, to labour in vain, to waste one's efforts; aver le budella in un -**e**, to be terrified; -**e** sfondato, spendthrift. -**ina** *f. dim.*, -**ino** *m. dim.* small basket, lunch-basket; work-basket. -**one** *m. augm.* large basket; -**one** da bottiglie, basket (with compartments for carrying bottles). -**uzzo**, -**uz·zolo** *m. pejor.* shabby basket; *m. dim.* small basket.

panific-are [A2s] *tr.* to make into bread; *intr.* (*aux.* avere), to make bread, to bake; *rfl.* to become bread, to turn into bread. -**atore** *m.* baker. -**azione** *f.* bread-making, baking.

panifi·cio *m.* bread-making, baking; bakehouse, bakery.

pani-one *m.*, -**uzza** *f.* See under **pania**.

paniẓẓ-are [A1] *tr.* to make into bread; *intr.* (*aux.* avere) to be made into bread. -**a·bile** *adj.* fit for making into bread. (-**ato** *part. adj.*) -**azione** *f.* bread-making, baking.

panm-issi·a *f.* (biol.) panmixis. -**it·tico** *adj.* panmictic.

pann-a¹ *f.* cream; — montata, whipped cream. †-**are** *tr.* to cream. -**arola** *f.* skimming ladle.

panna² *f.* (naut.) boom, sea defence across a harbour entrance, usually floating and capable of opening to allow entry of ships; position of a vessel hove to; — con mure a dritta o a sinistra, hove to on the starboard or port tack; — orziera, heaving to with a tendency to make to windward; — leggera, heaving to making leeway; essere in —, trovarsi in —, mettere in —, stare in —, far servire la —, to be or become hove to; essere in — sulla gabbia controbracciata, to back a topsail; †essere in — secca, to heave to under bare poles.

panna³ *f.* (motor.) breakdown; puncture; rimanere in —, to have a breakdown (of a car, bicycle, etc.).

pann-aiuolo *m.*, -**eggiare** [A3c]. See under **panno**.

pannell-o *m.* (carpen.) panel; (bldg.) riscaldamento a -**i** radianti, radiant heating (see also under **panno**). -**atura** *f.* panelling.

†**pan·nia** *f.* (bot.) reedmace, *Typha latifolia*.

pann-o *m.* cloth; — di lana, — lano, see pannolano; — lino, see pannolino; — da biliardo, billiard cloth; (piece of) cloth; coprire con un —, to cover with a cloth; bianco come un — lavato, white as a sheet; pigliare un — per il suo verso, to understand something as it is meant; *pl.* clothes; essa non ha -**i** per vestirsi, she has no clothes to put on; -**i** vecchi, old clothes; -**i** d'inverno, winter clothes; -**i** del bucato, dirty clothes, soiled linen, washing, laundry; (provb.) i -**i** sudici si lavano in casa, do not wash dirty linen in public; mettersi i -**i** delle feste, to dress in one's Sunday best, to put on one's best clothes; dovresti metterti nei miei -**i**, you ought to put yourself in my place; se io fossi nei tuoi -**i**, if I were you; non poteva star nei -**i**, he was beside himself (e.g. with joy); stringere i -**i** addosso a uno, to put pressure on, to press, to constrain someone; tagliare i -**i** addosso a uno, to speak ill of someone; portarne i -**i** laceri, to come off badly; so di che -**i** si veste, I know what stuff he is made of; (provb.) Iddio manda il freddo secondo i -**i**, God tempers the wind to the shorn lamb; film, skin, layer (e.g. skin on boiled milk); — dell'uovo, egg-skin (under the shell); — del bicchiere per l'acqua fredda, film of moisture condensed on the outside of a glass of cold water; (agric.) chestnut skin; — d'arazzo, tapestry, arras; — incerato, oilskin, oilcloth; †(naut., Venice) in —, in irons, hove to (cf. **panna**); (mus.) — rosso, a kind of Apulian tarantella allied to words of a Bacchanalian nature; — verde, a kind of tarantella allied to words of a pastoral nature. -**aiuolo** *m.* draper. -**eggiamento** *m.* drapery. -**eggiare** [A3c] *tr.* to drape; to adorn with hangings; *abs.* (paint.) to represent drapery. -**eggiato** *part. adj.* draped; *n.m.* drapery. -**eg·gio** *m.* drapery; draping. -**ello** *m. dim.* small linen or light woollen cloth; bit of cloth; cloth to cover dough while rising; (paint.; sculp.) panel, painted, decorated in bas-relief, inlay or otherwise. -**icello** *m.* small piece of cloth; -**icello** di un bambino, swaddling clothes; *pl.* rags, poor clothes; (fig.) -**icelli** caldi, inefficient remedies. -**icino** *m.pl.* linen, small garments; -**icino** d'Egitto, dimity, cotton lining. -**i·colo** *m.*, †-**i·culo** *m.* (anat.) -**icolo** adiposo, fatty layer. †-**iere** *m.* clothier; draper. -**ilino** *m.* linen (underclothes, towels, etc.); (eccl.) church linen collectively. -**ina** *f.* woollen cloth. -**ola** *f.* long line for fishing. -**olano** *m.* woollen cloth. -**olina·io** *m.* linen manufacturer. -**olino** *m.* linen cloth; linen. -**oso** *adj.* ragged; dulled; having a skin, scum or crust; vino -**oso**, crusted wine. †-**uc·cia** *f.* apron. -**ume** *m.* crust, skim, scum; film; lining membrane of an egg; blur on the eye.

pannoc·ch-ia *f.* (bot.) panicle; (agric.) maize cob; — della cipolla, onion (bulb); — del cavallo, horse's tail; (zool.) *Squilla mantis*, an edible crustacean, resembling a small lobster. -**ina** *f.* (bot.) -**ina** dei lidi, *Aeluropus litoralis*. -**iuto** *adj.* having a cob; tufted; cob-shaped.

panno-lano *m.*, -**lino** *m.* See under **panno**.

pannume *m.* See under **panno**.

panoftalmite *f.* (med.) panophthalmia.

pano·plia *f.* panoply.

panop·tici *adj. m.pl.* adaptable (of spectacles, for any eyesight).

panor-ama *m.* panorama; view; di quassù si gode un bel —, you get a lovely view from up here; (fig.) comprehensive view; — della letteratura italiana, general outlines of Italian Literature. **-a·mica** *f.* (cinem.; telev.) pan, panning, pan-shot; -amica verticale, tilt; -amica orizzontale, panning. **-amicare** [A 2 s] *tr.* (cinem.; telev.) to 'pan'. **-a·mico** *adj.* panoramic; (cinem.) schermo -amico, wide screen. (**-amicamente** *adv.*)

panotto *m.* (foundry) pig.

panşlav-işmo *m.* Pan-slavism. (**-ista** *m., f.*)

pantagrue·l-ico *adj.* pantagruelian. **-işmo** *m.* pantagruelism.

Pantalon-e¹ *pr.n.m.* (theatr.) Pantaloon, a 'mask' of Venetian comedy; (provb.) paga —, the people will pay, the taxpayer pays.

pantalone² *m.* (mus.) pantaleon, pantalon (a kind of dulcimer invented by Pantaleon Hebenstreit in the eighteenth century); German horizontal pianoforte with the hammers striking downwards.

pantalone³ *m.* pantaloon; *pl.* trousers; sports trousers; football-bags.

pantan-o *m.* bog, swamp; mi sono cacciato in un bel —, I have got into a fine mess; essere in un —, to be in a jam; *adj.* boggy, swampy. **-a** *f.* (orn.) greenshank, *Tringa nebularia*. **-eşco** *adj.* (*m.pl.* -eschi) bog-like. **-oşo** *adj.* boggy, swampy, miry; erbe -ose, marsh grasses, marsh plants.

pante-işmo *m.* pantheism. **-ista** *m., f.* pantheist. **-iş·tico** *adj.* pantheistic. **-isticamente** *adv.* pantheistically.

pa·nteo *adj.* (class. antiq.) having the attributes of several gods (e.g. of a statue).

pa·nteon *pr.n.m.* Pantheon (in Rome); *n.m.* pantheon.

panter-a *f.* (zool.) panther, *Panthera pardus*; birdnet; duck-trap; (Lombardy) fishnet; (mil. hist.) covered assault tower; (neol.) a sort of jeep or small lorry used by the Italian police. **-ana** *f.* (orn.) skylark. **-ina** *f.* fishnet permitted in certain Italian lakes. **-ino** *adj.* pantherine; (fig.) panther-like.

Pan·theon *pr.n.m.* See **panteon**.

†pantiera *f.* cuirass.

pantocra·tore *adj.* almighty; (Byz. art) il —, the Pantocrator (in mosaics).

panto·fol-a *f.* slipper; un paio di -e, a pair of slippers; in -e, slippered; baciare la — al papa, to kiss the Pope's toe. **-a·io** *m.* slipper maker, or seller; (fig., pol.) ultra-conservative. (**-a·ia** *f.*)

panto·graf-o *m.* (eng. drawing) pantograph; (electr.) pantograph trolley; (pop.) trolley of an electric locomotive or trolley-bus. **-are** [A 1 s] *tr.* (eng. drawing) to pantograph.

panto-mima *f.* (theatr.) pantomime; series of gesticulations; (iron.) play-acting, 'putting it on'; non gli dare retta, è tutta una —, don't take any notice of him, it's all put on. **-mi·mico** *adj.* pantomimic; like a pantomime. **-mimo** *m.* mimic actor; pantomime; mime.

pantrac·cola *f.* See **panzana**.

panunto *m.* See under **pane**.

Panurgo *pr.n.m.* Panurge (from Rabelais); rascal, swindler; i montoni di —, Panurge's sheep, (fig.) silly sheep.

†panza *f.* and derivs. See **pancia**.

panzan-a *f.* fib, nonsense, story; -e!, humbug! **-are** [A 1] *tr.* to amuse with idle tales. **-a·ria** *f.* cock and bull story. **-ella** *f.* bread dipped in water and cooked with oil and vinegar; toasted bread with garlic and fresh oil.

panze·a *f.* pansy, heartsease, *Viola tricolor* var. *hortensis*.

panzer-one *m.* (mil. hist.) breastplate, buckler. **-iera** *f.*, **-iere** *m.* (mil.) body armour; breastplate; muddy fringe around a dress; net to catch skylarks. **-uola** *f.* (mil. hist.) parapet.

panzirone *m.* See **panzerone**.

panzone *m.* (Rome). See **pancione**, under **pancia**.

Pa·ola *pr.n.f.* Paula.

Pa·ol-o *pr.n.m.* Paul; (numism.) paolo, old Tuscan and Papal silver coin of small denomination. **-ino** *pr.n.m.* Paulkin; fool; (joc.) Tuscan. **-otto** *m.* friar of an order founded by St Francis of Paola; member of missionary order founded by St Vincent de Paul; (fig., derog.) cleric; pious humbug.

paonazzo *adj., n.m.* violet; purple; peacock-blue; (eccl.) abito —, the violet dress of bishops.

†paone *m.* and derivs. See **pavone**.

papà *m. indecl.* daddy, papa; figlio di —, spoilt child, son of a rich man.

pap-a *m.* (eccl.) pope; andare a Roma e non vedere il —, to miss the most important thing; — nero, 'Black Pope' (said of the General of the Jesuits); — rosso, 'Red Pope' (said of the Prefect of Propaganda and also of the presumed head of international free-masonry); stare bene come un —, to live like a lord, to be in clover; entrarci come il — nelle minchiate, to have nothing to do with it, to be quite out of place. **-a·bile** *adj.* (of a prelate) having some chance of becoming pope; likely, promising (as a candidate for the papacy). **-ale** *adj.* papal, of the pope; *adv. phr.* alla -ale, plainly, frankly; *n.f.* (agric.) a kind of pear. **-alina** *f.* skull-cap; smoking-cap; (ichth.) sprat, *Clupea sprattus*. **-alino** *adj.* papal, attached to the pope; of the pope's party or household; soldati -alini, pope's soldiers, papal guard; *n.m.* supporter of the pope; *pl.* pope's men, papal troops. **-asso** *m.* (eccl.) priest of an Eastern rite; Orthodox (parish) priest, 'papa', 'papas'; †priest; holy man or religious leader of an unfamiliar faith (e.g. Christian priest from Saracen point of view, Moslem imam from Crusaders' point of view); (fig.) leader, captain; fare il -asso, to give oneself airs; (joc.) ringleader; fare il -asso, to act as leader; giuoco del -asso, follow-my-leader. **-ato**, **†-a·tico** *m.* (eccl.) papacy; (fig.) comfortable situation, soft job. **-eşco** *adj.* (*m.pl.* -eschi) popish; papistical. **-essa** *f.* 'popess', 'she-pope'; the legendary Pope Joan; woman of dominant influence at the papal court (e.g. Marozia or Theodora in the tenth century); (joc.) woman who is very well off; nickname for a pope who is considered weak; card in the game of 'minchiate'. **-etto** *m. dim.* (derog.) pope of little worth; (numism.) papetto, silver coin of Papal state of low denomination. **-ino** *m. dim.* (derog.) pope of little worth; the first card in the game of 'minchiate'; (billiards) miscue. **-işmo** *m.* Popery (from the standpoint either of an old-fashioned Protestant or of an opponent of the temporal power). **-ista** *m.* papist. **-i·stico** *adj.* popish, papistical (cf. **papismo**). **†-izzare** *intr.* to be pope, to reign as pope.

pap-a·io *f.* (bot.) papaya, pawpaw, *Carica papaya*. **-aina** *f.* (chem.) papain, vegetable pepsin.

pap-ale *adj.*, **-alina** *f.*, **-alino** *adj.*, etc. See under **papa**.

paparina *f.* (bot.) chickweed, *Stellaria media*.

paparino *m. dim.* of **papà**; Daddy, Daddikins.

papave·rico *adj.* somniferous, soporific, inducing drowsiness; listless; *n.m.* slacker, lazybones; tu sei il gran —!, you *are* a slacker!

papa·ver-o *m.* (bot.) poppy, *Papaver*; — cornuto, yellow horned poppy, *Glaucium flavum*; — domestico, opium poppy, *Papaver somniferum*; — officinale, *P. somniferum* var. *album*; (fig.) grossi -i, bigwigs. **-ato** *adj.* made with poppy-seed. **-ina** *f.* (chem.) papaverine.

†pape *excl.* of wonder and amazement, possibly derived from **padre** and being therefore an invocation of the Deity.

†papeio, **†pape·o** *m.* wick; (bot.) see **papiro**.

†papelito *m.* cheroot.

pa·per-a *f.* (orn.) see **papero**; young goose; (fig.) silly woman, 'goose'; mistake, blunder; (sport) kicking the ball into one's own goal; pigliare una —, to make a blunder; (theatr.; radio, etc.) 'fluff'. **-ina** *f.* (bot.) chickweed, *Stellaria media*. **-ino** *m.* young gosling. **-o** *m.* (orn.) gosling; (fig.) silly man; (fam.) i -i menano a bere le oche, go teach your grandmother to suck eggs. **-otto**, **-ot·tolo** *m.* fat gosling.

†papi(g)li-one *m.* butterfly. **†-otti** *m.pl.* hair-curlers.

papill-a *f.* (anat.) papilla. **-are** *adj.* (anat.) papillar, papillary. **-oma** *m.* (surg.) papilloma. **-oşo** *adj.* (anat.) papillose.

papir-o *m.* (bot.) papyrus, *Cyperus papyrus*; (univ.) freshmen's charter, a humorous decree issued by older students bestowing on first-year men the dignity of freshmen (cf. **matricola**); (joc.) paper, document; †sheet of paper; †wick. **-a·ceo** *adj.* (anat.; biol.) papyraceous. **-eto** *m.* papyrus plantation. **-ologi·a** *f.* papyrology. **-o·logo** *m.* papyrologist.

pap-işmo *m.*, **-ista** *m.*, **†-izzare** *vb.* See under **papa**.

papp-a *f.* pap, soaked bread; bread poultice; paste; una — di acqua e amido, starch mixed to a paste; diventare una —, (of macaroni) to be overcooked, to be boiled to a mush; mangiar la — in capo a uno, to have the whip-hand of someone; scodellare la — a uno, to explain something to someone in words of one syllable; voler la — fatta, to expect too much, to expect to be waited on; aver — (frullata) nel cervello, to be brainless; soffiare nella —, to play the spy; una — fredda, a mollycoddle. **†-acchione** *m.* greedy-guts; fool, simpleton. **-aceci** *m.*, *f. indecl.* see under **pappare**. **-agor·gia** *f.* double-chin; wattles of a turkey. **-arella** *f.* see **pappardella**.

pappafi·co *m.* (*pl.* -**chi**) hood; cowl; diver's helmet; imperial (beard); †(naut.) topgallantsail.

pappagall·o *m.* (orn.) parrot; fare il —, to talk like a parrot; ripetere a —, to repeat (in) parrot fashion; nel ripetere la lezione sono tanti -i, they repeat the lesson like so many parrots; (colloq.) rude youth who makes offensive remarks to women in the streets; (ichth.) green wrasse, *Labrus viridis.* -**are** [A I] *tr.* to copy, to imitate the words of. -**eri·a** *f.* flattery by imitation. -**escamente** *adv.* (in) parrot fashion, like a parrot. -**esco** *adj.* (*m.pl.* -**eschi**) parrot-like; parrot's, pertaining to parrots. -**escamente** *adv.* in parrot fashion. -**essa** *f.* hen-parrot; woman chatterbox. -**etto** *m. dim.* (pop.) budgerigar. -**ino** *m. dim.* (fig.) little parrot; child who repeats like a parrot. (-**uc·cio** *m. dim.*)

pappagor·gia *f.* See under **pappa.**

†**pappalardo** *m.* hypocrite; greedy-guts.

pappardella *f.* long, senseless speech; tit bit; *pl.* (cul.) 'lasagne' (i.e. 'pasta' in broad ribbon-like strips) seasoned with meat, esp. hare; stare in -**e**, to be in clover, to enjoy life; (fam., joc.) condotto delle -**e**, throat, gullet.

papp·are [A I] *tr.* to eat up. to gobble up; to gulp down; s'è -**ato** tutto, he has gobbled up everything; *intr.* (*aux.* avere), *rfl.* to eat one's fill; (fig.) to make illicit gains; -**a** tu che -**o** anch'io, there are pickings for both of us; se non c'è da —, non ne vuol sapere, if there's no rake-off he won't touch it. -**aceci** *m., f. indecl.* blockhead; useless person; lazy individual; mangiare a -**aceci**, to swallow, to devour, (fig.) to swallow, i.e. to believe. -**alasagne** *m., f. indecl.* lazy individual; silly person. †-**alecco** *m.* glutton; meal. †-**alefave** *m.* weak, ineffectual person. †-**amille·simi** *m.* pedant, bookworm; antiquarian. †-**astri·coli**, †-**astron·zoli** *m.pl.* edible root-crop. -**ata** *f.* feast, hearty meal; fare una buona -**ata**, to have a good feed. -**ataci** *m.* (ent.) gnat; sandfly, *Phlebotomus* spp.; (fig.) easy-going person; marito -**ataci**, *mari complaisant.* -**atore** *m.* greedy eater, guzzler, glutton. (-**atrice** *f.*) -**ato·ria** *f.* feasting; (provb.) tutti i salmi finiscono in gloria e tutte le feste in -**atoria**, all psalms end with the 'gloria' and all celebrations with a feast; (pop.) bellyful; (fig.) pickings, illicit gains. -**io** *m.* grand feast. †-**o** *m.* bread. -**one** *m.* great eater; (fig.) greedy, insatiable, voracious person. (-**ona** *f.*)

pappin·a *f.* hospital servant often entrusted with minor nursing duties, nursing assistant; †untrained lay hospital nurse; (joc.) scolding; pap; linseed poultice. -**o** *m.* hospital orderly, male nurse; (joc., mil.) medical corps troops.

papp·o[1] *m.* (bot.) pappus. -**oso** *adj.* (bot.) pappose, downy.

Pappo[2] *pr.n.m.* (Rom. antiq.) Pappus, 'Gaffer', a stock character in Atellan farce.

pappolata *f.* thin soup; overcooked, sloppy food; la — dei porci, pig-swill; (fig.) silly tedious talk.

pappolone *m.* tedious talker, great chatterer.

pappuc·cia *f.* See **babbuccia.**

pa·prica *f.* (bot.) paprika, *Capsicum.*

papuano *adj., n.m.* Papuan.

pa·pula *f.* (surg.) boil, pustule.

par[1] *adj.* abbrev. of **pari**, q.v.

par[2] *m.* See **paio.**

para[1] *f.* Brazilian rubber.

†**para**[2] *f.* refuge, shelter.

para-[3] *pref.* para, near. (For derivs. in which the stress falls on the second syllable, e.g. **para·basi**, see separate headings. See also compounds under **parare.**) -**assiale** *adj.* (scient.; anat.) paraxial. -**ba·nico** *adj.* (chem.) parabanic; acido -**banico**, parabanic acid, oxalyl urea. -**bellum** *m. indecl.* sub-machine gun. -**bioso** *f.* (biol.) parabiosis. -**bio·tico** *adj.* parabiotic. -**blasto** *m.* (anat.) parablast. -**bla·stico** *adj.* parablastic. †-**blema** *f.* (naut.) auxiliary tackle used as a sheet or tack as required. -**cantosi** *f.* (med.) paracanthosis. -**casei·na** *f.* (chem.) paracasein. -**cata·loge** *f.* (mus.) an irregular kind of chanting (ancient Greek music). -**ce·ntesi** *f.* (surg.) paracentesis. -**centrale** *adj.* (scient.) paracentral. -**ciano·geno** *m.* (chem.) paracyanogen. -**ci·meno** *m.* (Gk. gramm.) perfect tense. -**cinesi** *f.* (med.) paracinesia. -**ci·stico** *adj.* (anat.) paracystic. -**cistite** *f.* (med.) paracystitis. -**clasi** *f.* (geol.) paraclase; fault. -**cmasi** *f.* (med.) paracme. -**colpite** *f.* (med.) paracolpitis. -**cresolo** *m.* (chem.) paracresol. -**cromatosi** *f.* (med.) parachromatosis. -**cronismo** *m.* parachronism. -**cusi**, -**cusi·a** *f.* (med.) paracusia, paracusis. -**denite** *f.* (med.) paradenitis. -**dentale** *adj.* (med.) paradental. -**dentosi** *f.*

(med.) paradental disease. -**den·zio** *m.* (anat.) paradentium. -**di·dimo** *m.* (anat.) paradidymis, Geraldes's organ. -**difte·rico** *adj.* (med.) paradiphtherial. -**dissenteri·a** *f.* (med.) paradysentery. -**epa·tico** *adj.* (anat.) parahepatic. -**fimosi** *f.* (med.) paraphimosis. -**fisi** *f.* (med.) paraphysis; (bot.) paraphysis. -**fito** *m.* (med.) paraphyte. -**formaldeide** *f.* (chem.) paraformaldehyde, polyoxymethylene. -**frenite** *f.* (med.) paraphrenitis. -**ganglina** *f.* (pharm.) paragangline. -**gan·glio** *m.* (anat.) paraganglion. -**ge·nesi** *f.* (geol.) paragenesis. -**glossa** *f.* (med.) paraglossa. -**glossite** *f.* (med.) paraglossia. -**gnato** *m.* (med.) paragnathus. -**grafi·a** *f.* (med.) paragraphia. -**lali·a** *f.* (med.) paralalia. -**ldeide** *f.* (chem.) paraldehyde. -**lessi·a** *f.* (med.) paralexia. -**lipsi** *f.* (rhet.) paralipsis. -**ller·gico** *adj.* (med.) parallergic. -**logismo** *m.* paralogism, illogical reasoning; fallacy. -**logi·stico** *adj.* paralogistic. -**logiz·zare** [A I] *intr.* (*aux.* avere) to paralogize, to reason falsely. -**magne·tico** *adj.* (phys.) paramagnetic. -**me·cio** *m.* (zool.) *Paramecium.* -**metrite** *f.* (med.) parametrites. -**mnesi·a** *f.* (med.; psych.) paramnesia; *déjà vu.* -**nefrite** *f.* (med.) paranephritis. -**ninfo** *m.* (Gk. antiq.) paranymph; 'friend of the bridegroom'; 'best man'; matrimonial agent. **nucleare** *adj.* paranuclear. -**nu·cleo** *m.* (cyt.) paranucleus. -**pla·sma** *m.* (biol.) paraplasm. -**plegi·a**, -**plessi·a** *f.* (med.) paraplegia. -**ple·gico** *adj.* (med.) paraplegic, paraplectic. -**renale** *adj.* (anat.) pararenal. -**rettale** *adj.* (anat.) pararectal. -**sacrale** *adj.* (anat.) parasacral. -**rmoni·a** *f.* (mus.) that which is almost harmony. †-**rmo·nico** *adj.* (mus.) unessential (to the harmony). -**rtrema** *m.* (med.) almost complete luxation. -**salpingite** *f.* (med.) parasalpingitis. -**sceve** *f.* Parasceve; (Bibl.) eve of the Sabbath; day of preparation for the Sabbath, Friday; (eccl.) Good Friday. -**selene** *m.* (astron.) paraselene. -**sele·nico** *adj.* paraselenic. -**simpa·tico** *adj.* (anat.) parasympathetic; organi -**simpatici**, parasympathetic bodies. -**sinovite** *f.* (med.) parasynovitis. -**sinu·sale** *adj.* (anat.) parasinoidal. -**spadi·a** *f.* (med.) paraspadia. -**ssiticida** *m.* parasiticide. -**ssitismo** *m.* parasitism. -**ssito·geno** *adj.* (med.) parasitogenic, due to parasites. -**statale** *adj.* (neol.) para-statal; under State control, state-controlled; of public utility; ente -**statale**, public utility company, corporation, etc.; *n.m.* employees of public corporations, or sim. -**ti·fico** *adj.* (med.) paratyphoid. -**tifo** *m.* (med.) paratyphoid fever. -**tifoide·o** *adj.* (anat.) paratyphoid. -**tiro·ide** *f.* (anat.) parathyroid. -**tormone** *m.* (physiol.) parathormone, parathyroid hormone. -**trimma** *m.* (med.) intertrigo. -**vaginite** *f.* (med.) paracolpitis. -**vertebrale** *adj.* (anat.) paravertebral. -**vescicale** *adj.* (anat.) paravesical.

para·basi, †**parabase** *f.* (Gk. lit.) parabasis.

para·bol·a[1] *f.* parable; fable, invention; †figure, metaphor; †word. -**ano** *m.* chatterbox, prattler; *adj.* chattering. -**one**, †-**oso** *m. augm.* great chatterbox.

para·bol·a[2] *f.* (geom.) parabola, curve; compire una —, to decline, to begin to fall. -**o·ide** *m.* (geom.) paraboloid.

parabo·lic·o[1] *adj.* parabolic(al); relating to parables. -**amente** *adv.* parabolically; parlare -**amente**, to speak in parables.

parabo·lico[2] *adj.* (geom.) parabolic, relating to a parabola.

paraboloso *adj.* prating, talkative; *n.m.* a gossip.

parabrezza *m. indecl.* and all such compounds, see under **parare.**

paracleto, **para·clito** *m.* (theol.) Paraclete, Holy Ghost; (fig.) consoler.

paradell·a *f.*, -**o** *m.* long pole used in fishing.

paradigm·a *m.* (*pl.* -**i**) (gramm.) paradigm. -**a·tico** *adj.* paradigmatic, exemplary.

paradis·o *m.* paradise; — terrestre, earthly paradise; — celeste, celestial paradise; — artificiale, opium den, happiness sought in drugs, the drugs themselves; *Il — Perduto* di Milton, Milton's *Paradise Lost*; heaven; i santi del —, the saints of heaven; in — non ci si va in carrozza, you can't ride to heaven in a carriage; voler andare in — in carrozza, to expect to have the best of both worlds; perfect bliss; è un —, it's (like) heaven!; di —, heavenly, è una musica di —, it is heavenly music; (orn.) uccello di —, bird of Paradise; (geog.) Gran Paradiso, name of a mountain group, in W. Alpine region of Piedmont; volere entrare in — a dispetto dei santi, to go where one is unwelcome, to gate-crash; †(archit.) parvis, portico of a Gothic church; †(naut.) stateroom; ship with a cabin; living quarters in a ship; (Venice) palace adjacent to the dockyard assigned to one of the three superintendents; *adj.* (agric.) applied to certain kinds of fruit (e.g. 'uva -**a**', 'pera -**a**', etc.). -**e·a** *f.* (orn.) bird of Paradise. -**i·aco** *adj.* heavenly, celestial, paradisiac(al); *n.m.* (bot.) banana,

paradis-o (*cont.*)
plantain, *Musa sapientum*. **-iale** *adj.* see **paradisiaco**. **-ino** *m. dim.*
delightful spot, e.g. in the country.

paradoss-o *m.* paradox. **-ale** *adj.* paradoxical. **-are** [A I] *intr.* (*aux.*
avere) to speak in paradoxes. **-as·tico** *adj.* paradoxical. **-eggiare**
[A 3] *intr.* (*aux.* avere) to speak in paradoxes, to delight in paradox.
-ista *m., f.* paradoxer, paradoxist.

paraf-are [A I] *tr.* to initial (a treaty, an agreement, etc.). **-a** *f.*
flourish after a signature (cf. **para(f)fo**); initials, signature to a
document. **-atura** *f.* initialling (of a document).

parafern-a *f.* (leg.) parapherna, paraphernalia, free property of a
wife (C.C.). **-ale** *adj.* (leg.) paraphernal; beni -ali, paraphernalia;
free property of a wife (C.C.).

paraffina *f.* (chem.) paraffin, paraffin wax.

paraf(f)o *m.* paragraph sign; paraph, flourish after a signature.

parafras-are [A I] *tr.* to paraphrase. **-ato** *part. adj.* paraphrased.

para·fras-i, **-e** *f.* paraphrase. **-i·a** *f.* (med.; psych.) paraphrasia.

parafr-aste *m.* paraphrast, paraphraser. **-a·stic-o** *adj.* paraphrastic.
-asticamente *adv.* paraphrastically.

†**parafreniere** *m.* See **palafreniere**, under **palafreno**.

parag·gio *m.* (usu. *pl.*) part, quarter, neighbourhood; vicinity; credo
che egli abiti in questi paraggi, I think he lives somewhere about
here; (joc.) outlandish place, unusual place; come mai ti trovo
in questi paraggi!, I didn't expect to find you here!; (naut.) waters
in the vicinity of a harbour; i paraggi di Southampton, Southampton waters; lineage, degree, station; di gran —, of high degree.

pa·rago *m.* (ichth.). See **pagro**.

para-goge, **para·goge** *f.* (gramm.) paragoge. **-go·gico** *adj.* (gramm.)
paragogic.

paragon-e *m.* comparison; a — di, in — di, in comparison with,
compared with; fare un — (tra), to make a comparison (between);
sostenere il —con, to bear comparison with; senza —, unequalled;
i -i sono odiosi, comparisons are odious; pietra di —, touchstone;
paragon, model, example; test, trial; al — delle armi, by, in, the
test of arms; (gramm.) simile; (typ.) paragon type, two-line long
Primer. **-a·bile** *adj.* comparable; cose -abili tra loro, comparable
things. †**-anza** *f.* comparison; comparing; trial, test; model. **-are**
[A I c] *tr.* (*prep.* con, a) to compare; -a il tuo vestito col mio, compare your dress with mine; -ò l'insetto a una cicala, he compared
the insect to a cicada; non essere da -are con, not to be compared
to (with); -are due persone, to compare two people; lo -erei ad
un asino, I call him an ass; †to equal, to be the equal of, to be
comparable with; *rfl.* to compare oneself; to be compared; *recip.*
rfl. to be comparable; non sono da -arsi, they cannot be compared. (**-ato** *part. adj.*) **-ite** *f.* (geol.; miner.) paragonite.

para·graf-o *m.* paragraph sign, section mark; paragraph; subsection. **-are** [A I s] *tr.* to paragraph, to divide into paragraphs.
(**-ato** *part. adj.*)

paralipo·meni *m.pl.* paralipomena, continuation, supplement; (Bibl.)
Paralipomena (Septuagint and Vulgate name for the two books
of 'Chronicles').

para·l-isi *f.* (med.) paralysis; — agitante, Parkinson's disease,
paralysis agitans; — progressiva, creeping paralysis. †**-isi·a** *f.*
(med.) see **paralisi**. †**-iticare** *rfl.* to become paralysed. †**-iticato**
part. adj. paralysed. **-i·tico** *adj. n.m.* (med.) paralytic; (Bibl.)
miracolo del -itico, miracle of the man sick of the palsy (Matt. ix).
-izzare [A I] *tr.* (med.) to paralyse; (fig.) to paralyse, to slow down.
-izzato *part. adj.* paralysed.

parall-asse *f.* (astron.; opt.) parallax. **-at·tico** *adj.* parallactic.

parallel-a *f.* parallel line, parallel; a —, in parallel fashion, parallel;
(geom.) parallel, parallel rule; (eng.) parallel block; (naut.)
parallel ruler; (mil.) support trench; *pl.* (gymn.) parallel bars.
-amente *adv.* in parallel (fashion), parallel. **-epi·pedo**, **-epi·pede** *m.*
(geom.) parallelepiped; *adj.* balla -epipeda, square bale (e.g. of
cotton). **-ismo** *m.* parallelism; correspondence; equidistance;
(liter.) parallelism; (geom.) parallelism, parallel. **-o** *adj.* (geom.)
parallel; (mus.) quinte -e, consecutive fifths; *n.m.* parallel; (geog.)
parallel, circle, latitude; (electr.) in -o, in parallel; (fig.) comparison, parallel; non si può fare il -o tra cose diverse, you cannot
compare (draw a parallel between) different things. **-ogrammo** *m.*
(geom.) parallelogram; (mech.) -ogrammo delle forze, parallelogram of forces.

pa·ralo *m.* (naut. hist.) Athenian festival craft also used by emissaries.

paramento *m.* See under **parare**.

para·mese *f.* (mus.) paramese (note in ancient Greek music).

para·m-etro *m.* (math.; geol.) parameter. **-e·trico** *adj.* parametric.

paran-co *m.* (*pl.* **-chi**) (naut.) purchase, tackle, luff, fall; — di
abbandono, — di ritegno, — di rilievo, careening purchase;
— di candeletta, — di candelozza, main tackle; — di capone,
cat purchase; — di cima (al pennone), yard purchase; — a coda,
tail purchase; — differenziale, Weston's Purchase; — doppio,
double purchase; — su, — a orecchino, luff upon luff; — di
richiamo, inhaul, guide purchase; — semplice, luff; — di sicurezza,
preventer tackle; — volante, jigger, handy billy; (comm.) consegnare merce sotto —, to place goods alongside a ship, *or* to
deliver goods on dock under tackle; (eng.) pulley block, block
and tackle, hoist; — a catena, chain block. **-care** [A 2] *tr.* (naut.)
to haul or lift with a tackle. **-chetto** *m. dim.*, †**-chinetto**, †**-chino**
m. dim. (naut.) small luff, jigger, handy billy. **-cone** *m.* (naut.)
boat's fall.

paranete *f.* (mus.) paranete (note in ancient Greek music).

parangari·a *f.* (leg. hist.) feudal servitude; thraldom.

†**parangone** *m.* See **paragone**.

paran-oia *f.* (med., psych.) paranoia. **-o·ico** *adj. n.m.* (med., psych.)
paranoiac. **-o·ide** *adj.* (psych.) paranoid; complesso -oide,
paranoidism.

paranz-a *f.* (naut.) sailing trawler; fishing trawler with one large
triangular sail and a small mizzen; (Catania) small rowing boat;
trawl net; (Varano) stockade for catching fish. †**-ana** *f.* (naut.)
preparation for sea or for making sail. **-ella** *f.*, **-ello** *m.*, **-iella** *f.*
(naut.) small (20–30 ton) fishing trawler, very seaworthy. **-ellaro**
m. (naut.) trawler fisherman.

†**para·ola** *f.* word; fable, invention; parable.

par-are [A I] *tr.* **1.** To ADORN, to deck, to decorate; to prepare;
(litur.) to vest (a priest); — una chiesa a festa, to deck out, to
adorn, a church with bright hangings and flowers; — una chiesa
a lutto, to drape a church in black (usu. for a requiem); (naut.)
— le vele, to hoist the sails. **2.** To PARRY, to ward off, to keep
off; — una da, to shield a person from; to keep out (light); le
tende -ano il sole, the blinds (curtains) keep out the sun; il soldato
-ò il colpo con lo scudo, the soldier parried the blow with his
shield; l'ombrello -a la pioggia, the umbrella keeps off the rain;
— uno con l'ombrello, to shelter someone under one's umbrella;
venga qua, la -o io, come and shelter under my umbrella; to
prevent, to hinder, to catch, to stop; to avoid, to avert; to drive
away, to shoo; — le pecore al monte, to drive the sheep up the
mountain; — un cavallo, to stop a horse; (soccer) to save.
3. To STRETCH OUT, to hold out, to offer; -a il grembiule, che ti
darò le noci, hold out your apron for some walnuts; — la mano,
to hold out one's hand, to beg; — l'altra guancia, to turn the
other cheek; *intr.* (*aux.* avere) to lead (up) to, to aim at; (fam.)
to drive at; vediamo dove va a —, let's see what he is getting at;
rfl. to dress (up), to adorn oneself; il prete si -ò per la messa, the
priest vested for mass; to protect oneself, to take shelter; to
appear, to present oneself; mi si -ò dinanzi, he presented himself,
he came up to me. **-abordo** *m.* (naut.) fender, padding; -abordo
fisso, rope fender secured along the rubbing strake or padding
fender over the bows. **-abrezza** *m. indecl.* windscreen; wind-
shield. **-acadutare** [A I] *intr.* (*aux.* essere) to parachute. **-acadute**
m. indecl. (aeron.) parachute; lanciarsi col -cadute, to bale out;
corde di sospensione del -acadute, shroud lines. **-acadutista** *m.*
parachutist; reparti di -acadutisti, paratroops; *adj.* truppe
-acadutiste, paratroops. **-acaduti·stico** *adj.* relating to parachutes
or paratroops. **-acalli** *m. indecl.* corn-protector (for the foot).
-acaminetto, **-acamino** *m.* firescreen. **-acarro** *m.* stone marking
edge of a road; stone or iron placed to protect gateposts or door-
posts from the wheels of carriages; kerbstone. **-acenere** *m.* fireguard; fender. **-acera** *m.* one who collects and sells again the
wax from candles in church processions. **-acielo** *m.* canopy;
ceiling; roof. **-acolpi** *m. indecl.* bumper, buffer. **-acqua** *m. indecl.*
umbrella. **-afango** *m.* (*pl.* **-afanghi**) (motor., etc.) mudguard.
-afiamma *m. indecl.* fireproof bulkhead, fireproof partition.
-aful·mine *m.* lightning conductor. **-afumo** *m.* cover for a lamp-
chimney. **-afuoco** *m.* firescreen; fireguard. †**-aghiac·cio** *m.* (naut.)
ice guard or fender on the bows of a ship. **-agua·i** *m.* overall.
-aguanto *m.* tip, gratuity. **-aluce** *m.* (photog.) lenshood, focusing
hood. **-alume** *m.* lampshade; eyeshade. **-ama·niche** *m. indecl.*
sleeve-cover. **-amano** *m.* wrist-band, cuff; gauntlet; arm-sling.
-amarra *f.* (naut.) fluke guard on the bows of a ship, plating
protecting it from the anchor. **-amento** *m.* decoration, furnishing;

par‑are (*cont.*)

hanging(s), curtains; (liturg.) vestment; hanging (in church); (masonry) face, facing; †‑amenti di palafreno, trappings of a palfrey. **‑ameẓẓale** *m.* (naut.) hog, the beam or plate above the keel, to which the frames are secured; **‑amezzale laterale,** hog plate above the docking keels. **‑amine** *m.* (naut.) sweep, mine‑sweep; **‑amine per il dragaggio in corsa,** minesweeper's gear; **‑amine per il dragaggio di protezione,** paravane, P.V., towed by warships for self‑protection against mines. **‑amosche** *m. indecl.* fly‑net; wire gauze dish‑cover. **‑aoc·chi** *m. indecl.* goggles; eye‑shield; blinkers (for a horse); (photog.; opt.) eyepiece. **‑ao·lio** *m. indecl.* (eng.) splash guard; oil seal. **‑aọnde** *m. indecl.* (naut.) breakwater fitted on bow. **‑apalle** *m. indecl.* (mil.) butts. **‑apetto** *m.* parapet; balustrade; (window‑)sill; (naut.) bulwark; taffrail; gunwale; parapet; breakwater; (mil.) parapet, stone fortification or earth thrown up before a trench; chest guard, protective waistcoat; †breastplate. **‑api·glia** *m.* turmoil, commotion. **‑apiog·gia** *m. indecl.* umbrella. **‑apọlvere** *m. indecl.* dust cover. **‑asar·tie** *m. indecl.* (naut.) shroud plates, points where stays and shrouds are fixed to the hull. **‑asassi** *m. indecl.* (motor.) gravel guard. **‑aschegge** *m. indecl.* splinter guard. **‑aschiuma** *m.* (aeron.) spray strip (on a seaplane). **‑ascintille** *m. indecl.* (electr.) spark arrester. †**‑ascosa** *m.* (naut.) hog plates of the locking keels. **‑asọle** *m.* sunshade, parasol; awning. **‑aspalla** *m. indecl.* (mil.) parados, the rear protecting earthwork in a trench. **‑aspi·golo** *m.* (bldg.) staff angle. **‑aspruzzi** *m.* (techn.) splash‑preventer, baffle board; (motor.) wing, mudguard, splashguard. **‑asquadro** *m.* (naut. hist., seventeenth century) bulkhead. **‑ata** *f.* (fencing) parry; (fig.) star sulle **‑ate,** to be on one's guard; in **‑ata,** alert; vedere la mala **‑ata,** to perceive the danger, to see that things are going badly; vista la mala **‑ata** me n'andai, when I saw the bad turn things were taking I went away; (soccer) una bella **‑ata,** a fine save (by the goalkeeper); parade, display; sfilare in **‑ata,** to march past (on parade); abito di **‑ata,** full dress; parade‑ground; mettere in **‑ata,** to put on show, to exhibit; cloud‑banks on the horizon at sunrise or sunset; †(mil.) fortress defences such as traverses and mantlets; †(naut.) fender; scotsman, wooden gangway guard; †corde di **‑ata,** rope fenders; naval honour of manning ship; †manning the rigging; †dressing ship. **‑atasche** *m. indecl.* pocket‑flap. **‑atella** *f.* net for catching quails, etc.; see **paratia.** **‑ato** *part. adj.* decorated. decked; hung with curtains; prepared, ready; mal **‑ato,** in difficulties; warded off, parried, stopped; *n.m.* hangings, curtains, ornament; carta da **‑ato,** wall‑paper; (eccl.) hangings (in church): (liturg.) set of vestments; shelter, cover; *pl.* (naut.) chocks, docking blocks. **‑atọia** *f.* (hydr. eng.) sluice gate, sluice valve; gate valve; **‑atoia di presa,** inlet sluice. **‑atọre** *m.* decorator. (**‑atrice** *f.*) **‑atura** *f.* decoration; hangings; **‑aurti** *m. indecl.* shock‑absorber; (motor.; rlwy.) bumper, buffer; (watchm.) banking stop. **‑avento** *m.* screen; (motor.) windscreen. **‑aveste** *m.* (cycle) dress‑guard.

paraṣanga *f.* (Persian antiq.) parasang, measure of about three English miles.

parasceve *f.* See under **para**[3].

parassit‑a, paras(s)ito *m.* (Gk. antiq.) 'parasite', privileged guest at a religious or civil banquet; (class. antiq.) parasite, despised hanger‑on (a stock character in Gk. and Lat. comedy); parasite, hanger‑on, sponger; (biol.) parasite; *adj.* (electr.) parasitic, stray. **‑ag·gine** *f.* parasitical behaviour, sponging. †**‑a·rio** *adj.* see **parassitico. ‑iṣmo** *m.* (biol.) parasitism. **‑ologi·a** *f.* parasitology.

parassi·tico *adj.* parasitic.

parastra *f.* (archit.) pilaster.

para‑ti·a *f.* (naut.) bulkhead, partition; **—** di collisione, collision bulkhead (additional subdivisions of the fore‑peak); **—** a quartieri, expanded metal mess subdivisions; **—** stagna, watertight bulkhead. †**‑tiera** *f.* cuirass, armour; (fig.) shield; protection. †**‑ti·o** *m.* (naut.) see **paratia;** (mil.) group of defences covering a sector.

†**para·vol‑a** *f.* see **parabola.** †**‑oso** *adj.* loquacious, eloquent.

Parca *pr.n.f.* (Rom. myth.) Parca; fate; one of the three Fates.

parcella *f.* honorarium, fee; (leg.) solicitor's bill of costs; note of counsel's fees (C.C.P.).

†**par·cere** *tr.* to pardon; to save, to spare.

par‑co[1] *m.* (*pl.* **‑chi**) park; enclosure; paddock; yard; **—** automobilistico, car park; (naut.) **—** ancora, anchor yard; **—** di bestiame, enclosure in a cattle boat; **—** ittico, fishery; **—** di

legnami, timber pond; (mil.) **—** d'artiglieria, artillery park; **—** d'assedio, siege train; **—** minatori, mine‑yard; (comm.) **—** di deposito, dump, stockyard. **‑care** [A2] *tr.* to park (cars, guns). **‑chẹggio** *m.* parking; parking‑place, car park; **‑cheggio vietato,** no parking. **‑chi·metro** *m.* parking‑meter.

par‑co[2] *adj.* (*m.pl.* **‑chi**) sparing, frugal, moderate; parsimonious; **—** di lodi, sparing of praise; essere **—** di aggettivi, to use few adjectives. **‑camẹnte** *adv.* sparingly, frugally. **‑chẹzza** *f.* moderation, temperance. **‑cità** *f.* parsimony, parsimoniousness.

pard‑o *m.* (zool.) leopard, *Panthera pardus;* †a spotted feline animal. **‑ello** *m.* blockhead. **‑i·glio** *m.* Bardiglio (marble). †**‑ino** *adj.* pardine, pertaining to a leopard; made of leopard skin.

†**parecchiare** *vb.* and derivs. See **apparecchiare.**

parẹcchio *adj.* some, many; a good deal; a good many; several; a lot of; much; considerable; bevette **—** vino, he drank a good deal of wine; c'era parecchia gente, there were a good many people; **—** tempo fa, long ago, a long time ago; è **—** tempo che non ti vedo, I haven't seen you for quite a time; parecchie volte, many a time; †equal; †similar; *prn. m.* non avrai tutto, ma **—,** you won't get it all but you will get a certain amount; avete speso **—,** you have spent a lot; *pl.* parecchi mi hanno detto ciò, several people have told me so; *adv.* mi costa **—,** it costs me a good deal, it is rather expensive; ha lavorato **—,** he has worked pretty hard; mi piace **—,** I like it very much; di **—,** considerably; benchè avesse passato di **—** la sessantina, though he was well over sixty.

pareggi‑are [A3c] *tr.* to equal, to be equal to; nessuno lo **‑a** in questo, he has no equal in this; nessun poeta **‑a** Dante, no poet is equal to Dante; to equalize, to make equal; to level; to balance; **—** la strada, to level the road; **—** le partite, to share out equally, to give equal shares; **—** le spese con le entrate, to make expenses equal income, to balance income and expenditure; **—** i conti, to balance the accounts; **—** il bilancio, to balance accounts, to balance the budget; to put on the same footing, to obtain official recognition for; **—** una scuola, to get a school recognized by the Board of Education; *intr.* (*aux.* avere) to equalize, to draw (in a game); (vet.) to trim or pare the hoof of a horse before shoeing it; *rfl.* to compare oneself; *recip. rfl.* to be equal; to square accounts; le loro forze quasi si **‑ano,** their forces are almost equal. **‑a·bile** *adj.* comparable; that can be equalled. **‑amẹnto** *m.* levelling; balancing; equalizing, putting on an equality; **‑amento di una scuola,** official recognition of a school. **‑ato** *part. adj.* equalled, equalized; balanced; levelled; compared; (football) drawn; incontro **‑ato,** drawn match; officially recognized; scuola **‑ata,** school recognized by the Ministry of Education. (**‑atọre** *m.* **‑atrice** *f.*) **‑atura** *f.* levelling.

parẹggio *m.* equalization; balance, balancing; a **—** di, by, in, comparison with; (comm.) a **—,** in balance; (sport) a draw; **—** interno, home draw.

†**pare·glio** *adj.* equal; similar.

parego·rico *adj. n.m.* (pharm.) paregoric.

parella *f.* (eng.) dowel.

†**parem·bola** *f.* (gymn.) weight for putting.

parem‑i·a *f.* proverb. **‑iọgrafico** *adj.* parœmiographic. **‑io·grafo** *m.* collector of proverbs, parœmiographer. **‑iologi·a** *f.* parœmiology.

paren·chim‑a *m.* (biol.) parenchyma. **‑a·tico, ‑atọso** *adj.* (anat.) parenchymatous.

par‑eneṣi *f.* parænesis, parenesis, exhortation. **‑ene·tico** *adj.* parænetic, hortatory.

parent‑e *m., f.* relation, relative, kinsman (kinswoman); un lontano **—,** a distant relation; è un mio **—,** he is a relative of mine; siamo **‑i** stretti, we are closely related; il **—** più stretto, il **—** più prossimo, the next of kin; conoscenti e **‑i,** kith and kin, friends and relations; l'uno e l'altro **—,** the father and mother, the parents; *pl.* parents; i primi **‑i,** our first parents, Adam and Eve; (fig.) il sonno è **—** della morte, sleep is closely related to (is very like) death. **‑ado, ‑ato** *m.* relationship, kinship; kindred, kin, stock; lineage, parentage; relatives; relationship by marriage; marriage; essere di buon **‑ado,** to come of good stock; ha fatto un bel **‑ado,** he (she) has married very well, has made a good match; fu conchiuso il **‑ado** con grandi feste, the marriage was celebrated with great rejoicings. †**‑ag·gio,** see **parentado. ‑ale** *adj.* concerning relations; in, relating to, the family; società **‑ale,** family; †paternal. **‑ali** *m.pl.* (Rom. antiq.) Parentalia, feast of the dead; celebration (in honour of the illustrious dead); celebrare i **‑ali** di, to commemorate (by speeches lectures, etc.). †**‑anza** *f.* see **parentado.**

parent-e (*cont.*)

-**ato** *m.* see **parentado**. -**ela** *f.* relationship, kinship; affinity; relatives, relations, kin; (leg.) blood-relationship (of those descended from a common ancestor) (C.C.); gradi di -ela, degrees of consanguinity; -ela o affinità, relationship by blood or marriage (C.C.). †-**enza** *f.*, †-**eri·a** *f.* see **parentado** or **parentela**. †-**esco** *adj.* pertaining to a relative or kinship. †**e·vole** *adj.* affectionate, loving; affable, informal in speech. †-**ezza** *f.* see **parentado**.

paren·t-eṣi *f. indecl.* (gramm.) parenthesis; (fig.) lull, interval, pause; bracket(s) (marking a parenthesis); — quadre, square brackets; — tonde, round brackets; aprire (chiudere) una —, to put a bracket to mark the beginning (end) of a parenthesis; chiuso fra —, (enclosed) in brackets; fra (tra) —, incidentally, by the way; far —, to make a little digression, to say something by the way; (math.) brackets; togliere la —, to remove the brackets. -**e·tico** *adj.* parenthetic(al).

†**parento·rio** *adj.* See **perentorio**.

†**parenza** *f.* See **apparenza**.

par-ẹre [B 19] *intr.* (*aux.* essere) to seem, to appear; -e che sia stanco, he seems to be tired; -e che sia un buon diavolo, he seems to be a nice chap; a quanto -e, to judge from appearances, to all appearances; mi -e che faremmo meglio a partire, it seems to me (I think) we had better set out; che ve ne -e?, what do you think of it?; mi è - so di udire un rumore, I thought I heard a noise; mi -e di sì, I think so; è vero questo? mi -e, is that true? I think so; fate come vi -e, do as you please, do as you think fit; faccio quel che mi -e e piace, I do just as I like; che ti -e di quest'abito?, what do you think of this dress?; non ti paia strano ciò, don't think (consider) that strange; prendo solo quel tanto che mi -e, I only take what I think right (what seems to me to be just); -e che il tempo voglia rimettersi, it seems the weather may improve, the weather looks like picking up; to look, to look like; -e ammalato, he looks ill; -e un cigno, it looks like a swan; -e un nome tedesco, it sounds like a German name; -e miele, it tastes like honey; mi -e mill'anni di poterlo rivedere, I am longing to see him again; -e ieri, it seems like yesterday; ti -e!, don't mention it!; *n.m.* appearance; per un bel —, for the sake of appearances; opinion, judgement; advice; — consultivo, advisory opinion; vorrei sentire il vostro —, I should like to hear your opinion; m'inchino al vostro —, I bow to your judgement; io non condivido il vostro —, I do not share your opinion; a mio —, a — mio, in my opinion; mutar —, to change one's mind; essere del — che, to be of opinion that; domandare il — dell'assemblea, to take the consensus of opinion of the meeting; prendere un — da un avvocato, to take counsel's opinion; sentire il — di un avvocato, to consult a solicitor. -**erac·cio** *m. pejor.* bad or ill opinion. †-**e·vole** *adj.* apparent, seeming; visible. †-**imento** *m.* opinion.

parer-go *m.* (*pl.* -**ghi**) appendix, addendum; accessory; (archit. paint.) accessory ornament, adjunct; parergon; (numism.) ornament surrounding a figure or inscription.

pa-reṣi *f.* (med.) paresis. -**resteṣi·a** *f.* (med.) paraesthesis. -**reste·sico** *adj.* (med.) paraesthetic. -**re·tico** *adj.* (med.) paretic.

parẹssa *f.* peeress; (neol.) — a vita, life-peeress.

pareta·ria *f.* (bot.) parietaria, pellitory of the wall.

parẹt-e *f.*, †*m.* wall (inner wall of a house); -i dipinte, painted walls; -i ricoperte di carta, papered walls; egli non è felice che fra le -i domestiche, he is happy only when he is at home, he is only happy within his own four walls; vivere fra quattro -i, to lead a secluded life; internal surface; le -i di un vaso, the inside (inner surface) of a vase; le -i dello stomaco, the walls of the stomach; (anat.) paries; — toracica, chest wall; (vet.) see **muraglia**; shelter; obstacle; mettere una —, to put an obstacle, to block an opening; †net for catching birds. -**a·io** *m.* place for hanging nets to catch birds; nets for catching birds; (fig.) le case da giuoco sono grandi -ai, gambling houses are a great snare. -**a·ria** *f.* see **parietaria**. †-**i·o** *m.* see **parete**.

par-g-olo, †-**ulo** *m.* little child; baby. †-**olarità** *f.* see **pargolezza**. -**oleggiante** *part. adj.* childish, behaving like a child. -**oleggiare** [A 3 c] *intr.* (*aux.* avere) to talk or behave like a child. -**oletta** *f.* little girl; †young girl; young woman. -**oletto** *m.* little child; baby, babe; *adj.* tiny, small, little; -oletta damma, a young deer. †-**olezza** *f.* childhood; littleness. †-**olità** *f.* see **pargolezza**.

par-i, -**e** *adj. indecl.* equal, like, same; (of numbers) even; andar —, to match; (math.) even; (comm.; finan.) even; equal; alla —,

at par; alla — di cambio, at par of exchange; i due sono — per abilità, the two are equal in ability; sotto la —, below par; di — merito, of equal merit; non m'aspettavo un successo — a quello, I did not expect a success like that; di — età, of the same age; in — tempo, at the same time; (of a surface) even, level; — siamo, siamo — e patta, we are quits; e tutti —, and all quits, that's the end of it; portarsi alla — di, to catch up with; procedere di — passo, to proceed at the same rate; (racing) arrivo a — merito, dead heat; (tennis) quaranta —, deuce; (games) essere —, to draw; non era — al compito che gli fu affidato, he was not equal to the task that was entrusted to him; fu — alla bisogna, he was equal to the emergency; saltare a piè —, to make a clear jump; (fig.) saltare una pagina a piè —, to skip a whole page; di — passo con, together with; la superbia va di — passo con l'ignoranza, pride goes with ignorance; *n.m.* (sometimes abbrev. to **par** before a consonant) peer, equal; il — e l'impari, odd and even; giuocare a — e caffo, to play at odd and even; like, level; non troverete il suo —, you will not find his equal (peer, like); non ha —, he has no equal, he is unequalled; senza —, matchless, unequalled; bazzicate coi vostri —, mix with your equals; da — a —, as equals; un par mio, a man like me; (fam.) i — miei, the likes of me, people like me; osate parlare così a un — mio, dare you speak like that to a man like me?; i — del Regno Unito, the peers of the United Kingdom; moglie di un —, peeress; dignità, ordine dei —, peerage; (with several prepositions forming *adv.* phrases): tenere i conti in —, to keep the accounts up to date; mettersi in — coi pagamenti, to pay off arrears; al — di, like; nero al — del carbone, black as coal; al — di lui sono tutti bestie, compared with him they are all fools; del —, equally, as well, likewise, also; egli conosce del — il latino, he knows Latin as well, he knows Latin too; levarsela del —, to be neither in nor out of pocket, to break even; *adv.* si levò dal luogo — —, he went away very slowly; *n.f.* portarsi alla —, to catch up, to get up to date; †uscirne del —, to get off scot free; *n.m.pl.* (naut.) — di guardia, port watch. -**i·a** *f.* peerage. -**imẹnte**, -**imẹnti** *adv.* likewise, similarly; also; smoothly. -**ipennata** *f.* (bot.) paripinnate. -**isil·labo** *adj.* (gramm.) parisyllabic.

pari passu *adv. phr.* (Lat., leg.) *pari passu*, on an equality, without preference.

pa·ria[1] *m. indecl.* pariah, outcast, untouchable.

pari·a[2] *f.* peerage.

Pa·ride *pr.n.m.* (myth.) Paris (the Trojan prince).

pariet-ale *adj.* (anat.) parietal; (bot.) placenta —, parietal placenta. -**a·ria** *f.* (bot.) see **paretaria**.

parific-are [A 2 s] *tr.* to equalize, to make equal; to put on an equal footing. -**amẹnto** *m.* making equal; recognizing as equal. -**ato** *part. adj.* equal; (of a school) recognized by the Ministry; scuola -ata, recognized school. -**aziọne** *f.* equalization, balancing.

†**pariforme** *adj.* equal, similar, matching.

Parig-i *pr.n.m.* (geog.) Paris; moda di —, Paris fashion; guanto di —, condom, french letter; punta di —, wire nail. -**ina** *f.* Parisian woman, Parisienne; (circus) woman tight-rope walker; (typ.) pearl (type-size, equiv. to five-point). -**ino** *adj.* Parisian; (text.) seta -ina, suprammonium silk; *n.m.* Parisian; young dandy; (numism.) old French coin, parisis, parisee, denier (worth a twelfth of a sou); (fig.) a very small amount.

par-i·glia *f.* pair (esp. of horses); couple; — di pistole, brace of pistols; render la —, to give tit for tat; (naut.) pair of heavy tackles used for hoisting in boats, etc. -**iglina** *f. dim.* nice little pair (of horses).

parimẹnte *adv.* See under **pari**.

pa·rio *adj.* Parian; marmo —, Parian marble.

par-ipennato *adj.*, -**isillabo** *m.* See under **pari**.

parità *f.* parity, equality; a — di condizioni, conditions being equal; (sport) dead heat; (comm.) parity; — di cambio, par of exchange; — di carico, if the load is the same.

parita·rio *adj.* (admin.) combined, joint; commissione paritaria, joint commission.

parkerizẓ-are [A I] *tr.* (metall.) to parkerize. (-**ato** *part. adj.*) -**aziọne** *f.* (metall.) parkerizing.

†**parla·gio** *m.* (hist.) place where Parliament met.

parlament-are[1] [A I] *intr.* (*aux.* avere) to discuss, to parley, to arrange terms; (joc.) -erò io con l'oste, I shall arrange with the landlord; (mil.) to parley; bandiera per —, flag of truce; †(naut.) to hail.

parlament-are² *adj.* parliamentary; *n.m.* parliamentarian. **-armente** *adv.* in parliamentary fashion. **-a·rio** *adj.* parliamentary; (naut.) bastimento -ario, vessel calling for conditions; *n.m.* parliamentarian; (mil.) emissary officer having powers to treat; (naut.) ship carrying a flag of truce or calling for terms; †truce. **-arismo** *m.* (neol.) parliamentary system; faults of the parliamentary system. **-arista** *m.*, *f.* advocate (supporter) of parliamentary government. **-atore** *m.* one who parleys, negotiator. (**-atrice** *f.*)

parlament-o *m.* Parliament; membro del —, member of Parliament; (hist.) il lungo —, the Long Parliament; far —, to meet for discussion, to deliberate; (mil.) site of meeting and the convention drawn up between belligerents seeking an armistice; (naut.) hailing; exchange of communications by voice usually aided by megaphone or loud hailer; chiamare a —, to call (a ship) within hailing distance; (hist.) — subalpino, Parliament of the Kingdom of Sardinia, 1848–60; †speech, talk, talking. **-ino** *m. dim.* (joc.) petty parliament.

parl-are [A 1] *intr.* (*aux.* avere) to talk, to speak; to discourse; to make a speech; il bambino comincia a —, the baby is beginning to talk; non finisce mai di —, he never stops talking; — pel naso, to talk through one's nose; — alla muta, to talk by signs, to use the deaf-and-dumb language; — per figura, to speak in metaphors; — tra i denti, — stretto, to mumble, to speak indistinctly; — fuor de' denti, to speak plain; — fra sè, to talk to oneself; — a bassa voce, to speak in a low voice; — forte, — ad alta voce, to speak loudly; — in punta di forchetta, to speak mincingly; (teleph.) con chi -o?, who is that speaking?; qui -a il direttore, this is the manager speaking; — bene di uno, to speak well of someone; — male di uno, to speak ill of someone; — per qualcuno, in favore di qualcuno, to speak for someone, on behalf of someone; — con uno, to talk to someone; ho bisogno di -arti a quattr'occhi, I want to have a private talk with you; io con te non ci -o, I have nothing (more) to say to you; — di bottega, to talk shop; — dell'India, to speak of India, to give a talk about India; -ò contro quella proposta, he spoke against, he made a speech opposing, that proposal; — dalla cattedra, to lecture; — dal pulpito, to preach; — di politica, to talk politics; nel libro dove Cicerone -a dell'amicizia, in the book in which Cicero speaks (writes) about friendship; il giornale oggi -a di te, there's something about you in the paper today; — di questo e di quello, — della pioggia e del bel tempo, — del più e del meno, to speak of this and that, to talk about various things; — a torto e a traverso, to speak foolishly; — a cuore aperto, to speak frankly; di che state -ando?, what are you talking about?; ha fatto molto — di sè, he has been much talked about; non ne -iamo più, let's say no more about it; non se ne deve più —, there must be no more talk about it; ciò -a da sè, that speaks for itself; i fatti -ano, the facts speak for themselves; il creato -a di Dio, Creation speaks of God; (mus.) to speak, to emit sound; quando suona il violino, lo fa —, when he plays the violin he makes it talk; — al cuore, to speak to the heart, to move; — agli occhi, to make a striking (visual) impression, to be striking; — al deserto, — al vuoto, — in aria, to speak to the winds, to waste one's breath; a chi -o?, am I wasting my breath?; to talk, to reveal secrets; testimone che non vuol —, witness that will not talk; lo faremo —, we will make him (induce him to) talk; o che! -o turco?, can't you understand me?; — coi morti, to converse with the dead, i.e. to read old books; *tr.* to speak; — italiano, to speak Italian; qui si -a inglese, English spoken (here); *rfl.* to talk to oneself; *recip. rfl.* to talk to each other; to converse; to correspond; to keep company; *n.m.* talk; way of speaking; speech; dialect; words; language; dialect; ci fu un gran — di ciò, there was much talk about it; — furbesco, thieves' lingo; il — è proprio dell'uomo, speech is a human characteristic; questo è un — ambiguo, those are ambiguous words; il bel —, fine language; il — toscano, Tuscan dialect (speech). **-a·bile** *adj.* speakable, pronounceable. **-achiaro** *m. indecl.* outspoken person. †**-acocco** *m.* a game played with dice. †**-agione** *m.* speech, speaking, way of speaking. **-ante** *part. adj.* speaking, talking; ben -ante, eloquent; fatti -anti, facts that speak for themselves; prova -ante, convincing proof; bambola -ante, talking doll; confetti -anti, sugar almonds with a motto; un ritratto -ante, a lifelike portrait; a speaking likeness; una copia -ante, an exact copy, a lifelike reproduction; *part. adj.* (mus.) quasi -ante, almost in a speaking-voice; sala -ante, room with a whispering gallery; †loquacious, eloquent. †**-antiere**, †**-antieri** *m.*

gossip, chatterer. **-antina** *f.* tongue; talkativeness, loquacity; avere una buona -antina, to have a glib tongue; il vino gli ha fatto venire una gran -antina, the wine has loosened his tongue, has made him very talkative. **-antino** *adj.* talkative. †**-anza** *f.* see parlatura. **-ardo** *adj. n.m.* see parlatore. †**-aresco** *adj.* (mus.) canto -aresco, recitative. **-ata** *f.* speech, talk; una lunga -ata, a long speech; way of speaking; dialect; lo riconobbi alla -ata, I recognized him by the way he spoke; -ata siciliana, Sicilian accent or way of speaking Italian. **-atina** *f.* scolding, talking-to. **-ato** *part. adj.* spoken; lingua -ata, spoken language (as opposed to written); (radio) giornale -ato, a programme of various news features, including interviews, discussions, brains trusts, etc.; nodo -ato, clove hitch; *n.m.* (cinem.) sound-track; †discourse, speech; †words; †parliament. **-atore** *m.* speaker; good talker; ready speaker; orator; talkative person. (**-atora**, **-atrice** *f.*) **-ato·rio** *m.* parlour (esp. in a convent or school). **-atura** *f.* way of speaking; speech. †**-e·vole** *adj.* talkative, loquacious; non -evole, inexpressible. (**-iera** *f.*) **-iere**, **-iero** *m.* speaker; talker; gossip, chatterer. (**-iera** *f.*) **-ottare** [A 1] *intr.* (*aux.* avere) to whisper, to murmur, to converse very quietly. **-ucchiare** [A 4] *intr.* (*aux.* avere), *tr.* to speak brokenly; -ucchiare una lingua, to have a smattering of a language.

†**parl-asi·a** *f.* see paralisi. †**-a·tico** *adj.* see paralitico.

parlato¹ *part. adj.*, *n.m.* See under parlare.

†**parlato²** *m.* See prelato.

†**parl-eṣi·a** *f.* see paralisi. †**-e·tico** *adj.* see paralitico.

Parm-a¹ *pr.n.f.* (geog.) Parma. **-ense** *adj.* of Parma; l'archivio -ense, the archives of Parma. **-igiano** *adj.* Parmesan, of Parma; (cul.) alla -igiana, cooked or served with butter and Parmesan cheese; *n.m.* native or inhabitant of Parma; Parmesan cheese. (**-igiana** *f.*)

parma² *f.* (Rom. antiq.) parma, small round shield.

Parmigianino *pr.n.m.* nickname of the painter, Mazzola of Parma (1503–40).

Parnaso *pr.n.m.* See parnasso.

parnas·sia *f.* (bot.) grass of Parnassus, *Parnassia palustris*.

parnassiano *adj.* (lit. hist.) relating to the French literary review *Le Parnasse contemporain*, published by C. Mendès and P. Richard; characteristic of, relating to, the Parnassian school of French poetry; *n.m.* Parnassian.

parnas·sico *adj.* of or relating to Parnassus or poetry.

parnas·sio *m.* (ent.) Parnassus butterfly, *Parnassius apollo*.

Parnass-o *pr.n.m.* (geog.; myth.) Mt Parnassus; (fig.) poetry; salire in —, to write poetry; il — italiano, Italian poets, Italian poetry; (paint.) Il Parnasso Italiano, a celebrated picture by Raphael in the Vatican. **-esco** *adj.* (*m.pl.* **-eschi**) relating to Mt Parnassus; poetic.

paro¹ *adj.* See pari.

paro² *m.* See paio.

Paro³ *pr.n.f.* (geog.) Paros.

parocchetto *m.* See parrochetto.

parocchi *m. indecl.* See paraocchi, under parare.

†**parocismo** *m.* See parossismo.

†**pa·roco** *m.* See parroco.

parod-i·a *f.* parody; (mus.) parody (i.e. piece of music to which new words have been adapted). **-iare** [A 4] *tr.* to parody. (**-iato** *part. adj.*) **-iatore** *m.*, **-ista** *m.* parodist.

paro·dico¹ *adj.* (math.) parodic.

paro·dico² *adj.* pertaining to a parody.

pa·rodo *m.* (Gk. lit.) parodos, parode; parodist.

†**parof·fia¹** *f.* region; inhabitants of the same region.

†**parof·fia²** *f.* beauty, majesty, splendour.

parol-a *f.* word; term; speech; doctrine; maxim; promise; avere la —, to be allowed to speak, to have the floor, to be speaking; muovere la —, to begin to speak; parole; non ho -e per esprimere la mia gratitudine, I have no words to express my gratitude; in una —, in a word, to sum up; in —, in question; è una —!, it's just a lot of talk, it doesn't mean anything; sono -e!, you don't mean it!; coniare -e, to coin words; giuoco di -e, pun, play upon words; -e incrociate, crossword puzzle; onesto nelle -e e nei fatti, honest in word and deed; belle -e, fair words, flattering speech; far —, to speak; non far —, to hold one's tongue; rompere la — in bocca a uno, to interrupt a person; porre le -e in bocca a uno, to put the words into someone's mouth, to tell one what to say; (leg.) — per —, word for word, *verbatim*, il presidente dà la — alla difesa, the Court calls upon the defence (C.C.P.); — di codice, code word; libertà di —, freedom of speech; rivolgere la

parol-a (*cont.*)

— a uno, to address someone; mi rivolse la — in inglese, he addressed me in English; perdere la —, to lose the use of one'e tongue, to be tongue-tied, to be (struck) speechless; ricòrdati le -e che t'ho detto, remember my words, mark my words; è un uomo di poche -e, he is a man of few words; ti voglio dire mezza —, I want to have a little word with you; uomo di —, a man of his word; mantenere la —, to keep one's word (promise); gli diedi la mia —, I gave him my word; essere di —, to be as good as one's word; — da vecchia, old wives' tale, tall stories;—d'onore word of honour; — d'onore, non dissi altro, upon my honour I said nothing else; venire a -e, to have words, to quarrel; ebbi delle -e con lui, I had words with him; passare dalle -e ai fatti, to proceed from words to blows; restituire la — ad uno, to release one from a promise; prendere, pigliare qualcuno in —, to take someone at his word; rimangiarsi le -e, to eat one's words; (rel.) le sette -e, the Seven Words of Christ on the Cross; dire (scrivere) una — per, to recommend, to put in a word in favour of; dire una — al vescovo, to put in a word with the bishop; — d'ordine, password, word; la — d'ordine è 'presto', 'sharp's the word'; — fuori d'uso, obsolete word; — per —, verbatim, word for word; tradurre a —, to translate literally; -e in rima, -e rimate, rhyme(s), verse, poetry; arte della —, oratory; — piana, word accented on the last syllable but one; — sdrucciola, word accented on the last syllable but two; — tronca, word accented on the last syllable; -e di colore oscuro, obscure words, words difficult to understand. **-ac·cia** *f. pejor.* bad word, coarse word, swear word. **-a·io** *m.* talkative person; wordy speaker; *adj.* wordy, long-winded; loquacious; prosy. **-ȩtta** *f. dim.* saying; quip, witty saying. **-iere** *m.* 'lyrics' writer, author of words of popular songs. **-ina** *f. dim.* kind word; brief mention; -ine dolci, honeyed words; **-ọne** *m.*, **-ọna** *f. augm.* emphatic word; long word; usava certe -one!, he used such big words!; bombastic speech. **-uc·cia** *f. dim.* little word. **-uzza** *f. dim.* whispering, few whispered words.

parole *excl.* (pron. as Fr.) (poker) 'parole' (said when a player having the right to bet forgoes the privilege, which then passes to the person on his left).

parom-a *f.* (naut. hist.) lift of a yard; (Taranto) strop on a block; hemp or grassrope used by ropemakers. **-ella** *f.* (naut.) grassline supporting a net. **-era** *f.* (naut., Ven.) painter. **-esi** *f.pl.* (naut.) mooring lines.

paronichi·a *f.* (med.) whitlow, paronychia; (bot.) herb.

paro·n-imo *m.* (gramm.) paronym. **-imi·a** *f.* (gramm.) paronymy. **-i·mico** *adj.* (gramm.) paronymous.

paronoma·ṣia *f.* (gramm.) paronomasia.

paropsi·a *f.* (med.) paropsis.

par·oressi·a *f.* (med.) parorexia, perversion of the appetite. **-oṣmi·a** *f.* (med.) parosmia, parosphresis.

paross-iṣmo *m.* (med.) paroxysm. **-i·stico** *adj.* (med.) paroxysmal.

parossi·tono *adj.*, *n.m.* paroxytone, accented on the last syllable but one.

paro·tico *adj.* (anat.) parotic, parotid.

paro·t-ide *f.* (anat.) parotid gland. **-ide·o** *adj.* (anat.) parotid, parotic. **-ite** *f.* (med.) parotiditis. the mumps.

†parpaglione *m.* butterfly; **†**(naut.) awning; additional sail.

parra *f.* (orn.) jacana, lily-trotter (family Jacanidae).

Parra·ṣi-a *pr.n.f.* (geog.; myth.) Parrhasia, in Arcady. **-o** *adj.* relating to Parrhasia; bosco -o, Arcadian grove, (lit. hist.) garden meeting-place of the Arcadian Academy on the Janiculum.

parresi·a *f.* freedom of speech, parrhesy.

parri-cida *m.* parricide; traitor, regicide; *adj.* parricidal; **†**see **parricidio**. **-cidiale** *adj.* parricidal. **-ci·dio** *m.* parricide (action, crime); (leg.) murder of father; murder of a parent; murder of an ascendant or descendant (C.P.).

parrochȩtt-o *m.* (orn.) parakeet; (naut.) mizzen topsail; — doppio, lower and upper mizzen topsail; — basso, inferiore, lower topsail; — superiore, — volante, upper topsail; albero di —, mizzen topmast; pennone di —, mizzen topsail yard. **†-iero** *m.* (naut.) mizzen topman.

parro·c-chia *f.* (eccl.) parish; parish church; (locally) district administered by a rural dean; †diocese. **-chiale** *adj.* parochial; parish; chiesa -chiale, parish church; libri -chiali, parish register(s); †(eccl.) prete -chiale, parish priest. **-chialmȩnte** *adv.* parochially. **-chiano** *m.* parishioner; †(eccl.) parish priest.

par·roco *m.* parish priest.

---

†parrof·fia *f.* See **paroffia**.

parruc-ca *f.* wig; periwig; long hair; (fig.) scolding, wigging; (pop.) binge. **-chȩtto** *m.* (bot.) tulip, *Tulipa*; (orn.) see **parrocchetto**. **-chiere** *m.* hairdresser, barber; wig-maker. **-chino** *m. dim.* half-wig, transformation, toupée. **-cone** *m. augm.* large wig; (fig.) reactionary, old fogey; big-wig.

parsimo·nia *f.* frugality; parsimony; con —, sparingly; — di parole, taciturnity.

parso *part.* of **parere**, q.v.

partac·cia *f. pȩior.* See under **parte**.

part-e *f.* **1.** Part; le -i del corpo umano, the parts of the human body; — d'abbasso, backside; le -i del discorso, the parts of speech; le cinque -i del mondo, the five continents; una gran — di questo è vero, a great part of this is true; la maggior — di loro non ritornò, most of them did not return; per la maggior —, for the most part; in —, in part, partly; essi sono in — arrivati, some of them have come; — per —, in detail, point by point, item by item; di ricambio, spare parts; divise il libro in tre —, he divided the book into three parts (sections). **2.** Portion, share; ciascuno ebbe la sua —, each had his share; la — del leone, the lion's share; assumere la propria — di responsabilità, to share the responsibility; egli non ebbe nessuna — in quell'affare, he had no hand (he took no part) in that business; avere, prendere —, to participate, to take part, to share; voglio prendere — con voi all'impresa, I shall share with you in the undertaking; non volevo prender — alla discussione, I did not want to take part in the discussion; essere arte e — in una cosa, to be art and part in something, i.e. to take a full share, to be deeply concerned in something. **3.** (Leg.) Party; — attrice in causa, applicant; plaintiff (C.C.P.); — avversaria, the other side; — civile, civil party, i.e. party suing in criminal proceedings for damages or other relief under civil law (C.C.P.); — contraente, contracting party; — danneggiata, — lesa, injured party; — soccombente, — vittoriosa in giudizio, unsuccessful, winning, party in the action; — processuale, person of full legal capacity with *locus standi* (C.C.P.); — in causa, party to the action; per ambo le -i, for both sides. **4.** Part, side, quarter; egli stette dalla nostra —, he sided with us; uno per —, one for each side; mettere da —, to lay aside, to put by; mettere da — per qualcuno, to set aside for someone; mettere da — per la vecchiaia, to save for one's old age, to put by for a rainy day; lo tirai da una —, I took him aside; d'altra —, on the other side, on the other hand, besides; da una —,...dall'altra —, on the one hand,...on the other; il servizio è a —, service is extra; da una — all'altra, from side to side, from end to end, through; lo passarono da — a —, they pierced him through; (sport) — aperta, open side; — chiusa, blind side (rugby); da un anno a questa — non c'eravamo più veduti, we had not seen each other for a whole year; tenetevi da questa — della strada, keep on this side of the road; dall'altra —, on the other side; per — di madre, on his mother's side; da ambe (ambo) le -i, on both sides. **5.** District, region, part; io sono uno sconosciuto da queste -i, I am a stranger in these parts; non ero mai stato da queste -i, I had never been in this district; il suo nome è celebre in ogni —, his name is famous everywhere (in all regions); in qualche altra —, somewhere else; da che — vieni?, where do you come from?, what district do you come from?, from which direction do you come?; sapere da buona —, to know on good authority. **6.** (Mus.) Part, voice, melodic line; operatic role; singer (of an operatic role); -i estreme, outer parts; -i inferiori, lower parts; -i di mezzo, inner parts; -i superiori, upper parts; contrappunto a otto -i reali, counterpoint in eight real parts; -i buffe, singers of comic parts; colla —, direction to an accompanist to follow the free tempo of a soloist; (theatr.) part; ha fatto la — di Shylock, he has played (the part of) Shylock; fa le -i del caratterista, he plays character parts; actor (actress); le prime -i, the leading actors; (fig.) part, role; ha fatto una — nobile, he has played a noble part; ha fatto una — odiosa, he had an odious role. **7.** In Prepositional Phrases: egli prese la cosa in buona —, he took it in good part; prende tutto in mala —, he takes everything amiss; mettere, fare, dare uno a — di una cosa, to inform someone of something; non ero a — della faccenda, I was not acquainted with (I did not know anything about) the matter; ditegli da — mia che..., tell him from me that...; salutatelo da — mia, give him my kind regards, remember me to him; per — mia, as far as I am concerned; è molto gentile da — sua, it is very kind

part-e (*cont.*)

of him; a —, apart, aside; excepted; scherzi a —, joking apart; è un caso a —, it is a particular case, it is exceptional. **8.** (POL., ETC.) PARTY, faction; la — guelfa, the Guelph faction; uomo di —, party man, *or* partisan, one who is biased. **-ac·cia** *f. pejor.* shameful action; hostile reception; reproof; mi fece una -accia, he behaved badly towards me, he scolded me; (theatr.) badly written part, unsatisfactory role. **-emmezza** *f.* (naut.) shareholding by members of the crew in lieu of pay; †extra ration earned on account of special heavy duties; essere alla —, to serve on the basis of sharing profits from the catch, etc. **-icella** *f. dim.* small portion, particle; (gramm.) particle, suffix, conjunction, preposition; article; paragraph; (scient.) particle; -icella alfa, alpha particle; (leg.)—catastale, small parcel of land subject to land-tax.

partecip-are [A I s] *intr.* (*aux.* avere; *prep.* a) to participate, to partake, to take part; to share; to attend, to be present; — al dolore di uno, to share someone's sorrow, to condole with someone, to write a letter of condolence to someone, *or* to insert a notice in the obituary column of a newspaper; noi non -ammo al conflitto, we took no part in the conflict; — ai lavori di una commissione, to sit on a committee; non -ai all'adunanza, I did not attend the meeting; (*prep.* di) — di una cosa, to have something (of the nature) of a thing; †to converse, to mingle (with); *tr.* to announce, to notify; to communicate, to impart; to bestow, to grant; — una cosa ad una persona, to acquaint a person with something; Dio -a a tutti la sua grazia, God bestows his grace upon all. **-a·bile** *adj.* obtainable; communicable. **-amento** *m.* participating; participation. **-ante** *part. adj.* present, attending; partaking; sharing; bestowing, granting; non -ante al voto, non-voting; (eccl.) protonotari -anti, protonotaries *de numero participantium* (members of the highest college of prelates in the Roman Curia); *n.m.* participant, one taking part; partaker, sharer; person present; accomplice. **-anza** *f.* partaking; participation; (leg.) -anza agraria, a form of collective farm. **-ativo** *adj.* suitable for sharing; informative, notifying. (**-ato** *part. adj.*) **-atore** *m.* partaker, informant; announcer. (**-atrice** *f.*) **-azione** *f.* participation; sharing; announcement, notification; -azione di nozze, announcement of a wedding; (leg.) notification; participation; sharing of profit and loss; -azione ai difensori, notification of counsel (C.P.P.); -azione a banda armata, taking part in armed band; -azione a prestiti a favore del nemico, participation in loans for benefit of enemy (C.P.); associazione in -azione, association by way of participation (C.C.); †(mus.) temperament.

parte·cipe *adj.* participating, partaking, sharing; essere — di, to share; acquainted, informed; far — di, to acquaint with, to inform of; (leg.) participant; participating; assistenza ai partecipi di cospirazione, aid to those taking part in conspiracy (C.P.); A rende — B degli utili, A grants B share of profits (C.C.).

parteggi-are [A 3 c] *intr.* (*aux.* avere) to take sides; — per, to side with, to take the side of, to support. **-amento** *m.* taking sides. **-ante** *part. adj.* taking sides, supporting. **-atore** *m.* one who takes sides; partisan; factious person. (**-atrice** *f.*)

partemmezza *f.* See under **parte**.

†**partenere** *vb.* and derivs. See **appartenere**.

parte·n-io *m.* (bot.) feverfew, *Chrysanthemum parthenium*. **-ocarpi·a** *f.* (bot.) parthenocarpy, apomixis, parthenogenesis. **-oge·nesi** *f.* (biol.; myth.) parthenogenesis.

Partenone *pr.n.m.* (Gk. antiq.; archit.) Parthenon; (art) i marmi del —, (in England) the Elgin marbles.

Parte·nop-e *pr.n.f.* (class. myth.) Parthenope, esp. the siren associated with Naples; ancient name, sometimes still used, for Naples. **-e·o** *adj.* (poet.; pol.) Parthenopean, Neapolitan; La Repubblica -ea (*or* la Partenopea), the Neapolitan Republic, set up by the French in 1799.

partente *part.* of **partire**, q.v.; *adj.* departing, leaving, starting; *n.m.* person leaving; quanti sono i partenti con questo treno?, how many (passengers) are leaving by this train?; *pl.* the starters (horse-racing).

partenza *f.* departure; leaving; start(ing), setting out; punto di —, starting point, place of departure; (of ships) sailing; (rlwy.) in — per, leaving for; (naut.) departure, sailing; stare in —, essere in stato di —, to be ready to sail, to be about to sail; manifesto di —, clearance papers; preparativi per la —, stations for getting under way; segnale di —, starting gun, Blue Peter (Letter P of alphabetical code); (horse-racing) start; passing away, death.

†**part-e·vole** *adj.*, †**-i·bile** *adj.* divisible separable.

parterre *m. indecl.* (pron. as Fr.) flower-garden; (theatr.) pit.

partiac·qua *f.* (geog.) watershed.

particella *f. dim.* See under **parte**.

partici·p-io *m.* (gramm.) participle. **-ale** *adj.* (gramm.) participial; clausola -ale, participial clause.

pa·rtico *adj.* (class. antiq.) Parthian; Parthicus (title of general victorious in Parthia, e.g. the Emperor Trajan).

parti·cola *f.* (liturg.) particle, altar-bread, host; †(gramm.) particle; †part of an utterance, part of a construction.

particolar-e *adj.* particular; peculiar; especial, special; private; udienza —, private audience; per nessuna ragione —, for no particular reason; egli aveva ragioni -i, he had private reasons; un saluto —, a special greeting; adunanza —, special meeting; case -i, private houses; un sapore —, a distinctive flavour; (comm.) conti -i, personal accounts; (geog.) carte -i, inset, detailed maps; *n.m.* particular; detail; private individual, person; reproduction of part of a work of art; alcuni -i molto interessanti, some very interesting details; in —, in particular, particularly; su questo —, on this point; i beni dei -i, property in private ownership. **-mente** *adv.* particularly; in particular; in detail; †on one side; †apart. **-eggiamento** *m.* particularization. **-eggiare** [A 3 c] *intr.* (*aux.* avere) to particularize, to recount or describe in minute detail; *rfl.* to stand out, to be distinguished. **-eggiato** *part. adj.* detailed, particularized; circumstantial. **-ismo** *m.* particularism; (neol.) favouritism, partiality. **-ista** *m.* (theol.) Particularist, one who holds that Christ did not die for all men. **-ità** *f.* peculiarity; particular, detail; partiality. **-izzare** [A I] *tr.* to particularize, to describe in detail. **-izzato** *part. adj.* particularized, described in detail. **-izzazione** *f.* particularization, detailing.

partigian-o *adj.* partisan, partial; factious; spirito —, party spirit; legge -a, partial (unfair) law; *n.m.* partisan, follower, supporter; guerrilla or resistance fighter; partial judge. **-amente** *adv.* factiously; partially, unfairly. **-a** *f.* (mil. hist.) partisan. **-ello** *adj.*, *n.m. dim.* (derog.) partisan. **-eri·a** *f.* partisanship, partiality; factious action. **-esco** *adj.* (*m.pl.* -eschi) (derog.) partisan, factious. **-etta** *f.* (mil. hist.) half pike. **-etto** *m. dim.* young partisan; weak supporter. **-iere** *m.* (naut. hist.) pikeman in a galley; slave owner. **-one** *m.* (mil. hist.) halberd, heavy pike.

part-ire[1] [D I] *tr.* to divide; to separate; to share (out); to part with; — la famiglia, to bring discord into the family; — l'occhio da un oggetto, to take one's eye off a thing. **-i·bile**, †**-e·vole** *adj.* divisible, separable. †**-igione** *f.* division; discord, disunion. **-imento** *m.* division; separation; (of the hair) parting; (archit.) compartment; (paint.) section; gradation of colours; (mus.) counterpoint exercise written over a figured bass to facilitate the study of continuo-playing; (Provençal lit.) *jeu parti*. **-ita** *f.* panel, leaf (of a door, of the lid of a chest, etc.); shutter (of a window); una tavola con le -ite aperte, a folding table with the leaves opened out; (mil.) party, small group of soldiers; section employed on specific duty, reconnaissance, etc.; -ita d'onore, duel; -ita d'armi, duel (not for honour); game (of cards, etc.), round, rubber; fare una -ita, to make a four (at cards); fare -ita, to win; una — di calcio, a game of football; -ita di piacere, excursion, outing, party; essere della -ita, to be one of the party; (mus.) partita, suite; (comm.) lot, consignment; -ita semplice, single entry; -ita doppia, double entry; -ita scoperta, overdrawn account; (leg.) -ite di giro, clearing transactions (C.C.); (finan.) parcel; share; †part, division; †livery. **-itante** *part. adj.*, *n.m.* partisan, party member. **-itanza** *f.* (leg.) form of collective agricultural tenancy involving payment of rent in kind. **-ita·rio** *m.* (book-keeping) ledger. **-i·tico** *adj.* related to party politics. **-itivo** *adj.* (gramm.) partitive. **-ito** *part. adj.* divided, separated; parted (of hair, etc.); (bot.) foglia -ita, deeply divided leaf; (herald.) per pale; (Provençal lit.) giuoco -ito, *jeu parti, juoc partitz*, poem of debate; *n.m.* choice, alternative; prendere -ito, to take sides; prendere -ito pro o contro, to side with or against; prendere un -ito, to come to a decision, to make up one's mind; per -ito preso, having made up one's mind, of set purpose; mettere il cervello a -ito, to settle down, to become reasonable; (mil.) side; (pol.) party, il -ito del lavoro, the Labour party; (comm.) terms; (fig.) non accetto a nessun -ito, I will not accept on any terms, I won't do it at any price; (marriage) match, partner; egli è un buon -ito, he is very eligible as a husband, it would be a suitable match; mandare a -ito una cosa, to put a matter to the vote; advantage, profit, benefit; cercare di trarre

part-ire (*cont.*)
-ito da tutto, to try to turn everything to account; course, purpose, resolve; non sapeva a che -ito appigliarsi, he could not make up his mind to anything; tu t'inganni a -ito, you are utterly mistaken; situation, condition; mal -ito, sorry plight, predicament; ridursi a mal -ito, to get into a mess (into an awkward situation); all'estremo -ito, in desperate straits; femmina di -ito, prostitute; odds (in a game). **-itamente** *adv.* separately, distinctly; point by point. **-itone** *m. augm.* (marriage) excellent match; (pol.) very strong party. **-itore** *m.* distribution, divider; (math.) divisor; (hydr. eng.) divisor; (electr.) -itore di tensione, voltage divider, potentiometer; (photog.) -itore ottico, beam splitter. **-itura** *f.* (mus.) score, full score; mettere in -itura, to score. **-iturina** *f.* (mus.) miniature score. **-izione** *f.* partition; division; (mus.) groundwork, bearings, scale (in tuning keyboard instruments).

part-ire² [D 2] *intr.* (*aux.* essere) to go away, to depart, to leave; to set out; to start; to begin; (of a ship) to sail; lasciar — un colpo da un fucile, to fire a gun; le lettere che -ono, out-going letters; a — da domani, beginning, reckoning, from tomorrow; (fig.) — da, to depart from, to start from, to originate in, to rise from; un sospiro che -e dal cuore, a sigh from the heart; *rfl.* to leave, to depart; -irsi da, to part with, from, to give up, to depart from; to abstain, to cease; -irsi di questa vita, to depart this life, to die. **-ita** *f.* departure, ultima -ita, final parting, i.e. death. **-ito** *part. adj.* departed, gone away.

parti·tico *adj.* See under **partire¹**.

part-o¹ *m.* birth, childbirth; delivery; new-born baby; morire in (di) —, to die in childbirth; — gemino, double birth, birth of twins; essere di —, to be confined, to be in childbed; — laborioso, difficult birth; doglie del —, labour pains, pangs of childbirth; la freccia del —, the last severe pains of labour (a play upon words: 'the Parthian shot', see **parto²**); (fig.) parturition, creation, work; fruit, production, output (artistic or literary); — della fantasia, fruit of the imagination, work of fancy, fiction, fib; †foetus; †embryo; †gift presented to a mother after a birth; †laying of eggs; †mettere al —, to breed from. **-oriente** *adj.* parturient; in labour; *n.f.* woman in labour; ricovero per le -orienti, maternity home. **-orimento** *m.* delivery, birth, confinement. **-orire** [D 2] *tr.* to bear, to bring forth, to give birth to; to be delivered of; (of animals) to drop, to foal, to litter; (fig.) to produce, to originate, to cause, to give rise to; *intr.* (*aux.* avere) to be delivered; to be in labour. **-orito** *part. adj.* born, brought forth; (fig.) caused, originated. **†-urire** *vb.* and derivs. see **partorire**.

parto² *adj.*, *n.m.* Parthian; la freccia del —, the Parthian shot.

†partuta *f.* part, division; condition, plight.

paru·lide *f.* (med.) parulis.

†parut-a *f.* semblance, aspect, appearance; avere —, to become visible; fare —, to pretend. **†-o** *part.* of **parere**, q.v.

parven-te *adj.* seeming, apparent; visible; †*n.m.* appearance; opinion, view. **-za** *f.* appearance, aspect; apparition; (false) show, pretence.

parvità *f.* small amount, paucity; (moral theol.) — di materia, *parvitas materiae*.

†parv-o *adj.* small; slight, insignificant. **†-ezza** *f.* small amount, paucity. **†-ificare** *tr.* to reduce in size, to make small. **†-ificenza** *f.* paucity; meanness. **†-i·fico** *adj.* mean-spirited, ungenerous.

pa·rvol-o *adj.* (poet.) little, young; *n.m.* child, baby. **†-eggiare** *intr.* to behave like a child. **-etto** *adj.*, *m. dim.*, **-ino** *adj.*, *m. dim.* (poet.) tiny (babe).

†parvulità *f.* childhood; youth.

parzial-e *adj.* partial; incomplete; unfair, biased, one-sided; elezione —, by-election. **-mente** *adv.* partially, in part, partly; unfairly. **-eggiare** [A 3 c] *intr.* (*aux.* avere) to be partial, biased, unfair; to show favouritism. **-ità** *f.* partiality, favouritism; †faction. **-izzare** [A 1] *tr.* (techn.) to close, to shut down, to choke. **-izzatore** *m.* (eng.; motor.) shutter.

†parzion-a·bile *adj.* sharing, participating; involved, implicated; *n.m.* participant. **†-ale** *adj.* partial, biased; *n.m.* partisan, supporter; participant, sharer; essere fatto -ale di, to be made a party to. **†-evole** *adj.* see **parzionabile**. **†-iere** *adj.* participating, sharing.

†pascale *adj.* See **pasquale**, under **pasqua**.

pa·sc-ere [B 1 7] *intr.* (*aux.* avere) to graze; to pasture; *tr.* (of animals) to browse on, to feed on; (fig.) to eat; to feed; to nourish (also fig.); *tr.* to lead to pasture, to put out to grass; — la mente, to nourish the mind, to educate the mind; — la mola del mulino, to feed the press with olives; — di parole, — di erba trastulla, to feed with words or idle promises; — di promesse, to put off with promises; *rfl.* (*prep.* di) to feed (on); (fig.) -ersi d'illusioni, to cherish illusions; -ersi di vane speranze, to live on false hopes; -ersi di ragionamenti, to delight in argument. **-ente** *part. adj.* grazing, at pasture. **†-imento** *m.* grazing, feeding; pasture, food. **-iona** *f.* rich pasture, good grazing; meadow after the grass has been cut; (fig.) plenty, abundant food; prosperity. (**-itore** *m.* **-itrice** *f.*) **-iuto** *part. adj.* ben -iuto, well-fed, plump; così grasso e -iuto!, so sleek and fat!; (fig.) satisfied, complacent.

pasci-à *m. indecl.* pasha; (fig.) fare il —, stare come un —, to live like a lord. **-alato** *m.* pashalic, office, jurisdiction of a pasha.

pasciuli *m.* patchouli.

pasco *m.* see **pascolo**; Monte dei Paschi, name of a savings bank and building society in Siena.

pas·col-o, pasco *m.* pasture, meadow, grass; (leg.) pasturage; — abusivo, unlawful pasturage (C.C.); diritto di —, commoners' right of pasture (C.C.); (geog.) pasture-land; (fig.) food, nourishment; dare un segreto in — al pubblico, to make a secret a matter for general gossip; dare — alla maldicenza, to give occasion for scandal, to encourage gossip. **†-ante** *part. adj.* grazing. **-are** [A 1 5] *intr.* (*aux.* avere) to graze; to pasture; (fig.) -are di speranze, to feed on hope; *rfl.* (*prep.* a) (fig.) to revel in. **-ato** *adj.* (of land) good for grazing.

†pascore *m.* spring.

†pasm-o *m.* spasm; fainting fit. **†-are** *intr.* to faint. **†-asone** *m.* spasm; fainting fit; convulsion.

Pasqu-a *pr.n.f.* Easter; — degli Ebrei, Passover; — di rose, Whitsunday, Pentecost; — dei morti, All Souls' Day, 2 November; (hist.) Pasque veronesi, the massacre of French troops in Verona, 17 March 1797; (geog.) Isola della —, Easter Island; prender la —, to go to one's Easter duties, to make one's Easter communion; far (la) — in famiglia, to keep Easter, to spend Eastertide with one's own family; (fig.) far —, to make merry, to celebrate; contento come una —, as merry as a grig, as happy as a sand-boy; la — è venuta in domenica, it has happened just at the right time; †any day of religious festival; †— di Natale, Christmas; †non venire che per le -e, to go only on rare occasions. **-ale** *adj.* pertaining to Easter; Easter; agnello -ale, paschal lamb; (eccl.) precetto -ale, Easter duties. **-alino** *m.* (eccl.; joc.) parishioner who never comes to the sacraments except at Easter, 'Easter lamb'; *pl.* (eccl. hist.) Paschalites (Franciscan group, 1541–83). **-are** [A 6] *intr.* (*aux.* avere) to keep Easter, to celebrate Easter. **†-ata** *f.* day of solemnity, feast day. **†-eggiare** *intr.* to celebrate Easter.

Pasquin-o *pr.n.m.* name given to a celebrated antique statue in Rome (to which lampoons used to be affixed). **-are** [A 1] *tr.* to lampoon. **-ata** *f.* lampoon, pasquinade.

†passa *f.* (naut.) a short fathom (about 5 ft.); cf. **passo¹**.

passa·bil-e *adj.* passable, tolerable; fair, fairly good, not bad. **-mente** *adv.* passably, tolerably; rather well.

passaca·glia *f.* (mus.) passacaglia.

passa-cavallo *m.* (naut.) sluggish coasting craft used in the Levant under oars or sail. **-cavo** *m.* (naut.; aeron.; eng.) chock, fairlead.

passacore *m.* very sharp dagger.

passafili *m. indecl.* (text.) guiding slit.

†passa-gallo, -ga·glio *m.* (mus.) see **passacaglia**; guitarist's introduction to the verse of a popular song.

passag·g-io *m.* passing, passage; crossing; transit; transition; essere di —, to be passing through; (fig.) di —, in passing; far —, to pass, to proceed; uccelli di —, birds of passage; passing away, death; passage, extract, quotation; passage, way; corridor; gangway; — sotterraneo, subway; — pedonale, pedestrian crossing; thoroughfare; traffic; impedire il — della strada, to block the flow of traffic; lift; chiedere un —, to ask for a lift (in a car); — a livello, level-crossing; — tracciato da chiodi, studded crossing (for pedestrians); vietato il —, no thoroughfare; — interdetto, no entry; (leg.) right of way; — coattivo, right of way of necessity (C.C.); — in giudicato, point in legal procedure at which judgement becomes final (C.C.P.); passage money, fare (by ship); transit duty (customs); (astron.) transit conjunction; — al meridiano, meridian passage; (naut.) voyage; charter; crossing; — dell'equatore, crossing the line; (hist.) Crusade; — oltremare, passage to the Holy Land by Crusaders; (eccl. hist.)

passagg-io (*cont.*)

indulgenze per il —, Crusade indulgences; (geog.) — dei Dardanelli, (Strait of) the Dardanelles; — del nordest, North-east Passage; — del nordovest, North-west Passage; (eng.) — d'ispezione, manhole; (cinem.) velocità di —, film speed; (schol.) promotion; (scient.) transition; (soccer, rugby) pass; (rugby) — rovesciato, reverse pass; (mus.) passage; run; dissonanza di —, passing dissonance; nota di —, passing note. **-etto** *m. dim.* of **passaggio**, q.v.; small passage, hall; (mus.) short phrase executed in one breath, or in one bow. †**-iare** *intr.* (mus.) to sing passages.

passaiola *f.* stepping-stone.

passaman-o *m.* passing from hand to hand; lace trimming; braid. **-a·io** *m.* (text.) trimming manufacturer. **-eri·a** *f.* lace trimming articles, shop, or factory; (text.) trimming.

†**passamento** *m.* passing; passage; step; crossing; death; superiority.

passamezzo, passa e mezzo, passemezzo *m.* (mus.) Passamezzo, passymeasure, dance usually composed over a conventional ground bass.

passamontagna *m. indecl.* hood; woollen cap; Balaclava helmet.

passante *part.* of **passare**, q.v.; *adj.* passing; easily digestible; piercing; *n.m.* passer-by; pedestrian; stiletto; guard or keeper through which the end of a strap is passed.

passa-palle *m. indecl.* (mil.) bore-gauge. **-parola** *m. indecl.* (naut.) passing the word to inform the ship's company (usually a long message). **-piatti** *m. indecl.* serving-hatch. **-piede** *m.* (mus.) passepied, paspy.

passaporto *m.* passport; — marittimo, ship's passport; — collettivo, permit entitling a group of tourists to enter a foreign country without carrying individual passports.

pass-are [A I] *intr.* (*aux.* essere). **1.** To PASS; to pass through; to pass by; -a di qui, come this way; — da un luogo, to pass by or through a place; -erò da lui domani, I shall call at his place tomorrow; tutto -a, all things pass away; to pass over; to pass in; to pass along; to pass on; -a via!, go away!; merce che non può — in Italia, goods not allowed (to pass) into Italy; lascia — della dogana, ship's clearance inwards; to pass away, to die; il Tevere -a attraverso Roma, the Tiber flows through Rome; — sotto il ponte, to flow, to sail, etc. under the bridge; — per la mente a uno, to occur to one, to come to one's mind; un'idea mi -ò per la mente, an idea crossed my mind; — di mente, to be forgotten, to slip one's memory. **2.** To OCCUR, to happen, to come to pass; to elapse; che è -ato?, what happened?; trattative che -ano fra le parti, negotiations taking place between the parties; to come into, or go out of, fashion; la moda -a presto, fashion changes quickly; oggi è -ato in uso di dire male delle cose nostre, nowadays it has become a habit to run down our products. **3.** — a un esame, to pass (in) an examination; (schol.) — ad un'altra classe, to be promoted, to be moved up; — in seconde nozze, to marry again, to be married for the second time. **4.** To EXIST, to be; -a molta differenza, there is a great difference; (provb.) tra il dire e il fare -a il mare, it's easy enough to talk, *or* there's many a slip twixt the cup and the lip; — per, to be considered, to pass for; -a per un ragazzo intelligente, he is considered an intelligent boy. **5.** To PASS OVER, to pass off, to subside; l'ira gli è -ata, his anger has subsided; il temporale è -ato, the storm is over; la pioggia è -ata, the rain has stopped; il dolore è -ato, the pain has ceased. **6.** (ENG.) calibro -a, go gauge; calibro non -a, no-go gauge. **7.** (LEG.) la sentenza -a in giudicato, judgement becomes final (C.C.P.).

tr. **1.** To PASS, to surpass, to beat; to overtake; — oltre, to overrule; to pass, to spend (time); — l'inverno, to spend the winter; — la vita a lavorare, to spend one's life working; to cross, to pass over; — un fiume a nuoto, to swim across a river; il barcaiuolo lo -ò all'altra riva, the boatman ferried him across to the other bank; — il Rubicone, to cross the Rubicon. **2.** To PASS, to hand; to transfer; to put; gli -a mille lire al mese, he gives him a thousand lire a month; volete -armi il pane?, will you pass me the bread?; lo -ai in cantina, I put it in the cellar; (comm.) — al libro mastro, to post in ledger. **3.** -arla male, to have a bad time, to run into trouble; ne ho -ate tante, I have endured so many troubles; la -ai liscia, I got off scot free; ti faccio — un guaio, I am causing you a lot of trouble; (S. Ital.) ho -ato un guaio, I had had a lot of trouble. **4.** To EXCEED, to overstep, to go beyond; il vostro bagaglio -a il peso, your luggage is overweight; -a il chilogramma, it is (weighs) more than a kilogram;

10 libbre e -a, ten pounds and over; — i limiti del giusto, to go beyond what is right. **5.** To PIERCE, to transfix; con un colpo di spada gli -ò il petto, he pierced his breast with a sword thrust; (fig.) to cut to the quick, to wound; mi -a il cuore di doverlo mandar via, it wrings my heart to have to send him away. **6.** To PUT THROUGH, to pass into; — il filo per la cruna dell'ago, to put the thread through the eye of the needle, to thread the needle; to filter, to sift, to sieve, to strain; — le acque, to take the waters (cure of mineral waters); — per le armi, to execute by shooting; — a fil di spada, to put to the sword; — in rivista, to review (troops); dobbiamo — la cosa sotto silenzio, we must pass over it in silence; — a penna, to ink in; *rfl.* (*prep.* di) di without, to abstain (from), to dispense (with); (*dat.* of *prn.* 'si') -arsela bene, to get on well; to be well off; -arsela allegramente, to enjoy oneself.

passarino *m.* (naut.) seizing.

passat-a *f.* passage (action of passing); far le -e innanzi a una casa, to walk up and down in front of a house; look, glance; devo dare una — alla lezione, I must look over my lesson; volete dare una — a questi conti, per favore, will you look through these accounts, please?; dare una — a un libro, to glance through a book; una — di pioggia, a passing shower; a stroke or touch (of a pen or any tool); (bldg.) doorway; (eng.) cut (on a lathe); (mil.) penetrating power of a projectile; (naut.) turn, each of the turns of a rope round a bollard, etc., *or* of a seizing round a rope; trot (of a horse); (agric.) ridge, strip; (cul.) mash, purée; una — di patate, mashed potatoes; (mus.) link, bridge-passage, modulation; scolding; outburst; di —, in passing; di tutta —, completely, at any rate, always. **-ina** *f.* a slight application, a touch; brief glance; slight shower. **-ini** *m.pl.* (cul. Romagna) strings of grated bread and cheese, bound with egg and eaten in soup.

passatello *adj. dim.* See under **passato**.

passatempo *m.* pastime, amusement; game; hobby.

passat-o *part.* of **passare**, q.v.; *adj.* past, gone by; faded; over; l'anno —, last year; una bellezza -a, a faded beauty; frutta -a, overripe fruit; (cul.) carne -a, overdone meat; (gramm.) tempo —, past tense; *n.m.* past; time gone by; in —, in past times; nel —, formerly, in the past; come in —, as before; una donna che ha un —, a woman with a past; mettiamo una pietra sopra il —, let bygones be bygones; (gramm.) past tense; — prossimo, present perfect, perfect tense; ancestor, predecessor. **-ello** *adj.* elderly, getting on in years; overblown; fading. **-ista** *m.* (art) traditionalist; reactionary.

passatoia *f.* strip of carpet, runner; stair-carpet.

passatoio¹ *n.m.* foot-bridge; stepping-stone; stile; †(mil.) missile.

passatoio² *adj.* easy to walk on; easy to pass, digestible.

passatore *m.* traveller, passenger; ferryman; transgressor; Il Passatore, nickname of a famous bandit of Romagna; seafarer; — di mare, overseas traveller; †(naut.) bargee using a punt-pole; †(mil.) missile.

passatura *f.* darn; darning.

passavanti *m. indecl.* (naut.) flying bridge; fore and aft gangway; †provisional ship's papers; (theatr.) free pass.

passavi·a *m.* flying bridge.

Passa·via *pr.n.f.* (geog.) Passau.

passavivande *m. indecl.* service-hatch.

passavolante *m.* (mil. hist.) long-range culverin; dummy gun; raider.

passegger-o *adj.* transient, passing, fleeting; (mil.) truppe -e, transit troops; fortificazione -a, temporary defence; *n.m.* passenger; traveller; †ferryman. **-a** *f.* female passenger; (naut.) passenger ship.

passeggi-are [A 3 c] *intr.* (*aux.* avere) to walk, to take a walk, to go for a walk; — a cavallo, to ride, to go for a ride; — in carrozza, to go for a drive, to drive; (mus.) to perform ornaments; *tr.* to walk, ride or drive through; -ò tutto il giardino, he walked all round the garden; — un cavallo, to walk a horse; to take out (for a walk, ride or some amusement); to make fun of; (mus.) to ornament. **-amento** *m.* walk; ride. **-ata** *f.* walk; fare una -ata, to go for a walk; drive, ride; -ata a cavallo, ride on horseback; excursion; promenade, wide road; (mil.) -ata militare, route march; (colloq.) a 'walk-over'. **-ato** *part. adj.* traversed (in several directions); valle -ata dal fiume, valley traversed by the winding river; cavallo -ato, led horse; (mus.) ornamented. **-atore** *m.* walker; person out for a walk. **-atrice** *f.* street-walker; girl who waits to be picked up by men in cars.

passeggier-o, -e *adj., n.m.* See **passeggero**.

passeggio *m.* walk; drive; walking; promenade, public walk; sono stato a —, I have been out for a walk; (mus.) ornamentation; ornament.

passemezzo *m.* (mus.). See **passamezzo**.

passe-partout *m. indecl.* (pron. as Fr.) pass-key, master-key; *passe-partout* picture frame.

pas·ser-a *f.* (orn.) sparrow, esp. the Italian sparrow, *Passer italiae*; — di padule, reed bunting, *Emberiza schoeniclus*; — lagia, rock sparrow, *Petronia petronia*; — mattugia, tree sparrow, *Passer montanus*; — oltremontana, house sparrow, *P. domesticus*; — sarda, Spanish sparrow, *P. hispaniolensis*; — scopaiola, hedge sparrow, *Accentor modularis*; — solitaria, blue rock-thrush, *Monticola solitarius*; (ichth.) flounder, *Pleuronectes flessus*. **-a·cei** *m.pl.* (orn.) passerines. **-aio** *m.*, **-ina·io** *m.* twittering of sparrows, chirping. **-ìo** *m.* (*pl.* **-ìi**) twittering, chirping; chattering. **-o** *m.* see **passera**. **-otto** *m.* fledgling sparrow; tirare ai -otti, to make a blunder, to be wide of the mark; a -otto, foolishly.

passerella *f.* (naut.) gangplank; shore gangway; (bldg.) footbridge; (aeron.) catwalk.

passerino¹ *m.* (naut.) guard-rail; — di tempesta, lifeline.

passerino² *m. dim.* of **passero**, q.v., under **passera**.

passetto *m. dim.* See under **passo¹**.

passi·bil-e *adj.* liable, susceptible; (leg.) liable; — di multa, liable to fine; (theol.) passible. **-ità** *f.* susceptibility; (leg.) liability.

passic·cio *adj.* rather withered.

passiflora *f.* (bot.). See 'fior di passione' under **passione**.

passi·metro *m.* (eng.) dial gauge.

†passin-a *f.* (archit.) space between two triglyphs. **†-ata** *f.* series of triglyphs or joists.

passino *m. dim.* See under **passo¹**.

pas·sio *m.* (liturg.) Passion (the Gospel narrative as sung or said in Holy Week); (fig.) lungo quanto il —, interminable; (mus.) Passion.

passion-e *f.* passion, suffering; pain, distress; è una — sentirlo parlare, it is painful to hear him speak; (rel.) the Passion of Christ; the (narrative of the) Passion in the Gospels (esp. as sung or said in Holy Week); Domenica di —, Passion Sunday; 'passion', martyrdom of a saint or the literary record of this; (mus.) Passion; con —, in an impassioned manner; (philos.; gramm.) passivity; love; keen desire; sorrow; anxiety; aver — per, to be very fond of; ha preso — al disegno, he has taken a liking to drawing; the object of love; quella donna è stata la sua —, he has been passionately in love with that woman; la mia — è il viaggiare, I adore travelling; fomite di —, love-potion; (bot.) fior di —, passion flower, *Passiflora*. **-ale** *adj.* relating to suffering; relating to passion; impassioned; vehement; passionate; delitto -ale, crime of passion, *crime passionnel*; *n.m.* (eccl.) book containing the 'passions' of martyrs, martyrology, 'passional'. **-alità** *f.* passionateness; excitability; passion, passionate temperament. **†-are** *tr.* to inspire with passion; to cause suffering to; to put to death. **-a·rio** *m.* (eccl.) book containing the Passion narratives from the Four Gospels, 'passional'. **-ato** *part. adj.* passionate; impassioned; very fond, deeply in love; pathetic; troubled; martyred; partial, influenced by feeling or prejudice; giudizio -ato, partial (unfair) judgement; (mus.) impassioned; expressive. **-atamente** *adv.* passionately; with passion. **-cella** *f. dim.* (amorous) liking; 'crush'; flirtation. **-évole** *adj.* passionate; of passion. **-ista** *m.* (*pl.* **-isti**) (eccl.) Passionist (Father); *f.* (*pl.* **-iste**) Passionist nun.

†passire *tr.* See **appassire**.

passista *m.* See under **passo¹**.

passito *m.* raisin wine.

passiv-o *adj.* passive; unprofitable; (gramm.) passive; (chem.) passive; (comm.; leg.) cambiali -e, bills payable; (finan.) obbligazioni -e, passive bonds; *n.m.* liability; debit; deficit; (colloq.) loss; — previsto, liabilities expected to rank; (leg.) — del fallimento, liabilities of bankrupt; stato del —, statement of liabilities; rendiconto del — e dell'attivo, statement of affairs (in bankruptcy) (C.C.); (gramm.) passive (voice). **-amente** *adv.* passively. **-azione** *f.* (phys. chem.) passivation. **-ismo** *m.* (med.) passivism. **-ità** *f.* passivity; insensibility; (comm.) liabilities; (chem.; metall.) passivity.

pass-o¹ *m.* step, pace; stride; walk, gait; march; fare -i lunghi, to take long strides; fare un — avanti, to take a step forward, (fig.)

to make progress; fare due -i, to go for a short walk; ci sono dieci -i, it's only about ten yards; speed, rate, pace; al — (of vehicles), at walking pace, dead slow; (mil.) step; pace; march; — regolare, regulation pace; — di parata, parade march; a — di carica, at the double; — accelerato, — doppio, fast, rifle regiment pace; — di corsa, — di bersagliere, double, jog-trot; — d'oca, — di scuola, goose step; (Ital. hist.) — romano, a sort of goose-step adopted by the Fascist militia; andar di pari — con, to keep pace with; a — di lumaca, at a snail's pace; andare a buon —, to walk quickly, to go at a good pace; footfall, sound of a footstep, step, tread; riconobbi il suo — leggiero, I recognized her light footstep; riconobbi il suo — pesante, I recognized his heavy tread; footprint, footstep (also fig.); seguitare i -i d'uno, to follow in someone's footsteps; (fig.) un — avventato, imprudente, temerario, a rash step; fare il — più lungo della gamba, to bite off more than one can chew; un — falso, a false step, a mistake, a gaffe; un gran —, an important step, action, decision; passo passo, softly, gently; a — —, step by step, slowly; a — a —, little by little; di — in —, in succession; fare i propri -i, to take appropriate steps, action; dalla vita alla morte non c'è che un —, it is but a step from life to death; i primi -i, the first steps, the elements (of knowledge, etc.); nei peggiori -i, in one's worst moments; procedure; precedence; pigliare il — innanzi, to take precedence; (geog.) pass; inlet; straits, passage, entrance; il — di Calais, the Straits of Dover; aprirsi il — con la forza, to force a passage; aprirsi un — attraverso qualche cosa, to make one's way through something; passage, extract (from a book); -i scelti, selections; (mus.) passage; run; uccello di —, bird of passage; aspettare le quaglie al —, to wait for the quails where they pass; tenere il — ad alcuno, to bar someone's way; (text. weaving) shed; (cinem.) — d'immagine, frame gauge; pellicola a — ridotto, substandard film; — ridotto, substandard gauge; (rugby) — laterale. sidestep; (long measure) yard; (Rom. mil. hist.) passus, double step, five feet; (Ital. hist.) pace of different lengths in various provinces; (naut.) crossing of a river; barca da —, ferry; — della barca, boat ferry; channel; pass, canal; migration of fish in the spawning season; — dell'elica, pitch of a propeller; (aeron.) feathering screw; — crescente, increase of a screw pitch nearer the hub; †(Ven.) a fathom, 1·737 m.; †(Ven.) raft armed with guns. **-ac·cio** *m. pejor.* difficult or dangerous step. **-etto** *m. dim.* short step; †measure of length differing in various regions. **-ino** *m. dim.* child's step; passin passino, slowly; (neol.) coffee-strainer; †Florentine measure of length. **-ista** *m.* (sport) cyclist capable of maintaining high average speed over long distances.

pass-o² *adj.* dried; withered, shrivelled; uva -a, raisins; erba -a, dried grass, hay; salciuoli -i, withies cut for drying; *n.m.* raisin wine; drink made from any dried fruit. **-ola** *f.* (also *adj.*) raisins. **-olino** *adj.* dried (of grapes or other fruit).

passone *m.* stake, paling.

past-a *f.* (cul.) 'pasta'. NOTE: 'macaroni' is used in English as a general term, covering the various forms of 'pasta asciutta' (i.e. 'pasta' served comparatively dry, with a small quantity of sauce, gravy, oil or butter) and 'pasta' or 'minestra in brodo' (i.e. served in soup). The forms most commonly eaten as 'pasta asciutta' in N. Italy are: spaghetti, lasagne, tagliatelle, ravioli; in Naples, maccheroni. 'Minestra in brodo' is made in smaller shapes: seeds, stars, rings, etc., thin strips, 'tagliatelle' or 'vermicelli'. — fresca, 'pasta' made at home for immediate use; dough; — cresciuta, dough after rising; occorre dimenare molto la —, the dough should be thoroughly kneaded; pastry; piece of pastry, cake; — frolla, very light sweet pastry; — sfoglia, — spoglia, puff pastry; sweet, sweetmeat; bonbon; — reale, a kind of sweet pudding made with whipped white of egg; — di mandorle, almond paste; pulp, sausage-meat; paste (adhesive); wet plaster, clay; (paperm.) pulp, stuff; — meccanica, wood pulp; (chem.) — d'amido, starch paste; — di legno, wood pulp; special paste used as fish-bait; prendere la —, to take the bait; (fig.) nature, temperament, temper; constitution; un uomo di buona —, a good-natured man; un uomo di — frolla, a weakling; avere le mani in —, to have a finger in the pie; mettere le mani in —, to meddle in other people's affairs. **-ac·cio** *m. pejor.*, **-ac·cia** *f. pejor.* buon -accio, stupid person. **-a·io** *m.* maker or vendor of 'pasta'; (joc.) one very fond of 'pasta'. **-ella** *f.* batter; (fig.) trickery, fraud. **-etta** *f. dim.* batter of flour, water and oil; political fraud, gerrymandering. **-ifi·cio** *m.* 'pasta' factory. **-ina** *f. dim.* 'pasta' in

past-a (*cont.*)
small shapes for soup; cake, small pastry, tart; (bldg.) topping.
-one *m. augm.* large piece of dough; bran mash; mashed olives.
-ume *m.* (derog.) mess of 'pasta'; mash for poultry.

pastecca *f.* (naut.) snatchblock.

pasteggi-are [A3c] *intr.* (*aux.* avere) to eat at table; to have one's
meals; **-a a pernice**, he is having partridge for dinner; **vino da
-are**, table wine. **-a·bile** *adj.* (of wine) suitable to be drunk at meals.
-amento *m.* eating at table.

pastell-o *m.* (art) pastel, coloured crayon; pastel drawing; **a —**, in
pastel, pastel; (bot.) woad, *Isatis tinctoria*; see **pasticcio**. **-ista**
m., f. (art) pastel-painter.

paste·nula *f.* (ichth.)—**bianca**, forkbeard, *Phycis blennoides*;—**bruna**,
P. mediterranea.

pasticc-a *f.,* †**-o** *m.* pastille, lozenge, tablet (cf. **pastiglia**).

pasticceri·a *f.* pastrycook's shop, confectioner's; pastry; confectionery.

pasticci-are [A3] *tr.* to make a mess of; to bungle; **che cosa stai
-ando?**, what muddle is this you're making?; *intr.* (*aux.* avere)
to intrigue; *rfl.* to become smudged. **-ato** *part. adj.* messed up,
bungled; smudged; (cul.) **maccheroni -ati**, macaroni cooked with
cheese, butter and meat-gravy.

pastic·c-io *m.* pie; **— di mele**, apple-pie; **crosta di —**, piecrust; mess,
muddle; **che —!**, what a mess!; **bel —!**, a nice mess!; bad work;
embarrassment; **trovarsi nei -i**, to be in a fix; (mus.) medley;
(art) imitation, copy; bad picture. **-iere** *m.* pastry-cook, confectioner; (paint.) painter of copies or of inferior pictures. **-ino**
m. dim. tart; tartlet; small pastry; sweetmeat; cake; bun. **-ione**
m. augm. large pie; (fig.) bungler; meddler, mischief-maker.
-iotto *m.* sweet pastry, tart.

†**pastieri** *m.pl.* (naut.) cleat or stayshorn.

pasti·gli-a *f.,* **-o** *m.* pastille; paste imitation of precious stones;
(pharm.) tablet; (electr.) paste.

pastinaca *f.* (bot.) parsnip, *Pastinaca sativa*; (ichth.) sting-ray,
Dasybatus pastinacus; (fig.) **come il pesce —**, inconclusive, vague.

pastinac·cio *m.* (bot.). See **pastinaca**.

pa·stin-o *m.* tilth, ground prepared for planting. **-are** [A1s] *tr.* to
break up, to break down (the soil). **-ato** *part. adj.* (of soil)
crumbled, well-broken up. **-azione** *f.* breaking up ground, preparing the soil.

past-o *m.* meal; food; repast; fruit-pulp; lights (offal); **essere di
buon —**, to eat heartily; **vino da —**, table wine, wine in carafe
(as opposed to bottled wine); **a tutto —**, freely, abundantly; **stare
ai -i**, to eat only at meals; (fig.) affair; bargain; **dare in — al
pubblico notizie sensazionali**, to regale the public with sensational
news; **— gonfio**, fat, ruddy person. **-occhia** *f.,* **-rocchio** *m.* idle
talk, story, fib, nonsense; humbug; **non raccontar -occhie**, don't
talk nonsense. **-occhiata** *f.* silly thing, stupid action. **-occhione**
m. big, rather fat person. (**-occhiona** *f.*) **-one** *m. augm.* a large meal;
mash; (journ.) a survey or digest of foreign comments on political
events.

pastoia *f.* hobble, for hobbling horses or cattle; fetters; (vet.) see
pastorale, under **pastore**.

pastone[1] *m. augm.* See under **pasta**.

pastone[2] *m. augm.* See under **pasto**.

pastor-e *m.* shepherd; **bastone da —**, shepherd's crook; rough
countryman; leader, ruler; (rel.) shepherd of souls (esp. of a pope,
bishop, or parish priest); **il Buon —**, the Good Shepherd; (in
Protestant usage) minister, pastor; **— evangelico**, Protestant
clergyman. **-a** *f.* shepherdess; (vet.) see **pastorale**. **-ale** *adj.*
pastoral, of shepherds; bucolic; **in abito -ale**, dressed as a shepherd; **poesia -ale**, pastoral poetry; (mus.) pastoral (whether
referring to Christmas or in the general sense 'bucolic'); *n.m.* pastorale, composition for organ or other instruments representing the
shepherds' pipes at the Nativity; *n.m.* (eccl.) pastoral, bishop's
letter; bishop's pastoral staff, crosier; (vet.) pastern. **-almente**
adv. pastorally. **-eccio** *adj.* pastoral. **-ella** *f. dim.* young shepherdess; form of pastoral poem, originally Provençal; Arcadian
shepherdess; (mus.) see **pastorale**. **-elleri·a** *f.* (derog.) Arcadian
poetry. **-ello** *m.* (lit. hist.) Arcadian shepherd; (eccl.) carol recited
by children at the Christmas crib; *pl.* (hist.) the Pastouraux of
1251 or 1320. **-i·zia** *f.* sheep-rearing. **-i·zio** *adj.* pastoral; **sale
-izio**, salt for sheep, etc.

pastorizz-are [A1] *tr.* to pasteurize. **-ato** *part. adj.* pasteurized.
-azione *f.* pasteurization; pasteurizing.

pastos-o *adj.* soft; sticky; mellow; (paint.) soft, mellow; (of wine)
rather sweet; (mus.) flowing, mellifluous, euphonious (of a composition); mellow, full, well-modulated (of a voice). **-ità** *f.* softness, stickiness; (paint.) mellowness of light and colour, with
plastic effects; (mus.) flexibility, light and shade.

†**pastrana** *f.* See **pastrano**.

pastran-o *m.* overcoat, greatcoat; cloak with sleeves. **-a·io** *m.* cloak-
room attendant. **-ella** *f.* Inverness cloak.

pastricciano *m.* (bot.) rough chervil, *Chaerophyllum temulentum*;
parsnip, *Pastinaca sativa*; (fig., joc.) stupid person; simple good-
natured man.

pastroc·chio *m.* See under **pasto**.

pastume *m.* See under **pasta**.

pastur-a *f.* pasture, pasturage; (fig.) aliment, nutriment; (hunting)
dung of wild animals; †joke. **-ale** *adj., n.m.* (vet.) see **pastorale**,
under **pastore**. **-are** [A1] *tr.* to pasture, to put out to graze; to
lead to pasture; *intr.* (*aux.* avere) (fig.) to be a shepherd of souls,
to tend one's flock (as bishop or priest); *rfl.* to feed, to graze.
-ato *part. adj.* put out to pasture, out at grass. †**-e·vole** *adj.* ready
for grazing; abounding in pasturage.

patacc-a *f.* (numism.) old Spanish coin, coin of little value; **non
vale una —**, it isn't worth a brass farthing; large stain, spot of
dirt (on clothes); (joc., derog.) 'gongs', worthless decorations;
cheap, imitation-gold watch sold by a swindler for a high price.
-aro *m.* one who sells worthless watches. **-one** *m. augm.* Brazilian
coin, equivalent to three 'patacche'; (joc.) 'turnip' (watch); big,
clumsy person. (**-ona** *f.*)

†**pataf·fio** *m.* epitaph, sepulchral inscription.

pataffione *m.* solemn, sententious person; fat, clumsy person.

pata·gio *m.* (Rom. antiq.) *patagium*, gold edging on tunic.

Patag-onia *pr.n.f.* (geog.) Patagonia. **-one** *adj., n.m.* Patagonian.

patanfiona *f.* fat, coarse woman.

†**pa·tano** *adj.* patent, evident, manifest; large, gross.

pata-pu·m *excl.* (onom.) bang; thud. **-tra·c** *m. indecl., excl.* (onom.)
bang; crash; crack.

patarac·cia *f.* (ichth.) *Citharus linguatula*, a kind of flatfish.

patarasso *m.* See **paterasso**.

patarino *m.* (eccl. hist.) Patarin, Paterin; any heretic or unorthodox
person.

patat-a *f.* (bot.) potato, *Solanum tuberosum*; **-e tenere**, new potatoes;
-e all'insalata, **-e all'olio**, potato salad; **-e fritte**, fried potatoes,
chips; **-e lesse**, boiled potatoes; **spirito di —**, clumsy wit, silly
joke. **-a·io** *m.* potato merchant. **-ina** *f. dim.* new potato, little
potato; *pl.* chips, chip potatoes. **-ucco** *m.* clumsy, stupid person;
cape with hood; (joc.) Austrian (soldier).

patatra·c *excl.* See under **patapum**.

patavin-o *adj.* (hist.) Paduan, of Padua. **-ità** *f.* Patavinity, provincialism of expression as exemplified in Livy.

†**pate** *m.* See **padre**.

†**patefatto** *adj.* See **patente**.

patell-a *f.* (zool.) limpet, *Patella* spp.; (anat.) patella, knee-cap.
-are *adj.* (anat.) patellar. **-ari** *m.pl.* (Rom. myth.) **di patellarii**,
household gods. **-iforme** *adj.* (anat.) patelliform.

patema *m.* trouble, anxiety; pain, suffering; chagrin.

patena *f.* (liturg.) paten.

patent-e *adj.* open, wide open; clear, obvious, evident, self-evident,
manifest; patent; **ingiustizia —**, flagrant injustice; **lettera —**,
letters patent; (bot.) spreading, patent; *n.f.* licence, certificate,
diploma; **— di circolazione**, car licence; **— di abilitazione**, certificate of competence; **— di autista**, **— di guida**, driving licence;
charter; **— per la vendita degli alcoolici**, wine and spirit licence;
ha la — di maestro elementare, he is a certificated teacher, he has
a teaching diploma; **ha la — di levatrice**, she is a certified midwife;
(leg.) licence; **— di abilitazione** (per la guida di automobili),
driving licence; (naut.) **— bratta**, **— sporca**, invalid bill of health;
— di corsale, **— di corso**, letter of marque; **— di grado**, Master's
Certificate; (naut. hist.) **— di navigazione**, **— di navigabilità**,
precursors of 'Lloyd's Certificate'; (comm.) **— netta**, clean bill;
— di sanità — sanitaria, bill of health; **— sudicia**, foul bill.
-emente *adv.* evidently, obviously. **-ato** *adj.* patented; certificated; licensed, provided with a licence; holding a diploma, etc.;
qualified; **levatrice -ata**, certified midwife; **è uno sciocco -ato**,
he is an out and out fool. **-ino** *m. dim.* temporary shooting
licence.

pa·tera *f.* (Rom. antiq.) patera, shallow dish.

paterac·chio *m.* (joc.) friendly agreement; family relationship; marriage; contract.

pater-asso, -azzo *m.* (naut.) stay, wire or hemp lateral supports of all upper rigging.

†**patere**[1] *intr.* to be manifest, evident; pate, it is evident.

†**pa·tere**[2] *vb.* and derivs. See **patire**.

patereccio *m.* (med.) whitlow, paronychia.

paterfami·lias *m. indecl.* paterfamilias, head of a household.

paterino *m.* See **patarino**.

patern-o *adj.* paternal; father's; fatherly; la mia casa -a, my father's house; (hist.) il — governo, the Paternal Government, i.e. of the Grand Dukes of Tuscany after 1815. -**amente** *adv.* paternaliy, like a father. -**ale** *adj.* paternal; *n.f.* scolding, rebuke; fare una -ale ad uno, to talk to someone like a father, *or*, like a Dutch uncle. -**ità** *f.* paternity; fatherhood; (leg.) ricerca di, indagini sulla, -ità, investigation of, inquiries into, paternity (C.C.); -ità legale, adoptive fatherhood; (admin.) Christian name of father (in official documents to be filled in); la -ità di uno scritto, the authorship of a written article; aggiungere la -ità, to add the father's name; (eccl.) Vostra -ità, Your Paternity (very formal mode of address to a religious).

pater-noster *m. indecl.* (rel.) Paternoster, Lord's Prayer.

paternostro *m.* (rel.) Paternoster, Lord's Prayer; sapere come il —, to know by heart, to know as well as anything; il — della scimmia (della bertuccia), a string of oaths; paternoster (bead), large bead in a rosary; (naut.) deadeye; *pl.* (archit.) beads in an astragal, or sim. ornament; †aver detto il — di San Giuliano, to have secured a good lodging for the night.

pate·tic-o *adj.* pathetic; touching; un discorso —, a moving speech; mawkish; melancholy; (anat.) nervo —, pathetic nerve, fourth cranial nerve, patheticus; †(gramm.) punto —, exclamation mark; *n.m.* (the) pathetic; pathos. -**amente** *adv.* pathetically. -**one** *m.* melancholy person, one given to self-pity; writer or other who indulges in sentimentality. -**ume** *m.* sentimentality; drama, speech, etc. too heavily charged with feeling.

pati·bile *adj.* See under **patire**.

pati·bol-o *m.* gallows, scaffold; gibbet; place of execution; faccia da —, gallows-bird. -**are** *adj.* fit for the gallows, fit to be hanged; faccia -are, gallows-bird.

†**pa·tico** *adj.* See **epatico**.

patimento *m.* See under **patire**.

pa·tin-a *f.* varnish; glazing (on earthenware); patina (on old bronze or copper); coating (on the tongue); (tan.) dubbin; (metall.) patina; polish (on shoes); glaze (on paper). -**are** [A1s] *tr.* to glaze; to varnish; to dub (leather). -**ato** *part. adj.* glazed; varnished; carta -ata, glazed (glossy) paper, 'art paper'; (of leather) dubbed, prepared for polishing; -ato di grasso, coated with grease; lingua -ata, furred tongue. -**atore** *m.* glazer; varnisher. -**atura** *f.* glazing; varnishing.

pat-ire [D2] *tr.* to suffer; to bear, to stand, to endure; to go through, to experience; to undergo; quante angherie m'è toccato —!, how many wrongs I have had to endure!; — la fame, to be starving, to starve; mi fecero — la fame, they starved me; — di vettovaglie, to be short of food; — il caldo, to suffer from the heat; non posso — il freddo, I cannot bear the cold; — il mal di mare, to be seasick; non -irò questo affronto, I will not bear this insult; to allow, to permit; non -irò che egli t'insulti, I will not allow him to insult you; non lo posso — in casa mia, I won't have him in the house; *intr.* (aux. avere) to suffer; to grieve; si vede che ci -isce, you can see he is grieving about it; finire di —, to end one's sufferings, i.e. to die; to deteriorate, to suffer; (prep. di) to suffer (from); — d'insonnia, to suffer from insomnia; †to digest; *n.m.* suffering. -**i·bile**, †-**e·vole** *adj.* endurable; susceptible, liable to suffer. -**imento** *m.* suffering; pain; affliction. -**ito** *part. adj.* suffered; suffering; sickly; run down (in health); frutta -ita, overripe fruit, fruit going bad; *n.m.* (prep. per) languishing lover; boy friend, sweetheart; fan, admirer (of).

pat-oge·nesi *f.* (med.) pathogenesis. -**oge·nico** *adj.* (med.) pathogenic. -**o·geno** *adj.* pathogenous, pathogenic. -**ognomo·nico** *adj.* (med.) pathognomonic. -**ologi·a** *f.* pathology. -**olo·gico** *adj.* pathological. -**o·logo** *m.* pathologist.

patos, pathos *m. indecl.* pathos.

Patrasso *pr.n.m.* (geog.) Patras; (joc.) andare a —, to go to rest with one's fathers, to die; mandare a —, to send to the devil.

†**patre** *m.* See **padre**.

pa·tri-a *f.* native land, country; fatherland; home; morire per la —, to die for one's country; ritornare in —, to return home; in — e fuori, at home and abroad; madre —, mother country; pigliare per — un luogo, to make one's home in a place, to settle down there; (rel.) — celeste, heavenly country, home in heaven.

patri-arca *m.* (pl. -archi) patriarch; founder of a family; — di tribù, founder of a family or tribe; (Bibl., eccl.) patriarch. -**arcale** *adj.* patriarchal; venerable; (herald.) croce -arcale, double cross, Lorraine cross. -**arcalmente** *adv.* like a patriarch, venerably. -**arcato** *m.* patriarchy (as social institution); (eccl.) patriarchate (status, time of office, see or residence of a patriarch). †-**archi·a** *f.* (eccl.) patriarchate. -**ar·chio** *m.* patriarch's residence.

patri-cida *m.* parricide (person); *adj.* parricidal. -**ci·dio** *m.* (pl. -ci·dii) parricide (act).

patri·cio *m.* (hist.) title of a dignity instituted in the Roman Empire by Constantine; Imperial vicar.

patrigno *m.* step-father.

patrimo·ni-o *m.* patrimony, inheritance; heritage; estate; total assets; (fig.) a large sum of money; gli è costato un —, it cost him a mint of money; (leg.) — familiare, family estate (similar in some ways to English settled estate) (C.C.); — sociale, total assets of company or partnership (C.C.); imposta sul —, tax on total wealth (C.C.); (colloq.) estate duty, capital levy; — immobiliare, real estate; — mobiliare, personal estate, personalty; il — letterario di una nazione, the literary heritage of a nation; — eterno, eternal bliss, heavenly home; (hist.) capitano del —, standard-bearer of the Church. -**ale** *adj.* inherited, hereditary; patrimonial; (comm.) stato -ale, statement of assets and liabilities, balance sheet.

patrinato *m.* office of godfather.

patrino *m.* See **padrino**, under **padre**.

pa·tri-o *adj.* paternal; (leg.) -a potestà, paternal authority (C.C.); of (one's own) country; of one's home; native; domestic; amor —, love of one's country, patriotism; storia -a, national history. -**ota**, -**otta** *m.* patriot; compatriot, fellow-countryman; nostro -ota, our compatriot. -**ottardo** *m.* (neol., derog.) factious or insincere patriot. -**ot·tico** *adj.* patriotic. -**ottismo** *m.* patriotism. -**otto** *m.* see **patriota**.

patri·stica *f.* (eccl.) patristics, patristic studies.

patri·zi-o[1] *m., adj.* patrician. -**ato** *m.* class of patricians.

Patri·zi-o[2] *pr.n.m.* Patrick. -**a**, *pr.n.f.* Patricia.

†**patrizzare** [A1] *intr.* (aux. avere) to take after one's father.

patrocin-are [A1] *tr.* to defend, to support, to protect; to plead (a cause); to champion; — una candidatura, to support a candidature; (leg.) to act for; to appear for (C.C.P.). -**ante** *part. adj.* (leg.) representing, appearing for; *n.m.* -ante in cassazione, advocate with right of audience in Court of Cassation (C.C.P.). -**atore** *m.* (leg.) -atore legale, legal representative (in proceedings) (C.C.P.); -atore delle arti, delle lettere, patron of the arts, of letters. (-**atrice** *f.*)

patroci·nio *m.* protection, support; defence; (leg.) legal representation; — gratuito, legal aid (C.C.P.); (rel.) patronage, protection (of a saint).

patrologi·a *f.* (eccl.) patrology.

patron-ale *adj.*, -**ato** *adj.* See under **patrono**.

patroni·mic-o *adj.*, *n.m.* named after one's father, patronymic; family name. (-**amente** *adv.*)

patron-o, †-**e** *m.* (Rom. antiq.) patron; (leg.) advocate of party to legal proceedings; patron of ecclesiastical benefice; (eccl.) patron (saint); patron (of a living); †(naut.) master of a ship; †(Venice) -i d'arsenale, three dockyard superintendents recruited from the nobility who served for a month. †-**a** *f.* flagship of a galley squadron; 2nd flagship of a fleet under a 'capitano'. -**ale** *adj.* patronal. -**ato** *m.* patronage; charitable institution; (Rom. antiq.) status of patron; (eccl.) patronage (of benefice); regio -ato, king's right of patronage; -ato dei carcerati, prisoners' aid society; -ato scolastico, institution for helping poor scholars in elementary schools. -**a** *f.*, -**essa** *f.* patroness. †-**i·a** *f.* see **padronanza**.

patt-a *f.* (in games, etc.) draw, quits; far —, esser pari e —, to be quits, to be all square; (tailor.) palm; (naut.) palm (of an anchor); crows' foot; ormeggiarsi a — d'oca, to moor in the several splayed cables or anchors. -**are** [A1] *intr.* (aux. avere) to be quits, to be all square.

patteggiare [A3c] and derivs. See under **patto**.

pat·tin-o[1] *m.* skate; — a rotelle, roller-skate; (aeron.) skid; (eng.) sliding block; shoe; runner; pad; (eng.) stantuffo a —, slipper

pat-tino (*cont.*)
piston; (cinem.) pressure pad, film tension pad. **-ag·gio** *m.* skating; -aggio a rotelle, roller-skating; -aggio artistico, figure-skating. **-are** [A I] *intr.* (*aux.* avere) to skate. **-atore** *m.*, **-atrice** *f.* skater. **-o·dromo** *m.* skating-rink.

pattino² *m.* (Tusc.) a kind of pleasure boat consisting of two floats (cf. **sandalo**).

pattinsonag·gio *m.* (metall.) Pattinson process.

patt-o *m.* agreement; pact; compact; covenant; condition; treaty; il — atlantico, the Atlantic treaty; *pl.* terms; understanding; fare un —, to make, to conclude an agreement; venire a -i, to come to terms; a — che, on condition that; a nessun —, on no account, by no means; ad alcun —, somehow; a qualunque —, a tutti i -i, at any cost; rendersi a -i, to surrender on terms; (provb.) -i chiari, amici cari, clear agreements make good friends; — sociale, Social Contract; (theol.) l'Antico —, the Old Covenant; il Nuovo —, the New Covenant; (leg.) agreement; condition; pact; — commissario, covenant for forfeiture (in mortgage); — di riscatto, right to repurchase (C.C.). **-eggia·bile** *adj.* negotiable; that can be arranged; susceptible of agreement. **-eggiamento** *m.* bargaining; arrangement, compromise. **-eggiare** [A 3 c] *intr.* (*aux.* avere) to bargain, to negotiate; to discuss terms, to come to terms; to covenant; -eggiare con la propria coscienza, to come to terms with one's conscience, to still one's conscience; (provb.) chi ben guerreggia ben -eggia, a good fighter gets good peace terms; *tr.* to negotiate; to arrange the terms of; -eggiare un accordo, to negotiate an agreement; -eggiarono la resa, they arranged terms of surrender; †*recip. rfl.* to come to terms, to conclude an agreement. **-eggiato** *part. adj.* negotiated, agreed; (mil.) surrendered on terms; †enlisted. **-eggiatore** *m.* negotiator; party to a bargain; covenanter; *adj.* bargaining, negotiating. (**-eggiatrice** *f.*)

patton-a *f.* (cul.) polenta made of chestnut-flour; overcooked macaroni (sticking together). **-a·io** *m.* seller of 'pattona'; greedy eater of 'pattona'; †clumsy person.

pattone *m.* bump; slap.

pattu·gli-a *f.* (mil.) patrol; incontrare la —, to run into the patrol; essere di —, to be on patrol, to form part of a patrol. **-are** [A 4] *intr.* (*aux.* avere) to go on patrol.

pattu-ire [D 2] *tr.* to negotiate; to agree (upon); to arrange, to fix, to settle; — la vendita, to negotiate the sale; — la carrozza, to strike a bargain for (the hire of) the carriage; ciò non era stato -ito, that had not been settled; *abs.* to bargain. **-ito** *part. adj.* agreed (upon), settled, stipulated; le nozze -ite, the marriage that has been arranged.

pattum-e *m.* refuse, litter; dust-heap; mud; dirt; (agric.) rushes, fern, etc. as litter; (naut.) †mixture of pitch used for tarring the hull or rigging; †bait. **-a·io** *m.* scavenger, dustman. **-iera** *f.* dust-bin.

patull-are [A 4] *rfl.* (*acc.* of *prn.* 'si') to enjoy oneself, to take it easy; (*dat.* of *prn.* 'si') -arsi uno, to make fun of someone; *tr.* (poet.) to lull to sleep; lo -a il vento, the wind rocks his cradle.

†pa·tulo *adj.* open; wide; ample.

paturn-a, †**-ia** *f.* (usu. *pl.*) low spirits, melancholy; aver le -e, to be in the dumps.

†pa·uc-o *adj.* see **poco**. **†-ità** *f.* paucity.

paul-iani, **-iciani** *m.pl.* (eccl. hist.) Paulicians (dualistic sect). **-isti** *m.pl.* (eccl.) Paulists, Paulist Fathers.

pa·uperi·smo *m.* (neol.) pauperism, extreme poverty.

†pa·upero *m.* and derivs. See **povero**.

pau·r-a *f.* fear, dread; fright; tremar di —, to shiver with fright; aver — di, to be afraid of, to fear; sentirsi morire di —, to be frightened to death; senza —, fearlessly; niente —!, non aver —!, don't be afraid; per — di, for fear of; una terribile —, a terrible fright; metter — a, mettere in —, to frighten; aver — che, to fear, to suspect that; ho — che la colpa sia sua, I'm afraid it is his fault; anxiety, concern; ho — d'ingrassare troppo, I am afraid of getting too fat; da far —, awful, terrible, terribly; è brutta da far —, she is as ugly as sin; cause of fear, anxiety, disquiet; quella era la mia —, that is what I was afraid of. **†-are** *tr.* to frighten. **-etta** *f. dim.* alarm, apprehension. **†-ire** *tr.* to frighten. **-o** *m.* (Tusc.) assassin lurking in the Salaiuole woods near Florence. **-oso** *adj.* timorous, timid; (of a horse) shy, skittish; fearful; alarming, dreadful, frightful; è -oso anche della sua ombra, he is afraid even of his own shadow; un luogo -oso, a terrifying place; una vista -osa, a dreadful sight. **-osamente** *adv.* timidly; in fear and trembling; fearfully; dreadfully.

pa·us-a *f.* pause, stop; rest; (mus.) pause, rest; semibreve rest; pause-sign; facciamo una —, let us call a halt; slowness, hesitation. **†-a·bile** *adj.* capable of pausing or resting; non -abile, restless. **-are** [A I a] *intr.* (*aux.* avere) to pause, to stop; to show deliberation; (mus.) to rest.

pausa·rio *m.* (Rom. antiq.) *pausarius*, a kind of boatswain.

pavan-a¹ *f.* (mus.) Pavane, Pavan. **-i·glia** *f.* (mus.) see **pavana**.

†pavana² *adj. f.* lingua —, Paduan dialect.

†pavefatto *adj.* frightened, terrified.

pavent-are [A I] *intr.* (*aux.* avere) (poet.) to be afraid; (of animals) to be timid; †*tr.* to fear. **†-ato** *adj.*, **†-e·vole** *adj.* see **paventoso**. **†-o** *m.* see **spavento**. **-oso** *adj.* afraid, fearful; frightful, dreadful. **-osamente** *adv.* fearfully, timidly; frightfully.

pavese¹ *adj.* (geog.) of Pavia; (cul.) zuppa alla —, Pavia soup, i.e. soup containing lightly poached eggs; *n.m.* native of Pavia; district round Pavia; *f.* woman of Pavia.

pavese² *m.* (mil. hist.) pavise, a rectangular shield which protected a man completely; a soldier with such; (naut. hist.) painted wooden shield placed along the gunwale; alzare il gran —, to dress a ship overall, (fig.) to make a brave show; cf. **gala**. **†-a·io**, **†-aro** *adj.* bearing a shield; *n.m.* soldier carrying a shield; i -ai facevano da parapetto ai balestrieri, the shieldsmen acted as a screen for the archers; (naut.) dress of a ship; †strips of different colours used to decorate; coloured bunting, usually blue with red ornament; †hammock netting corners; -ai cerati, waterproof covers; -aio elettrico, illumination of ship's outline. **-are** [A I] *tr.* to dress (ship) overall *or* with masthead flags only; to decorate (a hall, a room, with flags, etc.). **-ata** *f.* (naut.) dressing of a ship; painted cloths along the side of a galley; the side of a galley.

pa·vid-o *adj.* timid, fearful; frightened; cowardly; shy. **-amente** *adv.* fearfully, timidly, timorously; in alarm; in a cowardly way; shyly.

†paviglione *m.* See **padiglione**.

paviment-o *m.* pavement; floor; — intavolato, parquet floor; (anat.) pavement. **-are** [A I c] *tr.* to pave; to floor; to macadamize, to metal (a road). **-ato** *part. adj.* paved; macadamized, metalled. **-atore** *m.* (bldg.) floor layer; paviour. **-azione** *f.* (work of) paving; laying a floor; flooring; paving; metalling. **-oso** *adj.* (anat.) epitelio -oso, pavement epithelium.

†pa·volo *m.* (numism.). See **paolo**.

pavon-e *m.* (-a, -essa *f.*) (orn.) peacock, peahen; (ichth.) red wrasse, *Labrus mixtus.* **-azzo** *adj.*, *n.m.* peacock-blue; violet; purple. **-azzetto** *adj. dim.* purplish, bluish; *n.m.* kind of white marble veined with purple. **-cella** *f.* (orn.) lapwing, *Vanellus vanellus.* **-eggiare** [A 3 c] *rfl.* to strut; to show off; to be as proud as a peacock. **-i·a** *f.* (ent.) -ia minore, Emperor moth, *Saturnia pavonia*; -ia maggiore, *S. pyri.* **-ic·cio** *adj.* see **pavonazzo**.

†pavore *m.* See **paura**.

pazien-te *adj.* patient, forbearing; suffering; *n.m.* patient, sick person (esp. if suffering acute pain or about to be operated upon; cf. **ammalato** and **malato**); sufferer; one undergoing punishment. **-temente** *adv.* patiently, with patience; forbearingly. **-tare** [A I] *intr.* (*aux.* avere) to wait; to have patience, to be patient. **-za** *f.* patience, forbearance; endurance; game of patience; aver -za, to be patient; abbia -za!, excuse me!; abbi -za, vieni qua, just a minute, come here; -za, se almeno fosse gentile, it wouldn't matter (it wouldn't be so bad) if only he had nice manners; m'ha fatto scappar la -za, he has made me lose my temper; se è impossibile, -za, if it's impossible, never mind!; (theol.) patience (as a virtue); (eccl.) scapular; (eccl.) girdle. **-zioso** *adj.* patient; long-suffering.

pazz-o *adj.* mad, insane, lunatic; wild; foolish; frenzied; un'idea -a, a foolish idea; ira -a, wild rage; brodo —, thin soup; acqua -a, thin, tasteless soup; watered wine, milk, etc.; *n.m.* madman, lunatic; ospedale dei -i, lunatic asylum; madness; dare nel —, to go mad; to fall into folly. (-a *f.*) **-amente** *adv.* madly, insanely, foolishly; excessively. **-acchione** *m.* hare-brained person, madcap. **-ac·cio** *m.* arrant fool. **-eggiare** [A 3 c] *intr.* (*aux.* avere) to play the fool, to act like a madman. **-erello** *m.* fool; silly person; madcap. **-erellone** *m.* jovial person given to playing the fool. **-eri·a** *f.* lunatic asylum; madness. **†-eric·cio** *adj.* slightly mad. **†-erone** *adj.* eccentric, odd; *n.m.* any strange, eccentric person. **-esco** *adj.* (m.pl. -eschi) crazy, foolish, wild. **-escamente** *adv.* foolishly, madly, wildly; like a lunatic. **-i·a** *f.* madness, lunacy, insanity; frenzy; folly; foolish act; mad idea; ha un ramo di -ia, he is a little crazy; commettere -ie, to behave foolishly; non farò

pazz·o (cont.)

la ~ia di seguirlo, I shall not be so foolish as to follow him; far qualche ~ia, to do something desperate. †~icone, †~ic·cio, a little mad. ~i(u)ola f. dim. foible, little eccentricity.

pe' contr. See **pei**.

pean·a, ~e, pea·n m. (pl. ~i, ~a) (Gk. myth.) Paean (title of Apollo); (Gk. antiq.; fig.) paean; song of triumph, battle, or joy; (prosod.) paeon.

peata f. (naut., Ven.) barge.

pebrin·a f. (silkb.) spotted disease, pebrine, caused by the sporozoa, Nosoma bombycis. ~oso adj. (silkb.) infected with spotted disease.

pe·cari m. (zool.) peccary, Dicotyles spp.

pecca f. fault, error; blemish; defect, flaw.

pecc·are [A 2] intr. (aux. avere) to sin; to transgress; to err; to be at fault; to offend; to be faulty, to be deficient, to be wrong; — contro il buon costume, to offend against (common) decency; in ciò ~a un poco, it is not quite right there; è un quadro che ~a nel colorito, there is a wrong use of colour in this picture; — di superbia, to be too proud; — di ingratitudine, to be ungrateful. ~a·bile adj. fallible, liable to err. ~abilità f. fallibility. ~adi·glio m. peccadillo, trifling offence. ~aminoso adj. sinful. ~aminosamente adv. sinfully. ~ante part. adj. sinning, sinful; faulty; (med.) peccant, morbid, unhealthy; †(med.) umori ~anti, peccant humours; n.m., f. sinner. †~ata f.pl. of peccato, q.v. ~ati·glio m. peccadillo. ~ato m. sin; fault; error; ~ato di lingua, grammatical mistake; (theol.) sin (mortal, venial, original, actual); il ~ato di Adamo, The Fall (of Adam and Eve), as subject of paintings or other representation; che ~ato!, what a pity!; è proprio un ~ato!, it's really a shame! ~atore m. (theol.) sinner; adj. sinful; sinning. (~atrice, ~atora f.) ~atuc·cio, ~atuzzo m. dim. peccadillo; slight fault, slip, trifling offence. †~o m. see peccato.

†**pec·chero** m. beaker, goblet; (herald.) covered cup.

pecchi·a f. bee. ~aiolo adj. (orn.) falco ~aiolo, honey buzzard, Pernis apivorus. †~are tr. to suck like a bee. ~olino m. dim. young adult bee. ~one m. drone; bumble-bee.

†**pec·ci·a¹** f. paunch, belly. †~ata f. blow on the belly. †~uto adj. big-bellied.

pecci·a² (bot.) spruce, Picea. ~olo m. (agric.) kind of fig.

pec·e f. pitch; — liquida, tar; — bianca, — nera, varieties of resin; — greca, hard resin, colophony; — da calzolai, cobbler's wax; fare la —, to get resin from the trees; nero come la —, pitch-black, pitch-dark; (fig.) macchiati di una stessa —, tarred with the same brush. ~etta f. dim. plaster (esp. for the head); stain, spot of dirt; nuisance, bore; mettere una ~etta a, to patch up. ~ioso adj. pitchy, smeared with pitch. ~iotto m. (orn.) nuthatch; (fig.) mess, bad job.

pechblenda f. (miner.) pitchblende.

Pechin·o pr.n.f. (geog.) Peking. ~ese adj. of, or relating to Peking; n.m., f. native, or inhabitant of Peking; (breed of dog) Pekingese.

pecile, pe·cile m. (Gk. antiq.) the Stoa Poikile (Painted Hall) at Athens.

Pecili pr.n.f. (geog.) Pe Chili.

Peciora pr.n.f. (geog.) Pechora.

pe·cor·a f. sheep; ewe; mutton; un branco di ~e, a flock of sheep; carne di —, mutton; (fig.) — nera, — segnata, black sheep; (derog.) essere una —, to be a coward; quegli uomini sono ~e, those men are like sheep (i.e. they follow blindly); (provb.) chi — si fa, il lupo lo mangia, if you behave like a sheep the wolf will eat you; le ~e bianche, privileged persons; (naut.) breaker, 'white horse'; (rel.) member of a (bishop's or priest's) flock, 'sheep'. ~ag·gine f. servility; stupidity, silliness, sheepishness; simple-mindedness; simplicity. ~a·io, †~aro m. shepherd (~a·ia f. shepherdess); uncouth countryman, boor. ~ame m. flock of sheep (also fig.). †~a·rio adj. pertaining to sheep. ~eccio adj. sheepish; n.m. maze, confusion; entrare nel ~eccio, to get into a maze, to get into difficulties. ~ella f. dim. little sheep; ~ella smarrita, lost sheep; (rel.) one of the flock, 'sheep', parishioner; (ichth.) rockling, Onos triciratus; pl. sea-foam, 'white horses'; fleecy clouds; (meteor.) cielo a ~elle, fleecy clouds, mackerel sky; (provb.) cielo a ~elle, acqua a catinelle, a mackerel sky means rain. ~esco adj. (m.pl. ~eschi) stupid, foolish, sheepish. ~escamente adv. foolishly, sheepishly. ~ile adj. of sheep, sheepish; n.m. sheepfold; sheep's dung. ~ino adj. sheep's; pelle ~ina, sheepskin; formaggio ~ino, sheep's milk cheese; carta ~ina, parchment; n.m. sheep's milk cheese; sheep's dung; lamb; †fare come il ~ino di Dicomano, to show one's hand, to reveal one's limitations, to appear at the

least opportune moment. ~o m. (zool.) wether, castrated male sheep. ~ona f. augm. big ewe. ~one m. augm. ram, big sheep; (fig.) blockhead; poor-spirited creature; studiare il ~one, to be ignorant. ~oso adj. (of country) rich in sheep. ~ume m. (fig.) servile flock; servility.

pe·ctico adj. (bot.; chem.) pectic.

pect·ina f. (chem.) pectin. ~oli·tico adj. (chem.) pectolytic.

pectis f. indecl. (mus.). See **pettide**.

peculato m. (leg.) peculation; embezzlement of public funds, etc. (C.P.).

peculiar·e adj. peculiar, special, particular. ~mente adv. peculiarly; especially. ~ità f. peculiarity.

pecu·lio m. savings, nest-egg; (leg.) — del condannato, prisoner's savings (C.P.); earnings (of a convict); gratuity (after service); (Rom. antiq.) peculium, private property of a slave or child; — castrense, peculium castrense, a son's gain during military service.

pecu·ni·a f. money; essere a corto di —, to be hard up. ~ale adj. see **pecuniario**. ~a·rio adj. (of) money; pecuniary; multa ~aria, money fine. ~ariamente adv. pecuniarily, in the matter of money. ~oso adj. wealthy; avaricious.

pedag·gi·o m. toll; ponte soggetto a —, toll-bridge; (naut.) canal tax; †(Genoa) tax on merchandise; †footing, a tribute exacted by seamen on those who climbed aloft for the first time or passed through the Straits of Gibraltar or across the equator. ~ere m. toll-collector.

pedagn·a f. (naut.) stretcher, foot-rest used in rowing. ~uolo m. stock or trunk of a young tree; plank-bridge, tree-trunk serving as a bridge over a ditch; billet of charcoal.

pedago·gic·a f. pedagogics. ~o adj. pedagogic(al). ~amente adv. pedagogically.

pedago·go m. (pl. ~ghi) pedagogue; teacher. ~gheri·a f. pedantry. ~gi·a f. pedagogy, education. ~gismo m. pedagogism. ~gista m. student of pedagogy (pedagogics). ~gizzare [A 1] intr. (aux. avere) (derog.) to play the pedagogue, to be pedantic.

pedal·e m. stock (of a vine), trunk (of a tree); stem; foot (of a stocking); pedal, treadle (of a sewing-machine); cobbler's leather strap; (motor.) — dell'acceleratore, accelerator; il freno a —, the foot-brake; — della frizione, clutch pedal; — d'innesto, clutch pedal; (motor-cycle) — d'avviamento, avviatore a —, kick-starter; (rlwy.) — a sega, rat-trap pedal; (mus.) pedal (of organ, piano, harp, etc.); organ-point, pedal-point; pedals only (indication to an organist not to play harmonies above the figured bass, cf. 'tasto solo' under **tasto**); — acuto, inverted pedal; — celeste, damping pedal; — del forte, sustaining pedal; — figurato, — fiorito, florid pedal; †handle; †foothill. ~are [A 1] intr. (aux. avere) to pedal; to work a treadle; to cycle. ~ata f. push on a pedal; stroke of a treadle. ~eggiare [A 3 c] tr., intr. (aux. avere) to pedal, to cycle; (mus.) to pedal. ~etto m. dim. (mus.) composition-pedal. ~iera f. pedal controls, pedal keyboard; (mus.) pedal-board; ~iera concava-radiale, concave radiating pedal-board; ~iera a ventaglio, radiating pedal-board. ~ino m. dim. (mus.) composition-pedal. ~ista m., f. pedaller, cyclist; ~ista audace, scorcher. ~izzare [A 1] intr. see **pedaleggiare**.

†**pedamento** m. hoarding, planking; trestles.

pedana f. foot-rest; fender; bedside rug; lining at the bottom of a gown, trousers, etc.; (motor.) running board; platform; (gymn.) springboard.

peda·neo adj. (Rom. hist.) un giudice —, a minor judge.

pedano m. trunk (of a tree); (carp.) mortise chisel.

pedant·e¹ m. pedant; fare il —, to be pedantic; finicking. ~eggiare [A 3 c] intr. (aux. avere) to play the pedant, to be pedantic. ~eri·a f. pedantry. ~esco adj. (m.pl. ~eschi) pedantic; (hist.) lingua ~esca; a learned jargon of Latin with Italian endings, in use in the sixteenth century. ~escamente adv. pedantically. ~essa f. blue-stocking. †~izzare vb. and derivs. see **pedanteggiare**.

†**pedante²** m. pedestrian, person on foot.

peda·rio adj., n.m. (Rom. antiq.) (senator) pedarius, (senator) with vote but no right to speak.

pedar(u)ola f. (naut.) tack of a sail.

pedata f. footprint; footstep; seguitare le pedate di uno, to follow in someone's footsteps; sound of a footstep; kick; cacciar fuori uno a pedate, to kick someone out; stair, step; (bldg.) tread.

†**pedemontano** adj., n.m. (geog.) Piedmontese; one who lives in the foothills of a range of mountains.

pederast-a *m.* pederast, sodomite. **-i·a** *f.* (leg.) sodomy.

pedestr-e, †**-o** *adj.* pedestrian; viaggio —, journey on foot; (mil.) milizia —, foot-soldiers, infantry; †scudiero —, shield-bearer on foot; (fig.) dull, monotonous; uninspired, pedestrian. **-eménte** *adv.* (fig.) dully; monotonously; in an uninspired and pedestrian way.

ped-iatra *m.* paediatrician. **-iatri·a** *f.* (med.) paediatrics. **-ia·trico** *adj.* paediatric. **-iatro** *m.* see **pediatra**. **-oco·mio** *m.* children's hospital.

pe·d-ica *f.* footprint; footstep. **-icciuolo** *m.* stalk (of fruits). **-icello** *m.* pedicel; (zool.; med.) *Sarcoptes scabiei*, the acarine parasite causing scabies. **-icolare,** †**-iculare** *adj.* (med.) pedicular. **-icoloso** *adj.* pediculous, lousy. †**-i·culo** *m.* see **pedicciuolo**. **-iculosi** *f.* (med.) pediculosis, infestation with lice. **-icure** *m., f.* chiropodist.

pedignon-e *m.* chilblain (on a foot). †**-e·vole** *adj.* suffering from chilblains (on feet).

pedilu·vio *m.* (med.) foot-bath; paddling (in sea).

pedin-a *f.* (chess) pawn; (draughts) man, piece; (fig.) avere una buona —, to hold a trump card; (joc.) woman of low social standing (as opposed to **dama**, q.v.); (sport) andare di —, (of birds) to run instead of flying (on a shoot). **(-aménto** *m.*) **-are** [A I] *tr.* to follow, to shadow, to trail, to stalk; to spy upon, to dog the steps of; *intr.* (*aux.* avere) to walk very slowly; (of birds) to run instead of flying (on a shoot).

pedino *m. dim.* of **piede**, q.v.

pedis·sequ-o *adj.* servile, fawning; clumsy; traduttore —, overliteral translator; *n.m.* lick-spittle. **-aménte** *adv.* servilely; clumsily; pedantically, literally, word for word.

†**peditato** *m.* (mil.) infantryman.

pedivella *f.* pedal crank (of a bicycle).

pedo *m.* shepherd's staff.

pedofili·a *f.* (med.) paedophilia.

pedoge·neşi *f.* (biol.) paedogenesis.

pedo·metro *m.* (techn.) pedometer.

pedon-e¹ *m.* pedestrian; *adj.* foot-passenger; †(mil.) foot-soldier; *adj.* strada **-a**, footpath. **-a** *f.* woman pedestrian; †(chess) see **pedina**. †**-ag·gio** *m.,* †**-a·glia** *f.* (mil.) foot, foot-soldiers. **-ale** *adj.* (reserved) for foot-passengers, pedestrian; traffico **-ale**, pedestrians; passaggio **-ale**, strisce di attraversamento **-ale**, pedestrian or zebra crossing. †**-cina** *f. dim.* of **pedona**, q.v.

†**pedone²** *m.* (agric.). See **pedale**.

†**pedon-e³,** †**-i** *adv.* on foot, walking.

†**ped-ota,** †**-oto,** †**-otto,** †**-otta** *m.* guide; pilot.

†**pedovare** *tr.* (mil.) to pillage (the countryside) on foot.

peduc·ci-o *m. dim.* little foot; trotter (of pig or other animal); (archit.) small pedestal; bracket, corbel; support, far — a, to support, to back up. **-a·io** *m.* seller of pig's trotters.

pedula *f.* climbing-boot (used in the Alps, made largely of canvas).

pedul-e *m.* stocking foot; in **-i**, in stocking feet, (fig.) barefoot, poverty-stricken; a light boot worn in the mountains; (cul.) omelet with slices of bread.

pedu·ncol-o *m.* (bot.) peduncle; (anat.) peduncle, pedunculus; **-i** cerebellari, pedunculi cerebri. **-are** *adj.* (anat.) peduncular. **-ato** *adj.* (bot.) peduncled; (anat.) pedunculate.

pegamo·ide *f.* (neol.) pegamoid, imitation leather.

Pe·gaş-o *pr.n.m.* (class. myth.) Pegasus. **-e·o** *adj.* (class. myth.) Pegasean; fonte **-ea**, Hippocrene, the Muses' spring; (fig.) poetic inspiration.

peg·gi-o *adv., adj. indecl.* worse, di male in —, from bad to worse; le cose vanno —, things are going from bad to worse; — che mai, worse than ever; tanto —, so much the worse; worst; alla —, at the worst, if the worst comes to the worst, somehow or other, very badly; *n.m.* the worst; temere il —, to fear the worst; *f.* worsening; defeat; the worst thing; avere la —, to get the worst of it. **-oraménto** *m.* worsening, deteriorating; aggravation; ci fu un **-oramento** nel tempo, the weather became worse and worse. **-orare** [A I c] *intr.* (*aux.* essere) to get worse, to become worse; *tr.* to make worse. **-orativo** *adj.* pejorative, depreciative; (gramm.) suffisso **-orativo**, pejorative suffix. **-orativaménte** *adv.* pejoratively. **-orato** *part. adj.* worse; worsened, deteriorated, grown worse. **(-oratóre** *m.* **-oratrice** *f.*) **-ore** *adj.* worse; (provb.) non v'è **-ore** sordo di chi non vuol sentire, there are none so deaf as those who do not wish to hear; *n.m., f.* the worst.

pegmatite *f.* (geol.) pegmatite.

pegn-o *m.* pledge; token; pawn; mettere a —, to pawn; tenere in —,

to hold in pawn; persona che presta denaro su pegni, pawnbroker; agenzia di —, pawnshop; conduttore di credito su —, pawnbroker; polizza di —, pawnticket; in — d'affetto, in token of affection; giuoco dei **-i**, forfeits; (leg.) il costituente del —, pledgor (C.C.); prestito contro —, su —, loan upon, secured by, pledge. **-orare** [A I c] *tr.* to pledge; to pawn.

pegola *f.* pitch.

pegù *m. indecl.* resin (evaporated).

pei, pel *contr.* of **per** with *def. art.* for the.

†**pela-cane,** †**-cucchino,** †**-gatti,** see under **pelare**.

pelagiano *adj.* (eccl. hist.) Pelagian (also *n.m.*).

pela·gico *adj.* (scient.) marine.

pe·la·go *m.* (*pl.* **-ghi**) sea, ocean; — di guai, sea of troubles; *pl.* †(poet.) depths of a river.

pelame *m.* See under **pelo**.

pela·mide *f.* (ichth.) see **palamita**; (zool.) a poisonous sea-snake.

pelandrone *m.* shirker, slacker.

pel-are [A I c] *tr.* to strip (the hair) from; to peel; to skin; to pluck (fowls); to pare; — le patate, to peel the potatoes; — un'arancia, to peel an orange; — un albero, to strip the bark off a tree; (fig.) una gatta da —, a hard nut to crack; ho altre gatte da —, I have other fish to fry; (fig.) to fleece; se vai in quell'albergo ti **-ano**, if you go to that hotel they will make you pay through the nose; è una tramontana che **-a**, it is a biting north wind; (provb.) a penna a penna si **-a** l'oca, every little helps; *rfl.* to lose one's hair, to go bald; to moult; (of trees) to lose their leaves, to become bare; (fig.) to tear one's hair; (of walls) to crack, to develop small cracks; (of plaster) to flake. †**-acane** *m.* tanner. †**-acucchino** *m.* coin of little value. †**-agatti** *m.* rogue, knave, trickster. **-agione** *f.* see **pelatura**. **-agrilli** *m.* miser, skinflint. **-amantelli** *m.* rogue, one who fleeces his customers. †**-amatti** *m.* rogue. **-aménto** *m.* stripping, peeling, plucking; (tanning) unhairing, dewoolling, fellmongering (of sheep pelts). †**-anibbi** *m.* twister, cheat. †**-apiedi** *m. indecl.* debt collector, extortioner. †**-apolli** *m.* useless person. †**-arella** *f.* gossip, slander. **-ata** *f.* pluck, plucking; stripping (in one action); (fig.) fleecing; scrounging; (colloq.) baldness, bald head. **-atina** *f. dim.* (pop.) ringworm; (of animals) mange; moulting. **-ato** *part. adj.* peeled, stripped, bare; testa **-ata**, bald head; (provb.) gallina **-ata** non fa uova, don't kill the goose that lays the golden egg; (of marble, other stone, or plaster) cracked. **-atoio** *m.* tool, or place, for plucking. **-atore** *m.* one who peels, skins or plucks; trickster, rogue. **-atrice** *f.* woman who peels, skins or plucks; (eng.) peeling machine. **-atura** *f.* peeling; stripping; paring; skinning.

pelargo·nio *m.* (bot.) pelargonium, cultivated geranium.

pell-e *f.* (anat.) skin; una ferita a fior di —, a graze; hide; leather, skin; conciare **-i**, to tan hides; — di camoscio, chamois-leather; — di capretto, kid; — greggia, raw hide; — conciata, dressed skin, dressed leather; — lucida, — verniciata, patent leather; legato in —, leather-bound; il serpente cambia la —, the snake casts its skin; salvare la —, to save one's skin; aver la — dura, to be thick-skinned; avere la — d'oca *or* di cappone, to have goose-flesh; far venire la — d'oca ad uno, to make a person's flesh creep; non capire nella — per contentezza, to be beside oneself for joy; (fam.) life; vendere cara la —, to sell one's life dear; ci giocherei la —, I would stake my life on it; amici per la —, friends for life; far la — ad uno, to kill someone; essere nella — d'uno, to be in someone (else)'s shoes; in —, superficially; (fam.) sort of person; tu non sai che — è costui!, you don't know what he is!; (iron.) che buona —!, what a scoundrel!; peel, rind; (paperm.) — d'aglio, onion skin; (bot.) carpet; surface; crust (of the earth); coat (of plaster, etc.); (art) patina; le **-i**, skin on coffee, milk, etc.; (carpen.) glasspaper; (text.) — di pesce, — di diavolo, coarse cotton cloth; — d'uovo, fine muslin. **-ac·cia** *f. pejor.* (fig.) stout, stubborn or cunning person; wicked man; naughty boy; è una **-accia** dura, he is a tough nut. †**-agione** *f.* complexion. **-agra** *f.* (med.) pellagra. **-agro·ide** *adj.* (med.) pellagroid. **-agro·geno** *adj.* (med.) pellagragenic. **-agroşo** *adj.* (med.) pellagrous; *n.m.* pellagrin. **-a·io** *m.* leather dresser; tanner; leather merchant; hide merchant; usurer (who 'flays' or 'fleeces' people). **-ame** *m.* hide, leather; skins; *pl.* (industr.) hides and skins. **-e·tica** *f.* loose growing skin (of a person); tough skin-like tissue in meat. **-etteri·a** *f.* (neol.) hides, leather; leather goods. **-ettiere** *m.* (neol.) leather merchant, dealer in leather goods. **-ionella** *f.* (ent.) clothes moth. **-olina** *f. dim.* film, thin skin.

pellegrin-o *adj.* vagrant; foreign; exotic, rare; novel; strange; i Padri ~i, the Pilgrim Fathers; usanze ~e, foreign customs; *n.m.* (rel.) pilgrim (originally one who visited the shrine of St James in Compostella, as distinguished from 'palmieri', palmers, who went on pilgrimages to the Holy Land, and from 'romei', who visited the shrines of the Apostles in Rome); traveller; tramp; (eng.) movimento al passo di —, intermittent feed motion; (ichth.) basking shark, *Cetohinus maximus*; *pl.* (fam.) lice. †-**amente** *adv.* strangely, in a foreign exotic way; like a pilgrim. ~**a** *f.* female pilgrim; pelerine, tippet; (zool.) see **pellerina**. ~**ag·gio** *m.* pilgrimage; andare in ~aggio, to go on a pilgrimage; visit to a place of commemoration; group of pilgrims. †-**a·io** *m.* part of a hospice where pilgrims or travellers were received; part of a hospital where sick patients were received. ~**ante** *part. adj.* travelling, vagrant, vagabond; *n.m.* vagrant. ~**are** [A1] *intr.* (aux. avere) to go on pilgrimage; to travel; to wander from place to place; (rel.) to be a pilgrim, a sojourner, on earth. ~**a·rio** *m.* pilgrims' hostel. ~**atore** *m.* pilgrim; traveller; sojourner. (~**atrice** *f.*) ~**azione** *f.* pilgrimage; long journey; peregrination. ~**ità** *f.* strangeness; rarity.

pellerin-a *f.* (zool.) scallop, *Pecten jacobaeus*. ~**ella** *f.* (zool.) *Chlamys opercularis* and *C. varia*, edible bivalves like small scallops.

pellerossa *m., f.* See **pellirosse**.

pellet-ica *f.*, ~**tiere** *m.* See under **pelle**.

pelletierina *f.* (pharm.) pelletierine.

pellicano *m.* (orn.) pelican, esp. the white pelican, *Pelecanus onocrotalus*; — riccio, Dalmatian pelican, *P. crispus*; (rel.) Christ as the 'Pelican of mercy' (esp. in reference to the Crucifixion or the Blessed Sacrament); †(chem.) vessel used in distillation; †(surg.) hook used in extracting teeth.

pellic·c-ia *f.* fur; fur coat or other garment; — di volpe, fox cape; — per carrozza, fur-lined carriage-rug; (zool.) fur. ~**eri·a** *f.* furs; furrier's shop; fur-trade. ~**ia·io**, ~**iaro** *m.* furrier. ~**iame** *m.* furs (in quantity). ~**iare** [A3] *tr.* to line (or trim) with fur. (~**iato** *part. adj.*) ~**iere** *m.* see **pellicciaio**. ~**ione** *m.* heavy fur coat; (joc.) scuotere il ~ione a, to thrash, to tan, to give a good hiding to; †to have sexual intercourse with. ~**iotto** *m.* short fur coat; dress trimmed with fur.

pellic-ella *f. dim.* of **pelle**, q.v.; thin skin, membrane; film. ~**ina** *f. dim.* of **pelle**, q.v.; fine skin; ~ina dell'uovo, egg-skin. ~**ino** *m.* corner of a sack; wallet, bag. ~**iuola** *f.* see **pellicola**.

pellionella *f.* See under **pelle**.

pelli·cola *f.* thin skin, membrane; il latte ha fatto la —, there is a skin on the milk; — del chicco di uva, grape-skin; (of fish, snake) scale; (photog.; cinem.) film; — su rocchetto, roll-film; un rotolino di —, a roll of film.

pellirosse *f.pl.* Red Indians; *sing.* un pellirossa, un pellerossa, a Redskin; una pellirossa, una pellerossa, a squaw, a Redskin woman; (derog., fig.) barbarian.

pellolina *f.* See under **pelle**.

pellu·cido *adj.* pellucid; transparent; (geol.) pellucid.

pel-o *m.* hair; di — rosso, red-haired; un — lungo, a long hair; (of animals) fur, coat; (of dogs) dal — raso, smooth-haired; con — ruvido, rough-haired, wire-haired; — di capra d'Angora, mohair; — di cammello, camel hair; (wool) — perduto, mother hair; caccia di —, hunting (of ground game); cavalcare a —, to ride bareback; un — di ciglio, an eye-lash; i ~i della barba, the hair of the beard; è un giovanotto di primo —, he is very young; non sono più di primo —!, I wasn't born yesterday!; (bot.) pubescence; thin crack (in a wall); il muro ha fatto —, the wall is cracked; vein (in marble); surface (of a liquid); a — d'acqua, on the surface of the water; hairsbreadth, very little; essere a un — di, to be within a hairsbreadth of; ci mancò un — che non cadesse, per un — non cadde, he was within a hairsbreadth of falling; non ci corre un —, there is no difference; le mie parole non lo smossero d'un —, my words did not deter him in the least; cercare il — nell'uovo, to be very fastidious, to seek to find fault, to look closely into something; a —, exactly; vi corrisponde a —, it matches exactly; andare al —, to do just as one likes; contro —, the wrong way, against the grain; avere il cuore con tanto di —, to be very hard-hearted; avere il — sullo stomaco, to be ruthless, to be unscrupulous; esser d'un — e d'una buccia, to have just the same character; lisciare il — a uno, to rub someone down the right way; non torcere un — a uno, not to hurt a hair of someone's head; fare il — e il contropelo, (of a barber) to shave with the

lie of the hair and then against it, (fig.) to indulge in malicious gossip; non ha ~i sulla lingua, he is very frank; ci lascerai il —, it will cost you dear. ~**ame** *m.* (zool.) the skin or coat of an animal, especially the fur. ~**one** *m. augm.* (text.) coarse cloth.

pelo-bate *m.* (zool.) toad-frog, *Pelobates* spp. ~**emi·a** *f.* (med.) pelohaemia.

pelori·a *f.* (bot.) peloria.

Pelor-o *pr.n.f.* (class.) Pelorus; (med. geog.) Peloro, name of a promontory near Messina (also called Capo di Faro). ~**itano** *adj.* (geog.) Peloritan, of Peloro.

pelos-o *adj.* hairy, hirsute; shaggy; rough-haired; (fig.) not disinterested; (bot.) fagiolo —, vernal whitlow grass, *Erophila verna*. ~**ella** *f.*, ~**etta** *f.* (bot.) mouse-ear hawkweed, *Hieracium pilosella*. ~**ina** *f.* (bot.) see **pelosella**; (silkb.) first sleep of silkworms. ~**ino** *m.* (joc.) barber. ~**ità** *f.* hairiness, shagginess.

pelot-a *f.* (sport) pelota, a Basque game somewhat resembling tennis or rackets, played in a large court with a ball and a racket of wickerwork fastened on the hand. ~**aro** *m.* player of pelota.

†**pelotone** *m.* (mil.). See **plotone**.

pelta *f.* (Gk. antiq.) light shield.

peltr-o *m.* pewter; metal; wealth. ~**a·io** *m.* tinsmith, worker in pewter. ~**ato** *adj.* tinned.

†**pelu·ia** *f.* See **peluria**.

pelu·ria *f.* downy covering; down, soft hair; (text.) floss silk; fluff; inner shell of chestnut; coperto di —, downy.

peluto *adj.* (pop.) hairy (cf. **peloso**).

peluzzo *m.* short, soft hair; fine cloth.

pelv-i *f.* (anat.) pelvis; grande —, pelvis falsa; piccola —, pelvis vera. ~**i·grafo** *m.* (med.) pelvigraph. ~**imetri·a** *f.* (med.) pyelometry. ~**i·metro** *m.* (med.) pyelometer.

pe·lvico *adj.* (anat.) pelvic.

pe·mfigo *m.* (med.) pemphigus, blister-like vesicular pimples on the skin; (ent.) *Pemphigus bursarius*, a common aphid causing conspicuous galls in the leaf petioles of poplar trees.

pen-a *f.* (leg.) penalty; punishment; applicazione, esecuzione di —, infliction, carrying out of punishment; la — inflitta, the sentence (C.P.); l'atto dell'infliggere la —, the passing of sentence (C.P.P.); sotto — di, on penalty of; la — di morte, la — capitale, death penalty; — pecuniaria, fine; scontare una —, to suffer punishment, to undergo a sentence; paga ora la — dei suoi peccati, he is now paying for his sins; pain, suffering, trouble, distress; sorrow; aver compagno al duol sana la —, two in distress makes sorrow less; pity; difficulty; mia madre era nella più grande —, my mother was extremely anxious; non stia in — per me, don't worry about me; darsi —, to be sorry or anxious, to take trouble; non si diede la — di scrivermi, he did not take the trouble to write to me; non ne vale la —, it is not worth while; non vale la — di leggerlo, it is not worth reading; perchè dovrei prendermi la — di spiegare questo?, why should I trouble to explain this?; mi fate —, I pity you; ciò mi fa —, that distresses me, I am sorry; a —, a gran —, a mala —, hardly, scarcely; può a mala — farsi capire, he can hardly make himself understood; lo conosco a mala —, I scarcely know him; (rel.) (ecclesiastical) penalty, punishment (spiritual or temporal); pain(s) of Hell or Purgatory. †-**ace** *adj.* retributive; painful. ~**ale** *adj.* (leg.) criminal; penal; clausola ~ale, penalty clause (C.C.); codice ~ale, criminal, penal code (C.P.); procedure ~ali, criminal, penal procedure (C.P.P.); *n.f.* (leg.) penalty; agreed liquidated damages (C.C.). ~**almente** *adv.* penally; (leg.) responsabile ~almente, criminally liable. ~**alista** *m.* (leg.) authority on criminal law. ~**alità** *f.* (leg.; sport) penalty. ~**alizzare** [A1] *tr.* to inflict a penalty on, to detract points from (e.g. in a motorcar rally). ~**ante** *part. adj.* undergoing punishment; suffering, in trouble. †-**anza** *f.* pain, grief, travail. ~**are** [A1c] *intr.* (aux. avere; *prep.* a) to suffer; to find it difficult, to be hardly able to wait (for); to take pains; ha finito di ~are, his sufferings are over; ~ava a farsi capire, he could hardly make himself understood; ~ai un poco a trovare la vostra casa, I had some difficulty in finding your house; *rfl.* to take pains, to take trouble. ~**arella** *f. dim.* light punishment; little trouble. ~**ato** *part. adj.* troubled, suffering, afflicted.

Penati *pr.n.m.pl.* (Rom. myth.) Penates, household gods; (fig.) home.

pencol-are [A1s] *intr.* (aux. avere) to hang over, to hang down; to dangle; to be unsteady; to totter; to waver, to hesitate. ~**ante** *part. adj.* dangling; wavering. ~**ìo** *m.* dangling. ~**one** *m.* totterer, unsteady walker.

pen·d-ere [B I] *intr.* (*aux.* avere) to hang, to hang down; to dangle; — di sotto a, to hang below, to show beneath; to overhang; to lean; to include, to be inclined (also fig.); to slope; (fig.) to be pending; to depend; un quadro -e dal muro, a picture hangs on the wall; — a sinistra, to lean over to the left; la torre di Pisa -e, the tower of Pisa leans over; — verso la valle, to slope down towards the valley; -eva verso il Comunismo, he showed a tendency towards Communism; vino che -e al dolce, slightly sweet wine; to be pending; -ono ancora le trattative, negotiations are still pending; — tra il sì ed il no, to be unable to make up one's mind; — dalla volontà altrui, to be dependent on someone else's wishes; — dalla bocca, dalle labbra, dalle parole, di uno, to hang upon someone's words. **-a·glio** *m.* (mil.) swordbelt strap; -aglio da forca, gallows-bird; *pl.* (bed) curtain, hangings. **-ente** *part. adj.* hanging (down); dangling; drooping; leaning; torre -ente, leaning tower; inclined, sloping; (fig.) pending, unsettled, outstanding; doubtful; undecided; †(gramm.) passato -ente, imperfect tense; (leg.) lite -ente, *lis pendens*, pending action; *n.m.* slope; pendant; ear-drop, drop ear-ring; fringe (e.g. of lace); †bed-curtain, hangings; †fruit (hanging) on the tree; †(naut.) pennant on the mainmast of a galley; vertical fishnet. **-enza** *f.* slope, gradient, declivity; la strada ha una forte -enza, the road is very steep; (fig.) affair pending; tutte queste -enze sono state regolate, all these affairs have been settled; outstanding balance; (leg.) pendency; -enza della lite, pendency of action (C.C.P.); -enza del termine, pendency of the term or due date (C.C.); (bldg.) tetto ad una sola -enza, lean-to roof; (radio) transconductance. **-evole** *adj.* pendulous, pensile. **-ice** *f.* slope, declivity; hill-side; †part of a city near the walls; †andare alle -ici, (of a city) to be destroyed; †mettere alle -ici, to sack, to destroy. **-ino** *m.* (electr. rlwy.) suspension wire. **-io** *m.* (*pl.* -ii) slope, declivity; incline; gradient; sul -io, on the slant; essere a -io, to slope; in -io, slopingly; †pigliar -io, to make off; †prendere altro -io, to find a new love.

pe·ndol-a *f.* pendulum clock. **-ina** *f. dim.* small pendulum clock.

pendolare[1] *adj.* pendulous, oscillating, swinging; (med.) movimento —, pendular movement.

pendol-are[2] [A I s] *intr.* (*aux.* avere) to swing, to swing to and fro; to be pendulous, to slope. **-amento** *m.* swinging to and fro; (eng.) hunting. **-one, oni** *adv.* dangling, hanging pendulously.

pe·ndol-o[1] *m.* pendulum; plumb-line; (mil.) — balistico, ballistic pendulum, used for calculating muzzle velocities; (naut.) pendulum in a torpedo, which together with the depth-keeping mechanism controls the horizontal fins; pendant. **-ino** *m. dim.* little pendulum; (orn.) penduline tit, *Remiz pendulinus*. **-one** *m. augm.* hangings; fringe; -oni del letto, bed curtains.

pe·ndolo[2] *adj.* See **pendulo**.

pendol-one[1], **-oni** *adv.* See under **pendolare**[2].

pendol-one[2] *m. augm.* See under **pendolo**[1].

pe·ndulo *adj.* pendulous; hanging; drooping; swinging; dangling; (fig.) stare in —, to be undecided; (anat.) pendulous.

pene *m.* (anat.) penis.

penello *m.* (naut.) fishtrap; narrow mole; groin (on the coast); flag or burgee, senior officer's pennant; wind direction indicator, 'windsock'; ancora a —, anchor catted or 'a cock bill' ready for letting go.

Pene·lop-e *pr.n.f.* (class. myth.) Penelope; (fig.) a woman who remains faithful to her husband during a long absence; tela di —, Penelope's web, (fig.) endless task. **-e·o** *adj.* of Penelope.

pene·se *m.* See **pennese**.

penetr-are [A I s] *intr.* (*aux.* essere; *prep.* in) to penetrate (into), to enter, to come in; to sink in; qui la luce non -a mai, light never penetrates here; *tr.* to penetrate, to pierce, to break into; to permeate, to pervade; to sink into; to fathom, to see through; le sue preghiere -arono il mio cuore, his pleading touched me to the heart; non riesco a — l'animo suo, I really cannot understand what is in his mind; il genio -a le più astruse verità, genius fathoms the most abstruse truths; *rfl.* to enter thoroughly (into a part); to identify oneself (with). **-abile** *adj.* penetrable; accessible, susceptible. (**-abilità** *f.*) **-ale** *adj.* innermost; *n.m.* innermost recess; secret room; il -ale del cuore, one's deepest feelings. **-amento** *m.* penetration, entering. **-ante** *part. adj.* penetrating; piercing; acute; searching; ferita -ante, deep wound; parole -anti, moving words. †**-anza** *f.* see **penetrazione**. **-ativa** *f.* insight, acute intelligence. **-ativo** *adj.* sharp, acute, penetrating. **-ato** *part.*

adj. pierced; understood; fathomed, pervaded, permeated; (fig.) essere -ato di, to be keenly aware of. (**-atore** *m.* **-atrice** *f.*) **-azione** *f.* penetration; (fig.) insight; intuition; -azione pacifica, peaceful penetration. †**-e·vole** *adj.* penetrating. **-o·metro** *m.* (chem. indust.) penetrometer.

penice *f.* (naut., Genoa) pinnace.

penicillina *f.* (pharm.) penicillin.

penichella *f.* (Rom.) fare la —, to have forty winks.

peninsulare *adj.* peninsular; l'Italia —, the Italian mainland.

peni·sola *f.* (geog.) peninsula; (fig.) la —, Italy, the mainland (as opposed to Sicily); — Balcanica, Balkan Peninsula; — dei Pescatori, Ribachi Peninsula.

peniten-te *adj.* (rel.) penitent; *n.m., f.* penitent; one who goes regularly to confession; *pl.pr.n.m., f.* Penitents (various groups or congregations). **-temente** *adv.* penitently, repentantly. **-za** *f.* (rel.) penitence; penance (as sacrament or as canonical punishment); †prender -za, to go to confession; Ordine della -za, Order of Penance; forfeit (party games); punishment, pain, trouble; (joc.) venga a far -za con noi, come and have a bite with us; (school) mettere in -za, to punish; (in games) forfeit. **-ziale** *adj.* (rel.) penitential (Psalms, works); *n.m.* person doing penance, or undergoing punishment; convict. †**-ziare** *tr.* to inflict punishment on; *rfl.* to submit to punishment. **-zia·rio** *adj.* penitentiary; *n.m.* reformatory; convict prison. **-ziere** *m.* (eccl.) penitentiary (priest); -ziere maggiore, Grand Penitentiary. **-zieri·a** *f.* (eccl.) penitentiary (tribunal); status or residence of priests with special faculties for confession.

penn-a *f.* feather; quill; plume; caccia di —, shooting game or other birds; metter le -e, to be fledged, to grow feathers, (fig.) to get ready to leave the nest; — d'oca, goose-quill, quill pen; — di struzzo, ostrich feather; farsi bello con le -e del pavone, to wear (be adorned with) borrowed plumes; levare a uno le -e maestre, to clip someone's wings thoroughly, to take away most of his property; occhio alla —!, look out!, take care!; pen; — stilografica, — a serbatoio, fountain pen; uomo di —, penman; scorso di —, slip of the pen; — a sfera, ball pen, ball-point pen; passare a —, to ink in; testo a —, manuscript; lasciare nella —, to leave unwritten; non sa tenere la — in mano, he cannot write; dar di — a qualche cosa, to cross something out; un frego di —, a (cancelling) stroke of the pen; (art) schizzo a —, pen and ink sketch; (fig.) writer; è una delle migliori -e italiane, he is one of the best Italian writers; (poet.) wing; le -e del vento, the wings of the wind; (mountain-) peak; cane da —, retriever (for wildfowl, feathered game); (eng.) — di martello, peen; (mus.) plectrum; quill (of harpsichord); (naut.) peak of a lateen or lugsail; head of a triangular sail; capelli della —, stu'nsail guys; imbroglio di —, ingiaro della —, peak bails; inghinatura della —, peak lashing; far la —, far l'uomo alla —, to be a masthead look-out; mettere, mandare alla —, to place or send aloft the masthead look-out. **-acchiera** *f.* plume on a helmet or horse's head; ornamental plume-holder. **-acchietto** *m. dim.* small plume, tuft of feathers. **-a·cchio** *m.* plume, bunch of feathers; cloud of smoke; (archit.) corbel, bracket; (bot.) -acchio rotondo, cotton grass, *Eriophorum scheucheri*; -acchi penzoli, broad-leaved cotton grass, *E. latifolium*; (naut.) windvane (usu. made of feathers); topsail or peak sail; palm of an anchor. **-acchino, -accino** *m.* (naut.) dolphin strike; vento del -acchino, martingale. **-acchiuto** *adj.* plumed, adorned with large feathers. †**-aggio** *m.* plumage. **-a·io** *m.* feather-dresser, one who sells feather ornaments for hats. **-ai(u)olo** *m.* quill-case, pen-case; pen-dealer; (derog.) scribbler, penny-a-liner. **-ata** *f.* penful (of ink); stroke of the pen; (agric.) bill-hook. **-atella** *f. dim.* light bill-hook. **-ato** *adj.* feathered; (bot.) pinnate; *n.m.* (agric.) bill-hook; *pl.* the feathered tribe, birds. **-ec·chio** *m.* distaff-ful (of flax, etc.).

pennell-o *m.* paint-brush, brush; (fig.) painter; un quadro del medesimo —, a picture from the same brush; l'arte del —, painting; fare una cosa a —, to do something extremely well; fatto a —, well-finished; stare a —, to fit to a 't', to fit like a glove; triangular flag; pennant; commodore pennant; windvane; avere, tenere l'occhio a —, to keep an eye on the wind; to keep a weather eye lifting; tenere il — per, to be sailing towards or making for; sotto un —, under the same flag; additional small anchor; ancora a —, anchor a cock bill, vertical, ready for letting go; — di mezzodì, noon flag, equivalent to time ball; a —, of a flag hoisted close up, usually the International code flag or

pennell·o (*cont.*)

answering pennant, signifying 'I can read and understand your signal'; groyne in a river; (opt.) pencil (of rays); (radio) beam. **-are** [A I] *intr.* (*aux.* avere) to paint, to work with a brush; (naut.) to back an anchor with a grapple to add to its resistance. **-ata** *f.* brush-stroke; brush-work; dare le ultime **-ate**, to put the last touches (to a picture); construction of a dyke on a river. **-ato** *part. adj.* touched up, painted, brushed. **-atura** *f.* brush-work; painting. **-eggiare** [A 3 c] *tr.* to paint, to colour; (fig.) to paint (by verbal description); *intr.* (*aux.* avere) to use the brush, to paint. (**-eggiato** *part. adj.*) **-eggiatore** *m.* painter; word-painter. (**-eggiatrice** *f.*) **-essa** *f.* large bristle-brush; wide, flat brush.

pennese *m.* (naut. hist.) victualling personnel (thirteenth to seventeenth centuries); Captain of the hold (early nineteenth century); supply rating; purser's staff; yeoman or storekeeper; — del nostromo, boatswain's storeman; — del capo-torpedinieri, torpedo gunner's yeoman; barca —, pilot boat.

pennetta *f.* (ichth.) fin.

pennin·a *f.* pen-nib, steel pen; (bot.) — del paradiso, *Stipa pennata.* **-er·vio** *adj.* (bot.) pinnately veined. **-o** *m.* pen-nib, steel pen.

Pennini *pr.n.m.pl.* (geog.) Pennines.

penniven·dolo *m.* scribbler; hack; ghost-writer.

pennolina *f. dim.* of penna, q.v.

pennon-e *m. augm.* of **penna**, q.v.; (mil.) pennant; colour; a number of soldiers under one flag; regimental flag (cavalry); plumes on a lance; (naut.) yard; — secco, bare poles, without sail; **-i stretti**, **-i bracciati di punto**, braced up yards; **-i imbrancati**, scandalized yards; **-i a segno**, yards braced up to the marks; (herald.) pennon. **-cello** *m. dim.* small flag; streamer; plume.

pen·nula *f.* fish-fin.

pennuto *adj.* feathered; fledged; *n.m.pl.* i pennuti, feathered folk, birds.

penombra *f.* (astron.) penumbra; (fig.) shadow, half-light; stare nella —, to stay in the shadow(s), to be retiring by nature; figure in —, figures in shadow.

penos-o *adj.* painful; troublesome; distressing; difficult; trying. **-amente** *adv.* painfully; with difficulty.

pens-are [A I] *intr.* (*aux.* avere) to think, to reflect, to meditate; **-a e ripensa**, gli venne finalmente in mente, he thought and thought and at last it occurred to him; — a, to think of (to direct thought to, to dwell upon); — a uno, to think of a person, to be considerate towards someone; — a, to provide for, to look after; to see to; ci **-erò**, I'll think it over; ci **-erò io**, I'll see to it, leave it to me; **-arci su**, think over it; un libro che fa —, a book that makes one think; dar da — a uno, to make one suspicious, apprehensive, to give a person food for thought; quella febbre ostinata mi dava molto a —, that persistent fever caused me much anxiety; — di, to think of, to hold a certain opinion of; che ne **-i**?, what do you think of it?; — bene di uno, to have a good opinion of someone; to believe; to consider; tu **-i** di farmi paura?, do you think you can frighten me?; non **-avo** che fosse possibile, I did not think it possible; to mean, to resolve, to intend; ho **-ato** di partire, I have made up my mind to go, non **-ava** di far del male, he meant no harm; **-avo** di partire oggi, I intended to start today; **-ate!**, just think of it!; lo fece senza —, he did it unthinkingly; digli di — ai casi suoi, tell him to mind his own business; **-a** a quello che stai facendo, mind what you are about; *tr.* to think out; to think over; to think about; to imagine; to meditate upon; to contrive; to plan; che **-ate**?, what are you thinking about?; non — a tutto il male che fa, he does not intend all the harm he does; ne **-a** sempre una nuova, he's always thinking up some new trick; una ne fa e cento ne **-a**, he has hardly finished one thing when he is planning a hundred more; — le sventure sofferte, to dwell upon misfortunes suffered; questo lo **-ò** già Aristotele, Aristotle had the same idea; lascio — a voi, I leave it to your imagination; *n.m.* thought. **-a·bile** *adj.* conceivable, imaginable, thinkable; non **-abile**, unthinkable. **-abilità** *f.* possibility; being conceivable. **-acchiare** [A 3] *intr.* (*aux.* avere) to be pensive; to give a thought now and then. **-amento** *m.* thinking, thought; idea; intention; solicitude; uneasiness. **-ante** *part. adj.* thinking; †thoughtful; *n.m., f.* one who thinks; (derog.) i ben **-anti**, Philistines. **-ata** *f.* thought; idea; una buona **-ata**, a good idea; †fuori di ogni **-ata**, quite unexpectedly. **-ativo** *adj.* thinking, thoughtful; prudent. **-ato** *part. adj.* considered; (of persons) prudent; thoughtful; †*n.m.* thought; thinking. **-atamente** *adv.*

deliberately, intentionally; on purpose, purposely; parlare **-ata-mente**, to speak after reflection. **-atoio** *m.* (Gk. lit.) the 'thinking-house' of Socrates in Aristophanes' *Clouds*; (joc.) entrare nel **-atoio**, to put on one's thinking-cap. **-atore** *m.* thinker; libero **-atore**, free-thinker. (**-atrice** *f.*) †**-azione** *f.* thought, thinking.

pensée *f. indecl.* (pron. as Fr.) (bot.) pansy, *Viola tricolor* var. *hortensis.*

pensiere[1] *m.* loop on a spinner's breast to hold the end of the distaff; bunch of wool or hemp to be spun.

†**pensiere**[2] *m.* See **pensiero.**

pensier-o *m.* thought; idea; un — gentile, a kind thought; fu un — geniale, it was a brilliant idea; essere assorto in un —, essere sopra —, to be absorbed in thought; lettore del —, thought-reader; veloce come il —, quick as thought; mind, way of thinking; giacchè siamo dello stesso —, since we are of one mind; opinion; system of thought, ideas, philosophy; il — del Vico, Vico's philosophy; mutar —, to change one's mind; intention; non avevo alcun — di andarmene, I had no intention of leaving; trouble: non si diede mai — di scrivere, he never took the trouble to write; anxiety, solicitude; care; stare in —, to be anxious, to be uneasy; l'educazione dei figli è un gran —, bringing up children occasions much anxiety; ciò gli dava molto —, that caused him great anxiety; la sua vita è sempre stata piena di **-i**, his life has always been full of worry; care. attention; mettere tutto il suo — in, to give all his attention to; object of care, of desire, etc; è tutto il suo —, it is all he thinks about, it is his chief preoccupation; non dà —, it is easy, it's no trouble; (theol.) peccati di —, sins of thought; (bot.) viola del —; see **pensée.** †**-ato** *adj.* thoughtful. **-oso** *adj.* thoughtful, pensive; serious, grave; sedate (also *n.m.*) (cf. **pensoso**).

pen·sil-e *adj.* hanging (down); suspended, pensile; giardini **-i**, hanging gardens; (electr.) quadro —, hanging switchboard. **-ina** *f.* projecting roof; arched roof of a railway station; roof of a railway platform; bus-shelter.

Pensilva·nia *pr.n.f.* (geog.) Pennsylvania.

pension-e *f.* pension; — per la vecchiaia, old-age pension; board; boarding-house; boarding-school; albergo con —, hotel providing board (as well as lodging); stare a —, to be a boarder, to live 'en pension'; — completa, full board and lodging; mezza —, dinner, bed and breakfast, but not lunch; †salary, stipend. **-ante** *m., f.* boarder. **-are** [A I c] *tr.* to pension (off). **-a·rio** *m.* pensioner; boarder, paying-guest; (hist.) Gran **-ario**, Prime Minister of Holland (1619–1794). **-ato** *part. adj.* pensioned (off); on a pension; *n.m.* pensioner; holder of a bursary; boarding-school.

†**pensivo** *adj.* See **pensoso.**

pensos-o *adj.* pensive, thoughtful; serious, grave; anxious; — più di sè che d'altrui, thinking of oneself rather than of others. **-amente** *adv.* thoughtfully; seriously, gravely; anxiously.

pensucchiare [A 3] *intr.* (*aux.* avere) to give an occasional thought (to something).

pent-a·colo *m.* five-pointed star, pentacle. **-acordo** *m.* (mus.) pentachord; five-stringed lyre; fifth. **-adecacordo** *m.* (mus.) fifteen-note scale; instrument of fifteen strings; fifteenth. **-adat·tilo** *adj.* (zool.) pentadactyl. **-ae·dro** *adj.* (geom.) pentahedral; *n.m.* pentahedron. **-afonale** *adj.* (mus.) pentatonic; scala anemitonica **-afonale**, tonal pentatonic scale. **-afoni·a** *f.* (mus.) concord of the fifth. **-agonale** *adj.* (geom.) pentagonal. **-a·gono** *m.* (geom.) pentagon. **-agramma** *m.* (mus.) five-line stave. **-agrammato** *adj.* (mus.) furnished with blank staves; carta **-agrammata**, music paper. **-alfa** *f.* (herald.) pentalpha. **-a·metro** *m.* (prosod.) pentameter. **-ano** *m.* (chem.) pentane. **-a·poli** *f.* (hist. geog.) Pentapolis, group of five towns. †**-apolitano** *adj., n.m.* Pentapolitan; sodomite. **-archi·a** *f.* pentarchy; (hist.) the five Great Powers of Europe, 1815–60. **-armo·nico** *adj.* (mus.) five-toned (ancient Greek music). **-asil·labo** *adj.* (prosod.) pentasyllabic; *n.m.* line verse, of five syllables. **-ate·uco** *m.* (Bibl.) Pentateuch. **-atlo** *m.* (Gk. antiq.) pentathlon; an event comprising five contests in the modern Olympic games, etc. **-a·tono** *m.* (mus.) pentatone, augmented sixth.

Pentecoste *pr.n.f.* (Jewish rel.) Pentecost, Feast of Weeks; (eccl.) Pentecost, Whitsuntide.

pente·lico *adj.* of Pentelicus, applied to the white marble from a mountain of that name, in Greece.

pent-ire [D I] *rfl.* (*prep.* di) to repent, to be sorry, to regret (something); non vi **-irete** mai di questo, you will never regret it; voleva farsi medico, ma poi se ne **-ì**, he wanted to be a doctor, but after-

pent·ire (*cont.*)

wards he changed his mind (he regretted it); ve ne -irete!, you'll be sorry! **-imento** *m.* repentance, regret; ebbi un -imento, I changed my mind; *pl.* corrections, alterations (e.g. made by a painter on a picture), second thoughts. **-ito**, **†-uto** *part. adj.* sorry, penitent, repentant; è -ito di quel che ha fatto, he is sorry for what he has done; *n.m.* penitent; ricovero delle -ite, asylum for reformed prostitutes. **†-uta** *f.* repentance, change of heart.

pentodo *m.* (radio) pentode.

pentol-a *f.* (two-handled) pot (of earthenware or metal); saucepan; potful, saucepanful, panful; deve lavorar molto per mantenere la — al fuoco, he has to work hard to keep the pot boiling; sappiamo che cosa bolle in —, we know what is brewing; (provb.) dura più una — fessa che una sana, a creaking gate hangs longest; (provb.) il diavolo insegna a far la —, ma non il coperchio, be sure your sins will find you out; cavar gli occhi della —, to skim the pot, (fig.) to take off the cream; fare la — a due manichi, to stand with hands on hips; portare a -e, to carry (e.g. a child) on one's shoulders, with legs astride one's neck; *pl.* (fam.) fat cheeks; (mil.) — di fuoco, primitive incendiary bomb consisting of a pot filled with combustibles, suitably primed; brazier used for illuminating trenches, walls or saps. **-a·io**, **†-aro** *m.* potter; seller of earthenware; fare come l'asino del -aio, to keep stopping to gossip. **-ata** *f.* potful, saucepanful, panful. **-ina** *f.*, **-ino** *m. dim.* small pot; kettle; modest family meal; accozzare i -ini, to eat together, each bringing his own food; tornare al -ino, to return to simple fare (after a period of overeating); -ino della colla, glue-pot; (joc.) soldier's képi or peaked cap. **-ine** *f.pl.* (bot.) grape hyacinth, *Muscari.* **-o** *m.* small, one-handled pot; saucepan. **-one** *m. augm.* large pot, boiler; (fig.) blockhead.

pentosano *m.* (chem.) pentosan.

pento·șio *m.* (chem.) pentose.

pentos·sido *m.* (chem.) pentoxide.

†pentut-a *f.* repentance, change of heart. **†-o** *part.* of pentire, q.v.

pe·nula *f.* (Rom. antiq.) *paenula,* (heavy) cloak; (eccl.) (primitive) chasuble.

penul·tim-o *adj.* last but one, penultimate. (**-amente** *adv.*)

penu·ri-a *f.* scarcity, lack, dearth, penury; (comm.) — di denaro sul mercato, pressure on the money market. **†-oso** *adj.* penurious; infertile.

penzol-are [A I S] *intr.* (*aux.* avere) to dangle, to hang down, to be suspended. **-ante** *part. adj.* hanging, dangling, suspended.

†pen·zolo *adj.* dangling, hanging, pendulous; *n.m.* hanging cluster, bunch (of grapes, etc.); (naut.) sling; — della candelizza, gantry.

penzolon-i, **-e** *adv.* dangling; drooping; stare -i, to dangle, to hang down; swinging; con le orecchie -i, with drooping ears; egli cammina con le braccia -i, he swings his arms as he walks.

pe-one *m.* (prosod.) paeon (metrical foot). **-o·nico** *adj.* (prosod.) paeonic.

peo·nia *f.* (bot.) peony, *Paeonia.*

peota *m.* (naut., Ven.) pilot; — pratico, harbour pilot; pilot boat (oars and sail); racing gig (eight oars).

pep-e *m.* pepper; — di Caienna, Cayenne pepper; (bot.) — cornuto, red pepper, *Capsicum annuum*; — d'acqua, waterpepper, *Polygonum hydropiper*; — di palude, pillwort, *Pilularia globulifera*; (fig.) non volli metterci nè sale ne —, I did not want to interfere; quel ragazzo è tutto —, that boy has all his wits about him. **-aiuola** *f.* pepper-box, pepper-pot. **-ato** *adj.* peppered; spiced; pan -ato, gingerbread; (fig.) peppery; pungent, witty; una risposta -ata, a witty reply; peppery, irritable; spicy, salacious. **-erino**, **†-erigno** *adj.* pepper-coloured; *n.m.* tufa. **-erone** *m.* capsicum, chilli; (fig., joc.) big nose; rosso come un -erone, (of the face) red as a turkey-cock. **-ino** *m.* quick-witted child; far -ino, to blow on the fingers of one hand gathered together.

pepiniera *f.* See vivaio.

pepita *f.* (mining) nugget.

peplo *m.* (Gk. antiq.) peplos, peplus.

pep·pola *f.* (orn.) brambling, *Fringilla montifringilla.*

pepsina *f.* (biol.; chem.) pepsin; (pharm.) pepsin; (pharm. veg.) papain (enzyme of papaw tree, *Carica papays*).

pep·t-ico *adj.* (physiol.) peptic; unità -ica, pepsin unit. **-izzazione** *f.* (chem.) peptization. **-o·geno** *adj.* (physiol.) peptogenic, peptogenous. **-o·lisi** *f.* (physiol.) peptolysis. **-one** *m.* (physiol.) peptone. **-o·nico** *adj.* peptonic. **-onizzare** [A I] *tr.* (med.) to peptonize. **-onizzazione** *f.* peptonization. **-onuri·a** *f.* (med.) peptonuria.

per *prep.* (*contr.* with *def. art.*; **pel**, **pello**, **pei**, **pegli**, **pella**, **pelle**; these forms are found, but are now little used). **1.** SPACE: through, by way of; passare — Roma, to go through Rome, to go by way of Rome; — mare e — terra, by sea and land; camminare — i campi, to walk through the fields; girare — il mondo, to travel the world over; entrare — la finestra, to enter by the window; un brivido — la schiena, a shiver up and down one's spine; (fig.) passare — la mente a, (of thought, idea) to pass through the mind of. **2.** TIME: through, during; — tutto l'inverno, throughout the winter; — tutta la vita, for life; — l'addietro, in the past; una volta — sempre, once for all; — ora, for now; — tutta la strada essa non fece che piangere, she did nothing but cry all the time we were on the road; (anticipation of a division of time) by; — domani, by tomorrow; partirò — settembre, I shall have left by the beginning of September; la casa s'appigiona — marzo, the house will be to let at the beginning of March; — la fine del mese, by the end of the month; — Natale, by Christmas (cf. under no. 4); alzarsi — tempo, to get up early. **3.** AGENCY: — giorno, *per diem,* by the day; — anno, *per annum,* yearly; (transport, communication) by; — ferrovia, by rail; — posta, by post; — telegrafo, by telegraph, by wire; condurre — mano, to lead by the hand; — lettera, by letter; — iscritto, in writing; by means of, by way of, through; lo manderò — mio fratello, I will send it by my brother; lo seppe — bocca d'altri, he heard it from someone else. **4.** DESTINATION, OBJECT, PURPOSE: for; partì — Roma, he set out for Rome; tende — finestre, window curtains (for windows); pasticche — la tosse, cough sweets; regali — Natale, Christmas presents; mandate — il medico, send for the doctor; siete pronto — il tè?, are you ready for tea? **5.** RELATIONSHIP: for, as for, in relation to; che è ciò — voi?, what is that to you?; — me non ci vado, as for me, I am not going; according to; — me non è un grande scrittore, in my opinion he is not a great writer. **6.** REASON, SAKE: through, on account of, owing to; non fosse — quello sarei felice, but for that I should be happy; dovette rimanere a Firenze — la sua malferma salute, he had to stay in Florence on account of his bad health; fu — colpa vostra che arrivai in ritardo, it was all through you that I was late; dimenticai le ingiurie — compassione, I forgot his insults through pity (because I was sorry for him); lo feci — voi, I did it for you; — amore, for love, for kindness' sake; — amor di Dio, for the love of God. **7.** EXCHANGE, VALUE: on account of, for the price of, to the value of; lo ebbi — poco, I got it for a song; l'ho venduto — mille lire, I sold it for a thousand lire; possiede quadri — mezzo milione, he has paintings worth half a million; non dite una cosa — un'altra, don't say one thing instead of another; lo pagai — il suo servizio, I paid him for his service. **8.** FUNCTION, CHARACTER: lo presi — servo, I took him on as a servant; l'hanno tenuto — sciocco, they considered him a fool; — che cosa mi prendete?, what do you take me for?; mi prendi — un Inglese?, do you take me for a fool?; padrone — padrone, as masters go. **9.** BEFORE AN INFINITIVE: to, in order to, for (the purpose of); venni — parlare con voi, I came to speak to you; sto — fare..., I am just going to...; essere — partire, to be on the point of leaving; — così dire, so to speak, as it were; è troppo astuto — essere ingannato, he is too clever to be cheated; cominciare — pulire la stanza, to begin by cleaning the room. **10.** BEFORE A PREPOSITION OR ADVERB: — di fuori, outside, on the outside; — lo meno, at least; — lo più, for the most; — poco, almost; ove — poco il cor non si spaura (Leopardi), wherein the heart is all but dismayed (cf. under No. 7); — di più, in addition; un pranzo — bene, a really good dinner; una signorina — bene, a respectable girl. **11.** EXCLAMATORY USES: — Bacco!, by Jove!; — l'appunto!, exactly!; — Dio!, by God! **11.** WITH NUMERALS: times, by; 4 per 3, 4 times 3, 4 by 3, 4×3; uno — uno, one by one; — uno, — due, by ones, by twos; — mille, by the thousand; cinque — cento, five per cent. **12.** CONCESSIVE USE: — quanto ricco, however rich; — gridare che faccia, however much he yells; — quanto abbia potere, however powerful he may be.

per-a[1] *f.* pear; (fig., fam.) head; grattarsi la —, to scratch one's head; cascare come le -e cotte, to die like flies, *or* to fall sound asleep, *or* to fall head over heels in love; (provb.) quando la — è matura, convien che caschi, when the apple is ripe, it must fall, everything comes to him who waits; pear-switch; pear-shaped rubber douche; bell-pull; end of a bell-clapper. **†-eto** *m.* pear-

per-a (*cont.*)

orchard. **-o** *m.* (bot.) pear-tree, *Pirus communis*; (fig.) fare —, to stand on one leg.

†**pera²** *f.* pocket; pouch.

†**peragrare** *tr.* to search (land, country); to wander through, to traverse.

per-avventura, -bene, -benino. See under **avventura**, etc.

†**per·rbio** *m.* pulpit.

perca *f.*, **per·chia** *f.* (ichth.) perch, *Perca fluviatilis*.

percall-e *m.* cotton cambric. **-ina** *f.* glazed cotton, percaline.

percentuale *f.* (comm.; leg.) percentage; — di servizio, service charge (in hotels and restaurants); *adj.* proportional per cent.

percep-ire [D2] *tr.* to perceive, to notice, to collect; to draw, to receive (salary, etc.); — una somma, to draw, to cash, to realize a sum of money. †**-enza** *f.* perception, awareness. **-i·bile** *adj.* perceptible, discernible, noticeable. (**-ito** *part. adj.*)

percett-i·bile *adj.* perceptible; non —, imperceptible. (**-ibilità** *f.*) **-iva** *f.* perceptive faculty, intelligence. **-ività** *f.* perceptiveness; intelligence. **-ivo** *adj.* perceptive; facoltà -iva, perceptive faculty, intelligence. **-o** *adj.* perceived; *n.m.* percept, thing perceived. **-ore** *m.* collector (of taxes or other payments). **-ori·a** *f.* tax-collector's office.

percezione *f.* perception; discernment; drawing, cashing, realizing (of money).

perchè. 1. As INTERROGATIVE: why?; — hai fatto così?, why did you do this?; — mai?, why on earth?; — così?, why so?; *n.m. indecl.* the reason why; non so il —, I don't know why; questo è il — del mio ritorno, this is why I returned; non posso indagare i — e i percome, I cannot go into the whys and wherefores; (provb.) il libro del — si stampò e si perdè, the book of 'why' was printed and lost (said to a child who keeps asking 'why?'). **2.** As CONJUNCTION (followed by *indic.*): because, since; — fai così?, why do you do that?; — mi piace, because I like to; — sì!, because I say so!; — no!, because it isn't, that's all! **3.** As CONJUNCTION (followed by *subjunc.*): so that, in order that; feci così — mi osservasse, I did that so that he would notice me; — trovassero tutto pronto, so that they should find everything ready; (with *neg.*)— non caschi, so that he doesn't fall, to stop him from falling.

†**per·chio** *m.* bolt.

per-ciò *conj.* therefore, so; for that reason. **-ciocchè** *conj.* since, as, for the reason that; for; †in order that.

†**perci·pere** *vb.* and deriv. See **percepire**.

per-clorato, -cloruro, -manganato and other formations, see under **iper-**.

percome *m. indecl.* (pop.) the wherefore; il perchè e il —, the why and the wherefore.

percorr-ere [C5] *tr.* to run through, or across; to cross, to traverse, to pass through, to travel through, or over; to cover (distance); to scour; -evamo una bellissima strada, we were running along a very fine road; avevamo percorso un lungo cammino, we had gone a long way; to glance through (a book, letter, etc.); to run through (a statement, argument, etc.); (of heavenly bodies) — le orbite, to run their courses. **-ente** *part. adj.* running through, traversing. **-enza** *f.* run; way; time taken by a journey; fare, cost of a journey.

percorso *part.* of **percorrere**, q.v.; *adj.* traversed, completed; *n.m.* run, stretch, distance; way, course; journey; (by sea) passage, voyage; route; distance covered; course; (eng.) travel, run; stroke; (atom. phys.) range; per tutto il —, for the whole journey; tracciare il — della nuova strada, to trace the route of the new road; (skiing) — misto, course involving flat ground and slopes; (show-jumping) — netto, clear round.

percoss-a *f.* blow; stroke; crash; (leg.) blow (C.P.); (mus.) clash, clashing. **-o** *part.* of **percuotere**, q.v.; *adj.* struck, beaten; lashed; hit; -o dal fulmine, struck by lightning; -o da spavento, terror-stricken.

percoti-mento *m.* striking, beating; blow. **-tore** *m.* one who strikes, striker. (**-itrice** *f.*)

percuo·t-ere [C15] *tr.* to strike, to beat, to hit; to knock; to bump; -ersi il petto, to beat one's breast; (leg.) — taluno, to strike someone (C.P.); to knock down; (fig.) to afflict; (mus.) — i piatti, to clash the cymbals; — la lira, to strike (or smite) the lyre; — le corde, to sweep the strings; †to kill; †to sacrifice; †— a, to be offensive to; *recip. rfl.* to hit (strike) one another; to fight. †**-ito·io** (mil.) hammer or striker of an old-fashioned gun or other explosive device. **-itura** *f.* striking; blow.

†**percu·pere** *tr.* to desire ardently.

†**percurvo** *adj.* curved, arched.

†**percuss-are** *vb.* and derivs. see **percuotere**. †**-ente** *adj.* striking, knocking, beating.

percuss-ione *f.* percussion; blow, striking; (mus.) strumenti a —, percussion instruments; †wound, contusion; †killing, death-blow. **-ivo** *adj.* (mus.) percussive. **-ore** *m.* person who strikes; (eng.) percussion pin, firing pin, striker; (mil.) striker, firing mechanism of a gun. †**-ura** *f.* blow.

percuziente *adj.* striking; *n.m.* striker.

per·d-ere [B1, C3] *tr.* to lose; to miss; — la pazienza, to lose patience; — la testa, to lose one's head, to get flurried, to lose control; — terreno, to lose ground; la nave e tutto l'equipaggio furon -uti, the ship was lost with all hands; — il treno, to miss the train; non -etti mai un pasto, I never missed a meal; — il turno, to miss one's turn; (colloq.) — la corsa, 'to miss the bus'; — di vista qualcuno, to lose sight of someone; (of hounds) — di naso, to lose the scent of; — la strada, to lose one's way; — un amico, to lose a friend (whether by death or cessation of friendship); to ruin; la sua avarizia lo -ette, his avarice was his downfall; (motor.; eng.) — colpi, to misfire; (aeron.) — quota, to lose height; — l'erre, to slur one's speech; (vulg.) — il tacco, (of a girl) to lose one's good name; to waste; — tempo, to waste time; ho -uto un giorno, I have wasted a day; ho -uto la fatica, my efforts have been wasted; *abs.* to waste (away); to run to waste; to leak; questo secchia -e, this bucket leaks, is leaking; to lose (money); — al giuoco, to lose at cards or gambling; to lose (value, interest, force, etc.); la storiella non -e nel racconto, the story does not lose in the telling; *intr.* (aux. avere) to be the loser, to lose (in battle, game, etc.); ci -o, I am giving it away; (provb.) chi -e ha sempre torto, the loser is always wrong; *rfl.* to lose oneself, to get lost, to lose one's way; mi ci -o, I can make neither head nor tail of it; to disappear, to go astray, to miscarry (of letters, etc.); to be spoilt, to be ruined; s'è -uto in un bosco, he lost his way in a wood; -ersi alla vista, to be lost to sight; una goccia che si -e nell'oceano, a drop in the ocean; figura che si -e nell'ombra, figure vanishing in the gloom; -ersi per una donna, to ruin oneself for a woman; -ersi in mare, to be shipwrecked; -ersi in, dietro, una cosa, to give all one's time to something; -ersi dietro a, to run after, to be taken up with. †**-a**, †**-anza** *f.* see **perdita**. **-e·ndosi** (*ger.*) (mus.) dying away. **-ente** *part. adj.* losing, *n.m.* loser; essere, rimanere -ente, to be the loser. **-enza** *f.* loss, losing; essere in -enza, to be the loser; †perdition, damnation. **-i·bile** *adj.* liable to be lost. **-ifiato** *adv. phr.* a -ifiato, at the top of one's voice; (mus., Malipiero) strumenti a -ifiato, wood-winds. †**-igione** *f.* perdition, damnation. **-igiornata**, **-igiorno** *adj.* idle; *n.m.* idler. **-ilegno** *m.* (ent.) goat moth, *Cossus cossus*. **-imento** *m.* losing, loss; waste; ruin; un -imento di tempo, a waste of time; andare a -imento, to be ruined; -imento dell'anima, perdition, damnation. **-itempo** *m.* waste of time; useless work, labour in vain. **-itore** *m.* loser; squanderer, waster. (**-itrice** *f.*) **-ito·rio** *adj.* transitory; easily lost. **-izione** *f.* loss, ruin; destruction; (theol.) perdition, damnation; andare in -izione, to lose one's soul.

perdice *m.* See **pernice**.

per-di·coli, -dinci, -dina *excl.* euphemistic for 'per Dio'.

per·dita *f.* loss; — di tempo, waste of time; profitti e perdite, profit and loss; vendere in —, to sell at a loss; a — d'occhio, as far as the eye can see; subire, toccare una —, to suffer (incur) a loss; (med.) haemorrhage; loss of blood; menstruation; (leg.) loss; — della cittadinanza, loss of citizenship (C.P.); — del diritto, loss of right or title; perdite emergenti, consequential loss; (comm.) — assoluta, total loss; — corpo e beni, total wreck; — per furto, pilferage; — con ricupero, salvage loss; (finan.) — in peso della moneta, abrasion of coin.

perdo·mito *adj.* (poet.) thoroughly tamed.

perdon-are [A1c] *tr.* to forgive, to pardon; to excuse; to spare; — un'offesa, to forgive, to pardon, an offence; — la persona colpevole, to forgive the guilty person; non posso -argli la sua negligenza, I cannot forgive him for his carelessness; il cielo vi -i, may Heaven forgive you; — la vita a uno, to spare someone's life; non la -ona a nessuno, he is hard on everyone, he will not take any excuses; -ate il disturbo, excuse me for the trouble I am causing you; *intr.* (aux. avere) -i!, excuse me!; per questa volta gli -erò, I will forgive him this time; che Dio gli -i, may God

perdon-are (*cont.*)
    forgive him; (with *neg.*) not to grudge; non -ò nè a spese nè a fatiche, he spared neither expense nor labour; non — a età, to make no allowance for age; -ate e sarete -ati, forgive, and you will be forgiven; malattia che non -a, incurable disease; *rfl.* to forgive oneself; non so -armi questo errore, I can't forgive myself for this mistake; *recip. rfl.* to forgive each other; -iamoci i nostri falli, let us overlook each other's faults. -a·**bile** *adj.* pardonable; excusable. -**ante** *part. adj.* forgiving; indulgent. †-**anza** *f.* see **perdono**; permission, leave, pardon. -**ato** *part. adj.* forgiven. -**atore** *m.* one who pardons readily, forgiving person; -atore dei debiti, indulgent creditor. (-**atrice** *f.*) -**evole** *adj.* indulgent, ready to forgive.

perdono *m.* pardon, forgiveness; ti chiedo —, se ti ho fatto male, forgive me if I have hurt you; (theol.) pardon, forgiveness (of sin); (eccl.) indulgence, esp. as attached to a particular church or pilgrimage; church or pilgrimage where indulgence may be gained (cf. the Breton 'pardon'); (leg.) — giudiziale, judicial pardon (C.P.).

†**perduellione** *f.* High Treason.

perdur-are [A 1] *intr.* (*aux.* avere, essere) to last, to endure; to persist; to persevere; to continue. †-a·**bile** *adj.* durable, lasting, eternal. -**abilità** *f.* persistence; durability. -**anza** *f.* persistence; long continuance. -**evole** *adj.* lasting; durable; continuous.

†**perdurre** *tr.* to lead; to guide; — ad effetto, to carry into effect, to realize.

perdut-o *part.* of **perdere**, q.v.; *adj.* lost; missing; missed; bewildered; ruined, destroyed; done for; uomo —, hopeless rake or drunkard; donna -a, fallen woman; animali -i, extinct animals; fatiche -e, lost labour, labour in vain; — d'animo, dismayed, terrified; di -a speranza, desperate; *adv.* camminare —, to walk blindly, without any choice of direction. -**amente** *adv.* desperately, hopelessly; madly; excessively, wildly.

†**perecotta·io** *m.* vendor of cooked pears.

peregrin-o *adj.* strange, foreign, uncommon; rare, precious; frasi -e, elegant expressions; (orn.) falco —, peregrine falcon; †*n.m.* peregrine falcon, peregrine; pilgrim. -**are** [A 1] *intr.* (*aux.* avere) to wander abroad, to travel; to rove, to roam. -**azione** *f.* peregrination, wandering; excursion, journey. -**ità** *f.* rarity, singularity; strangeness; elegance.

perenn-e *adj.* everlasting; perennial; perpetual; inexhaustible; acqua —, inexhaustible spring of water, nevi -i, perpetual snow; monumento più — del bronzo, monument more lasting than bronze; (bot.) perennial. -**emente** *adv.* perennially; eternally, perpetually. -**ità** *f.* perennity; perpetuity.

perent-o *adj.* (leg.) lapsed; barred through lapse of time. -**o·rio** *adj.* (leg.) termine -orio, mandatory period or term which cannot be extended (C.C.P.); final date (contrasted with 'termine comminatorio', q.v., under **comminatorio**); peremptory, decisive; imperious; *n.m.* peremptory notice. -**oriamente** *adv.* peremptorily.

perenzione *f.* (leg.) the barring (of e.g. right of action) through lapse of time.

perequ-are [A 6] *tr.* to equalize; to distribute equally; (leg.) to assess tax. (-**ato** *part. adj.*) -**atore** *m.* (leg.; comm.) assessor of taxes. -**azione** *f.* equalization; equal distribution; (leg.) assessment (of tax).

†**pererrato** *adj.* wrong, mistaken, ill-advised.

†**pereto** *m.* pear orchard.

perfett-o *adj.* perfect; complete; thorough; full; blameless; un gentiluomo —, a perfect gentleman; godere -a salute, to have perfect health; (mus.) accordo —, full chord; cadenza -a, perfect cadence, full close; consonanza -a, perfect consonance; tempo —, perfect time, i.e. division of the long into three breves in medieval music; (math.) numeri -i, perfect numbers; (ent.) insetto —, imago; *n.m.* perfection; (gramm.) perfect tense; passato —, past definite (historic) tense; più che —, pluperfect (past perfect) tense; *pl.* (eccl. hist.) Perfecti (Albigensian or Waldensian). -**amente** *adv.* perfectly; completely; wholly; fully; quite; avete -amente ragione, you are quite right; l'avevo -amente dimenticato, I had completely forgotten it; *excl.* exactly!, I quite agree! †-**are** *tr.* to perfect. -**i·bile** *adj.* perfectible. -**ibilità** *f.* perfectibility. -**ivo** *adj.* perfective, making perfect; (gramm.) perfective.

perfezion-e *f.* perfection; completion; faultlessness; excellence; finish; essa è la — in persona, she is perfection itself; (theol.) perfection; (mus.) perfection (in medieval mensural notation).

-a·**bile** *adj.* capable of improvement; capable of being perfected or completed; perfectible. -**abilità** *f.* perfectibility. -**amento** *m.* improvement; perfecting; completion; specialization; studi di -amento, specialized studies; borsa di -amento, bursary or scholarship for specialization; corso di -amento, specialization course. -**ando** *adj.* specializing, engaged in specialized studies; *n.m.* student who is following a specialized course. -**are** [A 1 c] *tr.* to perfect, to bring to perfection; to improve; to complete; (leg.) to execute (e.g. a formal contract); (comm.) -are una tratta, to accept a bill; *rfl.* to perfect oneself, to acquire a perfect knowledge (of); -arsi nel francese, to perfect one's knowledge of French. -**ativo** *adj.* finishing, designed to complete, to improve. -**atore** *m.* perfecter; improver; *adj.* perfecting. -**atrice** *f.*, *adj.* educazione -atrice, specialized education.

†**perfi·cere** *tr.* to perfect.

perfi·di-a *f.* perfidy, perfidiousness; treachery; wickedness; persistence in deceit, etc.; con —, perfidiously; †(mus.) persistent repetition of a figure. -**ante** *part. adj.* persistent (in evil); obstinate. -**are** [A 4] *intr.* (*aux.* avere) to be persistent (in evil); to be obstinate; to be perfidious. †-**ato** *adj.* (mus.) persistently repeated. -**oso** *adj.* perfidious; obstinate. -**osamente** *adv.* perfidiously.

per·fid-o *adj.* treacherous, perfidious; wicked; nasty; obstinate; persistent; tempo —, nasty weather; negro —, coal-black negro; (med.) malattia -a, malignant disease; *n.m.* treacherous, wicked, obstinate person. -**amente** *adv.* treacherously, perfidiously; wickedly. †-**ezza** *f.* see **perfidia**.

perfin-e *adv. phr.* alla —, last of all, at last, at length. -**o** *adv.* even.

perfinire *m.* witty or neat conclusion of a speech or article.

perfor-are [A 1 c] *tr.* to perforate, to pierce, to drill; to punch; to bore; — la pelle, to pierce the skin; — una montagna, to bore a tunnel through a mountain; — un biglietto, to punch a ticket; (eng.) to drill, to bore, to pierce, to punch, to perforate, to puncture. -a·**bile** *adj.* that can be perforated, pierced, etc. -**amento** *m.* perforating, perforation; piercing. -**ante** *part. adj.* piercing; (mil. hist.) armour-piercing. -**ato** *part. adj.* perforated, pierced, punched; calcolatore a schede -ate, punched card computer. -**atore** *m.* piercer, borer, drill; (telegr.) perforator. -**atrice** *f.* (eng.) rock drill; -atrice a stella, belt punch. -**azione** *f.* perforation, piercing; boring; tunnelling; (electr.) tensione di -azione, puncture voltage.

perfosfato *m.* (chem.; agric.) superphosphate.

†**perfran·gere** *tr.* to break up into several pieces; *rfl.* to be refracted (of light).

†**perfrequentare** *tr.* to frequent.

†**perfuntoriamente** *adv.* in a perfunctory manner, superficially.

perfus-ione *f.* (med.) perfusion, transfusion. -**o** *adj.* sprinkled.

pergam-ena *f.*, †-**ina** *f.* parchment; — vegetale, vegetable parchment; (paperm.) greaseproof paper; — da rocca, parchment or paper covering for the flax on a distaff; zucchero in —, refined sugar in long pieces; (archit.) lantern of a dome. -**ena·ceo** *adj.* parchment-like, of parchment. -**ena·io** *m.* parchment-maker. -**enata** *f.* parchment-paper. -**enato** *adj.* of, or like, parchment. †-**eno** *m.* see **pergamena**.

per·gamo *m.* (eccl.) pulpit.

†**per·gere** *intr.* to go.

†**pergiur-are** *vb.* and derivs. see **spergiurare**. †-**o** *m.* see **spergiuro**.

per·gol-a *f.* pergola; arbour; vine-trellis; (herald.) pall, pale; intergato in —, tierced pallwise. -**ato** *adj.* trellised; having a pergola; *n.m.* pergola, arbour; trellised vines, vines grown on a pergola; (bot.) great hedge bedstraw, *Galium mollugo*. -**ese** *f.* (agric.) Pergolese, a kind of grape (also *adj.*). -**eto** *m.* field of trellised vines.

†**per·golo** *m.* bench; seat in a theatre; pulpit.

peri[1] *f.* peri, good fairy (in Oriental tales).

peri-[2] *pref.* (scient.) peri —, around.

periambo *m.* (prosod.) pyrrhic.

peri-anto *m.*, -**a·nzio** *m.* (bot.) perianth.

periblema *m.* (bot.) periblem.

peri-car·dico *adj.* (anat.) pericardiac. -**car·dio** *m.* (anat.) pericardium. -**cardi·tico** *adj.* (med.) pericarditic. -**cardiotomi·a** *f.* (surg.) pericardiotomy. -**cardite** *f.* (med.) pericarditis.

pericar·pio *m.* (bot.) pericarp.

periciclo *m.* (bot.) pericycle.

perici·st-ico *adj.* (anat.) pericystic. -**ite** *f.* (med.) pericystitis.

Pe·ricle *pr.n. m.* Pericles.

†**periclit·are** *intr.*, *rfl.* to be in danger; to be likely to fail; to go astray; *tr.* to compromise; to endanger. †**-ante** *part. adj.* in danger.

pe·rico *m.* (bot.). See **iperico**.

pericol·are [A I s] *intr.* (*aux.* avere) to be in danger, to be unsafe; to threaten to fall; †to plot, to intrigue; †*tr.* to ruin; to damage. **-amento** *m.* danger, being in danger. **-ante** *part. adj.* in danger; unsafe; unsteady; tottering; likely to fall or fail. **-ato** *part. adj.* in danger. †**-atore** *m.* plotter, schemer. †**-azione** *f.* danger, peril.

peri·col·o *m.* danger, peril; si trovò in — di vita, his life was in danger; a mio rischio e —, at my own risk; venire in —, correre —, to run into danger, to run a risk; (fam.) non c'è —!, no fear!, not on your life!; (leg.) — inesistente, non-existent danger; delitto di comune —, crime to the common danger (C.P.); — di danno alle cose ipotecate, jeopardy of the security (C.C.); (comm.) -i di mare, perils of the sea; — imminente ed effettivo, danger pending and real. **-oso** *adj.* dangerous; perilous; risky; (econ.) mestieri -osi, dangerous trades; (leg.) persona socialmente -osa, person who is a danger to society (C.P.). **-osamente** *adv.* dangerously, perilously. **-osità** *f.* (leg.) danger; -osità sociale, danger to society (C.P.).

pericon·dr·io *m.* (anat.) perichondrium. **-ale** *adj.* (anat.) perichondrial. **-ite** *f.* (med.) perichondritis.

pericr·a·nico *adj.* (anat.) pericranial. **-a·nio** *m.* (anat.) pericranium.

periderma *m.* (bot.) periderm.

peri·dio *m.* (bot.) peridium.

periedo *m.* (geog.) inhabitant on the same parallel.

perie·gesi *f.* description of the globe; *pr.n.f.* title of a poem by Dionysius of Alexandria.

perieleşi *f.* (mus.) cadenza, vocal or instrumental flourish at the end of a piece.

perie·lio *m.* (astron.; geog.) perihelion.

periencefalite *f.* (med.) periencephalitis, meningitis.

†**perier·a** *f.*, †**-o** *m.* (mil. hist.) catapult machine for hurling boulders.

peri·feri·a *f.* periphery; boundary; outskirts. **-fe·rico** *adj.* peripheral; quartiere -ferico, suburb; (geom.) peripheral, circumferential.

perifleb·ite *f.* (med.) periphlebitis. **-i·tico** *adj.* (med.) periphlebitic.

perifocale *adj.* (scient.; med.) perifocal.

perifollicolite *f.* (med.) perifolliculitis.

perifraş·are [A I] *tr.* to periphrase, to express by circumlocution. (**-ato** *part. adj.*)

peri·frași *f.* periphrasis, circumlocution.

perifra·stic·o *adj.* periphrastic. (**-amente** *adv.*)

perigangliare *adj.* (anat.) periganglionic.

periga·strico *adj.* (anat.) perigastric.

perigastrite *f.* (med.) perigastritis.

perige·o *adj.*, *n.m.* (astron.) perigee.

perigi·nio *m.* (bot.) perigynium (mosses).

perigino *m.* (bot.) perianth (liverworts).

perigli·are [A I 5], **-o** *m.*, **-oso** *adj.* (poet.). See **pericolare**, etc.

perigo·nio *m.* (bot.) perianth.

perilinf·a *f.* (anat.) perilymph. **-angite** *f.* (med.) perilymphangitis.

perimento *m.* See under **perire**.

peri·metrale *adj.* (archit.) of a perimeter: muri -metrali, surrounding walls; (anat.) perimetric. **-metri·a** *f.* (archit.) perimetry. **-me·trico** *adj.* perimetric(al). **-me·trio** *m.* (anat.) peremetrium.

peri·metr·o *m.* perimeter; circuit; (scient.; archit.) perimeter. **-ite** *f.* (med.) perimetritis.

perimi·şi·o *m.* (anat.) perimysium. **-ale** *adj.* perimysial.

perineale *adj.* (anat.) perineal.

perine·o *m.* (anat.) perineum.

periodato *m.* (chem.) periodate.

perio·dic·o *adj.* periodic, recurrent; periodical; festa da ballo -a, regular ball (one of a series); stampa -a, periodical press; (math.) frazione -a, recurring fraction; (chem.) periodic; *n.m.* periodical, newspaper, magazine, review. **-amente** *adv.* periodically. **-ità** *f.* periodicity.

peri·od·o *m.* (gramm.) sentence; paragraph; — complesso, complex sentence; (mus.) sentence; (rhet., prosod.) period; period (of time); stage; spell; (geol.) period; (electr.) cycle; (med.) period, menstruation; (astron.) phase; (naut.) — d'un faro, characteristic of the light sent out by a lighthouse, the number and length of flashes or occultations; — naturale, period of a vessel's roll; — dell'onda, period of time between wave crests; — apparente, apparent time

between waves as observed from a ship under way; — di oscillazione doppio, time to complete a roll one way and back; — della marea, interval between succeeding high water, usually about 12 hr. 24 min.; — velico, sailing-ship era. **-ac·cio** *m. pejor.* (gramm.) clumsy sentence. **-are** [A I s] *intr.* (*aux.* avere) to compose (sentences); *n.m.* style of (literary) composition. **-eggiare** [A 3 e] *intr.* (*aux.* avere) to practise an affected style of composition. **-etto** *m. dim.* (gramm.) little sentence.

periople *f.* (vet.) periople, quick of the hoof of a horse.

peri·o·stio *m.*, †**-o·steo** *m.* (anat.) periosteum. **-ostite** *f.* (med.) periostitis. **-ostoşi** *f.* (med.) periostosis.

periostraco *m.* (zool.) periostracum.

perio·tico *adj.* (anat.) periotic.

peripate·tic·o, *adj.*, *n.m.* (philos.) Peripatetic; Aristotelian; (joc.) conversazione -a, walk and talk. **-a** *f.* (pop.) prostitute, street-walker. **-amente** *adv.* peripatetically. **-işmo** *m.* Peripateticism.

Peripato *pr.n.m.* Peripatus, the walk in the Lyceum where Aristotle taught.

peripezi·a *f.* vicissitude; change of fortune; (theatr.) dénouement; *pl.* ups and downs.

pe·riplo *m.* circumnavigation; long sea voyage.

peri·pneumoni·a *f.* (med.) peripneumonia. **-polmonite** *f.* (med.) peripneumonia.

per·ire [D 2] *intr.* (*aux.* essere) to perish, to be lost, to be destroyed; to die; to languish; to die out (of a race or family); to come to an end; (theol.) to be lost, to be damned. **-imento** *m.* perishing; ruin; (leg.) destruction (C.C.). **-ito** *part. adj.* perished; lost; ruined; -ito in mare, lost at sea, died at sea. **-ituro** *adj.* perishable; transient; non -ituro, imperishable.

peri·scio *adj.* (geog.) Hyperborean.

perisc·o·pico *adj.* (opt.) periscopic. **-o·pio** *m.* periscope; -opio di esplorazione, small periscope usually also fitted for anti-aircraft; -opio — di attacco, short and very slender periscope used when attacking.

perisperma *m.* (bot.) perisperm.

perispi·rito *m.* psychic aura.

perisplenite *f.* (med.) perisplenitis.

perispo·meno *m.* (Gk. gramm.) perispomenon.

perisporio *m.* (bot.) perispore.

†**perissema** *m.* filth, offscouring.

perissodat·tilo *adj.* (anat.) imparidigitate; *m.pl.* (zool.) perissodactyls.

perissologi·a *f.* (gramm.) perissology, pleonasm.

perist·alsi *f.* (physiol.) peristalsis. **-al·tico** *adj.* (physiol.) peristaltic.

peristi·lio *m.* (archit.) peristyle; colonnade.

peristoma·tiche *f.pl.* (bot.) peristome teeth (mosses).

peritale *adj.* See under **perito²**.

perit·are [A I] *rfl.* to hesitate, to be shy or backward; to have scruples; -arsi a chiedere un favore, to hesitate to ask a favour; non mi -ai a chiedergli questo, I had no scruples in asking him for this. **-anza** *f.* hesitation, shyness, scruples. †**-ezza** *f.* see **peritanza**. **-oso** *adj.* shy, hesitant; †slothful.

perite·cio *m.* (bot.) perithecium.

peritero *m.* (naut.) asdic, anti-submarine detecting instrument.

peritiflite *f.* (med.) perityphlitis.

perito¹ *part.* of **perire**, q.v.

perit·o² *adj.* expert; skilled, skilful; (comm.) -i stimatori, appraisers; — contabile, qualified accountant; *n.m.* (leg.) technical expert; expert witness (C.P.); technical assessor (C.C.P.); (comm.) surveyor; valuer. **-ale** *adj.* (leg.) done by, or having to do with, a technical expert; prova —, expert evidence. **-amente** *adv.* expertly, skilfully.

periton·e·o *m.* (anat.) peritoneum. **-ite** *f.* (med.) peritonitis.

peritoso *adj.* See under **peritare**.

perit·tero *adj.* (archit.) peripteral.

perituro *adj.* See under **perire**.

peri·zi·a *f.* skill, expert skill; dexterity; expert's opinion, report; examination; valuation; survey; — arbitrale, arbitration award; (comm.) survey; surveyor's report; (leg.) expert evidence; expert's report; falsa —, perjured expert evidence (C.P.); far fare una —, to cause an expert examination to be made. **-ale** *adj.* expert; responso -ale, expert judgement. **-are** [A 4] *tr.* to assess, to estimate, to appraise; (comm.) to survey; to value. **-ato** *part. adj.* assessed; estimate; value; (horse-racing) corsa -ata, a race, the finish of which is submitted to experts for adjudication, 'photo-finish'. **-ore** *m.* arbitrator; (leg.) expert umpire.

perizoma *m.* loincloth; †apron; †modesty, chastity.

perl-a *f.* pearl; pescatore di -e, pearl-diver; un vezzo di -e, a string of pearls; color —, pearly, pearl-colour; grigio —, pearl grey; denti di —, pearly teeth; -e artificiali, imitation pearls; -e giapponesi, cultivated pearls, (colloq.) 'howlers', slips, errors in daily or weekly press; (fig.) gettar -e ai porci, to cast pearls before swine; è una — di scolaro, he is a model schoolboy; una — di moglie, a treasure of a wife; (med.) capsule; (geog.) Fiume delle Perle, Canton River. **-a·ceo** *adj.* pearly. **-a·io** *m.* worker in pearl; dealer in pearls. **-ato** *adj.* pearly; nacreous; adorned with pearls; orzo -ato, pearl barley; (mus.) pearly, brilliant; (herald.) pearled. **(-etta** *f. dim.* **-ettina** *f. dim.*) **-i·fero** *adj.* yielding pearls; ostrica -ifera, pearl-oyster. **-ina** *f. dim.* seed-pearl; cerchio di -ine, circle of dots (round the edge of a coin); (carpen.) matchboard. **-inag·gio** *m.* (carpen.) matchboarding. **-inato** *adj.* (carpen.) matched, i.e. matchboarded. **†-ismaltato** *adj.* pearl-encrusted. **-ite** *f.* (metall.) pearlite. **-i·tico** *adj.* pearlitic. **(-ona** *f. augm.*) **-onac·cio** *m.* (derog.) large artificial pearl. **(-one** *m. augm.*)

perlomeno *adv.* at least, at the very least.

†perlucente *adj.* brilliant, of extreme brightness.

perlustr-are [A 1] *tr.* to search, to look through; to explore; to reconnoitre, to scout; to patrol. **-atore** *m.* policeman on patrol; scout. **-azione** *f.* reconnaissance; patrol; andare in -azione, to go on patrol.

permalos-o *adj.* irritable, touchy; peevish; *n.m.* irritable person; touchy individual; peevish person. **(-a** *f.*) **-ità** *f.* touchiness; irritability; peevishness.

perman-ere [B 25] *intr.* (*aux.* essere), to remain, to stay; to last, to persist; -e la causa del male, the cause of the disease still exists. **-ente** *part. adj.* permanent, lasting; standing; ondulazione -ente, permanent wave (waving); esercito -ente, standing army; colore -ente, fast colour; nevi -enti, perpetual snow; (anat.) dentatura -ente, permanent teeth; (admin.) organo -ente, standing body; (mil.) fortificazioni -enti, fixed defences; (leg.) giunta -ente, standing committee; (rlwy.) biglietto -ente, pass entitling to free travel for life; *n.m.* (rlwy.) permanent way; *n.f.* permanent wave. **-entemente** *adv.* permanently. **-enza** *f.* permanence, permanency; stay; residence; durante la mia -enza, during my stay; buona -enza!, have a nice time at home! (a reply sometimes made to the salutation 'buon viaggio!'); essere di -enza, to be a resident. **†-e·vole** *adj.* lasting, durable.

permang-anato *m.* (chem.) permanganate. **-a·nico** *adj.* (chem.) permanganic.

†permans-ivo, †-uro *adj.* lasting, durable.

perme-are [A 5] *tr.* to permeate. **-a·bile** *adj.* permeable. **-abilità** *f.* permeability. **-a·metro** *m.* (electr.) permeameter. **-anza** *f.* (electr.) permeance. **-ato** *part. adj.* permeated. **-azione** *f.* (phys.) permeation.

permess-o[1] *part.* of **permettere**, q.v.; *adj.* allowed, permitted; non è — di entrare, no admittance; se mi è — di dirlo, if I may say so; —?, may I come in?, *or* please, teacher, may I leave the room?; —!, excuse me!; *n.m.* permission, leave; leave of absence; licence; permit; — di caccia, game licence; andare in —, to go on leave; col vostro —, allow me; (leg.) permit; — di lavoro, labour permit; — di soggiorno, residence permit (C.P.); (comm.) clearance; — di partenza, ship's clearance outwards; — di navigazione, ship's passport; (finan.) — d'imbarcare, backed note; (comm.) — di sbarco, request note; (comm.) — di transito in cabotaggio, transire.

Permesso[2] *pr.n.m.* (myth.) Permessus, river valley sacred to the Muses near Mt Helicon.

permett-ere [C 20] *tr.* to allow, to permit; tempo -endo, weather permitting; to authorize; to admit; (theol.) to permit (evil); *rfl.* (*dat.* of *prn.* 'si') to allow oneself; to take the liberty; mi -erò un po' di riposo, I will allow myself a little rest; egli si permise di scrivermi questa lettera, he took the liberty of writing this letter to me; non posso -ermi il lusso di tenere un'automobile, I cannot afford to keep a car. **-ente** *part. adj.* Dio -ente, God willing; tempo -ente, weather permitting. **†-imento** *m.* permission.

permiano *adj.* (geol.) Permian.

per·mico *adj.* (geol.) See **permiano**.

†permischiare *vb.* and derivs. See **mischiare**.

permiss-i·bile *adj.* allowable, permissible. **-ione** *f.* permission, leave, licence. **-ivo** *adj.* permissive. **-ivamente** *adv.* by concession.

†permist-ione *f.* mixture. **†-o** *adj.* mixed, confused, muddled.

permittività *f.* (electr.) permittivity.

†per-mosso *adj.* stirred, moved. **†-motore** *m.* mover, motive force.

permut-are [A 1] *tr.* (leg.; comm.) to exchange; to transfer; (fig.) to remove, to rearrange, to permute; *rfl.* to transform oneself; to change. **-a** *f.* (leg.) barter (C.C.); exchange; commutation; transfer. **-a·bile** *adj.* exchangeable. **-abilità** *f.* permutability. **-amento** *m.* exchange; changing (**-ante** *part. adj.*) *n.m.* **†-anza** *f.* exchange, substitution. **-ativo** *adj.* favouring permutation or exchange. **-ato** *part. adj.* exchanged; bartered. **(-atore** *m.* **-atrice** *f.*) **-azione** *f.* exchange; transposition; (leg.) the act of bartering, or its effect; (math.) permutation.

pernambuco *m.* (dyeing) legno di —, Brazil wood.

pernic-e *f.* (orn.) partridge, esp. of the genus *Alectoris* (cf. **starna**, the correct name for the partridge *Perdix perdix*); — bianca, ptarmigan, *Lagopus mutus*; — di mare, pratincole, *Glareola pratincola*; — rossa, red-legged partridge, *Alectoris rufa*; — sarda, Barbary partridge, *A. barbara*; (med.) occhio di —, corn between the toes; †(mil.) eight-pounder gun. **-etta** *f. dim.*, **-iotto** *m. dim.* young partridge; (mil. hist.) granata -iotto, mortar bomb.

pernicios-o *adj.* pernicious; malignant; febbre -a, malignant fever. **-amente** *adv.* perniciously. **-ità** *f.* perniciousness.

pernicon-a *f.* (agric.) a kind of plum. **-e** *m.* a kind of plum-tree.

per·nio *m.* (Tusc.). See **perno**.

pern-o *m.* (techn.) pivot; fare — su, to be pivoted on; hinge; stud; support; axis; (watchm.) a — corto, without bit; a — lungo, with bit; (naut.) bolt (ship construction); holdfast (stag's horn on cleat); †ring bolt holding the ankle chain of a slave; nave —, pilot ship or guide in manœuvres; (mus.) tail-pin; (fig.) turning-point.

pernott-are [A 1] *intr.* (*aux.* avere) to stay overnight, to spend the night; — in orazione, to spend the night in prayer. **-amento** *m.* stay overnight, spending the night; indennità per il -amento, reimbursement of hotel expenses. **(-ante** *part. adj.*, *n.m.*, *f.*) **-ato** *part. adj.*, **-azione** *f.* see **pernottamento**.

pero *m.* See under **pera**[1].

per-ò *conj.* however; but, yet; still, nevertheless; therefore, on that account. **†-occhè** *conj.* because, for; as, since.

†perondino *m.* dandy, fop.

pe·ron-e *m.*, **peron-e** *m.* (anat.) fibula. **-eo** *m.* (vet.) fibula (of a horse).

peror-are [A 1] *tr.*, *intr.* (*aux.* avere; *prep.* presso) to plead; to defend (a case, a person); to perorate, to pronounce a peroration; to harangue. **(-ato** *part. adj.*) **-azione** *f.* peroration; summing up; pleading; defence; harangue.

peros·sid-o *m.* (chem.) peroxide. **-azione** *f.* (chem.) peroxidation.

†perpen·dere *tr.* to recognize, to realize, to deduce.

perpendi·col-o *m.* plumb-line, plummet; a —, perpendicularly, vertically. **-are** *adj.* perpendicular; vertical; *n.f.* (geom.) perpendicular; abbassare una -are, to drop a perpendicular. **-armente** *adv.* perpendicularly. **-arità** *f.* perpendicularity.

per·pero *m.*, **perpe** *m.* (numism.) bezant (gold coin of Byzantium); silver bezant (of Ragusa).

perpetr-are [A 1] *tr.* to perpetrate; to commit (crime); (joc.) — un nuovo romanzo, to perpetrate a new novel. **(-ato** *part. adj.*) **-atore** *m.* perpetrator. **(-atrice** *f.*) **-azione** *f.* perpetration, commission (e.g. of crime).

Perpe·tua *pr.n.f.* name of a character in Manzoni's *I Promessi Sposi*; (fig.) a priest's servant, housekeeper.

perpe·tu-o *adj.* perpetual; continuous; permanent, constant; for life; everlasting, eternal; (finan.) debito pubblico —, funded or consolidated debt; (leg.) irredeemable; perpetual; (mus.) see **moto**; (eng.) vite -a, perpetual screw, Archimedes screw; carcere —, life imprisonment, imprisonment for life; in —, perpetually, for ever, in perpetuity. **-amente** *adv.* continuously, perpetually. **-a·bile** *adj.* perpetuable; fit to be perpetuated. **-almente** *adv.* perpetually; for ever. **-are** [A 6] *tr.* to perpetuate; *rfl.* to last, to persist, to continue; to be perpetuated. **(-ato** *part. adj.*) **-atore** *m.* perpetuator. **(-atrice** *f.*) **-azione** *f.* perpetuation; perpetuating. **-ino** *m.* (bot.) everlasting, *Xeranthemum annuum*. **-ità** *f.* perpetuity; persistence.

Perpignano *pr.n.m.* (geog.) Perpignan; †fine woollen cloth from Perpignan.

perpless-o *adj.* perplexed; uncertain; puzzled, baffled. **-amente** *adv.* confusedly; with uncertainty. **-ità** *f.* perplexity, irresolution.

†perpolito *adj.* See **pulito**.

perquirente *adj.* investigating; *n.m.* investigator.

†**perqui·rere** *tr.* to seek out, to look for carefully.

perquiṣ-ire [D 2] *tr.* (leg.) to search; (comm.) to rummage. **-ito** *part. adj.* searched. **-itọre** *m.* investigator; detective. (**-itrice** *f.*) **-iziọne** *f.* perquisition, search; mandato di **-izione**, search warrant; diritto di **-izione**, right of search; **-izione** domiciliare, search of premises; **-izione** personale, search of the person (C.P.); (comm.) rummage.

perrocchẹtto *m.* (orn.). See **parrocchetto**.

perrucca *f.* See **parrucca**.

persa *f.* (bot.). See **persea**.

persale *m.* (chem.) per-salt.

perscrut-are [A 1] *tr.* to investigate; to search out; to explain. **-a·bile** *adj.* scrutable; open to investigation and explanation. (**-ato** *part. adj.*) **-aziọne** *f.* investigation, search.

per·sea *f.* (bot.) avocado pear, *Persea americana*.

persecu-tọre *m.* persecutor. (**-trice** *f.*) **-ziọne** *f.* persecution; (psych.) mania di **-zione**, delirio di **-zione**, persecution mania; pestering, importunity; (fam.) è una **-zione**!, it's a terrible bore!, it's a frightful nuisance!

persegu-ire [D 1] *tr.* to pursue; to follow; to continue; — uno scopo, to have an end in view; (leg.) to prosecute. **-ente** *part. adj.* pursuing; following; †*n.m.* pursuer. **-i·bile** *adj.* (leg.) prosecutable; un reato **-ibile** d'ufficio, offence liable to public prosecution as a matter of course (which may be set in motion by a 'denuncia', q.v.; see also **procedimento**) (C.P.P.). **-imẹnto** *m.* persecution. **-itare** [A 1 s] *tr.* to persecute; to pursue. **-itato** *part. adj.* persecuted; pursued, chased. **-itatọre** *m.* persecutor. (**-itatrice** *f.*) **-ito** *part. adj.* pursued, followed; continued, persisting.

persẹmolo *m.* (bot.). See **prezzemolo**.

Per·seo *pr.n.m.* (Gk. myth.) Perseus.

persever-are [A 1] *intr.* (*aux.* avere) to persevere; to be persevering; to persist; to insist. **-ante** *part. adj.* persevering; persistent. **-antemẹnte** *adv.* perseveringly; persistently. **-anza** *f.*, †**-an·zia** *f.* perseverance; persistence.

Persi *m.pl.* (ancient) Persians.

Per·si-a *pr.n.f.* (geog.) Persia, Iran; (bot.) sweet marjoram, *Marjorana hortensis*. **-ana** *f.* (outside) window-shutter, sun-shutter; **-ana** (alla) Veneziana, **-ana** avvolgibile, Venetian blind, jalousie. **-anina** *f. dim.* lower part of a window-shutter, opening on a hinge. **-ano** *adj., n. m.* Persian; il **-ano**, la lingua **-ana**, Persian, the Persian language. **-ca·ria** *f.* (bot.) persicaria, *Polygonum persicaria* and pale persicaria, *P. lapathifolium*. **-cata** *f.* peach jam. **-chino** *adj.* peach-blossom (colour); *n.m.* peach wine.

per·sico *adj.* Persian (of ancient Persia); golfo —, Persian Gulf; (ichth.) pesce —, perch, *Perca fluviatilis*; *n.m.* nero di —, peach black, made from carbonized peach-stones.

persino *adv.* even.

persi·st-ere [C 24] *intr.* (*aux.* avere) to persist; to persevere, to insist; to continue. **-ente** *part. adj.* persistent, persisting; persevering; obstinate; (geog.) nevi **-enti**, perennial snows. **-enza** *f.* persistence, persistency; perseverance; (opt.) persistence; **-enza** delle immagini, persistence of vision.

pers-o¹ *part.* of **perdere**, q.v. (altern. of **perduto**, but of less extensive use); *adj.* lost; wasted; tempo —, time wasted, lost time; cause **-e**, lost causes.

perso² *adj.* dark (colour); deep purple; †*n.m.* cloth of dark purple hue.

†**persol·vere** *vb.* and derivs. See **solvere**.

persọn-a *f.* **1.** PERSON, self; man, woman; *pl.* people; — grata, *persona grata*; di —, in —, personally, in person; lo pagherete di —, you shall pay for it personally, yourself; lo conosco di —, I am personally acquainted with him; per —, apiece, a head, per head; in — di, in the place of, representing; una terza —, a third party; ciascuna —, each person; quante **-e** c'erano?, how many people were there?; le **-e** di casa, the people in the house, the household, the family; le **-e** della Santissima Trinità, the three Persons of the Trinity; la mia umile —, my humble self; era lui in petto e in —, it was he himself in person; essa è l'eleganza in —, she is elegance itself; per ciò che riguarda la mia —, as for myself; per amore della vostra —, for love of your good self; lui è una brava —, ma lei è una donna detestabile, he is a good man, but she is a detestable woman. **2.** FIGURE; body; la ragazza ha una — molto graziosa, the girl has a very graceful figure; piccolo di —, short in stature; un dolore per la —, pain throughout one's body; togliere la — a, to kill; far forza nella —, to use physical force. **3.** (LEG.) — giuridica, artificial, juridical, legal person

contrasted with: — fisica, natural person; — giuridica pubblica, public body; riconoscimento, estinzione della — giuridica, incorporation, dissolution, of corporation; — incerta, unascertained person; — sensata, reasonable person; — interposta, nominee; — nominata, — da nominare, undisclosed principal (C.C.). **4.** (GRAMM.) person; prima, seconda, terza —, first, second, third person. **5.** WITH NEGATIVE: nobody, no one; non c'è —, there is nobody there; (with neg. implied) c'è stata mai — che abbia capito questo?, has anyone ever understood this? **-ac·cia** *f. pejor.* unpleasant person; ugly figure. **-ag·gio** *m.* personage; figure (in a picture, etc.); character (in a play, etc.); *pl.* dramatis personae. **-ale** *adj.* personal; carte **-ali**, personal papers, identity card, passport, etc.; biglietto **-ale**, non-transferable ticket; oggetti **-ali**, personal effects; (comm.) conti **-ali**, personal accounts; capitale **-ale**, personal capital; sostanze attive **-ali**, personal assets; garanzia **-ale**, personal security; *n.m.* staff, personnel; il **-ale** insegnante, the teaching staff; il basso **-ale**, servants, domestic staff; comitato del **-ale**, staff committee; figure, body; un bel **-ale**, a lovely figure. **-almẹnte** *adv.* personally, as for me; I am personally acquainted with him; (gramm.) usare **-almente** un verbo, to use a verb personally, i.e. with a personal subject. **-alismo** *m.* (philos.) personalism. **-alità** *f.* personality; personage; *pl.* well-known people; personality, gossip, remark about a person; (leg.) **-alità** giuridica, corporate existence; riconoscimento della **-alità** giuridica, incorporation (C.C.). **-alino** *m. dim.* pretty, slim figure. **-ato** *adj.* (bot.) personate. **-cina** *f. dim.* of **persona**; little person; trim little figure. **-eggiare** [A 3 c] *tr.* to act the part of, to impersonate. **-ificare** [A 2 s] *tr.* to personify; to impersonate; il padre **-ifica** la famiglia, the father represents the family. **-ificato** *part. adj.* personified; la bontà **-ificata**, goodness personified. **-ificaziọne** *f.* personification; personifying.

†**perspettiva** *f.* (art). See **prospettiva**.

perspic-ace *adj.* perspicacious, discerning; shrewd; keen; †clear. **-acemẹnte** *adv.* perspicaciously; shrewdly. **-a·cia** *f.* perspicacity; shrewdness. **-acità** *f.* perspicacity; keenness of vision; shrewdness.

perspi·cu-o *adj.* clear; transparent; perspicuous; evident; discorso —, lucid speech. **-amẹnte** *adv.* clearly, with perspicuity; lucidly. **-ità** *f.* perspicuity; clearness; transparency; lucidity.

persuad-ere [C 3] *tr.* to persuade, to convince; to influence; to induce; **-e** poco, he, it, does not inspire confidence; il suo modo di fare non mi **-e**, I don't like the way he behaves; lo persuasi a star zitto, I induced him to keep silent; *rfl.* to be convinced; to convince oneself, to persuade oneself; si persuase che la cosa stava così, he was convinced that that was the case; si **-a**!, you must admit it! **-ente** *part. adj.* convincing; persuasive. **-i·bile** *adj.* easily persuaded. (**-itọre** *m.* **-itrice** *f.*)

persuaṣ-o *part.* of **persuadere**, q.v.; *adj.* convinced; persuaded, resigned; sono — che, I am sure that. **-i·bile** *adj.* credible, convincing; persuasible. **-ibilmẹnte** *adv.* persuasively. **-iọne** *f.* persuasion; conviction; belief; di facile **-ione**, easily persuaded; a **-ione** di, at the instigation of. **-iva** *f.* persuasiveness. **-ivo** *adj.* persuasive; convincing. **-ivamẹnte** *adv.* persuasively; convincingly. **-ọre** *m.* persuader; instigator. **-o·rio** *adj.* (*m.pl.* **-orii**) by persuasion; of persuasive character.

†**persutto** *m.* See **prosciutto**.

†**perta** *f.* See **perdita**.

pertanto *conj.* on that account, therefore, consequently; non —, yet…not, not for all that, none the more for that; parlava molto, ma non — era eloquente, he talked a great deal but that does not mean that he was eloquent; ciò non —, notwithstanding this (in other uses 'non pertanto' is equivalent to 'nondimeno', q.v.).

†**pertenere** *vb.* and derivs. See **appartenere**.

†**perterrito** *adj.* See **atterrito**.

per·ti-ca *f.* pole, rod, perch; (agric.) rod or pole for measuring; (naut.) pole, stanchion; launching spar; (Rom. antiq.) *pertica*, ten-foot rod or measure; (fig.) spindle leg; tall, thin person. †**-care** *tr.* to beat with a rod; to measure. **-cata** *f.* blow, beating with rod or pole. **-cato** *m.* a group of rods or perches (of land) measured together. **-catọre** *m.* surveyor's assistant; measurer. **-caziọne** *f.* field measurement, surveying. **-chella**, **-chẹtta** *f. dim.* (naut.) punt-pole; (naut. hist.) awning stanchion of a galley; guardrail stanchion. **-chino** *m.* (mus.) super, understudy (in opera); unimportant solo passage (in opera); (theatr.) walking-on part, understudy; third horse added to help a pair. **-cọne** *m. augm.* long pole; (fig.) tall, thin man; tall soldier.

pertin·ace *adj.* pertinacious, persevering; battaglia —, hard-fought battle; peccatore —, persistent sinner. **-acemẹnte** *adv.* pertinaciously; perseveringly. **-a·cia** *f.* pertinacity; staying-power.

pertinen-te *adj.* pertinent, pertaining; belonging. **-za** *f.* pertinence, pertinency; (leg.) appurtenance; a right belonging to property or to an estate; competence; belonging; *pl.* appurtenances (C.C.).

†pertin·gere *intr.* to arrive, to approach.

pertọsse *f.* (med.) whooping-cough.

pertratt-are [A I] *tr.* to treat of, to examine; to treat, to handle, to deal with. (**-ato** *part. adj.*) **-aziọne** *f.* treatment, discussion.

†per-tratto *adj.* made, contrived; — di, made of. **†-trazione** *f.* prolonging; drawing out.

pertu·gi-o *m.* hole, aperture, opening, orifice; — della serratura, keyhole. **-are** [A 3] *tr.* to pierce, to make an aperture in, to perforate. (**-ato** *part. adj.*)

†pertun·dere *tr.* to knock, to hit, to bump.

perturb-are [A I] *tr.* to perturb, to agitate; to upset; to disturb, to trouble; *rfl.* to be perturbed. **-amẹnto** *m.* disturbance, disorder. **-ativo** *adj.* disturbing, upsetting. **-ato** *part. adj.* perturbed, agitated; upset. **-atọre** *m.* agitator. (**-atrice** *f.*) **-aziọne** *f.* disturbance, disorder; perturbation; (meteor.) disturbance.

†pertuso *m.* and derivs. See **pertugio**.

Per-ù *pr.n.m.* (geog.) Peru; (colloq.) valere un —, to be worth a fortune. **-uviano** *adj.*, *n.m.* Peruvian.

†perug·gine *m.* wild pear-tree.

Peru·g-ia *pr.n.f.* (geog.) Perugia. **-ino** *adj.* of Perugia; *n.m.* native of Perugia. **-ina** *f.* girl or woman of Perugia; name of a chocolate factory in Perugia.

Perugino *pr.n.m.* il Perugino, the painter, Pietro Vannucci (1446–1523).

pe·rule *m.* (bot.) bud-scales.

perusto *adj.* (poet.) burnt up; torrid.

perva·dere [C 3] *tr.* to pervade; to permeate; to penetrate; to run through.

†pervagare *tr.* to roam, to wander through; *intr.* to wander about.

pervaso *part.* of **pervadere**, q.v.; *adj.* (*prep.* di) pervaded (with, by); permeated; — di tristezza, full of sadness.

perven-ire [D 17] *intr.* (*aux.* essere; *prep.* a) to arrive; to reach, to attain; to come to, to come into the possession of; †— in fama, to acquire fame; †to happen; †to become; †to proceed; †(of plants) to thrive; †— a uno, to fall to the lot of someone, to be the responsibility of someone. **-uto** *part. adj.* come, arrived; lettera -uta al destinatario, letter delivered to the addressee.

pervers-o *adj.* perverse, wicked, bad; depraved; tempo —, bad weather; *n.m.* il —, the evil one, the devil. **-amẹnte** *adv.* perversely; wickedly. †**-are** *intr.* to toss about wildly as though possessed by an evil spirit; *tr.* to afflict, to torment. **-iọne** *f.* perversion; depravity. **-ità** *f.* perversity; perverseness; wickedness.

†perver·tere *vb.* and derivs. See **pervertire**.

pervert-ire [D I] *tr.* to pervert, to lead astray, to corrupt; †to change; †to substitute; *rfl.* to be perverted, to be led astray; to become depraved. **-imẹnto** *m.* perverting. **-ito** *part. adj.* depraved, spoilt; perverted; *n.m.* pervert; apostate; homosexual. **-itọre** *m.* perverter; seducer; *adj.* corrupting; subversive. (**-itrice** *f.*)

pervic-ace *adj.* obstinate. **-acemẹnte** *adv.* obstinately. **-a·cia** *f.* obstinacy; arrogance.

pervinca *f.* (bot.) lesser periwinkle, *Vinca minor*; — maggiore, greater periwinkle, *V. major*.

per·vio *adj.* open, accessible.

†perzare *tr.* to pierce.

pẹsa *f.* See under **pesare**.

pẹs-are [A I c] *tr.* to weigh, to assess the weight of; (horse-racing) to weigh in; (fig.) to ponder; to weigh, to weigh up; — il pro e il contro, to weigh the pros and cons; l'ho -ato alla prima occhiata, I weighed him up at the first glance; *intr.* (*aux.* avere, essere) to weigh (more or less heavy); to be heavy; to lie heavy; — su, to bear on, to press; (fig.) to carry weight; to be weighty; to be a burden; il bagaglio -a circa 100 libbre, the luggage weighs about 100 pounds; questo ragazzo -a molto, this boy is very heavy; la volta -a su pilastri, the arch is supported by pilasters; (fig.) so quanto -ano i suoi giudizi, I know what weight his opinions carry; la vita mi -a, my life is a burden (in this sense the auxiliary is always 'essere'); gli è -ato di doverlo licenziare, he was grieved to have to dismiss him; quel fatto -ava sulla sua coscienza, the fact weighed heavily on his conscience; la loro

ansia mi -a, their anxiety afflicts me; quella fanciulla vale quanto -a!, that girl is worth her weight in gold!; (of a horse) — alla mano, 'to take hold of the bit', 'to take the bit between its teeth'; *rfl.* to weigh oneself, to be weighed; to esteem oneself. **-a** *f.* weighing; weighing in; weighing-machine; weighbridge. **-abini** *m. indecl.* baby-scales. **-afiltro** *m. indecl.* (chem.) weighing bottle. **-ag·gio** *m.* (horse-racing) weigh-in. **-alet·tere** *m. indecl.* letter-scales. **-amẹnto** *m.* weighing. **-ante** *adj.* heavy; weighty; artiglieria -ante, heavy artillery; mani -anti, heavy hands (of one who is heavy-handed, a hard hitter); aria -ante, close atmosphere (air, weather); acqua -ante, heavy water; cibo -ante, indigestible food; lavoro, fatica -ante, heavy work; stile -ante, ponderous style, dull, heavy style; tiresome, troublesome, boring; è un individuo -ante, he is a tiresome individual; come sei -ante!, how tiresome you are!; terreno -ante, heavy soil; olio -ante, smoky oil (that will not give a clear flame). **-antemẹnte** *adv.* heavily; ponderously; weightily. **-antẹzza** *f.* heaviness; weight; dullness, tiresomeness. **-ata** *f.* weighing; amount weighed in one lot. **-ato** *part. adj.* weighed; pondered. **-atamẹnte** *adv.* with due consideration. **-atọre** *m.* weigher; inspector of weights and measures. **-atrice** *f.* weighing-machine; (rlwy.) -atrice per vagoni, wagon balance. **-atura** *f.* weighing; fee for weighing.

Pẹsaro *pr.n.f.* (geog.) Pesaro.

pes-ca[1] *f.* peach, fruit of the peach-tree, **pesco**, q.v.; marmellata di -che, peach jam; †volere la — monda, to want to get things without trouble; †blow with the fist, punch, bruise. **-ca·io** *adj.* of peaches (in the saying: Agosto -aio, August the month of peaches).

pẹsca[2], see under **pescare**.

pesc-are [A 2 c] *tr.* to fish (for), to catch; to fish out; (fig.) to pick up; — un'idea, to get an idea; *abs.* to go fishing, andò a — in Arno, he went fishing in the Arno; canna per —, fishing-rod; — con la lenza, to angle; (naut.) — un'ancora, to drag for an anchor; — una gomena, una catena, to recover a hawser or cable; to find; finalmente l'ho -ato!, at last I have found it!; vattel'a -a!, see if you can find it!; (rowing) — un granchio, to catch a crab, (fig.) to make a gaffe; — in aria, to haver, to achieve nothing; (cards) to take or pick up (a card) from the pack or 'pool' on the table; *intr.* (*aux.* avere) (naut.) to draw; to have a draught of; — davanti, to have a draught forward; — di dietro, to have a draught aft; il tubo -ava nell'acqua per due metri, the pipe went down more than six feet under water; (fig.) — nel torbido, to fish in troubled waters. **-a** *f.* fishing; fishery; catch (of fish); -a con la lenza, angling; -a della balena, whale-fishery; (naut.) barca da -a, fishing-boat; -a abusiva, illegal method of fishing (using dynamite, etc.); -a d'alto mare, -a di grande altura, deep-water fishing; -a alla deriva, drift-net fishing; -a a strascico, trawl fishing; fishing up (or out), recovery from sea, river, etc.; kind of lottery. **-ag·gio** *m.* (naut.) -aggio con carico, laden draught; -aggio senza carico, in ballast or light draught. **-agiọne** *f.* (naut.) draught; differenza di -agione, trim, or difference in draught between stem and stern; †fishing; †catch of fish. **-a·ia** *f.* dam, weir. **-ai(u)olo** *m. dim.* small weir. **-ante** *part. adj.* fishing; *n.m.* (naut.) main brace; spreader; cathead; cat pennant; (Venice) fisherman. **-ata** *f.* catch; draught (of fishes). **-ato** *part. adj.* caught, fished; found. **-atọre** *m.* fisherman, fisher; angler; -atore subacqueo, underwater fisher, skin diver, aqualung diver (man or woman); (naut.) cat tackle; bozza del -atore, cat pennant; nodo di -atore, fisherman's bend; (eccl.) l'anello del -atore, the Fisherman's Ring; (orn.) falco -atore, osprey; martin -atore, kingfisher. **-atọ·rio** *adj.* (*m.pl.* -atorii) (relating to) fishing, piscatorial. **-atrice** *f.* fisherwoman; *adj.* canna -atrice, fishing-rod.

pẹsc-e *m.* (ichth.) fish (for the numerous different types of fish, see under the secondary names); muto come un —, dumb as a fish; non essere nè carne nè —, to be neither fish, flesh, fowl nor good red herring; (provb.) chi dorme non piglia -i, the early bird catches the worm; colla di —, fish-glue, isinglass; nuovo —, simpleton, poor fish; non saper che -i pigliare, not to know which way to turn; (typ.) omission; *pl.* (astron.) i Pesci, the Fishes; (geog.) Fiume del —, Great Fish river; (theol.) the Fish, the Ichthus (as a symbol of Christ). **-aiola** *f.* (orn.) smew, *Mergus albellus*. **-ecane** *m.* shark; dog-fish; (fig.) *nouveau riche*; profiteer; tycoon. †**-eduovo** *m.* fritter. **-erello** *m.*, **-ẹtto** *m. dim.* pastry in the shape of a fish. **-iaiuola** *f.* fish-kettle; dish for serving fish. **-iaiuolo** *m.* fishmonger. **-iarello** *m.* see **pescetto**. **-iatello** *m. dim.*

pesc-e (*cont.*)

little fish. -**icoltura** *f.* pisciculture, fish-breeding. -**ino** *adj.* pertaining to fishes, piscine. -**io** *m.* (naut.) a goring cloth, bolt or strip of canvas at the edge of a sail cut on the cross. -**iolino** *m. dim.* small fish; (ent.) -**iolino argentato**, silverfish, *Lepisma saccharina*; *pl.* fry; (fig.) lively little boy; *pl.* small fry. -**iotto** *m.* fair-sized fish. -**itello** *m. dim.* little fish; (naut.) gusset in a sail. -**ivendolo** *m.* fish-hawker, fishmonger. (-**ivendola** *f.*) -**osità** *f.* abundance of fish. -**oso** *adj.* teeming with fish.

pescher-eccio *adj.* (pertaining to) fishing; barche -**ecce**, fishing-boats, industria -**eccia**, fishery, fisheries; well-stocked with fish, good for fishing; *n.m.* fishing-boat trawler. -**i·a** *f.* fish-market; †haul; †fishing.

peschiera[1] *f.* fish-pond; fishing-ground, fishery; weir.

Peschiera[2] *pr.n.f.* (geog.) Peschiera (fortress-town on Lake Garda).

pescianino *adj., n.m.* (agric.) (of) a variety of olive.

pesc-o *m.* (*pl.* **peschi**) (bot.) peach-tree, *Prunus persica*; wood of the peach-tree; †peach (the fruit). -**oso** *adj.* producing peaches; †occhi -**osi**, eyes swollen with crying; †black eyes (from blows). -**otto** *m.* punch that causes a black eye.

pes-o *m.* weight; burden; load; -**i e misure**, weights and measures; (leg.) detenzione di -**i illegali**, possession of illegal weights (C.P.); issare di —, to heave bodily; — **vivo**, live weight; — **morto**, dead weight; pigliar di —, to take the weight, to lift; levare di —, to lift up, to carry away bodily; rubare sul —, to give short weight; mettere un —, to add a counterpoise; (techn.) weighing machine; — **a bilico**, platform scale; (chem.) — **atomico**, atomic weight; (phys.) — **specifico**, specific gravity, relative density; serie di -**i**, set of weights (for a pair of scales); (comm.) — **lordo**, gross weight; — **lordo depurato della sola tara**, suttle weight; — **netto**, net weight; note di —, weight accounts; — **di spedizione**, shipping weight; distinta di —, weight note; rifazione di —, the tret; (finan.) weight; perdita in — **della moneta**, abrasion of coin; (sport) lancio del —, getto del —, putting the weight; (boxing) peso mosca, flyweight; — **piuma**, featherweight; — **gallo**, bantamweight; — **leggero**, lightweight; — **medio**, middleweight; — **mediomassimo**, light heavyweight; — **massimo**, heavyweight; (games) lead bias; (fig.) weight, importance; authority; burden, load; heaviness; queste considerazioni hanno grande —, these considerations carry great weight; sono cose di poco —, these are matters of little importance; il — della famiglia era troppo grave per lui, the burden of the family was too heavy for him; sentire il — degli anni, to feel the weight of years; — che grava sull'eredità, cost of maintenance that burdens the inheritance; aver due -**i e due misure**, to be unfair, to judge (or act) unfairly; *adj.* (dial.) heavy, weighty; aria -**a**, heavy, close atmosphere.

pesol-o *adj.* hanging, dangling. -**one** *adv.* dangling.

pessa·rio *m.* pessary.

pes·sim-o *adj.* very bad; worst; wicked; foul; horrible; awful; vita -**a**, wretched life; tempo —, nasty weather, foul weather; *n.m.* il —, the worst; è uno dei -**i**, he is one of the worst. (-**a** *f.*) -**amente** *adv.* very badly; the worst. -**ismo** *m.* pessimism. -**ista** *m., f.* pessimist. -**is·tico** *adj.* pessimistic. -**isticamente** *adv.* pessimistically.

pesta *f.* See under **pestare**.

pest-are [A I c] *tr.* to pound, to crush; to stamp (with the feet); to tread upon; to trample on; bada di non — **i fiori**, mind you don't tread on the flowers; alcuni furono -**ati a morte**, some were trampled to death; — **i piedi**, to stamp one's feet; — **i calli a uno**, to tread on someone's corns (also fig.); -**ai un serpe**, I trod on a snake; (vulg.) ti -**o il muso a forza di pugni**, I'll smash your face in; (bldg.) to tamp; (mus.) to thump (fig.) — **l'acqua nel mortaio**, to beat the inane, to do something useless; (fig.) to harp on, to keep repeating; — **una regola di grammatica**, to harp on, to drive home a grammatical rule. -**a** *f.* beaten track; footprint, footstep, trace; footfall; sulle -**e di**, on the track of; trovarsi nelle -**e**, to find oneself in difficulties; lasciare nelle -**e**, to leave in the lurch; †see **peste**. -**acolori** *m. indecl.* (paint.) colour-grinder (i.e. one who prepares colours in powdered form, for painting). -**amento** *m.* pounding, crushing; treading, stamping (feet). -**apepe** *m. indecl.* pepper-grinder, (derog.) pharmacist, chemist. -**asavori** *m. indecl.* small pestle and mortar. -**ata** *f.* pounding, crushing; chopped or crushed parsley, garlic, etc. with minced bacon; trampling, stamping. -**ato** *part. adj.* crushed, pounded, etc.; carne -**ata**, minced meat. -**atoio** *m.* pestle. -**atore** *m.* crusher,

pounder; chestnut-grinder. (-**atrice** *f.*) -**atura** *f.* pounding, crushing, grinding; trampling; (bldg.) tamping. -**ellata** *f.* crushing with a pestle. -**ello** *m.* (chem.; pharm.) pestle; (techn.) pounder; rammer; tamper. -**io** *m.* (*pl.* -**ii**) continued pounding, stamping, trampling. -**o** *apocop. part.; adj.* crushed, pounded; trampled; carta -**a**, papier mâché; occhi -**i**, bruised eyes, eyes dull through illness; buio -**o**, pitch darkness; (cul.) anything crushed or minced; -**o alla Genovese**, basil and garlic minced for seasoning.

pest-e *f.* plague; (vet.) — **bovina**, cattle plague, rinderpest; (fig.) pest; pestilence; stench; la — **lo colga!**, a plague on it!; le sette -**i**, a bad lot; (bot.) — **d'acqua**, Canadian pond weed, *Elodea canadensis*. -**erella** *f.* sporadic appearance of plague. -**i·fero** *adj.* pestiferous, pestilential; noxious. -**ilente** *adj.* pestilent; *n.m., f.* plague-stricken person. -**ilenza** *f.* pestilence, plague; stench. -**ilenziale** *adj.* pestilential. -**ilenzialmente** *adv.* pestilentially. -**ilenzioso** *adj.* pestilential; pernicious; tempo -**ilenzioso**, time of plague; *n.m.* (fig.) pestilential person, depraved person.

pest-ello *m.*, -**io** *m.* See under **pestare**.

†**pe·stio** *m.* chain, bolt on a door.

Pesto[1] *pr.n.f.* (geog.) Paestum.

pesto[2] *apocop. part.* See under **pestare**.

petacchina *f.* (numism.) Genoese coin; slipper.

pet-ac·chio, -**ac·cio** *m.* (naut. hist.) gun brig; bomb-ketch; small lightly armed vessel used for scouting or harbour protection.

petacci(u)ola *f.* (bot.) plantain, *Plantago major* and *P. lanceolata*.

pe·talo *m.* (bot.) petal.

petard-o *m.* (mil.) petard; mortar; grenade; (fire) cracker, Chinese cracker; — **natalizio**, Christmas cracker; fog-signal; (rlwy.) detonator. -**are**, -**iere** *m.* (mil.) bombardier.

pe·taso *m.* (Gk. antiq.) petasus; (broad-brimmed) hat; a version of this with wings, worn by Hermes.

petecchi-a *f.* miser; (agric.) disease of citrous fruit-trees; thin skin or tissue which covers chestnuts inside the shell. -**e** *f.pl.* red rash raised on the skin by some contagious or infectious diseases.

petente *m.* petitioner; *adj.* petitioning.

†**pe·tere**, †**petire** *tr.* to petition; to solicit, to seek from, to entreat.

petit-ore *m.* petitioner. (-**rice** *f.*) -**o·rio** *adj.* (leg.) petitioning; petitory; giudizio -**orio**, action on title (C.C.P.).

petizione *f.* (leg.) petition; (fig.) formal request; supplication; — **di principio**, begging the question; a —, on request.

peto *m.* (vulg.) fart; voler saper tutti i -**i**, to want to know all the ins and outs (all the details).

petonciano *m.* (bot.) egg plant, aubergine, *Solanum melongena*.

†**petr-a** *f.* and derivs. see **pietra**. †-**afatto** *adj.* petrified.

petrafen·dola *f.* hard Sicilian honey-cake.

petra·ia *f.* heap of stones; quarry.

Petrar-ca *pr.n.m.* Petrarch (Francesco di ser Petracco, 1304–74). -**cheggiante** *part. adj.; n.m.* imitator of Petrarch. -**cheggiare** [A 3 c] *intr.* (*aux.* avere) to write in the style of Petrarch. -**cheri·a** *f.* (derog.) servile or poor imitation of Petrarch. -**chesco** *adj.* (*m.pl.* -**cheschi**) Petrarchan, Petrarch's. -**chescamente** *adv.* in the style of Petrarch. -**chevole** *adj.* imitating Petrarch. -**chino** *m. dim.* little Petrarch, i.e. small edition of Petrarch's 'Canzoniere'. -**chista** *m.* Petrarchist, imitator of Petrarch.

†**petrata** *f.* blow with a stone; stoning.

petr-ella *f. dim.* of **pietra**, q.v.; small stone; stone mould, for casting pewter plates; non si può gettare in -**elle**, it is not easy to do. -**ello** *m.* (orn.) petrel. -**eo** *adj.* (bot.) growing on rocks. -**iera**, †-**era** *f.* stone-quarry; (mil. hist.) heavy sling on a catapult; mine or sap. -**iero**, -**iere** *m.* (mil.; naut.) petard; small gun; -**iero a braga**, breech gun.

petrific-are [A 2 s] *tr.* to petrify. -**ante** *adj.* petrifying. -**ato** *part. adj.* petrified, turned to stone. -**azione** *f.* petrification.

†**petri·fico** *adj.* petrifying.

petr-igno *adj.* of stone, stony. †-**ina** *f.* stone. -**ino** *adj.* stony, hard as stone.

petrografi·a *f.* (geol.) petrography.

petrol-iera *f.* (naut.) tanker, oil-tanker. -**iero**, -**iere** *adj.* relating to, working with petroleum; *adj., n.m.* incendiary; destructive, revolutionary; oil-man (petroleum industry). -**i·fero** *adj.* oil-bearing, rich in petroleum; pozzo -**ifero**, oil-well; azioni -**ifere**, valori -**iferi**, oil-shares; zona -**ifera**, oilfield; (geol.) petroliferous.

petro·lio *m.* paraffin (oil), kerosene; — **grezzo**, petroleum, crude oil; (chem.) etere di —, petrol ether; (eng.) motore a —, petroleum engine.

petrone m. augm. of **pietra**, q.v.; large stone; (orn.) corn bunting.

†**petrosa** f. stony terrain.

†**petros-ello** m., †**-illo** m. parsley.

petroso adj. stony, full of stones; stony, like stone, of stone.

pett-abotta f., **-ata** f., **-azzurro** m. See under **petto**.

pettegol-a f. woman who gossips, gossip; hussy; (orn.) redshank, *Tringa totanus*. **-are** [A I SC] intr. (aux. avere) to gossip. **-ata** f. gossip, chat. **-eggiare** [A 3 C] intr. (aux. avere) to gossip. **-ezzo** m., †**-ezza** f., †**-ezze** f.pl. trivial gossip, tittle-tattle; petty wrangling. **-io** m. frequent gossiping. **-o** m. gossiper, gossip, tatler; adj. gossiping, fond of gossiping, talkative; tale-bearing; ragazza **-a**, girl given to gossip. (**-ona** f., **-one** m. augm.) **-ume** m. trivial matters; gossip.

petticciuolo m. dim. of **petto**, q.v.

pet·tide f. (mus.) pectis, Lydian harp.

pettier-a f., **-e** m. See under **petto**.

petti·mio m. (bot.) dodder, *Cuscuta*.

pettina f. (chem.) pectine.

pettinac·cia f. (text.) noil.

pettinare [A I S] and derivs. See under **pettine**.

pet·tin-e m. comb; mascelle del —, comb-ends; — fitto, narrow-toothed comb, fine comb; (text.) — fitto, switch, fine hackle (for flax); — rado, — strigatoio, wide-toothed comb; — da donna, ornamental comb; — da cavallo, curry-comb; (naut.) comb-like ornament on the prow of a gondola; (zool.) scallop, *Pecten jacobaeus*; — opercolare, *Chlamys opercularis*, — vario, *C. varius*, kinds of scallops; (mus.) plectrum; (bot.) shepherd's needle, *Scandix pecten-veneris*; (provb.) tutti i nodi vengono al —, sooner or later one must pay for one's mistakes, *or* be sure your sins will find you out. **-a·io** m. comb-maker; comb-seller. **-are** [A I S] tr. to comb; to scratch; to card, to dress (wool); (text.) to comb; to hackle (flax); (fig.) to scold, to find fault with; l'ha **-ato** per benino, he gave him a good dressing down; **-are** la tigna, to waste favours on an ungrateful person; **-are** la terra, to hoe, to weed the ground; rfl. to comb one's hair. **-ata** f. (a) combing; darsi una **-ata** in fretta, to comb one's hair hurriedly; scolding. **-ato** part. adj. combed; carded; dressed; (fig.) polished. **-atore** m. hairdresser; (text.) **-atore** da lino, flax hackler. **-atrice** f. woman hairdresser; (text.) comber, comb tenter; combing machine; **-atrice** da lino, flax-hackling machine. **-atura** f. combing (hair, etc.); hairdressing; hair style; (text.) hackling (of flax); (naut.) cleaning hemp; picking oakum (part of punishment of cell prisoners was to pick 3 lb. of old rope daily). **-ella** f. dim. fine comb; small harpoon; (sculp.) claw-tool; wooden spatula (with serrated edges, for clay-modelling). **-ic·chia** f. very fine-toothed comb; †(naut.) lining of a hold. **-iera** f. comb-case. **-ino** m. dim. little comb (e.g. for moustache).

pett-o m. breast; tenere al —, to suckle; battersi il —, to beat one's breast; chest; un uomo dal — largo, a broad-chested man; malato di —, consumptive; stazione climatica per malati di —, sanatorium (for tuberculous patients); (harness) breastband; — a botta, see **petta(b)botta**; (tailor.) una giacca a un —, single-breasted coat; una giacca a due **-i**, un doppio —, a double-breasted coat; — di camicia, shirt-front; (mus.) voce di —, chest-voice; corde di —, chest-notes; (butcher.) brisket (NOTE: Italian butchers divide what English butchers call the brisket into: 'pancetta', 'petto grosso' and 'petto sottile'); (fig.) heart; pigliar di —, to undertake with enthusiasm, to put one's heart into; di tutto —, with all one's heart; animosi **-i**, brave hearts; aver — a una cosa, to have the heart (or strength) for a thing; dar di — a, to meet, to come up against; a — di, in comparison with, in contrast to; stare a — con, to stand comparison with; a — a —, face to face; (eccl., of the Pope) riservare in —, to keep (a new cardinal's name) in petto, i.e. to create (someone) a cardinal without publicly announcing his name; mettetevi una mano al —, put your hand on your heart (and tell me truly...). **-a(b)botta** f. breastplate. **-ata** f. (vet.) chest (of a horse); brisket (of an ox); place where the flow of water is obstructed; obstacle. **-azzurro** m. (orn.) bluethroat, *Cyanosylvia svecica*. **-iera** f. breast-collar (for a horse); †(naut.) breast hook, timber at bow or stern in wooden craft. **-iere** m. (orn.) see **pettirosso**. **-ino** m. dim. little chest; bib; dickey, detachable shirt-front; flannel chest-protector. **-irosso** m. (orn.) robin, red-breast, *Erithacus rubecula*; (typ.) printer's error. **-oc·cio** m. ample bosom, full breast. (**-one** m. augm.) **-orale** adj. pectoral, chest, breast; (anat.) pectoral;

(liturg.) croce **-orale**, pectoral cross; (leg.) giudizio **-orale**, summary judgement; n.m. breastplate; breast-collar; (of horse) breast-band; (liturg.) morse, pectoral. †**-oreggiare** tr., rfl. to shock, breast against breast; to oppose. **-orina** f. stiffened front, like a corset, worn by peasant-women; stomacher; †(naut.) after-mast frames (ribs) in wooden vessel. †**-orinale** m. blunderbuss. **-oruto** adj. proud, haughty; with one's chest thrown out; andar **-oruto**, to strut. **-orutamente** adv. proudly; with strutting gait.

†**pet·tora** f.pl. of **petto**, q.v.

petulan-te adj. brash, arrogant, self-important, bad-tempered, nagging; aggravating, unpleasant; provoking; saucy, impertinent (not 'petulant'). **-temente** adv. impertinently; arrogantly; saucily. **-za** f. arrogance; impertinence; sauciness, pertness; (leg.) per **-za**, out of insolence (C.P.).

petu·nia f. (bot.) petunia, *Petunia*.

peutingeriana adj. f. (Rom. antiq.) Tavola —, *Tabula peutingeriana*, Peutinger Table, ancient map once belonging to Conrad Peutinger (1465–1547).

pevera f. large wooden funnel for filling wine casks; †large cup.

pever-e m. pepper. †**-ada** f., †**-ata** f. highly peppered broth; a kind of sauce; (fig.) jest, prank. †**-o** m. a kind of stew (highly peppered).

peziol-o m. (bot.) see **picciuolo**. **-ato** adj. (bot.) stalked, petioled.

pezz-a f. piece (of cloth, etc.); patch; roll (of paper, cloth, or ribbon); linen cloth; — di flanella, flannel chest-protector; cutting, clipping (odd pieces of cloth, etc. left over from cutting out); barber's towel; polishing cloth, rag; swaddling-band; dressing (for wounds, etc.); bandage; length of time; gran —, buona —, lunga —, long time, long while; (comm.) merci alla —, piece goods; (finan.) coin, piece; (leg.) document; extract; (mil. hist.) piece of a suit of armour; helm; gauntlet; (mil.) piece of armour-plate on a gun-mounting; (naut.) strengthening or filling piece (wood); strap; metal plate joining two others; (agric.) piece, strip (of cultivated land); Roman square measure; (vet.) large spot or fleck of a different colour in the coat of a horse; (butcher.) extreme top back of round of beef. **-ac·cia** f. pejor. dirty rag; poor cloth. **-ami** m.pl. (text.) pieces. **-are** [A I] tr. (mining, etc.) to size, to classify, to grade. **-ato** part. adj. (mining, etc.) sized, classified, graded; (vet., of a horse's coat) flecked with spots, usually white. **-atore** m. (techn.) sizer, grader. **-atura** f. dappling, speckling, spotting; (of coal, etc.) di **-atura** grossa, large, in large lumps; (techn.) particle size. **-etta** f. dim. little price; (finan.) peseta.

pezzent-e m. beggar; ragamuffin; mendicant; adj. like a beggar; in rags; beggarly. **-eri·a** f. beggary; meanness; crowd of beggars. **-one** m. augm. pejor. ragamuffin.

pezz-o m. piece; portion, fragment; in **-i**, in bits, in pieces; fare a **-i**, to break to pieces; tagliare a **-i**, to cut up, to cut to pieces, to kill; a **-i** e (a) bocconi, piecemeal; un — di carta, a scrap of paper, a sheet of paper; — di terra, plot of land; uno al —, one apiece; — di legno, log, block of wood; (fig.) — da catasta, boorish person; tutto d'un —, solid, firm; uomo tutto d'un —, man of the greatest integrity, *or* a rigid, unyielding man; un bel — d'uomo, a fine figure of a man; un — grosso, a person of importance, a V.I.P.; un — di naso, a very big nose; — d'asino, ass (said of, or to, a person); — duro, ice (cream), iced pudding; stretch, period (of space or time); ho fatto un bel — di strada, I went a good long way; ti aspetto da un —, I have been waiting for you a long while; (eng.) part; — fuso, casting; — di ricambio, spare part; (naut.) timber, hull frame or mast strengthening; spare filling piece; **-i** di quartiere, bow frames; **-i** di volta, curved timbers; **-i** d'imbono, filling pieces; **-i** longitudinali, longitudinal frame; (mil.) gun; piece; batteria su sei **-i**, six-gun battery; giro del —, moving part of a gun; squadrare il —, to line up a gun; — reale, heavy gun; — da breccia, siege gun; article of clothing; article, piece (i.e. one of a number of similar objects); (mus.) piece, composition, number; — chiuso, separate number, detached movement (in opera); — concertato, — d'insieme, concerted piece; — lungo, bass-joint, long-joint (of bassoon); (journ.) regular feature; piece (of chessmen); (numism.) coins of various values formerly current in Leghorn and Parma; (bot.) spruce, *Picea abies*. †**-a·io** m. seller of scraps of leather. **-ame** m. scraps, lot of pieces, broken crockery, potsherds. **-is·simo** m. a very long while.

pezz(u)ol-a f. handkerchief; kerchief; small piece of cloth, rag; nappy; — da collo, scarf. **-ata** f. piece, portion; handkerchieful.

pezzuol-a (*cont.*)

-o *m.* piece, bit, fragment; -o di terra, small plot of land; -o di tempo, short space of time; a -i, piecemeal.

piacci-chic·cio *m.* sticky mud; wet clay. **-cone** *m.* (of a person) slow-coach; *adj.* slow and clumsy. **-coso** *adj.* sticky, dirty. **-cotto** *m.* clumsy darn (or patching), soiled work, botched work.

Piacen-za *pr.n.f.* (geog.) Piacenza. **-tino** *adj.* of Piacenza; *n.m.* native of Piacenza.

piac-ere [B 20] *intr.* (*aux.* essere; *prep.* a) to please, to be pleasing (to); finchè loro -e, to their heart's content; mi -e, -e a me, I like it; mi -e la musica di Beethoven, I like Beethoven's music; fate come vi -e, do as you like; il bello -e a tutti, everyone likes beautiful things; la fatica non -e, hard work is unpleasant; -cia a Dio!, please God!; come a Dio -que, as fate decreed, in God's good Providence; (foll. by *infin.* without *prep.*) dopo pranzo mi -e dormire, after lunch I like to have a nap; (foll. by a clause in subjunc.) non mi -e che egli venga qui, I don't like him to come here; mi -e che voi siate vicini a me, I like you to be near me; *impers.* (foll. by 'di' and *infin.*, as the true subject) -que al Re di nominare il Villari cavaliere dell'Annunziata, the king was pleased to create Villari knight of the 'Annunziata'; -que al Senato di fare così, the Senate chose to act thus; *rfl.* to congratulate oneself, to be pleased (about, with); -ersi di, to boast of; *n.m.* pleasure, delight; satisfaction, enjoyment; amusement; favour, kindness; per —, (if you) please; con —, with pleasure, readily; a —, at (one's) pleasure, at will, (mus.) a —, ad libitum, in free rhythm; trovar, aver —, to find, to take pleasure (in); ho il — di informarvi, I am glad to inform you; sarà per me un grande — il rivederlo, I shall be delighted to see him again; vuol farmi il — di aprire quella porta?, will you be so kind as to open that door?; fammi il — di non dire queste cose, don't talk such nonsense!; fammi il —!, stop it!; fammi il famoso — di star zitto!, just you be quiet!; (comm. corresp.) al — di leggervi, awaiting your reply. **-ente** *part. adj.* pleasing, pleasant, charming; gratifying; agreeable, nice. (**-entemente** *adv.*) **-enteri·a** *f.* flattery; coaxing. **-eretto** *m. dim.* little favour. **-erone** *m. augm.* great favour. **-eruc·cio, -eruzzo** *m.* little pleasure; small favour. **-eru·colo** *m.* favour of no importance. **-evolare** [A 1 sc] *intr.* (*aux.* avere) to make oneself agreeable (to), to flatter, to coax. **-evole** *adj.* pleasant, agreeable; graceful, pretty; favourable. **-evolmente** *adv.* graciously, courteously, pleasantly; agreeably; gracefully. †**-evoleggiare** *intr.* to jest; to be facetious; to indulge in pleasantry. **-evolezza** *f.* charm, courtesy; agreeableness, affability, pleasantness; gracefulness; jest, pleasantry; **-evolezza d'animo**, calmness, tranquillity. **-evolone** *adj.* vivacious, gay, jesting. **-imento** *m.* pleasure, liking; desire; è di vostro -imento?, is it to your liking?; se ti va, prendine a tuo -imento, if you like it, take as much as you want. **-iucchiare** [A 4] *intr.* (*aux.* essere) to give a little pleasure, to be rather pleasant. **-iuto** *part. adj.* pleased.

piag-a *f.* wound; sore; scar; blow; calamity, evil; plague; sad sight; painful memory; (of a person) bore; nuisance; la — dell'analfabetismo, the bane of illiteracy; le sette piaghe d'Egitto, the seven plagues of Egypt; (bot.) scar. **-ante** *part. adj.* wounding. **-are** [A 2] *tr.* to ulcerate, to produce a sore in (or on); to injure, to wound. **-ato** *part. adj.* wounded; hurt; full of sores; cuore -ato, love-sick; animo -ato, troubled mind. **-oso** *adj.* full of sores.

†**piagere** *vb.* and derivs. See **piacere**.

piaggeri·a *f.* See under **piaggiare**.

piag·g-ia *f.* slope, declivity; (poet.) seashore; coast. **-iata** *f.* coast. **-etta** *f. dim.* pleasant, gentle slope.

piagg-iare [A 3] *tr.* to flatter, to coax; to agree with in order to please; †*intr.* to coast; (fig.) to temporize. (**-iamento** *m.*) **-iatore** *m.* flatterer; wheedler. (**-iatrice** *f.*) **-eri·a** *f.* flattery; coaxing, wheedling.

†**pia·gnere** *vb.* See **piangere**.

piagn-iste·o *m.* long drawn out whining, crying, wailing; keening over the dead; lament. **-oloso** *adj.* mournful, tearful; miserable. **-one** *m.* hired mourner, mute (at a funeral); tearful person. (**-ona** *f.*) **-ucolamento** *m.* whining, whimpering; prolonged crying. **-ucolare** [A 1 s] *intr.* (*aux.* avere) to whimper, to whine, to cry. **-ucolio** *m.* whining, constant whimpering. **-ucolone** *m.* whimperer, cry-baby. (**-ucolona** *f.*) **-ucoloso** *adj.* tearful; whining; mournful.

piagoso *adj.* See under **piaga**.

piall-a *f.* (carpen.) plane; planing machine; — per scanalare, rabbet plane. **-ac·cio** *m.* (techn.) veneer. **-are** [A 1] *tr.* (eng.; carpen.) to

plane. **-ata** *f.* planing, stroke with a plane. **-ato** *part. adj.* (eng.; carpen.) planed; smooth(ed); polished; †*n.m.* plank of planed wood. **-atore** *m.* (carpen.) planer. **-atrice** *f.* planer, planing machine. **-atura** *f.* (eng.; carpen.) planing; shavings. **-ettare** [A 1 c] *tr.* (bldg.) to float; (carpen.) to jack-plane. **-etto** *m.* (carpen.) jack-plane; (bldg.) (for smoothing walls) float. **-ettone** *m.* (carpen.) jack-plane. **-one** *m. augm.* (fig.) sluggish person; idler; trifler; *adj.* coarse, rough, badly done.

†**pia·mero** *m.* (naut., Ven., sixteenth century) the inboard rower of a galley oar manned by three men.

pian-a *f.* level ground, level flower-bed; plain; (naut.) flat; shoal near the surface; shelf or bank conveniently deep for anchoring; (Venice) hog, the first timber above the keel; (vet.) canine tooth of a male horse; tush. **-ale** *m.* terrace; level ground; (rlwy.) flatcar; *adj.* (rlwy.) carro -ale, platform car, flatcar. **-are** [A 1] *tr.* to smooth, to iron, to press; to flatten; to level (ground, etc.). **-ato** *part. adj.* levelled; flat, smooth. **-atoio** *m.* (techn.) plane. **-atore** *m.* smoother, leveller; planisher; (techn.) planing machine. (**-atrice** *f.*) **-atura** *f.* smoothing, flattening, levelling. **-eggiante** *part. adj.* almost level; tending towards flatness. **-eggiare** [A 3 c] *intr.* (*aux.* avere) to be almost flat, level; to be even; (mus.) to soften the voice; *tr.* to equal, to balance. **-ella** *f.* flat roofing tile; (heelless) slipper; (bot.) -ella della Madonna, Lady's slipper, *Cypripedium calceolus*; (mil. hist.) flat helmet; képi or Uhlan's head-dress; (naut. hist.) flat-bottomed galley. **-ella·io** *m.* maker or seller of 'pianelle'; tiler. **-ellata** *f.* blow with a slipper (or tile). **-ello** *m.* (agric.) strip of ground between two rows of vines. **-ellone** *m. augm.* large tile.

piancito *m.* (Lomb.) pavement, paving; flooring, floor.

†**pianere** *m.* See **paniere**.

pianerot·tolo *m.* See under **piano**.

pianet-a¹ *m.*, †**-o** *m.* (astron.) planet. **-ino** *m. dim.* (astron.) asteroid. **-o·ide** *m.* (astron.) planetoid.

pianet-a² *f.* (liturg.) chasuble; (Bibl.) ephod. **-a·io** *m.* vestment maker.

pianeta³ *f.* destiny, fate, horoscope.

pian-etto *m.*, **-ezza** *f.*, **-oforte** *m.* See under **piano**.

pia·ng-ere [c 5] *intr.* (*aux.* avere) to weep, to cry, to mourn; — a lungo, a sazietà, to cry one's heart out; il bimbo s'addormentò dopo aver pianto a lungo, the child cried himself to sleep; — da un occhio solo, to pretend to cry; non posso —!, I can't say I'm sorry!; (fig.) to drip, to ooze; to bleed; la vite -e, the vine is bleeding; mi -e il cuore di vederlo soffrire così, my heart bleeds to see him suffer so; (of the nightingale, etc.) to lament, to sing or call mournfully; *tr.* to weep over, to mourn for, to cry for (or over), to be sorry for; to bewail; to deplore; — amare lagrime, to shed bitter tears, to weep bitterly; — miseria, to lament one's (pretended) poverty; to regret; -o la quiete del mio paese, I miss the quiet of my village; *rfl.* to grieve, to complain; -ersi d'alcuno, to complain about someone; *n.m.* weeping, tears, lament; il -ersi dell'usignuolo, the nightingale's lament. **-ente** *part. adj.* weeping, in tears, tearful; occhi -enti, tearful eyes; salice -ente, weeping willow; la -ente cipolla, the tearful onion (i.e. provoking tears); dame -enti, professional women mourners; *n.m.pl.* (eccl. hist.) weepers, Flentes (class of penitents in Early Church). **-evole** *adj.* tearful; lamentable. **-evolmente** *adv.* with tears, tearfully; mournfully. **-i** *m. indecl.* (Tusc.) fare il -i, to cry, to cry 'boo-hoo'. **-imento** *m.* weeping; tears. **-itore** *m.* weeper, mourner. (**-itrice** *f.*) **-iucchiare** [A 4] *intr.* (*aux.* avere) to weep quietly; to sob. **-olare** [A 1 s] *intr.* (*aux.* avere) to shed a few tears; to whimper. **-oloso** *adj.* whining, whimpering, sorrowful; plaintive.

pian-o *adj.* 1. LEVEL, flat; smooth; even; (techn.) tavola -a, plane table; a piè —, at ground level; humble, unassuming, simple, plain, clear, easy; -a dimostrazione, plain proof, clear demonstration; voce -a, low voice; in lingua -a, in plain language; faccenda -a, easy job; (gramm.) parola -a, a word accented on the last syllable but one; (mus.) soft, piano; canto —, plainsong; (horse-racing) flat; 200 metri -i, 200 metres sprint; (archit.) bozza -a, flat boss, flush corbel (or only slightly projecting); colonna -a, flat column, pilaster; nodo —, reef knot; (naut.) cavo —, hawser-laid rope; *adv.* softly, gently, quietly; in a low voice; slowly; parlate —, speak slowly; pian piano, very gently or slowly; bisogna andarci —, we (you) must go carefully; chi va — va sano e va lontano, slow and steady wins the race; (on a parcel) posa —!, with care, fragile; *n.m.* level ground, plain; ground,

pian-o (*cont.*)

bottom; basso —, lowland plain; vino di —, wine from the plain; recare al —, to raze to the ground, to level; — stradale, road surface; (poet.) il ceruleo —, the sea. **2.** PLANE; (geom.) fuori —, not in the same plane; (paint.) — prospettivo, perspective plane; in —, horizontally; in primo —, in the foreground; (cinem.; telev.) primo —, close shot, (radio) fading in; (mil.) — dell'artiglieria, gun level; — del pezzo, horizontal level of a gun; (naut.) — di galleggiamento, waterplane, plane through the waterline of a vessel; — di lancio, — di tiro, vertical plane through the axis of a torpedo tube or gun; (aeron.) plane; — alare, wing area; — di deriva, fin. **3.** (ARCHIT.) PLATFORM, staircase-landing, floor, storey; al primo —, on the first floor; casa a quattro -i, four-storey house; — terreno, see **pianterreno**, under **piano**; — nobile, first floor of a Renaissance palace; (fig., colloq.) avere appigionato l'ultimo —, to have a screw loose; shelf (e.g. of a bookcase); tray (e.g. of a tea-trolley); — della seggiola, seat of the chair; — di marmo, marble slab; (bldg.) murare per —, to lay stretchers (i.e. bricks with the long side exposed); — caricatore, loading platform. **4.** PLAN, large-scale map, chart; design, drawing; plan, scheme, project; (leg.) — regolatore, town-planning scheme (C.C.); — di guerra, plan of campaign. **5.** (BOT.) — fogliare, whorl. **6.** (HERALD.) terrace in base. **7.** (MUS.) See under **pianoforte**. **-amente** *adv.* quietly, softly, gently, smoothly; simply, plainly; slowly. **-eggiante** *part. adj.* (of landscape) slightly undulating. **-eggiare** [A 3 c] *intr.* (*aux.* avere) (aeron.) to glide; †*tr.* (mus.) to soften (the voice). **-erot·tolo**, **-erotto** *m.* (archit.) landing (above stairs); abitare sullo stesso -erottolo, to live on the same floor; small level space. **-etto** *m. dim.* (aeron.) stub plane. **-ezza** *f.* flatness, smoothness; flat part, flat ground, plain; clearness; ease, easiness; quietness, gentleness, slowness. †**-forte** *m.* see **pianoforte**. **-ificazione** *f.* planning; **-ificazione** demografica, planned parenthood. **-igiano** *m.* plainsman, lowlander, inhabitant of a plain; *adj.* dwelling in the plain. **-ino** *adv. dim.* quite slowly; softly; pian -ino, very slowly, very softly; *n.m. dim.* (mus.) small piano; upright piano, cottage piano, pianino; piano-organ, street-organ. **-ismo** *m.* (mus.) pianism, pianoforte-playing. **-ista** *m., f.* (mus.) pianist. **-is·tico** *adj.* (mus.) pianistic. **-ocon·cavo** *adj.* (geom.; opt.) plano-concave. **-oconvesso** *adj.* (geom.; opt.) plano-convex. **-oforte** *m.* (mus.) pianoforte, piano; -oforte a coda, grand piano; -oforte incrociato, -oforte obliquo, overstrung piano, cottage piano; -oforte quadrato, -oforte a tavolino, square piano; -oforte verticale, upright; pestare il -oforte, to thump the piano, to play badly; accompagnare col -oforte, to accompany on the piano. **-ola** *f.* (mus.) pianola, player-piano. **-oparallelo** *adj.* (opt.) plano-parallel. **-oro** *m.* (geog.) plateau, tableland. **-terreno** *m.* ground-floor. **-uzzo** *m.* (archit.) flat rib between flutings of a column.

piant-a *f.* **1.** PLANT; tree; shrub; — della seta, *Gomphocarpus fruticosus*; le male -e, weeds; †race, stock, lineage. **2.** (ANAT.) SOLE (of foot); dal capo alle -e, from head to foot; (of shoes) sole; muover le -e, to take steps, to proceed; voltar le -e, to turn round; -e ignude, barefoot. **3.** (ARCHIT.) GROUND PLAN; fare, levare, disegnare la —, to make, to draw the plan; — dei locali, plan of the premises; site (of a building); palazzo di —, detached house; di (sana) —, entirely, completely; inventato di —, completely new; togliere di (sana) —, to lift (take away, steal) bodily. **4.** PLAN (of a town, etc.), map; — stradale, road map; design, project; — degli impiegati, list of employees; impiegato in — stabile, employee on the regular staff; in —, on the establishment. **-acarote** *m. indecl.* story-teller, fibber. †**-adoso** *adj.* full of plants, cultivated. **-ag·gine** *f.* plantain, *Plantago major*. **-agione** *f.* (work of) planting; plantation. **-amento** *m.* planting. **-ana** *f.* (aeron.) pedestal. **-animale** *m.* (zool.) zoophyte. **-are** [A I] *tr.* to plant; -are per seme, to sow seeds; -are carote, to tell cock and bull stories; -are (layer (plants); andare a -are cavoli, to retire from public life, to retire to the country; to place, to put, to fix; to plunge; to thrust; to set up; (mil.) -are le tende, -are l'accampamento, to set up camp; — una tenda, to pitch a tent; -are i pezzi, to site the guns; -are l'ordinanza, to site a battery; -are la bandiera, to plant a flagpole or hoist a flag, to place markers; (eng.; bldg.) to drive, to ram; (comm.) to enter in the books; -are chiodi, to incur debts; -are gli occhi addosso ad uno, to stare at someone; (colloq.) to quit, to leave; mi -ò in mezzo alla strada, he left me in the middle of the road; ci -ò in asso, he left us in the lurch;

ha -ato a mezzo il lavoro, he downed tools in the middle of the job; -are baracca e burattini, to give up, to abandon a task; -are la questione, to pose the question; (colloq.) -are una grava, to make a complaint, to make a fuss, to cause trouble; -are un negozio, to found a business; -arle a uno, to cheat someone; (fam.) -ala!, stop it!; *rfl.* to stop dead; si -ò davanti allo specchio, he planted himself in front of the mirror; (mil.) to come to attention; to dig in, to entrench or consolidate a position; (of a horse or mule) to dig its heels in and refuse to budge. **-ata** *f.* planting; plants set at one time; row of plants. **-ato** *part. adj.* planted; -ato a olmi, planted with elm trees; (fig.) -ato come un palo, rooted to the spot; fixed; set up; uomo ben -ato, well-built man (well set-up). **-atoio** *m.* stake, post; dibble. **-atore** *m.* planter. (**-atrice** *f.*) **-atura** *f.* plants; planting; plantation. **-ella** *f.* outer sole of a boot. **-icella** *f. dim.* young plant, tiny plant. (**-icina** *f. dim.*). **-imi** *m.pl.* seedlings. **-ina** *f.* growing plant (ready for transplanting); (slang) policeman on point duty.

pianterreno *m.* See under **piano**.

piant-o[1] *m.* tears; weeping; lamentation; plaint; fare il —, to mourn (for the dead); fatto il —, at the end of mourning; scoppiare in —, to burst into tears; (eccl.) S. Maria del —, Our Lady of Compassion, of the Sorrows; (theol.) — eterno, eternal weeping, everlasting woe; (bot.) bleeding (of plants). **-oriso** *m.* laughter and tears together.

pianto[2] *part. of* **piangere**, q.v.; *adj.* wept, mourned, lamented; deplored; regretted.

pianton-e *m.* cutting, shoot (for planting); (mil.) orderly; watchman; essere di —, to be on orderly duty; mettersi di —, to take up a watching position; stare di —, to be at attention, to be on the alert; — dell'ufficio, guardroom orderly; (naut.) sentry; — al salvagente, lifebuoy sentry; — ammiraglio, — comandante, orderly; (archit.) mullion; (motor.) — di guida, steering column. **-aia** *f.*, **-aio** *m.* nursery (for plants), nursery-bed. **-are** [A I C] *tr.* to mount guard over, to guard. **-ato** *part. adj.* under guard. **-cello** *m. dim.* small shoot (of a plant).

pian-ura *f.* (geog.) plain, open plain; la — del mare, the surface of the sea, 'the watery plain'; (herald.) terrace in base. **-uzza** *f.* (ichth.) flounder, *Pleuronectes flesus*. **-uzzo** *m.* see under **piano**.

piarda *f.* moorings of a floating mill.

†**piare**[1] *intr.* (of birds) to cheep, to twitter.

†**piare**[2] *intr.* (agric. of chestnuts, melons, etc.) to put forth shoots.

piaristi *m.pl.* See under **pio**[2].

†**pias-entiero** *m.* one who is pleasing. †**-i·bile** *adj.* pleasing, charming.

piassava *f.* (bot.) piassaba.

piastr-a *f.* metal-plate; thin slab or sheet of wood, stone or glass; (techn.) plate; (electr.) plate, grid; (bldg.; eng.) — di appoggio, base plate; (rlwy.) tie plate; — di cemento armato, reinforced concrete slab; (mil.) armour plate, shield, sheath; (naut.) — di corazza, a sheet of armourplate; — a dentiera, rackplate (capstan); — di fondazione, keel plate; (zool.) scale, or any bone forming part of the dermal armour of a fish, etc.; (biol.) — equatoriale, — metafasica, metaphase plate; (finan.) piastre; (sport) — su ghiaccio, puck. **-aio** *m.* armourer, maker of plate-armour. **-ella** *f.* quoit; (prepared) slab of cheese; (aeron.) bounce; (bldg.) floor tile. **-ellare** [A I] *tr.* (bldg.) to tile; *intr.* (*aux.* avere) (aeron.) to bounce. **-ic·cio**, **-ic·cico** *m.* medley, hotchpotch; mess, sticky mess. **-icina** *f.* (mil.) -icina del focone, protective ring of a touch hole; (naut.) -icine della torpedine, bearing lugs welded to the sides of a torpedo. **-ina** *f. dim.* small metal plate; (text. mech.) sinker (of knitting machine); (anat.) platelet. **-i·ngolo** *m.* see **piastriccio**. **-ino** *m. dim.* small metal plate; disc; small coin. **-one** *m. augm.* large metal plate; breastplate; shirt-front; (fencing) plastron; flagstone; (zool.) plastron (of a tortoise or turtle). (metall.) slab.

†**piatà** *f.* See **pietà**.

piat-o *m.* action; proceedings; suit; litigation; lawsuit; dispute. †**-eggiare**, †**-ire** *intr.* to take action; to start proceedings; to quarrel, to dispute, to bicker; -ire il pane, to be short of bread. †**-itore** *m.* litigant; petitioner. (†**-itrice** *f.*)

†**piatoso** *adj.* See **pietoso**.

piatt-o *adj.* flat; pesce —, flat fish; even; plain; (fig.) dull, uninspired; †crouching, lurking; †hidden; *n.m.* flat part (e.g. of a sword); colpire di —, to strike with the flat of one's sword; plate, dish; lavare i -i, to wash up; — fondo, soup-plate; (food on a)

piatt-o (*cont.*)

dish, course (at a meal); — forte, main course (of a meal); primo —, first course (hors d'œuvre or soup); secondo —, meat course; (eccl.) — cardinalizio, *piatto cardinalizio*, allowance by pope to cardinals; scale (of a balance); turntable of a gramophone; the 'pot' (poker); (naut.) — idrostatico, hydrostatic valve, regulating the running depth of a torpedo; (metall.) strap iron; (aeron.) — volante, flying saucer; *pl.* (mus.) piatti, *or* piattiturchi, cymbals. **-a** *f.* pontoon; †(naut.) lighter, punt, ship's dinghy. **-abanda** *f.* (archit.) (flat) ceiling, architrave, plinth, low pedestal. **-aforma** *f.* (*pl.* **-aforme**) (archit.: artill.) platform; (geog.) -aforma continentale, continental shelf; (naut.) staging used round a ship during construction or painting, etc.; fighting top, gun-control platform on a mast, gun platform; -aforma di lancio, aircraft-launching platform; (rlwy.) turntable; (of tram) platform; (fig.) political platform, programme, policy. **-a·ia** *f.* plate-rack. **-a·io** *m.* crockery-seller, hawker of crockery. **-ello** *m.* plate of serviceable ware; tiro al -ello, clay-pigeon shooting; (eng.) cap; (aeron.) fare -ello, to make a pancake landing. (**-elletto**, **-ellino** *m. dim.*) **-erello** *m. dim.* small dish (for food). **-eri·a** *f.* crockery; crockery shop. **-ina** *f.* (metall.) strap. **-ino** *m.* saucer; small plate; tazza e -ino, cup and saucer; tasty little dish; *pl.* hors d'œuvre; (mus.) cymbals; (poker) the 'pot' (cf. **piatto**).

piat·tol·a *f.* (ent.) crab louse, *Phthirus pubis*, also used loosely, and in dialect, of cockroaches and other noisome insects; (fig.) bore, tiresome person; dull, inert person; (vulg.) avere il sangue di —, to have the guts of a louse. **-oso** *adj.* lousy.

piatton-e *m. augm.* of **piatto**, q.v.; large dish; flat (of a sword, etc.); (ent.) (Tuscan dial.) cockroach. **-are** [A I c] *tr.* to strike with the flat of the sword. **-ata** *f.* blow with the flat of a sword.

piazz-a *f.* square; market-place; business; affari di —, matters of business; vettura di —, cab, hackney coach, automobile di —, taxi(cab); mettere una cosa in —, to make something public; far — pulita, to make a clean sweep, to clear away everything; i ladri fecero — pulita, the thieves stole everything; town; il popolo è sceso in —, the populace poured out of their houses and started rioting; fortress; (comm.) market; prezzo di —, market price; sono questi i prezzi praticati sulla —?, are these the prices quoted on the market?; clearing (in a wood); bald patch (in hair); (joc.) andare in —, to go bald; ma va' a —!, don't bother me!; mob, rabble; †(naut.) well deck, midship space available for passengers; †— dell'arme, small-arms store; †— marittima, naval port, coastal command zone; (mil.) gun emplacement; square, parade or exercise ground; — d'arme, *place d'armes*; military enclosure or zone; fortress, fortress area, military command zone; †rallying ground; concentration point for all units; capitano, comandante della —, fortress commander; †garrison and weapons belonging to a fortress; tutta la —, the whole weight of artillery available; perdere —, to lose a fortress, (fig.) to lose ground; tener —, to hold a fortress; post, place, employment; ha trovato una buona —, he has found a good post; space, room; far —, to make room; letto a due -e, double bed; letto a una —, single bed; letto a una — e mezza, a large single bed; — del paretaio, meadow. **-aforte** *f.* fortress, fortified town. **-aiolata** *f.* street squabble, scene; row. **-aiuolo** *m.* street loafer; demagogue; *adj.* eloquenza -aiuola, popular oratory. (**-aiuola** *f.*) **-ale** *m.* large square; esplanade; open space in a town; yard; -ale per magazzinaggio, storage yard; (rlwy.) -ale di smistamento, marshalling yard. **-are** [A I] *tr.* to place, to plant; *rfl.* to plant oneself, to be placed (esp. of 2nd and 3rd in races). **-ata** *f.* public row; street quarrel; spero che non faranno una -ata, I hope they won't make a scene; bare patch of ground. **-ato** *part. adj.* (sport, racing) placed. **-eggiare** [A 3 c] *intr.* (*aux.* avere) to loaf about. †**-ese** *adj.* low, vulgar. **-etta** *f. dim.* small square; small clearing; small fortress. **-ino** *m.* loafer. **-ista** *m.* commercial traveller; salesman; agent; canvasser. **-(u)ola** *f.* (mil.) gun platform emplacement; (golf) 'tee'; (motor.) -uola di sosta, lay-by.

†**pica**[1] *f.* magpie.

pic-a[2] *f.*, **-acismo** *m.*, **-amalaci·a** *f.* (med.) pica.

pica[3] *f.* (dial., slang) binge; pigliare una —, to get drunk.

picador *m. indecl.* (bull-fighting) picador.

picato *adj.* (Rom. antiq.) with pitchy flavour (of wine).

pic-ca *f.* (mil. hist.) pike; regiment of pikemen; mezza —, half pike; abbassare la —, to lower the point for action; strascinare la —, to trail one's pike on the march; levare la —, to raise the point,

to surrender; posare la —, to rest the lance; lunghezza di una —, a pike's length; passo di —, pikeman's pace, slow step; (fig.) obstinacy, pig-headedness; *pl.* (cards) le -che, spades; (fig.) parere il fante di -che, to be vain, boastful; contare quanto il fante di -che, to be of no account; rispondere -che, to give a negative answer, a flat refusal; fare a —, to compete; pique, spite; tiff; mettere a —, to provoke, to irritate. **-cante** *part. adj.* sharp, pungent, piquant; stinging, cutting; pointed; spicy; racy; storielle -canti, racy (improper) stories; vino -cante, sparkling wine. **-cantino** *adj.* pleasantly sharp, piquant. **-care** [A 2] *intr.* (*aux.* avere) to prick, to sting; to pique, to nettle; (aeron.) to dive; *rfl.* to be offended, to be piqued; -carsi di, to plume or pique oneself on; si -ca di essere un abile parlatore, he thinks himself a clever speaker; -carsi con uno, to enter into competition with someone. **-caressa** *f.* (naut.) catting chain on pennant, used for securing an admiralty pattern anchor or slipping it when letting go. **-cato** *f.* blow with a pike. **-cati·glio** *m.* mince, minced meat. **-cato** *part. adj.* stung; piqued; frittura -cata, meat interlarded with small pieces of bacon, and fried; *n.m.* piqué (quilting).

Piccardi·a *pr.n.f.* (geog.) Picardy.

piccheggiare [A 3 c] *tr.* to tease, to taunt; *recip. rfl.* to make stinging remarks to each other; to retort, to bicker.

picchett-are [A I c] *tr.* to trim with dots and picot edging; to spot, to speckle; to picket; to mark out with stakes; (surv.) to stake; (mus.) to play staccato notes in one bow. **-ato** *part. adj.* trimmed with dots, etc.; (mus.) note -ate in su, staccato notes in one up-bow; note -ate in giù, staccato notes in one down-bow. (**-atore** *m.* **-atora** *f.* **-atrice** *f.*) **-atura** *f.* ornamental dots and picot edging; (surv.) staking; (mus.) flying staccato.

picchett-o *m.* stake, picket, -i delle tende, tent-pegs; (surv.) stake; (naut.) quartermaster's staff (including sentries, messengers, etc. on duty during the watch); stake used to mark out a road; (mil.) picket; — d'onore, guard of honour; (naut.) piquet; ufficiale di —, orderly officer; stanza del —, guardroom; (cards) piquet. **-iere** *m.* (mil. hist.) pikeman.

picchi-are [A 4] *tr.* to knock; to strike, to hit; to beat, to tap; — le mani, to clap one's hands; lo -arono di santa ragione, they beat him soundly; -ai un piede contro una pietra, I struck my foot against a stone; -ò leggermente col bastone contro la finestra, he tapped the window with his stick; — i piedi in terra, to stamp on the ground; aver -ato la testa da piccolo, to be a little queer in the head; *intr.* (*aux.* avere) to knock; — all'uscio, to knock at the door; to persevere; -a e ripicchia, by dint of perseverance; (aeron.) to dive; (motor.) — in testa, to pink; *rfl.* to strike oneself; -arsi il petto, to beat one's breast; *recip. rfl.* to come to blows, to hit one another. (**-amento** *m.* **-ante** *part. adj.*) **-apedelle** *m. indecl.* boiler-maker, coppersmith. **-apetto** *m.* hypocrite; †jewel pendant. **-ata** *f.* knock, knocking; tapping; blow; stroke; accident, blow (of fate); touch (i.e. request for a loan); (aeron.) dive; -ata verticale, nose dive. **-atello** *adj.* (joc.; slang) queer in the head, half-witted, pixillated; *n.m.* one who is queer in the head, etc.; name of an Italian dive-bomber. **-ato** *part. adj.* knocked; beaten; tapped; dotted, spotted, speckled. **-atoio** *m.* door-knocker. **-atore** *m.* hitter, striker; (boxing) hard hitter. †**-erella** *f.* beating; dare la -erella a, to beat; aver la -erella, to be very hungry. **-erellare** [A I] *tr.* to tap, to drum, to rattle; la pioggia -erellava sui vetri, the rain beat against the windows. **-erello** *m.* double-pointed sculptor's trimmer, used in working porphyry. **-ettare** [A I c] *tr.* to tap repeatedly, to drum; to spot, to speckle; to paint in little dabs or dots; (mus.) see **picchettare**. **-ettato** *part. adj.* spotted, speckled. **-ettatura** *f.* speckling. **-ettio** *m.* constant tapping; constant drumming.

pic-chi-o[1] *m.* knock, blow; knocking; ci fu un — alla porta, there was a knock at the door; diede un — sulla tavola, he thumped, banged with his fist, on the table; *adv. phr.* di —, all of a sudden. **-otto** *m.* door-knocker; stick for husking chestnuts. **-ottolare** [A I S] *intr.* (*aux.* avere) to rap with a door-knocker, to knock at the door. **-ottolio** *m.* rapping, continued knocking. **-ot·tolo** *m.* door-knocker.

pic·chio[2] *m.* (orn.) woodpecker; — cenerino, grey-headed woodpecker, *Picus canus*; — muraiolo, wall creeper, *Tichodroma muraria*; — muratore, nuthatch, *Sitta caesia*; — nero, black woodpecker, *Dryocopus martius*; — rosso maggiore, greater spotted woodpecker, *Dendrocopus major*; — rosso mezzano, middle spotted woodpecker, *D. medius*; — rosso minore, lesser

picchio (*cont.*)

  spotted woodpecker, *D. minor*; — tridattilo, three-toed woodpecker, *Picoides tridactylus*; — verde, green woodpecker, *Picus viridis*.

picchiol-a *f.* mildew on certain plants. **-are** [A I] *tr.* to spot, to speckle. (**-ato** *part. adj.*) **-ettare** [A I C] *tr.* to speckle. (**-ettato** *part. adj.*)

†**picchione** (numism.) an old Lombard coin.

picchiotto[1] *m.* See under **picchiare**.

picchiotto[2] *m.* (orn.) nuthatch, *Sitta caesia*.

†**pic·cia** *f.* row of loaves attached by thin kissing-crust; (Tusc.) piece.

†**piccicore** *m.* See **pizzicore**, under **pizzico**.

piccin-o *adj.* little, tiny; piccino piccino, teeny-weeny; of small account; mean; humble; andare —, to slouch along; farsi —, to try to escape notice, to hide behind others; grandi e -i, rich and poor; mente -a, narrow mind; vino —, light wine; *n.m.* little boy; povero —!, poor little mite!; il — dei fratelli, the smallest, youngest, of the brothers; i -i, the little ones, (of animals) the young; (of a dog) puppy. **-a** *f.* little girl. **-eri·a** *f.* pettiness, meanness; mean action; petty pedantry.

pic·ciol-o *adj.* (poet.) small, little, short, weak; vino —, light wine; †see **piccolo**; *n.m.* (numism.) an old Florentine coin; non vale un —, it's not worth a sou. **-ęzza** *f.* see **piccolezza**, **pochezza**.

piccion-e *m.* (orn.) pigeon; — gozzato, pouter pigeon; — marino, rock dove; — pavonino, fantail pigeon; — selvatico, rock dove, *Columba livia*; — tomboliere, tumbler pigeon; — torraiolo, semi-domesticated pigeon, 'London pigeon'; — viaggiatore, homing pigeon; tiro al —, pigeon shooting; (provb.) pigliare due -i a una fava, to kill two birds with one stone; (butcher.) a slice cut from the forward section of topside of beef or veal; (fig.) young innocent; -i della stessa colombaia, lovers living under the same roof. **-a·ia** *f.* pigeon house, dove-cote; (fig.) room on the top floor; loft; attic; (theatr.) gallery, spectators sitting in the gallery.

picciotto[1] *m.* (Neap., Sicil.) lad.

†**picciotto**[2] *m.* See **piccione**.

picciuol-o *m.* (bot.) petiole, pedicel; (fig.) debole sui -i, weak on one's pins. (**-ato** *part. adj.*) **-uto** *adj.* (of a kind of fig) with a large stalk.

picco *m.* (geog.) peak; a —, vertically; (naut.) gaff; Sampson post, derrick mast; essere a — corto, to be anchored at short stay; a —, up and down; a lungo —, long stay; tirarsi a —, virare a —, to shorten, to short stay; a —, to the bottom (in the sense of sinking); andare a —, calare a —, to sink; mandare a —, to sink (*tr.*); discesa a —, dive; (techn.) peak; pick-axe; (aeron.) (electr.) tensione picco-picco, peak-to-peak voltage; (fig.) witticism, stinging retort; sting, sharp taste.

pic·col-o *adj.* little, small; short; diminutive; -a lettera, small, lower-case, letter; su -a scala, on a small scale; in —, in miniature; in — tempo, in a short time; trifling, unimportant; narrow-minded, petty; humble, lowly; -a borghesia, lower middle-class; (leg.) — fallimento, (formerly) small bankruptcy (now dealt with under 'procedimento sommario'); — imprenditore, person carrying on trade, business or profession in small way (C.C.); (rlwy.) -a velocità, ordinary goods train (as opposed to 'grande velocità', express goods train); (electr.) circuito —, short circuit; (finan.) -e spese, petties; -a cassa, petty cash; giornale della -a cassa, petty cash book; -a avaria, petty average; (numism.) fiorino —, gold florin; — borghese, (of) lower middle-class; *n.m.* white-collar, *or* black-coated, worker; (eccl.) -e suore dei poveri, Little Sisters of the Poor; (geog.) Le Piccole Antille, Lesser Antilles; *n.m.* little boy, boy; child; *pl.* children, little ones; (radio) l'ora per i -i, children's hour; waiter's boy; (in hotels) lift-boy, call-boy; smallness; dare nel —, to be on the small side; small way (of life); (zool.) lesser horseshoe bat, *Rhinolophus hipposiderus*; (numism.) small coin. **-ęzza** *f.* smallness; pettiness; meanness, mean act; trifle.

picc-one *m.* pick, mattock; qui ci vuole il —, this should be demolished; (mil. hist.) large pile; opera del —, demolition work. **-ona·io**, †**-onaro** *m.* sapper; navvy, demolition worker. **-onare** [A I C] *intr.* (*aux.* avere) to wield a pick-axe. **-onata** *f.* blow with a pick-axe. **-oniere** *m.* sapper, miner, navvy.

piccos-o *adj.* touchy; peevish, irritable. **-ag·gine**, **-ità** *f.* peevishness, touchiness, irritability. **-ętto** *adj. dim.* rather touchy; inclined to be peevish.

piccozz-a *f.* hatchet; chopper; — da pompiere, fireman's axe; ice-axe. **-ino** *m.* carpenter's hatchet.

pi·cea *f.* (bot.) spruce, *Picea*.

pi·ceo *adj.* pitchy; pitch-black.

pich-pine *m.* indecl. (bot.) pitch pine, *Pinus taeda*.

pickl-are [A I] *tr.* (tanning) to pickle. **-ag·gio** *m.* (tanning) pickling. (**-ato** *part. adj.*)

picno·metro *m.* (phys.) specific gravity bottle, pyknometer.

picnoṣi *f.* (biol.) pycnosis.

picoli·t *m. indecl.* a wine resembling Tokay.

picozzo *m.* (vet.) central incisor teeth of a horse.

pi·cr-ico *adj.* (chem.) picric. **-ato** *m.* (chem.) picrate. **-otossina** *f.* (chem.) picrotoxin, cocculin.

pidoc·chi-o *m.* (ent.) louse, *Pediculus vestimenti* and *P. capitis*; also various other parasites of animals and plants; (fig.) upstart, *nouveau riche*. **-eri·a** *f.* stinginess, meanness; trifle. **-ọso** *adj.* lousy; (fig.) stingy, mean, miserly; dirty.

piè *m. indecl.* see **piede**; (zool.) — di pellicano, *Aporrhais pespelicani*; — d'asino, *Pectunculus glycimeris*, dog cockle.

pied-e *m.* (sometimes abbrev. to **piè**). **1.** FOOT (of a human being); da capo a -i, from head to foot; aver male ai -i, to be footsore; andare a -i, to go on foot, to walk; andare a quattro -i, to go on all fours; camminare a -i nudi, to walk barefoot; metter —, to set foot; in -i, standing; stare in -i, to stand; alzarsi in -i, to stand up; posto in -i, standing-room; cadere in -i, to fall on one's feet (also fig.); avere un — nella fossa, to have one foot in the grave; pestare i -i, to stamp (one's feet); corsa a -i, foot-race; guardie a -i, footguards; salto a -i giunti, standing jump; avere il — marino, to have gained one's sea-legs; lungo dieci -i, ten feet long; tenere il — in due staffe, to hold with the hare and hunt with the hounds; (leg.) a — libero, (*loosely*) on bail, (*strictly*) denunciato a — libero, summonsed to appear to answer charge; (fig. uses) a piè pari, with ease, at one's ease; saltare a piè pari, to skip through (e.g. a chapter), to glide over, to by-pass; saltò le difficoltà a piè pari, he dodged all the difficulties; procedere coi -i di piombo, to go slowly and carefully; darsi la zappa sui -i, to defeat one's own ends; mettere i -i al muro, puntare i -i, to be obstinate, to stick to one's guns; mettersi sotto i -i qualcuno, to run down someone; rimanere a -i, to be left behind, to be left standing, *or* (fig.) to miss the 'bus, to be left in the lurch; quel suo ragionamento non sta in -i, his argument will not hold water; ragionare coi -i, to talk through one's hat; un lavoro fatto coi -i, a very clumsy piece of work; cavarne i -i, to get out of a scrape; esser sempre tra i -i, to be always in the way; fuori dai -i!, get out of my way! **2.** GROUND; footing; foothold; stand; standard; prendere —, to gain ground; sul — di guerra, on a war-footing; sul — di venti miglia all'ora, at the rate of twenty miles an hour. **3.** (ZOOL.) FOOT (of any sort of animal); — biforcuto, cloven hoof; trotter. **4.** BASE, pedestal; leg, foot (of a chair, etc.), stalk, stem; (archit.) base (of a column, etc.); piè diritto, plain base (i.e. without mouldings); trestle; small easel; nota a piè di pagina, footnote; (naut.) — d'albero, piè d'albero, foot of a mast (lower portion above decks); — di bandiera, — di una randa, jack of a flag or sail; — di ruota, bottom of stem on sternpost; non c'è —, you can't touch bottom; — di pollo, knot, manrope knot, 'Matthew Walker' used for beckets or buckets; — di pollo, Southern Cross, Crux Australis; (mil.) — di asta, foot of a mast or pole; — di fucile, butt of a gun or rifle; — di lancia, heel of a spear, etc.; pied-arm!; order arms!; — di porco, barbed-wire stake, crowbar; (motor.) small end (of con rod); (rlwy.) flange (of rail); (mus.) foot (of organ-pipe); pedestal (of harp). **5.** (PROSOD.) METRICAL FOOT; subdivision of a 'canzone' (first or second half of the 'fronte'). **6.** (BOT.) — anserino, *Chenopodium murale*; — colombino, *Geranium columbinum*; — d'asino, *Ranunculus velutinus* and *R. bulbosus*; — di corvo, *Coronilla scorpioides*; — di gallo, *Eranthus hiemalis* and *Geranium molle*; — d'uccello, *Rhagadiolus stellatus*. †**-e·stile** *m.* (archit.) base. **piedistallo. -ilu·vio** *m. indecl.* foot-bath. **-impennato** *adj.* (poet.) 'with feet that fly on feathers'. **-ino** *m. dim.* little foot; (colloq.) fare -ino, to nudge with one's foot; pressure foot (of sewing-machine); (techn.) stem. **-istallo**, **-estallo** *m.* (archit.) pedestal; mettere su di un -istallo, to put on a pedestal; far da -istallo a, to help up, to hold up, to support. **-ritto** *m.* (archit.) plain pedestal (or base), impost.

pie·dica *f.* saw-horse.

pieficcato *adj.* (herald.) croce pieficcata, cross fitchy.

pieforcuto *adj.* (herald.) croce pieforcuta, cross forked in base.

piega *f.* See under **piegare**.

pieg·are [A 2] *tr.* to fold, to fold up; — in due, to fold in two; to bend, to flex; to subdue; — il capo, to bow, to bend one's head, (fig.) to consent, — la fronte, to bow; le sventure non l'avevano -ato, misfortunes had not subdued him; — l'ostinazione, to overcome resistance; — l'orecchio, to lend ear, to give one's attention; — le ginocchia, to bend the knee, to kneel, (fig.) to submit; *intr.* (*aux.* avere) to bend, to turn, to lean; to give way; to submit; la barca -ò su un lato e si capovolse, the boat leaned over to one side and capsized; la strada -a a sinistra, the road turns to the left; -a a destra e troverai una piazza, turn to the right and you will come upon a square; la fanteria nemica -ò, the enemy infantry gave way; non piegheremo mai, we will never submit; *rfl.* to become folded, creased or bent; to bend; to bow; to yield, to submit; si è -ato, he gave in, he yielded to persuasion; -arsi all'inevitabile, to bow to the inevitable. **-a** *f.* fold, crease, pleat; wrinkle; tuck; recess, inner part; bend; turn; formar pieghe, to crease; quest'abito non ti fa una -a, this coat fits you perfectly; (fig., e.g. of an argument) non fare una -a, to have no flaw, to be absolutely convincing, to be dead right; -a del terreno, fold in the ground; course; prendere la -a naturale, to follow the normal course; prendere una cattiva -a, to take a turn for the worse; le cose stanno prendendo una cattiva -a, things are going wrong; (of hair) wave; messa in pieghe, set; mettere in pieghe, to wave and set; (geol.) -a coricata, recumbent bed; pieghe disarmoniche, irregular folds; (mil.) hinge of a manœuvre; act of hinging; act of following back. **-a·bile** *adj.* flexible, pliable, folding, collapsible. **-ac·cia** *f. pejor.* (ugly) crease. **-afo·glio** *m. indecl.* (typ.) folding machine. **-amento** *m.* folding, bending, bend, curve; flexion; -amenti del busto, body-bending (exercises); lowering; depression; -amento della voce, inflection (of the voice), vocal inflection. **-ante** *part. adj.* bending, yielding. **-arota·ie** *m. indecl.* (rlwy.) jim crow, rail bender. **-ata** *f.* bend, turn; fold(ing). **-ato** *part. adj.* folded; bent; turned back, in retreat, retiring; sloping (of handwriting); (scient.) plicate; (herald.) embowed. **-atondino** *m. indecl.* (eng.) rod bender. **-atore** *m.*, **-atrice** *f.* (eng.) bending machine, bending press. **-atubi** *m. indecl.* (eng.) tube bender, pipe bender. **-atura** *f.* folding, bending; fold, bend; curve; turn; plaiting; (anat.) plication. **-one** *m.* (slang) 'heart-throb', 'lady-killer'.

†**pieg·g·io** *m.* pledge, guarantee; guarantor. †**-eri·a** *f.* surety.

pie-gheggiare [A 3 c] *intr.* (*aux.* avere) (paint.; sculp.) to drape, to represent drapery or folds in fabric. **-ghetta** *f. dim.* small pleat. **-ghettare** [A 1 c] *tr.* to pleat; to ruche; to smock. **-ghettato** *part. adj.* pleated; ruched; smocked. **-ghettatura** *f.* pleating; ruching; smocking. **-ghetto** *m.* small folder (esp. of paper); circular (letter). **-ghevole** *adj.* pliable, pliant; folding, flexible; supple; yielding, docile, compliant, submissive; sedia -ghevole, folding chair; ingegno -ghevole, versatile genius; -ghevole alle lusinghe, susceptible to flattery; adjustable; flexible; *n.m.* folder, brochure, leaflet. (**-ghevolmente** *adv.*) **-ghevolezza** *f.* pliability, flexibility; suppleness; submissiveness.

pie-go *m.* (*pl.* **-ghi**) cover, envelope; packet; wrapper; sotto —, under cover; in — separato, under separate cover; folder; folded sheets of paper. **-golina** *f. dim.* loose fold (in garments). **-golinare** [A 1] *tr.* to fold prettily.

piel-ite *f.* (med.) pyelitis. **-i·tico** *adj.* (med.) pyelitic. **-onefrite** *f.* (med.) pyelonephritis. **-opati·a** *f.* (med.) pyelonephrosis. **-oscopi·a** *f.* (med.) pyeloscopy.

piella *f.* (bot.). See picea.

pi-emi·a *f.* (med.) pyaemia. **-e·mico** *adj.* (med.) pyaemic.

Piemont-e *pr.n.m.* (geog.) Piedmont. **-ese** *adj., n.m., f.* Piedmontese; *m.* Piedmontese dialect. **-ite** *f.* (geol.) piedmontite, manganepidote.

piena *f.* See under **pieno**.

pien-o, pien-o *adj.* full; entire; complete; — fino a traboccare, full to overflowing; — zeppo, crammed full, full right up; full-bodied, fat; donna -a, pregnant woman; respirare a -i polmoni, to breathe deeply; luna -a, full moon; in — giorno, in broad daylight; a notte -a, at the dead of night; di -a estate, in the height of summer; — di macchie, full of spots; traduzione -a di errori, translation full of mistakes; perfect, utter; con — rispetto, with all respect; approvato a -i voti, passed unanimously; abundant;

(poet.) l'annata è -a, there is an abundant harvest; (fig.; fam.) sick, tired, 'fed up'; averne -e le tasche, to have had more than enough of things; — fino agli occhi, 'fed to the teeth'; (fig.) otre — di vento, wind-bag; muro —, solid wall (i.e. without a cavity); colpo (in) —, home-thrust, well-aimed blow; cogliere in —, to hit a bull's eye, to strike home; a —, fully, completely; a -e mani, liberally, abundantly; (herald.) plain; *n.m.* fullness; perfection; height; depth; full part; nel — della notte, at dead of night; dare il — a, to fill up, to top up; (motor.) fare il —, to fill up; (mus.) diapason chorus (of organ). **-a** *f.* flood, spate; overflow; crowd, throng; stream; andar contro la -a, to go against the stream; il fiume è in -a, the river is in flood; -a crescente, high tide, springs; (leg.) -a straordinaria, overflowing of banks (C.C.); abundance, fullness; (theatr.) far -a ogni sera, to play to a full house every night; ardour, warmth; -a degli affetti, warmth of feeling. **-amente** *adv.* fully, completely, totally; utterly; quite; esser -amente libero, to be quite free. **-erella** *f. dim.* small flood, spate. **-ezza** *f.* fullness; abundance; -ezza dei tempi, fullness of time; impetuosity; ardour. †**-itu·dine** *f.* plenitude. **-one** *m. augm.* large crowd; full house. **-otto** *adj. dim.* plump, rather fat, fleshy.

†**pientis·simo** *adj.* most gracious.

pie·ridi *f.pl.* (class. myth.) Muses; (ent.) cabbage whites and related butterflies (Fam. Pieridae).

Piero *pr.n.m.* Piers; Peter (cf. **Pietro**).

†**piet-a** *f.* anguish, pain; discomfort. †**-ade** *f.* see **pietà**.

pietà *f.* pity, mercy; compassion; piety; per —!, for pity's sake; senza —, pitiless, merciless; pitilessly; monte di —, pawn office (in Italy there are no pawnbroker's *shops*; the 'monti di pietà' are state-controlled); (art) the Virgin Mary holding the body of the dead Christ; libri di —, devotional books.

pietanz-a *f.* dish; portion, helping, plate(ful) of food; far —, to serve food. **-etta** *f. dim.* nice helping (of food). **-iera** *f.* dinner pail.

pie·tica *f.* See **piedica**.

piet-ismo *m.* (eccl. hist) Pietism (Lutheran movement begun c. 1670); (fig.) pietism, parade of piety. **-ista** *adj., n.m.* Pietist; pietist. **-i·stico** *adj.* pietistic, sanctimonious.

pietos-o *adj.* compassionate, merciful; piteous, pitiable; pitiful, sorry, wretched; loving, devoted; pious; menzogna -a, white lie, merciful lie; (provb.) il medico — fa la piaga verminosa, a merciful doctor makes the wound stink; — verso i parenti, devoted to one's relations; opera -a, work of piety, good deed; le armi -e, holy arms (of the Crusaders); guerra -a, holy war. **-amente** *adv.* compassionately, mercifully, pitifully, piteously; pitiably; piously.

pietr-a *f.* stone; — angolare, corner stone; posare la prima —, to lay the foundation stone; — preziosa, precious stone, gem; (geol.) — d'aquila, -e verdi, ferro-magnesian rocks; età della —, Stone Age; costruito in —, built of stone; — da taglio, freestone; — calcare, limestone; — per affilare, whetstone, grindstone; — focaia, flint; (watchm.) jewel; con —, jewelled; senza —, non-jewelled; — del focolare, hearthstone; — chilometrica, — miliare, milestone; — per affilare, whetstone; — lunare, moonstone; — da mulino, millstone; — sepolcrale, tombstone; — filosofale, philosopher's stone; — di paragone, touchstone; (med.) male della —, calculus, 'stones'; (mil. hist.) fucile a —, flintlock; (bot.) — fungaia, edible fungus, *Polyporus tuberaster*; (fig.) mettere una — su, to bury the remembrance of; cuore di —, stony heart, hard heart; mettiamo una — sul passato, let bygones be bygones; scagliare la prima —, to cast the first stone; — d'inciampo, (fig.) stumbling-block; — dello scandalo, stone of stumbling, stumbling-block; portar la sua — all'edifizio, to do one's bit, to help in a task; cavar sangue da una —, to draw blood from a stone, to extort money. **-a·ia** *f.* quarry; (geol.) -aia semovente, rock glacier. **-a·io** *m.* quarryman. **-ame** *m.* (archit.) dressed stone(s), for building; heap of stones. **-ante** *m.* (med.) person suffering from calculus. **-ata** *f.* blow with a stone. **-ella** *f. dim.* see petrella. **-iera** *f.*, **-iere** *m.* see petriero. **-ina** *f. dim.* flint (of a cigarette-lighter).

pietrificare [A 2 s] and derivs. See **petrificare**.

petri·fico *adj.* petrifying.

pietrino *m. dim.* small stone; marble (or other) doorstop; (eccl.) stone base with socket for crucifix, banner, etc.; *adj.* made of stone; †olio —, petroleum.

pietris-co *m.* rubble, ballast, gravel; (geol.; road bldg.) crushed stone. **-chino** *m.* (road bldg.) crushed stone.

Pietro *pr.n.m.* Peter; (geog.) Isola —, Peter Island; il successore di (San) —, (St) Peter's successor, the Pope; la navicella di San —, Peter's Bark, the Catholic Church; gabbar San —, to throw up a clerical career, to decide not to become a priest; — e Paolo, Smith and Jones, Tom, Dick (and Harry); (bot.) erba di San —, samphire, *Crithmum maritimum*; (zool.) orecchia di San —, ormer, *Haliotis lamellosa*; (ichth.) pesce di San —, John Dory, *Zeus faber*.

pietrolina *f. dim.* of **pietra**, q.v.; small stone, precious stone, gem.

pietrọs-o *adj.* stony; made of stone; cut out of stone; flinty; rocky; acque -ose, water springing from among rocks. **-ità** *f.* stoniness.

pietr-uzza *f. dim.* of **pietra**, q.v.; small precious stone, gem; *pl.* lapilli. **-uz·zole** *f.pl.* lapilli, gall-stones; grit.

piev-e *f.* (eccl.) parish church (usu. chief church of a district and one of ancient foundation); parish (district or people). **-anale** *adj.* (eccl.) of a parish priest. **-ani·a** *f.* (and pop. **piovani·a**) (eccl.) parish (of privileged status); status of *pievano*; parish priest's house, presbytery. **-ano** *m.* (eccl.) priest in charge of a 'pieve'; parish priest (usu. with some jurisdiction over less important local churches). **-anello** *m. dim.* humble, obscure, parish priest. †**-iale** *adj.* see **piviale**.

pieẓ-oelettricità *f.* (electr.) piezo-electricity. **-oelet·trico** *adj.* (electr.) piezo-electric. **-o·metro** *m.* (phys.) piezometer. **-ome·trico** *adj.* (phys.) piezometric. **-ooscillatọre** *m.* (radio) quartz oscillator.

†**pifa** *f.* (mus.) this word, appearing at the beginning of the MS. of Handel's Pastoral Symphony in the *Messiah*, is either a form of **piva**, q.v., or an abbrev. of **pifara**, q.v.

†**pifani·a** *f.* See **epifania**.

†**pi·fara** *f.*, **pi·faro** *m.* (mus.). See **piffero**.

†**pi·fera** *f.* (mus.) female piper.

piffer-are [A I S] *tr., intr.* (aux. avere) (mus.) to pipe. **-a·io** *m.*, **-aro** *m.* (mus.) wandering piper (usu. one coming into towns to play Christmas music). **-ata** *f.* (mus.) piping. **-atọre** *m.* (mus.) piper. **-ina** *f.* (mus.) small pipe, fife. †**-ello** *m.* (archit.) large T-square.

pif·fer-o *m.* (mus.) pipe, fife, flageolet, shepherd's pipe, rustic bagpipe; piper; (provb.) fare come i -i di montagna, che andarono per suonare e vennero suonati, many go for wool and come home shorn; (naut.) hulk; ship reduced to transport duty; (joc.) 'hook pot'. **-ọne** *m. augm.* (mus.) large 'piffero'. **-otto** *m.* (mus.) small 'piffero'.

pi·gamo *m.* (bot.) *Thalictrum angustifolium*.

pigaruolo *m.* a sort of fishing net.

†**piggiore** *adj.* and derivs. See **peggiore**.

†**pi·ghero** *adj.* See **pigro**.

pi·gia *m.* See under **pigiare**.

pigiama *m.* pyjama suit, pyjamas.

pigi-are [A 3] *tr.* to press, to crush, to squeeze; — l'uva, to press grapes; (bldg.) to tamp; *rfl.* to crowd, to crush. **-a** *m.* crush; un pigia pigia, a dense crowd, a tight squeeze. **-amẹnto** *m.* pressing, crushing, squeezing. **-ata** *f.* squeeze. **-ato** *part. adj.* pressed, squeezed; uva **-ata**, pressed grapes; come si era **-ati** in quella stanza!, how crowded that room was!; **-ati** come le acciughe, packed like sardines. **-atọio** *m.* wine-press. **-atọre** *m.* presser, squeezer. **-atrice** *f.* macchina **-atrice**, wine-press. **-atura** *f.* pressing (esp. of grapes); crushing; (bldg.) tamping.

pigino *m.* push-button.

pi·gi-o *m.* crushing, squeezing; crowd, throng; entrare, stare nel —, to embark on a risky undertaking, to volunteer; crusher, rammer. **-ọne** *m. augm.* crusher, for threshing chestnuts.

pigiọne¹ *m. augm.* See under **pigio**.

pigiọn-e² *f.* (leg.) rent (usu. of urban property) (C.C.); giorno del pagamento della —, rent day; prendere a —, to rent; dare a —, to let; (iron.) prendere a — una cosa, to treat something as one's own, to keep and use a borrowed object; pigliare, prendere a — un luogo, to make oneself at home somewhere, to frequent a place; avere il cervello a —, to be scatterbrained; stare a —, to be out of place. **-ale** *m., f.* (leg.) lessee, tenant; lodger; *adj.* tenant's; as a tenant. **-aluc·cio** *m. pejor.* bad tenant, unsatisfactory tenant. **-ante** *m.* tenant; lodger. **-uc·cia** *f. pejor.* miserable little rent.

pi·glia *m.* See under **pigliare**.

pigli-are [A 4] (more fam. than **prendere**, q.v.; the *part.* **pigliato** is considered inelegant, and in educated speech or formal writing **preso** is preferred). **I.** *tr.* **1.** To TAKE; — moglie, to take a wife; (of a horse) — il morso fra i denti, to take the bit between its teeth (also fig.); — la via, to take the road; — un bagno, to

take a bath; — appunti, to take notes; — le cose sul serio, to take things seriously; — possesso, to take possession; — fiato, to take breath; — la colla, to take the glue (i.e. to hold, to stick, to set); — un lavoro, to take on, to take up, a task; — una medicina, to take some medicine; **-ò** un brodo, he took some soup; **-arne**, to take punishment. **2.** To SEIZE, to catch; — topi, to catch mice; (provb.) figli di gatto **-ano** topi, like father like son; — pesci, to catch fish; (fig.) non saper che pesci —, not to know where to begin, *or* which way to turn; **-alo!**, catch him!; — un raffreddore, to catch cold; — fuoco, to catch fire; — la palle al balzo, to seize an opportunity; non mi ci **-a** più!, he won't catch me like that again! **3.** To STRIKE, to hit, to 'get'; tirò un sasso e lo **-ò** sulla testa, he threw a stone and got him on the head; che ti **-a**?, what's got into you?, what's wrong with you?; — nel bel mezzo, to hit in the very middle. **4.** (NAUT.) — i rilevamenti, to take bearings; — volta, to take a turn (with a rope); — largo, — mare, to stand off from land; — a nolo, to charter; — porto, to enter harbour; — terra, to land; — l'abbrivo, to get way on a ship. **II.** *intr.* (aux. avere) to take, to hold; (of cement, glue, etc.) to set; **-a!**, take!; che **-a**, **-a**, grab what you can, it's a free-for-all; (of plants) to take root; (of ideas) to catch on; to turn, to tend; **-a** a destra, take the turn to the right. **III.** *rfl.* (dat. of *prn.* 'si') to take on oneself; egli si **-ò** tutta la responsabilità, he took all the responsibility upon himself; **-arsi** un raffreddore, to get a cold; **-arsi** una sbornia, to get drunk; **-arsela** con uno, to get angry with someone; **-arsela** a male, to take offence; *recip. rfl.* to come to an understanding; si **-arono** a pugni, they came to blows. **-a** *m.* snatcher; policeman, 'copper'; catching, grabbing; è un **-a -a**, it's a 'free for all', grab what you can. **-a·bile** *adj.* seizable. **-amẹnto** *m.* taking, catching; **-amento** dell'aria, breathing, breathing-space. **-amọsche** *m. indecl.* (orn.) flycatcher, esp. the spotted flycatcher, *Muscicapa grisola*; (bot.) Venus's flytrap. **-ato** *part. adj.* (see note under **pigliare**) taken; caught. **-atọre** *m.* taker, receiver. (**-atrice** *f.*) **-avẹnto** *m.* ventilator.

pi·glio¹ *m.* hold; catch; taking hold; dar di — a, to get hold of, to seize, to take up; (cards) trick; †profit, gain.

pi·glio² *m.* look, aspect, bearing; action; mal —, threatening look, threat; ha un — simpatico, he has a charming way with him; con — severo, with a severe expression.

Pigmaliọne *pr.n.m.* Pygmalion.

pigment-o *m.* colouring matter, pigment. **-ali** *f.pl.* (zool.) eye spots. †**-a·rio** *m.* embalmer. **-aziọne** *f.* pigmentation.

pigm-ẹo *m.* (ethn.) pigmy; (fig.) nonentity (**-ẹa** *f.*); *adj.* razza **-ẹa**, pigmy race, race of pigmies.

pign-a *f.* (bot.) see **pina**; (archit.) stonework forming the top of a dome, cone-shaped ornament (usu. on a cornice), gable, cut-water of a bridge; large (cone-shaped) bunch of grapes; (naut.) grating; strainer on an inlet valve; rope making headplate; (zool.) *Phallusia mamillata*, a kind of sea squirt. **-atta** *f.*, †**-atto** *m.* pot, cooking-pot; **-atta** di fuoco, fire bomb, incendiary or illuminant. **-atta·io**, †**-attaro** *m.* potter. **-attẹlla** *f.* foot-warmer; warming-pan. **-attẹllo** *m. dim.* small cooking pot. **-attina** *f.*, **-attino** *m.* (mil.) torch; hand grenade; small bomb. †**-eta** *f.*, **-ẹto** *m.* pine-wood. **-ola** *f.* (bot.) see 'erba pignola' under **erba**, and **pinocchio¹**. **-olẹtto** *m. dim.* of **pignuolo**, q.v. **-olo** *m.* see **pignuolo**, below. **-ọne** *m.* (archit.) cut-water (of a bridge); dyke, embankment; (eng.) pinion; (for a chain) sprocket; **-one** conico, bevel pinion; (watchm.) **-one** di scappamento, escape wheel pinion. **-uolo** *m.* pine-seed; kind of black grape, and its wine; (fig.) stickler for discipline, martinet, pedantic upholder of regulations; *adj.* meticulous; pedantic.

†**pi·gnere¹** *vb.* and derivs. See **dipingere**.

†**pi·gnere²** *vb.* and derivs. See **spingere**, **pingere**.

pignor-are [A I] *tr.* (leg.) to attach; to distrain; to seize by way of distress (C.C.); to pledge; to pawn. **-a·bile** *adj.* (leg.) distrainable; liable to distraint or distress (C.C.). **-abilità** *f.* (leg.) liability to distraint, distress or attachment (C.C.). **-amẹnto** *m.* (leg.) attachment; distraint; distress; **-amento** di una rendita, attachment of an annuity; **-amento** delle cose, distraint of goods (C.C.); **-amento** di crediti verso terzi, attachment by garnishment (C.C.P.). **-ante** *m.* (leg.) distrainer; pawner; pledger (C.C.). **-ata·rio** *m.* distrainee. **-ati·zio** *adj.* (leg.) having in pawn or pledge; creditore **-atizio**, pawnee, pledgee (C.C.). (**-ato** *part. adj.*) **-aziọne** *f.* see **pignoramento**.

pignuolo *m.* See under **pigna**.

pig·o[1] *m.* (ichth.) *Leuciscus pigus*, a fresh-water fish related to the roach living in certain Italian rivers.

†**pigo**[2] *m.* deer.

pigol·are [A I S] *intr.* (*aux.* avere) to chirp, to chirrup, to cheep; to cry out; to give voice; (fig.) to complain, to grumble. **-aménto** *m.* chirping. **-ìo** *m.* (*pl.* **-ìi**) constant chirping, continual cheeping. **-óne** *m.* plaintive, whining person, grouser. (**-óna** *f.*)

pigr·o *adj.* lazy, indolent; slothful; sluggish; slow; dull; un ragazzo —, a lazy boy, a dull, inert boy; una corrente **-a**, a sluggish stream; sonni **-i**, idle dreams; (poet.) il — gelo, numbing frost; *n.m.* lazy boy or man. (**-a** *f.*) **-aménte** *adv.* lazily, sluggishly; indolently; slowly. **-ac·cio** *m. pejor.* lazy good-for-nothing. **-ęzza** *f.* sluggishness; slowness. †**-ire** *vb.* and derivs. see **impigrire**. **-i·zia** *f.* laziness, idleness, sloth; indolence. †**-izioso** *adj.* see **pigro**. †**-izire** *vb.* and derivs. see **impigrire**. **-óne** *adj. augm.* extremely lazy. †**-oso** *adj.* see **pigro**.

pïina *f.* (chem.) pyin.

pik *m. indecl.* measurement, 'foot' or 0·68 of a metre, used in Tripoli.

pil·a *f.* (archit.) pier (of a bridge), buttress; heap, pile; una — di libri, a pile of books; (electr.) battery, cell, pile; — a secco, dry battery; — atomica, atomic pile; — termoelettrica. thermopile; — di volta, galvanic battery; basin; font; — dell'acqua santa, holy-water stoup; (agric.) — da riso, beater for threshing rice; (paperm.) — olandese, hollander, beater; — delle ulive, olive press (esp. the kind of basin in which the olives are placed); horse (cattle) trough; (techn.) instrument used for melting coins; (watchm.) pillar; (herald.) pile; — movente, pile issuing from the dexter base; — rovesciata, pile issuing from the base; una — e due **-e** rovesciate, three piles one in chief between two in base. **-astrino** *m.* (bldg.) newel. **-astro** *m.* (archit.) pillar, pier, post, column; (scient.) rod. **-ętta** *f. dim.*; **-etta** dell'acqua santa, holy-water stoup; (eng.) footstep bearing; (bldg.) drain. **-iere** *m.* (archit.) pillar, pier of a bridge, pylon. **-óne** *m. augm.* large basin; ditch; (electr.) **-one** a traliccio, pylon; (archit.) pier supporting a dome, pier of a bridge; rammer; tower; *pl.* (text.) molino a **-one**, beetle (for beating flax); (aeron.) **-one** d'ormeggio, mooring mast; (sport) prop, support (rugby).

Pi·lade *pr.n.m.* See under **Oreste**.

Pilato *pr.n.m.* (Bibl.) Pilate; Ponzio —, Pontius Pilate; entrar come — nel Credo, to be out of place, to have no business somewhere, to have got somewhere accidentally or under false pretences; mandar da Erode a —, to send from pillar to post.

pilatro *m.* (bot.) pellitory of Spain, *Anacyclus pyrethrum*; Saint John's wort, *Hypericum*.

pilęggi·o *m.* (naut.) channel; dar —, to clear, to give clearance, permission to sail. **-are** [A3C] *intr.* (*aux.* avere) to sail; to take to sea; to go down channel.

pi·le·o *m.* (class. antiq.) pileus, (close-fitting) cap; *m.* (orn.) pileum; (bot.) pileus (of fungi); root-cap. **-ato** *adj.* wearing (having) a 'pileus'. **-orìza** *f.* (bot.) root cap.

pil·ętta *f.*, **-iere** *m.* See under **pila**.

pilla·c·chera, **-cola** *f.* splash of mud (on clothes, etc.); dirt (in the wool of sheep or goats); blemish; — sulla coscienza, load on one's conscience; *n.m.*, *f.* stingy person. **-cheróso** *adj.* muddy, splashed with mud.

pill·are [A I] *tr.* to pound; to tread, to ram, to ram down; (bldg.) to tamp. **-ato** *part. adj.* pounded; rammed down. **-o** *m.* (bldg.) tamper, rammer.

pilliere *m.* (ent.) dung beetle, sacred scarab.

pil·l·ola *f.* (pharm.) pill; (fig.) ingoiare una — amara, to swallow a bitter pill; indorare la —, to gild the pill; ridurre in **-ole**, to smash to bits; (ent.) gall (of a gall-forming insect); pebble. **-olare** *adj.* in the shape of a pill; for pills; of pills; massa **-olare**, pill mixture. **-olętta**, **-olina** *f. dim.* pillule, little pill. **-ora** *f.* large pebble; stone in a river-bed; †**pill**.

pillott·a *f.* solid leather-covered ball (for playing 'pelota'); the game 'pelota'. **-are** [A I] *tr.* to baste (meat). (**-ato** *part. adj.*) **-o** *m.* basting-ladle; dripping-pan.

pil·o *m.* (Rom. antiq.) *pilum*, throwing spear; truncated pillar (to mark a tomb); pier of a bridge (cf. **pila**). **-ano** *m.* (Rom. antiq.) *pilanus*, soldier using *pilum*.

pilocarpina *f.* (chem.; pharm.) pilocarpine.

pilóne *m. augm.* See under **pila**.

pilo·rcio *m.* clippings of skins or leather used as manure; miser.

pilo·rico *adj.* (anat.) pyloric.

pilor·o *m.* (anat.) pylorus. **-ectomi·a** *f.* (surg.) pylorectomy. **-ite** *f.* pyloritis. **-opla·stica** *f.* (surg.) pyloroplasty. **-oscopi·a** *f.* (surg.) pyloroscopy.

†**piloso**[1] *adj.* see **peloso**; lingua pilosa, evil tongue, slandering person.

†**piloso**[2] *m.* monster half man and half beast.

pilot·a, **-o** *m.* (naut.; aeron.) pilot; sailing master; — di bordo, ship's navigating officer; — di porto, harbour pilot; — reale, master, fleet navigating officer; bastimento —, pilot ship; battello —, pilot boat; corpo dei **-i**, pilot service; capo —, senior or chief pilot; (motor.) rider (of motorcycle); racing car driver; (techn.) impianto —, pilot plant; (ichth.) pesce —, pilot fish, *Naucrates ductor*; *pl.* (archit.) piles (for foundation). **-ag·gio** *m.* (naut.) pilotage, art of piloting, work of piloting; diritto di **-aggio**, pilotage dues; (aeron.) scuola di **-aggio**, flying-school. **-are** [A I] *tr.* (naut.) to pilot; to drive (cars, etc.); to ride (bicycles, etc.); to drive a car in a race; (aeron.) to fly. **-ino** *m. dim.* (naut.) apprentice (Merchant Service, equivalent of a midshipman); navigating officers' yeoman, 'tankie'.

pilucc·are [A2] *tr.* to pick (grapes from a bunch); to pluck, to pick out, to pick up; to pick (bones or morsels of food); to tear to bits; Dio ti pilucchi!, Devil take you!; (fig.) to fleece, to rob; (fig.) to pick up (trifles, profit, etc.); *rfl.* (joc.) to tear one's hair. (**-ato** *part. adj.*) **-atóre** *m.* picker, one who picks, pecks, plucks, etc. (**-atrice** *f.*) **-óne** *m. augm.* scrounger, beggar; 'picker up of unconsidered trifles'.

†**pimac·ci·o** *m.*, †**-uolo** *m.* See **piumaccio**.

pima·rico *adj.* (chem.) pimaric.

pimelite *f.* (med.) pimelitis.

pimelo·si *f.* obesity.

pimento *m.* (bot.) allspice, *Pimenta officinalis*; red pepper, *Capsicum frutescens* var. *longum*.

pimper-impera, **-impara**, **-impì** *m. indecl.* polvere del —, magical powder; (fig.) dust in one's eyes; illusion.

pimpinella *f.* (bot.) pimpernel.

pimpinna·colo *m.* See **pinnacolo**.

pimple·o *adj.* (poet.) of the Muses; *n.f.pl.* le Pimplee, the Muses.

pin·a *f.* (bot.) fir cone, pine cone; (of flesh) sodo come una —, firm; largo come una — verde, stingy, mean; (archit.) acroter in the form of a pine-cone (cf. **pigna**). †**-ato** *adj.* (Tusc.) grasso **-ato**, fat and plump.

pinac·cia *f.* (naut.) coastguard pinnace; ship or boat having oars and sail.

†**pina·colo** *m.* See **pinnacolo**.

pinacoteca *f.* picture-gallery.

pinastro *m.* (bot.) maritime pine, *Pinus pinaster*.

†**pinato** *adj.* See under **pina**.

†**pincerna** *m.* cup-bearer.

pin·cio[1] *m.* See **pinco**.

Pin·cio[2] *pr.n.m.* name of a hill and of a public garden in Rome.

pin·co *m.* (*pl.* **-chi**) (naut.) three-masted merchant vessel; — barbaresco, Barbary pirate vessel; (fig.) fool. †**-ca** *f.* a variety of cucumber; foolish woman. **-chellóne** *m.* silly man, stupid person. **-contag·gine** *f.* stupidity, silliness; stupid action. **-cóne** *m.* stupid person, fool; *adj.*, *adv.* **-con -cone**, very quiet(ly), crestfallen, subdued. **-copallino** *m.* chap, bloke.

Pin·d-aro *pr.n.m.* (Gk. lit.) Pindar. **-arésco** *adj.* Pindaresque, Pindaric. **-a·rico** *adj.* Pindaric (said either in praise of lofty style or in criticism of pompousness or abruptness); volo **-arico**, mixed metaphor. (**-aricaménte** *adv.*)

Pindo *pr.n.m.* (Gk. antiq.) Pindus, mountain of the Muses; (fig.) salire in (sul) —. to write poetry.

pin·eale, **-ęta** *f.*, **-ęto** *m.* See under **pino**.

pinella *f.* (cards) a 'two' which, like the jokers, can have any value in the game of canasta.

pin·gere[1] [C 5] *vb.* and derivs. See **spingere**.

†**pin·gere**[2] *vb.* and derivs. See **dipingere**.

pingu·e *adj.* fat; corpulent; rich; large; un uomo —, a fat man; **-i** pascoli, rich pastures; **-i** guadagni, fat profits; carico —, lucrative post; (class. antiq.) **-i** altari, altars reeking with the blood and fat of sacrifice. **-eménte** *adv.* richly. **-a·rio** *adj.* fat. **-ęzza** *f.* obesity; richness. **-e·dine** *f.* obesity, corpulence, fatness; fertility, richness.

pinguino *m.* (orn.) penguin; (colloq.) a kind of ice-cream.

pinite *f.* (miner.). See under **pino**[1].

pinn-a *f.* (zool.) fan shell, *Pinna nobilis*; (ichth.) fin; (aeron.) stub plane; side of the nose; (naut.) — di scaroccio, bilge keel (see also **penna**).

pinna·colo *m.* (archit.) pinnacle, battlement (on a tower).

pinnato *adj.* (bot.) pinnate.

pinni·pede *m.* (zool.) pinnipede (i.e. seal).

pin-o[1] *m.* (bot.) fir, pine; — cembro, Arolla pine, *Pinus cembra*; — comune, Scotch fir, (in recent botanical books) Scots pine, *P. silvestris*; — da fastelli, maritime pine, *P. pinaster*; — da pinocchi, stone pine, *P. pinea*; — delle Alpi, mountain pine, *P. mugo*; — d'Aleppo, Aleppo pine, *P. halepensis*; — d'Austria, Austrian pine, *P. nigra*; — di Gerusalemme, *P. halepensis*; — d'Italia, stone pine, *P. pinea*; — di Scozia, see **pino comune**; — domestico, see **pino d'Italia**; — marittimo, — selvatico, *P. pinaster*; — zimbro, see **pino cembro**; ago di —, pine-needle; — artificiale, artificial Christmas tree; (naut.) timber, deal, etc.; — di Plinio, — vulcanico, mushroom cloud (of volcanic origin); (poet.) ship; †torch; (geog.) Isola dei Pini, Pines Island. (anat.) pineal; ghiandola -eale, pineal body. -**eta** *pr.n.f.* name of a pine forest east of Ravenna. -**eto** *m.* pine-wood, pine forest. -**i·fero** *adj.* pine-bearing. -**ite** *f.* (miner.) pinite, matecite, sennite. -**olo** *m.* pine-seed. -**oso** *adj.* abounding in pine-trees.

†**pino**[2] *adj.* See **pieno**.

pinoc·ch-io[1] *m.* pine-seed. -**a·io** *m.* seller of pine-seeds. -**ata** *f.* sweet pastry containing pine-seeds. -**etto** *m.* dim. (bldg.) intonaco a -etto, pebble-dashing. -**ino** *m.* fine gravel; *adj.* (bot.) erba -ina, white stone-crop, *Sedum album*.

Pinoc·chio[2] *pr.n.m.* protagonist (and title) of a children's book by Collodi (Carlo Lorenzini).

pin-olo *m.*, -**oso** *adj.* See under **pino**[1].

pint-a[1] *f.* pint (measure of capacity varying in Italy from $\frac{1}{2}$ litre up to $2\frac{1}{2}$ litres at Modena); — inglese, English pint (0·568 litres).

†**pinta**[2] *f.* See **spinta**.

pinta·culo *m.* See **pentacolo**.

pinto[1] *part.* of **pingere**[1], q.v.

†**pint-o**[2] *part.* of **pingere**[2], q.v. †-**ore** *m.* see **pittore**

†**pintura** *f.* See **pittura**.

Pinturic·chio *pr.n.m.* nickname of Bernardino di Betto Biagio of Perugia, 1454–1513; †(fig.) worthless painter.

pinz-a *f.* (eng., of a lathe) collet; pliers; pincers; — per fili, wire nippers; *pl.* (surg.) forceps; -e da arteria, artery forceps; (chem.) -e da crogiuolo, crucible tongs; (zool.) pincers, chelae, etc. of Arthropods. -**ac·chio** *m.* (ent.) weevil. -**are** [A I] *tr.* to sting (esp. of wasps, etc.); to prick; to bite. -**ata** *f.* sting; prick; bite (of an insect). -**ette** *f.pl.* small pincers; tweezers (also **pinzettine**); (fig.) ci vuole le -ette, it's hard to get hold of, it's a ticklish job. -**imo·nio** *m.* olive oil with pepper and salt, as a dressing for celery, artichokes, etc. -**o** *m.* sting; bite; (ent.) sting or ovipositor; *adj.* full up, crammed; fat (esp. of a person); pieno -o, crammed full. -**uto** *adj.* having a sting; sharp pointed.

pinzo·cher-o *m.*, -**a** *f.* †(eccl.) tertiary; (fig.) sanctimonious person, pious humbug; over-devout person, over-zealous churchgoer; hypocrite. -**one** *m.* hypocrite. -**ona** *f.*)

piò[1] *m.* (*pl.* **pìi**) chirping (cf. **pigolìo**).

pi-o[2] *adj.* dutiful, obedient; pious, devout; compassionate; charitable; affectionate, loving; il — fondatore, the pious founder; hai fatto opera -a, you have done a good deed; non c'è un'opera -a in questa città?, is there no charitable institution in this town?; scuole -e, charity schools; (anat.) -a madre, pia, pia mater; Porta Pia, one of the city gates of Rome, named after Pope Pius VI. -**amente** *adv.* piously, religiously; compassionately. -**aristi** *m.pl.* (eccl.) Piarists.

Pio[3] *pr.n.m.* Pius; — Nono, Pius the Ninth.

†**pioba** *f.* See **pioggia**.

piocele *m.* (med.) pyocele.

piocianina *f.* (chem.) pyocyanin.

piocito *m.* (med.) pyocyte.

piocolpo *m.* (med.) pyocolpos.

pioderm-atosi *f.* (med.) pyodermatosis. -**ite** *f.*, -**atite** *f.* (med.) pyodermitis.

pio-ge·nesi *f.* (med.) pyogenesis, pus formation. -**ge·nico** *adj.* (med.) pyogenic, producing pus. -**rre·a** *f.* (med.) pyorrhoea.

piog·g-ia *f.* rain; stagione delle -e, rainy season; una — dirotta, heavy rain, downpour; una — leggera, light rain, drizzle; scroscio

di —, shower; una — di cenere, a rain of ashes; sotto la —, in the rain; — artificiale, downpour of rain obtained by bombarding clouds (a system frequently used in Italy during summer); (fig.) una — di congratulazioni, a flood (shower) of congratulations; (class. myth.) — d'oro, the shower of gold in which Zeus visited Danaë; — di lagrime, flood of tears; — di rimproveri, flood of reproaches; (geog.) piogge zenitali, summer rains; (astron.) — di stelle, meteorite shower; (fig.) far la — e il bel tempo, see under **bello**[1]. -**erella** *f.* dim. fine rain, drizzle; light shower.

pio·ide *adj.* (med.) pyoid, pus-like.

piolo *m.* stick; paling; stump; fermo come un —, stock-still.

piombico *adj.* (chem.) plumbic.

piomb-o *m.* lead; shot, bullet; (metall.) lead; — in pani, pig lead; (chem.; motor.) — tetraetile, tetraethyl lead, seal; plummet; filo a —, plumb-line, sounding-line, sounding lead, lead; a —, in —, vertical, plumb; fuori di —, out-of-plumb, out of perpendicular; (dress-making) hang, fall; a —, upright; height; depth; (rlwy.) — della dogana, seals placed by customs on goods in transit; (eccl.) — pontificio, papal seal (of lead); (typ.) type-metal, lead; (med.) malattia del —, saturnism, lead-poisoning; cadere di —, to fall suddenly, violently; andare con piedi (coi piè) di —, to proceed very cautiously; (fig.) — ai piedi, impediment; *pr.n.m.* i Piombi, prison of the Doges' Palace in Venice. -**ag·gine** *f.* (miner.) plumbago, graphite, black lead. -**a·io** *adj.* leaden, containing lead; pietra -aia, see **piombaggine**. -**aiuola** *f.* leaden ball, on a stick, whip, etc. -**ante** *part. adj.* falling heavily, plunging. -**are** [A I c] *tr.* to plumb; to affix a leaden seal to; (metall.) to coat with lead, to terne-plate; (rlwy.) -are un carro, to seal a goods-truck; (bldg.) to plumb; -are un dente, to stop (fill) a tooth; *intr.* (*aux.* essere) to fall heavily, suddenly; to fall (upon), to attack; -arono addosso al nemico, they fell upon the enemy; to plunge; to pounce; to sink like lead; (fig.) -are nella miseria, to sink into poverty; to arrive unexpectedly; mi è -ato a casa quel seccatore, I'm landed with that bore at home. -**ato** *part. adj.* leaded; leaden, like lead; mazza -ata, loaded stick, cosh; (chem.) plumbate; (metall.) lamiera -ata, terne-plate. -**atoia** *f.* bullet, ball of lead. -**atoio** *m.* (mil. archit.) orifice in the corbelling of the battlements of a castle used for throwing molten lead, stones or hot liquids on to the assailants. -**atore** *m.* (eccl.) 'Sealer' in Papal Chancery. -**atura** *f.* sealing; soldering; plumbing; leading. -**i·fero** *adj.* (miner.) plumbiferous, lead-bearing. -**inatore** *m.* cesspool emptier; plumber who frees the drains. -**inazione** *f.* taking soundings; unstopping drains, etc. -**ino** *m.* plummet, plumb-line; plumb; a -ino, with the plumb-line; (naut.) lead, handlead used in small boats for sounding; lead pellet used in a cable shackle; -ini della rete, sinkers in a net, fishing line, etc.; tool for clearing drains; (art) kind of pencil for sketching; *pl.* bobbins used in making pillow-lace; trina a -ini, pillow-lace; lead weights (to make a dress hang straight); leaden seal; (orn.) kingfisher; *adj.* leaden (in colour), lead-coloured. -**ito** *m.* (chem.) plumbite. -**one** *m.* (fam.) lazy man, slow-coach. -**osità** *f.* leadenness. -**oso** *adj.* leaden (in weight or colour); containing lead; (chem.) plumbous; acido -oso, plumbic acid.

pionier-e, -**o** *m.*, *adj.* pioneer; (mil.) sapper.

piopp-o *m.* (bot.) poplar, *Populus*; — comune, — nero, black poplar, *Populus nigra*; — bianco, — abele, white poplar, *P. alba*; — tremolo, aspen, *P. tremula*; — del Canadà, *P. deltoides*; timber from the poplar; tree grown for training vines; dormire come un —, to sleep like a log; (naut.) albero a —, polemast, formed by a single bole; group; (fam.) fool, stupid man; prete —, ignorant priest. -**a** *f.* see **pioppo**. -**a·ia** *f.* poplar grove, poplar plantation. -**ata** *f.* poplar (or other tree) supporting two or more vines. -**ato** *part. adj.* planted with poplars. -**eto** *m.* poplar wood. -**ino** *m.* (bot.) honey fungus, *Armillaria mellea*; *adj.* relating to the poplar.

†**piorno** *adj.* rainy.

piorre·a *f.* (med.) pyorrhoea.

piot-a *f.* sole of the foot; sod, turf; clump of earth clinging to the roots of a plant being transplanted. -**are** [A I] *tr.* to turf. (-**ato** *part. adj.*) -**atura** *f.* turfing.

†**piova** *f.* rain.

piovana *f.* (zool.) salamander.

piovanello *m.* (orn.) curlew sandpiper, *Calidris testacea*; — maggiore, knot, *C. canutus*; — pancia nera, dunlin, *C. alpina*; — tridattilo, sanderling, *Crocethia alba*; — violetto, purple sandpiper, *Calidris maritima*.

piov·ano¹ *adj.* relating to rain; acqua -ana, rainwater; (leg.) scarico delle acque -ane, discharge of rainwater (C.C.); *n.m.* (naut.) oilskin cap. **-asco** *adj.* (*m.pl.* **-aschi**) (relating to) rain; *n.m.* short shower(s).

piovan·o² *m.* see **pievano**. **-ato** *m.*, **-a·tico** *adj.* see **pievania**.

pio·v·ere [C27] *impers.* (*aux.* essere, avere) to rain; to drip; — a dirotto, to rain in torrents, to pour with rain; — a catinelle, to rain cats and dogs; sta per —, it is going to rain; pare che voglia —, it looks like rain; to drip, leak through the roof; in questa casa ci -e, this house has a leaking roof; (of a roof) to slope; (of a mountain) to slope down, to descend; (fig.) -ono quattrini da tutte le parti, money comes pouring in on all sides; -vero congratulazioni, there was a flood of congratulations; (fig.) -e sul bagnato, it never rains but it pours; tanto tonò che piovve!, it was bound to happen!; to arrive in numbers or unexpectedly; mi sono -uti in casa tutti i parenti, all my relations have descended on me; *tr.* to rain, to pour down (or out); to let fall, to shed; to hurl (stones, etc.); i meli -ono i bianchi petali, the apple-trees are shedding their white petals; il cielo piovve la guazza, a heavy dew fell from heaven; — fiamme di fuoco, to breathe forth, to throw out flames of fire; — grazie, to be profuse in thanks. **-ente** *part. adj.* hanging, sloping down; capelli -enti, flowing locks; *n.m.* coping; pitch, slope of a roof; tetto a un solo -ente, lean-to roof; tetto a due -enti, span roof. **-iccicare** [A3] *intr.* (*aux.* essere, avere) to drizzle. **-icolare** [A1s] *intr.* (*aux.* essere, avere) to drizzle. **-iggina·ia** *f.* drizzle. **-igginare** [A1s] *intr.* (*aux.* essere, avere) to drizzle. **-igginoso** *adj.* rainy, drizzling; inclined to rain; cielo -igginoso, rainy sky. **-i·schio** *m.* drizzle. **-iscolare** [A1s] *intr.* (*aux.* essere, avere) to drizzle. **-itore** *m.* (Rom. myth.) Pluvius, title of Jupiter as god of rain. **-itura** *f.* rainy season, rains. **-orno** *adj.* (of the sky) full of watery clouds; (poet.) dei pini s'udì l'aereo murmure -orno (Pascoli), the murmur of pines in the breeze sounded like rain. **-osità** *f.* (geog.) precipitation; wetness of weather. **-oso** *adj.* rainy, wet; (of wind) bringing rain; lavoro -oso, work in the rain; estate -osa, wet summer; *pr.n.m.* (hist.) Pluviose, fifth month of the French Revolutionary calendar. **-uta** *f.* fall of rain (quantity at one time). **-uto** *part. adj.* fallen, rained down; arrived suddenly; barba -uta, long, flowing beard.

pio·vra *f.* (zool.) octopus; (fig.) blood-sucker, vampire; person who causes ruin, downfall.

pip-a *f.* pipe; tobacco-pipe; caricar la —, to fill one's pipe; fumare la —, to smoke one's pipe, to smoke a pipe; pipe(ful); fumare due -e al giorno, to smoke two pipes a day; (joc.) big long nose; pipe (cask, measure for wine, etc.); (mil. slang) reprimand, 'rocket'. **-are** [A1] *intr.* (*aux.* avere) to smoke a pipe. **-ata** *f.* pipeful; smoke (of a pipe). **-atina** *f. dim.* a puff, a whiff (or two). **-atore** *m.* pipe-smoker. **-etta** *f. dim.* small pipe; (chem.) pipette.

pipelè *m. indecl.* (joc.) doorkeeper, porter, concierge.

piperazina *f.* (chem.) piperazine.

piper-idina *f.* (chem.) piperidine. **-ina** *f.* (chem.; pharm.) piperine.

pipetta *f.* See under **pipa**.

pip-i, pipì *m. indecl.* chirp, cheep; (baby word for **pisciare**) pee; far —, to pee. **†-iare**, **-ilare**, **-ire** [D2] to chirp, to cheep, to twitter.

pipistrell-o *m.* (zool.) bat; sleeveless cloak with large collar (like an Inverness cape); debtor (who tries to dodge his creditors); †(naut.) upper gudgeon on a rudder.

pipita *f.* pip (disease of fowls); hangnail; (joc.) aver la —, to have an impediment in one's speech, *or* to suffer from thirst; (agric.) tagliare le pipite, to cut off the tips (of plants or twigs).

pippion-e *m.* (orn.) nestling pigeon, squab; silly man, fool. **†-ata** *f.* stupid action.

Pippo *pr.n.m.* (abbrev. of **Filippo**) Philip, Pip; (fig.) far —, to play the spy.

pip·polo *m.* pip, grain, stone; pimple, any small excrescence.

pique-nique *m.* (pron. as Fr.) picnic; meal for which each pays his own share.

piquet *m.* (pron. as Fr.) piquet (card-game).

pira *f.* pyre, funeral pile; fire (for execution of criminals, for burning at the stake).

pirale *m.* (ent.) species of pyralid moths, esp. *Oenophthira pilleriana*, a pest of vines.

pira·mid-e *f.* (archit.) pyramid; — a gradini, step-pyramid; a —, in the shape of a pyramid; (geom.) pyramid; *pl.* (anat.) -i del Malpighi, Malpighi's pyramids; (fig.) — sociale, pyramid of society, social order (the lowest classes being the most numerous). **-ale** *adj.* pyramidal (in shape or size); (geom.) pyramidal; (anat.) osso -ale, pyramidal bone, carpal cuneiform bone; muscolo -ale, pyramidalis muscle; huge, enormous; sproposito -ale, huge blunder. (**-almente** *adv.*) **-are** [A1s] *tr.* to shape into a pyramid; *intr.* (*aux.* essere) to rise in the shape of a pyramid. **-ato** *part. adj.* formed into a pyramid. **-eggiare** [A3c] *intr.* (*aux.* essere) to rise in a pyramid. **-one** *m. augm.* of **piramide**; (chem.) pyramidon, amido-pyrine.

pirargirite *f.* (miner.) pyrargyrite, dark red silver ore.

pirat-a, †-o *m.* pirate; — della strada, road-hog, motorist who does not stop after an accident; *adj.* nave —, pirate ship. **-eggiare** [A3c] *intr.* (*aux.* avere) (naut.) to commit piracy, to pirate. **-eri·a** *f.* piracy; -eria letteraria, literary piracy, pirating; plagiarism. **-esco** *adj.* (*m.pl.* **-eschi**) see **piratico**.

pira·tic-o *adj.* piratic(al). **-amente** *adv.* piratically.

pirausta *m.* See **pirale**.

†pi·rchio *m.* miser.

pirelio·metro *m.* (meteor.) pyrheliometer.

pirene *m.* (chem.) pyrene.

Pirene·i *pr.n.m.pl.* (geog.) Pyrenees.

Pire·o *pr.n.m.* (geog.) the Piraeus.

pir-essi·a *f.* (med.) pyrexia, fever. **-et·tico** *adj.* (med.) pyrexial, pyretic. **-etro** *m.* (bot.) pellitory of Spain, *Anacyclus pyrethrum*; pyrethrum, *Chrysanthemum coccineum*; (chem.) pyrethrum.

piridina *f.* (chem.) pyridine.

pir-ite *f.* (miner.) pyrites; — di ferro, iron pyrites. **-i·tico** *adj.* (miner.) pyritic. **-itizzazione** *f.* (chem.) pyritization. **-itoso** *adj.* (miner.) pyritous.

piro- *pref.* (denoting fire). For derivs. in which the stress falls on the second syllable, e.g. piro·foro, see separate headings. **-bali·stica** *f.* (mil.) ballistics of firearms. **-barca** *f.* steamboat. **-boli·a** *f.* pyrotechny. **-catechina** *f.* (chem.) pyrocatechol. **-cloro** *m.* (miner.) pyrochlore. **-conducibilità** *f.* (phys.; electr.) pyroconductivity. **-cono·fobo** *m.* insecticide burnt to kill mosquitoes. **-corvetta** *f.* (naut.) steam corvette. Note: in the middle of the nineteenth century many classes of sailing ships were given auxiliary steam propulsion and the prefix piro- indicated this, as in 'pirofregata', 'pirovascello'. As sail gave way completely to steam the meaning altered to signify only steam propulsion as in 'piroscafo', etc. **-draga** *m.* (naut.) steam dredger. **-elettricità** *f.* (phys.) pyro-electricity. **-fosfato** *m.* (chem.) pyrophosphate. **-fosfo·rico** *adj.* (chem.) pyrophosphoric. **-fregata** *f.* (naut.) steam frigate (cf. Note under **pirocorvetta**). **-gal·lico** *adj.* (chem.) pyrogallic; acido -gallico, pyrogallic acid, pyrogallol. **-gal·lolo** *m.* (chem.) pyrogallol. **-genato** *adj.* (chem.) produced by the action of heat on organic substances. **-grafi·a** *f.* pyrography, poker-work. **-lusite** *f.* (miner.) pyrolusite. **-maca** *f.* (miner.) flint. **-magne·tico** *adj.* (phys.) pyromagnetic. **-magnetismo** *m.* (phys.) pyromagnetism. **-mani·aco** *adj.*, *n.m.* pyromaniac. **-mante** *m.* pyromantic. **-manzi·a** *f.* pyromancy, divination by fire. **-metallurgi·a** *f.* (metall.) pyro-metallurgy. **-metri·a** *f.* (phys.) pyrometry. **-morfite** *f.* (miner.) pyromorphite, green lead ore. **-schelmo** *m.* (naut.) steam launch, steam pinnace. **-scissione** *f.* (chem.) cracking. **-solfato** *m.* (chem.) pyrosulphate. **-ssenite** *f.* (miner.) pyroxenite. **-sseno** *m.* (miner.) pyroxene. **-ssilina** *f.* (chem.) pyroxylin, collodion cotton. **-tecni·a** *f.* pyrotechny. **-te·cnica** *f.* pyrotechny, pyrotechnics. **-te·cnico** *adj.* pyrotechnic; arte -tecnica, pyrotechny; (mil.) laboratorio -tecnico, pyrotechnical workshop; *n.m.* pyrotechnist, maker of fireworks. **-vascello** *m.* (naut.) steamship (cf. Note under **piro-corvetta**).

piroett-a *f.* pirouette. **-are** [A1c] *intr.* (*aux.* avere) to pirouette.

piro·foro *adj.* (chem.) pyrophoric; *n.m.* (ent.) firefly, *Pyrophorus noctilucus*.

piroga *f.* native dug-out canoe, pirogue.

piro·l-isi *f.* (chem.) pyrolysis. **-i·tico** *adj.* (chem.) pyrolitic.

pirolo *m.* (mus.) peg (of a stringed instrument).

piro·metro *m.* (phys.) pyrometer.

pirone *m.* peg; plug; crank; (naut.) cleat, belaying pin; capstan bar or hand lever; †bolt, copper or wooden pin used in ship construction; (mus.) wrest-pin (of harpsichord or pianoforte).

piropiro *m.* (orn.) sandpiper; — boschereccio, wood sandpiper, *Tringa glareola*; — culbianco, green sandpiper, *T. ochropus*; — piccolo, common sandpiper, *T. hypoleucus*.

piropo *m.* (miner.) pyrope.

piro·scafo *m.* (naut.) steamship, steamer; (pop.) any mechanically propelled vessel; — a ruote, paddle-steamer; — ad eliche, screw-steamer (cf. Note under **pirocorvetta**).

pirosi *f.* (med.) heartburn, pyrosis.

piro·tico *adj.* caustic.

pir·rica *f.* (Gk. antiq.) Pyrrhic dance, war-dance.

pirri·chio *adj., n.m.* (prosod.) pyrrhic (foot).

Pirro *pr.n.m.* Pyrrhus; vittoria di —, Pyrrhic victory.

pirroco·ride *m. Pyrrhocoris apterus,* a plant bug.

pirr-olo, -o·lio *m.* (chem.) pyrrole, azole.

pirro·n-ico *adj., n.m.* Pyrrhonic. **-ismo** *m.* Pyrrhonism. **-ista** *m.* Pyrrhonist, sceptic.

pirrot-ina, -ite *f.* (miner.) pyrrhotite, magnetic pyrite.

Pis-a *pr.n.f.* (geog.) Pisa; la torre pendente di —, the leaning tower of Pisa; dritto come la torre di —, crooked; il soccorso di —, help coming too late. **-ano** *adj.* Pisan, of Pisa; *n.m.* native of Pisa, Pisan. **(-ana** *f.*)

†**piscatore** *m.* See **pescatore**.

piscato·rio *adj.* relating to fishing and fishermen; piscatory; egloga piscatoria, piscatorial eclogue; (eccl.) l'anello —, the Fisherman's Ring.

pi·sci-a *f.* (vulg.) piss, urine. **-are** [A 3] *intr.* (aux. avere) (vulg.) to piss, to pass water, to urinate; (of a fountain, cask, etc.) to spout, to spurt; *tr.* -are sangue, to pass blood; -are denari, to throw (one's) money about. **-acane** *m.* (bot.) dandelion, *Taraxacum officinale.* **-a(l)letto** *m., f.* (vulg.) baby; one who wets the bed; ha fatto una -aletto, she has given birth to a girl; *m.* (bot.) dandelion, *T. officinale.* **-ancio, -arello** *m.* pale red wine. **-asangue** *m.* haematuria. **-ata** *f.* passing water, urination. **-atoio** *m.* urinal. **(-atura** *f.*) **-o** *m.* piss, urine. **-one** *m.* baby; child; one who wets the bed; person who passes water frequently. **-oso** *adj.* wet with urine, stinking (of urine); *n.m.* see **piscione**.

piscicoltura *f.* pisciculture, fish-breeding.

piscina *f.* fish-pond; swimming-pool; (Bibl.) la — probatica, the Pool of Bethesda; — battesimale, font (esp. for baptism by immersion); watering-trough; bath (for steeping various objects).

†**pi·scopo** *m.* See **episcopo**.

†**pisc-oso** *adj.* see **pescoso**. †**-ulento** *adj.* stinking of fish.

pisell-o *m.* (bot.) pea, *Pisum sativum;* — dei prati, meadow vetchling, *Lathyrus pratensis;* — quadrato, *L. sativus;* — selvatico, wild pea, *Pisum sativum* var. *arvense;* -i in scatola, tinned peas; si assomigliano come due -i, they are as like as two peas in a pod; verde —, pea-green; (fig.) fool, imbecile; i Piselli, nickname for adherents to the Partito Socialista dei Lavoratori Italiani (P.S.L.I.). **-ac·cio** *m. pejor.* see **pisellone**. **-a·ia** *f.,* **-a·io** *m.* pea-field; bed of peas. **-ata** *f.* dish of peas; pease-pudding. **-one** *m. augm.* great fool. **(-ona** *f.*)

pi·sol-o *m.* doze, nap, snooze. **-are** [A I S] *intr.* (aux. avere) to nod, to doze, to snooze. **-etto** *m. dim.,* **-ino** *m. dim.* little nap, snooze, 'forty winks'.

pisp-igliare [A 4] *intr.* (aux. avere) to whisper. **-i·glio** *m.* whisper, whispering. **-iglio** *m.* (*pl.* **-iglii**) continual whispering. **-illo·ria** *f.* whispering, chatter; boring speech; twittering of birds.

†**pispin-are** *intr.* to gush, to spout. †**-o** *m.* jet; spurt.

pi·spol-a *f.* (orn.) meadow pipit, *Anthus pratensis;* bird-catcher's whistle; uccellare a -e, to seek easy profit; non uccellare a -e, to look for big profits; raccontar -e, to talk nonsense; †see **fistola**. **-are** [A I S] *intr.* (aux. avere) to whistle to attract birds.

pissasfalto *m.* (miner.) maltha, pissasphalt.

pissi *m. indecl.* whispering; whisper; s'udiva un — —, one could hear whispering; dire il —, to pray softly, to mumble prayers; faceva i — —, he was whispering secrets.

pis·side *f.* (liturg.) ciborium; pyx; (bot.) pyxidium.

pissipissare [A I] *intr.* (aux. avere) to whisper.

pista *f.* race-track, ice-rink, (toboggan) run; (aeron.) runway, strip; — di rullaggio, taxiway; — di lancio, launching strip (esp. for gliders); (eng.) race (of bearings); area of activity of dances and other meetings; foot-prints; trail; scent; essere sulle -e di uno, to be on someone's track.

pistac·ch-io *m.* (bot.) pistachio nut, *Pistacea vera;* — falso, bladder-nut, *Staphylea pinnata;* — selvatico, *Pistacia terebinthus;* verde —, pale green. **-iata** *f.* cake made with pistachio nuts. **-ina** *f. adj.* pistachio-like (applied to a kind of small nut).

pistacite *f.* (geol.) epidote, pistacite.

pistagna *f.* (tailor.) coat-collar; facings; flounce.

†**pistello** *m.* See **pestello**.

†**pistilen·zia** *f.* and derivs. See **pestilenza**.

pistill-o *m.* (bot.) pistil, gynoecium. **-i·fero** *adj.* (bot.) pistil-bearing.

pistoc-co *m.* (*pl.* **-chi**) (mil. slang) alpenstock.

Pistoi-a *pr.n.f.* (geog.) Pistoia. **-ese** *adj., n.m., f.* (inhabitant) of Pistoia; (eccl. hist.) dottrine -esi, decrees of the Synod of Pistoia, 1786.

pistol-a¹ *f.* pistol; una pariglia di -e, a brace of pistols; — a due canne, double-barrelled pistol; — a spruzzo, spray gun; — mitragliatrice, sub-machine gun. **-enza** *f.,* **-enzioso** *adj.* see **pestilenza**. **-ese** *m.* (hist.) dagger, hunting-knife. **-etta** *f. dim.* small pistol. **-ettata** *f.* pistol-shot. **-etto** *m.* short pistol. **-one** *m. augm.* (mil. hist.) short carbine used by mounted troops.

pistola² *f.* pistole.

†**pi·stola³** *f.* see **epistola**; †(eccl.) ordinato a —, ordained subdeacon. **-otto** *m.* (joc. or derog.) short emphatic speech, striking peroration; sting in the tail of a letter.

piston-e *m.* (eng.) piston; ram, plunger; (motor.) corsa del —, stroke; archibugio, blunderbuss; (mus.) piston; corno a -i, valve-horn; cornetto a -i, cornet. **-cino** *m.* (mus.) combination-piston (of organ).

†**pistorese** *m.* See **pistolese**, under **pistola¹**.

pistorino *m.* See **bisturi**.

†**pistrino** *m.* mill; oven.

pistura *f.* chestnut waste (after grinding).

†**pitaf·fio** *m.* See **epitaffio**.

Pita·gor-a *pr.n.m.* Pythagoras. **-eggiare** [A 3 c] *intr.* (aux. avere) to follow Pythagoras (in doctrine), to Pythagorize. **-eismo** *m.* Pythagoreanism. **-eo** *adj.* Pythagorean; (anct. philos.) il pavone -eo, the peacock in the Pythagorean doctrine of transmigration (it being said, e.g., that the spirit of Homer passed into a peacock and thence into Ennius).

pitag-o·rico. Pythagorean; tavola -ica, multiplication table; vitto —, meatless diet; vegetarianism; silenzio —, silence lasting several years; *n.m.* Pythagorean. **-oricamente** *adv.* after Pythagoras. **-oricismo** *m.,* **-orismo** *m.* Pythagoreanism. **-orista** *m.* Pythagorean.

pitale *m.* (vulg.) chamber-pot; night-stool.

pitec-o *m.* (zool.) monkey, ape. **-o·ide** *adj.* (zool.) pithecoid.

pi·tia *f.* See **pizia**.

pi·tico *adj.* (Gk. antiq.) Pythian.

pitir-i·asi *f.* pityriasis. **-ia·sico** *adj.* (med.) pityriasic.

pitiusa *f.* (bot.) *Euphorbia pithyusa.*

†**pitizione** *f.* See **petizione**.

pitoc-co *m.* (*pl.* **-chi**) beggar; stingy person, miser; †coat; †cloak. **-ca** *f.* beggar woman. **-care** [A 2] *intr.* (aux. avere) to beg; *tr.* to beg (for). **-cheri·a** *f.* beggary; meanness; beggarly action.

pito·metro *m.* (aeron.) Pitot tube.

pit-one *m.* (zool.) python; (eng.) stud, centre bolt. **-onessa** *f.* pythoness: (Gk. antiq.) Pythia, priestess of Apollo; (Bibl.) witch (of Endor); fortune-teller, clairvoyante. **-o·nico** *adj.* pythonic, divinatory, soothsaying.

pitos *m. indecl.* (Gk. antiq.) jar or cask for wine, *pithos.*

pitta *f.* (bot.) century plant, American aloe, *Agave americana.*

pittare¹ [A I] *tr.* (of a fish) to nibble.

pitt-are² [A I] *tr.* (dial.; colloq.) to paint; to colour. †**-o** *m.* painting.

pit·tima¹ *f.* plaster; (fig.) bore.

pit·tima² *f.* (orn.) godwit; — minore, bar-tailed godwit, *Limosa lapponica;* — reale, black-tailed godwit, *L. limosa.*

pitt-ore *m.* painter, artist; graphic describer (in speech or writing); (derog.) — da chiocciole, — da sgabelli, inferior painter. **-orello** *m.* inferior painter, dauber. **-oresco** *adj.* (*m.pl.* **-oreschi**) of a painter; relating to painting, picturesque, painterly. **-orescamente** *adv.* picturesquely; in a painterly style. **-oressa** *f.* (joc.) see **pittrice**. **-o·rico** *adj.* pictorial; graphic; relating to painting or painters; arte -orica, art of painting, pictorial art. **-rice** *f.* woman painter, artist; *adj.* fantasia -rice, painter's fancy, pictorial imagination. **-ura** *f.* (art of) painting; picture, painting; word-painting, vivid description; (of a garment) sta come una -ura, it fits like a glove. **-urac·cia** *f. pejor.* daub. **-urare** [A I] *tr.* to paint, to decorate, to adorn with pictures or with plain colours; -urare una porta, to paint a door; *intr.* (aux. avere) to paint; (fig.) to use picturesque language; non scrive, ma -ura, he writes very vividly, he makes you see what he describes; *rfl.* to paint one's face, to make up. **-urato** *part. adj.* painted, vividly described; made-up (with cosmetics).

pitu·it-a *f.* (med.) phlegm, mucus. **-a·ria** *f.* (anat.) pituitary gland, hypophysis. **-a·rio** *adj.* pituitary. **-arismo** *m.* (med.) pituitarism. **-oso** *adj.* (med.) pituitous, mucous. **-rina** *f.* (pharm.) pituitrin.

più **1.** *adv.* MORE; with an *adj.* it has the force of the Eng. suffix -er, forming the comparative; — intelligente, cleverer; — costoso, more expensive, dearer; — bello, finer, more beautiful; voi siete — alto di me, you are taller than I; quel ragazzo è — alto che robusto, that boy is tall but not very strong; with *def. art.* it indicates either the comparative or the superlative (according to the context); il (la) — intelligente, the cleverer, *or* the cleverest; il — costoso, the most expensive, the dearest; il — bello, the finest, the most beautiful; l'Italia è la nazione — gloriosa del mondo, Italy is the finest nation in the world; with *adv.* — cortesemente, more courteously; — tardi, later; — su, higher (up); — giù, lower (down); — oltre, further, farther; — giù che sù, lower rather than higher; *superl. adv.* la poesia è l'arte che — mi consola, poetry is the art which brings me most comfort; fare a chi — corre, to run a race; non è il caso di fare a chi — mangia, it's not an eating contest; sempre —, — e —, more and more; — gli parlate — vi piace, the more you talk to him the more you like him; quanto — lo conosco, tanto — lo ammiro, the better I know him, the more I admire him; longer; non —, no longer, not any longer, no more, not again; mai —, never again; restate —?, are you staying any longer?; non lo vedo —, I can't see it any longer; non farlo —, don't do it again; non viene —, he isn't coming again, he won't come any more; non mangiare —, don't eat any more; non camminare —, don't walk any farther; non cammina —, he has stopped walking; with *prep.* costa di —, it costs more; mi piace di —, I like it better; molto di —, much more; in —, per di —, moreover, in addition, besides (*or*, in the same meaning, without *prep.*: —, il leone è fortissimo, moreover, the lion is very strong); — che mai, more than ever, absolutely; sono — che mai risoluto a procedere, I am more than ever resolved to go on (with it), I have fully made up my mind to go on; una cosa non — vista, something never seen before; erano non — di quattro, they were not more than four, they were only four; non — che, only; non ho — che un vestito, I have only one dress; (math.) plus; uno — uno fanno due, one and one make two; tre seggiole — una poltrona, three chairs and an armchair; dieci volte —, ten times as much; a — non posso, as much as I (you, he) possibly can, with all one's might, to the very utmost; tanto —, so much the more; tanto — che, insomuch as, even more so; da —, of more value, importance, etc.; credersi da — di altri, to think oneself better than others; per soprappiù, di soprappiù, into the bargain, in addition. **2.** *adj. indecl.* MORE; ci vuole — costanza, more perseverance is required; — nemici, — onore, the more enemies, the greater the honour; aver — quattrini di un altro, to have more money than someone else; numerous, many; ha — peccati sulla coscienza, he has many sins on his conscience; several; lo vidi — volte, I saw him several times; larger, greater; la — parte, the greater part, the majority. **3.** *n.m. indecl.* THE GREATER PART; per lo —, for the most part, mostly, generally; tutt'al —, at (the) most; il — è fatto, the greater part is done; il — delle volte, the majority of times, most times, mostly, generally; parlare del — e del meno, to speak of this and that; dal — al meno, more or less, approximately; *pl.* i —, the majority, most; i — la pensano così, most people think so; i — di questi piatti sono rotti, most of these plates are broken; andar nel numero dei —, to join the great majority, i.e. to die; †(gramm.) numero del —, plural number (math.) plus, plus sign; qui ci vuole un —, a plus sign is required here.

†piubicare *vb.* and derivs. See **pubblicare**.

pium-a *f.* feather; plumage; quill pen; leggiero come una —, light as a feather, (fig.) very fickle; un materasso di —, a feather mattress, feather bed; seggendo in —, sitting at ease (in bed or on cushions); animali di —, feathered creatures, birds; feather or down pillow, cushion, etc.; muff; down, also as fine hair, e.g. on the cheek; (fig.) essere una —, to be like a feather, light and agile; (boxing) peso —, featherweight; *pl.* (poet.) pinions, wings; le -e del desiderio, the wings of desire. **-ac·cio** *m.* feather pillow; cushion. **-accetto** *m. dim.* small feather pillow or cushion; pad, wad, wadding; †(naut.) tingle or any form of pad for hull repair; -accetto per palla, shot stopper. **-acciuolo** *m. dim.* small pillow or cushion; pad; (surg.) wad; (archit.) console, capital, esp. of an Ionic column; †(naut.) propeller shaft bearing plate; (vet.)

expression of pain on the face of a horse, with the lips lifted, as though sneezing (i.e. the expression that can be produced artificially by tickling with a feather). **-ag·gio** *m.* plumage. **-a·io** *m.* feather-dresser, seller of ornamental feathers. **-are** [A I] *tr.* to pluck. **-ata** *f.* feather-pill (for falcons); (vet.) tuft of feathers put up a horse's nose to make it sneeze. **-ato** *part. adj.* plumed; covered, adorned with feathers. **-etta** *f.* (bot.) plumule. **-ettato** *adj.* (herald.) plumetis. **-ino** *m.* down; down filling of quilts, pillows, etc.; eiderdown quilt; plumes of feathers; aigrette; powder-puff. **-osità** *f.* downiness, softness; featheriness. **-oso** *adj.* downy, feathery; soft like down; (biol.) cromosomi -osi, 'lamp brush' chromosomes.

pi(u)olo *m.* peg, post; rung of a ladder; scala a -i step-ladder; (gardening) dibber; pale, paling; low stone column; tenere a —, to keep waiting.

piuttosto *adv.* sooner; rather; instead; vorrei morire —, I'd rather die; deprime — che incoraggiare, he doesn't encourage, he depresses one; è — pigro, he is rather lazy.

†piu·vico *adj.* and derivs. See **pubblico**.

piv-a *f.* (mus.) pipe, bagpipe; Christmas pastoral for pipes or organ, pastoral symphony; tornarsene con le -e nel sacco, to fail, to return empty-handed. **-etta** *f.* (mus.) reed.

pivial-e *m.* (liturg.) cope, pluvial. **-ista** *m.* (liturg.) person wearing a cope (not necessarily a priest).

pivier-e¹ *m.* (orn.) plover; — dorato, golden plover, *Charadrius apricarius*; — tortolino, dotterel, *C. morinellus*. **-essa** *f.* (orn.) grey plover, *C. squatarola*.

†piviere² *m.* district of a 'pieve', q.v.

piv-o *m.* truculent, overbearing young man; buffoon. **-ello** *m. dim.* (slang) a young innocent.

Pi·zi-a *pr.n. f.* (Gk. antiq.) Pythia, priestess of Apollo. **-o** *adj.* (Gk. antiq.) Pythian.

pizz-a *f.* kind of savoury cake or pancake (varying in different districts of S. Italy). **-agallina** *f.*, **-aguerra** *f.* see under **pizzare**. **-aiuolo** *m.* maker and seller of the Neapolitan 'pizza'. **-eri·a** *f.* a special restaurant where 'pizza' is made and eaten.

pizz-are [A I] *tr., intr.* (*aux.* avere) to sting. **-agallina** *f.* (bot.) chick weed, *Stellaria media*. **-aguerra** *m., indecl.* mischief-maker.

pizzi-ca·gnolo *m.* pork-butcher; dealer in pickles, cheese, etc.; Italian warehouseman. **-cai(u)olo** *m.* Italian warehouseman; druggist; colour-merchant. **†-camorto** *m.* grave-digger. **-cheri·a** *f.* pork-butcher's shop; delicatessen.

pizzic-are [A 2 S] *tr.* to pinch, to nip; to sting, to bite; to hurt (with stinging words); to prick, to stimulate; (of a bird) to peck; — la lingua, to burn the tongue, to taste sharp; — un cavallo con gli speroni, to spur a horse; — un cavallo con lo sferzino, to use one's whip on a horse; (fig.) to extort (money); (slang) to arrest, to 'pinch'; se ti -o!, if I catch you!; (mus.) to pluck (strings); — il violino, to twang one's fiddle; *intr.* (*aux.* avere) to itch; to tingle; to smart; questa gamba mi -a, this leg of mine itches; mi sento tutto —, I feel itchy all over; sentirsi — le mani, to feel one's hands itching (i.e. with the desire to fight or hit someone); — di, to know a little about; -a di musica e di pittura, he knows a bit about, he dabbles in, music and painting; to smell of, to seem like; -a di eretico, he seems something of a heretic; -a di matto, he seems a bit mad. **-ante** *part. adj.* sharp; pungent; piquant. **-ata** *f.* sting; prick; pinch, pinching; plucking; una -ata di tabacco da fiuto, a pinch of snuff; -ata delle corde, plucking the strings; *pl.* little sweets, sugar plums. **-ato** *part. adj.* (mus.) pizzicato, plucked; *n.m.* (mus.) pizzicato movement.

pizzicheri·a *f.* See under **pizzicagnolo**.

piz·zi-co *m.* (act of) pinching, pinch; — al braccio, pinch on the arm; (fig.) tingling; small amount, pinch, smattering; (mus.) strumenti da —, plucked instruments. **-core** *m.* stinging, sting; tingling, tingle; itching, itch; smart; keen desire; mi viene il -core alle mani, I am itching to fight; un -core di poesia, a touch of poetry. **-corino** *m.* tickling; mi fai il -corino, you're tickling me. **-cottare** [A I] *tr.* to pinch; -cottare un cavallo, to flick a horse with a whip; *rfl.* to pinch oneself; *recip. rfl.* to bicker. **-cottata** *f.* (mus.) plucking (of strings). **-cotto** *m.* pinch, large pinch; nip; un -cotto di sale, a large pinch of salt; hard pinch (with the fingers); flick (with a whip); nick or ridge in a loaf of bread.

pizzo *m.* mountain peak; imperial, goatee (beard); whiskers; — spenzolone, side-whiskers; lace.

†pizzo·chero. See **pinzochero.**

†**pizzuga** *f.* tortoise; slow, inept individual.

pizzuolo *m.* (naut.) bow or stern sheets of a ship with fine lines, or of a galley.

pizzutello *m.* (agric.) a kind of grape.

plac-are [A 2] *tr.* to appease, to soothe, to placate; to calm; to allay, to alleviate; nulla vale a — il suo odio, nothing is able to appease his hatred; — gli stimoli della fame, to allay the pangs of hunger; *rfl.* to subside; to be appeased; to grow calm; il vento s'è -ato, the wind has dropped. **-abile** *adj.* easily appeased, placable; mild, forgiving; soothing. (**-abilmente** *adv.*) **-abilità** *f.* clemency; placability; mildness. **-amento** *m.* appeasement; soothing. **-ativo** *adj.* soothing, sedative. **-ato** *part. adj.* appeased, soothed, calmed; allayed, alleviated, mitigated. **-atore** *m.*, **-atrice** *f.*, *adj.* preghiera -atrice, prayer in mitigation, request for clemency. **-azione** *f.* appeasement; pacifying.

placc-a *f.* metal plate, plaque; — della porta, door-plate; metal badge; (watchm.) — d'appoggio, bearing plate; — di contro-perno, end-piece; (electr.) plate (of accumulator, valve, etc.); (anat.) plate, platelet; (zool.) — neurale, neural plate, medullary plate; (bot.) — cribrosa, sieve plate. **-are** [A 2] *tr.* (metall.) to plate; (sport, rugby) to tackle. **-aggio** *m.* tackling. **-ato** *part. adj.* plated. **-atore** *m.* plater; (sport) tackler. **-atura** *f.* (metall.) plating; -atura elettrolitica, electroplating.

placchetta *f.* (eng.) plate; bit (of tool); (watchm.) — di frizione, friction plate.

placebo *m. indecl.* approbation, approval; gridar —, to voice one's approbation; (med.) mock medicine (sugar and water, etc.) given to psychomatic patients and neurotics, placebo.

placent-a *f.* (anat.; bot.) placenta. **-are** *adj.* (anat.; bot.) placental. **-azione** *f.* (med.; anat.) placentation. **-iforme** *adj.* placentoid. **-ite** *f.* (med.) placentitis. **-oide** *adj.* (med.) placentoid.

placen·tula *f.* (bot.) placenta.

†**placere** *vb.* and derivs. See **piacere**.

pla·cid-o *adj.* calm, peaceful, tranquil; serene; mild, gentle; mare —, calm sea; vento —, light breeze; morte -a, peaceful death. **-amente** *adv.* calmly, peacefully, tranquilly; serenely; gently. **-ezza** *f.* serenity, placidity. **-ità** *f.* serenity, mildness; placidity, calmness; gentleness.

pla·cit-o *m.* judgement, decree; approval; (leg.) decree; order. **-are** [A I S] *tr.* to decree, to ordain.

plafond *m. indecl.* (pron. as Fr.), **plafon-e** *m.* (archit.) ceiling. **-iera** *f.* overhead lamp, ceiling light, glass ceiling bowl (for electric light).

plaga[1] *f.* expanse of sky, quarter of the heavens or of the globe; region, district; †shore (cf. **piaggia**).

plaga[2] *f.* affliction, plague.

plagale *adj.* (mus.) plagal.

plagas *Lat.* dire — di qualcuno, to speak ill of someone, to slander, to abuse.

†**plagere** *vb.* and derivs. See **piacere**.

plagiaulo *m.* (mus.) ancient Greek cross-flute.

pla·gi-o *m.* plagiarism; plagiary; commettere un — ai danni di uno scrittore, to plagiarize an author; (leg.) the crime of kidnapping or detaining a person by illegal force (C.P.); (Rom. law) *plagium*, kidnapping; †*adj.* (mus.) plagal. **-ario** *adj.*, *n.m.* plagiaristic; plagiarist; (Rom. law) *plagiarius*, kidnapper. **-ariamente** *adv.* plagiaristically.

plagio-cefali·a *f.* (med.) plagiocephaly. **-ce·falo** *adj.* plagiocephalic.

pla·id *m. indecl.* travelling rug, plaid.

plan-are [A I] *intr.* (*aux.* avere) (aeron.) to glide. **-ata** *f.* glide. **-è** *adj. indecl.* (aeron.) vol -è, glide. **-eur** *m. indecl.* (pron. as Fr.) (aeron.) glider.

plan·cia *f.* (naut.) bridge, navigating position; bow door of assault craft forming a gangway to the beach when lowered; flying bridge; method of swimming, using the arms close to the sides and the legs as in the crawl; (motor.; aeron.) dashboard.

plancton *m. indecl.* (biol.) plankton.

planeta·rio *adj.* (astron.; eng.) planetary; ingranaggio —, planetary gears; *n.m.* (eng.) crown wheel; (astron.) planetarium, orrery.

planfilm *m.* (photog.) non-curling film.

†**plan·gere** *vb.* and derivs. See **piangere**.

plani-metri·a *f.* (geom.) planimetry; (bldg.) location plan; (archit.) plan (of a building). **-me·trico** *adj.* (geom.) planimetric. **-metrica-mente** *adv.* on a horizontal plane. **-sfe·rio** *m.* (astron.) planisphere; star-map.

plani·metro *m.* planimeter.

†**plani·zie** *f.* smoothness of surface.

plankton *m. indecl.* See **plancton**.

planogameti *m.pl.* (bot.) planogametes.

plantare [A I] *adj.* (anat.) plantar; arcata —, plantar arch; muscolo —, plantaris muscle; (med.) supporto —, arch support.

†**planta·rio** *m.* nursery of young plants.

plaquette *f.* (pron. as Fr.) pamphlet, booklet.

plaṣm-a *m.* mould; (archit.) terracotta figure; (biol.) plasma; (phys.) plasma; (biol.) protoplasm; (miner.) plasma; †(mus.) graceful modulation of the voice. **-a·bile** *adj.* mouldable, plastic. (**-abilità** *f.*) **-are** [A I] *tr.* to mould, to form, to shape; to model; -are l'animo, la mente, to train the mind, to educate. **-a·tico** *adj.* (biol.) plasmatic. **-ato** *part. adj.* moulded, formed; created, imagined. (**-atore** *m.* **-atrice** *f.*) **-azione** *f.* moulding; forming; creation. **-odeṣmi** *m.pl.* (bot.) plasmodesmata. **-odiale** *adj.* plasmodial. **-o·dio** *m.* (biol.) plasmodium. **-o·liṣi** *f.* (biol.) plasmolysis. **-oliṣare** [A I] *rfl.* (biol.) to plasmolyse. **-oliṣa·bile** *adj.* plasmolysable. **-oliṣabilità** *f.* plasmolysability. **-oli·tico** *adj.* (biol.) plasmolytic. **-on** *m. indecl.* (pharm.) plasmon.

pla·stic-a, †**-e** *f.* (sculpt.) plastic art, modelling, casting; plastic material; †figure in relief, cast; plastic surgery. **-are** [A 2 S] *intr.* (*aux.* avere) (sculpt.) to model, to cast. (**-atore** *m.* **-atrice** *f.*)

pla·sti-co *adj.* plastic; arti plastiche, plastic arts; (chem. industr.) plastic, materie -che, plastics; argilla -ca, modelling clay; (paint.) in relief, plastic, quadri -ci, pictures of statuesque groups; materia -ca, plastic material, plaster, etc.; (geol.) plastic, incompetent (of beds); chirurgia -ca, plastic surgery; (fig.) plastic, pliant, supple; *n.m.* modeller; model; plastic; synthetic material. **-ità** *f.* plasticity. **-iẓẓante** *adj.* (chem.) plasticizing; *n.m.* plasticizer.

pla·stide *f.* (biol.) plastid.

plasti·dio *m.* (biol.) plastid.

plastific-are [A 2 S] *tr.* (industr.) to plasticize, to soften; to cover with a film of plastic material. **-ante** *part. adj.* plasticizing; *n.m.* plasticizer. **-ato** *part. adj.* (industr.) plasticized; with a plastic cover; libro con copertina -ata, book with a plastic cover. **-azione** *f.* plasticization.

plastilina *f.* (sculpt.) plastic composition resembling 'plasticine'.

plastro·n *m. indecl.* large made-up necktie; plastron, shirt front.

pla·tan-o *m.* plane-tree, *Platanus*. **-a·ria** *f.* Norway maple, *Acer platanoides*. **-ẹto** *m.* grove or wood of plane trees.

plat-e·a *f.* (archit.) foundations (extending under the whole of a building; platform supported by piles; bed of concrete; (theatr.) pit, spectators in the pit; *also* whole ground floor of an auditorium, i.e. stalls and pit; (oceanography) plateau; — continentale, continental shelf. **-eale** *adj.* low, vulgar; commonplace; (finan.) relating to the market; (comm.) debiti -eali, market loans or credit, sundry debts. **-ealmente** *adv.* vulgarly, commonly; coarsely; indecently, disgustingly. **-eare** [A 6] *tr.* (archit.) to lay underwater foundations. **-ea·tico** *m.* local tax, rate. (**-eato** *part. adj.*)

platelminti *m.pl.* (zool.) platyhelminthes.

pla·tina *f.* (text.) sinker; (typ.) platen, platen press.

pla·tin-o *m.* (chem.) platinum. **-are** [A I S] *tr.* to platinum-plate. **-ato** *part. adj.* platinum-plated; capelli -ati, platinum-blonde hair; bionda -ata, platinum blonde. **-atura** *f.* platinum plating. **-i·fero** *adj.* platinum-bearing, platiniferous. **-ocianuro** *m.* (chem.) platino-cyanide. **-o·ide** *adj.* (metall.) platinoid. **-otipi·a** *f.* (photog.) platinotype.

platirrino *m.* (zool.) platyrrhine (monkey).

Plat-one *pr.n.m.* Plato. **-o·nico** *adj.* of Plato; Platonic; dialoghi -onici, Plato's dialogues; amore -onico, Platonic love; (joc.; iron.) unreal, ideal, idealistic; impossible; *n.m.* Platonist, follower of Plato. **-onicamente** *adv.* Platonically. **-oniṣmo** *m.* Platonism; idealism. †**-oniṣta** *m.* Platonist.

†**platta** *f.* (mil. hist.) chest or fund available for advances on pay or for special allowances, administered by a council of officers.

plaud-ire [D I], †**-ere** *tr.* to clap, to applaud; to approve (of); -o la vostra proposta, I approve of your proposal. **-endo** *ger.* applauding, approving. **-ente** *part. adj.* applauding, approving.

pla·uṣ-o *m.* applause; approbation; praise; fare — a, to applaud; (in an examination) distinction; †(mus.) beat. **-i·bile** *adj.* acceptable, reasonable; praiseworthy; plausible. (**-ibilmente** *adv.*) **-ibilità** *f.* acceptability, reasonableness; plausibility, praiseworthiness.

†**pla·ustro** *m.* farm-wagon, ox-cart; (astron.) King Charles's wain.

Pla·ut-o *pr.n.m.* Plautus. **-ino** *adj.* Plautine; relating to Plautus. (**-inamẹnte** *adv.*)

pleb-e *f.* common people; lower classes; la — lavoratrice, the working class. **-ac·cia**, **-a·glia** *f.* mob, rabble. **-ani·a** *f.* (eccl.) small ecclesiastical district (cf. **pievania**). **-ano** *adj.* rural. **-eac·cio** *m.* pejor. low person, vulgar person. **-eamẹnte**, †**-eiamente** *adv.* vulgarly, coarsely. **-eiṣmo** *m.* vulgarism; vulgar action; vulgarity. **-e·o**, †**-e·io** *adj.* vulgar, plebeian; coarse; *n.m.* plebeian; patrizi e -ei, patricians and plebeians. †**-euscito** *m.* see **plebiscito**. **-iscita·rio** *adj.* unanimous; plebiscitary. **-iscito** *m.* plebiscite; common consent.

Ple·iade *pr.n.f.* (astron.) one of the Pleiades; le Pleiadi, the Pleiades; (Gk. myth.) Pleiades (daughters of Atlas); (Fr. lit. hist.) la Pléïade; (fig.) a select group; una — di eroi, a noble band of heroes.

†**pleia·ria** *f.* guarantee, pledge.

pleistoc-ene *m.* (geol.) the Pleistocene Age. **-e·nico** *adj.* Pleistocene.

plena·ri-o *adj.* plenary, complete, fully attended; seduta -a, plenary session; (theol.) plenary (indulgence). **-amẹnte** *adv.* plenarily.

plenil-unare *adj.* of the full moon, plenilunar(y); notte —. night of full moon, night when a full moon is shining. **-u·nio** *m.* full moon.

plenipotenz-a *f.* plenipotence; plenary power(s). **-iale** *adj.* plenipotential; plenipotentiary. **-ia·rio** *adj. n.m.* plenipotentiary.

plenitu·dine *f.* fullness, plenitude; nella — dei tempi, in the fullness of time.

pleo-croiṣmo *m.* (phys.) pleochroism. **-mazi·a** *f.* (zool.) the multimammate condition (in mammals). **-naṣmo** *m.* (gramm.) pleonasm. **-na·stico** *adj.* pleonastic. **-nasticamẹnte** *adv.* pleonastically.

pleroma *m.* (theol., esp. Gnostic) *pleroma*, spiritual fullness, plenitude of being, (sphere of) spiritual perfection.

pless-ifọrme *adj.* (anat.) plexiform. **-i·grafo** *m.* (med.) plexigraph. **-i·metro** *m.* (mus.) a kind of metronome; (med.) pleximeter. **-ime·trico** *adj.* (med.) pleximetric.

plesso *m.* (anat.) plexus; (geog.) — montuoso, mountain complex.

pletis-mografi·a *f.* (med.) plethysmography. **-mo·grafo** *m.* (med.) plethysmograph. **-mometri·a** *f.* (med.) plethysmometry. **-mo·metro** *m.* (med.) plethysmometer.

ple·t-ora *f.* (med.) plethora; (fig.) plethora, superabundance, glut. **-o·rico** *adj.* (med.) plethoric; mercato -orico, overstocked market; classe -orica, overlarge class.

pletta *f.* (archit.) interlaced ornament.

plettro *m.* (mus.) plectrum; †(poet.) violin-bow; (liter.) 'inspiration', poetic spirit.

ple·ur-a *f.* (anat.) pleura.

ple·ur-ico *adj.* (anat.) pleural. †**-isi·a**, †**-esi·a** *f.* see **pleurite**. **-ite** *f.* (med.) pleurisy. **-i·tico** *adj.* (med.) pleuritic. **-ocen·teṣi** *f.* (surg.) pleurocentesis. **-ocele** *m.* (med.) pleurocele. **-ocliṣi** *f.* (med.) pleuroclysis. **-odini·a** *f.* (med.) pleurodynia, pleuralgia. **-opolmonare** *adj.* (med.) pleuropulmonary. **-opolmonite** *f.* (med.) pleuropneumonia. **-orre·a** *f.* (med.) pleurorrhoea. **-oscopi·a** *f.* (med.) pleuroscopy. **-osco·pio** *m.* (med.) pleuroscope. **-otomi·a** *f.* (surg.) pleurotomy. **-oto·tono** *m.* (med.) pleurothotonos.

plian·t *adj. indecl.* sedia —, folding chair, deck chair.

plic-a *f.* (mus.) plica, a character (in medieval music) indicating a note succeeded by a grace-note; (anat.) plica. **-ata** *f.* (liturg.) folded chasuble. †**-a·tile** *adj.* pliable. **-azionẹ** *f.* (anat.) plication.

pli-co *m.* (*pl.* **-chi**) cover, envelope; folder; (postal) packet; in — separato, under separate cover.

Pli·ni-o *pr.n.m.* Pliny (the Elder or the Younger). **-ano** *adj.* relating to Pliny; lettere -ane, Letters of Pliny the Younger; pino di Plinio, *or* pino -ano, mushroom cloud following volcanic eruption; *n.m.* follower of Pliny.

plint-i *m.pl.* (herald.) billets. **-ato** *adj.* (herald.) billetty.

plinto *m.* (archit.) plinth.

plio-cene *m.* (geol.) Pliocene. **-ce·nico** *adj.* (geol.) Pliocene.

plo·ceo *m.* (orn.) weaver bird.

†**plo·ia** *f.* rain; outpouring, flowing forth; weeping.

plor-arẹ [A I] *intr.* (aux. avere) (poet.) to weep, to lament; to rain; (provb.) per la santa Candelora, o se nevica o se -a, dell'inverno siamo fora, come rain, come snow, by Candlemas we are past the winter. **-oṣo** *adj.* weeping; mourning.

ploto *m.* (orn.) darter, (Amer.) water turkey, *Anhinga* spp.

plotọne *m.* (mil.) platoon.

†**plumata** *f.* See **piumata**, under **piuma**.

plu·mbeo *adj.* leaden; lead-coloured; livid; (fig.) heavy, dull; boring.

plur-ale *adj.* plural; (gramm.) numero —, plural number; *n.m.* (gramm.) plural (number), plural form; al —, in the plural. **-almẹnte** *adv.* plurally. **-aliṣmo** *m.* pluralism. **-alità** *f.* plurality; majority; (leg.) -alità di domande, multiplicity of actions (C.C.P.). **-aliżżarẹ** [A I] *tr.* (gramm.) to put in the plural; to speak in plural form. **-igemellarità** *f.* (zool.) polyembryony. **-iloculare** *adj.* (bot.) plurilocular. **-imotọre** *adj. indecl.* (aeron.) multi-engined; *n.m.* multi-engined aircraft. **-inominale** *adj.* multi-number; proportional. **-ivalente** *adj.* (chem.) multivalent. **-ivocalità** *f.* (mus.) vocal polyphonic texture.

plu·rimo *adj.* multiple; voto —, plural vote; *pl.* very many.

†**plus-ore** *adj.* more. †**-quamperfetto** *adj.* (gramm.) pluperfect; (joc.) too perfect.

pluṣvalọre *m.* (econ.; comm.) plus-value.

Plutarco *pr.n.m.* Plutarch; Il — italiano, The Italian Plutarch, title used for a collection of biographies of famous Italians.

plu·teo *m.* (Rom. antiq.) *pluteus*, mobile semi-circular screen for besiegers; i plutei di Traiano, a marble bas-relief in the Roman forum; (mil. hist.) assault screen; mantlet, shield, revetment; (naut.) bulwark, palisade; case or set of shelves of a particular form used esp. for MSS; (zool.) pluteus larva (of echinoderms).

Pluto *pr.n.m.* (myth.) Plutus, god of riches.

plut-o·crate *m.* plutocrat. **-ocra·tico** *adj.* plutocratic. **-ocrazi·a** *f.* plutocracy.

Plutọn-e *pr.n.m.* (myth.) Pluto, god of the underworld. **-iano** *adj.* (myth.) Plutonian, of Pluto.

pluto·nio *m.* (miner.) plutonium.

†**plu·via** *f.* rain.

pluvi-ale *adj.* (of) rain; pluvial; acqua —, rainwater; *n.m.* (bldg.) drainpipe. **-lignọsa** *f.* (geog.) rainforest.

Plu·vi-o *pr.n.m.* (Rom. myth.) Giove —, *Iuppiter pluvius*, Jupiter as rain-bringer; *adj.* rainy. **-o·grafo** *m.* (meteor.) pluviograph, recording rain-gauge. **-ome·trico** *adj.* rain-measuring; (of, by a) rain-gauge. **-o·metro** *m.* (meteor.) rain-gauge. †**-oṣo** *adj.* rainy.

pneum-a *m.* (mus.) pneuma, jubilus, group of notes sung to final syllable of a sentence in plainchant; stroke indicating a breathing-place at end of a phrase; (Byzantine music) a rising interval. **-a·tica** *f.* (phys.) pneumatics. **-a·tico** *adj.* pneumatic; macchina -atica, air-pump; martello -atico, pneumatic hammer, compressed-air hammer; trapano -atico, pneumatic drill; posta -atica, express letter service (dispatched by pneumatic tube); fucile -atico, air-gun; *n.m.* (pneumatic) tyre. **-atoce·falo** *m.* (med.) pneumo-cranium. **-atocele** *m.* (med.) pneumatocele; pneumocele; pulmonary hernia. **-ato·fori** *m.pl.* (biol.) pneumatophores. **-a·todi** *m.pl.* pneumatodes. **-atologi·a** *f.* (philos.) pneumatology. **-ato·maci** *m.pl.* (eccl. hist.) Pneumatomachi, Pneumatomachists. **-atoṣi** *f.* (med.) pneumatosis. **-ectomi·a** *f.* (surg.) pneumonectomy, resection of the lung. **-obacillo** *m.* (med.) pneumobacillus, *Bacillus pneumoniae*. **-ocele** *m.* (med.) pneumatocele. **-ococcemi·a** *f.* (med.) pneumococcaemia. **-ococ·cico** *adj.* (med.) pneumococcal. **-ococco** *m.* (med.) pneumococcus. **-oconioṣi** *f.* (med.) pneumoconiosis. **-oenterite** *f.* (med.) pneumo-enteritis. **-oga·strico** *adj.* (anat.) pneumogastric. **-o·grafo** *m.* (med.) pneumograph. **-o·liṣi** *f.* (surg.) pneumonolysis. **-ometri·a** *f.* (med.) spirometry. **-o·metro** *m.* (med.) spirometer; (aeron.) pneumometer, speed indicator. **-oni·a**, **-onite** *f.* (med.) pneumonia. **-o·nico**, **-oni·tico** *adj.* (med.) pneumonia; pulmonary. **-orragi·a** *f.* (med.) pneumorrhagia, pulmonary apoplexy. **-orra·gico** *adj.* pneumorrhagic. **-otifo** *m.* (med.) pneumotyphus. **-otomi·a** *f.* (surg.) pneumotomy, incision into the lung. **-otorace** *m.* (med.) pneumothorax. **-otora·cico** *adj.* pneumothoracic.

Po *pr.n.m.* (geog.) the river Po.

po' *adv.* See **poco** or **poi**.

poana *f.* See **poiana**.

†**pocalissi** *f.* See **apocalisse**.

†**pocanza** *f.* See **pochezza**, under **poco**.

pocanzi *adv.* a short time ago (cf. **poco**).

†**poc·ci·a** *f.* breast. †**-are** *intr.* to suck; to get drunk. †**-atoio** *m.* see **poppatoio**. †**-oṣo** *adj.* full-breasted; stare -oso, to live in comfort.

pochade *f.* (pron. as Fr.) poor farce, low comedy.

po·co *adj.* (*m.pl.* **-chi**).   **1.** LITTLE, very little, small; *pl.* few; uomo di — ingegno, man of little intelligence; uomo di -che parole, man of few words; lago di -ca profondità, lake having little depth, rather shallow lake; scarce, insufficient; questo pane è —, this bread is not enough; (of a person) little, small, thin; quell'uomo è così — che tutti i lavori sono troppo gravi per lui, that man is so small that all the jobs are too heavy for him; (naut.) fondo —, shallow, shoalwater.   **2.** *indef. prn.* LITTLE; contentarsi del —, to be satisfied with little; sa di —, it has very little taste; — o niente, little or nothing; feci il — che potei, I did what little I could; sa un — di tutto, he knows a little of everything; cavare il — dal —, to get something (some profit, advantage) out of every little thing; un — (*or* un po'), a little, a certain amount, some; un po' di pane, some bread; un po' di buona volontà, a little (i.e. a fair amount of) good will; un buon —, a good deal; un altro —, a little more, some more; po' po', a lot; che po' po' di sfacciataggine!, what (confounded) cheek!; un — di buono, a good for nothing, uomo da —, 'good for nothing', insignificant person; roba da —, rubbish; non —, not a little, a lot; egli fece non — per la causa, he did not a little for the cause; *pl.* few; c'erano -chi dei suoi amici, few of his friends were there; alcuni -chi, some few; non -chi, not a few; questo è cibo per i -chi, this is food for the few (for connoisseurs); (fam.) -chi (i.e. 'denari'), little money; ha perso quei -chi che aveva, he has lost what little (money) he had.   **3.** *adv.* LITTLE, very little; not much; a short time, a little while; mi piace —, I don't like him much; nè punto nè —, not at all; a — a —, little by little, by degrees; lavoro — proficuo, work of little use; ingegno — pratico, not very practical mind; — simpatico, not very attractive, unattractive; rimasi assente da casa proprio —, I was away from home only a short time; fra —, in a short time, before long, shortly; — fa, poc'anzi, a short time ago; per —, for a short time, *or* for not much money; ci starò ancora per —, I shall stay here a little while longer; l'ebbi per —, I got it very cheap; in —, in a short time, *or* in short, in brief; un altro —, a little longer; un altro — ed ero finito, if it had gone on a little longer I should have been exhausted; ad ogni —, every now and then; da —, for a short time, ci sta da —, he has only been there a little while; vende a —, he sells things cheaply; almost, nearly, all but; per — (non) ci cascavo, I nearly fell into it; — manca che (non), almost, nearly, all but; — mancò che non cadessi, I very nearly fell down; 'ove per — il cor non si spaura' (Leopardi), wherein the heart is almost dismayed; per — che (foll. by *subj.*), however little; un po' per aver bevuto e un po' per lo spavento non era capace di ricordarsi quel che aveva visto, what with having drunk and what with his fright, he could not recollect what he had seen; *adv. phr.* un — (modifying or amplifying an imperative) just; assaggia un po' questo caffè!, just try this coffee!; senti un po', just listen to me!, look here!; va un po' a comprare del pane, just go and buy some bread, *or* I say, do go and get some bread; vediamo un po' questo libro, let's just have a look at this book; un po' più in su, a little higher (up); un po' più avanti, a little further on; un po' meno, a little less.   **-chẹt'o, -chettino** *m., adj. dim.* un -chetto, very little; ever so little; just a moment!; *adv.* very little; rather. **-chẹzza** *f.* smallness, narrowness; scantiness, scarcity; lack, insufficiency; -chezza d'ingegno, lack of talent; -chezza di mezzi, scanty means. **-chino** *m. dim.* just a little, a very little; è -chino, it's not enough; aspettami qui un -chino, wait for me here a little while; di denari ne ha proprio -chino, as to money he is very badly off; *pl.* few, very few. **-olino** *m.* see **pochino**.

†**po·c·olo, -ulo** *m.* drinking-cup.

†**pocrisi·a** *f.* See **ipocrisia**.

poculiforme *adj.* cup-shaped.

pod-agra *f.* (med.) gout, podagra. **-a·grico** *adj.* podagral, gouty. **-agrọso** *adj.* (med.) podagrous, gouty.

Podali·rio *pr.n.m.* (Gk. myth.) Podalirius (son of Asclepius); (ent.) a large swallow-tail butterfly, *Papilio podalirius.*

podartrite *f.* (med.) podarthritis.

podẹr-e[1] *m.* farm; agricultural holding (C.C.); estate; rendere quanto un —, to be very productive; un — in piano, a profitable holding (of any kind of property), a good investment. **-ale** *adj.* relating to a farm; casa -ale, farmhouse. **-ante** *m.* farmer; *adj.* farming. **-ẹtto** *m. dim.* smallholding, small farm. **-ino** *m. dim.* smallholding, very small farm.

†**podere**[2] *m.* See **potere**.

poderọs-o *adj.* powerful, mighty; very strong; †sufficient. **-amẹnte** *adv.* powerfully; †sufficiently.

podest-à, †**podẹ·sta** *m.* administrative head of a commune: mayor (not elected but nominated by central Government, as opposed to **sindaco**, q.v.); †*f.* power, authority. **-arẹssa** *f.* wife of the podestà, mayoress. **-ariato** *m.* office of podestà. **-arile, -erile** *adj.* of the 'podestà'. **-eri·a** *f.* town-hall; office of podestà; district governed by a podestà.

pode·zio *m.* (bot.) podetium.

†**po·dice** *m.* See **ano.**

po·d-io *m.* (archit.) podium; (Rom. antiq.) podium (of amphitheatre); (naut.) supporting structure for a ship's figurehead; (mus.) (conductor's) rostrum. **-ismo** *m.* (sport) walking; (naut.) clew of a sail. **-ista** *m., f.* (sport) walker. **-i·stica** *f.* (sport) walking. **-i·stico** *adj.* (sport) relating to walking. **-ofillọso** *m.* (vet.) corium of the wall of the hoof, in a horse. **-o·gino** *m.* elongated thalamus. **-ologi·a** *f.* farriery. **-olo·gico** *adj.* relating to farriery. **-o·metro** *m.* an instrument for measuring the hoof of a horse, before shoeing; instrument for measuring walking distances, pedometer. **-ovillọso** *m.* (vet.) corium of the sole (in a horse.

poe-ma *m.* (*pl.* **-mi**) poem, long poem (usu. epic); — in (di) scherno, satire; — in prosa, prose poem; il — sacro, il divino —, *The Divine Comedy* of Dante; (mus.) — sinfonico, symphonic poem, tone-poem; (fig.) è un vero —, it's a dream!, it's beautiful. **-mẹssa** *f.* dull, boring poem. **-mẹtto** *m. dim.* little poem; short poem.

poeṣ-i·a *f.* poetry; poem (i.e. lyric, not an epic, which is 'poema'); mettere in —, to put into verse; questa è —, this is untrue, this is fictitious; (paint.) representational picture (mythological, historical, etc.). **-i(u)ola** *f. dim.* little poem.

poet-a *m.* poet; il divino —, Dante; — di teatro, dramatist; — laureato, poet laureate; (hist.) — cesareo, court poet to the Emperor (esp. in Vienna); (fam.; joc.) dreamy person, person with his head in the clouds. **-a·bile** *adj.* suitable for poetic treatment. **-ac·cio** *m. pejor.* bad poet, poetaster. **-ante** *part. adj.; n.m.* versifier, writer of poetry, poet. **-are** [A I] *intr.* (*aux.* avere) to write poetry (or verse); to be a poet; *tr.* to put into verse; to express poetically. **-astro** *m.* poetaster. **-eggiare** [A 3 c] *intr.* (*aux.* avere) to write verse; to play the poet; to tend towards poetry, to be somewhat poetical; prosa che -eggia, poetical prose. **-ẹssa** *f.* poetess, woman poet; prophetess, sibyl.

poet-i·ca *f.* poetic(s), poetic theory; art of poetry; †book or treatise in which laws of poetry are defined. **-care** [A 2 s] *intr.* (*aux.* avere) to write poetry. **-cheri·a** *f.* (iron.; derog.) fancy, fantasy; poetic fancy. **-co** *adj.* poetic(al); of poetry or poets; immagine -ca, poetic image; licenza -ca, poetic licence; il -co alloro, the poet's crown (of laurel); opere -che, poetical works; senso -co, poetic sense, imagination; (of a subject) suitable for treatment in poetry, poetic; prosa -ca, poetic prose; imaginary; personaggio -co, fictitious character; (joc.) fantastic, fanciful, strange; *n.m.* professor of poetry; the poetic; dare nel -co, to tend towards poetry, to indulge in poetry. (**-camẹnte** *adv.*) **-cino** *m. dim.* minor poet. **-cizzare** [A I] *intr.* (*aux.* avere) to poetize, to write poetry; *tr.* to poeticize, to render poetical; to versify; to put into verse. (**-cizzato** *part. adj.*)

†**poetri·a** *f.* poetics; treatise on poetics.

poff-are, -arbacco, -areddio *excl.* good heavens!; poffar il cielo!, heavens above!

pog·gi-a *f.* (naut.) dipping line, used for dipping the fore end of a yard when tacking; leeward; due caviglie alla —!, wheel two spokes to leeward (down); da — e da orza, a — e ad orza, both down as well as up wind; — con orza!, both watches!, all hands! **-are** [A 3] *intr.* (*aux.* avere) (naut.) to shelter, to seek refuge in a harbour or protected waters; to blow from a certain quarter; to bear up (turn away from wind); -are sopra una nave, to bear down on a ship; -are stando alla cappa con tempo fortunale, to turn and run with a gale astern; -a!, bear up!; -a tutto!, helm hard up!; non -are!, nothing to leeward!; (mil.) to bear away; to change position; -are a destra, to incline to the right. **-ata** *f.* (naut.) alteration of course away from the wind; essere di -ata in un porto, to have taken shelter in a harbour. **-ero** *adj.* (naut.) carrying lee helm, i.e. ill-loaded or of faulty construction or dangerously rigged and sailed.

poggiare[1] [A 3] (naut.). See under **poggia.**

poggi·are² [A 3] *intr.* (*aux.* avere) to rise, to climb; *tr.* to rest, to lean, to place; -a il piede a terra, put your foot on the ground; questo muro -a su uno strato roccioso, this wall rests on a bed of rock; (fig.) tutto il suo ragionamento -a su false ipotesi, all his reasoning rests on false premises; *rfl.* to lean; -arsi a, to lean against. **-acapo** *m. indecl.* head-rest, antimacassar. **-apiedi** *m. indecl.* foot-rest. **-ata** *f.* rising ground, slope. **-atesta** *m. indecl.* see **poggiacapo**. **-ato** *part. adj.* rested, supported; resting; -ato a, leaning on, resting against.

pog·g-io *m.* hill, hillock, knoll; eminence; parapet; balcony; (archit.) podium. †**-iaiuolo** *m.* hillman. **-erello** *m. dim.* hillock; mound. **-ẹtto** *m. dim.* hillock, knoll; parapet, balcony. **-iọso** *adj.* hilly. **-i(u)olo** *m.*, †**-iuola** *f.* low hill; balcony, parapet, railing; small terrace; †sand dune.

†**pogo** *adv., m.* See **poco**.

poh *excl.* pooh!

poi *adv.* then; next; after all; da ora in —, henceforward; o prima o —, sooner or later; c'è — una piazza, then, after that, next, there is a square; e —?, what next?; promette molto ma — non mantiene, he is full of promises but when it comes to the point he doesn't keep them; non è — così stolto come noi lo credevamo, after all he is not so silly as we thought; questo — no!, I can't allow this!, I can't believe this!, this is too much!; afterwards, subsequently, later; di —, afterwards; quando — furono arrivati, after they had arrived; il giorno di —, next day, (on) the following day; l'anno del mai e il mese del —, never; (for emphasis) ti voglio tanto e — tanto bene, I love you so much; se — abbia ragione, vedrai tu, you'll soon see if he's right or not; io — non c'entro, after all it's nothing to do with me; *n.m.* the future, afterwards, the time to come; pensiamo al —, we must think of the future; il senno del —, wisdom after the event; (provb.) del senno del — son piene le fosse, everyone is wise after the event.

poiana *f.* (orn.) buzzard, *Buteo buteo*; — calzata, rough-legged buzzard, *B. lagopus*.

†**poiare** *vb.* and derivs. See **poggiare²**.

poichè *conj.* since, as, for; when, after; — non mi credete, non parlerò più, since you don't believe me, I will say no more; siate clementi, — dovrete essere giudicati anche voi, be merciful, for you too shall be judged; — egli ebbe finito, when he had finished; — mi ebbe detto questo, after he had told me this.

poiṣe *m.* (phys.) poise.

poker *m. indecl.* four of a kind (in poker).

†**pola** *f.* (orn.) jackdaw (*Paradiso* XXI, 35).

polacca *f.* Polish woman; (mus.) Polonaise; (naut.) three-masted vessel up to 200 or even 300 tons; (cul.) Russian salad.

polac-co *adj.* (*m.pl.* **-chi**) Polish; *n.m.* Pole; Polish, the Polish language. **-chino** *m. dim.* little Polish boy; bootee. **-cọne** *m.* (naut.) trysail, stormsail; foresail of a fishing boat.

polar-e *adj.* polar, pole; stella —, pole star, North star; circolo —, Arctic Circle; (math.) polar; coordinate -i, polar co-ordinates; *n.m.* (math.) polar (curve). **-mẹnte** *adv.* like the pole(s); -mente opposto, poles apart. **-imetrịa** *f.* (chem.) polarimetry. **-imẹtrico** *adj.* (chem.) polarimetric(al). **-imetro** *m.* (opt.) polarimeter. **-iscọpio** *m.* (opt.) polariscope. **-ità** *f.* (scient.) polarity. **-iẓẓare** [A I] *tr.* (scient.) to polarize; (fig.) to attract; -izzare l'attenzione del pubblico, to attract public attention; *rfl.* to get one's bearings; *recip. rfl.* to converge. **-iẓẓato** *part. adj.* polarized. **-iẓẓatore** *m.* **-iẓẓatrice** *f.*, also *adj.*) **-iẓẓazịone** *f.* (scient.) polarization; (opt.) togliere la -izzazione, to depolarize; (radio) -izzazione di griglia, grid bias. **-ogra·fico** *adj.* (chem.; phys.) polarographic. **-o·grafo** *m.* (chem.) polarograph. **-ogramma** *m.* (phys.; chem.) polarogram, polarographic curve.

pol-ca *f.* (mus.) Polka. **-chista** *m.* (mus.) composer of Polkas.

Polcinella¹ *pr.n.m.* see **Pulcinella**.

polcinella² *m.* (orn.) —di mare, puffin, *Fratercula arctica*.

polẹdro *m.* See **puledro**.

polẹggia *f.* See **puleggia**.

polemarco *m.* (Gk. hist.) polemarch.

pole·m-ica *f.* polemic, polemics; controversy; (theol.) polemics. **-ico** *adj.* polemic(al), controversial; *n.m.* controversialist. **-ista** *m.* controversialist. **-iẓẓare** [A I] *intr.* (*aux.* avere) to engage in controversy, to polemize.

polena *f.* (naut.) figurehead, decorative carving on the bow of a ship, frequently alluding to the ship's name. In galleys the carving often represented a wild beast, snake, dragon, etc.

polent-a *f.* (cul.) polenta, a kind of pudding made chiefly of maize flour; — di farina dolce, polenta made with chestnut flour. **-a·io**, **-aro** *m.* polenta seller; (joc.) great eater of polenta. **-ata** *f.* dish of polenta; eating polenta. **-ina** *f. dim.* linseed poultice. **-ọne** *m.* lazy person, sluggard; (joc.) Northern Italian, esp. Milanese or Bergamese.

polẹṣine *m.* (geog.) delta; *pr.n.m.* the Po delta.

poliaden-ịa *f.* (med.) polyadenia. **-ite** *f.* (med.) polyadenitis.

poliambulanza *f.* (med.; surg.) surgery, dispensary where first-aid treatment can be given.

poliante·a *f.* anthology.

polianto *m.* (bot.) tuberose, *Polianthes tuberosa*.

poli-archi·a *f.* government by many. (**-ar·chico** *adj.*)

poliar-monị·a *f.* (mus.) polyharmony. **-mo·nico** *adj.* (mus.) polyharmonic.

poliarticolare *adj.* (anat.) polyarticular, polyarthric.

poliar-trịte *f.* (med.) polyarthritis. **-trịtico** *adj.* polyarthritic.

poliba·ṣico *adj.* (chem.) polybasic.

poliboro *m.* (orn.) carrion-hawk, *Polyborus* spp.

police·falo *m.* (mus.) flute-melody imitating the hissing of the serpents in the Gorgon's hair.

policheti *m.pl.* (zool.) polychaete worms.

policit-e *f.* (med.) polycythaemia. **-e·mico** *adj.* polycythaemic.

policli·nic-a *f.* (med.; surg.) hospital (considered as a combination of several clinics). **-o** *adj.* relating to such a hospital.

policlora *f.* (ent.) large tortoiseshell butterfly, *Nymphalis polychloros*.

policordo *m.* (mus.) polychord.

policrom-a·tico *adj.* polychromatic, many-coloured. **-ị·a** *f.* (paint.) polychromy, art of decoration in various colours; variety of colours in a picture or decoration.

poli·cromo *adj.* (scient.) polychrome, polychromatic, many-coloured.

policro·nio *ad·.* long-lived.

polidattili·a *f.* (biol.) polydactylism.

polidemonịṣmo *m.* (anthropol.) polydaemonism.

poli-ẹdrico *adj.* (geom.) polyhedric. **-edro** *m.* (geom.) polyhedron.

poliennale *adj.* dated (of Government securities).

polie·stere *m.* (chem.) polyester; resina —, polyester resin.

poliesterificazịone *f.* (chem.) polyesterification.

poliesteṣị·a *f.* (med.) polyaesthesia.

polietilene *m.* (chem.) polyethylene, (pop.) polythene.

pol-ifagi·a *f.* (med.) polyphagia; bulimia. **-i·fago** *adj.* polyphagous, omnivorous.

polifase *adj. indecl.* (electr.) multiphase.

polifile·tico *adj.* (biol.) polyphyletic.

poli·fil-o *m.* one who has many friends; †one who writes or speaks using words from different languages. **-i·a** *f.* friendship with many; abundance of friends.

poli-fonị·a *f.* (mus.) polyphony. **-fo·nico** *adj.* (mus.) polyphonic. (**-fonicamẹnte** *adv.*) **-fonịṣmo** *m.* (mus.) polyphonism. **-fonista** *m.* (mus.) polyphonist.

polifrequen-te *adj.* (phys.) multifrequent. **-za** *f.* (phys.) multifrequency.

poli·gala *f.* (bot.) milkwort, *Polygala*.

poligalatti·a *f.* (med.) polygalactia, abnormally increased secretion of milk.

poliga·mico *adj.* See **poligamo**.

poli·gam-o *adj.* polygamous; (bot.) polygamous; *n.m.* polygamist. **-i·a** *f.* polygamy.

polige·n-eṣi, **-i·a** *f.* polygenesis, polygeny. **-ịṣmo** *m.* polygenism.

poliglott-o, **-a** *adj. n.m.* polyglot; *m.* (orn.) mocking bird, *Mimus polyglottos*.

poligo·n-io *adj.* polygonal. **-ale** *adj.* polygonal; (bldg.) muratura a giunti -ali, rag work, snail creep; *n.f.* (surv.) traverse.

poli·gono *m.* (geom.) polygon; — delle forze, polygon of forces; (bldg.) — funicolare, link polygon; (mil.) fort or fortified zone having many sides; rifle range; artillery range; — missilistico, — per missili, missile range, missile proving ground; (bot.) *Polygonum*.

poligr-afare [A I S] *tr.* to copy, to duplicate. **-afato** *part. adj.* duplicated (in many copies). **-afị·a** *f.* miscellany, miscellaneous writings; printing; polygraphy, cryptography; duplicating, printing from a stencil; master-copy; (duplicated) copy. **-a·fico** *adj.* polygraphic; officina -afica, duplicating office, printing works; Istituto -afico dello Stato (*or* il Poligrafico), the State printing works and stationery office in Rome; *n.m.pl.* i -afici, the printing operatives, the printing industry. (**-aficamẹnte** *adv.*)

poli·grafo *m.* polygraph; hectograph; duplicating machine; copying machine; versatile writer (sometimes derog.).

poli·m-ero *m.* (chem.) polymer; — elastico, elastomer. **-eri·a** *f.* (chem.) polymerism. **-e·rico** *adj.* (chem.) polymeric. **-erizzare** [A 1] *tr.* (chem.) to polymerize. **-erazione** *f.* polymerization.

poli·m-etro *adj.* see **polimetrico**; *n.m.* poem in several different metres. **-etri·a** *f.* use of various metres in one poem. **-e·trico** *adj.* in various metres, having several metres.

polimiosite *f.* (med.) polymyositis.

†**polimit-o** *m.* damask cloth; *adj.* woven in many colours. †**-a·rio** *m.* weaver of damask cloth.

Polim·nia *pr.n.f.* (myth.) Polyhymnia, Polymnia, the Muse of the sublime hymn.

polimorf-işmo *m.* (biol.; chem.) polymorphism. **-o** *adj.* polymorphous, polymorphic, multiform; (miner.) polymorphous.

Poline·şi-a *pr.n.f.* (geog.) Polynesia. **-ano** *adj.* Polynesian.

poli-ne·urico *adj.* (anat.) polyneural. **-neurite**, **-nevrite** *f.* (med.) polyneuritis, multiple neuritis.

polino·mio *adj.*, *n.m.* (math.) polynomial, multinomial.

poli-nucleare *adj.* (scient.) polynuclear. **-nucleoşi** *f.* (med.) polynucleosis.

po·lio *m.* (bot.) *Teucrium polium.* **-encefalite** *f.* (med.) poliencephalitis. **-mielite** *f.* (med.) poliomyelitis, 'polio.' **-ni·chia** *f.* (med.) polyonychia. **-pi·a** *f.*, **-psi·a** *f.* (med.) polyopy.

Poliorcete *pr.n.m.* (Gk. hist.) Poliorcetes, 'the Besieger', title of Demetrius 1 of Macedon.

poliploidi·a *f.* (biol.) polyploidy.

po·lip-o *m.* (zool.) polyp; (med.) polyp, polypus. **-a·io** *m.* dye derived from the polyp. **-o·o** *adj.* (med.; vet.) polypous.

polipropilene *m.* (chem.) polypropylene.

pol-ire [D2] *tr.* (techn.) to polish, to finish; (fig.) to polish (e.g. verses); to furbish. **-ito** *part. adj.* (techn.) polished, finished; (fig.) elegant, polished; un oratore -ito, a polished speaker.

polireme *f.* (naut. hist.) polyreme.

poliritmo *adj.* (mus.) polyrhythmic.

polis-arci·a *f.* (med.) polysarcia, obesity. **-ar·cico** *adj.* (med.) polysarcous, obese.

pol-i·semo *adj.* (gramm.) polysemous, having many meanings; having meanings other than the literal one. **-isenso** *adj.* polysensous, equiv. to polysemous, having meanings other than the literal one; *n.m.* quibble, pun, riddle.

polisil·labo *adj.* polysyllabic; *n.m.* polysyllable.

polisillogişmo *m.* (logic) argument comprising several syllogisms.

polisi·ndeto *m.* (gramm.) polysyndeton.

†**polisin-foni·a** *f.* (mus.) harmony. †**-fo·nico** *adj.* (mus.) harmonious.

polisinte·tico *adj.* polysynthetic.

poli·stilo *adj.*, *n.m.* (archit.) polystyle, (of a) building with many columns.

polistirolo *m.* (chem.) polystyrene.

†**poli·store** *adj.* learned in many things; *n.m.* man of wide learning.

politeama *m.* theatre; variety theatre; hippodrome.

polite·cnico *adj.* polytechnic; *n.m.* polytechnic, technical school (or college); school of engineering.

polite-ismo *m.* polytheism **-ista** *m.*, *f.* polytheist. **-i·stico** *adj.* polytheistic. (**-isticamente** *adv.*)

politene *m.* (chem.) polyethylene, (pop.) 'polythene'.

politenico *adj.* (biol.) polytene; cromosomi politenici, polytenic chromosomes.

politetrafluoroeti-lene *m.* (chem.) polytetrafluorethylene, PTFE. **-le·nico** *adj.* polytetrafluorethylene; resina -lenica, polytetrafluorethylene resin.

politezza *f.* high finish, polish; fineness; finesse.

poli·ti-ca *f.* politics; policy; political theory; — interna, domestic policy, home affairs; — estera, foreign policy; — della foglia di carciofo, artichoke-leaf policy, i.e. of doing one thing at a time; parlare di —, to talk politics; voi seguite una — sbagliata, you are pursuing a wrong policy; l'onestà è la miglior —, honesty is the best policy. **-cante** *m.* (derog.) (professional) politician; petty politician, 'politico'. **-cantişmo** *m.* political intrigue. **-castro** *m.* political schemer, petty politician.

poli·ti-co *adj.* political; politic; cautious; crafty; economia -ca, political economy, economics; lega -ca, body politic; scritti -ci, political writings (works); diritti -ci, political rights; ordinamento —, constitution, political order; malattia -ca, feigned illness;

pl. ordinamenti -ci, constitution, constitutional law(s); elezioni -che, parliamentary elections; corrispondente -co, political correspondent (of a newspaper); uomo -co, politician; l'uomo è un animale -co, man is a social animal; equilibrio -co, balance of power; *n.m.* politician; politic person; schemer, cunning individual. (**-camente** *adv.*) **-chino** *adj.* dabbling in politics; (fam.) cunning; *n.m.* dabbler in politics, petty intriguer; (fam. dim. of a child) cunning little rogue. **-cone** *m.* augm. schemer; cunning fellow; rogue. (**-cona** *f.*)

politipi·a *f.* (typ.) polytype.

politonal-e *adj.* (mus.) polytonal. **-ità** *f.* (mus.) polytonality.

poli·trico *m.* (bot.) polytrichum moss, *Polytrichum.*

politro·pico *adj.* (phys.; chem.) polytropic.

poli·tropo *adj.* crafty, full of tricks; clever (also *n.m.*).

politti·co *m.* (paint.) polyptych, a painting (or series) on several folding panels.

poli-uri·a *f.* (med.) polyuria. **-u·rico** *adj.* (med.) polyuric.

poli-valente *adj.* (chem.) polyvalent. **-valenza** *f.* polyvalence.

polivin-ile *m.* (chem.) polyvinyl. **-i·lico** *adj.* polyvinyl.

polivo·mere *m.* (agric.) multi-furrow plough.

poliz-i·a *f.* (leg.) police; — giudiziaria, judicial police (C.P.); — stradale, — di circolazione, traffic police; — tributaria, excise and revenue police; autorizzazione, provvedimento di —, police permit, police order (C.P.); i poteri di —, police powers (C.P.P.); Commissariato di —, Police Station; policing, public order; (leg.) la — dell'udienza, keeping order in Court (C.P.P.); police regulations; agente di —, guardia di —, policeman; — municipale, town (city) police; le banche hanno la loro —, the banks have their information service; — sanitaria, sanitary inspectors; — scientifica, scientific crime-detection. **-iesco** *adj.* (m.pl. -ieschi) relating to the police; misure -iesche, police precautions; romanzo -iesco, detective novel. **-iotto** *m.* policeman; detective; *adj.* cane -iotto, police dog.

po·lizz-a *f.* voucher; card, ticket; voting-paper; receipt form; note, bill; lottery ticket; (leg.) — di assicurazione, insurance policy; — di assicurazione sulla vita, policy of life assurance (C.C.); — di cambio, bill of exchange; — di pegno, pawn ticket (C.C.); (comm.) — aperta, open policy; — nominata, named policy; — valutata, valued policy; — di carico, bill of lading; — d'indennità, indemnity policy; — di restituzione del dazio, drawback debenture. **-a·rio** *m.* policy register; registrar of policies. **-ino** *m.* particular forms of banker's draft, of limited negotiability, issued by certain Italian banks (C.C.); customs note (of duty payable); (eccl.) card of church membership, in some times and places given by priest to parishioners for Easter communion. **-otto** *m.* bill, handbill; large ticket, etc.

polka *f.* (mus.). See **polca**.

poll-a *f.* spring (of water). †**-are** *intr.* (of a spring) to rise.

pollachiuri·a *f.* (med.) pollakiuria.

†**pollacco** *adj.*, *n.m.* See **polacco**.

poll-a·io *m.* fowl-house, hen-coop; poultry-yard; poultry; bird's roosting-place; essere a —, to have gone to bed (to roost); tener i piedi a —, to rest one's feet on a bar, stool, etc. **-ai(u)olo**, **-arolo** *m.* poulterer. **-ame** *m.* poultry. **-anca** *f.* young turkey-hen; pullet. **-anco** *m.* turkey, young turkey (-cock). **-a·rio** *m.* (Rom. antiq.) *pullarius*, keeper of sacred chickens. **-astra** *f.* pullet; (joc.) simple girl, pretty girl. **-astro** *m.* cockerel; (fam.) simple fellow, 'mug'; stripling. **-astrone** *m.* greenhorn; overgrown boy. (**-astrona** *f.*) **-strotto** *m. dim.* simpleton.

†**pollebbro** *m.* good-for-nothing.

polleri·a *f.* poultry market; poulterer's shop; poultry.

pol·lice *m.* (anat.) thumb; big toe; inch (unit of measurement used also in measuring screens of television sets); — per —, inch by inch, little by little; non cedere di un —, not to yield an inch.

pollicino[1] *m. dim.* of **pollo**, q.v.; chicken (cf. **pulcino**).

Pollicino[2] *pr.n.m.* Tom Thumb; (fig.) diminutive person.

pollicitazione *f.* (leg.) pollicitation, unaccepted promise.

polli-coltura, **-cultura** *f.* poultry-farming; poultry-breeding. **-cultore** *m.* poultry-farmer.

pollina *f.* fowls' droppings.

†**pollinaro** *m.* See **pollinaio**.

pol·lin-e *m.* (bot.) moth mullein, *Verbascum blattaria*; pollen.

pollino[1] *adj.* See under **pollo**.

pollino[2] *m.* swamp; bog; quicksand; floating island.

pollivendolo *m.* poulterer.

pọll-o *m.* (orn.) chicken, barndoor fowl; — sultano, purple gallinule, *Porphyrio porphyrio*; allevamento di -i, poultry-farm; — d'India, turkey; andare a letto coi -i, all'ora dei -i, to go to bed very early; alzarsi coi -i, to get up at cock-crow; — arrosto, roast chicken; — lesso, — bollito, boiled chicken; — d'allevamento, boiling fowl; brodo di —, chicken broth; (fig.) essere un — freddo, to be a poor fish; conoscere i propri -i, to know whom one has to deal with; cose da far ridere i -i, fit to make a cat laugh; essere un buon —, to be a 'mug'; essere come i -i di mercato, to be a mixture (i.e. some good, some bad); roba da gettare ai -i, rubbish; piede di —, Matthew Walker knot; piede di — coronato, crown knot; piede di — doppio, French shroud knot, double wall knot; piede di — semplice; single wall knot. **-ina** *f.* fowl excrement used as manure. **-ino** *adj.* relating to fowls, of fowls or poultry; pidocchio -ino, bird-louse; (fam.) occhio -ino, soft corn (on the toes).

pollọn-e *m.* (bot.) sucker, stolon; — selvatico stock (in grafting). **-ẹto** *m.* nursery bed of suckers, cuttings, etc.; plantation of young chestnut-trees grown to make stakes.

Pol·luce *pr.n.m.* (myth.; astron.) Pollux.

pollu-to *adj.* polluted, defiled. **-zione** *f.* (med.) pollution, involuntary emission of semen.

†polmento *m.* soup of lentils or broad beans; food.

polmọn-e *m.* (anat.) lung; (med.) — d'acciaio, iron lung; aver buoni -i, to have good lungs, to have a strong voice; (fig.) ci ho rimesso un —, ci ho consumato i -i, I have wasted my breath; (fam.) sputare i -i, to have a violent fit of coughing, *or* to speak very loud, to shout; (fig.) allargarsi i -i, to breathe freely (after anxiety); i parchi sono i -i di Londra, the parks are the lungs of London; (zool.) — marino, a kind of medusa; (naut.) — artificiale, aqua-lung; — idropneumatico, vent, servomotor operating the diving and blowing valves. **-ale, -are** *adj.* (anat.; med.) pulmonary. **-a·ria** *f.* (naut.) hulk, overflow ship or accommodation vessel. **-ati** *m.pl.* (zool.) pulmonate snails. **-ite, -i·a, †-e·a** *f.* (med.) pneumonia; inflammation of the lungs.

pol-o *m.* (geog.) pole, — artico, — nord, — boreale, North Pole; — antartico, — del sud, South Pole; — magnetico, Magnetic Pole; — negativo, negative pole, (crystal.) — negativo, antilogous pole.

polocito *m.* (biol.) polar body.

Polo·n-ia *pr.n.f.* (geog.) Poland. **-ẹse** *f.* (mus.) Polonaise.

polo·nico *adj.* See **polacco**.

polo·nio *m.* (chem.) polonium.

pọlp-a *f.* pulp; flesh; — di manzo, beef without bones; (anat.) — dentaria, dental pulp; (bot) pulp (of fruit); pith; (industr.) — di legno, wood pulp. **†-ac·cia** *f.* see **polpetta**. **-ac·cio** *m.* calf (of the leg); base of the thumb. **-acciuolo** *m.* fleshy part of the thumb or finger; meat (beef, etc.); pad, wad. **-acciuto** *adj.* plump, fleshy. **-astrello** *m.* fleshy tip of finger or thumb. **-ẹtta** *f.* (cul.) croquette, rissole, meat-ball; (fig.; fam.) far -ette di uno, to make mincemeat of someone; (cul.) -etta di mare, minced meat with fish liver, roasted; poisoned food. **-ettọne** *m.* hash, minced meat (sometimes eaten cold in slices); severe scolding; big book of little value. **-ọso** *adj.* pulpy, fleshy (esp. of fruit). **-uto** *adj.* fleshy, plump, gambe -ute, fat legs; terreno -uto, rich land; vino -uto, strong wine (with 'body').

pọlp-o *m.* (zool.) octopus; — bianco, *Ozoena aldrovandii*; — muschiato, *Eledone moscata*; — comune, *Octopus vulgaris*. **-ara** *f.* (naut.) octopus fishing tackle.

pọls-o *m.* (anat.; med.) pulse; tastare il — a uno, to feel someone's pulse, (fig.) to sound, to probe, someone; — frequente, quick, rapid pulse; wrist; stringere i -i a uno, to tie someone's wrists; legare uno ai -i, to tie someone by the wrists; (fig.) strength, nerve, energy; skill; gli manca il —, he hasn't the strength; lavoro di —, work requiring skill and strength; di —, clever, skilful, vigorous, strong; con — fermo, with a strong hand; orologio da —, wrist-watch; gemelli da —, cuff-links. **-eggiare** [A 3 c] *intr.* (aux. avere) to pulsate, to beat. **-ino, †-etto** *m. dim.* cuff, wristband; -ini alla moschettiera, double cuffs.

†polta *f.* See **polenta**.

polt-i·glia *f.* gruel, mush; ridurre in —, to cook to a mush; — per empiastro, poultice; mud, slush. **-iglioso** *adj.* mushy; muddy; slushy. **-ric·chio** *m.* mess.

pọltr-o *adj.* lazy; idle; inert. **-ac·chio** *m.* colt, foal. **-ire** [D 2] *intr.* (aux. avere) to lie lazily in bed; to be lazy; to live in idleness; to wallow; to be sunk in sloth.

poltrọn-a *f.* lazy woman; armchair, easy-chair; — a sdraio, chaise-longue; — a dondolo, rocking-chair; chair of office; (theatr.) stall. **-ag·gine** *f.* laziness. **-cello** *adj. dim.* rather lazy. **-cina** *f.* small easy-chair; (theatr.) back stall, reserved seat. **-e** *m.* lazy fellow, slacker; coward, poltroon; (zool.) sloth; *adj.* lazy; cowardly. **-eggiare** [A 3 c] *intr.* (aux. avere) to idle, to be lazy; to live in idleness; to loiter. **-eri·a** *f.* laziness, indolence, sloth; cowardice. **-ẹsco** *adj.* (m.pl. -ẹschi) lazy, indolent. **-escamẹnte** *adv.* lazily. **-is·sime** *f.pl.* (theatr.) front rows of the stalls, orchestra stalls. **-ite** *f.* (joc.) laziness (as a disease).

†poltruc·cio *m.* cold (cf. **puledro**).

†polvento *adv. phr.* a —, sheltered from the wind.

pọlver-e, †pọlve *f.* dust; powder; una nube di —, a cloud of dust; sollevare —, to raise the dust; spegner la —, to lay the dust (with water); fare la —, to do the dusting; gettar — negli occhi ad uno, to throw dust in someone's eyes; — da fucile, — pirica, gun-powder; in —, powdered, in powder form; zucchero in —, powdered sugar, castor sugar; caffè in — (or — di caffè), ground coffee; medicinal powder; — di vetro, powdered glass; — di riso, ground rice, or rice powder; — di Cipro, powder for the hair, face-powder; — di tabacco, snuff; — di Pimpirimpi, magic powder; mordere la —, to bite the dust; mandare, ridurre in —, to reduce to dust; (fig.) scuotere la — di dosso, to beat, to thrash; orologio a —, hour-glass; sand (formerly used for drying writing-ink); — d'oro, powdered gold (for making gold paint); (comm.) abbuono per —, tret; (text.) — di battitore, scutcher fly; — di ventilatore, fanny. **-ac·cio** *m. pejor.* (unpleasant) dust; fertilizer (in powder). **-a·ia** *f.* cloud of dust, dust blown by the wind. **-a·io** *adj.* raising dust, dusty. **-iera** *f.* (mil.) magazine, powder magazine. **-ifi·cio** *m.* powder-factory; powder-mill. **-ina** *f. dim.* (medicinal) powder; magic powder; (bot.) pollen. **-ino** *m.* sand-box (for drying ink); sand (for the same), pounce; mettere il -ino a, to approve (what is written), to pass; -ino di carbone, coal dust; -ino di miniera, slack; (mil. hist.) priming powder; powder flask; sand-glass; coal dust. **-io** *m.* (*pl.* -ii) cloud of dust, dust carried by the wind. **-ista** *m.* (techn.) worker in a powder-mill. **-iẓẓa·bile** *adj.* pulverizable. (**-iẓẓabilità** *f.*) **-iẓẓamẹnto** *m.* pulverizing, pulverization; destruction; pulverized matter. **-iẓẓare** [A I], **†-eggiare** *tr.* to pulverize; to powder; (of a liquid, in a spray, etc.) to atomize; (fig.) to destroy; *rfl.* to be reduced to powder; to be destroyed; to disappear. (**-iẓẓato** *part. adj.*) **-iẓẓatọre** *m.* (techn.) sprayer, spray, spray-gun, nozzle, atomizer; duster. **-iẓẓazione** *f.* (techn.) pulverization; spraying, atomizing. **-ọne** *m. augm.* great cloud of dust. **-ọso** *adj.* dusty; *n.m.* a kind of marble found near Pistoia. **-ulento** *adj.* powdery, pulverulent. **-ume** *m.* dust; heap of dust.

polv-i·glio *m.* fine powder; snuff, face-powder, medicinal powder, gunpowder; lavender-bag (sachet). **†-ino** *m.* down, light fluff. **-i·scolo** *m.* very fine dust, fine spray.

†polzella *f.* girl, maiden.

†poma *f.* See **pomo**.

pom-a·io, -a·rio, †-aro *m.* orchard; nursery for fruit trees. **†-aran·cio** *m.* (bot.) orange, *Citrus sinensis*. **-ata** *f.* pomade, pomatum; ointment, salve; brilliantine, cold-cream, etc. **-ato** *adj.* planted with fruit-trees; giardino -ato, orchard, fruit garden; (vet.) (of a horse's coat) pommelled. **-ello** *m.* (anat.) cheek bone; (eng.) knob, ball, handle. **-ettato** *adj.* (herald.) croce -ettata, cross pommeted, cross pommy.

pomer *m. indecl.* pom, pomeranian dog.

pomer-idiano *adj.* (of the) afternoon; alle 5 -idiane, at 5 p.m.; seduta -idiana, afternoon session. **-ig·gio** *m.* afternoon; di -iggio, in the afternoon; edizione del -iggio, evening (afternoon) edition.

pome·rio *m.* (Rom. antiq.) pomerium; (mil.) clearing intentionally left round a glacis.

pomẹto *m.* See under **pomo**.

pọmic-e *f.* (miner.) pumice. **-iare** [A 3] *tr.* to pumice, to sand; to rub, to smooth with pumice-stone. (**-iato** *part. adj.*) **-iatura** *f.* smoothing with pumice-stone; (techn.) sanding. **-iọso, †-oso** *adj.* bearing pumice; like pumice (-stone).

pomidoro *m.* (zool.; bot.). See under **pomo**.

Pomino *pr.n.m.* (geog.) Pomino, in Tuscany; wine from this district.

pommer *m. indecl.* (mus.) pommer (obs. species of oboe).

pom-o *m.* apple, *Malus silvestris*; — d'Adamo, lime, *Citrus auranti-folia*; Citron, *C. medica*; — di terra, potato; — di acajou, cashew

pom·o (*cont.*)
nut, *Anacardium occidentale*; — di sodoma, *Solanum sodomaeum*; -i al forno, baked apples; vino di —, cider; fruit; — vietato, forbidden fruit; (door-) knob; rounded top, head (of walking-stick, dagger, etc.), pommel (e.g. of a sword); orb (with cross, carried by emperor or king); rose (of watering-can); (anat.) — d'Adamo, Adam's apple, prominentia laryngea; (naut.) Turk's head, a large knot on the end of a rope; a stopper (chem.). -**eto** *m.* (apple-) orchard; fruit-garden. -**icultore** *m.* fruit-farmer; apple grower. -**icultura** *f.* fruit-farming. -**idoro** *m.* (*pl.* -idoro, -idori) (bot.) tomato, *Solanum lycopersicum*; salsa di -idoro, tomato sauce; rosso come un -idoro, (fam.) red as a beetroot; (zool.) -idoro di sabbia, *Cereactis aurantiaca*, and -idoro di scoglio, *Actinia equina*, two species of sea anemone. -**odoro** *m.* (*pl.* -odori) see **pomidoro**. -**ogranato** *m.* see **melagrano**. -**ologia** *f.* pomology. -**olo·gico** *adj.* pomologist. -**oso** *adj.* fruitful, rich in fruits; autunno -oso, fruitful Autumn.

pomolo *m.* (eng.) knob, ball handle.

Pomo̱na *pr.n.f.* (myth.) Pomona, goddess of fruit and fruit-trees.

†**pomonte** *m.* region beyond the hill.

pomp-a¹ *f.* pomp; ostentation, display; con gran —, with great pomp; -e funebri, funerals, funeral ceremonies, imprenditore di -e funebri, undertaker; a —, ostentatiously; far — di dottrina, to parade one's learning.

pomp-a² *f.* pump; — da incendio, fire-engine; — da (*or* per) bicicletta, bicycle pump; (med.) vomito a —, projectile vomiting; (mus.) tuning-slide. -**ag·gio** *m.* pumping; stazione di -aggio, pumping-station. -**are** [A I C] *tr.* to pump, to pump up. -**ata** *f.* pump-full; pumping. (-ato *part. adj.*) -**atura** *f.* pumping; swelling.

pompeggi-are [A 3 c] *intr.* (*aux.* avere) (poet.) to make a display, to show off; to attract attention, to strike the eye; -ava di gioielli, her jewellery made a fine show; la campagna -a nelle sue bionde messi, the country is bright with golden corn; *rfl.* to deck oneself out; to show off; to flaunt oneself; to strut.

Pompe-i *pr.n.f.* (hist. geog.) Pompeii. -**iano** *adj.*, *n.m.* Pompeian. (-iana *f.*)

pompelmo *m.* grape-fruit, pummelo, shaddock, *Citrus grandis*.

Pompe-o *pr.n.m.* Pompey, Pompeius. -**iano** *m.* partisan of Pompey.

pompier-e *m.* fireman; i pompieri, the fire-brigade; aiuto -i, fire-engine.

pom·pilo *m.* (ichth.) tunny, *Thunnus thynnus*.

pompo̱so *adj.* stately, ostentatious, magnificent; pompous; (mus.) ceremonious, majestic; viola -a, instrument invented by J. S. Bach. -**amente** *adv.* ostentatiously, pompously. -**ità** *f.* pomp; pomposity, pompousness; -ità di stile, affectation, pompousness.

ponc-e *m.*, -**ino** *m.* punch (drink); — al rum, rum punch.

po·ncio *m.* poncho, S. American cloak, as worn by Garibaldi.

ponder-are [A I C] *tr.* to ponder, to think over (or on), to weigh; — ogni parola, to weigh every word; to muse, to meditate upon; *intr.* (*aux.* avere) to meditate; to muse. -**a·bile** *adj.* ponderable; having weight; deserving consideration. -**abilità** *f.* ponderability. -**atezza** *f.* deliberation, circumspection; carefulness, habitual caution; un uomo di grande -atezza, a man who weighs matters carefully. -**ato** *part. adj.* considered, deliberate; careful; circumspect; discorso -ato, carefully thought out speech; giudizio -ato, considered judgement; persona -ata, cautious person; tutto -ato, all things considered. -**atamente** *adv.* deliberately, thoughtfully; with due consideration; deliberare -atamente, to consider thoroughly. -**atore** *m.*, -**atrice** *f.*, *adj.* giustizia -atrice, even-handed justice. -**azione** *f.* pondering, reflection; consideration; (gramm.) analysis, critical examination; (statist.) weighting. -**omotore** *adj.* (phys.) ponderomotive. (-omotrice *f.*) -**osità** *f.* gravity, ponderousness; weight. -**oso** *adj.* ponderous, heavy; laborious.

pond-o *m.* weight; load; burden; gravity, importance; †pound (weight); †mal di —, *or* †mal di -i, dysentery.

ponent-e *m.* west; andare verso —, to go west(wards); west wind; a —, facing westwards, on the west side; (geog.) Riviera di —, the Italian Riviera between Genoa and the French frontier; (eccl.) *ponens relator* (in causes of beatification). -**elibec·cio** *m.* wind from west-south-west. -**ello** *m.* light west wind. -**ema·estro** *m.* wind from west-north-west. -**ino** *m.* light westerly breeze; *adj.* western, of the west.

†**po·nere** *vb.* and derivs. See **porre**.

poney *m. indecl.* (zool.) pony.

poni-me̱nto *m.* placing, laying; — di mani, laying on of hands; †— del sole, sunset. -**tore** *m.* (paperm.) coucher (cf. **porre**).

†**ponsò** *m.* bright red, flame colour.

ponta·io *m.* See under **ponte**.

†**pontare** *tr.* to stop; to fix (cf. **appuntare**).

pont-e *m.* (archit.) bridge; stage; scaffolding; — ferroviario, railway bridge; — girevole, swing bridge; — levatoio, drawbridge; — di barche, bridge of boats; — di chiatte, pontoon bridge; — a schiena d'asino, humpbacked bridge; — pensile, — sospeso, suspension bridge; — sospeso da catene, chain-bridge; — pensile, *also* painter's cradle; bruciare i -i, to burn one's bridges; fare — a, to serve as a bridge across, (fig.) to give a leg up to, to support; (provb.) a nemico che fugge -i d'oro, give every facility to a retreating enemy; (naut.) deck; — di batteria, main deck, battery deck; — di comando, bridge: — di coperta, upper deck; — corazzato, armoured deck; — di corridoio, middle deck; — di sbarco, gangplank; — di stazza, lower deck; — di volo, flight deck (carriers); primo —, hold, the lowest deck; (Venice) — canale, sewer; (geom.) — dell'asino, *pons asinorum*; (geom.) giuoco del —, bridge; (watchm.) cock; — d'ancora, pallet cock; — del bilanciere, balance cock; — di forcella, pin pallet cock; (mus.) bridge-passage; (motor.) rear axle; (radio) — radio, radio link. -**a·io** *m.* scaffold-builder; toll-collector on a bridge. -**ata** *f.* stage of scaffolding; finire una -ata, to complete a stage (of building or painting). -**ato** *adj.* bridged. -**ecanale** *m.* aqueduct. -**eggio** *m.* (bldg.) scaffolding; staging; -eggio tubulare, tubular scaffolding. -**icello** *m. dim.* small bridge, foot-bridge; (mus.) bridge (of stringed instrument); sul -icello, with the bow close to the bridge; (watchm.) cock; (mil.) handguard on a sword, joining the basket to the hilt; trigger guard; (naut.) fiddles, bad weather table fittings used to prevent cutlery from sliding; chiodo a -icello, staple. -**icino** *m. dim.* (billiards) cue test. -**iere** *m.* (mil.) sapper in a bridge construction unit.

pont-e·fice *m.*, †-**i·fice** *m.* (Rom. hist.) pontifex; (Bibl.) Jewish High Priest; (eccl.) bishop; (now nearly always) the Supreme Pontiff, the Pope.

Po·ntici *pr.n.m.pl.* (geog.) Pontine Mountains.

†**po·ntico** *adj.* harsh, sharp, sour.

pontiere *m.* See under **ponte**.

pontific-ale *adj.* (Rom. hist.) pontifical, of a pontifex; (eccl.) pontifical, of a bishop or pope; messa —, pontifical High Mass (as sung by bishop or abbot); in —, in full pontificals; caso —, sin whose absolution is reserved to the Pope; *n.m.* pontifical, *pontificale*, book of ceremonies for bishops; pontifical function (normally Mass or Vespers). -**almente** *adv.* pontifically. -**are** [A 2 s] *intr.* (*aux.* avere) (eccl.; fig.) to pontificate. -**ato** *m.* (Rom. hist.; eccl.) pontificate.

pontifi·cio *adj.* (Rom. hist.) pontifical; (eccl.) papal, pontifical.

pontile *m.* (naut.) landing-stage, boat-wharf.

Pontine *pr.n.f.pl.* (geog.) the Pontine marshes.

ponto *m.* (poet.) sea; *pr.n.m.* (geog.) il Ponto Eusino, the Black Sea; †Ocean.

ponton-e *m.* (naut.) lighter, pontoon, dumb lighter; hulk; — armato, monitor; gunboat; — a biga, sheer hulk, floating crane; — per salpare, mooring lighter; — a sbarco carri armati, tank-landing craft (L.C.T.); (mil.) pontoon used for bridging. -**iere** *m.* (mil.) member of a bridge-building unit of sappers using pontoons.

†**pontura** *f.* See **puntura**.

ponz-are [A I C] *intr.* (*aux.* avere) to strain, to make an effort; *tr.* (fig.) to meditate upon; to think about (with a view to producing); ha -ato un romanzo, he has been thinking of writing a novel; (iron.) to produce after a great effort. -**amento** *m.* straining, effort; -amento del parto, straining in childbirth; (fig.) mental effort, cogitation. (-atore *m.* -atrice *f.*) -**atura** *f.* straining, prolonged effort.

Po·nzio *pr.n.m.* Pontius; — Pilato, Pontius Pilate.

†**ponzò** *m.* See **ponsò**.

popa¹ *m.* (Rom. antiq.) *popa*, priest's assistant at sacrifice.

popa² *f.* See **pupa**.

pope *m.* (Eastern Churches) pope, parish priest.

†**popin-a** *f.* tavern, inn. †-**one** *m.* glutton.

po·plit-e *m.* (anat.) poples, the back of the knee. -**e·o** *adj.* (anat.) popliteal; muscolo -eo, poplitaeus.

popo *m.* See **pope**.

popolano *adj.*, *n.m.* See under **popolo¹**.

popolar-e[1] *adj.* popular, enjoying popularity; render —, to make popular, *or* to popularize; common, prevalent; of the people, popular; canto —, folk-song, *or* popular song; relating to a crowd; adunata —, mass meeting; *n.m., f.* man, or woman, of the people. **-mente** *adv.* popularly; commonly, generally. **-ęsco** *adj.* (*m.pl.* **-ęschi**) common, vulgar, plebeian; favore **-esco**, popular favour, favour of the people; vocabolo **-esco**, vulgar word, dialect word, term used by common people. (**-escaménte** *adv.*) **-ità** *f.* popularity; acquistare **-ità**, to gain popularity; avido di **-ità**, eager for popularity. **-iẓẓare** [A I] *tr.* to popularize; to vulgarize; to make accessible to the common man. (**-iẓẓato** *part. adj.* **-iẓẓaẓióne** *f.*)

popol-are[2] [A I S] *tr.* to populate; to people; to colonize; to crowd; *rfl.* to become populated; to become peopled; to become crowded; Londra si **-a** sempre più di stranieri, London is becoming more and more crowded with foreigners. **-ato** *part. adj.* (*prep.* di) populated (with); un paese densamente **-ato**, a densely populated country; populous, crowded; strade **-ate**, crowded streets; scuole **-atissime**, overcrowded schools.

popolaẓióne *f.* population; censimento della —, population census; eccesso di —, overpopulation; populace, people; la — qui è molto laboriosa, the people here are very industrious; race, stock, people; le popolazioni germaniche, the Germanic races.

po·pol-o[1] *m.* people; nation; tribe; il — d'Israele, the children of Israel; il — eletto, the chosen people; un — bellicoso, a warlike nation; crowd, multitude, populace; il — gremiva la piazza, the square was swarming with people; il — minuto, the common people, the working class; è venuto su dal —, he has risen from the working class; (hist.) il — grasso, the (wealthy) middle class; medieval Florentine republic; capitano del —, magistrate in the Florentine republic; il — e il comune, all the inhabitants of a town; (fig.) lo sa il — e il comune, it is common knowledge; (eccl.) people of a parish; (provb.) a — pazzo prete spiritato, if you ask for trouble you'll get it, people only get what they deserve. **-ac·cio** *m. pejor.*, **-a·glia** *f. pejor.* mob, rabble, scum. **-ano** *adj.* of the people, democratic; *n.m.* man of the people; workman, artisan; commoner; (eccl.) parishioner. (**-ana** *f.*) **-aẓẓo** *m.* (derog.) rabble, vulgar herd. **-ino** *m. dim.* the common people, the lower classes; simple people; (numism.) a silver Florentine coin. **-óso** *adj.* populous; (fig.) abundant, numerous; (poet.) ella i ciliegi **-osi** miete (Pascoli), she gathers the plentiful cherries.

†**po·polo**[2] *m.* (bot.). See **pioppo**.

popón-e *m.* (bot.) melon, *Cucumis melo*, and other species; — amaro, colocynth, *Citrullus colocynthis*; (fig.) hump. **-a·ia** *f.* melon bed. **-a·io** *m.* melon-seller; see **poponaia**. **-cino** *m.pl.* (bot.) squirting cucumber, *Ecballium elaterium*. **-ella**, **-essa** *f.* (bot.) bottle gourd, *Lagenaria siceraria*. †**-eto** *m.* see **poponaia**.

popp-a[1] *f.* (anat.) breast; dare la — a, to suckle, to give the breast to, to breast-feed; levar la — a, to wean; bimbo da —, suckling, baby; volere ancor la —, to behave like a baby; swarm of bees; (agric.) — di Venere, a luscious kind of peach; †chest. **-aiola** *f.* feeding bottle. **-aióne** *m.* (agric.) sucker. **-ante** *part., n.m., f.* suckling; baby at the breast (also *adj.*). **-are** [A I] *intr.* (*aux.* avere) to suck (at the breast); *tr.* to suck up; (joc.) to 'lap up', to drink greedily; *rfl.* (*dat. of prn.* 'si') **-arsi** le dita, to suck one's fingers; **-arsi** tutto il vino, to drink up all the wine. **-ata** *f.* feed (from the breast or bottle). **-atina** *f.* teat. **-atóio** *m.* rubber (or otherwise artificial) teat; dummy; feeding-bottle; apparatus for drawing oil from a bottle. **-ellina** *f. dim.* small teat, nipple. **-ina** *f.* (agric.) shoot of a sucker; 'eye' of a plant. **-ino** *adj.* breast-shaped, well rounded (of apples, pears, etc.). **-uta** *f.*, *adj.* full-breasted, big-bosomed.

popp-a[2] *f.* (naut.) stern; — quadra, — tonda, square stern, rounded stern; albero di —, mizzen mast; dritto di —, ruota di —, sternpost; slancio di —, counter; da — a prua, fore and aft, from stern to stem; †per l'anca di —, on the quarter; in —, astern; andar in —, to run with sails filled; passare da —, to pass under the stern (of another ship); †dare la —, to escape; mollare in —, to make for shelter. **-avi·a** *f.* (naut.) *adv. phr.* a **-avia**, aft, astern, aloft. **-ęse** *adj.* (naut.) pertaining to the stern; *n.m.* stern moorings; mizzen shrouds. **-ętta** *f.* (naut.) sternsheet; stern locker, space between the backboard and the transom of a boat. **-iere** *m.* (naut.) quarterdeckman, sternsheetsman; stroke oar; (Venice) gondolier, stern oarsman. **-iero** *adj., adv.* (naut.) aft, astern, abaft the beam; caduta **-iera**, leech of a sail.

popu·l-eo *adj.* of the poplar-tree, poplar; having poplars, planted with poplars; fronda **-ea**, poplar leaf; (poet.) sul — Po, on the banks of the Po which are rich in poplars.

†**po·pulo** *m.* See **popolo**[1].

por *f. apocop.* See **porta**.

porca *f.* See under **porco**.

porcell-ana[1] *f.* (zool.) cowrie. **-ętta** *f. dim.* (zool.) small cowrie. **-ętto** *m.* (ent.) woodlouse, *Porcellio* spp.

porcellana[2] *f.* porcelain; china; articoli di —, porcelain ware, china ware; terra di —, china clay; (vet.) blue roan horse.

porcellana[3] *f.* (bot.) candytuft, *Iberis*; sweet alison, *Lobularia maritima*; purslane, *Portulaca oleracea*; — di mare, salt bush, *Atriplex halimus*.

porcello *m. dim. and derivs.* See under **porco**.

por-co *m.* pig, swine; (carne di) —, pork; boar; (ichth.) pesce —, — di mare, *Oxynotus centrina*, a kind of shark; *Murex trunculus*, a kind of whelk; — spino, hedgehog, *Erinaceus* spp.; porcupine, *Hystrix* spp.; sudicio come un —, dirty as a pig; mangia come un —, he eats like a pig; far l'occhio del —, to look askance; fa la vita del beato —, he lives to eat and drink and enjoy himself; perle buttate ai **-ci**, pearls cast before swine; (slang) jemmy; (eng.) piè di —, lever bar; *adj.* (vulg.) filthy; questa **-a** vita!, this wretched life!; **-a** miseria!, hell! **-caménte** *adv.* swinishly, piggishly; filthily. **-ca** *f.* (zool.) sow; (fig.) slut, dirty woman; unchaste woman; (agric.) ridge between two furrows. **-cacchióne** *m.* filthy person; foul-mouthed person. (**-cacchióna** *f.*) **-cacchiuolo** *m. dim.* boy with dirty habits, dirty little pig. **-cac·cio** *m. pejor.* (term of abuse) dirty pig, filthy swine. **-ca·io**, **-caro** *m.* swineherd; (fig.) pigsty, filthy place. **-caiuolo** *m.* swineherd. **-caręccia** *f.* (agric.) pig-farm; pigsty. **-cata** *f.* see **porcheria**. **-cella** *f.* (zool.) young sow, gilt. **-cellinac·cio** *m.* dirty boy, filthy brat. **-cellino** *m. dim.* piglet; sucking pig; star fermo e cheto come un **-cellino** grattato, to put up with everything; (fig.) dirty child; (zool.) **-cellino** d'India, guinea-pig; **-cellino** di mare, see 'porco di mare'; (zool.) **-cellino** di terra, woodlouse (also **porcelletto**). **-cello** *m.* young pig. **-cellóne** *m. augm.* (fig.) dirty person; immoral person. **-cellóna** *f.* slut. **-cellotto** *m.* fat young pig. **-cherec·cio** *adj.* of pigs; spiedo **-cherec·cio**, boar spear. **-cheri·a** *f.* dirt, filth; dirty trick; obscenity, indecency; lavoro che è una **-cheria**, botched work. **-cheriola** *f.* dirty trick. **-chętta** *f. dim.* (cul.) sucking pig roasted on a spit or in the oven, with spices. **-chętto** *m. dim.*, **-chettuolo** *m. dim.* (fig.) youth who behaves indecently. **-ciglióne** *m.* (orn.) water rail, *Rallus aquaticus*. **-cile** *m.* pigsty; wild boar's den; *adj.* porcine. **-cina** *f.* pork. **-cinello** (bot.) *Boletus scaber* (fungus). **-cino** *adj.* porcine, pig; piggish; carne **-cina**, pork; occhio **-cino**, pig's eye; (bot.) *B. edulis* (edible fungus); pan **-cino**, sow-bread, *Cyclamen*. **-cóne** *m.* (fig.) very dirty person, filthy person. (**-cóna** *f.*) **-concello** *m. dim.* dirty young man. **-cume** *m.* lot of pigs; (fig.) lot of dirt; filth; obscenities.

po·rfido *m.* (miner.) porphyry; *pl.* (geol.) porphyries; slab on which powders are ground, for paints, etc.

Porfiriani *pr.n.m.pl.* (philos.; eccl. hist.) Porphyrians.

porf-i·rico, **-i·reo** *adj.* of, or like, porphyry. **-ite** *f.* (miner.) porphyrite. **-iẓẓare** [A I] *tr.* (techn.) to grind with a porphyry grindstone. **-iẓẓaẓióne** *f.* (techn.) grinding, etc. **-oge·nito** *adj., n.m.* born in the purple, imperial; sovereign; (fig., of Christians) reborn in the blood of Christ.

†**por·f-iro**, †**-i·rio** *m.* See **porfido**.

por·g-ere [C 4] *tr.* to hold out, to offer, to give, to hand; to reach out, to stretch out; to bring; — aiuto, to give aid; **-igli** da bere, give him something to drink; **-imi** quel libro, hand me that book; **-ete** i miei ossequi a vostra madre, give my kind regards to your mother; — la mano a, to hold out one's hand to, to give one's hand to, (fig.) to give a helping hand to, to lend a hand; — la destra, to hold out one's hand; — orecchio, — ascolto, to listen; — l'attenzione, to pay attention; — la morte, to be deadly, to bring death; — paura a, to strike fear into, to be frightening; *abs.* to declaim, to recite; arte del —, elocution; *intr.* (*aux.* essere) to stick out; *rfl.* to offer oneself, to show oneself; si **-eva** pietoso ai mali altrui, he showed himself compassionate towards the misfortunes of others; se si **-e** l'occasione, if opportunity offers. **-imento** *m.* offering, offer; bringing. **-itóre** *m.* bearer, bringer, il **-itore** della presente è un mio vecchio amico, the bearer of this letter is an old friend of mine. (**-itrice** *f.*)

pornogr-afi·a *f.* pornography. **-a·fico** *adj.* pornographic.

por·o *m.* (anat.; bot.) pore. **-icida** *m.* (bot.) capsule opening by pores. **-osità** *f.* porousness, porosity. **-oso** *adj.* porous.

porpezite *f.* (miner.) porpezite.

por·por·a *f.* purple; crimson; (zool.) various kinds of dog whelk, etc.; (fig.) cardinalship; (med.) purpura; (herald.) purpure. **-a·io** *m.* (antiq.) purple-dyer, *purpurarius*. **-ato** *adj.* clothed in purple, wearing purple; *n.m.* (eccl.) cardinal. **-eggiante** *part. adj.* purplish. **-eggiare** [ʌ3c] *intr.* (aux. avere) to be purplish, to turn purple; to crimson. **-ino** *adj. dim.* (of lips, etc.) rosy; reddish; red. **-o** *m.* see **porpora**.

porr·ac·cia *f.* (bot.) — de' fossi, *Thelygonum cynocrambe*. **-a·ceo** *adj.* leek-coloured. **-andello** *m.* (bot.) *Allium ampeloprasum*, wild leek.

porre [B21] *tr.* (used mainly of objects one can carry personally, otherwise **mettere**, q.v.; usu. abbrev. to **por** before a consonant) to put, to set, to place; to lay; lo porrò sulla tavola, I will put it on the table; pose a terra il carico, he laid his load on the ground; — la prima pietra, to lay the foundation stone; (fig.) to set; — mente a, to put one's mind to; — in libertà, to set free; — in non cale, to set at naught; — un freno a, to check, to put a stop to; poniamo il caso che, let us suppose that; to agree, to arrange; ponemmo di ritrovarci il mese prossimo, we arranged to meet again next month; senza por tempo in mezzo, without delay; por mano a, to set one's hand to, to begin; non posi mente a quel che egli faceva, I did not notice what he was doing; — in disparte, to lay aside, to leave alone; — ad effetto, to make effective, to carry out; — un termine, to fix a limit; — termine a, to finish, to put an end to; — ai voti, to put to the vote; — a consiglio, to take advice; — nome a, to give a name to; — tributo a, to impose a tax on; — a oro, to gild; (agric.) — un terreno a vigna, to plant a piece of ground with vines, to plant a vineyard; — discosti, to space out (in planting trees, plants); †to shape, to draw; *rfl.* to place oneself, to set oneself; mi pongo a sedere, I'll take a seat; to proceed; si pose al lavoro, he set to work.

porrectus *m. indecl.* (mus.) porrectus (plainchant neum).

porr·o *m.* (bot.) leek, *Allium porrum*; wild leek, *A. ampeloprasum*; mangiare il — per la coda, to begin at the wrong end; predicare ai -i, to waste one's breath; piantare un —, to give a false impression, to deceive; (surg.) wart; (vet.) papilloma. **-etto** *m.* (vet.) see **porro**. **-ina** *f.* bulbous part of the leek; young chestnut-tree grown for its wood. **-oso** *adj.* warty, full of warts.

port·a¹ *f.* (†**porti** *m.pl.*). **1** THRESHOLD; opening; door; doorway; — principale, front door; — secondaria, back door; — di servizio, tradesmen's entrance; — segreta, private door, secret door; — a due battenti, double door; — volante, swing door; — imbottita, padded door; accompagnare uno alla —, to see a person to the door, to show out; mettere alla —, to turn out (of doors); sbattere la — in faccia a uno, to slam the door in someone's face; bussare alla —, to knock at the door; infilare la —, to hurry through the door; pigliare la —, to go out, to go away; essere — a — con, to be next door to; andare di — in —, to beg from door to door; aprire le -e a, to open one's doors to; chiudere la — a, to put an end to negotiations; (leg.) udienza a -e chiuse, hearing in Chambers (C.C.P.), trial in camera (C.P.P.); (admin.) riunione a -e chiuse, meeting *in camera*, in private, behind closed doors; secret session; vendere a -e chiuse, to sell lock, stock and barrel; (naut.) — stagna, watertight door. **2.** GATE, gateway; main gate of a city; fuori —, outside the city gate, beyond the city walls; (Rom. antiq.) *porta decumana* (in camp); (eccl.) — Santa, Holy Door (at St Peter's); (hist.) la Sublime —, the Sublime Porte; (fig.) dare la — a, to let in, to allow to enter; vietare la — a, to refuse admission to; (mil.) gateway; frontier gate or pass; (geog.) gate. **3.** EXIT; (mil. hist.) — di soccorso, sally port, secret exit, (naut.) escape hatch, (bus, etc.) emergency exit. **4.** (ANAT.) vena —, portal vein. **-ale** *m.* (archit.) portal, doorway. **-ella** *f. dim.* little door (of oven, etc.). **-ellino** *m.* (naut.) scuttle; (Merchant Navy) port-hole; **-ellino** quadrato, square port; **-ellino** di murata, ship's side-scuttle. **-ello** *m. dim.* little door, cupboard-door, etc.; postern gate; (art) shutter or folding cover for pictures; (naut.) square port, gun-port; †shot hole; †sweep port (for the oars of a galley); †masthole. **-eri·a** *f.* porter's lodge. **-icciuola** *f. dim.* little door, postern; oven-door, etc.; †(mil.) postern. **-iere** *m.* see under **portiera**.

porta·² *pref.* carrier, holder, etc.

†**porta·cqua** *m.* water carrier.

port-ae·rei *m. indecl.*, **-aeroplani** *m. indecl.* aircraft carrier. **-aghi** *m. indecl.* (med.) needle holder. **-ampolle** *m. indecl.* cruet-stand.

porta-baga·gli *m. indecl.* luggage-rack, luggage carrier, porter. **-bandiera** *m.* (mil.) standard-bearer. **-battente** *m. indecl.* (text.) swing beam. **-bigliętti** *m. indecl.* card-case, note-case. **-bombole** *m. indecl.* (eng.) cylinder holder. **-boz·zoli** *m. indecl.* (silkb.) cocoon holder. **-calze** *m. indecl.* stocking-bag. **-cannętte** *m. indecl.* (text.) cop holder. **-cappelli** *m. indecl.* hat-box. **-carte** *m. indecl.* brief-case, paper holder, map case. **-cartoc·cio** *m.* (mil.) cartridge carrier, charge holder; (naut. hist.) powder monkey, the boy employed in bringing charges up to the gun. **-catino** *m. indecl.* wash-stand. **-cęnere** *m. indecl.* ash-tray. **-cicche** *f.* (mil. slang) spittoon; (naut. slang) spitkid. **-collare** *m. indecl.* (naut.) cleat. **-corda** *m. indecl.* (naut.) line-throwing apparatus. **-cricco** *m. indecl.* (watchm.) ruota -cricco, pawl-bearing wheel. **-crostini** *m. indecl.* toast-rack. **-cuscinętti** *m. indecl.* (eng.) diestock. **-dolci** *m. indecl.* sweet-dish, sweetmeat holder. **-dol·lari** *m.* (joc.) *indecl.* wallet for bank-notes, note-case. **-elet·trodo** *m. indecl.* (electr.) electrode holder. †**-facelle** *m.* link-boy. †**-fasci** *m.* porter. **-feriti** *m. indecl.* stretcher-bearer. **-fiammi·feri** *m. indecl.* matchbox; match-holder. **-fiasca** *m. indecl.* (mil. hist.) hook holding the powder horn and shot pouch used with an arquebus. **-fiaschi** *m. indecl.* bottle carrier, basket, crate for carrying bottles. **-fiasco** *m.* (metall.) bottle holder, for the table; bottle-stand. **-fili** *m. indecl.* (text.) thread carrier. **-filiera** *f.* (eng.) diestock. **-fil·mine** *m. indecl.* (cinem.) film carrier (for filmstrips). **-filtri** *m. indecl.* (photog.) screen holder. **-fiori** *m. indecl.* flower-stand. **-fo·glio**, **-fo·gli** *m. indecl.* note-case, wallet; portfolio, pocket-book; letter-case; (pol.) portfolio; ministry, ministerial office; (comm.) effetti in -foglio, bills on hand. **-fortuna** *m. indecl.* mascot, lucky charm. **-freşa** *f.* (eng.) cutter holder. **-frotto** *m.* (motor.) jet block, jet carrier (of carburettor). **-garze** *m. indecl.* (med.) sterile-dressing container. **-gio·ie**, **-gioielli** *m. indecl.* jewel-case; trinket box. **-grù** *m. indecl.* davit socket. **-guidone** *m. indecl.* (mil.) colour-bearer. **-lam·pada** *f.* (electr.) lamp-holder; lamp socket. **-landre** *m. indecl.* (naut. hist.) wooden chocks supporting the chainplates abreast the masts of a sailing ship; wood to which a boat's lifting plates or rings are attached. **-lapis** *m. indecl.* pencil-holder. **-let·tere** *m. indecl.* postman; *f.* postwoman. **-licci** *m. indecl.* (text.) harness frame. **-lucerna** *f. indecl.* phantom-ship. **-mantello** *m.* suitcase, valise; (mil.) cavalry haversack to which the cloak is strapped. **-mic·cia** *m. indecl.* (naut.) portfire. **-monęte** *m. indecl.* purse. **-morso** *m.* (equit.) 'face leather', 'cheek piece', a leather strap attached to the bit. **-mu·sica** *m. indecl.* music-stand; music cabinet. **-naspi** *m. indecl.* hose holder; cassetta -naspi, fire-hose box. **-navętta** *m. indecl.* (text.) shuttle carrier. **-oculare** *m. indecl.* (opt.) eyepiece holder. **-pacchi** *m. indecl.* postman (for parcels); messenger boy; (bicycle) carrier; (motor.) carrier, luggage grid. **-penne** *m. indecl.* pen-holder. **-pennoni** *m. indecl.* (naut.) housing crutch or cradle. **-pet·tine** *m. indecl.* (text.) wraith holder. **-pitone** *m. indecl.* (watchm.) stud-holder; -pitone mobile, adjustable stud-holder. **-pranzi** *m. indecl.* tray, basket (or other container for sending out meals from a restaurant). **-provętta**, **-provętte** *m. indecl.* (chem.) test-tube stand; test-tube rack. **-provviste** *m. indecl.* carrello -provviste, trolley, dumb waiter. **-ritratti** *m. indecl.* photograph frame, portrait frame. **-riviste** *m. indecl.* newspaper rack. **-rulli** *m. indecl.* (text.) beam creel. **-ruota** *m. indecl.* (eng.; motor.) wheel carrier. **-sapone** *m. indecl.* soap-dish. **-satel·liti** *m. indecl.* (eng.; motor.) spider (e.g. of differential). **-scalmo** *m. indecl.*, **-scalmiera** *m. indecl.* (naut.) crutch socket; rowlock housing; -scalmiera di corsa, outrigger. **-scappamęnto** *m. indecl.* (watchm.) piastra -scappamento, escapement-bearing plate. **-scudi** *m. indecl.* (zool.) Scutigera. **-sigarętte** *m. indecl.* cigarette-case; cigarette-holder. **-si·gari** *m. indecl.* cigar-case. **-spazzature** *m. indecl.* dustpan. **-spaz·zole** *m. indecl.* (electr.) brush holder. **-spilli** *m. indecl.* pin-cushion. **-stecchini** *m. indecl.* toothpick holder. **-stendardo** *m. indecl.* standard-bearer. **-strumenti** *m. indecl.* instrument holder; (motor.) quadretto -strumenti, instrument panel. **-telaini** *m. indecl.* (cinem.) slide holder, slide-carrier. **-timbro** *m. indecl.* (watchm.) sounding spring-holder. **-tra·pano** *m. indecl.* (eng.) drill chuck. **-tubętti** *m. indecl.* (text.) bobbin carrier. **-(u)ovo** *m.* (*pl.* **-uova**) egg-cup. **-uten·sili** *m. indecl.* (eng.) tool holder; tool post, tool carrier. **-vaşi** *m. indecl.* (text.) can boy, can carrier; (naut.) chocks. **-vite** *m. indecl.* (watchm.) screw holder. **-vivande** *m. indecl.* see **portapranzi**. **-voce** *m. indecl.*

porta-bagagli (*cont.*)
speaking-tube (from floor to floor, in a house); (sport, etc.) megaphone; (fig.) mouthpiece, spokesman.

porta-finestra *f.* (*pl.* **porte-finestre**). French window.

port-are [A I] **I.** *tr.* **1.** To TAKE; to bring; to carry; — un bambino in collo, to carry a baby in one's arms; -ami il cappello e il bastone, bring me my hat and stick; -a questi libri nel mio studio, take these books to my study; -ale questo mazzo di fiori, take her this bunch of flowers; — in palma di mano, to praise highly; mi ha -ato in macchina, he brought me in his car; -ò la mano al cappello, he touched his hat; una polmonite lo -ò via, an attack of pneumonia carried him off; che il diavolo lo -i!, devil take him!; — via, to carry off; — via molto tempo, to take a long time; — acqua al mare, — legno al bosco, — vasi a Samo, — nottole ad Atene, to carry coals to Newcastle; (math.) to carry; scrivo 2 e -o 5, I put down 2 and carry 5. **2.** To WEAR, to have on; to bear; essa -ava un abito verde, she wore a green dress; non -a mai gioielli, she never wears jewellery; — il lutto, to be in mourning, to wear black; — gli occhiali, to wear spectacles; — l'ombrellino, to carry an umbrella; — la palma, to bear the palm; — la spada, to wear a sword; — la testa dritta, to hold one's head up; — i capelli lunghi, to wear one's hair long; — bene gli anni, to carry one's years well; — un nome illustre, to bear a famous name; (of an inanimate object) il libro -a questo titolo, the book bears this title; il documento -a la vostra firma, the document bears your signature. **3.** To BEAR, to suffer to feel; — la pena, to bear the penalty, to suffer punishment; -a con dignità la sua sventura, he bears his misfortune with dignity; — odio (a), to feel hatred (for), to hate; — amore a, to love; — rispetto a, to respect; la consuetudine non lo -a, custom does not allow it. **4.** To CAUSE, to bring about; to produce; to yield; ciò ha -ato un grave turbamento, that has been the cause of much trouble; i fatti -ano più delle parole, actions speak louder than words; — danno, to do harm; l'albero -a i frutti, the tree bears fruit; la pigrizia -a la miseria, laziness leads to poverty. **5.** To BRING FORWARD, to bring to light, to adduce, to allege; ci ha -ato buone notizie, he has given us some good news; — delle buone ragioni, to adduce good reasons; — le prove, to show (bring forward, adduce) proof; — un esempio, to put forward an example; to nominate, to put forward for an election. **6.** To LEAD, to conduct; — le pecore al pascolo to lead the sheep to pasture; — il cane a fare una passeggiata, to take the dog for a walk; tutte le strade -ano a Roma, all roads lead to Rome. **II.** *abs.* To CARRY, to have a range of (of a gun, voice, telescope, etc.); quel cannone -a a dieci chilometri, that gun has a range of about six miles; — male, to bring bad luck; — bene, to bring good luck; (naut.) to carry, to draw; far — le vele, to make the sails draw, i.e. to set the sails and steer so that the vessel is propelled; lascia —!, let draw!; -a pieno!, sail full and by! **III.** *rfl.* (*acc.* of *prn.* 'si') To Go. to betake oneself; to behave, to bear oneself; to be; to stand; to put oneself forward: -arsi deputato, to be a candidate for parliament; (*dat.* of *prn.* 'si') si è -ata la colazione, he has brought his lunch; -arsi le mani al volto, to put one's hands to one's face. **-a·bile** *adj.* portable; peso -abile, weight that can be carried; (fig.) bearable; (mus.) see 'organo -abile', under **organo**. **-amento** *m.* carriage, bearing; gait; conduct, deportment; (mus.) portamento, vocal glide. **-ante** *part. adj.* carrying, bearing; productive; onda -ante, carrier wave (radio); (mech.) load-bearing; *n.m.* gait (of a horse). **-antina** *f.* sedan-chair; carrying chair. **-antino** *m.* chair-man, litter-bearer. **-anza** *f.* bearing, gait; carrying capacity, load (of any vehicle); (aeron.) lift. **-ata** *f.* reach, range, compass, scope, span; capacity; importance, significance; purport; a -ata di, suited to; a -ata di mano, within reach; a -ata di voce, within call; a -ata d'orecchio, within hearing; fuori -ata, out of range; alla -ata di tutti, within reach of all; ciò supera la -ata delle loro menti, that exceeds their mental powers; non ha capito la -ata dell'osservazione, he has not understood the implication of the remark; uomo di grande -ata, very influential man; di prima -ata, of the first importance; (mil.) range (of gun); cannone di grande -ata, long-range gun; (naut.) range; cannocchiale di grande -ata, long-range telescope; capacity, carrying capacity; tonnage; -ata lorda, gross tonnage; -ata netta, net register tonnage; -ata di marinaro, dunnage; range, visibility; -ata di un faro, visibility of a lighthouse; (mus.) staff, stave; (eng.) capacity, carrying capacity, lifting capacity; (archit.)

capacity, maximum load (of bridge, etc.); produce, product income; (hydraul.) rate of flow; (at table) dish, course; il pranzo consisteva di tre -ate, dinner consisted of three courses. **-atic·cio** *adj.* transported; terreni -aticci, alluvial soil; *n.m.* alluvial soil, drift. **-a·tile** *adj.* portable; armi -atili, small arms; sedia -atile, sedan chair; (mus.) organo -atile. see under **organo**. **-ativo** *adj.* (mus.) organo -ativo, portative organ. **-ato** *part. adj.* carried, borne; (of clothes) worn, second-hand; -ato dall'ira, impelled by anger; -ato a, inclined, given to; sono -ato a pensare, I am inclined to think; è molto -ato alla ricerca scientifica, he is much given to scientific research; non ci sono -ato, I have no inclination for it; -ato di bocca, -ato in bocca, on everyone's lips, frequently mentioned; nominated, put forward for election, etc.), favoured; (mus.) note -ate, half-staccato notes; *n.m.* outcome, result, issue, effect, consequence; questo è un -ato della civiltà, that is a product of civilization. **-atore** *f.* porter; bearer; i -atori del feretro, the bearers of the coffin; (finan.) bearer; titoli al -atore, bearer bonds; (leg.) -atore legittimo, holder in due course (C.C.); †pilot; †sufferer, patient. **-atura** *f.* carriage; porterage; hair style; arrangement of the beard. **†-itore** *m.* boatman.

porte-enfant *m. indecl.* (pron. as Fr.). See **garde-enfant**.

†porte·ndere *tr.* to portend, to presage; to prognosticate.

portent-o *m.* prodigy, miracle, marvel; operare -i, to work wonders; questo ragazzo è un —, this boy is a prodigy; i -i della scienza, the marvels of science; un — di scienza, a prodigy of learning; omen, portent. **-oso** *adj.* prodigious, marvellous, wonderful, astonishing; memoria -osa, prodigious memory, wonderful memory. **-osamente** *adv.* prodigiously, marvellously, wonderfully, astonishingly; portentously.

po·rtic-o *m.* (archit.) portico, porch; *pl.* colonnade, arcade; (of a farmhouse) courtyard, terrace; (anct. hist.) il —, the Porch (as standing for Stoic philosophy). **†-ale** *m.* colonnade. **-ato** *adj.* having a colonnade; *n.m.* colonnade, arcade.

port-iera *f.* door-curtain; (motor.) door; portress; concierge; non c'è — per te, you are to be admitted freely; (eccl.) (sister) portress (in convent). **-iere**, **†-ieri** *m.* porter, doorkeeper, janitor, concierge; -iere dell'albergo, hotel porter; (soccer) goalkeeper. **-ina·io**, **†-inaro**, **†-iniero** *m.* porter, doorkeeper, janitor. **-ineri·a** *f.* porter's lodge.

portinsegna *m. indecl.* (mil.) ensign-bearer.

porto[1] *m.* carriage, transport; carrying, wearing; post (horse); cost of carriage; — della lettera, postage; — affrancato, postage prepaid; — pagato, franco, carriage paid; — dovuto, — assegnato, carriage forward, payable on delivery; (comm.) carriage; (leg.) act of carrying; — abusivo di armi, unlawful carrying of arms (C.P.); licenza di -- d'armi, licence to carry arms; — d'armi, gun licence; fu multato per — d'armi abusivo, he was fined for carrying arms without a licence.

porto[2] *part.* of **porgere**, q.v.

porto[3] *apocop. part.* of **portare**; cf. **portato**.

port-o[4] *m.* (naut.) harbour; port; dockyard; docks; anchorage, shelter; — di prima categoria, naval port; — di seconda categoria, commercial port (NOTE: these are further subdivided into 1st, 2nd, 3rd and 4th class according to their annual tonnage); — aperto, open anchorage; — d'armamento, commissioning or fitting-out port; — artificiale, — esterno, artificial harbour; — bacino, basin; — di barro, — con trave, harbour having a tidal bar; — bloccato, blockaded port; — bloccato dai ghiacci, icebound harbour; — canale, canal harbour; capitano di —, harbourmaster, Queen's harbourmaster, Master Attendant; capitaneria del —, docks office, Harbourmaster's offices; — capolinea, port of origin; — del carbone, coaling port or basin; — chiuso, blocked port; — commerciale, mercantile port; — di diga, harbour formed by breakwater; diritti di —, harbour dues; — di fiume. — fluviale, fluvial harbour; — franco, free port; — interno, inner harbour; — interrato, filled in or partially silted harbour; — di levata, sailing anchorage; — di marea, tidal harbour; — militare, — di guerra, naval port; — morto, abandoned harbour; — naturale, natural harbour; — netto, harbour free of obstructions; — omnibus, coasting and discharging port; — d'immatricolazione, port of Registry; — di pesca, — peschereccio, fishing port; — del petrolio, oil loading or bunkering port; — di rifornimento, replenishing and revictualling port; — di rifugio, refuge anchorage; — di rilascio, refitting and resting harbour; — sbarrato, defended port; — di scalo, port of call; — di sverno,

port-o (*cont.*)

— vernereccio, wintering port; — sportivo, yacht harbour; (comm.) lettera di —, consignment note; (fig.) un — di pace, a haven of rest; essere ormai in —, to be in port, to have reached one's goal; (fig.) condurre in —, to accomplish. **-olano** *m.* (naut.) sailing directions; handbook used in conjunction with a chart. **-olata** *f.* (Chioggia) fishing-master's boat. **-olatto** *m.* (Ven. **-olate** *f.*) (naut.) motorboat used for landing fish. **-uoso** *adj.* rich in harbours; paese **-uoso**, land of many ports. †**-ulano** *m.* see **portolano**; pilot (fourteenth century).

Porto[5] *pr.n.m.* (geog.) Oporto; port, port wine.

Porto-gallo *pr.n.m.* (geog.) Portugal; *n.m.* Portuguese orange. **-ghese** *adj.* Portuguese; la lingua **-ghese**, Portuguese (language); *n.m.* Portuguese (man, language); (slang) gate-crasher (e.g. in a theatre or football ground); *f.* Portuguese woman or girl.

portombrelli *m. indecl.* umbrella-stand.

porton-e *m. augm.* of **porta**[1], q.v.; gate, carriage-entrance; main door (of public buildings, etc.). **-cino** *m. dim.* house door, resembling a 'portone'.

portor-dini *m. indecl.* messenger.

Portorico *pr.n.m.* (geog.) Puerto Rico.

porto-rio *m.* (naut.) dues; passenger cargo or canal taxes.

portorolo-gio *m. indecl.* watch-stand; watch-pocket.

portu-ale *adj.*, **-a-rio** *adj.* (naut.) of a port, appertaining to a harbour; lavori **-ali**, harbour-works, engineering operations in a port; marinaio **-ario**, seaman employed on harbour duties; opere **-arie**, docks, lighthouses, etc.

Portuensi *pr.n.m.pl.* (eccl.) canons of the Portuensis Congregation.

portulaca *f.* (bot.) purslane, *Portulaca oleracea*.

†**portulano** *m.* See **porto**[4].

†**portunato** *m.* slave in charge of a ship's dinghy.

portuoso *adj.* See under **porto**[4].

porzi-one *f.* portion, part, share, helping, ration; fare le **-oni** giuste, uguali, to share out equally; ho avuto la mia —, I have had my share; mi dia due **-oni** di arrosto, give me roast beef for two; (leg.) — disponibile, proportion of his estate over which testator has power of testamentary disposition (C.C.). **-oncella**, **-oncina** *f.* small portion, tiny bit. †**-oniere** *m.* shareholder. **-un-cola** *f.* (eccl.) the Portiuncula at Assisi; the indulgence attached to this.

pos-a *f.* laying, placing; la — della prima pietra, the laying of the foundation-stone; pause, rest; senza —, without rest, without ceasing; non trovar —, to find no rest; (gramm.) accent, stress; la — della voce va sulla prima sillaba, the stress is on the first syllable; attitude, posture, pose; una — naturale, a natural attitude; (of a model) mettersi in —, to assume a pose; (fig.) la vostra filantropia è soltanto una —, your philanthropy is a mere pose; (photog.) exposure; time exposure; (bldg.) laying. **-are** [A1] *tr.* to place, to put; to lay; to set; -are la penna, to lay down one's pen; -ò il bambino nella culla, she laid the baby in the cradle; to lay aside; è ora di -are il pastrano, it is time to leave off an overcoat; — le armi, to lay down one's arms, to cease fighting; (techn.) to lay (cables, tracks, etc.); *intr.* (*aux.* avere) to rest, to stand; to stop, to cease to do anything more; to settle (down); to pose, to sit (for a portrait); lasciar -are la terra, to let the land rest, lie fallow; (archit.) to rest (on a base), -are in falso, to be out of perpendicular; questo edificio -a su roccia viva, this building has its foundations on living rock; (sculpt.; paint.) to pose; (fig.) to pose; il vostro amico -a a letterato, your friend poses as a literary man; non ha dove -are, he has nowhere to rest (his head), he can settle nowhere; il vino bisogna lasciarlo -are prima di travasarlo, wine should be left to settle before it is poured off; (poet.) to lie, to repose; ove -a il corpo di quel grande, where the body of that great man reposes; *rfl.* to alight; to settle; to rest; to sit; to perch; non trovava luogo dove -arsi, he could settle nowhere; non sa dove -arsi, he does not know where to put himself; la neve si -ò sulle cime più alte, the snow settled on the highest peaks; la rondine si -ò sul tetto, the swallow alighted on the roof; il suo sguardo si -ò sopra un oggetto strano, his gaze rested on a strange object; (provb.) chi altri tribola sè non -a, troubling others you upset yourself; *adv. phr.* piglia e -a, with frequent interruptions; *n.m.* (archit.; sculpt.) base, pedestal. **-acavi** *m. indecl.* (naut.) cablelayer. **-acenere** *m. indecl.* ash-tray. **-aferro** *m. indecl.* iron-stand, rest for a hot flat-iron. **-alume** *m. indecl.* lamp-stand. **-amento** *m.* laying; placing; rest; base; foundation. **-amine** *m. indecl.* (naut.) minelayer. **-amolle** *m.*

indecl. stand for tongs, fire-irons. **-ante** *part. adj.* resting, leaning; **-apiano** *m. indecl.* notice signifying 'handle with care', 'with care'; (person) slowcoach. **-apiede**, **-apiedi** *m. indecl.* foot-stool, foot-rest. **-areti** *m. indecl.* (naut.) netlayer. **-ata** *f.* cover (knife, fork and spoon, or any of these separately); metti una -ata in più, lay for one more (at table); rest, stop; (mil.) staying point; deposit (in a liquid), sediment; †inn. **-ato** *part. adj.* resting; at rest; seated; calm, rested; sedate; staid; l'uccello era -ato sul ramo più alto, the bird was perched on the highest branch; uomo -ato, staid man, prudent man. **-atamente** *adv.* calmly, sedately, quietly. **-atezza** *f.* composure; staidness; calm(ness), quietness; sedateness. **-atoio** *m.* perch. **-atore** *m.* poseur; affected person. (**-atrice** *f.*) **-atura** *f.* settling (of a liquid); sediment; base, support; †attitude, pose.

†**posca** *f.* vinegar and water; compress moistened with vinegar and water.

po-scia *adv.* (poet.) then, afterwards (cf. **poi**).

†**po-sciacchè** *conj.* after, when (cf. **poichè**).

†**poscon-dola** *f.* glade.

†**pos-cra-i** *adv.* the day after tomorrow. †**-crilli** *adv.* the day after the day after tomorrow. †**-qua-chera** *adv.* the day after the day after the day after tomorrow (words coined by Luigi Pulci in *Il Morgante*).

poscritt-a *f.*, **-o** *m.* postscript.

posdat-are *tr.* to post-date. (**-ato** *part. adj.*)

†**posdoman-i**, †**-e** *adv.* the day after tomorrow.

†**posdomattina** *adv.* the morning after tomorrow.

Posidone *pr.n.m.* (Gk. myth.) Poseidon.

posido-nia *f.* (bot.) *Posidonia oceanica*.

positiv-o *adj.* positive; real, certain; practical, matter of fact; uomo —, practical man, matter-of-fact person; prova -a, positive proof; fatti -ivi, real facts; esito —, favourable result; risposta -a, affirmative answer; (gramm.) positive; grado — degli aggettivi, positive degree of adjectives; (scient.; electr.) positive; (leg.) diritto —, positive (as opposed to 'natural') law; (math.) positive; filosofia -a, positivism; (mus.) organo —, choir organ; *n.m.* reality; what is certain; *adv. phr.* for sure, for certain; vengo di —, I'll come for sure. **-amente** *adv.* positively; for certain; without a doubt; †moderately. **-a** *f.* (photog.) positive. **-ismo** *m.* (philos.) positivism. **-ista** *m.*, *f.*, *adj.* positivist; realist. **-ità** *f.* positivity, positiveness.

posit-one *m.* (atom. phys.) positon. **-rone** *m.* see **positone**.

positura *f.* position, place, site; attitude, posture, pose.

posizione *f.* situation, position; quella casa è in una bella —, that house stands in a fine situation; ciò non è facile per un uomo nella mia —, that is not easy for a man in my position; (mil.) — di attenti, position of attention; prendere — contro una proposta, to take a stand against a proposal; (gramm.) position (of a vowel, with regard to the following consonants); (class. prosod.) sillaba lunga per —, syllable long by position; (mus.) position (on finger-board of stringed instruments); (naut.) position; state; fanali di —, position lights, two vertical white lights used by warships to indicate their position; — della nave, ship's position on the chart or in the ocean; — di sgombro, stowage position; linea di —, position line; triangolo di —, position triangle or cocked hat; — amministrativa, state of a ship, in full commission, reserve, etc.; — ausiliaria, state of retirement of an officer, classification in reserve; (fig.) — imbarazzante, embarrassing situation; in una — difficile, in a difficult situation; (leg.) far —, to examine, to question; status; (comm.) item; (finan.) — finanziaria, financial standing.

poslimi-nio, **postlimi-nio** *m.* (Rom. law) *postliminium*, rights of a returning captive.

pos(t)lu-dio *m.* (mus.) postlude.

†**poso** *m.* respite; idleness.

pos-ofoto-metro, **-o-grafo** *m.*, **-o-metro** *m.* (photog.). See **esposi-metro**.

po-sola[1] *f.* strap used with a pack-saddle for holding up the girth-strap (passed through the holes at the extremities of the girth-strap and fastened to the saddle); †(fig.) remorse; heavy burden. †**-atura** *f.* see **posolino**.

po-sol-a[2] *f.*, **-ino** *m.* (equit.; herald.) crupper.

posologi-a *f.* (med.) dosage, dose.

†**pospasto** *m.* dessert.

pos-porre [B21] *tr.* to place after; — una voce ad un'altra, to place one item, or heading, below another; to place lower down (in a list); — una persona di merito a un intrigante, to pass over a

pos·porre (*cont.*)

deserving person in favour of an intriguer; -pone la virtù alla ricchezza, he esteems virtue less than wealth; to postpone, to defer. **-ponimento** *m.* placing after, movement to a subsequent position. **-positivo** *adj.* (gramm.) postpositive, enclitic. **-posizione** *f.* deferment; postponement, adjournment; placing after; placing lower down. **-posto** *part. adj.* placed lower down; passed over, overlooked; postponed, deferred.

poss-a *f.* (poet.) power, strength, vigour; a tutta —, with might and main; con ogni sua —, with all his strength. **-anza** *f.* (poet.) power, might, dominion, puissance; strength.

possed-ere [B 28] *tr.* to possess, to own, to have; to hold; possiede diverse case, he owns several houses; possiedi una macchina?, have you got a car?; possiede molte buone qualità, he has many good qualities; — una lingua, to master, to be master of, a language; — un segreto, to be in possession of a secret; to have taken possession of; la -eva il demone della gelosia, she was possessed by the demon jealousy; *abs.* to have property; è uno che possiede, he is a man of property, he owns property. **-imento** *m.* possession, colony; estate, property; mi mostrò i suoi -imenti, he showed me his estate. **-itore** *m.* owner, possessor; master. **-itrice** *f.* owner, mistress. **-uto** *part. adj.* owned; possessed; dominated; obsessed; è -uto dalla passione del giuoco, he is dominated by a passion for gambling; -uto dal demonio, possessed of a devil.

possent-e *adj.* vigorous; powerful, mighty; potent; masterful; vino —, strong (potent) wine; *n.m.* powerful person, influential person. **-emente** *adv.* powerfully.

possess-ione *f.* possession; landed property; ownership; property, estate; entrare in — di, to enter into possession of. **-ioncella** *f. dim.* small estate, little property. **-ivo** *adj.* possessive; (gramm.) pronomi -ivi, possessive pronouns; aggettivo -ivo, possessive adjective. **-ivamente** *adv.* possessively.

possess-o *m.* (leg.) possession; occupation; (Scots law) seisin; sequestration; presa di —, seizure, taking of possession (C.C.P.); (leg.) — continuo, continuato, uninterrupted possession; — di stato, claim of (marital or filial) status; (C.C.) mutamento della detenzione in —, change of having and holding into possession (C.C.); accessione del —, taking of possession (C.C.); immissione in —, order or writ of possession; tenure; occupation, ownership; il quadro è in — di un mio amico, the picture is in the possession of a friend of mine; prendere — di, to take possession of; prender — della presidenza, to assume the presidency, to take office as president or chairman, to take the chair; cerimonia, funzione della presa di —, installation ceremony (of the president of the Chamber of Deputies); — della libertà, freedom, enjoyment of liberty; — delle sue facoltà, possession of one's faculties; essere in — di sè, to be in possession of oneself, to be self-possessed; — di una lingua, mastery of a language; sono in — della vostra lettera del 1° corr., I am in receipt of your letter of the 1st inst.; *pl.* property, estate; vasti -i, extensive landed property. **-ore** *m.* possessor; owner; proprietor; holder; -ore legittimo, rightful owner; (leg.) -ore di mala fede, a person who wrongfully and knowingly holds goods belonging to others (C.C.); terzo -ore, third-party in possession (C.C.); (comm.) holder. **-orio** *adj.* (leg.) giudizio -orio, action of possession; provvedimento -orio, order for possession (C.C.P.).

possi·bil-e *adj.* possible; feasible; credo che gli sarà — venire, I think he will be able to come; è — che egli riesca, it is possible that he will succeed; con la minore spesa —, as inexpensively as possible; al più presto —, as soon as possible; al —, as much as possible; nei limiti del —, as far as possible; (schol. philos.) intelletto —, possible (passive) intellect; *n.m.* that which is possible; farò tutto il —, I will do everything possible, I will do everything I possibly can. **-mente** *adv.* possibly; if possible; sciogliete nell'acqua, -mente calda, dissolve in water, hot if possible. **-is·simo** *adj. superl.* quite possible; very likely. **-ista** *adj.* within the realms of possibility, realistic; *n.m.* (pol.) one willing to compromise, possibilist. **-ità** *f.* possibility; power; vi sono diverse -ità, there are several possibilities; non c'è -ità che egli venga, it is impossible that he should come; non abbiamo la -ità di far questo, we have no power to do this; mettere una persona nella -ità di, to enable a person to.

possiden-te *adj.* owning (property); wealthy; (eccl.) frati, opere pie, -ti, religious communities, charitable institutions, owning property; *n.m.* landowner; man of property; owner of real estate. **-za** *f.* ownership, right of possession; estate, property; landowners, landlords.

post-a *f.* **1.** Post, post-office; mail, mails; — aerea, air-mail; — raccomandata, registered mail; — pneumatica, despatch of letters by pneumatic tube (in large cities only); — centrale, General Post Office; direttore delle -e, postmaster; ministro delle -e e telecomunicazioni, Postmaster-General; mandare, spedire, per —, to send by post; porta questo alla —, take this to the post; spese di —, postage; a — corrente, by return of post; fermo in —, *poste restante*; addetto al servizio delle Poste, Post Office employee (C.P.); place where the coach-horses were changed; mail-coach; andare in —, to post. **2.** Post (e.g. of a sentry); spot; rendezvous, meeting-place; darsi la —, to arrange to meet; 'hide-out', place where a hunter watches for game; stare alla —, to lie in wait; mettersi alla — di qualcuno, to be on the look out for someone; stall (for a horse, in stable). **3.** Placing, putting; (cards) stake; (math.) item (in an addition sum); (paperm.) 250 sheets; grande —, 500 sheets; (rel.) decade of the rosary (prayers or beads); (Tusc.) the placing of anything; (agric.) — degli ulivi, planting of olive-trees; — delle uova, placing of eggs under the hen; (mus.) — di voce, placing of the voice; nota di —, unprepared note; (comm.) posting. **4.** In Adverbial Phrases: a — (also **apposta**, q.v.), a bella —, on purpose, deliberately; a sua —, as he pleases; di —, quickly, directly. **-ale** *adj.* postal; post, mail; ufficio -ale, post office; timbro -ale, postmark; furgone -ale, mail-van; treno -ale, mail-train; francobollo -ale, postage-stamp; cartolina -ale, postcard; spese -ali, postage; biglietto -ale, letter-card; vaglia -ale, postal-order, money-order; pacco -ale, parcel, postal packet; spedire come pacco -ale, to send by parcel post; cassetta -ale, letter-box (pillar-box); casella -ale, post-office box; direttore di un ufficio -ale, postmaster; impiegato -ale, post-office clerk; unione -ale, postal union; ambulanza -ale, mail-van (on a train); cassa di risparmio -ale, post-office savings bank; *n.m.* mail-train; mail-boat, packet. **-are** [A 1] *tr.* to place, to post; to station; (mil.) to site, to place, to post (e.g. a gun, a lookout, a sentry); *rfl.* to place oneself, to take up one's position or station; *rfl.* (mil.) to take post, to take up position. **-ato** *part. adj.* posted, placed; stationed. **-azione** *f.* (mil.) emplacement (of a gun, radar, etc.).

post-bel·lico *adj.* post-war. **-combustione** *f.* (motor.) afterburning, reheating. **-com(m)unio** *m.*, †**-munione** *f.* (liturg.) post-communion (collect); (mus.) post-communion. **-universita·rio** *adj.* post-graduate.

postegg-iare [A 3 c] *tr.* to lie in wait for; to watch for; to park (car); †*intr.* to post, to travel (with post-horses). **-iatore** *m.* stall-holder (in a market); street-player or singer who takes up his stand in fixed places.

posteggio *m.* stand; cab-rank; tassa di —, market-dues (payment for a stand); parking-place; parking; — di automobili di piazza, taxi-cab rank.

postelegra·f-ico *adj.* postal and telegraphic; ufficio —, post-office, telegraph office; *n.m.* clerk or official of the postal and telegraphic service. **-o·nico** *adj.* postal, telegraphic and telephonic; pertaining to posts and telegraphs; spese -oniche, postages and telegraph expenses; *n.m.* post-office clerk.

postem-a *f.* (surg.) boil; abscess; (zool.) musk gland; (joc.) purse, savings, hoard; †heavy burden. **-oso** *adj.* having an abscess.

†**postemastro** *m.* postmaster (of horses).

posterg-are [A 2] *tr.* to turn one's back on, to scorn; to cast aside; to neglect; to defer; (leg.) — una ipoteca, to postpone a mortgage; †to endorse. **-ato** *part. adj.* scorned; neglected; deferred; †endorsed; †scudo -ato, shield carried on the back.

po·ster-i *m.pl.* descendants, posterity; passare ai —, to hand down to posterity. **-iore** *adj.* hind(er), back; posterior, subsequent; la parte -iore del duomo, the back of the cathedral; gamba -iore, hind leg; ruota -iore, back wheel; porta -iore, back door, postern; un fatto -iore, a subsequent event; scritti -iori later works. **-iormente** *adv.* subsequently, later on; at the back; from behind. **-iorità** *f.* posteriority. **-ità** *f.* posterity, descendants, issue; later times.

†**posteri·a** *f.* See **posterla**.

posterla *f.* postern.

postic·c-io *adj.* artificial; false, sham; fictitious; capelli posticci, false hair; denti -i, artificial teeth; volto —, mask; ponte —,

posticc·io (*cont.*)

temporary bridge; (agric.) terra -ia, earth recently moved to another place; *n.m.* (naut. hist.) second stroke oar of a galley (sixteenth century); second oarsman of the stroke oar (seventeenth century); ufficiale —, substitute officer, alternate; *pl.* gunwales of a galley; gunwale capping. **-iamęnte** *adv.* artificially. **-e** *f.pl.* sponsons or projections outside a ship. **-ia** *f.* (agric.) vineyard with regular lines of vines; (naut. hist.) office and position of an alternate, substitute or *locum tenens*. **-iata** *f.* row of trees, or other plants.

posticip-are [A I S] *tr.* to postpone, to defer; *intr.* (*aux.* avere) to come late. **-ato** *part. adj.* deferred, delayed; after the event; pagamento -ato, deferred payment, payment on delivery; (leg.) pigione -ata, rent payable in arrear. **-atamęnte** *adv.* after the proper time; when the work is finished; desidero pagare -atamente, I wish to pay for the work when it is finished. **-azione** *f.* (leg.) postponement; adjournment; delay.

po·stico *adj.*, *n.m.* (archit.) back, rear (of a building).

†**postiere** *m.* see postiglione; postmaster (of horses).

†**postieri** *adv.* the day before yesterday.

†**postierla** *f.* See posterla.

postigliọne *m.* postillion; *adv. phr.* alla —, in postillion style, postillion.

postill-a *f.* marginal note, note; gloss; (leg.) postil; rider; (poet.) le -e del viso, the features. **-are** [A I] *tr.* to annotate; to gloss, to write a note on. **-ato** *part. adj.* annotated; with notes; -ato da, with notes by. **-atọre** *m.* annotator, commentator, editor. (**-atrice** *f.*) **-atura** *f.* annotating; notes.

postime *m.* (agric.) planting; seedling plants; (plant) nursery.

postino¹ *m.* postman.

†**postino²** *m.* nursery for seedlings.

†**postione** *m.* posterior, behind.

post-ite *f.* (med.) posthitis, inflammation of the prepuce. **-i·tico** *adj.* posthitic.

postlu·dio *m.* See posludio.

postluminescenza *f.* (phys.; telev.) afterglow, persistence.

postmilitare *adj.* post-military; istruzione —, instruction continued after military service.

post-o¹, post-o *part.* of **porre**, q.v.; *adj.* situated, placed, put; set; giorno —, given day; supposed; ciò —, admitting that; — che (*or* postochè, *conj.*), supposing that, assuming that.

post-o², post-o *m.* **1.** PLACE; — d'onore, place of honour (cf. under no. 6); spot; position, site, situation; sul —, on the spot; arrivare sul —, to arrive on the scene; essere al proprio —, to be in the right place; rimettere i libri a —, to put the books back in their proper places; prendere il — di, to take the place of; tenere la lingua a —, to hold one's tongue; le mani a —!, keep your hands to yourself!; fare uno stare al suo —, to keep a person in his place; non vorrei essere al vostro —, I shouldn't like to be in your place. **2.** SEAT; place; room; space; occupare troppo —, to take up too much room; c'è sempre — per voi, there's always room for you; un'automobile a quattro -i (*or* un quattro -i), a four-seater car; un — d'avanti, a front seat; prenotare un —, book a seat; (theatr.) — di poltrona, stall; — di platea, pit-stall; in piattaforma, seat (or standing-room) on the platform; — in piedi, standing-room; — d'angolo, corner seat; — riservato, reserved seat. **3.** POST, appointment; situation, employment; — di segretario, appointment as secretary; — d'insegnante, teaching post; fare domanda per un —, to apply for a situation; cercare un —, to be looking for a job; occupare un ragguardevole —, to hold an important position. **4.** POST, station; — di primo soccorso, first-aid post; — di medicazione, dressing-station; (mil.) — d'avvertimento, reporting post or point; — di blocco, road block; — di osservazione, observation post; — di distribuzione, issue point; — di ascolto, listening post; — avanzato, outpost; — di comando, control or command post; — emittente, transmitting station; — ricevente, receiving station. **5.** (FINAN.) denari —, spot cash. **6.** (HERALD.) — d'onore, honour point. **-iciat·tolo** *m. dim.* (derog.) very small place (hamlet, village). **-icino** *m. dim.* little place; spot.

post-operato·rio *adj.* post-operative. **-prandiale** *adj.* post-prandial; discorso -prandiale, after-dinner speech. **-refrigerante** *adj.* (techn.) aftercooling. **-refrigeratọre** *m.* (techn.) aftercooler. **-refrigerazione** *f.* (techn.) aftercooling.

postremo *adj.* last.

postri·bolo, †**postri·bulo** *m.* brothel.

post-riscaldo *m.* (metall.) reheating. **-scriptum** *m. indecl.* see poscritto. **-trauma·tico** *adj.* (med.) neurosi -traumatica, accident neurosis.

postul-are [A I S] *tr.* to demand, to claim; to beg for, to apply for; (eccl.) to postulate, to name for office subject to the consent of a higher authority. **-ante** *m.* petitioner (e.g. for government post or church benefice); (eccl.) postulant (one not yet a novice). **-ato** *part. adj.* postulated; demanded; *n.m.* postulate; principle; i -ati del socialismo, the principles of socialism, socialist principles; (geom.) postulate. **-atọre** *m.* (eccl.) postulator; (liter., with fem. **-atrice**) petitioner.

po·stumo¹ *adj.* posthumous; *n.m.* posthumous child; (med.) consequence of an illness; i postumi dell'influenza, illness resulting from influenza.

Po·stumo² *pr.n.m.* Postumus.

postura *f.* place; position, site, situation; posture; bestowing (e.g. of a name); (mil.) posture (of an army); siting (of a camp); layout (of a fortification, etc.); †pondering, deliberation.

†**postutto** *adv. phr.* al —, after all.

pota·bil-e *adj.* fit for drinking; drinkable; acqua —, drinking-water. **-ità** *f.* fitness for drinking.

potag·gio *m.* soup.

potame·idi *f.pl.* river-nymphs, naiads.

pot-are [A I] *tr.* (hort.) to prune; to lop; — a corona, to cut all branches to equal length; — a vino, to prune (vines) lightly, in order to obtain more wine though of inferior quality. **-agione** *f.* pruning; pruning-time. **-ai(u)olo** *m.* pruning-knife, pruning-hook. **-amęnto** *m.* pruning, lopping. (**-ato** *part. adj.*, *n.m.*) **-atọio** *m.* pruning-knife, pruning-hook. **-atọre** *m.* pruner; pruning-knife. (**-atrice** *f.*) **-atura** *f.* pruning, lopping; prunings, clippings, lopped branches.

pot-assa *f.* (chem.) potash; — caustica, caustic potash. **-as·sico** *adj.* (chem.) of potassium; carbonate -assico, potassium carbonate. **-as·sio** *m.* (chem.) potassium.

pot-atọre *m.*, **-atura** *f.*, **-azione** *f.* See under potare.

†**poteca** *f.* See ipoteca.

poten-te *adj.* powerful, forcible, mighty; strong, potent; influential; un — alleato, a powerful ally; una medicina —, a potent medicine; vino —, strong wine; una ragione —, a cogent reason; (physiol.) potent; *n.m.* (usu. *pl.*) i -ti della terra, the powerful, those who have power on earth. **-temęnte** *adv.* powerfully, mightily; potently. **-tato** *m.* potentate, power; i -ati amici, friendly powers. **-za** *f.* power, might; strength, force, authority; faculty: -za militare, military strength; le grandi -ze, the great powers; riunione di quattro -ze, four-power meeting; (math.) power; alla seconda -za, to the power of 2; (eng.) power; -za al freno, brake horse-power; (philos.) potency, potentiality; -za pura, (mere) potentiality; in -za, in potency, potential, potentially; -ze dell'anima, powers, faculties of the soul; -za della stampa, power of the press; (herald.) croce -za, cross potent throughout. **-ziale** *adj.* potential; (gramm.) modo -ziale, optative (potential) mood; *n m.* (electr.) potential; (radio) -ziale base, grid bias. **-zialmęnte** *adv.* potentially; virtually. **-zialità** *f.* potentiality; power; capacity. **-ziamęnto** *m.* strengthening; development. **-ziare** [A4] *tr.* to potentiate. **-ziato** *adj.* having the faculty, potentiality; forza -ziata, effective power (force); (herald.) potent. **-zio·metro** *m.* (electr.) potentiometer; (radio) potentiometer, voltage divider.

pot-ęre¹ [B 22] *intr.* (*aux.* avere; essere is recommended when used with a dependent *infin.* of a *vb.* that takes essere: e.g. io sono potuto andare). **1.** ABILITY, to be able; non posso alzarlo, I can't lift it; non può venire, he is unable to come; se puoi, scrivimi, write to me, if you can; la verità non si può dire sempre, one cannot always tell the truth; vorrei — fare qualche cosa per voi I wish I could do something for you; è un uomo che può tutto, he is a man who is capable of anything; non posso farci nulla, I can't do anything about it; non -ei farlo, I could not, I was unable to, do it; farò quanto posso, I'll do all I can; si fa quel che si può, one does what one can; non ne posso più, I can't stand any more, I can't go on, I have had enough; a più non posso, to the utmost; gridare a più non posso, to shout at the top of one's voice. **2.** PERMISSION: non potè parlare, he was not allowed to speak; si può?, may I come in?; ci sei potuto andare?, were you allowed to go? (*or* were you able to go?); Mamma, posso andar fuori?, Mother, may I go out? **3.** PROB-ABILITY: può darsi, può essere, it may be; può darsi che egli

pot·ere (*cont.*)

sappia, it is possible that he knows, he may know; -ranno essere stati una decina, there may have been about ten; potrebbe arrivare oggi, he might come today; avrebbe -uto farlo, he might have done it (*or* he could have done it); potrebbe aver smarrito la strada, he might have lost his way; spero che egli possa riuscire, I hope he may succeed. **4.** EFFECTIVENESS: con lui non ce la possiamo, we are nowhere compared with him; l'esempio può più delle parole, actions speak louder than words, example is better than precept; da queste parti il vento ci può molto, the wind is very strong from this quarter; volere è —, where there's a will there's a way; (poet.) poscia più che il dolore potè il digiuno (Dante), then hunger achieved what grief could not.

potere² *m.* power; authority; sway, influence; ability; farò tutto quello che è in mio —, I will do everything in my power; a mio —, all I can; definire i poteri, to define powers; pieni poteri, full powers; — assoluto, absolute power; il partito che è ora al —, the party now in power; salire al —, to seize power, to rise to power; restare al —, to hold power; abuso di —, abuse of power; non ha il — di far ciò, he has no authority to do that; avere — su, to have power over; a tutto —, with all one's might, as much as possible; ciascuno faccia il suo —, let everyone do all he can; i pubblici poteri, the public authorities; il — civile, the civil power; il quarto —, the press (esp. political); (phys.; eng.; scient.) power, value, capacity; (phys.) — assorbente, absorptive power; — rotatorio specifico, specific rotation; (econ.) — d'acquisto, purchasing power; verifica dei poteri, checking of qualifications or credentials; (leg.) power; esercitare il — di fatto, to have the enjoyment (C.C.).

potest-à *f.* power; authority; la divina —, l'alta —, the Almighty; — di vita e di morte, power of life and death; (leg.) — maritale, marital authority; patria —, paternal authority (C.C.); *pl.* (theol.) Powers (order of angels). **-ariato** *m.* office of 'podestà'. **-ativo** *adj.* (leg.) condizione -ativa, potestative condition (C.C.). **-eri·a** *f.* see **podesteria**. **-essa** *f.* (joc.) wife of the 'podestà'.

†**potire** *tr.* to possess; to take possession of.

†**potis·simo** *adj.* strongest, most especial, principal; ragione potissima, very strongest reason.

†**poto** *m.* drinking.

†**potta¹** *f.* (anat.; vulg.) vulva.

potta² *f.* (zool.) — marina, see 'polmone di mare', under **polmone**.

potta³ *pr.n.m.* (joc.) the 'Podestà' of Modena in the *Secchia rapita* by Tassoni; (essere il — di Modena, to boast.

†**pottag·gio** *m.* See **potaggio**.

pottarga *f.* See **bottarga**.

pottinic·cio *m.* (vulg.) mud, mess, slush; (fig.) botching, clumsy work.

po·ver-o *adj.* poor; needy; unfortunate; humble; scanty; un — diavolo, a poor wretch (i.e. unfortunate, evoking pity); — me!, poor me!; un uomo —, a poor man (i.e. impoverished); — di materie prime, poor in, lacking, raw materials; un raccolto —, a poor harvest, a scanty harvest; (motor.) miscela -a, weak mixture; (fig.) una -a consolazione, an inadequate consolation; montagne -e di pascoli, mountains with little pasturage; fiume — di acqua, river with little water, shallow river; architettura -a, plain architecture (i.e. with little or no ornament); stile —, plain style; in lingua -a, in parole -e, in plain language (i.e. without flourish or circumlocution); il mio — parere, my humble opinion; (rel.) — di spirito, poor in spirit, (pop.) simple-minded, stupid; il — giovane si uccise, the unhappy youth committed suicide; la mia -a sorella, my late sister; (rel.) pregate per i -i morti, pray for the poor souls (in Purgatory); (eccl. hist.) i -i di Lione, the Poor of Lyons (Waldensians); i -i cattolici, the Poor Catholics (Waldensians who returned to the Catholic Church and founded a mendicant order in 1208); (rel.) i -i volontari, the poor by choice, those who have embraced poverty (said of all religious orders); once esp. of an Augustinian congregation); — in canna, destitute, 'down and out'; *adv. phr.* alla -a, poorly, scantily, wretchedly; *n.m.* poor man, pauper; beggar, mendicant; ricchi e -i, rich and poor. **-amente** *adv.* poorly, scantily, wretchedly. **-ac·cia** *f.*, **-assa** *f.*, **-azza** *f.* (zool.) *Venus gallina*, an edible bivalve. **-ac·cio** *adj. pejor.* poor man, poor fellow, poor creature, poor thing, poor devil. **-a·glia** *f.* poor people; (crowd of) beggars, mendicants; tutta la -aglia del paese si affollò intorno a me, all the beggars of the village crowded round me. **-ello** *m.* poor man, pauper; i -elli, the poor; poor creature, beggar; il -ello d'Assisi,

the Poor Man of Assisi, St Francis, *adj.* la gente -ella, the poor friars of St Francis. **-ellamente** *adv.* like a poor man. **-etto** *m.* poor fellow; -etto!, poor thing! (-etta *f.*) **-ino** *m. dim.* poor chap (esp. as *excl.* expressing compassion); *adj.* mercante di vino, mercante -ino, a wine merchant doesn't grow rich. **-one** *m. augm.* (iron.) man who wishes to appear poor. **-tà** *f.* poverty; want; scarcity; meanness; -tà di acque, scarcity of water; (leg.) certificato di -tà, poor person's certificate (C.C.P.); (theol.) poverty (evangelic, voluntary, holy, religious); le nozze di S. Francesco con la -tà, the marriage of St Francis with Lady Poverty.

pozione *f.* potion, decoction; una — calmante, a sedative.

poziọr-e *adj.* (leg.) having priority of title; having prior or better right; *n.m.* one who has priority of right or title. **-ità** *f.* (leg.) priority of right or title.

pọzz-a *f.* pool, puddle. **-ac·cia** *f. pejor.* large dirty puddle. **-an·ghera** *f.* muddy pool; puddle; duck-pond. **-etta** *f. dim.* little pool; dimple.

pọzz-o *m.* well; — artesiano, artesian well; acqua di —, well-water; (mine) shaft; tank; — dell'ascensore, lift-shaft; (fig.) fount, fountain; — petrolifero, oil-well; — nero, cesspool; il — di S. Patrizio, the widow's cruse; (fig.) è un — di scienza, he is a well of learning, a fountain of knowledge; avere un — di denari, to have pots of money; far vedere la luna nel — a uno, to delude someone; (naut.) well, well deck, hold; †wells, spaces in the bilges where the ship's pumps drained off excess water; †— della sentina, — della tromba, pump well; †— di bordo, fresh-water tank; — del bacino, drain in a dry dock; — caldo, hot well of a condenser; — della catena, cable locker; — dell'elica, propeller well; (mil.) shaft, mine, countermine; (cards) pack or 'pool' from which players take cards. **-etto** *m. dim.* (liturg.) font for immersion; (hydr.; bldg.) trap; -etto di raccolta fanghi, mud trap; (motor.) sump; (naut.) stern sheets of a boat; †cockpit; drinking fountain; -etto di depurazione, water filter. †**-ino** *m.* (archit.) wedge-shaped brick, used in an arch or a well-head. †**-uolo** *m.* pit.

Pozzuoli *pr.n.f.* (geog.) Puteoli.

Praga *pr.n.f.* (geog.) Prague.

pragmat-ișmo *m.* (philos.) pragmatism. **-ista** *m.* pragmatist. (**-i·stico** *adj.*)

pra·io *m.* (ichth.) *Pagrus pagrus*, a kind of sea bream.

pralina *f.* sugared almond.

prama *f.* (naut.) pram, small dinghy; flat-bottomed river craft; (Ven.) gun-lighter.

pramma·tica *f.* custom; customary manner; prescribed method; regular practice; di —, *de rigueur*; essere di —, to be customary; risposta di —, regulation answer; *adj. f.* (hist.) — sanzione, Pragmatic Sanction.

prana *m.* (Indian) breath of life, universal life-principle.

†**pran·d-ere** *intr.* to dine, to feast. †**-io** *m.* banquet, feast.

pra·nia *f.* (naut.). See **prama**.

†**pranso** *adj.* satisfied, replete, full.

pranz-o *m.* (N. Ital.) dinner; (Tusc. and S. Ital.) lunch; luncheon; mid-day dinner; ora di —, dinner-time, dinner hour *or* lunch-time; campanello che annunzia l'ora del —, dinner-bell; il — è pronto, dinner (lunch) is served; sala da —, dining-room; vestirsi per il —, to dress for dinner; — di amici, — con invitati, dinner-party; — di gala, banquet; — di Corte, Court banquet; dopo —, in the afternoon, after lunch; saltare il —, to dine with Duke Humphrey, to miss dinner. **-are** [A I] *intr.* (*aux.* avere) to dine; to have dinner; to have lunch; -are fuori di casa, to dine out; -are la sera, to dine in the evening, to have late dinner. **-atore** *m.* diner; one who cadges dinners. (**-atrice** *f.*) **-etto** *m. dim.* light dinner, plain dinner; light lunch; little dinner-party (with a few friends). **-one** *augm.* big dinner.

pra·ș-ino, **pras·s-ino** *adj.* leek-green.

prassi *f. indecl.* practice (as opposed to theory); routine procedure.

Prassi·tele *pr.n.m.* Praxiteles.

†**prata·glia** *f.* See **prateria**, under **prato**.

prataiola *f.* (orn.) gallina —, little bustard. **-aiuolo** *adj.* of the fields or meadows, field; *n.m.* mushroom, *Agaricus campestris*.

prat-are [A I] *tr.* to sow with grass. **-ellina** *f.* see **pratolina**, under **prato**. **-ense** *adj.* see under **prato**.

pra·tic-a *f.* practice, experience; practical knowledge; familiarity; intercourse; intrigue; training; business; matter, affair; la — val più che la teoria, practice is better than theory; la — è una grande maestra, experience is the best teacher; ha fatto una lunga —,

pratic-a (*cont.*)

he has had a long training; ha molta — del suo mestiere, he knows his job very well; ha molta — negli affari, he has a good knowledge of business; gli manca la — del mondo, he lacks knowledge of the world; fu messo a far — presso un chirurgo, he was apprenticed to a surgeon; far — in ospedali, to walk the hospitals; in —, in practice; mettere in —, to put into practice; misi in — i vostri consigli, I took your advice; acquistare —, to become proficient through practice, to learn by experience; lo si acquista con la —, it comes with practice; aver — di un autore, to be familiar with an author's works; da noi la — è questa, this is our practice, this is how we do it; business, matter, affair; studio questa —, I am studying this matter (*or* the papers concerning this matter); affidare una — a qualcuno, to leave a matter to someone; condurre una — segreta, to conduct an affair secretly; regolare una —, to settle a matter; è una bottega che ha molte pratiche, it is a shop that has many customers; (leg.; admin.) case; dossier; file (of documents); accantonare una —, to shelve a case; disincagliare una —, to reopen a case; (naut.) pratique, permission to enter harbour, having a clean bill of health; esame di —, extra Master's ticket; — del mare, seamanlike knowledge and ability; familiarity; *pl.* practical arrangements, means or steps; pratiche contro la procreazione, contraceptive practices (C.P.); (comm.) dealings, arrangements, steps; fare le pratiche per, to take steps to; ci sono le pratiche in corso, steps are being taken; osservare le pratiche religiose, to fulfil one's religious duties, to observe the forms of worship. **-ac·cia** *f. pejor.* undesirable companion, person to be avoided; empirical skill or knowledge.

prat-ichezza *f.* familiarity, intercourse; skill, practical knowledge. **-icona** *f. augm.* long training, experience.

pratic-are [A 2S] *tr.* to practise, to put into practice; to carry out; to exercise; to frequent, to associate with; — la medicina, to practise as a doctor; — le virtù cristiane, to practise Christian virtues; — una cura, to try a treatment; — un luogo, to haunt, to frequent, a place; — una persona, to be familiar with a person; (provb.) chi -a lo zoppo impara a zoppicare, he who walks with the lame learns to limp; to make, to open, to execute; — un buco, to make, to bore, a hole, — un'apertura, to make an opening; — la pace, to negotiate a peace treaty; — un matrimonio, to arrange a marriage; — prezzi, to quote prices; *abs., intr.* (*aux.* avere) è dottore in medicina ma non -a, he is a doctor of medicine but he does not practise; è credente ma non -a, he is a believer but he does not go to church; to be a companion (of), to be familiar (with); (provb.) dimmi con chi pratichi e ti dirò chi sei, tell me who your friends are and I will tell you what you are; (naut.) to have contact communication or access to the shore; non poter — con la terra, to be unable to communicate with land (e.g. owing to bad weather, unfriendly relations, or infectious disease). **-a·bile** *adj.* practicable; feasible; possible; practical; luogo -abile, place easy of access, scala -abile, convenient staircase; gente -abile. accessible people, people easy to get on with; strada -abile, road that is passable; (cinem.) treppiede -abile, ladder tripod; *n.m.* (theatr.) stage buildings; (techn.) catwalk. **(-abilmente** *adv.*) **-abilità** *f.* practicability, convenience. **-ante** *part. adj.* practising; *n.m., f.* apprentice; church-goer, practising Christian. **-ato** *part. adj.* frequented; carried out, put into practice.

pra·tic-o *adj.* practical; experienced; metodo —, practical method; persone pratiche, practical people; è un insegnante —, he is an experienced teacher; — di, familiar with, experienced in; non sono — del luogo, I do not know the place, I am a stranger here; è — del suo mestiere, he knows his trade; voglio vederlo all'atto —, I want to see him put to the test; efficient, serving its purpose; questa sveglia è molto -a, this alarm-clock is very useful; *n.m.* practitioner; expert; (naut.) lower-grade pilot; — locale, certified local pilot for small craft; — ufficiale, local pilot. **-amente** *adv.* practically; in practice; by practice. **-ità** *f.* convenience; practicalness, usefulness; -ità di un consiglio, practical character of a piece of advice. **-one** *m. augm.* expert; experienced worker; è un -one e niente più, he knows only the practical side of his trade, nothing else.

prat-o *m.* meadow; -i ridenti, smiling meadows; terreno coltivato a —, grassland; rompere un —, to plough up a meadow; (geog.) uncultivated land used for pasture; prati-pascoli, land where animals are pastured after hay-harvest; (bot.) regina dei -i, meadow-sweet, *Filipendula ulmaria*; (mil.) pelle di —, turf covering of a glacis, etc.; †sod used for dowsing red-hot shot. **-ello** *m. dim.* pretty little meadow; lawn. **-ense** *adj.* of the meadows, meadow; fiori -ensi, meadow flowers, field flowers. **-eri·a** *f.* grassland; prairie. **-ic·cio** *m.* paddock; lawn. **(-icello, icino** *m. dim.*) **-ile** *pr.n.m.* (hist.) Prairial, the ninth month of the French revolutionary calendar. **-i·o** *adj.* see **prativo**. **-ivo** *adj.* in grass; as a meadow; growing in meadows; terreni -ivi, grassland(s); piante -ive, meadow plants **-olina** *f.* (bot.) daisy, *Bellis perennis*. **-olino** *m.* mushroom, *Agaricus campestris*.

†**pra·tora** *f.pl.* of **prato**, q.v.

prav-o *adj.* wicked, depraved. **(-amente** *adv.*) **-ità** *f.* wickedness, depravity.

pre' abbrev. of **prete**, q.v.

preaccenn-are [A I] *tr.* to mention beforehand. **-ato** *part. adj.* aforesaid; mentioned before.

preaccensione *f.* (motor.) 'pinking'.

preaccusare [A I] *tr.* (leg.) to accuse before the event.

preadam-ita *m.* (theol.) Preadamite; supposed human predecessor of Adam or believer in the existence of such. **-i·tico** *adj.* before Adam, prehistoric; (joc.) ancient, primitive, antiquated.

preadattamento *m.* (biol.) preadaptation.

Prealpi *pr.n.f.pl.* (geog.) foothills of the Alps.

pream·bol-o *m.* preface, preamble; lasci stare i -i, don't beat about the bush; senza (tanti) -i, without more ado. **-are** [A I S] *intr.* (*aux.* avere) (joc.) to preface one's remarks, to be slow in coming to the point.

†**pream·bulo** *m.* See **preambolo**.

preamplific-atore *m.* (radio; telev.) preamplifier. **-azione** *f.* (radio; telev.) preamplification.

preannunzi-are [A4] *tr.* to announce in advance, to give notice of. **(-ato** *part. adj.*)

preannun·zio *m.* announcement; preliminary announcement; prediction.

preanticip-are [A I S] *tr.* to forestall, to anticipate. **(-ato** *part. adj.*)

preassiale *adj.* (anat.) preaxial.

preatas·sico *adj.* (med.) preataxic.

preauricolare *adj.* (anat.) pre-auricular, pro-otic.

preavvert-ire [D I] *tr.* to inform in advance. **(-ito** *part. adj.*)

preavvis-are [A I] *tr.* to inform in advance; to give early notice to; ci -arono, we were told in advance; (leg.) to give previous notice to. **(-ato** *part. adj.*) **-o** *m.* (leg.) warning, notice; -o di pagamento, notice of payment due; con -o di un mese, at a month's notice.

prebagno *m.* (photog.; techn.) preliminary bath.

prebend-a *f.* (eccl.) prebend; — teologale, — penitenziale, prebend held by the canon theologian or penitentiary; (fig.) easy money. **-a·rio** *m.* (eccl.) prebendary. †**-a·tico** *m.* (eccl.) prebend. **-ato** *adj.* (eccl.) holding a prebend; *n.m.* prebendaryship; prebendary.

pre-cambriano, -ca·mbrico *adj.* (geol.) Pre-Cambrian.

preca·mera *f.* (motor.) pre-combustion chamber.

precanceroso *adj.* (med.) precancerous.

precapillare *adj.* (med.) precapillary.

†**precare** *vb.* and derivs. See **pregare**.

†**prec-ari·a** *f.*, †**-azione** *f.* See **preghiera**.

preca·ri-o *adj.* precarious, temporary; uncertain; (leg.) precarious; detenzione -a, holding at will. **-età** *f.* precariousness.

precauzione *f.* precaution; care, caution; con la debita —, with due care; misure di —, precautionary measures; le precauzioni non sono mai troppe, you can't be too careful.

prece *f.* (poet.) prayer.

prece·d-ere [B I] *tr.* to precede, to come before, to go before; to lead; mio figlio mi -erà, my son will precede me; to be superior to; *intr.* (*aux.* essere) to come first; -e una descrizione del paese, first comes a description of the country; far —, to put first; il Manzoni fa — al suo romanzo una importante introduzione, Manzoni prefaces his novel with an important introduction. **-ente** *part. adj.* preceding; former, previous; *n.m.* precedent; senza -enti, unprecedented; (leg.) precedent. **-entemente** *adv.* previously, formerly; before. **-enza** *f.* precedence; priority; esso ha la -enza su tutti gli altri, it takes precedence of all others; ordine di -enza, order of precedence; con ordine di -enza superiore, of high priority; -enza assoluta, absolute priority; (leg.) precedence; priority; avere la -enza su, to take precedence of, to have priority over; (road traffic) diritto di -enza, right of way (equiv. to **priorità**, q.v.);

preced-ere (*cont.*)

dare la -enza, to give (right of) way; (rlwy.) priority; -enza di passaggio, right of way; in -enza, previously, formerly, *or* beforehand, in advance. (-uto *part.*)

precellen-te *adj.* excellent, of superior excellence; supreme. **-za** *f.* supremacy, superiority.

†**precelso** *adj.* See **eccelso**.

†**precen-tore** *m.* (eccl.) precentor. **-zione** *f.* (Rom. antiq.) *praecentio*, music before a battle or sacrifice.

precess-ione *f.* (eng.) precession, advance, lead; (astron.) — degli equinozi, precession of the equinoxes; †precedence. **-o** *adj.* past, gone by. †**-ore** *m.* (theol.) il -ore di Gesù, the Precursor, St John Baptist.

precett-o *m.* precept; maxim; un esempio val più di un —, example is better than precept; order; ubbidisci ai -i del tuo superiore, obey your master's orders; (theol.) precept (as distinct from counsel); -i della chiesa, precepts, commandments, of the Church; feste di —, holidays of obligation; -i evangelici, Gospel teaching (precepts); (leg.) notice of judgement for debt (C.C.P.); — per consegna o rilascio, notice of judgement for delivery up; mandato di — al terzo, garnishee order; — di polizia, police warning (C.P.); (mil.) reassignment (order). **-ante** *m.*, *f.* (leg.) party causing issue of 'precetto'; †preceptor, teacher. **-are** [A I] *tr.* to enjoin, to order, to summon; (leg.) to place under police supervision; to give formal warning to (C.P.); to serve formal notice of judgement for debt upon; -are il terzo, to garnishee (C.C.P.); (mil.) to preassign (a unit); to reallocate (duties in the field). **-ato** *part. adj.* (leg.) served with notice (in any sense of 'precetto'); *n.m.* addressee of 'precetto'; il terzo -ato, garnishee (C.C.P.). **-atore** *m.* one who formulates rules or precepts; (leg.) issuer of notice or warning (in any sense of 'precetto'). (**-atrice** *f.*) **-i·bile** *adj.* expressible as a maxim or precept; suitable for teaching. **-ista** *m.* writer who expounds an art (esp. rhetorical) in terms of rules and examples, teacher by precepts. **-i·stica** *f.* art of forming precepts. **-ivo** *adj.* preceptive, didactic; (leg.) carta -iva, list of rules ordered by Judge (C.P.P.). **-ivamente** *adv.* didactically, by precept. **-orato** *m.* tutorship. **-ore** *m.* tutor; teacher; preceptor.

†**prechiaro** *adj.* See **preclaro**.

preci·dere [C I] *tr.* to cut short, to cut off; — ogni via di scampo, to cut off every way of escape; — la carriera a uno, to cut short a person's career.

precin·gere [C 3] *tr.* to surround; to girdle; *rfl.* to gird oneself, to put a belt on.

precin-to *part.* of **precingere**, q.v.; *adj.* surrounded; girt; †*n.m.* precinct. **-zione** *f.* (Rom. antiq.) *praecinctio*, terrace between two rows of seats running round an amphitheatre.

preci·pit-e *adj.* headlong; steep, precipitous. **-a·bile** *adj.* (chem.) precipitable. **-abilità** *f.* (chem.) precipitability. **-a·mento** *m.* precipitation; fall. **-ante** *part. adj.* precipitating; *n.m.* (chem.) precipitant. **-are** [A I S] *tr.* to cast down headlong; to throw down; to hasten; to precipitate; Lucifero fu -ato dal cielo, Lucifer was flung headlong from Heaven; Iddio -ò Lucifero nell'inferno, God cast Lucifer into Hell; dovette -are la partenza, he had to hasten his departure; -are una decisione, to make a hasty decision; to hurry (the pace, time, beat in music, etc.); -are gl'indugi, to eliminate, to cut out, to reduce, delay; (chem.) to precipitate; *intr.* (*aux.* essere) to fall headlong, to crash; il muro -ò con grande rumore, the wall collapsed with a loud noise; l'apparecchio -ò al suolo, the plane crashed; (of snow, rain, etc.) to fall; (chem.) to be precipitated, to form a precipitate; to hasten, to hurry; to rush on, to come to a head; -a l'ora, time is flying; non -iamo, let's not hurry; gli eventi -ano, events are coming to a head; (fig.) to be ruined, (fam.) to come a cropper; ha fatto una speculazione sbagliata ed è -ato, he made a bad speculation and ruined himself; *rfl.* to rush, to run precipitately; to throw oneself down; si -ò fuori della stanza, he rushed out of the room. **-ato** *part. adj.* rash, hasty, precipitate; fallen, cast down; *n.m.* (chem.) precipitate. **-atamente** *adv.* precipitately; hastily. **-atore** *m.* (chem.; phys.) precipitator. (**-atrice** *f.*) **-azione** *f.* precipitancy, haste; precipitation, fall; -azioni atmosferiche, falls of rain, snow or hail; (chem.) precipitation; (meteor.) precipitation. **-evole** *adj.* precipitous, steep; (fig.) impetuous, hasty. **-evolissimevolmente** *adv.* (joc.) chi troppo in alto sal, cade repente (*or* sovente) -evolissimevolmente, i.e. pride goes before a fall. **-evolmente** *adv.* precipitously. **-ina** *f.* (med.) precipitin. **-oso** *adj.* hasty, precipitate, hurried; fuga -osa,

headlong flight; una pioggia -osa, a pelting rain; lavoro -oso, scamped work; precipitous; una rupe -osa, a precipitous cliff. **-osamente** *adv.* hastily, precipitately; correre -osamente, to run headlong.

precipi·zi-o *m.* precipice; headlong fall; ruin; (fig.) coming down in the world, loss of caste; essere sull'orlo del —, to be on the verge of ruin; correre a —, to run headlong; parlare a —, to speak hastily, without consideration; ce n'era un —, there was a flood.

preci·pu-o *adj.* chief, principal. **-amente** *adv.* chiefly, mainly; above all.

precis-o *part.* of **precidere**, q.v.; *adj.* precise, exact; punctual; definite, accurate; le sue -e parole, his exact words; questa è la parola -a, this is the proper (right) word; strict, bounden; è — dovere, it is one's bounden duty; — a pagare, punctual in paying; alle dieci -e, at ten o'clock sharp, on the stroke of ten; dovete essere -i in tutto, you must be exact in everything; —!, precisely!, quite so!; cut short; capelli -i, close-cropped hair; separated, interrupted; absolute; senza una -a necessità, without absolute necessity. **-amente** *adv.* precisely, exactly; concisely; *excl.* quite so! **-are** [A I] *tr.* to state precisely; to specify; to tell exactly; non potrei -arvi il luogo, I couldn't tell you the place exactly. **-ione** *f.* precision, accuracy, exactness; -ione di linguaggio, exactness of language; (techn.) bilancia di -ione, precision balance; (mil.) armi di -ione, precision weapons; tiro di -ione, accurate fire; strumenti di -ione, precision computers.

precitato *adj.* aforesaid, above mentioned; quoted above.

preclar-o *adj.* eminent, prominent; illustrious; noble; (of the dead) di memoria -a, of illustrious memory. **-amente** *adv.* eminently; illustriously. (**-ità** *f.*)

precl-u·dere *tr.* [C 3] to block; to debar; to prevent; to preclude; — la via ad uno, to block someone's way; — ogni dubbio, to preclude all doubt. **-uso** *part. adj.* blocked, closed; precluded.

†**preco** *m.* See **preghiera**.

precoc-e *adj.* precocious, early; premature. **-emente** *adv.* precociously, early, prematurely. **-ità** *f.* precociousness, precocity; la -ità va a danno della resistenza, early ripe, early rotten.

†**precogitare** *tr.* to think over beforehand.

†**preco·gnito** *m.*, *adj.* (that which is) known beforehand.

precognizione *f.* foreknowledge.

†**precogno·scere** *vb.* and derivs. See **preconoscere**.

precolombiano *adj.* (hist.) precolumbian (in America before Columbus).

precompresso *adj.* (eng.) prestressed.

preconcetto *adj.* preconceived; giudicare secondo idee preconcette, to judge according to preconceived notions; *n.m.* preconception, prejudice; bias; giudicare senza preconcetti, to judge without prejudice.

†**precone** *m.* herald.

preco·nio *m.* public announcement; (eccl.) preconization.

preconizz-are [A I] *tr.* to announce publicly; (eccl.) to preconize; to predict, to foretell. (**-ato** *part. adj.*) **-azione** *f.* (eccl.) preconization; eulogy, public praise.

preconosc-ere [B 9] *tr.* to foreknow, to have foreknowledge of; to foresee. **-enza** *f.* foreknowledge; prescience. **-imento** *m.* knowing beforehand. **-iuto** *part. adj.* foreknown, known beforehand.

precord-i *m.pl.* (†**preco·rdia** *f.pl.*) precordium, epigastric region. †**-iale** *adj.* (anat.) precordial, epigastric.

precorr-ere [C 5] *tr.* to anticipate; to be in advance of; to forestall; to outrun; precorse i tempi, he was in advance of his age; — gli avvenimenti, to anticipate, forestall, events; *intr.* (*aux.* essere) to hasten in advance; era precorso per dargli l'annunzio, he had come in advance to give him the news. **-ente** *part. adj.* preceding, running ahead. **-itore** *m.* precursor, forerunner. **-itrice** *f.* alba -itrice del giorno, dawn, harbinger of day.

precorso *part.* of **precorrere**, q.v.; *adj.* preceding; anticipated; past; l'anno —, last year, the preceding year.

precostitu-ire [D 2] *tr.* (leg.) to establish or set up previously. **-ito** *part. adj.* il giudice -ito per legge, judge preordained by law (I.C.); la prova -ita, documentary evidence dating before action brought.

precu·neo *m.* (anat.) precuneus.

†**precuo·io** *m.* See **procuoio**.

precursor-e *m.* forerunner, precursor; harbinger; †(mil.) quartermaster; (theol.) il —, the Precursor, the Forerunner, St John Baptist; *adj.* precursory, premonitory; segni -i della tempesta, harbingers of the storm, first signs of a coming storm.

pred-a *f.* object of pursuit, quarry; prey; uccello di —, bird of prey; booty; — di guerra, war booty, spoils of war; essere facile — del nemico, to fall an easy prey to the enemy; essere in — alla disperazione, to be a prey to despair; darsi in — a, to give oneself up to, to abandon oneself to; essere in — al vizio, to be a slave to vice; essere in — all'ira, to be overcome by rage; (leg.; naut.) prize; buona —, permissible prize; Tribunale delle -e, prize court, Admiralty court; il decimo della —, Captain's share (tenth); (mil.) booty, loot; porre in —, to put to sack; dare in —, to give over to plunder, to hand over to be sacked; (bldg.) masonry; (dial., Mantua) brick. **-ace** *adj.* predatory; (poet.) tempo -ace, destructive time, time the thief of youth, etc. **-amento** *m.* pillage, sack. **-are** [A I] *tr.* to plunder, to pillage, to sack; to prey upon. **-ato** *part. adj.* plundered, sacked, stripped. **-atore** *m.* plunderer, pillager; pirate; (zool.) predator. (**-atrice** *f.*) **-atorio** *adj.* predatory; (mil.) pertaining to looting; concerned with foraging; scrounging.

predecessore *m.* predecessor; forebear, ancestor; forerunner.

predell-a *f.* foot-rest, footboard; carriage-step; platform, dais; (liturg.) foot-pace (of altar); praying-stool; close-stool, commode; — di marmo, marble slab of a latrine; (paint.) predella (of an altar-piece); (equest.) the ends of the reins, where they are held in the hand. **-ina** *f.*, **-ino** *m. dim.* foot-stool; little chair; child's high chair; folding carriage-step; step, footboard; (motor.) running-board. **-one** *m. augm.* high stool. **-uccia** *f. dim.* little seat, esp. in the phrase: portare a -ucce, to give a hand-seat to.

predestin-are [A I] *tr.* to predestine; to destine, to mark out (for); (theol.) to predestinate, to predestine. **-ativo** *adj.* marking out, destining. **-ato** *part. adj.* destined, predestined, marked out (for). **-aziani** *m.pl.* (eccl. hist.) Predestinarians. **-azione** *f.* predestination; (theol.) predestination.

predetermin-are [A I S] *tr.* to predetermine, to foreordain. **-ato** *part. adj.* predeterminate, preordained. (**-atamente** *adv.*) **-azione** *f.* predetermination.

predetto *part.* of predire, q.v.; *adj.* aforesaid, above mentioned, foretold.

predial-e *adj.* (leg.) appendant; *n.f.* land-tax. **-ità** *f.* (leg.) appendance.

prediasto·lico *adj.* (med.) prediastolic; soffio — prediastolic murmur.

pre·dic-a *f.* (eccl. and fig.) sermon; †congregation hearing sermon; bastonare come sonare a —, to give a thorough good beating to, to thrash soundly; da quale pulpito viene la —, look who's talking!; (fam.) lecture; fare una —, to read a lecture, to scold; finiscila con codeste prediche!, stop sermonizing!; aver preso posto alla —, to have become an important person. **-a·bile** *adj.* (eccl.) worth preaching about, usable as sermon material; (philos.; *adj.*, *n.m.*) predicable. **-amento** *m.* sermon, preaching; (logic) predicament, category; esteem, consideration; essere in buono —, to be (held) in high esteem. **-ante** *part. adj.* preaching; (eccl.) frati -anti, Friars Preachers, Dominicans; *n.m.* preacher.

predic-are [A 2 S] *tr., intr.* (*aux.* avere) to preach, to proclaim; — a braccio, to preach extempore; (eccl.) to preach (sermon, gospel, crusade); — la quaresima, to preach (a course of) sermons through Lent; (dial., of ducks) to quack; †to preach to, to evangelize; -a bene e razzola male, he does not practise what he preaches; non dovete -arlo ai quattro venti, you must not proclaim it to the four winds; — al vento, to speak to the winds (the wall), to waste one's breath; to praise; (logic; gramm) to predicate. **-ato** *part.* proclaimed; praised; *n.m.* (gramm.) predicate; essere in -ato per un posto, to be a candidate for a post; in -ato di sindaco, standing for the mayoralty; non ho niente in -ato per ora, I have nothing in prospect for the present; parleremo questa sera della cosa in -ato, this evening we shall discuss the matter in question. **-atora** *f.* (joc.) woman given to sermonizing, or to curtain lectures. **-atore** *m.* preacher; one given to declamation; eulogist; (eccl.) preacher; frati -atori, Friars Preachers. (**-atrice** *f.*) **-atoressa** *f.* (joc.) see predicatora. **-ato·rio** *adj.* (*m.pl.* -atorii) predicatory, sermonizing; tono -atorio, sermonizing tone. **-azione** *f.* preaching; sermon; la -azione del vangelo, the preaching of the Gospel; sermonizing, good advice, reprimand; (gramm.; logic) predication.

†**predi·cere** *vb.* See predire.

predi-chetta *f.* admonition; scolding; fare una — a uno, to lecture someone. **-china** *f.*, **-chino** *m. fam.* gentle reproof, mild scolding. **-cozzo** *m. dim.* (fam.) admonition, scolding.

predic-imento *m.* prediction. **-itore** *m.* prophet; first speaker. (**-itrice** *f.*)

predigestione *f.* (physiol.) predigestion, preliminary digestion.

predil-etto *part.* of prediligere, q.v.; *adj.* favourite, dearest; il mio giuoco —, my favourite game; il suo amico —, his dearest friend; *n.m.* favourite, dearest, darling; pet; era il — della mamma, he was his mother's darling. (**-etta** *f.*) **-ezione** *f.* predilection, partiality; la sua -ezione era la caccia, his favourite occupation was hunting (shooting, etc.). **-i·gere** [C 13] *tr.* to prefer, to have a special liking for; to like better, to hold dear, dearer or dearest; fra i poeti -igo Dante, I like Dante best of all the poets.

predire [B 10] *tr.* to foretell, to predict, to forecast; questo vento predice pioggia, this wind is a sign of rain.

predirezionale *adj.* (motor.) incolonnamento —, instruction whereby cars should keep to their lane before turning left or right.

predis-porre [B 21] *tr.* to arrange in advance; tutto era stato -posto, everything had been arranged beforehand; to predispose; -ponilo in mio favore, predispose him in my favour; — a, to induce; queste letture -pongono al sonno, this reading induces sleep; la sana fatica -pone al buon riposo, healthy toil induces sound sleep; *rfl.* to prepare oneself; -porsi con l'animo, to prepare one's mind. **-posizione** *f.* predisposition, partiality; arrangement; (med.) predisposition, proneness. **-posto**, **-posto** *part. adj.* arranged, prepared; predisposed; (med.) predisposed, susceptible, prone.

predistillazione *f.* (industr.) predistillation.

predisti·n-guere [C 5] *tr.* to single out, to mark with especial distinction. **-to** *part. adj.* most distinguished.

†**pre·dito** *adj.* gifted; endowed.

predizione *f.* prediction, prophecy.

predomin-are [A I S] *intr.* (*aux.* avere) to predominate, to prevail; to take the first place; to be dominant, to dominate; qui -a lo stile gotico, the Gothic style predominates here; vuole —, he wants to dominate, to take first place; in lui -a l'ambizione, ambition is his chief characteristic; (followed by *prep.* 'su' or 'a') l'utile -a sul diletto (*or* al diletto), practical considerations prevail over pleasure; *tr.* to dominate, to sway, to master; -a tutti, he dominates everyone; l'ira lo -a, he is swayed by anger. **-ante** *part. adj.* predominant, prevailing; ruling; prevalent; vento -ante, prevailing wind; idea -ante, ruling idea, opinione -ante, prevalent opinion; over-riding. **-ato** *part. adj.* overcome, mastered; over-ruled. **-azione** *f.* supremacy.

predomi·nio *m.* predominance, supremacy, rule; prevalence; (chem.) excess.

predone *m.* robber; plunderer, marauder; pirate; — del mare, pirate.

pre-eleg·gere [C 12] *tr.* to elect; to pre-elect; to prefer. **-eletto** *part. adj.*, *n.m.* i -eletti di Dio, God's elect. **-elezione** *f.* pre-election, preference, predestination.

†**preeminenza** *f.* pre-eminence.

preesi·st-ere [B I] *intr.* (*aux.* avere) to pre-exist. **-ente** *part. adj.* pre-existent, pre-existing; condizioni -enti alla guerra, pre-war conditions; (leg.) pre-existent; debiti -enti non scaduti, debts owing but not due (C.C.). **-enza** *f.* pre-existence.

prefabbric-are [A 2 S] *tr.* (techn.; bldg.) to prefabricate. **-ato** *part. adj.* prefabricated.

prefato *adj.* aforesaid.

prefa·z-io *m.* (liturg.) Preface (in the Mass); (mus.) the music of a Preface in the Mass; (fig.) piantare sul bel del —, to leave in the lurch; †see prefazione. **-ione** *f.* preface, introduction. **-ioncella** *f. dim.* short preface.

†**prefenda** *f.* See prebenda

prefer-ire [D 2] *tr.* to prefer, to like better; to give preference to; -isco la poesia alla prosa, I like poetry better than prose; fra tutti voi -isco Maria, I like Mary best of you all; -ì morire piuttosto che tradire il segreto, he chose to die rather than reveal his secret; -isco andarmene, I would rather go; potete aspettarlo qui, se -ite, you can wait for him here if you prefer; i signori -iscono le bionde, gentlemen prefer blondes. **-enza** *f.* preference; dare la -enza a, to prefer; favouritism; usare -enza, to have favourites; avere la -enza su, to have the preference over, to be preferred to; a, in -enza di, rather than, in preference to; di -enza, preferably, for preference; leggo di -enza romanzi, I mostly prefer reading novels, I read mostly novels; (leg.) diritto di -enza, preferential right (C.C.); (finan.) capitali di -enza, preference stock; azioni di -enza, preference shares. **-enziale** *adj.* preferential, azioni -enziali, preference shares; tariffe doganali -enziali, preferential tariffs.

prefer-ire (*cont.*)

-i·bile *adj* preferable. -ibilmẹnte *adv.* preferably, for preference. (-ibilità *f.*) -i·colo *m.* (Rom. antiq.) *praefericulum*, sacrificial dish. -ito *part. adj.* preferred; (finan.) azioni -ite, preferred shares; *n.m.* favourite. -itọre *m.* one who shows a preference, one who has favourites. (-itrice *f.*)

prefett-o *m.* (Rom. antiq.) prefect, *praefectus* (military or civil official); (modern sense) the chief administrative officer and representative of the central government in a province; — di polizia, prefect of police, chief of police, police superintendent; (schol.) prefect; master; — degli studi, tutor, director of studies; — della biblioteca, chief librarian; (eccl.) prefect: — apostolico, Prefect Apostolic; (mil. hist.) — dell'oste, camp quartermaster; — del pretorio, captain of the Imperial guard; — dei fabbri, chief engineer; (naut. hist.) general of the galleys (sixteenth century); — marittimo (France), coastal district command. -ẹssa *f.* prefect's wife; woman holding a chief office; (joc.) weak or incompetent prefect. -ino *m.* (hist.) sub-prefect in papal Legations. -i·zia *f.* prefect's dress coat. -i·zio *adj.* prefect's, prefectoral. -ura *f.* prefecture; building containing the prefect's offices; (eccl.) -ura apostolica, prefecture Apostolic; (Rom. hist.) prefecture, *praefectura.*

pre·fica *f.* (Rom. antiq.) hired woman mourner; (fig.) whining or complaining person; (mus.) hired female mourner, female threnodist.

prefig·g-ere [C12] *tr.* to fix beforehand, to fix; to prefix; — un termine, to fix a term (limit); — una data, to arrange a date; *rfl.* (*dat.* of *prn.* 'si') to purpose, to intend, to design, to set before oneself; mi sono prefisso di parlargli domani, I intend to speak to him tomorrow; ecco lo scopo che ci siamo prefissi, this is the aim that we have in view. -imẹnto *m.* arrangement; purpose; intention.

prefigur-are [A1] *tr.* to prefigure. -amẹnto *m.* prefiguring; symbolizing. -ante *part. adj.* prefiguring, foreshadowing. -ato *part. adj.* prefigured, foreshadowed. -azịọne *f.* prefiguration; prototype.

prefiltro *m.* (techn.) initial filter, pre-cleaner.

prefin-ire [D2] *tr.* to predetermine. (-ito *part. adj.*) -izịọne *f.* predetermination.

prefiss-o *part.* of **prefiggere**, q.v.; *adj.* prefixed, fixed; established; appointed; all'ora -a, at the appointed time; *n.m.* (gramm.) prefix. -iọne *f.* prefixing; arranging.

preflorazịọne *f.* aestivation.

prefogliazịọne *f.* (bot.) vernation, prefoliation.

preform-are [A1c] *rfl.* to form beforehand. -ato *part. adj.* preformed; foreshadowed. -azịọne *f.* preformation.

pregangliare *adj.* (anat.) preganglionic.

preg-are [A2] *tr.* to ask, to pray, to beg, to request, to invite; — Dio, to pray (to God); sta -ando, he is praying; -o Dio che..., would to God that...; vi -o di considerare questo, I beg you to consider this, please consider this; ecco quello di cui lo -ai, that is what I requested of him; non potevo — voi di questo, I could not ask you to do this; mi -arono di andare da loro, they invited me to go to their house; lo preghi di entrare, ask him to come in; vi -o di dirmi..., please tell me...; -o!, don't mention it! (in answer to thanks), after you! (inviting someone to go first); farsi —, to stand on ceremony, to wait to be asked twice; si fece molto —, he took a lot of persuading; non farsi —, not to wait to be asked, to accept readily; via, accettate, non fatevi —, do accept, don't wait to be pressed; (in a threat) -a Dio che non ti capiti un'altra volta, just see that it doesn't happen again; preghi Dio di non capitarmi fra i piedi, God grant (let him mind that) he does not cross my path; to curse; — malanno su, to curse. †-a *f.* the sixteenth card of a pack of Minchiate cards which bore the figure of a woman in prayer. -adi·o *m.* (ent.) praying mantis. -ante *part., n.m., f.* one who prays, worshipper. -ato *part. adj.* requested, begged for; *n.m.* (Ven. **pregado**) in the Venetian Republic, Member of the Lesser Council or Senate. -atọre *m.* one who prays, worshipper. (-atrice *f.*)

pregẹvol-e *adj.* valuable, good; of worth; estimable; precious. -ẹzza *f.* value, goodness, worth.

preghier-a *f.* prayer; la — domenicale, the Lord's prayer; — della sera, evening prayer; dire, recitare le -e, to say one's prayers; libro di -e, prayer book; request, entreaty; viva —, earnest entreaty; rivolgere una — a, to make a request of; accogliere la — di uno, to grant one's request; fece il sordo alle mie -e, he turned a deaf ear to my entreaties; devo farvi una —, I must ask you a favour; — di essere brevi, speakers are requested to be brief. †-o *m.* see **preghiera**.

pregi-are [A3c] *tr.* to esteem, to value, to appreciate; to prize; to praise; to express esteem for; *rfl.* to have the honour, to beg to (in letters, etc.); mi -o d'informarvi, I beg to inform you, I have the honour to inform you; mi -o d'avervi come collega, I am honoured to have you as a colleague. -a·bile *adj.* estimable, valuable. -abilità *f.* worth, estimable qualities. -ato *part. adj.* esteemed, valuable, valued; autore molto -ato, highly esteemed author; (comm.) ho ricevuto la vostra -ata lettera del 10, I have received your favour of the 10th. -atis·simo *superl. adj.* highly esteemed; -atissimo signore, Dear Sir; al Pregiatissimo signor Peter Burbidge, Peter Burbidge, Esq. -atọre *m.* admirer, one who admires and appreciates. (-atrice *f.*)

pre·gi-o *m.* esteem; value, merit, good quality, excellence; essere di gran —, to be of great value; di nessun —, of no value, valueless; tenere in gran —, to hold in high esteem; essere in gran —, to be highly esteemed; ha molti pregi, he has many good qualities; ha pregi non comuni, he has unusual merits; (iron.) avrà dei pregi nascosti, no doubt he has hidden merits; mi faccio un — di avvertirvi, I venture to point out to you; (poet.) — della borsa, liberality; — della spada, valour.

†**pregione** *m., f.* and derivs. See **prigione**.

pregiud-icare [A2s] *tr.* to prejudge; to prejudice, to be prejudicial to; to harm, to injure; — il proprio avvenire, to prejudice one's future; — la salute, to be injurious to health, to harm one's health; — a, to prejudice in favour of; *rfl.* to harm oneself, to injure one's cause, prospects, etc.; to compromise oneself. -icante *part. adj.* prejudicial, compromising (also *n.m.*). -icativo *adj.* prejudicial, damaging, harmful. -icato *part. adj.* prejudged, settled, prejudiced; compromised; opinione -icata, fixed opinion, prejudice; mente -icata, prejudiced mind; suspected, suspect; *n.m.* (leg.) a person with a previous conviction (C.P.); (fam.) jailbird; suspect; i -icati politici sono tenuti sotto sorveglianza, political suspects are kept under supervision. †-i·cio *m.* see **pregiudizio**. -iziale *adj.* (leg.) una questione -iziale, preliminary question of law, *or* preliminary issue (C.C.P.); porre una questione -iziale, to raise a question which must be answered before the matter can be pursued further; prejudicial; having priority; *n.f.* (admin.) matter that must be settled before the main question. -izialmẹnte *adv.* prejudicially. -izịẹvole *adj.* (leg.) prejudicial. (-izievolmẹnte *adv.*) -i·zio *m.* prejudice, superstition; il -izio della iettatura, the superstition of the evil eye; i -izi popolari, popular superstitions (prejudices); harm, detriment; questa grandine è di -izio al raccolto, this hail is harmful to the crops; senza -izio di, without detriment to; tornare al -izio di, to be detrimental to; (leg.) prejudice.

pregn-ante *adj.* pregnant; (fig.) significato —, pregnant meaning; *n.f.* pregnant woman, expectant mother. -antemẹnte *adv.* pregnantly, meaningfully, meaningly. †-anza *f.* see **pregnezza** under **pregno**.

pregn-o *adj.* pregnant; latte —, milk of a pregnant woman; (fig.) full, filled, saturated; impregnated; rich (in), teeming (with); muro — d'umido, wall saturated with moisture; occhi -i di lagrime, tearful eyes; terreno — di acqua, sodden (waterlogged) ground; città -a di discordie, city teeming with quarrels. -ẹzza *f.* pregnancy; (med.) sopra -ezza, superfoetation.

pre-go *m.* (*pl.* -ghi) (poet.) prayer, request.

pregust-are [A1] *tr.* to have a foretaste of, to anticipate, to look forward to. -amẹnto *m.* foretaste. (-ato *part. adj.*) -atọre *m.* (hist.) taster. (-atrice *f.*) -azịọne *f.* foretaste; anticipation. †-o *m.* foretaste.

preignizịọne *f.* (motor.; aeron.) pre-ignition.

pre-indicato *adj.* before mentioned, aforesaid. -inserto *adj.* inserted before.

prein-ten·dere [C1] *tr., intr.* (*aux.* avere) to understand beforehand; to purpose, to mean. -tẹso *part. adj.* understood already, or beforehand; intended.

preinton-are [A1] *tr., intr.* (*aux.* avere) (mus.) to sing an intonation. -azịọne *f.* (mus.) intonation.

preintro-ducimẹnto *m.* previous or early introduction. -durre [B2] *tr.* to introduce beforehand.

†**pre-io** *m.* See **pregio**.

†**preïre** *tr.* to precede, to go before.

preï·sto·ria *f.* prehistory. **-sto·rico** *adj.* prehistoric; (joc.) antediluvian, ancient.

prelat-o *m.* (eccl.) prelate; (ichth.) *Dasybatus violaceus*, a kind of sting ray. **-ęsco** *adj.* (*m.pl.* **-ęschi**) (derog.) prelatic; prelate-like. **-ivo** *adj.* (leg.) carrying preferential right. **-i·zio** *adj.* of or relating to a prelate. **-ura** *f.* status, office, of prelate; body, group, of prelates; prelate's house.

prelazione *f.* (leg.) diritto di —, preferential right (C.C.); position of authority; †(eccl.) prelacy.

prelegato *m.* (leg.) preferential legacy (C.C.).

prelegge *f.* (leg.) colloq. term for 'Le disposizioni sulla legge in generale, General provisions of law' preceding C.C.

prelev-are [A I] *tr.* to draw, to withdraw, to take away, to take out; to deduct; — danaro da una banca, to draw money at a bank; — su, to deduct from. **-aménto** *m.* drawing money out; deduction. **-ato** *part. adj.* drawn, deducted. **-azione** *f.* (act of) drawing money out.

prelezione *f.* introductory lecture.

†**preliare** *intr.* to fight.

prelib-are [A I] *tr.* to have a foretaste of, to try in advance; to treat briefly by way of introduction. **-ato** *part. adj.* treated briefly in advance; choice, exquisite; excellent, delicious; vini -ati, exquisite wines; boccone -ato, exquisite titbit. **-atamente** *adv.* by way of introduction. **-azione** *f.* trying beforehand; foretaste; right to taste or try sample first.

prelievo *m.* (finan., neol.) drawing money out (cf. **prelevamento**, under **prelevare**).

preliminar-e *adj.* preliminary; introductory; progetto —, first draft; riunione — per le istruzioni, briefing meeting; *n.m.* (usu. *pl.*) element, principle; -i di pace, preliminaries of peace. **-mente** *adv.* preliminarily, as a first step.

prelodato *adj.* already mentioned with approval.

prelu·d-ere [C 3] *intr.* (*aux.* avere; *prep.* a) to write (or speak) an introduction; to be a prelude (to), to lead (to); quella rottura diplomatica preluse alla guerra, the breaking off of diplomatic relations was a prelude to war; la musica preluse al dramma, music paved the way for drama; — alla tempesta, to be a sign of a storm. **-iare** [A 4] *intr.* (*aux.* avere) (mus.) to prelude.

prelu·dio *m.* (mus.) prelude; (fig.) introduction, prelude; preparation; portent, forerunner.

premarinaro *adj.* istruzione premarinara, naval training prior to national service; (hist.) branch of cadet service in the Fascist régime known as Opera Nazionale Balilla, which also covered military training.

prematur-o *adj.* premature; (eng.) accensione -a, pre-ignition. **-aménte** *adv.* prematurely; è morto -amente, he died young.

premedit-are [A I s] *tr.* to premeditate, to design, to plan. **-ato** *part. adj.* premeditated, planned; (leg.) omicidio -ato, wilful murder attended by aggravating circumstance of premeditation (C.P.). **-atamente** *adv.* with design. **-azione** *f.* premeditation; design, intent, intention.

prementovato *adj.* before mentioned, aforesaid.

pre·m-ere [B I] *tr.* to press, to press upon, to weigh upon; -ete il bottone, press the button; -ete il bottone del campanello, ring the bell; essa -ette la mia mano, she pressed my hand; to press, to squeeze, to bear too heavily upon; eravamo -uti dal nemico, we were hard pressed by the foe; to crush; — un limone, to squeeze a lemon; — dell'uva, to crush, press, grapes; la scarpa -e troppo il piede, the shoe pinches, the shoe is too tight; — coi piedi, to press with one's feet, to tread on, to trample; (fig.) to repress; to restrain: — i moti del cuore, to repress one's feelings, to restrain one's emotions; *intr.* (*aux.* avere) to press, to push, to exert pressure; to weigh; la folla -eva da ogni parte, the crowd was pressing in from all directions; -ono su di lui perchè faccia testamento, they are urging him, bringing pressure to bear on him to make a will; non -ete troppo su questo tasto, don't harp too much on that string; to be pressing, to be urgent; questa lettera -e, this letter is urgent; non c'è più nulla che -a, there is nothing else that presses, nothing else is urgent; to matter, to be very important; mi -e l'avvenire di mio figlio, I am anxious about my son's future; mi -e di riuscire, it is very important that I should succeed, I am anxious to succeed; se la cosa vi -e, if it matters to you; se vi -e la sua vita, as you value his life; *impers.* mi -e di sapere se sei disposto a far ciò, I want to know if you are willing

to do that; se di me ti -e, if you care for me. **-ente** *part. adj.* pressing, urgent; necessità -ente, pressing need.

pre-męssa *f.* (logic) premise, premiss; previous statement; (leg.) premise. **-męsso** *part.* of **premettere**, q.v.; *adj.* stated in advance, already stated; ciò -messo, that being stated, when that has been said; (leg.) -messo che, whereas.... **-méttere** [C 20] *tr.* to say first of all, to state in advance; to premise, to put forward; dovete -mettere il nome al cognome, you must put your Christian name before your surname; to give preference to; (introducing a statement) -metto, mind you.

preme·stru-o *m.* (physiol.) premenstruum, premenstrual period. **-ale** *adj.* premenstrual.

premi-are [A 4] *tr.* to reward; to give (award) a prize to; fu -ato, he was awarded a prize; — la diligenza, to reward industry. **-a·bile** *adj.* deserving a prize; worthy of reward. **-ando** *adj.* deserving a prize; *n.m.* prize-winner. **-ante** *part. adj.* rewarding; giving prizes. **-ato** *part. adj.* rewarded; awarded a prize; numeri -ati, (lottery) winning numbers; *n.m.* prize-winner; -ato con medaglia d'oro, gold-medallist. **-atóre** *m.* prize-giver. (**-atrice** *f.*) **-azione** *f.* prize-giving, distribution of prizes.

premi-baderna *m. indecl.* (eng.) stuffing box. **-carta** *f. indecl.* paper grip (of typewriter). **-lamiera** *m. indecl.* (eng.) sheet holder, blank holder. **-stoppa** *m. indecl.* (eng.) stuffing box; anello -stoppa, packing gland.

pre·mice *adj.* easily crushed, soft; mandorla —, almond easy to crack (with the fingers).

première *f. indecl.* (neol., pron. as Fr.) first performance.

premilitare *adj.* (mil.) premilitary; istruzione —, premilitary training.

premiménto *m.* pressure; squeezing, pressing.

premin-ente *adj.* pre-eminent. **-enza**, †**-en·zia** *f.* pre-eminence, superiority; -enze ingiuste, unfair advantages.

pre·mi-o *m.* prize; reward; award; ottener — nell'altra vita, to be rewarded in the life to come; (finan.) premium; bonus; buoni a premi, premium bonds; — del credere, *del credere* commission; premi all'esportazione, export bounties or subsidies; (leg.) consideration money; premium; reward (C.C.); (sport) premio d'ingaggio, transfer fee; bounty, subsidy; istituire un —, to endow a prize; — Nobel, Nobel prize; — di consolazione, consolation prize.

†**premissione** *f.* placing before, preamble; mission sent before another.

pre·mit-o *m.* (med.) contraction, straining. **-ore** *m.* presser. (**-rice** *f.*) **-ura** *f.* pressing; juice, oil, etc. pressed out.

†**premi·zia** *f.* See **primizia**.

premodulazione *f.* (radio) premodulation.

premolare *adj., n.m.* (anat.) premolar.

†**premonire** *tr.* to prewarn; to have a premonition of.

premoni-tóre *adj.* premonitory; *n.m.* one who (something that) forewarns. (**-trice** *f.*) **-to·rio** *adj.* (*m.pl.* **-to·rii**) premonitory. **-zione** *f.* premonition; warning; (zool.) warning coloration; (psych.) precognition; (spiritualism) clairvoyance.

premor-ire [D 12] *intr.* (*aux.* essere) to die previously; — alla moglie, to predecease one's wife. **-ienza** *f.* (leg.) predecease. **-to** *part. adj.* having died previously; -to al fratello minore, having died before his younger brother.

premostrare [A I] *tr.* to show beforehand, to afford a preview.

premostratęse *adj., n.m.* (eccl.) Premonstratensian.

premozione *f.* (theol.) premotion.

premun-ire [D 2] *tr.* to fortify beforehand; to forearm; *rfl.* to be forearmed, to protect oneself; come posso -irmi contro le conseguenze?, how can I secure myself against the consequences?; dovete -irvi, you must take protective measures (precautions); -irsi di, to provide oneself with (means of defence, or sim.); -irsi d'un bastone, to provide oneself with a stick; -irsi di un certificato, to obtain a certificate. **-iente** *part.* protecting, fortifying (beforehand). **-ito** *part adj.* forearmed. **-izione** *f.* premunition; (rhet.) preparation (of hearers' minds).

premur-a *f.* urgency; solicitude; care, attention; kindness; eagerness; haste; cosa di —, urgent matter; aver —, to be in haste; aveva — di sistemare la cosa, he wanted to settle the matter as soon as possible; non c'è —, there is no hurry; devi aver — di questo, you must attend to this; dimostra una grande — per me, he shows great solicitude on my account; mi colma di -e, he is most attentive; grazie delle vostre -e, thank you for your kindness;

premur-a (*cont.*)

far — a, to beseech; mi fece — di andare, he entreated me to go. **-oso** *adj.* attentive, kind, thoughtful; careful; solicitous; eager, ready; polite; urgent, pressing; mostrarsi molto -oso, to be very kind. **-osamente** *adv.* attentively, solicitiously; thoughtfully; kindly; cordially; readily; hastily; politely.

†premutare *vb.* and deriv. See **permutare**.

premuto *part.* of **premere**, q.v.; *adj.* pressed; squeezed; (fig.) urged.

prenarcoṣi *f.* (med.) prenarcosis, basic anaesthesia.

prenarr-are [A I] *tr.* to relate beforehand. **-ato** *part. adj.* told beforehand, already narrated.

pre-na·scere [B 18] *intr.* (*aux.* essere; *prep.* a) to be born previously; — a, to be older than. (**-nato** *part. adj.*)

prenatale *adj.* (physiol.) prenatal, antenatal.

†prence *m.* See **principe**.

prèn·d·ere [C I] *tr.* (almost synonymous with **pigliare**; where there is any difference **pigliare** implies more violence or speed, and is used in preference to **prendere** in colloquial style). **1.** TO TAKE; to take up; to lay hold of, to pick up; prese la valigia e la posò sulla tavola, he picked up the suitcase and put it on the table; — con due dita, to pick up between two fingers; — per il manico, to hold (take hold of, pick up) by the handle; — la mano di una persona, to take a person's hand; — uno per il collo, to seize someone by the neck, (fig.) to swindle someone. **2.** TO CAPTURE, to seize; to take possession of; to catch; — il treno, to catch the train; — un autobus, to take a bus; — d'assalto, to take by storm, to storm; — una fortezza, to take (capture) a fortress; esser preso in trappola, to be caught in a trap; — un ladro, to catch a thief; il gatto -e i topi, the cat catches mice; to surprise, to catch, to fall upon, to attack; lo prese sul fatto, he caught him in the act; essere preso in flagrante, to be caught red-handed; prese il nemico alle spalle, he attacked the enemy in the rear by surprise; — a bastonate, to attack with a stick, to give a beating to; con un sasso lo prese in un occhio, he caught (hit) him in the eye with a stone; -erle (i.e. busse, percosse) to be hit, to take a beating; se ti -o!, if I catch you!; le -erete!, you'll catch it! **3.** TO TAKE AWAY, to steal; to remove; ha preso quel che c'era di buono, he took all that was any good; — possesso di, to take possession of, to get hold of; — il posto di, to take the place of. **4.** TO OCCUPY; questo scaffale -e troppo posto, this bookcase takes up too much room; to take for occupation; ho preso casa, I have taken a house; — alloggio, to take lodgings; — in affitto, to hire, to rent. **5.** TO TAKE UP, to take on; to engage; to assume; — un lavoro, to take on a job, to make a contract; — a soldo, to engage, to take into one's pay; — uno per guida, to engage someone as a guide; — una carica, to assume an office, to take a post; — un grado, to take (receive) a rank; — servizio, to take service; — al servizio, to take into one's service. **6.** TO USE, to need, to take; — tempo, to take one's time, to take time (e.g. for consideration); — tutta la giornata in visite, to spend the whole day visiting. **7.** TO MOVE (towards), to make for; — la destra, to turn to the right, to take the right-hand turning; — il mare, to put to sea; — il largo, to make for the open sea, (fig.) to clear out, to get away; — la montagna, to begin to climb the mountain; — la porta, to go out; — il volo, to take (to) flight, to begin to fly, (fig.) to flee; — le mosse, to start moving, (vulg.) to get going, to get cracking. **8.** TO BEGIN, to take (to); prese a dire..., he began to say...; prese a canticchiare un motivo, he took to humming a tune. **9.** TO TAKE OVER, to take on, to adopt, to derive, to borrow; — le abitudini da un popolo straniero, to take over customs from a foreign race; — l'argomento di un libro dalla realtà, to take the subject of a book from real life; — la corrente da un cavo, to receive the current from a cable; — un vocabolo da una lingua straniera, to borrow a word from a foreign language. **10.** TO PARTAKE OF; to have; — l'aria, to take the air; — il sole, to sun oneself; — le acque, to take the waters; — qualche spasso, to allow oneself some amusement; — il caffè, to have coffee; — un uovo, to have an egg; — una pillola, to take a pill; (liturg.) — la comunione, to take Holy Communion, to make one's communion; — la Pasqua, to make one's Easter communion, to go to one's Easter duties. **11.** TO TAKE WITH ONE, or in one's company; uscendo di casa prese l'ombrello, when he went out he took his umbrella; prendi con te Giacomino, take Jimmy with you; vieni a -ermi a casa, come and call for me; — all'arrivo, to meet on arrival; ti -erò all'ora dell'uscita, I shall

meet you when you come out; to take in marriage; — moglie to take a wife, to get married. **12.** TO CATCH (a disease); to acquire (a vice); — un raffreddore, to catch cold; prese il vizio del giuoco, he acquired the bad habit of gambling; — fuoco (*or* prendere), to catch fire; — una sbornia, to get drunk; — acqua, — la pioggia, to get wet (with rain). **13.** TO RECEIVE, to get, to have; — un dono, to receive a gift; — una pedata, to get a kick, to be kicked; — lezione, to have a lesson; questa stanza -e luce da due finestre, this room gets its light from two windows. **14.** TO RECEIVE, to get (money, etc.); to charge; to cost; il medico prese trecento lire per visita, the doctor charged three hundred lire a visit; vendendolo -erò mille lire, when I sell it I shall get a thousand lire; to earn; — diecimila lire alla settimana, to earn ten thousand lire a week; to win; — un terno, to win a treble on the 'lotto', (fig.) to have a stroke of luck; ho preso un paio di scarpe, I have got myself a pair of shoes. **15.** WITH VARIOUS COMPLEMENTS, ADVERBS, ETC.: — la larghezza di, to measure the width of; — le misure di, to measure; — il peso di, to weigh; to portray, to represent; il pittore lo prese di scorcio, the painter showed it foreshortened; il fotografo lo prese bene, the photographer took a good likeness; — una fotografia, to take a photograph; — copia, to take a copy, to copy; — in considerazione, to take into consideration; — in mala parte, to take ill; — alla lettera, to take literally; — forma, to take shape; — con le buone, to treat well; — uno per galantuomo, to take someone for (to consider one) an honest man; — uno per inglese, to take a person to be English; (colloq.) mi -i per un inglese?, do you think I am a B.F.?; per chi mi -ete?, what (whom) do you take me for?; to mistake; — una cosa per un'altra; — lucciole per lanterne, to mistake fireflies for lanterns, i.e. to be grossly mistaken; — un abbaglio, un granchio, to make a mistake, to 'drop a brick'; — amore, to fall in love; — coraggio, to take courage; esser preso d'amore per..., to fall in love with...; lo prese la paura, fear came over him, fear assailed (overcame) him; lo prese il capriccio della musica, he took a fancy for music; esser preso da rimorso, to be seized with remorse; esser preso da ira, to get into a rage; — meraviglia, to be amazed, to be surprised; — sospetto, to become suspicious; — pensiero, to become pensive; — una risoluzione, to take a resolve, to make up one's mind; — impegno, to pledge oneself, to give an undertaking; — pratica, to get practice, to practise, to exercise (oneself); — stanza, to settle, to establish oneself; — visione di, to see, to take a look at; — congedo, to take one's leave; — qualcuno in parola, to take someone at his word; — partito per, to side with, to take the part of; — mano, to get one's hand in, to practise; (of a horse) — la mano, to get out of hand (also fig., of a person); (eccl.) — il velo, to take the veil; — gli ordini (sacri), to take orders, to receive holy orders; — il fucile, to take up arms, to enlist; — il cappello, to take offence; — piede, to become fashionable; — radice, to take root; — a cuore, to take to heart, to care for, to take an interest in; — contatto con, to make contact with, to enter into close relations with; — atto di, to take note of, to place on record; — nota, to make a note (notes); — il toro per le corna, to take the bull by the horns; — di mira, to aim at, (fig.) to stare at; — la palla al balzo, to seize the opportunity; (aeron.) — quota, to gain height; — il volo, to take off; — su, to pick up; il treno si ferma a — su i passeggeri, the train stops to pick up passengers; prese su e se ne andò, he took up his things and left; *intr.* (*aux.* avere) to set, to congeal, to curdle; to take root; il cemento ha preso, the cement has set; to turn; — a sinistra, to turn to the left; to come upon, to happen (to); gli prese la febbre, he became feverish, he caught fever; gli prese il dolore, he was seized with pain; che gli prenda un accidente!, devil take him!; che cosa gli -e?, what is the matter with him?; *rfl.* (*acc.* of *prn.* 'si') to be taken; to be understood; (*dat.* of *prn.* 'si') to take for oneself, to allow oneself; -ersi una vacanza, to take a holiday; mi -o la libertà di offrirvi questo dono, I take the liberty of making you this present; -ersi un malanno, to catch a disease, to suffer a misfortune; se lo -a il diavolo!, devil take him (it)!; non voglio -ermene pensiero, I will not think of it; non -ertela, don't take it to heart; -ersela con qualcuno, to lay the blame on someone, to be angry with someone; -ersela calda, to feel anger or enthusiasm about something, (vulg.) to get het up; -ersela comoda, to take it easy; *recip. rfl.* -ersi a pugni, a botte, a schiaffi, to come to blows; fare a -ersi, to play catch (catching each other); to get

prend·ere (*cont.*)
married; to come to an agreement. **-i·bile** *adj.* seizable; fit to be taken; liable to capture. (**-ibilità** *f.*) **-imento** *m.* taking; capture. **-itore** *m.* receiver; payee; manager (of a lottery); capturer. (**-itrice** *f.*) **-itori·a** *f.* lottery office (agency).

preneopla·stico *adj.* (med.) preneoplastic.

prenom·e *m.* Christian name, first name, fore-name, given name; (leg.) baptismal, Christian or given name (C.C.). **-inato** *adj.* above mentioned, aforesaid.

prenot-are [A I] *tr.* to book, to engage; -are posti, to book seats; to bespeak, to order in advance; farsi -are, to put one's name down for, to bespeak, to order; *rfl.* (*dat.* of *prn.* 'si') to book, to bespeak; to put one's name down for. **-ato** *part. adj.* booked, engaged, bespoken. **-atore** *m.* subscriber. **-azione** *f.* booking (in advance); (leg.) priority notice.

prenozione *f.* foreknowledge, prescience; (philos.) prenotion; innate idea.

pren·sile *adj.* prehensile.

prensione *f.* prehension.

prenunzi-are [A 4] *tr.* to predict, to announce; to establish in advance. (**-ato** *part. adj.*) **-atore** *m.* prophet. (**-atrice** *f.*) **-azione** *f.* prediction, prophecy.

prenun·zio *m.* prediction.

†**prenz-e** *m.* see **principe**. †**-ezza** *f.* see **principessa**.

preoccup-are [A I S] *tr.* to occupy beforehand; to seize in advance; (fig.) to preoccupy, to make anxious, to trouble; to influence; — l'animo del giudice, to exert undue influence on the judge; questo sospetto mi -a la mente, this suspicion worries me; *rfl.* to be preoccupied; to be anxious, to be worried; non vi -ate!, don't worry!; essa si -ava della salute della figlia, she was anxious about her daughter's health; non -atevi della spesa, never mind the expense. **-ato** *part. adj.* already occupied; preoccupied; anxious, worried; (with *prep.* 'di', or 'per'): sono -ato di ciò, I am anxious about that; sono -ato per mio figlio, I am worried on account of my son; (with *prep.* 'da') preoccupied with, troubled by. **-azione** *f.* previous occupation; preoccupation; preconceived opinion; care; anxiety; uneasiness; worry; (rhet.) anticipation (of objections), prolepsis.

†**preonorato** *adj.* honoured above others.

preopinante *m.* first to express an opinion; previous speaker.

preordin-are [A I SC] *tr.* to order, to establish beforehand; to pre-arrange; to predetermine; to preordain; (theol.) to preordain, to predestine. **-amento** *m.* arranging beforehand; predisposition. (**-ato** *part. adj.*) **-azione** *f.* predetermination; predestination.

prepaleozo·ico *adj.* (geol.) pre-Palaeozoic.

prepar-are [A I] *tr.* to prepare, to make ready; — la tavola, to lay the table; — il letto, to make the bed; — il fuoco, to lay the fire; — la guerra, to make preparations for war, to mobilize; — da pranzo, to prepare the dinner; — una lezione, to prepare a lesson; — un esame, to read for an examination; — un ragazzo per un esame, to coach a boy for an examination; — una persona a ricevere qualche notizia, to prepare a person for some news; — il terreno, to prepare the ground (for sowing seed), (fig.) to pave the way; (chem.) to prepare (a substance); (mus.) — una dissonanza, to prepare a dissonance; *rfl.* to prepare, to get ready; -arsi a un viaggio, to make preparations for a journey; -arsi a un esame, to read for an examination; -arsi alla lezione. (of master or pupil) to prepare the lesson; (rel.) -arsi alla comunione, to make one's preparation for communion; (of a storm) to brew. **-amento** *m.* preparing, preparation; (mil.) preparatory work, bombardment, etc. **-ativo** *adj.* preparatory; *n.m.* preparation; -ativi della partenza, preparations for departure; (naut.) preparation; †(med.) purgative. **-ato** *part. adj.* prepared, ready; fit; -ato alla difesa, prepared for defence; *n.m.* (scient.; med.) preparation, prepared specimen; (chem.; pharm.) preparation, compound; *pl.* advance arrangements. **-atore** *m.* preparer. (**-atrice** *f.*) **-ato·rio** *adj.* (*m.pl.* **-ato·rii**) preparatory; scuola -atoria, preparatory school. **-azione** *f.* preparation; in — azione a, in preparation for; debita -azione, due preparation; parlare in pubblico senza -azione, to make an extempore speech; (scient.) preparation; making ready, setting up; (mining) dressing (of ore); (text.) slubbing, roving; (mus.) preparation (of a dissonance or of a shake); (mil.) logistic preparation, stocking and storing of military material and food; -azione di artiglieria, artillery preparation, the laying down of a barrage or curtain prior to an assault, 'softening up'; (rel.)

-azione alla Messa, preparation for Mass; priest's prayers before Mass; a card bearing the words of these. **-ucchiare** [A 4] *tr. freq. dim.* to make some little preparation now and then; (for an exam.) to read or work spasmodically.

prepatellare *adj.* (anat.) prepatellar; (med.) borsite —, housemaid's knee.

prepensare [A I] *tr.* to premeditate, to think over beforehand.

pre-pilo·rico *adj.* (anat.) prepyloric. **-placentare** *adj.* (anat.) pre-placental.

preponder-are [A I SC] *intr.* (*aux.* avere) to weigh more heavily; (fig.) to preponderate, to prevail, to have more power or influence. **-ante** *part. adj.* preponderant, predominant; prevailing. **-anza** *f.* preponderance, predominance; superiority; -anza dell'Inghilterra sui mari, English supremacy at sea; -anza della passione sulla riflessione. passion outweighing reason. **-azione** *f.* preponderance; excess weight; superior power.

pre-porre [B 21] *tr.* to place in front; to prefix; to prefer, to place over, to put at the head of; — al governo, to put at the head of the government; fu -posto alla difesa della città, he was put in charge of the defence of the city; to set above; questa pagina va -posta all'altra, this page comes before the other; (fig.) — una persona a un'altra, to prefer one person to another; vedersi — un altro, to see oneself superseded. **-positale** *adj.* (eccl.) of a provost. **-positivo** *adj.* (gramm.) prepositive; vocale -positiva, the first vowel of a diphthong. **-po·sito** *adj.* (eccl.) see **preposto**. **-positura** *f.* (eccl.) status of provost; provost's house. **-positurale** (eccl.) of a provost; chiesa -positurale, parish church whose priest has the rank of provost. **-posizione** *f.* placing before, prefixing; (gramm.) preposition.

prepossente *adj.* See **prepotente**.

pre-posto, -posto *part.* of **preporre**, q.v.; *adj.* put before, prefixed; put at the head (of); preferred; above; *n.m.* (eccl.) provost (dignitary in chapter; parish priest of privileged status; superior in some religious houses).

prepoten-te *adj.* overbearing, arrogant; tyrannical; insolent; powerful; irrepressible; desiderio —, irrepressible desire; *n.m.* overbearing person, insolent fellow; bully. (**-temente** *adv.*) **-za** *f.* supreme power; -enza del vero, sovereignty of truth; arrogance; insolence; ha commesso una -za, he is guilty of overbearing behaviour, he has abused his power; di, con -za, arrogantly; lo fece di -za, he did it arrogantly, he acted without any consideration for others; abuse of power; bullying.

pre-puberale *adj.* (med.) prepubescent. **-puziale** *adj.* (anat.) preputial. **-pu·zio** *m.* (anat.) prepuce, foreskin.

preraffael-ismo *m.* (paint.) Pre-Raphaelitism. **-ita, -ista** *adj., n.m.* (paint.) Pre-Raphaelite.

prerefrigeratore *m.* (motor.) precooler.

preriscald-are [A I] *tr.* (motor.) to preheat. **-amento** *m.* (industr.) preheating. **-ato** *part. adj.* **-atore** *m.* (industr.) preheater; feed heater (of a boiler). **-o** *m.* (industr.) preheating.

prerogativ-a *f.* prerogative, privilege; special virtue or property; ha la — di una memoria ferrea, he has the excellent gift of a cast-iron memory; (leg.) lesa —, offence to the prerogative (C.P.). **-amente** *adv.* by privilege.

prerompitore *m.* (rubber indust.) cracker.

prerotu·leo *adj.* (anat.) prepatellar; borsa prerotulea, prepatellar bursa.

†**prerutto** *adj.* precipitous, steep.

pres-a *f.* capture, seizure, taking; — della Bastiglia, taking of the Bastille; — di possesso, taking possession; — di possesso di un ufficio, taking office; catching (prey, etc.); cane da —, retriever; setter; taking hold (of), beginning; grasp, grip, hold; pinch; allentare la —, to release one's hold; venire alle -e con, to come to grips with, to fight, to wrestle with, to quarrel with; è alle -e col latino, he is wrestling with his Latin; essere alle -e coi creditori, to be in difficulties with one's creditors; pretext, occasion; dare — alle calunnie, to give rise to slander; (zool.) -e dello scorpione, pincers of a scorpion; (zool.) — dell'elefante, elephant's trunk; iron-holder (for holding a hot flat-iron); holder, knob, handle (of a saucepan-lid, or other lid, door-latch, etc.); — d'acqua, hydrant, fire-hydrant, water-cock, inlet, etc.; intake; — d'aria, air intake; (naut.) standpipe, hydrant, inlet valve; — di vapore, main or auxiliary stopcock on a boiler; bollard or any point capable of holding a hawser ashore; catch (of fish); †prize; fare —, to turn up (a rope); fare buona —, to secure (a rope); †far

pres-a (*cont.*)

la —, to take in prize; †riscattare una —, to arm and commission a prize ship; trovare una buona —, to find good holding ground; (of cement, etc.) setting; far —, to coagulate, (of plants) to take root; (photog.) exposure; shot; — di tempo, time exposure; (cinem.) take, shot; macchina da —, apparecchio da —, cine camera, (teleph.) jack; (eng.) drive; power take-off; engagement, meshing (of gears); (motor.) — diretta, top gear; (electr.) tap; take-off; plug socket; (electric light) point; pinch (of salt, snuff, etc.), mouthful, bite, bit (of food), drink, little glass, tot; dose (of medicine); (wrestling) hold; (boxing) — scorretta, unfair holding; (cards) trick; fare sette prese con atout quadri, to make seven tricks with diamonds as trumps; (comm.) — di possesso, attachment; sequestration; (agric.) allotment, piece of land, land measure (cf. **tavola**); (mus.) sign indicating a point of entry in a canon; (duelling) dar le -e, to give the enemy choice of weapons. **-ac·chio** *m.* cross-piece on the shaft of a spade. **-erella** *f. dim.* (med.) small dose. **-ina** *f. dim.*, **-ino** *m. dim.*, **-olina** *f. dim.* pinch; little taste; -ina di tabacco, pinch of snuff.

presa·g-io *m.* presage; presentiment, foreboding; prediction; omen; ne ebbi il —, I had a presentiment of it; lieti -i, happy omens, good omens. **-imento** *m.* presentiment. **-ire** [D 2] *tr., intr.* (*aux.* avere) to predict, to foretell, to presage; to bode, to augur, to portend; to have a presentiment, to foresee. (**-ito** *part. adj.*)

presa·go *adj.* (*m.pl.* **-ghi**) foreboding, presaging; essere — di, to foresee, to have a presentiment of; era — della sua sorte, he had a premonition of his destiny.

presame *m.* rennet, thistle-juice or other substance used to curdle milk; (bot.) cardoon, *Cynara cardunculus.*

presantificat-o *adj.* (theol.) presanctified, already consecrated; *n.m.pl.* (liturg.) messa dei -i, Mass of the Presanctified (on Good Friday).

presbiacusi *f. indecl.* deafness (due to old age).

presbi-ofreni·a *f.* (med.) presbyophrenia, senile dementia. **-opi·a** *f.* (opt.) presbyopia, long sight.

pre·sbite *adj., n.m., f.* (opt.) presbyopic.

presbiter-ale *adj.* priestly. **-ato** *m.* (eccl.) priesthood; order of cardinal priests. †**-essa** *f.* (eccl. hist.) presbyteress, *presbytera.*

presbiterian-ismo *m.* (rel.) Presbyterianism. **-o** *adj., n.m.* Presbyterian. (**-a** *f.*)

presbite·rio *m.* (liturg.; archit.) sanctuary of church, *presbyterium*, presbytery; (eccl.) priest's house, presbytery; †group or body of priests.

presbitismo *m.* long-sightedness, presbyopia.

Presburgo *pr.n.f.* (geog.) Bratislava.

prescegl-iere [B 27] *tr.* to select, to choose, to prefer. **-imento** *m.* selection, choice.

prescelto *part.* of **prescegliere**, q.v.; *adj.* selected; choice.

pre·scia *f.* (dial. S. Ital.) haste; in —, in haste, hurriedly.

†**presciare** *vb.* and derivs. See **pregiare**.

presci-ente *adj.* prescient. **-enza**, †**-en·zia** *f.* prescience, presentiment; (theol.) **-enza** divina, divine foreknowledge, prescience of God.

prescin-dere [C 21] *intr.* (*aux.* avere; *prep.* da) to leave out of consideration, to prescind from, to put aside; a — da ciò, quell'opera resta pur sempre bella, apart from that, this is indeed a fine work; prescindendo da, apart from.

†**presc-ire** *tr.* to know beforehand, to have foreknowledge of. †**-ito** *part. adj.* foreknown; foreordained; (theol.) reprobate; one whose damnation is foreknown by God.

presciutto *m.* See **prosciutto**.

†**prescri·bere** *vb.* and derivs. See **prescrivere**.

prescritt-i·bile *adj.* (leg.) prescribable; prescriptible; subject to prescription. **-ibilità** *f.* (leg.) prescriptibility. **-ivo** *adj.* (leg.) prescriptive.

prescritto *part.* of **prescrivere**, q.v.; *adj.* prescribed, established, fixed; obligatory; (on an invitation card, etc.) è — l'abito da sera, evening-dress; obsolete; (leg.) statute-barred; time-barred; *n.m.* prescript, ordinance.

prescr-i·vere [C 12] *tr.* to prescribe; to establish, to ordain; to fix; — una cura, to prescribe treatment; *intr.* (*aux.* avere) (leg.) to prescribe. **-ivimento** *m.* prescribing, prescription. **-izione** *f.* prescription; ordinance; directions; (med.) prescription; (leg.) -izione acquisitiva, positive prescription; -izione estintiva, negative prescription; legge di -izione, law of prescription; statute of limitation (C.C.); -izioni imposte dal giudice, rules ordered by Judge (C.P.).

presedere [B 28] and derivs. See **presiedere**.

pre-selettore *m.* (teleph.) pre-selector. **-selezione** *f.* (radio) pre-selection.

presell-a *f.* (metall.) fuller; (agric.) newly cultivated plot. **-are** [A 1] *tr.* (eng.) to caulk, to jag. **-atura** *f.* (eng.) caulking. **-o** *m.* (eng.) caulking tool.

†**presensione** *f.* See **presentimento**.

present-are [A 1] *tr.* to present, to offer; to introduce; to produce, to show; — un dramma, to present a play; -ategli i miei ossequi, present my compliments to him, give him my regards; -ato a pochi giorni fa, he was introduced to me a few days ago; — un progetto di legge al parlamento, to introduce a bill into Parliament; — un reclamo, to make a complaint; — un documento, to produce a document; — una sfida, to deliver a challenge; (naut.) to step (a mast); to run out (a gun); to face, to head, to present; — alla corrente, to ride to the tide; — il traverso, to present the beam, to be head on to the sea; (mil.) — le armi, to present arms; presentat-arm!, present arms!; — battaglia, to array one's forces before the enemy; — bersaglio, to offer a target; — alla battaglia, to muster for battle; to put on show; — la propria candidatura, to offer oneself as a candidate; *rfl.* to introduce oneself; to present oneself, to appear; to occur, to arise; to offer (itself, oneself); mi -ai al direttore, I appeared before the manager, *or* I introduced myself to the manager; -arsi alle autorità, to appear before the authorities; -arsi per un esame, to sit for an examination; -arsi come cameriere, to seek a situation as a waiter; (of an idea) -arsi alla mente di uno, to occur to one; quando si -a l'occasione, when opportunity offers; prendemmo il primo sentiero che ci si -ò, we took the first path that offered; simili difficoltà si -arono diverse volte, such difficulties arose several times; -arsi bene, to look well, to have a good appearance, *or* to promise well, to hold out good prospects. **-a·bile** *adj.* presentable; non -abile, unpresentable. (**-abilità** *f.*) **-ato** *part. adj.* presented; introduced; offered; *n.m.* (eccl.) cleric presented for benefice. **-atore** *m.* presenter, introducer; (theatr.; radio, etc.) compère; (comm.) -atore della cambiale, presenter of bill (C.C.). **-azione** *f.* presentation; introduction; lettera di -azione, letter of introduction; -azione dei documenti, production of the documents; (comm.) presentment; a -azione, on demand; tratta a -azione, cash order, draft on demand; (eccl.) Presentation of the B.V.M.: the feast of 21 November; a picture of this subject; (seldom used of the Presentation of Christ, which is normally called **purificazione** or **candelora**, feast of 2 February); name of several congregations of nuns; (paint.) -azione al Tempio, picture of the Presentation in the Temple either of the B.V.M. or (less usu.) of Christ (the famous Mantegna painting is of the latter).

present-e *adj.* present; il — volume, the present volume, this book; condizioni -i, present conditions; tener —, to bear in mind; nel — mese, in the current month; tempo —, present time, (gramm.) present tense; uomini -i, men of today; presente! (in answer to the calling of one's name at a roll-call), adsum!, present! (at funerals, whoever makes the official speech reads out the name of the deceased, whereupon the mourners shout 'presente!'); *adv. phr.* di —, presently; †immediately; *n.m.* present, gift; person present, member of the audience, spectator; eccettuati i -i, present company excepted; present (time); voi non vivete abbastanza nel —, you do not live enough in the present; al —, at present; per il —, for the present; (gramm.) present tense; al —, in the present; *adv.* at once; soon, presently. **-emente** *adv.* at present, now. **-a·neo** *adj.* instantaneous, immediate. **-ino** *m. dim.* little present, small gift. **-is·simo** *adj. superl.* actually present; of the moment; most imminent; highly favourable.

present-ire [D 1] *tr.* to have a presentiment of, to anticipate; to foresee; to forebode, to presage; -ì che la cosa non sarebbe riuscita bene, he had a presentiment that it would not turn out well. **-imento** *m.* presentiment, foreboding; misgiving. (**-ito** *part. adj.*)

presenz-a, †**-ia** *f.* presence; appearance, aspect; attendance; sight; si richiede la tua —, your presence is required; alla — di, in — di, in the presence of; un uomo di nobile —, a man of noble presence; (in advertisements) con —, of good appearance, of smart appearance; cercasi dattilografa con —, wanted, shorthand typist of smart appearance; non aver —, to be very thin; di —, in

presenz-a (*cont.*)

person; fare atto di —, to put in an appearance; gettone, medaglia di —, token (certificate) of attendance, attendance-fee; attendance (at a hospital, theatre, etc.); lista di —, attendance list; — di spirito, d'animo, presence of mind; (theol.) — di Dio, presence of God; (chem.) in —, present. **-iale** *adj.* present. in person. **-ialmente** *adv.* in person; assistere **-ialmente**, to attend personally. (**-ialità** *f.*) **-iare** [A 4] *tr.*, *intr.* (*aux.* avere) to attend, to be present (at); **-iare** un'adunanza, to attend a meeting; **-iare** agli esami, to be present at the examinations, to sit (take) the examinations.

presepe *m.* (poet.). See presepio.

presepio *m.* manger, crib, stall; hut; (rel.) Christmas crib (in church or at home); (art) painting or model showing the Nativity; day-nursery, crèche.

preserella *f. dim.* See under presa.

preserv-are [A I] *tr.* to preserve, to keep; to guard against; Iddio ti **-i** sempre da questi malanni, may God keep you from all these ills; — la sua salute, to take care of one's health. **-amento** *m.* preservation, keeping. **-ante** *part.* preserving; *adj.*, *n.m.* preservative. **-ativo** *adj.* preservative; (med.) contraceptive; preventative. **-ato** *part. adj.* preserved, kept. **-atore** *m.* preserver, preservative; *adj.* (**-atrice** *f.*) preservative; cura **-atrice**, preventive treatment. **-azione** *f.* preservation.

presiccio *adj.* See under preso.

preside *m.* principal (of school or sim.), headmaster, dean; (leg.) presiding judge.

president-e *m.* president, chairman; — del consiglio (dei ministri), premier, prime minister; — del consiglio d'amministrazione, chairman of the board of directors; (admin.) chiedere al — di prendere una decisione, to ask for a ruling; fare appello all'autorità del —, to invoke the chairman's authority; rimettersi al —, to leave the matter to the chairman's decision; — del consiglio della Corona, Lord President of the Council; — della Repubblica, President of the Republic; — della Camera dei Deputati, 'Speaker' of the Chamber of Deputies; il sindaco è — del Consiglio Comunale, the mayor is chairman of (presides over) the Town Council; — onorario, Honorary president; — effettivo, (active, actual) chairman; il — apre la seduta, the chairman opens the meeting; il — dà la parola al Professore Migliorini, the chairman calls upon Professor Migliorini to speak; il — richiama all'ordine, the chairman calls to order. **-tato** *m.* presidency; chairmanship; headmastership, principalship; duration of such offices. **-za** *f.* presidency, chairmanship; presidency (in the sense of house or staff of a president); tenne la **-za** per cinque anni, he was president for five years (chairman, in the case of a meeting, committee, board of directors, etc.); assumere la **-za**, to take the chair; essere alla **-za**, to act as chairman, to be in the chair; rivolgersi alla **-za**, to address the chair; ufficio di **-za**, general committee; inchinarsi dinanzi ad una decisione della **-za**, to bow to the chairman's decision. **-ziale** *adj.* presidential; of the chairman; il seggio **-ziale**, the chair; render nota una decisione **-ziale**, to give a ruling.

presidi-o *m.* (mil.) garrison; fortress troops; munire di —, to garrison; (fig.) defence, protection; a — di, in defence of. **-ale** *adj.* (mil.) pertaining to the garrison or fortress command. **-are** [A 4] *tr.* (mil.) to garrison (a fort or frontier, etc.). **-ario** *adj.* (mil.) belonging to, or attached to, a garrison. **-ato** *part. adj.* (mil.) garrisoned.

presied-ere [B 28] *intr.* (*aux.* avere) to preside, to be in the chair, to be chairman; to be at the head, to be in charge; — a un'assemblea, to preside at a meeting, to be chairman at (of) a meeting; chi pres(i)edeva?, who was in the chair?; presiede ai lavori stradali, he is in charge of work on the road(s); *tr.* — un'assemblea, to chair a meeting, to preside at a meeting; — il governo, to lead the government. **-ente** *part. adj.* presiding, in charge. **-uto** *part. adj.* (*prep.* da) presided over (by), under the chairmanship (of).

pres-ina *f. dim.*, **-ino** *m. dim.* See under presa.

presincronizzare [A I] *tr.* (techn.) to presynchronize.

†**presio** *m.* See pregio.

†**presistemazione** *f.* preference.

pres-o *part.* of prendere, q.v.; *adj.* taken, caught, captured; occupied; bound, imprisoned; posti tutti **-i**, all seats taken; — d'amore, in love; — da ira, seized with anger; — di meraviglia, moved to wonder; — dal colera, attacked by cholera; — di mira, aimed at; undertaken, taken up; la carriera **-a**, the career taken up; (naut.)

— dai ghiacci, caught in the icefloes, icebound; — dalla tempesta, caught in a storm, stormbound; partito —, prejudice, *parti pris*, a mind made up. **-iccio** *adj.* (orn.) uccello **-iccio**, bird trapped (as adult).

pressa *f.* press; pressure; crowd, crowding, throng, crush; far — intorno a uno, to crowd round someone; (dial. S. Ital.) haste, hurry; in haste; (eng.; techn.) press; — per balle, baler.

press-are [A I] *tr.* (techn.) to press; — a caldo, to hot-press; to test under pressure; (fig.) to press, to urge. **-acarte** *m. indecl.* paperweight. **-ante** *part. adj.* urgent, pressing; lettera **-ante**, urgent letter; necessità **-ante**, pressing need. **-antemente** *adv.* urgently. **-appoco**, see 'press'a poco', under presso. **-ato** *part. adj.* pressed; crushed; **-ato** dal bisogno, impelled by need. **-atoio** *m.* (techn.) pressing tool. **-atreccia** *f.* (eng.) stuffing box; (naut.) stern gland. **-atura** *f.* pressing; (industr.; techn.) pressing; (eng.) pressure test; †haste.

pressibil-e *adj.* compressible. **-ità** *f.* compressibility.

pressione *f.* pressure; — atmosferica, — dell'aria, atmospheric pressure, air pressure; alta —, high pressure; bassa —, low pressure; (hydraul.) — statica, static head; (of a boiler) mettere in —, to raise steam; (med.) — arteriosa, arterial pressure, blood pressure; fu fatta — su di lui, pressure was brought to bear on him; sotto la — della fame, driven by hunger.

press-o *adj.* near; essere — a fare..., to be about to do...; esser — a morire, to be at the point of death; †—, near, nearby, close; †— a quanto, about as much as; *prep.* (usu. followed by 'a') near, by, beside, with; essa era seduta — sua madre, she was sitting beside her mother; vieni qui — a me, come here by me; with, at the house of; il ragazzo abitava — mio padre, the boy was living in my father's house; (on an envelope) — la signora Gabrieli, c/o Mrs Gabrieli; with, in company with, in business with; lavoro da molti anni — il signor Bruni, I have been working with Mr Brown for many years; ha grande influenza — questa ditta, he has great influence with this firm; ambasciatore — la corte di San Giacomo, ambassador to the Court of St James; among, in the opinion of; — i sapienti tu passi per un facilone, among scholars you are considered a dilettante; — il popolo, in popular opinion, among the people; — a lui sei un nano, compared with him you are a dwarf; near (a place); — alla città, near the town; — Roma, near Rome; (time) near, close on; — al mattino, near morning; — a due anni, close on two years; *adv.* near, near-by, near at hand; è qui —, it is near-by, it is not far; abitava lì —, he lived close-by; *adv. phrs.* — che, almost; press'a poco, pressappoco, very nearly; a un di —, nearly, about; da —, nearby, from close at hand; *n.m.pl.* neighbourhood, vicinity; nei **-i** del mercato, in the neighbourhood of the market; nei **-i** di Roma, on the outskirts (in the environs) of Rome; pressure, push; (fig.) **-i** che fa la fortuna, the rubs that fortune gives. **-oché** *adv.* see above under *adv. phrs.*

press-oflessione *f.* (bldg.; eng.) combined compressive and flexural stress. **-ofusione** *f.* (foundry) die-casting. **-oio** *m.* (text.) presser, pressing machine. **-ore** *adj.* (cinem.) quadro **-ore**, pressure plate. **-orio** *adj.* (anat.) pressor. **-ostato** *m.* (eng.) thrust meter. **-ura** *f.* pressure; compression; oppression; affliction. **-urizzare** [A I] *tr.* (aeron.) to pressurize. **-urizzato** *part. adj.* (aeron.) pressurized; cabina **-urizzata**, pressurized cabin. **-urizzatore** *m.* (aeron.) pressurizer.

†**presta** *f.* See prestanza, under prestare.

prestabil-ire [D 2] *tr.* to lay down in advance, to establish in advance, to fix (beforehand). **-ito** *part. adj.* prearranged; appointed; fixed; all'ora **-ita**, at the appointed time; (opt.; photog.) lampada a fuoco **-ito**, prefocus bulb.

prestanome *m. indecl.* See under prestare.

prest-are [A I] *tr.* to lend; to give, to render (obedience), to attribute; — fede a, to believe, to give credence to; — fede a una persona, to trust a person; — ascolto, — orecchio, to give ear, to lend an ear; — aiuto, to lend a hand, to give a helping hand; — aiuto a, to help; — attenzione, to pay attention; — omaggio, to render homage; farsi —, to borrow; (leg.) — cauzione giudiziale, to put up a bond; — giuramento, to take the oath; *rfl.* (*prep.* a): to lend oneself to; to countenance; to be fit for; le mie gambe non si **-ano** a lunghe passeggiate, my legs are not fit for long walks; questo legno non si **-a** a essere intagliato, this wood does not lend itself to being carved; to be useful; to consent; si **-a** volentieri, he is always willing to lend a hand, he likes to make himself

prest·are (*cont.*)
useful; si ~ò a far questo, he consented to do this; to indulge (in); to give way (to); to lay oneself open; le obbiezioni alle quali si ~ano, the objections to which they are subject; — il fianco a, to expose oneself to. **~amento** *m.* tribute, tax. **~anome** *m.* (leg.) nominee; (fig.) dummy, man of straw; figurehead; 'guinea-pig' director of a company. **~ante** *part. adj.* excellent, eminent; outstanding; of noble presence, noble; commanding; è un uomo ~ante, he is a fine looking man. **~antemente** *adv.* excellently; eminently; nobly. **~antino, ~antino** *m.* (naut.) fore and after parts of the keelson, where the keel rises to meet stem or sternpost. **~anza,** †**~a·nzia** *f.* excellence, eminence; dignity of bearing; mi piace quella sua ~anza fisica, I like that commanding presence of his; loan; †tribute. **~ato** *part. adj.* lent; given, tendered; (of oath) sworn. **~atore** *m.* lender, moneylender; ~atore su pegno, pawnbroker; negozio di ~atore su pegno, pawnshop; ~atore dello Stato, investor in public Funds; (leg.) ~atore di lavoro, employee (C.C.). (**~atora, ~atrice** *f.*) **~azione** *f.* lending, loan; service; work done; tax, tribute, impost; (leg.) consideration; duty; service (C.C.); (sport; motor.) performance; (theatr.) engagement; performance.

†**prestere** *m.* poisonous serpent; typhoon.

prestevole *adj.* ready to help, willing.

prestezza *f.* readiness, alertness; speed, rapidity; skill.

prestidigit·atore *m.,* **~atrice** *f.,* **~azione** *f.* See **prestigiatore**, etc.

presti·gi·o *m.* sleight of hand, conjuring, illusion, trick; giuoco di —, conjuring trick; prestige; influence; authority. **~are** [A 4] *tr.* to deceive by conjuring; to delude. **~atore** *m.* conjurer, juggler; impostor. (**~atrice** *f.*) **~oso** *adj.* tricky, done by conjuring; illusory; having prestige, charming.

prestimo·nio *m.* (eccl.) benefice, endowment.

prestin·o¹ *m.* oven, baker's shop. **~a·io** *m.* (dial. Lomb.) baker, seller of 'pasta', rice, etc. (**~a·ia** *f.*)

prestino² *adv. dim.* See under **presto¹**.

pre·stito *m.* loan; — a breve scadenza ,short loan; — di guerra, war loan; contrarre un —, to incur a loan; sottoscrivere a un —, to subscribe to a loan; — a cambio marittimo, — alla grossa ventura, bottomry bond; — rimborsabile a domanda, call money; prestiti di giorno in giorno, day to day loans; conduttore di — su pegno, pawnbroker; affitti e prestiti lend-lease; dare a —, to lend; prendere, pigliare a (in) —, to borrow; presi questo libro in — da un mio amico, I borrowed this book from a friend of mine; biblioteca di —, lending library; biblioteca ammessa al —, library authorized to borrow books from other national libraries.

prest·o¹ *adj.* ready, prompt, quick; con mano ~a, ready-handed, readily, quickly; (mus.) very fast; *adv.* early; soon; quickly; in a short time; before long; più —, earlier, sooner; — o tardi, sooner or later; al più — possibile, as soon as possible; quanto più — è, meglio è, the sooner the better; far —, to be quick, to make haste; via, fate —, do make haste; presto!, quick!, hurry!; si fa — a dire!, that's easily said!; si fa — a criticare, it's easy to criticize; *adv. phr.* alla ~a, quickly. **~amente** *adv.* quickly, readily. **~etto, ~ino** *adv. dim.* rather early; rather quickly; fate ~ino!, be quick!; **~is·simo** *adj. superl.* very fast. **~issimamente** *adv.* very quickly; with the utmost presence of mind.

†**prest·o²** *m.* See **prestito**.

pre·sule *m.* (Rom. antiq.) *praesul*; one of the priestly college of Salii; president; patron; (eccl.) prelate.

pre·su·mere [C 8] *intr.* (*aux.* avere) to presume; to think, to believe; — falsamente, to make a false assumption; — di giudicare, to presume to judge; — di sè, to be presumptuous; — troppo di sè, to be conceited; ~e troppo della propria autorità, he relies too much on his own authority; non ~ete di saperne più di me, don't imagine you know more about it than I do. **~sumi·bile** *adj.* presumable. **~sumibilità** *f.* presumability. **~sumibilmente** *adv.* presumably. **~suntivo** *adj.* presumptive; foreseeable, calculable; (comm.) bilancio ~suntivo, budget, statement of anticipated income and expenditure. **~suntivamente** *adv.* presumptively. **~sunto** *part. adj.* presumed, anticipated, estimated; supposed; apparent; presumptive; (leg.) erede ~sunto, heir presumptive; morte ~sunta, presumed death (C.C.); prova ~sunta, presumptive evidence; danno ~sunto, estimated damage(s); spesa ~sunta, anticipated (estimated) cost. **~suntore** *m.* one who presumes. (**~suntrice** *f.*) **~suntuosag·gine** *f.* presumptuousness, self-conceit. **~suntuoso** *adj.* presumptuous, arrogant, (self-)conceited; impresa ~suntuosa, rash

undertaking; *n.m.* presumptuous (arrogant) person, conceited person. **~suntuosamente** *adv.* presumptuously, arrogantly. (**~suntuosità** *f.*) **~sunzione** *f.* presumptuousness; presumption, arrogance; presumption, conjecture; questa è una semplice ~sunzione, this is mere conjecture; (leg.) ~sunzione assoluta, irrebuttable presumption; ~sunzione legale, presumption of law; ~sunzione relativa, rebuttable presumption; ~sunzione semplice, presumption of fact (C.C.).

presuola *f.* (bot.) Lady's bedstraw, *Galium verum*.

presup·porre [B 21] to presuppose, to take for granted, to suppose; to conjecture; ~ponevo che egli non stesse bene, I supposed he was not well. **~positivo** *adj.* liable to presupposition. **~posizione** *f.* presupposition, conjecture, supposition. **~posto, ~posto** *part. adj.* presupposed; supposed; conjectured; *n.m.* presupposition; (leg.) preliminary assumption; premise.

presura *f.* capture, arrest; payment for making an arrest.

presu·ria *f.* (bot.) cardoon, *Cynara cardunculus*.

pret·e *m.* (rel.) priest (normally Catholic, sometimes Orthodox, rarely Jewish or pagan); (sometimes of Protestant clerics) clergyman; — luterano, Lutheran pastor; figlio di —, parson's son; Prete Gianni, Prester John; cardinale dell'ordine dei ~i, cardinal priest (NOTE: the words **prete** and **sacerdote** overlap a good deal, but **sacerdote** is rather more formal and dignified, and may be more respectful; it is also the word most used of non-Christian priests. **Prete** is more conversational and more popular; it is in itself quite respectful, but is often given a hostile tinge by anti-clericals, who prefer this word to **sacerdote**. **Prete**, not **sacerdote**, is regularly used of cardinal priests and of Priests of the Oratory and of the Mission); (provb.) dare da bere al — che il chierico ha sete, to ask for something one wants oneself pretending it is for another person; (techn.) wooden frame formerly used to raise the sheet and blankets, into which a warming-pan was slipped (see **monaca**); (ichth.) pesce —, stargazer, *Uranoscopus scaber*; (bot.) berretta da —, spindle tree, *Euonymus europaeus*. **~acchione** *m. augm.* big, fat priest. **~aglia** *f.* (derog.) a lot of priests. **~a·io, ~ai(u)olo** *adj.* clerical, pro-clerical, priest-ridden. **~ari·a** *f.* class, order of priests. †**~a·tico** *m.,* **~ato** *m.* priesthood. **~esco** *adj.* (m.pl. **~eschi**) (derog.) priestly. **~ino** *m.* young priest; cleric not yet a priest; seminarist; *adj.* priestly, priest's. **~ismo** *m.* (derog.) priestliness, priest-like talk, actions, etc. **~one** *m. augm.* big priest; pious humbug, hypocrite.

prete·nd·ere [C 1] *tr.* to claim; to profess; to pretend; to assert; to contend; to want, to require, to exact; la ~e a grand'uomo, he pretends to be a great man; noi non ~iamo di essere dei dotti, we do not profess to be scholars; ~evano di fare quel che a loro piaceva, they claimed to do what they liked; che cosa ~ete?, what do you want?; ~eva che andassi da lui a mezzanotte, he wanted me to go to his house at midnight; ~e d'essere salutato, he expects (requires) to be saluted; ~ete troppo da quel ragazzo, you expect (require) too much of that boy; ~erla a musicista, ~erla in musica, to claim to be an expert musician; to demand, to want; di quel candelabro ~eva mille lire, he wanted a thousand lire for that candelabrum; ~erebbe la mano di quella ragazza?, would he pretend to that girl's hand?; ~eva la corona, he claimed the crown; †to feign; *intr.* (*aux.* avere) to lay claim (to), to pretend (to); ~eva al trono, he claimed the throne; non poteva — a quel titolo, he could not pretend to that title; — in una eredità, to claim a share of an inheritance. **~ente** *part. adj., n.m.* claimant, (hist.) pretender; applicant; suitor, wooer; un ~dente al trono, a pretender to the throne; signorina assediata dai ~denti, young lady besieged by suitors. **~enza** *f.* pretension, claim.

prenten·sione *f.* pretension; arrogance; audace ~sione, bold claim; uomo di molte ~sioni, man of many pretensions; senza ~sione, unpretentiously; expectation, demand (with ref. to price). **~sionoso** *adj.* full of pretensions, demanding. **~zioso** *adj.* pretentious; full of pretensions, arrogant. (**~ziosamente** *adv.*)

preterintenzionale *adj.* (leg.) that goes beyond the intention; delitto —, crime going beyond the intention; omicidio —, manslaughter (C.P.).

preter·ire [D 2] *intr.* (*aux.* essere) to pass away; *tr.* to omit; to pass over (in silence). **~ito** *part. adj.* past; le cose ~ite, things past. **~izione** *f.* (leg.) passing-over of heir by testator; preterition (C.C.); (rhet.) paralipsis, preterition. **~met·tere** [C 20] *tr.* to omit, to pass over. **~naturale** *adj.* preternatural. (**~naturalmente** *adv.*)

preterito¹ *part.* of **preterire**, q.v.

preterito² *adj.* (gramm.) preterit(e); *n.m.* (gramm.) preterit(e) tense; past tense; (fam.) behind, bottom.

pretẹs-a *f.* pretension, claim; pretence; pretentiousness; essa non ha -e di eleganza, she has no pretensions to elegance; la sua — non fu considerata, his claim was not taken into consideration; egli lo fece con la — di aiutarci, he did it under pretence of helping us; non ha la — di passare per dotto, he does not set himself up as a scholar; aveva la — che lo aspettassimo, he wanted us to wait for him; ha molte -e, he expects a great deal; senza -e, unpretentious, unpretentiously; (in advertisements) indicare -e, state salary required; (leg.) claim; — temeraria, baseless claim (C.C.). -o *part.* of **pretendere**, q.v.; *adj.* claimed, demanded; maintained, asserted; diritti -i, rights maintained; claimed insistently; pretended, alleged, supposed.

pretẹsco *adj.* See under **prete**.

†**prete·smolo** *m.* See **prezzemolo**.

†**pretẹs·sere** *tr.* to affect, to assume, to feign.

pretest-a *f.* (Rom. antiq.) *(toga) praetexta.* **-ata** *f.* (Rom. lit.) *(fabula) praetextata, praetexta* (serious drama with Roman subject). **-ato** *adj.* (Rom. antiq.) wearing a *(toga) praetexta.*

pretest-o *m.* pretext, excuse; pretence; plea; col — di, under pretext of; trovare un — per, to find a pretext for, to show cause for; addurre come —, to allege as a pretext. **-are** [A I] *intr.* (aux. avere) to make excuses, to give a pretext; *tr.* to allege or give as a pretext, to pretend; -ando una emicrania mi ritirai in camera mia, pleading a headache I retired to my room.

pretọr-e *m.* (Rom. antiq.) praetor; (leg.) local stipendiary Magistrate (C.C.P. and C.P.P.). **-iano** *adj.* (Rom. hist.) of the praetorian guard; *n.m.* (usu. *pl.*) praetorian, member of the guard; (fig.) henchman, satellite, (armed) supporter.

pretọ·rio *adj.* (Rom. hist.) of a praetor, praetorian; nave pretoria, flagship; *n.m.* praetorium; †part of a house reserved to the master.

†**pretọ-sel·lo** *m.*, †**-se·molo** *m.* See **prezzemolo**.

prett-o *adj.* mere; pure, real; good, correct; parla il — toscano, he speaks pure Tuscan; due, direct; a — mezzogiorno, due South. **-amẹnte** *adv.* purely, correctly; really; merely, simply.

pretumorale *adj.* (med.) preneoplastic.

pretura *f.* (leg.) Local Magistrate's Court (C.C.P. and C.P.P.).

preval-ẹre [B 34] *intr.* (aux. avere, essere) to prevail; — su, to prevail over; il senso -e spesso sulla ragione. the senses often prevail over reason; — per numero, to prevail by (weight of) numbers; *rfl.* to avail oneself, to take advantage; non mi prevarrò di questi documenti, I will not avail myself of these documents; -ersi del bisogno altrui, to take advantage of another person's need. **-ente** *part. adj.* prevalent; prevailing; l'opinione -ente, prevalent opinion; (meteor.) il vento -ente, the prevailing wind. **-entemẹnte** *adv.* prevalently. **-enza** *f.* prevalence; preponderance; supremacy; majority; avere la -enza su, to prevail over; in -enza, chiefly, mostly; essere in -enza,to be preponderant, to be in the majority; -enza termometrica, rise in temperature; (of a pump) head.

prevaric-are [A 2 S] *intr.* (aux. avere) to betray one's trust; to act dishonourably, to abuse one's power or position; — dalla fede, to abandon the true faith; — dall'argomento, to wander from the point; l'ira lo fa —, anger makes him lose patience; *tr.* to transgress: — i comandamenti, to transgress, to break, the commandments. **-amẹnto** *m.* transgression. **-atọre** *m.* transgressor; defaulter; embezzler; *adj.* ufficiale -atore, defaulting officer, embezzler. **(-atrice** *f.*) **-aziọne** *f.* breach of trust, default; embezzlement; (leg.) corrupt act or omission by public official.

preved-ẹre [B 35] *tr.* to foresee; to expect; to forecast; to provide for; — un rialzo dei prezzi, to foresee a rise in prices; era da —!, it was to be expected!, I might have known!; (leg.) il contratto -e che..., the contract provides that...; la legge -e il caso, the law covers the case. **-i·bile** *adj.* foreseeable; ciò non era -ibile, that was not to be foreseen. **-imẹnto** *m.* foreseeing; prescience. **-uto** *part. adj.* foreseen; expected; ciò non poteva essere -uto, that could not be (have been) foreseen; (leg.) reati -uti dal codice, offences under the (criminal) code.

prevegg-ente *adj.* foreseeing; prescient; provident, prudent; far-sighted. **-enza** *f.* foresight; providence; forethought, prudence; far-sightedness.

†**prevẹnda** *f.* provender.

preven-ire [D 17] *tr.* to precede, to forestall, to anticipate, to meet; to provide against (loss, etc.); to ward off; to forewarn; to inform; to prevent; to avoid; lo -ni di pochi giorni, I preceded him by a few days; — un desiderio, to forestall a wish; — una domanda, to anticipate a question, to answer a question before it is asked; volevo scriverti, ma mi hai -uto, I was going to write to you, but you have forestalled me; Dio ci previene con la sua grazia, God prevents (i.e. goes before) us with his grace; desidero — ogni discussione, I wish to avoid all dispute; — una disgrazia, to guard against an accident; vi prevengo che non riceverete risposta, I warn you not to expect any reply; vi prevengo che se farete ciò..., I warn you that if you do that...; — con telegramma, to warn (advise, inform) by telegram; *recip. rfl.* cercar di -irsi, to see who can do something first. **-iente** *part. adj.* preceding, anticipating; (theol.) grazia -iente, prevenient grace. **-imẹnto** *m.* anticipation; prejudice. **-uto** *part. adj.* forestalled; prevented; avoided; warned; informed; *n.m.* (leg.) il -uto, the accused. **-ziọne** *f.* prepossession, prejudice; bias; suspicion; prevention, precautionary measure(s); warning; giudicare senza -zioni, to judge without prejudice; un giudizio dato senza -zioni, an unbiased judgement; (leg.) -zione degli infortuni, prevention of accidents (C.P.); priority (between pending actions); ricorso in -zione, application for leave to serve short notice (C.C.P.); in -zione, in anticipation; (naut.: mil.) preparative, warning order; comando di -zione, preparatory order.

preventiv-o *adj.* preventive; anticipated, estimated; (leg.) made or done before the event; bilancio —, budget; concordato (fallimentare) —, composition with creditors (C.C.); carcere —, carcerazione, detenzione -a, detention in custody pending trial (C.P.); *n.m.* (comm.) estimate, quotation, offer; *pro forma* invoice. **-amẹnte** *adv.* beforehand, in anticipation; previously; preventively; (leg.) il giudice -amente adito, judge first applied to (C.C.P.). **-are** [A I] *tr.* (comm.) to estimate; *intr.* (aux. avere) (comm.) to make an estimate, to quote. **-ista** *m.* (comm.; industr.) estimator.

preventri·glio *m.* (zool.) proventriculus.

preven-uto *part.*, **-ziọne** *f.* See under **prevenire**.

†**prevẹrt-ere**, †**-ire** *tr.* to disorganize; to upset; to rout.

previden-te *adj.* foreseeing, provident; prudent. **(-temẹnte** *adv.*) **-za** *f.* foresight; prudence; fondo, cassa di -za, benevolent fund; istituto di -za, provident institution; (leg.) social insurance, social security (C.C.); *pl.* acts of prudence; provision for the future; measures of security. **-ziale** *adj.* relating to, concerning, foresight; relating to measures of social security or insurance.

previ-o *adj.* previous; *indecl.* in *adv. phrs.* — avviso, upon notice; — smontaggio, after dismantling; — consultazione col segretariato, after consultation with the secretariat. **-amẹnte** *adv.* previously, beforehand.

previṣ-i·bile *adj.* see **prevedibile**. **-iọne** *f.* prevision, expectation; in -ione di, in anticipation of; forecast; -ione del tempo, -ioni meteorologiche, weather forecast; (finan.) bilancio di -ione, budget forecast; (leg.) nonostante la -ione dell'evento, although the outcome was foreseen (C.P.).

†**previssuto** *adj.* alive before; having previously lived.

previsto *part.* of **prevedere**, q.v.; *adj.* foreseen; anticipated; estimated; (comm.) passivo —, debts expected to rank.

†**pre·vite** *m.* See **prete**.

prevosto *m.* (eccl.). See **preposto**, under **preporre**.

prevulcaniẓẓaziọne *f.* (rubber industr.) prevulcanization.

†**pre·zio** *m.* See **prezzo**.

preziọṣ-o *adj.* precious, costly, valuable; metalli -i, precious metals; pietra -a, precious stone, gem, jewel; -i contributi, valuable contribution; -e informazioni, valuable items of information; precious, affected, elaborate, artificial; *n.m.* precious object, jewel; *pl.* jewellery; (lit. hist.) *précieux*, French writers of the early seventeenth century. **-amẹnte** *adv.* preciously; richly; like a precious thing, with great care; custodire un oggetto -amente, to cherish a thing with the utmost care. **-iṣmo** *m.* (lit. hist.) mannered writing characteristic of the seventeenth-century French school of *précieux*. **-ità** *f.* preciousness, costliness; preciosity, affectation; precious object, rarity; *pl.* museo ricco di -ità, museum rich in precious objects.

prezz-are [A I] *tr.* to value, to appraise; to prize, to appreciate; *rfl.* to congratulate oneself, to consider oneself honoured. **-a·bile** *adj.* valuable, estimable. **-ato** *part. adj.* prized; valued. **-atọre** *m.* valuer. **(-atrice** *f.*) **-ẹvole** *adj.* estimable; valuable.

prezzẹmolo *m.* (bot.) parsley, *Petroselinum crispum*; — indiano, ajowan, *Carum copticum*; — velenoso, fool's parsley, *Aethusa cynapium*; (fig.) — d'ogni minestra, nosey-parker, busybody.

prezz·o *m.* **1.** PRICE; cost; — di costo, cost price; — lordo, gross price; — netto, net price; — all'ingrosso, wholesale price; — al minuto, retail price; — corrente, current price; condizioni di —, price terms; — globale, inclusive price; — medio, average price, *or* turn of the market, mean market price, middle price; — minimo, reserve price; — ridotto per rivenditori, trade price; — al pubblico, retail price; — di copertina, published price (of books); — tutto compreso, all-in price; diminuzione repentina dei -i, recession, slump; -i di chiusure, closing prices; listino, distinta, dei -i, Stock Exchange quotations; vendere a poco —, to sell cheap, to sell at a low price; vendere sotto —, to sell below cost price; un articolo di poco —, a cheap article; a — d'affezione, at a fancy price; i -i salgono, prices are rising; un aumento di -i, a rise in prices; i -i scendono, prices are falling; una diminuzione di -i, a fall in prices; pattuire il —, to agree the price; (fig.) mettere a — la propria onestà, to accept bribes; non avere —, to have no price, to be beyond price, not to be had for money; contarla, pagarla a caro —, to pay dearly for something; a — dell'onore, at the cost of one's good name. **2.** FARE; terms; fee; rate; charge; — del biglietto di viaggio, train fare, bus fare, etc.; — dell'ingresso, admission fee; lavorare a poco —, to work for little reward, to be badly paid. **3.** VALUE, worth; non è il — dell'opera, it is not worth while; tenere in gran —, to hold in high esteem; dei tuoi consigli faccio gran —, I value your advice; cosa di poco —, thing of little worth; profit, gain. **-olare** [A I s] *tr.* (derog.) to hire; — sicari, to hire cut-throats. **-olato** *part. adj.* hired, mercenary; sold; stampa -olata, venal press.

pria *adv.* (poet.) before, formerly; *conj.* — che, before.

Pri·amo *pr.n.m.* (myth.) Priam.

Priap·o *pr.n.m.* (myth.) Priapus; (zool.) — marino, *Priapulus* spp. **-e·o** *adj.* (anct. rel.) of, relating to, Priapus; culto -eo, Priapic cult; (prosod.) Priapean (metre); *n.m.pl.* (class. lit.) Priapea. **-ismo** *m.* (med.) priapism. **-ite** *f.* (med.) priapitis, inflammation of the penis.

†pri·colo *m.* and derivs. See **pericolo**.

†prieg·a *f.*, **†-o** *m.* See **preghiera**.

†priegare *vb.* and derivs. See **pregare**.

†priego *m.* See **prego**

†prieta *f.* See **pietra**.

†priete *m.* See **prete**.

prigion·e *f.* prison; gaol, jail; l'hanno messo in —, he has gone to prison; imprisonment, detention; fu condannato a un anno di —, he was sentenced to a year's imprisonment; (mil.) prison; — militare, military detention quarters; — in caserma, barracks or guardroom cell; cinque giorni di — di rigore, five days close confinement on bread and water; (naut.) — da bordo, ships' cells; (fig.) prison; qui si sta come in —, it is like being in prison here; *m.* prisoner; andar —, to become a prisoner, to be taken prisoner. **†-are** *tr.* to imprison. **-cella** *f. dim.* close prison. **†-eri·a** *f.* imprisonment. **-i·a** *f.* imprisonment; detention; captivity. **†-iere** *m.* prisoner; warder. **-iero** *m.* prisoner; -iero di guerra, prisoner of war; far -iero, to take prisoner; essere fatto -iero, to be taken prisoner; scambio di -ieri, exchange of prisoners; (fig.) captive; (eng.) stud bolt; *adj.* soldati -ieri, prisoners of war; fare, condurre alcuno -iero, to take someone prisoner.

prill·are [A I] *tr.* to twirl, to whirl; *intr.* (aux. avere) to whirl, to spin. **-o** *m.* whirl, twirl, spin; whirling, spinning.

prima[1] *adv.* previously, before, beforehand, first; — tu, poi io, first you, then me; bisogna pensarci —, we must think about it first; si stava meglio —, we were better off before; le usanze di —, former customs; formerly, once; questa era — una chiesa, this was once a church; — si faceva così, formerly we used to do this; earlier, sooner; — o poi, sooner or later; quanto —, as soon as possible, very soon; dovreste alzarvi —, you ought to get up earlier; further back; due pagine —, two pages back; rather, preferably, sooner; vorrei — morire che vederli così, I would rather die than see them like this; — la morte che il disonore, rather death than dishonour; *prep. phr.* — di, before; — d'oggi, before today; — di lui, before him, preceding him; — di dormire, before going to sleep; — di tutto, first of all; *conj.* — che, before; — che parta, before he leaves.

prima[2] *f.* the first one; the first thing; the first time (**cosa**, **volta**, etc., being understood); (provb.) la — si perdona, la seconda si bastona, forgiveness the first time, a beating the second; (motor.) first gear, bottom gear; in —, in bottom; (fencing) prime; (liturg.)

Prime; first-class; viaggiare in —, to travel first-class; (schol.) first form; (theatr.) first night, first performance; (mus.) see **cantino**; (comm.) — di cambio, first of exchange; *adv. phr.* alla —, at once; sulle prime, in the beginning; a tutta —, at the very first; da —, see **dapprima**. **-acciuola** *f.* see **primaiuola**, under **primaio**.

primacci·o *m.* (dial. N. Ital.) pillow, feather-bed. **-ino** *m. dim.* small cushion. **-uolo** *m. dim.* pad.

primag·gio *m.* (comm.) primage.

†prima·io *adj.* first; *adv. phr.* alla primaia, firstly (cf. **primo**, **primiero**).

primaiuola *f.* woman at her first confinement; (agric.) ewe mated in spring.

primamente *adv.* See under **primo**.

primano *adj.* (Rom. army) of the first legion; *n.m.* soldier of the first legion.

prima·ri·o *adj.* primary; principal; medico —, chief physician (or surgeon) of a hospital; paramount; di -a importanza, of paramount importance; scuola -a, primary school; istruzione -a, primary (elementary) education; (scient.; chem.; electr.) primary; *n.m.* ospedaliero, top-ranking doctor in a small hospital or at the head of a large department in a large hospital. NOTE: this term is only used in hospitals run on public funds where appointment is by open competition. The hierarchy in hospitals is as follows: primario, aiuto, assistente. **-amente** *adv.* primarily; principally; firstly, first. **-ato** *m.* rank or post of a 'primario ospedaliero', q.v.

primasso *m.* (joc.) chief; primate.

primate *m.* (eccl.) primate; (zool.) primate.

primatic·cio *adj.* (agric.) early; premature.

primat·o *m.* pre-eminence, primacy; supremacy; acquistare il —, to gain supremacy; tenere il —, to be supreme; esercitare il — letterario, to be pre-eminent in literature; (leg.) supremacy of jurisdiction; (sport, etc.) championship, record; detenere un —, to hold a championship, to be a record-holder; conseguire un —, to win the championship. **-ista** *m., f.* record-holder; -ista mondiale di velocità sull'acqua, holder of the world water-speed record.

primaver·a *f.* spring, springtime; equinozio di —, vernal equinox; una giornata di —, a spring day; canzone di —, spring song; (provb.) una rondine non fa —, one swallow does not make a summer; (fig.) nella — della vita, in the springtime of life; (anct. rel.) — sacra, *ver sacrum*, 'spring offering' (custom by which in times of distress an Italian or Greek community consecrated to a god the beasts and human beings born in a particular spring, the former being sacrificed, the latter sent into exile at the age of twenty); (bot.) see **primaverina**. **-ile**, **†-esco** *adj.* vernal, spring; stagione -ile, springtime; fiori -ili, spring flowers; moda -ile, spring fashions. **-ina** *f.* (bot.) primrose, *Primula vulgaris*; cowslip, *P. veris*.

primaz·i·a *f.* (eccl.) status of primate, primacy; †supremacy. **-iale** *adj.* (eccl.) primatial; *n.f.* primatial church (e.g. St Mark's, Venice).

primeggiare [A 3 c] *intr.* (aux. avere) to excel, to be pre-eminent; to lead, to take the lead.

†primer·o, **†-ano** *adj.* See **primiero**.

primevo *adj.* primeval.

primice·r·io *m.* (eccl.) *primicerius* (chief dignitary in various ecclesiastical contexts). **†-ia** *f.* (eccl.) Mother Superior. **-i·a** *f.*, **-iato** *m.* (eccl.) status of *primicerius*. **-iale** *adj.* primicerial.

primiera *f.* (cards) primero, a card game, also termed 'bambara', a hand in which consists of four cards; a hand containing one card of each suit; andare a —, stare a —, to hold three cards of different suits, wanting only one of the fourth suit to make primero; (in the game of 'scopa' and 'scopone') to have four sevens, or three sevens and two sixes, or two sevens and three sixes, comprising at least one card of each suit; (fig.) voler — con tre carte, to cry for the moon, to want something impossible; (cul.) 'pasta' made in imitation of the markings of playing cards, used in soup.

primier·o *adj.* first, former, previous; *n.m.* (in the game of charades) first part of the chosen word. **-amente** *adv.* firstly, in the first place; first of all; above all; †in -amente, in the first place.

primige·nio *adj.* original, primigenial, primordial; la lingua primigenia, the original language.

primina *f.* (bot.) external integument.

prim·i·para *f.* primipara, woman bearing her first child; *adj.* primiparous. **-ipilare** *adj.* (Rom. antiq.) primipilar; *n.m.* centurion of this rank, esp. after retirement. **-ipi·lo** *m.* (Rom. army) *primipilus*, senior centurion in a legion; l'alto **-ipilo**, the 'high captain' of the Apostles, St Peter (Dante, *Para.* xxv). **-iscri·nio, -iscri·neo** *m.* (Rom. antiq.) *primiscrinius*.

primitiv·o *adj.* primitive, primal, original; primeval; pristine; early; crude, simple, credulous; senso **—**, original meaning; nome **—**, root word; uomo **—**, primitive man; (eng.) cerchio **—**, pitch centre; *n.m.* primitive man; (paint.) primitive (i.e. a pre-Renaissance painter). **-amente** *adv.* primitively; in the beginning; early. **-a** *f.* (eng.) pitch line.

primi·zia *f.* (usu. *pl.*) first fruits; early fruit; first shoot or branch from a stock; latest news, novelty; early extract of an unpublished work; †founder of a family.

prim·o *adj.* first; chief, foremost, principal, leading; old, ancient; prime; former; a **-a** vista, at first sight; di **-a** mano, first-hand; Giacomo **—**, James the First; i **-i** due, the first two; il **—** nato, the firstborn; **-i** anni, early years; dal **—** momento, from the very first; il **—** giorno dell'anno, New Year's Day; il **—** ministro, the Prime Minister; di prim'ordine, first-rate, first-class; una delle **-e** famiglie della città, one of the principal families of the town; **-a** mano di pittura, first coat of paint; numeri **-i**, prime numbers; staple; prime; materie **-e**, staple commodities, *or* raw materials; (gramm.) la **-a** persona, the first person; **—** caso, nominative case; la **-a** arte, the first art (of the seven, i.e. grammar); partirò col **—** treno, I shall leave by the next *or* first train; tornare ai **-i** amori, to return to one's early love; ritornò alla sua **-a** dimora, he went back to his former dwelling; non essere il **—** venuto, to be someone, not to be a nobody; **-a** copia, master-copy; minuto **—**, minute; (mus.) **-a** donna, leading soprano; arrivar **—**, to come in first (in a race); (mil.) first, senior; **—** capitano, captain; **—** tenente, lieutenant; **—** chirurgo, senior surgeon (naut.) **—** tenente di vascello, lieutenant (not 'first lieutenant' which is a position as opposed to a rank); **—** ufficiale, commanding officer; (theol.) **-a** colpa, original sin; (comm.) **-a** offerta, upset price; **-a** nota, waste-book; *prn.* first; former; fu il **—** a far ciò, he was the first to do that; il **—** di loro, the first of them; il **—** (di) maggio, the first of May; ai **-i** del mese venturo, at the beginning of next month; sul **—**, at the beginning; il **—** ...il secondo..., the former ...the latter...; leader, chief; (in a duel) principal; (math.) **—** d'arco, minute of arc; *adv.* first of all, firstly; **—** non chiaccherare, first of all, don't talk. **-amente** *adv.* at first, in the first place; chiefly. **-a** *f.* see **prima²**.

primoge·nit·o *adj.* firstborn, eldest; i frutti **-i**, the first-fruits; (eccl.) la figlia **-a** della chiesa, the eldest daughter of the Church, France; *n.m.* firstborn, eldest son; (Bibl.) i **-i** degli Egizi, the firstborn of Egypt; †favourite son. **-ato** *m.* primogeniture. **-ore** *m.* progenitor; the father of the race, Adam. **-rice** *f.* progenitrix. **-ura** *f.* (leg.) primogeniture; birthright.

pri·mola *f.* (bot.). See **primula**.

primor·d·io *m.* beginning, origin; outset; nei **-i**, in the beginning, at the outset; i primordi della civiltà, the dawn of civilization. **-iale** *adj.* primordial, primeval; primary; original; causa **-iale**, primary cause; indagini **-iali**, preliminary inquiries.

pri·mul·a *f.* (bot.) primrose, *Primula*; La **—** Rossa, *The Scarlet Pimpernel*.

princesse *f.* (pron. as Fr.) princess dress.

principal·e *adj.* principal; chief, main; la città **—** della regione, the chief town of the district; le **-i** caratteristiche, the chief features; (gramm.) la proposizione **—**, the main clause; il punto **—**, the main point; la linea **—**, the main line; l'ufficio, la sede **—** di una banca, the head office of a bank; porta **—**, front door, main gate or entrance; scala **—**, main staircase; i **-i** alberghi, the best hotels; *n.m.* manager, master, chief, 'boss'; senior partner; original (author, later imitated); main point, chief matter: ora veniamo al **—**, now we come to the main point; (comm.) principal; (mus.) open diapason (organ-stop); **—** chiuso, stopped diapason. **-mente** *adv.* principally, chiefly, mainly. **-ino** *m.* (mus.) choir diapason (organ-stop). **-issimamente** *adv.* most especially. **-ità** *f.* principalship.

prin·cip·e *m.* prince; **—** del sangue, prince of the Blood; **—** ereditario, Crown Prince; il **—** Consorte, the Prince Consort; **—** reggente, Prince Regent; **—** di Galles, Prince of Wales; il **—** Azzurro, Prince Charming; (text.) un Principe di Galles, a grey cloth of a distinctive pattern; a suit made of this material (for men or women); vivere da **—**, to lead a princely existence; (rel.) **—** degli Apostoli, prince of the Apostles, St Peter; **—** delle tenebre, prince of darkness, Satan; (eccl.) **—** della chiesa, prince of the Church, cardinal; *pl.* (Rom. army) *principes*, second line of soldiers; *adj.* chief, principal, first; edizione **—**, *editio princeps*, first edition; avvocato **—**, leading advocate; codice **—**, principal manuscript. **-are** [A I S] *tr., intr.* (*aux.* avere) to rule like a prince. **-ato** *m.* principality; il **-ato** del Galles, the Principality of Wales; sovereignty, supremacy; princedom; **-ato** ecclesiastico, clerical government, e.g. by a prince-bishop; **-ato** temporale, temporal government of the Pope; *pl.* (theol.) principalities (one of the nine angelic orders); †(eccl.) prelates. **-esco** *adj.* (*m.pl.* **-eschi**) princely; relating to, characteristic of, a prince; palazzo **-esco**, prince's palace; città **-esca**, (city) the seat of a prince; (fig.) princely; una mancia **-esca**, a lavish tip. **-escamente** *adv.* in princely style, like a prince. **-essa** *f.* princess. **-essina** *f. dim.* young princess, little princess. **-ino** *m. dim.* young prince. **-otto** *m.* princeling.

principi·are [A4] *tr.* to begin, to commence, to start, to initiate; **—** un lavoro, to begin a job; **—** una discussione, to start a discussion; *intr.* (*aux.* essere, avere) to begin, to commence, to start; l'estate è **-ata** col solstizio di giugno, summer began at the June solstice; ha **-ato** a lagnarsi da stamani, he began complaining early this morning; se **-iamo** così!, that's a bad beginning!; *n.m.* beginning, commencement: al **—** del mese, at the beginning of the month. †**-amento** *m.* commencement, beginning. **-ante** *part. adj.* beginning; inexpert; cavallo **-ante**, partly trained horse; *n.m., f.* beginner; novice; lezioni d'inglese per **-anti**, English lessons for beginners; (provb.) Dio ti salvi da un cattivo vicino e da un **-ante** di violino, Heaven preserve you from a bad neighbour and from a beginner on the violin. **-ativo** *adj.* beginning, serving to make a beginning. (**-ato** *part. adj.*) **-atore** *m.* initiator, founder, one who makes a beginning. (**-atrice** *f.*) **-atura** *f.* (techn.) beginning, commencement (e.g. of stockings and other knitting).

princi·p·io *m.* (*pl.* **-ii**) beginning, commencement; dal **—** alla fine, from beginning to end; lo spettacolo avrà **—** alle nove, the play will begin at nine o'clock; da **—**, at first, in the beginning; subito al **—**, at the very beginning; fin dal **—**, right from the start, from the very beginning; principle: **-ii** di economia politica, principles of political economy; **-ii** morali, moral principles; lo feci per **—**, I did it on principle; è un individuo senza **-ii**, he is an unprincipled person; in tutte queste macchine il **—** è lo stesso, in all these machines the principle is the same; **—** dell'universo, principle of the universe, First Cause; **—** attivo, active principle; (leg.) un **—** di diritto, a legal principle; un **—** di prova per iscritto, *prima facie* evidence in writing (C.C.); (logic) petizione di **—**, begging the question; (eng.) vite ad un **—**, single-threaded screw; *pl.* (Rom. antiq.) *principia*, a general's quarters.

princis·becco, (Tusc.) **-becche** *m.* (metall.) pinchbeck; di **—**, false, not real; (fig.) rimanere, restare di **—**, to be astounded.

†**Princisbech** *m.* See **princisbecco**.

priora *f.* (eccl.) prioress; (pop.) lady who organizes parish activities.

prior·e *m.* (eccl.) prior of a religious house; parish priest (esp. in Tuscany); senior cardinal deacon; †senior canon; (pop.) layman organizing parish activities; (hist.) prior, superior of the Knights of Malta, etc.; (joc.) star come un **—**, to live like a prior, i.e. to eat well and work little; (Ital. billiards) the largest of the 'birilli'. **-ale** *adj.* of a prior; of a priory. **-ato** *m.* priorship, magistracy; (eccl.) (in a religious house) priorship; (eccl.) (in a parish) status, and term of office, of a priest with title of 'prior'; durante il **-ato** di Don A., while Father A. was the parish priest; (hist.) priorship (of Knights of Malta). **-i·a** *f.* (eccl.) parish church (esp. in Tuscany) whose priest has the title of 'prior'; the house (presbytery) of such a priest: his ecclesiastical rank; his tenure of office; (eccl.) priorship of a religious house. **-ista** *m.* register and chronicle of priors (magistrates); (road traffic) diritto di **-ista**, right of way (equiv. to **precedenza**, q.v.).

priorità *f.* priority, precedence; (finan.) capitali con diritto di **—**, preference stock.

priscillianista *m.* (eccl. hist.) Priscillianist.

pris·co *adj.* (*m.pl.* **-chi**) ancient, early, old.

prism·a *m.* (geom.; opt.) prism. **-a·tico** *adj.* prismatic.

pri·spola *f.* See **pispola**.

prispolone *m.* (orn.) tree pipit, *Anthus trivialis*.

pri·stin-o *adj.* former; ancient; pristine; primitive; *n.m.* former state; rimettere qualche cosa in —, to restore something to its former condition. **-amȩnte** *adv.* formerly.

pritan-e·o *m.* (Gk. antiq.) Prytaneum, magistrates' hall, town hall. **-o** *m.* (Gk. antiq.) *prytanis*; ruler; head magistrate; (at Athens) member of presiding tribe.

priv-are [A I] *tr.* (*prep.* di) to deprive (of); — di libertà, to deprive of freedom; essere -ato del diritto di voto, to be deprived of the right to vote; — di vita, to kill; — di un divertimento, to deprive of a pleasure, enjoyment; to deny; non voglio -arti del piacere di…, I do not want to deny you the pleasure of…; to strip; — del suo denaro, to strip of one's money; fu -ato di tutto, he was stripped of everything; — della noia, to relieve of boredom; *rfl.* to deny oneself; to deprive oneself; si -a del necessario per suo figlio, she denies herself necessities for her son's sake; -arsi di una cosa, to get rid of a thing (to give it away, to sell it); re Lear si -ò di tutti i suoi possedimenti, King Lear stripped himself of all his possessions. **-amȩnto** *m.* depriving, denial; deprivation. **-ato** *part. adj.* deprived; bereft, stripped; -ato del comando, relieved of (his) command. **-azione** *f.* privation; suffering; loss, deprivation; lack, absence; soffersȩ molte -azioni, he suffered many privations; sente molto la -azione di suo padre, he feels the loss of, he misses, his father very much.

privatista *m.* See under **privato²**.

privativ-a *f.* monopoly, patent; sole right: — di Stato, State shop, selling tobacco, salt, government monopolies; (leg.) right to exclusive use; diritto di —, patent-right; generi di —, state monopoly goods (e.g. tobacco, salt, etc.); brevetto di —, letters patent. **-o** *adj.* privative, exclusive. **-amȩnte** *adv.* exclusively.

privato¹ *part.* See under **privare**.

privat-o² *adj.* private; personal; particular; scuola -a, private (i.e. non-State) school; proprietà -a, private property; aveva ragioni -e, he had personal reasons (private reasons); (leg.) diritto —, private law; scrittura -a, simple contract (C.C.); cassetta -a, (of a sovereign) privy purse; insegnamento —, private tuition; *n.m.* private person, (private) individual; in —, privately, in private; †privy; *adv.* vivere —, to live in retirement. **-ista** *m., f.* private pupil, private student, one educated privately.

priverno *m.* wine of Priverno (or Piperno).

†**privigno** *m.* stepson.

privile·gi-o *m.* privilege; monopoly; (leg.) lien; priority; preference; security; — generale sui mobili, general lien on personal property; — sopra gli immobili, charge on real property; — dell'albergatore, innkeeper's lien; ordine dei privilegi, order of priority of charges (C.C.); (comm.) charter; — dell'armatore, shipowner's lien; (eccl.) — del foro, *privilegium fori*, clerical right to be tried in a special court; (theol.) — sabatino, sabbatine privilege. **-ante** *part. adj.* bestowing a privilege. **-are** [A 3] *tr.* to privilege, to bestow a privilege on, to gift; -are una terra a una famiglia, to bestow an estate on a family; la natura lo ha -ato di una grande capacità inventiva, nature has endowed him with great inventive powers. **-ato** *part. adj.* privileged, favoured; gifted; uomini -ati, gifted men; (comm.) credito -ato, preferential, secured debt (C.C.); capitale -ato, preferred stock; (leg.) creditore -ato, secured creditor (C.C.); (eccl.) altare -ato, privileged altar; *n.m.* privileged person. (**-ata** *f.*)

privo¹ *adj.* (*prep.* di) devoid (of); destitute (of); lacking (in), wanting, without; — di senso comune, devoid of common sense; — di tutto, utterly destitute; — di coraggio, wanting in courage; — di notizie, without news; — della vista, blind; — di genitori, orphan(ed); campagna -a di alberi, treeless countryside; — di discernimento, wanting in judgement; — di utilità, useless; — di danaro, penniless.

privo² *apocop. part.* of **privare**, q.v., deprived, bereft, stripped.

†**prizzato** *adj.* speckled.

pro¹ *m.* advantage; benefit; profit; a — nostro, to our advantage; buon —!, good health!; (iron.) buon — vi faccia!, much good may it do you!; a che —?, what's the use?; far —, to do good (esp. of food); far — dell'esperienza altrui, to profit by other people's experience; lavorare a — degli altri, to work for others (for the benefit of other people).

†**pro²** *adj.* See **prode**.

pro³ *prep.* for, on behalf of; lotteria — mutilati, lottery on behalf of cripples (the disabled); — infanzia abbandonata, for waifs and strays; argomenti — e contro, arguments for and against; (also used in several Latin expressions): — forma, — tempore (as in

English), — domo sua, in one's own interest; *n.m.* il — e il contro, the pros and cons.

pro-⁴ *pref.* pro-; vice-.

proav-o *m.* great-grandfather; *pl.* ancestors, forebears. (**-a** *f.*)

†**proa·volo** *m.* See **proavo**.

prob-a·bile *adj.* probable; likely; ciò è molto —, that is most probable; non è — che venga, it is not likely that he will come, he is not likely to come; il costo —, the probable cost; ragioni -abili, acceptable reasons; (theol.) opinione —, probable opinion; †worthy of approval; *n.m.* probability; ha del —, it's not improbable. **-abilmȩnte** *adv.* probably; molto -abilmente, most probably, very likely. **-abiliore** *adj.* (theol.) more probable (opinion). **-abiliorismo** *m.* (theol.) probabiliorism. **-abiliorista** *m.* (theol.) probabiliorist. **-abilismo** *m.* (theol.; philos.) probabilism. **-abilista** *m.* (theol.; philos.) probabilist. **-abilità** *f.* probability, likelihood; chance; con ogni -abilità, in all probability; non c'è -abilità che essi vengano, there is no likelihood of their coming; non ha -abilità di vincere, he has no chance of winning; gradi della -abilità, degrees of probability; lontana -abilità, remote possibility; (math.) probability.

probante *adj.* decisive; questo è —!, that settles it!

proba·tico *adj.* (Bibl.) piscina probatica, the 'pool near the sheep-gate' of St John v. 2; pool of Bethesda.

probat-ivo *adj.* proving; tending to prove. **-o·rio** *adj.* (leg.) evidential; probative; avere efficacia -oria, to be, to constitute, evidence (C.C.); l'istruzione -oria, investigation of evidence (C.C.P.); documentazione -oria, vouchers; (fig.) that may be taken as evidence, indicative; compromising; non fare alcun cenno -orio, to be entirely non-committal, to give no sign one way or the other.

†**prob·brio** *m.* See **obprobrio**.

probità *f.*, **probiviri** *m.pl.* See under **probo**.

problem-a *m.* problem; question; risolvere un —, to solve a problem; -i sociali, social problems, social questions; (math.) sum; -i difficili, hard sums. **-aticità** *f.* problematic nature, uncertainty. **-a·tico** *adj.* problematic, problematical; uncertain. **-aticamȩnte** *adv.* problematically.

prob-o *adj.* upright; honest; just. **-amȩnte** *adv.* honestly, justly. **-ità** *f.* probity; uprightness, honesty; integrity; persona d'indiscutibile -ità, person of irreproachable integrity. **-iviri** *m.pl.* arbitrators; scrutineers; umpires.

probo·scide *f.* (zool.) proboscis; (of an elephant) trunk; (joc.) big nose, 'proboscis'.

procaccȩvole *adj.* See under **procacciare**.

†**procac·chia** *f.* (bot.) purslane, *Portulaca oleracea*.

procac·cia *m. indecl.* paid messenger (in country districts); rural postman who runs errands; carrier; remover.

procacci-are [A 3] *tr.* to procure; to get (by effort); to seek, to try; — il sostentamento ai propri figli, to procure sustenance for one's children; promise di -armi un impiego, he promised to get me employment; -ate di rendervi utili, try to make yourselves useful; (fig.) — dispiaceri alla famiglia, to bring trouble on one's family; *rfl.* (*dat.* of *prn.* 'si') to get; to procure; -arsi da vivere, to earn one's living; -arsi un impiego, to secure employment; -arsi noie, to get into trouble. **-amȩnto** *m.* procuring, getting; striving; (leg.) -amento di notizie, obtaining of information (C.P.). **-ante** *part. adj.* busy; meddlesome; *n.m., f.* busybody, meddler. (**-ato** *part. adj.*) **-atore** *m.* tout; busybody, meddler. (**-atrice** *f.*) **-(i)ȩvole** *adj.* industrious, eager for gain or advantage.

procaccin-o *m. dim.* of **procaccia**, q.v.; factotum; young man willing to run errands; fare il —, to be at everyone's beck and call. **-a** *f.* woman messenger; (rural) postwoman; errand-girl; woman who finds places for domestic servants.

procac-e *adj.* saucy, impudent, cheeky; provoking, tempting; challenging; sguardi -i, saucy looks. **-emȩnte** *adv.* impudently, saucily; shamelessly. **-ità** *f.* impudence, sauciness; provoking (alluring) behaviour.

procam·bio *m.* (bot.) procambium.

†**procci an-o** *adj.* near, close. †**-amȩnte** *adv.* nearly.

proce·d-ere [B I] *intr.* (*aux.* essere) to proceed, to go on; to act; — di buon passo, to walk at a good pace; se -iamo di questo passo arriveremo tardi, if we go on at this rate we shall be late; (fig.) ditemi come devo —, tell me how I ought to proceed; gli affari -ono abbastanza bene, business is going (on) pretty well; (*aux.* avere) to begin, to undertake, to start proceedings; (leg.)

proced-ere (*cont.*)

to proceed; — legalmente contro, to take proceedings against; ordine di non luogo a —, nonsuit; il chirurgo ha -uto all'operazione, the surgeon has proceeded to operate; — onestamente, to act decently; da che -e questo fatto?, how did this come about?; fiume che -e da un lago, river coming from a lake; (theol.) to proceed (said of the Son and of the Holy Ghost); *n.m.* conduct, behaviour; il vostro — non mi piace, I don't like your way of going about things; col — del tempo, in course of time. **-ente** *part. adj.* proceeding; coming from; going on; -ente da poco giudizio, arising from (coming from) poor judgement; -ente all'infinito, going on to infinity (for ever). **-enza** *f.* proceeding, going on; (theol.) procession. **-ibilità** *f.* (leg.) condition of being prosecutable (C.P.). **-imento** *m.* proceeding(s); course; conduct, dealing; -imento difficile, difficult proceeding; seguire il -imento naturale dei fatti, to follow the natural course of events; -imenti da villano, boorish conduct; (industr.) process; (theol.) procession; (leg.) proceeding; procedure; -imenti abbreviati, short (parliamentary) procedure (I.C.); -imento sommario, summary procedure (applied, e.g., in small bankruptcy); -imenti sommari, summary proceedings; -imenti speciali, (special or) short procedures (C.C.P.); -imento disciplinare, disciplinary measures; prosecution. NOTE: criminal proceedings may begin in four ways, according to gravity of charge: (1) public prosecution instituted by competent authority (cf. **perseguibile**) which may be set in motion by: **denuncia**, Formal Information; (2) richiesta di -imento, demand for prosecution; (3) istanza di -imento; application for prosecution; (4) **querela**, q.v., Information (C.P.P.). **-ura** *f.* procedure, practice; questa è la -ura comune, this is the common practice; (leg.) practice; proceedings; procedure; -ura coatta amministrativa, compulsory winding-up of companies; -ura fallimentare, bankruptcy proceedings (C.C.); regolamento di -ura, Rules of Procedure; aprire una discussione sulla -ura, to open a debate on procedure. **-urale** *adj.* procedural, relating to procedure. **-uto** *part. adj.* derived, coming (from); (fig.) gone forward.

proceleuṣma·tico *m.* (prosod.) proceleusmatic.

procell-a *f.* storm, tempest; (fig.) calamity. **-a·ria** *f.* (orn.) shearwater, petrel, esp. *Procellaria* spp.; *pl.* petrels, shearwaters, used collectively for family Procellariidae. **-oṣo** *adj.* stormy, tempestuous; mare -oso, tempestuous sea; tempi -osi, stormy times, unsettled times. **-oṣamente** *adv.* tempestuously, stormily.

†pro·ceri *m.pl.* magnates, patricians.

proceṣṣ-are [A I] *tr.* (leg.) to prosecute; (fig.) — uno, to draw a person out, to persuade a person to talk. **-a·bile** *adj.* (leg.) liable to prosecution. **-abilità** *f.* (leg.) liability to prosecution. **-ante** *adj.* (leg.) giudice -ante, trial judge. **(-ato** *part. adj.*)

proceṣṣion-e *f.* procession (esp. religious); una — di dimostranti, a procession of demonstrators; (colloq.) mena tutto il giorno gli amici a —, he trails round with his friends all day; succession; una — di visite, a string of visits; (theol.) — dello Spirito Santo, procession of the Holy Ghost; andare, camminare in —, to walk in procession; andare a —, to walk up and down. **-almente** *adv.* in procession, processionally. **-a·ria** *f.* (ent.) processionary caterpillar of the moth, *Thaumatopoea processionea*. **-cella** *f. dim.* short procession. **-evole** *adj.* going in procession.

proceṣṣ-o *m.* process; course; in — di costruzione, in process of construction; in — di tempo, in course of time; (industr.) process; (econ.) spese di —, process costs; (leg.) action; process; suit; trial; — penale, criminal trial; — di cognizione della causa, process of cognisance of action (C.C.P.); — verbale, minutes, written record of proceedings (see also under **verbale**); (anat.) processus, apophysis; — ciliare, ciliary processus; in — di stampa, in course of publication; nel — della guerra, in the course of the war, during the war. **-uale** *adj.* (leg.) having to do with an action, process or trial; questione -uale, preliminary issue; prejudicial question. **-ura** *f.* process; procedure.

procidenza *f.* (med.) procidentia, prolapse.

procinto *adv. phr.* in — di, on the point of; essere, trovarsi in — di, to be on the point of, to be about to; ero in — di partire, I was on the point of leaving.

Procione *pr.n.m.* (astron.) Procyon, α Canis Minoris.

proclam-a *m.* announcement; proclamation; ban; (leg.) pubblici -i, advertisements; public notices (C.C.P.); (eccl.) bann. **-are** [A I] *tr.* to proclaim, to promulgate; to announce publicly. **-ato** *part. adj.* proclaimed; promulgated. **-atore** *m.* proclaimer. **(-atrice** *f.*)

-azione *f.* proclamation; declaration; -azione dei diritti dell'uomo, Declaration of the Rights of Man.

procli·tico *adj.* (gramm.) proclitic.

procliv-e *adj.* inclined, disposed; prone; — all'ozio, inclined to idleness. **-ità** *f.* inclination, tendency, propensity, proclivity.

†proco *m.* suitor; *pl.* (Gk. lit.) i proci, the suitors of Penelope.

procolo¹ *m.* See **proquoio**.

pro·colo² *m.* (theatr., etc.) impresario.

procọmb-ere [B I] *intr.* [B def.] (poet.) to fall on one's face, to fall forward; to fall dead. **-ente** *adj.* (bot.) procumbent.

proco·nsol-e *m.* (Rom. hist.) proconsul; (fig.) authoritarian ruler. **-o** *m.* (Florentine hist.) 'proconsul'. **-are** *adj.* proconsular. **-ato** *m.* proconsulate, proconsulship.

procraṣtin-are [A I] *tr.* to postpone, to put off; to defer; — un'adunanza, to postpone a meeting; *intr.* (aux. avere) to procrastinate; to temporize; *n.m.* il — fa sciupare il tempo, procrastination is the thief of time. **-amento** *m.* procrastinating. **-ato** *part. adj.* postponed, deferred. **-atore** *m.* procrastinator, temporizer. **(-atrice** *f.*) **-azione** *f.* procrastination, temporizing; delay.

procre-are [A 6] *tr.* to procreate, to generate; to beget; to give birth to; to bring into the world. **-a·bile** *adj.* that can be procreated. **-amento** *m.* procreation. **-atore** *m.* procreator, begetter; origin; stock. **-atrice** *f.* mother. **-azione** *f.* procreation.

Pro·cride¹ *pr.n.f.* (myth.) Procris.

pro·cride² *f.* (ent.) *Procris ampelophaga*, a moth damaging vines.

proct-algi·a *f.* (med.) proctodynia, rectal pain. **-ite** *f.* (med.) proctitis, rectitis. **-odini·a** *f.* (med.) proctodynia, rectal pain. **-ologi·a** *f.* (med.) proctology. **-olo·gico** *adj.* (med.) proctological. **-opeṣṣi** *f.* (surg.) proctopexy. **-oṣco·pio** *m.* (med.) proctoscope; -oscopio operativo, operating proctoscope. **-oṣigmoidoṣco·pio** *m.* (med.) procto-sigmoidoscope. **-otomi·a** *f.* (surg.) proctotomy.

procura *f.* See under **procurare**.

procur-are [A I] *tr.* to procure, to get; to cause; mi ha -ato qualche noia, he has caused me some trouble; (provb.) dove manca natura, arte -a, art supplies the deficiencies of nature; (leg.) to procure; be the cause of; to cause; — allarme, to cause alarm (C.P.); *intr.* (aux. avere; *prep.* 'di', followed by *infin.*) to endeavour (to), to do one's best, to see if one can; to manage (to), to succeed (in); -ate di partire presto, arrange to leave early; *rfl.* (dat. of *prn.* 'si') to procure, to get; mi sono già -ato il libro, I have already procured the book; -arsi un malanno, to catch a disease; -arsi da vivere, to make a living; (leg.) l'aborto -atosi dalla donna, abortion procured by a woman upon herself (C.P.). **-a** *f.* (leg.) power of attorney; office of attorney; proxy; la -a generale, office of Attorney-General (C.C.P.); una -a generale, speciale, general, special Power of Attorney; -a institoria, deed appointing agent, factor, or manager; matrimonio per -a, marriage by proxy (C.C.); voto per -a, vote by proxy; firmare per -a, to sign per pro. **-ante** *part. adj.* procuring; *n.m.* attorney; proxy. **-ateṣṣa** *f.* (hist.) wife of the Procurator of St Mark's, Venice. **-ati·a** *f.* (hist.) building in St Mark's Square, Venice, formerly the residence of the Procurator; Procurators of St Mark, or their office; sotto le -atie, under the colonnades in St Mark's Square. **-ato** *part. adj.* procured; arranged; (med.) aborto -ato, abactio, abactus venter. **-atorato** *m.* office of attorney or procurator. **-atore** *m.* (leg.) attorney; holder of Power of Attorney; -atore legale, solicitor (with limited right of audience) (C.C.P.); -atore della Repubblica, public prosecutor; -atore generale, Attorney-General (C.P.P.); mi fece suo -atore, he made me his proxy; (eccl.) procurator (administering the temporal affairs of a religious house); (eccl.) -atore generale, procurator-general (representing a religious order or institute at Rome); (Rom. hist.) procurator. **-atoreṣṣa** *f.* wife of a 'procuratore'. **-atori·a** *f.* premises or office of the procurator of St Mark's. **-ato·rio** *adj.* (m.pl. -atorii) relating to an attorney or Procurator. **-azione** *f.* intercession; (hist.) office or rank of Procurator in the Republic of Venice; (eccl.) procuration, allowance for a bishop during visitation.

prod-a *f.* (naut.) foreshore; andar —, *or* andar proda proda, to hug the coast; venire a —, to come to land; prender —, to take the ground; toccar la —, to beach; †bow, stem; edge, border, side; — di un fosso, edge of a ditch; — del campo, side of the field; arrivare a —, to come to shore; (agric.) land on a slope; — del letto, bedside. **†-ano** *m.* (naut.) mast rope. **†-eggiare** *intr.* (naut.) to tack repeatedly. **†-eg·gio** *m.* (naut.) bowline. **-icella** *f. dim.* narrow bank or edge.

prod·e¹ *adj.* brave, valiant; bold; heroic; gallant (of a knight); — in armi, valiant in arms; *n.m.* brave man; valiant man; hero. **-emẹnte** *adv.* bravely, valiantly. **-ẹzza** *f.* gallantry, bravery, valour; boldness; brave action, deed of valour; (iron.) belle **-ezze!**, fine goings-on!; (fam.) bravado; *pl.* brave deeds.

prode² *m.* (poet.) good, benefit (cf. **pro¹**).

prodẹse *m.* See **provese**.

prodẹzza *f.* See under **prode**.

prodier-e *m.* (naut. hist.) forecastle hand; bowman, bow, bow oarsman. **-o** *adj.* (naut.) fore, foreward, 'forr'ard', 'fo'castle'; nave **-a**, leading ship.

prodig-alità *f.* prodigality; lavishness; (leg.) habitual extravagance; spendthrift conduct (C.C.). **†-alizzare** *tr.* to squander. **-almẹnte** *adv.* prodigally, lavishly. **-alọne** *m.* spendthrift, wastrel; reckless person. **-are** [A2s] *tr.* to lavish; to squander; to be prodigal of; to pour out; -are la vita per la patria, to give one's life for one's country; *rfl.* to give oneself heart and soul, to devote oneself; to do one's very best; si -ò in tutti i modi, he did all he could.

prodi·gi-o *m.* prodigy; marvel; miracle; quel ragazzo è un —, that boy is a genius; far prodigi, to work wonders, to work miracles; un — di architettura, a miracle of architecture, an architectural wonder; molti prodigi annunziarono la sua nascita, many strange events presaged his birth. **-osità** *f.* prodigiousness. **-ọso** *adj.* prodigious, miraculous; wonderful, marvellous; †monstrous. **-osamẹnte** *adv.* prodigiously, marvellously.

pro·di-go *adj.* (*m.pl.* **-ghi**) prodigal, lavish; liberal; la parabola del figliuol —, the parable of the Prodigal Son; — di parole, very talkative. (**-camẹnte** *adv.*)

†prodi-tore *m.* traitor. (**†-trice** *f.*)

prodito·ri-o *adj.* treacherous. **-amẹnte** *adv.* treacherously, by treachery.

prodittat-ọre *m.* dictator's deputy, pro-dictator. (**-oriale** *adj.*) **-ura** *f.* pro-dictatorship.

†prodizione *f.* treachery.

prodomo¹ *m.* (hist.) superior of the Knights of Malta.

pro·domo² *m.* (archit.) main door of an important building.

prodọtto¹ *part.* of **produrre**, q.v.; *adj.* produced; created; certificato —, certificate produced.

prodọtto² *m.* product; produce; prodotti nazionali, home products; il — delle nostre fatiche, the product of our labours; (agric.) — della terra, produce of the land; — agricolo, agricultural produce; lamb, calf, etc.; — principale, staple product, staple; — secondario, by-product; (leg.) produce; product; i prodotti agricoli, agricultural produce (C.C.); i prodotti industriali, industrial products (C.P.); (math.) product; (chem.) product; — finale, end product; prodotti chimici, chemicals; prodotti semilavorati, unfinished products, semi-manufactured products.

pro·dromo *adj.* premonitory; segni prodromi di tempesta, premonitory signs of storm, harbingers of (a) storm; (med.) prodromic, premorbid; premonitory; *n.m.* introductory speech; premonitory sign; symptom.

produc-ente *adj.* productive; (philos.) cagione —, efficient cause. **-i·bile** *adj.* producible. **-ibilità** *f.* (techn.) production capacity. **-imẹnto** *m.* production. **-itọre** *m.* producer. (**-itrice** *f.*)

†produ·cere *vb.* See **produrre**.

†produomo *m.* valiant and courageous man ('uomo prode').

pro-durre [B2] *tr.* to produce, to bring forth, to bear; to yield; to bring in; to show; to cause, to give rise to; to manufacture; l'Italia ha -dotto grandi artisti, Italy has produced great artists; questo terreno -duce molto grano, this land yields a good crop of corn; (fig.) il peccato -duce frutti amari, sin yields bitter fruit; le sue parole -dussero grande delusione, his words caused great disappointment; questi articoli non si -ducono in Italia, these articles are not made (manufactured, produced) in Italy; to cause, to occasion, to give rise to; l'ira -duce molti mali, anger is the cause of many evils; la nuova tassa -dusse grave scontento, the new tax caused serious discontent; (leg.) to bring forward, to cause, to produce; — documenti, to produce or exhibit documents (C.C.P.); — testimoni, to call, bring forward witnesses; — dei danni, to cause damage; †to prolong; *rfl.* to be produced; to happen; to occur; to appear, to make a public appearance; s'è -dotto da sè, it just happened; ciò si -dusse solo una volta o due, that only happened once or twice; egli si -dusse una profonda ferita, he wounded himself badly; -dursi sulla scena, to appear on the stage. **-dutti·bile** *adj.* producible. **-duttività** *f.*

productivity. **-duttivo** *adj.* productive; fruitful, fertile; spese **-duttive**, productive expenses, expenses that will yield a profit. **-duttọre** *m.* producer; manufacturer; *adj.* paesi **-duttori**, producing countries, exporting countries; (cinem.) producer. (**-duttrice** *f.*) **-duziọne** *f.* production; manufacture; output; yield; -duzione annua, yearly output; (leg.) production, la -duzione nazionale, the national production (C.C.); la -duzione di documenti, production of documents (C.C.P.); autore di scarsa -duzione, author with a small output; -duzione drammatica, dramatic work, theatrical production; (econ.) spese di -duzione, production costs; -duzione all'ingrosso, — in serie, mass production; †prolongation.

proe·mi-o *m.* foreword, preface, introduction, preamble; proem; dopo un — di scuse, after a preamble of excuses, after making a lot of excuses; senza —, without beating about the bush. **-ale** *adj.* introductory, prefatory. **-almẹnte** *adv.* by way of introduction. **-are** [A4] *intr.* (*aux.* avere) to write (or speak) an introduction; to preface one's remarks. **-zzare** [A1] *intr.* (*aux.* avere) see **proemiare**.

proenzima *m.* (biol.) proenzyme.

profan-are [A1] *tr.* to profane, to desecrate; to pollute; to contaminate; (eccl.) to profane, to desecrate (by sacrilege); to convert to secular use, to secularize (by regular procedure). **-amẹnto** *m.* profaning, desecrating. **-ato** *part. adj.* profaned, desecrated; polluted; contaminated. **-atọre** *m.* profaner, desecrater; polluter. (**-atrice** *f.*) **-aziọne** *f.* profanation, desecration.

profan-o *adj.* profane, secular; irreverent; ignorant, unskilled; (mus.) musica **-a**, secular music; (eccl.) chiesa **-a**, secularized church; *n.m.* (anct. rel.) uninitiated person, profane one; layman; outsider; bad judge; one unskilled in an art, etc.; sono un — in fatto di musica, I am no judge of music. **-amẹnte** *adv.* profanely; irreverently; ignorantly. **-ità** *f.* profanity; sacrilege; profane word or action; irreverence; ignorance.

profase *f.* (scient.) prophase.

profenda *f.* (ration of) fodder, provender.

pro(f)fer-ire [D2] *tr.* to utter, to pronounce; to proffer; to offer; — un giudizio, to utter (pronounce) a judgement; egli uscì senza — parola, he went out without uttering one word; essendogli caduti i denti, non -isce bene le parole, as he has lost his teeth he cannot pronounce his words properly; non poter — parole, to be unable to utter a word (through sickness, astonishment, shame, etc.); (mus.) — un intervallo, to sound an interval; *rfl.* to offer; si -ì di accompagnarci, he offered to accompany us. **-i·bile** *adj.* fit to be uttered; pronounceable. (**-ibilità** *f.*) **-imẹnto** *m.* uttering; pronunciation. **-ito** *part. adj.* uttered, pronounced; proffered. **-itọre** *m.* pronouncer; offerer. (**-itrice** *f.*) **-ta** *f.* offer, proffer. **-to** *part. adj.* uttered; proffered, offered.

proferimẹnto *m.* (biol.) proenzyme.

professa *f.* professed nun (cf. **professo**).

profess-are [A1] *tr.* to profess; to show; to practise; to teach; — una religione, to profess a religion; — amore, to declare one's love; — un'opinione, to profess an opinion; — la medicina, to practise medicine; — l'avvocatura, to practise at the Bar; (eccl.) — (i voti), to take one's vows, to make one's profession (as a religious); *abs.* to be a teacher, to teach, to be a professor; *rfl.* to profess (to be), to declare oneself; -arsi amico di uno, to profess to be someone's friend. **-ante** *part. adj.* professing; cattolico **-ante**, professing Catholic. **-ato** *part. adj.* professed, declared. **-atamẹnte** *adv.* professedly; by public profession.

professiọn-e *f.* profession; declaration; fare — di amicizia, to profess friendship; profession, calling; — di medico, medical profession; che — esercita suo padre?, what is his father?; (leg.) esercitare una —, to practise a profession; — intellettuale, learned profession (C.C.); (eccl.) religious profession, taking of (simple or solemn) vows; — di fede, profession of faith (esp. as sworn to by those taking ecclesiastical office); di —, by profession, professionally, *or* fully qualified; musicista di —, musician by profession, professional musician; giocatore di cricket di —, professional cricketer. **-ale** *adj.* professional; scuole **-ali**, technical schools; rischio **-ale**, occupational risk; (med.) malattia **-ale**, occupational disease; (leg.) professional. **-alismo** *m.* (sport) professional status, passare al -alismo, to turn professional. **-alità** *f.* (leg.) -alità nel reato, professionalism in crime (C.P.). **-ato** *adj.* professional; lo sport **-ato**, professional sport, professionalism in sport. **-ista** *m.*, *f.* professional man; professional (esp. in sport); libero **-ista**, free-lance.

professo *adj.* (eccl.) professed (religious), one who has taken vows; *n.m.* professed monk (friar, religious); ex —, with authority, with knowledge; explicitly.

professọr-e *m.* professor; schoolmaster; teacher; academic title indicating a degree one step higher than 'dottore'; — universitario, — aggregato, University Professor (or Lecturer, teacher); — incaricato, University Lecturer; — di liceo, secondary (grammar) schoolmaster; — di scienze, science master (teacher) (Note: this is a courtesy title readily accorded in Italy to anyone who teaches, or appears to be expert in, some art or science); (mus.) — d'orchestra, orchestral player; (joc.; iron.) ne sa quanto un —!, he is a walking encyclopedia!, he is a know-all!; †(rel.) avowed follower (of a way of life); — di povertà, one vowed to poverty. **-ale** *adj.* professorial; of, relating to, a professor or schoolteacher. **-ato** *m.* professorship; post of schoolteacher. **-ẹssa** *f.* schoolmistress; woman professor; (derog.) bluestocking. **-orino** *m.* young schoolmaster. **-o·rio** *adj.* (*m.pl.* **-orii**) professorial; master's. **-orọne** *m. augm.* famous professor; schoolmaster with a very good reputation.

profet-a *m.*, *f.* (Gk. antiq.) *prophetes*, prophet, interpreter of the god's will at an oracular shrine; (Bibl., theol.) prophet; il re —, the prophet king, David; (Moslem rel.) il —, the Prophet, Mohammed; — di sciagure, prophet of woe; (paint.) i -i di Michelangelo, the prophets painted by Michelangelo (round the ceiling of the Sistine Chapel); (medieval lit.) mistero dei -i, Mystery Play of the Prophets. **-ante** *part. adj.* prophesying; *n.m.*, *f.* prophet. **-are** [A I] *tr.*, *intr.* (*aux.* avere) to prophesy, to predict, to foretell. **-ẹssa** *f.* prophetess; sibyl.

profe·tic-o *adj.* prophetic. **-amẹnte** *adv.* prophetically.

profetizẓ-are [A I] *tr.*, *intr.* (*aux.* avere) to predict, to prophesy, to foretell. (**-ato** *part. adj.*)

profetti·zio *adj.* (leg.) profectitious; dote profettizia, wife's after-acquired property derived from an ancestor.

†**profetto** *m.* See **profitto**.

profezi·a *f.* prophecy, prediction; profezie di astrologi, astrologers' predictions; non tutte le profezie si sono avverate, not everything that was foretold came true.

profferire [D 2] and derivs. See **proferire**.

†**proffi·dia** *f.* See **perfidia**.

†**proffilare** *vb.* and derivs. See **profilare**.

proficiente *adj.* making progress, profiting; — negli studi, progressing in one's studies.

profici·scere *Lat. imp.* (rel.) *Proficiscere*, 'Go forth, Christian soul' (from prayers for the dying); (colloq.) essere al —, to be at death's door.

profi·cu-o *adj.* profitable; useful; of benefit; a chi è stato — questo delitto?, whom has this crime benefited?; occupazione -a, work that pays. **-amẹnte** *adv.* profitably; lavorare -amente, to earn money by one's work.

†**profigurato** *adj.* likened.

profilare [A I], see under **profilo**.

profil-assi *f.* (med.) prophylaxis. **-at·tico** *adj.*, *n.m.* (med.) prophylactic.

profil-o *m.* profile, outline, contour; side-face; section; visto di —, seen in profile; (archit.) outline of a vertical section of a moulding; (mil.) vertical section of a fort; (naut.) silhouette (of a ship); cross-sectional drawing; (eng.) contour, profile, cross-section, outline; (fig.) sketch, short study (esp. biographical); sotto questo —, from this point of view, from this angle. **-amẹnto** *m.* outlining, sketching; outline, profile. **-are** [A I] *tr.* to draw in profile (outline); to edge, to frame, to outline; to ornament the edge of; (eng.) to profile; *rfl.* to appear in profile; to appear; to stand out; le vette dei monti si -ano nel cielo, the mountain tops stand out against the sky. **-ato** *part. adj.* outlined; drawn in profile; viso -ato, sharp-featured face; naso -ato, sharp, fine, delicately modelled nose; edged, bordered; -ato d'oro, gold-(gilt-)edged; *n.m.* (eng.) section iron, section. **-atrice** *f.* (eng.) forming machine. **-atura** *f.* outlining, outline, profile; edging, edge, border, hem; (eng.) profiling, forming; -atura al tornio, profile turning. **-o·metro** *m.* (eng.) profilometer.

profitente *m.*, *f.* (eccl.) religious (monk, nun) making his (her) profession.

profitt-o *m.* profit; i -i della vendita, the profits from the sale; trarre — da, to profit by, to take (a mean) advantage of; a — di, for the benefit of; non mi fa —, it is not to my advantage; che — ne abbiamo avuto?, what good did it do us?; mettere a —, to profit by, to make good use of; mettere a — il tempo, to make good use of one's time; aver — da una medicina, to feel the benefit from taking a medicine; far — negli studi, to make progress in one's studies; (school marks) 8 in — e 6 in condotta, 8 for work and 6 for conduct; proceeds, income; — di un podere, income from a farm; non confessa tutti i suoi -i, he does not declare all his income; (comm.) — netto, net profit; conto dei -i e delle perdite, profit and loss account; — lordo, gross profit. **-a·bile** *adj.* profitable, useful. **-abilmẹnte** *adv.* profitably; usefully. **-are** [A I] *intr.* (*aux.* avere) to profit, to gain an advantage, to make a profit; to make good progress; to be useful, profitable, advantageous; con quel commercio -ava molto, he did very well out of that business; — di, to profit from, by, to make good use of; ha -ato dei miei consigli, he has profited by my advice; -a del tempo, make good use of your time; quel ragazzo -a poco degli studi, that boy makes little progress in his studies; -are a, to be useful to. **-atọre** *m.* profiteer. **-ẹvole** *adj.* profitable, useful, advantageous. (**-evolmẹnte** *adv.*)

†**profi·zio** *excl.* prosit!

†**profligare** *tr.* to defeat, to destroy.

proflu·vio *m.* flow; flood, torrent; abundance, plenty; un — di parole, a flood of words; un — di gente, a crowd of people, a great stream of people.

profond-are [A I C] *intr.* (*aux.* essere) to sink, to go down; la nave -ò negli abissi del mare, the ship sank to the bottom; *rfl.* to sink, to become absorbed; to go deeply (into a matter, with the mind); to be immersed; -arsi nella meditazione, to become absorbed in thought; *tr.* to sink; to ruin; to deepen; to plant or sink deeply; — le radici, to plant the roots deeply; — il canale, to deepen the canal. **-amẹnto** *m.* sinking; deepening; sounding. **-ato** *part. adj.* sunk; immersed; deepened; brought low; (iron.) -ato maestro, great master.

profond-ere [C 2] *tr.* to lavish, to pour out freely; to shower; to squander, to waste; — parole, to use a profusion of words; — tesori, to pour out one's treasure; *rfl.* to be lavish, to be profuse; si -eva in inchini, he bowed to everybody. **-itọre** *m.* squandeter. (**-itrice** *f.*)

profondità *f.* See under **profondo**.

profọnd-o *adj.* deep; profound; acqua -a, deep water; ferita -a, deep wound; azzurro —, deep blue; radici -e, deep roots; voce -a, deep voice, low-pitched voice; avere una voce di basso —, to have a deep bass voice; poco —, shallow; sonno —, deep sleep; quiete -a, perfect peace, complete quiet; umiltà -a, deep humility; passione -a, great passion; -a ignoranza, profound ignorance; — sapere, profound knowledge; essere — in una scienza, to have profound knowledge of a science, to be deeply learned in a science; — pensatore, profound thinker; mente -a, profound mind; dottrine -e, profound doctrines; poesia -a, deep, abstruse, difficult poetry; *n.m.* depth(s); deep; nel — della notte, at dead of night; nel — dell'inferno, in the depths of Hell; nel suo —, at the heart of it; mandare in —, to cast down, to ruin, to sink; *adv.* deeply, deep. **-amẹnte** *adv.* deeply, deep; profoundly; -amente radicato, deep-rooted; -amente sentito, deeply felt; dormire -amente, to sleep soundly; -amente addormentato, sound asleep; inchinarsi -amente, to make a deep bow; trattare -amente una questione, to treat a question profoundly. **-ẹzza** *f.* depth; profundity. **-i·metro** *m.* depth-gauge (used by divers). **-is·simo** *adj. superl.* mari -issimi, deepest seas; ossequio -issimo, profoundest respect. **-ità** *f.* depth; profundity; -ità di un pozzo, depth of a well; nelle -ità degli oceani, in the depths of the ocean; -ità della notte, dead of night; la -ità dell'anima, the depths of the soul; (naut.) depth; -ità dell'onda, amplitude of a wave; -ità della stiva, depth of the hold; -ità del timone, immersion of the rudder; linea di -ità, contour line, fathom line (20 metres or 10 fathoms, etc.); (aeron.) -ità dell'ala, thickness of a wing; timone di -ità, elevator, flipper.

†**profosso** *m.* (mil.) Provost, City governor; (naut.) senior rating responsible for cleanliness of a ship and execution of punishment.

pro·fu-go *adj.* (*pl.* **-ghi**) refugee; fugitive; famiglie -ghe, families of refugees, refugee families; *n.m.* refugee; fugitive; sussidio ai -ghi, relief for refugees.

profum-o *m.* scent, fragrance; il — dei fiori, the scent of flowers; mandar —, to give forth a fragrance, to smell sweet; (fig.) il — dell'innocenza, the fragrance of innocence, sweet air of innocence;

profum-o (*cont.*)

perfume; — liquido, liquid perfume; una boccetta di —, a bottle of scent; (iron.; joc.) smell, stink; †flattery, adulation. **-are** [A 1] *tr.* to scent, to perfume; to put scent on; — il fazzoletto, to put scent on one's handkerchief; *rfl.* to use scent, to perfume oneself (one's clothes, etc.). **-aménto** *m.* scenting, perfuming. **-ato** *part. adj.* sweet-smelling, fragrant; scented; fazzoletto -ato, scented handkerchief; (fig.) generous; munificent; expensive, dear. **-ata-ménte** *adv.* fragrantly; (fig.) generously, handsomely; dearly, expensively; pagare -atamente, to pay through the nose. **-atóre** *m.* one who uses scent; *adj.* fragrant. (**-atrice** *f.*) **-atuzzo** *adj. pejor.* scented (showing effeminacy). **-erì·a** *f.* perfumery (shop, or articles). **-iera** *f.* scent bottle; vessel for burning fragrant matter, perfume seller; †censer. **-iere**, †**-iero** *m.* perfumer, distiller of perfumes; maker of cosmetics; negozio di -iere, scent shop; vessel for burning fragrant matter. **-ino** *m.* scent bottle; faint scent; (fig.) fop.

profus-o *part.* of **profondere**, q.v.; *adj.* profuse; lavish. **-aménte** *adv.* profusely; lavishly; at great length. **-ióne** *f.* profusion; abundance; squandering; a -ione, in abundance; dare a -ione, to give lavishly; con -ione di sudore, with the sweat pouring off one.

†**progenerare** *vb.* and derivs. See **generare**.

progè·n-ie, †**-ia** *f.* progeny, offspring, issue, descendants; race, stock. **-itóre** *m.* ancestor, progenitor. **-itrice** *f.* progenitrix; ancestress; teorie -itrici di errori, theories giving rise to error.

progesteróne *m.* (chem.; physiol.) progesterone, corpus luteum hormone.

progètt-o *m.* plan, project; scheme; proposal; intention; per —, by design, on purpose; -i campati in aria, castles in the air; -i sfumati, schemes that have come to nothing; (leg.) — di legge, bill, draft law; -i di lavoro, working-drawings (C.C.). **-are** [A 1] *tr.* to plan, to design; to project. (**-ato** *part. adj.*) **-azione** *f.* planning, design, designing. **-ista** *m.* planner; schemer; author of a project; (eng.) designer, design engineer.

proglòt·tide *f.* (zool.) proglottid, segment of a tapeworm.

prognat-ìsmo *m.* (anat.) prognathism. **-o** *adj.* (anat.) prognathic.

Progne *pr.n.f.* (myth.) Procne; (poet.) swallow.

progno *m.* (geog., Ven.) gully.

pro·gnòsi *f.* (med.) prognosis.

prognòstic-ale *adj.* relating to forecasts; ominous. **-are** [A 2 s] *tr.* to predict; (med.) to prognosticate, to make a prognosis.

prognò·stico *m.* See **pronostico**.

programm-a *m.* programme; syllabus; prospectus; (pol.) platform, policy; manifesto; — giornaliero delle sedute, daily programme of meetings; stabilire il — dei lavori, to draw up the programme of work; line of conduct; plan; questo non era nel mio —, I had no intention of doing this; (leg.) prospectus (C.C.); (industr.) programme, schedule; — di fabbricazione, range of products; (mus.) musica a —, programme music; (sport) — delle corse, race-card. **-are** [A 1], **-atizzare** [A 1] *tr.* to put in a programme; (theatr.) to put on, to stage; -are spettacoli, to put on shows. **-a·tico** *adj.* relating to a programme; relating to policy. (**-ato**, **-atizzato** *part. adj.*) **-azióne** *f.* making up a programme; (cinem.) times of showing; di prossima -azione, 'coming shortly'; (industr.) programming, scheduling.

progred-ire [D 2] *intr.* (*aux.* avere, essere) to progress, to advance; to make progress; to improve, to develop; ho -ito nello studio, I have made progress in my studies; il ponte è molto -ito, the bridge is far advanced (in construction); il lavoro è -ito lenta-mente, the work has progressed slowly; to proceed, to go forward; le loro truppe non potevano —, their troops could not advance; — in bene, to get better; — in male, to get worse; *n.m.* progress, advance. **-iente** *part. adj.* progressing, progressive; civiltà -iente, progressive civilization. **-iménto** *m.* progressing, advance; progress. **-ito** *part. adj.* advanced, progressive, up-to-date.

progress-ióne *f.* progression, advance, progress; (math.) progression; (mus.) progression; sequence. **-ista** *m., adj.* (pol.) progressive. **-ivo** *adj.* progressive; tassa -iva, graduated tax; (eng.) stampo -ivo, follow die; (mil.) polvere -iva, powder made up so that the rate of burning accelerates as the bullet moves down the barrel. **-ivaménte** *adv.* progressively.

progrèsso *m.* progress; development, improvement; advance; fare (dei) progressi, to make progress, to improve, to develop; fare poco —, to make slow progress; siamo in via di —, we are making progress; in — di tempo, in the course of time.

proib-ire [D 2] *tr.* to forbid, to prohibit; ti -isco di parlare, I forbid you to speak; gli fu -ito l'ingresso, he was refused admittance; l'esportazione di queste merci è -ita, the export of these goods is prohibited; è rigorosamente -ito fumare, smoking strictly prohibited; to hinder, to bar, to impede; i venti ci -iscono di navigare, the winds make navigation impossible. **-itivìsmo** *m.* advocacy of prohibitive tariffs. **-itivo** *adj.* prohibitive, prezzi -itivi, prohibitive prices. **-ito** *part. adj.* forbidden, prohibited; -ito fumare, no smoking; -ito l'ingresso, no admittance; (leg.) giuochi -iti, illegal games; armi -ite, illegal weapons (arms); (comm.) merci -ite, prohibited goods; (Bibl.) il frutto -ito, the forbidden fruit; (eccl.) libri -iti, books on the Index; giorni -iti, abstinence days; tempi -iti, 'forbidden times', the periods of Advent and Lent, in which marriages are not completely forbidden but are shorn of the full festal ceremonial. **-itóre** *m.* forbidder. (**-itrice** *f.*) **-ito·rio** *adj.* (*m.pl.* **-itorii**) (leg.) that forbids or restrains. **-izióne** *f.* prohibition; con -izione di non farsi più vedere, being forbidden to show one-self again; (comm.) -izioni e restrizioni, prohibitions and restrictions. **-izionìsmo** *m.* prohibitionism, prohibition (of alcoholic beverages). **-izionista** *m.* prohibitionist.

proiett-are [A 1] *tr.* to project; to cast, to throw; i corpi -ano la loro ombra, bodies cast shadows; (geom.) to project; (cinem.) to project, to show, to screen; — una pellicola cinematografica, to show a film; *rfl.* to project, to protrude; to be cast, to fall; l'ombra della terra si -a talvolta sulla luna, the earth's shadow sometimes falls on the moon; *intr.* (*aux.* avere) (archit.) to project, to jut out. **-atóre** *m.* projector. (**-atrice** *f.*)

proiet·tile *adj.* projectile; *n.m.* projectile, missile, bullet; — illumi-nante, starshell.

proiettivo *adj.* (geom.) projective.

proiett-o *adj.* projected, thrown; *n.m.* (mil.) projectile; (archit.) projection. **-óre** *m.* projector; searchlight; head-lamp; flood-light; (radar) -ore di onda rotante, scanner. †**-ura** *f.* (archit.) see **proietto**.

proiezióne *f.* projection; casting, falling (of a shadow); (eng. drwg.) — all'americana, third-angle projection; (geom.) projection; — ortogonale, orthographic projection; (geog.) map-net; projection; — di Mercatore, Mercator's projection; proiezioni cinematografiche, moving pictures, films; — luminosa, lantern-slide; la conferenza sarà illustrata da proiezioni, the lecture will be illustrated with slides; conferenza con proiezioni, lantern lecture; (archit.) projection.

prola·bio *m.* (anat.) prolabium.

prolasso *m.* (med.) prolapse.

†**prolato** *adj.* uttered; ample.

prolat-óre *m.* utterer; publisher. (**-rice** *f.*)

prolattina *f.* (physiol.) prolactin.

prolazióne *f.* pronunciation; (mus.) prolation.

prole *f.* issue, offspring, progeny; — maschile, male issue; — numerosa, large family; senza —, childless, without issue; (of animals) young; (of plants) offshoots.

prolegato *m.* (Rom. hist.; eccl. hist.) prolegate.

prolegò·meni *m.pl.* prolegomena; preface.

pro-lèssi, **-lèpsi** *f.* (gramm.) prolepsis.

proletà·r-io *adj., n.m.* (Rom. hist.) proletarian. **-iato** *m.* proletariat; dittatura del -iato, dictatorship of the proletariat.

proliferativo *adj.* (med.) proliferative.

proliferazióne *f.* proliferation.

prolì·f-ero *adj.* prolific. **-icare** [A 2 s] *intr.* (*aux.* avere) to proliferate, to multiply. **-icazióne** *f.* procreation, prolification, fertility. **-icità** *f.* prolificness, fertility.

prolì·fico *adj.* prolific, fertile; (fig.) scrittore —, prolific writer.

prolìss-o *adj.* prolix; long-winded; (joc.) barba -a, flowing beard. **-aménte** *adv.* prolixly, tediously. **-ità** *f.* prolixity, long-windedness.

prò·lo-go *m.* (*pl.* **-ghi**) prologue, foreword; beginning of a dinner, hors d'œuvres; (mus.) prologue, explanatory first act of opera; (seventeenth century) a mythological introduction to an opera (not necessarily by the same composer) in which a compliment is proffered to an aristocratic personage in the audience. **-gheggiare** [A 3 c] *intr.* (*aux.* avere) (joc.) to say something by way of intro-duction, to be slow in coming to the point. **-ghetto** *m. dim.* short prologue.

prolu·dere [C 3] *intr.* (*aux.* avere) to make (write, speak) a prolusion; to pronounce an inaugural lecture.

prolunga *f.* See under **prolungare**.

prolung-are [A 2] *tr.* to prolong, to extend, to lengthen; to protract; to defer, to postpone; to delay; — una visita oltre il conveniente, to overstay one's welcome; (naut.) — una bordata, to continue on one tack; †to go alongside another ship, to grapple with the intention of boarding; *rfl.* to continue, to extend; la strada si ∼ oltre il ponte, the street continues beyond the bridge; ∼arsi in chiacchiere, to keep on chattering; ∼arsi su un argomento, to dwell upon a subject. **-a** *f.* (techn.) extension, extension-piece; (mil.) transporter, transport vehicle; †(naut.) breeching rope, limber rope. **-a·bile** *adj.* extendable. **-abilità** *f.* possibility of prolongation, of extension. **-amento** *m.* prolongation, extension, continuation; ∼amento di una strada, continuation of a street; ∼amento del servizio militare, extension of (the period of) military service; (gramm.) ∼amento d'una sillaba, lengthening a syllable. **-ato** *part. adj.* prolonged, extended, continued, lengthened; applausi ∼ati, prolonged applause. **-atamente** *adv.* at great length, with prolixity. **-atore** *m.* one who prolongs, defers, postpones, delays. (**-atrice** *f.*) **-azione** *f.* prolongation, continuation; (mus.) suspension, retardation.

proluṣ-ione *f.* inaugural lecture. **-o** *part.* of **proludere**, q.v.

prolu·vie *f.* flood.

promanare [A 1] *intr.* (aux. essere) to emanate; to flow forth.

promemo·ria *f. indecl.* memorandum, note; *aide-mémoire.*

†**promente** *adv.* See **prodemente**, under **prode**[1].

†**pro·mere** *tr.* to put forth; to express; to manifest.

promessa[1] *f.* See under **promesso**.

promess-a[2] *f.* promise; fare una —, to make a promise; mantenere, adempiere una —, to keep a promise; mancare ad una —, venire meno a una —, to break a promise; (leg.) — unilaterale, one-sided promise; — di matrimonio, promise of marriage; mancata —, breach of promise (C.C.); domandare la —, to ask for the fulfilment of the promise; liberare da una —, restituire una —, to free from a promise, to let off; (provb.) ogni — è debito, promises are made to be kept; — da marinaio, dicer's oath; pascere di ∼e, to put off with specious promises. †**-ione** *f.* see **promessa**.

promess-o *part.* of **promettere**, q.v.; *adj.* promised; (Bibl.) la terra ∼a, the Promised Land; betrothed; sposi ∼i, betrothed couple; *I Promessi Sposi, The Betrothed* (title of the novel by Alessandro Manzoni); *n.m.* fiancé. **-a** *f.* fiancée.

Prome·teo *pr.n.m.* Prometheus.

promett-ere [C 20] *tr.* to promise; mi promise di farlo, he promised me he would do so; sul Vangelo, to swear on the Gospel, to take one's Bible oath; — Roma e toma, *or* — mari e monti, *or* — la luna nel pozzo, to promise the moon; gli promise le busse, he promised him a beating; il cielo nero ∼eva un temporalaccio, the dark sky threatened a severe storm; *abs.* to promise, to give hope(s); la campagna ∼e quest'anno, the fields are promising this year; è un ragazzo che ∼e bene, he is a promising boy; — per un altro, to make oneself answerable for someone else, to pledge oneself for someone; *rfl.* (*acc.* of *prn.* 'si') to pledge oneself, to become engaged; (*dat.* of *prn.* 'si') to promise oneself (something), to look forward to; ∼ersi lunga vita, to promise oneself a long life, to look forward to a long life. **-ente** *part. adj.* promising; un ragazzo ∼ente, a promising boy; hopeful, giving rise to hope; annata ∼ente, promising year (for crops); cielo ∼ente, promising sky. **-itore** *m.* promiser; (provb.) gran ∼itore raro mantenitore, a too ready promiser rarely keeps his promises. (**-itrice** *f.*)

promice·lio *m.* (bot.) promycelium.

prominen-te *adj.* prominent, jutting out; zigomi ∼ti, prominent cheek-bones; terreno ∼, land on a projection (e.g. of hill or sea-coast). **-temente** *adv.* projecting, jutting out. **-za** *f.* prominence, protuberance; knoll, rise (in ground); embankment; un naso di maestosa ∼za, a majestically protuberant nose; (anat.) prominence, prominentia.

prominístro *m.* (hist.) under-secretary of State; — delle armi, Pope's War Minister.

promi·scu-o *adj.* mixed, promiscuous, common; (gramm.) genere —, common gender; matrimonio —, mixed marriage; scuola ∼a, mixed school; pascoli ∼i, common grazing-ground; (theatr.) attore —, versatile actor, character actor (also *n.m.*). **-amente** *adv.* promiscuously. **-ità** *f.* promiscuity; mixture; ∼ità di cibi, mixing foods, mixed diet; (leg.) rights of common enjoyed by commoners of more than one community; (gramm.) ∼ità del genere, community of gender.

promissa·rio *m.* (leg.) promisee.

promiss-ione *f.* (bibl.) terra di —, Land of Promise, Promised Land; (hist. Venice) Doge's edict; †permission. **-ivo** *adj.* promissory. **-ivamente** *adv.* as a promise. **-ore** *m.* promiser. **-o·rio** *adj.* (*m.pl.* **-orii**) promissory; (leg.) giuramento ∼orio, oath of fidelity, of office.

†**promo·bile** *adj.* See **mobile**.

promonto·rio *m.* (geog.) promontory, headland; cape; (joc.) big nose.

promoss-o *part.* of **promuovere**, q.v.; *adj.* promoted; successful; candidati ∼i, successful candidates; elenco dei candidati ∼i, pass-list; (mil.) promoted in rank; — dai ranghi, promoted from the ranks, ranker; officer; impresa ∼a da una società, enterprise promoted by a company.

promo-tore *m.* promoter, organizer; (leg.) — della società per azioni, company promoter (C.C.); *adj.* promoting, organizing; comitato —, promoters' committee, organizing committee. **-vendo** *adj.* ready for promotion. **-vi·bile** *adj.* deserving promotion. **-vimento** *m.* promoting; promotion. **-vitore** *m.* promoter. (**-vitrice** *f.*) **-zione** *f.* promotion; furtherance; advancement; fostering; †instigation.

promulg-are [A 2] *tr.* to publish; (leg.) — una legge, to promulgate an Act of Parliament; (fig.) to make public, to put forward, to proclaim, to issue. **-amento** *m.* promulgation, publication. (**-ato** *part. adj.*) **-atore** *m.* promulgator. (**-atrice** *f.*) **-azione** *f.* promulgation.

promuo·vere [C 15] *tr.* to promote; to induce; to stimulate, to encourage; to favour; to foster; to raise, to elevate, to move up; fu promosso capitano, he was promoted captain; essere promosso agli esami, to pass one's exams; — le arti, to promote the arts; — una festa di beneficenza, to promote a charity fête; — il vomito, to induce vomiting; — il sudore, to cause perspiration; — la febbre, to bring on a temperature; — una sottoscrizione, to open a subscription.

pro·nao *m.* (archit.) pronaos, vestibule of a temple; portico.

pron-are [A 1] *tr.* (anat.) to pronate. **-atore** *m.* (anat.) pronator. **-azione** *f.* (anat.) pronation.

Prone·a *pr.n.f.* (Gk. philos.) Pronoia; Divine Providence; (Gk. myth.) title of Athene as goddess of Forethought; (Ital. lit.) title of a poem by Cesarotti on Napoleon.

pronefro *m.* (zool.) pronephros.

†**pronesso** *m.* bowline (cf. **provese**).

pro-nipote, -nepote *m.* grand-nephew; *f.* grand-niece; great-grand-child; *m.pl.* descendants.

pron-o *adj.* prone; prostrate; bowed down; gettarsi — ad adorare, to prostrate oneself in adoration; (fig.) prone, inclined, ready, disposed; — al peccato, prone to sin; — all'amore, disposed to love. †**-ità** *f.* propensity, inclination.

pronom-e *m.* (gramm.) pronoun. **-inale** *adj.* (gramm.) pronominal; particelle ∼inali, unaccented forms of the pronouns, e.g. 'mi', 'ti', 'ci'. **-inalmente** *adv.* (gramm.) pronominally.

prono·stic-o *m.*, †**-a** *f.* prediction, forecast; omen; prognostic; — riguardante il tempo, weather forecast; concorso ∼i, football pools; schedina ∼i, entry form (for pools). **-amento** *m.* prediction; foretelling. **-are** [A 2 s] *tr.* to predict, to foretell, to forecast; to presage; queste nuvole ∼ano tempesta, these clouds presage a storm; tutto dà a ∼are che si sposeranno, all the indications are that they will get married. **-atore** *m.* forecaster, predictor, prophet; *adj.* sogni ∼atori, prophetic dreams. (**-atrice** *f.*) **-azione** *f.* prediction, forecast; omen.

pront-o *adj.* ready: siete ∼i?, are you ready?; tenere in —, to hold in readiness; sono — per partire, I am ready to start; — a tutto, ready for anything; quick, alert; ingegno —, ready wit; intelligenza ∼a, quick understanding; disegno —, quick (rapid) drawing; — all'ira, quick-tempered; prompt; immediate; ubbidienza ∼a, prompt obedience; azione ∼a, prompt action; (paint.) figure ∼e, lively figures; — i contanti, ready money; cash; confezione ∼a, ready-made clothes; (on a menu) piatti ∼i, *plats du jour*; — soccorso, first aid; (photog.) borsa pronto (*not* 'pronta'), ever-ready case; *excl.* (on the telephone) hello!; ∼i!, ready!, hold tight!, off we go!, right away!; (naut.) stand by!; ∼i a virare!, ready about! **-amente** *adv.* promptly, readily; without delay; quickly, rapidly. †**-are** *tr.* to solicit; to urge; *rfl.* to exert oneself. **-arello** *adj. dim.* rather quick, ready enough. **-ezza** *f.* readiness; quickness; ease; animation; promptitude; ∼ezza di spirito, ready wit, *or* presence of mind; ∼ezza d'ingegno, quick-wittedness, lively

pront-o (*cont.*)
intelligence; -ezza di parola, ready speech, fluency (in speech); -ezza del passo, quickness in walking; -ezza di mano, freedom, ease, in using one's hand(s); (paint.) liveliness; con -ezza, readily; impudence, effrontery. †-one *m.* (naut.) guy, stay, shroud.

prontua·rio *m.* handbook, reference book; — di frasi, phrase-book; — dei conti fatti, ready-reckoner.

pro·nub-a *f.* (Rom. antiq.) *pronuba*, matron attending a bride; (Rom. myth.) title of Juno as patroness of marriage. -o *m.* (Rom. antiq.) groomsman.

pronu·ncia *f.* See **pronunzia**.

pronunciamènte *m.* (pol.) *pronunciamiento*.

pronunciare [A 3] and derivs. See **pronunziare**.

pronun·zia *f.* pronunciation; un vocabolario della — inglese, an English pronouncing dictionary; accent, way of speaking; voice; si capisce alla — che è inglese, you can tell he's an Englishman by his accent; pronouncement; delivery; utterance; (leg.) — del giudice, judgement (C.C.P.); — della sentenza, delivery of judgement (C.P.P.).

pronunzi-are [A 4] *tr.* to pronounce; come -ate questa parola?, how do you pronounce this word?; to utter; non -ò una sola parola, he did not utter a single word; — un discorso, to deliver a speech; — una grande verità, to utter a great truth; — eletto, to declare elected; (leg.) — sulla causa, to give judgement in the action (C.C.P.); — una sentenza, to deliver a judgement; — sentenza di assoluzione, to acquit; — sentenza di condanna, to convict (C.P.P.); *rfl.* to pronounce oneself, to give one's opinion; non voler -arsi, to be unwilling to commit oneself; (admin.) la prego di -arsi, please signify. -a·bile *adj.* pronounceable; facilmente -abile, easy to pronounce. (-abilità *f.*) -aménto *m.* pronouncement. -ante *part. adj.* pronouncing. -ativo *adj.* pronouncing; uttering. -ato *part. adj.* pronounced; uttered, said; declared; pronounced, marked, decided; antipatia -ata, pronounced antipathy, evident dislike; naso molto -ato, very prominent nose; (mus.) well delivered; *n.m.* pronouncement, assertion; sentence; (leg.) -ato del Tribunale, judgement of the Court; il chiesto e il -ato, the relief sought and the terms of the judgement (C.C.P.). -atore *m.* pronouncer. (-atrice *f.*) -azione *f.* (gramm.) pronunciation; pronouncement, promulgation; (leg.) -azione di giudizio, judgement in the action; -azione interlocutoria, interlocutory order (C.C.P.).

propagand-a *f.* propaganda; advertising; far — per un corso di conferenze, to advertise a course of lectures; far — per un' elezione, to canvass for an election; (eccl.) (Congregation of) Propaganda. -are [A 1] *tr.* to advertise; to publicize; to make known; to extol. -ista *m.*, *f.* propagandist. -i·stico *adj.* relating to advertising; stampa -istica, advertising postage rate.

propag-are [A 2] *tr.* to propagate; to spread; — la fede cristiana, to propagate the Christian religion; — false notizie, to spread false reports; questi falsi allarmi vengono -ati ad arte, these false alarms are raised on purpose; (bot.) to propagate; *rfl.* to spread; to propagate; le male erbe si -ano rapidamente, weeds spread rapidly; le malattie contagiose si -ano facilmente, contagious diseases spread easily; (phys.) to travel; la luce si -a in linea retta, light travels in a straight line. -a·bile *adj.* propagable. (-abilità *f.*) -aménto *m.* propagation; spreading; diffusion. (-ato *part. adj.*)

propaggin-are [A 1 S] *tr.* (agric.) to propagate by layering; — la specie, to propagate the species; — le idee, to disseminate ideas; (hist.) to bury head downwards. -aménto *m.* (agric.) layering. -ato *part. adj.* layered; propagated. (-atore *m.* -atrice *f.*) -azione *f.* (agric.) layering; (hist.) burial head downwards (execution).

propa·ggine *f.* layer (shoot or twig of a plant); issue, offspring, descendants; seed; propagation; (of a plant) protendere le sue propaggini, to spread its branches wide; *pl.* (of a mountain chain) le ultime propaggini, the last outcrops; (fig.) distruggere il male nelle sue propaggini, to root out evil.

†**propago** *f.* race, stock.

propal-are [A 1] *tr.* to publish abroad; to divulge; — una notizia, to spread news. -atore *m.* divulger; -atore di notizie false, disseminator of false news, rumour monger. (-atrice *f.*) -azione *f.* divulgation; spreading.

propano *m.* (chem.) propane.

†**proparaless-e**, †-i *f.* See **paragoge**.

proparossi·tono *adj.*, *n.m.* (gramm.) proparoxyton.

†**prope** *adv.* nearby, near.

propede·utic-a *f.* propaedeutics, introductory study. -o *adj.* propaedeutic; introductory; biennio -o, two-year course (followed by all students of engineering in Italian Universities).

propellènte *m.* propellent (rocket propulsion); — liquido, liquid propellent; — solido, solid propellent.

†**propel·lere** *tr.* to chase away.

prope·ndere [B I] *intr.* (*aux.* avere; *prep.* a) to incline (towards); to lean; to have a propensity (for); — in favore di, to incline towards, to side with, to favour; l'animo suo -e al male, his mind has evil propensities; — per il sì, to be inclined to think so.

†**propens-are** *tr.* to think (over); to intend; *rfl.* to imagine to oneself.

propensiòne *f.* propensity; tendency; inclination, liking; -ione alla musica, per l'arte, propensity for music, art; aver -ione all'indulgenza, to be naturally indulgent.

propènso *adj.* inclined, ready; — a credere, inclined to believe, ready to believe; essere tutto — al servizio di una persona, to be disposed to do all one can for a person; essere — per, in favore di, to favour, to be inclined towards.

properispo·meno *adj.* (Gk. gramm.) properispomenon.

Proper·zio *pr.n.m.* Propertius.

propil-ammina *f.* (chem.) propylamine. -e *m.* (chem.) propyl. -ene *m.* (chem.) propene, propylene.

propile·o *m.* (archit.) propylaeum.

propi·lico *adj.* (chem.) propyl.

propin-are [A 1] *tr.* to give (to drink), to administer; to drink; — alla salute di, to drink the health of; — veleno, to administer poison. -a *f.* fee (esp. for examinations); -a d'esame, examiner's fee. -atore *m.* giver, administrator (of poison, etc.). (-atrice *f.*)

propinqu-o *adj.* neighbouring, near; related, akin. -ità *f.* propinquity; nearness, proximity; relationship, kinship.

†**pro·pio** *adj.* See **proprio**.

propio·nico *adj.* (chem.) propionic.

propi·zi-o *adj.* propitious; favourable; i fati furono propizi, the fates were propitious; (finan.) giorno —, red-letter day; (rel.) Dio è — agli umili, God is gracious to the humble; l'elemosina fa Iddio —, almsgiving wins God's favour; tempo —, favourable weather; è il tempo — per la potatura, it's the right time for pruning. -aménte *adv.* propitiously. -ante *part. adj.* (rel.) sacrifizio -ante, sacrifice of propitiation. -are [A 4] *tr.* to propitiate, to placate; *rfl.* (*dat.* of *prn.* 'si') to propitiate, to render favourable to oneself; cerca di -artelo, try to gain his favour. -atore *m.* propitiator. (-atrice *f.*) -ato·rio *adj.* (*m.pl.* -atorii) propitiatory; *n.m.* (Bibl.) Propitiatory, 'Mercy-seat', the golden covering of the Ark. -azione *f.* (rel.) propitiation, atonement; (Bibl.) giorno della -azione, Day of Atonement.

pro·poli *f.* (ent.) propolis, bee-glue.

propon-ènte *part. adj.* propounding; intending. -i·bile *adj.* proposable. (-ibilità *f.*) -iménto *m.* purpose; resolution; intention; mantenere in -imento, to adhere to a resolution, to keep one's resolve; fare -imento, to resolve, to make a vow; col -imento di tornar subito a casa, intending to go back home at once. (-itore *m.* -itrice *f.*)

†**propo·nere** *vb.* See **proporre**.

propòrre [B 21] *tr.* to propose; to propound; to put forward; l'uomo propone e Dio dispone, man proposes, God disposes; fu proposto per quell'ufficio, he was proposed for that office; (leg.) put forward; — una domanda in giudizio, to start legal proceedings; — un quesito, to put a question; — un disegno di legge, to bring in a bill; — uno ad esempio, to point out someone as an example; il prezzo che mi proponete è troppo alto, the price you ask is too high; — una donna di servizio, to recommend a servant; — un premio, to offer a prize; *rfl.* (*dat.* of *prn.* 'si') to purpose, to intend; to resolve; mi proponevo di fare un viaggio, I intended to go on a journey; ecco il fine che mi proponevo, that was the object I had in view; mi sono proposto di finire il lavoro entro questo mese, I have resolved to finish the work this month.

proporziòn-e *f.* proportion; ci deve essere una giusta — fra la pena e il delitto, there must be a proper relation between the punishment and the crime; il male ha assunto gravi -i, the evil has reached serious proportions; (math.) proportion; ratio; — geometrica, geometric proportion; — inversa, inverse proportion; in —, in proportion, in comparison; senza —, without comparison; mancante di —, out of proportion, disproportionate; (mus.) proportion (in the medieval theory of rhythm); (comm.) quota in —, *pro rata* share, share in proportion; scala di —, sliding-

proporzion-e (*cont.*)

scale. **-a·bile** *adj.* proportionable; -abile con, proportionable to. **-ale** *adj.* proportional; (math.) proportional; inversamente -ale, inversely proportional; rappresentanza -ale, proportional representation. **-almente** *adv.* proportionally; similarly; -almente alle sue forze, according to his strength. **-are** [A I c] *tr.* to proportion; to make to fit; to put into proper relation; dobbiamo -are le nostre spese alle nostre entrate, we must cut our coat according to our cloth. **-ato** *part. adj.* proportionate, proportioned; corpo -ato, well-proportioned body; braccio -ato alla gamba, arm in proportion with the leg; cappello -ato alla testa, hat fitting the head; l'aiuto non fu -ato al bisogno, help was inadequate. **-atamente** *adv.* proportionately; in proportion. (**-atore** *m.*, **-atrice** *f.*, *adj.*) **-evole** *adj.* proportionate. **-evolmente** *adv.* proportionately.

propo·sit-o *m.* purpose, intention; aim, object; design; subject; non potè mettere in esecuzione il suo —, he could not effect his purpose; — fermo, tenace, fixed intention; fare (il) — di, to intend to, to resolve to; buoni -i, good intentions; il suo — era di fare proseliti, his object was to make proselytes; cambiare (di) —, to change one's mind; avere fieri -i, to be planning great things; ciò non farebbe al nostro —, that would not meet our requirements; a questo — avrei molto da raccontarti, on that subject I have a good deal to tell you; che cosa hai da dire in —?, what have you got to say on the subject?; a che — dicesti questo?, in what connexion did you say this?; a — di, with reference to; a —, to the point, suitably, appropriately, pertinently, appositely, seasonably; tutto tornerà a —, everything will turn out all right; a — (as *adj.*) suitable; ho la persona a —, I know the very person you want; male a —, unsuitable, ill-timed, inopportune(ly); *adv. phr.* a —, by the way; a —, quando ritornerete?, by the way, when will you be back?; di —, on purpose, intentionally; lo fece di —, he did it deliberately; seriously, in earnest; s'è messo a studiare di —, he has started to work in earnest; (as *adj.*) uomo di —, reliable man (one who does not lightly change his mind); fuor di —, beside the point, inappropriate, impertinent; senza —, to no purpose. **-is·simo** *adj. superl.* (joc.) a -issimo, very much to the point, most apt.

proposi·tura *f.* (eccl.) status of 'provost'. Cf. **proposto**.

proposizi·one *f.* proposition; (gramm.) sentence, proposition; clause; — principale, main clause; enunciation of a theme; argument; prosthesis; (logic) premiso; (Bibl.) i pani della —, 'shewbread', the twelve loaves laid out on a table in the Temple.

propost-a *f.* proposal; — di matrimonio, proposal of marriage; offer; fare una —, to make a suggestion, (admin.) to table a proposal; approvare una —, to adopt a proposal; opporsi ad una —, to oppose a proposal; presentare una — di risoluzione, to submit a draft resolution; commissione delle -e, selection committee; offer (of employment); (leg.) — di legge, bill; offer; proposal; la — e l'accettazione, offer and acceptance (C.C.); — di transazione, proposal for compromise.

propost-o *part.* of **proporre**, q.v.; *adj.* put forward, proposed; *n.m.* purpose; (eccl.) 'provost'; head of a chapter, dean; parish priest of privileged status; †superior of religious house; †precentor (cf. **preposto**, **prevosto**); †(naut.) senior rating in a ship combining the duties of chief boatswain's mate and master-at-arms of a modern warship; di Marina, chief of dockyard police, also responsible for forced labour.

propre-fetto *m.* (Rom. hist.) proprefect. **-tore** *m.* (Rom. hist.) propraetor.

proprietà *f.* 1. (LEG.) OWNERSHIP; property; — assoluta, absolute, freehold property; — edilizia, property consisting of building(s); — fondiaria, landed property; — immobiliare, real property; — intellettuale, — letteraria, copyright; — indivisa, property held in undivided shares; — mobiliare, chattels, personal property; — nuda, reversionary property (C.C.); — tenuta in affitto, leasehold property; cessione della —, conveyance; diritto di —, right of property, ownership; violazione di diritto di —, trespass; (comm.) conti della —, estate accounts; — supposta, reputed ownership; questo libro è di mia —, this book is my property. 2. (CHEM.) PROPERTY; la — di sciogliere i grassi, the property of dissolving grease; il lauro ha — medicamentose, the laurel has medicinal properties. 3. PROPRIETY; essa fa ogni cosa con molta —, she does everything with great propriety; scrivere con grande — di vocaboli, to write with great propriety (of terms); vestire con —, to dress suitably (neatly and appropriately). **-a·rio** *m.*

(leg.) owner; proprietor; -ario legittimo, lawful owner; -ario rivierasco, riparian owner; -ario terriero, landowner; -ario di casa, landlord; -ari parziali, -ari di quota, part owners; (naut.) owner of a vessel; †(mil.) officer who raised and commanded a regiment. (**-a·ria** *f.*)

pro·pri-o *adj.* proper; (one's) own; peculiar, characteristic; odio —, self-hatred; amor —, self-love, self-esteem; appropriate; right, true, literal; exact; la -a famiglia, one's own family; a -e spese, at one's own expense; badare ai fatti propri, to mind one's own business; ha una casa -a, he has a house of his own; la parola -a, the proper word, the right word; nel significato — della parola, in the proper sense of the word; in senso —, non figurato, in the proper (literal), not the figurative meaning; nome —, forename, (gramm.) proper noun; (math.) frazione -a, proper fraction; la ragione è -a all'uomo, reason is characteristic of man; il difetto che gli è -, his characteristic failing; essa ci accolse con quella cortesia che le è -a, she welcomed us with her usual kindness; la chiesa non è il luogo più — per discorsi profani, church is not the most appropriate place for profane talk; neat, clean; of clean habits; vestir —, to be neat in one's dress; (techn.; scient.) inherent; stabilità -a, inherent stability; †propitious; *n.m.* quality, property, characteristic; one's own; il — dell'ape è fare il miele, the characteristic (proper function) of the bee is making honey; metterci del —, to put one's own money into it; in —, in person, at one's own expense; *adv.* quite, just; exactly; really, indeed; sto — bene, I am very well indeed; è — quello che ci occorreva, it is just what we needed; — così, just so; — allora, just then; — ora, just now; — all'ultimo momento, at the very last moment, in the nick of time; —?, really?; l'hai detto tu?, —!, did you say so?, yes, indeed!; è — un mariuolo, he is an utter scoundrel; feci — quel che voi mi dicesti, I did exactly what you told me; lo dice — lui!, he says it himself! **-amente** *adv.* properly; really; exactly; (gramm.) with propriety, in a literal sense. †**-are** *tr.* to assert positively.

propugn-are [A 5] *tr.* to fight for, to support; to plead for, to advocate; to champion, to defend; — una causa, to support (champion, fight for) a cause; — la concordia, to plead for peace; -ò l'abolizione della schiavitù, he fought for the abolition of slavery. **-a·colo** *m.* bulwark, outpost; bastion, outwork. **-atore** *m.* champion, supporter, defender; un strenuo -atore, a stout supporter; fu un valido -atore dei diritti degli oppressi, he was a valiant champion of the rights of the oppressed. (**-atrice** *f.*) **-azione** *f.* support, defence; championing.

propuls-are [A I] *tr.* to propel; (fig.) to reject, to repel, to rebut; — l'accusa, to rebut the accusation; *n.m.* il — dell'elice, the thrust of the propeller. (**-ato** *part. adj.* **-atore** *m.* **-atrice** *f.*) **-ione** *f.* (eng.) propulsion; a -ione autonoma, self-propelled; -ione a reazione, jet-propulsion. **-ivo** *adj.* (eng.) propulsive, propelling. **-ore** *m.* (eng.) propulsor; (fig.) motive force, thrust, urge; -ore del progresso, motive force of progress. **-o·rio** *adj.* (*m.pl.* **-o·rii**) propulsive, propelling; mezzo -orio, means of propulsion.

proquestore *m.* (Rom. antiq.) proquaestor.

†**proquo·io** *m.* drove of cattle; dairy-shed; sheepskin to kneel on while milking.

pror-a *f.* (poet.) ship; (naut.) bows, stem, head, eyes of a ship, forecastle, bow sheets; — dritta, vertical stempiece; — slanciata, raked stem; — acuta, fine-lined bows; — stellata, fine entry; — piena, — rigonfia, bluff bows; — a violino, swan bows; linea di —, lubbers' line, ship's head (compass); — vera, true course; — di bussola, — alla bussola, compass course; — magnetica, magnetic compass course; ruota di —, sternpiece; castello di —, forecastle; albero di —, foremast; barbetta di —, foremast turret; fardello di —, †fardo di —, quartiere di —, forecastle, seamen's quarters; buona guardia a —!, keep a good look out forrard!; —?, what is your course?; che —?, how is the ship's head?; aver la — al largo, to be heading to seaward. **-avi·a** *adv.* (naut.) ahead, for'ard, in the bows; a -avia, in the direction the ship is heading. †**-e·o** *adj.* (naut.) relating to the bows.

prorog-are [A 2] *tr.* (leg.) to adjourn; to extend; to postpone; to prorogue; to put off; to delay; to prolong; — il mandato, to extend the term of office; il termine è stato -ato, the period has been extended, the closing date has been deferred. **-a** *f.* (leg.) adjournment; delay; extension (of time); postponement; prorogation; respite; la -a di una causa, adjournment of a case; chiedere una -a per il pagamento, to ask for time to pay. **-a·bile**

prorog-are (*cont.*)
adj. subject to extension, liable to deferment; scadenza -abile, due date liable to deferment. **-abilità** *f.* -abilità del termine, possibility of extending the period. †**-ativa** *f.* arrogance; insolence; see **prerogativa.** **-ativo** *adj.* dilatory. **-ato** *part. adj.* delayed, postponed, extended, etc. **-azione** *f.* extension, deferment; prorogation.

prorǫmp-ere [C26] *intr.* (*aux.* avere) to break out, to burst out, to burst forth; to burst; — in una risata, to burst out laughing; — in pianto, to burst into tears; il sangue proruppe dalle vene, blood gushed from the veins; i nostri proruppero dalle trincee, our men rushed from the trenches. **-ente** *part. adj.* bursting out; gushing; lacrime -enti dal cuore, tears springing from the heart. **-imento** *m.* outburst; breaking forth.

prǫs-a *f.* prose; piece of prose; le -e, opere in —, prose works; scelta di -e, prose anthology; scrittore di -e, prose-writer; (theatr.) drama, legitimate theatre, straight theatre (i.e. not opera or vaudeville); teatro di —, theatre (as distinguished from an opera house); festival della —, drama festival; un uomo tutto —, a very prosaic man; — rimata, dull, unimaginative verse; amare in —, to love unromantically; la — della vita, the mundane things of life; (liturg.) prose; sequence. **-aicismo** *m.*, **-aicità** *f.* commonplace things; prosaicness, prosiness. **-a·ico** *adj.* prosaic; commonplace, matter-of-fact; uomo -aico, common man, vulgar individual; †scrittore -aico, prose-writer. **-aicaménte** *adv.* prosaically. **-aismo** *m.* prosiness. †**-ante** *m.* prose-writer. †**-are** *intr.* to write prose. **-asticità** *f.* prosiness. **-a·stico** *adj.* prosy, prosaic. **-atore** *m.* prose-writer. (**-atrice** *f.*) †**-eggiare** *intr.* to write prose. **-erella**, **-ętta** *f. dim.* (derog.) prose (writing) of little value. †**-etto** *m.* motto. **-ista** *m., f.* prose-writer.

prǫsa·pia *f.* race, stock, lineage; — di eroi, race of heroes; essere di nobile —, to be of noble birth.

proscę·nio *m.* (theatr.) proscenium; chiamare al — gli attori, to call the actors to take a curtain; palchi di —, boxes nearest to the stage.

prosci·m(m)ie *f.pl.* (zool.) lemurs.

prosciǫ·gl-iere [B26] *tr.* (leg.) to discharge; to dismiss charge against (distinguished from **assolvere**, to acquit) (C.P.P.); (theol.) to absolve (from sin); to release (from vow). **-imento** *m.* (leg.) discharge; dismissal of charge; -imento con sentenza istruttoria, discharge by examining magistrate (C.P.P.); absolution; remission; esami di -imento, elementary leaving examinations (successful pupils were formerly allowed to leave school at the end of the third year). **-itǫre** *m.* one who absolves; one who sets free. (**-itrice** *f.*)

prosciǫlto *part. adj.* (leg.) discharged; freed from criminal charge (C.P.P.); (theol.) absolved.

prosciug-are [A2] *tr.* to dry; to drain, to reclaim (by drainage, etc.); — il salame, to dry Italian sausage; il vento ha -ato la terra, the wind has dried the ground; — le paludi pontine, to drain and reclaim the Pontine Marshes; (agric.) to drain; *intr.* (*aux.* essere), *rfl.* to dry (up); mettere il granturco a -arsi nell'aia, to lay the maize to dry on the threshing-floor. **-aménto** *m.* drying (up); draining (land), reclamation; (agric.) draining. **-ato** *part. adj.* dried; drained, reclaimed.

prosciutt-o *m.* ham; bacon; aver gli occhi foderati di —, to be wilfully blind (*or* to show the red under-lid); aver gli orecchi foderati di —, to be hard of hearing; (provb.) levarsi la sete col —, to try unsuitable remedies; (joc.) violin. **-ato** *adj.* (cul.) cured, like ham; larded with ham.

proscr-i·vere [C26] *tr.* (leg.) to proscribe; to outlaw; to banish (also fig.). **-itto** *part. adj.* proscribed; banished, exiled; *n.m.* exile; outlaw. (**-ittore** *m.* **-ittrice** *f.*) **-izione** *f.* (leg.) proscription; banishment; -izione di un libro, proscription, prohibition of a book.

prosęcco *m.* name of a wine from the district of Istria.

prosecu-tivo *adj.* following up (or on); serving for continuation. **-zione** *f.* continuation; prosecution (e.g. of studies); (leg.) prosecution; pursuit; -zione della causa, prosecution of the action; mancata -zione, want of prosecution (C.C.P.).

prosęggi-are [A3c] *intr.* (*aux.* avere) to write in prose; to use a prosaic style. **-atore** *m.* prose-writer. (**-atrice** *f.*)

prosegretà·rio *m.* assistant secretary.

prosegu-ire [D1] *tr.* to continue, to go on with; to pursue; prosegui, go on; — la lettura, to continue (the reading); — il cammino,

to continue on one's way; (leg.) to prosecute; — un processo, to prosecute an action (C.C.P.); *intr.* (*aux.* avere, essere) to go on, to push on, to persist; Paolo ha -ito per Roma, Paul continued his journey to Rome; il piroscafo ha -ito (è -ito) per Genova, the steamer proceeded to Genoa; egli -ì nelle ricerche, he pursued his inquiries; — a cantare, to go on singing, to continue to sing; (on letters) far —, please forward. **-imento** *m.* continuation; resumption; buon -imento!, I hope you will continue to enjoy your (New Year or Christmas) holiday, *or* may the days to come be just as happy, etc., may you continue to do well (also, on leaving a railway-carriage, to fellow-travellers with whom one has conversed) I hope you have a good journey.

prosę·lit-o *m.* proselyte, convert; — del socialismo, convert to socialism. **-ismo** *m.* proselytism.

prosęnce·falo *m.* (anat.) prosencephalon.

prosęn·chima *f.* (bot.) prosenchyma.

Prosęr·pina *pr.n.f.* (myth.) Proserpine, Persephone.

prosettǫre *m.* (med.) prosector, dissector.

prosięguo *m.* (leg.) course; in — di tempo, in course of time, in due course.

prosillogismo *m.* (logic) prosyllogism.

prosin·daco *m.* acting mayor.

prǫsit (Lat.) *prosit!*; may it be fruitful!, may it be of benefit!; (fam.) good for you!, well done!

prosǫd-i·a *f.* prosody; scansion. **-i·aco** *adj.* (Gk. prosod.) prosodiac (metre: a particular sequence of syllables); (incorrectly) prosodic (connected with scansion in general).

prosǫ·dico *adj.* prosodic.

prosontuǫso *adj.* and derivs. (S. Ital.). See **presuntuoso.**

prosopografi·a *f.* description of persons (face, features); physiognomy.

prosopo-pe·a *f.* prosopopoeia; (fig.) affectation; affected gravity; avere molta —, to give oneself airs. **-pe·ico** *adj.* prosopopoeic(al).

prǫ·spęr-o *adj.* favourable, propitious, lucky, happy; prosperous, flourishing, thriving, prospering; campagne feconde e -e, fertile, flourishing fields; commercio —, flourishing business; — evento, happy event (i.e. birth); navigare con — vento, to sail before a fair wind; essere in -a salute, to enjoy very good health. **-aménte** *adv.* prosperously; favourably, happily. **-aménto** *m.* prospering, thriving; prosperity. **-are** [A1s] *intr.* (*aux.* avere) to thrive, to flourish; to be prosperous, to prosper; la vite -a in questo terreno, vines thrive in this soil; -ano gli affari, business is flourishing; *tr.* to favour, to make prosperous, to prosper; Dio vi -i!, God bless you! **-ęvole** *adj.* favourable, propitious; flourishing. **-evolménte** *adv.* favourably, propitiously. **-ità** *f.* prosperity; wealth; flourishing state; robust health; (a wish to one who sneezes) -ità!, God bless you! **-ǫso** *adj.* healthy, vigorous, lusty, sturdy; buxom; vecchiezza -osa, hale and hearty old age; thriving, flourishing. **-osaménte** *adv.* favourably, happily; lustily; vigorously; crescere -osamente, to grow big and strong.

prospęt·tic-o *adj.* (paint.) perspective, according to the principles of perspective. **-aménte** *adv.* perspectively, with perspective effect.

prospęttiv-a *f.* (paint.) perspective; le leggi della —, the laws of perspective; — aerea, aerial perspective; — lineare, linear perspective; in —, in perspective; (fig.) prospect; la — di un tristo avvenire, the prospect of an unhappy future; ha dinanzi a sè una brutta —, his prospects are gloomy; abbiamo in — un buon raccolto, we are expecting a good harvest; (hist. geog.) — della Neva, Nevsky Prospect, in Leningrad; view, prospect; una bella —, a fine view. **-ante**, **-ista** *m., f.* (paint.) one who observes the laws of perspective. **-o** *adj., n.m.* (paint.) (pittore) -o, scene painter (in theatre), landscape painter, one who observes perspective. **-aménte** *adv.* perspectively; prospectively, in prospect.

prospętt-o *m.* (archit.) front elevation, façade; prospect, view; un bel —, a fine view; di —, facing; guardare qualche cosa di —, to get a front view of something; figura di —, face seen from in front, full-face; (theatr.) palchi di —, boxes facing the stage; (fig.) prospect; ha in — una ricca eredità, he is in expectation of a substantial inheritance; prospectus; table, summary; — delle entrate, summary of income; — statistico della popolazione, statistical table of population (population statistics); (leg.) window with outlook (equiv. to **veduta**, q.v.); servitù di —, easement of outlook, prospect or view (C.C.); (finan.) prospectus. **-are** [A1] *tr.* to look out upon, to face, to overlook, to have a view of; la casa -ava la piazza, the house looked out upon the square;

prospett-o (*cont.*)
(fig.) to put before (one), to show; ti ho -ato soltanto un lato della questione, I have only put before you one side of the question; to envisage, to consider; — un'ipotesi, to envisage, to formulate, a hypothesis.

prospezione *f.* (geol.) prospecting.

prospiciente *adj.* looking out, commanding a view (over), facing; una casa — il mare, a house with sea view; — verso il giardino, looking towards the garden; — alla strada, overlooking the street.

prossen-eta *m.* (Gk. antiq.) *proxenetes*, broker, agent; (fig.) go-between (usu. disreputable); (incorrectly) *proxenos* (by confusion with **prosseno**, q.v.). **-e·tico** *m.* (Gk. antiq.) brokerage; (leg.) marriage-brokage.

prosseno *m.* (Gk. antiq.) *proxenos*; official friend or host of guests from abroad; representative of a foreign State.

pros·sim-o *adj.* very near, at hand; nearest, next; l'anno —, next year; in un — avvenire, in the near future; essere — alla partenza, to be on the eve of departure; la vittoria è -a, victory is at hand; — ai vent'anni, nearly twenty (years of age); la casa è -a alla chiesa, the house is very near the church; nei tempi a noi -i, in most recent times; parente —, close relation, next of kin; -a causa, immediate cause; (comm.) proximo; (leg.) — congiunto, near relative (C.P.); (gramm.) passato —, (present) perfect; trapassato —, past perfect, pluperfect; *n.m.* neighbour; fellow creature; non seccare il —, don't be troublesome; non conoscere nemmeno per —, not to know at all, to wish to have nothing to do with (a person); (as a collective noun) neighbours, human beings, people; (fam.) se ce n'era del —!, there weren't half a lot of people there! †**-a·io** *m.* next of kin. **-amente** *adv.* very soon, in a short time, presently; before long; very closely; segue -amente, he (it) follows very closely; (cinem.) coming shortly; *n.m.* (cinem.) un -amente, a trailer. **-ale** *adj.* (anat.) proximal. †**-ano** *m.* see **prossimaio**. **-iore** (leg.) *adj.* nearer; *n.m.* nearer relation. **-ità** *f.* proximity, nearness, vicinity; in -ità del mare, within a short distance of the sea; siamo in -ità delle feste, the holidays are near; eravamo in -ità del Natale, Christmas was approaching; close relationship; close resemblance; -ità di gusti, great similarity of tastes.

prostafe·reşi *f.* (astron.) equation of time.

pro·st-ata *f.* (anat.) prostate. **-atectomi·a** *f.* (surg.) prostatectomy, removal of the prostate. **-a·tico** *adj.* prostatic; ghiandola -atica, prostate gland. **-atismo** *m.* (med.) prostatism. **-atite** *f.* (med.) prostatitis.

prosten·dere [C I] *tr.* to stretch out; to extend; *rfl.* to stretch (oneself); to lie down; (fig.) to spread oneself; prostendersi in parole, to expatiate, to speak at considerable length.

prostern-are [A I] *tr.* to prostrate, to lay low, to cast down; *rfl.* to prostrate oneself; to bow down. **-azione** *f.* prostration; bowing down.

†**proster·nere** *tr.* to cast down, to prostrate; *rfl.* to stretch (oneself); to expatiate; to be cast down (discouraged), to humble oneself.

pro·s-teşi *f.* (gramm.) prosthesis. **-tetica** *f.* (surg.) prosthetics. **-te·tico** *adj.* (gramm.) prosthetic, prefixed; *adj.* (chem.) prosthetic.

pro·stilo *n.m.*, *adj.* (Gk. archit.) prostyle, portico of four columns at most.

prostitu-ire [D 2] *tr.* to prostitute; — l'ingegno, to prostitute one's talents; *rfl.* to prostitute oneself; to sell oneself; odio la gente che si -isce per danaro, I despise people who sell themselves for money; si -isce in adulazioni, he stoops to the basest flattery. **-ito** *part. adj.* prostituted. **-ta** *f.* prostitute; whore. (**-tore** *m.* **-trice** *f.*) **-zione** *f.* prostitution.

prostr-are [A I] *tr.* to prostrate; to dispirit, to cast down; to overwhelm; to weary, to fatigue; to exhaust; la fatica lo aveva -ato, he was dropping with fatigue; la triste notizia lo ha -ato, the sad news has overwhelmed him; la lunga malattia lo ha -ato, the long illness has pulled him down; *abs.* to fatigue, to be fatiguing; l'assiduo lavoro -a, continuous work is very exhausting; *rfl.* to prostrate oneself; -arsi ai piedi di alcuno, to fall at someone's feet, to kneel down before someone; gli si -ò ai piedi chiedendo grazia, he fell at his feet and begged for mercy. **-amento** *m.* kneeling down, falling down; prostration. **-ato** *part. adj.* prostrate, kneeling; dejected, dispirited; overwhelmed; exhausted; -ato dinanzi all'altare, prostrate before the altar; essere -ato dal dolore, to be prostrate with grief; -ato in letto, stretched out in bed. **-azione** *f.* prostration; dejection, depression; exhaustion.

prostro *apocop. part.* of **prostrare**, q.v.

†**prosu·mere** *vb.* and derivs. See **presumere**.

prosuo·cero *m.* father of father-in-law (or of mother-in-law).

†**prosutto** *m.* See **prosciutto**.

protagonist-a *m.*, *f.* (*m.pl.* -i, *f.pl.* -e) protagonist; (theatr., cinem.) leading role, main part, name part; leading actor or actress.

protallo *m.* (bot.) prothallus.

protamina *f.* (chem.) protamine.

pro·taşi *f.* (gramm.; rhet.) protasis.

protegg·g-ere [C I 2] *tr.* to protect, to shelter; to defend; to support, to patronize; Dio lo -a!, God protect him!, God keep him!; ha qualche santo in Paradiso che lo -e, some guardian angel is watching over him; — dal freddo, to shelter from the cold; — le lettere e le arti, to be a patron of arts and letters; prendere a —, to take under one's protection, to become a patron to; — le produzioni nazionali, to protect home products (with protective tariffs), to foster home industries (with subsidies). **-ente** *part. adj.* protecting, protective; pensilina -ente l'entrata, overhanging roof sheltering the entrance door. **-imento** *m.* protecting, protection. **-itore** *m.* protector, patron. (**-itrice** *f.*)

proteggicapez·zolo *m. indecl.* (med.) nipple shield.

prote·ico *adj.* (chem.) proteic, protein.

proteiforme *adj.* See under **proteo**.

prote-ina *f.* (chem.) protein. **-i·nico** *adj.* (chem.) relating to protein.

proten·dere [C I] *tr.* to stretch (out), to extend, to hold out; to spread; — le braccia implorando aiuto, to hold out one's arms in entreaty; — lo sguardo, to look far away; *rfl.* to stretch oneself; protendersi in avanti, to lean over, to lean out; protendersi dalla finestra, to lean out of the window.

Pro·te·o *pr.n.m.* (myth.) Proteus; (fig.) ever-changing person, one of Protean appearance or character; one who assumes various forms or disguises; dissembler; (zool.) olm, *Proteus anguinus*, a blind subterranean newt. **-iforme** *adj.* proteiform, protean, variable; dissimulating; ingegno -iforme, versatile talent. **-ismo** *m.* variability, versatility.

proteoli·tico *adj.* (chem.) proteolytic.

proter-andro *adj.* (biol.) proterandrous. **-o·gino** *adj.* (biol.) proterogynous.

proter·via *f.* arrogance; stubbornness; impudence.

proter·v-o *adj.* arrogant; stubborn, obstinate; impudent; impetuous; rash; vento —, raging wind. **-amente** *adv.* arrogantly; stubbornly; impudently.

pro·teşi, pro·teşi¹ *f.* (surg.) prosthesis; — dentaria, denture, false teeth. **-te·tico** *adj.* (surg.) prosthetic.

pro·teşi² *f.* (gramm.; rhet.) prosthesis.

pro·teşi³ *f.* (liturg.) prothesis, credence-table (in Eastern rites).

proteşo *part.* of **protendere**, q.v.; *adj.* outstretched; forward-looking; con le braccia protese, with outstretched arms; con lo sguardo —, straining one's gaze far ahead.

protesta *f.* protest; remonstrance; protestation, declaration; una — di fede, a protestation of faith; proteste d'amore, protestations of love; fare una —, to make a protest; una fiera — contro le violenze, an energetic protest against violence; il governo mandò una —, the government sent a remonstrance.

protest-are [A I] *intr.* (*aux.* avere), *tr.* to protest; — contro un atto d'ingiustizia, to protest against an act of injustice; -o la mia innocenza, I protest my innocence; -ava di non saper nulla, he protested that he knew nothing; — la guerra, to declare war; (leg.) to protest; (finan.) — una cambiale, to protest a bill (of exchange) (C.C.); *rfl.* to declare oneself, to plead, to protest (that one is); -arsi innocente, to plead innocent, to protest that one is innocent; si -ava mio amico, he declared that he was my friend. **-ante** *part. adj.*, *n.m.*, *f.* Protestant; pastore -ante, Protestant minister (pastor). **-antesimo, -antismo** *m.* Protestantism. **-ato** *part. adj.* protested; declared; (leg.; finan.) dishonoured, protested, noted (C.C.). **-atore** *m.* protester; remonstrator. (**-atrice** *f.*) **-ato·rio** *adj.* (*m.pl.* -atorii) concerning protestation. **-azione** *f.* protestation, declaration; -azione di affetto, protestation(s) of affection; (eccl.) the original 'protest' of Luther.

protesto¹ *m.* (leg.; finan.) protest; — cambiario, protest of a bill of exchange (C.C.).

†**protesto²** *m.* See **pretesto**.

prote·tico *adj.* See under **protesi¹**.

protett-o *part.* of **proteggere**, q.v.; *adj.* protected, sheltered; defended; supported, subsidized; patronized; luogo —, sheltered place; industrie -e, sheltered trades, protected industries; esporta-

protett-o (*cont.*)
zione -a, dumping; (naut.) incrociatore —, armoured cruiser; *n.m.* favourite, protégé. (**-a** *f.*) **-orale** *adj.* protector(i)al. **-orato** *m.* protectorship, protectorate; il -orato di Cromwell, Cromwell's Protectorate. **-ore** *m.* protector, patron; man who lives on the earnings of a prostitute; (hist.) Protector; -ore delle arti, patron of the arts; (rel.) Santo -ore, patron saint; (eccl.) Cardinale -ore, Cardinal Protector (of a religious order, etc.). **-rice** *f.* protectress, patroness; *adj.* Società -rice degli animali, Society for the Prevention of Cruelty to Animals. **-o·ria** *f.* (eccl.) protectorship (of Cardinal Protector).

protezion-e *f.* protection; patronage, favour; accordare — alle lettere, to grant patronage to literature; — delle industrie, protection of manufactures; misure di — antiaerea, air-raid precautions; condescension; un'aria di —, a patronizing air. **-iṣmo** *m.* (econ.) protectionism; special favour. **-ista** *m.* (econ.) protectionist.

protile *f.* (chem.) protyle.

†pro·tino *m.* stick, ready cudgel.

pro·tio *m.* (chem.) protium.

pro·tiro *m.* (Gk. archit.) prothyrum, vestibule.

protist-o *m.* (biol.) protistan. **-ologi·a** *f.* (biol.) protistology.

prot-o[1] *pref.* proto-. **-oatti·nio** *m.* (chem.) protoactinium, etatantalum. **-obromuro** *m.* (chem.) protobromide. **-ocano·nico** *adj.* (Bibl.) protocanonical. **-ocloruro** *m.* (chem.) protochloride.

proto[2] *m.* foreman in a printing-press; overseer.

protocollare[1] [A I] *tr.* (admin.) to file; to register; to record.

protocollare[2] *adj.* recording to, relating to, protocol.

protocoll-o *m.* protocol; register; register of documents, file, record; minutes of a diplomatic meeting; note of preliminary negotiations; essere a —, to be on record; mettere a —, to file, to record, to register; (leg.) protocol; minute book; record book; register; numero di —, reference number; carta —, foolscap paper. **-ista** *m.* keeper of record or register; filing clerk.

prot-odia·cono *m.* (eccl.) protodeacon, senior deacon (in Eastern Churches). **†-ofi·sico** *m.* see **protomedico** or **archiatra**. **-o·gino** *m.* (geol.) protogenic rock, protogeny. **-oguat·tero** *m.* chief scullion. **-oioduro** *m.* (chem.) proto-iodide. **-oli·tico** *adj.* (of the) Old Stone Age; età -olitica, Palaeozoic Age. **-ologi·a** *f.* (philos.) 'protology', study of first principle (used esp. by and of Gioberti). **-oma(e)stro** *m.* master-builder; foreman-printer (see **proto**). **-omar·tire** *m.* (theol.) protomartyr (esp. St Stephen). **-ome·dico** *m.* Court doctor, chief physician; physician to the Pope. **-one** *m.* (phys.) proton. **-onema** *f.* (bot.) protonema. **-o·nico** *adj.* (gramm.) protonic, preceding the accented syllable. **-onotariale** *adj.* (eccl.) protonotarial. **-onotariato** *m.* protonotaryship. **-onota·rio, -onotaro** *m.* (eccl.) protonotary; (hist.) Chancellor, Court Secretary; Pier della Vigna fu -onotario di Federico II, Pier della Vigna was Chancellor to Frederick II. **-opapa** *m.* (eccl.) protopope, archpriest (in Eastern Churches). **-oplaṣma** *m.* (biol.) protoplasm. **-oplaste** *m.* (theol.) primal creator, God. **-oplasto** *m.* (theol.) first created man, Adam. **-opsalte** *m.* (eccl.) *protopsaltes*, precentor, first cantor (in Eastern Churches). **-oquamquam** *m.* (joc.) wiseacre, know-all; fare il -oquamquam, to put on superior airs, to assume superiority. **-oscrinia·rio** *m.* (eccl. hist.) *protoscriniarius*. **-osolfuro** *m.* (chem.) protosulphide. **-ospata·rio** *m.* (Byz. hist.) *protospatharius*, Captain of the Guards. **-os·sido** *m.* (chem.) protoxide. **-o·tipo** *m.* prototype; model; egli è il -otipo dei gentiluomini, he is a perfect gentleman; (eng.) prototype. **-ovangelo** *m.* (eccl.) *Protoevangelium Jacobi*, the apocryphal Gospel of James; (theol.) *protoevangelium*, foreshadowing of the Gospel, the first promise of redemption in Gen. iii. 15. **-ozoi** *m.pl.* (zool.) protozoa.

protr-arre [B 33] *tr.* to protract, to prolong; to draw out, to lengthen; to defer, to postpone; — una discussione, to protract a discussion; — le vacanze, to prolong one's holidays; — la partenza, to put off one's departure. **-atto** *part. adj.* protracted; long drawn out; deferred, postponed. **-azione** *f.* protraction; deferment, postponement.

protuber-are [A I S] *intr.* (*aux.* essere) to bulge, to swell; to be protuberant. **-ante** *part. adj.* protuberant, bulging; prominent. **-anza** *f.* protuberance; prominence; swelling; (anat.) protuberance, eminence, apophysis; (joc.) hump (on the back).

protutore *m.* (leg.) deputy guardian (C.C.).

prov-a *f.* proof; trial, test; trying-on; examination; ordeal; evidence; token, pledge; a —, in —, on trial; prendo la macchina a —, I'll take the car on trial; in —, under test; lo sottoporrò a un'altra —, I will subject it to further trial (to another test); fare la — di un vestito, to try on a dress; a — della mia asserzione, in proof of my assertion; a — della mia stima, as a proof of my esteem; a — della mia amicizia, in token of my friendship; lo so per —, I know from experience; a — di bomba, bomb-proof; a — di fuoco, fire-proof; onestà a tutta —, well-tried honesty; fedeltà a tutta —, oft-proved loyalty; (hist.) — del fuoco, ordeal by fire; — delle armi, trial by combat, duel; una — di forza, a trial of strength; mettere alla —, to put to the test; far buona —, to stand the test; dar buona — di sè, to give a good account of oneself; — orale, oral examination; — scritta, written examination; subì le più dure -e, he underwent the severest trials; -e dolorose, sore trials, afflictions; (leg.) evidence; proof; — contraria, evidence in rebuttal, to the contrary; — documentale, documentary evidence; — indiziaria, circumstantial evidence; — piena, conclusive evidence; — testimoniale, parole evidence, witness' oral evidence (C.C.P.); assunzione delle -e, hearing of witnesses (C.C.P.); obbligo di fornire le -e, burden of proof; — ne sia che…, the proof is that…; -e vogliamo, non parole, we want facts, not words; (theatr.) rehearsal; — generale, dress rehearsal; la commedia è in —, the play is in rehearsal; (mus.) rehearsal; (choir) practice; (typ.) -e di stampa, proofs; foglio di —, specimen page, page-proof; (naut.) ship's trial; -e complementari, -e in mare, sea trials; -e sugli ormeggi, basin trials; -e di oscillazione, rolling trials; -e di massima potenza, full power trials; -e di resistenza, endurance trials; -e di stabilità, inclining trials; -e su base misurata, measured mile trials; -e per la ricerca del massimo raggio d'azione, economical speed trials; daily ration trial by the officer of the watch; — di fortuna, maritime accident, accident report. **-ẹtta** *f. dim.* of **prova**; little test; (chem.) test-tube; (mus.) operatic rehearsal with a reduced orchestra.

†provano *adj.* obstinate.

prov-are [A I] *tr.* to prove, to demonstrate; to test; to rehearse; to try; to try the effect of; to taste; to feel; to experience; — un fatto, to prove a fact; l'eccezione -a la regola, the exception proves the rule; dovete — la verità di ciò, you must demonstrate (give proof of) the truth of it; perchè non -ate a parlare in inglese?, why don't you try to speak English?; -ate di nuovo, try again; hai -ato ad essere dignitoso ed indifferente?, have you tried (the effect of) being aloof and dignified?; — una macchina (un'automobile), to test a car, to take a car out on trial (to try out); ogni macchina viene -ata prima che esca dal negozio, every machine is tested before it leaves the shop; avete mai -ato l'aspirina?, did you ever try aspirin?; -a queste castagne, try (taste) these chestnuts; — le scarpe, to try the shoes on; — un abito nuovo, to try on a new dress; (leg.) to prove; (theatr., etc.) to rehearse; tenne quel garzone un mese per -arlo, he kept that boy for a month on trial; ti -eremo, we will give you a trial, we will put you to the test; fu duramente -ato dalle disgrazie, he was sorely tried by misfortunes; — dolore, to feel pain; le fece — grandi dispiaceri, he caused her a great deal of trouble; — una grande difficoltà a imparare, to experience great difficulty in learning; potete immaginare la gioia che -ai, you can imagine how glad I was; — una delusione, to meet with a disappointment, to feel disappointed; *intr.* (*aux.* avere) (agric.; bot.) — bene, to take root, to become established, to grow well; l'ulivo -a molto bene in questi terreni, olive-trees do very well in this ground; *rfl.* (*acc.* of *prn.* 'si') to try, to endeavour; pròvati a scrivere queste parole, try to write (*or* try writing) these words; dovete -arvi a vincere la vostra paura, you must endeavour to overcome your fear; -arsi a camminare, to attempt to walk; -arsi a reggere un peso, to try to lift a weight; -arsi con qualcuno, to compete with someone, to strive, to have a trial of strength, with someone; (*dat.* of *prn.* 'si') to try, to try on; si -ò gli stivali, he tried on the boots; si -ò gli occhiali, he tried the spectacles. **-a·bile** *adj.* demonstrable, capable of proof; †probable. **-abilità** *f.* demonstrability. **-ante** *part. adj.* probative, affording proof; evidential. **-ato** *part. adj.* tried, experienced; tested; amico -ato, trusty friend; -ato in guerra; experienced in war; prova -ata, clear proof. **-atamẹnte** *adv.* decidedly; demonstrably; assuredly, surely. **-atọre** *m.* tester; one who accepts a challenge; *adj.* testing. (**-atrice** *f.*) **-atura** *f.* a kind of fresh buffalo cheese.

provenda *f.* food, provisions, provender; (Ancona) measure equiv. to 8·8 litres.

proven·ire [D 17] *intr.* (*aux.* essere; *prep.* da) to derive, to come (from); to originate (in); to arise; to be caused (by); questo treno proviene da Roma, this train starts at Rome; queste merci ~gono dalla Spagna, these goods originate in Spain; gravi malanni ~gono dal troppo bere, serious disorders are caused by drinking too much. **~iente** *part. adj.* (*prep.* da) originating (in); coming (from); caused (by). **~ienza** *f.* origin, place of origin, provenance, source; d'ignota ~ienza, of unknown origin; notizie di dubbia ~ienza, news from an unreliable source. (**~uto** *part. adj.*)

provento *m.* proceeds; income; i proventi saranno devoluti a opere di beneficenza, the proceeds will be devoted to charity; spese ogni suo —, he spent all his income; non avere altri proventi, having no other income.

Provenz-a *pr.n.f.* (geog.) Provence. **~ale** *adj.* Provençal; *n.m.* Provençal (man); Provençal (language). **~almęnte** *adv.* in Provençal style. **~aleggiante** *adj.* in Provençal style; lirica ~aleggiante, lyrical poetry on a Provençal model. **~aleggiare** [A 3 c] *intr.* (*aux.* avere) to write poetry in Provençal style, to imitate Provençal models. **~alesco** *adj.* (*m.pl.* **~aleschi**) in Provençal style, of Provençal origin; stile ~alesco, Provençal style. **~alismo** *m.* Provençalism (in speech, etc.). **~alista** *m.,f.* specialist in Old Provençal language and literature.

prover·bi-o *m.* proverb; saying; adage; come dice il —, as the saying goes; passare per —, to have become proverbial, to be very well known; per —, proverbially; (theatr.) short play with a proverb for title. **~ale** *adj.* proverbial; notorious; locuzione ~ale, proverbial saying; la loro volubilità è ~ale, their fickleness is notorious; la sua ostinazione è ~ale, he is obstinacy itself; quell'uomo è di un'ignoranza ~ale, that man is notorious for his ignorance. **~almęnte** *adv.* proverbially. **~are** [A 4] *tr.* to jeer at; to abuse, to scold; *recip. rfl.* to quarrel. **~atore** *m.* mocker; quarrelsome person. (**~atrice** *f.*) **~oso** *adj.* full of proverbs; jeering, mocking; parlare ~oso, jeering, abuse.

provęse *m.* (naut.) bow mooring, foremost hawser; mandar un — a terra, to run out a line (wire or hemp).

provętta *f. dim.* See under **prova**.

provętto *adj.* advanced (in years, knowledge, etc.); experienced, skilled, skilful; un insegnante —, an experienced teacher; età provetta, mature age; i più provetti, the oldest, the most advanced (in studies, skill, etc.); mano provetta, practised hand.

provianda *f.* See **provenda**.

provica·ri-o *m.* (eccl.) pro-vicar. **~ato** *m.* (eccl.) provicariate.

†**proviere** *m.* (naut.). See **prodiere**.

provinca *f.* (bot.). See **pervinca**.

provin·ci-a *f.* province (as an administrative unit the Italian 'provincia' corresponds approx. to an English county); district; abitare in —, to live in the provinces; (Rom. hist.) province (senatorial, imperial); (eccl.) province; †quarter of a city; †office, duties. **~alato** *m.* (eccl.) provincialate. **~ale** *adj.* provincial; usanze ~ali, provincial customs; strada ~ale, secondary road (maintained by a province); *n.m.,f.* provincial; modi da ~ale, provincial manners (not polished); (eccl.) (Father, Mother) Provincial. **~alismo** *m.* provincialism (in speech, dress, etc.); local turn of speech.

provino *m.* (mus.) preliminary rehearsal (esp. of ballet); (cinem.) screen-test; (techn.) sample, specimen, test-piece; (ballistics) proving chamber; proving gun; (chem.) test-tube.

provoc-are [A 2 s] *tr.* to provoke; to rouse; to stir up, to excite; to inspire; to cause; — l'ira di uno, to provoke someone to anger; — indignazione, to rouse indignation; — il riso, to cause laughter; — con l'ingiuria, to provoke with insults; — il popolo, to stir up the people; — il vomito, to cause vomiting; (admin.) to instigate. **~a·bile** *adj.* liable to provocation. (**~abilità** *f.*) **~amęnto** *m.* provoking, rousing, provocation. **~ante** *part. adj.* provoking; come sei ~ante!, how provoking you are!; parole ~anti, provocative words; provocative; seductive; inviting. **~antemęnte** *adv.* provokingly; provocatively; seductively; invitingly. **~ato** *part. adj.* provoked; roused; excited; caused. **~atore** *m.,* **~atrice** *f.* provoker; instigator; trouble maker; i ~atori del popolo, (public) agitators; i prepotenti chiamano ~atore chi si difende, tyrants call anyone who defends himself a disturber of the peace; *adj.* provoking, provocative; agente ~atore, agent provocateur; arroganza ~atrice, intolerable arrogance; lettera ~atrice, provocative letter. **~ato·rio** *adj.* (*m.pl.* **~atorii**) provocative; challenging; cartello ~atorio, challenge (to a duel). **~azione** *f.* provocation; challenge; emotional disturbance; (leg.) provocation (C.P.).

pro·vol-a *f.* a kind of fresh buffalo cheese. **~one** *m.* a kind of cheese, spherical or pear-shaped, made in S. Italy.

†**provol·vere** *rfl.* to prostrate oneself.

†**provosto** *m.* (eccl.). See **proposto**.

provved·ęre [B 35] *tr.* to provide, to supply; to furnish; to make provision; — il necessario per la famiglia, to provide for one's family; — i viveri ad un esercito, to supply an army with provisions; è stato ~uto tutto per la partenza, everything is ready for going away; to lay in a stock; ha ~uto grano e olio per tutto l'anno, he has made a provision of corn and oil for the whole year; l'orto ~e verdura per il nostro bisogno, the garden furnishes what greens we require; *intr.* (*aux.* avere; *prep.* a) to make provision, to provide; Dio ~erà, God will provide; to make arrangements (for); — all'educazione dei propri figli, to provide for one's children's education; provvidi a tempo a regolare i miei conti, I saw to the payment of my bills in time; ~erò io, I will see to it; devo — a tutto per il viaggio, I must think of everything for the journey; il — divino, Divine Providence; *rfl.* to provide oneself, to furnish oneself; ~ersi di passaporto, to provide oneself with a passport; *n.m.* providence; il — divino, Divine Providence. **~imento** *m.* provision; precaution; ~imento del necessario, providing what is needful; *pl.* measures; prendere ~imenti disciplinari, to take disciplinary measures; ~imenti igienici, hygienic precautions; (leg.) measure; order; provision; step; ~imento del giudice, Order of Court or judge (general term comprising interlocutory orders and judgements (C.C.P. and C.P.P.)); ~imento in rapporto alle misure di sicurezza, Order of Court in connexion with police measures (C.P.); ~imento legislativo, legislative measure; statutory provision. **~itorato** *m.* office of supervisor; local education office. **~itore** *m.* superintendent, supervisor; steward; manager; ~itore agli studi, (local, county) Director of Education; (mil.) quartermaster-general; (comm.) purveyor; ~itore della Real Casa, Purveyor to the Royal Household, by appointment to H.M. **~itori·a** *f.* superintendent's office; education office, office of 'provveditore'. **~uto** *part. adj.* provided, furnished; provided (with); una famiglia ben ~uta, a well-to-do family; †cautious, provident.

provviden-te *adj.* provident; far-seeing, prudent. **~temęnte** *adv.* providently; prudently. **~za** *f.* (theol.) (Divine) Providence; providence; prudence; fu una vera ~za, it was a real piece of luck; questa pioggia è una ~za, this rain is providential; quell'eredità è stata una ~za per noi, that legacy was providential for us; provision; che bella ~za!, what an abundance!; (leg.) ~za sociale, social welfare. **~ziale** *adj.* providential; soccorso ~ziale, providential help; uomo ~ziale, man sent by Providence. **~zialmęnte** *adv.* providentially.

prov·vid-o *adj.* provident, showing foresight; thrifty; istituzione ~a, provident institution. **~amęnte** *adv.* providently; with foresight.

provvigiǫne *f.* (leg.) (agent's) commission (C.C.); (*pl.*) somministrare provvigioni, to furnish supplies (C.P.); (comm.) poundage; allowance; fittage.

†**provvisare** *vb.* and derivs. See **improvvisare**.

provvisiǫn-e *f.* provision; providing, furnishing; victuals; (mil.) supply stores, victualling and ammunition; †(hist.) vicario di —, (equiv. to) minister of food supply; governmental board (Genoa); (leg.) provision; supply; — di denari, money bill or Act; pay, salary, income; †see **previsione**. **~ale** *f.* interim damages (C.C.P.); †*adj.* see **provvisorio**. **~are** [A 1 c] *tr.* to provide, to furnish (with salary, food, etc.); to pay, to provision; (mil.) ~are la batteria, to supply ammunition to a battery. **~ato** *part. adj.* provisioned; paid. **~cella** *f. dim.* small salary. **~iere** *m.* one responsible for provisions, victualler.

provvisǫre *m.* (hist.) president of the Genoese governmental board ('Provvisione'); Genoese commander-in-chief.

provviso·ri-o *adj.* provisional; temporary; interim; ad hoc; ponte —, temporary bridge; nel mondo tutto è —, nothing is permanent in this world; impiego —, temporary employment; governo —, provisional government; esercizio —, interim budget; (leg.) contratto —, ad referendum contract, contract to be considered further; esecuzione ~a, interim execution (C.C.P.); decidere a titolo —, to decide provisionally. **~amęnte** *adv.* provisionally, temporarily. **~età** *f.* provisional character, temporary nature.

provvist-a *f.* supply; abbiamo una nuova — di carbone, we have a new supply of coal; andare a fare le ~e per la famiglia, to go shopping, to do the family shopping; far le ~e per l'inverno, to

provvist-a (*cont.*)
lay in stocks for the winter; far — di salute, to build up one's health; (naut.) -e navali, stores; -e di bordo, ship's stores. **-o** *part.* of **provvedere**, q.v.; *adj.* (*prep.* di) provided (for, with); furnished (with); supplied; essere ben -o, to be well off, well-to-do; era -o di notevole ingegno, he was remarkably gifted; prepared (in mind), informed.

pro-zi·o *m.* great-uncle. **-zi·a** *f.* great-aunt.

pru-a *f.* (naut.) bows; da poppa a —, from stem to stern. **†-ato** *adj.* (naut.) by the head (said of a ship which trims with her bows too deep in the water). **-avi·a** *adv.* (naut.) for'ard; a -avia, towards the bows.

pruden-te *adj.* prudent, cautious; wise; careful; l'esperienza ci fa -ti, experience teaches us to be cautious; troppo —, overcareful, timid; giudicai — andarmene, I thought it wise to go away. **-temente** *adv.* prudently, cautiously; wisely. **-za** *f.* prudence; common sense; caution; soverchia -za, excessive caution, timidity; (theol.) prudence. **-ziale** *adj.* prudential; cautious; showing prudence. **-zialmente** *adv.* prudentially; with prudence.

pru-d-ere [B I def.] *intr.* (no compound tenses) to itch, to prick; sentirsi — le mani, to feel one's hands itching (i.e. to want to fight, or strike someone); mi -e il naso, my nose is tickling; sentirsi — la lingua, to itch to tell; toccare uno dove gli -e, to touch someone on the raw. **-ore** *m.*, **†-ura** *f.* itching.

prueggi-are [A 3 c] *intr.* (*aux.* avere) (naut.) to heave to; †to tack; †to yaw. **†-o** *m.* (naut.) act of tacking; method of heaving to; a -o, hove to; yaw.

prugn-o *m.* plum-tree. **-a** *f.* plum.

pru·gnolo *m.* (bot.) sloe, blackthorn, *Prunus spinosa*; — da siepe o da innesto, bullace, *P. insititia*.

prugnuolo *m.* (bot.) a kind of edible mushroom.

†pruina[1] *f.* See **brina**.

pruin-a[2] *f.* (bot.) bloom (e.g. on plums, cabbage leaves, etc.). **-oso** *adj.* (bot.) pruinose, frosted.

†pruna *f.* See **prugna**.

prun-a·ia *f.*, **-a·io** *m.* thorn-bush; thicket (properly of blackthorn); (provb.) una spina non fa un -aio, one thorn does not make a thicket; (fig.) trouble, difficulties, mess; mi son messo in un -aio, I have got into a mess. **-albo** *m.* (bot.) hawthorn, may, *Crataegus*. **-ata** *f.* blackthorn hedge. **-ella** *f.* (bot.) selfheal, *Prunella vulgaris*; a kind of liqueur. **-eto** *m.* blackthorn thicket; (fig.) difficulties.

prun-o *m.* (bot.) plum, *Prunus domestica*; — cocumile, *P. coco-milia*; — selvatico, sloe, blackthorn, *P. spinosa*; bramble, or any thorny shrub; thorn; mi è entrato un — in un piede, I've got a thorn in my foot; essere come un — in un occhio a, to be a thorn in the flesh to, to be a nuisance to; ogni — fa siepe, every little helps; discernere il — dal melarancio, to know what's what. **-oso** *adj.* thorny; prickly.

†pruovo *adv. phr.* a —, near, close; following close.

pruri-gin-e *f.* itching; tickling; (fig.) itch; excitement; (med.) prurigo. **-oso** *adj.* (med.) pruriginous; itching, itchy.

prurito *m.* (med.) pruritus; itch, itching; (fig.) bug, itch; — di amore, desire, lust.

†prusora *adv.* many times, several times, often.

Prus-si-a *pr.n.f.* (geog.) Prussia; blù di —, prussian blue. **-ana** *f.* Prussian woman or girl; long overcoat. **-ano** *adj., n.m.* Prussian.

prussiato *m.* (chem.) prussiate.

prus-sico *adj.* (chem.) prussic.

†psal·lere *intr.* to sing psalms.

psal-modi-a *f.* see **salmodia**. **-tero** *m.* see **salterio**.

psammite *f.* (geol.) psammite.

psammoma *m.* (med.) acervuloma.

pselaffesi·a *f.* (med.) pselaphesis.

psellismo *m.* (med.) psellism, stammering.

pse·ud-o *pref.* pseudo-. **-aca·cia** *f.* (bot.) acacia, *Robinia pseudo-acacia*. **-acu·si·a** *f.* (med.) pseudacousia. **-artro·si** *f.* (med.) pseudarthrosis. **-ogravidanza** *f.* (med.) pseudopregnancy, pseudo-cyesis. **-oit·tero** *m.* (med.) pseudoicterus, pseudojaundice. **-omel-anosi** *f.* (med.) pseudomelanosis. **-omembrana** *f.* (med.) pseudo-membrane. **-omor·fo** *adj.* (geol.) pseudomorphic. **-omor·fosi** *f.* (geol.) pseudomorphosis. **-o·nimo** *m.* pseudonym; pen-name. **-opo·dio** *m.* (zool.) pseudopodium. **-oprofeta** *m.* false prophet. **-osimmetri·a** *f.* (geol.) pseudosymmetry.

psic-agogi·a *f.* (anct. Gk. rel.) the guidance of souls down to the lower world; (anct. Gk. rel.) the summoning of souls up from the lower world; necromancy; (liter.) the guidance, persuasion or gratification of the mind, esp. through such arts as rhetoric and poetry. **-ago·gico** *adj.* guiding souls; conjuring up souls; fascinating the mind. **-agogo** *m.* (anct. Gk. rel.) guide of souls to the nether world (epithet of Hermes); conjurer up of souls, necromancer.

psican-a·lisi *f.* psychoanalysis. **-alista** *m., f.* psychoanalyst. **-ali·tico** *adj.* psychoanalytic.

psicasteni·a *f.* (med.) psychasthenia.

Psiche *pr.n.f.* (myth.) Psyche; (art) picture or statue representing Psyche; (psychology) psyche; cheval-glass.

psichi-atra *m.* (med.) psychiatrist. **-atri·a** *f.* (med.) psychiatry. **-a·trico** *adj.* psychiatric; ospedale -atrico, mental hospital, asylum.

psi·chico *adj.* psychic; psychical; fenomeni psichici, psychic phenomena.

psichismo *m.* (philos.) the life of the psyche in the widest sense; any theory which interprets external reality by analogy with psychological reality.

psico-dina·mica *f.* psychodynamics. **-dina·mico** *adj.* psychodynamic. **-grafi·a** *f.* psychography. **-gra·fico** *adj.* psychographic.

psico-logi·a *f.* psychology. **-lo·gico** *adj.* psychological. **-logicamente** *adv.* psychologically. **-logismo** *m.* (philos.) theory which makes psychology the key to philosophy in general. **-logista** *m.* (philos.) thinker who stresses or overstresses the importance of psychology as an explanation of reality.

psico·logo *m.* psychologist; romanziere —, psychological novelist, author of psychological novels.

psico-manzi·a *f.* divination by calling up spirits of the dead. **-metri·a** *f.* psychometry. **-moto·rio** *adj.* (physiol.) psychomotor. **-pati·a** *f.* psychopathy, mental disease. **-pa·tico** *adj.* psychopathic; *n.m.* psychopath. **-patologi·a** *f.* psychopathology.

psic-osi *f.* (med.) psychosis. **-o·sico**, **-o·tico** *adj.* (med.) psychotic. **-osoma·tico** *adj.* psychosomatic.

psicote·cnic-a *f.* industrial psychology. **-o** *adj.* psychotechnological; esame -o, psychotechnological fitness test.

psicoterapi·a *f.* (med.) psychotherapy.

psicro·metro *m.* (phys.) psychrometer, wet and dry bulb thermometer.

psilome·lano *m.* (geol.; miner.) psilomelane, manganese hydrate.

psil-osi *f.* (med.) psilosis; depilation. **-otro** *m.* depilant.

psittacosi *f.* (med.) psittacosis, parrot disease.

psor-i-asi *f.* (med.) psoriasis. **-ia·sico** *adj.* psoriatic.

pso·rico *adj.* psoric, scabious.

pss, pst *excl.* I say!, hi!; sh!

ptar·mica *f.* (bot.) sneezewort, *Achillea ptarmica*.

pte·rid-e *f.* (bot.) fern. **-ofite** *f.* (bot.) pteridophyte.

pter-i·gio *m.* (anat.) pterygium. **-igoide·o** *adj.* (anat.) pterygoid. **-odat·tilo** *m.* (zool.) pterodactyl.

ptial-ina *f.* (chem.; physiol.) ptyalin. **-ismo** *m.* (med.) ptyalism, excessive salivation.

ptilonorinco *m.* (orn.) bower bird, *Ptilonorhyncus*.

ptilosi *f.* (med.) ptilosis.

ptino *m.* (ent.) *Ptinus* spp., beetles infesting woollen goods, books and various stored products.

†ptisi *f.* expectoration.

ptomaina *f.* (chem.; med.) ptomaine.

ptosi *f.* (med.) ptosis, drop, prolapse.

pub·blica *f.* (numism.) copper coin current in the Kingdom of Naples (sixteenth to seventeenth centuries).

pubblicano *m.* (Rom. hist.; Bibl.) publican, tax-gatherer; (eccl. hist.) *pl.* Publicani, Populicani (Cathars).

pubblic-are [A 2 s] *tr.* to publish, to make public, to divulge; to bring out, to issue, to edit; — un libro, to publish a book; le lettere del Petrarca furono -ate da V. Rossi, Petrarch's letters were edited by V. Rossi; — un decreto, to issue a decree; — una legge, to promulgate a law; to present to the public, to put on the market; to make public property; to confiscate. **-a·bile** *adj.* fit for publication. **-amento** *m.* publishing, making public. **-ato** *part. adj.* published, issued, edited; recentissimamente -ato, just out. **-atore** *m.* publisher (in sense of one who first edits or publishes an old MS., etc.; cf. **editore**). (**-atrice** *f.*) **-azione** *f.* publication, publishing, issue; banns (of marriage); hanno fatto le -azioni, the banns have been published; (leg.) publication; -azione della sentenza, publication of judgement (C.C.P.; C.P.); pronouncement, manifesto; making public property, confiscation; published matter, publication.

pub·bli-co *adj*. public; national, state, government(al); debito —, national debt; giardini -ci, public gardens; strada -ca, public highway; fare una -ca protesta, to make a public protest; a spese -che, at public expense, at government expense; scuola -ca, state school, national school; — ministero, Public Prosecutor (etc.; see under **ministero**); — ufficiale, public official (C.P.); diritto —, international law; ente —, public body; -ca sicurezza, police; agente di -ca sicurezza, policeman; la forza -ca, armed police; opere -che, lavori -ci, public works; ministero dei lavori -ci, Office of Works; — ufficiale, civil servant; salute -ca, public health; l'opinione -ca, public opinion; vita -ca, public life (e.g. of politicians); atto, strumento —, deed, instrument under seal; far di -ca ragione, to publish, to call attention to, to invite comment on; *n.m.* public; people; audience; il — è il miglior giudice, the public is the best judge; il — dei lettori, the reading public; il — del teatro, the theatre audience, the spectators; parlò davanti a un folto —, he spoke before a crowded audience; esporsi al —, to make a public exhibition of oneself; in —, in public, publicly; mettere in —, to make public, to spread abroad. **-camente** *adv*. publicly, in public. **-cista** *m*. student of international law; free-lance writer; publicist. **-città** *f*. publicity; advertising; evitare la -città, to avoid publicity; piccola -città, small advertisements, small ads.; un po' di -città è necessario, some advertising is necessary; la -città è sempre costosa, advertising is always expensive; avviso di -città, advertisement (in newspaper, on placard, etc.); non è stata fatta sufficiente -città per i vostri prodotti, your products have not been sufficiently advertised; non facciamo -città!, don't let's make a scene! **-citario** *adj*. advertising; annunzio -citario, advertisement; *n.m.* advertising agent, publicity agent.

pube *m*. (†*f*.) (anat.) pubes.

pu·ber-e, †**-o** *adj*. (med.) pubescent; *n.m.* adolescent.

pubertà *f*. (med.) puberty.

pubescen-te *adj*. (bot.) pubescent. **-za** *f*. (med.) pubescence.

pu·b-ico *adj*. (anat.) pubic. **-iotomi·a** *f*. (surg.) pubiotomy.

†**puccetto** *m*. cuff, blow on the head with the hand.

puddell-are [A I] *tr*. (metall.) to puddle. **-aggio** *m*., **-atura** *f*. (metall.) puddling.

puddinga *f*. (miner.) pudding-stone, conglomerate.

pud-endo *adj*. (anat.) pudendal. **-enda** *f.pl.* (anat.) pudenda, external genital organs. **-ibondo** *adj*. modest, bashful; prudish; sguardo -ibondo, modest look, shy glance; un ragazzo -ibondo, a bashful boy.

pu·dic-o, **pudic-o** *adj*. modest, bashful; chaste. **-amente** *adv*. modestly. **-izia** *f*. modesty, decency, chastity.

pudore *m*. modesty; shame; offendere il — di uno, to offend someone's modesty; (leg.) decency; offese al —, offences against decency (C.P.); non ha — a chiedere, he is not ashamed to ask (to beg); non sentir — a dire, not to be ashamed to say; astenersi per —, to stay away (refrain, do without) out of shame; senza —, shameless; ha perduto ogni —, he has lost all shame (all sense of decency); falso —, false modesty.

puericultura *f*. care of children, child welfare.

puer-ile *adj*. childish, puerile; boyish; discorsi -ili, childish talk. **-ilmente** *adv*. childishly. **-ilità** *f*. childishness, puerility; childish trick; childhood. **-izia** *f*. childhood; boyhood, girlhood; amici fin dalla -izia, friends from childhood.

puer·per-a *f*. woman in childbed, newly delivered woman. **-ale** *adj*. puerperal; febbre -ale, puerperal fever.

puerpe·rio *m*. confinement, lying-in, esp. the time immediately following a birth; puerpery; (leg.) childbirth (C.C.).

puf *m. indecl.* (dressm.) pouffe, pad worn under women's dress; hair-pad; bustle.

pu·gil-e *m*. (sport) boxer; (Rom. antiq.) boxer (with *caestus*). **-ato** *m*. (Rom. antiq.) boxing (with *caestus*); (sport) boxing. **-atore** *m*. (sport) boxer. **-istica** *f*. boxing. **-istico** *adj*. (of) boxing; campione -istico, champion boxer, boxing champion.

pugillari *m.pl.* (Rom. antiq.) *pugillares*, writing-tablets (usu. of wood).

pugino *m*. (ent.) gnat (cf. **cugino**).

pu·gio *m*. (Rom. antiq.) *pugio*, dagger (esp. as worn by emperors or high officers).

Pu·glia *pr.n.f.* (geog.) Apulia; †whole of S. Italy.

pugn-a *f*. (poet.) fight, battle; restituire la —, to turn the tide of battle. **-ace** *adj*. pugnacious, warlike, bellicose; aggressive. (**-acemente** *adv*.)

pugnal-e *m*. dagger; colpo di —, stab; lavorar di —, to stab repeatedly; (fig.) blow; quella notizia fu un colpo di — al cuore, the news pierced him (me, etc.) to the heart; (mil.) — degli arditi, commando dagger. **-are** [A I] *tr*. to stab; lo -arono alla schiena, they stabbed him in the back. **-ata** *f*. stab; Cesare fu colpito da ventitré -ate, Caesar received twenty-three stab wounds; una -ata nella schiena, a stab in the back; (fig.) blow, bad news. **-atore** *m*. stabber, person handy with the dagger. (**-atrice** *f*.) **-etto** *m. dim.* small dagger, stiletto. **-ino** *m*. stiletto. **-otto** *m*. short dagger.

pugn-are [A 5] *intr*. (*aux.* avere) (liter.) to fight. **-ante** *part. adj*. fighting; schiere -anti, combat troops, fighting bands; *n.m.* fighter. **-ata** *f*. see under **pugno**. **-atore** *m*. fighter; one who struggles; wrestler. (**-atrice** *f*.)

†**pu·gnere** *vb*. and derivs. See **pungere**.

pugnitopo *m*. (bot.). See **pungitopo**, under **pungere**.

pugn-o *m*. (*pl.* -i *m*., -a *f*.) fist; punch, blow; stringere i -i, to clench one's fists; coi -i stretti, with clenched fists; mostrare i -i ad uno, to shake one's fist at someone; dare un — ad uno, to punch someone; un — sulla testa, a blow (punch) on the head; una scarica di -i, a rain of blows; fare a (ai) -i, to box, to fight, (fig.) to clash, to disagree, to be contrary, to contradict; questi colori fanno a -i fra di loro, these colours clash; (fig.) fare ai -i, to fight, to force one's way, to elbow one's way; si dovette fare ai -i per passare, you had to fight (to elbow your way) to get through (in, by); ciò fa a -i col buon senso, that is contrary to common sense; handful; hand(writing); un — di grano, a handful of corn; pugno a pugno, handful by handful, in handfuls, by handfuls; (fig.) un — d'uomini, a handful of men; rimanere con un — di mosche, to be left (to come away) empty-handed; lo scrisse di suo —, he wrote it with his own hand; la lettera era di suo —, the letter was in his handwriting; (fig.) tenere in —, to have in one's power; avevamo ormai la vittoria in —, victory was now within our grasp; serrare le -a, to die; — della briglia, bridle hand; — di ferro e guanto di velluto, an iron hand in a velvet glove (i.e. firm action taken in a gentle manner). **-ata** *f*. handful; punch. **-ello** *m*. small handful, fistful; handle, grip. **-ino** *m. dim.* little fist; children's game of placing one fist upon another.

†**pugnolare** *vb*. and derivs. See **pungolare**, under **pungolo**.

†**pugolare** *tr*. to whine for, to ask for peevishly or querulously.

pul-a *f*. chaff, husks; charcoal dust, slack coal. **-one** *m*. straw chaff.

pulc-e *f*. (ent.) flea, *Pulex* spp.; — penetrante, jigger, *Tunga penetrans*; — della vite, *Haltica ampelophaga*, a small beetle pest of vines; — delle nevi, *Entomobrya nivalis*, a collembolan found on snow fields; (fig.) ciò gli mise una — in un orecchio, that made him suspect something; (provb.) una — non leva il sonno, one shouldn't worry about trifles; chi dorme coi cani si alza con le -i, you can't touch pitch and not be defiled; noioso come una —, tiresome; morso di —, flea-bite; saper fare gli occhi alle -i, to be clever at close work requiring patience; color —, puce; (zool.) — di mare, sandhopper; — d'acqua, *Gammarus pulex*, the freshwater 'shrimp'. **-esecca** *f*. pinch; pull (of hair). **-iaio** *m*. nest of fleas, lot of fleas; quei cani hanno riddotto la casa un -iaio, those dogs have filled the house with fleas. **-ioso** *adj*. full of fleas, flea-ridden; *n.m.* lousy person, ragamuffin; (fig.) *nouveau riche*.

pulcell-a, **pulzella** *f*. maiden, damsel; la — d'Orléans, The Maid of Orleans (Joan of Arc). †**-ona** *f*. old maid.

†**pulcher·rimo** *superl*. of **pulcro**, q.v.

pulcia·io *m*. See under **pulce**.

pulcina·io *m*. See under **pulcino**.

Pulcinell-a *pr.n.m.* Punch, Punchinello ('mask' of Neapolitan comedy, introduced in the seventeenth century); il segreto di —, an open secret; fare il —, to play the fool, to fail to keep one's word; il carro di —, a wagonload of people, a car full of people; fare le nozze di —, to come to blows; (orn.) — di mare, see **polcinella**. **-ata** *f*. piece of buffoonery, silly behaviour; Punch and Judy show. **-ino** *m*. figure of Punch. **-otto** *m*. person dressed up as Punch.

pulcin-o *m*. (orn.) newly hatched chick, day-old chick; -i e chioccia d'oro, golden hen and chickens (a famous treasure in Monza Cathedral); ci entrò come un — bagnato, he came in like a drowned rat; (fig.) un — bagnato, a person feeling very sorry for himself; è come un — nella stoppa, he does not know which way to turn (he's like a frightened hen). **-aio** *m*. (joc.) chicken house; lot of chicks; house with a lot of children, big brood.

pulcioso *adj*. See under **pulce**.

†**pulc·ro** *adj.* beautiful. †-**ritu·dine** *f.* beauty.

puledr·o *m.* (zool.) unbroken colt, of horse, mule, etc.; — brado, colt raised in the field; — stallino, colt raised in a stable; (fig.) lively boy, 'young colt'. -**a** *f.* filly. -**a·ia** *f.* field or stable where colts are kept; (joc.) night nursery. -**otto** *m.* growing colt.

puleggia *f.* (eng.) pulley, sheave; — folle, idler, loose pulley.

puleggio[1] *m.* (bot.) penny-royal, *Mentha pulegium.*

puleggio[2] *m.* (naut.) sheave of a block or deadeye (rigging); †see **pileggio**.

puleżżo *m.* See **pileggio**.

pulica·ria *f.* (bot.) *Plantago psyllium.*

†**pu·lice** *f.* See **pulce**.

pul-ire [D 2] *tr.* to clean; to polish; to wash; — dalla polvere, to dust; — i mobili, to polish the furniture; — i vetri delle finestre, to clean the windows; — il piatto, to clear (up) one's plate, to leave a clean plate; (eng.) to polish, to buff; to scour; — a secco, to dry-clean; *rfl.* (acc. of *prn.* 'si') to wash (oneself), to clean oneself; to tidy oneself up; (*dat.* of *prn.* 'si') -itevi le mani, wash your hands; -irsi la bocca, to wipe one's lips; -irsi il naso, to blow one's nose; (fig.) to put on one's best manners, to become more polite. -**imento** *m.* cleaning; final polish, finishing touch(es); tirare a -imento, to put the finishing touches to, to perfect. -**isciorecchi** *m. indecl.* ear-pick. -**iscipenne** *m. indecl.* pen-wiper. -**iscipiedi**, -**isciscarpe** *m. indecl.* door-mat; scraper. -**ita**, -**itina** *f.* cleaning, clean; darsi una -ita al cappello, to give one's hat a brush; ho dato una -ita alle scarpe, I have polished (cleaned) my shoes. -**iteżża** *f.* cleanliness; polish; cleanness, neatness; propriety; politeness; -itezza nello scrivere, propriety in writing (in style). -**ito** *part. adj.* clean; neat; well-kept, tidy; avere le mani -ite, to have clean hands; avere la coscienza -ita, to have a clear conscience; biancheria -ita, clean linen; osso -ito, bare bone (stripped of flesh); la fece abbastanza -ita, he carried it off pretty well; fare piazza -ita, to make a clean sweep, to clear away everything or everybody, to eat up everything; polished; smooth; elegant; scrittura -ita, fair copy, (fig.) polished writing; parlare -ito, elegant speech; in -ita rima, in polished verse; polite, well-mannered; *n.m.* fair copy; consegnare il -ito, to hand over (send in) the fair copy; mettere a -ito, to make a fair copy (of); *adv.* scrivere -ito, to write neatly; mangiare -ito, to eat daintily. -**itamente** *adv.* cleanly, neatly, properly; politely; smoothly, quietly. -**itino** *adj. dim.* neat (in dress). -**itone** *adj. augm.* very particular as to dress and cleanliness. (-**itore** *m.*) -**itrice** *f.* (eng.) polishing machine, buffer; -itrice a nastro, belt grinder. -**itura** *f.* cleaning; polishing; dar l'ultima -itura a, to put the finishing touches to; cost of cleaning; -itura a secco, dry-cleaning; (eng.) polishing, buffing. -**izi·a** *f.* cleaning; cleanliness; tidiness; sweeping, dusting, scrubbing; fare la -izia, to do the housework; essa tiene molto alla -izia, she is very house-proud; fare -izia, to sweep, (fig.) to make a clean sweep, to clear everything away.

pulla·rio *m.* See **polla·rio**.

pullmann *f. indecl.* motor-coach; (rlwy.) pullman car.

pullover *m. indecl.* pullover; sweater; cardigan (used generally of almost any additional garment put on in cold weather).

pullul-are [A I S] *intr.* (*aux.* avere) to spring up, to shoot (of plants); to spread; to swarm, to pullulate; le male erbe -ano dappertutto, weeds spring up everywhere; i libri di quel genere -ano, there are lots of books of that kind; in questo libro -ano gli spropositi, this book is full of mistakes; (poet.) dal cielo roseo -a una stella (Pascoli), a star blossoms (springs to sight) in the rosy sky; *n.m.* era un gran — d'insetti, there were swarms of insects; (poet.) e d'un lieve — lo specchio segna dell'acque (Carducci), and marks the mirror of the waters with a (its) gentle bubbling. -**amento** *m.* springing up; pullulation; swarming. -**a·tico** *adj.* sprouting, disposed to sprout. -**azione** *f.* sprouting, springing; pullulation; swarming.

†**pulmento** *m.* See **polenda**.

pulo *m.* (geog.) doline, sink hole.

pulone *m.* See under **pula**.

pul·pito *m.* pulpit; (fig., iron.) montare in —, to preach, to sermonize; far del — teatro, to preach histrionically; da che — viene la predica!, the pot calling the kettle black!; †(theatr.) box.

puls-are [A I] *intr.* (*aux.* avere) to throb, to beat; to pulsate; gli -avano le tempie, his temples were throbbing; *tr.* to knock at (a door); (mus.) to play (an instrument). -**ante** *part. adj.* throbbing, beating; *n.m.* (watchm.) pusher; (eng.; electr.) push-button,

plunger; -ante da campanello, bell push; (photog.) -ante di scatto, shutter release. -**a·tile** *adj.* throbbing, beating, pulsatile. †-**a·tili** *m.pl.* (mus.) percussion instruments. -**atilla** *f.* (bot.) pasque flower, *Anemone pulsatilla.* -**ato·rio** *adj.* pulsatory. -**azione** *f.* beat, throb, throbbing, pulsation; (radio) angular velocity. †-**ione** *f.* see **impulsione**. †-**o** *adj.* see **espulso**. -**o·metro** *m.* (eng.) vacuum pump, pulsometer. †-**one** *m.* violent push or blow. -**oreattore** *m.* (aeron.) pulse-jet engine.

pult-a·ceo *adj.* pasty, like paste or soup. -**i·fago** *m.* (joc.) soup-eater, macaroni-eater. -**i·glia** *f.* paste; pulp; mush; liquid mud (cf. **poltiglia**).

pulverulento *adj.* covered with dust; il — scalpitamento dei cavalli, the dusty tramp of horses.

pulvinare *m.* (Rom. antiq.) *pulvinar*; couch or platform for images of the gods; imperial marriage-bed; imperial seat in circus.

pulvi·scol-o *m.* fine dust; fine spray; non un grano di —, not a speck of dust; (bot.) pollen; (text.) fly. -**are** [A I S] *tr.* (bot.) to pollinate; dusty; of (or like) pollen.

pulzell-a *f.*, -**etta** *f.*, -**ona** *f.* See **pulcella**.

puma *m.* (zool.) puma.

punch[1], **puncio** *m.* poncho.

punch[2] *m. indecl.* punch (drink).

†**punga** *f.* See **pugna**.

†**pungello** *m.* See **pungolo**.

pun·g-ere [C 5] *tr.* to prick; to sting; to pierce; una vespa mi ha punto, I have been stung by a wasp; mi punsi il dito con un ago, I pricked my finger with a needle; (fig.) fu punto dai miei rimproveri, he was stung by my reproaches; lo -eva la coscienza, his conscience pricked him; le mie parole lo punsero amaramente, my words wounded him deeply; l'avete punto sul vivo, you have stung him (pierced him) to the quick; mi -e un pensiero, an idea is troubling me; sentirsi —, to feel hurt; il freddo -e, the cold is piercing; — il cavallo, to set spurs to one's horse; *rfl.* to prick oneself; to get stung; mise la mano nell'ortica e si punse, he put his hand on the nettle and got stung. -**ente** *part. adj.* prickly; stinging; pungent; piquant; spine -enti, prickly thorns; freddo -ente, piercing cold; salsa -ente, piquant sauce; (fig.) biting, sharp, poignant; una satira -ente, a caustic (biting, pungent) satire; parole -enti, biting words, harsh words; *n.m.* spear. †-**etto** *m.* see **pungolo**. -**iglione** *m.* sting; (bot.) thorn; stinging hair; (fig.) spur, stimulus. -**imento** *m.* pricking, stinging; regret, compunction; incitement. -**itivo** *adj.* prickly; pungent; (fig.) wounding, offensive. -**itoio** *m.* pricker, prick; sharp instrument. -**itopo** *m.* (bot.) butchers' broom, *Ruscus aculeatus.* -**itore** *m.* pricker, stinger. (-**itrice** *f.*)

pun·gol-o *m.* goad; (fig.) spur, prick; il — dell'ambizione, the spur of ambition; il — della fame, the prick of hunger; stimulus; incentive; il — della novità, the excitement, attraction, of novelty. -**are** [A I S] *tr.* to goad; to urge.

puni·bile *adj.* and derivs. See under **punire**.

pu·nico[1] *adj.* (hist.) Punic, Carthaginian; le guerre puniche, the Punic Wars; fede punica, treachery; *n.m.* Carthaginian.

pu·n-ico[2] *m.* (bot.) pomegranate, *Punica granatum.* -**i·ce·o** *adj.* deep red, pomegranate red.

pun-ire [D 2] *tr.* to punish; to chastise, to correct; diritto di —, the right of punishment; — di morte, to punish by (with) death; to avenge. -**i·bile** *adj.* (leg.) liable to punishment; punishable. -**i·bilità** *f.* (leg.) condition or quality of being punishable (C.P.). -**imento** *m.* punishment; punishing. -**itivo** *adj.* punitive. -**ito** *part. adj.* punished. -**itore** *m.*, -**itrice** *f.* punisher, chastiser; *adj.* punitive, punishing; giustizia -itrice, punitive justice. -**izione** *f.* punishment, chastisement; penalty; passare senza -izione, to go unpunished; (leg.) punishment; (sport) calcio di -izione, free kick.

punt-a *f.* point; tip; corner; end; top, peak; la — di una spada, the point of a sword, sword-point; ferita di —, stab-wound, stab; la — della lingua, the tip of the tongue; queste scarpe hanno una — troppo pronunciata, these shoes are too pointed; camminare in — di piedi, to walk on tip-toe; con la — in alto, point upwards; (fig.) l'ho sulla — delle dita, I have it at my finger tips; parlare in — di forchetta, to speak affectedly; far la — a un lapis, to sharpen a pencil; non vede più in là della — del proprio naso, he can't see an inch in front of his nose, (fig.) he is narrow-minded; le -e dei campanili, the tops of the towers; le -e degli alberi, the tops of the trees, the tree-tops; (mountain-) peak; headland, promontory; stitch (in the side), sharp pain; ho una

punt-a *cont.*)

— al torace, I have a pain in my chest; — di petto, pleurisy; small amount, pinch, touch, trace, tinge; (of wine) prendere la —, to begin to go sour; una — d'invidia, a touch of envy; flying visit; feci una — a Como, I paid a flying visit to Como; piece of embroidery; point, tip (e.g. of picot edging); prendere una cosa di —, to take up (start, set about) something with enthusiasm; prendere una persona di —, to contradict someone, to 'take a person up' (on his words); a — di diamante, pyramid-shaped; ore di —, rush hour, peak hour; (techn.) di —, peak; pressione di —, peak pressure; — di Parigi, wire nail; (rlwy.) toe (of switch); (eng.) centre; — fissa, dead centre; bit, drill; (carpen.) — a guida, centre bit; — a succhiello, auger; — elicoidale, twist drill; di —, at the extremity, in front; i cavalli di —, (of four horses harnessed to a carriage) the leading pair of horses; — di petto, breast of beef, mutton, etc.; alla — del giorno, at break of day, at first light; cane da —, pointer (dog); (mil.) — di soldati, skirmish; thrust; wedge, salient, advanced post; ordinanze in —, spear formation, double echelon; — falsa, feint; †— d'ala, defensive outpost detached from the main bastion; (naut.) head; — del molo, head of the breakwater; — di vela, peak of a sail; bracciare di (in) —, to brace the yards close hauled; (naut. hist.) — di abbordaggio, boarding pike; (herald.) base. **-a·glia** *f.* (mil.) engagement, skirmish; tenere la -aglia, to hold one's own in action; (fig.) reggere una -aglia, to put up with something. **-aguzzo,** †**-aguto** *adj.* sharp-pointed. **-ale** *m.* metal tip (of a scabbard, sheath, etc.); ferrule (of umbrella, etc.); tag (of a shoe-lace); tongue (of a buckle); (shoem.) toe; ferrule, shoe; (eng.) push-rod; (naut.) height between decks; moulded depth of a ship measured amidships between the upper surface of the keel and the lower side of the upperdeck plating; vertical pillar supporting a deck (cf. **pontale**); (herald.) shape, crampet. **-aletto** *m.* (naut. hist.) after cabin pillar in a galley. **-alino** *m.* (motor.) valve cap. **-arella** *f. dim.* little point; move (in a specified direction); fare una -arella a destra, to move towards the right. **-azza** *f.* (bldg.) pile shoe. **-ina** *f.* pen-nib; drawing-pin; (cul.) form of 'pasta' used in soup; (mus.) gramophone needle; (shoem.) pin, heel pin; needle, stylus (of gramophone); (motor.) point (of sparking-plug); (vet.) small gall on the fetlock of a horse.

punt-are [A I] *tr.* to point, to aim, to direct (eyes, gaze); to fix, to direct; to level, to lay: -ò il dito verso di me, he pointed at me; — il cannocchiale a, to point the telescope at; (mil.) to aim, to lay (a gun); to head for, to direct troops towards; (eng.) to spot-weld; †(naut.) to prick the ship's position (cf. **punto**); il cane -ò la lepre, the hound pointed the hare; — i gomiti sulla tavola, to set one's elbows on the table; — i piedi a terra, to dig one's heels in, to refuse to budge; to bet, to wager, to lay, to punt; -ai dieci scellini sul favorito, I put ten shillings on the favourite; quanto -aste?, how much did you bet?; (mus.) to alter (a part) so as to make it easier to sing, to simplify; *intr.* (*aux.* avere) (naut.) to hoist sail, to set course; (fig.) — da, to set out from, to proceed from; to make an objection; — su alcune parole, to object to certain words. **-amento** *m.* (mil.) method of laying a gun. **-aruolo** *m.* see **punteruolo.** **-ata** *f.* thrust; part, number, instalment (of a serial story); stake, bet; (agric.) spit (spade's depth); renewal of the blade of a spade; measure equiv. to about 3 yards. **-ato** *part. adj.* speckled, dotted; linea -ata, dotted line; (mus.) dotted; *n.m.* (mus.) staccato. **-atore** *m.* (mil.) gun-layer; punter, gambler. (**-atrice** *f.*) **-atura** *f.* (eng.) spot-welding; (mus.) dotting; (mil.) laying of a gun.

punteggi-are [A 3 c] *tr., intr.* (*aux.* avere) (gramm.) to punctuate; (paint.) to dot; to draw dotted lines; (needlew., etc.) to prick out the lines of a design; to stitch; to mark with dots or points; to dot. **-amento** *m.* punctuation, dotting; series of dots; spots. **-ato** *part. adj.* dotted; speckled; linea -ata, dotted line; il mare era tutto -ato di barche, the sea was dotted with boats; punctuated. **-atura** *f.* punctuation; dotting; speckling; segni di -atura, punctuation marks.

punteggio *m.* dotting; pricking; marking; (sport) score.

puntell-o *m.* prop, support; wooden prop to fix a door; (bldg.) prop, shore, stay; (fig.) support, help, remedy; *pl.* props, beams, to shore up a wall; tener su a forza di -i, to prop up, to shore up, (fig.) to bolster up, to find support for; (naut.) docking shore; — poppiero, sternpost shore; †vertical deck pillar. **-are** [A I] *tr.* to prop, to shore up, to support, to buttress; -are con ragioni,

to give reasons in support of; (bldg.) to prop, to shore; *rfl.* to seek support; to assure oneself. **-amento** *m.* (bldg.) propping; shoring. **-ato** *part. adj.* propped (up), shored up; supported; trave -ata, beam serving as a prop. **-atura** *f.* (bldg.) propping, shoring, line of props or supports.

punterella. See **puntarella,** under **punta.**

punteri·a *f.* (mil.) fire direction; laying and training of a gun; tiro di —, point-blank aim; (naut.) hull fix sight; — di rapporto, director training, remote control laying; (eng.; motor.) tappet; (vet.) 'stamp', a sort of awl for making the hole for the nail in the hoof when shoeing a horse.

punteruolo[1] *m.* (eng.) drift, punch; awl; bodkin; stiletto; (provb.) far d'una lancia un —, to spoil, to reduce something almost to nothing.

punteruolo[2] *m.* (ent.) — del grano, grain weevil, *Calandra* sp.

punti·gli-o *m.*, †**-a** *f.* obstinacy; spite; lo fece per —, he did it out of spite; star sul —, to stick at trifles, to be awkward, to make things difficult; †punctiliousness. **-are** [A I] *intr.* (*aux.* avere), *rfl.* to be obstinate, to jib; to refuse to budge. **-oso** *adj.* obstinate, stubborn; spiteful. **-osamente** *adv.* stubbornly; spitefully.

punto[1] *part.* of pungere, q.v.; *adj.* pricked, stabbed, punctured; (fig.) goaded, spurred, incited.

punt-o[2] *m.* dot, spot, point, mark; — fermo, full stop; due -i, colon; — e virgola, semi-colon; — interrogativo, question-mark, mark of interrogation; — esclamativo, exclamation-mark; — e a capo, full stop, and new paragraph; mettere i -i sugl'i, to dot one's i's (also fig.); (needlew.) stitch; -i fitti, close stitching; — addietro, back-stitch(ing), 'point de sable'; — cieco, back-stitch; — in croce, cross-stitch; — a occhiello, button-hole stitch; — unghero, cross-stitch on canvas; mettere, dare un —, to stitch (up), to sew up; lasciare cadere un —, to drop a stitch; (provb.) un — dato in tempo ne salva cento, a stitch in time saves nine; (surg.) stitch; mettere i -i, to put in stitches; gli misero tre -i, he had three stitches in; *pl.* (med.) blackheads, (fig.) blemishes; (comm.) coupon, voucher; (leg.) point; — di diritto, in fatto, point of law, of fact; (naut.) — stimato, dead reckoning; (finan.) — dell'oro, specie point; — d'oro, gold point; (boxing) vincere ai -i, to win on points; (sport) fare -i, to score; (mus.) dot; (school, exam., etc.) mark; ottenere buoni -i, to get good marks; fare -i, to score; -i cardinali, points of the compass, cardinal points; (typ.) point, one of the 144 parts of the typographical scale; interlineatura a due -i, two-point leading; (mil.) point, position, aiming point; — di appoggio, point of support; — di atterraggio, landing place; — attuale, present position; — futuro, presumed future position; — in bianco, aiming mark, bull's eye, bull; di — in bianco, point blank, at point-blank range (also fig.); — di caduta, point of impact; — di mira, point of aim; — d'avvìo, release point; — d'incolonnamento, initial point; (eng.) — morto, dead centre; (naut.) fix, ship's position; fare il —, to fix the ship on the chart; — corretto, corrected fix; — estimato, estimated position; — di mezzodì, noon position; — osservato, observed (astronomical) position; — radiogoniometrico, wireless or radar fix; — rilevato, terrestrial fix; — stimato, — di stima, estimated position, dead reckoning; — di riferimento, reference position; — geodetico, geodetic position; (fig.) di — in bianco, directly, at once; dare, cogliere nel —, to hit the mark; in —, a —, in order; essere a buon —, to be in a satisfactory state, to have reached a desired end; mettere a —, to adjust; to tune up (of engines, etc.); mettere in — l'orologio, to set the clock (watch), to put the clock right; point, spot, place; position; (leg.) mettere al —, to settle (e.g. draft document); da questo — si vede Firenze, from this point you can see Florence; — di vista, view-point, point of view (usu. fig.); questo non è il mio — di vista, that is not my point of view; — di contatto, point of contact; — di partenza, starting-point; moment; arrivò in buon —, he came at the right moment; giunse in mal —, he came at the wrong moment; — critico, critical moment; state, condition; la cosa è al — di prima, the matter stands as before; fino a un certo —, to a certain extent, up to a point; in — di morte, at the point of death, at death's door; essere sul — di partire, to be on the point of leaving; a che — restammo?, where did we leave off?; fra un anno saremo al — d'oggi, a year from now we'll be just where we are today; — d'ebollizione, boiling-point; — di fusione, melting-point; — di rugiada, dew-point; — cieco, blind spot; far —, to leave off, to stop payment, to suspend payments; detail, item, particular,

punt-o (*cont.*)

particle; fornì la casa di tutto —, he fitted up the house in every particular; il — essenziale, the main point; in ogni —, on all points; veniamo al —, let us come to the point; voler vincere il suo —, to wish to carry one's point; — d'onore, point of honour; — per —, point by point; di — in —, in full detail; un — della *Divina Commedia*, a passage in the *Divine Comedy*; i quattordici -i di Wilson, (President) Wilson's Fourteen Points; — dell'ordine del giorno, item on the agenda; saperne un — più del diavolo, to be very crafty; fare il — su (di), to clarify, to limit, to define; se ha un — di amor proprio questa proposta l'offenderà, if he has a particle of self-respect that proposal will offend him; per un — non riuscì nel suo tentativo, he very nearly succeeded in his attempt; (provb.) per un — Martin perdè la cappa, for want of a nail the miller lost his mare; la pronuncia è il vostro — debole, pronunciation is your weak point. **-arello, -erello** *m. dim.* point (in a game, etc.). **-icolare** *adj.* pointed, shaped to a little point. **-ino** *m. dim.* mettere i -ini sugl'i, to dot the i's; *adv. phr.* a -ino, exactly, precisely. **-iscritto** *m.* laundry-mark, initials, etc. on linen; embroidery stitch. **-ofranco** *m.* free (customs) zone; bonded warehouse. **-olino** *m. dim.* little spot, dot; *pl.* dots (marking a break in a sentence). **-oncello** *m.* (mil. hist.) javelin. **-one** *m. augm.* (archit.) rafter; (mil. hist.) double echelon formation of troops; spur on salient bastion, (naut.) see **pontone**; point (e.g. of a sword); (bldg.) strut; *adv.* with the point.

punto³ *neg.* (as *adv.*, *adj.* or pronominal *adj.*) not at all; no, not any; non l'ho — veduto, I have not seen him at all; non ho — (*or* -a) fiducia in lui, I have *no* faith in him; non ho — (*or* -a) voglia di andarci, I have *no* desire to go; non ho quasi — denaro, I have hardly any money; non averne -i, to be penniless.

puntual-e *adj.* punctual; fu sempre —, he was always punctual, he always arrived on time; exact; lavoro —, accurate work; *n.m.* (naut.) standing part of a tackle (cf. **pontuale**). **-mente** *adv.* punctually; exactly, accurately. **-ità** *f.* punctuality; exactness; accuracy; -ità nel vestire, propriety in dress.

puntuazione *f.* punctuation.

puntun·ghero *m.* See 'punto unghero', under **punto**.

puntura *f.* prick; sting, (insect) bite; puncture; stabwound, stabbing pain; sento delle punture al capo, I have shooting pains in my head; stitch in one's side; (med.) injection; puncture.

puntuto *adj.* pointed, sharp.

punzecchi-are [A 4] *tr.* to prick, to sting, to bite; (fig.) to goad, to tease, to torment with pinpricks; to spur on; to tease playfully. **-amento** *m.* pricking, prickling; stinging; goading; teasing; pinprick (fig.); continui -amenti, continual pinpricks. **-ato** *part. adj.* pricked; stung; (fig.) goaded; *m.* pricking, prick; bite; goading; †(ent.) see **punteruolo**.

punzione *f.* stamp, punch mark; — del controllo, hall mark; †see **puntura**.

punzon-e *m.* (eng.) punch; (typ.) punch; hard punch. **-are** [A I c] *tr.* (eng.) to punch; (sport) to stamp, to affix an identification stamp or punch (on bicycles, before a race). **-atrice** *f.* (eng.) punching press, punching machine. **-atura** *f.* (eng.) punching, perforation; (sport) identification stamp or punch affixed on bicycles before a race. **-ista** *m.* (typ.) punch-cutter.

pupa¹ *f.* (ent.) pupa.

pup-a² *f.* baby; little girl; doll. **-etta** *dim.* newly-born baby (cf. **pupo**).

†**pupa**³ *f.* See **poppa**.

pup-attola *f.* doll; little child; tiny, doll-like woman. **-azza** *f.* (dial.) see **pupattola**. **-azzettare** [A I c] *tr.* to illustrate with caricatures; to caricature. **-azzetti** *m.* caricature. **-azzo** *m.* puppet.

pupill-a *f.* (anat.) pupil of the eye; (opt.) — d'uscita, object glass; con le -e asciutte, dry-eyed; è la — degli occhi della mamma, he is the apple of his mother's eye (cf. **pupillo**). **-are** *adj.* pupil(l)ary, of the pupil of the eye.

pupill-o *m.* (leg.) ward; (fig.) simpleton. **-a** *f.* (leg.) female ward. **-are** *adj.* relating to a ward or minor.

pupinizz-are [A I] *tr.* (teleph.) to pupinize. **-azione** *f.* (teleph.) coil loading.

pupo *m.* (Rome) doll; marionette, puppet; (dial.) child; little boy; l'opera dei pupi, puppet theatre; — del presepe, figure of a Christmas crib.

†**puppa** *f.* See **poppa**.

pupurrì *m. indecl.* pot-pourri.

pur-e *adv.*, *conj.* also, too; yet, still, even; however; somehow, anyhow; really, indeed; only; noi — andremo, we shall go too; un vestito di seta e un soprabito — di seta, a silk dress and a coat also of silk; era giovane, — era molto assennato, he was young, and yet he was very wise; volle fare di sua testa, he still chose to do it (to act) in his own way; (often abbrev. to **pur**): pur cantando, lo osservava, still singing, he watched him; pur facendo così, even if I (he, they, etc.) did that; ma — non si lasciava persuadere, however (and yet) he would not be persuaded; non —, not only *or* † hardly; non pur l'assaporò che gli dispiacque (Ariosto), he had hardly tasted it when he found it distasteful; non — uno, not even one; nè — (neppure), not even; senza nè — salutare, without even saying goodbye; l'ho — affermato, indeed, I have said so, I have even stated it; è — vero!, it is really true, indeed, it is true; pur che sia vero!, if only it be true!; pur di guadagnarsi il pane si adatterebbe a qualunque lavoro, if only he could earn a living he would turn his hand to anything; te lo do pur che tu vada via, I will give it you if only you will go away; pur di vederlo…, if only I could see him…; se —, if indeed, if only; entri —, do come in, please come in; faccia —!, please do!, make yourself at home!, please carry on!, don't mind me!; credete — che è un prezzo molto basso, you must see that the price is very low; sia —, granted, supposing that is so; e — (eppure), and yet, nevertheless; eppur si muove, and yet it *does* move, it moves all the same; o — (oppure), or, or else; lavorare o pure andarsene, work or clear out; fare o pure non fare?, is it to be done or not?; pur ora, just now, a moment ago; pur ieri, only yesterday. **-chè** *conj.* provided that, on condition that; if only; -chè paghi, può restare, as long as he pays, he can stay on. **-chessi·a** *adj.* any whatever, of any kind; (fam.) un cappello -chessia, any old hat.

purè *m. indecl.* (cul.) purée; — di patate, mashed potatoes; thick soup, 'cream'.

purezza *f.* purity; pureness; clearness; transparency, limpidity; sincerity, honesty; chastity; — dell'aria, clearness of the air; — di cuore, purity of heart; — della lingua, purity of the language; (art) — della linea, purity of line; (finan.) eccesso di —, betterness; mancanza di —, worseness.

purga *f.* See under **purgare**.

purg-are [A 2] *tr.* to purify; to purge; to cleanse, to clean, to clear, to clear out; (tanning) to bate, to puer; (silkb.) to scour; (rel.) to purge (away), to expiate, to atone for (one's sins); (Rom. antiq.) to lustrate, to purify ceremonially; (leg.) to purge; to free; — la terra dalle male erbe, to free the ground from weeds, to clear the ground of weeds; to expurgate; — uno scritto, to expurgate a text; *rfl.* to take an aperient; to purify oneself; to be purified; to purge oneself, to clear oneself. **-a** *f.* aperient; (pol.) purge; mettere in -a, to put in soak (for washing); (tanning) bating; -a di sterco di pollame, bating; -a di sterco di cane, puering; -a di crusca, drenching. **-abile** *adj.* capable of being cleansed, purged, etc. **-agione** *f.* (silkb.) scouring; †see **purgazione**. **-amento** *m.* purging, cleansing, purgation; (rel.) (spiritual) cleansing; purgation, expiation (of sins); excrement; menstruation. **-ante** *part. adj.*, *n.m.* laxative, aperient; (theol.) chiesa -ante, the Church suffering (in Purgatory); anime -anti, souls in Purgatory. **-antino** *m. dim.* mild laxative. **-antone** *m. augm.* strong purgative. **-ata** *f.* purge, purging. **-atezza** *f.* purity (of language, style, design, etc.). **-ativo** *adj.* (rel.) cleansing, expiatory; (mystical theol.) via -ativa, Purgative Way (preceding the Illuminative and the Unitive Way). **-ato** *part. adj.* cleansed, purified; orecchie -ate, sharp ears; expurgated; edizione -ata, expurgated edition; pure, correct; stile -ato, pure style. **-atamente** *adv.* with purity (of language, style). **-atoio** *m.* drain to carry water from a fountain; rain-water tank. **-atore** *adj.* purifying, cleansing; *n.m.* cleanser; vessel in which oil is collected; (archit.) rain-water tank, settling tank; drain carrying water from a fountain. (**-atrice** *f.*) **-atorio** *adj.* (*m.pl.* **-atorii**) purifying, cleansing; (theol.) purgatorial (pains); *n.m.* (theol.) Purgatory; anima del -atorio, soul in Purgatory; (fig.) torture, torment; (archit.) settling tank (for rain-water); part of an oil-press where impurities are deposited. **-atura** *f.* purgation, cleansing, disinfection; cost of cleansing, purifying, etc.; impurities. **-azione** *f.* purgation, purification; (leg.) purging; -azione delle ipoteche, clearing of mortgages (C.C.); (rel.) purgation, expiation (of sin); (eccl.) -azione canonica, canonical purgation (denial of a charge on oath and with witnesses).

purgo *m.* (*pl.* **purghi**) tank for rinsing; (fig.) mettere in —, to hold back (news, for confirmation or pending permission to release).

purific-are [A 2 s] *tr.* to purify, to cleanse; (rel.) to purify, to cleanse (ritually, spiritually); (liturg.) — una chiesa, to reconsecrate a church; (Rom. antiq.) to lustrate, to make a ritual purification of (a city or a body of people); *rfl.* to purify oneself; to be purified, to be cleansed. **-aménto** *m.* purifying; cleansing. **-ativo** *adj.* serving to purify or cleanse. **-ato** *part. adj.* purified; cleansed; refined. **-atoio** *m.* (liturg.) purificator. **-atore** *m.* purifier; (liturg.) purificator; *adj.* purifying; cleansing. (**-atrice** *f.*) **-azione** *f.* purification; cleansing; refining; (rel.) (spiritual) cleansing; (Jewish rel.) purification (after childbirth); (eccl.) la **-azione**, the Purification (of the B.V.M.), Candlemas (feast of 2 February); (eccl.) churching (of women); (liturg.) purification (of chalice at mass); reconsecration (of church); (art) picture representing the Purification of the Virgin Mary; purgation; -azione delle passioni, catharsis.

Purim *pr.n.m.* Purim (Jewish festival).

puriṣ-mo *m.* (ling.) purism, esp. in Italy in the first half of the nineteenth century. **-ta** *m., f.* purist.

purit-à *f.* purity; pureness; clearness; innocence; chastity; — del giglio, lily whiteness; (gramm.) purity (of diction, style). **-aniṣmo** *m.* puritanism. **-ano** *m.* (eccl. hist., fig.) Puritan; *adj.* puritanical.

pur-o *adj.* pure; unadulterated, unalloyed; neat (not diluted); mere, sheer, plain, clear; aria -a, pure air, clear air; cielo —, clear sky; vino —, unadulterated wine; matematica -a, pure mathematics; la -a verità, the plain truth; -a invenzione, sheer invention; un — capriccio, a mere caprice; fu un — caso, it was mere chance; una coscienza -a, a clear conscience; il — dovere, simple duty; (chem.) alcool —, absolute alcohol; (archit.) pure (unmixed in style); dorico —, pure Doric; linea -a, pure line (simple, clean); di razza -a, of pure breed, thoroughbred; un cavallo di razza -a, un cavallo di — sangue, a thoroughbred horse; (comm.) accettazione -a e semplice, general acceptance. **-aménte** *adv.* purely; sincerely; simply; merely, only; -amente e semplicemente, purely and simply.

purosangue *m. indecl.* thoroughbred.

purpu·reo *adj.* red; crimson; purple.

purtroppo *adv.* unfortunately; only to well.

purulen-to *adj.* purulent. **-za** *f.* purulence.

pus *m. indecl.* pus, matter.

puṣeiṣ-mo *m.* (eccl. hist.) Puseyism, Tractarianism. **-ta** *m.* (eccl. hist.) Puseyite, Tractarian.

puṣign-o *m.* late (or second) supper; snack eaten late at night. **-are** [A 5] *intr.* (*aux.* avere) to have supper or a snack late at night.

puṣilla·nim-e, -o *adj.* pusillanimous, faint-hearted, cowardly; *n.m.* coward. **-eménte** *adv.* faint-heartedly; like a coward. **-ità** *f.* pusillanimity; timidity; cowardliness.

puṣill-o *adj.* little, feeble; insignificant, of no account; humble; statura -a, insignificant stature; *n.m.* coward. **-ità** *f.* feebleness, weakness.

Pusta *pr.n.f.* (geog.) Puszta.

†pusterla *f.* See **posterla**.

pu·stol-a *f.* (vet.) pustule, carbuncle; (techn.) blister. **-ante** *adj.* blistering; gas -ante, blister gas. **-atura** *f.* (techn.) blistering. **-ẹtta, -ina** *f. dim.* pimple. **-oso** *adj.* pimply.

put-are [A I def.] *tr.* used only in the *phr.* -a caso (also **putacaso**), suppose, supposing; -a caso ch'io non tornassi, suppose I should not come back. **-ativo** *adj.* putative, reputed; (leg.) matrimonio -ativo, putative marriage (C.C.).

puteale *m.* (Rom. antiq.) *puteal*, stone curb round the mouth of a well or round a space of like shape (e.g. a *bidental*).

putera *f.* (bot.) stonewort, *Chara*.

pu·tid-o *adj.* stinking, fetid. **-ore** *m.* stink.

Putifarre *pr.n.m.* Potiphar.

putife·rio *m.* uproar, shindy, row; confusion, mess; stench, stink.

†putiglioso *adj.* See **putido**.

put-ire [D I] *intr.* (*aux.* avere) (geol.) to break down (of rock); †to stink; — a uno, to be abhorrent to someone. **-izza** *f.* (geol.) rotting of rock.

†putre *adj.* See **putrido**.

putr-e·dine, †-edo *f.* rottenness, rot; putrefaction, corruption; (fig.) moral corruption. **-edinoso** *adj.* rotten, putrid. **-efaciente** *part.* rotting, putrefying. **-efare** [B 14] *intr.* (*aux.* essere), *rfl.* to rot, to putrefy, to go bad; il pesce (si) -efà rapidamente ai calori estivi,

fish soon goes bad in hot weather. **-efatti·bile, †-efatte·vole** *adj.* liable to go bad; corruptible. **-efattivo** *adj.* liable to go bad. **-efatto** *part. adj.* rotten, putrefied, gone bad. **-efazione** *f.* putrefaction; in avanzata -efazione, in avanzato stato di -efazione, in an advanced state of decomposition. **-escente** *adj.* putrescent, rotting, going off. **-escenza** *f.* putrescence, putrefaction. **-esci·bile** *adj.* putrescible, liable to rot. **-idame** *m.* see **putridume**, under **putrido**.

pu·trid-o *adj.* putrid, rotten; legno —, rotten wood; acqua -a, filthy water, contaminated water; *n.m.* (fig.) corruption; 'C'è del — in Danimarca', 'Something is rotten in the State of Denmark'. **-ità** *f.* rottenness, putridity. **-ore, -ume** *m.* rottenness, rot; filth, garbage, mass of filth; il -ume delle fogne, the filth of the drains; questo luogo è un -ore, this is a filthy hole.

putrila·gin-e *f.* putrid matter, filth; decomposed matter (esp. in stagnant water). **-oso** *adj.* putrid.

putrire [D 2] *intr.* (*aux.* essere). See **imputridire**.

putrella *f.* beam; girder.

†putta *f.* girl; whore (cf. **putto**).

puttan-a *f.* whore, strumpet; prostitute; quel figlio di —, that son of a bitch (in Tuscany, a mild expression, equiv. to 'that man, that chap'). **-eggiare** [A 3 c] *intr.* (*aux.* avere) to play the whore; to be a prostitute; to solicit. **-eri·a** *f.* whoring. **-ẹsco** *adj.* (*m.pl.* **-ẹschi**) whorish, lewd. **-escaménte** *adv.* like a whore. **-e·ṣimo, -iṣmo** *m.*, **-i·a** *f.* prostitution. **-iere** *m.* whoremonger; one who frequents prostitutes.

putt-o *m.* child, little boy; (art) child, cupid, 'putto', amorino, little angel. **-eri·a** *f.* childishness. **-ino** *m. dim.* of **putto**; baby, little child (esp. painted or sculptured).

puzz-a *f.* pus; festering matter; stink, stench; dare —, to stink. **-acchiare** [A 4] and derivs. see **puzzicchiare**. **-are** [A I] *intr.* (*aux.* avere) to stink, to smell bad; -are d'aglio, to smell of garlic; -are di rinchiuso, to smell stale or stuffy (e.g. of a room that has been shut up); -are d'eresia, to smack of heresy; -are d'avaro, to be miserly; -a di pedante lontano un miglio, you can smell the pedant a mile off; ti -a la salute?, don't you care about your health?; ti -a il denaro?, does money mean nothing to you?; to be unbearable; a ognuno -a questo barbaro dominio (Machiavelli), this barbarous tyranny stinks in the nostrils of all men; non —, to be not bad, to be pleasant; dopo questa fatica, un bicchiere di vino non -erebbe, after this job a glass of wine would go down well. **-ato** *part. adj.* stinking; †putrified. **-ecchiare** [A 4] and derivs. see **puzzicchiare**. **-erello** *m. dim.* of **puzzo**; slight odour. **-icchiare** [A 4] *intr.* (*aux.* avere) to give off an unpleasant odour; to begin to smell. **-o** *m.* stench, stink; bad smell, offensive smell; festering matter; -o di uova fradice, smell of rotten eggs; -o di bruciato, smell of burning; senza -i, senza odori, having neither scent nor stink, i.e. having no decided opinions; (fig.) fuss, row, bother; fare un -o di una cosa, to make a fuss about something; -o di eresia, taint of heresy, suspicion of heresy.

puz·zola *f.* (zool.) polecat, *Mustela putorius*.

puzzolen-te, †-to *adj.* stinking, fetid; filthy; fiato —, bad breath, stinking breath; (provb.) il medico pietoso fa la piaga —, it is necessary to be cruel to be kind. **-teménte** *adv.* dirtily, filthily.

puz·zolo *m.* (bot.) *Rhamnus alaternus*, a kind of buckthorn.

puzz-one *m.* evil-smelling person, contemptible individual; carcass; (fig.) skunk. (**-ona** *f.*) **-ore** *m.* stink.

---

q *f.* (pron. **cu**) the letter Q; the consonant Q.

qua *adv.* here, in this place; di — e di là, on this side and on that; hither; — e là, here and there; in —, this way, towards this side; fatti in —, come nearer; di —, over here; il mondo di —, the world we live in, life; il di — di, the near side of; di — delle Alpi, this side of the Alps; più —, later, later on; da un mese in —, for a month now; †in —, up to now; †in — addietro, hitherto, formerly, until recently; †— entro, in this place; †— innanzi, soon, within a little.

qua qua qua (onomat.) quack quack.

quac·cher-o *m.* Quaker, 'Friend'; *adj.* Quaker; alla -a, in Quaker fashion, (fig.) without formality. **-iṣmo** *m.* Quakerism.

quac·quero *m. adj.* and deriv. See **quacchero**.

quaderlẹtto *m.* gusset.

quaderna *f.* See **quaterna**.

quadern·o *m.* note-book, copy-book, exercise-book; part (of a book published in parts); quire; (bookb.) quaternion; (comm.) — di cassa, cash-book; — degli oneri, memorandum of conditions; — di appalto, conditions of tender, contract or lease; (naut.) — di chiesola, log-book; fours (at dice); †(poet.) see **quadernario**; †see **quadrato**. **-ac·cio** *m.* rough-book; scrap-book. **-etto** *m. dim.* note-book. **-ale** *m.* (poet.) see **quadernario**; (naut.) four-stranded rope. **-a·rio** *adj.* quaternary; *n.m.* set of four; (poet.) stanza of four lines; one half of an octave (of a sonnet).

quadra *f.* (naut.) square sail; alla —, ship-rigged; (astron.; naut.) see **quadrante**, under **quadrare**; †carpenter's square; †kind, quality; †dare la — a, to flatter; to mock.

quadr-agena·rio *adj.* forty years old, forty-year-old; *n.m.* a forty-year-old man. **-age·sima**, **-age·sima** *f.* (eccl.) First Sunday in Lent; see **quaresima**. **-agesimale** *adj.* of Lent, Lenten. †**-age·simo** *adj.* fortieth. **-angolare** *adj.* (math.) quadrangular. †**-angolato** *adj.* square, quadrilateral. **-a·ngolo** *adj.* four-cornered; *n.m.* quadrilateral.

quadr-are [A I] *tr.* to square; to-adjust; — la testa a, to train to accurate reasoning; (comm.) to balance, to square; to reconcile; *intr.* (*aux.* essere, avere) to be-fitting, to fit in, to be suitable; non gli -a, it is not to his liking, it doesn't suit him. **-a·bile** *adj.* that may be squared; measurable. **-amento** *m.* squaring, adjusting; balancing. **-ante** *part. adj.* fitting, in place; *n.m.* (astron.; naut.) quadrant; quarter of a day; dial, face (of a clock); (hist.) Roman coin; pagare fino all'ultimo -ante, to pay up to the last farthing. **-ata·rio** *m.* (Rom. antiq.) stone-cutter. **-a·tico** *adj.* quadratic. **-atino** *m. dim.* small square; a -atini, checked, in squares; (naut.) gunroom; junior officers' or warrant officers' mess room. **-ato** *part. adj.* squared; square; (vet.) denti -ati, central incisor teeth of a horse; stocky, robust; firm; voce -ata, strong voice; lettera -ata, capital letter; sound, sensible; avere la testa -ata, to have one's head screwed on the right way; (math.) radice -ata, square root; metro -ato, square metre; otto a -ato, eight squared; (naut.) pontone -ato, lighter; *n.m.* square; (boxing) ring; (Rom. antiq.) unit of area; (naut.) upper portion of the shank of an anchor; wardroom; -ato sottufficiali, warrant officers' mess; -ato navale, old-fashioned type of pelorus; (mil.) square; defensive formation; quadrilateral defence; (typ.) quad, quadrat. **-atura** *f.* quarter of the moon; squaring; in -atura con, square with; (astron.) quadrature; (naut.) -atura del pennone, point where a yard is square sectioned, bunt; (archit.) caisson, square panel or section in any surface; (paint.) art of painting parts of buildings in perspective; (eng.) perpendicularity; (electr.) in -atura, wattless; (anat.) torso (of a living human being); (vet.) the trunk of an animal.

quadr-idiano *adj.* lasting four days. **-iennale** *adj.* four-yearly. **-ien·nio** *m.* space of four years. **-ifo·(g)lio** *m.* (bot.) *Marsilia quadrifolia*; (archit.) quatrefoil. **-iforme** *adj.* quadriform. **-i·foro** *adj.* (archit.) having four openings. **-ifronte** *adj.* four-faced; (mil.) ordinanza -ifronte, quadrilateral order of battle. **-iga** *f.* quadriga, a chariot drawn by four horses, esp. as represented in sculpture or on coins. †**-i·gamo** *adj., n.m.* thrice bigamous. **-iga·rio** *adj.* of or belonging to a quadriga. **-igato** *adj.* (numism.) stamped with the figure of a quadriga; *n.m.* coin so stamped. **-ige·mino** *adj.* (anat.) quadrigeminal; *n.m.* quadrigeminum.

quadri·gli·a *f.* (mus.) Quadrille; (mil.) commando or small independent fighting unit. **-ati** *m.pl.* see **quadriglio**; cloth of a check pattern. **-è** *m. adj. indecl.* (text.) check. **-o** *m.* (cards) quadrille.

quadr-ila·tero *adj.* four-sided; *n.m.* quadrilateral; (mil.) quadrilateral defensive position. **-ilingue** *adj.* quadrilingual; knowing four languages, speaking four languages; written in four languages. **-ilio·ne** *m.* quadrillion (in Italy, France and America, the fifth power of a thousand, i.e. 1 plus 15 ciphers; in Great Britain, the fourth power of a million, i.e. 1 plus 24 ciphers). **-ilit·tero** *adj.* quadriliteral, composed of four letters, four-lettered. **-ilungo** *adj.* oblong. **-ilustre** *adj.* twenty years old. **-imembre** *adj.* four-limbed. **-imestrale** *adj.* of four months; appearing every four months (e.g. of a periodical). **-imestralmente** *adv.* every four months. **-imestre** *adj.* four-monthly; lasting four months; *n.m.* period of four months. **-imotore** *adj.* four-engined; *n.m.* four-engined aircraft. **-ino·mio** *adj.* (math.) quadrinomial, consisting of four terms; *n.m.* quadrinomial expression. **-ipartire** [D I] *tr.* to divide into four parts. **-ipartito** *adj.* quadripartite; governo -ipartito, four-party coalition Government; *pr.n.m.* (Ital. pol. hist.) Il Quadripartito, the party alliance (Christian Democrats, Social Democrats, Liberals and Republicans) which governed Italy from 1947 to 1957. **-ipartitamente** *adv.* in four parts. **-ipartizione** *f.* quadripartition, division into or by four. **-iplegi·a** *f.* (med.) quadriplegia; paralysis of all four limbs. **-ireme** *f.* quadrireme. **-isil·labo** *adj.* quadrisyllabic; una parola -isillaba, a quadrisyllable. **-ittongo** *m.* double diphthong (as in 'muoia'). **-ivalente** *adj.* (chem.) tetravalent. **-i·vio** *m.* cross-roads; meeting of four roads; (medieval education) quadrivium; arti del -ivio, quadrivium; geometry, arithmetic, music and astronomy.

quadro[1] *adj.* square; spalle quadre, square shoulders; (naut.) vela quadra, square sail; robust, stocky; strong; sensible; †obstinate, stupid.

quadr-o[2] *m.* (paint.) a painting on boards or on canvas stretched on a frame; picture; (fig.) description; outline; dare un — della situazione, to outline the situation; un — della vita italiana, a general picture of Italian life; (archit.) caisson, square compartment in a ceiling; — per gli avvisi, notice-board; — nero, black-board; (techn.) panel; — di comando, control panel; — strumenti, instrument panel; (chess, draughts) square; each pip on a playing card where the pips are set out in square formation (as in seven, six, five and four); (cul.) type of 'pasta' for soup; square head-shawl; — sinottico, table, chart; (mil.) square defended by equal numbers of troops on four sides; regimental list, battle order; (cinem.) still; (telev.) frame; (cinem.; telev.) fuori —, out-of-frame; *pl.* (cards) diamonds; at 'scopa' equiv. to **ori**, q.v.; (herald.) delf, peat, square, billet. †**-aro** *m.* vendor of paintings. **-ello** *adj.* four-edged, four-sided (e.g. of a tool); *n.m.* quarrel, a square-headed arrow; weapon, or any tool, with a four-sided point; packing-needle; square flooring tile; square ruler; a piece sewn in between the fingers of a glove; gusset; (naut.) tabling piece, reinforcement of a sail; sailmaker's needle (square sectioned). **-eri·a** *f.* picture collection. **-ettato** *adj.* squared, chequered, check. **-ettino** *m. dim.* of quadro; a -ettini, squared, ruled in squares; chequered, check. **-etto** *m. dim.* of quadro; small tile; square of a chess-board or check pattern; square glass jar; (archit.) moulding, list, fillet; †(naut.) Admiral's flag, with the sovereign's colours and crest, hoisted in senior officer's galley. **-ettone** *m. augm.* large shot (for a gun). **-icello** *m. dim.* square base, pedestal. **-ino** *m. dim.* small square tile; (dial. Rom.) see **quattrino**. **-one** *m. augm.* of quadro; large brick slab or large flat block of stone for building; square-shaped torch of white wax; coarse linen. **-otta** *f.* square-ruled paper. **-otto** *m.* rather large picture; *pl.* (at dice) double fours. **-uccini** *m.pl.* (cul.) 'pasta' for soup in shape of squares. **-uc·cio** *m. pejor.* small, inferior picture; flooring-brick; (cinem.) -uccio di proiezione, film trap, projection aperture. **-u·mane** *m.* (zool.) member of the 'Quadrumani', arboreal monkeys. **-umvirato** *m.* (Ital. hist.) 'quadrumvirate', the four men appointed by Mussolini, 27 October 1922, to organize the 'March on Rome'. **-um·iro** *m.* (Ital. hist.) a member of the 'quadrumvirate'; (anct. hist.) one of the quattuorviri. **-u·pede** *m.* quadruped. †**-u·pedo** *adj., n.m.* see **quadrupede**. **-uplatore** *m.* (Rom. hist.) a quadruplator, informer among Romans who received a quarter of the confiscated goods if his information led to conviction; †usurer. **-uplicare** [A 2 S] *tr.* to quadruplicate; to multiply by four. **-uplicato** *part. adj.* quadruplicated; quadruplicate, fourfold. **-uplicatamente** *adv.* four times over. **-uplicazione** *f.* quadruplication. **-u·plice** *adj.* quadruple; quadripartite; senso -uplice, fourfold sense, esp. of Scripture. **-uplicità** *f.* quadruplicity, fourfold nature.

qua·druplo *adj.* four times as much; four times the size; (mus.) contrappunto —, quadruple counterpoint; *n.m.* quadruple.

quaggiù *adv.* here below, down here; in this world, in this life.

†**quaggiuso** *adv.* See **quaggiù**.

qua·gli·a *f.* (orn.) quail, *Coturnix coturnix*; — tridattila, Andalusian hemipode, *Turnix sylvatica*; re delle -e, corncrake, *Crex crex*; (fig.) buxom girl. †**-era·io** *m.* device for catching quails. †**-ere**, **-eri** *m.* instrument for making quail calls for purposes of decoy; aver pieno il -ere, to have plenty of money; non avere da sonare il -ere, to have no money. **-etta** *f. dim.* of quaglia; scraps of meat spitted and roasted; kebab.

quagli-are [A 4] *tr., rfl., intr.* (*aux.* essere) to curdle; to coagulate; to clot. **-a·bile** *adj.* coagulable. **-amento** *m.* curdling; coagulating; clotting. **-ata** *f.* curds; junket; rennet.

qua·glio *m.* (zool.; vet.) abomasum; rennet.

quairata *f.* (naut.) garboard strake.

qual·che *adj. indecl.* (NOTE: in mod. Ital. takes noun in singular even if meaning is plural; e.g. — libro, some books, *or* some book or other) some, several; a few; — volta, sometimes; in — luogo, somewhere; — cosa meno, something less, rather less; non lo vedo da — tempo, I haven't seen him for some time; — cosa, something; some, a certain; some sort of; un — segno, some sign or other. **-cheduno** *indef. prn.* somebody, someone. **-chessi·a** *indef. prn.* anybody, anyone. **-cosa** *indef. prn.* something; -cos'altro, something more; un milioncino e -cosa, a cool million or more; credere d'esser -cosa, to think oneself of some importance; aver -cosa al sole, to own land, to have a bit of property. **-coserella** *indef. prn. dim.* some little thing. **-cuno** *indef. prn. m.* anybody, someone, somebody; one or two, some (of them); c'è -cuno?, is anybody there? **-cuna** *indef. prn. f.* anyone (in *f.* context); one of them; avrà fatto -cuna delle sue, he's been up to his tricks again.

qual·e *adj., prn. interr.* what?; which?; *indef. adj.* what, what a; as, just as; tale —, such as, just as; tale e —, just alike, just the same, literally, (iron.) just as you say!, quite!; *rel. prn.* il — (*f.* la —, *m.pl.* i -i, *f.pl.* le -i) who; which; la qual cosa, which, a fact which; *excl.* — catastrofe!, what a catastrophe! **-mente** *adv.* in what way, in what manner, in what form. **†-esso** *indef. prn., adj.* see **quale**.

qual·ificare [A 2 s] *tr.* to qualify, to define, to call, to describe, to designate; *rfl.* to describe oneself; si -ifica facoltoso possidente, he describes himself as a wealthy landowner. **-ifica-** *f.* qualification; title; attribute; name, designation. **-ifica·bile** *adj.* qualifiable; describable; l'edificio -ificabile come una casa di campagna, the building which might be described as a rustic dwelling; eligible. **-ificante** *part. adj.* qualifying; defining; describing. **-ificativo** *adj.* qualifying, attributive. **-ificato** *part. adj.* qualified; named, entitled; endowed; distinguished, excellent; (leg.) ladro -ificato, robber, (pop.) unmitigated thief; furto -ificato, larceny with aggravating circumstances, compound larceny, robbery (C.P.); una maggioranza -ificata, a qualified majority (C.C.). **-ificatore** *m.* qualifier; (eccl.) qualificator, qualifier; *adj.* qualifying. (**-ificatrice** *f.*) **-ificazione** *f.* qualification; attribute, title; definition.

qualit·à *f.* quality; merit, capacity; accomplishment; condition; social standing; kind, species; in — di, in the capacity of, as; — di membro, membership. **-ativo** *adj.* qualitative.

†qualo[1] *m.* basket.

†qualo[2] *indef. prn. m.* See **quale**.

qual·ora *adv., conj.* when, whenever; if; in case; — egli scriva, in case he should write. **-si·a, -si·asi, si·ansi, -sisi·a, -sisi·ano, -sivo·glia, †-sivo·gliano** *indef. adj.* whichever, whatever; any. **†-unche** *indef. adj.* see **qualunque**. **-unque** *indef. adj. indecl.* (always takes sing.; cf. **qualche**) any, any whatever; whatever; a -unque costo, no matter what the cost; l'uomo -unque, the man in the street; una persona -unque, an ordinary person. **†-uno** *indef. adj.* see **qualunque**. **-volta** *adv., conj.* whenever; at whatever time; ogni -volta, every time, whenever.

quamquam *m. indecl.* stare sul —, spacciare il —, arrecarsi sul —, to assume an air of importance.

quando *adv.* when; at the time that; da — la vidi, ever since I saw her; da — è tornato?, how long has he been back?; fino a — resterai qui?, how long will you stay here?; resterò fino a — l'avrò rivisto, I shall stay until I have seen him again; di — in —, now and then, from time to time; — l'uno e — l'altro, sometimes one and sometimes the other; — prima, as soon as; while, whereas; †if, if by chance; *interr.* at what time?, when?; *n.m.* the time when, the moment; il dove e il —, the where and the when, the place and the time.

quandochessi·a *adv.* some day.

†quand-unque, †-unche, †-unqua *adv.* See **quando**.

quanquan *m.* See **quamquam**.

quanti·metro *m.* (radiology) dosimeter.

quantit·à *f.* quantity, number, amount, sum; abundance; una grande —, a large quantity, a great deal; in —, abundantly; (electr.) accoppiamento in —, connexion in parallel. **-ativo** *adj.* quantitative; *n.m.* (comm.) amount; quantity; il -ativo disponibile, the amount available.

quantizzato *adj.* (phys.) quantized.

quant·o *adj. interr.* how much, how many; — è durato?, how long did it last?; — costa?, how much is it?; -i ne abbiamo oggi?, what is the date?; ogni -i giorni?, how often?; *indef. prn., adj.*

quant·o (*cont.*)
as much; è — dire, it is as much as to say, it is as good as saying; tutto —, the whole, the lot; -e teste, tanti pareri, *quot homines tot sententiae*, there are as many points of view as heads; — sopra, the above; questo modello è — di meglio si può trovare sul mercato, this model is the best you can find on the market; *excl.* —!, what a lot!; *indef. rel. prn.* all that which; what; — dirò in sèguito, what I shall proceed to say; *n.m.* amount; (phys.) quantum; *adv.* how; how much; — prima, as quickly as possible; tanto —, as best we can; nè tanto nè —, nothing at all; — a, as regards, concerning; in — a, in regard to; in — che, as regards, as far as; per —, as far as; per — so, as far as I know; per — si possa tentare, however much one may try. **†-ochè** *adv.* see **quantunque**. **†-ochessi·a** *adv.* as much as may be. **†-unche** *conj.* see **quantunque**. **-unque** *conj.* although; though.

quant-um *m.* (*pl.* -a) (phys.) quantum; teoria dei -a, quantum theory.

quarant-a *card. num. indecl.* forty; quarantadue, 42; quarantaquattro, 44, etc.; (provb.) da — in là, mi duol qui, mi duol qua, from forty onwards, I begin to be all aches and pains; libro del —, libro dei — fogli, a pack of cards; (eccl.) i — santi, the Forty Martyrs (of Sebaste); — volte, many many times. **-amila** *card. num. indecl.* forty thousand. **-amille·simo, -amillęsimo** *ord. num., adj., n.m.* forty-thousandths. **†-ana** *f.* space of forty days. **-ano** *adj.* (agric.) maturing in forty days. **-ena** *f.* quarantine; period of forty days; (fig.) mettere una notizia in -ena, to wait a while before believing a piece of news; number of forty; (eccl.) indulgence of forty days, quarantine; (eccl. hist.) fast of forty days. **-en·ne** *adj.* forty-year-old; lasting forty years; *n.m.* forty-year-old. **-en·nio** *m.* period of forty years. **-e·şimo, -ęşimo** *ord. num., adj., n.m.* fortieth; (bookb.) 40mo. **-i·a** *pr.n.f.* (Ital. hist.) bench of forty magistrates under the Venetian and Florentine republics. **†-igiato** *adj.* valid. **-ina** *f.* set of forty; about forty; age of forty years; †(eccl.) Lent; †(eccl.) indulgence of forty days. **-ino** *adj.* (agric.) maturing in forty days. **-ore** *f.pl.* (liturg.) Forty Hours' Devotion, Quarant'Ore. **-otte·şimo, -ottęşimo** *ord. num., adj., n.m.* forty-eighth; (bookb.) 48mo. **-otto** *card. num., indecl.* forty-eight; *pr.n.m.* Il Quarantotto, (Ital. hist.) the rising(s) of 1848, esp. that of Milan. **-une·şimo, unęşimo** *ord. num., adj., n.m.* forty-first. **-uno** *card. num.* forty-one.

quare *m.* (Lat.) wherefore, cause, reason; non sine —, not without reason.

quarenti·gia *f.* See **guarentigia**.

quaręşim-a *f.* (eccl.) Lent; (fig.) sembra la —, he looks half-starved. **-ale** *adj.* of Lent, Lent(en); *n.m.* series of Lent sermons; (fig.) any much-repeated series of remarks; *pl.* special sweetmeats eaten in Lent. **-alista** *m.* Lent preacher.

quarnal-ara *f.* see **quarnale**. **-e** *f.* (naut.) four-stranded rope; fourfold purchase on tackle; jib.

†Quarquo·nia *pr.n.f.* (hist.) house of correction in Florence.

quarr-a *f.* Sardinian measure of 25·2 litres. **†-o** *m.* measure of length corresponding to a span; measure of weight corresponding to a dram.

quart-a *f.* (math.) quadrant (of a circle); (astrol.) space comprising three signs of the zodiac; one of the thirty-two points or sections of the compass; quarter of the moon; (leg.) an heir's lawful share; (mens.) unit of area, formerly in use, equivalent in Rome to 46·21 acres; dry measure varying according to the unit of which it is the quarter: one 'quarta' is equivalent to 73·6 litres in Rome, 29·2 litres in Genoa, 20·8 litres in Venice, 13·2 litres in Naples, 12·1 litres in Brescia, 7·9 litres in Modena; (linear measurement) a quarter of an ell; (mus.) fourth (interval); (eccl.) — canonica, — funerale, bishop's or priest's share of pious bequest; (fencing) quarte; farla di —, to deceive, to trick, to obtain something by a ruse. **-ab(u)ono** *m.* (carpen.) quarter round; a -abuono, crosswise. **-ale** *m.* quarter of an actor's monthly salary, usually paid in advance. **-ana** *f.* (med.) quartan ague. **-ana·rio** *adj.* suffering from quartan ague; *n.m.* sufferer from quartan ague. **-anella** *f.* mild attack of quartan ague. **-anello** *m.* (text.) material one part wool and three parts linen. **-ano** *m.* (schol.) fourth class; un forte -ano, a good Fourth (form, class); schoolchild in the fourth class. **-ara** *f.* measure of quarter of a barrel in Apulia. **†-a·rio** *m.* see **quartara**. **-aro** *m.* oil or wine measure, formerly in use, roughly equiv. to 5 litres (Milan 5·3 litres, Cagliari 5·6 litres); (numism.) coin of Genoese republic. **-aro·lo** *m.* measure of

quart-a (*cont.*)

capacity: formerly in use, equivalent in Rome to 14·6 litres, and in Bologna to 19·65 litres; Genoese gold coin; Venetian bronze coin; see **quarteruolo**. **-ato** *adj.* sturdy; (herald.) quartered. **-a·volo** *m.* ancestor (great-grandfather's grandfather). †**-eggiare** *tr.* (herald.) to quarter. **-eri·a** *f.* (Tusc.) four-year rotation of crops. †**-erone** *m.* quarter of any measure; quarter of the moon. †**-eruola** *f.* measure corresponding to a quarter of a bushel. **-eruolo** *m.* counter for games; (naut. hist.) fourth man at the oar of a galley.

quartier-e *m.* quarter, region, district of a city; (Tusc.) self-contained apartment; quarters, lodgings; (mil.) quarters; — d'inverno, winter quarters; barracks; — generale, headquarters; (mil.) quarter; chieder —, to ask for quarter; dar — a, to give quarter to, to spare; (naut.) each of the three parts of a boat: fore, amidships, aft; — di poppa, aft; — di prora, fore; — di mezzania, amidships; cambiare il — di prora, to swing the fore-yards; far —, to open out the angle between two ropes, spars, etc.; vogare a —, to row with one section only of the oars in a galley; (naut.) hatch; — di boccaporto, hatchway covering; (herald.) quarter; shield, coat of arms; back part of a horse's hoof; paddock, enclosure; †shelter, accommodation; †tomb, sepulchre; †quarter section, portion. **-ato** *adj.* (naut.) having blunt ends (of a ship). **-ino** *m.* small flat. **-mastro** *m.* (mil. hist.) barrackmaster.

quartigliere *m.* (mil.) barracks staff; camp cleaner; (naut.) sweeper, messdeck sweeper; (in prison) 'trusty', a good-conduct prisoner given special duties.

quarti·glio *m.* (cards) the game of 'tressette' arranged for four players.

quartilag·gio *m.* (psych.) quartile rank method.

quart-o[1] *ord. num.* fourth; la -a arma, the 'fourth arm', the air force in Italy (Note: this is to be distinguished from 'the fourth arm' in the United Kingdom, which means Civil Defence); il — potere, the Press; il — stato, the proletariat (as distinct from the nobility, the clergy and the bourgeoisie); la -a sponda, the coast of Tripolitania; (gramm.) il — caso, the accusative (from an order formerly adopted in Latin grammars); *n.m.* quarter; (Naples) oil measure of 6 decilitres (16th staio); (Palermo) measurement of area, 17 centiares (16th mondello); un — di vino, a quarter-litre of wine; quarter-of-an-hour; è il suo — d'ora, it is his time (of good luck, etc.); passare un brutto — d'ora, to pass through a bad moment; il — d'ora di Rabelais, the time for paying (of one who has no money); quarters, apartment; (herald.) quartering; — franco, an ordinary occupying a square space at the dexter chief of the shield; ha tutti i -i della nobilità, he has all the quarterings of nobility (i.e. all the four grandparents are of noble family); (vet.) back part of the hoof; crack in the hoof; (astron.) la luna è al primo —, the moon is in the first quarter; (butchering) quarter; cadere in —, cadere di —, to move very slowly (usu. of a beast of burden); piece, part; segment of a wheel; (mus.) — fagotto, double curtall; un quartetto d'archi in -i di tono, a string quartet in the quarter tone system; (bookb.) in —, quarto. **-etto** *m.* (mus.) quartet (whether composition or ensemble of performers); -etto d'archi, -etto per archi, string quartet; -etto per fiati, wind quartet; -etto con pianoforte, piano quartet; -etto delle arpe, Harp Quartet (Beethoven's op. 74); four players at billiards, two against two; -etto fisso, game in which the partners remain the same; -etto giro, game in which partners are changed each time. **-icciuolo** *m.* check in a pattern. **-icello** *m. dim.* barely a quarter; about a quarter of an hour; joint of lamb. **-icino** *m. dim.* a brief quarter of an hour; quarter of an animal, esp. a lamb. **-icroma** *f.* (mus.) hemidemisemiquaver. **-ina** *f.* (prosod.) quatrain; quarto; (Tusc.) staking on four numbers at 'lotto'; †measure of grain, a quarter of a 'sacco', less than a bushel. **-ino** *m.* (mus.) a kind of small clarinet; small wine-bottle, a carafe holding a quarter of a litre; measure of volume, about three-tenths of a litre; (finan. hist.) -ino di una lira, 25 centesimi. **-irolo** *m.* a Lombard variety of cheese; (agric.) grass left in the fields in September for cattle to graze on after it has been cut for the third time. †**-izione** *f.* (astron.) division of the heavens into four. **-obuono** *m.* see **quartabuono**, under **quarta**. **-odecimani** *m.pl.* (eccl. hist.) Quartodecimans. †**-ode·cimo** *ord. num.* fourteenth. **-oge·nito** *adj., n.m.* fourth-born. **-otondo** *m.* (archit.) a -otondo, arched. **-uc·cio** *m.* (mens.) 64th part of a 'staio' or 8th part of a 'fiasco'; Neapolitan measure of eight-tenths of a litre; Roman dry measure of 3·3 litres, oil measure of 0·129 litre; Roman measure of area of 288·82 sq. metres; Venetian measure of seven-tenths of a litre. **-u·ltimo** *adj., n.m.* last but three; fourth (syllable) from the end.

Quarto *pr.n.f.* (geog.) Quarto (in Sardinia, or near Genoa).

quarz-o *m.* quartz; -ialino, rock crystal; — citrino, false topaz; — violetto, amethyst. **-i·fero** *adj.* quartziferous. **-ite** *f.* quartzite. **-oso** *adj.* quartzose, quartzy.

quas-i *adv.* almost, nearly; approximately, round about; — dissi, — che dissi, I almost said; senza —, certainly, definitely, no mistake about it; — —, very nearly, 'for two pins'; — ci vado io, I've half a mind to go myself; (leg.) — contratto, quasi-contract; — che, nearly, almost. **-ichè** *conj.* as if. **-imente** *adv.* (Tusc.) very nearly; in the same way. **-imodo** *m.* (eccl.) Low Sunday, First Sunday after Easter.

quas-ia *f.* (bot.) quassia (wood), *Picraena excelsa*. **-ina** *f.* (chem.) quassin, quassite.

quas-sù *adv.* up here. †**-suso** *adv.* see **quassù**.

quatern-a *f.* set of four numbers; staking four numbers in the public lottery or in playing tombola; a win of four numbers; azzeccare una — al lotto, to win by backing four numbers on the 'lotto'. **-a·rio** *adj.* (geol.) Quaternary; (prosod.) quatrain, line of four syllables. **-ioni** *m.pl.* (math.) quarternions. **-ità** *f.* (theol.) quaternity; an aggregate of four.

quatr-iduano *adj.* four days old; morto —, having been dead four days. **-i·fido** *adj.* divided into four.

quatt-o *adj.* crouched, huddled up; squatting; cowering; — —, quiet as a mouse; *adv.* very softly, very quietly. (**-amente** *adv.*) **-ono**, **-oni** *adv.* crouching, cowering, squatting.

†**quattorde·cimo** *ord. num.* See **quattordicesimo**.

quattor-dic-i *card. num.* fourteen; †fourteenth. **-enne** *adj., n.m., f.* fourteen-year-old. **-e·simo**, **-e·simo** *ord. num.* fourteenth.

†**quattricroma** *f.* (mus.). See **quarticroma**, under **quarto**.

quattrin-o *m.* (numism.) the sixtieth part of a Tuscan lira, so called because equal to four 'denari' or 'piccioli'; the fourth part of a Neapolitan 'grano'; (fig.) a very small sum, a farthing; non vale un —, it is not worth a farthing; tirare al —, to be miserly; *pl.* (colloq.) money, dibs; far -i, to make money; fior di -i, bags of money. **-a** *f.* (bot.) herba quattrina, creeping Jenny, *Lysimachia nummularia*. **-a·io** *adj.* money-grabbing; *n.m.* money-grabber. **-a·ria** *f.* (bot.) see **quattrina**. **-ata** *f.* (Tusc.) farthing's worth; (fig.) row, quarrel; volerne una -ata da uno, to have a row with someone. **-ella** *f.* (bot.) see **quattrina**. **-ello** *m.* tiny sum, mite.

quattr-o *card. num.* four; dimostrare come — e — fanno otto, to explain the obvious, to demonstrate that 'two and two make four'; in — e quattr'otto, in a moment, in the twinkling of an eye; camminare per —, to march four abreast; farsi in — per, to do one's utmost to (for); (of a horse) fermarsi in —, to stop short; tra — mura, within four walls, privately; a — occhi, face to face, *tête-à-tête*; portar in —, to carry out feet first; fare il diavolo a —, to make the devil's own row; non dir — se non l'hai nel sacco, don't count your chickens before they are hatched; a few; dirgliene —, to tell a person a thing or two; — passi, a little stroll; mangiar — fave, to eat a few mouthfuls; sono — gatti a volerlo, very few people want it, only a minority believe in it; (mus.) a —, in four parts, for four voices; a — mani, for four hands, for pianoforte duet; (mil.) marciare per —, to march in fours; (rowing) — con, coxed four; — senza, coxswainless; (cards) — senza, four no-trumps; il giuoco dei — cantoni, a game resembling rounders. **-occhi** *m. indecl.* (orn.) goldeneye, *Bucephala clangula*; (ichth.) *Raia miraletus*, a kind of skate; (fam.) four-eyes, person wearing spectacles. **-ocentesco** *adj.* (*m.pl.* **-ocenteschi**) relating to the fifteenth century; (art) characteristic of fifteenth-century style. **-ocente·simo**, **-ocentesimo** *ord. num.* four-hundredth. **-ocentista** *m.* writer or artist of the fifteenth century; scholar whose field of expertise is some aspect of Italian life and culture in the fifteenth century. **-ocento** *card. num.* four hundred; (mil.) -ocento venti, gun (420 mm.), largest gun used in 1914–18 war; *n.m.* fifteenth century. **-ocromi·a** *f.* (typ.) four-colour printing. **-ofo·glie** (herald.) quatrefoil. **-omila** *card. num.* four thousand. **-opiedi** *m. indecl.* (zool.) see **quadrupede**. **-otem·pora** *f.pl.* (eccl.) Ember days.

quell-o *demons. adj.* (*m.pl.* **quei**, **quegli**; abbrev. in *m. sing.* to **quel** before an ordinary consonant; cf. rules governing the *def. art.*)

quell·o (*cont.*)

that; quel giorno, that day; quell'uomo, that man; -a lampada, that lamp (over there); o quel ragazzo!, oh that boy!; *indef. prn. m.* that man, that person; — lì, that man over there; — con gli occhiali, the man wearing glasses; — dell'automobile, the man who keeps talking about his car; è uno di -i, he is one of them; non sono più —, I am not the man I was; that, that thing; per — che ne so io, as far as I know about it; — che ti dissi, what I told you; quel che più mi piace, what I like best; — è vino!, that is something like wine!; sarà —, as you say. -a *indef. prn. f.* that woman; that thing; ne dice di -e!, he says such things!, the things he says!; hour, moment; in -a che, at the moment when.

quer·c·ia *f.* (bot.) oak, *Quercus*; (provb.) al primo colpo non cade la —, Rome was not built in a day; far —. to stand on one's head. -**eta** *f.* grove of oaks. -**e·tico** *adj.* (chem.) quercetic. -**etina** *f.* (chem.) quercetin. -**eto** *m.* grove of oaks. -**ino** *adj.* oaken, oak. -**iola** *f.* (bot.) wall germander, *Teucrium chamaedrys.* -**ioso** *adj.* abounding in oaks. -**ite** *f.* (chem.) quercite. -**itrina** *f.* quercitrin. -**itrone** *m.* (bot.) quercitron (bark), *Quercus tinctoria.* -**iuola** *f. dim.* of quercia; oak billet for burning, oak log; far -iuola, to stand on one's head. -**iuolo** *m.* see querciuola.

querel·a *f.* (poet.) complaint, lament; (leg.) Information (instituting criminal prosecution); criminal charge; summons; plaint; dare, proporre — a, to lay an information against, to summons; diritto di —, right to institute criminal proceedings, right of prosecution by Information; a — della persona offesa, upon Information laid by the injured party (C.P.) (cf. **procedimento**); — di falso, summons (in civil proceedings) challenging deed or public document relied on by other side (C.C.P.); contro —, counter-charge. -**ante** *m., f.* (leg.) plaintiff; Informant. -**antomani·a** *f.* mania for complaining. -**are** [A I] *tr.* (leg.) to lay an Information against, to summons; *rfl.* to complain; to lament; to wail bitterly; (leg.) to institute criminal proceedings (C.P.). -**ato** *part. adj.* (leg.) accused (in Information); *n.m.* defendant to prosecution instituted by Information. -**atore** *m.* (leg.) Informant; applicant. (-**atrice** *f.*) †-**ato·rio** *m.* complaint; *adj.* inquiring; questioning; *n.m.* inquirer, questioner.

querimo·nia *f.* complaint; lament; †whining, howling (of animals).

que·rul·o *adj.* querulous; complaining; peevish; mournful. †-**oso** *adj.* complaining; sorrowful, mournful, expressing complaint.

†**quesire** *tr.* to ask, to request.

quesito *adj.* un ragionamento —, a far-fetched argument; (leg.) un diritto —, an acquired right; *n.m.* problem, query, inquiry, question; porre un — per iscritto, to put a written question; *n.m.* †supplication, entreaty.

questi *pers. prn. m. sing.* he; this person, this man; the latter (cf. **questo**).

question·e *f.* question; la — trattata, the point under discussion; giungere alla — di fondo, to come to the substance of the matter; porre una — pregiudiziale, to raise a question which must be answered before the matter can be pursued further; (leg.) question; issue; dispute; inquiry; inquisition; quest; — principale, the main issue; — di diritto, question of law; — di competenza, question of jurisdiction (C.C.P.); — incidentale, interlocutory question; — pregiudiziale, pre-judicial question, question (e.g. of jurisdiction or practice) requiring determination before trial; exception; — preliminare, preliminary question (C.P.P.); — processuale, question of procedure; — di rito, point of practice; †interrogation under torture; †conflict, dispute. -**a·bile** *adj.* questionable. †-**ale** *adj.* subject to question. -**amento** *m.* questioning. -**are** [A I c] *intr.* (aux.) avere) to quarrel, to dispute, to argue; -are con, to dispute with; to raise a question; *tr.* (leg.) to question; to impugn. -**a·rio** *m.* questionnaire. -**ato** *part. adj.* questioned. -**atore** *m.* questioner; one who raises a question; disputant. (-**atrice** *f.*) -**cella**, -**cina** *f. dim.* minor question. -**eggiare** [A 3 c] *intr.* (aux.) avere) to keep raising questions. †-**e·vole** *adj.* see **questionabile**.

quest·o *demons. adj.* this; l'ho visto con -i occhi, I saw it with my own eyes; -e vostre pretese, these claims of yours; *indef. prn. m.* this man, this person; — qui, this man here; this thing; ti dirò solo —, I shall only say this to you; o — sì!, yes, that is true!; con —, con tutto —, despite all this; per —, for this reason. -**a** *f. indef. prn.* this woman; this girl; this thing; -a non me l'aspettavo, I didn't expect this; sentite -a!, listen to this!; oh -a è bella!, that's a good one!; this hour, this moment.

quest·ore *m.* (Rom. antiq.) quaestor; (leg.) police-superintendent, the Chief of Police in a province. NOTE: this corresponds to a far higher office in Italy than a police-superintendent in England. It is roughly equivalent to the Chief Constable of a county. -**o·rio** *adj.* (*m.pl.* -**orii**) pertaining to a quaestor; uomo -orio, Chief of Police (of Rome).

que·st·ua *f.* house-to-house collection or begging for alms, esp. for pious purposes; special collection in church. -**uante** *adj.*, *n.m.* (person) begging, esp. friar. -**uare** [A 6] *intr.* (aux.) avere) to go begging, to make a collection.

questur·a *f.* police station; police headquarters. -**ino** *m.* plain-clothes police officer, policeman.

queto *adj.* See **quieto**.

qui *adv.* here; in these parts, in this region; — presso, close by; — sopra, up here; — sotto, down here; fin —, up to here; in this spot; — mi fa male, I feel a pain here; (fig.) di —, whence; di — nasce, from this there arises; at this moment, at this point of time; di — a poco, in a short while from now; (comm.) — contra, *per contra*; herewith; — unito, enclosed herewith.

quia *m.* classical Latin for 'because', later Latin for 'that', used in Italian as *n.m.* to mean 'the reason why', 'the why and the wherefore'; stare contenti al —, (cf. Dante, *Purg.* III) be content with what one can understand; venire al —, to come to the point.

quibus *m. indecl.* See **conquibus**.

†**quic·i** *adv.* see **qui**. †-**entro** *adv.* in here. †-**iritta** *adv.* see **quiritta**.

†**quicumque** *m.* dare il — a, to give preference to, to give priority to.

quid *prn.* (Lat.) what; un certo —, a certain something, a *je ne sais quoi.*

quidam *prn.* (Lat.) a certain, some; un —, some person or other.

quidde *prn.* (Flor.). See **quid**.

quiddit·à *f.* essence, basic nature; (philos.) quiddity. -**ativo** *adj.* essential, fundamental.

quidem *adv.* (Lat.) certainly; bene —, all right, by all means.

quidern·o *m.* (pop.) see **quinterno**, under **quinto**. -**atore** *m.* workman who folds 'quinterni'.

quidità *f.* See **quiddità**.

quiescen·te *adj.* quiescent. -**za** *f.* quiescence, state of repose; (leg.) retirement; fondi di anzianità e di -za, superannuation and retirement funds (C.C.); dormant state; -za del diritto, dormancy of right.

†**quie·scere** *intr.* to be quiescent; to repose, to rest; *rfl.* to become tranquil.

†**quieta** *f.* See **quiete**.

quiet·are [A I] *tr.* to quiet, to still, to hush, to quieten; to soothe; †to satisfy, to appease; *rfl.* to be quietened; to calm down; to become tranquil; to be soothed; *intr.* (aux.) essere) to be quiet; to lie still. -**amento** *m.* quietening; soothing. -**anza** *f.* (comm.) receipt; discharge; release; quittance; -anza del titolo, stock receipt; contro -anza, against receipt. -**anzare** [A I] *tr.* to receipt. -**anzato** *part. adj.* receipted. -**anzatrice** *f.* receipting machine. †-**ativo** *adj.* calming, soothing. †-**azione** *f.* quiet; receipt.

quiete *f.* quiet; state of rest, repose; quietude, quietness; calm, stillness; respite.

quiet·o *adj.* quiet, still, tranquil; calm, peaceful; (fig.) acqua -a, still waters. (-**amente** *adv.*) -**ismo** *m.* (eccl. hist.) Quietism. -**ista** *m.* (eccl. hist.) Quietist. †-**itu·dine** *f.* see **quietudine**. -**one** *m.* person who pretends to be quiet; 'dark horse'. (-**ona** *f.*) -**u·dine** *f.* quietude, tranquillity.

qui·l·io *m.* (mus.) falsetto, high-pitched voice. -**iare** [A 4] *intr.* (aux.) avere) (mus.) to sing falsetto, to squeak.

quilisma *f.* (mus.) quilisma (plain-chant ornament).

quilla·ia *f.* (bot.) soap tree of Chile, *Quillaja saponaria.*

quina·rio *adj.* quinary; *n.m.* set of five; (prosod.) (line) of five syllables; (numism.) half of a Roman *denarius.*

†**quin·amonte** *adv.* far and away; over the hills and far away. †-**avalle** *adv.* way down below; over many a dale.

quinc·i *adv.* hence; parlare in — e quindi, to talk pedantically.

quinc·once *f.* quincunx; *adj.* (techn.) staggered. -**onciale** *adj.* quincuncial.

†**quindavalle** *adv.* way down below.

quindec·a·gono *m.* (geom.) quindecagon, fifteen-sided figure. -**emvirale** *adj.* pertaining to a quindecemvir. -**emvirato** *m.* office of quindecemvir. -**em·viro** *m.* (hist.) quindecemvir.

quinde·cimo *ord. num.* fifteenth.

quind-ena *f.* (eccl.) fortnight; — pasquale, period from Palm Sunday to Low Sunday. †**-en·nio** *m.* period of 15 years; (eccl.) *quindennium* (tax).

quindi *adv.* hence, from here; therefore, consequently.

quin·dic-i *card. num.* fifteen; oggi a —, fra — giorni, in a fortnight's time; — giorni, fortnight. **-ennale** *adj.* recurring every fifteen years; lasting fifteen years. **-enne** *adj., n.m., f.* fifteen-year-old. **-e·simo**, **-ęsimo** *ord. num.* fifteenth. **-imila** *card. num.* fifteen thousand. **-ina** *f.* set of fifteen; about fifteen; fortnight; fortnight's pay. **-inale** *adj.* pertaining to fifteen; fortnightly. **-ino** *m.* (numism.) Milanese bronze coin.

†**quindioltre** *adv.* nearby, near there.

†**quin-e** *adv.* there. †**-oltre** *adv.* nearby; near there.

†**quingente·simo** *ord. num.* See **quindicesimo**.

†**quinquage·cuplo** *adj.* fiftyfold.

quinquag-ena·rio *adj.* fifty years old; *n.m.* fifty-year-old; jubilee. **-e·sima**, **-ęsima** *f.* (eccl.) Quinquagesima (Sunday); †Whit Sunday, Pentecost. **-e·simo**, **-ęsimo** *ord. num.* fiftieth.

quinqu-an·golo *m.* pentagon, quinquangle. **-elustre** *adj.* recurring every 25 years; lasting 25 years. **-emestre** *adj.* of five months; parto -emestre, five months' birth. **-ennale** *adj.* five-yearly; piano -ennale, five-year plan. **-ennalità** *f.* period of five years, five-year term. **-enne** *adj., n.m., f.* five-year-old. **-en·nio** *m.* lustre, five-year period. **-eręme** *adj., m., f.* quinquereme. **-e·rzio** *m.* (antiq.) Pentathlon. **-esil·labo** *adj.* (prosod.) pentasyllabic. **-ilięne** *m.* quintillion.

quintale *m.* quintal, a hundred kilogrammes; †a hundredweight.

quintino[1] *m.* See under **quinto**.

Quintino[2] *pr.n.m.* Quentin; (provb.) esser peggio di San — che sonava a messa coi tegoli, to be worse off than St Quentin who was reduced to ringing for Mass with tiles.

quint-o *ord. num.* fifth; al — grado, in the highest degree; (provb.) essere la -a ruota del carro, to be the fifth wheel of the wagon, i.e. to be unimportant or superfluous; (joc.) abitare al — piano, to be almost deaf; *n.m.* (leg.) cessione del —, an assignment of a fifth of a debtor's wages or salary towards settlement of debt; (naut.) frame; cant timber; †fifth of a litre. **-a** *f.* (mus.) fifth (interval); **-e parallele**, consecutive fifths; falsa -a, diminished fifth, false fifth; *pl.* (theatr.) flies; wings; (fig.) dietro le -e, behind the scenes; fifth class (in school); (cinem.) aperture a -a, side curtain, fade-in. **-ade·cima** *f.* (astron.) fifteenth day after the new moon; luna in -adecima, full moon; (mus.) fifteenth (interval and organ-stop). †**-amente** *adv.* fifthly, in the fifth place. **-ana** *f.* tilting post, quintain; child's game of aiming at a melon or pomegranate; (herald.) quintain; (med.) quintan ague. **-ano** *m.* (mil.) section leader, having five men under him. **-arolo** *m.* fifth oarsman. **-a·volo** *m.* great-grandfather's great-grandfather. **-ello** *m.* (hist.) Venetian tax of five per cent on inherited property. **-eri·a** *f.* (agric.) five-course system of rotation. **-erna·rio** *adj., n.m.* see **quinario**. **-erno** *m.* quire; copy-book, strictly one made from folding five sheets of paper; (bookb.) quinternion. **-essenza** *f.* quintessence; sapere la -essenza, to know all about a thing. **-ętto** *m.* (mus.) quintet (whether composition or ensemble of performers); -etto con clarino, clarinet quintet. **-ile** *m.* (hist.) July, Quintilis; (astron.) quintile, quintile aspect. **-i·lio** *m.* (cards) a form of 'tressette' for five players. **-ilięne** *m.* quinquillion (cf. Note under **quadrilione**). **-ina** *f.* (at 'lotto') winning on five numbers. **-ino** *m.* fifth of a litre. **-ode·cimo** *ord. num.* fifteenth. **-oge·nito** *adj., n.m.* fifth-born. **-u·ltimo** *adj., n.m.* last but four. **-uplicare** [A2s] *tr.* to multiply by five. **-uplicato** *part. adj.* fivefold; multiplied by five. **-uplicatamęnte** *adv.* five times as much. **-u·plice** *adj.* fivefold.

qui·ntuplo *adj.* fivefold; *n.m.* quintuple.

Quir-ino *pr.n.m.* (myth.) Quirinus, Romulus. **-inale** *adj.* of Quirinus; *n.m.* Quirinal, one of the seven hills of Rome; the former Royal, now Presidential, palace at Rome; the former Italian Royal Court, nowadays the residence and offices of the President of the Italian Republic. **-iti** *m.pl.* (hist.) the citizens of Rome (i.e. those who had full Roman citizenship).

†**quiritt-a** *adv.* here precisely, just here. †**-o** *adv.* here.

quiscalo *m.* (orn.) grackle, *Quiscalus*.

quisqui·(g)lia *f.* trifles, scraps; small fry.

quissi·mile *something of the sort.

quistionare [A1c] and derivs. See **questionare**, under **questione**.

---

quistione *f.* See **questione**.

quitare [A1] and derivs. See **quietare**.

quivi *adv.* there; here; then.

†**quo·c-ere** *tr.* see **cuocere**. †**-o** *m.* see **cuoco**.

quodlibet *m. indecl.* (mus.) quodlibet.

†**quo·glio**, †**quo·io** *m.* See **cuoio**.

quondam *adj. indecl.* (Lat.) late, deceased; former, quondam.

†**quore** *m.* See **cuore**.

quorum *m. indecl.* quorum; il — è raggiunto, there is a quorum; verificare il —, to ascertain that there is a quorum.

quot-a *f.* (leg.) aliquot share; quota; portion; proportion; — in proporzione, pro rata; — sociale, member's share in company or partnership; — di conferimento, contributory share of company or partnership capital (C.C.); patto di — lite, champertous bargain between solicitor and client (C.C.); altitude, height; height above sea-level; (in maps) — 85, Hill 85; height; (aeron.) — di volo, flying height; acquistare —, to gain height; perdere —, to lose height; — di navigazione, cruising altitude; odds (in betting). **-are** [A1] *tr.* (comm.) to quote; to estimate. **-ali·zio** *adj.* quotatious. **-ato** *part. adj.* (comm.) quoted; (eng.) dimensioned (of a drawing); (industr.) efficient (of a worker); (fig.) talked of, mentioned; è molto -ato, he has a big reputation; un autore molto -ato, a well-known author. **-azione** *f.* (comm.; finan.) quotation; -azione di borsa, Stock Exchange price.

quotidian-o *adj.* daily; everyday; *n.m.* daily (newspaper). **-amęnte** *adv.* daily, everyday. **-eggiare** [A3c] *intr.* (aux. avere) to recur each day (of a fever).

quotizz-are [A1] *tr.* (comm.) to assess. (**-ato** *part. adj.*) **-azione** *f.* (comm.) assessment.

quoto *m.* quotient.

quou·sque *interr.* (Lat.) how long?; until when?

quoziente *m.* (math.) quotient; ratio; (soccer) quoziente reti, goal average; (pol.) quota; — elettorale, electoral quotient.

---

r *m., f.* (pron. **erre**) the letter R; the consonant R; gli manca l'—, he has a lisp; (fig.) perdere l'—, to become confused, to get fuddled.

rabagà *m. indecl.* political turncoat (from the name Rabagas, title-role of a comedy by V. Sardou (1872)).

rabar·baro *m.* rhubarb, *Rheum*; liqueur made from rhubarb.

rabattino *m.* (colloq., Tusc.) one who works hard and schemes to make money; 'trier', hard worker; toiler; *adj.* (usu. derog.) money-grubbing; industrious; hard-working.

rabballinare [A1] *tr.* to bundle together, to roll up, to make into a bundle.

rab-baruffare [A1] and derivs. see **abbaruffare**. **-bassare** [A1] and derivs. see **riabbassare**.

rabbat·tere [B1] *tr.* to push to (e.g. a door, window), to half-close, to set ajar; to leave ajar.

rabbatuffolare [A1s] and derivs. See **abbatuffolare**.

ra(b)bazza *f.* (naut.) housing of a topmast, heel of a topmast; portion between spectacle plates, square portion of a pole.

rabbellire [D2] *tr.* to beautify; to embellish (anew); to furbish up; *rfl.* to adorn oneself (cf. **abbellire**).

rabberci-are [A3] *tr.* to patch, to botch; to mend; (fig., colloq.) to patch up; -arla alla meglio, to make the best of a bad job. **-amęnto** *m.* patching; botching; mending. **-ato** *part. adj.* patched; botched; mended. (**-atore** *m.* **-atrice** *f.*) **-atura** *f.* patch; patching.

rabbi *m. indecl.* (Jewish rel.) Rabbi, Master; (fig., derog.) fare l'ave —, to be insincerely respectful (from the greeting of Judas to Christ at the moment of betrayal).

rab-bi-a *f.* (vet.) rabies, hydrophobia; (fig.) rage, anger; non ne posso più dalla —, I am beside myself with rage; gli fa — di dover aspettare, it makes him furious to be kept waiting; che —!, how maddening!; unreasoning, overmastering desire; frenzy; consuming passion; envy; (poet.) la — dei venti, the fury of the winds; †di —, nothing, signifying nothing; †non saperne di —, to know nothing about it.

rabbi·nico *adj.* rabbinical; studi rabbinici, rabbinics.

rabbin-o *m.* Rabbi, master of Hebrew law; il Gran Rabbino, the Chief Rabbi. **-eggiare** [A3c] *intr.* (aux. avere) to teach as a Rabbi, to interpret the scriptures. **-ișmo** *m.* Rabbinism. **-ista** *m.* Rabbinist, one who expounds the scriptures.

rabbiọs-o *adj.* (vet.) rabid, affected with rabies, mad; (fig.) furious; irascible, hot-tempered, choleric; mare —, raging sea; †excessive, violent, raging. **-a** *f.* (slang) rough brandy. **-amẹnte** *adv.* in a fury, in a fit of rage; furiously; madly.

rabbocc-are [A 2 c] *tr.* to fill up, to fill to the brim; to refill; (bldg.) to grout, to point. (**-ato** *part. adj.*) **-atura** *f.* filling to the brim; (bldg.; masonry) pointing.

rabbonacciare [A 3 c] *intr.* (*aux.* essere) (naut.) to set fair again; *rfl.* (of a person) to cease to be angry, to calm down; *tr.* to make calm or serene again.

rabbon-ire [D 2] *tr.* to pacify, to appease; to calm; *intr.* (*aux.* essere), *rfl.* to be pacified; to be quietened; to calm down; il tempo -isce, the weather is improving, the storm is passing. (**-ito** *part. adj.*)

rabbottonare [A 1 c] *tr.* to button (up) again.

†rabbrenciare *tr.* to restore, to repair.

rabbrevi-are [A 4] *tr.* to shorten again. (**-ato** *part. adj.*)

rabbriccic-are [A 2 s] *tr.* (colloq., Tusc.) to patch, to botch; *recip. rfl.* to patch it up. (**-ato** *part. adj.*)

rabbrivid-ire [D 2] *intr.* (*aux.* essere, avere) to shiver; — di freddo, to shiver with cold; (fig.) to shudder, to be horrified. **-ito** *adj.* shivering; -ito dal freddo, shivering with the cold.

rabbrunare [A 1] and derivs. See **abbrunare**.

rabbrusc-are [A 2] *intr.* (*aux.* essere), *rfl.* (of the sky) to become overcast; to darken; (of weather) to grow threatening; (of persons) to become gloomy; to become morose. (**-amẹnto** *m.* **-ato** *part. adj.*)

rabbruscolare [A 1 s] *tr.* to save up little by little; to put by.

†rabbruzz-are, †-olare *intr.*, *rfl.* to grow dark (of evening twilight).

rabbuff-are [A 1] *tr.* to rumple, to ruffle; to disorder, to disarrange; (fig.) to rebuke, to reprove, to reprimand; *rfl.* to become ruffled; (of weather) to grow stormy; (of the sea) to become rough. (**-amẹnto** *m.* **-ato** *part. adj.*) **-o** *m.* rebuke, reproof, reprimand; †calamity, misfortune, setback.

rabbui-are [A 4] *rfl.*, *intr.* (*aux.* essere) to grow dark; to become cloudy; to become overcast; (fig., of person) to become gloomy, sad; to grow sad again. to resume one's feeling of dejection; -arsi in volto, to take on a dejected or gloomy expression, *or* to glower. (**-ato** *part. adj.* (of the sky) dark; cloudy; (of person) gloomy; sad; glowering.

rabdar *m. indecl.* (Goldoni) police officer in Persia.

rabdoceli *m.pl.* (zool.) Rhabdocoela, Turbellarian worms.

rabdol-ogi-a *f.* rhabdology. **-o·gico** *adj.* rhabdological.

rabdom-ante *m.* dowser, water-diviner; rhabdomancer. **-an·tico** *adj.* rhabdomantic, relating to dowsing. **-anzi·a** *f.* dowsing, water-divining; rhabdomancy.

rabeleṣiano *adj.* Rabelaisian, characteristic of, or relating to, Rabelais.

rabẹs-co *m.* (*pl.* **-chi**) arabesque; scribble; hieroglyph. **-came** *m.* pattern of arabesques. **-care** [A 2] *tr.* to adorn with arabesques; (derog.) to doodle, to scribble, on. (**-cato** *part. adj.* **-catura** *f.*)

rabican-o *m.* black or bay horse flecked with white hairs; *pr.n.m.* name of Astolfo's horse in Ariosto's *Orlando Furioso*. **-ato** *adj.* (of a horse) having a black or bay coat flecked with white hairs.

ra·bid-o *adj.* rabid; (fig.) furious, raging, mad. **-amẹnte** *adv.* (fig.) furiously, madly.

rabino *m.* and derivs. See **rabbino**.

rabọso *m.* name of a red wine from Treviso.

ra·bula *m.* disreputable, bullying or pettifogging lawyer; legal quack.

raca *excl.* used only in the phrase: dir — a qualcuno, to insult someone (see *N.T.*, Matthew v, 22).

racanella *f.* (dial. Siena). See **raganella**.

raccapezz-are [A 1] *tr.* to find; to collect, to put together; to earn; *intr.* (*aux.* avere, with *adv.* ci) (fig.) to take in, to grasp, to understand; non ci -o proprio nulla, I don't understand it at all, I can't make head or tail of it; *rfl.* to find one's way; to understand, to make (it) out; non mi ci -o, I can't make head or tail of it. (**-ato** *part. adj.*)

rac-capigliare [A 4] and derivs. see **accapigliare**. **-cappellare** [A 1] and derivs. see **rincappellare**.

raccapricci-are [A 4] *intr.* (*aux.* essere, avere), *rfl.* to be horrified; gli spettatori -arono a quella vista, the audience were horrified at the sight; to feel one's hair stand on end; to shudder; to be shocked, to be disgusted; cose da far —, horrifying, blood-curdling things; (poet.) il vento fa — l'acqua, the wind ruffles the surface of the water. (**-amẹnto** *m.*) **-ante** *part. adj.* horrifying, blood-curdling. †**-e·vole** *adj.* see **raccapricciante**.

raccapric·ci-o *m.* horror, terror; disgust. †**-ore** *m.* see **raccapriccio**.

raccappriccire [D 2] and derivs. (Tusc.). See **raccappriciare**.

raccartocciare [A 3] *tr.* to wrap up; to curl up, to twist into a cone; *rfl.* to curl oneself (itself) up (cf. **accartocciare**).

raccatt-are [A 1] *tr.* to pick up (from the ground); to gather; — una maglia, to pick up a stitch; (fig.) to collect (phrases, gossip, scandal); to obtain; — tempo perduto, to make up for lost time; l'ho -ato per via, I met him in the street; (fam.) era da -arsi col cucchiaio, he was shattered. **-ace·nere** *m. indecl.* ash-tray; ash-pan. **-afieno** *m.* hay-raker (mechanical), horse-rake. (**-amẹnto** *m.*) **-apalle** *m. indecl.* (sport) ball-boy. **-atic·cio** *m. pejor.* rubbish, odds and ends, unconsidered trifles. (**-atore** *m.* **-atrice** *f.*) **-atura** *f.* (Tusc.; pop.) gathering, collecting, harvesting (esp. of fruit or nuts from the ground).

raccenciare [A 3] *tr.* to mend; to patch; to darn; *rfl.* to wear better clothes, to get out of one's old rags, to put on a better appearance; (fig.) to begin to prosper; to improve one's position.

raccen·dere [C 1] and derivs. (poet.). See **riaccendere**.

†raccennare *intr.* to signal again; to signal, to make signs (cf. **accennare**).

raccertare [A 1] *tr.* to ascertain; to confirm; *rfl.* to make sure; to confirm one's opinions; to reassure oneself (cf. **accertare**).

racchetare [A 1] *tr.* to pacify; to console; *rfl.* to be consoled, to cease to weep (cf. **acchetare**).

racchẹtt-a *f.* racket, racquet; — da neve, snow-shoe; (watchm.) regulator; (motor.) blade (of windscreen wiper). **-eri·a** *f.* (watchm.) regulating device; (mil.) Very rocket, flare. **-iere** *m.* (mil.) rocket gunner; (naut.) rocket-ship.

rac·chi-a *f.* (slang) plain woman; ugly woman; hag. **-ọna** *f. augm.* very ugly woman.

rac·chio *m.* (Tusc.) small, dried-up bunch of grapes left on the vine.

racchiocciolare [A 1 sc] *rfl.* to huddle, to crouch (cf. **acchiocciolare**).

racchiu·d-ere [C 3] *tr.* to enclose; to hold, to contain; la biblioteca -e molti tesori, the library contains many treasures; to include; to imply; questione che ne -e altre, a question which raises others; to shut up (e.g. a house); †to impede, to obstruct.

racciabattare [A 1] *intens.* of **acciabattare**, q.v.

racciarpare [A 1] *intens.* of **acciarpare**, q.v.

racco·gli-ere [B 7] *tr.* to collect, to gather; to pick up; to assemble; — notizie, to gather news; dobbiamo — insieme tutti i ragazzi, we must get all the boys together; — francobolli, to collect stamps; to harvest, to gather; to reap; (provb.) chi semina vento -e tempesta, sow the wind and reap the whirlwind; — le idee, to collect one's thoughts; — la sfida, to take up the gauntlet, to accept the challenge; — il parto, to act as midwife; to receive, to shelter; un ospizio che -e l'infanzia abbandonata, a foundling hospital; to receive, to obtain; la proposta raccolse pochissimi voti, the proposal obtained very few votes; to perceive, to take note of; — l'allusione, to recognize the quotation or reference; (naut.) — le vele, to take in sail; — le reti, to haul nets; — delle bandiere, to haul down flags without stowing; — della gala, to prepare a hoist of flags ready to do up; †— al vento, to bring (a ship) up into the wind; †see **serrare**; *rfl.* to gather together, to assemble; to settle down; to collect one's thoughts, to reflect; (of clouds) to gather, to collect; †(naut.) -ersi a terra, to land. **-cẹra** *f.* candle-holder, socket of a candlestick. †**-enza** *f.* see **accoglienza**, under **accogliere**. **-fochi** *m. indecl.* (paperm.) lay-boy. **-mẹnto** *m.* concentrated attention, absorption; pregare con -mento, to be absorbed in prayer; †welcome, reception. **-pọlvere** *m. indecl.* (industr.) dust-collector. **-tic·cio** *adj.* picked up here and there, gathered haphazard; *n.m.* haphazard collection. **-tọre** *m.* gatherer; collector; compiler; card-index; file, loose-leaf binder; rack, filing cabinet; accoucheur. **-trice** *f.* woman gatherer, collector, or compiler; (techn.) -itrice del cotone, mechanical cotton picker.

raccolt-a *f.* gathering, collecting; collection; harvest, crop; quantity, head (of water); mulino che macina a —, mill that works when there is a good head, or flow, of water; rally; chiamare a — il proprio partito, to rally one's party; chiamare a — le proprie energie, to rally one's energies; (leg.) — ufficiale di usi, officially published collection of customary usages (C.C.); (mil.) rally; sonare a —, to sound the rally; (derog.) group. **-ina** *f. dim.* -ina di poesie, little collection of poems.

raccolt-o *part.* of **raccogliere**, q.v.; *adj.* collected, assembled, gathered together, harvested; absorbed; meditative, thoughtful; concentrated; (of things) not large or sprawling, compact; slender, slim;

raccolt-o (*cont.*)

gambe -e, legs drawn up; (of houses, streets, etc.) quiet and convenient; dittongo —, true diphthong, i.e. counting as one vowel; *n.m.* harvest, crop. **-aménte** *adv.* meditatively, thoughtful; with concentration. **-ino** *adj. dim.* compact; casa -ina, cosy little house.

raccomand-are [A I] *tr.* to recommend (e.g. one person to another); to hand over (for safe keeping, protection or care); to secure, to make fast; (rel.) — l'anima a Dio, to recommend, to commend, one's soul (or another's soul) to God; (fig.) può — l'anima, he had better say his prayers, he is in a bad way; — una lettera, to register a letter; to inculcate, to insist upon; — l'ubbidienza, to insist upon obedience; — il segreto, to enjoin secrecy; vi -o che nessuno entri, see that no one comes in; (comm.) — una nave, to consign a ship; *rfl.* to commend oneself; to implore favour (grace, protection, pardon); to be a suppliant; disse -andosi, he said imploringly; mi -o, I beg you; (joc.) -arsi alle gambe, to take to one's heels, to run away; (fig.) è un libro che si -a da sè, it is a book that needs no recommendation; (stressing advice, command or request), mi -o!, mind you do!, please do!; scrivimi presto, mi -o, don't forget to write to me soon. **-a·bile** *adj.* recommendable; commendable; to be recommended. **-aménto** *m.* recommending; commending. **-ante** *part. adj., n.m.* recommending; introducer, sponsor. **-ata** *f.* registered letter; -ata a mano, letter sent by a messenger who is instructed to obtain a receipt for it; protégée. **-ata·rio** *m.* person to whom one is recommended, protector; (naut.) shipping agent; ship's agent; (comm.) consignee. **†-ativo** *adj.* to be recommended. **-ato** *part. adj.* recommended; placed under the protection (of); (of letters) registered; *n.m.* person recommended; il tuo -ato, the person you recommended; protégé; (mil. slang) -ato di ferro, one who avoids military service thanks to the protection of a powerful personage (cf. **imboscato**). (**-atóre** *m.* **-atrice** *f.*) **-ato·rio** *adj. (m.pl. -atorii)* lettera -atoria, letter of recommendation. **-azióne** *f.* recommendation; advice; lettera di -azione, letter of introduction; testimonial; (post) registration; tassa di -azione, registration fee; (rel.) -azione dell'anima, recommendation of a departing soul, prayers for the dying. **-i·gia** *f.*, **†-o** *m.* see **raccomandazione**.

raccomod-are [A I] *tr.* to repair, to mend; questi calzoni non si -ano più, these trousers are beyond repair; to adjust, to set to rights; to straighten; si -ò la cravatta allo specchio, he straightened his tie in front of the looking-glass; to put in order; (fig.) un vinetto che -a lo stomaco, a light wine that settles the stomach. **-aménto** *m.* mending, repair. (**-ato** *part. adj.* **-atóre** *m.* **-atrice** *f.*) **-atura** *f.* mending, repair(ing): cost of repair.

racconci-are [A 3 c] *tr.* to repair, to mend; to set to rights; (naut.) to refit (rigging); *rfl.* to tidy oneself, to make oneself presentable; (of weather) to change for the better .to turn fair; *recip. rfl.* to make it up with one another, to become friends again. **-aménto** *m.* see **racconciatura**. (**-ato** *part. adj.* **-atóre** *n.m.* **-atrice** *f.*) **-atura** *f.* mending, repair; -atura del Ministero, Cabinet reshuffle; clearing up (of weather).

raccóncio *adj.* repaired, mended; adjusted; *n.m.* repair; adjustment; settlement.

racconsol-are [A I] *tr.* to console; to comfort. **-ato** *part. adj.* consoled; comforted; con volto -ato, with an expression of renewed serenity.

raccont-are [A I c] *tr.* to tell, to relate, to narrate, to recount; -ano che…, they say that…; se ne -ano di belle sul suo conto, queer stories are told about him; se è vero tutto quel che si -a, if all tales be true; poterla —, to live to tell the tale; cose da -arsi a veglia, tall stories. **-a·bile** *adj.* fit to be told, fit to tell; suitable to relate. **-afa·vole** *m. indecl.* (joc.) romancer, story-teller. (**-ato** *part. adj.* **-atóre** *m.* **-atrice** *f.*)

raccónt-o[1] *m.* tale, story; — storico, historical novel; un breve —, a short story; narrative, narration; — di fate, fairy-tale; recital; report. **-ino** *m. dim.* little tale; children's story.

raccónto[2] *apocop. part.* of **raccontare**, q.v.; *adj.* (poet.) related, narrated, told.

raccoppiare [A 4 c] *tr.* to couple, to pair; to reunite (cf. **accoppiare**).

raccorci-are [A 3 c] *tr.* to shorten; *rfl.* to become shorter; (of days in autumn) to draw in. (**-aménto** *m.* **-ato** *part. adj.*) (Cf. **accorciare**.)

raccórcio *apocop. part.* of **raccorciare**, q.v.; *adj.* shortened, cut short; *n.m.* shortening, abbreviation.

raccorcire [D I c] and derivs. (Tusc.). See **raccorciare**.

raccord-are[1] [A I] *tr.* to join, to connect, to link; (eng.) to radius; *rfl., intr.* (aux. avere) to unite; to be brought together. **-ato** *part. adj.* joined, linked; ad angoli -ati, with rounded corners, dished.

raccordare[2] *vb.* and derivs. See **ricordare**.

raccord-o *m.* fastening together (e.g. with screws); connexion; union; joint; (rlwy.) junction; loop-line; branch line; (binario di) —, siding. **-eri·a** *f.* pipe fittings.

†raccorre *vb.* and derivs. See **raccogliere**.

†raccosciare *rfl.* to squat.

raccost-are [A I] *tr.* to bring together; to put side by side; to compare; — l'uscio, to close the door (i.e. to bring two shutters of a folding door together); *rfl.* to draw near, to approach, to come close together. (**-aménto** *m.* **-ato** *part. adj.*) (Cf. **accostare**.)

raccozz-are [A I] *tr.* to throw together; to put together; to scrape together, to collect with difficulty; *recip. rfl.* to meet, to unite; to join forces; to be in agreement. **-ato** *part. adj.* thrown together; collected, scraped together. (Cf. **accozzare**.)

rac-èmo *m.* bunch, cluster (of grapes, flowers); (bot.) raceme. **-emato** (chem.) racemate. **-e·mico** *adj.* (chem.) racemic; acido -emico, dl-tartaric acid. **-emi·fero** *m.* (bot.) racemiferous, bearing racemes; (of Bacchus) bearing grapes. **-emóso** *adj.* racemose.

Rachele *pr.n.f.* Rachel.

rachialgi·a *f.* (med.) rachialgia.

ra·chide *f.* (biol.) rachis; (bot.) midrib.

rachischi·si *f.* (med.) rhachischisis.

rachi·tico *adj.* suffering from rickets; (fig.) stunted, ill-grown, poorly developed; *n.m.* person suffering from rickets.

raci·mol-o *m.* small cluster within a bunch of grapes; (fig.) cluster, small group, knot (e.g. of people). **-are** [A I s] *intr.* (aux. avere) to pick the last little bunches of grapes, to glean in vineyards; *tr.* (fig.) to glean, to gather, to collect, to collect together. (**-ato** *part. adj.*) **-atóre** *m.* gleaner (also fig.). (**-atrice** *f.*) **-atura** *f.* gleaning in vineyards.

racquetare [A I] and derivs. See **acquietare**.

racquist-are [A I] *tr.* to regain; to recover; to obtain once more; *intr.* (aux. avere), *rfl.* to regain ground; to regain the initiative. (**-aménto** *m.* **-atóre** *m.* **-atrice** *f.*) **-o** *m.* regaining; recovery; reoccupation; reconquest. (Cf. **riacquistare**.)

rada *f.* (naut.) anchorage; roads; shelter; roadstead; — aperta, open anchorage; — di levata, sailing roads (of easy egress); — comune, — franca, free anchorage; — foranea, limited roads, outer anchorage; (iron.) campagna di —, non seagoing cruise; andare in —, to shift a ship to an outer anchorage; essere in —, to be at anchor in the roadstead.

radaménte *adv.* See under **rado**.

radan·ci-a *f.* (naut.) thimble. **-are** [A 3] *tr.* (naut.) to fit thimbles to (the roping of a sail or in an eyesplice).

radar *m. indecl.* radar. **-ista** *m.* radar operator or engineer.

radatura *f.* (text.) bare place in cloth; (fig.) bald patch.

radazz-a *f.* (naut.) mop; (slang) wart. **-are** [A I] *tr.* (naut.) to mop down, to swab.

raddens-are [A I] *tr.* to thicken, to make thicker; to condense further; *intr.* (aux. essere), *rfl.* to become thicker; to thicken; to condense. **-a·bile** *adj.* capable of being thickened. **-aménto** *m.* thickening, becoming thicker; condensing. (**-ato** *part. adj.* **-atóre** *m.* **-atrice** *f.*)

raddirizzare [A I] and derivs. See **raddrizzare**.

raddobb-o *m.* (naut.) hull repairs; bacino di —, refitting basin; base di —, refitting base. **-are** [A I] *tr.* (naut.) to refit.

raddolc-are [A 2] *intr.* (aux. essere) (of weather) to become milder.

†raddolciare *vb.* See **raddolcire**.

raddolc-ire [D 2] *tr.* to sweeten; (fig.) to soften, to soothe; to allay, to assuage; to mitigate; -ì la voce, he spoke more gently; (metall.) to soften; *intr.* (aux. essere), *rfl.* (of the weather) to become milder (cf. **raddolcare**); (fig.) to be soothed, to be allayed. **-iménto** *m.* sweetening; softening, assuaging. **-ito** *part. adj.* sweetened; softened, allayed, assuaged.

†raddomandare *vb.* and derivs. See **domandare**.

raddomanzi·a *f.* See **rabdomanzia**, under **rabdomante**.

raddoppi-are [A 4 c] *tr.* to double, to redouble; (gramm.) to reduplicate; (mus.) to double; *intr.* (aux. avere, essere), *rfl.* to double, to redouble; to increase, to occur more frequently; to become more intense; il vento ha (è) -ato, the force of the wind has doubled; il raccolto sarà -ato, the crop will be doubled; (of horses) to gallop. **-aménto** *m.* doubling, redoubling; (gramm.)

raddoppi-are (*cont.*)
reduplication; (sport) overlap. **-ata** *f.* (equit.) gallop. **-ato** *part.*
adj. doubled, redoubled; double; con sforzi -ati, with redoubled
efforts; al passo -ato, at the double; (gramm.) reduplicated; (bot.)
reduplicate. **-atamente** *adv.* doubly, in double measure. **-atura** *f.*
doubling; increasing; folding in two.

raddoppio *m.* double; doubling, redoubling; (rlwy.) binario di —,
double track.

raddotto *part.* of **raddurre**, *q.v.*; *n.m.* see **ridotto**.

raddrizz-are [A4] *tr.* to straighten, to put straight; to erect, to set
upright; (electr.) to rectify; (fig.) to put right; — le gambe ai
cani, to wash a blackamoor white, to attempt the impossible;
rfl. to straighten oneself, to draw oneself up; to stand up straight;
(of weather) to clear up, to become fine (cf. **addirizzare**). **-amento**
m. straightening; setting right; (electr.) rectification. (**-ato** *part.*
adj.) **-atore** *m.* (electr.) rectifier. **-atrice** *f.* (eng.) straightening
machine; *adj.* (radar) valvola -atrice (*or as n.f.*), rectifying valve.
-atura *f.* straightening.

raddurre [B2] *tr.* to reduce; to bring back; *rfl.* to be reduced; raddursi
a, to bring oneself to (e.g. do something distasteful) (cf. **ridurre**).

ra·d-ere [C3] *tr.* to shave; to file down; to scrape; to raze; — una
città al suolo, to raze a town to the ground; to erase, to scratch
out, to cancel; to graze; to brush against; to pass close to; (agric.)
to trim (a measure of grain) with a strickle; (naut.) to cut down
(masts and rigging of an old ship); — la sabbia, to touch bottom,
to 'feel'; — la superficie dell'acqua, to approach the surface;
†— il vento, to keep close to the wind; (mil.) to graze; *rfl.*
to shave, to shave oneself; *n.m.* il —, il -ersi, shaving. **-ente** *part.*
adj. grazing, passing very close; (sport) palla, pallone -ente, a ball
which keeps low; (mil.) con tiri -enti, grazing shot; tiro -ente,
flat trajectory; difesa -ente, flank shots; marcia -ente, advance
under cover; (aeron.) volo -ente, hedgehopping; (naut.) corrente
-ente, current following the coast; moto -ente, anti-clockwise
current of the Mediterranean; rotta -ente, coasting. **-enza** *f.*
grazing movement. **-i·bile** *adj.* that can be grazed or shaved.
-ima·dia *f.* scraper for a kneading-trough. **-imento** *m.* grazing;
scraping; erasing; erasure. **-itura** *f.* shaving; scraping; grazing;
material shaved, scraped or grazed off.

radi-are [A4] *intr.* (*aux.* avere, essere) to beam, to radiate, to emit
rays; *tr.* (admin.) to strike out (esp. from a list); to remove, to
erase; (leg.) to cancel; — una ipoteca, to cancel entry of mortgage
in Land Charges Register; (naut.) to withdraw from the seagoing
register. **-ante** *adj.* (poet.) radiant; (herald.) croce -ante, cross
rayonnant; *n.m.* (math.) radian. **-anza** *f.* (phys.) radiance. **-ato** *adj.*
radiate, shaped like a wheel or 'star'; struck out, erased; cancelled.
-atore *m.* radiator. **-azione** *f.* radiation; cancellation (esp. of a
mortgage); erasure, striking out.

ra·dic-a *f.* (pop.) root; root of a tooth; pipa di —, briar-pipe; (fig.)
fare le radiche, to strike root (cf. **radice**). **-ale** *adj.* (bot.) radical;
(fig.) radical; cura -ale, radical treatment; (pol.) partito -ale,
Radical party; (gramm.) parte -ale, root (-part of a word);
(anat.) vene -ali, great veins; *n.m.* (pol.) Radical, member of a
Radical party; (chem.) radical; *f.* (gramm.) root; una -ale greca,
a Greek root. **-almente** *adv.* radically; fundamentally. **-aleggiare**
[A3c] *intr.* (*aux.* avere) (pol.) to be inclined to radicalism. **-alismo**
m. (pol.) radicalism.

radic-are [A2s] *intr.* (*aux.* essere), *rfl.* to take root; (fig.) certe idee
qui non si -ano, some ideas do not take root here. **-amento** *m.*
taking root. **-ando** *m.* (math.) radicand. **-ante** *part. adj.* (bot.)
rooting. **-ata** *f.* (naut.) the whole system of knees and angle plates
supporting and strengthening the hull; -ata di corsia, staunchions
supporting fore and aft gangway in a galley. **-ato** *part. adj.*
rooted, that has taken root; (fig.) rooted, deep-rooted, deep-
seated. **-azione** *f.* rooting, taking root; radication.

radic·chi-o *m.* (bot.) chicory, *Cichorium intybus*, and endive, *C.
endiva.* **-ella** *f.* (bot.) dandelion, *Taraxacum officinale.* **-one** *m.*
(bot.) *Chondrilla juncea.*

radic-e *f.* (bot.) root; mettere, prendere —, to take root, to strike
roots; metter le -i al sole a un albero, to uproot a tree; (gramm.)
root; (fig.) root, fount, origin; la — di ogni male, the root of all
evil; (math.) root; — cubica, cube root; — quadrata, square
root; — quadrata dei valori medi al quadrato, root mean square,
R.M.S.

radicol-are *adj.* (anat.) radicular. **-ite** *f.* (med.) radiculitis.

radi-madi·a *f.*, **-mento** *m.* See under **radere**.

ra·di-o¹ *m.* radium. **-oattività** *f.* radio-activity. **-oattivo** *adj.* radioactive. **-ochi·mica** *f.* radio-chemistry. **-ocrono·metro** *m.* (atom.
phys.) radiochronometer. **-odermite** *f.* (med.) radiodermatitis.
-odiagno·stica *f.* (med.) X-ray diagnostics. **-oemanazione** *f.* (atom.
phys.) emanation, radon. **-ofo·sforo** *m.* (chem.) radiophosphorus.
-ografi·a *f.* radiography; X-ray, radiograph; (med.) -ografia mirata,
spot radiography. **-ogra·fico** *adj.* radiographic. **-ogramma** *m.* radiogram; (med.) radiograph, skiagram. **-olocalizzatore** *m.* radar.
-olocalizzazione *f.* radiolocation. **-ologi·a** *f.* (med.) radiology.
-o·logo *m.* (med.) radiologist. **-ometallografi·a** *f.* radiometallo-
graphy. **-ometro** *m.* (phys.) radiometer. **-omicro·metro** *m.* (phys.)
radiomicrometer. **-oscopi·a** *f.* (med.) radioscopy, screening.
-osco·pico *adj.* (med.) radioscopic. **-osensibilità** *f.* (med.) radio-
sensibility. **-otal·lio** *m.* (chem.) radium C. **-oterapi·a** *f.* (med.)
radiotherapy, actinotherapy. **-otera·pico** *adj.* (med.) radio-
therapeutical.

ra·di-o² *f.* wireless, radio; alla —, on the wireless, over the radio;
wireless (receiving) set; — a galena, crystal set; trasmettere per —,
to broadcast; musica trasmessa per —, broadcast music; giornale
—, (wireless) news, news bulletin; ascoltare la —, to listen in;
Radio Audizioni Italiana (R.A.I.), the Italian Broadcasting Corporation. **-oamatore** *m.* amateur wireless operator. **-oascoltatore** *m.*
(wireless) listener. **-oauditore** *m.* listener. **-oaudizione** *f.* broadcast.
-obus·sola *f.* (aeron. navig.) radiocompass. **-ocanale** *m.* radio
channel. **-ocomandato** *adj.* radio-controlled. **-ocomando** *m.* radio
control. **-ocomunicazione** *f.* wireless communication. **-ocro·naca** *f.*
running commentary (radio). **-ocronista** *m.* wireless commentator.
-diffondere [C3] *tr.* to broadcast. **-odiffusione** *f.* broadcasting;
broadcast. **-odisturbi** *m.pl.* atmospherics, statics. **-ofaro** *m.*
radio beacon. **-ofoni·a** *f.* radio-telephony, wireless telephony.
-ofo·nic-o *adj.* (mus.) having to do with, relating to broadcasting; cantanti -ofonici, broadcast singers, singers on the
wireless. **-o·fono** *m.* (phys.) radiophone. **-ofoto** *m.* radio picture.
-ofrequenza *f.* radio frequency. **-ogoniometrag·gio** *m.* direction
finding. **-ogoniometri·a** *f.* radiogoniometry. **-ogonio·metro** *m.*
radio direction finder. **-ogoverno** *m.* radio control. **-ogram-
mo·fono** *m.* radiogram. **-omontatore** *m.* radio mechanic. **-onavi-
gazione** *f.* (aeron.) radionavigation. **-oonda** *f.* radio wave.
-ora·rio *m.* weekly publication corresponding to the British *Radio
Times.* **-oricevitore** *m.* radio receiver. **-orilevamento** *m.* radio
bearing. **-oripetitrice** *f.* relay station. **-orumori** *m.pl.* atmospherics,
statics. **-osegnale** *m.* (aeron.) radio beacon; marker beacon.
-osonda *f.* (meteor.) radiosonde. **-otec·nica** *f.* wireless engineering,
radio engineering. **-otec·nico** *m.* wireless engineer; radio mechanic.
-otelefoni·a wireless telephone. **-otelefonista** *m., f.* radiotelephone operator. **-otele·fono** *m.* radiotelephone. **-otelegrafare**
[A1s] *tr., intr.* (*aux.* avere) to send (a message) by wireless-
telegraphy. **-otelegrafi·a** *f.* radio-telegraphy. **-otelegrafista** *m., f.*
radio-telegraph operator. **-otelegramma** *m.* radiotelegram. **-otele-
visione** *f.* see **televisione**. **-otrasmettere** [C20] *tr.* to broadcast.
-otrasmettitore *m.* radio transmitter. **-otrasmissione** *f.* broadcasting; broadcast; programme, item in a programme (broadcast).
-otrasmittente *f.* broadcasting station. **-ovisione** *f.* television;
televising; television programme.

ra·di-o³ *m.* (anat.) radius, forearm. **-ale** *adj.* (anat.) radial. **-ocar·pico**
adj. (anat.) radiocarpal.

radiol-ari *m.pl.* (zool.) radiolaria. **-o** *m.* (zool.) sea urchin.

radios-o *adj.* radiant; brilliant; beaming; shining; un mattino —,
a bright morning; (fig.) — di gioia, radiant with joy. **-ità** *f.*
radiance; brilliance.

raditura *f.* See under **radere**.

radium *m.* see **radio¹**. **-terapi·a** *f.* (med.) radium therapy.

rad-o *adj.* sparse, thinly scattered, rare; l'atmosfera -a, the upper
atmosphere; -i villaggi, scattered hamlets; capelli -i, thin hair;
rare, infrequent, occasional; nelle sue -e visite, on his occasional
visits; -e volte, rarely; le sorelle scambiavano -e parole, the sisters
exchanged a few words at intervals; di —, rarely; non di —, often,
frequently; ben di —, very seldom; *n.m.* thinly sown *or* planted
ground; c'è poco — nella nostra piantagione, there are not many
thin patches in our plantation; *adv.* seldom, rarely; seminar —, to
sow thinly. **-amente** *adv.* seldom, rarely. **-ezza** *f.* rareness; scantiness, thinness. †**-ità** *f.* rarity. **-one** *adj. augm.* very sparse; very thin
(esp. of textiles). **-ore** *m.* bare patch, thin place (in cloth, hair, field
or wood). **-ume** *m.* bare patch (in cultivation). **-ura** *f.* clearing
(in woods); glade; bare patch of ground; thin, worn part of cloth.

radòn *m. indecl.* (chem.) radon.

ra·dula *f.* (naut.) scrubber; hull scraper.

radun-are [A I] *tr.* (more pop. than **adunare**, q.v.) to assemble; to gather together; to collect; (naut.) — le rotte, to work up the dead reckoning (i.e. to calculate a ship's position); *rfl.* to assemble, to gather together in a group, to congregate. **-abile** *adj.* that may be assembled or gathered together; capable of being collected. **-amento** *m.* gathering, collecting; assembling. **-anza** *f.* assembly, gathering, reunion. **-ata** *f.* assembly, meeting, gathering; far -ata, to call together, to assemble. (**-ato** *part. adj.* **-atore** *m.* **-atrice** *f.*) **-o** *m.* rally; see also **radunata**.

radura *f.* See under **rado**.

ra·fano *m.* (bot.) horse-radish, *Armoracia rusticana*, and common radish, *Raphanus sativus*.

rafe *m.* (bot.) raphe, suture; (anat.) raphe.

raffa *f.* robbery with violence; rapine; o di riffa o di —, by hook or by crook, at all costs (even by violence); fare a ruffa —, to vie with each other in robbery and violence; (provb.) ciò che vien di ruffa — se ne va di buffa in baffa, ill-gotten gains never prosper.

†raffacci-are *tr.* (fig.) — qualcosa a uno, to fling something in someone's face; to bring up (e.g. memory of a wrong, or benefit forgotten). †**-o** *m.* reproof. (Cf. **rinfacciare**.)

Raffael·l-o *pr.n.m.* Raphael, un —, un quadro di —, a (picture by) Raphael; l'arcangelo —, the Archangel Raphael; *adj. phr.* alla -a, in the manner (style) of Raphael; capelli alla -a, berretto alla -a, hair, cap, in the style of Raphael (as shown in the well-known self-portrait in the Uffizi Gallery in Florence). **-eggiare** [A 3 c] *intr.* (aux. avere) to imitate Raphael, to paint in the manner of Raphael. **-esca** *f.* (usu. *pl.* **-esche**) frescoes, mural decorations like those by Raphael in the Stanze Vaticane at Rome; grotesques, arabesques. **-esco** *adj.* (*m.pl.* **-eschi**) Raphaelesque, in the style of Raphael; worthy of Raphael.

raffagottare [A I] *intens.* of **affagottare**, q.v.

raffardellare [A I] *intens.* of **affardellare**, q.v.

raffazzon-are [A I] *tr.* to do up, to touch up; to repair, to patch (up). (**-amento** *m.*) **-ato** *part. adj.* done up, refurbished; patched up; lavoro -ato, bungled piece of work. **-atore** *m.* botcher, bungler; clumsy adapter. (**-atrice** *f.*) **-atura** *f.* botching, clumsy adaptation.

rafferm-a *f.* confirmation; (mil.) re-engagement; avere due -e, to have two re-engagements; doppia -a, second re-engagement. **-are** [A I] *tr.* to confirm; to reassure; to renew (an appointment, engagement); to strengthen; to make firm (earth, ground); (paint.) to fix (colours); *rfl.* to become firm, fixed, assured; (of bread) to become stale; (mil.) to re-engage. (**-ativo** *adj.* **-atore** *m.* **-atrice** *f.* **-azione** *f.*) **-o** *apocop. part. adj.* made or become firm or hard; pane -o, stale bread.

raf·fia *f.* See **rafia**.

raf·fic-a *f.* squall; violent gust of wind; shower of hail; — di neve, scud of snow, sudden snowstorm; — di pallottole, hail of bullets; (aeron.) — discendente, air pocket; (fig.) — di insolenza, storm of abuse.

raffid-are [A I] *tr.* to reassure; to encourage; to give confidence to; *rfl.* (*prep.* a) to confide (in), to trust. **-ato** *part. adj.* reassured; encouraged. (Cf. **affidare**.)

raffievolire [D 2] *intens.* of **affievolire**, q.v.

raffigur-are [A I] *tr.* to recognize; to represent, to portray; to symbolize; *rfl.* (*dat.* of *prn.* 'si') to imagine. (**-abile** *adj.* **-amento** *m.*) **-ato** *part. adj.* recognized; represented, portrayed; symbolized.

raffil-are [A I] *tr.* to sharpen, to whet; to pare, to trim; — i capelli, to cut or trim the hair; to trim the edges of (cloth, paper, etc.); *intr.* (aux. avere) — sulle spese, to cut down expenses. **-ato** *part. adj.* sharpened; pared, trimmed; (bookb.) with cut edges. **-atoio** *m.* whetstone, strop (or other instrument for sharpening tools). **-atura** *f.* sharpening, trimming; *pl.* trimmings, shavings, clippings (esp. from pages of books trimmed by the bookbinder). (Cf. **affilare**.)

raffin-are [A I] *tr.* to refine; to purify; to remove the dross from; to make more elegant, refined, or pure; — il gusto, to refine one's taste; *rfl.* to become refined, to acquire refinement; to become more difficult to please or more exacting. **-amento** *m.* refining; purifying. **-atezza** *f.* refinement; subtlety. **-ato** *part. adj.* refined; gusto —, refined, cultivated taste; subtle, artful; malizia -ata, artful malice; (comm.; industr.) refined, pure; (chem.; industr.) raffinate; *n.m.* epicure, dandy, sybarite. **-atamente** *adv.* with refinement, refinedly. **-atoio** (metall.) refining furnace. **-atore** *m.*

refiner; (paperm.) beater. **-atrice** *f.* (paperm.) beater. (**-atura** *f.*) **-azione** *f.* refining; (chem.; industr.) refining. **-eri·a** *f.* refinery. †**-ire** *intr.* to become finer, to become refined; to become purified; *tr.* to refine, to purify; to sharpen (cf. **affinare**). **-o·sio** *m.* (chem.) raffinose, mellitriose.

raf·fi-o *m.* grappling hook; grapnel; di riffi o di raffi, by hook or by crook; tirar sù coi raffi, to achieve with difficulty.

raffitt-ire [D 2] *tr.* to thicken, to cause to grow thicker (e.g. hair, grass); to make more frequent; *intr.* (aux. essere), *rfl.* to grow thicker, to thicken; l'erba dopo il primo taglio -isce, after the first cutting the grass grows thicker; questa tela dopo lavata s'è -ita molto, this cloth has felted a good deal after washing; *recip. rfl.* (of persons) to draw closer together; -itevi un poco su coteste panche, close up a bit on those benches. **-ito** *part. adj.* thickened, grown thicker. (Cf. **affittire**.)

raffondare *intens.* of **affondare**, q.v.

†rafformare *tr.* to reform, to bring about a reformation in.

rafforz-are [A I] *tr.* to strengthen, to reinforce; — un suono, to sound louder, to make a louder note or noise; *rfl.* to grow stronger; (fig.) to fortify oneself. (**-amente** *m.* **-ato** *part. adj.*) (Cf. **afforzare, rinforzare**.)

raf-francare [A 2] *intens.* of **affrancare**, q.v. **-fratellare** [A I] see **affratellare**.

raffredd-are [A I c] *tr.* to cool; to chill; (fig.) to cool, to cool down, to cool off; *intr.* (aux. essere), *rfl.* to cool; to get cold; to cool down; la minestra si -a, the soup is getting cold; lascia che la minestra si -i un po', leave the soup to cool a little; (fig.) l'entusiasmo si -a, their enthusiasm is cooling down; to catch cold, to take a chill. **-amento** *m.* cooling (also fig.); (eng.) cooling; -amento ad acqua, water-cooling; -amento ad aria, air-cooling; -amento intermedio, intercooling; †(med.) cold, chill. **-ato** *part. adj.* cooled; gone cold; suffering from a cold (in the head, etc.); è -ato, he has a cold. **-atore** *m.* cooler; (motor.) radiator. **-atura** *f.* cooling; catching cold. **-ore** *m.* (med.) common cold, coryza.

raffren-are [A I] *tr.* to restrain, to check, to curb; to repress; *rfl.* to restrain oneself, to exercise restraint; to hold oneself in check. (**-amento** *m.* **-ativo** *adj.*) **-ato** *part. adj.* restrained; temperate. (**-atore** *m.* **-atrice** *f.*) (Cf. **frenare**.)

raffrescare [A 2] *intr.* (aux. essere) to cool off, to become cool; to grow cold; *rfl.* to catch cold; (Tusc.) pop. form of **rinfrescare**, q.v.

raffrign-are [A 5] *tr.* to botch, to cobble. **-o** *m.* bad sewing, botched work; scar, ill-healed wound.

raffront-are [A I c] *tr.* to bring face to face; to place together (side by side), to compare; — i margini d'una ferita, to draw the edges of a wound together; †to face again; †to reprove, to reproach; to behold face to face; *intr.* (aux. avere) to be alike, to agree; le due deposizioni -ano, the two statements are in agreement; *rfl.* to agree, to be in agreement; †non -arsi con sè, to be moody, to be uneven in temperament. **-amento** *m.* comparison. (**-ato** *part. adj.* **-atore** *m.* **-atrice** *f.*)

raffrònto *m.* comparison, comparing; placing side by side.

raffusolare [A I s] *tr. intens.* of **affusolare**, q.v., under **affusare**; †*intr.* (aux. essere), *rfl.* to dress up, to dress oneself gaudily.

ra·fia *f.* (bot.) raffia, i.e. leaf fibres of the palm *Raphia ruffia*.

ra·fio *m.* (bot.) raphid.

ra·gadi *f.pl.* (med.) rhagades, chaps; (vet.) 'broken knee'.

ragana *f.* (ichth.) weever fish, *Trachinus* spp.

raganella *f.* (zool.) tree frog, *Hyla arborea*, and other species.

ragazz-o *m.* boy, lad; ha quattro -i e una bambina, he has four boys and a girl; child; ho due -i, un maschio ed una femmina, I have two children, a boy and a girl; — di bottega, shop-boy, errand boy; è un buon —, he is a good boy, a good fellow; con tanto di barba, è sempre un ragazzo, old as he is, he is still a boy at heart; (pop.) boy-friend, young man; (also used referring to adults) avanti, -i!, come on, boys! **-a** *f.* girl; young woman; maid; nome di -a, maiden name; rimaner -a, to remain unmarried, to become an old maid; maidservant; shop-girl; waitress; barmaid; (pop.) girl-friend; (but with *poss. adj.* referring to a parent) daughter; (*pejor.*) -a squillo, call-girl. **-ac·cio** *m. pejor.* hooligan, lout. **-a·glia** *f.* (derog.) swarm of children, crowd, mob of boys; boys (i.e. stable-boys and other inferior servants). **-ame** *m.* see **ragazzaglia**. **-ata** *f.* boyish prank, childish action; non fare -ate, don't be foolish, don't behave like a child. **-ino** *m. dim.* little boy. (**-ina** *f.*) **-otto** *m.* big boy; young man, youth. **-ume** *m.* see **ragazzaglia**.

†**ragenzare** *tr.* to refurbish, to renew, to restore.

rag-gelare [A I] *intens.* or *repet.* of gelare, q.v. **-gentilire** [D 2] *intens.* of ingentilire or ringentilire, q.v. **-ghiacciare** [A 3] *intens.* of agghiacciare, q.v.

ragghiare [A 4] and derivs. See ragliare.

raggi-are [A 3] *intr.* (*aux.* avere, essere) to shine; to beam; to be radiant; to emit rays; (fig.) l'innocenza gli -ava sul volto, innocence shone in his countenance; -ava di felicità, he was radiant with happiness; (phys.) to radiate; *tr.* il sole -ava tanta luce, the sun radiated so much light; (fig.) il suo volto -ava tanta gioia, his face was so radiant with joy. (**-amento** *m.*) **-ante** *part. adj.* radiant; (phys.) calore -ante, radiant heat. **-ato** *part. adj.* radiate, arranged like rays (or spokes of a wheel); radiated; rayed.

raggiata *f.* (ichth.) ray, *Raia* spp.

raggiera *f.* See under raggio.

rag·gi·o *m.* ray, beam; gleam; un — d'intelligenza, a gleam of intelligence; — di speranza, ray of hope; (poet.) fame, glory; — della ruota, spoke of the wheel; (geom.) radius; (fig.) district; — d'affari, business circuit; (scient.) raggi X, X-rays; raggi ultravioletti, ultraviolet rays; (mil.) star shell; (naut.) — della coffa, crosstrees; — d'azione, radius of action; — di evoluzione, turning circle; †wreckage; (bot.) — midollare, medullary ray. **-era** *f.* halo; head-dress (e.g. of pins, as worn by peasant girls) resembling a halo; (liturg.) rays of a monstrance. †**-oso** *adj.* radiant, emitting rays.

raggiorn-are [A I c] *intr.* (*aux.* essere), *impers.* to dawn again, to become (day) light again; era appena -ato quando ci svegliammo, it was barely light when we woke; (poet.) pensa che questo dì mai non -a (Dante, *Purg.* XII, 84), think that this day will never dawn again; *tr.* (Tusc.) see aggiornare. (**-ato** *part.*)

raggir-are [A I] *tr.* to swindle, to cheat, to 'twist'; to get the better of; si lascia — da tutti, he lets everyone cheat him; *rfl.* to turn round and round, to go round and round; to prowl; (fig.) to beat about the bush; -arsi nel letto, to turn over and over in bed; -arsi su, to concern, to be concerned with; i suoi discorsi si -avano tutti su quell'argomento, everything he said related to that subject. **-amento** *m.* swindle; cheating; trick. (**-ante** *part. adj.* **-ata** *f.*) **-ato** *part. adj.* led round about; swindled, cheated; discorso -ato, involved speech. **-atore** *m.* swindler, trickster. (**-atrice** *f.*) **-evole** *adj.* turning easily; il -evole vento, the variable wind; easily turned; easily swindled, or cheated. **-o** *m.* trick; -i di ragazzi, boys' pranks; deception, cheating; pieno di -i, deceitful, sly; (leg.) trick; subterfuge (C.C.; C.P.). (Cf. aggirare.)

†**raggiu·gnere** *vb.* and derivs. See raggiungere.

raggiun·g·ere [C 5] *tr.* to reach, to get to, to arrive at; to catch up (with); to overtake; raggiunsi la vetta in poche ore, I reached (got to) the top in a few hours; avviatevi, chè vi -erò, go on and I will catch you up; to join; -erò mio fratello a Parigi, I shall join my brother in Paris; to rejoin; to achieve, to attain, to hit; — il bersaglio, to hit the target; la spesa -erà il milione, the expenditure will amount to a million lire; †to terminate, to complete; *rfl.* to be joined; *recip. rfl.* to meet, to join; to unite. **-i·bile** *adj.* attainable. **-imento** *m.* achieving, achievement; attaining, attainment; al -imento dell'età maggiore, on reaching one's majority.

raggiuntare [A I] *tr.* to stitch up again; to piece together (again) (cf. aggiuntare).

raggiunto *part.* of raggiungere, q.v.; *adj.* reached; caught up; overtaken; meeting, joined; con le sopracciglia raggiunte, with eyebrows meeting; attained, achieved; animale —, fat beast (esp. on kidneys).

raggiust-are [A I] *tr.* to mend, to repair; to repair again; to put in order; to settle; to see to; to beat, to belabour; *rfl.* to become adjusted; *recip. rfl.* to make peace, to become reconciled; to come to an agreement. (**-amento** *m.* **-ato** *part. adj.*) **-atura** *f.* mending; (cost of) repair; reparation. (Cf. aggiustare.)

raggomitol-are [A I s] *tr.* to rewind; to wind into a ball; to coil; to roll up; *rfl.* to curl (oneself) up, to roll oneself up; to bend (oneself) double. (**-amento** *m.*) **-ato** *part. adj.* rewound; coiled; curled up; bent double, stooping. (Cf. aggomitolare.)

raggracimolare [A I s] and derivs. See racimolare.

raggranch-iare [A 4] *tr.* to benumb; to contract or cause to shrivel with cold; *intr.* (*aux.* essere), *rfl.* to become numbed; to be shrivelled with cold. **-iato** *part. adj.* numb; shrivelled. **-ire** [D 2] *intr.* (*aux.* essere) to be numb, to shrivel with cold. (**-ito** *part. adj.*)

raggrandire [D 2] *intens.* of aggrandire, q.v.

raggranell-are [A I] *tr.* to gather, to scrape together, to scrape up; to collect; to glean; (fig.) — notizie, to gather news. (**-ato** *part. adj.*)

raggravare [A I] *intens.* of aggravare, q.v.

†**raggricchiare** *rfl.* to shrivel up; to shrink; to screw oneself up (with cold, etc.).

raggricciare [A 3] *intens.* of aggricciare, q.v.

†**raggrinchiare** *rfl.* to huddle (against the cold), to crouch.

raggrinz-are [A I], **-ire** [D 2] *tr.* to wrinkle; to crease; — il vestito, to crease one's dress; *intr.* (*aux.* essere), *rfl.* to become wrinkled; to become creased; una fronte -ita dagli anni, a forehead wrinkled with age. **-amento** *m.* wrinkling; creasing. **-imento** *m.* (photog.) wrinkling of film. **-ato**, **-ito** *part. adj.* wrinkled; creased; shrivelled; una mela -ita, a withered apple; (fig.) withered, faded; blighted. (Cf. aggrinzire.)

rag-groppare [A I] *intens.* of aggroppare, q.v. **-grottare** [A I] *intens.* of aggrottare, q.v. **-grovigliare** [A 4] *intens.* of aggrovigliare, q.v. **-grovigliolare** [A I s] *intens.* of aggrovigliolare, q.v. **-grumare** [A I] *tr.*, *rfl.* (techn.) to clot. **-grumazione** *f.* (techn.) clotting. **-grumolare** [A I s] *intens.* of aggrumolare, q.v.

raggrupp-are [A I] *tr.* to arrange in groups; to gather together; to regroup; (paint.; sculp.) to group; *rfl.* to form a group; to collect, to gather; to cluster. **-amento** *m.* grouping; group, cluster, knot. **-ato** *part. adj.* grouped, collected; clustered, clustering; involved, tied up together. †**-o** *m.* intrigue, complication. (Cf. aggruppare.)

†**raggruzzare** *rfl.* to crouch, to huddle.

raggruzzolare [A I s] *tr.* to put together, to scrape, to save (esp. money); *rfl.* to huddle, to curl oneself up.

ragguagli-are [A 4] *tr.* to equalize; to level; to level up to current costs or values; to compare; non possiamo — i due casi, we cannot compare the two cases; to inform; mi -ava di tutto, he kept me informed of everything; (comm.) — i conti, to post accounts in the ledger. **-a·bile** *adj.* comparable; capable of being equalized. **-amento** *m.* equalizing; comparing; levelling up to current costs or values. **-ativo** *adj.* tending to level or equalize. **-ato** *part. adj.* equalized; levelled; compared; taken equally into consideration; informed. **-atamente** *adv.* on the average; taking one thing with another; by and large; considerare la storia d'un paese -atamente alla storia universale, to set the history of a country in the context of universal history. (**-atore** *m.* **-atrice** *f.*) (Cf. agguagliare.)

raggua·glio *m.* comparison; (math.) tavole di —, comparative tables (of weights and measures, etc.); il —, conversion; piccolo in —, comparatively small; proportion; rate; al — del 10 per 100, at the rate of ten per cent (one in ten); information; report; (comm.) — del mercato, market report; *pl.* detailed information; ulteriori ragguagli, further details.

†**ragguardare** *vb.* and derivs. See riguardare.

ragguardevol-e *adj.* considerable; extensive; important; notable; worthy of respect. (**-mente** *adv.*) **-ezza** *f.* importance; notability.

†**ragguffato** *adj.* bundled up, wrapped up.

ra·gi-a¹ *f.* (bot.) Venetian turpentine; acqua (di) —, turpentine; (techn.) acqua — minerale, white spirit; (pop. Tusc.) fraud, deceit; †andare di —, to behave deceitfully, to be sly; †sapere la —, to be cunning and deceitful. **-oso** *adj.* resinous.

ra·gia² *m.*, **ragià** *m.* See raià.

ragion-are [A I c] *intr.* (*aux.* avere) to reason; to argue; to think; to be rational; to discourse; to talk; — tra sè e sè, to talk to oneself; con costui non si -a, it's no good arguing with him; — di, to discuss, to deal with, to treat of; non se ne -a, it is indisputable, there is no doubt about it; (Tusc.) costa un occhio il vino, la carne poi non se ne -a, wine is dear enough, meat is impossible; — con, to 'walk out' with, to have an understanding with (as between a man and a woman who are not engaged but thinking of becoming so); *tr.* to support with reasons; to argue (a case); to reason, to conclude, to deduce; †to compute; †to narrate; †to consider; †to esteem, to assess; †*rfl.* to be named, to be called; †-arsi con, to agree with; *n.m.* talk; argument. **-amento** *m.* reasoning; argument; -amento a priori, *a priori* reasoning; talk; discussion; discourse; lecture. (**-ante** *part. adj.*) **-ativo** *adj.* reasoning; facoltà -ativa, reasoning power, faculty of reason; of sound judgement, sensible, judicious. **-ato** *part. adj.* reasoned, explained, stated; explained and illustrated by examples; logical, reasonable; †endowed with reason. **-atamente** *adv.*

ragion-are (*cont.*)

rationally, by reasoning; reasonably; parlare -atamente, to talk sense. **-atore** *m.* reasoner, speaker; *adj.* reasonable; reasoning; un intelletto -atore, a logical mind. (**-atrice** *f.*) **-evole** *adj.* rational; reasonable; siate -evoli!, be reasonable!; proposta -evole, a reasonable (sensible) proposal; a prezzo -evole, at a reasonable (moderate) price. **-evolmente** *adv.* reasonably, with (good) reason; moderately. **-evolezza** *f.* reasonableness.

ragion-e *f.* reason; lume di —, the light of reason; perdere la —, to lose one's reason; c'è — di credere, there is reason to believe; a — egli si lagna, he complains with good reason; dovete dar — del vostro atto, you must give reasons for your action; vorrei sapere per quale — lo faceste, I should like to know (the reason) why you did it; reasonableness; ridurre alla —, to bring to reason; (*provb.*) nella felicità —, nell'infelicità pazienza, be reasonable in good fortune, patient in adversity; discourse, argument, proof; provare con —, to prove by argument, to give logical proof of; non intende —, he will not listen to reason; aver —, to be right; avete perfettamente —, you are quite right; dovetti dargli —, I had to admit that he was right; ebbe — del suo avversario, he got the better of his adversary; right; la — non è sempre completamente separata dal torto, right is not always quite distinct from wrong; questo ti appartiene di —, this belongs to you by right; chieder — a uno, to call someone to account; dare — del proprio operato, to give an account of one's (own) actions; volevo rendermi — del fatto, I wanted to satisfy myself about the fact; egli non sapeva rendersi — del fatto, he did not know how to explain the fact; rendere di pubblica —, to announce publicly, to make known; farsi una —, to resign oneself; di —, properly; come di —, quite properly, as a matter of course; ricorrerò a chi di —, I shall have recourse to the proper authorities; nature, quality, kind; animali d'ogni —, all sorts of animals; ratio, proportion, measure; sua madre gliele diede di santa —, his mother beat him soundly; a più forte —, all the more; in — di, at the rate of; (*leg.*) justice; motive; reason; right; a —, rightly; con —, with good reason; di —, of right; come di —, as is proper; dar — al convenuto, to find in favour of the defendant; dar — del fatto, to account for the fact; dar la —, to supply the reason; render —, to explain; render la —, to give the reason; far valere le proprie -i, to enforce one's rights; non saper far valere le proprie -i, to be unable to do oneself justice; sociale, style or firm (C.C.); (*comm.*) account; commercial concern; firm; house; creare una —, to establish a business; — sociale, firm name; registrazione delle -i sociali, registration of business names; dannare la —, to cancel an account; rendere —, to give account; a buona —, on good terms. **-eria** *f.* accountancy; book-keeping; accounting; ogni Ministero ha la sua -eria, every Ministry has its accountancy department. **-evole** *adj.* reasonable; judicious; moderate; prezzo -evole, moderate price; credible; well-founded. **-evolmente** *adv.* reasonably; judiciously; moderately; in all likelihood. **-evolezza** *f.* reasonableness; judiciousness; plausibility. **-iere** *m.* accountant; book-keeper; perito -iere, qualified accountant; †narrator. **†-io** *m.* long inconclusive argument or talk. **-issima** *f. superl.* (*colloq.*) avere ragione, -issima, to be right, perfectly right.

ragioso *adj.* See under **ragia**[1].

ragli-are [A4] *intr.* (*aux.* avere) to bray; (*fig.*) to talk like an ass; lasciali —!, pay no attention to the stupid things they say; *tr.* (*derog.*) to utter; — un discorso, to 'shoot off' a (stupid) speech. **-amento** *m.*, **-ata** *f.* braying, sound of braying; (*derog.*) stupid remark or speech. (**-atore** *m.* **-atrice** *f.*)

ra·glio *m.* braying; (*provb.*) — d'asino non arriva al cielo, a fool's words are not listened to by the wise.

ragn-a *f.* cobweb, spider's web, web; tela —, see **ragnatela**; bird-catcher's net; (*fig.*) snare, trap; cadere in una —, to fall into a trap; threadbare patch, thin patch; thin light cloud; (*naut.*) crow's foot (method of supporting a sail, awning or yard); †— del bompresso, net under a ship's bowsprit; rope network used to protect sails from chafing. **-a·ia** *f.* hedge or thicket suitable for bird-catching; arbour, grove. **-are** [A5] *intr.* (*aux.* avere, essere), *rfl.* to spread a net; to fall into a snare; (of clothes) to grow threadbare; (*naut.*) to fray; (of sky) to contain thin transparent clouds. **-atela** *f.*, **-atelo** *m.* (*zool.*) spider's web; cobweb; (*fig.*) inciampare nei -ateli, to be stopped by the smallest obstacle, to be unsteady on one's legs (through age or weakness); threadbare cloth, very thin material; very light cloud; †spider. **-ato** *part. adj.*

threadbare; thin as a spider's web; cielo -ato, mackerel sky, sky having very thin clouds. **-atura** *f.* threadbare condition; thin patch; thin, light clouds.

ragn-o *m.* (*zool.*) spider; (*ichth.*) weever fish; — bianco, — di mare, the greater weever fish, *Trachinus draco*; — nero, di grotto, *T. araneus*; — pagano, *T. radiatus*; also, less commonly, used for the common bass, *Morone labrax*; (*naut.*) — a vela, trawl net; (*fig.*) opera di —, something useless or insignificant; non cavare un — da un buco, to be completely unsuccessful. **-ola** *f.* (*ichth.*) lesser weever, *Trachinus vipera*. **-(u)olo** *m. dim.* small spider.

ragosta *f.* (*zool.*). See **aragosta**.

ragù *m. indecl.* ragout, stew; rich meat sauce served with *pasta*.

†ragunare *vb.* and derivs. See **radunare**.

Ragusa *pr.n.f.* (*geog.*) Dubrovnik (Yugoslavia), formerly Ragusa; Ragusa (town and province in Sicily).

raguse·o *adj.* Ragusan, of Ragusa; avaricious, grasping.

ra·i *m.pl.* of **raggio**, q.v.; (*poet.*) rays, beams; eyes; beaming glances.

ra·ia *f.* (*ichth.*) ray, *Raia* spp.

raià (rajà, rajah, ragià) *m. indecl.* rajah.

ra·id *m. indecl.* (*mil.*) raid; (*naut.*) raid; — remiero, pulling regatta; (police) round-up; (*sport*) race (esp. motor-racing); attack, raid (football, etc.).

ra·in-a *f.*, **-otto** *m.* (*ichth.*) carp, *Cyprinus carpio*.

ra·ion *m. indecl.* (*text.*) rayon.

ra·is *m. indecl.* (*naut.*) head of a tunny-fishing team; — di montagna, coastal look-out for tunny shoals; †captain of a privateer.

†ra·itro *m.* (*mil. hist.*) Reiter, German cavalry soldier (sixteenth and seventeenth centuries).

raling-a *f.* (*naut.*) roping of a sail, net or awning (hemp or wire); — d'antennale, — d'inferitura, yard roping; — di caduta, luff roping; — di bordame, — di cazzame, — di lunata, foot roping; ago di —, roping needle (curved); in —, into the wind. **-are** [A2] *tr.* (*naut.*) to sew roping on (a sail, etc.); to haul taut and stretch (a sail); to bring up into the wind; (command) -a la gabbia!, back the topsail!; *intr.* (*aux.* avere) (*naut.*) (of a sail) to be 'in irons', to flap in the wind.

rall-a *f.* (*eng.*) thrust block, thrust bearing; pivot; footstep bearing; — di controspinta, friction ring; — di estremità, step bearing; (*rlwy.*) centre pin socket; (*motor.*) fifth wheel (of trailer).

rallarg-are [A2] *tr.* to widen, to enlarge; to extend; to spread out; *intr.* (*aux.* essere). *rfl.* to widen; (of clouds) to become scattered, to open out; (of sky) to clear. (**-amento** *m.*) **-ato** *part. adj.* widened, enlarged, opened out; removed to a distance; out in the open sea (cf. **allargare**).

rallegr-are [A1] *tr.* to gladden, to cheer, to make glad; la notizia lo -ò, the news cheered him; *rfl.* to rejoice, to be glad; to be delighted; to cheer up; mi -o, I'm glad!; to congratulate; tutti si -arono con lui del risultato della mia impresa, everybody congratulated him on the result of my enterprise; (*agric.*) to flourish; (of a horse) to frisk, to prance. (**-amento** *m.*) **-ata** *f.* (of a horse) caper, prance. **-ativo** *adj.* cheering, gladdening. **-ato** *part. adj.* cheered, gladdened. (**-atore** *m.* **-atrice** *f.*) **-atura** *f.* gladness, cheerfulness; rejoicing; (of a horse) see **rallegrata**.

rallent-are [A1] *tr.* to relax, to slacken; to ease; to slow down; (*mus.*) to slacken (the speed); to lower (the pitch); *intr.* (*aux.* essere), *rfl.* to become slower; to become less frequent; to become less active; to slow down; to become slack; to become relaxed; to work loose. **-amento** *m.* slowing down, slackening speed; deceleration; lessening; relaxation. **-ando** *ger.* (*mus.*) rallentando, slowing down. (**-ato** *part. adj.*) **-atore** *m.* (*eng.*) decelerator; (*photog.*) restrainer; (*cinem.*) slow-motion camera; ora vi mostre-remo la stessa scena al -atore, now we shall show the same sequence in slow motion. (Cf. **allentare**.)

rallevare [A1] and derivs. (Tusc.) See **allevare**.

rallignare [A5] *intr.* (*aux.* essere) to take root again (also fig.); *rfl.* (of plants) to spring up again, to reproduce (itself, themselves) (cf. **allignare**).

rallino *m.* pivot; hinge.

rall-o *m.* (*orn.*) rail. **-idi** *m.pl.* (*orn.*) *Rallidae*, rails.

ral-luminare [A1] *intens.* of **alluminare**[1], q.v. **-lungare** [A2] *intens.* of **allungare**, q.v.

rally, rallye *m. indecl.* (pron. as Eng.) rally (esp. motor rally).

ram-a *f.* branch, spray, twig (esp. of fruit tree). **-accia** *f.* broom, besom. **-accio** *m. pejor.* stunted or twisted branch; rustling of branches; confused noise. **†-acciuto** *adj.* branchy, wide-branched,

ram-a (*cont.*)
many-branched. †**-ace** *adj.* epithet of a bird of prey caught for training while no longer a nestling.

Ramada·n *pr.n.m.* Ramadan (Mohammedan feast); (fig.) far —, to make a noise, to kick up a row.

rama·gli-a *f.* dead branches; clippings; prunings, loppings of trees. **-atura** *f.* pruning, lopping (of trees).

ram-a·io *m.* coppersmith; tinker. **-aiolata** *f.* ladleful. **-ai(u)olo** *m.* ladle; (fig.) tenere il -aiolo in mano, to rule the roost, to have the upper hand; †copper saucepan.

ramanzina *f.* scolding, reprimand, talking to; dare, fare, una — a uno, to lecture someone, to give someone a talking to.

ram-are [A 1] *tr.* to copper-plate; (agric.) to spray with copper sulphite. **-ato** *part. adj.* copper-plated; (agric.) sprayed with copper sulphite. **-atura** *f.* copper-plating; (agric.) spraying with copper sulphite.

ramarro *m.* (zool.) green lizard, *Lacerta viridis*; †aver l'occhio del —, to eye men amorously; †aver la bocca di —, to hang on tenaciously to what one has.

ram-ata *f.* sort of bat of woven withies or reeds for killing birds caught in nets at night; a —, in abundance. **-atare** [A 1] *tr.* to strike with a 'ramata'. **-atata, -ata** *f.* blow with a 'ramata'.

ramatura[1] *f.* arrangement of branches; branches.

ramatura[2] *f.* copper-plating.

ramazz-a basketwork sledge; (mil. slang) shell, grenade; see **ramaccia**, under **rama**. **-are** [A 1] *tr.* to drag on a basket-sledge.

ram-e *m.* (metall.; chem.) copper; — di cementazione, precipitated copper; — elettrolitico, electrolytic copper; (metall.) — granulare, feathered shot; — raffinato, touch copper; (miner.) — variegato, variegated copper ore; copper coin, copper engraving; età del —, Bronze Age; *pl.* copper cooking vessels. **-i·fero** *adj.* (miner.) cupriferous, copper-bearing.

rameggi-are [A 3 c] *tr.* (agric.) to stake, to provide (peas, beans, etc.) with sticks; *intr.* (*aux.* avere) (of antlers) to branch out. **-ato** *part. adj.* (agric.) staked; (of antlers) branching.

rame·ico *adj.* (chem.) cupric.

rameọso *adj.* (chem.) cuprous.

ramerino *m.* (bot., Tusc.) rosemary, *Rosmarinus officinalis*; pane di —, see under **pane**. (Cf. **rosmarino**.)

rami·a *f.* (bot.) Chinese vegetable silk, fibre of *Boehemeria nivea*; (text.) fibra di —, ramee fibre, China grass.

ramicciare [A 3]. See under **ramo**[1].

†**ramice** *m.* (med.) hernia, rupture.

ramicello *m. dim.* See under **ramo**[1].

ra·mico *adj.* (chem.) cupric.

ramiè *m.* (bot.; text.) See **ramia**.

rami·fero *adj.* See under **rame**.

ramific-are [A 2 s] *intr.* (*aux.* avere) to branch out, to grow branches; *rfl.* (fig.) to branch out, to ramify; il fiume si -a alla foce, the river branches (divides) to form a delta. **-ato** *part. adj.* ramified, ramifying, branching out. **-azione** *f.* ramifying; (bot.) branching, ramification; (fig.) ramification(s); extension.

rami·fico *adj.* branching, producing branches.

†**ramigno** *adj.* containing copper.

ramin-a *f.* flake or chip of copper (produced in working); copper waste; wire gauze. **-o** *m.* copper vessel; kettle; vase; copper engraving; -o bucato, creaming-ladle.

ramin-go *adj.* (*m.pl.* **-ghi**) (fig.) wandering, roving; fugitive; *n.m.* wanderer; refugee; fledgling. **-gare** [A 2] *intr.* (*aux.* avere) to wander, to rove, to roam.

ramino[1] *m.* See under **ramina**.

ramino[2] *m.* name of a card game.

rammagli-are [A 4] *tr.* (knitting) to graft; to repair ladders in (stockings); ho portato le mie calze a —, I have taken my stockings to be invisibly mended; (tanning) to remove shreds of flesh from (a hide). (**-ato** *part. adj.*) **-atura** *f.* (knitting) grafting; invisible mending (esp. of mesh or knitted garments). **-atrice** *f.* woman who repairs stockings, etc.; machine used in invisible mending of stockings.

†**rammarcare** *vb.* and derivs. See **rammaricare**.

rammaric-are [A 2 s] *tr.* to grieve; to vex; *rfl.* to grieve; to regret, to be sorry; mi -o molto di non poter far nulla per voi, I deeply regret that I cannot do anything for you; to complain; non avete nulla di cui -arvi, you have nothing to complain of; -arsi di gamba sana, to complain about nothing; (poet.) to moan.

-amento *m.* see **rammarico**. (**-atore** *m.* **-atrice** *f.*) **-azione** *f.* grief, bitterness; lamentation.

ramma·ri·co *m.* (*pl.* **-chi**) regret; sorrow, grief; vexation.

ram-massare [A 1] *intens.* of **amassare**, q.v. **-mattonare** [A 1 c] and derivs. see **ammattonare**. **-mazzolare** [A 1 s] and derivs. see **ammazzolare**.

rammemor-are [A 1 s] *tr.* to bring to mind; questo luogo mi -a la mia infanzia, this place reminds me, brings back the memory of, my childhood; *rfl., intr.* (*aux.* avere; *prep.* di) to remember, to call to mind. (**-ato** *part. adj.* **-atore** *m.* **-atrice** *f.*) **-azione** *f.* bringing to mind, reminding; memory.

rammend-are [A 1] *tr.* to darn; to mend. **-ato** *part. adj.* darned; mended. **-atore** *m.* mender; *adj.* serving to mend or darn. (**-atọra, -atrice** *f.* **-atura** *f.*)

rammendo *m.* darning; darn; ho molti rammendi da fare, I have a lot of darning to do; ricamo a —, net darning.

ramment-are [A 1] *tr.* to recall; to call to mind; nel viso -a molto suo padre, his face reminds one strongly of his father; to remember; devo -argli il suo impegno, I must remind him of his engagement; to mention; non — questo fatto dinanzi a lui, don't mention this when he is here; questa lapide -a i Caduti per la Patria, this stone commemorates the Fallen; *intr.* (*aux.* avere) (theatr.) to prompt; *rfl.* (*dat.* of *prn.* 'si') to remember, to recollect, to recall; non -arsi dal naso alla bocca, not to remember anything, to have a very bad memory. **-ato** *part. adj.* recalled, remembered; well-known, well-remembered, famous. **-atore** *m.* (theatre) prompter; (eccl.) prompter of a preacher. (**-atrice** *f.*)

rammodernare [A 1] *tr.* to modernize; to bring up to date; (clothes) to remodel (cf. **ammodernare** and **rimodernare**).

rammollare [A 1] *intens.* of **ammollare**[1], q.v.

rammoll-ire [D 2] *tr.* to soften; to soak; to melt; (fig.) to mollify; to make effeminate, to make soft; *rfl.* to become soft; to melt; *intr.* (*aux.* essere) to become childish; (fig.) to become effeminate or soft. **-imento** *m.* softening, -imento cerebrale, softening of the brain. **-ito** *part. adj.* softened; effeminate; feeble-minded; un vecchio -ito, an old man grown childish.

rammorbid-ire [D 2] *tr.* to soften; to mitigate; to make gentler; *intr.* (*aux.* essere), *rfl.* to grow soft; to become gentler. (**-imento** *m.* **-ito** *part. adj.*) (Cf. **ammorbidire**.)

rammort-o *m.* (tanning) layerway. **-are** [A 1] *tr.* (tanning) to tan in the layers.

rammor-zare [A 1] *intens.* of **ammorzare**[1], q.v. **-vidare** [A 1 s] see **rammorbidire**.

ramn-o *m.* (bot.) buckthorn, *Rhamnus*. **-etina** *f.* (chem.) rhamnetin, 7-methyl quercitin. **-ina** *f.* (chem.) rhamnin.

ram-o[1] *m.* branch; -i maestri, main branches; -i delle radici, branching roots; — d'ulivo, olive branch; (of a stag) antler; (fig.) avere un — di pazzia, to be a bit crazy; averne un —, to have a bee in one's bonnet, to have an idiosyncrasy; (anat.) ramus; (archit.) flight (of stairs, of a staircase); (herald.) -i di cervo, attires, antlers. **-icciare** [A 3] *tr.* to trim (a felled tree, or lopped branches). **-icello** *m. dim.* see **ramoscello**. **-olac·cio** (bot.) see *Rafano*; (colloq.) clown, buffoon; stupid person. **-olag·gio** *m.* (foundry) core assembly. **-oscello** *m.* twig, small branch. **-oso** *adj.* branching; full of branches; corna -ose, branching antlers; (herald.) attired. **-uto** *adj.* full of branches.

†**ramo**[2] *m.* See **rame**.

†**ramogn-a** *f.* buona —, good wishes. †**-are** *tr.* to wish a good journey to.

ramọso[1] *adj.* (chem.) cuprous.

ramọso[2] *adj.* See under **ramo**.

ramp-a *f.* paw with claws; (herald.) paw; steep ascent; steps; flight (of stairs); ramp; — missilistica, — per missili, missile ramp, missile range. **-ante** *part. adj.* climbing; (herald.) rampant; *n.m.* flight of stairs. **-are** [A 1] *intr.* (*aux.* avere) to climb; to paw the ground; *tr.* to claw, to maul, to wound with claws. **-aro** *m.* (mil.) ramp; glacis. **-ata** *f.* blow from a paw; steep ascent; upward slope of a road. **-icante** *part. adj.* climbing; creeping; (bot.) climbing; *n.m.pl.* (orn.) climbing birds, esp. the woodpecker, Picidae. **-icare** [A 2 s] *intr.* (*aux.* avere, essere) to climb. (**-icato** *part. adj.*) **-icatore** *m.* climber, mountaineer, mountain climber. (**-icatrice** *f.*) **-ichino** *m.* (bot.) climber; *adj.* climbing; (colloq.; joc.) fond of climbing about, restless; *n.m.* (orn.) short-toed tree-creeper, *Certhia brachydactyla*; -ichino alpestre, tree-creeper, *C. familiaris*. **-icọne** *m.* (naut.) grapnel, large grapple. **-inare** [A 1] *tr.* (naut.) to

ramp·a (*cont.*)

grapple. **-inato** *part. adj.* hooked, hook-shaped. **-inismo** *m.* (vet.) 'brushing' or 'speedy cut' in a horse. **-ino** *m.* hook; (fig., colloq.) attaccarsi a tutti i -ini, to seize upon any pretext; staple; tine of a fork; (writing) pot-hook; (naut.) grapple with three or four prongs used for dragging the sea-bed or for grappling the enemy; cable hook; paw with claws (esp. of a cat); (vet.) special iron nailed to a horse's hoof to prevent 'brushing'. **-onare** [A I c] *tr.* (naut.) to harpoon; *intr.* (*aux.* avere) to throw, use or fire a harpoon. **-one** *m.* harpoon; creeper (for picking up blocks of ice); 'dog' (for picking up logs); hob-nail. **-oniere** *m.* harpoon gunner, thrower; fisherman responsible for fish hooks, harpoons, etc., in a tunny fishery.

rampogn·a *f.* rebuke, reproof. **-are** [A 5 c] *tr.* to rebuke, to chide, to reprove; to upbraid; *recip. rfl.* to abuse one another. (**-amento** *m.* **-atore** *m.*, **-atrice** *f.*)

rampoll·are [A I c] *intr.* (*aux.* essere) (of a spring) to rise; (of water) to spring forth, to gush; (of a plant) to shoot; (fig.) — da, to spring, to arise, to originate, to have its source in. (**-amento** *m.* **-ante** *part. adj.*)

rampollo *m.* spring (of water); jet; (of trees) shoot; (fig.) son, descendant, scion.

rampon·e *m.*, **-iere** *m.* See under **rampa**.

ran·a *f.* (zool.) frog; — comune, edible frog, *Rana esculenta*; — rossa, *R. temporaria*; (colloq.) bad singer; boring chatterer; gonfio come una —, puffed up, conceited, suffering from a swelled head; (joc.) want of money; uomini-rana, frog-men; (swimming) nuoto a —, breast-stroke; (vet., of a horse) avere la —, to be a roarer; (ichth.) — pescatrice, angler fish, *Lophius piscatorius*. **-ettina** *f. dim.* (zool.) froglet, newly metamorphosed frog. **-ista** *m., f.* (sport) breaststroke swimmer.

ranca *f.* game leg, short leg.

ran·care [A 2], **-cheggiare** [A 3 c]. See **arrancare**[1].

ranci *m.pl.* (naut.) hammocks.

ranci·a *f.* (naut.) daily victualling list showing numbers in each mess.

ranciat·o *adj.* orange (coloured). †**-a** *f.* candied orange.

ran·ci·co *m.* (*pl.* **-chi**) bad taste in the mouth (after eating food fried in bad oil or butter); †*adj.* rancid.

ran·cid·o *adj.* rancid. **-ume** *m.* something rancid; (fig.) old-fashioned things; smettila di leggere questo -ume!, stop reading this out-of-date rubbish!

ran·cio[1] *adj.* orange-coloured; *n.m.* (bot.) marigold.

ran·ci·o[2] *m.* (mil.; naut.) mess, i.e. space and furniture occupied by an allotted number of men; mess, a number of men grouped for ration purposes under a serial number; ration; — degli ammalati, sick ration; meal; dinner; ora del —, dinner hour; sonare il —, to pipe dinner, to sound dinner call; (Genoa) fare —, to mess together; †— della gente, mess deck. **-ero** *adj.* (naut.; mil.) connected with the rations; capo -ero, head of a mess.

ran·co *adj.* (*m.pl.* **-chi**) lame, limping (cf. **ranca**).

ranc·ore *m.* grudge; rancour; serbar —, to bear a grudge; aver — contro uno, to have a grudge against someone; separarsi senza —, to part friends. **-ura** *f.* (rel.) (sin of) rancour, unforgivingness, uncharitableness.

rand·a *f.* border, edge; a —, barely, only just; a — a —, just touching; alla — del giorno, at peep of day; (naut.) spanker, mainsail of a cutter and similar sail on other masts of a schooner; — di cappa, — di fortuna, stormsail. †**-agine** *f.* wandering; andare -agine, to wander, to roam. **-agio** *adj.* stray; straying, wandering. **-are** [A 4] *tr.* to trace an arc or circle. †**-are** *intr.* (naut.) to work the spanker. **-eggiare** [A 3 c] *intr.* (*aux.* avere) (naut.) to cut across the bow or stern of another vessel; to hug a coastline. **-ellare** [A I] *tr.* to cudgel; to beat with a club. **-ellata** *f.* cudgelling. **-ello** *m.* cudgel, truncheon, club; packing-stick (to tighten cord by twisting); †(naut.) toggle used for mooring a galley. †**-ione** *m.* (orn.) gyrfalcon. **-one** *m.* vagrant, vagabond; big stick.

ranella *f.* (eng.) washer.

ranetta[1] *f. dim.* of **rana**, q.v.

ranetta[2] *f.* (agric.). See 'mela ranetta', under **mela**.

ranettina *f. dim.* See under **rana**.

ran·f·ia *f.* claw, talon (cf. **granfia**); **-ignare** [A 5] *tr.* to claw; to seize with claws or talons; to scratch. **-io** *m.* hook.

ranghinatore *m.* (agric.) side-delivery rake.

rangi·fero *m.* See **renna**.

rango *m.* (*pl.* **ranghi**) rank, degree, order; station, status; di primo —, of the first (highest) order; (mil.) file, line, array; *pl.* (fig.) ranks; rientrare nei ranghi, to leave public office.

†**ran·gol·a** *f.*, †**-o** *m.* care, anxiety, worry. †**-are** *intr.* to behave with solicitude, to act cautiously.

†**rangore** *m.* See **rancore**.

Rangùn *pr.n.f.* (geog.) Rangoon.

ranino *adj.* (anat.) ranine; arteria ranina, ranine artery, deep lingual artery.

ranista *m., f.* (sport). See under **rana**.

rann-aiuola *f.*, **-ata** *f.* See under **ranno**.

rannicchi-are [A 4] *rfl.* to crouch, to huddle; to cower; (fig.) -arsi nel suo guscio, to retire into one's shell; *tr.* to cause to crouch or to cower. **-ato** *part. adj.* crouching; -ato in, withdrawn into, shrunk into; con il capo -ato nelle spalle, with one's shoulders hunched.

rannid-are [A I], **-iare** [A 4] *intens.* of **annidare**, q.v.

rann·o *m.* lye (made with boiling water and wood-ash); — vergine (with water not boiling); — di mezzo, — di nitro, lye passed over quicklime (for softening olives); perdere il — e il sapone, to waste one's efforts, to take trouble for nothing; (text.) passaggio al —, scouring; far passare al —, to scour. **-aiuola** *f.* jar for lye; strainer. **-ata** *f.* boiling clothes with lye. **-oso** *adj.* with lye, like lye.

rannobilire [D 2] *intens.* of **annobilire**, q.v.

rannod-are [A I] *tr.* to tie; to join together again; (fig.) to renew; — una conoscenza, to renew an acquaintance; to reunite, to gather together again; — un ragionamento interrotto, to pick up the threads of an interrupted discussion. (**-amento** *m.* **-ato** *part. adj.*) (Cf. **annodare**.)

rannuvol-are [A I s] *intr.* (*aux.* essere), *rfl.* to become cloudy, to cloud over; to become gloomy, to grow dark; (fig.) egli si -ò in viso, his face darkened. (**-amento** *m.*) **-ata** *f.* sudden clouding over. **-ato** *part. adj.* cloudy, clouded over; (fig.) gloomy, dark, troubled. (Cf. **annuvolare**.)

ranoc·chi·o *m.*, **-a** *f.* (zool.) frog, especially the edible frogs, *Rana esculenta*, and *R. viridis*. **-aia** *f.* swampy ground, frog-pond; (orn.) heron, esp. the purple heron, *Ardea purpurea*. **-aio** *m.* frog-seller; one fond of (eating) frogs, frog-eater; (joc.) inhabitant of marshy country. **-esco** *adj.* (*m.pl.* **-eschi**) frog-like.

ran·tol·o *m.* (med.) rhoncus; death-rattle; (fig.) fino all'ultimo —, to the last gasp, to the bitter end; a loud or hoarse cry. **-are** [A I s] *intr.* (*aux.* avere) to breathe stertorously; to cry hoarsely. **-io** *m.* (*pl.* **ii**) frequent rattling in the throat. **-oso** *adj.* stertorous, rough (of breathing).

ra·nula *f.* (med.) ranula.

rap·a *f.* (bot.) turnip, *Brassica rapa*; cavar sangue da una —, to draw blood from a stone; (fig.) dunce, stupid individual; cuore di —, coward; non valere una —, to be good for nothing. **-accione** *m.* colza, cole-seed. **-aio** *m.* turnip-field; (fig.) confusion. **-aiola** *f.* (ent.) small white butterfly, *Pieris rapae*. **-one** *m.* silly individual, fool. **-uglio** *m.* turnip-field.

rapac·e *adj.* rapacious, greedy; predatory; (fig.) fiamma —, devouring flame; (orn.) uccelli -i, raptors; (herald.) lupo —, wolf erect. **-emente** *adv.* rapaciously, greedily; †rapidly. **-ità** *f.* rapacity; †rapidity.

rap·are [A I] *tr.* to crop the hair; farsi —, to have one's hair cropped; — il vello, to clip the fleece close to the skin. **-ata** *f.* crop (of hair cut close); close clipping (in sheep shearing). **-ato** *part. adj.* close-cropped; close-clipped.

rapè *m. indecl.* rappee, coarse snuff.

raperino *m.* (orn.) serin.

raperon-zolo *m.*, **-zo** *m.* (bot.) rampion, *Campanula rapunculus*.

raperu·giolo *m.* (orn.). See **raperino**.

ra·pida *f.* rapid (in a river).

ra·pid·o *adj.* swift; rapid; quick; speedy; — come il pensiero, quick as thought; treno —, express train (to travel by which one has to pay a supplementary fare); un'occhiata -a, a quick glance; †rapacious; *n.m.* express (train); speed. (**-amente** *adv.*) **-ità** *f.* speed, rapidity, quickness, swiftness.

rapin·a *f.* robbery; plundering; pillage; rapine; abduction; uccello di —, bird of prey; plunder, stolen property; violence (of storm, tempest, flood); (leg.) robbery with violence. **-are** [A I] *tr.* to rob, plunder, pillage; to abduct, to kidnap. (**-atore** *m.* **-atrice** *f.* **-eri·a** *f.*) **-oso** *adj.* swift, precipitous; morte -osa, sudden death. **-osamente** *adv.* violently, with violence; swiftly.

rap·ire [D 2] *tr.* to carry off; to steal; to seize, to snatch; (of persons) to abduct, to kidnap; to rape; (fig.) to ravish, to enrapture, to entrance, to fill with delight. **-imento** *m.* carrying off; abduction; rape; ravishment; (mystical theol.) rapture, ecstasy. **-ito** *part. adj.* carried off, stolen, seized; abducted; (fig.) enraptured, entranced, ravished with delight. **-itore** *m.* plunderer; *adj.* plundering. (**-itrice** *f.* also as *adj.*)

rapone *m.* See under **rapaio**.

rapon·tico *m.* (bot.) rhubarb, *Rheum rhaponticum*.

raponzolo *m.* See **raperonzolo**.

rapp-a¹ *f.* (mil.) tassel or pompom of coloured wool on a cap; (eccl.) bunch of dried flowers for altar.

rappa² *f.* (usu. *pl.*) (vet.) broken knee; †wrinkle, crease.

rappaci-are [A 3] *tr.* to reconcile. (**-ato** *part. adj.*) **-ficare** [A 2 s] *tr.* to reconcile; to pacify; *recip. rfl.* to be reconciled; to make it up. **-ficamento** *m.* pacifying; reconciling. (**-ficato** *part. adj.*) **-ficazione** *f.* pacification; reconciliation.

†rappadore *m.* plunderer; brigand (cf. **rapinatore**, under **rapinare**).

rappall-are [A 1], **-ottolare** [A 1 s] *intens.* of **appallottolare**, q.v.

rapparecchiare [A 4 c] *intens.* of **apparecchiare**, q.v.

rappattum-are [A 1] *tr.* to reconcile; to bring together again; *recip. rfl.* to be reconciled; to make it up. (**-ato** *part. adj.*)

†rappell-are *tr.* to recall; to reappeal; to challenge again; to touch up, to improve on. **†-o** *m.* appeal; senza **-o**, without delay.

†rappennecchiare *rfl.* to huddle, to crouch.

rappezz-are [A 1] *tr.* to patch, to patch up; (provb.) cattivo è quel sacco che non si può **—**, it's never too late to mend; (fig) to piece together, to put together. **-amento** *m.* patching; piecing together. (**-ato** *part. adj.* **-atore** *m.* **-atrice** *f.*) **-atura** *f.* patching; piecing together; patchwork.

rappezzo *m.* patching (up); patch; patched work; lavoro fatto di **-i**, patchwork; (fig.) feeble excuse; insufficient remedy; (foundry) scab.

rappiacevolire [D 2] *intens.* of **appiacevolire**, q.v.

rappiastr-are [A 1] *tr.* to replaster; to patch up; *recip. rfl.* (fig.) to 'patch it up'. **-iccicare** [A 2 s] *tr.* to stick again (cf. **appiastrare** and **appiastricciare**).

rappiattare [A 1] *intens.* of **appiattare**, q.v.

rappicc-are [A 2] *tr.* to join again; to fasten again; **—** il fuoco, to start a fire again, to relight; **—** un discorso, to start a speech again, to resume a discussion; **—** l'amicizia con, to renew friendship with; *intr.* (*aux.* avere) to set (of plaster, mortar); *rfl.* to become rekindled, to catch light again. (**-amento** *m.* **-ato** *part. adj.*) **-atura** *f.* sticking (pasting) up again; replastering; patching up. **-icare** [A 2 s] *tr., rfl.* to stick again.

rappigli-are [A 4] *tr., rfl.* to set, to curdle, to coagulate; (of blood) to clot, to coagulate; (fig.) to catch cold. (**-amento** *m.*) **-ato** *part. adj.* curdled; clotted.

rappisolare [A 1 s] *rfl.* See **riappisolare**.

†rappoggiare *vb.* and derivs. See **appoggiare**.

rapport-are [A 1] *tr.* to report; to relate; to tell (sometimes by way of accusation, causing trouble); to transfer (a design); to reproduce; (archit.) **—** un pezzo, to introduce a new piece (by way of repair or restoration); **—** documenti, to produce documents; (Tusc.) **—** la colpa, to attribute blame to; **—** grazie, to return thanks; †to bring, to bring back; †to bring about; †to attain; †to relate, to recite; *rfl.* (*prep.* a) to refer (to); (Tusc.) **-arsi** al parere di uno, to be guided by someone's opinion. (**-amento** *m.* **-ato** *part. adj.*) **-atore** *m.* reporter; tale-bearer, informer, spy; (geom.) protractor; (archit.) pantograph; isometric protractor. (**-atrice** *f.*) (Cf. **riportare**.)

rapporto *m.* report; denunciation; information; statement; secondo un **—** ufficiale, according to an official statement; farò un **—** contro di te al Direttore, I will report you to the Manager; (leg.) far **—** del reato, to report the offence (C.P.); connexion, relation(s); intercourse; non c'è alcun **—** fra quello che tu dici e quello che è accaduto, there is no connexion between what you are saying and what has happened; mettersi in **—** con, to get in touch with; (leg.) **—** di causalità, relation of cause and effect (C.P.); **—** di lavoro, relations between employer and worker (C.C.); **-i** giuridici, legal relations (C.C.); **-i** internazionali, international relations; **-i** amichevoli, friendly relations; **-i** sessuali, sexual intercourse; in **—** a, with reference to; sotto tutti i rapporti, in every respect; (comm.) account; **—** d'affari, dealings; (naut.) letter of proceedings; **—** d'avaria, captain's protest; (mil.) mettersi

a **—**, to demand a hearing; chiamare a **—**, to call for report; gran **—**, full meeting; (math.) ratio; (eng.) **—** di trasmissione, gear ratio; (atom. phys.) **—** di rallentamento, moderating ratio; (embroidery) ricamo a **—**, appliqué work.

rappozzare [A 1] *intens.* of **appozzare**, q.v.

rappren·dere [C 1] *tr., rfl.* to set, to curdle, to coagulate (cf. **rappigliare**).

rappresa·gli-a *f.* reprisal; retaliation; fare **-e**, to retaliate, to make reprisals; per **—**, by way of retaliation. **-are** [A 4] *tr.* to make reprisals upon, to retaliate against; to confiscate by way of reprisal.

rappresent-are [A 1] *tr.* to present; to represent; to show; to be agent for; to deputize for; (theatr.) to perform; **—** una commedia, to perform a play, to put on a comedy; **—** una parte, to act a part; to portray; to symbolize; **—** una parte notevole in società, to play an important part in society; non **—** niente, to be of no importance; to describe, to expound; *rfl.* (acc. of prn. 'si') to be represented; (admin.) invitare a farsi **—**, to invite the sending of a representative; accettare di farsi **—**, to agree to send a representative; (dat. of prn. 'si') to imagine, to picture oneself; *impers.* (theatr.) questa settimana si **-a** *La Travia a, La Traviata* is on this week. **-a·bile** *adj.* capable of being represented; presentable; representative; (theatr.) capable of being performed, suitable for stage performance. **-ante** *part. adj.* representing; portraying; (theatr.) scenico **-ante**, actor; *n.m.* representative, agent; delegate, deputy; (leg.) representative; (comm.) agent; representative, proxy; **-ante** esclusivo, sole agent or representative. **-anza** *f.* representation; agency; in **-anza**, as representative, as agent; **-anza** esclusiva, sole agency; (pol.) **-anza** proporzionale, proportional representation; **-anza** ponderata, balanced representation; (leg.) representation; **-anza** dell'incapace, representation of person under disability (C.C.); assembly; **-anza** nazionale, national assembly or representation. **-ativo** *adj.* representative; le arti **-ative**, the representative arts; persona **-ativa**, a person representative or typical (of an age, party, class); sistema **-ativo**, representative system, a system of election; (mus.) expressive, illustrative. (**-ativamente** *adv.*) **-ato** *part. adj.* presented; performed; shown; una commedia mai **-ata**, a play never performed before. (**-atore** *m.* **-atrice** *f.*) **-azione** *f.* representation; (theatr.) performance; **-azione** diurna, matinée; sacra **-azione**, mystery, miracle-play; (theol.) (symbolic) representation; description; mental image; (leg.) representation; legal personal representatives (collectively); i discendenti succedono per **-azione**, descendants succeed by representation; una **-azione** meccanica, a mechanical representation (C.C.).

rappreso *part.* of **rapprendere**, q.v.

rapprossimare [A 1 s] *intens.* of **approssimare**, q.v.

rapsod-i·a *f.* (Gk. lit.) rhapsody; recitation or composition of epic; portion of an epic convenient for one recitation; medley (in verse); (mus.) rhapsody. **-ista** *m.* rhapsodist; author of a poetic medley.

rapsodo *m.* (Gk. lit.) rhapsode; bard reciting his own poems; minstrel reciting the poems of others; professional reciter.

rapu·glio *m.* See under **rapaio**.

rar-o *adj.* rare; uncommon; exceptional; di **-a** bellezza, of rare beauty, uncommonly beautiful; scanty, thinly scattered; nuvola **-a**, thin cloud, light cloud; popolazione **-a**, sparse population; **-a** avis, rare bird (also fig.); *adv. phr.* di **—**, seldom, rarely. **-efa·bile** *adj.* rarefiable. **-efacimento** *m.* rarefaction. **-efare** [B 14] *tr.* to rarefy; (chem.) to dilute; **-efare** il terreno, to loosen the ground. (**-efatti·bile** *adj.*, **-efattivo** *adj.*) **-efatto** *part. adj.* rarefied; (fig.) subtle, refined. **-efazione** *f.* (phys.) rarefaction, rarefying; dilution. **-ezza** *f.* rarity; scarcity. **-ificato** *part. adj.* rarefied. **-ità** *f.* rarity; unusualness; scarcity; curiosity; uncommon object; questa è una **-ità**, this is a curiosity; (text.) thinness.

ras *m. indecl.* Abyssinian feudal chief, ras; (fig.) one who gives himself airs, a bumptious man.

rasa¹ *f.* (ichth.) ray (a common dialect form of **razza**, q.v.).

†rasa² *f.* See **ragia**.

ras-are [A 1] *tr.* to level; to smooth; to shave; **—** la siepe, to clip the hedge. **-amento** *m.* levelling; smoothing; (eng.) shim adjustment to a given clearance. **-ato** *part. adj.* smooth; clean-shaven; (text.) sateen. **-atura** *f.* shaving; smoothing; what is removed by shaving or smoothing off; (techn.) shavings, chips (of leather, etc.).

raschi-are [A 4] *tr.* to scrape; **—** via, to scrape off, to scrape away; (surg.) to curette; (naut.) **—** la carena, to scrape the bottom or

raschi-are (*cont.*)

hull; *intr.* (*aux.* avere) to clear one's throat; to cough (e.g. to attract attention); *rfl.* -arsi in gola, to clear one's throat. **-a·bile** *adj.* capable of being scraped away. **-amento** *m.* scraping; (surg.) curettage. **-ao·lio** *m. indecl.* (motor.; eng.) scraper-ring. **-archivi** *m. indecl.* (joc.) antiquary. **-ata** *f.* scrape; (joc.) darsi una -ata, to give oneself a scrape, i.e. to shave. (-ato *part. adj.*) **-atoio** *m.* (eng.) rabble, scraper, burnisher. **-atore** *m.* scraper; (archaeol.) side-scraper. **-atrice** *f.* (text.) stripping machine, fibre-extracting machine. **-atura** *f.* scraping, scrape; *pl.* scrapings; scratch; erasure.

raschiett-o *m.* (eng.) scraper; erasing knife. **-are** [A I c] *tr.* (eng.) to scrape.

raschin-o *m.* eraser, scratching knife; foot-scraper; (tanning) unhairing knife, scudding knife. **-are** [A I] *tr.* (eng.) to scrape.

ra·schio *m.* clearing one's throat; irritation in the throat.

ra·scia *f.* coarse serge (from Rashka in Yugoslavia) funeral hangings for doors.

rasciug-are [A 2] *tr.* to dry; to dry up; (joc.) — una bottiglia, to drink a bottle dry; — le tasche, to empty one's pockets, i.e. to spend all one's money; *rfl.* to dry oneself; to become dry or dried up; to wipe off one's perspiration; (iron., in locutions suggesting that one is lazy or is making a fuss about nothing) to pretend to work hard. (-amento *m.* -atura *f.*) (Cf. asciugare.)

rasciutt-o *adj.* dried up; dry; una bottiglia -a, an empty bottle. **-are** [A I] and derivs. see **rasciugare**.

rasent-e *prep.* (freq. followed by prep. 'a') along by; close to; — al muro, close to the wall; — a terra, (passing) close to the ground. **-are** [A I] to pass close to; to come near to; -are il patibolo, to cheat the gallows; (fig.) -are il codice penale, to sail close to the wind; questo -a la pazzia, this borders on madness.

rasetta *f.* (ichth.) *Raia punctata*, and other small rays.

rasier-a *f.* strickle, a straight-edge for levelling the top of a measure of grain; (carpen.) scraper (consisting of a short, broad blade for smoothing a board after it has been rasped). **-are** [A I] *tr.* to scrape, to smooth.

ras-o *part.* of **radere**, q.v.; *adj.* shaven; smooth; un cane dal pelo —, a short-haired dog; terreno —, levelled ground; campagna -a, bare country (level and treeless); misura -a, full measure (to the brim, i.e. level, not heaped); pieno —, full to the brim; (cul.) level; cucchiaino —, level teaspoonful; far tabula -a di, to sweep away, to make a clean sweep of; (naut.) nave -a, ship whose top hamper has been cut down or dismasted, or flush decked ship; alla -a, dismasted or with upper batteries struck down; a —!, order to sail full and by, or close to the wind with sails filling; — al vento, close to the wind; — che portino!, sail close!; †— d'acqua, waterline; cancelled; — di, deprived of; — di ogni baldanza (Dante), without any haughtiness; (embroidery) punto —, satin stitch; *adv.* close; *quasi prep.* — terra, close to the ground; *n.m.* satin; — di lana, wool satin, wool-backed satin; — operato, brocaded satin; — turco, Turkey twill; measure of length (about 60 cm.) formerly in use in the Kingdom of Sardinia. **-etto** *m.* sateen. **-ile** *adj.* easily scraped away.

rasoi-o *m.* razor; — di sicurezza, safety razor; dar la striscia al —, to strop the razor; attaccarsi ai rasoi, to try anything (however dangerous), to try desperate remedies; camminare sul filo d'un —, to walk on a razor's edge; che taglia come un —, razor-sharp. **-ata** *f.* razor-cut; tra una -ata e l'altra, while shaving.

rasp-a *f.* scraper; rasp; — mezzo tonda, half-round rasp; — per ebanisti, cabinet rasp. (-amento *m.*) **-ante** *part. adj.* rasping; vino -ante, sour wine. **-are** [A I] *tr.* to rasp, to scrape, to file down; to wear away; (of water) to erode; to scratch; to make scratching or scraping sounds; -are la gola, to irritate, to tickle, to burn the throat; il cavallo impaziente -a il terreno, the impatient horse paws the ground; il pollo -a, the chicken scratches about; (fam.) to pinch, to steal; to achieve; armeggia tutto il giorno e non si sa quel che -i, he fusses about all day and doesn't seem to get anything done; to scrawl, to scribble; to rummage; -a nel cassetto, look in the chest. **-atic·cio** *m.* scribble, scrawl; inferior workmanship. **-atino** *m.* very dry or sharp wine. **-ato** *part. adj.* rasped. **-atura** *f.* rasping, raspings, scrapings; (fig.) -atura di gallina, scrawl, scribble. **-erella** *f.* (bot.) common horsetail, *Equisetum arvense*. **-ino** *m.* smoothing file. **-io** *m.* (*pl.* ii) continued rasping, scraping, scratching.

rasp-o *m.* grape-stalk; sour taste (as of grape-stalks); mange (in

dogs); baker's rake. **-ollare** [A I c] *tr.*, *intr.* (*aux.* avere) (agric.) to glean (the vines). (-ollatura *f.*) **-ollo** *m.* small bunch of grapes passed over in the general picking.

rasseg-are [A 2] *intr.* (*aux.* essere), *rfl.* to form a layer of cold fat, to congeal; to set again (e.g. of butter after melting). (-amento *m.*) **-ato** *part. adj.* gone cold (therefore appearing greasy); (fig.) stale; sorriso -ato, forced smile.

rasseghio *m.* skin of fat formed or forming on cold soup or gravy.

rassegna *f.* (mil.) display; review; passare in —, to pass in review; (naut.) discharge (as being unfit); review, criticism, report; (printed periodical) review; recapitulation; facciamo una —, let us review the facts, to recapitulate; passare in — le cause, to review the causes.

rassegn-are [A 5 c] *tr.* to resign; — le demissioni, to hand in one's papers, to resign; to review, to mention, to enumerate; libro che -a i fatti avvenuti, a book giving an account of the events; (mil.) to check over; to review, to inspect; to take a census of; *rfl.* to resign oneself; to submit; dobbiamo -arci, we must accept the inevitable; to sign (oneself); mi -o vostro devotissimo, I am yours truly. **-amento** *m.* (military) review; resignation. **-atario** *m.* †(canon law) resignee. **-ato** *part. adj.* handed in, consigned, resigned; essere -ato al (proprio) destino, to be resigned to one's fate. **-atamente** *adv.* resignedly, with resignation. (-atore *m.* -atrice *f.*) **-azione** *f.* resignation, submission, meekness; eroica -azione, fortitude.

rassembrare [A I] (poet.) see **rassomigliare** or **radunare**.

†rassemprare *tr.* to copy, to make a copy of; to draw.

rasseren-are [A I c] *tr.* to clear; questo vento -erà il cielo, this wind will clear away the clouds; (fig.) to cheer up, to bring back serenity to; *intr.* (*aux.* essere), *rfl.* to clear up, to become bright again; il cielo (si) -ò verso tramonto, towards sunset the sky cleared; (fig.) to cheer up, to recover one's serenity; to brighten up; la notizia lo fece —, the news cheered him. **-amento** *m.* clearing; clearing up, brightening; (fig.) cheering up; recovery of one's serenity. **-ato** *part. adj.* cleared up; rendered serene again; cheered, in better spirits.

rassestare [A I] *intens.* of **assestare**, q.v.

rassett-are [A I] *tr.* to arrange, to rearrange; to tidy up; to set in order; to adjust; to patch (up), to mend; to put right; *rfl.* to make oneself tidy, to tidy oneself up; (equit.) -arsi in sella, to settle oneself in the saddle. (-amento *m.*) **-apiatti** *m. indecl.* potmender. **-ato** *part. adj.* rearranged; tidied; adjusted; mended; set right; patched up. (-atore *m.* -atora *f.* -atrice *f.*) **-atura** *f.* tidying up, arranging; arrangement; mending; setting to rights. (Cf. **assettare**.)

rassicur-are [A I] *tr.* to reassure; *rfl.* to assure oneself; to be reassured; to reassure oneself; to make certain. **-ante** *part. adj.* reassuring. **-ato** *part. adj.* reassured; (made) sure; tranquillized. (-atore *m.* -atrice *f.*) **-azione** *f.* (often *pl.*) assurance, reassurance.

rassod-are [A I] *tr.* to harden; to make firm; il freddo intenso -a il terreno, the severe cold makes the ground hard; to dry; to consolidate; to strengthen; la disgrazia -ò la loro amicizia, the misfortune cemented their friendship; *intr.* (*aux.* essere), *rfl.* to harden; to set; to dry; to become stronger; to be consolidated; to be confirmed. (-ato *part. adj.*) (Cf. **assodare**.)

†rassodi·a *f.* (mus.). See **rapsodia**.

rassomigli-are [A 4] *intr.* (*aux.* essere), *rfl.* to be like, to resemble, to bear a resemblance; -a alla madre, he is like his mother; to appear like; mi -a a persona che sia stata molto malata, he looks to me like someone who has been very ill; *tr.* -a lo zio, he looks like his uncle; to compare; lo -ò a demonio, he said he was like a devil; *recip. rfl.* to resemble each other; i due fratelli si -ano, the two brothers are very much alike. **-amento** *m.* resemblance; comparison. **-ante** *part. adj.* like, alike; bearing a resemblance; ritratto -ante, a good likeness. **-anza** *f.* likeness; resemblance; comparison. **-ativo** *adj.* (gramm.) expressing likeness; imitative. (-atore *m.* -atrice *f.*)

rassottigli-are [A 4] *tr.* to make thinner; to diminish, to reduce; to make finer, sharper; (fig.) to sharpen; — la mente, l'ingegno, to sharpen one's wits; *rfl.* to grow thin; to become smaller; to become finer, sharper. **-amento** *m.* fining, sharpening. **-ato** *part. adj.* thinner; made finer, sharper; diminished, reduced. (Cf. **assottigliare**.)

rastello *m.* and derivs. See **rastrello**.

†rastiare *vb.* and derivs. See **raschiare**.

rastiatore *m.* (text.) stripping knife.

rastrell-are [A 1] *tr.* to rake; to rake away; (fam.) to steal, to 'lift'; to search, to ransack; to gather up, to collect; to rake (e.g. the fire of a furnace or boiler); (mil.) to search (a ground) for snipers, etc.; to 'comb'; (naut.) to sail close to; to drag (an object) alongside or astern of a ship; *intr.* (*aux.* avere) to smell the bottom, to sweep the bottom. **-amento** *m.* raking; searching, search. **-ata** *f.* rake (i.e. one movement of the rake); rakeful, quantity of hay, etc. gathered up by a rake. **-atura** *f.* raking. **-iera** *f.* rack; hay-rack (e.g. in stables); gun-rack; plate-rack; (fam., joc.) false teeth; set of teeth; (text.) creel; (naut.) arms rack; capstan bar rack; **-iera** di caviglie, **-iera** di manovre, cleat rail (generally forming a square at the foot of the mast and holding belaying pins); (mus.) pipe-rack (of organ).

rastrell-o *m.* (agric.) rake; rail, railing; (text., etc.) rake; (mil.) outer defences such as dragon's teeth; menare il —, to take, to sack, to loot; (naut.) gantline or clothes line; shell fish dredge; grab dredger; boiler rake or slice.

rastrem-are [A 1] *tr.* (archit.) to reduce gradually the diameter of a column as it rises, to taper; (eng.) to taper, to scarf; *intr.* (*aux.* essere), *rfl.* to taper. **-ato** *part. adj.* tapered; tapering; (eng.) raccordo **-ato**, reducing coupling. **-atrice** *f.* (eng.) taper swaging machine. **-azione** *f.* tapering, reduction in scale.

rastro *m.* rake; (mus.) rastrum, music-pen (with five points for drawing the stave).

rasura *f.* scraping, grazing, shaving; erasure; tonsure.

rat-a *f.* instalment; comprare, vendere, a **-e**, to buy, to sell, by instalments, on hire-purchase; proportion; a, per, pro —, proportionately; rate, share. **-eale** *adj.* periodical; by instalments; compra a pagamento **-eale**, purchase by periodical payments (C.C.), hire-purchase. **-ealmente** *adv.* periodically; by instalments. **-eare** [A 6], **-izzare** [A 1] *tr.* to divide into instalments; **-eare** un pagamento, to arrange payment by instalments. **-eazione** *f.* division into instalments.

ratafià, ratafi·a *m. indecl.* ratafia (liqueur).

rata·nia *f.* (bot.) rhatany, *Krameria* spp.

†**rate** *f.* raft.

rat-eale *adj.*, **-eare** [A 6]. See under **rata**.

ratelo *m.* (zool.) ratel, *Mellivora capensis*.

ra·teo *m.* (finan.) calculation of interest for broken period; proportionate part of interest accrued to date or of sum overpaid.

†**ratiabizione** *f.* (leg.) ratification.

raticon-e, -i *adv.* andar —, to wander about.

ratiera *f.* (text.) dobby.

rati·fica *f.* ratification; sanction, approval.

ratific-are [A 2 s] *tr.* to ratify; (leg.) to ratify; to confirm; *rfl.* to declare, to make a declaration; to confirm one's statement. (**-ato** *part. adj.*) **-azione** *f.* ratification; confirmation; approval.

†**rati·lia** *f.* vessel, craft.

ratin-are [A 1] *tr.* (text.) to frieze. **-atrice** *f.* friezing machine. **-atura** *f.* friezing.

†**rati·o** *adj.* wandering, errant.

†**ratire** *intr.* to give forth a death-rattle.

Ratiṣbona *pr.n.f.* (geog.) Ratisbon, Regensburg.

ratito *adj.* (Rom. numism., of a coin) bearing a raft.

ratizzare [A 1], **-o** *m.* See under **rata**.

rato *adj.* (leg.) decided; approved; affirmed; confirmed; ratified; agreed; — e fatto, agreed and affirmed; — e fermo, acknowledged and affirmed; (canon law) matrimonio —, *matrimonium ratum*.

ratta *f.* (archit.) either end of a column; — da piedi, foot of a column with cavetto (cf. **imoscapo**); — di sopra, top of a column under the capital (cf. **sommoscapo**).

rattaccon-are [A 1 c] *tr.* to heel (boots and shoes); to mend, to patch. (**-amento** *m.* **-ato** *part. adj.*)

rattemp(e)r-are [A 1, A 1 s] *tr.* to moderate; — lo sdegno, to moderate one's anger; *rfl.* to restrain oneself, to keep calm; to exercise restraint. (**-amento** *m.* **-ato** *part. adj.*)

†**ratten·dere** *tr.* to expect; to await.

ratten-ere [B 32] *tr.* to hold back; to keep in; to retain; — le lagrime, to keep back one's tears; to restrain; — in mente, to remember; *rfl.* to hold oneself in, to exercise restraint; **-ersi** a, to hold on to; **-ersi** alla corda, to hold on to the rope; c'è da **-ersi**, there is need for circumspection. (**-imento** *m.*) **-itoio** *m.* restraint; curb; dam. **-uta** *f.* retaining, retention; catch-pit (for stagnant water); keeping back; amount deducted or kept back (e.g. from wages). **-uto**

part. adj. restrained; held back; cautious. **-zione** *f.* retention, holding back; restraint; circumspection.

rattęzza *f.* speed, rapidity; steepness (cf. **ratto²**).

ratticida *adj.* rodenticidal; *n.m.* rodenticide.

rattin-a *f.* ratteen. **-are** [A 1] and derivs. See **ratinare**.

rattivo *adj.* swift; rapacious.

rattizzare [A 1] and derivs. See **attizzare**.

ratto¹ *m.* rapine; theft; abduction, kidnapping, rape; il — di Elena, the abduction of Helen; il — delle Sabine, the rape of the Sabines; (leg.) abduction; — o violenza carnale, abduction or rape (C.C.); abduction by force or fraud (C.P.); (theol.) ecstasy.

ratto² *adj.* (usu. poet. or lit.) swift, quick, ready; *adv.* swiftly; — vola il tempo, time flies swiftly. (**-amente** *adv.*)

ratto³ *m.* (zool.) rat.

ratton-e, -i *adv.* secretly, slyly; ratton rattoni, stealthily.

rattopp-are [A 1] *tr.* to patch, to mend; to cobble; (fig.) to revise, to correct; (motor.) to patch (tyres); (naut.) to repair, to patch (canvas). **-amento** *m.* patching, mending. **-ato** *part. adj.* patched, mended; cobbled; (fig.) patched up. (**-atore** *m.* **-atrice** *f.* **-atura** *f.*)

rattoppo *m.* patch; mend; (motor.) patch on a tyre.

rattor·cere [C 5] and derivs. (poet.). See **attorcere**.

†**trattore** *m.* ravisher; kidnapper; extortioner.

rattralci-are [A 3] *intr.* (*aux.* avere) (agric.) to tie up the tendrils of young vine shoots (also *tr.*). (**-atura** *f.*)

rattrapp-ire [D 2] *tr.* to cause to contract; to paralyse; to benumb; il freddo mi ha **-ito** le mani, my hands are numb with cold; *intr.* (*aux.* essere), *rfl.* to become contracted, stiff, numb or paralysed; to shrink, to contract. **-imento** *m.* shrinking; numbing; (fig.) paralysis. **-ito** *part. adj.* numb, benumbed; stiff; avevo le mani **-ite**, my hands were numb; paralysed.

rat-trarre [B 33] *tr.* to cause to contract; to paralyse; *intr.* (*aux.* essere), *rfl.* to become stiff, numb or paralysed. **-traimento** *m.* contraction, convulsion; paralysis. **-tratto** *part. adj.* drawn together; stiff, paralysed; rimaner come **-tratto**, to stand stock still, to seem paralysed; mano **-tratta**, hand half-clenched; (fig.) avere le mani **-tratte**, to be close-fisted, grasping.

rattrist-are [A 1] *tr.* to grieve, to make sad, to sadden; to afflict; *rfl.* to grow sad, to grieve; (of plants) to droop. **-amento** *m.* affliction; grieving; grief, sadness. **-ante** *part. adj.* sad (i.e. inducing sadness, sorrow or grief); spettacolo **-ante**, distressing sight, sorry spectacle. **-ato** *part. adj.* sad (i.e. feeling sadness, sorrow or grief); sorry, sorrowful, grieved. (Cf. **attristare**.)

rattrist-ire [D 2] *tr.* to depress; questa pioggia ci **-isce**, this rain is very depressing; (of plants) to stunt, to cause to languish; *intr.* (*aux.* essere) to droop, to languish, to be enfeebled; la mancanza d'aria e di sole fa — le piante, the lack of air and sunlight causes plants to languish; *rfl.* to become gloomy; to be depressed; to become enfeebled; to languish, to droop. **-ito** *part. adj.* depressed; drooping; enfeebled.

†**trattura** *f.* rape.

ra·u-co *adj.* (*m.pl.* **-chi**) hoarse; harsh (of voice); strident. (**-camente** *adv.*) **-ce·dine** *f.* hoarseness.

†**trauge·o** *adj.* Ragusan; usurious.

Ra·ulo *pr.n.m.* Ralph.

raumiliare [A 4] and derivs. See **umiliare**.

raunare [A 1 a] and derivs. (pop.). See **radunare**.

†**trauncin-ato**, †**-uto** *adj.* hooked at one end.

ravagliat-ọre *m.* a kind of plough. **-ura** *f.* (agric.) the action of drawing earth from a furrow and replacing it on both sides.

rava·glio *m.* (ichth.) — bogo, Spanish bream, *Pagellus bogaraveo*.

†**travaglione** *m.* See **variecella**.

ravanastro·n *m. indecl.* (mus.) ravanastron, a kind of oriental violin.

ravan-ello *m.* (bot.) radish, *Raphanus sativus*. **-ẹse** *m.* (bot.) spelt (a grain similar to wheat).

ravanẹto *m.* (geog.) heap of rubble; steep slope below a marble quarry, used for tipping waste or blocks for loading.

†**tra·vano** *m.* See **ravanello**.

ravastina *f.* Sicilian method of fishing by night; net used in this method.

raveggiuolo *m.* See **ravigiuolo**.

Ravenn-a *pr.n.f.* (geog.) Ravenna. **-ate** *adj.* of Ravenna; *n.m.* inhabitant of Ravenna; district round Ravenna; *f.* woman of, from, Ravenna.

raver-u·schio, -usto *m.* (agric.) a kind of grape used to give colour to wine.

ravigi(u)olo *m.* a kind of soft cheese, made from goat's or sheep's milk.

ravi(u)oli *m.pl.* (cul.) ravioli, small, lightly cooked patties with 'ricotta', minced meat, spinach or other filling.

ravizzọne *m.* (bot.) rape, cole, *Brassica napus* var. *oleifera*; olio di —, colza oil.

†ravo *adj.*, *n.m.* dark yellow, deep gold.

ravvalor-are [A I c] *tr.* to strengthen, to reinforce; to enhance the value of. (**-ato** *part. adj.*) (Cf. **avvalorare**.)

ravved-ẹre [B I] *rfl.* to reflect upon the error of one's ways and repent; to acknowledge one's faults or mistakes; to mend one's ways; to reform. **-imẹnto** *m.* repentance; amendment; reform. **-uto** *part. adj.* repentant; amended; reformed.

ravvelenare [A I c] and derivs. See **avvelenare**.

ravvenare [A I c] *intr.* (*aux.* essere) (of a spring) to flow again.

ravversare [A I] *tr.* to tidy (up), to set in order; *rfl.* to tidy oneself.

ravvi-are [A I] *tr.* to set going again, to start again; to put on the right road again; (comm.) to set in order, to straighten, to adjust, to tidy; — una matassa arruffata, to disentangle a skein; *rfl.* (*acc.* of *prn.* 'si') to tidy oneself (clothes, hair); ora che ti sei -ato possiamo andare, now you have made yourself tidy we can go; (*dat.* of *prn.* 'si') -arsi i capelli, to tidy, to comb, one's hair. (**-amẹnto** *m.*) **-ata** *f.* tidying up; darsi una -ata, ai capelli, to run a comb through one's hair. **-ato** *part. adj.* tidied, set in order; set right; started afresh.

ravvicin-are [A I] *tr.* to bring closer; to bring together again; to reconcile; to compare; *rfl.* to draw closer; to come together again; to be reconciled. **-amẹnto** *m.* drawing nearer. (Cf. **avvicinare**.)

ravvigorire [D 2] and derivs. See **rinvigorire**.

ravvilire [D 2] *intens.* of **avvilire**, q.v.

ravvilupp-are [A I] *tr.* to entangle, to hem in; to confuse; *rfl.* to become tangled, entangled, entwined. (**-amẹnto** *m.*) **-ato** *part. adj.* entangled, entwined; confused; dramma -ato, play with a complicated plot. (Cf. **aviluppare**.)

ravvin-cidire [D 2] see **invincidire**. **-to** *part. adj.* see **avvinto**.

ravviṣ-are [A I] *tr.* to recognize; lo -ai subito, I knew him at once; to perceive, to see; (fig.) qui si -a la mano del maestro, here we recognize the master's hand. (**-a·bile** *adj.* **-ato** *part. adj.*)

ravviv-are [A I] *tr.* to revive; to give new life to; to restore to life (or consciousness); to enliven; (fig.) — il fuoco, to stir (draw up) the fire; (text.) to revive; (eng.) to dress (a grinding wheel); *rfl.* to revive, to be revived; to brighten up, to cheer up. (**-amẹnto** *m.* **-ante** *part. adj.* **-ato** *part. adj.* revived; *pr.n.m.pl.* (lit. hist.) I Ravvivati, members of an academy of Siena. **-atọre** *m.* one who revives or restores; (eng.) grinding wheel dresser (also **-atrice** *f.*). **-atura** *f.* (eng.) dressing, trueing.

ravvọlg-ere [C 5] *tr.* to wrap up; to wrap round and round; l'infermiera gli ravvolse una benda al braccio, the nurse wrapped a bandage round his arm; to rewind; *rfl.* to wrap oneself up (as in a cloak), -ersi in, to wrap oneself (up) in; (fig.) -ersi in un sacco, to become a monk or friar; to go round and round; to twist and turn; to roam; (of wine, etc.) to 'turn'. **-imẹnto** *m.* wrapping up; turning, twisting; (fig.) tortuousness, trickery, deceit. (**-itọre** *m.* **-itrice** *f.* **-itura** *f.*)

ravvọlt-a *f.* wrapping up; turn; tortuousness. **-are** [A I] *tr.* to wrap up; to involve. (**-ato** *part. adj.* **-atura** *f.*)

ravvọlto *part.* of **ravvolgere**, q.v.; *adj.* wrapped up; coiled; contorted; twisted; (fig.) involved, confused; *n.m.* bundle; parcel.

ravvoltolare [A I s] *tr.* to wrap up; *rfl.* to wrap (roll) oneself up (in cloak, blankets, etc.); ravvoltolarsi per terra, to roll on the ground; ravvoltolarsi nel fango, to wallow in the mire (cf. **avvoltolare**).

rayo·n *m. indecl.* (text.) rayon.

raz *m. indecl.* (naut.) — di marea, tidal wave.

raziale *adj.* See **razziale**, under **razza**.

raziocin-are [A I] *intr.* (*aux.* avere) to reason, to argue logically. (**-ante** *part. adj.*) **-ativo** *adj.* ratiocinative. **-aziọne** *f.* ratiocination, reasoning; series of arguments.

raziọci·nio *m.* reasoning; reason; ratiocination; good sense, judgement.

raziona·bil-e[1] *adj.* rational. **-ità** *f.* rationality; use of reason. **-mẹnte** *adv.* rationally, logically.

raziona·bile[2] *adj.* that can be rationed (cf. **razionare**).

razional-e *adj.* rational; (philos.) rational; in accordance with reason; endowed with reason; creatura —, rational (reasonable)

creature; rationalist(ic); (math.) rational; (mus.) intervallo —, rational interval; *n.m.* (Bibl.) breastplate, pectoral, of the High Priest; (liturg.) *rationale*, episcopal humeral or ornament; — liturgico, the *Rationale divinorum officiorum* of Durandus; (Rom. antiq.) *rationalis*, accountant or treasurer. (**-mẹnte** *adv.*) **-iṣmo** *m.* rationalism; -ismo teologico, theological rationalism. **-ista** *m., f.* rationalist. **-iṣ·tico** *adj.* rationalistic. **-ità** *f.* rationality; reason. **-iẓẓare** [A I] *tr.* (industr.) to rationalize, to place on a sound financial footing, to render efficient. **-iẓẓaziọne** *f.* (industr.) rationalization.

raziọn-e *f.* ration. **-amẹnto** *m.* rationing. **-are** [A I c] *tr.* to ration; †see **raziocinare**.

razz-a[1] *f.* race, breed; la — umana, the human race, mankind; di buona —, of good stock; di — pura, thoroughbred, (fig.) first-rate; un cavallo di — pura, a thoroughbred; di — incrociata, cross-bred; far — da sè, to inbreed, (fig.) to be stand-offish, unsociable; barriera di —, colour bar, racial discrimination; di ogni —, of all kinds; che — d'uomo è?, what sort of a man is he?; che — di briccone!, what a scoundrel!; — di vipere!, generation of vipers! **-iale** *adj.* racial. **-iṣmo** *m.* racialism. (**-ista** *adj.*, *n.m., f.*)

razza[2] *f.* (ichth.) ray, skate; — bavosa, *Raia macrorhynchus*; — monaca, *R. oxyrhynchus*; — chiodata, *R. clavata*; — grigia, *R. fullonica*; — marginata, *R. alba*; — stellata, — macchiettata, picchiettata, *R. asterias*; — baraccola, — occhiuta, *R. miraletus*; — scuffina, *R. radula*.

razza[3] *f.* spoke (of a wheel).

razza·ia *f.* strip of sandy or stony ground.

razza·io *m.* See under **razzo**.

razzama·glia *f.* See **razzumaglia**.

razz-are [A I] *tr.* to trim after pruning or lopping; to tie or chain up (a wheel by the spokes, when going downhill); to scrape; to scratch; *intr.* (*aux.* avere) to shine brightly; to emit rays of light; il sole cade -ando infocato (Pascoli), the sun sets with a blaze of fiery rays; *rfl.* (of the skin) to show streaks of inflammation. **-ante** *part. adj.* shining, radiating, radiant. **-ato** *part. adj.* streaked, marked with rays (or like rays); inflamed. **-atura** *f.* streakiness; streak of inflammation; pruning. **-ente** *adj.* (of wine) sharp; piquant; burning. **†-eggiare** *intr.* to shine, to emit rays.

razz-ia *f.* raid, plundering raid; plunder; requisition, depredation; round-up of suspects; name of an insecticide powder. **-iare** [A 4] *tr.* (neol.) to raid, to make a raid upon; to plunder; to requisition. (**-iatọre** *m.* **-iatrice** *f.*)

razzin-a·ia *f.*, **-ẹto** *m.* See **razzaia**.

razz-o *m.* rocket; lesto come un —, like a shot; (mil.) rocket; (aeron.) — ausiliario di decollaggio, take-off rocket, jato unit; (mus.) run, division; spoke (of a wheel); †ray of light. **-a·io** *m.* rocket-maker; (agric.) a kind of black olive. **-ẹse** *m.* a kind of Ligurian wine.

razzol-are [A I s] *intr.* (*aux.* avere) to scratch about (of fowls); (provb.) chi di gallina nasce convien che -i, what's bred in the bone comes out in the flesh; predicar bene e — male, not to practise what one preaches; (agric.) to weed; *tr.* to rummage for; che cosa -i in quel cassetto?, what are you rummaging for in that chest? **-ante** *part. adj.* scratching; *n.m.pl.* le -anti, fowls. (**-ata** *f.* **-atọre** *m.* **-atrice** *f.*) **-atura** *f.* scratching; rummaging. **-ìo** *m.* continual scratching or rummaging.

razzuffare [A I] and derivs. See **riazzuffare**.

razzuma·glia *f.* rubble.

rẹ[1] *m. indecl.* king; il Libro dei —, The Book of Kings; III Re, I Chronicles; IV Re, II Chronicles; i — Magi, the three Wise Men, the Magi, the Three Kings; (class. antiq.) — (sacerdote), *rex sacrorum*; — del convito, president of a banquet; — d'armi, king-at-arms; (chess) king; (ichth.) — degli aringhi, *Chimaera monstrosa*, rabbit fish; (cards) — di cuori, di quadri, di fiori, di picche, king of hearts, of diamonds, of clubs, of spades; — travicello, King Log; il — dei vini, the king (prince) of wines, i.e. the best of all; (orn.) — degli edredoni, king eider, *Somateria spectabilis*; — di macchia, wren; — di quaglie, corncrake, *Crex crex*. **-u·ccio** *m. dim.* baby prince.

re[2] *m.* (mus.) re (i.e. the second degree of the scale); the note D; the key of D.

re[3] *f.* (leg.) matter; — familiare, claim for a home and maintenance; *prep.* in the matter of, re.

rea *f.* (text.) ramee fibre, China grass.

reag·ire [D 2] *intr.* (*aux.* avere) to react; to show opposition; accettare una condizione senza —, to accept a condition without raising any objection or making difficulties. **-ente** *part. adj.* reacting; *n.m.* (chem.) reagent.

real-e[1] *adj.* real; actual; senso —, literal meaning; (mus.) fuga —, real fugue; (leg.) diritto —, real right, right *in rem*. **-mente** *adv.* really; in reality; in fact, indeed; (mus.) really, i.e. according to the rules of real fugue.

real-e[2] *adj.* royal; fiume —, river having tributaries, that flows into the sea; (orn.) aquila —, golden eagle, *Aquila chrysaëtos*; cigno —, mute swan, *Cygnus olor*; gabbiano —, herring gull, *Larus argentatus*; (mil.) guardia —, royal guard; pezzo —, artillery; galera —, flagship; *n.f.* (mil.) guard of a royal residence; (naut.) large mesh portion of a fishing net; *n.m.* (numism.) real, a Spanish coin; *n.m.pl.* i Reali, the King and Queen; the Royal Family; *I -i di Francia*, *The Kings of France* (title of a book formerly extremely popular, based on the *Chansons de Geste*, by Andrea da Barberino). **-ista** *m.*, *f.* royalist; più -ista del re, out-Heroding Herod.

realgar *m. indecl.* (chem.) realgar, red arsenic.

real-ismo *m.* (philos.) realism; (arts and literature) realism. **-ista** *m.*, *f.* realist. **-i·stico** *adj.* realistic. **-ità** *f.* see realtà. **-izzare** [A 1] *tr.* to make real; to implement; -izzare una promessa, to keep a promise; -izzare uno scopo, to achieve one's aim or object; (comm.) to realize, to convert into cash; to sell; -izzare titoli, to sell shares; *rfl.* to come true; to come to pass; un libro intorno al -izzarsi dei sogni, a book about dreams that come true. **-izza·bile** *adj.* realizable; (finan.) convertible. **-izza·tore** *m.* practical man; one who gets things done; (theatr.) -izzatore delle luci, manager of stage lighting. **-izzazione** *f.* carrying into effect; realization; di difficile -izzazione, difficult to achieve; -izzazione scenica, performance shown on the stage or screen; (comm.) conto di -izzazione, realization account; (techn.) embodiment (of an invention); (mus.) la -izzazione del basso continuo, the realization of the continuo-part.

realista[1] *m.*, *f.* See under **reale**[2].

realista[2] *m.*, *f.* See under **realismo**.

realmente *adv.* See under **reale**[1].

realtà *f.* reality; truth, true state of affairs; in —, in reality, in fact.

reame *m.* realm; kingdom.

reato *m.* crime; offence; commettere un —, to commit a crime; — di diffamazione, slander; — di sangue, wounding, assault; — di stampa, libel; (leg.) criminal offence; i reati si distinguono in delitti e contravvenzioni, criminal offences are divided into crimes and contraventions (C.P.); — di diffamazione, criminal defamatory libel; corpo del —, substance of the offence, *corpus delicti*.

reattanza *f.* (rad.) reactance; (electr.; acous.) reactance; (electr.) reactor, impedance coil, choke.

reatt-ivo *adj.* reacting; (chem.) reactive; *n.m.* (psych.) test; — attitudinale, aptitude test. **-ore** *m.* nuclear reactor; jet aircraft; jet engine; (electr.) reactor, reactance, impedance coil, choke; (atom. phys.) -ore a catena, chain reactor.

reazion-e *f.* reaction; response; opposition; (pol.) reactionary tendencies, reaction; revolt; (bldg.) reaction, supporting pressure; (chem.; med.) reaction; (aeron.) aeroplano a —, jet plane; motore a —, jet engine; momento di —, restoring moment; (electron.) reaction, feedback. **-a·rio** *m. adj.* (pol.) reactionary.

rebab *f. indecl.* See **ribeca**.

rebbi-o *m.* prong (of pitch-fork or table-fork). **-are** [A 4] *tr.* to strike with the prongs of a fork; to beat, to thresh. **-ata** *f.* action of striking or moving with a fork; threshing.

rebechino *m.* See **ribeca**.

rebo-ante *adj.* sonorous, resounding; (fig.) bombastic. **-ato** *m.* roaring; (fig.) bombast.

rebuffo *m.* (naut.) slip wire; ormeggiare di —, to reeve a slip wire *or* to secure with both ends of a rope inboard; di —, 'Chinese fashion', 'arsy versy'.

rebus *m. indecl.* riddle, conundrum; picture-puzzle; enigma. **-i·stico** *adj.* (joc.) like a riddle, enigmatical.

†rebutto *m.* onset.

recalcitrante *adj.* (herald.) kicking.

recalcitrare [A 1] and derivs. See **ricalcitrare**.

recalescenza *f.* (metall.) recalescence.

†recamo *m.* (naut.) tackle, purchase having two swivel blocks.

recanatẹse *adj.* (geog.) of or relating to Recanati; *n.m.* inhabitant of Recanati; il grande —, Giacomo Leopardi, *or* Beniamino Gigli (both of whom were born there).

recapit-are [A 1 s] *tr.* to deliver; to hand; ufficio delle lettere non -ate, dead-letter office; (comm.) to deliver; to hand over; *intr.* (*aux.* avere; *prep.* a) a) to attend; to refer (to); †to happen again.

reca·pito *m.* address, office; dov'è il vostro —?, where is your office?, what is your business address?; far — in un luogo, to use a place as an accommodation address; pronto —, prompt delivery; aver —, to have a ready market; dar — alle sue faccende, to arrange one's business; (comm.) acknowledgement; delivery; *pl.* effects; securities; (naut.) -i marittimi, ship's papers; bills of trading.

recapitolare [A 1 s] and derivs. See **ricapitolare**.

rec-are [A 2] *tr.* to bring, to carry, to take; — una lettera, to be the bearer of a letter; — in dote, to bring as a dowry; — una notizia, to bring news; ciò gli recherà dolore, that will cause him sorrow; — ad effetto, to carry out; — a termine, to accomplish; to finish; — a buon fine, to bring to a successful conclusion; to render; — a moneta italiana, to express in, *or* change into, Italian money; to translate; i poemi ossianici -ati in italiano dal Cesarotti, Ossian's Poems translated into Italian by Cesarotti; — a luce, to make known, to publish; — a lode, to consider praiseworthy; — a biasimo una cosa a qualcuno, to consider a person should be blamed for something; *rfl.* (acc. of prn. 'si') to go, to come, to betake oneself; (dat. of prn. 'si') -arsi addosso, to take upon oneself; -arsi in grembo, to take (or hold) on one's lap; -arsi ad onore, to consider (it) an honour, to take as a compliment; -arsi a cuore, to take to heart; -arsi a coscienza, to have scruples (about); -arsi ad ingiuria una cosa, to be offended at, by, something; -arsi a mente, to bear in mind, to remember. **-ata** *f.* helping; course (of food at a meal). **-ato** *part. adj.* brought; fetched; ascribed. (**-atore** *m.* **-atrice** *f.*) **-atura** *f.* carriage, transport; (cost of) carriage.

rec·chia[1] *f.* (agric., Tusc.) ewe that has not yet lambed.

rec·chia[2] *f.* (dial., S. Ital.) ear (cf. **orecchio**).

rece·d-ere [B 1] *intr.* (*aux.* essere, avere) to withdraw; to retire. (**-imento** *m.*)

†recelare *tr.* to hide.

recens-ione *f.* review; fare la — di un libro, to review a book; copia da —, review copy; critical examination (of a text); examination by a censor; (paint.) cissing. **-ire** [D 2] *tr.* to review. (**-ito** *part. adj.*) **-ore** *m.* reviewer. (**-itrice** *f.*)

recent-e *adj.* recent; late; new; di data —, of recent date; le -i guerre, the late wars; di —, recently, lately. (**-emente** *adv.*) **-is·sime** *f.pl.* latest news; stop press.

†rece·pere *vb.* See **ricevere**.

rec-ere [B 1] *tr.* to retch, to vomit; — un segreto, to reveal a secret; (fig.) mi fai —, you make me sick. **-i** *adv.* (Tusc.) a capo -i, head downwards.

recessione *f.* recession; receding.

recesso *m.* recess; (fig.) negli intimi recessi del cuore, in the inmost recesses of the heart; — ombroso, shady nook; (leg.) withdrawal; receding; l'accesso e il -- dell'onda, the movement of the wave as it approaches and withdraws, undertow.

recetta·colo *m.* and derivs. See **ricettacolo**, etc.

recettiv-o *adj.* receptive; facoltà, potenza -a, ability to learn; mente -a, mind quick to learn (but not otherwise intelligent). **-ità** *f.* receptivity.

recezione *f.* reception; receipt; induction, admission (to an office, academy, etc.); (comm.) receipt.

†reche·rere *vb.* and derivs. See **richiedere**.

†rechinare *vb.* and derivs. See **inchinare**.

reciara *f.* (naut.) large fishing-net used in winter.

reciclare [A 1] *tr.* (chem. eng.) to recycle.

reci·d-ere [C 3] *tr.* to cut off; to cut; to cut short, to curtail; — la strada, to take a short cut; (agric.) to replough; *rfl.* to split, to tear, to rip; (of the skin) to crack (cf. **reciso**).

recidiv-o *adj.* relapsing; falling into bad ways again; recidivous; *n.m.* backslider; old offender, recidivist; (leg.) persistent offender; person convicted of second or subsequent offence (C.P.). **-a** *f.* relapse; backsliding; recidivism; recurrence; (med.) relapse; (leg.) relapse into crime; aggravating circumstance consisting of the commission of a second or subsequent offence (C.P.). **-are** [A 1] *intr.* (*aux.* essere) to relapse. **-ità** *f.* recidivism.

recin·-gere [C5] to enclose; to fence in. (-**gimento** *m.*) -**to** *part. adj.* enclosed, fenced in, railed off; *n.m.* enclosure; surrounding wall; city walls; (finan.) -**to alle grida**, floor of Stock Exchange where dealings are done vocally; *pl.* precincts.

recinzione *f.* fence; (bldg.) enclosure.

reciot(t)o *m.* kind of Veronese sparkling red wine.

†**re·cipe** *m.* prescription.

†**reci·pere** *vb.* and derivs. See **ricevere**.

recipiente *adj.* suitable; **vaso poco —**, vessel of small capacity; *n.m.* vessel; recipient; container.

reci·proc-o *adj.* reciprocal, mutual; **— beneficio**, mutual benefit; (leg.) mutual; **accordo —**, mutual agreement; (math.) reciprocal; *n.m.* (math.) reciprocal; (prosod.) **versi -i**, reciprocal, recurrent, verses. -**amente** *adv.* mutually, reciprocally; **aiutarsi -amente**, to help each other; (leg.) mutually; (math.) reciprocally, in reciprocal proportions. -**anza** *f.* reciprocity. -**are** [A2s] *tr.* to alternate; to reciprocate; (of tide) to ebb and flow. (-**ato** *part. adj.*) -**azione** *f.* ebb and flow; (of pendulum) oscillation. -**ità** *f.* reciprocity; (leg.) mutuality.

reciṣ-o *part.* of **recidere**, q.v.; *adj.* cut off; cut away; **fiori -i**, cut flowers; (fig.) resolute; sharp; **un 'no' —**, a definite 'no'; **una risposta -a**, an abrupt answer; (herald.) couped. -**amente** *adv.* resolutely, decidedly; sharply. -**ione** *f.* resection; cutting out, cut (in a speech or article); (fig.) abruptness, curtness; uncompromising tone or quality. -**ura** *f.* crack (in the skin), chap.

re·cita *f.* performance; **prima —**, first performance, first night; recitation; recital.

recital *m. indecl.* (sometimes pron. as Eng.) (mus.) recital.

recit-are [A1s] *tr.* to recite; (theatr.) to perform, to act, to play; **stasera -ano una commedia del Pirandello**, there's a Pirandello play on at the theatre this evening; **pare che -i**, he is acting, he is playing a part (i.e. is insincere, or overemphatic); **— le preghiere**, to say one's prayers; to read aloud; to declaim; (mus.) to sing. -**a·bile** *adj.* suitable for performance. -**amento** *m.* reciting; recitation; performance. -**ante** *part. adj.* acting; *n.m.* actor; amateur actor; **discorre che pare un -ante**, he talks like an actor. -**ativo** *adj.* (mus.) **stile -ativo**, recitative style; *n.m.* (mus.) recitative; -**ativo secco**, -**ativo semplice**, plain recitative; -**ativo obbligato**, -**ativo strumentato**, accompanied recitative. -**ato** *part. adj.* acted, played; recited; narrated; performed. -**atore** *m.* actor; elocutionist, reciter; gossip. (-**atrice** *f.*) -**azione** *f.* recitation; recital; reading; acting; elocution; dramatic art; **scuola di -azione**, dramatic school, school of elocution.

recitic·cio *m.* vomit; (fig.; derog.) badly made thing; little misshapen person (cf. **recere**).

reciuto *part.* of **recere**, q.v.

reclam-are [A1] *intr.* (aux. avere) to complain, to protest; to raise objections; **— contro**, to complain of, to protest against; **— presso alcuno**, to make a complaint to someone; *tr.* to claim, to ask for, to demand; (leg.) to claim; to demand delivery of; to complain of. (-**ante** *part. adj.*, *n.m.*, *f.*) -**ato** *part. adj.* claimed; demanded. -**azione** *f.* complaint; claim. -**o** *m.* formal complaint; complaint (claim or protest) in writing; (leg.) -**o al collegio**, appeal to Bench (C.C.P.); -**o di stato**, claim of filial status (C.C.).

reclam-e *f. indecl.* (pron. as Fr.) publication; publicity. -**ista** *m.* (neol.) self-advertiser. -**i·stico** *adj.* (pertaining to) advertising.

reclin-are [A1] *tr.* to recline; **— la testa**, to bow one's head; **— gli sguardi**, to lower one's eyes, to look down; *intr.* (aux. avere) to bend back. -**ato** *part. adj.* **col capo -ato**, with bent (bowed) head. -**azione** *f.* (surg.) reclination.

recluṣ-ione *f.* seclusion; (eccl.) **suore di —**, enclosed nuns; (leg.) imprisonment with hard labour; penal servitude (C.P.). NOTE: there are four kinds of penal detention according to gravity of offence, roughly equatable; *arresto* to imprisonment with hard labour, in special division; *detenzione* to imprisonment with hard labour; *reclusione* to penal servitude; *ergastolo* to penal servitude for life. -**o** *m.* recluse; prisoner; *adj.* (eccl.) **monache -e**, enclosed nuns. -**o·rio** *m.* prison.

recluta *f.* See **re·cluta**.

re·clut-a *f.* recruit; novice. -**amento** *m.* recruiting. -**are** [A1s, A1] *tr.* to recruit, to enrol; to call up; to engage; -**are del personale temporaneo**, to recruit temporary staff.

†**recolere** *tr.* to commemorate with awe and reverence.

Recolletti *pr.n.*, *m.pl.* (eccl. hist.) Recollects.

recon·dit-o *adj.* hidden, concealed; secret; recondite. -**o·rio** *m.* (liturg.) altar-cavity, *sepulchrum*.

re·cord *m. indecl.* (sport, etc.) record; (athletics) **— stagionale**, best performance or time for the season. -**man** *m. indecl.* holder of the (a) record; one who breaks (makes) a record.

recrimin-are [A1s] *tr.* to recriminate; (leg.) to bring a counter-charge against; (fig.) to reproach; *intr.* (aux. avere) to make recriminations. -**atore** *m.* recriminator; (leg.) one who returns a charge against his accuser. (-**atrice** *f.*) -**azione** *f.* (leg.) counter-charge; (fig.) recrimination; reproach; complaint(s).

recrudescenza *f.* recrudescence; **una — di freddo**, a return of cold weather.

recto *m. indecl.* face, recto (of page, document, etc.).

recu·bito *m.* recumbent position.

†**reculare** *vb.* and derivs. See **rinculare**.

recuper-are [A1s] and derivs. see **ricuperare**. -**atore** *m.* (eng.) recuperator. -**ato·rio** *adj.* (leg.) which restores to possession. -**azione** *f.* (leg.) recovery by Order of Court.

recu·pero *m.* (watchm.) **mobile del —**, split-second runner.

†**recusare** *vb.* and derivs. See **ricusare**.

red-a[1] *f.*, **-e** *m.* see **erede**. †**-are** *vb.* and derivs. see **ereditare**.

reda[2] *f.* (Rom. antiq.) *rheda*, four-wheeled carriage.

redan·cia *f.* (naut.) thimble (metal eyelet); bight (in a rope).

redargu-ire [D2] *tr.* to reproach, to scold; to find fault with. (-**i·bile** *adj.*) (-**ito** *part. adj.*) -**izione** *f.* reproach, scolding; blame.

red-atore *m.*, -**atrice** *f.* See **erede**.

red-atto *part.* of **redigere**, q.v.; *adj.* written up; written out; drawn up; compiled; edited. -**attore** *m.* compiler, writer; editor; journalist; **è -attore di un giornale**, he is on the editorial staff of a newspaper; -**attore capo**, sub-editor; (leg.) draftsman. (-**attrice** *f.*) -**azione** *f.* drawing up; writing up; compilation; editing; editorial staff; editor's office; version; **il Boccaccio fece tre -azioni della vita di Dante**, Boccaccio wrote three versions of his Life of Dante; (leg.) drawing up; drafting; (admin.) **comitato di -azione**, drafting committee.

redazza *f.* (foundry) swab (cf. **radazza**).

†**red·dere** *vb.* and derivs. See **rendere**.

†**redd-ire** *intr.* to return. †-**ita** *f.* return. †-**ito** *part. adj.* returned.

red·dit-o *m.* income; revenue; annuity; net profit; **imposta sul —**, income-tax; **— imponibile**, gross income. -**iere** *m* profiteer. -**i·zio** *adj.* profitable; paying; lucrative; yielding an income; **impiego -izio**, profitable employment.

reden-to *part.* of **redimere**, q.v.; *adj.* redeemed; ransomed; freed, liberated; **terre italiane -te**, Italian provinces regained. -**tore** *m.* (theol.) Redeemer. -**torista** *m.* (eccl.) Redemptorist (priest); *f.* (*pl.* -**toriste**) (eccl.) Redemptoristine (nun). -**trice** *f.*, *adj.* redeeming; liberating; **guerra -trice**, war of liberation; (theol.) **grazia -trice**, redeeming grace; **opera -trice**, redemptive work, work of redemption. -**zione** *f.* ransom; redemption; -**zione degli schiavi**, manumission; liberation (e.g. from foreign rule); -**zione dalla soggezione economica**, setting free from economic dependence; **per altra via non c'è -zione**, there is no other way out; **senza -zione**, inescapably; (theol.) Redemption; (leg.) redemption.

†**redetare** *vb.* and derivs. See **ereditare**.

redib-ito·rio *adj.* (leg.) redhibitory; **vizio —**, redhibitory defect; **azione -toria**, action for annulment of contract (C.C.). -**izione** *f.* (leg.) redhibition.

redi·gere [C32] *tr.* to draw up (a document); to compile; to write (up), to compose; to edit; (leg.) to draft; (admin.) **— il processo verbale**, to draw up the minutes.

redi·m-ere [C9] *tr.* to redeem, to ransom; to set free, to liberate; to rescue, to save; (leg.) to redeem; *rfl.* to redeem oneself; to free oneself. -**i·bile** *adj.* redeemable; *n.m.* **il -ibile**, that which is redeemable. (-**ibilità** *f.*)

redim-ire [D1] *tr.* (poet.) to crown. -**ito** *part. adj.* (poet.) crowned; garlanded.

re·dina *f.* See **redine**.

re·dine *f.* rein; **tirare le redini**, to rein up, to draw rein; (fig.) **prendere le redini del governo**, to assume the reins of government.

redingote *f.* (a corruption of 'riding-coat') morning-coat, frock-coat; (formerly) a double-breasted, wide-skirted coat, worn by women as well as men.

redintegrare [A1s] and derivs. See **reintegrare**.

Redipu·glia *pr.n.f.* (geog.) name of one of the largest Italian war cemeteries of the 1915–18 war (near Monfalcone).

†**redire** *intr.* to return.

†**redit·à** *f.*, **-ag·gio** *m.* see **eredità**. †**-iere** *m.* see **erede**.

†**re·dit-o** *m.* return; *adj.* returned. †**-uro** *adj.* about to return; destined to return.

redivivo *adj.* alive again, returned to life; un Caruso —, a singer with a voice so like Caruso's he seems to be Caruso come to life again.

red-o *m.* calf; foal. (**-a** *f.*)

re·dola *f.* narrow path (in garden or fields)

redol-ire [D 2] *intr.* (*aux.* avere) (poet.) to smell sweet; to be fragrant, to give forth a sweet perfume. **-ente** *part. adj.* sweet scented; pleasantly odorous; redolent.

re·dova *f.* (mus.) Redowa, Bohemian dance similar to the Mazurka.

re·dox *adj. indecl.* (chem.) redox.

re·duce *adj.* returned, returning (from war, exile, expedition); *n.m.* ex-serviceman, veteran; survivor.

†**redu·cere** *vb.* and derivs. See **ridurre**.

reduplic-are [A 2 s] *tr.* to redouble; to reduplicate. **-ativo** *adj.* tending to reduplicate. (**-ato** *part. adj.*) **-azione** *f.* redoubling; reduplicating; (gramm.) reduplication.

†**redurre** *vb.* and derivs. See **ridurre**.

redutta·sio *m.* (chem.) reductase.

ref-e *m.* thread (hemp, flax); a — doppio, with a double thread, (fig.) with violence; cucire a — doppio, to act with alacrity, *or* to deceive, to act with duplicity; esser cucito a — doppio, to be a close friend; cucire a — scempio, to be foolish; campare, vivere refe refe, to make a bare living. **-aiuolo** *m.* one who sells thread, haberdasher.

referenda·rio *m.* (leg.) referendary; (eccl. hist.) *referendarius*; (derog.) tale-bearer; spy.

referen·dum *m. indecl.* referendum.

referenza *f.* testimonial, reference; (admin.) numero di —, reference number (cf. **riferimento**).

†**referire** *vb.* and derivs. See **riferire**.

referto *m.* report (esp. a doctor's report to the police) (C.P.).

†**refetto** *m.* refreshment, food.

re·fettoriere *m.* person in charge of a refectory, kitchen-manager. **-fetto·rio** *m.* refectory, dining-hall; canteen. **-fezionare** [A 1 c] *intr.* (*aux.* avere) to take, or serve, a light meal. **-fezione** *f.* light repast.

†**ref·iciare**, †**-iziare** *tr.* to refresh, to feed, to give refreshment to; *rfl.* to take refreshment.

†**refl·esso** *m.* see **riflesso**. †**-are** *vb.* and derivs. see **riflessare**.

†**reflet·tere** *vb.* and derivs. See **riflettere**.

refluire [D 2] *intr.* (*aux.* avere, essere) to flow back; to ebb.

re·fluo *adj.* ebbing, flowing back; (med.) sangue —, blood reflux.

re·folo *m.* (naut.) puff of wind; puffy, wind with unchanged direction.

refondere [C 2] *tr.* (metall.) to recast, to remelt.

†**refragare** *intr.* to be opposed; to vote in opposition; to be contrary.

†**refran·gere** *vb.* and derivs. See **rifrangere**.

refratta·ri-o *adj.* refractory; resistant; fireproof; *n.m.* (mil.) refuser of military service; unwilling conscript; conscientious objector; (eccl. hist.) non-juring priest at period of French Revolution; (techn.) refractory, fireproof; mattone —, firebrick; (med.) refractory. **-età** *f.* (techn.) refractoriness.

refratto·metro *m.* (phys.; opt.) refractometer.

refrattore *m.* (astron.) refractor, refraction telescope.

refrenare [A 1] and derivs. See **raffrenare**.

refriger-are [A 1 s] *tr.* to cool; to refresh; to refrigerate; *rfl.* to become cool, to cool down; to feel refreshed. (**-amento** *m.*) **-ante** *part. adj.* cooling, refreshing; (eng.) refrigerant, cooling; *n.m.* (eng.) coolant; (chem.) condenser; refrigerator; refrigerant. (**-ativo** *adj.*) **-ato** *part. adj.* cooled; refreshed; magazzino **-ato**, cold store. **-atore** *m.* (eng.) refrigerator, cooler; **-atore** intermedio, intercooler. **-azione** *f.* cooling; refrigeration.

refrige·rio *m.* (feeling of) coolness; refreshment, relief; †solace.

refurtiva *f.* (leg.) the stolen property; ricuperare la —, to recover the stolen goods.

refus-o *m.* (typ.) wrong fount, misprint, literal. **-are** [A 1] *intr.* (*aux.* avere) (typ.) to insert the wrong letter when correcting proofs. **-ione** *f.* (techn.) remelting; (finan.) refunding, paying back.

†**refutare** *vb.* and derivs. See **rifiutare**.

rega·glia *f.* See **rigaglia**.

regal-are [A 1] *tr.* to give (as a present), to make a present of; ha **-ato** un bambino al marito, she has borne her husband a son; to sell for a song, to sell dirt cheap, to 'give away'; (of food) to

season, to serve attractively; (iron.) — un pugno, to give a punch; *rfl.* (*dat.* of *prn.* 'si') to make oneself a present of; to allow oneself. **-a·bile** *adj.* suitable for a gift; (of a person) ready, open, willing to receive gifts. **-ato** *part. adj.* given (as a present); given away (i.e. sold very cheap); favoured; (of food, dishes) excellent, exquisite; frutta **-atissima**, exquisite fruit. **-atamente** *adv.* lavishly.

regal-e *adj.* regal, kingly; royal; *n.m.* (mus.) regal. **-mente** *adv.* regally; royally. **-i·a** *f.* (leg.) the royal rights of a sovereign; regalia; payments in kind (chickens, eggs., etc.) from farmer to landlord; gratuity; (comm.) primage. **-ità** *f.* royalty; (theol.) la **-ità** di Cristo, the kingship of Christ.

regalo *m.* present, gift; donation; dare in —, to give as a present; fare un —, to give a present; — di nozze, wedding-present; avere una cosa in —, to get a bargain; favour; mi farete un vero — se verrete da me, I shall be very much obliged if you will come to my house; (iron.) bel —!, that's a nice thing!; il — che fece Marzo alla nuora, tre noci e una nocciuola, a paltry gift; a —, suitably; magnificence, pomp, display, bribe; handsel; earnest money; (in apposition, *indecl.*) due buoni regalo, two gift tokens, two gift coupons.

re·gamo (bot.) wild marjoram, *Origanum vulgare.*

regat-a *f.* boat-race; regatta. **-are** [A 1] *intr.* (*aux.* avere) to take part in a regatta.

rege *m.* (poet.) king.

regesto *m.* chronological register of ancient documents (public or private).

†**regge** *f.* portal; (eccl.) doorway, gateway into choir or side-chapel; altar-rails.

reg·g-ere [C 12] *tr.* to hold (up, upright or straight); to bear, to support, to carry; — un peso, to bear a weight; questi muri **-ono** il tetto, these walls support the roof; è così debole che le gambe non lo **-ono** più, he is so weak that he cannot stand on his feet; (fig., colloq.) — il lume, — il moccolo, 'to play gooseberry' (i.e. to be a third party in the presence of a couple who would prefer to be alone); to guide, to rule, to govern; to hold in, to restrain; — un cane pel collare, to hold in a dog by the collar; colei che **-eva** i miei primi passi, she who guided my first steps; egli resse il governo in un periodo difficile, he was at the head of the government during a difficult period; (provb.) non è buon re chi non **-e** sè, he is not a good king who does not govern himself; (gramm.) to govern; to stand, to bear, to put up with; stoffa impermeabile che **-e** l'acqua, waterproof material; un vino robusto che **-e** l'acqua, strong wine that will stand (the addition of) water; non **-e** la celia, he can't stand a joke; — il vino, to take (to hold) one's drink (i.e. without getting drunk); — il cibo, to digest one's food; *intr.* (*aux.* avere) — del pari con, to hold one's own with; *rfl.* to stand; incapace di **-ersi** (in piedi, in gambe), not able to stand; non mi **-evo** più, I couldn't stand any longer; **-ersi** a galla, to keep afloat; to hold (on); si **-a** alla ringhiera, hold on to the rail; (of business) to keep going, to be doing fairly well; (fam.) **-ersi** la pancia, to hold one's sides, to be bursting with laughter; to be ruled, to have a government; **-ersi** a repubblica, to be governed as a republican government; il suo governo non si resse a lungo, his government did not last long; (naut.) to withstand the sea; *intr.* (*aux.* avere) to bear; to stand, to resist; — al freddo, to stand the cold; il ghiaccio **-e**, the ice bears; ho sofferto troppo, non **-o** più, I have suffered too much, I can stand no more; — con uno, to put up with a person, to bear to live with a person; questa tua idea non **-e**, this idea of yours won't stand examination; — alla prova, to stand (up to) the test; — al martello, to stand hammering; — al fuoco, to be fire-resisting; to last, to hold; se il tempo **-e**, partiremo, if the weather holds we shall go; (naut.) — alla vela, to have a (certain) capacity for carrying sail; — il mare, to withstand the sea; (comm.) to be seaworthy. **-ente** *part. adj.* holding; bearing up; resisting; ruling; (naut.) seaworthy, stiff, stable; *n.m.* regent; rector; governor; prefect; manager (temporary); principal (of a school). **-enza** *f.* regency; †resistance. **-etta** *f.* metal strap, hoop. **-ettone** *m.* large hoop.

reg·g-ia *f.* (*pl.* **-ie**) royal palace; palatial residence.

reggi·bile *adj.* that can be held; capable of being resisted; governable; capable of resisting (cf. **reggere**).

reggi-braca *m. indecl.* hip strap (of horse harness). **-calze** *m. indecl.* suspender-belt. **-catinelle** *m. indecl.* washstand. **-lume** *m .indecl.* lamp-stand; lamp-bracket. **-moc·colo** *m.* candle-holder; (colloq.) 'gooseberry' (i.e. a third party in the presence of a couple who

reggi-braca (*cont.*)
would prefer to be alone). **-pan·cia** *m. indecl.* belt; (for a horse) surcingle, girth. **-penne** *m. indecl.* pen-stand, pen-rack. **-petto** *m. indecl.* brassière; (for a horse) breast-collar, breast-strap. **-posata, -posate** *m. indecl.* knife- (or fork-) rest. **-seno** *m. indecl.* see **reggipetto. -spinta** *m.* (eng.; naut.) thrust bearing, thrust block. **-testa** *m. indecl.* head-rest. **-tirelle** *m. indecl.* trace-strap (of harness).

reggimento *m.* government, rule; control; behaviour; (mil.) regiment; (naut.) see **stabilità**, under **stabile**; (gramm.) object; construction (of a word governed by a verb or a preposition).

Reg·g-io *pr.n.f.* (geog.) Reggio Emilia; Reggio Calabria. **-iano** *adj.* of Reggio Emilia; *n.m.* native of Reggio Emilia; district round Reggio Emilia; (cul.) a sort of cheese, similar to Parmesan. (**-iana** *f.*) **-ino** *adj.* of Reggio Calabria; *n.m.* native of Reggio Calabria; district round Reggio Calabria. (**-ina** *f.*)

†**reggiola** *f.* (naut.) stringer, internal strengthening of the hull, weatherboard; *pl.* (naut.) boarded shelter in a fishing craft.

reggitore *m.* ruler; administrator; governor; manager; (naut.) stirrup or guide rope; lashing.

regìa *f.* board of excise; shop for sale of excisable goods; — dei tabacchi, tobacco monopoly; tobacco-shop; (theatr.; cinem.) production (cf. **regista**).

re·gia *f.* See **reggia** or **regio**.

regic-ida *m., f.* (*pl.* **-idi**) regicide (person); *adj.* regicidal. **-i·dio** *m.* (*pl.* **-idii**) regicide (act).

regilla *f.* (Rom. antiq.) *tunica regilla*, bride's tunic.

regime *m.* régime, government; in the years 1922–44 the word was used for 'il — fascista', the Fascist Régime; diet; essere a —, to be on a diet; (eng.) speed, rating; (techn.) pressione di —, working pressure; (naut.) range correction, to be applied to allow for temperature, gun wear, etc.; (meteor.) climatic data; — della pioggia, rainfall averages; — equatoriale, tropical conditions; — mediterraneo, Mediterranean climate; — delle pressioni atmosferiche, pressure conditions; (leg.) — patrimoniale della famiglia, law of family property (C.C.); — impositivo, system of taxation.

regina *f.* queen; — madre, Queen Mother; — vedova, Dowager Queen; la — dell'Adriatico, the Queen of the Adriatic, i.e. Venice; — delle tenebre, queen of the underworld, i.e. Proserpina; ape —, queen bee; (theol.) — del cielo, degli angeli, Queen of heaven, of angels, the B.V.M.; (liturg.; mus.) Salve —, (the antiphon) Salve Regina; (chess) queen; (bot.) erba della —, *Nicotiana tabacum*, the tobacco plant; — della notte, night-flowering cactus, princess of the night, *Selenicereus pteranthus* and other species; uva —, fine white grape of vine called 'alamanna' (introduced by Alamanna Salviati); pasta —, cheese-cake; acqua della —, spirits of camphor; Regina Coeli, name of a prison in Rome.

regino *adj.* velo —, bolting cloth.

re·gi-o *adj.* royal; via, strada **-a**, the king's highway; (hist.) — esercito, Italian Army; **-a** marina, Royal (Italian) Navy; (leg.) regius; royal; kingly; decreto —, royal decree; (med.) morbo —, King's evil, scrofula, struma; (chem.) acqua **-a**, aqua regia; *n.m.pl.* King's men (troops, party, esp. in Neapolitan history). **-amente** *adv.* royally.

†**regioire** *vb.* and derivs. See **gioire**.

region-e *f.* region, district; regional Government. (NOTE: in Italy, a region comprises several provinces, e.g. Veneto is a region, Venezia, Verona, etc. are provinces in the Veneto region. Certain government institutions, e.g. Courts of Appeal, are found in regional capitals, not in provincial capitals. Since 1945, 'regione' also means a district which has been granted local autonomy on the lines of Northern Ireland, i.e. they still send representatives to the Central Parliament in Rome, but also have local parliaments of their own. 'Regioni' in this sense are at present Val d'Aosta, Alto Adige (provinces of Bolzano and Trento), Sicily and Sardinia. Friuli-Venezia Giulia has been granted regional status; Umbria and Venezia Euganea (1960) are seeking it.) (geog.) region, tract of country having uniform (meteorological, climatic) characteristics; le **-i** del cielo, the four quarters of heaven (i.e. North, South, etc.); la — dei laghi, the lake district; la — addominale, the abdominal region; una — agricola, an agricultural district; realm, domain; la — dell'arte, the realm of art. **-ale** *adj.* regional; district. **-almente** *adv.* regionally. **-alismo** *m.* provincialism, regionalism. **-alista** *m.* local patriot, regionalist. (**-ali·stico** *adj.*) **-a·rio** *n.m.* (eccl. hist.) *regionarius*.

regista *m.* (theatr.; telev.) producer; (cinem.) director.

registr-are [A 1] *tr.* to register; to record; to enter; la storia non **-a** simili crudeltà, history does not record such cruelties; tutte le perdite sono state **-ate**, all losses have been entered; (comm.) to enter; to book; to register; to record; **-are** a mastro, **-are** a libro, to post; (leg.) to register; to journalize; to record; to enter; **-are** un atto, to register a deed; **-are** fonograficamente, to record phonographically (C.C.); (mus.) to choose organ-stops; (eng.) to regulate, to adjust; (radio; cinem.; telev.) to record. **-a·bile** *adj.* liable or subject to registration; fit to be recorded; (eng.) adjustable. (**-ato** *part. adj.*) **-atore** *m.* (also as *adj.*; *f.* **-atrice**) register, indicator, recorder; **-atore** delle lettere, letter file; **-atore** di cassa, cash register; **-atore** di velocità, speedometer; **-atore** a nastro, **-atore** magnetico, tape-recorder; (person) registrar; recorder. **-atura** *f.* registration; registration fee; (mus.) chorus of organ-stops. **-azione** *f.* registration; (leg.) spese di **-azione**, registration charges; **-azione** fonografica, phonographic recording; (comm.) **-azione** a mastro, posting; entry; (mus.) registration; gramophone recording; **-azione** a nastro, tape-recording; (eng.) adjustment, regulation, setting. **-oteca** *f.* recordings library (radio, cinema, television).

registro *m.* register; — dello stato civile, register of births, marriages and deaths, (and with capital R) Registry Office; ufficiale del Registro, registrar; ufficio di Registro, registrar's office; tassa di —, stamp duty; essere a —, to be on record; mettere a —, to record, to enter; (leg.) register; registry; ufficio del —, Registry of Deeds (office where deeds and documents affecting interest in real property are registered in order to be valid); ricevitore del Registro, registrar; — d'ipoteche, Register of charges; Pubblico Registro Automobilistico, government offices in each provincial capital, at which all motor vehicles have to be registered and which allots them numbers; imposta di —, registration and transfer duty; (comm.) register; book; — mercantile, register of shipping; — dei membri, — dei soci, register of members; — dei carichi, cargo book; (naut.) log, register, ship's book; Registro Italiano Navale, the equivalent of Lloyd's Register; Libro —, the annual publication of R.I.N.; naviglio di —, registered shipping; tonnellata di —, registered ton; cargo register; — dei cronometri, chronometer log; — delle leve marittime, register of seamen; — matricolare della nave, ship's book; — delle partenze, sailing register in a port; †— di disciplina, punishment book; (eng.) adjustment, regulation; — a madre e figlia, counterfoil book; (mus.) register (of voice, organ or harpsichord); organ or harpsichord stop; registri di fondo, foundation stops; registri di ripieno, mutation stops; (fig.) cambiar —, mutar —, to change one's tune, to alter one's ways; *pl.* records.

regiudicata *f.* (leg.). See **reiudicata**.

regn-are [A 5 c] *intr.* (*aux.* avere) to reign; (fig.) qui **-a** il silenzio, here silence reigns; to prevail, to predominate; nelle basse valli **-ano** le nebbie, mist prevails in the low valleys; questa moda **-ò** a lungo, this fashion prevailed for a long time; to flourish; in quelle terre **-a** l'ulivo, the olive-tree flourishes in that (kind of) country; *tr.* to rule, to dominate. **-ante** *part. adj.* reigning, ruling; dominant; prevailing; venti **-anti**, prevailing winds; *n.m.* king, sovereign, monarch, ruler; *pl.* king and queen. (**-ato** *part. adj.* **-atore** *m.* **-atrice** *f.*)

regn-o *m.* kingdom; il — Unito, the United Kingdom; (hist.) il Regno d'Italia, the Kingdom of Italy; il Regno Cisalpino, the Kingdom established by Napoleon in N. Italy; il Regno delle due Sicilie, the Kingdom of Naples; il — vegetale, the vegetable kingdom; (rel.) kingdom; — delle tenebre, kingdom of darkness, Hell; i tre **-i**, the three realms of departed spirits, Heaven, Hell and Purgatory; †(eccl.) papal tiara, triple crown; il — animale, the animal kingdom; (fig.) il — dei ghiacci eterni, the region (realm) of eternal ice; la casa è il — della donna, the house is woman's domain; reign; sotto, durante, il — di Vittorio Emanuele II, in, during, the reign of Victor Emanuel II; the royal crown; col — in testa, wearing the crown. **-i·colo** *m. adj.* subject; one living in a kingdom.

re·gol-a *f.* rule (esp. in gramm., prosody, the arts); l'eccezione conferma la —, the exception proves the rule; — aurea, golden rule; — empirica, rule of thumb; di —, usually, as a rule; è di —, it is customary; example, model; la sua vita può servire di — a molti, his life may serve as an example to many; ciò ti servirà di —, that will serve for your guidance; per tua norma e —, for your

regol-a (*cont.*)

guidance; order; quel ragazzo tiene i suoi libri in —, that boy keeps his books tidy; aver le carte in —, to have one's papers in order, (fig.) to have nothing to fear from the police, etc., to have a clear conscience; moderation; bere senza —, to be an immoderate drinker; use, custom, right, propriety; è di — che la persona più giovine saluti per prima la più anziana, it is proper for a younger person to greet an elder first; a — del mondo, in the ordinary course of events; in tutte le -e, in any case, in every way; (admin.) essere in —, to be in order; (leg.) rule; — dell'Aia, Hague Rules; (eccl.) rule (of religious life); — di San Benedetto, Rule of St Benedict; †religious community; (mus.) — armonica, monochord or harmonic canon; — dell'ottava, rule of the octave; *pl.* (med.) menses.

regola·bile *adj.* See under **regolare**.

regolamentare[1] *adj.* relating to regulations; non bisogna superare la velocità —, you must not exceed the regulation speed; della misura —, of regulation size; le ore regolamentari, the regulation hours; prescribed; nella forma —, in the prescribed form; (leg.) il potere —, power to make administrative regulations (C.C.); (admin.) è — questa mozione?, would this motion be in order?

regolamentare[2] [A I] *intr.* (*aux.* avere) to lay down regulations; *tr.* to control by regulations.

regolamento *m.* regulation; rule; by-law; (leg.) administrative regulation (a source of 'diritto'); I regolamenti esecutivi, statutory rules (C.C.); — di procedura; rules of procedure; the act of regulating; — di confini, fixing of boundaries (C.C.); — di competenza, appeal against judgement on point of jurisdiction (C.C.P.); (comm.) settlement; balance; — di conti, settlement of accounts; — d'avaria, average-statement; (admin.) commissione per il —, standing orders committee; — interno, rules of procedure, internal regulations; — provvisorio, provisional regulations; un'infrazione al —, an infringement of the rules; applicare il —, to apply the rules of procedure; richiamo al —, call to order; conformarsi al —, to conform to the rules; richiamare i termini del —, to recall the terms of the rules; sospendere il —, to waive the rules.

regol-are[1] [A I s] *tr.* to regulate; to settle; ho -ato quell'affare, I have settled that matter; to direct, to control; (comm.) to settle; — i conti, to balance the accounts, to settle one's debts, (fig.) to get one's own back, to avenge an insult, etc.; *rfl.* to behave, to act; ora so come -armi, now I know what to do, now I know what line to take; devi -arti come le circostanze consigliano, you must act as circumstances suggest. **-a·bile** *adj.* capable of being regulated; (eng.) adjustable, variable. **-atęzza** *f.* moderation; orderliness. **-ato** *part. adj.* orderly, regular; (well) regulated; temperate; appetito non -ato, unrestrained, unchecked appetite. **-atamente** *adv.* regularly; in an orderly manner; moderately. **-atore** *m.* (**-atrice** *f.*) regulator; one who makes rules or regulations; (archit.) dam; (eng.) governor; regulator; controller; damper (of a boiler, etc.); control; -atore a galleggiante, ball cock; *adj.* regulating; piano -atore, redevelopment plan, redevelopment project; town-planning scheme; il piano -atore prevede la demolizione della mia casa, my house will be demolished under the town-planning scheme; idea -atrice, dominating idea. **-azione** *f.* regulation; control; (eng.) adjustment; -azione di precisione, fine adjustment.

regolar-e[2] *adj.* regular; formazione —, regular formation; passo —, even pace; statura —, medium height; ora —, suitable time; venti -i, prevailing winds (at certain periods); (gramm.) regular; (mil.) esercito —, regular army; (eccl.) regular (clergy); chierici -i, Clerks Regular; ora —, canonical hour. **-mente** *adv.* regularly; properly; duly; according to rule or normal procedure; ricevetti -mente la vostra lettera, I duly received your letter; (eccl.) regularly, canonically. **-ità** *f.* regularity; punctuality; prova di -ità, endurance trial (motor-racing, cycling, etc.). **-izzare** [A I] *tr.* to regularize; to legalize, to render legal, esp. of relationship of long standing between a man and a woman. (**-izzato** *part. adj.* **-izzazione** *f.*)

regoli·zia *f.* See **liquirizia**.

re·gol-o[1] *m.* ruler, rule; (set-) square; — calcolatore, slide-rule; thin strip of wood; straightedge; (metall.) regulus; (archit.) fillet; (chess) file, line of squares on a chessboard; bars (for windows, cages, etc.); (comm.) rule. **-ętto** *m. dim.* small stick, strip of wood; (archit.) fillet.

re·golo[2] *m.* petty king; (myth.) basilisk; (orn.) goldcrest, *Regulus regulus*.

re-gredire [D 2] *intr.* (*aux.* avere, essere) to go back, to turn back; to recede, to regress, to retrogress. (**-grediente** *part. adj.*) **-gressione** *f.* regress, regression, recession, decadence; (med.) remission. **-gressivo** *adj.* regressive; retrograde; metodo —, analysis. **-gressivamente** *adv.* regressively. **-gresso** *m.* regress, retrogression; decadence; exit, way out; way back; (leg.) recourse (C.C.); regress; re-exchange; (canon law) regress; (mus.) regressus, that part of a responsory which is repeated after the verse (in Gregorian music); (chem.) refrigerante a -gresso, reflux condenser; (naut., etc.) propeller slip (i.e. difference between the theoretical advance of a screw and the actual horizontal speeds); (rlwy.) switchback, back shunt; (logic) regressive reasoning, i.e. from particular to universal, from effect to cause.

†re·gula *f.* See **regola**.

re-ietto *adj.* rejected, repudiated; cast out; forsaken; — dalla fortuna, forsaken by fortune; *n.m.* outcast; castaway; un — dalla società, an outcast from society, a 'down and out'. **-iezione** *f.* (leg.) dismissal; refusal.

reimpianto *m.* (med.) reimplantation.

reimpiego *m.* (leg.) reinvestment; — del prezzo, reinvestment of purchase money (C.C.).

†reina *f.* See **regina**.

reincanto *m.* (leg.) new auction (after abortive sale) (C.C.P.).

reincarnazione *f.* reincarnation.

reincro·cio *m.* (biol.) backcross.

reinfe-ttare [A I] *tr.* to reinfect. **-zione** *f.* reinfection.

reinoculazione *f.* (med.) reinoculation.

reintegr-are [A I s] *tr.* to reinstate; to indemnify; fu -ato dei danni, he was indemnified for the damage; to restore; con la sua saggia amministrazione -ò il patrimonio, by his wise management he restored his fortune; — la battaglia, to resume the attack, to regain the initiative; *rfl.* to be restored; to regain one's position; to make up a quarrel, to become friends again. **-amento** *m.* restoration; reinstatement; indemnification. **-anda** *f.* (leg.) possessory or recovery action. **-ativo** *adj.* relating to reinstatement, restoration, compensation. (**-ato** *part. adj.*) **-azione** *f.* reinstatement, restoration; compensation, indemnification; (leg.) recovery; refund; reimbursement; azione di -azione, action for recovery of possession (C.C.).

reinvestitura *f.* See **rinvestitura**, under **rinvestire**.

reità *f.* guilt; guiltiness.

reiter-are [A I s] to reiterate, to repeat. **-a·bile** *adj.* repeatable. **-amento** *m.* reiterating, repeating. **-ato** *part. adj.* reiterated, repeated; colpi -ati, repeated blows. **-atamente** *adv.* repeatedly, again and again. **-azione** *f.* reiteration, continued repetition; (rhet.) repetition.

reiudicata *f.* (leg.) *res judicata*; a thing or matter adjudged; a point decided by authority; (colloq.) foregone conclusion.

relais *m. indecl.* (pron. as Fr.) (wireless) relay.

relativ-o *adj.* relative; respective; in senso —, non assoluto, in a relative, not in an absolute sense; essa ascoltò le tristi notizie con -a compostezza, she heard the sad news with relative composure; (relating to a particular matter) pertinent; con le -e prove, with the relative proofs; la -a spesa, the appropriate expenditure; — alla domanda, proportioned to the demand; (gramm.) pronome —, relative pronoun; proposizione -a, relative sentence (clause). **-amente** *adv.* relatively, comparatively; -amente a, with regard to. **-ismo** *m.* relativism. **-i·stico** *adj.* (phys.) relativistic. **-ità** *f.* (phys.) relativity.

rela-tore *m.* reporter; rapporteur; (leg.) giudice —, rapporteur of Bench (who leads their consideration of case in Judges' Chambers) (C.C.P.); (mil.) ufficiale —, overseeing officer; (pol.) — di maggioranza, Government spokesman; — di minoranza, Opposition spokesman. **-trice** *f.* female reporter; (naut.) nave -trice, guide.

relazion-e *f.* report; compilare una —, to draw up a report; — ufficiale official report; saper per — d'altri, to know, to learn, from hearsay; (comm.) report; (admin.) — di gestione, report on the management; — sullo stato dei lavori, progress report; — interinale, interim report; (naut.) — del capitano, ship's report; relation, connexion; non c'è — fra i due, there is no connexion between the two; in — a, with regard to; *pl.* relations, intercourse; connexions; rompere le -i, to break off relations; siamo in buone

relazion-e (*cont.*)

-i, we are on good terms; contacts; acquaintances; -i commerciali, business relations; relation, relationship, kinship; acquaintanceship; (mus.) falsa —, false relation.

relè *m. indecl.* See **relais**.

releg·are [A 2 s] *tr.* to relegate; to confine; to banish, to exile. -**amento** *m.* relegating; confining; banishing, exiling. -**ato** *part. adj.* relegated; confined; banished, exiled; -ato in un'isola, banished to an island. -**azione** *f.* relegation; confinement; exile, banishment. (-**atore** *m.* -**atrice** *f.*)

religi·one *f.* religion; sacredness; la — della patria, fervent patriotism; (fig.) cult; devotion; con —, with reverent care, religiously; (colloq.) non c'è più —, the world is going to the dogs; (eccl.) monastic life, religious life; entrare in (nella) —, to enter religion, to become a monk (friar, nun, religious); religious order or congregation; military order (e.g. of Knights of Malta or St Stephen); †religious house. †-**onario** *m.* one professing a religion. -**osa** *f.* nun, (woman) religious. -**osità** *f.* piety, devotion, religious feeling; conscientiousness. -**oso** *adj.* religious, pious, devout; sacred; monastic; scrupulous, conscientious; *n.m.* religious (the most general term for one who has taken vows, whether monk, friar, or member of a more recent society or congregation). -**osamente** *adv.* piously, devoutly, religiously; (fig.) scrupulously, with great care.

relinga *f.* See **ralinga**.

†**relin·quere** *tr.* to leave; to relinquish.

†**reliquato** *m.* (leg.) residuum.

reli·qui·a *f.* relic; *pl.* relics, remains; le -e di Roma antica, the ruins of ancient Rome; le -e del passato, relics of the past; (eccl.) relic. -**ario** *m.* (eccl.) reliquary; (joc.) (of a bemedalled person) pare un -ario, he looks like a Christmas-tree.

relitt-o *part.* of **relinquere**, q.v.; *adj.* left, relinquished; abandoned; *n.m.* derelict, dereliction; derelict land, left by sea or river; piece of land left by official expropriation; stump (e.g. of a tree); *pl.* waifs and strays; (naut.) sea relict; wreckage, cargo or corpses thrown up on to a shore, jetsam; (leg.) — del *de cuius*, deceased's estate; — di aeromobili, wreckage of aircraft (C.C.).

reluttività *f.* (electron.) reluctivity.

rema *f.* (naut.) capstan, winch; (Sicily) whirlpool.

†**rema·io** *m.* See **remolaio**.

remancipazione *f.* (Rom. antiq.) *remancipatio*, form of divorce.

rem·are [A 1] *intr.* (*aux.* avere) to row; to paddle. (-**ante** *adj.*, *n.m.*) †-**ata** *f.* stroke (of rowing); row, rowing. †-**ato** *part. adj.* (poet.) oared, furnished with oars; rowed. -**atore** *m.* rower; oarsman. -**atora** *f.*, -**atrice** *f.* oarswoman.

rembata *f.* (naut. hist.) forecastle or bow platform of a galley.

remea·bile *adj.* that can be retraced; non —, see **irremeabile**.

remegg·io *m.* (naut.) complement of oars; (naut. hist.) rowing-space; (poet.) il — delle ali, the beating of wings. -**iare** [A 3 c] *intr.* (*aux.* avere) (poet.) to row; (of birds' wings) to beat, to flap. -**·o** *m.* continued beating (of oars or wings), flapping.

†**remiero** *m.*, *adj.* See **rematore**, under **remare**.

remig·are [A 2 s] *intr.* (*aux.* avere) to row; to strike with the legs in swimming; (of birds) to fly, to beat their wings. (-**amento** *m.*) -**ante** *part. adj.* rowing; beating; *n.m.* rower, oarsman; *f.pl.* (orn.) remiges. -**ata** *f.* (in rowing) stroke; striking; rowing. -**atore** *m.* see **remitore**, under **remare**. (-**atrice** *f.* -**azione** *f.*)

reminiscenza *f.* memory, remembrance; recollection; reminiscence; musica che è una raccolta di reminiscenze, music which is very reminiscent.

remi·pede *m.* (naut.) propeller blade; (sport) pedalo, foot-pedalled pleasure dinghy; †rower standing as in a gondola.

remiss·i·bile *adj.* pardonable, remissible. (-**ibilmente** *adv.*) -**ione** *f.* remission (of debt, sin), forgiveness; (of prisoners) setting free, liberation; senza -ione, unpardonably, without forgiveness, *or* without mercy; submission; giving up; payment of damages; remedy, way out; non c'è -ione, bisogna partire, there is nothing for it, we must go; (joc.) non ci fu -ione, lo fecero sedere e pranzare con loro, there was no getting out of it, he had to sit down and dine with them; -ione d'animo, weakness (of will), lack of energy; (mus.) slackness (of a string). -**ivo** *adj.* remissive; submissive, meek; humble; mild, gentle; (leg.) remitting; releasing; discharging. (-**ivamente** *adv.* -**ività** *f.*)

remisso·ria *f.* (leg.) order of discharge; (eccl.) dismissorial letter.

†**remita** *m.* See **eremita**.

remittenza *f.* (med.) remission.

rem-o *m.* oar; -i accoppiati a padella, -i accoppiati a pariglia, oars on the same thwart, sculls; — di governo, steering oar; -i di punte alternate, oars as in a whaler; sweep; girone del —, loom; ginocchio del —, shaft; pala del —, blade; — a posticcio, out-rigger; — semplice, one-man oar; un colpo di —, a stroke; (naut. hist.) condannare al —, cacciare al —, to condemn to the galleys; pena del —, condemnation to the galleys; †gente di —, crew; †uomini di —, rowers; †— di galea, — a galloccia, galley sweep; †— sensile, — a zenzile, one-man oar used standing; †— al terzaruolo, — al quartaruolo, — al quintaruolo (phrases indicating the number of men to an oar); (naut. commands) -i a mare!, oars down!; -i a prua!, bows! (order given before going alongside for bowmen to lay in their oars and pick up their boat-hooks); alza -i!, toss oars! (vertical, saluting); arma -i!, oars out!; agguanta -i!, hold water! (to stop the way); prepara i -i!, stand by oars!; leva -i!, oars!, cease rowing, keep the oars out and horizontal; rientra -i!, lay in the oars!; fila -i!, way enough! (oars are allowed to trail). †-**ola·io**, †-**olaro** *m.* ship's carpenter responsible for making, repairing and looking after oars.

re·mol-o *m.*, -**ino** *m.* tornado, hurricane (W. African particularly); (naut.) squall; circular storm; vortex; (vet.) whorl (of hair).

re·mora *f.* delay, impediment; (ichth.) pilot fish, *Echeneis remora*; (naut.) wake, slick (calm water produced astern or by a drifting ship).

remoto *adj.* remote, distant; far-off; controllo —, remote control; secluded; luogo —, lonely spot; (gramm.) passato —, past definite.

†**re·mpiere** *vb.* and derivs. See **riempire**.

†**remulco** *m.* See **rimorchio**.

remuner·are [A 1 s] and derivs. See **rimunerare**.

ren-a *f.* sand; sands; i bimbi giocano sulla —, the children are playing on the sands; portar — al lido, to carry coals to Newcastle; spendere i quattrini come la —, to spend money like water; (techn.) stillare a —, to distil on a sand-bath; †arena. -**accio** *m.* sand-bank; sandy barren ground. -**aio** *m.* sand-bank; sand-pit; sandy ground. -**ai(u)olo** *m.* sand-digger; sand merchant. -**are** [A 1 c] *tr.* to rub with sand, to clean with sand; to sprinkle with sand. -**ata** *f.*, -**atura** *f.* rubbing, polishing or sprinkling with sand. -**ato** *part. adj.* sanded. -**ella** *f.* (med.) gravel (in the urine); (bot.) asara bacca, *Asarum europaeum*. -**iccio** *m.* silt. -**ischio** *adj.* sandy; *n.m.* sandy soil. -**osità** *f.* sandiness. -**oso** *adj.* sandy; full of sand (cf. **arena**).

renale *adj.* See under **rene**.

Renan·i·a *pr.n.f.* (geog.) Rhineland. -**o** *adj.* pertaining to the Rhine.

ren·d·ere [C 1] *tr.* to give back; to restore, to pay back; — la vista ai ciechi, to restore sight to the blind; — la parola a uno, to release someone from a promise; to give in exchange; — bene per male, to return good for evil; — pan per focaccia, to give tit for tat; — il saluto, to return, to acknowledge, a greeting; to give up; — l'anima a Dio, to give up the ghost; — l'estremo respiro, to breathe one's last; — il pranzo, to be sick after dinner, to bring up one's dinner; to bring in, to yield; i suoi capitali -ono poco, his capital brings in but little; il podere -e trenta barili di vino, the farm yields thirty barrels of wine; to produce, to give, to pay; i faggi -ono molt'ombra, beech-trees give a great deal of shade; la penna non -e, the pen does not flow; — conto di, to give an account of, to explain, to justify; — un buon servizio a uno, to do someone a good turn; — omaggio, to pay homage; — gli onori, to do the honours, (mil.) to present arms; — testimonianza, to give evidence; — grazie, to give, to return, thanks; Dio ve ne -erà merito, God will reward you; — ragione, to administer justice, to settle a matter; to express; — un'idea, to express an idea; il pittore non ha reso l'espressione del vostro viso, the painter has not caught the expression of your face; — un personaggio sulla scena, to render a character on the stage; to translate; — in italiano, to translate, to put, into Italian; (foll. by *adj.*) to render, to make; l'età lo aveva reso sospettoso, old age had made him suspicious; — uno felice, to make someone happy; (rel.) — la Pasqua, to make one's Easter duties; *abs.* to pay; il delitto non -e, crime does not pay; a buon —, hoping to make due returns some time; *rfl.* to render oneself, to make oneself; -ersi impopolare, to make oneself unpopular; -ersi certo, to make sure; -ersi conto di, to realize; non si rese conto delle difficoltà, he did not realize the difficulties; to become; si rese

rend·ere (*cont.*)

necessaria un'operazione, an operation became necessary; to yield, to give, to give way; è una stoffa che si ~e, it is material that gives; ~ersi in un luogo, to go, to repair, to a place; ~ersi monaca, to become a nun; ~ersi a Dio, to be converted; ~ersi in colpa, to confess oneself in the wrong. **~ẹvole** *adj.* pliant, yielding; compliant; productive. **~i·bile** *adj.* that should be paid, given up, given back. **~icọnto** *m.* statement of accounts, account; report; (leg.) rendering of account; *pl.* minutes; notes, memoranda. **~imẹnto** *m.* rendering, giving up, yielding; productive capacity; (leg.) ~imento del conto, accounting, rendering of account; (comm.) yield; (eng.) efficiency; macchina di gran ~imento, very efficient machine; massimo ~imento, peak efficiency; output; ~imento globale, overall efficiency; ~imento termico, thermal efficiency. (**~itọre** *m.* **~itrice** *f.*) **~uto** *part. adj.* rendered; restored; given up; given back (cf. **reso**).

ren·dit·a *f.* income; interest; revenue; vivere di ~, to live on an income; imposta sulla ~, income-tax; ~ pubblica, interest on government stock; mangiar le ~e in erba, to spend your money before you get it; (leg.) annuity; ~ semplice, annuity secured by charge on real property; ~ fondiaria, annuity secured by assignment of real property; ~ perpetua, perpetual annuity; ~ vitalizia, life annuity; ~ dello Stato, Government annuity (C.C.); *pl.* rents and profits; (finan.) government or public stock; ~ ammortizabile, redeemable stock; ~ perpetua, undated, unredeemable stock; ~ nominativa, registered stock; ~ al portatore, government bond; †tribute.

ren·e *m.* (*m.pl.* **~i**) (anat.) kidney; ~ adiposo, fatty kidney; ~ mobile, floating kidney; *f.pl.* the small of the back; loins; voltar le ~i, to turn one's back; dar le ~i a, to run away from; il fil delle ~i, the spine; avere le ~i rotte, to be tired out, to be exhausted; sentirsela giù per le ~i, to feel it in one's bones, to know instinctively. **~ale** *adj.* (anat.) renal, of the kidney. **~iformȩ** *adj.* (techn.) kidney-shaped; (bot.) reniform. **~ella** *f.*, **~i·schio** *m.* see under **rena**.

renẹtta *f.* See **ranetta**.

re·nio *m.* (chem.) rhenium.

reniten·te *adj.* unwilling, reluctant, disinclined; uncooperative; essere ~ alla leva, to fail to register for military service; (leg.) recalcitrant (C.P.P.); *n.m.pl.* the shirkers. **~za** *f.* unwillingness, reluctance, repugnance; failure to comply with the law (esp. laws governing National Service); (leg.) ~za dell'imputato, refusal of accused to appear (C.P.P.).

renn·a *f.*, **~e** *m.* (zool.) reindeer, *Rangifer tarandus*; (geog.) Lago delle Renne, Reindeer Lake.

rennina *f.* (biochem.) rennin.

Reno[1] *pr.n.m.* (geog.) Rhine; vino del ~, Rhine wine, hock.

Reno[2] *pr.n.m.* (geog.) Reno, formerly a tributary of the Po, now flowing into the Adriatic north of Ravenna.

renọne[1] *m.* (zool.). See **renna**.

renọne[2] *m.* See **rene**.

renọne[3] *m.* coarse sand (cf. **rena**).

renọso *adj.* and deriv. See under **rena**.

rensa *f.* Rheims linen.

†**rentennare** *intr.* to resound, to reverberate.

renun·zia *f.* See **rinunzia**.

Renzo *pr.n.m.* (abbrev. of **Lorenzo**) Laurie.

re-o *adj.* accused; guilty; wicked; evil, cruel; fell; ~ destino, cruel fate; (leg.) guilty; *n.m.* (leg.) offender (C.P.). **~amẹnte** *adv.* wickedly; (leg.) guiltily.

reobar·baro *m.* See **rabarbaro**.

reob·așe *f.* (physiol.) rheobase. **~a·șico** *adj.* rheobasic.

re-ọforo *m.* (electr.) rheophore; (radio) socket, jack. **~ọ·grafo** *m.* (electr.) rheograph. **~ologi·a** *f.* (phys.) rheology. **~olọ·gico** *adj.* rheological. **~ometri·a** *f.* (electr.) rheometry. **~ome·trico** *adj.* rheometrical. **~ọ·metro** *m.* (electr.) rheometer. **~omorfișmo** *m.* (geol.) rheomorphism. **~oscọ·pico** *adj.* (electr.; phys.) rheoscopical. **~oscọ·pio** *m.* rheoscope. **~osta·tico** *adj.* (electr.) rheostatic. **~o·stato** *m.* (electr.) rheostat; ~ostato di avviamento, starting rheostat. **~ostrizịọne** *f.* (electr.) rheostriction; pinch effect. **~ọtano** *m.* (metall.) rheotan. **~otattịșmo** *m.* (biol.) rheotaxis. **~ọ·tomo** *m.* (electr.) rheotome. **~otropịșmo** *m.* (biol.) rheotaxis, rheotropism.

Reparata *pr.n.f.* Santa ~, a virgin who suffered martyrdom under Decius. In early times, down to the year 1298, she was the patron Saint of Florence. Her day is 8 October.

reparto *m.* distribution; department; capo ~, head of (a) department; (in a factory) department, shop, bay; (comm.) ~ straordinario di utili, bonus; (mil.) unit.

repel·l·ere [C23] *tr.* to repel, to repulse. **~ente** *part. adj.* repellent, repulsive; forza ~ente, power of repulsion. **~enza** *f.* (paint. techn.) crawling.

repenta·glio *m.* peril, danger; risk; mettere a ~, to jeopardize; mettere a ~ la vita, to risk one's life; stare a ~, to put up a brave stand.

repent·e *adj.* sudden; unexpected; sheer, steep; via, strada ~, steep road; *adv. phr.* di ~, suddenly, all of a sudden. **~emẹnte** *adv.* abruptly, with startling suddenness. **~ino** *adj.* sudden, unexpected; pioggia ~ina, sudden shower; (comm.) diminuzione ~ina dei prezzi, slump. **~inamẹnte** *adv.* suddenly, all of a sudden, unexpectedly.

†**re·pere** *intr.* to twine; se corpo in corpo repe, if one body interpenetrates another (Dante, *Para.* II, 39).

reper·ire [D2] *tr.* (admin.) to find, to trace. **~i·bile** *adj.* that can be found; available; il dottore è ~ibile al suo studio, the doctor may be seen at his surgery. **~ibilità** *f.* availability. (**~ito** *part. adj.*)

reperto *n.m.* (leg.) thing found in a search and produced during a trial; findings of a coroner or medical expert.

repertọ·rio *m.* collection; index; directory; (fig.) non è del mio ~, I don't know it; (theatr.) repertory; (leg.) indexed register; ~ notarile, Notary's Register.

†**repleto** *adj.* replete.

replezịọne *f.* (vet.) plenalvia; †repletion.

re·pli·ca *f.* reply; repartee, retort; objection; bisogna ubbidire senza ~, one must obey without question; (theatr.) repeat performance; molte ~che, a long run; repetition; orologio con la ~, repeater (watch); (paint.) copy, replica; (leg.) reply; replication (final written pleading on both sides, in civil action); rinunciare alle memorie di ~, to agree to close the pleadings (C.C.P.); (comm. correspondence) in ~ a, in reply to; (cinem.) retake. **~care** [A2s] *tr.* to repeat, to do again, to say again; ~care un'esperienza, to replicate an experiment; ~care le stesse parole, to say the same words over again; (theatr.) to repeat, to perform again; il dramma fu ~cato molte sere, the play had a long run; to object; non ho nulla da ~, I have no objection; to contradict; c'è poco da ~care, there is little to be said against it; *abs.* to reply; mi scrisse, ma io non ~cai, he wrote, but I did not answer; to repeat; vedo che non mi avete capito, ~cherò, I see you don't understand, I will repeat (it). **~ca·bile** *adj.* repeatable. **~camẹnto** *m.* repeating, repetition; reply; (gramm.) anadiplosis. **~cativo** *adj.* replying; repetitive. **~cato** *part. adj.* replied; repeated. **~catamẹnte** *adv.* repeatedly. **~cazịọne** *f.* (gramm.) repetition.

replo *m.* (bot.) replum.

reportage *m. indecl.* (pron. as Fr.) (journ.) report.

repren·dere [C5] and derivs. See **riprendere**.

reprens·i·bile *adj.* blameworthy, worthy of reproach, reprehensible. **~iọne** *f.* reproach.

repress-iọne *f.* repression; putting down, quelling; (leg.) ~ della violazione delle leggi, stamping-out of lawbreaking (C.P.). (**~ivo** *adj.*) **~o** *part.* cf. **reprimere**, q.v.; *adj.* suppressed, restrained; repressed; *n.m.* thwarted person; frustrated person (esp. sexually), refoulé. (**~ọre** *m.* **~ọra** *f.*)

reprim·ere [C18] *tr.* to suppress; to check, to restrain, to repress; *rfl.* to exercise restraint, to restrain, to check oneself. **~enda** *f.* reprimand; fare una ~enda a, to reprimand. **~ente** *part. adj.* restraining. **~i·bile** *adj.* repressible.

reprobare [A1]. See **riprovare**.

re·probo *adj.* bad, wicked; (theol.) reprobate (also *n.m.*).

reps *m. indecl.* (text.) repp.

repub·(b)li·ca *f.* the common good; the State; republic; (Brit. hist.) la ~ inglese, the British Commonwealth; reggersi a ~, to have a republican government; (joc.) la Repubblica tascabile, the 'pocket Republic', i.e. San Marino; (fig.) ~ letteraria, ~ delle lettere, men of letters, the literary world; ~ medica, the medical profession; (fam.) confusion, disorder. **~cano** *adj.*, *n.m.* republican; (orn.) sociable weaver-bird, *Philetairus socius*. **~canamẹnte** *adv.* in republican fashion. (**~canįșmo** *m.*) **~china** *f. dim.* (Ital. hist.) the Fascist Republic of Salò (1943–5). **~chino** *adj.* (Ital. hist.) relating to the above; *n.m.* one who swore allegiance to same.

repudiare [A4] and derivs. See **ripudiare**.

repugnare [A5] and derivs. See **ripugnare**.

repulisti *Lat.* fare ~ di, to make a clean sweep of.

repulsióne f. (phys.; biol.) repulsion.

repulsóre m. (rlwy.) buffer.

reput-are [A 1 s] tr. to deem, to judge, to consider, to think; lo ~ai mio dovere, I deemed it my duty; non lo ~o un grand'uomo, I do not consider him a great man; rfl. to consider oneself; ~arsi fortunato, to count oneself fortunate; ~arsi a onore, to consider (it) an honour. **~ato** part. adj. esteemed; è molto ~ato, he is highly esteemed. **~azióne** f. reputation; godere buona ~azione, to have, to enjoy, a good reputation.

re·qui·e f. rest, peace; non ebbe un momento di —, he didn't have a moment's rest; senza —, incessant(ly); m., f. (rel.) requiem (mass); any prayer for the dead; gli dirò un (una) —, I will say a prayer for him (for his soul); (liturg.; mus.) messa di —, requiem (mass).

re·quiem m., f. indecl. (liturg.) requiem (mass).

†requi·rere tr. to search for, to seek.

requiṣ-ire [D 2] tr. to requisition, to commandeer. **~ito** part. adj. requisitioned; n.m. requisite, requirement; pl. particulars, documents required, etc.; (leg.) ~iti del contratto, essential elements of contract (C.C.). **~ito·ria** f. (leg.) final speech by the prosecution; ~itoria scritta del Pubblico Ministero, prosecution's statement of charges against accused and penalty called for (C.P.P.). **~izióne** f. requisition; request; demand.

reṣa f. surrender; giving up, giving back; — dei giornali invenduti, return of unsold newspapers; yield; podere di poca —, farm that yields little; (comm.) rendering; delivery; alla — dei conti, on the rendering of accounts; (mil.; naut.) surrender; patti della —, surrender terms.

resarcire [D 2] and derivs. See **risarcire**.

†resca f. See **lesca**.

rescind-ere [C 21] tr. to cut into pieces; (leg.) to rescind; to annul, to cancel; — un contratto, to rescind or cancel a contract. **~i·bile** adj. (leg.) rescindable.

†re·scio m. fire-rake.

resciss-ióne f. (leg.) rescission; annulment, cancelling; indennità di — del contratto, compensation for termination of contract; (surg.) resection; — del colon, colectomy. **~o·rio** adj. (leg.) rescissory.

rescritto m. (hist.; eccl.) rescript.

resecare [A 2 s] (agric.) to cut out (e.g. branches), to cut away; (surg.) to resect.

reṣéda f. (bot.) mignonette, *Reseda odorata* and other species of *Reseda*.

reṣerpina f. (chem.; pharm.) reserpine.

resezióne f. (surg.) resection.

†res-i·a f. see **eresia**. **†~iarca** m. see **eresiarca**.

residén-te adj. resident; la popolazione —, the resident population; lying (as sediment); n.m., f. resident; i ~ti, the residents, the local inhabitants; m. Resident Minister, agent of Governor; part. residing; — a Roma, residing, living, in Rome. **~teménte** adv. permanently. **~za** f. residence, domicile; essere di ~za, to be in residence, to be at home; cambiamento di ~za, change of abode; official residence; office; (leg.) home; permanent address; residence (the place where a person has his habitual abode or dwelling, equivalent to 'dimora abituale' and distinguished from 'domicilio' where a person has the principal centre of his interests (C.C.)); (eccl.) residence; (liturg.) throne for monstrance at Exposition (with or without special baldacchino). **~ziale** adj. residential (i.e. requiring residence); zona ~ziale, residential area.

reṣi·du-o adj. left over, remaining; n.m. rest, residue, remainder; (comm.) balance; surplus; fondo ~i, surplus fund; (leg.) residue, the surplus of a testator's or intestate's estate after discharging all his liabilities; (math.) remainder; (chem.) residue(s). **~ale** adj. remaining, residual; n.m. remainder, residue. **~are** [A 6] tr. to reduce (a debt) by instalments; to arrange payment of by instalments; intr. (aux. essere) to be left (over), to remain. **~a·rio** adj. (leg.) residuary. **~ato** part. adj. reduced to a small balance; n.m.pl. ~ati di guerra, surplus war-stores; Azienda Rilievo e Alienazione Residuati (A.R.A.R.), Government Office responsible for sale of surplus war-stores.

reṣilién-te adj. (eng.; bldg.) resilient. **~za** f. (eng.; bldg.) resilience.

re·ṣin-a f. resin; rosin; (paperm.) colla di —, rosin size, acid size; — minerale, fossil resin; amber; (chem.) — vinilica, vinyl resin; — ossidata, epoxy resin. **~a·ceo** adj. resinous. **~ato** adj. treated with resin; n.m. (chem.) resinate, abietate. **~i·fero** adj. resinous.

~ificare [A 2 s] tr. to make resinous; (techn.) to resinify, to gum; rfl. to become resinous. **~ificazióne** f. (techn.) resinification. **~ite** f. (miner.) opal. **~o·ide** adj. resinoid, resin-like; n.m. resinoid, thermo-setting resin. **~óso** adj. resinous, like resin, containing or producing resin.

resipiscén-te adj. acknowledging mistakes; resipiscent. **~za** f. repentance, recognition of errors; resipiscence.

reṣi·pola f. See **erisipela**.

reṣi·ṣt-ere [C 1] intr. (aux. avere) to hold out; to bear up; to stay; with prep. 'a': to resist, to withstand, to endure; to stand up to (e.g. a test); — alle suppliche di un amico, to resist, to withstand, a friend's entreaties; — a ingiuste pretese, to oppose unlawful claims; — alla prova, to stand the test; — al fuoco, to be fireproof; non ci ~o più, I can't go on, I can't stand any more. **~ente** part. adj. resistant, resisting; strong; (of colours) fast; ~ente a tutte le intemperie, proof against the severest weather, weatherproof; ~ente al fuoco, fireproof. **~enza** f. resistance; endurance; durability; opporre ~enza, to offer resistance; ~enza alla fatica, endurance (of fatigue); (sport) endurance; prove di ~enza, endurance trials; (electr.) resistance; resistor; (electron.) ~enza di polarizzazione, bias resistor; (motor.) ~enza allo scarico, exhaust back-pressure; (bldg.) ~enza elastica, elastic strength; prova di ~enza, endurance test, reliability test; (naut.) ~enza di attrito, skin friction; (aerodyn.) ~enza aerodinamica, drag; ~enza relativa, lift/drag ratio; (eng.) ~enza all'urto, impact strength, shock resistance; ~enza di attrito, frictional resistance; strength, resistance; proofness; ~enza a compressione, compressive strength; ~enza a fatica, endurance limit, fatigue limit; (mech.) ~enza alla flessione, flexural strength; ~enza alla rottura, tensile strength; (mil.) resistance; (leg.) resistance; ~enza a un pubblico ufficiale, use of force or threats towards a public official; (Ital. hist.) la Resistenza, the underground resistance (anti-Fascist) movement in Italy (and elsewhere) at the end of the Second World War.

reṣistività f. (electr.) resistivity; — di massa, mass resistivity.

reṣistóre m. (electr.) resistor; — a decadi, decade resistor.

reṣ-o part. of **rendere**, q.v.; adj. restored, returned; rendered, made; — muto dallo stupore, struck dumb with astonishment; yielded. **~ocontista** m. reporter; report-writer; précis-writer. **~ocónto** m. report; account; ~oconto stenografico, verbatim record; statement; (comm.) ~oconti periodici, statements of account.

resorcina f. (chem.) resorcinol, resorcin.

†respi·gnere vb. and derivs. See **respingere**.

respin-g-ere [C 5] tr. to repel, to drive back; to repulse; — il nemico, to drive back the enemy; — l'assalto, to repel the attack; to reject; — un'offerta, to reject an offer; — una domanda, to refuse a request; — un candidato, to fail a candidate; fu respinto agli esami, he failed his examination; to return, to restore; (post) da ~ersi al mittente, return to sender. **~ente** adj. repellent; n.m. cutwater (of a bridge); embankment; (rlwy.) buffer. **~iménto** m. repelling; rejecting. (**~itóre** m. **~itrice** f.)

†respinta f. (mil.) recoil; reverse; repulsion, backthrust; (fig.) rejection, refusal; repulse.

respinto part. of **respingere**, q.v.; adj. rejected; repelled, driven back; sent back; (in an exam.) failed, (fam.) ploughed, plucked.

respir-are [A 1] intr. (aux. avere) to breathe; lasciami —, poi ti racconterò, let me get my breath, then I'll tell you; — a pieni polmoni, to take a deep breath; (fig.) to breathe (freely), to have a breathing space, to feel relief; (bot.) to respire; tr. — l'aria fresca, to breathe fresh air; — l'aria nativa, to be at home (on one's native heath); — l'aria della caserma, to live in barracks, to be a soldier; to breathe back again; to give forth, to exhale. **~a·bile** adj. breathable; fit to breathe. (**~abilità** f.) **~ativo** adj. favouring respiration; giving relief. **~atóre** m. respirator; (naut.) breathing-pipe vent; Davis escape apparatus in a submarine; schnorkel; generic term for any system permitting underwater breathing, whether diving bell, diver's suit or oxygen mask; aqualung. **~ató·rio** adj. (m.pl. **~ato·rii**) respiratory; apparato ~atorio, breathing apparatus. **~azióne** f. breathing; respiration; difficoltà di ~azione, shortness of breath; (comm.) pagare a ~azione, to pay by instalments; (med.) ~azione artificiale, artificial respiration; (bot.) respiration.

respiro m. breath; togliere il — a uno, to take a person's breath away, or (fig.) to pester someone; trarre un lungo —, to take a deep breath; trattenere il —, to hold one's breath, not to dare to breathe; esalare l'ultimo —, to breathe one's last; (mus.) semi-

respiro (*cont.*)

quaver rest; rest, pause, breathing space; delay, respite; senza —, promptly; pagare a —, to pay when it is convenient; accordare un — di sei mesi, to grant six months' respite; (techn.) gas vent.

†**respitto** *m.* See **rispetto**.

†**respo** *m.* See **cespo**.

responsa·bil-e *adj.* responsible; non siete — di ciò, you are not responsible for that; — davanti a Dio, responsible before God; — verso la famiglia, responsible for one's family; answerable; liable (esp. comm.); direttore — di un giornale, editor of a newspaper. -**ità** *f.* responsibility; mi prendo la -ità di farlo, I take the responsibility of doing it; fatelo sotto la vostra -ità, do it on your own responsibility; (leg.; comm.) liability; -ità civile per fatto illicito, legal liability for tort (C.C.); -ità per dolo, responsibility for criminal intent (C.P.); -ità limitata, limited liability.

responsione *f.* (comm.) rent.

responsivo *adj.* answering; lettera responsiva, (written) reply.

respons-o *m.* answer (esp. of an oracle); formal answer, decision; reply; (leg.) opinion; judgement; †(liturg.) response, responsory. -**oriale** *m.* (liturg.) *responsoriale*, antiphoner. -**o·rio** *m.* (liturg.) responsory.

†**responsura** *f.* response.

†**resquitto** *m.* rest, quiet, peace.

ressa *f.* crowd, throng; far —, to crowd, to throng; le ore di — e di fretta, the rush hours; insistence, pressure; (comm.) — agli sportelli per immediato pagamento, run on a bank.

ressi *f. indecl.* (med.) rhexis.

resta¹ *f.* (bot.) awn; onion skin; fish-bones.

resta² *f.* string (of onions, garlic, figs); (naut., Ancona) trawl rope, trawl line.

resta³ *f.* rest for a lance; con la lancia in —, with lance in rest; la — della lancia, the heel of the lance.

†**resta⁴** *f.* delay, pause; hiatus.

rest-are [A I] *intr.* (*aux.* essere) to stay, to remain; questo -i fra noi, this must be confidential; -a a vedere, it remains to be seen; — fedele, to remain faithful; — offeso, deluso, to be offended, disappointed; to be left, to be left over; non mi -avano che dieci sterline, I had only ten pounds left; ci -a molto da fare, a dire, we still have a lot to do, there is still much to be said; non -a da me, it is not my fault (that this is not done); to cease, to leave off; essa non -ava di parlare, she never stopped talking; — indietro, to lag behind, to fail to make progress; — d'accordo, to be in agreement; — in asso, to be left in the lurch; — morto, to be killed, to die a violent death; — sotto una macchina, to be run over by a car; to be situated, to stand, to lie; quel paesino -a in fondo alla valle, that little village lies at the bottom of the valley; (naut.) to bear; to be, to remain; — all'ancora, to remain at anchor; — in calma, to be becalmed; — a picco, to be at short stay (anchor ready for weighing); — di prua, to be ahead; — pel traverso, to be abeam; (comm.) to cease; to stop. -**abu·e** *m. indecl.* (bot.) restharrow, *Ononis spinosa*. -**ante** *part. adj.* remaining; *n.m.* remainder, rest; *pl.* the rest.

restaur-are [A I a] *tr.* to restore; to renovate; to repair; — un quadro, to restore a painting; to re-establish; — l'ordine, to restore order; *rfl.* to be restored; to recover. (-**a·bile** *adj.*) -**amento** *m.* restoring, making good, restoration. -**ativo** *adj.* restorative. -**ato** *part. adj.* restored; renovated; repaired. -**atore** *m.* (-**atrice** *f.*) restorer, esp. of pictures, statues, etc.; *adj.* scuola -atrice di virtù, school for building up character, reform school. -**azione** *f.* restoration (of works of art), restoration (of a dynasty); recovery, restoration (to health); (hist.) restoration; la Restaurazione, the Restoration after Napoleon.

resta·uro *m.* restoration work (on buildings, works of art); la casa ha bisogno di qualche —, the house needs some repair; far dei restauri, to carry out repairs.

†**resti·a** *f.* (naut.) scend, backwash at entrance of a harbour.

resti·o *adj.* reluctant, unmanageable, restive; un cavallo —, a restive horse; a jibbing horse; disinclined; sono — ad accettare queste condizioni, I am loath to accept these terms; *n.m.* restiveness, reluctance; impediment (in speech); hesitation.

restitu-ire [D 2] *tr.* to return, to give back; to restore; vi -irò il danaro domani, I shall pay you back the money tomorrow; lo -irono nel suo grado, they restored him to his former rank; *rfl.* to return, to go back; -irsi in un luogo, to return to a place. -**i·bile** *adj.* returnable; repayable. -**ito** *part. adj.* returned, restored; paid

back. (-**tore** *m.* -**trice** *f.*) -**to·rio** *adj.* (*m.pl.* -**to·rii**) (leg.) restitutory. -**zione** *f.* restitution; return; restoration; repayment; a buona -zione, hoping to be able to repay your kindness; -zione di un testo, critical editing of a text; recall (from exile); (astron.) completion of orbit; (leg.) restitution; (comm.) -zione del dazio, drawback.

rest-o *m.* remainder, rest, residue; (money) change; (math.) remainder; *pl.* remains; -i mortali, mortal remains, corpse; (of a building) remains, ruins; (comm.) balance; remainder; il — del carlino (literally, 'change from a penny'), name of the leading newspaper in Bologna; (fig.) se ciò non ti basta ti darò il — (del carlino), if that is not enough I'll give you what you deserve; (bowls) fare un —, to knock away one's opponent's bowl and put one's own in its place; *adv. phr.* del —, however, besides; del —, avresti dovuto dirmelo, besides, you ought to have told me. -**one** *m.* (vet.) a quiet placid horse; a kind of sporting dog used in shooting game (e.g. setter, pointer).

†**restoppia** *f.* straw, after threshing.

restremare *vb.* and derivs. See **rastremare**.

restrin·g-ere [C 5] *tr.* to tighten, to bind tighter; to squeeze; to narrow; to restrict; to straighten; to reduce, to diminish; — le spese, to cut down expenditure, expenses; (archit.) — la colonna, to taper the column; *rfl.* to tighten; to contract; to shrink; questa stoffa non si -e, this material does not shrink; -ersi nelle spalle, to shrug one's shoulders; la strada si -e, the road narrows; to decrease; -ersi nelle spese, to reduce expenses; to restrain oneself; non poter -ersi di piangere, to be unable to restrain one's tears; -ersi alla volontà di altri, to give way to someone else, to do as someone else wishes; *recip. rfl.* to draw closer together; (to pupils on school benches) -etevi!, sit closer together! -**imento** *m.* narrowing, contracting; tightening; shrinking; (med.) stricture. -**itivo** *adj.* restrictive. (-**itore** *m.* -**itrice** *f.*)

restrittiv-o *adj.* restrictive; (leg.) interpretazione -a, strict interpretation; leggi -e, restrictive laws; (comm.) girata -a, restrictive endorsement. (-**amente** *adv.*)

restrizione *f.* restriction; limitation; curtailing; senza —, unrestricted, unreservedly; — mentale, mental reservation.

resultare [A I] and derivs. See **risultare**.

†**resu·mere** *vb.* and derivs. See **riassumere**.

resupino *adj.* (poet.) supine.

resur·gere [C 5] (poet.). See **risorgere**.

†**resurressi** *m. indecl.* Resurrection.

retag·gio *m.* heritage, inheritance.

†**retare¹** *vb.* and derivs. See **ereditare**.

retare² [A I c]. See under **rete**.

ret-e *f.* net; netting; network; gettare le -i, to cast (fishing) nets; prendere pesci con la —, to net fish; wire-netting; string-bag; — per i capelli, hair-net; — stradale, network of roads, roads, road-system; (fig.) trap; rimanere alla propria —, to be caught in one's own toils, hoist with one's own petard; (sport) net of goal; actual goal scored; (soccer) a -i inviolate, a -i bianche, said of a team against whom no goal is scored in a given match; (tennis) gioco a —, net-play; (mil.) forage net; (naut.) net; — guardatesta, d'impagliettatura, splinter net, nettings; — d'arrembaggio, — da bordaggio, boarding net; — del bompresso, bowsprit net; — parasiluri, torpedo net; fishing net; maglia di —, mesh; panno di —, panel; armare la —, to make up a net; -i da posta fissa, permanent nets; -i da circuizione, encircling nets (seine, etc.); -i da posta a corrente, drift nets; -i a strascico, trawl or dragnets; calare la —, gettare la —, to shoot the net; salpare la —, to haul the net, to recover; (techn.) crivello di — metallica, wire sieve; network, system; (electr.) grid; mains; tensione di —, mains voltage; — metallica, wire netting; wire gauge; (rlwy.) luggage-rack; (zool.) omentum; (paint.) squared lines on paper or other surface to aid in spacing a design; punto in —, filet-work, filet embroidery. -**are** [A I] *tr.* (naut.) to net; (paint.) to square (paper or other surface, for drawing or painting); *intr.* (*aux.* essere) (paint, etc.) to crack (of surface of painting, plaster, gilding and the like, in a network of little cracks). -**ata** *f.* cast of a net; catch (of fishes, birds, criminals); round-up; bargain; network, netting (in any material). -**ato** *part. adj.* reticulated, netted (i.e. made of netting); *n.m.* reticulation; network. -**atura** *f.* (paint.) squaring (paper or other surface for painting). -**icella** *f.* little net; hair-net, snood; (rlwy.) -icella per le valige, luggage-rack; (anat.) reticulum; (bot.) reticulation;

ret·e (*cont.*)

(chem.) wire gauge; gas mantle. **-ina** *f. dim.* fine net (tissue); hair-net; (meteor.) reseau; gas mantle. **-ino** *m. dim.* little net, fine net; silk net, gold tissue, net embroidered with pearls; net embroidery, net darning; punch work; net used in a 'paretaio', q.v.; (text.) skimmer; a perforated ladle used in skimming the hot water used in preparing silk; (bldg.) wire grating to protect a window; (angling) landing-net. **-one** *m. augm.* larger net of the 'paretaio', q.v.

†**re·tena** *f.* See **retina²**.

retene *m.* (chem.) retene.

reten-tiva *f.*, **-zione** *f.* See **ritentiva, ritenzione**.

reticen-te *adj.* reticent; reluctant or refusing to speak. **-za** *f.* reticence; puoi parlar senza -za, you may speak frankly; withholding of information (usu. *pl.*); (rhet.) figure suggesting meaning while pretending to withhold it; (gramm.) punti di -za, omission marks; (leg.) non-disclosure (C.C.).

re·tico¹ *adj.* Rhaetian; vino —, wine made at Verona of grapes from the Alto Adige; (geol.) Rhaetic.

†**re·tico²** *adj.* See **eretico**.

reticol-are¹ [A I S] *tr.* to reticulate; *intr.* (*aux.* avere) (paint.) to draw squares on a surface for copying or spacing a design. **-amento** *m.* reticulating. **-ato** *adj.* reticulate, reticulated; (archit.) reticular; *n.m.* reticular masonry; barbed wire fence; (mil.) barbed wire defences; wire frame used at artillery proving range. **-azione** *f.* reticulation.

reticolare² *adj.* reticular; reticulated.

reticolite *f.* (med.) reticulitis.

reti·colo *m.* (scient.) reticulum, network; (zool.) reticulum, honeycomb (in stomach of ruminants); (mil.) wire entanglement; (phys.) — cristallino, crystal lattice; (astron.) reseau; (opt.) hair line, cross-hair, graticule; — di diffrazione, diffraction grating.

†**reti·culo** *m.* See **reticolo**.

retiforme *adj.* (scient.) retiform, net-like.

retina¹ *f. dim.* See under **rete**.

re·tin-a² *f.* (anat.) retina. **-acolo** *m.* (anat.) retinaculum. **-amento** *m.*, **-atura** *f.* (paint. techn.) checking. **-oscopi·a** *f.* (med.) retinoscopy. **-osco·pico** *adj.* (med.) retinoscopical. **-osco·pio** *m.* (med.) retinoscope.

retinenza *f.* retentive force.

retinite *f.* (med.) retinitis; (miner.) pitchstone.

re·tore *m.* (anct. hist. and fig.) rhetor; rhetorician.

reto·ric-a *f.* rhetoric; oratory, eloquence. **-ale** *adj.* see **retorico**. **-are** [A2 S] *intr.* (*aux.* avere) to teach rhetoric; (derog.) to speak with affected elegance. **-astro** *m.* (derog.) rhetorician. **-o** *adj.* rhetorical; figure retoriche, figures of speech; (iron.) è una figura -a, that is a mere figure of speech; *n.m.* teacher of rhetoric. **-ume** *m.* (derog.) bad rhetoric; stilted language.

†**retorta** *f.* (chem.) retort, alembic.

retrat·til-e *adj.* retractable; retractile; carrello non —, non-retractable undercarriage. **-ità** *f.* (scient.) retractability; liability to shrink. **-ito** *m.* (leg.) -ito successorio, right of co-heirs to buy in (C.C.).

retribu-ire [D 2] *tr.* to pay, to repay; to recompense, to reward; (leg.) to remunerate (C.C.). **-ito** *part. adj.* bene -ito, well-paid; ferie -ite, holidays with pay; *n.m.* i meglio -iti, the best, most highly, paid workers. (**-itore, -tore** *m.*, **-trice** *f.*) **-zione** *f.* reward, recompense; remuneration, pay; retribution; (theol.) -zione di vita eterna, the reward of eternal life; (leg.) remuneration.

retrivo *adj.* backward, behind the times; reactionary; *n.m.* reactionary.

retro¹ *adv.* behind; (poet.) ire — a, to follow; vedi —, see back; segue —, continued on back; *n.m.* back; back-room; (of a coin) reverse; negozio con —, shop with a room at the back.

retro-² *pref.* rear; back. **-ammira·glio** *m.* see **contrammiraglio**; nave -ammiraglio, rear-admiral's flagship. **-andare** [A 7] *intr.* (*aux.* essere) to retrace one's steps. **-attivo** *adj.* (leg.) retroactive; (leg.) retrospective; that relates back. (**-attivamente** *adv.* **-attività** *f.*) **-azione** *f.* retroaction; (leg.) retrospective effect; -azione dell'accettazione, relation back of acceptance (C.C.). **-bocca** *f.* (anat.) pharynx. **-bottega** *f.* back-room (behind a shop). **-bugigat·tolo** *m.* little back-room; lumber-room. **-bulbare** *adj.* (anat.) retrobulbar. **-ca·mera** *f.* back-room (leading from a bedroom). **-camerino** *m.* little back-room. **-ca·rica** *f.* (mil.) breechloading. **-cecale** *adj.* (anat.) retrocaecal. **-cedente** *part. adj.* receding;

retrogressive; (med.) retrocedent. **-ce·dere** [B I] *intr.* (*aux.* avere, essere) to go back, to withdraw, to retreat; (leg.) to reassign; to reconvey; (mil.) to disrate, to demote. **-cedimento** *m.* withdrawal; retrogression. **-cervicale** *adj.* (med.) retrocervical. **-cessione** *f.* withdrawal; retrocession, retrogression; restitution; (sport) relegation (soccer or any game in which teams are divided qualitatively into divisions); (canon law) waiving of right to bestow benefice; (med.) retrocession, 'striking inwards', 'going in' (of an eruption); (mil.) downgrading. **-cesso** *part. adj.* (mil.) disrated. **-co·lico** *adj.* (med.) retrocolic. **-datare** [A I] *tr.* to antedate. **-datato** *part. adj.* antedated, backdated. **-faringe·o** *adj.* (anat.) retropharyngeal. **-flessione** *f.* (med.) retroflexion. **-flesso** *adj.* (med.) retroflexed, retrocurved. **-gradare** [A I] *intr.* (*aux.* avere) to withdraw, to recede; (astron.) to retrograde. **-gradazione** *f.* (astron.) retrogradation; retrogression. **-grado** *adj.* retrograde; backward; reactionary; (astron.) moto -grado, retrograde motion. (prosod.) versi -gradi, reciprocal lines (scanning backwards as well as forwards). **-gressione** *f.* retrogression. **-guar·dia** *f.* (mil.) rearguard, afterguard. **-mar·cia** *f.* (eng.) reversing, reverse motion, reverse gear; (motor.) in -marcia, in reverse. **-peritoneale** *adj.* (anat.) retroperitoneal; spazio -peritoneale, retroperitoneum. **-peritonite** *f.* (med.) retroperitonite. **-posto** *adj.* (scient.) retroposed. **-pulsione** *f.* (med.) retropulsion. **-scena** *f.* (theatr.) backstage; *m.* (fig.) what goes on behind the scenes; backstairs business; underhand dealing; mi piacerebbe conoscere tutto il -scena, I should like to know what is behind all that. **-scritto** *adj.*, *n.m.* (something) written on the back, on the next page(s); see below. **-spettivo** *adj.* retrospective; *n.m.* retrospect; (cinem.) flashback. **-stante** *adj.* standing behind; territorio -stante, hinterland. **-stanza** *f.* back-room. **-tarsale** *adj.* (anat.) retrotarsal, at the back of the eyelid. **-terra** *m.* hinterland. **-trarre** [B 33] *tr.* to antedate; to commit an anachronism. **-trazione** *f.* anachronism. **-treno** *m.* rear wheels of car or lorry. **-uterino** *adj.* (med.) retrouterine. **-vaccinazione** *f.* (med.) retrovaccination. **-ven·dere** [B I] *tr.* to resell (to the original vendor). **-ven·dita** *f.* resale to vendor; col patto di -vendita, under agreement to take back goods at the same price. **-versione** *f.* (med.) retroversion; retranslation. **-vi·e** *f.pl.* (mil.) supply lines; area behind the front line. **-visore** *m.* (motor.) driving mirror.

†**retrorso** *adv.* backwards.

retroso *m.* backwash, back-current.

retta¹ *f.* (geom.) straight line.

retta² *f.* dar — a, to pay attention to, to listen to; to consent to, to take notice of, to heed; date — a me, mark my words; (pop. Tusc.) da' — come si bisticciano!, just listen to them bickering!

retta³ *f.* charge, terms (for board and lodging); vorrei sapere qual'è la — completa, I should like to know what are the inclusive terms; mezza —, half-board; fees (e.g. at a boarding-school); (naut.) — d'altezza, position line (used in obtaining an astronomical position).

retta⁴ *f.* resistance; durability; questo panno farà poca —, this cloth will not wear well.

rettan·gol-o *m.* (geom.) rectangle; oblong; court (e.g. for tennis); *adj.* (geom.) right-angled; triangolo —, right-angled triangle. **-are** *adj.* rectangular; oblong.

†**rettare** *intr.* to creep; *tr.* (mil.) to sweep with gunfire.

rettezza *f.* See under **retto**.

retti·fica *f.* correction, rectification; adjustment; (eng.) grinding.

rettific-are [A 2 S] *tr.* to rectify, to correct; to straighten; to adjust; — l'aria, to purify the air; — il proprio voto, to change one's vote; (geom.) to rectify; (chem.) to rectify; (eng.) to grind; to reface, to reseat (e.g. a valve). **-amento** *m.* rectifying; correcting. **-ato** *part. adj.* corrected; rectified; (chem.) alcool -ato, rectified alcohol. **-atore** *m.* (radio) detector; -atore a cristallo, crystal detector. **-atrice** *f.* (eng.) grinder, grinding machine; -atrice frontata, face grinder. **-azione** *f.* rectification; correction; amendment; adjustment; (geom.; chem.; leg.) rectification; (radio) rectification; -azione integrale, full-wave rectification; (eng.) grinding; -azione ad umido, wet grinding.

rettifilo *m.* straight road; straight (part, of road or track); straight line (e.g. of wall); *pr.n.m.* (at Naples) Corso Umberto.

ret·tile *m.* (zool.) reptile; (fig., of a person) 'snake in the grass'; vile wretch.

rett-o *part.* of **reggere**, q.v.; *adj.* straight; upright; (fig.) straightforward, upright, honest; just; correct, right; la -a pronunzia,

rett·o (*cont.*)
the correct pronunciation; (gramm.) caso —, nominative case; (astron.) ascensione -a, right ascension; (anat.) muscolo — dell'adome, rectus; *n.m.* (anat.) rectum; (geom.) right angle; (in books, esp. MS.) recto; (fig.) rectitude, honesty, justice. **-am̧ente** *adv.* honestly, justly, with justice; correctly; straight. **-ęzza** *f.* rectitude. **-ili·neo** *adj.* straight; rectilinear; (fig.) straightforward, perfectly honest; (geom.) rectilinear; *n.m.* straight road; (horse-racing, athletics) the straight. **-itu·dine** *f.* rectitude, straightforwardness, uprightness, honesty. **-ocele** *m.* (med.) rectocoele. **-opessi** *f.* (surg.) proctopexy. **-ouretrale** *adj.* (anat.) recto-urethral. **-outerino** *adj.* (anat.) recto-uterine; scavo -outerino, Douglas's cul-de-sac. **-ovaginale** *adj.* (anat.) recto-vaginal. **-ovescicale** *adj.* (anat.) rectovesical; scavo -ovescicale, rectovesical pouch.

rettor·e *m.* ruler; governor; rector; head, president; Rettore Magnifico, vice-chancellor (of a University); preside —, headmaster (of a secondary school); (eccl.) rector (Superior in some communities or institutions; parish priest or chaplain in some places). **-ato** *m.* rectorship, rectorate. **-ęssa** *f.* (joc.) rector's wife. **-i·a** *f.* (eccl.) church served by rector, or benefice held by him.

retto·ric-a *f.*, **-o** *adj.* See retorica, retorico.

retto-scopi·a *f.* (med.) proctoscopy. **-sco·pio** *m.* (med.) proctoscope.

rettotomi·a *f.* (surg.) proctotomy.

†reubar·baro *m.* See rabarbaro.

reuc·cio *m. dim.* See under re.

reucliniano *adj.* Iotacist (pronunciation of ancient Greek).

re·um-a *m.* (med.) rheumatism; cold, catarrh. **-atalgi·a** *f.* (med.) rheumatalgia, rheumatic pain. **-a·tico** *adj.* (med.) rheumatic. **-atiẓmo** *m.* (med.) rheumatism. **-atiẓzare** [A1] *tr.* to give rheumatism to, to cause rheumatism in; *rfl.* to get rheumatism. **-atiẓzato** *part. adj.* suffering from rheumatism, rheumatic.

†re·uma *f.* tidal junction.

revel·l-ere [C23] *tr.* (med.) to disperse. **-ente** *part. adj.* (med.) causing dispersion.

revellino *m.* See rivellino.

†reverberare *vb. and derivs.* See riverberare.

reveren-do *adj.* (eccl.) Reverend; *n.m.* (pop., esp. in vocative) buon giorno, —!, good morning, Father!; ti aspetta il —, the priest is waiting for you. **-dis·simo** *adj.* (eccl.) Right Reverend (NOTE: the title *Reverendissimo* (abbrev. 'Rev.mo') is given to prelates (e.g. abbots and monsignori) and implies in itself a certain rank. *Molto reverendo* (abbrev. 'M.R.') is merely a polite amplification of the 'reverendo' due to simple priests; on an envelope, 'M.R. Don Pietro Bianchi' is the proper equivalent of 'The Rev. Peter White'). **-te** *adj.* reverent, respectful. **-za** *f.* see riverenza, under riverire. **-ziale** *adj.* reverential.

†reverire *vb. and derivs.* See riverire.

reversale *f.* (comm.) reversal.

reversi·bil-e *adj.* (techn.) reversible. **-ità** *f.* (techn.) reversibility. (For other uses, see **riversibile**.)

reversino *m.* card-game in which the lowest number of points wins (cf. 'misère' in whist).

reversiọne *f.* (biol.) reversion to type.

revin·dica *f.* (leg.) action for recovery of property.

reviṣ-iọne *f.* revision; ufficio tecnico di —, (in the Ministry of Works) Office for supervising Public Works; (eng.) overhaul; (leg.) review; retrial; rehearing; (comm.) — dei conti, auditing of accounts. **-ionare** [A1c] *tr.* (eng.) to overhaul, to recondition. **-ǫre** *m.* reviser; (typ.) -ore di bozze, a slightly higher grade than 'correttore di bozze', proof-reader, implying the right to revise or 'edit' a text; press-censor; (leg.) -ore ufficiale dei conti, certified Public accountant (C.C.); (comm.) -ore di conti, auditor, comptroller.

revivaliẓmo *m.* revivalism.

revivific-are [A2] see revivificare, under rivivere. **-aziọne** *f.* (chem.) revivification; reduction to metallic form.

reviviscenza *f.* revival; reawakening.

re·voca *f.* (leg.) revocation; — di procura, revocation of a power of attorney; — di promessa, withdrawal of promise (C.C.).

revoc-are [A2s] *tr.* to recall; to revoke, to repeal; — a dubbio, to consider doubtful; (leg.) to revoke; to cancel; to annul. **-a·bile** *adj.* revocable. **-abilità** *f.* (leg.) revocability. (**-ato** *part.*) **-ato·rio** *adj.* (leg.) azione -atoria, action for revocation (C.C.). **-aziọne** *f.* revocation; (leg.) -azione del testamento, revocation of will (C.C.).

revol·ver *m. indecl.* revolver; (eng.) turret; tornio a —, capstan lathe. **-are** [A1s] *tr.* to shoot (at) with a revolver. **-ata** *f.* revolver-shot.

revuls-iọne *f.* (med.) revulsion. **-ivo** *adj.* (med.) revulsive.

rex-iẓmo *m.* (pol.) rexism (in Belgium). **-ista** *m., f.* rexist.

rezia·rio *m.* (Rom. hist.) retiarius.

†rezza *f.* (naut.) trammel net.

ręẓzo *m.* shade; cool breeze; stare al —, to take one's ease in the shade.

ri-. Like **r-** or **ra-**, this prefix indicates repetition or intensification, but not always. Sometimes verbs to which it has been added are virtually unchanged in meaning. If such a word is not found below, it should be sought under the first letter following the prefix.

riabbaiare [A4] *intr.* (*aux.* avere) to bark again; to bark in answer to a bark, to bark back.

riabbassare [A1] *tr.* to lower again; to lower still more.

riabbat·tere [B1] see **rabbattere**; *recip. rfl.* to meet each other again.

riabbracciare [A3] *tr.*, *recip. rfl.* to meet again after a long time.

riabbrunare [A1] *rfl.* to go into black again (for mourning).

riabilit-are [A1s] *tr.* to rehabilitate; to redeem; (leg.) to rehabilitate; to restore a forfeited right to; to discharge from bankruptcy; to relieve from incapacity; to qualify again; *rfl.* to recover one's reputation. **-ato** *part. adj.* rehabilitated; (comm.) fallito -ato, certificated, discharged bankrupt. **-aziọne** *f.* (leg.) rehabilitation; restoration of a forfeited right; (comm.) -azione del fallito, discharge of a bankrupt.

riaccomodare [A1s] *tr.* to mend (again); *recip. rfl.* to make up a quarrel, to become friends again.

riacconciare [A4c] *and derivs.* See **racconciare**.

riaccostare [A1] *tr.* to approach again; *recip. rfl.* to become reconciled (with each other), to renew friendly relations; *rfl.* (eccl.) riaccostarsi ai sacramenti, to return to the sacraments (cf. **raccostare**).

riaccreditare [A1s] *tr.* to credit; to confirm; *rfl.* to regain credit or esteem.

riacolite *f.* (miner.) rhyacolite.

riacquist-are [A1] *tr.* to recover; — la salute, to be restored to health; to buy back, to regain by purchase; *rfl.* to recover (oneself); to recover one's senses. **-a·bile** *adj.* available for repurchase; that can be recovered, recoverable. (**-ato** *part. adj.*) **-o** *m.* recovery; repurchase; thing repurchased; reacquisition.

riadatt-are [A1] *tr.* to restore to order; to put in its place; *rfl.* to readapt oneself; to yield again.

riaddormentare [A1] *tr.* to put to sleep again; *rfl.* to fall asleep again.

riaddossare [A1] *tr.* to lay, to put (a burden on someone); — la colpa ad uno, to blame someone again; *rfl.* (*dat.* of *prn.* 'si') riaddossarsi nuovi carichi, to assume fresh responsibilities, to saddle oneself with additional burdens.

riaffacciare [A3] *rfl.* to look out again, to show oneself again (e.g. at a window); to reappear.

riaffittare [A1] *tr.* to let again, to relet; to sublet; (leg.) to relet; to re-lease (esp. rural property).

riagganciare [A4] *tr.*, *abs.* to replace (telephone receiver); to hang up.

riagire [D2] *and derivs.* See **reagire**.

rialeṣare [A1] *tr.* (eng.) to rebore.

riallentare [A1] *tr.* to slow down again; — il passo, il corso, to go (walk, drive) still slower.

rialto *m.* height, eminence, rise; raised embroidery; unusually good meal; fare un —, to have a feast; (Venice) il Ponte di Rialto, the Rialto Bridge; (archit.) steps, raising a building above the street level.

rialz-are [A1] *tr.* to raise, to lift up (again); to heighten; — la testa, to raise one's head, (fig.) to become powerful or bold again; (naut.) to lift (a ship or boat); (dyeing) to top; (comm.) — il prezzo, to raise the price; *intr.* (*aux.* essere) or *rfl.* (of barometer) to rise; to raise oneself, to go up; to get better in health; to have a feast; (comm.) to recover. **-am̧ento** *m.* lifting up, raising; heightening; rise; (naut.) lift of the hull approaching the bow or stern. (**-ato** *part. adj.*) **-atura** *f.* (agric.) tying up vine-shoots. **-ista** *m.* (comm.) bull; long; long in stock. **-o** *m.* rise; i prezzi sono in -o, prices are rising; (comm.) giuocare al -o, to buy or sell bull; il cambio è in -o, the exchange is on the rise; -o improvviso e rapido, boom; (leg.) -o fraudolento di prezzi, fraudulent raising of prices (C.P.); (naut.) see **rialzamento**.

riam-are [A1] *tr.* to love in return; — uno, to return a person's affection; le vuol bene, ma non è -ato, he is fond of her, but she does not love him. (-**ante** *part. adj.* -**ato** *part. adj.*) -**icare** [A2] *tr.* to reconcile, to make friendly again; *rfl.* (*prep.* a, con) to become friends again with.

riammagliare [A4] *tr.* to repair ladders in (e.g. in stockings).

riammal-are [A1] *intr.* (*aux.* essere), *rfl.* to fall ill again, to have a relapse. -**amento** *m.* relapse.

riammettere [C20] *tr.* to readmit (to membership); to admit again.

riammiss-i·bile *adj.* eligible for readmission. -**ione** *f.* readmission; readmittance.

riammobiliare [A4] *tr.* to refurnish; to add some new furniture (in a house or rooms).

riand-are [A7] *intr.* (*aux.* essere) to go again; to go back; *quasi-tr.* (poet.) — i sempiterni calli (Leopardi), to traverse still that never-ending track; *tr.* to recall, to call to mind; to go over again in one's mind. -**amento** *m.* going back (again); going over again, recalling, repetition, reciting.

rianim-are [A1s] *tr.* to revive, to restore to life; *rfl.* to recover (oneself), to regain consciousness, to revive; to take heart again; to cheer up; (of streets) to become busy (full of people) again. -**ato** *part. adj.* revived. (-**azione** *f.*)

riannodare [A1] *tr.* to knot or tie again; to renovate.

riapertura *f.* reopening; beginning; torneremo alla — delle scuole, we shall come back when the school term begins; (leg.) — del fallimento, reopening of bankruptcy (C.C.).

riappalt-are [A1] *tr.* to make a fresh contract; to let out on sub-contracts. -**atore** *m.* contractor who allots work on subcontract. -**o** *m.* subcontract.

riappellare [A1] *tr.* (leg.) to appeal again.

riappezzare [A1] *tr.* to piece together (again).

riappigionare [A1c] *tr.* to relet; to sublet.

riappisolare [A1s] *rfl.* to nod off to sleep again (cf. **appisolare**).

riapprendere [C1] *tr.* to learn again; *rfl.* to be learnt again; (of fire) to catch again.

riapr-ire [D3] *tr.* to reopen; (fig.) — l'animo alla speranza, to feel one's hopes revive; — una ferita, to reopen a wound, to arouse painful memories; *rfl.* to reopen. -**itura** *f.* see **riapertura**.

riar·d-ere [C3] *tr., intr.* (*aux.* essere) to burn (again), to burn up; to scorch, to dry up; to consume; (chem.) to reignite. (-**imento** *m.*)

riarm-are [A1] *tr., rfl.* to rearm, to refit; to equip; (naut.) to recommission (a ship); (archit.) to strengthen, to reinforce; (of a musical instrument) to renew strings or other parts; (techn.) to refit; to recock. (-**amento** *m.* -**ato** *part. adj.*) -**atura** *f.* (archit.) strengthening. -**o** *m.* rearmament; increasing armed forces.

riarso *part.* of **riardere**, q.v.; *adj.* dry, parched; thirsty; (fig., of land) burnt up.

riassett-are [A1] *tr.* to rearrange; to set in order; *rfl.* to settle down; (of accounts) to balance. (-**ato** *part. adj.*)

riassetto *m.* rearrangement; order; balance.

riassicur-are [A1] *tr.* (leg.) to reinsure; to reassure. -**anza** *f.* see **riassicurazione**. -**atore** *m.* (leg.) reinsurer (C.C.). (-**atrice** *f.*) -**azione** *f.* reinsurance; (leg.) contratto di -azione, reinsurance contract (C.C.).

riassorbimento *m.* (physiol.) resorption; (surg.) dispersion.

riassu·mere [C8] *tr.* to resume, to take up again; to take back (into service), to re-employ; to summarize, to sum up; to recapitulate; (leg.) to resume.

riassunt-ivo *adj.* recapitulatory. -**o** *part.* of **riassumere**, q.v.; *adj.* resumed, summed up, summarized; *n.m.* summary, recapitulation; abstract; (leg.) brief.

riassunzione *f.* resumption; taking back (or up) again; re-employment; (leg.) Summons for transfer of action from one Court to another; Summons for rehearing after Cassation (C.C.P.).

riattacc-are [A2] *tr.* to attach again; to attack again; — i cavalli al carro, to harness the horses to the cart (again); -ami questo bottone, sew this button on for me; — il discorso, to resume one's speech, to begin talking again; *abs.* to put horses to a carriage; (teleph., pop.) to 'hang up', to hang up the receiver; to begin again, to be 'at it' again; svegliarsi e — subito, to wake up and fall asleep again instantly; *rfl.* to adhere again, to stick again; to be connected (with); -arsi alla speranza, to become hopeful again; to become attached again. (-**amento** *m.* -**ato** *part. adj.*)

riatt-are [A1] *tr.* to repair, to recondition, to make fit for use again. (-**amento** *m.* -**ato** *part. adj.*)

riattiv-are [A1] *tr.* to bring into use again; (rlwy.) to put back into service; to reopen (a line) that has been closed, to bring into normal working again (after an accident, landslide, etc.); il traffico è stato -ato, trains are again running normally; (chem.) to reactivate. (-**ato** *part. adj.*) -**azione** *f.* (chem.) reactivation.

riaugurare [A1sa] *tr.* to repeat, or reciprocate, good wishes.

riavallare [A1] and derivs. See **riavvallare**.

riavere [B3] *tr.* to get back, to recover; to restore; *rfl.* to recover (oneself), one's strength, vigour, health, self-control); to make a good recovery; to make good one's losses. -**uta** *f.* recovery; (sport) return match, 'revenge'. -**uto** *part. adj.* regained, recovered; restored (to health, vigour); re-established, set up, on a sound financial footing once more.

riavvallare[1] [A1] *rfl., intr.* (*aux.* essere) (of earth) to be washed down; to subside, to sink.

riavvall-are[2] [A1] *tr.* (comm.) to reguarantee. -**o** *m.* (comm.) re-guarantee.

riavvicin-are [A1] *tr.* to approach again; to compare; to resume friendly relations with; to reconcile; *rfl.* to be reconciled; to become friendly. (-**ato** *part. adj.*)

riavvitare [A1] *tr.* (eng.) to retighten.

riavvolg-ere [C5] *tr.* to rewind. (-**imento** *m.*)

riazione *f.* See **reazione**.

riazzuffare [A1] *recip. rfl.* to come to blows again.

ribaciare [A3] *tr.* to kiss again; to kiss in return.

†**ribadare** *rfl., intr.* to take very great care.

ribad-ire [D2] *tr.* to clinch, to rivet, to fix; (fig.) to confirm; to support (a statement) with additional reasons; — qualcosa nella testa a uno, to impress something on someone; *rfl.* (*acc.* of *prn.* 'si') to be clinched; to be riveted; (eng.) martello da — automatico, rivet gun; (fig.) to hold on to one's job, to be well 'dug in'; (*dat.* of *prn.* 'si') to impress upon one's mind, to take particular note of. (-**imento** *m.*) -**ito** *part. adj.* clinched, riveted; confirmed; fixed; *n.m.* (eng.) rivet; -ito a testa cilindrica, cheese-head rivet; -ito a testa piatta, flat-head rivet. -**itore** *m.* riveter (person). -**itrice** *f.* riveter, riveting machine. -**itura** *f.* riveting.

ribald-o *m.* scoundrel, rascal; †freebooter; *adj.* rascally; (colloq.) shockingly bad, very inferior. -**a·glia** *f.* pack of scoundrels, gang of ruffians. -**are** [A1] *intr.* (*aux.* avere) to behave like a scoundrel; †to be a freebooter. -**eri·a** *f.* rascality, scoundrelism; knavish trick; dirty trick; (colloq.) very bad work, mess, trash.

ribalenare [A1c] *intr.* (*aux.* avere) to flash again; (fig.) — alla mente, to come back to one (to one's memory) in a flash.

riballare [A1] *intr.* (*aux.* avere) to dance again.

ribalt-are [A1] *tr.* to overturn, to upset; to tip; *intr.* (*aux.* essere, avere), *rfl.* to overturn, to roll over; to be upset. -**a** *f.* lid; trap-door; folding bed or table (folding against a wall); (theatr.) foot-lights; front of stage; presentarsi alla -a, to take a (curtain) call; (fig.) tornare alla -a, to return to public life; il problema è tornato alla -a, the question has again become important, has come up again. -**a·bile** *adj.* tipping, tilting. -**amento** *m.*, -**atura** *f.* upsetting, overturning. (-**ato** *part. adj.*) -**i·bile** *adj.* tipping; seggiolino -ibile, tip-up seat. -**one** *m. augm.* fare un -one, to overturn; dare un -one a, to upset, to knock over.

ribalz-are [A1] *intr.* (*aux.* essere, avere) to bounce; (of sound) to echo; è -ato in sella, he leapt into the saddle. (-**amento** *m.*) -**o** *m.* bounce; (of light) reflection; (of sound) echo, reverberation.

riband-ire [D2] *tr.* to recall from banishment; to promulgate, to proclaim, again; to banish again. -**imento** *m.* recall from banishment. (-**ito** *part. adj.*)

ribass-are [A1] *tr.* to reduce (a price); il padrone -ò l'affitto di casa, the landlord reduced the rent; *intr.* (*aux.* essere) (of prices) to fall, to drop. (-**ato** *part. adj.*) -**ista** *m.* (finan.) bear. -**o** *m.* fall (in price); reduction; sale; vendere a -o, to sell off; concedere un -o, to allow a discount; grandi -i ferroviari, railway tickets issued at reduced rates, cheap fares; rebate; giuocare al -o, to buy or sell shares at a discount; -o improvviso, slump; tendenza al -o, sagging; aggiudicazione al -o, Dutch auction; essere in -o, to be at a discount, (of shares) to be down, (fig.) to be under a cloud, to have lost esteem, authority or importance.

ribat·t-ere [B1] *tr.* to beat again; to knock again (at a door); (money, medals) to coin, strike again; to clinch (a nail), to rivet; — la palla, to return the ball; — le costure, to press the seams (with an iron), *or* to turn back a seam; to whet, to sharpen; to reflect; (of light) to strike, to fall upon; (mus.) to repeat (the same note);

ribatt-ere (*cont.*)

to perform notes in a detached manner, to articulate; to refute (an argument); to confute; *intr.* (*aux.* avere) to insist; to reply, to retort; (mil.) to fall back, to retreat; (artill.) to recoil; (naut.) flapping (of sails or flags); (agric.) to draw earth into ridges; (paint.) to execute a pendant; to paint a similar picture on another wall. **-imento** *m.* beating; **-imento delle ali**, beating of wings; reflection (of light); echo; (paint.) companion picture; retort; confutation. **-ino** *m.* (eng.) rivet. **-itore** *m.* riveter; confuter; (tennis) receiver. (**-itrice** *f.*) **-itura** *f.* clinching; riveting; renewed beating (e.g. of wool in a mattress); (of light) reflection; (of sound) reverberation; seam; turning, pressing a seam. **-uta** *f.* reply, retort; (mus.) a vocal ornament consisting of the accelerated alternation of two adjacent notes (seventeenth century); (sport) return. **-uto** *part. adj.* clinched, riveted; beaten back (or again); materasse **-ute**, remade mattresses (i.e. with wool freshened by beating); returned; (of light) reflected; (of argument, etc.) refuted; *n.m.* seam. **-utamente** *adv.* insistently (cf. **ribattitura**).

ribattezz-are [A I] *tr.* to rename; (joc.) to mistake a (person's) name; (joc., of wine) to add more water to. (**-amento** *m.* **-ato** *part. adj.*) **-anti** *m.pl.* Anabaptists, Baptists (esp. in sixteenth century). (**-atore** *m.* **-atrice** *f.*)

ribatt-imento *m.*, **-ura** *f.*, **-uta** *f.* See under **ribattere**.

ribat·tito *m.* (naut.) back-draught (on a sail); masking of one sail by another causing a back-draught and flapping.

ribe-ca, ribe-ba *f.* (mus.) rebec. **-chino** *m.* small rebec. **-chista** *m., f.* rebec-player.

ribell-are [A I] *tr.* to rouse, to cause to rebel; to stir up rebellion; *rfl.* (*prep.* contro) to rebel, to rise (against); to protest, to raise an objection. **-amento** *m.* rebellion. **-ante** *part. adj.* rebellious; rebelling; in rebellion; *n.m., f.* rebel.

ribell-e *m.* rebel; *adj.* rebellious, rebel; truppe **-i**, rebel troops; angeli **-i**, rebel angels, devils; disobedient, refractory; tela — all'ago, cloth very difficult to sew; malattia —, stubborn disease, illness which is difficult to cure. **-ione** *f.* rebellion, revolt, insurrection, sedition; **-ione d'animo**, access of anger.

ribened-ire [D 10] *tr.* (eccl.) to reconsecrate, to rebless; to reconcile (with the church), to restore to communion. (**-etto** *part. adj.*) **-izione** *f.* (eccl.) reconsecration; reconcilement.

ribere [B 4], **ribevere** [B 4] *tr., abs.* to drink again, to keep on drinking.

ribes *m. indecl.* (bot.) currant (black, white or red), *Ribes*.

ribo·bol-o *m.* popular catchword, catch-phrase; witty saying (esp. in Florent. dial.). **-are** [A I s] *tr.* to obscure (meaning) by using slang or catch-phrases; to use Florentine slang. **-ista** *m., f.* person who uses Florentine slang. **-one** *m.* one fond of using 'riboboli' to deceive or mystify.

ribocc-are [A 2 c] *intr.* (*aux.* essere) to overflow. **-ante** *part. adj.* overflowing, full to overflowing.

riboc-co *m.* (*pl.* **-chi**) overflow; *adv. phr.* a —, overflowing, superabundant; spropositi a —, too much nonsense.

riboflavina *f.* (chem.) riboflavine.

riboll-ire [D I] *intr.* (*aux.* avere) to boil (again); to get hot by fermentation; il vino **-e**, the wine is working; (of earth) to be hot (as in a hot-bed), to be very fertile; (fig.) sentiva **-irsi** il sangue, his blood boiled; mi **-ono** le impertinenze che mi ha detto, I am still upset by his insolent remarks; *tr.* to boil up again; to boil for a long time. **-ente** *part. adj.* boiling; agitated; seething. (**-imento** *m.*) **-io** *m.* bubbling, sound of boiling. **-itic·cio** *m.* coffee, etc. boiled up again. **-itivo** *adj.* inducing fermentation. **-ito** *part. adj.* boiled up again; saper di **-ito**, to taste stale. **-itura** *f.* reboiling; something boiled up again.

ribone *m.* (ichth.) *Pagellus erythrinus*, Spanish bream.

ribo·sio *m.* (chem.) ribose.

ribotta *f.* spree; revelry; 'party'.

ribottalare [A I s] *tr.* (tanning) to redrum, to restock.

ribrezzo *m.* disgust; horror; shudder; shivering, trembling; mi fa — il solo verderlo, the mere sight of him makes me shudder.

ributt-are [A I] *tr.* to throw again; to hurl back; to bring up, to vomit; to repel; to disgust; to rebut, to confute; *intr.* (*aux.* avere) (of a wound) to bleed again; to suppurate; (bot.) to sprout; *rfl.* to throw oneself down (through weariness); to fall ill again; to lose heart, to be downcast; to abhor. (**-amento** *m.*) **-ante** *part. adj.* disgusting, shocking, revolting. **-ato** *part. adj.* repelled; disgusted; refuted; refused. **-o** *m.* repulsion; refusal; remains, refuse; vomit.

ribuzz-are [A I] *tr.* (techn.) to strike with a drive-bolt. **-o** *m.* (techn.) drive-bolt.

ricacci-are [A 3] *tr.* to drive (away or back); to repel; **-ò l'urlo in gola**, he smothered his cry; voglio **-argli in gola** la sua menzogna, I will make him shut his lying mouth, *or* eat his words; (paint.) — di scuri, to throw into relief by shading; *rfl.* to plunge again; to hide oneself again. (**-amento** *m.* **-ato** *part. adj.*)

ricad-ere [B 5] *intr.* (*aux.* essere) to fall down (again); to relapse; — ammalato, to fall ill again; — nel vizio, to relapse into vice; — nella miseria, to become destitute; (of tapestry, hair, dress) to hang, to fall; to come (to), to fall (upon); tutte le colpe **-ono** su di lui, he gets all the blame; (leg.) to revert; to have a reversionary interest. (**-ente** *part. adj.*) †**-i·a** *f.* annoyance, nuisance; relapse. **-imento** *m.* relapse; fall. †**-ioso** *adj.* annoying. **-ucità** *f.* (leg.) reversion. **-uta** *f.* relapse; fare una **-uta**, to have a relapse; (of clothes, etc.) hang; (atom. phys.) fall-out; †(naut.) deep, deeper water beyond a shoal. **-uto** *part. adj.* fallen (again), relapsed; malato **-uto**, patient suffering a relapse; fallen upon evil days (i.e. from wealth to poverty); (eccl.) relapsed (heretic).

†**ricagnato** *adj.* See **rincagnato**.

rical-are [A I] *intr.* (*aux.* essere) to come down, go down (again); *tr.* to lower again; to strike (a yard or topmast; i.e. to lower upper rigging only); to lower, to house (topmasts); to recaulk. **-ata** *f.* sinking down again; la **-ata** del parlare fiorentino, the sing-song drawl of Florentine speech. (**-ato** *part. adj.*)

ricalc-are [A 2] *tr.* to press down, to tread down; — il cammino, le proprie orme, to retrace one's steps; — le orme di uno, to follow in someone's footsteps; — la carica, to reload (firearms); (metall.) to upset; (eng.) to cold-head; (paint.) to transfer (a design), to copy, to reproduce (a drawing by mechanical means); to imitate, to copy; (naut.) to caulk, to drive home the tow between seams. **-a·bile** *adj.* (esp. of drawing) transferable, that can be reproduced. **-ata** *f.* pressing down; transfer, copy. **-ato** *part. adj.* imitated, modelled (on); un programma **-ato** su quello del Ministero, a policy based on that of the Ministry. **-atoio** *m.* apparatus for making transfers. **-atura** *f.* transfer; copy made from a tracing; (eng.) saldatura per **-atura**, upset welding; (metall.; eng.) upsetting; heading; **-atura** a caldo, hot-heading; **-atura** a freddo, cold-heading; **-atura** sflangiata, lopsided upset.

ricalcitr-are [A I s] *intr.* (*aux.* avere) to kick (esp. of horses); to resist; to be recalcitrant. (**-amento** *m.*) **-ante** *part. adj.* recalcitrant; restive. **-azione** *f.* recalcitrance; resistance.

rical-co *m.* (*pl.* **-chi**) transfer (drawing); cast; (eng.) saldatura a —, upset welding.

ricalo *m.* (foundry) depression.

ricam-are [A I] *tr.* to embroider; (fig., iron.) to embroider (a tale), to add fanciful details. **-ato** *part. adj.* embroidered; (fig., iron.) faccia **-ata**, pock-marked face. (**-atore** *m.* **-atora**, **-atrice** *f.*) **-atura** *f.* embroidery work; cost of embroidery. **-o** *m.* embroidery; **-o** a puntura, punch work, embroidery with punch stitch; **-o** a impuntura, embroidery with overstitching; **-o** a rammendo, embroidery on net or with darning stitch; **-o** a rapporto, embroidery with back-stitching; (fig.) il **-o** dei marmi di San Marco, the rich inlaid marbles of Saint Mark's; (fig.) frills, embroidery.

ricambi-are [A 4] *tr.* to reciprocate, to return, to repay (greeting, act of courtesy, injury); to exchange; (eng.) — un pezzo, to replace a part, to fit a spare. (**-ato** *part. adj.*)

ricam·bio *m.* exchange (of greetings, presents); reciprocation, return (of affection); in — di, in return for; (biol.) metabolism; (comm.) re-exchange; (eng.) pezzo di —, spare part; pezzi di —, spares; (motor.) ruota di —, spare wheel.

ricant-are [A I] *tr., intr.* (*aux.* avere) to sing again; to repeat; — su tutti i toni, to keep repeating the same thing (e.g. advice, warnings, etc.); to recant. **-amento** *m.* (joc.) chorus, refrain. (**-ato** *part. adj.*) **-azione** *f.* recantation; (mus.) palinode. **-o** *m.* (mus.) repeated song; palinode, or song of retraction.

ricapitol-are [A I s] *tr.* to sum up, to summarize; to recapitulate. **-ando** *ger.* used as *adv.*: in short. (**-ato** *part. adj.*) **-azione** *f.* recapitulation, summing up; summary.

†**ricapo** *adv. phr.* di —, again (cf. 'da capo' under **capo**).

ricarburazione *f.* (metall.) recarburization.

ricardare [A I] *tr.* (text.) to recard.

rica·rica *f.* (watchm.) rewinding; a — automatica, self-winding.

ricaric-are [A2s] *tr.* to reload, to recharge; to load more fully; (of clock, watch) to rewind; to reship; *rfl.* to take up a burden (or task) again. (-am**e**nto *m.* -ato *part. adj.*)

rica·ri·co *m.* (*pl.* -**chi**) heavy load.

ricasc-are [A2] *intr.* (*aux.* essere) to fall again; (provb.) l'asino dov'è cascato una volta, non ci -a la seconda, once bitten, twice shy; to relapse; — a dir sempre lo stesso, to keep repeating oneself; (of curtains, etc.) to hang. (-am**e**nto *m.*) -**ante** *part. adj.* falling, hanging, limp, flabby; panno -ante, cloth that hangs well. -**ata** *f.* relapse; fall; una bella -ata di tende, full, ample, well-hung curtains. -**ate**zza *f.* flabbiness, limpness. (-ato *part. adj.*)

ricas-co *m.* (*pl.* -**chi**) flounce; (archit.) pendentive, boss (of a vault).

ricatt-are [A1] *tr.* to make good one's losses; to recover expenses; (leg.) to hold to ransom; to demand money with menaces; to blackmail; *rfl.* to avenge an injury; to take one's revenge. -am**e**nto *m.* recovery, 'getting one's own back'; revenge. (-ato *part. adj.* -at**o**re *m.* -atrice *f.*) -**o** *m.* ransom; blackmail; revenge; (leg.) demanding money with menaces; blackmail.

ricav-are [A1] *tr.* to draw, to extract; to obtain, to get; — i numeri del lotto, to get 'lotto' numbers (from the indication of dreams, etc.); — utile, to obtain some benefit; da questa stoffa si può — un vestito, you can get a dress out of this material; ecco quel che si -a!, now we're getting at the truth! -ato *part. adj.* obtained; stanza -ata da un corridoio, room made out of a passage; *n.m.* profit, advantage, proceeds, gross receipts (takings).

ricavo *m.* proceeds; yield; return; (comm.) — netto, net yield.

Riccardo *pr.n.m.* Richard.

ricche**zza** *f.* wealth, riches; ricchezze improvvise, wealth of the new rich; è una —, it is very valuable; earnings; income; imposta di — mobile, income-tax; abundance; richness; — del suolo, richness, fertility, of the soil; source of wealth; la voce è la — del cantante, the singer's capital is his voice; (geog.) resource; (leg.) — privata, private property; — pubblica, public property; — mobile, personal property, (Scot.) moveables; — mobiliare, personalty; — immobiliare, real property, realty, (Scot.) heritables; imposta di — mobile, income-tax; (mil.) weight of metal in barrel of a gun or rifle.

ric·cio[1] *m.* (zool.) hedgehog, *Erinaceus europaeus*; sea urchin; — di mare, *Psammechinus microtuberculatus* and/or *Arbacia aequituberculata*; — di mare granulare, *Sphaerechinus granularis*; — marino comune, — melone, *Echinus melo*; (bot.) — di dama, Martagon lily, *Lilium martagon*; also prickly husk of chestnut.

ric·ci·o[2] *m.* curl, curly lock (of hair); ferro da ricci, curling-tongs, curling-iron; curl of wood shavings; (mus.) scroll (of a violin); (mil.) barbed wire knife rest; (cinem.) loop (of film); *adj.* curly; cavolo —, curly kale; (text.) a —, terry; oro —, gold thread; argento —, silver thread. -**arello** *m.* (cul., Siena) almond cake. -**uto** *adj.* curly.

ric·ci·ol-o *m.* curl (e.g. of hair); (eng.) burr; turning (from lathe). -**ina** *f.* curly endive; curly-headed girl. -**ino** *m.* little curl; curly-headed boy. -**ute**zza *f.* curliness. -**uto** *adj.* curly.

ricc-o *adj.* (*m.pl.* **ricchi**) rich, wealthy; ample; precious; magnificent; — di, rich in, abounding in; un libro — di aneddoti, a book full of anecdotes; (mil.) heavily armoured; *n.m.* rich man; — sfondato, very rich man; *pl.* i ricchi, the rich. -**ame**nte *adv.* richly. †-**omanno** *m.* landowner. -**one** *m. augm.* very wealthy man.

ricerca *f.* search, investigation; research; (leg.) investigation, inquiry; (comm.) request; demand; viva —, brisk demand; (chem.) research; †(mus.) fantasia.

ricerc-are [A2] *tr.* to search for, to seek; to investigate; to inquire into; to search (records, archives); — le fibre del cuore, to touch the very heart; freddo che -a le ossa, cold that penetrates to the bones; to examine carefully; to look through; — uno dal capo ai piedi, to look a person up and down; (mining) to prospect; (paint.) to touch up, to strengthen (an outline); (poet.) to touch, to try; †— le corde della lira, to touch or sweep, to run the hand over, the strings of the lyre; — le orecchie, to delight the ears (with music); *rfl.* to examine, to feel (by running the hands over) one's body, to search one's conscience, mind or heart; *n.m.* (mus.) ricercare; prelude; fugue without episodes; difficult passage; exercise. -**ata** *f.* act of search, investigation or research; (mus.) ricercare. -**ate**zza *f.* extreme care; elegance; affectation. -**ato** *part. adj.* sought; in great demand; -ato dalla polizia, wanted by the police; affected; far-fetched; elegant, refined; (mus.) fuga -ata,

fugue in which the subject is treated in the most scientific manner. -**ata**mente *adv.* on purpose; affectedly. -**at**o**re** *m.* researcher; searcher. (-atrice *f.*)

ricerco *apocop. part.* of ricercare, q.v.; (poet.) sought after; precious.

ricesso *m.* (poet.) bay.

ricett-a *f.* (chem.) recipe, formula; (pharm.; med.) prescription; (cul.) recipe, receipt; (comm.) -e lorde, gross receipts; means, expedient; (cul.) recipe, receipt. -**a·rio** *m.* book of prescriptions, pharmacopœia; book of recipes, cookery-book.

ricetta·colo *m.* refuge, shelter; receptacle; (bot.) receptacle, thalamus; (anat.) receptaculum; †(naut.) compass corrector pockets, corrector magnet holders in a compass binnacle; bilges.

ricett-are [A1] *tr.* to give shelter to, to shelter; to provide refuge for; to hide; (leg.) to receive (esp. stolen property); (med.) to prescribe, to write a prescription; *rfl.* to take shelter; to hide. -**ame**nto *m.* providing shelter; shelter, refuge. -**ante** *part. adj.* sheltering, harbouring. -**ato** *part. adj.* sheltered, taken in; hidden. -**at**o**re** *m.* receiver, one who receives; receiver of stolen goods. (-atrice *f.*) -**azi**o**ne** *f.* sheltering, receiving; (leg.) receiving (esp. of stolen property). -**ivit**à *f.* receptivity, sensitivity; (med.) receptiveness. -**ivo** *adj.* receptive, sensitive; mente -iva, receptive mind, i.e. learning easily, possibly without discrimination.

ricetta·rio *m.* See under **ricetta**.

ricetto *m.* refuge, harbour, shelter; dar — a, to give shelter to, to shelter, to receive; — di acque, pond, cistern.

rice**v-ere** [B1] *tr.* to receive; to accept; — una buona accoglienza, to be well received; andiamo a — i nostri ospiti, let's go and welcome our guests; la signora Bruni -e il mercoledì, Mrs Brown is at home (to visitors) on Wednesdays; il cardinale non -e oggi, the cardinal gives no audience today; to take; to get; questa stanza -e luce da una sola finestra, this room gets its light from one window; dolore che non -e conforto, pain that cannot be eased; to experience, to feel; — diletto, to be delighted; to accept patiently, to suffer, to put up with; (comm.) cambiale da —, bill receivable; — il salario, to get one's wages, to be paid; (eccl.) — la comunione, to receive communion, to make one's communion. -**i·bile** *adj.* acceptable, admissible. -**ibilit**à *f.* acceptability. -**ime**nto *m.* receiving; receipt; al -imento di questo dono, on receiving this gift; reception; sala di -imento, reception room; welcome; -imento di un nuovo socio, admission of a new member. -**it**o**re** *m.* receiver; customs and excise officer; -itore del registro, registrar; (comm.) -itore di merce, consignee; (teleph.; radio) receiver; -itore acustico, sounder. -**it**o**ri·a** *f.* receiving office, for collection of taxes, lottery money, etc.; -itoria del registro, Registry Office; -itoria postale e telegrafica, sub-post office. -**uta** *f.* receipt; quittance; -uta a saldo generale, receipt in full; accusare -uta di, to acknowledge receipt of; -uta in carta bollata, stamped receipt; -uta di spedizione, shipping receiving note; raccomandata con -uta di ritorno, registered letter for which a receipt is to be returned to the sender; return, sending back; (vulg.) fare la -uta, to 'bring up', to vomit. -**uto** *part. adj.* accepted, received; admitted; welcomed; *n.m.* what has been received.

ricezio**ne** *f.* (med.) reception; see recezione.

richiam-are [A1] *tr.* to call again; chiamai e -ai, ma nessuno rispose, I called again and again, but no one answered; to call back; poi quand'ella se n'andava, la -ò per domandarle..., then, as she was going, he called her back to ask her...; to recall (from exile, or office abroad); — in vita, to restore to life; — l'attenzione di uno su qualche cosa, to call someone's attention to something; lo spettacolo -a molta folla, the performance draws great crowds; — alla memoria, to call to mind; mi -a alla mente che, he reminds me that; to refer back; (neol.) to rebuke, to scold; (mil.) — alle armi, to call up; (admin.) — all'ordine, to call to order; — un oratore al rispetto delle convenienze, to call a speaker to order; *rfl.* to appeal; to complain; to lodge a complaint; (neol.) -arsi a, to claim kinship with, to boast descent from. -**a·bile** *adj.* liable to recall. -**ata** *f.* call; recall; (aeron.) pull-out; (typ.) -ata di correzione, proof mark. -**ato** *part. adj.* recalled, called back; *n.m.pl.* (slang) i -ati, the few remaining hairs on a balding head drawn across to cover the bald patch. (-at**o**re *m.* -atrice *f.*)

richiamo *m.* decoy; allurement; call; udire il — della primavera, to hear the call of spring; order to retire; admonition, warning; — verbale, verbal warning; complaint; reproof; appeal; draw; (leg.) — di documenti, call for production of documents (C.P.P.); (comm.) call; (admin.) incorrere in un — all'ordine, to be called

richiamo (*cont.*)
to order; reference, reference mark; (eng.) molla di —, restoring spring; (naut.) paranco di —, overhauling tackle; *pl.* allurements, allure.

richie·d-ere [C 19] *tr.* to ask again (for); mi richiese il libro, he asked me again for the book; to request; to demand; to require; ciò -e attenzione, that requires attention; un compito che -e abilità, a task that calls for skill; to need, to require; queste piante -ono terreno calcareo, these plants need chalky soil; (of a person) esser richiesto, to be sought after, to be invited; (of goods) to be in demand; to call, to invite (to a meeting, conference); — alla battaglia, to defy, to offer battle to; (leg.) to request, to demand, to apply for, to petition; *impers.* to be necessary; si -e la presentazione del passaporto, passports must be shown. **-ente** *part. adj.* applying; (teleph.) calling; *n.m., f.* applicant. (**-itore** *m.* **-itrice** *f.*) **-uto** *part. adj.* see **richiesto.**

richiesta *f.* request; demand; a —, if requested, on request; a — generale, by general request; c'è molta — di questo articolo, this article is in great demand; un esemplare viene spedito dietro —, specimen sent free on application; fare la prima — di matrimonio, to call the banns (for the first time of asking); (comm.) — d'approvvigionamento, inquiry; (leg.) application; request; summons (esp. on part of Pubblico Ministero, equivalent to 'istanza' of other parties; see also under **procedimento**); maestro delle richieste, Officer of the Court of Requests.

richiesto *part.* of **richiedere**, q.v.; *adj.* required, asked for; sought after; in demand; necessary; desirable; — del parere, asked for (his) opinion; called, invited (to a meeting); (teleph.) called; (leg.) requested; applied for; demanded; required; †— di battaglia, challenged.

richin-are [A 1] *tr., rfl.* to bend, to bow again, to bend right over; †-arsi a, to pay one's respects to. (**-ato** *part. adj.*) **-o** *adj.* bent, curved, bowed; -o dagli anni, bent under the weight of years.

richiu·d-ere [C 3] *tr.* to close; to shut again; to shut up (in); to close again; to receive; to shelter; lo richiuse tra le sue braccia, she held him closely in her arms; — una finestra, to have a window walled up; *abs.* to lock the door(s); to lock up; *rfl.* to close, to shut again; la ferita si richiuse, the wound closed up. (**-imento** *m.*)

richius-o *part.* of **richiudere**, q.v.; *adj.* closed, shut up. **-ura** *f.* (techn.) reclosure.

ri·cin-o *m.* (bot.) castor-oil plant, *Ricinus communis*; olio di —, castor oil. **-ina** *f.* (chem.) ricinine, ricidine. **-oleato** *m.* (chem.) ricineolate. **-ole·ico** *adj.* (chem.) ricinoleic.

ricinto *m.* See **recinto.**

ricitare [A 1] *tr.* (leg.) to resummon, to summons again.

†**riciurmare** *intr.* (naut.) to change crews; *tr.* (naut.) see **riarmare.**

†**riclamare** *intr.* to lodge a complaint (cf. **richiamare**).

ricocitura *f.* See under **ricuocere.**

rico·gl-iere [B 7] *tr.* to gather, to pick (esp. fruit); to harvest; to catch again; cerca che non ti ricolga più, mind I don't catch you again; *rfl.* to take shelter; to compose oneself; *recip. rfl.* to gather together again. **-imento** *m.* gathering, collecting. **-itore** *m.* gatherer (esp. of chestnuts); collector (of taxes, of news). **-itrice** *f.* -itrice del parto, midwife. **-itura** *f.* gathering (chestnuts); chestnut gathering time; redemption of pledges.

ricognit-ivo *adj.* (leg.) confirmatory; tending to remove doubt. **-ore** *m.* (aeron.) scout, spotter plane, reconnaissance aircraft.

ricognizione *f.* recognition; reward; (leg.) acknowledgement (C.C.); (mil.; naut.; aeron.) reconnaissance; apparecchio da —, reconnaissance plane; (naut.) inspection; muster or checking of stores; verbale di —, report, muster list.

ricolata *f.* (paint. techn.) sagging.

ricollegare [A 2] *tr.* to join again, to connect again; *rfl.* ricollegarsi a, to be connected with; to be linked, to be reconciled; *recip. rfl.* to join together again.

ricollocare [A 2] *tr.* to place again; to replace; *rfl.* (of a woman) to marry again.

ricolm-are [A 1 c] *tr.* to fill up (again); to load, to overload; (of fields) to flood. (**-amento** *m.*) **-ato** *part. adj.* filled up; loaded; *n.m.* alluvial soil. (**-atura** *f.*)

ricolmo *apocop. part. adj.* brimful; full to overflowing; overloaded.

ricolor-are [A 1 c], *tr.* to paint again, to give more colour to; *rfl.* to regain one's colour. (**-ato** *part. adj.*) **-ire** [D 2] *tr.* (paint.) to touch up, to restore. (**-ito** *part. adj.*)

ricolta *f.* (mil.) retreat; fatigue party; †harvest (cf. **raccolta**).

ricolto *part.* of **ricogliere**, q.v.; *adj.* gathered, collected; withdrawn; noted, accepted; *n.m.* see **raccolta.**

ricominci-are [A 3] *tr.* to begin again, to start again; to recommence; si -a!, they're at it again!; o che si -a?, what, again? **-amento** *m.* beginning again, fresh start. **-ato** *part. adj.* recommenced, begun again.

ricom-mettere [C 20] *tr.* to commit again; — un errore, to repeat a mistake; to join, to put together again; — i pezzi di un vaso, to mend a vase. (**-messo** *part. adj.*) **-mettitura** *f.* mending, joining; mark of a join.

ricompar-ire [D 1] *intr.* (*aux.* essere) to reappear; finalmente il sole -ve, at last the sun broke out again; (of a newspaper) to resume publication. **-sa** *f.* reappearance; -sa in scena, return to the scene; una -sa del colera, a fresh outbreak of cholera. (**-so** *part. adj.*)

ricompensa *f.* reward; recompense; in — di, in recompense for, as a return for.

ricompens-are [A 1] *tr.* to reward; to recompense; to requite. **-a·bile** *adj.* deserving of recompense; rewardable. **-ato** *part. adj.* rewarded; requited. (**-atore** *m.* **-atrice** *f.*)

ricomperare [A 1 sc] and derivs. See **ricomprare.**

ricom·p-iere, **-ire** [D 6] *tr., rfl.* to fill up again; to make good a loss. **-imento** *m.* addition, supplement.

ricom-porre [B 21] *tr.* to put together again; — una macchina, to reassemble a machine; to recompose; to reconstruct; (typ.) to reset; — il viso, to compose one's features; *rfl.* to be put together again; to be reconstructed; (fig.) to recover oneself, to regain one's composure. **-ponimento** *m.* recomposing, reordering; composing again. **-posizione** *f.* recomposition; (leg.) -posizione fondiaria, land resettlement (C.C.); (chem.) resynthesis. **-posto**, **-posto** *part. adj.* recomposed, composed again; reassembled; reconstructed; put together again.

ricompra *f.* (comm.) repurchase, buying-in.

ricompr-are [A 1 c] *tr.* to buy back; to buy another; to trade in; si è -ato una macchina, he has bought another car; (comm.) to buy in, to repurchase; to be worth more; lo -a cento volte, he is worth a hundred of him; to pay twice over (or more than the original cost); la casa l'ho -ata abbondantemente, the house cost me much more than it was worth; to regain; con quest'azione ha -ato la mia stima, by so doing he has regained my good opinion; (theol.) to redeem; *rfl.* to redeem oneself. **-a·bile** *adj.* redeemable. **-amento** *m.* buying back; (theol.) redemption. **-ato** *part. adj.* bought back; exchanged. (**-atore** *m.* **-atrice** *f.* **-azione** *f.*)

†**ricomu·nica** *f.* (eccl.) reconciliation.

ricomunic-are [A 2 s] *tr.* (eccl.) to restore to communion, to reconcile, to absolve from excommunication; *intr.* (*aux.* avere) to re-establish communication, relations; *rfl.* (eccl.) to be reconciled with the Church; to go to communion again. †**-azione** *f.* (eccl.) reconciliation.

riconcentr-are [A 1] *tr.* to reconcentrate; to regroup; (chem.) to reconcentrate; to concentrate further; *rfl.* to compose oneself in thought, to meditate. **-amento** *m.* regrouping; concentration; absorption. **-ato** *part. adj.* reconcentrated; regrouped; absorbed.

riconcili-are [A 4] *tr.* to reconcile; *rfl.* to be reconciled; (eccl.) to make one's peace (with God); to be reconciled (with the Church); to make one's confession (esp. soon after a previous confession); *recip. rfl.* to be reconciled one with another. **-a·bile** *adj.* reconcilable. **-amento** *m.* reconciling. **-ato** *part. adj.* reconciled. (**-atore** *m.* **-atrice** *f.*) **-ato·rio** *adj.* (*m.pl.* **-atorii**) reconciliatory. **-azione** *f.* reconciliation, reconcilement; (eccl.) reconciliation (with God, with the Church); confession (esp. soon after a previous confession).

ricondens-are [A 1] *tr.* to condense again (or further); *rfl.* to become thicker. (**-ato** *part. adj.*)

ricond-ire [D 2] *tr.* to season again. (**-ito** *part. adj.*)

†**ricon·dito** *adj.* See **recondito.**

ricondott-a *f.* bringing back; †(mil.) recall to the colours. **-o** *part.* of **ricondurre**, q.v.; *adj.* brought back; reduced.

†**ricondu·cere** *vb.* and derivs. See **ricondurre.**

riconducimento *m.* bringing back; reduction (cf. **ricondurre**).

ricon-durre [B 2] *tr.* to bring back, to take back; to lead back; lo -dussero a casa, they brought him home again; — all'ovile la pecora smarrita, to bring back the sheep that had strayed; (mil.) to recall; †to reappoint; *rfl.* to go (to some particular place) again; to go back. (**-duttore** *m.* **-duttrice** *f.*) **-duzione** *f.* (leg.) renewal of agricultural lease or tenancy.

riconferma *f.* confirmation; reconfirmation; avere la — dell'incarico, to have one's reappointment confirmed.

riconferm-are [A I c] *tr.* to confirm (again), to reconfirm; *rfl.* to show (prove) oneself once more. **-a·bile** *adj.* that can be confirmed. (**-ato** *part. adj.*) **-azione** *f.* confirmation; reconfirmation.

riconfort-are [A I] *tr.* to strengthen again, to refresh, to revive; to put fresh heart into; to console; *rfl.* to take heart again; to be consoled. (**-ato** *part. adj.* **-atore** *m.* **-atrice** *f.*)

riconforto *m.* encouragement; refreshment; consolation.

riconfront-are [A I c] *tr.* to confront anew. (**-ato** *part. adj.*)

ricongelamento *m.* (phys.) regelation.

ricon-giun·gere [C 5], †**-giu·gnere** *tr.* to join again, to reunite; *rfl.* (*prep.* a) to rejoin; to be reunited (with); **-giungersi al marito**, to go to live with one's husband again; *recip. rfl.* to meet again; to be joined together again. **-giungimento** *m.* rejoining; reunion; meeting. **-giunto** *part. adj.* joined together again; reunited. **-giunzione** *f.* rejoining; reuniting.

riconosc-ere [B 9] *tr.* to recognize, to acknowledge; **si travestì per non farsi —**, he disguised himself so as not to be recognized; **-o il bene che mi hai fatto**, I acknowledge the good you have done me; **— il proprio errore**, to admit one's mistake; **riconobbero le sue fatiche**, they rewarded him for his pains; (leg.) to acknowledge; **— un figlio naturale, un debito**, to acknowledge a natural son, a debt; **— una persona giuridica**, to incorporate a corporation (C.C.); (mil.) to reconnoitre; to recognize (friend or foe); to review; (naut.) to confirm; to recognize (a ship), to acknowledge (a signal); **— la costa**, to make a landfall, to survey the coast; **— un pericolo**, to verify a danger (reef, rock, etc.); **— un porto**, to check up the condition, to take soundings, etc., of a harbour; *rfl.* to acknowledge (oneself, one's faults); to confess; to be grateful; to be recognizable; **non si -e più**, it is no longer recognizable, it is completely altered. **-ente** *part. adj.* grateful, thankful. **-enza** *f.* gratitude; financial reward; (theatr.) recognition; †knowledge. **-i·bile** *adj.* recognizable. (**-i·bilmente** *adv.*) **-imento** *m.* recognition, acknowledgement; confession; identification; mark serving for recognition or identification; **segno di -imento**, identification mark; **-imento di un debito**, acknowledgement of a debt; **in -imento di**, in recognition of, as a reward for; (leg.) acknowledgement; **-imento della persona giuridica**, incorporation (C.C.); (theatr.) recognition; (naut.) landfall. **-itivo** *adj.* relating to recognition. **-itore** *m.* one who recognizes; one who makes a reconnaissance; *adj.* grateful; rewarding. (**-itrice** *f.*) **-iuto** *part. adj.* noticed; acknowledged; confessed; (leg.) acknowledged; admitted; **creditore -iuto**, judgement creditor.

riconquist-a *f.* recovery, reconquest. **-are** [A I] *tr.* to recover, to regain; to reconquer. (**-ato** *part. adj.*)

riconsegn-a *f.* redelivery; handing back; (leg.) **verbale di —**, Memorandum of reconsignment (esp. after sequestration). **-are** [A sc] *tr.* to redeliver; to hand back; to restore. (**-ato** *part. adj.*)

riconsigli-are [A 4] *tr.* to advise again; to induce, to lead; *rfl.* to decide, to make up one's mind; (poet.) **ogni animal d'amar si -a**, (Petrarch) every creature's thoughts turn again to love. (**-ato** *part. adj.*)

riconsol-are [A I c] *tr.* to console anew. (**-ato** *part. adj.*)

ricont-are [A I c] *tr.* to count again, to recount; to retell. †**-o** *m.* summary; epilogue.

riconvalidare [A I s] *tr.* to make valid again; to ratify (again).

riconven-ire [D 17] *tr.* (leg.) to sue by cross-action; to bring a counter-action against. **-uto** *part. adj.* (leg.) claimed by cross-action; *n.m.* person sued by cross-action. **-zionale** *adj.* (leg.) **causa, domanda -zionale**, cross-action (C.C.). **-zione** *f.* (leg.) cross-action; reconvention; †(fig.) reproof

riconver-tire [D I] *tr.* to reconvert; to turn; (rel.) to reconvert; *rfl.* to repent again; to reform; to mend one's ways again. (**-tito** *part. adj.*) **-sione** *f.* reconversion.

ricoperto *part.* of **ricoprire**, q.v.; *adj.* covered up, completely covered; coated; hidden; **mobili ricoperti**, upholstered furniture; **— di**, covered with, full of; coated, plated; **— d'oro**, gold-plated.

rico·pi-a *f.* fresh copy. **-are** [A 4] *tr.* to copy; to copy again; to copy out, to make a fair copy of; to imitate. (**-ato** *part. adj.* **-atore** *m.* **-atrice** *f.*) **-atura** *f.* copying; copying out; cost of copying; copy, reproduction.

ricopr-ire [D I] *tr.* (*prep.* di, con) to re-cover; to cover up; **— gli occhi**, to conceal, to hide; to mask; **— gli occhi**, to hide one's eyes; **— con buone opere i falli di prima**, to make up for earlier

faults by good deeds; to supply lavishly (e.g. with money); to overwhelm (with attention); **— un incarico**, to hold an official position; (mil.) to cover, to protect; to defend with walls; (techn.) to coat, to plate, to face; *rfl.* to cover oneself (again); **-irsi di penne**, to grow feathers; **-irsi della spesa**, to cover one's expenses; **-irsi col mantello d'altri**, to excuse oneself by blaming someone else; **-irsi di gloria**, to win great glory; (techn.) to become coated. (**-itore** *m.* **-itrice** *f.*) **-itura** *f.* covering up; re-covering.

ricorcare [A 2] *tr.* to lay down again; (agric.) to layer; *rfl.* to lie down again.

ricord-are[1] *tr.* (mus.) to restring; (sport) **far — una racchetta**, to have a racket restrung. **-ato** *part. adj.* restrung.

ricord-are[2] [A I] *tr.* to recall; **— i bei giorni**, to recall happy times; to remember; **— poco e male**, to have a bad memory; to remind of; **mi -a suo padre**, he makes me think of his father; **lo -a nell'espressione degli occhi**, he is like him in the expression of the eyes; **gli -ai l'invito di domani**, I reminded him of the invitation for tomorrow; **-atemi alla vostra moglie**, remember me to your wife; to mention, to record; to commemorate; **una lapide che -a i caduti**, a stone commemorating the fallen; *rfl.* (*prep.* di) to remember; **non vi -ate di me?**, don't you remember me?; **ora mi -o**, now I remember; **se ben mi -o**, if I remember correctly; **Dio s'è -ato di noi**, God has not forgotten us; **-arsi di uno nelle orazioni**, to remember someone in one's prayers; †*impers.* **mi -a che**, I remember that. **-a·bile** *adj.* memorable, worth remembering; worthy of mention. **-anza** *f.* memory; **giorno di lieta -anza**, day of happy memories; **a perpetua -anza di**, to the everlasting memory of; **a mia -anza**, within my memory. **-ativo** *adj.* aiding memory; **facoltà -ativa**, faculty of memory; memorable; commemorative. **-ato** *part. adj.* recalled, recollected; remembered; mentioned, cited. (**-atore** *m.* **-atrice** *f.*) **-evole** *adj.* mindful; **sempre -evole di**, ever mindful of; memorable. **-evolmente** *adv.* unforgettably; memorably.

ricord-o *m.* memory, recollection; remembrance; keepsake, souvenir; **vivere di -i**, to live on one's memories, to live in the past; memento; **terrò questo libro per vostro —**, I will keep this book in memory of you; a record (written); **abbiamo un sicuro — del fatto**, we have an indisputable record of the fact; **-i autobiografici**, memoirs; **prendere —**, to make a note; monument, memorial; **un — marmoreo**, a marble memorial; mark, trace (left by disease or wound); (paint.) note, sketch. **-ino** *m. dim.* little souvenir; keepsake; brief note.

ricoric-are [A 2 s] *tr.* to lay down again; (agric.) to layer; to earth up; *rfl.* to go to bed again, to lie down again; (of the sun) to set. (**-ato** *part. adj.*)

ricorre [B 7] (poet.). See **ricogliere**.

ricorreg·gere [C 12] *tr.* to correct again; to revise; *rfl.* to mend one's ways, to reform.

ricorr-ere [C 5] *intr.* (*aux.* avere or essere) to recur; (of anniversary, festival) to come round again, to fall; **domani -e il compleanno di mia madre**, tomorrow is my mother's birthday; (archit., of frieze, cornice, etc.) to run, to be continued, to be repeated; to have recourse (to), to apply (to); **quando è a corto di quattrini -e a sua madre**, when he is short of money he applies to his mother; **ricorse a questo espediente**, he had recourse to this expedient; to complain, to make a complaint; (naut.) to check carefully all seams and caulking; (leg.) **— (in)**, to resort (to), to apply (to), to have recourse (to); *tr.* to traverse again, to pass through again; **l'esercito corse e ricorse il paese**, the army overran the country in all directions, *or* overran the country again and again. **-ente** *part. adj.* recurrent, recurring; (of anniversary) falling, occurring; (archit.) running (round); (math.) recurring; *n.m.* (leg.) appellant; applicant; (admin.) petitioner. **-enza** *f.* recurrence; occasion; festival; **luttuosa -enza**, sad anniversary; **-enze festive**, bank holidays. **-imento** *m.* recurrence; recourse, appeal; frequent return.

ricor-retto *part.* of **ricorreggere**, q.v.; *adj.* corrected; revised. (**-rettore** *m.* **-rettrice** *f.*) **-rezione** *f.* correcting, correction; passage corrected.

ricorsa *f.* running back, *or* over again; **una — alla lezione**, another run through the lesson; (of pendulum) return, oscillation; (comm.) new loan incurred for keeping down interest.

ricorso *part.* of **ricorrere**, q.v.; *adj.* returned; recurrent; *n.m.* return, recurrence; appeal, complaint; application; **far — a**, to have recourse to; (leg.) appeal; application; interlocutory application

ricorso (*cont.*)
to Court or judge (C.C.P.); far —, to make an application; far — in appello, to appeal; petition; recourse; (admin.) petition; presentare un —, to file a petition; senza —, without recourse, *sans recours*; (archit.) repeated ornament; *pl.* (physiol.) i ricorsi, menses.

ricostitu-ire [D2] *tr.* to reconstitute, to reform; to re-establish; *rfl.* to be reconstituted; to reform; to recover. **-ente** *part. adj.* restorative; (med.) tonic; *n.m.* tonic, revitalizer; body-builder. **-ito** *part. adj.* reconstituted, re-established; restored. **-zione** *f.* reconstitution, re-establishment, restoration.

ricostru-ire [D2] †**-rre** *tr.* to rebuild; to reconstruct; to retread (a tyre); (fig.) to reconstruct; to recast (a sentence). (**-ito** *part. adj.* **-ttore** *m.* **-ttrice** *f.*) **-zione** *f.* rebuilding; reconstruction; (comm.) reorganization (of a firm); retreading (of tyres).

ricott-a *f.* kind of cottage cheese; fatto di —, soft, flabby, like jelly. **-aio** *m.* seller of 'ricotta', or one very fond of eating it. **-ella** *f.* (cul., Apulia) 'ricotta' made in little rolls.

ricotti *m.pl.* (silkb.) husks.

ricott-o *part.* of ricuocere, q.v.; *adj.* subjected to new or continued heat; letame —, well-rotted manure (of straw and dung); (techn.) annealed; — completamente, soft annealed. **-ura** *f.* (techn.) annealing; stress relieving.

ricover-are [A1s] *tr.* to shelter, to give shelter to; to receive; to admit (to hospital); (leg.) to place under care (esp. in asylum) (C.P.); *rfl.* to take shelter; to find refuge. (**-amento** *m.*) **-ato** *part. adj.* sheltered, received; *n.m.* inmate (of a charitable institution). (**-atore** *m.* **-atrice** *f.*) **-azione** *f.* recovery.

rico·vero *m.* refuge, shelter; — di mendicità, poor-house; casual-ward; (leg.) the placing under care; ordine di —, committal order (e.g. to reformatory) (C.P.); (med.) — in ospedale, admission to hospital.

ricoverto *adj.* See ricoperto.

ricre-are [A6] *tr.* to re-create, to re-elect; to restore; to refresh, to relieve; spettacolo che -a l'occhio, a sight for sore eyes; *rfl.* to take recreation; to amuse oneself; egli si -a giocando a tennis, his recreation is tennis. **-ativo** *adj.* recreational; amusing, pleasant; letture -ative, light reading. (**-ato** *part. adj.* **-atore** *m.* **-atrice** *f.*) **-atorio** *adj.* (*m.pl.* **-atorii**) recreational; *n.m.* day nursery, kindergarten; recreation room. **-azione** *f.* recreation; ora della -azione, playtime, break.

ricred-ere [B1] *rfl.* to change one's mind; to recant; to realize one's mistake; to become disillusioned; to be undeceived, to have one's eyes opened. †**-ente** *m.* (rel.) recreant, unbeliever or feeble believer. **-uto** *part. adj.* cowardly; compliant; *n.m.* turn-coat.

ricresc-ere [B9] *intr.* (*aux.* essere) to grow, to increase again; to rise; il prezzo dei metalli è -iuto, metal prices have risen again; le acque dell'Arno -ono, the Arno is rising; (cul.) to rise, to swell. **-ente** *part. adj.* growing (again); swelling; likely to swell. **-enza** *f.* swelling, growth, excrescence. **-imento** *m.* new growth; increase, rise. (**-iuto** *part. adj.*)

ricrescita *f.* increase; swelling; new growth; (econ.) — dei prezzi, rise in prices; (agric.) — delle erbe, fresh growth of grass, after-math.

†**ricrinare** *vb.* and derivs. See reclinare.

ricristallizz-are [A1] *tr.* to recrystallize. **-azione** *f.* recrystallization.

ricrociata *adj. f.* (herald.) croce —, cross crosslet.

rictus *m. indecl.* rictus.

ricuc-ire [D1] *tr.* to sew up (again); (fig.) to string together (e.g. phrases, platitudes). (**-imento** *m.*) **-ito** *part. adj.* sewn up (again); imbiancato e -ito, washed and mended. (**-itore** *m.* **-itrice** *f.*) **-itura** *f.* sewing up (again), mending; seam; (fig.) stringing together.

ricuoc-ere [C1] *tr.* to cook again, to boil up again; (techn.) to anneal. **-itura** *f.* second cooking (baking, boiling).

ricuper-are [A1s] *tr.* to recover, to regain; — l'appetito, to recover one's appetite; — il tempo perduto, to make up for lost time; to recuperate; to reclaim; to ransom; to rescue; (naut.) to recover, to hoist in, to haul taut, to shorten in; — l'imbando, to adjust a list; — una nave, to refloat a ship; — per mano, — con mano sopra mano, to haul hand over hand; — catena, to heave in cable; to recover, to salvage; (naut. command) -a!, order to the leadsman to haul in the lead line; *rfl.* to be regained, to be recovered; to find refuge, to take shelter. **-abile** *adj.* recoverable. (**-abilità** *f.* **-amento** *m.* **-ato** *part. adj.*) **-atore** *m.* (mil.) recuperator

(recoil); (eng.) recuperator (also **recuperatore**); *pl.* (leg.) recuperatores, judges who received applications from parties to a recovery action. (**-atrice** *f.*, *adj.*) **-atorio** *adj.* (*m.pl.* **-atorii**) serving to rescue or recuperate; relating to salvage; (leg.) recoverable; obtainable by judgement or trial. **-azione** *f.* recovery, regaining, getting back.

ricu·pero *m.* salvage; recovery; rescue; objects salvaged; (leg.) recovery; repurchase; diritto di —, right of repurchase; — di debiti, debt collection; — delle spese, recovery of costs; (comm.) perdita con —, salvage loss; (football, etc.) replay of an inter-rupted match or of one postponed owing to bad weather; (cycle racing) repêchage.

ricurv-are [A1] *tr.* to bend (again). **-o** *adj.* bent, curved; crooked; naso -o, hooked nose.

ricusa *f.* refusal; rejection; (leg.) see ricusazione, under ricusare.

ricus-are [A1] *tr.* to refuse; to deny, to reject; (leg.) to challenge (a judge, juror, etc.) upon any suspicion of partiality; (naut., of the wind) to head, to shift unfavourably for a ship; (of a ship) to be unable to tack; *rfl.* to refuse; -arsi di venire, to refuse to come. **-a** *f.* refusal; rejection; (leg.) see ricusazione. **-abile** *adj.* that can be refused; deniable. (**-abilità** *f.* **-ante**, **-ato** *part. adj.*) **-azione** *f.* (leg.) challenge to judge, juror, etc.; exception.

rid-acchiare [A4] *intr.* (*aux.* avere) to giggle; to snigger. **-anciano** *adj.* prone to laughter; laughable, funny; novella -anciana, humorous story. **-arello** *adj.* merry, laughing.

ridag·gio *m.* (naut.) setting up, hauling taut of standing rigging.

rid-are [A8] *tr.* to give back, to return; to give again; *intr.* (*aux.* avere, essere) — giù, to fall ill again, to have a relapse; — fuori, to return, to break out again; gli ha -ato il suo solito male, his old trouble has come back again; dagli e ridagli, after much labour, at long last, after trying repeatedly; dagli, ridagli, non mi riusciva, do what I could, I found it impossible; *rfl.* to give, devote, oneself again (see dare). (**-ato** *part. adj.*)

ridarell-a *f.*, **-o** *adj.* See under ridere.

ridd-a *f.* round dance, reel; wild dance; whirl; confusion; whirling crowd of dancers. **-are** [A1] *intr.* (*aux.* avere) to dance a round; to dance in a ring. **-oni** *adv.* in a round; whirling.

ri·d-ere [C3] *intr.* (*aux.* avere) to laugh; — di qualcuno, to laugh at someone; non c'è niente da —, there is nothing to laugh at; non è cosa da —, it is not a laughing matter; ci sarà da —, there will be some fun; — alle spalle di uno, to make fun of someone behind his back; — a crepapelle, to split one's sides with laughter; — sotto i baffi, to laugh up one's sleeve; far — i polli, to make a cat laugh; lo dissi per —, I said it in jest, I said it for fun; badate, che non -o, mind, I'm not joking; (provb.) -e bene chi -e l'ultimo, he who laughs last laughs best; (fig.) to shine brightly, to seem gay; gli -ono gli occhi, his eyes shine (are lit up) with joy; tutta la natura -e, all nature seems gay; to smile; la fortuna gli -e, fortune smiles upon him; (of shoes, sheets, etc.) to be worn out, to be torn, threadbare, to be in holes; *rfl.* (*dat.* of *prn.* 'si') -ersela, to laugh it off; me la -o, I just laugh at it; me la -o di lui, I don't care a brass button (a fig, a jot) for him; *tr.* (poet.) to laugh at, to mock, to scorn; *n.m.* laughter; laughing; scoppiare dal —, to burst out laughing; non potei trattenermi dal —, I couldn't help laughing. **-arella** *f.* (pop.) giggle. **-ente** *part. adj.* laughing, smiling; bright, gay; merry; delightful. **-erello**, **-arello** *adj.* easily moved to laughter; giggling. **-evole** *adj.* laughable, funny; ridi-culous. **-evolmente** *adv.* laughably. **-one** *m.* one prone to laughter.

ridest-are [A1] *tr.* to reawaken, to revive; to stir up; to wake up again; to arouse; *rfl.* to wake up (again); to be revived; to be rekindled. (**-amento** *m.* **-ato** *part. adj.*)

ridettare [A1] *tr.* to dictate again.

ridetto *part.* of ridire, q.v.; *adj.* said again, repeated; †predicted, foretold.

ridicchiare [A4] and derivs. See ridacchiare.

ridic-i·bile *adj.* repeatable, fit to be repeated. **-imento** *m.* repetition, saying again; †prophecy. **-itore** *m.* one who repeats things; informer, spy. (**-itrice** *f.*)

ridi·col-o *adj.* ridiculous; funny; un compenso —, paltry com-pensation; pretese -e, extravagant pretensions (claims); *n.m.* ridicule; absurdity; ridiculousness; non vedeva il — della cosa, he did not see how ridiculous it was; gettare il — su qualcuno, to make someone ridiculous, to make someone a laughing-stock; mettere in —, to ridicule, to make fun of. (**-amente**, **-mente** *adv.*) **-aggine** *f.* absurdity; quei pregiudizi sono -aggini, those pre-

ridicol-o (*cont.*)

judices are absurd. **-ẹzza** *f.* ridiculousness, absurdity; foolishness; dire mille -ezze, to talk a lot of nonsense; non stare a ringraziarmi per una -ezza simile, don't bother to thank me for such a trifle.

ridimandare [A I] and derivs. See **ridomandare**.

ridimension-are [A I c] *tr.* (cinem.) to reshape, to remodel; *tr., abs.* (pol.) to make a few changes in a political programme; to reshuffle, to rethink; to adapt; (comm.) — una ditta, to reorganize a firm. (**-ato** *part. adj.*)

ridintornare [A I c] *tr.* (paint.) to outline afresh, to go over the outlines of.

ridipin·gere [C 5] *tr.* (paint.) to repaint, to retouch.

ridire [B 10] *tr.* to repeat, to say again, to tell again; *intr.* (*aux.* avere) to repeat maliciously what has been told in confidence; to object, to find fault; trovar da — su qualche cosa, to object to something; trova sempre da — su quello che io faccio, he always finds fault with what I do; *rfl.* to change one's mind, to recant.

ridisciogliere [B 27] *tr.* (chem.) to redissolve.

ridi-tọre *adj., n.m.* See **derisore**. (**-trice** *f.*)

ridiven-ire [D 17], **-tare** [A I] *intr.* (*aux.* essere) to become again. (**-uto, -tato** *part. adj.*)

ridivi·dere [C 3] *tr.* to divide again; to subdivide.

ridolẹre [B 11] *intr.* (*aux.* essere), *rfl.* to ache again, to be painful again.

ridomandare [A I] *tr.* to ask for again; to inquire about again.

ridon-are [D I] *tr.* to give back; to restore; to give again; — la libertà a uno, to set someone free again. **-ato** *part. adj.* restored; given again. (**-atọre** *m.* **-atrice** *f.*)

ridond-are [A I c] *intr.* (*aux.* essere, avere) to be superabundant; to overflow; to redound; ciò -a a suo onore, that redounds to his credit; to result; (naut.) (of the wind) to shift in favour of the ship's course, to free; il vento -a, the wind is favouring (i.e. blowing conveniently for the course desired), the wind is free. **-amẹnto** *m.* redundancy, overflowing. **-ante** *part. adj.* redundant, superfluous. (**-antemẹnte** *adv.*) **-anza** *f.* redundance, superabundance, superfluity.

ridọppio *m.* more than double; pagare a —, to pay more than double, to pay far too much.

ridor-are [A I] *tr.* to gild again. (**-ato** *part. adj.*)

ridormire [D I] *intr.* (*aux.* avere) to sleep again.

ridosso *m.* shelter; sheltered place; (fig.) a — di, sheltering behind; avere a —, to have behind one; (naut.) lee, shelter, screen; protection offered by land or breakwater, etc., to shipping; protection against rain, wind or waves; a —, behind; close by; Genova ha le montagne a —, Genoa has mountains rising behind it, Genoa lies in the shelter of the mountains.

ridọtta *f.* See **ridotto,** *n.m.*

†ridottare *tr.* to fear greatly.

ridọtto *part.* of **ridurre**, q.v.; *adj.* reduced; — in pessimo stato, mal —, reduced to a very bad state, in very poor circumstances; adjusted, corrected; in proporzioni ridotte, on a small scale; forced, compelled; (cinem.) substandard; *n.m.* private room, card-room, parlour; — del teatro, foyer, theatre bar, theatre restaurant; (mil.) redoubt; (naut.) enclosure, enclosed zone in a ship; — corazzato, armoured belt.

†ridoventare *vb.* and derivs. See **ridiventare**.

riducchiare [A 4] *intr.* (*aux.* avere) to smile, to chuckle (without the malice or silliness implied by **ridacchiare**, q.v.).

riduc-ente *part. adj.* reducing; (welding) fiamme -enti, reducing flame; *n.m.* (chem.) reducing agent. **-i·bile** *adj.* reducible; prezzo -ibile, price subject to reduction; -ibile a miti consigli, amenable to counsels of mildness. **-imẹnto** *m.* reduction. (**-itọre** *m.* **-itrice** *f.*)

†ridu·cere *vb.* See **ridurre**.

ridurre [B 2] *tr.* to reduce; to bring back; — il gregge all'ovile, to lead the flock back to the fold; — alla memoria, to call to mind; to convert, to change; — un convento a caserma, to turn a monastery into a barracks; — la casa un inferno, to make the house a hell; — in pezzi, to break to pieces; — un brano italiano in latino, to translate a piece of Italian into Latin; to adjust, to adapt; to restrict; — il potere in un solo, to restrict power to one person; — un ragazzo, to discipline a boy, to make him docile; (mus.) to adapt, to arrange; (chem.) to reduce, to deoxidize; — in cenere, to ash; (metall.) to reduce, to smelt; (mil.) to reduce; †(naut.) to work up the dead reckoning of; *rfl.* to repair (to), to retire, to go; ridursi in campagna, to retire to the

country; to take refuge; to be reduced; questa stoffa, lavandola, si riduce di un terzo, when it is washed this material shrinks by a third; si ridusse a prendere in prestito pochi scellini, he was reduced to borrowing a few shillings; non credevo che si sarebbe ridotto a questo, I did not think it would come to this; to become smaller or worse; dopo la malattia s'è ridotto un cencio, since his illness he has become a mere skeleton.

ridut-tọre *m.* reducer; — di pressione, pressure reducing valve; (chem.) reducing agent, reducer; (electr.) — di potenziale, potential divider; (watchm.) mobile —, reduction gear; *adj.* reducing; sostanza -trice, reducing substance.

riduzione *f.* reduction; bringing back; discount; (theatr.) adaptation; (comm.) — del fino della moneta, debasement of currency; (mus.) adaptation, arrangement, reduction; (chem.; math.; surg.) reduction; (hist.) reduction (of Jesuits in S. America); (biol.) — gametica, reduction division.

riecco *excl.* here (it) is again!; rieccoli!, here they are again!

†rie·dere *intr.* to return; to turn out, to result.

riedific-are [A 2 se] *tr.* to rebuild. **-amẹnto** *m.* rebuilding. **-ato** *part. adj.* rebuilt. (**-atọre** *m.* **-atrice** *f.*) **-azione** *f.* rebuilding.

rieduc-are [A 2 s] *tr.* to re-educate; to rehabilitate; to give special training to. **-ato** *part. adj.* re-educated; rehabilitated. **-azione** *f.* re-education; rehabilitation.

ri-eleg·gere [C 12] *tr.* to re-elect. **-eleggi·bile** *adj.* eligible for re-election. (**-eleggibilità** *f.*) **-eletto** *part. adj.* re-elected. **-elezione** *f.* re-election.

riem·p·iere, riemp-ire [D 6] *tr.* to fill, to fill up, to fill in; — la bottiglia, to fill the bottle; la notizia mi -ì di gioia, the news filled me with joy; dovete — questo modulo, you must fill up this form; — un animale morto, to stuff a dead animal; (cul.) to stuff; *rfl.* to be filled; to cram oneself (with food), to eat too much; to become pregnant. **-iente** *adj., n.m.* filling, filler. **-imẹnto** *m.* filling up; filling; stuffing; (mil.) replacements (to bring up to strength); (naut.) filling pieces strengthening scantlings; filling (hull construction); filler; pezzi di -imento, filling pieces. **-ita** *f.* fill. **-itivo** *adj.* filling; expletive; pleonastic; (techn.) materia -itiva filling material, filler; *n.m.* pleonasm; expletive; filling, stuffing; (paint. techn.) extender. (**-ito** *part. adj.*) **-itọio** *m.* (naut.) see **riempitore**; *pl.* (naut.) strengthening pieces under the sternboard. **-itọre** *m.* filler; (naut.) sternpost; sternpost filling pieces; oak. **-itura** *f.* filling; stuffing; pleonasm. **-iuto** *part. adj.* filled, filled up; stuffed; (archit.) maniera -iuta (a cassa), timber-frame building.

rientr-are [A I] *intr.* (*aux.* essere) to go in again, to come in again; to re-enter; to go home; — in città, to return to town; — nel proprio, — nei suoi, — nelle spese, to recover what one has lost or spent; -arci, to make a small profit; — nei propri diritti, to be reinstated in one's rights; — in possesso, to regain possession; — in sè, to come to oneself, to recover one's senses, to take a more reasonable view of a matter; (of wood, cloth, etc.) — in sè, to shrink; to withdraw; to curve inwards; to be included; (mil.) to return to one's base, to withdraw to one's own lines; (typ.) far —, to indent; *tr.* (naut.) to get in, to take in (sail, flags, ropes, ensign-staffs, fenders, etc.); to hoist aboard; — la forza di vele, to shorten sail; — remi, to lay in the oars; (naut. command) -a!, order given by the officer of the watch on completion of the call on a boatswain's pipe when sounded as an honour. **-a·bile** *adj.* that can be re-entered; (photog.) collapsible (lens); (aeron.) retractable (undercarriage). **-amẹnto** *m.* re-entering; recession; re-entrant. **-ante** *part. adj.* receding; withdrawn; hollow, sunken; recessed; (mil) re-entrant **-anza** *f.* (typ.) indent, indentation; (techn.) recess, undercut. **-ata** *f.* return, retreat; withdrawal; (mil.) act of returning to base, withdrawal to one's own lines; (naut.) tumble-home (i.e. decreasing beam of a ship above the waterline for added stability). **-ato** *part. adj.* returned; withdrawn; suppressed; speranze -ate, vanished hopes; occhi -ati, deep-set eyes; impresa -ata, unexecuted project, enterprise that has come to nothing; (silkb.) bachi -ati, rusty silkworms. **-atọre** *m.* (shoem.) laster.

rientro *m.* shrinkage; revenue; return on money invested; recovery; (silkb.) rust (a disease of silkworms).

riepilog-are [A 2 s] *tr.* to recapitulate, to summarize; -ando, in short. **-amẹnto** *m.* recapitulating. **-azione** *f.* recapitulation, summarizing, summing-up.

riepi·lo-go *m.* (*pl.* **-ghi**) summary, recapitulation, epitome.

†**rieri**, †**rietro** *adv.* behind.

riesame *m.* (leg.) re-examination.

riescire [D 16] and derivs. See **riuscire**.

riespọrre [B 21] *tr.* to expose again; to exhibit again.

riesport-are [A 1] *tr.* (comm.) to re-export. **-aziọne** *f.* re-exportation.

riesposiziọne *f.* (mus.) recapitulation.

riesp-ọsto, **-osto** *part.* of **riespọrre**.

ries·sere [B 13] *intr.* (*aux.* essere) to be present again; ci sono ristato l'altro giorno, I was there (again) the other day; ci risiamo!, here we go again!

rievoc-are [A 2 s] *tr.* to call up (again), to conjure up (again); to recall. (**-ato** *part. adj.*) **-aziọne** *f.* recalling; tribute (obituary).

†**riezza** *f.* wickedness (cf. **rio²**).

rifabbric-are [A 2 s] *tr.* to rebuild; to make again. **-a·bile** *adj.* suitable for rebuilding, that can be rebuilt. **-amẹnto** *m.* rebuilding. **-ato** *part. adj.* rebuilt.

rifac-i·bile *adj.* that can be made again; that can be done again; repeatable. **-imẹnto** *m.* remaking; remodelling; restoration; -imento di danni, compensation for damage; revision, adaptation, rewriting. (**-itọre** *m.* **-itrice** *f.* **-itura** *f.*)

ri-fare [B 14] *tr.* to do again; to remake; to make again; — il letto, to make the bed; to rebuild; to renew; — di sana pianta, to do all over again; — la strada, to retrace one's steps; (motor. slang) to overhaul; (cul.) to cook again, to serve up again; to imitate; -fà benissimo la tua voce, he can imitate your voice perfectly; — la mobilia di, to refurnish; †— il padre, to name a son after his father; *rfl.* (*acc.* of *prn.* 'si') to recover one's strength, one's health; to cover one's losses; to make good; -farsi del tempo perduto, to make up for lost time; to get one's own back, to be revenged; -farsi da capo, to begin all over again; -farsi da, to begin at (a certain point, e.g. in a story); non saper da che parte -farsi, not to know where to start, where to turn, how to go on; (*dat.* of *prn.* 'si') -farsi lo stomaco, to give one's stomach a treat, to eat something more tasty (than the last dish); -farsi l'occhio, to feast one's eyes; -farsi una verginità, to start afresh, *or* to pretend to be innocent (cf. **fare**).

rifaṣ-are [A 1] *tr.* (electr.) to correct the power factor of. **-amẹnto** *m.* (telev.) phasing; (electr.) power-factor correction. (**-ato** *part. adj.*) **-atọre** *m.* (electr.) phase modifier.

rifasci-are [A 4] *tr.* to bind, to bind round and round; to swaddle; †(naut.) to repair the hull. **-ata** *f.* binding. **-ato** *part. adj.* bound. **-atura** *f.* (work of) binding.

rifa·scio *adv. phr.* a —, in disorder, pell-mell; andare a —, to go to rack and ruin.

rifatt-o *part.* of **rifare**, q.v.; *adj.* done again, remade; re-elected; restored, rebuilt; villano —, upstart; (cul.) rechauffé, cooked again, served up again (differently); (typ.) reset. **-i·bile** *adj.* that can be done again; capable of repair or restoration. **-ura** *f.* restoration; repair; rebuilding (or cost of the same).

rifaziọne *f.* restoration; rebuilding; compensation for damage.

rifen·d-ere [C 21] *tr.* to split again, to cut in pieces; (metall.) to draw. **-itọio** *m.* (metall.) wiredrawing mill.

rifer-ire [D 2] *tr.* to report, to relate, to tell; to ascribe, to attribute; — grazie, to return thanks to; (leg.) to refer back (C.C.); *rfl.* to refer, to relate; ciò che si -isce a lui, what relates to himself; mi -isco al recente accordo, I refer to the recent agreement; — al giudizio di un arbitro, to refer (appeal) to the decision of an umpire. **-ente** *part.*; *n.m.* reporter; referendary. **-i·bile** *adj.* referable; reportable. **-ibilmẹnte** *adv.* -ibilmente a, with reference to, with regard to, concerning. **-imẹnto** *m.* reference; con -imento a, with reference to *or* on the basis of; returning; -imento di grazie, giving thanks; avere un -imento, to have something to go by; (leg.) reference back; (mil.) punto di -imento, reference point. **-ito** *part. adj.* reported; related; ascribed (to). **-itọre** *m.* reporter; tale-bearer. (**-itrice** *f.*)

riferm-are [A 1] *tr.* to refasten; to stop again; to confirm; to strengthen; *rfl.* to renew an engagement (of service). **-ato** *part. adj.* shut; confirmed; re-engaged.

rifermo *adj.* See **rifermato**, under **rifermare**.

rifẹss-o *part.* of **rifendere**, q.v.; *adj.* split again; (herald.) croce -a, cross patonce.

riffa¹ *f.* raffle.

riff-a² *f.* violence; di —, at all costs, come what may; di — o di raffa, by hook or by crook. **-ọso** *adj.* violent, liable to commit an outrage.

rifiancare [A 2] *tr.* to strengthen (a building, etc.) at the sides.

rifiat-are [A 1] *intr.* (*aux.* avere) to breathe, to breathe freely; to have time to breathe; ho tanto lavoro da fare che non -o più, I have so much to do that I have no time to breathe; non —, not to breathe a word; non -ò, he kept absolutely mum; (colloq.) guai a te se -i!, if you say one word you're for it! **-amẹnto** *m.* breathing. **-ata** *f.* (a) breath; sigh of relief; pause; (colloq.) 'breather'. **-atọna** *f. augm.* great sigh of relief.

rificc-are [A 2] *tr.* to fix again (or more thoroughly); si -ò il cappello in testa, he put his hat back on his head; *rfl.* to get stuck in; in quel posto non ce lo volevano più, ma tanto ha fatto che ci si è -ato, they did not want to keep him in that post, but he succeeded in getting stuck in. (**-ato** *part. adj.*)

rificolọna *f.* paper lantern (carried on a stick); slut; woman who is a gad-about.

rifig·gere [C 12] *tr.* to refix; (eng.) to mesh, to engage.

rifigliare [A 4] *intr.* (*aux.* avere) to produce (more) offspring; (of a wound) to suppurate again.

rifil-are [A 1] *tr.* to spin again; to trim; to trim to size; (fig.) to report (words spoken); — un colpo, to deal a blow; -ò una moneta falsa, he passed a bad coin. (**-ato** *part. adj.*) **-atọre** *m.* reporter, tale-bearer, spy. **-atrice** *f.* woman who carries tales; (techn.) trimming machine.

rifin-ire [D 2] *tr.* to finish, to put the finishing touch to; to exhaust, to wear down, to wear out; non -iva di ringraziarmi, he never stopped thanking me, he kept on thanking me; *intr.* (*aux.* avere; *prep.* a) to be satisfactory (to); non ci -isce, we are not quite satisfied with it; *rfl.* to be exhausted; to become worn out. **-itẹzza** *f.* exhaustion (esp. from fasting). **-ito** *part. adj.* exhausted, worn out; -ito morto, dead tired; hard up, in financial difficulties; ben -ito, accurately finished off. **-itọre** *m.* (joc., with pun on 'diffinitore') padron -itore, person who finished everything off. **-itura** *f.* finishing off; (techn.) finishing, trimming. **-iziọne** *f.* finishing off; finish; mandare in -izione, to finish up, to consume completely.

rifior-ire [D 2] *intr.* (*aux.* avere, essere) to bloom again; to flourish again; to resume activity; to be renewed; to become mouldy, rusty, or spotty; (joc.) to get tipsy, to be 'lit up'; *tr.* to embellish; to make up (a road), to dress with gravel; (paint.) to touch up, to brighten (a picture). **-ente** *part. adj.* blooming, flourishing (again). **-imẹnto** *m.* new flourishing; revival; (paint.) ornament; embellishment; (roads, paths) making up with gravel. **-ita** *f.* bloom, reflorescence. **-ito** *part. adj.* blooming again; restored to health; spotted with mould, stains, rust, pimples. **-itura** *f.* reflorescence; embellishment; dressing of gravel; spots or stains of mould or grease.

rifischi-are [A 4] *intr.* (*aux.* avere) to whistle again; to hiss again; to whistle in reply; *tr.* to tell (tales); non andare a -arglielo subito, don't go straight away and tell him. **-ọne** *m.* tale-bearer, sneak.

rifisso *part.* of **rifiggere**, q.v.

rifitt-a *f.* refixing. **-o** *part.* of **rifiggere**, q.v.

rifiutare¹ *tr.* to sniff again.

rifiut-are² *tr.* to refuse, to decline; to reject; non mi -i questo favore, don't deny me this favour; to refuse to recognize; — la moglie, to repudiate one's wife; — il sole, to be unable to stand the sun; la fortuna -a i timidi, fortune favours the brave; (naut.) il vento -a, the wind fails, the wind heads; un porto che -a il vento, a sheltered harbour; (naut.) la nave -a di virare, the ship cannot tack; *rfl.* to refuse oneself; non -arsi mai, to be always willing to help, never to spare oneself; to refuse, to decline; -arsi di venire, to refuse to come. **-a·bile** *adj.* refusable. **-amẹnto** *m.* refusing. **-ato** *part. adj.* refused, rejected; declined. **-atọre** *m.* refuser, denier; *adj.* refusing, rejecting. (**-atrice** *f.*)

rifiuto *m.* refusal, rejection; renunciation; (fig.) il gran —, shirking of responsibility (with ref. to the abdication of Pope Celestine V); reject, person or thing rejected; *pl.* refuse, waste matter; -i di carta, waste-paper; i -i della società, the scum of society; dead letters; merce di —, rubbish, trash; (comm.) refusal; — di accettazione, non-acceptance; (industr.) waste, refuse, effluent; (text.) — di pettinatura, topping; -i radioattivi, radioactive waste; (naut.) materiali di —, below standard materials.

rifless-o *part.* of **riflettere**, q.v.; *adj.* reflected; (paint.) lume —, reflected light; (med.) atto —, reflex action, reflex; — tendineo, tendon reflex; *n.m.* reflexion; reflex (action); per —, indirectly;

rifless-o (*cont.*)

di —, by reflex action; indirectly, on the rebound. **-amẹnte** *adv.* indirectly, by reflexion. **-i·bile** *adj.* worth thinking about; important. (**-ibilità** *f.*) **-iọne** *f.* (phys.) reflection, reflectivity; (fig.) reflexion; deliberation; donna senza **-ione**, thoughtless woman; senza **-ione**, thoughtlessly, inconsiderately; fare un po' di **-ione**, to reflect a little; ha fatto alcune utili **-ioni**, he made some useful observations; artista di **-ione**, intellectual (self-conscious) artist; le **-ioni** di un saggio, a wise man's meditations. **-ivo** *adj.* reflecting; raggi **-ivi**, reflecting rays; (fig.) thoughtful, reflective; (gramm.) reflexive. (**-ivamẹnte** *adv.*)

riflẹt·t-ere [C 19] *tr.* to reflect, to throw back; (fig.) l'occhio **-e** i moti dell'anima, the eye reflects the workings of the mind; ciò non **-e** il caso nostro, that is not representative of our case; *intr.* (*aux.* avere) to reflect, to consider; senza —, thoughtlessly, off-hand; **-ete** bene prima di decidere, think well before you decide; ci **-erò**, I will think it over; *rfl.* to be reflected. **-ente** *part. adj.* reflecting. **-o·metro** *m.* (opt.) reflectometer. **-ọre** *m.* reflector; spotlight, searchlight; floodlight. **-uto** *part. adj.* thoughtful, considerate; reflected. **-utamẹnte** *adv.* after reflection; thoughtfully.

riflu-ire [D 2] *intr.* (*aux.* avere or essere) to flow again, to flow back; to ebb; merci che rifluiscono sul mercato, goods coming on to the market again.

riflusso *m.* reflux, refluence; ebb; — del mare, ebb-tide, low-tide; il flusso e il — del mare, the ebb and flow of the tide; backwash; (med.) afflux of blood to a given part of the body; (chem.) refrigerante a —, reflux condenser.

rifluttuare [A 6] *intr.* (*aux.* essere) to float back.

rifocill-are [A 1] *tr.* to revive; to refresh; — lo stomaco, to have something to eat, to take some refreshment; *rfl.* to eat something, to take refreshment. **-amẹnto** *m.* refreshment. (**-ato** *part. adj.*)

rifoderare [A 1 s] *tr.* to reline, to put new lining in.

rifoll-are [A 1] *tr.* (eng.) to upset. **-amẹnto** *m.*, **-atura** *f.* (eng.) upsetting.

ri·fọl-o *m.* (naut.) see refolo. **-are** [A 1 s] (naut.) see rifoleggiare. †**-atore** *m.* ramrod. **-eggiare** [A 3 c] *intr.* (*aux.* essere) to be subject to gusty winds.

rifond-are [A 1 c] *tr.* to found again; to rebuild; (archit.) to repair the foundations. **-ato** *part. adj.* refounded; re-established. (**-azione** *f.*)

rifọnd-ere [C 2] *tr.* (metall.) to recast; (comm.) to refund, to reimburse; (fig.) to recast (e.g. an essay, article); — acqua alla caldaia, to fill up, to refill, the boiler with water; — olio alla lampada, to refill the lamp (with oil). (**-i·bile** *adj.* **-itọre** *m.* **-itrice** *f.*) **-itura** *f.* (vet.) overfeeding of horses.

riforb-ire [D 2] *tr.* to refurbish; — le armi, to prepare weapons, to rearm; *rfl.* to be refurbished. **-ito** *part. adj.* refurbished.

rifọrma *f.* reform; correction; emendation; (eccl. hist.) reform (of religious orders, etc.); Reformation; — cattolica, Catholic Reform, Counter-Reformation; (leg.) — di sentenza, amendment, rectification of judgement (C.C.P.); (mil.) retirement, reduction, casting (owing to sickness or defect); (naut.) discharge (as being unfit, disabled or supernumerary).

riform-are [A 1 c] *tr.* to re-form, to form anew; to reform, to amend; to correct; (eccl. hist.) to reform; (mil.) to pay off, to pension, to cast; (naut.; mil.) to discharge unfit or condemn as substandard or supernumerary; — le spese, to cut down (reduce) expenses; to transform; *rfl.* to be restored to one's (its) former shape; to be reformed, corrected, amended. **-a·bile** *adj.* (eccl.) revocable (decree, etc.). **-amẹnto** *m.* reforming. **-ativo** *adj.* reformative, reforming. **-ato** *part. adj.* re-formed; corrected; modified; reformed; (mil.) turned down; retired; not accepted; *n.m.* a 'C3' man, a man unfit for acceptance into the services; *pl.* (eccl.) members of a reformed religious order (e.g. Franciscans, Carmelites); members of a Reformed Church, Protestants. **-atọre** *m.* reformer; i principi **-atori**, the reforming princes (in the eighteenth century, Carlo III at Naples, Giuseppe II in Lombardy, Leopold I in Tuscany). (**-atrice** *f.*) **-ato·rio** *adj.* (*m.pl.* **-atorii**) (leg.) reformatory. **-azione** *f.* reformation; new formation. **-ịsmo** *m.* reformism, doctrine and policy of reformists. **-ista** *m.* reformist (Socialist advocating reform rather than revolution).

riforn-ire [D 2] *tr.* to supply (with), to provide (with); — la lampada di olio, or — l'olio alla lampada, to refill the lamp with oil; *rfl.* to provide oneself (with); to take in a fresh supply (of); — di benzina, to get some petrol, to fill up with petrol. **-imẹnto** *m.*

supply, provision(s); (motor.) stazione di **-imento**, filling station; (mil.) provision, supply (ammunition, etc.); replenishments, replacements (of aircraft, etc.); (cycle-racing) point where the competitors are handed refreshments, etc. as they pass. **-ito** *part. adj.* supplied, provided; filled up. **-itọre** *m.* (rlwy.) water tank.

rifoss-are [A 1] *tr.* to ditch, to drain with new ditches. (**-ato** *part. adj.*)

rifọsso *m.* (mil. hist.) double trenching; secondary trench.

rifran·g-ere [C 5] *tr.* (phys.) to refract; to break up, to throw back; *rfl.* (phys.) to be refracted; (of sound) to be echoed; (of echo) to be thrown back; (of sight) to be dazzled. **-ente** *part. adj.* (phys.) refractive; (opt.) refracting. **-enza** *f.* (phys.) refringence. (**-i·bile** *adj.*, **-ibilità** *f.*) **-imẹnto** *m.* refraction.

rifranto *altern. part.* of **rifrangere**, q.v.; *adj.* crushed, broken up again (cf. **rifratto**).

rifrattiv-o *adj.* (phys.) refractive; refracting. **-ità** *f.* (phys.) refractivity.

rifratt-o *altern. part.* of **rifrangere**, q.v.; *adj.* refracted; *n.m.* refraction. **-o·metro** *m.* (phys.) refractometer. **-ọre** *m.* refractor.

rifrazịọne *f.* (phys.; opt.) refraction; (phys.) indice di —, refractive index.

rifredd-are [A 1 c] *tr.* to cool (after cooking); to chill; *intr.* (*aux.* essere), *rfl.* to get cold (esp. of food). **-ato** *part. adj.* cooled; chilled; got cold.

rifrẹddo *adj.* cold; pollo —, cold chicken; *n.m.pl.* cold meats, ham, tongue, etc.

rifrịg·g-ere [C 12] *tr.* to fry again; (fig.) to serve up again (arguments, etc., i.e. to say the same thing again in different form); *intr.* (*aux.* avere) to be fried too long; (fig., of an unmarried girl) to be on the shelf. (**-imẹnto** *m.* **-itọre** *m.* **-itrice** *f.*)

rifriggolato *adj.* (Tusc., pop.) refried; saper di —, to taste stale, as though it has been fried up.

rifritt-o *part.* of **rifriggere**, q.v.; *adj.* fried up again; (fig.) repeated many times; son cose queste fritte e **-e**, these things have been said a thousand times; *n.m.* smell of frying, smell of stale fat; saper di —, to taste rancid, stale; seasoning of fried herbs. **-ume** *m.* food fried up again, (fig.) rehash (of, e.g., literary composition, articles). **-ura** *f.* food fried again; (fig.) rehash (of previous publications).

rifrugare [A 2] *tr.* to rummage (in), to search again (in).

rifrust-are [A 1] *tr.* to thrash again; to rummage, to search; **-ò** tutti i vecchi giornali che aveva in casa, he searched through all the old newspapers he had in the house; ha **-ato** tutte le osterie per cercarvi il vin buono, he ransacked all the inns to find good wine; to recall things forgotten; ma guarda che cosa è andato a —!, just look what he has raked up! **-a** *f.* search, research. (**-ato** *part. adj.* **-atọre** *m.* **-atrice** *f.*) †**-o** *m.* severe blow.

rifrutt-are [A 1], **-ificare** [A 2 s] *intr.* (*aux.* avere) to bear, to fructify (again). **-o** *m.* (comm.) interest upon interest; compound interest.

rifugg-ire [D 1] *intr.* (*aux.* essere) to flee again, to run away again; — da, to be averse from, to shrink from, to be reluctant to; to take refuge; erano **-iti** tutti in cantina, they were all hiding in the cellar; †*tr.* to avoid. **-imẹnto** *m.* avoidance, aversion. **-ito** *part. adj.* fugitive, fleeing; avoided, disliked.

rifugi-are [A 3] *rfl.* to take refuge, to take shelter, to seek shelter; ci **-ammo** sui monti, we took to the mountains for safety; (fig.) **-arsi** nella preghiera, to seek solace in prayer. **-ato** *part. adj.* sheltered; admitted (as a refugee); *n.m.* refugee; i **-ati** politici, political refugees.

rifu·gio *m.* refuge, retreat, shelter, asylum; — sotterraneo, dug-out, underground shelter; — contraereo, air-raid shelter; — di malfattori, haunt of criminals; (naut.) shelter; porto di —, shelter; camera di —, escape chamber of a submarine; (theol.) — dei peccatori, Refuge of sinners, *Refugium peccatorum* (title of the B.V.M.).

riful·g-ere [C 30] *intr.* (*liter.*, *aux.* essere, avere) to shine, to be resplendent; to be refulgent; to be clear, to be apparent; rifulse la sua innocenza, his innocence shone forth for all to see. **-ente** *part. adj.* resplendent, brightly shining; refulgent.

rifumare [A 1] *tr.*, *intr.* (*aux.* avere) to smoke again; cominciò a — la pipa, he relit his pipe.

†**rifusare** *vb.* and derivs. See **rifiutare**.

rifuṣ-o *part.* of **rifondere**, q.v.; *adj.* remelted; *adv. phr.* (fig.) a —, in abundance; refunded. **-i·bile** *adj.* capable of being remelted. **-iọne** *f.* remelting; (fig.) recasting (of written composition), alteration; reimbursement, refund; refunding.

rifut-ativo *adj.* refutative, tending to disprove. **-azione** *f.* refutation.

riga *f.* line; row; stripe, streak; tirare una — col lapis, to draw a line with the pencil; scrivere poche righe, to write a few lines; saper leggere tra le righe, to read between the lines; falsa —, see under **falso**; alla terza — a cominciare dal basso, three lines from the bottom; tutti su una —, all in a row, all in line; la — dei capelli, the parting in one's hair; farsi la —, to part one's hair; (mil.) file; rompere le righe, to break file; (mus.) line (of the stave); uscir fuori della —, to achieve distinction; mettersi in — con alcuno, to compete with someone; rimettere uno in —, to put someone in his place, to reduce someone to obedience; ruler; straightedge; — a forma di T, T-square; (typ.) a line of type; rule, stick; slug; — bianca, blank line; (as measure) em-quad; mezza —, en-quad; (la pagina) cresce una —, one line too many on the page.

rigabello *m.* (mus.) portative organ.

riga·glia *f.* (usu. *pl.*) giblets; trifles, leavings; tip, small occasional earnings.

†**rigagn-a** *f.*, **-o** *m.* See **rigagnolo**.

riga·gnolo *m.* rivulet; trickle, thin stream; gutter; pescare pel —, to labour in vain.

rigame *m.* See under **rigare**.

ri·gamo *m.* (bot.) wild marjoram, *Origanum vulgare*.

rig-are [A2] *tr.* to rule (lines); — per traverso, to draw lines across; to score; grosse lagrime gli -arono il viso, great tears ran down his face; — la terra di sangue, to streak the ground with blood; (fig.) — dritto, to go straight; to irrigate, to furrow; (mil.) to rifle; †to underline. **-ame** *m.* ruling, lines; stripes; (archit. and stone masonry) fluting; (mil.) rifling. **-ata** *f.* ruling, line; tap (with a ruler or the like); (mus.) stave. **-atino** *m.* striped material (linen or cotton); (Tusc.) streaky bacon. **-ato** *part. adj.* irrigated, watered; fronte -ata di sudore, forehead bathed in sweat; lined, ruled; striped; (mil.) rifled; (eng.) scored (e.g. of car cylinder); †(naut.) vento -ato, strong steady wind; *n.m.* print, design (on striped material). **-atoni** *m.pl.* (cul.) a kind of 'pasta' marked with tiny flutings. **-atore** *m.* one who rules lines; (agric.) harrow. (**-atrice** *f.*) **-atura** *f.* ruling; la -atura è troppo larga, the lines are too widely spaced; drawing, cutting lines; (eng.) scoring, rifling; (mil.) form or nature of rifling.

rigaste *f.pl.* (Verona) riverside street, embankment.

rigatt-eri·a *f.* old clothes; junk. **-iere** *m.* old clothes dealer; rag and bone merchant; huckster, broker.

rigaudon *m. indecl.* See **rigodone**.

Rigel *pr.n.m.* (astron.) Rigel, β Orionis.

rigener-are [A1s] *tr.* to regenerate; to generate again; (theol.) to regenerate; *rfl.* to reproduce (oneself, itself); to grow again. **-amento** *m.* reproduction. (**-ante** *part. adj.* **-ato** *part. adj.* **-ativo** *adj.*) **-atore** *m.* regenerator; (industr.) heat exchanger; -atore dei capelli, hair restorer; *adj.* regenerating; (theol.) regenerative. (**-atrice** *f.*) **-azione** *f.* regeneration, reproduction; (radio) positive feedback; (motor.) retreading (of a tyre); (theol.) regeneration.

rigente *adj.* (poet.) cold, numb, stiff with cold.

rigermogli-are [A4c, A4] *intr.* (*aux.* essere, avere) to bud again, to sprout again; (fig.) to flourish again; to spring up again. (**-ante** *part. adj.*)

rigerm-oglio, -oglio *m.* sucker.

rigett-are [A1] *tr.* to throw again; to throw back; to throw away; to hurl, to fling back; to return; to reject; — un consiglio, to turn down advice; — una preghiera, to reject an entreaty; to postpone; to fail (in an examination); fu -ato in latino, he failed in Latin; (metall.) to recast; (leg.) to cast ashore; to throw up (C.C.); *abs.* to sprout again; gli ulivi hanno -ato, the olive-trees have put out fresh shoots; to vomit; *rfl.* to throw oneself again; -arsi al vizio, to plunge into vice again. **-a·bile** *adj.* rejectable, returnable. **-amento** *m.* rejection, throwing back; vomit; fresh sprouting. (**-ante** *part. adj.*) **-ato** *part. adj.* rejected; sent back; flung back. (**-atore** *m.* **-atrice** *f.*)

rigetto *m.* rejection; reject, throw-out; (geol.) throw; *pl.* (leg.) rigetti del mare, jetsam.

rigge *f.* (naut.). See **riggia**.

rig·gia *f.* (naut.) fore and aft struts under the foretop or crow's nest to which shrouds are secured.

righellina *f. dim.* of **riga**, q.v.

righello *m.* See under **rigo**.

righett-a *f.* (archit.) string course; cornice. **-are** [A1c] *tr.* to rule, to line; to stripe.

righiacciamento *m.* (rlwy.) adding fresh ice (to a railway truck).

righino *m.* (typ.) reglet, blank part of a line at end of paragraph; short line; (naut.) rubbing strake on a boat.

ri·gid-o *adj.* stiff (esp. with cold); very cold, rigorous (of climate, etc.); rigid; una sbarra -a, a rigid bar; (fig.) rigid; -a economia, rigid economy; strict, rigorous, austere; modi -i, stiff manners; (eng.) non-flexible; (geol.) rigid, competent (of a bed); *n.m.* rigour; extreme cold; questa sera fa —, it is very cold this evening. **-amente** *adv.* rigorously, strictly; obstinately. **-ezza** *f.* strictness, rigour, severity; rigidity; stiffness. **-ità** *f.* rigidity; severity; austerity; (electr.) strength; -ità dielettrica, dielectric strength; (med.) rigidity.

rigiocare [A2] *tr., intr.* (*aux.* avere) (sport) to play again, to replay.

rigir-are [A1] *intr.* (*aux.* essere, avere) to go round about; to walk again; gira e -a, finalmente l'ho trovato, finally, after going round and round, I found it; *tr.* to twist (again); to turn; — la chiave, to give the key another turn; essa lo -a come vuole, she twists him round her little finger; to stir; to surround; un largo viale -a tutta la città, a broad avenue runs all round the town; — tutto il paese, to go round the whole village; — il discorso, to change the subject; — una frase, to turn a phrase, a sentence; — denari, to invest money, to employ money in trade; to deceive; to misrepresent; to consider; sono brutte cose, comunque tu le -i, it's a nasty business, however you look at it; to turn to one's advantage; -arsela, to manage, to do well out of one's business; se la -ino come meglio possono, let them do the best they can; *rfl.* to turn round; to walk about. **-amento** *m.* turning round. **-ata** *f.* (a) turn. **-ato** *part. adj.* surrounded. **-atore** *m.* one who turns or twists; manager, leader; swindler, 'twister'. (**-atrice** *f.*) **-atorello** *m.* (slang) a tricky customer. **-evole** *adj.* easily turned, turning easily. **-io** *m.* continual turning; prowling. **-o** *m.* turning, winding; going to and fro; traffic; buying and selling; trick, subterfuge; -o di parole, rigmarole; -i di parole, circumlocution; far troppi -i di parole, to beat about the bush.

†**rignare** *vb.* and derivs. See **ringhiare**.

ri·go *m.* (*pl.* **-ghi**) line (drawn on paper), line (of writing or printing); scrivimi un — appena puoi, drop me a line as soon as you can; (mus.) line (of the stave); -ghi finti, -ghi addizionali, leger lines (cf. **riga**). **-ghello** *m.* ruler, straightedge, set-square.

rigodone *m.* (mus.) rigaudon, rigadoon.

rigogli-o *m.* exuberance, rankness (of vegetation); luxuriance; in pieno —, in full bloom; il — della giovinezza, the bloom of youth; (archit.) height (of an arch); top, point. **-oso** *adj.* luxuriant; exuberant; in full bloom; full of vigour; salute -osa, exuberant health. (**-osamente** *adv.*)

rigo·golo *m.* (orn.) golden oriole, *Oriolus oriolus*.

rigoletto *m.* (mus.) a kind of round dance; *pr.n.m.* title of an opera by Verdi, in which the title role is that of a clown of that name.

rigolino *m. dim.* of **rigo**, q.v.; little line.

ri·golo *adj.* (Gallicism) funny, ridiculous.

rigolone *m.* (mus.). See **rigodone**.

rigonfi-are [A4c] *tr.* to blow up (again); — il pallone, to blow up the balloon again; *intr.* (*aux.* essere), *rfl.* to swell; (of the sea) to become rough. **-amento** *m.* swelling; tumour; (techn.) bulging, buckling. (**-ato** *part. adj.*)

rigonfio *adj.* swollen, distended; blown up; *n.m.* swelling, tumour; (naut.) prora rigonfia, bluff-bowed.

rigore *m.* extreme cold, rigour; stiffness; (fig.) rigour, severity, strictness; a — di termine, in the strict sense of the term; è di — l'abito nero, evening dress is obligatory; di —, binding; (mil.) prigione di —, detention; (naut.) punishment; arresti di —, close arrest; (comm.) giorni di —, days of grace; hardness, inflexibility; (med.) rigor, rigidity; rigor (shiver); (sport) penalty; calcio di —, penalty kick.

rigor-go *m.* (*pl.* **-ghi**) overflow, gushing out; slight vomiting. **-gare** [A2c] *intr.* (*aux.* avere) to overflow; to gush forth.

rigor-ismo *m.* rigour, rigorousness, strictness; austerity. **-ista** *adj.* rigorist; strict, rigorous; scrupulous; austere; *m.*, *f.* stickler for discipline or etiquette, etc. **-i·stico** *adj.* relating to rigorism. **-ismo** *m.* rigorism.

rigoros-o *adj.* rigorous; strict; severe; (mus.) contrappunto —, strict counterpoint. **-amente** *adv.* rigorously; strictly. **-ità** *f.* strictness, rigorousness; severity.

rigovern-are [A 1] *tr.* to clean, to clean up; to set in order; — i piatti, to wash up, to wash the dishes, (joc.) to eat up (food), to leave a clean plate; (of horses) to groom, to curry; *abs.* to wash up, to do the washing up. **-ata** *f.* washing up, quick clean. (**-ato** *part. adj.*) **-atura** *f.* washing up; washing-up water, dish-water.

riguadagn-are [A 5] *tr.* to earn again; to win back, to recover; to win again; — la stima di uno, to regain someone's good opinion; — la città, to return to the town; — il tempo perduto, to make up for lost time. (**-ato** *part. adj.*)

riguard-are [A 1] *tr.* to look again at, to look over; voglio — la lezione, I want to look over my lesson; to look at attentively; to look at closely; guarda e -a, non ti vedevo, look as I would, I could not see you; to examine carefully, to revise; il lavoro è stato -ato, the work has been revised; to concern; ciò -a me solo, that concerns me alone; ciò non ti -a, that is not your business; to consider; to esteem; to hold in regard; *intr.* (*aux.* avere; *prep.* a) to consider, to have regard (to); — ai poverelli, to have consideration for the poor; — a un fine, to keep an end in view; to look out (upon), to have a view (over); casa che -a in una piazza, house that looks out on to a square; *rfl.* (*prep.* da) to look out (for), to guard (against); to beware (of); bisogna -arsi dalle correnti d'aria, one must beware of draughts; to take care (of); to abstain; -arsi dal bere, to abstain from drinking. **-amento** *m.* look, look over; consideration; circumspection, caution. **-ante** *part. adj.* pertinent; concerned. **-ata** *f.* look, glance; look over. **-ato** *part. adj.* revised; considered; circumspect, wary; on one's guard; looked after, preserved. **-atore** *m.* watcher, observer. (**-atrice** *f.*) **-evole** *m.* respectable, worthy of respect; considerable, remarkable. **-evolmente** *adv.* considerably, remarkably.

riguard-o *m.* regard; respect, consideration; care (esp. for one's health); fare —, to be careful; starsi in —, to be on one's guard; senza — a spesa, without considering the expense; aver poco — per uno, to have little consideration for someone; aver — di, to be rather afraid of, †to mind, to object; persona di —, a most respectable person; per — alla vostra famiglia, out of respect for your family; aver — di, to have regard to, to relate to; in — a, with regard to; per giusti -i, for good reasons; look; benigno —, a kind look; outlook; — a oriente, looking towards the East; (comm.) al — di, re, relating to; *prep.* — (a), concerning, as regards. **-oso** *adj.* careful; circumspect; respectful; considerate, thoughtful; poco -oso, thoughtless. **-osamente** *adv.* thoughtfully; respectfully; carefully, circumspectly.

riguarnire [D 2] *tr.* (eng.) to reline (e.g. a brake).

rigurgit-are [A 1 s] *intr.* (*aux.* avere) to overflow; to regurgitate; to gush out; (fig.) to swarm, to be packed; la piazza -ava di gente, the square was packed with people. **-amento** *m.* overflowing, overflow; backwash. **-ante** *part. adj.* overflowing; swarming; mare -ante di mostri, a sea teeming with monsters. **-ato** *part. adj.* (hydr. eng.) stramazzo -ato, submerged weir.

rigur·gito *m.* backwash, regurgitation; flowing back; overflowing.

rigustare [A 1] *tr.* to taste again.

rilagnare [A 5] *rfl.* to complain again.

rilampeggiare [A 3 c] *intr.* (*aux.* avere) to flash, to lighten again.

rilanci-are [A 3] *tr.* to throw again; to fling again; to hurl back; (poker) 'to raise'; (at an auction) to make a higher bid for. (**-ato** *part. adj.*)

rilan·cio *m.* another throw, throwing again; (at an auction) higher bid.

rilasci-are [A 4] *tr.* to leave again; to let go again; to release; tutti gli arrestati furono -ati, all the arrested men were released; (leg.) to release; to issue; — un passaporto, to issue a passport; — una ricevuta, to give a receipt; — un permesso, to grant permission; (comm.) to deliver, to consign; — una cosa a un prezzo minore, to sell a thing, to let it go, at a lower price; — un'offesa, to waive, to condone, an offence; to ease; to amuse; — l'animo, to relax, to have mental relaxation; *rfl.* to relax, to become slack; to weaken; to go limp; *recip. rfl.* to part, to separate; to leave one another again; *tr.* (naut.) to abandon (a course); — una nave, to release a ship after holding or searching her; †to ease, to check, to pay out (cable, etc.); *intr.* (naut.) to shelter, to seek refuge; to be forced to abandon a course; †to veer. **-amento** *m.* slackening, relaxation; weakening. (**-ato** *part. adj.*)

rila·scio *m.* release; concession; granting; agreed deduction (of pay, etc.); weakening; delivery; (leg.) — di una copia, issue of copy;

(naut.) porto di —, base, storing port; — forzato, unforeseen call or delay in harbour; navigazione di —, calling for orders only.

rilass-are [A 1] *tr.* to slacken, to loosen; to relax; to weaken; †see **rilasciare**; *rfl.* to slacken; to ease up; to become loose. **-amento** *m.* slackening; relaxation; weakening, weariness. **-ante** *part. adj.* laxative. **-atezza** *f.* laxity, looseness; lack of enthusiasm. **-ativo** *adj.* laxative. **-ato** *part. adj.* relaxed; lax, loose. **-atamente** *adv.* laxly; languidly. (**-atore** *m.* **-atrice** *f.*)

rilecc-are [A 2] *tr.* to lick again; (fig.) to put the finishing touches to, to polish up. **-ata** *f.* lick; (fig.) a finishing touch. **-ato** *part. adj.* over-revised, too carefully finished; (of person) all dressed up; affected. (**-atura** *f.*)

rileg-are [A 2] *tr.* to bind again; to tie again; (of books) to bind; (of gems) to set. (**-amento** *m.*) **-ato** *part. adj.* bound again; tied again; (of books) bound. **-atore** *m.* bookbinder. (**-atrice** *f.*) **-atura** *f.* binding; bookbinding; cost of binding.

rileg·gere [C 12] *tr.* to re-read, to read again; leggere e —, to read over and over again; to revise.

rilento *adv. phr.* a —, slowly; andare a —, to go carefully, to proceed with caution, *or* to progress slowly; (comm.) pagare a —, to be slow in paying.

riless-are [A 1] *tr.* to boil (up) again. **-ato** *part. adj.* boiled (up) again; twice cooked.

rilev-are [A 1] *tr.* to take up again; to take off again; to take away; to pick up; to point out, to draw attention to; to notice; non -ai il fatto, I did not notice the fact; — la temperatura di uno, to take someone's temperature; to understand, to realize; to learn, to obtain knowledge of; to take over; -arono l'azienda, they took over the business; to raise again; questa notizia ci ha -ato le speranze, this news has raised our hopes; to relieve; verrò a -arti alle cinque, I will come and take your place at five o'clock; (naut.) to take a compass or relative bearing of; to observe; to take an azimuth of; to relieve (the watch, sentry, leadsman, etc.); †to shift, to recognize, to raise and refloat; (mil.) to take the bearings of; to note the direction and disposition of (e.g. the enemy's position and forces); to relieve; far — le vedette, to have the look-out relieved; (art) to throw into relief; (fig.) — il petto, to throw one's chest out; (archit.) to draw an elevation (or plan); — la pianta di un edificio, to draw the plan of a building; to survey, to plot (for purposes of map-making); *intr.* (*aux.* avere) to rise (with yeast); to work (of liquid in fermentation); to amount to something, to be of consequence; (art) to stand out, to be in relief; *rfl.* to get up again, to stand up again; to rise again; (fig.) to get on one's feet again, to make good; (art) to stand out, to be in relief. **-a·bile** *adj.* (leg.) admitting of legal relief. (**-abilità** *f.*) **-amento** *m.* relief; relieving; survey; (archit.) elevation; drawing (of a plan); (art) prominence; (geol.) prospecting; (naut.) bearing; -amento (alla) bussola, compass bearing; -amento magnetico, magnetic bearing (i.e. corrected for compass deviation due to magnetism of the ship); navigare in linea di -amento, to keep station on a bearing; -amento ortodromico, -amento radiogonio-metrico, wireless bearing; -amento polare, relative bearing (measured in degrees from 0° to 180° either side of a ship); -amento vero, true bearing (corrected for declination and variation); linea di -amento, bearing line; prendere i -amenti, to take bearings in order to get a fix; (radar) bearing. **-ante** *part. adj.* considerable, important; prominent; weighty; spese -anti, heavy expenses. **-anza** *f.* (leg.) consequence(s); importance (C.C.). **-ata·rio** *m.* successor (in a business), purchaser. **-atic·cio** *adj.* self-made, risen from the ranks. **-ato** *part. adj.* raised (again); prominent, elevated; considerable; in relief; (comm.) taken over; *n.m.* height, elevation; high ground; high bank; embankment; (raised) pavement; figure in relief. (**-atamente** *adv.*) **-atore** *m.* one who raises or relieves; relief; field-worker (research, statistics, etc.); †-atore degli uomini, Redeemer of mankind. (**-atrice** *f.*) **-atura** *f.* protuberance, excrescence.

rilevi *m. indecl.* (naut.). See **rilievo**.

rilevo *m.* (pop., Tusc.) rearing; bringing up; child or creature reared.

rilievo *m.* relief, prominence; survey; (bookb., etc.) lavoro a —, embossed work; (needlw.) ricamo in —, raised embroidery; (sculpt.) relief; di —, di tutto —, tondo —, standing out, detached; alto —, high relief; mezzo —, middle relief; basso —, low relief; (paint.; mil.; leg.) relief; (mil.) dare — alla sentinella, to change the sentry; (naut.) bearing; (aeron. navig.) punto d'incontro dei -i,

rilievo (*cont.*)

fix; (fig.) mettere in —, to point out, to draw attention to; di grande —, outstanding, prominent; cose di —, matters of importance; cosa di nessun —, matter of no importance; dar — a, to stress, to give importance to; pubblicare con grande —, to put into headlines; relief map or topographical drawing; elevation, high ground; (fam., Tusc.) leavings (of a meal); (comm.) salvo -i, 'E & O.E' (errors and omissions excepted).

rilisciare [A 3] *tr.* repet. of **lisciare**, q.v.

rilitigare [A 2 s] *intr.* (*aux.* avere) repet. of **litigare**, q.v.

rillo *m.* harrow (without teeth, used after sowing maize).

rilodare [A 1] *tr.* repet. of **lodare**, q.v.

riluccicare [A 2 s] *intr.* (*aux.* avere) repet. of **luccicare**, q.v.

rilu·c-ere [C def.] *intr.* (having no *past part.*, it has no compound tenses) to shine, to be resplendent; to glisten; to be shining, to gleam; to glitter; -ono le stelle, the stars are shining brightly; (provb.) non è tutt'oro quel che -e, all is not gold that glitters; (fig.) to be brilliant, to be outstanding, to shine. -**ente** *part. adj.* shining; glittering; occhi -enti, shining eyes; resplendent; (fig.) illustrious; brilliant. -**entezza** *f.* brilliance, brightness, splendour; lustre.

rilustrare [A 1] *tr.* repet. of **lustrare**, q.v.

rilutt-are [A 1] *intr.* (*aux.* avere) to resist, to be reluctant; to object. -**ante** *part. adj.* reluctant; unwilling; uncooperative; unresponsive. -**anza** *f.* reluctance; con -anza, reluctantly; (electr.) reluctance; -anza specifica, reluctivity.

riluttività *f.* (electr.) reluctivity.

rim-a¹ *f.* rhyme; fare —, to rhyme; — piana, feminine rhyme; — tronca, masculine rhyme; — al mezzo, internal rhyme; — baciata, rhymed couplets; terza —, a three-line system of rhyming used by Dante in the *Divina Commedia*; ottava —, heroic stanzas of eight lines (as used by Ariosto in *Orlando Furioso*); (fig.) rispondere ad uno per le -e, to pay someone back in his own coin, (in fourteenth century) to reply to a sonnet by writing another with the same rhymes; volete che ve la canti in —?, do you want me to tell you straight out?; *pl.* poems; collection of poems. -**eri·a** *f.* (joc.) a lot of rhymes.

rima² *f.* crack, fissure; opening, slit.

rimacchiare¹ [A 4] *tr.* to stain again; to soil again (cf. **macchiare**).

rimacchiare² [A 4] *intr.* (*aux.* avere) to write a few lines of verse.

rimacinare [A 1 s] *tr.* to grind again, to regrind (cf. **macinare**).

rimaledire [B 10] *tr.* repet. of **maledire**, q.v.

rimalmezzo *f.* See 'rima al mezzo', under **rima¹**.

rimand-are [A 1] *tr.* to send again; to send back; to send away, to dismiss; to postpone, to put off, to defer; (in examinations) to refer; (mil.) to defer (a call-up); — una classe di leva, to discharge a national service class; to refer; — a una pagina, to refer to a page; (fig.) -arla giù, to swallow (e.g. an insult, one's words); — da Erode a Pilato, to send from pillar to post. -**ato** *part. adj.* sent again; sent back; postponed, deferred; rejected; (in an examination) referred (e.g. in a particular subject).

rimando *m.* sending back; postponement; (in ball games) return; (tennis) colpo di —, return of service; di —, in reply; cosa egli chiedeva da te, e cosa tu di — pretendevi da lui?, what did he ask of you and what did you expect of him in return?; reference (to another page, etc.); (eng.) intermediate control, hook-up.

rimaneggi-are [A 3 c] *tr.* to change, to alter; to rehandle; to remodel; to rearrange; to recompose, to readjust. -**amento** *m.* rehandling; remodelling; rearrangement, alteration; readjustment, revision, revised edition. (-**ato** *part. adj.*)

riman-ere [B 2 s] *intr.* (*aux.* essere) to stay, to remain; — a casa, to keep indoors, to stay at home; gli rimase un figlio, he had one son left, one son survived; to be left over; to stop, to leave off (e.g. in a story); dove siamo rimasti?, where did we get to?; (following 'ci') to die; cadde da un albero e ci rimase, he fell out of a tree and was killed; — sotto (una macchina), to be run over; — ucciso, to be slain; to remain speechless, or bewildered; a vederlo, son rimasto!, when I saw him I didn't know what to say, or do; — male, to be in trouble; sono rimasto molto male, I was very upset; — a corto di, to run short of; sono rimasto senza benzina, I have run out of petrol; to be situated; -e a destra del Duomo, it is (situated) to the right of the Cathedral; to agree; rimasero che loro avrebbero pagato le spese, they agreed that they would pay expenses; foll. by *prep.* 'a'; to be attributed to, to be owned by; to depend upon; se -esse a me, sarei già partito,

if it depended on me, I should have gone already; to cease; la lotta fratricida non -e mai, the fratricidal strife never ceases; †non -e da (per) lui, it is not his fault. -**ente** *part. adj.* remaining; left over; gli scolari -enti, the rest of the pupils; *n.m.* rest, remainder; residue; essere del -ente, to be left over; person succeeding, successor; *pl.* i -enti, the people who are left or who remain, those remaining; *adv. phr.* nel -ente, nevertheless, for the rest, moreover. -**enza** *f.* (comm.) residue; remainder; -enza a saldo, balance due; (electr.) remanence; hysteresis.

rimangi-are [A 3] *tr.* to eat again; to eat some more of; — una promessa, to go back on one's word; (Tusc.) to browbeat; *rfl.* (dat. of prn. 'si') to recant; si -a quello che ha detto, he has gone back on what he said, he has retracted what he said. (-**ato** *part. adj.*)

rimar-care [A 2] *tr.* (Gallicism) to mark again; to note, to notice, to draw attention to. -**ca·bile**, -**che·vole** *adj.* remarkable, important.

rimarco *m.* (Gallicism) remark; note; reproof, censure.

rim-are¹ [A 1] *tr.* to compose in rhyme, to write in verse; to rhyme; sto -ando un sonetto, I am composing a sonnet; *intr.* (*aux.* avere) to write poetry; — d'amore, to write love-poems; to rhyme, to be in rhyme. -**ante** *part. adj.* rhyming; in rhyme. -**a·rio** *m.* dictionary of rhymes; concordance to a particular poetical work giving a list of rhymes; -**ato** *part. adj.* rhyming; in rhyme; rhymed; parole -ate, verses. -**atore** *m.* versifier, poet. (-**atrice** *f.*)

†**rimare²** *tr.* to investigate.

rimargin-are [A 1 s] *tr.* to draw edges together (esp. of a wound); to heal (also fig.); *rfl.*, *intr.* (*aux.* essere) (of wounds) to heal. (-**ato** *part. adj.*)

rima·rio *m.* See under **rimare¹**.

rimarit-are [A 1] *tr.*, *rfl.* to remarry. (-**ato** *part. adj.*)

†**rimas-a** *f.* remaining, staying behind. †-**o** *part.* of **rimanere** (cf. **rimasto**); *n.m.* remainder.

rimastic-are [A 2 s] *tr.* to masticate again, to chew thoroughly; to ruminate, to chew the cud of; (fig.) to meditate upon, to ponder, to turn over in one's mind; — le parole, to mumble. (-**ato** *part. adj.*) -**atura** *f.* remasticating; ruminating; pondering.

rimasto *part.* of **rimanere**, q.v.; *adj.* left, left over, remaining; surviving; — al verde, without money, 'broke' (cf. under **candela**); — fuori, shut out; — di stucco, 'thunderstruck', astonished.

rimas·u·glio *m.* remainder, residue; l'ultimo — di vigore, the last ounce of strength; *pl.* scraps, left-overs, leavings. -**u·gliolo** *m.* (pop., Tusc.) see **rimasuglio**.

rimbacuccare [A 2] *tr.* to wrap up again, or more thoroughly; *rfl.* to wrap oneself up again; to wrap oneself up warmly.

rimbaldanzire [D 2] *tr.*, *intr.* (*aux.* avere) repet. and intens. of **imbaldanzire**, q.v.

†**rimbald-era** *f.* clamorous greeting. †-**ire** *tr.* to encourage, to cheer.

rimballare¹ [A 1] *tr.* to pack up again.

rimballare² [A 1] *intr.* (*aux.* avere) to bounce, to be shaken up; to jog.

rimbalz-are [A 1] *intr.* (*aux.* essere, avere) to rebound; to bounce back; to bounce; (mil.) to ricochet; *tr.* to send back, to return (e.g. a ball); to reflect. (-**ato** *part. adj.*) -**a·toio** *m.* surface favouring rebound. -**atura** *f.* rebounding, rebound. -**ello** *m.* game of ducks and drakes; fare, giocare a -ello, to play ducks and drakes. -**ino** *m.* game played by bouncing coins against a wall. -**o** *m.* rebound; bounce; di -o, on the rebound, (fig.) indirectly; (mil.) colpo di -o, ricochet; (telev.) relay television.

rimbambinire [D 2] *intr.* (*aux.* essere) to become babyish; to grow childish.

rimbamb-ire [D 2] *intr.* (*aux.* essere) to enter one's second childhood, to grow childish in old age. -**imento** *m.* becoming childish; second childhood. -**ito** *part. adj.* grown childish again; un vecchio -ito, an old man in his second childhood. -**olire** [D 2] (pop. Tusc.) see **rimbambire**.

rimbarbarire [D 2] *tr.*, *intr.* (*aux.* essere) repet. of **imbarbarire**, q.v.

rimbarbogire [D 2] *intr.* (*aux.* essere) to enter upon one's dotage, to become a dotard.

rimbarc-are [A 2] *tr.* to put on board ship again; *rfl.*, *intr.* (*aux.* essere) to re-embark. -**ato** *part. adj.* re-embarked; trave -ata, curved beam; (fig.) vecchio -ato dagli anni, old man bent under the weight of years. -**o** *m.* re-embarkation, re-embarking.

rimbastire [D 2] *tr.* repet. of **imbastire**, q.v.

†**rimbatto** *m.* (naut.). See 'salto di vento', under **vento**.

rimbecc-are [A 2 c] *tr.* to answer back; to retort; — il colpo, to return blow for blow; — la palla, to return the ball; *recip. rfl.* to peck one another; (fig.) to bicker. (**-ato** *part. adj.*)

rimbęc-co *m.* (*pl.* **-chi**) retort, smart reply; risponde sempre di —, he always has an answer; pecking at one another; bickering.

rimbecill-ire [D 2] *intr.* (*aux.* essere) to become more and more stupid, to grow sillier. (**-ito** *part. adj.*)

rimbellire [D 2] *tr.* to make beautiful, to embellish; to make beautiful again or more beautiful still; *intr.* (*aux.* essere), *rfl.* to become beautiful; to grow more beautiful (**-ito** *part. adj.*)

†**rimbeltempire** *intr.* (of weather) to become fine, to clear up.

†**rimberciare** *tr.* to patch.

rimbiancare [A 2] *tr.* to whiten again (cf. **imbiancare**); *intr.* (*aux.* essere) (pop., Tusc.) to become white; to turn white.

†**rimbiondare** *vb.* and derivs. See **rimbiondire**.

rimbiondire [D 2] *tr.* to make fair or blonde; *intr.* (*aux.* essere) to become fair, to turn blonde.

rimbocc-are [A 2 c] *tr.* to turn up (e.g. one's sleeves, trousers, etc.); to fold in (e.g. the top of a sack); — il lenzuolo, to turn down the sheet; (needlw.) to turn up, to put a hem in; to fill up (e.g. a half-empty bottle); il vento -a il fumo nella cappa del camino, the wind blows the smoke down the chimney; (mil.) to spike or blow up; — le artiglierie nemiche, to spoil the enemy's guns, by firing them with the muzzle choked and thus causing it to split, i.e. to tulip; (agric.) — la terra, to turn over the soil; — la siepe, to trim the hedge; †to overturn, to upset; †to spill; †to overflow. (**-amęnto** *m.*) **-ato** *part. adj.* turned up; tucked up; folded back, in; turned down; (fam.) poorly, not very well; (herald.) turned up. **-atura** *f.* tuck; turn-up; turn down; fare la -atura nel letto, to turn down the sheet or bedclothes.

rimbǫc-co *m.* (*pl.* **-chi**) turn-up; tuck, wide hem; †overflow; †disturbance.

rimbomb-are [A I c] *intr.* (*aux.* avere) to thunder, to roar; la voce del cannone -a, the cannon roars; to reverberate, to re-echo; to resound; una voce che -a, a booming voice. **-amęnto** *m.* thundering, roaring; reverberation. **-ante** *part. adj.* thundering, booming; reverberating; periodi -anti, resounding periods. **-io** *m.* (*pl.* **-ii**) continued roaring; rumbling.

rimbǫmb-o *m.* roar; thundering; reverberation; (fig., joc., of speeches, etc.) noise, bombast. **-ǫso** *adj.* noisy, loud, resounding.

rimbors-are [A I c] *tr.* to repay; to refund, to pay back, to reimburse; to put back into a sack or bag; *rfl.* to reimburse oneself; to obtain repayment. **-a·bile** *adj.* repayable; payable. (**-abilità** *f.*) **-amęnto** *m.* reimbursing. **-ato** *part. adj.* reimbursed; refunded.

rimbǫrso *m.* repayment; reimbursement; refund.

rimbosc-are [A 2 c] *tr.* to replant with trees; to carry out reafforestation in; *rfl.* to take to the woods, to hide in a forest. **-amęnto** *m.* reafforestation. **-ato** *part. adj.* replanted with trees.

rimbosch-ire [D 2] and derivs. see **rimboscare**. **-imęnto** *m.* (agric.) afforestation.

rimbręnci-o, -olo *m.* rag, tatter; scrap. **-olǫso** *adj.* ragged, in tatters; hanging in shreds.

rimbrividire [D 2] *intr.* (*aux.* essere, avere) to shiver, to shudder.

†**rimbroc·cio** *m.* reproof.

rimbrodolare [A I s] *tr.* (fam., Tusc.) to try to conceal, to cover up; to make excuses for; †to daub; †to soil.

rimbrott-are [A I] *tr.* to scold, to reproach, to rebuke; to taunt; *recip. rfl.* to reproach one another, to indulge in mutual recriminations. (**-ato** *part. adj.* **-atǫre** *m.* **-atrice** *f.*) **-ęvole** *adj.* scolding; full of reproaches; taunting.

rimbrotto *m.* reproach, rebuke; *pl.* fault-finding.

rimbrun-are [A I] *intr.* (*aux.* essere) to get darker. **-ire** [D 2] *intr.* (*aux.* essere), *rfl.* to get darker; (fig.) to become gloomy. **-ito** *part. adj.* darkened; darker.

rimbruscolare [A I s] *tr.* to scrape together.

rimbruttire [D 2] *intr.* (*aux.* essere) to grow ugly again; to grow uglier.

rimbuc-are [A 2] *tr.* to drive into a hole (again); to put in the wash again; *intr.* (*aux.* essere), *rfl.* to go into a hole (again); to hide. (**-ato** *part. adj.*)

rimbucciare [A 3] *rfl.* (of an animal) to grow clean or healthy skin again.

rimbuire[1] [D 2] *intr.* (*aux.* essere) to become darker.

rimbuire[2] [D 2] *intr.* (*aux.* essere) to become more 'ox-like', i.e. stupid.

rimbussolare [A I s] *tr.* to shake up again (in a ballot-box, etc.); (joc.) to beat; *abs.* (Tusc.) to shake numbers, lottery tickets, etc. in a container.

rimbuzzare [A I] *rfl.* (fam., Tusc.) to eat too much; rimbuzzarsi di, to stuff oneself with.

rimedi-are [A 4] *intr.* (*aux.* avere; *prep.* a) to provide a remedy (for); (provb.) a tutto si -a fuorchè alla morte, while there's life there's hope; — al tempo perduto, to make up for lost time; *tr.* to remedy, to cure, to put right; to mend; vediamo se si -a, let's see if it can be mended; to put together, to make up; lavora tanto da — il pranzo, he works enough to earn his dinner; — appena il necessario per vivere, to scrape a living; -arla, to rub along, to make just enough to live on; *abs.* come si -a?, what can we do to put things right? **-a·bile** *adj.* remediable; non è più -abile, nothing can be done about it now; è cosa -abile, it can be put right, mended, remedied. **-ato** *part. adj.* remedied; mended; put right; put together hastily or carelessly; una cena -ata, a 'scratch' supper. (**-atǫre** *m.* **-atrice** *f.*)

rimedicare [A 2 s] *tr.* repet. of **medicare**, q.v.

rime·dio *m.* remedy; cure; non c'è —, it can't be cured, *or* it can't be helped, there's no way out of it; che non ha —, irremediable, incurable; medicine, medicament; precaution; (leg.) — di legge, remedial law; advantage, behoof; il re fece fare una badia per — dell'anima di suo padre, the king built an abbey for the repose of his father's soul.

†**rimedire** *tr.* to ransom; to procure.

rimeditare [A I s] *tr.* repet. of **meditare**, q.v.

rimembr-are [A I] *tr.* (poet.) to recall, to remember; *intr.* (*aux.* avere), *impers.* to be remembered, to come to one's mind; mi -a, I remember; *rfl.* (acc. of *prn.* 'si'; *prep.* di) to remember, to recall. **-ante** *part. adj.* (poet.) mindful. **-anza** *f.* remembrance; memory; recollection; parco delle -anze, field or garden of remembrance (war memorial). (**-ato** *part adj.*)

rimen-are [A I] *tr.* to bring again; to bring back; to handle; (Tusc.) to knead, to mix thoroughly; *rfl.* to be bustling and stirring; *n.m.* un gran -arsi, a great stir. (**-amęnto** *m.*) **-ata** *f.* handling; mixing, kneading. (**-ato** *part. adj.*) **-io** *m.* (*pl.* **-ii**) continued stirring; far -io, to do one's best, to exert oneself. †**-o** *m.* return.

rimendare [A I] and derivs. See **rammendare**.

rimenio *m.* See under **rimenare**.

rimeri·a *f.* See under **rima**[1].

rimerit-are [A I s] *tr.* to recompense, to reward; to requite; to repay, to pay back. **-a·bile** *adj.* that can be repaid; benefici che non sono -abili, favours that cannot be repaid. **-amęnto** *m.* recompense, reward; requital. **-ato** *part. adj.* recompensed, rewarded; requited; repaid, paid back.

rime·rito *m.* recompense; reward.

rimęscere [c def.] *tr. repet.* of **mescere**, q.v.

rimescol-are [A I sc] *tr.* to mix up; to stir; to stir up; to stir again; to rummage among; (cards) to shuffle; (fig.) sono cose che fan — il sangue, these things make one's blood run cold *or* make one tingle with excitement; *rfl.* to interfere (in); to be upset; (of the sea) to get rough; (of emotion) to be aroused; appena sentivo la sua voce, che mi si -ava il sangue, as soon as ever I heard his voice, my heart leapt for joy. **-amęnto** *m.* mixing up; stirring up; (cards) shuffling; shivering, quivering. **-anza** *f.* mixture, blend. **-ata** *f.* mixing; stir. (**-ato** *part. adj.*) **-io** *m.* (*pl.* **-ii**) continued (or frequent) mixing, stirring, shaking up; bustling; confusion; -io di gente, moving, jostling crowd; thrill, agreeable feeling of excitement.

rimęscolo *m.* (pop., Tusc.) emotional upset, agitation.

rimęssa *f.* remission; sending back; return; (motor., etc.) — in marcia, restarting; (watchm.) bascula di — a zero, fly-back lever; (tennis, etc.) return; (football) — laterale, throw-in; (rugby) line-out; (leg.) remittance; entry (in current account) (C.C.); (comm.) consignment; delivery; remittance; transfer; — di valori, remittance; *pl.* -e degli emigranti, remittances from emigrants abroad; †(naut.) see **resa**; (mil.) vehicle park; shed; coach-house; — di automobili, garage; — per aeroplani, hangar; mews, stables; — delle vacche, cow-house, cow-shed; store, provisions; harvest.

rimessiǫne *f.* remission; (leg.) — della causa al collegio, setting-down of case for trial; — al primo giudice, sending back of case to Court of first instance; — in termine, reopening of time for entering appearance (C.C.P.).

rimessitic·c-io *m.* (agric.) root-sucker; gettare -i, to send out root-suckers; (genealogy) inferior strain introduced into a family.

rimẹss-o *part.* of **rimettere**, q.v.; *adj.* returned, (put, come) back; restored, recovered; un ammalato —, a patient who has recovered; il negozio è tutto — a nuovo, the shop has been completely done up; remitted; slow; placid; careless; submissive, mild, meek; (mus.) intervallo —, diminished interval; *n.m.* (paint.) retouching; (techn.) lavoro di —, marquetry, inlaid work. **-amẹnte** *adv.* submissively, mildly, meekly.

rimest-are [A I] *tr.* to stir (up) again; to shake up; (fig.) to raise again; è inutile — queste vecchie questioni, it is useless bringing up these old matters again. **†-a** *f.* stirring up; reproof. **-ato** *part. adj.* brought up again; stirred up. **-atọre** *m.* agitator. (**-atrice** *f.*)

rimẹtt-ere [C 20] *tr.* to put back; to put on again; to put in again; — insieme, to put together again; — a nuovo, to renew, to make like new again; — in discussione, to bring up for discussion again; to refer, to submit; ~iamo la questione ad un arbitro, let us submit the question to arbitration; to remit, to forgive; -i a noi i nostri debiti, forgive us our trespasses; to entrust; to lose; ci ho rimesso mille lire, I have lost a thousand lire (by the transaction); ci ho rimesso la salute, I have ruined my health (by so doing, thereby); — in salute, to restore to health; — lo stomaco a, to sharpen the appetite of; — il cibo, to vomit; — i fossi, to clear the ditches; — in piedi, to restore, to revive, to re-establish; — in giuoco, to bring into play again; — in palla, to restore; — la palla (al giuocatore), to return the ball (to the player); to correct; — l'orologio, to put the clock right; — una gamba, to set a (fractured) leg; to supply replacements for; — il tempo perduto, to make up for lost time; — il sonno perduto, to catch up on one's sleep; to postpone, to defer; to abate, to diminish; to lower; — la voce, to lower one's voice; (comm.) to remit, to consign; to hand over; to deliver; (gambling) — su, to lay another stake; *intr.* (*aux.* avere) to put up, to put by; to garage; (of plants) to sprout, to shoot again; to do inlaid work, to do marquetry; *rfl.* (acc. of *prn.* 'si') to set oneself again; ~ersi in via, to set out again; to place oneself again; to be restored; ~ersi a letto, to go back to bed; ~ersi in salute, to get well again; (of weather) ~ersi a buono, to clear up, to become fine again; ~ersi da, to recover from (e.g. fear, confusion, excitement); to resign oneself, to refer (to), to submit (to); ~ersi a, to rely on; ci ~iamo in tutto a voi, we leave it all to you, we rely on you; (dat. of *prn.* 'si') ~ersi i guanti, to put on one's gloves again. **-ag·gio** *m.* (text.) draft, pass; drawing-in, linking the warp yarn into chain. (**-itọre** *m.* **-itọra**, **-itrice** *f.*) **-itura** *f.* putting back, etc.; setting (a fracture).

rimir-are [A I] *tr.* to stare at, to gaze at; to behold; to look with admiration at; to gaze at again; (fig.) to keep one's eye on. (**-ato** *part. adj.*)

rimischiare [A 4] *repet.* of **mischiare**, q.v.

rimiṣurare [A I] *tr. repet.* of **misurare**, q.v.

rimmelensire [D 2] *intr.* (*aux.* essere) to become sillier, to grow more stupid (cf. **melenso**).

rimminchion-ire [D 2] *intr.* (*aux.* essere) to become silly or foolish; è cosa da far —, it's enough to drive you silly. **-ito** *part. adj.* grown silly or foolish; *n.m.* fool.

rimoderare [A I s] *tr. repet.* of **moderare**, q.v.

rimodern-are [A I s] *tr.* to modernize; to remake, to remodel; *rfl.* to undergo modernization; to become up to date, to move with the times. **-amẹnto** *m.* modernization; remaking, remodelling. **-ato** *part. adj.* modernized; brought up to date; remade, remodelled on modern lines. **-atọre** *m.*; *adj.* modernizing. (**-atrice** *f.*) **-atura** *f.* modernization; modernizing; redecoration in modern style.

rimodulazịọne *f.* (electr.) remodulation.

rimond-are [A I c] *tr.* to clean; to clear out (drains, ditches, etc.); to clean again; (hort.) to lop; (fig.) to purify; *rfl.* to clear oneself out, to clear one's complexion. **-amẹnto** *m.* cleaning out, clearing. **-ato** *part. adj.* clean, cleaned out; cleared; bare; shaven. (**-atọre** *m.* **-atrice** *f.*) **-atura** *f.* cleaning up; clearing out; refuse; rubbish cleared away; (hort.) prunings.

rimọndo *apocop. part.* of **rimondare**; *adj.* clean; cleared; (hort.) lopped.

rimọnta *f.* (mil.) remounting, renewal of cavalry; (shoem.) resoling; (eng.) reassembly; (mining) slant.

rimont-are [A I c] *intr.* (*aux.* avere) to remount, to get on horseback again; (*aux.* essere) to go up again; — su per le scale, to go upstairs again; to go back; questa istituzione -a al medio evo, this institution goes back to the Middle Ages; (naut.) — al vento, to work up to windward; *tr.* to remount; to go up again; — le scale, to go upstairs (again), to remount the stairs; to put together again, to reassemble (watch, machine); — una pendola, to wind up a clock; (sport) — i concorrenti, to catch up, to overtake, other competitors; (mil.) to remount; — soldati, to restore horses to dismounted troops; — cavalieri, to remount a cavalry unit, i.e. to provide fresh horses; (eng.) to reassemble, to refit; (naut.) to go against (tide, current, wind); — una costa, to work up a coast; — un promontorio, to round a headland; — il fiume, to go up river; — la rada, to go up harbour; — il timone, to ship the rudder. (**-ato** *part. adj.*)

†rimorbid-are, -ire *vb.* See **rammorbidire**.

rimor·chi-o *m.* (naut.) tow; vessel or object towed; cable, wire, or hemp used for towing; banchina da —, towpath; — bersaglio, target-towing craft; braca da —, towing pennant; fanale di —, towing light; a —, in tow, avere a —, to have in tow; chiedere —, to ask for a tow; dare —, to take in tow, to give tow; essere a —, trovarsi a —, to be in tow; lasciare il —, mollare il —, to cast off tow, to slip; prendere a —, to carry out the operation necessary for towing; (motor.) trailer; — a pianale, flat bed trailer; (fig.) avere una donna a —, to have a woman in tow; (comm.) spese di —, towage; trailer; cavo di —, towrope, towline; gancio di —, towing hook, pintle hook. **-amẹnto** *m.* towing. **-are** [A 4] *tr.* (naut.) to tow; (motor., etc.) to tow, to take in tow, to drag along; (fig.) to lug; già ci -amo dietro otto valige, we're already lugging eight cases along with us; (joc.) -are una donna, to have a woman tagging along. (**-ato** *part. adj.*) **-atọre** *m.* (naut.) tug, towing vessel. **-atrice** *adj. f.* (naut.) una nave -atrice, a towing vessel.

rimor·d-ere [C 3] *tr.* to bite again; to sting again; (fig.) to torment, to prick; mi -e la coscienza di non aver fatto ciò, my conscience keeps pricking me for not having done that; to rebuke; to reprove; *abs.* to occasion remorse. **-ente** *part. adj.* tormenting; causing remorse. **-imẹnto** *m.* remorse; -imento di coscienza, pricking of conscience.

†rimore *m.* See **rumore**.

rimọrso *part.* of **rimordere**, q.v.; *adj.* bitten again; stung again; tormented; *n.m.* remorse; provare il —, to feel remorse; non ho -i, I have no regrets.

rimọrto *adj.* dead as a door-nail; withered away, shrivelled up.

rimọsso *part.* of **rimuovere**, q.v.; *adj.* removed; taken away; †remote.

rimostr-are [A I] *tr.* to show again; to redemonstrate; to make known again; *abs.* to remonstrate. **-ante** *part. adj.* stating a case; remonstrating; *n.m.pl.* (eccl. hist.) Remonstrants. **-anza** *f.* remonstrance; fare una -anza a, to remonstrate with; complaint; representation; †demonstration.

rimọt-o *adj.* remote; distant; secluded. **-amẹnte** *adv.* remotely; distantly.

rimo·v-ere [C 15] see **rimuovere**. **-ente** *part. adj.* deterrent. **-i·bile** *adj.* removable. **-imẹnto** *m.* removal; dismissal. **-itọre** *m.* remover. (**-itrice** *f.*)

rimoziọne *f.* removal; removing; dismissal; (school) expulsion, suspension; (mil.) — dal grado, reduction of rank; (leg.) removal; — dei sigilli, removal of seals.

rimpacchettare [A I c] *repet.* or *intens.* of **impacchettare**, q.v.

rimpaciare [A 3] and derivs. (Tusc.). See **rappaciare** and **rappacificare**.

rimpadronire [D 2] *rfl. repet.* of **impadronire**, q.v.

rimpaginare [A I s] and derivs. See **impaginare**.

rimpagli-are [A 4] *tr.* to pack in straw again; to reseat (a straw-seated chair). (**-ato** *part. adj.* **-atọre** *m.* **-atrice** *f.* **-atura** *f.*)

rimpall-are [A I] *intr.* (*aux.* avere) (billiards) to cannon. **-o** *m.* (billiards) cannon.

rimpalud-are [A I] *rfl.* to revert to marshland. (**-ato** *part. adj.*)

rimpannucci-are [A 3] *tr.* to clothe better; *rfl.* to wear better clothes; to improve one's material prosperity. (**-ato** *part. adj.*)

rimpantan-are [A I] *rfl.* to sink in the mud again; (fig.) to return to vicious habits. (**-ato** *part. adj.*)

rimparare [A I] *tr. repet.* of **imparare**, q.v.

†rimparo *m.* (mil.) bastion.

rimpast-are [A I] *tr.* to knead again; to mix up again; (fig.) to recompose; to rearrange, to reconstitute; to recast; to revise. (**-ato** *part. adj.*) **-o** *m.* recomposition, reshuffle; -o ministeriale, Cabinet reshuffle.

rimpasticci-are [A 3] *tr.* to botch again; to make a mess of again; to think up excuses for. (**-amẹnto** *m.* **-ato** *part. adj.*)

rimpatri-are [A4] *intr.* (*aux.* avere or essere), *rfl.* to return home (to one's native land or town); *tr.* to repatriate, to send home (to one's own country or town). (**-ato** *part. adj.*)

rimpa·trio *m.* repatriation, return home; restitution, return to one's own country of territory formerly belonging to it; (leg.) — con foglio di via obbligatorio, compulsory repatriation (esp. to birthplace) by police (C.P.).

†**rimpecciare** *tr.* to bump into, to hurtle against.

rimpegnare [A5c] *tr. repet.* of **impegnare**, q.v.

rimpennare [A1] *tr. repet.* of **impennare**, q.v.

†**rimpetta·io** *adj.* opposite.

rimpettinare [A1s] *tr.* (techn.) to put back into the carding machine.

rimpett-ire [D2] *intr.* (*aux.* essere), *rfl.* to swell with pride. **-ito** *part. adj.* full of pride, bursting with pride or conceit.

rimpetto *adv.* opposite; face to face; *prep. phr.* di — a, opposite, facing (cf. **dirimpetto**).

rimpiaccic-are [A2s], **-ottare** [A1] *tr.* (Tusc.) to stick, to bung, together.

rimpiallacciare [A3] *tr.* (techn.) to veneer again.

rimpian·gere [C5] *tr.* to regret; to lament; †to sympathize with.

rimpianto *part.* of **rimpiangere**, q.v.; *adj.* regretted; lamented; il — Signor Bruni, the late Mr Brown; *n.m.* regret; il —, the late lamented, the dear departed.

rimpiastr-are [A1], **-icciare** [A3] *tr. repet.* of **impiastrare, impiastricciare**, q.v.

rimpiatt-are [A1] *tr.* to hide, to conceal; *rfl.* to creep away and hide; (fig.) può andare a -arsi, he is quite put in the shade. (**-ato** *part. adj.*) **-erello, -ino** *m.* (Tusc.) hide and seek; fare a -ino, to play hide and seek.

rimpiazz-are [A1] *tr.* (Gallicism) to replace, to substitute. (**-ato** *part. adj.*) **-o** *m.* substitute, replacement.

rimpiccin-ire [D2] *tr.* to dwarf; *intr.* (*aux.* essere) to become smaller. (**-ito** *part. adj.*)

rimpicc(i)ol-ire [D2] *tr.* to make smaller; *rfl.* to lessen, to decrease. (**-imento** *m.* **-ito** *part. adj.*)

rimpiegare [A2] *tr. repet.* of **impiegare**, q.v.; (finan.) to reinvest.

rimpie-go *m.* (*pl.* **-ghi**) see **impiego**; (finan.) reinvestment.

rimpigrire [D2] *intr. repet.* of **impigrire**, q.v.

rimpincon-ire [D2] *intr.* (*aux.* essere) (vulg.) to become silly, stupid. (**-ito** *part. adj.*)

rimpinguare [A6] *tr. repet.* of **impinguare**.

rimpinz-are [A1] *tr.* to stuff, to cram; *rfl.* (*acc.* of *prn.* 'si') to stuff oneself; to overeat; (*dat.* of *prn.* 'si') -arsi la testa di romanticherie, to stuff one's head with romantic ideas. (**-amento** *m.* **-ato** *part. adj.*)

rimpiombare [A1c] *tr. repet.* of **impiombare**, q.v.

rimpippiare [A4] *intr.* (*aux.* essere), *rfl.* to eat too much, to stuff.

rimpiumare [A1] *rfl.* to grow fresh feathers.

rimpollare [A1] *intr.* (*aux.* essere) to sprout again from the root.

rimpolp-are [A1c] *intr.* (*aux.* essere), *rfl.* to put on flesh, to grow fat; to become rich; *tr.* to fatten; (fig.) to enrich, to adorn. (**-ato** *part. adj.*)

rimpolpett-are [A1c] *tr.* to cover up (e.g. an indiscreet remark); to recast, to adapt; un dramma francese -ato all'italiana, a French play in an Italian adaptation; to scold, to rate soundly; *rfl.* to adapt oneself, to make oneself tidy. (**-ato** *part. adj.*)

†**rimpolsare** *tr.* to reinvigorate.

rimpoltronire [D2] *tr. repet.* or *intens.* of **impoltronire**, q.v.

rimpoverire [D2] *tr., intr. repet.* or *intens.* of **impoverire**, q.v.

rimpozzare [A1] *intr.* (*aux.* essere) (of water, etc.) to lie in pools, to have no outlet.

†**rimprocciare** *vb.* and derivs. See **rimproverare**.

†**rimproperare** *vb.* and derivs. See **rimproverare**.

rimprosciuttire [D2] *intr.* (*aux.* essere) to become lean, thin, or withered-looking.

rimprover-are [A1s] *tr.* to reprove, to rebuke, to reproach; mi -ò la mia ostinazione, he reproved me for my obstinacy; mi -i a torto, you are wrong to reproach me; to taunt with; — un favore, to remind of a favour for which one is ungrateful; to reprimand, to scold; l'insegnante -ò severamente il ragazzo, the teacher reprimanded the boy severely; (*prep.* a) to grudge (to); mi -a anche un tozzo di pane, he grudges me even a crust of bread; *rfl.* (*prep.* di) to reproach oneself (with); to repent (of); non aver nulla da -arsi, to have nothing to reproach oneself with. **-amento** *m.* reproof; reproach. **-abile** *adj.* blameworthy. (**-ato** *part. adj.* **-atore** *m.* **-atrice** *f.*)

rimpro·vero *m.* reproof, reproach; reprimand, rebuke; blame; fare dei rimproveri a, to reproach, to rebuke.

rimpulizz-ire [D2] *tr.* to clean (up); to tidy; to whitewash, to redecorate; *rfl.* to make oneself clean and tidy. (**-ito** *part. adj.*)

rimugin-are [A1s] *tr.* to turn over and over; to stir; (fig.) to keep on turning over in one's mind; *abs.* to rummage, to turn things upside down; mi sono sentito — tutto, I was quite upset. (**-ato** *part. adj.*)

†**ri·mula** *f.* crack, fissure.

rimuner-are [A1s] *tr.* to reward, to recompense, to remunerate; che -a, rewarding, profitable, remunerative. **-amento** *m.* rewarding; remunerating. **-ativo** *adj.* rewarding, remunerative, profitable. (**-ato** *part. adj.*) **-atore** *m.* one who rewards or remunerates. (**-atrice** *f.*) **-ato·rio** *adj.* (*m.pl.* **-atorii**) remunerative. **-azione** *f.* recompense, remuneration; reward; -azione del lavoro, remuneration for one's work.

rimun-ire [D2] *tr.* to refurnish; †to refurbish. (**-ito** *part. adj.*)

rimuo·v-ere [C15] *tr.* to move again; to remove; to clear away; to put away; fu rimosso dalla carica, he was deprived of his office; to keep away; deserto che -e ogni pianta, desert that allows no plant to grow; to deter; dobbiamo -erlo da tale proposito, we must deter him from such a purpose; (leg.) to remove; to take off; †to seduce; *rfl.* to withdraw; -ersi da alcuno, to dissent from someone; non -ersi, to stand firm, to persist, not to yield.

rimur-are [A1] *tr.* to brick up again; to rebuild. (**-ato** *part. adj.*)

rimut-are [A1] *tr.* to change again; to change; le prove più convincenti non riuscirono a -arlo, the clearest proofs did not succeed in shaking his opinion; *rfl.* to change one's mind. **-abile** *adj.* changeable; fickle. (**-abilità** *f.*) **-amento** *m.* change; change of mind. **-ato** *part. adj.* changed; corrected, emended. **-azione** *f.* change (of opinion, etc.); alteration; correction. **-evole** *adj.* changeable, fickle.

rinacerb-ire [D2] *tr.* to embitter; quella notizia ha -ito il suo dolore, that piece of news has aggravated his grief; *intr.* (*aux.* essere), *rfl.* to become embittered. (**-ito** *part. adj.*)

rinald-esca, -essa *n.f. adj.* (agric.) kind of grape and vine.

Rinaldo *pr.n.m.* Reginald; Rinaldo of Montalbano, hero of several epic poems in old French and later Italian imitations.

rin-algi·a *f.* (med.) rhinalgia. **-al·gico** *adj.* (med.) rhinalgic.

rinanimire [D2] *tr.* to give new courage to; to reanimate; *rfl.* to take heart.

rinarrare [A1] *tr. repet.* of **narrare**, q.v.

rina·sc-ere [B18] *intr.* (*aux.* essere) to be born again; to grow again; to spring up again; to revive; to return; -e la primavera, Spring is returning; ciò fece — l'antico odio, that revived the old hatred; mi sentii —, I felt a new man; uomini di quella specie oggi non -ono più, men like that are no longer born nowadays. **-ente** *part. adj.* growing again, reviving; returning.

rinasciment-o *m.* revival; *pr.n.m.* (hist.) Renaissance. **-ale** *adj.* relating to the Renaissance.

rina·scit-a *f.* revival, renaissance. **-uro** *adj.* about to be born again.

rinato *part.* of **rinascere**, q.v.; *adj.* restored (to life, vigour, health), revived; reborn.

rincacciare [A4] *tr.* to drive back; to repel.

rincagn-are [A5] *rfl.* to scowl; to flatten one's nose. **-ato** *part. adj.* naso -ato, snub-nose.

rincalcagnare [A5] *tr.* (colloq., Tusc.) to follow on the heels of.

rincalc-are [A2] *tr.* to pull down; si -ò il cappello fin sugli occhi, he pulled his hat well down over his eyes. (**-ato** *part. adj.*)

†**rincalcettare** *tr.* to silence by retort or mockery.

rincalor-ire [D2] *tr.* to warm up (again); *intr* (*aux* avere) to produce heat; to cause intestinal irritation; *rfl* to warm up, to get heated; si -ì quando entrò in quell'argomento, he warmed up when he got on to that subject. (**-ito** *part. adj.*)

rincalz-are [A1] *tr.* to press upon; to follow closely; (agric.) to plant firmly (by pressing down earth or stones), to earth up; — un letto, to tuck up the sides of a bed; to prop, to fix; — un tavolo, to fix a table (by putting a wedge under one leg); (joc.) andare a — i cavoli, to go to 'push up the daisies'. **-amento** *m.* support. **-ata** *f.* an act of reinforcement, support, earthing up, etc. (**-ato** *part. adj.*) **-atore** *m.* (agric.) ridger, ridging plough. (**-atrice** *f.*) **-atura** *f.* earthing up.

rincalzo *m.* reinforcement, support; andare di —, to support, to reinforce; a — di ciò che ho detto, in support of what I said; (mil.) truppe di —, support troops, auxiliaries; reserves; (sport) member of a reserve team, as opposed to 'titolare', member of first team.

rincamminare [A 1] *rfl.* to start walking again, to resume one's way.

†rincanata *f.* threatening rebuke, warning.

rincantucci-are [A 3] *tr.* to drive into a corner; to corner; to retire, to withdraw; *rfl.* to hide in a corner. (**-ato** *part. adj.*)

rincappell-are [A 1] *tr.* to pour old wine (on pressed grapes or new wine); (fig.) to cap; to catch (a cold, etc. on top of another); *rfl.* to get worse; il raffreddore mi si è -ato, my cold has got worse. (**-ato** *part. adj.*) **-azione** *f.* rebuke.

rincar-are [A 1] *tr.* to increase the price of; — gli affitti, to increase the rents; — la dose, to increase the quantity, (fig.) to punish more severely, to 'rub it in'; *intr.* (*aux.* essere) to become dearer. **-ire** [D 2] *tr.* see **rincarare**; *intr.* (*aux.* essere) to become dearer.

rincarn-are [A 1], **-ire** [D 2] *tr.*, *intr.* (*aux.* essere) to make (to become) fatter; to put on flesh; *rfl.* to put on flesh (of a wound) to heal; (of a graft in plant) to take, to grow; (of toe-nails) to grow in. **-imento** *m.* putting on flesh; (of a wound) healing; (of toe-nail) growing in. **-ato**, **-ito** *part. adj.* fatter; grows fleshy; unghia -ita, ingrowing toe-nail.

rincaro *m.* rise in prices; il — dei viveri, the rising cost of living (cf. **rincarare**).

rincart-are [A 1] *tr.* to wrap up in paper (again); — panni, to press clothes between sheets of stout paper; *intr.* (*aux.* essere) (of sheep) to grow fresh wool. (**-ato** *part. adj.*) **-o** *m.* erratum card bound into a book.

rincas-are [A 1] *tr.* to take home; *intr.* (*aux.* essere), *rfl.* to return home; rincasandosi, on the way home. (**-ato** *part. adj.*)

rincassare [A 1] *tr. repet.* of **incassare**, q.v.

rincatenare [A 1 c] *tr. repet.* of **incatenare**, q.v.

rincavall-are [A 1] *tr.* to put on horseback again, to remount; *rfl.* to get a remount. (**-ato** *part. adj.*)

rincav-are [A 1] *tr. repet.* of **incavare**, q.v. **-ato** *part. adj.* (pop.) deep sunk.

†rinceff-are *tr.* to reproach (with). **†-o** *m.* reproach.

rincentrare [A 1] *tr.* to bring into a central position (again).

†rinceppare [A 1] (mil.) — un cannone, to remount a gun; (naut.) — ancora, to restock an anchor.

rincerott-are [A 1] *tr.* to patch up; to adapt. (**-ato** *part. adj.*)

rinchin-are [A 1] *tr.* to bend right down, to bow down; *rfl.* to bow humbly; (fig.) to confess a fault, to give way, to give in. (**-ato** *part. adj.*)

rinchiocciolire [D 2] *intr.* (*aux.* essere) to draw into one's shell like a snail.

rinchite *f.* (ent.) weevil, of the genus *Rhynchites*.

rinchi-u·dere [C 3] *tr.* to shut up; to lock up; to shut in; to enclose; *rfl.* to shut oneself in; to lock oneself in; (fig.) -udersi in un monastero, to enter a monastery, to become a monk. (**-udimento** *m.*) **†-usa** *f.* cloister. **-uso** *part. adj.* shut up; locked in; enclosed; imprisoned; hidden; -uso nella gabbia, caged; (rel.) enclosed; *n.m.* enclosure; enclosed space; close room; saper di -uso, to smell close, to smell fusty; aria -usa, stale air; (rel.) enclosed monk, member of an enclosed order.

rinciprignire [D 2] *intr.* (*aux.* essere) intens. of **inciprignire**, q.v.

rincitrullire [D 2] *tr.*, *intr.* (*aux.* essere), *rfl. repet.* or *intens.* of **incitrullire**, q.v.

rincivil-ire [D 2] *tr.* to make civilized (again); *intr.* (*aux.* essere) to become civilized; to improve in manners. **-ito** *part. adj.* civilized; good-mannered; better-mannered. (Cf. **incivilire**.)

rincoll-are [A 1] *tr.* to paste (or glue) together again; *intr.* (*aux.* essere), *rfl.* (of water) to flow over a dam (or weir). (**-ato** *part. adj.*)

rincollo *m.* (of water) damming.

rincominci-are [A 3] *tr.* to begin again, to recommence. (**-amento** *m.* **-ato** *part. adj.*)

rincontr-are [A 1 c] *tr.* to meet (again); to encounter; *intr.* (*aux.* essere) to come about, to happen; *recip. rfl.* to meet each other (again). **-ato** *part. adj.* met, met with; encountered.

rincontro *m.* encounter, meeting; coming face to face; (agric.) vineprop; (herald.) head caboshed; *adv.* gli veniva —, he came towards him; *adv. phr.* a, di, —, opposite.

†rincoppellare *tr.* (metall.) to recupel.

rincor-are [A 1] *tr.* to encourage; to cheer; *rfl.* to be encouraged; to take heart again. **-amento** *m.* encouragement. **-ato** *part. adj.* encouraged; cheered up.

rincorbellire [D 2] *intr.* (*aux.* essere) (fam.) to grow stupid.

rincorpor-are [A 1 s] *tr.* to reincorporate; (mil.) to re-form; *rfl.* to be reincorporated. **-amento** *m.* reincorporation; (mil.) re-formation of troops. **-ato** *part. adj.* reincorporated; (mil.) re-formed (of troops).

rincorrere [C 5] *tr.* to chase, to pursue; to run after; (fam.) — le ragazze, to run after girls; *recip. rfl.* to chase each other; fare a rincorrersi, to play 'tig'.

rincorsa *f.* run, sprint; prender la —, to dart, *or* to take a run (in order to jump); di —, at a run, at a rush.

rincottatura *f.* (tanning) wrinkling (of a hide).

rincresc-ere [B 9] *intr.* (*aux.* essere; *prep.* a) to cause regret or displeasure (to); to cause sorrow (to); to be a matter of regret (to); sono cose che -ono, these are very regrettable matters; *impers.* mi -e di non potervi aiutare, I am sorry I can't help you; mi -e che tua moglie non stia bene, I'm sorry your wife isn't well; vieni qua un momento se non ti -e, come here a minute, do you mind?; non vi -a avvisarci se non venite, please be good enough to let us know if you are not coming. **-evole** *adj.* regrettable; unpleasant; annoying. **-evolmente** *adv.* with regret; unhappily. **-imento** *m.* regret; sentire -imento, to feel regret; con mio grande -imento, to my great regret. **-ioso** *adj.* regrettable; disagreeable; unwilling, reluctant, lazy.

rincrespare [A 1] *tr.*, *rfl. repet.* or *intens.* of **increspare**, q.v.

rincrociare [A 3 c] *tr. repet.* of **incrociare**, q.v.

rincrostare [A 1] *tr. repet.* of **incrostare**, q.v.

rincrudel-ire [D 2] *tr.* to make more cruel; *intr.* (*aux.* essere) to become more cruel; to behave more cruelly. (**-ito** *part. adj.*)

rincrud-ire [D 2] *tr.* to aggravate; to increase the pain of; to embitter; *intr.* (*aux.* essere), *rfl.* to become sharper, to become colder, to grow more severe; la stagione si è -ita, the weather has worsened; l'aria verso sera -isce, the air gets keener in the evening. **-imento** *m.* aggravation; (of weather) becoming colder or more severe. (**-ito** *part. adj.*)

rincul-are [A 1] *intr.* (*aux.* essere, avere) to draw back, to shrink back, to recoil; to back away; (of a horse) to back; (naut.) to go astern; to go stern first; — sotto vela, to make a sternboard; **†**— sui remi, to back on the oars. **-amento** *m.* recoiling; **†**(naut.) -amento del vento, see 'giro cattivo', under **giro**. **-ato** *part. adj.* drawn back, recoiled; (of a horse) volta -ata, backing; (herald.) rearing, forcene. **-o** *m.* drawing back, recoil; (mil.) recoil; freno di -o, recoil cylinder.

rincuo·cere [C 15] *tr.* (cul.) to cook thoroughly, to cook right through; (metall.) to reheat.

rincup-ire [D 2] *intr.* (*aux.* essere), *rfl.* to cloud over; to become gloomy; (fig.) il suo volto a quelle parole si -ì, at those words his face clouded over. (**-ito** *part. adj.*)

rincurv-are [A 1], **-ire** [D 2] *tr.*, *intr. repet.* or *intens.* of **incurv-are**, **-ire** q.v.

rindebitare [A 1 s] *tr. repet.* of **indebitare**, q.v.

rindolcire [D 2] *tr.*, *intr. repet.* or *intens.* of **indolcire**, q.v.

rindossare [A 1] *tr.* to put on (clothes) again; (dressm.) to have a second fitting of; (agric.) to cover with earth (cf. **indossare**).

rindurire [D 2] *tr.*, *intr. repet.* of **indurire**, q.v.

rinegare [A 2 c] *tr. repet.* or *intens.* of **negare**, q.v. (cf. **rinnegare**).

rinett-are [A 1] *tr.* to clean again; to clean out; to clean thoroughly; to make smooth and fair; (foundry) to trim (a casting); (fig.) to purify; *rfl.* to be cleaned; (fig.) to purify oneself. (**-amento** *m.*) **-ato** *part. adj.* cleaned again; made clean and fair. (**-atore** *m.* **-atrice** *f.*) **-atura** *f.* cleaning; thorough cleaning; clearing out. (Cf. **nettare**.)

rinfacci-are [A 3] *tr.* (*prep.* a) to throw (in the face of), to cast (in the teeth of); to bring up a grievance (against); to reproach with; sempre mi -a l'aiuto che mi prestò, he always taunts me with the help he gave me; (naut., of the wind) to head. **-amento** *m.* reproach. (**-ato** *part. adj.*)

rinfac·cio *m.* reproach; bitter taunt.

rinfagottare [A 1]. See **affagottare** or **infagottare**.

rinfanciull-ire [D 2] *intr.* (*aux.* essere) to become childish, to enter one's second childhood. (**-ito** *part. adj.*)

rinfarcire [D 2] *tr. repet.* or *intens.* of **infarcire**, q.v.

rinferr-are [A I] *tr.* to repair (e.g. tools) with iron tips; to reshoe (a horse); *rfl.* (fig.; joc.) to recover strength. (*-ato part. adj.*)

rinfervor-are [A I s] *tr.* to rouse to fresh enthusiasm; *rfl.* to warm up again, to become more enthusiastic (*-ato part. adj.*)

rinfiammare [A I] *tr. repet.* of **infiammare**, q.v.

rinfian-care [A 2] *tr.* (archit.) to support at the sides; to prop; (fig.) — un'ipotesi, to support an hypothesis. **-camento** *m.* support, reinforcement. (*-cato part. adj.*) **-cheggiare** [A 3 c] *tr.* to support. (*-cheggiato part. adj.*) **-co** *m.* (*pl. -chi*) support, flanking; (archit.) abutment.

rinficosecch-ire [D 2] *intr.* (aux. essere) (Tusc.; colloq.) to grow thin, to become shrivelled and wrinkled like a dried fig. (*-ito part. adj.*)

rinfidare [A I] *rfl.* (prep. a) to be trustful; to confide (in).

rinfier-ire [D 2] *intr.* (aux. essere) to grow fierce or violent again; to grow more fierce or violent; (fig.) to become more agonizing or acute. (*-ito part. adj.*)

rinfignolire [D 2] *intr.* (aux. essere) to become pimply; to have boils.

rinfil-are [A I] *tr.* to rethread; (fig.) to reel off without a mistake, to have pat. (*-ato part. adj.*)

rinfiorare [A I c] *tr., rfl. repet.* of **infiorare**, q.v.

rinfittire [D 2] *intr. repet.* or *intens.* of **infittire**, q.v.

rinfoc-are [A 2 d] *tr.* to rekindle; to inflame. (*-amento m.*) **-ato** *part. adj.* rekindled; inflamed.

rinfocol-are [A I s] *tr.* to rekindle; to excite again; to stir up; to revive; *rfl.* to burst into flame again (of embers or glowing coals). **-amento** *m.* rekindling; stirring up. (*-ato part. adj.*)

rinfoder-are [A I s] *tr.* to resheathe; to reline; (naut.) — una nave, to recopper a ship's bottom; (fig.) to hold one's tongue concerning; -ò le sue domande, he refrained from asking questions. (*-a·bile adj. -ato part. adj.*)

rinformare [A I c] *tr. repet.* of **informare**, q.v.

rinforz-are [A I] *tr.* to strengthen; to reinforce; (archit.) to prop up, to reinforce, to stiffen; — la disciplina, to tighten discipline, to enforce discipline, to be stricter; to confirm, to clinch (an argument); (naut.) to strengthen (a yard), to support (a mast); (mil.) to reinforce, to strengthen (a fortification) with troops, etc.; to double (sentries, guards, lookouts, etc.); to increase the fire power of; (naut.) il vento -a, the wind is freshening; (photog.) to intensify. **-amento** *m.* strengthening, reinforcement. **-ato** *part. adj.* strengthened, reinforced; accelerated; (naut.) squadra -ata, increased squadron.

rinforzo *m.* strengthening, reinforcement; prop, support; fare un — a, to strengthen, to reinforce, to act as a support to; (bldg.; eng.) bracing, stiffening; (mil.) reinforcement (materials or troops); strengthening (e.g. at the breech end of a gun).

rinfranc-are [A 2] *tr.* to hearten, to reassure; to encourage; *rfl.* to be reassured, to take heart again, to pluck up courage; to recover oneself, to be oneself again; to make good one's losses. (*-amento m. -ato part. adj.*)

rinfranchire [D 2] *rfl.* to be reassured; to improve, to become more skilful; — nell'aritmetica, to become quicker at figures.

rinfranco *m.* reassurance; extra support, reinforcement.

rinfran·-gere [C 5] *tr.* to break up, to break to pieces; *rfl.* to break into pieces, to break up; to be broken up. **-to** *part. adj.* broken up; *n.m.* (text.) hessian, sackcloth.

rinfratire [D 2] *intr.* (aux. essere) see **infratire**; (of silkworms) to become diseased and die.

rinfresc-are [A 2] *tr.* to cool, to make cooler; to refresh; la pioggia ha -ato l'aria, the rain has cooled the air; — la memoria a qualcuno, to refresh someone's memory; to rest, to give rest to; to replenish; to renew; to restore; — una piaga, to reopen a wound; (naut.) to wash down; — la gomena, — la manica, to freshen the nip; (mil.) to cool (a gun) with a wet ramrod; — la battaglia, to renew hostilities; (paint.; sculp.) to restore; (agric.) to turn over, to open up, with the plough; *intr.* (aux. essere) to become cool; to be cooling, to be refreshing; *rfl.* to become cooler, to cool down; to refresh oneself; to take refreshment; (of the wind) to freshen. **-amento** *m.* cooling; freshening; (fig.) refreshing; rest; refreshment; (mil.) the water and vinegar used to souse the ramrod; the operation of cooling; provisions, restocking; fresh troops, reinforcements. **-ante** *part. adj.* cooling; refreshing; *n.m.* a mild laxative. **-ata** *f.* cooling; lowering of temperature; sprinkling or dashing with water; aperient; (naut.) steady increase in wind (generally for a short period). **-ativo** *adj.* refreshing; cooling. **-ato** *part. adj.* cooled; refreshed; rested; restored; renewed;

replenished. **-atoio** *m.* ventilator; water-cooler. **-atura** *f.* cooling (down); refreshing; cooler weather; autumn; (paint.; sculp.) restoration, touching up.

rinfres-co *m.* (*pl. -chi*) light refreshments (at receptions, on trains, etc.); liqueur; rest; aid; (naut.) tabling or strengthening piece; — di vele, additional sails set; †fresh provisions.

rinfrign-are [A 5] *tr.* to cobble up, to sew badly, to pucker. **-ato** *part. adj.* puckered; wrinkled. **-o** *m.* pucker; scar. **-olito** *adj.* badly sewn up; puckered.

rinfrinzell-are [A I] *tr.* to sew up badly, to pucker. **-ato** *part. adj.* clumsily mended; puckered.

rinfronz-ire [D 2] *intr.* (aux. essere, avere) to grow fresh leaves; *rfl.* to adorn oneself with ribbons, etc.; to titivate oneself. **-olare** [A I s], **-olire** [D 2] *intr.* (aux. essere), *rfl.* to titivate oneself, to get oneself up (esp. of an elderly woman).

rinfurbire [D 2] *intr.* (aux. essere) (Tusc., colloq.) to become cunning; to increase in cunning.

rinfus-o *adj.* confused, mixed up; (vet.) cavallo —, a horse lame with laminitis; *adv. phr.* alla -a, higgledy-piggledy, in great confusion; (comm.) sold 'loose', not packed; merce alla -a, goods shipped in bulk, unpacked (e.g. grain, etc.).

ringabbiare [A 4] *tr. repet.* of **ingabbiare**, q.v.

ringagliard-ire [D 2] *tr.* to strengthen; to reinvigorate; (chem.) to strengthen (a reagent); *intr.* (aux. essere), *rfl.* to become stronger; to gain new strength. (*-imento m. -ito part. adj.*) (Cf. **ingagliardire**.)

ringall-ettare [A I c], **-uzzare** [A I]. See **ringalluzzire**.

ringalluzz-ire [D 2] *intr.* (aux. essere), *rfl.* to be elated, to be proud, to be 'cocky'; to be cheeky; *tr.* to make proud. **-ito** *part. adj.* cocky, self-assured.

ringambare [A I] *tr.* to fit with a new leg or shank; *intr.* (aux. essere), *rfl.* to get about again, to get on one's feet again.

ringangherare [A I s] *tr.* to replace on hinges; to put together again (e.g. a watch); (fig.) to piece together, to recall with difficulty.

†ringavagnare *tr.* to regain, to take again.

ringentil-ire [D 2] *tr.* to civilize, to make more polite; to cultivate; l'arte -isce l'animo, art cultivates the mind; to render amiable; *intr.* (aux. essere), *rfl.* to become civilized, polite, cultured. (*-ito part. adj.*)

ringhi-are [A 4] *intr.* (aux. avere) to snarl; to growl. **-ante** *part. adj.* snarling.

ringhiera *f.* rostrum, platform; balcony; (naut.) guard rail; (archit.) rail, railing; banisters; scendeva adagio adagio le scale, tenendosi alla —, he came slowly down the stairs, holding on to the banisters.

rin·ghi-o *m.* snarl; growl. **-oso** *adj.* snarling; bad-tempered; *n.m.* bad-tempered man.

ringhiottire [D 2] *tr. repet.* of **inghiottire**, q.v.

ringiallire [D 2] *tr., intr.* (aux. essere) to turn yellow; to turn yellow again (more expressive than **ingiallire**, q.v.)

†ringioire *intr.* to rejoice.

ringiovan-ire [D 2] *tr.* to make younger, to rejuvenate; to cause to look younger; (agric.) — un prato, to renew, to reseed, a meadow; *intr.* (aux. essere) to grow young again; to look younger; to regain a youthful appearance; to recover one's freshness and vigour (also of plants). **-imento** *m.* (med.) rejuvenescence. **-ito** *part. adj.* rejuvenated; looking younger.

ringoiare [A 4] *tr.* to swallow again; to eat again; (fig.) to withdraw (an accusation); *abs.* to eat one's words (cf. **ingoiare**).

†ringone *m.* ravine.

ringorgare [A 2 c] *intr.* (aux. essere), *rfl.* to form whirlpools; to swirl (cf. **ingorgare**).

ringor-go *m.* (*pl. -ghi*) whirlpool; swirling flood.

ringrana *f.* (metall.) roasting furnace.

ringran-are [A I] *tr.* (agric.) to sow with grain for the second year running; (watchm.) to seal in; †(mil.) to unspike (a gun). **-atic·cio** *m.* field sown with corn for two years in succession. **-ato** *part. adj.* sown with corn for the second year in succession. **-o** *m.* sowing corn for a second year.

ringrand-ire [D 2] *tr.* to enlarge further; to make bigger; (fig.) to make proud; *rfl.* to be enlarged; to be made bigger; (fig.) to get big ideas, to become proud. (*-imento m. -ito part. adj.*)

ringrassare [A I] *tr. repet.* or *intens.* of **ingrassare**, q.v.

ringrazi-are [A 4] *tr.* to thank (sometimes implying refusal or non-acceptance); — il nonno del regalo, to thank grandpa for the present; — di cuore, to thank with all one's heart; sia -ato Dio!,

ringrazi·are (*cont.*)
God be thanked!; (iron.) non ha che — se stesso di ciò, he has only himself to thank for that. **-amento** *m.* thanks; expression of thanks; gradisca i miei -amenti, accept my thanks; con tanti -amenti, with many thanks; -amento dell'assemblea, vote of thanks; (rel.) thanksgiving (esp. after mass or communion).

ringrett·ire [D 2] *tr.* to make mean or shabby; to reduce in importance; to demean. (**-ito** *part. adj.*)

ringrinz·are [A 1], **-ire** [D 2] and derivs. See **raggrinz·are**, **-ire**.

ringross·are [A 1] *tr.* to enlarge again; to increase again; (pop.) to enlarge; to increase; *intr.* (*aux.* essere), *rfl.* to increase; to grow greater; to be enlarged. (**-amento** *m.* **-ato** *part. adj.* **-atura** *f.*) (Cf. **ingrossare**.)

ringrosso *m.* increase; enlargement; thickening; (eng.) boss; (text.) slobbing.

ringuiggiare [A 4] *intr.* (*aux.* avere) (mil. hist.) to repair the handle of a shield; to grasp the handle of a shield; (fig.) to take up arms.

ringurgitare [A 1 s] and derivs. See **rigurgitare**.

rinite *f.*, †**rini·tide** *f.* (med.) rhinitis.

†**trinmillare** *rfl.* to increase a thousandfold.

rinnalz·are [A 1] *tr.* to raise again; to raise higher; *rfl.* to rise further; to grow higher. (**-amento** *m.*) **-ato** *part. adj.* high; raised; in relief.

rinneg·are [A 2 c] *tr.* to deny; to disown; — la religione, to give up, to renounce, one's religion; — Cristo, to deny Christ; — Dio, to swear profanely, to blaspheme; — la pazienza, to lose patience; — il mestiere, to forsake one's trade. (**-amento** *m.*) **-ato** *part. adj.* disowned; denied; refused recognition; *n.m.* renegade; -ato politico, turncoat. **-atore** *m.* **-atrice** *f.*) **-azione** *f.* denial; disowning.

rinnervare [A 1] *rfl.* (poet.) to grow strong again.

rinnest·are [A 1] *tr.* to graft again; to reinoculate, to revaccinate; to put together again. (**-amento** *m.* **-ato** *part. adj.*)

rinnesto *m.* new graft; new grafting.

rinnobilire [D 2] and derivs. See **annobilire**.

rinnov·are [A 1 d] *tr.* to renew; — le scuse, to apologize again; — gli applausi, to applaud again, to keep on clapping; — l'aria, to let in some fresh air, to provide ventilation; — le lenzuola, to change the sheets on a bed; — una cambiale, to renew a bill; — un contratto di fitto, to renew, or to grant a new, lease; to renovate; (naut.) — il fasciame, to carry out hull repairs; (paint.) to restore; (Tusc.) to put on for the first time; — un vestito, to wear a new dress; *intr.* (*aux.* essere) (of the moon) to be new; *rfl.* to be renewed; to be repeated; to begin again; to break out or occur again; to be renovated; to be restored or repaired. **-a·bile** *adj.* renewable; capable of being renovated. (**-abilità** *f.*) **-amento** *m.* renewal; return; revival, reawakening; renovating. **-ativo** *adj.* tending to renew. **-ato** *part. adj.* renewed; renovated; restored; repeated. (**-atore** *m.* **-atrice** *f.*) **-azione** *f.* renewal; renovation; restoration; (comm.) -azione di cambiale, renewal of a bill.

rinnovell·are [A 1] *tr.* to renew; to repeat; to refresh; to revive; to call to mind; *intr.* (*aux.* essere), *rfl.* to be renewed; to change. **-amento** *m.* renewal; fresh growth. (**-ato** *part. adj.* **-atore** *m.* **-atrice** *f.* **-azione** *f.*)

rinnovo *m.* renewal; renovation; (agric.) fresh ploughed land; (Tusc., of clothing) farsi un —, to get some new clothes; a new dress; new shoes, etc.

rinnuovo *m.* See **rinnovo**.

rinobilitare [A 1 s] *tr.* to confer new honour on (cf. **nobilitare**).

rinoceronte *m.* (zool.) rhinoceros.

rinofaring·e *f.* (anat.) rhinopharynx. **-ite** *f.* (med.) rhinopharyngitis.

rin·o·fima *m.* (med.) rhinophyma. **-ofoni·a** *f.* (med.) rhinophonia. **-ofo·nico** *adj.* rhinophonic.

rino·geno *adj.* (med.) rhinogenous, originating in the nose.

rino·lali·a *f.* (med.) rhinolalia, nasal speech. **-laringite** *f.* rhinolaryngitis. **-lite** *f.*, **-lito** *m.* rhinolith. **-li·tico** *adj.* rhinolithic.

rino·log·o *m.* (med.) rhinologist, nose specialist. **-i·a** *f.* (med.) rhinology.

rinom·are [A 1] *tr.* to celebrate; to praise. **-a·bile** *adj.* worthy of renown. **-anza** *f.* renown, fame. †**-ata** *f.* fame, renown. **-ato** *part. adj.* renowned, famous, celebrated; well known. †**-e·a** *f.* fame, renown.

rinomin·are [A 1 s] *tr.* to name again; to renominate; to reappoint. (**-ato** *part. adj.*)

rinopla·stica *f.* (surg.) rhinoplasty.

rinor·ragi·a *f.* (med.) epistaxis, nose-bleeding, rhinorrhagia. **-ra·gico** *adj.* rhinorrhagic. **-re·a** *f.* (med.) rhinorrhoea. **-re·ico** *adj.* rhinorrhoeic.

rinos·copi·a *f.* (med.) rhinoscopy. **-co·pico** *adj.* rhinoscopical. **-co·pio** *m.* rhinoscope.

rinot·are [A 1] *tr.* to note again; to take fresh notes. (**-ato** *part. adj.*) **-ificare** [A 2 s] *tr.* to notify again.

rinquart·are [A 1] *tr.* to multiply by four; to divide into quarters; (agric.) to sow four times with the same crop; *intr.* (*aux.* avere) (billiards) to strike three cushions and then score; *rfl.* to be divided, to divide, into four parts. (**-ato** *part. adj.*) **-atura** *f.* (agric.) cultivation for the fourth time.

rinquattrinare [A 1] *rfl.*, *intr.* (*aux.* essere) to be in funds again; *tr.* to supply with (more) money.

rinsacc·are [A 2] *tr.* to put into a bag again; to shake down in a bag (to settle the contents); *intr.* (*aux.* avere), *rfl.* to be shaken up (e.g. on horseback); to shrug one's shoulders; to dress badly (as in a sack). **-amento** *m.* putting in a bag; shaking a bag; shaking-up (e.g. on horseback). **-ato** *part. adj.* put into a sack; dressed as in a sack. (**-atura** *f.*)

rinsaldare [A 1] and derivs. See **risaldare**.

rinsangu·are [A 6] *tr.* to put fresh blood into; (fig.) to give new strength to; *rfl.* to get fresh strength; to recover; era mezzo rovinato, ma ora spera di -arsi, he was almost ruined, but now he hopes to recoup. (**-ato** *part. adj.*) **-inare** [A 1] *tr.* to stain with blood again; *rfl.* to get fresh blood; to recover; (fig.) to make good one's losses. **-inato** *part. adj.*

rinsan·ire [D 2] *intr.* (*aux.* essere) to recover one's health; to recover one's sanity. (**-ito** *part. adj.*)

rinsav·ire [D 2] *intr.* (*aux.* essere) to return to reason; to recover one's wits; to become sensible again. (**-imento** *m.* **-ito** *part. adj.*)

rinsegn·are [A 5] *tr.* to teach again; †to bring fresh news of. (**-ato** *part. adj.*)

rinselv·are [A 1] *rfl.* to revert to woodland; to take to the woods again; *tr.* to reafforest. **-atichire** [D 2] *intr.* (*aux.* essere) to grow wild again. (**-ato**, **-atichito** *part. adj.*)

rinserr·are [A 1] *tr.* to shut up again; to conceal, to hide; *rfl.* to shut oneself up; to hide. **-ato** *part. adj.* shut up; hidden; withdrawn, in retirement; *n.m.* house, room, etc. which is shut up; odore di -ato, close, musty smell.

rinsonare [A 1 d] *intr.* (*aux.* essere, avere) to resound; to roar.

rinsudiciare [A 3] *tr.* to make dirty again; *rfl.* to become dirty again.

rintagli·are [A 4] *tr.* to carve; to recarve; to carve over the lines of (a drawing). (**-ato** *part. adj.*)

rintallo *m.* (bot.) sucker.

rintan·are [A 1] *rfl.* to shut oneself up; to re-enter a den; (fig.) to hide; *tr.* to chase into a den. **-ato** *part. adj.* hiding in a den; shut up, shut away; hidden.

rintasare [A 1] *tr.* repet. of **intasare**, q.v.

rintegolare [A 1 s] *tr.* to repair the roof of; to retile.

rintegr·are [A 1] *tr.* to make good, to restore to proper condition; (comm.) to renew, to restore; *rfl.* to recover; to be restored. (**-amento** *m.* **-ato** *part. adj.* **-atore** *m.* **-atrice** *f.*) **-azione** *f.* restoration; recovery. (Cf. **reintegrare**.)

rintempire [D 1] *intr.* (*aux.* essere) (Tusc.) to become fine again (of weather).

rintenerire [D 2] *tr.*, *rfl.* repet. of **intenerire**, q.v.

rinterr·are [A 1] *tr.* to fill with earth again; to bury again. (**-amento** *m.* **-ato** *part. adj.*)

rinterro *m.* bank; ridge; silting up.

rinterrogare [A 2 s] *tr.* repet. of **interrogare**.

rinterz·are [A 1] *tr.* to treble; to repeat twice; (agric.) to sow with the same crop three times; *intr.* (*aux.* avere) (billiards) to strike two cushions and then score. **-ato** *part. adj.* trebled; triple; (prosod.) sonetto -ato, sonnet with a third line inserted after every second line of the regular form; (agric.) piantagioni -ate, triple plantations, i.e. with three lines of trees (vines, bushes).

rinterzo *m.* (billiards) stroke by which a player strikes two cushions and then scores.

rintiepidire [D 2] *tr.* repet. of **intiepidire**, q.v.

rintocc·are [A 2 c] *intr.* (*aux.* essere, avere) to toll; (of a clock) to strike; to ring; le parole gli -avano nell'anima, the words rang through his mind. (**-amento** *m.*)

rintoc·co *m.* (*pl.* **-chi**) tolling; knell; chime of a bell; sonare a -chi, to sound the alarm; blast of a horn.

rintonacare [A2s] *tr. repet.* of **intonacare**, q.v.

rinto·nico *adj.* (Gk. lit.) of or like the burlesque dramas of Rhinthon (third century B.C.); dramma —, mock heroic play, parody.

rintopp-are [A1] *tr.* to stumble against, to run into; to patch; to mend; *recip. rfl.* to meet each other, to run into each other; to come across each other. **-aménto** *m.* stumbling (into); meeting.

rintoppo *m.* meeting, encounter; obstacle; *adv. phr.* di —, by way of contrast, *or* in return.

rintracci-are [A3] *tr.* to trace; to track; to track down; to succeed in tracing or finding. **-a·bile** *adj.* that can be traced, traceable. (**-abilità** *f.*) **-aménto** *m.* tracking, tracing; investigation. (**-ato** *part. adj.*)

†**rintramet·tere** *tr.* to cross-plough.

rintrincer-are [A1] *tr.* to entrench (again). **-aménto** *m.* (mil.) entrenchment, emergency earthworks thrown up to cover a breach in a defensive position. **-ato** *part. adj.* (mil.) well entrenched.

rintron-are [A1] *tr.* to shake; to deafen, to stun; l'esplosione -ò tutta la casa, the explosion shook the whole house; quel vocione mi -a, I find that loud voice deafening; *intr.* (*aux.* essere, avere) to thunder, to boom; to resound. **-aménto** *m.* deafening, stunning; booming, thundering. **-ante** *part. adj.* deafening; booming. **-ato** *part. adj.* deafened, stunned. (Cf. **intronare**.)

rintro·nico *m.* angry retort; rispondere per —, to give tit for tat.

rintrono *m.* deafening noise.

rintuono *m.* thundering; booming; reverberation.

rintuzz-are [A1] *tr.* to blunt; to dull; to check; to cause to abate; to reduce, to lessen; *rfl.* to shrink, to cower. (**-aménto** *m.*) **-ato** *part. adj.* blunted; obtuse; cowering.

rinunciare [A3] and derivs. See **rinunziare**.

rinun·zia *f.* renunciation; — all'impiego, retirement; (leg.) disclaimer; waiver; surrender; clausola di —, waiver clause; valore di —, surrender value; (canon law) renunciation (e.g. of benefice).

rinunzi-are [A4] *tr.* to renounce; to give up; — a parlare, to waive one's right to speak; (canon law) to renounce, to resign; *intr.* (*aux.* avere; *prep.* a) to renounce; — al trono, to abdicate; to abstain (from); (rel.) -are al mondo, to renounce the world (esp. in baptismal vows), (fig.) to enter a convent; (leg.) to disclaim; to relinquish; to renounce; to waive. **-ante** *part. adj.* renouncing; *n.m.* renouncer; *pl.* (eccl. hist.) members of sects renouncing all property. **-ata·rio** *m.* (leg.) person in whose favour disclaimer, etc. operates. (**-ato** *part. adj.*) **-atóre** *m.* person making disclaimer, etc. (**-atrice** *f.*) †**-azione** *f.* see **rinunzia**.

rinutr-ire [D2] *tr.* to feed again; to feed up. **-iménto** *m.* tonic food. (**-ito** *part. adj.*) **-izione** *f.* feeding up; nourishment.

rinvangare [A2] *tr.* (fig.) to dig up again, to rake up, to recall; non — il passato, to let bygones be bygones.

rinvaṣ-are [A1] *tr.* (agric.) to repot; to transfer (a liquid) from one vessel to another. (**-ato** *part. adj.*) **-ellare** [A1] *tr.* to pour (wine) from one vessel to another.

rinvecchign-ire [D2] *intr.* (*aux.* essere) to age prematurely, to come to look prematurely old. **-ito** *adj.* shrivelled; wizened; looking much older.

rinven-ire [D17] *tr.* to discover, to find (out); to bring round (from a faint); (metall.) to draw, to temper; *intr.* (*aux.* essere) to recover one's senses; to come to oneself; to revive, to recover; (of wood) to swell (with water); to become soft; le frutta secche -gono nell'acqua tiepida, dried fruits become soft and swell in warm water; *rfl.* to remember; to find one's way. **-i·bile** *adj.* to be found, traceable. **-iménto** *m.* discovery; recovery; (metall.) drawing, tempering. **-uto** *part. adj.* found, discovered; recovered; come to one's senses; (of fruit, etc.) soaked; (fig.; fam.) soaked, wet through; (metall.) drawn, tempered.

rinverd-ire [D2] *tr.* to make green again; to revive; (tanning) to soak; *intr.* (*aux.* essere) to grow green again; to revive (also fig.). **-iménto** *m.* growing green again; (tanning) soaking. (**-ito** *part. adj.*)

rinverg-are [A2] *tr.* to find again after a long search; (naut.) — una bandiera, to bend on a flag anew; †*intr.* to bend new sails to a yard. (**-ato** *part. adj.*)

rinverminire [D2] *intr.* (*aux.* essere) to deteriorate, to rot; to become maggoty.

rinverniciare [A3] *tr. repet.* of **inverniciare**, q.v.

rinvert-ire [D1] *tr.* to invert; to convert, to change; to turn about; *rfl.* to turn (oneself) round, to turn back. (**-iménto** *m.* **-ito** *part. adj.*)

rinverẓ-icare [A2s] *intr.* (*aux.* essere) to grow green again. **-icolare** [A1s], **-icolire** [D2] *intr.* (*aux.* essere), *rfl.* to grow green again; (fig.) to cheer up. **-ire** [D2] see **rinverzicare**.

†**rinvesci-are** *intr.* to tell secrets. †**-ardo** *m.* blabber.

rinvest-ire [D1] *tr.* to reinvest; to install again; to cover (flasks, etc.) with a straw jacket; to strengthen (a wall) with a kind of coating; (mil.) to lay siege to again; †to reclothe. **-iménto** *m.* reinvesting; reinstallation (in a position of authority); recovering with straw; (mil.) -iménto di fortezza, the investment, or besieging of a fortress. (**-ito** *part. adj.*) **-itura** *f.* recovering (flasks) with straw; reinvestiture.

rinvi-are [A4] *tr.* to send back; — a casa, to send home; to put off, to postpone, to defer, to adjourn; (admin.) — la seduta, to adjourn the meeting; — alla commissione competente, to refer to the appropriate committee; — alla fine, to place at the end of the agenda; (leg.) to adjourn; to postpone; — una causa ad altro giudice, to order retrial by another judge; — a nuovo ruolo, to adjourn to next (civil) sittings, to next (criminal) sessions; to order a new trial of. (**-ato** *part. adj.*)

rinvigor-ire [D2] *tr.* to invigorate, to strengthen; *intr.* (*aux.* essere), *rfl.* to revive; to gain new strength, to grow strong again. **-iménto** *m.* strengthening; invigoration. **-ito** *part. adj.* strengthened; revived, restored.

rinviliare [A4] and derivs. See **rinvilire**.

rinvi·lio *m.* reduction; cheapening; depreciation, fall in price.

rinvil-ire [D2] *tr.* to cheapen; to lower the price of; *intr.* (*aux.* essere) to become cheaper; to be reduced in price. (**-ito** *part. adj.*)

rinvi·o *m.* sending back; return; (watchm.) setting wheel; cross reference; chiedere, proporre, il — della sessione, to move, propose, the adjournment of the session; (eng.) transmission, gear; — a cinghia, belt drive; (leg.) postponement, adjournment; cassazione con —, quashing of judgement and order for new trial.

rinvit-are[1] [A1] *tr.* to invite again; to invite in return. **-o** *m.* repeated invitation.

rinvitare[2] [A1] *tr.* (eng.) to screw up again.

rinvi·vere [C16], **rinvivire** [D2] *intr.* (*aux.* essere) (Tusc., fig.) to come to life again; to regain strength; un vino che fa —, a wine that 'revives a corpse'.

rinvol·gere [C5] *tr.* to wrap up again; *rfl.* to wrap oneself up (again); to roll about, to wallow.

rinvol·golo *m.* bundle; package.

rinvolt-are [A1] *tr.* to wrap up again; to wrap round and round. **-ato** *part. adj.* wrapped up; (fig.) enveloped, entangled.

rinvolto *part.* of **rinvolgere**, q.v.; *adj.* wrapped up, enveloped; capelli rinvolti, hair in ringlets; *n.m.* bundle, package.

rinvoltolare [A1s] *tr.* to wrap round and round, to wrap up thoroughly; *rfl.* to roll about, to wallow.

rinvoltura *f.* wrapping up; wrapping materials; (fig.) entanglement; intrigue; (rhet.) euphemism.

rinzaff-are [A1] *tr.* (bldg.) to fill up chinks in, to give the first rough coat of plaster to. (**-ato** *part. adj.* **-atura** *f.*) **-o** *m.* plastering rough-cast.

rinzepp-are [A1] *tr.* to fill right up; (fig.) to pad; *rfl.* to eat too much, to stuff. (**-aménto** *m.* **-ato** *part. adj.*) **-atura** *f.* (techn.) wedge, quoin. (Cf. **inzeppare**.)

rinzocco *m.* duplicated plinth.

rinzuppare [A1] *tr. repet.* or *intens.* of **inzuppare**, q.v.

rio[1] *m.* stream, brook; — di lagrime, flood of tears; (at Venice) canal, lane with a canal in the centre; †river.

rio[2] *adj.* wicked; guilty; *n.m.* wickedness; guilt.

rioccup-are [A1s] *tr.* to reoccupy; *rfl.* to occupy oneself again. (**-aménto** *m.*) **-ato** *part. adj.* reoccupied. **-azione** *f.* reoccupation.

riolite *f.* (miner.) rhyolite.

rion-e *m.* quarter (of a city); ward, district; non conosco questo —, I don't know this part of the city. **-ale** *adj.* relating to a quarter, ward, etc. not of the city-centre; un teatro -ale, a theatre in one of the outlying districts of a city; (fig.) cheap, shoddy.

rioperare [A1s] *tr.* (surg.) to operate again on; *intr.* (*aux.* avere) to work again, to act again; (surg.) to operate again.

riordin-are [A1s] *tr.* to rearrange; to put in order again; to re-organize; to order again; — il carbone al carbonaio, to order more coal from the coal merchant; (mil.) to re-form; *rfl.* to get into order again; (mil.) -arsi il fronte, to re-form one's front. **-aménto** *m.* rearrangement; reordering; re-forming. **-ato** *part.*

riordin-are (*cont.*)
adj. rearranged; reorganized; reordered; (mil.) re-formed. (**-atore** *m.* **-atrice** *f.*) **-azione** *f.* rearrangement; reorganization; re-ordering; (eccl.) reordination.

riorganizz-are [A1] *tr.* to reorganize; to rearrange. (**-amento** *m.*) **-ato** *part. adj.* reorganized. **-azione** *f.* reordering; reconstruction, reorganization.

riorl-are [A1] *tr.* to hem; to rehem. (**-ato** *part. adj.*)

rioscillare [A1] *intr.* (*aux.* avere) to reoscillate, to oscillate again.

riosservare [A1] *tr. repet.* of **osservare**, q.v.

rioterrà *m. indecl.* (Venice) a street formed by filling in a canal.

†**riott-a** *f.* quarrel. †**-are** *intr.* to dispute.

†**riot·tolo** *m.*, †**rioz·zolo** *m.* rivulet, brook.

riottos-o *adj.* litigious; quarrelsome; refractory; sulky. (**-amente** *adv.*) **-ità** *f.* quarrelsomeness; sulkiness.

ripa *f.* bank; canal wharf on left bank of the Tiber in Rome; steep bank, precipice; (orn.) uccelli di —, waders; (agric.) — del solco, edge of furrow; †beach, coast.

ripacific-are [A2s] *tr.* to pacify again; to reconcile; *rfl.* to become reconciled, to reconcile oneself; *recip. rfl.* to become reconciled to one another. (**-ato** *part. adj.*)

ripag-are [A2] *tr.* to pay again; to repay; to pay back; to recompense; to replace (at one's own expense). (**-ato** *part. adj.*)

ripar-are¹ [A1] *tr.* to repair, to mend; to make good; — il tempo perduto, to make up for lost time; — un esame, to take an exam again after failing; (Tusc.) — le spese, to meet expenses, to foot the bill; (naut.) to refit; — vele, to refit sails; — alberi, to refit masts; to shield, to shelter; to parry; *intr.* (*aux.* avere; *prep.* a) to provide (for), to remedy, to make good; to see (to), to make arrangements (for); *rfl.* to take shelter. **-a·bile** *adj.* repairable; mendable; reparable; defensible; città **-abile**, city prepared for defence. (**-abilità** *f.*) **-amento** *m.* repair; remedy; restoration; defence. **-ata** *f.* hurried repair(s); tenere alla **-ata**, to keep under cover. **-ato** *part. adj.* protected, sheltered; repaired, restored; safe; parried. (**-atore** *m.*, *adj.* **-atrice** *f.*) **-azione** *f.* repair(s); reparation; satisfaction; (archit.) repair(s); restoration; esami di **-azione**, autumn examination for candidates who failed in summer.

riparare² [A1] *intr.* (*aux.* essere) to repair, to make away; to escape.

†**riparare³** *tr.* to hinder, to stay; *rfl.* to dwell.

riparella¹ *f.* (bot.) purple loosestrife, *Lythrum salicaria.*

riparella² *f.* (eng.) washer.

ripa·rio *adj.* riparian, living on river banks; *n.m.* (zool.) shore crab, *Carcinus maenas*; (geog.) Dora riparia, a tributary of the Po.

riparlare [A1] *intr.* (*aux.* avere) to speak again; ne riparleremo, we shall see, just wait and see; *recip. rfl.* to talk things over, to discuss differences (with a view to settlement).

riparo *m.* shelter, protection, cover, defence; mettersi al —, to get under cover; al —, in safety; remedy; senza —, beyond repair, beyond redemption; è perduto senza —, it is irretrievably lost; non c'è —, there is nothing to be done about it; metter — a un inconveniente, to put a stop to a nuisance; fence, embankment (of mountain stream, etc.); (eng.) guard, apron, protective casing, bumper, fender; (mil.) fortification; bastion; †defensive work thrown up to cover a breach; †dwelling.

ripartire¹ [D1] *intr.* (*aux.* essere) to leave again; to set out again, to start again (cf. **partire**).

ripart-ire² [D1] *tr.* to share; to divide; to distribute; to separate, to part. **-i·bile** *adj.* divisible. **-imento** *m.* division, distribution; compartment. **-ito** *part. adj.* distributed; separated; (herald.) per pale, the sinister also per pale. **-itamente** *adv.* in fair shares. **-itore** *m.* one who shares or divides; (teleph.) distribution frame. (**-itrice** *f.*) **-izione** *f.* division; distribution; sharing out; break-down (of document); (comm.) allotment; assessment; (bankruptcy) **-izione** dell'attivo, distribution of assets. **-o** *m.* distribution; compartment, department; share; (mil.) unit.

ripa·sc-ere [B17] *tr., intr.* (*aux.* avere) to graze, to feed; to satisfy; *rfl.* to feed; to be satisfied. (**-iuto** *part. adj.*)

ripass-are [A1] *tr.* to cross again (or over) again; to pass through (or over) again; to look over again, to revise; to go over in one's mind; to iron (with a smoothing-iron); — un rasoio, to strop a razor; to pass through again (needle, thread, etc.); to sieve, to sift, to strain; to beat, to hit; (paint.; sculp.) to touch up, to retouch; to put the finishing touches to; — ad inchiostro, to ink in (a drawing); (eng.) to overhaul, to regrind, to reface, to rectify, to adjust;

— al trapasso, to redrill; (comm.) — i conti, to review the accounts; (joc.) to strike, to beat, again; to check (money), to recount; *intr.* (*aux.* essere) to pass again; to call again; — col ferro sulla biancheria, to iron the laundry. **-ata** *f.* passing again; repassing; **-ata** col ferro, ironing; **-ata** ai vestiti, looking over clothes (to see if mending is needed); dare una **-ata** ai mobili, to give the furniture a polish; rebuke; (joc.) una buona **-ata**, a good beating. **-ato** *part. adj.* (paint.) touched up. (**-atore** *m.* **-atrice** *f.*) **-atura** *f.* (eng.) overhauling, rectification, regrinding, resetting. **-o** *m.* return (e.g. of birds of passage); repetition; revision.

ripasseggiare [A3c] *intr.* (*aux.* avere) to go out walking again; passeggiare e —, to walk up and down.

ripa·tic-a *f.* (leg.) riparian right. **-o** *m.* wharf, quay, dock (on river or canal).

ripatire [D2] *tr. repet.* of **patire**, q.v.

ripatri-are [A4] *intr.* (*aux.* avere), *rfl.* to go home (to one's own country); *tr.* to repatriate, to send back home. (**-ato** *part. adj.*) **-azione** *f.* return home, repatriation. (Cf. **rimpatriare**.)

ripavimentazione *f.* (roadm.) resurfacing.

ripens-are [A1] *intr.* (*aux.* avere) to think again; to think over; devo **-arci**, I must think it over; ora che ci **-o**, now that I think of it; ci ho **-ato**, I have changed my mind; *tr.* to recall; — con, to compare with; *rfl.* (acc. of *prn.* 'si') to change one's mind; (dat. of *prn.* 'si') to recall to mind. **-amento** *m.* thinking things over; change of mind. (**-ato** *part. adj.*)

ripense *adj.* riparian.

ripent-ire [D1] *rfl.* to repent (again); to regret; to change one's mind. **-imento** *m.* repentance; regret. **-ite** *n.f.pl.* (eccl.) Penitent Sisters, Penitents. (Cf. **pentire**.) **-ito** *part. adj.* repented.

ripercorrere [C5] *tr.* to run over again, to travel through again. (Cf. **percorrere**.)

ripercoss-a *f.* see **ripercussione**. **-o** *part.* of **ripercuotere**, q.v.; *adj.* struck again; remi **-i** nell'acqua, oars striking the water again; echoed, reflected, returned.

riperc(u)o·t-ere [C15] *tr.* to strike again, to beat; to send back, to throw back; to reflect; (mus.) to reiterate; to shake, to trill; *rfl.*, *intr.* (*aux.* essere) to echo, to be reflected, to reverberate, to be given back, to come back. (**-imento** *m.*)

ripercussione *f.* repercussion; reflection; echo, reverberation; (mus.) repercussion, reiteration; shake, trill, tremolo.

riper·dere [C28] *tr. repet.* of **perdere**, q.v.

riperdonare [A1] *tr. repet.* of **perdonare**, q.v.

riperquisito *adj.* (comm.) rerummaged.

ripes-are [A1] *tr.* to weigh again; to think over. **-ata** *f.* reweighing. (**-ato** *part. adj.*) (Cf. **pesare**.)

ripesc-are [A2c] *tr.* to fish out again; to pick up, to pull out, again; to find (again), to discover (after search); dove hai **-ato** questa notizia?, where did you get hold of this piece of news?; to recall; (pop., Tusc.) to beat. **-amento** *m.* picking up; finding; discovery. **-ata** *f.* (pop., Tusc.) beating. (**-ato** *part. adj.* **-atore** *m.* **-atrice** *f.*)

ripesco *m.* (*pl.* **ripeschi**) intrigue, secret love affair.

ripet-ere [B1] *tr.* to repeat; to recite, to say, tell again; fare — una lezione, to hear a lesson; (theatr.) to rehearse; — un esame, to take an exam again (after failing); to contradict; to recall; to derive; la mitologia romana **-e** le sue origini da quella greca, Roman mythology derives its origin from Greek (that of Greece); (leg.) to claim; to demand repayment or return of; to repeat; (naut.) — i segnali, to hoist the same flags as the admiral; to repeat back; to check back; *rfl.* to repeat oneself; to recur; sono scuse che si **-ono** troppo spesso, these excuses recur too frequently. **-ente** *part. adj.* repeating; *n.m., f.* pupil remaining in the same class for a second year; (leg.) claimant of repayment or return. **-imento** *m.* repetition. **-itore** *m.* repeater; private tutor, coach; one who 'knows all the answers', ready-witted person; (teleph.) repeater; (acoust.) echoer; (eng.) repeater; (rlwy.) **-itore** di segnali, signal repeater; (astron.) repeating circle; *adj.* †(naut.) bastimento **-itore**, see 'nave ripetitrice'. **-itrice** *f.*; *adj. f.* (naut.) nave **-itrice**, repeating ship; bandiera **-itrice**, repeating flag, repeater; 1st, 2nd or 3rd repeater used to convey the same meaning or figure as the 1st, 2nd or 3rd flag in the same hoist. **-itura** *f.* (derog.) repetition. **-izione** *f.* repetition; revision; private lesson; recitation; rehearsal; (mountaineering) ascent following a route already used; (leg.) request; claim; demand for return;

ripet·ere (*cont.*)
recovery (C.C.); (mil.) fucile a -izione, repeating gun, repeater; orologio a -izione, repeater; (mus.) repetition; rehearsal. **-uto** *part. adj.* repeated; recalled. **-utaménte** *adv.* repeatedly.

ripezzare [A I] and derivs. See **rappezzare**.

ripianare [A I] *tr.* to level; (accounts) to balance; to settle; (agric.) to level (ground) after ploughing.

ripian·gere [C 5] *intr.* (*aux.* avere) to weep again; *tr.* to mourn again.

ripiano *m.* landing (of a staircase); level space; terrace; a ripiani, terraced, in terraces; shelf.

ripicca *f.* See **ripicco**.

ripicchi·are [A 4] *tr.*, *intr.* (*aux.* avere) to knock again; to beat, to strike again; *rfl.* (fam.) to titivate oneself, to dress up. **-ata** *f.* knocking again; polishing up. **-ato** *part. adj.* knocked; beaten, struck; dressed up, smart.

ripic·chio *m.* repercussion.

ripicco *m.* pique; resentment; per —, out of pique; è stato un —, it was done out of pique; †revenge.

ri·pid-o *adj.* steep; precipitous. **-aménte** *adv.* steeply. **-ęzza** *f.* steepness.

ripidolite *f.* (miner.) ripidolite.

ripieg-are [A 2] *tr.* to fold again; to fold up; to bend again; (fig.) — le ali, to draw in one's horns, to become less eager; — le cuoia, to die; (naut.) to furl; *intr.* (*aux.* avere) (mil.) to withdraw, to give way, to retreat; to make shift; vedremo di —, we shall seek a remedy; *rfl.* to fold; to bend; to become bent; to withdraw into oneself; l'anima si -a in se stessa, the soul communes with itself; to sink; -arsi nel vizio, to fall into vice; (of light) to be reflected; (mil.) -arsi a sinistra, to incline to the left. **-aménto** *m.* folding, folding again; bending; tortuousness; reflection (in thought); (mil.) withdrawal, retreat. **-ata** *f.* folding, fold. **-ato** *part. adj.* folded up; bent low; (scient.) plicate; (naut.) furled. **-atura** *f.* double fold; folding; lap.

ripie-go *m.* (*pl.* -ghi) expedient; makeshift; remedy; per —, as the best way out; pretext, excuse. **-ghęvole** *adj.* pliable; flexible.

ripie·n-o, ripięn-o *adj.* (*prep.* di) full up, quite full; replete, stuffed (with); (fig.) filled; caramelle -e, soft-centred sweets; (herald.) croce -a, cross voided; *n.m.* filling; pad; padding; feeling of repletion; pleonasm; (cul.) stuffing; (archit.) curtain wall; (text.) weft, woof; (mus.) full sound (made by multiplication of voices or instruments, or by all stops of an organ); filling up, ripieno; part or instrument or voice which helps to make up the full ensemble; accompaniment (opposed to **concertino**, q.v., in a concerto grosso); diapason chorus (of organ); violino da —, second violin; registri di —, mutation stops; †fullness, fullness of spirit. **-a** *f.* (mining) gob, goaf, waste-filling. **-ęzza** *f.* repletion; surfeit; (of river) fullness, flood; (agric.) a disease of mulberry-trees. **-ista** *m.*, *f.* (mus.) ripienist, rank-and-file player.

ripigli-are [A 4] *tr.* to take again, to catch again; to recover, to regain; (of hair) to shorten; to curl up; (knitting) to pick up (a dropped stitch); to darn (a hole); to resume, to begin again; — il filo del discorso, to take up the thread of a speech again; to repeat; to reply; (naut.) to make up; to square off; to haul taut, to belay; †to take up, to reprove; *intr.* (*aux.* avere) to come to oneself; to recover, to revive; *rfl.* to resume, to go on again; to begin again; to correct oneself; -arsi con, to start fighting again; †see **rappigliare**. **-aménto** *m.* resumption. (**-ato** *part. adj.*) **-atura** *f.* taking (up) again; resuming.

ripiglino *m.* game of cat's cradle; game of throwing up a pebble, etc. and catching it on the back of the hand; (fig.) fare -ino, to get one's own back, *or* to 'break even'.

ripi·glio *m.* reproof.

†**ripinta·glio**. See **repentaglio**.

†**ripire** *intr.* to climb.

†**ripitare** *tr.* to oppose.

†**ripo·nere** *vb.* and derivs. See **riporre**.

ripopol-are [A I s] *tr.* to repopulate; to repeople; *rfl.* to be repopulated. **-aménto** *m.* repeopling; repopulating. (**-ato** *part. adj.*)

ripọrre [B 2 I] *tr.* to replace; to put back; to place, to lay (again); to put on again; to put away; to hide; — le speranze in, to place one's hopes in; to deposit; to store; to put back (in former state); to repair, to restore; *rfl.* to place oneself again; riporsi a sedere, to sit down again; riporsi a leggere, to resume one's reading; to hide; to withdraw; to take a back seat.

ripọrt-are [A I] *tr.* to bring back; to take back; to carry back; to relate; — un passo, to quote a passage; — grazie, to return thanks; — una buona impressione, to receive a good impression; — un premio, to carry off a prize; — una ferita, to receive a wound; (math.) to carry; (accountancy) to carry forward; (eng.) to add (material), e.g. by welding; (paint.) to transfer; — in grande, to enlarge; *rfl.* (*prep.* a) to go back (also fig., in thought); to refer (to), to appeal (to). (**-abile** *adj.* **-aménto** *m.*) **-ato** *part. adj.* brought back; reported; (eng.) added, inserted; *n.m.* (leg.) one party to 'riporto' transaction. **-atore** *m.* relater, reporter; (math.) proportional scale; (leg.) other party to 'riporto' transaction. (**-atrice** *f.*) **-atura** *f.* transfer, reproduction (of a drawing and sim.).

ripọrto *m.* relationship; ornament, esp. of gold or silver embroidery; (leg.) contango contract (C.C.); (eng.) materiale di —, added material; — di terra, embankment; neve di —, drift snow; (comm.) amount carried or brought forward; (finan.) premio di —, contango; giorno del —, making-up day; fare il —, to receive backwardation; pagare il —, to pay contango.

ripọṣ-are [A I] *tr.* to put back, to put down again; to lay down again; to rest; — la voce, to rest one's voice; *intr.* (*aux.* avere) to rest; to sleep; to die; to be at rest; to be buried; — sugli allori, to rest on one's laurels; to trust; -iamo in te, we rely on you; *rfl.* to rest; to cease work; to take time off; to enjoy peace and quiet. †**-aménto** *m.* resting, rest. **-ante** *part. adj.* restful; soothing; pleasant; restful (of colour); tonalità -ante, restful shade; †*n.m.* retired official. †**-anza** *f.* retirement. **-ata** *f.* rest, pause, stop; (mil.) halt, usually a ten-minute rest every hour during a march. **-ato** *part. adj.* rested; calm, placid, quiet, peaceful; deposited (at the bottom of a liquid); settled. **-ataménte** *adv.* calmly, peacefully; quietly, placidly. **-atoio** *m.* landing (of a staircase); resting place. (**-atore** *m.* **-atrice** *f.*)

ripoṣito·rio *m.* (Rom. antiq.) tray for food.

ripoṣizióne *f.* putting on one side; reservation; deposition.

ripọṣo *m.* rest, repose; resting place; quiescence, lethargy; buon —!, sleep well!; giorno di —, day off; (theatr.) questa sera —, no performance tonight; collocare a —, to retire, to put on the retired list; a —, retired; fare la domanda di —, to send in one's resignation; (agric.) in —, lying fallow; landing (of a staircase); (in a carriage) arm-rest; (mil.) —!, stand easy!; a —, in retirement; (phys.) in —, at rest; (archit.) capital (of a column, as that on which an arch rests); (mus.) accordo di —, chord of resolution, cadence-chord.

ripọst-o, ripọst-o *part.* of **riporre**, q.v.; *adj.* put back, put away; — nel fodero, sheathed; hidden; secret; *n.m.* (mil.) store (victualling, clothing or small-arms); (naut.) pantry; in —, in secret. **-aménte** *adv.* secretly; with reserve. **-i·glio** *m.* repository; locker; hiding place; lumber-room; i -igli del cuore, the secret places (innermost recesses) of the heart; (naut.) stowage for small articles in a ship.

ripreda *f.* recovery of booty.

ripregare [A 2] *tr.* to entreat again; pregare e — qualcuno, to beg and implore someone.

ripre·mere [B I] *tr.* to press again; †see **reprimere**.

ripremiare [A 4] *tr.* to award another prize to; to reward again.

ripren·d-ere [C I] *tr.* to take back; to take up again; to retake, to recapture; to resume; to get back; ho ripreso il mio danaro, I have got my money back; — le armi, to take up arms again; — una maglia, to pick up a stitch; to strike, to attack again; lo riprese la febbre, he became feverish again; — fiato, to rest, to get one's breath; — il cammino, to set out again; — il pennello, to start painting again; — a gridare, to start shouting again; to criticize, to blame, to admonish; to reply, to retort; (cinem.) to film; (naut.) to make up; to square off; to haul taut, to belay; — il posto, to regain station; *rfl.* to correct oneself; to recover; to resume (the thread of one's speech); *intr.* (*aux.* avere) to recover (consciousness, strength, vigour); il fuoco ha ripreso, the fire has burnt up again. (**-ente** *part. adj.*) **-iménto** *m.* reproof. (**-itóre** *m.* **-itrice** *f.*)

riprens·i·bile *adj.* reprehensible; blameworthy. (**-ibilménte** *adv.* **-ibilità** *f.*) **-ióne** *f.* reproof; disapproval, blame; (vet.) laminitis. **-ivo** *adj.* critical, reproving, reprehensive. **-ivaménte** *adv.* critically, reprehensively. **-óre** *m.* critic, censor, reprover. (**-óra** *f.*) **-o·rio** *adj.* (*m.pl.* -orii) critical, reproving, blaming.

ripreṣ-a *f.* resumption, recommencement, renewal; a più -e, several times over; (photog.) shot, exposure; le riprese sottomarine, underwater shots; (cinem.) take; macchina da —, apparecchio da —, camera, ciné camera; (telev.) — diretta, live television; (sport) second half (of any game divided into two periods); (boxing) round; (mil.) renewal of hostilities, of a truce or parley; (naut.) recapture of a prize, N.F. prize; (prosod.) *ripresa*, refrain, esp. in the *ballata*; (mus.) repeat; repeat-mark, repeat-sign; refrain; reprise; recapitulation; revival (of opera or play); (horse-racing) acceleration; *pl.* (archit.) toothed wall-end. †-a·glia *f.* reprisal.

ripreṣent-are [A1] *tr.* to present again; to introduce (again); *rfl.* to present oneself again; to offer again. (**-ato** *part. adj.* **-atore** *m.* **-atrice** *f.*)

ripreṣo *part.* of **riprendere**, q.v.; *adj.* taken (back, up) again; reflected, echoed; censured, blamed, reproved; (comm.) pagamento a quattrini -i, net payment of proceeds.

ripreṣso *part.* of **ripremere**, q.v.

†**ripresso** *m.* See **ribrezzo**.

riprillare [A1] *tr.* to spin, to twirl (again).

†**ripriṣo** *part.* See **ripreso**.

ripristin-are [A1] *tr.* to restore; to renew; to re-establish; to re-instate; — la circolazione, to get traffic moving again (e.g. after an accident); (comm.) to reinstate; (bldg.) to make good. **-amento** *m.* restoration, renewal. (**-ato** *part. adj.* **-atore** *m.* **-atrice** *f.*) **-azione** *f.* restoration, renewal. **-o** *m.* see **ripristinamento**.

†**riprobare** *tr.* to disapprove.

riproduc-i·bile *adj.* reproducible. **-imento** *m.* reproducing, reproduction. (Cf. **riprodurre**.)

ripro-durre [B2] *tr.* to reproduce; to produce again; — una scena dal vero, to reproduce a scene from life; — a colore, to reproduce in colour; — con la stampa, to take a print of; (journ.) to print, to carry; *rfl.* to reproduce one's kind; to be reproduced; to recur; to return. **-duttivo** *adj.* reproductive. **-duttore** *m.*; *adj.* reproducing; organi -duttori, organs of reproduction; *m.* reproducer; -duttore acustico (gramophone) pick-up; -duttore fonografico, record player; (of animals) sire. (**-duttrice** *f.*) **-duzione** *f.* reproduction (act or result); copy; replica.

ripromętt-ere [C20] *tr.* to promise again; — di alcuno, to give a guarantee on someone's behalf; *rfl.* (*dat.* of *prn.* 'si') to hope (for); -ersi di venire, to hope to be able to come, to count on being able to come; -ersi da, to expect of, from. **-itore** *m.* surety, guarantor. (**-itrice** *f.*)

ripromissione *f.* guarantee; promise; (Bibl.) terra della —, the promised land.

ripro-porre [B21] *tr.* to propose again; (leg.) — un'azione, to start an action over again. **-ponibilità** *f.* (leg.) -ponibilità di un'azione, possibility of an action being started over again (C.P.P.).

riprova *f.* new proof; new evidence; confirmation; (leg.) stare alla —, to undergo cross-examination; (math., etc.) proof.

riprov-are [A1] *tr.* to try again, to test again; to experience again; to obtain confirmation; to disprove; provando e -ando, by trial and error; to refuse; to reject; — agli esami, to fail, to reject (a candidate); to disapprove, to blame. **-amento** *m.* reprobation; reproof; blame. **-ato** *part. adj.* disapproved; rejected; failed (in examination); (theol.) reprobate, damned; proved again; confirmed; tested by experiment (or experience). **-atore** *m.* reprover, blamer; rejector. (**-atrice** *f.*) **-azione** *f.* reprobation; rejection; (theol.) reprobation. **-ęvole** *adj.* blameworthy, censurable; despicable; shameful. (**-evolmente** *adv.*)

†**ripruova** *f.* See **riprova**.

ripua·rio *adj.* riparian; (leg.) leggi ripuarie, Ripuarian laws.

ripubblic-are [A2s] *tr.* to republish, to publish again; to reissue. **-a·bile** *adj.* fit for republication. **-ato** *part. adj.* republished; reissued. **-azione** *f.* republication, reissue.

ripudi-are [A4] *tr.* (leg.) to disavow; to disclaim; to disown; to reject; to repudiate. (**-a·bile** *adj.*) **-ato** *part. adj.* disowned; rejected; repudiated; la -ata, the repudiated wife. (**-atore** *m.* **-atrice** *f.*)

ripu·dio *m.* disowning; repudiation; rejection; fare il —, to divorce one's wife; — del mondo, retirement, withdrawal from the world.

ripugn-are [A5] *intr.* (*aux.* avere; *prep.* a) to be contrary (to); le sue parole -ano all'evidenza, his words are contrary to the evidence; — al buon senso, to be contrary to common sense; to be repugnant to; cibo che -a allo stomaco, repugnant food; †to fight. **-ante**

part. adj. repugnant; disgusting; -ante da, opposed to, contrary to, contradictory to; that cannot be reconciled, incompatible. (**-antemęnte** *adv.*) **-anza** *f.* repugnance; aversion; -anza dello stomaco, nausea; reluctance; imcompatibility.

ripul-ire [D2] *tr.* to clean again; to clean; to tidy; to clear away; to purge; to polish, to revise; to make a clean sweep of; to eat up; (needlw.) to finish off; (in a game) to sweep the board; — uno, to clean a person out, to take (or win) all his money; — dalle erbacce, to weed; *rfl.* to clean oneself (up), to tidy oneself; to smarten oneself up. **-imento** *m.* clearing out; cleaning (up); refining. **-isti** *m. indecl.* see **repulisti**. **-ita** *f.* cleaning up; clearance; clearing away; bracco di -ita, dog sent through a covert to clear the last of the game; revising, polishing; touching up. **-ito** *part. adj.* clean; polished; finished off; tidy; smart. (**-itore** *m.* **-itrice** *f.*) **-itura** *f.* cleaning; clearing; waste, refuse.

ripullulare [A1] *intr.* (*aux.* avere or essere) to spring up again; to swarm, to pullulate again; *tr.* to cause to spring up again (cf. **pullulare**).

ripuls-a *f.* refusal, rejection, repulse; ebbe una —, he met with a refusal, he was repulsed. **-are** [A1] *tr.* to repulse, to refuse; to reject; to deny. (**-ato** *part. adj.* **-atore** *m.* **-atrice** *f.*) **-azione** *f.* rejection; confutation. **-ione** *f.* repulsion; aversion; repugnance; (mech.) repulsion. **-ivo** *adj.* repulsive; repellent. **-o** *adj.* rejected; repulsed; *n.m.* (naut.) see **regresso**.

ripuntatore *m.* (agric.) subsoiler.

ripurg-are [A2] *tr.* to purify; to revise, to correct. **-amento** *m.* purging; purifying. **-ativo** *adj.* purgative. **-ato** *part. adj.* purged; purified; revised, corrected. **-atura** *f.* (metall.) remelting of pig-iron.

ripur-go *m.* (med., usu. *pl.* **-ghi**) lochia.

riputare [A1 def.] and derivs. See **reputare**.

riquadr-are [A1] *tr.* to square; to dress (stone); to true, to true up; to measure (surface); — le stanze, to redecorate walls with a cornice or border, etc.; *intr.* (*aux.* avere) to be square; to be true; to measure; questa stanza -a venti metri, this room measures twenty square metres; non mi -a, it doesn't seem right to me. **-ato** *part. adj.* squared; true, quite square; marked, or arranged, in squares; scarpe -ate in punta, square-toed shoes; (math.) squared; *n.m.* square. **-atura** *f.* squaring; square; (naut.) square portion of the loom of an oar or of the bunt of a yard. **-o** *m.* (naut.) see **battente**; square; (archit.) panel, coffer; rectangular panel; inset (of diagrams, photographs, etc.).

riqualificazione *f.* restatement of policy.

riregistr-are [A1] *tr.* (acoust.) to re-record. (**-ato** *part. adj.*) **-azione** *f.* (acoust.) re-recording.

risa *f.pl.* of **riso**, q.v.; †*f. sing.* laugh; laughter.

risacca *f.* (naut.) backwash.

risa·i-a *f.* paddy-field, rice-field, rice-plantation; building for threshing and polishing rice. **-uola** *f.* worker in paddy-fields. (**-uolo** *m.*)

risald-are [A1] *tr.* to resolder; to mend; to consolidate; (of a wound) to cause to heal; to solder. **-amento** *m.* soldering; mending. **-ato** *part. adj.* resoldered; soldered; mended. **-atura** *f.* resoldering; soldering; mending; consolidation; solder; cement.

risal-ire [D13] *intr.* (*aux.* essere) to go up again; to go back; to rise again; to travel upstream; (fig.) bisogna — al medio evo per trovare esempi, we must go back to the Middle Ages to find instances; to go back (to), to date back (to); il barometro -e, the barometer is rising; (of prices) to keep rising; (archit.) to project; *tr.* to ascend (again); — le scale, to go upstairs again; — un fiume, to go upstream. **-imento** *m.* rising again; projection. **-ita** *f.* projection, prominence; fresh ascent. **-ito** *part. adj.* (derog.) risen in the world; upstart.

risalt-are [A1] *tr.* to jump over (across) again; — il fosso, to jump over the ditch again; *intr.* (*aux.* avere or essere) to spring up again; to stand out, to be prominent; il giallo -a sul turchino, yellow stands out against dark blue; far —, to make conspicuous; (archit.) to project; to stand out; to be prominent; (fig., of person) to be prominent; to be conspicuous; (of truth) to be self-evident. **-amento** *m.* standing out, prominence, relief. (**-ato** *part. adj.*) **-azione** *f.* (rare) prominence; rebound.

risalto *m.* prominence; relief; vividness; (archit.) projection; relief; (mil.) crown, beak on the handle of a sword; glacis; counterscarp; dar — a, to enhance, to lay emphasis on, to make prominent; senza —, inconspicuous.

risalut-are [A I] *tr.* to salute again; to return a greeting to, to greet in return. (**-ato** *part. adj.* **-azione** *f.*)

risan-are [A I] *tr.* to heal, to cure; to restore to health; — il cervello a, to teach sense to, to knock sense into; to reclaim; — l'aria, to clear the air; — lo spirito a, to restore the serenity of; *intr.* (*aux.* essere), *rfl.* to recover; to be restored to health. **-a·bile** *adj.* curable; capable of reformation; (of land) reclaimable. **-amento** *m.* cure; recovery; reformation; improvement; slum clearance; (of land) reclamation. **-ato** *part. adj.* healed, cured; (of land) reclaimed; (made) healthy, salubrious. **-atore** *m.* healer; *adj.* healing; reforming. (**-atrice** *f.*)

risanci-ano, -one *adj.* See **ridanciano**.

risap-ere [B 26] *tr.* to get to know; to hear about; to find out; se la cosa si risà, if the matter leaks out; to know well; *intr.* (*aux.* avere) to smell, to taste. **-uto** *part. adj.* known, very well known; una cosa **-uta**, a thing that everyone knows.

risarc-ire [D 2] *tr.* to repair; to mend; to make good; to restore; (leg.) to compensate (for); to indemnify; to make good; — uno della perdita, to compensate someone for his loss; — il danno, to make good the damage; — i danni, to pay damages. **-i·bile** *adj.* repairable; reparable; that can be compensated or made good; indemnifiable; (leg.) for which compensation is claimable; for which there is liability for damages; danno **-ibile**, injury sounding in damages. **-imento** *m.* repair; restoration; compensation; (leg.) **-imento dei danni**, compensation; damages; indemnity; reparation. (**-ito** *part. adj.*)

risat-a *f.* laugh; burst of laughter; scoppiare in una —, to burst out laughing; che **-e!**, how we (they) laughed!; rispondere con una —, to reply with a laugh. **-ina** *f. dim.* sly laugh, laugh up one's sleeve; snigger.

risa·zi-o *adj.* sated; sazio e —, more than satisfied. **-are** [A 4] *tr.* to satisfy very fully (cf. **saziare**).

riscald-are [A I] *tr.* to warm; to heat; — per mezzo di una stufa, to heat by means of a stove; to overheat; to heat again; to heat up; (fig.) to excite; *intr.* (*aux.* essere) (of weather) to become milder; (of wine, etc.) to ferment; to generate heat; *rfl.* to warm oneself; to get warm; to get hot; (fig.) to get excited; to get heated; **-arsi a freddo**, to feign enthusiasm, to be moved without cause. **-amento** *m.* heating; charge for heating (e.g. on hotel bills); **-amento centrale**, central heating; **-amento a pannelli radianti**, radiant heating; excitement, irritation; (med.) feverishness; heat spots. **-ata** *f.* warm; warming up. **-ato** *part. adj.* heated; warm; warmed up; in a perspiration; angry, excited; (of food) saper di **-ato**, to taste as if warmed up; (fig.) minestra **-ata**, stale ideas, *or* a decision, previously rejected, subsequently adopted. **-atore** *m.* heater; **-atore a immersione**, immersion heater. (**-atura** *f.*) **-o** *m.* heat; sudden access of passion; irritation; **-o di testa**, fancy, caprice; (tanning) sweating; (tailoring) lining for extra warmth.

riscarnare [A I] *tr.* (tanning) to reflesh.

riscatt-are[1] [A I] *tr.* to ransom; to redeem; to liberate; to set free; (leg.) to redeem; to pay off; to buy back; *rfl.* to redeem oneself; to free oneself, to vindicate oneself. **-a·bile** *adj.* redeemable. (**-ato** *part. adj.* **-atore** *m.* **-atrice** *f.*) **-o** *m.* ransom; redemption; liberation; recovery; (leg.) payment off; redemption; surrender; diritto di **-o**, right of redemption; valore di **-o**, surrender value (of insurance policy) (C.C.); (theol.) redemption, ransom, ransoming.

riscattare[2] [A I] *intr. repet.* of **scattare**, q.v.

ri-scegliere [B 27] *tr.* to choose carefully; to choose again; to make another choice. (**-sceglimento** *m.*) **-scelta** *f.* more careful choice; further or subsequent choice; restricted selection. **-scelto** *part. adj.* very choice, carefully selected.

†**riscerre** *vb.* and derivs. See **risceglieere**.

rischiar-are [A I] *tr.* to light up; to illumine, to illuminate; — la via, to light the way; to make lighter, to lighten; — la voce, to clear one's voice; to elucidate, to explain; to enlighten; (agric.) to thin out; *rfl.*, *intr.* (*aux.* essere) (of the sky, weather) to clear; to clear up; (of water) to clear, to become clear; to clarify; (of colour) to become light, bright. **-amento** *m.* lighting up; clearing up; brightening; clarification; elucidation. **-ato** *part. adj.* lighted up; illumined. (**-atore** *m.* **-atrice** *f.*)

rischiare [A 4]. See under **rischio**.

rischiar-ire [D 2] *intr.* (*aux.* essere), *rfl.* (of sound, voice, etc.) to clear, to become clear. **-imento** *m.* clearing (up). **-ito** *part. adj.* cleared, clear.

ri·sch-io *m.* risk, hazard; correre il —, to run the risk; a — di

ventura, come what may; mettersi a — di, to risk; (comm.) i **-i** della guerra, war risks; la merce viaggia a — del destinatario, goods sent at consignee's risk; a — di mare e di gente, against risk of storms and theft (in a maritime contract); a — del compratore, at buyer's risk. **-iare** [A 4] *tr.* to risk, to expose to risk; to venture; to hazard; *intr.* (*aux.* avere) to run a risk; to run risks; **-iò di rompersi il collo**, he ran the risk of breaking his neck. **-ioso** *adj.* risky, full of risk; dangerous; hazardous; rash, daring, ready to take risks.

risciacqu-are [A I] *tr.* to rinse again; to rinse well; to rinse out; to swill; (provb. phr.) — i suoi cenci in Arno, to revise an Italian work in conformity with Florentine usage (as Manzoni revised his novel); (techn.) to rinse, to flush out; *rfl.* (*acc.* of *prn.* 'si') to wash (oneself) in clean water; to splash; (*dat.* of *prn.* 'si') (fig.) **-arsi la bocca di uno**, to speak ill of someone. **-amento** *m.* rinsing. **-ata** *f.* rinse, rinsing; (fig.) reproach, rebuke; scolding; fare una **-ata** a uno, to scold someone. **-ato** *part. adj.* rinsed; (colloq.) very wet. **-atoio** *m.* (techn.) rinsing vat; spillway. **-atore** *m.* rinser. **-atrice** *f.* rinser; rinsing machine. **-atura** *f.* rinsing; rinse; (fig.) **-atura in Arno**, a rinse in the Arno (a phrase referring to Manzoni's revision of his novel); rinsing water; dish-water; **-atura di bicchieri**, bad, weak wine; **-atura di piatti**, bad soup; (fig.) bad essay, worthless writing; (techn.) rinse.

risciac·quo *m.* gutter (to take water across a road); shallow ditch; (med.) mouthwash, rinse.

riscintillante *adj. intens.* of **scintillante**, q.v.; sparkling, brilliant; star-spangled.

risciò *m. indecl.* rickshaw.

†**risco** *m.* See **rischio**.

ri·scolo *m.* (bot.) saltwort, *Salsola kali* and *S. soda*.

riscont-o *m.* (leg.) rediscount; *m.* contabile attivo e passivo, book-keeping practice on entering debits and credits. **-are** [A I c] *tr.* (leg.) to rediscount.

riscontr-are [A I c] *tr.* to meet; to go to meet; to find, to notice; to verify, to check; to compare; (comm.) to reply to; to rediscount; (typ.) to check (corrections) on proofs; *recip. rfl.* to meet; to cross; le nostre lettere si **-arono**, our letters crossed; to match, to correspond; to be consistent. **-a·bile** *adj.* that may be found; questo errore è **-abile** in molte altre opere, this mistake is to be found in many other works; that can be checked. **-amento** *m.* meeting, finding; checking; collation. **-ata** *f.* check. **-ato** *part. adj.* met; collated, verified; found. **-atore** *m.* checker; **-atore di conti**, auditor; inspector. (**-atrice** *f.*)

riscontro *m.* opposition; correspondence; checking; collation; (typ.) last checking of proofs before printing; mettere a —, to compare; belle parole che non trovano — nei fatti, fine words that are not accompanied by deeds; reply; in — alla vostra lettera, in reply to your letter; far degno — a, to be a match for; draught (of air); (eng.) calibro di —, reference gauge, master gauge; (mus.) clash; (leg.) proof or check of witnesses; requital, reciprocation; trovar — d'amore, to find one's love requited; (Tusc.) meeting, encounter; receipt, acknowledgement, reply; confirmation.

riscoprire [D 8] *tr. repet.* of **scoprire**, q.v.

riscorr-ere [C 5] *tr.* to run through; to look over; to read through; to revise; to have another look through; to go over in one's mind. (**-imento** *m.*)

riscoss-a *f.* recovery; redemption; redress; liberation; insurrection; †(mil.) support given by the second line to the leading column; schiera di —, reserve column; †ransom. **-ione** *f.* collection (of payment, rent, tribute, tax); encashment; *pl.* takings. **-o** *part.* of **riscuotere**, q.v.; *adj.* received, collected; recovered; liberated; restored. **-one** *m.* violent start, jerk, shock.

risco·tere *vb.* and derivs. See **riscuotere**.

riscri·vere [C 12] *tr.* to rewrite; to write again; to transcribe, to copy.

riscuo·t-ere [C 15] *tr.* to rouse; to awaken; to receive payment of; to cash (a cheque); to redeem, to take out of pawn; to get back, to obtain again, to receive back; *rfl.* to give a start, to start; to come to, to rouse oneself; to take revenge, to get one's own back; to free oneself. **-i·bile** *adj.* payable; receivable. (**-ibilità** *f.* **-imento** *m.*) **-itore** *m.* knocker-up; receiver; **-itore delle imposte**, tax-collector. (**-trice** *f.*)

riscurare [A I] *intr.* (*aux.* essere) (paint.) to become darker.

risdal·lero *m.* (numism.) thaler, rix-dollar.

risec-are [A 2] *tr.* to cut away (branches, etc.); — le spese, to cut down expenses; to remove, to extirpate. (**-ato** *part. adj.*)

risecc-are [A2c] *tr.* to dry up again; *intr.* (*aux.* essere), *rfl.* to dry up; to wither. (**-ante** *part. adj.* **-ato** *part. adj.*)

risecch-ire [D2] *intr.* (*aux.* essere) (Tusc., pop.) to dry up, to become dry; questo pane *-isce* facilmente, this bread soon becomes stale. *-ito part. adj.* dried up, very dry; stale; (fig.) dull, uninteresting, dry.

risęc-co *adj.* (*m.pl.* **-chi**) dry; dried up; withered.

rised-ęre [B28] *intr.* (*aux.* avere) to sit again (for all other meanings see **risiedere**).

risega *f.* (masonry) set-off; (mil. fortif.) step, decrease in thickness of a protecting wall or armour plate; weal (on flesh, as result of tight binding); roll of fat (on person's flesh).

riseg-are [A2] *tr.* to saw off; to cut away, to cut down; (archit.) to form a set-off in. (**-ato** *part. adj.*) **-atura** *f.* cutting away, cutting down; sawdust; notch (in wood).

risęgna *f.* assignment; transfer; review.

risegn-are [A5c] *tr.* to mark again; †to sign in approval of, to ratify. (**-ato** *part. adj.*)

riseguitare [A1s] *tr. repet.* of **seguitare**, q.v.

riselciare [A3c] *tr. repet.* of **selciare**, q.v.

risella *f.* rice of very poor quality.

†**risembrare** *tr.* to resemble; to imitate.

riseminare [A1s] *tr. repet.* of **seminare**, q.v.

risens-are [A1] *intr.* (*aux.* essere), *rfl.* to recover one's senses; to come round. (**-ato** *part. adj.*)

risent-ire [D1] *tr.* to hear again; to feel again, to feel acutely; to feel the effect of; to suffer, to experience; *intr.* (*aux.* avere; *prep.* di) to show traces; to resound, to echo (with); (bldg.) to crack (e.g. as an after-effect of an earthquake); *rfl.* to wake up; to recover one's senses, to come to; *-irsi di*, to feel the effects of, to show resentment at, to be offended by; (of plants) to recover, to begin to flourish. **-imęnto** *m.* resentment; con *-imento*, resentfully; (med.) after-effect; (bldg.) crack (e.g. in a wall); (paint.; sculp.) expression of feeling (by attitude). **-itęzza** *f.* susceptibility, touchiness. **-ito** *part. adj.* heard again; felt again; experienced; awakened, awake; conscious; resentful, angry; vigorous, lively; loud; muscoli *-iti*, prominent muscles; (paint.) bold, lively (of manner, style); *adv.* resentfully, with resentment.

riseppell-ire [D2] *tr.* to bury again. **-imęnto** *m.* reburial, removal to a fresh burial place. **-ito** *part. adj.* reburied.

riserb-are [A1] *tr.* to keep, to reserve; to save. **-atęzza** *f.* reserve, reservedness. **-ato** *part. adj.* hidden, secret; reserved. (Cf. **riservare**.)

riserbo *m.* reserve, reservedness; reticence, circumspection; discretion; restraint; senza —, unreservedly; custody; sotto buon —, in safe keeping.

riseri·a *f.* rice mill.

riserr-are [A1] *tr.* to shut again; to close, to compress; to keep safe; *rfl.* to shut oneself up. (**-amęnto** *m.*) **-ata** *f.* shutting up; enclosing; enclosure. **-ato** *part. adj.* shut again; shut up, closed; puzzo di *-ato*, close, musty smell.

riserv-a *f.* exception; restriction; senza —, without restriction, without reserve; stock; di —, reserve, stand-by; (leg.) reservation; reserve; (eccl.) reservation (of benefice); (mil.) reserve force; reserve; appartenere alla —, to be in reserve; ufficiale di —, officer on the reserve list; passare alla —, to be placed on the reserve list; (naut.) reserve; navi alle *-e*, ships in reserve and out of commission; — di galleggiabilità, — di spinta, reserve buoyancy; — di stabilità dinamica, righting moment, metacentric height; †squadron kept as reinforcement; (comm.) reserve fund held by insurance companies to meet abnormal claims; — occulta, hidden reserve(s); reserve; rest; — metallica, gold and silver reserve held against issued nominal money; senza —, without reserve; fondo di —, reserve fund; passivo di —, reserve liability; — d'oro, gold reserve; reserve, spares, spare parts; store (also as place); (fishing or shooting) preserve; aver di —, to hold in reserve; superior quality of wine or spirits of a given vintage. **-are** [A1] *tr.* to keep, to reserve, to set aside; to put off; to book (a seat); *-iamo* questa discussione ad altro momento, let us put off this discussion till another time; una grande sorpresa mi era *-ata*, a great surprise was awaiting me; *rfl.* to reserve oneself; to keep for oneself; to delay until a suitable occasion; mi *-o* di farlo più tardi, I propose doing it at a later time; (comm.) ci *-iamo* di mandarvi il preventivo col prossimo corriere, we shall send you the estimate by next mail. **-atęzza** *f.* circumspection, caution. **-ato** *part. adj.* reserved; private; confidential; personal (on a letter); (theol.) caso *-ato*,

reserved case; peccato *-ato*, reserved sin. **-atamęnte** *adv.* reservedly, with reserve; in private. (**-atore** *m.* **-atrice** *f.*) **-ista** *m.* (mil.) reservist.

riservire [D1] *tr. repet.* of **servire**, q.v.

risgridare [A1] *tr. repet.* of **sgridare**, q.v.

risguard-are [A1] *tr.* to regard; to look at; to respect; to concern; *intr.* (*aux.* avere; *prep.* a) to show consideration (to); to be retrospective; to refer, to have reference (to). **-amęnto** *m.* regard; consideration. **-ante** *part. adj.* regarding; concerning. **-o** *m.* regard; respect, consideration; (bookb.) end paper; †view, window, light; *pl.* anxiety, solicitous regard.

risi·bil-e *adj.* ridiculous; laughable; †capable of laughter. **-ità** *f.* ridiculousness.

ri·sic-o *m.* (pop.) risk; andai a — di cadere, I nearly fell. **-are** [A25] *tr.* (pop.) to risk; *intr.* (*aux.* avere) to take risks; (provb.) chi non *-a* non rosica, nothing venture nothing gain. **-ato** *part. adj.* risked. **-atore** *m.* (naut., Leghorn) member of a salvage undertaking. **-oso** *adj.* risky, hazardous; (of a person) daring, venturesome.

risicoltura *f.* rice-growing, rice-cultivation.

risie·d-ere [B28] *intr.* (*aux.* avere) to reside; to be resident; to have one's flat; to be situated, to lie; (canon law) to reside; (theol.) — nei cieli, to dwell, to be, in Heaven; (of a liquid) to settle. **-ente** *part. adj.* residing; resident; situate. **-enza** *f.* (liturg.) see **residenza**.

†**risigallo** *m.* (miner.) realgar.

†**ri·sima** *f.* See **risma**.

risi·pol-a *f.* (med.) erysipelas. **-ato** *adj.* (med.) suffering from erysipelas. **-oso** *adj.* (med.) erysipelatous.

rişma *f.* (of paper) ream; quality; tutti della stessa —, all of the same quality; gente d'ogni —, people of all kinds.

ris-o¹ *m.* (*pl.* **-a** *f.*) laugh, laughter; crepare, sbellicarsi dalle *-a*, to split one's sides with laughing; (provb.) il — fa buon sangue, 'laugh and grow fat'; smile, pleasant expression, gaiety; brightness, splendour; (med.) — sardonico, risus sardonicus. **-arella** *f.* uncontrollable laughter; fit of the giggles. **-olino** *m. dim.* smile; little laugh.

ris-o² *m.* (bot.) rice, *Oryza sativa*. **-otto** *m.* (cul.) dish of rice cooked with gravy or mushrooms, scampi, etc.; *-otto* alla milanese, risotto flavoured with saffron; (theatr.) claque; compagnia del *-otto*, people paid to applaud in a theatre.

risoffiare [A4c] *tr. repet.* of **soffiare**, q.v.

risognare [A5c] *tr. repet.* of **sognare**, q.v.

risol-are [A1] *tr.* (shoem.) to resole. **-ato** *part. adj.* (shoem.) resoled. **-atura** *f.* (shoem.) resoling.

risolcare [A2c] *tr. repet.* of **solcare**, q.v.

risollev-are [A1] *tr.* to raise again, to lift up again; to raise, to improve; to comfort; to rouse again; *rfl.* to be cheered, comforted (again), to take fresh courage. (**-ato** *part. adj.*)

risolto *part.* of **risolvere**, q.v.; *adj.* solved; resolved.

risolu·bile *adj.* soluble; solvable; resolvable.

risolut-o *part. adj.* dissolved; melted; faded away; resolved; decided; (paint.; sculp.) maniera *-a*, bold, decided style; (agric.) terreno —, light soil, loose earth. **-amęnte** *adv.* resolutely; without hesitation; †safely, surely. **-ęzza** *f.* resolution; con *-ezza*, resolutely, deliberately. **-ivo** *adj.* (med.) resolutive, laxative; (leg.) resolutive; resolutory; revoking a prior obligation; clausola *-iva*, determination clause; (opt.) potere *-ivo*, resolving power; (math.) formula *-iva*, formula for solving a problem.

risoluzięne *f.* resolution; decision; prendere una —, to make up one's mind; solution (solving or dissolving); commissione per le risoluzioni, resolutions committee; progetto di — comune, draft joint resolution; — sostitutiva, substitute resolution; (leg.) annulment; avoidance; cancellation; determination; discharge; rescission; resolution; revocation; termination; solemn judgement; (med.) resolution; clearing up (e.g. of an abscess); (mus.) resolution; solution (of a canon); (paint.) softness, flabbiness; †analysis.

risol·v-ere [C14] *tr.* to solve; to dissolve; to resolve; — una questione, to settle a question; (mus.) to resolve; to solve (a canon); (leg.) to annul; to cancel; to determine; to make void; to rescind; to resolve; to revoke; to terminate; (agric.) to break up the ground, to plough, to harrow, to dig; to determine, to decide; to induce, to persuade; *intr.* (*aux.* avere) (med.) to resolve (e.g. of an abscess), to clear up; (of weather) to change; *rfl.* to dissolve, to melt; to break up, to disintegrate; to resolve, to decide, to make

risolv-ere (*cont.*)
up one's mind; to be reduced, to end; le sue promesse si risolsero in nulla, his promises ended in (came to) nothing. **-ente** *part. adj.* resolvent; resolving. **-enza** *f.* (opt.) resolution. **-i·bile** *adj.* soluble; resolvable; that can be dissolved (fig.). **-imento** *m.* solution (in a liquid); resolution, decision.

rison-are [A I d] *intr.* (*aux.* essere, avere) to resound; to ring; to echo; to be famous; -arono gli applausi, applause rang out; *tr.* to ring again; to play (music) again; to utter; to celebrate (fame, name). **-amento** *m.* reverberation, resonance. **-ante** *part. adj.* resonant, resounding, sonorous. (**-antemente** *adv.*) **-anza** *f.* resonance, echo; sound, voice, sonority; (phys.) entrare in -anza, to resonate; (fig.) il discorso ebbe molta -anza, the speech gave rise to a great deal of discussion; (mus.) resonance, sustaining-power. **-atore** *m.* resonator.

risone *m.* (agric.) paddy.

risorcina *f.* See **resorcina**.

risorg-ere [C 5] *intr.* (*aux.* essere) to rise again; to spring up again; to be restored (to health, strength, consciousness); to flourish again; mi risorse il dubbio, my doubts returned; (rel.) to rise from the dead, to be resurrected; *tr.* to raise again; to bring back to life; to reinvigorate. **-ente** *part. adj.* springing up again, resurgent.

risorgiment-o *m.* revival, resurgence, renaissance; *pr.n.m.* (hist.) the period in the nineteenth century, and the movement which then took place, by which Italy acquired independence and unity; (theol.) — della carne, resurrection of the body. **-ale** *adj.* relating to the (Italian) Risorgimento.

risorgiva *f.* (geog.) Vauclusian spring; spring-line.

risorsa *f.* resource; uomo di molte risorse, very resourceful man; risorse naturali, natural resources.

risorto¹ *part.* of **risorgere**, q.v.; *adj.* resuscitated; risen again; new.

†risorto² *m.* direct dominion, feudal right or jurisdiction; tribute.

risospin·g-ere [C 5] *tr.* to push back; to shove again; mi risospinse verso la porta, he pushed me back towards the door. **-imento** *m.* push backwards.

risospinto *part.* of **risospingere**, q.v.; *adj.* repelled; pushed back.

risospirare [A I] *tr.*, *intr. repet.* of **sospirare**, q.v.

risotterrare [A I] *tr. repet.* of **sotterrare**, q.v.

risotto *m.* See under **riso²**.

risottomettere [C 20] *tr. repet.* of **sottomettere**, q.v.

risovven-ire [D 16] *impers.* to come to mind, to be remembered; *intr.* (*aux.* essere; *prep.* a) to come again to the help (of); far — a, to remind; *rfl.* to remember; to recollect. **-imento** *m.* recollection; memory, help.

rispalmare [A I] *tr. repet.* of **spalmare**, q.v.

rispar·gere [C 4] *tr. repet.* of **spargere**, q.v.

risparmi-are [A 4] *tr.* to save; to spare; — le forze, to husband one's strength; — il fiato, to save one's breath; non mi —, don't spare me (i.e. I'll do all I can to help); *abs.* to economize; — a uno una cattiva notizia, to spare someone a bad piece of news; *rfl.* (*acc.* of *prn.* 'si') to spare oneself; (*dat.* of *prn.* 'si') -arsi la fatica di, to save oneself the effort of. **-ato** *part. adj.* saved; spared. **-atore** *m.* saver, one who saves; *adj.* saving, thrifty; poco -atore, rather thriftless. (**-atrice** *f.*)

rispar·mio *m.* saving; vive dei suoi risparmi, he lives on his savings; per — di tempo, in order to save time; senza —, without stint; fare risparmi, to economize; (comm.) savings; Cassa nazionale di —, Post Office Savings Bank; libretto di — postale, (equiv. of) Post Office Savings bank book; cassa di —, building society; piccolo —, small savings account, bearing interest, with a bank. Note: Italian banks issue 'libretti di risparmi', i.e. for unlimited amounts, at a low rate of interest, and 'libretti di piccolo risparmio', which pay a higher rate of interest, but with a maximum limit.

rispecchi-are [A 4] *tr.* to reflect; to mirror; *rfl.* to be mirrored. **-ato** *part. adj.* reflected; mirrored.

risped-ire [D 2] *tr.* to send again; to ship again; to send back; to forward. (**-ito** *part. adj.*)

rispett-are [A I] *tr.* to respect; to have regard for; to honour; to concern, to regard; *rfl.* to have self-respect. **-a·bile** *adj.* respectable; estimable; worthy; considerable; (joc.) big. (**-abilità** *f.* **-ato** *part. adj.*) **-ivo** *adv.* respective; own; particular; tornarono alle -ive case, each of them returned to his own house; †respectful. **-ivamente** *adv.* respectively, relatively; -ivamente a, relating to; in regard to.

rispett-o *m.* respect; la morte non porta — nè ai giovani nè ai vecchi, death respects neither young nor old; regard; i miei -i a sua madre, my regards to your mother; passar sopra i -i umani, to defy conventions; per — umano, for fear of what people may say; con — parlando, excuse my mentioning it (*or* them; used esp. when one mentions one's feet); — a, in respect of, as regards; per ogni —, in every respect; in every way; al — con, as compared with; cavallo di —, remount, spare horse; (naut.) spare, reserve; ancora di —, sheet anchor; vele di —, stormsail; albero di —, jurymast; abeti di —, spars; ala di —, trysail; linea di —, limit of territorial waters; (theol.) — umano, human respect; (comm.) account; giorni di —, days of grace; (poet.) love poem in a stanza of eight or six lines (a popular art-form, esp. of the Tuscan countryside). **-oso** *adj.* respectful; †circumspect. **-osa** *n.f.* (euphem.) prostitute (after Sartre's *La Putain Respectueuse*). **-osamente** *adv.* respectfully.

rispian-are [A I] *tr.* to level thoroughly; to make plain, to explain. (**-ato** *part. adj.*)

†rispiarmare *vb.* and derivs. See **risparmiare**.

†rispi·gnere *vb.* and derivs. See **respingere**.

rispigol-are [A I s] *tr.* to glean thoroughly; (fig.) to scrape together, to collect. **-amento** *m.* gleaning; culling, collecting (e.g. of words, phrases). (**-ato** *part. adj.*)

rispinta *f.* push back, repulse.

†rispitto *m.* See **rispetto**.

risplen·d-ere [B I] *intr.* (*aux.* essere, avere) to shine; to glitter; to be brilliant; to be famous; *tr.* to radiate; to shine with. **-ente** *part. adj.* shining; glittering; resplendent. **-entemente** *adv.* splendidly; with great brilliance. †**-enza** *f.* splendour, resplendence. †**-e·vole** *adj.* brilliant; exciting admiration; beautiful. †**-imento** *m.* brilliance, splendour. †**-ore** *m.* splendour.

rispond-ere [C 11] *intr.* (*aux.* avere; *prep.* a), to answer, to reply (to); — a traverso, to answer at cross-purposes; — al nome di, to answer to the name of, *or* to answer in the name of; — a uno scopo, to answer a purpose; (mil.) — evasivamente, to reply by evasion; (naut.) to reply, to answer (a signal); to acknowledge (a salute); (mus.) to answer; (leg.) to give an opinion; to respond, to comply; (cards) to respond (with the play expected); to pay what is due; (of a horse) to obey (the bridle); to correspond; (of windows, rooms) to look; — a mezzogiorno, to have a southern aspect; (agric.) to give a proper return; to answer back, to make objections; obbedire e non —, to obey without question; — di, to answer for, to be responsible for, to be guarantor for; — dei danni, to be liable in damages (C.C.); to answer, to utter in reply; — poche parole, to answer in a few words; (cards) — picche, to reply with spades, (fig.) to give an abrupt refusal, to refuse a request; *recip. rfl.* to correspond; to answer each other. **-ente** *part. adj.* answering; corresponding; proportionate, in harmony. **-enza** *f.* correspondence; relation, agreement, harmony; repercussion; reply. †**-e·vole** *adj.* answering, corresponding. **-iero** *adj.* inclined to answer back; impertinent. (**-itore** *m.* **-itrice** *f.*)

risponsa·bile *adj.* and derivs. See **responsabile**.

risposare [A I] *intr.* (*aux.* avere) to marry again, to remarry.

rispost-a, rispost-a *f.* answer, reply; (mus.) answer; — reale, real answer; — del tuono, tonal answer; (mil.) reply to a recognition signal or any other message; counter, counter measure, 'riposte'; (fencing) counterblow, (leg.) botta e —, blow and counterblow, (fig.) quick repartee; (leg.) memoria di —, pleading in answer (C.C.P.); (comm.) — dei premi, declaration of options; giorno di —, contango; (electron.) response; — complessiva, overall response. **-ac·cia** *f. pejor.* rude answer. **-o** *part.* of **rispondere**, q.v.; *adj.* answered. **-uc·cia** *f.* (derog.) perfunctory answer.

†risquittire *tr.* (hawking) to adjust the feathers of.

†risquitto *m.* rest, respite.

riss-a *f.* brawl; fare —, to brawl; fray; polemic. **-ai(u)olo** *adj.* quarrelsome; ready to fight; *n.m.* quarrelsome person. **-ante** *part. adj.* fighting; *n.m.* fighter; quarreller, brawler. **-are** [A I] *intr.* (*aux.* avere), *recip. rfl.* to brawl, to quarrel; to fight. (**-atore** *m.* **-atrice** *f.*) **-oso** *adj.* quarrelsome.

ristabil-ire [D 2] *tr.* to re-establish; to restore; *rfl.* to be re-established; to be restored; -irsi in salute, to be restored to health. **-imento** *m.* restoration; re-establishment; recovery. (**-ito** *part. adj.*)

ristagn-are¹ [A 5] *intr.* (*aux.* avere) to stagnate, to become stagnant, to revert to marsh; (of blood) to congeal, to cease flowing; *tr.* to make stagnant; to stanch. (**-amento** *m.*) **-ante** *part. adj.* stagnant.

ristagn-are (*cont.*)
-**ativo** *adj.* styptic; restricting or stopping the flow. -**o** *m.* ceasing to flow; stagnation; marsh; stagnant pool; (fig.) stagnation, slackness; (comm.) slack period.

ristagn-are[2] *tr.* (techn.) to retin, to solder. (-**ato** *part. adj.*) -**atura** *f.* retinning; soldering; cost of soldering.

ristamp-are [A I] *tr.* to reprint. -**a** *f.* reprint, reprinting; impression; terza -**a**, third impression. -**a·bile** *f.* fit for reprinting. -**ato** *part. adj.* reprinted. (-**atore** *m.* -**atrice** *f.*)

ristare [A 9] *intr.* (*aux.* essere) to stay again; to stay; to stop, to cease, to leave off; — nell'atto di, to stop in the very act of; to hesitate; non — dal chiedere, don't hesitate to ask; *rfl.* to stop; non ristarsene, to keep at it, to persevere.

ristaurare [A I a] and derivs. See **restaurare**.

ristill-are [A I] *tr.* to redistil. (-**ato** *part. adj.*)

ristimare [A I] *tr. repet.* of **stimare**, q.v.

ristoppiare [A 4 c] *tr., intr.* (*aux.* avere) to cut and gather stubble; to glean; to repeat a corn crop on the same ground.

ristorare [A I] *tr.* to restore; to refresh; to feed; to replenish; to reward, to compensate for; to make amends for; *rfl.* to refresh oneself; to eat something; to rest. (-**a·bile** *adj.*) -**amento** *m.* refreshment; restoration. -**ante** *part. adj.* refreshing, restorative; *n.m.* restaurant; (rlwy.) vagone -**ante**, dining car. -**ativo** *adj.* refreshing; *n.m.* restorative. -**ato** *part. adj.* refreshed; restored; compensated. -**atore** *m.* restorative, cordial; restaurant-keeper; (rlwy.) refreshment room; *adj.* refreshing. (-**atora**, -**atrice** *f.*) -**azione** *f.* restoration, repair; compensation; refreshment.

ristorn-o *m.* rebound. -**are** [A I c] *intr.* (*aux.* essere) to bounce back, to rebound.

ristoro *m.* refreshment; relief; rest; posto di —, rest-room; reparation; compensation; (iron.) per —, besides, into the bargain.

ristrett-o *part.* of **ristringere**, q.v.; *adj.* narrow, limited, restricted, confined; close together; un uomo di vedute -**e**, a narrow-minded man; ditemi il prezzo —, tell me your lowest price; (cul.) brodo —, clear soup, consommé, *or* soup made with very little water; caffè —, a small cup of very strong coffee (as opposed to 'caffè lungo'); †conclusion. -**amente** *adv.* strictly, narrowly, closely. -**ezza** *f.* narrowness; poverty; vivere in -**ezza**, to live in straitened circumstances. -**is·simo** *adj. superl.* (comm.) prezzo -**issimo**, lowest possible price; *n.m.* summary, précis; in -**issimo**, very briefly; -**issimo** di gente, small group of people; lowest price. †-**iva** *f.* (typ.) mould; forme. -**ivo** *adj.* restrictive, limiting; (gramm.) particella -**iva**, restrictive particle. -**ivamente** *adv.* strictly, rigorously; to a limited extent.

†**ristri·gnere** *vb.* and derivs. See **ristringere**.

ristrin·gere [C 5] *tr.* to grasp, to clasp again; to draw close again; to restrict; to retighten; (fig.) — l'amicizia, to renew friendship; *recip. rfl.* to sit closer together, to squeeze up.

ristrofinare [A I] *tr. repet.* of **strofinare**, q.v.

ristucc-are [A 2] *tr.* (bldg.) to replaster; (fig.) to cloy, to disgust; to tire, to weary; (fam.) to make 'fed up'. -**amento** *m.* disgust, boredom. (-**ato** *part. adj.*) -**atura** *f.* plastering; mending, or cost of same; join or mark of mending (e.g. in furniture).

ristuc-co *adj.* (*m.pl.* -**chi**) tired, weary; bored; 'fed up'.

ristudiare [A 4] *tr. repet.* of **studiare**, q.v.

ristuzzicare [A 2 s] *tr. repet.* or *intens.* of **stuzzicare**, q.v.

risuc·chi-o *m.* eddy, suction; (naut.) swirl, downward pull experienced in a whirlpool, in the wake of a ship, or when a vessel sinks; (aeron.) downwash; (foundry) shrinkage. -**are** [A 4] *tr.* to suck back; to absorb again; (fig.) to listen to or endure with boredom; dovetti -**are** tutto il racconto, I had to listen to the whole boring story again. (-**ato** *part. adj.*)

risud-are [A I] *intr.* (*aux.* avere) to sweat again; to drip; (of leaves) to be dripping with moisture; (of walls) to sweat. (-**amento** *m.*)

risult-are [A I] *intr.* (*aux.* essere) to result; to spring; to follow; to emerge; to come out; ciò -**erà** dai documenti, that will appear from the documents; la sua colpa -**ò** da vari fatti, his guilt was proved by various facts; *impers.* mi -**a** che sta per partire, I hear, I am told, I understand, he is just going away; non mi -**a**, ma sarà come voi dite, I have no information about it, but no doubt you are right; ti -**a** nulla del latrocinio in via del Senato?, do you know anything about the burglary in Parliament Street? -**a·bile** *adj.* likely to result; probable. -**amento** *m.* consequence, result. -**ante** *part. adj.* resultant, resulting; (mech.; math.) resultant; forza -**ante**, resultant force. -**anza** *f.* result; issue. -**ato** *part. adj.*

resulted, resulting; *n.m.* result; issue; outcome; (finan.) -**ato** negativo, bankruptcy.

risuonare [A I d] and derivs. See **risonare**.

risurrezione *f.* resurrection; revival; (theol.) resurrection.

risuscit-are [A I s] *tr.* to resuscitate; to revive; — dall'oblìo, to call back from oblivion; (theol.) to raise from the dead; *intr.* (*aux.* essere) to revive; to rise; (theol.) to rise again, to rise from the dead. -**amento** *m.* resurrection; resuscitation. -**ato** *part. adj.* resurrected; revived; pale and thin (as if raised from the dead). (-**atore** *m.* -**atrice** *f.*) -**azione** *f.* resuscitation.

risvegli-are [A 4 c] *tr.* to wake up; to rouse; to waken; to revive; questo -**ò** la mia curiosità, this aroused my curiosity; — l'ira di uno, to excite someone's anger; *rfl.* to wake up again; to revive. -**amento** *m.* awakening; rousing; coming to life. -**ativo** *adj.* rousing. -**ato** *part. adj.* awakened; awake; revived. -**atore** *m.* awakener; knocker-up; *adj.* rousing. (-**atrice** *f.*)

risveglio *m.* awakening; al mio —, when I awoke; che doloroso —!, what a sad awakening!; — della coscienza pubblica, awakening of public conscience; revival; — del commercio, trade revival.

risvolta *f.* turn back; lapel (of coat); cuff; †(mil.) revolver.

risvolt-are [A I] *intr.* (*aux.* avere) to turn back; to reverse. -**a·bile** *adj.* reversible (of cuffs, collars, etc.).

risvolto *m.* lapel, facing, cuff; flap (of book cover); (eng.) welt.

ritagli-are [A 4] *tr.* to cut again; to cut away; to cut out; to clip off; — l'olio, to draw the oil off the dregs and separate it into different vessels according to quality. (-**ato** *part. adj.*) -**atore** *m.* cutter; seller of remnants (cloth). (-**atrice** *f.*) -**uzzare** [A I] *tr.* to cut into little bits.

rita·glio *m.* cutting, clipping, piece cut out; — di giornale, newspaper cutting; (of cloth) remnant; lapel; *pl.* clippings; nei ritagli di tempo, in odd moments, in one's spare time; a —, (by) retail.

ritard-are [A I] *tr.* to delay; to defer, to postpone; to retard; (mus.) to slow down; to suspend; *intr.* (*aux.* avere, essere) to be late; (of a clock) to be slow; to delay. -**a·bile** *adj.* that can be delayed, deferred, postponed. -**amento** *m.* delaying; deferment; postponement; delay; slowing down. -**ando** *ger.* (mus.) ritardando, slowing down. -**ante** *part. adj.* retarding; delaying, deferring; *n.m.* (chem.) retarder. -**anza** *f.* delay, retarding. -**ata·rio** *m.* late-comer; lingerer; unpunctual person; defaulter (in payment). -**ativo** *adj.* delaying; causing lateness. -**ato** *part. adj.* retarded; delayed; late; (eng.) ad azione -**ata**, delayed-action; (mus.) nota -**ata**, suspended note, retarded note. -**atore** *m.* laggard; (techn.) retarder; (eng.) time-lag device; †late-comer. (-**atrice** *f.*) -**azione** *f.* delaying; delay.

ritardo *m.* delay; lateness; slowness; lag; in —, late; (of a train) avere un forte —, to be very late, to be greatly behind schedule; avere dieci minuti di —, to be ten minutes late; riguadagnare, rimettere il —, to make up (lost) time; (mus.) suspension, retardation; (eng.) deceleration; (astron.) retardation.

ritavolare [A I 5] *tr.* (surv.) to measure the area of (a piece of ground).

ritegno *m.* reserve; reservedness; restraint; impediment; avere — a, to hesitate to, to be reluctant to, to shrink from; fu costruita una diga a — delle acque, a dam was built to keep back the water(s); muro di —, retaining wall; (eng.) valvola di —, non-return valve.

ritemp(e)r-are [A I, A I s] *tr.* to retemper; to strengthen; — le forze, to restore one's strength; to resharpen; *rfl.* to recover one's strength; to find new strength. -**ato** *part. adj.* strengthened; -**ato** dal dolore, grown strong through grief; -**ato** nelle sventure, tempered by misfortune.

riten-ere [B 32] *tr.* to detain; to withhold; to stop, to hold back; to hold; to regard, to consider; to think; non lo -**go** un amico, I do not regard him as a friend; non -**go** che sia mio dovere, I don't consider it my duty; to remember (what has been learnt); to own, to possess; to keep; to accept (gift, invitation, etc.); to acquire; *rfl.* to restrain oneself; to stop, to stay; to consider oneself. -**ente** *part. adj.* restraining; (mus.) checking the speed. †-**enza** *f.* restraint; reserve; support. -**imento** *m.* restraint; obstacle; stay; acceptance. -**itore** *m.* harbourer; receiver; keeper; holder; *adj.* retaining, retentive. (-**itrice** *f.*) -**uta** *f.* deduction; stoppage; -**uta** sui salari, deduction from wages; hold; guiding-rope. -**uto** *part. adj.* retained; restrained; maintained; deducted; reserved; (mus.) ritenuto, slackening the speed.

ritentare [A I, A I c] *tr., intr.* (*aux.* avere) to try again; *imp., quasi adv. phr.* tenta ritenta, try, try again (after repeated attempts); to tempt again.

†**ritentire** *intr.* to resound.

ritentiv-a *f.* memory, retentive faculty; (phys.) hysteresis. **-o** *adj.* retentive.

ritenzione *f.* reserve; restraint; deduction; (med.) — di urina, urine retention; impediment; arrest, detention; possession; (leg.) diritto di —, right of retention (C.C.).

rites·s-ere [B I] *tr.* to weave again; to retell (story); to recompose; to do again. (-**itura** *f.* -**uto** *part. adj.*)

ritin·gere [C 5] *tr.* to dye again; to paint again; to dip again; (eccl.) ritingersi l'abito col minio, 'to dye one's cassock red', i.e. to be made a cardinal.

ritint-o *part.* of ritingere, q.v.; *adj.* dyed; repainted; (of hair) dyed; tinted. **-ura** *f.* dyeing; tinting.

ritir-are [A I] *tr.* to withdraw; to retract; to take back, to revoke; — una promessa, to take back one's promise; to shorten, to diminish; to import; to send for; to draw; to accept delivery of; — il premio, to carry off the prize, to receive the award; to collect; to fetch; — la posta, to take one's post or mail out of a locker or letter box; to draw (as salary); (comm.) to withdraw; to cancel; — moneta, to withdraw money (from circulation); — un ordine, to cancel an order; — una cambiale, to pay a bill; — dalla circolazione, to demonetize; to withdraw (a book) from circulation (as a result of a libel action or by order of the police); *rfl.* to retire, to withdraw, to retreat; to go away, to depart; to go home; to shrink; (mil.) to retreat, to withdraw, to fall back; (leg.) to retire from a sitting or hearing; *intr.* (*aux.* avere) to shrink; to take after, to resemble. **-amento** *m.* withdrawal; tapering; shrinking; -amento verso il principio, return to the beginning; retirement. **-ata** *f.* withdrawal; retirement; (mil.) retreat, withdrawal; departure; tenersi aperta la -ata, to keep open a line of retreat; battere in -ata, to beat a retreat; (naut.) retreat; withdrawal; breaking off action; punteria in -ata, cannoni in -ata, stern guns; combattimento in -ata, running fight, escaping; tiro in -ata, fire abaft the beam; formazione in -ata, retreating order; portelli in -ata, stern posts; suonare la -ata, to sound the recall, to beat the retreat; -ata dei franchi, return of libertymen; tiro della (di) -ata, sunset gun, recall gun (in Italy also a gun fired when leave is up); †paranco di -ata, gun tackle; latrine, closet, lavatory; pretext; excuse for withdrawal; place of retirement, refuge. (-**atamente** *adv.*) **-atezza** *f.* retirement; retiringness; reserve. **-ato** *part. adj.* withdrawn; retired; reserved; at home again; (mil.) withdrawn, re-entrant; fianco -ato, withdrawn wing; re-entrant bastion. **-o** *m.* withdrawal; andai alla posta per il -o della corrispondenza, I went to the post-office to fetch my letters; camera di -o, private boudoir; retirement; retreat; non voleva abbandonare il suo -o, he did not want to leave his retreat; convent; penitentiary; return home; in -o, retired, pensioned; shrinkage, contraction; confiscation; il -o della patente, confiscation of driver's licence; (metall.) piping.

†**ritmeg·gio** *m.* rhythmic pattern.

rit·mic-a *f.* rhythmic(s). **-o** *adj.* rhythmical, rhythmic; (mus.) rhythmic, rhythmical; accento -o, rhythmical accent; movimento -o, measured motion (in dancing); *n.m.* rhythmicist. **-amente** *adv.* rhythmically, in rhythm.

ritm-o *m.* rhythm; measure; verse; in pieno —, in full swing; rate, pace; — metabolico, basal metabolic rate; (mus.) rhythm; — di tre battute, three-bar rhythm; (archit.) harmonious proportions. **-are** [A I] *tr.* to beat out (rhythm); i tamburi -ano i canti, the drums beat out the ryhthm of the songs. †**-eggiato** *adj.* (mus.) arranged in rhythm, rhythmized. †**-o·ide** *m.* (mus.) free rhythm, recitative.

rito *m.* rite, ceremony; usage; custom; è di —, it is customary, prescribed by custom; (liturg.) Rite (Roman, Ambrosian, Coptic, Mozarabic); (eccl.) Congregazione dei Riti, Congregation of Rites.

ritocc-are [A 2 C] *tr.* to touch up; — una corda, to bring up an old subject; (paint.) — a secco, to touch up a fresco when the plaster is dry; to touch up; — i prezzi, to revise prices; *intr.* (*aux.* avere) to insist; *rfl.* to tidy oneself; (of a horse) to overreach (to strike the forefeet with the hind). **-ata** *f.* touch; retouching, touching up; finishing touch; correction. **-ato** *part. adj.* (paint.) touched up; altered, revised, corrected. (-**atore** *m.*) **-atura** *f.* retouching, touching up.

ritoc·co *m.* (*pl.* -**chi**) retouch; touch; finishing touch; correction; adjustment; revision, increase (of taxes, rlwy. fares, etc.); (photog.) retouching; *apocop. part.* of ritoccare, q.v.

ritogli·ere [B 27] *tr.* to take back, to take again; to take away, to take off; -erne un altro, to take another; to set free, to save; *rfl.* to take oneself off; -ersi da, to free oneself from.

ritond-are [A I C] *tr.* to round off; to make round. **-ato** *part. adj.* rounded (off).

ritone *m.* (Gk. antiq.) rhyton, drinking-cup.

ritonfare [A I C] *intr.* (*aux.* essere) to plunge, to fall again; (fig., iron.) ritonfa!, there we go again!, haven't we had enough of that?

ritor·c-ere [C 5] *tr.* to twist again; to retort, to rebut (e.g. an accusation); (text.) to double, to twist; *rfl.* to twist backwards, to get twisted. **-i·bile** *adj.* that can be twisted; that can be rebutted. **-imento** *m.* rebuttal; (text.) doubling, twisting. **-itoio** *m.* (text.) doublling frame, twister. **-itore** *m.*, **-itrice** *f.* (text.) twister, doubler. **-itura** *f.* striking again; (text.) doubling; twisting; doubling mill; throwing (of silk); (knitting) cabling.

†**rito·rica** *f.* See rettorica.

ritorn-are [A I C] *intr.* (*aux.* essere) to return; to come back; to go back; to become once more; — sopra, — su, to go over again (in one's mind); to recover (from illness, etc.); to recur; to occur; to redound; ne -a a onore, it brings glory; *rfl.* to turn back; to go back; *tr.* to give back, to bring back, to return; — da, to turn from, to lead away from. **-a·bile** *adj.* returnable; leading back. **-ata** *f.* return; (eccl.) return of a procession; outdoor procession (esp. in Octave of Corpus Christi). **-ato** *part. adj.* returned; recovered.

ritornell-o *m.* (poet.) refrain; (mus.) ritornello, ritornel; symphony (i.e. instrumental introduction or passage between the vocal sections of an aria); orchestral tutti (in a concerto); refrain; repeat, repetition; repeat-mark, repeat-sign; (fig.) repetition; non fa che ripetere il solito —, he is always harping on the same string; fare —, to beg again. **-ato** *adj.* (poet.) having a 'ritornello' or refrain.

ritorno *m.* return; fare —, to go back, to return; via del —, way back; biglietto di andata e —, return ticket; di —, on returning; essere di —, to be back; (sport) partita di —, return match; girone di —, second half of the season; (telev.) flyback, retrace; (comm.) vuoti di —, return of empties; carico di —, homeward cargo; spese di —, back charges; merci di —, returned goods; cavalli di —, horses back from a job; (fig.) carrozza di —, stale news, stories coming back to the one who first told them; recurrence, repetition; (electron.) — acustico, acoustic feedback; (naut.) hauling part of a rope; bozzello di —, leading block; fiamma di —, paying off pennant, (techn.) blowback of a flame; (motor.) — di fiamma, backfire; (eng.) return, reversion, recovery.

†**ritorre** *vb.* See ritogliere.

ritorsione *f.* retort, retorting; fare una —, to turn an opponent's arguments against him; retaliation.

ritort-o *part.* of ritorcere, q.v.; *adj.* twisted, contorted; folded up; via -a, tortuous path (way, road); (fig.) retorted, rebutted; turned against the originator; (text.) doubled, twisted; filo —, yarn; (text.) doubled yarn, folded yarn; (archit.) volute; *n.m.* (text.) yarn. **-a** *f.* withy; cord; bond; chain; subterfuge; (naut.) see **torticcio**; (mus.) crook (of a brass instrument). **-i·glio** *m.* twisted thread; tangle.

ritor·t-ola *f.* bond; expedient, excuse; (provb.) aver più — che fastelli, to be over-ready with excuses, to have more withies than faggots; trovar la sua — ad ogni fascio, to have an answer to everything, a remedy or trick for every occasion. **-ura** *f.* convolution(s), contortion.

ritossire [D I] *intr.* (*aux.* avere) to cough again; to answer by a little cough.

ritradurre [B 2] *tr.* to retranslate; to revise the translation of.

ritraente *adj.* representing; reproducing; depicting, portraying.

ritran·gol-o *m.*, **-a** *f.* (comm.) the repurchase of the sold article at a lower price.

ritrarre [B 33] *tr.* to draw back; to draw again; to withdraw; to turn away; — l'attenzione di uno, to divert someone's attention; to get, to obtain; to reproduce, to represent; (paint.) to portray, to make a portrait of; to copy, to reproduce (a drawing, etc.); to depict; to extract (information, etc.); to obtain payment, to collect; — dalla banca, to withdraw from the bank; to report (on someone or something); to bring back (an answer, etc.); to conclude, to understand; *intr.* (*aux.* avere) to approach; to resemble; — da, to take after; *rfl.* to draw back; to withdraw; to give up (an enterprise); to portray oneself.

ritrasmęttere [C 20] *tr.* to retransmit; to rebroadcast.

ritrasmissione *f.* retransmission, rebroadcast.

ritratt-are¹ [A I] *tr.* to treat again; to resume an exposition of; to retract, to recant, to recall; to withdraw; to report; (comm.) to retract, to return; *rfl.* to withdraw one's words, to retract what one has said; to recant. †-a *f.* (naut.) see riflusso. **-ȧ·bile** *adj.* retractable. (**-abilità** *f.*) (**-ato** *part. adj.* **-atore** *m.* **-atrice** *f.*) **-azione** retraction; recantation; withdrawal; rehandling; shortening; (comm.) **-azione di documenti**, discovery of documents.

ritratt-are² [A I] *tr.* to make a portrait of; to photograph; farsi —, to have one's photograph taken; *rfl.* to portray oneself; to have one's portrait made or photograph taken. (**-ato** *part. adj.*)

ritrat·tile *adj.* retractile; (aeron.) carro —, retractable undercarriage.

ritratt-o *part.* of ritrarre, q.v.; *adj.* drawn back; reported; represented, portrayed; *n.m.* portrait, picture; image; essa è proprio il — della salute, she looks the very picture of health; è proprio il — di suo padre, he is the very image of his father; account (of historical events, conditions, etc.); (finan.) fare — di, to sell, to liquidate; (leg.) — litigioso, transfer of a disputed credit. **-ista** *m.*, *f.* (paint.) portrait painter; *adj.* relating to portrait painting.

ritra·vio *m.* (paperm.) pulp-agitator, hog.

ritrazione *f.* retraction, diminution; contraction.

ritręcine *m.* throwing net, circular net having lead pellets around the periphery, which when cast over the water descends like a parachute; mill-wheel (set horizontally); (fig.) andare a —, to go to the dogs, to rush headlong to ruin.

†**ritrep·pio** *m.* flounce.

ritrinciato *adj.* (herald.) croce ritrinciata, cross ending in four fusils.

ritrit-o *adj.* hashed, minced; (fig.) trite. **-are** [A I] *tr.* to pulverize, to mince finely. (**-ato** *part. adj.*)

ritroncato *adj.* (herald.) per fess, the base also per fess.

ritrosa *f.* bag-net; net for birds; tuft of hair that will not lie down.

ritros-o *adj.* moving backwards, retrograde; averse; reluctant; bashful, shy; — alle nuove dottrine, slow to respond to new ideas; *adv. phr.* a —, backwards; against the grain; — della corrente, against the stream; *n.m.* eddy, backwash; turn-back at the mouth of a lobster pot; slow or shy person; fare il —, to feign reluctance. **-amente** *adv.* reluctantly; with aversion. **-ag·gine** *f.* shyness; reluctance. **-i·a** *f.* shyness; aversion; reluctance; repugnance; awkwardness, stubbornness. †-ità *f.* see ritrosia.

ritrov-are [A I] *tr.* to find again, to recover; (comm.) — il conto, to agree the account; to retrace (a path), to follow (footsteps); to go back over, to go over again (drawing, etc.); to find; to discover; to meet, to visit; to recognize; -o nel viso di lui le sembianze paterne, I can see his father's features in his face; *rfl.* to find oneself; to be; attualmente mi -o a Parigi, I am in Paris at present; to happen to be; mi -ai al fatto, I was present on the occasion; to come to one's senses, to awake; to feel at home; non mi ci -o, I don't see my way, I don't quite know where I am; ci si -a sempre bene in compagnia di gente onesta, one always feels at ease in the company of good people; come si -a?, are you happy where you are?, how do you feel in that place?; *recip. rfl.* to meet. **-a·bile** *adj.* to be found; recoverable. **-amento** *m.* finding; meeting; discovery; (theatre) recognition. **-ata** *f.* finding; discovery; invention. **-ato** *part. adj.* found (again); met; *n.m.* invention; contrivance, device; lie; cunning trick; meeting; meeting-place. **-atore** *m.* discoverer; inventor, deviser. (**-atrice** *f.*)

ritrovo *m.* meeting, gathering; meeting-place, resort, haunt; punto di —, rendezvous, meeting-place; the 'local'; — notturno, night club; (mil.) meeting-place, rendezvous, post; sentry post.

ritt-o *adj.* straight; standing; upright, erect; (provb.) sacco vuoto non sta —, one cannot work on an empty stomach; nè per —, nè per rovescio, in no wise; *n.m.* right side (opp. to wrong); (coin or medal) obverse, 'heads'; straight line; vertical line, upright; prop; (mining) pit prop; *adv.* straight; quite; †qui —; just here. **-a** *adj.* right; *n.f.* right hand. †**-orove·scio** *adv.* back to front; upside down.

ritual-e *adj.* ritual; customary; (archit.) architettura —, ecclesiastical architecture; *n.m.* ritual. (**-mente** *adv.*) **-ismo** *m.* (rel.) interest in ritual; ritualism; High Church movement in England. **-ista** *m.*, *f.* (rel.) expert on ritual; liturgiologist; ritualist; High-Churchman; Anglo-Catholic.

rituffare [A I] *tr.* repet. of tuffare.

ritur-are [A I] *tr.* to recork; to stop up again; to obstruct again; *rfl.* to become blocked again. **-amento** *m.* stopping up; stoppage.

riun·gere [C 5] *tr. repet.* or *intens.* of ungere, q.v.

riunione¹ *f.* meeting, gathering; prender parte a una —, to attend a meeting; — preliminare per le istruzioni, briefing meeting; — non ufficiale, unofficial meeting; — della tavola rotonda, round table meeting, — a porte chiuse, meeting *in camera*; — di certi specialisti, panel meeting; (leg.) — di procedimenti, consolidation of actions (C.C.P.); (mil.) recall, rallying signal; (naut.) punto di —, rendezvous.

Riunione² *pr.n.f.* (geog.) Réunion.

riun-ire [D 2] *tr.* to reunite, to bring together again; to unite, to join, to combine, to gather; to reconcile; (mil.) to re-form, to revise, to review, orders, plans, state, etc.; (naut.) to rejoin; (equestr.) — un cavallo, to 'collect' a horse; *rfl.* (acc. of prn. 'si') to come together again, to be reunited; to join; to meet; to be joined, combined; (*dat.* of prn. 'si') **-irsi i capelli**, to tidy one's hair. (**-imento** *m.* **-ito** *part. adj.*) **-itrice** *f.* (text.) lapping machine.

riunto *part.* anointed, oiled, greased (again); (fam.) pidocchio —, ciuco —, upstart.

riurt-are [A I] *tr.* to knock again; to knock in reply; *recip. rfl.* to bump together. (**-amento** *m.* **-ato** *part. adj.*)

rius-are [A I] *intr.* (aux. essere) to be in use again, to be used; ora -ano i calzoni larghi, wide trousers are now being worn again; *tr.* to use again. (**-ato** *part. adj.*)

riusc-ire [D 16] *intr.* (aux. essere) to go out again; to go out; to come out; la strada riesce in piazza del Duomo, the street leads to the Cathedral Square; to reach; to succeed; to become, to turn out to be; l'impresa -ì, the undertaking was successful, turned out well; to be able; non -irete mai a persuaderlo, you will never be able to persuade him; non riesco a capire, I am at a loss to understand; — su, to look out on; la finestra riesce sul giardino, the window looks out on to the garden; non capisco a che cosa egli voglia —, I can't understand what he is driving at; *impers.* non mi riesce di farlo, I can't manage (to do) it; gli -ì fatto, he succeeded in doing it. **-i·bile** *adj.* likely to succeed; possible, feasible. (**-ibilità** *f.*) **-ita** *f.* result, event; success; quest'abito ha fatto una buona -ita, this dress has worn well; il ragazzo non fece nessuna -ita, the boy did not get on at all; way out, issue, exit. **-ito** *part. adj.* issued; successful.

riutilizzazione *f.* (industr.) re-utilization; (atom. phys.) reprocessing.

riva *f.* bank; shore; andare in — al mare, to go to the seaside; mantenersi a —, to hug the shore; sotto —, close to the bank; street running alongside a river or canal, e.g. Riva degli Schiavoni at Venice; essere a —, to have arrived; venire a —, to reach the end; — del mare, seashore; (naut.) shoreline; — banchinata, quay; a —, aloft; a —!, order to go aloft; avere tutto il cotone a —, to have all sail spread; avere la bandiera a —, to fly the flag; ancora a —, anchor in sight; parata a —, manning the yards, placing men aloft on masts and yards; (agric.) terrace facing south.

rivaccinare [A I] *tr. repet.* of vaccinare.

†**rivag·gio** *m.* See riva.

rival-e *m.* rival; competitor; *adj.* rival; (Bologna) net used in river fishing. **-eggiare** [A 3 C] *intr.* (aux. avere; *prep.* di) to be the rival (of); to emulate; to compete (with), to vie (with).

rivalęre [B 34] *rfl.* (*prep.* su qualcuno, di qualche cosa) to recover (health, money, property); to make good one's losses.

rivalità *f.* rivalry; emulation.

rivalsa *f.* (comm.) indemnity; reimbursement; redraft; cross bill; second draft; re-exchange.

rivalut-are [A I] *tr.* to revalorize, to revalue. **-azione** *f.* revalorization, revaluation.

rivang-are [A 2] *tr.* to dig up again; (fig.) to recall, to rake up, to revive; non rivanghiamo il passato, let bygones be bygones. (**-ato** *part. adj.*) **-atura** *f.* digging up again; (fig.) recalling, raking up again.

rived-ęre [B 35] *tr.* to see again; a rivederLa (arrivederLa), goodbye, see you again soon; to revisit; to look over, to examine (again), to revise, to correct; to edit (a text); la maestrina -eva i compiti delle sue scolarette, the schoolmistress was marking, going over her pupils' exercises; lasciarsi —, to put in another appearance, to go back; làsciati — qualche volta, come and see us now and then; (eng.) to overhaul; (comm.) — il conto, to examine an account; to audit; *recip. rfl.* to meet again; a rivederci (arrivederci), goodbye, see you again (soon). **-i·bile** *adj.* revisable; (mil.) recluta -ibile, recruit due for examination the following year.

rived-ere (*cont.*)

-**imento** *m*. reviewing, revising, revision. -**itorato** *m*. inspectorate; office of revisor or checker. -**itore** *m*. see **revisore**. (-**itrice** *f*.) -**itura** *f*. (techn.) inspection; †revision, correction. -**uta** *f*. quick second glance; hurried revision. -**uto** *part. adj.* seen again; revised; corrected.

riveggente *part.* of **rivedere**, q.v.; *adj.* revising.

rivel-are [A 1] *tr.* to reveal, to disclose; to show, to display; (theol.) to reveal; (radio) to detect; *rfl.* to reveal oneself; to show oneself (to be); to be revealed. (-**a·bile** *adj.* -**abilità** *f*.) -**ante** *part. adj.* revealing. -**ativo** *adj.* revealing, designed to reveal. -**ato** *part. adj.* revealed; shown (to be); (theol.) revealed (truth, dogma). -**atore** *m*. revealer; (metall.) -atore di incrinature, crack detector; (photog.) developer; (radio) detector; coherer; *adj.* revealing. (-**atrice** *f*.) -**azione** *f*. revelation, disclosure; manifestation; (theol.) revelation; (comm.) -azione di documenti, discovery of documents; (techn.) detection.

rivellino *m*. (mil. hist.) ravelin, detached outer work.

rivelto *adj.* (agric.) uprooted; *n.m.* root torn up.

rivend-ere [B 1] *tr.* to resell; to retail; to sell again; to repeat; la -o come l'ho sentita, I repeat it as I heard it; to surpass, to beat hollow; per quel che sia prosperità, l'Olanda ci -e, in commercial prosperity Holland is streets ahead of us. †-**eri·a** *f*. trickery, fraud. -**i·bile** *adj.* suitable for resale. (-**ibilità** *f*.) -**itore** *m*. seller, retailer; prezzo ridotto per -itori, trade price. (-**itora** *f*. -**itrice** *f*.) -**u·gliolo** *m*. seller of second-hand goods. -**uto** *part. adj.* sold; resold.

rivendic-are [A 2 s] *tr.* to vindicate; to claim (successfully); to recover; to avenge again; (leg.) to sue for recovery; to vindicate; to exercise right of rivendication; *rfl.* to vindicate oneself; to take revenge (again). (-**ato** *part. adj.*) -**atore** *m*. vindicator. (-**atrice** *f*.) -**azione** *f*. vindication; (techn.) patent claim; (leg.) rivendication.

rivendita *f*. resale; small retail shop; sconti di —, trade discount.

rivendugliolo *m*. See under **rivendere**.

riven-ire [D 1 8] *intr.* (aux. essere) to come back; to come again; ora mi riviene, now I remember; — nel suo grado, to be re-instated; — in, to come into possession of; to result in. (-**uto** *part. adj.*)

riverber-are [A 1 s] *tr.* to reflect; to echo; to throw back, to reverberate; *intr.* (aux. essere), *rfl.* to be reflected; to be a reflection; to reverberate. -**ato** *part. adj.* reflected, cast back. -**atoio** *m*. (metall.) roof of reverberatory furnace. -**azione** *f*. reverberation; radiation; reflection.

river·bero *m*. reverberation; reflection; glint, gleam (of reflected light); reflector; di —, by reflection, indirectly; (phys.) reverberation; (metall.) forno a —, reverberatory furnace.

river-ente *adj.*, -**enza** *f*. See under **riverire**.

river-ire [D 2] *tr.* to respect; to revere, to venerate; to pay one's respects to; -isca per me sua madre, please give my kind regards to your mother; -isco, goodbye (or other salutation in formal circumstances, generally used by those in humble condition when speaking to superiors). -**ente** *part. adj.* reverent; respectful. (-**entemente** *adv.*) -**enza** *f*. act of reverence; bow; respectful salutation; fare una -enza, to bow, to make a low bow; fate le mie -enze al signore, please give my respects to your husband (cf. **reverenza**). -**enziale** *adj.* see **reverenziale**. -**enzina** *f*. *dim.* (fam.) little bow, as made by a child. -**enzone** *m*. *augm.* low bow, deep bow. -**enzioso** *adj.* ceremonious, given to much bowing. -**ito** *part. adj.* respected, revered; mio -ito signore, my dear sir; (iron.; joc.) i miei -iti dubbi, I don't think! (-**itore** *m*. -**itrice** *f*.)

rivernici-are [A 3] *tr.* to repaint. (-**ato** *part. adj.*) -**atura** *f*. repainting.

riversale *f*. (eccl.) promise made by both parties in a mixed marriage.

rivers-are [A 1] *tr.* to pour (out, in), to pour out again; to upset, to overturn; to turn (clothes); — la colpa su altri, to throw (cast, put) the blame on others; to inflict a reverse upon, to defeat; (cinem.; radio) to dub; *intr.* (aux. essere) (of a pan, etc.) to boil over; *rfl.* to pour, to flow; to overflow; to rush; to throng, to go in crowds. -**amento** *m*. pouring, outpouring; flowing, overflow. -**ato** *part. adj.* turned, turned over, round, back.

riversi·bil-e *adj.* (leg.) reversionary; alienable. -**ità** *f*. (leg.) condizione di -ità, provision for reversion; stipulare la -ità, to reserve the reversion; patto di -ità, reversionary clause (C.C.).

riversione *f*. reversion; return; (leg.) reversion; (scient.) reversal.

rivers-o *adj.* turned back; reversed; on one's back, supine; cadere —, to fall on one's back; occhi -i, eyes staring out of one's head;

(archit.) gola -a, cyma reversa, ogee (moulding); arco —, ogee arch; *n.m.* overturning, upsetting; wrong side, back; contrary; back-hander, blow with the back of the hand; disaster.

†**river·tere** *tr.* to overturn; to turn back. †-**ire** *tr.* to convert; to turn.

†**rivesciare** *vb.* and derivs. See **rovesciare**.

rivest-ire [D 1] *tr.* to dress (again); to fit out (with clothes), to provide a new outfit; — le armi, to take up arms again; to invest (in an office); to line (a garment); to cover; (mil.) to revet (a trench, etc.); to face; to put an outer cover or lining of stone, etc. (on an earthwork); (bldg., etc.) to coat, to cover, to face, to line; — con mattonelle, to tile; — con pannelli, to panel; — con isolante, to lag; — un muro, to plaster a wall, cover a wall with marble, etc.; — un terreno, monte, to reafforest a piece of land, a mountain; *rfl.* to dress oneself again; to change one's clothes; to put on new clothes; to be reclothed, recovered; *rfl.* (theol.) — di carne, to be clothed in flesh again, to resume one's body. -**imento** *m*. dressing again; reclothing, recovering; (techn.) lining, coating; facing; covering, upholstery; (aeron.) cowling; (mil.) revetment. -**ito** *part. adj.* dressed again; dressed better; villano -ito, peasant grown rich; lined; covered; (metall.) covered, plated; alto forno -ito, blast furnace with chamber hearth. -**itura** *f*. covering; -itura dei fiaschi, (straw) covering of bottles.

rivett-are [A 1 c] *tr.* to rivet. -**ato** *part. adj.* riveted. -**atrice** *f*. riveting machine.

rivett-o *m. dim.* of **rivo**; rivulet; rivet; — a maschio, screw rivet; — spaccato, split rivet. -**ino** *m. dim.* small rivet; (mil.) guard on the basket of a sword handle.

rivier-a¹ *f*. coast; uccelli da —, waterfowl; a caccia e a —, for birds and other small game; da bosco e da —, adaptable; (tanning) reparto di —, wet shop, beamhouse; †river; †countryside. -**asco** *m.* (*pl.* -**aschi**) inhabitant of the Riviera; coast-dweller.

Riviera² *pr.n.f.* (geog.) Riviera; sheltered coast of sea or lake; — di Levante, coast from Genoa to Spezia; — di Ponente, coast from Genoa to Mentone; — del Garda, west bank of Lake Garda.

†**rivilicare** *tr.* to think over minutely, to ponder carefully.

rivin·cere [C 5] *tr.* to win again; to win back; to defeat (after being defeated oneself); — i contradittori, to convince, to confute, one's adversaries.

rivin·cita *f*. revenge; recovery; return match.

rivinto *part.* of **rivincere**, q.v.; *adj.* recovered; won back.

rivirare [A 1] *tr.* (naut.) to tack or go about again.

†**riviscello** *m.* See **ruscello**.

rivisit-are [A 1 s] *tr.* to revisit; to pay a return visit to; to revisit in one's thoughts; (fig.) to reconsider, to think over. (-**ato** *part. adj.*)

rivissuto *part.* of **rivivere**, q.v.

rivist-a *f*. review; magazine; revision; (mil.) review, inspection; march-past, parade; il re passava la — al campo di Marte, the King held the review at the military parade-ground; — della guardia, checking the sentries, etc.; (naut.) naval review; — di vestiario, kit muster; (theatr.) music-hall entertainment, show, revue. -**aiolo** *adj.* relating to, characteristic of, music-hall; (fig.) gaudy, showy, superficial.

rivisto *part.* of **rivedere**, q.v.; *adj.* reviewed; revised; seen again (cf. **riveduto**).

rivi·v-ere [C 16] *intr.* (aux. avere, essere) to live again; to return to life; to revive; to be revived; *tr.* to live over again; to experience again. -**ificare** [A 2 s] *tr.* to revivify; to reinvigorate. -**iscenza** *f*. (theol.) reviviscence (cf. **reviviscenza**).

rivo *m.* stream; little stream; brook; flow (of water, blood, tears, etc.); flow (of eloquence); flood (of ideas, information, etc.).

rivocare [A 2 s] and derivs. See **revocare**.

rivog-are [A 2] *intr.* (aux. avere) to sail again; *tr.* (fam., joc.) to give, to deal (a blow, kick, etc.); — una liretta, to spend a lira or so. (-**ata** *f*.)

rivolere [B 36] *tr.* to want again; to want back; to continue to want; non lo rivuole, he doesn't want it any more, he doesn't want it back.

rivol·g-ere [C 5] *tr.* to turn; to turn back; to turn over; — la parola ad uno, to address someone; to turn over in one's mind, to think over, to meditate upon; to convert, to turn aside, to distract; *rfl.* to turn round; to turn (towards), to apply; a chi devo -ermi per informazioni?, to whom should I apply for information?; si -a al vigile, ask a policeman; to apply oneself, to give one's

rivolg-ere (*cont.*)
mind (to); to change one's mind, to be converted; to pray; si rivolse a Dio, he prayed to God; (of wine, milk, etc.) to turn (sour); (of stars, etc.) to revolve; (leg.) -ersi al tribunale, to apply to the court. -i**mento** *m.* change, aversion, upheaval; disturbance; avere -imento di stomaco, to feel sick; revolution.

ri·volo *m.* stream, little brook; rivulet.

rivolta *f.* turn; turning; le rivolte della fune, the coils of the rope; turn back (of cuff, glove, etc.); — dei cartocci, rim of cartridges; — del mondo, world's end, rim, 'edge' of the Earth; (archit.) volute; turn; revolt, insurrection, rebellion; aversion, rivulsion.

rivolt-are [A I] *tr.* to turn (again); to turn over, to turn inside out, upside down; — un vestito, to turn a garment (reversing the material); (fig.) — la frittata, to hedge, to give one's words a different meaning; — la colpa a un altro, to cast the blame on someone else; (mus.) to invert (chords, intervals or counterpoint); *rfl.* to turn; to turn round and round (over and over); to revolt, to rebel; (of wine, etc.) to turn, to go bad; mi si -ò lo stomaco a tale vista, my stomach heaved at the sight; to direct oneself; to be directed; to turn for help; *intr.* (*aux.* essere) to turn back. -**ante** *part. adj.* turning; revolting, disgusting. -**ata** *f.* turn; (agric.) dare una — alla terra, to turn over the soil. -**ato** *part. adj.* turned, turned out; giubba -ata, turncoat; revolted; (herald.) contournee. (-**atore** *m.* -**atrice** *f.*) -**atura** *f.* turning (coat, etc.), cost of turning. -**ella** *f.* revolver; †little lane. -**ellata** *f.* revolver shot.

rivolto *part.* of rivolgere, q.v.; *adj.* turned; — a, turning to, looking at; disposed towards; inclined to; directed, addressed, referred to; *n.m.* (mus.) inversion; turning (of clothes).

rivolt-olare [A I S] *tr.* to turn, to turn over and over; to turn upside down; *rfl.* to roll about, to wallow. -**olìo** *m.* continual turning; stirring; turning upside down. -**olone** *m.* somersault; fare -oloni, to turn somersaults. -**oloni** *adv.* turning over and over.

rivoltoso *adj.* rebellious; mare *m.* choppy, rough sea; *n.m.* rebel; revolutionary.

rivoluzion-e *f.* revolution; — delle stagioni, succession, round, revolution of the seasons; (scient.) revolution, cycle; (hist.) revolution; confusion, disturbance. -**are** [A I C] *tr.* to cause to revolt; to revolutionize; to upset (e.g. an established order). -**a·rio** *adj.*, *n.m.* revolutionary. -**arismo** *m.* revolutionary ideas or tendencies.

rivotare[1] [A I] *intr.* (*aux.* avere), *tr.* to vote again.

ri-votare[2] [A I], **ri-vuotare** [A I d] *tr.* to empty again. (-**votatura** *f.*) -**vuoto** *adj.* quite empty.

rivuls-ione *f.*, -**ivo** *adj.* see revuls-ione, -ivo.

riz-ine *f.pl.* (bot.) rhizoids. -**obi** *m. pl.* (bot.) root-tubercle bacillus, *Rhizobium leguminosarum.* -**o·idi** *m.pl.* (bot.) rhizoids. -**oma** *f.* (bot.) rootstock, rhizome. -**o·tomo** *m.* (bot.) herbalist, druggist.

rizome·lico *adj.* (anat.) rhizomelic.

rizz-are [A I] *tr.* to erect; to set up; — la bandiera, to hoist, to run up, the flag; (fig.) — la cresta, to take courage; — baracca, to quarrel; *rfl.* to spring erect; (of hair) to bristle. -**a** *f.* (naut.) lashing; -e delle ancore, anchor lashings; -e delle imbarcazioni, holding down chains. -**aculo** *m.* (ent.) a species of ant, *Cremato-gaster scutellaris.* (-**amento** *m.* -**ata** *f.* -**ato** *part. adj.*)

rizzo *m.* (zool.) sea urchin (cf. riccio).

ro *excl.* See under bi.

roano[1] *adj.*, *n.m.* roan (horse).

Roano[2] *pr.n.f.* (geog.) Rouen.

rob, robbo *m.* (hist. pharm.) rob; fruit conserve, syrup.

rob-a *f.* things; goods; (provb.) la — va alla —, money breeds money; '— del comune, — di nessuno', public property is no one's property; furniture; cloth, material; clothes, belongings, 'things'; — d'inverno, winter clothes, winter things; thingummy, what-you-may-call-it; — da mangiare, something to eat; — da cani, only fit for dogs (to eat); bella —!, a fine piece of work!; — da chiodi, rubbish; ha detto — da chiodi!, he has talked a lot of nonsense (or scandal)!; qui c'è —!, that is important!, this is something good!; aver — in corpo, to have something on one's mind; (iron.) è una bella roba!, he's a fine one! -**ac·cia** *f. pejor.* worthless stuff, rubbish. -**etta** *f. dim.* (derog.) stuff, things of little value; inferior goods; (techn.) inferior flour, seconds. -**ic·cia** *f. dim.* a little something. -**icciuola** *f. dim.* un poco di -icciuola, a snack; simple dress. -**ina** *f. dim.* dress (or other garment); linen. -**one** *m. augm.* robe (of state, academic, etc.). -**uc·cia**, -**u·cola** *f. dim.* things of very little value or importance.

robbi-a *f.* (bot.) — domestica, madder, *Rubia tinctorum*; (dyeing) madder; *pr.n.m.* Luca della Robbia, Florentine sculptor (1399–1482) famous especially for his terracotta reliefs covered with enamel.

†**rob·bio** *adj.*, *n.m.* red; (mil.) 'red tab'.

Roberto *pr.n.m.* Robert.

robinetto *m.* See rubinetto.

robi·n-ia *f.* (bot.) false acacia, locust, *Robinia pseudo-acacia.* -**ina** *f.* (chem.) robinin.

robio·la *f.* cheese of Brianza, Lombardy.

robivecchi *m. indecl.* (Florent.) second-hand dealer.

robo *m.* (bot.) durum wheat, hard wheat (used for macaroni and spaghetti), *Triticum durum.*

roboante *adj.* See reboante.

rob-one *m.*, -**uc·cia** *f.*, -**u·cola** *f.* See under roba.

roborante *adj.* (med.) tonic, roborant.

†**roborare** *vb.* and derivs. See corroborare.

ro·bot *m. indecl.* robot, automaton.

roburite *f.* (explos.) roburite.

robust-o *adj.* strong; robust, sturdy; vigorous (also fig.); pithy (of style). (-**amente** *adv.*) -**ezza** *f.* strength; sturdiness; vigour.

rocag·gine *f.* See under roco.

Rocambol-e *pr.n.m.* (pron. as Fr.) bold adventurer, hero of novels by Ponson du Terrail. -**esco** *adj.* (*m.pl.* -**eschi**) bold, adventurous; typical of Rocambole.

roc-ca[1] *f.* (mil.) citadel; fort; fortress built on high ground governing a commanding position; (fig.) stronghold; (geog., in proper names) having such a fortress; rock; — del camino, chimney stack. -**cacannuc·cia** *pr.n.f.* imaginary village of no importance; che credi, che Roma sia -cacannuccia?, do you think Rome is a little one-horse town? -**caforte** *f.* stronghold (also fig.). -**cale** *adj.* relating to a fortress; *n.m.* (mil.) bastion, outer ward (also fig.). -**chetta** *f. dim.* small fortress; tower (occurring also in geog. names). -**chigiano** *m.* castellan, keeper of a fortress.

roc-ca[2] *f.* distaff; (text.) reel; oil-lamp with long handle; wine-glass with long stem. -**cata** *f.* as much wool as a distaff will hold. -**cafuoco** *m. indecl.* (naut.) rocket. -**chello** *m.* (naut.) lower portion of a topmast overlapping the mast. -**chellone** *m.* lazy person. -**chetta** *f.* little distaff; †(mil.) rocket (cf. razzo).

roccetto *m.* (Tusc.). See rocchetto[2].

rocchett-o[1] *m.* reel; spool; (text.) bobbin; (cinem.) reel; — avvolgitore, take-up spool; (watchm.) — dei minuti, cannon pinion; (eng.) — a denti, sprocket; (electr.) coil; (motor.) — d'accensione, ignition coil; — di induzione, induction coil. -**iera** *f.* (text.) warp winder.

rocchetto[2] *m.* (liturg.) rochet.

roc·ch-o *m.* short cylindrical object of wood or stone; section of a column, or tree trunk; jet of water; cylindrical or rounded piece of meat (e.g. sausage), or fish (e.g. rock-fish, eel, etc.); roll of hair; 'tubby' person. -**are** [A4] *tr.*, *intr.* (*aux.* avere) to form into rolls.

roc·ci-a *f.* rock; cliff; (geog.) — montonata, *roche moutonnée*; (geol.) — di letto, bedrock; — eruttiva, igneous rock; (techn.) lana di —, mineral wool; (naut.) submerged reef; crust, incrustation (of tartar on teeth, of dirt, etc.). -**atore** *m.* (neol.) rock-climber, esp. in the Dolomites. -**oso** *adj.* rocky; incrusted, grimed with dirt; (naut.) rocky (nature of bottom).

rocco *m.* (*pl.* **rocchi**) (chess) rook, castle; (herald.) chess rook; †(eccl.) crosier, bishop's crook.

roc·colo *m.* fine net for bird-catching; (mil.) trap or deception; tirar il —, to spring the trap (also fig.).

ro-co *adj.* (*m.pl.* -**chi**) hoarse; *n.m.* mal del —, a disease of poultry, croup. -**cag·gine** *f.* hoarseness. -**chezza** *f.* hoarseness.

rodamina *f.* (chem.; text.) rhodamine.

rod-are [A I] *tr.* (motor.) to run in. -**ag·gio** *m.* (motor.) running in; in -aggio, being run in.

Ro·dano *pr.n.m.* (geog.) Rhône.

rod-ano·geno *m.* (hist. chem.) thiocyanogen. -**anuro** *m.* (hist. chem.) sulphocyanide, thiocyanate.

ro·deo[1] *m.* (ichth.) bitterling, *Rhodeus amarus.*

rode·o[2] *m.* rodeo.

ro·d-ere [C 3] *tr.* to gnaw; to nibble; (joc.) datemi qualche cosa da —, give me something to eat; to corrode, to consume, to waste away; to erode; — un osso duro, to do something difficult; — il freno, to chafe (e.g. with impatience); (chem.) to attack, to cor-

rod·ere (*cont.*)

rode, to eat away; *rfl.* to chafe, to be worried; -ersi d'invidia, to be consumed with envy; *recip. rfl.* -ersi l'un l'altro, to hate one another. **-ente** *part. adj.* gnawing; consuming; stinging; *n.m.* (dyeing) mordant, striker. **-i·bile** *adj.* **-ibiscotto** *m.* (joc.) 'biscuit-nibbler' (i.e. sailor). **-ilegno** *m. indecl.* (ent.) goat moth, *Cossus ligniperda.* **-imento** *m.* gnawing, nibbling; (fig.) anxiety, uneasiness, worry; (archit.) erosion, corrosion. **-io** *m.* continual gnawing, nibbling; sound of nibbling. (**-itore** *m.* **-itrice** *f.*)

Roderico *pr.n.m.* Roderick.

Rodi *pr.n.f.* (geog.) Rhodes. **-ese** *adj., n.m.f.* Rhodian.

ro·dico *adj.* (chem.) rhodic (cf. rodio²).

rodigino *m.* inhabitant of Rovigo.

ro·dio¹ *adj.* see **rodiese**, under **rodi**; (leg. hist.) diritto —, Rhodian law; a code of maritime law made by the people of Rhodes.

ro·d-io² *adj.* (bot.) radice -ia, *n.m.* (chem.) rhodium. **-ite** *f.* (ent.) the wasp causing bedeguar galls on roses, *Rhodites rosae*; (metall.) rhodite, rhodium gold. **-izonato** *m.* (chem.) rhodizonate. **-izo·nico** *adj.* (chem.) rhodizonic. **-odendro** *m.* (bot.) *Rhododendron ferrugineum* and *R. hirsutum*, and cultivated species of *Rhododendron.* **-onite** *f.* (miner.) rhodonite, fowlerite.

rodìo *m.* See under **rodere**.

rodi-ota *m.*, **-otto** *m.* Rhodian, inhabitant of Rhodes.

rodoge·nesi *f.* (biochem.) rhodogenesis.

Rodolfo *pr.n.m.* Rudolph; Ralph.

Rodomont-e *pr.n.m.* heroic character in 'Orlando Furioso'. **-ata** *f.* rodomontade. **-eri·a** *f.* boastfulness, braggadocio. **-esco** *adj.* (*m.pl.* **-eschi**) boastful, bragging.

rodopsina *f.* (biochem.) rhodopsin.

roegarze *f.* kind of round dance.

roella *f.* (ichth.). See **rovella**.

†**rof·fia** *f.* encrustation, grime; murkiness.

rogantino *m.* See **rugantino**.

rog-are [A2] *tr.* (leg., of Notary Public) to draw up; to attest; — un atto, to draw up a deed; *rfl.* to be attested, verified or witnessed. **-ato** *part. adj.* drawn up; attested; witnessed; verified; examined. **-atore** *m.* attestor, attester; (Rom. hist.) *rogator*, 'polling-clerk'. **-ato·ria** *f.* (leg.) *commission rogatoire*, rogatory commission, commission issued to another Court (esp. abroad) requesting some judicial action such as taking of evidence; letter of request; evidence obtained on commission. **-ato·rio** *adj.* (*m.pl.* **-atorii**) (leg.) rogatory. **-azione** *f.* rogation; *pl.* (liturg.) Rogations; Rogationtide.

roggia *f.* (N. Ital.) artificial canal; irrigation channel.

roggio *adj.* russet, reddish; *n.m.* rust colour, russet.

roggiolo *m.* black bread.

roggiol-ona, **-one** *f.* (agric.) kind of chestnut.

ro·gito *m.* (leg.) the drawing-up and attestation by Notary Public of execution of deed, will, etc.; notarial deed, will, etc.; *pl.* notary's authority to draw up such documents.

rogn-a *f.* (med.) itch, scabies; (vet.) itch; mange; sheep scab; — follicolare, follicular mange; (agric.) fungus disease in olive trees; itch; worry; trouble; (vulg.) che hai? ti pizzica la —?, what's the matter? can't you stop fidgeting?; cerca qualcuno chi gli gratti la —, he's asking for a hiding; cercare —, to pick a quarrel to ask for trouble. **-oso** *adj.* (vet.) scabby; (fig.) dirty, diseased; *n.m.* one who has the itch.

rognon-e *m.* kidney. **-ata** *f.* (cul.) kidneys en casserole. **-cini** *m.pl.* (cul.) kidneys.

rogo¹ *m.* pyre; fire; condannare al —, to condemn to be burnt, to send to the stake; salire il —, to go to the stake; †death.

rogo² *m.* See **rogito**.

†**rogo³** *m.* (bot.). See **rovo**.

Rolando *pr.n.m.* Roland.

roll-are [A1] *intr.* (*aux.* avere) (naut.) to roll; *tr.* to roll, to roll up; — le tende, to roll up the blinds or awnings. **-ata** *f.* (naut.) a roll; rolling; -ata lenta, slow rolling; -ata viva, rapid rolling. **-ìo** *m.* (naut.) roll; il -ìo di una nave smorzato dalle chiglie, the rolling of a ship reduced by bilge keels.

Roma *pr.n.f.* (geog.) Rome.

Romagn-a *pr.n.f.* (geog.) Romagna, region of Italy between the Po and the Marches (formerly a Papal State). **-(u)olo** *adj.* of Romagna; *n.m.* inhabitant of Romagna; (text.) coarse undyed woollen cloth. (**-(u)ola** *f.*)

roma·ico *adj., n.m.* Modern Greek, Romaic.

romana¹ *f.* testing balance.

romana² *f.* of **romano**, q.v.

roman·cio *m., adj.* (ling.) Romansch.

Romani·a¹ *pr.n.f.* (geog.) Rumania.

Rom-a·nia² *pr.n.f.* the Roman world, Roman Empire; (geog. hist.) Eastern Peloponnese under Venetian domination; (ling.) area where Romance languages are spoken; (lit.) name of a literary review devoted to the Romance languages. **-a·nico** *adj.* Romanic, Romance; (archit.) Romanesque; (lit.) lingue -aniche, Romance languages. **-anina** *pr.n.f.* (mus.) la Romanina, the nickname of two celebrated opera-singers: (1) Giovanna Albertini who flourished in first half of eighteenth century, and (2) Marianna Benti Bulgarelli (1684–1734), friend of Metastasio. **-anino** *pr.n.m.* (paint.) Girolamo Bresciano (1485–1556); *n.m.* (numism.) coin minted by the popes at Avignon. **-anismo** *m.* idiom of the Roman dialect; (eccl.) obedience to the Holy See; acceptance of the authority of Rome. **-anista** *m.* Romanist; expert in Roman law or Romance languages and literature. **-anità** *f.* Romanity, Roman character; the spirit and ideals of ancient Rome recalled or revived; (eccl.) clericalism; devotion, loyalty, to the Holy See; support of papal policy. **-ano·logo** *m.* Romanist, one learned in Roman law or Romance languages and literature.

roman-o *adj.* Roman; (hist.) la questione -a, the Roman question, concerning the temporal power of the pope; numeri -i, Roman numerals; (typ.) caratteri -i, characters resembling Roman letters in inscriptions (cf. 'caratteri tondi' under **tondo**); chiesa -a, Roman Church (i.e. strictly, the Church of the diocese of Rome; more widely, the whole Church in communion with Rome); lingua -a, Old Provençal; (archit.) arco —, round arch, (in England) Norman arch; stile —, composite order; (vet.) spada -a, feather line at the junction of two hair currents; fare alla -a, to go Dutch (i.e. each paying his share); candela -a, Roman candle (firework); lattuga -a, cos lettuce; (Ital. hist.) saluto —, Fascist salute; passo —, a kind of goosestep adopted by the Fascist militia; *n.m.* Roman; i -i, the Romans; (mus.) lettere di Romano, Romanian letters (indications of expression in plainchant MSS.); Enotrio Romano, pseudonym of Giosue Carducci; (paint.) Giulio Romano (1492–1546), a disciple of Raphael. **-a** *f.* Roman woman, Roman girl; cos lettuce. **-amente** *adv.* in the Roman fashion (esp. of ancient Rome); morì -amente, he died like a Roman. **-ato** *m.* (archit.) Roman cornice (as a rounded arch over a window). **-ella** *f.* (poet.) kind of **rispetto**, q.v. **-esca** *f.* (mus.) galliard; the name of a conventional ground bass. **-esco** *adj.* (*m.pl.* **-eschi**) modern Roman; of Rome; *n.m.* Roman dialect. **-esimo** *m.* (ling.) Romanism.

roman·ti-co *adj., n.m.* Romantic; romantic. **-camente** *adv.* romantically. **-cheri·a** *f.* romantic attitude, notions; una ragazza senza -cherie, a girl with no romantic nonsense about her, a sensible girl. **-cismo** *m.* romanticism; romance; *pr.n.m.* (lit. hist.) il Romanticismo, the Romantic Movement. **-cume** *m.* (derog.) romantic notions, romantic nonsense.

romanz-o *adj.* romance (neo-Latin languages, esp. Old French); *n.m.* romance (composition in a Romance language); il Romanzo della Rosa, *Le Roman de la Rose*; romanticized history; novel; — fiume, excessively long novel. **-a** *f.* ballad, romance; (mus.) romance (a simple air *or* an instrumental slow movement of romantic character). †**-are** *tr.* to embroider in the telling, to tell as a romance. **-atore** *m.* author of romances of chivalry. (**-atrice** *f.*) **-eggiare** [A3c] *tr., intr.* (*aux.* avere) to romance; to compose romances. **-ero** *m.* Spanish collection of romances, Romancero. **-esco** *adj.* (*m.pl.* **-eschi**) romantic; adventurous; extravagant; avere del -esco, to be far-fetched. **-escamente** *adv.* romantically; adventurously. **-etta** *f.* (mus.) a short romance. **-etto** *m. dim.* short novel; romance; romantic love-affair. **-evole** *adj.* romantic; suitable to a novel. **-iere** *m.* novelist; collection of romances, ballads.

romb-a *f.* see **rombo¹**. **-ante** *part. adj.* booming, roaring, thundering. **-are** [A1c] *intr.* (*aux.* avere) to roar; to buzz; il vento -a, the wind is howling. **-azzo** *m.* noise, roar, row.

romb-etto, -icello *m. dim.* (ichth.) see **rombo²**; -etto di grotta, top-knot, *Phrynorhombus unimaculatus.*

rombice *m.* (bot.). See **romice**.

romb-ico *adj.* (geom.) rhombic. **-ododecaedro** *m.* (cryst.) rhombo-dodecahedron. **-oe·drico** *adj.* rhombohedral. **-oedro** *m.* rhombo-hedron. **-oidale** *adj.* (geom.) rhomboid(al). **-o·ide** *m., adj.* rhomboid.

rombo[1] *m.* buzzing (of bees or sim.); (sound of) fluttering, beating of wings; far —, to pay attentions (to), to court; roaring, thundering, booming.

rombo[2] *m.* — chiodato, — grande, — maggiore, turbot, *Rhombus maximus*; — liscio, brill, *Rh. laevis*; — bastardo, — d'arena, *Platophrys podas*.

rombo[3] *m.* (naut.) point of the compass; — di bussola, compass course (uncorrected); — magnetico, magnetic course (corrected for variation); — vero, true course (corrected for variation and deviation); assegnare il —, dar il —, to set the course; governare per il —, to steer a given compass course. NOTE: the points are subdivided as follows: quarto di Levante per Greco, East by North, and these in turn are divided into 'quartini' or quarter points, 'mezze quarte', half points; (math.) rhombus; rhomb, lozenge, diamond; (geog.) linea di —, rhumb line.

rombol-are [A I sc] *intr.* (aux. avere) to sling (with a sling). **-atore** *m.* slinger.

rome·o[1] *adj.* relating to the pilgrim routes; la strada romea, the road from Venice to Rome.

Rom-e·o[2] *pr.n.m.* Romeo; pilgrim (esp. to Rome). **-eag·gio** *m.* pilgrimage (esp. to Rome).

romice *m.* (bot.) broad-leaved dock, *Rumex obtusifolius*.

romit-o *m.* hermit; *adj.* solitary; lonely; withdrawn. **-ag·gio** *m.* hermitage; hermit's life. **-ano** *m.* (eccl.) Augustinian hermit, Austin Friar; solitary; rustic. **-o·rio** *m.* hermitage; lonely place.

romore *m.* and derivs. See **rumore**.

romp-ere [C26] *tr.* to break; **-ersi** l'osso del collo, to break one's neck; il fiume in piena ruppe gli argini, the river in spate broke its banks; — zolle, to break up clods; — il digiuno, to break one's fast; to interrupt; — gl'indugi, to put an end to delays; **-ersi** le gambe, to become very tired; (fam.) — le scatole a uno, to bother someone; (provb.) cuor forte **-e** la cattiva sorte, a brave heart wards off ill fortune; — la folla, to clear a way through the crowd; (phys.) — l'atomo, to split the atom; (mil.) — il nemico, to defeat the enemy; — le file, to break ranks; (naut.) — l'andana, to break bulk; — in mare, to wreck, to shipwreck; — amicizia con, to break off a friendship with; — la legge, to break (transgress) the law; to break up, to break down (materials with various tools); — l'incanto, to break the charm, to be more daring than others; — una lancia in favore di uno, to break a lance on someone's behalf, to defend someone; — la testa, to deafen or bore with noise or chatter; **-erla** con qualcuno, to fall out with someone; non **-etemi** le tasche, don't bother me; *abs.* (sport) to break the gait (trotting races); *intr.* (aux. avere) to break; (phys., of a ray) to be refracted; to be shipwrecked; — in pianto, to burst into tears; il cielo **-eva** a oriente, the sky cleared in the east (i.e. the clouds were breaking); (of day, dawn) to break; (of a river) to overflow, to break its banks; *rfl.* (acc. of prn. 'si') to break, to be broken; **-ersi** con uno, to break with someone; (of weather) to turn wet, to break; (naut.) **-ersi** su di una costa, to be cast ashore; (dat. of prn. 'si') **-ersi** la testa, to rack one's brains; **-ersi** le corna, to labour in vain. **-ente** *part. adj.* breaking, breaking in (or out); (naut.) bozza **-ente**, parting stopper; *n.m.* (naut.) see 'frangente', under **frangere**. **-iballe** *m. indecl.* bale-breaker; (fig., vulg.) bore, tiresome person. **-icapo** *m. indecl.* trouble; 'headache' (in fig. sense); troublesome person; puzzle. **-icollo** *adj.* breakneck; a **-icollo**, at breakneck speed; dangerous; ruinous; *n.m.* ruinous bargain, business; vendere a **-icollo**, to sell for a song; dangerous spot; a **-icollo**, precipitous; dare-devil; thoughtless person. **-icordoni** *m. indecl.* bore, troublesome person. **-ifiamma** *m. indecl.* (eng.) flame trap. **-ighiac·cio** *m. indecl.* ice-breaker; (aeron.) mechanical de-icer. **-imento** *m.* breaking; break; rupture; shipwreck; breach (of law, etc.) **-imento** di capo, troublesome person or thing, trouble; **-imento** di tasche (di scatole, di stivali), trouble, annoyance; †(naut.) shipwreck. **-isca·tole**, **-istivali**, **-itasche** *m. indecl.* (colloq.) bore, troublesome person. **-itore** *m.* breaker; **-itore** di tasche, bore, troublesome person. (**-itrice** *f.*) **-one** *m.* (fam.) clumsy person, smasher, one who breaks dishes, etc.) (**-ona** *f.*)

Ro·m-ulo *pr.n.m.* Romulus. **-u·leo** *adj.* Romulian, relating to Romulus, founder of Rome. **-u·lide** *m., adj.* Roman (as descendant of Romulus).

ron-ca *f.* (mil. hist.) halberd, or similar weapon having a spike as well as a cutting blade; (agric.) billhook; pruning hook. **-care** [A2c] *tr.* (agric.) to trim or clear with a billhook; to hoe. **-cato** *part. adj. n.m.* tunny-cleaning knife. (**-catura** *f.*) **-cheggio** *m.* (agric.) trimming, clearing (with a billhook). **-chetta** *f. dim.*, **-chetto** *m. dim.* (agric.) pruning-knife.

roncaso *m.* (orn.) hazel hen.

†roncheggiare *intr.* to snore.

ronchiare [A4c] *intr.* (aux. avere) to growl.

ronchi-one *m.* rock, crag; block of stone. **-oso** *adj.* rugged; knotted, gnarled.

ronc-i·glio *m.* hook. **-iglione** *m.* big hook; billhook. **-inato** *adj.* hooked (in shape); (bot.) runcinate.

ronco[1] *m.* (med.) rhoncus, râle.

ronco[2] *m.* blind alley, cul-de-sac; esser nel —, to be in a tight place.

ronco[3] *m.* (ichth.) — spinoso, spiny shark, *Echinorhinus brucus*.

roncol-a *f.* (agric.) pruning-hook, billhook. **-o** *m.* large knife with a blade like a billhook.

roncone *m.* reaping-hook; (mil. hist.) spear having a hook; (ichth.) stickleback, *Gasterosteus aculeatus*.

rond-a *f.* (mil.) rounds, night rounds patrol; far la —, to do the rounds; cammino di —, covered walk, portion of a sentry's beat; rounds, night rounds; — ai depositi di munizione, magazine rounds; — in mare, harbour patrol; — esterna, external inspection (of a ship, to ensure darkening, or for another specific purpose); (paint.) La Ronda di Notte, the Night Watch (a famous picture by Rembrandt). **-are** [A I c] (mil.) *intr.* (aux. avere) to carry out the rounds; *tr.* to inspect (sentries, etc.). **-inare** [A I] *intr.* (aux. avere) (mil.) to do a short round. **-ino** *m.* (mil.) guard commander, corporal or soldier in charge of the watch.

ronde *m.* round hand (writing).

rondella *f.* (eng.) washer; — di spinta, thrust washer; — elastica, spring washer.

rondello *m.* (mus.) roundel, roundelay; (mil.) space left for sentries to do their rounds, 'catwalk'.

†ron·dina *f.* See **rondine**.

rondin-e *f.* (orn.) swallow, *Hirundo rustica*; (provb.) una — non fa primavera, one swallow does not make a summer; — di mare, tern, *Sterna* spp., especially common tern, *Sterna hirundo*; — di mare codalunga, Arctic tern, *S. macrura*; — di mare del Mac-Dougall, roseate tern, *S. dougallii*; — di mare gambe nere, gull-billed tern, *Gelochelidon nilotica*; — di mare maggiore, Caspian tern, *Hydroprogne caspia*; — di mare zampe nere, gull-billed tern; — montana, crag martin, *Ptyonoprogne rupestris*; — rossiccia, red-rumped swallow, *Hirundo daurica*; a coda di —, swallow-tailed; abito a coda di —, evening dress-coat, 'tails'; (ichth.) pesce —, — di mare, flying gurnard, *Dactylopterus volitans*. **-ella** *f. dim.* little swallow; (ichth.) flying fish, *Exocoetus volitans*. **-otto** *m.* young swallow.

rondino[1] *m.* (ichth.) ray's bream, *Brama rayi*.

rondino[2] *m.* See under **ronda**.

rond-ò *m. indecl.* (mus.) rondo, rondeau; (prosod.) rondeau; (neol.) small round open space at the end of an avenue. **-iletta** *f.*, **-inetta** *f.*, **-ino** *m.*, **-oletto** *m.* (mus.) short rondo.

rondone *m.* (orn.) swift, *Apus apus*; — alpino, Alpine swift, *A. melba*; — pallido, pallid swift, *A. pallidus*; (joc.) porta dei rondoni, window; andar di —, to go swimmingly.

roneograf-i·a *f.* mimeographing, roneographing. **-are** [A I S] *tr.* to roneograph. (**-ato** *part. adj.*)

ronfa *f.* (cards) game similar to 'primiera', q.v., played in Italy in the sixteenth and seventeenth centuries; point, sequence in the game of 'ronfa'; accusare la — giusta, to call the full 'ronfa', (fig.) to speak out, to tell the whole truth.

ronfi-o *m.* snore, snoring. **-are** [A4c] *intr.* (aux. avere) to snore loudly; (fig.) il mare **-ava**, one could hear the dull roar of the sea.

†ronne *m.* an abbreviation R', which stood for the Latin termination -*rum* and which used to be placed after Z in the alphabet mounted on board and formerly used in schools (known as the 'crocesanta', q.v.); (fig.) dall'a al —, from a to z, from beginning to end; essere al —, to have reached the end (cf. **conne**).

ronz-are [A I c] *intr.* (aux. avere) to buzz; to hum; (of arrows) to whirr, to whistle; (of bullets) to whistle; to whine; mi **-ano** gli orecchi, I have a singing in my ears; (fig.) un'idea mi **-a** per il capo, an idea keeps running through my head; — intorno a qualcuno, to hang round someone. **-amento** *m.* buzzing, humming. **-atore** *m.* buzzer (cf. **cicala**); (orn.) humming-bird. (**-atrice** *f.*) **-io** *m.* continued buzzing, hum, buzz, murmur; (radio; electr.) hum.

Ronzinante *pr.n.m.* Rosinante, name of Don Quixote's horse.

ronzin-o *m.* nag, jade; packhorse. **-one** *m.* big horse; stallion.

ronz-o *m.* (poet.) buzz, hum, murmur; il — dell'alte sfere (Pascoli), the music of the heavenly spheres. **-one** *m.* (ent.) cockchafer, May bug, *Melolontha vulgaris*; (fig.) admirer; quella ragazza ha intorno molti -oni, that girl has a lot of admirers.

ror-are [A I] *tr.* to bedew; to refresh. (**-ato** *part. adj.*)

rora·rio *m.* (Rom. hist.) *rorarius*, light-armed skirmisher.

ro·rido *adj.* dewy; bedewed; — di morte, showing cold sweat in death.

rosa[1] *f.* (Tusc.) itch; erosion; bank, land, etc. eroded; 'nibble', small profit.

ros-a[2] *f.* (bot.) rose, *Rosa*; — canina, dog rose, *Rosa canina*; — delle Alpi, alpenrose, alpine rose, *Rhododendron ferrugineum* and *R. hirsutum*; (eccl.) — d'oro, Golden Rose; (archit.) rose-window, rosace; (zool.) — di mare, sea anemone; (mus.) soundhole, rose, knot (of lute or similar instrument); (naut.) — della bussola, compass rose; — nautica, — del (di) pilota, master's course computer; — dei venti, compass card (reprinted in suitable positions on a chart); (mil.) fare la —, to pepper (with shot); fresca come una —, fresh as a daisy; (provb.) non c'è — senza spine, there is no rose without a thorn; acqua di -e, rosewater; all'acqua di —, 'milk-and-water', tepid; vino —, vin rosé; Pasqua di -e, Whitsuntide; — Croce, Rosicrucians (Rosacroce *m.* the highest rank in Freemasonry); (techn.) -e d'Olanda, Dutch rose, diamond chips; (bot.) mela —, rose apple, *Eugenia jambos*; (butcher.) section which forms part of round, topside or silverside in English butchering; *adj. indecl.* pink, rosy; *n.m.* the colour pink; il — ti sta bene, pink is becoming to you. **-a·ceo** *adj.* rosy, rose-coloured; (med.) gotta -acea, rosacea. **-a·io** *m.* (bot.) rose plant, rose bush, rose; †see **rosario**. **-ali·a** *f.* (mus.) rosalia, real sequence; (med.) german measles, rubella. **-anilina** *f.* (chem.) rosaniline. **-arino** *m.* little wreath. **-a·rio** *m.* (rel.) rosary (whether prayers or beads); dire il -ario, to say one's rosary; (fig.) sfilò (tutto) il -ario, he came out with a string of abuse. **-asecca** *adj.* dried rose-leaf colour. **-ato** *adj.* rosy; acqua -ata, rose-water.

Rosa[3] *pr.n.f.* Rose; Rosa.

†**rosata** *f.* See **rugiada**.

rosbif(fe) *m. indecl.* roast beef.

†**ro·scido** *adj.* See **rugiadoso**, under **rugiada**.

roseggiare [A 3 c] *intr.* (no compound tenses) to be or to appear red.

roseina *f.* (chem.) rosein, fuchsine, magenta, aniline red.

rosellina *f.* (bot.) turban and Persian buttercups, *Ranunculus asiaticus*.

†**rosellire** *vb.* and derivs. See **rosolare**.

ro·ş-eo *adj.* rosy; rose-coloured; crimson. **-e·ola** *f.* (med.) rose-rash, roseola; blush (for shame).

roseto *m.* rose-garden; rose-bud.

rosetta *f. dim.* of **rosa**[2], q.v.; little rose; rosette; ring or earring with rosette of diamonds; (eng.) washer; collar; -etta elastica, spring washer; -etta per cordami, grummet thimble; (vet.) star (on a horse's forehead); a kind of paring knife; (mus.) diminutive of **rosa**, q.v.

rosetto *m.* (ichth.) red sea-bream, *Pagellus erythrinus*.

rosign(u)olo *m.* See **usignuolo**.

rosi-care [A 2 s] *tr.* to gnaw, to nibble; (provb.) chi non risica non -ca, nothing venture nothing have. **-cante** *part. adj.* gnawing; *n.m.pl.* (zool.) rodents. **-catura** *f.* gnawing; itching. **-cchiamento** *m.* nibbling, gnawing. **-cchiare** [A 4] *tr.* to nibble, to gnaw. **-cchio** *m.* continual gnawing, nibbling.

Rosina *pr.n.f.* Rosina; name of a gambling apparatus in the form of a revolving sphere.

rosmarino *m.* (bot.) rosemary, *Rosmarinus officinalis*.

rosminiano *adj., n.m.* (eccl., philos.) Rosminian.

roso *part.* of **rodere**, q.v.; *adj.* gnawed, nibbled; eaten; worn away; eroded.

ro·şola *f.* (vet.) a kind of paring knife.

rosolac·cio *m.* (bot.) field poppy, *Papaver rhoeas*; (joc.) cockade.

rosol-are [A I S] *tr.* (cul.) to brown; (fig.) to scold severely; *rfl.* to roast, to roast oneself; lì non ti riscaldi, ti -i, you will not just get warm there, you will be roasted. (**-ato** *part.*, **-atura** *f.*)

rosoli·a *f.* (med.) German measles, rubella.

roso·lico *adj.* (chem.) rosolic; acido —, rosolic acid, aurin.

rosolida *f.* (bot.) sundew, *Drosera rotundifolia*.

roso·li-o *m.* rosolio, a liqueur or cordial made with many different flavourings. **-era** *f.* liqueur set; small bottle for holding rosolio.

ro·şolo *m.* (cul.) browning produced by roasting or baking (cf. **rosolare**).

rosone *m.* (archit.) rose window; (typ.) tail-piece; (electr.) rosette (to hold hanging light filament).

rospo *m.* (zool.) toad, *Bufo vulgaris*; — smeraldino, *Bufo viridis*; (ichth.) coda di —, — di fango, angler fish, *Lophius piscatorius*, also a less common Mediterranean species, *L. budegasa*; (fig.) unsociable person; boor; slanderous pamphlet; ingoiare un —, to swallow a bitter pill; (vet.) male del —, chronic ulcer on a horse's leg.

rossetto *adj., n.m.* See under **rosso**.

ross-o *adj.* red; — come un gambero cotto, red as a boiled lobster; diventar —, to blush *or* to flush; si fece tutta -a in viso, she blushed bright red; capelli -i, red hair; pesce —, goldfish; di sangue —, fiery, passionate; livrea -a, red livery of the Italian Royal House; (paint.) terra -a, red ochre; camicia -a, red-shirt (uniform of Garibaldi's followers); Croce -a, Red Cross; (agric.) barba -a, a kind of grape; *n.m.* red, the colour red; un — acceso, a fiery red; vedere tutto in —, to see red; — d'uovo, yolk of egg; (provb.) di sera bel tempo ne mena, a red sky at night is shepherd's delight; (herald.) gules; (techn.) — di anilina, fuchsine; — di piombo, (miner.) red lead; -i e neri, socialists and clericals; (hist.) i Rossi, redshirts, followers of Garibaldi, *or* Communists, 'Reds'. **-ac·cio** *adj. pejor.*; *n.m.* (derog.) red-haired person, 'carrots'. **-astro** *adj.* reddish, dark red. **-eggiante** *part. adj.* reddish; turning red. **-eggiare** [A 3 c] *intr.* (aux. avere) to be reddish; to appear red; le viti -eggiano d'uva matura, the vines are purple with ripe grapes. **-ellino** *adj., n.m.* (agric.) term for certain kinds of olive, fig and grape. **-ello** *adj.* tinged with red; fico -ello, a kind of fig; *n.m.* red patch, flush. **-etta** *f.* (zool.) *Pteropus melanotus*, the edible flying fox. **-etto** *adj.* bright red; *n.m.* rouge; -etto per le labbra, lipstick; darsi il -etto, to put on rouge and (or) lipstick. **-ezza** *f.* redness; flush. **-ic·cio** *adj.* reddish; *n.m.* russet, rust colour. **-igno** *adj.* reddish, slightly red (also *n.m.*). **-ino** *adj.* auburn; *n.m.* person with auburn hair. **-one** *m.* (agric.) kind of grape. **-ore** *m.* red, redness; flush, blush; shame; ho -ore di te, I am ashamed of you; modesty; quella fanciulla non ha -ore di nulla, that girl is shameless; il -ore era sparito dalla sua faccia, the blush had faded from his face, (or fig.) he had become shameless; *pl.* blushes.

rosta *f.* rough home-made fan; fly whisk; (of a turkey, etc.) far la —, to fan out its tail; fanlight over a door; semicircular trench at the foot of a chestnut tree serving to retain water; trench or bank to retain fallen chestnuts on a steep slope; strengthened river-bank.

rostic·c-io *m.* clinker; trellis; person shrivelled or deformed; *pl.* (techn.) iron slag. **-iana** *f.* cake made with oil. **-iere** *m.* cook-shop keeper. **-ieri·a** *f.* cook-shop; snack-bar.

†**rosto** *m.* and derivs. See **arrosto**.

rostr-o *m.* beak, bill; muzzle; snout; (anat.) sphenoid process; (Rom. antiq.) ship's beak; *pl.* Rostra, speaker's platform (in the Forum); rostrum. **-ale** *adj.* (Rom. hist.) rostral. **-ato** *adj.* beaked; pointed, having points; (Rom. antiq.) rostrated; nave -ata, beaked ship; corona -ata, naval crown; colonna -ata, *columna rostrata*.

ros-ume *m.* nibblings; residue from gnawing or chewing by cattle, silkworms, etc. **-ura** *f.* gnawing; erosion.

rota *f.* see **ruota**; (eccl.) la (Sacra) —, the (Sacred) Rota.

rota·bile *adj.* See under **rotare**.

rotacişmo *m.* (ling.) rhotacism, excessive use or peculiar pronunciation of *r*.

rota·ia *f.* rut, wheel-track; rail; (rlwy.) — a due funghi, bullhead rail; — a canale, grooved rail; (naut.) scalo a -aie, slipway having rails; (in convents) turn-sister, *sœur tourière*.

rotang *m. indecl.* (bot.) rattan cane (stems of various climbing palms).

rot-are [A I] *tr.* to rotate, to whirl round; (hist.) to break on the wheel; *intr.* (aux. avere) to revolve, to wheel, to rotate; to run on wheels; to roll; (eng.) to slew (of a crane). **-a·bile** *adj.* fit for carriages; strada -abile, carriage road, (rlwy.) permanent way; *n.f.* carriage road. (**-abilità** *f.*) **-ante** *adj.* rotating, rotary; revolving; (herald.) pavone -ante, peacock in his pride; *n.m.* (anat.) amatorial muscle, any of the muscles which assist the eye to ogle. **-ariano** *adj.* relating to the Rotary Club, Rotarian (also *n.m.*). **-ata** *f.* blow from a wheel. **-ativa** *f.* rotary printing press. **-ativo** *adj.* (eng.) rotary, rotating; (finan.) credito -ativo,

rot-are (*cont.*)
renewable credit. **-ato** *part. adj.* wheeled, having wheels; on wheels; rolling. **-atore** *m.* rotator; -atore di fionda, slinger; *n.m.pl.* (anat.) rotator muscles; rotatores; (zool.) rotifers. (**-atrice** *f.*) **-ato·rio** *adj.* (*m.pl.* **-atorii**) rotatory; circular; circolazione -atoria, (traffic sign) roundabout; *n.m.* (anat.) rotator muscle. **-azionale** *adj.* (scient.) rotational. **-azione** *f.* rotation; senso di -azione, direction of rotation; (agric.) -azione agraria, rotation of crops; (eng.) momento di -azione, torque; (phys.) -azione atomica, atom spin.

rote-are [A 6] *intr.* (*aux.* avere) to rotate, to wheel; to whirl; (of a peacock) to display the tail; *tr.* to whirl; to roll; — gli occhi, to roll one's eyes; *n.m.* the sound of wheels; un — di carrozza risonò nella strada, the sound of carriage wheels was heard in the street. **-a·bile** *adj.* rotatable; (rlwy.) materiale -abile, rolling stock. **-amento** *m.* rotating, wheeling; rolling. (**-ante** *part. adj.*) **-azione** *f.* rotation; wheeling.

roteggi-o *m.* running, rolling along (of carriages); system of wheels; — dell'orologio, wheels of the clock. **-are** [A 3 c] *intr.* (*aux.* avere) see **roteare**.

rot-ella *f. dim.* small wheel; roller; rowel (of a spur); pattino a -elle, roller-skate; -elle matte, castors (on furniture); (mil. hist.) archibugio a —, arquebus having a ratchet; — a scudo, buckler and/or targe; (mus.) rotary valve (in brass instruments); any small ring or circular mark; (anat.) patella, knee-cap; — metrica, measuring tape, tape measure; (herald.) — di sperone, mullet. (**-elletta** *f. dim.*) **-ellina** *f. dim.* (game) roulette. **-ello** *m.* (poet.) roll of linen cloth (Pascoli). **-i·feri** *m.pl.* (zool.) rotifers. **-ina** *f. dim.* little wheel; routine. **-ino** *m.* small wheel; (mil.) machine-gun pan; *pl.* fore-wheels of a carriage (being smaller than the rear wheels). **-ismo** *m.* (eng.) gears, gearing, mechanism.

rotenone *m.* (chem.) rotenone, nicouline.

roto-calco *m.* (typ.) rotogravure press; rotogravure, paper printed by such method; popular illustrated magazine. **-calcografi·a** *f.* (typ.) rotogravure. **-compressore** *m.* (naut.) rotary compressor, blower. **-galvanostegi·a** *f.* (electrochem.) barrel-plating. **-grafi·a** *f.* (typ.) rotogravure. **-incisione** *f.* (typ.) intaglio printing.

ro·tol-o *m.* roll; — di stoffa, roll of cloth; (photog.) — di pellicola, roll film; *adv. phr.* a -i, rolling down; (fig.) andare a -i, to fail, to go to rack and ruin; mandare a -i, to ruin, to overthrow; (eng.) cuscinetto a —, antifriction bearing; (S. Italy) a measure of weight, equiv. to 2 lb. **-amento** *m.* rolling; (eng.) cuscinetto a -amento, antifriction bearing. **-are** [A 1 s] *tr.* to bowl, to roll; -are il sasso di Sisifo, to weary oneself at an impossible task; *intr.* (*aux.* essere) to roll down; *rfl.* to roll, to wallow; -arsi in terra, to roll on the ground. (**-ato** *part. adj.*) **-etto** *m. dim.* little roll, small packet. **-io** *m.* the sound of wheels. **-one** *m. augm.* andar giù a -oni, to tumble down, to go rolling down. **-oni** *adv.* rolling, head first.

rotonave *f.* (naut.) rotorship, wind-driven vessel designed by Flettner in 1925 employing a rotating mast.

roto·nda *f.* (archit.) rotunda, round building (e.g. the Pantheon at Rome); terrace of a sea-bathing establishment; (naut.) a bellying sail comparable to the modern 'Genoa'.

rotond-are [A 1 c] *tr.* to make round; to round off; — un conto, to reduce an account to a round sum; (sculp.) — una figura, to round off a figure. **-eggiante** *part. adj.* roundish; filling out, becoming round. **-eggiare** [A 3 c] *intr.* (*aux.* essere) to fill out, to become round; *tr.* to round, to make round. (**-eggiato** *part. adj.*)

rotond-o *adj.* round; rotund; plump; spherical; cylindrical; circular; (naut.) nave -a, broad-beamed ship; (poet.) tavola -a, (King Arthur's) Round Table, (fig.) 'round table' discussion; stile —, rotund style; periodo —, well-turned period; somma -a, round sum; cifra -a, round number; *n.m.* round, round part; curve (naut.) stern; — di poppa, curve of the stern. **-amente** *adv.* roundly; rotundly; luna illuminata -amente, moon shining full and round; sbagliarsi -amente, to be completely mistaken. **-astro** *adj.* roundish, roughly circular. **-ità** *f.* roundness; rotundity; (archit.) di tutta -ità, in full relief, in the round; (paint.) fullness of outlines; (rhet.) rotundity (of a period).

rotore *m.* (eng.) rotor; (electr. eng.) — ad anelli, slip-ring rotor; (naut.) rotor, cylindrical rotating mast (cf. **rotonave**).

rotta¹ *f.* (mus.) rotte, rote, crwth, crowd.

rott-a² *f.* break; breach; a — di collo, at breakneck speed; rent, rip; break (in the weather), rain, thunderstorm; venire alle -e con,

to quarrel with, to break with; (naut.) breach in a canal or river bank; (mil.) rout; andare in —, fuggire in —, to escape in confusion; ricevere una —, to suffer defeat; (poet.) la — di Roncisvalle, the defeat of Roncesvalles. **-ame** *m.* fragment(s); scrap(s); -ame di vetro, cullet; *pl.* wreckage; -ami di ferro, scrap-iron.

rott-a³ *f.* route; course; — di collisione, course (of a torpedo) to obtain a hit; — corretta, adjusted course (after fixing); — falsa, simulated course; — di sicurezza, searched channel; — vera, true course; servizio di —, plotting table; tracciatore di —, plotting table; ufficiale di —, navigating officer; in — per, heading for, on a course for, sailing towards; tracciare la —, to lay down the course; torna in —!, get back on your course!; va in —!, keep to your course! (comm.) way; foglio di —, way bill; fuori —, off course (also fig.); †essere in — con, to be on bad terms with. **†-iere** *m.* (naut.) book equivalent to *Ocean Passages of the World*.

rottame *m.* See under **rotta²**.

rott-o *part.* of **rompere**, q.v.; *adj.* broken; fractured; broken off; interrupted; vita -a, a vicious life; very tired; ho le gambe così -e dalla fatica che non posso più camminare, my legs are so tired they won't carry me any further; nave -a, shipwreck; ceci -i, split peas; (mus.) intervallo —, spread chord, broken chord; — a, inured to, trained to; — alla fatica, inured to fatigue; esser — a un mestiere, to know a trade thoroughly; — ad ogni vizio, thoroughly vicious; strade -e, impassable roads; tempo —, rainy, stormy weather; piovere a cielo —, to pour cats and dogs; (comm.) prezzo —, cut price; *n.m.* break; rupture; rent, tear; fragment; uscirsene pel — della cuffia, to have a narrow escape, to escape 'by the skin of one's teeth'; (archit.) intermittent moulding, as in the 'billet' and various 'decorated' mouldings; *pl.* fractions; mille lire e -i, a thousand lire odd. **-o·rio** *m.* (surg.) cautery; split; (fam.) annoyance, bother.

rottura *f.* breakage, break; breaking off; rupture, fracture, split; (phys.) — dei raggi, refraction of rays; (of river) breaking its banks, overflowing; (eng.) failure, breakdown; — per, di, fatica, fatigue failure; (leg.) breach; — di un contratto, breach of a contract; buono per —, breakage; (mil.) breach; (naut.) see **naufragio**; rotture di gamella, mess breakages; carico di —, breaking strain; (archit.) break in moulding; indentation (cf. **rotto**); arco a —, arched opening breaking an expanse of wall; (surg.) fracture; †rupture; †hernia; — dei confini, violation of the frontiers; rupture, breaking off (of diplomatic relations); outbreak (of war); (fam.) — di tasche, — di capi, annoyance, trouble.

ro·tula *f.* (anat.) patella; little wheel; rowel (of a spur).

roulotte *f.* (pron. as Fr.) caravan.

roulottina *f.* (neol.) shopping bag mounted on wheels.

routang *m. indecl.* (bot.). See **rotang**.

routier *m.* (pron. as Fr.) road-cyclist.

rova·io *m.* north wind; (colloq.) dar dei calci al —, to be hanged.

rovano *adj.* (of a horse) roan; rust coloured, reddish.

rovella *f.* (ichth.) Spanish bream, *Pagellus bogaraveo*.

rovello *m.* anger, rage.

rovent-e *adj.* red-hot; burning, scorching; very hot. **-are** [A 1] *tr.* to make red-hot (cf. **arroventare**). **-ire** [D 2] *tr., intr.* (*aux.* essere) to make, to become, red-hot.

rover-e *f.* (bot.) common oak, *Quercus robur*; oak (timber). **-eto** *m.* oak wood, plantation.

Roveret-o *pr.n.m.* (geog.) Rovereto. **-ano** *adj.* of Rovereto; il filosofo -ano, Rosmini.

†roversato *adj.* See **rovesciato**, under **rovesciare**.

rove·scia *f.* wrong side; revers; lapel; facing; cuff (turned back).

rovesci-are [A 3] *tr.* to overturn; to upset; to turn inside out; — il governo, to put the government out of office; — le tasche, to turn out one's pockets; †(naut.) — il bordo, to go about; (mil.) to overthrow; *rfl.* to throw oneself (down); si -ò dalla finestra, he threw himself out of the window; si -ò sulla poltrona, he threw himself on to the sofa; to be overturned; to pour back; (of a boat) to capsize. **-a·bile** *adj.* (eng.) tipping, tip-up. **-amento** *m.* overthrow, overturning; upsetting; reversal; subversion; (of a boat) capsized, capsizing. **-ante** *part. adj.* upsetting; overflowing, pouring. **-ato** *part. adj.* overthrown; upset; overturned; (turned) inside out; (turned) upside down; -ato indietro, all'indietro, thrown back, held back (e.g. of a person's head); reversed; subverted; (herald.) in base; issuing from the base; reversed; (archit.) gola -ata, ogee moulding, cyma reversa. (**-atore** *m.* **-atrice** *f.*)

rovescina *f.* (cards) a game in which one wins by losing.

rovescino *m.* (text.) ribbing.

rove·sci·o *adj.* turned upside down, inside out; cadere —, to fall backwards; giacere —, to lie on one's back; cono —, inverted cone; (archit.) gola -a, ogee moulding, cyma reversa; (tanning) ferro —, unhairing knife; scudding knife; *adv. phr.* alla -a, inversely, upside down; *n.m.* wrong side; il — della medaglia, the reverse of the medal, (fig.) the other side of the question; *adv. phr.* a —, upside down, back to front, backwards; al —, the wrong way round; fare tutto al —, to do everything wrong; (of bedclothes) the part turned back at the top; rovesci di fortuna, reverses of fortune, bad luck; rovesci finanziari, financial disasters, losses, reverses; (naut.) recurvature; pezzo di —, curved plating whose curvature is inverted to its neighbour; backhaul, any line or tackle working in opposition to another or idle until the vessel goes about; — del timone, trailing edge of the rudder; *pl.* brails; (mus.) inversion, contrary motion; retrograde motion, cancrizans; fall; ruin; downpour; un — di pioggia, a heavy shower of rain; — di pugni, hail of blows; — di sassi, shower of stones; blow with the back of the hand; cuff, slap; (tennis) backhand stroke; *pl.* (agric.) crop ploughed in for manure. **-one** *m. augm.* heavy reversal; -one d'acqua, heavy rain; heavy blow with back of the hand; blow with the flat of a sword; (tennis) backhand stroke. **-one, -oni** *adv.* on one's back.

roveto *m.* bramble thicket; briar; (generically) undergrowth; (Bibl.) il — ardente, the burning bush.

†**rovigliare** *tr.* to rummage.

†**roviglione** *m.* (ichth.) gurnard.

rovin-a *f.* fall; collapse; ruin; landslide; queste spese non saranno la tua —, these expenses will not ruin you; death; slaughter; *pl.* ruins. **-ac·cio** *m.* (bldg.) old (used) brick-end; bit of ruined wall. **-ante** *part. adj.* crumbling, falling; ruinous. **-are** [A1] *intr.* (aux. essere) to fall crashing, to crash down; to crumble; la valanga -ò a valle, the avalanche crashed down the mountainside; (fig.) i nostri affari -ano, our business is going to rack and ruin; non -erà il mondo per così poco, the world will not come to an end for such a trifle; to rush, to dash; *tr.* to ruin; to bring down; to demolish; le piogge -eranno le olive, the rain will spoil the olives; (fig.) la sua prodigalità lo -ò, his extravagance ruined him; (provb.) le acque chete -ano i ponti, still waters run deep; to harm, to hurt, to injure; *rfl.* (acc. of prn. 'si') to ruin oneself; to be ruined; mi si -arono le scarpe in quella passeggiata, my shoes were ruined on that walk; (dat. of prn. 'si') -arsi la salute, to ruin one's health. **-atic·cio** *adj.* somewhat ruined; falling into decay. **-ato** *part. adj.* ruined; spoilt; 'done for', 'down and out'. **-atore** *m.* destroyer; ravager. (**-atrice** *f.*) **-io** *m.* downfall; crumbling; crashing; noise of falling. **-oso** *adj.* violent; furious, impetuous; ruinous; tempesta -osa, violent storm; fuga -osa, headlong flight; (fig.) spese -ose, ruinous expenses. **-osamente** *adv.* ruinously; violently; piovere -osamente, to rain in torrents.

rovist-are [A1] *tr.* to rummage, to search in; to ransack; -ò ogni angolo della casa, he searched in every corner of the house; — le tasche, to turn out one's pockets; *abs.* to make a noise of rummaging. (**-ato** *part. adj.* **-atore** *m.* **-atrice** *f.*) **-io** *m.* continued sound of rummaging; rustling.

†**rovisto** *adj.* See **rubesto**.

rovo *m.* (bot.) blackberry, bramble, *Rubus fruticosus* agg.; (agric.) bacchette di —, sticks of briar, or bramble used to make trays on which to dry fruit; il — di Mosè, Moses's burning bush.

roʒʒa *f.* jade; vicious old horse; rogue.

roʒʒ-o *adj.* rough, rude; crude; clumsy; without refinement; mura -e, unplastered walls; tela -a, unbleached linen; (ling.) voiced (of s or z); primitive, simple; rustic. **-amente** *adv.* roughly, clumsily, rudely. **-ezza** *f.* roughness; clumsiness; boorishness. **-one** *adj.* boorish; rude. **-otto** *adj.* rather clumsy; somewhat boorish. **-ume** *m.* rough things; roughness; rough appearance. **-uolo** *m.* a kind of fishing-net.

ruba *f.* sack, pillage; mettere a —, to pillage; andare a —, to sell like hot cakes.

rubacchi-are [A4] *tr.* to pilfer. **-ato** *part. adj.* pilfered; scrounged; picked up here and there; lavoro -ato, odd jobs. (**-atore** *m.* **-atrice** *f.*)

rubacuori *m. indecl.* See under **rubare**.

rub-are [A1] *tr.* to steal; — sul (*or* nel) peso, to give short weight; — a man salva, to steal impudently; — al giuoco, to play unfairly, to cheat at cards; (provb.) ladro tanto chi -a quanto chi tiene il sacco, the thief and the receiver are tarred with the same brush; a casa del ladro non ci si -a, there's honour among thieves; — una donna, to seduce a woman; — il mestiere a uno, to do someone out of a job, to put someone out of business; — il cuore a uno, to steal someone's heart; — il tempo a uno, to waste a person's time; — ore al lavoro, to idle, to waste time; — un bambino, to kidnap a child; (naut.) — il vento, to steal the wind (used of one vessel overtaking another, or when obstacles intervene). **-acuori** *adj., n.m., f. indecl.* dangerous beauty; (joc.) lady-killer, heart-breaker; sguardi —, irresistible glances. **-amento** *m.* stealing, theft; (mus.) -amento di tempo, rhythmic freedom. **-apaga, -apaghe** *m. indecl.* an employee not worth his pay; a lazy and stupid employee. **-ari·a** *f.* see **ruberia**. **-ato** *part. adj.* stolen; roba -ata, stolen goods, *or* goods sold very cheap, 'given away'; snatched away by untimely death; quattrini -ati, money not honestly earned; tempo -ato, time wasted, (mus.) free rhythm, rubato (i.e. lengthening some notes and shortening others so as not to alter the duration of a whole phrase); (typ.) -ato spazio, space gained on a page by reducing space between paragraphs, adjusting text, etc. **-atore** *m.* thief; robber; brigand; -atore di cuori, lady-killer; uccelli -atori, birds of prey. (**-atrice** *f.*)

rub·bia *f.* See **robbia**.

rubb-io *m.* (*pl.f.* **-ia**) old corn-measure, chiefly used in Rome, *c.* 280 litres; old measure of area at Rome and in the Papal States; aver danari a -ia, to have bags of money.

rubec·chio *adj.* (Tusc. dial.) glowing, fiery-red, ruddy.

rub-efacente *m.* (med.) rubefacient. **-efazione** *f.* (miner.) surface redness of ferruginous minerals. **-ellite** *f.* (miner.) rubellite.

†**rubello** *m.* and derivs. See **ribelle**.

ruberi·a *f.* theft, robbery; fraud; mettere a —, to sack; to rob; è una —, it is sheer robbery; prey; booty; †rape.

rubesto *adj.* (N. Ital.) robust (cf. **robusto**).

rubia·ria *f.* (ent.) humming-bird, hawk moth, *Macroglossa stellatarum*.

†**rubicante** *adj.* glowing, red, fiery.

rubicondo *adj.* ruddy, rubicund; rosy-red.

Rubicone *pr.n.m.* (geog.) the river Rubicon, near Rimini, forming in Caesar's time the boundary between Cisalpine Gaul and Italy proper; passare il —, to cross the Rubicon, as Caesar did in 49 B.C., thus defying the Senate; (fig.) to take an irrevocable step.

rubi·dio *m.* (chem.) rubidium.

rubi·gli-a *f.* (bot.) wild pea, *Pisum sativum* var. *arvense*. **-one** *m.* (bot.) *Lathyrus sativus*.

rubinetto[1] *m.* tap; aprire il —, to turn on the tap; cock; — a due vie, two-way cock; — di spurgo, drainage cock.

rubinetto[2] *m. dim.* of **rubino**, q.v.

rubino *m.* (miner.) ruby; — del Brasile, pink topaz; — d'Ungheria, purple-red garnet; — di Boemia, fire-red garnet; — di Siberia, red tourmaline; (jewell.) — artificiale, boule; (watchm.) jewel; ruby-colour; (agric.) a kind of red grape and wine.

rubiola *f.* (agric.) a kind of reddish grape.

rubizzo, rubiʒʒo *adj.* hale; florid; healthy looking.

rublo *m.* (finan.) rouble.

†**trubo** *m.* See **rovo**.

†**trubore** *m.* redness; blush (cf. **rossore**).

rubric-a *f.* (miner.) rubrica; red pencil; rubric, title, chapter heading in red ink; subsection, subheading; — dell'ordine del giorno, item on the agenda; index-book; address-book; — telefonica, telephone-book; (journ.) page, feature, column; — femminile, woman's hour, woman's page; (eccl.) rubric. **-are** [A2] *tr.* to mark in red; to mark in an index. **-ista** *m.* (eccl.) rubrician. †**-o** *adj.* painted, raddled.

ru-ca *f.* (bot.) *Eruca sativa*; (ent.) caterpillar. **-chetta** *f.* (bot.) *E. sativa*, salad rocket; also *Diplotaxis muralis*. **-chettone** *m.* (bot.) white mustard, *Sinapis alba*.

†**trucolare** *vb.* and derivs. See **ruzzolare**.

rud-e *adj.* rough; coarse; rude; materia —, raw material; parole -i, rough words; — trattamento, rough usage; modi -i, coarse manners, rudeness; un colpo —, a hard blow; stile —, clumsy, unpolished style; lavoro —, hard work. **-emente** *adv.* roughly; coarsely; rudely; harshly. **-ezza** *f.* coarseness; rudeness.

ru·der-e, -o *m.* ruin; *pl.* remains; i -i del Colosseo, the ruins of the Colosseum; (fig., of an old person) è ormai un -e, now he's only a shadow of his former self.

rudiment-o *m.* rudiment; i primi -i di una scienza, the rudiments, the first principles, the elements, of a science. **-ale** *adj.* rudimentary.

†**ru·ere** *intr.* to rush headlong.

ruff-a *f.* scramble; fare la —, to throw things to be scrambled for; fare a — raffa, to catch as catch can, to steal, to snatch; roba che vien di — raffa, ill-gotten goods (cf. provb. under **raffa**). **-ata** *f.* snatch, snatching. **-ello** *m.* (text.) tangle of wool; bunch, tuft. **-ellone** *m.* dishevelled person. **-i** *adv. phr.* o di -i o di raffi, by hook or by crook.

ruffian-o *m.* pander, pimp; procurer; go-between; (vet.) cavallo —, teaser (stallion or jackass used to test whether a mare is on heat). **-a** *f.* procuress. **-are** [A I] *tr.* to procure (for immoral purposes), to pander. **-ato** *part. adj.* earned by procuring. **-eccio** *m.* pimping, procuring, pandering; procurer's trick. **-eggiare** [A 3 c] *intr.* (*aux.* avere) to pander, to pimp. **-eri·a** *f.* procuring, pandering. **-esco** *adj.* (*m.pl.* -eschi) pandering; relating to pimping or procuring. **-esimo** *m.* procuring (as a trade).

Ru·fina *pr.n.f.* (geog.) Rufina near Pontassieve (Tuscany); name of the wine of Rufina.

rufolare [A I s] and derivs. See **grufolare**.

rufolino *adj.* (agric.) infested by moles.

rug-a[1] *f.* wrinkle; crease. **-ato** *adj.* wrinkled; creased.

ruga[2] *f.* (ent.) caterpillar.

ruga[3] *f.* (bot.) rue, *Ruta.*

†**ruga**[4] *f.* (Ven.) shopping-street.

Rugantin-o *pr.n.m.* (Rome) name of a puppet character, made famous by Gaetano Santangelo in the early part of the nineteenth century but known already in the eighteenth; a weak bully; il — di Modena, Francesco IV d'Este (so called by Giuseppe Giusti). **-ata** *f.* act of swaggering; bragging; bullying.

rugbista *m.* (sport) rugby-player.

ruggero[1] *m.* (mus.) dance composed over a conventional ground bass.

Ruggero[2] *pr.n.m.* See **Ruggiero**.

rugghiare [A4] *intr.* (*aux.* avere) to roar; to murmur; to bubble (esp. sound of boiling saucepan).

rug·ghio *m.* roar; bubbling; rumbling (in intestines).

Ruggiero *pr.n.m.* Roger.

rug·gin-e *f.* rust; far la —, to rust, to go rusty; (provb.) chi si frega al ferro, gli s'appicca la —, you can't touch pitch without being defiled; filth, pollution; (on the teeth) tartar; stain; (on corn) rust, blight, mildew; disease of silkworms; (fig.) bad blood; rancour; aver della — con qualcuno, to bear someone a grudge. **-a** (bot.) rust fungus, *Puccinia graminis*; rust-colour; †verdigris; *adj.* rust-coloured; pera -a, russet pear. **-ire** [D 2] *intr.* (*aux.* essere), *rfl.* to rust. (**-ito** *part. adj.*) **-osità** *f.* rustiness, rust. **-oso** *adj.* rusty, rust-coloured; denti -osi, teeth coated with tartar; mele -ose, russet apples. **-uzza** *f.* rancour.

rugg·ire [D I] *intr.* (*aux.* avere) to roar; to howl; il vento -iva, the wind was howling; (of a person) to roar, to rage; (of saucepan) to boil, to bubble; (of intestines) to rumble; *tr.* to shout, to roar; — vendetta, to cry vengeance. **-ente** *part. adj.* roaring, howling, rumbling. **-io** *m.* see **ruggito**, *n.m.* **-ito** *part.* roared, shouted; *n.m.* roar; il -ito del leone, the lion's roar; howl(ing); bubbling; rumbling.

rugiad-a *f.* dew; (fig.) balm; le sue parole furono — al mio cuore, his words were balm to my heart; pasqua — (dial. for 'pasqua rosata', which is rare for 'pasqua delle rose'), Whitsuntide; (bot.) — del sole, sundew, *Drosera rotundifolia*; (phys.) punto di —, dew-point. **-oso** *adj.* dewy, bedewed; guance -ose, cheeks bedewed with tears; fresh, flourishing; unctuous, hypocritical.

rugliare [A4] *intr.* (*aux.* avere) to growl; to rumble; to roar; il vento ruglia, the wind is howling; (of pigeons) to coo.

ruglione *m.* (ichth.) gurnard.

rugos-o *adj.* wrinkled; crinkled; (bot.) rugose. **-ità** *f.* rugosity; roughness, unevenness.

ruin-a *f.*, **-oso** *adj.* See **rovin-a, -oso**.

†**ruire** *intr.* to rush headlong (cf. **ruere**).

ruletta *f.* roulette.

rull-are [A I] *intr.* (*aux.* avere) (of drums) to roll; (aeron.) to taxi; (naut.) see **rollare**; *tr.* to roll (with a roller); (agric.) to roll, to harrow. **-aggio** *m.* (aeron.) taxi-ing. **-amento** *m.* roll; rolling. **-ante** *part. adj.* rolling; (mus.) cassa -ante, tenor drum. (**-ato** *part. adj.*) **-atrice** *f.* (eng.) burnishing machine. **-atura** *f.* (eng.) rolling. **-io** *m.* roll, rolling; (naut.) see **rollìo**.

rull-o *m.* roll, beating (of drums); (naut. hist.) roll of drum used to start an exercise; call on a bugle in lieu of a drum used to end an exercise; (eng.) roller; — conico, tapered roller; catena a -i, roller chain; cuscinetto a -i, roller bearing; (photog.) — di gomma, squeegee; skittle, ninepin; dare nei -i, to begin to roll. **-etto** *dim.* little roll; (typ.) roller for running off proofs. **-ino** *m.* (eng.) cuscinetto a -ini, needle roller bearings.

†**rumare** *vb.* and derivs. See **ruminare**, under **rumine**.

rumen-o *adj., n.m.* Roumanian. (**-a** *f.*)

ru·min-e *m.* (zool.) rumen. **-ale** *adj.* (Rom. hist.) fico -ale, *ficus ruminalis*, the fig-tree under which Romulus and Remus were suckled by the she-wolf. **-ante** *part. adj.* ruminating; *n.m.pl.* (zool.) ruminants. **-are** [A I s] *intr.* (*aux.* avere) to ruminate; *tr.* (fig.) to think over, to ponder, to meditate upon. **-ato** *part. adj.* pondered, thought over. (**-atore** *m.* **-atrice** *f.*) **-atura** *f.* rumination; cud; pondering, consideration.

rumor-e *m.* noise; din; clamour; uproar; outcry; levarsi a —, to create a disturbance; metter il campo a —, to raise the alarm, to cause great excitement; fame; il mondan —, earthly fame; far —, to become famous, to be much talked about; rumour; lontano dai -i del mondo, far from the madding crowd; *Molto — per nulla, Much Ado about Nothing.* **-eggiante** *part. adj.* rumbling; muttering; noisy; un uditorio -eggiante, a restless audience; una folla -eggiante, a noisy crowd. **-eggiare** [A 3 c] *intr.* (*aux.* avere) to make a noise; to rumble; to talk loudly; to murmur; to create a disturbance; *tr.* to incite; to put about a rumour; to stir up; to murmur against; to shout down. (**-eggiatore** *m.* **-eggiatrice** *f.*) **-io** *m.* noise; continued sound of talking, etc., murmur. **-ista** *m.* (cinem.; radio) sound effects man. **-osità** *f.* noise, noisiness. **-oso** *adj.* noisy; loud; risata -osa, loud laughter; facondia -osa, noisy eloquence.

run-a *f.* (*pl.* -e, -i *m.*) rune.

†**runci·glio** *m.* See **ronciglio**.

ru·nico *adj.* runic; alfabeto —, runic alphabet; iscrizione runica, runic inscription.

runite *f.* (miner.) graphic graphite.

ruol-o *m.* (mil.) muster list; nominal list; (naut.) stationing bill of a ship's company; — di anzianità, seniority list; passare il —, mettere a —, to muster; — per l'abbandono della nave, abandon ship station list; — per l'assalto di combattimento, quarter bill; — di bordo, a complete table showing the station and duty of every officer and man in a warship for all the most important occasions; — degli impiegati dello stato, lists of state employees; — delle tasse sul patrimonio, rent-roll; (school) insegnante di —, regular teacher, permanent member of staff; impiegato di —, clerk on the staff; di —, on the permanent staff (as opposed to 'd'incarico', temporary); class-list; class, category; (leg.) list; cause-list (C.C.P.); calendar (C.P.P.). **-ino** *m.* (mil.) -ino di marcia, marching order or list; -ino tascabile, duplicate copy of marching list held by each company commander.

ruota *f.* wheel; — di fune, coil of rope; (motor.) — anteriore, front wheel; — posteriore, rear wheel; — dentata, cog wheel; — d'ingranaggio, gear wheel; — di ricambio, spare-wheel; — del mulino, mill wheel; — a pale, paddle wheel; — idraulica, water wheel, mill wheel; (agric.) — limitatrice di profondità, gauge wheel (of plough); (fig.) la — della fortuna, the wheel of Fortune; ungere le ruote, to grease the wheels; essere la quinta (*or*, l'ultima) — del carro, to be the least important member of a team or group; (provb.) l'ultima — del carro è quella che cigola, the worst wheel of the cart makes the most noise; il pavone fa la —, the peacock spreads its tail; pare un tacchino quando fa la —, he struts like a turkey-cock; fare la —, to show off, to pay court to a woman, *or* to wheel round, to turn about, (of birds, aeroplanes) to wheel, to circle; (watchm.) — dei minuti, cannon pinion; (naut.) wheel, steering wheel; — a pala, — a paletta, paddle, paddle wheel; piroscafo a ruote, paddle-steamer; — di cavo, cable drum; — del timone, — di governo, steering wheel; — di prora, stempiece; — di poppa, sternpost; ancorare a —, to anchor with one anchor (swinging berth); subire il supplizio della —, to be broken on the wheel; — di Issione, Ixion's wheel; turning-box (for gifts, etc. used in convents, or for foundlings); lottery wheel or urn; (in convents) turn; (leg.) circuit; panel; rota; (anat.) kneecap, patella.

ruotare [A I] and derivs. See **rotare**.

ruotino *m.* little wheel; (aeron.) — di coda, tail wheel.

ruotismo *m.* (watchm.) — di minuteria, minute work; ponte del —, train wheel bridge; (eng.) gearing, mechanism.

ruotone *m. augm.* large wheel, great wheel; — del mulino, the driving wheel of a mill.

rup-e *f.* rock; cliff; la — Tarpea, the Tarpeian Rock. **-estre** *adj.* rocky; belonging to, flourishing among rocks; flora -estre, rock plants. (**-icella** *f. dim.*) **-i·cola** *f.* (orn.) cock of the rock, *Rupicola crocea.*

ru·pia¹ *f.* (med.) rupia.

rupi·a² *f.* (finan.) rupee.

rural-e *adj.* country; rural; scuola —, country school; economia —, rural economy; politica —, agrarian policy; *n.m.* countryman; *pl.* i -i, country people. **-izzare** [A I] *tr.* to countrify, to ruralize.

ruscell-o *m.* brook, stream. **-amento** *m.* (geog.) sheet-wash. **-etto** *m. dim.* brooklet; -etto orgoglioso, low-born person who becomes haughty in success.

ru·schio *m.* (bot.) privet, *Ligustrum vulgare.*

rusco *m.* (bot.) butcher's broom, *Ruscus aculeatus.*

ruspa *f.* search; andare alla —, to collect chestnuts after the harvest; scratching of hens; (agric.) scraper; bullock-sledge.

rusp-are [A I] *intr.* (*aux.* avere) to scratch about; to rummage; to glean chestnuts. **-ante** *part. adj.* scratching, searching; (hist.) *pl.n.m.* members of the household of Giangastone, Grand Duke of Tuscany, who were paid a 'ruspone' a day (cf. under **ruspo**). **-atore** *m.* gatherer, esp. of late chestnuts. (**-atrice** *f.*)

rusp-o *adj.* rough, rugged; moneta -a, freshly minted coin; *n.m.* (numism.) Florentine sequin; what is found by scratching about. **-ezza** *f.* roughness. **-olina** *f.* (agric.) rake for collecting chestnuts. **-one** *m.* (numis.) Florentine coin worth 3 sequins; *pl.* money, riches; salute e -oni, health and wealth.

russ-are [A I] *intr.* (*aux.* avere) to snore; †to sleep deeply. **-amento** *m.* snoring. **-io** *m.* prolonged snoring. †**-o** *m.* snoring; deep sleep.

Rus·s-ia *pr.n.f.* (geog.) Russia. **-o** *adj.*, *n.m.* Russian; (cul.) insalata -a, Russian salad. (**-a** *f.*)

russo¹ *adj.*, *n.m.* See under **Russia**.

†**russo²** *m.* See under **russare**.

ru·stia *f.* (bot.) small scabious, *Scabiosa columbaria.*

ru·sti-co *adj.* rustic, (of the) country; danze -che, country dances; mobili -ci, plain, simple furniture; mobilia -ca, rustic garden furniture; un uomo —, an unsociable man; maniere -che, rudeness; parlata -ca, countryman's speech; (archit.) lavoro —, rustic work; facciata -ca, rustic façade, unplastered; casa -ca, country cottage (sometimes like a Swiss chalet); la vita -ca, the simple life; *adv. phr.* alla -ca, simply, roughly, with simplicity; *n.m.* countryman; rustic; cottage; qui c'è la villa e là il —, here is the farmhouse and there is the labourer's cottage; *I Rustici (I Rusteghi), The Misanthropes,* title of a comedy by Goldoni; (archit.; bookb.) rustic style; rough and ready building. **-camente** *adv.* roughly, rudely; (archit.) lavorato -amente, in rustic style, with rough finish. **-cag·gine** *f.* rudeness; roughness; simplicity (in manners). **-cale** *adj.* rustic; rural; poesie -ali, poems of country life; *n.m.* coat for country wear. **-calmente** *adv.* rustically, rurally. **-cano** *adj.* (of the) country; rustic; *Cavalleria Rusticana,* 'Rustic Chivalry' (title of a short story by Verga and an opera by Mascagni). **-chetto** *adj. dim.* simple, rather rough. **-chezza** *f.* rusticity; rudeness; shyness, sullenness. **-cità** *f.* rusticity; shyness, bashfulness; simplicity; ignorance.

rut-a *f.* (bot.) rue, *Ruta graveolens*; — canina, *Scrophularia canina*; — caprina, *Hypericum hircinum*; — sfrangiata, *Ruta chalapensis*; — di muro, wall rue, *Asplenium ruta-muraria.* **-ale** *adj.* of rue. **-ato** *adj.* (pharm.) compounded with rue.

rutang *m. indecl.* (bot.). See **rotang**.

rut-ene *m.* (geog.) Ruthenian. **-e·nico** *adj.* Ruthenian; (chem.) ruthenic. **-e·nio** *m.* (chem.) ruthenium.

rutherford *m. indecl.* (atom. phys.) rutherford.

ru·til-e, -o *m.* (miner.; chem.) rutile; *adj.* reddish; fair, bright. **-ante** *adj.* (poet.) rutilant, shining; brilliant; (chem.) vapore -ante, nitrogen peroxide; (med.) bright red (said of arterial blood). **-are** [A I S] *intr.* (*aux.* avere) to rutilate, to shine, to sparkle.

rutina *f.* (chem.) rutin, eldrin.

rutt-o *m.* belch; far -i, to belch. **-are** [A I] *intr.* (*aux.* avere) to belch; *tr.* to belch forth; -are ingiurie, to spit out insults; -are fiamme, to belch forth flames. (**-atore** *m.* **-atrice** *f.*) **-eggiare** [A 3 c] *intr.* (*aux.* avere) to belch frequently. **-ile** *m.* (bot.) mericarp. **-ore** *m.* (electr.) contact breaker, trembler. **-ura** *f.* (electr.) breaking.

ru·vid-o *adj.* rough (to the touch); pelle -a, rough skin; harsh; coarse; (fig.) rough, rude, coarse; modi -i, rudeness, rough manners. **-amente** *adv.* roughly, harshly; rudely; vestito -amente, dressed in coarse garments. **-ezza** *f.* roughness; harshness; rudeness. **-ità** *f.* roughness, rudeness; ruggedness, scabrousness.

ruvi·stico *m.* (bot.). See **ligustro**.

ruzza *f.* contest; dispute; rough and tumble.

ruzz-are [A I] *intr.* (*aux.* avere) to romp, to frolic, to gambol; to make a noise. **-amento** *m.* romping; noisy play. **-ante** *part. adj.* romping, gambolling; *pr.n.m.* Il Ruzzante, name given to Angelo Beolco, sixteenth-century writer of comedies in Paduan dialect. **-o** *m.* romping; noise of romping; playfulness, frolicsomeness; caprice; quarrel, tiff; cavare il -o di capo a uno, to knock the nonsense out of someone.

ruz·zol-a *f.* spinning-disk, bowled like a hoop or with a string. **-are** [A I S] *intr.* (*aux.* essere, avere) to tumble; to roll down, to roll; far -are un cerchio, to trundle a hoop; *tr.* to roll; -are macigni dalla vetta, to roll down boulders from the top of the hill; -are le scale, to tumble downstairs. **-ata** *f.* tumble. **-io** *m.* (*pl.* -ii) continued rolling, tumbling. **-one** *m.* tumble, fall; fare il -one, to tumble down, (fig.) to fall from office, etc.; fare le scale a -oni, to fall down the stairs. **-oni** *adv.* tumbling down, headlong.

---

s *f.* (pron. esse) the letter S; the consonant S; the sibilant S; fatto a S, twisted like an S, S-shaped.

sa' *abbrev.* of **santo**, q.v.

Saba *pr.n.f.* (Bibl., geog.) Sheba, Saba; la Regina di —, the Queen of Sheba.

sabadi·gl-ia *f.* (bot.) sabadilla, *Schoenocaulon officinalis.* **-ina** *f.* (chem.) sabadilline, cevadilline.

sabal *m. indecl.* (bot.) palmetto, *Sabal.*

saba·tico *adj.* sabbatical; anno —, sabbatical year.

sabatino *adj.* See under **sabato**.

sa·bat-o *m.* Saturday; — inglese, Saturday afternoon off; (iron.) — che viene!, *à la venue des coquecigrues,* i.e. never; (provb.) non c'è — senza sole, non c'è donna senz'amore, every dog has its day; Dio non paga il —, i.e. punishment will catch up with the wicked in the end; (Jewish rel.) Sabbath (not used of Christian Sunday); via del —, Sabbath day's journey; (eccl.) — santo, Holy Saturday. **-ari** *m.pl.* (rel. hist.) Sabbatarians. **-ino** *adj.* pertaining to Saturday; born on a Saturday; *n.m.* Saturday's child; observer of Saturday as the Sabbath. (**-ina** *f.*) †**-izzare** *intr.* to keep the Sabbath; *tr.* to keep as a Sabbath.

saba·udo *adj.* (hist.) of Savoy; of the House of Savoy; *n.m.pl.* descendants of the House of Savoy; (comm.) Lloyd —, name of a Genoese shipping firm now merged in the Società 'Italia'.

sabba *m.* witches' sabbath; — classico, sabbath of Hellenic spirits in Goethe's *Faust,* Part II.

sab·b-ia *f.* sand; -ie mobili, quicksand; (zool.) canale della —, stone canal (of echinoderm). **-ia·ia** *f.* sandpit. **-iare** [A 4] *tr.* (eng.) to sandblast. **-iatrice** *f.* sandblasting machine, sander. **-iatura** *f.* (eng.) sanding; sandblasting. **-iera** *f.* (rlwy.) sandbox; (paperm.) button-trap, sand-catcher. **-io** *m.* (Tusc.) sandy soil capable of cultivation. **-ione** *m.* gravel; sandy soil; †large sandy stretch or plain. **-ioso** *adj.* sandy.

sabelliano *adj.*, *n.m.* (rel. hist.) Sabellian.

sabel·lico *adj.* (hist.) Sabellic, Sabine.

sab-e·o *m.* (rel.) Sabaist. **-eismo** *m.* (rel.) Sabaism.

sabin *m. indecl.* (acoust.) sabin.

Sabina¹ *f.* of Sabino, q.v.; il ratto delle Sabine, the rape of the Sabines.

sabina² *f.* (bot.) savin, *Juniperus sabina.*

Sabino *pr.n.m.* (hist.) Sabine; *adj.* Sabine.

†**saborra** *f.* and derivs. See **zavorra**.

sabot-are [A I] *tr.* to sabotage; to damage wilfully; to wreck; (fig.) to botch; to thwart. **-ag·gio** *m.* sabotage; (leg.) malicious damage; wanton destruction (esp. of employer's property) (C.P.). (**-ato** *part. adj.*) **-atore** *m.* saboteur. (**-atrice** *f.*)

sac-ca *f.* bag; satchel; wallet; — da viaggio, travelling-bag, Gladstone bag; kitbag; — da notte, pyjama-case, nightdress-case; — da piedi, foot-muff; (mil.) sack; haversack, ration-bag; (geog.) bay, cove; (aeron.) — d'aria, air pocket; (metall.) — di alto forno, bosh. **-cagno** *m.* (slang) knife. **-ca·ia** *f.* place (e.g. in a granary) where sacks are hung up; sackful; (med.) fare -caia, to

sac·ca (*cont.*)
fester, (fig.) to let one's resentment rankle or fester. **-capane** *m.*
see **tascapane**. **-cheri·a** *f.* sacking-works; supply of sacks. **-chętta**
f. dim. nosebag. **-chettare** [A I c] *tr.* to sandbag; to hit with a
sandbag.

sacc-arato *m.* (chem.) saccharate; *adj.* saccharated. **-a·rico** *adj.*
saccharic. **-ari·fero** *adj.* sugar-producing. **-arificare** [A2] *tr.* to
saccharify. **-arificazione** *f.* saccharification. **-arimetri·a** *f.*, **-aro-**
metri·a *f.* (chem.) saccharimetry. **-ari·metro** *m.*, **-aro·metro** *m.*
saccharimeter. **-arina** *f.* (chem.) saccharin, glucoside. **-arina·ceo**
adj. saccharine. **-arinato** *adj.* saccharinated, flavoured with
saccharin. **-arino** *adj.* saccharine, sugary. **-aro·ide** *adj.* (miner.)
saccharoidal. **-aro·metro** *m.* (chem.) saccharometer. **-aromiceti**
m.pl. (bot.) yeasts, Saccharyomycetes. **-aro·sio** *m.* (chem.)
saccharose, sucrose.

†saccardo *m.* (mil. hist.) camp follower.

saccat-a *f.* sackful; sack (of); a saccate, by the sack, in sackloads;
(agric.) measure of land (as much as is needed to sow a sackful
of grain, about 5600 sq. metres); (naut.) flapping or whipping of
sails. **-ura** *f.* (meteor.) secondary depression.

saccella·rio *m.* (eccl. hist.) *saccellarius*.

saccent-e *adj.* presumptuous, pretentious; *n.m.* wiseacre, know-all;
pedant; fare il —, to parade one's knowledge; *f.* blue-stocking.
-emęnte *adv.* pretentiously. **-eri·a** *f.* presumption; smattering of
knowledge; arrogant parade of learning; pretentiousness;
pedantry. **-one** *m.* wiseacre; pedant.

saccheggi-are [A3c] *tr.* to sack; to pillage; to plunder; to despoil;
to plagiarize; to pocket. **-amęnto** *m.* sacking; plundering;
plagiarizing. **-ato** *part. adj.* sacked; pillaged; plagiarized. **-atore**
m. pillager, plunderer; *adj.* pillaging, plundering. (**-atrice** *f.*)

sacchęggio *m.* sacking, sack, plunder; dare il — a, to sack, to pillage;
(leg.) looting; pillage (C.P.).

sacch-eri·a *f.*, **-ętta** *f.*, **-ettare** [A I c]. See under **sacca**.

sacchętto *m.* See under **sacco**.

†sacci-amento *m.* knowledge. **†-uto** *adj.* pretentious, affecting
knowledge; pedantic.

sac·co *m.* (*pl.m.* **-chi**; Tusc. **-che** *f.* in sense of 'full sacks') sack;
bag; pouch; — postale, mailbag; — di carbone, sack of coal;
— di grano, sack of grain; — da montagna, rucksack; — a terra,
sandbag; — a pelo, sleeping-bag; a **-chi**, in sackfuls, by the sack-
load, in abundance; quattrini a **-chi**, pots, bags, of money;
sackcloth; avere un — di cose da fare, to have a pile, heap, of
things to do; un — d'ingiurie, a heap of insults; gliene ha detto
un —, he spoke his mind; un — e una sporta, a sackful and then
some; ago da —, packing-needle; sack-like clothing; (fig.) andare
con la testa nel —, to be blind, to be unaware of what's going on;
mettere nel —, to override; colmare il —, to go to the limit; to do
one's worst; la gatta nel —, a pig in a poke; cogliere uno con la
mano nel —, to catch a person red-handed; farina del suo —,
one's own, what one is familiar with; andarsene con le pive nel —,
to come away empty-handed; (mil.) sack; mandare a —, mettere
a —, to put to the sack; sacchi di, a, terra, sandbags for defensive
purposes; (naut.) — dei marinai, sailors' kitbag; palliasse used
by galley slaves; coil, piece of a fishing net; belly of a sail either
ill cut or ill set; (mus.) butt, double joint (of bassoon); (anat.)
sac; (bot.) — embrionale, embryo-sac. **-chętto** *m. dim.* of **sacco**;
(naut., etc.) housewife (pron. 'husif'); shalloon bag containing
cordite charge; Turk's head on the end of a heaving line. **-coc·cia**
f. pocket; wallet; (fig.) averne piene le **-cocce**, to be thoroughly
fed up (with, about). **-cocciata** *f.* pocketful. **-coccione** *m.* (Rome)
heavy drinker, guzzler. **-co·fori** *m.pl.* (eccl. hist.) saccophori.
-coleva *m.* (naut.) Greek or Sicilian sponge-fishing boat; Greek
trader, 30–60 tons, carrying a bellying sail. **†-comaneggiare** *tr.*
see **saccomannare**. **†-comannare** *tr.* to sack, to plunder, to pillage,
to loot. **†-comanno** *m.* see **saccardo**; sack, sacking, plundering; plunderer; ruffian. **-cone** *m.* palliasse, straw mattress;
-cone elastico, **-cone a molla**, sprung mattress; (anat.) saccule.

sac·culo *m.* (anat.) saccule.

sacello *m.* (Rom. antiq.) *sacellum*, shrine; (eccl.) chapel, shrine.

sacerdot-e *m.* (rel.) priest (Christian or non-Christian); sommo —,
the pope; (fig.) — di Temide, magistrate, judge (cf. **prete**). **-ale**
adj. priestly, sacerdotal; (canon law) beneficio **-ale**, benefice
tenable only by a priest. **-almęnte** *adv.* in priestly fashion; as a
priest. **†-are** *tr.* to 'priest', to ordain priest. **†-a·tico** *m.* priesthood. **-ęssa** *f.* priestess; (fig.) **-essa** di Venere, courtesan.

sacerdo·zio *m.* (eccl.) priesthood; clergy; (fig.) priesthood, ministry,
mission (of culture, science, etc.); **†**(eccl.) benefice.

†sa·coma *f.* See **sagoma**.

sacra *f.* See **sagra**.

sacral-e *adj.* (rel.) sacral; (anat.) sacral. **-ità** *f.* (rel.) sacral character.

sacrament-o *m.* (**†***pl.* **-a** *f.*) oath; (theol.) sacrament; **-i** dei morti,
sacraments of the dead (of those not in a state of grace, i.e.
baptism and penance); **-i** dei vivi, sacraments of the living (i.e. the
other five); il Santo —, il Divin —, the Blessed Sacrament; (fig.)
con tutti i **-i**, with all proper ceremonies, properly, thoroughly,
well and truly; **†**holy thing; **†**taking of the veil. **-ale** *adj.* (theol.)
sacramental (grace, character, confession); (fig., joc.) conventional; parole **-ali**, ritual words, consecrated formula; *n.m.pl.*
sacramentals (rites, or blessed things, outside the seven sacraments, e.g. a bishop's blessing, holy water, etc.). (**-almęnte** *adv.*)
-are [A I] *tr.* (eccl.) to administer a sacrament to (someone), esp.
Holy Communion to the dying; *intr.* (*aux.* avere) to swear; *rfl.* to
receive a sacrament, esp. the Viaticum. **-a·rio** *m.* (liturg. hist.)
sacramentary; *pl.* (eccl. hist.) sacramentarians. **-ato** *part. adj.*
(theol.) consecrated; Gesù **-ato**, Christ in the Blessed Sacrament.
-ine *f.pl.* (eccl.) Sacramentines (nuns of Perpetual Adoration).

sacr-are [A I] *tr.* (liter.) to consecrate, to hallow, to dedicate; to
ordain. **-a·rio** *m.* (Rom. antiq.) shrine, sacrarium; (liturg.)
piscina, sacrarium; (liturg.) small chapel; (fig.) shrine, sanctum;
nel **-ario** della famiglia, in the bosom of one's family; **†**sacristy;
†tabernacle; **†**sanctuary, presbytery; (fig.) sanctuary. **-ato** *part.*
adj. consecrated; **†**prete **-ato**, ordained priest; **†**monaca **-ata**,
professed nun; *n.m.* consecrated ground; churchyard; space
before church; oath.

sacrest-ano *m.*, **-i·a** *f.* See **sagrest-ano**, **-ia**.

sacrific-are [A2s] *tr.* to sacrifice; to offer (to God); **†-are** la messa,
to offer mass; (fig.) to renounce, to forgo; to give up; *rfl.* to
sacrifice oneself; to make sacrifices; to be unselfish; to make a
martyr of oneself. **-ante** *part. adj.* (rel.) sacrificing; *n.m.* sacrificer.
-ato *part. adj.* sacrificed; (rel.) devoted, unselfish, mortified (e.g.
of a life); **†**hallowed; (eccl. hist.) *n.m.pl.* sacrificati. **-atore** *m.*
sacrificer. **-azione** *f.* sacrificing, sacrifice.

sacrifi·cio *m.* sacrifice; offering; (theol.) il — divino (incruento), the
holy (bloodless) sacrifice, the Mass; (rel.) offrire in — a Dio i
dolori, to offer up one's sufferings; privation; act of self-denial;
— di tempo, waste of time, loss of time; a costo di grandi sacrifici,
at the cost of much self-denial, at the cost of many privations;
fare dei grandi sacrifici, to put in a lot of effort, to take trouble.

sacrifi·zio *m.* (Tusc.). See **sacrificio**.

sacrile·gio *m.* (rel.) — (personale, locale, reale), sacrilege (against
persons, places, things); (leg.) sacrilege; larceny from a church.

sacri·le-go *adj.* (m.pl. **-ghi**) sacrilegious, profane; lingua **-a**, blasphemous, impious, tongue, (fig.) shameless scandalmonger;
n.m. sacrilegious person. **-gamęnte** *adv.* sacrilegiously, profanely.

Sacripante *pr.n.m.* Sacripante, a Saracen King (character in Ariosto's
Orlando Furioso); (fig.) blusterer; bully.

sacris, in (Lat. phr.) (eccl.) essere *in sacris*, to be in (holy) orders.

sacrist-a *m.* (eccl.) sacristan (chiefly of the Sacristan to the Pope).
-ano *m.* see **sagrestano**.

sacr-o¹ *m.* sacred; holy; inviolate; (archaeol.) Via **-a**, the Via Sacra
in ancient Rome which runs through the Forum from the Colos-
seum to the Capitol; (lit.) il poema —, the *Divine Comedy*; il —
fonte, the fountain of Hippocrene, poetic inspiration; i **-i** bronzi,
church bells; solemn, awestruck; (iron.) blessed, wretched,
accursed; (naut.) ancora **-a**, sheet anchor. **-osanto** *adj.* sacrosanct.

sacr-o² *m.* (anat.) sacrum; *adj.* (anat.) osso —, sacrum. **-algi·a** *f.*
(med.) sacralgia. **-ococ·cice** *m.* (anat.) sacrococcyx.

sacro³ *m.* (orn.) Saker falcon, *Falco cherrug*.

†sada *f.* a leek-green precious stone.

†sadda *f.* See **sada**.

†saddisfare *vb.* and derivs. See **soddisfare**.

sad(d)uce-o *adj.* (rel. hist.) Sadducean; *n.m.* Sadducee.

sa·d-ico *adj.* sadistic. **-işmo** *m.* sadism.

saęppol-a *f.* (Tusc. euphem. for **saetta**, q.v.) che ti venga una —!,
devil take you!; (bot.) Canadian fleabane, *Erigeron canadensis*.
†-are *tr.* (agric.) to cut (a vine) down to the root. **-o** *m.* (agric.)
epicormic shoot of vine; **†**crossbow for shooting small birds.

saętt-a *f.* arrow; dart; thunderbolt, flash; (colloq.) restless child,
imp, trial; che — di ragazzo!, that child's never still an instant!;

saett·a (*cont.*)

correre come una —, to run like the wind; naso a —, pointed nose; ti pigli una —, devil take you!, curse you!; (with *neg.*) nothing; neanche una —, not a sausage; non ci capisco una —, I can't make head or tail of it; (ichth.) beaked carp, *Chondrostoma saetta*; (math.) sagitta, versed sine; (sculp. tool) punch; (liturg.) hearse (frame for candles at Tenebrae). **-ame** *m.* collection of arrows, quantity of arrows. **-ella** *f. dim.* of **saetta**; (techn.) bit, point of auger. **-i·a** *f.* (naut. hist.) brigantine (48–80 oars); a fast sailing-ship; a ship's boat, generally the captain's gig; (liturg.) hearse (candle-frame). **-iere** *m.* bowman, archer. **-iforme** *adj.* (bot.) sagittate. **-one** *m. augm.* large arrow; (bldg.) brace, strut; (aeron.) strut; (zool.) Aesculapian snake, *Coluber longissimus*. **-ume** *m.* see **saettame**. **-uzza** *f. dim.* small arrow; (eng.) drill bit.

saett·are [A 1 c] *tr.* to shoot with an arrow; to fling, to lance, to dart; il sole -a raggi roventi, the sun darts its fiery rays; — occhiate pungenti, to dart ferocious glances; *recip. rfl.* to shoot at one another with arrows. **-amento** *m.* shooting (with arrows); archery; shot; -amento di parole, volley of words. **-ante** *part. adj.* shooting; il -ante Apollo, the archer Apollo. **-ata** *f.* shot (with an arrow); bow-shot; spazio di una -ata, length of a bow-shot. **-ato** *part. adj.* shot; lanced, darted, flung. **-atore** *m.* archer; *adj.* arco -atore, bow. **-atrice** *f.* huntress; *adj.* caccia -atrice, hunting with bow and arrows.

safena *f.* (anat.) saphena, saphenous vein.

saf·f·ico *adj.* Sapphic; amori -ici, Lesbianism; (prosod.) Sapphic (line, stanza). **-ica** *f.* (prosod.) Sapphic ode, poem in Sapphics. **-ismo** *m.* (med.) Sapphism, Lesbianism.

†**saffiro** *m.* See **zaffiro**.

Saffo *pr.n.f.* Sappho.

safranina *f.* (chem.) safranine.

saga *f.* saga; †twitch.

sag·ace *adj.* sagacious; shrewd; clever, smart; cane —, dog with a good nose. **-acemente** *adv.* shrewdly; cleverly. **-a·cia** *f.* see **sagacità**. **-acità** *f.* sagacity; shrewdness; cleverness, smartness; (of a dog) a good nose.

sa·gari *f. indecl.* (archaeol.) war-axe, axe of the Amazons.

sagenite *f.* (miner.) sagenite.

sagg̣etto *m. dim.* of **saggio²**, q.v.

sagg̣ezza *f.* wisdom; prudence; sound judgement; experience (cf. **saggio¹**).

saggi·are [A 3] *tr.* to test, to sample; to try, to taste; (of a cook) — la minestra, to taste the soup; — il vino, to wine-taste; (scient.) to test, to assay; **-ato** *part. adj.* tested; sampled; tried; tasted. **-atore** *m.* tester; (hist.) title of a polemical treatise by Galileo (Rome, 1623). **-atura** *f.* testing, test. **-avino** *m. indecl.* wine-taster.

saggin·a *f.* (bot.) great millet, *Sorghum vulgare*. **-ale** *adj.* of millet; *n.m.* dried millet stem; (orn.) curlew sandpiper, *Calidris testacea*; -ale piccolo, dunlin, *C. alpina*. **-are** [A 1] *tr.* to fatten. **-ato** *part. adj.* fattened; mixed with sorghum. **-ella** *f. dim.* of **saggina**; (bot.) erba -ella, Aleppo-grass, *Sorghum halepense*; (orn.) see **sagginale**.

sag·gi·o¹ *adj.* wise; prudent; wary; shrewd; judicious; experienced; sensible; sage; sapient; (of a child) good, well-behaved; *n.m.* wise man; sensible person; sage; cosa da —, wise thing, sensible thing. **-amente** *adv.* wisely; prudently; shrewdly; judiciously; sensibly; sagely.

sag·g·io² *m.* test; trial; dare — di sè, to prove one's worth; sample; taste; essay; monograph; exam-paper, script; — degli studenti, end of term performance (e.g. music recital, etc.); (leg.) rate; — dell'interesse, rate of interest (C.C.); — del cambio, rate of exchange. **-ista** *m., f.* essayist, essay writer. **-i(u)olo** *m. dim.* little taste, nip; scales for weighing coins; (chem.) specimen bottle, weighing bottle.

†**sagire** *tr.* to occupy, to seize.

sagittale *adj.* (anat.) sagittal; (bot.) see **saettiforme**.

Sagitta·rio *pr.n.m.* (astron.) Sagittarius.

sagliente *m.* (mil.) see **saliente**; (herald.) salient.

†**sagnare** *tr.* to pierce with a lance, to cause to bleed.

sago¹ *m.* See **sagù**.

sago² *m.* (poet.). See **sa·io**.

†**sago³** *adj.* See **presago**.

sa·gola *f.* (naut.) strand of a rope, leadline, hogline, halyard; — intrecciata, sennet, plaited rope.

sa·gom·a *f.* (archit.) profile, section of a design; moulding; (techn.) outline, shape; counterweight of a steelyard; (bldg.) strickle;

(rlwy.) standard clearance gauge; — limite, maximum movement dimensions; clearance limit; — di carico, loading gauge; (road transport) overall bulk or dimensions; (fig.) shape, outline, figure; — del viso, profile, lines of a face; target shaped like a human; (slang) che —!, what a queer chap! **-are** [A 1 s] *intr.* (*aux.* avere) (archit.) to make a moulding; *tr.* to draw in profile or section; to mould or shape; to carve. (**-ato** *part. adj.*) **-atura** *f.* (eng.) profile turning.

sagra *f.* (rel.) feast, esp. of the consecration of a church; festival; commemoration, commemorative ceremony; la — dell'uva, the grape festival; (paint.) picture representing a religious festival or ceremony.

sagramento *m.* and derivs. See **sacramento**.

sagr·are [A 1] *tr.* see **sacrare**; *intr.* (*aux.* avere) (*vulg.*) to curse, to swear. **-ato** *m.* (eccl.) consecrated ground; space, square, in front of a church; churchyard; (pop.) curse, oath; tirare un -ato, to curse, to utter an oath.

sagrest·ano *m.* (eccl.) sacristan; sexton; — del Papa, sacristan to the pope (a Domestic Prelate). **-ana** *f.* (eccl.) sextoness; sister sacristan (in convent). **-i·a** *f.* (eccl.) sacristy.

sagrì *m. indecl.* (ichth.) — moretto, *Etmopterus spinax*, a kind of dogfish (cf. **zagrino**); shagreen.

sagrificare [A 2 s] and derivs. See **sacrificare**.

sagri·fi·cio *m.*, **-le·gio** *m.* See **sacrificio, sacrilegio**.

sagrino *m.* See **zagrino**.

sagri·sta *m.* see **sacrista**. **-sti·a** *f.* see **sagrestia**, under **sagrestano**.

sagro¹ *adj.* See **sacro¹**.

sagro² *m.* (ichth.) See **zagrino**.

sagro³ *m.* (orn.). See **sacro²**.

†**sagro⁴** *m.* cannon.

sagù *m. indecl.* (bot.) sago.

Sahara *pr.n.m.* (geog.) Sahara.

sahlite *f.* (miner.) sahlite.

sa·ia *f.* (text.) twill; — alla rovescia, reversed twill; †(naut.) bunting.

sa·ica, saic·ca *f.* (naut. hist.) caique, Turkish sailing craft or boat under oar.

saime *m.* fat; grease.

saina *f.* (naut.) seine fishing net.

sa·i·o *m.* (man's) gown; (eccl.) religious habit; (Rom. antiq.) sagum (worn by soldiers and slaves); (mil.) cloak. **-one** *m. augm.* long gown.

sa·iride *m.* (ichth.) saury pike, *Scomberesox saurus*.

saisseti·a *f.* (agric.; ent.) black scale, *Saissetia* spp.

sal·a¹ *f.* hall; lounge; room; giuochi di —, parlour games; — da pranzo, dining room; — d'aspetto, — d'attesa, waiting room; — di lettura, reading room; — di scrittura, writing room; — da ballo, ballroom, dance-hall; — di scherma, *salle d'armes*; — da concerto, concert hall; (hosp.) — operatoria, operating theatre; (leg.) — di udienza, Court, court room; (theatr.) auditorium; — del comitato, committee room; (radio; telev.) — di riproduzione, reproduction channel; — controllo, control room; (comm.) — di mostra, sales room, stock room; (mil.) — di convegno, officers' mess; — di disciplina, correction establishment, guard-room, *or* (slang) glasshouse; (naut.) — nautica, chart house; — d'armi, arsenal in Venice; — d'armi di bordo, small arms magazine; — delle sagome, — dei garbi, — a tracciare, hull designing workshop (full scale). **-ẹtta** *f. dim.* of **sala**; little room; (merchant navy) warrant officers' mess.

sala² *f.* (bot.) pendulous sedge, *Carex pendula*, great reedmace, *Typha latifolia*.

sala³ *f.* (eng.) axle, axletree; — montata, pair of wheels and axle.

sala⁴ *m. indecl.* abbrev. of **salamelecco**, q.v.

salac·ca *f.* (ichth.) shad, *Alosa alosa*, (cul.) smoked and dried shad; (joc.) sword; dog-eared and tattered book; very thin and withered person. **-cata** *f.* (joc.) 'swipe with wet fish'; a cut with a sword. **-chino** *m. dim.* of **salacca**; tattered little book; tap with the fingers.

salac·e *adj.* salacious; spicy, risqué; pungent; lascivious. **-ità** *f.* salaciousness; lasciviousness.

†**sala·i·a** *f.* salt-market. **-uolo** *m.* vendor of salt.

salamalecche *m.* See **salamelecco**.

salamandr·a *f.* (zool.) salamander; — pezzata, *Salamandra maculosa*, spotted salamander; — nera, *S. atra*, Alpine salamander. **-ina** *f.* (zool.) *Salamandrina perspicillata*, a kind of newt.

salamanna *f.* (agric.) name of a kind of white grapes, first grown by Alamanno Salviati.

salam-e *m.* (cul.) sausage, salami; (fig.; colloq.) dolt, blockhead. (-**ẹtto**, -**ino** *m. dim.*)

salamelec-co (*pl.* -**chi**) deep bow; obsequious salutation; exaggerated compliment; salaam.

†**salamistr-o** *m.* pedant; wiseacre. †-**eri·a** *f.* pedantry; tiresome assumption of superior knowledge.

salamo·i-a *f.* brine; pickle; (fig.) è una —!, che —! (said, e.g., of soup, etc., that is too salt); (tanning) salato in —, wet-salted. -**are** [A4] *tr.* to put in brine; to pickle; to marinate. (-**ato** *part. adj.*)

†**Salamone** *pr.n.m.* See **Salomone**.

salangana *f.* (orn.) edible birds' nest swiftlet, *Collocalia* spp.

salano *m.* (leg.) quasi —, perpetual leaseholder.

salapu·zio *m.* dandyprat, 'minimus', dwarf, pigmy.

sal-are [A1] *tr.* to salt; to season with salt; to add salt to; to sprinkle salt on; (fig.; colloq.) to 'cut', to miss, to skip; — una lezione, to cut a lecture or class; — la scuola, to play truant from school. -**ante** *part. adj.* bacini -anti, salt baths. -**ata** *f.* salting, adding of salt; dare una -ata a, to salt, to add a pinch of salt to. -**atino** *m.* salt biscuit. -**ato** *part. adj.* salted; too salt; seasoned; spiced; (fig.) expensive; (fig.) pagarla -ata, to pay dearly for it; pungent; parole -ate, witty, pungent, remarks; (geog.) Lago Salato, Great Salt Lake; *n.m.* salami, salted meat; salt pork; *adv.* costare -ato, to be very expensive. -**atore** *m.*, -**atrice** *f.* (industr.) salter. (-**atura** *f.*)

sala·ri-o *m.* wages; pay; salary; (industr.) — a cottimo, piece wage; (hist.) the ration of salt and other food given to soldiers, functionaries, etc., as payment for their services. -**ale** *adj.* of, relating to, salaries; accordo -ale, agreement concerning salary or wages. -**are** [A4] *tr.* to pay, to pay wages to; to remunerate. -**ato** *part. adj.* paid; wage-earning; salaried; hired; giornalista -ato, hired journalist; *n.m.* wage-earner; salaried work.

salass-are [A1] *tr.* (med.) to let blood from, to bleed; *abs.* (fig.) to overcharge, to 'bleed', to 'squeeze dry'; *rfl.* to cut an artery, to open one's veins. (-**ato** *part. adj.*) -**atore** *m.* (surg.) blood-letter. -**atura** *f.* (surg.) blood-letting. -**o** *m.* (surg.) blood-letting; (vet.) lancet; (joc.) extortion of money; heavy expenditure; very heavy bill; fare un -o a, to extract money from.

†**sa·lav-o** *adj.*, †-**oso** *adj.* dirty, stained.

salbanda *f.* (geol.) salband.

salc-e *m.* (bot.) see **salcio**. -**erella** *f.* (bot.) purple loosestrife, *Lythrum salicaria*; pale persicaria, *Polygonum persicaria*. -**ia·ia** *f.* (bot.) willow faggot, rivet. -**iaiola** *f.* (orn.) Savi's warbler, *Locustella luscinioides*.

salcic·cia *f.* (pop.). See **salsiccia**.

sal·c-io *m.* (bot.) willow, *Salix*. -**ẹto** *m.* grove of willows, willow-grove. -**igno** *adj.* made of willow; (Tusc., pop.) knotty; (of meat) tough; (of a person) unmanageable, intractable, stubborn, cross-grained. -**(u)olo** *m.* (agric.) willow sprig used in grafting vines.

salcra·ut, salcra·uti, salcrautte *m. indecl.* (cul.) sauerkraut.

salda¹ *f.* (laundry, etc.) starch; (chem.) — d'amido, starch paste.

†**salda²** *f.* (agric.) field left in winter to provide spring pasture.

sald-are [A1] *tr.* to consolidate; to strengthen; (comm.) to balance; to pay, to settle; to effect settlement; (med.) to heal, to knit, to cicatrize; (eng.) to weld (see also under **saldatura**). -**a·bile** *adj.* (eng.) weldable; -abile a dolce, capable of being soldered; -abile a forte, brazable. -**amẹnto** *m.* consolidating, strengthening; (med.) healing, cicatrization; (eng.) welding; soldering; brazing; wiping (see also under **saldatura**). -**ativo** *adj.* strengthening; (fig.) healing. -**ato** *part. adj.* consolidated; strengthened; joined; (fig.) healed; (med.) healed, cicatrized; (eng.) welded; soldered; brazed; wiped. -**atoio** *m.* (eng.) soldering iron; -atoio a benzina, -atoio a fiaccola, blowlamp soldering iron. -**atore** *m.* strengthener; (eng.) welder. -**atrice** *f.* welder; welding machine; -atrice per ribaditura, rivet welder. -**atura** *f.* strengthening; (fig.) healing; (med.) healing (of a wound); (eng.) welding; -atura ad arco, arc welding; -atura ad arco annegato, submerged arc welding; -atura a fuoco, forge-welding; -atura al maglio, hammer welding; -atura a percussione, percussion welding; -atura a punti, spot welding; -atura a resistenza, resistance welding; -atura a ricalco, upset welding; -atura a ricoprimento, lap welding; -atura a scintillio, flash welding; -atura a sovrapposizione, lap welding; -atura a spinta, push welding; -atura autogena, autogenous welding; -atura col cannello, blowpipe welding; -atura continua, seam welding; -atura continua a rulli, roll seam welding; -atura continua multipla, multiple seam welding; -atura di imbastitura, tack

welding; -atura di testa, butt welding; -atura elettrica, electric welding; -atura elettrica progressiva, electrical sequence welding; -atura ossidrica, oxy-hydrogen welding; -atura per ricalcatura, upset welding; -atura plastica continua, mash seam welding; -atura provvisoria, tack welding; -atura sopratesta, overhead welding; -atura super-rapida, ultra-speed welding; weld, welded joint; cordone di -atura, seam; bead; senza -atura, weldless; soldering; -atura dolce, -atura tenera, soft welding; -atura forte, hard soldering, brazing; lega per -atura dolce, soft solder; lega per -atura forte, hard solder; soldered joint.

sald-o *adj.* firm; sound; solid; robust; steady; rigid; — appoggio, firm support; stare —, tenersi —, to hold steady, to stand firm; mettere in —, to make firm, to fix; (fig.) staunch, steadfast; constant; -e ragioni, sound reasons; argomento —, valid argument; — come l'acciaio, true as steel; (comm.) balanced; fare —, to settle; mettere un libro in —, to balance the books; *n.m.* (comm.) balance; remainder; fare i -i, to balance; merce di —, balance of goods; settlement; ti do mille lire a — dei nostri conti, I give you a thousand lire in settlement of our account; — morto, dormant balance. -**ẹzza** *f.* firmness; stability; solidity; soundness.

sale *m.* salt; un pizzico di —, a pinch of salt; amaro di —, over-salted, too salt; dolce di —, lacking salt, needing salt, (of a person) not quite all there; per due centesimi di — guastar la minestra, to spoil the ship for a ha'p'orth of tar; saper di —, to taste salt, (fig.) to taste bitter; (poet.) l'alto —, the sea; (chem.) salt; — ammoniaco, sal-ammoniac; (pharm.) — inglese, Epsom salts; (fig.) mother-wit; good judgement; aver — in zucca, to have one's head screwed on the right way; wit; pungency; — attico, Attic salt, (fig.) wit; rimanere di —, to be struck dumb, to be dumb-founded; io son rimasto di — quando l'ho saputo, you could have knocked me down with a feather when I heard it.

†**salebroso** *adj.* brackish; rough, jolting.

saleg·gia *f.* (bot.) corn salad, lamb's lettuce, *Valerianella*.

†**saleggiare** *vb.* and derivs. See **salare**.

salep *m. indecl.* (bot.) name of several wild orchids and of the mucilaginous meal made from their tubers; (chem.) salep.

salesian-o *adj.*, *n.m.* (eccl.) Salesian (priest, cleric or laybrother). -**a** *f.* (eccl.) Salesian sister.

salẹtto *m.* (zool.) sandhopper, *Orchestia littorea*.

salgemma *m.* rock salt, common salt.

sali-are *adj.* (Rom. antiq.) of the Salii, Salian. -**ato** *m.* (Rom. antiq.) priesthood of the Salii.

sali·bile *adj.* See under **salire**.

sa·lic-e *m.* (bot.) see **salcio**. †-**ale** *m.* willow-bed. -**astro** *m.* (bot.) white, silver willow, *Salix alba*. -**ella** *f.* (bot.) purple willow, *S. purpurea*. -**ilato** *m.* (chem.) salicylate. -**ile** *m.* (chem.) salicyl. -**i·lico** *adj.* (chem.) salicylic. -**iloso** *adj.* (chem.) acido -iloso, salicylaldehyde. -**ina** *f.* (chem.) salicin.

sa·lico *adj.* (hist.) Salic; legge salica, Salic law; *n.m.* Corrado il —, Emperor Conrad (1027).

salicor·nia *f.* (bot.) marsh samphire, *Salicornia*.

saliente *part.* of **salire**, q.v.; *adj.* rising, mounting; increasing; la marea —, the rising tide; (fig.) la corruzione —, the mounting tide of corruption; projecting, salient; (fig.) notable, important; *n.m.* (mil.) salient.

saliera *f.* salt-cellar (for the table).

sal-i·fero *adj.* containing salt. -**ifica·bile** *adj.* (chem.) salifiable. -**ificare** [A2s] *tr.* (chem.) to salify; *intr.* (*aux.* essere) to form a salt. -**ificazione** *f.* (chem.) salt formation.

†**saligastro** *m.* See **salicastro**.

saligenina *f.* (chem.) saligenin, salicyl alcohol.

†**saligno¹** *adj.* willow-like.

saligno² *adj.* salt, salty; saline; (miner.) marmo —, sweaty marble.

sa·lii *m.pl.* (Rom. antiq.) Salii (priests of Mars at Rome, of Hercules at Tibur).

†**salimbacca** *f.* small saucer-shaped piece of wood for receiving the seal on bags of salt or other merchandise; disk pendant from a patent of privilege; wooden bowl.

†**salimpanco** *m.* See **saltimbanco**.

salina *f.* salt-works; salt pan; crude salt; †salt-cellar.

salincervo *m.* See under **salire**.

salin·dia *f.* (bot.) mock orange, *Philadelphus coronarius*.

salino *adj.* containing salt; (chem.) saline.

sal-ire [D1] *intr.* (*aux.* essere) to ascend; to rise; to go up; — (su) per le scale, to go upstairs; — sul monte, to go up the hill; (naut.)

sal-ire (*cont.*)

— a riva, to climb the rigging, to go aloft; (of prices) to rise, to mount; — al trono, to ascend to the throne; — al paradiso, to go to Heaven; — in grado, — di grado, — in onore, — in fama, to get on in the world, to make a name for oneself; (iron.) — in cattedra, — sul pulpito, to pontificate; — sul Parnaso, to write poetry; — sulla nave, to embark; — da uno, to go and visit someone, to drop in on someone; *tr.* to mount; (provb.) questo mondo è fatto a scale, chi la scende e chi la -e, life has its ups and downs, *or* some people have all the luck; (radio; telev.) far —, to fade up. **-i·bile** *adj.* passable; climbable. **-incervo** *m.* children's game rather like leap-frog. **-iscendi** *m. indecl.* going up and down; ups and downs; alternation; (of a door) latch; lume a -iscendi, lamp with an adjustable shade; strada a -iscendi, hilly street, street all ups and downs, undulating road. **-ita** *f.* ascent; upward slope; rising ground; fare la -ita, to climb the hill; (comm.) rise; ascending; climb; height; gradient; (archit.) -ita di volta, springing of a vault. **-ito** *part. adj.* risen; gone up; ascended; increased. †**-ito·io** *m.* ladder, scaling ladder. (**-ito·re** *m.* **-itrice** *f.*)

Salisburgo *pr.n.f.* (geog.) Salzburg.

saliv-a *f.* saliva; attaccato colla —, stuck on with spit. **-ale, -are¹** *adj.* salivary; glandule -ali (-ari), salivary glands. **-are²** [A I] *intr.* (*aux.* avere) to salivate. **-azione** *f.* (physiol.) salivation.

salizada *f.* (Ven. dial.) shopping street.

salizono *m.* (Apulia) stone block for building.

Sallu·sti-o *pr.n.m.* Sallust. **-ano** *adj.* Sallustian; (Rom. antiq.) orti -ani, the gardens of Sallust.

salma *f.* corpse, dead body; mortal remains; heavy burden; (poet.) living body (regarded as the burden borne by the soul); measure of volume; measure of area; (dial. Sicily) unit of measurement (equiv. to 275·1 litres).

salmarino¹ *m.* (chem.) common salt, sea salt.

salmarino² *m.* (ichth.) *Salvelinus* sp., a species of char found in the Po basin.

salmastr-a *f.* (naut.) stopper. **-are** [A I] *tr.* (naut.) to put stoppers on (sail or cable). †**-atore** *m.* (naut.) cable hand.

salmastr-o *adj.* salt, brackish; also *n.m.* **-a·ia** *f.* brackish soil. **-oso** *adj.* brackish; terreno -oso, soil impregnated with salt water.

salmata *f.* long discourse, boring speech; scolding, 'dressing-down'.

salmeggi-are [A 3 c] *intr.* (*aux.* avere) (mus.) to sing psalms; to chant. **-amento** *m.* psalm-singing. **-atore** *m.*, **-atrice** *f.* (mus.) psalm-singer.

salmeri·a *f.* (mil.) baggage train; pack animals; transport.

salmerino *m.* (ichth.). See **salmarino²**.

salmì *m. indecl.* (cul.) salmi, ragout; lepre in —, jugged hare.

†**salmisi·a** *excl.* touch wood!, God help us!, Heaven preserve us!

salm-o *m.* psalm. **-ista** *m.* psalmist. **-odi·a** *f.* (mus.) psalmody. **-odiare** [A 4] *intr.* (*aux.* avere) to sing psalms; (fig.) to speak in a monotonous way, to intone. **-o·dico** *adj.* (mus.) psalmodic. †**-odo** *m.* (mus.) psalm-singer.

salmone *m.* (ichth.) salmon, *Salmo salar*; (metall.) rame in salmoni, pig copper; (naut.) pig iron or lead ballast used in submarines and elsewhere; sinker used for mooring a small float.

salnitro *m.* (chem.) saltpetre.

salolo *m.* (chem.) salol, phenyl salicylate.

Salomè *pr.n.f.* Salome.

Salomone *pr.n.m.* Solomon; il giudizio di —, the judgement of Solomon; (geog.) Isole —, Solomon Islands.

salone *m.* hall; large hall; saloon; reception-room; aprire i saloni, to hold receptions; barber's saloon; auditorium (of a cinema); (rlwy.) vettura —, Pullman car.

Salonicco *pr.n.f.* (geog.) Salonika.

salott-o *m.* drawing-room; sitting-room, parlour; reception-room; drawing-room suite; — letterario, salon. **-iere** *m.* man-about-town; (colloq.) lounge-lizard. **-iero** *adj.* relating to drawing-rooms; (derog.) gossipy; frivolous and fashionable. **-ino** *m.dim.* parlour.

salpa *f.* (ichth.) *Box salpa*.

salpare [A I] *intr.* (*aux.* avere) (naut.) — a braccia, to weigh by hand; to weigh, to recover (a torpedo, mine or net); — l'àncora, — il ferro, to weigh the anchor, 'the pick'; — con la barca, — pei capelli, — a capelli, to weigh (a kedge anchor) using a boat; — con la margherita, to weigh by deck tackle; salpa!, order to weigh when the cable is 'up and down'; to sail; — da Napoli per Genova, to sail from Naples for Genoa; (fig., joc.) to start, to leave, to set out.

†**salpetra** *m.* See **salsapietra**.

salping-e *f.* (anat.) salpinx, Fallopian tube. **-ectomi·a** *f.* (surg.) salpingectomy. **-ite** *f.* (med.) salpingitis. **-i·tico** *adj.* salpingitic. **-otomi·a** *f.* (surg.) salpingotomy. **-ovarite** *f.* (med.) salpingo-ovaritis.

salprunella *f.* (pharm.) sal-prunella.

sals-a *f.* sauce; gravy; — di pomodoro, tomato sauce; — verde, parsley sauce; (fig.) cucinare in tutte le -e, to cook up (the same old thing) in different ways; (joc.) — di San Bernardo, good appetite; (provb.) l'appetito non vuol —, hunger needs no sauce. **-iera** *f.* sauce-boat; gravy-boat.

salsamento *m.* and derivs. See under **salso**.

salsapar-i·glia *f.*, **-illa** *f.* (bot.) sarsaparilla, *Smilax sarsaparilla*; — nostrale, *S. aspera*.

salsapietra *f.* (chem.) saltpetre, nitre.

salse·din-e *f.*, **-oso** *adj.* See under **salso**.

salsic·ci-a *f.* pork sausage; sausage-meat; force-meat; un rocchio di —, a sausage; fare — di, to chop up into tiny pieces, to mince; to trample on; (mil.) powder train made up in canvas, to any required length. **-a·io** *m.* pork-butcher, vendor of sausages. **-one** *m. augm.* of **salsiccia**; a kind of large fat sausage. **-otto** *m.* a kind of long salami; a single sausage.

salsiera *f.* See under **salsa**.

sals-o *adj.* salt, salty; salted; acqua -a, salt water; lago —, salt lake; pungent; spiced; *n.m.* saltiness, salt. **-amenta·ria** *f.* preserved food shop. **-amenta·rio** *m.* delicatessen-vendor; sausage-vendor; pork-butcher. **-amento** *m.* salted food; kippered fish; sausage; preserved meat. **-e·dine** *f.* saltiness; grado di -edine, degree of salt; (fig., colloq.) nella -edine, in the 'briny'. **-edinoso** *adj.* brackish. **-ug·gine** *f.* salinity, saltiness, brackishness; salt liquor. **-ugginoso** *adj.* salt, salty, brackish; salt tang; saltiness. **-ume** *m.* salt pungent smell; salt tang; saltiness; salted meat.

salt-are [A I] *intr.* (*aux.* avere) to jump, to leap (the action of leaping up and down only is implied, no movement from one place to another; cf. below, with *aux.* 'essere'); to spring, to vault; — a piè pari, — a piè giunti, to jump with both feet together; — su un piede, to hop on one foot; — per allegrezza, — per gioia, to leap for joy; (*aux.* essere) to jump (from one place to another); — giù dal letto, to leap out of bed; — dalla finestra, to jump out of the window; — in mare, to leap into the water (but: if 'to jump up and down in the water' is meant, the *aux.* is 'avere'); — in testa, (of an idea) to pop into one's head; — agli occhi, to be immediately evident; — fuori, to come forward, to appear from nowhere; — fuori con una proposta, to come out with a suggestion; — in aria, to go up, to blow upwards, to blow up, to explode; (electr.) to blow (of a fuse); è -ato una valvola, a fuse has gone; — in bestia, to lose one's temper; — da una cosa all'altra, to jump from one thing to another, to lack concentration, to be butterfly-minded; — di palo in frasca, to switch from one subject to another; gli -ò il grillo (la mosca), he lost his temper; le -ò il ticchio, she was seized with a sudden whim; (mus.) — da una nota all'altra, to move by leap from one note to another; *tr.* to jump, to jump over; to clear; — il Rubicone, to cross the Rubicon; to leave out; — due righe, to jump two lines, to skip two lines. **-abecca** *f.* (pop.) grasshopper; (joc.) cammina che pare una -abecca, he walks in a very jerky manner. **-abeccare** [A 2 c], **-abellare** [A I] *intr.* (*aux.* avere) to leap and skip like a cricket; to go hop skip and jump. **-acavalla** *f.* (ent.) grasshopper. **-afossi** *m. indecl.* two-wheeled carriage. †**-aimpanca** *m.* see **saltimbanco**. **-aleone** *m.* spring made of thin brass or other wire coiled in a very fine spiral. **-amartino** *m.* (pop.) grasshopper, cricket; jumping toy; toy leaded at the bottom which rights itself; (fig.) restless child; (mil. hist.) small handy gun (4-pounder). †**-amiaddosso**, †**-amindosso** *m.* ragged garment, wretched-looking coat; (of a person) one who waits helplessly for things to turn up. **-ando** *ger.* (mus.) see **saltato**. **-ante** *part. adj.* (mus.) see **saltato**. **-arello** *m.* (mus.) see **saltato**, and also **salterello**. **-ante** *part. adj.* jumping, leaping; punto -ante, blood spot in an egg. **-arupi** *m. indecl.* (zool.) klipspringer, *Oreotragus saltator*. **-ato** *part. adj.* jumped, cleared; skipped, omitted; overtaken; (cul.) patate -ate, sauté potatoes; (mus.) sautillé, jeté, ricochet (bowing). **-atoia** *f.* (naut.) fish-net into which fish are made to jump. **-atoio** *m.* perch (in a bird-cage). **-atore** *m.* jumper, leaper; tumbler, acrobat; hurdler; dancer; rope-dancer; (of a horse) jumper; *m.pl.* (ent.) grasshoppers, locusts, crickets, etc. (**-atrice** *f.*) **-azione** *f.* exercise of jumping; (archaeol.) games, leaping and wrestling.

saltell-are [A I] *intr.* (*aux.* avere) to hop; to skip along; to hop, skip and jump; to dart in and out, to peep; (of the thoughts) to flit; (of the pulse) to palpitate; (of the heart) to beat rapidly. **-ante** *part. adj.* skipping, tripping; un passo -ante, a light tripping step; col cuore -ante, with a wildly beating heart. **-ọne, -ọni** *adv.* skipping along; andar -oni, to trip along.

saltello *m. dim.* of salto, q.v.; (pop.) grasshopper.

salterell-are [A I] *intr.* (*aux.* avere) to hop and skip; to hop on the tips of the toes. **-o** *m.* little hop; jumping cracker; (pop.) grasshopper; (mus.) Saltarello (dance similar to the Galliard); country dance similar to the Tarantella; rhythmic figure of three notes characteristic of the Saltarello (dotted quaver, semiquaver and quaver); jack, saltarello (of harpsichord).

salte·rio *m.* (mus.) psaltery; (Bibl.) Psalter; †primer; reading-book including psalms.

†saltero *m.* See salterio.

salticchiare [A 4] *intr.* (*aux.* avere) to jump lightly on tip-toe.

saltimban-co *m.* (*pl.* -chi) mountebank; tumbler; juggler; acrobat; impostor, charlatan.

saltimbọcca *m. indecl.* (cul.) a thin slice of veal and a thin slice of ham wrapped together and first braised, then stewed in anchovy sauce.

saltimpalo *m.* (orn.) stonechat, *Saxicola torquata*.

saltin-palo, -selce *m.* (orn.) See saltimpalo.

salt-o *m.* jump; leap; prendere un —, fare un —, to jump, to leap, to give a spring; camminare a -i, to jump along; spiccare un —, to give a leap, to spring; faccio un — in farmacia, I'll just pop over to the chemist's; a -i, jerkily, without continuity; — di vento, change of wind; di —, rapidly; di primo —, immediately, without any preliminaries; in quattro -i, no sooner said than done; (gymnastics, diving) — mortale, somersault; — mortale all'indietro, backwards somersault; — in lungo, long jump; — in alto, high jump; — con l'asta, pole-vault; — al cavallo, vault (over a vaulting horse); (fig.) — nel buio, leap in the dark; omission; — di tre righe, three lines left out; — di temperatura, sudden rise in temperature; (hydr.) head; — utilizzabile, available head; — non utilizzato, lost head; — di pressione (eng.) pressure stage (of a turbine); *pl.* rapids, falls, cataracts; (mus.) — per —, by leap; (eccl.) l'ordinarsi per -i, ordination *per saltum*; (agric.) wood, uncultivated land. **-ua·rio** *adj.* without continuity; jerky; desultory; intermittent. **-uariamẹnte** *adv.* at intervals.

salu-bre *adj.* healthy; wholesome; salubrious, health-giving. **-bre-mẹnte** *adv.* healthily; with attention to health. **-ber·rimo** *adj. superl.* of salubre; clima -berrimo, most salubrious climate. **-brità** *f.* healthiness; healthfulness; salubrity; wholesomeness.

Saluen *pr.n.f.* (geog.) Salween.

salum-e *m.* salt meat; salt provisions; preserved food. **-a·io** *m.* pork-butcher; dealer in salt-provisions. **-eri·a** *f.* delicatessen (shop). **-iere** *m.* wholesale pork-butcher. **-ifi·cio** *m.* delicatessen factory.

salunta *f.* (pop. Tusc.) (cul.) fried bread; bread and dripping.

†saluta *f.* See salute.

salutar-e¹ *adj.* salutary; beneficial; wholesome; healthful; arte —, medicine, the medical profession; (fig.) una lezione —, a salutary lesson; †*n.m.* (theol.) salvation. **-mẹnte** *adv.* in a salutary way, with a salutary effect.

salut-are² [A I] *tr.* to salute; to greet; to bow to; to acknowledge; to welcome; to send regards to; to say goodbye to; — con la mano, to wave to; — con l'inchino, to bow to; — con il sorriso, to smile at; — cavandosi il cappello, to take one's hat off to; — alcuno re, to proclaim someone king; (rel.) to pay homage to, to greet with due devotion, to say a prayer to; (mil.) to salute; — colle armi, to present arms; — col cannone, to fire a gun salute; — le bandiere, to salute the flags; *recip. rfl.* to greet one another; non -arsi più, to have broken off relations, to be no longer on speaking terms. **†-amento** *m.* see salutazione. **-ante** *part. adj.* greeting. **-ato** *part. adj.* greeted; *n.m.* person greeted. **-atọre** *m.* one who greets. (**-atrice** *f.*) **-ato·rio** *m.* (eccl. hist.) salutatorium. **-aziọne** *f.* salutation; greeting; message; (rel.) -azione angelica, the Angelic Salutation, the Hail Mary.

salut-e *f.* health; well-being; come sta di —?, how are you feeling?, how are you in health?; essere in (buona) —, to be in good health, to enjoy good health; non ha —, he's not very strong, he does not enjoy good health; conservarsi in —, to keep well; utile alla —, good for one's health; essere il ritratto della —, to be the picture of health; schizzare —, crepare di —, to be bursting with health; bere alla — di, to drink to the health of, to propose

the health of, to drink a toast to; casa di —, sanatorium, *or* nursing-home, (euphem.) casa di —, mental home; *excl.* —!, good health!; — e figlioli maschi!, God bless you! (said to someone who sneezes); welfare; safety, refuge; (rel.) salvation; †salutation. **-ẹvole** *adj.* health-giving. **-evolmẹnte** *adv.* healthily; salutarily; safely. **-i·fero** *adj.* health-giving; good for the health; cibo -ifero, health-food; (theol.) saving, availing to salvation. **-ista** *m.* health crank, health maniac; (rel.) Salvationist, member of the Salvation Army.

salutẹvole¹ *adj.* See under salute.

salutẹvole² *adj.* See under saluto.

salut-o *m.* greeting; bow; salutation; tanti -i (a), kindest regards (to); con i miei più cordiali -i, with all good wishes, with kindest regards; (comm.) distinti -i, yours truly; rendere un —, to return a bow, to greet in return; amico di —, bowing acquaintance; levare il — a, to fail to greet, to pass by, to 'cut'; (mil.) salute; (naut.) — alla voga, salute under oars; tossing the oars (vertically) for a senior officer or horizontally in the position known as 'oars' for other occasions; — con le vele, salute under sail by letting fly the sheets; (fencing) salut; (liturg.) Benediction (service). **-ẹvole** *adj.* welcoming, friendly. **-are** [A I] and derivs. see above

salva *f.* (mil.) gun salute; tiro di —, blank round; salvo; — di batteria, battery fire; volley; — di applausi, round of applause; (agric.) ewe-sheep.

salv-acondọtto *m.* safe-conduct; permit. **-adana·io, -adanaro** *m.* money-box. **-afiaschi** *m. indecl.* wicker basket for wine bottles. **-agente** *m. indecl.* (naut.) lifebuoy; -agente anulare, cork lifebuoy; -agente automatico, ship's lifebuoy fitted with automatic release (carrying calcium flares); -agente collettivo, Carley float, spanner raft, etc.; vedetta, piantone, al -agente, lifebuoy sentry; (road traffic) traffic island, pedestrian refuge in middle of street-crossing; (rlwy.) 'cow-catcher'; (motor.) any similar safety device placed laterally between front and rear wheels. **-aguardare** [A I] *tr.* to safeguard; to protect; to defend; *rfl.* to safeguard oneself. **-aguar·dia** *f.*, **-aguardi·a** *f.* safeguard; protection; (mil.) piquet, prisoner's escort. **-amotọre** *m.* (electr.) overload cut-out. †**-aroba** *f. indecl.* see guardaroba. **-atacco** *m.* (*pl.* -atacchi) (shoem.) tip (on heel). **-avọce** *m.* (mus.) echeion, resonator (cf. **echeo**).

†salvag·gio *m.* and derivs. See **selvaggio**.

salv-are [A I] *tr.* to save; to rescue; to deliver; to preserve; to reserve; (sport) to save; (rel.) to save; Dio ti -i, God save you (a traditional form of greeting preserved in the Italian version of the Ave Maria: Dio ti -i, Maria, Hail Mary); *rfl.* to save oneself; to escape, to flee; to make off. **-amẹnto** *m.* saving; portare a -amento, to save, to carry to safety; †andare a -amento, to make for harbour in bad weather; essere arrivati in -amento, to have reached shelter; †fare il -amento, to salvage. †**-anza** *f.* salvation. **-atag·gio** *m.* rescue; salvage; operazioni di -ataggio, rescue, *or* salvage operations; battello di -ataggio, lifeboat; diritti di -ataggio, salvage dues; (comm.) perdita con -ataggio, salvage-loss; (naut.) apparecchio di -ataggio, lifesaving apparatus; -ataggio autonomo, Davis submerged escape; cintura di -ataggio, lifebelt; razzo di -ataggio, lifesaving rocket carrying a line and employed with a breeches-buoy; società di -ataggio, salvage company. **-ato** *part. adj.* saved; rescued; salvaged. **-atọre** *m.* rescuer; deliverer; (theol.) Saviour. (**-atrice** *f.*) †**-ato·rio** *m.* refuge, sanctuary, asylum. **-aziọne** *f.* salvation; (rel.) salvation; andare a, in, (luogo di) -azione, to go to Purgatory, to go to Heaven; società di -azione, Salvation Army.

salvarsan *m.* (med.) salvarsan. **-iẓẓato** *adj.* (med.) salvarsanized.

salvastrella *f.* (bot.) salad burnet, *Poterium sanguisorba*.

†salvatichezza *f.* shyness.

salva·tico *adj.* See selvatico.

salvatọre¹ *m.* see under salvare.

Salvatọre² *pr.n.m.* Salvador.

salv-e *excl.* (Lat. *2nd sing. imp.*) Hail! esp. in the liturg. antiphon, -e Regina, Hail, holy Queen; (colloq.) so long!, cheerio! **-eregina** *f.* (liturg. mus.) the antiphon Salve Regina, due -eregine, two Salves. **-ete** *excl.* (Lat. *2nd pl. imp.*) Hail!

salvẹzza *f.* See under salvo.

sal·via *f.* (bot.) garden sage, *Salvia officinalis*.

salviett-a *f.* (table-) napkin, serviette; towel. **-ina** *f. dim.* of salvietta; paper napkin.

†salv-ificante *adj.*, †**-i·fico** *adj.* saving, leading to salvation. †**-i·gia** *f.* see **salvezza**, under salvo.

salv-o¹ *adj.* safe; secure; unhurt; unscathed; arrivare sano e —, to arrive safe and sound; mettere in —, to put in a safe place, to rescue, to put by; ebbe -a la vita, he escaped with his life; mettersi in —, to reach safety, to save oneself; rubare a man -a, to steal everything one can lay hands on; essere in —, to be safe; mettere in —, to put safely away, to stow safely away. **-amẹnte** *adv.* safely; without injury. **-ẹzza** *f.* safety; salvation; una via di -ezza, a way out (of difficulty or danger); †(naut.) gavitello di -ezza, lifebuoy; ancora di -ezza, sheet anchor.

salvo² *prep.* save, except; barring; apart from; — il vero, if I mistake not; — notizie contrarie, unless we hear to the contrary; — l'onore, *sauf l'honneur*; (leg.) pagamento — buon fine, due payment reserved (C.C.); (comm.) — venduto, subject to being unsold; — errori ed omissioni, errors and omissions excepted; *conj.* — che, except that; (foll. by *subj.*) unless.

†salvocondotto *m.* See **salvacondotto**.

sa·mar-a *f.*, **-i·dio** *m.* (bot.) samara.

Samarcanda *pr.n.f.* (geog.) Samarkand.

sama·rio *m.* (chem.) samarium.

Samaritan-o *pr.n.m.*, *adj.* (Bibl.) Samaritan; (fig.) a kind person. **-a** *f.* (Bibl.) la -a, the woman of Samaria; lady member of volunteer nursing association.

†sambra *f.* room.

sam-buca *f.* (mus.) sambuca, sambuke, sambugue, Chaldean harp; (poet.) bagpipes; (mil. hist.) ladder for scaling the defences of besieged coastal towns. **-bu·cina** *f.* (mus.) female singer who accompanied herself on the sambuca at Roman banquets.

sambu-co *m.* (*pl.* **-chi**) (bot.) elder, *Sambucus nigra*; — di montagna, *S. racemosa*; (naut.) sambuc, type of dhow used in the Indian Ocean and Arab waters.

sambudello *m.* black-pudding (blood sausage).

†sameto *m.* See **sciamito**.

Samo *pr.n.f.* (geog.) Samos; portare vasi a —, to carry coals to Newcastle; *m.* white wine; liquid made from dried figs used for adulterating Marsala wine.

Samoiedi *pr.n.m.pl.* (geog.) Samoyedes.

samolo *m.* (bot.) brookweed, *Samolus valerandi*.

samoro *m.* (naut.) Rhine barge.

Samotra·cia *pr.n.f.* (geog.) Samothrace.

sampier-o, sampietr-o *m.* fig, or plum, ripening by 29 June, the feast of St Peter; (ichth.) John Dory, *Zeus faber*. **-ino** *adj.* (eccl.) of St Peter's, Rome; *n.m.* (usu. *pl.*) workman permanently employed on the fabric of St Peter's; †coin of Pius VI.

sampogna *f.* and derivs. See **zampogna**.

Samuele *pr.n.m.* Samuel.

san-a·bile *adj.*, **-abilità** *f.* See under **sanare**.

sanale *m.* (bot.). See **sagginale**.

san-are [A 1] *tr.* to heal; to be healing; to cure; to remedy; to rectify; — irregolarità, to regularize a position; — luoghi acquitrinosi, to reclaim marshland; — un'industria, to put an industry on its feet again; (leg.) to indemnify; to make good; to ratify; to rectify; — la nullità, to make good the fatal defect (C.C.P.); to remedy; *rfl.* to get better, to recover; (of a wound) to heal. **-a·bile** *adj.* curable; remediable; facilmente -abile, easily cured. **(-abilità** *f.*) **-amẹnto** *m.* cure; curing; remedying. **-ativo** *adj.* healing; curative. **-ato** *part. adj.* healed; cured; remedied. **-atọre** *m.* healer; *adj.* healing; curative. **(-atrice** *f.*) **-ato·ria** *f.* (leg.) act of indemnity; indemnity; making good; ratification; rectification; remedy. **-ato·rio** *adj.* (*m.pl.* **-atorii**) sanatory; remedial; (leg.) sentenza -atoria, amending order; order of indemnity; order of rectification; *n.m.* Sanatorium. **-azione** *f.* healing; cure; totale -azione, complete cure; (canon law) -azione nella radice, *sanatio in radice*.

sanbenito *m.* (eccl. hist.) sanbenito; (fig.) penitential status.

sanchẹtto *m.* (ichth.) scald fish, *Arnoglossus laterna*.

sanc-ire [D 2] *tr.* to sanction; to enforce; to ratify; to decree. **-ito** *part. adj.* (leg.) sanctioned; enforced; decreed; ratified.

sancta sanctorum *m. indecl.* (Lat., Bibl.) Holy of Holies; (liturg.) tabernacle; sanctuary; (fig.) shrine, sanctum.

sanctus *m. indecl.* (liturg.) Sanctus (of the Mass); (mus.) Sanctus; organ-playing during the Canon after the Sanctus.

sanculott-i *m.pl.* (hist.) sansculottes, French revolutionaries. **-idi** *m.pl.* sansculottids, five days added to the French Republican calendar at the end of each year.

san·d-alo¹ *m.* (bot.) — rosso, red sandal wood, *Pterocarpus santalinus*; — bianco, sandal wood, *Santalum album*; (naut.) flat-

bottomed craft used in Mediterranean and shallow inland waters. **-olina** *f.* fishing net used on rivers. **-olino** *m. dim.* (naut.) lighter; canoe. **-olo** *m.* (naut.) shooting punt (Venice); †large sailing craft on Barbary coast.

san·dalo² *m.* sandal; *pl.* (liturg.) sandals; (vet.) 'boot' (for a horse).

sandracca *f.* (miner.) realgar; (bot.) sandarac (powdered resin of *Tetraclinis articulata*).

Sandro *pr.n.m. dim.* of **Alessandro**.

sanẹse *adj.* See **senese**.

sanfedista *m.* (usu. *pl.*) (hist.) Sanfedist.

sangiacc-ato *m.* (pol. hist.) sanjak, one of the administrative districts of a Turkish vilayet. **-o** *m.* head of a sanjak.

sangimignano *m.* wine from the region of San Gimignano.

sangiovann-i *adj. indecl.* (agric.) mela —, substance added to meal; erba —, *Sedum maximum*, *S. telephium*, and *Hypericum perforatum*. **-ita** *m.* Knight of the order of St John.

sangiov-ẹse, -ẹto *m.* (agric.) kind of grape harsh to the taste but good for vintage.

†sangri·a *m.* See **salasso**.

sangu-e *m.* blood; fare —, to bleed, to be bleeding; spargere il — per la patria, to shed one's blood for one's country; spargimento di —, bloodshed; reato, delitto, di —, crime involving bloodshed; non si può cavar — da una rapa, you can't get blood from a stone; battersi all'ultimo —, to fight to the death; assetato di —, blood-thirsty; il riso fa buon —, laughter is good for one's health; (theol.) il — prezioso, the Precious Blood; (eccl.) Congregazione del preziosissimo —, Congregation of the Most Precious Blood; (zool.) — di turco, dog cockle, *Glycimeris glycimeris*; (fig.) cattivo —, bad blood, rancour; guastarsi il —, to suffer annoyance; avere a —, to hold dear; non avere buon — con, to feel an antipathy towards; quell'uomo non mi va a —, I don't like that man; le andai a —, she took a liking to me; sudare —, to sweat blood; succhiare il — di uno, to bleed someone white; non avere — nelle vene, to be cold-blooded; avere il — caldo, to be hot-blooded; avere il — bollente, to be hot-headed, to be violent; tuffo di —, shock, violent emotion; sentirsi rimescolare il —, to suffer a violent emotion; a — freddo, in cold blood; a — caldo, in hot blood; piangere lagrime di —, to shed bitter tears; lineage, line, origin, family; essere di — nobile, to be of noble birth; di puro —, pure-blooded; cavallo di —, thoroughbred horse; essere di — gentile, to be of gentle birth, to be well-connected, to be of good family; la voce del —, family instinct; avere qualche cosa nel —, to have an inborn aptitude for something; sentirsi qualcosa nel —, to have a presentiment about something; (joc.) — turchino, — blu, blue blood; relationship, relations; il — non è acqua, blood is thicker than water; odio di —, blood-hatred; il — non stinge, blood will out; i figlioli sono — mio, my children are my own flesh and blood; color —, blood-red; faccia di latte e —, milk and roses complexion; *excl.* — di Giuda!, Judas!; ('sangue di Giuda' is also the name of a red wine from Stradella in Lombardy); — d'un cane!, hell!; (bot.) — di drago, see **drago**. **-idọtto** *m.* (anat.) blood-vessel. **-i·fero** *adj.* sanguiferous; vasi -iferi, blood-vessels. **-ificare** [A 2 s] *intr.* (aux. essere) to form blood, to turn into blood. **-ificatọre** *adj.* (*f.* **-ificatrice**) blood-forming. **-ificazione** *f.* (physiol.) sanguification, haematopoiesis. **-igna** *f.* blood-stone; (paint.) red crayon drawing; in -igna, in red (pencil or crayon). **-igno** *adj.* sanguine; full-blooded; di carnagione -igna, red-faced; arancia -igna, blood-orange; blood-red; (physiol.) sanguine, plethoric; *n.m.* colour of blood; blood-red colour. **†-igrondante** *adj.* dripping with blood. **-ina** *f.* see **sanguigna**. **-inac·cio** *m.* black-pudding, blood sausage. **-inante** *part. adj.* bleeding. **-inare** [A 1 s] *intr.* (aux. avere) to bleed; gli -ina il naso, his nose is bleeding; mi -ina il cuore, my heart bleeds; *tr.* to stain with blood. **-ina·rio** *adj.* bloody; sanguinary; blood-thirsty; *n.m.* killer, homicidal maniac. **-inella** *f.* (bot.) crab-grass, *Digitaria sanguinalis* and *Andropogon ischaemum*; red millet, *Digitaria ischaemum*. **-inẹnte** *adj.* see **sanguinante**; (poet.) guerra -inente, bloody war. **-i·neo** *adj.* blood-stained; bloody; colore -ineo, blood-red; *n.m.* (med.) plethoric subject. **-infrola** *m.* (ichth.) minnow, *Phoxinus laevis*. **-inità** *f.* (leg.) consanguinity; blood-relationship. **-inolente, -inolento** *adj.* see **sanguinante**; mixed with blood; mani -inolente, 'hangman's hands'. **-inọso** *adj.* bloody; profusely bleeding; sanguinary; cruel; blood-thirsty. **-inosamẹnte** *adv.* in a bloodthirsty manner. **-isuga** *f.* (zool.) leech; (fig.) blood-sucker.

†**sanicare** *vb.* and derivs. See **sanare**.

sanidin-a *f.*, **-o** *m.* (miner.) sanidine.

sa·nie *f.* (med.) sanies.

sanificare [A 2 S] and derivs. See **sanare**.

sanit-à *f.* soundness; good health; tornare in —, ricuperare la —, to recover one's health; — di mente, sanity, mental health; Ministero della — Pubblica, Ministry of Health; (mil.) medical service including pharmacists and their offices and hospitals; truppe di —, compagnie di —, equivalent of Royal Army Medical Corps; (naut.) patente di —, bill of health; (leg.) sanity; sound judgement; soundness of mind. **-a·rio** *adj.* sanitary; concerning health; misure **-arie**, health measures; cordone **-ario**, sanitary cordon (line of posts, etc. placed round an area affected by infectious diseases); (med.) ufficiale **-ario**, officer of health; (mil.) sanitary; corpo **-ario** militare, equivalent of Royal Army Medical Corps (see also under **sanità**).

sanmisi·a *excl.* See **salmisia**.

sann-a *f.*, **-uto** *adj.* See **zann-a**, **zann-uto**.

†**sanni·tr-io** *m.*, †**-o** *m.* See **salnitro**.

san-o *adj.* sound; healthy; well; wholesome; health-giving; — e fresco, spry; — e salvo, safe and sound; — e vivo, alive and kicking; — come un pesce, in the best of health; servarsi —, to keep well; rifarsi —, to get well again; mente **-a** in corpo —, 'mens sana in corpore sano'; non di **-a** mente, insane; aria **-a**, healthy air; cibo —, healthy food; — allo stomaco, good for the stomach; frutta **-a**, sound fruit; honest, upright; consiglio —, sound advice; principii **-i**, sound principles; affetti **-i**, healthy emotions, sound natural impulses; dottrina **-a**, sound learning; entire, whole; dolersi di gamba **-a**, to complain about nothing; di **-a** pianta, from top to bottom; pane —, a whole loaf; scarpe **-e**, new shoes, shoes newly heeled and soled; un mese —, an entire month, an unbroken month; healed; una ferita **-a**, a wound that has healed; †andate —, farewell. **-amente** *adv.* healthily; wholesomely; vivere **-amente**, to lead a healthy life.

sanrocchino *m.* See **sarrocchino**.

sansa *f.* residue of olives that have been pressed several times and from which completely black olive-oil is extracted, used for industrial purposes or, compressed into 'briquettes', as fuel or cattle-food.

san·scrit-o *m.*, *adj.* Sanskrit. **-ista** *m.* Sanskrit scholar.

sanseviera *f.* (text.) fibra di —, bowstring hemp.

sansimonismo *m.* (econ., etc.) Saint-Simonism.

San Simon Squarzavele *pr.n.m.* (Ven. naut.) St Simon-Tear-Sail, feast of 28 October marking the beginning of autumn gales.

Sansone *pr.n.m.* Samson; (fig.) superman; he-man.

†**sansuga** *m.* See **sanguisuga**, under **sangue**.

†**santà** *f.* See **sanità**.

santabar·bara *f.* (naut.) magazine, hold for gunpowder (see also under **barbara**[1]).

†**santacroce** *f.* chart of the alphabet (cf. **crocesanta**).

†**santa·gio** *m.* slow-moving, leisurely person.

santalena *f.* (zool.) limpet (of various species); (numism.) Byzantine coin impressed with the cross of St Helena.

santalina *f.* (chem.) santalin.

santamari·a *f.* (rel.) Our Lady; (bot.) costmary, *Chrysanthemum balsamita*; acqua di —, infusion of costmary used for treating tobacco; (orn.) uccel — (*m.*), kingfisher, *Alcedo atthis*.

sant-arello, **-erello** *m.* See under **santo**.

Sant'Elmo *pr.n.m.* (naut.) fuoco di —, St Elmo's fire, an electrical discharge producing a glowing light on masts and yards of wooden ships.

santific-are [A 2 S] *tr.* to sanctify, to make holy, to hallow; to keep holy; to keep, to observe (feasts of the Church); to reverence (the name of God); to canonize; to offer to God, to dedicate, to consecrate; *rfl.*, †*intr.* to become holy. **-amento** *m.* hallowing; sanctifying. **-ante** *part. adj.* sanctifying; (theol.) grazia **-ante**, sanctifying, habitual, grace. **-ato** *part. adj.* sanctified, made holy, hallowed; kept holy; dedicated; *n.m.* person or thing made holy, hallowed or dedicated. (**-atore** *m.* **-atrice** *f.*) **-azione** *f.* sanctification; hallowing; observance (of feasts); offering. **-etur** *m.*, *f.* (from the Lat. vb. in the Paternoster) pious hypocrite.

santimo·ni-a *f.* holiness; sacredness; sanctimoniousness. **-ale** *adj.* devout; sanctimonious.

Santippe *pr.n.f.* Xanthippe (wife of Socrates); (fig.) shrew, scold, nagging woman.

santità *f.* sanctity, holiness; sainthood; saintliness; (as title) Sua — Giovanni XXIII, John XXIII; morire in odore di —, to die in the odour of sanctity; sacredness; uprightness, probity, integrity.

sant-o *adj.* (rel.) holy, blessed, sacred; lo Spirito —, the Holy Spirit, the Holy Ghost; acqua **-a**, holy water; la **-a** fede, our holy faith; il — Padre, the Holy Father; la **-a** Sede, the Holy See; vino —, altar wine (also name of several ordinary white wines); lunedì —, Monday in Holy Week; giovedì —, Maundy Thursday; venerdì —, Good Friday; anno —, Jubilee year; il Sant'Uffizio, the Inquisition; la terra **-a**, the Holy Land; **-e** parole, sacred (edifying) words; **-e** verità, truths of the faith; Saint (in this sense alone, the adjective now changes as 'buono' or 'bello' does: in old Ital. it often remained unchanged); san Pietro, St Peter; san Gregorio, St Gregory; santo Stefano, St Stephen; sant'Antonio, St Antony; santa Chiara, St Clare; sant'Agata, St Agatha; (in vaguer senses) diritti **-i** della patria, sacred rights of one's country; verità **-e**, solemn truths; parole **-e**, gospel truth (said esp. of something unpalatable); **-a** bastonata, salutary thrashing; tutto il — giorno, the whole blessed day; (mild excl.) **-a** Madonna!, good heavens!; — Dio!, good Lord!; fatemi il — piacere d'andar via di qui, for heaven's sake please get out; di **-a** ragione, quite rightly; picchiare uno di **-a** ragione, to give someone a sound beating; erba **-a**, (kind of) snuff; *n.m.* holy one; holy thing; il — dei **-i**, God; Christ; the Holy of Holies; il **-issimo**, the Blessed Sacrament; saint; saint's day; saint's picture or statue; — patrono, patron saint; Tutti i **-i** (*or* i **-i**) (Ognissanti), All Saints' Day; (at Padua) la basilica del —, St Anthony's church; non sapere a che (qual) — votarsi, not to know what to do, to be at one's wits' end; aver qualche — dalla sua, to have powerful protection or great luck; saintly person; avere una pazienza da —, to have the patience of a saint; non è uno stinco di —, he's not an edifying character; passata la festa, gabbato lo —, promises are forgotten as soon as one has got what one wanted; non ci ho il — con lui, I can't get on with him, I can't bear him; †church (surviving in the phrases, mettere in —, to church a woman, and entrare in —, to be churched); (mil. slang) password. (**-amente** *adv.*) **-arello**, **-erello** *m.*, **-arella**, **-erella** *f.* (fig.) little saint; (iron.) prig, prude; religious humbug. †**-ese** *m.* priest or other person responsible for care of a church. **-essa** *f.* prig; prude. **-ino** *m.* small print of a saint, 'holy picture' to be slipped into a prayer-book or the like. **-is·simo** *adj. superl.* holiest; il **-issimo** Sacramento, the Blessed Sacrament. **-occhieri·a** *f.* sham piety, hypocrisy. **-oc·chio** *m.* hypocrite. †**-oc·cio** *adj.* simple-minded; (slang) la **-occia**, the Church. **-one** *m.* Moslem hermit or holy man; pious hypocrite.

santolina *f.* (bot.) lavender cotton, *Santolina chamaecyparissus*.

san·tolo *m.* godfather.

santonina *f.* (bot.) *Artemisia cina*; (chem.; pharm.) santonin, santonic lactone.

santoreggia *f.* (bot.) summer savory, *Satureja hortensis*, and winter savory, *S. montana*.

santua·ri-o *m.* (rel., fig.) sanctuary, holy place; shrine; pilgrimage church; (liturg.) sanctuary; (Bibl.) Holy of Holies; †*adj.* holy. †**-a** *f.* (rel.) relic.

†**sant-ula** *f.* godmother; 'gossip'. †**-us·se** *m.* pious humbug.

Santuzza *pr.n.f.* Santuzza in Mascagni's opera *Cavalleria Rusticana*; black head-shawl (as worn by Santuzza).

†**sanza** *prep.* See **senza**.

sanzion-e *f.* sanction; approval; — prammatica, pragmatic sanction; (leg.) sanction (in all senses); decree; *pl.* (hist.) the sanctions enforced against Italy by the League of Nations during the Abyssinian War. **-are** [A 1 C] *tr.* to sanction; to approve; (leg.) to sanction; to apply sanctions against.

sapa *f.* new wine, evaporated and condensed by boiling, used as seasoning.

sap-ere [B 26] *tr.* to know; so una cosa sola, che non so nulla, I know only one thing, that I know nothing; non ne voglio — più nulla, I don't want to hear any more about it; chi lo sa?, who knows?; non lo so, I don't know; averlo **-uto**!, if only I had known!; — a memoria, to know by heart; si sa, of course, naturally; — a menadito, to have at one's finger-tips; to have knowledge of; to have learnt, to have studied; — l'italiano, to know Italian; — la lezione, to know one's lesson, to have studied one's lesson; — di, to have a smattering of; — di lettere, to have (had) some education; la sa lunga, he knows a lot, no flies on him; *abs.* to

sap-ere (*cont.*)
know, to possess knowledge; 'il maestro di color che sanno', the master of those who have knowledge (i.e. Aristotle, Dante's *Inf.* IV, 131); (foll. by *inf.*) to know how (to), to be able (to); — ballare, to know how to dance; sa guidare?, do you drive?; saprei girare Roma al buio, I could find my way round Rome in the dark; to have the gift of; — persuadere, to know how to coax, to be persuasive; *intr.* (*aux.* avere, *prep.* di) to smell (of); to taste (of); to savour (of); (fig.) non — di nulla, to be insipid; mi sa mille anni che torni, I am longing for his return; mi sa male che torni, I am sorry he is coming back; mi sa che..., I have a presentiment that, my impression is; *n.m.* knowledge; learning; il saper fare, know-how. †-e·vole *adj.* knowable; knowing. -uta *f.* knowledge (of a fact); a mia -uta, as far as I know; per -uta, by hearsay. -utello *m.* (derog.) 'Mr Know-all'. (-utella *f.*) -uto *part. adj.* known; -uto e risaputo, hackneyed, 'hoary'; knowledgeable, pretentious about knowledge; wise; *n.m.* know-all, wiseacre; fare il -uto, to show off one's knowledge.

sa·pid-o *adj.* flavoursome, tasty, pleasing to the taste. -ità *f.* sapidity.

sapien-te *adj.* wise; learned; knowledgeable; informed; skilled, skilful; sapient; *n.m.* wise man, sage; scholar; savant; well-informed person. -temente *adv.* wisely; learnedly; skilfully. -tessa *f.* (derog.) blue-stocking; female pedant. -tone *m. augm.* of sapiente; (iron.) great scholar; wiseacre. -za *f.* wisdom; learning; knowledge; name of University at Rome, Pisa; (theol.) wisdom; la somma -za, the supreme Wisdom, God; (Bibl.) the Book of Wisdom. †-zia *f.* see sapienza. -ziale *adj.* concerning wisdom; (Bibl.) libri -ziali, Sapiential Books.

sapindo *m.* (bot.) soap nut, *Sapindus saponaria.*

sapino *m.* (bot.) Aleppo pine, *Pinus halepensis.*

†**sa·pio** *adj.* See savio.

sapon-e *m.* soap; — da barba, shaving-soap, shaving-stick; — da toletta, toilet-soap; bolla di —, soap-bubble; (fig.) gas and gaiters; empty promises; rimetterci il ranno e il —, to carry out a useless task; dare il — a, to flatter, to 'soft-soap'; pigliare il —, to be responsive to flattery; (chem.) soap; (joc.) learned man, wiseacre; maestro —, Mr Know-all (cf. sapere). -a·ceo *adj.* saponaceous, soapy; (bot.) erbe -acee, plants used as soap. -a·ia *f.* (bot.) see saponaria; *pl.* (ent.) cuckoo-spit insects (Fam. Cercopidae). -a·io, -aro *m.* (techn.) soap-maker. -a·ria *f.* (bot.) soapwort, bouncing Bet, *Saponaria officinalis*; (miner.) saponite. -ata *f.* soap-suds; lather; (of a horse) fare la -ata, to be lathered in sweat, to be in a fine lather; (fig.) flattery, 'soft soap'. -ato *adj.* soapy; acqua -ata, suds, lather. -eri·a *f.* (industr.) soap works. -etta *f.* (cake of) toilet soap; flat pocket watch. -etto *m.* toilet soap; -etto liquido, liquid soap. -iera *f.* soap-dish. -ifica·bile *adj.* (chem.) saponifiable. -ificare [A2s] *tr.* (chem.) to saponify. -ificazione *f.* (chem.) saponification; numero di -ificazione, saponification value. -ifi·cio *m.* (industr.) soap works. -ina *f.* (chem.) saponin. -ite *f.* (miner.) saponite, bowlingite. -oso *adj.* soapy; slippery; resembling soap.

sapor-e *m.* flavour; taste; relish; savour; di mezzo —, neither one taste nor the other; dare — al sale, to teach one's grandmother to suck eggs; (fig.) savour, pungency; motto che non ha —, insipid remark, pointless joke; non avere amore nè —, to be lifeless, to be dull, to be stodgy; avere — di antiquato, to have an old-fashioned appearance. -ire [D2] *tr.* to flavour. -ito *adj.* savoury; tasty; salty; un po' -ito, a little too salt; dormitina -ita, refreshing nap; piquant; lively; witty; rimprovero -ito, sharp reproof; (of prices) high; conto -ito, stiff bill. -itamente *adv.* deliciously; with relish; with zest; with gusto; dormire -itamente, to have a deep refreshing sleep; ridere -itamente, to laugh delightedly. -oso *adj.* tasty; (fig.) witty; pungent. (-osamente *adv.*)

sapoti·glia *f.* (bot.) sapodillo, *Achras zapota.*

†**sappiente** *adj.* See sapiente.

saprof-ito *m.* (bot.) saprophyte. -i·tico *adj.* (bot.) saprophytic.

saputa *f.* See under sapere.

saputo *part. adj., n.m.* See under sapere.

Sara[1] *pr.n.f.* Sarah, Sara.

†**sara**[2] *f.* fabulous fish, possibly a sawfish.

†**sarabachino** *m.* carriage with seating arrangement similar to that of Irish jaunting car.

sarabanda *f.* (mus.) Saraband, Sarabande; (fig.) laughing and shouting, uproar.

saracca *f.* (ichth.) shad; see salacca.

sarac·chio *m.* (bot.). See saraccio.

sarac·cio *m.* (bot.) *Ampelodesmon tenax.*

saracco *m.* (techn.) (carp.) ripsaw; — a dorso, backsaw; — con costola, tenon saw.

saraceno *m., adj.* Saracen; (bot.) grano —, buckwheat, *Fagopyrum esculentum.*

saracin-o *m., adj.* (pop.) see saraceno; quintain; (fig.) butt, object of ridicule; *pl.* grapes beginning to turn purple. -esca *f.* rolling shutter; (hist.) portcullis; (hydraul.) gate valve; (herald.) portcullis; *adj. f.* see saracinesco. -esco *adj.* (*m.pl.* -eschi) Saracen; porta -esca, portcullis.

saraco *m.* (ichth.). See sparo.

†**sara·gia** *f.* See ciliegia.

†**sarago** *m.* (ichth.) See sargo.

Saragozza *pr.n.f.* (geog.) Saragossa.

†**sarament-o** *m.* oath. †-are *tr.* to swear on oath.

sarc-asmo *m.* sarcasm; sarcastic remark; meno -asmi!, a little less sarcasm! -a·stico *adj.* sarcastic. -asticamente *adv.* sarcastically, with sarcasm.

sar·chi-o *m.* (agric.) a light hoe. -are [A4] *tr.* (agric.) to hoe, to weed with a hoe. -amento *m.* (agric.) weeding. -ata *f.* (agric.) hoeing. -ato *part. adj.* hoed; weeded; (herald.) croce -ata, cross voided throughout. -atore *m.* (agric.) hoer. -atrice *f.* (agric.) mechanical hoe. -atura *f.* (agric.) hoeing. -ella *f.* garden hoe. -ellare [A1] *tr.* to weed with a hoe. -ello *m.* garden hoe.

†**sar·cina**[2] *f.* bundle; burden.

sarcina[1] *f.* (chem.) sarcine, hypoxanthine.

†**sarcire** *tr.* to overdecorate; to adjust, to repair, to mend.

sarc-ite *f.* (med.) myositis. -ocele *m.* (med.) sarcocele. -ocolla *f.* (chem.) sarcocolla. -o·fago *m.* (*pl.* -o·faghi) sarcophagus. -ologi·a *f.* (med.) sarcology, myology. -oma *m.* (med.) sarcoma. -omatosi *f.* (med.) sarcomatosis. -omatoso *adj.* sarcomatous. -opte, -opto *m.* (zool.) the mite, *Sarcoptes scabiei*, which causes scabies in man. -osina *f.* (chem.) sarcosine, methyl glycocoll.

sarcra·uti *m.pl.* See salcraut, etc.

sar·cula *f.* (agric.) Bolognese variety of grape.

sarda[1] *f.* (miner.) sard, cornelian.

sarda[2] *f.* (ichth.) pilchard (adult sardine), *Clupea pilchardus*; — papalina, sprat, *C. sprattus*; palamita —, *Sarda mediterranea*; (colloq.) essere pigiati come -e, to be packed like sardines. -ella *f.* (ichth.) sardine, *Clupea pilchardus.* -ellina *f.* (ichth.) sprat, *C. sprattus.* -ina *f.* (ichth.) -ina comune, sardine, young *C. pilchardus.*

sardana *f.* a Catalan dance.

Sardanapal-o *pr.n.m.* (Assyr. hist.) Sardanapalus; (fig.) effeminate king given to luxurious living. -esco *adj.* (*m.pl.* -eschi) effeminate and luxurious.

Sardegn-a *pr.n.f.* (geog.) Sardinia; (hist.) regno di —, Kingdom of Sardinia, the territory governed by the House of Savoy from 1718 until the Unification of Italy (Piedmont, Savoy, Sardinia). -olo *adj.* (of animals only) Sardinian (cf. sardo).

sard-ella *f.*, **-ina** *f.* See under sarda.

sar·d-io *m.*, †**-one** *m.*, †**-o·nica** *f.* See sardonice.

sard-o *adj.* Sardinian; *n.m.* Sardinian; Sardinian language. (-a *f.*) -esco *adj.* (*m.pl.* -eschi) Sardinian-like, Sardinian in type. †-igna *f.* (geog.) see Sardegna; dump for carcases and putrefying meat.

sardo·nice *m.* (miner.) sardonyx.

sardo·nico[1] *adj.* sardonic; ghigno —, sardonic sneer; (med.) riso —, risus sardonicus.

sardo·nico[2] *m.* See sardonice.

sargasso *m.* (bot.) sargasso, *Sargassum*, a kind of seaweed.

†**sargente** *m.* See sergente.

sar·gia *f.* cretonne; flowered curtain material; bedspread, coverlet.

sargo *m.* (ichth.) various species of edible marine fish; — maggiore, — rigato, *Sargus sargus*; — comune, *S. vulgaris*; — dall'anello, *S. annularis*; — d'Istria, *Puntazzo puntazzo.*

sa·riga *f.* (zool.) opossum.

sariss-a *f.* (class. antiq.) sarissa, Macedonian pike. -o·foro *m.* soldier with sarissa.

sarment-o *m.* (bot.) vine branch, twig, tendril; brushwood. -oso *adj.* (bot.) having many twigs or tendrils.

sarpa *f.* (ichth.). See salpa.

†**sarpare** *vb.* and derivs. See salpare.

sarrocchino *m.* short weather-proof cloak as formerly worn by pilgrims (from the name of San Rocco, 1295–1327).

sarrus(s)o·fono *m.* (mus.) sarrusophone.

†**sarta·gine** *f.* frying-pan.

sar·t-ia, ~a *f.* (naut.) stay, shroud; ~ie maggiori, lower rigging; ~ie minori, upper rigging. **-iame** *m.* (naut.) standing rigging; cordage. **-iare** [A4] *tr.* (naut.) to walk back, to render or ease away; ~iare un paranco, to overhaul a tackle; (naut. comm.) sartia!, check away! (NOTE: with true nautical inconsequence 'to check' means 'to ease out'). **-iole** *f.pl.* (naut.) upper standing rigging. †**-ione** *m.* (naut.) spanker boom lifts.

sart-o *m.* tailor; — da donna, ladies' tailor. **-a** *f.* seamstress; dressmaker. **-ina** *f.* young girl apprenticed to a dress-maker's. **-ori·a** *f.* tailoring; tailor's workshop; clothing factory. **~o·rio** *adj.* (anat.) muscolo ~orio, sartorius.

sassafrasso *m.* (bot.) sassafras, *Sassafras officinale.*

sass-a·ia *f.*, **-ai(u)ola** *f.*, **-ai(u)olo** *adj.*, **-ata** *f.* See under **sasso**.

†**sassamino** *m.* See sesamino.

sassella *f.* red wine of the Valtellina region.

sassello *adj.* (orn.) tordo —, redwing, *Turdus musicus.*

sas·seo *adj.* turned to stone; stone-like.

sassi·fraga *f.* (bot.) saxifrage; (pharm.) sassafras.

sass-o *m.* stone; rock; pebble; tirare ~i, to throw stones; tombstone; (fig.) cuore di —, heart of stone; rimanere di —, restare di —, to be dumbfounded; mountain; cliff; (geog.) il Gran Sasso d'Italia, Mount Corno, the highest peak of the Apennines. **-a·ia** *f.* dam; barrier of stones; stony ground; heaps of stones. **-ai(u)ola** *f.* volley of stones; hurling of stones; battle of stones; fare la ~aiuola a, to stone. **-ai(u)olo** *adj.* (orn.) colombo ~aiuolo, rock dove. **-ata** *f.* blow from a stone; tirare una ~ata, to throw a stone; prendere a ~ate, to stone; cogliere con una ~ata, to hit with a stone, to throw a stone at, and hit; dare il pane e la ~ata, to take away with one hand what you give with the other. **-a·tile** *adj.* (orn.) see sassai(u)olo; (bot.) pianta ~atile, rock plant. **-eto** *m.* stony ground. **-etto** *m. dim.* of sasso, pebble. **-ificare** [A2s] *tr.* to change into stone, to petrify. **-ofrasso** *m.* (bot.) sassafras, *Sassafras officinale.* **-olino** *m.* pebble; *pl.* gravel. (miner.) sassolite; a kind of liqueur produced at Sassuolo (Emilia). **-olite** *f.* (miner.) sassolite. **-one** *m. augm.* of sasso. **-oso** *adj.* stony; terreno ~oso, stony ground; resembling stone. **-uolo** *m. dim.* of sasso; (geog.) cliff, rock.

sasso·fono *m.* (mus.) saxophone.

sas·sola *f.* (naut.) baler, baling pan, used to eject water from the bottom of a boat.

sassone¹ *m. augm.* of sasso, q.v.

sas·sone² *adj., n.m.* Saxon, gli anglo-sassoni, the Anglo-Saxons.

Sasso·nia *pr.n.f.* (geog.) Saxony.

Sata·na *pr.n.m.* (poet.). See Satana.

Sa·t-ana *pr.n.m.* Satan. **-anasso** *m.* devil; bad-tempered person; restless child, imp; (zool.) black saki monkey, *Pithecia satanas.* **-aneggiare** [A3c] *intr.* (aux. avere) to kick up a shindy; to curse and swear. **-a·nico** *adj.* Satanic.

Satanno *pr.n.m.* (poet.). See Satana.

satel·l-ite *f.* (Rom. hist.; pol.) satellite; (fig.) follower; hired ruffian, assassin; (astron.) satellite, moon; (phys.) satellite; sputnik; (eng.) planetary gear, planet wheel; (eng.) ingranaggio a ~iti, planetary gear. **-i·zio** *m.* (Rom. hist.) office and function of a satellite.

satin *m. indecl.* (pron. as Fr.) satin. **-are** [A1] *tr.* to satin, to give a glossy surface to. **-ato** *part. adj.* satiny, satin-like; carta ~ata, hot-pressed paper, glazed paper, paper having a satin finish.

sa·tir-a *f.* satire; satirical writing; satirical comment, mocking remarks; mettere in — uno, to mock someone; dare la — a, to mock, to make fun of; fare la —, to speak mockingly, to write mockingly. **-eggiante** *part. adj.* satirizing, satirical. **-eggiare** [A3c] *tr.* to satirize. **-o·grafo** *m.* writer of satires, satirist.

sati·ric-o¹ *adj.* satirical; relating to satire; *n.m.* satirical writing, satirical vein; satire; satirist. **-amente** *adv.* satirically.

sati·rico² *adj.* satyr-like; (Gk. lit.) dramma —, satyr play, satyric play (like the *Ichneutae* of Sophocles or the *Cyclops* of Euripides).

sa·tir-o¹ *m.* satyr; (fig.) lascivious person. **-esco** *adj.* (m.pl. ~eschi) satyr-like; orecchi ~eschi, faun-like ears; lascivious. **-escamente** *adv.* in satyr-like fashion; lasciviously. **-i·asi** *f.* (med.) satyriasis. **-ista** *m.* (theatr. hist.) actor who danced the role of satyr.

†**sa·tiro²** *m.* satirist.

†**satisfare** *vb.* and derivs. See soddisfare.

sativo *adj.* (agric.) terreno —, cultivated land; piante sative, cultivated plants.

†**sato** *m.* a Hebrew measure, equivalent to about seven quarts.

satoll-a *f.* filling meal, full meal; bellyful; (fig.) more than one can stand, more than enough, bellyful. **-amento** *m.* satiating; full meal, 'blow out'; (agric.) manuring. **-are** [A1c] *tr.* to sate, to satiate; to fill, to stuff (with food); (agric.) to manure. **-ato** *part. adj.* satiated; replete; stuffed. **-o** *adj.* satiated, sated; satisfied; replete; overfed; ventre ~o, full stomach; (provb.) corpo ~o non crede al digiuno, the well-fed body has no notion of hunger.

†**sa·toro** *adj.* See saturo.

sa·trapa *m.* See satrapo.

sa·trap-o *m.* (Pers. hist.) satrap; (fig.) bigwig; ostentatiously wealthy individual, fare il —, to lord it over others. **-essa** *f.* (fig.) woman rolling in riches. **-i·a** *f.* (Pers. hist.) satrapy, dignity, function or province of a satrap. **-one** *m. augm.* man of importance.

satur-are [A1s] *tr.* (chem.) to saturate; *rfl.* to become saturated; (fig.) to saturate; †to satiate. **-a·bile** *adj.* saturable. **-abilità** *f.* saturability, capacity for saturation. **-ato** *part. adj.* (chem.) saturated; idrocarburo ~ato, saturated hydrocarbon; (fig.) ~ato di propaganda, saturated with propaganda. **-azione** *f.* (chem.) saturation; †satiety. **-ità** *f.* (chem.) saturation, saturation-point.

satur·nio *adj.* (poet.) relating to Saturn; of Saturn; Saturnia terra, Italy; (prosod.) verso —, Saturnian verse (pre-classical Latin verse-form of doubtful scansion).

Saturn-o *pr.n.m.* (myth.) Saturn; (astron.) Saturn; l'anello (usu. *sing.*) di —, the rings (usu. *pl.*) of Saturn; Saturn, the alchemic name for lead; (chem.) sale di —, zucchero di —, sugar of lead, salt of Saturn, hydrated lead acetate. **-ale** *adj.* pertaining to Saturn; riotously merry. **-ali** *n.m.pl.* (Rom. antiq.) Saturnalia; (fig.) period of licence and orgiastic living. **-ali·zio** *adj.* (Rom. antiq.) pertaining to the Saturnalia. **-ino** *adj.* saturnine; sombre; (astron.) Saturnian; (med.) colica ~ina, lead colic, Devonshire colic. **-i·smo** *m.* (med.) saturnism, plumbism, lead poisoning. †**-ità** *f.* see saturnismo.

sa·turo *adj.* saturated; full; (chem.) saturated; (eng.) vapore —, saturated steam.

sa·uri *m.pl.* (zool.) lizards.

sa·uro *adj.* (vet.) bay, roan; *n.m.* bay or roan horse.

savana *f.* (geog.) American prairie.

savanella *f.* (geog., Emilia) small drainage ditch.

savanna *f.* (bot.) savanna(h).

†**savere** *vb.* and derivs. See sapere.

Save·rio *pr.n.m.* Xavier.

savina *f.* (bot.). See sabina.

sa·vi-o *adj.* wise; experienced; judicious; skilled; sage; (of a child) good; fare — di, to inform of; *n.m.* sage; legal adviser to the civic administration (e.g. at Venice); Libro dei sette Savi, Book of the Seven Sages; fare il —, to behave sensibly. **-amente** *adv.* wisely; prudently; sagely. **-ezza** *f.* wisdom; prudence.

Savo·i-a *pr.n.f.* (geog.) Savoy; (hist.) la Casa di —, the House of Savoy; i Savoia, the family of the House of Savoy; (mil. hist.) avanti —!, battle cry used by Italian troops (before 1945) going in to attack or 'over the top'. **-ardo** *adj.* of Savoy; *n.m.* inhabitant of Savoy, Savoyard; (cul.) a kind of biscuit. **-no** *m.* Member of the House of Savoy.

savonarola *f.* a kind of folding chair (in use in the sixteenth century).

savon-ea *f.* (bot.) emulsion of sweet almonds. **-ina** *f.* (bot.) red valerian, spur valerian, *Kentranthus ruber.*

savonnette *f.* (pron. as Fr.) (watchm.) cassa —, hunter case.

savore *m.* (cul.) sharp sauce; sauce made of walnuts, etc.; any semi-liquid mixture; †savour.

savorra *f.* (naut.). See zavorra.

sax *m. indecl.* (mus.) saxhorn.

sazi-are [A4] *tr.* to satisfy; to satiate; — la fame, to satisfy one's hunger; to content; le patate ~iano, potatoes are filling; — il desiderio, to satisfy one's desire, to appease one's longing; *rfl.* to satisfy oneself; to eat one's fill; non si ~a mai, he is never satisfied. **-a·bile** *adj.* capable of being satisfied; facilmente ~abile, easily satisfied. **-abilmente** *adv.* satisfyingly. **-abilità** *f.* satiability. **-amento** *m.* satisfaction; contenting, satisfying. **-età** *f.* satiety; sino a ~età, ad nauseam, ad lib.; fullness after eating; mangiare a ~età, to eat one's fill; pane a ~età, as much bread as one wants. **-evolag·gine** *f.* surfeit, disgust (with overeating). **-evole** *adj.* (of food) cloying; stodgy; (fig.) tiresome. (**-evolmente** *adv.*) **-evolezza** *f.* satiety; disgust; nausea.

sa·zio *adj.* satiated; sated; full (up); (fig.) wearied, sick; tired, non essere mai —, to be never satisfied; (colloq.) essere — di, to be fed up with.

sbaccan-are [A I] *intr.* (*aux.* avere) to make a hullabaloo. **-eggiare** [A 3 c] *intr.* (*aux.* avere) to kick up a shindy. **-ìo** *m.* hullabaloo. **-one** *m.* brawler, rowdy individual.

sbaccell-are [A I] *tr.* to shell (peas, etc.). (**-ato** *part. adj.*) **-atura** *f.* shelling.

sbacchett-are [A I c] *tr.* to beat (rugs, etc.); to hit with a stick; to shake, to flap (in order to get the dust out of). **-ata** *f.* beating (of rugs, etc.); dare una **-ata** a, to beat. (**-ato** *part. adj.*) **-atura** *f.* beating, shaking (of rugs, etc.); groove for the ramrod of a fowling-piece. (Cf. bacchett-a, -are.)

sbacchi-are [A 4] *tr.* to bang; to slam; — l'uscio sul viso a uno, to slam the door in a person's face; non sapere dove — il capo, not to know which way to turn; to be desperate; *intr.* (*aux.* avere) to bang, to slam; l'uscio **-a**, the door is banging. **-amento** *m.* banging, slamming. **-ata** *f.* bang, slam. **-ato** *part. adj.* slammed, banged.

sbac·chio *m.* bang; slam.

sbaciucchi-are [A 4] *tr.* to kiss repeatedly; to slobber over; *recip. rfl.* to slobber over one another. (**-amento** *m.* **-atore** *m.* **-atrice** *f.*) **-one** *m.* slobberer. (**-ona** *f.*)

sbadacchi-are [A 4] *tr.* (bldg.) to prop up, to shore up. (**-ato** *part. adj.*) **-atura** *f.* (bldg.) propping, shoring.

sbadac·chio *m.* (bldg.) horizontal strut; (mining) stull.

sbadat-o *adj.* careless; heedless; inattentive; *n.m.* inattentive or careless person. (**-a** *f.*) **-amente** *adv.* carelessly; heedlessly; inattentively. **-ag·gine** *f.* carelessness; negligence; heedlessness. **-one** *m.* careless, heedless, individual. (**-ona** *f.*)

sbadigli-are [A 4] *intr.* (*aux.* avere) to yawn; to gape; to be wide open; *tr.* to utter amid yawns, to yawn. **-amento** *m.* yawn; yawning. **-ante** *part. adj.* yawning; bored; weary; gaping. **-ato** *part. adj.* uttered amid yawns; versi **-ati**, verses written without care or sincerity. **-ella** *f.* (colloq.) continual yawning, a fit of yawning.

sbadire [D 2] *tr.* (techn.) to undo, to unrivet, to release.

sbaf-are [A I] *intr.* (*aux.* avere; *prep.* da) to scrounge (from), to sponge (on); *tr.* (Tusc.) to eat greedily. **-atore** *m.* scrounger. (**-atrice** *f.*) **-o** *adv. phr.* a **-o**, without paying; vivere a **-o**, to scrounge a living.

†**sbagagliare** *tr., intr.* to unpack.

sbagli-are [A 4] *tr.* to mistake; to miscalculate; **-arla**, to be mistaken; — strada, to miss one's way; ha **-ato** me con mio fratello, he mistook me for my brother; **-ai** il treno di Roma con quello di Milano, I took the wrong train, getting mixed up between the one for Milan and the one for Rome; (mil.) — il passo, to be out of step, to break step; — un occhio, to squint; *intr.* (*aux.* avere) to make a mistake; to be mistaken; to err; to miss (a shot). **-ante** *part. adj.* in error, mistaken. **-ato** *part. adj.* mistaken; miscalculated; wrong; erroneous; è tutto **-ato**, it's all wrong, it is full of mistakes. **-atamente** *adv.* mistakenly; erroneously.

sba·glio *m.* mistake; blunder; error; fault; per —, by mistake.

†**sbaiaffare** *intr.* to prate, to prattle.

sbaiocc-are [A 2] *intr.* (*aux.* avere) to spend money lavishly, to have a good time; *rfl.* **-arsela**, to go gay, to spend recklessly.

sbaionett-are [A I c] *tr.* to bayonet. (**-ato** *part. adj.*)

†**sbaire** *intr.* to be bewildered, to be dismayed, to experience terror.

sbaldanz-ire [D 2] *tr.* to humble; to make less 'cock-a-hoop', to take the conceit out of. **-ito** *part. adj.* humbled; less arrogant.

†**sbaldeggiare** *tr.* to inspire with courage.

†**sbaldire** *tr.* to cheer, to encourage; *intr.* to feel cheered, to take courage.

†**sbaldore** *m.* See baldore.

sbaldoriare [A 4] *intr.* (*aux.* avere) to have a gay time, to spend recklessly.

sbalestr-are [A I] *intr.* (*aux.* avere) (fig.) to miss the target; to be wide of the mark; to be a long way from the truth; to wander from the point; *tr.* to fling, to hurl; — un'occhiata a, to dart a glance at; to drive, to thrust; to remove, to send away, to get rid of; to send from pillar to post; (vet.) — le gambe, to 'dish' (a vice of movement in horses); *rfl.* to be ruined, to crash; to lose one's grip of affairs. (**-amento** *m.*) **-ato** *part. adj.* wide of the mark; unbalanced; rash; wild. (**-atamente** *adv.*)

sball-are [A I] *tr.* to unpack; to unbale; (colloq.) **-arle** grosse, to talk big, to tell tall stories; — certe fandonie, to 'lay it on', to exaggerate, to pull one's leg; *intr.* (*aux.* avere) (games, sport, etc.) to overshoot; (vulg.) 'to kick the bucket'. (**-amento** *m.*) **-ato** *part. adj.* unpacked; thrown away; unbalanced; unsettled; exaggerated; (vulg.) dead. (**-atamente** *adv.*) **-onata** *f.* tall story. **-one** *m.* one who exaggerates; teller of tall stories. (**-ona** *f.*)

sballott-are [A I] *tr.* to toss up and down in one's arms; to toss about; to push around; fare —, to jolt, to jerk, to make jump up and down. **-amento** *m.*, **-ìo** *m.* tossing up and down; jerking, jolting.

sbalord-ire [D 2] *tr.* to stun; to knock unconscious; to bewilder; to amaze; to strike dumb with astonishment; to dumbfound; *intr.* (*aux.* avere) to be dumbfounded; c'è da —, it is enough to drive one out of one's senses. **-imento** *m.* amazement, astonishment, stupefaction; bewilderment. **-itag·gine** *f.* bewilderment; awkwardness, embarrassment. **-itivo** *adj.* bewildering; astonishing; stupefying; staggering, amazing. (**-itivamente** *adv.*) **-ito** *part. adj.* stunned; amazed; dumbfounded; staggered.

sbaluginare [A I S] *intr.* (*aux.* essere, avere) to glitter.

sbalz-are [A I] *tr.* to fling; to hurl; to throw down; to cast out; to send away; *intr.* (*aux.* essere) to bounce; to spring (down); to dart; to leap; (mus.) to move by leap. **-amento** *m.* hurling down; removal, removing; flinging away; overthrow; dismissal. **-ata** *f.* bounce; leap; spring; dare una **-ata**, to bounce; to leap. **-ato** *part. adj.* flung down; hurled; cast out; removed; dismissed.

sbalzell-are [A I] *intr.* (*aux.* avere) to bounce up and down; *tr.* to jolt. **-ìo** *m.* continual jolting. **-one** *m.* violent jerk. **-oni** *adv.* bouncing up and down.

sbalzo *m.* bound; spring; leap; bounce; dare uno —, to leap, to spring; sudden change; — di temperatura, sudden change in temperature; dare in sbalzi, to go leaping about; a sbalzi, by leaps and bounds, by fits and starts; di —, with a spring, with a leap; (techn.) projecting part; cogliere la palla di —, to make good use of an opportunity; a —, overhanging, cantilever; (bldg.) trave a —, cantilever, semi-girder; (electr.) surge; — di temperatura, — termico, temperature jump.

sbambagiare [A 4] *intr.* (text.) to fray.

sbanc-are[1] [A 2] *tr.* (bldg.) to remove earth from; (naut.) to unship thwarts from; *intr.* (*aux.* avere) (naut.) to unship thwarts of a boat. **-amento** *m.* (bldg.) earth-moving, excavation; (naut.) unshipping of thwarts. (**-ato** *part. adj.*) (From banco q.v.)

sbanc-are[2] [A 2] *intr.* (*aux.* avere) (in gambling) to break the bank; *tr.* (in gambling) to win the bank from; (fig.) to overcome, to get the better of. **-ato** *part. adj.* sold up, ruined (from banca, q.v.).

sbanchettare [A I c] *intr.* (*aux.* avere) to go to, or to give, a great many banquets; to be a diner-out.

sband-are [A I] *tr.* to disband; to disperse; — una folla, to break up a crowd; *intr.* (*aux.* avere) (naut.) to have a list, to be listing; far —, to list; *rfl.* to disperse; to be disbanded; (motor.) to (side) skid. **-amento** *m.* disbandment, disbanding; dispersal; (motor.) skid; (naut.) list; coppia di **-amento**, listing moment; (fig.) disturbance, 'twist' (e.g. of character or mind). **-ata** *f.* (motor.) skid. **-ato** *part. adj.* disbanded; dispersed; luogo **-ato**, uncultivated area. **-atamente** *adv.* dispersedly.

sbandeggi-are [A 3 c] *tr.* to banish. **-amento** *m.* banishment. **-ato** *part. adj.* banished. (**-ato** *part. adj.*)

sbandell-are [A I] *tr.* to take from its hinges; to remove the hinges from. **-ato** *part. adj.* unhinged.

sbandier-are [A I] *intr.* (*aux.* avere) to wave flags; to hang out flags; *tr.* to display; (fig.) to show off; to parade, to make a display of; — le sue ricchezze, to make a display of one's wealth. **-amento** *m.* (iron.) flag-waving. **-ata** *f.* waving of flags; wave with a flag. **-ato** *part. adj.* decorated with flags; (fig.) displayed, paraded.

sband-ire [D 2] *tr.* to banish, to exile; to chase away; to send away; to dismiss; †to proclaim. **-imento** *m.* banishment; exile, exiling; place of exile; renunciation; dismissal. **-ito** *part. adj.* banished; exiled; †proclaimed; *n.m.* exiled person, exile; outlaw.

†**sbando** *m.* disbandment.

†**sbandolare** *tr.* to undo (e.g. a skein).

sbando·metro *m.* (aeron.) bank indicator.

†**sbandonare** *vb.* See abbandonare.

sbaragli-are [A 4] *tr.* to throw into confusion; to rout; to disperse; *rfl.* to disperse, to disband, to scatter. **-amento** *m.* routing; dispersal. (**-ato** *part. adj.*)

sbaraˑglio *m.* rout; confusion; turmoil; mettere allo —, to rout, to throw into confusion; risk, jeopardy; mettersi allo —, to take foolish risks.

†**sbarattare** *tr.* to scatter, to disperse, to put to flight, to rout; see **barattare**.

sbarazz-are [A I] *tr.* (*prep.* di) to free (from), to clear (of); — le stanze, to clear the rooms; — le pareti, to strip the walls (of pictures, etc.); — la tavola, to clear the table; — il terreno, to clear the ground (also fig.); *rfl.* to free oneself; to rid oneself (of). -**ato** *part. adj.* cleared; freed (from), free (of).

sbarazzin-o *m.* street urchin; also *adj.* (-**a** *f.*) -**ata** *f.* prank.

sbarb-are [A I] *tr.* to uproot; — le male erbe, to weed, to pull up weeds; — un dente, to pull out a tooth; (fig.) -**arla**, to succeed, to pull a thing off, to get what one wants; (eng.) to shave; *rfl.* to shave (oneself). -**atello** *m.* young man, youth, shaver. -**ato** *part. adj.* uprooted; with roots exposed; pulled up; pulled out; shaven; clean-shaven; (naut.) batteria -**ata**, uncovered battery; *n.m.* beardless youth; clean-shaven man. -**atrice** *f.* (eng.) shaving machine; (agric.) hummeller (for barley). -**atura** *f.* (eng.) shaving (e.g. of gears).

†**sbarbazz-are** *tr.* to scold. †-**ata** *f.* scolding.

sbarbic-are [A 2 S] *tr.* to uproot; (fig.) to eradicate. (-**amento** *m.* -**ato** *part. adj.*)

sbarbific-are [A 2 S] *rfl.* (joc.) to shave (oneself). -**ato** *part. adj.* (joc.) tutto -**ato**, all clean and shaven.

sbarc-are [A 2] *tr.* to disembark; to put ashore; to unload (grain); (joc.) to save from the wreck; to pass, to spend; to get through; — la vita, to be able barely to make ends meet, to 'rub along'; abbiamo -**ato** l'estate discretamente, we spent quite a pleasant summer; — il lunario, to scrape a living; *intr.* (*aux.* essere) to disembark; to go ashore; to land; (colloq.) to get down (from a carriage or car); *rfl.* -**arsela**, to get through as best one can, to manage. -**amento** *m.* disembarking. -**ato** *part. adj.* disembarked; (naut.) †ufficiale -**ato**, non-seagoing officer; †marinaio -**ato**, non-seagoing rating. -**atoio** *m.* (naut.) landing place.

sbar-co *m.* (*pl.* -**chi**) disembarkation; landing; unloading; ponticello da —, gangplank; truppe da —, landing parties, Royal Marines, assault troops.

sbard-are [A I] *tr.* (mil. hist.) to remove the trappings from (a horse). (-**ato** *part. adj.*) -**ellare** [A I] *tr.* to break in (a horse) using a large saddle. -**ellato** *part. adj.* (of a horse) broken in by this method; †(fig.) exorbitant; immense; reckless.

sbarello *m.* tipping-lorry (used for carrying earth).

sbarr-a *f.* bar; barrier; (rlwy.) bar, road barrier; — a bilico, bascule barrier (e.g. of level crossing); — levatoria automatica, self-acting bascule barrier; (gymn., etc.) bar; (naut.) — del timone, tiller; (mil.) entrenchment, barricade, boom; (vet.) bar gag; (leg.) presentarsi alla —, to appear before the Court (as the accused), to appear in the dock; (techn.) wheel guard; (of a typewriter) — spaziatrice, space bar; (electr.) — collettrice, bus bar; (mus.) bar-line; double bar; (herald.) bend sinister; interzato in —, tierced per bend sinister. -**amento** *m.* barring; barricading; blocking; (hydraul.) barrage, weir; -**amento** mobile, frame weir; (mining) brattice; (naut.) barrage, mine barrage, minefield; boom, river or harbour defence; (mil.) barrage, method of blocking; ditch, road block; forte di -**amento**, blockhouse; campo di -**amento**, minefield; tiro di -**amento**, barrage fire. -**are** [A I] *tr.* to bar; to place a barrier across; to block; to barricade; (comm.) to cross; -**are** un assegno, to cross a cheque; to unbar; to open wide; -**are** gli occhi, to open one's eyes wide; -**are** le braccia, to hold open one's arms; †to launch. -**ata** *f.* (mil.) trench; riparo di -**ate**, stockade. -**ato** *part. adj.* barred; blocked; barricaded; (comm.) assegno -**ato**, crossed cheque; assegno non -**ato**, open cheque; unbarred; wide open; (herald.) bandy sinister. -**etta** *f. dim.* of sbarra; (typ.) short hyphen, tilde. †-**o** *m.* see **sbarra**; uproar.

sbarullare [A I] *tr., abs.* (archit.) to remove the support (used in construction) from an arch.

†**sbasire** *vb.* and derivs. See **basire**.

†**sbasoffiare** *intr.* to guzzle, to eat greedily.

sbass-are [A I] *tr.* to make lower, to shorten; to reduce; to bring down (prices). -**amento** *m.* lowering, sinking; reducing. -**ato** *part. adj.* lowered, shortened; reduced, sunk, sunken. -**o** *m.* (comm.) discount; fall; decline; drop.

sbastigliata *f. adj.* (Alfieri) Parigi —, Paris de-Bastillized.

sbatacchi-are [A 4] *tr.* to flap; to bang; to knock about; to slam; *intr.* (*aux.* avere), *rfl.* to toss about, to fling oneself about, to be restless; to rattle; to flap about; to swing to and fro. -**amento** *m.* banging, bang; slamming, slam; swinging to and fro; clattering, clashing. -**ata** *f.* bang; slam. -**ato** *part. adj.* -**atore** *m.* -**atrice** *f.*)

sbatacchio[1] *m.* continual banging; clatter.

sbatacˑchio[2] *m.* (mining) stull.

sbattagliare [A 4] *intr.* (*aux.* avere) (of bells) to ring loudly.

sbatˑt-ere [B I] *tr.* to shake; to toss; to hurl, to fling; to flap; to bang; — la porta, to slam the door; — uova, to beat eggs; — i piedi, to stamp one's feet; — i panni, to beat (rugs, etc.); to fend off; to resist; (fig.) — la malinconia, to shake off a feeling of depression; *rfl.* to toss (oneself) about, to fling (oneself) about; to be restless; to struggle; *intr.* (*aux.* avere) to bang, to slam; imposte che -**ono**, shutters banging; to flutter, to 'chatter'; (naut.) to flap (sails or slack rigging); †fa —!, luff! †-**imentare** *tr.* (paint.) to shade, to put in shadows. -**imento** *m.* banging; slamming; battering; clattering; (paint.) shadow; (mus.) answering, response (of one choir to another); (naut.) action of flapping. -**itura** *f.* banging; bang; crashing; crash; flapping; shaking; shake. -**itutto** *m. indecl.* whipping machine, whisk, beater. -**uta** *f.* bang; slam; dare una -**uta** ai panni, to give the clothes a shake out. -**ute** *f.pl.* (naut.) the flaps. -**uto** *part. adj.* banged; knocked about; battered; bashed; (fig.) depressed; worn out; run down.

sbattezz-are [A I C] *tr.* to induce (a person) to abjure the Christian religion; (fig., joc.) to change the name of; *rfl.* to abjure the Christian religion; (fig., joc.) mi ci -**erei**!, *or* c'è da -**arsi**!, I swear it's true!, *or* I bet it isn't true!. (-**ato** *part. adj.*)

sbatˑtito *m.* banging; battering; slamming; †passion; †suffering.

sbatufolare [A I S] *tr.* (Tusc.) to maul, to handle, to finger.

†**sbaudire** *tr.* to cheer.

sbaulare [A I S] *tr., abs.* to unpack.

sbavagliare [A 4] *tr.* to ungag, to remove a gag from.

sbav-are [A I] *intr.* (*aux.* avere) to slobber, to slaver; to dribble; (of froth, etc.) to bubble forth; *rfl.* to slobber all over oneself; to dribble slobber down one's chin; (eng.; metall.) to burr; to trim; to clean (a casting). -**amento** *m.* slobbering, slavering; dribbling; (eng., metall.) burring, trimming, cleaning. (-**ato** *part. adj.*) -**atore** *m.* (eng.; metall.) trimmer. -**atrice** *f.* (eng.) burring machine, snagging machine. -**atura** *f.* slobber; slaver; dribble; slime, slimy track (of a snail); (paperm.) deckle-edge; (typ.) inky smudge left by badly cut letters; (eng.) trimming, burring (a casting); trimming, snagging (a drop-forged article); burr (as removed in this operation); flash (rough edges on a drop-forged article). -**one** *m.* slobberer.

†**sbavigliare** *vb.* and derivs. See **sbadigliare**.

sbeccucci-are [A 3] *tr.* to break the spout of. -**ato** *part. adj.* spoutless, with broken spout; bricco -**ato**, jug with the spout knocked off.

†**sbeffa** *f.* See **beffa**.

sbeff-are [A I] *tr.* to mock cruelly; to deride (stronger than **beffare**, q.v.). -**amento** *m.* cruel mocking; deriding. -**ato** *part. adj.* mocked, derided, set upon with cruel mockery. (-**atore** *m.* -**atrice** *f.*) -**atura** *f.* cruel mockery.

sbeffeggi-are [A 3 C] *tr.* to make fun of, to poke fun at maliciously, to dig at, to 'get at' (stronger than **beffeggiare**, q.v.). -**amento** *m.* mocking; making game of. -**ato** *part. adj.* mocked; made fun of. (-**atore** *m.* -**atrice** *f.*)

sbellic-are [A 2] *tr.* to split open; to disembowel; *rfl.* -**arsi** dalle risa, to split one's sides with laughter. -**ato** *part. adj.* split open; disembowelled. -**atamente** *adv.* ridere -**atamente**, to laugh fit to burst.

sbend-are [A I] *tr.* to unbandage. -**ato** *part. adj.* unbandaged.

sberˑcia *f.* (colloq. Tusc.) duffer; incompetent (individual); allo sport sono una —, I'm a rabbit at games.

sberciare[1] [A S] *intr.* (*aux.* avere) to shoot wide of the mark; *tr.* to mock, to satirize, to lampoon.

sberciare[2] [A 3] *intr.* (*aux.* avere) to shriek, to yell.

†**sbergo** *m.* See **usbergo**.

sberleff-o *m.*, -**e** *m.* grimace; expression of scorn or mockery; †scar on the face.

sberlingacciare [A 3] *intr.* (*aux.* avere) to make merry, to hold festival (cf. **berlingaccio**).

†**sberna**, †**sberˑnia** *f.* (hist. costume) cloak (sixteenth century).

sberrett-are [A I c] *rfl.* to take off one's cap, to lift one's cap. **-ata** *f.* greeting, sign of respect (by raising one's cap); fare una grande -ata, to take off one's cap with a flourish. (**-ato** *part. adj.*)

sbertare [A I] *tr.* to mock, to mimic; to find fault with.

sbertucci-are [A 3] *tr.* to crush, to crumple; to rumple; to spoil the shape of; (fig.) to mock; to crush; — un autore, to comment unintelligently on an author. **-ato** *part. adj.* crushed; rumpled; (fig.) mocked.

†sbeucchiare *vb.* and derivs. See **sbevazzare**.

sbevacchiare [A 4] *intr.* (*aux.* avere). See **sbevazzare**.

sbevazz-are [A I] *intr.* (*aux.* avere) to tipple; to 'indulge'. **-amento** *m.* drinking bout. **-atore** *m.* toper, boozy individual. (**-atrice** *f.*)

†sbe·vere *vb.* and derivs. See **bere**.

sbev-icchiare [A 4], **-ucchiare** [A 4]. See **sbevazzare**.

†sbezzicare *vb.* and derivs. See **bezzicare**.

sbiadato[1] *adj.* (of a horse, etc.) kept off oats.

†sbiadato[2] *adj.* See **sbiadito**, under **sbiadire**.

sbiad-ire [D 2] *intr.* (*aux.* essere) to fade; to turn pale; to grow pale, to pale; *tr.* to fade, to cause to fade; to take the colour out of; to make look pale. **-imento** *m.* fading. **-ito** *part. adj.* faded; pale; washed-out; bellezza -ita, faded beauty; stile -ito, insipid style, colourless style; dull.

sbianca *f.* (text.) bleaching.

sbianc-are [A 2] *intr.* (*aux.* essere), *rfl.* to turn white; to fade; to grow pale; *tr.* to whiten; to whitewash; (text.) to bleach. **-amento** *m.* (scient.) bleaching, whitening. **-ato** *part. adj.* whitened; whitewashed; white; pale; pallid; (text.) bleached. **-atrice** *f.* (text.) bleaching agent.

sbianchire [D 2] *tr.* see **sbiancare**; (tanning) to whiten (a cutting process).

sbiasci-are [A 3] *tr., intr.* (*aux.* avere) to mumble. (**-ato** *part. adj.*) **-atura** *f.* mumbling; (text.) fault in cloth where the scissors have failed to bite.

sbicchier-are [A I] *tr.* to sell by the glass (e.g. wine); *intr.* (*aux.* avere) to drink in company; to 'have a glass'. **-ata** *f.* a drink in company, a drink together.

sbie·co *adj.* (*m.pl.* **-chi**) oblique; awry; di, a, per —, askew, *or* on the cross; crooked; edgeways; guardare di —, to look askance at, *or* to look at angrily, scornfully; (photog.) presa di —, angle shot; (techn.) tagliato a —, chamfered, bevelled. **-camente** *adv.* crookedly; aslant; obliquely. **-care** [A 2] *tr.* to distort; to look askance at; to straighten; *intr.* (*aux.* avere, essere), *rfl.* to be crooked. **-cata** *f.* crookedness, slant. **-cato** *part. adj.* crooked; straightened.

†sbietolare *intr., rfl.* to weep copiously (like a beetroot), to indulge in grief.

sbiett-are [A I c] *tr.* to pull away the wedges from, to release; (naut.) to unwedge, to remove the wedges from; *intr.* (*aux.* essere) to trip, to take a false step; to miss one's footing; — per le scale, to fall on the stairs. (**-ato** *part. adj.* **-atura** *f.*)

sbigonciare [A 3 c] *intr.* (*aux.* essere, avere) to overflow (from a vat or tub); (Tusc.) (of produce) to be in great abundance; (joc.) to need larger shoes, to bulge out of one's shoes (cf. **bigoncia**).

sbigott-ire [D 2] *tr.* to terrify; to dismay; to demoralize; *intr.* (*aux.* essere), *rfl.* to be dismayed; to lose heart; to be discouraged. **-imento** *m.* dismay; consternation; terror; discouragement. **-ito** *part. adj.* dismayed; terrified; discouraged; demoralized; faint-hearted; timid, timorous. (**-itore** *m.* **-itrice** *f.*)

sbilanci-are [A 3] *tr.* to unbalance; to throw off balance; to unsettle; to derange; *intr.* (*aux.* avere) to overbalance; to be weighed down on one side; to lose one's balance; *rfl.* (fig.) to commit oneself; to make too many promises; to take on too many commitments; to spend beyond one's means. **-amento** *m.* loss of balance; loss of equilibrium; unsettling; derangement; (eng.) unbalance. **-ato** *part. adj.* thrown off balance; out of equilibrium.

sbilan·ci·o *m.* lack of balance; loss of equilibrium; disproportion; (finan.) deficiency; deficit; (med.) imbalance. **-one** *m.* augm. of **sbilancio**; leap; sudden rise; (of a horse) fare uno -one, to give a sudden leap; *adv. phr.* a -oni, by leaps and bounds.

sbilen-co *adj.* (*m.pl.* **-chi**) crooked; bandy-legged; bow-legged; (vet.) pigeon-toed (of a horse); (fig.) versi -chi, limping verses. **†-are** *tr.* to trip up; *intr.* (of wood) to warp.

†sbillacco *adj.* See **bislacco**.

sbiluci-are [A 3] *intr.* (*aux.* avere) to peer, to look searchingly and

with curiosity; to ogle; to leer at. **-one** *m.* one who peers and stares; one who ogles.

†sbiobbo *adj.* stunted, twisted; rickety.

sbirbare [A I] *intr.* (*aux.* avere) to have a gay time; to lead an idle life; sbirbarsela, to have a good time, to be always amusing oneself.

sbirci-are [A 3] *tr.* to eye; to watch closely; to cast sidelong glances at; to watch out of the corner of one's eye; *intr.* (*aux.* avere) to give sidelong glances; to be watchful; to look closely. **-ata** *f.* sidelong glance. **-ato** *part. adj.* eyed; closely watched.

sbir·cio *m.* sidelong glance; quick look, 'squint'.

sbirichinare [A I] *intr.* (*aux.* avere) to play childish tricks, to get up to pranks.

sbirr-o *m.* (pop.) see **birro**; (naut.) strop. **-a** *f.* domineering woman. **-a·glia** *f.* (derog.) gang of police-spies. **-eggiare** [A 3 c] *intr.* (*aux.* avere) to behave in a bullying or threatening manner. **-eri·a** *f.* police force; residence of police. **-esco** *adj.* (*m.pl.* **-eschi**) bullying, threatening; of, relating to, or resembling a police-spy. **-i·glia** *f.* see **sbirraglia**.

sbittare [A I] *tr.* (naut.). See **disbittare**.

sbizzarire [D 2] *tr.* to satisfy the whim of; *rfl.* to indulge one's whims, to have one's own way, to have what one fancies.

sbizzire [D 2] *intr.* (*aux.* essere), *rfl.* to give way to one's caprices; to indulge in a show of temper.

sbloccare [A 2] *tr.* (mil.) to lift the siege, to lift the blockade (of); (econ.) to release; — il credito, to release a blocked or frozen credit; (techn.) to clear.

sblocco *m.* lifting of blockade; (econ.) release, defreezing; — dei fitti, decontrolling of rents.

sbocc-are [A 2 c] *intr.* (*aux.* essere; *prep.* in) (of a river, etc.) to flow (into); to have its outlet (in); to fall (into); (of a street) to open (into), to lead (to); to debouch; to come out (on to); to emerge; to overflow; to burst forth, to break through; (naut.) to leave a canal *or* to come out of a fiord, etc.; *tr.* to break the rim of (a jug, vase, etc.); — un fiasco, to pour a few drops from the top of a flask. **-amento** *m.* outflow; outfall; outlet; mouth (of a river, etc.). **-ata** *f.* outflowing. **-atag·gine** *f.* coarseness of speech, foul language. **-ato** *part. adj.* with rim or lip broken (e.g. of a jug); foul-mouthed, coarse; cavallo -ato, horse with a hard mouth; (mil.) cannone -ato, 'tuliped' gun. **-atamente** *adv.* coarsely, lewdly; parlare -atamente, to be foul-mouthed. **-atoio** *m.* outlet. **-atura** *f.* the removing of the layer of oil from the top of a flask of wine; (artill.) defect of a gun (tulip effect of muzzle).

sbocci-are[1] [A 3] *tr.* (bowls) to knock away (the bowl of an opponent). (**-ato** *part. adj.*)

sbocci-are[2] [A 3] *intr.* (*aux.* essere) to bud; to blossom; to open (of flowers); (fig.) to begin to develop; to blossom. **-ato** *part. adj.* (of a flower, etc.) in bud, open; in bloom, blossoming. (Cf. **bocciare**.)

sboc·cio *m.* bud; blossom; bloom; fiori di —, flowers in bud; (fig.) sul primo —, in the flower of youth, in early youth; giovinetto di primo —, young man in the prime of youth.

sboc-co *m.* (*pl.* **-chi**) outlet; opening; mouth; way out; discharge; — della fogna, outfall; (geog.) outlet; river mouth; (comm.) market; channel of trade; (med.) — di sangue, bleeding from the mouth.

sbocconcell-are [A I] *tr.* to nibble; to masticate slowly; to bite little pieces off; to cut in small pieces; to split up into small sections; to break the edge off, to chip (esp. crockery, etc.). **-ato** *part. adj.* nibbled; chipped; split up, divided, fragmented. **-atura** *f.* nibbling; chip; splitting up; division, fragmentation.

†sbociare *tr.* to report, to publish.

sboffo *m.* (dressm.) puff, fullness; maniche con gli sboffi, puff-sleeves.

†sbofonchiare *vb.* and derivs. See **bofonchiare**.

†sboglientare *intr.* to boil furiously; to seethe.

sbolgiare [A 3] *intr.* (*aux.* essere) (of clothing) to bag, to bulge, to be baggy.

sbolinato *adj.* (naut.) untrimmed, slack (of a sail, etc.); untidy, carelessly dressed (of a sailor); (fig.) unmethodical.

sboll-are [A I c] *tr.* to unseal, to break the seal of. (**-ato** *part. adj.*)

sboll-ire [D 2] *intr.* (*aux.* essere, avere) to go off the boil; (fig.) to die down, to calm down; l'ira gli è -ita, his anger has simmered down. **-ito** *part. adj.* off the boil; no longer boiling; (fig.) calmed; furia -ita, fury that has abated.

ş̣bolognare [A 5] *tr.* (colloq.) to palm off on; mi sbolognò cento lire false, he palmed off a dud 100-lire coin on me.

ş̣bombare [A I c] *tr.* to reveal, to let out; to disclose indiscreetly; — una notizia, to let out a piece of news; *intr.* (*aux.* avere) to exaggerate, to 'lay it on', to 'tell the tale'.

ş̣bombazzare [A I] *intr.* (*aux.* avere) see **sbombare**; †to drink excessively.

†sbombettare *intr.* to tipple.

ş̣bombọne *m.* (Tusc., colloq.) teller of tall stories, leg-puller; exaggerator.

†sbontadiato *m.* good-for-nothing.

ş̣bonzol-are [A I sc] *intr.* (*aux.* avere) to droop, to be weighed down; to trail; (archit.) to crack (through subsidence); *rfl.* (colloq.) -arsi dalle risa, to laugh fit to burst. **-ante** *part. adj.* weighed down, trailing, pendulous. **-ato** *part. adj.* weighed down, burdened; †*n.m.* rupture.

†sborchiare *tr.* to remove the studs from.

ş̣bord-are [A I] *tr.* to dismantle; to break up; (naut.) to lift a deck or sideplating of. **-ato** *part. adj.* dismantled; broken up; (text.) skirted. **-atura** *f.* (text.) skirting.

ş̣bordonata *f.* (mus.) droning.

ş̣bor·nia *f.* (colloq.) drunkenness; 'binge'; prendere una —, to get drunk; smaltire una —, to sleep off a binge; (fig.) infatuation.

ş̣borni-are[1] [A 4] *rfl.* (colloq.) to get drunk; to go on a binge. **-ato** *part. adj.* drunk. **-ọne** *m.* tippler, toper; drunkard.

ş̣borniare[2] [A 4] *tr.* (Tusc., colloq.) to perceive faintly, to see hardly at all; to peer at; senza occhiali non sbornio nulla, I can't see a thing without my glasses.

ş̣borr-are [A I c] *tr.* to take the stuffing out of; to squeeze (a spot, boil, etc.). **-ato** *part. adj.* emptied of stuffing; limp; enfeebled; sagging.

ş̣bors-are [A I c] *tr.* to disburse; to pay out. **-amento** *m.* disbursement; paying out. **-ato** *part. adj.* disbursed; paid out.

ş̣bọrso *m.* disbursement; outlay; payment.

ş̣bosc-are [A 2] *tr.* to deforest; to cut down trees from. **-amento** *m.* deforesting; clearing of trees. **-ato** *part. adj.* deforested; cleared of trees.

†sbotrare *intr.* to stray from the right path; to give away secrets; *tr.* to jot down; to write fluently, with facility.

ş̣bott-are [A I c] *tr.* (*aux.* essere) (colloq. Tusc.) to burst out, to burst forth; to tell everything; — in un pianto dirotto, to burst out sobbing. **-ata** *f.* outburst; -ata di riso, burst of laughter.

ş̣botton-are [A I c] *tr.* to unbutton; to undo; *rfl.* to unbutton oneself, to unbutton one's clothing; (fig.) to let oneself go, to become communicative; to unbosom oneself. **-ato** *part. adj.* unbuttoned. **-atura** *f.* unbuttoning; confiding; revealing. **-eggiare** [A 3 c] *intr.* (*aux.* avere) to speak abusively, to 'let fly'.

ş̣bọẓẓach-ire [D 2] *intr.* (*aux.* essere) to grow strong; to gain strength; *tr.* to rough-hew; to civilize; to refine. **-ito** *part. adj.* improved in strength, developed; (fig.) refined, 'with the corners rubbed off'.

ş̣boẓẓ-are [A I c] *tr.* to sketch out; to outline; to rough-hew; (paint.) to make a rough sketch of; (sculp.) to boast; (carp.) to rough-plane; (masonry) to scabble; †*intr.* (naut.) to cast off. **-amento** *m.* outlining; roughing out; (masonry) boasting. **-ato** *part. adj.* outlined; roughed out; (eng.) rough-shaped; -ato di macchina, rough-machined; (masonry) dressed; *n.m.* (metall.) intermediate forging. **-atore** *m.* (sculp.) stone-mason. **-atura** *f.* (sculp.) boasting; (metall.) intermediate forging; (eng.) rough-turning, rough-machining; †(naut.) operation of casting off and letting go. **-ino** *m.* (carp.) jack plane.

ş̣bọẓẓo *m.* rough outline; (paint.) sketch; (sculp.) boasting, bozzetto.

ş̣boẓẓolare [A I s] *intr.* (*aux.* essere) (ent.) to come out of the cocoon; (silkb.) to remove the cocoons from the mulberry leaves.

ş̣bracalato *adj.* (fam.) sloppily dressed; with trousers slipping down.

ş̣brac-are [A 2] *tr.* to take the trousers off, to strip the pants off; to debag; (naut.) to unstrop; *rfl.* to take one's trousers off; (colloq.) -arsi per, to show too much solicitude about; (vulg.) -arsi dalle risa, to laugh fit to burst. **-ato** *part. adj.* without one's trousers; with one's trousers falling down; (fam.) risa -ate, loud guffaw; feckless; sloppy; slipshod. **-atamente** *adv.* sloppily, carelessly; in a slipshod way; excessively.

ş̣braccettare [A I c] *tr.* to lead on one's arm, to take on one's arm; *recip. rfl.* to walk arm in arm.

ş̣bracci-are [A 3] *tr.* to carry on one's arm; — lo scudo, to put on one's shield; *intr.* (*aux.* avere) to gesticulate with one's arms; *rfl.* to bare one's arms; to roll up one's sleeves; (fig.) to work hard, to get through a lot of work; to go to great lengths; to do one's utmost; to make strenuous efforts. **-ata** *f.* shove with the arms, elbowing. **-ato** *part. adj.* bare-armed; with one's sleeves rolled up.

ş̣brac·cio *m.* throw, throwing movement; space to throw.

†sbracceri·a *f.* lavishness; boastfulness (cf. **sbraciare**).

ş̣braci-are [A 3] *tr.* — il fuoco, to poke the fire, to open up a fire so that the live coals burn more brightly; — il caldano, to stir the brazier; *intr.* (*aux.* avere) (of sparks) to leap from the living coals; (fig., pop. Tusc.) to spend lavishly, to make a show with one's money; to swagger, to boast. **-ata** *f.* stir, poke; dare una -ata al fuoco, to give the fire a poke. **-onata** *f.* (pop., Tusc.) swaggering; boastful action; lavish spending. **-ọne** *m.* (pop., Tusc.) swaggerer, boaster. (**-ọna** *f.*) **-atọio** *m.* game similar to poker, 'brag'.

sbracio *m.* lavishness; overspending.

†sbraire *vb.* and derivs. See **braire**.

ş̣brait-are [A I] *intr.* (*aux.* avere) to shout loudly, angrily. **-amento** *m.* loud shouting; bawling. **-io** *m.* continual loud shouting; bawling; uproar. **-ọne** *m.* bawler; shouter. (**-ọna** *f.*)

ş̣bramare [A I] *tr.* to satisfy; — gli occhi, to look one's fill, to feast one's eyes; — le voglie, to have one's desire; *rfl.* to satisfy one's longing.

ş̣bramino *m.* (techn.) machine for pearling rice.

sbran-are [A I] *tr.* to tear to pieces, to rend; to lacerate; to destroy; *rfl.* to destroy oneself; *recip. rfl.* to rend one another. **-amento** *m.* tearing, rending; lacerating. **-ato** *part. adj.* rent; torn to shreds; lacerated; destroyed. **-atore** *m.* (**-atrice** *f.*)

ş̣branc-are [A 2] *tr.* to take from the flock; to separate; to detach; *rfl.* to scatter; to stray; to leave the flock; (mil.) to disband, to break away, to fall out (from motives of negligence, cupidity, cowardice, etc.). **-amento** *m.* separating from a flock; detaching; scattering; straying. **-ata** *f.* part of a flock that has strayed. **-ato** *part. adj.* strayed; pecora -ata, sheep that has strayed; scattered; separated.

ş̣brancicare [A 2 s] and derivs. (pop.). See **brancicare**.

ş̣brandellare [A I] and derivs. See **sbrindellare**.

ş̣brano *m.* tearing, rending; (Tusc.) tear, rent, wrench.

ş̣bratt-are [A I] *tr.* to clean; to clear; to tidy, to put in order; — la tavola, to clear the table; — le strade, to sweep the streets; — il paese dal nemico, to clear the enemy out of the country; *intr.* (*aux.* essere) to clear out, to be off; -ate di qui!, clear out of here! **-ata** *f.* clean, cleaning, sweeping; diamo una -ata a questa stanza, let's give this room a clean. **-ato** *part. adj.* cleaned; cleared. **-o** *m.* cleaning; clearing; clean; polish up; dare lo -o a, to clean; avere lo -o, to be cleaned up; (naut.) see **bratto**.

ş̣bravata *f.* See **bravata**, under **bravo**.

ş̣bravazz-are [A I] *intr.* (*aux.* avere) to swagger; to brag, to boast; to bluster. **-ata** *f.* bragging, boasting; boast; swaggering; blustering, bluster. **-ọne** *m.* swaggerer; blusterer. (**-ọna** *f.*)

ş̣brecc-are [A 2 c] *tr.* to chip the edge of; to chip. **-ato** *part. adj.* chipped; una tazza -ata, a chipped cup.

ş̣brecci-are [A 3 c] *tr.* (mil.) to breach (with sustained activity), to 'hammer away at' (a weakened position). (**-ato** *part. adj.*)

ş̣brẹndol-o *m.* shred; rag; tatter. **-are** [A I sc] *intr.* (*aux.* essere, avere) to fall to rags; to hang in tatters. **-ọne** *m.* ragamuffin; tatterdemalion. (**-ọna** *f.*)

ş̣bresciare [A 4] *tr.* (tanning) to flesh over the beam.

†sbriccare *tr.* to fling, to throw, to hurl.

ş̣bricchi *excl.* (Tusc.) sbricchi sbricchi, quanti? (said in a guessing game when a person is asked to guess how many objects another holds in his hands).

†sbricco *m.* rascal.

ş̣briciare [A 3] *rfl.* (poet.) to crumble; *tr.* to crush.

ş̣bri·cio *adj.* poor, wretched; shabby; poorly dressed.

ş̣briciol-are [A I s] *tr.* to crumble; (fig.) to crush; to annihilate; to shatter; *rfl.* to crumble; to fall to pieces, to turn to crumbs. **-amento** *m.* crumbling; crushing. **-ato** *part. adj.* crumbled; crushed. **-atura** *f.* crumbling; crumbled pieces.

ş̣brig-are [A 2] *tr.* to dispatch; to finish off; to expedite; — una faccenda, to hurry an affair through; — una questione, to solve a question; — un cliente, to rush through an interview with a client; — una persona, to comply quickly with a person's wants,

sbrig-are (*cont.*)
to settle a person's affairs; *rfl.* to hurry; to make haste; sbrìgati!, hurry up!; (*prep.* di) to get rid (of). **-aménto** *m.* dispatch; haste; expedition; hurry. **-ativo** *adj.* quick; expeditious; quickly done; quickly made. **-ativaménte** *adv.* quickly, speedily; expeditiously. **-ato** *part. adj.* finished quickly; hurried through; via **-ata**, quick way, short cut; hastened; dispatched; (iron.) **-ato dai medici**, helped out of this world by doctors.

sbrigli-are [A4] *tr.* to unbridle; (fig.) to relieve; to loosen; to set free, to liberate; †*intr.* to pull on the reins. **-aménto** *m.* unbridling; loosening; releasing, release. †**-ata** *f.* pull on the reins; (fig.) pull-up, reproof. **-atézza** *f.* unruliness; unbridled behaviour. **-ato** *part. adj.* unbridled; (fig.) loosened; set free; unchecked; unlicensed; gioventù **-ata**, unruly youth; sprightly, lively, spirited; brilliant. **-ataménte** *adv.* freely; unrestrainedly. **-atura** *f.* unbridling; loosening; sprightly behaviour.

sbrin-are [A1] *tr.* to defrost. **-aménto** *m.* defrosting (e.g. of a refrigerator). **-ato** *part. adj.* defrosted. **-atóre** *m.* defroster (of a refrigerator). **-atura** *f.* see sbrinamento.

sbrindell-are [A1] *tr.* to tear to shreds; to tear into strips. **-ato** *part. adj.* in shreds, tattered and torn. **-óne** *m.* ragamuffin. (**-óna** *f.*)

sbrividire [D2] *tr.* to stop (someone, something) from shaking or shivering; — le mani, to warm, to 'thaw', hands that were trembling with cold.

†**sbrizzare** *vb.* and derivs. See sprizzare.

†**sbrobbiare** *tr.* to speak ill of, to heap opprobrium upon.

sbroc-co *m.* (*pl.* **-chi**) (silkb.) waste removed from silk fibre after removal from the cocoon. **-care** [A2] *tr.* (silkb.) to clean (silk fibre) after its removal from the cocoon; (agric.) to strip (a branch) of its twigs and leaves. **-catura** *f.* (silkb.) cleaning silk fibre. **-cóne** *m.* (shoem.) pegging tool.

sbroccolare [A1s] *tr.* to nibble the tender branches of, to browse on.

sbrodare [A1] and derivs. See sbrodolare.

sbrodol-are [A1s] *tr.* to spill soup down; to spot, to spatter (with food); (fig.) to spin out, to draw out; — un discorso, to make a long, wordy speech; *rfl.* to spill food down oneself, to be a messy eater. **-ato** *part. adj.* soup-stained; spotted (with food); (fig.) un discorso **-ato**, a long-winded speech. **-óne** *m.* messy eater, slobberer.

sbrogli-are [A4] *tr.* to disentangle; to untangle; to extricate; to clear; *intr.* (*aux.* avere) (naut.) to let go the brails; *rfl.* (*acc.* of *prn.* 'si'; *prep.* da) to get clear of; to get finished with; to get out of (a difficulty, etc.); to release oneself, to get free; (*dat.* of *prn.* 'si') **-arsela**, to get out of a difficult situation. **-aménto** *m.* disentangling; extricating; clearing. **-ato** *part. adj.* disentangled; untangled; extricated; freed.

sbro·glio *m.* small book for making rough notes.

sbroncare [A2]. See sbronconare.

sbronciare [A3] and derivs. See sbroncire.

sbroncire [D2] *intr.* (*aux.* essere) to sulk, to pout.

sbroncon-are [A1c] *tr.* (agric.) to clear (land), to dig the stumps from. (**-ato** *part. adj.*)

sbro·sci-a *f.* (Tusc.) tasteless beverage; (fig.) long boring speech. **-atura** *f.* (techn.) spent silk dye-liquor used for dyeing leather.

†**sbrotare** *vb.* See sbotrare.

†**sbrucare** *vb.* See brucare.

sbruff-are [A1] *tr.* (*prep.* di) to bespatter, to besprinkle; to spurt; to squirt (with); (fig.) to attempt to bribe; to tell tall stories to. **-ata** *f.* spurt; squirt. **-ato** *part. adj.* spurted; bespattered; (cul., Naples) insalata alla **-ata**, salad seasoned by the primitive method of taking oil and vinegar into one's mouth and squirting it out on to the salad; (fig.) bribed. **-o** *m.* squirt; spurt; gush; (fig.) bribe; pigliare lo **-o**, to take bribes. **-óne** *m.* braggart. (**-óna** *f.*)

†**sbruttare** *tr.* to enhance, to transform from ugliness to beauty.

sbuc-are [A2] *intr.* (*aux.* essere; *prep.* da) to emerge; to come forth; to issue; to come out (of, from); *tr.* to draw out; to pull out; to dislodge; to start (a fox, etc.). (**-ato** *part. adj.*)

sbucci-are [A3] *tr.* to skin, to peel; to pare; to shell; to husk; (fig.) to have a smattering of; to get a superficial knowledge of; to skim through; **-arla**, to get out of a difficulty, to wriggle out; — uno, to 'skin a person alive'; *rfl.* (*acc.* of *prn.* 'si') to scrape oneself; to take the skin off oneself; (ent.) to moult; (*dat.* of *prn.* 'si') **-arsi** il ginocchio, to graze one's knee; **-arsela**, to get out of a difficulty, to wriggle out. **-afatiche** *m. indecl.* idler; one who

evades work. **-aménto** *m.* peeling; shelling. **-apatate** *m. indecl.* (cul.) potato-peeler. **-ato** *part. adj.* peeled; skinned; shelled; cleaned. **-atura** *f.* peeling; shelling; stripping; graze, scratch. **-óne** *m.* idler, loafer.

†**sbuccicare** *tr.* to peel, to skin.

†**sbuccinare** *vb.* and derivs. See buccinare.

sbudell-are [A1] *tr.* to disembowel; to gut; — un pollo, to draw a chicken; to stab, to knife; *rfl.* to receive injuries to the abdomen; *recip. rfl.* to knife each other. **-aménto** *m.* disembowelling; gutting; knifing, stabbing. **-ato** *part. adj.* disembowelled; gutted; knifed, stabbed. (**-atóre** *m.* **-atrice** *f.*)

sbuff-are [A1] *intr.* (*aux.* avere) to snort; to puff; to pant; to puff and blow; to fume; (of wind) to rage, to bluster; *tr.* to give forth, to belch forth, to puff; — fumo, to puff forth smoke. **-aménto** *m.* puffing; snorting; panting. **-ante** *part. adj.* puffing, panting. **-ata** *f.* puff. (**-ato** *part. adj.*) **-o** *m.* puff; snort; gust.

†**sbufonchiare** *vb.* and derivs. See bofonchiare.

†**sbuggerare** *vb.* and derivs. See buggerare.

sbugiardare [A1] *tr.* to convict of lying; to give the lie to; to catch out in a lie.

sbullett-are [A1c] *tr.* to untack; *rfl.* to come untacked; (agric., of corn) to blister. (**-ato** *part. adj.*) **-atura** *f.* untacking; loosening.

sburr-are [A1] *tr.* (techn.) to skim (milk).

†**sbusare** *tr.* to 'skin', to win (at gambling) all the money of (an opponent).

sbuzz-are [A1] *tr.* (colloq. Tusc.) to draw (fowl); to gut (fish); to disembowel; — un tumore, to lance a tumor; *rfl.* to burst; (of an abscess, etc.) to burst.

scab·bi-a *f.* (med.) scabies; (vet.) scabies, scab. **-ósa** *f.* (bot.) field scabious, *Knautia arvensis*, and other allied plants. **-óso** *adj.* rough; (med.) scabious, affected with scabies; (vet.) pecora **-osa**, a scabby sheep.

†**scabello** *m.* See sgabello.

scabino *m.* (hist. leg.) *scabinus, wardeus.*

scabbióso *adj.* See under scabbia.

scabr-o *adj.* rough; rugged; harsh. **-ézza** *f.* roughness; ruggedness; harshness; (fig., of style) inequality, unevenness, roughness.

scabrós-o *adj.* rugged; unequal; knotty; uneven; (fig.) passo **—**, difficult passage (in an author); affare **—**, scabrous affair, *or* difficult or delicate situation. (**-aménte** *adv.*) **-ità** *f.* roughness; ruggedness; unevenness; inequality; (fig.) scabrousness.

scacato *adj.* (techn.) pale, washed out.

scacazzare [A1] *intr.* (*aux.* avere) (vulg.) to shit; *tr.* to foul, to defile.

scaccato, scaccheggiato *adj.* chequered; check; patterned like a chess-board; chequerboard; (herald.) checky.

scacchi-are [A4] *tr.* (agric.) to prune; to pollard. (**-ato** *part. adj.*) **-atura** *f.* (agric.) pruning; pollarding.

scacch-iera *f.* chessboard; draughtboard. **-iere** *m.* (mil.) terrain; disposizione a **-iere**, ordinanza a **-iere**, échelon formation; (English hist. and finan.) Court of the Exchequer; Cancelliere dello **-iere**, Chancellor of the Exchequer. **-ista** *m., f.* chess-player. **-i·stico** *adj.* pertaining to chess; un torneo **-istico**, a chess tournament.

scac·cia *m. indecl.* (sport) beater.

scacci-are [A3] *tr.* to drive out; to chase away; to expel; to send packing; to dismiss; to 'sack'; to dispel. **-acani** *m. indecl.* blank pistol for frightening dogs off. **-adia·voli** *m. indecl.* (mil. hist.) long-range gun throwing an incendiary projectile. **-afumo** *m. indecl.* (artill.) air blast used in conjunction with a wash-out squirt to clear smoke and smouldering cordite from the breach of a gun after it has fired; (naut.) automatic blow through, operating after a gun has fired. **-aménto** *m.* chasing away; expulsion; dismissal; exile, banishment; rebuff. **-amósche** *m. indecl.* fly-swatter. **-ante** *part. adj.* repellent; rebuffing. **-apasta** *m. indecl.* (paperm.) banger, fillet. **-apensieri** *m. indecl.* pastime; distraction; (mus.) Jew's harp. **-ata** *f.* chasing away; expulsion; dismissal; dispelling. **-ato** *part. adj.* driven out, off; chased away; expelled; dismissed; 'sacked'; exiled, banished; dispelled; *n.m.* exile; outlaw, bandit. (**-atóre** *m.* **-atrice** *f.*) **-óni** *m.pl.* (sport) beaters.

scac-co *m.* (*pl.* **-chi**) square; check; a **-chi**, checked, chequered; flanella grigia a **-chi**, grey-checked flannel; vedere il sole a **-chi**, to see the sun reflected through barred windows, (joc.) to be in prison; subire un grave **—**, to suffer a heavy loss; tenere uno in **—**, to keep someone in check; *pl.* chess. **-comatto** *m.* (chess) checkmate; (mil.) check, block, enclosure.

†**scaciato** *adj.* bianco —, cheese-white, white as cheese.

scad-ere [B I] *intr.* (*aux.* essere) to decline; to sink; to fall off; to decrease; to devolve; (leg.; comm.) to fall due; to expire; to mature; (naut.) to fall to leeward, to drift; to make leeway; — sottovento bordeggiando, to lose ground in spite of tacking; †to fall behind. **-ente** *part. adj.* declining; falling; sinking; going off; fading; poor in quality, below standard; (leg.; comm.) falling due; expiring; consigliere **-ente**, retiring director. **-enza** *f.* (leg.; comm.) maturity; expiration; run; prompt; a breve **-enza**, short dated; a lunga **-enza**, long dated; a vista **-enza**, at sight; cambiali a breve **-enza**, short bills; media **-enza**, average due date; giorni di **-enze**, term days; a breve **-enza**, (fig.) in a short while, before long; a lunga **-enza**, in the long run. **-enza·rio** *m.* (comm.) bill book. **-imento** *m.* decline; falling off; decay, decadence. **-uto** *part. adj.* declined; unhappy; fallen low; run down in health; due; expired; matured; azioni **-ute**, forfeited shares.

†**scaf-a** *f.* boat. †**-are** *intr.* to scull.

scafandro *m.* (naut.) diving apparatus (suit, helmet, bell, etc.); — autonomo e indipendente, breathing apparatus, aqualung; special chamber in which living creatures can live during travel in space-ships; space-suit.

†**scafarda** *f.* basin; bowl.

scaffal-e *m.* bookcase; set of bookshelves; rack; (typ.) composing-frame. **-are** [A I] *tr.* to shelve (books); to fit (a room) with shelves. **-ata** *f.* bookshelf full of books, bookshelf; una **-ata** di romanzi, a bookshelf of novels. **-atura** *f.* putting on to shelves; fitting with shelves; shelving; set of shelves. **-etto** *m. dim.* small shelf; dumb waiter.

†**scaffare**[1] *intr.* to fall from horseback.

†**scaffare**[2] *intr.* to play at odd and even.

†**scafi·glio** *m.* a measure for corn.

scafo *m.* (naut.) hull; — esterno o leggiero, outer hull of a submarine; — resistente, pressure hull; boat, yacht, etc.; caricare a —, to charter 'hull only'; (comm.) hull; ossatura di —, hulk.

scafo-cefali·a *f.* (med.) scaphocephaly. **-cefa·lico** *adj.* scaphocephalic. **-ce·falo** *m.* scaphocephalus.

scafo·id-e *adj.* (anat.) scaphoid. **-ite** *f.* (med.) scaphoiditis.

†**scaggiale** *m.* See **scheggiale**.

scagion-are [A I c] *tr.* to excuse; to exculpate; to justify; *rfl.* to justify oneself. (**-ato** *part. adj.*)

sca·gli-a *f.* (zool.) scale (of a reptile); (archit.) tetto a **-e**, roof covered with small overlapping tiles; (sculp.) chip, flake; (meteor.) scale; (of stone) scabbing; (mil. hist.) mixture of iron shot, grapeshot, chainshot, etc.; crust, coating, layer; (derog., iron.) avere la —, to have a layer of dirt, to be in need of a wash. **-ame** *m.* quantity of scales; heap of flakes, chips, etc.; (bldg.) backing brick. **-etta** *f. dim.* splinter (usu. of stone). **-ona** *f.* (vet.) a mare which has canine teeth. **-osa** *f.* (zool.) scaly. **-oso** *adj.* scaly. **-(u)ola** *f. dim.* of **scaglia**; (miner.) scaglia; (bot.) canary grass, *Phalaris canariensis*; **-uola pelosa**, *Koeleria pubescens*.

scagli-are [A 4] *tr.* to scale; to flake; (sculp.) — il marmo, to chip the marble; to fling, to hurl; to throw; — ingiurie, to hurl insults; *rfl.* to fling oneself, to hurl oneself; **-arsi contro con parole**, to inveigh against; †(naut.) to come off the ground, to refloat. **-amento** *m.* scaling; flaking; hurling; (geol.) flaking. (**-ato** *part. adj.* **-atore** *m.*) **-atrice** *f.* (industr.) flaking machine. **-atura** *f.* (metall.) spalling.

scaglion-e *m.* large step; mountain terrace; (archit.) step, tread (of a staircase); ornamental step (as in a monument); (mil.) armband; a —, in echelon; (vet.) canine teeth of a horse; (herald.) chevron; — in sbarra, chevron issuing from the flank. **-are** [A I c] *tr.* (mil.) to draw up (troops) in echelon formation. **-ato** *part. adj.* (mil.) drawn up in echelon formation; (of ground) in terraces; (herald.) chevronny.

scagn-are [A 5] *intr.* (*aux.* avere) (of a dog) to yelp; to bay, to give tongue. **-o** *m.* yelp, yelping; baying.

scagno[1] *m.* See under **scagnare**.

†**scagno**[2] *m.* high-backed chair; stool, campstool; (comm.) office; counter.

scagnolo *m.* (vet.) side bone.

scagnozz-o *m.* impoverished priest in search of employment; mediocre person, mediocrity, failure, broken-down hack; *adj.* impoverished; broken-down; mediocre; poor, wretched, sorry. **-a** *f.* lazy, idle woman. **-are** [A I] *intr.* (*aux.* avere) (Florence) to go in search of alms or employment (as a priest).

scal-a[1] *f.* staircase; stairs; step; — mobile, escalator, moving staircase; (archit.) staircase, flight of stairs; — bramantesca, external staircase in two wings leading to a central platform; — a chiocciola, lumaca, spiral staircase; — cordonata, ramp with shallow steps at wide intervals; — a volo, — libera, free staircase (i.e. without balustrade or handrail); — a collo, staircase with one side resting against a wall; tromba, pozzo della —, tromba delle **-e**, well of stairs; — a piuoli, ladder; — di fune, — di corda, rope ladder; — a libretto, steps (for reaching library shelves); — porta, — volante, firemen's ladder; (naut.) ladder; — di banda, boat ladder or ship's ladder; — del comandante, Captain's ladder; — reale, starboard gangway; — di bocca porto, hatch ladder; — comune, port gangway; — di combattimento, sea gangway; — biscaglina, Jacob's ladder, chain gangway, jumping ladder; (mil.) scaling tower; (Bibl.) — di Giacobbe, Jacob's ladder; (eccl.) — Santa, the Scala Santa at Rome; (gymn.) — svedese, horizontal bars.

scal-a[2] *f.* scale; proportion; su larga —, su vasta —, on a large scale; su piccola —, on a small scale; order, sequence, series; (mus.) scale, gamut; key; — esatonale, whole-tone scale; — pentatonale, pentatonic scale; (geol.) scale; (geog.) — di mare, whirlpool; (paint.) la — dei colori, the scale of colours (as in the spectrum); (comm.) — di proporzione, — mobile, sliding scale; (econ.) — mobile, cost-of-living index; (radio) — parlante, tuning dial; (naut.) — di marea, tide gauge; — di Beaufort, Beaufort scale. **-i·metro** *m.* (surv.) scale, computing scale.

Scala[3] *pr.n.* (hist.) della Scala, the Scala family, the Scaligers.

Scala[4] *pr.n.f.* Il Teatro alla Scala, the Scala Opera House in Milan.

†**scal-abrino** *m.* rascal, rogue, cunning person. †**-abrone** *m.* see **calabrone**.

scalandrone *m.* (naut.) gangway; landing-stage brow.

scalappiare [A 4] *tr.* to loose from a slip-knot; *intr.* (*aux.* essere) to get free from a slip-knot; (fig.) to escape from a trap (cf. **calappio**).

scal-are[1] [A I] *tr.* to scale; to climb; — le mura di una città, to scale the city walls; to scale down; to graduate; to reduce by degrees; to diminish gradually; — un debito, to pay off a debt in instalments; debito a —, deferred payment; (mil.) to scale, to assault (walls, towers, etc.); (aeron.) to stagger. **-amento** *m.* scaling; climbing; graduating; scaling down; (aeron.) stagger. **-ata** *f.* scaling, climbing; (mil.) scaling, assault; andare alla **-ata**, to undertake a scaling operation; dare la **-ata** a, to scale; (fig.) dare la **-ata** al potere, to make a bid for power; (comm.) dare la **-ata** a una banca, to hold majority shares of a bank to control it. **-ato** *part. adj.* scaled; climbed; graduated; in steps; graded; letture **-ate**, graded reading passages; (fig.) figliuoli **-ati**, children nicely spaced (as to ages in a single family); (paint.) colori ben **-ati**, well-graded colours. **-atore** *m.* climber; mountain climber; rock climber; racing-cyclist specializing in hill-work. (**-atrice** *f.*)

scalare[2] *adj.* pertaining to stairs, staircase or ladder.

scalar-e[3] *adj.* graduated; proportional; done to scale; (comm.) interesse —, diminishing interest. **-mente** *adv.* (mus.) scalewise.

scalariforme *adj.* ladder-shaped; in steps.

scalarmente *adv.* See under **scalare**[3].

scalbatra *f.* (ichth.) rudd, *Scardinius erythrophthalmus*.

scalcagn-are [A 5] *tr.* to wear (shoes) down at the heel; *intr.* (*aux.* avere) to thump with the heels in walking. **-ato** *part. adj.* down at heel; shabby.

scalc-are [A 2] *tr.* to carve (meat, poultry). **-ato** *part. adj.* carved. **-atore** *m.* carver; carving knife. (**-atrice** *f.*)

scalciare [A 3] *intr.* (*aux.* avere) to kick, to be a kicker (e.g. of a mule, etc.).

scalcin-are [A I] *tr.* (bldg.) to knock the plaster off. **-atura** *f.* (bldg.) removal of plaster; bare patch where plaster has broken away. **-azione** *f.* (bldg.) removal of plaster.

scal-co *m.* (*pl.* **-chi**) (hist.) steward; carver; coltello da —, carving knife; (naut.) steward, storekeeper; place where the tow is falling out of a seam (uncaulked). **-cheri·a** *f.* (hist.) stewardship; carving.

scald-are [A I] *tr.* to heat; to warm; to heat up, to warm up; — il latte, to heat the milk; to inflame; to scald; — la testa a, to put ideas into the head of, to excite; — le panche, to sit idle at school; *rfl.* (*acc.* of *prn.* 'si') to warm oneself; to get warm; to become excited, to excite oneself; to become impassioned; non ti —, keep cool, don't get excited, don't get upset, don't worry; (*dat.* of *prn.* 'si') **-arsi** le mani, to warm one's hands; **-arsi** la serpe in seno, to nurture a snake in one's bosom. **-abagno** *m. indecl.* bath-

scald-are (*cont.*)
heater, geyser; **-abagno ad immersione**, immersion heater. **-acolla** *m. indecl.* (carpen.) glue pot. **-aletto** *m. indecl.* warming-pan. **-amani**, **-amano** *m. indecl.* hand-warmer; children's game of putting hand upon hand. **-amento** *m.* heating; warming. **-apanche** *m. indecl.* lazy boy at school. **-apiatti** *m. indecl.* plate-warmer. **-apiedi** *m. indecl.* foot-warmer; hot-water bottle; (rlwy.) underseat heater. **-aran·cio** *m. indecl.* food-warmer. **-aseg·giole** *m. indecl.* idler, lazy-bones. **-ata** *f.* heating; warming; dare una **-ata** alla stanza, to warm, to heat the room (for a short while). (**-ato** *part. adj.* **-atore** *m.* **-atrice** *f.*) **-avivande** *m. indecl.* chafing-dish; dish-warmer. †**-eggiare** *tr.* to heat; to warm. **-ino** *m.* foot-warmer; brazier.

scaldo *m.* skald, scald, an ancient Scandinavian poet.

scale·a *f.* (archit.) flight of steps (usu. before a church or other large building).

scalen-o *adj.* (geom.) scalene; (anat.) scalene; muscolo **—**, scalenus. **-oe·drico** *adj.* (geom.) scalenohedral. **-oe·dro** *m.* (geom.) scalenohedron. **-otomi·a** *f.* (surg.) scalenotomy.

†**scalentare** *tr.* to make red hot; to scald.

scal-e·o *m.* (Tusc.) steps, pair of steps; step-ladder; library steps; stand for holding vases of flowers. **-era** *f.* (archit.) see 'scala bramantesca', under **scala**[1].

scaless-are [A 1] *intr.* (*aux.* avere) to go for joy-rides, to go joy-riding. **-ata** *f.* joy-ride; joy-riding. (Cf. **calesse**.)

scalett-a[1] *f. dim.* of **scala**[1], q.v.; **— a lumaca**, spiral stair; (archit.) steps outside the east end of a church; (techn.) set of holes or projections for fixing adjustable shelves, etc. **-are** [A 1 c] to construct in steps, to build steps into; **-are una collina**, to hew out steps up a hill; to indent (margin, heading, etc.). **-ato** *part. adj.* built in steps; stepped; with steps; indented; inset.

scaletta[2] *f. dim.* of **scala**[2]; (mus.) short scale, run.

†**scalfare** *vb.* and derivs. See **scaldare**.

scalfarotto, scalferotto *m.* foot-muff.

†**scalficcare** *vb.* and derivs. See **scalfire**.

scalf-ire [D 2] *tr.* to scratch; to graze; to wound slightly. (**-ito** *part. adj.*) **-itura** *f.* scratch; graze.

scali·gero[1] *adj.* (mus.) of the Scala Opera House in Milan.

Scali·gero[2] *pr.n.m.* (hist.) member of the Della Scala family, Scaliger; *pl.* (pop.) gli Scaligeri, the Veronese.

scali·metro *m.* See under **scala**[2].

scalin-o *m.* step; stair; rung. **-ata** *f.* flight of steps; (archit.) wide interior staircase; **-ata monumentale**, imposing staircase; (aeron.) formazione a **-ata**, echelon formation. **-ato** *adj.* (herald.) croce **-ata**, cross degraded, cross with each arm ending in degrees.

scallare [A 1] *tr.* to open a pathway through (cf. **calle**).

scalman-a *f.* chill, cold; prendere una **—**, to catch a chill; (fig.) craze, enthusiasm; prendere una **—** per, to develop a craze for. **-are** [A 1] *rfl.* to catch a chill; to get overheated and subsequently chilled; (fig.) to fluster; to worry; to fuss; to wear oneself out; fare le cose senza **-arsi**, to take things in one's stride. **-ata** *f.* hurry; pother, fuss, to-do; ho fatto una **-ata** per arrivare in tempo, I have had a fearful rush to get here in time. **-ato** *part. adj.* suffering from a cold or chill; (fig.) overheated; flustered; out of breath; tutto **-ato**, all hot and bothered. **-atura** *f.* cold; chill; (fig.) fussing; hurrying; pother.

scalm-o *m.* (naut.) rowlock; thole pin; **— a bocca di granchio**, incurving rowlock; **— doppio**, crutch; **— a portello**, rowlock having a poppet; scantling, complex of metal or wooden frames and plates which go to make up a portion of the hull structure. †**-ata** *f.* (naut.) bulwark, nettings. †**-atura** *f.* (naut.) ship's side; strakes where the oars of a galley were supported. **-iere** *m.* (naut.) crutch; **-iere girevole**, **-iere a forcella**, **-iere mobile**, portable crutch (usually brass); porta **-iere**, metal lining of the crutch hole. †**-eri·a** *f.* (naut.) see **scalmata**. **-otto** *m.* (naut.) intermediate frames, light upperwork plates; bulwark; bulkhead.

scal-o *m.* (naut.) port of call; fare **— a**, to call at; **— d'approdo**, calling port; **— capolinea**, port of departure; **— facoltativo**, optional calling port; **— intermedio**, port called at between the start and end of a voyage; landing place; **— merci**, commercial quay; **— passeggieri**, passenger quay; slip, slipway; **— di alaggio traversale**, broadside slip; **— avanzato**, **— vivo**, submerged portion of a slip; **— di raddobbo**, refitting slip; nave allo **—**, ship on the slips; (rlwy.) **— merci**, goods station, freight yard; (aeron.) intermediate stop; volo senza **—**, non-stop flight. **-oc·cio**

m. (naut. hist.) the tiers which permitted three men to work on a galley oar, hence also the name of the type of oar or sweep.

scalogna *f.* bad luck; evil eye; (pop.) che **—**!, what bad luck! **-ato** *adj.* pursued by misfortune. **-one** *m.* one who brings bad luck.

scalogno *m.* (bot.) shallot, *Allium ascalonicum*.

scalona *f. augm.* of **scala**[1], q.v.; long staircase.

scalone *m. augm.* of **scala**[2], q.v.; grand staircase.

scalopp-a, **-ina** *f.* (cul.) escalope; **— di vitello**, *escalope de veau*.

scalpell-o *m.* chisel; scalpel; **— pneumatico**, rock drill, pneumatic drill; l'arte dello **—**, sculpture. **-are** [A 1] *tr.* to chisel; (sculp.) to cancel, to cut away (with the chisel). **-ino** *m.* (sculp.) stone-mason; stone-cutter; (derog.) è uno **-ino** e nulla più, he's only a chiseller (i.e. he is no sculptor).

scalpicci-are [A 3] *intr.* (*aux.* avere) to shuffle one's feet; to tramp; *tr.* to frequent, to tread. **-amento** *m.* shuffling; tramping; sound of footsteps. **-ato** *part. adj.* frequented, trodden.

scalpiccio *m.* continual shuffling of feet; tread of feet; sound of footsteps; scraping with feet; tramping; tramp, tramp.

scalpit-are [A 1 s] *intr.* (*aux.* avere) to paw the ground; **— su**, to trample over; †*tr.* to trample on. (**-amento** *m.*) **-ante** *part. adj.* trampling, galloping; zoccoli **-anti**, pounding hoofs. **-ato** *part. adj.* frequented, trodden, trampled down.

scalpitio *m.* continual trampling; thud of feet.

scalpore *m.* altercation, squabble; row; **— di sciabole**, rattling of sabres; fare **—**, to cause a sensation, to get talked about, *or* to make a fuss, to shout, to raise a loud complaint; tanto **—** per una sciocchezza, a lot of fuss about nothing.

†**scalpro** *m.* See **scalpello**.

scaltr-ire [D 2] *tr.* to sharpen the wits of; to make shrewd, to make knowing; to smarten; *rfl.* to become shrewd; to learn from experience; to become cunning; s'è **-ito** abbastanza, he has learned a thing or two. **-imento** *m.* development in sagacity; smartening of wits; shrewd action; astuteness. **-ito** *part. adj.* smartened (of wits); shrewd, astute; experienced; expert; knowing; cunning; †polished. **-itamente** *adv.* shrewdly; knowingly; cunningly.

scaltr-o *adj.* smart, sharp; alert, awake; astute, shrewd; cunning; crafty; artful. **-amente** *adv.* astutely, shrewdly; cunningly; craftily; artfully. **-ezza** *f.* astuteness, shrewdness; expertness; cunning; craftiness.

†**scalvare** *tr.* to render bald; to lop.

scalz-are [A 1] *tr.* to remove shoes and stockings from; to remove the shoes of; to make barefoot; (techn.) **— un muro**, to under-wash a wall; (fig.) to undermine; **— l'autorità**, to undermine the authority; to remove, to dismiss; **— un dente**, to pull out a tooth; *rfl.* to take off one's shoes and socks; to go about barefoot; (eccl.) to become a discalced religious. **-acane**, **-acani** *m. indecl.* a down-and-out; impoverished, shabby person; mediocrity; quack. **-amento** *m.* taking off of shoes and stockings; (fig.) undermining. **-ato** *part. adj.* barefoot; without shoes or stockings; (vet.) cavallo **-ato**, a horse with hooves which don't shoe easily; (fig.) undermined, threatened; deprived of support. (**-atore** *m.* **-atrice** *f.*) **-atura** *f.* divesting of shoes and socks; pulling off of top-boots; (bldg.) cavity under a wall caused by washing out; (fig.) undermining, threatening.

scalzo *adj.* barefoot, barefooted; andare **—**, andare con i piedi scalzi, to go barefoot; a piedi scalzi, in bare feet; poor; impoverished; (eccl.) *adj.*, *n.m.* discalced (religious, esp. Carmelite); religious who goes barefoot or wears sandals.

†**scamato** *m.* See **camato**.

scambi-are [A 4] *tr.* to exchange; **— regali**, to exchange presents; **— parola**, to exchange a few words; to change; **— le carte in mano**, to shift one's ground; **— moneta**, to change money, to give change for money; (comm.) to trade; to exchange; to mistake; **— una persona per un'altra**, to mistake one person for another; **— il cappello**, to take the wrong hat; *rfl.* to be exchanged; *recip. rfl.* to exchange with each other; to exchange with one another; **-arsi qualche parola**, to have a few words together; **-arsi il saluto**, to greet one another; to be confused, mistaken, for one another. **-amento** *m.* exchanging; exchange; mistaking; mistake, confusion. **-ato** *part. adj.* exchanged; changed; mistaken, confused; occhio **-ato**, swivel eye. **-atore** *m.* (techn.) exchanger; **-atore di calore**, heat exchanger; (chem.) **-atore di ioni**, ion exchanger. **-evole** *adj.* reciprocal; mutual. (**-evolmente** *adv.*) **-evolezza** *f.* reciprocity; mutualness.

scambiẹtt-o m. dim. of **scambio**, q.v.; caper; quick movement of the feet; quick change of step (in dancing). **-are** [A I c] intr. (aux. avere) to caper; to make certain quick changes of step (in dancing).

scam·b-io m. exchange; in —, in exchange; barter; (comm.) trade; libero —, free trade; (mil.) — dei prigionieri, handing over or exchange of prisoners; (biol.) crossing over; (chem.) — di base, base exchange; (chem.) — ionico, ion exchange; error, mistake; confusion; togliere in —, to mistake; substitute; replacement; andare in —, to go as a replacement, to go instead; temporary employee; successor; (rlwy.) points, switch; (rlwy.; trams) — aereo, aerial frog, trolly frog; adv. (Tusc.) — di venire, instead of coming; (S. Ital.) senza eleganza ma, —, con penetrante chiarezza, ungracefully but, on the other hand, clearly and forcibly; instead, on the contrary. **-ista** m. (comm.) trader; libero -ista, free trader; (rlwy.) pointsman.

scamerare [A I s] tr. (leg.) to release; to release from sequestration.

scamerita f. (butcher.) fillet of pork.

scamici-are [A 3] rfl. to take one's jacket off; to be in one's shirt sleeves. **-ato** part. adj. in shirt sleeves; jacketless; (fig., colloq.) subversive in politics; n.m. vulgarian; dangerous radical.

scammellata f. camel-ride, journey on camel-back.

†scamoiare intr. to run away, to flee.

scamọne m. (butcher.) rump; (leatherm.) butt.

sca(m)mon·e·a f. (bot.) scammony, *Convolvulus scammonia*. **-eato** m. (pharm.) medicament containing scammony resin. **-ina** f. (chem.) jalapin, scammonin.

†scamorza f. See **scamozza**.

scamosci-are [A 3] tr. to chamois, to oil-tan. **-ato** part. adj. chamois, oil-tanned. **-atọre** m. chamois leather manufacturer; oil-tanner.

scamọ·scio adj. pelle scamoscia, chamois leather; (zool.) chamois, *Rupicapra rupicapra*.

scamozza f. a kind of cheese.

scamozz-are [A I c] tr. to truncate; to lop the head off; to pollard. **-ato** part. adj. truncated; with head lopped off; pollarded. (**-atura** f.)

†scamoz·zolo m. tiny piece, little bit.

scampa f. (zool.) squat lobster, *Galathea strigosa*; — falsa, *G. rugosa*.

scampafọrca m. indecl. gallows-bird.

scampagn-are [A 5] intr. (aux. avere) to go for a trip to the country; to spend a holiday in the country; to rusticate. **-ata** f. trip to the country; day in the country; picnic; fare una -ata, to go for a day's outing.

scampan-are [A I] intr. (aux. avere) to ring the bells; to chime; to peal; (of a skirt) to be full, to spread out; (motor.) to slap (of a piston); n.m. ringing of bells; peal. **-acciata** f. derisive 'serenade' (see **scampanata**). **-amẹnto** m. (motor.) piston-slap. **-ata** f. peal of bells; derisive 'serenade' with rough instruments for e.g. an ill-matched couple (an expression of social disapproval comparable to the 'skimmity-ride' in Hardy's *Mayor of Casterbridge*). **-ìo** m. continual ringing of bells, incessant chiming.

scampanell-are [A I] intr. (aux. avere) to ring a bell. **-ata** f. ringing of a bell; ring at a door-bell. **-ìo** m. continual loud ringing of bells.

scamp-are [A I] tr. to save; to rescue; to liberate, to free; Dio ce ne -i e liberi!, Heaven forbid!; -arla bella, to have a lucky escape, to escape by the skin of one's teeth; intr. (aux. essere) to come through, to survive; — da una malattia, to come through an illness; to be a survivor; — al naufragio, to be a survivor of a shipwreck; — alla strage, to escape massacre. **-amẹnto** m. rescuing; escaping; survival. **-ato** part. adj. rescued; saved; surviving; n.m. survivor. **†-avi·a** m. (naut.) captain's gig or fast ship's boat.

scampar-ella f. (zool.) squat lobster, *Galathea strigosa*. **-ello** m., **-ẹtto** m. See **scampa**.

scampo m. rescue; liberation; escape; safety; (zool.) Dublin Bay prawn, *Nephrops norvegicus*; — morte, squat lobster, *Galathea rugosa*; pl. (cul.) scampi.

scam·polo m. remnant, piece of cloth left over from a roll; (fig.) — di tempo, spare moment, time left over; (fig.) little person; — d'uomo, undersized man.

†scamuffare vb. and derivs. See **camuffare**.

†scamuz·zolo m. See **scamozzolo**.

†scana f. See **zanna**.

scanal-are [A I] tr. to groove; to channel; (archit.) to flute; (eng.) to spline; intr. (aux. avere) to issue from a canal; (fig.) to cut through red tape. **-ato** part. adj. grooved; (archit.) colonna -ata, fluted column; (herald.) invecked, invected. **-atura** f. grooving; groove; (archit.) flute, fluting; (eng.) spline.

scancellare [A I] and derivs. See **cancellare**.

†scanceri·a f. See **scansia**.

scancìo m. oblique line; adv. phr. di (a, per) —, askew, awry; obliquely; tagliare a —, to cut on the cross; guardare di —, to look askance at.

scanda·gli-o m. (naut.) sounding machine, lead line; sounding; depth of water; — acustico, — ad eco, echo sounding; — comune, — a sagola, lead line; (naut.) — contatore, — a decolorazione, — idrostatico, — a pressione, — a molinello, — meccanico, variants of Thompson's Sounding Gear; — ultrasonoro, — ultra-custico, echo sounding gear; livello di riferimento degli scandagli, chart datum; andare allo —, essere allo —, to proceed on the lead; compiere lo —, to sound; gettare, rotare, lanciare lo —, to heave the lead line; gridare lo —, to call the sounding; navigare sullo —, to be in soundings (under 100 m. or about 55 fathoms); getta lo —!, take a cast!; cessa lo —!, stop soundings; ricupera —!, haul in the line!; ripiglia lo —!, continue sounding!; rientra gli scandagli!, lay in the leads; (fencing) tentative action or move; (comm.) gauge; gauging-rod; (fig.) probe, test. **-are** [A 4] tr. (naut.) to sound; — a!, sound; take a cast!; (fig.) to probe, to test, to sound. **-atọre** m. (naut.) leadsman. **-atrice** f. (naut.) macchina -atrice, sounding machine. **-ẹtto** m. (naut.) handlead, small lead weight.

scandalida f. (bot.) *Tetragonolobus maritimus*.

scan·dal-o m. scandal; calumny; gossip; disgrace, shame; far —, to shock (the public); fare uno —, to stir up scandal; dare — a, to scandalize; mettere —, to spread scandal; gridare allo —, to cry shame. **-izzare** [A I] tr. to scandalize; to outrage; to shock; rfl. to be scandalized; to be shocked. **-izzato** part. adj. scandalized; shocked; corrupted. **-izzatọre** m. scandalous person; one whose behaviour shocks; outrager. (**-izzatrice** f.) **-ọso** adj. scandalous; shocking; outrageous. **-osamẹnte** adv. scandalously; shockingly; outrageously.

scandella f. (bot.) two-rowed barley, *Hordeum distichon*; spelt, *Triticum spelta*.

scan·d-ere[1] [B def.] intr. (poet.) to ascend. **-ẹnte** part. adj. ascending; (bot.) climbing by means of thorns, as roses and brambles.

scan·dere[2] [B def.]. See **scandire**.

scanderọna f. (bot.) clary, *Salvia sclarea*.

†scandescenza f. See **escandescenza**.

scan·dicus m. indecl. (mus.) scandicus (plainchant neume of three ascending notes).

scandi·glio m. a measure of broken stones, i.e. an amount which will cover one square metre to a depth of 25 centimetres.

Scand-ina·via pr.n.f. (geog.) Scandinavia. **-inavo, -i·navo** adj., n.m. Scandinavian. (**-inava, i·nava** f.)

scan·dio m. (chem.) scandium.

scandire [D 2] tr. (lit.) to scan (verse); to pronounce carefully, to articulate; to pronounce distinctly, to articulate.

†scan·dol-a f. shingle, wooden roofing-tile. **†-aro** m. roofer; †captain's cabin in a galley.

†scan·dolo m. See **scandalo**.

scanellare [A I] and derivs. See **scannellare**.

†scanfarda f. chamber pot.

†scangè m. stuff of iridiscent hue, a 'shot' fabric.

†scanidato adj. white.

scann-are [A I] tr. to cut the throat of; to butcher; (fig.) to bleed, to extort money from; (butcher.) to stick (of pig, etc.); (text.) to unwind, to unreel; (hydraul.) — un fosso, to tap a ditch (e.g. for irrigation). **-abecco** m. (techn.) butcher's knife. **-abu·e** m. (lit. hist.) nickname of Aristarchus, adopted by G. Baretti in his *Frusta Letteraria*. **†-ade·o** m. shameless profiteer; pious humbug. **-afosso** m. open culvert; (mil. hist.) culvert from the citadel to the moat. **†-agallo** m. (naut.) scullion. **-amẹnto** m. throat-cutting; butchery. **†-aminestre** m. braggart, swaggering soldier. **-apane** m. indecl. good-for-nothing; person good only at filling his stomach. **-ato** part. adj. butchered, slaughtered; (fig.) bled, robbed; n.m. down-and-out, impoverished person. **-atọio** m. (pop.) slaughterhouse, shambles; (fig.) shop where exorbitant prices are charged; gambling-house. **-atọre** m. cut-throat; assassin; moneylender. (**-atrice** f.) **-atura** f. throat-cutting; butchering, slaughter; sticking (of pigs, etc.). **-auo·mini** m. indecl. moneylender; usurer.

scannell-are [A I] *tr.* to groove; (archit. and applied arts) to flute; (text.) to unwind, to unreel. **-amento** *m.* (art) flute; fluting; (text.) unreeling. (**-ato** *part. adj.*) **-atura** *f.* grooving; channel moulding; (archit.) fluting.

scannello[1] *m.* portable writing-desk; small bench; stool; †(mus.) bridge (of a stringed instrument).

scannello[2] *m.* (butcher.) large cut of beef between the round and the inner part of the hind quarters.

scanno *m.* bench; seat; (eccl.) scanni del coro, choir stalls; (geog.) lake-shore terrace; dune; (naut.) bar; shoal water or sandbank at the entrance to a river, harbour, etc.; captain's seat or cabin in a galley.

†scannonezzare *vb.* and derivs. See **cannoneggiare**.

scanon-icare [A 2 s] *tr.* (eccl.) to deprive of a canonry; *rfl.* to cease to be a canon. **-izzare** [A I] *tr.* to uncanonize, to unsaint.

†scanoscente *adj.* See **sconoscente**.

scans-are [A I] *tr.* to avoid; to shun; to escape, to escape from; to remove; *rfl.* to move aside; to withdraw; to get out of the way; to move to one side. **-afatiche** *m. indecl.* slacker, shirker. **-amento** *m.* avoidance; withdrawing, moving aside. **-arote** *m.* bollard by a doorway to prevent damage by cart wheels. **-ato** *part. adj.* avoided; shunned; escaped. (**-atore** *m.* **-atrice** *f.*)

scansi-a *f.* bookcase; set of shelves; cupboard.

scansione *f.* scansion, scanning (of verse); articulation, distinct utterance (of words, syllables); †manual of prosody; (telev.) scanning.

scanso *m.* avoidance; *prep. phr.* a — di, (in order) to avoid; a — di pericoli, to avoid danger; excuse; pretext; †(naut.) lull, let up of wind or rain.

scantinare [A I] *intr.* (*aux.* avere) (mus.) to go out of tune; (fig.) to speak out of turn, to be indiscreet, to let something slip; to stray from the path of virtue; to fail to fulfil an obligation.

scantinato *m.* cellar, basement.

†scan-tolo *m.* doorpost.

scanton-are [A I c] *tr.* to round the corners of; to cut off the corners of; (fig.) to avoid, to give the slip to; to dog's-ear (a page of a book); *intr.* (*aux.* avere) to turn a corner; (fig.) to take a wrong turning; *rfl.* to break off at the corners. **-amento** *m.* trimming off corners; avoiding; avoidance; dog's-earing; turning a corner. **-ato** *part. adj.* avoided, shunned; dog's-eared. **-atura** *f.* rounding of corners, cutting off corners; avoiding, avoidance; giving the slip; dog's-earing.

scantucci-are [A 3] *tr.* to cut the edges off; — il pane, to cut the crusts off bread. **-ato** *part. adj.* having the edges removed; pane **-ato**, bread with the crusts cut off.

scanzonato *adj.* free and easy; easy-going; informal.

scapaccion-e *m.* clout on the head; slap, smack; prendere a **-i**, to clout, to slap; passare a —, to get in free (at a theatre, etc.); passare agli esami a —i, to pass exams by sheer good luck. **-are** [A I c] *tr.* to clout; to slap.

scap-are [A I] *tr.* to decapitate, to behead; to cut off the head of; *rfl.* (fig.) to lose one's head; to worry; to rack one's brains. **-amento** *m.* decapitating, beheading; worry, fret, anxiety. **-atag-gine** *f.* heedlessness; recklessness; thoughtless action; light-headed behaviour. **-ato** *part. adj.* decapitated, beheaded; (fig.) irresponsible, thoughtless; flighty; *adv. phr.* alla **-ata**, thoughtlessly; recklessly. (**-atamente** *adv.*) **-atone** *m.* thoughtless person; flighty person. (**-atona** *f.*)

scapecchi-are [A 4 c] *tr.* (text.) to hackle (flax). (**-ato** *part. adj.*) **-atoio** (text.) hackle, hackler; **-atoio** di sgrosso, rougher hackler, long ruffer. **-atore** *m.* (text.) flax hackler. **-atrice** *f.* (text.) flax hackling machine. **-atura** *f.* (text.) hackling (of flax).

†scapestrare *intr.* to live dissolutely; *rfl.* to slip one's head out of the halter; (fig.) to rush to one's ruin.

scapestrat-o *adj.* wild; dissolute; reckless; cavallo —, unbroken horse; *adv. phr.* alla **-a**, wildly; dissolutely; *n.m.* madcap; scapegrace; dare-devil. (**-amente** *adv.*) **-aggine** *f.* dissoluteness; dissolute life; wild behaviour; recklessness; rash action.

scapezz-are [A I c] *tr.* to prune; to lop; to pollard. **-amento** *m.* pruning; lopping; pollarding. **-o** *m.* pruning; lopping; pollarding; section; fragments; stump.

†scapezzone *m.* See **scapaccione**.

scapigli-are [A 4] *tr.* to dishevel; to ruffle, to rumple; *rfl.* to become dishevelled; to rumple one's hair; (fig.) to lead a dissolute life. **-ata** *f.* (bot.) love-in-a-mist, *Nigella damascena*. **-ato** *part. adj.*

dishevelled; ruffled, rumpled; (fig.) dissolute; disorderly; irregular; unconventional (also *n.m.*) **-atura** *f.* dissoluteness; loose living; free and easy manners; bohemianism; (lit. hist.) La Scapigliatura, an Italian literary clique of the middle of the nineteenth century composed chiefly of writers of N. Italy.

scapit-are [A I s] *intr.* (*aux.* avere) to suffer loss, to lose; in questo affare ci -o, I lose by this transaction; — di credito, to lose credit; — nella stima, to go down in (people's) esteem. †**-amento** *m.* see **scapito**.

sca-pito *m.* loss; detriment; damage; *prep. phr.* a — di, to the detriment of, at the sacrifice of; tutta questa attività sportiva va a — dello studio, so much time spent on sport means that one's work suffers; (comm.) loss.

scapo *m.* (archit.) shaft of a column; imo —, base of a shaft; (bot.) scape.

scapocchi-are [A 4] *tr.* to take off the head of. **-ato** *part. adj.* headless, lacking a head.

sca-pol-a *f.* (anat.) scapula. **-are** *adj.* (anat.) scapular; cingolo **-are**, shoulder girdle; *n.m.* (rel.) scapular.

scapol-are [A I s] *intr.* (*aux.* avere; *prep.* a) to escape; to flee; **-arsela**, to do a bunk; *tr.* to get out of, to avoid, to escape; **-arla bella**, to escape by the skin of one's teeth; (metall.) to strike (when die-stamping), to fuller; (naut.) to let (a rope or cable) run free; to double (a cape, shoal, etc., i.e. when a ship has passed some danger); to avoid (a gale, etc.). **-atura** *f.* (metall.) striking, fullering.

scapolite *f.* (miner.) scapolite, wernerite.

sca-pol-o *adj.* single, unmarried (of a man); free, untrammelled; *n.m.* bachelor; appartamento da —, bachelor flat; (naut. hist.) freeman in a galley. **-one** *m.* crusty old bachelor; gay bachelor.

scapolopessi *f.* (surg.) scapulopexy.

scapon-ire [D 2] *tr.* to make docile, to persuade, to coax. **-ito** *part. adj.* persuaded; won over.

scapp-are [A I] *intr.* (*aux.* essere) to escape; to flee; to run away; to be off; to take to one's heels; to hurry away; — a casa, to hurry home; — dalla prigione, to break out of prison; — di mano ai birri, to elude the police; to be bursting; — dall'impazienza, to be bursting with impatience; — a ridere, to burst out laughing; to slip out; m'è **-ata**!, I said it without meaning to!; — dalla mente, to slip one's memory; **-arsene**, to take to one's heels. **-a** *adv. phr.* a **-a** e fuggi, in a great hurry, all in a rush. **-amento** *m.* escaping, escape; (watchm.) escapement; **-amento** a caviglie, pin escapement; **-amento** a cilindro, cylinder escapement; (motor.; aeron.) exhaust; **-amento** libero, open cutout; tubo di **-amento**, exhaust pipe; (mus.) escapement (in pianoforte action); escape (of gas). **-ante** *part. adj.* escaping; fleeing; (Tusc.) maniche **-anti**, very short sleeves. **-ata** *f.* escape; flight; run; dare una **-ata** al farmacista, to run over to the chemist's; escapade; outing; brief visit; excursion; outburst; *bon mot*; *adv. phr.* di **-ata**, hastily. **-ato** *part. adj.* escaped; fled; missing; cavallo **-ato**, run-away horse. **-atoia** *f.* subterfuge; evasion; pretext; bluff; clausola **-atoia**, escape clause. **-atore** *m.* fugitive; *adj.* fleet, fast; cavallo **-atore**, fast horse. **-atrice** *f.*) **-avi-a** *m. indecl.* hurry, rush; *adv. phr.* fare le cose a **-avia**, to do things in a tearing hurry; (naut. hist.) warship armed with a bow chaser (under Ferdinand III).

scappell-are [A I] *rfl.* to raise one's hat; *tr.* to greet, to lift one's hat to; (orn.) to unhood (a hawk); (naut.) to unrig (a mast); to take off (ropes, shrouds, etc.); to take off (the cable) from the bits. **-ata** *f.* salutation, greeting (by raising one's hat); bow. (**-ato** *part. adj.*) **-atura** *f.* flourish of one's hat; gesture of exaggerated respect.

scappellott-o *m.* cuff; slap; prendere a **-i**, to cuff, to slap; passare con lo —, to get in free; to pass (an exam) owing to the indulgence of the examiners; (cinem.; eng.) trasporto a —, dog movement, plunger movement. **-are** [A I] *tr.* to cuff; to slap.

†scapperuc-cio *m.* hood.

scap-pia *f.* broken stones, rubble.

†scappiare *tr.* to unloose.

†scappino *m.* sole of a stocking; 'mask' (see **maschera**) of the Commedia dell'Arte, representing a crafty servant (the origin of Molière's Scapin); cunning individual.

scapponata *f.* meal of capons; (Tusc.) peasants' feast in celebration of the birth of an eldest son.

scappottare [A I] *intr.* (*aux.* avere) (at piquet and other games) to save a capot.

scappucciare[1] [A3] *tr.* to remove the hood from; to lift the hood off.

scappucci·are[2] [A3] *intr.* (*aux.* avere) to stumble; to trip; (fig.) to blunder. **~ata** *f.* stumble; dare una ~ata, to stumble; (fig.) blunder.

scappuc·cio *m.* stumble; (fig.) blunder; mistake.

†**scaprestare** *vb.* and derivs. See **scapestrare**.

scapricciare [A3] *tr.* to gratify the whim of; *rfl.* to indulge oneself, to gratify one's whims.

scapriccire [D2]. See **scapricciare**.

scapruggin·are [A1s] *tr.* (techn.) to break (a cask) by tearing the ends from the notches in the staves. **~ato** *part. adj.* (techn.) (of barrels) with the ends forced out of the notches.

scapsulazione *f.* (med.) decapsulation.

scarabat·tol·o *m.*, **~a** *f.* (Tusc.) showcase; china cabinet; geegaw, knick-knack; snowshoe.

scarabe·o *m.* (ent.) scarab beetle; — rinoceronte, Rhinoceros beetle, *Oryctes* spp.; (archaeol.) scarab.

scarabillare [A1] *tr.* (mus.) to strum on, to thrum (a plucked instrument).

scarabina *f.* (ichth.) shad, *Clupea alosa*.

scarabocchi·are [A4] *tr.* to scribble on, to scrawl over; — un libro, to scribble on a book; to scribble; ho ~ato una risposta, I've scribbled a reply; to jot down. **~ato** *part. adj.* scribbled; scrawled; scribbled on; scrawled over. **~atore** *m.* scribbler. (**~atrice** *f.*) **~atura** *f.* scribbling, scribble; scrawl. **~one** *m.* scribbler. (**~ona** *f.*)

scaraboc·chio *m.* scribble; scrawl; doodle blot.

scarac·chi·o *m.* phlegm. **~are** [A4] *intr.* (*aux.* avere) to cough up phlegm, to spit phlegm. **~one** *m.* person who coughs and hawks up phlegm.

scarafag·gio *m.* (ent.) — delle cucine, cockroach, *Blatta orientalis*; — della patata, Colorado beetle, *Leptinotarsa decemlineata*.

†**scarafaldone** *m.* hired ruffian or assassin.

†**scaraffare** *tr.* to seize and rush away with.

scaramanzi·a *f.* magic to offset the power of the evil eye.

scaramazza *adj. f.* perla —, blister pearl.

†**scarami·a** *f.* (naut.) caulker's tool-box; also used as a stool.

scaramuc·ci·a[1] *f.* (mil.) skirmish; (fig.) brush; polemical discussion, controversy. **~are** [A3] *intr.* (*aux.* avere) to skirmish; †*rfl.* to defend oneself. **~atore** *m.* (mil.) skirmisher.

Scaramu·ccia, Scaramuzza *pr.n.m.* (theatr.) character of a swaggering soldier in the Commedia dell'Arte, Scaramouche.

scaravent·are [A1] *tr.* to hurl, to fling; — un pugno, to let fly with one's fist; *rfl.* to hurl oneself; to hurtle. (**~ato** *part. adj.*)

scarbon·are [A1c] *tr.* to remove charcoal from (the pit). **~atura** *f.* removing charcoal from the pit.

scarcer·are [A1s] *tr.* to release from prison; to set free. **~amento** *m.* setting free; freeing from prison. **~ato** *part. adj.* released from prison; set free; 'out'. **~azione** *f.* release from prison; setting free; liberation.

†**scarciume** *m.* vile or putrid thing or person.

†**scarco** *adj.* See **scarico**.

scarda *f.* (bot.) sea-lettuce, *Ulva*.

scardaccione *m.*, **scardac·cio** *m.* (bot.) creeping thistle, *Cirsium arvense*; teasel, *Dipsacus fullonum*.

scardare [A1] *tr.* to husk (chestnuts).

scardass·are [A1] *tr.* (text.) to card. (**~ato** *part. adj.*) **~atore** *m.* (text.) carder. **~atura** *f.* (text.) carding. **~o** *m.* (text.) card.

scardiccione *m.* (bot.). See **scardaccione**.

scardinare[1] [A1s] *tr.* to take (e.g. a door) off its hinges; to unhinge; (fig.) to render unstable; to undermine (cf. **cardine**).

scardinare[2] [A1s] *tr.* (text.; hatmaking) to card (fur).

scar·dola *f.* (ichth.) rudd, *Scardinius erythrophthalmus*.

scardon·are [A1c] *tr.* (techn.) to deburr. **~amento** *m.* (techn.) deburring. (**~ato** *part. adj.*)

scar·dova *f.* (ichth.) a freshwater fish related to the rudd, *Scardinius scardafa*.

scarducciare [A3] *tr.* to strip (artichokes) of prickly foliage.

scarduffare [A1] *tr.* to ruffle, to rumple; *rfl.* to become ruffled; to get dishevelled.

†**scareg·gi·o** *m.* annoyance; disgust. †**~oso** *adj.* disgusting, revolting.

scar·gia *f.* (bot.) water soldier, *Stratiotes aloides*.

sca·rica *f.* unloading; discharge (of firearms); motion (of the bowels); (electr.) discharge, flashover, jump spark; scariche elettriche, the electric chair; (fig.) load, heap; flood; — di ingiurie, flood of insults.

scaric·are [A2s] *tr.* to unload; to discharge; — il ventre, to empty the bowels; (finan.) to discharge; (naut.) to discharge, to unload, to unship; — le merci, to discharge cargo; to trice up the yards when going about; — di, to relieve of; to shoot (a gun); to let fly (an arrow); to unburden; to lighten; — addosso a, to unload on to; (fig.) to put on to; *rfl.* to get wound down, to run down (of a spring, etc.); to relieve oneself; to acquit oneself; to deliver oneself; to discharge; to flow. **~abarili** *m. indecl.* children's game of lifting each other standing back to back, arms entwined; (fig.) fare a ~abarili, essere uno ~abarili, to throw the responsibility on someone else, to 'pass the buck'. **~ala·sino** *m. indecl.* children's game of carrying each other pick-a-back. **~amento** *m.* unloading; discharging; (comm.) lighterage; (rlwy.) piano di ~amento, unloading platform. **~ato** *part. adj.* unloaded; discharged; relieved; unburdened; run down; not wound up; (comm.) discharged; fallito ~ato, discharged bankrupt. **~atoia** *f.* spring-trap. **~atoio** *m.* unloading place, dump; depot; (hydr. eng.) ~atoio delle acque, spillway; (archit.) gutter. **~atore** *m.* unloader; docker; dumper; lighterman; (text.) doffer (of carding machine); (hydr.) ~atore d'acqua, water trap; ~atore di superficie, spillway; (electr.) discharger, arrester; ~atore a corna, horn gap arrester; ~atore ad intervallo, surge gap; (archit.) gutter; (mus.) wind trunk (of organ). (**~atrice** *f.*) **~atura** *f.* unloading; discharging.

scari·co *adj.* (*m.pl.* ~chi) unloaded; not loaded; empty; not wound up, run down; discharged; (fig.) clear, serene, untroubled; occhi ~chi, clear eyes; cielo —, clear sky, cloudless sky; lightened; unburdened; colore —, light colour; (of a horse) — di gamba, swift, nimble; (colloq.) capo —, madcap; *n.m.* unloading; —, dump, rubbish-dump, refuse-tip; baroccio di —, dust cart; (bldg.) arco di —, relieving arch; tubo di —, drainpipe; evacuation, motion (of the bowels); extenuation, justification, excuse; a suo —, in his defence; testimoni di —, witnesses for the defence; lightening, unburdening; a — di coscienza, to ease one's conscience; (comm.) bolletta di —, unloading bill; iniziare lo —, to break bulk; mandato di —, freight release; (leg.) — coattivo, compulsory drainage (C.C.); demurrage, unloading time; cargo discharged; (eng.) undercutting (of a cog); (motor.) exhaust; collettore di —, exhaust manifold; tubo di —, exhaust pipe.

scarific·are [A2s] *tr.* (surg.; agric.) to scarify. (**~ato** *part. adj.*) **~atore** *m.* (surg.) scarifier; (civ. eng.; agric.) scarifier, rooter, ripper. **~azione** *f.* (surg.) scarification.

scariola *f.* (bot.) prickly lettuce, *Lactuca serriola*.

scarite *m.* (ent.) *Scarites arenarius*, a large beetle living on sandy beaches round the Mediterranean.

scarlatt·o *adj.* scarlet; farsi — in viso, to turn scarlet, to blush a bright red; rosso —, bright scarlet; *n.m.* scarlet, the colour scarlet; scarlet cloth; doctor's gown; (provb.) dare — per bigello, to give as good as one receives; cucire lo — al velluto, to join things that do not go well together. **~ina** *f.* (med.) scarlatina, scarlet fever. **~ino** *adj.* scarlet; (med.) febbre ~ina, scarlet fever. **~ino·ide** *adj.* (med.) similar to scarlatina.

scarle·a, scarleggia *f.* (bot.) *Salvia sclarea*.

scarlin·a, ~e *f.* (bot.) *Lupsia Galactites*, a species of thistle.

†**scarma·glia** *f.* See **schermaglia**, under **scherma**.

†**scarman·a** *f.* see **scalmana**. †**~ato** *adj.* see **scalmanato**.

scarmigli·are [A4] *tr.* to ruffle; to rumple; *rfl.* to tear one's hair (with grief, rage, etc.). **~ato** *part. adj.* ruffled; dishevelled. (**~atura** *f.*)

Scarmiglione *pr.n.m.* Scarmiglione, one of the devils in Dante's *Inferno*, Canto XXI (cf. **scarmigliare**).

†**scarmo** *m.* See **scalmo**.

scarn·are [A1] *tr.* to strip the flesh from; (tanning) to flesh; *rfl.* to grow thin, to lose flesh. **~amento** *m.* stripping of flesh; (tanning) fleshing. **~ato** *part. adj.* stripped of flesh; (tanning) fleshed, thin, emaciated; †flesh-coloured. **~atoio** *m.* (tanning) fleshing knife. **~atrice** *f.* (tanning) fleshing machine. **~atura** *f.* (tanning) fleshing.

scarnascial·are, scarnescial·are [A1] *intr.* (*aux.* avere) to hold carnival; to live riotously, to make merry. **~ata** *f.* revelry, merry-making; orgy.

scarnicciare [A3] *tr.* (tanning) to flesh.

scarnific·are [A2s] *tr.* to tear flesh from; to lacerate. **~ato** *part. adj.* torn, mutilated, mauled. (**~azione** *f.*)

scarn·ire [D2] *tr.* to strip the flesh from; to make lean; (foundry) — l'anima, to scrape the core of a mould. **~ito** *part. adj.* stripped of flesh; made lean; thin, emaciated. **~itoio** *m.* (bookb.) paring knife. **~o** *adj.* thin; lean; viso ~o, lean countenance, thin face; (fig.) meagre.

scarnovalare [A I]. See **scarnascialare**.

scarọgna *f.* See **scalogna**.

scarognare [A 5 c] *intr.* (*aux.* avere) to slack, to work half-heartedly.

scarognire [D 2] *tr.* to cure of laziness, to wake up, to jerk up; *rfl.* to pull oneself together, to stop slacking.

scarola *f.* (bot.). See **scariola**.

†**scaronzare** [A I] *intr.* (*aux.* essere) (naut.) to drift, to be set (by a current).

scarp-a *f.* shoe; ‑e col tacco alto, high-heeled shoes; ‑e con la fibbia, buckle-shoes; ‑e da passeggio, walking-shoes; ‑e coi laccetti, lace-up shoes; ‑e alte, boots; ‑e rotte, shoes in need of repair; ‑e che ridono, ‑e che hanno fame, shoes with the soles flapping; (colloq.) fare le ‑e a, to carry tales about, to report (a person) to his superiors, to ‘tell on’; mettere le ‑e al sole, to ‘turn one’s toes up’, to die; morire con le ‑e ai piedi, to die a violent death; non aver ‑e ai piedi, to run barefoot, to be very poor; rimetterci anche le ‑e, to have had all one’s trouble for nothing; aver le ‑e solate di bucce di cocomero, to slip and slide, to be unable to stand up; è meglio consumar le ‑e che le lenzuola, it’s better to wear out than rust out; avere il giudizio sotto le suole delle ‑e, to have no sense; ‑e grosse e cervello fino, i.e. a peasant is often more intelligent than he looks; drag (on a carriage wheel); skid (on a car wheel); (archit., of a wall) a —, inclined, sloping, with projecting footings; escarpment; (eng.) head (of spring or spoke); (electr.) — polare, pole shoe; (mining) — di trivellazione, spudding shoe; (bldg.) scarp; muro di —, scarp wall; (naut.) —dell’ancora, anchor bed; (ichth.) see **carpa**. ‑a·io *m.* street-vendor of shoes and slippers. ‑ante *m.* (pop.) Conventual Franciscan. ‑are [A I] *tr.* to build in escarpments; to attach a skid to; to attach a drag to; (naut.) to bed down (an anchor). ‑aro *m.* see **scarpaio**. ‑ata *f.* slap with a slipper; (bldg.) escarpment; scarp; (rlwy.; civ. eng.) embankment, slope; (geog.) ‑ata continentale, continental shelf. ‑ato *part. adj.* built in escarpments; sloping; fitted with a skid; fitted with a drag. ‑atore *m.* thief; poacher. ‑ẹtta *f. dim.* of **scarpa**; baby’s shoe; ‑ette da ballo, dancing-shoes, pumps, ballet-shoes; (zool.) small cuttlefish. ‑icciare [A 3] and deriv. see **scalpicciare**. ‑ina *f. dim.* of **scarpa**; baby’s shoe. ‑inare [A I] *intr.* (*aux.* avere) (slang) to walk, to wear out shoe-leather, to tramp. ‑inata *f.* long tramp. ‑ino *m. dim.* of **scarpa**; dainty shoe; evening shoe; dancing shoe. ‑oncello *m.* leather bootee, (woman’s) snowboot. ‑ọne *m. augm.* of **scarpa**; ski-boot; (colloq.) boor, lout, clodhopper; *pl.* Alpine troops.

scarpello *m.* (pop.). See **scalpello**.

scarpiọne (zool.). See **scorpione**, or **scazzone**.

†**scarrier-a** *f.* gente di —, vagabonds; comprare, vendere per —, to buy or sell in some irregular way or by some lucky chance. †‑are *intr.* to run about; to career about.

scarroc·cio *m.* (naut.) drift, leeway; †error on course made good; angolo di —, drift angle, difference between course steered and made good; pinna di —, leeboard; andare in —, to go adrift; to be adrift.

scarrozz-are [A I] *tr.* to take out for a drive in a carriage; *intr.* (*aux.* avere) to go for a drive in a carriage. ‑ata *f.* drive in a carriage. ‑io *m.* continual rumble of carriage wheels; coming and going of carriages.

scarrucol-are [A I s] *intr.* (*aux.* avere) to run (of a rope, etc. on a pulley); to reeve; (joc.) to trill, to sing a cascade of notes; *tr.* to unreeve. ‑amẹnto *m.* reeving, strand (of belt or rope). ‑ante *part. adj.* reeving, passing (over a pulley). ‑ato *part. adj.* unreeved, slipped off pulley. ‑io *m.* running of pulley-block; (joc.) trill, cascade of notes. ‑ọne *m.* slip; blunder.

scarruff-are [A I] *tr.* (Tusc., fam.) to dishevel; to rumple; to ruffle. ‑ato *part. adj.* dishevelled; rumpled; ruffled; tutto ‑ato, *or* coi capelli ‑ati, dishevelled, with ruffled hair.

scarsell-a *f.* purse, wallet; (pilgrim’s) scrip; avere il granchio alla ‑ella, to be miserly; (mil. hist.) mail apron. ‑ac·cio *m.* (mil. hist.) apron covering from belt to knees. ‑are [A I] *tr.* (naut., Genoa) to serve (a rope). ‑atura *f.* (naut.) parcelling. ‑ọna *f. augm.*, ‑ọne *m. augm.* large bag or sack.

scars-o *adj.* scarce; scanty; scant; slight, trifling; inadequate; poor; rare; short; insufficient; veste ‑a, tight, short dress; raccolto —, poor harvest; tempi ‑i, times of poverty; annata ‑a, lean year; acque ‑e, low level of water; — a quattrini, short of money, hard up; — d’ingegno, lacking in intelligence; nutrimento —, insufficient nourishment; tre miglia ‑e, a bare three miles; peso —,

short weight; misura ‑a, short measure; thin, spare, lean; luce ‑a, faint light; colpo —, blow that does not get home; mean, careful, stingy; — nel parlare, grudging; — a credere, slow to believe; (naut.)vento —, light airs, insufficient wind; *adv.* andare —, to be mean, to be careful with money; *n.m.* scarcity; famine. (‑amẹnte *adv.*) ‑eggiare [A 3 c] *intr.* (*aux.* essere) to be scarce; to be in short supply; (naut., of the wind) to back, *or* to veer (to the detriment of a ship); (*prep.* a) to be in need (of), to be short (of), ‑eggiare a denari, to be short of money; (*prep.* di) to be deficient (in); ‑eggiare di buon senso, to lack common sense; (*prep.* in) to be mean (with), to be grudging (of), to grudge; ‑eggiare nelle lodi, to stint praise. ‑ẹzza *f.* scarcity, scarceness; shortage; lack; insufficiency; ‑ezza d’ingegno, lack of intelligence; ‑ezza di mezzi, insufficient means. ‑ità *f.* scarcity; c’è grande ‑ità di frutta, fruit is very scarce.

scartabell-are [A I] *tr.* to turn over (the pages of a book), to leaf through, to thumb, to skim, to skip; to go through the documents in (a case, or file). (‑ato *part. adj.* ‑atore *m.* ‑atrice *f.*)

scartafac·cio *m.* scribbling block; rough paper; (joc.) magnum opus; (comm.) waste book.

scart-are [A I] to unwrap, to remove the paper from; to discard; to reject; to put on one side; to set apart, to be discarded; (mil.) — uno alla leva, to fail someone in the medical test for military service; (cards) to discard; (comm.) — moneta, to garble coin; *intr.* (*aux.* avere) (of a horse) to swerve, to side-step; (of a car) to skid; (football) to dribble; (naut.) to set; *rfl.* to be set laterally off one’s course. ‑amẹnto *m.* discarding; swerving; skid; (rlwy.) gauge; ‑amento normale, standard gauge; ‑amento ridotto, narrow gauge; (motor.) track; (fig.) a ‑amento ridotto, in dribs and drabs; meanly. ‑ata *f.* discarding; rejection; reproof; (of a horse) swerve; (of a car) skid. ‑ato *part. adj.* discarded; rejected; *n.m.* (mil.) reject from military service, ‘C3’. ‑atore *m.* (techn.) sorter. ‑o *m.* discarding; putting aside; roba di ‑o, stuff to be thrown out; (cards) gli ‑i, the cards discarded; a form of the game of charades in which a new word is found by discarding a letter or syllable of a previous one, e.g. ve[na]le, vele; *pl.* refuse, scrap, waste; (fig.) mettere fra gli ‑i, to attach no importance to; swerve; skid; (post office) sorting; (football) dribbling; (naut.) set. ‑occiare [A 3] *tr.* to unwrap; to take the wrappings off; (agric.) to strip (maize). (‑occiatura *f.*) ‑oc·cio *m.* (colloq.) wrapping, wrapper; (archit.) cartouche; scroll-ornament; (mil.) cartridge case. ‑ozzo *m.* (mil.) see **scartoccio**.

scartof·fia *f.* (derog.) rubbishy old papers.

scas-are [A I] *tr.* to turn out (lodger, tenant); to evict; *intr.* (*aux.* avere) to move house. ‑ato *part. adj.* homeless; turned out of house and home; evicted; without a roof to one’s head.

sca·şimo *m.* (Tusc., fam.) smirk (cf. **spasimo**).

scass-are[1] [A I] *tr.* to unbale; to unpack; to force open, to break open; — la serratura, to force the lock; (agric.) to break up (ground). ‑a *f.* (naut.) base, footing of a mast; bed plate of an engine, boiler or capstan; (Venice) shortening of a reefed sail. ‑ata *f.* unpacking, unbaling; breaking open; forcing; (agric.) breaking up of ground. ‑ato *part. adj.* unpacked, emptied; forced open; cancelled, deleted; (agric.) broken up, newly dug; (colloq.) broken-down, dilapidated (esp. of old vehicles); *n.m.* (agric.) ground newly dug. ‑atore *m.* unpacker, unloader; one who breaks in, or forces, a lock; house-breaker. (‑atrice *f.*) ‑atura *f.* unpacking, unloading, emptying (of packing-cases, bales, etc.). ‑ọne *m.* (colloq.) dilapidated old lorry.

scassare[2] [A I] *tr.* to cancel, to delete (cf. **cassare**).

scassettare [A I c] *tr.* to empty (boxes, drawers, etc.); (Tusc. colloq.) to clean out (of money); mi hai scassettato, you’ve left me without a bean.

scassin-are [A I] *tr.* to pick the lock of; to force the lock of; to break up (earth); — le lastre della strada, to dig up the path, to take up the paving stones; *n.m.* house-breaking. (‑ato *part. adj.*) ‑atore *m.* house-breaker. (‑atura *f.*)

scasso *m.* breaking open; forcing; breaking into; burglary; forcible entry; (leg.) forcing of lock, chest, cash-box, etc., in order to commit larceny; (naut.) tabernacle, aperture in the deck allowing the mast to be held in position.

†**scastagnare** *intr.* to be evasive; to break one’s word; to behave dishonestly.

scatafa·scio *adv. phr.* andare in —, to go to pieces.

scatapecchiamẹnto *m.* slum-clearance.

scatapu·z-ia, -za, *f.* (bot.) catapuzia, caper spurge, *Euphorbia lathyris.*

scataro·scio *m.* (pop.) downpour, deluge.

scatarr-are [A I] *intr.* (*aux.* avere) to expectorate, to cough up phlegm. **-ata** *f.* act of expectorating; fare una -ata, to cough up phlegm. **-one** *m.* person with a heavy cough. (**-ona** *f.*)

scatarzo *m.* (text.) floss silk.

scaten-acciare [A 3] *intr.* (*aux.* avere) to unbolt a door, to draw back the bolts; to rattle chains. **-ac·cìo** *m.* continual rattling of chains.

scaten-are [A I] *tr.* to unchain; (fig.) to let loose; to unleash; to give rise to; to set off; *rfl.* to free oneself from chains; to be set free; (fig.) to be unleashed; to break loose; to break out; to burst forth. **-amento** *m.* unchaining; freeing; unleashing; loosing; setting free. **-ato** *part. adj.* unchained; freed; let loose; diavolo -ato, devil let loose; venti -ati, violent tempest; (mus.) cracked (referring to a broken lute or guitar), 'coming off the glue'. **-io** *m.* rattling of chains.

sca·tol-a *f.* box; tin; can; — da cappelli, hat-box; — di fiammiferi, match-box; box of matches; — per i biscotti, biscuit tin; — di biscotti, box (or tin) of biscuits; — di tabacco, tobacco jar; carne in -a, tinned meat; lettere di —, block capitals; (eng.) box, casing, housing; (mus.) — armonica, musical box; (mil.) — di mitraglia, pellet chamber; (anat.)—cranica, cranium; *pl.*(euphem.)testicles; (fig.) rompere le -e a, to importune, to be a nuisance to, to bore. **-a·io, -aro** *m.* box-maker. **-ame** *m.* tinned food (collectively). **-ino** *m. dim.* of **scatola**; -ino per gli occhiali, spectacle-case; -ino delle gioie, jewel-case; sembrare uscito da uno -ino, to look as though just turned out of a bandbox.

scatol-ogi·a *f.* scatology. **-o·gico** *adj.* scatological; (fig.) filthy.

scatramare [A I] *tr.* to de-tar, to de-pitch.

scatt-are [A I] *intr.* (*aux.* essere, avere) to spring up; — in piedi, to spring to one's feet, to leap up; (of a spring) to be released, to go off; (of a gun) to go off; to burst out; — a dire, to burst out saying; (of the hour) to strike; (of time) to go by; to differ, to diverge; (Tusc.) non ci -a nulla, it's all the same; ci è -ato poco che..., it almost happened that...; *abs.* (cinem.) to shoot; *tr.* to mistake; to miss out; senza — una nota, without playing a wrong note; (photog.) to release; to take, to snap. **-adata** *m. indecl.* (watchm.) date jumper. **-afasi** *m. indecl.* (watchm.) moon phase jumper. **-agiorni** *m. indecl.* (watchm.) day jumper. **-amesi** *m. indecl.* (watchm.) month jumper. **-apaletto** *m. indecl.* (watchm.) bolt jumper. **-ato** *part. adj.* released, sprung; gone off. **-atoio** *m.* (eng.) trigger, trip, release. **-atore** *m.* spring release; (watchm.) jumper.

scattivare [A I] *tr.* (Tusc.) to cut away the bad pieces from (fruit, etc.); to patch, to mend (e.g. clothing).

scatt-o *m.* (eng.) release, click, trip, slip hook; kick; (cinem.) movimento a —, intermittent feed; periodo di —, feed stroke; (photog.) release; — flessibile, cable release; (sport) spurt (esp. in cycling); (fig.) outburst, access, fit; impulse; convulsive movement; sudden jerk; parlare a -i, to talk jerkily; avere degli -i, to have sudden inspirations. **-ino** *m.* (watchm.) stop; jumper. **-osità** *f.* (techn.) snap (property of rubber, etc.).

scatur-i·gine *f.* spring, source, fount; (geog.) centre of a spring; — di petrolio, petroleum well; (fig.) origin. **-iginoso** *adj.* (of land) well watered.

scatur-ire [D 2] *intr.* (*aux.* essere) to spring; to gush; to spout; to rise; (fig.) to arise, to ensue; to originate. (**-ente** *part. adj.*)

scautismo *m.* (pop.). See **scoutismo**.

scavalc-are [A 2] *intr.* to dismount; to put up, to lie (for the night); *tr.* to unhorse; to stride over, to surmount, to clamber over; to oust; to supplant; to be promoted over; (in reading) to skip; (in knitting) — una maglia, to cross one stitch over another; (mil.) to damage (a gun) by smashing its trunnions so that it drops. **-amento** *m.* dismounting; unhorsing; straddling; striding over; crossing; promotion. **-ato** *part. adj.* dismounted; unhorsed; crossed; ousted, supplanted; passed over; *n.m.* (knitting) part of the work where stitches have been crossed over, cast-off section. (**-atore** *m.* **-atrice** *f.*)

scavallare [A I] *intr.* (*aux.* avere) to run free, to run wild; to gallop about.

scav-are [A I] *tr.* to excavate; to dig out; to discover by digging; to dig; — una buca, to dig a hole; to hollow out; -arsi la fossa con le proprie mani, to dig one's own grave, to do oneself harm; — un pozzo, to sink a well; to wear out, to wear holes in (clothing);

(fig.) to discover; to nose out; to come by, to come upon; to hunt out; dove l'hai -ato?, where on earth did you find that? **-afossi** *m. indecl.* ditch digger (man); *f. indecl.* trencher (machine). **-amento** *m.* excavating; digging; hollowing; excavation; hole. **-apozzi** *m. indecl.* well-sinker. **-ato** *part. adj.* excavated; dug out; hollowed; (of clothing) in holes, worn; (fig.) discovered; guance -ate, hollow cheeks, sunken cheeks. **-atore** *m.* excavator; digger; miner. **-atrice** *f.* excavator, power shovel, earth mover, muck shifter. **-atura** *f.* hole; cavity; earth dug up. **-azione** *f.* excavation, excavating; digging.

scavezz-are [A I c] *tr.* to take the halter off; to break, to fracture; -arsi il collo, to break one's neck; (techn.) to lop branches from close to the trunk. **-acollo** *m.* headlong fall; rash undertaking; (fig.) reckless individual; scamp; daredevil; madcap, tomboy; turbulent or gay young person; *adv. phr.* a -acollo, at a breakneck pace; headlong; precipizio a -acollo, sheer drop. **-ato** *part. adj.* freed from the halter; broken, fractured; truncated; sawn off; (artill.) fucile -ato, sawn-off gun easily carried and concealed, in two parts; (naut.) spring; nave -ata, ship having its back broken. **-atura** *f.* freeing from a halter; breaking, fracturing.

scavezzo *part. apocop.* of **scavezzare**, q.v.; *m.* (mus.) clavicembalo a tasti scavezzi, harpsichord with short keys divided so as to distinguish between enharmonic notes.

scavigliare [A 4] *tr.* to remove (silk) from the throwing frame.

scavitolare [A I s], **scavizzolare** [A I s] *tr.* to hunt about for, to rummage out; — pretesti, to seek excuses; *intr.* (*aux.* avere) to rummage.

scavo *m.* excavation; digging; tunnelling; hole; cavity; hollow; worn patch (in clothing); *pl.* (archaeol.) excavation, dig; visitare gli scavi, to visit the site of excavation; gli scavi di Pompei, the ruins of Pompeii; direttore degli scavi, archaeologist in charge of an excavation; (anat.) — pelvico, pelvic cavity.

scazonte *adj.* (prosod.) scazontic (verse); *n.m.* scazon.

scazzone (ichth.) sea scorpion, *Cottus* spp.

scazzottare [A I] *tr.* (fam.) to punch, to hit with the fists.

scea *f.* (metall.) crude iron; far la —, to open the lower tap of the smelting furnace to run off the crude molten iron.

†**sced-a** *f.* gibe; grimace; rough draft; sample of cloth; model. †**-ardo** *m.* scoffer. †**-are** *tr.* to scoff. †**-ario** *m.* sampler.

scegl-iere [B 7] *tr.* to choose; to select; to nominate; to pick (out); — in isposa, to take to wife; c'è da —, there's enough to pick and choose; sono tutti uguali, non c'è da —, they're all the same, there's nothing to choose between them; (techn.) to sort. **-itic·cio** *m.* residue, remains; left-overs. **-itore** *m.* chooser; (industr.) sorter. **-itrice** *f.* (industr.) sorter.

sceic-co *m.* (*pl.* **-chi**) sheikh.

sceller-ag·gine, -atag·gine, -atezza *f.* wickedness; evil; villainy; atrocity. **-ato** *adj.* wicked, evil; villainous; cruel; (joc.) fearful, awful; *n.m.* villain; wretch. (**-atamente** *adv.*)

scellino *m.* shilling (English or Austrian).

†**scelo** *m.* crime.

scelotirbe *f.* (med.) scelotyrbe.

scelta *f.* choice; pick; option; libera —, free choice; di sua —, as he chooses; a —, according to choice, to taste; preference; selection; (duelling) — delle armi, choice of weapons; (comm.) option; fare —, to choose; promozione a —, promotion by merit; prima —, best quality, prime grade; seconda —, inferior quality, second grade.

scelt-o *part.* of **scegliere**, q.v.; *adj.* chosen; picked; selected; choice; select; distinguished; elegant; exquisite; noble; praiseworthy; (mil.) guardia -a, picked sentry, picked men for guard duty; corpo —, 'corps d'élite', picked troops; puntatore —, marksman, crack shot. **-amente** *adv.* with distinction; elegantly; exquisitely. **-ezza** *f.* choiceness; distinction; exquisiteness. **-ume** *m.* residue; remnants, left-overs.

scem-are [A I c] *tr.* to diminish; to lessen; to reduce; — il prezzo, to lower the price; *intr.* (*aux.* essere) to diminish; to lessen; to be reduced; to ease off; to drop; to be lowered; (of the moon) to be on the wane; (of the tide) to be going out; — di pregio, to go down in people's estimation; — di autorità, to lose authority. **-a·bile** *adj.* reducible; capable of being diminished. **-amento** *m.* reduction; diminution; abatement; -amento della luna, waning of the moon. **-ato** *part. adj.* reduced; diminished; abated; lowered; weakened; luna -ata, waning moon. (**-atore** *m.* **-atrice** *f.*)

scẹm-o *adj.* diminished; reduced; lacking; half-full; half-empty; (fig.) — di forze, lacking in strength; mentally defective, half-witted; *n.m.* reduction; diminution; half-wit; idiot; (knitting) casting-off; part of the work where stitches have been cast off. **-enza** *f.* stupidity; half-witted behaviour; half-wittedness, idiocy.

scẹmpi-o¹ *adj.* simple; single; cucire col filo —, to sew with single thread; consonante -a, single consonant; calza -a, plain knitting; fiore —, single flower; silly, simple, foolish. (**-amẹnte** *adv.*) *n.m.* simpleton. **-ag·gine** *f.* foolishness, stupidity. **-are** [A 4 c] *tr.* to use single; to divide, to split; -are le consonanti, to pronounce double consonants as though they were single. (**-amẹnto** *m.*) **-ato** *part. adj.* divided; single; stupid, silly, simple. (**-atamẹnte** *adv.*) **-ọne** *m.* blockhead.

scẹmpio² *m.* slaughter; havoc; fare — di, to slaughter, (fig.) to destroy, to create havoc amongst.

scen-a *f.* scene; (theatr.) stage; theatre; scene, set; dietro le -e, behind the scenes, backstage; pittore di —, scene-painter; andare in —, to go on (to the stage); calcare le -e, to tread the boards, to live as an actor; mettere in —, to put on, to produce; direttore di —, producer; fare —, to play a part; re di —, stage king; colpo di —, *coup de théâtre*, sensational turn in the action of a play; — muta, mime; (mus.) scena, extended operatic soliloquy employing both recitative and aria; (fig.) scene, row; fare delle -e, to make scenes; la — politica, the political scene; venire in —, to come on the scene; dietro le -e, behind the scenes. **-a·rio** *m.* (theatr.) stage; scenery, set, backcloth, flats; scenario; (fig.) panorama, vista. **-arista** *m.* (cinem.) scenarist, script-writer. **-ata** *f.* scene, row; quarrel; fare una -ata, to make a scene, to kick up a row, to 'create'.

scẹnd-ere [C 1] *intr.* (*aux.* essere, avere) to descend; to go down; to come down; to run down; to flow down; to sink; to drop; to decline; to slope; — da cavallo, to dismount; — dalla nave, to disembark; — a, to put up at, to stay the night at; — a pettegolezzi, to stoop to gossip; to be descended; — dall'aristocrazia, to be descended from the aristocracy; — al cuore, to touch the heart, to move; *tr.* — le scale, to descend the stairs; — il monte, to go down the hill; (dial., S. Ital.) to hand down, to lift down; -imi quel libro, hand me down that book. **-ente** *part. adj.* descending; *n.m.* (phys.) falling body. **-i·bile** *adj.* practicable for the (downward) climber, easy to descend. **-iletto** *m. indecl.* bedside mat or carpet.

sceneggi-are [A 3 c] *tr.* (theatr.) to arrange in acts and scenes; to adapt for the stage. **-amẹnto** *m.* (theatr.) arrangement (of a play); adaptation. **-ato** *part. adj.* (theatr.) arranged, adapted. **-atọre** *m.* (theatr.) adapter (of other work) for the stage; (cinem.) scenarist, script-writer. **-atura** *f.* (theatr.) adaptation, arrangement; (cinem.) scenario.

sce·n-ico *adj.* scenic; theatrical; apparato —, stage properties; effetto —, stage effect; palco —, stage; *n.m.* (theatr.) actor; (hist.) gladiator. **-icamẹnte** *adv.* scenically. **-ografi·a** *f.* (theatr.) scene-painting (or designing); stage decoration; perspective; (cinem.; telev.) art direction. **-ogra·fico** *adj.* (theatr.) scenic, scenery, stage (as *adj.*). **-o·grafo** *m.* (theatr.) scenery designer; scene painter; (cinem.; telev.) art director. **-opegi·a** *f.* (Jewish rel.) Feast of Tabernacles. **-otec·nica** *f.* (theatr.) stage management. **-otec·nico** *adj.* (theatr.) relating to stage-management; *n.m.* stage-manager.

†**scentrare** *vb.* and derivs. See **discentrare**.

†**scentre** *adv. phr.* a mio —, to my knowledge.

scepsi *f.* (philos.) scepsis.

scerb-are [A 1] *tr.* (Tusc.) to weed. **-amẹnto** *m.*, **-atura** *f.* weeding.

sceriffo *m.* sheriff; (hist.) shereef.

scer·n-ere [C 2 8] *tr.* to discern; to distinguish; to make out, to see clearly; to choose, to select; to separate (out). **-imẹnto** *m.* discerning, distinguishing; discernment; recognition. †**-ire** *vb.* and derivs. see **scernere**.

†**scerpare** *tr.* to destroy, to lay waste.

scerpellọne *m.* gross blunder.

†**scer·pere** *tr.* to rend, to tear, to lacerate.

scervell-are [A 1] *tr.* to drive to distraction; *rfl.* to rack one's brains. **-ato** *part. adj.* mentally fagged; brainless, hare-brained.

scẹsa *f.* descent; slope, declivity; downward path; (fam.) — di testa, whim, caprice, mad idea; prendersi la — di testa di, to take it into one's head to; gli è venuto la — di testa di comprare una macchina, he has this mad idea of buying a car.

scẹso *part.* of **scendere**, q.v.; *adj.* descended; (fig.) declining; in decline; sole —, setting sun; *prep.* (Tusc.) down; — la scala, down the stairs.

†**scetterare** *intr.* to play the 'cetera', q.v.

scet·t-ico *adj.* (philos.) Sceptic (school, philosopher); sceptical; *n.m.* Sceptic; sceptic. **-icamẹnte** *adv.* sceptically. **-icịsmo** *m.* Scepticism; scepticism.

scẹttr-o, scẹttr-o *m.* sceptre; royal authority; mastery, ascendancy; tenere lo —, to rule, (joc.) to rule the roost; deporre lo —, to abdicate, to lay down the crown. **-ato** *adj.* sceptred; sovereign.

scever-are [A 1 sc] *tr.* to sever; to divide; to part; to separate; to distinguish; — il bene dal male, to know good from evil; *rfl.* to be separated; to disperse, to disband. **-amẹnto** *m.* separating; separation. **-ato** *part. adj.* severed; divided; separated; distinguished; routed; dispersed.

scẹvro *adj.* (foll. by *prep.* di) free (from); exempt (from); — di colpa, free from blame; — d'errore, innocent of error; — d'impurità, free from impurity; argomento scevro di fondamento, argument totally without foundation.

scevrò *m.* (i.e. Fr. **chevreau**) kid; guanti di —, kid gloves.

sched-a *f.* slip of paper; index card; form; application form; counterfoil; — di associazione, membership ticket; — per votazione, voting-paper, ballot-paper; urna per le -e, ballot-box; -e valide, valid ballot-papers; si terrà conto delle -e bianche o nulle, declared abstentions will be taken into account; deporre una — nell'urna, to deposit a voting-paper in the ballot-box; schedule; list; form, card; — di biblioteca, library catalogue; -e del personale, staff cards; (admin.) — di segnalazione, notification-form. **-are** [A 1] *tr.* to compile notes concerning, to annotate (on cards); to index. **-a·rio** *m.* card-index; catalogue (on cards); card-index drawer; filing cabinet. **-ato** *part. adj.* indexed; filed; scheduled; (leg.) donna -ata in Questura, woman known to the police. **-atura** *f.* indexing; filing. **-ina** *f. dim.* of **scheda**; -ina del Totocalcio, football pools coupon.

†**schedone** *m.* See **schidione**.

†**sche·dula** *f.* counterfoil; ticket (cf. **cedola**).

scheelite *f.* (miner.) scheelite.

schẹggi-a *f.* splinter; flake; chip; (provb.) la — ritrae dal ceppo, he is a chip off the old block; (mil.) — di granata, shell splinter; *pl.* canister; †framework (Dante, *Purg.* XXVI, 87). **-are** [A 3 c] *tr.* to splinter; (industr.) to chip; *rfl.* to splinter, to go into splinters. **-amẹnto** *m.* splintering; splitting. **-ato** *part. adj.* splintered; split asunder; cleft. **-atura** *f.* splintering; splinters; chips, chippings.

schẹggi-o *m.* rocky precipitous slope. **-ọso** *adj.* liable to splinter; brittle.

schei *m.pl.* (dial. Lomb., fam.) money; centesimi; sono senza —, I'm broke.

Schelda *pr.n.f.* (geog.) Scheldt.

schele·trico *adj.* pertaining to a skeleton; apparato —, body frame; thin as a skeleton; skeleton-like; (fig.) lacking in substance; thin, bare, meagre; prosa scheletrica, unadorned prose.

sche·letr-o *m.* skeleton; ridotto uno —, reduced to a skeleton; (zool.) skeleton; also used of the carcase of an animal; (geog.) texture (of soil); (naut.) frames of a ship being broken up; (techn.) framework, skeleton; skeleton outline, plan. **-ame** *m.* (naut.) 'bones' of old ships rotting or being broken up. **-ire** [D 2] *tr.* to make thin; to reduce to a skeleton; *rfl.* to grow very thin; to grow as thin as a skeleton; to become nothing but skin and bone. **-ito** *part. adj.* very thin; reduced to a skeleton.

†**schelmo** *m.* See **palischermo**.

scheltro *m.* (mil.) banner pole; lance.

schem-a *m.* scheme; plan; design; outline; project; diagram; (leg.) draft; (rhet.) figure; (Kantian philos.) schema (*pl.* schemata). **-aticità** *f.* simplicity, schematicness. **-a·tico** *adj.* schematic; diagrammatical; figura -atica, chart, plan; orderly; regular. **-atịsmo** *m.* (philos.) schematism; schematic method. **-atizzaziọne** *f.* reduction to a simpler form.

†**schencire** *intr.* to move obliquely; *tr.* to avoid.

†**schenella** *f.* See **schienella**.

schepsi *f.* See **scepsi**.

†**scherag·gio** *m.* (Florence) ditch or sewer to collect the rainwater.

scherano *m.* brigand; bandit; cut-throat, assassin; †*adj.* brigand-like.

scherm-a *f.* fencing; swordsmanship; tirare di —, fare la —, to fence; sala di —, *salle d'armes*; maestro di —, fencing master; gara, torneo di —, fencing competition; accademia di —, fencing

scherm·a (*cont.*)
display; (fig.) polemic; skirmish; †uscire di —, to get out of practice. **-a·glia** *f.* skirmish; duel; combat; controversy; polemic; -aglia di parole, brush, argument, set-to; (mil.) defence-works. †**-a·glio** *m.* fencing; defence.

scherm·are [A 1] *tr.* to fence; (techn.) to screen, to shield. **-ag·gio** *m.* (techn.) screening, shielding. (**-ato** *part. adj.*)

scherm·ire [D 2] *intr.* (*aux.* avere) to fence; *rfl.* to defend oneself; to put up a defence; to protect oneself; -irsi da, to parry; to ward off; †*tr.* to ward off. **-idore** *m.* (poet.) fencer, parrier; defender. **-itore** *m.* fencer. (**-itora, -itrice** *f.*)

scherm·o *m.* screen; protection; shield; defence; farsi — di, to shelter behind; (photog.; cinem.) screen; filter; diva dello —, film star; (techn.) baffle; (lit. hist.) donna dello —, screen lady, the woman who served as a blind to divert the attention of the world away from the poet's true love; †weapon; †fencing (cf. **scherma**). **-ogra·fico** (med.) accertamento -ografico, X-ray check-up; unità mobile di accertamento -ografico, mobile chest X-ray unit, mass radiography unit.

†**schermu·gio.** See **scaramuccia**[1].

†**scherna** *f.* See **scherno**.

schern·ire [D 2] *tr.* to scorn; to despise; to deride; to sneer at; to scoff at; to jeer at. **-evole** *adj.* scornful; derisory; sneering; parole -evoli, jeering remarks; worthy to be scorned; ridiculous; beneath contempt. (**-evolmente** *adv.*) **-ito** *part. adj.* scorned; scoffed at, derided; despised; -ito e beffato, mocked and derided. **-itore** *m.* scoffer; sneerer, jeerer; *adj.* sneering; derisory. (**-itrice** *f.*)

scherno *m.* scorn; derision; mockery; avere a —, to hold in scorn; essere lo — di, to be despised by; to be derided by; sneer; taunt; fare scherni a, to sneer at, to taunt.

†**scheruolo** *m.* (zool.) squirrel (cf. **scoiattolo**).

scherz·are [A 1] *intr.* (*aux.* avere) to joke; to jest; non -o!, I really mean it!; non si -a, this is no joking matter; to romp; to frolic; — sul vero, to prevaricate; — con la morte, to trifle with death; — alle spalle di uno, to laugh behind a person's back; — di tutto, — su ogni cosa, to be facetious, to be forever making fun of everything; (poet., e.g. of light) to play, to smile. **-ando** *ger.* (mus.) playfully, jestingly, freakishly. **-ante** *part. adj.* joking; playful, frolicsome; venticello -ante, playful little breeze. **-atore** *m.* humorist, joker, jester; one who loves a joke; facetious person; *adj.* joking; humorous. (**-atrice** *f.*) **-eggiare** [A 3 c] *intr.* (*aux.* avere) to joke; to trifle. **-evole** *adj.* playful; whimsical; joking, jesting. **-evolmente** *adv.* jokingly, in jest.

scherz·o *m.* joke; jest; per —, in fun; senza —, senza -i, seriously, joking apart; non reggere allo —, to be unable to take a joke; un brutto —, a dirty trick; whim, caprice; trick; freak; — della fortuna, freak of fate; -i d'acqua, ornamental waterworks; (mus.) scherzo, a playful movement—originally an accelerated minuet but later in any time-signature; -i musicali, light Italian canzonets of the seventeenth century; (lit.) light essay, humorous writing. **-oso** *adj.* joking; jesting; facetious; humorous; playful; frolicsome. **-osamente** *adv.* jokingly, jestingly.

schete *f.* (naut.) very long net; seine net as used in Liguria (the net is laid out in a straight line at first with one end moored; the other end is then towed round in a wide sweep); also **schetta** or **schetto**.

schet·tin·o *m.* roller-skate; un paio di -i, a pair of roller-skates. **-ag·gio** *m.* roller-skating. **-are** [A 1 s] *intr.* (*aux.* avere) to roller-skate.

†**schezz·a** *f.* see **scheggia**. †**-ale** *adj.* see **scheggiale**.

schi *m. indecl.* and derivs. See **sci**.

schiac·cia *f.* weighted trap; (fig.) rimanere alla —, to be caught in a trap, to be trapped (e.g. by falling masonry).

schiacci·are [A 3] *tr.* to crush; to squash; to squeeze; to flatten; to smash; to tread on, to trample on; to run over; — con argomenti, to override with argument; — noci, to crack nuts; — una questione, to hush a matter up; — un sonnellino, to have a nap, to have forty-winks; (Tusc., fam.) — uno studente all'esame, to plough a candidate; — moccoli, to curse. **-amento** *m.* crushing; squashing; flattening; (geog.) -amento della terra ai poli, flattening of the earth at the poles; (motor.) -amento d'un pneumatico, deflation of a tyre. **-anoci** *m. indecl.* nutcracker, nutcrackers. **-ante** *part. adj.* crushing; overriding; utterly convincing. **-apatate** *m. indecl.* (cul.) potato-masher. **-ata** *f.* crushing; squashing; flattening; squeeze; (cul.) flat cake of dough cooked in olive oil;

-ata unta, flat cake of dough, cooked in olive oil with bacon, egg-yolks and sugar. **-ato** *part. adj.* crushed; squashed; squeezed; flattened out; run over; cracked; damaged; di forma -ata, flat, flattened; naso -ato, flat nose; (archit.) arco -ato, four-centred, three-centred, segmental arch (i.e. any kind of 'flattened' arch). **-atura** *f.* crushing; squashing; flattening; squeezing. **-(u)ola** *f.* crimping iron; young pea-pod; *pl.* curling tongs.

schiaccino *m.* See **schiaccianoci**, under **schiacciare**.

schiacciolare [A 1 s] *tr.* to crush, to crumple.

schi·ade *f.* (anat.) see **ischiade**. **-a·dica** *f.* (pop.) see **sciatica**.

schiaffare [A 1] *tr.* to fling; to chuck; to stuff away; to throw carelessly; (fig. joc.) — dentro, to put in prison, to 'put inside'; †to slap; *rfl.* to fling oneself; schiaffarsi in poltrona, to drop down into an armchair.

schiaffeggi·are [A 3 c] *tr.* to slap; to smack; to box the ears of; to cuff; to slap the face of; *recip. rfl.* to slap each other's face; to box each other's ears. (**-ato** *part. adj.* **-atore** *m.* **-atrice** *f.*)

schiaffo *m.* slap in the face; smack; box on the ears; cuff; (billiards) cannon off the cushion; pigliare uno —, to get slapped; (fig.) insult, blow; — senza mano, humiliation; (cinem.; eng.) trasporto a —, dog movement, plunger movement.

schi·agrafi·a *f.* (med.) skiagraph; radiograph; skiagraphy, radiography. **-agramma** *m.* (med.) skiagram. **-ametri·a** *f.* (med.) skiametry. **-a·metro** *m.* (med.) skiameter. **-ascopi·a** *f.* (med.) skiascopy, retinoscopy.

schiamazz·are [A 1] *intr.* (*aux.* avere) to cackle; to squawk; to raise a din; to shout; to clamour. **-atore** *m.* brawler, hoodlum. (**-atrice** *f.*) **-io** *m.* continual cackling; constant squawking; continual uproar. **-o** *m.* din, uproar; shouting; brawling; cackling; squawking.

†**schianc·iana** *f.* (geom.) diagonal. †**-i·o** *adj.* oblique.

schiant·are [A 1] *tr.* to break; to split; to shatter; to wrench away; to snap off; to tear; — l'uscio, to break down the door; (fig.) — il vestito, to be bursting out of one's dress, to wear too tight a dress; *intr.* (*aux.* essere) to burst; to split; — dalle risa, to split one's sides with laughter; mangiare fino a —, to eat fit to burst; (pop.) to 'peg out'; — dalla fatica, to drop with fatigue; *rfl.* to burst, to split; le si -a il cuore, her heart is breaking; (of a shoe-lace, etc.) to snap. (**-ato** *part. adj.* **-atura** *f.*) **-o** *m.* crash; burst; lo -o del fulmine, the crack of lightning; wrench; ripping, tearing, sound of ripping; break; noise of a break; (fig.) pang; affliction; sudden blow; fu uno -o, it was a wrench; che -o di cuore!, what a sad blow!; *adv. phr.* di -o, suddenly; violently.

†**schianza** *f.* scab; dirty mark, stain.

schiapp·a[1] *f.* kindling, kindling wood; stake; (fam.) duffer, booby; rabbit (at games). **-are** [A 1] *tr.* to chop up for firewood, to split into kindlings; *rfl.* to split. (**-ato** *part. adj.* **-atura** *f.*) **-ino** *m.* (fam.) duffer, booby; rabbit (at games).

schiappa[2] *f.* (tanning) side.

†**schiappa**[3] *f.* close-fitting coat, tight at the waist, worn by young men (fifteenth century).

schiar·are [A 1] *tr.* to illumine; to light up; to explain, to clarify; (laundry) — i panni, to give clothes a second rinsing; — la voce, to clear one's voice; *intr.* (*aux.* essere), *rfl.* (of liquid) to clear; (of weather) to clear up, to lighten. **-ato** *part. adj.* illumined; clarified; cleared, clear; faccia -ata, countenance lightened of an expression of doubt or anxiety. (Cf. **rischiarare**.)

schiare·a *f.* (bot.). See **scarlea**.

†**schiari·a** *f.* (naut.) clearing; (in a wood) clearing, glade.

schiar·ire [D 2] *tr.* to lighten; to illuminate; to illumine; to let light in on; to clarify; to explain; to clear up; to thin out; — i capelli, to lighten the colour of one's hair; *intr.* (*aux.* essere) to grow brighter; (of the weather) to clear up, to lighten; (of light, day) to dawn; (of colours) to show up more vividly; *rfl.* to clear; to become clear; to brighten; to light up; to grow lighter; (of hair) to become fairer; (of a wood) to be thinned out. **-imento** *m.* clarifying; elucidating; per uno -imento, on a point of clarification; clearing up, brightening. **-ita** *f.* turn for the better (in weather), bright interval; una -ita nelle relazioni politiche, improved political relations. **-ito** *part. adj.* brightened; cleared up; clarified; illumined; elucidated; colorito -ito, improved colouring, brighter and rosier cheeks. **-itoio** *m.* (industr.) clarifying tank. †**-o** *m.* light grey.

schiass·are [A 1] *intr.* (*aux.* avere) to make a din, to shout, to brawl. **-ata** *f.* din, uproar; scene, row (cf. **chiasso**).

schiatta *f.* race, line, stock; family; cavalli di buona —, thoroughbred horses; (of fruit) quality.

schiatt-are [A I] *intr.* (*aux.* essere) (vulg.) to burst, to 'bust'; to 'peg out'; — dalla rabbia, to be boiling with rage; c'è da —, it's enough to make one boil; — dalle risa, to split one's sides with laughter. †-**one** *m.* thick-set, robust young man. (†-**ona** *f.*)

schiattire [D 2] *intr.* (*aux.* avere) (of hounds) to bay, to give tongue; to yelp (cf. **squittire**).

schiava¹ *f.* See under **schiavo**.

†**schiava²** *f.* (agric.) a kind of white grape.

schiavacciare [A 3] *tr.* to unbolt (a door); to lift the latch of; *intr.* (*aux.* avere) to rattle keys, to jingle a bunch of keys.

†**schiav-are, -ellare** *tr.* to take the pin out of (e.g. a hinge); to undo, to unfasten.

†**schiavina¹** *f.* See under **schiavo¹**.

schiavina² *f.* See under **schiavo²**.

schiav-o¹ *m.* slave; captive slave; traffico degli -i, slave trade; -i negri, negro slaves; essere fatto —, to be taken into slavery; (fig.) slave, devoted admirer; uno — delle abitudini, a slave to habit; è — della moglie, he is at his wife's beck and call; *adj.* enslaved; subject; subjugated; in fief; (comm.) — di dogana, duty unpaid. -**a** *f.* woman slave; tratta delle -e bianche, white slave traffic. †-**ag·gio** *m.* slavery (cf. **schiavitù**). -**esco** *adj.* (*m.pl.* -**eschi**) pertaining to a slave; slave-like; vesti -esche, slave's clothing. †-**ina** *f.* slaves' prison. -**ista** *m.* slaver; slave-owner; advocate of slavery. -**itù** *f.* slavery; enslavement; subjection; subjugation; -itù del fumare, enslavement to smoking.

†**schiav-o** *adj.*, *n.m.* Slav, Slovonic (cf. **slavo**); †*pl.* name of cold winds blowing from Slavonic countries. -**ina** *f.* (hist.) pilgrim's dress, a long, flowing over-garment, falling to the calf, unbelted (thirteenth to sixteenth centuries); (vet.) sheep pox; †covering for a bed. -**one** *m.* (hist.) Slovene soldier in the service of the Venetian Republic. -**onesca** *f.* a kind of dance.

†**schiazzama·glia** *f.* rabble (cf. **marmaglia**).

†**schiazzata** *f.* spurt, squirt, jet.

schiccare [A 2] *tr.* to pick (e.g. grapes), to pluck.

schiccher-are¹ [A I s] *tr.* to bedaub; to scribble over; to dash off; to 'spill', to blab, to blurt out; to rattle off (e.g. verse). -**acarte, -afogli** *m. indecl.* scribbler; dauber. -**amento** *m.* scribbling; scribble; daubing; daub. -**ato** *part. adj.* scribbled (on); daubed (over); dashed off; rattled off; blurted out. (-**atore** *m.* -**atrice** *f.*) -**atura** *f.* scribbling; scribble; daubing; daub. -**ìo** *m.* continual scribbling; frequent daubing.

schiccher-are² [A I s] *tr.* to guzzle; to gulp down; *intr.* (*aux.* avere) to tipple. (-**ato** *part. adj.*) -**one** *m.* guzzler; tippler. (-**ona** *f.*)

†**schicchiriare** *intr.* (Tusc., joc.) to crow long and loud.

schiccolare [A I s] *tr.* to pick (grapes) (cf. **schiccare**).

schidion-e *m.* (roasting) spit; (eng.) spindle. -**are** [A I c] *tr.* to roast on a spit; to run through with a spit, to spit. -**ata** *f.* row of poultry, etc. on a spit.

schien-a *f.* spine; backbone; back; il fil della —, the small of the back; colpire alla —, to stab in the back; avere molti anni in sulla —, to be getting on in years; breaking work, heavy labour; (colloq.) rompersi la —, to work oneself to death; (fam.) mettersi di — a, to throw oneself into (a job), to put one's back into; voltare la — a, to turn one's back on; curvare la —, to bow, to make obeisance; trasportare a — di mulo, to transport on muleback; (of a road) a — di mulo, a — d'asino, hog's back; (geog., Lomb.) — d'asino, gentle slope of irrigated meadow; — di monti, mountain-chain; (of a horse) giuocare di —, to buck, to kick out with the hind legs. -**ale** *m.* back (of chair, bench, pew, etc.); addossato allo -ale, supported against the back, leaning against the back (of a chair, etc.); (tailor.) back (of a jacket, etc.); (cul.) 'marrow' from bones of the spine; (mil. hist.) back half of a cuirass (opposite of breastplate); (naut.) backboard. -**ella** *f. dim.* (joc.) the hump, sulks. -**uto** *adj.* broad-backed; gibbous.

†**schiencire** *vb.* and derivs. See **schencire**.

schier-a *f.* band; troop; group; company; rank; flock (of birds); una — di formiche, a swarm of ants; la volgare —, the common herd; fare —, to form a crowd; una — di scioperanti, a crowd of unemployed; a —, in a crowd, in crowds, in flocks; (mil.) array, line of troops; muovere le -e, to move one's forces; -e invitte, undefeated lines or forces; andare fuori di —, to go out of the line; (naut.) squadron fleet.

schier-are [A I d] *tr.* to line up; (mil.) to draw up in line or lines; *rfl.* to deploy one's forces; -arsi in ordine di battaglia, to draw up in fighting order; to array oneself; -arsi dalla parte di, to side with, to take sides with, to be on the side of. -**amento** *m.* lining up; marshalling; (mil.) deployment, disposition of the forces in lines; (sport) line-up, team; (naut.) order and disposition of a squadron or fleet; assumere uno -amento, to assume a formation. -**ato** *part. adj.* lined up; marshalled; arrayed; (mil.) truppe -ate, troops drawn up in line.

schierazzo *m.* (naut.) Turkish trading vessel.

schieric-are [A 2 s] *tr.* (eccl.) to unfrock (priest); *rfl.* (eccl.) to unfrock oneself. -**ato** *part. adj.* unfrocked; *n.m.* unfrocked priest; apostate cleric.

schiett-o, schiett-o *adj.* frank; open; sincere; open-hearted; blunt, downright; plain, unadorned; simple; pure; genuine; undiluted; unadulterated; (of fruit) sound; di sangue —, pure-blooded; la -a pronunzia fiorentina, the pure Florentine accent; la -a verità, the plain truth; una -a risposta, a frank reply, a plain answer; a dirla -a, to speak plainly; *adv. phr.* alla -a, frankly, plainly; (archit.) membro architettonico —, plain architectural feature (i.e. smooth, without carving); *adv.* frankly; parlare —, to speak plainly. -**amente** *adv.* frankly, plainly, openly; sincerely; purely, simply. -**ezza** *f.* frankness; openness; sincerity; genuineness; plainness; simplicity; uomo di rara -ezza, man of rare integrity.

†**schifa** *f.* See **schifo¹**.

schif-are [A I] *tr.* to loathe; to hold in abhorrence; to feel disgust for; †to shun; †to avoid; †— biasimo, to avoid blame; †— fatica, to avoid effort; *intr.* (*aux.* avere) — da, to shun, to avoid; — di, to be loth to, to be reluctant to; *rfl.* (*prep.* di) to feel repugnance (for), to be disgusted (by). †-**alpoco (a'l poco)** *m.* person who is fussy or faddy. -**ano·ia** *m.* lazybones; idler; (hist.) Palazzo Schifanoia, a palace of the Estensi at Ferrara. -**ato** *part. adj.* loathed, held in loathing, abhorred; †shunned; †avoided.

schif-o¹ *m.* disgust, loathing; nausea; avere a —, to loathe; to shun; to abhor; to feel repugnance for; fare — a, to disgust, to inspire with loathing; *adj.* revolting, disgusting; loathsome; revolted, disgusted; reluctant, unwilling, shy; delicate-minded; fastidious; queasy; fare lo —, to show exaggerated fastidiousness. -**ezza** *f.* disgust; loathing; disgusting thing; object of loathing; abomination. -**iltà** *f.* repugnance; nausea, queasiness; delicacy of stomach; reluctance; shyness; scruples; delicacy of mind. -**iltoso** *adj.* faddy, fussy; easily nauseated; -iltoso nel mangiare, faddy about one's food. -**osità** *f.* loathsomeness; nastiness. -**oso** *adj.* disgusting, revolting; nauseating; loathsome; filthy; un avaro -oso, an 'old Shylock'. (-**osamente** *adv.*)

†**schifo²** *m.* (naut.) skiff; †ship's boat, galley's boat.

†**schimbe·scio** *m.* See **sghimbescio**.

schindare [A I] and derivs. See **sghindare**.

schindilesi *f.* (anat.) schindylesis.

†**schinella** *f.* See **schienella**, under **schiena**.

schiniere *m.* (mil. hist.) greave, shin-guard.

schino *m.* (bot.) pepper tree, *Schinus molle*.

schiocca *f.* (naut.) stern port, after hatch; (Naples) decorated stern-board.

schiocc-are [A 2] *tr.* to crack; to snap; — la frusta, to crack the whip; — la lingua, to click one's tongue; — le labbra, to smack one's lips; — le dita, to snap one's fingers, *or* to crack one's knuckles; — le mani, to clap one's hands; — un bacio, to give a loud smacking kiss; -arla a, to play a trick on; (cards) — la primiera, to lay down the 'primiera' (or 'premiera') in the game of 'scopa'; *intr.* (*aux.* avere) to make a cracking noise, to crack; to crackle; to hiss; to snap; fare — la frusta, to crack the whip; bacioni che -ano, loud, smacking kisses. -**ata** *f.* crack; crack of a whip; snap; smacking noise; smack. (-**ato** *part. adj.*)

schioc-co *m.* (*pl.* -**chi**) crack; snap; smacking noise; smack.

schioccolare [A I s] and derivs. See **chioccolare**.

schiod-are [A I] *tr.* to draw out a nail from; to unfasten; to prise open; to unlock; to unrivet; (fig.) — la bocca a uno, to unseal someone's lips, to make someone talk; (mil.) to unspike (a gun); (naut.) to unshackle (taking the pin out of a cable shackle); to unbolt (armour plates). -**ato** *part. adj.* unfastened; prised open; unlocked. -**atura** *f.* drawing out of nails; unlocking; unfastening.

schiom-are [A I] (poet.) to dishevel; to ruffle the tresses of. -**ato** *part. adj.* dishevelled; ruffled.

†**schioppa** *f.* See **schioppo** or **schioppetto**.

schioppętt-o *m. dim.* of **schioppo**, q.v.; (mil. hist.) very short carbine. **-ata** *f.* shot, gunshot; gunshot wound; fare alle -ate, to shoot at one another. †**-eri·a** *f.* number of carbines or soldiers armed with carbines. **-iere** *m.* (mil. hist.) soldier armed with carbine; manufacturer of carbines.

schioppo *m.* (mil. hist.) carbine (slightly shorter than a musket); (pop., colloq.) gun; a un tiro di —, within gunshot.

†**schiostrare** *rfl.* to leave one's convent.

†**schiovamento** *m.* dislocation (of a limb, etc.).

†**schiovolare** *tr.* to dislocate.

schipetaro *m.* Albanian.

†**schippire** *intr.* to slip away, to make a swift escape.

†**schiragua·ito** *m.* sentry on night duty.

†**schir-atto** *m.*, †**-at·tolo** *m.* See **scoiattolo**.

schiribilla *f.* (orn.) little crake, *Porzana parva*; — grigiata, Baillon's crake, *P. pusilla*.

schiribizz-o *m.* whim, caprice; freakish fancy. **-oso** *adj.* capricious; full of freaks and fancies.

Schiro *pr.n.f.* (geog.) Scyros.

schiṣ-are [A I] *tr.* (math.) to reduce (a fraction); (billiards) — la palla, to give the bias or spin (sidespin, backspin, topspin). **-o** *adj.* (Tusc.) oblique; askew; (math.) reduction (of a fraction); residual fraction; *adv. phr.* a —, di —, per —, obliquely, askew; alla -a, on the slant; (billiards) prendere la palla di —, see 'schisare la palla'.

schiṣma *m.* (mus.) schisma, a minute musical interval.

schiṣo *adj.* See under **schisare**.

schist-o *m.* (geol.) schist, shale; olio di —, shale oil; -i oliosi, oil shale. **-oce·falo** *m.* (med.) schistocephalus. **-o·cito** *m.* (biol.) schistocyte. **-ocitọsi** *f.* (med.) schistocytosis. **-osità** *f.* (geol.) schistosity. **-oso** *adj.* (geol.) schistose.

schitarr-are [A I] *intr.* (*aux.* avere) (mus.) to twang the guitar, to thrum. **-amento** *m.* (mus.) guitar-playing, guitar-twanging.

schiu·d-ere [C 3] *tr.* to open; to unclose; — gli occhi, to open one's eyes; — le labbra al sorriso, to part one's lips in a smile; to unfold; to explain; to reveal; †to exclude; *rfl.* to open; to be capable of being opened; non si -e, it won't open. **-imento** *m.* opening; unfolding; hatching.

schium-a *f.* foam; froth; lather; scum; (fig.) dross, dregs; la — della società, the scum of society; (miner.) — di mare, sepolite, meerschaum; estintore a —, foam extinguisher. **-ai(u)ola**, **-ar(u)ola** *f.* skimming-spoon; (Parma) fishing-net. **-are** [A I] *tr.* to skim; to remove the scum from; *intr.* (*aux.* avere) to froth; to lather. **-atọio** *m.* see **schiumaiuola**. **-atọri** *m.pl.* (naut.) -atori di mare, sea rovers. **-o·geno** *adj.* foaming. **-oso** *adj.* frothy; foamy; in a lather; covered in scum.

schiusa *f.* opening; unfolding; (zool.) hatching (of an egg).

schiuso *part.* of **schiudere**, q.v.; *adj.* opened; disclosed; open; hatched; pulcini appena schiusi, day-old chicks; uovo —, egg from which a bird has hatched.

schiv-are [A I] *tr.* to avoid; to shun; to keep away from; — di parlare, to avoid speaking; *rfl.* to be avoided; to stay away; *recip. rfl.* to avoid one another. **-a·bile** *adj.* avoidable. **-afatiche** *m. indecl.* shirker; slacker; lazybones. (**-ato** *part. adj.*)

schivazzo *m.* (naut., derog.) heavy skiff.

schivo *adj.* shy; bashful; retiring; coy; fastidious; — di, averse from; essere — delle lodi, to dislike praise; è — di mostrarsi al pubblico, he is shy of making a public appearance.

schizo-freni·a *f.* (med.) schizophrenia, split mind. **-fre·nico** *adj.*, *n.m.* (med.) schizophrenic.

schizolite *f.* (geol.) schizolite.

schizz-are [A I] *intr.* (*aux.* essere) to squirt, to spurt, to gush; to leap; to dart; — fuori, to jump out; to leap out of bed; (of sparks) to fly; (of liquid) to be effervescent, to fizz; (of varnish, etc.) to flake; *tr.* to spurt; to shoot; — veleno, to dart poison, (fig.) to give vent to one's wrath; — la bile, to vent one's spite; — salute, to be bursting with health; (*prep.* di) to spatter (with); — d'inchiostro, to splash with ink; (art) to sketch; †to put out the eyes of. **-amento** *m.* spurting, squirting. **-ata** *f.* spurt, gush; splash; plop; (art) sketching; sketch. **-ato** *part. adj.* spurting; spattered; (art) sketched; drawn; (vet.) cavallo -ato, a horse castrated by twisting and compressing the testicles. **-atọia** *f.* (techn.) burner jet. **-atoiata** *f.* amount of flow through a jet. **-atọio** *m.* syringe; squirter; pump.

schizzętt-o *m. dim.* of **schizzo**, q.v. (art) small sketch; study; (med.)

---

syringe; (joc.) pop-gun. **-are** [A I c] *tr.* to splash, to spot, to spatter; *rfl.* to become spattered. **-ata** *f.* spattering; (med.) shot, injection. (**-ato** *part. adj.*) **-atura** *f.* (med.) injection.

schizzignọso *adj.* (pop.). See **schizzinoso**.

schizzinọs-o *adj.* squeamish; fastidious; fussy, faddy; hard to please; di gusto —, faddy about food. (**-amẹnte** *adv.*)

schizzo *m.* squirt, spurt; dart, dash; leap; jet; splash; a few drops, squeeze; uno — di limone, a few drops of lemon-juice; bicchiere di vermut con lo — di limone, glass of vermouth with a dash of lemon-juice; caffè con lo —, coffee with liqueur; splash, mudspot; leap; plop; (art) sketch; drawing; study; (fig.) outline, plan; rough draft; (colloq.) lively, vivacious individual; di primo —, immediately, straight away; (med.) injection, shot.

sci *m. indecl.* ski; ski-ing.

sci·a *f.* (naut.) wake; navigare nell'altrui —, to follow in the wake of another ship; (aeron.) roach (sheet of water thrown up by seaplane); (fig.) track, footsteps; trail; wake; string of consequences.

scià *m. indecl.* Shah.

†**sciabà** *m. indecl.* Sabbath; festival.

sciabęcco *m.* (naut. hist.) Xebec, three-masted Mediterranean warship later used for trading.

scia·bi-ca *f.* (naut.) seine net, large trawl net, and also the name of the type of boat used; fare —, to sag (of a rope taking the shape of the loop of a net); (orn.) moorhen, *Gallinula chloropus*. **-care** [A 2 s] *intr.* (*aux.* avere) (naut.) to drag the bottom, to use a bottom sweep; to trawl. **-chella** *f.* (naut.) very small-mesh seine net. **-co** *m.* (naut.) -co di fondo, small one-man net sometimes having a canvas cod-end. **-cọne** *m.* (naut.) trawl net; (fig.) two-faced individual. **-goto** *m.* (naut.) seine fisherman. **-gotta** *f.* (naut.) (Ancona) small trawl net.

†**sciabla** *f.* See **sciabola**.

sciablọna *f.* (eng.) template, former.

scia·bol-a *f.* sabre; — di cavalleria, cavalry sabre; — d'onore, sword of honour; governo della —, military despotism; (fig.) gambe a —, bow-legs; (ichth.) pesce —, scabbard fish, *Lepidopus caudatus*. **-are** [A I s] *tr.* to slash with a sabre; to mow down, to cut down, with sabres. **-ata** *f.* sabre-cut; (fig.) slashing, savage criticism. **-atọre** *m.* swordsman.

sciabord-are [A I c] *tr.* to shake (a liquid); to splash up and down, to stir round (in a liquid); *intr.* (*aux.* avere) (of waves) to lap, to wash; *rfl.* to heel over, to collapse. **-ìo** *m.* continual shaking, tossing; -ìo del mare sulla costa, beating of the waves on the beach.

sciacallo *m.* (zool.) jackal, *Canis aureus*; (fig.) jackal; opportunist (esp. one who takes advantage of an accident, earthquake, etc., in order to steal).

sciacma *m.* (zool.) chacma baboon, *Papio chacma*.

sciacqu-are [A 6] *tr.* to rinse; to rinse out, to rinse through; — i piatti, to wash up; *rfl.* (*acc.* of *prn.* 'si') to be rinsed; (*dat.* of *prn.* 'si') -arsi lo stomaco, to take only liquids; -arsi la bocca, to rinse one's mouth; (fig.) -arsi la bocca sul conto di, to speak ill of. **-abọcca** *m. indecl.* throat-spray. **-abudella** *m. indecl.* (pop.) weak wine; swill; watery beverage; bere a -abudella, to drink on an empty stomach. **-adenti** *m. indecl.* mouth-rinse; (joc.) breakfast; snack. **-adita** *m. indecl.* finger-bowl. **-amẹnto** *m.* rinsing, sluicing. **-ata** *f.* rinse. **-atọio** *m.* mill-race. †**-ato·rio** *m.* andarsene, andare, in -atorio, to be ruined. **-atura** *f.* rinsing, sluicing; rinsing water; slops; -atura di bicchieri, poor wine. **-ino** *m.* dishwater; down-and-out. **-ìo** *m.* continual rinsing; splashing; washing. (Cf. **risciacquare**.)

sciac·qu-o *m.* rinsing of the mouth; mouthwash. **-ọne** *m.* (bldg.) W.C. cistern.

Sciaffusa *pr.n.f.* (geog.) Schaffhausen.

sciaguatt-are [A I] *tr.* (pop., Tusc.) to shake (liquid) to splash; to stir round (in a liquid); — i panni, to move clothes up and down in water, to rinse the washing; *intr.* (*aux.* avere) to be too big; veste che -a, dress that is too loose or too large for the wearer. **-amẹnto** *m.* shaking, splashing; sluicing. **-ato** *part. adj.* shaken, splashed; well rinsed; sluiced.

sciagur-a *f.* calamity, misfortune, disaster; mishap; essere perseguitato dalla —, to be dogged by one misfortune after another; che —!, what a disaster!; ho il presentimento d'una —, I have a feeling something terrible is going to happen. **-atag·gine** *f.* spiteful action, mean behaviour, caddish trick. **-ato** *part. adj.*

sciagur-a (cont.)
unfortunate, unlucky; ill-starred; wretched; unhappy; calamitous; tempi -ati, calamitous times; wicked, evil; spiteful; n.m. wretch; unlucky individual; unhappy man; evil person; spiteful person. **-atamẹnte** adv. unluckily; unhappily; unfortunately. †**-oso** adj. see **sciagurato**.

scialacqu-are [A 6] tr. to lavish, to waste; to pour out profusely; to dissipate; to spend extravagantly; rfl. (acc. of prn. 'si') to be poured out; to spend money lavishly; to live riotously, to indulge in extravagances; (dat. of prn. 'si') -arsela, to waste one's substance in riotous living. **-amẹnto** m. lavishing; extravagant spending; outpouring; waste, extravagance. **-ato** part. adj. lavished; wasted; poured out profusely; spent lavishly. **-atamẹnte** adv. lavishly; profusely; wastefully; extravagantly. **-atọre** m. waster; spendthrift; prodigal. (**-atrice** f.) **-io** m. constant extravagance; continual lavishing.

scialac·qu-o m. waste; extravagance; lavish spending; profusion; adv. phr. a —, in profusion. **-ọne** m. spendthrift; prodigal. (**-ọna** f.)

†**scialappa** f. (bot.). See **gialappa**.

scial-are [A I] intr. (aux. avere) to spend money extravagantly; to buy whatever one wants; to waste one's substance; to lead a dissipated life; — in teatri, in divertimenti, in pranzi, to have a gay time going to theatres, banquets; non c'è da —, there's none too much, there's none to waste; in fatto d'ingegno ha poco da —, he is not overburdened with brains. **-amẹnto** m. wasting; squandering; extravagance. **-ante** part. adj. wasteful; extravagant. (**-atọre** m. **-atrice** f.) **-o** m. lavishness; waste; profusion; fare -o, to spend lavishly; non c'è -o di nulla, not a penny is wasted. **-ọne** m. spendthrift. (**-ọna** f.)

†**scialb-are** tr. to whitewash. †**-ato** part. adj. whitewashed; (Bibl.) sepolcro -ato, whited sepulchre. †**-atura** f. whitewashing; whitewash.

scialbo adj. pale; faint, dim; wan; faded; colourless; (fig.) feeble; una prova scialba, a feeble attempt; †n.m. whitewash.

†**scialenguato** adj. See **scilinguato**.

†**scialiva** f. See **saliva**.

scialle m. shawl; scarf.

sciallo m. See **scialle**.

scialo m. See under **scialare**.

scialoliti·aṣi f. (med.) sialolithiasis.

scialolito m. (med.) sialolith.

scialorre·a f. (med.) sialorrhoea, excessive salivation.

scialuppa f. (naut.) sloop, longboat, seaboat; gettar una — a mare, to lower or drop a seaboat.

sciaman-iṣmo m., **-i·stico** adj. See under **sciamano**.

sciamann-are [A I] tr. (pop.) to use clumsily; to handle carelessly; to crumple; rfl. to be untidy; to be slovenly (e.g. in dress). **-ato** part. adj. slovenly; careless, untidy; clumsy; adv. phr. alla -ata, carelessly, clumsily. **-ọne** m. untidy, slovenly person. (**-ọna** f.)

sciamanno m. veil or special material formerly worn by Jews on their hats, to distinguish them from Christians.

sciaman-o m. (rel.) shaman. **-iṣmo** m (rel.) shamanism. **-i·stico** adj. (rel.) shamanistic, relating to shamanism.

sciam-are [A I] intr. (aux. avere, essere) to swarm (e.g. of bees); (fig.) to leave one's abode; to emigrate. **-ante** part. adj. swarming; (fig.) crowding, in crowds. **-atura** f. swarming.

sciam-e, †**-o** m. swarm (of bees); (fig.) crowd, host.

sciamit-o, scia·mito m. samite; (bot.) chaff flower, Achyryanthes.

sciamma m. burnous.

Sciampagn-a pr.n.f. (geog.) Champagne; m. champagne (wine). **-ino** m. a sweet fizzy drink containing some alcohol; mock champagne.

†**sciampannare** tr., intr. to spend lavishly, to squander.

†**sciampiare** tr. to widen, to enlarge, to extend.

sciampo m. indecl. shampoo.

scianc-are [A 2] tr. to dislocate the hip of; rfl. to dislocate oneself, to become hipshot. **-ato** part. adj. hipshot; crippled, lame; (fig.) rickety, unsteady; lopsided; governo -ato, unstable government; n.m. cripple. **-atamẹnte** adv. limpingly; lopsidedly.

scianto m. (pop., Tusc.) rest, recreation; dáre lo —a, to let (children, etc.) out for a break, or rest.

sciantung m. indecl. (text.) shantung.

scia·p-ido, sciapo adj. silly, stupid; insipid. **-idire** [D 2] intr. (aux. essere) to become tasteless; to become stupid, silly.

sciapito adj. See **scipito**.

sciara f. (Sicily) land on the slopes of Mt Etna, with subsoil of lava on which only bushes grow.

sciarab-à, -àn m. (dial. Neap.) charabanc.

sciarad-a f. charade; — incatenata, charade in which the final syllable of a component word is identical with the first syllable of the succeeding word, e.g. amo, moro, rosa, amorosa. **-ista** m., f. one good at charades; person taking part in a game of charades.

†**sciarda** f. mala —, blackguard.

sci-are[1] [A 4] intr. (aux. avere) (naut.) to back the oars; (naut. comm.) scia!, back!; a dritta scia!, a sinistra voga!, back starboard!, give way port!; †mettere a —, to do a sternboard. **-ata** f. (naut.) action of backing the oars.

sci-are[2] [A 4] intr. (aux. avere) to ski. **-atọre** m. skier. (**-atrice** f.)

Sciari pr.n.f. (geog.) Shari, Cleari.

sciarp-a f. sash; scarf; sash; (naut.) shell of a block; blue sash worn by officers with full dress or as a badge of office by the Officer of the Watch, whilst on duty (in the British Royal Navy a sword-belt is worn for the same purpose).

†**sciarpellare** intr. to keep one's eyes wide open, to prise one's eyes open with the fingers.

sciarrano m. (ichth.) sea perch; — gigante, Serranus gigas; — comune, — cabrilla, — listato, S. cabrilla; — scrittura, Serranellus scriba; — sacchetto, Paracentropristis hepatus.

†**sciarr-are** tr. to disband; to scatter; rfl. to altercate, to fall into discord. †**-ata** f. quarrel; 'scene'. †**-ato** part. adj. quarrelling; parted; (mil.) truppe -ate, troops in disorder.

†**sciartrosa** f. chartreuse (liqueur).

sciascopi·a f. See **schiascopia**.

scia·tic-a f. (med.) sciatica; woman suffering from sciatica. **-o** adj. (anat.) sciatic; n.m. sufferer from sciatica.

scia·tọre m., **-trice** f. See under **sciare**[2].

sciatta f. (naut.) trading vessel, small craft (cf. **chiatta**).

sciatt-are [A I] tr. to crumple; to spoil; (dial., Marches) to weaken. **-ato** part. adj. crumpled; spoiled; †excepted.

sciatt-o[1] adj. slovenly, untidy, careless; slatternly; clumsy; weak, wretched. (**-amẹnte** adv.) **-ag·gine** f. slovenliness, untidiness; awkwardness. **-eri·a** f. slovenliness; defective object; silliness. **-ino** m. careless person; clumsy individual. (**-ina** f.) **-io** m. slovenly work. **-ọna** f. slut; slattern. **-ọne** m. slovenly man, sloven.

†**sciatto**[2] m. lament for the dead.

†**sciau·r-a** f. see **sciagura**. †**-ato** adj. see **sciagurato**.

scia·vero m. (timber) slab, outside plank cut from trunk; (text.) remnant, scrap; piece of waste wood (from sawing); scrap of leather, cloth, etc.

sciavog-a f. (naut.) backing the oars. **-are** [A 2] tr. (naut.) to back.

sci·bile adj. knowable; n.m. knowledge; tutto lo — umano, all human knowledge, all that man can know.

sci(b)bole·t m. indecl. shibboleth.

†**scicche** adj., n.m. chic.

sciccheri·a f. elegance, smartness; chic.

†**sciccome** adv. See **siccome**.

scient-e, †**-re** adj. aware; conscious; learned. **-emẹnte** adv. knowingly, wittingly, consciously.

scienti·fic-o adj. scientific; insegnamento —, science teaching; scholarly; rivista -a, learned journal. **-amẹnte** adv. scientifically; in a scholarly way.

scienz-a f. knowledge; la — del bene e del male, the knowledge of good and evil; di certa —, of certain knowledge; sapere di propria —, to know for certain, at first-hand; science; la pura —, pure science; la — applicata, applied science; le -e, the sciences; learning; lore; (theol.) — infusa, infused knowledge; (joc.) non ho mica la — infusa, I am not omniscient, you can't expect me to know everything; (lit. hist.) la gaia —, poetic composition in Old Provençal. †**-iale** adj. pertaining to knowledge; pertaining to science. **-iato** adj. learned; n.m. scientist; scholar, learned man. †**-iuola** f. knowledge; learning.

†**scien·zia** f. See **scienza**.

sciffoniera f. chiffonier (furniture); chest of drawers.

†**scifrare** vb. and derivs. See **decifrare**.

†**scigna** f. See **scimmia**.

†**scigrigna** f. stripe; mark of a lash.

sci-iṣmo m. ski-ing. **-i·stico** adj. (relating to) ski-ing.

scilacc-a *f.* slap; tap, rap; blow; blow with flat of a sword; †sword. **-are** [A 2] *tr.* to slap; to tap, to rap; to hit with the flat of a sword. **-ata** *f.* slap; rap. (**-ato** *part. adj.*)

sciliato *adj.* See **scilivato**.

scilingua *f.* (Tusc., pop.). See **siringa**.

scilingu-a·gnolo *m.* (anat.) tongue-string; (fig.) tongue, speech; avere lo — sciolto, to have a ready tongue; il vino gli aveva sciolto lo —, wine had loosened his tongue. **-are** [A 6] *intr.* (*aux.* avere) to stutter, to stammer; to lisp. **-ato** *part. adj.* stuttering, stammering; *n.m.* stutterer. (**-atamente** *adv.*) **-atura** *f.* stuttering; stammer; impediment in one's speech; inability to speak clearly.

sciliva *f.* (pop.). See **saliva**.

scilivato *adj.* stodgy, ill-cooked (of bread); stale-smelling.

scill-a[1] *f.* (bot.) squill, *Urginea maritima*. **-itina** *f.* (chem.) scillitin.

Scill-a[2] *pr.n.f.* (geog.) Scylla; (myth., fig.) fra — e Cariddi, between Scylla and Charybdis. **-e·o** *adj.* of Scylla, Scyllean.

scil·lio *m.* (ichth.) dogfish; — gattuccio, *Scyllium canicula*; — gatto-pardo, *S. stellare*; — bocca nera, *Galeus melanostomus*.

†**scillo·ria** *f.* (joc.) gumption, sense.

†**scilocco** *m.* See **scirocco**.

sciloma *m.* (joc.) sermon, wordy discourse.

†**sciloppo** *m.* See **sciroppo**.

†**scima** *f.* (archit.). See **cimasa**.

scimitarr-a *f.* scimitar. **-ata** *f.* blow with a scimitar.

sci(m)·mi-a *f.* (zool.) a monkey, ape; (as an insult) brutta —, ugly brute; far la — a, to imitate, to ape; (mil.) graphic recorder used for testing gun-barrels for defects (similar to a pantograph). **-ata** *f.* mimicry; monkey trick. †**-a·tico** *adj.* ape-like. **-eggiare** [A 3 c] *tr.* to ape, to mimic. **-eggiato** *part. adj.* aped, mimicked; subject to mimicry. (**-eggiatore** *m.* **-eggiatrice** *f.*) **-eggiatura** *f.* mimicry, aping. **-esco** *adj.* (*m.pl.* **-eschi**) simian; monkey-like. †**-o** *m.* see **scimmia**. **-ottare** [A 1] *tr.* to ape, to mimic. **-ottata** *f.* mimicry. (**-ottato** *part. adj.*) **-otto** *m.* young monkey; person ugly as a monkey; fare lo **-otto** a, to ape, to mimic.

scimpanzè *m. indecl.* (zool.) chimpanzee, *Pan satyrus*.

scimunit-o *adj.* silly, foolish, stupid; *n.m.* fool, blockhead. (**-amente** *adv.*) **-ag·gine** *f.* silliness, foolishness; stupid action.

scinco *m.* (zool.) skink, *Scincus officinalis*.

scin·d-ere [C 21] *tr.* to sever; to separate; to split; to divide; to tear; — le vesti, to rend one's garments; (scient.; techn.) to resolve. **-i·bile** *adj.* (leg.) divisible. **-ibilità** *f.* (leg.) divisibility.

scin·gere [C 5] *tr.* (poet.) to ungird, to loosen; to doff; to take off; *rfl.* to loosen one's belt; to lay aside one's sword; to undress; to free oneself.

scintill-a *f.* spark; sparkle; fare **-e**, to give off sparks *or* to sparkle; (motor.) — di accensione, ignition spark; (fig.) la — del genio, the spark of genius; la sacra —, the sacred spark (of inspiration); (med.) scintillation. **-are** [A 1] *intr.* (*aux.* avere) to give off sparks; to sparkle; to scintillate; to shine; to twinkle. **-amento** *m.* sparkling; twinkling; scintillation. **-ante** *part. adj.* sparkling; twinkling; scintillating; bright. **-azione** *f.* scintillation; twinkling; (astron.) scintillation, twinkling. **-io** *m.* sparkling; twinkling; flashing. **-o·metro** *m.* (astron.) scintillometer. **-osco·pio** *m.* (phys.) scintilloscope.

scinto[1] *part.* of **scingere**, q.v.; *adj.* (poet.) ungirt; loosened.

scint-o[2] *m.* (rel.) Shinto. **-oismo** *m.* Shintoism.

Scìo[1] *pr.n.f.* (geog.) Chios; (fig.) andare a —, to get lost; mandare a —, to dismiss, to kill.

scìo[2] *m.* See **ischio**.

sciò *excl.* shoo!

scioccato *adj.* (med.) suffering from shock; (neol., fig.) shocked.

scioc-co *adj.* (*m.pl.* **-chi**) insipid, tasteless; (fig.) silly, stupid, foolish; nonsensical; inane; fatuous; *n.m.* fool. (**-camente** *adv.*) **-cag·gine** *f.* foolishness, silliness. **-cheggiare** [A 3 c] *intr.* (*aux.* avere) to behave like a fool. **-cherello** *adj. dim.* rather silly; *n.m.* silly goose. **-cherellone** *m. augm.* fool; ass. **-cheri·a** *f.* foolish action or remark. **-chezza** *f.* foolishness, silliness; stupidity; inanity; fatuousness; nonsense; foolish action; stupid remark; mistake; trifle. **-chino** *adj. dim.* (e.g. of child) foolish; *n.m.* foolish little thing, little fool. (**-china** *f.*) **-cone** *m. augm.* utter fool; idiot.

scio·gl-iere [B 27] *tr.* to undo, to untie; to loose, to loosen; to let loose, to release; to set free; to disband; to unleash; to unfurl; to solve; to dissolve; to melt; to resolve (doubt); to fulfil (vow, promise, obligation); to utter; to raise (hymn, song); (med.) to

---

resolve; (leg.) to determine; to dissolve; to release; to sever; — una locazione, to determine a lease; — un contratto, to dissolve a contract; — una società, to dissolve a partnership or company; — la comunione, to sever tenancy in common (of real property), common ownership (of personal property), community of goods (of husband and wife); †(naut.) to sail; to weigh; (poet.) — le vele, to set sail; †— i terzaruoli, to shake out a reef; *rfl.* to free oneself, to release oneself; to melt, to dissolve; **-iersi** in lagrime, to melt into tears; (of a meeting) to break up; (of a joint or muscle) to lose its stiffness. **-i·bile** *adj.* solvable; soluble; that can be dissolved; that can be loosened. **-iente** *part. adj.* solvent. **-ilingua** *m. indecl.* tongue-twister. **-imento** *m.* solution, dissolving; disbanding; breaking up; dissolution; melting; termination; (leg.) determination; dissolution; release; severance; (comm.) dissolution; **-imento** di una società, dissolution of partnership or company; (med.) **-imento** di corpo, diarrhoea; (eccl.) dissolution (of a religious order); (theatr.) dénouement, catastrophe; (paint.; sculp.) movement; (naut.) breaking up of ice in a river, etc. **-itore** *m.* liberator; solver. (**-itrice** *f.*)

scïo-grafi·a *f.* the art of telling the time of the day or night from the shadow cast by the sun or moon; (archit.) section (drawing), part elevation. (**-gra·fico** *adj.*)

scïolina *f.* ski wax (rubbed on skis to make them slide better).

†**scï·olo** *adj.* sciolist(ic); *n.m.* wiseacre.

sciolta *f.* (med.) diarrhoea.

sciolt-o *part.* of **sciogliere**, q.v.; *adj.* untied, unbound, loose; quaderno a fogli **-i**, loose-leaf notebook; free; easy; nimble; disengaged; burro —, melted butter; discorso —, prose; versi **-i**, blank verse; avere la lingua **-a**, to have a ready tongue; a briglia **-a**, at full gallop, headlong; — nel sonno, sound asleep; in dissolution; destroyed, broken up; solved; (comm.) loose, not packed, wrapped or bottled; vini **-i**, wines from the wood; (chem.) dissolved; †(naut.) vela **-a**, a free sail, without boom or yard at the foot; (mus.) in free style; detached; dissonanze **-e**, unprepared dissonances. **-amente** *adv.* freely, easily, nimbly; fluently. **-ezza** *f.* ease; fluency; freedom (of movement); agility, nimbleness; camminare con **-ezza**, to walk with an easy gait; absence of affectation or inhibition. **-ura** *f.* (archit.) looseness in masonry.

†**sciol·vere** *vb.* and derivs. See **asciolvere**.

sciomanzi·a *f.* necromancy.

†**scion-e** *m.* (naut.) squall, hurricane, whirlwind; (Tusc.) tingle 'fishing' on a spar. **-ata** *f.* (naut.) tornado (African coast).

†**scionnare** *rfl.* to wake up.

sciop *m. indecl.* beer-glass.

scioper-are [A 1 s] *intr.* (*aux.* avere) to strike, to go on strike. **-ag·gine** *f.* idleness, laziness. **-ante** *part. adj.* on strike, striking; *n.m.* striker. **-atac·cio** *m. pejor.* loafer; slacker. **-atag·gine** *f.* idleness (due to a strike); (fig.) laziness. **-atezza** *f.* unemployment. **-ativo** *adj.* out of work; on strike. **-ato** *part. adj.* out of work, unemployed; lazy; *adv. phr.* alla **-ata**, idly, lazily; *n.m.* lazy person; idler, loafer. (**-atamente** *adv.*)

scioper-o *m.* strike; far —, to strike, to go on strike; — a singhiozzi, a kind of intermittent strike on alternate days, etc.; — lampo, lightning strike; — a catene, series of strikes in various branches of industry; — di regolamento, go-slow strike (i.e. adhering literally to regulations); — di protesta, token strike; — a braccia incrociate, — bianco, sit-down strike; diritto di —, right to strike; — di solidarietà, sympathetic strike; — della fame, hunger-strike; **-i** e serrate, strikes and lock-outs.

†**sciopino** *m.* accident (in the course of work).

Scïo·podi *pr.n.m.pl.* (myth.) Sciapodes.

†**scioppa** *f.* See **stoppa**.

†**sciopr-are** *vb.* and derivs. see **scioperare**. †**-o** *m.* see **sciopero**.

†**sciorare** *intr.* to flow freely away; *tr.* see **sciorinare**.

sciorina *f.* (ichth.) grey mullet, *Mugil chelo*.

sciorin-are [A 1] *tr.* to hang out to dry; to air (clothes); (naut.) — le brande, to air bedding; to spread out, to display; (fig., Tusc.) to babble forth, to rattle off; to disclose, to divulge; *intr.* (*aux.* essere) (of liquid) to run away, to pour out. (**-amento** *m.*) **-ato** *part. adj.* hung out; displayed; spread out; poured out.

sciorlo *m.* (miner.) schorl, black tourmaline.

†**sciorre** *infin.* See **sciogliere**.

†**scioverare** *vb.* and derivs. See **sceverare**.

†**sciovernare** *rfl.* to pass the winter.

scïovi·a *f.* (neol.) ski-lift.

sciovin-ismo *m.* chauvinism. **-ista** *m.* chauvinist; *adj.* chauvinistic.

†**scipare** *tr.* to spoil; — il sangue, to curdle the blood; *rfl.* to miscarry (cf. **sciupare**).

†**scipidire**, †**scipire** *intr.* to become insipid, to lose flavour.

†**sci·pido** *adj.* See **scipito**.

scipit-o *adj.* insipid, tasteless; lacking savour; dull. (**-aménte** *adv.*) **-ag·gine** *f.* silliness, fatuity; dullness; insipidity. **-ezza** *f.* tasteless-ness, insipidity; dullness; silliness, fatuity.

scipp-o *m.* (slang) bag-snatching; (Naples) theft accompanied by violence. **-are** [A I] *tr.* (slang) to 'pinch'. **-ista** *m.* bag-snatcher.

†**scire**[1] *tr.* to know.

†**scire**[2] *intr.* See **uscire**.

sciringa *f.* (mus.). See **siringa**.

scirocc-o *m.* (geog.) Sirocco, Scirocco; guardare verso —, to look to the south-east; (naut.) south-east wind; direction south-east; applied to any hot damp wind regardless of direction and even sometimes when dry and scorching; also to denote close, 'stuffy' weather, even when there is no wind; sou'wester hat. **-ale** *adj.* of S(c)irocco; sultry. **-ata** *f.* south-east gale, lasting usually three to six days.

Scirone *pr.n.m.* (Gk. myth) Sciron, the brigand killed by Theseus; (Gk. antiq.) Sciron, the wind blowing from the Scironian cliffs.

sciropp-o *m.* syrup; (pharm.) — per la tosse, linctus; (joc.) — di cantina, wine. **-are** [A I] *m.* to candy with syrup; to sweeten; to sip, to savour; (fig., joc.) to console. **-ato** *part. adj.* sweetened; preserved in syrup; *n.m.* syrup. **-etto** *m. dim.* light syrup, fruit-juice drink, sherbet. **-oso** *adj.* syrupy.

scirpo *m.* (bot.) bulrush, *Holoschoenus paluster*.

scirr-o *m.* (med.) scirrhus. **-oso** *adj.* scirrhous.

scism-a *m.* (eccl. and fig.) schism. **-a·tico** *adj., n.m.* schismatic. (**-aticaménte** *adv.*)

scis·s-ile *adj.* fissile, liable to split up; (miner.; geol.) scissile. **-ione** *f.* splitting, split; division; cleavage; secession; (biol.) fission; riproduzione per **-ione**, reproduction by fission; (atom. phys.) fission; **-ione** nucleare, nuclear fission; soglia di **-ione**, fission threshold; (atom. phys.) suscettibile di **-ione**, fissionable. **-iparità** *f.* (biol.) fissiparity; reproduction by fission, fissipation.

sciss-o *part.* of **scindere**, q.v.; *adj.* divided, separated; cleft; split; torn; open-necked. **-ura** *f.* cleft, split; division; furrow; dis-sension, disagreement; break; (anat.) fissure; **-ura** di Rolando, sulcus centralis; (vet.) crack in a horse's hoof.

scist-o *m.*, **-oso** *adj.* See **schist-o**, **-oso**.

sci·tal-a, **-e** *f.* (Gk. antiq.) cudgel; *scytale* (staff used by Spartans for sending dispatches in cipher).

scito *m.*, *adj.* Scythian; †term used to denote any people in the far north.

sciuga-mano *m.*, **-toio** *m.* See **asciuga-mano**, **-toio**.

sciuma *m.* See **sciamma**.

†**sciuno** *adj.* undefended; unprepared, ill-equipped; unprovided.

sciuntag·gio *m.* (electr.) shunting.

sciup-are [A I] *tr.* to spoil, to damage, to mar; to hurt; to injure; to ruin; to waste, to consume, to squander; — il tempo, to waste one's time; *rfl.* to be spoiled, to spoil; to be ruined; (of material, etc.) to get crumpled; to become run down in health. **-acarte** *adj., n.m. indecl.* scribbler. **-acchiare** [A 4] *tr.* to spoil bit by bit; to damage slightly. †**-ateste** *m. indecl.* incompetent teacher. **-ato** *part. adj.* spoiled, damaged; injured; ruined; wasted; squandered; run down in health. **-atore** *m.* waster; squanderer. (**-atrice** *f.*) **-inìo**, **-io** *m.* constant waste; wastage; (comm.) abbuono per **-ìo**, tret. **-o** *m.* waste; fare **-o** di, to waste; damage; dissipation. **-one** *m.* waster, squanderer; spendthrift. (**-ona** *f.*)

sciuscià *m.* (neol.) Neapolitan shoeblack (corruption of 'shoeshine').

sciverto *m.* (naut., Genoa) curving of a plate or frame.

sci·vola *f.* steep slide; water course or duct set on a steep incline.

scivol-are [A I s] *intr.* (essere, avere) to slip, to slide; to glide; far — un biglietto, to slip a note (into someone's hand, etc.); (fig.) — su, to pass over (a subject) lightly; (aeron.) — sull'ala, to sideslip; (mus.) — sulla tastiera, to glide over the keys, to play a glissando (cf. under **glissare**). **-ante** *part. adj.* slipping; gliding. **-ata** *f.* slide; sliding. **-atoio** *m.* slip (for seaplanes); slipway.

sci·vol-o *m.* slip, slide (for tobogganing, etc.); (aeron.) runway; slip (for seaplanes); (techn.) chute, pair of skids; (mus.) slide-trill, glide. **-etto** *m.* (mus.) slide-trill, glide. **-one** *m. augm.* bad fall.

sclamare [A I] and derivs. See **esclamare**.

sclarea *f.* (bot.) clary, *Salvia sclarea*.

scler-a *f.* (anat.) sclera, sclerotic coat. **-anto** *m.* (bot.) knawel, *Scleranthus*. **-ema** *m.* (med.) sclerema. **-en·chima** *f.* (bot.) sclerenchyma. **-ite** *f.* (med.) scleritis, sclerotitis. **-oma** *m.* (med.) scleroma. **-o·metro** *m.* (eng.) hardness testing machine; sclero-meter; **-ometro** a sfera, ball hardness testing machine. **-onissi** *f.* (surg.) scleronyxis. **-osante** *adj.* (med.) sclerosing. **-osi** *f.* (med.) sclerosis. **-o·tica** *f.* (anat.) sclerotic coat, sclerotic. **-o·tico** *adj.* sclerotic. **-otomi·a** *f.* (surg.) sclerotomy. **-o·zio** *m.* (bot.) sclerosis.

†**scluso** *adj.* See **escluso**.

†**scob·bia** *f.* See **sgobbia**.

scocca *f.* (motor.) body; mono —, monocoque, single shell.

scocc-are [A 2 c], [A 2] *intr.* (aux. essere) to shoot out; to go off; to dart, to fly; (of a catch, trap, etc.) to spring; (of the hours) to strike; **-ano** le sei, it is striking six; (of thread) to run off the spindle; *tr.* to shoot (esp. an arrow); to shoot off, to let fly; to throw, to fling; to dart; — un bacio, to give a smacking kiss; (of a clock) to strike; l'orologio **-ava** le nove, the clock was striking nine; (fig.) **-are** un epigramma, to come out with an epigram on the spur of the moment; *n.m.* beginning, start; allo — della prima decade di aprile, in the early part of April. **-ante** *part. adj.* shooting, darting; **-anti** baci, smacking kisses. **-ato** *part. adj.* shot; sprung; let fly; struck; flung.

scocchiumare [A I] *tr.* to remove the bung from (a cask).

scocci-are [A 4] *tr.* to break (pots, eggs, etc.); (fig., pop.) to harass, to bother; to bore; (naut.) to unhook, to unreeve; — la rete, to cast off the lashings in order to haul in a net; *rfl.* (of fishes) to get free from a hook. **-aménto** *m.* breaking; (fig., pop.) harassing. (**-ato** *part. adj.*) **-atore** *m.* bore. (**-atrice** *f.*) **-atura** *f.* breakage; (fig., pop.) bother, nuisance.

scoccigliare [A 4] *tr., intr.* (aux. avere) to move crockery noisily, to clash or rattle crockery.

scoc-co *m.* (*pl.* **-chi**) shooting off, letting fly; (of a bow) twang; (of a kiss) smack; (of a clock) stroke, striking; allo — di mezza-notte, on the stroke of midnight.

scoccolare [A I s] *tr.* to pluck (berries), to strip (a plant) of berries; †to scribble off, to dash off; †(derog.) to utter, to give vent to.

†**scoccoveggiare** *vb.* and derivs. See **coccoveggiare**.

scocuzzolare [A I s] *tr.* to decapitate, to cut off the top of.

scod-are [A I] *tr.* to dock. **-ato** *part. adj.* docked; tailless.

scodell-a, †**scudella** *f.* (Tusc., C. Italy) soup-plate; soup-plateful; far le **-e**, to serve out the soup; (N. Italy, Ven.) bowl; porridge-bowl; fare — delle mani, to cup one's hands together; †(naut.) bed-plate of a capstan; *pl.* scales of a balance. **-aio** *m.* maker or vendor of crockery. **-are** [A I] *tr.* to dish out, to serve up (esp. soup); (fig., pop.) to 'dish out', to pour forth (promises, excuses, etc.); to produce. **-ata** *f.* helping (of food), plateful; bowlful. **-ato** *part. adj.* dished out, served up. **-ina** *f.* (bot.) wall pennywort, *Umbilicus rupestris*; (zool.) limpet, *Patella coerulea*; (numism.) concave coin, value 5 paoli. **-ino** *m.* small bowl; scale of balance; (eng.) cup; cap; retainer; *pl.* (fam.) dimples (in the cheeks).

scodinzol-are [A I s] *intr.* (aux. avere) (of an animal) to wag its tail; (fig., joc., of a woman) to sway the hips when walking (cf. **sculettare**). **-io** *m.* tail-wagging.

†**scoffacciare** *tr.* to squash flat (cf. †**cofaccia**, metathesis of **focaccia**, q.v.).

scoffin-a *f.*, **-are** [A I]. See **scuffin-a**, **-are**.

†**scoffone** *m.* woollen coverlet; woollen stocking.

†**sco·glia** *f.* outer covering, skin (cf. **spoglia**).

sco·gli-o[1] *m.* rock; cliff; gli scogli bianchi di Dover, the white cliffs of Dover; (oceanog.) reef; (fig.) difficulty; stumbling-block. **-era** *f.* reef of rocks; rocky cliff; **-ere** coralline, coral reefs. **-etto** *m. dim.* rocky islet. **-oso** *adj.* rocky; full of rocks; (fig.) difficult; dangerous.

sco·glio[2] *m.* (zool.) *Murex* spp., a kind of whelk; — brandare, *M. brandaris*; — troncato, *M. trunculus*.

scoglion-are [A I c] *tr.* (vulg.) to ridicule; to insult. **-ato** *part. adj.* ridiculed; insulted; (slang) 'shattered', in despair, profoundly depressed; discouraged.

†**scognominato** *adj.* nicknamed.

scoiat·tolo *m.* (zool.) squirrel, *Sciurus* spp.; (electr.) gabbia di —, squirrel cage.

scola[1] *f.* shuttle.

†**scola**[2] *f.* See **scuola**.

†**scola·io** *m.* See **scolaro**.

scol-are¹ [A I] *tr.* to drain; to leave to drip; to pass through a strainer; *intr.* (*aux.* essere) to drip, to drain off, to run off. **-afritto** *m. indecl.* frying-basket. **-amento** *m.* draining, dripping. **-andino** *m.* colander. **-ato** *part. adj.* drained off; drained; well drained. **-atoio** *m.* drain, drain-pipe; sink; strainer; drip pan; *adj.* serving to drain. **-atura** *f.* draining; dripping; drains, drips, dregs. **-atrice** *f.* (industr.) dewatering machine. **-azione** *f.* (med.) see **scolo**. **-io** *m.* constant dripping; draining away.

†**scolare**² *m.* See **scolaro**.

scolar-o *m.* schoolboy; pupil; scholar; student; disciple, follower. (**-a** *f.*) †**-eggiare** *intr.* to behave like a schoolboy (-girl). **-esca** *f.* the pupils in a class or school; students, student-body. **-esco** *adj.* (*m.pl.* **-eschi**) relating to schools and schoolchildren; gergo **-esco**, schoolboy slang; *adv. phr.* alla **-esca**, in schoolboy fashion. (**-escamente** *adv.*)

scolasticheri·a *f.* (derog.) pedantry.

scola·stic-o *adj.* scholastic; relating to school; anno **—**, school year; doveri **-i**, school tasks, homework, etc.; aula **-a**, schoolroom; ispettore **—**, inspector of schools; (admin.) gioventù **-a**, children of school age; (mus.) stile **—**, strict style, academic style, learned style; (philos.) scholastic; *n.m.* schoolman, scholastic philosopher; schoolmaster; (hist.) teacher of rhetoric; head of a (medieval) school; (eccl.) canon theologian. **-amente** *adv.* scholastically. **-a** *f.* scholastic philosophy and theology, scholasticism. **-ag·gine** *f.* (derog.) pedantic scholasticism. **-ismo** *m.* scholasticism. **-ità** *f.* scholastic quality; pedantry. **-ume** *m.* (derog.) pedantic minutiae.

scolecite *f.* (miner.) scolecite.

scoletta¹ *f. dim.* of **scuola**¹, q.v.; kindergarten; first year's Latin class.

scoletta² *f. dim.* of **scola**¹, q.v.; little shuttle; fuse; (naut., Leghorn) dead-eye.

scoliaste *m.* scholiast.

sco·lice (zool.) scolex (of a tapeworm).

sco·lio *m.* (textual criticism) scholium, gloss; (Gk. antiq.) scolion, drinking song.

scoli-osi *f.* (med.) scoliosis, curvature of the spine. **-o·tico** *adj.* (anat.) scoliotic.

scollacci-are [A 3] *rfl.* to wear a dress that is too décolleté. **-ato** *part. adj.* wearing a dress that is too décolleté; immodest; (fig.) licentious. **-atura** *f.* décolletage; immodesty in dress; (fig.) licentiousness.

scoll-are¹ [A I] *tr.* to unglue, to take off (something glued or pasted on); *rfl.* to come off, to come unstuck. **-ato** *part. adj.* unstuck; testa **-ata**, scatterbrained person. **-atura** *f.* ungluing; coming unstuck (cf. **colla**).

scoll-are² [A I] *tr.* to cut the neck-hole in (a garment); **—** a punta, to make a V-neck; **—** a quadro, to cut a square neck; **—** un fiasco, to break the neck off a flask; *rfl.* to wear a low-necked dress. **-amento** *m.* (surg.) décollement. **-ato** *part. adj.* low-necked, cut low in the neck; wearing a low-necked garment; camicia **-ata**, open-necked shirt; scarpa **-ata**, court shoe, shoe leaving the instep uncovered; *n.m.* neck-opening; (naut., Leghorn) gunwale. **-atura** *f.* neck-opening; cutting out the neck of a garment (cf. **collo**).

scolleg-are [A 2] *tr.* to disconnect, to separate. **-amento** *m.* disconnexion, untying, uncoupling; lack of continuity; (rhet.) asyndeton. (**-ato** *part. adj.*)

scollettare [A I c] *tr.* (agric.) to top (e.g. sugar-beet).

scollinare [A I] *intr.* (*aux.* avere) to walk in the hills; to take to the hills.

scoll-o *m.* neck-opening (of a garment). **-ino** *m.* neck-handkerchief, neckerchief, square.

†**scollorire** *rfl.* to give vent to rage.

scolmare [A I c] *tr.* to remove the top from; to remove excess from; to level (cf. **colmo**).

sco̧lo *m.* drain; drain-pipe; drainage; liquid that drains away; (leg.) acque di **—**, drainage water; (U.S.) seepage; (geog.) drain, run-off; (naut.) canale di **—**, scupper; (med.) blennorrhoea; (slang) gonorrhoea.

scolopendr-a *f.*, **-i·a** *f.*, **-i·o** *m.*, **-o** *m.* (bot.) hart's tongue fern, *Phyllitis scolopendrium*.

scolo·pio *m.* (eccl.) Piarist, member of the Pauline Congregation.

scolor-are [A I c] *tr.* to cause to fade; to discolour; to deprive of colour; to remove colour from; *rfl.* to fade; to become dis-

coloured; to grow pale. **-amento** *m.* fading; discoloration. **-ato** *part. adj.* faded; discoloured.

scolor-ire [D 2] *tr.*, *intr.* (*aux.* essere) to lose colour; to grow pale. (**-imento** *m.*) **-ina** *f.* ink eradicator; stain remover. **-ito** *part. adj.* colourless; pale.

scolp-are [A I c] *tr.* to excuse; to exculpate; to justify; *rfl.* to make excuses, to defend oneself; to justify oneself. (**-ato** *part. adj.*)

scolp-ire [D 2] *tr.* (sculp.) to carve; to sculpt, to sculpture; to cut, to chisel; to engrave; (fig.) **—** nella memoria a, to the memory of; **—** le parole, to pronounce one's words distinctly. **-ito** *part. adj.* carved; sculptured, sculpted; chiselled; engraved; (fig.) impressed; distinct. **-itamente** *adv.* distinctly. †**-itore** *m.* see **scultore**. **-itura** *f.* groove (e.g. in a tyre tread).

scolt-a *f.* (mil.) sentry, nightwatchman; fare la **—**, to be on sentry go; patrol, round; (naut.) lower deck sentry (usually unarmed); †harbour watchman. †**-are** *vb.* and derivs. see **ascoltare**.

scoltell-are [A I] *tr.* (agric.) to weed with a knife; to cut (for gathering); to knife, to wound with a knife; *recip. rfl.* to fight with knives. **-ato** *part. adj.* cut (and gathered). (**-atore** *m.* **-atrice** *f.*)

scolt-o *adj.*, **-ura** *f.* See **scult-o**, **-ura**.

scombaciare [A 3] *tr.* to prise asunder, to part.

†**scombat·tere** *vb.* and derivs. *intens.* of **combattere**, q.v.

†**scombavare** *intr.* to slobber.

†**scomberello** *m.* long scoop or ladle.

†**scombiatare** *vb.* and derivs. See **accommiatare**.

scombiccher-are [A I s] *tr.*; *intr.* (*aux.* avere) (pop.) to scribble. **-ato** *part. adj.* scribbled; scribbled on or over. **-atore** *m.* scribbler. (**-atrice** *f.*)

scombin-are [A I] *tr.* to disarrange; to upset; (typ.) to distribute. **-ato** *part. adj.* disarranged; upset; (fig.) confused, muddled. **-azione** *f.* disarranging; upsetting.

scombro *m.* (ichth.) mackerel; **—** comune, common mackerel, *Scomber scomber*; **—** macchiato, **—** occhi grossi, Spanish mackerel, *S. colias*.

scombu·glio *m.* disorder, confusion.

scombui-are [A 4] *tr.* to upset; to derange; to confuse; to disturb; to overwhelm. **-amento** *m.* disorder, confusion, disturbance. **-ato** *part. adj.* disturbed, upset.

scombussol-are [A I s] *tr.* to confuse (with regard to direction); to upset; to disturb; to derange. (**-amento** *m.*) **-ato** *part. adj.* confused; disturbed; deranged. **-io** *m.* continual disturbance; confusion.

scomment-are [A I] *tr.* (naut.) to open the seams of. **-ato** *part. adj.* (naut.) bastimento **-ato**, neglected ship.

scom-messa *f.* bet, wager; stake; fare una **—**, to bet, to lay a wager; (leg.) debito di giuoco o **—**, gaming debt or wager (C.C.). **-messo** *part.* of **scommettere**², q.v.; *adj.* wagered; staked.

scommett-ere¹ [C 20] *tr.* to bet, to wager, to stake; (fig.) scommetto che, I bet that, I am certain that; *intr.* (*aux.* avere) to bet, to gamble. **-itore** *m.* gambler; one who bets. (**-itrice** *f.*)

scommett-ere² [C 2] *tr.* to undo, to untie; to disconnect; to take apart; (fig.) to cause division between. **-imento** *m.* undoing; disconnecting. **-itura** *f.* lack of cohesion, state of being disconnected.

†**scommezzare** *vb.* and derivs. See **dimezzare**.

†**scommiatare** *vb.* and derivs. See **accommiatare**.

†**scommossa** *f.* agitation, commotion; upheaval.

scommosso *part.* of **scommuovere**, q.v.; *adj.* violently shaken; mare **—**, rough sea.

scommovimento *m.* violent shaking.

scommuo·vere [C 15] *tr.* to shake violently (cf. **commuovere**).

scomod-are [A I s] *tr.* to trouble, to inconvenience, to disturb; *rfl.* to put oneself out, to trouble oneself. (**-ato** *part. adj.*)

sco·mod-o¹ *adj.* inconvenient; uncomfortable, troublesome; stare **—**, to be uncomfortable. **-amente** *adv.* uncomfortably; inconveniently; unfortunately. **-ità** *f.* discomfort; inconvenience.

sco·modo² *m.* discomfort; inconvenience; trouble; gli diedi una mancia per lo **—**, I gave him a tip for his trouble.

scompagin-are [A I s] *tr.* to disarrange; to upset, to throw into disorder; (typ.) to distribute. **-amento** *m.* disarrangement, upsetting. **-ato** *part. adj.* disarranged; upset; in disorder; in confusion; (typ.) distributed. **-atura** *f.* disarrangement; disorder, confusion. **-azione** *f.* action of disarranging, upsetting.

scompa·gine *f.* lack of order, disorder.

scompagn-are [A 5] *tr.* to part, to separate (a pair, companions, etc.); *rfl.* (*prep.* da) to part (from); *recip. rfl.* to separate, to part (from one another). **-amento** *m.* separating, parting; dividing. **-ato** *part. adj.* parted, separated. **-atura** *f.* parting, separating. **-o** *adj.* odd, not matching.

scompar-ire [D 2] *intr.* (*aux.* essere) to disappear, to vanish; to fade away; to retire, to quit the scene; to cut a poor figure; to look insignificant; (euphem.) to depart this life, to pass away. **-sa** *f.* disappearance; (euphem.) death; woman who has passed over. **-so** *part. adj.* disappeared, vanished; extinct; (euphem.) deceased; *n.m.* deceased person.

scompart-ire [D 1] *tr.* to divide up; to share out; to allot. **-imento** *m.* division; dividing up; sharing out; (rlwy.) compartment; (archit.) partition; gli -imenti dell'Inferno di Dante, the divisions of Dante's Hell; (naut.) -imento stagno, watertight compartment; (paint.) panel, section (of a polyptych, etc.). **-ito** *part. adj.* divided up; shared out; allotted; partitioned. **-itamente** *adv.* separately, distributively. (**-itore** *m.* **-itrice** *f.*) **-o** *m.* compartment, section.

scompens-o *m.* (techn.) lack of compensation; (med.) decompensation. **-are** [A 1] *tr.* (eng.; phys.) to decompensate.

scompiac-ere [B 15] *intr.* (*aux.* essere; *prep.* a) to be disobliging; to be unaccommodating. **-ente** *part. adj.* disobliging; unaccommodating; unhelpful, uncooperative. **-enza** *f.* disobligingness; unresponsiveness; lack of co-operation. **-iuto** *part. adj.* hurt, rebuffed.

scompigli-are [A 4] *tr.* to disarrange, to upset, to throw into disorder; to ruffle; to discompose; to trouble; *rfl.* to become upset; -arsi per un nonnulla, to make a fuss about nothing. **-a·bile** *adj.* liable to be upset; precarious. **-amento** *m.* disorder, confusion; upsetting. **-ato** *part. adj.* upset; confused, disordered; perturbed; matassa -ata, tangled skein. **-atamente** *adv.* confusedly; in disorder. **-atore** *m.* disturber, agitator. (**-atrice** *f.*)

scompi·gl·io *m.* confusion, disorder; fuss; mettere tutto in —, to throw everything into confusion; discord; quarrel; mettere lo — in una famiglia, to cause dissension in a family. **-io** *m.* continual fuss, confusion; continual discord, dissension.

scompisci-are [A 3] *tr.* to piss upon, to wet (upon); to make a mess of; *rfl.* to piss oneself; (fig.) -arsi dalle risa, to split one's sides with laughter. (**-ato** *part. adj.*)

scomplet-are [A 1] *tr.* to render incomplete; — una collezione, to break up, to sell part of, a collection. (**-ato** *part. adj.*)

scompleto *adj.* incomplete, broken.

†**scompo·n-ere** *vb.* see **scomporre**. **-ente** *part. adj.* decomposing; analytical. **-i·bile** *adj.* decomposable. **-imento** *m.* decomposition; -imento del cadavere, dissection of the corpse.

scom-porre [B 21] *tr.* to break up; to take to pieces; to analyse; to decompose, to disarrange; to discompose; to trouble, to worry; to agitate; (eng.) — un motore, to strip an engine; (rlwy.) — un treno, to split up a train; (mech.) — una forza, to resolve a force; — in fattori, to factorize; (typ.) to distribute; *rfl.* to decompose; to be troubled, to be upset; to be worried, to worry; to lose one's temper; senza -porsi, remaining quite composed, without turning a hair. **-positivo** *adj.* liable to decomposition; analytical. (**-positore** *m.* **-positrice** *f.*) **-posizione** *f.* breaking up; breaking down; analysis; decomposition; perturbation; disorder; (mech.) resolution (of a force); (chem.) decomposition; (electron.) -posizione dell'immagine, image scanning.

scompost-o, scompost-o *part.* of **scomporre**, q.v.; *adj.* in pieces, broken up; discomposed, disordered, untidy; slack; unseemly; non stare -o, don't loll; troubled; confused; (equit.) uncollected. (**-amente** *adv.*) **-ezza** *f.* disorderliness.

scomput-are [A 1] *tr.* to deduct, to subtract; — un debito, to pay off a debt. **-a·bile** *adj.* deductible. (**-ato** *part. adj.*)

scom·puto *m.* deduction, subtraction; amount to be deducted.

scomunare *tr.* to divide, to disunite.

scomu·nic-a *f.* (eccl.; fig.) excommunication; aver la — (addosso), to be always in trouble, to be very unlucky, to be 'under a curse'; (joc.) expulsion from a political party. **-are** [A 2 s] *tr.* to excommunicate; to prohibit; (joc.) to expel (e.g. from a political party). **-ato** *part. adj.* excommunicate(d); sacrilegious; profane; prohibited; forbidden; (fig., colloq.) faccia -ata, ugly mug; *n.m.* excommunicated person. (**-atore** *m.*) **-azione** *f.* sentence of excommunication, anathema.

†**scomunione** *f.* See **scomunica**.

---

†**scomuz·zolo** *m.* tiny particle, morsel, crumb.

scona *f.* (naut.) schooner.

sconcac-are [A 2] *tr.* (vulg.) to foul, to dirty; (fig.) to besmirch. (**-ato** *part. adj.* **-atore** *m.* **-atrice** *f.*)

†**sconcacciare** *vb.* and derivs. See **scacciare**.

sconcaten-are [A 1] *tr.* to disconnect; to unchain, to loose; to unbind the chain of. **-amento** *m.* disconnecting; unchaining. (**-ato** *part. adj.*)

†**sconcennatamente** *adv.* in disorder; improperly.

sconcert-are [A 1] *tr.* to disconcert; to baffle; to perturb, to upset; to trouble; to derange. **-amento** *m.* disconcertedness. **-ato** *part. adj.* disconcerted; perturbed; troubled; disturbed; disorderly; (mus.) out of tune. **-atamente** *adv.* disconcertedly; perturbedly.

sconcerto *m.* disturbance (esp. of stomach), sickness; (mus.) false intonation; confused performance.

sconcezza *f.* See under **sconcio**.

sconchiu·dere [C 3] and derivs. See **sconcludere**.

sconci-are [A 3 c] *tr.* to spoil, to mar; to deform; *rfl.*, †*intr.* to miscarry, to have a miscarriage. **-atura** *f.* marring; abortion; (fig.) work badly done.

sconc-io *adj.* indecent; obscene; filthy, nasty; deformed; ill-shapen; †untidy, disorderly; *n.m.* indecent, obscene thing. **-iamente** *adv.* indecently; obscenely; filthily; nastily. **-ezza** *f.* indecency; obscenity; filth; nastiness.

sonclu·dere [C 3] *tr.* to break off; — un contratto, to break a contract.

sconclus·ionato *adj.* inconclusive; inconsequent; rambling. **-o** *part.* of **sconcludere**, q.v.; *adj.* broken off; inconclusive.

sconcord-are [A 1] *intr.* (*aux.* avere) to disagree; not to go well together, not to match. **-ante** *part. adj.* discordant, out of harmony. **-anza** *f.* clash (of colours, etc.); disharmony; dissonance; disagreement; (gramm.) breach of a rule of concord.

sconcorde *adj.* discordant; not in agreement; dissident.

sconcor·dio *f.* disagreement.

†**scon·dere** *vb.* and derivs. See **nascondere**.

†**scondescen·dere** *vb.* and derivs. See **scoscendere**.

scondito *adj.* not seasoned; †insipid; †inane.

scon-facente, †-face·vole *adj.* unsuitable.

sconferm-a *f.* contradiction. †**-are** *tr.* to contradict.

sconfess-are [A 1] *tr.* to disavow; to disown; to repudiate. **-ato** *part. adj.* **-ione** *f.* disavowal; disowning; repudiation; (comm.) disclaimer.

sconficc-are [A 2] *tr.* to pull out, to extract; to remove. **-a·bile** *adj.* that can be extracted; removable. (**-amento** *m.*) **-ato** *part. adj.* pulled out, extracted; removed. **-atura** *f.* pulling out, extraction; mark left after extraction; removal.

sconfid-are [A 1] *intr.* (*aux.* avere), *rfl.* to lose trust, to be no longer confident; to lose hope. **-ato** *part. adj.* distrustful; no longer confident; not hopeful. **-ente** *part. adj.* distrustful. **-enza** *f.* distrust, loss of confidence; discouragement.

sconfig·g-ere[1] [C 12] *tr.* to defeat; to discomfit. **-imento** *m.* defeat; discomfiture. (**-itore** *m.* **-itrice** *f.*)

sconfig·gere[2] [C 12] and derivs. See **sconficcare**.

sconfin-are [A 1] *intr.* (*aux.* avere, essere) to break bounds; to trespass; to cross the frontier; (fig.) to exceed the limits (of); to digress widely. **-amento** *m.* breaking of bounds; trespass; escape. **-ato** *part. adj.* excessive, extravagant; boundless, unlimited.

sconfitt-a *f.* defeat; discomfiture; toccare una —, to suffer defeat; (fig.) avere una —, to be defeated. **-o** *part.* of **sconfiggere**[1], q.v.; *adj.* defeated; discomfited; (fig.) ruined.

†**sconfon·dere** [C 2] *intens.* of **confondere**, q.v.

sconfort-are [A 1] *tr.* to dishearten, to discourage; to distress; to dissuade; *rfl.* to become disheartened; to lose courage; to distress oneself. **-ante** *part. adj.* discouraging; disheartening; distressing; disturbing. **-ato** *part. adj.* discouraged; disheartened, downcast; distressed; disturbed. **-atore** *m.* 'Job's comforter'. (**-atrice** *f.*) **-evole** *adj.* see **sconfortante**.

sconforto *m.* discouragement; depression; distress; sorrow; dejection; mi prese lo —, my spirits sank; essere pieno di —, to be disheartened; un momento di —, a moment of depression.

scongegnare [A 5 c] *tr.* to take to pieces; to separate the parts of.

scongiun·g-ere [C 5] *tr.* to disjoin; to disconnect. **-imento** *m.* disjoining; disconnecting.

†**scongiura** *f.* See **scongiuro**, under **scongiurare**.

scongiur-are [A 1] *tr.* to entreat, to implore, to beseech; lo -avano a desistere, they implored him to desist; mi -ò di non partire, he implored me not to leave; to exorcize; to avert. **-amento** *m.* entreaty, beseeching; exorcism. **-ato** *part. adj.* entreated, implored. (**-atore** *m.* **-atrice** *f.*) **-azione** *f.* exorcism; curse. **-o** *m.* entreaty; invocation; exorcism; incantation, charm; fare gli -i contro la iettatura, to ward off the evil eye; (eccl.) exorcism.

sconness-o *part.* of **sconnettere**, q.v.; *adj.* disconnected; desultory; pensieri -i, wandering thoughts. **-amente** *adv.* disjointedly; desultorily. **-ione** *f.* disconnectedness, want of connexion; desultoriness.

sconnet·tere [C 19] *tr.* to disconnect; to fail to connect.

sconocchi-are [A 4] *tr.* to take from the distaff; to strip (the grain) from maize; *intr.* (*aux.* avere) to finish spinning a distaff-full. (**-ato** *part. adj.*) **-atura** *f.* taking from the distaff; what remains on the distaff.

sconosc-ere [B 9] *tr.* to fail to recognize; to refuse to recognize; to slight; to disregard; to be ignorant of; to underrate; to fail to appreciate; (mil.) to refuse recognition of (an undesirable deserter); *intr.* (*aux.* avere) to be ungrateful. **-ente** *part. adj.* ignorant; ungrateful, thankless; *n.m.* gli -enti, ungrateful people. **-entemente** *adv.* ungratefully, thanklessly. **-enza** *f.* ingratitude, ungratefulness; †ignorance. **-imento** *m.* refusal to recognize (a claim, right, etc.). **-iuto** *part. adj.* unknown; disregarded; unappreciated; -iuto a se stesso, unaware of one's own worth; *n.m.* unknown person; stranger. (**-a** *f.*) **-iutamente** *adv.* secretly; unbeknown.

sconquass-are [A 1] *tr.* to smash; to shatter; to break up; to destroy. (**-amento** *m.*) **-ato** *part. adj.* smashed, shattered; salute -ata, broken health. (**-atore** *m.* **-atrice** *f.*) **-o** *m.* destruction; smashing; smash; ruin; crash; tumult.

sconsacr-are [A 1] *tr.* (rel.) to profane; to desecrate; to degrade; to unfrock (a priest); to turn (a church) to a secular purpose. (**-ato** *part. adj.*) **-azione** *f.* (rel.) profanation; desecration; deconsecration.

sconsenso *m.* (pop.). See **consenso**.

sconsent-ire [D 1] *intr.* (*aux.* avere) to dissent. **-imento** *m.* dissent.

†sconsertato *adj.* See **sconcertato**, under **sconcertare**.

†sconserto *adj.* untwisted (cf. **conserto**).

sconsider-ato *adj.* thoughtless, heedless; inconsiderate; feckless; rash. **-atamente** *adv.* thoughtlessly, heedlessly; inconsiderately; fecklessly; rashly. **-azione** *f.* thoughtlessness; lack of consideration.

sconsigli-are [A 4] *tr.* (*prep.* da) to dissuade (from); to deter, to discourage; è un'impresa da -arsi a chiunque, it is something everyone ought to be dissuaded from doing. **-a·bile** *adj.* inadvisable. **-atezza** *f.* rashness; inconsiderateness; thoughtlessness. **-ato** *part. adj.* ill-advised; indiscreet; rash; foolish. **-atamente** *adv.* unadvisedly; rashly. (**-atore** *m.* **-atrice** *f.*)

sconsi·glio *m.* dissuasion.

sconsol-are [A 1] *tr.* to dishearten; to depress; to sadden. **-ante** *part. adj.* discouraging; disheartening; saddening, sad. **-atezza** *f.* disconsolateness; sadness. **-ato** *part. adj.* disheartened; saddened; sad; unhappy; depressed; disconsolate. **-atamente** *adv.* disconsolately. **-ato·rio** *adj.* depressing; sad. **-azione** *f.* grief; affliction; sadness.

scont-are [A 1 c] *tr.* to discount (also fig.); to deduct; to take off; to pay off (by instalments); to expiate, to atone for; to pay for; — una sentenza, to serve a sentence in prison; — il carcere, to do time; (comm.) to discount; — una cambiale, to discount a bill. **-a·bile** *adj.* (comm.) discountable. **-amento** *m.* paying (off, for, etc.); atoning, expiation. **-ante** *part. adj.* discounting; paying (off). **-ato** *part. adj.* discounted; paid (off, for); atoned, expiated. **-atore** *m.* (comm.) discounter.

scontent-o¹ *adj.* discontented, dissatisfied; disappointed; *n.m.* discontent; dissatisfaction. **-are** [A 1] *tr.* to dissatisfy; to displease; to disappoint; *rfl.* to be dissatisfied, disappointed. (**-ato** *part. adj.*) **-ezza** *f.* discontent; dissatisfaction; disappointment; sadness.

†scontento² *adj.* not contained; unconfined; unrestrained.

scontes·s-ere [B 1] *tr.* to undo (weaving); (fig.) to unweave; to analyse. **-itura** *f.* weaving partly undone; unweaving. (**-uto** *part. adj.*)

scontinu-are [A 6] *tr.* to discontinue. **-ato** *part. adj.*

scont-o¹ *m.* deduction; rebate; discount; allowance; (comm.) tassa ufficiale di —, bank rate; corso di —, market rate of discount; — commerciale, — rivendita, trade discount; (fig.) a — delle mie colpe, 'for my sins'. **-ista** *m.* (comm.) discounter.

sconto² *apocop. part.* of **scontare**, q.v.

scontor·-cere [C 5] *tr.* to contort, to twist; *rfl.* to twist oneself up; to perform contortions; to writhe. **-cimento** *m.* contortion; writhing. **†-ci·o** *m.* twisting, contorting. **-to** *part. adj.* contorted, twisted; deformed. (Cf. **contorcere**.)

†scontra *f.* encounter (cf. **incontro**).

scontraffare [B 14] *tr.* to imitate; to counterfeit, to forge.

†scontrappesare *rfl.* to lose balance, to overbalance.

scontr-are [A 1 c] *tr.* to meet, to encounter; to collate, to compare; to run across, to fall in with; †(naut.) to reverse the wheel or rudder; scontra!, meet her! (i.e. check the swing); *recip. rfl.* to encounter one another; to meet in battle; to collide, to come into collision, to run into each other; to crash. **-amento** *m.* encounter; collision. **-ata** *f.* encounter. (**-ato** *part. adj.*) **†-azzo** *m.* skirmish.

scontrino *m.* See under **scontro**.

scontr-o *m.* encounter; collision; crash; (mil.) action, engagement; *pl.* (eng.) tappet; (naut.) capstan pawls. **-ino** *m.* check; ticket; receipt; voucher; -ino di ricevuta, receipt note. **-osag·gine**, **-osità** *f.* peevishness; irritability, bad temper; moroseness; coyness. **-osetto** *adj. dim.* rather peevish, touchy; also *n.m.* (**-osetta** *f.*) **-oso** *adj.* cantankerous; ill-tempered; peevish; touchy; irritable; sulky; reluctant, coy; also *n.m.* (**-osa** *f.*)

sconturb-are [A 1] *tr.* to disturb thoroughly, to upset; *rfl.* to be deeply disturbed; to be upset, to torment oneself. (**-ato** *part. adj.*) **-o** *m.* disturbance; trouble; upset.

sconven-ire [D 17] *intr.* (*aux.* essere) to be unsuitable; to be improper. **†-enza** *f.* see **sconvenienza**. **-evole** *adj.* unseemly; indecorous; improper; indecent. **-evolmente** *adv.* improperly, indecorously; in an unseemly manner. **-evolezza** *f.* unseemliness; breach of good manners. **-iente** *part. adj.* impolite, unseemly; improper; unsuitable. (**-ientemente** *adv.*) **-ienza** *f.* unsuitableness; impropriety; unseemliness; indecency; improper conduct; breach of good manners.

sconvertire [D 1] *tr.* to pervert from newly acquired faith.

sconvo·l-gere [C 14] *tr.* to upset; to overturn; to turn upside down; to throw into confusion; to derange. **-gimento** *m.* upset; overturning; confusion; perturbation. (**-gitore** *m.* **-gitrice** *f.*) **-to** *part. adj.* upset; deranged; mare -to, rough sea; (fig.) emotionally upset; perturbed.

scooner *m. indecl.* (naut.) schooner.

scooter *m.* (motor.) scooter. **-ista** *m., f.* scooter rider.

scopa¹ *f.* (bot.) besom heath, *Erica scoparia*; — di fastella, tree heath, *E. arborea*; — marina, tamarisk, *Tamarix*.

scopa² *f.* broom; besom; birch (for thrashing); stiff, bushy hair.

scop-a³ *f.* popular Italian card game for two or four players, played with forty cards (dealt three at a time, four being put on the board at the outset); fare —, to sweep the board. **-ista** *m., f.* player of the game of 'scopa'.

scopai(u)ola *f.* (orn.) corncrake, *Crex crex*; passera —, hedge sparrow, *Prunella modularis*; (bot.) broom-corn, *Sorghum vulgare* var. *technicum*.

scop-are [A 1 c] *tr.* to sweep; (fig.) to pillory, to put to shame; to make a clean sweep of; (vulg.) to have sexual intercourse with; (naut.) to sweep down. **-a(m)mare** *m. indecl.* (naut.) studding-sail (pron. stuns'l). **-amestieri** *m. indecl.* one who frequently changes his trade. **-ata** *f.* sweep; sweeping. **-ato** *part. adj.* swept. **-atoio** *m.* (mil.) besom, broom made of twigs used for sweeping out a battery. **-atore** *m.* sweeper; road-sweeper; (mil.) see **scopatoio**; (text.) alley boy, jag-about; *pl.* (eccl.) -atori segreti, floor-sweepers in papal household; (eccl. hist.) flagellants. **-atrice** *f.* woman sweeper; (text.) alley girl, jag-about. **-atura** *f.* sweeping.

scoparina *f.* (chem.) scoparin.

scopazza *m.* (bot.) witch's broom.

scopera·gnola *f.* (orn.) whitethroat.

scoperchi-are [A 4] *tr.* to uncover; to remove the lid from; to lift the top of; †(vet.) to skin (an animal), to flay. **-ato** *part. adj.* uncovered; with the lid off. **-atura** *f.* uncovering; (butcher.) flank; breast (of mutton).

scoperta *f.* discovery; finding out; disclosure, revelation; unmasking; contrivance, invention; (mil.) investigation, reconnaissance, search; (naut.) exploration; nave da scoperte, exploring ship; servizi di —, semaphore, coast watching service; †marinaio di —, lookout; number shown on dice; †clearing, glade.

scopert-o *part.* of **scoprire**, q.v.; *adj.* uncovered; exposed; bare; unprotected; open; manifest; clear; †(naut.) undecked; ponte —, upper deck (cf. **coperta**); cantiere —, uncovered dock; giocare a carte -e, to put one's cards on the table; a capo —, bareheaded; *adv.* openly; *n.m.* open space, esplanade; open air; allo —, in the open; rimanere allo —, to make a bad debt; overdraft; margin; vendere allo —, to sell short; comprare allo —, to buy short; trarre allo —, to draw in blank; credito allo —, open credit. **-aménte** *adv.* openly. **-ura** *f.* openness; bareness; revelation; manifestation.

scopéto *m.* heath (cf. **scopa¹**).

scop-étta *f. dim.* of **scopa²**, q.v.; small broom or brush. **-ettóni** *m.pl.* Dundreary whiskers, (fam.) 'mutton-chops'.

scopina *f.* (bot.) *Erica carnea.*

scopino *m.* See **spazzino**.

scopista *m., f.* See under **scopa**.

scopo *m.* purpose; object; aim; end; target; design; — precipuo, main object; adatto allo —, fit for the purpose; senza —, aimless; chiederne lo —, to ask what it's for; (admin.) scope, terms of reference; — di una disposizione, scope of a provision; (mil.) target; aim; falso —, laying mark for indirect fire.

sco·pola *f.* (aeron.) air pocket causing bumpy flying conditions.

scopolamina *f.* (pharm.) scopolamine.

†sco·polo *m.* See **scoglio**.

scopóne¹ *m.* (bot.) tree heath, *Erica arborea.*

scopóne² *m.* game of cards for four players similar to 'scopa', q.v., in which all forty cards are dealt except four which are put on the table; — scientifico, the same game except that all forty cards are dealt.

†scoppettiere *m.* See **schioppettiere**, under **schioppo**.

scoppi-are¹ [A4] *intr.* (aux. essere) to burst, to explode; to break out; to erupt; — in lacrime, to burst into tears; — di rabbia, to be bursting with rage; — dalle risa, to split one's sides with laughing. **-a·bile** *adj.* liable to burst; explosive. (**-abilità** *f.*) **-aménto** *m.* exploding; bursting. **-ante** *part. adj.* bursting, exploding. **-ata** *f.* explosion; burst. **-ato** *part. adj.* broken out; burst; cracked, (herald.) split. **-atura** *f.* bursting; breaking out; crack (in the skin).

scoppi-are² [A4c] *tr.* to uncouple; *rfl.* (of a pair) to separate. **-ato** *part. adj.* uncoupled; parted, separated (cf. **coppia**).

scop·pio¹ *m.* burst; bursting; explosion; bang; crack (e.g. of a whip); outbreak; (fig.) pang; heartbreak; blow, affliction; (eng.) motore a —, internal combustion engine; atomic explosion; accertamento degli scoppi, detection of atomic explosions; — del carro, the traditional firework display outside the Duomo of Florence on Easter Eve, when a spark is carried by an artificial bird resembling a dove, sliding down a wire to set off a firework display on the 'carro', a heavy cart carrying a tiered tower.

scoppiett-are [A1c] *intr.* (aux. avere) to crackle; to flicker; to crack, to snap; — di arguzie, to keep up a running fire of witticisms, to sparkle with wit. **-aménto** *m.* crackling, crackle; snapping. **-ante** *part. adj.* crackling; snapping; (of flames) flickering, snapping. **-ino** *m.* crack, little explosion. **-io** *m.* continual crackling; uno -io di motti arguti, a running fire of repartee.

scoppiettiere *m.* (mil. hist.) fusilier.

scoppiétto *m. dim.* of **scoppio¹**, q.v.; shot; (fig.) quip.

†scop·pio¹ *m.* See **schioppo**.

†scop·pio² *m.* See **scoglio¹**.

scop·pola *f.* slap, smack; box on the ears.

scopr-ire [D8] *tr.* to uncover, to lay bare, to bare; to disclose; to unveil; to discover, to find out; to detect; to descry; to sight (e.g. land); to reveal; to expose, to show; (fig.) — il proprio giuoco, to put one's cards on the table; — un altare per ricoprirne un altro, to rob Peter to pay Paul; (mil.) — il fianco, to leave one's flank exposed; (naut.) to sight (land or sail); to uncover guns, etc.; — la chiglia, to expose the keel; — la carena, to expose the hull; (sculp.) to carve out, to chisel; *abs.* (mil.) to study the lie of the land; mandare avanti a —, to send out scouts to get a good view from a vantage point; *rfl.* to uncover oneself; to undress; to raise one's hat; to put off winter clothing; to expose oneself; to betray oneself; to reveal one's thoughts; (mil.) to disclose one's position, to come out into the open; (naut.) to emerge as the tide falls; to roll or list. **-i·bile** *adj.* discoverable. **-iménto** *m.* uncovering; exposure, discovery; revelation; unveiling. **-itóre** *m.* discoverer; inventor. (**-itóra**, **-itrice** *f.*) **-itura** *f.* uncovering; discovery.

†sco·pul-o *m.*, **†-oso** *adj.* See **scogli-o**, **-oso**.

scoragg-iare [A3], **-ire** [D2] *tr.* to discourage, to dishearten; *rfl.* to lose heart, to become disheartened. **-iaménto** *m.*, **-iménto** *m.* discouragement; depression. **-iante** *part. adj.* discouraging. **-iato**, **-ito** *part. adj.* disheartened, discouraged; depressed, in low spirits.

scor-are [A1] *tr.* to cause acute depression or profound dejection in. **-aménto** *m.* acute depression, profound dejection. **-ato** *part. adj.* profoundly disheartened; acutely depressed; utterly disheartened.

scorbacchi-are [A4] *tr.* to put to shame; to hold up to contempt. **-ato** *part. adj.* held in contempt; disgraced, put to shame. **-atura** *f.* holding in contempt; shame, disgrace.

scorbellato *adj.* rude, ribald.

scor·bia *f.* and derivs. See **sgorbia**.

scor·bio *m.* See **sgorbio**.

scor·b-uto *m.* (med.) scurvy, scorbutus. **-u·tico** *adj.* scorbutic, affected with scurvy.

†scorcare *intr.* to rise, to arise.

scorc-iare [A3c], **-ire** [D2] *tr.* to shorten; to make shorter; to curtail; to abbreviate; (art) to foreshorten; *intr.* (aux. essere) (art) to be foreshortened; *rfl.*, *intr.* (aux. essere) to shorten, to grow shorter; (of days in autumn) to draw in. **-iaménto** *m.* shortening. **†-iapino** *m. indecl.* (naut.) small fleet tender. **-iato** *part. adj.* shortened, abbreviated; (herald.) couped. **-iataménte** *adv.* briefly; in short. **-iatóia** *f.*, **-iatóio** *m.*, **-itóia** *f.*, **-itóio** *m.* short-cut (also fig.). (**-iatóre** *m.* **-iatrice** *f.* **-iatura** *f.*)

scórcio¹ *m.* (paint.; archit.) foreshortening; di —, foreshortened, in perspective; grimace; end, close; tail-end; sullo — del secolo, towards the end of the century; in questi scorci di tempo, in these brief moments; (photog.) — dal basso, worm's eye view; — dall'alto, bird's eye view.

scórcio² *apocop. part.* of **scorciare**, q.v.

scorcire [D2] and derivs. (Tusc.). See **scorciare**.

scord-are¹ [A1] *tr.*, *rfl.* (*prep.* di) to forget; non me ne -erò mai, I shall never forget it; (bot.) non-ti-scordar-di-me, forget-me-not, *Myosotis palustris* and *M. pyrenaica.* **-ato** *part. adj.*, *n.m.* forgotten. **-évole** *adj.* (*prep.* di) forgetful, unmindful (of). **-óne** *m.* forgetful person, scatterbrain. (**-óna** *f.*)

scord-are² [A1] *tr.* (mus.) to mistune; to untune; *intr.* (aux. avere) (mus.) to be out of tune; *rfl.* (mus.) to go out of tune. **-anza** *f.* false intonation. **-ato** *part. adj.* (mus.) out of tune; †(paint.; sculp.) out of proportion. **-atura** *f.* (mus.) scordatura, intentional mistuning of a string for the purpose of an unusual effect.

scor·dio *m.* (bot.) water germander, *Teucrium scordium.*

scorégg-ia *f.* leather strap; (vulg.) fart, wind. **†-ale** *m.* leather belt. **-are** [A3c] *intr.* (aux. avere) (vulg.) to fart, to break wind.

scor·fano *m.* (ichth.) sea scorpion (an edible sea fish); — bastardo, *Sebastes dactylopterus*; — rosso, — maggiore, *Scorpaena scrofa*; — bruno, — rascasso, *S. porcus*; (fig., fam.) ugly person.

scor·g-ere [C5] *tr.* to perceive; to discern; to descry; to notice; uscì senza farsi —, he stole out unnoticed; to escort, to accompany; †to guide, to direct. **-iménto** *m.* perception, notice; discernment. **-itóre** *m.* one who notices; †guide. (**-itrice** *f.*)

sco·ri-a *f.* dross; skimmings; (metall.) slag, dross; scum; -e Thomas, basic slag; — fusa galleggiante, floss; scale; (boiler, etc.) clinker. **-ficare** [A2s] *tr.* to scorify, to slag. (**-ficato** *part. adj.*) **-ficatóio** *m.*, **-ficatóre** *m.* scorifier. **-ficazióne** *f.* scorification.

scorn-are [A1] *tr.* to dishorn; (of a bull) to gore; to toss; (fig.) to put to shame; to hold up to ridicule. **-abécco** *m.* (bot.) *Cistus salvifolius* and *Pistacia terebinthus.* **-ata** *f.* butt, toss, blow (with horns). **-ato** *part. adj.* dishorned; gored; tossed; (fig.) put to shame, ridiculed; contemptible. **-atura** *f.* dishorning, breaking the horns (of). **-eggiare** [A3c] *intr.* (aux. avere) to butt (of goats, etc.).

scornici-are [A3] *tr.* to remove from a frame; *intr.* (aux. avere) to construct frames. **-aménto** *m.* framing; unframing. **-ato** *part. adj.* unframed; without cornice. (**-atóre** *m.*) **-atrice** *f.* (carpen.) matching machine, planing and moulding machine. **-atura** *f.* frame, framing; cornice.

scorn-o *m.* shame, ignominy; disgrace; avere a —, to scorn, to hold in contempt; avere — di, to be disgraced by.

scoron-are [A1c] *tr.* to uncrown; to dethrone; to poll (a tree); — un dente, to remove the crown of a tooth; *intr.* (aux. avere) (joc.) to keep saying rosaries, to be everlastingly praying; *rfl.* to lay down one's crown; to lose the crown of a tooth. **-ato** *part. adj.* uncrowned; dethroned; (of a tree) polled.

scorpacciata *f.* bellyful; fare una —, to eat one's fill; (fig.) overdose, excess; fare una — di romanzi, to have an orgy of novel-reading.

scorpena *f.* (ichth.). See scorfano.

scorpi-one *m.*, †**scor·pio** *m.* (zool.) scorpion, *Scorpio* spp.; — acquatico, water scorpion, *Nepa* sp.; (astron.) Scorpio, the Scorpion; (mil.) tank fitted with chains used to clear a passage through a minefield; †balister; †cat-o'-nine-tails, spiked rod; (fig.) ugly, malicious person. -**uro** *m.* (bot.) *Scorpiurus.*

scorpor-are [A I s] *tr.* (leg.) to disembody; to disincorporate; to separate from the mass; to spend from capital; to draw off, to separate (money) from capital (of estate); to set apart or distribute (an interest or share) under a will; †*rfl.* to exert oneself. -**ato** *part. adj.* separated, disincorporated; expended. -**azione** *f.* (leg.) drawing-off, separation (of money) from capital; distribution of an interest or share under a will.

scor·poro *m.* outlay; heavy expense; (iron.) un bello —!, what a waste of money!; (leg.) disincorporation; sum or share drawn or set apart from capital of estate.

scorrazz-are [A I] *intr.* (aux. avere) to run (about); to rove; (mil.) to make raids; *tr.* (mil.) to raid, to overrun. (-ato *part. adj.*)

scorredare [A I] *tr.* to deprive of a trousseau.

scorreg·gere [C 12] *tr.* to make incorrect; †to render indecent or licentious.

scorreg·gia *f.* See scoreggia.

scorr·ere [C 5] *intr.* (aux. essere) to flow; to glide; to roll, to slide; to run smoothly; (of time) to pass quickly, to fly; to elapse; to overflow; to slip, to make a slip; le parole -ono dal suo labbro, he speaks glibly; una penna che -e, a pen that writes well, smoothly, in which the ink flows well; uno stile che -e, a fluent style; un rasoio che -e bene, a sharp razor; *tr.* to travel through, to run over; to scour, to raid; to run one's eye over, to glance over; — un libro, to glance through a book. -**ente** *part. adj.* running, flowing; acque -enti, running water. -**eri·a** *f.* raid, incursion. -**imento** *m.* flowing; sliding; rolling; (eng.) sliding, slide; slip, slippage; (phys.) -imento molecolare, creep.

scorrett·o *adj.* incorrect; improper; unbecoming; indecent. -**amente** *adv.* incorrectly; improperly. -**ezza** *f.* incorrectness; error; impropriety; commettere una -ezza, to do something improper or unseemly.

scorrevol-e *adj.* fluent; flowing; gliding; sliding; grooved; pezzo — in un altro, piece which slides smoothly into another; porta —, sliding-door; (of liquid) thin, running; (eng.) smooth-running; — su cuscinetti a sfere, mounted on roller-bearings; (watchm.) rocchetto —, clutch wheel; (mus.) flowing, fluent. -**mente** *adv.* smoothly; flowingly; fluently. -**ezza** *f.* fluency; (eng.) smoothness (of running).

scorrezion-e *f.* incorrectness; error; mistake; slip. -**cella** *f. dim.* little slip, slight mistake.

scorr-ibanda, †**-iban·dola** *f.* incursion, raid; (fig.) excursion, digression.

scorridore *m.* (mil. hist.) outrider, forerunner; soldier sent ahead of troops with considerable latitude of action; †(naut.) duty boat; harbour launch; scourer of the seas; †brook; †vagabond; idler.

scorrimento *m.* See under scorrere.

†**scorrotto** *m.* mourning, grief.

†**scorrubbi-are** *rfl.* to fly into a rage. †-**ato** *adj.* enraged. †-**oso** *adj.* angry; testy.

scorrucci-are [A 3] *rfl.* (pop.) to get very angry. †-**ante** *adj.* simmering with rage. -**ato** *part. adj.* angry, in a rage. (Cf. corrucciare.)

scorruc·cio *m.* anger, rage; vexation.

scors-a *f.* excursion, trip; (fig.) glance, rapid examination; hurried skimming through a book; date una — a questi conti, just look over these accounts; — di lingua, slip of the tongue; — di penna, slip of the pen. -**erella** *f. dim.* little jaunt. †-**ivo** *adj.* see scorsoio. -**o** *part.* of scorrere, q.v.; *adj.* run (through); past, last; vite -a, overgrown vine; †decayed; *n.m.* slip; mistake, error. -**oio** *adj.* sliding, running; nodo, laccio -oio, slipknot, running-knot.

scorta *f.* escort; guide; convoy; (mil.) escort; sotto buona —, under good guard; provision; subvention; (comm.) stock, stores; (agric.) scorte vive, livestock; scorte morte, dead stock (implements); (naut.) nave da —, escort vessel; nave di —, escorting vessel.

scort-are[1] [A I] *tr.* to escort, to convoy. -**ato** *part. adj.* escorted, accompanied.

†**scort-are**[2] *tr.* to shorten, to abbreviate; (art) to foreshorten; *rfl.* to become shorter; *intr.* (art) to be foreshortened. †-**ato·ia** *f.* see scorciatoia, under scorciare.

scortecci-are [A 3 c] *tr.* to peel, to strip, to bark; — il pane, to take the crust off bread; *rfl.* to be stripped; to be peeled; (paint.) to peel (off). -**amento** *m.* stripping, peeling, barking. (-ato *part. adj.*) -**atrice** *f.* (techn.) debarking machine. -**atura** *f.* stripping, barking; peeled surface; bare patch.

†**scorteggiare** *vb.* and derivs. See scortare[1].

scortes-e *adj.* rude, impolite; uncivil; discourteous; unkind. -**emente** *adv.* rudely; unkindly; discourteously; unkindly. -**i·a** *f.* rudeness; incivility; discourtesy; unkindness; discourteous action.

scortic-are [A 2 s] *tr.* to skin, to flay; to graze (e.g. skin); (fig.) to fleece; (at interviews, etc.) to 'grill'; to shell (peas, etc.); scorticherebbe un pidocchio, he would skin a flea, he is a skinflint; tanto fa male chi tiene quanto chi -a, an accessory (or instigator) is as guilty as the doer (of an evil deed). -**agatti** *m. indecl.* (derog.) incompetent surgeon, 'sawbones'. -**amento** *m.* skinning, flaying; (fig.) fleecing. -**a·ria** *f.* trawl-net. -**ata** *f.* (butcher.) action of cutting up carcases; tearing, tear, rent. -**ativo** *adj.* serving for the process of skinning. -**ato** *part. adj.* skinned; flayed; (fig.) fleeced. -**atoio** *adj.* serving for the process of skinning; *n.m.* flaying knife; knacker's yard; (joc.) moneylender's office. -**atore** *m.* skinner; (fig.) skinflint; usurer. (-atrice *f.*) -**atura** *f.* abrasion, scratch; skinning; (fig.) extortion. -**avillani** *m. indecl.* extortionate landlord.

scortichino *m.* skinning-knife; flayer; (joc.) student of anatomy, 'sawbones'; (fig.) extortioner, usurer.

†**scortificare** *vb.* and derivs. See scorticare.

†**scortilla** *f.* harlot.

†**scortinare** *intr.* (mil.) to demolish a curtain.

†**scortire** *vb.* See scortare.

scorto[1] *m.* (art) foreshortening.

scorto[2] *part.* of scorgere, q.v.; *adj.* distinct; clearly seen.

scorto[3] *apocop. part.* of scortare[1], q.v.; *adj.* guided, escorted.

scor-za, -za *f.* bark; rind, peel, skin; crust (of bread); (fig.) outside, exterior; essere di — dura, to be tough, to be thick-skinned; human body, 'mortal coil' (as container of the soul); non valere una —, to be worthless, not to be worth a fig; a — a —, through and through; (joc.) soldier's uniform. -**zare** [A I] *tr.* to peel; to strip, to bark; *rfl.* to be stripped; to be peeled; to shed skin, to peel. (-zato *part. adj.*) -**zatrice** *f.* (paperm.) barking machine. -**zatura** *f.* peeling, stripping; barked part (of a tree). -**zone** *m.* tough individual; boor; thick-skinned person; stubborn person. -**zoneri·a** *f.* rudeness, boorishness. -**zoso** *adj.* with thick bark; thick-skinned (e.g. oranges). †-**zuto** *adj.* covered by a rind.

scorzone[1] *m.* (zool.) Aesculapian snake, *Coluber longissimus*; (ichth.) *Spondyliosoma orbicularis*, a kind of sea bream.

scorzone[2] *m.* See under scorza.

scorzonera *f.* (bot.) black salsify, *Scorzonera hispanica.*

scosa *f.* (naut. hist.) curvature of ship's timbers in a galley; bilge keel, docking keel.

sco-scendere [C I] *tr.* to break; to split; to cleave; *intr.* (aux. essere), *rfl.* to fall; to crash down; to collapse; to slide down; to slope, to split. -**scendimento** *m.* collapse; fall (of rock, etc.), landslide; crag; †cleft. -**sceso** *part. adj.* broken; split; collapsed; rugged; precipitous; steep.

scosci-are [A 4] *tr.* to take the legs off (chicken, etc.); *rfl.* to spread one's legs widely; (fig.) to tire oneself by climbing or walking, to be run off one's legs. (-ata *f.* -ato *part. adj.*)

scoscienziato *adj.* conscienceless.

sco·scio *m.* 'splits' (as done by dancers, acrobats, etc.); (tailor.) fork, crutch; †precipice, broken place.

scoss-a *f.* shock; shake; shaking; jerk; jolt; pull; — elettrica, electric shock; sharp shower; sudden loss or damage. -**are** [A I] *tr.* to shake; to shock. -**ata** *f.* shaking. (-ato *part. adj.*) -**erella** *f. dim.* -erella di acqua, short, sharp shower. -**o** *part.* of scuotere, q.v.; *adj.* shaken; shocked; moved, excited, roused; broken, weakened; -o dalla sella, thrown; cavallo -o, riderless horse. -**one** *m.* severe shock; violent shake; jolt; a good shaking; heavy shower.

scost-are [A I] *tr.* (prep. da) to remove; to put aside; to put out of the way; to detach, to move away (from); to shove off; *rfl.* to stand aside; to get out of the way; to stand back; to withdraw; to leave; to depart; to make way; to swerve; (fig.) -arsi dall'argo-

scost-are (*cont.*)

mento, to wander from the subject; *intr.* (*aux.* essere) to stand some distance away; to stand out (from). **-a** *excl.* (as word of command) shove off!; (naut.) -a prua!, bear off forward. **-amento** *m.* removal, separation; distance apart. (**-ato** *part. adj.*)

scostolare [A I] *tr.* to remove a rib from.

scostumat-o *adj.* dissolute, licentious; low; ill-mannered. **-amente** *adv.* dissolutely, licentiously. **-ezza** *f.* coarse manners; evil living; dissoluteness; licentiousness.

sco·tano *m.* (bot.) wig tree, Venetian sumach, *Cotinus coggigria*; (dyeing) fustic.

scotenn-are [A I] *tr.* to scalp; to skin (a pig). (**-ato** *part. adj.*) **-atoio** *m.* scalping-knife; flaying-knife.

†**sco·t-ere** *vb.* and derivs. see **scuotere.** **-imento** *m.* shaking; jolting; tossing. **-ipa·glia** *m. indecl.* (agric.) part of a threshing-machine. **-io** *m.* continued shaking. **-itoia** *f.* (paperm.) duster, rag duster, thrasher. **-itoio** *m.* shaker; salad-basket; (mining) washing vat. (**-itore** *m.* **-itrice** *f.*)

Scot-i *pr.n.m.pl.* (hist.) Scots (esp. Celts of Ireland). **-ista** *m.* (philos.) Scotist, follower of Duns Scotus. **-i·stico** *adj.* pertaining to the philosophy of Duns Scotus.

scotodini·a *f.* (med.) dizziness accompanied by dimness of sight.

scotofobi·a *f.* (med.; psych.) scotophobia.

sco·tol-a *f.* (text.) scutch, scutcher. **-are** [A I S] *tr.* (text.) to scutch; to swingle (flax). (**-ato** *part. adj.*) **-atoio** *m.* (text.) scutching-frame, swingle bench. **-atrice** *f.* (text.) scutching-machine, swingling-machine. **-atura** *f.* (text.) scutching; swingling (of flax).

scotom-a *m.* (med.) scotoma, blind spot in the visual field; — scintillante, teichopsia. †**-a·tico** *adj.* scotomatous.

scott-a¹ *f.* (naut.) sheet. **-ame** *m.* (naut.) set of sheets; -ame d'una vela, sheets, tackle appertaining to a sail. **-are** [A I] *intr.* (*aux.* avere) (naut.) to trim the sheets, to take in the sheets. **-iere, -iero** *m.* (naut.) sailor responsible for the sheets. **-ina** *f.* (naut.) topsail, topgallant sail-sheet; jigger, tackle having one double and one single block; filar le -ine, to ease the sheets; tesare le -ine a baciare, to haul taut 'two blocks'.

scotta² *f.* whey.

scott-are¹ [A I] *tr.* to scorch; to burn; to scald; (rubber industry) to scorch, to precure; (fig.) to sting; to nettle; to offend, to hurt, to irritate; *intr.* (*aux.* avere) to scorch, to burn; il sole -a, the sun is scorching hot. **-amento** *m.* scorching, burning, scalding. **-ante** *part. adj.* scalding hot, scorching; (fig.) burning; stinging; highly controversial. **-ata** *f.* scalding; light cooking; heating up; burn; scald. **-ato** *part. adj.* (fig.) burning with resentment. **-atura** *f.* burn; scald; burning; parboiling; scalding (infusion in hot water); blister; sunburn; (rubber industr.) scorching, precuring; (surg.) cauterizing; (eng.) damage due to burning; fire damage. **-iere** *m.* (mining) dump for ore.

scottare² [A I] See under **scotta¹.**

scotto¹ *m.* bill, score, reckoning; share (of a bill), scot; meal; pagare lo —, to pay the consequences; la speranza non paga lo —, hopes butter no parsnips.

scotto² *part.* of **scuocere**, q.v.; *adj.* overdone, too much cooked.

†**scotto³** *adj.* (geog.) Scotch, Scottish; *n.m.* Scot; Scotch tweed.

†**scott-obrinzi** *m.*, **-obrunzi** *m.* strolling-player.

†**scovacciare** *tr.* to rouse from a lair.

scov-are [A I] *tr.* to drive out, to dislodge; to rouse (game); to find, to discover. **-amento** *m.* driving out; rousing; discovering; discovery, find. (**-ato** *part. adj.*)

†**scoverchiare** *vb.* and derivs. See **scoperchiare.**

scovol-o *m.* (eng.) swab, tube brush; (mil.) ramrod; pull-through. **-are** [A I C] *tr.* to clean (a gun). **-atore** *m.* (mil.) gun cleaner. **-ino** *m.* pipe cleaner.

†**scovrire** *vb.* and derivs. See **scoprire.**

sco·zia¹ *f.* (archit.) Scotia, trochilus.

Sco·zia² *pr.n.f.* (geog.) Scotland; filo di —, strong cotton yarn of especially good quality.

scozz-are [A I] *tr.* to shuffle (cards). **-ata** *f.* shuffle, shuffling. (**-ato** *part. adj.*)

scozzese *adj.* Scotch; Scottish; stoffa —, tartan, plaid; vestito —, kilt; passo —, slow step, solemn pace; doccia —, alternate hot and cold showers, (fig.) playing fast and loose, blowing alternately hot and cold; (mus.) danza —, Schottische, German Polka; *n.m.* Scot, Scotsman; *f.* Scotswoman.

scozzon-e *m.* horse-breaker, trainer. **-are** [A I C] *tr.* to break in, to

train (horses); (fig.) to break in, to introduce to a new subject of study; to initiate. **-ato** *part. adj.* (of horses) broken in, trained; (fig.) initiated; well-trained, experienced, wise. **-atore** *m.* see **scozzone. -atura** *f.* breaking in, training; initiation.

†**scralla** *f.* game of peg-top.

scrann-a *f.* high-backed chair; seat; bench; (iron.) sedere a —, to pronounce *ex cathedra* (cf. Dante, *Paradiso* XIX, 79). †**-o** *m.* see **scranna.**

screanzat-o *adj.* unmannerly; ill-bred; impolite, rude, discourteous; crude, uncouth; coarse; una mano -a, a large, coarse hand; *n.m.* unmannerly person; boor. **-amente** *adv.* impolitely, rudely; roughly, crudely.

screato *adj.* stunted; weakly; ill-grown, underdeveloped.

scred-ere [B I] *tr.*, *intr.* (*aux.* avere; *prep.* da) to recant (from); to cease to believe. **-ente** *part. adj.* distrustful, incredulous; *n.m.* (rel.) unbeliever.

scredit-are [A I SC] *tr.* to discredit; to bring into disrepute; *rfl.* to be discredited; to incur disgrace. **-ato** *part. adj.* discredited; in disrepute.

scredito *m.* discredit; disrepute.

screm-are [A I] *tr.* to skim; to separate (cream from milk). **-ato** *part. adj.* skimmed; separated. **-atrice** *f.* (agric.) milk separator, skimming machine. **-atura** *f.* (agric.) milk separation, skimming.

†**scremento**, †**-i·zio** *m.* See **escremento.**

†**scremire** *vb.* and derivs. See **schermire.**

†**screp-are**, †**-azzare** *vb.* and derivs. See **crepare.**

screpol-are [A I S] *rfl.*, (Tusc.) *intr.* (*aux.* essere) to crack; to chap; *tr.* to cause to crack or chap. **-ato** *part. adj.* cracked; chapped. **-atura** *f.* crack; chap; fissure.

†**scre·pol-o** *m.* see **screpolatura,** under **screpolare.** †**-oso** *adj.* see **screpolato.**

†**scre·scere¹** *intr.* to decrease, to grow smaller, to diminish in stature.

†**scre·scere²** *intr.* to grow excessively.

scre·zi-o *m.*, **-a** *f.* variegation; speckling; (fig.) variance, difference; friction; disagreement; c'è uno — fra quei due, those two don't see eye to eye. **-are** [A 4] *tr.* to variegate; to speckle. **-ato** *part. adj.* variegated, speckled; (herald.) patterned; †overornamented. **-atura** *f.* variegation, speckling.

scri·a *m.* (orn.) the smallest bird in a nest.

scrib-a *m.* (Bibl.) Scribe, interpreter of the Law; gli -i e i farisei, the Scribes and Pharisees; (derog.) scribbler; †scribe, copyist. **-acchiare** [A 4] *tr.*, *intr.* (*aux.* avere) to scribble. **-acchiatore** *m.* scribbler. (**-acchiatrice** *f.*) **-acchino** *m.* scribbler.

scribivendolo *m.* (derog.) journalistic hack, writer who 'sells his pen' to the highest bidder.

scricchiare [A 4] *intr.* (*aux.* avere) to creak, to grate.

scric·chio *m.* creaking, squeaking.

scricchiol-are [A I S] *intr.* (*aux.* avere) to creak; to grate; to squeak; (of ice) to crack, to crackle; to make a scrunching sound. **-amento** *m.* creaking; grating; squeaking; scrunching, scrunch. **-ata** *f.* creak; squeak. **-io** *m.* continued creaking, grating; (med.) crepitation.

scric·ciolo, scric·cio *m.* (orn.) wren, *Troglodytes troglodytes*; (fig., e.g. of a little child); essere uno —, to be tiny; avere il cervello di uno —, to have the brain of a rabbit; mangiare quanto uno —, to eat as much as a sparrow.

scrign-o *m.* †**-a** *f.* strong-box, money-box; jewel-case; casket; †thump. †**-uto** *adj.* hunchbacked; humpbacked; naso -uto, hooked nose.

†**scrim-a** *f.*, †**-a·glia** *f.* and derivs. See **scherma.**

†**scrimin-ale** *m.*, †**-ato·io** *m.* comb.

scriminatura *f.* parting (of the hair).

†**scrimire** *vb.* and derivs. See **schermire.**

scri·molo *m.* (extreme) edge, rim.

†**scrina** *f.* See **scriminatura.**

scrin-are [A I] *tr.* to clip (mane or tail of a horse). **-ato** *part. adj.* hairless; capelli -ati, hair fallen out; cavallo con la coda -ata, horse with docked tail.

scrinia·rio *m.* (eccl.) *scriniarius*, archivist (of papal chancery).

scri·o *adj.* (usu. doubled) (Tusc.) pure; acqua scria scria, just water, water and nothing else.

scristian-are [A I] *tr.* to dechristianize; *rfl.* to lose the Christian faith. **-ire** *tr.*, *intr.* (*aux.* essere) to unchristianize; to lose one's faith; to lose patience; mi farai -ire, you will make me angry. **-izzare** [A I] *tr.* to dechristianize. (**-izzato** *part. adj.*)

scriteriato *adj.* lacking in judgement, lacking criteria, without standards.

†**scriticato** *adj.* uncritical.

scritta *f.* written contract, legal document; marriage lines; stracciare la —, to break the contract; inscription; notice, placard, poster; fascia board; †writing; †book.

scritt·o *part.* of scrivere, q.v.; *adj.* written; handwritten, manuscript; in writing; sta —, it is written, it is down in black and white; inscribed; (fig.) fated, bound to happen; — a registro, registered; *n.m.* script; writing; written document; handwriting; per iscritto, in writing; *pl.* literary works, writings; essays. **-oio** *m.* study, office; writing-desk; -oio a saracinesca, roll-top desk; (comm.) counting-house. **-ore** *m.* writer; author; (eccl.) *scriptor* (in papal chancery). **-rice** *f.* authoress; woman writer. **-orello**, **-oretto** *m. dim.* (derog.) scribbler, insignificant author. **-ori·a** *f.* clerk's office; secretary's office; writing-desk. **-o·rio** *adj.* relating to writing; materie -orie, writer's material, copy. **-oru·colo** *m.* (derog.) petty scribbler. **-uc·cio** *m.* (derog.) insignificant piece of writing.

scrittur·a *f.* writing; handwriting; avere una bella —, to write a good hand; retta —, correct spelling; senza —, illiterate; — a macchina, typewriting; (leg.) document; agreement; contract; — privata, written paper or instrument signed but not under seal, simple contract (distinguished from 'atto pubblico', formal contract under seal); — privata autenticata, simple contract attested by Notary Public; -e contabili, commercial books (C.C.); — formale, — pubblica, deed; — rogata da notaio, deed attested by Notary Public; (comm.) posting; entry; *pl.* bookkeeping; doppia, double entry; tenere le -e, to keep the books, to keep the accounts; text, reading; (theatr.) engagement, contract; (Bibl.) la (Sacra) —, (Holy) Scripture; le (Sacre) -e, the (sacred) Scriptures. **-a·bile** *adj.* (book-keeping) suitable for entry; (theatr., etc.) suitable for engagement. **-ale** *adj.* scriptural; *n.m.* clerk; book-keeper; copyist, scribe. **-are** [A 1] *tr.* (book-keeping) to enter; (theatr., etc.) to engage; to sign on, to sign up; (comm.) to post; to journalize. **-a·rio** *m.* (rel. hist.) Scripturarian, Scripturist. **-ato** *part. adj.* (theatr., etc.) engaged, signed on; under contract. **-azione** *f.* copying; clerical work. **-etta** *f. dim.* short document, deed. **-ista** *m.* biblical scholar.

scrivacchiare [A 4] and derivs. See scribacchiare, under scriba.

scrivani·a *f.* writing-desk; bureau; writing-cabinet; †office.

scrivan·o *m.* clerk; copyist, scribe; amanuensis; — pubblico, public letter-writer; (eccl.) — di confraternita, secretary of a religious guild; (naut.) second in command of small coasters; apprentice after having done seaman's time. **-ello** *m. dim.* (derog.) junior clerk, office-boy; copyist. **-eri·a** *f.* (derog.) pen-pushing.

scri·v·ere [C 12] *tr., abs.* to write; — a matita, to write in pencil, to pencil; come si -e questa parola?, how do you spell this word?; — a macchina, to typewrite, to type; — in versi, to write poetry; — per il teatro, — per le scene, to write for the stage; — sui giornali, to write for the papers; — in un registro, to enter, to record; — nel libro della memoria, to impress on the memory; — nel cuore, to take to heart; — a casa, to write letters home; (mil. slang) far — a casa, to deprive of rank, pay, etc.; to ascribe; te lo -o a lode, I ascribe it to your credit; to describe, to tell, to relate; to inscribe; †to conscript; *n.m.* writing; l'occorrente per —, writing-materials; macchina da —, typewriter. **-ente** *part., n.m., f.* writer. **-i·bile** *adj.* capable of being written; fit to be written. **-icchiare** [A 4], **-ucchiare** [A 4] *tr., intr.* (*aux.* avere) (colloq.) to write with difficulty, to write very little, or with painful slowness and labour. †**-imento** *m.* writing. **-iritto** *m.* writing-desk at which the user stands to write.

†**scrivo** *adj.* See scrio.

†**scriziato** *adj.* See screziato, under screzio.

†**scrizione** *f.* See iscrizione.

†**scrob·a** *f.*, †**-o** *m.* deep pit, ditch.

scrobi·colo *m.* (anat.) scrobiculus.

scroc·care[1] [A 2] *tr.* to scrounge, to sponge, to cadge; mi ha -ato un pranzo, he got me to stand him a dinner; — la paga, to get paid for nothing. **-catore** *m.* scrounger, sponger, cadger. (**-atrice** *f.*) **-cheri·a** *f.* scrounging, sponging, cadging. **-cone** *m.* scrounger, sponger, cadger.

†**scroccare**[2] *vb.* and derivs. See scoccare.

scrocchi·are[1] [A 4] *intr.* (*aux.* avere) to creak; to crackle. **-ante** *part. adj.* creaking; crackling.

scrocchi-are[2] [A 4] *tr.* to lend out on interest; to pawn. **-atore** *m.* moneylender; pawnbroker.

scroc·chio[1] *m.* creak; cracking, crackling.

scroc·chi-o[2] *m.* pawnbroking; dare a —, to pawn. **-etto** *m. dim.* pawnbroker's profit. **-one** *m.* moneylender, usurer.

scrocc-o[1] *m.* sponging, scrounging; a —, gratis, gratuitously. **-one** *m.* sponger, scrounger; swindler, sharper. (**-ona** *f.*)

scrocco[2] *m.* spring; coltello a —, clasp-knife; (bldg.) spring catch.

scrocco[3] *m.* crackle; crunch, scrunch.

scroc-ellare [A 1] *tr.* to mark with a little cross (e.g. to cut a little cross in the skins of chestnuts, for roasting). **-iare** [A 4] *tr.* (naut.) to sway a yard into a vertical position (i.e. uncrossed).

scrofa, scrofa *f.* sow; (slang) loose woman; †see scrofola.

scro·fano *m.* (ichth.). See scorfano.

scro·fol-a *f.* (med.) scrofula, struma, king's evil. **-are** *adj.* scrofulous. **-a·ria** *f.* (bot.) water betony, *Scrophularia aquatica.* **-ide** *f.* (med.) scrofuloderma. **-osi** *f.* (med.) scrofula. **-oso** *adj.* scrofulous; *n.m.* sufferer from scrofula.

†**scrogolare** *tr.* to munch, to crunch.

scroi *m.pl.* clogs, heavy wooden shoes worn by farm labourers, etc. for walking through mud.

scroll-are [A 1] *tr.* to shake, to toss; to shrug; — la testa, to shake one's head. **-amento** *m.* shaking; tossing. **-ata** *f.* shake; toss of the head; shrug of the shoulders. (**-atina** *f. dim.* **-ato** *part. adj.*) **-atura** *f.* shaking; tossing; shake; toss.

scroll-o *m.* shake, shaking; vibration. **-one** *m. augm.* violent shaking; jerk, jolt.

scrosci-are [A 4] *intr.* (*aux.* avere, essere) to hiss; to bubble; to splash; to crash; (of rain) to pelt; (of dry leaves, etc.) to crackle; to creak; to rumble; to roar. **-ante** *part. adj.* pioggia -ante, pelting rain; applausi -anti, thunderous applause; risate -anti, loud bursts of laughter.

scro·scio *m.* heavy shower; thunderclap; thundering, rumbling; bubbling; piovere a —, to pour with rain, to rain in torrents; bollire a —, to boil over; crackling; creaking; roar; storm; outburst; uno — di applausi, a burst of clapping, thunderous applause; (med.) crepitus.

scrost-are [A 1] *tr.* to remove the crust from, to peel; (techn.) to descale, to scrape, to strip; — le pareti, to strip the walls; *rfl.* to lose the crust; to flake; la parete si -a, the plaster is peeling off the wall. **-amento** *m.* peeling; stripping; removing of plaster. **-ato** *part. adj.* stripped; peeled; affresco -ato, uncovered fresco. **-atura** *f.* stripping; peeling; (techn.) descaling, scraping, stripping; cleaning (of pictures); surface uncovered; wall that has been stripped.

scrot-o *m.* (anat.) scrotum. **-ale** *adj.* (anat.) scrotal.

scrubber *m. indecl.* (chem. eng.) scrubber, absorption tower.

scrud-ire [D 2] *tr.* to warm, to take the chill off; (text.) to soften (silk fibre). **-imento** *m.* (text.) softening (of silk fibre). (**-ito** *part. adj.*)

scrudolire [D 2] and derivs. See scrudire.

†**scrunare** *tr.* to break the eye (of a needle).

†**scrupo** *m.* chessman.

scru·pol-o, †**scru·pulo** *m.* scruple; qualm; uomo senza -i, unscrupulous man; onesto sino allo —, scrupulously honest; si fa — di chiedere un favore, he hesitates to ask a favour; non avere — a, to be quite ready to; (theol.) scruple; scruple (weight); three minutes (time). **-eggiare** [A 3 c] *intr.* (*aux.* avere) to be scrupulous, to have scruples; to hesitate. **-oso** *adj.* scrupulous, meticulous; full of scruples; exact. **-osamente** *adv.* scrupulously. **-osità** *f.* scrupulousness.

scrut-are [A 1] *tr.* to investigate; to inquire into; to search; to pry into; to scrutinize; to peer at; to examine minutely. **-a·bile** *adj.* open to investigation; that will stand scrutiny. (**-ato** *part. adj.*) **-atore** *m.* investigator; (comm.) scrutineer; teller (of votes); designare gli -atori, to appoint tellers; *adj.* inquisitive; searching; scrutinizing; closely observant. (**-atrice** *f.*) **-inamento** *m.* investigation; scrutiny; ballot. **-inare** [A 1] *tr.* to investigate; to scrutinize; to hold a ballot. **-i·nio** *m.* counting of the votes after the close of the poll (in Italy this is done on the day after polling-day); addition of examination marks; fare lo -inio trimestrale, to check the term's marks; (eccl. hist.) scrutiny (of catechumens).

scuccumedra *f.* nag.

scuccutret·tola *f.* (orn.). See cutrettola.

scuc·ire [D I] *tr.* to unpick (sewing); to unstitch; *rfl.* to come unstitched. **-imẹnto** *m.* (naut.) lo -imento delle lamiere, the opening up of a ship's seams. **-ito** *part. adj.* unstitched; unpicked; (fig.) incoherent, disconnected. **-itura** *f.* seam that has come unstitched; unstitching, unpicking; qui c'è una -itura, the stitches have come undone here.

scud·ale *adj.*, **-a·io** *m.*, etc. See under **scudo**[1].

†**scudella** *f.* See **scodella**.

scuderi·a *f.* stable (esp. racing or royal); stables (collectively); garzone di —, groom; ragazzo di —, stable-boy; coach-house; tram-depot; (mil.) stables, regimental stable, remount depot; (naut.) stabling rigged up in a ship; (sport) racing-car organization; la — Ferrari, Ferrari racing-car organization.

scudẹtto *m. dim.* See under **scudo**[1].

scudier-o, **-e**, †**-i** *m.* squire; equerry; groom; *adj. phr.* alla -a, suitable for riding, connected with riding; calzoni alla -a, riding breeches; stivali alla -a, top-boots, riding-boots; guanti alla -a, gauntlets with cuffs of a different colour.

scudi·sci-o *m.* (†**-a** *f.*) riding-whip, switch; lash, thong. **-are** [A 3] *tr.* to lash, to whip. **-ata** *f.* whipping, thrashing. (**-ato** *part. adj.*)

scud-o[1] *m.* shield; gunshield; (fig.) defence, protection; defender, protection; (herald.) escutcheon; (coin) scudo, écu; escudo; (herald.) — accartocciato, Renaissance shield; — incavato, targe à bouche; — femminile, lozenge; (naut.) ship's nameplate, embossed stern, etc.; †bagli di —, beams at the stern, sternport. **-ale** *adj.* relating to a shield; like a shield; forma -ale, shield-shape; *n.m.* gunshield. **-a·io** *m.* shield-maker; *adj.* shield-bearing. †**-are** *tr.* to defend with a shield. **-ato** *adj.* armed with a shield; (mil.) carrying or protected by a shield, shielded; artiglieria -ata, artillery fitted with a gunshield. **-ẹtto** *m. dim.* small shield; key-hole guard; (mil.) flash pan of a gun; (sport) shield; the top place in the first division of the Football League, so-called because during the following season the players of the team which has gained that place wear a 'scudetto' as a badge; (hortic.) innesto a -etto, eye-graft, grafting by inoculation. **-icciuolo** *m.* (hortic.) innesto a -icciuolo, see 'innesto a -etto'; strip of white linen worn with half-mourning; †(mil.) holder for the primer of a mortar. **-ifọrme** *adj.* (scient.) scutiform.

Scudo[2] *pr.n.m.* (astron.) Scutum, the Shield of Sobieski.

scuf·fi-a *f.* cap, coif, caul; (fig.) drunkenness, intoxication; (mil. hist.) soft bonnet worn under a helmet; sock used for holding missiles launched by a petard, etc.; (naut.) far —, to capsize. **-otto** *m. dim.* little cap; (dial., Milan) slap, smack, cuff.

scuffiare [A 4] *tr.*, *intr.* (*aux.* avere) to gobble, to 'scuff'.

scuffin-a *f.* (techn.) tinker's rasp. **-are** [A I] *tr.* to grate, to rasp, to file. (**-ato** *part. adj.*)

scugnizzo *m.* street urchin (originally of Naples but now used to denote 'waifs and strays' in general); (fig.) naughty boy.

sculacci-are [A 3] *tr.* to smack (on the bottom), to spank. **-ata** *f.* smack, smacking, spanking; (fig.) a 'kick in the pants'. **-ato** *part. adj.* smacked, spanked. (**-atura** *f.*) **-ọne** *m. augm.* resounding smack; good spanking.

sculda·scio *m.* (hist.) head of a territorial division under the Longobards, equiv. to Roman *centenarius*.

sculettare [A I c] *intr.* (*aux.* avere) (vulg.) to waddle, to waggle one's bottom when walking.

†**scul·pere**, †**scultare** *vb.* and derivs. See **scolpire**.

scultellatura *f.* (tanning) flay mark.

sculto *adj.* (poet.) carved, sculptured.

scult-ọre *m.* sculptor; — in legno, wood-carver; *adj.* vividly descriptive. **-rice** *f.* sculptress, woman sculptor; also *adj.* **-o·rio** *adj.* sculptural; statuesque; stile -orio, vivid descriptive style. **-ura** *f.* sculpture, carving; (piece of) sculpture.

sc(u)oi-are [A 4] *tr.* to skin, to flay. (**-ato** *part. adj.*) **-atura** *f.* flaying, skinning.

scuol-a[1] *f.* school; schoolhouse; schoolroom, classroom; class; — elementare, primary school; — media, secondary school; — serale, evening school; — pareggiata, private school, the certificates, diplomas, etc. of which are accepted as being equal to those of State schools; — promiscua, co-educational school; (motor.) — guida, driving school; riapertura delle -e, beginning of term; — professionale, technical school; — di belle arti, — di disegno, art school; (eccl.) -e pie, Pious Schools, schools for the poor founded by St Joseph Calasanctius in 1597,

and the religious order of Clerks Regular (Piarists) who administer them; (mil.) — di Modena, Officer Cadet College; — di Parma, Small Arms School; — di Caserta, Customs Officers' School; (naut.) nave —, training ship; (paint.) school (of painting), e.g. — umbra, Umbrian School (similarly 'school' of music, poetry, etc.); dare a —, to teach, to keep school; marinare la —, to play truant; servire di —, to be an example; gli fu — il dolore, grief taught him a great deal.

scuola[2] *f.* See **spola**.

scuo·t-ere [C 19 d] *tr.* to shake; to shake off; — il giogo, to shake off the yoke; — le spalle, to shrug one's shoulders; to agitate, to move; to startle; to disturb; to assail; to rouse, to excite; to disregard; to weaken, to impair; *rfl.* to rouse oneself; to wake up; to stir; to be startled; (fig.) to be moved. **-imẹnto** *m.* shaking, tossing; buffeting; agitation. **-ipa·glia** *m. indecl.* (agric.) shaker (of threshing box). (**-itọre** *m.* **-itrice** *f.*)

scup·cina *f.* (Serbian hist.) Skupshtina.

†**scurare**[1] *tr.* to cleanse; to scour.

†**scurare**[2] *vb.* and derivs. See **oscurare**.

scur-e, †**-a** *f.* axe, hatchet; condannato alla —, sent to the block, condemned to death by decapitation; (mil.) — dei guastatori, sapper's hatchet, small axe used by demolition squad. (**-ella**, **-etta** *f. dim.*)

scur-ẹtto *m.*, **-ẹzza** *f.* See under **scuro**.

scuria-ta, †**-da** *f.* switch, riding-whip.

scurios-are [A I c] *intr.* (*aux.* avere) to be inquisitive, to pry. **-ire** [D 2] *tr.* to satisfy the curiosity of; *rfl.* to be inquisitive, to seek to satisfy one's curiosity.

†**scuri·scio** *m.* See **scudiscio**.

scur-o *adj.* dark; dim; rosso —, dark red, deep red; obscure; gloomy; occhio —, troubled, lowering looks; *n.m.* dark, darkness; allo —, in shadow; vestito di —, wearing dark (subfusc) clothes; window-shutter; (fig.) essere allo —, to be in the dark (i.e. ignorant); (paint.) shadow; shaded part of a picture. **-ẹtto** *adj. dim.* rather dark, darkish; *n.m.* inside window-shutter, small shutter. **-ẹzza** *f.* darkness; obscurity. **-ic·cio** *adj.* darkish. **-ire** [D 2] *tr.* to darken; to obscure; to tone down; *rfl.*, *intr.* (*aux.* essere) to darken, to grow dark; *impers.* tra poco -isce, it will soon be getting dark. †**-ità** *f.* darkness; (fig.) obscurity.

†**scurra** *m.* buffoon.

scurril-e *adj.* scurrilous; licentious, lewd. (**-mẹnte** *adv.*) **-ità** *f.* scurrility; licentiousness.

scus-are [A I] *tr.* to excuse; to pardon, to forgive; to justify; — uno con l'età giovanile, to excuse a person on grounds of youth; *rfl.* to excuse oneself; to refuse, to decline, an invitation; to justify oneself; -arsi con, to apologize to; -arsi d'essere arrivato tardi, to apologize for being late. **-a** *f.* apology; excuse; pretext; chiedere -a, to beg pardon; chiedere -a di, to apologize for; lettera di -a, letter of apology; magre -e, lame excuses; meschina -a, poor excuse; negligenza che non ammette -a, carelessness for which there is no excuse. **-a·bile** *adj.* pardonable, excusable. **-abilmẹnte** *adv.* pardonably, excusably. (**-abilità** *f.*) **-ante** *part. adj.* (leg.) circostanza -ante, extenuating circumstance (C.P.). **-ato** *part. adj.* excused; forgiven; justified; avere uno per -ato, to hold a person excused. (**-atọre** *m.* **-atrice** *f.* **-ato·rio** *adj.*) †**-e·vole** *adj.* see **scusabile**.

scuss-o *adj.* destitute; bare; plain; verità -a, plain (naked) truth; acqua -a, plain water; pane —, dry bread; *adv.* plainly; parlare scusso scusso, to speak out, not to beat about the bush.

Scu·tari *pr.n.f.* (geog.) Scutari.

†**scutati** *m.pl.* shield-bearers, soldiers carrying shields (cf. **scudo**).

scutell-a·ria *f.* (bot.) *Scutellaria peregrina*. **-arina** *f.* (chem.) scutellarin.

scuter·zola *f.* (zool.) polecat, *Putorius putorius*.

scu·tica *f.* lash, whip.

†**scuti·fero** *adj.* shield-bearing.

scu·tulo *m.* brass plate or plaque; (med.) scutulum.

șdamare [A a] *intr.* (*aux.* avere) (draughts) to open up the back row.

șdare [A 8] *rfl.* (*prep.* da) (fam., Tusc.) to give up; to become lazy; to lose inclination (for); si è -ato dalla musica, he has given up music; *abs.* to become disheartened.

șdazi-are [A 4] *tr.* (comm.) to clear through the customs. **-a·bile** *adj.* ready for clearance. **-amẹnto** *m.* clearing of goods through the customs, clearance. (**-ato** *part. adj.*)

ṣdebit-are [A I S] *rfl.* to get out of debt, to pay off one's debts; to pay a debt; to discharge one's obligations; to fulfil one's commitments; to reciprocate, to return a favour; -arsi d'una promessa, to keep a promise; *tr.* to clear from debt; to release from an obligation. (-ato *part. adj.*)

ṣdegn-are [A SC] *tr.* to disdain; to scorn; to loathe, to abhor; to refuse; to take a strong dislike to (esp. food); (of the stomach) to refuse to digest; non lo -ò per marito, she was quite willing to take him as a husband; to irritate; to enrage; *rfl.* (*prep.* di) to get angry, to be offended; to refuse; (of a wound) to become inflamed, not to heal; (of the stomach) to refuse food; (of plants) to grow weakly, to fade, not to flourish. -amento *m.* disdaining; see sdegno. -ato *part. adj.* indignant; angry; annoyed; disdained; loathed. (-atore *m.* -atrice *f.*)

ṣdegno *m.* indignation; anger; wrath; scorn, disdain; contempt; muovere a —, to rouse the indignation of, to anger; prendere —, to take offence; *pl.* moments of irritation; outbursts of scorn or indignation.

sdegnos-o *adj.* scornful; disdainful; haughty; indignant; irascible, touchy. -amente *adv.* scornfully; indignantly; disdainfully. -aggine *f.* scorn, contempt. -ità *f.* haughtiness; scornfulness; contempt.

ṣdent-are [A I] *tr.* to pull out the teeth of; to break the teeth of (a comb, saw, etc.); *rfl.* to lose one's teeth; to break one's teeth. -ato *part. adj.* toothless; having teeth missing, or broken off; *n.m.pl.* (zool.) Edentata. -atura *f.* breaking or pulling out of teeth; loss of teeth; (mil.) damage or wear of the rifling of a gun.

†**ṣdetta** *f.* See disdetta.

ṣdiacci-are [A 3] *tr.* (fam. Tusc.) to take the chill off; to thaw; *intr.* (*aux.* essere) (of the temperature, etc.) to grow a little warmer.

ṣdiavolare [A I S] *intr.* (*aux.* avere) to make the devil's own row.

†**ṣdice·vole** *adj.* See disdicevole.

ṣdigiun-are [A I] *tr.* to put on to food again after a fast; *rfl.* to break one's fast. -o *m.* breakfast.

†**ṣdilacciare** *vb.* and derivs. See slacciare.

ṣdilinqu-ire [D 2] *rfl.*, (Tusc.) *intr.* (*aux.* essere) to swoon, to faint; to droop, to grow feeble; (fig.) to become foolishly sentimental; *tr.* to enfeeble, to weaken. -imento *m.* swoon, fainting fit; (fig.) languishing; mawkishness, false sentiment. -ito *part. adj.* enfeebled; soft, mawkish; lackadaisical.

ṣdimenticare [A 2 S] and derivs. *intens.* of dimenticare, q.v.

†**ṣdimet·tere** *vb.* and derivs. See smettere, dimettere.

ṣdimezzare [A I] and derivs. (pop.). See dimezzare.

ṣdipanare [A I] *tr.* to unravel; to unwind.

ṣdipin·gere [C 5] *tr.* to paint out, to cancel what has been painted.

ṣdiragnare [A 4] *tr.* to clear of cobwebs, spiders' webs.

ṣdire [B 10] and derivs. See disdire.

ṣdiren-are [A I], -ire [D 2] *rfl.* to wear oneself out.

ṣdiricci-are [A 3] *tr.* to husk (chestnuts). (-ato *part. adj.* -atura *f.*)

†**ṣdiridito** *adj.* emaciated, thin, wan.

†**ṣdisocchiare** *tr.* to put out the eyes of.

ṣdogan-are [A I] *tr.* to clear through the customs. -amento *m.* clearing through the customs, clearance. (-ato *part. adj.*) -azione *f.* clearance.

ṣdog-are [A 2] *tr.* to remove a stave (or staves) from a cask. (-ato *part. adj.*)

ṣdolcinat-o *adj.* sickly; too sweet; sugary; (fig.) mawkish; maudlin; affected; *n.m.* maudlin person; mealy-mouthed or affected person. -ezza *f.* mawkishness; affectation. -ura *f.* mawkish or maudlin behaviour; affected words; sentimentality.

ṣdolenz-ire [D 2] *tr.* to remove numbness from, to restore circulation to, to revive. (-ito *part. adj.*)

†**ṣdolere** *intr.* to cease to grieve; *tr.* to cause to cease grieving.

†**ṣdonnare** *rfl.*, *intr.* to cease to be master or leader.

†**ṣdonneare** *intr.* to cease to hold converse with one's beloved.

ṣdonnino *adj.*, *n.m.* (vet.) blue roan.

ṣdonzellare [A I] *rfl.* (joc., derog.) sdonzellarsela, to lead a life of idle pleasure.

ṣdoppi-are [A 4 c] *tr.* to uncouple; to separate a pair; to split, to divide; to reduce from double to single; to use one instead of two. -amento *m.* uncoupling; -amento della personalità, creation of a split personality; -amento della coscienza, hallucinatory feeling of oneself as two persons. -ato *part. adj.* uncoupled; separated; divided into two.

ṣdorare [A I] *tr.* to ungild, to remove gilding from.

ṣdoss-are [A I] *tr.* to take off, to put off, to remove from the back of. (-ato *part. adj.*)

ṣdotto[1] *adj.* (of plants) sickly; podere —, neglected farm.

†**ṣdotto**[2] *adj.* glad, rejoiced.

ṣdottor-are [A I c] *tr.* to deprive of a doctor's title and privileges; *intr.* (*aux.* avere) to pose as a learned man. -amento *m.* posing as a learned man; tiresome display of learning. (-ante *part. adj.* -ato *part. adj.*) -eggiare [A 3 c] *intr.* (*aux.* avere) to sermonize, to pontificate.

ṣdra·ia *f.* chaise-longue; couch.

ṣdrai-are [A 4] *rfl.* to lie down, to stretch oneself at ease; to loll; *tr.* to stretch out at full length. -ata *f.* lying down, fare una -ata, to lie down for a while. -ato *part. adj.* lying down; stretched out; -ato in una poltrona, lolling in an armchair.

ṣdrai-o *adv.* a —, full-length; sedia a —, deck-chair *or* chaise-longue; poltrona a —, easy chair; mettersi a —, to lie down, to stretch out; *n.m.* cradle (for working underneath a car). -one, -oni *adv.* lying down, reclining, lolling; starsene -oni sulla spiaggia, to lie at full length on the beach.

ṣdramba *f.* (tanning) tow, cotton waste, etc. used as a duster.

ṣdrucciol-are [A I S] *intr.* (*aux.* avere, essere) to slip, to slide; to skate; (of water) to glide, to flow down; — su di un argomento, to touch lightly on a subject; (of time) to fly. -amento *m.* slipping, sliding. -ante *part. adj.* slippery. -ativo *adj.* liable to slip, slippery. (-ato *part. adj.*) -ente *adj.* slippery. -evole *adj.* slippery; memoria -evole, bad, unretentive memory. (-evolmente *adv.*) -ìo *m.* frequent slipping.

ṣdruc·ciol-o *adj.* slippery; sliding; parola -a, proparoxytone, word accented on third last syllable; verso —, line ending with a proparoxytone, having therefore one syllable more than the usual number; *n.m.* slippery place; slip; slide; mettere una cosa a —, to slide a thing along; (prosod.) 'verso sdrucciolo', q.v.; slippery slope, steep path; scala a —, ramp; (fig.) si va verso un brutto —, we are riding for a fall. -one *m.* slip, fall; fare gli -oni, to slide (on ice). -one, -oni *adv.* sliding, slipping. -oso *adj.* slippery.

ṣdru·cio *m.* tear, rent, rip; cut; laceration; — del porco, cutting up the pig (for salting); (fig.) — della borsa, heavy expense.

ṣdruc-ire [D 2] *tr.* to tear, to rend, to rip; to unstitch; to cut; to lacerate. -ito *part. adj.* rent, worn out, threadbare; unstitched; split; occhi -iti, staring (wide-open) eyes; leaky; barca -ita, foundered boat; *n.m.* tear, rent; large cut. (-itore *m.* -itrice *f.*) -itura *f.* unstitching; rent; rip.

ṣdrumare [A I] *tr.* (neol.) to 'bash', to batter, to lay flat.

†**ṣducare** *tr.* to deprive of a dukedom.

ṣdur-ire [D 2], -are [A I] *tr.* to soften, to make tender.

se[1] *conj.* (often occasions doubling of a following consonant, thereby combining two words as one, e.g. 'se bene' becomes 'sebbene', 'se pure' becomes 'seppure', etc.). **1.** IF; (follow. by *indicative*) — vuoi, if you wish; — lo tempo permetterà, if weather permits, weather permitting; — sarai buono ti racconterò una storia, if you are good I will tell you a story; non so — loro verranno, I don't know if they will come; — non è vero è ben trovato, if it isn't true it's a good tale anyway; (follow. by *subjunctive*) — fossi in te, if I were you; oh — potessi!, if only I could!; — non venisse morivo di fame, if he hadn't come I should have died of hunger; — non fosse per, if it were not for, but for; dubitava — dovesse venire, he wondered if he ought to come; non sono sicuro — fosse lui, I am not sure if it was he; come — non lo sapesse, as if he didn't know. **2.** USED EMPHATICALLY, WITH SUPPRESSION OF MAIN VERBS: — lo so! (i.e. 'tu mi domandi — lo so'), of course I know!; — l'ho visto io!, but I saw him myself!; — è caldo? Scotta!, is it hot? It's scalding!; — ha pazienza!, is he patient!, of course he's patient! **3.** USED IN CONJUNCTION WITH OTHER PARTS OF SPEECH: — no, if not, otherwise, or else; — non altro, at least, if nothing else; — non —, except that, if it were not that; — non che (*or* sennonché), unless; — bene (*or* sebbene), though, although (follow. by *subj.*); — bene sia tardi, although it is late; — bene avesse ottant'anni, although he was eighty years old; (pop., follow. by *indicative*); — bene non vuol venire, although he doesn't want to come. **4.** *n.m. indecl.* IF; tutti questi — e ma, all these ifs and buts; va bene ma qui c'è un gran —, all right, but there's a serious condition attached to it.

†**se**[2] *adv.* as, so (in a formula of adjuration often used by Dante, e.g. '— tu mai nel dolce mondo reggi', as you hope to return, by all your hopes to return, to the sweet world, *Inf.* x, 82).

se[3] *prn. rfl. conjunct.* (form of **si**, q.v., used before 'lo', 'la', 'li', 'le', 'ne') oneself; itself; himself; herself; themselves.

sè[4] *prn. rfl. disjunct.* oneself; itself; himself; herself; themselves; fare da —, to act alone, to do (something) on one's own; ognuno per —, everyone for himself; essere fuori di —, to be beside oneself; uscire di —, to lose consciousness; tornare in —, to come to oneself, to regain consciousness; contento di —, self-satisfied, pleased with oneself; aver fiducia in —, to be self-confident; diceva fra —, he said to himself; pensare tra — e —, to think to oneself; la cosa va da —, that goes without saying; fare parlare di —, to get oneself talked about; *n.m.* self; il — di una volta, one's former self.

se[5] *abbrev.* of 'sei', from **essere**, q.v.

†**se'** *card. num.* See **sei**.

seba·ceo *adj.* (physiol.) sebaceous.

seba·cic·o *adj.* (chem.) sebacic, decanedioic. **-ato** *m.* (chem.) sebacate.

sebaste *m.* (ichth.) *Sebastes dactylopterus*, an edible marine fish.

Sebastiano *pr.n.m.* Sebastian.

sebbene *conj.* although, though (cf. 'se bene', under **se**[1]).

seb·o *m.* (physiol.) sebum. **-oraggi·a** *f.* (med.) seborrhagia, seborrhoea. **-orag·gio** *adj.* (med.) seborrhoeic. **-orre·a** *f.* (med.) seborrhoea. **-orre·ico** *adj.* (med.) seborrhoeic.

sec·are [A2] *tr.* to cut; (fig.) to glide, to cut, to streak (through the air or on water); (geom.) to cut, to intersect; to divide (an angle). **-ante** *f.* (geom.; trig.) secant. (**-ato** *part. adj.*)

secc·a *f.* shoal, sandbank; reef; reef bar; extra low water (tidal); — di sabbia, sandbank; — cieca, hidden shoal (below water); — frangente, breaking shoal (where the breakers disclose its presence); — allo scoperto, reef, sandbank breaking the surface; (naut.) arenarsi sulla —, to go aground; cadere su di una —, to run into a shoal; dare nella —, to be cast ashore; lasciarsi in sulle secche, to run aground, (fig.) to find oneself stranded. **-ag·gine** *f.* dryness; (fig.) weariness; trouble, annoyance. **-agginoso** *adj.* troublesome, annoying; *n.m.* dry branches, etc. **-agione** *f.* (agric.) drying up, effects of drought. **-agno** *adj.* (agric.) arid, dried up (ground); *n.m.* (naut.) series of shoals. **-a·ia** *f.* dry twigs, branches, etc. **-aione** *m.* dry branch; heel of a vine-cutting. **-anic·cio** *adj.* thin, wiry person. **-arello** *m.* see **seccherello**.

secc·are [A2] *tr.* to dry, to dry up; to wither; to desiccate; to weary, to bore, to bother, to annoy, to vex; — una palude, to drain a swamp; — un pozzo, to empty a well; (naut.) to pump out the bilges; to dry the decks; *rfl.* mettere le vele a -arsi, to hoist sails to dry; *intr.* (aux. essere) and *rfl.* to dry (up); to wither; to get thin; to get bored; to be weary. **-a·bile** *adj.* easily dried, drained, etc.; liable to be bored. **-amento** *m.* drying (up); desiccation; (fig.) annoyance. **-ante** *part. adj.* tiresome, boring; troublesome; colore -ante, quick-drying paint. **-arec·cia** *f.* (agric.) aridity; drought. **-ata** *f.* drying (of figs, etc.); (fig.) bore, annoyance. **-atasche** *m. indecl.* bore (person). **-atic·cio** *adj.* partly dried; legna -aticcia, dry wood (dry enough to burn well); colore -aticcio, quick-drying paint; (of animal) dry (of milk); (of a person) very thin; *n.m.* thin, wiry person; dried-up thing. **-ativo** *adj.* drying; (chem.) siccative; olio -ativo, drying oil. **-ato** *part. adj.* dried (up); dry, withered; tired, wearied; sick; bored, annoyed; stufo e -ato di tutto, bored and fed-up with everything. **-atoio** *m.*, **-atoia** *f.* drying-room; oast-house (esp. for chestnuts); squeegee. **-atore** *m.* bore. (**-atora**, **-atrice** *f.*) **-atura** *f.* drying (esp. of chestnuts); annoyance, nuisance; trouble.

secch-ereccio, †**-eric·cio** *adj.* almost dry, fairly dry; *n.m.* dryness; drought. **-erello** *adj. dim.* thin, dried-up looking; *n.m.* crust of dry bread. **-eri·a** *f.* stinginess, parsimony; meanness; (paperm.) drying end. **-ezza** *f.* dryness; (fig.) thinness; (art) stiffness; (ascetic theol.) spiritual dryness, aridity.

secchi·a *f.* bucket, pail; 'La Secchia Rapita', title of a mock-heroic poem by A. Tassoni; piovere a -e, to rain cats and dogs; fare come le -e, to go up and down; old liquid measure, at Udine 10·7 litres. **-are** [A4] *intr.* (aux. avere) to swot. **-ata** *f.* bucketful. **-ello** *m. dim.*, **-erella** *f. dim.* small pail (or bucket). **-ona** *f.*, **-one** *m. augm.* large bucket; (metall.) ladle; (mining) tub; (slang) swot.

secchio *m.* bucket; large milk-pail; churn; fire-bucket; bucket of a well; stable bucket; — per carbone, coal-scuttle.

secci·a *f.* stubble; fagioli fatti sulla —, vetches grown in stubble-fields. **-a·io** *m.* (agric.) stubble field.

secc·o[1] *adj.* (*pl.* **-chi**) dry; dried; dried up; withered; parched; wizened; thin, spare, gaunt, lean; mean, stingy; distinct; sharply defined; harsh; un colpo —, one sharp blow; una risposta -ca, a curt answer; unadorned, bald (of style, etc.); (cul.) carne -ca, smoked and salted pork; (comm.) a titolo —, ex coupon, ex dividend; denari -chi, hard cash; stufa -ca, furnace or other apparatus for heating by hot air; sorgente -ca, spring run dry; (chem.) analisi per via -ca, dry way analysis, (metall.) dry assay; (naut.) cappa -ca, stormsail; grappo —, squall without rain or cloud; essere in panna -ca, to be under bare poles; — di vele, having lost all canvas in bad weather; palata a —, a 'dry' stroke of an oar; (cards) avevo l'asso di fiori —, I had the ace of clubs bare; terno —, (lotto) stake placed on three numbers without any other combinations; *n.m.* dryness; dry portion; dry place; dry ground; dry weather; drought; thin, gaunt or wizened person; lasciare in —, to leave in the lurch; rimanere al —, to be left penniless; (naut.) andare in —, to ground; mettere, tirare a —, to slip, to haul up on a slip to dock; dare in —, to beach; restare in, a, —, to dry out; (fig.) rimanere in —, to be left alone in some difficulty; (paint.) pittura a —, painting on dry plaster; muro a — dry wall; (fig.) mangiare a —, to eat without drinking; *adv.* harshly, curtly; stiffly; *adv.* coldly; stiffly; bluntly; gruffly. **-camente** *adv.* drily, coldly; stiffly; bluntly; gruffly. **-cac·cio** *adj. pejor.* very thin, 'skinny'. **-chic·cio** *adj.* partly dried; rather dry. **-chiginoso** *adj.* full of dry wood (and sim.). **-core** *m.* dryness (esp. of air, weather); drought. **-cume** *m.* dry things (branches, leaves, etc.); dryness; *pl.* dried fruits. **-cura** *f.* see **seccore**.

secco[2] *apocop. part.* of **seccare**, q.v.

secent-esimo *ord. num.* six-hundredth. **-ismo** *m.* seventeenth-century mannerism of style; gongorism, euphuism; baroque. **-ista** *m., f.* writer or artist of the seventeenth century; scholar specializing in seventeenth-century history or culture. (**-i·stico** *adj.*) **-o** *m.* see **seicento**.

secer·nere [C28] *tr.* to separate; to distinguish; (scient.) to secrete.

sece·spita *f.* (Rom. antiq.) *secespita*, sacrificial knife.

session·e *f.* secession; Guerra di Secessione, American Civil War. **-ista** *m.* (*pl.* **-isti**) secessionist, separatist.

Seciuàn *pr.n.f.* (geog.) Szechwan.

seco *prn.* (poet.) with him, with her, with them.

se·col·o *m.* century; age, era; time; nel nostro —, in our time; è da un — che non ti vedo, I haven't seen you for ages; (rel.) il —, the world; ritirarsi dal —, to leave the world (for the cloister); Padre Paolo, al — A.B., Father Paul, in the world A.B. (known as A.B. before he became a monk); this (the present) world, this (the present) life; l'altro —, the world (life) to come; dal cominciamento dei -i, from the beginning of time; per tutti i -i dei -i, for ever and ever; parlare ai -i, to speak for posterity; nella notte dei -i, in the dim past; l'immortale —, the next world, the future life; l'universo —, the universe; (joc.) essere fuori del —, to be out of one's wits. **-are** *adj.* age-old; age-long; hundreds of years old; time-honoured; (rel.) secular; lay; worldly; (scient.) secular, long-term; foro -are, civil court; abito -are, civilian clothes; beni -ari, worldly wealth; †unlettered; *n.m.* layman; *pl.* laity. **-armente** *adv.* secularly; in a worldly manner. **-aresco** *adj.* (*m.pl.* **-areschi**) secular, lay; worldly. **-arescamente** *adv.* in a worldly manner. **-arità** *f.* permanence; secularity; secularism. **-arizzare** [A1] *tr.* to secularize; to laicize; (eccl.) to secularize. (**-arizzato** *part. adj.*) **-arizzazione** *f.* secularization.

seconda *f.* See under **secondo**[1].

second·o[1] *ord. num., adj.* second; la -a volta, the second time; al — piano, on the second floor; Vittorio Emanuele II ('Secondo'), Victor Emmanuel II; — volume (abbrev. vol. II), volume II; minuto —, second; di -a mano, at second hand; mobili di -a mano, second-hand furniture; informazione di -a mano, information derived from second-hand sources; substitute, another such, just such another; per noi è una -a madre, she is a second mother to us; di -a qualità, of inferior quality; di — grado, second-rate; — a nessuno, second to none, first-rate; ulterior; senza — fine, with no ulterior motive; following, subsequent, later; (cul.) piatto —, or -a mensa, main dish on a menu, entrée; dessert; (gramm.) — caso, genitive case; (mus.) lower (of two vocal or instrumental parts); -a donna, second lady (in opera); (theatr.) -a parte, supporting role; -a galleria, upper circle; (vet.) morso —,

second-o (*cont.*)

permanent dentition; (naut.) — nostromo, second coxwain, second mate; (poet.) favourable, propitious; *n.m.* second, the one following the first; (duelling, boxing) second; (of time) second; due -i e sarò con voi, I'll be with you in two ticks; (watchm.) lancetta dei -i, second-hand; ruota dei -i, fourth wheel and pinion; (naut.) second-in-command, mercantile first officer (immediately after a captain). **-a** *f.* second (person, woman, girl, thing, etc.), the one following the first; second grade, second class; second division; (motor.) second (gear); (rlwy.) second class; viaggiare in -a, to travel second; (med.) afterbirth; (finan.) -a di cambio, second of exchange, second copy of bill of exchange; second via; (mus.) second (interval); comandare in -a, to be second in command; (mil.) comandante in -a, second-in-command; vino di -a, second-grade wine, inferior quality wine; *adv.* secondly, in the second place; *adv. phr.* a -a, following the stream; (fig.) andare a -a, to go well, to be favourable; *prep. phr.* a -a di, according to, in accordance with. **-amento** *m.* seconding; supporting; support. **-are** [A I C] *tr.* to second; to support; to back up; to favour; to be propitious to; -are i capricci di, to indulge the whims of; -are la moda, to follow the fashion; *intr.* (*aux.* avere) (med.) to get rid of the afterbirth, to expel the placenta. **-ario** *adj.* secondary; minor; side; (rlwy.) linea -aria, branch line; (eng.) albero -ario, driven shaft; (paint.; astron.) lume -ario, reflected light. **-ariamente** *adv.* secondarily. **-ato** *part. adj.* seconded; supported; favoured. **-atore** *m.* seconder. (**-atrice** *f.*) **-ina** *f.* (anat.) amniotic sac; (agric.) cow that has calved twice. **-ino** *m.* under-gaoler; (vet.) permanent dentition. **-ogenito** *adj.* second-born, younger; *n.m.* second son. (**-ogenita** *f.*) **-ogenitura** *f.* status and rights of a second son. **-onato** see **secondogenito**.

secondo² *prep.* according to; in accordance with; — me, in my opinion; — quel che ha detto, according to what he has said; — natura, in accordance with nature, true to nature; — il caso, according to circumstances; verrai anche tu? secondo, will you come too? it depends; following; — la corrente, with the stream; — la moda, following the fashion, after the fashion; *conj.* — che, according as; — che mi piaccia o no, according to whether I wish to or not.

secrétaire *m.* (pron. as Fr.) writing-desk.

secret-o¹ *m.*, **-amente** *adv.*, **-ario** *m.* See **segreto**, etc.

secret-o² *part.* of **secernere**, q.v.; *adj.* secreted; *n.m.* (physiol.) secretum, secretion. **-ina** *f.* (biochem.) secretin. **-ore** *m.* (physiol.) secretory. **-orio** *adj.* (physiol.) secretory.

secrezione *f.* (physiol.) secretion.

secutore *m.* (Rom. antiq.) *secutor*, (kind of) gladiator.

†**secuzione** *f.* See **esecuzione**.

†**sed** *conj.* See **se¹**.

se·dan-o *m.* (cul.) celery; (bot.) wild celery, *Apium graveolens*; lovage, *Levisticum officinale*. **-ina** *f.* (bot.) -ina d'acqua, *Apium nodiflorum*, *Berula erecta*, and *Sium latifolium*.

sed-are [A I] *tr.* to assuage; to allay; to appease, to calm; to quell. **-ante** *part. adj.* sedative, calming. **-ativo** *adj.*, *n.m.* sedative. **-ato** *part. adj.* assuaged, allayed; calmed; quelled; sedate, calm. **-atamente** *adv.* sedately, calmly. (**-atore** *m.* **-atrice** *f.*)

sede, sède *f.* seat; residence; office; un'antica — del sapere, an ancient seat of learning; — centrale, head-office; la — di un'organizzazione, the headquarters of an organization: (eccl.) see; la Santa —, la — Apostolica, the Holy See; — vacante, *sede vacante*; (eng.) seat, seating; (mil.) station, command, headquarters; (leg.; comm.) office; seat; residence; centre; session; sitting; — legale, registered office, (admin.) deliberare in — di bilancio, to debate the budget, (comm.) to consider the accounts; liquidare in separata —, to settle at a separate session; (fig.) in — tecnica, from the technical point of view; (gramm.) — dell'accento, place of the accent, accented syllable.

sed-ère [B 28] *intr.* (*aux.* avere) to be seated; to be sitting; mettere a —, to seat; offrire da — a, to offer a seat to; tenere a — sulle ginocchia, to hold (e.g. a child) on one's lap; posti a —, seats; alzarsi da —, to get up from one's seat; a —!, be seated!, sit down!; chi in piedi e chi a —, some were standing and others were sitting down; scrivere a —, to write sitting down; — a mensa, to sit at table; — in trono, to be on the throne; — sulla cattedra di S. Pietro, to be Pope; Londra siede sulle rive del Tamigi, London is on the river Thames; (leg.) to sit; to be in office; — su un Consiglio, to serve on a Board; to reside, to have

one's abode; *rfl.* to sit down, to take a seat; *n.m.* sitting; sitting down; being seated; backside, posterior, seat; seat (of a chair, etc.); †chair. **-entario** *adj.* sedentary; *n.m.* person of sedentary habits; *pl.* (naut. slang) non sea-going personnel; (mil.) fortress troops; disabled personnel re-employed in suitable non-combatant posts. **-ente** *part. adj.* sitting, seated; reigning; situated; residing; (herald.) sejant affronté.

se·d-ia *f.* chair, seat; — a bracciuoli, armchair; — a dondolo, rocking-chair; — a sdraio, deck-chair; — pieghevole, camp-stool, folding-chair; (post-)chaise; — volante, litter; — rullante, sedan-chair; — elettrica, electric chair; — di posta, post-chaise; (eccl.) — gestatoria, gestatorial chair; †(eccl.) see. **-iario** *m.* sedan chair-man; (eccl.) carrier of gestatorial chair.

sedicente *adj.* self-styled, would-be; pretended.

se·dic-i *card. num.* sixteen; sixteenth; umpteen; *n.m.* (joc.) bottom, 'sit-upon' (cf. **sedere**). **-enne** *adj.* sixteen years old; *n.m.*, *f.* sixteen-year-old. **-esimo** *ord. num.* sixteenth; (typ.) signature of sixteen pages, 16mo.; (paperm.; bookb.) in -esimo, sixteenmo, 16mo. **-iangolare** *adj.* (geom.) sixteen-sided. **-ina** *f.* group of about sixteen; set of sixteen. **-ino** *m.* (numism.) old Bolognese coin (16 quattrini); *pl.* (joc.) officials in Tuscany at the time of the Grand Dukes (paid on the 16th of the month).

sed-ile *m.* seat, chair; bench; — allungabile, sliding-chair; — girevole, swivel-chair; — pieghevole, folding-chair; (fig.) far — di botti, to stand idle; seat (in a carriage); (archit.) seating (of an arch). **-ime** *m.* seating; sediment, dregs.

sediment-o *m.* sediment, deposit; dregs, lees; (geol.) deposit, sediment; *pl.* (industr.) foots (in oil). **-ario** *adj.* relating to sediment, of sediment; (geol.) sedimentary. **-azione** *f.* (geol.; chem.) sedimentation. **-oso** *adj.* sedimentary; forming a deposit; formed by deposit.

sedi-olina *f.* see **seggiolina**. **-one** *m. augm.* see **seggiolone**. **-tore** *m.* sitter. (**-trice** *f.*) **-(u)olo** *m.* sulky (light two-wheeled carriage); seat (in a carriage).

sedizi-one *f.* sedition; disagreement. **-oso** *adj.* seditious; turbulent; *n.m.* rebel; rioter. **-osamente** *adv.* seditiously.

sedo *m.* (bot.) stonecrop, *Sedum*.

sedotto *part.* of **sedurre**, q.v.; *adj.* seduced; fascinated; corrupted.

seduc-ente *part. adj.* seductive; charming, fascinating; tempting. **-i·bile** *adj.* seducible; corruptible. **-imento** *m.* allurement; seduction. †**-itore** *m.* see **seduttore**.

†**sedu·cere** *vb.* See **sedurre**.

†**se·dul-o** *adj.* sedulous. †**-ità** *f.* sedulousness.

sedurre [B 2] *tr.* to seduce; to entice; to lure; to corrupt; to tempt; to fascinate; to please; to charm; to allure.

seduta *f.* sitting; meeting; session; togliere la —, to adjourn the meeting; — solenne d'inaugurazione, formal opening sitting; — segreta, secret session; — d'apertura, opening session, sitting or meeting; — di chiusura, final session; tenere —, to be in session, to be sitting; in —, in session; la — è aperta, the sitting is open, is called to order; riprendere la —, to resume the sitting; voto per alzata e —, vote by sitting and standing; prendere una decisione — stante, to decide forthwith, to decide in the session; (paint.; sculpt.) sitting (of a model).

sedut-ore *m.* seducer; tempter; enticer; *adj.* seductive; corrupting. **-trice** *f.* temptress; also *adj.* †**-torio** *adj.* seductive; alluring; tempting.

seduzione *f.* seduction; temptation; cedere alla —, to yield to temptation; allurement; charm; — di Eva da parte del serpente, temptation of Eve by the serpent.

seenne *adj.* six years old; of six years' duration; *n.m.*, *f.* six-year-old.

seg-a *f.* saw: — a nastro, band saw; — circolare, circular saw; — da traforo, fretsaw; a denti di —, serrated; — di pietra, toothless saw (for cutting stone); saw-shaped object; toothed edge of a wall; (hist.) poll-tax; fare la —, to play a game resembling cat's cradle, *or* to play truant, *or* (slang) to masturbate; (ichth.) sawfish, *Pristis antiquorum*; (mil.) defence such as concrete blocks; road block, 'dragon's teeth'; (vulg.) masturbation. **-abile** *adj.* fit for sawing. **-accio** *m.* ripsaw. **-aiuolo** *m.* (slang) addict to masturbation.

segal-e, -a *f.* (bot.) rye, *Secale cereale*; — cornuta, ergot (sclerotium of *Claviceps purpurea*). **-aio** *m.* rye-field. **-ata** *f.* maslin. **-ato** *adj.* rye-like. **-igno**, †**-ino** *adj.* of rye; like rye; (of person) slender; wiry.

seg·are [A2] *tr.* to saw, to saw off; to mow, to reap; to cut; (geom.) to cut, to intersect; — le onde, to cleave the waves; — il mare, to plough through the sea, to cut through the water; (joc.) — il violino, to scrape the violin. **-a·bile** *adj.* that can be sawn through. **-amento** *m.* sawing; (math.) see **segmento**. **-ante** *part. adj.* sawing, cutting; *n.f.* (geom.) see **secante**, under **secare**. **-antino** *m.* sawyer. **-astoppia** *m.* farm labourer; reaper. **-ata** *f.* sawing. **-atic·cio** *adj.* fit for sawing (up). **-ato** *part. adj.* sawn (up, off); cut with a saw; *n.m.* mown grass (etc.). **-atore** *m.* sawyer; (agric.) mower; †*adj.* (naut.) fondo -atore, bad holding ground where cables may part and anchors are lost, foul anchorage. **-atrice** *f.* sawing machine. **-atura** *f.* sawing; mowing; mowing time; cost of sawing (or mowing); sawdust; dare la -atura, to sweep a floor after sprinkling sawdust; saw-mark, cut made by a saw in wood, etc. **-avec·chia** *f.* dummy filled with dried fruits, which is carried round in Romagna in mid-Lent. †**-avene**, †**-aveni** *m.* cut-throat, assassin; tyrant.

†**se·geta** *f.* corn for horses, etc.

†**seggenza** *f.* seat.

seggetta *f.* See under **seggio**.

seg·gi·o *m.*, †**-a** *f.* seat; chair (official); throne; togliere di —, to remove from office, to deprive of authority (rank); tenersi in —, to hold one's place in office; (eccl.) (bishop's) throne; see; — di San Pietro, St Peter's chair; — (di canonico), (canon's) stall; (fig.) place, office; authority; seat (in Parliament or on municipal council); i comunisti hanno ottenuto otto seggi, the Communist party has won eight seats; — elettorale, polling station; (leg.) seat; bench. **-etta** (**seggetta**) *f. dim.* small chair; commode, close-stool; sedan-chair, portable chair. **-ovi·a** *f.* chair-lift.

seg·giol·a *f.* chair; (eccl.) — apostolica, papal throne; (eng.) seating. **-a·io** *m.* chair-maker; seller or mender of chairs. **-etta** *f. dim.*, **-ina** *f. dim.* small chair. **-ino** *m.* baby's chair; (aeron.) pilot's seat. **-one** *m. augm.* arm-chair, easy-chair; baby's high chair; -one a libro, folding-chair.

seggiovi·a *f.* See under **seggio**.

Seghedino *pr.n.m.* (geog.) Szeged.

segheri·a *f.* saw-mill; lumber-mill.

seghettato *adj.* serrated (of leaves); notched like a saw, having a saw-edge.

seghetto *m. dim.* hand-saw (cf. **sega**).

seghidi·glia *f.* See **seguidilla**.

segment-o *m.* (geom.) segment; (motor.) piston ring; — per freni, brake lining. **-ale** *adj.* segmentary; segmental. **-azione** *f.* (geom.; zool., etc.) segmentation.

segn-acarte *m. indecl.*, **-acaso** *m. indecl.*, **-achilo·metri** *m. indecl.* See under **segnare**.

segn-a·colo, †**-ac·chio** *m.* mark; sign; emblem; (rel.) la Croce è il -acolo del cristiano, the Cross is the Christian's emblem; il — della vita, baptism.

segnal-e *m.* signal; sign; token; omen; — di pericolo, distress signal; — orario, time-signal; — indicatore, signpost, fingerpost; — di traffico, traffic signal; — luminoso, illuminated sign; — prescrittivo, warning-sign; cifrario per i -i, code of signals; brutto —, bad omen, bad sign; (naut.) beacon, daymark; signal; — d'aiuto, — di soccorso, distress signal; — di altezza della marea, tide gauge signal; — d'esecuzione, executive signal; — di evoluzione, manœuvring signal; (rlwy.) — d'allarme, communication cord; †— di fuggire, signal to escape or scatter; — d'intelligenza, acknowledging signal; abbassare un —, ammainare —, to haul down a hoist; alzare un —, to hoist a signal; alzare a metà —, to hoist at the dip; alzare un — a metà l'intelligenza, to hoist or keep the answering pennant at the dip whilst decoding or checking a signal; -i di presagio di tempesta, -i di presagio meteorologico, storm signals; -i di ricognizione, recognition signals; †sign of the Zodiac. **-are** [A1] *tr.* to signalize; to point out; to notify; to signal; to mark; to draw attention to; to mention; (naut.) to signal; -are con bandiere, to make a flag signal; to report; -are il nemico, to report sighting the enemy; to mark; -are una secca, to put daymarks on a shoal; -are un canale, to put buoys in a channel; *rfl.* to distinguish oneself. **-amento** *m.* signalling; signal; (naut.) -amenti marittimi, system of marking, buoyage beacons, etc. **-ato** *part. adj.* distinguished; prominent; eminent; remarkable; noticed; mentioned. **-atamente** *adv.* markedly, signally; notably; eminently. **-atore** *m.* signaller; (rlwy.) signalman; signalling apparatus; indicator; (naut.) signalling apparatus; signalman; warrant officer in charge of the navigating stores; (aeron.) -atore

a ventaglio, fan marker. **-azione** *f.* signalling; signal; (fig.) recommendation; cabina di -azione, signal-box; -azioni luminose, traffic lights, illuminated signals; -azione visiva, visual signalling; -azioni stradali, road-traffic signals; notification; -azione dell'ispettorato, notification by the inspectorate; scheda di -azione, notification form; (naut.) method or operation of signalling; -azione acustica, sound signalling; -azione con bandiera a mano, semaphore; †telegram. **-e·tica** *f.* system of signs; -etica orizzontale (verticale), system of signs on surface of road (on posts); science of identification marks, finger-prints, etc. **-e·tico** *adj.* relating to signs or distinguishing marks; dati -etici, identification marks.

segn-are [A5c] *tr.* to mark; to note, to note down, to enter (in a register); to indicate, to show; to mark out, to trace, to draw, to sign; to seal; — i confini, to mark the boundaries; to scratch; — nella memoria, to make a mental note of; — di propria mano, to sign with one's own hand; — il passo, to mark time; — a dito, to point the finger of scorn at; (sport) to score; (comm.) — a debito, to debit; (rel.) to make the sign of the cross on someone (e.g. on a baby); †to bless (with the sign of the cross); *rfl.* to cross oneself; to make the sign of the cross; -arsi bene, to begin the day well; -arsi male, to get out of bed on the wrong side; to be astonished. **-acarte** *m. indecl.* book-marker, book-mark. **-acaso** *m. indecl.* (gramm.) preposition as case-sign. †**-accento** *m.* (gramm.) sign indicating an accent. **-achilo·metri** *m. indecl.* taximeter. **-alibro** *m.* (*pl.* **-alibri**) book-marker; book-mark. **-ali·nee** *m. indecl.* (sport) linesman. **-ata·rio** *m.*, *adj.* signatory. **-atasse** *m. indecl.* post-office stamp indicating insufficient postage. **-ato** *part. adj.* marked; signed; scratched; sentiero -ato, (well-)beaten path; -ato da Dio, (of a person) deformed, hunchbacked, squint-eyed, etc.; *n.m.* guàrdati dai -ati, beware of deformed people (as bringers of bad luck); pecora -ata, black sheep, marked man, watched by the police, etc. **-atamente** *adv.* markedly; especially; chiefly. **-atoio** *m.* marker (tool). **-atore** *m.*, **-atrice** *f.* marker (person); indicator; scorer; signatory; *adj.* serving to indicate; freccia -atrice, weathervane. **-atura** *f.* marking, stamp(ing); signing; (typ.) signature; (eccl.) (papal) *signatura.* **-avento** *m. indecl.* (aeron.) wind sleeve, wind cone, wind sock.

†**segni·zie** *f.* laziness, indolence.

segn-o *m.* mark; sign; trace; target; un — di distinzione, a mark of distinction; i -i dei tempi, the signs of the times; il dolore ha lasciato -i evidenti sul suo volto, sorrow has left visible traces in his face; tirare a —, to shoot at a mark; tiro a —, target-practice; cogliere, dare, nel —, to hit the bull's eye; (fig.) le sue parole andarono a —, her words struck home; aim, point; essere fatto a —, to be the object of; limit; avete passato il —, you have overshot the mark, you have gone too far; fare — a una persona, to beckon to a person; fare — una persona a qualcuno, to point a person out to someone; fino a un certo — ci posso credere, up to a point I can believe it; siam ridotti a — che..., we are fallen so low that...; stare a —, to render obedience; far stare uno a —, to bring someone to book, to make him toe the line; sample; token; in — d'amicizia, as a token of friendship; trace, track, vestige; sulla sabbia c'erano i -i dei piedi nudi, there were the tracks of bare feet in the sand; i -i di Roma, the vestiges of (ancient) Rome; signal; standard; symbol; i santi -i (Tasso), the holy standard(s); scratch, scar; spot; gli lasciò un — in un braccio, he left a scar (bruise, mark) on one of his arms; (on a car) scratch; -i caratteristici, identification marks (on the body); (typ.) sign, imprint (of a typewriter's type); degree, measure; all'ultimo —, al massimo —, in the very highest degree; per filo e per —, in all details, in full; motion, nod, wave, gesture; fare un — di assentimento col capo, to nod assent; un — di mano, a wave of the hand; mark, sign, symbol; i -i dello zodiaco, the signs of the Zodiac; -i d'interpunzione, punctuation marks; (math.) sign; — di addizione, plus sign; — di eguaglianza, sign of equality; — meno, minus sign; — più, plus sign; — contrario, opposite sign; -i algebrici, algebraical symbols; (mus.) dal —, repeat from the sign; (med.) sign; symptom; (mil.) unit flag, distinguishing pennant; (naut.) a —, close up (said of a flag or sail or any hoist when it is as high as it will or should go); (comm.) mark; sign; — di grado di differenza, hallmark; (rel.) -i sacri, sacred signs; symbol; farsi il — della croce, to cross oneself; (of an illiterate person) fare il — della croce, to make a cross (in place of signature); fare un — di croce su una cosa, to say goodbye to a thing, to put it out of one's mind.

†**segnor-e** *m.*, †**-i·a** *f.* See **signor-e, -ia**.

sęg-o[1] *m.* (*pl.* **sęghi**) tallow; suet. **-oso** *adj.* tallowy, greasy; (cul.) rich.

†**sego**[2] *prn., prep.* See **seco**.

sęgolo *m.* pruning-hook.

segon-e *m. augm.* of **sega**, q.v.; two-handed saw. **-ato** *adj.* sawn with a 'segone'.

Sego·via *pr.n.f.* (geog.) Segovia; fine cloth of Segovia; (joc.) candele di —, tallow-candles (cf. **sego**[1]).

segreg-are [A 2 S] *tr.* to segregate; to isolate; to secrete; *rfl.* to withdraw, to retire in isolation. (**-amento** *m.*) **-ante** *part. adj.* celle **-anti**, cells for solitary confinement. **-ato** *part. adj.* isolated; solitary; vivere **-ato**, to live an isolated life; malato **-ato**, patient in an isolation ward or hospital. **-azione** *f.* segregation; seclusion; isolation; retirement; 'apartheid'; **-azione cellulare**, solitary confinement.

†**segrenna** *f.* thin, undersized person, weakling; gossiping woman.

segręta *f.* dungeon; (mus.) wind-chest (of organ); (liturg.) Secret (prayer between Offertory and Preface); (mil. hist.) inner protective headshield worn under the helmet and made of very thin steel.

†**segret-ale** *m.*, †**-ano** *m.* See **segretario**.

segret-a·rio *m.* secretary; confidential clerk; — particolare, private secretary; sotto —, undersecretary; — comunale, town clerk; — generale assistente, Assistant Secretary-General; — generale, Secretary-General; Vice — generale, Assistant Secretary-General; 'il — galante', title of various collections of model love-letters; il Segretario Fiorentino, i.e. Machiavelli who was Secretary of the 'Dieci di libertà e di pace'; (eccl.) (Cardinal) — di Stato, (Cardinal) Secretary of State; — consistoriale, Consistorial Secretary; (orn.) secretary bird, *Sagittarius serpentarius*. **-a·ria** *f.* woman secretary, female secretary. **-ariale** *adj.* secretarial. **-ariato** *m.* secretariat(e); secretaryship; **-ariato dei poveri**, public assistance bureau. **-ariesco** *adj.* (*m.pl.* **-arieschi**) (usu. derog.) clerk-like. **-eri·a** *f.* secretary's office; secretarial staff; writing desk; (university) Registry; (naut.) office (of Captain's or Admiral's secretary).

segręt-o *adj.* secret; hidden; private; tener —, to keep secret; fondi **-i**, secret-service money; onta **-a** di famiglia, family skeleton, skeleton in the cupboard; Consiglio —, Privy Council; *n.m.* secret; essere a parte del —, to be in the secret; il — di Pulcinella, an open secret; secret lock; secret drawer; secrecy, confidential nature; — professionale, professional discretion; violare il — di, to violate the secrecy of; (mus.) wind-chest (of organ); privacy; in —, in secret, secretly; sembrava sereno ma nel — soffriva, he seemed happy but secretly he was suffering. **-amẹnte** *adv.* secretly; in private; †on one side, apart. **-ẹzza** *f.* secrecy; con tutta **-ezza**, with great secrecy. **-ino** *m.* spring door-lock. **-ume** *m.* (derog.) furtive secrecy; a lot of unimportant secrets.

seguace *m.*, *f.* follower; adherent; disciple; supporter; (poet.) tributary; *adj.* (poet.) following; l'ombra — del corpo, the shadow accompanying the body; l'edera —, clinging ivy; pliant, yielding, flexible.

seguenza *f.* See under **seguire**.

†**seguestro** *m.* See **sequestro**.

segu·gio *m.* bloodhound; (police) sleuth.

seguidilla *f.* a Spanish dance, Seguidilla; (mus.) seguidilla.

segu-ire [D I] *tr.* to follow; to accompany; to imitate; to obey; — la corrente, to go with the stream; — le orme di uno, to follow in someone's footsteps; — la propria via, to go one's own way; — il consiglio di qualcuno, to take someone's advice; le cose devono — il loro corso, things must take their course; to keep; — con l'occhio, to keep an eye on; *abs.* to follow; to ensue; to happen; che **-iva** nei sotterranei del palazzo?, what was happening in the palace dungeons?; to result; to continue; **-e** al prossimo numero, to be continued in our next; **-e** a tergo, please turn over; come **-e**, as follows; ne **-e** che la colpa fu vostra, it follows that the fault was yours; casi che **-ono**!, it's the sort of thing that always happens! **-ente** *part. adj.* following, next; ensuing; succeeding; continuous; (mus.) basso **-ente**, continuo, thorough-bass. **-enza** *f.* (mus.) sequence (i.e. ascending or descending repetition of a figure); see **sequenza**. **-imento** *m.* following; sequel. **-ito** *part. adj.* accompanied, followed; continuous; (mil.) canna **-ita**, smooth-bored barrel; *n.m.* event, occurrence.

seguit-are [A I SC] *tr.* to continue; to follow up, to pursue; *intr.* (*aux.* avere; *prep.* a) to go on, to keep on, to continue; to persevere; to persist; **-iamo** lo stesso, let us continue notwithstanding; (iron.) **sèguita!**, go on!, don't mind me!; *impers.* (*aux.* essere) è **-ato** a piovere, it has continued to rain, it has gone on raining; to follow as a consequence; al delitto ha **-ato** il rimorso, after the crime remorse set in; da questo **-a** che tu hai ragione, from this it follows that you are right. **-ante** *part. adj.* continuing. **-ato** *part. adj.* followed; pursued; supported. **-atore** *m.* follower, imitator. (**-atrice** *f.*)

seguito[1] *part.* of **seguire**, q.v.

sęguito[2] *m.* suite, train, attendants, followers, retinue; set; documenti che fanno — alla tesi, documents which form part of, an appendix to, the thesis; sequence, series; un — di disgrazie, a series of misfortunes; andare in —, to run on (in series); run; (typ.) andare di —, to run on; sequel, continuation; consequence; manca il —, it ends here; non ebbe —, it went no further; la cosa ebbe un —, there was a sequel to that; il — al prossimo numero, 'to be continued in our next'; in —, afterwards, *or* consequently; in — a questo, on this, as a consequence of this, owing to this; di —, uninterruptedly, immediately afterwards; (comm.) non possiamo dar — alla vostra ordinazione, we cannot execute your order; facendo — al nostro colloquio, following our interview, with reference to our conversation; facendo — alla nostra lettera, further to our letter; (sport) cane da —, tracker dog; dare alla palla il —, to put a top-spin on the ball.

sei[1] *card. num.* six; ha — anni, he is six years old; alle — di mattina, at six o'clock in the morning; tiro a —, six-in-hand, coach and six; *n.m.*, *indecl.* the number six; il — del mese, the sixth of the month; un — facce, a cube; il — di quadri, the six of diamonds. **-centenne** *adj.* six hundred years old. **-cente·simo**, **-centęsimo** *ord. num.* six-hundredth. **-centismo** *m.* seventeenth-century style and mannerisms; Euphuism, Gongorism, etc. **-centista** *m.* seventeenth-century writer; specialist in seventeenth-century history, art, literature, etc. (**-centi·stico** *adj.*) **-cento** *card. num.* six hundred; *n.m. indecl.* il **-cento**, the seventeenth century; (med. pharm.) **-cento sei**, Salvarsan, arsphenamine. **-mila** *card. num.* six thousand.

sęi[2] *pres. indic.* 2nd pers. sing. of **essere**, q.v.

Seicelle *pr.n.f.pl.* (geog.) Seychelles.

seino *m. dim.* of **sei**[1], q.v.; (joc., at dice, etc.) double six.

seismo *m.* (geol.) seismism, movements of the earth's crust viewed collectively.

se·iu-ga *f.* (Rom. antiq.) six-horse chariot. **-ghi** *m.pl.* team of six horses drawing chariot.

se·lace *m.* (ichth.) — gigante, basking shark, *Cetorrhinus maximus*.

sela·cio *m.* (ichth.). See **selace**.

sęlc-e *f.* shingle; pebble; (miner.) flint. **-ia·io** *m.* pavior. **-iare** [A 3] *tr.* to pave. **-iata** *f.* pavement; flagstones. **-iato** *part. adj.* paved; *n.m.* pavement; paved street. **-iatore** *m.* paver, pavior. **-iatura** *f.* paving. **-ioso** *adj.* flinty.

Selene *pr.n.f.* (myth.) Selene.

seleniato *m.* See under **selenio**.

sele·nico *adj.* (chem.) selenic; (miner.) seleniferous.

sele-n·io *m.* (chem.) selenium; (electr.) cellula al —, selenium cell, photo-electric cell. **-iato** *m.* (chem.) selenate. **-ioso** *adj.* (chem.) selenious. **-ita** *m.*, *f.* 'Selenite', a supposed inhabitant of the moon. **-ite** *adj.* lunar; (miner.) selenite, gypsum. **-i·tico** *adj.* (miner.) selenitic. **-ito** *m.* (chem.) selenite. **-iuro** *m.* (chem.) selenide. **-ocen·trico** *adj.* (astron.) selenocentric. **-ografi·a** *f.* (astron.) selenography. **-ogra·fico** *adj.* selenographic(al). **-o·grafo** *m.* selenographer. **-otografi·a** *f.* topography of the moon.

selett-o *adj.* select; distinguished. **-ivo** *adj.* selective, having the faculty to select; characterized by choice or selection; (radio) selective. **-ivamẹnte** *adv.* selectively. **-ività** *f.* (radio) selectivity. **-ọre** *m.* selector; (radio; electr.; teleph.) selector; (eng.) selector, sorter; *adj.* selecting, selective. (**-rice** *f.*)

selezion-e *f.* selection; choice; (musical) selections; (industr.) grading; (radio) selection, selectivity; (motor.) gearshift, changing gear. **-amento** *m.* sorting. **-are** [A I C] *tr.* to select; to pick out; to sort, to grade. **-ato** *part. adj.* selected; graded; choice. **-atore** *m.* selector (e.g. a football selector); sorting machine; *adj.* selecting; selective. **-atrice** *f.* (techn.) grader, grading machine; *adj.* selecting; selective; giuria **-atrice**, selection committee.

selfinduzióne *f.* (electr.) self-induction.

selgiucido *adj.* (hist.) Seljukian, relating to Turkish dynasties (eleventh to thirteenth centuries).

sell-a *f.* saddle; cavallo da —, saddle-horse; levare la — a un cavallo, to unsaddle a horse; star bene in —, to sit well, have a good seat; votar la —, to be thrown, to fall from one's horse; rimanere in —, to keep one's seat, (fig.) to remain in control; — all'inglese, †— alla turchesca, English saddle, i.e. without saddle-bows; — alla buttera, — alla maremmana, saddle with saddle-bows; (of a horse) tra due -e, middle-sized, (of a person) of medium height, *or* middle-aged; (butcher.) — di agnello, saddle of lamb; (geog.) saddle; (meteor.) trough; (anat.) — turcica, pituitary fossa. **-a·io**, †**-aro** *m.* saddler. **-are** [A I] *tr.* to saddle. **-ato** *part. adj.* saddled; saddle-backed; (fig.) ready. **-atura** *f.* saddling; saddlery; (motor.) upholstery. **-eri·a** *f.* saddler's shop; harness-room; (motor.) upholstery works. **-ino** *m. dim.* small saddle of draught horse's harness; saddle (of bicycle or motorcycle).

sellaite *f.* (miner.) sellaite, native magnesium fluoride.

sel·lero *m.* (pop.). See **sedano**.

selmo *m.* (zool.) brittle star, *Ophiothrix fragilis*.

seltz *m. indecl.* acqua di —, soda-water. **-o·geno** *m.* soda-water maker.

sęlv-a *f.* wood; forest; (fig.) una — di vascelli, a forest of ships; una — di capelli, luxuriant hair; anthology, 'treasury'; versi a —, poem in various metres; rough draft, preliminary sketch, 'notes' for a literary composition. **-aggina** *f.* (sport; cul.) game. **-ag·gio** *adj.* wild; savage; uncivilized; primitive; untutored; wild, boisterous; extremely shy; surly; *n.m.* savage. (**-aggiamęnte** *adv.*) **-aggiume** *m.* game; wild animals, plants; wildness. †**-ano** *adj.* see **silvano**. **-astrella** *f.* (bot.) see **salvastrella**. **-aticac·cio** *adj. pejor.* uncouth. **-atichęllo**, **-atichętto** *adj. dim.* rather shy; somewhat uncouth. **-atichęzza** *f.* wildness; rudeness; lack of manners; rough untutored behaviour. **-a·tico** *adj.* wild; uncultivated; untamed; vivere -atico, to live in the wild, to run wild; rustic; rude; uncouth; lonely, uninhabited; essere -atico ad alcuna cosa, to be averse to, from, something; *n.m.* woodland, forest; smell of wild animals, smell of game. **-aticotto** *adj. dim.* rather rough and wild. **-aticume** *m.* wild things; wildness; roughness. **-ato** *adj.* wooded; afforested. **-ereccio**, †**-arec·cio** *adj.* relating to woodland. **-icoltóre**, **-icultóre** *m.*, **-icoltura**, **-icultura** *f.* see **silvicoltore**, etc. **-óso** *adj.* wooded, woody; (fig.) testa -osa, shaggy-head, bushy head of hair; (poet., joc.) mento -oso, hairy chin.

selz *m. indecl.* See **seltz**.

sema·f-oro *m.* instrument used for signalling, semaphore; semaphore or lookout station; (rlwy.) signal, semaphore; (road) traffic light(s). **-o·rico** *adj.* semaphoric; posto -orico, semaphore station, Lloyds Signal Station. **-oricamęnte** *adv.* by semaphore. **-orista** *m.* semaphorist; signaller.

sema·io *m.* See under **seme**.

sem-an·tica *f.* (ling.) semantics. **-an·tico** *adj.* (ling.) semantic. **-aşiologi·a** *f.* (ling.) semasiology. **-aşiolo·gico** *adj.* (ling.) semasiological. **-aşio·logo** *m.* semasiologist.

semata *f.* See under **seme**.

sema·tico *adj.* sematic; emblematic; relating to signs or symbols.

sembian-te *m.* semblance; appearance, aspect, mien; countenance; far — di, to pretend, to make a show of; far — di nulla, to feign indifference; in —, seemingly; nel primo —, at first sight; avere — di, to look like, to appear to be; ha — di vetro, it looks like glass; d'un —, alike, similar in appearance. **-za** *f.* look; appearance; aspect; features; di belle -ze, good-looking; sotto le -ze del vero, with an appearance of truth.

†**sembiare** *vb.* and derivs. See **sembrare**.

†**semble·a** *m.* meeting, encounter (cf. **assemblea**).

sembr-are [A I C] *intr.* (aux. essere) to seem, to appear; to appear to be; to look like; to resemble; to sound like; to taste like; to feel like; -a molto stanco, he seems to be very tired, he looks very tired; *impers.* -a che voglia piovere, it looks like rain; -ava piovesse, it looked like rain; -a che tutto vada bene, everything seems to be going well; mi -a che tu abbia sbagliato, I think you have made a mistake; che ti -a?, what do you think of it?; mi -a vergognoso agire in questo modo, I think it is a shame to act in this way; -a di no, it seems not, it doesn't seem so, it doesn't look like it. †**-anza** *f.* see **sembianza**, under **sembiante**.

sęm-e *m.* seed; — da bachi, silkworm eggs; -i duri, peas, beans, lentils, etc.; (of apple, pear, etc.) pip; (cards) suit; (biol.) semen; (bot.) — santo, — santonina, worm seed, *Artemisia cina*; (fig.) race, breed; del — di Adamo, of the seed of Adam; mal — bad breed; germ, origin; cause; source; il — della discordia, the seeds of dissension. **-a·io** *m.* dealer in silkworm eggs; seller of roasted gourd seeds; seedsman. **-ata** *f.* extract of melon or similar seeds for making a cooling drink; the drink made from these seeds; barley-water. **-ini** *m.pl. dim.* (cul.) seed-shaped 'pasta', used in soup.

semeio·tica *f.* (med.) semeiotics, semeiology.

se·mel *m. indecl.*, (Tusc. pop.) **semelle** *m.* (cul.) a soft roll made of fine flour.

Sę·mele *pr.n.f.* (myth.) Semele.

se·men *m. indecl.* (bot.; chem.) semen. **-contra** *f.* (bot.) wormseed, *Artemisia cina*.

semęnta *f.* sowing (esp. of corn); seed time.

semęnt-are [A I C] *tr.* to sow. **-a·bile** *adj.* (of seed) fit to be sown. **-ativo** *adj.* (of land) fit for sowing. **-ato** *part. adj.* sown; *n.m.* sown field. **-atóre** *m.* sower. (**-atrice** *f.*)

semęnt-e *f.* seed (for sowing); seed-corn. **-ina** *f.* (bot.) worm seed, *Artemisia cina*. **-ino** *adj.* for sowing; giornate -ine, good sowing days; *n.m.* small plough, used to prepare for sowing; pippin, fruit from a seedling. **-ire** [D 2] *intr.* (aux. essere) to run to seed, to go to seed. **-ivo** *adj.* (for) sowing.

semęnz-a *f.* seed; roasted pumpkin seeds; in —, run to seed; (fig.) origin; descent; race, progeny, offspring. **-a·io** *m.* (agric.) seed-bed; seed-store; seed-merchant. **-ina** *f.* see **sementina**, under **semente**.

semestr-e *m.* half-year, six months; semester; pago a -i, payment half-yearly; *adj.* half-yearly, belonging to the half-year. **-ale** *adj.* half-yearly. **-almęnte** *adv.* every six months.

semi- *pref.* half-, semi-, demi-. **-ala** *f.* (aeron.) wing, main plane. **-al·bero** *m.* (eng.) axle shaft. **-anello** *m.* (eng.) half-ring. **-an·golo** *m.* (geom.) half angle. **-asse** *m.* (eng.) axle shaft, drive shaft; (math.) semiaxis. **-biscroma** *f.* (mus.) hemidemisemiquaver. **-breve** *f.* (mus.) semibreve; *adj.* (gramm.) half-short (syllable). **-cadenza** *f.* (mus.) half close, imperfect cadence. †**-capro** *m.* satyr. †**-cavallo** *m.* centaur. **-cer·chio** *m.* (geom.) semicircle. **-chiuso** *adj.* (techn.) semi-enclosed. **-ciclo** *m.* (electr.) half-cycle. **-circolare** *adj.* semicircular; *n.m.* (anat.) semicircular canal. **-cir·colo** *m.* semicircle; protractor; (mus.) broken circle (indicating imperfect time in which the breve is divided into two semibreves). **-circonferenza** *f.* (geom.) semi-circumference. **-conduttore** *m.* (electr.) semi-conductor. **-corda** *f.* (geom.) semichord. **-cotto** *adj.* (text.) seta -cotta, half-boiled silk, souple. **-croma** *f.* (mus.) semiquaver. **-cu·pio** *m.* hip-bath. **-cuscinętto** *m.* (eng.) half-bearing. **-dia·metro** *m.* (geom.) semi-diameter. **-dia·pason** *m. indecl.* (mus.) diminished octave. **-diapente** *f.* (mus.) diminished fifth. **-diates·saron** *m. indecl.* (mus.) diminished fourth. **-di·o** *m.* (*pl.* **-dei**) demigod; (fig.) atteggiarsi a -dio, to pose as a demigod. **-di·polo** *m.* (radio; telev.) half dipole. **-di·tono** *m.* (mus.) diminished third. **-diurno** *adj.* almost daily. **-dóppio** *m.* (liturg.) semi-double; (bot.) semi-double. **-duro** *adj.* (miner.; metall.) semi-hard. **-finale** *adj.*, *n.f.* (sport) semifinal. **-finalista** *m.*, *f.* (sport) semifinalist. **-flo·sculo** *m.* (bot.) ray flower. **-fluido** *adj.* **-fręddo** *m.* ice-cream mixed with whipped cream and biscuits; (phys.) semifluid. **-fusa** *f.* (mus.) semiquaver. **-gǫla** *f.* (mil. hist.) half of a protecting bastion. **-go·tico** *adj.* resembling Gothic; (palaeogr.) scrittura -gotica, bastard (Gothic) script. **-gratuito** *adj.* half-price. **-lavorato** *adj.* (industr.) semi-manufactured, partly finished. **-li·quido** *adj.* (phys.) semiliquid. **-luna** *f.* half-moon; (zool.) -luna grigia, grey crescent. **-lunare** *adj.* semilunar, half-moon shaped; (anat.) osso -lunare, semilunar bone, lunate bone, os lunatum; valvole -lunari, semilunar valves. **-lu·nio** *m.* (astron.) time of half-moon. †**-metallo** *m.* semimetal, non-malleable metal. **-me·topa** *f.* (archit.) space of half a metope. **-mi·nima** *f.* (mus.) crotchet. **-morto** *adj.* half-dead; feeble; obsolescent. **-nfermità** *f.* (med.) partial infirmity, the state of being a semi-invalid, partial disablement; (leg.) -nfermità mentale, partial insanity; condition of diminished responsibility; non-exemptive insanity; (statutory) mental disorder. **-nterrato** *m.* (bldg.) basement, semi-basement. **-nudo** *adj.* half-naked. **-onciale** *adj.* (palaeogr.) semiuncial. **-ǫnda** *f.* (electron.) half-wave. **-opale** *m.* (miner.) semi-opal. **-permea·bile** *adj.* (phys.) semipermeable. **-pilastro** *m.* (archit.) pilaster protruding

semi- (*cont.*)

only slightly from a wall. **-protetto** *adj.* (techn.) semi-protected; semi-enclosed. **-ri·gido** *adj.* (techn.) semirigid, semiflexible. **-ri·mor·chio** *m.* (motor.) semitrailer. **-secolare** *adj.* recurring every half-century; fifty years old. **-sfera** *f.* hemisphere. **-sfe·rico** *adj.* hemispheric(al). **-sonne** *adj.* half-asleep. **-spinale** *adj.* (anat.) semispinalis. **-spinato** *m.* (anat.) semispinalis muscle. **-stonato** *adj.* (mus.) not quite in tune. **-tendinoso** *adj.* (anat.) muscolo -tendinoso, semitendinosus. **-tonare** [A I] *intr.* (*aux.* avere) (mus.) to move in semitones. **-tonato** *part. adj.* (mus.) chromatic. **-to·nico** *adj.* (mus.) semitonic. **-tono** *m.* (mus.) semitone; -tono cromatico, chromatic semitone; -tono diatonico, diatonic semitone; (photog.) carta a -tono, half-tone paper. **-trillo** *m.* (mus.) upper mordent; short trill. **-tuono** *m.* (mus.) see **semitono**. **-valenza** *f.* (chem.) semi-valency. **-vivo** *adj.* half-dead. **-vocale** *f.* semivowel. **-volata** *f.*, **-volo** *m.* (tennis, etc.) half-volley; (herald.) demi-vol, a wing.

semin-a *f.* seed; sowing; seed-time. **-ale** *adj.* seminal; relating to seed; (fig.) cause seminali, root causes, origins.

semin-are [A I sc] *tr.* to sow; — un campo a grano, to sow a field with corn; (fig.) to scatter, to spread; to disseminate; — zizzania, to sow discord. **-amento** *m.* sowing; scattering; disseminating. **-ata** *f.* seed sown; sowing. **-ativo** *adj.* fit for sowing; *n.m.* land fit for seed; *pl.* (geog.) arable lands. **-ato** *part. adj.* sown; strewn; (fig.) scattered, spread; disseminated; (herald.) semy, powdered; -ato di stelle, semy of mullets; *n.m.* sown field (land, ground); (fig.) uscire dal -ato, to digress, to wander from the subject, (fam.) to take leave of one's senses. **-atoio** *m.* seed-drill; (hand) seed-sower. **-atore** *m.* sower. **-atrice** *f.* woman sower; sowing machine, seeder, drill. **-atura** *f.* sowing. †**-azione** *f.* see **seminatura**.

semina·r-io *m.* (eccl.) seminary; university department which provides practical training; seminar; *adj.* (anat.) vasi -i, seminal vesicles. **-ista** *m.* (eccl.) seminarist; (fig., iron.) young innocent. **-i·stico** *adj.* of a seminary; educazione -istica, seminary education.

seminativi *m.pl.* (geog.). See under **seminare**.

seminella *f.* (mil.) powder train (used in lieu of a slow-match).

semin-i·fero *adj.* (anat.) seminiferous. **-i·o** *m.* germ; seeding, scattering, sowing; (fig.) un -io di denari, a squandering of money.

semino *m. dim.* See under **seme**.

semi-ografi·a *f.* abbreviation; conventional sign, shorthand (writing). (**-ogra·fico** *adj.* **-o·grafo** *m.*) **-ologi·a** *f.* treatise on symbols; (med.) semeiology. **-olo·gico** *adj.* (med.) semeiological. **-o·logo** *m.* (*pl.* **-o·loghi**) semeiologist.

semio·tic-a *f.*, **-o** *adj.* See **semeio·tic-a**, **-o**.

†**se·mita¹** *f.* path.

sem-ita² *m.*, *f.* (*m.pl.* **-iti**, *f.pl.* **-ite**) Semite. **-i·tico** *adj.* Semitic. **-itista** *m.*, *f.* Hebrew scholar; student of Semitic languages.

semol-a *f.* bran; (fig.) freckles. **-ata** *f.* bran-mash (for horses). **-atrice** *f.* (flourmilling) purifier. **-ino** *m.* semolina; coarse snuff; (agric.) middlings. **-oso** *adj.* full of bran; (fig.) covered with freckles, freckled.

†**semoto** *adj.* separate, separated.

semoven-te *adj.* (motor.; techn.) self-propelled; automatic; (leg.) beni -ti, self-moving property (i.e. animals); (mil.) cannone —, self-propelled gun. **-za** *f.* mobility; power to move.

†**sem·pice** *adj.* and derivs. See **semplice**.

Sempione *pr.n.m.* (geog.) the Simplon Pass (and Tunnel).

sempitern-o *adj.* everlasting, eternal, perpetual; *adv. phr.* in —, for ever. **-amente** *adv.* everlastingly, for ever and ever. **-are** [A I] *tr.* to make perpetual.

semplic-e *adj.* simple; ordinary; cittadino —, private citizen; soldato —, private soldier; ragioni -i, plain, straightforward reasons; plain; homely; unpretentious; unadorned; simple, unsophisticated; anima —, simple soul; unaffected, artless; inexperienced; — come una colomba, guileless as a dove; easy; natural; mere; sheer; stare alla — parola di, to rely on the mere word of; puro e —, pure and simple; per una combinazione pura e —, by mere chance; una — proposta, a tentative suggestion, merely a suggestion; easy, not difficult, simple; è —!, it's easy!, it's simple!; un problema —, an easy problem; single; occhiale —, eye-glass, monocle; consonante —, single consonant; (mus.) intervallo —, simple interval (i.e. less than an octave); (comm.) tenuta di libri in partita —, single-entry book-keeping; interesse —, simple interest; (leg.) furto —, simple larceny; plain theft; (canon law) benefizio —, simple benefice (without cure of souls); (phys.)

simple; (archit.) plain, without ornament; portico —, porch, portico with a single row of columns; (math.) frazione —, simple fraction; *adv. phr.* alla —, simply, clearly; *n.m.pl.* simples (herbs). **-emente** *adv.* simply; plainly; merely. **-ello** *adj. dim.* artless; simple-minded. **-ione** *m.* simpleton. **-ioneri·a** *f.* ingenuousness. **-iotto** *m.* simpleton (also *adj.*). **-ismo** *m.* over-simplification. **-ista** *m.* herbalist; one who oversimplifies. **-i·stico** *adj.* relating to oversimplification. **-ità** *f.* simplicity, plainness; naturalness; ease; unpretentiousness; artlessness; -ità di vita, simple living. **-izzare** [A I] and derivs. see **semplificare**.

semplific-are [A 2 s] *tr.* to simplify; to make simple. **-ato** *part. adj.* simplified. (**-atore** *m.* **-atrice** *f.* also *adjs.*) **-azione** *f.* simplification.

sempr-e *adv.* always; on all occasions; still; yet; per —, for ever, for good (and all); — che, provided that, whenever; — più, more and more; — meno, less and less; — avanti, keep on!; piove —, it is still raining; *or* piove — in Inghilterra, it is always raining, it always rains, in England; — meglio, still better; — più, still more; il suo stato è — grave, his condition is still serious. **-everde** *adj.*, *n.m.* evergreen. **-evivo** *m.*, **-eviva** *f.* (bot.) house leek, *Sempervivum tectorum*; (numism.) Milanese silver coin (sixteenth century).

Sempro·nio *pr.n.m.* Sempronius; (fig.) hypothetical person: Tizio, Caio e —, Smith, Brown and Robinson, *or* Tom, Dick and Harry.

†**sen** *prep.* See **senza**.

sena *f.* (bot.) senna, *Senna*; — falsa, bladder senna, *Colutea arborescens*; (dice, dominoes) double-six; (naut.) drift net.

se·nap-a, **-e** *f.* mustard; (bot.) — nera, black mustard, *Brassica nigra*; — bianca, white mustard, *Sinapis alba*; — selvatica, — de' campi, charlock, wild mustard, *S. arvensis*; (fig.) gli venne la — al naso, he grew angry. **-ato** *adj.* seasoned with mustard; carte -ate, mustard plasters. **-iera** *f.* mustard-pot. **-ina** *f.* (chem.) sinapine. **-ino** *m.* mustard (powder). **-ismo** *m.* mustard poultice, mustard plaster; (fig.) intolerable annoyance.

Sena·rio¹ *pr.n.m.* (geog.) Mount Senario (in Tuscany).

sena·rio² *m.* (prosod.) line of six syllables, Latin verse of six feet; also *adj.*

senarmontite *f.* (miner.) senarmontite.

senata *f.* (naut.) seine net.

senat-o *m.* (Rom. antiq.) Senate; (leg.) senate; Upper House of the Italian Parliament; (in U.S.A., universities) Senate; Senate house. **-oconsulto** *m.* (Rom. antiq.) *senatus consultum*; (pol.) views expressed in the Italian Senate. **-orato** *m.* senatorship. **-ore** *m.* senator; -ore a vita, senator elected for life; infornata di -ori, batch of senators, i.e. all those elected at one time. **-oressa** *f.* senator's wife. **-oriale** *adj.*, **-orio** *adj.* senatorial; relating to, characteristic of, a senator. **-rice** *f.* woman senator.

†**sendo** *ger.* See **essendo**, under **essere**.

sene (poet.) *adj.* aged, old; *n.m.* old man, elder.

Se·neca *pr.n.m.* Seneca.

senescen-te *adj.* senescent. **-za** *f.* senescence.

senes-e *adj.* Sienese; of Siena; (paint.) scuola —, School of Siena (esp. in the time of Duccio di Buoninsegna, thirteenth to fourteenth centuries); *n.m.* Sienese; Sienese dialect; the district round Siena; *f.* Sienese woman. **-ismo** *m.* Sienese idiom or form.

†**senett-a** *f.*, †**-ù** *f.*, †**-ute** *f.* old age.

sen-ile *adj.* senile; of old age; asilo —, old folks' home. **-ilmente** *adv.* in a senile way. **-ilità** *f.* senility.

seniore *adj.*, *n.m.* elder, senior; *pl.* (sport) seniors, senior class.

Senna¹ *pr.n.f.* (geog.) Seine.

senna² *f.* (bot.). See **sena**.

senn-o *m.* (good) sense, judgement; wisdom; far —, to become wise; in —, in one's senses; perdere il —, to lose one's wits; esser fuori di —, to be out of one's senses; da —, in earnest; fare a suo —, to do as one thinks best, to rely on one's own judgement; (provb.) del — di poi son piene le fosse, it is easy to be wise after the event; — naturale, mother-wit; il — antico, the wisdom of the ancients. **-eggiare** [A 3 c] *intr.* (*aux.* avere) to be wary. **-ino** *m.* good sense; clever child (or young person); -ino d'oro, affected person.

sennonchè *conj.* See under **se¹**.

seno *m.* bosom; breast; tenere al —, to hold to the breast, to suckle; in —, in one's arms; scaldare la serpe in —, to cherish a snake in one's bosom; lap; womb; (of a dress) bodice; (fig.) heart, centre; depth; in — a, among, in, within; nel — di una valle,

seno (*cont.*)

deep in a valley; in — alla propria famiglia, in the bosom of one's family; in — alla commissione, in committee, among the members of the committee; (comm.) in — a questa lettera, enclosed herewith; (math.) sine; (eng.) piano —, sine plates; (geog.) inlet, bay; cove; (anat.) sinus.

senof·obi·a *f.* xenophobia, hatred of foreigners. **-o·fobo** *m.* xenophobe.

Senofonte *pr.n.m.* Xenophon.

sens·ale *m.*, †**-a·io** *m.* (comm.) broker; middleman; — di effetti, di cambiali, bill broker; — di fondi pubblici e titoli di credito, stock- (and share-) broker; — marittimo, shipping agent; — di pesci, fish auctioneer (S. Italy); go-between; † — di sicurtà, insurance broker;† — di matrimonii, marriage-agent.

sensat·o *adj.* sensible; prudent, judicious; wise; (leg.) la persona -a, the reasonable man (C.C.); *n.m.* sense datum, data. **-amẹnte** *adv.* sensibly; prudently; judiciously; wisely; ora parli -amente, now you are talking sense. **-ẹzza** *f.* sound sense; judgement; prudence, discretion.

sensazion·e *f.* sensation; feeling; excitement, stir; dramma a —, sensational play. **-ale** *adj.* sensational; thrilling; exciting. **-alismo** *m.* sensationalism.

sens-eri·a, -ari·a *f.* brokerage; agency.

sensi·bil·e *adj.* sensitive; susceptible; — alle ingiurie, touchy; sentient; sensible, aware; tender-hearted; noticeable, appreciable; palpable; perceptible; (photog.) sensitized; (radio, etc.) sensitive; *n.f.* (mus.) leading note. **-mẹnte** *adv.* noticeably, perceptibly, appreciably; sensitively. **-ità** *f.* sensitiveness; feeling, sensibility; touchiness; delicacy; questo offende la sua -ità, this hurts his feelings; (scient.) sensitivity; (photog.) speed. **-izzare** [A I] *tr.* (photog.) to sensitize. **-izzatore** *m.* (photog.) sensitizer. **-izzazione** *f.* (photog.) sensitization.

sensile *adj.* (naut.) small, short, junior; (Naples) corda —, small rope; remo —, short-bladed oar used by a standing rower or in a galley; galea —, galley commanded by a junior captain.

†**sensione** *f.* feeling, sensation.

sens-ịsmo *m.* (philos.) sensationalism. **-ista** *m.* (philos.) sensationalist, sensist.

sensit-iva *f.* sensitiveness, sensibility; (bot.) sensitive plant, *Mimosa pudica*. **-ività** *f.* sensitivity, sensitiveness. **-ivo** *adj.* sensitive; sensory; of the senses; sensual; †*n.m.* clairvoyant, psychic person. (**-ivamẹnte** *adv.*) **-ogramma** *m.* (photog.) sensitogram. **-ometri·a** *f.* (photog.) sensitometry. **-ome·trico** *adj.* sensitometric. **-o·metro** *m.* (photog.) sensitometer, sensitivity meter.

sens-o *m.* (†*pl.f.* **sen·sora**) sense: i cinque -i, the five senses; perdere i -i, to lose consciousness; ricuperare i -i, to come to one's senses again; con tutti i -i, with full awareness; privo di -i, senseless, unconscious; buon —, common sense; — di responsabilità, sense of responsibility; che — c'è a parlare in questo modo?, what is the sense of talking like that?; sense, meaning, import; in un certo —, in a sense; in tutti i -i, in every sense; doppio —, double meaning; è un non —, it is nonsense; tradurre a —, to give the sense of, to translate freely; rispose in — affermativo, he answered in the affirmative; a — di, in accordance with; a — di legge, according to the law; sensation; feeling; sentiment; judgement; understanding; far —, to cause an unpleasant sensation, to create a disagreeable impression; mi fa —, it disgusts me, I find it repulsive; direction; way; in — giusto, in the right direction; nel — opposto, in the opposite direction; in ogni —, in every direction, (fig.) in every way; una strada a — unico, a one-way street; circolazione in — unico, one-way traffic; — vietato, no entry; — orario, clockwise direction; — antiorario, anti-clockwise direction. **-o·rio** *m.* organ of sense; **-orio comune**, nerve centre; *pl.* (anat.) sensory nerves; *adj.* sensory. **-uale** *adj.* sensual; sensuous; istinto -uale, sense instinct. **-ualmẹnte** *adv.* sensually; voluptuously; with the senses; sensitively. **-ualịsmo** *m.* hedonism; sensuality; (philos.) sensationalism. **-ualista** *m.* (philos.) sensationalist, sensist. **-uali·stico** *adj.* sensual; sensualistic. **-ualità** *f.* sensuality; voluptuousness; sensual act or words; (art) sensuousness.

†**sentac·chi·o** *m.* (of dogs, and other animals) a keen sense of smell, 'a good nose'. (†**-oso** *adj.*)

†**sent·are** *intr.*, *rfl.* to sit down. †**-ata** *f.* session.

sentenz·a *f.* opinion; judgement; aphorism; maxim; pronouncement; pithy saying; sputare, trinciare -e, to be sententious; (rel.)

la Gran Sentenza, the Last Judgement; (leg.) judgement; decision; order (of Court or judge); — arbitrale, arbitrator's award (C.C.P.); — di rinvio a giudizio, order of committal for trial; proscioglimento con — istruttoria, discharge by (order of) examining magistrate; — di proscioglimento pronunciato nel giudizio, dismissal of charge at trial; — di assoluzione, acquittal; — di condanna, conviction; — penale di condanna all'ergastolo, conviction and sentence to penal servitude for life (C.P.P.); *rarely* sentence: e.g. — di morte, death sentence; pronunciare —, to pronounce judgement; — della corte, decision of the Court; notificare la —, to record the judgement; ricorrere in appello contro la —, to appeal against the decision. **-iale** *adj.* of or relating to maxims; un libro -iale, a book of maxims. **-iare** [A4] *tr.* to judge; to criticize; (leg.) to pass judgement (on), to pronounce judgement (on); to record a sentence (on); *intr.* (*aux.* avere) to decide; to criticize; to pronounce an opinion, to talk sententiously; (leg.) to decide; to give a decision; to give judgement; to make an order. **-iato** *part. adj.* judged; decided; condemned. (**-iatore** *m.* **-iatrice** *f.*) **-ieggiare** [A3c] *intr.* (*aux.* avere) to talk sententiously. **-iọna, -ọna** *f. augm.* long-winded judgement. **-iọso** *adj.* sententious; aphoristic; epigrammatic; critical. **-iosamẹnte** *adv.* learnedly; judiciously; sententiously. **-iuola** *f. dim.* pithy saying; maxim, epigram.

sentier·o, †**-e** *m.* footpath, pathway; track; way; (fig.) allontanarsi dal retto —, to go astray.

sentiment·o *m.* (†*pl.f.* **-a**) feeling, sentiment; sense; opinion; meaning; esprimere i propri -i, to express one's feelings; il — generale, the general feeling; animato da buoni -i, inspired by noble sentiments; avere il — della propria responsabilità, to have a sense of responsibility; — artistico, artistic sense; — di sè stesso, proper pride, sense of one's own worth; perdere i -i, to lose one's senses, to lose consciousness; — fondamentale, sixth sense; good sense; judgement; intelligence; uomo di molto —, very sensible man; cavallo di —, intelligent horse; †meaning, significance. **-ale** *adj.* sentimental; mawkish; lettera -ale, loveletter; *n.m.,f.* sentimentalist. **-almẹnte** *adv.* sentimentally. **-alịsmo** *m.* sentimentalism; sentimentality. **-alità** *f.* sentimentality; mawkishness. **-alọne** *m. augm.* a great sentimentalist, a very mawkish person. (**-ọna** *f.*)

sentina *f.* (naut.) sump well; bilge; (fig.) sink (e.g. of iniquity).

sentinella *f.* sentry; sentinel; guard; watch; posto di —, sentry box; (fig.) fare la —, to stand and wait a long time for somebody; (naut.) — sottomarina, echo-sounder, underwater apparatus which emits signal warning ships that they are in shallow water.

sent·ire [D I] *tr.* to feel; to hear; to listen to; to learn; to be conscious of; to smell; to scent; to taste; — freddo, to feel (the) cold; — dolore, to feel pain; — fame, to be hungry; — riconoscenza, to feel gratitude; non — nulla, to feel nothing; non ci -e, he doesn't hear, he is deaf; — un concerto, to listen to a concert; (pop.) — la Messa, to attend Mass; farsi —, to make oneself heard, to make people listen; stammi a —, listen to me; lo -ii parlare, I heard him speak(ing); non ho mai -ito parlare di ciò, I have never heard of it; ho -ito dire che..., I have heard that...; vuol — questo vino?, will you taste this wine?; -immo odore di gas, we smelt gas; (as amplification of passive) si sentì dire che..., he was told that...; (naut.) to answer; la nave -e il timone, the ship answers (obeys); *abs.* to listen; *intr.* (*aux.* avere) to taste of, to smack of; to smell of, to be redolent of; questo vino -e di tappo, this wine is corked; — di muffa, to smell musty; (fig.) -e di malandrino, he seems to be a ruffian; -e troppo di sè, he thinks too much of himself; *rfl.* to feel; -irsi male, to feel ill; -irsi disposto (a), to feel inclined (to); mi -o di farlo, I feel like doing it; non mi -o di fare il lavoro, I do not feel up to the work; non -irsela, not to feel fit; -irsi innocente, to know that one is innocent; *n.m.* feeling; uomo di alto —, man of noble sentiments; impression (of something heard); non fa un bel —, it makes a bad impression. **-ito** *part. adj.* heard; -ito e risentito, heard again and again; il -ito dire, hearsay; per -ito dire, by hearsay; felt; cordial, sincere, deep; warm; strong. **-itamẹnte** *adv.* cordially, heartily; sincerely; deeply, warmly; (comm.) Vi ringraziamo -itamente della Vostra lettera, we thank you for your letter. **-ọre** *m.* sense, feeling, inkling; sign; rumour; aver -ore di un complotto, to get wind of a plot; (poet.) scent, odour.

Senuss-i·a *pr.n.f.* Senussi (Islamic confraternity); Senussiism. **-ita** *m.* Senussite. **-o** *m.* Grand Senussi.

senza[1] *prep.* without; (before a *disjunct. pers. prn.* foll. by 'di'); — di me, without me; — di te, without you, etc.; — esitazione, without hesitation; senz'altro, without fail, infallibly, certainly; senz'altro!, of course!, rather!; — fine, endless; — testa, thoughtless(ly); — tregua, incessant(ly); farne —, to go without, to do without (it); — forse, certainly, doubtless; — numero, innumerable, countless; — meno, without fail; — complimenti, make yourself at home, do whatever you like, don't stand on ceremony (also used ironically when someone has committed a 'gaffe'); — tanti complimenti, speaking frankly; (sport, rowing) quattro —, cox-less four. SYNTACTICAL CONSTRUCTIONS: — che egli ci veda, without his seeing us; — essere visti, without being seen; *n.m.* (bridge) un —, due —, tre —, one No Trumps, two No Trumps, three No Trumps; (comm.) — fondi, no funds; — conti, no account; cambiale — girata, original bill; — ricorso, *sans recours*, without recourse; — riserva, ex all; — cupone, ex coupon; — dividendo, ex dividend; — diritto all'estrazione, ex drawing; — interesse, ex interest; — diritto alle azioni nuove, ex new; — diritto, ex rights; — pregiudizio, without prejudice.

senza[2] *pref.* lacking; equiv. to Eng. suffix -less. **-brache** *pr.n.m.* 'sans culottes'. **-pa·tria** *m. indecl.* stateless person; displaced person. **-tetto** *m. indecl.* homeless person, one without a roof to his head; (leg.) legge per i -tetto, law to aid those left homeless (e.g. by war).

senziente *adj.* sentient.

sepa *f.* (zool.) *Seps chalcides*, a lizard with reduced legs, resembling a slow-worm.

se·palo *m.* (bot.) sepal.

separ-are [A I S] *tr.* to separate, to sever; to part, to divide; to disjoin, to disunite; *rfl.* to become separated; to be severed; to separate, to part; to part company. **a·bile** *adj.* separable. (**-abilità** *f.*) **-amento** *m.* separating. †**-anza** *f.* see **separazione**. **-atezza** *f.* separateness. **-atismo** *m.* (pol.) separatism. **-atista** *m.* (pol.) separatist. **-ativo** *adj.* separative; (gramm.) disjunctive. **-ato** *part. adj.* separated; severed; divided; parted; separate; distinct; conto -ato, separate account; vivere -ati, to live apart; coniugi -ati, husband and wife legally separated. **-atamente** *adv.* separately; apart. **-atore** *m.* (techn.) separator; trap; -atore di polvere, dust trap. **-azione** *f.* separation; parting; severance; disjunction; linea di -azione, line of demarcation; (chem.) analysis; (med.) secretion; (leg.) -azione giudiziale dei beni, judicial separation of property; -azione giudiziale personale, judicial separation of husband and wife, divorce *a mensa et thoro*; -azione consensuale, (legal) separation by mutual consent (C.C.); -azione legale, legal separation.

separasab·bia *m. indecl.* (paperm.) button-trap, sand-catcher, sand table.

séparé *m. indecl.* (pron. as Fr.) private room in a restaurant.

†**se·pari** *adj.* See **dispari**.

sepe *f.* (zool.). See **sepa**.

sepiment-o *m.* (biol.) septum. **-ato** *adj.* (biol.) septate.

sepiol-a *f.* (zool.) see **seppiola**. **-ite** *f.* (miner.) sepiolite, meerschaum.

sepolcr-o *m.* sepulchre; grave; il Santo —, the Holy Sepulchre; — di famiglia, family vault; (eccl.) canonici del —, Canons of the (Holy) Sepulchre; (liturg.) 'sepulchre', altar of repose; visitare, fare, i -i, to visit such an altar in several churches (on Maundy Thursday or Good Friday); -i imbiancati, whited sepulchres; (leg.) grave (esp. underground); burial-place (distinguished from 'tomba', tomb, which is used esp. of burial-place above ground); violazione di tomba o di —, violation of tomb or grave (C.P.). **-ale** *adj.* sepulchral; monumenti -ali, tombs; pietra, lapide -ale, gravestone, tombstone. **-eto** *m.* cemetery; (ancient) burial-ground.

sepolt-o *part.* of **seppellire**, q.v.; *adj.* buried; (fig.) — nel sonno, in a deep sleep; hidden away; *n.f.pl.* le -e vive, strictly enclosed nuns. **-ura** *f.* funeral, burial, interment; burial-place; entrare in -ura, to die; (eccl.) privare della -ura, to refuse (church) burial to, to deprive of (Christian) burial; (leg.) luogo di -ura, burial-ground (C.P.).

sepparola *f.* dummy cuttlefish, used as a decoy in fishing for cuttlefish.

seppell-ire [D 2] *tr.* to bury, to inter; to cover with earth; (fig.) to cover (up), to hide; to consign to oblivion; *rfl.* (fig.) to bury oneself, to hide. **-imento** *m.* burial; -imento in mare, burial at sea. **-ito** *part. adj.* see **sepolto**. **-itore** *m.* grave-digger, sexton.

seppi·a *f.* (zool.) cuttlefish, *Sepia officinalis*; (paint.) nero di —, sepia; (photog.) copia —, sepia print. **-are** [A 4 c] *tr.* (techn.) to pounce, to polish with cuttle-bone.

seppietta *f.* (zool.). See **seppiola**.

seppiola *f.* (zool.) *Sepiola rondeleti*, a small edible cuttlefish; — grossa, *Rossia macrosoma*, a small edible cuttlefish, inferior as food to the true 'Seppiola', *S. rondeleti*.

seppure *conj.* even though, even if; — viene lui, non lo voglio vedere, even if he does come, I won't see him; — ci hai colpa ti perdono, even if you are to blame I forgive you.

sep-si *f.* (med.) sepsis. **-sina** *f.* (chem.) sepsine. **-ticemi·a** *f.* (med.) septicaemia.

sequaro *m.* (naut.) belay, turn up, turns for lowering; alare a —, to hoist hand over hand (with the end taken in and held in a cleat, etc.); ammainare a —, to veer or walk back from a stagshorn as in lowering a boat.

sequela *f.* succession, sequence; una lunga — di disgrazie, a long series of misfortunes.

sequenz-a *f.* (liturg.) sequence; †far —, to cross oneself at the beginning of the Gospel; (fig.) succession, sequence; (mus.) sequence (plain-chant jubilus issuing from the Gradual to which metrical words have been added); (poker) —, 'straight'; (cinem.; telev.) sequence. **-iale** *m.* (liturg.) sequencer.

sequestr-o *m.* (leg.) attachment; distraint; distress; seizure; sequestration; stoppage; ordinare il —, to issue a distringas notice, to make a sequestration order; levare il —, to lift a distress; — conservativo, protective sequestration, receivership; — giudiziario, judicial attachment; disporre il — giudiziario, to order appointment of receiver; sotto —, in the hands of a receiver, under sequestration; — convenzionale, deposit of property with stakeholder or trustee, by agreement, voluntary sequestration; — della merce, attachment, sequestration of goods; mandato di —, seizure notes; embargo; kidnapping; — di persona, false imprisonment (C.P.); seizure of person; (surg.) sequestrum, necrosed bone fragment. **-a·bile** *adj.* liable to distraint; seizable. (**-abilità** *f.*) **-amento** *m.* distraining; seizing; attaching; sequestration. **-are** [A I] *tr.* (leg.) to distrain; to attach; to seize; to sequestrate; to take into judicial possession; — il corpo del reato, to take charge of the *corpus delicti* (C.P.); to isolate; to confiscate. **-ata·rio** *m.* bailiff; custodian; sequestrator; receiver appointed by Court; -atario convenzionale, bailee, custodian, stakeholder, trustee (C.C.). **-ato** *part. adj.* seized; secluded; isolated. (**-atore** *m.* **-atrice** *f.*) **-azione** *f.* sequestration; (med.) isolation of cases; formation of dead bone. **-otomi·a** *f.* (surg.) sequestrotomy.

sequo·ia *f.* (bot.) Wellingtonia, big tree, *Sequoia gigantea*.

sera *f.* evening; night; buona —!, good evening!; abito da —, evening dress; a, di —, in the evening; studiare la —, to study in the evenings; la — vado a spasso, in the evenings I go for a walk; sul far della —, at nightfall; mattina e —, always, from morning till night, continuously; (poet.) l'ultima —, death; (provb.) ogni dì vien —, the longest day comes to an end (cf. **serata**).

seracco *m.* (geog.) sérac, ice-block.

sera·fico *adj.* (theol.) seraphic; il padre —, the Seraphic Father, St Francis of Assisi; il dottore —, the Seraphic Doctor, St Bonaventure; l'ordine —, the Franciscans.

serafino *m.* (theol.) seraph; il — d'Assisi, St Francis of Assisi.

†**serafo** *m.* See **serafino**.

seral-e *adj.* evening; studio —, preparation; scuola —, evening school, night school, evening institute, Institute of Further Education. **-mente** *adv.* in the evening; every evening.

serape·o *m.* (Egyptol.) Sarapeum, Serapeum.

serat-a *f.* evening; le lunghe -e invernali, the long winter evenings; evening-party; (theatr.) evening performance; — d'onore, benefit night; — di gala, gala performance; — d'addio, last performance (of a run). **-ac·cia** *f. pejor.* rough, nasty (rainy, windy) night; very unpleasant evening. **-ante** *adj., n.m., f.* (theatr.) beneficiary of a benefit night. **-ona** *f. augm.* (theatr.) very good (successful, profitable) night, 'good house'.

serb-are [A I] *tr.* to keep; to put aside, to reserve; to save up; to preserve; — fede, to keep faith; — un segreto, to keep a secret; — un posto a qualcuno, to keep a place for someone; — rancore, to bear a grudge; — un dolce ricordo, to cherish a fond memory; *rfl.* to be saved up, to be reserved; to hold oneself ready; -arsi in buona salute, to keep well; to remain; -arsi fedele, to remain faithful. (**-ato** *part. adj.*) **-atoio** *m.* reservoir; store; tank; -atoio

serb·are (*cont.*)
a sbarramento, reservoir formed by a dam; -atoio della benzina, petrol tank; magazine (of rifle, etc.); barrel (of fountain-pen); (naut.) air-bottle (torpedo). (-**atore** *m.* -**atrice** *f.*)

Ser·bia *pr.n.f.* (geog.) Serbia, Servia (now part of Yugoslavia).

serbo[1] *m.* keeping; custody; reserve; mettere in —, to put by; tenere in —, to keep in store, to hold in reserve.

serb-o[2] *adj.* Serbian; *n.m.* Serb, Serbian. (-**a** *f.*)

serdaro *m.* (Turkish, Egyptian hist.) sirdar (military chief).

serenella *f.* (bot.) lilac, *Syringa vulgaris.*

seren-o *adj.* serene, cloudless, clear; un fulmine a ciel —, a bolt from the blue; bright; calm, tranquil, dispassionate; equable, good-tempered; pietra -a, bluish sandstone (used for building); (med.) gotta -a, amaurosis; *n.m.* clear sky; starlit sky; dormire al —, to sleep in the open. -**amente** *adv.* serenely; tranquilly; calmly. -**are** [A I c] *tr.* (poet.) to calm, to tranquillize; *intr.* (*aux.* avere) (mil., etc.) to bivouac, to camp out; *rfl.* (of weather) to clear up, to become fine; (fig.) to grow calm. -**ata** *f.* (mus.) serenade, serenata, alfresco concert; cantare, fare, portare una -ata a, to serenade; (joc.) mock serenade, whistling, cat-calls, etc. (-**ato** *part. adj.* -**atore** *m.* -**atrice** *f.*) -**is·simo** *adj., n.m.* (hist.) Serene Highness (title given to ruling princes and to Doges). -**is·sima** *f.* La Serenissima, the Venetian Republic; (fig.) Venice. -**ità** *f.* serenity; cloudlessness; equability; calm, peace, tranquillity.

sergent-e *m.* (mil.) sergeant; (mil. hist.) — di battaglia, battalion commander (sixteenth century); infantry general (seventeenth century); inspector and commander-in-chief; — maggiore di battaglia, assistant chief of staff (seventeenth century); †(naut.) captain of a gun; quartermaster (in the Italian Navy, also a rank in the ancillary branches, engineers, wireless operators, etc.); sergeant of the guard; agent, representative, factor; policeman; (carpen.) cramp. †-**ina** *f.* (mil.) lance or pike carried by sergeants and officers.

†**sergozzone** *m.* See **sorgozzone**.

seriazione *f.* (math.) seriation.

se·ri·co *adj.* (of) silk; silky; silken; (ent.) verme —, silkworm. -**ce·o** *adj.* (poet.) silky. -**ci·geno** *adj.* baco -cigeno, silkworm; glandula -cigena, silk-gland; (text.) porro -cigino, spinning-nipple. -**cina** *f.* (text.) sericin(e), silk gum. -**ciparo** *adj.* (of an insect) silk-spinning. -**colite** *f.* (min.) sericite. -**colo** *adj.* silk-producing, sericultural. -**coltore**, -**cultore** *m.* silk-producer. -**coltura**, -**cultura** *f.* sericulture, silk culture. -**gra·fico** *adj.* (typ.) pertaining to silkscreen printing.

se·rie *f. indecl.* series, succession; range; set; una — di conferenze, a course of lectures; (comm.) set; cambiale in —, set of bills; (electr.) in —, in series parallel; condensatore in —, series capacitor; (math.; chem.) series; (industr.) produzione in —, mass production; modello di —, current model; una (macchina) fuori —, a special model (car); (soccer, etc.) division; (tennis, etc.) testa di —, seed; (mus.) la — armonica, the harmonic series; per —, scalewise.

seri·fero *adj.* silk-producing.

seri·m·etro *m.* (text.) serimeter. -**e·trico** *adj.* (text.) serimetric; misurazione -etrica, serimeter test.

se·ri·o *adj.* serious, earnest, steady; grave; thoughtful; stern; important; weighty; trustworthy; reliable; virtuous; una ragazza -a, a virtuous girl; responsible; genuine, bona fide; sul —, in earnest, seriously; dici sul —?, do you mean it?, are you serious (in earnest)?; sì, sul —, yes, really; prendere sul —, to take seriously, to consider important; (mus.) opera -a, grand opera, tragic opera, heroic opera. -**amente** *adv.* seriously; earnestly; gravely; sternly; occupato -amente, engaged in important business. -**età** *f.* seriousness; gravity; trustworthiness; con -età, seriously, gravely; mettersi in -età, to become serious, to put joking aside; (comm.) integrity, good standing. -**ume** *m.* gravity, seriousness.

serio-co·mico *adj.* serio-comic. -**giocoso** *adj.* at once grave and gay.

seriola *f.* (ichth.) *Seriola dumerilii*, 'yellow tail', a prime edible fish of the Mediterranean.

†**serios-o** *adj.* difficult; weighty, important. (-**amente** *adv.*) (Cf. serio.)

serìr *m. indecl.* (geog.) stony desert.

serizzo *m.* (miner.) gneiss.

serment-o *m.*, -**oso** *adj.* See **sarment-o**, -**oso**.

†**sermocinare** *intr.* to speak solemnly, to moralize, to 'preach'.

sermollino *m.* (bot.) garden thyme, *Thymus vulgaris*; — selvatico, — cedrato, wild thyme, *T. serpyllum.*

sermon-e[1] *m.* speech; discourse; talk; (rel.) sermon; il — sulla Montagna, the Sermon on the Mount; (fig.) admonition, reproof, lecture (scolding); (poet.) light satire in verse; i -i di Orazio, Horace's Satires; †language, †idiom. -**are** [A I c] *intr.* (*aux.* avere) to moralize; to lecture, to preach. -**a·rio** *m.* (eccl.) collection of (specimen) sermons. -**atore** *m.* preacher; poeta -atore, didactic poet. (-**atrice** *f.*) -**cino** *m. dim.* short sermon; rebuke; piece of prose or poetry recited by a child at the Crib (presepio). -**eggiare** [A 3 c] *intr.* (*aux.* avere) to sermonize, to preach.

†**sermone**[2] *m.* See **salmone**.

sermontana *f.* (bot.) *Laserpitium siler.*

†**seroc·chia** *f.* See **sirocchia**.

serofagi·a *f.* (rel.) xerophagy, strict abstinence (in Eastern Churches).

serolone *m.* (ichth.) See **seghettone**.

sero·tin-o, †-**e** *adj.* (agric.) ripening late; tardy; serotinous; (fig.) late in the day.

serpa *f.* box(-seat) of a coach; (naut.) see **serpe**.

serpante *m.* (naut.) heads sweeper; bathroom cleaner.

serp-e *m.* (zool.) snake; or **serpente**; (fig.) allevare la — in seno, to cherish a serpent in one's bosom; (provb.) le cose lunghe diventano -i, delays are dangerous; a —, winding; (mus.) wing (of bassoon); (naut. hist.) finials round the bows, decoration; the eyes of a ship, foremost part of deck; heads (Venice). -**a·io** *m.* snake-pit; brood of snakes; place infested by snakes; neglected farm. -**aro** *m.* snake-charmer. -**ato** *adj.* snake-coloured.

serpegg·iare [A 3 c] *intr.* (*aux.* avere) to wind; to meander; to creep; (of an epidemic, etc.) to spread; il malcontento -iava fra la popolazione, discontent was spreading among the people; (of the lips) to curl; *tr.* (mil.) to zig-zag (as in building defences, trenches, etc.); (naut.) to steer a bad course, to weave; *tr.* (naut.) — due corde, to snake down two ropes. -**iamento** *m.* winding; meandering; (rlwy.) shunting. -**iante** *part. adj.* winding, meandering; tortuous; sinuous; spreading unnoticed; (herald.) entwined around. -**iato** *part. adj.* crossed sinuously, with windings; snake-coloured. -**ìo** *m.* constant winding.

serpellino *m.* See **scerpellino**.

serpent-e[1] *m.* (zool.) snake, serpent; — a sonagli, rattlesnake, *Crotalus* spp.; (naut.) — di mare, sea serpent; (fig.) sensational scoop, *or* improbable news item; l'antico —, the old serpent, Eve's tempter; malicious and deceitful person; — tra l'erba, snake in the grass; (astron.) Serpens; Hydra; (mus.) serpent. †-**are** *tr.* to molest, to annoy by importunity. -**a·ria** *f.* (bot.) *Dracunculus vulgaris.* -**a·rio** *m.* (astron.) Serpentarius, Ophiuchus; (orn.) secretary bird, *Sagittarius serpentarius.* -**ato** *adj.* snake-infested. -**ello** *m. dim.* little snake, young snake, (of child) imp, little devil; malicious person; (naut.) worming, small rope wound round a larger following the lay. -**i·fero** *adj.* producing snakes, inhabited by snakes, snake-infested; (herald.) croce -ifera, cross gringolee. -**iforme** *adj.* snake-like; in the form of a serpent. -**ile** *adj.* serpentine, snaky. -**ina** *f.* (mil. hist.) serpentine, a small gun like a culverin; (geol.) serpentine; (bot.) bistort, *Polygonum bistorta*; winding road, with hairpin bends; coil (pipe), worm pipe; (surg.) tourniquet; *pl.* (vet.) broken knees. -**ino** *adj.* serpentine, snaky; tortuous; sinuous; danza -ina, snake-dance; (vet.) lingua -ina, tongue lolling out of an animal's mouth, (fig.) venomous tongue; (bot.) *Oxalis corniculata*; (geol.) serpentine; *n.m.* (industr.) coil, pipe coil; (mil. hist.) port-fire used for carrying a lighted fuse. -**inoso** *adj.* (miner.) serpentinous. -**one** *m. augm.* large serpent; (mus.) serpent. -**oso** *adj.* infested by snakes; (fig.) snaky. †-**ire** *tr.* to wind round.

†**serpente**[2] *part.* of **serpere**, q.v.

†**ser·pere** *intr.* See **serpeggiare**.

serpi·gin-e *f.* (med.) ringworm, serpigo. -**oso** *adj.* (med.) serpiginous.

serpillo *m.* (bot.) wild thyme, *Thymus serpyllum* agg.

serpolina *f.* (zool.) *Seps chalcides*, a lizard with reduced legs, similar to a slow-worm.

serpone *m. augm.* of **serpe**, q.v.; (fig.) il vecchio —, the old serpent (i.e. the devil).

serqu-a *f.* dozen (of eggs, apples, nuts, etc.); a lot, lots. -**ettina** *f. dim.* nice little lot.

serr-a[1] *f.* dyke, embankment; narrow gorge; enclosed place; waistband, belt; crowd, crush, press; greenhouse, glasshouse; conservatory; — calda, hothouse; fiore di —, hothouse plant (also fig.); — per viti, vinery; — per palme, palm house. -**adella** *f.* (bot.) serradella, *Ornithopus sativus.*

serra² *f.* chain of mountains.

†**serra³** *f.* See **sega**.

serra·gli·o *m.* enclosure; cage for wild beasts; menagerie; harem, seraglio; (archit.) keystone. **-ere** *n.m.* zoo-keeper, lion-tamer.

serrama·nico *m.* See under **serrare**.

serrame *m.* lock; fastening; †chest, coffer.

serrano *m.* (ichth.) *Serranus gigas, Serranellus cabrilla*, and other sea perch.

serr-are [A I] *tr.* to lock; to lock up; to shut, to close, to close up; to squeeze; to clench; — un dado, to tighten a nut; to hold tightly; to bind, to harden (of, e.g., ice, snow, etc.); to conclude; il giorno che -a la vita, the last day of one's life; — un patto, to conclude an agreement; to hide, to keep in; — un dolore nel cuore, to hide one's grief in one's heart; — la stalla quando sono fuggiti i buoi, to lock the stable-door when the horse has bolted; (mil.) — le fila, to close the ranks; (naut.) — la voga, to quicken the stroke; †— il vento, see under **stringere**; — il letto del fiume, to dam the river; *intr.* (*aux.* avere) to fit tight; to close properly (of window, door, etc.); queste maniche -ano troppo nel gomito, these sleeves are too tight at the elbow; un -a -a, a crush, crowd, press, *or* headlong flight, pushing and shoving; *rfl.* (*prep.* a) to stand close (to); -arsi al muro, to put one's back to the wall; -arsi addosso a, to close with (in attack). **-abozze** *f.pl.* (naut.) anchor stoppers. **-acarte** *m. indecl.* filing-cabinet. **-afila** *f.* (naut.) tail of the line. **-afilo** *m.* (radio; electr.) terminal; connector. **-afune** *m. indecl.* cable clip. **-ag·gio** *m.* (eng.) gripping, nipping, clamping. **-ama·nico** *m.* spring-knife, jack-knife, clasp-knife. **-amento** *m.* locking; lock; (bldg.) window frame, door frame; (med.) stypsis; (radio) jamming. **-anda** *f.* furnace (or oven) door; (bldg.) rolling gate, rolling shutter. **-apennoni** *m.pl.* (naut.) brails. **-apezzi** *m. indecl.* (eng.) chuck. **-aporta** *m. indecl.* door-spring (for automatic closing). **-ata** *f.* fence; enclosure; dam; (hist.) -ata del Maggior Consiglio, a restrictive law affecting the constitution of the Venetian Republic (1297); (industr.) lock-out. **-atina** *f.* (naut.) gust of northerly or north-westerly wind. **-ato** *part. adj.* close, compact; concise; succinct; serried; shuttered; locked-up; ice-bound; fiumi -ati di ghiaccio, rivers frozen over; tempo -ato, threatening weather; trotto -ato, rapid trot; (of workman) locked-out; (eng.) tight (e.g. of bolt). **-atamente** *adv.* closely; concisely. (**-atore** *m.* **-atrice** *f.*) **-atura** *f.* lock; door-lock; buco della -atura, keyhole; -atura di sicurezza, safety lock; -atura a doppia mandata, double lock; -atura a colpo, a scatto, a sdrucciolo, spring-lock; fastening, clasp; (archit.) keystone.

serra·tola *f.* (bot.) saw-wort, *Serratula tivedoria*.

serretta *f.* (bot.). See **serratola**.

serrettame *m.* (naut.) bottom boards, inner frames, longitudinals, stringers, the whole complex of inner frames.

Serse *pr.n.m.* Xerxes (Ahasuerus).

serto *m.* garland, wreath; — dei Cesari, imperial crown; (fig.) — nuziale, wedding garland (i.e. collection of poems written in celebration of a wedding); (astron.) igneo —, ring of Saturn.

ser·tula *f.* (bot.) — campana, melilot, *Melilotus*.

serv-a *f.* domestic servant (derog.); romanzo da —, cheap sensational novel, 'penny dreadful'; — di Pilato, ugly woman; essere il figlio della —, to be neglected; **-ag·gio** *m.* servitude, slavery; bondage; serfdom. **-ai(u)olo** *m.* seducer of (maid-)servants. **-etta** *f. dim.* young servant; (theatr. hist.) soubrette.

†**servare** *vb.* and derivs. See **serbare**.

servent-e *m.,* **-ese** *f.* See under **servire**.

†**servi·gio** *m.* favour, kindness, service; business (cf. **servizio**).

servil-e *adj.* servile; slavish; menial; (hist.) guerra —, servile war (esp. that of Spartacus, 73–71 B.C.); (gramm.) verbi -i, auxiliary verbs of mood; (theol.) timore —, servile fear. **-mente** *adv.* servilely; slavishly; menially. **-ità** *f.* servility; servile action or behaviour.

serv-ire [D I] *tr.* to serve; to assist; to wait on; to attend to; to serve up; to be of use to, for; il pranzo è -ito, dinner is served; vuoi che ti -a un po' di carne?, may I help you to some meat?; (eccl.) — una chiesa, to serve a church (by officiating there); — la Messa, to serve Mass (by answering and assisting the priest); (mil.) — un pezzo di artiglieria, to serve a gun (i.e. to form part of a gun crew); *intr.* (*aux.* avere, essere) to be of use; to serve; non -e, it is no use; tanto -e!, that's enough!; — di scusa, to be a pretext, to serve as an excuse; — a, to be useful for; scarpe che -ono bene a camminare sui sassi, shoes that are suitable for walking on

stony ground; — da, to take the place of, to serve as; questa stanza -e da ripostiglio, this room serves as a lumber-room; (*aux.* avere) — a tavola, to wait at table; (mil.) to serve (in the forces, etc.); — a cavallo, to serve in the cavalry; — nell'artiglieria, to serve in the artillery; — sotto la bandiera, to serve under the flag; *rfl.* (*prep.* di) to make use (of), to use; si -ì di lui per far carriera, he made use of him to make his own way in the world; to help oneself (at table): sèrviti di carne, help yourself to meat; -irsi da, to deal with (i.e. tradesmen); ci -iamo da un fornaio qui vicino, we get our bread at a baker's nearby. **-ente,** †**-iente** *part. adj.* serving; (in-) waiting; (hist.) cavaliere -ente, gentleman-in-waiting; see also **cicisbeo**; (leg.) fondo -ente, servient tenement (C.C.); *n.m.* servant, attendant; lay-brother; serving-table; (tennis) server; (mil.) orderly; assistant; member of a gun crew; *f.* maid, servant. **-entese** *m.,f.* sirvente, a kind of poem, originating with the troubadours, usually of political, religious or satirical character. **-i·bile** *adj.* usable, serviceable. †**-iente** *m.* (mil.) see **servente. -ita** *m.* (eccl.) Servite. **-ito** *part. adj.* served; deserved; (poker) 'no cards'. **-itorame** *m.* (derog.) servants; 'hangers-on', flatterers. **-itore** *m.* servant, domestic servant; civil servant; -itore della patria, one who serves his country; hall-stand (with hat-pegs); -itore muto, -itore inglese, dumb-waiter; servitor vostro!, I am at your service!; -itore umilissimo, your humble servant. (**-itrice** *f.*) **-itoresco** *adj.* (*m.pl.* **-itoreschi**) (derog.) servile. (**-itorescamente** *adv.*) **-itù** *f.* servitude, slavery; bondage; serfdom; servants (collectively), domestic staff; serving a sentence (in prison); (theol.) worship, service (of God, of idols); (leg.) easement; servitude; service; right; -itù reale, real servitude; -itù prediale, *servitium praediale*, praedial, predial servitude, servitude pertaining to land; personal service owed by tenant in fee; -itù di luce, easement of light; -itù coattiva, -itù volontaria, easement created by operation of law, by grant; -itù attiva, profit-a-prender (C.C.).

servi·zi-o *m.* service; favour; kindness; (rel.) service (in Catholic use, chiefly of funerals or of High Mass attended by state dignitaries; in Protestant use, of the normal 'divine service'); — funebre, last offices; (mil.) service; durata del —, length of service; cose che concernano il —, service matters; — di guardia, turn of duty; prestar —, to join a service; — permanente effettivo (abbrev. S.P.E.), regular army; (naut.) service; duty; servicing, serving; fresh-water service (pipe system); service at sea, Departmental service; — attivo, active service; turni del —, duty roster; entrare in —, to commission; — delle artiglierie, gunnery department; (tennis) serve, service; employment; (comm., etc.) supply; running; far —, to trade, to ply, to run (of a ship, bus, etc.); fuori —, out of commission; department; — acquisti, purchasing department; duty; attendance, waiting (hotel, etc.); personale di —, staff (hotel, etc.); donna di —, charwoman, daily help; — compreso, service charge (NOTE: the service charge is divided among the staff, but the waiter expects a 'mancia' for himself); set (dishes, utensils); — da tavola, dinner-service; — da tè, tea-set (service); turn-out (carriage, etc.); scala di —, backstairs; mettere a —, to put out to service; andare a —, to go into domestic service; essere a —, to be in service; mezzo —, domestic help by the day; job, place (as a domestic servant); (rlwy.) — diretto, through service; far —, to run, to function, to operate, to run; essere di —, to be on duty; turno di —, turn of duty; riprendere il — di uno, to return to duty, *or* to start functioning again; mettersi al — di uno, to place oneself at someone's disposal; ricambiare un —, to return a favour. †**-ale** *m.* enema. **-ente** *m.* (naut.) gun servant. **-evole** *adj.* obliging; willing; helpful; serviceable; useful, handy.

servo *adj.* servile; base; (eng.) comando —, servo control; *n.m.* servant; manservant; slave; (theatr.) scene-shifter; (eccl.) Servite; — di Dio, servant of God, holy person; — dei servi di Dio, servant of the servants of God (papal title); (hist.) — della gleba, serf.

servo-comando *m.* (eng.) servo control. **-freno** *m.* (eng.; motor.) brake booster. **-meccanismo** *m.* (eng.) servo-mechanism. **-motore** *m.* (eng.) servomotor. **-sostegno** *m.* (mining) -sostegno pneumatico, airleg. **-sterzo** *m.* (motor.) power-assisted steering. **-val·vola** *f.* (eng.) servo-valve.

se·sam-o (bot.) sesame, *Sesamum indicum*; apriti —!, Open Sesame. **-o·ide** *adj.* (anat.) sesamoid; *n.m.* (anat.) sesamoid bone. **-oide·o** *adj.* (anat.) sesamoid.

†**sescalco** *m.* See **siniscalco**.

se·scuplo *adj.* sixfold, sextuple.

se·ṣia *f.* (ent.) name for the principal genus of clearwing moths which mimic wasps and bees.

seṣino *m.* old copper coin, of several parts of Italy.

sesqui- *pref.* sesqui-; one and a half times; sixfold, 3:2, or similar ratio. **-al·tera** *f.* (mus.) sesquialtera (organ-stop); -altera maggiore, ¾ time; -altera minore, ⅜ time. **†-alterare** *tr.* [A I s] (mus.) to sesquialterate, to dot, to add half the time-value. **-al·tero** *adj.* (math.) sesquialter, in the proportion of 1½ to 1; (mus.) of the proportion of 3:2. **-doppio** *adj.* (math.) sesquiduple, in the proportion of 2½ to 1. **-os·sido** *adj.* (chem.) sesquioxide. **-pedale** *adj.* sesquipedalian; (fig.) big-sounding; polysyllabic. **-plano** *adj.* (aeron., of a biplane) having lower wings smaller than the upper; (iron.) enormous, too big. **-quarto** *adj.* one and a quarter times as much. **-terzo** *adj.* one and a third times as much.

sessa *f.* (geog.) seiche, 'tidal' phenomenon occurring in large lakes.

sessagena·rio *adj.* sixty years old; *n.m.* sexagenarian.

sessage·ṣim-a *f.* (liturg.) Sexagesima. **-o** *adj.* sixtieth.

†sessa·gono, **†sess-an·golo** *adj.*, *n.m.* hexagon(al). **†-angolare** *adj.* hexagonal.

sess-anta *card. num.* sixty; *n.m. indecl.* the number sixty; (hist.) Il Sessanta, i.e. 1860, the year of the establishment of the Kingdom of Italy. **-antamila** *card. num.* sixty thousand. **-antaquattre·ṣimo** *adj.* sixty-fourth; *n.m.* (typ.) 64ᵐᵒ, sixty-fourmo. **-antenne** *adj.* sixty years old; *n.m.* sexagenarian. **-anten·nio** *m.* period of sixty years. **-ante·ṣimo** *ord. num.*, *adj.* sixtieth; *n.m.* sixtieth part. **-antina** *f.* three score; age of sixty or thereabouts; the sixties; essere sulla -antina, to be about sixty. **-antino** *m.* kind of maize (which ripens in sixty days). **-antune·ṣimo, -ante·ṣimo primo** *ord. num.*, *adj.* sixty-first.

sess-ennale *adj.* six-yearly; recurring every six years. **-enne** *adj.* six years old (cf. **seenne**). **-en·nio** *m.* period of six years.

ses·sile *adj.* (scient.) sessile.

session-e *f.* minutes of a session; convocare in — straordinaria, to convene in special session; (leg.) session; sitting(s). **-a·rio** *m.* (leg.) a record book of attendances and consultations kept by solicitor for client.

sessitura *f.* tuck (in clothes); hem.

sesso¹ *m.* sex; il — gentile, the fair sex; il — forte, the male sex; di — femminile, female; di — maschile, male.

†sesso² *m.* seat, backside.

ses·sola *f.* (naut.) bailer (cf. **sessa**).

sessual-e *adj.* sexual; relating to sex. **(-mente** *adv.*) **-ità** *f.* sexuality.

sesta¹ *f.* (naut.) camber (of a deck); *pl.* made-up model, generally full size in light material.

sesta² *f.* (liturg.) sext; (mus.) sixth (interval); (fencing) sixte; leg of a compass; *pl.* pair of compasses; aver le seste negli occhi, to have a good eye for measurements; a seste, with precision; arte della —, architecture.

sester·zio *m.* (Rom. antiq.) *sestertius*, sesterce.

sest-o¹ *ord. num.* sixth; (gramm.) — caso, ablative case; *n.m.* sixth; sixth part; (typ.) sexto; (mus.) sixth; (naut.) armare in —, to reeve a threefold purchase, i.e. with six parts; (hist.) 'quarter' of a city ward. **-angolare** *adj.* hexagonal. **-an·golo** *m.* hexagon. **-ano** *m.* (Rom. hist.) soldier of the Sixth Legion. **-ante** *m.* sextant; (Rom. antiq.) *sextans* (weight and coin). **-a·rio** *m.* (Rom. antiq.) *sextarius* (measure). **-etto** *m.* (mus.) sextet, sestet. **-iga** *f.* coach-and-six. **-ile** *adj.*, *n.m.* (astron.) sextile; aspetto -ile, sextile aspect; *pr.n.m.* (Rom. antiq.) Sextilis (earlier name for August). **-ina** *f.* (prosod.) (strictly) sestina, a poem like Dante's 'Al poco giorno ed al gran cerchio d'ombra', where in each of six-line stanzas (and in the three-line envoi) the same end-words recur in changing order: ABCDEF, FAEBDC, etc.; (more widely) a rhyming six-line stanza, esp. one of the type ABABCC; format of small notepaper; (mus.) sextolet, sextuplet. **-ino** *m.* (mus.) clarinet in A flat; (hist.) Milanese copper coin issued by Maria Theresa; small-sized brick. **-ode·cimo** *ord. num.* sixteenth. **-oque** (joc., a play upon *in jure utroque*) dottorarsi in -oque, to become learned in all the laws. **-ul·timo** *adj.* sixth-last; sixth from the end. **-upla** *f.* (mus.) sextuplet. **-u·plice** *adj.* having six parts.

sesto² *m.* order, orderliness, good order; mettere a —, dare — a, to put in order; essere fuori di —, to be out of order; right size or shape; (typ., etc.) format; (archit.) curvature of an arch; rib of a vault; arco a tutto —, round-headed arch; arco a — acuto, pointed arch.

se·stuplo *adj.* sixfold, sextuple.

sęt-a *f.* silk; — greggia, raw silk; — cruda, unbleached silk; — da cucire, sewing silk; — vegetale, rayon, artificial silk (esp. rayon); — gloria, mercerized cotton; (fig.) capelli di —, silky hair; camminare sopra un filo di —, to go gingerly. **-a·ceo** *adj.* silky, like silk. **-aiuolo, -arolo** *m.* silk merchant, mercer; silk weaver; silk manufacturer. **-eri·a** *f.* silk goods; silk factory. **-icoltura** *f.* silk production. **-icoltore** *m.* silk farmer. **-ifi·cio** *m.* silk farm; silk mill; silk factory. **-ino** *m.* fine sewing-silk; silk hangings used in churches for festivals.

setac·ci-o *m.* see **staccio**. **-are** [A 3] *tr.* to sieve, to sift, to bolt. **(-ato** *part. adj.*) **-atura** *f.* sifting.

sęt-e, †-a *f.* thirst; aver —, to be thirsty; cavarsi, levarsi la —, to quench one's thirst; (fig.) longing, eager desire; greed; aver — di sangue, to be bloodthirsty; levarsi la — col prosciutto, to apply a remedy worse than the disease, to make matters worse; (poet.) drought. **†-ardente** *adj.* causing great thirst.

sętol-a *f.* bristle; coarse hair; hog's bristle used for threading; chap, crack in the skin; crack in horse's hoof; (zool.) seta, chaeta. **-are** [A I sc] *tr.* to brush. **-aio** *m.* brush-maker; vendor of brushes. **-inare** [A I] *tr.* to brush with a clothes-brush. **-inata** *f.* a brushing with a clothes-brush. **-ino** *m.* clothes-brush; hat-brush; whisk. **-one** *m.* (bot.) horse-tail, *Equisetum*; (vet.) sand-crack. **-oso** *adj.* bristly, bristling; cracked, chapped. **-uto** *adj.* (derog.) bristly; sacco -uto, sackcloth, hairshirt.

setone *m.* (vet.) seton.

setta *f.* sect; faction; secret society; fare —, to conspire.

sett-a·gono, -an·golo *m.* (geom.) heptagon. **-angolare** *adj.* heptagonal.

settale *adj.* (anat.) septal, septile.

settant-a *card. num.* seventy; *n.m.* the number seventy; (hist.) Il —, the year 1870, in which Rome was established as the capital of the Kingdom of Italy; (Bibl.) i —, the translators of the Septuagint. **-adue** *card. num.* seventy-two; *n.m.pl.* (Bibl.) i -adue, the Seventy-Two disciples (cf. Lk. x. 1; in some texts, Seventy). **-enne** *adj.* seventy years old; seventy-year-long; *n.m.*, *f.* septuagenarian. **-e·ṣimo, -eṣimo** *ord. num.* seventieth; *n.m.* seventieth; seventieth part. **-ina** *f.* age of seventy or thereabouts; the seventies; essere sulla -ina, to be about seventy years of age.

sett-a·rio *adj.* sectarian; parochial; party; spirito —, party spirit; *n.m.* member (of sect or party); follower; partisan. **†-atore** *m.* member, partisan; sectary.

sett-e *card. num.* seven; i — savi, the seven sages; i — pianeti, the seven planets (of the Ptolemaic system: Moon, Mercury, Venus, Sun, Mars, Jupiter, Saturn); (theol.) le — virtù, the four cardinal and three theological virtues; (rel.) i — dolori di Maria, the Seven Dolours (Sorrows) of Our Lady (feast of 15 September); avere — spiriti come la gatta, to have nine lives like a cat; *n.m.* the number seven; (cards, etc.) the seven; (fig.) — vostro!, good for you!; — bello, point won at 'scopa' by player or team of two players securing the seven of diamonds; (rlwy.) 'il Sette Bello', name of the super de luxe Milan-Rome express; tear in clothing shaped like the number 7; *pl.* i —, the seven (people, etc.); i — a Tebe, The Seven against Thebes. **-ecentęsco** *adj.* (*m.pl.* **-ecentęschi**) relating to the eighteenth century; poesia -ecentesca, eighteenth-century poetry. **-ecente·ṣimo, -ecentęṣimo** *ord. num.* seven-hundredth; *n.m.* seven-hundredth; seven-hundredth part. **-ecentista** *m.*, *f.* eighteenth-century writer, artist, etc., specialist in eighteenth-century studies. **-ecento** *card. num.* seven hundred; *n.m.* the number 700; il -ecento, the eighteenth century. **-emila** *card. num.* seven thousand. **-ino** *m.* (mus.) septet.

†setteggi-are [A 3 c] *intr.* (*aux.* avere) to conspire; to form a sect. **†-ante** *part. adj.*, *n.m.*, *f.* sectarian, partisan. **†-atore** *m.* partisan, follower (cf. **setta**).

settembr-e *m.* September; (hist.) festa del 20 —, commemoration of the liberation of Rome, 20 September 1870 (abolished at the time of the Concordat). **†-ec·cia, -ęsca, -i·a** *f.* autumn. **-ino** *adj.* of, relating to, September; lana -ina, wool clipped in September; fichi -ini, figs ripening in September. **-ista** *m.* Septembrist (referring to events in France in September 1792).

settem·plice *adj.* sevenfold; repeated seven times; septuple.

†settena *f.* (eccl.) seven-day penance.

settena·rio *m.* period of seven days or seven years; (poet.) line of seven syllables; (med.) septan; *adj.* septenary; (mus.) misura settenaria, septuple time, seven-beat time.

settenn·ale *adj.* septennial, recurring every seven years. **-ato** *m.* (leg.) septennate. **-e** *adj.* seven years old; seven-year-long.

setten·nio *m.* period of seven years.

settentrion-e *m.* north; Septentrion. **-ale** *adj.* north, northern; northerly; l'Italia -ale, Northern Italy; *n.m.* northerner; †constellation of Ursa Major.

sett-envirale *adj.* (Rom. antiq.) septemviral. **-envirato** *m.* (Rom. antiq.) septemvirate. **-en·viri** *m.pl.* (Rom. antiq.) *septemviri.*

†sette·ṣimo *m.* (eccl.) seventh-day requiem, 'week's mind'.

sett-icida *adj.* (bot.) septicidal. **-icla·vio** *m.* (mus.) system of seven clefs (i.e. treble, soprano, mezzo soprano, alto, tenor, baritone and bass). **-icorde** *adj.* (mus.) seven-stringed; *n.m.* (mus.) heptachord (also **setticordo**). **-iforme** *adj.* having seven forms, sevenfold; (theol.) sevenfold (of the Holy Ghost and His gifts). **-ifra·gio** *m.* (bot.) septifragal.

set·tic-o *adj.* (med.) septic. **-emi·a** *f.* (med.) septicaemia; (vet.) **-emia dei suini**, swine erysipelas. **-e·mico** *adj.* (med.) septicaemic.

setti·duo *adj.* (of) seven day(s); *n.m.* period of seven days, week.

†set·tile (art, of a mosaic) made of large pieces of stone of various colours; (agric.) ready for cutting.

set·tima *f.* See under **settimo**.

settiman-a *f.* week; di — in —, week in week out; ogni quattro -e, every fourth week; una — oggi, today week; fine di —, week-end; — entrante, next week; week's wages; riscuotere la —, to receive one's week's wages; (eccl.) — santa, Holy Week; (Bibl.) — mosaica, week of years, seven years. **-ale** *adj.* weekly; week's; giornale -ale, weekly journal, weekly; *n.m.* weekly; week's pay. **-almente** *adv.* weekly, by the week; every week.

set·tim-o *ord. num.* seventh; (theol.) il — sacramento, the seventh sacrament, marriage; *n.m.* seventh; seventh part. **-a** *f.* (eccl.) seventh-day requiem, 'week's mind'; (mus.) seventh (interval). **†-ello** *adj.* bambino -ello, seventh months' child. **-estre** *adj.* seven month's, seven-months-long. **-ino** *m.* (mus.) septet; seven months' child.

settino *m.* (mus.) See under **sette**.

settinsulare *adj.* relating to the seven Ionian islands; (hist.) governo —, the British protectorate of the Ionian islands, terminated in 1860.

settiẓo·nio *m.* (Rom. antiq.) a *septizonium*, esp. that built by Severus, A.D. 203; the seven planetary spheres (of the Ptolemaic system).

setto[1] *m.* (anat.) septum; (eng.) baffle; — deviatore, deflecting baffle plate.

†setto[2] *adj.* separated, distinct; cut off.

settore *m.* sector; section; quadrant; area; field of activity; (mil.) sector, an area or division of military responsibility; portion of a battle-front; fire-sector of a battery; (geom.) sector; (eng.) sector, quadrant; (surg.) prosector.

settotraṣverso *m.* (anat.) diaphragm.

settu-agena·rio *adj.*, *n.m.* septuagenarian. **-age·ṣima** *f.* (liturg.) Septuagesima. **-age·ṣimo**, **-ageṣimo** *ord. num.* seventieth; *n.m.* (the) seventieth. **-plare** [A I], **-plicare** [A 2 s] *tr.* to multiply by seven.

set·tuplo *adj.* sevenfold, septuple.

seudo- *pref.* See **pseudo-**.

†severare *vb.* and derivs. See **sceverare**.

Severna *pr.n.f.* (geog.) Severn.

sever-o *adj.* severe; strict; austere; stern; rigorous; harsh; rough; studi -i, serious, scholarly, work; colore —, subdued, quiet colour, subfusc. **-amente** *adv.* severely; strictly, austerely; sternly; rigorously; harshly. **-ità** *f.* severity, strictness; sternness; harshness.

sevi·zi-a *f.* (usu. *pl.*) cruelty; ill-treatment; usare -e contro, to maltreat. **-are** [A 4] *tr.* to ill-treat; to torture.

ṣevo[1] *m.* See **sego**.

ṣevo[2] *adj.* cruel; ferocious.

sezion-are [A I c] *tr.* (micro.) to section; to dissect. **-amento** *m.* (electr.; eng.; micro.) sectioning. **-ato** *part. adj.* sectioned; (bot.) foglia -ata, compound leaf. **-atore** *m.* (electr.) isolating switch. **-atrice** *f.* (electr.) isolator.

sezione *f.* section; part; (archit.) section; sectional drawing; (naut.) subdivision (of a flotilla or squadron); section of a ship, cross-section; — diametrale, profile; unit, working party, team; (surg.) dissection; (geom.) section; cross-section; cross-sectional area; — piana, plane section; — conica, conic section; intersection; (astron.) intersection of the equator and the zodiac; division;

department; group; (schol.) — classica, classical side; (leg.) division; court; capo di —, head of division; — elettorale, electoral division; — di polizia, police station; (mil.) section, small military unit or subdivision, usually specialized; sezioni mitragliatrici, machine-gun sections; (aeron.) wing, a portion of a flight; (eccl.) — di benefizio, division of a benefice.

sezza *f.* See **sessa**.

†sezz-o *adv. phr.* da —, at the end, last. **†-a·io**, **†-ano** *adj.* last.

sfabbricare [A 2 s] *tr.* to demolish; to destroy the fabric of.

sfaccend-are [A I] *intr.* (*aux.* avere) to be busy; to bustle; avere sempre da —, to be always busy; — per casa, to be busy about the house. **-ato** *adj.* idle, unoccupied; *n.m.* idler, loafer. (**-ata** *f.*)

sfaccett-are [A I c] *tr.* (jewel.) to facet. (**-ato** *part. adj.*) **-atura** *f.* (jewel.) cutting; cut; facet; facets.

sfacchin-are [A I] *intr.* (*aux.* avere), *rfl.* to toil, to drudge, to slave; to work like a black. **-ata** *f.* heavy work, back-breaking labour; tough job.

sfacci-are [A 3] *tr.* to face, to smooth, to cut; (eng.) to face (on a lathe); †*intr.*, *rfl.* to be impudent. **-atag·gine** *f.* impudence, cheek; effrontery; avere la -ataggine di, to have the effrontery to; impudent behaviour; shamelessness; ci vuole una bella -ataggine!, what cheek! **-atello** *adj. dim.* rather cheeky. **-atezza** *f.* impudence, effrontery; la -atezza dei colori, boldness of colours. **-ato** *adj.* impudent; shameless; (art) colori -ati, bold colours; luce -ata, dazzling light; (of a horse) having a large 'blaze' on its forehead; (techn.) faced; faceted. **-atamente** *adv.* impudently; shamelessly. **-atura** *f.* (vet.) 'blaze', white patch on a horse's forehead; (eng.) facing.

sfacelo *m.* collapse, ruin, breakdown; disaster; essere in —, to be crumbling to pieces; (med.) sphacelation, gangrene, necrosis.

sfacimento *m.* decay; ruin; weakening; undoing.

sfagliare [A 4] *tr.* (cards) to discard; *rfl.* (*prep.* di) to get rid of.

sfa·glio *m.* discarding; cards discarded; (vet.) 'shying' in a horse.

sfagno *m.* (bot.) bog-moss, *Sphagnum.*

sfald-are [A I] *tr.* to cut into slices; to cause to flake or scale; *rfl.* to exfoliate, to flake, to scale. **-a·bile** *adj.* (miner.; geol.) spathic. **-abilità** *f.* (geog.) non-resistance. **-amento** *m.* flaking; (geol.) cleavage. (**-ato** *part. adj.*) **-atura** *f.* flaking; scaling; (miner.) flaking, exfoliation; (metall.) scaling; flaw; (geol.) cleavage. **-ellare** [A I] *tr.* (text.) to card; *rfl.* to break into pieces, to crumble.

sfalerite *f.* (miner.) sphalerite, blende.

†sfallare *vb.* See **sfallire**.

sfallire [D 2] *intr.* (*aux.* avere) to err, to be at fault; to fail (cf. **fallire**).

sfaloppare [A I] *intr.* (*aux.* avere) (silkb.) to remove bad cocoons.

sfals-are [A I] *tr.* to parry, to ward off; (bldg.; eng.) to offset, to stagger; (bldg.) to joggle (bricks in a wall). **-amento** *m.* (eng.) stagger. (**-ato** *part. adj.*)

sfam-are [A I] *tr.* to feed; to provide food for; to appease the hunger of; to satisfy; *rfl.* to appease one's hunger. **-ato** *part. adj.* fed; satisfied; appeased.

†sfanfanare *tr.* to destroy; to undo.

sfang-are [A 2] *intr.* (*aux.* avere) to splash through mud; (fig.) to drudge, to toil; to get out of the mud; (fig.) to get out of the mire; to get out of difficulties; *tr.* to clean mud from; (fig.) -arla, to get out of the difficulty, to scrape through; *rfl.* (*acc.* of *prn.* 'si') to clean mud from oneself; (*dat.* of *prn.* 'si') (fig.) -arsela, to get out of a scrape. **-ato** *part. adj.* (mining) de-slime. **-atrice** *f.* mud-clearing machine (for the streets). **-atura** *f.* street-cleaning, removing mud.

sfare [B 14] *tr.* to undo; to dissolve; to melt; to take apart; †not to do; *rfl.* to decompose; to melt; (of bubble, blister, etc.) to burst; †sfarsi di, see 'disfarsi di' under **disfare**.

sfarfall-are [A I] *intr.* (*aux.* avere) to come out of the cocoon; to flutter about, to flit; (fig.) to lack concentration; (of flowers) to fall, to drop, to shed their petals. **-amento** *m.* fluttering; (motor.) wobble (of wheels); -amento delle valvole, valve floating; (cinem.) flicker. **-atura** *f.* emerging from the cocoon; fluttering, flitting. **-io** *m.* continual flitting; (cinem.; telev.) flicker. **-one** *m.* blunder.

sfarin-are [A I] *tr.* to grind to flour; to reduce to powder; to pulverize; *rfl.* to be reduced to powder; to crumble; (of potatoes) to be overcooked. **-a·bile** *adj.* reducible to powder. **-amento** *m.* crumbling; (paint industry) chalking. **-ante** *part. adj.* (techn.) crumbling. **-ato** *part. adj.* (of pears) sleepy; (of potatoes) overcooked.

sfarẓ-o, sfarz-o *m.* pomp; magnificence; ostentation, display; splendour; brilliance; luxury; sala addobbata con —, luxuriantly furnished room; illuminato con —, brilliantly lit. **-osità** *f.* ostentation, display; vain pomp. **-ọso** *adj.* magnificent; splendid; brilliant; gorgeous, sumptuous; luxurious; ostentatious. (**-osamẹnte** *adv.*)

sfaṣ-are [A I] *tr.* (electr.) to dephase; (motor.) to upset the timing of (an engine). **-amẹnto** *m.* (electr.) phase displacement. **-ato** *part. adj.* (electr.) out of phase; (motor.) with faulty timing; (colloq., fig.) 'mental', deranged, off one's head, 'not quite all there'; *n.m.* (telev.) phase shift.

sfasci-are [A 3] *tr.* to unbind (esp. bandages); to undo; to dismantle; to demolish; (naut.) to break up; to unlay a cable; (mil.) to dismantle; to knock down or raze fortifications or walls; *rfl.* to break down, to collapse; to crash; to come undone, unwound. **-amẹnto** *m.* unwrapping, unbinding; unwinding; dismantling; collapse, ruin. **-ato** *part. adj.* unwrapped; unbandaged. (**-atọre** *m.* **-atrice** *f.*) **-atura** *f.* removing of bandages, etc. **-ume** *m.* ruins; rubbish, litter; (fig., of a person) wreck; (geol.) -ume meteorico, talus.

sfa·scio *m.* collapse; (Tusc.) cadere di —, to fall one's full length.

sfat-are [A I] *tr.* to discredit, to unmask, to expose; — una tesi, to explode a theory; to 'debunk'. **-amẹnto** *m.* discrediting; unmasking; exposure. **-ato** *part. adj.* discredited; unmasked; exposed; (of a theory, etc.) exploded; 'debunked'.

sfaticato¹ *adj.* lazy, unwilling; *n.m.* idler, slacker; shirker.

sfaticat-o² *adj.* (Tusc.) *intens.* of **affaticato**, q.v.; (N. Italy) idle, lazy; *n.m.* slacker.

sfatto *part.* of **sfare**, q.v.; *adj.* undone; unmade; letto —, unmade bed; ruined; flabby; gone to pieces; overcooked.

sfavill-are [A I] *intr.* (*aux.* avere, †essere) to sparkle; to shine; to glitter; (fig.) to be radiant; i suoi occhi -avano di gioia, his eyes shone with pleasure. **-amẹnto** *m.* sparkle; glitter; brilliance. **-ante** *part. adj.* sparkling, radiant, brilliant; (fig.) occhi -anti, shining eyes, sparkling eyes. **-io** *m.* continual sparkling, glittering, flashing.

sfavọr-e *m.* disfavour; disapproval; disgrace. **-ẹvole** *adj.* unfavourable; adverse; contrary. (**-evolmẹnte** *adv.*) **-ire** [D 2] and derivs. see **disfavorire**.

sfebbr-are [A I] *tr.* to bring down the temperature of; *rfl., intr.* (*aux.* essere) to be cured of a fever. **-ato** *part. adj.* free from fever, no longer feverish.

sfederare [A I S] *tr.* to take (a pillow) out of a pillow-case.

sfegat-are [A I S] *rfl.* to exert oneself to the utmost; to wear oneself out; to work oneself into a passion; to become frantic; to rage; to bawl and yell. **-ato** *part. adj.* passionate; raging, frantic; ardent. (**-atamẹnte** *adv.*)

sfen·d-ere [B I] *tr.* to split; *rfl.* (of metals, stone) to scale, to split into layers; to crack. **-imẹnto** *m.* splitting; cracking. **-itura** *f.* split; crack.

sfe·nio *m.* (anat.) sphenion.

sfen-o *m.*, **-a** *f.* (miner.) sphene, titanite.

sfeno·id-e *adj.* (anat.) sphenoid; *n.m.* sphenoid, sphenoid bone. **-ale** *adj.* (anat.) sphenoid, sphenoidal.

sfeno-tribo *m.* (surg.) sphenotribe. **-trissi** *f.* (surg.) sphenotresia.

sfer-a *f.* sphere; globe, orb; circle; — celeste, sky, heaven(s); — terrestre, Earth; — dell'aria, atmosphere; (fig.) nelle alte -e, in exalted circles; — d'azione, sphere of action; (geom.) sphere; (football) ball; (liturg.) orb (of monstrance); (eng.) cuscinetto a -e, ball bearing; penna a —, ball pen; (watchm.) hand; — delle ore, hour hand; — dei minuti, minute hand; (naut.) — celeste, star globe. †**-ale** *adj.* see **sferico**.

sfe·r-ico *adj.* spherical; (geom.) spherical. **-icamẹnte** *adv.* spherically. **-icità** *f.* sphericity, quality of being spherical; (geom.) sphericity. **-istẹrio** *m.* (Gk. antiq.) ball-court; (neol.) sports ground. **-i·stica** *f.* (Gk. antiq.) (art of) ball-play. **-oidale** *adj.* (geom.) spheroidal. **-o·ide** *m.* (geom.) spheroid. **-oidizzare** [A I] *tr.* (metall.) to spheroidize. **-oidizziọne** *f.* (metall.) spheroidizing. **-omachi·a** *f.* (antiq.) ball game(s). **-o·metro** *m.* (techn.; scient.) spherometer. **-osiderite** *f.* (miner.) spheroidal siderite.

sferire [D 2] *tr.* (naut.) to unreeve (a tackle); — un segnale, to unbend a hoist; — la gala, to undress ship.

sferr-a *f.* piece of old iron; worn horseshoe; clout; *pl.* cast-off clothing. **-acavallo** *m.* (bot.) horseshoe vetch, *Hippocrepis comosa*. **-are** [A I] *tr.* (vet.) to remove the shoes from (a horse), to unshoe; to free (a prisoner) from irons, from chains; to draw a weapon

from a wound; to deliver a kick, an attack, etc.; *rfl.* (vet.) to cast a shoe; to break loose (from chains); to jerk away. (**-ato** *part. adj.*) †**-ato·ia** *f.* see **ferratoia**. **-atura** *f.* removal of horseshoes; casting shoes. **-avec·chie** *f.pl.* old horseshoes, scrap iron. **-uzzare** [A I] *intr.* (*aux.* avere) (colloq.) to sit and knit, to 'knit away'. **-uzzato** *adj.* (of limestone, etc.) overbaked.

sfervorato *adj.* having lost fervour; disheartened; cooled off, cooled down; become indifferent.

sferz-a *f.* whip, lash, scourge; (fig.) sotto la — del sole, under the merciless rays of the sun; rebuke, censure; whiplash; — di rose, flattery, blandishments. **-are** [A I] *tr.* to whip, to lash; to thrash; to flog, to scourge; (fig.) il sole -a, the sun beats down upon; to lash out at; to censure, to rebuke; †(naut.) to take a cloth out of (a sail, for repairs, etc.). **-ata** *f.* cut with a whip; thrashing; (fig.) sharp rebuke. **-ato** *part. adj.* whipped; thrashed; flogged, scourged; rebuked, censured. **-atọre** *m.* flogger; flagellant. (**-atrice** *f.*) **-ina** *f.* (naut.) towing line of a dragnet; (Viareggio) float line. **-ino** *m.* lash at the end of a whip; whipcord; (naut.) small cord used for whippings; mackerel line.

sfẹso *m.* leather sole sewn part way through.

sfẹsso *part.* of **sfendere**, q.v.; *adj.* split; *n.m.* crack, split; (vet.) gape of the mouth (of a horse).

sfiaccolag·gine *f.* weariness; weakness.

sfiaccolare [A I S] *intr.* (*aux.* avere) (of candle, lamp, etc.) to flare; to gutter.

sfiaccolato *adj.* worn out, jaded; enfeebled.

sfiammare [A I] *intr.* (*aux.* avere) to blaze, to burn away (esp. of faulty charcoal-burning).

sfianc-are [A 2] *tr.* to break; to destroy; to break through the sides of; (fig.) to exhaust by overwork; *intr.* (*aux.* essere) to give way; to cave in; to burst; *rfl.* to overwork; to exhaust oneself. **-amẹnto** *m.* overwork, strain; bursting; distension; giving way; (med.) straining (of the heart). **-ato** *part. adj.* burst; strained; distended; worn out, exhausted; (vet.) hollow flanked (of a horse).

sfiat-are [A I] *intr.* (*aux.* avere) to exhale; (*aux.* essere) (of gas, air) to escape, to leak; *rfl.* to talk oneself breathless; dovetti -atarmi per persuaderlo, I had hard work to persuade him. **-amẹnto** *m.* breathing out; escape (of gas, etc.). **-ato** *part. adj.* out of breath, breathless, panting; weak, feeble. **-atọio** *m.* vent(-hole); ventilation shaft; (mil.) countermine; (eng.) relief valve; breather; (bldg.) ventilation opening; (zool.) blow-hole of a whale. (**-atọre** *m.*) **-atura** *f.* exhalation; escape (of gas, etc.); hole (allowing escape or leak). **-i·o** *m.* deflating (of bellows). **-o** *m.* vent(-hole); escape (of gas, air); (bldg.) breather pipe.

sfibbi-are [A 4] *tr.* to unbuckle; to unfasten, to unclasp; to unbutton; (fig.) to utter, to let fly (insults, oaths, etc.); *rfl.* to let oneself go, to speak without reserve; to unbutton oneself. (**-amẹnto** *m.*) **-ato** *part. adj.* unbuckled; unbuttoned. **-atura** *f.* unfastening; unbuttoning; unbuckling.

sfibr-are [A I] *tr.* to weaken, to enervate; to unnerve. (**-amẹnto** *m.*) **-ante** *part. adj.* enervating, exhausting. **-ato** *part. adj.* enervated; weakened; unnerved. **-atọre** *m.* (paperm.) wood-grinding machine; (text.) machine for fibre extraction. **-atura** *f.* (paperm.) wood grinding. **-inare** [A I] *tr.* (med.; chem.) to defibrinate, to defibrinize.

sfid-are¹ [A I] *tr.* to challenge; — a duello, to challenge to a duel; — al biliardo, to challenge to a game of billiards; lo -o a ripeterlo, I challenge him to say it again; (fig.) to defy; to face, to brave; to withstand; — i secoli, to defy the ravages of time; *abs.* to be certain, to be sure; to be confident; -o io!, of course!, you bet!; ci sarò, -o io!, I'll be there, I can tell you!; -o! come no?, naturally! why ever not?; —! come avrebbe potuto?, naturally he didn't! how could he?; *recip. rfl.* to challenge each other; si sono -ati a duello, they have challenged each other to a duel. **-a** *f.* challenge; raccogliere la —, to accept the challenge; defiance; con aria di —, with a defiant air, in a challenging manner. **-ante** *part. adj.* challenging; *n.m., f.* challenger. **-ato** *part. adj.* challenged; defied; braved, faced. **-atọre** *m.* challenger; *adj.* challenging. (**-atrice** *f.*)

†**sfid-are²** *intr.* to lose confidence, to become diffident. **-ato** *adj.* (Tusc.) diffident; no longer confident.

sfidu·ci-a *f.* mistrust, distrust; avere — di, to mistrust, to distrust; lack of confidence; votare la —, to pass a vote of no-confidence. **-are** [A 3] *tr.* to discourage; to dishearten; to undermine the confidence of; *rfl.* to lose confidence, to lose heart; to become

sfiduci·a (*cont.*)
discouraged. **-ato** *part. adj.* discouraged; disheartened; disappointed, disillusioned. (**-atamente** *adv.*)

sfienare [A 1] *tr.* to take out (straw) from a corn-sheaf.

sfigliol·are [A 1 s] *intr.* (*aux.* avere) (agric.; bot.) to throw out new shoots. **-atura** *f.* new shoots.

sfig·m·ico *adj.* (med.) sphygmic, pertaining to the pulse. **-ocardio·grafo** *m.* (med.) sphygmocardiograph. **-ocardiogramma** *m.* (med.) sphygmocardiogram. **-ocrono·grafo** *m.* (med.) sphygmochronograph. **-o·fono** *m.* (med.) sphygmophone. **-ografi·a** *f.* (med.) sphygmography. **-o·grafo** *m.* (med.) sphygmograph. **-ogramma** *m.* (med.) sphygmogram. **-oide·o** *adj.* (med.) sphygmoid, pulse-like. **-omanometri·a** *f.* (med.) sphygmomanometry. **-omano·metro** *m.* (med.) sphygmomanometer. **-osco·pio** *m.* (med.) sphygmoscope.

sfigur·are [A 1] *tr.* to disfigure; to deform; *intr.* (*aux.* avere) to cut a poor figure, to make a bad impression; to be unsuitable; to look out of place. **-ato** *part. adj.* disfigured; deformed.

sfilac·cia *f.* loose threads; †(naut.) strand of a cable.

sfilacci·are [A 3] *tr.* to fray out; (text.) to unravel; *rfl.* to become frayed; to fray; to unravel. **-amento** *m.* (text.) fibre extraction. **-ato** *part. adj.* frayed. **-atrice** *f.* (text.) rag grinding machine breaker. **-atura** *f.* unravelling; fraying out; (text.) rag grinding.

sfilaccic·are [A 2 s] *tr., rfl.* to fray out; to unravel. (**-ato** *part. adj.*) **-atura** *f.* fraying out; frayed part of cloth.

sfil·are [A 1] *tr.* to unthread (a needle); to unstring (beads, etc.); to unhitch; to slip off; — l'arrosto, to take the roast (meat) off the spit; — la tela, to draw out threads (for drawn-thread work, for darning, etc.); — una sigaretta, to slip a cigarette out of a packet; (fig.) — tutto il rosario, to say all possible evil of a person; *intr.* (*aux.* avere) (mil.) to defile (on a narrow front); to march past (on parade); (naut.) — in rivista, to steam past in review order; *rfl.* to come unthreaded; to come unstrung; le perle si sono -ate, the pearls have come off their string; (of a person) to become exhausted. **-amento** *m.* unthreading; unstringing; (mil.) march past; (naut.) long line of ships. **-ata** *f.* file; row; procession, march past; assistere alla -ata di un corteo, to watch a procession; fashion parade. **-ato** *part. adj.* unthreaded; unstrung; loose; (of knives, etc.) blunted, blunt; (of a person) exhausted, done-up; *adv. phr.* alla -ata, a few at a time, in succession; *n.m.* drawn-thread work; †(mil.) tow, woolly head used in loading or cleaning a gun. **-atura** *f.* unthreading; unstringing; (in a stocking) ladder; (of road, wall, ditch) straightening, realignment.

sfil·eggiare [A 3 c] (*aux.* avere) (naut.) to flap (of a sail); fare — una vela, to bring a sail into the wind. **-eggio** *m.* (naut.) action and effect of being 'in the wind' or 'in irons'.

sfiloşofare [A 1 s] *intr.* (*aux.* avere) (derog.) to philosophize; *rfl.* (joc.) to abandon philosophy.

sfilz·are [A 1] *tr.* to detach from a string, series, file, etc. (cf. **infilzare**); *rfl.* to become detached. (**-ato** *part. adj.*)

†**sfingardag·gine** *f.* See **infingardaggine**.

sfinge *f.* sphinx; volto di —, sphinx-like countenance; (ent.) hawk moth, *Sphinx* spp.

sfin·ire [D 2] *tr.* to exhaust, to wear out; *intr.* (*aux.* essere) to faint, to swoon; *rfl.* to become exhausted; to tire oneself out; to faint, to swoon. **-imento** *m.* exhaustion, extreme weakness, faint, swoon. **-itezza** *f.* exhaustion, extreme weakness. **-ito** *part. adj.* exhausted; worn out; haggard.

sfint·ere *m.* (anat.) sphincter. **-e·rico** *adj.* (anat.) sphincterial. **-erodini·a** *f.* (med.) sphincteralgia. **-erotomi·a** *f.* (surg.) sphincterotomy.

sfiocc·are [A 2] *tr.* to make into tassels; to unravel so as to form a tassel; *rfl.* to become unravelled; (of a cloud) to break up into little flakes or tufts. **-amento** *m.* loosening into tassels, tufts or flakes; (text.) pulling (cotton). **-ato** *part. adj.* tasselled; unravelled. **-atura** *f.* (text.) loosening (of cotton).

sfiocco *m.* edge of material frayed as into tassels.

sfiond·are [A 1 c] *tr.* to sling, to throw from a sling; (fig.) — fandonie, to talk nonsense, to tell a lot of tall stories. **-atore** *m.* slinger. (**-atrice** *f.*) **-atura** *f.* slinging; †gross lie.

sfior·are [A 1 c] *tr.* to touch lightly; to graze, to brush, to skim over; to caress; un sorriso che -a il labbro, a smile hovering about the lips; (fig.) — un argomento, to touch on a subject; — un libro, to skim through a book; — il latte, to skim milk; (fig.) to skim, to take the best of. **-amento** *m.* touching, grazing, caressing.

(**-ato** *part. adj.*) **-atore** *m.* overflow(-pipe); (hydr.) spillway; **-atore** a stramazzo, weir; (mining) baffle board (in ore-washing machine). (**-atura** *f.*)

sfior·ire [D 2] *intr.* (*aux.* essere) to fade; (of a flower) to drop its petals; to wither, to decay. **-ito** *part. adj.* faded; overblown. **-itura** *f.* fading; decay.

sfioro *m.* (mining) overflow (cf. **sfioratore**, under **sfiorare**).

sfioss·are [A 1] *tr.* to form the arch of (shoes). (**-ato** *part. adj.* **-atura** *f.*)

sfirena *f.* (ichth.) — comune, spet, *Sphyraena spet.*

sfissare [A 1] *tr.* to cancel (e.g. an arrangement), to 'unfix'.

sfitt·are [A 1] *tr.* to leave untenanted; *rfl.* to remain unlet. **-ato** *part. adj.*, **-o** *adj.* unlet, empty, free.

sfittonare [A 1 c] *tr.* to pare a horse's hoof down to the quick.

sfi·zio *m.* amusement, joke; pastime.

sfocat·o¹ *adj.* (photog.; opt.) out of focus; (of eyes) astigmatic; dull, dim. **-ura** *f.* (photog.) fuzziness.

†**sfocato²** *adj.* See **sfogato**, under **sfogare**.

sfoci·are [A 3] *tr.* to widen the mouth of (river or stream); *intr.* (*aux.* essere; *prep.* in) to flow out (into); to debouch. **-amento** *m.* clearing, widening (of a river's mouth). (**-ato** *part. adj.*) **-atura** *f.* work or cost of clearing a river's mouth.

sfocon·are [A 1 c] *tr.* to poke (the fire); (mil.) to spike, to damage or enlarge the touch hole of; to remove an obstruction from (the fire hole); *rfl.* (of a gun) to wear away through use. (**-ato** *part. adj.*)

sfoder·are [A 1 s] *tr.* to unsheath; (fig.) to display; — citazioni, to show off one's knowledge by repeatedly quoting writers. (**-amento** *m.* **-ato** *part. adj.*)

sfog·are [A 2] *tr.* to give vent to, to let out; to give free play to; to disclose; — la piaga, to open the wound (to allow pus to escape); -ò la sua stizza sul poveraccio, he vented his ill-humour on the poor devil; *rfl.* to relieve (give vent to) one's feelings; -arsi con uno, to unbosom oneself to someone; -arsi contro uno, to tell someone what you think of him; *intr.* (*aux.* essere) (of smoke, water, etc.) to escape, to get out, to flow away; (of a wound) to suppurate; (of clouds) to break in rain. **-amento** *m.* see **sfogo**. **-ato** *part. adj.* vented; let loose; allowed free; rami -ati, freely growing branches. **-atamente** *adv.* unrestrainedly, unreservedly; passionately. **-atoio** *m.* outlet; air-hole, ventilation shaft; vent.

sfoggi·are [A 3] *intr.* (*aux.* avere) to show off, to be ostentatious, to dress smartly; *tr.* to flaunt, to display, to show off. **-amento** *m.* see **sfoggio**. **-ato** *part. adj.* lavish, ostentatious, showy; excessive; (archit.) architettura -ata, overornate architecture. **-atamente** *adv.* lavishly; flauntingly.

sfog·gio *m.* display: luxury, abundance; ostentation, show, parade; — di dottrina, di erudizione, parade, display, of learning.

sfo·gli·a *f.* (metall.) scale; (cul.) pasta —, puff-pastry; sfoglie del granturco, dried maize leaves; (ichth.) a common dialect form of **sogliola**, q.v. **-ame** *m.* (metall.) scale.

sfogli·are [A 4] *tr.* to strip off (leaves, petals), — il granturco, to strip maize; to cut into thin flakes; — un libro, to turn over the pages of a book, to open uncut pages of a book with a paper-knife, *or* to glance through a book; (cards) to draw one by one from a pack; *rfl.* to shed leaves; to flake off. (**-amento** *m.*) **-ata** *f.* rapid glance (through a book); (cul.) flaky pastry. **-atella** *f. dim.* (cul.) little turn-over of puff-pastry. **-ato** *part. adj.* stripped (of leaves, petals); libro -ato, book of which the pages have been opened, *or* book which has been glanced through; flaked; (archit.) shaped like leaves or scrolls, foliate. **-atoio** *m.*, **-atrice** *f.* leaf-stripping machine. **-atura** *f.* stripping (of leaves); flaking (of iron under the hammer). **-azione** *f.* falling of leaves in autumn. **-ettare** [A 1 c] *tr.* to turn the pages of, to glance through idly. (**-ettato** *part. adj.*)

sfo·gli·o *m.* see **sfoglia**. **-oso** *adj.* flaky, liable to flake or scale.

sfognare [A 5 c] *intr.* (*aux.* essere) to go down the drain, to drain away; to overflow from the drain; †to be born; *tr.* to unstop (a drain).

sfo·go, **sfo·go** *m.* (*pl.* **-ghi**) vent, outlet; relief; (fig.) fare i suoi -ghi con uno, to unbosom oneself to someone, to unburden one's mind by confiding in or gossiping with someone; outburst; (fig.) valvoletta di —, safety-valve; free play; (med.) eruption; (archit.) maximum height (of arch, vault, etc.); (comm.) dare — a un affare, to conclude a deal; dare — a una lettera, to act on a letter, to deal with a letter; merce che non trova —, goods that do not sell.

†**sfoiare** *rfl.* to satisfy one's lust.

sfolgor-are [A I sc] *intr.* (*aux.* essere, avere) to flash; to blaze; occhi che -ano, flashing eyes; to flame; il sole -ava, the sun was blazing; to move, to act, like lightning; *tr.* to blaze forth; to flash forth. **-amento** *m.* flashing; blazing; blaze. **-ante** *part. adj.* resplendent; blazing; flashing; glittering; ingegno -ante, brilliant mind. **-ato** *part. adj.* resplendent, splendid; dazzling; excessive, rash; spese -ate, lavish expenditure. **-atamente** *adv.* like lightning; with extreme brilliance; dazzlingly. **-eggiamento** *m.* blazing; flashing; glittering. **-eggiare** [A 3 c] *intr.* (*aux.* essere, avere) to flash; to glitter. **-io** *m.* blaze; flashing; glitter; uno -io di gioielli, a blaze of jewels; refulgence; radiance; splendour.

sfoll-are [A I] *intr.* (*aux.* essere, avere), *rfl.* (of a crowd) to disperse, to thin out; to break up; to become less crowded; il teatro -ò lentamente, the theatre emptied slowly; to be evacuated; *tr.* to clear (a crowd); to empty; to evacuate; (rlwy.) — un binario, to clear a line. **-agente** *m. indecl.* truncheon. **-amento** *m.* dispersing; break up (of crowd, meeting, etc.); reduction of staff; evacuation. **-ato** *part. adj.* dispersed; scattered; emptied, empty (of a hall, etc.); deserted; evacuated; *n.m.* evacuee. (**-ata** *f.*)

sfond-are [A I c] *tr.* to wear a hole in; to knock the bottom out of; to break; to break down; to demolish; to break open, to burst open; to stave in; — la linea principale di difesa, to break through the main line of defence; to go deeply into; — poco, to be shallow-minded; — lo stomaco, to lie heavy on the stomach, to cause indigestion, (fig., of a discourse) to be boring; (fig.) — una porta aperta, to explain the obvious; (archit.) to make a recess in (a wall); *intr.* (*aux.* avere) to make headway; (mil.) to break through; †(paint.) to appear in the background; *intr.* (*aux.* essere) to give way; to sink; si sentiva — sotto i piedi la terra, he felt the ground giving way beneath his feet; *rfl.* to burst at the bottom; to become worn through. †**-agiaco** *m.* armour-piercing weapon. **-amento** *m.* breaking; bursting open; staving in; knocking out of the bottom; (mil.) -amento del fronte, breaking through. **-asto·maco** *m. indecl.* boring speech, sermon, etc. **-ato** *part. adj.* broken; burst; worn out, worn into holes; ruinous, in ruins; bottomless, boundless; (fig.) ricco -ato, rolling in money; (paint.) having depth, having background in perspective; *n.m.* (archit.) door or window space, opening; (paint.) perspective view showing considerable distance. **-atoio** *m.* (mil.) spike, instrument used for spiking a gun. (**-atore** *m.* **-atrice** *f.*) **-atura** *f.* breaking; bursting; see **sfondamento**.

sfondo *m.* (paint.) recess in wall or ceiling (intended for a painting); background; view; (theatr.) — della scena, back of the stage; backcloth; (mech.) socket; (eng.) gap (between teeth of a cogwheel).

sfontanare [A I] *tr.* to pour forth; to spurt; (fig.) — denari, to spend money like water.

sforacchi-are [A 4] *tr.* to bore, to drill holes in; to pierce. (**-ato** *part. adj.*) **-atura** *f.* boring of holes; holes bored.

sforbici-are [A 3] *tr.* to cut (with scissors), to snip; to cut out. (**-ato** *part. adj.*) **-atura** *f.* press-cutting.

sform-are [A I c] *tr.* to deform; to disfigure; to destroy the shape of, to pull out of shape; (foundr.) to shake out, to remove the mould from; *abs.*, *rfl.* to lose shape; (fig., fam.) to lose patience, to forget oneself, to be rude. **-ato** *part. adj.* deformed; disfigured; disproportioned; shapeless; ugly; (shoem.) removed from the last; *n.m.* shape, vegetables, pudding, etc., cooked as a mould. **-atamente** *adv.* excessively, without restraint. **-atura** *f.* (sculp.) casting (in a mould); (foundr.) shake-out.

sformo *m.* (eng.) taper in a die to allow the finished article to come out.

sfornaciare [A 3] *tr.* to take out of the furnace.

sforn-are [A I c] *tr.* to take out of the oven; to dish up, to serve out; (fig.) — un libro nuovo, to bring out a new book. **-ata** *f.* batch. (**-ato** *part. adj.*) **-atura** *f.* removal from the oven; dishing-up, serving out.

sforn-ire [D 2] *tr.* (*prep.* di) to strip (of); to deprive (of); to leave (without); to dispossess; *rfl.* to run short (of); to become dispossessed (of); to be stripped (of). **-ito** *part. adj.* stripped; deprived; dispossessed; destitute; unprovided; (mil.) -ito di artiglierie, short of artillery; -ito del porto d'armi, not having a firearms permit.

†**sfortificare** *tr.* (mil.) to dismantle.

sfortun-a *f.* bad luck; misfortune. **-ato** *part. adj.* unlucky; unfortunate; (provb.) fortunato al giuoco -ato in amore, lucky at cards unlucky in love. **-atamente** *adv.* unfortunately; unhappily; as ill luck would have it.

†**sfortunio** *m.* See **infortunio**.

sforz-are [A I] *tr.* to force; to compel; to constrain; to urge; (naut.) to drive; — di vele, to crowd with sail; (mil.) to force (a pass or defence); to occupy; †to weaken; *rfl.* (*prep.* di) to strive (to); to make every effort (to); mi -ai di riuscire, I did everything I could to succeed; si -a di capire, he tries very hard to understand; to strain oneself. **-amento** *m.* force, violence; compulsion; (mus.) extension (in violin fingering). **-ando** *ger.* (mus.) with strong accentuation. **-ato** *part. adj.* forced; coerced; excessive; unnatural; under pressure; vino -ato, wine made in vessels hermetically closed; (mil.) taken by force, cleared of enemy forces; expunged; (leg.) forced; galera -ata, hard labour. **-atamente** *adv.* under compulsion; by force; violently. (**-atore** *m.* **-atrice** *f.*) **-atura** *f.* forcing, compulsion; something forced; exaggeration; caricature; artificiality.

sforz-o *m.* effort; endeavour; exertion; fare ogni —, to strive hard; senza —, without (any) effort; (eng.) stress; — di flessione, bending stress; — di taglio, shearing stress; strain; (mil.) thrust, blow, attack; weight of the attack; (naut.) working or labouring of a ship in bad weather.

sfoss-are [A I] *tr.* to remove from a ditch or pit; (tanning) to remove (hides) from the pit, to 'haul'. (**-ato**[1] *part. adj.* **-atura** *f.*)

sfossato[2] *adj.* (of eyes) deep-set.

sfottere [B I] *tr.* (pop.) to tease; to make fun of.

sfracass-are [A I] *tr.* to shatter. (**-amento** *m.* **-ato** *part. adj.*)

sfracell-are [A I] *tr.* to shatter; to smash; *rfl.* to smash oneself up, to get badly hurt; to be shattered, smashed; -arsi in pezzi, to be smashed to pieces. **-amento** *m.* shattering, smashing. **-ato** *part. adj.* shattered; smashed.

sfragi·stica *f.* sphragistics (specialized study of seals or rings).

sfranare [A I] and derivs. See **franare**.

sfrances-are [A I c] *tr.* to free from French habits; to rid of gallicisms; *intr.* (*aux.* avere) (joc.) to speak French badly; *rfl.* to rid oneself of French ways. (**-ato** *part. adj.*)

sfranchire [D 2] *tr.* to free; to give ease or confidence to; *rfl.* to acquire facility; to gain confidence; to become less timid; to grow bolder.

sfrangi-are [A 3] *tr.* to fray out, to make into a fringe. **-amento** *m.* (eng.) feathering, having a rough edge. (**-ato** *part. adj.* **-atura** *f.*)

sfrantum-are [A I] *tr.* to shatter, to break to pieces. (**-ato** *part. adj.*)

sfrascare [A 2] *tr.* to cut out boughs and foliage from; to take out silk cocoons from; *intr.* (*aux.* avere) (of foliage) to rustle.

sfraso *m.* (finan.) misappropriation of funds; residue of tickets left unsold; fragment.

sfrat-are [A I] *tr.* to unfrock (friar or monk); *rfl.* to unfrock oneself; to leave a religious order. (**-ato** *part. adj.*)

sfratt-are [A I] *tr.* to expel, to turn out; to dismiss; (leg.) to evict. **-o** *m.* expulsion; dismissal; eviction; (leg.) intimazione di -o, notice to quit (C.C.P.).

sfrecciare [A 3] *intr.* (*aux.* essere) to flash past; to speed past; to whizz past.

sfredd-are [A I c] *tr.* to cool; to chill. (**-ato** *part. adj.*) **-ire** [D 2] *intr.* (*aux.* essere), *rfl.* to get cool; to get cold.

sfreg-are [A 2] *tr.* to rub; (text.) to dress (flax); *rfl.* to rub oneself (cf. **fregare**). **-acciare** [A 3] *tr.* to rub lightly; to draw little strokes on; to scrawl on. **-ac·ciolo** *m.* scrawl. **-amento** *m.* rubbing; (text.) dressing (of flax). **-ata** *f.* rub. **-ato** *part. adj.* rubbed; carta -ata, lined paper. **-atore** *m.* (text.) rubbing gear. (**-atura** *f.*) **-olare** [A I s] *tr.* to rub gently. **-olata** *f.* (text.) dressed; light rubbing; gentle friction.

sfregi-are [A 3 c] *tr.* to disfigure; to deface; to slash; (fig.) to disgrace; to sully. **-ato** *part. adj.* disfigured; defaced; (fig.) disgraced; sullied; *n.m.* 'scarface'. (**-atore** *m.* **-atrice** *f.*)

sfregio *m.* disfigurement; gash, cut, scar; slash; (fig.) slur, affront; disgrace.

sfregolare [A I s]. See under **sfregare**.

sfren-are [A I c] *tr.* to let loose; to give rein to; to let fly; *rfl.* to let oneself go; to throw off all restraint. **-amento** *m.* letting loose; letting fly. **-atag·gine** *f.* licence; licentiousness. **-atezza** *f.* looseness, wildness; profligacy; licentiousness. **-ato** *part. adj.* unbridled, unrestrained; excessive; wild; dissolute; unlicensed;

sfren-are (*cont.*)

licentious. **-atamente** *adv.* wildly; unrestrainedly; immoderately; dissolutely. **-ellare** [A I] *tr.* (naut.) to cast off, to unlash; *intr.* (*aux.* avere) to take off the tiller ropes, to remove thole pin grommets; to dip the oars in the water when getting under way.

sfrido *m.* (industr.) wastage; scrap.

sfrig·gere [C5] *intr.* (*aux.* essere) to hiss (cf. **sfriggolare**).

sfri(g)golare [A I s] *intr.* (*aux.* avere) to hiss, to splutter, to sizzle (as in frying).

sfringuell-are [A I] *intr.* (*aux.* avere) to twitter, to warble; to chatter; to blab. **-ino** *m.* chatterbox; indiscreet talker.

sfriṣ-are [A I] *tr.* to graze (at billiards, etc.). **-o** *m.* graze, grazing stroke (at billiards).

sfrittellare [A I] *intr.* (*aux.* avere) to cook fritters; *tr.* to spatter with grease (e.g. in frying); *rfl.* to become spattered with grease (with frying).

sfrogiato *adj.* (of a horse) having wide nostrils.

sfrollato *adj.* very soft; (of meat) high.

sfrombol-are [A I s] *tr.* to throw from a sling. **-ata** *f.* blow with missile from a sling.

sfrond-are [A I c] *tr.* to strip of leaves; (fig.) to remove superfluities from; to curtail; to diminish the reputation of; *rfl.* (of a plant) to lose its leaves. (**-amento** *m.*) **-ato** *part. adj.* stripped of leaves; curtailed; diminished in reputation. **-atoio** *m.* (silkb.) leaf stripper. (**-atore** *m.* **-atrice** *f.*) **-atura** *f.* (agric.) stripping of leaves.

sfrontat-o *adj.* shameless; impudent; cheeky; unblushing. **-amente** *adv.* impudently, cheekily; shamelessly; unblushingly. **-ag·gine** *f.* shamelessness. **-ezza** *f.* effrontery; impudence; shamelessness.

sfronzare [A I c] *intr.* (*aux.* avere) (bookb.) to trim the edges of the leaves (also *tr.*); (agric., of sown corn) to form the blade.

sfrottolare [A I s] and derivs. *intens.* of **frottolare**, q.v.

sfrusc-iare [A 3] *intr.* (*aux.* avere) to rustle. **-io** *m.* continuous rustling.

sfrutacchione *m.* (zool.) a name for various kinds of snake.

sfrutt-are [A I] *tr.* (agric.) — il suolo, to overwork the soil, to exhaust the soil; (fig.) to overwork; to exploit; to take advantage of; to sweat; to speculate on; — le circostanze, to profit by circumstances; (leg.) — i guadagni di una prostituta, to live on the immoral earnings of a woman (C.P.). **-amento** *m.* exploitation; working to exhaustion; overworking; abuse; (mining) working of a deposit; (leg.) -amento di prostitute, living on earnings of prostitution. **-ato** *part. adj.* exhausted; exploited; worked out; rendered sterile; (of labour) sweated. **-atore** *m.* exploiter; profiteer; sweater (of labour); (leg.) souteneur. (**-atrice** *f.*)

sfucin-are [A I] *tr.* to take from the forge; to take from the oven; to serve up; (fig.) to bring out, to produce. †**-ata** *f.* large quantity. (**-ato** *part. adj.*)

sfugg-ire [D I] *tr.* to escape; to avoid; to shun; *intr.* (*aux.* essere; *prep.* a) to escape; to slip; to slip out; to pass unnoticed; — all'attenzione di uno, to escape a person's notice; m'è -ito il suo nome, his name escapes me, I have forgotten his name; la lettera gli -ì di mano, the letter slipped from his hand; nulla gli -e, nothing escapes him; — a una promessa, to break a promise; lasciarsi — una occasione, to miss an opportunity; lasciarsi — un segreto, to let a secret out; (art; archit.) to recede, to be foreshortened, to diminish in perspective. **-ente** *part. adj.* fleeing; evasive; sguardi -enti, shifty looks; fronte -ente, receding forehead. **-evole** *adj.* fleeting, transitory; ephemeral; slippery. **-evolmente** *adv.* fleetingly. **-evolezza** *f.* transitoriness. **-imento** *m.* escape; slipping away; (art) recession, receding (in perspective). **-ita** *f.* short visit; little jaunt; trip; fare una -ita a, to pay a short visit to, to go away for a few days to; *adv. phr.* alla -ita, di -ita, hastily, stealthily, in passing, incidentally. **-ito** *part. adj.* escaped; disappeared; -ito all'attenzione, unnoticed; -ito alla mente, forgotten; vestito -ito, coat (dress) that has become too short or too tight.

sfum-are [A I] *intr.* (*aux.* essere) to smoke, to evaporate; to fade away; to disappear, to vanish; (fig.) to end in smoke, to come to nothing; *tr.* to evaporate, to boil away; (art, of colour) to shade off, to graduate; (of line, shadow) to soften, to stump; (of sound) to diminish gradually, to fade; (radio, recording, etc.) to fade down. **-amento** *m.* shading; evaporation; fading away; trace. **-ante** *part. adj.* vanishing; fading; (of colours) shading off, graduated. **-atezza** *f.* (art) delicacy of shading or gradation. **-ato** *part. adj.* evaporated; vanished; lost; (fig.) gone up in smoke;

(art) soft, mellow, delicately shaded; pittore -ato, painter who uses soft colours and shaded outlines; colore -ato, pale colour; luce -ata, soft light; *n.m.* shading; (art) sfumato, gradation; (photog.) soft focus. **-atamente** *adv.* delicately, with nice gradation; little by little, by degrees. **-atura** *f.* (paint.) shading, gradation of colours; light wash of colour; shade, nuance; touch (of colour, etc.); slight suggestion, hint; trace. **-ino** *m.* (art) stump.

sfunare [A I] *rfl.* (naut.) to untie, to cast off.

sfuocato *adj.* (opt.; photog.) out of focus.

sfuri-are [A 4] *intr.* (*aux.* avere), *rfl.* to fly into a passion, to give vent to one's anger; *tr.* to vent, to give vent to (anger, etc.). **-ata** *f.* outburst (of passion, anger); scolding; burst of energy; per gli esami fece una -ata, he worked like fury for his exams; spasm (of pain, illness); -ata di pioggia, sudden heavy shower; (pop.) fare una -ata a uno, 'to blow a person up'.

sfuṣo *adj.* (pop.) loose, unpacked (esp. of cigarettes).

ṣgabbi-are [A I] *tr.* to take out of bond; †*rfl.* -arsi di, to get rid of; (euphem.) to kill. **-ato** *part. adj.* cleared, freed from bond.

ṣgabell-are [A I] *tr.* to take out of bond; †*rfl.* -arsi di, to get rid of; (euphem.) to kill. **-ato** *part. adj.* cleared, freed from bond.

ṣgabell-o *m.* stool; bench (with no back); (fig.) farsi — di uno, to make use, to make a convenience, of somebody. **-ata** *f.* blow with a stool. **-one** *m.* ledge, shelf, bracket.

ṣgabuẓẓino *m.* small room; lumber-room; recess, closet; poky hole; (mil.) officers' dug-out.

ṣgagliard-are [A I] *tr.* to weaken, to enfeeble. (**-ato** *part. adj.*) **-ire** [D 2] *tr.*, *rfl.* to weaken, to grow weak. (**-ito** *part. adj.*)

ṣgaid-are [A I] *tr.* (dressm.) to cut on the cross. **-ato** *part. adj.* cut on the cross. (**-atura** *f.*)

†**ṣgalante** *adj.* ungallant.

ṣgalera *f.* (bot.) cardoon, *Cynara cardunculus.*

ṣgall-ettare [A I c] *intr.* (*aux.* avere) to play the wit; to be sprightly, to show off (like a cockerel). **-ettio** *m.* continual showing off. †**-inacciare** [A 3] *intr.* (*aux.* avere) (mus.) to screech. †**-uzzare** [A I] *intr.* to make merry.

ṣgamb-are [A I] *tr.* to break the stalk of; *intr.* (*aux.* avere) to stride along; to walk fast; *rfl.* to walk oneself off one's legs, to tire oneself by walking. **-ata** *f.* (pop.) long walk; run. **-ato** *part. adj.* without a stalk; calze -ate, very short socks; run off one's legs, tired out. **-ettare** [A I c] *intr.* (*aux.* avere) to walk with short quick steps; to trip along; (of a child) to toddle; to frolic; to kick the legs about; to gambol; to frisk; to caper. (**-ettata** *f.*) **-etto** *m.* caper; jump; dare lo -etto a, to trip up (esp. at football); (fig.) to oust. **-olio** *m.* frolicking. **-ucciato** *adj.* without stockings, bare-legged.

ṣganasci-are [A 3] *tr.* to dislocate the jaw of; (Tusc.) to unhinge; — un libro, to break the back of a book; *rfl.* to dislocate one's jaw; -arsi dalle risa, to split one's sides with laughing; (joc.) to exercise one's jaws (i.e. to eat). **-amento** *m.* dislocation; pulling to pieces. **-ante** *part. adj.* riso -ante, boisterous laughter. **-apo·poli** *m. indecl.* (joc.) dentist. **-ata** *f.* roar of laughter; boisterous laugh. **-ato** *part. adj.* broken-jawed; broken, rickety; ramshackle. **-one** *m.* box on the ear.

ṣganci-are [A 3] *tr.* to uncouple; to unhook; to release; — bombe, to drop bombs; *rfl.* to be uncoupled; to be unhooked; to be released; (fig.) to make off, to decamp. **-abombe** *m. indecl.* (aeron.) bomb release. (**-amento** *m.* **-ato** *part. adj.*)

ṣganci·o *m.* See **schiancio**.

ṣgangher-are [A I s] *tr.* to unhinge; to dislocate; to undo; to pull to pieces; *rfl.* to become unhinged; to become dislocated; to come undone; to come to pieces. **-amento** *m.* unhinging; dislocating. **-ato** *part. adj.* unhinged; disjointed; awkward; loose; ramshackle, rickety; coarse, immoderate. **-atamente** *adv.* disjointedly; awkwardly; immoderately; ridere -atamente, to laugh boisterously.

ṣgann-are [A I] *tr.* to undeceive; *rfl.* to be undeceived; to learn the truth. (**-amento** *m.* **-ato** *part. adj.*)

ṣgarb-o *m.* discourtesy; rudeness, incivility; offence; bad grace. **-atag·gine** *f.* rudeness; unmannerliness. **-atezza** *f.* rudeness; unmannerliness; roughness; awkwardness, clumsiness. **-ato** *adj.* rude; unmannerly; rough; awkward, clumsy. (**-atamente** *adv.*) **-eri·a** *f.* rudeness; discourteous act or words.

ṣgargarizzare [A I] and derivs. *intens.* of **gargarizzare**, q.v.

ṣgargi-are [A 3] *intr.* (*aux.* avere) to show off, to cut a dash. **-ante** *part. adj.* showy; gaudy; (of colour) 'loud', violent.

†**ṣgari·glio** *m.* See **sgherro**.

sgarr-are [A I] *intr.* (*aux.* avere) to err, to be mistaken; to go wrong; (of a clock) to gain; to lose; — (di) cinque minuti al giorno, to gain, *or* to lose five minutes a day; *tr.* to mistake; parole che non -avano il segno, words that struck home; (of a person) non — mai un minuto, to be always dead on time. **-aménto** *m.* error.

sgarz-a[1] *f.* (tanning) slicker. **-are** [A I] *tr.* (tanning) to shave, to slicker-whiten.

sgarza[2] *f.* (orn.) heron, esp. 'sgarza ciuffetto', squacco heron, *Ardeola ralloides*.

sgarza[3] *f.* (Tusc.). See **cipero**.

sgattaiolare [A I] *intr.* (*aux.* essere) to wriggle out; to slip away.

sgavazzare [A I] *intr.* (*aux.* avere) to revel, to carouse.

sgelare [A I] and derivs. See **disgelare**.

sgessare [A I] *tr.* to knock the plaster from.

sghęmb-o *adj.* crooked; oblique, slanting; (fig.) odd, queer, comical; (geom.) rette -e, right angles not in the same plane; *n.m.* crookedness; slant; *adv. phr.* a —, aslant, obliquely; crookedly; colla cravatta a —, with one's tie askew; andare a —, to walk crabwise. **-are** [A I c] *intr.* (*aux.* avere) to slant; to be oblique.

sgheronato *adj.* cut aslant; shaped like a gore or gusset; sottana sgheronata, gored skirt.

sghęrro, **sghęrro** *m.* hired ruffian, assassin; *adj.* ruffianly.

sghiacciare [A 3] (pop., Tusc.) See **sdiacciare**.

sghiaiatóre *m.* gravel-trap, ditch to catch the gravel washed down by a river.

sghignare [A 5] and derivs. *intens.* of **ghignare**, q.v.

sghignazz-are [A I] *intr.* (*aux.* avere) to laugh scornfully; to guffaw. **-aménto** *m.* derisive laughter. **-ata** *f.* burst of derisive laughter; hoot, guffaw. **-io** *m.* continual guffaws.

†**sghignoso** *adj.* See **schizzinoso**.

sghilęmbo *adj.* (colloq., Tusc.). See **sghembo**.

sghimbe·scio *m.* oblique line; *adv. phr.* a, di, —, obliquely (cf. **sghembo**).

sghind-are [A I] *tr.* (naut.) to unrig a yard or topmast (generally implying also its striking down to the deck). **-ato** *part. adj.* (naut.) tutto -ato, unrigged, completely unready for sea; (fig., of a person) ill turned-out.

sghiribizzo *m.* and derivs. (pop.). See **ghiribizzo**.

†**sgiudiziato** *adj.* lacking in judgement.

sgnaccare [A 2] *tr.* (mil. slang) to hunt, to chase; — in prigione, to cast into prison.

sgnauli·o *m.* See **gnauli·o**.

sgobbare [A I] *intr.* (*aux.* avere) to become hunchbacked; to work (too) hard, to slave; (slang) 'to swot'.

sgobb-o *m.* hard work, grind; lavoro di —, drudgery. **-óne** *m.* hard worker; drudge; unintelligent but hard-working student; (slang) swot. (**-óna** *f.*)

sgocciol-are [A I sc] *tr.* to pour out in drops; to drain to the last drop; *intr.* (*aux.* avere, essere) to drip, to trickle; (of a secret) to leak out. (**-aménto** *m.* **-ato** *part. adj.*) **-atóio** *m.* eaves; cornice over a window; drip-stone; cup or other vessel to catch drops; frame to hold, e.g. photographic plates, to allow dripping; (paperm.) ass, drainer. **-atura** *f.* dripping, dropping; scattered drops; dregs; (fig.) very end; (archit.) gutter (of roof). **-io** *m.* constant dripping.

sgocciolo *m.* dripping; last drop; (fig.) very end; last little bit, fag-end; essere agli sgoccioli, to have almost none left (e.g. of money, etc.), to be at the end of one's tether.

sgol-are [A I c] *rfl.* to tire one's throat; to shout oneself hoarse; *tr.* (art) to cut mouldings in (esp. in woodwork). **-ato** *part. adj.* hoarse (with talking); †see **scollato**.

sgomarello *m.* ladle used for molten iron.

sgomb(e)r-are [A I s] *tr.* to clear; to remove; to sweep away; to evacuate; — il passo a, to make way for; — la mente dalle preoccupazioni, to free one's mind from anxieties; (naut.) — la coperta, to clear the decks; — la fronte, to clear the arc of fire; (mil.) to abandon a position, to retreat to a safe position; (comm.) to clear; *intr.* (*aux.* avere) to go away; to pass; to depart; to move house; to clear out. (**-aménto** *m.* **-ato** *part. adj.*) **-atóre** *m.* furniture remover; *adj.* relating to removal. (**-atrice** *f.*) **-atura** *f.* removal, move; customary or periodic time for removing; cost of removal.

sgombero, **sgombro**[1] *apocop.* of **sgomb(e)rare**, q.v.; *adj.* clear; free; empty; untenanted; *n.m.* clearing; freeing; removal; emptying.

sgombro[2] *m.* (ichth., pop.) mackerel. See **scombro**.

sgoment-are [A I c], †*-ire* *tr.* to terrify; to dismay; to alarm; to discourage; *rfl.* to be frightened, alarmed, dismayed. **-aménto** *m.* alarm. (**-ato**, †*-ito part. adj.*)

sgoment-o *apocop. part.*; *adj.* frightened, alarmed, dismayed; discouraged; *n.m.* dismay; alarm, fright; terror; discouragement. **-óne** *m.* person easily frightened or discouraged. (**-óna** *f.*)

sgomin-are [A I c, A I] *tr.* to throw into disorder; to disperse, to rout; (mil.) to defeat, to disperse, to rout. **-ato** *part. adj.* thrown into confusion; routed. **-io** *m.* rout, dispersal; utter confusion.

sgomitolare [A I s] *tr.* to unwind (e.g. a ball of wool); *rfl.* (of ball of wool, etc.) to come unwound, to unwind (itself).

sgomm-are [A I c] *tr.* to unstick; to remove gum from; (text.) to degum. **-ato** *part. adj.* unstuck; (text.) degummed. **-atura** *f.* unsticking; (text.) degumming, scouring.

sgonfi-are [A I sc] *tr.* to deflate; to reduce, to bring down; to empty of air; to flatten out; (fig.) to annoy, to vex; to bore; *rfl.* to be deflated; (of a swelling) to go down; (of pride, etc.) to be pricked; to go flat; to collapse. **-aménto** *m.* deflating. **-ato** *part. adj.* deflated; pallone -ato, pricked balloon (also fig.). **-atura** *f.* deflation.

sgonfi-o *part. apocop.* of sgonfiare, q.v.; *adj.* deflated; flattened; gone soft and flabby; pricked; punctured; *n.m.* bubble; (dressm.) puff. **-otto** *m. dim.* (dressm.) small puff; (cul.) pastry puff.

sgonnell-are [A I] *intr.* (*aux.* avere) (of a woman) to gad about, to be flighty. **-óna** *f.* gad-about, flighty woman.

sgorbia *f.* gouge, chisel; (techn.) kind of mould used in tile-making; (surg.) gouge.

sgor·bi-o *m.* blot; scrawl; crossing out; daub; (of a person) a 'fright', a 'sight'. **-are** [A 4] *tr.* to blot; to daub, to stain; to scrawl on. **-ato** *part. adj.* blotted; daubed; scrawled on. (**-atóre** *m.* **-atrice** *f.*) **-atura** *f.* scrawl(ing); blot; stain.

sgorg-are [A 2 c] *intr.* (*aux.* essere) to gush; to gush forth; to spout; to spring; to well up; to flow; il fiume -a nel mare, the river flows into the sea; *tr.* to disgorge; to pour out. **-aménto** *m.* gushing; spouting; pouring forth. **-ante** *part. adj.* gushing; flowing; spouting. **-ata** *f.* gush; discharge. **-atóio** *m.* spout. (**-atóre** *m.* **-atrice** *f.*)

sgor-go *m.* (*pl.* -ghi) pouring; gush; *adv. phr.* a —, abundantly, freely.

sgottare [A I c] *tr.* to pump out, to bale out.

sgovern-o *m.* misgovernment; mismanagement. **-are** [A I] *tr.* to misgovern; to mismanage. (**-ato** *part. adj.*)

sgozz-are [A I c] *tr.* to cut the throat of; (fig.) to bleed (by usury). (**-ato** *part. adj.*) **-atóre** *m.* cut-throat. (**-atrice** *f.*) **-atura** *f.* (butcher's) kosher slaughtering; (fig.) slaughter. **-ino** *m.* usurer.

†**sgradare** *vb.* and derivs. See **digradare**.

sgradévol-e *adj.* unpleasant; disagreeable. **-ménte** *adv.* unpleasantly; disagreeably.

sgrad-ire [D 2] *tr.* to be displeased with; not to welcome; vi prego di non —, be pleased to accept; *intr.* (*aux.* essere; *prep.* a) to be displeasing or unwelcome (to). **-ito** *part. adj.* unpleasant; unwelcome; undesirable; disagreeable.

sgraffa *f.* (typ.) paragraph sign; brace.

sgraffi-are [A 4] *tr.* to scratch; to steal; (colloq.) to 'pinch'; (art) to draw on plaster with a pointed tool. (**-ato** *part. adj.*) **-atóre** *m.* scratcher; plaster-decorator. **-atura** *f.* scratch. **-gnare** [A s] *tr.* (colloq.) to steal, to 'pinch'; to carry off. (**-gnato** *part. adj.*)

sgraf·fio *m.* scratch; implement used for drawing on a plastered wall by scratching the white plaster to show a black layer underneath.

sgraffire [D 2] *tr.* see **sgraffiare**; *intr.* (*aux.* avere) (art) to do graffito work.

sgrammatic-are [A 2 s] *intr.* (*aux.* avere) to be ungrammatical. **-ato** *part. adj.* ungrammatical; full of grammatical mistakes. **-atura** *f.* mistake in grammar. **-óne** *m.* (derog.) person who habitually makes mistakes in grammar. (**-óna** *f.*)

sgran-are [A I] *tr.* to shell (peas, etc.); to hull; to husk; — il rosario, to say one's rosary, (iron.) to utter a string of oaths; — paternostri, to say prayers; (eng.) to crash gears; (text.) to gin (e.g. cotton); (naut.) to disengage (cable from a capstan); to devour, to eat with great relish; — gli occhi, to open one's eyes wide; *rfl.* to crumble; to fall to dust; (sport) to spread out (of runners, cyclists, etc.). (**-a·bile** *adj.* **-aménto** *m.*) **-ato** *part. adj.* shelled, hulled, husked; (of grapes, etc.) separated from the stalk; occhi -ati, staring eyes. **-atóio** *m.* machine for shelling, hulling, etc.

sgran-are (*cont.*)

-**atore** *m.* see **sgranatoio.** -**atrice** *f.* (text.) gin; -atrice a cilindri, roller gin; opificio delle -atrici, gin house, ginnery. -**atura** *f.* shelling; hulling; husking; (text.) ginning (of cotton).

sgranchiare [A 4] and derivs. See **sgranchire.**

sgranch-ire [D 2] *tr.* to stretch; *rfl.* (acc. of prn. 'si') to stretch oneself to action; (dat. of prn. 'si') sgranchirsi le gambe, to stretch one's legs. (-**ito** *part. adj.*)

sgranell-are [A I] *tr.* to pick (grains) from the ear; to pick (grapes) from the bunch. (-**amento** *m.* -**ato** *part. adj.*) -**atoio** *m.* machine or tool for picking grapes, ginning cotton, etc. -**atura** *f.* picking; separating; (text.) ginning.

sgranocchiare [A 4] *tr.* to munch, to eat with enjoyment.

sgrappolatoio *m.* wooden grating on which grapes are separated from their stalks.

sgrass-are [A I] *tr.* to remove grease from, to skim the fat off; (techn.) to degrease. (-**ato** *part. adj.*) -**atore** *m.* (techn.) degreaser. -**atura** *f.* (techn.) degreasing.

†**sgratare** *intr.* to be displeasing.

sgraticciare [A 3] *tr.* to take (trelliswork, etc.) to pieces; — una siepe, to thin out and tidy a hedge.

sgrav-are [A I] *tr.* to relieve of weight; to unload; to lighten; — la coscienza a, to relieve the conscience of; mi hai -ato da un gran pensiero, you have taken a great load off my mind; *rfl.* (acc. of prn. 'si') to be relieved of a burden; to unburden oneself; -arsi del feto, to give birth; (dat. of prn. 'si') -arsi la coscienza, to ease one's conscience. -**amento** *m.* lightening, alleviation; relief. -**ato** *part. adj.* unburdened, lightened. (-**atore** *m.* -**atrice** *f.*) †-**idanza** *f.* birth, delivery. -**idare** [A I s] *intr.* (*aux.* essere) to be delivered (of a child); to miscarry.

sgra·vio *m.* relief; alleviation; lightening; — delle imposte, reduction in taxation; per — di coscienza, for conscience sake; clearing of alluvial gravel, sand, etc. from rivers; evacuation (of the bowels).

†**sgra·zia** *f.* and derivs. See **disgrazia.**

sgraziat-o *part. adj.* awkward, clumsy; ungainly, ungraceful; graceless; †wretched, unfortunate; *n.m.* awkward or clumsy person. (-**a** *f.*) -**amente** *adv.* awkwardly, clumsily. -**aggine** *f.* clumsiness; ungainliness.

sgretol-are [A I sc] *tr.* to grind; to pound; to crumble; to crush to bits; to crunch; — i denti, to grind one's teeth; *rfl.* to crumble; to fall to pieces; to disperse gradually (e.g. of a crowd). (-**amento** *m.*) -**ato** *part. adj.* ground; pounded; crumbling; crushed; rocce -ate dalle acque, rocks broken up by the action of water. -**io** *m.* continual grinding, pounding, etc. -**oso** *adj.* crumbly; friable.

sgricchiare [A 4] *intr.* (*aux.* avere) to giggle; to chuckle.

sgridacchiare [A 4] *tr.* to grumble at; to scold a little; to chide.

sgrid-are[1] [A I] *tr.* to scold; to rebuke; to reprimand; to rail at. -**ata** *f.* scolding; rebuke; reprimand. -**ato** *part. adj.* scolded; rebuked; reprimanded. (-**atore** *m.* -**atrice** *f.*)

†**sgridare**[2] *tr.* to banish, to exile (cf. **grida**).

sgrigiato *adj.* tinged with grey.

sgrigiolare [A I s] *intr.* (*aux.* avere) to creak (e.g. of new shoes); to emit a crunching sound.

sgri·gli-o *m.* creaking sound. -**olare** [A I s] *intr.* (*aux.* avere) to creak.

sgri·gliolo *m.* creak; crunching sound.

†**sgrigno** *m.* and derivs. See **scrigno.**

sgrillettare [A I c] *tr.* to pull the trigger of (a firearm); *intr.* (*aux.* avere) (of a trigger) to be released, to go off; (cul.) to sputter, to spit.

sgrin·fia *f.* (pop.). See **grinfia.**

sgromm-are [A I c] *tr.* to cleanse (e.g. casks) of incrustation. (-**ato** *part. adj.* -**atura** *f.*)

sgrond-are [A I c] *intr.* (*aux.* essere) to drip; to trickle; *tr.* to put to drip; to leave to drain. -**atoio** *m.* perforated board where bottles are set to drip, bottle-rack. (-**atura** *f.*) -**io** *m.* continual dripping.

sgrondo *m.* dripping; mettere a —, to set to drip; terreno a —, sloping, well-drained ground.

sgroppare[1] [A I] *tr.* to unknot; to untie; to disentangle (cf. **groppo**).

sgropp-are[2] [A I] *intr.* (*aux.* avere) (of a horse) to kick out with both hind legs. -**ata** *f.* a horse's kick with both hind legs; (cycle racing) fare una -ata, to make a great effort when going uphill. -**onare** [A I c] *intr.* (*aux.* avere) (of a horse) to buck; *rfl.* to make one's back ache by bending over work. -**onata** *f.* bucking movement (cf. **groppa**).

sgross-are [A I] *tr.* to whittle down; to reduce to proper size or shape; (sculp.) to rough out, to rough-cast; (eng.) to rough; — al tornio, to rough-turn. -**amento** *m.* whittling down; roughing out. (-**ato** *part. adj.*) -**atore** *m.* (eng.) rougher. -**atura** *f.* (eng.) roughing.

sgrott-are [A I] *tr.* to hollow-out; to dig (a trench); — vino, to take wine from the cellar; *intr.* (*aux.* essere) to cave in, to subside. -**amento** *m.* hollowing out; cavity. (-**ato** *part. adj.* -**atura** *f.*)

sgrovigli-are [A 4], -**olare** [A I s] *tr.* to disentangle; to untie.

sgrugn-are [A 5] *tr.* (fam.) to punch on the snout. -**ata** *f.* punch on the snout; grunt; parlare a -ate, to speak in a series of grunts. -**o** *m.* (fam.) punch on the snout.

sgrupp-are [A I] *tr.* to remove or release from a group. (-**ato** *part. adj.*)

sguaiat-o *adj.* ill-mannered; awkward; rude; shameless; unpleasant, disagreeable; *n.m.* lout. -**amente** *adv.* rudely; awkwardly. -**aggine** *f.* rudeness; coarseness; awkwardness; slovenliness; shamelessness; stupidity.

sguain-are [A I] *tr.* to unsheathe; to draw (a sword). (-**ato** *part. adj.*)

sgualcire [D 2] and derivs. (pop.). See **gualcire.**

sgualdrina *f.* strumpet, trollop.

sguan·cia *f.* (equit.) cheek piece.

sguan·cio *m.* (bldg.) splay, embrasure.

sguar·dia *f.* (bookb.) end-paper.

sguard-o *m.* look, glance; — fisso, stare; fin dove arriva lo —, as far as the eye can see; al primo —, at first sight, at the first glance; bello —, beautiful view; dare uno — a, to glance at; gettare uno — sopra, to cast one's eye over.

sguarn-ire [D 2] *tr.* to strip of trimmings; (mil.) to leave undefended or without means of defence; to withdraw the garrison from; to reduce the garrison of; (naut.) to disarm (a ship), to pay off, to unrig; to unreeve (a tackle, etc.); †to unbit (the cable); *rfl.* (naut.) to become dismasted by storms, etc. -**ito** *part. adj.* stripped (of trimmings, defences, etc.); devoid of trimmings; undefended.

sguat·ter-o *m.* scullion; scullery-boy. -**a** *f.* scullery-maid.

sguazzare [A I] *intr.* (*aux.* avere) to splash about, to shake (of liquid in a vessel); to wallow; to paddle about; to squelch; (fig.) — nell'oro, to be rolling in money; — in un vestito, to be 'lost' in a coat or dress that is much too big for one; *tr.* to ford; to lead (cattle) into the water; to fritter away, to use wastefully.

sgub·bia *f.* (pop.) see **sgorbia**; (techn.) gouge.

sguerciare [A 3] *rfl.* to strain one's eyesight.

†**sguerciato** *adj.* (naut.) crank (said of a vessel either badly loaded or ill constructed).

sguercire [D 2] *intr.* (*aux.* essere), *rfl.* to strain one's eyesight; to peer, to squinny.

sguerguenza *f.* (fam., Tusc.) prank, trick; naughtiness; bad behaviour.

sguernire [D 2] and derivs. See **sguarnire.**

†**sguiggiare** *tr.* to remove the sandal-strap from; (fig.) to rob.

sguinc-iare [A 3] *tr.* to cut obliquely, to cut on the cross. (-**ato** *part. adj.*) -**i·o** *adj.* oblique, slanting; askew.

sguinzagli-are [A 4] *tr.* to unleash, to let off the lead; to let loose; — dietro a, to set on the track of. (-**ato** *part. adj.*)

sguisciare [A 3] and derivs. (fam. Tusc.). See **sgusciare.**

sguizzare [A I] and derivs. See **guizzare.**

sgusci-are [A 3] *tr.* to shell; to hull; to husk; *intr.* (*aux.* essere) to slip away, to steal away; to slough, to cast, to shed (a skin); to become hollow (like a shell or pod). -**ata** *f.* pile of pods or shells. -**ato** *part. adj.* (of peas, beans, etc.) shelled; (archit.) shell-shaped, hollowed out; *n.m.* hollow, shell (carved or modelled). -**atura** *f.* shelling; hollowing out.

sgu·scio *m.* chaser's gouge; notch, hollow.

shunt *m. indecl.* (as Eng.) (electr.) shunt. -**are** [A I] *tr.* (electr.) to shunt.

si *rfl. prn. conjunct.* himself; herself; itself; oneself; themselves; *recip.* each other, one another; *indef. prn.* one; people; we; they; — dice, they say, it is said; — dice da tutti, everyone says; in Inghilterra — beve molto tè, in England they drink a lot of tea; — parte dunque?, shall we set off then?; (corresponding to an English passive voice): — parla inglese, English spoken; questi articoli — vendono solo a dozzine, these articles are only sold by the dozen; — affittano appartamenti, flats to let; (with 'noi' added when implying 'we') noi — stava facendo due chiacchiere, we were just having a little chat; (pleonastic) poco mancò, che egli non — morisse, he very nearly died.

sì[1] *affirm. particle* yes; rispondere di —, to answer yes, to give an affirmative answer; (in response to a knock on the door) come in!; — davvero!, yes indeed!; ma —!, yes, of course; forse che — forse che no, maybe or maybe not; accennare di —, to nod assent; voto per 'sì' e per 'no', vote by 'yes' and 'no'; mi par di —, I think so; (in marriage ceremony) —, I will; mangiare un giorno — e l'altro no, to get a meal only every other day; *adv. phr.* — e no, about, more or less; si vedeva — e no, it was dimly visible; ricevetti — la tua lettera, ma..., I did get your letter, but...; mi ha detto — che sarebbe venuto, he certainly told me he would come; e — che, and yet; *n.m.* yes, affirmative answer; la lingua del —, Italian.

sì[2] *adv.* so; thus; — fatto (*or* **siffatto**), such; era pieno — d'ignoranza, — di superbia, he was both ignorant and full of pride.

sì[3] *m.* (mus.) te (i.e. the seventh degree of the scale); the note B; the key of B.

sia...sia *conj.* both...and; either...or; whether...or; sia che...sia che, whether...or. (Cf. **essere**.)

sialadenite *f.* (med.) sialadenitis.

sialagogo *adj.* (med.) sialogogic; *n.m.* (med.) sialogogue.

sialorre·a *f.* (med.). See **scialorrea**.

Sia·m *pr.n.f.* (geog.) Siam.

siamẹse *adj.* Siamese; fratelli siamesi, Siamese twins, (fig.) inseparable companions; *n.m., f.* Siamese.

sibar·ita *m., f.* (Gk. antiq.) Sybarite; (fig.) sybarite. **-i·tico** *adj.* sybaritic. **-iticamẹnte** *adv.* sybaritically, in voluptuous ease.

Sib·e·ria *pr.n.f.* (geog.) Siberia (also fig., to denote a very cold climate); va in —!, go to hell! **-eriano, -e·rico** *adj., n.m.* Siberian (also fig.).

sibil·are [A I s] *intr.* (*aux.* avere) to whistle; to hiss; to whizz; to wheeze. **-ante** *part. adj.* hissing; (gramm.) *adj., n.f.* sibilant. (**-atọre** *m.* **-atrice** *f.*) **-io** *m.* continued whistling, hissing, etc.

sibill·a *f.* (class. antiq.) Sibyl; (pop.) fare la —, to predict lottery numbers, to interpret dreams, etc.; (derog.) crafty old woman; giuoco della —, see **sibillone**. **-ino** *adj.* (class. antiq.) Sibylline; libri -ini, Sibylline Books; (fig.) mysterious, ambiguous, oracular. **-ọne** *m.* a literary guessing-game, using cryptic answers; trouble-maker, malicious gossip.

si·bilo *m.* hiss; whistle; (med.) singing in the ears; (telev.) beat frequence, C.W. interference; *pl.* wheezing.

sica *f.* (Rom. antiq.) *sica*, (curved) dagger.

sicambro *adj., n.m.* (hist.) Sigambrian.

sicano *adj.* (ethn.) Sicilian.

sica·rio *m.* assassin, hired ruffian, cut-throat.

siccativo *adj.* see **seccativo**; (chem.; industr.) olio —, drying oil.

sicchè *conj.* so that; with the result that; so; then; — vieni o rimani?, are you coming then, or not?

siccidesẹrta *f.* (geog.) hot desert.

sic·ciolo *m.* See **cicciolo**.

siccità *f.* drought, dryness; aridity; dry weather; (fig.) dryness; (of style) flatness.

siccọme *adv., conj.* as; conveniva aspettare — feci, it was necessary to wait, as I did (and so I did); since, for the reason that.

Sici·li·a *pr.n.f.* (geog.) Sicily. **-ana** *f.* Sicilian woman, Sicilian girl; (mus.) Siciliana, a rustic dance of Sicily in $\frac{6}{8}$ time characterized by the rhythmic figure known as 'saltarello', q.v. **-anismo** *m.* Sicilianism, Sicilian dialect form. **-ano** *adj., n.m.* Sicilian; (hist.) i vespri -ani, the Sicilian Vespers (1282); (agric.) grano -ano, maize.

sicinni, sicin·nide *f.* (Gk. antiq.) Sicinnis, Satyr-dance.

siclo *m.* (Jewish antiq.) shekel (silver coin).

sicofant·e, -a *m.* spy, informer; sycophant.

sico·moro, sicomoro *m.* (bot.) sycamore (of the Bible), *Ficus sycamorus*; sycamore, *Acer pseudoplatanus*.

sicọsi *f.* (med.) sycosis.

sicumera *f.* pomposity; complacency; self-satisfied air.

sicura *f.* See under **sicuro**.

sicur·o *adj.* safe; secure; sure; confident, assured; reliable, trustworthy; notizia -a, news from a reliable source; bold; skilful; (comm.) sound; affari -i, sound business; titoli -i, securities; puoi esser — di lui, you may depend on him; *adv.* undoubtedly, certainly; of course; quite so; naturally; *n.m.* safety; shelter; certainty; al —, in safety; (iron.) essere al —, to be in prison; giocare al —, to play safe; di —, for sure, certainly. **-a** *f.* safety-catch, safety-bolt. **-amẹnte** *adv.* certainly; for sure; boldly, firmly,

steadfastly; in safety. **-ẹzza** *f.* safety, security; certainty; assurance; ispirare -ezza, to inspire confidence; valvola di -ezza, safety-valve; lampada di -ezza, safety-lamp, Davy lamp; rasoio di -ezza, safety-razor; uscita di -ezza, emergency exit; (aeron.) coefficiente di -ezza, safety-factor; cassetta di -ezza, safe; cassette di -ezza, safe deposit; -ezza pubblica, public safety; Pubblica Sicurezza, Police; l'autorità di pubblica -ezza, police authority; agente di pubblica -ezza, policeman; misura di -ezza, precautionary measure; provvedimento di -ezza, security measure; (mil.) covering units, flank, rearguard or forward; -ezza del tiro, accuracy of fire; angolo di -ezza, safety arc; -ezza della canna, test or proving of gun barrel. **†-tà** *f.* see **sicurezza**.

sicut erat (Lat. phrase, sometimes Italianized as **sicutera**) 'As it was in the beginning'; tornare al —, to return to the *status quo*.

sidecarista *m.* (sport) motor-cyclist engaged in side-car racing.

siderale *adj.* See **sidereo**.

siderazịọne *f.* (med.) sideration, sudden or unexpected attack.

side·reo *adj.* of or pertaining to the stars; sidereal; tempo —, sidereal time.

siderite *f.* (miner.) siderite, chalybite.

sider·urgi·a *f.* iron metallurgy; the iron and steel industry. **-ur·gico** *adj.* pertaining to the iron and steel industry.

†sido *m.* intense cold; assideration.

Sidọne *pr.n.f.* (geog.) Sidon.

sidro *m.* cider.

Sien·a *pr.n.f.* (geog.) Sienna, Siena; (paint.) terra di —, sienna; (provb.) per forza —!, inevitably! **-ẹse** *adj., n.m., f.* see **senese**.

sienite (miner.) syenite.

siẹp·e, †-a *f.* hedge; — viva, — naturale, quickset hedge; — morta, — artificiale, fence, hedge or barrier made with cut branches; barrier, hurdle; obstacle; wall; far —, to line a road (e.g. of people watching a procession), *or* to form a barrier; (provb.) ogni pruno fa —, every little helps; (athletics) corsa di -i, hurdle-race, steeplechase; tre chilometri -i, three thousand metres steeplechase. **-a·glia** *f.*, **-a·ia** *f.* thick, overgrown hedge. **-are** [A I] *tr.* to fence in, to hedge round; to enclose.

siẹr·o, -e *m.* serum; (agric.) whey. **-ọsa** *f.* (anat.) serosa. **-osità** *f.* (med.) serosity. **-ọsite** *f.* (med.) serositis. **-ọso** *adj.* (anat.) serous. **-oterapi·a** *f.* (med.) serotherapy.

siesta *f.* siesta, afternoon nap.

siffatt·o *adj.* such, of such a nature; (usu. *pejor.*) gente -a, people of that sort. **†-amẹnte** *adv.* in such a manner, in such wise.

sifil·ico·mio *m.* hospital for venereal diseases. **-ide** *f.* (med.) syphilis. **-i·tico** *adj., n.m.* syphilitic. **-iẓẓare** [A I] *tr.* (med.) to syphilize, to infect with syphilis. (**-iẓẓato** *part. adj.*) **-iẓẓaẓịọne** *f.* (med.) syphilization, infection with syphilis. **-o·ide** *adj.* (med.) syphiloid. **-o·logo** *m.* (med.) syphilologist, specialist in venereal diseases. **-oma** *m.* (med.) syphiloma.

sif·o·id·e *adj.* (anat.) xiphoid, ensiform; *n.f.* xiphoid cartilage. **-oide·o** *adj.* (anat.) xiphoid, ensiform.

sifọn·e *m.* siphon, syphon; — per acqua di selz, sodawater siphon; waterspout; (hydr. eng.) trap, drain trap; U-bend; (zool.) siphon (e.g. of a mollusc); (Byz. hist.) tube containing 'Greek fire'. **-are** [A I C] *tr.* to siphon. **-ato** *part. adj.* siphoned; furnished with a siphon. **-atọre** *m.* (Byz. hist.) siphonator, 'gunner' propelling 'Greek fire'. **-oma** *m.* (surg.) siphonoma.

si·gar·o *m.* cigar; — leggero, dolce, mild cigar. **-a·ia** *f.* woman employed in a tobacco factory. **-a·io** *m.* cigar maker; cigarette maker; itinerant cigar and cigarette-seller. **-ẹtta** *f.* cigarette; (mil. slang) rifle cartridge, round. **-ẹtto** *m. dim.* special type of small cigar. **-iera** *f.* cigar-case.

sigill·o *m.* seal; signet; stamp; mark; (fig.) impression; ho il — alla bocca, my lips are sealed; (leg.) seal; rimozione dei -i, removal of seals; libro di -i, seal book; (eccl.) — della confessione, seal of the confessional; (bot.) — di Salomone, Solomon's seal, *Polygonatum*. **-are** [A I] *tr.* to seal; to close; (colloq.) to round off; to stop up; to mark, to stamp; (leg.) to seal; *intr.* (*aux.* avere) to fit well. **-ato** *part. adj.* sealed; closed; terra -ata, bole, fine ferruginous clay. **-atura** *f.* sealing; seal. **-ografi·a** *f.* sphragistics.

Sigịṣmọndo *pr.n.m.* Sigismund, Siegmund.

sigi·zia *f.* See **sizigia**.

sigl·a *f.* initials, monogram; abbreviation; signet; (radio, television) — musicale, signature tune. **-are** [A I] *tr.* to initial, to mark with a monogram.

sigm·a *m.* sigma, letter of the Greek alphabet; (anat.) sigmoid flexure. **-o·ide** *f.* (anat.) the mitral valve of the heart. **-oidectomi·a** *f.* (surg.) sigmoidectomy. **-oide·o** *adj.* sigmoid; colon -oideo, sigmoid flexure. **-oidite** *f.* (med.) sigmoiditis. **-oidopessi** *f.* (surg.) sigmoidopexy. **-oidoscopi·a** *f.* (surg.) sigmoidoscopy. **-oidosco·pio** *m.* (med.) sigmoidoscope.

signi·fero *m.* (hist.) standard-bearer; *adj.* (astron., of the zodiac) sign-bearing.

signific·are [A 2 s] *tr.* to mean, to signify; to symbolize; to denote; to imply; to indicate; to intimate; to notify, to inform; to make known; non -a niente, it doesn't mean anything, *or* it doesn't matter, it doesn't signify. **-amento** *m.* signifying; implying. **-ante** *part. adj.* expressive, significant; indizio -ante, revealing circumstance. **-antemente** *adv.* significantly; expressively. †**-anza** *f.* significance. **-a·tici** *m.pl.* (eccl. hist.) Significatists. **-ativo** *adj.* significant; expressive; full of significance, meaningful; noteworthy. **-ativamente** *adv.* significantly; expressively. **-ato** *part. adj.* signified; denoted; implied; made known; *n.m.* meaning, sense, import; purport; signification; **-ato ambiguo**, double meaning. **-atore** *m.* one who signifies; *adj.* indicative, significant. (**-atrice** *f.*) **-azione** *f.* signification, sense, purport; indication.

signor·e *m.* gentleman; c'è un — che chiede di Lei, there is a gentleman asking for you; (as a title, equiv. to Mr, it is always written 'signor' when followed by the name and always preceded by the def. art. unless it is in the vocative); il signor Rossi è qui, Mr Rossi is here; signor Rossi! può venire un momentino?, Mr Rossi, can you spare a moment?; il Rossi è un signore, Rossi is a gentleman; (in letters) Egregio Signore, Dear Sir; il signor capitano, the captain; vivere da —, to live like a lord; fare il —, to put on airs; il Signore, the Lord; Nostro Signore, Our Lord; (hist.) principe —, ruling prince. **-a** *f.* lady (as a title, equiv. to Mrs, it is always preceded by the def. art. unless it is in the vocative); la -a Rossi è qui, Mrs Rossi is here; -a Rossi! può venire un momentino?, Mrs Rossi, can you spare a moment?; wife; mi saluti la Sua -a, remember me to your wife. **-eggiare** [A 3 c] *tr.* to rule; to master; to dominate; to govern; to sway; to lord it over; castello che -a il paesaggio, castle that dominates the landscape; i colli -ano le valli, the hills tower above the valleys; *intr.* (*aux.* avere) to rule, to be master; to be domineering. (**-atore** *m.* **-atrice** *f.*) **-ello** *m. dim.* lordling. **-esco** *adj.* (*m.pl.* **-eschi**) lordly, pretentious, magnificent. (**-escamente** *adv.*) **-etto** *m. dim.* petty tyrant. **-one** *m. augm.* grand gentleman. (**-ona** *f.*) **-otto** *m.* country squire.

signor·i·a *f.* Lordship; Ladyship; lordship, dominion, rule; (hist.) governing body of a medieval commune; è in — delle passioni, he is at the mercy of his emotions; (in official communications) Vostra — (abbrev. V.S.), you. **-ile** *adj.* gentlemanlike, ladylike; lordly; courtly; (fig.) first-rate, really good; un albero -ile, a first-rate hotel; aristocratic; un pranzo -ile, a sumptuous meal. (**-ilmente** *adv.*) aristocratically. **-ilità** *f.* refined manners; distinction; courtly behaviour.

signorin·a *f.* young lady (as a title, equiv. to Miss, always preceded by the def. art. unless in the vocative); la — Rossi è qui, Miss Rossi is here; — Rossi! può venire un momentino?, Miss Rossi, can you spare a moment?; spinster, girl, unmarried woman. **-o** *m.* young gentleman.

signor-nò, -sì *excl.* (mil.) no sir!; yes sir! (negative or positive replies to a command requiring acknowledgement).

signor-one *m.*, **-otto** *m.* See under **signore**.

sigrino *m.* See **zagrino**.

sil *m. indecl.* (Rom. antiq.) *sil*, ochre.

Sila *pr.n.f.* (geog.) name of a mountain ridge and forest in Calabria.

silag·gio *m.* (agric.) silage.

silano *m.* (chem.) silane.

silema *m.* (bot.) xylem.

Sileno *pr.n.m.* (class. myth.) Silenus.

silente *adj.* (poet.) silent (cf. **silenzioso**, under **silenzio**).

silen·zi·o *m.* silence; ridurre al —, to silence; passare sotto —, to pass over in silence; —!, be quiet!, silence!; (motor.) zona di —, street or quarter of a town in which motorists are forbidden to sound horns; (mil.) segnale del —, 'lights out'; (eccl.) (monastic) silence; *silentium*; dispensare il (dal) —, to allow talking (esp. in refectory); (liturg.) saying of certain prayers in a very low voice. **-are** [A 4] *tr.* (motor.) to fit with a silencer. **-a·rio** *m.* (Byz. hist.) silentiary; (eccl.) religious bound to strict silence, e.g. Trappist.

-atore *m.* (motor.) silencer. **-oso** *adj.* silent; quiet; noiseless. **-osamente** *adv.* silently; quietly; noiselessly.

†**silere** *intr.* to be silent.

silermontano *m.* (bot.) *Laserpitium siler*.

si·lfide *f.* sylph; ballet dancer.

si·lfio *m.* (bot.) *Silphium*; *Thapsia garganica*; double coconut, coco de mer, *Ladoicea sechellarum*.

silfo *m.* sylph, spirit of the air.

si·lic·e *f.* (miner.) silica; (chem.) gelo di —, silica gel. **-atare** [A I] *tr.* to silicify, to petrify. (**-atato** *part. adj.*) **-atazione** *f.* silicification, petrification. **-ato** *m.* (chem.) silicate; **-ato di soda**, sodium silicate, waterglass. **-azione** *f.* silicification; petrification. **-e·o** *adj.* (chem.; miner.) siliceous. **-icole** *f.pl.* (bot.) silicaphyte, silica-loving plants. **-iuro** *m.* (chem.) silicide. **-izzare** [A I] *tr.* to silicify, to petrify. (**-izzato** *part. adj.*) **-one** *m.* (chem.; techn.) silicone. **-osi** *f.* (med.) silicosis. **-o·tico** *adj.* (med.) silicotic.

sil-i·cio *m.* (chem.) silicon. **-i·cico** *adj.* (chem.) silicic.

si·liqua¹ *f.* (zool.) razor shell, *Ensis siliqua*.

si·liqu·a² *f.* (bot.) siliqua, pod; (Rom. antiq.) *siliqua* (weight and coin). **-astro** *m.* (bot.) Judas tree, *Cercis siliquastrum*.

sil·lab·a *f.* syllable; non dir —, not to say a word. **-a·rio** *m.* spelling-book, elementary reading-book; primer. **-are** [A I s] *tr.* to articulate; to pronounce by syllables; domandi ad un Italiano 'come si scrive Verona', e lui risponderà 'Ve-ro-na', cioè sillabando, ask an Italian how he spells Verona and he will reply 'Ve-ro-na', that is, by articulating the syllables (not by spelling out the letters). **-arista** *m.* author of a spelling-book. **-azione** *f.* articulation of syllables; syllabification.

silla·bico *adj.* syllabic; (Gk. gramm.) aumento —, syllabic augment.

sillabismo *m.* syllabism.

sil·labo *m.* syllabus; index; (eccl.) syllabus; list of theological errors condemned (by Pius IX, 1864, and Pius X, 1907).

sillepsi, sillessi *f.* (gramm.) syllepsis.

sillimanite *f.* (miner.) sillimanite, fibrolite.

sil·log·e *f.* (lit.) collection (of writings, books, works); anthology; sylloge. **-ismo** *m.* syllogism. **-i·stica** *f.* syllogistic, reasoning by syllogisms. **-i·stico** *adj.* syllogistic. **-isticamente** *adv.* syllogistically, by syllogisms. **-izzante** *part. adj.* syllogizing. **-izzare** [A I] *tr.*, *intr.* (*aux.* avere) to syllogize; to reason syllogistically. **-izzato** *part. adj.* syllogistic; expressed in syllogisms.

silo *m.* granary; silo; conservazione nei sili, ensilage; (industr.) silo, bunker, bin.

silobal·samo *m.* wood of the balm tree.

siloè *m. indecl.* aloes (of the Bible), *Aquillaria agallocha*.

silo·fon·o *m.* (mus.) xylophone. **-ista** *m.* (mus.) xylophonist, xylophone-player.

siloglit·tica *f.* fine wood-carving.

sil-ografi·a *f.* woodcut. **-ogra·fico** *adj.* xylographic. **-o·grafo** *m.* xylographer.

silol-ogi·a *f.* study of wood and trees. (**-o·gico** *adj.*)

silor·gano *m.* (mus.) piano-action xylophone.

silos *m. indecl.* See **silo**.

siloteca *f.* museum containing specimens of wood, sections of trees, etc.

siluetta *f.* (art) silhouette.

siluriano *adj.* (geol.) Silurian; *n.m.* (geol.) Silurian system.

silu·rico *adj.* (geol.). See **siluriano**.

silur·o *m.* torpedo; (ichth.) catfish, *Silurus* spp. **-amento** *m.* torpedoing (also fig.). **-ante** *part. adj.*, *n.f.* torpedo-boat; aero-silurante, torpedo-carrying aircraft. **-are** [A I] *tr.* to torpedo; (fig.) to cashier; (colloq.) to 'sack'; -are una legge, to throw out a bill, to reject a law; *intr.* (*aux.* avere) to fire torpedoes. (**-ato** *part. adj.* **-atore** *m.* **-atrice** *f.*) †**-iera** *f.* torpedo-boat (cf. **silurante**). **-ifi·ci·o** *m.* torpedo factory. **-ipe·dio** *m.* (naut.) torpedo firing range. **-ista** *m.* (naut.) torpedoman. **-otto** *m.* (naut.) small (18 in.) torpedo.

silv-ano *adj.* sylvan; rural; luogo —, wooded place, wood; *pr.n.m.* (Rom. myth.) Sylvanus. **-estre** *adj.* wild; rustic; of the woods.

Silvestr-o *pr.n.m.* Sylvester; il san —, New Year's Eve. **-ine** *f.pl.* (eccl.) Sylvestrine nuns. **-ini** *m.pl.* (eccl.) Sylvestrine monks.

Sil·via¹ *pr.n.f.* Sylvia.

sil·via² *f.* (orn.) warbler, *Sylviidae* spp.; esp. — di Rüppell, Rüppell's warbler, *Sylvia rüppelli*.

sil·via³ *f.* (bot.) wood anemone, *Anemone nemorosa*.

silvicul-tore *m.* forester. **-tura** *f.* forestry, silviculture.

silvina *f.* (miner.) sylvine.

Sil·vio[1] *pr.n.m.* Sylvius.

sil·vio[2] *m.* (typ.) 14-point type, 'English'; (anat.) scissura di —, division between lobes of the brain.

silvite *f.* See **silvina**.

sima *f.* (archit.) small concave moulding, cavetto.

simaruba *f.* (bot.) quassia, *Picraena excelsa*.

simble·faro *m.* (med.) symblepharon.

simbi-onte *m., f.* (biol.) symbiont. **-o·tico** *adj.* (biol.) symbiotic. **-oṣi** *f.* (biol.) symbiosis.

sim·bola *f.* (eccl. hist.) common meal; agape.

simboleggi-are [A 3 c] *tr.* to symbolize; to stand for, to represent; to typify. (**-amento** *m.* **-ato** *part. adj.*)

simbo·lic-a *f.* symbolism, use and study of symbols; typology. **-o** *adj.* symbolic, symbolical; prezzo -o, nominal price. **-amente** *adv.* symbolically, by symbols.

sim·bol-o *m.* symbol; emblem; type; (theol.) Creed (Apostles', Nicene, Athanasian). **-iṣmo** *m.* symbolism. **-ista** *m.* symbolist. **-iẓẓare** [A I] and derivs. see **simboleggiare**.

simbologi·a *f.* See **simbolica**.

Simeone *pr.n.m.* Simeon.

simfilo *m.* (zool.) inquiline.

†**si·mia** *f.* See **scimmia**.

simiano *adj., n.m.* (agric.) variety of plum, ripening in July.

simigliare [A 4] and derivs. See **somigliare**.

si·mil-e *adj.* like; alike; such; similar; sono -i come due gocce d'acqua, they are as like as two peas; una — occasione, such an opportunity; un — problema, a problem of the kind; (geom.) similar; triangoli -i, similar triangles; *n.m.* like; fellow; i nostri -i, our fellow-creatures; (provb.) ogni — ama il suo —, birds of a feather flock together. **-mente**, †**-emente** *adv.* similarly, likewise; in like manner; as well as. **-are** *adj.* similar; homogeneous. **-arità** *f.* similarity; homogeneity. **-igravura** *f.* (typ.) half-tone engraving; autotype. **-itudina·rio** *adj.* with likeness; rich in similes. **-itu·dine** *f.* likeness; similarity; similitude; simile. **-oro** *m.* pinchbeck, imitation gold.

simità *f.* See under **simo**.

simmetri·a *f.* symmetry.

simme·tr-ico *adj.* symmetric(al). **-icamente** *adv.* symmetrically. **-iẓẓare** [A I] *tr.* to symmetrize. **-izzato** *part. adj.* symmetrical.

sim-o *adj.* flat-nosed. **-ità** *f.* flatness of the nose.

Simon-e *pr.n.m.* Simon; (Bibl.) Simon Mago, Simon Magus. **-eggiare** [A 3 c], **-iẓẓare** [A I] *intr.* (*aux.* avere) to practise simony. (**-eggiatore** *m., adj.* **-eggiatrice** *f.*) **-i·a** *f.* simony. **-i·aco** *adj.* simoniacal. **-iacamente** *adv.* by means of simony.

simpati·a *f.* liking; attraction; sympathy; le nostre simpatie e le nostre antipatie, our likes and dislikes; avere una — per, to have a weakness for; giudicare per —, to be partial in one's judgements; acquistò subito la — generale, he at once made himself popular with everybody; successo di —, personal success; — del popolo, popularity; (paint.) — dei colori, harmony of colours; (mus.) sympathetic resonance.

simpa·t-ico *adj.* nice, pleasant, agreeable; congenial; likeable; riesce -ica a tutti, everyone likes her, she is liked by everybody; inchiostro —, invisible ink; (anat.) sympathetic, thoracolumbar. **-icamente** *adv.* nicely; pleasantly; agreeably; endearingly. **-icopati·a** *f.* (med.) sympathicopathy, disease of the sympathetic nervous system. **-iẓẓare** [A I] *intr.* (*aux.* avere) to take a liking (to); -izzarono subito, they took an immediate liking to one another; -izzare con uno, to come to like someone.

simpieẓo·metro *m.* (phys.) sympiezometer.

simpo·dio *m.* (bot.) sympodium.

simpo·ṣ-io *m.* banquet; symposium. **-i·aco** *adj.* relating to a symposium. **-iarco** *m.* symposiarch.

simul-acro, †**-agro** *m.* simulacrum; image; semblance; shadowy likeness; mere pretence, sham; (techn.) mock-up.

simul-are [A I s] *tr.* to feign, to simulate, to sham; (mil.) — il passo, to mark time; *intr.* (*aux.* avere) to dissemble; to sham. **-amento** *m.* pretence; shamming. **-ativo** *adj.* simulating; sham. **-ato** *part. adj.* feigned, pretended; false; sham; (leg.) counterfeit; faked; pro forma; fictitious; asta -ata, mock auction; vendita -ata, fictitious sale. (**-atamente** *adv.*) **-atore** *m.* simulator; hypocrite. (**-atrice** *f.*) **-ato·rio** *adj.* (m.pl. -atorii) feigned, pretended; counterfeit, false. **-aẓione** *f.* pretence, simulation; (leg.) simulation (consisting of making fictitious contract, C.C.); -azione di reato, simulation of

offence (consisting of falsely reporting an offence to have been committed, or faking signs of one, C.P.).

simulta·ne-o *adj.* simultaneous; lezione -a, collective lesson (to several classes). (**-amente** *adv.*) **-ista** *m., f.* simultaneous interpreter (at conferences, congresses, etc.). **-ità** *f.* simultaneousness.

simùn *m. indecl.* (meteor.) simoom.

sinagoga *f.* synagogue; Jews as gathered together; the Jewish religion; the Jewish race; (derog.) gathering; babel.

sinalbina *f.* (chem.) sinalbin.

sinalefe *f.* (gramm.) synaloepha.

sinallagm-a *m.* (leg.) mutual agreement; reciprocal obligation. **-a·tico** *adj.* synallagmatic; imposing mutual obligations; reciprocally binding.

sinapina *f.* (chem.) sinapine.

sin-apse *f.* (anat.) synapse. **-apsi** *f.* (biol.) synapsis. **-ap·tico** *adj.* synaptic.

sinaptaṣi·a *f.* (chem.) synaptase, emulsin, amygdalase.

sinap·tico *adj.* See under **sinapse**.

sinartroṣi *f.* (med.) synarthrosis.

sinassi *f.* (liturg.) synaxis.

†**sinatantochè** *conj.* See under **sino**.

sincarpo *m.* (bot.) compound fruit, syncarp.

sincer-o *adj.* pure; genuine, true; sincere, unfeigned; frank, candid, honest; voglio esserti —, I'll be honest (candid) with you; clear, open; healthy; vino —, unadulterated wine. **-amente** *adv.* sincerely, truly; candidly, honestly; really. **-are** [A I] *tr.* to persuade, to convince; to assure; to absolve, to acquit; *rfl.* (*prep.* di) to satisfy oneself (about), to make sure (of). **-ato** *part. adj.* assured, certain; acquitted. **-atore** *m.* informer, informant, reliable witness. (**-atrice** *f.*) **-aẓione** *f.* assurance. **-ità** *f.* sincerity; truth; candour. (**-one** *adj., n.m.* **-ona** *f.*)

sinche *f.* kind of net used in tunny fishing.

sinchè *conj.* See **finchè**.

sin·chiṣi *f.* (gramm.; med.) synchysis.

sinci·pit-e *m.* (anat.) sinciput. **-ale** *adj.* (anat.) sincipital.

sinciẓiale *adj.* (biol.) syncytial.

sinclinale *adj.* (geol.) synclinal, syncline.

sincondroṣi *f.* (anat.) synchondrosis.

sin·cop-e *f.* (med.; mus.) syncope; (gramm.; mus.) syncopation. **-ale** *adj.* (med.) syncopal. **-are** [A I s] *tr.* gramm.; music) to syncopate. **-ato** *part. adj.* syncopated; (mus.) syncopated. **-atura** *f.* syncopation.

sin·craṣi *f.* (gramm.) syncrasis.

sin-cre·tico *adj.* syncretic. **-cretiṣmo** *m.* (philos.) syncretism. **-cretista** *m.* syncretist.

sincrociclatone *m.* (atom. phys.) synchrocyclotron.

sincron-i·a *f.* (phys.) synchrony. **-iṣmo** *m.* synchronization, synchronizing; (electr.) synchronism; uscire di -ismo, to fall out of step; (telev.) framing control. **-iẓẓare** [A I] *tr.* to synchronize. **-iẓẓato** *part. adj.* synchronized; (electr.) synchronized, in step; non -izzato, out of step; (motor.) marce -izzate, syncromesh. **-iẓẓatore** *m.* (electr.) synchronizer; (aeron.) Constantinesco gear (permitting a machine-gun to fire between the blades of a propeller). **-iẓẓaẓione** *f.* synchronization, synchronizing.

sincro·nico *adj.* synchronous.

sin·cron-o *adj.* synchronous; contemporary, contemporaneous. **-osco·pio** *m.* (electr.) synchronoscope.

sincrotone *m.* (atom. phys.) synchroton.

sin·dac-o *m.* mayor, Lord Mayor; syndic; auditor; (comm.; leg.) auditor; -i e revisori dei conti, auditors and certified Public Accountants (C.C.); (eccl.) procurator. **-a·bile** *adj.* subject to inspection, censure or audit; verifiable. (**-abilità** *f.*) **-ale** *adj.* mayoral; auditorial; associazioni -ali, trade unions, friendly societies (and sim. recognized by the Government); (leg.) collegio -ale, board of auditors. **-aliṣmo** *m.* syndicalism; trade-unionism. **-alista** *m.* syndicalist, trade-unionist. **-amento** *m.* inspection, audit. **-are** [A 2 s] *tr.* to audit, to inspect, to censure. **-ato** *m.* syndicate; trade union; -ati operai, trade unions; association; inspection, audit; mayor's (term of) office; (leg.) -ato finanziario, financial syndicate; -ato industriale, manufacturers' consortium, combine; (comm.) -ato industriale, trust. **-atore** *m.* inspector, auditor, controller. (**-atrice** *f.* **-atura** *f.* **-aẓione** *f.*)

sindat·til-e *adj.* (orn.) syndactylous. **-o** *m.* (med.) syndactylus; *adj.* (med.) syndactylous. **-i·a** *f.* (med.) syndactylia, syndactylism, syndactyly.

sinde·reṣi *f.* (philos.) synteresis, synderesis; conscience; perdere la —, to talk nonsense, to rave.

sindeṣm-ologi·a *f.* (anat.) syndesmology. **-oṣi** *f.* (med.) syndesmosis.

sin·done *f.* shroud, winding-sheet; (eccl.) la santa —, the Holy Shroud (at Turin).

sin·dr-oma, -ome *f.* (med.) syndrome. **-o·mico** *adj.* (med.) syndromic.

sinechi·a *f.* (surg.) synechia, adhesion (esp. of the iris to the lens capsule or the cornea).

sinecura *f.* sinecure.

sined·doche *f.* (gramm.) synecdoche.

sine·drio *m.* Sanhedrin; Synedrion; (also *adj.*).

sine·reṣi *f.* (gramm.; chem.) syneresis.

siner-ge·tico *adj.* (med.) synergic. **-gi·a** *f.* (med.) synergy. **-giṣmo** *m.* (med.) synergy. **-iṣti** *m.pl.* (eccl. hist.) synergists.

sin·fiṣi *f.* (anat.) symphysis.

sin·fito *m.* (bot.) comfrey, *Symphytum*.

sinfon-i·a *f.* (mus.) symphony (in all senses); overture; — avanti l'opera, opera-overture. †**-eggiare** *(intr.)* to play in tune. **-iale** *adj.* symphonic. †**-iare** *(intr.)* to play in concert.

sinfo·n-ico *adj.* (mus.) symphonic. **-ista** *m.* (mus.) symphonist, symphony-composer.

sinforosa *f.* large hat with ribbons tied under the chin; (fig.) old woman who pretends to be young and dresses as such.

singalęse *adj.* of or pertaining to Ceylon, Sinhalese; *n.m., f.* Sinhalese.

sing-e·neṣi *f.* (scient.) syngenesis. **-ene·tico** *adj.* (geol.) syngenetic.

†**singhiottire** *vb.* See **singhiozzare**.

singhiozz-are *intr.* (aux. avere) to sob; to hiccup. **-ìo** *m.* continued hiccuping or sobbing.

singhiọzz-o *m.* sob; hiccup; avere il —, to have hiccups; to hiccup; (mus.) hocket. **-oso** *adj.* mingled with sobs, sobbing.

singolar-e *adj.* singular; peculiar; particular; odd, queer, quaint; unique; single (combat); *n.m.* (gramm.) singular; (tennis) singles. **-męnte** *adv.* particularly, especially; singularly; individually. **-eggiare** [A 3 c] *intr.* (aux. avere) to be outstanding, to excel. **-ità** *f.* singularity; peculiarity; uniqueness; queerness, oddity; peculiar circumstance(s); originality; distinction. **-izzare** [A 1] *tr.* to make singular; to pick out; *rfl.* to stand out; to be peculiar. (**-izzato** *part. adj.*)

sin·gol-o *adj.* single, individual; tutti e -i, all and every; le -e prove, the separate proofs; *n.m.* individual; (sport) singles; (rowing) single sculls; per —, individually, singly.

singrafa *m.* (leg.) syngraph, written contract signed by all parties.

singulto *m.* hiccup; sob.

†**sinib·bio** *m.* wind-driven snow.

sinighella *f.* See **sirighella**.

sinigrina *f.* (chem.) sinigrin, sinigroside, potassium myronate.

siniscal-co *(pl. -chi)* (hist.) seneschal. **-cato** *m.*, **-chi·a** *f.* office or jurisdiction of a seneschal.

sinistr-o *adj.* left, left-hand; crooked; sinister, ominous; inauspicious; grim; lurid; contrary, unfavourable; *n.m.* accident, mishap; disaster; deputy (M.P.) of left-wing party; a left (boxing). **-a** *f.* left hand; left side; left (position and politics); left wing; (herald.) sinister; (naut.) port; accosta -a!, steer to port!; tutto a -a!, hard a port! (wheel). **-ale** *adj.* (on the) left, belonging to the left; leftist; †(naut.) pertaining to the port watch. **-amęnte** *adv.* ominously, unfavourably; lo guardava -amente, he gave him sinister looks. **-are** [A 1] *intr.* (aux. avere) (of a horse) to jib, to shy; *rfl.* to put oneself out. **-ato** *part. adj.* injured (in an accident); having suffered disaster; bombed out; *n.m.* victim of accident, disaster, bombing, etc. **-ogira** *adj.* (phys.) laevorotatory. **-orso** *adj.* (zool.) sinistral (of a gastropod shell); (bot.) left-handed, sinistrorse; (techn.) left-handed, anticlockwise.

siniżeṣi *f.* (gramm.) syneresis, synizesis; (med.) synezesis.

sin-o *adv.* even; lo ammiravano — i nemici, even his enemies admired him; *prep.* — qui, up to here; (foll. by *prep.* 'a') till, until; up to, as far as; (leg.) — a nuovo ordine, indefinitely (cf. **fino**). †**-atantochè** *conj.* until. **-chè** *conj.* see **finchè**.

si·nod-o *m.*, †*f.* (eccl.) synod; council; Santo —, (Orthodox) Holy Synod; (astrol.) †synod. **-ale** *adj.* synodal, synodical; età -ale, Tridentine age (the mature age required by canon law for a priest's housekeeper, etc.). **-almęnte** *adv.* synodically, synodally. **-a(t)·tico** *m.* synodaticum, synodal.

sino·dico *adj.* synodical; lettere sinodiche, synodal letters; (astron.) synodic.

sino·logo *m.* Sinologist, Sinologue.

sino·nim-o *adj.* synonymous; *n.m.* synonym. **-amęnte** *adv.* synonymously. **-i·a** *f.* synonymy; synonymousness. **-izzare** [A 1] *intr.* (aux. avere) to synonymize; to abound in synonyms.

sin-o·pia *f.* sinopite, sinoper, sinople; red ochre, rubric. **-o·pico** *adj.* sinopic; like red ochre.

sinorchidi·a *f.* (med.) synorchism.

sin-ossi *f.* synopsis. **-ot·tico** *adj.* synoptic; in tavole -ottiche, in tabular form; *n.m.pl.* (Bibl.) i -ottici, the Synoptic gospels.

sinostoṣi *f.* (med.) synosteosis.

sino·vi-a *f.* (anat.) synovia, synovial fluid. **-ale** *adj.* synovial; membrana -ale, synovial capsule. **-ina** *f.* synovin. **-ite** *f.* (med.) synovitis.

sintagm-a *f.* (gramm.; rhet.) syntagma.

†**sintanto** *conj.* — che, as long as; until.

sin-tassi *f.* syntax. **-tat·tico** *adj.* syntactic; regole -tattiche, rules of syntax. **-tatticamęnte** *adv.* syntactically.

sinterizz-are [A 1] *tr.* (techn.) to sinter. (**-ato** *part. adj.*) **-azione** *f.* (techn.) sintering.

sin·teṣi *f.* synthesis; di —, synthetic; résumé, summary; †tunic, loose gown, the synthesis worn in ancient Rome.

sinte·t-ico *adj.* synthetic; fibre -iche, man-made fibres; (poet.; paint.) generalized, using only outlines. **-icamęnte** *adv.* synthetically. **-izzare** [A 1] *tr.* to synthesize, to synthetize. (**-izzato** *part. adj.*)

sinto *m.* (rel.). See **scintoismo**.

sin·tom-o *m.* symptom; sign, token; (med.) symptom. **-a·tico** *adj.* symptomatic. **-atologi·a** *f.* (med.) symptomatology. **-atolo·gico** *adj.* (med.) symptomatological.

sinton-i·a *f.* (radio) tuning. **-iṣmo** *m.* (electr.) syntony. **-izza·bile** *adj.* (radio) tunable. **-izzare** [A 1] *tr.* (radio) to tune (in). (**-izzato** *part. adj.*) **-izzatore** *m.* (radio) tuner. **-izzazione** *f.* (radio) tuning (in).

sintoṣi *f.* (med.) symptosis.

sinuọs-o *adj.* sinuous, winding; concave; (fig.) tortuous. (**-amęnte** *adv.*) **-ità** *f.* bend, bending, sinuosity; curl or curving (of the lips).

sinuṣ-ale *adj.* (anat.) sinusal. **-ite** *f.* (med.) sinusitis.

sinuṣo·id-e *f.* (geom.) sine curve, sine wave. **-ale** *adj.* (geom.) sinusoidal.

Si·on *pr.n.f.* (Mount) Zion, Sion, Jerusalem. **-iṣmo** *m.* Zionism. **-ista** *m.* Zionist.

sione *m.* (naut., Taranto) coral or sponge bed known only to certain fishermen; marker used by crabbers and lobsterpot fishermen.

sior *m.* (dial.) see **signore**. **-a** *f.* see **signora**.

†**sipa** *affirm. particle* (Bologn.) yes.

sipa·rio *m.* curtain; (fig.) veil; covering; (theatr.) curtain, dropcurtain; cala il —, the curtain falls; (fig.) il — di ferro, the Iron Curtain.

Sira *pr.n.f.* (astron.) Sirrah (and Andromeda).

Siracuṣa *pr.n.f.* (geog.) Syracuse.

Sire *pr.n. m.* Sire (form of address to a king).

siren-a *f.* (myth.) siren; mermaid; siren, hooter; (naut.) — da nebbia, foghorn; (mus.) — acustica, acoustic siren (instrument for measuring vibration-frequencies); (slang) male prostitute.

Si·r-ia *pr.n.f.* (geog.) Syria. **-i·aco** *adj.*, *n.m.* Syriac. **-iano** *adj.*, *n.m.* Syrian.

siri·aṣi *f.* (med.) siriasis, heat-stroke.

si·rima *f.* (prosod.) second half of a *canzone* stanza (cf. **fronte**).

siring-a *f.* (Gk. myth. and antiq.) Syrinx; (mus.) Panpipes, syrinx; (med.) syringe; (eng.) grease gun; (cul.) kind of syringe used in shaping pasta; pasta —, pipe-shaped pasta, usually sweet; icingtube; (bot.) lilac, *Syringa vulgaris*. **-are** [A 2] *tr.* to syringe; (med.) to give an injection to. (**-atura** *f.*) **-omielite** *f.* (med.) syringomyelitis. **-otomi·a** *f.* (surg.) syringotomy. **-o·tomo** *m.* (surg.) syringotome.

siring-e *f.* (anat.) syrinx; (orn.) syrinx, the vocal organ of birds. **-ite** *f.* syringitis. **-otomi·a** *f.* (surg.) syringotomy.

Si·rio[1] *pr.n.m.* (astron.) Sirius.

si·rio[2] *adj.* See **siriaco**, under **Siria**.

sirma *m.* See **sirima**.

Sir·mia *pr.n.f.* (geog.) Mitrovica.

Sirmione, (poet.) **Sir·mio** *pr.n.m.* (geog.) Sirmione.

†**siroc·chia** *f.* sister.

siroppo *m.* See **sciroppo**.

sirratte *m.* (orn.) Pallas's sangrouse, *Syrrhaptes paradoxus*.

sirte *f.* (geog.) network of reefs and sandbanks.

Sirti *pr.n.f.pl.* (geog.) the Syrtes (of the coast of Libya).

Sir·tica *pr.n.f.* (geog.) Sidra.

†**sirventese** *f.* See **serventese**.

sisal *f.* (text.) sisal.

sisalano *adj.* (text.) *Canapa sisalina,* sisal hemp.

si·ṣaro *m.* (bot.) skirret, *Sium sisarum.*

Si·ṣifo *pr.n.m.* (Gk. myth.) Sisyphus.

si·ṣmico *adj.* seismic.

sism-o *m.* earthquake, earth tremor. **-ografi·a** *f.* seismography. **-o·grafo** *m.* seismograph. **-ogramma** *m.* seismogram. **-ologi·a** *f.* seismology. **-olo·gico** *adj.* seismological. **-o·logo** *m.* seismologist. **-o·metro** *m.* seismometer.

sissarcoṣi *f.* (anat.) syssarcosis.

sissignọr-a, sissignọr-e *excl.* yes, madam; yes, sir; (in colloq. usage 'sissignora' also means 'yes, sir', used emphatically).

sissitura *f.* tuck (to shorten a garment).

†**sissi·zio** *m.* banquet of male guests only, syssitia.

sistal·tico *adj.* (med.) systolic, systaltic.

sistem-a *m.* system; method; rule; mutar —, to change one's way of life; arrangement; (comm.) — bancario, banking; (mus.) stave; system (i.e. number of staves united by one brace); — armonico, harmonic system; — massimo, greater perfect system (ancient Greek music); — metrico decimale, metric system; (soccer) 'third back' game. **-are** [A I s] *tr.* to arrange; to regulate; to settle; to put in order; -are un conto, to settle an account; to find a place for; to put in position; to accommodate; to put up (e.g. for the night, etc.); (iron.) to 'settle', to 'fix'; (euphem.) to kill; *rfl.* to settle (down, in); to make one's arrangements; (fig.) to marry. **-a·tica** *f.* branch of science concerned with classification. **-a·tico** *adj.* systematic; polso -atico, regular pulse. **-aticamẹnte** *adv.* systematically; lavorare -aticamente, to work methodically. (**-atọre** *m.* **-atrice** *f.*) **-azione** *f.* regularization; arrangement; settlement; lay-out; set-up; accommodation. **-ista** *m., f.* (neol.) one who follows a system in compiling football-pool coupons, etc.

si·stilo *m., adj.* (archit.) systyle (of building characterized by colonnade where the intervals are twice the diameter of the columns).

Sist-o¹ *pr.n.m.* Sixtus. **-ino** *adj.* Sistine, Sixtine; Cappella Sistina, Sistine Chapel.

sisto² *m.* (class. antiq.) xystus.

si·st-ole *f.* (med.) systole. **-o·lico** *adj.* (med.) systolic; soffio -olico, systolic murmur.

sistro *m.* (mus.) sistrum, rattle.

†**sitare** [A I] *intr.* (aux. avere) to give off a bad odour.

sitibọndo *adj.* thirsty; (fig.) thirsting, eager; — di vendetta, thirsting for revenge.

†**sitiofobi·a** *f.* (med.) sitiophobia.

†**sitire** *intr.* to be thirsty; *tr.* to thirst for.

sito¹ *m.* place, site, spot; position; *adj.* situated; placed; sited.

sit-o² *m.* musty smell. **-erello** *m. dim.* disagreeable odour.

sitol-ogi·a *f.* sitology; study of food grains. **-o·gico** *adj.* sitological.

sitosterolo *m.* (chem.) sitosterol.

situ-are [A 6] *tr.* to place, to site; to set. **-ato** *part. adj.* situated; sited; set; placed; located, positioned. **-azione** *f.* situation; position; condition, state (of affairs); list, schedule; (comm.) -azione bancaria, bank return; essere all'altezza di una -azione, to be worthy of a position of responsibility, to be able to cope with a situation; (mil.) effective strength, number of fighting units available at a given moment as opposed to ration strength.

Siua *pr.n.f.* (geog.) Siwa.

siviera *f.* (foundry) ladle.

Sivi·glia *pr.n.f.* (geog.) Seville; a kind of snuff.

†**siziente** *part.* of †**sitire**; *adj.* thirsty.

sizi·gia *f.* (astron.; geog.) syzygy; maree sizigie, the extremes of the tides, spring and neap tides; (Gk. antiq.) squadron of four war-chariots.

si·zio *m.* (Bibl.) 'I thirst'; *n.m.* (fig.) essere al —, to be at the last gasp; tornare al —, to get back to work, to return to a heavy job.

†**sizza** *f.* cold blast of wind, esp. the tramontana.

ski *m.pl.* See **sci**.

ṣlabbr-are [A I] *tr.* to damage the edge, brim or mouth of; to enlarge, to open out (a wound, pipe, orifice, etc.); — una bottiglia, to break off the neck of a bottle; *intr.* (aux. essere) to overflow, to spill over, to brim over; (of a wound) to gape; *rfl.* (of a bottle, jug, etc.) to get chipped at the spout or brim. (**-ato** *part. adj.*) **-atura** *f.* chipping; chipped edge; chip, crack.

ṣlacci-are [A 3] *tr.* to unlace, to untie; (fig.) to set free, to liberate *rfl.* to come untied or unlaced; to free oneself. (**-ato** *part. adj.*)

ṣlalom *m. indecl.* (ski) slalom, descent over fixed course marked by flags.

ṣlam *m. indecl.* (cards, bridge) grande —, grand slam; piccolo —, little slam.

ṣlamare [A I] *intr.* (aux. essere) (of ground) to fall; to collapse (in a landslide).

ṣlanare [A I] *tr.* (tanning) to de-wool, to fellmonger.

ṣlanci-are [A 3] *tr.* to hurl, to fling; to throw; *rfl.* to rush; to hurl oneself; (fig.) to be bold or daring; to begin impetuously. **-ato** *part. adj.* tall and slim, slender; graceful; well-built.

ṣlan·c-io *m.* rush; dash; bound; jump; start; impulse, élan, outburst; di primo —, at the first impulse; pieno di —, full of go; prendere lo —, to take a run, to make a dash; (mus.) prendere di — una nota, to attack a note with impetuosity (or with fire), to make a brilliant attack upon a note, to dash at a note; (naut.) rake; — di prua, rake of the stern.

ṣlappol-are [A I s] *tr.* (techn.) to deburr. (**-ato** *part. adj.*) **-atrice** *f.* (text.) burring machine. **-atura** *f.* (text.) burring, burr extraction.

ṣlarg-are [A 2] *tr.* to enlarge; to widen; — la folla, to disperse the crowd; *rfl.* to open out (also fig.); to spread out; to lay aside one's reserve. **-amẹnto** *m.* enlargement; widening; spreading out. **-ando** *ger.* (mus.) broadening the tempo. (**-ato** *part. adj.*) **-atura** *f.* widening; enlarging.

ṣlar-go *m.* (*pl.* **-ghi**) widening.

ṣlatin-are [A I] *intr.* (aux. avere) (derog.) to use Latin quotations, to show off one's Latin. **-ata** *f.* (derog.) long string of Latin quotations.

ṣlatt-are [A I] *tr.* to wean. **-amẹnto** *m.* weaning. **-ato** *part. adj.* weaned. **-atura** *f.* weaning.

ṣlavat-o *adj.* pale, colourless; washed out; wan; (paint.) pallid, lacking colour; dull, insipid; uninteresting. **-ura** *f.* anything colourless, pale or washed-out looking; patch where colour has faded.

ṣlavina *f.* avalanche; landslide; snowslide.

ṣlav-o *adj., n.m.* (geog.) Slav. **-iṣmo** *m.* (pan)slavism. **-ista** *m., f.* student of slavonic languages; slavophil. **-iẓẓare** [A I] *tr.* to slavonicize. **-o·filo** *m., adj.* Slavophil. **-o·fobo** *m., adj.* Slavophobe.

†**ṣlazzerare** *intr.* to spend lavishly, to fork out money.

ṣleal-e *adj.* unfaithful; unfair, dishonest; disloyal; concorrenza —, unfair competition; giuoco —, foul play; **-mẹnte** *adv.* unfairly; disloyally. **-tà** *f.* disloyalty; unfaithfulness; unfairness.

†**ṣleanza** *f.* See **slealtà**, under **sleale**.

ṣleg-are [A 2] *tr.* to unbind; to untie, to unfasten, to undo; to loose; to loosen; (fig.) to release; *rfl.* to come undone; to work loose; (fig.) to be released. **-amẹnto** *m.* loosening, untying. **-ato** *part. adj.* loose; unbound; unfastened, untied, undone; disconnected. **-atamẹnte** *adv.* loosely. **-atura** *f.* unfastening; lack of connexion, looseness.

Ṣle·ṣia *pr.n.f.* (geog.) Silesia.

ṣlingottatrice *f.* (metall.) ingot stripper.

ṣlitt-a *f.* sledge, sleigh; sled; slide; (mil.) gun-carriage, gun-cradle; (eng.) slide; — trasversale, cross slide. **-amẹnto** *m.* sliding; skidding; (techn.) skidding, slipping; slippage. **-are** [A I] *intr.* (aux. avere, essere) to sledge; to slide; to slip; (motor.) to skid; (eng.) to slip (of a belt); (comm.) far -are una commessa, to hold back an order. **-ata** *f.* (motor.) skid. **-ọne** *m.* (eng.) ram. **-ovi·a** *f.* (neol.) sledge-lift.

ṣlivoviz *m. indecl.* plum-brandy, made in Friuli, Dalmatia and Slovenia.

ṣlo-ca *m.* (*pl.* **-chi**) (prosod.) sloka, a couplet in Sanskrit verse.

ṣlog-are [A 2] *tr.* to dislocate, to displace; *rfl.* to become, to get, dislocated. **-amẹnto** *m.* dislocating, dislocation. **-ato** *part. adj.* dislocated. **-atura** *f.* dislocating, dislocation.

ṣloggi-are [A 3] *tr.* to dislodge; *intr.* (aux. avere) to decamp, to clear out; to retire; (mil.) to dislodge the enemy; to evacuate a position. (**-amẹnto** *m.* **-ato** *part. adj.*)

ṣlog·gio *m.* (leg.) eviction; diffida di —, notice to quit.

ṣlomb-are [A I c] *tr.* to break the back of; to wear out; to exhaust; *intr.* (aux. essere), *rfl.* to hurt one's back; to knock oneself up; to exhaust oneself; (fig.) to become enfeebled. **-ato** *part. adj.* exhausted; nerveless; flaccid; enervated.

ṣlontan-are [A I] *tr.* to remove; to move away; *rfl.* to withdraw to a distance; to take oneself off. **-amẹnto** *m.* removing; taking away. (**-ato** *part. adj.* **-atọre** *m.* **-atrice** *f.*)

Ṣlovac·chia *pr.n.f.* (geog.) Slovakia.

ṣlovacc·o *adj., n.m.* Slovak. (*-a f.*)

ṣloven·o *adj., n.m.* Slovene, Slovenian. (*-a f.*)

ṣlumac·are [A2] *intr.* (*aux.* avere) to leave a trail (like a snail). *-atura f.* snail's trail; shiny mark.

ṣlung·are [A2] *tr.* to prolong; to lengthen; *rfl.* to stretch; †to withdraw; †to go far away. (*-ato part. adj.*) *-atore m.* one who prolongs or stretches; †*adj.* (anat.) stretching muscle (cf. **estensore**). (*-atrice f.*)

ṣlustrare [A1] and derivs. See **dilustrare**.

ṣmacc·are [A2] *tr.* to put to shame; to vilify. *-ato part. adj.* put to shame; vilified; (fig.) excessive; nauseous; dolce *-ato*, nauseously sweet, sickly.

ṣmacchi·are[1] [A3] *tr.* to remove stains from; to clean; to scour. *-ato part. adj.* cleansed of spots and stains. *-atore m.* (dry-)cleaner; scourer; detergent; cleanser; stain-remover, spot-remover. *-atori·a f.* cleaning-works. *-atura f.* (dry-)cleaning; scouring; removing of stains.

ṣmacchiare[2] [A4] *tr.* (agric.) to clear of brushwood, trees, etc.; †*rfl.* to come out from one's place of hiding in the 'macchia', q.v.

ṣmac·co *m.* (*pl.* *-chi*) affront; insult; shame; disgrace; humiliating defeat; mortification.

ṣmagare [A2] and derivs. See **dismagare**.

ṣmagli·are [A4] *tr.* to undo (pull out) knitting; to undo the meshes of (e.g. a net); to take (fishes) out of a net; to break the links of (e.g. a chain-mail, chain); to ladder (a stocking); (fig.) to discourage; *rfl.* to come out unravelled (of a stocking) to ladder; *intr.* (*aux.* avere) to shine brightly; to sparkle. *-ante part. adj.* shining; brilliant; dazzling; gaudy. *-ato part. adj.* unravelled, undone, broken (of net, knitting, chain-mail, etc.); (of a stocking) laddered. *-atura f.* break (in mesh, etc.); ladder (in a stocking); (med.) vibex.

ṣmagnetizẓ·are [A1] *tr.* to demagnetize; to 'wipe', to 'wash' (of tape-recordings); (electr.) to degauss. (*-ato part. adj.*) *-azione f.* demagnetization; degaussing.

†**ṣmago** *m.*, †**ṣmai** *m.* dismay.

ṣmagrante *m.* (techn.) thinner.

†**ṣmagrare** *vb.* and derivs. See **smagrire**.

ṣmagr·ire [D2] *intr.* (*aux.* essere) to grow thin, to lose weight; *tr.* to make thin; — un fiume, to reduce the flow of a river; — un terreno, to exhaust a piece of land (by overcropping). *-imento m.* emaciation; loss of weight; exhaustion. (*-ito part. adj.*)

ṣmalizi·are [A4] *tr.* to make crafty. *-ato part. adj.* crafty, cunning.

ṣmall·are [A1] *tr.* to remove from the husk; *rfl.* to come out of the husk (esp. of walnuts, chestnuts, etc.). (*-ato part. adj.*)

ṣmalt·are [A1] *tr.* to enamel; — a vetrino, to glaze; (fig., poet.) to adorn. (*-amento m.* *-ato part. adj.*) *-atore m.* enameller; (photog.) glazing apparatus. (*-atrice f.*) *-atura f.* enamelling; *-atura a vetrino*, (pot-)glazing; coat of enamelling; (photog.) gloss; estrema *-atura*, high gloss. *-ina f.* (miner.) smaltite, smaltine, grey cobalt. *-ino m.* smalt, Azure Blue, Saxony Blue.

ṣmalt·ire [D2] *tr.* to sell off; to get rid of; to digest; to sleep off; — un'ingiuria, to swallow an insult. *-imento m.* selling off; sale. *-ito part. adj.* disposed of; finished with; liquidated. *-itoio m.* drain, sewer; sump.

ṣmalt·o *m.* enamel, enamel-work; glaze; artificial stone; pavement; cuore di —, heart of stone; (paint.) colour, paint (for mixing with oil, water, etc.); verniciatura a —, enamel paint; — alla nitrocellulosa, nitrocellulose lacquer; (anat.) enamel (of the teeth). *-ista m.* enameller, enamelist. *-ite f.* (miner.) see **smaltina**.

ṣmammolare [A1s] *rfl.* (fam., Tusc.) to laugh heartily; to have the time of one's life.

ṣmanacci·are [A3] *intr.* (*aux.* avere) (fam.) to applaud vigorously, to clap loudly. *-ata f.* loud applause. *-one m.* enthusiastic member of an audience, one who applauds loudly. (*-ona f.*)

ṣmancer·i·a f. affectation, simpering; mincing manner; mawkishness. *-oso adj.* affected, mincing; mawkish.

ṣmangi·are [A3] *tr.* to eat away; to corrode; to wear down; (typ.) to eliminate (a short line) by taking it up into the previous line. (*-ato part. adj.*) *-atura f.* corroding; corrosion.

ṣmangiucchiare [A4] and derivs. See **mangiucchiare**.

ṣma·nia f. craze; rage; frenzy; eager desire; impatient longing; dare nelle smanie, to give way to frenzied behaviour; restlessness; mettere la — addosso a, to induce restlessness in; †menare smanie, to behave in a frenzied way.

ṣmani·are [A4] *intr.* (*aux.* avere) to rave; to be delirious; to be restless; to talk wildly; to desire ardently; to be restless; (*prep.* 'di', foll. by *infin.*) to desire ardently to; -avo di rivederla, I was longing to see her again. (*-amento m.*) *-ante part. adj.* raving; wild, delirious; crazy. *-atamente adv.* madly; ravingly; eagerly.

ṣmanic·are [A2s] *tr.* to break the handle of; *rfl.* to lose its handle; mi si è -ato il coltello, the handle has come off my knife. *-ato part. adj.* lacking a handle; having a handle broken off.

ṣmanierato *adj.* unmannerly.

ṣmani·gli·a f., *-o m.* handle; handlebar; bracelet. *-are* [A4] *tr.* (naut.) to unshackle (cable or anchor).

ṣmanios·o *adj.* filled with eager longing; madly desirous; frenzied. *-amente adv.* restlessly; frenziedly; madly.

†**ṣmannata f.** troop, band.

ṣmantell·are [A1] *tr.* (industr., etc.) to dismantle; (mil.) to dismantle; to destroy the defences, walls, etc. of; (naut.) to dismast, to smash up the superstructure of; to break up (a ship, in order to recover the metal). *-amento m.* dismantling; demolition; (industr.) dismantling. *-ato part. adj.* dismantled; (naut.) dismasted. (*-atore m.* *-atrice f.*)

†**ṣmanzier·e m.**, †*-a f.* amorous person. †*-oso adj.* amorous; lustful.

ṣmaragdite f. (miner.) smaragdite.

ṣmarcare [A2] *tr.* (sport) to mark.

ṣmargiass·o m. bully; blusterer; braggart. *-are* [A1] *intr.* (*aux.* avere) to bluster; to brag; to hector, to play the bully. *-ata f.* bluster; bragging; bullying; rodomontade. *-eri·a f.* boasting; swagger, bravado.

ṣmargin·are [A1s] *tr.* (bookb.) to trim the margins of; (typ.) to remove the margins of (printing plates, blocks, etc.). *-ato part. adj.* (bookb.) cropped; (bot.) foglie *-ate*, emarginate leaves.

ṣmarra f. (pop.) see **marra**. *-are* [A1] *tr.* to hoe. *-atura f.* hoeing.

ṣmarr·ire [D2] *tr.* to mislay; to lose; to mislead; to bewilder, to confuse; — la vista a, to dazzle; *rfl.* to lose one's way; to go astray; to be bewildered; to become confused; to be upset; to be worried. *-imento m.* sense of being lost; bewilderment; loss; error; miscarriage; -imento di titoli al portatore, loss of bearer securities. *-ito*, †*-uto part. adj.* mislaid; lost; strayed; la pecorella *-ita*, the lost sheep; ufficio di oggetti *-iti*, lost-property office; bewildered, confused; con l'occhio *-ito*, with a bewildered look. *-itamente adv.* confusedly; bewilderedly.

ṣmartellare [A1] *intr.* (*aux.* avere) to keep singing on one note.

ṣmascell·are [A1] *rfl.* to dislocate one's jaw; (fig.) to split one's sides with laughter. (*-amento m.*) *-ato part. adj.* (of a jaw) dislocated. *-atamente adv.* (of laughing) uproariously, 'fit to bust'.

ṣmascher·are [A1s] *tr.* to unmask. *-amento m.* unmasking. *-ato part. adj.* unmasked; not wearing a mask. (*-atore m.* *-atrice f.*)

†**ṣmascolinato** *adj.* effeminate; emasculated.

ṣmass·are [A1] *tr.* to remove from the mass. *-amento m.* (bldg.) clearing.

ṣmatassare [A1] *tr.* to separate (skeins) from a bundle; to undo (a skein); to disentangle.

ṣmatton·are [A1c] *tr.* to demolish (by removing paving-stones, bricks or tiles). *-ato part. adj.* demolished; pavimento *-ato*, broken pavement. *-atura f.* removal of bricks or tiles; break in a pavement.

†**ṣmegliare** *vb.* See **sgarrare**.

ṣmegma m. (anat.) smegma.

ṣmel·are [A1] *tr.* to take off the honey from (combs, hives). (*-ato part. adj.* *-atore m.*) *-atrice f.* honey separator. (*-atura f.*)

ṣmembr·are [A1] *tr.* to dismember; to partition, to split up. *-amento m.* dismemberment; splitting up. *-ato part. adj.* dismembered; partitioned, split up. (*-atore m.* *-atrice f.*) *-atura f.* dismemberment.

ṣmemor·are [A1s] *intr.* (*aux.* avere) to lose one's memory. *-atag·gine f.* forgetfulness; loss of memory; bewilderment; stupidity. *-atezza f.* absent-mindedness. *-ato part. adj.* forgetful; absent-minded; scatter-brained; silly; stupid; †forgotten; *n.m.* person who has lost his memory. *-atamente adv.* absent-mindedly.

ṣmemoriato *adj.* (pop.) See **smemorato**, under **smemorare**.

ṣmenc·ire [D2] *intr.* (*aux.* essere) (fam., Tusc.) to grow feeble; to become flabby; *tr.* to enfeeble; to make soft and flabby. *-ito part. adj.* soft and flabby.

†**ṣmenomare** *vb.* and derivs. See **menomare**.

ṣmensol·are [A1s] *tr.* (archit.) to shape into a bracket. *-ato part. adj.* bracket-shaped.

†**smensurato** *adj.* See smisurato.

sment·ire [D 2] *tr.* to deny; to contradict; to give the lie to; to refute; to belie; *rfl.* to contradict oneself; to be unworthy of oneself; la sua onestà non si -ì mai, his honesty never failed; to break one's word. **-ita** *f.* denial; contradiction; refutation; disproof. **-ito** *part. adj.* denied; contradicted. (**-itọre** *m.* **-itrice** *f.*)

smerald·o *m.* emerald; emerald green. **-are** [A 1] *tr.* to make emerald green. **-ino** *adj.* of, relating to, emeralds; emerald green.

†**smerare** *tr.* to purify.

smerci·are [A 3] *tr.* (comm.) to sell off; to dispose of; to deal in; to trade in; to sell. (**-ato** *part. adj.*)

smer·cio *m.* sale (of goods); avere, trovare —, to sell.

smerd·are[1] [A 1] *tr.* to foul, to befoul; (fig.) to smirch. (**-ato** *part. adj.*)

smerd·are[2] [A 1] *tr.* to cleanse of filth; — un bambino, to change, to clean, a baby. (**-ato** *part. adj.*)

smergo *m.* (orn.) sawbilled duck, genus *Mergus*; — maggiore, goosander, *Mergus merganser*; — minore, red-breasted merganser, *M. serrator.*

smerigli·are[1] [A 4] *tr.* to rub with emery; to grind (glass); to polish; (eng.) to grind, to lap. **-ato** *part. adj.* polished; (eng.) lapped; ground; (glassm.) frosted; carta -ata, emery paper. **-atọre** *m.* (eng.) lap. **-atrice** *f.* (eng.) lapping machine; polishing machine; (carpen.) sandpapering machine, sanding machine. **-atura** *f.* (eng.) grinding, lapping; (carpen.) sandpapering, sanding.

smerigliare[2] [A 4]. See under smeriglio[2].

smeri·gli·o[1] *m.* emery; polvere di —, emery powder; tela —, emery cloth. **-ọso** *adj.* (of marble) very hard, difficult to work.

smerigli·o[2] *m.* (orn.) merlin, *Falco columbarius*; (mil. hist.) falconet (small 4-pounder gun). **-are** [A 4] *tr.* (mil. hist.) to shoot with the falconet.

†**smeritare** *vb.* and derivs. See demeritare.

smerl·are [A 1] *tr., intr.* (aux. avere) (needlew.) to trim with purl, buttonhole or picot edging; to embroider the edges (of); (of paper) to cut an indented edge. **-ato** *part. adj.* fazzoletto -ato, lace-edged (or embroidered) handkerchief; torre -ata, embattled (crenellated) tower. (**-atura** *f.*) **-ettare** [A 1 c] *tr.* (needlew.) to embroider at the edge with lace or scalloped embroidery. **-uzzare** [A 1] *tr.* to cut (paper) making a scalloped or indented edge.

smerlo[1] *m.* (needlew.) purl, picot edging; scallop; indented edge.

smerlo[2] *m.* (orn.). See smeriglio[2].

smẹsso *part.* of smettere, q.v.; *adj.* (of clothes) cast-off, left-off; (derog.) former; prete —, unfrocked priest; out of practice.

smẹt·tere [C 20] *tr.* to leave off; to give up; (colloq.) to 'drop'; to stop; smẹttila!, stop it!; *intr.* (aux. avere; *prep.* di) to leave off; to stop; to give up; ho smesso di fumare, I have given up smoking.

smezz·are [A 1] *tr.* to halve; to cut in half; to divide. (**-amẹnto** *m.*) **-ato** *part. adj.* cut in the middle; in half; halved; divided.

†**smiacio** *m.* See smagio.

smicciare [A 3] *tr.* to disarm (by removing a fuse).

smidoll·are [A 1] *tr.* to remove the marrow from; to remove the pith from; to remove the crumb from (a loaf); *rfl.* to lose strength. **-ato** *part. adj.* hollowed out; weakened; albero -ato, hollow tree; (bot.; anat.) non-medullary.

smielatrice *f.* (agric.) honey separator.

smilac·e *f.* (bot.) *Smilax aspera.* **-ina** *f.* extract of sarsaparilla.

smilitarizz·are [A 1] *tr.* to demilitarize. (**-ato** *part. adj.* **-aziọne** *f.*)

†**smillantare** *vb.* and derivs. See millantare.

smilzo *adj.* thin, slim; slender; spare.

†**smimorato** *adj.* See smemorato, under smemorare.

smin·are [A 1] *tr.* to clear of mines. (**-amẹnto** *m.* **-ato** *part. adj.*)

sminchion·are [A 1 c] *tr.* to ridicule, to make a fool of. **-ato** *part. adj.* ridiculed; made a fool of; also *n.m.*

sminu·ire [D 2] *tr.* to diminish, to lessen; *rfl.* to be diminished; (fig.) to belittle oneself. **-endo** *gerund.* (mus.) diminuendo, becoming softer. **-imẹnto** *m.* diminishing; diminution; lessening. **-ito** *part. adj.* diminished; enfeebled; minished; (mus.) diminished (interval). (**-itọre** *m.* **-itrice** *f.*)

sminuzz·are [A 1] *tr.* to mince, to hash; to cut up; to hew; to break into little pieces; to pull, to pluck, to bits; (paperm.) to break (rays); to chop (wood); (fig.) to chew over, to discuss in minute detail; *rfl.* to break into tiny fragments; to turn to powder; to turn to spray. (**-amẹnto** *m.* **-ato** *part. adj.*) **-atọre** *m.* mincer, mincing-machine. **-atrice** *f.* (industr.) chipping machine, chipper. **-atura** *f.* mincing; mince; hash. **-olamẹnto** *m.* crushing, grinding,

pulverizing. **-olare** [A 1 s] *tr.* to crush, to grind; to pulverize; (fig.) to analyse in minute detail; *rfl.* -olarsi per la gioia, to go into ecstasies.

Smirn·e *pr.n.f.* (geog.) Ismir (Smyrna). **-e·o** *adj.* relating to Ismir, Smyrnaean, Smyrniote; *n.m.* (poet.) il cieco -eo, Homer.

smir·nio *m.* (bot.) *Smyrnium perfoliatum.*

smist·are [A 1] *tr.* to sort (letters); *tr.* (rlwy.) to shunt, to switch; (soccer, rugby, etc.) to pass. **-amẹnto** *m.* sorting; (rlwy.) shunting; posto di -amento, clearing-station, clearing-house, marshalling-yard; ospedale di -amento, casualty clearing-station. (**-ato** *part. adj.*)

†**smisurare** *intr.* to be measureless, infinite, boundless.

smisurat·o *adj.* immense, boundless; enormous; excessive. **-amẹnte** *adv.* immensely, enormously. **-ẹzza** *f.* immensity, enormousness.

smithsonite *f.* (miner.) calamine, smithsonite.

smobili·are [A 4] *tr.* to empty of furniture. **-ato** *part. adj.* unfurnished.

smobilit·are [A 1 s] *tr.* (mil.) to demobilize. (**-ato** *part. adj.*) **-aziọne** *f.* demobilization.

smocci·are [A 3] *tr.* to remove nasal mucus from; to wipe the nose of. **-care** [A 2 s] *intr.* (aux. avere) to snivel; *tr.* to soil with mucus.

smoccol·are [A 1 s, A 1 sc] *tr.* to snuff, to snuff out; *intr.* (aux. avere) (fam.) to swear, to curse; (joc.) to steal. (**-ato** *part. adj.*) **-atọio** *m.,* **-atọie** *f.pl.* snuffers. (**-atọre** *m.*) **-atura** *f.* snuffing, snuffing out.

smod·are [A 1] *intr.* (aux. avere), *rfl.* to be intemperate, to act without proper moderation. **-ato** *part. adj.* excessive, immoderate; intemperate; exaggerated. **-atamẹnte** *adv.* immoderately, excessively; intemperately. (Cf. trasmodare.)

smoder·are [A 1 s] *intr.* (aux. avere), *rfl.* to be intemperate, to exceed proper limits. (**-amẹnto** *m.*) **-atẹzza** *f.* excess; lack of moderation; intemperance; exaggeration. **-ato** *part. adj.* immoderate, excessive; intemperate; exaggerated. **-atamẹnte** *adv.* immoderately, excessively; intemperately; to excess. **-aziọne** *f.* see smoderatezza.

†**smoggiare** *intr.* to abound, to overflow the bushel (cf. moggio).

smoking *m. indecl.* dinner jacket.

smolendare [A 1] *tr.* (of a miller) to take the multure on, to take a toll in kind for grinding.

smollare [A 1] *tr.* to soak (clothes) before washing; to take out of soak.

smollic·are [A 2 s] *tr.* (of bread) to crumble; *rfl.* (of stone) to be friable. **-ato** *part. adj.* crumbled.

smonac·are [A 2 s] *tr.* to remove from a convent or monastery; *rfl.* to leave the cloister, to cease to be a nun or monk. (**-ato** *part. adj.*)

smont·are [A 1 c] *tr.* to take down; to bring down; — le scale, to go downstairs; to unhorse, to unseat; (mil.) to overthrow, to capsize, to strip, to take down (e.g. a gun); — la cavalleria, to dismount the cavalry; — di guardia, to withdraw a guard; (naut.) — il timone, to raise the rudder; to take to pieces, to dismantle, to disassemble; (jewellery) to remove from mounting; (fig.) to discharge; to deflate; *intr.* (aux. essere) to dismount; to get out; to alight; to go down; (of colours) to fade; (of prices) to drop; to go off duty, to stop work; l'infermiera di notte -a alle 8.15, the night nurse goes off duty at 8.15 a.m.; †see tramontare; *rfl.* to lose enthusiasm, to cool off (fig.); (naut., of the rudder) to be unshipped. **-a·bile** *adj.* (eng.) detachable; collapsible; that may be dismantled or taken to pieces. **-ag·gio** *m.* (eng.) disassembly, dismantling, stripping. **-ato** *part. adj.* dismounted; (eng.) dismantled, knocked down. **-atura** *f.* (eng.) dismantling, disassembling, taking to pieces.

smorb·are [A 1] *tr.* to heal; to purify; to disinfect. (**-ato** *part. adj.*)

smor·fi·a *f.* grimace; affected smile or gesture; languishing look; pose; wry face; avere, fare una —, to pull a face, to grimace. **-ata** *f.* (pop.) see smorfia. **-ọso** *adj.* affected; mincing; skittish; wheedling. **-osamẹnte** *adv.* affectedly; mincingly; skittishly.

†**smorire** *intr.* to turn pale.

smort·o *adj.* pale; wan; listless, lifeless; dull; dim; (of colour) mat; (of metal) unpolished, tarnished; (of flowers) withered; dead; (of shade, forest, etc.) dark; bleak. **-ẹzza** *f.* pallor. **-ire** [D 2] *intr.* (aux. essere) to turn pale; to lose brightness; to fade. **-ito** *part. adj.* pale; wan; dull; faded.

smorz·are [A 1] *tr.* to extinguish; to dim; to shade; to appease, to quench; to slake; to tone down; to abate, to moderate; (techn.) to triturate (ore); to quench (steel); to damp (vibrations, etc.); (naut.) — l'abbrivo, to reduce a ship's way; †— una vela, to take in a sail; *rfl.* to be extinguished; to fade away; to grow faint. **-amẹnto** *m.* extinguishing; toning down; (electr.) damping; (phys.)

smorz-are (*cont.*)
damping, attenuation; (radio; telev.) damping, decrement. **-ando** *gerund.* (mus.) fading away. **-ato** *part. adj.* extinguished; attenuated; toned down; (electr.; teleg.) damped. **-atoio** *m.* (mus.) damper (of pianoforte). **-atore** *m.* (eng.; techn.) damper, shock absorber; (motor.) -atore di scappamento, silencer. **-atura** *f.* attenuation; toning down; shading.

smorzo *m.* extinction; toning down; shading; appeasement; (mus.) damper (of pianoforte); damping-pedal, soft pedal.

smoss-o *part.* of **smuovere**, q.v.; *adj.* displaced, removed, shifted; disturbed; agitated; piede —, dislocated foot, sprained ankle; terreno —, tilled ground, ploughed land; terra di fresco -a, freshly turned earth. **-a** *f.* motion; movement; shift, shifting.

smostacciata *f.* contemptuous facial expression.

smott-a *f.* fall of earth (in landslide). **-amento** *m.* landslide. **-are** [A 1] *intr.* (*aux.* essere) to slip, to fall (of earth). **-atura** *f.* see **smotta**.

smozz-are [A 1] *tr.* to lop off; to chip off; to chop off. (**-ato** *part. adj.*) **-atura** *f.* lopping; chopping off; piece lopped off.

smozzic-are [A 2 sc] *tr.* to cut to pieces; to mutilate; to maim; to clip; to cut short. (**-amento** *m.*) **-ato** *part. adj.* cut to pieces; mutilated; maimed; cacio -ato dai topi, cheese nibbled by mice; *n.m.* maimed man, cripple. (**-atura** *f.*)

†**smucciare** *intr.* to slip away; to run away; *tr.* to cut obliquely.

smun·g-ere [C 5] *tr.* to drain; to suck dry; to milk dry; (fig.) to exhaust; to render pale and wan; to fleece; — denari a, to extort money from; *rfl.* to be drained; to be sucked dry; to run dry; (fig.) to become exhausted. **-itore** *m.* extortioner; sponger. (**-itrice** *f.*)

smun-ire [D 2] *tr.* to leave undefended. **-ito** *part. adj.* undefended, unprotected; defenceless.

smunto *part.* of **smungere**, q.v.; *adj.* pale, wan; emaciated; haggard; exhausted; lean, thin, scraggy; impoverished; — di denari, fleeced.

smuo·v-ere [C 15] *tr.* to shift; to displace; to move, to stir; to set in motion; to affect, to excite; to deter, to dissuade; — il terreno, to till the soil, to plough the land; — la città, to create a disturbance in the city; — il corpo, to move the bowels; *rfl.* to move; to be moved; to be swayed; non si smosse, he did not budge. **-itore** *m.* agitator. (**-itrice** *f.*) (**-itura** *f.*)

smur-are [A 1] *tr.* to demolish the walls of; (naut.) to ease sheets, to partially spill the sail; -a e imbroglia!, brail up! (the easing of sheets is understood in the English command).

smuṣ-are [A 1] *tr.* (Tusc., fam.) to smash the face of, to hit in the face; *intr.* (*aux.* avere) to make a face, to grimace (indicating disgust or contempt). **-ata** *f.*, **-atura** *f.* smack in the face; grimace.

smuss-are [A 1] *tr.* to blunt; to round off the corners of; (fig.) to smooth, to soften; (eng.) to bevel, to chamfer; *rfl.* to get blunt; to be blunted. **-amento** *m.* blunting; bevelling. **-ato** *part. adj.* bevelled, chamfered, blunt. **-atura** *f.* (techn.) bevelling, chamfering; bevel; chamfer. **-ettino** *m.* chamfering chisel. **-o** *apocop. part.*; *adj.* bevelled, chamfered; blunted at the corners; broken; (fig.) softened; *n.m.* bevel; chamfering chisel, chamfer.

†**snamorare** *vb.* and derivs. See **disinnamorare**.

†**snaṣ-are** *tr.* to cut off the nose of. (**-ato** *part. adj.*)

snatur-are [A 1] *tr.* to alter the nature of, to change; to distort; to misrepresent; *rfl.* to change one's nature; to alter, to change completely; *intr.* (*aux.* essere) to degenerate; to denature. **-amento** *m.* alteration (of nature); denaturalization; perversion. **-atezza** *f.* unnaturalness; inhumanity. **-ato** *part. adj.* unnatural; cruel; monstrous; madre -ata, mother who neglects or abandons her children. (**-atamente** *adv.*)

snazionaliẓẓ-are [A 1] *tr.* to denationalize. **-ato** *part. adj.* **-azione** *f.* denationalization.

snebbi-are [A 4] *tr.* to clear fog from; to dispel the mist from; (fig.) — la mente, to clear the mind; *intr.* (*aux.* essere), *rfl.* to become clear (esp. of the sky). **-ato** *part. adj.* clear; free from fog or mist; orizzonte -ato, horizon free of mist.

sneghittire [D 2] *tr.* to make smart, to smarten up; to make brisk; *rfl.* (colloq.) to pull oneself together; to 'pull one's socks up'.

snell-o *adj.* nimble; brisk; active; quick, swift; agile; slim, slender; (archit.) colonne -e, slender columns; architettura -a, architecture free of heaviness, elegant style of architecture; stile —, easy, rapid, style. **-amente** *adv.* nimbly; briskly; swiftly. **-ezza** *f.* agility; nimbleness; quickness, swiftness; slimness; slenderness.

snerv-are [A 1] *tr.* to exhaust; to enfeeble; to enervate; (colloq.) to annoy, to get on the nerves of; to cut the tendons of, to remove a tendon from; — di denaro, to keep very short of money; *rfl.* to become exhausted, enfeebled, enervated. **-amento** *m.* nervous exhaustion; enervation, weakness; (phys.; eng.) yielding; (mech.) sollecitazione di -amento, yield stress; (eng.; bldg.) resistenza allo -amento, yield strength. **-ante** *part. adj.* enervating; exhausting. **-atezza** *f.* debility, weakness; prostration. **-ato** *part. adj.* exhausted; enervated; faint, weak; flabby; dull. (**-atamente** *adv.* **-atore** *m.*) **-atrice** *f.* (eng.) strain-relieving machine.

†**snicchiare** *vb.* and derivs. See **snidare**.

snid-are [A 1] *tr.* to dislodge; to drive out; to drive from the nest; to drive from shelter; — una lepre, to rouse a hare; (mil.) to eject (the enemy) from a strong point, to 'winkle out'; *intr.* (*aux.* essere), *rfl.* to come out (from a shelter). (**-ato** *part. adi².*)

snob *m. indecl.* snob; member of the 'smart set'; *adj. indecl.* smart, fashionable; ti sei comprato un cappello molto —, that's a very smart hat you're wearing. **-iṣmo** *m.* snobbery; affectation; snobbishness. **-i·stico** *adj.* snobbish; di stampo -istico, snobbish.

snobbare [A 1] *tr.* to snub.

snocciol-are [A 3 s] *tr.* to remove the kernel from, to stone; (fig.) to talk glibly about; to 'spout'; to rattle off; to pay out readily. **-atamente** *adv.* glibly; freely. (**-ato** *part. adj.*) **-atoio** *m.* tool for stoning olives, cherries, plums, etc.

snod-are [A 1] *tr.* to untie; to loosen; to unravel; to undo; to stretch, to loosen up, to exercise, to make supple; *rfl.* to come loose, to come untied; to become supple; (of a snake, etc.) to wriggle; la strada si -a nella valle, the road winds through the valley. (**-amento** *m.*) **-ato** *part. adj.* untied; loosened; flexible, supple; (eng.) articulated; (of a joint) dislocated, put out; metro -ato, folding meter-rule. **-atamente** *adv.* freely, loosely; flexibly. **-atura** *f.* loosening, untying; flexing; suppleness, articulation; pivoting. **-evole** *adj.* supple.

snodo *m.* (eng.) articulation, articulated joint; — a sfera, ball joint.

snudare [A 1] *tr.* to bare, to lay bare; to unsheathe.

†**so¹** *poss. prn., adj.* See **suo**.

†**so²** *prep.* See **su**.

so³ *1st pers. sing. pres. indic.* of **sapere**, q.v.

†**soatto** *m.* See **sogatto**.

soav-e *adj.* sweet, soft; mild; gentle; profumo —, sweet scent; voce —, soft, sweet, voice; vino —, smooth wine, *also* a dry white wine from Soave, near Verona; pendio —, gentle slope; (paint.) gentle, restrained; *adv.* (mus.) gently, delicately, sweetly. **-emente** *adv.* sweetly, softly, gently; morire -emente, to die peacefully. **-eolente** *adj.* (poet.) sweet smelling. **-ità** *f.* sweetness; softness; gentleness.

sobbalz-are [A 1] *intr.* (*aux.* avere) to jolt; to jerk; to bounce; to jump up; to leap; to give a start; to throb; — di gioia, to jump for joy. **-o** *m.* start, jump; jolt; jerk; svegliarsi di -o, to wake up with a start.

sobbarcare [A 2] *tr.* to impose a burden on; to lay heavy responsibility on; — una società a grandi spese, to burden a company with heavy expenditure; *rfl.* to take on responsibility; (*prep.* a) sobbarcarsi a, to assume the burden of.

†**sobbarcolare** *rfl.* to tuck up one's gown, etc. to avoid being encumbered.

†**sobbillare** *vb.* See **sobillare**.

sobboll-ire [D 2] *intr.* (*aux.* avere) to simmer, to boil gently; (fig.) to come out in a heat rash; l'ira -iva nel suo cuore, he was seething with suppressed anger. (**-imento** *m.*) **-ito** *part. adj.* simmering; fieni -iti, fermenting hay; (fig.) ira -ita, suppressed anger; *n.m.* spots on the skin, rash, pimples.

sobbor-go *m.* (*pl.* -ghi). See **borgo**.

†**sobbu·glio** *m.* See **subbug·lio**.

sobill-are [A 1] *tr.* to instigate; to incite (to rebellion, etc.); to stir up; †to suborn. (**-amento** *m.* **-ato** *part. adj.*) **-atore** *m.* instigator. **-azione** *f.* instigation, incitement; †suborning.

†**sobranzare** *vb.* and derivs. See **sovranzare**.

so·bri-o *adj.* temperate, moderate, sober; stile —, restrained style of writing. (**-amente** *adv.*) **-età** *f.* temperance, moderation, sobriety.

†**socceneric·cio** *adj.* (of bread) baked under the ashes.

†**socchiamare** [A 1] *tr.* to call softly.

socchiu·dere [C 3] *tr.* to half close, to leave ajar; to draw to.

socchiuso *part.* of **socchiudere**, q.v.; *adj.* half-closed, half-open; ajar.

soc·cid-a *f.* (leg.) contract for agistment of cattle owned by 'soc-cidante'; — **parziaria**, the like contract, of cattle owned severally by the parties (C.C.); partner to an agistment contract. **-ante** *m.* bailor of cattle in agistment. **-a·rio** *m.* agistor.

soc·cio *m.* agistor; see **soccida**; cattle kept under a contract of agistment.

socco *m.* (class. antiq.) sock, the light shoe worn by actors in comedy; calzare il —, to don the sock, i.e. to write a comedy.

soccoda·gnolo *m.* crupper (strap).

soccomb-ere [B I] *intr.* (*aux.* essere; *prep.* a) to succumb; to give way; to yield (to); to be overcome (by); to die. **-ente** *part. adj.* yielding, giving way; rimanere **-ente**, to get defeated (in sport), to get the worst of it; (leg.) la parte **-ente**, the losing party, the loser. **-enza** *f.* (leg.) position of loser; consequences of losing.

soccorr-ere [C 5], †**-ire** *tr.* to help; to assist; to relieve; to succour; *intr.* (*aux.* avere, essere) to come to mind; *recip. rfl.* to help one another. **-evole** *adj.* helpful; charitable. **-evolmente** *adv.* helpfully; charitably. **-i·bile** *adj.* suitable for help; fortezza **-ibile**, fortress that can be relieved. **-itore** *m.*, **-itrice** *f.* helper; help; member of a rescue team; *adj.* helpful; carità **-itrice**, charity, benevolence.

soccorso *part.* of **soccorrere**, q.v.; *adj.* helped, relieved; succoured; *n.m.* help, aid; prestare —, to lend aid; succour; assistance; relief; *pl.* (mil.) reinforcements; (provb.) il — di Pisa, tardy relief, help coming too late; pronto —, first aid, *or* casualty ward in a hospital; posto di primo —, first-aid station; società di mutuo —, (mutual) benefit society; uscita di —, emergency exit; gridare al —, to call for help; helper; help.

socco·scio *m.* (butcher.) fillet of rump steak.

soccotrino *m.* (bot.) Socotrine aloes, *Aloë succotrina*.

so·cer-a *f.*, **-o** *m.* See **suocer-a**, **-o**.

socia·bil-e *adj.* sociable; (zool.) gregarious. **-ità** *f.* sociability; companionableness; (zool.) gregariousness.

social-e *adj.* social, corporate; (zool.) animale —, social animal (esp. man and insects); economia —, sociology; patto —, social contract; ordine —, social order; assistente —, welfare officer; (leg.; comm.) belonging to, or having to do with, a 'società', q.v.; attivo —, partnership assets; ragione —, style or firm, firm name; statuto —, partnership articles, company's articles of association; sede —, head office, registered office; capitale —, capital of company of partnership; patrimonio —, partnership property; quota —, share of capital of partnership; (Rom. hist.) guerra —, Social War. **-mente** *adj.* socially, in society; sociably.

social-ismo *m.* socialism. **-ista** *adj.*, *n.m.*, *f.* socialist; **-ista** della 3ª internazionale, communist. **-i·stico** *adj.* socialistic; socialist. **-isto·ide** *m.* one favourable to socialism, 'fellow-traveller'.

socialità *f.* brotherhood; umana —, brotherhood of man; sociability.

socializz-are [A I] *tr.* to socialize, to collectivize, to nationalize. (**-atore** *m.* **-ato** *part. adj.* **-atrice** *f.*) **-azione** *f.* socialization; nationalization.

societ-à *f.* society; community; companionship, fellowship; club; di —, amateur, private; party; company, firm; partnership; in con, in partnership with; tenere —, to receive (company, guests); abito di —, evening dress; la — elegante, the fashionable world; — delle nazioni, League of Nations; (comm.; leg.) company; corporation; partnership; society; — anonima, (former appellation of) limited liability company (now called 'società per azioni', q.v.); — anonime esercenti un servizio pubblico, public utility companies; — commerciale, company or partnership with commercial objects; — co-operativa, co-operative society; — edilizia, building and contracting company; — fiduciaria e di revisione, trust company; — finanziaria, holding company; — immobiliare, property company; — mobiliare, finance company; — occulta, secret partnership; — operaia, trade union; — semplice, partnership with non-commercial objects; — straniera, foreign company; — a responsabilità limitata, partnership with limited liability; private or proprietary company; — di assicurazione, insurance company or society; — di investimento, investment company; — di mutua assicurazione, mutual insurance society; — di mutuo soccorso, Friendly Society; mutual benefit society; — di previdenza sociale, provident society; — in accomandita semplice, limited partnership; — in accomandita per azioni, limited partnership with shareholders; — in nome collettivo, (general, unlimited) partnership; — per azioni, company limited by shares; joint-stock company; limited liability company; public company; — per azioni controllata, subsidiary company controlled by another; — per azioni familiare, family company; certificato d'iscrizione della S. per azioni, certificate of incorporation; contratto di —, Memorandum of Association; domicilio legale della —, Registered Office (cf. **sede**); company's address for service; statuto di —, Articles of Association; costituire una —, to form a company. **-a·rio** *adj.* (sport) relating to a club or a society.

socievol-e *adj.* sociable; companionable; social. (**-mente** *adv.*) **-ezza** *f.* sociability.

socinian-ismo *m.* Socinianism, Socinian heresy. **-o** *adj.* (leg.) cautela **-a**, election allowed to legitimate heir in certain cases of insufficiency of Testator's estate (C.C.); *n.m.* Socinian.

so·cio *m.* member; associate; fellow; partner; (leg.; comm.) — accomandante, limited partner, sleeping partner, special partner; — accomandatario, unlimited partner, general partner; — anziano, senior partner; — fondatore, original member of incorporated company, foundation member of club or society; — gerente, managing partner; — occulto, secret partner; — promotore, original partner; — sovventore, contributing member; registro dei soci, list, register, of members.

sociol-ogi·a *f.* sociology. **-o·gico** *adj.* sociological. (**-ogicamente** *adv.*) **o-logo** *m.* sociologist.

So·cr-ate *pr.n.m.* Socrates. **-a·tico** *adj.*, *n.m.* Socratic (philosopher, method). **-aticamente** *adv.* Socratically.

soda *f.* soda; sodium carbonate; soda-water; — caustica, caustic soda; bicarbonato di —, sodium bicarbonate.

soda·glia *f.* untilled land.

sodal-e *m.* fellow, companion, colleague. **-i·zio** *m.* association; brotherhood; guild.

sod-are[1] [A I] *tr.* to consolidate; to strengthen, to make firm; to make solid; — panno, to full cloth. (**-ato** *part. adj.*) **-atura** *f.* fulling (cloth).

sodare[2] [A I] *tr.* (leg.) to guarantee.

so(d)dis-fare [B 14] *tr.* to satisfy; to gratify; to fulfil; to comply with; to meet, to answer; to discharge; — un obbligo, to discharge an obligation; — un'offesa, to give satisfaction for an insult; *intr.* (*aux.* avere; *prep.* a) to satisfy; — al proprio dovere, to do one's duty; — a Dio, to please God; †to be sufficient; *rfl.* to satisfy oneself; to be satisfied. **-facente** *part. adj.* satisfactory; satisfying. (**-facemente** *adv.*) **-facimento** *m.* satisfaction; compliance; fulfilment; discharge (of debt or obligation). **-fattivo** *adj.* satisfactory. **-fatto** *part. adj.* satisfied, gratified, pleased, content; mal **-fatto**, discontented, dissatisfied; debito **-fatto**, debt discharged. †**-fatto·rio** *adj.* satisfactory. **-fazione** *f.* satisfaction; gratification; consolation, pleasure; approval; con nostra grande **-fazione**, much to our satisfaction; incontrare la piena **-fazione** di qualcuno, to meet with someone's full approval; reparation; **-fazione** per le armi, settling of a quarrel by means of a duel; chiedere **-fazione**, to challenge to a duel.

†**Sod·doma** *pr.n.f.* See **Sodoma**.

sodezza *f.* solidity, firmness; compactness; massiveness; steadiness; — nelle avversità, steadiness in adversity; ingegno senza —, unstable genius; (archit.) — dell'ordine dorico, solidity (massiveness) of the Doric order; †hardness.

so·d-ico *adj.* (chem.) of sodium; solfato —, sodium sulphate. **-io** *m.* (chem.) sodium; solfato di **-io**, sodium sulphate.

sod-o *adj.* solid, firm, substantial; strong; massive; compact; hard; heavy; uovo —, hard-boiled egg; grano —, whole grain (unground); terreno —, untilled land; star —, to stand firm, to stand one's ground; *adv.* parlar —, to speak clearly and firmly; picchiar — (*or* darle **-e**), to hit hard; dormir —, to sleep soundly; lavorare —, to work hard, to do sound work; *n.m.* firm ground; mettere in —, to establish; (archit.) solid block; foundation; (fig.) posare sul —, to rest on a firm foundation; sul —, seriously. **-amente** *adv.* firmly, solidly; steadfastly; soundly; studiare **-amente**, to study diligently, to work hard and methodically.

So·dom-a *pr.n.f.* (Bibl.) Sodom; †sodomy. **-i·a** *f.* sodomy. **-ita** *m.* sodomite.† **-itare** *intr.* to practise sodomy. **-i·tico** *adj.* sodomitical.

sofà *m. indecl.* sofa; settee; couch.

soffer-ente *adj.* suffering; ailing, unwell, sickly; — del petto, consumptive; patient, enduring; — del freddo, enduring (standing) cold. **-entemente** *adv.* patiently; painfully. **-enza** *f.* suffering, pain; patience, endurance; (comm.) dishonour; sufferance; cambiale in **-enza**, unmet, unpaid, dishonoured bill; lasciare una tratta in **-enza**, to let a bill lie over; merci in **-enza**, restricted goods. **-ire** [D 2] and derivs. see **soffrire**.

sofferm-are [A I] *tr.* to detain; *rfl.* to stay a while, to pause for a moment; -arsi su, to linger over, to dwell upon. **-ata** *f.* pause, short stay; stop; (med.) intermission (of pulse, etc.). (**-ato** *part. adj.*)

sofferto *part.* of **soffrire**, q.v.; *adj.* suffered, endured; (leg.) carcere —, period spent in detention or under arrest; *n.m.* (leg.) computare il —, to take into account the time spent under arrest.

†soffi *m. indecl.* shah (of Persia).

soffi-are [A 4] *intr.* (*aux.* avere) to blow; — sul caffè perchè si raffreddi, to blow on one's coffee to cool it; — sulla candela, to blow out the candle; — nel fuoco, to blow the fire, (fig.) to stir up strife; to breathe; to puff, to pant; *tr.* to blow out; to blow; — il fumo in faccia a uno, to blow the smoke in someone's face; (of a cat) to spit; to fan (flames); (draughts) to huff; to whisper, to prompt; to tell tales (secretly); *rfl.* (*dat.* of *prn.* 'si') to prime; -arsi il naso, to blow one's nose; -arsi le dita, to blow on one's fingers (to warm them). **-amento** *m.* blowing; puffing; breath; -amento di maldicenza, breath of scandal. **-ante** *part. adj.* blowing, puffing; macchina -ante, mechanical bellows, blower; *n.m.* blower. **-ata** *f.* blast, blow; puff; breath (of wind). **-ato** *part. adj.* blown, driven; neve -ata dal vento, driven snow, snow-drift; (chem.; industr.) blown; l'industria del vetro -ato, the glass-blowing industry; olio di lino -ato, blown linseed oil. **-atoio** *m.* bellows. **-atore** *m.* person blowing; (fig.) inciter; (eng.) blower, jet; (electr.) -atore magnetico, magnetic blow-out (for electric arc); (theatr.) prompter. **-atrice** *f.* blower. **-atura** *f.* blowing; blow; blowing one's nose; non dimenticare di farti una buona -atura di naso, don't forget to give your nose a good blow; (glassm.) -atura del vetro, glass blowing; (foundry) blow-hole (in a casting).

†sofficcare *tr.* to conceal.

sof·fic-e *adj.* soft; soft to the touch; gentle; light; tender; yielding; guanciale —, soft pillow; (agric.) terreno —, well-tilled soil; *n.m.* softness; dormire nel —, to sleep soft. **-emente** *adv.* softly; gently; lightly.

soffieggiare [A 3 c] *intr.* (*aux.* avere) to keep puffing and blowing; to puff and pant.

soffieri·a *f.* bellows; mechanical bellows used for a furnace.

soffietto *m.* See under **soffio**.

†soffig·gere *tr.* to thrust underneath; to hide.

soff-io *m.* puff; breath; breathing; blowing; con un — spense la candela, he blew out the candle; breath of wind; breath of air; whiff; — violento, blast, gust; (fig.) in un —, in an instant, in a twinkling; passato come un —, gone in a flash; il — animatore, the breath of life; inspiration; (of a cat) spitting; (med.) murmur; (radio) — microfonico, microphone hiss; †spy's report. **-ietta·io** *m.* bellows-maker. **-ietto** *m.* bellows; (journalistic) puff; -ietto editoriale, blurb; †spy; †hood of a carriage. **-ino** *m.* game of wager played by blowing a coin off the back of the hand; †fare a -ino, to play the spy. **-ione** *m.* bellows-pipe, bellows; forge-blower; (geog.) fumarole, jet of boiling vapour; (bot.) dandelion, *Taraxacum officinale*; (mil. hist.) gun; portfire used for firing a gun; conceited, puffed-up person; (joc.) spy; (pop.) prompter (cf. **soffiatore**, under **soffiare**).

soffitt-a *f.* garret, attic; lumber-room; (archit.) soffit; lower part of a cornice. **-are** [A I] *tr.* (archit.) to provide with soffit(s); to make the ceiling of. **-ato** *part. adj.* having a soffit; having a ceiling; *n.m.* see **soffitto**[1].

soffitto[1] *m.* (archit.) ceiling; soffit; false ceiling; (aeron.) ceiling.

†soffitto[2] *part.* of **soffiggere**, q.v.

soffoc-are [A 2 s] *tr.* to suffocate; to strangle; to smother; to stifle; to choke; to extinguish; to repress; to suppress; to quell; to hush up; — l'odio, to repress hatred; — una sommossa, to suppress a rebellion; — uno scandalo, to hush up a scandal; (mil.) to douse (a powder train); to neutralize (the enemy position) by concentrated fire; (naut.) to spill the wind in (a sail) by brailing up; *intr.* (*aux.* avere) to feel suffocated; qui si -a, it's suffocating in here. **-amento** *m.* suffocating; choking; quelling. **-ante** *part. adj.* suffocating; stifling; stuffy, close; sultry; oppressive. **-ato** *part. adj.* suffocated; strangled; choked; stifled; morì -ato, he was strangled, *or* he was suffocated (by accident). **-atamente** *adv.* stiflingly; chokingly; suffocatingly. **-atore** *m.* strangler; *adj.* suffocating. (**-atrice** *f., adj.*) **-azione** *f.* suffocating; suffocation; choking; repressing; suppressing; (med.) asphyxia.

soffogare [A 2] and derivs. (pop.). See **soffocare**.

†soffoggiata *f.* bundle carried under the arm and hidden by a cloak.

†sof-fol·cere, **†-folcire**, **†fol·gere**, **†-folgire**, *tr.* to support; *rfl.* to lean. **†-folto**, **†-fulto** *part. adj.* supported; sustained.

†soffondare *vb.* and derivs. See **affondare**.

soffondere [C 5] *tr.* to suffuse.

†sofforare *tr.* to pierce a hole in from underneath.

†soffornato *adj.* sunk, cavernous.

†soffran·gere *tr.* to break into small pieces.

†soffratt-a *f.* dearth; scarcity; famine; dire need. **†-oso** *adj.* scarce.

soffreddare [A I c] *tr., rfl., intr.* (*aux.* essere) to cool, to cool down.

†soffreddo *adj.* cool.

soffreg-are [A 2] *tr.* to rub gently; **†***rfl.* to creep up obsequiously and ask for favour, etc. **-amento** *m.* gentle rubbing. (**-ato** *part. adj.*)

†soffretta *f.* See **soffratta**.

soffrig·gere [C 12] *tr., intr.* (*aux.* avere) to fry lightly; (joc.) to grumble, to complain.

soffr-ire [D I] *tr.* to suffer; to endure, to bear, to stand; — il dolore, to suffer pain; non lo posso —, I can't bear him; to put up with; to allow; non -e la critica, he won't accept criticism; *intr.* (*aux.* avere) to suffer; to be a sufferer; — di, to suffer from, with; — di nevralgia, to suffer from neuralgia; to grieve; to take harm, to deteriorate; il commercio -ì grandemente, trade was badly hit. **-ibile** *adj.* endurable, bearable, sufferable.

soffritto *part.* of **soffriggere**, q.v.; *adj.* lightly fried; *n.m.* onions lightly fried with celery, carrots, parsley, etc.; (Naples) zuppa di —, soup made from pig's entrails served with tomato sauce and toast.

soffuso *part.* of **soffondere**, q.v.; *adj.* suffused; — di rossore, suffused with blushes; sprinkled; — di sudore, wet with sweat.

Sofia[1] *pr.n.f.* Sophia.

sof-ia[2] *f.* (liter.) wisdom; (theol.) the Divine Wisdom, Sophia. **-isma**, **-ismo** *m.* sophism. **-ista**, **†-isto** *m.* sophist. **†-isteri·a** *f.* sophistry. **-i·stica** *f.* sophistry; dialectic. **-isticag·gine** *f.* pedantry; hair-splitting. **-isticamento** *m.* cavilling; adulterating. **-isticare** [A 2 s] *intr.* (*aux.* avere) to argue sophisticatedly, to cavil; *tr.* to adulterate; to sophisticate. **-isticato** *part. adj.* adulterated. **-isticazione** *f.* (comm.) adulteration; sophistication. **-isticheri·a** *f.*, **†-isteri·a** *f.* subtlety; cavilling; pedantry, hair-splitting. **-i·stico** *adj.* sophistic; pedantic; meticulous (**-isticamente** *adv.*)

So·fia[3] *pr.n.f.* (geog.) Sofia (Bulgaria).

sofo *m.* (poet.) sage, wise man; i sette sofi della Grecia, the seven sages of Greece.

So·focle *pr.n.m.* Sophocles.

so·fora *f.* (bot.) *Sophora japonica*, a leguminous papilionate.

†sofrone·tico *adj.* wise, prudent.

†sofroniste·rio *m.* house of correction.

†soga *f.* leather strap, thong; cord, rope.

sog-atto, **-at·tolo** *m.* (Tusc.) leather strap; thong of cowhide.

†sogello *m.* See **suggello**.

soggettiv-o *adj.* subjective; (gramm.) costruzione -a, construction comprising a dependent clause with its subject in the nominative case. **-amente** *adv.* subjectively. **-ismo** *m.* subjectivism. **-ista** *m., f.* subjectivist. **-ità** *f.* subjectivity.

soggett-o *adj.* subject, subjected; subordinate; liable; amenable; — a modificazione, subject to alterations; *n.m.* subject; subject matter, topic; cambiamo —, let's change the subject; (derog.) individual; è un cattivo —, he is a bad lot; (med.) patient, subject; (theatr.) commedia a —, improvised comedy; recitare a —, to act extempore; (mus.) subject, theme; contrappunto a —, fugal counterpoint, imitative counterpoint; (archit.) theme; (leg.) — di diritto, person who can sue and be sued; — di processo, (collectively) the parties to an action. **-ac·cio** *m. pejor.* bad lot; scamp, scallywag. **-amente** *adv.* submissively; in subjection. **-amento** *m.* subjection. **-are** [A I] *tr.* to subject; to subdue; *rfl.* to subject oneself. **-ato** *part. adj.* subjected. (**-atore** *m.* **-atrice** *f.*) **-ista** *m., f.* (cinem.) script-writer.

soggezione *f.* subjection; awe; timidity; shyness; embarrassment; uneasiness; constraint; sentirsi in —, provar —, to feel uneasy; porre in —, to overawe; avere — di, to stand in awe of; dare — a, to embarrass; — all'estero per le materie prime, dependence on foreign countries for raw materials.

sogghign-are [A 5] *intr.* (*aux.* avere) to smile contemptuously; to grin maliciously; to laugh derisively; to laugh up one's sleeve; to sneer; to jeer. (**-atore** *m.* **-atrice** *f.*) **-o** *m.* grin; grimace; leer; ironic smile; sneer.

soggiac-ere [B 15] *intr.* (*aux.* essere; *prep.* a) to be subject (to); to be liable; to succumb; to yield; to put up (with), to lie down (under). **-ente** *part. adj.* liable (to); subject. **-enza** *f.* (geol.) layer, bed. **-imento** *m.* liability, subjection.

soggiog-are [A 2] *tr.* to subjugate; to bring into subjection; (fig.) to subdue. **-amento** *m.* subduing; subjugation; subjection. **-ante** *part.* subjugating; *n.m.* conqueror. **-ato** *part. adj.* subjugated; in subjection; (fig.) subdued. (**-atore** *m.* **-atrice** *f.*) **-azione** *f.* subjugation; subjection.

soggiornare [A 1 c] *intr.* (*aux.* avere) to stay, to sojourn; to reside; †*tr.* to house, to give shelter to; †to air, to ventilate.

soggiorno *m.* stay, sojourn; resort; residence; carta di —, permesso di —, residence permit; tassa di —, visitors' tax; indennità di —, subsistence allowance; stanza di —, living-room; bed-sitting-room; casa di —, holiday home; †(mil.) stage, staging-point, halt; †senza —, without delay.

soggiu·gnere *vb.* and derivs. See **soggiungere**.

soggiun·g-ere [C 5] *tr.* to say in addition, to add; to subjoin. **-imento** *m.* subjoining; addition; remark.

soggiuntivo *adj., n.m.* (gramm.). See **congiuntivo**.

soggiun-to *part.* of soggiungere, q.v.; *adj.* added; subjoined. **-zione** *f.* addition (e.g. of more words), further remarks.

soggol-o, †**-a** *f.* wimple; chinstrap; (harness) throatband; dewlap.

sogguard-are [A 1] *tr.* to eye shyly; to eye slily, to peer up at; *recip. rfl.* to look furtively or askance at one another; to steal glances at one another. (**-ato** *part. adj.*)

sogguat-are [A 1] *tr.* to eye with suspicion, scorn, fear, etc.; to look askance at; *recip. rfl.* to eye one another suspiciously. (**-ato** *part. adj.*)

so·gli-a¹ *f.* threshold; varcare la —, to cross the threshold; sill; (door) step; window-sill; (geol.) sill; (naut.) top strake; — del ponte, foundation of piers of a bridge; gun'l capping; gunport; (scient.) threshold; — di udibilità, audibility threshold; *pl.* (fig.) threshold; verge. †**-aio** *m.*, †**-are** *m.* threshold.

so·glia² *f.* (ichth.). See **sogliola**.

so·glio¹ *m.* throne; (poet.) palace; court.

†**so·glio²** *m.* liquid measure of capacity (54·6 litres, Mantua).

so·gliola *f.* (ichth.) sole; — vera, Dover sole; — volgare, *Solea solea* — turca, *S. klenii*; — occhiuta, *S. ocellata*; — gialla, solenette, *S. lutea*; — pelosa, *Monochirus hispidus*.

sogn-are [A 5 c], [A 5] *tr., intr.* (*aux.* avere) to dream; to dream of, about; to dream up; mi pareva di —, I thought I was dreaming; to daydream, to muse; — ad occhi aperti, to be in a fool's paradise *or* to indulge in idle fancies; passare il tempo -ando, to dream away one's time; to long for; -avo una villetta in campagna, it was my dream to have a little cottage in the country; *rfl.* (*dat.* of *prn.* 'si') to imagine, to fancy (to oneself); non me lo sono mai -ato, I never (even) dreamt of it; tu ti -i!, you're dreaming!; avevi promesso di venire stasera, o me lo sono -ato?, did you say you would come this evening, or did I dream it?; (pop.) to dream of; stanotte mi sono -ato mia madre, last night I dreamt of my mother. **-ato** *part. adj.* dreamt of; imagined; longed for, desired. **-atore** *m.* dreamer; visionary; *adj.* dreaming. (**-atrice** *f.*)

sogn-o, sogno *m.* dream; vision; reverie; fancy; illusion; far-fetched idea; — ad occhi aperti, illusion, waking dream, daydream; un — che si è avverato, a dream come true; in un mondo di -i, in dreamland; apparire in —, to appear in a dream; libro dei -i, book of dreams, *or* book indicating lucky lotto numbers; fable; imagined vision, fantasy; *Un — di una notte di mezza estate*, *A Midsummer Night's Dream*; questo è —!, that is fantastic!; neppure per —!, by no means!, on no account; è un —!, it's heavenly!, it's a dream!

so·ia¹ *f.* (bot.) soya bean, *Glycine max*.

†**so·ia²** *f.* exaggerated praise, flattery, adulation mixed with mockery.

soigneur *m. indecl.* (pron. as Fr.) (boxing) second.

sol¹, †**solle** *m.* (mus.) soh (i.e. the fifth degree of the scale; the note G; the key of G).

sol² *m. indecl.* (scient.) sol.

sola *f.* See under **solo**.

†**solacci-are** *vb.* and derivs. see **sollazzare**, under **sollazzo**. †**-o** *m.* see **sollazzo**.

sola·io *m.* (bldg.) floor (comprising the ceiling of one room and the floor of the room above); stratum; loft.

solamente *adv.* See under **solo**.

solan-acee *f.pl.* (bot.) family of plants of Solanaceae. **-ina** *f.* (chem.) alkaloid found in damp potatoes. **-io·ide** *adj.* (med.) solanoid.

solano *m.* (bot.) — nero, black nightshade, *Solanum nigrum*.

solare¹ *adj.* relating to the sun, solar; sistema —, solar system; i raggi solari, the sun's rays; luce —, sunlight; macchie, facole solari, sunspots; orologio —, sundial; (leg.) lastrico —, sun-terrace (C.C.); (med.) chiodo —, sunstroke, touch of the sun; (anat.) plesso —, solar plexus.

solare² [A 1] and derivs. See **risolare**.

sola·rio *m.* sun parlour; sun terrace.

solarizzazione *f.* (photog.) solarization.

solat-a *f.* long spell in hot sunshine; sunstroke. **-io** *m* (pop., Tusc.) part facing south; sunny spot; *adj. phr.* a -io, with a south(ern) aspect; *adj.* sunny, facing south.

solatro *m.* (bot.) black nightshade, *Solanum nigrum*; — maggiore, deadly nightshade, *Atropa belladonna*; — spinoso, *Solanum sodomaeum*.

†**sola·zio** *m.* See **sollazzo**.

solc-are [A 2 c] *tr.* to plough; to dig; (fig.) to furrow, to line; — l'acqua, to plough through the water; — i mari, to navigate, to sail, the seas; to streak across; to line. **-a·bile** *adj.* ploughable. **-ata** *f.* furrow; wake; track. **-ato** *part. adj.* ploughed; furrowed; fronte -ata, wrinkled brow. **-atore** *m.* ploughman. **-atura** *f.* ploughing, furrowing; furrow; scoring, grooving.

sol-co *m.* (*pl.* **-chi**) furrow; track; (fig.) uscir dal —, to leave the beaten track; streak; straight line; (oceanography) furrow; (of a ship) wake; (of disc recordings) groove; *pl.* (geol.) cracks, crevices (in rocks). **-co·metro** *m.* (naut.) log, patent log, pitometer.

soldanella *f.* (bot.) sea bindweed, *Convolvulus soldanella*.

†**soldano** *m.* and derivs. See **sultano**.

soldare [A 1] *tr.* (mil.) see **assoldare**; (naut.) to hire, to charter; to hire, to commission.

soldat-o *m.* soldier; fare il —, to be a soldier, to be in the army, to do one's military service; (Tusc.) andar —, to go into the army; (mil.) other rank; (fig.) — di Cristo, priest; *pl.* troops, army. **-ac·cio** *m. pejor.* rough, brutal soldier. **-a·glia** *f.* (derog.) mob of soldiers; brutal and licentious soldiery. **-esca** *f.* soldiery; troops; undisciplined soldiers. **-esco** *adj.* (*m.pl.* **-eschi**) soldierly; soldier's; soldier-like; military. **-escamente** *adv.* in soldierly manner. **-essa** *f.* **-essa** dell'Esercito della Salute, Salvation Army lass. **-ina** *f.* woman camp-follower. **-ino** *m. dim.* young soldier; private soldier; toy-soldier, tin-soldier. **-one** *m.* veteran, old soldier.

soldinella *f.* (bot.) — acquatica, pennywort, white rot, *Hydrocotyle vulgaris*.

sold-o *m.* coin of small value (about 5 centesimi); (fig.) penny, copper; non spendere un —, not to spend a penny; non vale un —, it isn't worth a farthing; essere al — di, to be in the pay of; (mil.) militia, mercenary; andare al —, to 'take the shilling', to join up, to go into the army; prendere il —, to enlist, to engage; †uomo di —, mercenary, paid soldier; *pl.* money; non aver -i, to have no money; è un uomo che ha fatto -i, he is a man who has made his pile. **-ino** *m.* (hist.) small silver coin (Milan sixteenth century); (bot.) Christ thorn, *Paliurus Spina-Christi*. **-one** *m.* copper coin; mettere in -oni, to change for coppers, (fig.) to explain in detail.

sol-e *m.* sun; la levata del —, sunrise; al primo —, at sunrise; il tramonto del —, sunset; orologio a —, sundial; aprire gli occhi alla luce del —, to see the light of day, to be born; aver qualcosa al —, to possess land; fare una cosa alla luce del —, to do a thing openly; farsi bello del — d'agosto, to take undeserved credit; (joc.) andare a veder il — a scacchi, to go to prison; (herald.) sun in splendour; sunshine; sunlight; un raggio di —, a ray of sunshine; un occhio di —, a gleam of sunlight; è chiaro come il —, it's as clear as daylight; colpo di —, sunstroke; occhiali da —, sun-glasses; cappello da —, sun-hat, sun-helmet, sun-bonnet; ombrellino da —, parasol; stare al —, to be, to stay, in the sun; riscaldarsi al —, prendere il —, to sunbathe, to sit, to lie, in the sun; pieno di —, sunny, full of sunshine; (fig.) sun; dawning or rising hopes of achievement of an ideal. **-icello**, **-icino** *m. dim.* weak sunlight; pale, feeble sun; winter sunshine; not much of a sun.

soleare *m.* (anat.) soleus, solearis.

sol-ecchio *m.*, †**-ic·chio** *m.* shield from the sun's rays; canopy; fare —, †farsi il —, to shade one's eyes from the sun or other bright light.

solec-iṣmo *m.* solecism, grammatical mistake; pieno di -ismi, full of grammatical errors. **-iẓẓare** [A I] *intr.* (*aux.* avere) to commit grammatical errors.

soleggi-are [A 3 c] *tr.* to sun, to expose to the sun; to spread in the sun; to dry in the sun; *intr.* (*aux.* avere) to bask in the sun. **-ato** *part. adj.* sunny; exposed to the sun; bright; una camera -ata, a sunny bedroom.

soleina *f.* (techn.) rosin spirit.

solenn-e *adj.* solemn; very great; grave; formal; abito —, ceremonial dress; voto —, formal vote; (colloq.) thorough; terrific; un — imbroglione, a downright swindler; una — indigestione, a fearful attack of indigestion. **-emente** *adv.* solemnly; gravely; formally; with ceremony. **-ità** *f.* solemnity; formality; gravity; impressiveness; ceremony; rite; (leg.) solemn form. **-iẓẓamento** *m.* solemnizing. **-iẓẓare** [A I] *tr.* to solemnize; to celebrate. **-iẓẓato** *part. adj.* solemnized.

soleno·id-e *m.* (elect.) solenoid. **-ale** *adj.* (electr.) solenoidal.

ṣo·leo *adj., m.* (anat.) soleus.

solere [B 30] *intr.* (*aux.* essere) to be in the habit of; to be wont to, to be accustomed to; suole andare, he usually goes, he is in the habit of going; soleva dire, he used to say, he was wont to say; ero solito andare, I used to go (cf. **solito**); *impers.* come suole accadere, as usually happens; suol piovere sulla fine della settimana, it usually rains towards the end of the week.

soleretta *f.* (mil. hist.) footguard (in metal).

solert-e, †**-o** *adj.* diligent, industrious; active; enterprising; ingenious; careful, attentive. (**-emente** *adv.*)

soler·zia *f.* diligence; industriousness; attention to detail, care.

solętt-a[1] *f.* sole of stocking, stocking-foot; (shoem.) insole; (archit.) ceiling of reinforced concrete; (watchm.) — del cricco, click sole. **-are** [A I c] *tr.* to furnish (a shoe) with a sock. (**-ato** *part. adj.*) **-atura** *f.* cork serving as sock (i.e. a loose inner sole).

solętt-a[2] *f.,* **-o** *m.* See under **solo**.

solfa *f. indecl.* (mus.) sol-fa, tonic sol-fa; battere la —, to beat time, (fig.) to repeat oneself continually; cantare a uno la —, to teach someone a lesson; †la — degli Ermini, Double Dutch, gibberish.

solf-amato *m.* (chem.) sulphamate. **-a·mico** *adj.* (chem.) sulphamic. **-a·mide** *f.* (chem.) sulphamide. **-ami·dico** *adj.* (chem.) sulphamidic; *n.m.pl.* (pharm.) i -amidici, the sulfa drugs. **-amile** *m.* (chem.) sulphamyl. **-ami·lico** *adj.* (chem.) sulphamylic. **-ami·nico** *adj.* (chem.) sulphaminic. **-anila·mide** *f.* (chem.) sulphanilamide. **-antimoniale** *adj.* (chem.) sulphantimonial. **-antimoniato** *m.* (chem.) sulphantimonate. **-antimo·nico** *adj.* (chem.) sulphantimonic.

†**solfanaria** *f.* See **solfatara**.

solfanell-a·io *m.* matchseller. **-o** *m.* (sulphur-)match.

solf-ara *f.* (miner.) sulphur deposit (esp. in Sicily). **-atara** *f.* (geog.) volcano or fumarole which gives off sulphur gas.

solf-are [A I c] *tr.* (agric.) to apply sulphur to. **-ato** *part. adj.* (agric.) treated with sulphur; *n.m.* (chem.) sulphate. **-azione** *f.* (electr.) sulphation (of battery plates).

solfatiẓẓare [A I] *rfl.* to sulphate.

solfeggi-are [A 3 c] *tr., intr.* (*aux.* avere) (mus.) to sol-fa. **-amento** *m.* (mus.) sol-fa, tonic sol-fa. **-ante** *part., n.m.,* **-atore** *m.* (mus.) sol-faist, tonic sol-faist. (**-atrice** *f.*)

solfeggio *m.* (mus.) solfeggio, vocal exercise.

ṣolf-o *m.* sulphur (cf. **zolfo**). **-erino** *m.* sulphur match; †bright red, a colour fashionable after the battle of Solferino (1859). **-idrato** *m.* (chem.) hydrosulphide. **-i·drico** *adj.* (chem.) hydrosulphurous; acido -idrico, sulphuretted hydrogen, hydrogen sulphide. **-i·fero** *adj.* sulphur-bearing. †**-ina·io** *m.* (sulphur) matchseller. **-inile** *m.* (chem.) sulphinyl. †**-ino** *m.* sulphur match; *adj.* sulphur-coloured. **-ito** *m.* (chem.) sulphite. **-ocianuro, -ocianato** *m.* (chem.) sulphocyanide, thiocyanate. **-onare** [A I c] *tr.* (chem.) to sulphonate. **-onato** *part. adj.* (chem.) sulphonated. **-onazione** *f.* (chem.) sulphonation. **-o·nico** *adj.* (chem.) sulphonic. **-o·nio** *m.* (chem.) sulphonium. **-oricinato** *m.* (chem.) sulphoricinoleate; (techn.) -oricinato di soda, Turkey Red Oil, sulphonated castor oil. **-o·rico** *adj.* (chem.) sulphuric; acido -orico, sulphuric acid. **-orile** *m.* (chem.) sulphuryl; cloruro di -orile, sulphuryl chloride. **-oroṣo** *adj.* (chem.) sulphurous. **-oṣale** *m.* (chem.) thio salt. **-uro** *m.* (chem.) sulphide; -uro di carbonio, carbon disulphide.

†**solic·chio** *m.* See under **solecchio**.

solic-ello, -ino *m. dim.* See under **sole**.

ṣo·lid-o *adj.* solid; firm; compact; substantial; strong; safe; sound;

un uomo —, a man of substance, *or* a reliable person; colori -i, fast colours; *n.m.* solid; (geom.) solid, solid figure, solid body; (leg.) in —, jointly and severally; obbligazione in —, joint and several liability (C.C.). **-amente** *adv.* solidly; firmly; (leg.) jointly and severally. **-ale** *adj.* joint; dichiararsi -ale, to declare oneself in agreement; (eng.) -ale con, integral with, forming one piece with; (leg.) joint and several; obbligazione -ale attiva, liability of debtor to his creditors jointly and severally; obbligazione -ale passiva, joint and several liability of debtors to their creditor (C.C.). **-are** [A I s] *tr.* to solidify; to make firm, to strengthen. **-a·rio** *adj.* (leg.) joint and several. **-ariamente** *adv.* (leg.) jointly and severally. **-arietà** *f.* (leg.) joint and several liability; loyalty; solidarity. (**-ato** *part. adj.*) **-eẓẓa** *f.* solidity; firmness.

solidific-are [A 2 s] *tr.* to solidify. **-a·bile** *adj.* solidifiable. **-ante** *part. adj.* solidifying; *n.m.* (techn.) solidifier, hardener. (**-ato** *part. adj.*) **-azione** *f.* (phys.) solidification.

solidiṣmo *m.* (med. hist.) solidism, solidistic pathology.

solidità *f.* solidity; firmness; strength; steadiness; substantiality; (techn.) proofness, fastness; — alla luce, fastness to light; fastness (of a dye).

solidun·guli *m.pl.* (zool.) Perissodactyls (horses, etc.).

soliflusso *m.* (geog.) solifluxion, soil-creep.

soli·gliolo *m.* luminary, little sun.

solilo·quio *m.* soliloquy; facile ai soliloqui, given to talking to oneself.

solin-a *f.* sunny place. **-are** [A I] *tr.* to sun, to expose to the sun; *intr.* (*aux.* avere) to bask in the sun. (**-ato** *part. adj.*)

solin-go *adj.* (*m.pl.* **-ghi**) lonely; solitary; alone. **-gamente** *adv.* solitarily; in lonely fashion; all alone.

solino *m.* (Tusc.) detachable collar; — duro, stiff collar, — rovesciato, (turn-down) double collar; (naut.) sailor's collar; (bldg.) cemented coiner.

†**ṣo·lio** *m.* See **soglio**[1].

soli·pede *m.* (zool.) perissodactyl.

solipsiṣmo *m.* (philos.) solipsism.

sol-ista *m., f.,* **-i·stico** *adj.* See under **solo**.

solita·ri-o *adj.* solitary, lonely; alone; secluded; deserted; un luogo —, a lonely spot; (orn.) passero —, blue rock-thrush, *Monticula solitarius*; (zool.) verme —, tapeworm; (naut.) onda -a, tidal wave or wave caused by a ship, especially in restricted waters; *n.m.* hermit; solitary; recluse; un paio di solitari, a pair of solitaire ear-rings; solitaire, patience; fare un —, to play patience; (pol.) independent. **-amente** *adv.* alone, by oneself; solitarily.

ṣo·lit-o *part.* of **solere**, q.v.; *adj.* era — venire ogni mattina, he used to come every morning; è — di levarsi di buon'ora, it is his habit to rise early; *adj.* usual, habitual, customary; è la -a storia, it is the usual story; siamo alle -e!, as usual!, it's the same old thing!; *n.m.* the usual thing; custom, habit; what usually happens; è accaduto il —, the usual thing has happened; secondo il suo —, as he usually does; più tardi del —, later than usual; più del —, oltre al —, more than usual; *adv. phr.* al —, di —, as a rule, usually; come al —, as usual.

solitu·dine *f.* solitude, loneliness; solitary place; seclusion; wilderness.

soli·va-go *adj.* (*m.pl.* **-ghi**) (poet.) wandering alone.

solivo *adj.* (poet.) sunny.

solla *f.* blister (on the foot).

sollazz-o *m.* pleasure; amusement, recreation, pastime, sport; entertainment; essere di —, to give pleasure, to be amusing. **-are** [A I] *tr.* to amuse, to entertain; to divert; to provide with recreation; *rfl.* to amuse oneself; to enjoy oneself. (**-ato** *part. adj.*) **-ęvole** *adj.* amusing, entertaining; pleasant; merry, jolly. (**-evolmente** *adv.*)

sollęcciola *f.* (bot.) sorrel, *Rumex acetosa*; groundsel, *Senecio vulgaris*.

sollecit-are [A I s c] *tr.* to hasten; to urge; to request; to entreat; to press; — il passo, to quicken one's pace; (comm.) to write to again on receiving no reply; — la consegno, to urge delivery; (mech.) to stress; (theol.) to tempt (esp. to unchastity); (leg.) to solicit. **-amento** *m.* hastening, urging; entreaty; request. **-ativo** *adj.* pressing; urgent. **-ato** *part. adj.* urged, pressed; harassed; (mech.; bldg.) stressed, under strain. **-atore** *m.* petitioner, suppliant; proposer, instigator; tempter; (industr.) progressman. **-atrice** *f.* temptress. **-ato·ria** *f.* pressing letter (for payment, for an answer, etc.); begging letter. **-atura** *f.* urgency. **-azione** *f.*

sollecit-are (*cont.*)

entreaty, solicitation; pressure; urging; repeated request; (theol.) temptation (esp. to sin of lust); (mech.; bldg.) stress; (mech.) -azione di compressione, compressive stress; -azione di flessione, bending stress; -azione di rottura, breaking strain; -azione di taglio, shearing stress; -azione di tensione, tensile stress; -azione di torsione, torsional stress.

sollecit-o *adj.* prompt, speedy; ready; eager; solicitous; having the habit of early rising; (provb.) uomo — non fu mai povero, cf. early to bed and early to rise makes a man healthy, wealthy and wise; troppo — del benessere materiale, too fond of material comforts; — della gloria, intent on achieving fame or glory; (comm.) reminder that an answer has not been received, or an invoice not paid, etc. **-amente** *adv.* quickly, promptly, readily; eagerly; diligently. **-u·dine** *f.* speed, readiness, promptness; diligence; dispatch; solicitude, care; eagerness; desire; (comm.) con cortese -udine, (equiv. to) at your earliest convenience.

solleone *m.* Dog-days (period when the sun is in Leo).

solletic-are [A 2 sc] *tr.* to tickle; (fig.) to excite; to flatter; to prompt; — l'appetito, to tempt the appetite. (**-amento** *m.*) **-ato** *part. adj.* tickled; (fig.) excited; flattered; prompted.

solleti·co *m.* (*pl.* **-chi**) tickling; fare il — a, to tickle; temere, sentire il —, to be ticklish; (fig.) stimulus; il — della curiosità, the prick of curiosity; il — dell'ambizione, the spur of ambition.

sollev-are [A 1] *tr.* to lift; to raise; to heave up; — una questione, to raise a question; to relieve, to comfort; — uno da un peso, to relieve someone of a burden; — un animo afflitto, to comfort someone in affliction; (eng.) to hoist, to lift; *rfl.* to rise; to rebel; to get up (e.g. after an illness). **-a·bile** *adj.* capable of being raised. **-amento** *m.* relief, comfort; rising, tumult; (geol.) upcast; (eng.) lifting, hoisting; meccanismo di -amento, lifting gear; (aeron.) take-off. **-ato** *part. adj.* raised; exalted, eminent; di spirito -ato, uplifted in spirit; relieved, alleviated; stirred up; rebellious; in high spirits; light; pane -ato, well-risen bread; *n.m.pl.* insurgents, rebels. **-atore** *m.* comforter, reliever; agitator, leader of revolt; (eng.) hoist; (agric.) power lift; *adj.* lifting, raising; (anat.) muscolo -atore, levator muscle. **-atura** *f.* raising; rousing; (art) high relief; protuberance. **-azione** *f.* rising, revolt, insurrection, rebellion; sedition; rise, rising; elevation.

sollievo *m.* relief; un sospiro di —, a sigh of relief; alleviation; comfort; portare — a, to relieve.

†**sollimo** *m.* See **sublime**.

sollione *m.* See **solleone**.

†**sollo** *adj.* soft; mild; yielding.

solluchar-are [A 1 s] *tr.* to move, to touch emotionally; *rfl.* to be moved, touched; to go into raptures. (**-ato** *part. adj.*)

sollu·chero *m.* thrill; emotional excitement; rapture; (fam.) andare in —, to go into ecstasies, to be enraptured.

solmisazione, solmizzazione *f.* (mus.) solmization.

sol-o¹ *adj.* alone; sta sempre —, he is always alone; vivere troppo —, to live too much alone; tutto —, all alone; only; noi -i, we only, only ourselves; sono — a lavorare, I am the only one working; ingresso ai -i membri, members only (admitted); unique, sole; credo in un — Dio, I believe in one God; una -a volta, once only; avere un figlio —, to have only one son; la mia unica e -a speranza, my one and only hope; l'uomo non vive di — pane, man does not live by bread alone; single, one; camera con un — letto, single-bedded room; giacca a un — petto, single-breasted coat; una moltitudine animata da un — proposito, a multitude inspired with a single purpose; mere; un — cenno, a mere hint; *n.m.* (the) only man; (a) person alone; fare da —, to do (a job, etc.) by oneself; (the) only thing; *adv.* only; uno —, one only; — egli mancò, he alone was not there, he only was missing; — che, provided that; (mus.) solo. **-a** *f.* (the) only woman, (the) only girl; (the) only thing; quella -a, that one only; (leg.; comm.) sola, document drawn up in a single original; -a di cambio, sole of exchange. **-amente** *adv.* only; merely; solely; se non -amente, excepting only; -amente lo scorno!, only think of the disgrace! **-etto** *adj. dim.* all alone; se ne stava lì sola -etta, she was there all by herself; tutto -etto, solo -etto, all on one's own, all by oneself, all alone. **-ista** *m.,f.* (*pl.* **-isti**) (mus.) soloist. **-i·stico** *adj.* (mus.) solo; strumento -istico, solo instrument.

solo² *m.* See **suolo**.

Solone *pr.n.m.* Solon (Athenian legislator); il senno di —, the wisdom of Solon.

solreut, solreutte *m.* (mus.). See **gisolreut**.

solsti·zi-o *m.* (astron.) solstice. **-ale** *adj.* (astron.) solstitial.

soltanto *adv.* only; merely; solely; non — lui ma anche lei, not only he, but she as well; 'ho scritto due pagine'. 'Soltanto?', 'I've written two pages'. 'Is that all?'

†**solto** *adj.* See **sciolto**.

solu·bil-e *adj.* soluble; — in acqua, water-soluble; (surg.) tumore —, reducible tumour. **-ità** *f.* solubility.

solutivo *adj., n.m.* laxative.

soluto *part.* of **solvere**, q.v.; *adj.* loose; (fig.) solved; (med.) corpo —, bowels open; (chem.) in solution, dissolved; digiuno —, broken fast; terreno —, loose soil, tilled land; *n.m.* solute.

soluzione *f.* solution; substance dissolved; (phys.; chem.) solution; (photog.; chem.) — madre, — di riserva, stock solution; decision, conclusion; (math.) solution; — di continuità, interruption, break; (leg.) discharge.

solv-ato *m.* (chem.) solvate. **-azione** *f.* (chem.) solvation.

sol·v-ere [C 14] *tr.* (poet.) to dissolve; to solve; to liquefy; (fig.) — il cuore a, to melt the heart of; — il digiuno, to break one's fast. **-ente** *part. adj.* (leg.; comm.) solvent; (chem.) *adj., n.m.* solvent; (leg.) payer; (med.) laxative, purgative. **-enza** *f.* (leg.; comm.) solvency. **-i·bile** *adj.* (comm.) solvent. **-ibilità** *f.* (leg.; comm.) solvency.

soma¹ *m.* (Vedic rel.) soma.

som-a² *f.* burden; load; weight; bestia da —, beast of burden; cavallo da —, pack-horse; (dry measure) load (of various quantities); a -e, in abundance. **-aro** *m.* ass, donkey; (fig.) ass, fool.

Soma·lia *pr.n.f.* (geog.) Somaliland.

so·mal-o *adj.* relating to Somaliland; *n.m.* Somalian (-a *f.*).

Somaschi *pr.n. m.pl.* (eccl.) Somaschi (religious order founded in 1532, of which the main object is the education of poor children); padri —, members of this order.

soma·t-ico *adj.* (med.; biol.) somatic. **-ologi·a** *f.* (med.) somatology. **-olo·gico** *adj.* somatological. **-oscopi·a** *f.* (med.) somatoscopy. **-osco·pico** *adj.* somatoscopic.

someggi-are [A 3 c] *tr.* to transport by pack-horse, mule or donkey; animali da —, beasts of burden, pack-animals. **-a·bile** *adj.* transportable by pack-animal; artiglieria -abile, mountain artillery. (**-ato** *part. adj.*)

som-iere, -iero *m.* ass; beast of burden; (mus.) wind-chest (of organ); falso —, pipe-rack (of organ).

somigli-are [A 4] *tr.* to resemble, to be like, to be similar to; -a il fratello, he is like his brother; to compare; — la vita ad un viaggio, to compare life to a journey; *intr.* (*aux.* avere; *prep.* a) to resemble, to be similar (to); -a alla mamma, he takes after his mother; *recip. rfl.* to resemble each other. **-ante** *part. adj.* (*prep.* a) similar, like; resembling; un ritratto -ante, a good likeness; è -ante allo zio, he resembles his uncle; *adv.* similarly; *n.m.* the same; fare il -ante, to do likewise. **-antemente** *adv.* similarly, likewise. **-anza** *f.* resemblance, likeness, similarity.

somm-a *f.* (math.) addition; sum; operazione di —, adding operation; segno di —, plus sign; total; (comm.) — lorda, gross amount; — in uscita, outlay; amount; conclusion; gist; fare una —, to cast up; tirare le -e, to cast up accounts, (fig.) to settle a matter; tirate le -e, all things considered; comprehensive treatise, e.g. the Summa of St Thomas Aquinas; la — delle opere di un artista, an artist's 'œuvre'; *adv. phr.* in —, in short, after all; (fam., joc.) in — delle -e, in conclusion, finally. **-amente** *adv.* in the highest degree, highly; extremely; exceedingly. **-ista** *m.* (medieval philos.) summist, writer of a *summa*; (eccl.) summist in papal chancery, *sommista*.

so(m)macco *m.* (bot.) sumach, *Rhus coriaria*; (tanning) sumach.

somm-are [A 1 c] *tr.* to add up; to sum up; to reckon; (math.) to add; *intr.* (*aux.* essere; *prep.* a) to amount (to). **-ato** *part. adj.* added up; tutto -ato, all included, *or* all things considered; *n.m.* see **somma**. (**-atore** *m.* **-atrice** *f.*) **-ato·ria** *f.* (math.) summation. **-ato·rio** *m.* (*pl.* **-atorii**) sum of the terms of a series. **-azione** *f.* adding up; summing up; (opt.; photog.) -azione cromatica, chromatic addition.

somma·ri-o *adj.* summary, compendious; brief; scant; (leg.) summary, *n.m.* summary, synopsis; epitome; précis; (in books) 'Contents', table of contents. **-amente** *adv.* in short; (leg.) summarily.

sommer·g-ere [C 4] *tr.* to submerge; to sink; to flood, to swamp; (fig.) to overwhelm; *intr.* (*aux.* essere), *rfl.* to sink; (of submarine)

sommerg-ere (*cont.*)
to submerge, to dive. **-i·bile** *adj.* submergible; (naut.) pompa -ibile, submersible pump; *n.m.* (naut.) submarine. **-imento** *m.* submergence, submersion, sinking; (naut.) diving. (**-itore** *m.* **-itrice** *f.*)

sommers-o *part.* of **sommergere**, q.v.; *adj.* submerged, sunk; (fig.) overwhelmed. †**-are** *vb.* and derivs. see **sommergere**. **-ione** *f.* submersion, sinking; flooding; burying.

sommess-o *adj.* subdued; soft, low; humble; modest; submissive. **-amente** *adv.* in a subdued tone; softly; humbly; modestly. **-ivo** *adj.* submissive, humble. **-ivamente** *adv.* submissively; humbly.

sommettere [C 20]. See **sottomettere**.

somministr-are [A 1] *tr.* to provide, to supply; to administer; — i sacramenti, to administer the sacraments; — una medicina, to give a medicine; (leg.) to purvey; to supply. **-amento** *m.* supplying; administering. **-ativo** *adj.* serving to supply. **-ato** *part. adj.* supplied, provided, given; supplied with, provided for. (**-atore** *m.* **-atrice** *f.*) **-azione** *f.* supply; vision; (leg.) contract of purveyance; supply.

sommissione *f.* submission; compliance; obedience; respect for one's betters.

somm-o *adj.* highest; very great; topmost; supreme; excellent, sublime; le **-e** spighe, the tallest ears of corn; per **-i** capi, under the chief headings; *n.m.* summit, top; a — della scala, at the top (head) of the stairs; al —, in the highest degree. **-amente** *adv.* highly; extremely; exceedingly. **-ità** *f.* summit, top; sublime height(s); a supremely great man.

†**sommom·mol-o** *m.* blow under the chin; kind of rice fritter. †**-a·io** *m.* seller of fritters.

†**sommormorare** *intr.* to murmur under one's breath.

sommoscapo *m.* (archit.) top of a column (below the capital).

sommoscio *adj.* (agric.) going soft; uva sommoscia, over-ripe grapes.

sommoss-a *f.* uprising; riot; revolt; sedition; †instigation. **-o** *part.* of **sommuovere**, q.v.; *adj.* troubled, excited; acque **-e**, troubled waters.

sommov-imento *m.* agitation; stirring up; revolt; movement. (**-itore** *m.* **-itrice** *f.*)

sommozzatore *m.* skin diver; underwater swimmer; frogman; deep-sea diver.

sommuo·vere [C 15] *tr.* to stir up, to agitate; to disturb, to trouble; to excite, to rouse; to instigate.

sona·bile *adj.* See under **sonare**.

sonacchiare [A 4] and derivs. See under **sonare**.

sona·gl-io *m.* bell; sheep-bell; rattle; (fig.) fool; serpente a **-i**, rattlesnake; bubble (or splash) of rainwater; little drop of oil or fat floating on a liquid. **-iare** [A 4] *intr.* (*aux.* avere) to ring the bells (by shaking, cf. **sonagliera**). **-iata** *f.* shake of the bells. **-iato** *adj.* (herald.) belled. **-iera** *f.* collar or string of bells; jingling. **-ino** *m. dim.* little bell; *pl.* (bot.) *Briza maxima*, quaking grass.

son-are [A 1 d] *tr.* to ring; to play; to blow; to sound, to strike; — il piano, to play (on) the piano; — a orecchio, to play by ear; l'orologio ha **-ato** le cinque, the clock has struck five; (fam.) **-arle** a uno, to give someone a thrashing; to ring for; — la Messa, to ring for Mass; — a morto, to toll a knell; — la ritirata, to sound the retreat; to mean, to signify; le sue parole suonano minaccia, his words convey a threat; (fam.) gliel'ho **-ata**, I told him straight; *intr.* (*aux.* avere) to ring; to strike; to sound; to resound; to re-echo; suona strano, it sounds strange; mi suona male, I don't like the sound of it; suonano le sei, it is striking six; le sue parole suonano ancora nell'orecchio, his words are still ringing in my ears; battuto qui il muro suona, the wall sounds hollow when you tap it here. **-a·bile** *adj.* playable; fit for playing, ringing, etc.; sonorous. **-acchiare** [A 4] *tr.* to strum; to play a little. (**-acchiatore** *m.* **-acchiatrice** *f.*) **-ante** *part. adj.* ringing; sounding; sonorous, resonant; high-sounding; mare **-ante**, the sounding of the waves; fiume rapido e **-ante**, swift, roaring river; parole **-anti**, resonant words, (fig.) impressive speech; moneta, denaro **-ante**, ready cash. **-ata** *f.* ring, ringing; (mus.) sonata. **-atina** *f.* (mus.) sonatina. **-ato** *part. adj.* struck; è **-ata** l'ora, the hour has struck; ha sessant'anni **-ati**, he is well over sixty. **-atore** *m.* player; performer; executant; musician; ringer; **-atore** di violino, violinist; **-atore** ambulante, strolling musician. (**-atrice** *f.*) **-atura** *f.* ringing; playing; **-atura** delle campane, bell-ringing (or cost of this).

sonco *m.* (bot.) sow thistle, *Sonchus*.

---

sond-a *f.* sounding line, sounding-rod, sounding-apparatus; (med.) sound, probe; (techn.) sound, probe, feeler; (mining) drill; (meteor.) pallone —, meteorological balloon **-a·bile** *adj.* soundable. **-ag·gio** *m.* sounding; (mining) drilling, boring. **-are** [A 1 c] *tr.* to sound; to probe; to gauge; to feel; (fig.) to attempt to find out reactions of; **-are** una ferita, to probe a wound. (**-ato** *part. adj.*) **-atura** *f.* sounding.

sondelo *m.* (zool.) shrew.

sondro *m.* (bot.) *Pistachia lentiscus*.

soneri·a *f.* striking mechanism (of a clock); burglar alarm.

sonett-o *m.* sonnet; — caudato, sonnet with a tail, i.e. having an additional tercet (or more) placed after the usual fourteen lines; — doppio, — rinterzato, double sonnet, having a short line (settenario) added after the first and third lines of each quatrain, and after the second line of each tercet, making twenty lines in all; †little sound; †tune, air. **-ante** *m.*, *adj.* (derog.) sonneteer, writer of sonnets. **-are** [A 1 c] *tr.* to write sonnets to (or about); to jeer at. **-essa** *f.* sonnet with a tail (cf. 'sonetto caudato'). †**-iere** *m.* sonneteer. **-ista** *m.*, *f.* sonneteer, sonnet-writer.

sonicchiare [A 4] *tr.*, *intr.* (*aux.* avere) to strum, to play badly.

son-icino *m.* slight sound. **-io** *m.* prolonged, tiresome strumming.

so·nico *adj.* (phys.; acoust.) sonic.

so·nito *m.* (poet.) sound, noise.

sonnacchi-oni *adj. indecl.*, *adv.* dozing, nodding off to sleep. **-oso** *adj.* sleepy, drowsy; (fig.) sluggish, dull. **-osamente** *adv.* sleepily, drowsily; (fig.) sluggishly.

sonnam·bul-o *m.* sleepwalker, somnambulist. **-a** *f.* woman sleepwalker; fortune-teller. **-ismo** *m.* somnambulism, sleepwalking.

sonnecchiare [A 4 c] *intr.* (*aux.* avere) to doze, to slumber; to nod off to sleep; Omero sonnecchia Homer nods.

sonn-o, sonn-o *m.* sleep; aver —, to be asleep; aver un gran — addosso, to be very sleepy; — profondo, sound sleep; addormentarsi d'un — profondo, to fall into a deep sleep; avere il — leggero, to be a light sleeper; prender —, to go to sleep; riattaccare il —, to go to sleep again; dormire d'un — solo, to sleep through the night; vinto dal —, overcome with sleep; parlare nel, tra il —, to talk in one's sleep; perdere il —, to become wakeful; rimettere il — perduto, to catch up on one's sleep; rubare le ore al —, to go short of sleep; mi mette —, it makes me sleepy; l'ultimo —, il — eterno, death; il — invernale, winter sleep (of animals); (med.) malattia del —, sleeping-sickness; *pl.* (fig.) peace of mind; a pensarci perdo i miei **-i**, thinking about it keeps me awake at night. **-ellino** *m. dim.* nap; doze; little sleep; fare un **-ellino**, to have a nap, to doze off. **-iferare** [A 1 s] *intr.* (*aux.* avere) to doze; to drowse. **-i·fero** *adj.* somniferous; narcotic; soporific; *n.m.* narcotic; sleeping-draught. **-ilo·quio** *m.* talking in one's sleep. **-i·loquo** *m.* one who talks in his sleep. (**-i·loqua** *f.*) **-olento**, †**-olente** *adj.* somnolent; drowsy; heavy with sleep. **-olenza** *f.* somnolence; drowsiness; sleepiness.

†**sonnottare** *intr.* to pass the night.

sono[1] *1st pers. sing.*, *3rd pers. pl. pres. indic.* of **essere**, q.v.

†**sono**[2] *m.* See **suono**.

sono·metro *m.* (mus.) sonometer.

sonor-o *adj.* sonorous; resonant; high-sounding; sounding; l'espressione **-a** di alti concetti, the expression in sound (the musical expression) of sublime ideas; film —, sound-film; onda **-a**, sound-wave; risa **-e**, loud laughter; schiaffo —, resounding slap; (phon.) voiced, sonant; colonna **-a**, vibrating column of air, (cinem.) sound-track. **-amente** *adv.* sonorously; fischiato **-amente**, loudly hissed. **-ità** *f.* sonorousness, sonority; resonance. **-izzare** [A 1] *tr.* (cinem.) to add a sound-track to. (**-izzato** *part. adj.*) **-izzazione** *f.* (cinem.) addition of a sound-track.

†**son·tico** *adj.* turbid.

sontuos-o *adj.* sumptuous; luxurious; lavish. **-amente** *adv.* sumptuously; luxuriously; lavishly.

soperchiare [A 4] and derivs. (pop.). See **soverchiare**.

soper·ch-io *m.* (pop.) see **soverchio**; (provb.) il — rompe il coperchio, cf. the last straw breaks the camel's back. **-i·a** *f.* insolence, overbearing conduct; outrage; imposition.

†**sopersedere** *vb.* and derivs. See **soprassedere**.

sop-ire [D 2] *tr.* to calm; to appease; to lull; to allay; to soothe. **-imento** *m.* lulling to sleep; soothing, alleviation; drowsiness. **-ito** *part. adj.* calmed; appeased; lulled; allayed; soothed. (**-itore** *m.* **-itrice** *f.*) **-ore** *m.* drowsiness; light sleep; gentle sleep; lethargy, torpor; coma. **-ori·fero** *adj.* soporific.

soppal·co *m.* (*pl.* **-chi**) (archit.) garret, attic (room); lumber-room.

soppann·are [A I] *tr.* to line (a garment) with 'panno'. (**-ato** *part. adj.*) **-o** *m.* lining; sock (of a shoe).

soppass·o *adj.* (of fruit) half-dried, partly dried; calcina -a, half-dried plaster, half-dried mortar. †**-are**, †**-ire** *intr.* (of fruit) to dry partly.

sopped·a·neo *m.* footstool, foot-mat. †**-iano** *m.* socle, low pedestal running round a bed.

soppęlo *m.* (Tusc., butcher.) cut of meat near the shoulder.

sopperire [D 2] *intr.* (*aux.* avere; *prep.* a) to provide (for, e.g. an unforeseen contingency); to cope (with); to make up (for); — a spese, to face expenses, to undertake expenditure.

soppes·are [A I c] *tr.* to weigh in one's hand; (fig.) to ponder, to think over. (**-ato** *part. adj.*)

soppęso *adj.* held in the hand; *prep. phr.* di —, in one's hands; in one's arms; alzar di —, to raise bodily. (Cf. 'di peso', under **peso.**)

soppestare [A I] *tr.* to pound a little (i.e. not to powder).

soppiano *adv.* softly; *adv. phr.* di —, under one's breath.

soppiant·are [A I] *tr.* to supplant; to oust; to dispossess; †to trip up. **-amento** *m.* supplanting; ousting. (**-ato** *part. adj.* **-atore** *m.* **-atrice** *f.*)

soppiatt·o *adj.* concealed; *adv. phr.* di —, secretly; stealthily; entrare di — a, to creep into. †**-are** *tr.* to conceal. **-one** *adj.* sly; *n.m.* sly-boots; *adv.* stealthily, slyly. (**-ona** *f.*)

sopport·are [A I] *tr.* to bear; to endure, to tolerate; to withstand; to stand, to put up with; non posso — la sua presenza, I can't bear the sight of him; — un danno, to suffer an injury; to support; to hold up, to bear on one's shoulders; — le spese, to bear the expense; to prop up; to substantiate, to bear out; to second; *rfl.* to be borne, to be endured; è difficile a -arsi, it is difficult to bear. **-a·bile** *adj.* bearable, endurable; tolerable; non -abile, intolerable. **-abilmęnte** *adv.* bearably. **-abilità** *f.* bearableness. **-amento** *m.* bearing; supporting; tolerating; enduring. (**-ante** *part. adj.*) **-ato** *part. adj.* borne; endured; supported. (**-atore** *m.* **-atrice** *f.*) **-azione** *f.* bearing; supporting; tolerance; endurance; forbearance; †permission. **-ęvole** *adj.* bearable. (**-evolmęnte** *adv.*)

sopporto *m.* support; stand, mounting; bracket; (eng.) — a ruote, roller bearings; (fig.) toleration; grace, patience; (watchm.) d'albero, stem cock. (Cf. **supporto.**)

soppressa *f.* (techn.) press.

soppress·are [A I] *tr.* (techn.) to press; †to oppress; abolished. (**-ato** *part. adj.*)

soppressiǫne *f.* suppression; abolition; — delle congregazioni religiose, suppression of religious houses; doing away with, dispensing with; (teleph.) absorption; — di impulsi, digit absorption; (med.) suppression; (leg.) — di testamento, destruction of Will (C.C.); — di cadavere, doing away with dead body; — di stato, suppression of civil status of newly-born child, concealment of birth (C.P.).

soppress·o *part.* of **sopprimere**, q.v.; *adj.* suppressed; abolished; done away with. **-ivo** *adj.* tending to suppress; abolitionary. **-ọre** *m.* (radio) suppressor.

soppri·mere [C 18] *tr.* to suppress; to abolish; to do away with; (euphem.) to kill.

†**sopprior·e** *m.* subprior. †**-a** *f.* subprioress.

sǫpra¹ *prep.* **1.** OVER; saltare — il muro, to jump over the wall; volare — la città, to fly over the city; una spada pendeva — il suo capo, a sword hung over his head; una finestra che guarda — il mare, a window looking out over the sea; (fig.) passare — una cosa, to pass over a thing, to pay little attention to something; vegliare, regnare, trionfare —, to watch, reign, triumph over. **2.** ABOVE; — le nuvole, above the clouds; un villaggio — Firenze, a village above Florence; — il livello del mare, above sea-level; Bolzano resta sulla linea del Brennero, — Trento, Bolzano lies on the Brenner line, above Trent; — tutto, above all; — venti, above, more than, twenty; — ogni cosa, above, more than, anything. **3.** BEYOND; le terre — il Garda, the villages beyond Lake Garda; — la sessantina, beyond (over, more than) sixty years of age; è — la mia comprensione, it is beyond (above) my understanding. **4.** ON, UPON; metti il libro — la tavola, put the book on the table; la bomba cadde — un ospedale, the bomb fell on a hospital; fondato — validi argomenti, founded on valid reasoning; portato — una barella, carried on a stretcher; gettarsi — uno, to fall on, to attack, someone; *prep. phr.* — a, on, on top

of; mettere una cosa — a un'altra, to put a thing on top of another; (fig.) mettiamoci una pietra —, let's forget the whole thing; contarci —, to count on; gli furono tutti —, they all attacked him; — di (follow. by *pers. prn.*), on, upon; rimanere — di sè, to be lost in thought; prendere — di sè, to take on oneself. **5.** AFTER; vino da bere — il dolce, wine to be drunk after the sweet; disgrazia — disgrazia, disaster upon disaster, one disaster after another. **6.** NEXT TO, ON TOP OF; portare lana — la carne, to wear wool next to the skin; on the surface of; — la terra, on the face of the earth. **7.** ON THE SUBJECT OF; notizie — gli ultimi avvenimenti, information about recent events; insegnamento —, instruction in, about; parlare — lo stesso argomento, to speak on the same subject; piangere —, to cry about. **8.** *adv.* ABOVE; come —, as above; — ricordato, mentioned above; up; upstairs; è andato —, he has gone up; dev'essere —, he must be upstairs; un mobile che non va —, a piece of furniture which won't go (is too big to go) up the stairs; on the top, on the outside; è d'oro soltanto —, it is gold only on top; abito di —, top-coat. **9.** *adv. phr.* di —, upstairs, up above; la famiglia di —, the family on the floor above; per di —, up above; sopra sopra, one above the other, ranged, in layers; al di —, up yonder, up above; *used with* '*ci*': scrivici — il tuo nome, write your name on it; riflettiamoci —, let us reflect on it; beviamoci —, let's have a drink on it; ti consiglio di dormirci —, I advise you to sleep on it (before deciding about a matter, etc.). **10.** *prep. phr.* al di — di, above. **11.** *n.m.* THE UPPER SIDE; the top.

sopra-² *pref.* (for words in which the stress falls on the 'a' of 'sopra', e.g. **sopra·bito**, see separate entries) super-; sur-; extra-; above-; upper. **-bbanda** *f.* (mil.) trunnion cover; (naut.) upper half of a bearing (propeller shaft). **-bbastare** [A I] *intr.* (*aux.* essere) to be more than sufficient. **-bbollare** [B I] *tr.* to overstamp, to add fresh stamps, postmarks, etc.; to surcharge. **-bbondare** [A I c] and derivs. see **sovrabbondare.** **-bbordo** *adv.* (naut.) aboveboard, on or above the upper deck. **-bbuono** *adj.* excellent, more than good; (slang) 'super'. **-bbusto** *m.* bodice. **-ccaldo** *adj.* overheated; *n.m.* superheated steam. **-calza** *f.* overstocking; gaiter. **-cami·cia** *f.* overshirt, blouse. **-canale** *m.* (naut.) bottom board. **-ccapellini** *m.pl.* (cul.) fine vermicelli for soup. **-ccapo** *m.* anxiety, worry; superintendent; (joc.) horns; (games) overhand stroke or throw. **-ccaricato** *adj.* (herald.) charged. **-ccarta** *f.* outside of a folded sheet of paper; paper wrapper; cover; envelope; address on an envelope; (colloq.) si vede dalla -ccarta, you can see at a glance. **-ccassa** *f.* watchcase; (naut.) keelson; inner hull (double bottom). **-cceleste**, **-iale** *adj.* (theol.) supercelestial. **-ccennato** *part. adj.* above-mentioned, aforesaid. **-cchiamare** [A I] *tr.* (med.) to call in (for a second opinion). **-cchi·glia** *f.* (naut.) hog (between the keel and the keelson). **-ccielo** *m.* (top of) canopy, tester. **-cci·glio** *m.* (*pl.* **-cci·glia** *f.*) eyebrow; frown, scowl; (archit.) architrave, door-jamb. **-ccin·ghia** *f.* surcingle. **-ccinto** *adj.* girt, girded. **-cciò** *m.* superintendent; wiseacre. **-(c)citato** *adj.* above-mentioned, quoted above. **-ccoda** *f.* (orn.) upper tail coverts. **-ccollo** *m.* overload, excess; (naut.) supercargo. **-ccolǫnnio** *m.* (archit.) architrave. **-ccolǫre** *m.* top-coat (of paint). **-ccon·solo** *m.* (hist.) magisterial title in the Venetian Republic. **-(c)coperta** *f.* counterpane, coverlet; (book) cover; binding; envelope, wrapper; (naut.) upperwards, deck house; double awning. **-(c)copertina** *f.* dust-jacket (of a book). **-ccopiato** *adj.* quoted, copied out, above. **-(c)cornice** *f.* (archit.) ornament at the top of the cornice. **-ccorrente** *adv.* upstream; *n.f.* overflow; (naut.) a warm current or stratum above a cold layer of sea. **-ccorrere** [C 5] *intr.* (*aux.* avere, essere) to overflow; to win (in a race). **-ccorsi·a** *f.* (naut.) reinforced deck of a flying bridge; †fore and aft deck in a galley. **-ccorso** *m.* upper course. **-ccoscienza** *f.* burden on the conscience. **-c(c)osta** *f.* (anat.) strengthened frame, interframe or additional rib. **-c(c)ostale** *adj.* (anat.) supracostal. **-cotta** *f.* (hist.) surcoat. **-cręscere** [B 9] *intr.* (*aux.* essere) to grow excessively. **-culo** *m.* (poultry) Pope's nose, parson's nose. **-cuoco** *m.* chef, head-cook. (**-cuoca** *f.*) **-cuto** *adj.* oversharp, too sharp. **-daziare** [A 4] *tr.* to surcharge (with duty). **-da·zio** *m.* extra customs duty, overcharge. **-ddare** [A 8] *tr.* to give more, to give abundantly. **-ddente** *m.* milk tooth remaining alongside of a permanent tooth; extra tooth. **-(d)dętto** *adj.* aforesaid, above-mentioned. **-dditato** *adj.* aforesaid, above-mentioned. **-ddotale** *adj.* in addition to a dowry. **-ddotare** [A I] *tr.* to give in addition to a dowry; to endow. **-ddote** *f.* gift by a

sopra- *(cont.)*

husband to augment the dowry. **-desidera·bile** *adj.* highly desirable. **-diletto** *adj.* well-beloved, dearest. **-dito** *m.* (mus.) close position of fingers in order to obtain the diminished fifth on the violin. **-dolce** *adj.* very sweet. **-dominante** *f.* (mus.) submediant. **-dotto** *adj.* extremely learned. **-dovere** [B12] *adj.* more than required, excessive. **-ddragante** *m.* (naut.) transom board. **-ebollizione** *f.* superheating (of liquids). **-elevare** [A1s] and derivs. see **soprelevare.** **-elevazione** *f.* high ground, terrace; plateau; (archit.) elevation, walls above ground (as opposed to footings and foundations); (rlwy.; roadb.) superelevation, cart; (leg.) superstructure built on to top story of building. **-esaltare** [A1] *tr.* to extol excessively. **-esposto,** **-esposto** *adj.* set out above, aforesaid. **-fac·cia** *f.* surface. **-ffacimento** *m.* overwhelming, overpowering; oppression. **-ffare** [B14] *tr.* to overcome, to overpower; to overwhelm; to dominate. **-ffatto** *part. adj.* overcome, overwhelmed; oppressed. **-ffazione** *f.* defeat; oppression, tyranny. **-ffa·scia** *f.* outer bondage. **-ffilare** [A1] *tr.* to hem. **-ffilo** *m.* hem. **-ffino** *adj.* con arte -ffina, with extreme ability. **-ffinestra** *f.* (archit.) small window over a main door or window, fanlight or grille over a door. **-ffusione** *f.* (chem.; geog.) supercooling. **-ffuso** *adj.* supercooled. **-ggale·a** *f.* (naut. hist.) admiral's galley. **-gittare** [A1] *tr., intr.* (aux. avere) (sewing) to whip, to overcast. **-ggitto** *m.* (sewing) whipping; punto a -ggitto, whip-stitch. **-ggiun·gere** [C5] *intr.* (aux. essere) to arrive, to turn up; to happen, to occur; to ensue; to come (over, upon); stava per guarire quando gli -ggiunse la febbre, he was on the way to recovery when he developed a fever; *tr.* to overtake; to come upon; †to add. **-ggiunta** *f.* unexpected arrival; per -ggiunta, into the bargain, in addition, moreover. **-ggiunto** *part. adj.* arriving late; overtaken; notizie -ggiunte, later news, news just received; -ggiunto dalla tempesta, overtaken by the storm. **-(g)gravare** [A1] *tr.* to overload heavily. **-grave** *adj.* extremely heavy; very grave. **-gra·vio** *m.* extra burden. †**-gguar·dia** *f.* (mil.) chief watchman; senior of a scouting group. **-indicato** *adj.* above-mentioned. **-indotto** *part. adj.* added, superimposed. **-intendere** [C3] and derivs. see **soprintendere.** †**-liminare** *m.* (archit.) architrave. †**-limitare** *m.* (archit.) architrave. **-llegato** *adj.* cited above; aforesaid. **-llode** *f.* high praise. **-llog·gia** *f.* (archit.) open gallery, loggia on an upper floor. **-luminosità** *f.* (telev.) bloom. **-(l)luogo** *adv.* on the spot; *adj. indecl.* (comm.; finan.) consegna -luogo, spot delivery; *n.m.* (leg.) judicial inspection of the scene of, the crime, etc., investigation on the spot. **-mare** *m.* (naut.) sea surface; *adv.* above water; †overseas. **-marino** *adj.* (naut.) surface. **-mentovato,** **-menzionato** *adj.* mentioned above, aforesaid. **-messo** *part.* see **soprammesso.** **-metallo** *m.* (eng.) machining allowance. **-mma·nica** *f.* (usu. *pl.*) cuff(s), oversleeve(s). **-mmano** *m.* (sewing) whipstitch; (fencing, etc.) overhand stroke; *adv.* overhand; *adj. indecl.* of superior quality, first-rate. **-mmattone** *m.* (archit., bricklaying) wall one brick thick, with bricks placed as 'headers'. **-mmercato** *m.* surplus; *adv. phr.* per -mmercato, into the bargain, in addition, besides. **-mmesso** *adj.* superimposed, placed over, denti -mmessi, overlapping teeth; (techn.) clinker-built. **-mmettere** [C20] *tr.* to place over, to place above. **-mmisura** *adv.* exceedingly; immoderately. **-mmo·bile** *m.* knick-knack; ornament. **-mmodo** *adv.* exceedingly, extremely. **-mmondano** *adj.* supermundane; supernatural. **-mmontare** [A1] *intr.* (aux. essere) to superabound; to be excessive. **-mmurare** [A1] *tr., intr.* (aux. avere) to build up, to carry a wall higher. **-nnarrato** *adj.* above-related. **-nnarrazione** *f.* continuation; appendix. **-nna·scere** [B18] *intr.* (aux. essere) to supervene; to follow, to arise. **-nnaturale** *adj.* supernatural; felicità -nnaturale, heavenly bliss; virtù -nnaturale, sublime virtue; *n.m.* (theol.) the supernatural (the realm of grace); divinity; divine Providence; (poet.) the supernatural (element) in poetry, etc. **-nnaturalmente** *adv.* supernaturally. **-nnome** *m.* nickname; †surname. **-nnominare** [A1s] *tr.* to nickname, to give a nickname to. **-nnominato** *part. adj.* nicknamed; known as, called. **-nn(u)otare** [A1] *intr.* (aux. avere) to float. **-nnotato** *adj.* mentioned above; aforesaid. **-nnumera·rio** *adj.* supernumerary. **-nnu·mero** *adj.* supernumerary; *adv.* excessively; in -nnumero, supernumerary. **-nolo** *m.* (comm.) primage. **-ordina·rio** *adj.* supernumerary, additional; extra. **-ornato** *m.* (archit.) entablature, frieze and cornice. **-pagare** [A2] *tr., intr.* (aux. avere) to overpay; to pay 'through the nose'. **-passag·gio** *m.* fly-over bridge (over road or railway), railway bridge. **-pensiero** *adv.* absent-mindedly; *quasi-*

adj. lost in thought; era -pensiero, he was thinking about something. **-pontino** *adj.* (anat.) suprapontine. **-ppaga** *f.* bonus (added to pay). **-pparto** *m.* (med.) afterbirth. **-ppensiero** *adj. indecl.* absentminded; lost in thought. **-ppeso** *m.* overweight; per -ppeso, for good measure. **-ppetto** *m.* (mil. hist.) surcoat worn over armour or cuirass. **-ppigliare** [A4] *tr.* to take more. **-ppiù** *m.* extra; addition; per -ppiù, in addition; essere di -ppiù, to be extra; (typ.) spare copies printed in excess of those ordered by the publisher; *adv.* besides; in addition. **-pporta** *m.* (archit.) ornamental panel over a door. **-pportare** [A1] *tr.* to carry up, *or* over. **-pporto** *m.* (archit.) ornamental panel over a door (inside a building). **-pposizione** *f.* superposition. **-pposta** *f.* (vet.) white line on a horse's hoof; (mus.) podatus, pes (in plainchant notation). **-pposto,** **-pposto** *adj.* superposed, superimposed. **-ppren·dere** [C1] see **sorprendere;** to take too much; to draw an advance of pay, on account. **-prezzo** *m.* enhanced price; surcharge; appreciation, increase in price or value; (leg.) price over par; emettere azioni ad un -prezzo, to issue shares at a premium (C.C.). **-profitto** *m.* excess profit(s). **-pu·bico** *adj.* (anat.) suprapubic. **-r·bitro** *m.* (leg.) chief referee. **-r·co** *m.* (archit.) arch over another arch. **-riferito** *adj.* aforesaid, above-mentioned. **-rragionare** [A1c] *tr.* to continue the argument about. **-rrenale** *adj.* see **surrenale.** **-rren·dere** [C1] *tr.* to repay with interest, to give back more than you get. **-rrivare** [A1] *intr.* (aux. essere) to supervene; to occur, to happen. †**-rronda** *f.* (mil.) additional rounds, exceptional inspection. **-sale** *m.* (chem.) higher salt. **-saturare** [A1s] *tr.* (phys.) to supersaturate. (**-saturato** *part. adj.*) **-saturazione** *f.* supersaturation. **-sa·turo** *adj.* (phys.) supersaturated. **-sberga** *f.* (mil. hist.) hauberk. **-sbergato** *adj.* wearing a vest over the hauberk. **-scal·mio** *m.* (naut. hist.) distance between banks of oars. **-scapolare** *adj.* (anat.) suprascapular. **-scarpa** *f.* overshoe, galosh. **-schiena** *f.* (harness) backstrap. **-scritta** *f.* superscription; address (on envelope); (typ.) title (of chapter, etc., in a book). **-scritto** *adj.* aforesaid, said; above-mentioned; *n.m.* see **soprascritta.** **-sensi·bile** *adj.* supersensual. **-senso** *m.* higher (allegorical) meaning. **-smalto** *m.* enamel; enamel-work. **-sostanziale** *adj.* supersubstantial; *n.m.* the fourth heaven, the heaven of the sun (in the Ptolemaic system). **-spalle** *m. indecl.* (mil.; naut.) harness, leather strap slung over the shoulders to assist men in hauling on drag-ropes or towing-lines. **-spen·dere** [C1] *intr.* (aux. avere) to overspend. **-spesa** *f.* overspending. **-squadra** *adj. f.* (math.) obtuse, more than a right angle, over 90°. **-ssagliente** *adj.* †(naut.) supernumerary (of sailors in assault troops). **-ssalire** [D1] *tr.* to attack suddenly, to fall upon. **-ssalto** *m.* sudden attack; sudden movement, start; di -ssalto, with a start, on a sudden. **-ssa·turo** *adj.* (geog.) supersaturated. **-ssedenza** *f.* delay, waiting, procrastination. **-ssedere** [B28] *intr.* (aux. avere) to delay, to suspend action; to wait; -ssedere a, to put off, to defer; -ssedere ad una decisione, to postpone a decision. **-ssegnare** [A5c] *tr.* to sign above; to countersign. **-ssegno** *m.* (additional) mark; countersign. **-ssella** *f.* saddle-cloth. **-ssello** *m.* (extra) load on a pack-saddle; per -ssello, in addition; into the bargain. **-ssicurazione** *f.* (leg.) overinsurance. **-ssenno** *m.* shrewdness; cunning. **-sin·daco** *m.* chief magistrate. **-sso·glio** *m.,* **-sso·glia** *f.* (archit.) architrave, lintel; raised edge of a weir, etc.; (naut.) batten, hatch batten. **-ssoldo** *m.* (mil.) allowance, additional pay, bonus; -ssoldo di guerra, danger money; (comm.) extra pay. **-ssoma** *f.* extra load. **-(s)sostanza** *f.* (philos.) supersubstantial being. **-(s)sottana** *f.* overskirt, extra skirt. **-sstalli·a** *f.,* **-sstallo** *m.* (agric.) prolonged rest, in stall or byre; (naut.) demurrage; delays of a ship in port. **-stante** *adj.* overhanging; impending; *n.m.* watchman; overseer; superintendent. **-stantemente** *adv.* with deliberation. **-stare** [A9] *intr.* (aux. avere; *prep.* a) to be at the head, to superintend; to be superior (to); *tr.* to dominate; to overcome; to delay, to put off; to cease. **-struttura** *f.* superstructure; (naut.) superstructure, any construction above the upper deck, such as the forecastle poop, deck cabin or bridges. **-suola** *f.* road pad, track shoe (of a tractor). **-suolo** *m.* top-soil. **-sviluppo** *m.* (photog.) overdevelopment. **-tara** *f.* (comm.) super tare. **-tassa** *f.* (leg.) extra tax payable as penalty; (finan.) surtax, supertax; additional fee; (comm.) surtax; extra charge for postage due. **-tenda** *f.* second curtain, overcurtain. **-terra** *adv.* above ground; at ground level. **-ttieni** *m. indecl.* extension of time, for payment. **-ttutto** *adv.* above all; especially; principally; *n.m.* overcoat; overall. **-umano** *adj.* see **sovrumano.** **-vanzare** [A1] *tr.* to surpass, to pass; *intr.* (aux. essere) to protrude,

sopra- *(cont.)*

to project, to jut out; to be left over; to be excessive. **-vanzo** *m.* surplus, remainder, balance, residue; di -vanzo, in excess, left over, remaining. **-vvedęre** [B 35] *tr.* to examine, to observe closely. **-vveduto** *part. adj.* circumspect, wary. **-vvegliare** [A 4] *tr.* to watch over, to watch carefully; to superintend. **-vveglianza** *f.* surveillance. **-vvęn·dere** [B 1] *tr.* to sell dearer. **-vvenire** [D 17] *intr.* (*aux.* essere) to arrive, to come up, to come on the scene; to happen, to occur; quando -vvenne la notte, when night fell; (leg.) to supervene; to come to light or into existence subsequently (C.C.); *tr.* to overtake, to come upon suddenly, to surprise. **-vveniente** *part. adj.* occurring; arriving. **-vvenienza** *f.* occurrence; (leg.) supervention; subsequent coming to light or into existence; -vvenienze attive, passive, contingent assets, liabilities. **-vvenimęnto** *m.* sudden arrival. **-vvenuta** *f.* unexpected arrival; attack; la -vvenuta tempestiva dei rinforzi, the timely arrival of (the) reinforcements. **-vvenuto** *part. adj.* occurred, arrived; persone -vvenute, new arrivals; overtaken; -vvenuto dalla morte, overtaken (struck down) by death; *n.m.* one who has arrived unexpectedly. **-vvento** *adv.* (naut.) windward, to windward, upwind; *n.m.* (naut.) windward position; prendere il -vvento, to get to windward; avere il -vvento, to have the weather gauge; (fig.) advantage; superiority; upper hand. †**-vventame** *m.* (naut.) the weather side; side to windward of a flag; direction of prevailing winds. **-vventamęnto** *m.* method of getting to windward. **-vventare** *intr.* (naut.) to work to windward (of); to obtain the weather gauge; to seek the weather gauge; *tr.* to dash against; *rfl.* to rush at, to fall upon, to attack. †**-vventatore** *m., adj.* (naut.) of a ship which works well to windward. **-vventazione** *f.* action of beating to windward. **-vveste** *f.* overall; cape, outer garment; surcoat. **-vvestire** [D 1] *tr.* to put an overall on, to cover up, to clothe. **-vvia** *f.* upper road; fly-over road. **-vvin·cere** [C 5] *tr., intr.* (*aux.* avere) to overcome; to be victorious. **-vvinto** *part. adj.* overcome; -vvinto dal sonno, overcome with sleep. **-vvissuto** *adj.* surviving; *n.m.* survivor. **-vvivente** *part. adj.* surviving; *n.m.* survivor. **-vvivenza** *f.* survival; continued existence; right of succession to a post; (leg.) survivorship. **-vvi·vere** [C 16] *intr.* (*aux.* essere) to survive, to continue to exist; -vvivere a, to outlive, to survive; -vvivere un anno, to live for another year; -vvivere a sè stesso, to outlive one's fame. **-vvi·volo** *m.* house leek, *Sempervivum tectorum.* **-vvolta** *f.* (archit.) upper arch.

sopra·bito *m.* light overcoat.

soprac·queo *adj.* above-water.

†**sopra·nimo** *adv.* spiritedly; passionately; inimically.

sopran-o *m.* (mus.) soprano voice, treble voice; soprano part, top part; soprano singer. (NOTE: the gender remains masculine.) **-ino** *m.* (mus.) voice higher than soprano.

sopreccitare [A 1 S] and derivs. See **sovreccitare.**

sopredific-are [A 2 S] *tr.* to build, to raise; — su salde fondamenta, to build on firm foundations. (**-ato** *part. adj.*) **-azione** *f.* building; raising; building up.

soprelev-are [A 1 S] *tr.* to raise higher; to build another story on to; (techn.) — la tensione di una corrente elettrica, to raise the tension of an electric current. (**-ato** *part. adj.*) **-azione** *f.* high ground; terrace; (archit.) elevation; new story added to an existing building.

sopr-espǫsto, -espǫsto *adj.* See **sovrespǫsto.**

†**sopresso** *prep.* over, above.

soprindicato *adj.* indicated (mentioned) above.

soprinsęgna *f.* embroidery, necklace, or other device worn over a coat-of-arms.

soprinten·d-ere [C 1] *intr.* (*aux.* avere; *prep.* a) to be superintendent (of); to be responsible (for); to have charge (of); to superintend; — ai lavori, to be works superintendent, to superintend the work. **-ente** *part., n.m.* superintendent. **-enza** *f.* superintendence; supervision; Government office. **-itǫre** *m.* person in charge; overseer; superintendent. (**-itǫra, -itrice** *f.*)

soprosso *m.* (surg.) bony outgrowth; (vet.) splint; (pop.) any hard lump or excrescence forming near a bone; (fig.) annoyance, trouble.

soprumano *adj.* See **sovrumano.**

soprumerale *m.* (rel. vestment) superhumeral, esp. the ephod of the Jewish High Priest.

soprun·ghia *f.* (vet.) ring bone.

sopruş-o *m.* abuse of power, act of tyranny; insult, injury, outrage. †**-are** *intr.* to abuse one's power.

soqquadr-o *m.* disorder, confusion; ruin; mettere a —, to throw into confusion; (eng.) jamming due to misalignment. **-are** [A 1] *tr.* to turn upside-down; to throw into confusion; *intr.* (*aux.* avere) (eng.) to jam because of misalignment. **-ato** *part. adj.* turned upside-down; thrown into confusion.

sǫr[1] *m.* (pop.) see **signore. -a** *f.* (pop.) see **signora**; sister; -a morte, death.

†**sor[2]** *prep.* See **sopra[1].**

sor- *pref.* sur-.

Sorabi *pr.n.m.pl.* (ethn.) Sorbs.

sorante *adj.* (herald.) rising.

soratǫre *m.* (mus.) waste-pallet (of organ).

sorb-a *f.* (bot.) sorb, sorb-apple, *Sorbus domestica*; service-berry; (provb.) conoscer le -e dai fichi, to know what's what (cf. **sorbo**).

sorbętt-o *m.* ice-cream; iced-drink; (fam.) diventare un —, to be frozen, to feel very cold. **-iera** *f.* container in which ice-cream, etc. is stirred, and which is placed in the freezing compartment of a refrigerator. **-iere** *m.* ice-cream vendor.

sorb-ire [D 2] *tr.* to sip; to suck; to absorb; (fig.) to swallow; *rfl.* (*dat.* of *prn.* 'si') to put up with; la conferenza era molto noiosa ma ho dovuto -irmela tutta, the lecture was very boring, but I had to sit through the whole thing. **-i·bile** *adj.* fit to be sipped or swallowed; bearable. **-illare** [A 1] *tr.* to sip.

sorb-ite *f.* (chem.) sorbitol; (metall.) sorbite. **-i·tico** *adj.* (metall.) sorbitic.

sorbo *m.* (bot.) service tree, *Sorbus domestica*; — degli uccellatori, — selvatico, mountain ash, rowan, *Sorbus aucuparia*; — montano, white beam, *Sorbus aria.*

sor·bola *f.* (zool.) — di mare, file shell, *Lima inflata.*

Sorbona *pr.n.f.* Sorbonne (University of Paris).

†**sorbottare** *tr.* to thrash.

sǫrc-io *m.* (zool.) mouse. **-elli** *m.pl.* (mil.) mole, fire vents in a mine. **-ętto** *m. dim.* little mouse. **-ino, -igno** *adj.* mouse-coloured, mousey; of, relating to, a mouse; denti -ini, teeth like a mouse's; *n.m. dim.* little mouse, mousie; (vet.) mouse-coloured coat (of a horse).

†**sorcotto** *m.* surcoat; smock.

sord-ag·gine *f., -ęzza* *f.* See under **sordo[1].**

†**sorde** *f.* filth.

sor·did-o *adj.* dirty; sordid; mean, niggardly; ignoble. **-amęnte** *adv.* meanly; sordidly; in a niggardly way; vivere -amente, to live like a miser. **-ęzza** *f.* dirt; dirtiness; meanness; sordidness.

sǫrd-o[1] *adj.* deaf; — come una campana, deaf as a post; — da un orecchio, deaf in one ear; (fig.) unresponsive; inexorable; stifled; strangled; inarticulate; ebbe una -a esclamazione, he uttered a stifled cry; teatro —, theatre with bad acoustic properties; (mus.) toneless, dull; (of a voice) hollow; (of sound) rumbling, low; colore —, dull colour; (phon.) unvoiced; underhand, secret; mi faceva una guerra -a, he opposed me secretly; -a ostilità, underhand opposition; (bot.) mazza -a, reed mace, *Typha*; *adv. phr.* alla -a, secretly; stealthily, silently; *n.m.* deaf person; i -i, the deaf; (provb.) non c'è peggio — di chi non vuol capire, there are none so deaf as those who don't want to hear; fare il —, to pretend to be deaf. **-amęnte** *adv.* dully; noiselessly; secretly. **-acchiǫne** *m.* one who feigns deafness. (**-acchiǫna** *f.*) **-ag·gine** *f.* partial or temporary deafness; hardness of hearing. **-astro** *adj.* rather deaf, almost deaf; hard of hearing. **-ellina** *f.* (mus.) a kind of bag-pipe. **-ęzza** *f.* see **sordità. -ina** *f.* subdued sound; (mus.) a kind of clavichord; mute, damper; (fig.) con la -ina di, muted by, muffled by; *adv. phr.* alla -ina, noiselessly; stealthily, on the sly. **-ino** *m.* (mus.) mute, damper; bird-whistle (to attract thrushes). **-ità** *f.* deafness. **-ǫne** *m.* (orn.) Alpine accentor, *Prunella collaris.* **-omutismo** *m.* deaf-mutism. **-omuto** *adj.* deaf and dumb; *n.m.* deaf-mute. **-otto** *adj., n.m.* slightly deaf (person).

sǫrdo[2] *m.* (math.) surd.

sore·dio *m.* (bot.) soredium.

sorell-a *f.* sister; — di latte, foster-sister; (myth.) le nove -e, the Muses; le tre -e, the Parcae; (fig.) arti -e, sister arts (painting and sculpture); (eccl.) sister, nun (cf. **suora**). **-astra** *f.* step-sister; half-sister. **-ęvole** *adj.* sisterly. **-ina** *f. dim.* little sister.

sorello *m.* (ichth.) horse mackerel, *Trachurus trachurus.*

sǫrg-ere [C 5] *intr.* (*aux.* essere) to rise; to stand up; to rise up; to arise; to emerge, to proceed; — da, to spring from; (naut.) to refloat; — sulle ancore, to lie at anchor; †*tr.* to raise; *n.m.* rise, rising; il — del sole, sunrise. **-ente** *part. adj.* rising; *n.f.* spring; fountain; source; origin, cause; -enti termali, hot springs; -ente

sorg·ere (*cont.*)

   di petrolio, oil well. **-imento** *m.* arising; (astron.) rising; -imento apparente, -imento visibile, visible rising; -imento vero, true astronomical rising.

sorgiv·o *adj.* (of a) spring; acqua -a, spring water. **-a** *f.* spring (of water).

sorgo *m.* (bot.) *Sorghum.*

†**sorgozzone** *m.* See sergozzone.

sori *m.* (miner.) bornite, peacock copper ore, erubescite.

Sor·i·a *pr.n.f.* (geog.) Syria. **-iano** *adj.* Syrian; gatto -iano, cypress-cat (i.e. cat having black stripes and no patches on a silver-grey background, as distinguished from a tabby cat, 'gatto tigrato', which has black stripes and black patches on a tawny background); (vet.) zebra marked (of a horse's coat).

†**so·rice** *m.* See sorcio.

sorite *m.* (logic) sorites.

sormont-are [A1C] *tr.* to surmount; to rise above; to surpass; to overcome; to top; to overflow; †*intr.* to rise. **-amento** *m.* surmounting. **-ato** *part. adj.* surmounted; surpassed; overcome. (**-atore** *m.* **-atrice** *f.*)

sornac·chi·o *m.* phlegm. **-are** [A4] *intr.* (aux. avere) to cough up phlegm.

sornion-e *adj.* sly, crafty, artful; surly; *n.m.* slyboots, sneak. (**-a** *f.*)

sor-o *m.* (bot.) sorus. **-o·sio** *m.* (bot.) multiple fruit.

sororale *adj.* sisterly.

†**sorore** *f.* sister.

sorpass-are [A4] *tr.* to surpass, to outdo, to excel; (motor.) to pass, to overtake; to jump over, to clear; *rfl.* to surpass oneself, to excel oneself. **-ato** *part. adj.* surpassed; outdone; overtaken; démodé; old-fashioned. **-o** *m.* (motor.) overtaking; vietato il -o, no overtaking; (eng.) by-pass.

sorpren·d-ere [C1] *tr.* to deceive; to take advantage of; to overtake; to swindle; to take by surprise; la notte ci sorprese per via, night overtook us while we were on the road; to surprise, to cause surprise to; vederlo qui mi -e davvero, I really am surprised to see him here; *rfl.* (prep. di) to be surprised (at, by); non c'è da -ersene, there is nothing to be surprised at, no wonder; oramai non mi -o più di nulla, nothing surprises me any longer. **-ente** *part. adj.* surprising, astonishing; strange. **-entemente** *adv.* surprisingly.

sorpres-a *f.* surprise; astonishment; con mia grande —, greatly to my surprise; sudden trick; taking of someone off his guard; stratagem; police raid; raid; *adv. phr.* di—, unexpectedly. **-o** *part.* of sorprendere, q.v.; *adj.* surprised; caught; -o in flagrante, caught in the act; -o dalla morte, overtaken by death.

sorra *f.* tunny in oil; best part of tunny; shoulder (e.g. of mutton).

†**sorrecchiare** *vb.* and derivs. See orecchiare.

sorreg·gere [C12] *tr.* to hold up, to support, to sustain; to prop up; (fig.) to sustain; to encourage; *rfl.* to stand upright; to be able to stand; sorreggersi contro, to lean against (for support).

sorretto *part.* of sorreggere, q.v.; *adj.* supported; propped up; sustained.

sorri·d-ere [C3] *intr.* (aux. avere; *prep.* a) to smile (at, on); to be favourable (to); gli -eva la vita, life seemed good to him; to please; mi -e l'idea, the idea appeals to me; — di, to smile at, about, to find amusing. **-ente** *part. adj.* smiling. **-entemente** *adv.* smilingly; rispose -entemente, he answered with a smile.

sorriso *part.* of sorridere, q.v.; *adj.* smiled upon, gladdened; parole sorrise, words spoken with a smile; smile; *n.m.* smile; fare un —, to give a smile; un — a fior di labbra, a half-hearted, faint, smile; (fig.) beauty, radiance; il — della natura, smiling nature.

sors-o *m.* draught, drink, drop; non si trovava un — d'acqua, not a drop of water was to be found; bere a -i, to sip; a -i a -i, drop by drop, little by little. **-are** [A1C] see sorseggiare. **-ata** *f.* drink, draught, gulp. **-atina** *f.* a little drop. **-eggiare** [A3C] *tr., intr.* (aux. avere) to sip; to savour.

sort-a, †**-e** *f.* kind, sort; ogni — di, all kinds of; sensa spesa di —, without any expense whatever; (colloq.) farne di ogni —, to make all kinds of mistakes; quality; brand, make; quale — di sigarette desidera?, what brand of cigarettes do you want?; mandatemi un esemplare per —, send me a sample so that I can see what kind it is.

sort-e, †**-a** *f.* lot, fate, destiny, fortune; chance, luck; augury; per —, by chance; tirare a —, to draw lots; far decidere alla —, to leave to chance; toccare in — a uno, to fall to the lot of someone; per buona —, luckily; per mala —, as ill-luck would have it; avere

la — di, to have the luck to; far buon viso a cattiva —, to make the best of a bad job; †(finan.) principal; *pl.* augury, fortune (foretold); oracle; tirar le -i, to tell fortunes; destiny; le -i del mondo, the future of mankind. **-eggiare** [A3C] *tr.* to draw by lot; to assign by lot; to elect by lot; furono -eggiati i premi, (the) prizes were drawn for. **-eggio** *m.* drawing (of lots), draw; fu fatto il -eggio, lots were drawn, the draw took place. **-ile·gio** *m.* witchcraft; sorcery; spell. **-i·lego** *m.* sorcerer; *adj.* spell-binding. **-ire** [D2] *tr.* to draw (in a lottery); to allot, to assign; to have, to receive, to get (by chance, good fortune, inheritance); to be endowed with; l'impresa non ha -ito l'esito che ci aspettavamo, the undertaking has not produced the result that we expected; [D1] *intr.* (aux. essere) to be drawn (in a lottery), to come out; sono -iti i numeri che hai giuocato, your numbers have been drawn; to fall to one's lot; gli -ì di ottenere, he was successful in obtaining. **-ita** *f.* (mil.) sortie (ground); postern; -ita cieca, night sortie; postern-gate; sallyport; (mus.) entrance aria; (theatr.) entrance; opera-cloak; (fig.) sally, witty remark. **-ito** *part. adj.* drawn (by lot); allotted; received.

sorto *part.* of sorgere, q.v.; *adj.* risen, raised; sprung.

sorvegli-are [A4] *tr.* to watch over; to superintend; to keep under observation; to keep an eye on; *intr.* to keep watch; to act as superintendent; *rfl.* to keep a watch on oneself; to exercise self-control. **-ante** *part., n.m.* watchman, caretaker; keeper; overseer; attendant; inspector, superintendent. **-anza** *f.* surveillance, watchful care, supervision; superintendence; (leg.) giudice di -anza, superintending judge; supervisory judge (of care of infants, etc., C.C.P.); -anza vigilato, surveillance of person (esp. of full age and capacity) by police (C.P.). **-ato** *part. adj.* watched, kept under observation, supervised. (**-atore** *m.* **-atrice** *f.*)

sorvol-are [A1] *tr.* to fly over; to fly higher than; to rise above; to pass over; (fig.) to touch lightly upon; *intr.* (aux. essere) to fly higher; to pass over; (fig.) -ò sulla questione, he glossed over the question.

so·sia *m.* double (of a person; from a character in Plautus's *Amphitryon*); è il mio —, he is my double.

†**soso** *adv.* See su.

†**sospecciare** *tr.* to look up at; to look at furtively.

sospen·d-ere [C1] *tr.* to hang up; to suspend; (fig.) to stop, to put a stop to; to suspend, to adjourn, to defer, to put off; — la lettura, to interrupt the reading; — uno studente, to rusticate an undergraduate; (leg.) to stay; to stop; to suspend; — il processo, to stay proceedings; la prescrizione rimane sospesa, prescription does not run (C.C.); — il pagamento, to stop payment; — un assegno, to stop a cheque; (canon law) — a divinis, to suspend (from the exercise of sacred functions). **-i·bile** *adj.* suspensible. **-imento** *m.* suspending, suspension. **-itore** *m.* support; suspensor; *adj.* suspending; hanging. (**-itrice** *f.*)

sospens-ione *f.* suspension; lume a —, hanging lamp; uncertainty; interruption; adjournment; pause; temporary stoppage; (leg.) — dell'esecuzione, stay of execution; — del processo, stay of proceedings (C.C.P.); — della prescrizione, interruption of prescription; (comm.) stop; — dei pagamenti, suspension of payments; (chem.) suspension; (mus.) suspension; (canon law) — a divinis, suspension (from the exercise of one's orders); (mil.) — d'armi, di ostilità, cease fire, armistice, suspension of hostilities; (eng.; motor.) suspension; — anteriore, front-wheel suspension; — anteriore indipendente, independent front-wheel suspension; — cardanica, gimbals (of a compass); (gramm.; liter.) suspense. **-iva** *f.* delay; adjournment. **-ivo** *adj.* suspensive; relating to, indicating, causing delay, suspense or uncertainty; (typ.) puntini -ivi, dots (showing interruption of a sentence). **-ivamente** *adv.* with delay; hesitatingly. **-o·rio** *adj.* suspensory; *n.m.* (anat.) suspensory ligament or muscle; suspensory bandage; (naut.) chain sling or lift of a yard.

sospes-o *part.* of sospendere, q.v.; *adj.* hanging; hanging up; (chem.) in suspension; (agric.) mantenere il terreno —, to keep the soil loose; (archit.) ponte —, suspension bridge; (fig.) uncertain, in suspense; irresolute; rimaner col cuore —, to be in serious doubt, to be anxious; suspended; deferred, adjourned; causa -a, case adjourned; pagamenti -i, interrupted payments; treni -i, trains not running; (mus.) suspended; †suspicious; *n.m.* suspense; —, in suspense; tenere in —, to keep in suspense; in abeyance; tenete in — questa faccenda per pochi giorni, let this matter lie for a few days; (comm.) tenere un conto in —, to nurse an account.

sospett-are [A I] *tr.* to suspect; to distrust; to doubt; to surmise; lo -avano morto, they feared he was dead; *intr.* (*aux.* avere; *prep.* di) to be suspicious (of). **-a·bile** *adj.* arousing suspicion, suspect; open, liable, to suspicion; dubious. **-abilità** *f.* liability to suspicion; dubiousness. (**-ato** *part. adj.*)

sospett-o *adj.* suspect, suspicious; uomini non -i, men above suspicion; doubtful, risky, dangerous; allegare — un giudice, to suspect the impartiality of a judge; *n.m.* suspicion; dare —, to arouse suspicion; fear; mistrust; diffidence; timidity; (of a person) suspect; †trace, indication; clue. (**-amente** *adv.*) **-oso** *adj.* full of suspicion, naturally suspicious; wary, cautious; diffident; arousing suspicion, suspect; mercanzie -ose, doubtful goods, goods that are suspect. **-osamente** *adv.* suspiciously; diffidently.

†**sospicciare** *vb.* See **sospettare**.

sospin·g-ere [C 5] *tr.* to push; to push on; to impel; to stimulate; to goad; to urge, to drive, to drive on; — da, to drive away from; -emmo lo sguardo oltre la siepe, we peered over the hedge; *rfl.* to urge oneself. **-imento** *m.* push; shove; impulse; urge.

sospint-a *f.* push; (mil.) drive forward without pause (sustained). **-o** *part.* of **sospingere**, q.v.; *adj.* pushed, driven; urged; ad ogni piè -o, at every step, at every moment.

sospir-are [A I] *intr.* (*aux.* avere) to sigh; to breathe out; — per, to sigh for, to long for; — per la lontananza di, to grieve at the absence of; *tr.* to sigh for; to long for; to hanker after; to regret, to lament. **-ante** *part. adj.* sighing; longing; *n.m.* suitor. **-ato** *part. adj.* desired, longed for. (**-atore** *m.* **-atrice** *f.*) †**-e·vole** *adj.* full of sighs; accompanied by sighing.

sospir-o *m.* sigh; gasp; long-drawn breath; lament; desire (i.e. something longed for); il — dell'anima, the heart's desire; (mus.) short pause (see under **canone**); *pl.* air-holes, vents; mi costa molti -i, I'm longing for it, *or* it troubles me; rese l'ultimo —, he breathed his last; (cul.) chocolate (covered) biscuit or cake. **-one** *m.* long-drawn sigh, deep sigh. **-oso** *adj.* sighing, full of sighs; plaintive. **-osamente** *adv.* sighing, with sighs, sighingly; plaintively.

So·spita *pr.n.f.* (Rom. myth.) Sospita ('Preserver', cult-name of Juno).

sossello *m.* (archit.) raised step in front of a building.

sossopra *adv.* upside-down, topsy-turvy; mettere —, to turn topsy-turvy.

sosta *f.* rest, halt, pause; stay; cessation; respite; il dolore non gli dà — un minuto, the pain does not give him a minute's respite; (mil.) lull, armistice; (motor.) parking; divieto di —, no parking; (naut.) time in harbour, duration of visit; (leg.) giorni di —, demurrage days.

sostantiv-o *adj.* substantive; substantival; *n.m.* noun, substantive; battere il —, to emphasize the noun (in speaking a sentence). **-amente** *adv.* substantively; substantivally, as a noun. **-are** [A I] *tr.* to use as a noun; to substantivize. (**-ato** *part. adj.*)

sostanz-a *f.* substance; essence; matter; property; patrimony; — alimentare, foodstuff; — organica, organic matter; — colorante, dye, dyestuff; sacrificare la — per l'apparenza, to sacrifice the substance for the shadow; (phil., theol.) substance; persona fornita di —, person of substance, man of means; ha ereditato tutte le -e paterne, he has inherited all his father's property; (leg.; comm.) -e attive personali, personal estate; -e mobili, personalty; -e materiali infruttifere, dead securities; la — del discorso, the essential points of the speech; in —, to sum up, in conclusion; di —, substantial; cibo di —, nourishing food. **-iale** *adj.* substantial; essential; well-founded; *n.m.* essential; important (point, matter, etc.); substance. **-ialmente** *adv.* substantially; fundamentally. **-ialità** *f.* substantiality; solidity, importance. **-iare** [A 4] *tr.* to substantiate; to make substantial; *rfl.* to gain substance; to be substantiated. †**-ie·vole** *adj.* substantial. **-ioso** *adj.* substantial, nourishing; terra -iosa, rich soil; (fig.) profitable, elevating.

sostare [A 9] *intr.* (*aux.* avere) to stop, to halt; to rest; — all'ombra, to rest in the shade; to pause; to stay; — dal lavoro, to take a break from work; to desist.

sostegno *m.* support, prop; bracket; column; — per lampada, lamppost; muro di —, sustaining wall; fulcrum; pivot; (archit.) weir, lock (e.g. on a canal); (fig.) support; il — della famiglia, the family support; argomento a — di, argument in support of.

sosten-ere [B 32] *tr.* to support, to hold up; to uphold; to sustain; to make out, to maintain; -go che, I maintain that; -eva di essere più giovane, she made herself out to be younger; to stand, to

bear; to afford; (theatr.) — una parte, to act, to perform, a part; to dam, to confine, to contain (water); (mus.) — l'arco, to withhold the bow; — il canto, to support the melody; — la voce, to sustain the voice; (comm.) — la merce, to keep up the price of goods; — la piazza, to support the market, to keep up the market price; (mil.) to support, to sustain; (naut.) to withstand; — un fortunale all'ancora, to ride out a storm at anchor; to maintain, to affirm; sostiene che ciò è vero, he maintains that to be true; — di affermare, to dare to affirm; — il vino, to have a good head for wine, to carry one's liquor; — gli esami, to take, to sit for, the examination(s); †*intr.* to endure, to hold out; *rfl.* to support oneself; to maintain oneself; to sustain oneself; (mil.) to hold on (to a position); (naut.) -ersi al mare, to remain at sea. **-ente** *part. adj.* supporting; tenacious. †**-enza** *f.* tolerance; endurance. **-i·bile** *adj.* sustainable; maintainable; supportable; bearable, tolerable. (**-ibilità** *f.*) **-imento** *m.* support; assistance; resistance. **-itore** *m.* sustainer, maintainer, supporter; defender; socio -itore, member contributing to support of club. (**-itrice** *f.*)

sostent-are [A I] *tr.* to support; to maintain; to sustain; (mus.) — la voce, to sustain the voice; *rfl.* to support oneself; si -a con poco, he can live on very little; non ha di che -arsi, he has nothing to live on. **-a·bile** *adj.* maintainable. **-amento** *m.* sustenance; support; procurarsi il -amento, to get one's living; (aeron.) see **sostentazione**. **-ativo** *adj.* sustaining; nourishing. (**-ato** *part. adj.* **-atore** *m.* **-atrice** *f.*) **-azione** *f.* support; maintenance; (aeron.) aerodynamic lift; resistenza di -azione, wing resistance; -azione negativa, down load.

sostenut-o *part.* of **sostenere**, q.v.; *adj.* supported; suffered; reserved; stiff, distant (in manner); haughty; (of style) elevated, high-flown, precious; (mus.) sostenuto, sustained; (comm.) steady, unchanged; prezzi -i, prices remaining high, or stable; (aeron.) — dall'aria, airborne (i.e. 'up'); *n.m.* (herald.) a pale supported by a bar. **-ezza** *f.* reserve; reservedness; gravity; stiffness, haughtiness.

sostitu-ire [D 2] *tr.* to substitute; — una parola a un'altra, to substitute one word for another; — con, to replace by; to take the place of; -ì per un mese il segretario, for a month he was acting-secretary; to supplant; to supersede; (motor.) — gli spessori dei freni, to reline the brakes; (leg.) to substitute. **-ente** *part. adj.* **-i·bile** *adj.* replaceable. (**-ibilità** *f.*) **-ito** *part. adj.* substituted; changed; (leg.) neonato -ito, changeling child; (chem.) substituted; replaced (by a deputy); *n.m.* (leg.) substitute; remainderman; person entitled under gift over (C.C.). **-to** *m.* deputy, substitute; 'locum' (tenens); representative; (eccl.) surrogate (in Roman Congregations); (naut.) substitute (flag); primo -to, first substitute (i.e. repeat of first flag in a hoist). **-tore** *m.* deputy, substitute, representative. (**-trice** *f.*) **-zione** *f.* change; substitution; replacement; in -zione di, in place of; (chem.) substitution; (leg.) substitution; -zione ordinaria dell'erede, designation of another person to succeed as heir on failure of appointed heir; devise or bequest with contingent gift over; -zione fedecommissaria, devise or bequest to tenant-for-life and remainderman; (loosely) entail (C.C.); -zione di persona, impersonation (C.P.).

sostra *f.* (mil.) coal and wood store.

sostrato *m.* substratum; subsoil; lower layer; (fig.) fund; hidden depths; (philos.) matter; substance.

sostruzione *f.* (archit.) foundations, substructure, substruction.

sota·dico *adj.* (liter.) Sotadic.

soti·aco *adj.* (astron.) Sothic.

sottace-re [B 20] *tr.* to suppress (truth, evidence, information); to keep quiet about.

sottaceto *m.* (cul.) pickle.

sott-affusto *m.* (mil.) undercarriage; lower portion of gun-mounting. †**-aguzzino** *m.* (naut.) boatswain's mate. **-ambasciadore** *m.* Deputy Ambassador.

sottan-a *f.* petticoat; skirt; underskirt; sempre cucito alla — della mamma, tied to his mother's apron-strings; (fig., joc.) 'skirt'; woman, women; c'entra di mezzo la —, there's a woman in the case; (eccl.) cassock; (mus.) see **sottanella**. **-ella** *f. dim.* petticoat; underskirt; (mus.) small mean, lesser mean (lute-string); (rel.) haircloth worn penitentially as girdle. **-iere** *m.* womanizer. **-ina** *f.*, **-ino** *m.* under-petticoat; child's frock; tu-tu, ballet skirt.

sottangente *f.* (math.) subtangent.

sottano *adj.* (Sicily) lower; Petralia sottana, lower Petralia; †placed below; †inferior; †*n.m.* undergarment.

sottarchivista *m.*, *f.* assistant keeper of records.

sottar·co *m.* (*pl.* **-chi**) (archit.) underside of an arch or vault.

sottasta *f.* (naut.) pillar placed under a mast for support.

sott·ecchi, -ecche, †-ecco *adv.* stealthily, by stealth; secretly; guardare di —, to peer up at, to steal a glance at, *or* to eye warily; sorridere di —, to smile slyly.

sotten·dere [C I] *tr.* (geom.) to subtend.

sottentr·are [A I] *intr.* (*aux.* essere) to creep in, to slip in; to go in beneath; — a, to take the place of. (-am̱ẹnto *m.* -ato *part. adj.*)

sotterfu·gio *m.* subterfuge; pretext, excuse; evasion; *adv.* di —, by subterfuge; vedersi di —, to meet secretly.

sotterr-a *adv.* underground; (of the sun) andare —, to set; voler nascondersi —, to wish that the earth would open and swallow one; mettere —, to bury; *adv. phr.* di —, from under the earth. **-a·neo, †-ano** *adj.* underground; subterranean; corridoio -aneo, underground gallery; Roma -anea, the catacombs in Rome; poco -aneo, just below street level; molto -aneo, deep underground; (fig.) voce -anea, cavernous voice; *n.m.* cave; cellar; vault; dungeon; underground; (archit.) cellar, basement.

sotterr-are [A I] *tr.* to bury; to inter; to cover up; (agric.) to earth up; — i semi, to sow the seed deep; (fig.) to hide; to put away; to spend; to consume; in quell'impresa ci ha -ato un patrimonio, he has sunk (and lost) a fortune in that undertaking; *rfl.* to hide (oneself); to ruin oneself, to be ruined, to be done for. (-a·bile *adj.*) **-am̱ẹnto** *m.* burial, interment. **-am̱orti** *m. indecl.* grave-digger. (-ato *part. adj.* -atore *m.* -atrice *f.*) †-ato·rio *m.* burial; place of burial. †-atura *f.* burial; covering with earth.

sottẹs-o *part.* of **sottendere**; *adj.* (geom.) subtended. **-a** *f.* (geom.) chord, subtended side.

†sottesso *prep.* See **sotto**.

†sottigliare *vb.* and derivs. See **assottigliare**.

sottigliẹzza *f.* fineness; thinness; (of air) lightness, purity; (of the voice) shrillness, sharpness; (of vision) sharpness, keenness; (theol.) subtility (of spiritual bodies); (of mind, intelligence, arguments) subtlety, acuteness, ingenuity; sophistry; close attention; insight; precision, refinement.

†sottigliume *m.* fine work; refinement; cavilling, hair-splitting.

sottil-e *adj.* thin, fine, slender; corda —, cord; aria —, pure (light) air; polvere —, fine dust; (naut.) flotta —, light fleet or forces (destroyers, M.T.B., etc.); spiaggia —, shallow beach; fiume —, shallow river, stream; orecchio —, sharp ear (hearing); terra —, light (friable) soil; subtle, sharp, sly; (schol. philos.) dottor —, Doctor Subtilis, Duns Scotus, (by ext.) anyone oversubtle; weak; failing; mal —, consumption; *n.m.* slender (fine, thin) part; ridurre al —, to reduce to extremity; trarre il — dal —, to make a little money out of everything; subtlety; pel —, narrowly; guardare pel —, to scrutinize. **-mẹnte, †-emente** *adv.* thinly, finely; delicately; (fig.) subtly; artfully; cunningly; minutely; esaminare -mente, to examine very closely. **-ità** *f.* fineness, delicacy; thinness; daintiness; subtlety, acuteness, ingenuity. **-izzamẹnto** *m.* use of subtlety; hair-splitting; subtilization. **-izzare** [A I] *intr.* (*aux.* avere) to make subtle distinctions, to split hairs; *tr.* to introduce subtleties into; to subtilize; to examine minutely. (-izzato *part. adj.*) **-izzatore** *m.* hair-splitter; sophist.

sottinfermier-e *m.* hospital assistant, undernurse. (-a *f.*)

sottinsù *adv. phr.* upside down; di —, from beneath, upwards; *n.m.* (paint.) picture designed to be seen from below, or from underneath.

sottinten·d-ere [C I] *tr.* to understand (what is not expressed); to leave unexpressed; to imply; to guess; to divine; si -e, of course!, obviously! **-ente** *part.*; *n.m.* submanager, assistant superintendent, surveyor, inspector, etc. **-enza** *f.* assistant managership. **-imẹnto** *m.* understanding; implicit meaning.

sottintẹs-o *part.* of **sottintendere**, q.v.; *adj.* understood, not expressed; *n.m.* implication; thing implied or understood; senza -i, without mental reservations; parlare per -i, to hint, to give hints.

sọtto *prep.* **1.** UNDER, underneath; beneath, below; — un albero, under a tree; — terra, underground; — il cielo, beneath the sky, under heaven; restare — un'automobile, to be run over by a car; mettere — i piedi, to trample on, (fig.) to spurn; — il monte, at the foot of the mountain; — la finestra, beneath the window; — il livello del mare, below sea-level; (requiring 'a' or 'di' before a personal pronoun) — a noi, — di noi, below us, beneath us. **2.** THIS SIDE OF; tre miglia — Firenze, three miles this side of Florence; una signora — i quaranta, a lady of under forty; — il Natale, this side of, before, Christmas; — la raccolta, near harvest-time; — gli esami, near examination time *or* during the

exams. **3.** LESS THAN, below, short of; — il quintale, under the hundredweight; — zero, below zero; — la pari, below par; — il chilometro, less than a kilometer. **4.** SERVING, under, in the service or command of; subject to, under the dominion of; combattè — Garibaldi, he fought under Garibaldi; — la bandiera italiana, under the Italian flag; studiò — Mario Praz, he studied under Mario Praz; — la guida di, under the guidance of. **5.** CONCEALED UNDER, in the guise of; — la maschera dell'amicizia, in the guise of friendship; — lo pseudonimo di, under the pseudonym of; — il colore, under the pretext. **6.** UNDER THE STRESS OR INFLUENCE OF; — l'impulso dell'ira, impelled (driven) by anger; — l'azione del narcotico, under the influence of the narcotic; — pena di morte, on pain of death; — minaccia di, under threat of. **6.** FROM; — un certo punto di vista, from a certain point of view; — un nuovo aspetto, from a new angle. **7.** *adv.* DOWN; (of the sun) andar —, to set, (at cards, games) to lose; restar —, to lose, to get the worst of it, to be inferior; (fam.) dar —, to get down to it, to set to; dargli —, to attack him, to set about him; —, ragazzi, al lavoro!, now boys, get on with your work!; (bridge) andare quattro mani —, to go four hands down; (naut. command) down! (helm); below, at the bottom; abita —, he lives down below (on a lower floor); (mil.) chiamare — (abbrev. of 'sotto le armi'), to call up; andare —, to be called up.

sọtto- *pref.* sub-, under-. (Before a vowel the final *o* is often elided, e.g. **sottispettore**; for words in which the accent falls on the second syllable, e.g. **sottor·dine**, see separate entries.) **-alimentazịọne** *f.* undernourishment. **-ammi·raglio** *m.* (naut.) commodore (1914–18 war). **-archivista** *m.* assistant keeper of records. **-ascelle** *m. indecl.* dress-shield. **-banda** *f.* (mil.) trunnion cap; (naut.) bearing plate. **-barba** *f.* (vet.) chin (of a horse). **-bicchiere** *m.* glass-stand, mat, saucer. **-bọccia** *m.* decanter-stand. **-botti·glia** *m.* slide (e.g. saucer on which a bottle of port is moved round at table). **-bordo** *adv.* (naut.) a beam under the lee, alongside. **-bosco** *m.* undergrowth. **-cancelliere** *m.* vice-chancellor. **-capo** *m.* assistant manager, assistant chief; -capo stazione, under-station-master; -capo di Stato Maggiore, Assistant Chief of Staff; (naut.) coxswain, petty officer, yeoman. **-capoverso** *m.* sub-subparagraph. **-cchiello** *m.* (shoem.) facing. **-ccipitale** *adj.* (anat.) sub-occipital. **-ccupazịọne** *f.* unremunerative or part-time employment. **-celeste** *adj.* (theol.) subcelestial (esp. of human souls contrasted with angelic spirits). **-chiave** *adv.* under lock and key. **-chi·glia** *f.* (naut.) linea di -chiglia, building line under the keel plate. **-coda** *m.* crupper. **-comitato** *m.* subcommittee. †-co·mito *m.* (naut.) boatswain's mate. **-complesso** *m.* (eng.) sub-assembly. **-coperta** *f.* underblanket; *adv.* (naut.) between decks; below hatches. **-corrente** *f.* undercurrent; longitudinal section of a river-bed; *adj.* forming an undercurrent, flowing below another current. **-correre** [C 5] *intr.* (*aux.* avere, essere) to form an undercurrent, to flow beneath. **-cuta·neo** *adj.* subcutaneous, hypodermic. **-cute** *adv.* (med.) subcutaneously. **-diminutivo** *adj.*; *n.m.* double diminutive. **-divi·dere** [C I] and derivs. see **suddividere**. **-dominante** *f.* (mus.) subdominant. **-dorsale** *adj.* (anat.) subdorsal. **-durale** *adj.* (anat.) sub-dural. **-eccitazịọne** *f.* (electr.) under-excitation. **-espọrre** [B 21] *tr.* (photog.) to underexpose. **-esposizịọne** *f.* (photog.) underexposure. **-fa·scia** *m. indecl.* printed matter (posted open, under a wrapper). **-fattoriale** *adj.* (math.) subfactorial. **-fluviale** *adj.* (of water) from the undercurrent, flowing deep below the surface (therefore purer). **-fọndo** *m.* (radio; telev.; cinem.) background; in -fondo, faded under, held under; (bldg.) foundation, base. **-fru·tice** *m.* (bot.) see **suffrutice**. **-gamba** *adv.* carelessly, quickly; prendere una cosa di -gamba (or di sotto gamba), to take a thing in one's stride. **-ge·nere** *m.* sub-genus. **-gola** *f.* (archit.) moulding running below dentils or similar ornament; chin-strap, collar, ruff; gorget, wimple. **-gọmma** *adj. indecl.* (electr.) rubber-insulated. **-grondale** *m.* (archit.) drip-stone moulding. **-gruppo** *m.* (chem.) sub-group. **-introdotte** *f.pl.* (eccl. hist.) *subintroductae*. **-lettura** *f.* contatore di -lettura, check-meter. **-limitare** *m.* threshold. **-lineare** [A 6] *tr.* to underline; (fig.) to emphasize. **-lineato** *part. adj.* underlined; emphasized; *n.m.* words or passage underlined. **-linguale** *adj.* sublingual. **-lume** *m.* mat to stand a lamp on. **-lunare** *adj.* sublunary. **-mano** *adj.* secret (also 'sotto mano'); *adv.* within reach; at hand; di -mano, secretly; *n.m. indecl.* note-pad, writing-pad; bonus, gratuity. **-mare** *adj.* submarine; *adv.* at the bottom of the sea; *n.m. indecl.* the bottom of the sea, sea-floor. **-marino** *adj., n.m.*

sotto- *(cont.)*

submarine. **-mascellare** *adj.* (anat.) submaxillary. **-mastro** *m.* assistant keeper of an arsenal. **-me·dia** *m.* less than half marks. **-mediante** *f.* (mus.) submediant. **-messo** *part.* of **sottomettere**, q.v.; *adj.* subjected; subdued; submissive, obedient; respectful. **-mettere** [C 20] *tr.* to subdue; to subject; to vanquish; to reduce to obedience; **-mettere i buoi al giogo**, to put the oxen to the yoke; **-mettere ad analisi**, to subject to analysis; *rfl.* to submit, to acquiesce; to yield, to give in; **mi -metto ai vostri voleri**, I bow to your wishes. **-minare** [A 1] *tr.* to undermine. (**-minato** *part.* *adj.*) **-missione** *f.* submission; subjection, subjugation; submissiveness; humility, meekness; resignation. **-mucosa** *f.* (anat.) submucosa. **-mul·tiplo** *m.* (math.) sub-multiple. **-murare** [A 1] *tr.* (bldg.) to underpin. **-murata** *f.* (archit.) foundation, footing of walls. **-murazione** *f.* (bldg.) underpinning. †**-mutanza** *f.* (gramm.) hypallage, metonymy. **-normale** *adj.* subnormal; *n.f.* (math.) subperpendicular. **-notato** *part.* *adj.* mentioned below. **-pan·cia** *f.*, *m.* girth-strap, belly-band. **-paranco** *m.* (naut.) deck cargo, goods consigned on deck (F.O.B.). **-passag·gio** *m.* underpass, underbridge; subway. **-piede** *m.* under-strap of a spur, *or* of trousers (passing under the instep); (shoem.) insole; (motor.) car-mat; †door-mat; †step of a carriage. **-piombo** *adj.* *indecl.* (electr.) lead-sheathed (of cable). †**-pontuale** *m.* (naut.) risings. **-porre** [B 21] *tr.* to submit, to subject; to expose; **-porre a**, to place under, to put under; **-porre un progetto al giudizio di uno**, to submit a plan to someone's judgement; **il clero fu sottoposto alla legge generale**, the clergy were placed under (made subject to) the ordinary law; **-porre le uova alla gallina**, to set the eggs under the hen; **sottopose molte province**, he subjugated many provinces; (leg.) to submit; to place under; *rfl.* (*prep.* a) to submit (to). **-por·tico** *m.* (archit.) portico; prostyle; arcade. **-posizione** *f.* subjection; submission; placing under. **-posto, -posto** *part.* of **sottoporre**, q.v.; *adj.* placed under or below; subject, subjected; **-posto a pericoli**, exposed to dangers; **-posto a terremoti**, liable to earthquakes; *n.m.* subject, dependent, subordinate. **-prodotto** *m.* (industr.) by-product. **-protesto** *m.* (comm.) under protest. **-raffreddamento** *m.* (phys.) supercooling. **-scala** *m.* (archit.) space or room under a staircase; cupboard under the stairs; tiny room, 'hole'. **-scapolare** *adj.* (anat.) subscapular. **-scatto** *m.* (mil.) trigger-plate. †**-scritto** *part.* of **sottoscrivere**, q.v.; *adj.* signed; undersigned; (finan.) subscribed; *n.m.* undersigned; (joc.) l'**umile -scritto**, 'yours truly', the present writer. **-scrittore** *m.* signatory; subscriber. (**-scrittrice** *f.*) **-scrivente** *part.*, *n.m.*, *f.* signatory, the undersigned. **-scri·vere** [C 12] *tr.* to sign; to subscribe; to underwrite; (leg.) **-scrivere un testamento**, to sign a Will; **-scrivere il capitale sociale**, to subscribe a company's capital; *intr.* (*aux.* avere; *prep.* a) to assent; to agree; to adhere; to subscribe; (comm.) **-scrivere a un prestito**, to subscribe to a loan; *rfl.* (*prep.* a) to subscribe; to sign, to append one's signature, to bind oneself by signing. **-scrizione** *f.* signature; subscription; subscription list, list of adherents; inscription (below a statue, etc.); (leg.; comm.) signature; subscription; underwriting; **-scrizioni di testamento**, signature of Will; **domanda di -scrizione di azioni**, application for shares. **-segreta·rio** *m.* undersecretary. **-sezione** *f.* subsection. **-sopra** *adv.* upside-down; topsy-turvy; **mettere -sopra**, to overturn, (fig.) to throw into confusion; *adj.* *indecl.* in a turmoil, confused; *n.m.* *indecl.* utter chaos, confusion, turmoil. **-spe·cie** *f.* (biol.) subspecies. **-squadra** *adj.* *indecl.* acute-angled, pointed; **tetto -squadra**, steep-pitched roof. **-squadro** *m.* goldsmiths' and silversmiths' term for an oblique cavity corresponding to a sharp projection in the mould; (sculp.) a similar deep cavity; (foundry) undercut. **-stante** *part.* *adj.* lying, situated below; **i piani -stanti**, the floors below; subordinate, inferior. **-stare** [A 9] *intr.* (*aux.* essere; *prep.* a) to be below; to occupy a subordinate position; to submit, to give in, to yield; to be subject (to); to endure; to obey. **-stazione** *f.* (electr.) substation. †**-stra·glio** *m.* (naut.) forestay. **-struttura** *f.* (techn.) infrastructure, substructure. **-suolo** *m.* (agric., etc.) subsoil; underground; **una stazione del -suolo**, a station on the underground; (bldg.) basement. **-tangente** *f.* (geom.) subtangent. **-tenente** *m.* (mil.) second-lieutenant; (naut.) **-tenente di vascello**, sublieutenant. **-terra** *m.* *indecl.* subterranean space; underground room; *adj.* *indecl.* see **sotterra**. **-tipo** *m.* (zool.) sub-phylum. **-ti·tolo** *m.* subheading, subtitle. **-valutare** [A 1] *tr.* to undervalue. **-vaso** *m.* saucer (e.g. for flower-pot). **-vela** *adv.* (naut.) under sail. (NOTE: a ship is not under sail, even with all sail set, if it is being

propelled by any other means). **-ventare** [A 1] *tr.* (naut.) to weather; to pass to windward; *rfl.* to pass to leeward. **-vento** *m.* (naut.) lee, leeward; **cadere -vento**, to drift, to fall to leeward; **navigare -vento**, to pass or sail to leeward of; (geog.) **Isole di Sottovento**, Leeward Islands; (fig.) **essere -vento**, to be in an unfavourable position. **-veste** *f.* undergarment; waistcoat. **-vita** *f.* an undergarment resembling a camisole; †waistcoat. **-voce** *adv.* in a low voice, softly; in an undertone.

sottorbitale *adj.* (anat.) suborbital.

sottor·dine *m.* (biol.) sub-order; *adv.* *phr.* in —, in subjection; subordinately; **questione passata in —**, matter which has become of minor importance.

sottos·sido *m.* (chem.) suboxide.

sottraendo *m.* (math.) subtrahend.

sottrarre [B 33] *tr.* (*prep.* da, a) to subtract, to deduct; to withdraw; to remove, to take away; to rescue; **— alla morte**, to rescue from death; to embezzle; to conceal (from); to abstract; (math.) to subtract, to deduct; *rfl.* (*prep.* a) to get out (of), to escape (from); to evade; to withdraw (from); **sottrarsi al proprio dovere**, to shirk one's duty.

sottratt·o *part.* *adj.* (*prep.* a) subtracted, taken away, deducted; stolen; saved, freed (from); †*n.m.* theft. **-ore** *m.* subtractor; deliverer. (**-rice** *f.*)

sottrazione *f.* subtraction; deduction; removal; withdrawal; **— di sangue**, blood-letting; **— di danaro**, theft of money; (leg.) **— di beni**, abstraction of property; (math.) subtraction.

sottufficiale *m.* (mil.) warrant officer; (naut.) petty officer. (NOTE: the same anomaly exists in Italian and Royal Navy as opposed to the army. In both armies the warrant officers do not mess with officers whereas they do in their respective naval messes.)

sovent-e *adv.* often, frequently; **più —**, oftener, more frequently; *adj.* frequent; **-i volte**, oftentimes; *adv.* *phr.* **di —**, often. **-emente** *adv.* frequently.

soverchi-are [A 4] *tr.* to surpass, to overcome; to overflow; to overwhelm; to browbeat; †to surmount; *intr.* (*aux.* avere) to be in excess; to be superfluous; to rise in flood; to protrude; to stick out. **-amento** *m.* exceeding, surpassing, overwhelming. **-ante** *part.* *adj.* excessive, overwhelming; crushing; *n.m.* overbearing person, browbeater. **-anza** *f.* excess, superabundance, superfluity; insolence; outrage. **-ato** *part.* *adj.* surpassed; overcome; browbeaten; outraged. **-atore** *m.* overbearing person; oppressor; transgressor; *adj.* overbearing. (**-atrice** *f.*) **-eri·a** *f.* overbearing conduct; insolence; outrage; imposition.

sover·chi-o *adj.* excessive, superfluous; immoderate; **— caldo**, extreme heat; *n.m.* excess, surplus; superabundance; **averne di —**, to have too much; (fig.) overbearing conduct, insolence; abuse of power; *adv.* excessively, too much; *adv.* *phr.* **di —**, too; **di —buttiroso**, too rich in butter. **-amente** *adv.* excessively, too much; immoderately. †**-e·vole** *adj.* insolent; excessive.

sovero *m.* (bot.). See **sughero**.

sove·sci-o *m.* (agric.) mulch, green manure. **-are** [A 3] *tr.* to dig in (a crop) as green manure.

sovra¹ *prep.* See **sopra¹**.

sovra-² *pref.* cf. **sopra²**. **-bbondante** *part.* *adj.* superabundant; superfluous, excessive. (**-bbondantemente** *adv.*) **-bbondanza** *f.* superabundance; redundancy; glut. **-bbondare** [A 1 c] *intr.* (*aux.* essere) to be superabundant; (*aux.* avere; *prep.* di, in) to abound greatly (in). **-bbondevole** *adj.* superabundant. **-bbondevolezza** *f.* excess, superabundance. **-ccaricare** [A 2 s] *tr.* to overload, to overburden; (techn.) to overload; *intr.* (*aux.* avere) to exaggerate, to 'lay it on'. **-cca·rico** *m.* excessive burden; overload; overweight; supercargo; (techn.) overload; (philately) overprint; *adj.* overburdened; overloaded; **-ccarico di lavoro**, overworked. **-ccennato** *adj.* above-mentioned. **-cculto** *m.* (theol.) hyperdulia. **-coperta** *f.*, **-copertina** *f.* *dim.* book-cover, dust-jacket. **-corrente** *f.* (electr.) over-current. **-cuti** *m.pl.* (mus.) very high notes. **-ddetto** *adj.* see **sopraddetto**, under **sopra²**. **-eccitare** (electr., etc.) over-excitation. **-elongazione** *f.* (telev.) overshoot, overswing. **-eminente** *adj.* pre-eminent. **-eminenza** *f.* pre-eminence. **-ente** *m.* (philos.) Supreme Being. **-esporre** [B 21] *tr.* (photog.) to overexpose. **-esposizione** *f.* (photog.) overexposure. **-esposto, -esposto** *part.* *adj.* (photog.) overexposed. **-ffollate** *adj.* overcrowded. **-limentare** [A 1] *tr.* (eng.; motor.) to supercharge, to boost. **-limentato** *part.* *adj.* (motor.) supercharges. **-limentazione** *f.* (eng.) supercharging, boosting; (fig.) overfeeding. **-lluvionato** *adj.* (geog.) covered with

sovra- (*cont.*)

alluvium. **-metallo** *m.* see **sprametallo**. **-modulato** *adj.* (electron.) overmodulated. **-modulazione** *f.* (electron.) overmodulation. **-nnaturale** *adj.* see **soprannaturale**, under **sopra²**. **-ppeso** *m.* (sport; comm.) overweight, excess weight. **-pporre** [B21] *tr.* (*prep.* a, su) to place upon; to lay on top (of); to superimpose (on); to apply (to); (geom.) to superpose; (eng.) to overlap; †to add; *rfl.* to be superimposed; to place oneself (above); to get the better (of); to make oneself master (of). **-pposizione** *f.* laying, placing, on top; superimposing; (geom.) superposing; (eng.) overlap. **-pposto**, **-pposto** *part. adj.* (*prep.* a) superimposed (on); laid (on); uno strato è -pposto all'altro, one layer rests on the other; †placed before. **-pressione** *f.* (phys.) overpressure, pressure in excess of atmospheric pressure. **-produzione** *f.* (industr.) overproduction. **-scaldato** *adj.* see **surriscaldato**. **-sollecitazione** *f.* (mech.) over-stress. **-stampare** [A1] *tr.* (typ.) to overprint. **-stampato** *part. adj.* (typ.) overprinted; (philately) francobolli -stampati, overprinted stamps. **-stare** [A9] *intr.* (*aux.* avere; *prep.* a) to hang (over); to impend; to threaten; to overhang; to lie high above; to dominate; to be superior (to). **-struttura** *f.* superstructure. **-tassa** *f.* (comm.) surcharge. **-tensione** *f.* (electr.) excess voltage, overvoltage.

sovran-o *adj.* sovereign; supreme; rupe -a, towering cliff; onore —, supeme honour; diritto —, sovereign right, sovereign's right; *n.m.* sovereign, reigning prince, princess; king, queen; †(mus.) see **soprano**. **-a** *f.* sovereign, queen; (numism.) sovereign. **-amente** *adv.* royally; majestically; supremely; un'opera -amente bella, a supremely beautiful work. **-eggiante** *part. adj.* domineering; dominant, supreme. **-eggiare** [A3c] *intr.* (*aux.* avere) to exercise sovereign power; to be supreme; *tr.* to rule over; to domineer over. **-ità** *f.* sovereignty; supremacy.

†**sovresso** *prep.* on, upon.

sovr-imporre [B21] *tr.* to superimpose; to lay (an additional burden) upon. **-imposta** *f.* additional tax. **-impressione** *f.* (photog.) super-impression. **-intelligenza** *f.* (philos.) apprehension of a higher order of reality. **-intelligi·bile** *adj.* beyond human understanding. **-inten·dere** [C1] and derivs. see **soprintendere**. **-umanità** *f.* quality of being superhuman. **-umano** *adj.* superhuman. (**-umanamente** *adv.*)

sovvag·gio *m.* See **sovvaggiolo**.

sovvag·giolo *m.* pad (of straw, etc. used in packing); padding; bulge.

sovvallo *m.* (Tusc.) surplus; reserve; mettere a —, to put on one side; a —, in abundance; di —, in addition; †reinforcement, support.

sovven-ire [D17] *tr.* to help, to assist; to aid (esp. financially); to subsidize, to support; — di consigli, to help by means of advice; *intr.* (*aux.* essere; *prep.* a) to supply, to find a remedy (for); — al bisogno, al difetto, to supply a need, lack, to make good a deficiency; *impers.* to come to mind; to occur (to); (*prep.* di) non mi sovviene del nome, I can't remember the name; mi fai — di quei giorni, you remind me of those days; (also used *rfl.* but this is considered a Gallicism); *n.m.* memory, recollection, remembrance. †**-enza**, **-ienza** *f.* aid, help. †**-evole** *adj.* helpful, ready to help. †**-i·bile** *adj.* that can be helped; that can be recollected; memorable. **-imento** *m.* assistance, relief; recollection. **-itore** *m.* one who helps. (**-trice** *f.*) **-tore** *m.* financial backer. (**-trice** *f.*) **-uto** *part. adj.* helped, aided; subsidized, supported.

sovvenzion-e *f.* subvention; subsidy; (naut.) -i marittime, maritime subsidies. **-are** [A1c] *tr.* (comm.) to finance; to subsidize. (**-ato** *part. adj.*)

sovvernare [A1] *intr.* (*aux.* avere) to pass the winter; to hibernate (cf. **svernare**).

sovvers-ione *f.* overthrow; destruction; subversion. **-ivismo** *m.* subversive activities. **-ivo** *adj.* subversive; tending to subversion; *n.m.* revolutionary; extremist. **-ivamente** *adv.* subversively.

sovverso *adj.* overthrown; destroyed; †corrupt.

sovvert-ire [D1] *tr.* to subvert; to overturn, to overthrow; to upset; to cause unrest among; to undermine the loyalty of; †to corrupt; †to pervert. **-imento** *m.* subversion, subverting; overthrow; upsetting. **-ito** *part. adj.* subverted; overthrown; †perverted; †corrupt. **-itore** *m.* subverter; †perverter; *adj.* tending to subvert. (**-itrice** *f.*)

†**sovvol·gere** *vb.* and derivs. See **sovvertire**.

†**so·zio** *m.* and derivs. See **socio**.

sozzare [A1c] and derivs. See **insozzare**.

sozz-o *adj.* filthy, dirty; nasty; foul; loathsome; vile; polluted; -i guadagni, ill-gotten gains; — di sangue, smeared with blood. **-amente** *adv.* dirtily; filthily; foully; loathsomely. **-ezza** *f.* dirtiness, filthiness; dirty, filthy, foul or loathsome thing or action. **-ume** *m.* filth; filthy thing(s). **-ura** *f.* filth; foulness; loathsomeness; pollution; filthy house.

spacc-are [A2] *tr.* to split; to crack; to break open; to chop, to cleave; — la legna, to chop wood; (tan.) to split; — in due un capello, to split hairs; (of a clock, watch) — il minuto, — i sessanta, to keep perfect time; (fam.) to bash; *rfl.* (*acc.* of *prn.* 'si') to split, to crack; to burst; (*dat.* of *prn.* 'si') -arsi la testa, cadendo, to fall and cut one's head open. **-afiamma** *f. indecl.* device in a lamp for dividing the flame. **-alegna**, **-alegne** *m. indecl.* wood-cutter. **-amento** *m.* splitting; cleaving; bursting; cracking. **-amontagne**, **-amonte**, **-amonti** *m. indecl.* braggart. **-apietre** *m. indecl.* stone-breaker. **-ata** *f.* splitting; (tan.) skiver; split; (fencing) lunge; (gym.) splits. **-ato** *part. adj.* split; cleft; (fig.) clear, evident; pure and simple, complete, unadulterated; bugiardo -ato, arrant liar; (of pronunciation) articulated; (herald.) per fess; *n.m.* (archit.) section. **-atamente** *adv.* clearly; decidedly. (**-atore** *m.*) **-atrice** *f.* (tan.) splitting machine. **-atura** *f.* split; cleft, crack, fissure, crevice; splitting.

spacchettare [A1c] *tr.* to undo (a parcel); to remove wrappings from.

spacchino *m.* (pop.). See **spaccapietre**, under **spaccare**.

spacci-are [A3] *tr.* to sell; to sell out; to sell off; to get rid of; to dispose of; to dispatch, to kill; — una faccenda, to dispatch a piece of business; to circulate, to spread, to give out (news, rumour, etc.); -arle grosse, to spin yarns, to tell tall stories; *rfl.* -arsi per, to give oneself out to be, to pass oneself off as; to hurry, to make haste; spàcciati!, be quick!; -arsi da uno, to be rid of someone. **-a·bile** *adj.* readily saleable; easily disposed of. **-afosso** *m. indecl.* (mil. hist.) heavy gun firing grape for sweeping a moat. **-amento** *m.* sale; dispatch. **-ativo** *adj.* quick, expeditious, efficient; suitable for sale. **-ato** *part. adj.* sold; dispatched; set free; declared; -ato dai medici, despaired of by the doctors, *or* (joc.) 'done in' by doctors; matto -ato, stark mad; done for; ruined; dead; è bell'e -ato, it's all over with him; dar per -ato, to consider finished. **-atamente** *adv.* quickly, immediately; with dispatch. **-atore** *m.* seller; distributor; -atore di frottole, spreader of false news; -atore di monete false, coiner, forger. (**-atrice** *f.*)

spac·cio *m.* sale; selling; merce che non trova —, goods which do not sell; avere pronto —, to sell readily; shop (esp. tobacco-shop); — di vino, wine-shop; dispatch; — di biglietti, booking-office; dare — a, to dispatch, (euphem.) to kill.

spac-co *m.* (*pl.* -chi) split, crack, cleft; opening; break; innesto a —, cleft grafting; tear, rent; farsi uno — nei calzoni, to tear one's trousers. **-conata** *f.* bragging, braggadocio. **-cone** *m.* braggart, boaster; bully. (**-cona** *f.*)

spad-a *f.* sword; — a doppio taglio, two-edged sword; incrociare le -e con, to cross swords with; sguainare la —, to draw one's sword; rimettere la — nel fodero, to sheathe one's sword, (fig.) to make peace; passare a fil di —, to put to the sword; — corta, dagger; uomo di —, swordsman, (fig.) military man; buona —, good swordsman; a — tratta, vigorously, impetuously, freely; brandire la —, to threaten war; dritto come una —, straight as a die; (vet.) junction of hair streams on the neck of a horse; (ichth.) ribbon fish, *Trachypterus iris*; pesce —, swordfish, *Xiphias gladius*; — argentina, Argentine, *Argentina sphyraena*; — rossa, red band fish, *Cepola rubescens*; (text.) — di lancio, picking stick (of a loom). **-acciuola** *f.* (bot.) *Gladiolus*. **-a·io**, **-aro** *m.* sword-maker; (hist.) sword-bearer; a — tratta, vigorously, impetuously, freely; **-ata** *f.* sword-cut; sword-thrust. **-erella** *f.* (bot.) *Gladiolus*. **-erno** *m.* triple fish-hook. **-iforme** *adj.* (bot.) ensiform. **-ino** *m. dim.* dress-sword; dirk. **-ista** *m.* swords-man. **-ona** *adj. f.* (agric.) pera -ona, a kind of conference pear. **-one** *m. augm.* broadsword; cavalry sword; -one a due mani, two-handed sword; (iron.) menare lo -one a due gambe, to run away.

spa·dic-e *m.* (bot.) spadix. **-eo** *m.* (vet.) strawberry roan.

spadone¹ *m. augm.* of **spada**, q.v.

spadone² *m.* eunuch.

spadron-are [A1c], **-eggiare** [A3c] *intr.* (*aux.* avere) to swagger; to be domineering; to be arrogant.

spa·dul-a *f.* (naut.) see **spata**. †**-are** *tr.* to drain (a swamp).

spaesato *adj.* out of one's own country or region; (fig.) out of one's depth; lost, bewildered.

spaghetti *m.pl.* See under **spago**.

spagin-are [A I s] *tr.* (typ.) to alter the paging of. (**-ato** *part. adj.* **-atura** *f.*)

†**spagiri·a** *f.* term in alchemy for the analysis and the composition of metals and alloys.

spagli-are[1] [A 4] *tr.* to remove straw from; to unpack from straw covering; *intr.* (*aux.* avere) (of animals) to scatter straw, to kick straw about; to feed on straw. (**-ato** *part. adj.*) **-atore** *m.* unpacked (from straw coverings). (**-atrice** *f.*) **-atura** *f.* removal of straw.

spagliare[2] [A 4] *intr.* (*aux.* avere) (of water) to flood, to overflow.

spa·gli-o *m.* flood, pool of flood-water; seminare a —, to sow broadcast; (of a horse) sudden convulsive movement. **-one** *m.* (mil. hist.) mantlet.

spagliucol-are [A I s] *intr.* (*aux.* avere) to scatter wisps of straw. **-io** *m.* continual scattering or blowing about of straw.

Spagn-a *pr.n.f.* (geog.) Spain; cera di —, see **ceralacca**; (bot.) (erba) —, lucerne, *Medicago sativa*. **-olagine** *f.*, **-olata** *f.* bravado, braggadocio. **-oleggiare** [A 3 c] *intr.* (*aux.* avere) to adopt Spanish manners; to use Spanish expressions. **-olesco** *adj.* (*m.pl.* **-oleschi**) (derog.) un fare **-olesco**, a haughty manner or way of behaving. **-oletta** *f.* window-bolt; spool or reel (esp. of cardboard) of silk or cotton; †(kind of) cigarette; (mus.) Spagnoletta, an Italian dance of Spanish origin. **-olismo** *m.* Spanish idiom, Hispanicism; Spanish fashion (esp. in Italian literature and painting in the seventeenth century). **-uola** *f.* Spanish woman, Spanish girl; Spanish influenza (epidemic of 1918–19). **-uolo** *adj.* Spanish; *n.m.* Spaniard; Spanish; (dog) spaniel.

Spagnoletto *pr.n.m.* José de Ribera (1588–1656), disciple of Caravaggio.

spagnottare [A I] *intr.* (*aux.* avere) to eat (bread), to relieve one's hunger (cf. **pagnotta**).

spa·go *m.* (*pl.* **-ghi**) string, twine; un gomitolo di —, a ball of string; packthread; a piece of string; (provb.) tre fili fanno uno — e tre -ghi fanno una corda, i.e. strength lies in unity; cobbler's thread; (fam.) tirare lo —, to be a cobbler; (fig.) dare — a uno, to give a person rope, i.e. to allow him greater freedom, etc.; (fig., colloq.) fear, 'blue funk'. **-ghettini** *m.pl.* (cul.) fine spaghetti. **-ghetto** *m. dim.* thin string; (fig., colloq.) fear, 'wind up'; *pl.* (cul.) spaghetti.

spai-are [A 4] *tr.* to separate (a pair); to unmatch, to uncouple. **-amento** *m.* separating a pair, uncoupling; disparity. **-ato** *part. adj.* (of a pair) separated; unmatched, uncoupled; scarpe **-ate**, odd shoes.

spa·lace *m.* (zool.) mole-rat, *Spalax* spp.

spalanc-are [A 2] *tr.* to open wide, to throw open; — gli occhi, to open one's eyes wide, to stare; *rfl.* to open wide; la porta si -ò, the door was flung open. **-amento** *m.* flinging wide. **-ato** *part. adj.* wide open; la guardò con gli occhi **-ati**, he stared wide-eyed at her. **-atamente** *adv.* gapingly; widely; too openly.

spal-are[1] [A I] *tr.* to shovel away; — il grano, to winnow the corn (with a kind of shovel); *intr.* (*aux.* avere) (naut.) to rest on the oars; to keep the oars horizontal; to feather the oars; (command) **-a!**, oars! **-ata** *f.* action of shovelling; a shovelful. (**-ato** *part. adj.*) **-atore** *m.* snow-shoveller, man who clears away the snow; **-atore** meccanico, snow-plough. **-atura** *f.* work or cost of shovelling away snow or earth.

spalare[2] [A I] *tr.* (agric.) to remove props or stakes from.

Spa·lato *pr.n.f.* (geog.) Split.

spalc-are [A 2] *tr.* to take away scaffolding from; to cut away the lower branches from; *intr.* (*aux.* avere) (colloq.) to stand out, to excel; ingegno che **-a**, outstanding ability. **-ata** *f.* piece of bravado; reproof given with assumed dignity. (**-ato** *part. adj.*)

spalco *m.* distinction, excellence; *adj. phr.* di —, outstanding, striking, brilliant.

spald-o *m.* projection, balcony; (hist.) battlements; bastion; (mil. hist.) rampart, sentry walk on a bastion. **-are** [A I] *tr.* (mil. hist.) to fortify with a glacis or counterscarp.

spall-a *f.* **1.** SHOULDER; portare a —, to carry on one's shoulder; dare di — a, tenere, fare — a, to help, to give a helping hand to, to support; stringersi nelle -e, alzare, scrollare le -e, to shrug one's shoulders; lavorare di -e, to do heavy work such as hoisting weights, (fig.) to shove one's way forward pushing with one's shoulders, to shoulder one's way along; voltar le -e a, to turn one's back on; buttarsi una cosa dietro le -e, to discard, to take

no further notice of something; prendere sulle proprie -e, to shoulder (e.g. a responsibility); avere la famiglia sulle -e, to have to support one's family; avere un certo numero di anni sulle -e, to begin to feel one's age; vivere alle -e di uno, to live at someone's expense. **2.** *pl.* BACK; cogliere alle -e, to catch unprepared, to fall upon suddenly; dire una cosa dietro le -e di uno, to say things behind someone's back; ridere alle -e di uno, to laugh at someone behind his back; alle -e di, following behind; ero proprio alle tue -e, I was just behind you; ha la moglie che gli sta sempre alle -e, his wife supports him, helps him on, stands behind him, in everything; avere le -e al muro, to have one's back to the wall; mettere uno con le -e al muro, to get someone with his back to the wall, to drive him into a corner; mettersi con le -e al muro, to resist, to dig one's heels in. **3.** (OF A GARMENT) SHOULDER; (butcher.) — di montone, shoulder of mutton; clod sticken (of beef); — di San Secondo, salted shoulder of pork; (bldg.) abutment; (naut.) break of a deck; shoulder of a gun; — del timone, trailing part of a rudder; — di fiume, bank of a river not cultivated; †half deck; †flare of a hull; (mil.) buttress, abutment; il fucile in —, gun on shoulder, rifle at the shoulders; spall'arm!, shoulder arms!; (mus.) violino da —, first violin, leader (because, being seated on the left side of the platform, he turns his shoulder to the conductor); (sport, 'pallone') player standing nearest the wall for the return; (eng.) web (of a crankshaft). **-accia** *f. pejor.* big, ugly shoulder; *pl.* (vet.) shoulder galls. **-accio** *m. pejor.* see **spallina**; (hist.) shoulder-piece of armour. **-amento** *m.* (eng.) shoulder. **-are** [A I] *tr.* (pop.) -are un cavallo, to put a horse's shoulder out. **-ata** *f.* push, heave, with the shoulder(s); shrug of the shoulders. **-ato** *part. adj.* finished, done for; **-ato** per debiti, ruined financially; cause **-ate**, lost causes; (of a horse) with a shoulder out of joint. **-eggiamento** *m.* help, support, backing. **-eggiare** [A 3 c] *tr.* to support, to back (usu. illicitly); *recip. rfl.* (usu. iron.) to give mutual support. **-etta** *f. dim.* parapet, embankment; retaining-wall; (archit.) splay of a window (where the wall is cut away obliquely to allow space for the shutters). **-iera** *f.* back (of a chair, bench, sofa, etc.); head or foot of a bed; side of a child's cot; (hortic.) espalier, raised bed, row of plants trained against a wall; grassy bank; (naut. hist.) half deck where poop ladders rested in a galley; stroke thwarts of a galley; naval honour like manning the side; (naut.) backboard; (mil.) cradle of a gun; cordon of soldiers. **-iere** *m.* (naut.) stroke; *pl.* men on the stroke oar. **-ieretta** *f. dim.* low wall, edging of steps or garden path. **-ina** *f.* (mil.) epaulette; bagnare le -ine, to have a drink to celebrate one's promotion; shoulder strap or epaulet of an apron. **-ino** *m. dim.* (Tusc.) see **spallina**; porter (who carries bundles on his back). **-uccia** *f. dim.* narrow, hunched, shoulder; far **-ucce**, to shrug one's shoulders. **-ucciata** *f.* shrug of the shoulders. **-uto** *adj.* broad-shouldered.

spalm-are [A I] *tr.* to smear (with oil, grease, etc.); — di burro, to butter; (naut.) to clean and tar (the hull); *rfl.* to smear oneself; to rub ointment, etc., on one's body. **-amento** *m.*, **-ata** *f.* (naut.) careening and tarring down. **-ata** *f.* smearing, oiling; blow with a cane on the palm of the hand. (**-ato** *part. adj.*) **-atore** *m.* (naut.) caulker; tarring brush; †*adj.* careening (e.g. of a ship). **-atura** *f.* smearing, greasing, tarring; (naut.) tar, bottom composition. **-o** *m.* (naut.) tar, bottom composition.

spalto *m.* glacis; bastion; embankment.

spaludare [A I] and derivs. See **spadulare**.

spampan-are [A I] *tr.* (agric.) to strip (a vine) of its leaves; *rfl., intr.* (*aux.* essere) (of roses, etc.) to shed petals, to drop; (fig.) to spread, to expand; to boast. (**-amento** *m.*) **-ata** *f.* stripping, shedding leaves or petals; (fig.) boasting, boast. **-ato** *part. adj.* (of flowers) overblown; (fig.) fallen into excess or absurdity. **-atura** *f.*, **-azione** *f.* (agric.) stripping of vines.

†**spampinare** *vb.* and derivs. See **spampanare**.

span-are [A I] *tr.* to remove earth from around the root of (a plant); to break the thread of (a screw); *rfl.* (eng.) to become stripped of thread (of a screw). (**-ato** *part. adj.*)

spanci-are [A 3] *tr.* (joc.) to disembowel; (dressm.) to reduce the fullness of; *intr.* (*aux.* avere) (of a wall) to bulge; *rfl.* -arsi dalle risa, to burst with laughing. **-ata** *f.* bellyful; fare una **-ata**, to eat 'fit to burst'; blow on the belly. (**-ato** *part. adj.*)

spanconare [A I c] *rfl.* (agric., of dry ground) to crack.

span·d-ere [C 5] *tr.* to shed; to scatter, to spread; — odore, to give off a smell; — false notizie, to spread false news; to spill; to slop;

spand-ere (*cont.*)

(poet.) — lacrime, to shed tears; *intr.* (*aux.* avere) to leak, to drip; (fig.) spendere e —, to squander money; *rfl.* to spread out; to be scattered; to be diffused; to be dispersed. **-ente** *part. adj.* spreading; *n.m.* sprinkler; (paperm.) loftsman. **-iconcime** *m.* (agric.) fertilizer-spreader, muck-spreader. **-ifieno** *m. indecl.* (agric.) tedder. **-imento** *m.* spreading; scattering; shedding; diffusion; (agric.) fertilizzazione a -imento, top dressing. **-itoio** *m.* (paperm.) drying-room. (**-itore** *m.* **-itrice** *f.* **-itura** *f.*)

spani-are [A I] *tr.* to free (a bird) from a trap or bird-lime; to remove limed twigs from; *rfl.* to get free (from bird-lime or from entanglement). **-ato** *part. adj.* freed from bird-lime, etc.; *n.m.* trap of limed twigs.

spanierare [A I] *tr.* to empty (e.g. fruit) from a basket.

spanna *f.* span (of the hand); lungo una —, a span wide; avere la vista corto una —, to see no further than the end of one's nose.

spann-are¹ [A I] *tr.* to skim (milk), to cream. **-ato** *part. adj.* skimmed; latte -ato, skim milk. **-atoia** *f.* skimmer. **-atura** *f.* skimming.

spannare² *intr.* (*aux.* avere) to dismantle the 'ragna' (a type of bird-net); also *tr.*

†**spannare³** *tr.* to clean, to cleanse (cf. **appannare**).

spannoc·chi-a¹ *f.* corn-cob. **-are** [A4] *tr.* to strip, to husk (corn-cobs). (**-ato** *part. adj.*) **-atura** *f.* maize harvest, gathering of the cobs.

spannoc·chi-a² *f.* (zool.) *Penaeus kerathurus*, a large edible prawn (also **-o** *m.*).

spanopne·a *f.* (med.) spanopnoea.

spantan-are [A I] *tr., rfl.* to get out of a bog; (fig., usu. joc.) to get out of the mire. (**-ato** *part. adj.*)

spanto *part.* of **spandere**, q.v.; *adj.* spread; scattered; spilt; poured forth; (colloq.) vedersela spanta, to realize that one is done for.

spappagallare [A I] *intr.* (*aux.* avere) (derog.) to chatter like a parrot; to jabber.

spappato *adj.* (of textiles) having the starch or dressing washed out.

spappol-are [A I s] *tr.* to pulp, to reduce to pulp; *rfl.* to go to a pulp, to become mushy; (fig.) -arsi dalle risa, to laugh fit to burst. **-a·bile** *adj.* that can be pulped. **-ato** *part. adj.* pulped; reduced to pulp; soft, mushy.

sparadrappo *m.* (med.) sticking plaster, strapping.

sparaghella *f.* See **sparagella**, under **sparagio**.

spa·rag-io *m.* (bot.) garden asparagus, *Asparagus officinalis* var. *altilis*; un mazzo di -i, a bunch of asparagus; (cul.) -i, asparagus. **-ella** *f.* (bot.) wild asparagus, *A. acutifolius.* **-ia·ia** *f.* asparagus bed; woman asparagus seller. **-ia·io** *m.* asparagus seller.

sparaglione *m.* (ichth.). See **sparo²**.

sparagn-o *m.* (pop.) saving. †**-are** *tr.* to spare; *intr.* to go short.

spar-are¹ [A I] *tr.* to shoot (a firearm) to discharge, to fire; — calci a, to kick; — fandonie, to talk nonsense, to exaggerate; -arle grosse, to 'shoot a line'; *intr.* (*aux.* avere) to fire, to shoot. **-afucile** *m. indecl.* braggart; *pr.n.m.* name of a character in Verdi's *Rigoletto.* (**-amento** *m.*) **-apane** *m. indecl.* (Tusc., pop.) idler, loafer, good-for-nothing. **-ata** *f.* discharge, shot; volley; boasting, swaggering; exaggeration. **-ato** *part. adj.* (of firearms) discharged; (of person or missile) shot; *adv. phr.* alla -ata, freely, openly. **-atore** *m.* shooter; boaster, swaggerer. (**-atrice** *f.*) **-ato·ria** *f.* shooting, shooting affray; exchange of shots. **-avento** *m.* draughty place.

spar-are² [A I] *tr.* to rip open; to gut; to cut lengthwise; *rfl.* to be ripped open; to split; (fig.) to sweat one's guts out. **-adrappo** *m.* adhesive tape. **-ato** *part. adj.* ripped open; split lengthwise; gutted; *n.m.* front opening of coat, waistcoat, etc.; -ato inamidato, starched shirt-front.

spar-are³ [A I] *tr.* (eccl.) to unvest; to remove hangings from. **-ato** *part. adj.* (eccl.) unvested; chiesa -ata, church without hangings.

†**sparavieri** *m.* See **sparviere**.

sparecchi-are [A4c] *tr.* — la tavola, to clear the table; *abs.* to clear away after a meal; †(fig.) to eat everything set before one. (**-amento**, **-ato** *part. adj.*)

sparecchio *m.* clearing away after a meal; clearance (of the food); (vulg.) fare — di, to make a clean sweep of, to 'collar'.

spareggiare [A3c] and derivs. See **sparigliare.**

spareggio *m.* inequality, disparity; deficit; difference; (sport) play-off, *repêchage*, 'decider'.

†**sparere** *vb.* and derivs. See **sparire.**

sparetamento *m.* (mining) slabbing.

spar·g-ere [C4] *tr.* to spread, to scatter, to strew; — al vento, to scatter to the wind; — la voce, to spread the rumour; — denari,

to squander money; — spie, to send out spies; to disseminate, to issue (e.g. printed publications); to sow (seed); to shed; — il sangue, to shed blood; to sprinkle; — di lagrime, to wet with one's tears; *rfl.* to be scattered; to spread; la voce si sparse in un baleno, the news spread like lightning. **-imento** *m.* spreading, scattering; shedding; -imento di sangue, bloodshed; pouring out; (med.) -imento di fiele, jaundice. **-ipolvere** *m. indecl.* (techn.; agric.) duster, dust spreader. **-itore** *m.* scatterer; -itore di sangue, one guilty of shedding blood. (**-itrice** *f.*)

spar·golo *adj.* (agric., of a bunch of grapes) thin, scanty.

sparigli-are [A4] *tr.* to break up (a pair), to separate, to unmatch; (cards) technique at the game of 'scopa' consisting in taking two or more cards which add up to seven with a single card in one's hand, e.g. to take the two of diamonds and the five of spades on the table with the seven of hearts in one's hand (cf. under **apparigliare¹**). (**-ato** *part. adj.*)

spar-ire [D2] *intr.* (*aux.* essere) to disappear; to vanish; to fade away; — via, to go off, to die away, to perish; far —, to make disappear, to suppress, (euphem.) to kill; (iron.) far — a, to relieve of, to steal from; gli hanno fatto — tutte le provviste, they have run through all his provisions. **-imento** *m.* see **sparizione**. **-ito** *part. adj.* vanished; gone. **-izione** *f.* disappearance, vanishing; death.

sparl-are [A I] *intr.* (*aux.* avere; *prep.* di) to speak ill (of); to slander, to backbite, to talk scandal about. **-amento** *m.* malicious gossip; backbiting. **-atore** *m.* backbiter; scandalmonger. (**-atrice** *f.*)

sparlotto *m.* (ichth.). See **sparo²**.

sparnazz-are [A I] *tr.* (pop.) to scatter; (fig.) to squander; *intr.* (*aux.* avere) (of fowls) to flap their wings (cf. **starnazzare**). **-amento** *m.* scattering. (**-ato** *part. adj.*)

sparo¹ *m.* shot, discharge, report; detonation, explosion; si udì uno —, a shot was heard.

sparo² *m.* (ichth.) gilthead, *Sargus annularis*; — acuto, — puntazzo, *Puntazzo puntazzo.*

sparo³ *m.* (Tusc.). See **sparato**, under **sparare².**

sparpagli-are [A4] *tr.* to scatter, to disperse; to disseminate; to spread about; to squander; *rfl.* to be scattered, to spread out. **-amento** *m.* scattering; dispersal; squandering. **-ato** *part. adj.* scattered; dispersed; squandered; disordered. **-atamente** *adv.* in disorder, helter-skelter.

sparpa·gl-io *m.* scattering, complete disorder. **-io** *m.* frequent or continuous scattering. **-one** *m.* untidy person. (**-ona** *f.*)

spars-o *part.* of **spargere**, q.v.; *adj.* scattered; loose; (of hair) loose, ruffled, in disorder; (of blood) shed; pagine -e, loose leaves (phrase commonly used as title of a book consisting of short articles, essays, etc. of an author, originally published in various reviews, etc.); (bot.) foglie -e, alternate, spiral; rime -e, collected poems; — di rugiada, sprinkled with dew, dewy; campo — di cadaveri, field strewn with corpses; (mil.) ordine —, open order, skirmishing order; notizie -e, news spread abroad; rami -i, spreading branches; tubo —, pipe opening out at the end. **-amente** *adv.* sparsely, here and there; thinly; disconnectedly.

Spart-a *pr.n. f.* (geog.) Sparta. **-ano** *pr.n.m., adj.* Spartan; (fig.) brave, Spartan-like. **-anamente** *adv.* in Spartan fashion, like a Spartan.

Spar·taco *pr.n.m.* Spartacus.

sparte *adv. phr.* (Flor.) a —, on one side, apart, aside.

spart-e·a *f.* (bot.) see **sparto¹**; (text.) fibra di —, esparto fibre. **-eïna** *f.* (chem.) sparteine, lupinidine. **-eri·a** *f.* (industr.) esparto goods.

spart-ire [D2] *tr.* to divide, to separate; — i capelli, to part one's hair; (archit.) to partition; (mus.) to score, to put into score; — il tempo, to play (or sing) in time; to share; (fig.) non aver nulla da — con, to have nothing in common with. **-iacque** *m. indecl.* (geog.) watershed. **-i·bile** *adj.* divisible. **-imento** *m.* dividing; partition; -imento delle acque, watershed. **-ineve** *m. indecl.* snowplough. **-ito** *part. adj.* separated; partitioned; *adv. phr.* alla -ita, disconnectedly, in disorder; *n.m.* (mus.) score, full score. **-itamente** *adv.* separately; one by one. **-itoio** *m.* sluiceway. **-itore** *m. adj.*, **-itrice** *f. adj.* (techn.) separating. **-itraf·fico** *m.* isola -itraffico, traffic island; white line in centre of road; strip of grass dividing carriage-ways on an autostrada; colonnina -itraffico, traffic bollard marked 'keep left' in England. **-itura** *f.* partition; distribution; division; (mus.) score, full score. **-izione** *f.* partition, distribution, division; (of the hair) parting

sparto¹ *m.* (bot.) esparto grass, *Stipa tenacissima, Lygeum spartum,* etc.; (techn.) esparto fibre; (text.; paperm.) esparto.

†**sparto**[2] *part.* of **spargere**, q.v.; outspread (cf. **sparso**); divided (cf. **spartito**).

sparut-o *adj.* lean, thin; spare; emaciated. **-ẹzza** *f.* leanness, thinness.

sparvier-e *m.*, **-o** *m.* (orn.) sparrowhawk, *Accipiter nisus;* — levantino, Levant sparrowhawk, *A. brevipes;* (provb.) drizzare il becco allo —, to perform the impossible; (bldg.) mortar-board, hod; (naut.) large circular net. **-ato** *adj.* hawk-like, swift.

spa·sim-o *m.* spasm, convulsion; pang; (rel.) Madonna dello —, Our Lady of Sorrows; (paint.) name of Raphael's painting of the Agony of Jesus. **-ante** *part. adj.* suffering, racked with pain; *n.m.* (iron., joc.) suitor, aspirant to a girl's hand. **-are** [A I s] *intr.* (*aux.* avere) to suffer agonies, to be racked with pain; to long ardently; -are per una persona, to be in love with a person. **-ato** *part. adj.* in convulsions, in great pain; deeply in love. **-atamẹnte** *adv.* passionately, ardently; agonizingly. **-ọso** *adj.* agonizing; moto -oso, spasmodic movement.

spasm-o *m.* (med.) spasm. **-o·dico** *adj.* (med.) spasmodic, spastic; (fig.) spasmodic, convulsive. **-o·lişi** *f.* (med.) spasmolysis. **-oli·tico** *adj.* (med.) spasmolytic.

†**spas-o** *adj.* spread out; wide open; intent, attentive. †**-a** *f.* wide flat basket.

spass-are [A I] *tr.* to amuse; to divert; to provide amusement for; (naut.) to unreeve (a tackle); *rfl.* (*acc.* of *prn.* 'si') to amuse oneself; (*dat.* of *prn.* 'si') -arsela, to enjoy oneself, to have a good time. †**-amento** *m.* amusement, diversion.

spasseggiare [A 3c] *intr.* (*aux.* avere) (pop.) to go out for a walk (cf. **passeggiare**).

spassẹggio *m.* (pop.). See **passeggio**.

spassion-are [A I c] *rfl.* to give vent to one's feelings, to unbosom oneself; to attain calm of mind. **-atẹzza** *f.* impartiality; tranquillity. **-ato** *part. adj.* dispassionate, impartial. **-atamẹnte** *adv.* dispassionately, impartially.

spass-o *m.* pastime, amusement, recreation; darsi agli -i, to give oneself up to amusements; andare a —, to go for a walk; pigliarsi, prendersi — di qualcuno, to make fun of someone; menare a —, to make fun of, *or* to make empty promises to, to 'lead up the garden path'; mandare a —, to dismiss, to send away; essere, stare a —, to be out of work; ha il marito a —, her husband has lost his job, is unemployed. **-ọso** *adj.* amusing.

spast-are [A I] *tr.* to remove dough or 'pasta' from; to ungum, to unpaste; *rfl.* (*acc.* of *prn.* 'si') to come unstuck; (*dat.* of *prn.* 'si') -arsi le mani, to clean one's hands after making bread, pastry, etc. (-**ato** *part. adj.*).

spa·stic-o *adj.*, *n.m.* (med.) spastic. (-**a** *f.*) **-ità** *f.* (med.) spasticity.

spastoi-are [A 4c] *tr.* to unshackle, to set free; *rfl.* to free oneself; spastoiarsi dai pregiudizi, to rid oneself of prejudice. (-**ato** *part. adj.*).

spata[1] *f.* (bot.) spathe.

†**spata**[2] *f.* See **spada** or **spatola**.

spaternostrare [A I] *intr.* (*aux.* avere) to mutter endless prayers, to go through a string of prayers.

spa·tico *adj.* (miner.) spathic, spathose.

spat-o *m.* (miner.) spar; — calcare, calcite, calcspar; — d'Islanda, Iceland spar; — pesante, heavy spar, barytes. **-ofluore** *m.* (miner.) fluorspar. **-ọso** *adj.* (miner.) spathose.

spa·tola *f.* spatula; ladle; scutcher; putty knife; Harlequin's wooden sword; — d'Arlecchino, slap-stick; (bldg.) flat trowel; (naut., Neap.) stick used for thrashing hemp; (orn.) spoonbill, *Platalea leucorodia.*

spatriare [A 4] and derivs. See **espatriare**.

spa·tula *f.* See **spatola**.

spaurac·chi-o *m.* scarecrow; bogey; bugbear. †**-are** *vb.* and derivs. see **spaurire**.

†**spaurare** *vb.* and derivs. See **spaurire**.

spaur-ire [D 2] *tr.* to frighten, to terrify, to alarm; *rfl.* (*prep.* di) to be frightened, to be terrified (by); to take alarm (at); (of a horse) to shy. **-imẹnto** *m.* fright; alarm. **-ito** *part. adj.* frightened; terrified; pale with fright.

spavald-o *adj.* arrogant; defiant, insolent; aggressive; *n.m.* insolent person; arrogance; braggart; ha dello —, there is something insolent, aggressive, etc. about him. (-**a** *f.*) **-amẹnte** *adv.* arrogantly; defiantly, insolently; aggressively. **-eri·a** *f.* effrontery, impudence; defiance; insolence; aggressiveness; boastfulness, boast.

spava·nio *m.*, **spave·nio** *m.* (vet.) spavin.

spavent-are [A I] *tr.* to frighten, to terrify; to scare off; to appal; la morte non -a il forte, death has no terrors for the brave; *intr.* (*aux.* avere; *prep.* di), *rfl.* to take fright (at); to be terrified (by); (of a horse) to take fright, to shy. **-a·bile** *adj.* frightful, terrible. †**-ac·chio** *m.* see **spauracchio**. **-ato** *part. adj.* frightened, terrified, fearful. **-atore** *m.* terrifying person; fearsome object. **-atrice** *f.*) **-ẹvole** *adj.* terrifying, frightening; terrible, appalling; awful; huge, enormous; horrible. **-evolmẹnte** *adv.* frightfully; awfully, dreadfully; enormously. **-evolẹzza** *f.* frightfulness.

spavent-o *m.* terror; fright; fear; mettere — in, incutere — a, to frighten; (vet.) — di bue, spavin (of cattle); *adv. phr.* a —, fearfully. **-osità** *f.* (pop.) frightfulness. **-ọso** *adj.* frightening, alarming; frightful, terrible; horrible; monstrous; fearful; †full of fear; †(of a horse) timid, skittish. **-osamẹnte** *adv.* frighteningly; fearfully.

spaziale *adj.* spatial; of, relating to, space; tenuta —, space suit (cf. **spazio**).

spazi-are [A 4] *intr.* (*aux.* avere) to range, to roam freely, to rove; to wander at large; to soar; (fig.) to expatiate; *tr.* (typ., etc.) to space, to white. **-ante** *part. adj.* ranging, roving, wandering. (-**ato** *part. adj.*) **-atura** *f.* (typ.) space, letter. **-eggiare** [A 3c] *tr.* (typ.) to space. (-**eggiato** *part. adj.*) **-eggiatura** *f.* (typ.) spacing of words, letters, etc.; -eggiatura normale, normal spacing.

spazient-ire [D 2] *rfl.* (pop.) to lose patience. **-ito** *part. adj.* out of patience. (Cf. **impazientire**.)

spa·zi-o *m.* (†*pl.f.* -a) space; room; fare, dare —, to make room; distance; (typ.) (blank) quad, quadrat; uno — bianco, a blank space; space of time, interval; avere —, to have time; senza —, without delay; dopo breve —, after, in, a short time; nello — di un'ora, in an hour's time; lo — percorso, the distance covered; (mus.) space (between lines of stave); *pl.* space (beyond the earth's atmosphere); (vet.; zool.) spazi interdentari, diastema. **-osità** *f.* spaciousness. **-ọso** *adj.* spacious, vast; ample; wide, broad; large; roomy. **-osamẹnte** *adv.* spaciously, widely, amply; si sta -osamente, there is plenty of room.

spazz-are [A I] *tr.* to sweep, to clean; to sweep away; (fig.) la pestilenza -ò via migliaia di persone, the plague carried off thousands of people; (motor.) to scavenge; (mil.) to sweep away (e.g. the enemy defences); — i nemici, to disperse the enemy; — il terreno, to sweep or rake the ground; (naut., of a wave) to sweep away, to carry away. **-acamino** *m.* chimney-sweep. **-acampagna** *f.* (mil. hist.) canister gun. **-aforno** *m. indecl.* oven-mop, oven-brush. **-amento** *m.* sweeping, cleaning (esp. of streets). **-amine** *m. indecl.* (naut.) minesweeper. **-aneve** *m. indecl.* snow-plough (esp. on railway); macchina -aneve, motor snow-plough; (ski-ing) a technique in braking. **-ata** *f.* action of sweeping, sweep; dare una -ata a, to sweep. **-atamburi** *m. indecl.* (text.) card brusher. **-atina** *f. dim.* a little light sweeping or dusting. **-ato** *part. adj.* swept; -ato via, swept away. **-atoio** *m.*, **-atore** *m.* sweeper; (techn.) scavenger. **-atrice** *f.* woman sweeper; mechanical sweeper; (mil.) pull-through. **-atura** *f.* sweeping; sweepings, refuse, dirt; cassetta della -atura, dustpan; buttare nella -atura, dustcart; trattare come la -atura, to treat like dirt; metal filings, dust from coral, ivory, etc. **-atura·io** *m.* sweeper, dustman, scavenger. **-ẹtta** *f.* (mil.; eng.) tube brush. **-ino** *m.* road-sweeper; †crossing-sweeper.

spazzo *m.* level or levelled ground; flat open space; †pavement.

spaz·zol-a *f.* brush; — da capelli, hair-brush; — da panni, clothes-brush; — da scarpe, shoe-brush; frond (of a palm-tree); horse-hair; capelli tagliati a —, hair *en brosse;* baffi tagliati a —, tooth-brush moustache; — metallica, — di fili d'ottone, wire-brush; (electr.) brush; (motor.) rotor arm; (teleph.) wiper (of selector). **-are** [A I s] *tr.* to brush. **-ata** *f.* brush, (act of) brushing. (-**ato** *part. adj.*) **-ino** *m. dim.* small brush; -ino per i denti, toothbrush; -ino per le unghie, nail-brush; (mil. slang) batman.

speaker *m. indecl.* (pron. as Eng.) (radio) announcer.

spec·chia *f.* (geog. Apulia) cairn of stones cleared from field by farmers; (archaeol.) bronze-age tomb.

specchi-are [A 4] *rfl.* (*prep.* in) to be reflected; to look at one's reflection; to look at oneself in a mirror; -arsi in alcuno, to model oneself on someone. **-amento** *m.* contemplation of one's reflection. **-ato** *part. adj.* reflected, mirrored; (fig.) flawless, spotless, blameless; upright; probità -ata, transparent honesty; di costumi -ati, of exemplary conduct (morals). **-atura** *f.* looking at oneself in the mirror.

spec·chi-o *m.* mirror, looking-glass; guardarsi nello —, to look at oneself in the glass; — molato, bevelled mirror; — a tre facce, triple mirror; — ustorio, — ardente, burning-glass; scrittura a —, mirror-writing; pulito come uno —, as clean as a new pin; — d'acqua, sheet of water; sorgere a — dell'acqua, to be situated on the water's edge; (prov.) acqua torbida non fa —, still waters run deep; gli occhi sono lo — dell'anima, the eyes are the mirror of the soul; model, pattern; uno — di virtù, a model of virtue; farsi — di, to model oneself on; list, register (of attendances, etc.); handbook; summary, survey, table; analysed list, schedule; (motor.) — retrovisore, driving mirror; (bot.) — di Venere, Venus's looking-glass, *Specularia speculum*; (naut.) — di mare, glass-bottomed bucket used for searching the sea bottom when fishing for octopus, etc.; (of a steam-engine) — del cassetto di distribuzione, slide; face, port face; (geol.) slickensides. **-a·io**, †**-aro** *m.* mirror-maker; vendor of mirrors. **-era** *f.* large mirror; looking-glass; dressing-table mirror; dressing-table. **-etto** *m. dim.* hand-mirror; facet (of cut glass); piece of quartz mounted behind a precious stone; synopsis, summary, table, schedule; -etto per le allodole, apparatus with a number of little mirrors, used for attracting skylarks, (fig.) false inducements; essere (come) uno -etto per le allodole, to bait simple-minded people by appearing to be what one is not; *pl.* (vet.) splotches or specks of a lighter or darker colour on a horse's coat.

spe·ci-e¹ *f. indecl.* species; sort, kind; variety; description; l'origine della —, the origin of species; (schol. philos.) species (sensible or intelligible); merci di ogni —, goods of every description; è una — di rappresentante, he is a sort of agent; nella —, in the particular case; in ispecie, especially; sotto — di, with the pretext of; appearance, form, shape; ornament; beauty; in — umana, in human shape; mutare —, to change appearance; fare —, to impress, to make a show, *or* to make all the difference, to matter, to show, *or* to be surprising; (theol.) species (of bread and wine); spice, aroma; *pl.* simples. **-ale** *adj.* special, particular; peculiar; singular; frutta -ale, choice fruit(s); *n.m.* (post) bag of registered letters or parcels. **-almente** *adv.* especially, specially, particularly. **-alista** *m., f.* specialist; riunione di certi -alisti, panel meeting; (leg.) special commissioner; special examiner; (naut.) technician (rating). **-alità** *f.* speciality; peculiarity; (comm.) special line or class of goods; -alità medicinali, proprietary medicines; (mil.) specialization; -alità d'arma, Special Branch; (frequently used as a euphemism to cover duties of a secret department); (naut.) category, branch (e.g. torpedo, gunnery, etc.). **-alizzare** [A I] *tr.* to specify, to particularize; *rfl.* (*prep.* in) to specialize (in). **-alizzato** *part. adj.* specified; particularized; specialized; (of a worker) skilled; operaio non -alizzato, unskilled worker. **-alizzazione** *f.* specialization.

spe·cie² *adv.* especially, particularly.

speci·fic-o *adj.* specific; (phys.) calore —, specific heat; peso —, specific gravity; (comm.; leg.) esecuzione -a del contratto, specific performance; (med.) malattia -a, specific disease; *n.m.* specific. **-a** *f.* detailed list; memorandum; specification. **-amente** *adv.* specifically; (phys.) una sostanza -amente più grave, a substance of higher specific gravity. **-amento** *m.* specifying. **-are** [A 2 s] *tr.* to specify. **-ativo** *adj.* specifying, serving to specify. **-ato** *part. adj.* specified. **-azione** *f.* specification; (gramm.) complemento di -azione, specifying complement, genitive; (leg.) formation of a new species of property out of someone else's material by converting it into a different form; (Scot.) specification (C.C.). **-ità** *f.* specific quality.

specill-o *m.* (med.) probe, specillum; (chem.) glass rod. **-are** [A I] *tr.* to probe.

specimen *m. indecl.* (typ.) specimen page; specimen binding.

specios-o *adj.* specious; singular; †beautiful. (**-amente** *adv.*) **-ità** *f.* speciousness; †beauty.

spe·co *m.* (*pl.* -**chi**) cave, den; cavern; grotto; (eccl.) sacro —, St Benedict's grotto at Subiaco; (astron.) observatory, lookout; — vesuviero, seismographic observatory on Mount Vesuvius. **-are** [A I s] and derivs. See **speculare**.

spe·colo *m.* (surg.) speculum; †mirror.

speculare¹ *adj.* mirror-like, specular; (metall.) ghisa —, spiegeleisen.

specul-are² [A I s] *tr.* (surg.) to examine (e.g. with a speculum); (fig.) to speculate upon, to investigate; *intr.* (*aux.* avere) to speculate, to meditate; to observe; (finan.) — in, su, to speculate in; — sul rialzo, to buy bull; — sul ribasso, to sell bear. **-a·bile** *adj.* fit (object) for speculation or observation. **-amento** *m.* observation; speculation. **-ante** *part. adj.* speculating; observant; speculative. (**-antemente** *adv.*) **-ativa** *f.* speculative faculty. **-ativo** *adj.* speculative; scienze -ative, pure science(s); *n.m.* theorist. **-ativamente** *adv.* speculatively. **-ato** *part. adj.* speculated upon; meditated. (**-atamente** *adv.*) **-atore** *m.* speculative philosopher; (finan.) speculator; stock jobber; -atore insolvibile, -atore espulso, lame duck; †*pl.* (Rom. antiq.) Emperor's bodyguard; scouts. (**-atrice** *f.*) **-azione** *f.* speculation; inquiry; meditation; (finan.) speculation; venture; valori di -azione, speculative stocks; -azione oltre il capitale disponibile, overtrading; per -azione, as a speculation.

†**spe·culo** *m.* See **specchio**.

spe·culum *m.* (surg.) speculum.

spedal-e *m.* (Tusc., pop.) hospital. **-esco** *adj.* (*m.pl.* -**eschi**) relating to hospitals. **-iere** *adj.* of, relating to, a hospital; *n.m.* director of a hospital; hospital officer, nurse; (eccl.) -iere di S. Giovanni di Dio, Brother Hospitaller of St John of God; †guest. **-ino** *m.* medical student; house surgeon, houseman; *adj.* of, relating to, a hospital; febbri -ine, hospital fevers (i.e. caught in hospital). **-ità** *f.* hospital treatment. (Cf. **ospedale** and derivs.) **-izzare** [A I] *tr.* to hospitalize. (**-izzato** *part. adj.*)

spedantire [D 2] *tr.* to rid of pedantry.

sped-are [A I] *rfl.* to become footsore; to be walked off one's feet; *tr.* (naut.) to weigh (anchor). **-ato** *part. adj.* footsore; walked off one's feet; (naut.) ancora -ata, anchor aweigh. **-atura** *f.* footsoreness.

†**spedicare** *tr.* to unfetter.

spediente *m.* See **espediente**.

sped-ire [D 2] *tr.* to perform, to execute, to carry out with dispatch; to expedite; to send; to post; to forward; to ship; to draw up, to settle, to arrange finally; (of a pharmacist) — una prescrizione, to make up a prescription; (eccl.) to draw up (bulls, briefs, etc.); (leg.) — causa, — lite, to try and set action down for judgement (C.C.P.); †*intr.* to be expedient; *rfl.* to hasten, to hurry, to make haste, to be quick. **-imento** *m.* performing, execution; lo -imento della prescrizione, the making-up of the prescription. **-itezza** *f.* quickness; readiness; expedition; dispatch. **-itivo** *adj.* expeditious, prompt. **-ito** *part. adj.* sent; quick, prompt, easy, fluent; free, unimpeded; beyond hope, done for; -ito dai medici, given up by the doctors; *adv.* quickly, promptly, with dispatch, speedily; fluently. (**-itamente** *adv.*) **-itore** *m.* sender; consignor, shipper; forwarding agent. (**-itrice** *f.*) **-izione** *f.* sending, dispatching; dispatch; forwarding; consignment; shipping; shipment; peso di -izione, shipping weight; -izione contro assegno, charges forward; bolletta di -izione, ricevuta di -izione, consignment note; bollettino di -izione, dispatch note; casa, agenzia di -izione, shipping (forwarding) agency; (leg.) -izione della causa, trial and setting-down of action for judgement; -izione in forma esecutiva, official issue of judgement or order warranting levy of execution; ruolo di -izione delle cause, cause list (C.C.P.); contratto di -izione, contract of forwarding agency (C.C.); (eccl.) 'expedition'; the drawing up of a papal brief, etc.; the document when drawn up. **-izioniere** *m.* forwarding-agent; (eccl.) (Apostolic) Expeditor, Expeditioner.

†**spe·glio** *m.* See **specchio**.

spegn-are [A 5 c] *tr.* to take out of pawn; *rfl.* to free oneself from a pledge. **-ato** *part. adj.* redeemed; released.

spegn-ere, spe·gn-ere [C 7] *tr.* to extinguish, to put out; to blow out; to turn out, to turn off; to switch off; to quench; to allay; — la farina, to mix flour with water; — la polvere, to lay the dust; to check, to put a stop to; to put an end to; to destroy; to kill; to uproot; (techn.) — la calce, to slake lime; — il forno, to damp down (or put out) the furnace; (motor.) — il motore, to switch off the engine; (metall.) to quench; (leg.) — un debito, to pay off a debt; — un'ipoteca, to discharge a mortgage; (naut.) l'abbrivo, to check the way; *rfl.* to be extinguished; to go out; to fade away; to diminish; to vanish; to pass away, to die; si spense dolcemente, he passed away peacefully. **-iarco** *m. indecl.* (electr.) arc eliminator. **-i·bile** *adj.* extinguishable. **-imento** *m.* extinguishing, putting out; extinction; (elect.) blow-out. **-imoc·colo** *m.* candle-snuffers. **-itoio** *m.* fire-extinguisher. **-itorce** *m.* torch-extinguisher. **-itore** *m.* extinguisher; -itore d'incendii, fireman. (**-itrice** *f.*) **-itura** *f.* extinguishing.

spelacchi-are [A4] *tr.* to pull out the hair of; (fig.) to fleece; *rfl.* to lose one's hair; to go bald. (**-aménto** *m.*) **-ato** *part. adj.* nearly bald; peeled, stripped of skin; stripped of leaves; mangy, shabby; (fig.) fleeced.

†**spelagare** *tr.* to rescue from the sea; (fig.) to rescue from trouble; *intr.* to get out of trouble (cf. **pelago**).

spela·ia *f.* (text.) floss silk.

spel-are [A1] *tr.* to strip of hair; to shear; *intr.* (*aux.* essere) to lose one's hair; to moult. **-aménto** *m.* (tanning) unhairing, dewoolling, fellmongering (of sheep pelts). **-ato** *part. adj.* stripped of hair; shorn; moulting; barba -ata, thin, ragged, beard. **-atura** *f.* stripping of hair. **-azzare** [A1] *tr.* (text.) to sort and clean (wool). (**-azzato** *part. adj.*) **-azzatura** *f.* (text.) sorting and cleaning wool. **-azzino** *m.* (text.) wool-sorter, fellmonger.

spelda *f.* (Tusc.). See **spelta**.

spel-e·o *m.* cave; (rel.) *spelaeum*, cave of initiation (esp. Mithraic). **-eologi·a** *f.* speleology. **-eo·gico** *adj.* speleological. **-eo·logo** *m.* speleologist. **-erpe** *m.* (zool.) *Spelerpes fuscus*, a cave-dwelling newt.

spell-are [A1] *tr.* to skin, to flay, to excoriate; (fig.) to fleece, to extort money from; *rfl.* to rub one's skin off, to get skinned; le si -ano le mani, the skin is peeling off her hands; (of upholstery) to become threadbare. **-aménto** *m.* excoriation. (**-ato** *part. adj.*) **-atura** *f.* skinning; abrasion. **-icciare** [A3] *tr.* to tear the skin, or fur; to skin; (fig.) to treat roughly; *recip. rfl.* (of dogs, etc.) -icciarsi a morsi, to tear each other's fur, to bite each other, to fight. **-icciata**, **-icciatura** *f.* skinning, tearing of fur or hair; (fig.) severe reproof, 'skinning'. **-uzzicare** [A2s] and derivs. see **spilluzzicare**.

†**spellire** *tr.* to declare; to expound; to articulate, to say clearly.

spelónca *f.* cave; den; cavern; (fig.) large, gloomy house.

spelta *f.* (bot.) spelt, *Triticum spelta*; two-rowed barley, *Hordeum distichon*.

speme *f.* (poet.) hope.

spen·d-ere [C1] *tr.* to spend; to expend; to lay out; to consume; to use up; to employ, to make use of; spesi un'ora per convincerlo, it took me an hour to persuade him; — monete contraffatte, to pass counterfeit coins; *abs., intr.* (*aux.* avere) to spend; to make purchases, to go shopping; (provb.) chi più -e meno -e, the best is not the cheapest, don't spoil the ship for a ha'p'orth of tar; è un uomo che -e, he is free with his money; non badare a —, to spend freely; — in erba, to spend on the security of a future crop; — e spandere, to squander one's money; *rfl.* to give one's services; to take trouble, to exert oneself. **-accióne** *m.* (fam., derog.) spendthrift. (**-accióna** *f.*) **-eréccio** *adj.* lavish, prodigal; extravagant. **-i·bile** *adj.* (for) spending; spendable; moneta -ibile, current coin (legal tender); persona -ibile, helpful person (who allows his name to be used, gives his services, etc.). **-ibilità** *f.* currency, validity, negotiability. **-icchiare** [A4] *tr., intr.* (*aux.* avere) to spend in driblets. **-itóre** *m.* spender; spendthrift; one who spends on behalf of another. (**-itóra**, **-itrice** *f.*)

spen·dita *f.* spending; putting into circulation; (leg.) — di monete false, passing false coins.

†**spene** *f.* See **speme**.

spen·gere [C7] and derivs. (Tusc.). See **spegnere**.

spennac·chi-o *m.* ostentatious, large plume. **-ato** *adj.* plucked, featherless; moulting; ruffled; like a plucked fighting-cock; (fig.) vecchio -ato, bald-headed old man; disordered, uncared for; (mus.) spinetta -ata, broken-down spinet. **-era** *f.* plume; tuft of feathers.

spenn-are [A1] *tr.* to pluck, to strip of feathers; (fig.) to fleece; *rfl.* (of birds) to moult; (mus.) to unquill (a harpsichord). **-acchiare** [A4] *tr.* to pluck, to pull out (some of the) feathers from; (fig.) to fleece; *rfl.* to moult. **-ato** *part. adj.* plucked; moulting; shabby; rimaner -ato, to be put out of countenance.

spennell-are [A1] *tr.* to give a coat of paint to; — la gola con tintura di iodio, to paint the throat with iodine. **-ata** *f.* stroke of the brush. (**-ato** *part. adj.*) **-atura** *f.* painting; brushwork.

spennoc·chia *f.* (vet.) cracked knees (of a horse).

†**spensare** *vb.* and derivs. See **dispensare**.

spensier-ato *adj.* thoughtless; careless; carefree; heedless; alla -ata, thoughtlessly, carelessly, *or* free from care. **-atag·gine** *f.* thoughtlessness. **-atamente** *adv.* thoughtlessly. **-atézza** *f.* thoughtlessness. **-ito** *adj.* freed from care, relieved of worry; carefree.

spénto, spento *part.* of **spegnere**, q.v.; *adj.* extinguished, put out;

no longer alight, out; extinct; lifeless, dead; spent; colore —, dull colour; rubbed out, cancelled; finished; — di allegrezza, bereft of gaiety; (techn.) calce spenta, slaked lime.

spenzol-are [A1s] *intr.* (*aux.* avere) to dangle, to hang down; (archit.) to project, to overhang; *tr.* to dangle. **-ato** *part. adj.* dangling; overhanging. **-óne, -óni** *adv.* dangling.

spera[1] *f.* (poet.) sphere; globe; heavenly sphere; sky; una — di sole, a ray of light; (Tusc.) hand-mirror; (naut.) sea-anchor; (med.) suppository.

†**spera**[2] *f.* See **speranza**, under **sperare**[2].

sperare[1] [A1] *tr.* (pop.) to look through (an object) against the light; — le uova, to candle eggs; †*intr.* to be transparent.

sper-are[2] [A1] *intr.* (*aux.* avere) to hope; -iamo per giorni migliori, let us hope for better times; -o di sì, I hope so; -o di riuscire, I hope to succeed; — in, to rely on; -ano nel vostro aiuto, they rely on your help; — in Dio, to trust in God; *tr.* to hope for; to expect; -o un aiuto, I am hoping for help; non si può — altro che danno, we can only expect harm to come of it; (provb.) rosso di sera, buon tempo si -a, red sky at night is shepherd's delight; †to consider probable. **-a·bile** *adj.* to be hoped for; è -abile che, it is to be hoped that. **-anza** *f.* hope; expectation; confidence; trust; non dà molte -anze, it doesn't inspire great hopes; giovane di belle -anze, young man of promise; color della -anza, hope's colour (i.e. green); senza -anza, hopeless; finchè c'è vita c'è -anza, while there's life there's hope; vivere di -anza, to live on hopes; -anza di vittoria, hope of victory; un filo di -anza, a ray of hope; (theol.) hope (as a theological virtue); (naut.) ancora di -anza, sheet anchor; (geog.) Capo di Buona Speranza, Cape of Good Hope. **-anzini** *m.pl.* (iron.) clerical optimists (expecting return of the Pope's temporal power). **-anzóso** *adj.* (often joc.) hopeful. **-anzuola** *f. dim.* faint hope, slender hope. **-ato** *part. adj.* expected, hoped for; non -ato, unexpected, unhoped for, unlooked for.

sper·d-ere [C3] *tr.* to disperse, to scatter; to drive away; to remove; to lose; to nullify; -a il cielo l'augurio!, Heaven forbid!; (vulg.) Dio vi -a!, Devil take you!; *rfl.* to disperse, to be scattered; to get lost, to go astray; to disappear, to vanish. **-iménto** *m.* dispersal; loss, disappearance; †miscarriage; †abortion. **-itóre** *m.* scatterer, destroery (**-itrice** *f.*) **-uto** *part. adj.* lost; dispersed; missing; ill at ease; bewildered; mi sentivo -uto fra quella gente rumorosa, I felt uncomfortable among those noisy people; wandering; wild; un luogo -uto, a wild place.

†**spereggiare** *intr.* to shine brightly.

sperequazióne *f.* disproportion; (finan.) gap; (geog.) inequality.

sperga *f.* (ichth.) grouper, *Serranellus cabrilla*; (orn.) see **svasso**.

†**sper·gere** *tr.* to sprinkle.

spergiur-are [A1] *intr.* (*aux.* avere) to commit perjury, to perjure oneself; *tr.* —il vero, to lie on oath; — il nome di Dio, to swear falsely by God. **-a·bile** *adj.* giuramento -abile, false oath, oath sworn falsely, perjury. **-aménto** *m.* perjuring. **-ato** *part. adj.* perjured, sworn falsely, invoked in a false oath. (**-atóre** *m.* **-atrice** *f.*) **-azióne** *f.* perjury. **-o** *adj.* perjured; *n.m.* perjury; perjurer. (**-a** *f.*)

spericol-are [A1s] *rfl.* to take fright. **-ato** *part. adj.* daring; (Tusc.) afraid; *n.m.* one taking a risk.

†**sperienza** *f.* See **esperienza**.

speriment-o *m.* experiment; per modo di —, by way of experiment (cf. **esperimento**). **-ale** *adj.* experimental; (agric.) campo -ale, trial plot. (**-alménte** *adv.*) **-are** [A1c] *tr.* to test; to try; to make trial of. **-ato** *part. adj.* experienced, expert; skilful; well-tried, tested. (**-atóre** *m.* **-atrice** *f.*)

sperm-a, †**-o** *m.* sperm. **-acéti** *m.* spermaceti. (**-ace·tico** *adj.*) **-a·tico** *adj.* (anat.) spermatic; cordone -atico, spermatic cord. **-atorre·a** *f.* (med.) spermatorrhœa. **-atozo·o** *m.* spermatozoon. **-oderma** *m.* (bot.) spermoderm; seed-pod.

spernuz·zola *f.* (orn.) great tit.

†**spero**[1] *m.* See **specchio**.

†**spero**[2] *f.* See **speranza**.

speron-e *m.* spur; (archit.) abutment; (vet.) 'feathers' on a horse's feet; (naut.) ram; (mil.) buttress; (geol.) spur; (herald.) rotella di —, mullet. **-a·ia** *f.* prick with a spur; spurs. †**-ara** *f.* (naut.) small sailing coaster. **-are** [A1c] (mil.) to buttress; (naut.) to ram. **-ata** *f.* spurring; ramming. **-ato** *part. adj.* spurred. **-ella** *f.* (bot.) *Delphinium ajacis, D. orientale, D. peregrinum, Galium aparine.* †**-iera** *f.* (naut.) small sailing coaster. **-iere** *m.* (orn.) peacock-pheasant, *Polyplectrum* spp.

sperper-are [A I S] *tr.* to squander, to dissipate; to scatter. **-amento** *m.* dissipation, squandering, scattering. (**-ato** *part. adj.* **-atore** *m.* **-atrice** *f.*) **-io** *m.* continual waste.

sper·pero *m.* waste; dissipation, squandering.

sperpe·tua *f.* (pop.) bad luck; misfortune; querulous complaint.

sperso *part.* of **sperdere**, q.v.; *adj.* scattered; bewildered; lost; cane —, stray dog.

spersonalizz-are [A I] *tr.* (psych.) to depersonalize. (**-ato** *part. adj.*) **-azione** *f.* (psych.) depersonalization.

spertic-are [A 2 S] *rfl.* (of a tree) to shoot up, to grow too tall; (fig.) to exaggerate. **-ato** *part. adj.* overgrown, too tall; excessive in length or height; (fig.) extreme, exaggerated, excessive, overdone; lodi -ate, fulsome flattery. **-atamente** *adv.* excessively; fulsomely.

†**spe·rula** *f.* little sphere.

spes-a *f.* expense; cost; *pl.* expenses; expenditure; -e di gestione, running expenses; (leg.) costs; disbursements; out-of-pocket expenses; -e compensate, each side bearing its own costs; -e funebri, funeral expenses; -e irripetibili, disallowed costs; solicitor and client costs; -e legali, legal costs; -e liquidate, taxed costs; -e processuali, Court fees, stamps and incidental charges paid down by every party to an action; -e ripetibili, recoverable costs; party and party costs; -e voluttuarie, expenses for mere ornament, unnecessary expenses; -e di causa, costs of action; -e per gli sponsali, expenses in contemplation of marriage; liquidazione delle -e di giudizio, taxation of costs; nota -e, bill of costs; -e d'imballaggio, (cost of) packing; -e di trasporto, carriage; -e postali, postage; -e di viaggio, travelling expenses; -e di magazzinaggio, storage, warehousing expenses; -e accessorie, additional charges; -e comprese, including costs; senza —, exclusive of costs; fattura e —, charge for making and accessories; franco -e, free of charge; francare la —, to save costs; esente da —, free of charge; -e di ammortamento, depreciation; -e diverse, sundry charges; -e di bollo, stamp charges; -e generali, overheads; -e piccole, -e minute, petties; -e di facchinaggio, porterage; -e di processo, process costs; -e di fondazione, -e d'impianto, -e di costituzione, promotion money; -e di vendita, selling costs; fare la —, *or* le -e, to do the shopping; è uscita per la —, she has gone out shopping; questa è stata una — forte, that was very expensive; far fronte a una —, to meet an expense; non badare a -e, not to count the cost; stare sulle -e, to be put to considerable expense; essere sulle -e, to live at one's own expense; far le -e a uno, to keep, to support someone; a proprie -e, at one's own expense, (fig.) to one's cost; è più la — che l'impresa, it is not worth while, you will not see your money back; fare le -e di una serata, to be the life and soul of a party; fare le -e della compagnia, to be the laughing-stock of the party; fare le -e di una conversazione, to keep a conversation going, *or* to be talked about, criticized. **-are** [A I] *tr.* to pay the expenses of; to pay the keep of; non mi pagano ma mi -ano di tutto, I don't receive a salary, but they pay all my expenses. **-ato** *part. adj.* paid for, met; receiving payment for expenses; *n.m.* expense, expenditure.

speso *part.* of **spendere**, q.v.; *adj.* spent; expended

spessartina *f.* (miner.) spessartite, spessartine, manganese garnet.

spess-o *adj.* thick; — cinquanta centimetri, fifty centimetres thick; dense; compact; closely spaced; occurring frequently; -i errori, frequent errors; -i casi, many instances; -e volte, often; *adv.* often, frequently (also **-amente** *adv.*). **-eggiamento** *m.* frequency, frequent occurrence. **-eggiare** [A 3 c] *tr.* to repeat; to reiterate; *intr.* (*aux.* avere, essere) to happen often; to be a frequent occurrence; to become frequent; -eggiavano i lampi, there were frequent flashes of lightning, *or* the flashes of lightning grew more and more frequent. (**-eggiato** *part. adj.*) **-ezza** *f.* thickness; density. **-i·metro** *m.* (eng.) thickness gauge, feeler gauge. **-ire** [D 2] *tr.* to thicken; to condense; (tan.) to firm; *intr.* (*aux.* essere) to thicken, to become thick or thicker. **-ito** *part. adj.* thickened; condensed. **-ore** *m.* thickness; avere lo -ore di, to be as thick, or as wide, as; (archit.) mattone messo in -ore, header.

spetezz-are [A I C] *intr.* (*aux.* avere) (vulg.) to fart. (**-amento** *m.*)

†**spetrare** *tr.* (poet.) to soften, to mitigate the stoniness of.

spetta·bil-e *adj.* worthy of respect, respected; (on an envelope, etc.) (Alla) Spett. Ditta ..., Messrs ..... **-ità** *f.* importance, eminence.

spetta·col-o *m.* spectacle; sight; scene; entertainment, play; show; performance; tassa -i, entertainment tax; (fig.) dare — di, to display, to show off; dare — di sè, to make an exhibition of

oneself. **-are** *adj.* spectacular; theatrical; (fig.) amazing. **-oso** *adj.* spectacular; showy; gaudy; sensational; imposing; (joc.) terrific. **-osamente** *adv.* spectacularly.

spett-are [A I] *intr.* (*aux.* essere; *prep.* a) to belong (to); to be the duty, concern (of); -a a lui regolare la faccenda, it is his duty to settle the matter; l'educazione dei figli -a ai genitori, parents are responsible for the education of their children; to be the right, privilege (of); non -a a te di giudicare, you have no right to judge; mi -ano dieci mila lire, I am owed 10,000 lire; to be the turn (of); -a a voi pagare, it is your turn to pay. **-ante** *part. adj.* (*prep.* a) due, belonging (to); concerning. **-anza** *f.* concern, business; competence; property; sum owing to a person; essere di -anza (di), to be one's duty; non è di mia -anza, it is beyond my authority; palazzo di sua -anza, house belonging to him; (mil.) daily assignment of duties; *pl.* fees. **-ativa** *f.* see **aspettativa**.

spett-atore *m.* spectator; onlooker, bystander; essere — del disastro, to witness the accident; *m.pl.* (theatr., etc.) audience; (also *adj.*). **-atrice** *f.* (woman) onlooker; *adj.* la folla -atrice, the crowd of onlookers, the spectators, the audience.

spettegolare [A I SC] *intens.* of **pettegolare**, q.v.

spettin-are [A I S] *tr.* to ruffle the hair of; *rfl.* to become dishevelled; to rumple one's hair. **-ato** *part. adj.* dishevelled; uncombed; unkempt.

spettorare [A I S] *rfl.* to expose one's bosom; †*intr.*, *tr.* see **espettorare**.

spettr-o *m.* spectre, ghost, apparition; phantom; (phys.) spectrum; — di assorbimento, absorption spectrum. **-ale** *adj.* spectral, ghostly; unearthly, eerie, weird; (phys.) spectral; analisi -ale, spectrum analysis. **-ofotometri·a** *f.* (opt.) spectrophotometry. **-ofoto·metro** *m.* (opt.) spectrophotometer. **-ografi·a** *f.* (phys.) spectrography. **-o·grafo** *m.* (phys.) spectrograph; -ografo a reticolo, lattice spectrograph; -ografo di massa, mass spectrograph. **-ogramma** *m.* (phys.) spectrogram. **-ometri·a** *f.* (phys.) spectrometry. **-ome·trico** *adj.* (phys.) spectrometric. **-o·metro** *m.* (phys.) spectrometer. **-omicrosco·pio** *m.* (phys.) spectromicroscope. **-oscopi·a** *f.* (phys.) spectroscopy; -oscopia di massa, mass spectroscopy. **-osco·pico** *adj.* (phys.) spectroscopic; microscopio -oscopico, spectromicroscope. **-osco·pio** *m.* (phys.) spectroscope.

spe·zi-e *f. indecl.* (usu. *pl.*) spice, spices. **-ala** *f.* sister dispenser (in a convent); apothecary's (or grocer's) wife. **-ale** *m.* druggist, chemist; chemist's shop; grocer; grocer's shop; a lettere di -ali, in large clear letters, in block capitals; cose che non vendono gli -ali, things too rare to be bought and sold; †*adj.* see **speciale**. **-eri·a** *f.* druggist's shop; grocer's shop; *pl.* spices.

spezz-are [A I] *tr.* to break in pieces; to fragment; to shatter; to break up; to chop up, to split, to divide; — il viaggio, to break the journey; (mus.) — il basso, to divide the bass (i.e. to play a variation of it in shorter notes); (mil. hist.) — una lancia, to break a lance; *rfl.* to break, to be broken; to be shattered; mi si -a il cuore, my heart is breaking; non posso mica -armi in due, I can't be in two places at once. **-a·bile** *adj.* breakable; fragile. (**-abilità** *f.*) **-amento** *m.* breaking; fragmenting; break-up; -amento della legna, chopping of wood; -amento di corrente, interruption of the flow of a stream or river; †(mil.) break in a fortified line. †**-antenne** *m.* (naut.) dismasting wind, gale. †**-aspade** *adj. indecl.* (mil. hist.) swordproof. **-ata** *f.* (drawing) broken line. **-atino** *m.* (cul.) meat cut up small and stewed or braised. **-ato** *part. adj.* broken; interrupted; legna -ata, chopped wood; (phys.) refracted; (archit.) arco -ato, broken (incomplete) arch; (agric.) terra -ata, separate plots of ground; *adv. phr.* alla -ata, bit by bit, with interruptions; *n.m.pl.* small change. **-ata·mente** *adv.* brokenly, piecemeal, bit by bit; by fits and starts, spasmodically; with interruptions. **-atore** *m.* breaker; cutter. (**-atrice** *f.*) **-atura** *f.* breaking; breakage; section, fragment. **-ettare** [A I C] *tr.* to cut into small pieces; to mince, to hash. (**-ettato** *part. adj.* **-ettatura** *f.*)

†**spezzo** *m.* remnant.

spezzone *m.* bomb stick; incendiary bomb; (metall.) crop end.

spia *f.* spy; informer; observer; tell-tale; indication, sign, clue; (in a door) judas; (electr.) lampada —, pilot lamp; (eng.) inspection window; — olio, oil window; (electr.; eng.) — luminosa, warning light; (naut.) coloured yarn in rope denoting dockyard in which it was made (e.g. blue for Castellammare, or for Portsmouth in British Royal Navy, etc.).

spiacci-care [A 2 S] *tr.* (Tusc., fam.) to squash, to crush; to flatten; to bust, to smash; un giorno o l'altro gli -co il muso, one day

spiacci-care (*cont.*)
or other I'll bash his face in for him. **-cato** *part. adj.* squashed, crushed; flattened; smashed. **-chìo** *m.* continual crushing, smashing, etc.; crushed things; smashed objects.

spiac-ẹre [B 20] *intr.* (*aux.* essere; *prep.* a) to displease; to be displeasing (to); to cause displeasure (to); mi -e che non sia venuto, I am sorry he did not come. **-ente** *part. adj.* unpleasant, disagreeable; displeasing; (pop.) sorry, regretful. **-ẹvole** *adj.* unpleasant, disagreeable; unfortunate; incidente -evole, regrettable incident. (**-evolmẹnte** *adv.*) **-evolẹzza** *f.* unpleasantness, disagreeableness. **-imẹnto** *m.* feeling of displeasure.

spiaggẹtta *f. dim.* of **spiaggia**, q.v.; small portable writing-desk (which slopes, like a shore).

spiag-gi-a *f.* beach; shore; seaside resort; — sottile, shallow beach; a —, sloping gently; buttato sulla —, cast ashore; (techn.) (leg.) beach (i.e. land inland of foreshore, 'lido del mare', q.v., under **lido**, which serves as way of access and landing place from the sea (C.C.)). **-ata** *f.* stretch of beach.

spiamẹnto *m.* See under **spiare**.

spian-are [A 1] *tr.* to level, to smooth, to smooth out; to plane (wood); to bulldoze; to roll out (pastry); to iron, to press; — i mattoni, to trim the clay in making bricks; — un fucile contro, to level a gun at, to aim at; — una lancia, to couch a lance; — una fortezza, to demolish a fortress; — al suolo, to raze to the ground; (at table) — ogni cosa, to clear the table, to eat up everything; (fig.) — difficoltà, to smooth away difficulties; to explain; — il senso, to make the meaning plain; (mus.) — la voce, to sing with even tone; *intr.* (*aux.* essere; *prep.* su) to rest evenly (upon); to stand level; *rfl.* to stretch out; to lie down. **-amẹnto** *m.* levelling; smoothing; demolition; explanation; (radio) filtro di -amento, ripple filter. **-ata** *f.* levelling; smoothing; levelled ground; esplanade; (mil.) parade ground; (mil. hist.) clearing before the fortress walls; open space between the city and citadel. **-ato** *part. adj.* levelled; smoothed; ironed; explained, made plain; (mus.) smoothly; canto -ato, even, sustained singing; *n.m.* level space (smaller than **spianata**, q.v.). **-atoia** *f.* pastryboard. **-atoio** *m.* rolling-pin. **-atore** *m.* leveller; (mil.) sapper, pioneer. **-atrice** *f.* (bldg.) bulldozer; (eng.) straightening machine. **-atura** *f.* levelling; demolition; smoothing. **-azione** *f.* explanation, making plain; smoothing, levelling.

spiano *m.* levelling; smoothing; (hist.) the flour supplied by the 'Abbondanza' (an official board in Florence which supplied flour to bakers at a fixed price); *adv. phr.* a tutto —, profusely, lavishly; lavorare a tutto —, to work full out.

spiantano *m.* (zool.) a crab that is due to moult.

spiant-are [A 1] *tr.* to uproot; — un palo, to dig out a post; to demolish, to ruin, to destroy; *rfl.* to go to rack and ruin. **-amẹnto** *m.* uprooting; ruin, destruction. **-ato** *part. adj.* uprooted; destroyed; ruined; negozio -ato, bankrupt business; also *n.m.* **-atore** *m.* uprooter; gardener's trowel. (**-atrice** *f.*)

spianto *m.* ruin; destruction; dare lo — a, to ruin, to destroy; andare a —, to go to rack and ruin.

spi-are [A 4] *tr.* to spy upon; to pry into; to spy out; to watch; to inquire into; — le mosse di una persona, to keep a close watch on a person's movements; to look carefully or anxiously for; -ava l'occasione di vendicarsi, he was waiting for an opportunity to revenge himself; — i segreti della natura, to investigate the secrets of nature; (mil.) to spy, to spy out, to reconnoitre. **-amẹnto** *m.* spying; watching; observation. **-arola** *f.* spy-hole, peep-hole. **-ata** *f.* spying; secret information or report laid by a spy; secret accusation or denunciation; fare una -ata a, to denounce. **-ato** *part. adj.* spied upon; watched, kept under observation. **-atoio** *m.* (mil.) spy-hole, peep-hole. **-atore** *m.* watcher; (mil.) look-out; scout; skirmisher; (aeron.) pathfinder. (**-atrice** *f.*)

spiattell-are [A 1] *tr.* to declare openly; to tell flatly; to blab. **-ato** *part. adj.* declared openly; said plainly, flatly; dirle -ate, to blab, to keep nothing back; *adv. phr.* alla -ata, flatly, openly, plainly. **-atamẹnte** *adv.* openly; dire -atamente, to blurt out.

spiazz-are [A 1] *intr.* (*aux.* essere) (joc.) to go bald, to develop bald patches. **-ata** *f.* clearing; open space; bare patch; (joc.) bald patch. **-atella** *f. dim.* little bare, bald, patch. (**-ato** *part. adj.*) **-o** *m.* open space; clearing (e.g. in a wood).

spica¹ *f.* forte, tang, the end of the blade (of sword, knife, etc.) that is fixed in the handle.

†**spica²** *f.* See **spiga**.

spicanardi *m.pl.* (bot.) spikenard, *Nardostachys jatamansi*.

spiccace *adj.* (of fruit, poet.) of which the flesh comes away easily from the stone.

spicc-are [A 2] *tr.* to detach, to cut off; to pluck, to pick (off); to articulate, to pronounce distinctly; — bene le parole, to pronounce one's words distinctly; to bring out clearly (e.g. sense, meaning); (leg.) — un mandato di cattura, to issue a warrant for arrest; (comm.) — una tratta, to draw a bill; (mil.) to detach; — un salto, to take a leap; — il volo, to fly up, to rise, to take off in flight, (fig.) to take flight; — un muro, to begin to construct a wall; — il bollore, to begin to boil; — guadagno, to make a profit; to despatch; *intr.* (*aux.* avere) to be striking, to be conspicuous; to stand out, to excel; *rfl.* to drop off; to become detached; la mela si -ò dal ramo, the apple fell from the branch; la polpa si -a dal nocciolo, the flesh comes away from the stone easily; †to take one's leave. **-amẹnto** *m.* detachment, separation; -amento di volo, taking flight. **-ante** *adj.* striking, conspicuous; (of colours) bright, striking. **-ato** *part. adj.* distinct; clear; notable, remarkable; strong; una -ata tendenza, a marked tendency; (mus.) spiccato (style of staccato bowing in which the bow rebounds from the string); *n.m.* (bldg.) base course. **-atamẹnte** *adv.* distinctly; conspicuously, notably, outstandingly. **-atoio** *adj.* slipstone (of peach, plum, etc. which comes away easily from the stone).

spic-chi-o *m.* section, segment; gore; — di un'arancia, 'pig' of an orange; quarter (of apple, pear, etc.); — d'aglio, clove of garlic; — d'una noce, lobe of a walnut; (fig.) — di luna, crescent of the moon; slice; a 'spicchi', in slices, sliced; fare a spicchi, to slice; (eccl.) peak of biretta; (archit.) section of a ribbed vault. **-are** [A 4] *tr.* to divide into segments, sections, etc.; to slice. (**-ato** *part. adj.*)

spicci-are [A 3] *intr.* (*aux.* essere) to spurt out, to gush forth; to dash away; *tr.* to detach; to tear off; to dispatch, to expedite; -atemi quella faccenda, get this rushed through for me; (of money) to give small change for; *rfl.* (*acc.* of *prn.* 'si') to make haste, to be quick; spicciati!, be quick!; to become detached; to work loose; (*dat.* of *prn.* 'si') -arsi una cosa, una persona, to get rid of, free of, something or someone; (mil. slang) -arsela, to be in a hot spot, to be in a jam. **-ativo** *adj.* expeditious, quick; (of a person) energetic; colpo -ativo, finishing blow, *coup de grâce*. **-ato** *part. adj.* dispatched; finished.

spiccic-are [A 2 s] *tr.* to detach, to tear off; to unstick; to articulate; to pronounce clearly; *rfl.* to come off, to come unstuck; to be torn off; to tear oneself away. **-ato** *part. adj.* detached; torn off; distinct. (Cf. **appiccicare**.)

spic-c-io *adj.* expeditious, quick, prompt; cosa -ia, something quickly done; risoluzione -ia, quick decision, snap judgement; andare per le -e, to go straight to the point, to waste no time (or words); free; non ha un momento —, he hasn't a free moment; avere le mani -e, to have one's hands free; moneta -ia, loose change (also *n.m.pl.*).

spic-ciol-o *adj.* broken up small; moneta -a, small change; (fig.) per dirla in moneta -a, to put it plainly; soldato —, private soldier; *n.m.* small coin; non avere uno —, to be penniless; *pl.* loose change, small change. **-ame** *m.* quantity of small change; quantity of little things, bits and pieces. **-are** [A 1 s] *tr.* to change into smaller money. **-ato** *part. adj.* moneta -ata, small change, scattered coins; *adv. phr.* alla -ata, little by little, a few at a time. **-atura** *f.* (agric.) picking, stripping.

spicc-o *m.* relief; vividness; fare —, to stand out, to catch the eye; *adj.* (of peach, plum, etc.) coming away easily from the stone.

spicile-gio *m.* scrap-book, miscellany; selection; (agric.) gleaning.

spicin-are [A 1] *tr.* to break into small pieces, to grind; to eat up; *rfl.* to crumble. (**-ato** *part. adj.*) **-io** *m.* crumbling; ruin.

spi-co *m.* (*pl.* **-chi**) (vet.) hairs going in a different direction from the main stream, in the coat of a horse.

spi-cole *f.pl.* (zool.) the skeleton of a sponge.

†**spi-culo** *m.* point of an arrow.

spider *m. indecl.* two-seater sports car.

spidẹtto *m.* tapered end of spoke of wheel.

spidocchiare [A 4] *tr.* to delouse, to rid of lice; (fig.) to lift from poverty; *rfl.* to delouse oneself, (fig.) to lift oneself out of poverty.

spied-o *m.* (kitchen) spit; spear, boar-spear; spike for keeping papers on; (herald.) boar-spear. **-ata** *f.* spitful; thrust with a spit or spear. **-ino** *m.* skewer.

spieg-are [A 2] *tr.* to spread out; to unfold; to lay out; to display; to unfurl; (naut.) to set (sail); (mil.) to deploy; to extend over a wide front; (mus.) — la voce, to sing with full voice, to increase the volume of the voice; to explain; to justify; to interpret; — una poesia, to interpret, expound, comment on, a poem; ti spiegherò come devi fare, I will explain what you must do; *rfl.* to be unfolded; to spread; (of a flower) to open; to be unfurled; la bandiera -ava al vento, the flag floated, waved, in the breeze; to explain oneself, to make oneself understood; mi -o, let me explain, I'll explain; non so se mi -o?, need I say more?; non so -armi, I don't know how to express myself; to reveal one's thoughts, feelings, etc.; to construe; *recip. rfl.* to be frank with one another. **-a·bile** *adj.* explicable; justifiable; understandable; ben -abile, easy to understand. (**-abilità** *f.*) **-amento** *m.* spreading out; unfolding; explanation; (naut.; mil.) -amento di forze, deployment of forces; (aeron.) fune di -amento, rip cord (of parachute). **-ativo** *adj.* explanatory. **-ato** *part. adj.* spread; opened; unfolded; (of an army) deployed; con le bandiere -ate, with flags flying; a voce -ata, at the top of one's voice; explained, interpreted. (**-atamente** *adv.*) (**-atore** *m.* **-atrice** *f.*) **-atura** *f.* unfolding, spreading (out). **-azione** *f.* explanation, interpretation; solution; answer.

spiegazz-are [A 1] *tr.* to crease, to crumple. (**-ato** *part. adj.*)

spieggiare [A 3 ic] *intr.* (*aux.* avere) to keep spying, to snoop.

†spiemontizzare *intr.* (Alfieri) to drop Piedmontese expressions, habits, etc.

†spiet-à *f.*, **†-anza** *f.* lack of pity, mercilessness; cruelty; coldness.

spietat-o *adj.* pitiless, ruthless; cruel; implacable; obdurate. **-amente** *adv.* pitilessly, ruthlessly; cruelly; implacably; obdurately. **-ezza** *f.* ruthlessness, cruelty; inhumanity.

spiffer-are [A 1 s] *intr.* (*aux.* avere) to pipe, to play the pipe (or other wind instrument); (of the wind) to whistle through a crack or small aperture; -a un vento dalla finestra, there's a piercing draught coming in through the window; *tr.* to report, to tell (what one has seen or heard); to declare openly; to blurt out. (**-amento** *m.*) **-ata** *f.* (mus.) piping. (**-ato** *part. adj.*)

spif·fer-o *m.* (colloq.) piercing draught. **-one** *m.* telltale. (**-ona** *f.*)

spig-a *f.* ear (of corn, etc.) (bot.) spike; — banca, cock's foot, *Dactylis glomerata*; — tonda, Yorkshire fog, *Holcus lanatus*; (am)mattonato a —, herring-boned brickwork; tessuto a —, twill, twilled cloth; punto a —, herring-bone stitch; (astron.) spica Virginis. **-acel·tica** *f.* (bot.) *Valeriana celtica*. **-ame** *m.* a quantity of ears of corn. **-are** [A 2] *intr.* (*aux.* essere, avere) (of corn) to come into ear; (of lettuce, etc.) to run to seed. **-ato** *part. adj.* (of corn) in the ear; (of cloth) twilled, twill. **-atura** *f.* (of corn) forming ears, or the appropriate season for this.

spighetta *f.* braid; trimming; (bot.) spikelet.

spigion-are [A 1 c] *rfl.* to be unlet, to be empty. (**-amento** *m.*) **-ato** *part. adj.* unoccupied; casa -ata, empty house; (fig.) avere l'ultimo piano -ato, to be weak in the top story, to be empty-headed.

spigliat-o *adj.* easy, free and easy; nimble, graceful; self-possessed. (**-atamente** *adv.*) **-ezza** *f.* ease, self-possession; agility, nimbleness.

spignorare [A 1 c] *tr.* to release from sequestration, distraint or pawn (cf. **pignorare**).

spigo *m.* (bot.) lavender, *Lavandula*.

spi·gola *f.* (ichth.) bass, *Morone labrax*.

spigol-ame *m.* quantity of ears of corn; gleanings. **-amento** *m.* gleaning. **-are** [A 1 s] *tr.* to glean. **-atore** *m.* gleaner. (**-atrice** *f.*) **-atura** *f.* gleaning; late pickings (of cotton crops); *pl.* (fig.) gleanings (e.g. of news items).

†spigolistro *m.* hypocrite; pedant.

spi·gol-o *m.* corner; corner of a field; edge (of a step); (mil.) salient. **-one** *m. augm.* large tile ('embrice') for roof-ridges.

spigonardo *m.* (bot.) *Lavandula dentata*.

spigon-e *m.* (naut.) studdingsail yard; any lengthening pole on mast or yard; (Liguria) lower portion of fishnet; (Sicily) fishing-craft. **-etto** *m. dim.* (naut.) stu'nsail yard on fore or mizzen mast.

spigoso *adj.* (agric.; of corn) ripening well, well eared.

spigrire [D 2] *tr.* to rouse to action; *intr.* (*aux.* essere), *rfl.* to shake off laziness; to rouse oneself.

spilite *f.* (miner.) spilite.

spilla *f.* brooch; tie-pin.

spillaccherare [A 1 s] *tr.* to brush the mud from; *rfl.* to brush oneself.

spill-o *m.* pin; hair-pin; — di sicurezza, — da balia, safety-pin; testa di —, pinhead; piccolo come un capo di —, about the size

of a pin's head; cuscinetto per -i, pin-cushion; — da cravatta, tie-pin; tacchi a —, stiletto heels; bradawl for tapping a cask; hole made with bradawl; thin jet of wine, water or other liquid; pig-sticker; piercer, gimlet; stabber; (mil.) spike used for breaking up cordite charges; (eng.) valvola a —, needle valve; colpo di —, pin-prick; uccidere a colpi di —, to worry to death, to torment; *pl.* (bot.) -i di Dama, thrift, sea pink, *Armeria maritima*. **-a·io** *m.* pin-maker; seller of pins. **-an·cola** *f.* (zool.) tadpole. **-are** [A 1] *tr.* to pierce; to broach; to tap (cask); to draw (wine, blood); to get (with difficulty, in small quantities); -are denaro a, to squeeze money out of; *intr.* (*aux.* avere) to pour, to spill. **-a·tico** *m.* (leg.) pin-money. (**-ato** *part. adj.*) **-atura** *f.* tapping, broaching, piercing. **-etta** *f.* pin. **-etto** *m. dim.* small pin; tongue (of a buckle); (mil.) rimer, vent cleaning tool; -etto di onore, shooting prize (silver or gold pin, equiv. to spoon given in U.K.). **-ettoni** *m.pl.* (bot.) shepherd's needle, *Scandix pecten-veneris*. **-oncetti**, **-oncini** *m.pl.* (cul.) kind of 'pasta' used in soup. **-oncioni** *m.pl.* (cul.) 'pasta' like the above, but larger. **-one** *m.* hat-pin; brooch; tie-pin; (foundry) vent wire; *pl.* (cul.), see spilloncini.

spi(l)luzzic-are [A 2 s] *tr.* to nibble, to peck at; to earn, to make small profits. **-amento** *m.*; nibbling; making of small profits. (**-ato** *part. adj.*) **-o** *adv. phr.* a spillùzzico, in dribs and drabs.

spilo *m.* (med.) naevus; (bot.) hilum.

spilorc-io, **spilor·c-io** *adj.* stingy, mean, niggardly; miserly, close-fisted; sordid; *n.m.* niggardly or miserly man. (**-iamente** *adv.*) **-eri·a** *f.* niggardliness, stinginess, meanness; miserliness; tight-fistedness. **-ia** *f.* niggardly woman; (naut.) floating grass line at the top of a net.

spiluccare [A 2] and derivs. See **piluccare**.

spilungon-e *adj.* tall and lanky; tall and lanky person, spindle-shanks. (**-a** *f.*)

spin *m. indecl.* (atom. phys.) spin.

spin-a *f.* (bot.) spine, thorn; — alba, *Centaurea calcitrapa*; — Cristi, *Lycium europaeum*; *L. porci*, *Poterium spinosum*; thorn, prickle; fish-bone; senza -e, thornless, (of fish) boneless, boned; disegno a — di pesce, herring-bone pattern; avere una — nel cuore, to have an aching heart; stare, essere sulle -e, to be on thorns, to be agitated, very anxious; corona di -e, crown of thorns, (fig.) series of troubles; (provb.) non c'è rosa senza -e, there is no rose without a thorn; avere il pesce senza la —, to get something too easily; senza — e senz'osso, without any trouble (or expense); (wasp's) sting; prick (of fortune), annoyance, trouble; bung-hole (of a cask); birra alla —, draught beer; (archit.) rib (of a vault); (text.) twill; — da quattro, four-harnessed twill; (eng.) pin, peg; — cilindrica, parallel pin; — di riferimento, dowel; — di sezione non circolare, cotter; — di sicurezza, shear pin; — conica, taper pin; (electr.) plug; — con interruttore, switch plug; (naut.) ring-bolt; (Taranto) keel; †centreline of keel; †passare per la —, to keelhaul, a punishment consisting of pulling the guilty under the ship; bilges of a boat, lowest internal portion. **-a·io** *m.* thicket (of thorn-bushes). **-ale** *adj.* spinal, of the backbone.

spin-ace *m.*, **-acio** *m.* (bot.) spinach, *Spinacia oleracea*; — della N. Zelanda, New Zealand spinach, *Tetragonia expansa*; — fragifero, strawberry blite, *Chenopodium capitatum*; *pl.* (cul.) spinach; (fig.) mangiar -aci, to act the spy. **-acione** *m.* (bot.) orach, *Atriplex hortensis*.

spinacene *m.* (chem.) squalene.

spinapesce *m.* herring-bone brickwork; a — (also 'a spina di pesce'), herring-bone(wise), zigzag; mattoni posti a spina di pesce, herring-bone brickwork.

spin-are[1] [A 1] *tr.* (eng.) to dowel; to broach. (**-ato** *part. adj.*) **-atura** *f.* (eng.) broaching. **-atrice** *f.* (eng.) broaching machine.

spin-are[2] *m.*, **-arello** *m.* (ichth.) stickleback, *Gasterosteus aculeatus*.

Spina·rio *pr.n.m.* (sculp.) name of a well-known ancient bronze figure representing a boy taking a thorn from his foot (in the British Museum; copy in Rome in the Museo Capitolino).

spinarolo *m.* (ichth.) piked dogfish; — comune, *Squalus fernandinus*; — imperiale, *Acanthias vulgaris*.

spinato *adj.* thorny; filo di ferro —, barbed wire; (of cloth) twilled; boned, filleted (i.e. having spine or bones removed); (herald.) engrailed; — allargato, engrailed, échancré.

spinell-a *f.* (vet.) ring bone; (miner.) see **spinello**. **-o** *m.* (ichth.) piked dogfish, *Acanthias vulgaris*; (miner.) spinel; -o nobile, ruby spinel, balas ruby.

spineto *m.* thicket (of thorn bushes).

spinętt-a *f.* *dim.* of **spina**, q.v.; (text.) braid 'a spina'; (watchm.) — di limitazione, curb pin; (mus.) spinet; virginal. **-a·io** *m.* (mus.) spinet-maker; virginal-maker.

spingarda *f.* (mil. hist.) a kind of catapult; small gun; mortar.

spingare [A 2] *intr.* (*aux.* avere) to kick.

spin·g·ere¹ [C 5] *tr.* to push; — l'uscio, to push open the door; to thrust, to shove; to drive; to propel; to force; (fig.) — l'occhio, lo sguardo, to cast one's eyes (to some distance); to incite, to induce; to impel; chi lo spinse a far ciò?, who induced him to do that?; (mus.) — l'arcata, to play an up-bow; *rfl.* to push forward; -ersi nel bosco, to penetrate into the wood; to venture; to dare. **-imento** *m.* push, thrust. **-itoio** *m.* (eng.) pusher. (**-itore** *m.* **-itrice** *f.*)

†**spin·gere²** *tr.* to clean the paint off.

spinite *f.* (vet.) louping ill; (med.) tabes.

spin-o *m.* (bot.) — bianco, hawthorn, may, *Crataegus*; — cervino, — merlo, buckthorn, *Rhamnus cathartica*; — di Giuda, *Gleditsia triacanthos*; — gatto, *Paliurus spina-Christi*; — nero, blackthorn, sloe, *Prunus spinosa*; — quercino, *Rhamnus saxatilis*; — spine (of a hedgehog, etc.); *adj.* prickly; (bot.) uva -a, gooseberry, *Ribes grossularia*; (zool.) porco —, hedgehog. **-oc·chio** *m.* (ichth.) stickleback, *Gasterosteus aculeatus*. **-one** *m.* (cloth) serge; a variety of sporting dog. **-osità** *f.* prickliness; thorniness; (fig.) awkwardness, ticklishness, delicacy (e.g. of a situation). **-oso** *adj.* prickly; thorny; (fig.) difficult; ticklish; perplexing, troublesome; knotty; awkward; *n.m.* hedgehog. **-otto** *m.* (eng.) gudgeon pin, piston pin.

spi·nola *f.* (ichth.) a common dialect name for the bass, *Morone labrax* (cf. **spigola**).

spinoz-iano *m.* (philos.) Spinozist; *adj.* Spinozistic. **-ismo** *m.* Spinozism.

spint-a *f.* push, shove; thrust; — del vento, force of the wind; dare una — a uno, to give someone a shove; calcolare la —, to calculate the thrust; — di galleggiamento, flotation; (naut.) thrust; — di galleggiamento, flotation; (naut.) thrust; cuscinetto di —, thrust block; (naut.; aeron.) — assiale, propeller thrust, (eng.) end thrust, axial thrust; (archit.) thrust; (fig.) stimulus, inducement; temptation; (econ.) — al rialzo, boost in the market; (joc.) -e o sponte, willy-nilly. **-arella**, **-erella** *f.* *dim.* little push. **-eggiare** [A 3 c], †**-eare** *tr.* to keep pushing. **-one** *m.* *augm.* violent shove.

spintarisco·pio *m.* (phys.) spinthariscope.

spinto *part.* of **spingere**, q.v.; *adj.* pushed; pushed on; led on, induced; impelled; driven; inclined; (of a joke, etc.) risqué.

spinter-o·geno *m.* (motor.) distributor. **-o·metro** *m.* (electr.) spark gap; (electr.; radio) -ometro rotante, rotary spark gap.

spin·tria *m.* (Rom. antiq.) *spintria*, (male) sexual pervert.

spinza-go *m.* (*pl.* **-ghi**) (orn.) avocet.

spiomb-are [A 1 c] *tr.* to remove lead from; to bring tottering down; to unseal, to break the seals of; *intr.* (*aux.* avere, essere) (of walls, etc.) to bulge or lean from the vertical; to weigh as heavy as lead. **-ato** *part. adj.* stripped of lead; (fig.) heavy as lead, leaden; peso -ato, leaden weight. **-atoio** *m.* (mil. hist.) machicolation. (**-atore** *m.*)

spiọn-e *m.* master-spy; secret agent. (**-a** *f.*) **-ag·gio** *m.* espionage; secret service. **-cello** *m.* (orn.) water pipit, *Anthus spinoletta*; -cello marino, rock pipit, *A. s. petrosus*. **-cino** *m.* peep-hole, judas. **-eggiare** [A 3 c] *intr.* (*aux.* avere) to be engaged in espionage.

spio·v·ere [C 27] *impers.* (*aux.* essere) to stop raining; *intr.* (*aux.* essere) to flow, to run away. **-ente** *part. adj.* flowing; running away (of water), draining; baffi -enti, drooping moustache; capelli -enti, flowing locks; *n.m.* watershed. **-imento** *m.* **-uto** *part. adj.* falling, hanging down; capelli -uti, long hair, flowing locks.

spi·pola *f.* (orn.). See **pispola**.

spippolare¹ [A 1 s] *tr.* to pick off (e.g. grapes from the bunch, corn grains from the cob).

spippolare² [A 1 s] *tr.* to warble; (fig.) to write, to compose (songs, verses, etc.); to rattle off fluently, without hesitation.

spira *f.* coil; spiral; loop; turn (of a screw, of a coil); convolution; curl (of smoke); coil (of a spring); — ornamentale, scroll; (gramoph. record) groove; fatto a —, coiled, in coils, spiral.

spira·bile *adj.* See under **spirare**.

†**spira·colo** *m.* See **spiraglio**.

spira·glio *m.* air-hole, vent; aperture; draught, breath of air; small skylight; peep, glimmer; faintest sign; uno — di speranza, a ray of hope; gleam; (naut.) skylight; glass let into deck to give light below.

spiral-e *adj.*, *n.f.* spiral; fatto a —, coiled, spiral; (math.) spiral; — di Archimede, Archimedean spiral; (watchm.) molla —, hairspring. **-mente** *adv.* spirally; attorcere -mente, to coil, to wind on a coil. **-ina** *f.* (electr.) pigtail (connexion).

spir-are [A 1] *intr.* (*aux.* avere) to breathe; to breathe out; to exhale; (theol.) to breathe forth (cf. below, under *tr.*); (of wind, breeze, etc.) to blow; (*aux.* essere) to breathe one's last, to expire, to pass away; (of a period) to expire, to come to an end; *tr.* to breathe out; to give off; to exhale; to inspire; (poet.) to breathe; (theol.) to breathe forth (said of the Procession of the Holy Spirit); *n.m.* expiry, expiration, end; (comm.) allo — del tempo stabilito, on expiration of the time agreed upon. **-a·bile** *adj.* (of air) fit to breathe, breathable. **-ame** *m.* air-hole, vent; crack. **-amento** *m.* breathing, breath; outlet, vent; breathing space; inspiration. **-ante** *part. adj.* breathing; (fig.) parere vivo e -ante, to seem almost alive (e.g. of a figure in a painting, etc.); blowing; (gramm.) consonanti -anti, fricative consonants; inspiring; expiring, dying, on the point of death; l'anno -ante, the closing year. **-ato** *part. adj.* breathed out; exhaled; inspired; expired; ended; (comm., etc.) 31 -ato mese, 31st ult. **-atore** *m.* inspirer; *adj.* inspiring. (**-atrice** *f.*) **-azione** *f.* inspiration; (theol.) spiration.

spir-ea *f.* (bot.) spiraea, *Spiraea*. **-ema** *m.* (biol.) spireme (a stage in mitosis).

spirillo *m.* (bact.) spirillum.

spiri·t-ico *adj.* spiritualistic; seduta spiritica, spiritualistic séance. **-ismo** *m.* spiritualism. **-ista** *m.*, *f.* spiritualist. **-i·stico** *adj.* spiritualistic.

spi·rit-o *m.* breath of life; spirit; ghost; mind; soul; wit; uomo di —, witty man; courage; temper; boldness; prontezza di —, ready wit; presenza di —, presence of mind; — depresso, low spirits; humour; head, leader, inspiration; egli fu lo — della rivolta, he was the leading spirit of the rebellion; — d'osservazione, power of observation; (theol.) — santo, Holy Spirit, Holy Ghost; lo — di Dio, the Spirit of God; spirituality; darsi allo —, to devote oneself to spiritual things; filosofia dello —, mental philosophy; nutrire lo — con buone letture, to nourish (improve) one's mind by good reading; uomo povero di —, humble, (pop.) stupid; opinion, feeling; — di corpo, *esprit de corps*, corporate feeling, loyalty; — di parte, party spirit; lo — pubblico, public spirit; alcohol; una tassa sugli -i, a tax on spirits; lampade a —, spirit lamp; — di legno, methyl alcohol; — denaturato, methylated spirits; (Gk. gramm.) breathing; †(naut.) — della corrente, strongest part of the current. **-ale** *adj.* spiritual; holy, divine; inspired; soulful. **-are** [A 1 s] *intr.* (*aux.* essere) to be possessed (by a demon, etc.); -are dalla paura, to be beside oneself with fear; (colloq.) -are dalla fame, dal freddo, to be shivering with hunger, cold. **-ato** *part. adj.* possessed (by an evil spirit); crazy, mad; terrified; (colloq.) ragazzo -ato, imp of mischief; *n.m.* one possessed by an evil spirit; entrò come uno -ato, he entered like one possessed. (**-atamente** *adv.*) **-ello** *m.* *dim.* sprite, elf, goblin; (of a child) imp; (liter.) spirit; power; soul; (ent.) plume moth, *Pterophorus* spp.

spiritọs-o *adj.* alcoholic, spirituous; (of wine) strong; alcoholic; witty; vivacious; ingenious; '-a invenzione', witty device (i.e. lie, after Goldoni's *Il Bugiardo*); (mus.) with spirit, in a lively manner. **-amente** *adv.* wittily; brightly; in a sprightly manner. **-ag·gine** *f.* forced wit, witticism. **-ità** *f.* wit, wittiness; witticism; vivacity; alcoholic strength.

spiritual-e *adj.* spiritual; intellectual; (rel.) spiritual (reading, exercises, relationship); padre —, 'ghostly father', confessor; *n.m.* (rel.) spiritual power of the church, 'spirituals'. **-mente** *adv.* spiritually, mentally; (rel.) spiritually, in a spiritual sense, by spiritual means. **-ismo** *m.* (philos.) any philosophy upholding 'spiritual values'; anti-materialism. **-ista** *m.*, *f.* (philos.) anti-materialist; (eccl. hist.) francescano -ista, Franciscan Spiritual. **-ità** *f.* spirituality, mental quality or character.

spiritualizz-are [A 1] *tr.* to spiritualize; *rfl.* to become spiritualized. (**-ato** *part. adj.*)

spiro *m.* (poet.) breath; spirit, soul; †(theol.) il Santo Spiro, the Holy Spirit.

spiroch-eta *f.* (bact.) spirochaete. **-e·tico** *adj.* (bact.) spirochaetal.

spir-oidale, **-o·ide** *adj.* spiral. **-ometri·a** *f.* (med.) spirometry. **-o·metro** *m.* (med.) spirometer.

spirt-o *m.*, **-ale** *adj.* (poet.). See **spirit-o**, **-uale**.

spitarello *m.* (ichth.) stickleback, *Gasterosteus aculeatus*.

spittinare [A 1] *intr.* (*aux.* avere) to sing (of certain birds, e.g. robins).

spium-are [A 1] *tr.* to pluck, to strip of feathers; (fig.) to fleece; *rfl.* to moult; to lose feathers; (of a flower) to lose its petals. **-acciare** [A 3] *tr.* to shake up (bed, pillows, cushions). **-acciata** *f.* shaking, shake-up (of pillows, etc.). (**-acciato** *part. adj.*) **-ato** *part. adj.* plucked, stripped of feathers; (fig.) fleeced.

spiz·zi-co *m.* (*pl.* **-chi**) pinch; *adv. phr.* a —, little by little, in driblets. **-care** [A 2 s] *tr.* to pinch, to nibble; to take a little of. (**-cato** *part. adj.*) (**-catura** *f.*)

splan·cnico *adj.* (anat.) splanchnic, visceral.

splancno-logi·a *f.* (med.) splanchnology. **-tomi·a** *f.* (surg.) splanchnotomy, dissection of the viscera.

splateamento *m.* (bldg.) levelling.

spleen *m. indecl.* (med.) spleen; †melancholy, depression.

splen-algi·a *f.* (med.) splenalgia, splenalgy. **-al·gico** *adj.* (med.) splenalgic.

splen·d-ere [B 1] *intr.* (*aux.* essere, avere) to shine, to be resplendent; to sparkle, to glitter; to be illustrious, to be a shining light. **-ente** *part. adj.* bright, shining; resplendent. **-entemente** *adv.* brightly; resplendently.

splen·did-o *adj.* bright, brilliant, dazzling; splendid, gorgeous, magnificent; glistening, shining; munificent; *n.m.* munificent and lavish person; fare lo —, to live in splendour, on a grand scale. **-amente** *adv.* brilliantly; dazzlingly; splendidly. **-ezza** *f.* splendour, magnificence.

splendore *m.* brightness, brilliance; splendour; magnificence, grandeur; ha una figlia che è uno —, he has a daughter who is a beauty; *pl.* splendour; magnificence; sono finiti gli splendori, the days of splendour are over.

splen-e *m.* (anat.) spleen. **-ectomi·a** *f.* (surg.) splenectomy. **-e·tico** *adj.* (med.) splenetic, melancholic; (fig.) ill-tempered. **-ite** *f.* (med.) inflammation of the spleen. **-izzazione** *f.* (med.) splenization. **-oblasto** *m.* (physiol.) splenoblast. **-ocito** *m* (anat.) splenocyte. **-ocleisi** *f.* (med.) splenocleisis. **-oide** *adj.* (anat.) splenoid. **-o·lisi** *f.* (med.) splenolysis. **-omegali·a** *f.* (med.) splenomegaly, enlarged spleen, splenocele. **-opati·a** *f.* (med.) splenopathy, disease of the spleen. **-orragi·a** *f.* (med.) splenorrhagia. **-otomi·a** *f.* (surg.) splenotomy.

sple·nico *adj.* (anat.) splenic, pertaining to the spleen.

sple·nio *m.* (anat.) splenium; muscolo —, splenius.

Spluga *pr.n.m.* (geog.) Splügen; Passo dello —, Splügen Pass.

spoc·chia *f.* (colloq.) bumptiousness.

spodest-are [A 1] *tr.* to dispossess, to deprive of power or property; to dethrone; to depose; *rfl.* to divest oneself of power or property; to renounce power, etc. **-amento** *m.* dispossession; dethronement. **-ato** *part. adj.* dispossessed; dethroned; deposed.

†**spo·dio** *m.* ivory black, spodium, from calcined ivory; cinders from a smelting furnace.

spod-o·geno *adj.* (physiol.) spodogenous. **-o·fago** *adj.* (physiol.) spodophagous. **-umeno** *m.* (miner.) spodumene, hiddenite.

spoet-are [A 1] *tr.* to deprive of the title of poet; *intr.* (*aux.* avere) (joc.) to keep writing or reciting poetry; *rfl.* to give up writing poetry. **-izzare** [A 1] *tr.* to take away the poetic quality of; to disillusion; to disenchant; *rfl.* to lose one's ideals. (**-izzato** *part. adj.*)

spo·gli-a *f.* (of a snake) slough; (of a wild beast) skin; (of a human being) mortal remains; spoil, booty; le -e del Partenone, the Elgin Marbles; (of an onion) skin or layer; (sculp.) plaster jacket used in casting; (of pastry) case, shell; (eng.) angolo di —, rake; angolo di — superiore, top rake. **-amento** *m.* spoliation, plundering; deprivation; stripping; divesting; undressing. **-are** [A 4] *tr.* (*prep.* di) to divest (of); to despoil, to plunder; to deprive (of); (of a snake) to cast, to slough; (eccl.) — l'abito, to leave a religious order; (liturg.) — l'altare, to strip the altar; (eng.) to relieve, to back off; (eng.) to strip down, to dismantle; (foundry) to shake out; (leg.) to deprive; to dispossess; *rfl.* to undress (oneself), to strip (oneself); to divest oneself (of); to give up; to renounce; si- ò di ogni prevenzione, he put aside all prejudice; to lose; to shed; gli alberi si -ano delle loro foglie, the trees are shedding their leaves; (eccl., of a priest) to unvest. **-arello** *m.* strip-tease act or show. **-a·rio** *m.* (Rom. antiq.) *spoliarium* (in the amphitheatre). **-ato** *part. adj.* divested (of), deprived (of), stripped; casa -ata, unfurnished, empty, house; fiasco -ato, flask stripped of its straw covering; alberi -ati, bare trees, leafless trees; vino -ato, clear wine (having shed its sediment); undressed. **-atoio** *m.*

dressing-room; (in a factory) locker-room; (at school, etc.) cloak-room. **-atore** *m.* despoiler, plunderer; one who culls words, phrases, etc. (e.g. for a dictionary); scrutineer; also *adj.* (**-atrice** *f.*) **-atura** *f.* (pop.) undressing, stripping; spoliation, plundering. **-azione** *f.* spoliation, plundering, pillaging; misappropriation; (leg.) disseisin.

spo·glio *adj.* bare, stripped, naked, undressed; denuded; — di pregiudizi, free from prejudice; *n.m.* cast off clothing; (of snake, etc.) slough; culling, selection; lo — delle riviste, culling of bibliographical and other data from journals; scrutiny; — dei voti, counting of the votes; procedere allo —, to count the votes; stripping, undressing; (leg.) dispossession.

spol-a *f.* (text.) shuttle; spool; cop; (fig.) far la — fra, to go to and fro, to ply, between, to maintain a shuttle service between; †(naut.) small craft. †**-adora** *f.* (text.) reel. **-atore** *m.* (text.) bobbin boy, layer-on. **-atrice** *f.* (text.) bobbin layer-on; bobbin winder (machine); (electr.) coil winder. **-etta** *f.* fuse (of explosive device); -etta ad azione ritardata, delayed-action fuse; -etta a tempo, time fuse; -etta a tempo e percussione, combination fuse; shuttle (of a sewing-machine). **-ettiera** *f.* (text.) winding-machine. **-etto** *m.* bobbin (of a shuttle).

spolia·rio *m.* See **spoglia·rio**, under **spoglia**.

spoliazione *f.* spoliation, plundering.

spolino *m.* See **spoletto**.

spolitic-are [A 2 s] *intr.* (*aux.* avere) to talk politics (without special knowledge). (**-ante** *part. adj., n.m.*)

spollaiare [A 4] *rfl.* to shake oneself (like a bird, shaking its feathers).

spollon-are [A 1 c] *tr.* to remove side-shoots or suckers from (vines, fruit trees, etc.); *intr.* (*aux.* essere, avere) to grow fresh shoots, to sprout. **-ato** *part. adj.* (**-atura** *f.*)

spolmonare [A 1 c] *rfl.* to get out of breath (with talking); to shout or talk oneself hoarse; mi spolmonavo a spiegare, I made myself hoarse trying to explain, I explained till I was blue in the face; fare — uno to make a person talk himself breathless.

spolp-are [A 1 c] *tr.* to strip of flesh; (fig.) to fleece, to strip of every penny. (**-amento** *m.*) **-ato** *part. adj.* stripped of flesh, fleshless; mere skin and bone; (Tusc.) cotto -ato, madly in love.

spolpo *apocop. part.* of **spolpare**, q.v.; tisico —, in the last stages of tuberculosis.

spoltr-ire [D 2], **-onire** [D 2] *tr.* to cure of laziness; to rouse; *rfl.* to shake off laziness, to rouse oneself. (**-ito**, **-onito** *part. adj.*)

spoltroneggiare [A 3 c] *intr.* (*aux.* avere) to idle, to loaf, to do nothing but laze about.

spolver-are [A 1 sc] *tr.* to dust; to brush; (iron.) — le spalle a uno, to beat someone; (fig.) to make a clean sweep of; to eat greedily, to eat up everything; to steal, to carry off; (art) to pounce; to dust, to sprinkle; — di zucchero, to dust with sugar; *rfl.* to dust, brush, oneself; to be pulverized, to turn into powder or dust. **-agio·ie** *m. indecl.* cleaner of a jeweller's windows and showcases. **-ata** *f.* action of dusting; dare una -ata a, to give a flick of a duster to. (**-ato** *part. adj.*) **-atura** *f.* dusting; cleaning; powdering (with fine flour, face powder, charcoal dust); (fig.) smattering. **-ina** *f.* dustcoat; overall. **-ino** *m.* duster; -ino di penne, feather duster; powder; fine sand, esp. such as was formerly used to dry ink-writing; sand-box; (art) pounce-box; dust-coat; overall. **-io** *m.* cloud of dust. **-izzare** [A 1] *tr.* to powder, to dust; to pulverize; (art) to pounce. (**-izzato** *part. adj.*) **-izzatore** *m.* (surg.) see **polverizzatore**. †**-izzo**, †**-ezzo** *m.* pounce-bag; apparatus for sprinkling powdered charcoal, chalk, etc.

spolvero *m.* dusting; dust raised by dusting; — di carbone, coal dust; (art) pounce-paper; pounce, powdered charcoal; uno — di zucchero, a sprinkling of sugar; (fig.) mere show, superficiality.

spomiciare [A 3] and derivs. *intens.* of **pomiciare**, q.v.

spond-a *f.* bank; edge, border; side of a cart or lorry; (sea) coast; (geog.) la quarta —, the North African coast; parapet; quay, embankment; (bldg.) side wall; (leg.) -e ed argini, embankments and dykes; (mil.) gun carriage, gunmounting; side; (fig.) l'altra —, the other side (e.g. in party politics); means of protection; (billiards) cushion. †**-ella** *f.* (mil.) rear end of a flint in a flintlock. **-eruola** *f.* (carpen.) rabbet plane.

spond-e·o *m.* (prosod.) spondee. **-a·ico** *adj.* (prosod.) spondaic.

spon·dilo[1] *m.* (zool.) thorny oyster, *Spondylus* spp.

spon·dil-o[2] *m.* (anat.) spondyl(e), vertebra. **-artrite** *f.* (med.) spondylarthritis. **-ite** *f.* (med.) spondylitis. **-osi** *f.* (med.) spondylosis.

†**sponga** *f.* (zool.). See **spugna**.

†**spongat-a** *f.*, †**-o** *m.* kind of cake with marzipan filling; kind of ice with whipped cream, flavoured with rum.

spongiforme *adj.* spongy; (scient.) spongiform, spongioid.

spongio-blasto *m.* (physiol.) spongioblast. **-blastoma** *m.* (med.) spongioblastoma. **-plasma** *m.* (biol.) spongioplasm.

spongiọs-o *adj.* spongiose, spongy. **-ità** *f.* sponginess; (anat.) -ità midollare, medullar spongiosa.

†**spons-a** *f.* see **sposa**. †**-a·glia** *f.* see **sposalizio**. †**-o** *m.* see **sposo**.

sponsale *adj.* wedding (*adj.*), matrimonial, nuptial; *n.m.pl.* nuptials, wedding; betrothal; marriage contract; (leg.) spese per gli sponsali, expenditure incurred in contemplation of marriage.

sponta·ne-o *adj.* spontaneous; natural, unaffected; sincere; un-premeditated; involuntary; not forced, i.e. voluntary; combustione ~a, spontaneous combustion; (chem.) ossidazione ~a, spontaneous oxidation, autoxidation. **-amẹnte** *adv.* spontaneously; voluntarily. **-ità** *f.* spontaneity, spontaneousness; (leg.) spontaneity in making up for an offence (one of the ordinary extenuating circumstances) (C.P.).

sponte *adv.* (Lat.) see **spontaneamente**; *adv. phr.* — o spinte, willy-nilly.

spopol-are [A 1 s] *tr.* to depopulate; to empty (of people); *abs.* to draw crowds (i.e. leaving all other places empty). **-amẹnto** *m.* depopulation. **-ato** *part. adj.* depopulated, deserted, empty. **-aziọne** *f.* see **spopolamento**.

spopp-are [A 1] *tr.* to wean. **-amẹnto** *m.*, **-atura** *f.* weaning. **-ato** *part. adj.* weaned.

spora *f.* (biol.) spore.

Spo·radi *pr.n.f.pl.* (geol.) the Sporades, islands of the Greek archipelago.

spora·dic-o *adj.* sporadic, scattered, rare; (fig.) sporadic. (**-amẹnte** *adv.*)

sporan·gio *m.* (bot.) sporangium.

sporcacciare [A 3], **sporcare** [A 2]. See under **sporco**.

sporcheri·a *f.* See **porcheria**.

sporchettare [A 1 c] *tr.* (agric.) to break the ground in furrows (between two 'porche', see **porca**).

sporchẹzza *f.* dirtiness, filth(iness), (esp. fig.) filthiness.

sporchi·zia *f.* See **sporcizia**.

sporci·zia *f.* dirt, filth; filthiness; disgraceful conduct, indecency; turpitude; filthy language.

sporc-o *adj.* (*m.pl.* **sporchi**) dirty; foul; filthy; soiled; (naut.) tempo —, dirty weather; àncora ~a, foul anchor (where the cable has fouled the flukes or some other object has been hooked up); carena ~a, foul bottom; spiaggia ~a, costa ~a, dangerous coast, strewn with rocks; (leg.) avere la fedina ~a, to have a police record; patente ~a, endorsed licence; (fig.) parole sporche, dirty talk, obscene language; coscienza ~a, bad conscience; l'ha fatta ~a, he has behaved disgracefully. (**-amẹnte** *adv.*) **-acciare** [A 3] *tr.* to make filthy. **-acciọne** *m.* filthy person; loathsome creature; *adj.* filthy, disgusting. **-are** [A 2] *tr.* to dirty, to soil; to foul; to make a mess on; to besmirch; to slander; *intr.* (*aux.* avere) (of a dog, etc.) to mess, to dirty; *rfl.* (*acc. of prn.* 'si') to get dirty, to dirty oneself; (*dat. of prn.* 'si') -arsi le mani, to soil one's hands. **-ato** *part. adj.* dirtied, dirty, soiled; (fig.) onestà ~ata, sullied honour. (**-atọre** *m.* **-atrice** *f.*)

spor·g-ere [C 5] *intr.* (*aux.* essere) to jut out, to project; *tr.* to stretch out, to hold out; to put out; to put forward; to present; to hand out; — in su, to hold up, to stretch up; — querela, to lodge a complaint; (leg.) to lay an information; to institute; to start; *rfl.* to lean out; to jut out; to stand out, to protrude; to reach, to stretch; -ersi avanti, to reach forward; (archit.) *intr.*, *rfl.* to project. **-ente** *part. adj.* projecting, protruding, jutting; overhanging; prominent; chiodo a testa -ente, button-headed nail. **-enza** *f.* protrusion, projection; jutting point; overhang; (fig.) appianare le -enze, to rub off the corners. **-imẹnto** *m.* projection; †projecting building.

spori·cida *m.* sporicide.

spor-i·dio *m.* (bot.) sporidium. **-ocarpo** *m.* (bot.) sporocarp. **-ogo·nio** *m.* (bot.) sporogonium.

†**sporre** *vb.* and derivs. see **esporre**; (colloq.) to 'sport', to wear.

sport *m. indecl.* (pron. as Eng.) sport; per —, for pleasure, as an amateur; gli sport subacquei, underwater sports. **-ivo** *adj.* sporting; good at sport; vestiti -ivi, sports clothes; *n.m.* one who is good at sport; spectator, patron of sport; sportsman. (**-iva** *f.*) **-ivamẹnte** *adv.* sportingly.

sport-a[1] *f.* hamper; basket; shopping-basket; con la — al braccio, with her shopping-basket on her arm; (eccl.) — vescovile, bishop's travelling allowance; (colloq.) un sacco e una —, great amount; gliene dissi un sacco e una —, I gave him a piece of my mind; cappello a —, wide-brimmed straw-hat. **-ata** *f.* hamperful, basketful.

sporta[2] *f.* (bldg.) knee rafter.

sportare [A 1] *tr.*, *intr.* (*aux.* essere) (archit.) to project; to stand out, to jut out.

sportell-o *m.* wicket gate; shutter; hatch; small door (in a large door or gate); door of a coach, railway carriage or motor-car; (in a prison) wicket (for warder to look through); counter, cash-desk; booking-office, ticket-window; (of a bank) chiudere gli -i, to suspend payment; clock-case; flap. **-ato** *part. adj.* fitted with a little door, hatch, flap, etc. **-ino** *m.* little door; hatch; †fall-front of breeches.

sporto *part.* of **sporgere**, q.v.; *adj.* outstretched; leaning out; *n.m.* (archit.) projection; balcony; penthouse; shutter of a shop-front opening outwards; — del camino, chimney-piece; stall for display of goods in front of a shop; (leg.) balconi o altri -i, balconies or other projections (C.C.).

spor·tula *f.* (Rom. antiq.) *sportula*, dole from patron to client; (hist.) conventional fee to a judge.

spo·rula *f. dim.* of **spora**, q.v.

spọṣa *f.* betrothed, bride-to-be (in case of impending marriage); spouse, wife; abito da —, wedding-dress; (eccl.) — di Dio, — di Gesù, (the) Bride of Christ, the Church; una — di Gesù, a bride of Christ, a nun. **-ali·zio** *m.* wedding. **-amẹnto** *m.* marriage, wedding. **-are** [A 1] *tr.* to marry; to wed; Giovanni ha -ato Maria, e Lucia ha -ato Antonio, John married Mary and Lucy married Anthony; to give in marriage; il babbo non la vuol -are a Filippo, her father doesn't want to marry her to Philip; li ha -ati il vescovo, they were married by the bishop; †to betroth; (fig.) to embrace, to espouse; -are la poesia alla musica, to wed poetry to music; (eccl.) -are la chiesa di S. Giuseppe, to become parish priest of S. Giuseppe; -are Gesù, to become a nun; *rfl.* (*acc. of prn.* 'si'; *prep.* a, con) to get married (to), to marry; -arsi con un ricco signore, to marry a wealthy man; -arsi alla povertà, to take a vow of poverty; (*dat. of prn.* 'si') me lo -o di mio genio, I am marrying him of my own free will, because I want to; se la -a domani, he's marrying her tomorrow; (fig., Tusc.) -arsi di, to espouse; *recip. rfl.* to marry each other; (poet, e.g. of rivers) to mingle, to flow together. **-atore** *m.* (joc.) man who marries; (provb.) amanti molti e -atori pochi, many lovers but few husbands. **-ina** *f.* young bride; young wife; (eccl.) girl just taking the veil; (orn.) Carolina duck, wood duck, *Aix sponsa.* **-ino** *m.* young husband; newly married man. **-o** *m.* bridegroom, husband-to-be (in case of impending marriage); novelli -i, newly married couple; *I Promessi Sposi, The Betrothed* (title of a novel by Alessandro Manzoni); (rel.) il mistico -o, lo -o della Chiesa, the mystic Bridegroom, the Church's Bridegroom, Christ.

sposs-are [A 1] *tr.* to exhaust; to fatigue; to tire out; to enfeeble, to weaken. **-amẹnto** *m.* exhaustion; prostration; (agric.) exhaustion (of fertility of the soil). **-atẹzza** *f.* exhaustion; prostration; weakness. **-ato** *part. adj.* exhausted; fatigued, weary; prostrated. **-atamẹnte** *adv.* exhaustedly; wearily; feebly. (**-atọre** *m.* **-atrice** *f.*)

spossess-are [A 1] *tr.* (*prep.* di) to dispossess, to deprive (of); *rfl.* to deprive oneself (of); to renounce. (**-ato** *part. adj.*) **-iọne** *f.* (leg.) disseisin.

spost-are [A 1] *tr.* to displace; to move, to shift; to change, to alter; to unsettle; — una parola in una frase, to change the position of a word in a sentence; (techn.) to offset; (mus.) to transpose; *rfl.* to move, to shift; (fig.) to become unsettled. **-afo·glio** *m. indecl.* (paperm.) laying machine. **-amẹnto** *m.* displacement; movement; change in position; shifting; unsettling; (chem.) displacement; (geol.) throw (of a fault); -amento d'aria, blast (caused by a bomb); (med.) -amento del cuore, ectopia cordis; (naut.) see **dislocamento**. **-ato** *part. adj.* displaced, moved; shifted; changed; ad un'ora -ata, at an unusual hour; unsettled; mentally deranged; (techn.) offset; (mus.) transposed; *n.m.* person who does not fit in, misfit; one who follows his own bent; one who lives on his wits, having no regular employment; mentally deranged person. **-atura** *f.* displacement; misplacement; altering; moving; unsettling.

spostacin·ghia *m. indecl.* (eng.) belt fork, belt shifter.

sprang-a *f.* bar; cross-bar; bolt; arm of a balance; rail; rivet for mending china. -**are** [A2] *tr.* to bar, to bolt; to rivet (e.g. crockery); (archit.) to tie (with metal rods); to deal (blows, kicks), (of horses) -**are calci**, to kick. -**ato** *part. adj.* riveted; tied (with metal); barred, bolted. -**atura** *f.* barring; riveting.

spranghętta *f. dim.* of **spranga**, *q.v.*; (mus.) bar-line; (fig.) painful feeling of tightness in the head, like a tight band round the forehead.

sprazz-o *m.* splash; spray; flash; gleam, beam (of light); — d'intelligenza, gleam of intelligence; — d'ingegno, brain-wave. -**are** [A1] *tr.* to splash. (-**ato** *part. adj.*)

sprec-are [A2] *tr.* to waste; to squander, to dissipate; — il tempo, to waste one's time; — il fiato, to waste one's breath. (-**amento** *m.*) -**ato** *part. adj.* wasted; è fiato -**ato**, it's a waste of breath; sono tutte fatiche -**ate**, it's a lot of labour for nothing. -**atore** *m.* one who wastes and squanders; wastrel. (-**atrice** *f.* -**atura** *f.*)

spre-co *m.* (*pl.* -**chi**) waste, squandering; dissipation; con tutti i loro -chi non avranno più un soldo, they have squandered so much (money, etc.) they are probably penniless; far — di, to waste, to squander; far — della vita, to waste one's life. -**cone** *m.* (colloq.) squanderer, waster; wastrel. (-**cona** *f.*)

spregi-are [A3] *tr.* to despise; to disdain; *rfl.* to despise oneself; to neglect oneself, to be indifferent to one's own person or interests. -**amento** *m.* disdain, contempt. -**ativo** *adj.* disdainful; disparaging; derogatory. -**ato** *part. adj.* despised, disdained; scorned; neglected. -**atore** *m.* despiser, scorner. (-**atrice** *f.*)

spre·g·io *m.* contempt, scorn, disdain; contemptuous action; fare degli -i, uno —, a, to treat contemptuously; avere in molto —, to hold in great contempt. -**evole** *adj.* contemptible, despicable; mean. -**evolmente** *adv.* despicably, contemptibly. -**ioso** *adj.* scornful. (-**iosamente** *adv.*)

spregiudic-are [A2s] *rfl.* to rid oneself of prejudice; bisogna -**arsi**, one must keep an open mind; *tr.* to rid of prejudice. -**atezza** *f.* freedom from prejudice, open-mindedness. -**ato** *part. adj.* unprejudiced; open-minded; con mente -**ata**, with an unprejudiced mind; *n.m.* fair-minded, open-minded man; (derog.) freethinker, *or* one who holds no beliefs. -**atamente** *adv.* in an unprejudiced way, without prejudice.

sprella *f.* (bot.) horse-tail, *Equisetum*.

spre·m-ere [B1] to squeeze; to press; (laundry) — i panni, to wring the clothes; — un limone, to squeeze a lemon; (fig.) — il sugo da, to get the substance out of; — denari da uno, to squeeze money out of a person; †to express. -**ilimoni** *m. indecl.* lemon-squeezer. -**itoio** *m.* instrument for squeezing. -**itore** *m.* squeezer; (eng.) cilindro -**itore**, squeezing roller, press roller. -**itura** *f.* squeezing, pressing, (laundry) wringing. -**uta** *f.* squeeze; squash; -uta di limone, -uta di arancia, juice of a lemon, juice of an orange, lemon squash, orange squash. -**uto** *part. adj.* squeezed; pressed; limone -**uto**, squeezed lemon, (fig.) one who has been sucked dry.

spret-are [A1] *tr.* to unfrock (a priest); *rfl.* to be unfrocked, to abandon the priesthood. -**ato** *part. adj.* unfrocked.

sprete *m.* (Tusc.) ex-priest.

sprezz-are [A1] *tr.* to despise, to disdain, to scorn; to slight. -**a·bile** *adj.* despicable; non -**abile**, not to be disdained. -**amento** *m.* disdain, scorn. -**ante** *part. adj.* contemptuous; scornful; disdainful; haughty; *n.m.*, *f.* haughty, disdainful person; fare lo, la, -ante, to have a haughty and contemptuous manner, to look down on other people. -**ato** *part. adj.* despised, scorned; spurned; neglected. -**atore** *m.* despiser, scorner; *adj.* scornful; contemptuous. (-**atrice** *f.*) -**atura** *f.* (as defined by Castiglione in *Il Cortegiano*) perfect manners combined with ease and naturalness of bearing (indicative of the courtier's disdain or lack of anxiety to prove his good breeding); (in general) ease of manner, the ability to do the right thing, to dress well, etc., without apparent effort; studied carelessness; (fig.) -**atura** del verso, gracefulness, ease, in verse-writing.

sprezzo *m.* disdain; scornful, superior manner. (Cf. **disprezzo**.)

sprigion-are [A1c] *tr.* to release (from prison); to set free; to exhale, to emit, to give off; *rfl.* to be released; to be set free; to issue, to be given off. -**amento** *m.* release; exhalation. (-**ato** *part. adj.*)

sprill-are [A1] *intr.* (*aux.* essere) to spurt; to spout. -**o** *m.* jet; spout; spurt.

†**sprimacciare** *vb.* and derivs. See **spiumacciare**.

springare [A2] and derivs. See **spingare**.

sprizz-are [A1] *intr.* (*aux.* essere) to issue in a gentle spray; *tr.* to sprinkle; to emit; — scintille, to send forth a shower of sparks. -**ato** *part. adj.* (*prep.* di) sprinkled, sprayed; spotted; speckled. -**o** *m.* spurt; spray; dash (of flavouring, essence, etc.); flesh.

sproc-co *m.* (*pl.* -**chi**) shoot, sprout; twig. -**catura** *f.* (vet.) bruise on the sole of a horse's hoof.

sprofferta *f.* See **profferta**.

sprofond-are [A1c] *intr.* (*aux.* essere) to sink; to founder, to go to the bottom; to give way, to collapse; il pavimento -**ò**, the floor gave way; *rfl.* to sink; to give way; to sink back; -**arsi in una poltrona**, to sink into an armchair; -**arsi nel fango**, to sink into the mud; -**arsi in riverenze**, to bow with exaggerated courtesy; -**arsi in un libro**, to immerse oneself, to become absorbed, in a book; *tr.* to sink (cf. **affondare**). -**amento** *m.* sinking, foundering; collapse; †profound discouragement. -**ato** *part. adj.* sunk; deep; -**ato in una valle**, deep in a valley; (fig.) immersed, absorbed; -**ato nella meditazione**, deep in meditation; collapsed; ruined; *adv.* out and out, extreme; ricco -**ato**, extremely rich; buio -**ato**, pitch dark.

sprolo·quio *m.* tedious speech; empty words; nonsensical tirade; ama fare sproloqui, he likes talking for talking's sake.

†**sprolungare** *vb.* and derivs. See **prolungare**.

spromettere [C20] *intr.* (*aux.* avere) to break a promise.

spron-e *m.* spur; dar di — a, to spur on; (fig.) stimulus, spur, incentive; *adv. phr.* a spron battuto, at the gallop, (fig.) at top speed; (of a cock) spur; (of a bee) sting; *pl.* (of a dog) dew claws; (vet.) feathers on a horse's feet; †(naut.) see **sperone**; (mil. hist.) redoubt ward; (archit.) footing (of a wall); cutwater (of a bridge); groyne or weir (projecting from a bank, not crossing a river); (bldg.) scarp buttress; raking shore; (bot.) — di cavaliere, forking larkspur, *Delphinium consolida*. -**aglia** *f.*, -**aia** *f.* wound from a spur; spur-gall. -**aio** *m.* spur-maker; smith. -**amento** *m.* setting spurs to one's horse; (fig.) spurring on. -**are** [A1c] *tr.* to set spurs to; (fig.) to incite, to stimulate; to urge; to stir up; to goad. -**ata** *f.* touch of the spur; spur-gall; (fig.) incitement; sharp reminder. -**ato** *part. adj.* spurred; (fig.) spurred on, incited, urged. (-**atore** *m.* -**atrice** *f.*) -**ella** *f.* rowel (of a spur). -**etto** *m. dim.* little spur (esp. cockspur).

spropiare [A4] and derivs. (pop.). See **spropriare**.

sproporzion-e *f.* disproportion, want of proportion. -**ale** *adj.* disproportionate. -**almente** *adv.* disproportionately. -**alità** *f.* disproportionateness. -**are** [A1c] *tr.* to make disproportionate, to disproportion. -**ato** *part. adj.* disproportionate; -ato al valore, out of proportion to the value. -**atamente** *adv.* disproportionately.

spropo·sit-o *m.* mistake, blunder; *gaffe*, *faux pas*; absurdity; (fam.) swear word; excessive amount; di pasta mangiano uno —, they eat a vast amount of 'pasta'; costa uno —, it costs an excessive amount; *adv. phr.* a —, inopportunely, irrelevantly; foolishly. -**are** [A1s] *intr.* (*aux.* avere) to blunder, to make mistakes; to talk nonsense; *tr.* to render enormous. -**ato** *part. adj.* full of blunders; mistaken; absurd; excessive; (joc., derog.) enormous, out of all proportion. (-**atamente** *adv.*) -**one** *m. augm.* serious blunder; blunderer, one who often makes mistakes. (-**ona** *f.*)

spropri-are [A4] *tr.* (*prep.* di) (pop.) to dispossess; to despoil; *rfl.* to be dispossessed; spropriarsi di tutto per, to give up everything for (cf. **espropriare**). (-**ato** *part. adj.*)

spro·prio *m.* dispossessing; despoiling; excessive expenditure.

sprovved-ere [B35] *tr.* (*prep.* di) to deprive (of); to leave unprovided (with); *rfl.* to allow oneself to be deprived (of) or unprovided (with). -**utezza** *f.* unpreparedness. -**uto** *part. adj.* destitute; not equipped; unprovided; incautious; *adv. phr.* alla -**uta**, unexpectedly; †fortuitous. -**utamente** *adv.* incautiously.

sprovvist-o *altern. part.* of **sprovvedere**, *q.v.*; *adj.* destitute; unprovided; lacking; — di denari, without any money, penniless; una bottega sempre -**a di tutto**, a shop that is always out of (stock of) everything; *adv. phr.* alla -**a**, unexpectedly; cogliere qualcuno alla -**a**, to take someone unawares. (-**amente** *adv.*)

†**sprungeg·gi·o**, †-**olo** *m.* (bot.). See **pungitopo**.

spruzz-are [A1] *tr.* (*prep.* di) to spray, to sprinkle (with); to splash (with); — d'acqua, to sprinkle with water; (*prep.* a) to sprinkle (on); gli spruzzarono un po' d'acqua sul viso, they sprinkled a little water on his face; *impers.* (of rain) to drizzle. -**aglia** *f.* sprinkling; fine spray; drizzle, fine rain. -**amento** *m.* spraying; sprinkling; (radio) sputtering (inside a valve). -**ata** *f.* spraying, sprinkling; splash; light shower. -**ato** *part. adj.* sprayed, sprinkled;

spruzz-are (*cont.*)
splashed. **-atọio** *m.* sprinkler. **-atọre** *m.* sprayer, sprinkler; pulverizer; atomizer, vaporizer; sprayer, spray; (motor.) jet (of carburettor); -atore compensatore, auxiliary jet. **-atura** *f.* spraying; sprinkling; -atura a caldo, hot spraying; -atura del disotto della carrozzeria, underbody spraying. **-erellato** *adj.* sprinkled. **-ẹtta** *f.* (chem.) wash-bottle. **-ẹtto** *m.* sprayer, sprinkler.

spruzz-o *m.* spray; sprinkling; verniciatura a —, spray painting; uno — di pioggia, a few spots of rain, drizzle; -i del mare, sea-spray; doccia a —, shower-bath; jet, spurt; gush; drenching wave. **-olare** [A I s] *tr.* to spray, to sprinkle; *impers.* (of rain) to drizzle. **-olata** *f.* light shower; splash. **-olato** *part. adj.* splashed, sprinkled; speckled. **-olìo** *m.* continuous sprinkling, splashing.

spruz·zol-o *m.*, **-ino** *m.* *dim.* little splash.

spudorat-o *adj.* shameless, impudent; menzogna -a, bare-faced lie. **-amẹnte** *adv.* shamelessly, impudently. **-ẹzza** *f.* shamelessness, impudence; immodesty.

spugn-a *f.* (zool.) sponge; (bot.) — vegetale, loofah, dried fibrous framework of the fruit of *Luffa aegyptiaca*; (chem.) — di platoni, platinum sponge; bagnarsi con una — imbevuta d'acqua fredda, to sponge oneself with cold water; (fig.) passare la — sopra a, to wipe out, to cancel; gettare la —, to throw up the sponge; essere, bere, come una —, to drink like a fish; divenire una —, to get wet through, to be soaked; tell-tale, gossip; Turkish towelling; *pl.* (archit.) stones with sponge-like surface, used for ornament. **-ata** *f.* wipe with a sponge. **-atura** *f.* sponging, sponge down. **-olo** *m.* (bot.) morel, *Morchella esculenta*. **-ọne** *m.* (miner.) crude gypsum (from Volterra). **-osità** *f.* sponginess; *pl.* sponges, spongy substances. **-ọso** *adj.* spongy; spongiose; sponge-like.

spul-are [A I] *tr.* to winnow (corn); to hull (chestnuts, etc.); to fan. (**-ato** *part. adj.*) **-atọio** *m.* winnowing-fan. (**-atura** *f.*)

spulci-are [A 3] *tr.* to rid of fleas; (fig., derog.) to go through with a fine tooth-comb; *rfl.* to get rid of fleas; il cane sta -andosi, the dog is scratching for fleas. (**-ato** *part. adj.* **-atura** *f.*)

spuleẓẓare [A I c] (pop., Tusc.) *intr.* (*aux.* essere) to run away, to make off.

spul-ire [D 2] *tr.* (techn.) to polish; to grind (glass). **-ito** *part. adj.* polished; ground; vetro -ito, frosted glass.

spum-a *f.* foam, froth; la — del mare, sea foam; — di marosi, surf; — di sapone, lather. **-ante** *part. adj.* foaming; (of wine) sparkling; (fig.) -ante d'ira, foaming with rage; *n.m.* sparkling wine. **-are** [A I] *intr.* (*aux.* avere) to foam, to froth; to lather. **-ata** *f.* patch of foam; splash of foam. **-eggiante** *part. adj.* foaming, frothing; (of wine) sparkling. **-eggiare** [A 3 c] *intr.* (*aux.* avere) to foam, to froth, to sparkle. **-i·fero** *adj.* foaming, full of foam. **-ọne** *m.* sweet comprising white of egg or whipped cream; a kind of ice-cream. **-osità** *f.* frothiness. **-ọso** *adj.* frothy, foamy, foaming; merletti -osi, foamy lace.

spungiọne *m.* (miner.) a yellowish tufaceous rock.

spunt-are [A I] *tr.* to blunt; to break the point of; to remove the tip of; to trim; — i baffi a, to clip the moustache of; to undo, to unpin; (fig.) to overcome; -arla, to win through, to succeed; to remove, to erase, to strike out; to tick, to mark with a tick, etc.; (mil.) to dislodge; (aeron.) to switch the motor on and off, to make and break contact; *rfl.* to become blunted; (of a pencil, etc.) to lose its point; to come unpinned, to come unfastened; (fig.) to become less acute or sharp; to become less efficacious; *intr.* (*aux.* essere) to appear, to poke out, to come into view, to peep out; (of the sun) to rise; (of teeth) to come through; (of the day) to break, to dawn; (of tears) to start, to well up; †(fig.) to start; †to get going; *n.m.* appearance, appearing; allo spuntar del giorno, at daybreak. **-asi·gari** *m. indecl.* cigar-cutter. **-ato** *part. adj.* blunted; just appearing, come through; speranza -ata, a gleam of hope, a dawning hope; (mus.) diminished. **-atrice** *f.* (eng.) chamfering machine. **-atura** *f.* blunting; removal, of the tip; stump, end; -ature di sigari, cigars sliced for pipes; -ature del baccalà, heads and tails of dried cod; (butcher.) -atura di lombo, a cut low down beneath rump and sirloin; -atura di costa, a cut low down beneath sirloin and ribs of beef; (eng.) chamfering; (metall.) crop end. **-ellare** [A I] *tr.* to remove props from (cf. **puntello**). (**-ellato** *part. adj.*) **-ino** *m.* snack, light refreshment.

spunt-o¹ *m.* starting point, point of departure; rise, origin, impulse, start; dare lo — a, to give rise to; (sport) spurt; (theatr.) cue; (mus.) initial word (given by prompter in opera-theatre); (of

wine) acidity. **-erbo** *m.* (shoem.) toecap. †**-iera** *f.* (naut.) timber gantry used on drifters in the Adriatic. **-ọne** *m. augm.* large spike; (naut.) bearing off spar; (mil.) pike, half-pike, halberd.

spunto² *apocop. part.* of **spuntare**, q.v.; *adj.* blunted, blunt.

spunzọn-e *m.* (Tusc.) large spike (cf. **spuntone**); punch poke. **-are** [A I c] *tr.* to prod; to nudge; (fig.) to goad, to urge on. **-ata** *f.* prod, push. (**-ato** *part. adj.*)

†**spurare** *tr.* to polish.

†**spur·cido** *adj.* filthy; squalid.

spurg-are [A 2] *tr.* to clean, to clear out; to purge; — i bronchi, il petto, il catarro, to clear one's chest of phlegm; — il naso, to clear one's nose (e.g. after a heavy cold); (techn.) to drain, to bleed; also *rfl.* (**-amẹnto** *m.*) **-ato** *part. adj.* cleared; cleaned out. **-azione** *f.* clearing; clearing out.

spur-go *m.* (*pl.* **-ghi**) mucus, etc. cleared away; — sanguigno, discharge of blood; cleaning out of ditch, duct, gutter, etc.; drain, drainage; (hydraul.) bleeding; drainage plug; *pl.* rubbish, matter, cleared away.

spu·rio *adj.* spurious, illegitimate; figlio —, bastard; not genuine; not authentic; (anat.) costole spurie, false ribs.

sputare [A I] and derivs. See under **sputo**.

sput-o *m.* spit, spittle; spitting; — sanguigno, blood spitting; (colloq.) appiccicato con lo sputo, stuck on with spit; pane e —, dry bread; fatto con lo —, weak, lacking resistance; stimare una persona uno —, to consider a person a weakling or of no account; (med.) sputum. **-acchiare** [A 3] *intr.* (*aux.* avere) to spit out phlegm; *tr.* to spit upon; lo -acchiò in faccia, he spat in his face. **-acchiera** *f.* spittoon. **-acchino** *m.* (ent.) cuckoo spit insects (Fam. Cercopidae). **-ac·chio**, †**-a·glio** *m.* spittle, phlegm. **-apẹpe** *m. indecl.* witty but spiteful talker, clever sarcastic speaker. **-are** [A I] *intr.* (*aux.* avere) to spit; -are addosso a, in, su, to spit at, on; (fig.) -are su, to despise; vietato -are, do not spit, no spitting; *tr.* to spit out; -are i polmoni, to 'cough up one's lungs', i.e. to have a hacking cough; -are sangue, to spit blood, *or* (fig.) to sweat blood; -are veleno, -are bile, to spit bile, to speak spitefully; -are sentenze, to talk sententiously; -are tondo, to speak solemnly; (of a door, window) -are vento, to let in a draught. **-asẹnno** *m. indecl.* pompous person. **-asentẹnze** *m. indecl.* sententious person. **-ata** *f.* spitting. **-ato** *part. adj.* spat out; (pop.) real, evident; una bugia -ata, a downright lie; è suo padre nato e -ato, he is the spit and image of his father. **-atọndo** *m. indecl.* (derog.) pompous ass. (**-atọre** *m.* **-atrice** *f.*) **-avelẹno** *m.* (bot.) squirting cucumber, *Ecballium elaterium*. †**-azuc·chero** *m.* hypocritical flatterer.

squac·quer-a *f.* diarrhoea; liquid excrement. **-are** [A I s] *intr.* (*aux.* avere) to have diarrhoea; *tr.* (vulg.) to blurt out. **-ato** *part. adj.* soft and damp; (of laughter, voice, sound) uproarious, noisy, loud. **-atamẹnte** *adv.* uproariously; ridere -atamente, to guffaw.

squadern-are [A I] *tr.* to turn over the leaves of (a book); to display; aprii il dizionario e glielo -ai, I opened the dictionary and put it under his nose, handed it to him to see for himself; mi -ò la tua lettera, he handed me your letter to read; (bookb.) to unstitch; *rfl.* to be dispersed, to be scattered. **-ato** *part. adj.* opened, displayed before one; (bookb.) unbound, unstitched. (**-atọre** *m.* **-atrice** *f.*)

squadra¹ *f.* square; fuori di —, out of square; — a T, T-square; — fissa, set square; (eng.) strap; (naut.) square portion of mast or yard; (herald.) canton charged with another.

squadr-a² *f.* team; group; squad; — di soccorso, breakdown gang; (sport) — calcistica, football team; (mil.) a lined-up unit or squadron; uscire di —, to get out of line; company, squad, section; part of a company; unit under a corporal (i.e. section); half a platoon; a section of customs men; a security squad; — volante, flying squad; detachment; (naut.) squadron. **-ac·cia** *f. pejor.* bad set, gang. **-iere** *m.* foreman, group leader. **-i·glia** *f.* squadron; squad; (naut.) flotilla. **-igliere** *m.* (mil.) soldier belonging to a squadron. **-iṣmo** *m.* (Ital. hist.) organization and methods of the Fascist bands. **-ista** *m.* (Ital. hist.) member of a Fascist squad.

squadr-are [A I] *tr.* to square; to make square; to look at squarely; — uno da capo a piedi, to look a person up and down; (techn.) to square, to dress, to true; *intr.* (*aux.* avere; *prep.* a) to square (with); (fig.) to suit, to go well with, to be acceptable to; è un'idea che non mi -a, it is an idea that does not appeal to me. **-ato** *part. adj.* squared; examined closely, looked up and down. **-atọre** *m.* stone-cutter. **-atura** *f.* squaring, dressing, alignment. **-i·glia** *f.* small square.

squadr·o *m.* (eng.) square; (surv.) cross-head; (naut.) clinometer, instrument for measuring the list or sag of a ship; (ichth.) monk-fish, *Squatina squatina.* **-ino** *m.* (tech.) brick trimmer. **-olina** *f.,* **-olino** *m.* (ichth.) see **squadro**.

squadrone¹ *m. augm.* of **squadro**, q.v.; *augm.* large set square used in ship-building.

squadron·e² *m.* (mil.) squadron (of cavalry, generally 100); large squadron (200 men); cavalry sabre; — volante, reconnaissance troops; †(naut.) squadron of ships. **-are** [A 1 c] *intr.* (*aux.* avere) (mil.) to form squadrons; *rfl.* to form up one's forces; to array. (**-ato** *part. adj.*) **-cello** *m. dim.* (mil.) platoon (25 to 30 men). **-cino** *m. dim.* (mil.) small unit; patrol; small sword or dirk.

squagli·are [A 4] *tr.* to melt; to melt down, to liquefy; *rfl.* to melt; (fig., joc.) to steal away, to make off. (**-amento** *m.*) **-ato** *part. adj.* melted (down); (fig., joc.) gone, disappeared.

squa·glio¹ *m.* melting (down or away); disappearance; (Rome) drinking chocolate.

squa·glio² *m.* (ichth.) chub, *Squalus cephalus.*

squali·fic·a *f.* (sport) foul, disqualification; suspension (of a player for misconduct); — del campo, temporary closing of a (football) ground owing to disorderly conduct of spectators. **-are** [A 2 s] *tr.* to rate as of inferior quality; to disqualify. (**-ato** *part. adj.*) **-azione** *f.* disqualification.

squallente *adj.* (liter.). See **squallido**.

squal·lid·o *adj.* dismal, dreary, cheerless; wretched; gloomy, grim; barba -a, unkempt beard; wan, deadly pale; having the pallor of death. **-ezza** *f.* dreariness, gloom; wretched appearance; -ezza del cadavere, deathly pallor of the corpse.

squallore *m.* pallor; wretched appearance; dreariness, cheerlessness, gloom; squalor.

squalo *m.* (ichth.) name of various sharks; — feroce, *Carcharias ferox*; — nasuto, *Lamna cornubica*, porbeagle shark; — massimo, *Cetorhinus maximus*, basking shark; — rostrato, juvenile basking shark.

squam·a, †**squamm·a** *f.* (zool.) scale (of fish, etc.); (bot.) scale, scale leaf; (mil. hist.) scale armour; overlapping plates; (metall.) scale beaten off metal by hammering at the forge. **-are** [A 1] *tr.* to scale, to remove scales from; *rfl., intr.* (*aux.* essere), to scale; to flake (off). **-ato** *part. adj.* formed (or made to look) like scales. **-i·gero** *adj.* having scales, scaly. **-oso** *adj.* scaly; flaky.

squarci·are [A 3] *tr.* to rend, to tear, to rip; — la bocca, to open one's mouth as wide as possible; il sole -a le nuvole, the sun is breaking through the clouds; — il velo del mistero, to pierce, to penetrate, the veil of mystery; *rfl.* to be torn asunder; to part; le nubi si -ano, the clouds are dispersing. †**-acuori** *f. indecl.* (joc., of a woman) breaker of hearts. **-agola** *adv. phr.* a -agola, at the top of one's voice, with a loud yell. **-amento** *m.* rending, tearing; ripping. **-asacco** *adv. expr.* guardare a -asacco, to scowl at. **-ata** *f.* tear; rending; rip. **-ato** *part. adj.* torn, rent; voce -ata, loud, bawling voice; pronunzia -ata, coarse, unrefined accent (too loud, emphatic, aspirated, guttural, etc.); (vet.) bocca -ata, large, well-formed mouth (of a horse). (**-atore** *m.* **-atrice** *f.*) **-atura** *f* rending, tearing; tear; split; wound.

squar·cio *m.* tear, rent; gash; hole; leak; piece torn off; (from a book) passage, excerpt, extract.

†**squarcion-e** *m.* swaggering, blustering person. (†**-a** *f.*)

squarquo·i·o *adj.* (pop., Tusc.) decrepit; età squarquoia, old age. **-a** *f.* fat old woman.

squart-are [A 1] *tr.* to quarter; to tear to pieces; to cut up; to chop up; (fig.) — lo zero, to be punctilious, to split hairs; — i minuti, not to waste a minute. **-amento** *m.* quartering; cutting up. **-anu·voli** *adj., n.m. indecl.* bumptious (person). **-aspic·cioli** *adj., n.m. indecl.* miser(ly). **-ato** *part. adj.* quartered; cut up; chopped. **-atoio** *m.* chopper, butcher's cleaver. (**-atore** *m.* **-atrice** *f.*) (**-atura** *f.*) **-o** *m.* quartering; cutting up; legne di -o, chopped wood for making charcoal; (hist.) condannato allo -o, condemned to be (hung, drawn and) quartered. **-avento** *adj., n.m. indecl.* blustering (person). **-one** *m.* log (of wood split from a trunk).

squartucciare [A 4] *intr.* (*aux.* avere) to sell wine by the glass (cf. **quartuccio**).

†**squasimo(d)de·o** *m.* simpleton; *excl.* (corruption of 'spasimo di Dio!').

squass-are [A 1] *tr.* to shake violently; to rock; — l'asta, to brandish one's spear; — il capo, to shake one's head (in disapproval or disagreement); — le spalle, to shrug one's shoulders; *rfl.* to shake

(be shaken) violently; to totter. **-amento** *m.* violent shaking; shock. **-ato** *part. adj.* violently shaken; rocked. **-o** *m.* violent shaking; shock.

†**squa·tin-o** *m.,* †**-a** *f.* (ichth.). See **squadro**, under **squadra²**.

†**squatrare** *vb.* and derivs. See **squartare**.

squattrin-are¹ [A 1] *tr.* to leave penniless; to count out penny by penny; *intr.* (*aux.* avere) to spend lavishly; to shower money about; to make a display of wealth; *rfl.* to beggar oneself. **-ato** *part. adj.* penniless; *n.m.* penniless person, beggar; sposare uno -ato, to marry a man without a penny.

squattrin-are² [A 1] *tr.* to scrutinize, to examine minutely; to peer at, to squinny at. **-ata** *f.* squinnying. (**-ato** *part. adj.*)

†**squero** *m.* (naut., Ven.) covered yard or boatshed.

squilibr-are [A 1] *tr.* to unbalance, to throw out of balance; to unsettle; to embarrass; *rfl.* to lose one's balance; (fig.) to get into difficulties. **-ato** *part. adj.* unbalanced; deranged, insane; (eng.; electr.) unbalanced; *n.m.* unbalanced person, one mentally deranged. **-azione** *f.* (eng.) unbalance.

squili·brio *m.* lack of balance; — mentale, mental derangement; difference; inequality; (eng.; electr.) unbalance.

squilla¹ *f.* (bot.) squill, *Urginea scilla.*

squill-a² *f.* bell, small bell, harness-bell, cow-bell; angelus(-bell), ringing of the angelus. **-ante** *part. adj.* shrill; ringing sharp and clear; riso -ante, ringing laugh; pealing; (of trumpets) blaring. (**-antemente** *adv.*) **-are** [A 1] *intr.* (*aux.* avere) to ring; to peal; to blare; to sound shrilly; to resound; (mus.) to blare, to sound (of trumpets). **-ato** *adj.* (herald.) with bell.

squill-o *m.* ring, ringing; sound, note; blast; peal; uno — di tromba, a trumpet-blast; dare gli -i, to give the three trumpet-blasts (sign for dispersal like reading the Riot Act); ragazza —, 'call girl'; (mus.) blast, blare, fanfare (of trumpets). **-one** *m. augm.* big bell.

squinant-o, -e *m.* (bot.) geranium grass, camel's hay, *Cymbopogon schoenanthus.*

squinanzi·a *f.* (vet.) quinsy.

†**squinci** *adv.*; *adv. phr.* in — e squindi, affectedly, mincingly.

squin·cio *adj.* (pop., Tusc.) aslant, askew; *n.m.* cloth cut on the cross.

squintern-are [A 1] *tr.* to take (a book) to pieces (cf. **quinterno**); to turn over the pages of (a book); (fig.) to disarrange. **-ato** *part. adj.* (of a book) taken to pieces; (fig.) disarranged.

squisit-o *adj.* delicious, delicate; of rare quality, exquisite. **-amente** *adv.* exquisitely; very delicately; elegantly. **-ezza** *f.* delicacy; elegance; rare quality, perfection, excellence; refinement.

†**squitterire** *vb.* and derivs. See **squittire**.

†**squittinare** *vb.* and derivs. See **scrutinare**.

squittire [D 2] *intr.* (*aux.* avere) to yelp; to squeal; to squeak; to squawk.

sradic-are [A 2 s] *tr.* to uproot; — un dente, to take a tooth out; (fig.) to eradicate, to extirpate. **-amento** *m.* uprooting; (fig.) eradicating. **-ato** *part. adj.* uprooted; (fig.) extirpated; (herald.) eradicated. **-atore** *m.* uprooter; extirpator. (**-atrice** *f.*)

sragion-are [A 1 c] *intr.* (*aux.* avere) to reason falsely; to talk irrationally, to talk nonsense. **-amento** *m.* false reasoning; irrational talk, nonsense. **-ato** *part. adj.* falsely reasoned; irrational, nonsensical. **-atore** *n.m., adj.* rambling, inconsequent (person, argument, etc.). (**-atrice** *f.*) **-evole** *adj.* see **irragionevole**.

sralingare [A 2] *tr.* (naut.) to take the roping off (a sail); *intr.* (*aux.* avere) to have the canvas blown out of its roping.

sregionalizz-are [A 1] *tr.* to deregionalize, to deprive of regional characteristics. (**-ato** *part. adj.*)

sregol-are [A 1 s] *tr.* to throw into disorder; to upset. **-amento** *m.* disordering, upsetting. **-atezza** *f.* disorder; intemperance, excess; dissipation, debauchery. **-ato** *part. adj.* disordered; intemperate, immoderate; dissolute; (motor.) out of tune; (eng.) out of adjustment. **-atamente** *adv.* intemperately; excessively. **-azione** *f.* disorder; (eng., motor.) the state of being out of order; 'trouble'.

srotolare [A 1 s] *tr.* to roll off.

†**srugginire** [D 2] *tr.* to derust, to remove the rust from.

†**sruvidire** [D 2] *tr.* to dress, to polish; to soften.

sss! *excl.* sh!

st!, sst! *excl.* pst!; sh!

sta·¹ abbrev. of **stai**, *imp. 2nd pers. sing.* of **stare**, q.v.

†**sta·²** *f.* See **estate**.

†**sta·³** *m.* See **staio**.

stabaccare *intr.* (*aux.* avere) (joc., derog.) to take snuff.

sta·bat *m.* (liturg., mus.) the liturgical sequence *Stabat Mater* or any of its musical settings.

stab·bi·o *m.* (agric.) manure, dung; compost; fold, pen. **-are** [A4] *intr.* (*aux.* essere) (agric.; of animals) to be in a stall, fold or pen; to be folded in the fields (with a view to manuring the ground); *tr.* to stable; to pen, to fold; to manure. **-ato** *part. adj.* manured (naturally, by animals); *n.m.* piece of land thus manured. **-atura** *f.* manuring, folding (with a view to manuring). **-uolo** *m.* sty, pigsty; small shed or fold for sheep.

sta·bil·e *adj.* stable, steady, firm, fixed; durable, lasting; permanent; personale in pianta —, permanent staff; un'offerta —, a firm offer; beni -i, real estate; entrare in beni -i, to buy property; colore —, fast colour; ripa —, flood-resisting river embankment; dimora —, permanent address, fixed abode; (of weather) tempo —, set fair; salute —, constant good health; (naut.) naviglio —, craft having good stability; (mus.) direttore —, permanent conductor; orchestra —, permanent orchestra; (theatr.) compagnia —, repertory company; *adv. phr.* in modo —, steadily; *n.m.* landed property; building; house; *f.* theatrical company permanently engaged by a theatre. **-mente** *adv.* regularly, permanently, always. **-ità** *f.* stability; steadiness; firmness; -ità della ripa, resistance (to flood) of the river-embankment; -ità dell'impiego, permanence of employment; (naut.) stability.

stabil·ire [D2] *tr.* to establish; to ascertain; to fix; to settle; to arrange; to determine upon; — di andare, to decide to go; — il da farsi, to decide what is to be done; — un dividendo, to declare a dividend; to assign; to state; to decree; — che, to lay it down that; *rfl.* to establish oneself; to settle. **-imento** *m.* establishment; stabilization; settlement; factory, mill; workshop, works; -imento siderurgico, ironworks, steelworks; foundation; -imento penale, prison, penal settlement; -imento balneare, bathing establishment, public baths; (naut.) -imento del porto, lunitidal interval at springs. **-ito** *part. adj.* firm, steady, settled; fixed, constant. **-itamente** *adv.* firmly; in settled fashion. (**-itore** *m.* **-itrice** *f.*) **-itura** *f.* (bldg.) final coat of white plaster.

stabilizz·are [A1] *tr.* to stabilize; (comm.) to peg. **-ante** *part. adj.* stabilizing; (aeron.) momento -ante, righting moment, restoring moment. (**-ato** *part. adj.*) **-atore** *m.* (naut.) stabilizer, gyroscopically controlled fins which help to decrease the roll of a ship; (aeron.) tail plane; (electr.; chem.) stabilizer. **-azione** *f.* stabilization.

stabul·a·rio *m.* public kennel for stray dogs; pound (for cattle); †guardian of cattle. **-azione** *f.* stall-feeding; stabling.

†**stacca** *f.* (mil.) ring, socket, rack for flagpoles; lanyard on a lancer's shoulder for holding the stave when the butt is in the holster.

stacc·are [A2] *tr.* (*prep.* da) to take off; to detach; to pull off; — con un morso, to bite off; to remove; to unhook; — i quadri dai muri, to take the pictures down from the walls; to separate, to sever; to unyoke (e.g. oxen); to pronounce distinctly, to articulate; (mus.) to detach; (electr.) to cut out, to disconnect; (rlwy.) to uncouple, to unhitch; (comm.) to give; to issue; (fig.) non — lo sguardo da una persona, not to take one's eyes off a person; — la corsa, to start running; — la volata, to take off (in flight); — il bollore, to come to the boil; *rfl.* to come off, to come loose, to withdraw, to retire (from); to leave; to come unstuck; non si poteva — dal suo figliolino, he could not tear himself away from his little son; to stand out; to differ, to be different; (cycling, racing, etc.) -arsi da, to outdistance, to break away from; *intr.* (*aux.* avere) to come off, to come away clean; (art) to stand out (against a particular background); (colloq.) to cease work; gli operai -ano alle sei, the men knock off at six. **-a·bile** *adj.* detachable. (**-abilità** *f.* **-amento** *m.*) **-ata** *f.* ancient square measure (just over half a hectare). **-atezza** *f.* separateness, disjunction. **-ato** *part. adj.* detached, separate; orecchi -ati, prominent ears; separated; distinct; interrupted, broken up; (mus.) staccato, detached; (electr.) cut out, disconnected, dead. **-atamente** *adv.* separately; interruptedly; brokenly. **-atore** *m.* detacher, separator. (**-atrice** *f.*) **-atura** *f.* detaching, cutting off.

stacch·eggiare [A3c], **-ettare** [A3c] *intr.* (*aux.* avere) to clatter with one's heels in walking.

staccino *m.* calico or linen cloth with check or striped pattern.

stac·ci·o *m.* sieve, hair-sieve; passare allo —, to sift, to sieve; farina a tutto —, finely sifted flour; (techn.) cucchiaio a —, sieve spoon. **-a·io** *m.* maker or vendor of sieves. **-are** [A3] *tr.* to sift, to sieve; to bolt; to riddle; to screen; (fig.) to sift, to examine minutely.

-ata *f.* action of sifting; a sifting, i.e. amount sifted in one operation; (joc.) proceedings of the Crusca Academy. **-ato** *part. adj.* sifted, sieved; bolted; riddled; screened. **-atura** *f.* action of sifting; siftings; bran. **-onata** *f.* hurdle (esp. for horse-jumping); (carpen.) stockade. **-uolo** *m.* enclosure for partridges, pigeons, etc.

stac·co *m.* (*pl.* **-chi**) separation, detachment; gap, space; piece detached; ticket; — d'abito, d'un vestito, piece of cloth for a suit, dress-length; (art) fare —, to stand out, to be prominent; (fig.) fare — con, to be in contrast to, to stand out against; (comm.) counterfoil; (cinem.; telev.) — netto, 'cut' (cf. **staccare**).

stachidrina *f.* (chem.) stachydrine.

stachio·sio *m.* (chem.) stachyose.

stader·a *f.* steelyard (balance); — a ponte, weighbridge. **-a·io** *m.* steelyard maker or seller; controller of weights and measures. **-ante** *m.* retailer of meat (in small quantities).

sta·dia *f.* (surv.) stadia, levelling staff.

sta·dio *m.* (class. antiq.) stade, stadium (measure of about 200 yards), furlong; (class. antiq.) running-track, racecourse, stadium; (sport) stadium, sports ground; (fig.) phase, stage.

staff·a *f.* stirrup; bicchiere della —, stirrup cup; vuotar le -e, to fall off horseback; (fig.) perdere le -e, to lose one's temper; tenere il piede in due -e, to hold with the hare and hunt with the hounds; -e per arrampicarsi, climbing irons (e.g. on a post or pylon); (of a carriage, etc.) footboard; (eng.) strap, clip, clamp, bracket; (foundry) moulding-box, flask; (anat.) stapes; (mus.) balancing swell pedal (of organ); gut loop (attaching tailpiece to the button or pin of violin); — del crescendo, crescendo pedal (of organ); †(naut.) -e delle landre, strengthening plate where shrouds are secured; †strop; †footrope. **-ale** *m.* step of a spade. **-arda** *f.* large heavy stirrup. **-are** [A1] *intr.* (*aux.* avere) to lose one's stirrups; -are da un piede, to lose one of one's stirrups; *tr.* (techn.) to stirrup; *rfl.* to have one's foot held in the stirrup when thrown (also 'rimanere staffato'). **-ato** *part. adj.* entangled in the stirrup; essere -ato corto, to ride with shortened stirrups, with racing stirrups. **-atore** *m.* (foundry) moulder. **-eggiare** [A3c] *intr.* (*aux.* avere) see **staffare**. **-etta** *f. dim.* small bolt or bar; clamp; latch-holder; courier, dispatch-rider; (fig.) fare da -etta, to fetch and carry; a -etta, immediately; (rlwy.) locomotiva -etta, pilot engine; (sport) corsa a -etta, relay race. **-iere, -iero** *m.* groom, footman, lackey. **-one** *m.* (of a carriage) footboard.

staffil·e *m.* stirrup-leather; whip; strap, thong; scourge. **-amento** *m.* beating, thrashing. **-are** [A1] *tr.* to beat with a leather thong; to thrash. **-ata** *f.* beating, thrashing; (fig. `stinging reproof; biting criticism. (**-ato** *part. adj.* **-atore** *m.* **-atrice** *f.*) **-atura** *f.* beating, thrashing.

stafil·ino *adj.* (anat.) staphyline, pertaining to the uvula; muscolo —, staphylinus. **-ite** *f.* (med.) uvulitis. **-ococ·cia** *f.* (med.) staphylococcia. **-ococco** *m.* (bact.) staphylococcus. **-oma** *m.* (med.) staphyloma. **-optosi** *f.* (med.) uvulaptosis. **-otomi·a** *f.* (surg.) uvulotomy. **-o·tomo** *m.* (surg.) uvulotome.

stafisa·gria *f.* (bot.) stavesacre, *Delphinium staphysagria*.

stag·gi·o *m.*, **-a** *f.* prop; stay, stay-rod; pole for hanging bird nets; one of the two stringers of a ladder; measuring rod; upright bar of a cage; back leg (forming also high back) of a chair; moveable bar of an embroidery frame; †(naut.) stay; forestay; †top gallant yard; (Ven.) spars used as spreaders on trawlers. **-are** [A3] *tr.* (agric.) to prop up (trees overloaded with fruit). **-ato** *part. adj.* (agric.) propped.

stagion·e *f.* season, time of year; nel colmo della —, at the height of the season; i prezzi fuori —, off-season charges; — morta, slack time; mezza —, spring or autumn; frutto di —, fruit in season; cattiva —, bad weather; (mus.) — lirica, opera season; *adv. phr.* alla —, as occasion offers; †tutta —, always. **-ale** *adj.* seasonal. **-amento** *m.* seasoning (of wood, etc.); keeping for ripening (of fruit). **-are** [A1c] *tr.* to season; to mature, to keep to ripen; *intr.* (*aux.* essere), *rfl.* to mature, to ripen; to be seasoned. **-ato** *part. adj.* seasoned; weathered; ripe, mature; (fig., joc.) well-preserved. (**-atore** *m.* **-atrice** *f.*) **-atura** *f.* seasoning; ripening. **-evole** *adj.* seasonable.

Stagirita *pr.n.m.* the Stagirite, name for Aristotle as a native of Stagira.

stagli·are [A4] *tr.* to hack; to cut unevenly; to hew; to lop; to keep a tally of; *rfl.* -arsi su un fondo, to stand out distinctly against a background. **-ato** *part. adj.* hacked; unevenly cut; notched (on a tally).

sta·glio *m.* rough reckoning; rough estimate; vendere a —, to sell as a job-lot.

stagna *f.* See under **stagno²**.

stagn-are¹ [A 5] *intr.* (*aux.* avere) to be stagnant; to stagnate; to gather, to lie, to collect; to cease to flow, to be stanched; *tr.* to stanch, to stop the flow of. **-amento** *m.* stanching; stagnating. **-ante** *part. adj.* stagnant. **-ato** *part. adj.* stanched; stagnant; stagnating; lying stagnant.

stagn-are² [A 5] *tr.* to tin, to solder; to make watertight. **-ata** *f.* tin, can; packet wrapped in tin-foil; lining with tin; soldering. **-ato** *part. adj.* soldered; ferro -ato, tin-plate. **-atura** *f.* covering with tin; soldering.

stagno¹ *m.* stretch of stagnant water; pond, pool.

stagn-o² *m.* tin; tin-ware; — battuto, tin-foil. **-a** *f.* tin-can; tin-box. **-a·io**, †**-aro** *m.* tin-smith; tinker. **-ina** *f.* tin-can. **-ino** *m.* light tin-plate; tin-smith, tinker. **-(u)ola** *f.* tin-foil; tin-can. **-(u)olo** *m.* tin-can; *pl.* counterfeit coins containing tin.

stagno³ *adj.* proof; waterproof, watertight; airtight; — alla luce, lightproof; (naut.) nave stagna, seaworthy ship, 'tight little ship'; paratia stagna, watertight bulkhead; porta stagna, watertight door.

sta·i-o *m.* (*pl.* **sta·i** *m.*, **sta·ia** *f.*) bushel (measure varying in different parts of Italy); a -a, in plenty; cappello a —, top hat; colmare lo —, to complete the job; (*m.pl.* **stai**) containers or units of measurement. **-a** *f.* amount of a product contained in a 'staio'. **-ata** *f.* bushelful; bushel; ground that can be sown with a bushel of corn. **-one** *m.* 3 bushels, or 2 bushels. **-oro** *m.* (*pl.* **-ora** *f.*) area of ground that can be sown with one bushel of corn. **-uolo** *m. dim.* at Rome, a measure of area (equiv. to 1284 square metres).

stalagm-ite *f.* (geol.) stalagmite. **-i·tico** *adj.* stalagmitic. **-itiforme** *adj.* shaped like a stalagmite.

stalatt-ite *f.* (geol.) stalactite. (**-i·tico** *adj.*) **-itiforme** *adj.* shaped like a stalactite, stalactitic.

†**stalentag·gine** *f.* unwillingness, reluctance.

stall-a *f.* stable; horsebox; cowshed; quantity of horses or cattle in a stable; pigsty; sheepfold; (provb.) serrar la —, perduti i buoi, *or* chiudere la — quando sono fuggiti i buoi, to lock the stable door after the horse has bolted; (fig.) una casa che pare una —, a house like a pigsty; (myth., fig.) spazzare le -e di Augia, to cleanse the Augean stables. †**-aggiare** *tr.* to stable. **-ag·gio** *m.* stabling. **-are** [A 1] *intr.* (*aux.* essere) (of horses, cattle) to be stabled, to be in a stall; (of sheep) to be folded. **-ata** *f.* herd (housed in one cow-house), stable (i.e. a number of horses in a stable). **-a·tico** *m.* stabling; (agric.) stable manure. **-ereccio** *m.* stables, stabling; *adj.* relating to stabled animals, folded sheep, etc. **-iere** *m.* stableman, stable-boy, groom; †cavallo **-iere**, stallion. **-ino** *adj.* stable-born, stable-reared; *n.m. dim.* pen, esp. breeding-pen for goats or sheep. **-i·o**, **-ivo** *adj.* (of a horse) kept in the stable. **-one** *m.* stallion; (mil.) remount depot; stable-boy. **-uc·cio** *m.* pigsty.

stallare¹ [A 1] and derivs. See under **stalla**.

stall-are² [A 1] *intr.* (*aux.* avere) (naut.) to wait the tide; to anchor owing to weather; *tr.* — la corrente, to head up into the current without drifting; — il vento, to remain at anchor without dragging, to 'hold'. **-ato** *part. adj.* †(naut.) marea -ata, slack water. **-i·a** *f.* (naut.) delay in harbour; -ia regolare, -ia ordinaria, normal loading time or stop-over; -ia irregolare, -ia straordinaria, demurrage.

stallo *m.* (eccl.) choir stall; †bishop's throne; (fig.) seat of honour; residence; (chess) stalemate; (aeron.) stall.

stalloggi *m.pl.* (bot.) *Aristolochia.*

stamaiuol-a *f.*, **-o** *m.* See under **stame**.

stamane *adv.* (poet.). See **stamani**.

sta-mani, -mattina *adv.* this morning.

stambec-co *m.* (*pl.* **-chi**) (zool.) ibex, *Capra hircus*; †(naut.) see **sciabecco**. †**-china** *f.* (mil. hist.) balister used by mounted troops. †**-chino** *m.* (mil.) light infantryman; balister used by him.

stamberga *f.* wretched little room; dog-hole; hovel; garret.

stambur·gio *m.* dark little room.

stambur-are [A 1] *intr.* (*aux.* avere) to beat the drum; to drum, to keep drumming; *tr.* to proclaim; (iron.) to laud to the skies. **-amento** *m.* beating of drums. **-ata** *f.* roll of drums, drumming; (fig.) long-winded speech. (**-ato** *part. adj.*)

stam-e *m.* (text.) fine carded wool; (fig.) thread of life; (bot.) stamen. **-aiuola** *f.* (text.) weaver's beam. **-aiuolo** *m.* (text.) wool chandler. **-enale** *m.* see staminale. **-igna** *f.*, **-ina** *f.* (text.; naut.) bunting. **-inale** *m.* (naut.) scantling; frame. **-ino·ide** *m.* (bot.) staminode.

stamp-a *f.* **1.** PRINT; printing; presswork; machining; — chiara, clear print; errore di —, misprint; a —, in print; esser sotto —, esser in corso di —, to be in the press, to be printing; mandare alle -e, send to (the) press; dare alle -e, to print, to publish; bozze, prove, di —, printer's proofs; — a rilievo, relief printing; engraving; print; negozio di -e, print-shop; *pl.* (on an envelope, etc.), printed matter. **2.** PRESS; addetto stampa, press attaché; la — periodica, the periodical press, periodicals; la — estera, the foreign press; fu invitata la —, the press (i.e. journalists, representative of the press) was invited; sezione —, press department; tribuna riservata alla —, press gallery; ritagli di —, press cuttings. **3.** (FIG.) SORT, class; uomo della vecchia —, old-fashioned type of man; type, character; gente di quella —, people of that type. **4.** MOULD, form; (sculp.) punch; (cul.) pastry-cutter, wafer-cutter, etc.; (fig.) se n'è persa la —, they don't make them like that any more. **-one** *m.* (typ.) printer's proof.

stampanino *m.* (techn.) die-cutter.

stamp-are [A 1] *tr.* to stamp, to press; to impress; to print; to publish; si -i, imprimatur, passed for printing; to imprint; stàmpati bene in mente che, get it into your head that; — un bacio, to imprint a kiss; (photog.) to print; to stamp out, to cut out; to mould; to punch; (of coins, etc.) to strike; (eng.) — a freddo, to press; — a caldo, to drop-forge, *or* to swage; — un ferro da cavallo, to stamp the nail holes in a horseshoe; (fig.) to coin, to invent, to improvise. **-a·bile** *adj.* printable, fit to be printed. **-ag·gio** *m.* (eng.) pressing, presswork; forging; swaging; striking (a coin); forming; -aggio profondo, deep drawing; (rubber indust.) polvere di -aggio, moulding powder. **-ante** *part. adj.* printing. **-atello** *m.* block capital(s); (typ.) heavy type. **-ato** *part. adj.* printed; impressed; imprinted; stamped; struck; published; parlare come un libro -ato, to talk like a book; tessuti -ati, (cotton) prints; (eng.) forged; swaged; pressed; *n.m.* (comm.) printed heading, form; (leg.) printed matter; (eng.) forging; presswork. **-atore** *m.* printer; nome dello -atore, imprint; stamper; engraver; machine-minder. **-atrice** *f.* printing-press. **-atura** *f.* printing.

stampella *f.* crutch; (mus.) hurdy-gurdy.

stamp-eri·a *f.* printing-works, printing-house. **-etta** *f.* stamping-die. **-i·glia** *f.* rubber or metal stamp; placard; board with winning lottery numbers; (printed) form; fly-leaf; (comm.) -iglia di sotto-scrizione, form of application. **-igliare** [A 4] *tr.* to stamp, to mark with a (rubber) stamp. (**-igliato** *part. adj.*) **-igliatore** *m.* stamp; numbering machine. **-igliatura** *f.* serial number; stamping, printing.

stamp-ina *f.* printer's proof; stencil-copy. **-inare** [A 1] *tr.* to stencil, to print with a stencil; to stamp. **-ino** *m.* stencil; stencil plate; stamp (for making an impression); punch (for punching holes); printer's proof. **-ista** *m.* (eng.) diesinker.

stampita *f.* (lit. hist.) Provençal song (estampida); †long, boring speech; †*pl.* complaints, reproaches.

stampo *m.* stamp; mould; (cul.) — per dolci, jelly mould; (eng.) die; drop-forging die; matrix; punch; swage; — per chiodi, rivet set; — per coniatura, minting die; nail hole in a horseshoe; (fig.) kind, sort, type, class.

stampone *m.* See under **stampa**.

stan-are [A 1] *tr.* to drive (an animal) from its den; (fig.) to dislodge, to drive out; sta sempre in casa ed è difficile -arlo, he is always indoors and it's difficult to get him to go out. **-ato** *part. adj.* driven into the open; dislodged.

stan-co *adj.* (*m.pl.* **-chi**; *prep.* di) tired; weary; fatigued; exhausted; worn out; — morto, tired out, dead tired; sick (of); bored (with); annoyed; (poet.) al giorno —, at close of day. **-camente** *adv.* wearily; exhaustedly. **-ca** *f.* (naut.) slack water; (of a river) time of year when water is low; (fig.) backwater. **-ca·bile** *adj.* easily tired. **-camento** *m.* fatigue; tiring (out). **-care** [A 2] *tr.* to tire, to fatigue, to weary; to exhaust; to bore; *rfl.* (*prep.* di, a) to get tired, to grow weary (of). **-cato** *part. adj.* tired, exhausted; worn out; bored. **-cheggiare** [A 3c] *tr.* to irritate; to bore; to annoy. **-chetto** *adj. dim.* rather tired. **-chevole** *adj.* tiring, tiresome, wearisome. **-chezza** *f.* tiredness, weariness, fatigue.

stand *m. indecl.* stand (at an exhibition, at a race-meeting, etc.).

standard *adj., n.m. indecl.* model; (techn.) standard. **-izzare** [A I] *tr.* to standardize. (**-izzato** *part. adj.*) **-izzazione** *f.* (techn.) standardizing; standardization.

†**stanforte** *m.* woollen cloth (manufactured at Stamford).

stan·ga *f.* bar, barrier; cross-bar; swing-bar; shaft; pole; lever; (of a horse-drawn vehicle) shaft, thill; (of a plough) beam; (industr.) — di ghiaccio, ice block; essere la — di mezzo, to receive knocks from both sides (as when one intervenes in a quarrel). **-gare** [A 2] *tr.* to bar; to prop, to stay with a prop; to give a blow with a bar; (fig.) to ill-treat. **-gata** *f.* blow with a bar or pole; (fig.) dare a uno una ~gata, to treat someone very badly; (vulg.) prendere una ~gata, to take a nasty knock. **-gato** *part. adj.* barred; very poor, distressed. **-ghetta** *f.* small bar; small pole; bolt of a lock; vertical line of division in writing or print; (mus.) bar-line; curved ear-piece of spectacles; occhiali a ~ghetta, spectacles, *or* lorgnette; bolt (of lock); (equit.) bit. **-gonare** [A I c] *tr.* to puddle (molten metal). (**-gonato** *part. adj.*) **-gone** *m.* heavy bar; stirring-pole (for puddling).

Stanisla·o *pr.n.m.* Stanislaus, Stanislas.

stann-ato *m.* (chem.) stannate. **-ite** *f.* (miner.) stannite, tin pyrites, bell-metal ore. **-ito** *m.* (chem.) stannite. **-oso** *adj.* (chem.) stannous.

stan·nico *adj.* (chem.) stannic.

stanotte *adv.* tonight; last night.

stante *part.* of stare, q.v.; existing; current; present; this; seduta —, instanter; poco —, soon after; *n.m.* column, prop, support; bracket, corbel; (stone) door-jamb; *prep.* in view of, considering; *conj.* — che, as, since, seeing that. †**-emente** *adv.* instantly.

stant-i·o, †**-ivo** *adj.* stale; not fresh; stuffy.

stantuff-o *m.* (eng.) piston; plunger; — a disco, flat piston; — tuffante, plunger, drowned piston; stelo di —, piston-rod. **-ata** *f.* piston-stroke.

stanz-a, †**-ia** *f.* (place of) residence; room; apartment; un appartamento di sette -e, a seven-roomed flat; (mil.) quarters; essere di — a, to be stationed at; il reggimento è di — a Milano, the regiment is stationed at Milan; †stare alle -e, to be encamped; †lunga —, long delay; — di compensazione (bankers' clearing-house); *pl.* (Tusc.) meeting-rooms, club; (paint.) Le -e del Vaticano, a suite of rooms at the Vatican painted in fresco by Raphael; (prosod.) stanza (esp. in *ottava rima*); verse; le Stanze, short title of a poem by Poliziano in honour of Giuliano dei Medici; †instance; †place; †staying, stay. **-iale** *adj.* permanent; stable; (mil.) standing; permanent, fixed; commissione -iale, standing committee. **-ialmente** *adv.* permanently. **-iamento** *m.* deliberation; decree; (of funds) setting apart, assignment, appropriation, allocation; †sojourn, stay. **-iare** [A 4] *tr.* to appropriate, to allocate, to set (funds) aside for a special purpose; to assign, to appropriate; *intr.* (aux. avere) to deliberate, to decree; (mil.) to live in married quarters. **-ia·rio** *adj.* permanent. (**-iato** *part. adj.*) (**-iatore** *m.* **-iatrice** *f.*) †**-i·bolo** *m. dim.* (Tusc., joc.) little room. **-ina** *f. dim.* nice little room. **-ino** *m.* little room; dressing-room; privy, closet; lumber-room; (theatr.) box. **-one** *m. augm.* large room; orangery, greenhouse. **-uola** *f. dim.* moderate-sized room.

stapazzina *f.* (orn.) black-eared wheatear, *Œnanthe hispanica*.

stap-ede *m.* (anat.) stapes. **-edectomi·a** *f.* (surg.) stapedectomy. **-ediano** *adj.* (anat.) stapedial. **-e·dio** *adj.* (anat.) stapedial; muscolo -edio, stapedius.

stapp-are [A I] *tr.* to uncork; *abs.* to open a bottle; to have a drink; to drink a toast; — gli orecchi a uno, to clear wax from a person's ears, (fig.) to make a person listen. (**-ato** *part. adj.*)

†**sta·pula** *f.* store; market; depot.

starda *f.* (orn.). See otarda.

stare [A 9] *intr.* (aux. essere)   **1.** STATE, CONDITION, etc.: to be; come sta?, how are you?; sta male, he is not well; il fatto sta che, the fact is that; le cose stanno così, that is how things are, how matters stand; stando così le cose, that being so; lasciare —, to let be, to leave alone; sta scritto così, this is what is written; tutto sta che conosca a fondo il mestiere, the great thing is that he should know his job thoroughly; — seduto, to be sitting down; — tranquillo, to be calm; — a dieta, to be on a diet; — comodo, to be comfortable; — solo, to be alone; — in due, to be in two minds, to be undecided; — fresco, to be in for trouble or disappointment; (S. Italy) dove sta la mia penna?, where is my pen?; (leg.) — del credere, to be 'del credere' agent.   **2.** TO REMAIN, to keep; to stay; — in casa, to stay at home; andare a — con, to go to stay with; — zitto, to keep silent;

— fermo, to keep still; dobbiamo andare o —?, ought we to go or stay?; sta' quanto ti pare, stay as long as you like; non starò che un'ora, I shall only stay, be, an hour; state lì, stay there; (cards) sto, I stay, I pass; †to last.   **3.** TO LIVE, to reside, to dwell; to be situated; dove sta di casa, Lei?, where do you live?, what is your address?; — da sè, to live on one's own; — tutto l'anno in campagna, to live in the country all the year round; andarono a — in via Roma, they went to live in the Via Roma; sta in riva a un lago, it lies on the bank of a river; sta in cima a un monte, it is situated on the top of a hill; — come un principe, to live like a prince.   **4.** TO STAND; — in piedi, to stand (on one's feet), to be standing; — di, in, guardia, to stand guard; — piantato sull'uscio, to stand in the doorway; — saldo, to stand firm, to stand fast; — dietro a, to stand over, to stand behind.   **5.** IN COMPOUND TENSES FOLLOWED BY 'DA': to have gone to see; sono stato dal dentista, I have been to the dentist; la moglie era stata dalla sarta, his wife had gone to visit her dressmaker.   **6.** TO DELAY, to wait; stette un po', poi scrisse la lettera, he waited, delayed, hesitated, for a little, then wrote the letter; starà poco a tornare, he won't be long coming back; (poet.) nè per questo stette d'andare, nor did he on this account delay his steps (cease walking).   **7.** FOLLOWED BY PREPOSITION 'A': — a quello che si è detto, to stand by what has been said; — alle parole di qualcuno, to rely on someone's promise, word; — ai patti, to stand by an agreement, to keep a bargain; — alle regole, to abide by the rules; la moglie gliene fa di tutti i colori, ma lui ci sta, his wife behaves outrageously but he puts up with it; vorremmo fargli un regalo se ci stai anche tu, we'd like to make him a present if you will join us in it; saper — allo scherzo, to know how to take a joke; — a uno, to fall to the lot of, to be the right, duty, etc. of; sta a te, it depends on you; tutto sta a (nell') arrivarci prima, it all depends on our getting there first; è una cosa che mi sta a cuore, it is a thing I care a great deal about; to suit; non ti sta (bene) il cappello, the hat doesn't suit you; ti sta a pennello, it fits you, suits you, perfectly.   **8.** FOLLOWED BY PREPOSITION 'A' AND INFINITIVE: — a vedere, to wait and see; (iron., in protest against an unreasonable claim or position) o! sta a vedere che non dovrò parlare con mio padre, I suppose I mustn't talk to my own father now; — a sentire, to wait to hear; — ad ascoltare, to listen, to pay heed.   **9.** FOLLOWED BY PREPOSITION 'PER' AND INFINITIVE: — per partire, to be on the point of going; stavo per dire, I was just about to say; questa è, sto per dire, un'infamia, this, I must say, I would even say, is a disgrace.   **10.** FOLLOWED BY OTHER PREPOSITIONS. su: — sulle generali, to keep to generalities; — sulle spese, to live away from home and so incur additional expenses; — sulle sue, to stand on one's dignity; — sulla sua, to mind what one is doing, to be careful not to commit oneself. in: non — in sè dalla gioia, to be beside oneself with joy; se stesse in me, if it depended on me; sta appunto in questo l'ingiustizia, the injustice consists precisely in this.   **11.** FOLLOWED BY 'BENE': sta bene!, all right!, very well!; ti sta bene, it serves you right; il vestito ti sta bene, the dress suits you; — bene con uno, to be on good terms with someone; — bene a denaro, to have enough money.   **12.** FOLLOWED BY GERUND: to be in the act of; stavamo parlando, we were (just) talking; il treno che sta arrivando al binario numero 2, the train now arriving at platform 2; sto leggendo il tuo libro, I am reading your book.   **13.** WITH PLEONASTIC REFLEXIVE PRONOUN AND ENCLITIC 'NE': starsene con le mani in mano, to be idle, to do nothing; starsene di mangiare, to stop eating.   **14.** †TO DO NOTHING.   **15.** *n.m.* STANDING; STAY.

†**starlo·maco** *m.* astrologer.

starn-a *f.* (orn.) partridge, *Perdrix perdrix*. **-are** [A I] *tr.* to draw, to clean out (partridge or other game bird as soon as shot). (**-ato** *part. adj.*) **-azzare** [A I] *intr.* (aux. avere) (of birds) to flutter, to flap their wings on the ground, to dust; *tr.* -azzare le ali, to flap their wings; †to squander. **-otto** *m. dim.* young partridge.

starnutare [A I] and derivs. See starnutire.

starnut-ire [D 2] *intr.* (aux. avere) to sneeze. **-i·glia** *f.* sneezing-powder. **-o** *m.* sneeze; sneezing; fare uno ~o, to give a sneeze, to sneeze; (fig.) è come fare uno ~o, it's as easy as winking.

†**staro** *m.* See staio.

staroccare [A 2] *intr.* (aux. avere) (in the game of 'tarocchi') to play the highest trumps.

starolare [A I] *tr.* (tan.) to dewarble.

stasa *f.* (eng.) plate gauge.

stasare [A I] *tr.* to unstop, to clear (ears, nose, etc.); (eng.) to clear, to free (e.g. a blocked pipe).

stasẹra *adv.* this evening; tonight.

stasi *f.* (med.) stasis; inactivity, stoppage; (finan.) standstill; gli affari hanno raggiunto un periodo di —, business has come to a standstill, *or* business is slack.

†**stasire** *intr.* to go into ecstasy.

stassẹra *adv.* (pop.). See **stasera**.

statale *adj.* See under **stato²**.

statare [A I] *intr.* (aux. avere) (pop., Tusc.) to spend the summer; *tr.* (agric.) to leave in summer fallow.

sta·ta·rio *adj.* steady; static; stable; fixed; commedia stataria, play involving little movement; (mil.) milite —, steady soldier; battaglia stataria, static battle or warfare (not fluid); (leg.) see **sommario**.

stat·e *f.* (pop., Tusc., poet.) see **estate**. †**-ereccio** *adj.* relating to summer. **-ino** *adj.* summer; frutte -ine, summer fruits; (orn.) summer visitor.

†**state·a** *f.* See **stadera**.

statere *m.* (anc. numism.) stater.

sta·tica¹ *f.* (mech.) statics.

sta·tica² *f.* (bot.) sea-lavender, *Limonium.*

sta·tic-o¹ *adj.* static; immobile; steady; casa -a, solidly built house; commedia -a, play involving little action; (scient.) static; momento —, static moment. **-amẹnte** *adv.* statically; (eng.) -amente determinato, statically determinate. **-iṣmo** *m.* static quality, immobility; (phys.) statism.

†**sta·tico²** *m.* hostage.

stati·metro *m.* (eng.) thrust meter.

stat-i·stica *f.* statistics; collection of statistics; treatise on statistics. **-i·stico** *adj.* statistical; media -istica, mean in statistics.

stativo *m.* stand (for an instrument, etc.); (photog.) tripod.

stato¹ *part.* of **stare** or **essere**, q.v.

stat-o² *m.* **1.** STATE, condition; situation; frame (of mind); plight; repair, order, fettle, trim; in buono —, in good condition, in good repair; position, posture; status; profession, occupation; mutar —, to change one's condition, i.e. to marry, *or* to change one's occupation; — libero, bachelorhood, spinsterhood; alla tua età bisogna farsi uno —, you are old enough to think of settling down; record; — di servizio, record of service; ufficiale di — civile, registrar of births, marriages and deaths; account, return, list; (phys.) state; (techn.) condition; serviceability. **2.** (LEG.) — civile, legal status; civil status; atti, registri dello — civile, records, register of births, marriages and deaths, of vital statistics (C.C.); — giuridico, status, juridical status, legal standing; — di assedio, martial law; — di bisogno, necessitous situation; — di famiglia, family status, family situation, state of family; — di graduazione, list of creditors in order of preference, order of priority; — di insolvenza, insolvency; — di necessità, state of necessity; — di pericolo, jeopardy of the person; in — di ubriachezza, under the influence of drink; possesso di —, claim of (marital or filial) status. **3.** (POL.) STATE; government; Chiesa e —, Church and State; — cuscinetto, buffer State; uomo di —, statesman; Segretario di —, Secretary of State; ragione di —, the interests of the State; funzionario di —, civil servant; gli -i Uniti, the United States; (hist.) gli -i Pontifici, the Papal States; -i Generali, States General; il terzo —, the third estate; colpo di —, *coup d'état.* **4.** (MIL.) — di guerra, state of war; — d'assedio, state of siege; — maggiore generale, General Staff; capo di — maggiore, Chief of Staff. **-ale** *adj.* (of the) State, government; impiegati -ali, civil servants, state employees; (comm.) obbligazione -ale, government bond; *n.m., f.* civil servant. **-erello** *m. dim.* small state; (hist.) gli -erelli balcanici, the little Balkan States. **-ino** *m. dim.* prospectus; synopsis; short list; (in some Italian universities) ticket to be produced by a student before an examination, being a receipt of exam. fee and a proof of his being on the list. **-ista** *m.* statesman; student of statecraft. **-iẓẓare** [A I] *tr.* to nationalize. (**-iẓẓato** *part. adj.*) **-iẓẓazione** *f.* nationalization. **-olatra** *m.* believer in State action, believer in bureaucracy. **-olatri·a** *f.* exaltation of the State, belief in bureaucracy.

statolder *m. indecl.* (hist.) Stad(t)holder (in the Netherlands). **-ato** *m.* office of Stadtholder.

statọre¹ *adj.* (Rom. myth.) Stator (title of Jupiter).

statọre² *m.* (electr.; eng.) stator.

statoreattọre *m.* (eng.) ram-jet engine; — a risonanza, resojet engine.

statosco·pio *m.* (techn.) statoscope.

sta·tu-a *f.* statue; — a bassorilievo, figure in low relief; (fig.) fare la —, parere una —, to stand like a statue (motionless or silent). **-a·rio** *adj.* statuesque; suitable for statuary; (fig.) rigidezza -aria, rigidity of a statue; *n.m.* sculptor. **-ino** *adj.* statuesque.

statu-ire [D 2] *tr., intr.* (aux. avere) to decree, to make a decree; to ordain; †to erect. **-ito** *part. adj.* patti -iti, agreements reached.

statunitense *adj.* relating to, belonging to, the United States of America; *n.m., f.* American (of the U.S.A.).

statura *f.* stature, height, size; (fig.) grandeur, eminence, stature.

statut-o *m.,* †**-a** *f.* statute; constitution; articles of association; (leg.) by-laws; — costitutivo di società, memorandum and articles of association; — di associazioni, by-laws, rules and regulations of associations; — di società, articles of association of company; (hist.) festa dello —, first Sunday in June (no longer celebrated, now replaced by 'festa della Repubblica', 2 June); 'Constitution Day'; *pl.* rules of a club, etc. **-ale** *adj.* statutory. **-a·rio** *adj.* statutory; constitutional.

staurolite *f.* (miner.) staurolite, staurotide.

staurosco·pio *m.* (phys.) stauroscope.

stàvolo *m.* (geog.) temporary shelter in the mountains.

Sta·zio *pr.n.m.* Statius.

stazio·grafo *m.* (naut., etc.) station pointer.

stazion-e *f.* station; — balneare, watering-place; — climatica, health resort; — di monta, stud farm; — ferroviaria, railway station; depot; (motor.) — di rifornimento, petrol station, filling station; (naut.) action station; — di direzione del tiro, fire control station; — di lancio, torpedo room; — di punteria generale, gun control station; — di governo, wheelhouse, tiller flat, steering position; station, post; — navale, naval station abroad delimited geographically; also the ships composing the squadron; (radio) — transmittente, broadcasting station; — di tappa, refuelling or revictualling port or base; (eccl.) 'stational' church in Rome, or visit to such; one of the Stations of the Cross; †shop. **-are** [A I c] *intr.* (aux. avere) to stand, to stay; (of vehicles) to park, to be parked; †to be stationed; (naut.) to be stationed or appointed to a colony or a foreign station. **-amẹnto** *m.* standing, staying; parking space; -amento per quattro auto pubbliche, rank for four taxis. **-a·rio** *adj.* stationary; civiltà -aria, unprogressive civilization; condizioni -arie, stable (unchanging) conditions; *n.m.* (naut.) a ship on a foreign station.

stazza *f.* (naut.) tonnage; volume in ship exclusive of machinery and crew space; tonnellata di —, ton equal to 100 cubic feet; — lorda, gross tonnage; — netta, net tonnage; — di registro, register tonnage; certificato di —, tonnage certificate (canal dues, etc.).

stazz-are [A I] *tr.* to measure, to gauge; (naut.)— la nave, to measure or calculate the ship's tonnage. (NOTE: net tonnage is obtained by deducting engine and crew space as well as certain deckhouse volume from the gross tonnage.) **-amẹnto** *m.* measuring. (**-ato** *part. adj.*) **-atọre** *m.* gauger; (naut.) perito -atore, expert measurer, Lloyd's agent. **-atura** *f.* (naut.) the whole operation of measuring and calculating tonnage.

stazz-o *m.* station, stand; post; roadstead; fold (standing) for sheep; (Sard.) house in a rural district. **-ọna** *f.* (Corsica) prehistoric monument similar to a dolmen. **-ọne** *m. augm.* large stand; shop.

†**stazzonare** *tr.* to mishandle; to maul.

ste-arato *m.* (chem.) stearate. **-a·rico** *adj.* (chem.) stearic; made of tallow; candela -arica, tallow candle. **-arina** *f.* (chem.) stearin.

steat-ite *f.* (miner.) steatite, soapstone. **-oma** *m.* (med.) steatoma, lipoma durum. **-opi·geo** *adj.* fat-rumped. **-ọsi** *f.* (med.) fatty degeneration, steatosis.

steca, ste·cade *m.* (bot.) *Lavandula stoechas.*

stẹc-ca *f.* small stick; slat; rib (of fan, umbrella, etc.); splint; paper-knife; (billiards) cue; piece of whalebone (e.g. in corsets); (sculp.) modelling tool; (motor.) dipstick; (eng.) splice bar; (rlwy.) fish-plate; (agric.) foot-rest on a spade; (mus.) fare una —, to fluff a note; (neol., comm.) package containing ten packets of American cigarettes. **-cac·cia** *f.* (billiards) miscue. †**-cadente, -cadenti** *m. indecl.* see **stuzzicadenti, stecchino.** **-ca·ia** *f.* camp-shedding; oblique wooden wall in a stream to direct water to a mill; pen for sheep. **-care** [A 2] to fence, to surround with a palisade; to rail off; to put in splints; to cut with a paper-knife;

stec·ca (*cont.*)
(cul.) to stuff with pieces of bacon; (mil.) -care il campo, to stake out a camp; (rlwy.) to fish; (mus.) to fluff (a note). **-cata** *f.* palisade, fence, stockade; wall. **-cato** *part. adj.* fenced; palisaded; *n.m.* fence; paling; palisade; (mil.) the stockade forming the perimeter of a camp; (racing) rails. **-catura** *f.* (rlwy.) fishing. **-cherino** *m.* (bot.) *Hydnum imbricatum* (edible fungus). **-chetto** *m.* small stick; (fig.) short rations; stare a -chetto, to go short, to be on short commons; tenere qualcuno a -chetto, to keep someone short of food or money. **-china** *f. dim.* of stecca. **-chino** *m. dim.* toothpick; little stick; †match. **-chire** [D2] *tr.* to kill outright; *intr.* (*aux.* essere), *rfl.* to grow thin, to dry up; to go stiff (with cold). **-chito** *part. adj.* dead; dried up, parched; extremely thin; secco -chito, as thin as a lath; morto -chito, stone dead. **-co** *m.* (*pl.* **-chi**) stick; dry twig; wooden pin, peg; thorn; toothpick; bar of a cage; (fig.) very thin person; (ent.) stick insect, *Bacillus rossii*; (sculp.) modelling tool; sottile come uno -co, thin as a lath; campare con uno -co unto, to live on next to nothing. **-coluto** *adj.* full of thorns, full of sticks; like a stick. **-cona·ia** *f.* enclosure, stockage. **-conare** [A1c] *tr.* to fence in; *rfl.* (mil.) to form close lines. **-conata** *f.* enclosure, stockade. **-conato** *part. adj.* fenced in; stockaded; *n.m.* enclosure; stockade. **-cone** *m. augm.* of stecco; large stake, paling.

stechio·metri·a *f.* (chem.) stoichiometry. **-me·trico** (chem.) stoichio-metric(al) (also **stoichio-**).

stedesc·are [A2] *tr., rfl.* to degermanize. (**-ato** *part. adj.*)

Ste·fan·o *pr.n.m.* Stephen; (fam.) stomach, belly, 'little Mary'; empirsi lo —, to fill one's belly; da Natale a Santo —, from 25 to 26 December, i.e. one day; (hist.) corona di Santo —, St Stephen's crown, i.e. the Hungarian monarchy. **-iano** *adj.* of St Stephen; ordine -iano, order of St Stephen. **-ite** *f.* (miner.) stephanite, brittle silver ore.

ste·gola *f.* plough-handle.

†stela *f.* See stele.

stele *f.* (art hist.) stele; pillar with inscriptions.

stell·a *f.* star; — del dì, the Sun; — del mattino, morning star; — polare, Pole Star; — cadente, — filante, shooting-star, falling star; (fig.) paper streamer; rowel (of a spur); asterisk; la bandiera delle -e e delle striscie, the Stars and Stripes; veder le -e, to see stars (i.e. as the result of a blow); portare alle -e, to laud to the skies; salire alle -e, to rise steeply (of prices); film star, etc.; (vet.) 'star' on a horse's forehead; (orn.) -e del pavone, eyes of a peacock's tail; (zool.) — di mare, starfish; — di sabbia, *Astropecten aurianticus*; (bot.) — delle Alpi, edelweiss, *Leontopodium alpinum*; (electr.) collegamento a —, star connexion, Y-connexion; stella-triangolo, star-delta; (naut.) fining of a vessel towards bow and stern; altezza della —, lift of the keel; (herald.) mullet; — con sei punte, mullet of six points; — radiante, mullet irradiated. **†-adi·a** *f.* nectar. **-ante** *part. adj.* shining like a star; star-spangled. **-are** [A1c] *tr., rfl.* to shine like a star; to fill with stars; to spangle; *adj.* stellar; star-shaped. **-ato** *part. adj.* starry, starred; starlit; bandiera -ata, star-spangled banner; linea -ata, line of asterisks; (bot.) stellate; (electr.) tensione -ata, Y-voltage; (naut.) bastimento -ato, ship having fine lines; ossature -ate, quinti -ati, V-shaped sections; (embroidery) punto -ato, cross-stitch; *n.m.* starry sky; starlight; (naut.) transverse section fore and aft; †space allocated to members of the crew of a small craft. **-atura** *f.* (naut.) vice or defect of timbers in construction; system and method of fining away the hull towards bow and stern during construction. **-eggiare** [A3c] *tr.* to embroider in cross-stitch; to star, to sprinkle with stars; *intr.* (*aux.* avere) to scintillate. **-eggiato** *part. adj.* dotted with stars, starry; (vet.) cavallo -eggiato (*or* cavallo -ato), horse having a star or blaze on its forehead. **-etta** *f. dim.* asterisk; small star; (mil.) distinctive of rank; star; rimetterci la -etta, to risk or to lose one's rank or seniority; *pl.* (rel.) metal tags on penitential scourge. **-ettare** [A1c] *tr.* (typ.) to insert asterisks in (e.g. to mark the beginning of a paragraph or note) as reference to a footnote, etc. **-icchi** *m.pl.*, **-icchini** *m.pl.* (Tusc., cul.) 'pasta' cut in the form of little stars, served in soup. **-i·fero** *adj.* star-bearing (of the heaven of the fixed stars). **-ificato** *adj.* crowned, encircled, with stars. **-ina** *f. dim.* asterisk; (bot.) -ina odorosa, woodruff, *Asperula odorata*. **-ino** *m.* (numism.) Tuscan silver coin issued by Duke Cosimo dei Medici; *adj.* (bot.) fieno -ino, *Setaria verticillata*. **†-o·grafo** *m.* writer on astronomy. **-oncino** *m.* (newspaper) paragraph; *pl.* (cul.) 'pasta' cut in shape

of stars. **-one** *m. augm.* big star; (fig.) lo -one d'Italia, Italy's star (of fortune); the dog-days, great heat.

stellite *f.* (metall.) stellite.

stelo *m.* (bot.) stalk, stem, bole; axis; support; (eng.) shaft; — della valvola, valve stem, valve spindle; — dello stantuffo, piston rod; web (of rail).

stemm·a *m.* (herald.) bearing; coat of arms, armorial bearings, shield; (hist.) arms of Savoy in the centre of the monarchic Italian flag. **-ato** *part. adj.* armigerous.

stemper·are [A1s], **stemprare** [A1] *tr.* to dilute; to dissolve; to mix; — la calcina, to slake lime, to mix mortar; (fig.) to water down, to conceal in verbiage; (techn.) to deprive (a metal) of temper; to distemper (with water paint); — un lapis, to blunt (wear down the point of) a pencil; †to treat harshly; *rfl.* to melt; to grow blunt; -arsi in lagrime, to burst into tears. **-amento** *m.* melting, dissolving; changing; (chem.) dilution. **-ato** *part. adj.* dissolved; melted; (of paints, etc.) mixed; caldo -ato, excessive heat; (fig.) immoderate, intemperate; dissolute; aria -ata, stuffy atmosphere, bad air; (mus.) tamburo -ato, slack drum. **-atamente** *adv.* immoderately, excessively.

stempi·are [A4] *rfl.* to go bald. **-ato** *part. adj.* going bald.

†stendale *m.* See standardo.

standard·o *m.* standard, banner; (naut.) — reale, Royal Standard; (mil.) cavalry banner, pennant; (eccl.) banner (of parish or guild); (bot.) vexillum, standard; (herald.) standard. **†-iere** *m.* standard-bearer.

stendare [A1] *intr.* (*aux.* avere) to remove an awning, sun-blind, etc.; to strike tents (camp).

sten·d·ere [C1] *tr.* to extend, to stretch; to lengthen; to spread out, to lay out; to hang out (e.g. washing); — le reti, to spread, to set, to lay, the nets; — la mano, to hold out one's hand; — la gamba, to stretch one's leg; (slang) — le gambe, to 'turn up one's toes', i.e. to die; — il passo, to lengthen the pace; — il tappeto sul pavimento, to lay the carpet; — la tovaglia, to lay the table-cloth; to smooth, to smooth out; to lay on (colour, varnish, etc.); — l'arco, to release the bowstring; (naut.) — un'àncora, to lay out an anchor (kedge); — un cavo, — una cima, — un ormeggio, to put out, to send out, to lay out a hawser; — un guardiano per poppa, to let go a stream anchor; — una lenza, to shoot a fishing-line; — un paranco, to overhaul a luff (separating the blocks); — di rebuffo, to send out a hawser on its reel and bring the ends back; — la tela (della vela), to stretch the canvas, to haul taut the sheets; †— la vela, to sheet home the sail; (text.) to tenter; (admin.) — il processo verbale, to draw up the minutes; — il verbale, to make, draw up, a report, to set out in writing; *rfl.* to stretch oneself; to spread, to extend. **-imento** *m.* stretching, spreading, laying; setting down in writing; (text.) tentering. **-itoio** *m.* (agric.) drying-room; (text.) tenter. **-itore** *m.* (paperm.) loftsman.

stenebrare [A1s] *tr.* to illuminate, to light up; (fig.) to enlighten.

sten·o *m.*, **-oalino** *m.* (biol.) stenohaline.

stenocardi·a *f.* (med.) angina pectoris.

stenodattilo·graf·o *m.*, **-a** *f.* shorthand-typist. **-i·a** *f.* shorthand-typing.

stenograf·are [A1s] *tr.* to write in shorthand, to take down (in shorthand). (**-ato** *part. adj.*)

sten·o·grafo *m.* shorthand writer, stenographer. **-ografi·a** *f.* short-hand, stenography. **-ogra·fico** *adj.* (in) shorthand. **-ograficamente** *adv.* in shorthand, stenographically.

stenosco·pio *m.* (photog.) pinhole camera.

sten·osi *f.* (med.) stenosis. **-osato** *adj.* (med.) stenosed. **-o·tico** *adj.* (med.) stenotic.

stent·are [A1, A1c] *intr.* (*aux.* avere) to be in need; to find it hard; to be hardly able; to have difficulty (in, over); sono tanti anni che -ano, they have felt the pinch for many years; — a credere, to find it hard to believe; -a a camminare, he is hardly able to walk; — in prigione, to languish in prison; *tr.* to have difficulty over; — il pane, to hardly get enough to eat; — la vita, to find difficulty in earning a living; fare — il pagamento, to keep one's creditors waiting; *rfl.* to strive, to exert oneself; to endeavour, to take a good deal of trouble. **-acchiare** [A4] *intr.* (*aux.* avere) to be shiftless; to suffer want through idleness. **-amento** *m.* hardship, privation; difficulty. **†-arolo** *m.* (naut.) stern cabin beam supporting rafters, etc. **-atezza** *f.* difficulty; straitened circumstances, poverty; stunted growth. **-atino** *adj. dim* of stentato, q.v. **-ato** *part. adj.* difficult, hard; straitened; stunted, scrubby; (of style) laboured; vita -ata, hard life, life of poverty; pane -ato,

stent-are (*cont.*)
hard-earned bread; *n.m.* difficulty, awkwardness; effort, constraint. **-atamęnte** *adv.* with difficulty; vivere -atamente, to live in straitened circumstances, to be poor. **-atura** *f.* awkwardness, constraint, laboured quality.

Stenterell-o *pr.n.m.* a 'mask' of the Florentine theatre (nineteenth century), usually a servant, thin, sly but rather stupid. **-ata** *f.* action or saying characteristic of 'Stenterello'; play in which this character appears. (**-ęsco** *adj.*)

stent-o, stęnt-o *m.* hardship; suffering; privation; difficulty; effort, toil; vivere fra gli -i, in mezzo agli -i, to live in poverty, to have a wretched existence; vita di -i, life of privation and hardship; pittura in cui si vede lo —, laboured painting; *adv. phr.* a —, hardly, with difficulty; trattenne a — le lagrime, he could hardly keep back his tears; crescere a —, to be backward in growth, to be stunted; senza —, without difficulty; *adj.* stunted. **-acchiare** [A4], **-icchiare** [A4], **-ucchiare** [A4] *intr.* (*aux.* avere) to have a struggle to make ends meet. **-ino** *adj.*, sickly, ailing; frail; also *n.m.* **-ume** *m.* laboured production; poor specimen.

stento·reo *adj.* stentorian.

stęppa *f.* (geog.) steppe.

steppage *m.* (med.) steppage, steppage gait.

ster-co *m.* (*pl.* **-chi**, †**ster·cora** *f.*) excrement, dung. **-cora·ceo** *adj.* (med.) stercoraceous. **-corale** *adj.* (med.) stercoral. **-cora·rio** *adj.* pertaining to dung, or stable-manure; (ent.) scarabeo -corario, dung beetle; *n.m.* (orn.) skua; -corario maggiore, great skua, *Catharacta skua*; -corario mezzano, Pomarine skua, *Stercorarius pomarinus*; *pl.* (eccl. hist.) Stercoranists.

stere *m.* See **stero**[1].

stereo·bate *m.* (archit.) stereobate.

stereochi·mica *f.* stereochemistry.

stere-ofoni·a *f.* stereophony. **-ofo·nico** *adj.* stereophonic. **-ografi·a** *f.* stereography. **-ogra·fico** *adj.* stereographical. (**-ograficamęnte** *adv.*) **-ogramma** *m.* (opt.) stereogram. **-oisomeri·a** *f.*, **-oisomerişmo** *m.* (chem.) stereoisomerism. **-o·metra** *m.* surveyor, quantity surveyor. **-ometri·a** *f.* (geom.) stereometry, solid geometry. **-ome·trico** *adj.* (geom.) stereometrical. (**-ometricamęnte** *adv.*) **-oscopi·a** *f.* stereoscopy. **-osco·pico** *adj.* stereoscopic. **-oscopicamęnte** *adv.* stereoscopically. **-osco·pio** *m.* stereoscope. **-otelemetrista** *m.* (naut.) rangetaker using stereoscopic rangefinder. **-otele·metro** *m.* (opt.) stereo-rangefinder. **-otipare** *tr.* (typ.) to stereotype. **-otipato** *part. adj.* stereotyped, stereotype. **-otipi·a** *f.* (typ.) stereotypy. **-otipista** *m.* (typ.) stereotyper. **-o·tipo** *m.* stereotype. **-otomi·a** *f.* (geom.) stereotomy.

sterg-a·io *m.* (agric.) windrow (of hay or other forage). **-are** [A2] *tr.* to windrow, to gather into windrows. **-ata** *f.* see stergaio.

sterigmo *m.* (bot.) sterigma.

ste·ril-e *adj.* sterile, barren, unfruitful, unproductive; useless; vain; (miner.) barren, waste; *n.m.* (miner.) waste. **-męnte** *adv.* barrenly; unfruitfully; sterilely; vainly. **-ęzza** *f.* sterility. **-ire** [D2] *intr.* (*aux.* essere), *rfl.* to become sterile, barren, unproductive; *tr.* to make barren, to exhaust the fertility of (land); (fig.) to exhaust the creative faculty (of the mind). **-ità** *f.* barrenness, sterility; scantiness, poorness (of harvest, crops); -ità d'ingegno, lack of creative (intellectual) power. **-ito** *part. adj.* exhausted, unfruitful, barren.

sterilizz-are [A1] *tr.* to make barren, unproductive; to sterilize. **-ante** *part. adj.* sterilizing, disinfectant. **-ato** *part. adj.* sterilized, sterile. **-atóre** *m.*, **-atrice** *f.* sterilizer. **-azióne** *f.* sterilization.

sterlęto *m.* (ichth.) sterlet, *Acipenser ruthenus*.

sterlina *f.* (finan.) pound (sterling); due sterline, £2; (Libya) Libyan pound.

sterline-are [A6] *tr.* (typ.) to remove leads from (a page of type). (**-ato** *part. adj.*) **-atura** *f.* (typ.) removal of leads.

stermin-are [A1s] *tr.* to ravage, to destroy; to demolish; to exterminate; to root out; to extirpate. **-a·bile** *adj.* exterminable; interminable. **-amęnto** *m.* extermination; (Bibl.) -amento dei primogeniti, slaying of the firstborn of Egypt. **-ato** *part. adj.* exterminated, destroyed; boundless; endless, limitless; immense. **-atamęnte** *adv.* boundlessly; endlessly; limitlessly; immensely, enormously. **-atęzza** *f.* boundlessness; immensity. **-atóre** *m.* destroyer; exterminator; *adj.* destroying, destructive. (**-atrice** *f.*) **-azióne** *f.* destruction; extermination.

stermi·nio *m.* extermination, massacre; destruction; enormous quantity, endless stream.

sterna *f.* (orn.) tern; — codalunga, Arctic tern, *Sterna macrura*; — comune, common tern, *S. hirundo*; — del Dougall, — del Macdougall, roseate tern, *S. dougallii*; — maggiore, Caspian tern, *Hydroprogne caspia*; — zampenere, gull-billed tern, *Gelochelidon nilotica*.

stern-algi·a *f.* (med.) sternalgia. **-al·gico** *adj.* (med.) sternalgic.

†**ster·n-ere**, †**-ire** *tr.* to distend, to stretch out; to level; to explain; to bed down.

stern-o *m.* (anat.) sternum, breastbone. **-ale** *adj.* sternal. **-o·pago** *m.* (med.) sternodymus.

sternuto *m.* See **starnuto**, under **starnutire**.

stero[1] *m.* cubic metre.

†**stero**[2] *m.* lodging.

ster-o·ide *adj.* (chem.) steroid. **-olo** *m.* (chem.) sterol. **-óne** *m.* (chem.) sterone.

sterp-o *m.* (†-e *f.*) shoot from an old stump or from roots left in the ground; stump; thorn-bush; dry twig; terreno pieno di -i, land overgrown with brushwood. **-a·glia** *f.* brushwood, undergrowth. **-a·gnola** *f.* (orn.) Dartford warbler. **-a·gnolo** *m.* thicket, tangle of weeds. **-a·io** *m.* thicket, brake. **-ame** *m.* heap of brushwood. **-amento** *m.* rooting out, weeding, clearing ground. **-are** [A1] and derivs. (pop.) see estirpare. **-arola** *f.* (orn.) see sterpazzola. **-ata** *f.* cutting, clearing (of brushwood). **-azzola** *f.* (orn.) whitethroat, *Sylvia communis*; -azzola di Sardegna, spectacled warbler, *S. conspicillata*. **-azzolina** *f.* (orn.) subalpine warbler, *S. cantillans*. (**-ato** *part. adj.*) **-ęto** *m.* thicket, thorn-brake. **-ic·cio** *m.* see sterpaglia. **-igno** *adj.* like a stump or offshoot; overgrown with brushwood; full of stumps and weeds. **-olino** *m.* young shoot. **-óne** *m.* nasty stump; bastard. **-óso** *adj.* overgrown with brushwood; full of stumps.

sterquili·n(i)o *m.* manure-heap, dung-heap; cesspool.

sterr-are [A1] *tr.*, *abs.* to dig out, to dig trenches for foundations; to excavate; to level down. **-amento** *m.* digging; excavation. **-ato** *part. adj.* dug out; levelled; excavated; (of a road) unmetalled; *n.m.* place where earth has been dug out; unmetalled road, dust road. **-atóre** *m.* digger, navvy. **-atura** *f.* (foundry) knock-out.

sterro *m.* muck-shifting; (bldg.) digging (up or out); excavation; earth dug out, spoil; ditch; hole (dug in the ground); strada a —, unmetalled road; materiale di —, excavated material, spoil.

stertor-e *m.* (med.) stertor. **-óso** *adj.* stertorous. (**-osamęnte** *adv.*)

sterz-are[1] [A1] *tr.* to divide into three parts; to divide proportionately; — un bosco, to thin out a wood; (paint.) to tone down (colours); — tabacchi, to blend tobaccos; *rfl.* to take turns at work, to work in shifts; to share out one's work or income. (**-amento** *m.* **-ato** *part. adj.*)

sterz-are[2] [A1] *intr.* (*aux.* avere) to swerve; *tr.* (motor.) to steer. **-ata** *f.* (motor.) massimo angolo di -ata, steering lock. (**-ato** *part. adj.* **-atura** *f.*)

sterzo *m.* (eng.) steering; (motor.) steering-wheel; meccanismo di —, steering-gear; — reversibile, steering with castor action; tutto —!, full lock!; (rlwy.) steering-truck; — girevole, flexible axle; gig; *adv. phr.* di sotto —, secretly, indirectly.

stęsa *f.* spread; display; — di merci, display of goods; spreading, smear(ing); una — di vernice, a coat of varnish.

stęs-o *part.* of **stendere**, *q.v.*; *adj.* stretched out; extended; spread; smeared; written down, drawn up (in writing); expanded, 'up' (of a folding hood); (naut.) vento —, steady wind; *n.m.* (Tusc.) net-drying ground; (Taranto) -i di macchie, bundles of twigs used on the oyster beds. **-amęnte** *adv.* at length, in detail; diffusely. **-are** [A1c] *tr.* (naut.) to ease (a rope); to walk back; to slacken. (**-ato** *part. adj.*)

stes·sere [B1] *tr.* to unweave; to unravel.

stęss-o *adj.* same; very; la -a mattina, the same morning; la mattina -a, that very (same) morning; oggi —, this very day; con uno — treno, by (one and) the same train; io —, I myself; lui —, he himself; lei -a, she herself; noi -i, we ourselves; è la gentilezza -a, *or* la -a gentilezza, he is kindness itself; lo — Manzoni, Manzoni himself, even Manzoni; *n.m.* the same (thing); per me fa lo —, it's all the same to me; *f.pl.* the same things; essere sempre alle -e, to be always up to the same old tricks; *adv. phr.* lo —, notwithstanding; andremo lo —, we shall go all the same (cf. **medesimo**).

stesura *f.* drawing up, drafting; version; draft.

steto-scopi·a *f.* (med.) stethoscopy; auscultation. **-sco·pico** *adj.* stethoscopic. **-sco·pio** *m.* (med.) stethoscope.

Stettino *pr.n.m.* (geog.) Szczecin (Stettin).

sti·a[1] *f.* hen-coop; fattening pen for poultry; hutch.

sti·a[2] *1st, 2nd, 3rd pers. pres. subj.* of **stare**, q.v.; *imp.* — seduto, don't get up, don't bother to get up.

†**stiac·ci·a** *f.*, **-are** [A4]. See **schiacci-a**, **-are**.

stiaccino *m.* (orn.) whinchat, *Saxicola rubetra*.

†**stiaffare** *vb.* and derivs. See **schiaffare**.

stian·ci·a *f.* (bot.) reedmace, bulrush, *Typha.* **-a·io** *m.* worker who puts straw casing on wine bottles. **-are** [A4] *tr.* to put straw casing on (wine bottles). (**-ato** *part. adj.*)

sti·ano *3rd pers. pl. pres. subj.* of **stare**, q.v.

sti·b·ico *adj.* antimonic. **-iato** *adj.* containing antimony. **-ina** *f.* (miner.) stibnite, antimony glance.

sti·bi·o *m.* (chem.) antimony. **-ato** *adj.* antimonial, containing antimony; tartaro -ato, tartar emetic.

sticcare [A2] *intr.* (aux. avere) to luff; — a raso, to sail close hauled; non —!, no higher!

stiepid-ire [D2] *tr.* to warm; to take the chill off. (**-ito** *part. adj.*)

†**stific-are** *tr.* to signify. †**-anza** *f.* significance.

stigadosso *m.* (bot.) See **steca**.

Stige *pr.n.m.* ((geog.; myth.) Styx.

sti·gio *adj.* Stygian.

stigliare [A4] *tr.* (text.) to scutch, to swingle (flax, etc.).

stigm-a *m.* (pl. **-ate** *f.*) stigma; stamp, brand; mark; (scient.) stigma; †*pl.* **-e** *f.* (rel.) stigmata. (Cf. **stimmate**.) **-a·tico** *adj.* (opt.; photog.) stigmatic. **-atismo** *m.* (opt.; photog.) stigmatism. **-atiẓẓare** [A1] *tr.* to stigmatize. (**-atiẓẓato** *part. adj.*)

stignare [A5] *tr.* to cure of ringworm, etc; also *rfl.*

stilb *m. indecl.* (phys.; opt.) stilb.

stil-e[1] *m.* writing-style, stylus; engraving tool; (for sound recordings) stylus; beam (of a balance); (surg.) probe, stylet; (mil.) spike used for putting a gun out of action; dagger; (agric.) handle of a scythe, spade, etc.; pole round which a hay- or straw-stack is built; (archit.) pit-prop, timber used in building. **-etta** *f.* stab, wound. **-ettare** [A1c] *tr.* to stab, to wound with stiletto, dagger or knife. **-ettato** *part. adj.* stabbed with stiletto; spada -ettata, pointed sword for piercing. **-ẹtto** *m.* small dagger, stiletto; *pl.* (bot.) water soldier, *Stratiotes aloides.* **-ifọrme** *adj.* styliform, needle-like.

stil-e[2] *m.* style; (calendar) style of reckoning; (sport) form, style; — libero, free style (swimming); in grande —, in grand style, on a large scale, in the grand manner; clausola di —, standard clause. **-are** [A1] *tr.* to draw up; to pen; to word; (comm.) to charge; (leg.) -are un contratto, to draft a contract; -are un tratto, to draw a bill. (**-ato** *part. adj.*) **-ista** *m.* stylist. **-i·stica** *f.* rhetoric; stylistic(s); treatise on literary style. **-i·stico** *adj.* stylistic; rhetorical. **-iẓẓare** [A1] *tr.* to stylize. **-iẓẓato** *part. adj.* stylized; showy; formal. **-ogra·fico** *adj.* stylographic(al); inchiostro -ografico, fountain-pen ink; una penna -ografica, *or* una -ografica, a fountain-pen.

still-a *f.* drop; a — a —, drop by drop; just a spot, a little taste, very small quantity. **-amẹnto** *m.* dripping, dropping; oozing. **-are** [A1] *tr.* to drip, to ooze, to exude; to distil; (chem.) see **distillare**; to instil, to infuse; (fig.) -are negli orecchi a, to suggest to; *intr.* (aux. avere) to drizzle, to spot with rain, to drip; *rfl.* -arsi il cervello, to rack one's brains. **-ato** *part. adj.* oozed, exuded; drawn up (in writing); dictated, suggested, 'inspired'. **-atọio** *m.* dropper, dripper. (**-atọre** *m.* **-atrice** *f.*) (**-aẓiọne** *f.*) **-ici·dio** *m.* dripping, leak(ing), e.g. from a roof (also fig., of any gradual process); (archit.) drain to catch rainwater from a roof, gutter; (leg.) dropping of rainwater from eaves of house; stillicidium; (med.) stillicidium; drip. **-ino** *m.* small saver, one who saves trifling sums. **-o** *m.* (chem.) still; (Tusc.) dodge; clever ruse; campar di -i, to live on one's wits; (cards) the ace, two or three of any suit.

stilo[1] *m.* (for sound recordings) stylus (see also **stile**[1]).

stil-o[2] *m.* (archit.) rustic column, term, terminus; shaft (of a column); (bot.) style. **-ata** *f.* (archit.) colonnade, esp. supporting a bridge. **-ita**, **-ite** *m.* (*pl.* -iti) (eccl.) stylite, pillar-saint; S. Simone -ita, St Simeon Stylites. **-o·bate** *m.* (archit.) stylobate.

stilogra·fica *f.* See under **stile**[2].

stilo·ide *adj.* (anat.) styloid.

stilopo·dio *m.* (bot.) stylopodium.

stima *f.* See under **stimare**.

stim-are [A1] *tr.* to value; to reckon; to esteem, to appreciate; to judge, to consider, to think, to deem; to estimate, to appraise;
— a occhio e croce, to make a rough estimate of; — al di sopra del valore reale, to overestimate; (leg.; comm.) to appraise; to estimate; to value; — i danni, to assess the damage; non — un fico, to consider worthless, not to give a fig for; (naut.) to estimate a ship's position; *rfl.* to esteem oneself; to consider oneself, to think oneself; si -a molto, he has a very good opinion of himself. **-a** *f.*, †**-o** *m.* esteem; estimation; respect, consideration, valuation; (leg.) appraisal; estimate; valuation; (naut.) punto di -a, estimated position; errore della -a, difference between estimated and observed position; (agric.) -e vive, estimated value of livestock; -e morte, estimated value of implements, tools, hay, straw, fertilizers, etc.; successo di -a, *succès d'estime*; †*adv. phr.* senza -a, extraordinarily. **-a·bile** *adj.* estimable, respectable; esteemed. (**-abilità** *f.*) **-amẹnto** *m.* valuation; appreciation, esteem. **-ativa** *f.* judgement, critical faculty. (**-ativo** *adj.*) **-ato** *part. adj.* esteemed, valued; estimated; (leg.) appraised; assessed; valued; (naut.; radar) punto -ato, posizione -ata, dead reckoning; (naut.) cammino -ato, estimated run. **-atis·simo** *adj. superl.* (in letters) esteemed. **-atọre** *m.* valuer; appraiser; admirer. (**-atrice** *f.*) (**-aẓiọne** *f.* esteem; estimation; valuation.

stimma *m.* (bot.). See **stigma**.

stim·mat-e *f.pl.* (rel.) the Five Wounds of Christ; the stigmata of certain saints; brand (on a convict); scar; (med.) stigmata; le — del vaiuolo, pockmarks. **-iẓẓare** [A1] and derivs. see **stigmatiẓẓare**, under **stigma**.

†**stimo** *m.* See **stima**.

stimol-are [A1s] *tr.* to goad, to urge on; to stimulate; to incite; to whet; to excite, to encourage; to drive; — l'appetito, to whet one's appetite; (med.) to stimulate. **-ante** *part. adj.* stimulating; *n.m.* (med.) stimulant. **-ativo** *adj.* stimulating; *n.m.* stimulant. **-ato** *part. adj.* stimulated; goaded; excited; incited. **-atọre** *m. adj.* stimulating. (**-atrice** *f.*) **-ato·rio** *adj.* stimulating. **-aẓiọne** *f.* stimulation; incitement. **-ọso** *adj.* pricking, stinging; troublesome.

sti·molo *m.* goad; spur; stimulus, incentive; incitement, encouragement; annoyance; (med.) stimulus.

stinare [A1] *tr.* to draw from a vat, tub, etc.

Stin-che *pr.n.f.pl.* (hist.) name of an old prison in Florence, for debtors and life prisoners. **-cai(u)olo** *m.* prisoner in the 'Stinche'.

stin-co *m.* (*pl.* **-chi**) (anat.) shin-bone, tibia; (butcher.) polpa di —, shin of beef; (slang) allungare gli -chi, to 'turn up one's toes', i.e. to die; non è uno — di santo, he is far from being a saint, *or* he's no gentleman; (vet.) cannon bone; (cul.) — di morto, a sweetmeat made with almonds. **-cata** *f.* blow on the shin; (fig.) rebuke, 'bad mark'. **-catura** *f.* bruise on the shin.

stin·gere [C5] *tr.* to fade, to discolour; (fig.) to obscure, to deface; *intr.* (aux. essere) *rfl.* to fade, to lose colour; (fig.) to change character; (industr.) to crock, to have the colour rubbed off.

stinto[1] *part.* of **stingere**, q.v.; *adj.* faded.

†**stinto**[2] *m.* See **istinto**.

†**sti·o** *adj.* see **estivo**; (agric.) lino —, summer flax, sown in March.

stip-a[1] *f.* brushwood, firewood; stubble; (bot.) — delle fate, esparto grass, *Stipa pennata*; †hedge. **-are** [A1] *tr.* to clear of undergrowth. (**-ato** *part. adj.* **-atọre** *m.* **-atrice** *f.*)

stip-a[2] *f.* heap; crowd, throng. **-are** [A1] *tr.* to crowd, to pack closely; to heap up; li -arono in cortile, they crowded them into the courtyard. **-ato** *part. adj.* crowded, pressed together; eravamo così -ati che non si poteva respirare, we were so crowded we couldn't breathe.

stipen·di·o *m.* salary; pay; (mil.; naut., etc.) essere agli stipendi, to be on the pay-roll; beccarsi lo —, not to earn one's pay. **-are** [A4] *tr.* to pay a salary to; to engage, to employ, to hire, to take on. **-ato** *part. adj.* salaried, stipendiary; taken on, engaged; *n.m.* employee; clerk; stipendiary; (leg.) magistrato -ato, stipendiary magistrate.

stip-ẹto *m.* ground overgrown with brushwood. **-ino** *adj.* overgrown with heather.

sti·pit-e, †**-o** *m.* post; upright of a cross; shaft (of a column); (bot.) stem (of palms), phylum; (bldg.) pier, jamb; doorpost; (fig.; family) stock; (leg.) common ancestor (C.C.).

stip-o *m.* cabinet; chiffonier. **-etta·io** *m.* cabinet-maker. **-ẹtto** *m. dim.* small cabinet; casket; jewel-case; (naut.) locker, rack, chest; -etto per le bandiere, flaglocker; -etto dei ranci, mess rack.

sti·pola *f.* (bot.) stipule.

stipsi *f.* (med.) constipation, stypsis.

stipul-are [A I s] *tr.* to stipulate; to lay down; to draw up, to arrange; to settle, to agree; (leg.) — un contratto, to draw up, enter into, a contract in legal form. **-ante** *part. adj.* stipulating; *n.m.* (leg.) obligee; party in whose favour provision of contract is made (C.C.). (**-ato** *part. adj.*) **-azione** *f.* stipulation, agreement, arrangement; (leg.) act of drawing up contract; contract so made; contractual provision.

stira *f.* (tan.) breaking iron; fleshing knife, scudding knife.

stiracchi-are [A 4] *tr.* to stretch, to pull, to tug; (fig.) to distort, to twist, to force, to wrench; — il prezzo, to haggle; *abs.* to haggle, to bargain, to quibble; — la vita, to rub along somehow, to manage to live. **-a·bile** *adj.* stretchable; liable to distortion. **-amento** *m.* pulling, tugging; (fig.) cavilling, haggling. **-atezza** *f.* sophistry; quibbling. **-ato** *part. adj.* forced, distorted. **-atamente** *adv.* with distortion, forcing (of meaning), sophistically; with haggling. **-atura** *f.* forced interpretation; cut price (forced down by haggling). (**-eri·a** *f.*)

stir-are [A I] *tr.* to stretch (out); to iron; to press; ferro da, per, —, smoothing iron, flat-iron; (naut.) to stretch; — un cavo, to stretch a hawser; (techn.) to stretch; (text.) to draw (in carding); *rfl.* to stretch (oneself). **-acalzoni** *m. indecl.* trouser-press. **-amento** *m.* pulling, stretching, drawing; contraction; (med.) traction; (text.) drawing; draft (of carding machine); (techn.) stretch; (metall.) limite di -amento, yield point. **-ato** *part. adj.* ironed, pressed; stretched; spesato, imbiancato e -ato, boarded and lodged, washed and ironed, i.e. 'all found'; (metall.) lamiera -ata, expanded metal. **-atoio** *m.* ironing-blanket; ironing-board; (text.) drawing frame; gill box. **-atora**, **-atrice** *f.* laundress; ironer. (**-atore** *m.*) **-atori·a** *f.* laundry. **-atura** *f.* ironing, pressing, stretching; (text.) drawing (in carding). **-eri·a** *f.* laundry; cleaners. **-izzire** [D 2] *rfl.* to stretch (to relieve stiffness, numbness); (fam.) to loosen up. **-o** *m.* ironing; pronto per lo -o, ready for ironing; (text.) draft, draught; (naut.) initial stretching (of a new hawser).

stir-ene *m.*, **-olo** *m.* (chem.) styrene.

Sti·ria *pr.n.f.* (geog.) Styria.

†**stirice** *m.*, †**stirce** *m.*, †**stiric·chio** *m.* (naut.) forecastle or stemcabin lobby, cable locker.

stirizzire [D 2]. See under **stirare**.

stirolo *m.* See under **stirene**.

stirp-e *f.* race, stock; extraction, birth; offspring, issue; descent; di nobile —, of noble birth; (leg.) stirps; per -i, *per stirpes* (C.C.); delitto contro la sanità della —, crime against the health of race (C.P.). †**-eto** *m.* see **sterpeto**.

sti·ti·co *adj.* styptic; constipated; astringent; (fig.) sour-tempered, surly; strict, stern; miserly, stingy; mean. **-camente** *adv.* strictly; costively. **-cag·gine** *f.* pedantry; meanness. †**-care** *tr.* to make constipated. **-chezza** *f.* (med.) constipation.

stiva¹ *f.* (agric.) plough-handle.

stiv-a² *f.* (naut.) hold, space between the ship's inner bottom and the lowest deck; hold, one of many cargo spaces; — del vino, wine store (spirit room); capo —, captain of the hold; correnti di —, longitudinal stringers (supporting beam); fondo di —, bottom of the hold; aggiustare la —, to trim the cargo; appoppare, approrare la —, to trim by the stern or by the bows; dare a —, †to punish (a sailor) by ducking him repeatedly as in keelhauling; essere in —, to be well trimmed; levare la —, †to lose trim due to shift of cargo; mettere in —, †to trim; trovar la —, †to achieve a good trim; mezza —, half-deck; rompere la —, to break bulk, to open a hold and start discharging; sistemare la —, to trim, to load correctly; rovistare la —, to search, to rifle the hold. **-ag·gio** *m.* (naut.) stowage; cargo disposition, loading plan; time a cargo remains in the hold; buono -aggio, correct loading; cattivo -aggio, faulty loading; legni di -aggio, dunnage placed between casks. **-atore** *m.* stevedore.

stival-e *m.* boot, riding-boot; ungere, lustrare gli -i ad uno, to lick someone's boots; -i alla scudiera, top-boots, Wellington boots; mezzo —, ankle-boot, half-boot; (joc.) Italy; per tutto lo —, all over Italy; (vulg.) dottore dei miei -i!, doctor my foot!; (mil.) shin guard; (derog.) fool. **-a·io** *m.* bootmaker. **-ata** *f.* kick (with a boot), booting. **-ato** *part. adj.* booted, wearing boots; il gatto -ato, Puss-in-Boots; booted, kicked with boots. **-eri·a** *f.* boot factory. **-etto** *m. dim.* bootee; ankle-boot; half-boot; skating-boot; (theatr.) buskin; (vet.) 'brushing boot'. **-one** *m. augm.* top-boot, jack-boot; fishing-boot. **-otto** *m. dim.* ankle-boot; half-boot.

stiv-are [A I] *tr.* to stow (away); to cram, to pack; to heap up; — alla rinfusa, to stow in bulk; (foundry) to ram; (naut.) to strike down, to load; — alla rinfusa, to load in bulk (grain, coal, etc.); — in verde, to load a moist cargo, *or* to load into a damp hold; — zavorra, to take in ballast. **-amento** *m.* packing, cramming; heaping up. **-ato** *part. adj.* stowed away; packed, crammed; -ati come acciughe, packed like sardines. **-atore**, **-adore** *m.* stevedore; trimmer. **-atrice** *f.* (foundry) moulding machine.

†**stiviere** *m.* boot (cf. **stivale**).

stizz-a¹ *f.* anger; vexation; irritation; ill-humour; quando gli monta la —, non bada più a quel che dice, when he gets angry he does not mind what he says; (vet.) mange (of dogs). **-erella** *f. dim.* irritation, slight vexation. **-ire** [D 2] *intr.* (*aux.* essere), *rfl.* to get angry; to fly into a passion; non -irti, don't be cross; *tr.* to make angry, to vex. **-ito** *part. adj.* angry, cross, vexed. **-osac·cio** *adj.* very irritable; choleric; spiteful. **-oso** *adj.* irascible, irritable; petulant; spiteful; (-oso) (vet.) mangy. (**-osamente** *adv.*)

stizz-a² *f.* candle-snuff. †**-are** [A I] *tr.* to snuff (candles).

sto¹ *adj.*, *prn.* (colloq.). See **questo**.

sto² *1st pers. sing. pres. indic.* of **stare**, q.v.

Stoa *pr.n.f.* (Gk. antiq., philos.) Stoa; the porch in Athens where Zeno taught; the teaching of Zeno; Stoicism.

stoccafisso *m.* dried cod, stockfish; (fig.) thin, gaunt person.

Stoccarda *pr.n.f.* (geog.) Stuttgart.

stoc-co¹ *m.* (*pl.* **-chi**) dagger; rapier; swordstick; bastone a —, swordstick; (naut.) dirk; — corto, dagger; (eccl. hist.) sword blessed by the Pope; †uomo di —, stout fellow, resolute man. **-cata** *f.* stab, dagger-thrust; rapier thrust; (fig.) sudden demand for money, request for a loan; tirare una -cata a uno, to touch someone for some cash. **-catore** *m.* one who asks for loans. **-cheggiare** [A 3 c] *tr.* to wound with the dagger; *intr.* (*aux.* avere) to use a dagger; (fig.) to be on one's guard.

stoc-co² *m.* (*pl.* **-chi**) (agric.) pole of a strawstack; stalk of maize; fare lo —, (of maize) to form the cob.

Stoccolma *pr.n.f.* (geog.) Stockholm.

stock-vaccino *m.* (med.) stock-vaccine.

stoff-a *f.* cloth, material; (of silk, wool, etc.) stuff; (fig.) character, nature, quality; in quello ragazza c'è —, there's good stuff in that girl; c'è in quel mascalzone la — di un galantuomo, that rascal has the makings of a decent chap. †**-o** *m.* material; matter; quality, value.

†**stogare** *rfl.* to remove one's toga.

†**stog·gio** *m.* flattery; unctuous behaviour.

†**sto·ia** *f.* See **stuoia**.

stoi-are [A 4] *tr.* to cover with (rush) mats. **-ata** *f.* (archit.) ceiling having matting, reeds or canes covered with plaster.

stoichio-metri·a *f.* (chem.) stoichiometry. (**-me·trico** *adj.* (chem.) stoichiometrical (also **stechio-**).

sto·ic-o *n.m.* Stoic; *adj.* stoical. **-amente** *adv.* stoically. **-ismo** *m.* Stoicism; stoicism.

stoino *m. dim.* of **stuoia**, q.v.; small mat; sun-blind.

stoke *m. indecl.* (pron. as Ital.) (phys.) stoke.

stola *f.* (Rom. antiq.) *stola*, lady's long tunic: (liturg.) stole; (eccl.) diritti di —, incerti di —, stole fees; robe, dress; — dell'innocenza, robe of innocence; aver la — sui piedi, to be at death's door; (fur) stole.

stol-co *m.* (*pl.* **-chi**) (orn.) blackcock.

sto·lid-o *adj.* dull, stupid; risata -a, stupid laughter; stolid; *n.m.* stupid person; vecchio —, silly old fool. (**-amente** *adv.*) **-ag·gine** *f.* stupid behaviour; stolid action or utterance. **-ezza** *f.*, **-ità** *f.* stupidity; stolidity.

stollo *m.* (agric.) pole of a straw- (*or* hay-) stack; stare come uno —, to be rooted to the spot; lungo come uno —, lanky.

stolone *m.* (liturg.) vertical orphrey on cope; (bot.) stolon.

stolt-o *adj.* foolish, silly; stupid; *n.m.* fool. **-amente** *adv.* foolishly; stupidly. **-ezza** *f.* foolishness, silliness; folly; stupidity; è -ezza credere questo, it is silly to believe that. **-ilo·quio** *m.* silly talk. **-i·zia** *f.* foolishness; act of stupidity.

stoma *m.* stoma.

stoma·chico *adj.* stomachic.

sto·ma-co *m.* (*pl.* **-chi**) (anat.) stomach; un'arcata di —, sforzi di —, retching, vomiting; a — vuoto, on an empty stomach; avere uno — debole, to have a weak stomach, to have a delicate digestion; avere uno — di ferro, to have a cast-iron stomach, to be able to

stoma·co (*cont.*)

eat anything; dare di —, to be sick; dare allo — a, to sicken, to nauseate; rimanere nello —, to lie heavy on the stomach; (fig.) quella tua cattiva azione m'è rimasta nello —, your bad behaviour sticks in my gullet; (cul.) tripe; (fig.) cheek, impudence; courage, strength; willingness; contro —, against the grain, unwillingly. **-cac·cio** *m.* upset stomach. **-cag·gine** *f.* stomach upset, disturbance; nausea. **-cale** *adj.* good for the stomach, digestible; (anat.) gastric, stomachic; digestione -cale, gastric digestion. **-care** [A2s] *tr.* to upset the stomach of; to sicken; to disgust; *intr.* (*aux.* avere; *prep.* a) to upset the stomach; to sicken, to cause vomiting; to arouse disgust; *rfl.* (*prep.* di) to be sickened, disgusted (by); to become sick (of). **-cato** *part. adj.* sickened, nauseated, disgusted; †satiated. **-cazione** *f.* disgust; nausea. **-chevole** *adj.* disgusting, loathsome, revolting. (**-chevolmente** *adv.*) **-chino** *m. dim.* weak stomach; †stomacher. **-coso** *adj.* disgusting, nauseating. **-cuc·cio** *m.* (person with a) delicate stomach. **-cuzzo** *m. dim.* (derog.) delicate stomach; aver gli -cuzzi, to have indigestion.

stoma·tica *f.* (usu. *pl.*) (bot.) guard cell.

stoma·tico *adj., n.m.* stomachic, tonic.

stomat-ite *f.* (med.; vet.) stomatitis. **-opla·stica** *f.* (surg.) stomatoplasty. **-ologi·a** *f.* (med.) stomatology. **-osco·pio** *m.* (med.) stomatoscope.

stomos·side *f.* (ent.) *Stomoxys calcitrans*, a biting fly.

stonac-are[1] [A2s] *tr.* to remove plaster from (walls, etc.). **-ato** *part. adj.* stripped of plaster (cf. **intonaco**).

stonacare[2] [A2s] *tr.* (joc.) to unfrock (cf. **tonaca**).

ston-are [A1] *intr.* (*aux.* avere) (mus.) to sing (or play) out of tune; (of colours) to clash; to disagree, to be out of place, to be out of harmony; *tr.* to disconcert, to disturb. **-amento** *m.* (mus.) false intonation. **-ato** *part. adj.* out of tune; false (note); out of place; disconcerted, bewildered; (mus.) out of tune; è -ato, he can't sing (or play) in tune. **-atura** *f.* (mus.) false intonation; lack of harmony, of agreement; incongruity. **-azione** *f.* (mus.) singing (or playing) out of tune. **-i·o** *m.* (mus.) false intonation.

stop *m. indecl.* (naut.) stop; (used when taking astronomical observations or when lining up guns, or timing a ship's speed); dare uno —, prendere uno —, to take the time or give the instant of an observation; (teleg.) stop; (road-sign) Halt! major road ahead; (fam.) red tail-light of a car.

stopp-a *f.* (text.) tow; — da calafato, oakum; (fig.) questa carne è —, this meat is very tough (like leather); uomo di —, man of no account, 'man of straw'; far la barba di — a uno, to play a trick on someone; (pop.) bout of drunkenness. **-abuchi** *m. indecl.* wad (of tow, etc.); (fig.) stop-gap. **-ac·cio** *m.* wad, wadding; (mil.) wad, pull-through. **-a·glio** *m.* quantity of wads or wadding. **-a·gnolo** *adj.* tow-like. **-aiuolo** *m.* (mil.) wad-maker, employee in an arsenal. **-are** [A1] *tr.* to plug, to stop up with tow; *intr.* (*aux.* avere) to stop; *rfl.* (fam.) to get drunk. **-ato** *part. adj.* plugged, stopped up; (neol.) stopped; (fig.) drunk, tight; (mus.) stopped. **-atore** *m.* caulker. **-eggiare** [A3c] *tr.* to rub or polish with oakum. **-ettina** *f.* finely-combed tow. **-inare** [A1] *tr.* to fire with a fuse, to light with match, taper, etc.; (mil.) to fuse, to insert a slow match in; -inare usci, finestre, to plug doors, windows (to stop draughts). **-inato** *part. adj.* fired; candelotto -inato, lighted candle. **-iniera** *f.* portable metal lighter; holder for a taper. **-ino** *m.* wick; wax taper; (agric.) sulphur candle for fumigating casks; (text.) slubbing, roving; (mil.) wick, fuse. **-oso** *adj.* (of meat) tough, stringy; lacking juice; (bot.) covered with tuffed hairs or filaments, stupeous, stupose, stuppeous.

stop·pi-a *f.* (agric.) stubble; stubble field; mettere — in aia, to carry coals to Newcastle; esser la grandine sulla —, to produce much noise with little damage; stumps, etc. remaining in a wood when trees are cut down. **-onac·cio** *m. pejor.* thistles, rank weeds. **-one** *m.* (bot.) field thistle, *Cirsium arvense*, and teasel, *Dipsacus fullonum*.

stopp-one, -oso *adj.* See under **stoppa**.

storace *m., f.* (chem.; pharm.) styrax, oriental sweet gum; — liquida, liquid amber orientalis; (bot.) *Styrax officinalis*.

†storare *vb.* and derivs. See **ristorare**.

†storberi·o *m.* disturbance.

stor·c-ere [B1] *tr.* to twist, to distort, to wrench; to wrest; to dislocate; to sprain; to untwist, to unravel (fig.), to alter, to misrepresent; *rfl.* to twist, to writhe; to be distorted, crooked; -ersi dalle risa, to be doubled up with laughter. **-icollo** *m.* (orn., fig.) see **torcicollo**. **†-ileggi** *m. indecl.* (derog.) dishonest lawyer. **-imento** *m.* twisting, contortion; distortion; dislocation. **-itura** *f.* twisting; dislocation; slipped disk; -itura del collo, crick in the neck; (text.) untwisting.

stord-ire [D2] *tr.* to stun; to daze, to bewilder; to stupefy; to make dizzy; *rfl.* to be dazed, to be bewildered; to stupefy oneself; cercava di -irsi bevendo, he tried to drown his sorrows in drink; *intr.* (*aux.* essere) to be amazed; -isco a sentirti parlare così, I am dumbfounded at hearing you speak like this; cose che fanno —, astonishing things. **-imento** *m.* dizziness, dazed condition, stupefaction; il mio -imento era dovuto alla mancanza di sonno, my dullness was due to lack of sleep; deafening noise. **-itag·gine** *f.* mistake, stupid action, folly; è di una -itaggine incredibile, he is unbelievably scatter-brained. **-itezza** *f.* folly, stupidity; carelessness, inattention. **-itivo** *adj.* dumbfounding; bewildering. **-ito** *part. adj.* amazed, bewildered; stunned; giddy; thoughtless; foolish; scatter-brained; numbed; *n.m.* fool, scatter-brain. (**-itamente** *adv.*)

sto·ri-a *f.* **1.** STORY, tale; è la solita —, it's the same old story; sono tutte -e, it's all lies; -e!, humbug! **2.** HISTORY; — naturale, natural history; — della terra, historical geology; (paint.; sculp.) historical picture, epic representation, etc. **-a·io, -aro** *m.* seller of epic poems or tales. **-ale** *adj.* historical, legendary. **-are** [A4] and derivs. (pop.) see **istoriare**. **-ella** *f. dim.* of storia; short story; fable, fanciful story; fib, lie. **-etta** *f. dim.* of storia; tale; novelette. **-ografi·a** *f.* historiography; written history, chronicles, records. (**-ogra·fico** *adj.*) **-o·grafo** *m.* historian; historiographer.

sto·ri-co *adj.* historical; scienze -che, humane studies; (gramm.) historic; *n.m.* historian. **-camente** *adv.* historically. **-ci·smo** *m.* tendency to consider all human actions in relation to their historical background.

storione *m.* (ichth.) sturgeon, *Acipenser sturio*.

†storlomi·a *f.* astronomy.

†stormento *m.* See **strumento**.

storm-o *m.* host, crowd; flock, swarm; pack (of hounds); uno — d'uccelli, a flock of birds; (mil.) formation, group; (aeron.) flight, a formation of aircraft; campana a —, alarm-bell; (mus.) suonare a —, to ring the alarm. **-eggiare** [A3c] *intr.* (*aux.* avere) to swarm; to gather; to ring the tocsin. **-ire** [D2] *intr.* (*aux.* avere) to rustle.

†stornac·chi-o *m.* phlegm. **†-are** *intr.* to spit.

storn-are [A1c] *tr.* to avert; to divert; to turn aside, to turn back; to ward off; to deter; to dissuade; (leg.) to misapply; to misappropriate; (comm.) to cancel; to misapply; to annul; (comm.) to transfer; — una somma, to transfer an amount (in bookkeeping, from one account to another), to change the appropriation of a sum of money; *intr.* (*aux.* essere) to turn back, to come back; to be diverted. **-ato** *part. adj.* averted; diverted; (leg.) somme -ate, misapplied funds; (comm.) somme -ate, amounts transferred.

stornello[1] *m.* (orn.) see **storno**[1]; grey coat (of horse); grey horse; *adj.* capo —, grey hair, grizzled head.

stornell-o[2] *m.* (prosod.) stornello, a ditty of three lines, the first having five syllables and rhyming with the third. **-are** [A1] *intr.* (*aux.* avere) to compose or sing 'stornelli'.

†stornimento *m.* dizziness, giddiness.

storn-o[1] *m.* (orn.) starling, *Sturnus vulgaris*; — nero, spotless starling, *S. unicolor*; — roseo, rose-coloured starling, *S. roseus*; (vet.) a horse's coat, with white spots on a dark background (as in the Andalusian breed); *adj.* grey, dappled grey; 'La cavalla -a' (Pascoli), 'The grey mare'.

storn-o[2] *m.* (comm.) transfer; *adj.* (vet.) capo —, giddiness in a horse, 'gid' in sheep.

storpi-are [A4, A4c] *tr.* to cripple, to maim, to mangle; to mar, to spoil; — un lavoro, to bungle a job; — il (un) nome, to get the (a) name wrong. **-amento** *m.* crippling; maiming; bungling; -amento di parole, mispronunciation of words. **-ato** *part. adj.* crippled; (paint.; sculpt.) botched, badly executed; badly pronounced; wrongly spelled; *n.m.* cripple. (**-atamente** *adv.* **-atore** *m.* **-atrice** *f.*) **-atura** *f.* crippling, maiming; bungling; something spoilt, damaged, bungled.

stor·pio, stọrpio *adj.* crippled, maimed; *n.m.* cripple; damage, maiming.

stort-o *part.* of **storcere**, q.v.; *adj.* crooked, twisted, deformed; curved, bent; (of eyes) squinting; (of legs) bandy; (fig.) false, erroneous; idee -e, wrong ideas. **-aménte** *adv.* crookedly; mistakenly; falsely. **-a** *f.* twist, twisting; wrenching, distortion; sprain, rick; (of a river) bend; (chem.) retort; (mil.; naut.) cutlass, curved sword, sabre, scimitar. **-ame** *m.* crooked timber. **-étta** *f. dim.* curved dagger (historical in Europe, contemporary in Asia). **-ézza** *f.* crookedness; falseness. **†-igliato** *m.*, **-ilato** *m.* (vet.) distortion of the hoof in horses. **-ignac·colo** *m.* (vulg.) deformed child. **-ina** *f.* small retort or similar vessel. **-ini** *m.pl.* (cul.) kind of short, crooked spaghetti. **-ura** *f.* deformity; crookedness; false idea, mistake; -ura morale, delinquency.

stoscanizzare [A I] *tr.* to de-Tuscanize.

†sto·scio *m.* rushing fall.

stovaina *f.* (pharm.; med.) Stovaine.

stovi·gli-e *f.pl.* crockery, pottery, earthenware; kitchen utensils; pots and pans; — da cucina, kitchenware; — da portata, tableware. **-a·io** *m.* dealer in earthenware and crockery, potter. **-eri·a** *f.* crockery, earthenware; domestic hardware.

stozz-o *m.* gouge. **-are** [A I] *tr.* (eng.) to slot. **-atrice** *f.* (eng.) slotter, slotting machine. **-atura** *f.* slotting.

stra- *pref.* (equiv. to Lat. *extra*) indicating: **1.** INTENSITY, superiority or excess; **2.** MISCALCULATION, disproportion, error, distortion. **-balzaménto** *m.* tossing about; jolting. **-balzare** [A I] *intr.* (*aux.* essere, avere) to jump about; to toss (about); *tr.* to jolt. **-balzo** *m.* jolt; *pl.* jolting; (fig.) ups and downs. **-balzoni** *adv.* by jolts, jerkily; camminare -balzoni, to stagger. **-bastare** [A I] *intr.* (*aux.* essere) to be more than enough, to be fully sufficient. **†-bello** *adj.* extremely beautiful. **†-bene** *adv.* extremely well. **-benedire** [B I0] (pop.; iron.) mandare a far -benedire, to commend to the devil. **-bere** [B4] *intr.* (*aux.* avere) to drink too much. **-biliare** [A4] *intr.* (*aux.* avere), *rfl.* to be astonished, to be amazed, to marvel. **-biliante** *part. adj.* amazing. **-biliato** *part. adj.* amazed. **-bi·lio** *m.* amazement. **†-bilire** see **strabiliare**. **-boccare** [A2c] *intr.* (essere or avere) to overflow, to be superabundant. **-boccaménto** *m.* overflowing, excess; ruin. **-boccante** *part. adj.* overflowing, excessive. **-boccato** *part. adj.* superabundant, excessive. **-boccataménte** *adv.* with (to) excess; immoderately. **-bocchévole** *adj.* overflowing; superabundant; excessive; †impetuous. **-bocchevolménte** *adv.* excessively, without restraint. **-canare** [A I] *rfl.* to work like a navvy; to lead a dog's life. **-cannare** [A I] *tr.* (text.) to cop, to rewind. **-cannatura** *f.* (text.) copping, rewinding. **-cantare** [A I] *intr.* (*aux.* avere) (mus.) to bawl, to shout. **-ca·rico** *adj.* (*m.pl.* **-chi**) overloaded, overburdened. **-cicalare** [A I] *intr.* (*aux.* avere) to talk too much. **-collare** [A I] *intr.* (*aux.* essere) to fall over; to topple. **-contento** *adj.* (pop.) overjoyed. **-cottare** [A I] *tr.* to stew in a 'stracotto'. **-cotto** *part.* of **stracuocere**, q.v.; overcooked; well-done; (fig., fam.) drunk; -cotto d'amore, in love; *n.m.* stew of beef or veal. **-cuo·cere** [C I5d] *tr.* to overcook. **-doppio** *adj.* more than double; (bot.) fiore -doppio, double flower. **-dotale** *adj.* (leg.) belonging to wife as her separate property. **-fare** [B I4] *intr.* (*aux.* avere) to overdo things, to do too much. **-fatto** *part. adj.* over-ripe. **-felice** *adj.* overjoyed. **-fine** *adj.* superfine. **-giudiziale** *adj.* (leg.) extra-judicial; done out of Court; liquidazione -giudiziale del danno, out-of-Court settlement of damages. **-giudizialménte** *adv.* (leg.) out of Court. **-godere** [B I6] *tr.* (fam.) to enjoy excessively. **-gonfio** *adj.* extremely swollen. **-grande** *adj.* outsize; exceptionally large. **-lodare** [A I] *tr.* to over-praise. **-lunare** [A I] *tr.* to open (one's eyes) wide, to roll. **-lunato** *part. adj.* (of the eyes) staring wildly; rolling. **-maledire** [B I0] *tr.* to curse from the bottom of one's heart. **-maturo** *adj.* over-ripe. **-orzare** [A I] *rfl.* (naut.) to luff suddenly, to reach involuntarily into the wind. **-orzata** *f.* (naut.) luff, coming into the wind. **-pagare** [A2] *tr.* to overpay. **-parlare** [A I] *intr.* (*aux.* avere) to talk too much; to rave; to talk scandal. **-per·dere** [C I] *intr.* (*aux.* avere) to suffer excessive losses. **-pieno** *adj.* overfull; overflowing. **-piombare** [A I c] *intr.* (*aux.* essere, avere) to be out of the perpendicular; to be out of true. **-piombo** *m.* overhanging; (archit.) overhang, projection, bulge. **-poggiare** [A3c] *intr.* (*aux.* essere) (naut.) to bear away suddenly, to broach to. **-poggiata** *f.* (naut.) fall away from the wind, act of broaching. **-potente** *adj.* overpowering; excessively powerful. **-potenza** *f.* excessive power. **-ripaménto** *m.* flooding, overflowing. **-ripare** [A I] *intr.* (*aux.* essere, avere) (of a river, etc.) to overflow, to flood, its banks. **-ripato** *part. adj.* in flood; overflowing. **†-servire** *tr.* to serve

extremely well. **-sibilare** [A I s] *rfl.* to be indifferent, not to care. **-sonare** [A I] *intr.* (*aux.* avere) (mus.) to sound out of tune or out of time; (of an organ) to cipher. **-vacato** *adj.* (typ.) crooked (the forme not having been placed straight in the press). **†-valicare** *tr.* to cross, to ford, hurriedly. **-vasare** [A I] *intr.* (*aux.* essere), *rfl.* to overflow (from a vessel). **-vec·chio** *adj.* very old; (of food) mature, ripe; vino -vecchio, vintage wine; un formaggio grana -vecchio, a grana cheese which has matured for two years. **-vecchióne** *adj. augm.* (usu. ref. to food, wine, etc.) mature, ripe; un formaggio grana -vecchione, a grana cheese which has matured for four years. **-vedere** [B35] *tr.*, *intr.* (*aux.* avere) to see very clearly; to view mistakenly; to take a biased view (of); -vedere per uno, to treat someone as a favourite. **-vin·cere** [C5] *intr.* (*aux.* avere) to win easily, to achieve complete victory; to abuse one's victory. **-vinto** *part. adj.* easily won. **-visare** [A I] *tr.* and derivs. see **travisare**. **-vi·zio** *m.* intemperance; excess; fare -vizio nel mangiare, to overeat. **†-vizzo** *m.* (lit. hist.) annual feast of the Crusca Academy. **-vol·gere** [C5] *tr.* to roll; to twist; to upset; -volgere gli occhi, to roll one's eyes; -volgere le membra, to contort, to twist one's limbs; (fig.) to distort, to twist; *rfl.* to be overturned, upset; to be contorted, twisted; to become distorted. **-volgiménto** *m.* twisting; contortion; distortion; -volgimento di mente, mental agitation. **-volto** *part.* of **stravolgere**; *adj.* twisted; contorted; distorted; crooked; convulsed; agitated; upset; overturned; (of eyes) wild; †*n.m.* cripple.

stra·b·ico *adj.* squinting; cross-eyed; *n.m.* person with a squint. (-ica *f.*) **-ismo** *m.* strabismus, squint. **-o·metro** *m.* (med.; opt.) strabometer, deviometer. **-otomi·a** *f.* (ophth. surg.) strabotomy.

strac-ca *f.* fatigue; *adv. phr.* alla —, wearily, indifferently, lazily; *pl.* breeching-straps of a pack-saddle; braces; shoulder-straps. **-cadenti** *m. indecl.* hard biscuit. **-cag·gine** *f.* weariness, slackness. **-cale** *m.* breeching-strap of a pack-saddle, girth; (fig.) portar lo -cale, to be an ass; *pl.* braces (trouser suspenders). **-caménto** *m.* weariness, fatigue. **-care** [A2] *tr.* to tire out, to fatigue; to weary, to wear out; to bore; †(naut.) to be cast ashore, to be cast away, to be thrown upon a shore; *rfl.* to tire oneself out. **-cato** *part. adj.* tired out, weary. **-catoia** *f.* weariness, exhaustion. **-catoio** *adj.* tiring, wearisome. (-catore *m.* -catrice *f.*) **†-catura** (naut.) relict, jetsam. **-chezza** *f.* weariness, fatigue; (of dies, type, stamps, etc.) wear, worn condition. **-chic·cio** *adj.* rather weary. **-chino** *m.* soft white cheese (of Lombardy).

stracceri·a *f.* rags, rag.

stracci-are [A3] *tr.* to tear, to rend; — i capelli, to tear one's hair; to tear up; to scratch; †to vituperate; †*intr.* to deviate from the track; *rfl.* (*acc.* of *prn.* 'si') to get torn; to split up, to break; (*dat.* of *prn.* 'si') -arsi i capelli, to tear one's hair. **-a·bile** *adj.* that can be torn; fragile. **-abrache** *m. indecl.* (bot.) *Smilax aspera*. **-afo·glio** *m.* notebook, scribbling-block; (eccl.) lowest rank of membership in the Florentine Misericordia. **-a·io** *m.*, **-aiolo** *m.* rag (and bone) merchant, old-clothes man. **-aménto** *m.* tearing. **-apane** *m. indecl.* poetaster. **-asacco** *adv. phr.* guardare a -asacco, to look askance at. **-ato** *part. adj.* torn, ragged, in rags; (fig.) nazione disunita e -ata, nation without unity torn with strife. (-atore *m.* -atrice *f.*) **-atura** *f.* tearing, tear; laceration.

strac·ci-o *adj.* torn, in rags; (paperm.) carta -a, waste; *n.m.* rag, tatter; rent, tear; scrap; — di cucina, cleaning-rag, floor-cloth, polishing-cloth; rimendare uno —, to mend, to darn, to patch, a tear; non aveva neppure uno — per coprirsi, he hadn't a rag to his back; (text.) lana da stracci, shoddy; gli stracci van sempre all'aria, the weakest goes to the wall; uno — di marito, a poor sort of husband. **-one** *adj.* ragged, dressed in rags, very poor; *n.m.* ragamuffin, tatterdemalion. **-uc·cio** *m. dim.* rag; shred. **-uolo** *m.* scrap; -uolo di carta, scrap of paper.

strac-co *adj.* (*m.pl.* **-chi**) tired out; worn out; — morto, dead tired; exhausted; pesce —, stale fish; (fig.) poor; weak; feeble; stale; tepid; *n.m.* weariness, exhaustion. **-aménte** *adv.* wearily.

strad-a *f.* street; road; way; — principale, main street; — maestra, main road; — nazionale, arterial road; — provinciale, main road maintained by Provincial Council; — comunale, secondary road maintained by Communal Council; — secondaria, by-road; — laterale, — di circonvallazione, by-pass (road); — di deviazione, loop road; — carrozzabile, — rotabile, carriage road (fit for wheeled traffic); — ferrata, railway; — mulattiera, mule-

strad-a (*cont.*)

track; — pubblica, highway; — vicinale, country lane; regolamento della —, rule of the road; codice della —, traffic laws, highway code; parte centrale della —, roadway; per istrada, on the road, in the street; — facendo, on the way, walking along; porta di —, street door; l'uomo della —, the man in the street; domandare la —, to ask the way; trovare la propria —, to find one's way; smarrire la —, to lose one's way; mettere sulla buona —, to put on the right road (also fig.); fare molta —, to go a long way; farsi — nel mondo, to make one's way in the world; (fig.) non vedo nessun'altra — aperta davanti a me, I see no other course open to me; (mil.) strategic route; distance between columns; — delle ronde, inspection route; — coperta, covered (protected) route; tunnelled route (as on Monte Grappa); essere fuori di —, to be off the beaten track, (fig.) to be on the wrong track, to be following a mistaken course; (fig.) andare per la propria —, to go one's own way, to mind one's own business; fermarsi a mezza —, to stop short, to fail to persevere; tagliare la — a uno, to block someone's way, to obstruct one's career; (fig.) trovar la — giusta, to go the right way to work; gettarsi alla —, to take to the road (i.e. to become a highwayman). **-ale** *adj.* of the road(s), road; incidenti -ali, road accidents; codice -ale, highway code; regolamento -ale, rule of the road; Polizia -ale, Road Patrol; manutenzione -ale, upkeep of the roads; lavori -ali, roadworks; pianta -ale, road map; *n.m.* avenue; road. **-amento** *m.* direction, putting on the right road; entering on a course (of study, business, etc.). **-are** [A 1] *tr.* to direct, to put on the right road; (fig.) to start in life, to put (someone) in the way of learning a profession or making a career; *rfl., intr.* (*aux.* avere) to take the road, to set out. **-a·rio** *m.* itinerary. **-ato** *part. adj.* put on the road, started off; successive, in succession. **-ellina** *f. dim.*, **-ellino** *m. dim.* narrow lane. **-ella** *f. dim.*, **-ello** *m. dim.* little road; -ella cieca, blind alley. **-ętta** *f. dim.*, **-icciuola** *f. dim.* lane, alley; path. **-iere** *m.* customs officer (for local customs). **-ino** *m. dim.* lane; (techn.) road member. **-iota** *m.* (mil. hist.) Levantine light cavalryman; Macedonian mercenary or Slav soldier in Venetian pay (sixteenth century); leather helmet. **-ista** *m.* (sport) road cyclist (as distinct from track cyclist). **-one** *m. augm.* wide road, main road.

stradiva·rio *m.* (mus.) Strad, violin made by Stradivarius.

strafil-are [A 1] *tr.* (naut.) to lash up (a hammock); to make up and secure (a sail or awning). **-ag·gio** *m.* (naut.) hammock lashing. (**-ato** *part. adj.*) **-atura** *f.* (naut.) operation of lashing up.

strafizzeca *f.* (bot.) stavesacre, *Delphinium staphisagria*.

straforare [A 1 c] *tr.* and derivs. See **traforare**.

straforo *m.* piercing; perforation; small hole; lavoro di —, filigree work; *adv. phr.* di —, stealthily, secretly.

strage *f.* slaughter, massacre; havoc, disaster; (fam.) mass, abundance; la — degli innocenti, the slaughter of the Innocents; i gitani fecero una — di uva, the gipsies played havoc among the grapes; è stata una —, it has been a disaster; gli esaminatori hanno fatto —, the examiners have failed a large number of candidates; di pesche, quest'anno ce n'è una —, there is a very heavy crop of peaches this year.

stra·gl-io *m.* (naut.) stay, forestay; — di maestra, mainmast forestay; — d'alberetto, top-gallant stay; vela di —, staysail. **-iętto** *m. dim.* (naut.) top-gallant stay.

†**stragno** *adj.* See **estraneo**.

†**straïnare** *vb.* and derivs. See **strascinare**.

stralci-are [A 3] *tr.* to prune, to cut off shoots from (vines, etc.); to lop off; to slash; (fig.) to remove, to take off; to cut out; to clear up, to settle; to reach a compromise concerning; (comm.) to clear (stock). (**-ato** *part. adj.*) **-atura** *f.* pruning, cutting out, etc.

stral·cio *m.* pruning, etc.; excerpt, extract, passage (of article, book, etc.); clearance, clearance sale; (comm.) oddment, clearance line, remnant, job line; (parliament) una legge —, a short Act passing principal provisions of longer Bill.

stral-e *m.* (poet.) arrow, dart; wound. (**-ętto** *m. dim.*)

strallogi *m.pl.* (bot.) birthwort, *Aristolochia clematitis*.

stram-a·glia *f.*, **-aiolo** *m.* See under **strame**.

stramare [A 1] *tr.* to feed with hay, straw, etc.; to look after, attend to (animals).

stramazzo[1] *m.* (hydr. eng.) weir, overfall; (naut.) fender; recoil cushioning made up of old rope and canvas; (Venice) bitt pin; (Venice) -i dello scalo, chocks on a slipway; †straw mattress.

stramazz-o[2] *m.* heavy fall; dare uno — in terra, to fall heavily to the ground. **-are** [A 1] *tr.* to fell, to knock down; to knock senseless; *intr.* (*aux.* essere) to fall heavily; -are da cavallo, to fall from one's horse, to be thrown. **-ata** *f.* heavy fall. **-ato** *part. adj.* (fallen) senseless; giacere -ato, to lie stunned; (fig.) -ato dal dolore, overwhelmed with grief. (**-atore** *m.* **-atrice** *f.*) **-one** *m.* heavy fall; violent blow.

stramba *f.* See under **strambo**.

stramb-o *adj.* crooked; odd, queer; unusual, strange, eccentric. **-a** *f.* rope or cord of esparto grass, etc., grass used for plaiting; (naut.) sennet, plaited rope. **-amente** *adv.* crookedly; queerly, oddly; strangely. **-are** [A 1] *intr.* (*aux.* avere) to behave strangely; to be twisted; (of wood) to warp; to make ropes of plaited grass (cf. **stramba**); †(naut., of a wind) to be fickle. **-eri·a** *f.* oddity, eccentricity; eccentric utterance or action. **-ęzza** *f.* eccentricity. **-uchina** *f.* (naut., Brescia) fresh-water fishing-net with very small mesh.

strambott-o *m.* (lit. hist.) strambotto, a folk-lyric of 8 or 6 lines; (fig.) poem of no great value; long rigmarole. **-are** [A 1] *intr.* (*aux.* avere) to sing 'strambotti'.

stram-e *m.* straw, hay; litter; fodder; †victuals. **-a·glia** *f.* straw, litter. **-eggiare** [A 3 c] *intr.* (*aux.* avere) (of animals) to eat straw, hay, etc.

stramo·nio *m.* (bot.) thorn-apple, *Datura stramonium*.

stramortire [D 2] and derivs. (pop.). See **tramortire**.

strampal-ato *adj.* odd, queer; eccentric; unusual, bold; illogical; un modo — di ragionare, an illogical way of arguing; *n.m.* queer person; eccentric. **-atag·gine** *f.* queer action, manner, speech. **-ateri·a** *f.* queer action; eccentric utterance; oddity, eccentricity. **-atone** *adj.* very queer, quite illogical. **-eri·a** *f.* eccentric action; odd behaviour; queer pronouncement.

†**stran-are**, †**-eggiare** *tr.* to ill-treat; *intr.* to behave strangely.

stranezza *f.* See under **strano**.

strangol-are [A 1 s] *tr.* to strangle, to throttle, to choke; to suffocate; (fig.) to oppress, to harm; †to cut the throat of; (naut.) to lash, to seize, to rack; to spill or brail up (a sail); to choke the luff of (a rope) in a block; — le sartie, to rack down the rigging; — una vela, to stop a sail bellying and flapping; *rfl.* to shout or scream one's head off; to choke; to hang oneself. †**-acani** *m. indecl.* (naut.) brails. **-agab·bie** *m. indecl.* (naut.) buntlines. **-amento** *m.* strangling, strangulation; choking. **-ato** *part. adj.* strangled, throttled; choked; (med.) strangulated. **-atoio** *adj.* likely to cause strangulation (fig.) 'cut-throat', swindling. **-atore** *m.* strangler; (metall.; eng.) straight peen (hammer); †(naut.) throat brail; (**-atrice** *f.*) *adj.* strangling; choking; oppressive. **-ato·rio** *adj.* (*m.pl.* -atorii) causing strangling; liable to cause choking. **-atura** *f.* strangling; strangulation; choking, pressure; restriction; (naut.) act and effect of brailing up; (Genoa) crossing of two hawsers. **-azione** *f.* strangulation; suffocation.

stranguglioni *m.pl.* (vet.) strangles.

strangur-i·a *f.* (med.) strangury. **-iare** [A 4] *intr.* (*aux.* avere) (med.) to suffer from strangury.

strani-are [A 4] *tr.* (*prep.* da) to alienate, to estrange (from); to draw away (from); to distract; *rfl.* to drift away (from); to become estranged. **-ato** *part. adj.* estranged; separated; †alien.

stranier-o, **-e** *adj.* foreign; *n.m.* foreigner; università per -i, university for foreign students (e.g. at Perugia); stranger; (leg.) alien; ufficio -i, Aliens' Office.

stra·nio *adj.* (poet.) foreign; strange.

stran-o *adj.* strange, queer; odd, unusual; eccentric; peculiar, curious; singular; contrade -e, wild, lonely country, una -a coincidenza, an odd coincidence; strano!, che strano!, strange!, how strange!; †*n.m.* stranger; foreigner. **-amente** *adv.* strangely, queerly; oddly. **-ęzza** *f.* strangeness, oddity; queerness; singularity; whimsicality.

straordina·ri-o *adj.* extraordinary, unusual, uncommon, exceptional; special, extra; ora di —, ore -e, lavoro —, overtime; misure -e, emergency measures; outside the curriculum; professore —, visiting or temporary lecturer; (finan.) dividendo —, cash bonus; (leg.) assemblea -a, special (general) meeting; *n.m.* temporary clerk, teacher, lecturer. **-amente** *adv.* extraordinarily, uncommonly; not usually; as an exceptional case. **-ato** *m.* temporary position. **-età** *f.* extraordinariness, singularity; rarity.

strapazz-are [A 1] *tr.* to ill-use, to ill-treat; to overwork; to scold, to abuse, to swear at; to mishandle, to bungle, to botch; — un

strapazz-are (*cont.*)
lavoro, to botch a job; — un autore, to misinterpret a writer; — una sonata, to play a sonata badly; *rfl.* to overwork, to wear oneself out. **-amẹnto** *m.* rough usage; overwork; fatigue. **-ata** *f.* scolding, reprimand, rebuke. **-ato** *part. adj.* ill-used, overworked, scolded, harassed; uova -ate, scrambled eggs. (**-atamẹnte** *adv.* **-atọre** *m.* **-atrice** *f.*) **-o** *m.* rough usage; common use; fatigue; excess; over-work; vestito da -o, working clothes; vita di -i, hard life; fare -o di, to spoil, to ill-use; gli -i della giovinezza, the excesses of youth; scrittore da -o, scribbler, author of little merit; lingua da -o, coarse, vulgar language; rebuke, reprimand; *adj.* stark staring mad. **-ọne** *m.* rough handler (of persons or things); *adj.* fatiguing, harassing. (**-ọna** *f.*) **-ọso** *adj.* fatiguing, tiring; tiresome; neglected. **-osamẹnte** *adv.* roughly, inconsiderately.

strapontino *m.* See **strapuntino**, under **strapunto**.

strapp-are [A I] *tr.* (*prep.* a) to snatch, to tear; to rip; to pull away, to pluck (from); to wrench, to wring; to extort; to tear up; to tear out, to tear off, to tear away; — un dente, to pull out a tooth; — a uno la verità, to get the truth out of someone; — le lagrime a, to move to tears; — il cuore a, to wring the heart of; — la vita, il pane, to make a bare living; *rfl.* (*acc.* of *prn.* 'si') to tear, to get torn; to tear oneself away; (*dat.* of *prn.* 'si') -arsi il cuore, to break one's heart; -arsi i capelli, to tear one's hair. **-a·bile** *adj.* liable to tear; detachable. **-acchiare** [A4] *tr.* to tear here and there. **-alana** *f.* (bot.) *Xanthium italicum.* **-amẹnto** *m.* tearing; ripping; snatching; wringing; (aeron.) fuso di -amento, rip panel. **-ata** *f.* sharp tug; pull; snatch; wrench; (mus.) plucking, thrumming. **-ato** *part. adj.* torn (out, off, away); snatched; uprooted; (herald.) erased. **-atọre** *m.* snatcher. (**-atrice** *f.*) **-atura** *f.* snatching, wrenching; tear; pull. **-o** *m.* tear, rent; pull; wrench; jerk; (weight-lifting) snatch; -o a due braccia, two-handed snatch; (fig.) wrench; il lasciare la casa fu un grande -o, leaving home was a great wrench; questo fu uno -o al cuore per la povera madre, this wrung the poor mother's heart; fare uno -o al regolamento, to make an exception to the rule; -o muscolare, pulling a muscle; a -i, by fits and starts, jerkily. **-ọne** *m. augm.* great rent; violent tug.

strapunt-o *m.* quilt. **-ino** *m.* small, long, narrow mattress; (motor.; theatr., cinem., etc.) folding seat.

†**strarre** *vb.* and derivs. See **estrarre**.

Strasburgo *pr.n.f.* (geog.) Strasbourg.

strascic-are [A2s] *tr.* to drag, to trail; to shuffle; — i piedi, to drag, to shuffle, one's feet; — le parole, to drawl one's words; — il lavoro, to drag out one's work, to go slow; (fig.) — l'abito, to trail one's coat; *intr.* (*aux.* avere) to shuffle along; to drag one's feet; (of a gown, etc.) to trail on the ground; *rfl.* to drag oneself along; to shuffle. (**-amẹnto** *m.*) **-ante** *part. adj.* dragging; trailing on the ground. **-ata** *f.* dragging, trailing; -ata della voce, drawl. **-ato** *part. adj.* dragged, trailing; voce -ata, drawling voice; (mus.) canto -ato, drawling; (cul.) cavolo -ato, cabbage dragged round the pan with a fork, while cooking in sauce.

strascichi·o *m.* dragging or shuffling noise.

stra·sci·co *m.* (*pl.* -chi) trailing, dragging; trail; following; escort; train; lo — della veste della sposa, the train of the bride's dress; sledge; sequel; aftermath; gli -chi del tifo, the after-effects of typhus; lasciar lo — come le lumache, to leave a trail, like snails, i.e. to leave things about untidily, *or* to leave a bad impression, *or* to leave debts behind one; — nel piatto, leavings on the plate, what is left on the dish; — (nel bicchiere), dregs; (naut.) rete a —, trawl-net. **-cọne** *m.* person who drags his feet or shuffles along; loafer, idler. (**-cọna** *f.*)

strascin-are [A I] *tr.* to drag, to drag along the ground; — al male, to lead into evil ways; *intr.* (*aux.* avere) (mus.) to drawl, to drag; (vet.) to 'go short' (a vice of movement in horses); *rfl.* to be dilatory; to drag oneself along. **-amẹnto** *m.* dragging. **-ato** *part. adj.* dragged. **-atamẹnte** *adj.* with delays and difficulties, dilatorily. **-atura** *f.* dragging. **-io** *m.* continued dragging; sound of dragging.

stra·scino *m.* dragging; drag-net; trammel(-net); (agric.) home-made harrow; (naut.) casting-net; ground net; (mus.) portamento, slurring; hawker of meat; ignorant physician or surgeon; sledge, truck, trailer.

strasecolare [A I s] and derivs. See **trasecolare**.

strasso *m.* (jewellery) paste, strass.

stratagemma *m.* stratagem; expedient, trick, plot, device; ricorrere a uno —, to resort to a deception.

strat-ega, -ego *m.* (*pl.* -eghi) strategist; — da tavolino, — da caffè, armchair strategist; (hist.) strategus; *adj.* strategical. **-egi·a** *f.* strategy. **-e·gico** *adj.* strategic, strategical; †(naut.) nave -egica, flagship. **-egicamẹnte** *adv.* strategically.

strat-o *m.* (geol.) stratum, layer; (of paint, etc.) coat, layer, coating; (naut.) water baffle in a ship's boiler; layer of water, usually clearly defined by a change of temperature, salinity or direction of current; (meteor.) stratus; — tagliuzzato, fractostratus; (fig.) — della società, class. **-ificare** [A2s] *tr.* (geol.) to stratify; *intr.* (*aux.* essere), *rfl.* to lie in layers, to be stratified. **-ificato** *part. adj.* stratified; in layers; (miner.) foliated. **-ificazione** *f.* (geol.) stratification; (metall.) stratification, banding. **-ifọrme** *adj.* stratiform, disposed in strata. **-igrafi·a** *f.* (radiol.) planigraphy. **-ocu·mulo** *m.* (meteor.) strato-cumulus. **-ografi·a** *f.* (geol.; radiol.) stratography. **-osfera** *f.* stratosphere. **-osfe·rico** *adj.* relating to the stratosphere; (fig., iron.) lofty and sublime.

stratt-a *f.* pull, tug, jerk; a -e, by jerks. **-ọne** *m. augm.* violent pull; wrench; a -oni, by fits and starts.

†**stratto**[1] *adj.* extracted; abstracted; strange, extravagant.

†**stratto**[2] *adj.* separated, divided; descending, inclined.

stravag-ante *adj.* queer, odd; eccentric; fantastic; whimsical; extravagant; excessive; †rime -anti, additional poems (not included in the poet's own collection). **-antemẹnte** *adv.* oddly, strangely; funnily, queerly, extravagantly. **-anza** *f.*, †**-an·zia** *f.* oddness; wild fancy, wild imagining; fare delle -anze, to do odd things; sudden change of weather; freak of nature; extravagance.

strazi-are [A4] *tr.* to torture; to tear to pieces; to lacerate; to cause havoc among, in, to; to wound, to hurt, to spoil; to ruin; (fig.) — il cuore a, to rend the heart of; musica che -a gli orecchi, music that pierces one's ear-drums. **-amẹnto** *m.* torture; havoc, destruction. **-ante** *part. adj.* heartrending; dolore -ante, agonizing pain, heartrending grief; grido -ante, piercing shriek; exhausting, exacting. **-ato** *part. adj.* tormented; torn; il paese era -ato da discordie, the country was torn by strife. **-atọre** *m.* tormentor; *adj.* tormenting. (**-atrice** *f.*)

stra·zio *m.* havoc, destruction; laceration; torment, torture; fare — di, to tear to pieces; è uno — assistere a questo spettacolo, it is torture to watch this; fare — del nome di una persona, to destroy a person's reputation; fece — del suo patrimonio, he squandered his inheritance; scorn, ridicule; (typ.) waste resulting from trimming sheets of paper to reduce them to required format; 'maculature'.

strebbiare [A4c] and derivs. See **strubbiare**.

strecciare [A3c] *tr.* to unplait. (**-ato** *part. adj.*)

strefol-are [A I s] *tr.* (naut.) to unlay (a rope); *intr.* (*aux.* essere) to slip out (away), to slink away unnoticed. **-amẹnto** *m.*, **-ata** *f.* (naut.) act of unlaying; quantity of unlaid rope or dunnage. (**-ato** *part. adj.*) **-atura** *f.* (naut.) effect of unlaying. **-atọre** *m.* (naut.) person or instrument employed for unlaying rope.

strẹ-ga *f.* witch, sorceress; caccia alle -ghe, witch-hunt; (fig.) hag; ugly, disagreeable woman; *pr.n.f.* (trademark) Strega, a liqueur made at Benevento; (Florent.) taper; punto a —, herring-bone stitch; (bot.) erba —, see under **erba**. **-gacchiola** *f.* (derog.) (of a woman) ugly old witch. **-gamẹnto** *m.* spell, witchcraft. **-gare** [A2c] *tr.* to cast a spell on, to bewitch; to charm, to bewitch (inspiring love). **-gato** *part. adj.* bewitched; wan, emaciated. **-gheri·a** *f.* witchcraft; witches' sabbath. **-ghino** *m.* (gas) lamp-lighter's torch.

†**strẹg·ghia** *f.* See **striglia**.

strẹg-o *m.* wizard; miser; very thin man. **-ọne** *m.* wizard, sorcerer; witchdoctor. **-onec·cio** *m.*, **-oneri·a** *f.* witchcraft, sorcery; spell. **-o·nia** *f.* (bot.) see 'erba strega' under **erba**.

strẹgua, strẹ·gua *f.* rate; standard; measure; way; alla — comune, by ordinary standards; alla stessa —, on a par, on a level; trattare tutti alla stessa —, to treat everybody alike; giudicare uno alla — di un altro, to judge one person by another; alla — di, in the light of; †quota, levy.

strem-are [A I] *tr.* (*prep.* di) to exhaust, to drain (of); to reduce, to bring to the end of resources. **-ato** *part. adj.* exhausted; drained; -ato di forze, reduced to extreme weakness.

stremenzire [D2] and derivs. See **striminzire**.

strem-o *adj.* (pop., poet.) see **estremo**; extremely poor; †vita -a, hard life; †(eccl.) -a unzione, extreme unction; *n.m.* extremity, very end; nello — d'Europa, in the uttermost parts of Europe; ridursi allo —, to be reduced to poverty. **-ità** *f.* (pop., poet.) see **estremità**.

strenna, strẹnna *f.* New Year's gift; — di Natale, Christmas present; collection of poems, prose, essays, etc. published at the beginning of the year.

stre·nu-o *adj.* strenuous; valorous; valiant, gallant. **-amẹnte** *adv.* strenuously; valiantly. **-ità** *f.* strenuousness; valour.

stre·pere [B def.] *intr.* (poet.). See **strepitare**, under **strepito**.

stre·pit-o *m.* din, noise; uproar, shouting, clamour; lo — del treno, the rumbling of the train; lo — d'armi, the clash of arms; se ne andò senza fare —, he went away quietly, without making a fuss; (fig.) fare —, to get talked about, to make a stir; (mus.) noise, verve, spirit. **-amẹnto** *m.* see strepito. **-are** [A 1 s] *intr.* (*aux.* avere) to shout and yell; to complain loudly; che cos'hai da -are?, what are you shouting about?, why are you making a fuss?; fece quel che doveva senza -are, he did what he had to do without making a song about it. **-ìo** *m.* continuous clamour; ceaseless shouting and yelling. **-ọso** *adj.* noisy, loud, uproarious; clamorous; applausi -osi, loud applause; successo -oso, roaring success; fatto -oso, much talked of occurrence; (mus.) noisily; notizia -osa, astonishing piece of news; promesse -ose, lavish promises. **-osamẹnte** *adv.* noisily; uproariously; clamorously.

strepto-cocco *m.* (med.) streptococcus. **-coccemi·a** *f.* streptococcaemia. **-coc·cico** *adj.* streptococcal. **-coccọsi** *f.* (med.) streptococcicosis. **-micina** *f.* (med.; pharm.) streptomycin.

strẹtta *f.* See under **stretto**.

strettire [D 2] *tr.* (techn.) to cramp, to squeeze, to restrict.

strẹtt-o *part.* of **stringere**, q.v.; *adj.* tight; narrow; pinched; near, close; restricted; strict; intimate; private, secret; scarpe troppo -e, shoes that are too tight; coi pugni -i, with clenched fists; lo tenevo —, I held it fast; uno — passaggio, a narrow passage; tenere — a denari, to keep short of money; avaro e —, close-fisted, mean; — dal bisogno, constrained by want; fortuna -a, reduced circumstances; un parente —, a near relation; è nostro — dovere, it is our bounden duty; -a disciplina, strict discipline; in -i rapporti, in close touch, in close connexion; di -a necessità, strictly necessary; lo — significato delle parole, the precise meaning of the words; sunto —, brief summary, précis; (gramm.) vocale -a, close vowel; (fig.) essere di manica -a, to be straitlaced; (naut.) vento —, heading wind; (mus.) battuta -a, accelerated beat; tempo -o, quickening tempo; (vet.) — di budella, herring-gutted, 'tucked up' (of a horse); *adv.* strictly, tight(ly); narrowly; closely; meanly; *n.m.* (geog.) strait(s); lo Stretto di Gibilterra, the Straits of Gibraltar; narrows; — delle montagne, mountain pass; stare allo —, to be in a tight corner; colto allo —, caught in a difficulty; urgency; meanness; avere dello —, to be rather mean; (knitting) slipped stitch passed over a knitted stitch, *or* two stitches knitted together; (mus.) stretto, close imitation in a fugue; (agric.) wine made from the dregs of pressed grapes. **-amẹnte** *adv.* strictly; è -amente proibito, it is strictly forbidden, prohibited; -amente necessario, strictly, absolutely, necessary. **-a** *f.* grasp, grip, hold; clasp, squeeze, embrace; pressure; una -a di mano, a handshake; una -a al cuore, a pang in one's heart; dare una -a alla cinghia, to tighten one's belt; fu preso nella -a di una folla, he was caught in the press of a crowd; alla -a del freddo, when the cold was most intense; *pl.* straits, difficult position; essere alle -e, to be at the end of one's tether; lo mettemmo alle -e e finì col parlare, we pressed him hard and at last he talked; (agric.) pressing (of olives, etc.); (geog.) mountain pass; dry wind from the south; (mus.) rapid finale. **-ẹzza** *f.* narrowness; tightness; closeness; scarcity; per la -ezza di tempo, owing to the very limited time available, for lack of time; *pl.* straits, straitened circumstances, poverty. **-ọia** *f.* tight bandage; narrow passage; (fig.) difficulty, 'tight spot'. **-ọio** *m.* (agric.) press; screw-press; (fig.) press (of people); crowded, narrow place. **-ọre** *m.*, **†-ora** *f.* tight bandage. **-ura** *f.* narrowness; tightness; pressure; urgent need; straits.

stri-a *f.* (archit.) rib of the fluting of a column; (anat.) stria; -e midollari, stria medullaris; (astron.) stria; stripe, thin streak; furrow. **-are** [A 4] *tr.* to streak, to stripe. **-ato** *part. adj.* streaked; chequered; (techn.) striated; (anat.) striate, striated. **-atura** *f.* streaking; (anat., etc.) striation.

strib·bia *f.* (text.) slub-catcher.

stribbiare [A 4] and derivs. See **strubbiare**.

†stribuire *tr.* see **distribuire**; to lay waste, to plunder.

stricco *m.* (naut.) Spanish Burton, a purchase utilizing two single blocks and a hook on the bight of the rope between them, giving a power ratio of 3.

stricnin-a *f.* (chem.; pharm.) strychnine. **-ịsmo** *m.* (med.) strychninism.

stri·d-ere [B 1] *intr.* (*aux.* avere) to creak; to make a scraping sound; to screech, to shriek; to squeak; to chirp, to chirrup; (of snakes, etc.) to hiss; (of colours) to clash, to jar. **-ente** *part. adj.* shrill, sharp; jarring; strident; creaking; rasping; ali -enti, whirring wings; (of colours) clashing; un contrasto -ente, a violent contrast. **-ìo** *m.* prolonged creaking, screeching, etc.

stridire [D 1] (poet.). See **stridere**.

strid-o *m.* (*pl.* **-a** *f.* of the human voice, otherwise **-i** *m.*) shrill cry; shriek, screech. **-ọre** *m.* creaking, shrieking; (of teeth) gnashing, grating; scraping (sound); piercing cold, biting wind; (med.) stridor. **-ulanti** *m.pl.* (ent.) stridulating organs of a cicada or a grasshopper.

stri·dulo *adj.* shrill, piercing; strident.

strig-are [A 2] *tr.* to unravel; to disentangle; *rfl.* to come unravelled; to extricate oneself; (*dat.* of *prn.* 'si') -arsene, to get out of a difficulty; -arsela tra loro, to come to terms. (**-ato** *part. adj.*)

strige *f.* (orn.) owl.

†strig·gine *m.* cold, unpleasant weather.

stri·gile *m.* (antiq.) strigil.

stri·gli-a *f.* currycomb. **-are** [A 4] *tr.* to currycomb; (fig.) to scold, to rebuke; *rfl.* (joc.) to titivate oneself; to brush oneself up. **-ata** *f.* currycombing; (fig.) scolding. (**-ato** *part. adj.*) **-atore** *m.* groom. **-atrice** *f.* lady-groom. **-atura** *f.* currycombing; dust from the currycomb; (fig.) scolding.

stri·gol-o *m.* scream, shrill cry; (zool.) omentum; *pl.* offal; (bot.) — selvatico, corn gromwell, *Lithospermum arvense*. **-are** [A 1 s] *intr.* (*aux.* avere) to scream, to shriek, to cry.

Strigo·nia *pr.n.f.* (geog.) Esztergom.

stri·gope *m.* (orn.) owl-parrot or kakopo, *Strigops*.

strill-are [A 1] *intr.* (*aux.* avere) to shriek, to scream; to cry out; to complain loudly; che cosa ha da —?, what is he complaining about?; che avrà che -a così?, what's the matter with him, shrieking like that?; *tr.* to cry out, to shriek. **-ante** *adj.* shrill. **-ata** *f.* loud scream; loud protest; violent scolding.

strill-o *m.* scream; loud protest; fare uno *m*, to give a shriek; gli -i dei ragazzi, the shrieks and yells of the children. **-ọne** *m.* newspaper seller; one who calls his wares; one who habitually shrieks and yells, person with a loud voice. (**-ọna** *f.*) **-ọzzo** *m.* (orn.) corn bunting, *Emberiza calandra*.

striminz-ire [D 2] *tr.* to stunt, to pinch; *rfl.* to become stunted; to lace (oneself) too tightly. **-ito** *part. adj.* stunted; withered, shrivelled.

strimpell-are [A 1] *tr.* to strum (on), to thrum; — il violino, to scrape the violin. **-amẹnto** *m.* strumming, thrumming; scraping (on a violin), etc. **-ata** *f.* strum; scrape. (**-ato** *part. adj.*) **-atore** *m.* strummer. (**-atrice** *f.*) **-atura** *f.* strumming. **-ìo** *m.* continued strumming. **-o** *m.* sound of strumming, etc.; the instrument strummed or scraped upon. **-ọne** *m.* strummer; scraper (of stringed instrument). (**-ọna** *f.*)

†strina *f.* intense cold; cold wind.

strin-are [A 1] *tr.* to singe. **-ato** *part. adj.* singed; scorched; dried up; *n.m.* singeing; puzzo di -ato, smell of singeing. **-atura** *f.* singe, mark of singeing; smell of singeing.

string-a *f.* lace, shoelace; tag of a bootlace; non vale una —, it's not worth a pin. **-a·io** *m.* bootlace seller; haberdasher. **-are** [A 2] *tr.* to lace; (fig.) to restrict; to draw together; to condense, to make concise. **-atẹzza** *f.* tightness; neatness; (fig.) conciseness; terseness. **-ato** *part. adj.* tightly laced; close-fitting; neat in one's dress; (fig.) concise; terse. **-atamẹnte** *adv.* concisely; without wasting words.

strin·g-ere [C 5] *tr.* to draw tight, to tighten; to press, to squeeze, to grasp, to clasp; to clench; to bind together; — la mano ad uno, to shake hands with someone; — un'alleanza, to make an alliance; — amicizia, to form a friendship; to constrain, to compel; — uno con le spalle al muro, to press someone to an immediate decision; necessità mi -e, necessity compels me; il tempo -e, time presses; to besiege; — d'assedio una città, to lay siege to a town; — un trattato, to conclude a treaty; to close (a speech, discussion); — la bocca, to shut one's mouth; — un vestito, to take in a dress (coat); — le ciglia, to look narrowly; — il passo, to quicken one's pace; (eng.) to tighten (e.g. a nut); — i freni, to apply the brakes (also fig.); (naut.) — il vento, to sail close to the wind, to sail full and by;

string·ere (*cont.*)
(mus.) — i tempi, quickening the speed; *impers.* (used adverbially) stringi stringi, after all, when all's said and done; stringi stringi, il senso è questo, when you get down to it, this is what it really means (cf. 'strizza strizza'); *intr.* (*aux.* avere) to be tight, to fit tightly; questa giubba -e nelle spalle, this coat is tight at the shoulders; (naut.) to sail close hauled; *rfl.* to draw close, to close up, to squeeze closer together; -ersi al muro, to hug the wall, to keep close to the wall; -ersi nelle spalle, to shrug one's shoulders; (fig.) -ersi nelle spese, to cut down expenses; -ersi in amicizia con, to form a friendship with. **-ente** *part. adj.* pressing, urgent; compelling; cogent, conclusive. **-enza** *f.* urgency. †**-ibordo** *m.* (naut.) shipwright's clamp used for bending strakes into position. **-ilabbro** *m.* (vet.) gag. **-imento** *m.* tightening, pressing; squeezing; contraction. (**-itore** *m.* **-itrice** *f.*) **-itubo** *m. indecl.* (eng.) pipe wrench, Stillson. **-itura** *f.* squeezing; contraction; (agric.) pressing (of olives, etc.).

strino *m.* (Tusc., dial.) cold wind; (Umbria) intense cold (also **strinone**).

†**strione** *m.* and derivs. See **istrione**.

stripp·are [A I] *intr.* (*aux.* avere) to gorge oneself, to stuff, to overeat. **-apelle** *adv. phr.* (vulg.) mangiare a -apelle, to eat one's bellyful. **-ata** *f.* bellyful; feast; fare una -ata di, to have a vast helping of. **-o** *m.* gorging; guzzling; overeating. **-one** *m.* greedy-guts. (**-ona** *f.*)

stri·sci·a *f.* strip; stripe; streak; streamer; — di acqua, narrow channel, thin stream of water; (razor-)strop; — di scorrimento, tread (of a tyre); trail; (naut.) zone; — del 50 %, 50 % probability zone; (artill.) fall of shot zone; *pl.* (cul.) strips of 'pasta' for soup; (motor.) strisce di attraversamento pedonale, pedestrian-crossing, *or* zebra-crossing; †(naut.) lift, mastrope; strong local current. **-aiuola** *f.* (orn.) ashy-headed wagtail, *Motacilla flava cinereocapilla.* **-amento** *m.* stroking; grazing, skimming; trailing, dragging, shuffling; creeping, crawling; (fig.) flattery, fawning. **-ante** *part. adj.* creeping, crawling; (fig.) cringing, fawning; obsequious; (eng.) sliding; (bot.) creeping; *n.m.* sliding bow (of pantograph); *m.pl.* reptiles. **-are** [A4] *tr.* to graze, to skim; to creep along by; to drag; to trail; to slur; to cut or tear into strips; (mil.) to graze, to creep alongside; *intr.* (*aux.* avere) to creep, to crawl; to glide, to slide, to slip; to bow and scrape; to cringe; (mil.) -are lungo il ciglio, to creep along the ridge; (mus.) to glide, to perform a glissando; *rfl.* to crawl, to creep; -arsi contro, to rub oneself against; to clean oneself up, to dress oneself up; -arsi a, to fawn on, to suck up to, to creep round. **-ata** *f.* rub, rubbing; stroking; sliding; (fig.) flattery, buttering-up. **-ato** *part. adj.* trailed; grazed; skimmed; slurred; valzer -ato, gliding waltz. **-atura** *f.* rub, rubbing; stroking; trailing; slurring (of speech); (fig.) obsequious behaviour.

stri·sci·o *m.* dragging; shuffling; gliding; (scient.) smear (for microscope work); colpire di —, to graze. **-one** *m. augm.* large streak or strip; -one pubblicitario, (sport) streamer marking end of cycle race.

†**stris·simo** *adj. superl.* (abbrev. of **illustrissimo**, q.v., used iron.).

stritol·are [A I s] *tr.* to crush; to grind down; to break into small pieces; to destroy; to smash; (fam.) se ti piglio ti -o, if I catch you I'll make mincemeat of you; (fig.) to crush (by argument, etc.); *rfl.* to be broken into pieces; (fig.) to go to bits. **-abile** *adj.* fragile, liable to be broken or crushed. **-amento** *m.* grinding; crushing; smashing. **-ato** *part. adj.* ground down; crushed; broken to bits. (**-atore** *m.* **-atrice** *f.*) **-atura** *f.* crushing, grinding; smashing. (**-azione** *f.*)

strizione *f.* (techn.) contraction in area.

strizz·are [A I] *tr.* to squeeze; to wring (out); to press; — l'occhio, to wink; *impers.* (used adverbially) -a a -a, after all, when you get down to it (cf. 'stringi stringi', under **stringere**). **-alimoni** *m. indecl.* lemon-squeezer. **-ata** *f.* squeeze; wring, wringing; -ata d'occhio, wink. (**-ato** *part. adj.*) **-atura** *f.* squeeze; wringing; pressing, compressing. **-one** *m.* hard squeeze, wring; sharp pain; extreme cold.

stro·bil·o, -e *m.* (bot.) cone; (zool.) the chain of proglottids of a tapeworm.

strobo·sco·pico *adj.* (phys.) stroboscopic. **-sco·pio** *m.* (phys.) stroboscope.

strof·a, †-e *f.* stanza, strophe; verse.

strofanto *m.* (bot.) *Strophanthus.*

stro·fico *adj.* pertaining to strophes, strophic.

strofin·are [A I] *tr.* to rub; — con un cencio, to polish, to wipe, with a rag; *rfl.* -arsi a, to rub oneself against; (fig.) -arsi ad alcuno, to fawn on someone. **-ac·cio** *m.* dishcloth; rag; duster; floorcloth. **-amento** *m.* rubbing; wiping. **-ata** *f.* a rub; a wipe. (**-ato** *part. adj.*) **-io** *m.* continued rubbing; elettricità di -io, frictional electricity, tribo-electricity.

stro·folo *m.* (med.) strophulus.

stro·fulo *m.* See **strofolo**.

strogolare [A I s] *intr.* (*aux.* avere) to poke about in the trough, to wallow; (fig.) to eat piggishly.

stro·laga *f.* (orn.) diver; — maggiore, great northern diver, *Gavia immer*; — mezzana, black-throated diver, *G. arctica*; — minore, red-throated diver, *G. stellata.*

strolog·are, strolagh·are [A2] *tr.* to predict, to foretell; *intr.* (*aux.* avere) to tell fortunes, to cast horoscopes, to read the stars; to study, to muse, to think; to rack one's brains. (**-ato** *part. adj.*) †**-i·a** *f.* see **astrologia**.

strom·a *m.* (bot.; anat.) stroma. **-a·tico** *adj.* stromatic, stromal.

stromb·are [A I c] *tr.* (archit.) to make an embrasure of (an opening in a wall); to splay. (**-ato** *part. adj.*) **-atura** *f.* funnel-shaped end of a pipe; (archit.) embrasure; (bldg.) splay, splayed jambs.

strombazz·are [A I] *tr.* to trumpet, to noise abroad; to proclaim, to announce proudly; non bisogna — le proprie virtù, you shouldn't blow your own trumpet. **-ata** *f.* trumpet blast, trumpeting; (fig.) puff. **-ato** *part. adj.* trumpeted, noised abroad; loudly praised. **-atore** *m.* boaster, one who blows his own trumpet. (**-atrice** *f.*)

strombett·are [A I c] *tr., abs.* to play (badly) on the trumpet; to keep blowing a trumpet; (fig.) to boast, to blow one's own trumpet. **-ata** *f.* trumpet-blast, trumpeting; noise, fuss; boasting. **-ato** *part. adj.* (fig.) published with trumpet blasts. (**-atore** *m.* **-atrice** *f.*) **-iere** *m.* trumpeter, bugler. **-io** *m.* trumpeting, continued blowing of a trumpet.

strombo[1] *m.* (archit.) embrasure (esp. one to hold window-shutters); (bldg.) splay, splayed jambs.

strombo[2] *m.* (zool.) *Strombus* spp., large marine gastropods; (ichth.) used also in Ligurian and other dialects for mackerel and related fish.

stromeierite *f.* (miner.) stromeyerite.

†**stromento** *m.* See **strumento**.

stronc·are [A2c] *tr.* to break off; — un ramo, to break off a branch; to break; to smash; to maim; — la resistenza nemica, to break the enemy's resistance; to criticize harshly; i critici hanno -ato il libro, the book has been slashed by the critics; (gramm.) to truncate (a word) by dropping the last syllable; to divide into syllables; *rfl.* (acc. of prn. 'si') to be broken; (colloq.) -arsi dalle risa, to burst with laughing; (dat. of prn. 'si') -arsi la gamba, to break one's leg; (fig.) -arsi le mani e le braccia, to wear one's fingers to the bone. **-amento** *m.* cutting off; breaking; maiming. **-ato** *part. adj.* broken; mezzo -ato, weak, tired. **-atoio** *adj.* (of trees) easy to lop. **-atura** *f.* breaking off; smashing; maiming; (fig.) destructive criticism, savage review; (gramm.) apocope; division into syllables.

stron·co (*pl.* **-chi**) *apocop. part.* of **stroncare**, q.v.; (pop. Tusc.) l'hai —, you've bust it; *adj.* crippled, maimed; broken; worn out; *n.m.* cripple. **-chino** *n.m.* crippled child; also *adj.* **-cone** *m.* stump.

stronfi·are [A4c] *intr.* (*aux.* avere) to snort; to puff; to pant. **-one** *m.* one who snorts or puffs; (fig.) one puffed up with pride. (**-ona** *f.*)

stron·gil·o *m.* (zool.) *Strongylus* spp., parasitic nematode worms. **-osi** *f.* (ent.) strongylosis.

†**stronzare** *tr.* to cut short, to diminish; to restrict excessively (cf. **stroncare**).

stron·zi·o *m.* (chem.) strontium. **-ana** *f.* (chem.) strontia, strontium oxide. **-a·nico** *adj.* (miner.) containing strontia. **-anite** *f.* (miner.) strontianite.

stronzo *m.*, **stronzolo** *m.* (vulg.) turd.

stropicci·are [A3] *tr.* to rub; to scrub; to scrape; — i denti, to clean one's teeth; — i piedi, to drag one's feet, to shuffle; *rfl.* to rub oneself; (fig.) -arsi a, to fawn on; (dat. of prn. 'si') -arsi le mani dalla gioia, to rub one's hands with delight. **-amento** *m.* rubbing; -amento di piedi, shuffling of feet. **-apanni** *m. indecl.* wash-house. **-ata** *f.* rub; scrub(bing). (**-ato** *part. adj.*) **-atoio** *m.* wash-house. **-atura** *f.* rubbing, scrubbing; (joc.) dressing-down, scolding. **-one** *m.* toady, sycophant. (**-ona** *f.*)

stropicci·o *m.* rubbing, scrubbing; continued shuffling; (fig.) bickering; rubbing shoulders with undesirables.

stropp-are [A 1] *tr.* (naut.) to strop, to put a hemp rope round (a bale or block, etc.); to attach (an oar) to its tholepin. (**-ato** *part. adj.*)

stroppo *m.*, **strop·polo** *m.* sling; (naut.) strop.

stro·sci-a *f.* channel made by rain or any water on the ground. **-are** [A 4] *intr.* (*aux.* avere) to swish, to hiss (of heavy rain or other falling water). **-o** *m.* swish, hiss (of falling water, rain, etc.).

strozz-a *f.* throttle, gullet, throat; windpipe; †(naut.) navel pipe, cable pipe heading through the deck to the cable locker. **-alino** *m.* (bot.) flax dodder, *Cuscuta epilinum.* **-amento** *m.* throttling, strangling; choking; (road traffic) un -amento della circolazione, a traffic bottleneck; (techn.) throttling. **-apreti** *m. indecl.* pears and plums of a sour variety; sour (or very dry) wine; (fam.) small fichu; *pl.* form of 'pasta' in large pieces (Neap. **strangolapreti**). **-are** [A 1] *tr.* to strangle, to throttle; to choke; to tie up (sausages, etc.); (fig.) to fleece, to rob, to extort usury; to stifle, to suppress; (techn.) to throttle; (naut.) to nip (the cable) with a compressor; to brail up (a sail). **-ato** *part. adj.* strangled, throttled; choked; vaso -ato, narrow-necked vase; voce -ata, choking voice; (med.) ernia -ata, strangulated hernia. **-atoio** *adj.* sharp-tasting; narrow-necked; tight; *n.m.* (naut.) a compressor or cable clench operating in the navel pipe; †-atoio ad ingranaggio, -atoio a bilico, controller or bow stopper. **-atore** *m.* strangler. (**-atrice** *f.*) **-atura** *f.* strangling, choking; narrowing, narrow part; usury; bottleneck. **-iere** *m.* (hist.) falconer. **-inag·gio** *m.* usury. **-ineri·a** *f.* behaviour of a usurer. **-inesco** *adj.* (*m.pl.* **-ineschi**) relating to usury. **-ino** *m.* trap that strangles in a loop of wire on a spring; (fig.) grasping moneylender.

strubbi-are [A 4] *tr.* to wear out, to be hard on (clothes, etc.); to waste, to run through, to use up. (**-ato** *part. adj.*)

strub·bi-o *m.* wear and tear (esp. of clothes). **-one** *m.* one very hard on clothes. (**-ona** *f.*)

strucc-are [A 2] *rfl.* to remove one's make-up; seta da -arsi, cloth or tissue for removing make-up. (**-ato** *part. adj.*)

strucin-are [A 1] *tr.* (pop., Tusc.) to wear out; to wear holes in. (**-ato** *part. adj.*) **-io** *m.* wear and tear (esp. of clothes).

strudel *m. indecl.* German pastry-cake with apple-filling.

strufaz·zolo *m.* small piece of meat.

†**struf·folo** *m.* small bundle of straw used for polishing marble.

strug·g-ere [C 12] *tr.* to destroy; to consume; to melt; to liquefy; to wear away; to waste; to afflict; *rfl.* to be destroyed; to be consumed; to melt; to turn to liquid; (fig.) to be consumed (with desire, envy, etc.); to pine; to languish; si -eva di conoscerlo, she was longing to make his acquaintance; -ersi di, per, uno, to pine for, to be in love with; -ersi in lagrime, to melt into tears; to be afflicted, to be distressed. **-ibuco** *m. indecl.* useless, thankless task; fare a -ibuco, to wear oneself out for nothing. **-icuore** *m. indecl.* heartache; heartbreak; (cards) beggar-my-neighbour. **-imento** *m.* melting; liquefaction; destruction; tender feeling, longing; pining; torment; boredom; sentivo un -imento di rivederla, I felt a great longing to see her again; che -imento non poter far nulla per aiutarlo!, how agonizing not to be able to do anything to help him! **-isto·maco** *m. indecl.* bore. **-itore** *m.* destroyer; *adj.* destroying, destructive. (**-itrice** *f.*)

strull-o *m.* silly, stupid; *n.m.* simpleton. **-ata** *f.* silliness, stupidity. **-eri·a** *f.* silliness, foolishness.

strum-a *f.* (med.) scrofula; goitre. **-a·tico** *adj.* (med.) strumous. **-ectomi·a** *f.* (surg.) strumectomy. **-oso** *adj.* strumous.

strument-o *m.* tool, implement; instrument (also fig.); (admin.) depositare gli -i di ratifica, to deposit the instruments of ratification; (leg.) instrument; — di misura, measuring instrument; (mus.) instrument. **-a·io** *m.* instrument-maker. **-ale** *adj.* instrumental; errore -ale, error due to an instrument; (gramm.) caso -ale, instrumental case (e.g. in Sanskrit, Russian, etc.); (mus.) instrumental. **-almente** *adv.* instrumentally. **-are** [A 1 c] *tr.* (mus.) to orchestrate; (leg.) to draw up. (**-ato** *part. adj.* **-atore** *m.* **-atrice** *f.*) **-atura** *f.*, **-azione** *f.* (mus.) orchestration, instrumentation. **-ista** *m., f.* (mus.) instrumentalist.

strumite *f.* (med.) strumitis.

strumosità *f.* (med.) being affected with goitre.

strusci-are [A 3] *tr.* to rub; to chafe; to wear out; *rfl.* -arsi a contro, to rub oneself against, (fig.) to fawn upon, to flatter. **-amento** *m.* rubbing; chafing; wearing out. **-ata** *f.* a rub, a wipe.

stru·sci-o *m.* rubbing; wearing out, wear and tear. **-one** *m.* person hard on his clothes; flatterer, toady; (also *adj.*). (**-ona** *f.*)

strusa *f.* (text.) flock silk, curley.

strutta *f.* (techn.) rendering, melting (cf. **struggere**).

strutt-o *part.* of **struggere**, q.v.; *adj.* melted (down), liquefied; consumed; wasted away, destroyed; *n.m.* lard.

struttur-a *f.* structure; construction; form, shape; (gramm.; prosod.) form, construction. **-ale** *adj.* structural. (**-almente** *adv.*)

†**struzione**[1] *f.* See **distruzione**.

†**struzione**[2] *f.* See **destituzione**.

struzz-o *m.* (orn.) ostrich, *Struthio camelus*; (fig.) stomaco di —, stomach of an ostrich (said of a hearty eater with perfect digestion, or of a ruthless person, without scruples or remorse). **-a** *f.* (naut.) sprit.

Stuardo *pr.n.m.* Stuart; Stewart; (hist.) Maria Stuarda, Mary Stuart.

stuc-care [A 2] *tr.* (bldg.) to stucco; (eng.) to putty; to stop (a surface); (fig.) to surfeit, to bore; *rfl.* to paint one's face; to become surfeited; bored. (**-camento** *m.*) **-cato** *part. adj.* (bldg.) stuccoed; (eng.) puttied; (fig.) bored, surfeited. **-catore** *m.* plasterer, worker in stucco, maker of plaster-casts; (fig., joc.) bore, tiresome person. (**-catrice** *f.*) **-catura** *f.* plaster-work. **-chevolare** [A 1 s] *tr.* to bore; to surfeit; to sicken; to disgust. **-chevole** *adj.* tedious, boring, sickly; insipid. **-chevolmente** *adv.* insipidly; tediously, boringly. **-chevolezza** *f.* tiresomeness; affectation; artificiality; insipidity. **-china·io** *m.* seller or maker of plaster statuettes; (bldg.) stucco decorator. **-chino** *m.* plaster statuette, figurine; (fig., fam.) insipid-looking girl, 'wax-doll'.

†**stuc·cio** *m.* See **astuccio**.

stuc-co[1] *m.* (*pl.* **-chi**) plaster, stucco; stucco-work; plaster-figure; plaster-cast; rimanere di —, to be dumbfounded; uomo di —, dull stick; (eng.; motor.) stopping (before spraying nitrocellulose); (bldg.) putty, filler. **-coso** *adj.* chalky, plaster-like.

stuc-co[2] *apocop. part.* of **stuccare**; *adj.* (*m.pl.* **-chi**) disgusted, sick (of); — e ristucco di, sick to death of. **-coso** *adj.* boring, tiresome.

student-e *m.* student; university student; undergraduate; la vita di —, student life; pupil; — di Liceo, grammar-school pupil. **-esca** *f.* student body, students. **-esco** *adj.* (*m.pl.* **-eschi**) relating to students; students', student; gergo -esco, students' slang. **-essa** *f.* woman student.

studi-are [A 4] *tr.* to study; — la musica, to study music; — la scherma, to learn, to be learning, fencing; to receive instruction in; to observe; to watch closely; to read; to examine; to survey; — le parole, to watch one's words, to be careful what one says; †— il passo, to hasten one's steps; (techn.) to design; *intr.* (*aux.* avere) to study, to work; non -a, he doesn't work, he doesn't get on with his work; — bene, to work well, to be a good student or pupil; — in, to be a student, pupil, at; -a nel Liceo, he goes to the grammar-school; *rfl.* (*prep.* a, di) to try, to endeavour, to do one's best (to); to take pleasure (in). **-a·bile** *adj.* capable of being studied. **-acchiare** [A 4] *tr.*, *abs.* to study listlessly, to make a pretence of studying. **-ato** *part. adj.* studied; carefully prepared; deliberate; affected; -ato dal naturale, drawn (photographed, etc.) from nature. **-atamente** *adv.* studiedly, deliberately; designedly; affectedly.

stu·di-o *m.* study, subject of study; preparation; (results of) study; monograph; — complessivo, survey; studi classici, classical studies; fare gli studi regolarmente, to pursue a regular course of studies; uomo di —, scholar, studious man; examination; care, pains; mette grande — in tutto, he takes great pains in everything; office, study; studio; lo — di un avvocato, a lawyer's office, chambers; (artist's, photographer's) studio; (doctor's) consulting room; (cinem.; radio, telev.) studio; (art) study; — di figura, figure study; (mus.) study, étude; (fig.) inclination, affection; vocation; a bello —, on purpose, deliberately, with every intention; †zeal. **-arello** *m. dim.* small study, short article. **-etto** *m. dim.* small study (room), little office. **-(u)olo** *m. dim.* small study (room); †cabinet, cupboard. **-oso** *adj.* studious; diligent; -oso di, desirous of; *n.m.* scholar; research worker. **-osamente** *adv.* studiously; diligently; deliberately, on purpose; †eagerly.

stuell-o *m.* (surg.) tent, drain. **-are** [A 1] *tr.* (surg.) to tent, to drain (a wound).

stuf-a *f.* stove; — a petrolio, oil stove; tubo da —, stovepipe; hot bath; — a vapore, vapour bath; (techn.) stove, oven; (cul.) in —, in casserole; (bot.) hot-house, stove; (agric.) far la — alle botti, to cleanse wine-casks with boiling water. **-ai(u)ola** *f.* casserole, stew-pan. **-are** [A 1] *tr.* to stew; (silkb.) to stifle; (fig.) to bore, to weary; *rfl.* (fig.) to grow weary, to get bored; mi -o a far sempre questo lavoro, I get sick of always doing the same job. **-ato** *part.*

stuf-a (*cont.*)
adj. stewed, braised; maccheroni ‑ati, cooked macaroni lightly baked in the oven; *n.m.* stew, stewed meat. **‑atura** *f.* (silkb.) stifling. **‑o** *apocop. part.* of **stufare**; *adj.* tired, sick, fed up, bored.

stultilo·quio *m.* stupid speech; empty, senseless talk.

stu(m)·mia *f.* (Tusc.) scum.

stuo·i-a *f.* mat, matting; — di giunco, rush mat(ting); (bldg.) kind of matting or trellis to hold the plaster of a ceiling; lath; (needlew.) a kind of cross-stitch. **‑are** [A4] *tr.* (bldg.) to lath. (**‑ato** *part. adj.*) **‑atura** *f.* (bldg.) lathing, lathwork.

stuol-o *m.* troop; group; band; host; crowd; flock; uno — di mosche, a swarm of flies; (naut.) fleet; array; convoy. **†‑addensato** *adj.* numerous, abundant.

stupe‑facente, †‑faciente *adj.* stupefying, narcotic; astonishing; *n.m.* narcotic; drug; traffico degli ‑facenti, drug traffic. **‑fare** [B14] *tr.* to stupefy; to surprise, to astonish; *rfl.* (*prep.* di) to be astonished (at). **‑fattivo** *adj.* (med.) narcotic. **‑fatto** *part. adj.* astonished, surprised; viso ‑fatto, look of astonishment; stupefied; insensible, unconscious. **‑fazione** *f.* surprise, astonishment; stupefaction; insensibility.

stupend-o *adj.* stupendous; magnificent, splendid, marvellous. **‑amente** *adv.* stupendously; magnificently; marvellously.

stu·pid-o *adj.* stupid; silly; foolish; *n.m.* dolt, blockhead, fool. **‑amente** *adv.* stupidly. **‑ag·gine** *f.* act of stupidity; nonsense; non dire ‑aggini, don't talk nonsense; sono ‑aggini, that's all nonsense. **‑ire** [D2] *intr.* (*aux.* essere), *rfl.* to become stupid; *tr.* to render stupid; to stupefy. **‑ità** *f.* utter stupidity; obtuseness.

stup-ire [D2] *intr.* (*aux.* essere) to be amazed, to be astonished; cose da fare —, astonishing things; to be greatly surprised; also *rfl.*; non c'è da ‑irsi, there's nothing to be astonished at; *tr.* to amaze, to astonish; †to gaze on with amazement. **‑ito** *part. adj.* amazed, astonished; greatly surprised. **‑ore** *m.* amazement, astonishment; essere uno ‑ore, to be a wonder, a marvel; fare ‑ore, to amaze, to astonish; stupor.

stupr-o *m.* rape; †adultery. **‑are** [A1] *tr.* to rape. (**‑ata** *part. adj.* **‑atore** *m.*)

stura¹ *f.* (zool.) fan shell, *Pinna nobilis*.

stur-a² *f.* opening (of a bottle), uncorking; (fig.) beginning, lead, opening; prendere la —, to lead off, to begin, to open the discussion, etc.; dare la — a, to begin talking about, to start on, to give vent to. **‑are** [A1] *tr.* to uncork; to open; ‑are gli orecchi a qualcuno, to open someone's ears. **‑abotti·glie** *m. indecl.* corkscrew, bottle-opener. (**‑amento** *m.*) **‑ato** *part. adj.* uncorked, opened.

sturbare [A1] and derivs. See **disturbare**.

sturbo *m.* (of the stomach) upset. (Cf. **disturbo**.)

†sturmento *m.* See **strumento**.

†stutare *tr.* to deaden; to kill.

stuzzi-care [A2s] *tr.* to stir; to poke; — il fuoco, to poke the fire; to stir up; to prod; — una piaga, to probe a wound; to arouse, to whet; to excite, to provoke; to incite; to tease; — i denti, to pick one's teeth; (provb.) non — il cane che dorme, let sleeping dogs lie. **‑cadenti** *m. indecl.* toothpick. **‑camento** *m.* poking; prodding; stirring up, whetting; teasing. **‑cante** *part. adj.* stimulating; irritating; appetizing. **‑cato** *part. adj.* poked; prodded; stirred up; aroused, whetted; excited. **‑catore** *m.* exciter; inciter; provoker; teaser, tease. (**‑catrice** *f.*) **‑chino** *m.* (fam.) tease, irritating person; meddler; appetizer, appetizing dish; snack, titbit. **‑corecchi** *m. indecl.* earpick.

su *prep.* (*contr.* with *def. art.* **sul, sulla, sui, sugli, sull'**; before a vowel, **sur**, though this is no longer used in modern Italian). **1.** ABOVE, over; on, upon; mille metri sul livello del, sul, mare, a thousand metres above sea-level; about, on; un volume sulla musica moderna, a book on modern music; riferire —, to report on; sull'istante, on the instant, at once; balletto — musiche di Scarlatti, ballet based on music by Scarlatti; fatto — misura, made-to-measure; pitturato — tre mani, painted in three coats; otto persone — dieci, eight persons out of ten. **2.** ON, towards; in the direction of; up to; marciare — Berlino, to march on Berlin; sull'esempio di, following the example of. **3.** ABOUT, towards, near, close to; sulla cinquantina, about fifty years old; sull'imbrunire, about dusk, near twilight; sul punto di, about to, sul partire, about to leave; *adv.* UP, upwards; andiamo —, let us go up, *or* upstairs; tirar —, to bring up, to rear; (mus.) arcata in —, up-bow; metter — casa, to set up house; pochi metri più —, a few yards

further up; un poco più —, a little higher up; un poco più — del ginocchio, a little above the knee; devi scriverci — l'indirizzo, you must write the address on it; da domani in —, from to-morrow; dal primo piano in —, from the first floor up; (with other *preps.*) facevo assegnamento — di lui, I relied on him; di sul letto, (from) off the bed; levare di sul fuoco, to take off the fire; in — quel punto, at that point; — di ciò, thereupon; — per up, up among; *adv. phr.* — per giù, poco — poco giù, approximately, by and large; in — e in giù, up and down; sul serio, in earnest; (fam.) — di sopra, upstairs; di —, from above; *excl.* —!, up!; —poltronaccio!, come on, lazy-bones!; —!, coraggio!, come, pull yourself together! *n.m.* tutto quel — e giù, all that going up and down. **‑accennato** *adj.* before mentioned, aforesaid.

sua·cia *f.* (ichth.) — comune, *Citharus linguatula*; — cianchetta, *Arnoglossus laterna*; — fosca, *A. grohmanni*, scaldfish.

Suada *pr.n. f.* (myth.) Suada, goddess of persuasion.

suad-ere [C3] (poet.) see **persuadere**. **‑ente** *part. adj.* persuasive, winning. **‑itore** *m.* persuader, flatterer; *adj.* persuasive, winning, wheedling. **†‑o** *adj.* persuasive; conducive.

†suas-o *part.* of **suadere**, q.v.; *adj.* persuaded, won over. **†‑ione** *f.* persuasion.

suasiv-o, ‑o·rio *adj.* (poet.) persuasive, winning, flattering.

†suave *adj.* and derivs. See **soave**.

sub¹ *prep.* (Lat., used in certain expressions) — divo, — Jove, under a clear sky, in the open air; *pref.* as in **subentrare, subalpino**, etc., q.v.

sub² *m. indecl.* (abbrev. of **subacqueo**, q.v.).

subaccoll-are [A1] *tr.* to delegate by subcontract; to subcontract. **‑ata·rio** *m.* subcontractor. (**‑ato** *part. adj.*) **‑o** *m.* subcontract.

suba·cido *adj.* (chem.) subacid.

subac·que-o, †suba·queo *adj.* submarine, underwater; cacciatore —, underwater fisherman; also *n.m.* (**‑a** *f.*)

subacuto *adj.* (med.) subacute.

subaffitt-are [A1] *tr.* to sublet. (**‑ato** *part. adj.*) **‑o** *m.* sublease; sublet, subletting; underlease; (esp. of rural property, at a 'fitto' or 'canone di affitto', C.C.). **‑ua·rio** *m.* subtenant, undertenant.

subal·bido *adj.* (poet.) whitish.

subalpino *adj.* subalpine, Piedmontese; *n.m.pl.* the Piedmontese.

subaltern-o *adj.* subordinate, subaltern; inferior; dependant; (logic) subaltern; *n.m.* (mil.) subaltern (officer); (naut.) gunroom officer, midshipman, sublieutenant. **‑are** [A1] *tr.* to subordinate. **‑ato** *part. adj.* subordinate(d).

subanale *adj.* (anat.) sub-anal.

subappalt-are [A1] *tr.* to subcontract. (**‑ato** *part. adj.*) **‑atore** *m.* subcontractor. (**‑atrice** *f.*) **‑o** *m.* subcontract (for supplies, work or services at agreed price or rate).

subappennino *adj.*, *n.m.* (geog.) sub-apennine.

subast-a *f.* auction; forced sale. **‑are** [A1] *tr.* to sell by auction.

subato·mico *adj.* (phys.) subatomic.

sub·bi-a *f.* stonemason's chisel; chisel. **‑are** [A4] *tr.* to chisel, to work (with a chisel); (fam.) to beat, to knock about. (**‑ato** *part. adj.*)

subbilioso *adj.* slightly bilious.

sub·bi-o *m.* (text.) beam (of loom); montare sul —, to beam. **‑olo** *m.* sculptor's chisel.

subbollire [D2] and derivs. See **sobbollire**.

subbu·glio *m.* hubbub, turmoil; confusion; upheaval; mettere in —, to throw into confusion.

subcla·vio *m.* See **succlavio**.

subcommittente *m.* (leg.) one who lets a subcontract (C.C.).

subconduttore *m.* (leg.) sublessee; subtenant (under 'sublocazione', q.v.).

subcontra·rio *adj.* (logic) subcontrary.

subcontratto *m.* (leg.) subcontract.

subcosciente *adj.*, *n.m.* subconscious.

subcro·nico *adj.* (med.) subchronic.

sub·dol-o *adj.* cunning, crafty; deceitful; shifty; underhand; arti ‑e, underhand tricks. (**‑amente** *adv.*)

†subdurre *vb.* and derivs. See **sedurre**.

subeco·nom-o *m.* assistant bursar. **‑ato** *m.* assistant bursar's office.

subecume·nico *adj.* (geog.) inhabitable temporarily.

subemendamento *m.* (admin.) amendment to an amendment.

subenfite·usi *f.* (leg.) subemphyteusis.

subentr-are [A1] *intr.* (*aux.* essere; *prep.* a) to take the place (of), to replace; to succeed. **‑ante** *part. adj.* succeeding, following; l'inquilino ‑ante, the next tenant. **‑ato** *part. adj.* following, succeeding.

suber-ificazióne *f.* (bot.) suberization. **-iẓẓato** *adj.* (bot.) suberized.

†**su·bero** *m.* See **sughero.**

subfornitóre *m.* (comm.) subcontractor.

subietto *adj.* (poet.) lying below; in or relating to a valley; †*n.m.* see **soggetto.**

subingresso *m.* (leg.) subrogation.

subintestazióne *f.* subheading.

sub-íre [D2] *tr.* to undergo; to suffer, to endure; — una condanna, to be condemned; to be convicted; — una sconfitta, to suffer a defeat. **-íto** *part. adj.* suffered, undergone; experienced; (sport) il 'Milan' ha segnato 61 gol, contro 36 -iti, the Milan team scored 61 goals, conceded 36.

subiss-áre [A1] *tr.* to overthrow, to ruin, to raze to the ground; (fig.) to overwhelm; *intr.* (*aux.* essere) to collapse, to fall into ruins; *rfl.* to be ruined; to sink. **-aménto** *m.* ruin, overthrow. **-ativo** *adj.* ruinous, destructive. (**-áto** *part. adj.*) **-atóre** *m.* destructive, ruinous, overwhelming. (**-atrice** *f.*) **-o** *m.* ruin, collapse; confusion; great mass, heap; overwhelming quantity; (fig.) outburst; shower, flood; un -o d'applausi, a thunderous outburst of clapping.

su·bit-o *adj.* sudden, prompt, ready; hasty; *adv.* immediately; quickly; at once, directly; soon; — dopo le quattro, soon after four (o'clock); ritorno —, I shall be back in a moment; giunse — dopo, he arrived just afterwards; di —, suddenly, all of a sudden; *conj.* — che, no sooner than, as soon as; *n.m.* moment, instant; in un —, in a moment; su quel —, at that moment, just then. **-aménte** *adv.* suddenly, all at once; unexpectedly; immediately. **-eẓẓa** *f.* suddenness; unexpectedness.

subita·ne-o *adj.* sudden; uomo —, hasty man; †discorso —, impromptu speech. **-aménte** *adv.* suddenly; unawares. **-ità** *f.* suddenness.

subita·rio *adj.* (Rom. hist.) hastily raised (army), emergency (troops).

subiteẓẓa *f.* See under **subito.**

†**sublato** *adj.* carried off; abstracted.

sublim-áre [A1] *tr.* to raise up, to exalt; (phys.) to sublime; (psych.) to sublimate; *rfl.* to exalt oneself; (psych.) to be sublimated. **-aménto** *m.* exaltation; sublimation. **-áto** *part. adj.* exalted; sublimated; *n.m.* (chem.) sublimate; -ato corrosivo, corrosive sublimate. **-atúra** *f.* sublimation. **-azióne** *f.* sublimation.

sublim-e, †**-o** *adj.* sublime, exalted; extremely high; excellent; (math.) calcolo —, higher calculus; stile —, exalted style; poesia —, sublime poetry; *n.m.* (the) sublime; supreme excellence; *adv.* sublimely. **-eménte** *adv.* sublimely. **-ità** *f.* sublimity, loftiness; supreme excellence; magnificence; (the) sublime.

sublinguale *adj.* (anat.) sublingual, hypoglossal.

subloc-áre [A2] *tr.* to sublet. **-atário** *m.* (leg.) sublessee; subtenant. (**-áto** *part. adj.*) **-atóre** *m.* (leg.) sublessor. **-azióne** *f.* (leg.) sublease; subletting (esp. of personal property, urban property and furnished premises, hired or let at a 'pigione', q.v.; C.C.).

sublunare *adj.* sublunary.

sublussazióne *f.* (med.) subluxation.

submicróne *m.* (scient.) submicron.

subnavigante *m.* (naut. slang) submarine; submariner.

subnormale *adj.* See **sottonormale.**

suboceà·nico *adj.* underwater, submarine; telegrafia suboceanica, submarine telegraph, ocean telegraph.

subodor-áre [A1c] *tr.* to get wind of, to suspect. (**-áto** *part. adj.*)

subordin-áre [A1s] *tr.* to subordinate. **-aménto** *m.* subordinating; dependence; subordination. **-áto** *part. adj.* subordinate; -ato a, subject to; (gramm.) proposizione -ata, subordinate clause; *n.m.* subordinate. (**-áta** *f.*) **-ataménte** *adv.* subordinately; -atamente all'approvazione, subject to approval. **-azióne** *f.* subordination; dependence, dependency; obedience; (mil.) reduction in rank.

suborn-áre [A1] *tr.* to suborn. (**-áto** *part. adj.*) **-atóre** *m.* suborner. (**-atrice** *f.*) **-azióne** *f.* (leg.) subornation.

subos·sido *m.* (chem.) suboxide.

Subo·tica *pr.n.f.* (geog.) Szabadka, Maria-Theresiopoli.

subsannare [A1] *intr.* (*aux.* avere) to mock, to ridicule.

subscapolare *adj.* (anat.) infrascapular.

subsin·crono *adj.* (electr.) subsynchronous.

subso·nico *adj.* (aeron.) subsonic.

substanziale *adj.* and derivs. See **sostanziale.**

substrato *m.* (geol.) substratum (cf. **sostrato**).

substratosfera *f.* substratosphere.

subtercuta·neo *adj.* **sottocutaneo.**

subu·cula *f.* (Bibl.) priestly tunic.

suburbano *adj.* suburban.

suburbica·rio *adj.* (eccl.) suburbicarian.

subur·bio *m.* See **sobborgo.**

Suburra *pr.n.f.* (Rom. antiq.) Subura, a busy and disreputable district in ancient Rome; (fig.) slum, unsavoury quarter.

subverso *adj.* See **sovverso.**

succagogo *m.* (med.) succagogue.

succe·d-ere [C22] *intr.* (*aux.* essere; *prep.* a) to succeed, to follow; alla tempesta successe il bel tempo, fine weather followed the storm; Vittorio Emanuele II -ette a Carlo Alberto, Victor Emmanuel II succeeded Charles Albert; to follow as a consequence; to occur, to happen, to befall; gli è successa una grave disgrazia, a serious misfortune has befallen him; che cosa -e?, what is happening?; sono cose che -ono, things like this are always happening, these things happen; *recip. rfl.* to occur in succession, to follow one another; lampi e tuoni si -evano ininterrottamente, lightning and thunder alternated continuously; *n.m.* succession; il -ersi degli avvenimenti sconvolse i suoi piani, the sequence of events upset his plans; un -ersi di disastri, a run of misfortunes. **-a·neo** *adj.* substituted, substituting; surrogate, deputy; *n.m.* substitute.

succenturiato *adj.* (med.) placenta succenturiata, accessory placenta.

success-o *part.* of **succedere,** q.v.; *adj.* following, substitute(d); occurred; *n.m.* result; success; event, occurrence; course (of time). **-i·bile** *adj.* (leg.) capable of succeeding; entitled to succeed; in line of succession; *n.m.* (leg.) person entitled to inherit under will or on intestacy. **-ibilità** *f.* (leg.) eligibility to inherit. **-ióne** *f.* succession, inheritance; course (of time); la -ione degli avvenimenti, the course (order) of events; prossimo alla -ione, next in order of succession; offspring, descendants; (leg.) diritto di -ione, right of succession; diritti, tassa di -ione, estate duty; imposta di -ione, succession duty; -ione legittima, -ione ab intestato, intestate succession, legal succession; -ione testamentaria, succession under will, testamentary succession; apertura della -ione, opening, vesting, of succession; liquidare la -ione, to wind up the estate. **-ivo** *adj.* subsequent; next; following; il giorno -ivo, next day; vedi punto 6 -ivo, see point 6 below. **-ivaménte** *adv.* subsequently; afterwards. **-óre** *m.* successor; heir; *adj.* following, succeeding, next. (**-óra** *f.*) **-o·rio** *adj.* (*m.pl.* **-orii**) (leg.) having to do with succession.

succhi-áre [A4] *tr.* to suck; to sip; to suck in, to suck up; to drink in; (fig.) — il sangue a, to suck the blood of; pareva che volesse -armi dagli occhi il segreto, he gazed at me as though he hoped to read the secret in my face; *rfl.* (*dat.* of *prn.* 'si') to 'swallow', to put up with, to 'take'. **-aménto** *m.* sucking; sipping. (**-áto** *part. adj.*) **-atóio** *m.* (ent.) tongue of a bee; (bot.) haustorium. **-atóre** *m.* sucker; *pl.* (zool.) Suctoria. (**-atrice** *f.*)

succhiell-o *m.* gimlet, auger; — a cucchiaio, pod gimlet; (chem.) — per campionatura, sampling borer. **-a·io, -áro** *m.* gimlet maker (or seller). **-aménto** *m.* boring of holes. **-áre** [A1] *tr.* to bore holes in. **-ina·io** *m.* gimlet-maker (or seller). **-ináre** [A1] *tr.* to bore slightly, to bore (little holes). (**-ináto** *part. adj.*) **-íno** *m.* small gimlet; (fig.) one who works secretly for his own ends.

succhieruola *f.* suction rose (of pump intake).

suc·chio[1] *m.* gimlet, auger, drill; (mil.) screwhead on a ramrod.

suc·chi-o[2] *m.* (bot.) sap, juice; — di limone, lemon juice, lemon squash; (chem.) suspension; solution; small whirlpool. **-óne** *m.* (agric.) sucker; parasite; (fig.) parasite, bloodsucker.

succi-áre [A3] *tr.* to suck, to suck up; to eat greedily; -arsi le dita, to lick one's fingers (in eating); *tr., rfl.* (pop.) to put up with, to endure. **-abrodo** *m.* (joc.) good-for-nothing, inept individual. **-acapre** *m.* (orn.) nightjar, *Caprimulgus europaeus.* **-afióri** *m.* (orn.) honey-sucker (fam. Meliphagidae). **-amalati** *m. indecl.* (derog.) paid nurse, one who lives at the expense of sick people. **-amele** *m.* (bot.) broomrape, *Orobanche crenata.* **-aménto** *m.* suction, sucking; absorption. **-aminestre** *m. indecl.* see **succiabrodo. -ane·spole** *m.* silly person; (in Goldoni) a stupid servant as a comic character. **-arupe** *m. indecl.* (ichth.) sucker-fish, *Lepadogaster* spp. **-asangue** *m. indecl.* bloodsucker, exploiter. **-ata** *f.* suck; dare una -ata a, to have a suck of. (**-áto** *part. adj.*) **-atóre** *m.* sucker, one who sucks. (**-atrice** *f.*) **-avíno** *m.* drinker.

succi·dere [C3] *tr.* to cut down low, to cut back (plants); *rfl.* to crack, to split.

succ·inato *m.* (chem.) succinate. **-i·nico** *adj.* (chem.) succinic. **-inile** *m.* (chem.) succinyl. **-inite** *f.* (miner.) succinite.

†**succineric·cio** *adj.* See **soccenericcio.**

succin·gere [C5] *tr.* to gird, to tuck up (clothes) under a girdle; — i lombi, to gird (up) one's loins.

suc·cino *m.* amber.

succint-o *part.* of **succingere,** q.v.; *adj.* tucked up, short; (fig.) succinct, brief, concise; scanty; in —, briefly, in short; *n.m.* précis, summary, résumé; †belt, girdle. **-amente** *adv.* succinctly, briefly, concisely.

suc·cio *m.* suck; sucking; mark of sucking or kissing.

suc·ciol-a *f.* boiled chestnut (in the skin). **-a·io** *m.* boiled-chestnut seller. **-ata** *f.* dish of boiled chestnuts.

succiso *part.* of **succidere,** q.v.; *adj.* cut, cut off.

succitato *adj.* quoted above, aforesaid.

succla·vio *adj.* (anat.) subclavian; muscolo —, subclavius muscle.

suc·co *m.* (*pl.* **-chi**) juice; sap; (physiol.) — gastrico, gastric juices; (fig.) essence, substance, spirit. **-cosità** *f.* juiciness; pithiness. **-coso** *adj.* juicy; sappy; pithy. **(-cosamente** *adv.*)

†**Succole** *pr.n.f., pl.* (astron.) the Pleiades.

succonti·nuo *adj.* (med.) intermittent.

succrescere [B9] *intr.* (*aux.* essere) to grow shoots low down (on a plant).

suc·cubo *m.* succubus.

succulento *adj.* succulent, juicy; substantial; pithy.

succursale *adj.* helpful; *n.m.* branch office, branch; *n.f.* (eccl.) chapel of ease.

succussione *f.* (med.) succussion.

succuta·neo *adj.* (anat.; med.) subcutaneous, hypodermic.

su·cid-o *adj.*, **-ume** *m.* See **sudici-o, -ume.**

sud *m., adj., indecl.* south: verso —, southward(s); (geog.) polo —, South Pole; (astron.) Croce del —, Southern Cross; il — ovest africano, South-west Africa; sud-africano, South African; America del —, South America; — tirolese, German-speaking inhabitant of Alto Adige.

sud-are [A1] *intr.* (*aux.* avere) to perspire, to sweat; to feel hot; come -o!, how hot I feel!; to exude (moisture), to ooze; (fig.) to toil, to drudge; le pareti della grotta -avano, the walls of the cave were covered with moisture; *tr.* to sweat; — sangue, to sweat blood; — freddo, to break into a cold sweat; *rfl.* -arsi una cosa, to earn something by the sweat of one's brow. **-acchiare** [A4] *intr.* (*aux.* avere) to perspire slightly. **-acchiata** *f.* slight sweat. **-a·mina** *f.*, **-a·mini** *m.pl.* (med.) sudamina. **-ante** *part. adj.* sweating; con -anti pene, with toil and sweat; (Rom. antiq.) meta-ante, *meta sudans.* **-a·rio** *m.* shroud; (eccl.) Veil of Veronica, 'vernicle'. **-ata** *f.* sweat, sweating; fare una -ata, to sweat profusely. **-atic·cio** *adj.* damp with perspiration. **-ato** *part. adj.* wet with sweat, bathed in sweat; sweated over, toiled over; carte -ate, -ate carte, writings that have entailed prolonged and laborious study; pane -ato, bread earned by the sweat of one's brow. **-atamente** *adv.* with (toil and) sweat; quattrini -atamente raccolti, hard-earned gains (money). **-atore** *m.*, **-atrice** *f.* one who perspires freely; (fig.) hard worker; busybody. **-ato·rio** *adj.* (*m.pl.* **-atorii**) inducing perspiration; *n.m.* (Rom. antiq.) *sudatorium,* sudatory.

suddecan-o *m.* (eccl.) subdean. **-ato** *m.* status of subdean.

suddeleg-are [A2s] *tr.* to (sub)delegate. **(-ato** *part. adj.*) **-azione** *f.* subdelegation; office of subdelegate.

suddetto *adj.* aforesaid, above-mentioned; il —, the said (person), the same.

suddia·con-o *m.* (eccl.) subdeacon. **-ato** *m.* (eccl.) subdiaconate.

suddialetto *m.* subdialect.

suddistin·-guere [C6] *tr.* to make a further distinction in. **(-to** *part. adj.*) **-zione** *f.* subdistinction.

sud·dit-o *adj., n.m.* subject (person); — della legge, subject to the law. **-anza** *f.* subjection; citizenship.

suddivi·dere [C3] *tr.* to subdivide; to split up.

suddivis-i·bile *adj.* divisible, capable of further division. **(-ibilità** *f.*) **-ione** *f.* subdivision; division; very small division (or compartment); (comm.) split; (mil.) territorial command dependent on higher authority; (naut.) subdivision of a ship to produce numerous watertight compartments.

suddiviso *part.* of **suddividere,** q.v.; *adj.* subdivided; further divided; (chem.; phys.) finemente —, finely divided.

Sudeti *pr.n.m.pl.* (geog.) Sudetes.

su·dic-io *adj.* dirty, filthy; foul, indecent; guadagni -i, filthy lucre;

discorsi -i, dirty (filthy) talk; aver la camicia -ia, to have on a dirty shirt, (fig.) to have a bad conscience; azione -ia, dirty trick; (comm.) patente -ia, foul bill; scorpacciate -e, gluttonous feasting; copia -ia, rough copy; (paint.) colore —, dirty colour; dull, muddy or dark colour; *n.m.* dirt, filth. **-iamente** *adv.* dirtily; indecently; vestito -iamente, ill-dressed. **-eri·a** *f.* dirtiness, filthiness; filthy mess; indecency; dirty trick; dire delle -erie, to use foul language; miserliness. **-etto** *adj. dim.* rather dirty. **-ezza** *f.* dirtiness, filthiness. **-ione** *m.* dirty (filthy) person. **(-iona** *f.*) **-iume** *m.* dirt, filth (in quantity); dirty things; obscenity; (in raw wool) yolk.

sudor-e *m.* sweat, perspiration; essere tutto in —, to be in a sweat; promuovere il —, to promote perspiration; frutto dei propri' -i, fruit of one's labour; col — della fronte, by the sweat of one's brow; gli venivano i -i della morte, he was in great distress (or pain); — freddo, cold sweat; mi vengono i -i freddi al solo pensarci, it makes me shudder even to think of it; (bot.) flux. **-azione** *f.* perspiration. **-i·fero** *adj.* promoting perspiration; sudorific; ghiandole -ifere, sweat glands; *n.m.* sudorific. **-i·fico** *adj.* sudorific. **-i·paro** *adj.* (anat.) sudoriparous.

sud-ovest *m. indecl.* south-west; (naut.) sou'wester (wind).

suesposto *adj.* above-stated.

suffetto *m.* (hist.) substitute.

suffici-ente *adj.* sufficient, enough; la tua parola sarà —, your word will suffice; abbiamo tempo più che —, we have time enough and to spare; capable; adequate; capacious; (in a school report) fair, very fair; tessuto —, hard-wearing cloth; *n.m.* sufficiency, enough; ha il — per vivere, he has enough to live on; †(of a person) able, capable; fare il -ente, to have a high opinion of oneself. **-ente·mente** *adv.* sufficiently, enough. **-enza** *f.* sufficiency; sufficient quantity; aptitude; ability; complacency; haughtiness; (school) pass-mark; a -enza, enough, sufficiently.

suffisso *m.* (gramm.) suffix.

†**suffocare** *vb.* and derivs. See **soffocare.**

†**suffol·cere** *vb.* and derivs. See **soffolcere.**

sufformativo *adj.* formative in secondary degree.

suffrag-are [A2] *tr.* to support, to assist; — la tesi, to maintain the thesis; (theol.) to pray for (the dead), to help (the dead) by prayers or good works. **-aneità** *f.* (eccl.) suffraganship, suffragan status. **-a·neo,** †**-ano** *adj.* (eccl.) suffragan (bishop); priest with vote in chapter. **-ante** *part., n.m.* supporter, voter (in favour); (eccl.) one who votes for a canonization. **-ato** *part. adj.* supported, assisted. **-atore** *m.* supporter; *adj.* supporting, favouring; (rel.) preghiera -atrice, prayer of intercession. **-azione** *f.* support; voting; (theol.) prayers (for the dead).

suffra·g-io *m.* vote, suffrage; approval, support; eletto per — di popolo, elected by popular vote; suffragi espressi, votes cast; il diritto di —, the (right to) vote; (theol.) (spiritual) help (esp. to the dead); messa in — di uno, mass said for, on behalf of, someone; (theol., *pl.*) 'suffrages', prayers (or good works) offered for the dead; -i comuni, prayers for all the faithful departed; -i particolari, prayers for a particular dead person. **-etta** *f.* suffragette. **-ista** *m., f.* suffragist.

suffru·tice *m.* (bot.) shrub, bush.

†**suffulto** *part.* of **soffolcere,** q.v.

suffumic-are, suffumig-are [A2s] *tr.* to fumigate. **-amento** *m.* fumigation. **(-ato** *part. adj.*) **-azione** *f.* fumigation.

suffumi·gio *m.* fumigation; vapour, exhalation produced for purposes of magic; inhalant.

suffus-o *adj.* see **soffuso. -ione** *f.* (med.) suffusion; cataract.

sugare [A2] and derivs. See **asciugare** or **succhiare.**

†**sugatto** *m.* See **sogatto.**

suggell-o *m.* seal; pledge; (leg.) apporre i -i a, to seal; (fig.) aveva il — della morte in viso, his face bore the marks of death. **-amento** *m.* sealing (up). **-are** [A1] *tr.* to seal; to seal up; to stamp; questo -ò la nostra amicizia, this sealed our friendship; *intr.* (*aux.* avere) to fit closely, to close. **-ato** *part. adj.* sealed; closed, close, tight. **-atamente** *adv.* closely, tight. **(-atore** *m.* **-atrice** *f.*) **-atura** *f.* seal(ing); stamp.

sug·gere [C def.] *tr.* to suck; to sip; to absorb; †dare — a, to give suck to.

sugger-ire [D2] *tr.* to suggest; to prompt; to advise; (theatr.) — la parte a un attore, to prompt an actor; non occorre che tu mi -isca quel che devo fare, there's no need for you to tell me what to do; †to proffer. **-imento** *m.* prompting; suggestion; hint;

sugger-ire (*cont.*)
  pl. advice. **-ito** *part. adj.* suggested; inspired; given by prompting. **-itore** *m.* (theatr.) prompter; buca del -itore, prompter's box; (fig.) non aver bisogno di -itore, to have no need to be told, to know what one is about. (**-itrice** *f.*)

suggest-ione *f.* (hypnotic) suggestion; instigation; temptation; (psych.) suggestion; (leg.) undue influence (upon testator); la — di una folla in tumulto, exciting influence of riotous crowd (C.P.). **-iona·bile** *adj.* suggestible. **-ionabilità** *f.* suggestibility. **-ionante** *part. adj.* hypnotic. **-ionare** [A I c] *tr.* to hypnotize. **-ionato** *part. adj.* hypnotized; unduly influenced. **-ivo** *adj.* stimulating; interesting; picturesque; luogo -ivo, romantic spot; domanda -iva, leading question.

suggesto *m.* (Rom. antiq.) *suggestus*; raised place, tribune; raised seat.

sug·gio *m.* (naut.) launching cradle bracket; chain plate; strengthening where shrouds and stays are secured.

suggrun·dio *m.* (Rom. antiq.) *suggrunda*, eaves.

†**sughera** *f.* (bot.). See **sughero**.

su·gher-o *m.* cork oak, *Quercus suber*; cork (stopper); testa di —, empty head; cork linoleum; something made of cork; cork float. **-ato** *part. adj.* corked, furnished with cork; scarpe -ate, cork-soled shoes; (paperm.) carta -ata, cork paper. **-ello** *m.* (ichth.) horse mackerel, *Trachurus trachurus*. **-eta** *f.*, **-eto** *m.* plantation of cork-trees. **-iera** *f.* cork-container (for an ice-box). **-oso** *adj.* cork-like; (scient.) suberose.

†**sugliardo** *adj.* dirty; repulsive.

sugn-a *f.* lard; (lubricating) grease. **-oso** *adj.* containing lard; greasy.

su·go *m.* (*pl.* **-ghi**) juice; sap; gravy; sauce; — finto, mock gravy, or sauce made without meat; (fig.) essence, substance; purpose; interest; una vita senza —, a dull life; non c'è —, there's no pleasure, point, in it; non so che — ci sia a parlare con lei, I don't know what pleasure there can be in talking to her; (Tusc.) liquid manure. **-gos·ità** *f.* juiciness; tastiness. **-goso** *adj.* juicy; succulent; tasty; (fig.) pithy; full of substance. (**-gosamente** *adv.*)

suicid-a *adj.* (*m.pl.* **-i**) suicidal; *n.m.* suicide (person); *f.* (*pl.* **-e**) woman suicide. **-are** [A I] *rfl.* to commit suicide.

suici·dio *m.* suicide, self-murder; — morale, moral, political or social suicide.

†**suil·lio** *m.* swine; *adj.* (joc.) swine-like.

suindicato *adj.* above-mentioned, aforesaid.

suino *adj.* of, pertaining to, swine; carne -a, pork; *n.m.* swine; hog; (fig., as term of abuse) swine; — verticale, two-legged swine.

sui-şmo *m.* egoism. †**-sta** *m., f.* egoist. †**-tà** *f.* egoism.

suite *f.* (decl. and pron. as Fr.) (mus.) suite; (art) set of drawings, etc.

sula *f.* (orn.) gannet, *Sula bassana*.

sulfami·dico *m.* (pharm.) sulphonamide, sulpha drug.

sulfocianuro *m.* (chem.) sulphocyanide, thiocyanate.

sulfon-ale *m.* (pharm.; chem.) sulphonal, sulphonmethane. **-alişmo** *m.* (med.) sulphonalism. **-ato** *m.* (chem.) sulphonate.

†**sul·fure** *m.* See **zolfo**.

sulfu·re-o *adj.* sulphureous; sulphurous; (composed of, pertaining to) sulphur; (fig.) temperamento —, irascible disposition. **-ità** *f.* sulphureousness.

sulla *f.* (bot.) French honeysuckle, *Hedysarum coronarium*.

sullo *m.* (ichth.) *Puntazzo puntazzo*, an edible marine fish.

sullodato *adj.* above-mentioned, already praised.

sullunare *adj.* sublunary.

sultan-o *m.* Sultan; (poultry) sultan; (colour) deep red. **-a** *f.* Sultana; divan; (naut.) large caique; **-ato** *m.* Sultanate. **-ina** *f.* sultana (raisin); kind of divan. **-ino** *m.* (numism.) sultanin, an old Turkish gold coin.

su·mere [B def.] (liturg.) (of priest) to receive (host and chalice), to make one's communion.

Sum-eri *pr.n.m.pl.* (hist.) Sumerians. **-e·rico** *adj.* Sumerian.

summen-tovato, -zionato *adj.* above-mentioned.

†**summessione** *f.* See **sommissione**.

Sunn-a *pr.n.f.* Sunna, sayings attributed to Mohammed. **-ita** *m.* Sunnite, 'orthodox' Mohammedan.

sunt-o *m.* summary, précis, recapitulation. **-eggiare** [A 3 c] *tr.* to summarize, to make a brief summary of.

suntu-a·rio *adj.* sumptuary. **-osità** *f.* magnificence, sumptuousness. **-oso** *adj.* sumptuous, lavish, magnificent. (**-osamente** *adv.*)

sunzione *f.* (liturg.) reception, receiving (of host and chalice); (priest's) communion.

suo *poss. adj.* (*m.pl.* **suoi**, *f.* **sua**, *pl.* **sue**) his, her, its; one's own; — padre, his, her, father; il — babbo, his, her, daddy; — fratello, his, her, brother; i suoi fratelli, his, her, brothers; la sua signora, his wife; son parole sue, those are his very words; proper; ogni cosa ha il — tempo, there is a time for everything; a — tempo, in due course; (fam.; poet.) their; *poss. prn.* his, her, its; di —, of his own accord; vuole dir la sua, he will have his say; star sulle sue, to be on one's guard; star sul suo, to stand, insist, on one's rights; i suoi, one's people, one's own family; ha fatto una delle sue, he has played one of his usual tricks, he has behaved as one might expect; spende del —, he is spending his own money; ha qualche santo dalla sua, he's a lucky man, he must have a lucky star, *or* he has powerful protection somewhere.

suo·cer-o, †**so·cero** *m.* father-in-law. **-a** *f.* mother-in-law; scold, nagging woman; mal della -a, pain in the funny-bone (when knocked); (bot.) -a e nuora, wild pansy, *Viola tricolor*; -a e nuora, cruet, twin joined bottles of oil and vinegar (twisted so that the mouths are pointing in opposite directions). **-ona** *f.* (fam.) domineering woman.

suol-a *f.* sole (of boot or shoe); (naut.) timber on a slipway forming the bearing surface of the cradle; (metall.) hearth; (mining) floor; (shoem.) sole; — interna, insole. **-o** *m.* (vet.) sole of the foot (of a horse). **-atura** *f.* (shoem.) soling. **-etta** *f.* (shoem.) insole.

suolo[1] *m.* See under **suola**.

suolo[2] *m.* ground, soil; il patrio —, one's native soil (land); cadere al —, to fall to the ground; radere al —, to raze to the ground; floor; tenne gli occhi fissi al —, he kept his eyes fixed on the ground (floor); (naut.) bottom of a keelless vessel; (geog.) — alluviale, leached soil; layer, stratum; †floor of a building.

suonare [A I d] and derivs. See **sonare**.

suoneri·a *f.* (watchm.) alarm; striking mechanism (of a clock); — elettrica, electric bell.

suon-o *m.* sound; note, ringing; — di campane, ringing of bells; (mus.) sound; -i armonici, harmonics, overtones; le parole e il —, words and music; cantare un —, to sing a song; (clock) alarm, striking mechanism of a clock; buzzing, singing, in the ears; (aeron.) muro del —, sound barrier.

suora *f.* (eccl.) nun, sister. NOTE: the final *a* is regularly dropped before a proper name. If no proper name is used, 'suora' as vocative is replaced by 'sorella'. Buon giorno, Suor Maria (Suor Anna), good morning, Sister Mary (Sister Anna). But 'Buon giorno, sorella', good morning, sister.

suovetauri·lia *m.pl.* (Rom. antiq.) *suovetaurilia*, triple sacrifice.

super *Lat. pref.* used in certain compounds, e.g. **superuomo**, superman.

super-are [A I S] *tr.* to surpass, to excel; to overcome; — l'avversario, to get the better of one's opponent; to get through, to get over; — un esame, to pass an examination; — una malattia, to recover from an illness; to exceed; -a per velocità qualunque altra macchina, it is superior in speed to any other machine (*or* car), its speed exceeds that of any other car; to pass over, to get over, to climb over; — un muro, to climb over a wall; — sè stesso, to surpass oneself; *intr.* (*aux.* essere) to be too big; to be too many; to be excessive; (naut.) to gain (when ship's pumps are sufficient to counteract a leak). **-a·bile** *adj.* surmountable, superable; surpassable. **-amento** *m.* overcoming; excelling. **-ato** *part. adj.* overcome, surpassed; (of an exam) passed. (**-atore** *m.* **-atrice** *f.*)

super·bia *f.* pride, arrogance; haughtiness; presumption; montare, levarsi, in —, to grow proud, to put on airs; mettere —, to become conceited; gonfio di —, swollen with pride; (theol.) pride (as a deadly sin).

super·b-o, †**-io** *adj.* proud; arrogant, haughty; presumptuous; andar — di, to be arrogant about, to be conceited about; superb, splendid; extremely high, topmost, le -e vette, the topmost peaks; *n.m.* proud man. **-a** *f.* proud woman; la Superba, Genoa; *pl.* the proud, proud people. **-amente** *adv.* proudly; haughtily; arrogantly; superbly, magnificently. **-ioso** *adj.* haughty. †**-ire** *vb.* and derivs. see **insuperbire**.

supercentri·fuga *f.* (eng.) supercentrifuge.

supercompensazione *f.* (psych.) overcompensation.

supereroga-to·rio *adj.* supererogatory. **-zione** *f.* (theol.) supererogation.

superessenziale *adj.* (theol.) superessential.

supereterodina *f.* (radio) superheterodyne.

superfecondazióne *f.* (biol.) superfecundation.

superfetazióne *f.* (med.) superfoetation; (gramm.) pleonasm; superfluity.

superfi·c-ie *f. indecl.* (or *pl.* **-i**) surface; surface area; area; outside; — interna, inner surface (e.g. of a vault); vedere le cose alla —, to take a superficial view; (leg.) diritto di —, superficial tenure (of building as separate tenement from 'suolo', soil) (C.C.); (naut.) surface; — bagnata della carena, wetted surface; — velica, sail area. **-iale** *adj.* superficial; hasty; conoscenza -iale, superficial knowledge, smattering; (phys.) tensione -iale, surface tension. **-ialmente** *adv.* superficially; hastily; lightly, on the surface. **-ialità** *f.* superficiality; surface; smattering (of knowledge).

superfluidità *f.* (phys.) superfluidity.

super·flu-o *adj.* superfluous, redundant; unnecessary; spese -e, needless expense(s); gratuitous; (mus.) intervallo —, augmented interval; *n.m.* surplus. **-amente** *adv.* superfluously, excessively. **-ità** *f.* superfluity; excess.

superfosfato *m.* (chem.; agric.) superphosphate.

superillustre *adj.* See **sovraillustre**.

superimpregnazióne *f.* (biol.) superimpregnation, superfecundation.

superinfóndere [C2] *tr.* to pour in from above; to infuse.

superinfuso *part.* of **superinfondere**, *q.v.*; *adj.* infused from on high; virtù superinfusa, strength (virtue) from on high.

superiór-e *adj.* superior; upper, higher; piano —, flat above, upper floor; gli arti -i, the upper limbs, the arms; Italia —, Northern Italy; corso — del fiume, upper reaches of the river; corpi -i, heavenly bodies, stars; secoli -i, earlier ages (centuries); il compito è — alle mie forze, the task is beyond my strength; — a ogni elogio, beyond praise; è un uomo —, he is a highly gifted man; qualità —, better quality; ufficiale —, field officer; ordine —, order of a superior office; istruzione —, higher education, university education (teaching); scuole -i, colleges, places of higher education; *n.m.* person of higher rank, superior, superior officer; senior; (eccl.) (Father) Superior; *pl.* one's betters; the authorities. **-mente** *adv.* above; on the upper side; in a higher degree; †formerly. **-a** *f.* (eccl.) (Mother) Superior. **-ato** *m.* (eccl.) status, office, of Superior. **-ità** *f.* superiority; con aria di -ità, with a superior air; vinto dalla -ità del numero, beaten by superior numbers.

superlativ-o *adj., n.m.* superlative; al —, in the superlative. **-amente** *adv.* superlatively, in the highest degree.

superlazióne *f.* superlative condition; hyperbole.

supernale *adj.* See under **superno**.

supern-o *adj.* (poet.) celestial, divine; supreme; supernal. **-amente** *adv.* from on high, from heaven. **-ale** *adj.* supernal; la città -ale, the heavenly city, paradise.

Supernova *pr.n.f.* (astron.) Supernova.

su·pero *adj.* (poet.) upper, superior; il Mare —, the Adriatic; (bot.) ovario —, superior ovary; *n.m.pl.* the powers above, the gods; (comm.) superi di cassa, cash over.

superpesante *adj.* (techn.) extra heavy.

superpolia·mide *f.* (chem.) superpolyamide.

superposizióne *f.* supremacy, overlordship.

superreazióne *f.* (radio) super-reaction, super-regeneration.

superso·nico *adj.* (aeron.) supersonic.

super·stite *adj.* surviving; *n.m.,* *f.* survivor.

superstizi-óne *f.* superstition. **-osità** *f.* superstitiousness, superstition. **-oso** *adj.* superstitious; credulous. (**-osamente** *adv.*)

superumerale *m.* (Bibl.) ephod; (eccl.) (monastic) scapular.

superuomo *m.* superman.

supervac-a·neo, †-**ano** *adj.* superfluous, unnecessary.

supervis-ióne *f.* (cinem.) supervision. **-ore** *m.* (cinem.) supervisor.

supin-o *adj.* lying on one's back; supine (also fig.); cadere —, to fall on one's back; fare il viso —, to look blank; mani -e, hands held palms uppermost; errore —, gross mistake; obbedienze -a, slavish obedience; *adv. phr.* alla -a, on one's back; *n.m.* (gramm.) supine. **-amente** *adv.* supinely, carelessly, indolently; slavishly; -amente ignorante, crassly ignorant. **-are** [A1] *tr.* (anat.) to supinate. **-atore** *adj.* (anat.) supinator. (**-atrice** *f.*) **-azióne** *f.* (anat.) supination, turning the hand palm uppermost.

†**suppa** *f.* See **zuppa**.

sup·paro *m.* (Rom. antiq.) *supparum*, linen garment.

supped-a·neo *m.* see **soppedaneo**. †-**iano** *adj.* see **soppidiano**.

suppellet·tile *f.* furniture; usu. *pl.* articles of furniture; household goods; equipment; fittings; (eccl.) ornaments, furnishing, of a church; (archaeol.) archaeological material.

suppergiù *adv.* (also **su per giù**) approximately, nearly; by and large; roughly speaking; ripetè — le stesse parole, he repeated practically the same words; avere — la stessa età, to be about the same age.

supplemént-o *m.* supplement; addition; extra; appendix; supplementary volume (or part of a journal); (geom.) supplement; (rlwy.) additional fare payable on 'rapidi' and 'trains de luxe'; (comm.) — di dichiarazioni doganali, post entry. **-are** *adj.* supplementary, additional; (geom.) angolo -are, supplementary angle; (comm.) assicurazione -are, overinsurance; ore -ari, overtime.

suppl-ente *adj.* supplementary; maestro, professore —, schoolteacher on supply, temporary master; substitute, deputy; locum tenens. **-enza** *f.* temporary post, supply work; substitution.

suppletiv-o *adj.* supplementary. (**-amente** *adv.*)

suppleto·rio *adj.* supplementary; (leg.) giuramento —, interrogatory; question(s) to be answered on oath, put to party by Court, in civil action (C.C.P.).

sup·plica *f.* petition; supplication, entreaty.

supplic-are [A2s] *tr.* to beg, to implore, to entreat, to beseech. **-a·bile** *adj.* fit to be begged for. **-ante** *part. adj.* suppliant; *n.m., f.* petitioner, suppliant. **-ato** *part. adj.* begged, implored; *n.m.* favour, boon, object of a petition. **-atore** *m.* petitioner, suppliant; also *adj.* (**-atrice** *f.*) **-ato·rio** *adj.* (*in pl.* **-atorii**) of a petition; lettera -atoria, begging letter, letter of entreaty. **-azióne** *f.* supplication, prayer; entreaty; (Rom. antiq.) *supplicatio.*

sup·plic-e *adj., n.m.* suppliant. **-emente** *adv.* suppliantly, entreatingly.

supplichévol-e *adj.* suppliant, imploring, entreating; *n.m.* petitioner (in writing). **-mente** *adv.* suppliantly, with entreaties.

suppl-ire [D2] *intr.* (*aux.* avere; *prep.* a) to take the place (of); — a un bisogno, to meet a need; to make up (for); -isce con la diligenza alla scarsezza d'ingegno, he makes up for lack of brains by hard work; †to be sufficient; *tr.* to take the place of; to make up for; to deputize for; to replace temporarily. **-imento** *m.* deputizing; supplying; supplement. **-ito** *part. adj.* replaced; impiegato -ito da un collega, clerk temporarily replaced by a colleague.

suppli·zi-o *m.* punishment; torture, torment; questo è il — di Tantalo!, this is most tantalizing!; andare al —, to go to execution. **-are** [A4] *tr.* to torture; to execute. (**-ato** *part. adj.*)

sup-pórre [B21] *tr.* to suppose, to assume; to imagine; non -poneva neppur lontanamente che, he had not the faintest suspicion, the slightest idea, that; to infer, to take (for example or hypothesis); lo -pongo, I suppose so; †to substitute; to place under (as support); † — le fiamme, to stir up the fire. **-poni·bile** *adj.* possible to suppose, imaginable.

support-o *m.* (eng.) bearing; mounting; holder. †-**are** *vb.* and derivs. see **sopportare**.

suppositiv-o *adj.* hypothetical, conjectural. (**-amente** *adv.*)

supposíti·zi-o *adj.* (leg.) supposititious. **-amente** *adv.* suppositiously, by substitution.

†**suppositó·rio** *m.* (med.) suppository.

supposizióne *f.* supposition; nella — che, on the supposition that; (leg.) supposition; fraudulent substitution of another person or thing for the genuine one; — di parto, act of registering suppositious birth (C.P.).

supposta *f.* (med.) suppository.

suppósto *part.* of **supporre**, *q.v.*; *adj.* supposed, conjectured; substituted; (leg.) proprietà supposta, reputed ownership (C.C.); reato —, supposed offence (C.P.); *conj.* — che, supposing, supposing that; *n.m.* supposition; †(mus.) a kind of appoggiatura.

suppur-are [A1] *intr.* (*aux.* avere) (med.) to suppurate; to come to a head. **-a·bile** *adj.* (med.) liable to come to a head, capable of suppurating. **-amento** *m.* (med.) suppuration. **-ativo** *adj., n.m.* (med.) suppurative, suppurant. **-ato** *part. adj.* suppurating; *n.m.* pus. **-ato·rio** *adj.* (med.) suppurant. **-azióne** *f.* (med.) suppuration.

suprém-o *adj.* highest, supreme; greatest; crowning, paramount; il bene —, the greatest good; l'Essere —, the Supreme Being; il tribunale —, the highest (supreme) court; una donna di -a bellezza, a supremely beautiful woman; in grado —, in the highest degree; i -i conforti della religione, the last consolations of religion; il — addio, the last goodbye; (theol.) giudizio —, Last Judgement. **-amente** *adv.* supremely; in the highest degree; most. **-azi·a** *f.* supremacy, highest authority.

sur *prep.* used in place of **su** for euphony before a word beginning with a vowel (now antiquated).

sur-a[1] *f.* (anat.) calf, sura; calf bone, fibula. **-ale** *adj.* sural.

Sura[2] *pr.n.f.* Sura, chapter of the Koran.

Sura[3] *pr.n.f.* (geog.) Surat, in India.

surclassare [A I] *tr.* (sport) to outclass.

surcontre *f. indecl.* (pron. as Fr.) (cards, bridge) 'redouble'.

surdimensionato *adj.* (techn.) oversize.

†**sur·gere** *vb.* See **sorgere**.

surmenage *m. indecl.* (pron. as Fr.) overwork, ill-usage.

suro *m.* (ichth.) horse mackerel, *Trachurus trachurus*.

surreal-işmo *m.* surrealism. **-ista** *m., f.* surrealist. **-i·stico** *adj.* surrealist.

surrenale *adj.* (anat.) suprarenal.

sur-retti·zio *adj.* surreptitious; (leg.) obtained by suppression of truth or fraudulent misrepresentation. **-rettiziamẹnte** *adv.* surreptitiously. †**-rezione** *f.* (leg.) surreption; want of good consideration.

surriferito *adj.* above-mentioned, aforesaid.

surriscald-are [A I] *tr.* (techn.) to overheat; to superheat. **-amẹnto** *m.* (techn.) overheating; superheating. **-ato** *part. adj.* (techn.) vapore -ato, superheated steam. **-atọre** *m.* (eng.) superheater.

surro *m.* (ichth.). See **suro**.

sur·roga *f.* substitution.

surrog-are [A 2] *tr.* (*prep.* a) to take the place (of), to replace; to substitute (for). (**-a·bile** *adj.* **-abilità** *f.*) **-amẹnto** *m.* substituting. **-ante** *part. adj.* replacing; *n.m., f.* supply, substitute. **-ato** *part. adj.* substituted; replaced; *n.m.* deputy; temporary substitute; -ato del caffè, coffee ersatz, substitute. **-ato·rio** *adj.* (leg.) of, having to do with subrogation. **-azione** *f.* substitution; (leg.) subrogation.

survolt-ag·gio *m.* (electr.) additional voltage, boosting voltage. **-ọre** *m.* (electr.) positive booster; -ore devoltore, positive and negative booster. **-rice** *f.* (electr.) voltage booster.

Susanna *pr.n.f.* Susan; (Bibl.) Susanna; (joc.; iron.) far, parer, la casta —, to play the innocent.

suscettanza *f.* (electr.) susceptance.

suscett-i·bile *adj.* (*prep.* di) susceptible, capable (of); touchy, easily offended. **-ibilità** *f.* susceptibility; touchiness; bada di non offendere la sua -ibilità, be careful not to hurt his feelings. **-ività** *f.* susceptibility, receptivity; (phys.) susceptibility. **-ivo** *adj.* receptive; susceptible.

suscit-are [A I s] *tr.* to arouse, to stir up, to provoke; to give rise to; — curiosità, to arouse curiosity; — proteste, to give rise to claims, to draw protests; (poet.) to raise (up). **-amẹnto** *m.* arousing, stirring up, creation. **-ato** *part. adj.* aroused; stirred up; provided. (**-atọre** *m.* **-atrice** *f.*)

susin-a *f.* plum; — secca, prune; (fig.) — acerba, misfortune. **-o** *m.* (bot.) plum, *Prunus domestica*; plum-tree.

†**suso** *adv.* up, upwards.

†**susorniare** *intr.* to grumble; to murmur.

suspiciọne *f.* (leg.) suspicion (obsolete except in expression); per legittima —, for legitimate fear of no fair trial.

sussecutiv-o *adj.* subsequent; successive. **-amẹnte** *adv.* successively, subsequently, after(wards).

sussegu-ire [D I] *intr.* (*aux.* essere; *prep.* a) to be subsequent (to), to succeed, to follow; al lampo -e il tuono, thunder follows the lightning; *recip. rfl.* to follow one another, to occur in quick succession. **-ente** *part. adj.* subsequent, following; next (following); (geog., of streams) subsequent. (**-entemẹnte** *adv.*) **-enza** *f.* succession.

†**sussi** *m. indecl.* a primitive form of quoits; essere il —, to be ʈ butt, or to be a mere figurehead.

sussi·di-o *m.* help, aid, reinforcement(s); subsidy, grant ̶ ̶ ̶ ̶ention; grant in aid; dole; — di disoccupazione, unemploᵧ̲ment benefit; — di malattia, sickness benefit; †suggestion. **-are** [A 4] *tr.* to subsidize, to help (esp. with money); to aid, to assist. **-a·rio** *adj.* subsidiary, auxiliary, reserve; (naut.) motore -ario, auxiliary motor; (eccl.) capella -aria, side chapel; *n.m.* notes, commentary. **-ariamẹnte** *adv.* subsidiarily. **-ato** *part. adj.* aided, subsidized. **-atọre** *m.* helper, supporter, benefactor. (**-atrice** *f.*)

sussie-go *m.* (*pl.* **-ghi**) imposing air, hauteur, stiff attitude, exaggerated dignity; trattare uno con —, to treat someone condescendingly; mettersi in —, to stand on one's dignity.

sussi·st-ere [C] *intr.* (*aux.* essere, avere) to exist; to subsist; non —, to be non-existent. **-ente** *part. adj.* existent; substantial. **-enza** *f.* subsistence; existence; victualling.

†**sussolano** *m.* (naut.) East wind.

sussult-are [A I] *intr.* (*aux.* avere) to start; to tremble; il suo cuore -ò a quel grido, his heart beat violently at that cry; — di gioia, to jump for joy; il terreno -ò sotto i nostri piedi, the earth trembled beneath our feet. **-o** *m.* start, jump; leap; tremor; ebbi un -o, I gave a start; -i terrestri, earth tremors. **-o·rio** *adj.* jerky; jumpy; (of the earth) rumbling.

sus(s)urr-are [A I] *tr.* to whisper; to murmur; — un nome, to whisper a name; — segreti, to whisper secrets; to mention privately; to breathe in secret; non lo -erei a nessuno, I wouldn't breathe a word about it to anyone; *intr.* (*aux.* avere) to whisper, to talk quietly, to murmur; (of bees, etc.) to hum; (poet.) to rustle. **-amẹnto** *m.* whispering; murmuring; (poet.) rustling. (**-ato** *part. adj.*) **-atọre** *m.* whisperer; murmurer; grumbler. **-azịọne** *f.* murmuration. **-ino** *m. dim.* child (e.g. at school) who keeps chattering, 'talker'. (**-ina** *f.*) **-ịo** *m.* continual murmuring, whispering; buzz of conversation; rustling. **-o** *m.* whisper; murmur; hum; buzz; grumbling. (**-ọne** *m. augm.*)

sust-a *f.* (mechanical) spring; (naut.) halyard; purchase; tackle; (Ven.) brace or lift on a yard (cf. **sosta**); *pl.* ear-pieces of a pair of spectacles. †**-ino** *m.* (naut.) small guy or downhaul.

†**sustante** *adv. phr.* in —, standing up.

†**sustanz-a** *f.*, †**-ia** *f.* and derivs. See **sostanza**.

†**sustentare** *vb.* and derivs. See **sostentare**.

†**sustitu-ire** *vb.*, **-zione** *f.* See **sostitu-ire**, **-zione**.

†**suto** *part.* of **essere**, q.v.

sutra *f.* (Sanskrit lit.) Sutra.

sutro *m.* (orn.) spotted crake.

sutur-a *f.* (surg.) suture; (anat.) suture, synarthrosis. **-ale** *adj.* (anat.) sutural. **-are** [A I] *tr.* (surg.) to suture. (**-ato** *part. adj.*)

†**su·vero** *m.* See **sughero**.

†**suvvi** *adj.* up there, up aloft.

suzzac·chera *f.* (Tusc.) (fig.) tiresome job; †vinegar with sugar.

suzzare [A I] *tr.* (fam., Tusc.) to dry (with a cloth or sponge); to mop up; to absorb; — una bibita, to drink a beverage slowly.

şvag-are [A 2] *tr.* to amuse, to divert; non ci vuol molto a -arlo, it is easy to distract his attention; *rfl.* to while away the time, to amuse oneself; to find distraction; ho bisogno di -armi, I need some amusement; to stray, to wander from the path. **-amẹnto** *m.* diversion, distraction, relaxation, amusement. **-atag·gine** *f.* love of amusement; lack of concentration; absent-mindedness. **-atẹzza** *f.* absent-mindedness. **-ativo** *adj.* amusing, recreative; diverting. **-ato** *part. adj.* absent-minded, inattentive; heedless, thoughtless; relaxed; *n.m.* absent-minded person; pleasure-seeker. (**-ata** *f.*)

şva-go *m.* (*pl.* **-ghi**) amusement, diversion, relaxation, recreation; play; abbiamo bisogno di un po' di —, we need a little relaxation; ai bambini fanno male troppi -ghi, too many amusements are bad for children.

şvaligi-are [A 4] *tr.* (usu. joc.) to ransack, to rifle, to plunder; (slang) to clean out; le hanno -ato la casa, they took everything she had in the house; — i libri di altri scrittori, to plagiarize other writers, to 'lift' from other people's writings. **-amẹnto** *m.* plundering. (**-ato** *part. adj.*) **-atọre** *m.* plunderer. (**-atrice** *f.*)

şvalorizz-are [A I] *intr.* (*aux.* essere) (finan.) to depreciate. (**-ato** *part. adj.*) **-azịọne** *f.* (finan.) depreciation.

şvalut-are [A I] *tr.* to undervalue, to depreciate, to devalue. (**-ato** *part. adj.*) **-azịọne** *f.* (neol.) depreciation; devaluation; undervaluation.

şvampare[1] [A I] *intr.* (*aux.* essere, avere) (of flame, heat, steam, etc.) to blaze forth; to burst out; to escape; to evaporate; to be consumed, to go up in smoke.

şvampare[2] [A I] *intr.* (*aux.* essere) to die down; to diminish; to cool.

şvan-ire [D 2] *intr.* (*aux.* essere) to vanish, to disappear; to come to nothing; to lose flavour, quality or strength; to evaporate; to be dispersed; to cool down; to pass. **-ẹvole** *adj.* evanescent. **-imẹnto** *m.* vanishing; fading away. **-itic·cio** *adj.* evanescent. **-ito** *part. adj.* vanished; empty; enfeebled; affare -ito, abortive affair; avere la memoria -ita, to have no longer so good a memory as one had; senile, wandering.

şvano *m.* door or window-opening; recess, cavity.

şvantag·gi-o *m.* disadvantage, drawback; detriment; prejudice; a — di, to the disadvantage of. **-ọso** *adj.* unfavourable, detrimental; disadvantageous; prejudicial. (**-osamẹnte** *adv.*)

şvan·zica *f.* (numism.) zwanziger, Austrian coin, value 20 kreuzer.

ṣvapor-are [A I c] *intr.* (*aux.* essere) to evaporate; (fig.) to vanish, to disappear, to fade away; to die down, to cool; *tr.* to (make) evaporate. **-a·bile** *adj.* volatile, liable to evaporate. **-amẹnto** *m.* evaporation. **-ata** *f.* (joc.) trip in a steamboat. **-ato** *part. adj.* (fig.) una ragazzina ~ata, a silly empty-headed little girl. **-aziọne** *f.* evaporation. **-eggiare** [A 3 c] *intr.* (*aux.* essere) to keep evaporating; to boil away. **-ire** [D 2] *intr.* (*aux.* essere) to vaporize, to become vaporized.

ṣvari-are [A 4] *tr.* to change; to divert; to cause to vary; *intr.* (*aux.* avere, essere); to vary, to change; to waver; to change colour; to be unstable. **-amẹnto** *m.* varying. **-ante** *part. adj.* various, varied; varying. **-atẹzza** *f.* variety. **-ato** *part. adj.* various, varied; diverse. **-atamẹnte** *adv.* variously.

ṣva·ri-o *m.* difference; variation. **-ọne** *m.* blunder.

ṣvaṣ-are [A I] *tr.* (hortic.) to plant out; to repot; (eng.) to flare; to countersink. **-amẹnto** *m.* planting; repotting; (eng.) countersinking; (techn.) widening, flare. **-ato** *part. adj.* planted; repotted; (eng.) countersunk. **-atura** *f.* planting out; potting; funnel; (eng.) countersinking; flare (of a tuyère); (bldg.) hollow, -atura muraria, embrasure.

ṣvasso *m.* (orn.) grebe; — collorosso, red-necked grebe, *Podiceps griseigena*; — cornuto, Slavonian grebe, *P. auritus*; — maggiore, great crested grebe, *P. cristatus*; — piccolo, black-necked or eared grebe, *P. caspicus*.

ṣva·stica *f.*, **ṣva·stika** *f.* swastika.

ṣvecchi-are [A 4 c] *tr.* to renew, to freshen up; to modernize; to prune (removing old wood). **(-amẹnto** *m.* **-ato** *part. adj.*) **-atura** *f.* renewal; modernization; pruning.

ṣveccia-tọio, **-tọre** *m.* sieve (esp. for sifting and grading corn); shelling machine.

ṣvedese *m.* Swede; Swedish (language); *f.* Swedish woman or girl; *adj.* Swedish; fiammifero —, safety match.

ṣvẹgli-a *f.* awakening; reveille; alarm-bell; dare la —, to sound the alarm; alarm-clock; calibro a —, alarm-watch; (mus.) reveille, an obsolete wind-instrument. **-amẹnto** *m.* (rare) awakening; waking. **-are** [A 4 c] *tr.* to awaken, to wake, to wake up; -atemi presto, call me early; (fig.) to rouse, to animate, to excite; -are l'appetito, to stimulate the appetite; *rfl.* to wake, to wake up; to be awakened; (of a wind) to rise; (of vegetation) to grow quickly. **-arino** *m.* alarm clock; memorandum, reminder. **-ata** *f.* awakening. **-atẹzza** *f.* wakefulness, liveliness; quickness, vivacity; readiness; -atezza d'ingegno, quick-wittedness. **-ato** *part. adj.* awake; wideawake; quick-witted. **-atọio** *m.* awakener, alarm. **-atọre** *m.* awakener, alarm. **(-atrice** *f.*)

ṣvẹgli-o *adj.* awake; wideawake, vigilant; quick-witted; clever. **-ọne** *m.* (mus.) a large **sveglia**, q.v.

ṣvel-are [A I] *tr.* to unveil, to reveal, to disclose; *rfl.* to unveil, to reveal oneself. **-amẹnto** *m.* unveiling, disclosure; revelation. **-ato** *part. adj.* unveiled; bare; revealed, disclosed. **-atamẹnte** *adv.* openly. **-atọre** *m.* unveiler; revealer. **(-atrice** *f.*)

ṣvelen-are [A I c] *tr.* to remove poison from; *rfl.* to give vent to one's malice. **(-ato** *part. adj.*) **-ire** [D 2] *tr.* to remove the poison from; (fig.) -ire una satira, to take the venom (the sting) out of a satire; *rfl.* to give vent to one's anger, hatred, etc., to vent one's spite.

†**ṣvelicare** *vb.* and derivs. See **svelare**.

†**ṣvellato** *adj.* flowing (of hair, or mane).

ṣvel·l-ere [B 31] *tr.* to uproot; to pluck out, to tear out; (fig.) to extirpate, to eradicate; *rfl.* to tear oneself away. **-imẹnto** *m.* uprooting; eradication.

ṣvelocipedare [A I] *intr.* (*aux.* avere) to cycle, to ride a velocipede; to pedal away.

ṣvelto[1] *part.* of **svellere**, q.v.

ṣvelt-o[2] *adj.* slender, svelte; lively, brisk; quick-witted, smart; — di mano, light-fingered; — di lingua, talkative; camminare con passo —, to walk quickly; *adv.* rapidly; parla —, he talks very fast. **-ẹzza** *f.* slenderness; grace; quickness, agility, nimbleness; -ezza di mente, nimble-mindedness, cleverness; -ezza di mano, sleight of hand. **-ire** [D 2] *tr.* to make slender; to liven up, to smarten up; to make supple; *rfl.* to smarten oneself up; to become livelier; to become slim. **(-ito** *part. adj.*)

ṣven-are [A I] *tr.* to bleed to death; (fig.) to bleed (by extortion of money); *rfl.* to open one's veins. **-amẹnto** *m.* bleeding; blood-letting. **-ato** *part. adj.* bled, suffering from loss of blood; morire -ato, to bleed to death; impoverished. **-atura** *f.* bleeding; (vet.) gape of the mouth (of a horse).

ṣvẹnd-ere [B I] *tr.* to sell off (below cost), to clear; -e la casa, he is selling the (his) house for a song (or, for what it will fetch). **(-uto** *part. adj.*)

ṣvẹndita *f.* selling-off; underselling.

ṣvenẹvole *adj.* See under **svenire**.

ṣve·nia *f.* sentimental affection; wheedling; simpering; *pl.* languishing gestures, simpering.

ṣven-ire [D 17] *intr.* (*aux.* essere), *rfl.* to faint, to swoon; sentirsi —, to feel faint; †(of light) to fade, to go out. **-ẹvole** *adj.* languishing; sentimental; simpering, affected. **(-evolmẹnte** *adv.*) **-evolẹzza** *f.* affectation; sentimentality; simpering; languishing behaviour. **-imẹnto** *m.* (med.) faint, fainting, syncope. **-uto** *part. adj.* in a faint, in a swoon; unconscious.

ṣventagli-are [A 4] *tr.* to wave, to flap; to scatter; to spread out; *rfl.* to fan (oneself). **(-ato** *part. adj.*)

ṣvent-are [A I] *tr.* — una mina, to frustrate a mine by countermining; un vulcano può — la forza del terremoto, a volcano may diminish, like a safety-valve, the force of the earthquake; (fig.) to frustrate, to foil, to baffle, to thwart; — una trama, to foil a plot; — un disegno, to thwart a plan; (naut.) — una vela, to empty a sail; †(agric.) to winnow; *intr.* (*aux.* essere) (of gas, air, etc.) to escape; (mil.) to unload the shot leaving a blank charge in the gun; *rfl.* to fan oneself, to give oneself air; (of a sail) to empty itself of wind. **-atag·gine** *f.*, **-atẹzza** *f.* thoughtlessness, heedlessness, carelessness; light-headedness; thoughtless action. **-ato** *part. adj.* foiled, frustrated; misfired; thoughtless, careless; light-headed, scatter-brained; *adv. phr.* alla -ata, thoughtlessly; *n.m.* thoughtless person. **(-ata** *f.* **-atamẹnte** *adv.*)

ṣvẹn·tol-a *f.* fan; fire-fan; winnowing fan; (pop.) slap; *pl.* big ears, flapping ears. **-amẹnto** *m.* waving, fluttering, flapping; fanning. **-are** [A I s] *tr.* to unfurl, to fly (e.g. a flag); to wave, to flap; *intr.* (*aux.* avere) to wave, to flap, to fly, flutter; *rfl.* to fan oneself. **-ata** *f.* fanning; flutter (esp. of a fan). **-ato** *part. adj.* waved, waving; fluttering. **-io** *m.* continued waving, fluttering.

ṣventr-are [A I] *tr.* to disembowel, to rip open; to open up; (of fish) to gut; (of poultry) to draw; to demolish, to gut a house; to widen (a street); to clear (slums); *intr.* (*aux.* avere) to eat too much, to eat fit to burst; *rfl.* to wound oneself in the belly. **-amẹnto** *m.* disembowelling, gutting; drawing (poultry); demolition; widening. **-ata** *f.* evisceration; free action of the bowels, evacuation. **-ato** *part. adj.* disembowelled, gutted, drawn; gluttonous. **-aziọne** *f.* (med.) eventration.

ṣventur-a *f.* misfortune; mishap; bad luck; per mia —, unfortunately for me; compagno di —, companion in misfortune; colpo di —, stroke of bad luck. **-ato** *adj.* unfortunate, unlucky; hapless; *n.m.* unlucky man; poor wretch. **-ata** *f.* unfortunate woman. **-atamẹnte** *adv.* unfortunately, unluckily.

ṣvenuto *part.* of **svenire**, q.v.

ṣverdire [D 2] *intr.* (*aux.* avere) to fade; to wither (of green leaves, etc.).

ṣvergin-are [A I s] *tr.* to ravish, to deprive of virginity; to deflower; (fig.) to initiate; to use for the first time; (poet.) — la spada, to blood one's sword. **-amẹnto** *m.* deflowering. **-ato** *part. adj.* ravished, deflowered; (fig.) used for the first time. **-atọre** *m.* ravisher; first lover.

ṣvergogn-are [A I c] *tr.* to disgrace, to humiliate; to put to shame, to shame; to defame; fu -ato in pubblico, he was publicly disgraced. **-ag·gine** *f.* shamelessness; impudence. **-amẹnto** *m.* disgracing; humiliating; †impudence. **-atẹzza** *f.* impudence, shamelessness; piece of impudence. **-ato** *part. adj.* shameless, impudent; put to shame, abashed. **-atamẹnte** *adv.* shamelessly, impudently.

ṣvergol-are [A I s] *tr.* (aeron.) to warp; (eng.) to twist, to warp. **-amẹnto** *m.* (eng.; aeron.) twist, warp; -amento positivo, wash-in; -amento negativo, wash-out. **(-ato** *part. adj.*)

ṣvern-are[1] [A I] *intr.* (*aux.* avere) to spend the winter; (silkb.) to winter; (bot.) to overwinter. **-amẹnto** *m.* spending the winter, wintering; (of silkworm eggs) wintering.

ṣvern-are[2] *intr.* (*aux.* essere) (of winter) to end; (of spring) to begin; *intr.* (*aux.* avere) (of birds) to sing in springtime.

ṣverre [B 31]. See **svellere**.

ṣverz-a *f.* stick; splinter (of wood, glass, etc.). **-are** [A I] *tr.* to splinter; to split (wood) into sticks; to mend with small pieces of wood; *rfl.*, *intr.* (*aux.* essere) to splinter, to split up. **(-ato** *part. adj.*) **-ino** *m.* cord at the end of a whiplash.

ṣvesci-are [A 3 c] *tr.* to blurt out; to blab. **(-ato** *part. adj.*) **-atọre** *m.*, **-ọne** *m.* windy gas-bag, person who blabs. **(-atrice** *f.* **-ọna** *f.*)

svescic-are [A2] *tr.* to raise a blister on, to blister; *rfl.* to blister. **-ato** *part. adj.* blistered.

svest-ire [D1] *tr.* to undress; to take off; to strip; to divest; (fig.) to lay aside; *rfl.* to undress (oneself); -irsi nudo, to strip naked. **-ito** *part. adj.* undressed; stripped; -ito di pelo (e.g. of cottonseed) freed from hairs.

svett-are [A1] *tr.* to poll, to pollard, to trim the tops of (hedges, etc.); — un bastoncino, to whittle a stick; — i capelli, to trim hair; *intr.* (*aux.* avere) (of trees, plants) to wave their tops; to loom, to be visible, to show (at a height); to be silhouetted. (**-amento** *m.*) **-ato** *part. adj.* pollarded, pollard; cut off at the top; il Vesuvio -ato, the truncated cone of Vesuvius. **-atura** *f.* pollarding.

Sve·via *pr.n.f.* (hist. geog.) Swabia.

svevo *adj.*, *n.m.* Swabian; Italo Svevo (Ettore Schmitz, 1861–1928).

Sve·zia *pr.n.f.* (geog.) Sweden.

svezz-are [A1c] *tr.* to wean; to rid of a habit; *rfl.* (*prep.* di) to be weaned; to break oneself (of). (**-ato** *part. adj.*)

†svezzese *adj.*, *n.m.* See svedese.

svi-are [A4] *tr.* to turn aside; to lead astray; (rlwy.) to switch; *rfl.* to go astray; to run off the lines; to go away, to take another direction. **-amento** *m.* deviation; turning aside; running off the lines; leading (or going) astray; (rlwy.) derailment. **-ato** *part. adj.* strayed, astray; wandering; misguided; boschi -ati, pathless woods; *n.m.* misguided person; one who has gone astray. (**-ata** *f.*) **-atoio** *m.* (rlwy.) cross-switch. **-atore** *m.* false guide. (**-atrice** *f.*)

svicolare [A1s] *intr.* (*aux.* essere, avere) to turn into an alley; to turn a corner; to dodge, to slip away; *rfl.* (*dat.* of *prn.* 'si') (fam.) svincolarsela, to 'skip'.

svign-are [A5] *intr.* (*aux.* essere) (fam.) to sneak away, to slip away; to make off; (*dat.* of *prn.* 'si') -arsela, to sneak off; appena mi vide arrivare se la -ò, as soon as he saw me coming he did a bunk.

svigor-ire [D2] *tr.* to weaken, to enfeeble; to attenuate; *intr.* (*aux.* essere), *rfl.* to become enfeebled; to deteriorate. **-imento** *m.* weakening, enfeeblement; loss of vigour. (**-ito** *part. adj.*)

svil-ire [D2] *tr.* to debase; to depreciate; to reduce (prices). **-imento** *m.* depreciation, debasement. **-ito** *part. adj.* debased; depreciated.

svillaneggi-are [A3c] *tr.* to abuse, to revile; to insult; *recip. rfl.* to abuse one another. **-amento** *m.* reviling; abuse. (**-ato** *part. adj.* **-atore** *m.* **-atrice** *f.*)

svilupp-are [A1] *tr.* to loose, to undo; to untie; to extricate; to develop, to amplify; — un argomento, to enlarge on a subject; — una trama, to work out a plot; — un attacco, to develop (carry out) an attack; (photog.) to develop; *rfl.*, *intr.* (*aux.* essere, avere) to develop, to grow; to increase; gli si -a l'intelligenza, his intelligence is developing; si -ò un incendio, a fire broke out; *rfl.* to free oneself, to break away; to shake off; si -ò dalle mani degli assalitori, he broke away from, shook off, his assailants. **-a·bile** *adj.* capable of development. **-ato** *part. adj.* untied, loosed; extricated; free; developed; well-grown; malattia -ata, fully developed disease (so as to be capable of diagnosis). **-atore** *m.* person who develops, etc.; (photog.) developer.

sviluppo *m.*. development; spread; growth; increase; età dello —, adolescence, the years of growth; nel suo pieno —, fully developed; (photog.) developing, development; exposition, treatment (of a subject); development, expansion (of business, etc.); (chem.) evolution (of a gas); (math.) development, expansion; (mus.) development, development-section.

†svi·mero *m.* four-wheeled carriage.

svin-are [A1] *intr.* (*aux.* essere) to draw the wine from the vat. (**-ato** *part. adj.* **-atore** *m.* **-atrice** *f.*) **-atura** *f.* drawing the wine from the fermenting vat into casks; the time when the wine-making is completed.

svincol-are [A1s] *tr.* to release, to free; to disengage; to redeem (from pawn, mortgage); to clear (from customs). **-amento** *m.* liberation, release, redemption. (**-ato** *part. adj.*)

svin·colo *m.* release, liberation, clearance; prendere uno —, to get a crick in one's neck (or pain in any joint, from sudden movement).

sviolin-are [A1] *tr.* (fam., joc.) to sing the praises of. (**-ata** *f.* **-atura** *f.*)

svirare [A1] *tr.* and derivs. (naut.). *See* devirare.

svis-are [A1] *tr.* (joc.) to scratch the face of; to disfigure; (fig.) to misrepresent, to distort. (**-amento** *m.* **-ato** *part. adj.*)

sviscer-are [A1s] *tr.* to eviscerate, to disembowel; (fig.) to exhaust; to examine thoroughly; *rfl.* to be disembowelled; (fig.) to exhaust

oneself; to pine, to languish. **-amento** *m.* disembowelling; (fig.) thorough examination; exhaustive research; -amenti di cuore, effusive demonstration, unburdening of one's soul. **-atezza** *f.* ardent love, passion; deep affection; devoted attachment. **-ato** *part. adj.* eviscerated, gutted; (fig.) passionate, ardent; deep; tender; heartfelt; devoted; sincere; amico -ato, bosom friend. (**-atamente** *adv.*) **-atore** *m.* one who treats a subject exhaustively. (**-atrice** *f.*)

svista *f.* oversight; mistake; per una —, by mistake.

svit-are [A1] *tr.* to unscrew; (eng.) to unscrew, to screw out. **-ato** *part. adj.* unscrewed; (iron.) having a screw loose, barmy. **-atura** *f.* unscrewing.

svitellare [A1] *tr.* (agric.) to remove a calf from (its mother).

sviticchi-are [A4] *tr.* to disentangle; to disentwine. (**-ato** *part. adj.*)

svituper-are [A1s] *tr.* to vituperate, to abuse. (**-ato** *part. adj.*)

svivagn-are [A5] *tr.* to cut off the selvedge from. **-ato** *part. adj.* frayed (as being without selvedge).

sviziare [A4] *tr.* (*prep.* di) to cure (of a bad habit); to reform; *rfl.* to cure oneself (of bad habits); reform, to turn over a new leaf.

Sviz·zer-a (la) *pr.n.f.* (geog.) Switzerland; — Italiana, Canton of Ticino. **-o** *adj.*, *n.m.* Swiss; doorkeeper; (papal) Swiss guard; sportsman. **-a** *f.* Swiss woman or girl.

svoci-ferare [A1s] *intr.* (*aux.* avere) to vociferate, to shout; *tr.* to divulge (a secret). **-nare** [A1] *intr.* (*aux.* avere) to keep on shouting, to shout and yell.

svogli-are [A4c] *tr.* (*prep.* di) to make disinclined (for); to make indifferent (to); *rfl.* to take a dislike (to); to become indifferent (to); si è -ato dallo studio, he has lost the will to work. (**-amento** *m.*) **-atag·gine** *f.* listlessness, indifference; laziness. **-atezza** *f.* listlessness; laziness; indifference; disinclination; è d'una -atezza senza pari, his laziness is unequalled; -atezza di stomaco, lack of appetite. **-ato** *part. adj.* listless; lazy; unwilling, loath; disinclined; without appetite; (also *n.m.*). (**-atamente** *adv.*) **-one** *m.* lazybones. (**-ona** *f.*)

svol-are [A1] *intr.* (*aux.* avere) to fly; to flit; to flutter. (**-amento** *m.*)

svolazz-are [A1] *intr.* (*aux.* avere) to fly, to flutter; to flit; to fly here and there; to hover. **-amento** *m.* flying about, flitting; fluttering. **-ante** *part. adj.* flitting; fluttering; waving, -ante al vento, flying in the wind; fickle, unstable. (**-atore** *m.* **-atrice** *f.*) **-etto** *m. dim.* (painted, drawn) streamer, scroll, flourish. **-io** *m.* flitting about; continued fluttering; whirring of wings. **-o** *m.* flutter; flitting; (dress) flounce; streamer; (paint, MS.) streamer, scroll, flourish; ornamental initial letter; (typ.) swash letter.

svol·g-ere [C14] *tr.* to unroll, to unwind; to open out, to display; to unfold; to develop; to work out; to complete; (techn.) to uncoil, to unwind, to unreel; — un tema, to write an essay; — un programma, to carry out a programme; to perform; — da, to dissuade from; *rfl.* to turn back; to go away; (of plants) to begin to grow; to develop, to take shape; to take place; to go on; to happen, to occur; la vita si -e tranquilla, life pursues the even tenor of its way; to make progress, to progress; (chem.) to be evolved (of a gas). **-imento** *m.* development; unfolding; expansion; course; treatment (of a subject); working out; lo -imento dei fatti, the course of events; lo -imento di un tema, the treatment of a subject; (cinem.) film feed; (mus.) development, development-section. **-itore** *m.* developer; (text.) uncoiler; (cinem.) rocchetto -itore, pay-out spool. **-itrice** *f.* (cinem.) bobina -itrice, pay-out spool.

svolt-a *f.* turn; turning; turning-point; corner; winding; (fig.) cross-roads, turning-point; (archit.) curve (e.g. in a river embankment). **-are** [A1] *tr.* to unroll; to turn, to twist; to dissuade, to make (a person) change his mind; *intr.* (*aux.* avere) to turn, to change direction; to deviate. **-ata** *f.* turn, turning; corner. **-ato** *part. adj.* unrolled; turned; twisted; dissuaded; †distorted, crooked. (**-atore** *m.* **-atrice** *f.*) **-atura** *f.* turning; unrolling. **-icchiare** [A4] *rfl.* to turn slightly; to twist (oneself).

svolt-o *part.* of svolgere, q.v.; *adj.* unfolded; unwrapped; developed; fully treated; dissuaded; frank; dislocated; *n.m.* turn, turning (cf. **svolta**).

svoltol-are [A1s] *tr.* to roll; *rfl.* to roll about, to tumble, to wallow; -arsi nel fango, to wallow in the mud. **-amento** *m.* rolling about; tumbling; wallowing. **-one** *m.* tumbling; wallowing.

svot-are [A1d] *tr.* (*prep.* di) to empty out completely; to clear out; *intr.* (*aux.* avere) to empty one's bowels; *rfl.* to be emptied (of). **-amento** *m.* thorough emptying; clearing. (**-ato** *part. adj.*)

swattato *adj.* (electr.) wattless.

T, t *f.*, *m.* (pron. **ti**) the letter T; the consonant T; fatto a —, T-shaped; ferro a —, T-iron; ferro a doppio —, T-beam.

ta *onomat.* pom; ta ta ta ta, pomptypom, etc.

†**ta'** *abbrev.* of **tai**, obsolete *pl.* of **tale**, q.v.

tabac-co *m.* (*pl.* -**chi**) (bot.) tobacco plant, *Nicotiana*; tobacco; — da pipa, pipe tobacco; — da fiuto, — da naso, snuff; fiutare —, to take snuff; presa di —, pinch of snuff; rivendita di sale e -chi, State tobacco-shop (selling also salt, quinine and postage-stamps); *adj. indecl.* color —, tobacco-coloured (dark brown); snuff-coloured (buff). -**ca·io** *m.* tobacconist. (-**ca·ia** *f.*) -**care** [A 2] *intr.* (*aux.* avere) to take snuff. -**cheri·a** *f.* tobacco-shop, tobacconist's. -**chiera** *f.* snuff-box; (anat.) -chiera anatomica, tabatière anatomique. -**china** *f.* woman worker in a tobacco factory. -**cone** *m.* (derog.) fusty person who continually takes snuff. (-**cona** *f.*) -**coso** *adj.* tobacco-stained.

taba-cosi *f.*, -**gismo** *m.* (med.) tabacosis, tabacism.

tabari·n *m. indecl.* nightclub.

tabarro *m.* cloak; loose overcoat; (mil.) cavalry cloak; (hist.) tabard.

tabasci·r *m. indecl.* tabasheer (concretion found in bamboo stems and used medicinally).

tab-e *f.* (med.) tabes; †(fig.) rottenness. †-**efatto** *adj.* putrid; tabefied. -**e·tico** *adj.* (med.) tabetic, tabic, tabid.

tabell-a *f.* schedule, table; board carried by sandwich-man; list; in forma di —, in tabular form; — dell'orario ferroviario, railway timetable (displayed on boards); — dei prezzi, price-list; (leg., etc.) disporre in -e, to tabulate; (comm.) — degli interessi, interest table; (naut.) — di armamento, Quarter Bill; — di deviazione, deviation card; (rel.) votive picture; rattle replacing bells in Holy Week; clapper, rattle; (vulg.) sonar le -e dietro a, to mock, to jeer at. -**are** *adj.* tabular. -**a·rio** *adj.* (Rom. antiq.) letter-carrying; letter-carrier. -**iera** *f.* (industr.) time-card rack. -**ionare** [A I c] *tr.* (leg.) to attest; to authenticate. -**ionata** *f.* (leg.) notary's office, profession and cypher. (-**ionato** *part. adj.*) -**ione** *m.* (Rom. antiq.) *tabellio*, notary; (joc.) lawyer. -**one** *m. augm.* poster, placard; (sport) score-board; (eccl. hist.) list of persons incurring censure, posted up at S. Bartolommeo, Rome.

taberna·colo *m.* (Bibl.) tabernacle; Festa dei Tabernacoli, Feast of Tabernacles; (eccl.) small shrine (with statue, picture, etc.) esp. at roadside; (liturg.) tabernacle; (fig.) the body as 'this fleshly tabernacle'; sanctuary; — dell'anima, tabernacle (temple) of the soul, i.e. the body; †(naut.) tabernacle, binnacle, compass housing; †tent; †pavilion.

†**tabes·cere** *intr.* to contract a wasting disease (cf. **tabe**).

tabe·tico *adj.* See under **tabe**.

tabi *m.* tabby, silk taffeta.

ta·b·ico *adj.* (med.) tabetic, tabic, tabid (cf. **tabetico**, under **tabe**). -**i·fico** *adj.* tending to tabefy; producing tabes; pestilential.

tablino *m.* (Rom. antiq.) *tab(u)linum* (archives).

tablò *m. indecl.* (pron. as Fr. 'tableau') tableau; (also used elliptically, as in English, to draw attention to a striking scene or situation).

tablo·ide *m.* tablet, tabloid.

Tabo·r *pr.n.m.* (geog.) (Mount) Tabor. -**iti** *m.pl.* (rel. hist.) sect of Hussites who gave the biblical name Mount Tabor to a hill near Prague.

tabù, tabu *m.*, *adj. indecl.* taboo.

ta·bul-a (*Lat. n.f.*) writing-tablet; (fig.) essere — rasa, to be a complete ignoramus, to have a blank mind; far — rasa, to start afresh; fare — rasa di, to make a clean sweep of, to carry off. -**are** *adj.* tabular. -**a·rio** *m.* (Rom. antiq.) *tabularium*, archives.

tabulatore *m.* (techn.) tabulator (in a typewriter).

tac *onom.* sound of a little sharp blow; the ticking of a clock; tic —, tick-tock.

tacc-a *f.* notch; scratch; nick; cut; mark; blemish; — di una stadera, notch, graduation, on the long arm of a steelyard; — di una freccia, notch of an arrow; (typ.) nick; (comm. hist.) tally; (leg.) — di contrassegno, tally (C.C.); (fig.) size, height; quality; di una —, della stessa —, of the same kind; (mil.) notch on sight; — di mira, backsight notch; (watchm.) — di frizione, clam notch; (geog.) limestone hill; *adv. phr.* (Tusc., fam.) tacca tacca, little by little, bit by bit. †-**are** *tr.* to mark; to notch, to nick. -**ata** *f.* (naut.) keel blocks, chocks, beams supporting a ship in dry dock; †marking; notching; notch; nick.

taccagn-o *adj.* stingy, niggardly; miserly; †disputatious; *n.m.* miser, skinflint; è un vero —, he's a real old miser. (-**one** *adj.*, *n.m.* -**ona** *f.*)

taccamacca *f.* balsam poplar, *Populus gileadensis*; (pharm.) tacamahaca.

†**taccare** *vb.* See under **tacca**.

tacch-eggiare [A 3 c] *tr.* (typ.) to lay-guide; (slang) to shoplift. (-**eggiato** *part. adj.*) -**eggiatrice** *f.* female shoplifter. -**eggio** *m.* (typ.) lay-guiding; (slang) shoplifting.

tacch-erella *f.* slight fault; avere le sue -erelle, to have one's little failings. -**ietta** *f.* (naut.) cleat. -**iettare** [A I c] *intr.* (*aux.* avere) to clatter noisily with one's heels in walking. -**iettio** *m.* tapping of heels on a pavement; sound of machine-gun fire, etc.; rattle, clatter. -**ietto** *m.* (naut.) fid; -ietti di scala, ladder treads.

tac·chete *onom.* See **taffete**.

†**tac·chia** *f.* chip, wood-shaving.

tacchin-o *m.* (orn.) turkey, *Meleagris gallopavo*; rosso come un —, red as a turkey-cock; sembrare un — quando fa la ruota, to be as proud as a turkey-cock. -**a** *f.* hen turkey. -**otto** *m.* young turkey.

tac·ci-a *f.* stain on a person's reputation; charge, imputation; blemish, stain; senza —, unblemished. -**a·bile** *adj.* (*prep.* di) chargeable (with), liable to the imputation (of). -**are** [A 3] *tr.* (*prep.* di) to accuse (of), to charge (with), to tax (with); to impute; — uno di negligenza, to accuse someone of negligence; — uno di ladro, to call someone a thief. (-**ato** *part. adj.*)

tac·ci-o *m.* (Tusc.) rough estimate of the value of a sum total; fare un —, to settle in the gross, (fig.) to finish, to settle (e.g. a controversy, an undertaking, etc.). -**aiolo** *m.* (Tusc.) one who takes on employment on a rough estimate of total payment.

tac-co[1] *m.* (*pl.* -**chi**) heel (of a shoe); scarpe coi -chi alti, high-heeled shoes; -chi a spillo, stiletto heels; far rifare, aggiustare, i -chi, to have one's shoes heeled; (joc.) battere, alzare, il —, to run away, to take to one's heels; (typ.) lay-mark; (mil.) gun quoin; (aeron.) chock.

†**tacco**[2] *m.* (dial. Tusc.). See **tacchino**.

tac·cola[1] *f.* (orn.) jackdaw, *Corvus monedula*; (Lomb.) 'mange-tout' pea, a kind of pea eaten with the pod.

tac·col-a[2] *f.* slight fault; flaw; trifling incident. -**are** [A I S] *intr.* (*aux.* avere) to chatter, to prate. -**ata** *f.* idle chatter, prating.

tac·colo *m.* (Tusc., fam.) small debt; avere qualche —, to owe a little money here and there.

taccon-e *m. augm.* of **tacco**[1], q.v.; big heel; battere il —, to make off with all speed; (shoem.) patch; (prosod.) stop-gap in a line of verse, cheville. -**are** [A I c] *tr.* (shoem.) to sole (sewing a double sole on shoes); to patch. -**ata** *f.* (shoem.) patching; patch. -**ato** *part. adj.* (shoem.) with hand-sewn soles.

taccuino *m.* note-book; memorandum-book; pocket-diary; †calendar.

tac-ere [B 20] *intr.* (*aux.* avere) to be silent, to remain silent; to stop speaking; to say nothing, to hold one's tongue, to keep quiet; far —, to silence; — di, to say nothing about, to make no mention of, to pass over, not to speak of; (provb.) chi -e acconsente, silence signifies consent; (poet.) to fall silent; (of the sun, etc.) not to shine, to cease to shine; (of eyes) not to weep, to cease weeping; *tr.* to be silent about, to pass over in silence; to keep back, to withhold, to keep secret; to leave out, to omit, to leave unsaid; racconterò il fatto, -endo i nomi, I will tell the story leaving out the names; (mus.) -e, tacet; *rfl.* (liter., poet.) to cease speaking; *n.m.* keeping silent; mettere in —, to hush up; silence. -**ente** *part. adj.* (poet.) silent; tacit; †dumb, mute. -**iuto** *part. adj.* passed over in silence; hushed up.

tach-eografare [A I S] *tr.* to write by tachygraphy. -**eo·grafo** *m.* tachygraph, one who practises tachygraphy. -**eometri·a** *f.* (surv.) tachymetry. -**eo·metro** *m.* (surv.) transit, tacheometer. -**icar·dia** *f.* (med.) tachycardia. -**icar·dico** *adj.* (med.) tachycardiac. -**ifagi·a** *f.* (med.) tachyphagia. -**ifilassi·a** *f.* (med.) tachyphylaxis. -**ifrasi·a** *f.* rapid speech of the insane. -**ifreni·a** *f.* (med.) tachyphrenia. -**igrafi·a** *f.* tachygraphy. -**ilali·a** *f.* (med.) tachylalia. -**i·metro** *m.* tachymeter; (cycl.) cyclometer. -**ipessi·a** *f.* (techn.) quick-freezing. -**ipne·a** *f.* (med.) tachypnoea. -**isterolo** *m.* (chem.; physiol.) tachysterol.

tachina *f.* (ent.) tachinid fly.

ta·cit-o[1] *adj.* silent; tacit; not expressed; implied; secret; -a intesa, tacit understanding; la guardò —, he looked at her in silence; (poet.) -a notte, silent night; (leg.) accordo —, implied agreement; consenso —, implied consent; (comm.) socio —, sleeping partner; *adv.* tacitly, silently, in silence. -**amente** *adv.* in silence; tacitly; secretly. -**are** [A I S] *tr.* (leg.; comm.) -are un debito, to pay off

tacit·o (*cont.*)
something on a debt; -are un creditore, to satisfy a creditor, to keep a creditor quiet by part payment. (-ato *part. adj.*)

Tạcit·o² *pr.n.m.* Tacitus. -**eggiare** [A 3 c] *intr.* (*aux.* avere) to write in the style of Tacitus. -**iano** *adj.* Tacitean, in the style of Tacitus. -**ista** *m.* admirer or imitator of the style of Tacitus.

taciturn·o *adj.* taciturn; uomo —, man of few words; non-committal; reserved; sulky; (poet.) fiume —, river flowing silently. -**amẹnte** *adv.* taciturnly. -**ità** *f.* taciturnity.

taciuto *part.* See under **tacere**.

tael *m.* tael (Chinese weight or coin).

tafana·rio *m.* (joc.) backside, bottom.

tafan·o *m.* (pop.) horsefly; (fig.) nuisance; bloodsucker; (joc.) l'ora dei -i, noon. -**are** [A 1] *tr.* to bite, to sting; *intr.* (*aux.* avere) (fam.) to 'be into everything', to buzz about aimlessly.

tafefobi·a *f.* (med.; psych.) taphephobia, fear of being buried alive (also **tafofobia**).

tafferi·a *f.* dish, shallow bowl; flour-bin; — da pane, bread-bin.

taffer·ụglio *m.,* †-**ụgia** *f.* brawl, scuffle; skirmish.

taffẹtà *f.* See **taffettà**.

taf·fẹte *onom.* imitative of noise of bumping or falling; *excl.* bump!; bang!; quand'ecco, —!, capita proprio il lupo, when suddenly boo!, the wolf appeared.

taffett·à *m.* taffeta; — inglese, court plaster; †coif. †-**ano** *m.* see **taffettà**.

†**taf·fi·o** *m.* sumptuous feast, lavish banquet. †-**are** *intr.* to feast.

tafià *f.* See **ratafià**.

tafofobi·a *f.* (med.; psych.) taphophobia, fear of being buried alive (also **tafefobia**).

ta·gli·a *f.* (agric.) cutting (esp. of olive-trees); act of cutting; feeble or foible of a sword; (eng.) tackle, hoisting tackle; (leg.) — di contrassegno, tally (C.C.); (comm.) credit note or slip; fine; ransom; price on a person's head; figure, build, height; una — slanciata, a slim figure; (fig.) stature; †see **taglio**.

Tagliamẹnto *pr.n.m.* (geog.) name of a river in Friuli.

tagli-are [A 4] *tr.* to cut; to cut off; to cut up; to cut out; to hew; to lop, to crop, to trim; to clip; farsi — i capelli, to get one's hair cut; — un ascesso, to lance an abscess; — l'uva, to gather the grapes; — le biade, to reap the corn; — a fior di terra, to cut down to the ground; — il male alla radice, to strike at the root of the evil; — i viveri, to cut off supplies; — la strada a uno, to bar someone's way, to cut off someone's route; — le parole in bocca a uno, to prevent a person from finishing what he wants to say; — i panni addosso a, to speak ill of; — la testa al toro, to settle a question once and for all; — le gambe a uno, to cut the ground from under a person's feet; (of fog or other bad atmosphere) si potrebbe — col coltello, you could cut it with a knife; (naut.) — le funi, to slip the cable; (fig.) — la corda, to slip away; — la rotta a, to cross the bows of (another ship); (cards) to cut; to ruff, to trump; (surg.) to amputate, to resect; to dissect; (paint.) — con bianco, to break down with white; *intr.* (*aux.* avere) (of knife, scissors) to cut; (of a blunt knife) -a come cuce, it won't cut butter; vento che -a, biting wind; avere una lingua che -a e cuce, to have a caustic tongue; (fig.) — per i campi, to cut across the fields; per — corto, to cut a long story short. -**a·bile** *adj.* that can be cut. -**abọrse** *m. indecl.* see **borsaiuolo**. -**aboschi** *m. indecl.* woodcutter, woodman. -**abuchi** *m. indecl.* (mining) casing cutter. †-**acantoni** *m. indecl.* braggart, swaggering soldier. -**acarta** *m. indecl.* paper-cutting machine. -**acarte** *m. indecl.* paper-knife; letter-opener. -**acavo** *m. indecl.* cable-cutter, rope knife. -**ac·qua** *m. indecl.* (bldg.) cut-water, nosing (of a bridge or pier). -**afiamma** *m. indecl.* (eng.) flame trap. -**afili** *m. indecl.* wire-cutters. -**afilm** *m. indecl.* (cinem.) film-cutter. -**afuoco** *m.* (bldg.) fire barrier. -**alẹgna** *m. indecl.* woodcutter; wood-chopper. -**amare** *m. indecl.* (naut.) stem. -**amẹnto** *m.* cutting; cut; (math.) intersection; †killing, doing to death. -**ando** *m.* detachable coupon; warrant; slip; foglio di -andi, coupon sheet. -**ante** *part. adj.* cutting, sharp; *n.m.* cutter, cutting edge. -**apasta** *m. indecl.* (cul.) implement for cutting home-made 'pasta' into various shapes. -**apẹsce** *m. indecl.* fish-slice; fish-knife. -**apietra** *m. indecl.* small chisel. -**apietre** *m. indecl.* stone-cutter, stonemason. -**apiote** *m. indecl.* turf-cutter. -**arẹte** *m. indecl.* net-cutter. -**ata** *f.* cut; cutting; mowing, reaping, gathering (e.g. of grapes); felling (of trees); una -ata di capelli, a haircut; (mil.) a clearing of timber (to ensure field of fire); digging of

ditches; (sport, tennis, etc.) cut, slice; (fencing) coupé; †barrier of felled trees, branches, etc. -**atella** *f.,* -**atello** *m.* (usu. *pl.*) (cul.) thin strips of 'pasta'; -atelli verdi, the same coloured with spinach. -**atini** *m.pl.* (cul.) thin strips of 'pasta' resembling 'tagliatelli' but smaller. -**ato** *part. adj.* cut; cut out; cut away; (of a person) -ato bene, well built; -ato coll'accetta, clumsy, ungainly; (of clothing) -ato addosso a, a perfect fit for; (fig.) -ato per, 'cut out' for; -ato all'antica, not adaptable to new ways; (herald.) per bend sinister; manica mal -ata, anglice maunch. -**atọio** *m.* (techn.) cutter. -**atọre** *m.* cutter; -atore di legna, -atore di boschi, woodman, woodcutter; -atore di pietre, stonecutter; (techn.) cutter. -**atrice** *f.* (dressm.) cutter (woman); (eng.) cutting machine; -atrice ad arco, arc cutting machine. -**atubi** *m. indecl.* (eng.) pipe-cutter. -**atura** *f.* cutting, cut, cutting out; felling, pruning (of trees); intersection; *pl.* clippings. -**avento** *m. indecl.* (aeron.; motor.) windscreen; (mil.) nose, nose-cap, ballistic cap of projectile; †(naut.) stormsail. -**avetri** *m. indecl.* glass-cutter. -**eggiare** [A 3 c] *tr.* to impose a fine or tribute on; †to place a ransom on. -**ente** *adj.* cutting; sharp; keen; poco -ente, blunt; (fig.) lingua -ente, sharp, spiteful, tongue; freddo -ente, biting cold; (art) clear-cut; well defined; *n.m.* cutting edge, cutting point; (bldg.) cut-water, fore-starling (of a bridge). -**ere**, †-**ero** *m.* chopping-board; cutting bench; trencher; (hist.) communal dish; stare a -ere con uno, to eat out of the same dish with someone; (archit.) abacus. -**erina** *f.* (eng.) shears, shearing machine; (paperm.) -erina verticale, guillotine. -**erini** *m. pl.* (cul.) see **tagliatini**.

ta·gli·o *m.* cutting; (of trees) felling; — raso dei boschi, felling of all the trees in the woods; — saltuario, felling of chosen trees here and there; — dell'erba, mowing; (tailor.) cut; maestro di —, cutter; un — di stoffa, a length of material (suitable to be made up by a tailor or dressmaker); — dei capelli, haircut; (bldg.) ashlar; (mil.) arma da —, sword, etc.; (cards) cut; (surg.) incision; section; resection; — del braccio, amputation of the arm; — cesareo, caesarean section; (butcher., etc.) cut; pesce da —, fish sold in cutlets; — di vini, blending of wines; vino da —, wine with high percentage of alcohol suitable for mixing with lighter wines; (fig.) dare un — a una conversazione, to cut short a conversation; fare dei tagli in, to make cuts in, to cut; stature, height, build; di — mezzano, of medium height or build; ragazzo di un bel —, fine upstanding young man; (fig., derog.) gente di quel —, people of that sort; edge; — di tavola, table-edge; a due tagli, double-edged (also fig.); (bookb.) edge; — di testa, top edge; — dorato, top edge gilt; — inferiore, bottom edge; (eng.) (of a blade) cutting edge, edge; slot (in the head of a screw); sollecitazione di —, shearing stress; (finan.) denomination; carta moneta di piccolo, (grosso) —, low, (high) denomination paper money; (archit.) crack, fissure; opening; (art) — dolce, copper engraving; †(mus.) leger line; oblique or horizontal stroke (as abbreviation in musical notation); *pl.* (geog.) whirlpools; *adv. phr.* di —, edge-wise; per —, aslant, slantwise; venire, cadere, in —, to occur opportunely. -**ẹtto** *m.* rule-cutter. -**olini** *m.pl.* (cul.) thin strips of 'pasta' served in soup; small piece, slice (of meat, etc.). -**(u)ola** *f.* trap; preso alla -ola, caught in the trap; tendere la -ola, to set the trap. -**(u)olo** *m.* bit, piece; (Tusc.) cut (of meat); chisel; -olo a freddo, cold chisel. -**uzzamento** *m.* mincing, hashing, cutting into little bits. -**uzzare** [A 1] *tr.* to cut into little bits; to cut into shreds, to shred; to mince; to hash. -**uzzato** *part. adj.* shredded; minced; hashed; (meteor.) cumulo -uzzato, fractocumulus; strato -uzzato, fractostratus. †-**uzzo** *m.* little bit; shred; clipping.

taglịọne¹ *m.* talion; legge del —, law of retaliation, of 'an eye for an eye and a tooth for a tooth', *lex talionis*.

taglịọne² *m. augm.* of **taglio**, q.v.; (eng.) large hoisting tackle.

tagli-uola *f.,* -**uzzare** [A 1] and derivs. See under **taglio**.

Tago *pr.n.m.* (geog.) Tagus.

taicu·n *m. indecl.* (Japanese hist.) tycoon, title of the shogun (not used figuratively).

Ta·ide *pr.n.f.* Thaïs.

Tailan·d·ia *pr.n.f.* (geog.) Thailand. -**ẹse** *adj., n.m., f.* relating to inhabitant of Thailand.

tailleur *m. indecl.* (pron. as Fr.) tailor-made coat and skirt.

ta·it *m. indecl.* (also written **tight**) tight-fitting coat; morning coat.

taitan·o *adj.* relating to Tahiti; *n.m.* Tahitan. (-**a** *f.*)

Taitù *pr.n.f.* name of the Empress of Abyssinia (1854–1914); (provb.) woman of dark complexion.

takigoto *m.* (mus.) takigoto, a kind of Japanese dulcimer.

tal *adj.* See **tale**.

†**talabalacco** *m.* Moorish war-drum.

†**talacimanno** *m.* (Moslem rel.) muezzin.

talalgi·a *f.* (med.) talalgia.

talamence·falo *m.* (med.) deutencephalon.

ta·lam-o *m.* (poet.) bridal bed, nuptial couch; bride-chamber; condurre al —, to wed; (bot.) receptacle, torus, thalamus; (anat.) thalamus; — ottico, optic thalamus; †(naut.) stern cabin. †**-ita** *m.* rower in the lowest tier of a galley.

†**talano** *adj., n.m.* See **catalano**.

talar-e *adj.* ankle-length, reaching the heels; (eccl.) abito —, cassock, (religious) habit; veste —, cassock; *n.m.pl.* (myth.) talaria, Mercury's winged sandals.

talass-archi·a *f.* see **talassocrazia**. **-iti** *m.pl.* (zool.) turtles. **-obiologi·a** *f.* marine biology. **-o·crate** *m.* thalassocrat, ruler of the sea. **-ocrazi·a** *f.* thalassocracy; supremacy at sea; wealth derived from sea-power. **-ofobi·a** *f.* (med.) pathological fear of the sea. **-ografi·a** *f.* thalassography, oceanography. **-ogra·fico** *adj.* relating to thalassography, oceanographic. **-o·grafo** *m.* oceanographer. **-o·metro** *m.* sounding-line. **-oterapi·a** *f.* (med.) sea cure.

talchè *conj.* so that; see also 'tale che', under **tale**.

talchite *m.* (miner.) steatite.

talc-o *m.* (miner.) talc, talcum, soapstone; (bot.) — celeste, forget-me-not, *Myosotis palustris*; talc, talcum, french chalk. **-oschisto** *m.* (miner.) talc schist. **-oso** *adj.* talcous.

tal-e *adj.* (*m.pl.* **tali**, †**tai**). **1.** SUCH; -i cose non capitano mai, such things never happen; provò una — paura, he got such a fright; siamo a tal punto, we have reached such a point; similar; non è più —, he is no longer the same; non credevo che fosse —, I didn't think he (it) was like that; — il padre, — il figlio, like father, like son; (with correlative 'quale') è ancora — quale, it is still as it was; (comm.) — quale (*or* talequale), same as sample; (joc.) sentii una tal quale paura!, I had such a fright! **2.** *demonstr. prn.* SUCH (A) ONE; un —, a certain person; quel —, the above-mentioned man, the man you know of; il signor Tal dei Tali, Mr So and So; i -i, those people. **3.** *adv.* So; — che (*or* talchè), so that, to such an extent that. **-mente** *adv.* so; -mente che, so that, so much that, in such a way that, to such an extent that. **-ora**, †**-otta** *adv.* sometimes. **-uno** *demonstr. prn.* someone; *pl. adj.* certain. **-volta** *adv.* sometimes; at times; -volta...tal'altra, at some times...at other times.

ta·lea, **tale·a** *f.* (agric.) cutting; shoot; scion.

tale·d *m. indecl.* (Jewish rel.) tallith, prayer-scarf.

Taleggio *pr.n.m.* (geog.) Taleggio (near Bergamo); (cul.) a kind of cheese made at Taleggio.

talent-o *m.* (antiq.) talent (weight or sum of money of varying amount); parabola dei -i, parable of the talents; talent; aptitude; gift; genius; intelligence; (iron.) bel —!, very clever!; persona di —, gifted, talented, person; will; a suo —, at his pleasure; di suo —, of his own accord; — di mangiare, desire to eat; non mi va a —, it is not to my liking; mal —, ill-will, grudge, hatred. **-ac·cio** *m. pejor.* cunning, cleverness; freakishness. **-are** [A I] *intr.* (*aux.* essere; *prep.* a) to please, to be to one's liking; fai sempre quel che meglio ti -a, you always do just as you please. **-one** *m. augm.* (joc., iron.) genius. †**-oso** *adj.* desirous.

Talete *pr.n.m.* Thales.

Tali·a *pr.n.f.* Thalia, one of the three Graces; Thalia, the Muse of comedy and satire; (astron.) Thalia.

†**taliano** *adj., n.m.* See **italiano**.

talismano *m.* talisman; amulet.

talla[1] *f.* kind of beer made in Abyssinia.

talla[2] *f.* (poet.) shoot, scion.

tal·lero *m.* (numism.) thaler.

talleto *m.* See under **tallo**.

tal·l-io *m.* (chem.) thallium. **-ico** *adj.* (chem.) thallic. **-oso** *adj.* (chem.) thallous.

tall-o *m.* (bot.) thallus; sprout; cutting; graft; grass running to seed; (fig.) rimettere il —, to be reinvigorated, to feel young again. **-eta** *f.*, **-eto** *m.* nursery plot (planted with cuttings). **-ire** [D 2] *intr.* (*aux.* essere, avere) to sprout; to run to seed. **-o·fita** *f.* (bot.) thallophyte.

tallol·lio *m.* (techn.) tall oil.

tallon-e *m.* heel; il — di Achille, Achilles's heel, Achilles's tendon; (archit.) cyma reversa, ogee (moulding); footing of a wall; (agric.)

landside (of plough); (typ.) knib; (comm.) counterfoil, stub (from which the 'talloncino', q.v., is detached); (motor.) bead. **-ag·gio** *m.* (rugby) heeling. **-are** [A I c] *tr.* (cycling, long-distance running) to pursue closely; (rugby) to heel. (**-ato** *part. adj.*) **-atore** *m.* (rugby) hooker. **-cino** *m. dim.* receipt-form; detachable slip; voucher; cut-out coupon.

talloso *adj.* (chem.). See under **tallio**.

talmà *f.* gaberdine; raglan overcoat.

talmente *adv.* See under **tale**.

Talm-ùd *pr.n.m.* Talmud. **-udista** *m.* one who studies the Talmud. **-u·dico** *adj.* Talmudic.

talo *m.* scarp, escarpment; steep slope.

taloc·ci·a *f.* (bldg.) float. **-ato** *m.* (bldg.) floated coat.

tal-ora, †**-otta** *adv.* See under **tale**.

talp-a, †**-e** *f.* (zool.) mole; — comune, *Talpa europaea*; — cieca, *T. caeca*; (fig.) dullard; (naut.) diving-bell; *adj. indecl.* color —, mole-coloured.

talposi·metro *m.* (phys.) vapour-pressure thermometer.

tal-uno *prn.*, **-volta** *adv.* See under **tale**.

†**tamanto** *adj.* of such and such a size and description.

tamarice *f.* (bot.) tamarisk, *Tamarix* spp.; — minore, *Myricaria germanica*.

tamarindo *m.* (bot.) tamarind, *Tamarindus indica*.

†**tamarisco** *m.* (bot.). See **tamarice**.

tamaro, **ta·maro** *m.* (bot.) black bryony, *Tamus communis*.

tambarello *m.* (ichth.) bonito, *Auxis thazard*.

†**tambascià** *m.* merry-making.

tambellone *m.* large-sized brick, used in building bakers' ovens, chimneys, etc.

†**tambene** *adv.* as, that is.

tambouri·n *pr.n.m.* (mus.) Tambourin (French dance).

tamb-u·cio *m.*, **-ug·gio** *m.* (naut.) hatch cover, canvas weather screen.

tambu·r *m. indecl.* (mus.) tamboura, a kind of Oriental guitar.

tambur-o *m.* (mus.) drum; drummer; — basco, tambourine; — grande, — grosso, bass drum; — militare, side-drum, military drum, snare drum; — rullante, tenor drum; (mil.) — maggiore, drum-major; la mazza del — maggiore, bandmaster's staff; sul —, in the field, (fig.) immediately, without delay; service or disciplinary drumhead; chamber, drum, magazine (of revolver); pistola a —, (toy) 'cap-gun'; pill-box; any low and round defensive structure; (naut.) chronometer box; — del timone, rudderhead; — della ruota, paddlebox; (archit.) tambour (esp. of a cupola); (hist.) drum, drum-shaped receptacle (at Florence) into which anonymous letters of information were put; (ichth.) drum, *Pogonias chromis*. †**-ac·cio** *m.* (mus.) bass drum. **-ag·gine**, †**-agione** *f.* (hist.) accusation made by letters placed in the 'tamburo' (see above). **-a·io** *m.* maker or vendor of drums. **-amento** *m.* drumming; beating of drums. **-are** [A I] *tr.* to beat (a drum or drums); (joc.) to beat, to thrash; (hist., Flor.) to accuse anonymously, to denounce (by means of a letter placed in a drum-shaped receptacle; cf. under **tamburo**). (**-ato** *part. adj.*) **-azione** *f.* (hist.) anonymous accusation. **-eggia** *f.* (mil.) thunder of guns. **-eggiamento** *m.* (mil.) drumming. **-eggiante** *part. adj.* (mil.) fuoco -eggiante, drumfire. **-eggiare** [A 3 c] *intr.* (*aux.* avere) (mil.) to thunder (of guns). **-ellare** [A I] *intr.* (*aux.* avere) to drum; -ellava colle dita sulla vetrata, he drummed with his fingers on the pane. **-ello** *m. dim.* (mus.) little drum; tabor, timbrel; tambourine; name of a game resembling tennis played with tambourines (in many parts of Italy this is the traditional national game). **-etto** *m. dim.* stool; (naut.) bow locker, sail cupboard; †circular platform on the forecastle of a galley; †deck locker used for small arms usually kept on the fore side of a mast; (mus.) little drum. **-i·glia** *f.* (mus.) a kind of Moorish drum. **-inare** [A I] *tr.* to beat (drums); (mus.) tambourine; small drum; toy drum; (mil.) drummer-boy; -ino maggiore, drum-major; (ichth.) *Rhinobatus rhinobatus*; *pl.* (bot.) quaking grass, *Briza media*. **-ino** *m.* see **tambourin**. **-lano** *m.* clothes-dryer, linen-airer (shaped like a drum); coffee-roaster; †(naut.) paddle-box. **-one** *m. augm* big-drum; bass-drum.

tamerice *f.* (bot.) see **tamarice**; (pharm.) acqua delle tamerici, purgative mineral-water from Montecatini.

†**ta·mero** *m.* See **tamarindo**.

Tamigi *pr.n.m.* (geog.) Thames.

†**tami·gi-o** *m.* sieve. †**-are** *tr.* to sieve.

ta·mina *f.* See **tamaro**.

†**Tamisi** *pr.n.f.* (geog.). See **Tamigi**.

†**tamorletto** *m.* (naut.) paddlebox.

†**tampagno** *m.* (naut.) pin of a block.

tampoco *adv.* (joc., otherwise †) nè —, not even; non si degna nè — di scrivere, he is too high and mighty even to write.

tampon-e *m.* (surg.) tampon; (chem.) buffer; soluzione —, buffer solution; (eng.) pad, buffer, shock-absorber; (rlwy.) buffer; (motor.; aeron.) — di vapore, vapour lock; (watchm.) — ammortizzatore, buffer; pad; ink-pad (for rubber stamps); blotting-pad plug, stopper, bung. **~amento** *m.* (surg.) tamponade, tamponing. **~are** [A I C] *tr.* to plug, to stop, to bung; to dab; to bump, to collide with (esp. in motoring); (of a train) to strike the buffers of; to plug, to stopper; (foundry) to lute; (surg.) to plug, to tampon. (**~ato** *part. adj.*) **~atura** *f.* plugging.

tam-tam, tan-tan *m. indecl.* (mus.) tam-tam, Chinese gong.

tamu·lico *adj.* (geog.) Tamilian, Tamulic, relating to the Tamils of S.E. India and Ceylon.

tana *f.* den; (fig.) study; hole, lair; hole (in clothes, wall, etc.); (zool.) *Tupaia* spp., tree shrews.

tanacet-o *m.* tansy, *Tanacetum vulgare*. **~ina** *f.* (chem.) tanacetin.

tana·gli-a *f.* (usu. *pl.*) pincers; nippers; pliers; tongs; (fig.) levare una cosa con le **~e**, to obtain a thing with great difficulty; (dent.) forceps; (mil. hist.) tenaille, outer fortification having a scissor formation or in the shape of callipers; grab; (naut.) grappling hook. (Cf. **tenaglia**.) **~are** [A 4] *tr.* to torture with pincers; to pinch; to nip; (mil. hist.) to fortify with a tenaille. **~etta** *f. dim.* nippers. **~one** *m. augm.* large, two-handed pliers; (mil.) double-handed tongs. **~ozze** *f.pl.* cobbler's pliers.

Ta·nagra¹ *pr.n.f.* (geog.) Tanagra (in Boeotia); *f.* (sculp.) Tanagra, Greek terracotta statuette from Tanagra.

ta·nagra² *f.* (orn.) tanager, *Thraupidae* spp.

tanana·i *m. indecl.* hubbub, din, row.

Ta·naro *pr.n.m.* (geog.) a river in Piedmont, tributary of the Po.

tanat-ofobi·a *f.* (med.) thanatophobia, pathological terror of death. **~ologi·a** *f.* thanatology. **~olo·gico** *adj.* thanatological. **~o·metro** *m.* thanatometer.

tanca¹ *f.* (Sardinia) byre, fold; water-tank carried on mule-back.

tanca² *f. tanka*, the classic form of Japanese poem.

Tancredi *pr.n.m.* Tancred.

tandem *m. indecl.* tandem bicycle; (eng.) tandem; a —, in tandem; (of horses in harness) marciare in —, to drive tandem. **~ista** *m., f.* tandem cyclist.

†**tando** *adv.* then, at that time.

tanè *adj., n.m.* tawny (colour), tan.

†**tanfanare** *tr.* to beat, to hit; to ill-treat; to torment.

tanf-o *m.* stench; nasty smell; musty smell; sapere di —, to have, give off, a musty smell. **~ata** *f.* gust, whiff of an unpleasant odour.

tan·g-ere [C def.] *tr.* (poet.) to touch. **~ente** *part. adj., n.f.* (geom.) tangent; portion; quota; share. **~enza** *f.* (geom.) tangency; (aeron.) ceiling. **~enziale** *adj.* (geom.) tangential. **~i·bile** *adj.* tangible, palpable. (**~ibilità** *f.*)

Tan·ger-i, Tanger-i *pr.n.f.* (geog.) Tangier. **~ino** *adj.* relating to Tangier; *n.m.* inhabitant of Tangier; (bot.) see **mandarino**.

tangheggio *m.* (naut.) pitching of a ship.

tan·ghero *m.* boor, bumpkin.

tangi·bile *adj.* See under **tangere**.

tango *m. indecl.* (dance) Tango.

tangone *m.* (naut.) boomkin, bumpkin.

tanguina *f.* (chem.; pharm.) tanghinin.

tannato *m.* (chem.) tannate.

tan·nico *adj.* (chem.) tannic.

tann-ino *m.* tannin. **~ofor·mio** *m.* tannoform, methylene ditannin.

tannoni *m.pl.* (zool.) *Triops* (*Apus*) *cancriformis*.

tantafer-a, ~ata *f.* rigmarole, twaddle.

tanta·lico *adj.* (chem.) tantalic.

Tan·tal-o *pr.n.m.* (mythol.) Tantalus; sottoporre al supplizio di —, to tantalize; (chem.) tantalum. **~ato** *m.* (chem.) tantalate. **~i·fero** *adj.* (miner.) tantaliferous. **~io** *m.* (chem.) tantalum. **~ite** *f.* (miner.) tantalite.

tantième *m.* (pron. as Fr.) percentage; (Post-Office) gratuity proportional to length of service; (publishing) additional royalty paid to an author after a given number of copies have been sold.

tantino *adv. dim.* See under **tanto**.

tant-o¹ *adj.* **1.** SO MUCH; — pane, so much bread; **~a** gente, such a lot of people; just so much, just a lot of; è **~a** robaccia, it's just so much rubbish; such great; **~a** miseria, such great poverty; so great a; come conviene a — signore, as befits so great a gentleman; *pl.* so many; **~i** ragazzi, so many boys; **~e** ragazze, so many girls; *emphatic uses:* **~e** grazie!, many thanks!; grazie **~e**!, thank you so much!; ho avuto **~e** e poi **~e** disgrazie, I have had a whole heap of misfortunes; lasciò **~i** mai debiti, he left a great many debts. **2.** *adv.* So; so much; — meglio, so much the better; ti amo —!, I love you so much!; me ne rallegro —, I am so delighted about it; — bello, so lovely; — brutto, so ugly; tre volte —, three times as much; una volta —, once and for all, *or* once in a way, just this once; — per cominciare, just to begin with, just to set things going; — più, all the more; — meno, all the less; non mi piace più che —, I don't care for it particularly; (with correlative 'quanto') as; è — buona quanto è bella, she is as good as she is beautiful. **3.** *indecl. prn.* SO MUCH, such a lot; un — ogni mese, so much every month; fece — che..., he did so much that...; *elliptically* (with 'tempo', 'spazio', etc. understood) è — che aspetta, he has been waiting so long; di — in —, from time to time; ha già speso —, he has already spent so much; *emphatic uses:* — di, as much as this, a great lot of, etc.; gli costò —, it cost him a good deal; lo guardò con — d'occhio, he stared at him so hard; aveva — di barba, he had a great long beard; mi venne incontro con — di bastone, he came towards me with a great big stick; con — di velluto, all tricked out in velvet. **4.** *pers. prn. pl.* **~i** dicono, so many people, a lot of people, say; **~e** portano tacche a spillo, a lot of women, so many women, wear stiletto heels; *elliptical uses:* ne ha fatte **~e** (i.e. 'birichinate', pranks), he has got up to a few tricks in his time; ha in mano (di documenti, di prove) **~i** da mandarlo in prigione, he has enough (evidence) to send him to prison; **~i** ne guadagna e **~i** ne spende (i.e. money), he spends as much as he earns; **~i** al mese, on such and such a date; dieci uomini non son **~i** a farlo, ten men are not enough to do the job; *conj.* — che, so that, whilst; — più che, all the more (so) that; anyhow; meglio spender tutto, — si muore, you had better spend it all since 'you can't take it with you'; è inutile che tu dica, — una volta o l'altra dovrai pagarla, whatever you may say, sooner or later you will have to pay. **~inino** *m. dim.* teeny weeny bit. **~ino** *m.* a little; a ogni **~ino**, every little while; in un **~ino**, very soon, presently. **~one** *m. augm.* di tantino si fa **~one**, 'mony a mickle maks a muckle'.

†**tantosto¹** *adv.* immediately.

†**tantosto²** *m.* buttered eggs on toast.

tantr-a *m. indecl.* (Ind. rel.) Tantra. **~ismo** *m.* Tantrism.

taoismo *m.* (Chinese rel.) Taoism.

tapin-o *adj.* wretched, miserable; humble, poor; (naut.) naviglio —, craft having a low freeboard. **~are** [A I] *intr.* (aux. avere) to lead a wretched life; *rfl.* to be afflicted; to be vexed. **~ello** *adj. dim.* wretched, miserable.

tapioca *f.* tapioca.

tap-iro *m.*, **~i·rio** *m.* (zool.) tapir.

tappa *f.* stop, halting-place; stage; rest; stage, lap (mainly cycle-racing); (mil.) staging area; comando di —, headquarters; di — in —, by stages.

tapp-are [A I] *tr.* to stop up, to stop, to cork; to plug; to bung; — una botte, to bung a cask; — la bocca a uno, to stop a person's mouth; — uno in un luogo, to confine someone, to shut someone up, in a place; *rfl.* (acc. of *prn.* 'si') to shut oneself up; to muffle oneself up; **~arsi** in casa, to shut oneself in, to keep to the house; (dat. of *prn.* 'si') **~arsi** gli orecchi, to stop one's ears. **~abuchi** *m. indecl.* stop-gap. **~ato** *part. adj.* stopped-up, muffled-up; shut-up; rimasi **~ato** in casa tutto il giorno, I stayed in all day; (mus.) canna **~ata**, stopped organ-pipe.

tap·pete *onom., excl.* See **tacchete**.

tappet-o *m.* carpet, rug; mat; — del letto, bedside mat; chenille table-cloth; — erboso, carpet of grass, lawn; — verde, green baize table, gaming-table, diplomatic conference table; mettere sul —, to table (e.g. a resolution), to propose, to put forward (e.g. a subject for discussion). **~are** [A I C] *tr.* to carpet. **~ino** *m. dim.* rug; mat.

tappezz-are [A I] *tr.* (*prep.* di) to hang with tapestry; to upholster; to paper (a wall); (fig.) to plaster (with); — di fiori, to carpet, to spread, with flowers. (**~ato** *part. adj.*) **~eri·a** *f.* tapestry; hangings, soft furnishings; wall-paper; upholstery; upholsterer's shop; fare **~eria** in un ballo, to be a 'wall-flower'. **~iere** *m.* upholsterer; decorator; paper-hanger; house-furnisher; tapestry-maker.

tappo *m.* stopper, plug, bung; cork; — in bocca, 'mum's the word'; (zool.) — vitellino, yolk plug (of an embryo); (naut.) short stopper; muzzle cover, tompion; (joc.) — da botte, fat little man.

tar-a *f.* (comm.) tare; — extra, super tare; — media, average tare; — reale, actual tare; — d'uso, customary tare; — legale, estimated tare; sopra —, super tare; (med.) hereditary defect; (fig.) defect, blemish; taint. **-are** [A 1] *tr.* (comm.) to tare; to ascertain or allow for tare; (techn.) to calibrate; to rate; †to examine. (**-ato** *part. adj.* **-atore** *m.*) **-atura** *f.* (techn.) calibration; rating.

tarabus·o *m.* (orn.) bittern, *Botaurus stellaris.* **-ino** *m.* (orn.) little bittern, *Ixobrychus minutus.*

tarabusto *m.* (mil.) lynch pin; †short-barrelled gun.

tarall·o *m.* sort of ring-shaped biscuit, †(naut.) pan —, ship's biscuit, hard bread, hard tack. **-ino** *m. dim.* small sweet ring-shaped biscuit.

tarando *m.* (zool.) reindeer, *Rangifer tarandus.*

taran·tar-a, tarantar-à *m.* (mus.) taratantara, trumpet-blast, trumpeting, fanfare. **-izzare** [A 1] *intr.* (aux. avere) to trumpet.

tarantass *f. indecl.* four-wheeled Russian travelling carriage without springs.

tarant-ella *f.* (zool.) see **tarantola**; (mus.) Tarantella (dance); (fig.) fare la —, to make a fuss. **-ello** *m.* slice cut from a tunny-fish; make-weight, scrap thrown in as an extra with a purchase of provisions. **-ismo** *m.* (med.) tarantism, choreomania.

taran·tol-a *f.* (zool.) tarantula spider; — muraiola, *Tarentola mauritanica,* a kind of gecko; il male della —, St Vitus's dance. **-ato** *adj.* bitten by a tarantula. **-ina** *f.* (zool.) *Spelerpes fuscus,* a kind of newt. **-ismo** *m.* (med.) chorea, tarantism.

tarapatà *m.* (mus.) rub-a-dub, drumming, tattoo.

tar-are [A 1], **-atore** *m.* See under **tara**.

taras·sico *m.* (bot.) dandelion, *Taraxacum officinale.*

taratatà *m.* (mus.) rub-a-dub, drumming, tattoo.

tarbo·fide *m.* (zool.) *Tarbophis fallax,* a small snake.

tar·chia *f.* (naut.) spritsail.

†tarchiano *adj.* heavy and clumsy.

tarchiato *adj.* thickset; sturdy; strongly-built.

tardi *adv.* See under **tardo**.

tard-o *adj.* slow; sluggish, lazy; tardy, late; slow-witted; — di mente, slow-witted; dull; grave; slow; weary; a -i passi, with slow, dragging steps; -a vecchiaia, extreme old age; i -i anni, the evening of life; ore -e, evening (hours); delayed; i più -i posteri, the most distant (future) generations. **-amente** *adv.* slowly; wearily; lazily. **-anza** *f.* delay; slowness; tardiness. **-are** [A 1] *intr.* (aux. avere) to delay; to be late; ha -ato una settimana a rispondere, he has delayed replying for a week; -are a tornare, to delay one's return; stasera -ano, they will be, are, late tonight; (aux. essere) to be late; to seem late, to seem to take a long time; la guarizione è -ata, recovery has seemed very slow; quanto mi -a di rivederlo!, how I long to see him again!; *tr.* to delay; to hold back. **-ato** *part. adj.* delayed; late. **-ezza** *f.* slowness; dullness; tardiness; lateness. **-i** *adv.* late; too late; (provb.) meglio -i che mai, better late than never; chi -i arriva male alloggia, last come, last served; tosto o -i, sooner or later; al(la) più -i, at the latest; ieri sul -i, late last night; far -i, to be late, to come late, to stay out late; si fa -i, it is getting late; slowly; camminare -i, to walk slowly, to dawdle. **-ità** *f.* slowness; laziness; dullness. **-ivo** *adj.* slow, late; backward; slow to develop, ripen or mature; frutto -ivo, late fruit; scuse -ive, tardy apologies. **-ona** *f.* (fam.) old maid.

targ-a *f.* targe, shield; coat of arms; name-plate, door-plate; (motor.) number-plate; (archit.) tablet; ornamental plaque; (Tusc.) large slice. **-are** [A 2] *tr.* (motor., admin.) to affix a number-plate to. **-ato** *part. adj.* bearing a number-plate. **-atura** *f.* affixing of number-plates (on cars, motor cycles, etc.). **-ona·io** *m.* shield-maker; name-plate maker. **-one** *m. augm.* large shield; large name-plate.

targhetta *f. dim.* of **targa**, q.v.; (watchm.) hand-setting bolt; (techn.) name-plate; tag.

targone[1] *m. augm.* See under **targa**.

targone[2] *m.* (bot.) tarragon, *Artemisia dracunculus.*

tarì *m. indecl.* (numism.) medieval coin (Sicily, etc.); coin of the Kingdom of the Two Sicilies (equal to 2 carlini).

ta·rida *f.* (naut. hist.) large vessel used for transport in the Middle Ages, three-masted and defensively armed.

tariff-a *f.* (leg.; comm.) charge; duty; fee; rate; scale; table of charges, tariff; — doganale, rate of customs duty, table of customs duties, customs tariff; -e differenziali, differential rates, (rlwy.) sliding scale (on the Italian State Railways); -e preferenziali, preferential rates; — di cottimo, rates for piecework; — giudiziaria, judicature fee; — delle sentenze, judgement fees; -e notarili, scale of notarial fees; -e professionali, professional fees and charges; — telefonica, postale, telegrafica, telephone, postal, telegraph charges (rates); — ferroviaria, railway rates, fares. **-ale** *adj.* according to a scale of charges. **-are** [A 1] *tr.* to impose a scale of charges upon; to fix a tariff on; to rate. (**-ato** *part. adj.*) **-a·rio** *m.* scale of charges. (**-ato** *part. adj.*)

tarino *m.* See **tarì**.

tarlatana *f.* tarlatan, stiffened muslin.

tarl-o *m.* (ent.) clothes-moth, *Tinea pellionella,* also woodworm of various kind; dust left by woodworm; (fig.) gnawing of conscience, remorse; worrying doubt; consuming anxiety; il — della gelosia, the gnawing pangs of jealousy; avere il — con, to feel rancour towards. **-are** [A 1] *intr.* (aux. essere), *rfl.* to be worm-eaten; to be moth-eaten; *tr.* (of woodworm) to gnaw. **-ato** *part. adj.* worm-eaten; moth-eaten; dente -ato, decayed tooth. **-atura** *f.* worm-hole; dust from worm-holes.

tarm-a *f.* (ent.) clothes-moth. **-are** [A 1] and derivs. see **intignare**.

tar·mica *f.* (bot.) sneezewort, *Achillea ptarmica.*

taroc-co *m.* (usu. *pl.* **-chi**) (cards) the Italian game of tarot or 'tarocchi'; a trump card in the game of tarot. **-care** [A 2] *intr.* (aux. avere) to play a trump card when one has no card of a low value to throw away; (fig., fam.) to grumble, to mutter angrily. **-chista** *m., f.* player of tarot or 'tarocchi'. **-cone** *m.* grumbler. (**-cona** *f.*)

tarogatò *m.* (mus.) tárogató (Hungarian reed-instrument).

tarolo *m.* (ent.) warble fly, *Hypoderma bovis*; (tanning) — aperto, warble hole.

tarozzo *m.* (naut.) strand of rope; ratline(e); sheerstrake, metal bar at foot of shrouds; — da branda, hammock stretcher; — da vela, — da fiamma, sail batten.

†tarpagnuolo *m.* trickster, swindler.

tarpano *adj.* boorish; rustic; rough, uncouth; *n.m.* boor; rough, uncouth person.

tarp-are [A 1] *tr.* to clip; to pare; to trim; (fig.) — le ali a, to clip the wings of. **-ato** *part. adj.* clipped; pared; trimmed. **-atura** *f.* clipping; (fig.) cut, abridgement.

tarp-e·o *adj.* (Rom. topography) Tarpeian; rupe -ea (*or* 'la Tarpea'), the Tarpeian Rock (near the Capitol); †monte -eo, the Capitol itself.

tarpigna *f.*, **tarpina** *f.* (bot.) dodder, *Cuscuta.*

Tarqui·nio *pr.n.m.* (Rom. hist.) Tarquin; Tarquinius.

Tarragon-a *pr.n.f.* (geog.) Tarragona. **-ese** *adj., n.m., f.* Tarragonese.

tarsale *adj.* See under **tarso**.

tars-i·a, tar·s-ia *f.* inlaid woodwork, tarsia; marquetry; — di metallo, inlaid metalwork; (fig.) mosaic of quotations, plagiarism. **-iare** [A 4] and derivs. see **intarsiare**.

tar·sico *adj.* (anat.) tarsal.

tars-o *m.* (anat.) tarsus (of the foot); tarsus (of the eyelids); -i palpebrali, tarsal plates; (zool.) tarsus; (miner.) a very hard white marble. **-ale** *adj.* (anat.) tarsal. **-algi·a** *f.* (med.) tarsalgia, metatarsalgia.

Tarta·glia *pr.n.m.* (theatr.) name of a character who stutters (Neapolitan comedy).

tartagli-are [A 4] *intr.* (aux. avere) to stutter; to stammer; *tr.* to stammer out, to falter out; to stutter out; to mumble; (fig.) — una lingua, to speak a language badly. **-amento** *m.* stuttering; stammering. (**-ato** *part. adj.*) **-one** *m.* stutterer; stammerer. (**-ona** *f.*)

tartan-a *f.* (naut.) single-masted trading craft; trawl-net; †two-masted coastal trading ship; †three-masted warship; (joc.) big fat woman. **-etta, -ina** *f. dim.* small trawl-net, seine.

Tartari·a *pr.n.f.* (geog.) Tartary.

tarta·rico *adj.* Tartaric, relating to the Tartars.

tar·tar-o[1] *adj.* Tartar, Tartaric, of the Tartars; lingua -a, Tartar; *n.m.* Tartar, Mongol. **-esco** *adj.* (*m.pl.* **-eschi**) Tartaric, of the Tartars.

Tar·t-aro[2] *pr.n.m.* (class. myth.) Tartarus; Hell. **-areo** *adj.* Tartarean; infernal.

tar·tar-o[3] *m.* (physiol.) tartar; cremore di —, cream of tartar. **-ato** *m.* (chem.) see **tartrato**.

tartaruga *f.* (zool.) tortoise; turtle; — comune, *Thalassochelys caretta*; — franeia, *Chelone mydas*; (fig., of person) sluggard, slow-coach, snail; camminare a passo di —, to go at a snail's pace; guscio di —, tortoise-shell; pettine di —, tortoise-shell comb.

tartass-are [A I] *tr.* to vex; to ill-treat; to bully; dopo averlo -ato per bene all'esame, lo bocciarono, after a gruelling viva they failed him; — uno strumento, to treat an instrument badly, to strum, to scrape, to thump on an instrument. **-amẹnto** *m.* ill-treatment; vexing; bullying. (**-ato** *part. adj.*)

tartina *f.* open sandwich; slice of bread with butter and jam, paste, etc.

tartrato *m.* (chem.) tartrate.

tartuf·folo *m.* (zool.) *Echinus microtuberculatus*, a kind of sea-urchin.

tartuf-o¹ *m.* (bot.) truffle, *Tuber aestivum*; Jerusalem artichoke, *Helianthus tuberosus*, Piedmont or garlic-scented truffle, *Tuber magnatum*; cane da -i, dog trained to hunt for truffles, (fig.) person who always turns up at the right moment, when there is something good to eat or a bottle of wine has been opened. **-a·ia** *f.* truffle-ground. **-a·io** *m.* truffle-seller. **-ato** *adj.* served with (seasoned with) truffle. **-icultura** *f.* artificial cultivation of truffles.

tartufo² *m.* (zool.) — di mare, *Venus verrucosa*, an edible bivalve.

Tartufo³ *pr.n.m.* Tartuffe; (fig.) hypocrite.

†tarullo¹ *m.* fool, simpleton.

†tarullo² *m.* blasphemer.

tas-ca *f.* pocket; — dei calzoni, trouser-pocket; — in petto, breast-pocket; — a toppa, patch-pocket; starsene con le mani in —, to stand with one's hands in one's pockets, to idle; metter mano alla —, to put one's hand in one's pocket (also fig.); rovesciare le -che, to turn out one's pockets; mettere in —, to pocket; avere in —, to have in one's pocket, (fig.) to have ready, to be ready with; orologio da —, pocket-watch; case (for instruments or papers); un portafogli a due -che, a notecase with two pockets (compartments); a me non vien nulla in —, I am not in pocket, I don't gain anything; entrare in — a uno, to be always in someone's pocket, i.e. to molest, to importune, to be always hanging round someone; rompere le -che a, to annoy; averne piene le -che, to have had enough of; (anat.) — del Douglas, pouch of Douglas. **-ca·bile** *adj.* suitable for the pocket; edizioncina -cabile, small pocket edition; vocabolario -cabile, pocket dictionary; (naut.) corazzata -cabile, pocket battleship. **-capane** *m.* (mil.) haversack; †(naut.) breadholster. **-cata** *f.* pocketful. **-chino** *m. dim.* waistcoat pocket; ticket-pocket; purse for small change. **-cone** *m. augm.* big pocket; breast-pocket (inside coat or overcoat).

taso¹ *m.* incrustation; tartar.

†taso² *m.* harness; trappings.

tass-a *f.* tax; fee; — d'ingresso al museo, entrance fee to the museum; — d'iscrizione, entrance fee (to join a club, society, etc.); (leg.; comm.) duty; fee (payable for a public service rendered to payer); impost; tax; — di registro, registration fee; — addizionale, sopra —, surtax; — graduale, graduated duty, scale fee; — proporzionale, *ad valorem* duty; — di successione, estate duty; — progressiva sul patrimonio, tax on whole estate rising on sliding scale; — di ricchezza mobile, income-tax; — sul reddito, — fondiaria, land-tax; — di bollo, stamp duty; — d'esercizio, trading-licence tax; esente da —, free of tax; sgravio di —, tax relief; — spettacoli, entertainment-tax; — di ancoraggio, groundage; — indiretta, indirect tax; — di pedaggio, toll; — sui cani, dog licence; — sull'alcool, duty on spirits; postage; — pagata, pre-paid postage; — di frequenza, (at a school) tuition fee. **-a·bile** *adj.* taxable; assessable; subject to duty. (**-abilità** *f.*) **-a·metro** *m.* taximeter. **-are** [A I] *tr.* (*prep.* di) to tax; to assess; to fix a tariff on; (fig.) to tax, to accuse. **-ativo** *adj.* (leg.) compulsory; definite; definitive; exact; explicit; final; mandatory; positive; precise. **-ativamẹnte** *adv.* compulsorily; definitely, etc. **-ato** *part. adj.* taxed; assessed; (of letters) surcharged; accused, charged (with); definite. **-atore** *m.* assessor. **-aziọne** *f.* taxation; assessment; rating; charges.

tassell-o *m.* peg; wedge; dowel; (metall.) dolly block; (foundry) loose section of pattern; sample plug taken from cheese, etc. **-are** [A I] *tr.* to put in plugs, wedges, etc.; (cheese) to sample (taking out a 'tassello'); to tessellate; to do mosaic work. (**-atura** *f.*) **-ato** *part. adj.*; *n.m.* mosaic; tessellated (pavement, etc.).

tass-ì *m. indecl.* taxi-cab, taxi. **-ista** *m.* taxi-driver.

tas·sia *f.* (bot.) *Thapsia garganica*.

tassid-ermi·a *f.* taxidermy. **-ermista** *m.* taxidermist. **-er·mico** *adj.* taxidermal.

tass-o¹ *m.* (techn.) a form of anvil with no horns; (eng.) dolly; — da pianare, planishing stake. **-ẹtto** *m. dim.* stake (of a tinker).

tass-o² *m.* (bot.) yew, *Taxus baccata*. **-ina** *f.* (chem.) taxine. **-obarbasso** *m.* (bot.) Aaron's rod, *Verbascum thapsus*.

tasso³ *m.* (zool.) badger, *Meles meles*; (fig.) dormire come un —, to sleep like a dog.

tasso⁴ *m.* rate; rate of interest; — di sconto, rate of discount, bank-rate.

tassobarbasso *m.* See under **tasso²**.

tasson-omi·a *f.* (biol.) taxonomy. **-o·mico** *adj.* taxonomic.

tast-are [A I] *tr.* to feel; to touch; to try; to probe; to sound; — il polso a uno, to feel a person's pulse; — il muro col martello per trovare un vuoto, to tap the wall with a hammer to find a hollow place; prima di tentare il guado, -ate il fondo con una pertica, before attempting the ford try the bottom with a pole; (fig.) — il terreno, to explore the ground, to find how the land lies; — uno, to sound a person; (mus.) to touch, to finger, to play (the keys). **-amẹnto** *m.* feeling; touching; sounding. **-ata** *f.* touch; dare una -ata a, to touch, to feel. (**-ato** *part. adj.*) **-atore** *m.* **-atrice** *f.*) **-atura** *f.* touch; feeling; sounding; (mus.) keyboard; fingerboard. **-eggiare** [A 3 c] *tr.* to touch; to try again; to tap; (mus.) to finger; *intr.* (*aux.* avere) to grope. (**-eggiato** *part. adj.*) **-eggiatura** *f.* (mus.) fingering. **-iera** *f.* (techn.; mus.) fingerboard; keyboard, manual, row of keys; (mus.) sulla -iera, with the bow over the fingerboard (opposite of 'sul ponticello', q.v.); (naut.) diving controls in a submarine. **-ierista** *m.* (typ.) Monotype or Linotype keyboard operator; (fig.) an unknown hero. **-ino** *m. dim.* of **tasto**; meddler; one who wants to touch everything. **-o** *m.* touch; feel; riconoscere al -o, to recognize by the touch; andare al -o, to go by (the) touch; si sente al -o che è lana, you can tell it is wool by the feel of it; key; tapper; (teleg.) touch; trial shaft (pit) for excavation; (fig.) subject; toccare un -o delicato, to touch on a delicate subject; certi -i non vanno toccati, there are certain subjects that must not be touched upon; toccare il -o giusto, to strike the right note; (mus.) key (i.e. part of keyboard); fingerboard; fret; sul -o, with the bow over the fingerboard; -o solo, an indication to play the bass alone without improvising harmonies above it. **-ọne, -ọni** *adv.* by groping, gropingly; andar -oni, to feel one's way, to grope; (pop.) a -oni, gropingly.

tata¹ *excl.* (infant.) ta-ta! (goodbye); fare —, to say ta-ta.

tat-a², -o *m.* (dial.) daddy; (Tusc.) older sister; older brother.

†tattamellare *intr.* to gossip.

tattame·o *m.* slow-moving person.

†tat·tera *f.* trifle, something of no account; defect; excrescence.

tat·tic-a *f.* (mil.) tactics (also fig.); questo non è buona —, this is not good tactics. **-o** *adj.* (mil.) tactical; movimento -o, tactical move (also fig.); *n.m.* tactician. **-ọne** *m. augm.* (fig.) clever tactician, cunning person. (**-ọna** *f.*)

tat·til-e *adj.* tactile. **-ità** *f.* tactility.

tatt-o *m.* touch; the sense of touch; morbido, soffice al —, soft to the touch; (text.) fee, handle; (fig.) tact; una persona piena di —, a tactful person; non avere —, to have no tact, to be tactless; (mus.) touch; beat, tactus.

tatù *f. indecl.*, **tatuṣa** *f.* (zool.). See **armadillo**.

tatu-are [A 6] *tr.* to tattoo. **-ag·gio** *m.* tattooing, tattoo. **-ato** *part. adj.* tattooed.

ta·u *m.* letter (T) of the Greek alphabet; (hist.) squire in the Order of St Stephen in the time of the Grand Dukes of Tuscany, who bore a T-shaped cross on the breast; (herald.) cross formy.

ta·umat-urgi·a *f.* thaumaturgy, miracle-working; magic. **-ur·gico** *adj.* thaumaturgic, wonder-working; miraculous. **-urgo** *m.* (*pl.* **-urghi**) thaumaturge, worker of marvels or of miracles; (rel.) wonder-working saint.

†taupino *adj.* See **tapino**.

Ta·uro¹ *pr.n.m.* (astron.) Taurus.

ta·ur-o² *m.* (poet.) bull. **-iatri·a** *f.* (vet.) cow doctoring, veterinary care of bovines. **-ifọrme** *adj.* (class. myth.) tauriform. **-ina** *f.* (chem.) taurine, amino-ethionic acid. **-ino** *adj.* bull-like; collo -ino, bull-neck. **-ocolla** *f.* strong glue. **-omachi·a** *f.* bull-fight.

taut-o·crono *adj.* (math.) tautochronous. **-ologi·a** *f.* tautology. **-olo·gico** *adj.* tautological. **-omeri·a** *f.* (chem.) tautomerism. **-ome·rico** *adj.* (chem.) tautomeric. **-omerịṣmo** *m.* (chem.) tautomerism.

tavell-a *f.* (bldg.) hollow flat tile, hollow flat block. **-ato** *adj.* (bldg.) consisting of hollow flat blocks.

tavern-a *f.* public-house; andare per le -e, to pub-crawl; restaurant (once of a humble kind, now often fashionable); †shop. **-a·io**, **-aro** *m.* innkeeper, public-house keeper, landlord, host. **-iere** *m.* public-house keeper, innkeeper, landlord; †frequenter of taverns.

ta·vol-a *f.* **1.** BOARD; plank; — da stirare, ironing-board; — di salvezza, raft; panel; painting; slab, tablet; — di marmo, marble tablet; (archit.) flat slab of abacus; (mus.) belly, table (of violin); — (armonica), sounding-board (of pianoforte); (of gems) facet; (theatr.) *pl.* boards, stage. **2.** TABLE; — da pranzo, dining-table; — di cucina, kitchen-table; apparecchiare la —, to lay the table; — allungabile, draw-leaf table; — a ribalta, folding table; biancheria da —, table linen; sedersi a —, to sit down to table; servire a —, to wait at table; in —, on the table, served; — comune, table d'hôte; — calda, snack bar serving hot as well as cold dishes; meals; per la — vado dalla zia, I take my meals at my aunt's; — da giuoco, card-table; mettere le carte in —, to put one's cards on the table; la Tavola Rotonda, the Round Table (Arthurian, and fig.); (admin., etc.) riunione della — rotonda, round-table meeting; (geog.) Montagna della Tavola, Table Mountain; Baia della Tavola, Table Bay. **3.** TABLE, list; index; -e dei logaritmi, logarithm table; — pitagorica, — di moltiplicazione, multiplication table; plate, illustration; indice delle -e, list of plates (in book); -e geografiche, maps; (paint.) picture painted on wood; panel-painting; (liturg.) — dell'uffizio, ordo; (leg.) table, a slab inscribed with laws; a code of law; (Bibl.) le -e della legge, tables of the law (brought by Moses from Sinai); (Rom. hist.) leggi delle 12 -e, the Twelve Tables. **4.** †MEASURE OF AREA. **-ac·cio** *m. pejor.* plank bed, bare board (esp. in prisons and guard-rooms). **-ame** *m.* planking, scaffolding. †**-are** *adj.* in the form of a square or rectangle; *vb. tr.* to board up; to cover with planking; to measure land; *intr.* to game, to play at table. **-ata** *f.* table set for dinner; guests round the table; tenere allegra la -ata, to keep the table amused. **-ato** *m.* plank-floor; wooden floor; planking; wooden partition; (bldg.) floor-board; (geog.) tableland. †**-eggiare** *intr.* to wait at table; to sit at table after a meal. †**-ella** *f. dim.* of tavola; palette. **-ello** *m.* goldsmith's or silversmith's bench. **-etta** *f. dim.* small board, small plank; slab; -etta di cioccolata, bar, slab, of chocolate; small table; dressing-table; camerino da -etta, dressing-room; (archit.) architect's drawing-board; (surv.) plane table; (paint.) small picture; (class. antiq.) writing-tablet; (naut.) -etta del solcometro, rotor of a patent log; †-etta dei garbi, shipbuilder's drawing instrument. **-iere** *m.* chess-board; draughts-board; card-table; backgammon-board; (geog.) tableland; il Tavoliere di Puglia, the plain between the Gargano, the Gulf of Manfredonia and the Apennines.

ta·vol-o *m.* (a non-Tuscan form of **tavola**, q.v., or of **tavolino**, q.v.). **-ino** *m. dim.* little table; café-table; desk, writing-table; uomo di -ino, man of studious habits; -ino da lavoro, work-table; -ino da fumare, smoker's companion; -ino da notte, bedside-table. **-one** *m. augm.* large table; thick board or plank; (naut.) -one da sbarco, brow, gang-plank. **-ozza** *f.* (paint.) palette; (mus.) pallet (of organ).

taxi *m. indecl.* See **tassì**.

taxis *m. indecl.* (med.) taxis, tropism.

tazz-a *f.* cup; mug; — da tè, tea-cup; una — di tè, a cup of tea; — di fontana, basin of a fountain; (eng.) bucket, skip; pot; (anat.) poculum. **-etta** *f.* (bot.) polyanthus narcissus, *Narcissus tazetta*. **-iera** *f.* rack for cups. **-ina** *f. dim.* small cup.

te[1] *pers. prn. disjunct.* thee; you; a —!, over to you!, it's your turn; — stesso, yourself.

te[2] *pers. prn. conjunct.* form of **ti**[1], q.v., before **lo**, **la**, **li**, **le** or **ne**.

tè *m. indecl.* (bot.) tea plant, *Thea sinensis*; tea; — leggero, weak tea; — carico, strong tea; l'ora del —, tea-time; sala da —, tea-room, tea-shop; casa da — (in China and Japan), tea-house, (in Italy) brothel; thé dansant; servizio da —, tea-service, tea-set; vassoio da —, tea-tray; (bot.) — svizzero, speedwell, *Veronica officinalis*; tea rose, *Rosa odorata*.

te' *abbrev.* of **tene** (**tieni**), take!

tea *adj. f.* (bot.) rosa —, tea rose, *Rosa odorata*.

teak *m. indecl.* (bot.) teak, *Tectona grandis*.

te-an·drico *adj.* (theol.) theandric. **-antropi·a** *f.* (rel.) anthropomorphism. **-antro·pico** *adj.* anthropomorphic.

teatin-o, **-a** *adj.* and *n.m.*, *f.* (eccl.) Theatine (clerk regular or nun).

teatr-o *m.* theatre; andare a —, (Tusc.) al —, to go to the theatre; il — mi piace, I like going to the theatre; stage; — di prosa, legitimate stage; — di varietà, music-hall; — piccolo, — dei pupi, puppet-theatre; — aperto, open-air theatre; audience; 'house'; mercoledì sera era magnifico —, on Wednesday evening there was an excellent house; dramatic works, plays, drama; (mus.) — dell'opera, opera-theatre, opera-house; gente di —, theatrical people, theatricals, actors, etc.; lecture-theatre; (fig.) seat, centre; il — della guerra, the theatre of war. **-a·bile** *adj.* dramatic, suitable for the stage. **-ale** *adj.* theatrical; spettacolo -ale, theatrical performance; dramatic; gesto -ale, theatrical, dramatic, gesture. **-alme̜nte** *adv.* theatrically. **-alità** *f.* theatricality. **-ante** *m.*, *f.* actor, actress; theatrical person; one given to posing and declaiming. **-ino** *m. dim.* puppet-show; il -ino di Pulcinella, Punch and Judy show. **-one** *m. augm.* large theatre; full house.

tebaina *f.* (chem.; pharm.) thebaine, paramorphine.

Tebaldo *pr.n.m.* Theobald (cf. **Teobaldo**).

Teb-e *pr.n.f.* (geog.) Thebes, city of Boeotia; (Gk. lit.) 'I sette a —', the 'Seven against Thebes' (of Aeschylus); novella — (Dante, *Inf.* XXXIII), the modern Thebes (i.e. Pisa); Thebes, city of ancient Egypt. **-a·ide** *pr.n.f.* Thebaid. **-ano** *adj.* Theban.

†**tebertino** *m.* See **travertino**.

Tebro *pr.n.m.* (poet.). See **Tevere**.

tec *m. indecl.* kind of hydromel (mead) made in Abyssinia.

teca *f.* case; casket; (anat.) theca.

te̜cca *f.* (dial. Tusc.) little spot, stain, fault.

†**tec·chio** *adj.* large; gross.

te̜ccola *f.* See **tecca**.

teck *m. indecl.* (carpen.) teak.

tec·n-ico *adj.* technical; direttore —, production manager; Istituto —, Technical School; *n.m.* technician; anyone working on the production side of a works. **-ica** *f.* technique; technical knowledge; engineering. **-icame̜nte** *adv.* technically. **-icişmo** *m.* technicality; technique. **-icolor** *m. indecl.* (cinem.) technicolour. **-i·grafo** *m.* (eng.) drawing machine. **-ologi·a** *f.* technology; technical terminology. **-olo·gico** *adj.* technological. **-o·logo** *m.* technologist. **-opati·a** *f.* (med.) occupational disease.

te̜co (*contr.* of **te** and **con**) with thee; with you. (Common in Tusc., otherwise literary or archaic.)

teda *f.* (class. antiq.) torch, esp. at marriage ceremonies; †pine-wood torch.

†**te(d)deo** *m.* See **tedeum**.

tede̜s-co *adj.*, *n.m.* (*m.pl.* **-chi**) German; German-speaking (including Austrians, German Swiss, etc.); antico —, Old High German; basso —, Low German; (fig.) parlar —, to speak 'double-Dutch'. **-came̜nte** *adv.* in the German way. **-cante** *adj.*, *n.m.* pro-German. **-cac·cio** *m. pejor.* brutal German, a 'Hun'. **-cheggiare** [A 3 C] *intr.* (*aux.* avere) to Germanize. **-cheri·a** *f.* (derog.) Germanism; (joc.) Germany, Germans. **-co·filo** *adj.* Germanophil. **-cofobi·a** *f.* Germanophobia. **-co·fobo** *m.* Germanophobe. **-co̜ne** *adj. augm.* German of the Germans, very obviously German; also *n.m.* **-cume** *m.* (derog.) German ideas, things, people.

tede·um *m.* Te Deum.

te·di-o *m.* tedium, tediousness; weariness. **-are** [A 4] *tr.* to weary; to bore. **-osità** *f.* tediousness; tiresomeness. **-o̜so** *adj.* tedious; tiresome; wearisome. (**-osame̜nte** *adv.*)

tef *m. indecl.* (bot.) teff, *Eragrostis abyssinica*, kind of grass grown for fodder.

tefr-ina *f.*, **-oïte** *f.* (miner.) tephroite, manganous orthosilicate.

†**tega** *f.* pod.

tegam-e *m.* pan; frying-pan; uova al, nel, —, fried eggs; panful; (glassm.) crucible, melting-pot. **-ata** *f.* panful. **-ino** *m. dim.* shallow pan; small frying-pan.

te̜gli-a *f.* baking-pan; pie-dish; (chem.) crucible; (pop.) large, flat hat. **-ata** *f.* panful. (**-one** *m. augm.*)

teg·mine *m.* (bot.) integument.

tegn-ente *adj.* tenacious; holding; firm; (fig.) stingy; grasping. **-enza** *f.* tenacity; firmness.

te̜gola *f.* roofing-tile.

te̜gol-o *m.* (curved) roofing-tile; (fig.) un — sulla testa, an unpleasant surprise; (provb.) chi ha -i di vetro, non tiri sassi al vicino, those

tegol·o (*cont.*)
who live in glass-houses shouldn't throw stones; cotto come un —, 'pickled', very drunk, *or* madly in love; gli manca un —, he has a screw loose; (eccl.) cappello a —, (kind of) clerical hat. **-a·ia** *f.* tile-works, tilery, kiln. **-ata** *f.* blow from a falling tile. **-ato** *m.* tiling, tiled roof; *adj.* (herald.) roofed.

tegument-o *m.* (anat.) tegument; (bot.) integument. **-ale** *adj.* tegumental. **-are** *m.* (bot.) cuticle. **-a·rio** *adj.* tegumentary; integumentary.

te-iera *f.* tea-pot. **-ina** *f.* (chem.) theine, caffeine, guaranine.

te-iṣmo *m.* theism (sometimes opposed to deism, sometimes not). **-ista** *m.* theist. **-i·stico** *adj.* theistic.

tẹl-a *f.* cloth; linen; — di cotone, calico; — bianca, bleached linen; — greggia, unbleached linen; — da asciugamani, towelling; — per doccia, shower curtain; — da lenzuola, sheeting; — per federe, per materasse, ticking; — da imballaggio, bagging, canvas; — d'Olanda, hollands (linen); — da aeroplani, aeroplane fabric; — (in)cerata, — impermeabile, water-proof canvas; (paint.) canvas; picture painted on canvas; (bookb.) legatura in mezza —, half-cloth binding; (theatr.) curtain; (anat.) — coroidea, choroid membrane; (naut.) net; canvas; hatch cover; — da vele, sail-cloth supplied in 'bolts'; battello di —, canvas boat; — di ragno, spider's web; (fig.) web; plot, intrigue; la — di un romanzo, the plot of a novel; (pop., joc.) far —, to make off. **-ag·gio** *m.* quality of cloth; weave, web; (naut.) quantity of canvas required to make up a sail. **-ame** *m.* (naut.) the complete outfit of canvas, a suit of sails. **-arina** *f.* skin (on boiled milk, etc.). **-eri·a** *f.* linen goods; negoziante di -erie, linen-draper. **-ẹtta** *f. dim.* **-etta** d'oro, cloth of gold.

tel-a·io *m.* loom; frame; — a mano, hand-loom; — meccanico, power-loom; — a manovella, crank-loom; — per maglieria, knitting-frame; — da ricamo, tambour, embroidery-frame; (paint.) frame (on which canvas is stretched for painting); — di finestra, window-frame, sash; — di bicicletta, bicycle-frame; — d'automobile, motor-car frame, chassis; mettere sul —, to start a job, to put in train; (typ.) matrix-case of Monotype caster. **-aino** *m.* lantern slide; frame; (motor.) -aino finestrino, window-frame.

telamọne *m.* (archit.) telamon.

Telchini *pr.n.m.pl.* (Gk. antiq.) Telchines (gnomelike beings, craftsmen and sorcerers, said to have lived in Rhodes).

tele- *pref.* equiv. to Eng. 'tele-'. (For derivatives in which the stress falls on the second syllable, e.g. **tele·fono**, see separate entries.) **-abbonato** *m.* television licence-holder. **-avviatọre** *m.* (electr.) contactor, starter. **-ca·mera** television camera. **-comando** *m.* remote control. **-comunicazịọne** *f.* telecommunication. **-controllo** *m.* (industr.) remote control. **-cronista** *m.* television announcer. **-diffọndere** [C] *tr.* to televise, to telecast. **-fe·rica** *f.* (eng.) cableway, telpherage; ski-lift, *téléférique*. **-fe·rico** *adj.* pertaining to a cableway. **-fonare** [A I S] *tr.*, *intr.* (aux. avere) to telephone, to ring up. **-fonata** *f.* telephone call; -fonata interurbana, trunk call. **-fonato** *part. adj.* sent, received, by telephone. **-foni·a** *f.* telephony. **-fo·nico** *adj.* telephonic; cabina -fonica, call-box, telephone kiosk; centralino -fonico, telephone exchange. **-fonista** *m., f.* (telephone) operator; telephonist. **-foto** *m., f.* telephoto; signalling by lights; wire picture (journalism, etc.). **-fotografi·a** *f.* telephotography; telephoto, picture by wire. **-ge·nico** *adj.* (of an actor, television personality, etc.) who comes over well on television. **-giornale** *m.* television newsreel. **-grafare** [A I S] *tr.* to telegraph; to wire; to cable. **-grafato** *part. adj.* telegraphed, wired. **-grafi·a** *f.* telegraphy; telegraph office; -grafia senza fili, wireless telegraphy. **-gra·fico** *adj.* telegraphic; palo -grafico, telegraph-pole; ufficio -grafico, telegraph office. **-graficamẹnte** *adv.* telegraphically, by telegraph. **-grafista** *m.* telegraphist; (mil.) member of the Corps of Signals. **-gramma** *m.* telegram; wire; -gramma con risposta pagata, reply-paid telegram; -gramma cifrato, telegram in code, cipher telegram. **-lente** *f.* (photog.) telephoto lens. **-metri·a** *f.* range-finding; use of a telemeter. **-me·trico** *adj.* telemetric(al). **-metrista** *m.* (mil.; naut.) rangetaker. **-obbiettivo** *m.* (photog.) telelens, long-distance lens; telephoto lens. **-ologi·a** *f.* (philos.) teleology. **-olo·gico** *adj.* teleological. **-pati·a** *f.* telepathy; presentiment; thought-reading. **-pa·tico** *adj.* telepathic. **-ruttọre** *m.* (electr.) remote-control switch. **-schermo** *m.* television screen. **-sco·pico** *adj.* telescopic(al); visible only through a telescope; stelle -scopiche, telescopic stars. **-sco·pio** *m.* telescope; a -scopio,

telescopic (in the sense of 'collapsible'). **-scrivente** *m.* teleprinter. **-selezione** *f.* (teleph.) system whereby trunk-calls can be dialled. **-sịṣmo** *m.* (geol.) shock produced by distant earthquake. **-spetta-tọre** *m.* televiewer. **-steṣi·a** *f.* telaesthesia. **-termo·metro** *m.* (techn.) remote indication thermometer. **-vedẹre** [B 35] *tr.* to look in, to view (on television). **-visịọne** *f.* television. **-viṣivo** *adj.* relating to television, television; tubo -visivo, picture tube. **-viṣore** *m.* television set.

tele·fono *m.* telephone, phone; fili del —, telephone wires; parlare per —, to speak on the telephone, to telephone; elenco degli abbonati al —, telephone directory; numero del —, telephone number; chiamare al —, to ring up.

tele·grafo *m.* telegraph (apparatus); telegraph office; — sottomarino, telegraph (submarine) cable; (mil.) — campale, field telegraph; — ottico, semaphore; — senza fili, wireless; viti a —, vines trained on wires.

tele·metro *m.* (photog.) distance meter; (photog.; mil.; naut.) rangefinder; (mil.; naut.) — stereoscopico, stereoscopic rangefinder.

teleri·a *f.* See under **tela**.

†te·let-a *f.*, **†-e** *f.* (Gk. antiq.) sacred rite.

telẹtta¹ *f. dim.* See under **tela**.

telẹtta² *f.* See toletta.

teli·fono *m.* (zool.) false scorpion, *Thelyphonus caudatus*.

tellina *f.* (zool.) *Tellina* spp., edible marine bivalve.

†tellure *m.* the terrestrial globe.

tellu·r-ico *adj.* telluric, terrestrial; (scient.) telluric; magnetismo —, tellurism. **-io** *m.* (chem.) tellurium. **-oṣo** *adj.* (chem.) tellurous. **-uro** *m.* (chem.) telluride.

tẹlo¹ *m.* length of material (cf. **tela**).

telo² *m.* (poet.) arrow; dart; javelin; lance; — tridentato, Neptune's trident; un tratto di —, (distance of) a dart's flight.

telofaṣe *f.* final phase.

†telo·nio *m.* counter; work-bench.

tẹma¹, tema *f.* (poet.) fear.

tem-a² *m.* theme; subject; uscir di —, to wander from the subject; tenersi al —, to stick to the point; (school) exercise, composition; (gramm.) stem; (mus.) theme, subject; — fondamentale, leitmotiv. **-a·tica** *f.* (mus.) thematic idiom. **-a·tico** *adj.* thematic; (gramm.) of the stem, relating to the stem; (mus.) thematic.

temenza *f.* See under **temere**.

temera·ri-o *adj.* rash; foolhardy; reckless; (leg.) litigante —, rash litigant; lite -a, rash action; pretesa -a, baseless claim without reasonable cause (C.C.); (hist.) Carlo il Temerario, Charles the Bold. **-amẹnte** *adv.* rashly; recklessly. **-età** *f.* temerity, rashness, recklessness.

tem-ẹre [B I] *tr.* to fear; to be afraid (of), to dread; to shrink from; to hesitate; certi animali -ono il freddo, certain animals cannot stand the cold; *intr.* (aux. avere; *prep.* di) to be anxious (about); to be in doubt (concerning); -o delle mie forze, I mistrust my strength; -o di lui, I fear for him; — della vittoria, to be doubtful of victory; — della cattiva accoglienza, to fear a bad reception; -o che venga, I am afraid he may come; -o che non venga, I fear he won't come. **-ente** *part. adj.* fearful; anxious. **-enza** *f.* fear; dread; anxiety; shyness. **-erità** *f.* temerity, rashness, foolhardiness. **-i·bile** *adj.* to be feared. **-uto** *part. adj.* feared; dreaded.

Temi, Te·mide *pr.n.f.* (Gk. myth.; astron.) Themis.

†temmi·rio *m.* (Gk. antiq.) (demonstrative) proof.

te·molo *m.* (ichth.) grayling, *Thymallus thymallus*.

†tem-ore *m.*, **†-oṣo** *adj.* See timore, etc.

tẹmpa *f.* rounded summit of a hill.

tempani *m.pl.* (vet.) Hydrops amni (of mares).

†tempell-a *f.* clapper. **†-are** *intr.* to rattle a clapper; to hesitate; *tr.* to keep in doubt.

tem·per-a, tẹmper-a *f.* (paint.) tempera; distemper; far la — dei colori, to mix paints with water and gum or white of egg; picture painted in tempera; (metall.) hardening; quenching; tempering; (of sound) timbre; (fig.) temper, temperament.

temper-are [A I S, A I SC] *tr.* to temper; to mitigate; to moderate; (paint.) to mix (colours) for tempera painting; to blend; (metall.) to harden; to quench; (glassm.) to temper; (fig.) to whet; †to govern; †(naut.) — le vele, to trim the sails; *rfl.* to be temperate; to exercise self-control; -arsi nel bere, to be temperate in drinking. **-a·bile** *adj.* (metall.) hardenable. **-abilità** *f.* (metall.) hardenability. **-alapis, -amatite** *m. indecl.* pencil-sharpener. **-amẹnto** *m.* tempering; temper; disposition; temperament; just proportion; mix-

temper·are (*cont.*)
ture; arrangement; compromise; expedient; assuagement; mitigation, air-conditioning; (mus.) temperament, tuning; -amento equabile, equal temperament. **-ante** *part. adj.* temperate; moderate; soothing. **-anza** *f.* temperance; moderation; Società di -anza, Temperance Society. **-ativo** *adj.* moderating; soothing. **-ato** *part. adj.* tempered; temperate, moderate; terra -ata, land not too dry; zona -ata, temperate zone; (mus.) Il clavicembalo ben -ato, The Forty-Eight (Preludes and Fugues of Bach), The Well-tempered Clavichord (Klavier); (metall.) hardened; *adv.* temperately, moderately. (-**atamente** *adv.*) **-atore** *m.* moderator; temperer. (-**atrice** *f.*) **-atura** *f.* (phys.) temperature; -atura ambiente, ambient temperature, room temperature; tempering; sharpening; †(mus.) temperament, tuning.

tempe·rie *f.* mild or seasonable weather; equable climate; temperature; mixture in the right proportions.

temperin·o *m.* pen-knife. **-ata** *f.* cut with a pen-knife.

tempest·a *f.* storm; bad weather; tempest; thunderstorm; squall; — di neve, snowstorm, blizzard; — di vento, gale, hurricane; (fig.) shower; — di proiettili, shower of missiles; — di palle, hail of bullets; — in un bicchier d'acqua, storm in a teacup; acqua e non —!, that's too much!, enough is as good as a feast; †time. **-ante** *part. adj.* raging; storming. **-are** [A I] *intr.* (*aux.* avere) to rage; to storm; *tr.* (*prep.* di) to vex, to annoy, to harass; to importune; -are di domande, to harass with questions; to shake; to pull about, to toss about; to knock furiously; cominciò a -are la porta di pugni, he began to hammer on the door with his fists; to pelt (with); to shower (with); -are qualcuno di colpi, to shower blows on someone; -are di baci, to shower kisses upon. **-ato** *part. adj.* beaten; shaken; decked, adorned; spangled; -ato di gemme, studded with jewels. **-ivo** *adj.* timely; opportune; seasonable. **-ivamente** *adv.* timely; seasonably; opportunely; in time. **-ività** *f.* timeliness, seasonableness. **-oso** *adj.* stormy; tempestuous; violent; vehement; boisterous; cavallo -oso, restive horse; 'Tarantella Tempestosa', title of a tarantella by Alfred Reynolds; *Cime Tempestose, Wuthering Heights*; †changeable. **-osamente** *adv.* tempestuously; violently; boisterously; furiously; †anxiously. **-io** *m.* (Tusc., fam.) noise; fury.

tem·pi·a *f.* (anat.) temple; *pl.* head; hair at the temples. **-ale** *m.* (text.; eng.) template, temple; -ale automatico, mechanical temple; †temple.

tem·pi·o, tempi·o *m.* (*pl.* **templi**) temple; church; (rel.) pagan temple; the Jewish Temple; modern Jewish synagogue; Protestant church; (poet. or rhetorical, of a Catholic church) (great) church, 'fane'; order of Knights Templar. **-ere** *m.* Guardian of the Holy Sepulchre; *pl.* Knights Templars. **-etto** *m. dim.* little temple; shrine.

templare *m.* Templar; Knight Templar.

†**templo** *m.* (poet.). See **tempio**.

temp·o *m.* time; nello stesso —, at the same time; — propizio, favorevole, propitious, favourable, moment; times, days; il buon — antico, the good old times; il — presente, the present; il fattore —, the time factor; lasciare il — di riflettere, to grant time for reflection; (leg.; comm.) time; delay; term; period; concedere —, to allow time, to grant delay; prolungare il —, to extend the time, to extend the period; a — fisso, at a stated time; a — utile, in due course, in due time; in — di guerra, in wartime; in — di notte, in the night-time, by night; a suo —, in due course; a — debito, at the right time; proprio al — giusto, in the very nick of time; di — in —, from time to time; da molto —, long since, for a long time (in the past); da qualche —, some time ago, for some time (in the past); da quanto —?, how long ago?; ti do una settimana di —, I give you a week; con l'andar del —, in the long run; molto — prima, long before; per —, early, betimes; in questi ultimi -i, lately, of late; fino a quel —, until then; di notte —, at night-time, in the night; logoro dal —, time-worn; venerabile per il —, time-honoured; con i -i che corrono, as times go, in these days; (provb.) chi ha — non aspetti —, make hay while the sun shines; dar — al —, to let time pass, to mark time; darsi bel —, to have a jolly good time; uomo di buon —, man who is intent on pleasure; riacquistare il — perduto, to make up for lost time; precorse i suoi -i, he was in advance of his times, he was born before his time; questo libro ha fatto il suo —, this book has had its day; non ha resistito al collaudo del —, it did not stand the test of time; ingannare il —, to while away the time; ammazzare il —, to kill time; (motor.) stroke of an engine; motore a due -i, two-stroke engine; (gramm.) tense; — composto, compound tense; (cinem.) reel; (boxing) round; (soccer, etc.) half; (telev.) base dei -i, time base; (radar; math.) asse dei -i, abscissa axis, *x*-axis; (mus.) tempo, speed; time; movement; a —, in time; — ordinario, common time; — a due -i, two-four time; — a tre -i, three-four time; — rubato, see **rubato**, under **rubare**; (sport) record-time; period, age; — medio, Middle Age(s), *or* mean time; uomo di gran —, man of considerable age; ai suoi bei -i, in his youth (hey-day); season; — della mietitura, harvest time; vestito di mezzo —, between-season dress; weather; bel —, fine weather; brutto —, bad weather; che — hai avuto?, what sort of weather did you have?; — inglese, dull, cloudy weather *or* drizzle; (provb.) rosso di sera, buon — si spera, red sky at night is shepherd's delight. **-ac·cio** *m. pejor.* bad weather. †**-aiuolo** *m.* sucking pig. **-ino** *adv. phr.* per -ino, early, fairly early in the morning; (iron.) bad weather. **-is·simo** *adv. phr.* per -issimo, very early. **-ista** *m., f.* (mus.) good timekeeper; (fig.) one who senses a favourable moment; opportunist. **-one** *m. augm.* gaiety; a good time. **-u·scolo** *m.* infinitesimal division of time.

tem·pora *f.pl.* Ember days; le quattro —, the four Ember weeks.

temporal·e¹ *adj.* (rel.) temporal (life, goods, punishment); worldly; †secular, lay; relating to time; un lungo intervallo —, a long interval of time; (gramm.) temporal; of time; avverbio —, adverb of time; *n.m.* (eccl.) the temporal power (of the Pope); †sucking pig. **-mente** *adv.* temporally. **-ista** *m.* supporter of the temporal power of the Pope. **-alità** *f.* temporality, temporalty; †(rel.) worldliness; *pl.* (eccl.) temporalities.

temporal·e² *m.* thunderstorm. **-esco** *adj.* (*m.pl.* **-eschi**) stormy.

temporale³ *adj.* (anat.) temporal, relating to the temples.

tempora·ne·o *adj.* temporaneous, temporary; transitory; provisional; seasonal; pertaining to time, temporal. **-amente** *adv.* temporaneously, temporarily; transitorily. **-aneità** *f.* temporaneousness, temporariness.

tempora·ri·o *adj.* temporary; transient. **-amente** *adv.* temporarily.

temporeggi·are [A 3 c] *intr.* (*aux.* avere) to temporize; to gain time; to procrastinate; to mark time; *tr.* to postpone, to put off. **-amento** *m.* temporizing; delaying tactics; procrastinating. **-ante** *part. adj.* temporizing; time-serving. **-atore** *m.* temporizer; (hist.) Fabio il -atore, Fabius Cunctator; procrastinator.

†**temporile** *m.* sucking pig.

†**temporino** *adj.* precocious, developing early.

tempra, **tempr·a** *f.*; **-are** [A I]. See **temper·a**, **-are**.

tempu·scolo *m.* See under **tempo**.

temuto *part.* See under **temere**.

tenac·e *adj.* tenacious; adhesive; tough; retentive; persevering; firm of purpose, constant; †avaricious. **-emente** *adv.* tenaciously; perseveringly; †avariciously.

tena·c·ia *f.* tenacity; perseverance, firmness of purpose; retentiveness. **-ità** *f.* cohesiveness; toughness; stickiness.

tena·colo *m.* (surg.) tenaculum.

tena·glia *f.* and derivs. See **tanaglia**.

ten-algi·a *f.* (med.) tenalgia, painful tendon. **-al·gico** *adj.* tenalgic.

†**tencione** *m.* and derivs. See **tenzone**.

tend·a *f.* awning; curtain; hanging; blind; tirare la —, to draw the blind; tent; bell-tent; — da bagno, bathing-tent; grande — da campo, marquee; piantare la —, to pitch one's tent; levare le -e, to strike camp; dormire sotto la —, to sleep under canvas; ritirarsi sotto la —, to retire to one's tent (i.e. like Achilles, usu. with an implication of sulking); la statua è ancora avvolta in una —, the statue has not yet been unveiled; (theatr.) see **sipario**; (naut.) awning; far le -e, to spread awnings; rullare e serrare le -e, to make up and stow awnings; togliere le -e, to furl awnings. **-ag·gio** *m.* (text.) curtaining (material); *pl.* soft furnishings. **-ale** *m.* large tent; awning; marquee; †(naut.) stern awning in a galley. **-aletto** *m.* (naut.) boat's awning; †poop awning. **-ame** *m.* collection of awnings, curtaining, etc.; negozio per -ami, shop where canvas, etc. for awnings, blinds, tents, etc. is sold. **-ato** *part. adj.* tented; furnished with tents; pitched, erected, stretched (of tents or awnings). **-ina** *f.* curtain; blind; (photog.) otturatore a -ina, focal plane shutter; (cinem.) otturatore a -ina, slit shutter. **-one** *m. augm.* large tent; large awning; (fig., Tusc.) veil, curtain; -one di nebbia, curtain of mist. **-o·poli** *f.* a camp settlement, encampment; holiday camp.

tendenza *f.* and derivs. See under **tendere**.

ten·der *m. indecl.* (rlwy.) tender.

ten·d-ere [C I] *tr.* to stretch, to stretch out; to hold out; — i panni ad asciugare, to hang out the clothes to dry; — la mano, to hold out one's hand; — le braccia, to open, to hold out, one's arms; to strain; to draw tight; — gli orecchi, to strain one's ears; — il collo, to crane one's neck; to tighten, to pull tight, to make taut; — l'arco, to bend the bow; to lay; to spread; — una trappola, to set a snare; — una insidia, to lay a trap; — lo sguardo a, to direct one's glance towards; — la mente a, to give one's mind to; — il cammino verso, to direct one's steps towards; *intr.* (*aux.* avere; *prep.* a) to tend (towards), to aim (at); to lead (to); to be inclined (towards); il colore delle pareti ‑e al verde, the colour of the walls is verging on green; questo vino ‑e al dolce, this wine is on the sweet side; per natura ‑e all'ozio, he is naturally inclined to be lazy; to lead; to be conducive (to). **‑ente** *part. adj.* tending; di colore ‑ente al giallo, verging on yellow; di natura ‑ente alla malinconia, naturally inclined towards melancholy. **‑enza** *f.* tendency; trend; bent; inclination; leaning; propensity; liking; love; (leg.) ‑enza a delinquere, criminal tendency; (comm.) ‑enza al rialzo, upward trend; ‑enza al ribasso, downward trend, sagging; ‑enza a cadere in disuso, obsolescence. **‑enzioso** *f.* tendentious, partial, biased. **‑enziosamente** *adv.* tendentiously. **‑enziosità** *f.* tendentiousness. **‑icatena** *m. indecl.* chain tightener. **‑icin·ghia** *m. indecl.* (eng.) belt-stretcher, belt-tightener. **‑icin·golo** *m.* front idler (of a tractor). **‑ifeltro** *m.* (paperm.) rullo ‑ifeltro, hitch roll, stinting roll. **‑itoio** *m.* drying-room; drying-place, shed, etc.; clothes-horse; clothes-line post. **‑itore** *m.* person who is engaged in spreading, stretching, etc.; (fig.) ‑itore d'insidie, layer of snares; (techn.) shackle; turnbuckle (for tightening wires, etc.); *adj.* nodo ‑itore, Matthew Walker knot. (**‑itrice** *f.*)

ten·d-ine *m.* tendon; sinew; — d'Achille, Achilles's tendon. **‑i·neo** *adj.* (anat.) tendinous.

tendo-sinovite *f.* (anat.) tendosynovitis. **‑vaginale** *adj.* (anat.) tendovaginal. **‑vaginite** *f.* (med.) tendovaginitis.

te·nebr-e *f.pl.* darkness; gloom; obscurity; al cader delle —, at nightfall; i ciechi vivono nelle —, the blind live in darkness; il Re delle —, the king of the dark regions, Satan; (fig.) ignorance; intellectual blindness; avvolto nelle —, wrapped in obscurity; (liturg.) (ufficio delle) —, (office of) Tenebrae; la panca delle —, butt, general victim; far le — addosso a, to beat; confusion and clamour. **†‑are** *vb.* and derivs. see **ottenebrare**. **‑ato** *part. adj.* obscured, darkened. **‑i·a** *f.* extensive obscurity; gross darkness; (astron.) the dark space between the planets. **†‑icoso** *adj.* dark, shadowy. **‑i·o, ‑ione** *m.* (ent.) mealworm, *Tenebrio* spp. **‑one** *m.* one who speaks obscurely; gloomy person, pessimist; reactionary; obscurantist. **‑ore** *m.* darkness; gloom. **‑osità** *f.* darkness, gloom; dimness of vision; secrecy. **‑oso** *adj.* gloomy; dark; sombre; obscure; secret; confused; disturbing; occhio ‑oso, weak eye, poor vision; *n.m.* darkness, gloom. (**‑osamente** *adv.*)

tenente *part.*, *n.m.* and derivs. See under **tenere**.

ten·ere [B 32] *tr.* to hold; to hold on to; to hold back; to restrain; to keep; to keep back; to have; to gain, to win; to obtain; — il fiato, to hold one's breath; non c'è verso di ‑erlo, there's no holding him; — a bada, to hold at bay, to keep at bay; — il cappello in testa, to keep one's hat on; — in ordine, to keep in order; — d'occhio qualcuno, to keep an eye on someone; — la promessa, to keep one's promise; — un diario, to keep a diary; — la destra, to keep to the right (in traffic); — presente, to bear in mind; (fig.) to hold, to consider, to regard; to think; — una persona in grande stima, to hold a person in high esteem; to contain, to hold, to take; to take up (of space), to occupy; — un'adunanza, to hold a meeting; — una conferenza, to give a lecture; — la cima, to reach the summit, to be at the top; — una regola, to observe a rule; (comm.) — i libri, to keep books, to keep accounts; — un conto in sospeso, to nurse an account; (mus.) — una nota, to sustain a note; (mil.) to garrison, to defend; to hold; (naut.) — una barca sui paranchi, to have, to keep, a boat at her falls; — a rimorchio, to have in tow; — il blocco a, to blockade; — il giornale, to write up the log; — le mure a dritta, to be on the starboard tack; — testa a una nave, to hold one's own against an enemy ship; *abs.* tieni!, take that!, *or* here, take it!; *intr.* (*aux.* avere) to be lasting; (of colours) to be fast, to be fadeless; — fermo, duro, to hold on, to hold fast; to be valid; non c'è scusa che ‑ga, no excuse will hold water; — a, to keep to; — all'argomento, to keep to the point; to be anxious

(about), to care (about); non ci ‑go, I don't care to; — a fare bella figura, to care about making a good impression; ‑go a dirvi, I must tell you; I am bound to tell you; — per uno, to side with someone; — da, to take after, to resemble; tiene dallo zio, he takes after his uncle; (naut.) — fermo sopra un cavo, to keep a cable taut; *rfl.* to hold oneself; to consider oneself; ‑ersi onorato, to consider oneself honoured; to keep (oneself); ‑etevi a destra, keep to the right; ‑ersi in equilibrio, to keep one's balance; ‑ersi in contatto con, to keep in touch with; ‑ersi sulle gambe, in piedi, to keep standing, to be able to stand, to stand; non potersi —, to be unable to refrain; non potei ‑ermi dal ridere, I couldn't help laughing; ‑ersi di una cosa, to boast of something; (naut.) ‑ersi nelle acque d'una nave, to follow in the wake of a ship; ‑ersi all'àncora, to remain at anchor; ‑ersi nell'asse di un canale, to keep to the middle of a channel; ‑ersi a bordi corti, to tack and tack again; ‑ersi in crociera, to keep the seas; ‑ersi fuori del tiro dei cannoni, to keep out of range; ‑ersi a galla, to keep afloat; ‑ersi al largo, to keep in the offing; ‑ersi a mezzo picco, to remain at short stay; ‑ersi a picco, to have the anchor 'up and down'; ‑ersi a picco lungo, to be at long stay. **‑ente** *part. adj.* holding; keeping; lasting; †tenacious; *n.m.* (naut.) lieutenant; second in command of small craft; primo ‑ente di vascello, first-lieutenant (an indication of seniority in a ship); (mil.) lieutenant; ‑ente colonello, lieutenant-colonel; ‑ente generale, lieutenant-general; *pl.* (herald.) supporters. **‑enza** *f.* (mil.) office of lieutenant; district under a lieutenant. **‑i·bile** *adj.* tenable; una posizione non più ‑ibile, a position that is no longer tenable. **‑imento** *m.* holding; piece of land; (hist.) ward, district (of a city). **‑itore** *m.*, **‑itrice** *f.* holder; keeper; ‑itore di bisca, keeper of a gambling-house; ‑itore di una pensione, boarding-house keeper; (comm.) ‑itore dell'asta, auctioneer; *adj.* (naut.) that holds well; fondo ‑itore, good holding ground; melma ‑itrice, good holding, good anchorage.

te·ner-o *adj.* tender; soft; uovo —, lightly-boiled egg; sapone —, soft soap; pliable; dai ‑i anni, from one's early years; sensitive; affectionate; un uomo di cuore —, a tender-hearted man; — dell'onore, jealous of one's honour; (vet.) — di bocca, tender-mouthed (of a horse); *n.m.* tender part; (fig.) weak or soft side (of character, etc.). **‑amente** *adv.* tenderly; fondly; affectionately; †feebly; weakly. **‑ello** *adj.* tender; very young. **‑ezza** *f.* tenderness; softness; fondness, love, affection; *pl.* caresses, loving words; gestures or actions of tenderness; (iron.) affectation; cajolery; infatuation; (paint.) softness; delicacy. **‑one** *adj. augm.* oversoft, flabby; sentimental. **‑otto** *adj.* (joc.) plump and tender; soft-hearted. **‑ume** *m.* soft part, tender part; soft bones and cartilage; (fig.) mawkish sentimentality.

tenesmo *m.* (med.) tenesmus.

te·nia *f.* (archit.) taenia, tenia (in the Doric order); (zool.) tapeworm, *Taenia* spp.

teniere *m.* stock of a crossbow, arquebus, or musket.

tenimento *m.* See under **tenere**.

tenne *f.* (zool.) a kind of python.

ten·n-is *m. indecl.* lawn tennis; tennis; — ad anello, deck tennis; — da tavola, table tennis, ping-pong; giocare al —, to play tennis. **‑ista** *m., f.* tennis-player. **‑i·stico** *adj.* pertaining to tennis.

tenon·e (carpen.) tenon; (watchm.) stud. **‑atrice** *f.* (carpen.) tenon machine.

ten-oplasti·a *f.* (surg.) tenoplasty. **‑opla·stico** *adj.* tenoplastic. **‑orrafi·a** *f.* (surg.) tenorrhaphy, tendon repair. **‑osite** *f.* (med.) tenositis, tendinitis. **‑otomi·a** *f.* (surg.) tenotomy. **‑o·tomo** *m.* (surg. instr.) tenotome.

tenor·e *m.* tenor, proceeding; se continui su questo — andrai in rovina, if you go on at this rate you will be ruined; il — di vita delle classi lavoratrici, the standard of living of the working classes; a — di legge, according to the law; tenour; contents; il telegramma è del seguente —, the telegram reads as follows; il — della vostra lettera ci ha molto stupiti, we were greatly surprised at the tone of your letter; bearing; manner; parlò in questo —, he spoke in this way, in such a manner; system; grade; standard; (chem.; miner.) content, percentage; — di ceneri, ash content; (mus.) tenor voice; tenor part; tenor singer; counter-tenor (lute-string); open diapason (of organ). **‑eggiare** [A 3 c] *intr.* (*aux.* avere) (mus.) to sing tenor; (of a baritone) to sing like a tenor. **‑ino** *m.* (mus.) light tenor. **†‑ista** *m.* (mus.) tenor singer. **‑uc·cio** *m. pejor.* (mus.) inferior tenor.

ten·orrafi·a *f.*, **-otomi·a** *f.*, **-o·tomo** *adj.* See under **tenoplastia**.

tenosinovite *f.* See **tendosinovite**.

tenovagin·ale *f.*, **-ite** *f.* See **tendovaginale**, etc., under **tendosinovite**.

tensa *f.* (Rom. antiq.) *tensa*, ritual carriage for statues of the gods.

ten·sile *adj.* tensile, ductile; †(mus.) strumenti tensili, stringed instruments.

tensioattivo *adj.* (phys.) surface-active, surfactant.

tensio·metro *m.* tensiometer; potentiometer.

tensione *f.* tension; strain, tightness; — mentale, mental strain; — d'animo, absorption, nervous or emotional tension; — d'anima, exaltation; (eng.; bldg.) tension; assoggettabile a —, tensile; causante —, tensive; (eng.) stress, strain; (phys.) — di vapore, vapour pressure; — superficiale, surface tension; (electr.) voltage, tension; ad alta —, high tension; — a vuoto, no-load voltage; — della rete, mains voltage; (electron.) — base di griglia, grid bias; (electr.) stretch; sotto —, live.

tensivo *adj.* tensional.

tensore *m.* (math.) tensor.

tent·a *f.* (surg.) probe; †attempt. **-acolare** *adj.* tentacular. **-a·colo** *m.* tentacle; munito di -acoli, tentacled.

tent·are [A 1, A 1 c] *tr.* to try, to attempt; to tempt; — la sorte, la fortuna, to try one's luck; — il terreno, to test, to try, the ground; (foll. by prep. 'di' and infin.) -ai di persuaderlo, I tried to persuade him; (foll. by prep. 'a') fui -ato a rivelare il segreto, I was tempted to reveal the secret; (mil.) to risk, to accept or force action; — battaglia, to engage in battle; (theol.) to tempt; (surg.) to probe; to feel; to sound; to interrogate, to question; *abs.* to try; to make an effort; -iamo!, let's try!; -a ancora, try again; *n.m.* trying, attempting; il — non nuoce, there's no harm in trying; *adv. phr.* -a e ritenta, try how you will, no matter how one tries. **-a·bile** *adj.* attemptable; tentare il -abile, to try everything possible. **-amento** *m.* tempting. **-ativo** *m.* attempt, try; endeavour; trial; a mezzo di -ativi, by trial and error; (leg.) attempt; come ultimo -ativo, as a last shift (resource), in the last resort; *adj.* tentative. **-ativamente** *adv.* tentatively. **-ato** *part. adj.* tried, attempted; tempted; (leg.) delitto -ato, attempted crime. **-atore** *m.* tempter; *adj.* tempting. **-atrice** *f.* temptress. **-azione** *f.* temptation; cedere alla -azione, to yield to temptation; avrei una gran -azione di dirglielo sul naso, I am greatly tempted to tell him so to his face; (theol.) temptation.

†**tentellare** *intr.* See **tintinnare**.

Tentenna *pr.n.m.* (joc.) waverer, irresolute person; (hist.) il re —, satirical nickname of Charles Albert of Savoy.

tentenn·are [A 1 c] *tr.* to shake; — il capo, to shake one's head; *intr.* (aux. avere) to oscillate; to swing; to waver; to hesitate; to totter, to stagger; to be unsteady. **-amento** *m.* shaking; waggling; wavering, vacillation; hesitation; dopo molti -amenti partì con loro, after humming and hawing a good deal he went off with them; tottering; staggering. **-ata** *f.* shake, knock. (**-ato** *part. adj.* **-atore** *m.* **-atrice** *f.*) **-ino** *m.* waverer, irresolute person; coward; *pl.* (bot.) quaking grass, *Briza media*. **-ìo** *m.* continued shaking; wavering to and fro. **-one** *m. augm.* waverer; irresolute person; vecchio -one, old dodderer. (**-ona** *f.*) **-one**, **-oni** *adv.* quaveringly; hesitatingly.

tenton·e, **-i** *adv.* gropingly, feeling one's way; hesitatingly; andare a -i, to grope one's way; cercare a -i, to grope for.

te·nu·e *adj.* thin, fine, tenuous; small; slight; slender; — guadagno, meagre profit; luce —, faint light; (of fluid) watery; una purgante —, a mild laxative; (anat.) intestino —, small intestine; (gramm.) pronunzia —, soft pronunciation; *n.f.* (gramm.) tenuis. **-emente** *adv.* tenuously; slightly; delicately. **-ità** *f.* tenuousness; smallness; thinness; tenuity.

tenut·a *f.* estate, farm; holding (of land); capacity; possession; (provb.) chi è in —, Dio l'aiuta, possession is nine points of the law; — dei libri, book-keeping; (eng.) seal; — a labirinto, labyrinth seal; — a liquido, wet seal; — a secco, dry seal; a — d'aria, airtight; a — di olio, oil-tight; staying-power (horse-racing); road-holding (motor-cars); (mus.) power of sustaining; sustained note; (mil.) fort, fortress, command zone; dress, uniform, kit; — tropicale, tropical dress; — di servizio, — di fatica, fatigue dress; — grande, full dress; — piccola, undress uniform; — di marcia, battledress; (ichth.) black bream, *Spondyliosoma cantharus*. **-a·rio** *adj.* (leg.) holding; possessing; *n.m.* (leg.) holder; owner; landed proprietor. **-ella** *f. dim.* small (piece of) property.

-o *part. adj.* kept; owned; held; considered; obliged, bound; -o a dichiarare, bound to declare; (leg.) -o per legge, bound by law; (mus.) tenuto, slightly prolonged, dwelt upon; (rugby) tackled.

†**tenza** *f.* See **tenzone**.

tenzon·e *f.* (poet.) combat; contest; singolar —, single combat; (lit. hist.) tenson, poetical contest. **-are** [A 1 c] *intr.* (aux. avere) (poet.) to dispute; to contend; to be at strife.

Teobaldo *pr.n.m.* Theobald.

teobromina *f.* (chem.) theobromine, 3, 7-dimethylxanthine.

teocr·a·tico *adj.* theocratic. (**-aticamente** *adv.*) **-azi·a** *f.* theocracy.

teodice·a *f.* (theol.) theodicy.

teodolite *m.* (surv.) theodolite.

Teodor·o *pr.n.m.* Theodore. **-a** *pr.n.f.* Theodora.

Teodo·și·o *pr.n.m.* Theodosius. **-a** *pr.n.f.* Theodosia. **-ano** *adj.* Theodosian.

teofani·a *f.* (rel.) theophany.

Teofilan·tropi *pr.n.m.pl.* (hist.) Theophilanthropists, a sect of Deists that arose in France in 1796.

teofillina *f.* (chem.) theophylline.

Teo·filo *pr.n.m.* Theophilus.

Teofrasto *pr.n.m.* Theophrastus.

teo·goni·a *f.* theogony. (**-go·nico** *adj.*)

teo·l·ogo *m.* theologian; canonico —, canon theologian. **-ogale** *adj.* theological; le virtù -ogali, the theological virtues (faith, hope, charity). **-ogare** [A 2] *intr.* (aux. avere) (derog.) to theologize, to talk theology. **-ogastro** *m.* (derog.) theologaster, bogus theologian. **-oghessa** *f.* (joc.) woman theologian. **-ogi·a** *f.* theology (dogmatic, moral, pastoral, ascetic, mystical). **-o·gico** *adj.* theological, relating to theology. **-ogicamente** *adv.* theologically. **-ogizzare** [A 1] *intr.* (aux. avere) to theologize, to write or speak like a theologian.

teoman·i·a *f.* (med.) religious mania. **-i·aco** *m.* religious maniac; *adj.* suffering from religious mania. (**-i·aca** *f.*)

†**teorba** *f.* (mus.) See **tiorba**.

teorem·a *m.* (math.) theorem; — di Pitagora, Pythagoras' theorem. **-a·tico** *adj.* theorematic.

teor·i·a *f.* theory; hypothesis; speculation; doctrine; (Gk. antiq.) sacred embassy; procession, cortège; file, series. **-e·tico** *adj.* theoretic, theoretical; speculative. (**-eticamente** *adv.*)

teo·ric·a *f.* theory. **-o** *adj.* theoretic; theoretical; *n.m.* theorist. **-amente** *adv.* theoretically; in theory; by deduction.

teoro *m.* (Gk. antiq.) *theoros*, sacred envoy.

teo·șof·o *m.* theosoph, theosophist. **-i·a** *f.* theosophy. **-ista** *m.*, *f.* theosophist.

te·palo *m.* (bot.) tepal.

tepefatto *adj.* warmed, made tepid.

tep·ente *adj.* tepid, warm. †**-ere** *intr.* to be warm.

tepida·rio *m.* (antiq.) tepidarium.

†**tepidicare** *tr.* to warm, to make warm.

te·pido *adj.* and derivs. See **tiepido**.

tepore *m.* warmth; pleasant warmth; lukewarmness; tepidity; mildness (of weather).

teppa[1] *f.* (bot.) *Thuidium tamariscinum* (moss).

tepp·a[2] *f.* (Milan) lowest classes; rabble; mob; hooligans. **-ișmo** *m.* hooliganism. **-ista** *m.* young hooligan, ruffian; 'teddy-boy'.

teralite *f.* (miner.) theralite.

terap·e·utica *f.* therapeutics. **-e·utico** *adj.* therapeutic. **-i·a** *f.* therapy.

terat·ologi·a *f.* teratology. **-olo·gico** *adj.* teratological. **-oma** *m.* (med.) teratoma.

ter·b·io *m.* (chem.) terbium. **-ina** *f.* (chem.) terbia.

†**ter·chio** *adj.* boorish, rustic.

Terebinto[1] *pr.n.m.* (geog.) Terebinthos.

tereb·into[2] *m.* (bot.) *Pistacia terebinthus*. **-ene** *m.*, **-entene** *m.* (chem.) terebene, terebenthene. †**-entina** *f.* see **trementina**.

terebrante *adj.* (med.) (of pain) terebrant, terebrating, piercing.

tere·dine *f.* (zool.) ship worm, *Teredo navalis*.

Teren·z·io *pr.n.m.* Terence. **-ano** *adj.* (lit. hist.) in the style of the Latin author, Terence.

Teres·a *pr.n.f.* Teresa. **-ano** *adj.* (hist.) T(h)eresian, of the Empress Maria Theresa; (eccl.) of St Teresa of Avila (used esp. of the Carmelites of her reform).

te·rete *m.* (anat.) ligament of the head of the femur, ligamentum teres.

tergale *m.* See under **tergo**.

terge·mino *adj.* triple; *n.m.* triplet.

ter·g·ere [C def.] *tr.* to wipe; to wipe off; to wipe away; to scour; to clean; to polish; — le lacrime, to dry one's tears. **-icristallo** *m. indecl.* (motor.) windscreen wiper. **-ivetro** *m. indecl.* see **tergicristallo.**

terg·o *m.* (*pl.* **-a** *f.*) back (of man or beast); stare a — a, to stand behind; dare il —, to turn one's back (i.e. to run away); voltare il —, to turn one's back (i.e. to show lack of interest, or disrespect); (*pl.* **terghi** *m.*) reverse side, back; scrivere a — di un foglio, to write on the back of a sheet of paper; vedi a —, please turn over, see over. **-ale** *m.* ornamental chair-back. **-iversare** [A I] *intr.* (*aux.* avere) to tergiversate; to answer evasively; †(mil.) to turn away from the enemy. **-iversatore** *m.* tergiversator; †(mil.) fugitive from battle. (**-iversatrice** *f.*) **-iversazione** *f.* tergiversation; evasiveness; pretext, excuse. †**-iversore** *m.* (mil.) soldier who runs from battle.

teriac·a *f.* (pharm.) theriac. **-ale** *adj.* theriacal.

term·e *f.pl.* hot baths; hot springs; spa, mineral springs; (Rom. antiq.) *Thermae*; — di Caracalla, Baths of Caracalla. **-ale** *adj.* thermal; stazione **-ale,** spa.

ter·mico *adj.* (phys.) thermal, thermic; (geog.) equatore —, heat equator; resistenza termica, heat proofness.

Termido·r·o *pr.n.m.* (hist.) Thermidor, month of the French revolutionary calendar (19 July to 17 August). **-iano** *adj.* Thermidorian. **-ista** *adj.* Thermidorian; *n.m.* one who took part in the overthrow of Robespierre on the 9th Thermidor (27 July) 1794.

terminale *adj., n.m.* See under **termine.**

termin·are [A I S] *tr.* to finish; to end; to terminate; to wind up; to bound, to mark the boundary of; *intr.* (*aux.* essere) to end, to finish, to cease; -are con, to have a common boundary with, to march with; l'Italia -a con la Francia, la Svizzera, etc., Italy is bounded by France, Switzerland, etc.; (gramm.) -are con, in, to end in; †see **determinare. -a·bile** *adj.* terminable; vita **-abile,** life destined to end. **-ante** *part. adj.* terminating, ending. **-ativo** *adj.* limiting. **-ato** *part. adj.* limited; terminated; defined; finished. **-atamente** *adv.* definitely; precisely. (**-atore** *m.* **-atrice** *f.*) **-atura** *f.* terminating. **-azione** *f.* end; close, conclusion; termination, ending; (mus.) ending (of a psalm-tone); turn (of a trill).

Ter·mine[1] *pr.n.m.* (Rom. myth.) Terminus, god of boundary-marks.

ter·min·e[2], †**-o** *m.* term; limit; boundary; bound; space; end; time; date; aim; object; una questione di -i, a technical point; — per la presentazione dei documenti, dead line for the presentation of documents; (leg.) rimozione dei -i, extension of time; a — di legge, according to law; -i del contratto, terms of contract; contraddizione in -i, contradiction in terms; decorrenza di -i, expiration of time; prolungare il —, to extend the time; a — fisso, at a fixed time; — di prescrizione, period of prescription; — comminatorio, comminative time-limit (failure to observe which may incur penalty); — essenziale, agreed period, where time is of essence of contract; — giudiziale, period fixed by Court; — legale, period fixed by law; — ordinatorio, period fixed by order of Court; — perentorio, mandatory period (that cannot be curtailed or extended), absolute time-limit; -i processuali, time-limits in judicial proceedings; (comm.) obbligazione a —, dated stock; — della consegna, term of delivery; a — for the account; consegne a —, fixtures; — fisso, terminable; term (of a bill); cambiale a breve —, short-dated bill; prestito a breve —, short money; — utile, prescribed time; (sculp.) term; terminus; *pl.* (naut.) poop ornamentation, frequently brass dolphins; (gramm.) complemento di —, dative, dative case; in piccolo —, in a short (space of) time; chiedere maggior —, to ask for more time; in — di 24 ore, within 24 hours; entro il più breve — possibile, as soon as possible; (logic) term; — medio, middle term; mezzo —, compromise; expedient; (math.) term; algebraical expression; — medio, mean; word, expression; technical term; ogni arte ha i suoi -i, every craft has its technical terms; si espresse in questi -i, he expressed himself in these terms; a rigor di -i, strictly speaking; *pl.* terms, conditions (of an agreement); state, condition; condursi a cattivi -i, to be going from bad to worse. **-ale** *adj.* terminal; boundary; sasso **-ale,** boundary stone; final; aerostazione **-ale,** airline terminal; (anat.; bot.) terminal; *n.m.* (electr.) terminal. **-etto** *m. dim.* (sculp.) small term, terminus.

terminol·ogi·a *f.* terminology. **-o·gico** *adj.* terminological.

ter·mite[1] *f.* (zool.) termite, white ant.

termite[2] *f.* (chem.; metall.) thermit.

term-obaro·metro *m.* (phys.) thermobarometer. **-ocaute·rio** *m.* (surg.) thermocautery. **-ochi·mica** *f.* thermochemistry. **-ocoperta** *f.* electric blanket. **-ocroṣi** *f.* (phys.) thermochrosy. **-odina·mica** *f.* thermodynamics. **-oelettricità** *f.* (phys.) thermo-electricity. **-oelet·trico** *adj.* thermo-electric; coppia **-oelettrica,** thermo-electric couple, thermocouple. **-o·faro** *m.* heating-pad. **-o·grafo** *m.* thermograph. **-oindurente** *adj.* (chem.) thermohardening. **-oio·nico** *adj.* (electron.) thermionic; valvola **-oionica,** thermionic valve, vacuum valve. **-ologi·a** *f.* (phys.) thermology. **-omano·metro** *m.* thermomanometer. **-ome·trico** *adj.* thermometric. **-o·metro** *m.* thermometer; **-ometro** a bulbo bagnato, wet-bulb thermometer; **-ometro** ad alcool, spirit thermometer. **-opila** *f.* (phys.) thermopile. **-opla·stico** *adj.* (chem.) thermoplastic. **-oregolatore** *m.* (techn.) thermoregulator. **-oregolazione** *f.* (techn.) thermoregulation. **-osco·pio** *m.* (phys.) thermoscope. **-osifone** *m.* radiator; riscaldamento a **-osifone,** central heating by hot water. **-osta·bile** *adj.* not affected by changes of temperature. **-osta·tico** *adj.* (techn.) thermostatic. **-o·stato** *m.* thermostat; **-ostato** antincendi, pyrostat. **-oterapi·a** *f.* (med.) thermotherapeutics, heat treatment. **-otera·pico** *adj.* thermotherapeutic.

Termo·pil-e, -i *pr.n.f.* (geog.; hist.) Thermopylae.

termos *m. indecl.* thermos, thermos flask.

terna *f.* short list (of three candidates for a post); tern, trio, triplet; (electr.) group of three overhead cables in a power transmission line.

Terni *pr.n.f.* (geog.) name of city in Umbria; Tivoli Terni, the name of ornamental fountains at Tivoli.

tern·o *adj.* relating to the number three; threefold; *n.m.* group of three; winning draw by three numbers out of five in the game of lotto; giocare un — secco, to back three numbers at lotto, to win only if all three turn up; giocare un — ambato, to back three numbers to win if two out of the three turn up; (fig.) stroke of luck. **-ale** *m.* (naut.) jigger or small purchase; †sail rope; (prosod.) triplet, tercet, 'terzina', group of three lines of verse. **-a·rio** *adj.* ternary; triple, threefold; (mus.) tempo **-ario,** triple time; (prosod.) triplet, tercet, 'terzina', group of three lines of verse; word of three syllables; line of verse of three syllables; (Rom. coin) *ternarius.*

terpin·a *f.* (chem.) terpin. **-olo** *m.* (chem.) terpinol.

terr·a *f.* **1.** EARTH; world; la rotazione della —, the rotation of the earth; movimenti della —, earthquakes; tutta la —, the whole world, the entire inhabited earth; (myth.) Earth as goddess, Gaea, Ge, Tellus; nè in cielo nè in —, neither in heaven nor on earth; su questa —, on this earth, (fig.) in this world, in this life; le gioie della —, earthly joys; (euphem.) volare dalla — al cielo, to depart this life. **2.** LAND; shore; coast; vento di —, land-wind; braccio di —, promontory; — emersa, land-surface; per — e per mare, by land and sea; — di nessuno, no-man's-land; — ferma, mainland, (hist.) the provinces on the mainland under Venetian rule; — promessa, promised land; forze di —, land forces; scendere a —, to land; fra —, inland; dare in —, to run aground. **3.** GROUND; floor; per —, on the ground, on the floor; dormire in —, to sleep on the ground; a fior di —, close to the ground; mettere piede a —, to dismount; cadere a, per, —, to fall to the ground, to fall on the floor; dormire per —, to sleep on the ground; lampada da —, standard lamp; a —, down, low, (of a battery) flat; pneumatico a —, flat tyre; (fig.) andare per —, to be a failure; (in an exam.) rimanere a —, to fail; (mus.) battuta in —, downbeat; (electr.) mettere a —, to earth. **4.** SOIL, earth; — fertile, rich soil; — vegetale, loam; pomo di —, potato; tagliare una pianta fra le due **-e,** to cut off a plant below the surface of the soil; movimenti di —, earthworks, excavation, embankments. **5.** CLAY; — bianca, china clay; — di porcellana, kaolin; ware, pottery; lavori di — cotta, terracotta figures; stoviglie di —, earthenware; — smaltata, majolica, faïence; — di Siena, Sienna clay. **6.** LAND, estate, property; proprietario di **-e,** landowner; avere un po' di — al sole, to have a little property; (hist.) Giovanni senza —, John Lackland. **7.** COUNTRY; village; locality; region; la propria —, one's native country; **-e** lontane, foreign parts; †city. **8.** *adj. indecl.* terra terra, *terre à terre,* ordinary, mediocre; *adv.* terra terra, close to the ground. **9.** *pr.n.f.* (GEOG.) Terra di Baffin, Baffinland; — di Edoardo VII, King Edward VII Land; — del Fuoco, Tierra del Fuego; — di Francesco Giuseppe, Franz Joseph Land; — di Graham, Grahamland; — dell'Imperatore Guglielmo, Kaiser Wilhelm Land; — Nova, see **Terranova.**

terr-a (*cont.*)

(**-ac·cia** *f. pejor.*) **-acotta** *f.* terracotta; terracotta figure; vasi di -acotta, earthenware. **-ac·queo** *m.* (geog.) land and water surface (of the earth); *adj.* (geog.) terraqueous. **-acre·polo** *m.* see **cicerbita**. **-afęrma** *f.* land, dry land; continent. **-ag·gio** *m.* (mil.) throwing up of earthwork defences. **-a·glia** *f.* (*pl.* **-a·glie**) pottery; earthenware; -aglia durissima, crockery. **-agliare** [A4] *tr.* (mil.) to counterscarp. **-a·glio** *m.* (mil.) terracing; glacis, counterscarp. **-agliolo** *m.* (mil.) labour used in earthwork construction; entrenching tool. **†-agno** *adj.* ground-level. **-a·gnolo** *adj.* (of plants) creeping; (vet.) 'daisy-cutting' (of horses). **-amare, -amara** *f.* (miner.; hist.) terramare; *pl.* terramares, prehistoric settlements in the Po valley. **-amari·coli** *m.pl.* inhabitants of the terramares. **-ame** *m.* rubble, plaster, etc.; heaps of earth. **-apienare** [A1] *tr.* to earth-fill. **-apieno** *m.* (mil.) glacis; platform; terrace; embankment, bank; level surface; open space. **-asanta** *f.* (geog.) Holy Land. **-a·rio** *m.* terrarium. **-aticante** *m.* farmer, tenant-farmer. **-a·tico** *m.* rent (which may be in kind); lease, contract of a tenant-farmer. **-ato** *m.* embankment; terrace; flat roof; *adj.* earthed up. **-azza** *f.* (archit.) flat roof with parapet; balcony; terrace. **-azzano** *m.* villager, inhabitant of a small town; countryman; *adj.* relating to a village or small town. **-azziere** *m.* navvy; labourer. **-azzino** *m.* (archit.) balcony; (agric.) coltivazione a -azzini, cultivation in terraces. **-azzo** *m.* (archit.) loggia, balcony; terraced roof; (herald.) mount in base. **-emotato** *adj.* devastated by earthquakes; *n.m.* region, area, devastated by earthquakes. **-emoto** *m.* earthquake; -emoto di scoscendimento, subsidence; (fig.) lively, disturbing person; 'bombshell'. **-enac·cio** *m. pejor.* ground-floor in bad condition. **-estre** *adj.* of the earth, earthly; terrestrial; land; superficie -estre, surface of the earth; il globo -estre, the terrestrial globe; paradiso -estre, earthly paradise; battaglia -estre, land battle; (bot.) edera -estre, ground ivy, *Glechoma hederacea.* **-estrità** *f.* earthiness. **-ętta** *f.* dim. little town; (paint.) fine clay used in preparing priming. **-icciato** *m.* humus, compost. **-ic·cio** *m.* mould, loam, humus. **-iccuola** *f. dim.* small castle, town, village; poor soil. **-i·colo** *adj.* (of animals) living on the ground. **-icurvo** *adj.* bent (towards the ground). **-iera** *f.* (eccl.) out-sister (in convent). **-ier** *m. indecl.* terrier (dog). **-iero** *adj.* proprietario -iero, landowner; proprietà -iera, property, land, estate. **-i·geno** *adj.* (poet.) earthborn. **-igno** *adj.* living underground; living in the earth; earthy. **-ina** *f.* earthenware dish, pie-dish; soup-tureen; bowl. **-olina** *f. dim.* fine earth, such as ochre and others used in making paints. **-ọne** *m.* (agric., Apulia) smallholder; (N. Italy) Southerner (a derogatory term denoting all Southern Italians, esp. those who emigrate to the North). **-o·nia** *pr.n.f.* (derog.) Southern Italy. **-ọso** *adj.* earthy; muddy. **-u·cola** *f.* barren soil; hamlet; small village.

Terranova *pr.n.f.* (geog.) Newfoundland; *n.m.* Newfoundland dog.

terrẹn-o *adj.* earthly, worldly; incarico —, 'mortal coil', the body, the flesh; situated on the ground; pian —, ground-floor; *n.m.* ground; soil; land; field; site; guadagnare, acquistar —, to gain ground, to make progress (also fig.); (mil.) contrastare il —, to dispute ground; vantaggio del —, vantage ground, natural feature giving advantage; studiare il —, to study the lie of the land; scendere nel —, to go into battle, to come on to the ground, to take the field (for a duel, etc.); — incolto, waste, uncultivated, land; — acquitrinoso, boggy, marshy, ground; due giornate di —, land requiring two days' work; proprietario di -i, landowner; — per fabbricare, — fabbricabile, building site; tastare il —, to test, to explore, the ground, (fig.) to get information; preparare il —, to prepare the ground (usu. fig.); portare la questione su un altro —, to take the question into another sphere. (**-amẹnte** *adv.*)

terri·bil-e¹ *adj.* terrible; dreadful; awful; formidable; fearful; frightful; (joc.) milizia —, territorial army. **-mẹnte** *adv.* terribly; dreadfully; awfully; fearfully, frightfully. **-ità** *f.* awfulness; dreadfulness, frightfulness; awesomeness; formidableness.

†terri·bile² *m.* See **turibolo**.

terri·fic-o *adj.* terrific. **-ante** *part. adj.* terrifying; frightful; appalling. **-are** [A2s] *tr.* to terrify; to frighten; to appal. (**-ato** *part. adj.*)

territo·ri-o *m.* territory; district; — nazionale, Italian territory; (geog.) Territori del Nord, Northern Territories. **-ale** *adj.* territorial; (leg.) giurisdizione -ale, territorial jurisdiction; imposta -ale, land-tax; (mil.) milizia -ale, territorial militia.

terror-e *m.* terror; dread; fright; terror (one who inspires terror); (hist.) Terror (period of the French Revolution); — bianco, White Terror (in S. of France under the restored Monarchy). **-ịsmo** *m.* terrorism. **-ista** *m.* terrorist. (**-i·stico** *adj. neol.*) **-iẓẓare** [A1] *tr.* to terrorize; to terrify. **-iẓẓato** *part. adj.* terrorized; terrified, frightened out of one's wits.

tersẹzza *f.* See under **terso**.

Tersi·cor-e *pr.n.f.* (Gk. myth.; astron.) Terpsichore. **-e·o** *adj.* Terpsichorean, relating to dancing.

Tersite *pr.n.m.* (Gk. lit.) Thersites; (fig.) scurrilous talker; slanderer.

ters-o *part.* of **tergere**, q.v.; *adj.* terse; clear; polished. **-amẹnte** *adv.* tersely. **-ẹzza** *f.* terseness; polish, elegance.

terun·cio *m.* (Rom. coin) *teruncius.*

terzar(u)olo *m.* (naut.) reef; matafioni di —, reef points; nodo di —, reef knot.

terzera *f.* (bldg.) purlin.

terz-i·glio *m.*, **-ino** *m.* See under **terzo**.

terz-o *ord. num.* third; — anno, third year at school or university; (eccl.) terz'ordine, Third Order; (gramm.) — caso, dative; la Terza Italia, Modern Italy (distinguished from ancient Roman Italy, and the Italy of the intervening period of division into smaller states); il — Stato, the Third Estate; -a Roma, the Fascist name for modern Italy; (prosod.) -a rima, rhymed verse linked in groups of three lines as in the *Divina Commedia*; decimo —, thirteenth; vigesimo —, twenty-third; (leg.) — arbitro, umpire (in arbitration); — paese, neutral country; *n.m.* the third (in a series); a third (fraction); third party; — incomodo, unwanted third party, intruder, one playing gooseberry; in mano di -i, in possession of a third party; (leg.) third party; i -i di buona fede, third parties in good faith; con efficacia contro qualunque —, good against all the world; (comm.) buono del —, treasury bill; (archit.) spring of an arch; †(mil.) regiment; *adv.* thirdly, in the third place. **-a** *f.* (liturg.) Terce; (hist.) terce, the first three hours after sunrise; mezza -a, mid-terce; (mus.) third (interval); -a di Picardia, Tierce de Picardie; (herald.) three bars, tierce; (at school, etc.) third form, third class; -a elementare, the third class in an elementary school; (leg.) — di cambio, third of exchange. **-amẹnte** *adv.* thirdly; third. **-ana** *f.* (med.) tertian fever. **-anella** *f.* (med.) tertian fever; (bot.) scarlet pimpernel, poor man's weather glass, *Anagallis arvensis.* **-arda** *f.* (numism.) coin of first Milanese Republic, worth one-third of a soldo. **-are** [A1] *tr.* (mil.) to check the gauge of (a gun). **-arolare** [A1d] *tr.* (naut.) to reef. **-aruolo** (mil.) *adj.* munizione -aruola, heavy calibre rifle ammunition. **-avo, -a·volo** *m.* great-great-grandfather. **-eri·a** *f.* (leg.) agricultural tenancy under which a tenant receives one-third of the produce (cf. **mezzadria**). **†-eruolo** *m.* (mil.) small arquebus. **-ętta** *f.* (mil.) short pistol. **-ettata** *f.* (mil.) single shot from pistol. **-ętto** *m.* trio (of persons or things); (prosod.) see **terzina**; (mus.) vocal trio; triplet. **-ettino** *m. dim.* (mus.) short 'terzetto'. **-iare** [A4] see **terzare**. **-ia·rio** *adj.* (eccl.) tertiary; (geol.) Tertiary, Cenozoic, Cainozoic; *n.m.* (eccl.) (member of) a Third Order; (leg.) farmer who retains one-third of his produce, paying two-thirds as rent. **-i·glio** *m.* card game played among three players in which the highest card is the three, followed by the deuce and the ace. **-ina** *f.* (mus.) triplet; (prosod.) tercet, group of three lines as unit of 'terza rima'. **-ino** *m.* bottle holding one-third of a 'fiasco'; (soccer) back; -ino destro, right back; -ino sinistro, left back; (mus.) E flat clarinet; flute in E flat, third flute (now obs.). **-ode·cimo** *ord. num.* thirteenth. **- oge·nito, -onato** *adj., n.m.* third-born, third in a family. **-ọne** *m.* packing canvas; wrapper, gunny bag; (naut.) drinking-water cask in a sailing ship. **-ul·timo** *adj., n.m.* last-but-two, antepenultimate. **-uolo** *m.* (orn.) tiercel (falconer's term for a kind of hawk); †(naut.) see **terzaruolo**.

tẹs-a *f.* tension, stretching; — dell'arco, bending of the bow; spreading, laying (e.g. of nets); place where nets are spread to catch birds; visor; brim (of a hat); cappello a larghe -e, broad-brimmed hat; †measure of length (roughly equiv. to the span between two arms outstretched). **-are** [A1c] *tr.* (naut.) to haul, to stretch; to haul taut. **-ata** *f.* (eng.; bldg.) span. **-ato** *part. adj.* stretched; (naut., of rigging) -ato a ferro, set up bar taut.

tesaurizz-are [A1] *tr.* (usu. joc.) to hoard. (**-ato** *part. adj.*) **-atore** *m.* hoarder. (**-atrice** *f.*)

teṣa·uro *m.* (poet.). See **tesoro**.

te·schio, tẹschio *m.* skull; cranium; (sculp.) bucrane, bucranium.

Tese·o *pr.n.m.* (myth.) Theseus.

teṣ·i *f.* thesis; proposition; commedia a —, play with a moral; in — generale, as a general rule; (prosod.) thesis; (univ.) — di laurea, degree thesis. **-ina** *f. dim.* oral dissertation as part of degree examination.

†Tesi·fone *pr.n.f.* See **Tisifone**.

Tesmo·fo·rie *pr.n.f.pl.* (Gk. antiq.) Thesmophoria. **-teta** *m.* (Gk. antiq.) thesmothete, thesmothetes.

teṣ·o *part.* of **tendere**, q.v.; *adj.* taut; tight; stretched, spread out; (fig.) alert, attentive; (of nerves) overstrung; rapporti -i, strained relations; (naut.) vento —, breeze (corresponding to force three on the Beaufort scale).

teṣor·o *m.* treasure; treasury; (as term of affection) darling; ciao —, goodbye my darling; buoni del —, treasury, exchequer bonds; far — di, to set great store by, *or* to treasure up for future use, to benefit by; (eccl.) treasury of a church (housing relics, precious vestments, etc.); (leg.) Ministero del Tesoro, the Treasury. **-eggiare** [A3c] *intr.* (*aux.* avere) to hoard; to amass treasure; *tr.* to hoard, to accumulate; to set great store by. (**-eggiato** *part. adj.*) **-eggiatore** *m.* hoarder. (**-eggiatrice** *f.*) **-eri·a** *f.* treasury; exchequer; Treasurer's Office. **-etto** *m. dim.* precious object(s). **-ierato** *m.* treasurership, office of treasurer. **-iere** *m.* treasurer; (eccl.) treasurer (as guardian of relics, church plate, etc.). **-iẓẓare** [A1] *intr.* (*aux.* avere) to hoard, to amass treasure, wealth. (**-iẓẓato** *part. adj.*)

Tespi *pr.n.m.* Thespis, traditional father of Greek tragedy; il carro di —, travelling theatre.

Tessa·glia *pr.n.f.* (geog.) Thessaly.

tes·salo *adj., n.m.* Thessalian.

tessell-a *f.* a small tessera. **-are** [A1] *tr.* to tessellate. **-ato** *part. adj.* tessellated.

tes·ser-a *f.* (Rom. antiq.) tessera; (archit.) tessera (used in mosaic); card, ticket; pass; tally; — annonaria, ration-card; — di riconoscimento, identity-card; — di partito, party membership-card. **-are** [A1s] *tr.* to ration (a commodity); to provide with a membership-card. **-a·rio** *m.* (Rom. hist.) *tesserarius*, soldier entrusted with watchword (*tessera*). **-ato** *part. adj.* rationed; *n.m.* member (of a party, etc.).

tes·s·ere [B1] *tr.* to weave; la ragna -e la tela, the spider spins its web; l'uccello -e il nido, the bird builds, makes, its nest; (fig.) to compose; — le lodi, l'elogio, di qualcuno, to sing someone's praises; to plot; (provb.) l'uomo ordisce e la fortuna -e, cf. man proposes and God disposes. **†-iera** *f.*, **-itora** *f.* see **tessitrice**. **-itore** *m.* weaver; (orn.) weaver bird, Ploceidae spp. **-itori·a** *f.* cloth (weaving) factory; weaving-shed. **-itrice** *f.* woman weaver. **-itura** *f.* weaving; -itura a maglia, hosiery knitting; -itura meccanica, power-loom weaving; weaving-mill; (mus.) tessitura, lie (of a vocal part); texture; composition. **-uto** *part. adj.* woven; composed; *n.m.* cloth, fabric; (text.) woven material; fabbrica di -uti, weaving-mill, cloth-mill; fabbricante di -uti, cloth manufacturer; negoziante di -uti, draper; negozio di -uti, draper's shop; (biol.) tissue; (fig.) tissue, web; un -uto di menzogne, a tissue of lies.

tes·sile *adj.* textile; industria —, textile industry; fibre tessili, man-made fibres.

test-a *f.* 1. HEAD; in —, on one's head; dar di — in, to bump one's head against; (of wine, success, etc.) dare alla — di uno, to go to a person's head; lavata di —, reprimand; lavare la — all'asino, to do something quite useless; colpo di —, rash act; tenere la — a posto, to keep one's head; perdere la —, to lose one's head; mettersi in —, to take into one's head; tenere — a to make headway against, to oppose successfully; brains, wits; — quadra, good head, clever, well-balanced man; — di legno, blockhead; — dura, thickhead; (mus.) voce di —, head-voice; note di —, head-notes. 2. HEAD, top; alla — di, at the head of; marciare in —, to march at the head; (tennis) — di serie, 'seed'; (mil.) van, leading column; — di ponte, bridgehead; — di sbarco, beach-head; (motor.) valvole in —, overhead valves; battere in —, to pink; (naut.) head, end, cap, top; — d'una nave, eyes of a ship; — dell'armata, leading ship; — del calcatorio, rammerhead; — a fungo, mushroomhead; — carica, torpedo warhead; — da esercizio, torpedo collision head; — di moro, mast spectacle plate; — del timone, rudder-head; earthenware pot; potsherd; (ent.) — di morto, death's head hawk moth, *Acherontia atropos*. **-ac·cio** *m.* thing made of potsherds; Monte -accio, hill over 100 feet high on left bank of

the Tiber in Rome, composed of ancient potsherds. **-a·gnolo** *m.* hoop, securing either end of a barrel. **-a·io** *m.* seller of lambs' heads and offal. **-ata** *f.* head; top; heading; -ata di un campo, edge of a field (towards the road); (geog.) -ata di valle, head of a valley; (typ.) -ata di pagina, head-line, running head; (mil.) earthwork thrown up before an uncompleted defence position; (eng.; motor.) head, cylinder head. **-a·tico** *m.* (hist.) poll-tax. **-icciuola** *f. dim.* little head (esp. lamb's or kid's head after it has been severed by the butcher). **-iera** *f.* head-stall (harness); (mil. hist.) headguard and harness on horse's head; (naut.) -iera della vela, head of a sail; model head (for wig-making, etc.); chair-back. **-ina** *f.*, **-ino** *m.* little head (e.g. of a doll); (cul.) -ina di vitello, calf's head; (fig.) flighty person. **-olina** *f.* little head; (fig.) girl; una -olina sventata, a flighty girl, a scatter-brained girl. **-ona** *f. augm.* large head; big face. **-onac·cio** *m.* stubborn, obstinate, person. **†-oncello** *m.* tip. **-one** *m. augm.* large head; (fig.) stubborn, obstinate, person; blockhead; (numism.) teston, testoon, name given to various coins in the fifteenth and sixteenth centuries in Italy, France and England; (ichth.) giant goby, *Gobius capito*.

testa·cei *m.pl.* (zool.) shelled molluscs.

testament-o *m.* (leg.) testament; will; disporre per — di, to devise (real property), to bequeath (personalty); — olografo, holograph will; — congiuntivo o reciproco, joint or mutual will; omologazione, verificazione, di un —, probate; (Bibl.) Nuovo —, New Testament; arca del —, Ark of the Covenant; Testament, as name of a poem or collection of poems); — politico, last words of a statesman. **-a·rio** *adj.* (leg.) testamentary; given or made by will; disposizione -aria, bequest; devise; testamentary disposition; senza disposizione -aria, intestate.

testard-o *adj.* obstinate, stubborn; headstrong; also *n.m.* (**-a** *f.*) **-amente** *adv.* obstinately, stubbornly. **-ag·gine** *f.* obstinacy, stubbornness; headstrong behaviour.

test-are [A1] *intr.* (*aux.* avere) to make a, one's, will; †to attest. **-a·bile** *adj.* (leg.) disposable by will, bequeathable, devisable; †attestable. **-abilità** *f.* (leg.) disposability by will; †attestability. **-ante** *m.*, *f.* testator. **-ato** *part. adj.* attested. **-atore** *m.* (leg.) testator; **-atrice** *f.* (leg.) testatrix. **†-azione** *f.* (leg.) attestation.

teste *m.* (leg.) testimony; teste; witness.

†testè *adv.* just now; a moment ago; lately.

testerec·cio *adj.* obstinate; stubborn; battaglia testereccia, hard-fought battle.

testi·col-o *m.* (anat.) testicle, testis; (bot.) orchid. (**-are** *adj.*)

testific-are [A1s] *tr.* (leg.) to testify; to bear witness to; to declare, to attest; to certify. **-ativo** *adj.* testificatory; testifying; serving as evidence. (**-ato** *part. adj.*) **-atore** *m.* (leg.) testifier; witness. (**-atrice** *f.*) **-azione** *f.* (leg.) testification.

te·stile *adj.* See **tessile**.

testimon-e *m.* (leg.) witness (esp. independent witness giving oral evidence in Court); — di vista, — di veduta, — oculare, eye-witness; — auricolare, ear-witness, hearsay witness; ricusare un —, to challenge a witness; esaminare un —, to examine a witness; — a carico, witness for the prosecution; — a discarico, witness for the defence; senza —, without any evidence or witness; indennità ai -i, conduct money; banco del —, witness-box; fare da —, to act as a witness. **-iale** *adj.* testimonial; serving as evidence; (leg.) prova -iale, parole evidence, oral evidence of witness(es); scrittura -iale, written evidence; esame -iale, examination of witness; (eccl.) lettere -iali, certificate of ordination (from bishop). **-ianza** *f.* deposition of independent witness; testimony; proof by a witness; evidence given; falsa -ianza, false evidence; dar -ianza, to give evidence; in -ianza, in witness; -ianza a difesa, witness for the defence; rendere -ianza, to witness; (Bibl.) arca della -ianza, Ark of the Covenant, Ark of (the) Testimony. **-iare** [A4] *intr.* (*aux.* avere) to bear witness; to give evidence; -iare con giuramento, to give evidence under oath. **-iato** *part. adj.* witnessed; attested; proved.

†testimoni *m.pl.* (euphem.) testicles.

testimo·nio *m.* evidence; dare falso —, to give false evidence; fare —, to act as a witness; firmare come —, to sign as a witness; dire —, to testify; citare —, to summon witness.

testo¹ *m.* flower-pot; earthenware pot-lid; terracotta disc.

testo² *m.* text; libri di —, text-books; critica del —, textual criticism; authority; questo libro fa —, this is the most authoritative book on the subject; (fig.) il Palazzi non fa —, Palazzi's dictionary is

testo (*cont.*)
not necessarily right all the time; (typ.) original, 'copy' from which an edition is set; (leg.) — della legge, legal text-book, text of the Act; — unico, Consolidation Act; *pl.* Roman Law Pandects, Institutions, Codex.

†**testo**[3] *part.* of tessere, q.v. (cf. **tessuto**).

testone *m. augm.* See under **testa**.

†**test-ore** *m.*, †**-rice**. See tessit-ore, -rice, under **tessere**.

testual-e *adj.* textual; precise; queste furono le sue -i parole, these were his exact words; critica —, textual criticism. **-mente** *adv.* exactly, precisely; textually.

testuc·chio *m.* (bot.) field maple, *Acer campestre*.

†**test-udo** *f.*, †**-u·dine** *f.* See **testuggine**.

testug·gin-e *f.* (zool.) tortoise (used also sometimes of turtles); — terrestre, — comune, *Testudo graeca*; — moresca, *T. ibera*; — marginata, *T. marginata*, — palustre, — d'acqua dolce, *Emys orbicularis*; passi di —, tortoise pace; tortoise-shell; (mil. hist.) testudo; (astron.) Lyra; (archit.) vault; ceiling; cupola. **-ato** *adj.* (archit.) testudinate.

†**testu·nia** *f.* (archit.). See **testuggine**.

testura *f.* texture; structure.

te·t-ano *m.* (med.) tetanus, lockjaw. **-ani·a** *f.* (med.) tetany. **-a·nico** *adj.* tetanic.

teter·rimo *adj. superl.* of **tetro**, q.v.; horrible, dreadful.

Teti, Te·tide *pr.n.f.* (Gk. myth.; astron.) Thetis; (zool.) *Tethys leporina*, a large pelagic sea slug.

te·tico *adj.* (mus.) thetic, stressed, on the strong beat.

Te·tide *pr.n.f.* See under **Teti**.

tetr-acloruro *m.* (chem.) tetrachloride. **-acordo** *m.* (mus.) tetrachord; instrument of four strings; fourth. **-adimite** *f.* (miner.) tetradymite. **-adramma** *m.* (Gk. antiq.) tetradrachm. **-ae·drico** *adj.* (geom.) tetrahedral. **-aedrite** *f.* (miner.) tetrahedrite, grey copper ore, fahlerz. **-ae·dro** *m.* (geom.) tetrahedron. **-aetile** *m.* (chem.) tetraethyl; (motor.) -aetile di piombo, tetraethyl lead, T.E.L. **-afoni·a** *f.* (mus.) tetraphony. **-a·gono** *m.* (geom.) tetragon, quadrilateral; (astrol.) tetragon, the quadrate aspect; *adj.* (fig.) firm, steadfast; unflinching; four-square. **-agonale** *adj.* tetragonal; four-square. **-ago·nico** *adj.* tetragonal, belonging to a quadrangle. **-agonismo** *m.* (geom.) squaring the circle. **-agramma** *m.* (theol.) tetragram. **-agram·mato** *adj.* (theol.) four-lettered (of the name of God in Hebrew). **-alogi·a** *f.* tetralogy, group of four plays, or operas (esp. Wagner's 'Das Rheingold', 'Die Walküre', 'Siegfried', 'Götterdämmerung'). **-ametile** *m.* (chem.) tetramethyl. **-a·metro** *adj.*, *n.m.* (prosod.) tetrameter. **-aodonte** *m.* (ichth.) cowfish, *Tetraodon* spp. **-arca** *m.* (*pl.* **-archi**) (Rom. hist.) tetrarch. **-arcato** *m.* tetrarchate. **-archi·a** *f.* tetrarchy. **-a·stico** *adj.* (prosod.) of four lines; *n.m.* quatrain; tetrastich. **-a·stilo** *adj.* (archit.) having four columns; *n.m.* tetrastyle. **-a·tono** *m.* (mus.) tetratone, augmented fifth. **-avalente** *adj.* (chem.) tetravalent.

tetr-o *adj.* gloomy; dismal; dark; sad. (**-amente** *adv.*) **-ag·gine** *f.* gloom; sadness.

tetro·bolo *m.* (numism.) tetrobol; silver coin of ancient Greece.

tetrodo *m.* (electron.; radio) tetrode.

tetros·sido *m.* (chem.) tetroxide.

tett-a *f.* teat, nipple; breast. **-are** [A I C] *tr.* (fam.) to suckle. **-arella** *f.* teat; -arella di gomma, rubber teat (of a baby's feeding-bottle). **-ina** *f. dim.* teat of a baby's bottle.

tett-o *m.* (archit.) roof; house-top. NOTE: roofs are distinguished as 'a due, tre, quattro acque' according to the number of sloping sides carrying off the rain water; thus, a 'tetto a padiglione', a four (sloping) sided roof, more or less pyramidal in shape, is a 'tetto a quattro acque'; a 'tetto a capanna', a single-ridged roof, is a 'tetto a due acque'; — a punta, high-pitched roof; — a terrazza, flat roof; — morto, foundation of an open terrace; cameretta, stanza, a —, attic, garret, top-floor room; (fig.) house, home; non aver pane nè —, to be without food and shelter; senza —, homeless; i senza —, people without homes; — paterno, father's house, home; (provb.) quattrin sotto il —, quattrin benedetto, it is good to be able to earn your living indoors; non credere dal — in sù, not to believe in heaven, in another world; (astron.) — girante, revolving dome; (geol.; mining) — del filone, back (of lode); (naut.) — mobile, roof built over a hulk or ship under construction, sliding roof (e.g. in motor-car); (mil.) — portatile, transportable overhead screen. **-aiuolo**

m. (zool.) topo -aiuolo, sorcio -aiuolo, black rat, *Rattus rattus*; (fig.) topo -aiuolo, person living alone. **-ino** *m. dim.* hood, roof of driver's cab. **-oia** *f.* shed, penthouse; roof of station, market, etc.; open building; roofing, shelter. **-o·nica** *f.* (geol.) tectonics, structural geology. **-o·nico** *adj.* (geol.) tectonic. **-uc·cio** *m. dim.* (derog.) cottage, hovel; acque del -uccio, mineral water of Montecatini (Tuscany); (aeron.) canopy.

tettola *f. dim.* of **tetta**, q.v.

te·ucro *m.*, *adj.* (poet.) Trojan.

te-urgi·a, -ur·gica *f.* (rel.) theurgy. **-ur·gico** *adj.* theurgic. **-urgo** *m.* theurgist.

Teutoburgo *pr.n.m.* (geog.) Selva di —, Teutoburger Wald.

te·ut-one *pr.n.m.* Teuton; *pl.* Teutons, an ancient German tribe; (modern) Germans. **-o·nico** *adj.* Teutonic.

Te·vere *pr.n.m.* (geog.) Tiber.

thaf *m. indecl.* (bot.). See **tef**.

thè *m. indecl.* (bot.). See **tè**.

thera *m.* wine of the Greek island Santorin (Thera).

thermos *m. indecl.* See **termos**.

thora *f.* (Bibl.) Torah; Mosaic Law; Pentateuch.

ti[1] *pers. prn. conjunct.* 2nd sing. acc., dat. thee, to thee; you, to you.

ti[2] *m.* T, name of 18th letter of the Italian alphabet; (naut.) bagli a —, angle frames, T-shaped cross-section.

tialismo *m.* (med.) ptyalism.

Tian Scian *pr.n.m.* (geog.) Tien Shan.

tiara *f.* tiara (of the ancient Persians; of the Jewish High Priest; of the Pope); jewelled head-dress as worn by women, tiara.

ti·aso *m.* (Gk. antiq.) *thiasos*, Bacchic revel or band of revellers.

Tibaldo *pr.n.m.* Theobald (cf. **Tebaldo, Teobaldo**).

tiber-ino *adj.* of the Tiber; (Rom. myth.) dio —, Tiber, Tiberinus, as god of the river. **-i·nidi** *f.pl.* (myth.) nymphs of the Tiber.

Tibe·rio *pr.n.m.* (Emperor) Tiberius; (fig.) a cruel man, a 'Tiberius'.

Tibe·t *pr.n.m.* (geog.) Tibet. **-ano** *adj.*, *n.m.* Tibetan.

ti·bi-a *f.* (anat.) tibia, shin-bone; (mus.) tibia (ancient flute or modern organ-stop). **-ale** *adj.* (anat.) relating to the tibia; *n.m.* (mil. hist.) shin armour; (sport) shinguard.

†**tibiare** *vb.* and derivs. See **trebbiare**.

†**tibi·cin-e** *m.*, †**-a** *f.* flautist; *adj.* l'arte -a, the art of flute-playing.

Tibisco *pr.n.m.* (geog.) Tisza.

tibo *m.* (Sicily) sweet made of flour and grape-juice.

Tibull-o *pr.n.m.* Tibullus. **-iano** *adj.* Tibullian.

tibu·rio *m.* (archit.) cupola (on an octagonal base, as in Lombard style).

tiburtino *adj.* Tiburtine, of Tivoli; *n.m.* (geol.) travertine.

Tibur·zio *pr.n.m.* Tiburtius.

tic[1], **tic-che** *m. indecl.* tick, ticking; beat; il — toc dell'orologio, the ticking of the clock; il cuore mi faceva — toc, I felt my heart going pit-a-pat. **-chettare** [A I C] *intr.* (aux. avere) to tick; to click. **-chettio** *m.* ticking, beating; clicking; tapping.

tic[2] *m. indecl.* (med.) tic, facial spasm, prosopospasm.

†**tica** *f.* bread-bin.

tic·chi-o *m.* (med.) see **tic**[2]; (fig.) caprice, whim, fancy; gli saltò il — di uscire con tutta questa neve!, he took it into his head to go out in all this snow!; mannerism, trick; (vet.) shambling gait (in a horse). **-olato** *adj.* speckled. **-olatura** *f.* (agric.) scab.

†**tico** *prn. contr.* with *prep.* See **teco**.

tico·nico *adj.* (geog.) Tychonic.

tielismo *m.* See **tialismo**.

tient-ammente *m. indecl.* (joc. for 'tienti a mente') blow by way of reminder. **-ibene** *m. indecl.* (naut.) manrope, gangway canvassed handrail; -ibene dell'argano, swifter; bottone di -ibene, diamond knot.

tie·pid-o *adj.* lukewarm; warm. **-amente** *adv.* tepidly; coolly; without enthusiasm; lazily. **-a·rio** *m.* (Rom. antiq.) *tepidarium*. (**-etto** *adj. dim.*) **-ezza** *f.*, **-ità** *f.* tepidness; tepidity; lukewarmness, coolness; laziness.

†**tiepore** *m.* See **tepore**.

†**tiera** *f.* company; row, file.

tifa *f.* (text.) lana di —, reed mace, typha wool.

tifl-ite *f.* (med.) typhlitis. **-o·grafo** *m.* typhlograph (instrument enabling the blind to write). **-ope** *m.* (zool.) a very small snake, *Typhlops vermicalis*.

tif-o *m.* (med., etc.) typhus; (sport.) support, encouragement, enthusiasm for one's team; fare il — per, to be a fan of, (sport)

tif-o (*cont.*)
to be a supporter of; (vet.) dysentery in cattle. **-o·ide** *f.*, **-oide·a** *f.*
(med.) typhoid fever. **-oide·o** *adj.* (med.) typhoid. **-oso** *adj.*
(med.) typhous; *n.m.* fan; (sport) supporter.

†**ti·folo** *m.* shriek, yell.

tif·one *m.* typhoon; hurricane. (**-o·nico** *adj.*)

tight *m. indecl.* See **tait**.

ti·gli-o¹ *m.*, **-a** *f.* (bot.) lime, *Tilia*; (art) lime-wood used in intaglio
work.

ti·gli-o² *m.* (text.) staple; di — lungo, long-stapled; di — lunghissimo,
fancy-stapled; fibre; bast; vein (in stone). **-oso** *adj.* fibrous; (of
meat) tough, stringy.

tign-a *f.* (med.) ringworm, tinea; (vet.) mange; itch; (Tusc., pop.)
miser; (Rome, etc.) pig-headed, obstinate individual. **-a·mica** *f.*
(bot.) *Anthemis tinctoria, Helichrysum stoechas, Inula viscosa.*
†**-are** *vb.* and derivs. see **intignare**. **-oso** *adj.* scabby; suffering
from ring-worm; (vet.) mangy; (Tusc., pop.) miserly; (Rome,
etc.) obstinate (also *n.m.*). **-(u)ola** *f.* (ent.) term for moths of
various species; **-uola del grano**, grain moth, *Tinea granella*;
-uola dei panni, clothes moth, *T. biselliella*.

tigr-e¹ *m.*, †**-a** *f.*, †**-o** *m.* (zool.) tiger, *Panthera tigris*; (zool.)
— sciabola, sabre-toothed tiger; (fig.) fierce, cruel person; avere
un cuore di —, to be cruel and relentless. **-ato** *adj.* striped;
streaked; (of a horse) dappled; gatto **-ato**, tabby cat. **-esco** *adj.*
(*m.pl.* **-eschi**) tigerish. **-ino** *m. dim.* tiger-cub. **-otto** *m.* young
tiger.

Tigre² *pr.n.m.* (geog.) Tigris.

†**tigu·rio** *m.* See **tugurio**.

tilde *m.* the diacritic sign tilde.

tilland·sia *f.* (text.) fibra —, vegetable hair, Spanish moss, *Tillandsia
usneoides.*

timballo *m.* (mus.) kettledrum, naker; (cul.) timbale, — di maccheroni, timbale (with macaroni); — di riso, timbale with rice.

†**timbaro** *m.* (numism.) coin of Valenzia.

tim·brico *adj.* (mus.) pertaining to tone-colour.

timbr-o¹ *m.* official stamp; rubber stamp; — postale, postmark;
(comm.) — a secco, blank stamp; (leg.) seal; (herald.) crest.
-are [A I] *tr.* to stamp, to postmark. **-ato** *adj.* stamped; post-
marked. **-atura** *f.* stamping.

timbro² *m.* timbre (of voice, etc.); (mus.) timbre, tone-colour; jingle
(of tambourine); (watchm.) sounding spring.

ti·mel-e *f.* (Gk. antiq.) thymele. **-e·a** *f.* (bot.) *Cneorum tricoccum,
Daphne mezereum, D. laureola, D. gnidium.*

ti·mico *adj.* (anat.) thymic.

ti·mid-o *adj.* timid; nervous; shy, bashful; davanti a me è sempre —,
he is always shy with me; diffident; *n.m.* timid, nervous person;
shy person; fare il —, to be shy. **-amente** *adv.* timidly; shyly.
-ezza *f.* timidity; nervousness; shyness, bashfulness; diffidence.
-ità *f.* see **timidezza**.

tim-o¹ *m.* thyme, *Thymus vulgaris*. **-olo** *m.* (chem.) thymol.

timo² *m.* (anat.) ghiandola —, thymus gland (part of the 'sweetbreads').

†**timologi·a** *f.* See **etimologia**.

timon-e *m.* (naut.) rudder; — accoppiato, double rudder; — com-
pensato, balanced rudder; — prodiero, bow rudder; — a dritta!,
starboard rudder!; leva —!, ease the rudder!; —!, wheel, watch
your course!; via —!, alla via —!, steady!; (of cart, coach, etc.)
shaft, pole; plough-head; (of bicycle) handle-bar(s); (fig.) helm;
head, direction; cavalli del —, shaft horses; (aeron.) elevator,
flipper; (of submarine) hydroplane. **-ato** *adj.* having a rudder,
helm, pole, shaft, etc. **-eggiare** [A 3 c] *tr.* to steer; (fig.) to govern;
intr. (*aux.* avere) (naut.) to make unnecessary use of the rudder.
-ella *f.* four-wheeled gig, buggy (pulled by one horse); (mil.)
limber waggon shaft. †**-eri·a** *f.* (naut.) navigating personnel. **-iera**
f. (naut.) steering position, wheelhouse. **-iere** *m.* (naut.) helmsman,
quartermaster, sea dutyman; (rowing) cox. †**-ista** *m.* (naut.) see
timoniere.

timor-e *m.* fear; awe; — panico, panic; (rel.) timor di Dio, fear of
God; aver — di, to be afraid of; per — che fuggisse, for fear he
should run away; — filiale, filial fear, respect for one's parents;
(leg.) — reverenziale, reverential fear. **-ato** *adj.* respectful;
scrupulous; (rel.) **-ato** di Dio, God-fearing, devout, pious. **-oso**
adj. timorous, fearful; cowardly; timid; essere **-oso** di, to fear, to
be afraid of; scrupulous; gente onesta, **-osa** di Dio, decent God-
fearing people; †frightening. **-osamente** *adv.* timidly, fearfully.

Timote·o *pr.n.m.* Timothy.

tim·pan-o *m.*, *pl.* **-i** (mus.) kettledrums, timpani; (archit.) tympanum;
pediment; (anat.) tympanum, ear-drum; (fig.) rompere i **-i** a uno,
to deafen a person, to shout; essere di **-i** grossi, to be hard of
hearing; †(anat.) mesentery. **-etto** *m.* (mus.) little drum, timbrel;
(cul.) **-etto** di maccheroni, small timbale of macaroni (cf. **timballo**).
-ismo *m.* (med.) tympanites. **-ista** *m.*, *f.* (mus.) timpanist, kettle-
drummer. †**-i·stria** *f.* (mus.) female timpanist, timbrel-player.
-ite *f.* (med.) tympanites, tympanism, meteorism. **-i·tico** *adj.*
(med.) tympanitic.

tin-a *f.* small vat; tub; (naut.) tar barrel; †sail locker, deep locker;
†leadline cupboard. **-ac·cio** *m.* large vat. **-a·ia** *f.* vat-room;
cellar. **-ella** *f. dim.* tub; small vat used with oil-press.

tinca *f.* (ichth.) tench, *Tinca tinca*; (anat.) muso di —, cervix of
uterus; (fig., derog.) swarthy, dark-complexioned person; testa
di —, fool, blockhead; non dare nè in tinche nè in ceci, to come
to nothing.

tincal *m. indecl.* (miner.) tincal, native borax.

†**tincione** *f.* See **tenzone**.

tincone *m.* (med.) inguinal lymphadenopathy.

tinello *m.* (Tusc.) small cask for carrying grapes; tub let into the
ground to collect oil from the press; (hist.) small dining-hall in
a castle or palace (usu. at disposal of permanent guests such as
poets, artists and other protégés); (Ven.) dining-room; (mil.)
pantry; (neol.) dining recess; (fig.) board; avere il —, to have free
board; a tutto —, all found.

tin·g-ere [C 5] *tr.* to dye; to paint; to stain; — leggermente, to tinge;
to tint; to tincture; to stain (by accident), to blot, to spot; to
dirty; *rfl.* (*acc.* of *prn.* 'si') to be tinged, dyed, etc.; to use make-up;
(poet.) **-ersi** di rossore, to blush; (*dat.* of *prn.* 'si') **-ersi** i capelli,
to dye one's hair; **-ersi** le labbra, to use lipstick. **-itura** *f.* dyeing
(of material, etc.); cost of dyeing.

tinnire [D 2] and derivs. See **tintinnare**.

tinnosco·pio *m.* (naut.) pole fitted with rungs erected on the coast
for tunny lookouts.

tin·nulo *adj.* jangling, twanging.

tin-o *m.* (*pl.* **-i**, †**-a**) vat; tub; vendere al —, to sell (must) as soon
as it comes from the vat; (chem.; techn.) colorante al —, vat dye;
(industr.) vat, tub; carta da —, mould-made paper, hand-made
paper; (metall.) shaft (of blast furnace); — a muro, brick-built
vat or cistern; (provb.) rosso la mattina, mettere le **-a**, red sky
at morning is shepherd's warning. **-ozza** *f.* tub; wash-tub; bath-
tub, bath; (text.) rinsing vat.

tint-a *f.* dye; hue, colour; tint; tinge; shade; colouring; perdere
la —, to fade; sciogliere la —, to 'run'; — solida, fast dye;
— chiara, light dye, light tint; un quadro a **-e** calde, a picture
painted in strong colours; dipingere a **-e** fosche, to paint in dark
colours (also fig.); un dramma a **-e** forti, a sensational play;
touch; strain; tutti della stessa —, all of the same kind; ce n'è
di tutte le **-e**, there are some of all sorts, of all parties, opinions,
etc.; (iron.) e di che —!, and how!; (fig.) tincture, veneer (e.g. of
learning), superficial knowledge. **-arella** *f.* sun-tan; farsi la **-arella**,
to sun-bathe; fare, prendere, una bella **-arella**, to achieve a lovely
tan. **-eggiare** [A 3 c] *tr.* to tint, to tinge; to tincture; (bldg.) to
colour-wash (a wall). (**-eggiato** *part. adj.*) **-eggiatura** *f.* tinting;
tincturing; (bldg.) colour-washing. †**-illano** *m.* fine cloth.

tintìn *m. indecl.* (onom.) ding-dong; tinkling.

tintinn-are [A I], **-ire** [D 2] *intr.* (*aux.* essere, avere) to tinkle; to ring;
to jingle; to cllnk. **-a·bolo**, **-a·bulo** *m.* bell; tintinnabulum.
-amento *m.* tinkling, jingling, clinking. **-ante** *part. adj.* tinkling,
jingling, clinking. **-ìo** *m.* continuous tinkling, jingling, clinking.
-o *m.* bell; ringing; sound, resonance; hum; buzzing.

†**tintinto** *m.* ding-dong.

tint-o *part.* of **tingere**, q.v.; *adj.* dyed; stained; tinged; tinted; con
le mani **-e** di sangue, with blood-stained hands; acqua **-a**, dirty
water, or wine much watered down: questa è acqua **-a**!, this is
nearly all water! **-ore** *m.* dyer. **-ori·a** *f.* dyeing; dye-house, dye-
works, dyeing and dry-cleaning plant. **-o·rio** *adj.* relating to
dyeing; materie **-orie**, dyestuffs; chimica **-oria**, the chemistry of
dyestuffs. **-ura** *f.* dyeing; dye; tint; colour; (fig.) tincture, smattering; colouring, bias.

tio-cianato *m.* (chem.) thiocyanate, sulphocyanide. **-fene** *m.* (chem.)
thiophene. **-solfato** *m.* (chem.) thiosulphate, hyposulphite. **-ure·a**
f. (chem.) thio-urea. **-lo** *m.* (chem.) thiol.

tiorb-a *f.* (mus.) theorbo. **-ista** *m.*, *f.* (mus.) theorbo-player.

ti·pic·o *adj.* typical; perfect of its kind; locale —, 'old-world' restaurant or inn; vini -i, locally-known types of wine in any given district; (theol.) 'typical', symbolical. **-aménte** *adv.* typically; figuratively.

tip-o *m.* type; specimen; model; standard; (derog.) guy; un bel —, a queer character, a funny chap; (leg.) su — di campione, by standard of sample; (comm.) make, brand; (biol.) phylum; (typ.) type; coi -i di, printed by; (finan.) — di moneta, monetary standard; — argento, standard silver. **-o·fono** *m.* (mus.) dulcitone, typophone. **-ofotografi·a** *f.* phototype. **-ofotogra·fico** *adj.* phototypic. **-ofoto·grafo** *m.* phototype operator. **-ografi·a** *f.* typography; printing; printing-house; printing-works. **-ogra·fico** *adj.* typographical; letterpress; (relating to) printing; industria -ografica, printing trade. **-ograficaménte** *adv.* typographically. **-o·grafo** *m.* printer, typographer. **-olitografi·a** *f.* (techn.) printing-works which prints in litho as well as letterpress. **-ometri·a** *f.* (techn.) calibration. **-o·metro** *m.* (typ.) line gauge. **-o·tono** *m.* (mus.) tuning-fork, pitch-pipe.

tip tap, tip·pete, tap·pete *onom.* tap, tap; noise of tapping.

tipt-ologi·a *f.* typtology, interpretation of table-rapping; communication by tapping, tapping-code. **-olo·gico** *adj.* relating to table-rapping, or to tapping-codes. **-o·logo** *m.* expert in tapping-codes.

ti·pula *f.* (ent.) daddy-long-legs, *Tipula* spp.

tira *adv. phrs.* See under **tirare**.

tiran·nic·o *adj.* tyrannical; arbitrary; high-handed. (**-aménte** *adv.*)

tiran·nide *f.* tyranny (as a method of rule); despotism; absolute rule.

tirann-o *m.* (Gk. hist.) tyrant, absolute ruler; (fig.) tyrant; — dei burattini, puppet-tyrant; (orn.) tyrant-bird, kingbird, *Tyrannus* spp.; *adj.* tyrannical, tyrannous. **-a** *f.* tyrannical woman. **-eggia-ménto** *m.* tyrannizing; oppression. **-eggiare** [A 3 c] *tr.* to tyrannize over; to oppress; *intr.* (*aux.* avere) to play the tyrant; to rule with a rod of iron. **-eggiato** *part. adj.* tyrannized over; oppressed; living under tyranny. **-ello** *m. dim.* petty tyrant. **-eri·a** *f.* tyranny. **-ęsco** *adj.* (*m.pl.* -ęschi) tyrannous; despotic. **-escaménte** *adv.* tyrannically; despotically; oppressively. **-i·a** *f.* tyranny; despotism; oppression; †(naut.) backwash. **-icida** *m.* tyrannicide; *adj.* tyrannicidal. **-ici·dio** *m.* tyrannicide.

tir-are [A 1] *tr.* **1.** To PULL; to draw; to drag; i buoi -ano l'aratro, the oxen pull the plough; il cavallo -a la carrozza, the horse pulls the carriage; lo -ai per il vestito, I pulled him by his jacket; to draw, to attract; — su, to pull up, (fig.) to bring up, to rear; — avanti la famiglia, to support one's family, to have a family to support; — giù, to pull down, to drag down, to take down, to demolish; — fuori, to pull out, to draw out, to bring forth, to put forth; — una linea, to draw, to trace, a line; — acqua dal pozzo, to draw water from the well; — un dente, to draw, to pull, a tooth; *abs.* — a sorte, to draw lots; (typ.) to print, to print off; — una bozza, to pull a proof; (naut.) to haul; — a rovescio, to pay out, to ease. **2.** To STRETCH, to lengthen, to draw out; — le parole, to distort words; — miglior senso, to give a more favourable interpretation to; — il collo a, to wring the neck of; — il vino, to clarify wine; — a lustro, to polish, to shine; — l'arco, to draw one's bow; (text.) — la seta, to reel silk; — in grosso, to spread; banco a — in grosso, spread-board, spreader; (chem.) — a secco, to evaporate to dryness. **3.** To OBTAIN, to get; to draw; to arrive at; to derive; — lo stipendio, to draw one's salary; — mille lire (al giuoco), to win a thousand lire (at gambling, cards, etc.); — una conclusione, to draw a conclusion; — la somma, to add up (a sum, bill, etc.). **4.** To ATTRACT, to draw; to take; to absorb; terra che -a l'acqua, ground which sucks up the water; legname che -a la vernice, (unsized) wood which drinks in the paint. **5.** To THROW (with violence); to fling, to chuck; — sassi, to throw stones; gli -ò addosso una secchia d'acqua, he threw a bucket of water over him; — calci, to kick; — frecce, to shoot arrows; — bombe, to drop bombs, to throw bombs; — colpi di coltello, to deliver knife-wounds; — pugni a, to punch; — schiaffi a, to slap; — morsi e graffi a, to bite and scratch; — baci, to throw kisses; — sospiri, to yawn; — giù, to throw down, to jot down; -ò giù qualche verso, he scribbled down a few lines of verse; — giù bestemmie, to let out a stream of curses; — giù legnate, to administer some resounding whacks. **6.** *intr.* (*aux.* avere; *prep.* a) To TEND, to vee (towards); to be inclined (to); to aim (at); to verge (on); to draw on; -a ai quattrini del nonno, he is helped by, has access to, his grand-

father's money; — indietro, to draw back; — via, to go on, to proceed; -a via!, go on!, go ahead!; — di lungo, to go straight on; — in lungo, to delay, to be long-winded; — avanti, to get on fairly well; come va? Si -a avanti, how are things with you? I'm getting on fairly well; (of firearms, etc.) to go off; (aeron.) to take off; (of wind) to blow; cannocchiale che -a venti miglia, telescope with a range of twenty miles; — sul prezzo, to haggle about the price; *with prep.* '*di*': to wield; — di spada, to wield one's sword; — di scherma, — di fioretto, to fence. **7.** *rfl.* (*acc.* of *prn.* 'si') To DRAW; -arsi più vicino, to draw nearer; -iamoci intorno alla tavola, let us draw up round the table; -arsi indietro, to withdraw, to draw back; -arsi da parte, in disparte, to draw to one side; -arsi su, to draw oneself up, to pull oneself up; -arsi su per, to train as, to go in for; si -a su per fare l'avvocato, he is going in for the law; (mus.) tromba da -arsi, slide-trumpet; (*dat.* of *prn.* 'si') -arsi dietro, to drag after one; si -a dietro tutti gli altri, he is the leader of all the others, they all do whatever he does; -arsi dietro la famiglia, to have one's family tagging along behind. **-a** *adv. phr.* fare a tira tira, to wrangle; to dispute; giocare a -a e molla, to play fast and loose (cf. **tiremolla** and **tirammolla**); *n.m.* un tira tira, wrangling; pull, hold, attraction. **-abaci** *m. indecl.* kiss-curl. **-abozze** *m. indecl.* (typ.) small press for pulling proofs. †**-adentro** *m. indecl.* (naut.) inhaul. **-afondi** *m. indecl.* cooper's edge-screw. †**-afuori** *m. indecl.* (naut.) outhaul. **-ag·gio** *m.* draught, drawing; questa stufa ha poco -aggio, this stove does not draw well; (bot.) water absorption by root; (typ.) printing-off. **-a·glia** *f.* see **draglia**. **-agliatòri** *m.pl.* (mil.) French *tirailleurs*, marksmen. **-ali·nee** *m. indecl.* drawing-pen; ruling-pen. **-aloro** *m. indecl.* gold wire drawer. **-aman·tici** *m. indecl.* organ-blower. **-aménto** *m.* drawing; dragging; pull; extraction. †**-a(m)molla** *m.* (naut.) veer and haul, operation of paying out one end of a hawser whilst hauling in the other. **-ammolle** *m. indecl.* (mil.) gunmaker's implement for easing the hammer-springs. **-ante** *part. adj.* drawing; carrying; attractive; *n.m.* (naut.) -ante d'acqua, draught; hauling part of a rope; (agric.) hitch (of plough); (eng.) tie rod, stay rod; stay; -ante a fune, guy rope; -ante a vite, stay bolt; (motor.) -ante trasversale, track rod; (of overhead cables) cross-wire; (motor.) -ante longitudinale, drag link; (mus.) leather brace (of bass drum); -ante d'aria, draught; (archit.) tie-beam; boot-tag (for pulling on). **-apalle** *m. indecl.* (surg.) bullet forceps. **-apiedi** *m. indecl.* (hist.) assistant (esp. to a hangman); fare da -apiedi, to render degrading service; (joc.) secretary, assistant; amanuensis. **-apranzi** *m. indecl.* serving-lift, service-hatch; cf. **calapranzi**. **-astivali** *m. indecl.* boot-jack, shoe-horn. **-ata** *f.* pull; draw; -ata di campana, ring; -ata (*or* tiratina) d'orecchi, ear-pulling, (fig.) scolding; extent, length, run (of buildings, etc); tirade; long speech; scolding; -ata di penna, stroke of the pen; in una -ata, at a stretch; (fam.) draught (in drinking); blow; hit (in shooting); (mus.) vocal glide, slide; (poet.) group of lines with one rhyme (cf. **lassa**). **-atappi** *m. indecl.* corkscrew. **-atęzza** *f.* tension. **-ato** *part. adj.* stretched, drawn tight; carried, brought, delivered; drawn, pulled, extracted; carried through; printed; (fig.) stingy, close-fisted, niggardly. **-atore** *m.* (mil.) marksman; valente -atore, crack shot; -atore scelto, picked shot. (**-atrice** *f.*) **-atura** *f.* drawing; pull(ing); printing; impression, edition; circulation (book, paper); number of copies to be printed, 'run'; -tura a parte, off-print; prima -tura, first impression, (text.) spreading. **-atutti, -atutto** *m. indecl.* (mus.) composition pedal (or piston) which brings the full organ into play.

tiratròn *m. indecl.* (electr.) thyratron.

tir·chi·o *adj.* stingy, niggardly, mean; miserly; *n.m.* miser, skinflint. **-eri·a** *f.* meanness, stinginess, niggardliness; mean action. (**-óne** *adj.*)

tirella *f.* (equestr.) trace.

tiremmolla *m. indecl.* something alternately tight and slack; (naut.) see **tirammolla**; (fig.) indecision, hesitation; wavering; waverer; fare a —, to blow hot and cold.

†**Tireno** *pr.n.m.* (geog.). See **Tirreno**.

tirętto *m.* drawer.

tirillóne *m.* (pop., dial.) lazy hulking good-for-nothing.

†**tirini** *m.pl.* smugglers.

tirinnanzi *m.* go-between, pandar.

ti·rio *adj.* (geog.) Tyrian, relating to Tyre; also *n.m.*

tiritera *f.* rigmarole; long-winded yarn; endless tale or speech.

tiritessi *m. indecl.* (dial., Pisa) confusion, rushing to and fro.

tiritombolo *m. indecl.* tumble; bump; noise of a fall.

tiro[1] *m.* draught; throw, cast; shooting; shot; firing; fire; range; (billiards) stroke; — con l'arco, archery; — al piccione, pigeon shooting; — al piattello, clay-pigeon shooting; un —, a segno, a rifle-range; società del — a segno, rifle-club; (mil.) shot, fire; — della freccia, bowshot; — a polvere, powder charge; — all'aria, blank shot; — a cartoccio, separate charge; — di prova, ranging shot; — a palla piena, fire with live rounds; — di sbarramento, barrage fire; — giusto, correct shot; — esatto, accurate shot; (naut.) fire, shot; rosa di —, theoretical fall of shot zone. NOTE: in Italy this is taken as 99·3% of rounds fired and consequently the zone is slightly larger than the British equivalent which is based on 90% and gives an average spread of 200 yards; †— di affermazione, warning shot; — ad affondare, hit on waterline; — d'allarme, signal round, alarm signal; — di cannone di partenza, recall gun; — della diana, morning gun; — di collaudo, proving shot; — di punto in bianco, hull fixed shot (horizontal); centrale di —, transmitting station; a —, within range; essere a un — di sasso, to be within a stone's throw; se mi viene a — gli darò uno schiaffo!, if I can get my hand on him I'll box his ears!; sul —, on the stroke, on the dot; (cul.) essere a —, to be done to a turn; trick; un brutto —, a dirty trick; giuocare un — a, to play a trick on; cavallo da —, draught-horse; — a quattro, four-in-hand (carriage); — a sei, carriage and six; (vet.) broken wind (of a horse).

Tiro[2] *pr.n.m.* (geog.) Tyre; *n.m.* Tyrian purple.

†tiro[3] *m.* poisonous beast; viper.

tiroci·n-io *m.* apprenticeship; novitiate; (leg.) contratto di —, articles of apprenticeship. **-ante** *m.* apprentice; beginner; tyro.

tiro·id-e *adj.* thyroid; glandola —, thyroid gland; also *n.f.* **-e·o** *adj.* laryngeal. **-ina** *f.* (chem.) thyroidin, iodothyrin. **-ite** *f.* (med.) thyroiditis.

Tirol-o *pr.n.m.* (geog.) Tyrol. **-ese** *adj., n.m., f.* (geog.) Tyrolese; *f.* (mus.) Tyrolienne.

tiron-e *m.* (Rom. hist.) tyro, recruit; (fig.) beginner. **-iano** *adj.* (Rom. antiq.) Tironian; note **-iane**, Tironian notes (shorthand system).

tirosina *f.* (chem.) tyrosine.

Tirreno *pr.n.m.* (geog.) Tyrrhenian (Sea); the western coast of Italy as opposed to the Adriatic; *m.pl.* Tyrrhenians, Etruscans; *adj.* la Riviera tirrena, the Italian Riviera.

tirs-o *m.* (Gk. antiq.) thyrsus; (bot.) thyrse, spike-like panicle. **-i·gero** *adj.* (Gk. antiq.) thyrsus-bearing.

Tirte·o *pr.n.m.* (Gk. lit.) Tyrtaeus; (fig.) patriotic poet, esp. of narrative poems celebrating heroic deeds.

tirucchiare [A4] *tr.* to tug gently; to pull feebly.

tiṣana *f.* infusion, decoction, tea (of herbs, etc.); — d'orzo, barley-water.

Tiṣbe *pr.n.f.* Thisbe.

tiṣ-i *f.* tuberculosis, phthisis. **-ichello** *m. dim.* tubercular-looking person. (**-ichella** *f.*) **-ichęzza** *f.* tubercular condition; emaciation; extreme weakness. **-ichino** *m. dim.* puny child, 'poor little mite'. **-iologi·a** *f.* (med.) the study of tuberculosis. **-io·logo** *m.* doctor specializing in tuberculosis.

tiṣic-o *adj.* tubercular; morir —, to die of tuberculosis; emaciated; wretched, puny; feeble, stunted; *n.m.* tubercular patient, person suffering from tuberculosis. **-uc·cio**, **-uzzo** *adj.* sickly; run down in health; (of plants) stunted.

Tiṣi·fone *pr.n.f.* Tisiphone.

titanato *m.* (chem.) titanate.

Tita·nia *pr.n.f.* Titania.

tita·n-ico *adj.* titanic, gigantic; (chem.) titanic. **-i·fero** *adj.* (chem.; miner.) titaniferous.

tita·n-io *adj.* (poet.) of a Titan, of the Titans; la titania lampa, Titan's lamp (i.e. the sun); *n.m.* (chem.) titanium. **-ite** *f.* (miner.) titanite, sphene.

Titano *pr.n.m.* (class. myth.) Titan; (fig.) giant, titan.

titill-are [A1] *tr.* to titillate. **-amento** *m.* titillating. **-ato** *part. adj.* titillated. **-atore** *m.* titillator; (motor.) tickler (of carburettor). **-ato·rio** *adj.* titillating, causing titillation; l'ortica **-atoria**, the stinging nettle. **-azione** *f.* titillation.

titi·ma·glio *m.*, **-malo** *m.* (bot.) spurge, *Euphorbia*.

Tit-o *pr.n.m.* Titus; Tito. **-ino** *m.* follower of Tito; Yugoslav.

ti·tol-o *m.* title; title-page, heading; name; qualification, evidence; proof; right; status; a — personale, in a personal capacity; **-i** accademici, degrees, diplomas, academic qualifications; **-i** di studio, educational qualifications; (leg.) title; — nominativo, registered title; a — di benefizio, beneficially; tenuta a — di enfiteusi, leasehold; — di proprietà, title-deed; a — oneroso, for valuable consideration; atto a — gratuito, voluntary deed; *pl.* bonds; stock; stock-exchange securities; **-i** privilegiati, preference stock; **-i** in porta, securities in hand; **-i** nominativi, registered stock; **-i** di primo ordine, gilt-edged securities; **-i** al portatore, active, bearer bonds; **-i** differiti, deferred bonds, stock; **-i** cumulativi, cumulative stock; **-i** di second'ordine, second-rate securities; **-i** pubblici, government stock; **-i** negoziabili, negotiable documents; certificate; claim; fineness (coins); precious metal in alloy; grade; (chem.) titre, strength; (text.) number, count (of yarn); inscription, votive tablet; (eccl.) title; *titulus*; dot of the letter *i*, tittle; abbreviation sign used in MSS.; elenco dei **-i**, list of documents; a — di, in virtue of, by right of, as; a — privato, privately; a — di amicizia, as a mark of good feeling; mi ha dato dei brutti **-i**, he has called me names; †epitaph. **-are** [A1s] *tr.* to call, to entitle; to call names; (chem.) to titrate; (text.) to number; *adj.* titular; regular; rightful; nominal; *n.m.* (eccl.) titular (as subject of the dedication of a church or as priest of certain Roman churches); (regular) holder (of an office); owner; occupant; person entitled; i **-ari**, the best team a club (soccer, rugby, etc.) can put in the field. **-arità** *f.* (leg.) titularity. **-ato** *part. adj.* entitled, called; titled; *n.m.* person of title, titled person. **-azione** *f.* (chem.) titration; (text.) numbering, counting. **-eggiare** [A3c] *tr.* to bestow a title (on). **-etto** *m.* (typ.) sub-title, text in smaller type below main title. **-ografi·a** *f.* (iron.) publication (of books, articles, etc.) for the purpose of obtaining a degree, diploma or title. **-one** *m. augm.* overlong, inflated title.

Titon-e, -o *pr.n.m.* (class. myth.) Tithonus.

titub-are [A1s] *intr.* (*aux.* avere) to hesitate, to falter; to waver. **-ante** *part. adj.* hesitant, irresolute; perplexed, undecided, faltering. **-antemęnte** *adv.* irresolutely; with hesitation. **-anza** *f.* irresoluteness; hesitancy; senza perdere un attimo in **-anze**, without hesitating or dithering a moment; perplexity. **-azione** *f.* hesitation; irresolution; (med.) titubation.

tixotr-o·pico *adj.* (phys.) thixotropic. **-opi·a** *f.* (phys.) thixotropy.

Tizian-o *pr.n.m.* Titian. **-esco** *adj.* (*m.pl.* **-eschi**) (paint.) Titianesque; (of hair) auburn, Titian.

Ti·zio *pr.n.m.* (Gk. myth.) Tityus; (Rom. name) Titius; —, Caio e Sempronio, Tom, Dick and Harry; un —, a certain person, someone or other; un — qualunque, a nobody.

tizz-o *m.* brand, firebrand; smoking coal. **-ona·io** *m.* (techn.) stokehole. **-one** *m.* brand; firebrand; nero come un **-one** spento, black as coal; **-one** d'inferno, scoundrel. **-oniere** *m.* (mil. hist.) blow-match carrier.

tlasp-i *m. indecl.* (bot.) name of several small cruciferous plants, e.g. shepherd's purse, *Capsella bursapastoris*. **-o** *m.* (bot.) candytuft, *Iberis sempervirens* and *I. semperflorens*.

tmeṣi *f.* (gramm.) tmesis.

to'!, toh! *excl.* I say! (surprise); look here!; hallo!; here!; take it!; —, metti il giornale a posto, take the paper and put it back in its place.

†toba *f.* cavern, cave.

Tobi·a *pr.n.m.* Tobias, Toby.

toboga *f.* toboggan, sledge.

Tobru·ch, Tobru·k *pr.n.m.* (geog.) Tobruk.

toc *onom.* See **tic**[1].

tocca[1] *f.* silk tissue enriched with gold.

tọcca[2] *f.* (Tusc.) hole in the road; gap in a pavement; unevenness in a path.

†tocca[3] *f.* kerchief.

†tocca[4] *f.* touchstone.

Tocca·i *pr.n.f.* (geog.) Tokay; *n.m.* (wine of) Tokay.

tocc-are [A2c] *tr.* to touch; to feel; to finger; to tap; to hit, to strike; to press (bell, etc.); to call at, to touch at (a port); (mus.) to play (an instrument); to beat, to strike (drum, etc.) as a signal; (mil.) — la raccolta, to sound the rally; †— il buttasella, to sound the call 'boot and saddle'; — il cavallo, to whip a horse; (to a cabman, etc.) tocca! tocca!, hurry!; to goad (oxen); — il polso a, to feel the pulse of; — con mano, to feel, to try, test, explore by feeling; — la mano a, to shake hands with, to give one's hand to; (fig.) to move, to affect, to touch; to please, to impress; to con-

tocc·are (*cont.*)

cern; to injure; to offend; to touch on, to allude to; to meddle with; to adjoin; to reach; — lo stipendio, to draw one's salary; — pugni, to receive blows; -arle, -arne, to take some (bad) knocks; se non sei buono, le toccherai!, if you're not a good boy you'll catch it!; (paint.) to draw; to touch up, to retouch; *intr.* (*aux.* essere; *prep.* a) to befall; to fall to the lot (of); to be the duty (of); to be the turn (of); a chi -a?, whose turn is it?; -a a te (di, a) parlare, it is your duty to speak; (*aux.* avere; *prep.* su) to hint at, to touch upon; (sport) to touch down (rugby); *recip. rfl.* to meet, to touch; gli estremi si -ano, extremes meet; *adv. phr.* a -a non -a, so near and yet so far. -a·bile *adj.* tangible; touchable. -aferro *m.* children's game in which safety from capture consists of touching a piece of iron; *excl.* an expression uttered on seeing or hearing about anything supposed unlucky, cf. Eng. 'touch wood!'. -alapis *m. indecl.* pencil-holder. †-aleva *m.* (mil.) roll of drums or bugle call; beat to quarters. -amano *m.* (*pl.* -amani) handshake; tip, secret gratuity; (bot.) field madder, *Sherardia arvensis.* -amento *m.* touch, touching; contact. -ante *part. adj.* touching, feeling, making contact; moving; regarding, concerning. -apoma *m. indecl.* children's game resembling 'Puss in the corner'. -asana *m.* remedy, quick cure; panacea. -ata *f.* touch; dare al cavallo una -ata con la frusta, to give the horse a touch of the whip; (fig.) dare una -ata a, to touch upon, to allude to; (mus.) toccata. -atina *f. dim.* tap, pat, touch; dare una -atina di cappello, to touch one's hat (in salutation); (mus.) short toccata. -ato *part. adj.* touched; (fencing) touché; busse -ate, blows received; -ato in sorte, fallen to one's lot, received in the draw. (-atore *m.* -atrice *f.*) -atutto *m., f. indecl.* person who cannot refrain from touching things.

toccheggiare [A 3 c] *intr.* (*aux.* avere) to toll; *tr.* to pat; to tap.

toccheggio *m.* tolling of bells.

tocchettare [A I c] *intr.* (*aux.* avere) (soccer) to make a series of short passes.

toc·co[1] *m.* (*pl.* -chi) toque; cap or hat without brim.

toc·co[2] *m.* (*pl.* -chi) lump; piece; hunk; figure; un bel — di ragazza, a handsome girl, a fine figure of a girl; (provb.) un poco e un poco fa un —, 'mony a mickle maks a muckle'. -chetto *m. dim.* bit, morsel; tit-bit.

toc·co[3] *m.* (*pl.* -chi) blow, stroke; toll (of bell) udivo i -chi della campana, I heard the bell tolling; al —, at one o'clock; (leg.) settlement time; touch, stroke; con pochi -chi di pennello mi fece il ritratto, with a few strokes of the brush he painted my portrait; (mus.) touch; fare al —, to play a sort of game whereby one person of a party is selected on a count of fingers. -chetto *m. dim.* accidental blow, tap, touch. -cone *m.* meddlesome person, one who wants to touch everything. (-cona *f.*)

toc·co[4] *apocop. part.* of toccare, q.v.; *adj.* (*m.pl.* -chi) touched; moved; sembra — nel cervello, he seems a bit touched; struck; received; hinted at.

toco *m.* (orn.) toucan, *Ramphastidae* spp.

todaro *m.* (zool.) *Todarodes sagittatus*, a kind of squid.

toddi *m. indecl.* toddy, a fermented drink made in India from the sap of palm-trees.

toeletta *f. toilette,* costume.

tofa *f.* (zool.) *Tritonium nodiferum,* a large whelk.

to·fana, tofana *adj.* acqua —, poisonous drink containing arsenic, also called **acquetta.**

tofo *m.* (med.) tophus, uratoma.

tog·a *f.* (Rom. antiq.) toga (the characteristic peacetime dress of the Roman citizen); cedan le armi alla — (from Cicero's 'cedant arma togae'), let the art of war give place to the arts of peace; (leg.) gown; robes. -ale *adj.* of the toga. -ato *adj.* (Rom. antiq.) wearing the toga; i -ati, 'the toga'd race', the Romans; stile -ato, grandiloquent style; Gallia -ata, Cisalpine Gaul; Commedia -ata, *fabula togata;* gowned, wearing an academic gown; (leg.) robed.

to·gli·ere [B 7] *tr.* (*prep.* a, da) to take; to; prendi!, here, take it, *or* here you are!; to take (off), to take away (from); — di mezzo a, to take out of the way, to get rid of; — dal mondo, to kill; to carry away, to carry off; to seize; to steal; to appropriate (a thought, form of expression, etc.); — uno alla morte, to save someone's life; to free; Dio lo tolse dalle sue pene, God freed him from his sufferings; to prevent; to hinder; — gli orecchi a, to deafen; — il saluto a uno, to cease to acknowledge someone; ciò non -e che sia una brava persona, that does not prevent him

from being a worthy person; tolga Dio!, God forbid!; — di terra, to pick up; — di peso, di sana pianta, to pick right up, to lift bodily, to take right away; — dentro, to put in, to take in, to receive; to accept; to elect, to appoint (to an office); — in moglie, to take to wife, to marry; to buy; to get; to prefer; — di, to endeavour to, to undertake to; *rfl.* to get off; to get away; -ersi d'impiccio, to get out of a scrape; -ersi da, to leave off, to desist (from). -mento *m.* taking, taking away; theft. -tivo *adj.* removing, erasing.

Tognino *pr.n.m.* (mil. slang, 1918) Austrian soldier.

Togno *pr.n.m.* abbrev. form of **Antonio**, q.v.

toh *excl.* See **to'.**

Toka·i *pr.n.f.* (geog.). See **Toccai.**

told·a *f.* (naut.) upperdeck; †maindeck of a galley. -o *m.* (naut.) awning (Viareggio).

Tolem·eo *pr.n.m.* Ptolemy. -aico *adj.* Ptolemaic.

toletta *f.* dressing-table; mirror; toilet; toilet-table; dressing-room; gabinetto di —, lavatory, W.C.; far —, to dress, to wash, to do one's hair, to make up; sala di —, hairdresser's (shop, saloon); *toilette;* process of dressing one's hair; costume, style of dress (in this sense often **toeletta**).

toller·are [A I s] *tr.* to tolerate; to bear; to endure; to allow; to suffer. -a·bile *adj.* tolerable, bearable; passable, fairly good. -abilmente *adv.* tolerably; fairly, moderately. -abilità *f.* (leg.) tolerance; supera la normale -abilità, it is beyond normal toleration. -ante *part. adj.* tolerant; indulgent; mal -ante, intolerant. -anza *f.* tolerance; toleration; endurance; patient waiting; indulgence; casa di -anza, legally registered and licensed brothel (cf. Fr. 'maison de tolérance'); (rlwy.) allowance, clearance; (eng.) tolerance; (comm.) -anza di un tanto per cento, allowance of so much per cent. -ato *part. adj.* tolerated. (-atore *m.* -atrice *f.*) -azione *f.* toleration, tolerance.

†**tol·lere** *vb.* and derivs. See **togliere.**

tol·lero *m.* thaler (cf. **tallero**).

†**tolo** *m.* (archit.) tholus, dome.

tolom·aico *adj.* see **tolemaico.** -aïti *m.pl.* Ptolemaists, followers of Ptolemy, Egyptian philosopher. -(m)e·a *pr.n.f.* part of the ninth circle of Hell, in Dante's *Inferno,* abode of those who, like Ptolemy, king of Egypt, betrayed guests.

Tolone *pr.n.f.* (geog.) Toulon.

Tolos·a *pr.n.f.* (geog.) Toulouse. -ano *adj.* of Toulouse; also *n.m.*

tolsto·iano *adj.* Tolstoyan, relating to Leo Tolstoy. -ismo *m.* Tolstoyism (pacifism, Christian Socialism).

tolt·o *part.* of togliere, q.v.; *adj.* taken away, removed; stolen; — di sè, beside oneself, out of one's mind; *n.m.* thing(s) taken; il mal —, stolen goods, *or* ill-gotten gains. †-a *f.* taking, capture; seizure; extortion; theft; wife.

tol·ù *m. indecl.* (bot.) (balsam of) tolu, *balsamum tolutanum* (obtained from *Myroxylon toluifera*). -uene *m.* (chem.) toluene. -uolo *m.* (chem.) toluol.

toma[1] *f.* (in the phrase) promettere Roma e —, to make boundless promises; capire Roma per —, to mishear, to misunderstand.

toma[2] *f.* (N. Italy) fall.

†**toma**[3] *f.* a solitary or sheltered place.

toma·ia *f.* (shoem.) upper, vamp.

†**tomare**[1] *intr.* to fall headlong.

†**tomare**[2] *tr.* to seize.

tomb·a *f.* tomb; grave; vault; muto come una —, as silent as the grave; (fig.) death; (leg.) tomb (esp. above ground, distinguished from sepolcro, q.v.). -ale *adj.* (of a) tomb; pietra -ale, tombstone. -one *m. augm.* vault; vortex, whirlpool.

tombacco *m.* (metall.) tombac.

†**tomb·are**[1] *intr.* to fall. †-ata *f.* fall; (naut.) height of masts; vertical height of a square sail.

†**tombare**[2] *intr.* (of the voice) to resound.

tombino *m.* drain (in road); manhole cover.

tombol·a[1] *f.* tombola, lotto, housey-housey. -ata *f.* a game of tombola.

tombola[2] *f.* fall; far —, to fall; *excl.* (joc.) the devil!

tombol·o[1] *m.* tumble, headlong fall. -are [A I sc] *intr.* (*aux.* essere) to fall headlong, to tumble; *tr.* to tumble down; -are le scale, to fall down the stairs; †(naut.) to turn (a sail or yard) end for end. †-ata *f.* fall. -ato *part. adj.* fallen.

tombol·o[2] *m.* lace pillow; plump, tubby person; (text.) lavoro al —, braiding; lavorare al —, to braid.

tombol-o³ *m.* (geog.) tombolo, connecting bar; small dune. **-eto** *m.* dunes, shore with sand-hills.

toment-o *m.* (anat.) tomentum. **-oso** *adj.* (bot.) tomentose.

tom-ismo *m.* Thomism, the doctrine of St Thomas Aquinas. **-ista** *m.* Thomist. **-istico** *adj.* pertaining to Thomism, Thomistic.

Tommaso *pr.n.m.* Thomas; (fig.) essere, fare come san —, to be a doubting Thomas.

tommy *m. indecl.* (colloq.) a British soldier.

tom-o¹ *m.* volume; tome; part of a book; (colloq.) un bel —, a 'queer fish', a 'card'; essere — da, to be fool enough to.

†tomo² *m.* fall, tumble.

tomolo *m.* (S. Italy) measure of capacity equiv. to *c.* 45 litres.

†tomolto *m.* See **tumulto**.

Tompu·s *pr.n.m.* (Tom Pouce) 'Tom Thumb', midget; (joc.) undersized boy or man.

ton *m. onom.* dong; ton ton, ding-dong.

to·nac-a *f.* tunic; (eccl.) habit (of a religious); (eccl., rare) cassock (of secular priest); modelling clay; (anat.) tunica; gettare la — alle ortiche, to leave a monastic order. **-ella** *f. dim.* (liturg.) (strictly) tunicle (worn by subdeacon); (loosely) dalmatic (worn by deacon). **-one** *m. augm.* long coat or gown; person wearing clothes too long.

tonal-e¹ *adj.* (mus.) tonal. **-ità** *f.* shade of colour; (mus.) tonality.

Tonale² *pr.n.m.* (geog.) an Alpine pass between Trentino and Val Camonica.

ton-are [A I d] *intr.* (impers., aux. essere; pers., aux. avere) to thunder; to boom; (fig., of person) to thunder; to roar; to rail; *n.m.* thundering; booming. **-ante** *part. adj.* thundering, roaring; polvere -ante, gunpowder; voce -ante, loud, booming, sonorous voice. (**-ato** *part. adj.*) **-atore** *m.* thunderer; Giove il gran -atore, Jupiter the Great Thunderer. (**-atrice** *f.*)

tona·rio, tona·rium, tona·rius *m.* (mus.) tonarium, tonary (collection of liturgical music arranged according to Gregorian tones).

Tonchino *pr.n.m.* (geog.) Tonkin.

tonchi-o *m.* (ent.) pea, bean 'weevil' (not true weevils); — dei piselli, pea weevil, *Bruchus pisorum*; — dei fagioli, bean weevil, *B. fabae*; — della lenticchia, lentil weevil, *Laria lentis*; (of a boy) mite, puny child; brat. **-are** [A 4 c] *intr.* (aux. essere) to become infested with weevils.

tond-are¹ [A I c] *tr.* to round, to turn on a lathe. **-ato** *part. adj.* rounded off. **-atura** *f.* rounding off.

†tondare² *tr.* to trim, to cut.

tondeggi-are [A 3 c] *intr.* (aux. essere) to be roundish; *tr.* to round off; to make round; *n.m.* (paint.) roundness; effetto del —, appearance of roundness. **-amento** *m.* roundness. **-ante** *part. adj.* roundish; round. **-ato** *part. adj.* rounded (off).

tond-ere [B I] *tr.* to shear (sheep); to trim, to prune; — una siepe, to trim a hedge; †— i capelli, to cut hair. (**-itore** *m.* **-itrice** *f.*) **-itura** *f.* shearing; trimming. **-uto** *part. adj.* shorn; stripped; reduced to poverty.

tond-o *adj.* round; faccia -a, round face; (fig.) testa -a, fool; (archit.) cupola -a, round dome; arco —, round arch, semicircular arch; full; complete; cifra -a, a round number, whole number; luna -a, full moon; voce -a, full, sonorous voice; (sculp.) in full relief, standing out; di — rilievo, in full relief; mezzo —, in half relief; (typ.) carattere —, roman type; (naut.) collo —, a complete turn of a rope round a bollard, etc.; *adv.* fully, frankly, plainly; parlar chiaro e —, to speak out, to express one's opinion frankly; sputar —, to speak with affected gravity; *adv. phr.* alla -a, around; *n.m.* ring, circle; round; danzare in —, to dance in a ring, to dance a round; circumference; menare il bastone a —, to whirl a stick round, *or* to deal blows all round; mezzo —, semicircle; (paint.; sculp.) tondo, round picture; work on a circular ground; round or oval table; plate, saucer; round tray; globe, sphere; (typ.) roman (type), as opposed to italic; (naut.) turn, round turn. **-ello** *m. dim.* twisted straw placed on a bucket or tub to prevent splashing; round stick of charcoal; round joint of meat. **-ezza** *f.* roundness. **-ino** *m.* (dinner) plate; saucer; (archit.) astragal; (metall.) rod; (paint.) tondo; medallion; small round or oval painting. **-one** *m.* simpleton; unsquared beam; (dance) round.

tonfan-o, -e *m.* deep pole in a stream; pot-hole; †drinking vessel.

ton·fete *onom.* bump!

tonf-o¹ *m.* thud; bang; noise; il — della porta che si chiude, the sound of the door closing; splash; plunge; heavy fall. **-are** [A I c] *intr.* (aux. essere) to make a splash; to thump.

†tonf-o² *m.* (Florent.) stocky, corpulent person. **†-etto** *m. dim.* plump little person.

to·nica¹ *f.* (mus.) tonic, keynote.

†to·nica² *f.* See **tonaca**.

tonicella *f.* See tonacella, under **tonaca**.

to·nic-o *adj.* (mus.) tonic; (gramm.) accento —, tonic accent; (med.) tonic; crampi -i, tonic spasms; *n.m.* (med.) tonic; (gramm.) tonic accent. **-a** *f.* (mus.) tonic, key-note. **-ità** *f.* tonicity.

tonific-are [A 2 s] *tr.* to tone up; to invigorate. **-ante** *part. adj.* invigorating. **-ato** *part. adj.* toned up; invigorated. **-azione** *f.* toning-up; invigoration.

†tonista *m., f.* one who dresses and behaves in accordance with the *bon ton*.

tonitruante *adj.* booming; noisy; voce —, loud, booming voice.

†toni·truo *adj.* See **tonitruante**.

tonn-ara *f.* tunny nets; tunny-fishing ground. **-arioto, -aro(t)to** *m.* tunny fisherman. **-ato** *adj.* vitello -ato, veal cooked with mashed tunny, etc.

tonn-eggiare [A 3 c] *tr.* (naut.) to kedge; *intr.* (aux. essere) to shift berth by means of ropes, etc.; *rfl.* to wind or shift one's berth without use of engines. (**-eggiato** *part. adj.*) **-eggio** *m.* (naut.) act of kedging; rope used for kedging. **-ellaggio** *m.* (naut.) tonnage; -ellaggio di dislocamento, displacement tonnage (of a warship); -ellaggio di stazza, register tonnage (mercantile); (comm.) diritti di -ellaggio, tonnage dues. **-ellata** *f.* (naut.) ton (equiv. to 1000 kg., as against long ton, equiv. to 1016·057 kg., or short ton, equiv. to 907·185 kg.); -ellata metrica, metric ton; (mil.) improvised defence or barricade formed by filling casks with earth or stone. **-elletto** *m.* (mil. hist.) small barrel used as a container for stones and shot to be fired from a mortar. **-ello** *m.* (mil. hist.) drum used to improvise field defences; ton; liquid measure. **-ellotto** *m.* fairly large barrel; see **tonnello**.

tonn-o *m.* (ichth.) tunny fish (of various species); — comune, *Thunnus thynnus*, common tunny; — alalunga, *T. alalunga*, long-finned tunny; — bonita, palamida, *Gymnosarda pelamis*, bonito; — tonnina, *Euthynnus allitteratus*. **-ina** *f.* pickled tunny (back); far -ina, to cut in pieces; (ichth.) a small species of tunny, *Euthynnus allitteratus*.

ton-o *m.* tone; tune; accent; stress; — di voce, tone of voice; (fig.) dare il — alla conversazione, to give the tone to the conversation; in — grave, in a serious tone; cambiar —, to change one's tune; style; manner; in — con, in keeping with; stare in —, not to exceed the limits, to be decorous; levar di —, to confuse; esser fuori di —, to be amazed; darsi —, to make oneself important, to give oneself airs; rispondere a —, to answer to the point; (paint.) tone; (mus.) tone (interval), major second; quarti di —, quarter-tones; tone (pitch), note; dare il —, to give the note; psalm-tone; tone (timbre), tone-colour; (med.) tonus, tone, tonicity; (meteor.) see **tuono**. **-ometri·a** *f.* (mus.) tonometry. **-o·metro** *m.* (mus.) tonometer. **-otecni·a** *f.* (mus.) tonotechnics (art of making clockwork musical instruments).

tonsill-a *f.* (anat.) tonsil. **-are** *adj.* (anat.) tonsillar. **-ite** *f.* (med.) tonsillitis. **-ectomi·a** *f.*, **-otomi·a** *f.* (surg.) tonsillotomy. **-o·tomo** *m.* (surg. instr.) tonsillotome.

†tonso *adj.* pressed out, squeezed.

tonsore *m.* (joc.) barber, hairdresser.

tonsur-a *f.* (eccl.) tonsure. **-are** [A I] *tr.* to tonsure. **-ato** *part. adj.* tonsured; *n.m.* cleric.

tontina *f.* (comm.) tontine.

tonto *adj., n.m.* stupid, dull; fare il finto —, to pretend to be a fool.

top-a¹ *f.* female rat (cf. topo); (naut. Ven.) flat-bottomed boat. **-a·ia** *f.* rat's nest; place infested with rats; hovel. **-ato** *adj.* mousey, mouse-coloured (esp. of horses).

topa² *f.* (S. Italy vulg.) female genitals; prostitute.

topa·zi-o *m.* (miner.) topaz. **-olite** *f.* (miner.) topazolite.

topia·ri-a *f.* the topiary art. **-o** *adj.* topiary.

to·pica *f.* (rhet., as title of a treatise by Aristotle or as name of a work of the same nature) topics.

to·pico *adj.* topical; (med.) topical, local; (rhet.) topic, topical, relating to commonplaces; (fig.) uomo —, man who lives always in his own immediate locality, a solitary; (joc.) gross, coarse; fare una topica, to commit a blunder.

topinamburo *m. indecl.* (bot.) Jerusalem artichoke, *Helianthus tuberosus*.

top-o *m.* (zool.) rat; — d'acqua, water-rat, water-vole, *Arvicola amphibius*; — campagnolo, vole rat, *A. terrestris*; — delle chiaviche, brown rat, *Rattus norvegicus*; — comune, black rat; — nero, — tettaiolo, *R. rattus*; (bot.) orecchia di — canuta, *Eritrichium nanum*; (naut. Ven.) — col filo, boat with weatherboards; a coda di —, rat-tailed (pointing of a rope or other object such as a rubbing strake); (fig.) — di biblioteca, bookworm; — d'albergo, hotel-rat, i.e. thief preying on hotels. -esco *adj.* (*m.pl.* -eschi) (joc.) rat-like, mousey; insidie -esche, underhand tricks. (-etto *m. dim.*) -ina·ia *f.* hovel (cf. **topaia**, under **topa**¹). -ino *m. dim.* (joc.) active little child; *pl.* (cul.) small dumplings; (orn.) sand martin, *Riparia riparia*; *adj.* mouse-coloured. -ofobi·a *f.* (med.; psych.) topophobia. -olino *m.* (zool.) mouse; -olino delle case, house mouse, *Mus musculus*; -olino campagnolo, long-tailed field mouse, *Apodemus sylvaticus*; -olino delle risaie, -olino delle messi, harvest mouse, *Micromys minutus*; *pr.n.m.* 'Mickey Mouse'; *pr.n.f.* name of a small Fiat car.

top-ografi·a *f.* topography. -ografico *adj.* topographic(al); carta -ografica, map. (-ograficamente *adv.*) -ografo *m.* topographer.

toponomas·tic-a *f.* toponymy, study of place-names. -o *adj.* indice -o, index of place-names.

topotesi·a *f.* (geog.) plotting positions; (rhet.) description of an imaginary place.

toporagno *m.* (zool.) shrew; — alpino, *Sorex alpinus*; — comune, *S. araneus*.

topp-a *f.* lock (of door, chest, etc.); keyhole; patch; piece let in; mettere una — a, to patch (also fig.); (paint.) touching up; final touch; (verse) cheville, stop-gap; (cards) 'spot the lady'. -ato *adj.* piebald.

top·pete *onom., excl.* bang!; bump!

toppo *m.* stump; block of wood; log.

torac-e *m.* (anat.) thorax, chest. -en·tesi *f.* (surg.) thoracentesis. -otomi·a *f.* (surg.) thoracotomy. -opla·stica *f.* (surg.) thoracoplasty.

tora·cico *adj.* thoracic.

torb-a¹ *f.* peat. -iera *f.* peat-bog. -oso *adj.* peaty.

†torba² *f.* floodwater (cf. **torbida**).

Torbato *pr.n.m.* name of a Sardinian wine.

torbernite *f.* (miner.) torbernite.

torbida *f.* flood water; muddy stream; (mining) pulp, ore-pulp.

torbid-o *adj.* turbid; muddy; troubled; gloomy; cloudy; (of liquid) thick, clouded; nuvoli -i, dark clouds; confused; angry; c'è del — in tutto questo, there is something wrong ('fishy') in all this; (fig.) dirty, nasty, obscene; *n.m.* gloom; trouble, disorder, disturbance; pescare nel —, to fish in troubled waters; *pl.* (revolutionary) disturbances, trouble(s). (-amente *adv.*) -anza *f.* turbidity; gloominess. -ezza *f.* turbidness; gloominess; dimness. -ic·cio *adj.* somewhat turbid, not quite clear. -idi·metro *m.* (chem.) turbidimeter. -ità *f.* turbidity, turbidness; confusion. -ume *m.* turbid or muddy things (collectively).

torb-iera *f.*, -oso *adj.* See under **torba**¹.

torbo¹ *adj., n.m.* See **torbido**.

†torbo² *m.* See **turbine**.

Torcello¹ *pr.n.m.* (geog.) name of an island in the Venetian lagoon.

†torcello² *m.* (mus.) regal, portative organ.

tor·c-ere [c 5] *tr.* to twist; to wring; to turn; — il collo a, to wring the neck of; — il collo, to pretend to be devout; — il naso, to turn up one's nose; — la bocca, to make a wry mouth; — lo sguardo, to avert one's eyes; non oserà -erti un capello, he will not dare to touch a hair of your head; to distort; to wrench; (laundry) to wring; *intr.* (*aux.* avere) to wind, to turn, to twist; *rfl.* to turn, to revolve; to bend; to twist; to writhe; -ersi dalle risa, to split one's sides with laughing. -ente *part. adj.* twisting; (mech.) momento -ente, torque. -ibudello *m.* (med.) volvulus. -icollo *m.* stiff neck, torticollis; (orn.) wryneck, *Iynx torquilla*; (fig.) hypocrite, pious humbug. -ifecciola *f.*, †-ifec·cio *m.*, -ifecciolo *m.* jelly-bag, bag for straining juice from fruit. -igliare [A 4] *tr.* to twist. -imento *m.* twisting; twist; (med.) -imento d'intestini, torsion of intestines, volvulus. -inaso *m. indecl.* (vet.) barnacle-bit, twist. -itoio *m.* (text.) throwing machine. -itore *m.* twister; winder. (-itrice *f.*) -itura *f.* twisting.

torcetto *m. dim.* See under **torcia**.

tor·chi-o *m.* (in modern typ. usage) a hand-press; stampato in —, printed on a hand-press; (fig.) printing press in general; uscire dai torchi, to be published; è uscito dai torchi della C.U.P. un nuovo dizionario italiano-inglese, a new Italian-English dictionary has been published by the C.U.P.; essere sotto il —, to be in the press, i.e. printing; (joc.) far gemere i torchi, to have a work in course of publication, *or* to print rubbish; — da uva, — per le uve, wine-press; (techn.) wax-candle; candlestick. †-are *tr.* to press; to print. -atura *f.* pressing. (-ello *dim.*) -etto *m. dim.* printing-frame; (photog.) -etto per stampare, printing-frame; (cinem.) -etto per incollare, splicer.

tor·c-ia *f.* candle; torch; taper. -etto *m. dim.* small torch or candle, taper; small press; serrame a -etto, window-catch; fastening. -iere *m.*, †-iera *f.* large candlestick; torch-bearer.

torci-budello *m. indecl.*, -collo *m.*, etc. See under **torcere**.

torciere *m.* See under **torcia**.

†torcimanno *m.* See **turcimanno**.

tor·col-o *m.* press; — da rame, press for printing copper-engravings; (mus.) torculus (plain-chant neum). -a·io *m.* see **torcoliere**. -are *m.* press. -etto *m. dim.* small press; bookbinding press; hand vice; knee-clamp. -iere *m.* printer, pressman. -otto *m.* Venetian carnival mask.

tord-o *m.* (orn.) thrush, esp. the song thrush, *Turdus ericetorum*; — bottaccio, song thrush; — migratore, American robin, *T. migratorius*; — sassello, redwing, *T. musicus*; (ichth.) — di mare, corkwing, *Crenilabrus pavo*. -ela *f.* (orn.) mistle thrush, *Turdus viscivorus*. -iglione *m.* (mus.) Tordion (sixteenth-century dance of French origin). -ino *m.* (vet.) a horse's coat with dark spots on a lighter background, dapple.

tor·e·o *m.* bull-fight. -eadore *m.* toreador. -ero *m.* bull-fighter.

tore·utica *f.* toreutic(s), sculpture in relief.

†toric·cia *f.* she-goat.

Torin-o¹ *pr.n.f.* (geog.) Turin. -ese *adj.* of Turin, Turinese; *n.m.* inhabitant or native of Turin; district round Turin; *f.* woman, girl, from Turin.

torino² *m.* (dial. Tusc.). See **torello**, under **toro**.

to·r-io *m.* (chem.) thorium. -ina *f.* (miner.) thorianite. -ite *f.* (miner.) thorite.

tor-ismo *m.* (pol.) Toryism. -ista *m.*, *f.* (pol.) Tory.

torlo *m.* yolk (of egg); (fig.) centre; essere un — d'uovo, to be a model (e.g. of a well-kept farm, house, etc.).

torma *f.* (Rom. hist.) *turma*, squadron of cavalry; crowd; swarm; herd; (mil. hist.) mounted platoon (thirty men having three decurions).

tormalina *f.* (miner.) tourmaline.

tormenta *f.* snowstorm, blizzard; †storm at sea.

torment-o *m.* torment; torture; (leg.) instrument of torture; punishment by torture; torture; (theol.) torment (of hell); (fig.) pain, agony; annoyance, trouble; che —!, what a trial!, *or* how anxious (I was, etc.)!; buffeting; pains of love; *pl.* (mil. hist.) artillery; engines of war. -are [A 1 c] *tr.* to torture, to torment; to rack, to plague; to worry, to vex; to tease; to hurt, to damage; *rfl.* to torment oneself; to worry; (rel.) to scourge oneself penitentially; *intr.* (*aux.* essere) to torment oneself; to worry. -a·ria *f.* (mil. hist.) multiple-barrelled gun. -ato *part. adj.* tormented; tortured; worried; afflicted; (of landscape) broken. (-atore *m.* -atrice *f.*) -illa *f.* (bot.) tormentil, *Potentilla erecta*. -one *m.* (ent.) grub of a cockchafer, *Melolontha vulgaris*. -oso *adj.* tormenting; troublesome, vexing, worrying; acutely painful. (-osamente *adv.*)

†tornabona *f.* (bot.) the tobacco-plant, so-called after Niccolò Tornabuoni who, when Ambassador to France, sent some seeds of the plant to his nephew in Tuscany.

torn-are [A 1 c] *intr.* (*aux.* essere). **1.** To RETURN; to go back; to come back; ho preso questa deliberazione e non -o indietro, I have made up my mind and will not go back on my decision; — di moda, to come back into fashion; — in sè, to come to one's senses; — a dire, to say again; — a lavorare, to go back to work, to resume work; — a galla, to return to the surface, to bob up again; (of food) — a gola, to repeat. **2.** To TURN OUT, to prove to be; questo -a a suo onore, this does him credit; — a bene, to turn out well, to succeed; se ti -a comodo, if it is convenient to you; il conto -a, the account is correct; versi che non -ano, lines which do not scan; vestito che -a bene, dress that looks well, is becoming. **3.** To TURN (INTO), to become; — febbricitante, to turn feverish; — in, to be changed into. **4.** (Tusc.) To GO (for the first time, esp. to a new house or place of work); è -ato di casa in Via Ricasoli, he has gone to live in Via Ricasoli; è -ata colla Contessa B., she has gone into service, has got a job, with

torn-are (*cont.*)

Countess B. **5.** *tr.* To TURN, to turn round; to bring back; to reduce; to change. **-aconto** *m.* profit; benefit; utility; lo farà solo se ci troverà il -aconto, he will only do it if he finds it pays him. **-ado** *m.* (meteor.) tornado, whirlwind. †**-agusto** *m.* (cul.) appetizer. †**-aletto** *m.* valance round a bed. **-ante** *adj.* turning; curving; *n.m.* zig-zag, winding road. **-asole** *m.* (chem.) litmus; carta al -asole, litmus paper; (bot.) *Chrozophora tinctoria.* **-ata** *f.* return; sitting (of an assembly), meeting; (poet.) envoy. **-ato** *part. adj.* returned; ben -ato!, welcome back!, glad to see you again!; †changed; *n.m.* il ben -ato, welcome; dare il ben -ato a, to welcome. †**-avira** *m.* (naut.) swifter used for weighing anchor.

torneare [A 6] and derivs. See under **torneo**.

tornello *m.* (mil. hist.) surcoat; aproned vest reaching the knees.

torn-e·o *m.* tournament; tourney; jousting; assault-at-arms; †tour. **-eamento** *m.* see torneo. **-eare** [A 6] *intr.* (*aux.* avere) to joust, to tilt; to wheel round; *tr.* to surround. **-eato** *part. adj.* surrounded. **-eatore** *m.* jouster, one who takes part in a tournament.

tornes-e *m.* (numism.) a coin first issued in Tours and subsequently used in Italy and given different values; in the Kingdom of Naples its value was two centesimi. **-ello** *m.* Venetian coin made of copper or bronze alloy.

tornichetto *m.* turnstile.

torn-io *m.* (techn.) lathe; — a revolver, turret lathe, capstan lathe; †wheel (instrument of torture). **-iero** *adj.* of, relating to, a lathe. †**-igliato** *adj.* turned on a lathe.

torn-ire [D 2] *tr.* (eng.) to turn (on a lathe); — a spoglia, to hack off; (fig.) to shape; to polish; — una frase, to turn a phrase, to polish a sentence. **-imento** *m.* turning; shaping. **-ito** *part. adj.* turned; shaped; (fig.) shapely; well-turned, polished. **-itore** *m.* turner; potter. (**-itrice** *f.*) **-itura** *f.* turning; (fig.) shaping; polishing; shavings; filings.

torno¹ *m.* See tornio.

torno² *m.* period; in quel —, thereabouts; in quel — di tempo, about that time.

torno³ *prep.* round, about; — la casa, about the house; *adv.* torno torno, all round; levarsi una cosa di —, to get rid of a thing.

tor-o¹ *m.* bull; (fig.) strong, thick-set person; (astron.) Taurus; tagliar la testa al —, to cut the Gordian knot, to settle the question. **-ello** *m.* young bull. **-ino** *m.* (dial. Tusc.) see torello. **-oso** *adj.* bull-like; thick-set; sinewy, robust.

toro² *m.* (poet.) nuptial couch, marriage bed; (leg.) separazione del —, judicial separation.

toro³ *m.* (archit.) torus, a moulding semicircular in section round the base of a column; (geom.) torus; (on river embankments) a projection slightly above the normal height of the water; l'Adige ha superato il —, the Adige is in flood. NOTE: this should not be confused with 'guardia' which indicates the danger-line above which serious flooding may be expected.

torpe·din-e *f.* (naut.) torpedo, mine, depth-charge; aerial mine; (for self-propelled torpedo see **siluro**); (ichth.) electric ray, *Torpedo* spp.; — occhiata, — occhiatella, *T. ocellata;* — marezzata, — marmorata, — marmoreggiata, *T. torpedo;* — nera, — grande, — del Nobili, *T. nobiliana.* **-iera** *f.* (naut.) torpedo-boat; barca -iera, M.T.B. **-iere** *m.* (naut.) torpedo-man. (NOTE: this includes electricians as in the British Navy but is more commonly used for minelaying personnel.) **-oso** *adj.* (naut.) see **minato**.

torped-o *f. indecl.* sports-car; racing-car. **-one** *m.* motor-coach.

†**tor·p-ere** [B 1] *intr.* to be sluggish; to be numb. †**-ente** *part. adj.* numb; stiff; sluggish.

tor·pid-o *adj.* torpid; sluggish; dull. **-amente** *adv.* torpidly, sluggishly, dully. **-ezza** *f.* torpidity, torpor; sluggishness, dullness. **-ità** *f.* lethargy; sluggishness; numbness.

torpiglia *f.* (ichth.). See torpedine.

torpore *m.* torpor, numbness; (fig.) sluggishness; dullness, stupidity.

†**torqu-e** *m.*, †**-e·o** *m.* necklace, torque. **-ato** *adj.* torquated; (Rom. antiq.) wearing a chain or collar.

torre¹ [B 7]. See togliere.

torr-e² *f.* tower; — di Babele, tower of Babel, confusion of tongues; (radio) — di antenna, aerial mast; (chess) rook; — di controllo, control-tower (of an airport); (naut.) — barbetta, turret; — binata, twin turret; — di comando, armoured control post; — di vedetta, watchtower, semaphore station; (mil. hist.) assault tower fitted with a ram or fighting platform. **-acchione** *m.* big

tower; ancient ruined tower. **-aiuolo** *adj.* (orn.) piccione -aiuolo, domestic pigeon. **-azzo** *m.* big tower; il Torrazzo di Cremona, the bell-tower of the cathedral of Cremona. **-eggiante** *part. adj.* towering. **-eggiare** [A 3 c] *intr.* (*aux.* avere) to tower; *tr.* to surround with towers. **-etta** *f. dim.* turret, small tower; (naut.) conning tower (of a submarine); -etta di osservazione, observation chamber, diving-bell; -etta di telemetraggio, rangefinder tower; game of chance; (cinem.) -etta girevole, turret; (zool.) see **torricella**. **-icella** *f.* turret; pinnacle; (zool.) *Cerithium vulgatum*, a marine gastropod. **-icellato** *adj.* (herald.) with turrets. **-iere** *m.* tower-keeper. **-iero** *adj.* (of a) tower. **-igiano** *m.* guardian of a tower. **-ione** *m.* strong, embattled tower. †**-ito** *adj.* see **turrito**.

torre-fare [B 14] *tr.* to toast; to roast. **-fatto** *part. adj.* toasted; caffè -fatto, roasted coffee. **-fazione** *f.* toasting, torrefaction; (metall.) roasting.

torreggiare [A 3 c]. See under **torre²**.

torren-te *m.* torrent, stream; un — di luce, a flood of light; la pioggia cadeva a -ti, it was raining in torrents. **-tizio** *adj.* like a torrent, torrential. **-ziale** *adj.* torrential. (**-zialmente** *adv.*)

torr-etta *f.*, **-icella** *f.* See under **torre²**.

†**torriare** *tr.* to fortify with towers.

†**torri·bolo** *m.* See turibolo.

tor·rido *adj.* torrid; burning; scorching; (geog.) zona torrida, torrid zone.

torrier-e *m.*, **-o** *adj.* See under **torre²**.

torrone *m.* nougat; sweetmeat made with roasted almonds.

†**torsello** *m.* pad; pin-cushion.

torsi-o·grafo *m.* (phys.) torsiograph. **-o·metro** *m.* (text.) twist counter; (eng.) torque meter. **-ione** *f.* torsion; twist; contortion; (fig.) mental anguish; (text.) twist; *pl.* gripes, colic.

torso *m.* (anat.) torso, trunk; (sculp.) torso; (bot.) core of an apple, pear, etc.; stalk of a cabbage or other plant bearing flowers only near the top.

torsolo *m.* (bot.). See torso.

tort-a¹ *f.* cake; pie; tart; — di frutta, fruit-tart; — di mele, apple-tart, *or* apple-pie; (fig.) mangiar la — in capo ad alcuno, to be taller than, *or* superior to, someone. **-aio** *m.* pie-man, maker or vendor of pies. **-ellaio** *m.* maker and seller of 'tortelli'. **-ellini** *m.pl.* a form of 'past'asciutta' filled with spinach, etc. and 'ricotta' and eggs; -ellini di Bologna, the same made with ham, parmesan cheese, etc. **-ello** *m.* the same with filling of peas (or other vegetable), eggs with sugar and white wine.

tort-a² *f.* twist, twisting; (colloq.) fare la —, to pull wires, to form a clique; (herald.) roundel; — bisante, roundel per fess. **-ale** *m.* round wooden tray with two handles, used in olive-pressing.

tort-o¹ *part.* of **torcere**, q.v.; *adj.* twisted; crooked; twisty; tortuous; costumi -i, crooked behaviour, improper conduct; (herald.) arched in base. †**-amente** *adv.* obliquely, crookedly; unjustly; guardare -amente, to look askance at; crossly, sullenly. **-ezza** *f.* twistiness; crookedness. †**-icchiare** *intr.* to frequent crooked ways. **-iccio** *adj.* (naut.) twisted, laid up; cavo -iccio, cable-laid rope. **-igliere** *m.* (herald.) torse, crest-wreath. **-iglione** *m.* (ent.) weevil; spiral; rifled gun-barrel; Damascus-twist; ribbon; ostrich feather; (Orvieto) serpent-shaped sweetmeat made with almonds; name of an old country dance; *adj., adv. phr.* a -iglione, spiral, spirally. **-iglioso** *adj.* twisted; contorted. **-ile** *adj.* (archit.) twisted. †**-ire** *tr.* to twist; *intr.* to defecate. **-izza** *f.* (naut.) mastrope; †forestay. **-izzo** *m.* (naut.) kink in a cable. **-oio** *m.* bar for twisting rope. **-orato** *adj.* (herald.) semy of roundels.

torto² *m.* wrong; avere —, to be wrong, to be in the wrong, to be mistaken; non ha tutti i torti, he is not wholly in the wrong, *or* there is something in what he says; hai — di parlare così, you are wrong, you do wrong, to talk like that; avere — marcio, to be dead wrong; confessare i propri -i, to confess one's faults; fare — a, to wrong, *or* to be unworthy of; injury; injustice; dare — a, to put the blame on, *or* to prove in the wrong; *adv.* a —, wrongly; wrongfully.

tor·tol-a *f.* (orn.) see **tortora**. **-ino** *adj.* (orn.) dove-like; piviere -ino, dotterel, *Charadrius morinellus*.

tor·tor-a *f.* (orn.) turtle-dove, *Streptopelia turtur;* — dal collare, Barbary dove, *S. risoria;* — dal collare orientale, collared dove, *S. decaocto.* **-ella** *f. dim.* of **tortora**; color -ella, dove-colour.

†**tor·tore** *m.* See tortora.

tortor-e¹ *m.* club, cudgel. **-ata** *f.* blow with a cudgel.

†**tortore²** *m.* (hist.) executioner; torturer.

tortoreggi-are [A 3 c] *intr.* (*aux.* avere) to coo (like a dove); (fig.) to bill and coo. **-aménto** *m.* cooing; billing and cooing.

tor·trice *f.* (ent.) — dell'uva, *Sparganothis pilleriana*, a caterpillar pest of grapes; — della quercia, *Tortrix viridana*, a pest of oak-trees.

tortuọs-o *adj.* tortuous, crooked; twisting; curving; winding, meandering; (fig.) underhand, not straight. (**-aménte** *adv.*) **-ità** *f.* tortuousness; sinuosity; le -ità del fiume, the winding course of the river.

tortur-a *f.* torture; mettere alla —, to put to torture; (fig.) torment; agony; vexation; †twisting. **-are** [A I] *tr.* to torture; (fig.) to torment; to vex; *rfl.* (acc. of prn. 'si') to torment oneself; (*dat.* of prn. 'si') -arsi il cervello, to rack one's brains. (**-ato** *part. adj.*)

tọrv-o *adj.* surly; grim; threatening. **-aménte** *adv.* surlily; grimly.

†torzione *f.* See **storsione**.

torzóne *m.* lay brother; (fig.) ignorant, boorish, friar.

tọṣa *f.* (N. Italy) girl; girl-friend.

toṣ-are [A I] *tr.* to clip; to shear; (bookb.) to trim; (joc.) farsi —, to get one's hair cut. **-aménto** *m.* clipping; shearing. **-ato** *part. adj.* clipped; shorn; testa -ata, cropped head; moneta -ata, clipped coin. **-atóre** *m.* shearer; clipper (of coins). **-atrice** *f.* clipper, hair-clippers; sheep-shearing machine. **-atura** *f.* shearing; la -atura delle pecore, sheep-shearing; material shorn; clippings; (joc.) haircut.

Toscana *pr.n.f.* (geog.) Tuscany.

tosca·nico *adj.* (archit.). See **etrusco**.

toscan-o *adj.* Tuscan; lingua -a in bocca romana, Tuscan as spoken by a Roman (traditionally supposed to be the best Italian); architettura -a, Tuscan architecture (reckoned to begin with Brunelleschi); (paint.) scuola -a, Tuscan School (i.e. from Giotto to Michelangelo); (archit.) stile, ordine, —, Tuscan order; vini -i, Tuscan wines (Chianti, Pomino, Montepulciano, etc.); *adv. phr.* alla -a, in the Tuscan manner, with a Tuscan accent; *n.m.* Tuscan; the Tuscan language; a type of cheap and very strong cigar. **-a** *f.* Tuscan woman. **-aménte** *adv.* in Tuscan style. **-eggiante** *part. adj.* affecting Tuscan style. **-eggiare** [A 3 c] *intr.* (aux. avere) to resemble Tuscan, to verge on Tuscan; to imitate the Tuscan style, to affect a Tuscan accent. **-eri·a** *f.* (derog.) Tuscanism(s). **-eṣimo** *m.* see **toscanismo**. **-iṣmo** *m.* Tuscanism. **-ità** *f.* Tuscan quality of language. **-iẓẓare** [A I] *tr.* to Tuscanize; to render Tuscan; *intr.* (aux. avere) see **toscaneggiare**. (**-iẓẓato** *part. adj.*)

†tosco¹ *adj., n.m.* See **toscano**.

tosco² *m.* (poet.) poison; †poisonous.

†tosolare *vb.* See **tosare**.

toṣóne *m.* fleece; (herald.) Il Toson d'oro, the Golden Fleece; l'Ordine del Toson d'Oro, the Order of the Golden Fleece.

tọss-e, †-a *f.* cough; un colpo di —, a fit of coughing; nodo di —, prolonged fit of coughing; pastiglie per la —, cough drops, lozenges; decotto per la —, linctus, cough mixture; — asinina, — canina, whooping-cough. **-icchiare** [A4] *intr.* (aux. avere) to cough slightly and often; to cough (as a signal). **-icolọso** *adj.* inclined to be bronchial; often troubled by a cough. **-icóne** *m.* *augm.* heavy cough, troublesome cough.

tos·sic-o *adj.* toxic; poisonous; gas —, poison gas; *n.m.* poison; distasteful food; gall. **-a·ria** *f.* (bot.) *Gratiola officinalis*. **-ità** *f.* (med.) toxicity. **-oden·dro** *m.* (bot.) poison ivy, *Rhus toxicodendron*. **-ologi·a** *f.* toxicology, study of poisons. **-olo·gico** *adj.* toxicological. **-o·logo** *m.* toxicologist.

tossic-olọso *adj.*, **-óne** *m.* *augm.* See under **tosse**.

tossiemi·a *f.* (med.) toxaemia.

tossilag·gine *f.* (bot.) coltsfoot, *Tussilago farfara*.

tossina *f.* (med.) toxin.

toss-ire [D I] *intr.* (aux. avere) to cough. **-iménto** *m.* coughing.

†tosso *m.* (naut.) rope holding the shrouds together near the masthead.

†tost-a *f.* speed. **†-ano** *adj.* speedy, swift.

tost-are [A I] *tr.* to roast (coffee, almonds, etc.); to toast. **-apane** *m. indecl.* (electric) toaster. (**-ato** *part. adj.*) **-atura** *f.* roasting; toasting. **-icchiare** [A4] *tr.* to roast slightly. **-ino** *m.* coffee-roaster (machine).

tosto¹ *adj.* hard; (of bread) stale; uovo —, hard-boiled egg; stare —, to stand firm; faccia -a, cheek, impudence.

tost-o² *adv.* quickly; hurriedly; soon; o — o tardi, sooner or later; far —, to be quick; — che, as soon as; (provb.) chi — si risolve, tardi si pente, decide in haste and repent at leisure.

total-e *adj.* total; whole, entire; absolute; gross; *n.m.* total; sul —, on the whole. **-ménte** *adv.* totally; wholly; entirely; utterly. **-ità** *f.* totality; entirety; whole sum; mass. **-ita·rio** *adj.* complete; absolute; whole; (pol.) totalitarian. **-itariṣmo** *m.* (pol.) totalitarianism. **-iẓẓare** [A I] *tr.* to add up; to count (all together); (sport) la squadra italiana ha -izzato trenta punti, the Italian team scored thirty points. **-iẓẓatóre** *m.* totalizator.

to·tano¹ *m.* (zool.) squid, *Loligo vulgaris*, (fig.) simpleton, stupid individual.

to·tano² *m.* (orn.) — moro, spotted redshank, *Tringa erythropus*.

totem *m. indecl.* fetish; totem. **-iṣmo** *m.* fetishism; totemism.

†toto *adj.* See **tutto**.

totocal·cio *m.* football pool(s).

totoma·glio *m.* (bot.). See **titimaglio**.

tottavilla *f.* (orn.) woodlark, *Lullula arborea*.

tournée *f.* (pron. as Fr., *pl.* **tournées**) (theatr.) tour; — in provincia, provincial tour (cf. **giro**).

tova·gli-a *f.* table-cloth; stender la —, to put the cloth on the table; levar la —, to clear away, to clear the table; (liturg.) altar-cloth; — di comunione, communion-cloth. **-olino** *m.* bib; small napkin. **-(u)olo** *m.* napkin; tray-cloth; anello del -uolo, napkin-ring.

tozz-o¹ *m.* piece, morsel, bit; un — di pane, crust of bread. **†-olare** *intr.* to beg one's bread.

tozz-o² *adj.* stocky; thick-set; stumpy; squat; edificio —, squat building; (naut.) barchetta -a, small boat. **-otto** *adj.* *dim.* rather stocky; *n.m.* very thick brick.

tra¹ *prep.* between, among; NOTE: 'tra' is preferred to 'fra' if the following word begins with 'f'; and conversely. — la folla, among the crowd; from among, out of, of; preferire una persona — le altre, to prefer (favour) one person out of a number; il migliore — tutti, the best of all; — tutto fanno 100 lire, all together it makes 100 lire; — bella e buona non so qual fosse più (Dante, *Purg.* XXIV, 13–14), if she was more virtuous or more fair I knew not; — per la debolezza e per la paura, what with weakness and what with fear; — oggi o domani, either today or tomorrow.

tra-² *pref.* beyond, across, over.

†tra³ *pref. intens.* See **stra**.

†trabacca *f.* awning; tent; shed.

trab-acco *m.*, **-ac·colo** *m.* (naut.) brig (Adriatic); fishing-boat.

†trabald-are *tr.* to bully, to ill-treat. **†-eri·a** *f.* bullying.

traball-are [A I] *intr.* (aux. avere) to stagger; to totter; to sway; to reel; to lurch; (of small children) to toddle; come -a quest'autobus!, how this bus shakes!; (of a broken table) to be unsteady; †to dance on and on. **-ante** *part. adj.* staggering; tottering; lurching. **-ìo** *m.* continual staggering, tottering, lurching, etc. **-óne** *m.* *augm.* stagger; lurch; fall; (of a vehicle) jolt; *adv. phr.* a -oni, staggering; jolting.

trabaltare [A I] and derivs. See **ribaltare**.

trabalz-are [A I] *tr.* to shift; to remove; *intr.* (aux. essere) to jolt; to jerk; to rebound. **-ato** *part. adj.* removed, transferred. **-óne** *m.* jolt; *adv. phr.* a -oni, jerkily.

trabante¹ *m.* (hist.) member of the bodyguard of the German Emperor, or of the Grand-Duke of Tuscany.

trabante² *m.* (astron.) satellite.

†trabat·tere *intr.* to depart in haste; *tr.* to knock down with violence.

†trabe *f.* See **trave**.

tra·be-a *f.* (Rom. antiq.) *trabea.* **-ato** *adj., n.m.* (Rom. antiq.) (person) wearing the *trabea* (esp. knight or consul); (Lat. lit.) commedia -ata, *trabeata.*

trabeazióne *f.* (archit.) trabeation, entablature.

trabe·cola *f.* (anat.) trabecula.

trabic·col-o *m.* kind of clothes-horse or domed cradle for drying clothes over a brazier; or for supporting bed-clothes over a warming-pan; rickety vehicle; rickety piece of furniture. **-a·io** *m.* maker, seller, repairer of 'trabiccoli'.

trabocc-are [A 2 c] *intr.* (aux. avere, essere) to brim over, to overflow; la pentola ha -ato, the pot has boiled over; il latte è -ato, the milk has boiled over (run over); il fiume -a sopra gli argini, the river overflows its banks; quella fu la goccia che fece — il vaso, that was the last straw that broke the camel's back; (fig.) la bilancia -ò in favore di lui, the balance tipped in his favour; far — la nave, to capsize the boat; *tr.* to hurl to the ground; to cast down; to destroy (city, castle, etc.). **-aménto** *m.* overflow; excess; (of scales) weighing down; ruin, destruction. **-ante** *part. adj.*

trabocc·are (*cont.*)
overflowing, superabundant; peso -ante, overweight. †-**antemęnte** *adv.* like a flood; in excess. -**ato** *part. adj.* cast down; overthrown; dead; superabundant, excessive.

†**trabocchello** *m.* See **trabocchetto**.

trabocchętto *m.* pitfall, snare, trap.

trabocchęvol-e *adj.* overflowing, superabundant; excessive; †precipitous, hazardous. (-**męnte** *adv.*)

trabọc·co *m.* (*pl.* -**chi**) overflowing; overflow; flood; downfall, ruin; stare sul —, to be on the edge of a precipice; (mil. hist.) a kind of catapult, mortar.

tracann-are [A I] *tr.* to gulp down; to drink at one draught; *abs.* to swill; *rfl.* (*dat.* of *prn.* 'si') -arsi un bicchiere di vino, to gulp down a glass of wine. (-**ato** *part. adj.* -**atọre** *m.* -**atọra**, -**atrice** *f.*)

tracapello *m.* (bot.) dodder, *Cuscuta*.

traccagnotto *adj.* (N. Italy, fam.) squat; dumpy; sturdy; stocky.

traccheggi-are [A 3 c] *intr.* (*aux.* avere) to dally; to delay; (mil.) to skirmish; *tr.* to delay; to hold up. (-**atọre** *m.* -**atrice** *f.*) -**atura** *f.* delay.

traccheggio *m.* delaying; procrastination; annoyance; (boxing) shadow-boxing.

trac·chete *onom.* crash!

trac·ci-a *f.* trace; trail; track; spoor; (foot-)step, footprint; mark; vestige; (fig.) outline, general plan; non rimane — dell'edificio, no trace of the building is left; il dolore gli aveva lasciato le sue tracce sul viso, sorrow had left its mark on his face; seguire le tracce di uno, to follow in someone's footsteps; le tracce viscose di una lumaca, the slimy trail of a snail; la — di un componimento, the outline of a composition; essere in —, to be on the track (of), on the trail; perdere la —, to lose the way; far la —, to draw the line (outline); — della polvere, train of gunpowder; (mil.) track, the enemy's tracks; (bot.) leaf trace bundle. -**amęnto** *m.* tracing, marking out; sketching. -**are** [A 3] *tr.* to trace, to lay out, to mark out; to map out; to draw, to sketch; to outline; -are a grandi linee, to outline, to make a rough plan of; (naut.) to lay off (a course or bearing); *intr.* (*aux.* avere) to lay down a full-scale ship's plan. -**ato** *part. adj.* traced, drawn; *n.m.* trace; tracing; line; outline; seguire il -ato, to follow the tracings; stabilire il -ato della nuova strada, to establish (fix) the line of the new road. -**atọre** *m.* tracer; (naut.) designer; apparecchio -atore, plotting machine; marinaio -atore, plotter. (-**atrice** *f.*) -**atura** *f.* tracing; radar plotting.

†**trace** *adj.*, *n.m.* See **tracio**.

trache·a *f.* (anat.) trachea, windpipe; (ent.) trachea (of an insect); *pl.* (bot.) spiral vessel. -**ale** *adj.* tracheal; trachean. -**ite** *f.* (med.) tracheitis. -**otomi·a** *f.* (surg.) tracheotomy.

trachino *m.* (ichth.) weever; — ragno, *Trachinus araneus*; greater weever; — dragone, *T. draco*; — raggiato, — rigato, *T. lineatus*; — vipera, *T. vipera*, lesser weever.

trach-ite *f.* (miner.; geol.) trachyte. -**i·tico** *adj.* trachytic.

Tra·cia *pr.n.f.* (geog.) Thrace.

tracim-are [A I] *intr.* (*aux.* essere) (hydr. eng.) to overflow. -**ante** *part. adj.* (hydr. eng.) diga -ante, drowned dam.

tra·cio *adj.* Thracian; il — cantore, Orpheus; *n.m.* Thracian.

tracoll-a *f.* shoulder-belt; (mil.) bandolier; *adv. phr.* a —, slung over the left shoulder; (naut.) sciarpa a —, method of wearing the blue sash diagonally from right shoulder to left side for officers on duty. (NOTE: the sash is worn from the opposite shoulder by chiefs of staff or flag-lieutenants.) -**are** [A I] *intr.* (*aux.* essere) to stagger; to fall; to overbalance; to collapse; far -are la bilancia, to turn the scale (also fig.). -**ato** *part. adj.* -**o** *m.* collapse; breakdown; downfall; ruin; dare il -o alla bilancia, to turn the scale; -o finanziario, financial collapse; l'angoscia di quei giorni diede il -o alla sua salute, the anxiety of those days undermined his health.

tracom-a *m.* (med.) trachoma. -**atọso** *adj.* (med.) trachomatous.

tracot-ante *adj.* overbearing, overweening, arrogant; *n.m.* swaggerer. (-**antemęnte** *adv.*) -**anza** *f.* arrogance, haughtiness.

†**tracutag·gine** *f.* heedlessness.

†**tracut-amęnto** *m.* indifference; negligence. †-**ato** *adj.* heedless.

†**tra·dere** *tr.* to inform; to betray.

trad-ire [D 2] *tr.* to betray; to deceive; to be unfaithful to; to reveal; — l'ospitalità, to fail in one's duty as a host; se la memoria non mi -isce, if my memory does not deceive me; *rfl.* to betray oneself, to give oneself away. -**imęnto** *m.* betrayal; treason, treachery;

a -imento, treacherously, stealthily; (leg.) betrayal; treason; alto -imento, high treason. -**ito** *part. adj.* betrayal; deceived; revealed. -**itọre** *m.* traitor; betrayer; deceiver; (provb. expr.) traduttore -itore, i.e. no translation does justice to the original; vino -itore, wine which is more intoxicating than it seems; *adj.* treacherous; deceitful. (-**itọra** *f.*, -**itrice** *f.*) -**itoręsco** *adj.* (*m.pl.* -**itoręschi**) traitor-like.

tradizion-e *f.* tradition; per —, by tradition, traditionally; (theol.) tradition; (leg.) delivery; tradition; †betrayal. -**ale** *adj.* traditional; existing. -**almęnte** *adv.* traditionally. -**alismo** *m.* traditionalism. -**alista** *m.*, *f.* traditionalist.

tradọtta *f.* special train, troop train; leave train.

tradọtto *part.* of **tradurre**, q.v.; *adj.* translated; turned; expressed; †handed down.

traducian-ismo *m.* (eccl. hist.) Traducianism. -**o** *m.* Traducian.

traduci·bile *adj.* translatable; expressible.

tra-durre [B 2] *tr.* to translate; to turn; to express; to interpret; — il proprio pensiero, to express one's thought; — in atto, to carry out, to bring to effect; to summon, to take; to transfer; — in prigione, to take to prison; — davanti al giudice, to bring before the magistrate; — in lingua povera, to express in simple language. -**duttọre** *m.*, -**duttrice** *f.* translator; (leg.) -duttore giurato, sworn translator, interpreter. -**duzione** *f.* translation; rendering, version; (leg.) translation; -duzione dei detenuti, transfer of prisoners.

traente *m.* (finan.) drawer (cf. **trarre**).

†**tra·ere** *vb.* See **trarre**.

trafel-are [A I] *intr.* (*aux.* avere) to breathe heavily; to be out of breath. -**ato** *part. adj.* breathless, out of breath.

traferro *m.* (electr.) air gap.

traffic-are [A 2 s] *tr.*, *intr.* (*aux.* avere), to deal, to trade, to traffic; to do business (in); (often in pejor. sense of illicit trading); — in stupefacenti, to traffic in drugs; -a i capitali, he trades on his capital; -a in grano, he deals in corn, he is a corn-dealer; — le coscienze, to trifle with principles, to prostitute one's mind; (fig.) to be busy; andare -ando, to be busily engaged; (naut.) to traffic; — con la terra, to have communication with the shore. -**a·bile** *adj.* negotiable. -**ante** *part. adj.* trafficking, dealing; *n.m.* dealer, trader, trafficker. -**ato** *part. adj.* negotiated; bought and sold. -**atọre** *m.* trader, dealer; broker; tradesman, shopkeeper. (-**atrice** *f.*)

traffichino *m.* meddler; contriver; dealer.

traf·fi-co *m.* (*pl.* -**chi**, -**ci**) trade; dealing, trading; traffic; commerce; market; place of business; capo —, head of a business house; (motor.) traffic; — stradale, road traffic; (naut.) traffic; harbour movements; comando difesa —, harbour defence organization; †nave da —, transport, merchantman.

†**trafiere** *m.* (mil. hist.) a kind of stiletto.

trafig·g-ere [C 12] *tr.* to transfix, to pierce through; to wound; (fig.) to grieve; to give pain to; la notizia mi trafisse il cuore, the news pierced my heart. -**ente** *part. adj.* piercing; painful. -**imęnto** *m.* piercing through; wound; pain. (-**itọre** *m.* -**itrice** *f.*) †-**itura** *f.* see **trafittura**, under **trafitto**.

trafil-a *f.* (eng.) drawbench; — per fili, wire-drawing machine; — per tubi, tube-drawing machine; die, die-plate, drawplate; extruder; (fig.) a whole series, string; succession; unceasing round; routine; channel of negotiations, etc., formal procedure. -**are** [A I] *tr.* (metall.) to draw. -**ato** *part. adj.* (metall.) drawn; -ato a caldo, hot-drawn. -**atọre** *m.* (metall.) drawer, wire-drawer. -**atrice** *f.* (metall.) drawbench; -atrice per fili, wire-drawing machine. -**atura** *f.* (metall.) drawing; -atura in fili, wire-drawing; (rubber industr.) straining. -**eri·a** *f.* (metall.) drawing mill, wire-drawing mill, wire mill. †-**iera** *f.* (mil.) calibrator; barrel gauge.

trafilętto *m.* (journ.) paragraph, short notice; satirical notice, lampoon.

†**trafine** *m.* exile, banishment.

†**trafisso**. See **trafitto**, under **trafitta**.

trafitt-a *f.* stab wound; (fig.) pang; stabbing pain; cutting remark. †-**ivo** *adj.* stabbing. -**o** *part.* of **trafiggere**, q.v.; *adj.* transfixed; pierced through; wounded; col cuore -o, hurt to the quick; *n.m.pl.* (vet.) colic spasms. -**ura** *f.* piercing, stabbing, stab; pang; stabbing pain.

trafor-are [A I c] *tr.* to bore through; to pierce; to perforate; to tunnel; (needlew.) to embroider with openwork. -**ato** *part. adj.* pierced; perforated; montagna -ata, mountain bored by a tunnel;

trafor-are (*cont.*)
legno ~ato, fretwork; adorned with filigree work; (needlew.) embroidered with openwork. **-atore** *m.* borer. **-atrice** *f.* boring-machine; piercing-machine. **-azione** *f.* boring; perforating; tunnelling (cf. **traforo**).

†trafor-ello *m.* rogue, knave, scoundrel. **†-elleri·a** *f.*, **†-eri·a** *f.* roguery, knavery.

trafọro *m.* piercing; boring through; tunnel(ling); perforation; arte del —, lavoro in, di, —, fretwork; sega da —, fretsaw; (jewell.) filigree work; (needlew.) openwork; †hiding-place. (Cf. **traforare**.)

trafug-are [A 2] *tr.* to steal, to purloin; to carry off secretly; to kidnap; *rfl.* to steal away, to slip away. **-amẹnto** *m.* stealing, purloining; carrying off. **-ato** *part. adj.* stolen; (of persons) kidnapped. **-o** *m.* stealing, theft, robbery; di ~o, by stealth.

†trafuggire *vb.* and derivs. See **fuggire**.

†trafurello *m.* see **traforello**; (naut.) harbour launch, customs cutter.

trage·d-ia *f.* tragedy; (fig.) disaster; (iron., etc.) che —!, what a pity!; non far ~ie, don't make a fuss; se non trova pronta la cena fa una —, if he doesn't find his evening meal ready he makes a scene. **-ia·bile** *adj.* tragic, suitable (as a subject) for a tragedy. **-iante** *m.*, *f.* tragic actor or actress; playwright; (fig.) a person who assumes a tragic pose; **-io·grafo** *m.* tragic poet, tragedian, author of tragedies.

tragedo *m.* tragic poet.

†trage·mati *m.pl.* candied fruit.

tragett-are[1] *tr.* (metall.) to cast; to quench. (**-ato** *part. adj.*) **-atore** *m.* (metall.) gunfounder.

†tragettare[2] *vb.* See **tragittare**.

†tragetto *m.* See **tragitto**, under **tragittare**.

traghett-are [A 1 c] *tr.* to ferry across. (**-ato** *part. adj.*) **-atore** *m.* ferryman. (**-atrice** *f.*) **†-iere** *m.* ferryman. **-io** *m.* (Tusc.) bustle, coming and going; noise of a crowd.

traghẹtto *m.* passage, crossing (esp. by ferry); (Ven.) mooring-place for gondolas, etc.; gondola which ferries passengers from one side of a canal to the other; cross-Channel steamer; ferryboat; car-ferry; †(fig.) short-cut; trick.

tra·gic-o *adj.* tragic, tragical; relating to tragedy; poeta —, tragedian; *n.m.* tragedian. **-amẹnte** *adv.* tragically.

tragi-commẹ·dia *f.* tragicomedy. **-co·mico** *adj.* tragicomic.

tragitt-are [A 1] *tr.* to ferry across; farsi —, to be ferried across; — un fiume, to cross a stream; †flourish, to brandish. (**-ato** *part. adj.*) **-atore** *m.* ferryman. **-o** *m.* ferry; crossing; †short-cut.

trago *m.* (anat.) tragus.

traguard-are [A 1] *tr.* to look askance at; to sight (with a sight-vane). **-o** *m.* (astron.; math.) sight; (sport) finishing line, finishing tape; tagliare il ~o, to breast the tape, to come in first; (in cycle-racing) a prize awarded to the competitor who is first past an intermediate point in the course; valore ~o, target figure; (mil.) backsight; (naut.) azimuth ring; azimuth, bearing plate, transit; ~o per le regate, starting line.

tra·gula *f.* (Rom. antiq.) a kind of javelin.

Traiano *pr.n.m.* Trajan.

†traiettare *vb.* and derivs. See **tragittare**.

traietto·ria *f.* trajectory; (geog.) trajectory; (aeron.) — di discesa, glide path; (of a missile) — libera, with engines switched off, or burned out.

†traiezione *f.* (gramm.). See **trasposizione**.

†tra·ina *f.* (naut.) drag rope; (mil.) powder trail.

train-are [A 1 a] *tr.* to drag, to draw, to haul; to tow; farsi —, to go somewhere unwillingly, to 'have to be dragged'. **-ato** *part. adj.* drawn, dragged.

tra·ino *m.* drawing, dragging, haulage; truck; sledge; waggon-load; load; luggage; baggage train; (mil.) draught; trailer; towing; tow; (vet.) 'trifle' (a gait of the horse); (Tusc.) heavy weight, drag.

†traire *vb.* and derivs. See **tradire**.

tralasci-are [A 3] *tr.* to leave out, to omit; to leave off, to cease, to discontinue, to put aside; to neglect; — di (foll. by *infin.*) to cease, to break off; ~o di scrivere, I lay down my pen. **-amẹnto** *m.* omission; interruption. **-ato** *part. adj.* omitted; interrupted; abandoned.

†tralat-are *vb.* see **trasportare**, **tradurre**. **†-i·zio** *adj.* taken over, transferred; borrowed, adopted.

†tralazione *f.* See **traslazione**.

†tralce *m.* See **tralcio**.

tral·ci-o *m.* vine-shoot; vine-branch; shoot (of any climbing plant); (anat.) — ombelicale, stump of the umbilicus. **-a·ia**, **-aiuola** *f.* two vine-shoots fastened to a pole; collo della ~aia, part of a vine resting on the branch of a tree.

tralic·ci-o *m.* trellis; trelliswork; (eng.; carpen.) trellis; lattice; trestle, trestlework; — metallico, wire netting; (text.) ticking (used for covering mattresses, etc.). **-are** [A 3] *tr.* (bldg.) to strut.

tralice *adv. phr.* in —, obliquely; tagliare in —, to cut on the cross.

tralign-are [A 5] *intr.* (*aux.* avere, essere) to degenerate; †to deviate. **-amẹnto** *m.* degenerating; falling-off.

tralu·c-ere [B 1 def.] *intr.* (not used in compound tenses) to shine; la gioia ~e dagli occhi, her eyes shine with joy; to shine through; to be transparent. **-ente** *part. adj.* translucent; transparent.

†tralunare *vb.* and derivs. See **stralunare**.

tram *m. indecl.* tram; tramway (cf. **tranvai, tranvia**).

tram-a *f.* (text.) weft, woof; (telev.) raster; (fig.) design; scheme; plot; intrigue; *pl.* tissues. **-icella** *f. dim.* (naut.) line used for joining nets.

trama·glio *m.* drag-net; trammel.

tramagnino *m.* (theatr., from the brothers Tramagnini of Bologna) knock-about comedian, clown; actor skilled in sword-play, etc.

tramand-are [A 1] *tr.* to hand down; to hand on; to transmit; to give forth, to exhale. **-amẹnto** *m.* handing down, transmitting. **-ato** *part. adj.* handed down; transmitted; exhaled. (**-atore** *m.* **-atrice** *f.*)

tram-are [A 1] *tr.*, *intr.* (*aux.* avere) to plot, to scheme; to weave. (**-ato** *part. adj.*) **-atore** *m.* plotter, schemer. (**-atrice** *f.*)

†trambasciare *intr.* to be sore distressed.

†trambedue *prn.* See **ambedue**.

trambust-o *m.* turmoil; confusion; bustle; — di stomaco, disturbed digestion, upset stomach. **†-are** *tr.* to upset, to throw into confusion. **-io** *m.* frequent disturbances; continued turmoil.

tramelogẹ·dia *f.* (lit. hist.) tragedy with some characteristics of light opera (Alfieri's description of his *Abele*).

tramen-are [A 1] *tr.* (Tusc., fam.) to turn topsy-turvy; to move here and there; to rummage; †to handle, to deal with. **-io** *m.* continual bustle or stir, hurried activity; rummaging.

†tramendu-e, **†-i**, **†-ni** *prn.* See **ambedue**.

tramescolare [A 1 s] and derivs. See **rimescolare**.

†tramess-a *f.* interposition; digression; tit-bit; side-dish.

†tramessione *f.* See **intromessione, intermissione**.

†tramesso *m.* dish served between two main courses; diversion or entertainment offered between courses.

tramest-are [A 1] *tr.* to turn topsy-turvy; to untidy; *intr.* (*aux.* avere) to make everything untidy; to rummage. (**-ato** *part. adj.*) **-io** *m.* confusion, untidiness; bustling about.

tramẹttere[1] [C 20] *tr.* to insert; to interrupt; *rfl.* to intervene; to interfere, to meddle.

†tramet·tere[2] *vb.* and derivs. See **trasmettere**.

tramẹzza *f.* partition; (shoem.) slip-sole.

tramezz-are [A 1] *tr.* to partition off; to separate; to intersperse; — i fogli di un libro con pagine bianche, to interleave a book; to interrupt; *rfl.* to intervene. **-amẹnto** *m.* division; interruption; senza ~amento, uninterruptedly. **-ato** *part. adj.* partitioned; separated.

tramẹzz-o *m.* partition; (naut.) bulkhead; (archit.) — tra navata e coro, rood screen; interval; senza —, without interruption; †in quel —, meanwhile, in the meantime; *prep.* between; non mangiare — ai pasti, don't eat between meals; among. **-ẹtto** *m. dim.* small partition; short interval. **-ino** *m.* sandwich-man.

tramicella *f. dim.* See under **trama**.

tramischiare [A 4] and derivs. See **frammischiare**.

†tramissione *f.* See **trasmissione**.

tra·mite *m.* path; way; course; means; medium; per il — di una banca, through a bank; (admin.) per il — gerarchico, through official channels.

tramog·gi-a *f.* hopper; feed-box; (agric.) — del seme, seed-box; (metall.) — di colata, runner, running herd; (naut.) hopper; coalshute; barca a —, mud hopper; †cable passage; finestra a —, prison or convent window opening into a sort of hopper-shaped screen. **-a·io** *m.* workman at a hopper.

tramontan-a *f.* north wind; north; North pole; (fig.) perdere la —, to lose one's way, to become bewildered. **-ata** *f.* period in which the wind blows from the north. **†-o** *adj.* ultramontane; northerly; *n.m.* northerner; †north wind.

tramont-are [A I c] *intr.* (*aux.* essere) (of sun, moon, etc.) to set; to go down; (fig.) to decline, to fade; to pass away; la bellezza -a presto, beauty soon fades. **-amento** *m.* setting; decline. **-ante** *part. adj.* setting; declining. **-ato** *part. adj.* set; faded; passed away; gloria -ata, vanished glory.

tramonto *m.* setting; sunset; (paint.) sunset; (fig.) decline; la sua potenza è al —, his power is on the wane.

tramort-ire [D I] *intr.* (*aux.* essere) to faint, to swoon. **-imento** *m.* swoon, faint; fainting. **-ito** *part. adj.* fainted, in a swoon; unconscious; stunned.

tram·pol·o *m.* stilt; camminare sui -i, to walk on stilts, (fig.) to be in difficulties, to be in poor health. **-ieri** *m.pl.* (orn.) wading-birds, waders. **-ino** *m.* spring-board; diving-board; (fig.) far da -ino a uno, to help someone on in his career.

tramuta *f.* (pop.) transferring.

tramut-are [A I] *tr.* to transfer; to transplant; to rebottle; to transmute. (**-ato** *part. adj.*) **-azione** *f.* transferring; transplanting; transmutation.

tram-va·i *m. indecl.*, **-vi·a** *f.* See **tranvai**.

†tranare *vb.* and derivs. See **trainare**.

tran·ci·a *f.* slice; rasher; (eng.) shears; shearing machine; — a ghigliottina, guillotine shears; — da banco, bench shears; (miner.) — inclinata, rill slice, slice. **-acerchi** *m. indecl.*, **-areg·gie** *m. indecl.* bale hoop cutter. **-are** [A 3] *tr.* (eng.) to shear. **-atura** *f.* (eng.) shearing.

tranell-o *m.* trap; snare; plot; catch, tricky difficulty. **†-are** *tr.* to trap, to snare. **†-eri·a** *f.* trickery; plot.

tranghiott-ire [D 2] *tr.* to gulp down; to devour. **-ito** *part. adj.* swallowed; devoured; -ito dalle onde, engulfed by the waves.

trangla *f.* (herald.) barrulet.

trangosci-are [A 4] *intr.* (*aux.* essere) to be in anguish, to be very distressed. **-ato** *part. adj.* in great distress, sore distressed. **†-oso** *adj.* stricken with grief.

trangugi-are [A 3] *tr.* to gulp down, to bolt; to swallow up; — il pranzo, to bolt one's dinner; — il patrimonio, to run through one's heritage; — un boccone amaro, to swallow a bitter pill. **-amento** *m.* gulping down; swallowing up. **-ato** *part. adj.* gulped down; swallowed up. (**-atore** *m.* **-atrice** *f.*)

Tran·i *pr.n.f.* (geog.) Trani. **-ese** *adj.*, relating to, inhabitant of, Trani; *n.m.*, *f.* inhabitant, native of Trani.

tranne *prep.* except, save, but; tutti — uno, all but one.

tranquill-are [A I] *tr.* to calm, to soothe; to quiet; to tranquillize; — i creditori, to satisfy one's creditors; *rfl.* to calm oneself; **†***intr.* to be tranquil. **-amento** *m.* soothing; per -amento di coscienza, to satisfy one's conscience. **-ante** *part. adj.* soothing; tranquillizing; *n.m.* tranquillizer, sedative. **-ato** *part. adj.* soothed; calmed; quietened.

tranquill-o *adj.* quiet, peaceful; calm; still; tranquil; serene; undisturbed, untroubled; mare —, calm sea; coscienza -a, easy conscience; sta —, don't worry; lascialo —, leave him alone. **-amente** *adv.* calmly; peacefully; tranquilly. **-ità** *f.* calm, peace, peacefulness, tranquillity; quiet; -ità d'animo, peace of mind. **-izzare** [A I] *tr.* to calm; to soothe, to tranquillize; to quiet. (**-izzato** *part. adj.*)

trans- *pref.* beyond, across.

transalpino *adj.* transalpine (i.e. to the north of the Alps).

transatlan·tico *adj.* transatlantic; *n.m.* Atlantic liner; (fig.) lobby in the Italian Parliament.

transatto *part.* of **transigere**; *adj.* transacted, settled; (leg.) lite transatta, compromised action, *or* settled dispute.

transazione *f.* (leg.) compromise; settlement; transaction; — amichevole, amicable agreement; — estragiudiziale, extrajudicial compromise, settlement out of Court; (comm.) composition; — a contanti, cash settlement on composition; arrangement; deal; venire a una —, to come to an arrangement.

transconduttanza *f.* (electr.) transconductance, mutual conductance.

transcristallino *adj.* (metall.) transcrystalline.

transduttore *m.* (electr.) transducer.

tran·seat *Lat.* (fam.) all right!, so be it!

†transegna *f.* outer garment.

transenna *f.* (archit.) grille, screen.

transetto *m.* (archit.) transept.

transeunte *adj.* (leg.) transitory; (fig.) transient, fleeting.

transfinito *adj.* (math.) transfinite.

transgranulare *adj.* (metall.) transgranular.

Transiberiana *pr.n.f.* the Trans-Siberian railway.

transi·g-ere [C 32] *tr.* (leg.) to compromise; to come to an agreement concerning; to compound; to settle amicably; — una lite, to compromise an action; *intr.* (*aux.* avere) (comm.) to compound; — coi creditori, to compound with creditors; to come to terms; to yield; to compromise. **-ente** *part. adj.* yielding; indulgent.

transillumin-atore *m.* (med.) transilluminator. **-azione** *f.* (med.) transillumination.

†transire *intr.* to cross over; to go by, to pass; to enter; to die.

transistore *m.* (electr.; radio) transistor; (pop.) pocket wireless set.

transit-are [A I s] *intr.* (*aux.* essere) to pass (across, through, over). **-a·bile** *adj.* passable. **-abilità** *f.* possibility of transit. **-ivo** *adj.* (gramm.) transitive. **-ivamente** *adv.* (gramm.) transitively.

tran·sit-o *m.* transit; diritto di —, right of way; vietato il —, no thoroughfare; (comm.) bolletta di —, transit bond; permesso di — in cabotaggio, transire; (astron.; astrol.) transit; (eccl.) transitus, dormition, death (of saint); (paint.) death scene (of B.V.M. or saints); (mil.) a tutto —, to the last man. **-o·rio** *adj.* transitory, transient; temporary; (gramm.) transitional (sentence); (leg.) disposizioni -orie, transitional provisions. **-oriamente** *adv.* transitorily; temporarily. (**-orietà** *f.*)

transizione *f.* transition; governo, ministero, di —, temporary, 'caretaker', 'stop-gap' government; (leg.) tassa di — della proprietà, conveyancing stamp duty; (geol.) rocce di —, transition rocks; (mus.) bridge-passage; passage (from one key to another).

translu·cid-o *adj.* translucent. **-ità** *f.* translucence.

transmodulazione *f.* (electr.) cross-modulation.

trans-o·nico *adj.* (aeron.) transonic. **-onoro** *adj.* sounding through, not sound-proof.

transpaci·fico *adj.* transpacific.

transumanza *f.* (ethnology, etc.) transhumance.

transunto *m.* (leg.) abstract; excerpt.

transura·nico *adj.* (atom. phys.) transuranic.

transustanzi-are [A 4] *tr.* (theol.) to transubstantiate. (**-ato** *part. adj.*) **-azione** *f.* (theol.) transubstantiation.

†transvedere *vb.* and derivs. See **travedere**.

tran tran *m. indecl.* routine, daily round.

tran-va·i *m.*, **-vi·a** *f.* tram, tramcar; tramway, tramline. **-via·rio** *adj.* relating to the tramway. **-viere** *m.* tram-driver; tram-conductor. **-viera** *f.* tram-conductress.

trapalare [A I] *intr.* (*aux.* avere) to shovel.

Tra·pan-i *pr.n.f.* (geog.) name of a town and province in Sicily. **-ese** *adj.* relating to Trapani; *n.m.*, *f.* inhabitant of Trapani.

tra·pan-o *m.* (eng.) drill; drilling machine; — a colonna, upright drilling machine; — ad arco, bow drill; — motorizzato, power drill; (carpen.) auger; (surg.) trepan. **-amento** *m.* drilling; (surg.) trepanning. **-are** [A I s] *tr.* to drill; (surg.) to trepan. **-ato** *part. adj.* drilled; (surg.) trepanned; (art) intaglio -ato, perforated carving. **-atrice** *f.* (eng.) drilling machine. (**-atura** *f.* **-azione** *f.*) **-ino** *m. dim.* -ino elettrico, electric hand drill. **-io** *m.* constant drilling.

trapass-are [A I] *tr.* to pierce, to pass through, to transfix; -ò l'avversario con la spada, he ran his opponent through with his sword; — un muro, to make a hole through a wall; (fig.) — il cuore a, to pierce the heart of, to wound deeply; to overstep; to pass over, to pass by; to neglect; *intr.* (*aux.* essere) to pass, to pass on; to pass away; to die; l'eredità -a di padre in figlio, the inheritance passes down from father to son. **-a·bile** *adj.* that can be overlooked, passed by; passing, transitory. **-amento** *m.* passing (by, over, away); lungo -amento di tempo, long period of time; trespass; transgression; death; transmigration. **-ante** *part. adj.* passing; transient; perishable; transparent. **-ato** *part. adj.* dead, deceased; passed; changed; *n.m.* i -ati, the dead; è un -ato, he is finished, his day is done; (gramm.) past perfect, pluperfect (tense). (**-atore**, **-atrice** *f.*) **-o** *m.* passage, pass(ing); lungo -o di tempo, long period of time; death, decease; (comm.) transfer; -o di azioni, transfer of shares; fare un -o, to transfer; -o per girata, transfer by endorsement; (leg.) -o della proprietà, conveyance of the property; -o di proprietà, transfer of ownership; -o di un diritto, assignment of a right; atto di -o, deed of transfer; (vet.) half-canter.

trapelare[1] [A I c]. See under **trapelo**.

trapel-are[2] [A I c] *intr.* (*aux.* essere) to trickle forth; to ooze out, to leak out; to stream feebly out; (fig.) to leak out, to become known, to appear; lasciare — il segreto, to let the secret out. **-amento** *m.* leakage; infiltration.

trapel-o *m.* spare horse or other draught animal (e.g. to help up a hill); (theatr.) understudy; walking-on part, extra; (naut.) hook-rope. **-are** [A I C] *intr.* (*aux.* avere) to be used, to function, as a 'trapelo'.

†**trapens-are** *intr.* to think earnestly, to be thoughtful and pre-occupied. †**-ato** *adj.* thoughtful, lost in thought.

trape·z-io *m.* circus trapeze; (math.) trapezium; *n.m.* (anat.) trapezius (muscle); *adj.* (math.) trapezoid. **-oidale** *adj.* trapezoidal; (eng.) cinghia **-oidale**, V-belt. **-o·ide** *m.* (math.) trapezoid; (anat.) trapezium (bone); *adj.* trapezoidal.

†**trapez·zio** *m.* See **trapezio**.

trapiant-are [A I] *tr.* to transplant; *rfl.* to be transplanted; (fig.) to transplant oneself, to emigrate. **-amento** *m.* see **trapianto**. (**-ato** *part. adj.*) **-atoio** *m.* gardener's trowel. (**-atore** *m.* **-atrice** *f.*) **-o** *m.* transplanting.

†**traponimento** *m.* displacement; transposition.

traponte *m.* (naut.) between-deck.

†**traporre** *vb.* See **trasporre**, **interporre**.

†**traportare** *vb.* and derivs. See **trasportare**.

Trapp-a¹ *pr.n.f.* the Trappist order, so called from the Abbey of La Trappe in Normandy. **-ista** *m.* (eccl.) Trappist; (fig.) hermit.

†**trapp-a²** *f.* (naut.) **—** di boccaporto, hatch-bar; **-e** per carenare una nave, relieving tackles; **-e** delle tende, awning ropes. †**-ato** *adj.* (naut.) tende **-ate**, sloped awnings.

trappeso *m.* Neapolitan weight, 0·89 gramme.

trappeto *m.* oil-press.

trappista *m.* See under **trappa¹**.

trap·pol-a *f.* trap, snare; pitfall; **—** da topi, rat-trap; (fig.) deception, snare. **-are** [A I S] *tr.* to trap; to (en)snare; **-are** denari, to get money by dishonest means; to dupe, to deceive. **-atore** *m.* cheat, swindler. (**-atrice** *f.*) **-eri·a** *f.* cheating, trickery; deception. (**-ina** *f. dim.*) **-ino** *m.* spring-board; †(naut.) sounding apparatus for recovering a core; hollow at the bottom of the lead; *pr.n.m.* (theatr.) a character in the Commedia dell'arte. **-one** *m.* trickster. (**-ona** *f.*)

†**trapporre** *tr.* See **trasporre**, **interporre**.

†**trapun·gere** *tr.* to pierce through.

trapunt-a *f.* quilt; quilted doublet; (mil. hist.) quilted coat worn under armour, gipoun. †**-are** [A I] *tr.* to embroider; to quilt. **-o** *adj.* embroidered, stitched; †faccia **-a**, shrivelled, puckered, face (Dante, *Purg.* XXIV, 20–1); *n.m.* embroidery, quilting; quilt.

†**traripare** *vb.* and derivs. See **straripare**.

†**trarom·pere** *vb.* and derivs. See **interrompere**.

trarre [B 33] *tr.* to draw, to pull, to drag; to pull to; la curiosità lo trasse qui, curiosity brought him here; **—** un sospiro, to heave a sigh; **—** in inganno, to deceive; mi trasse dalla miseria, he rescued me from poverty; to derive, to obtain; non ne posso **—** alcun senso, I can't make any sense of it; (comm.) to draw; **—** a vista, to draw at sight; (text.) **—** la seta, to reel silk; *intr.* (*aux.* essere) to betake oneself; **—** da, to take after, to resemble; *rfl.* (*acc. of prn.* 'si') to draw; mi trassi in disparte, I drew aside; trarsi da un impiccio, to get out of a scrape; (*dat. of prn.* 'si') trarsi le scarpe, to draw off one's shoes; trarsi la voglia di, to satisfy one's desire for; *n.m.* throw; lontano un trar di pietra, a stone's throw away.

†**trarupare** *vb.* and derivs. See **dirupare**.

trasalire [D I] *intr.* (*aux.* avere, essere) to leap, to give a start; to jump about; **—** di gioia, to jump for joy; far **—**, to startle.

†**trasandare** *intr.* to jump along, to proceed by jumps.

trasand-are [A 7] *tr.* to neglect. **-amento** *m.* neglect. **-ato** *part. adj.* neglected; uncared for; slovenly; shabby.

†**trasatt-are** *rfl.* to take possession of, to appropriate. †**-o** *adv. phr.* in **-o**, suddenly, without warning.

trasbord-are [A I C] *tr.* to tranship; to transfer, to change to another train, etc.; (comm.) **—** merci, to break bulk. **-ato** *part. adj.* transhipped; transferred. (**-atore** *m.* **-atrice** *f.*)

trasbordo *m.* transhipment; transfer; (comm.) lascia passare per **—**, transhipment pricking note; certificato di **—**, transhipment shipping bill.

tra-scegliere [B 27] *tr.* to pick out; to choose carefully, to select. **-sceglimento** *m.* picking and choosing; selection. **-scelta** *f.* careful selection. **-scelto** *part. adj.* picked out, selected; choice.

trascend-ere [C I] *tr.* to transcend; to surpass; to rise above; †to rise faster than, to rise past; *intr.* (*aux.* essere) to go too far, to

go to excess; to descend, to stoop (e.g. to disgraceful or comic actions); **—** alle mani, to come to blows. **-entale** *adj.* transcendental. **-entalmente** *adv.* transcendentally. **-entalismo** *m.* transcendentalism. **-ente** *part. adj.* transcendent, surpassing; infinite. **-enza** *f.* transcendence, transcendency. **-imento** *m.* transcendence; excess.

trascin-are [A I S] *tr.* to drag, to drag along; to pull; to trail; to carry; to bear; (chem.) to entrain; (eng.) **—** il motore, to turn over the engine; (fig.) to carry away, to fascinate; **—** la vita, to drag out a wretched existence; *rfl.* to drag oneself along. **-amento** *m.* dragging; pulling along; (cinem.) **-amento** del film, film feed. (**-ato** *part. adj.*) **-atore** *m.* one who drags, pulls, etc.; (chem.) entrainer. **-ìo** *m.* continued dragging, drawing; trailing.

trascolare [A I] *intr.* (*aux.* essere) to trickle through; to drip through a filter.

trascolor-are [A I C] *intr.* (*aux.* essere), *rfl.* to change colour; to grow pale; to blush; *tr.* to change the colour of; to discolour. **-amento** *m.* discoloration; change of colour. **-ato** *part. adj.* discoloured; pale; blushing.

trascorr-ere [C 5] *tr.* to spend, to pass (time); **—** le vacanze in campagna, to spend a holiday in the country; to run over, to run through; to skim (book, pages, etc.); to travel through, to go about, to wander about, to roam (country); to pass over, to leave aside, to omit to mention; **—** i limiti, to overstep the boundary; †to run past; *intr.* (*aux.* essere) to pass (of time), to elapse; sono trascorse due ore da quando sei arrivato, two hours have elapsed since you arrived; (*aux.* avere) to go too far, to run to excess. **-evole** *adj.* fleeting; transient; going too far, immoderate. **-imento** *m.* passage, passing; per **-imento**, in passing, cursorily. (**-itore** *m.* **-itrice** *f.*)

trascorso *part.* of **trascorrere**, q.v.; *adj.* past; passed over; spent; elapsed; *n.m.* fault, wrong-doing; oversight, mistake; piccolo **—** perdonabile, peccadillo.

†**trascotato** *adj.* See **tracotato**.

trascritto *part.* of **trascrivere**, q.v.; *adj.* transcribed, copied; (leg.) recorded; registered. **-scrittore** *m.* transcriber. (**-scrittrice** *f.*)

trascri·vere [C 12] *tr.* to transcribe; to copy; (leg.) to copy from the original; to record; to register; **—** all'ufficio delle ipoteche, to register (a mortgage) with the Land Registry; (comm.) **—** al libro mastro, to post.

trascrizione *f.* transcript(ion), copy; (leg.) registration; **—** di un atto, registration of a deed.

trascur-are [A I] *tr.* to neglect; to disregard; to ignore; to slight; to overlook; to be indifferent (to, about); to be careless about; **—** di fare, to fail to do; **-iamo** qui di elencare..., we shall not bother to enumerate here.... **-abile** *adj.* negligible; (math.) negligible. **-ag·gine** *f.* indifference; negligence. **-anza** *f.* carelessness; thoughtlessness; neglect. **-atag·gine** *f.* carelessness. **-atezza** *f.* negligence; carelessness; slovenliness. **-ato** *part. adj.* neglected; uncared for; careless; negligent; slovenly. **-atamente** *adv.* carelessly. (**-atore** *m.* **-atrice** *f.*)

†**trascutare** *vb.* and derivs. See **trascurare**.

trasduttore *m.* (electr.) transductor, transducer.

trasecol-are [A I S] *intr.* (*aux.* essere, avere) to be amazed, astonished; to be startled; to be shocked; to start, to show surprise. **-amento** *m.* amazement, astonishment. †**-ato** *part. adj.* amazed, astonished; startled.

trasent-ire [D I] *tr.* to hear vaguely; to learn by hearsay; to get wind of; to mis-hear. (**-ito** *part. adj.*)

trasfer-ire [D 2] *tr.* to move, to remove; to transfer; to shift, to change; **—** il proprio domicilio, to change one's address; to translate; (leg.) to assign; to convey; to transfer; **—** la proprietà, to transfer property; (comm.) to transfer; **—** azioni, to transfer shares; **—** per mezzo di girata, to transfer by endorsement; †to move to a distance; *rfl.* to move, to go. **-i·bile** *adj.* transferable; (leg.) non **-ibile**, not negotiable. **-imento** *m.* transfer; removal; transference; change; (leg.) assignment; conveyance; transfer; **-imento** in bianco, blank transfer. **-ito** *part. adj.* transferred, removed. **-ta** *f.* transfer; essere in **-ta**, to be on duty away from home, to be absent on official business; (comm.) indennità di **-ta**, travelling allowance; il giudice è andato in **-ta**, the judge has gone on circuit; travelling expenses; gli pagarono la **-ta**, his travelling expenses were paid; (sport) 'away'; giocare in **-ta**, to play 'away'.

trasfigur-are [A I] *tr.* to transfigure; to transform; *rfl.* to be transformed. -**amento** *m.* transfiguring; transforming. -**ato** *part. adj.* transfigured; transformed; changed. -**azione** *f.* transfiguration; transformation; metamorphosis; a painting representing the Transfiguration of Christ; (eccl.) the Transfiguration and its feast (6 August, commemorating also the victory of the Christians over the Turks in 1456). -**ire** [D 2] *tr., rfl.* to change for the worse. (-**ito** *part. adj.*)

trasfond-ere [C 2] *tr.* to transfuse; to pour from one vessel into another; (fig.) to instill. -**i·bile** *adj.* transfusible. -**imento** *m.* see **trasfusione**.

†**trasforare** *vb.* and derivs. See **traforare**.

trasform-are [A I C] *tr.* to change, to transform; (rugby) to convert; *rfl.* to be transformed; to be changed, to change. -**a·bile** *adj.* transformable; convertible. (-**abilità** *f.*) †-**amento** *m.* changing, change; see **trasformazione**. -**ativo** *adj.* transformative. -**ato** *part. adj.* transformed; changed; *n.m.* one who has been changed or transformed; (lit. hist.) Accademia dei Trasformati, name taken by several learned academies in Renaissance Italy. -**atore** *m.* one who transforms; (electr.) transformer; *pl.* (eccl. hist.) Metamorphists. (-**atrice** *f.*) -**azione** *f.* transformation; conversion; evolution. -**ismo** *m.* (biol.) theory of the transformation and evolution of species (as opposed to the doctrine of special creation, esp. in relation to the origin of Man); (political) transformism. -**ista** *m.* transformist; quick-change artist; trimmer, political weathercock.

trasfus-ione *f.* transfusion; decanting; (med.) — del sangue, blood transfusion. -**o** *part.* of **trasfondere**, q.v.; *adj.* transfused; decanted; poured off; instilled.

†**trasgogliare** *tr.* to strangle; to suffocate.

trasgred-ire [D 2] *tr.* to transgress; to infringe, to break (law, etc.); to violate; *intr.* (*aux.* avere; *prep.* a) to transgress, to commit transgression; — a una legge, to break a law; — a un ordine, to disobey an order. -**imento** *m.* see **trasgressione**. -**itore** *m.* transgressor. (-**itrice** *f.*) -**ito** *part. adj.* transgressed, violated, broken.

trasgress-ione *f.* transgression; infringement; disobedience; (leg.) breach; trespass; — della legge, breach of the law; — d'un contratto, breach of a contract; †digression; †betrayal. -**ore** *m.* transgressor.

traslare [A I] *intr.* (eng.) to travel, to effect a movement of translation; *tr.* to remove from temporary to permanent burial ground.

traslat-o *adj.* transferred; figurative, metaphorical; *n.m.* metaphor; trope. -**amente** *adv.* figuratively, metaphorically. -**are** [A I] and derivs. see **trasportare**. -**ivo** *adj.* (leg.) atti -ivi, deeds of transfer.

traslazione *f.* removal; transfer; — di vocabolo, use of a word in a new sense; (astron.) translation; (leg.) transfer; conveyance; — di dominio, transfer of ownership; demise; (eccl.) translation (of bishop, relics, feast, Holy House of Loreto); †see **traduzione**.

traslitterazione *f.* transliteration.

trasloc-are [A 2] *tr.* to move, to transfer; *intr.* (*aux.* avere) to move, to remove, to change one's address. -**amento** *m.* see **trasloco**. (-**ato** *part. adj.*)

traslo-co *m.* (*pl.* -**chi**) removal; fare —, to move house; furgone per -chi, removal van, pantechnicon.

traslu·cid-o *adj.* (phys.) translucent, pellucid. -**ità** *f.* (phys.) translucence, translucency.

†**trasmare** *adv.* overseas.

trasmeato·rio *adj.* serving as a passage.

trasmesso *part.* of **trasmettere**, q.v.; *adj.* handed on; handed down; transmitted; sent, conveyed; broadcast; (leg.) — in eredità, passed by succession.

trasmett-ere [C 20] *tr.* to pass on, to hand on; to transmit; to send; to convey; — per radio, to broadcast; (leg.; comm.) to convey; to transfer; — la proprietà, to convey ownership; — titoli, to transfer securities; †to transport. -**itore** *m.* transmitter; *adj.* transmitting, sending, ufficio -itore, transmitting office, forwarding office; (naut.) transmitter, telegraph; -itore d'ordine, order transmitter. (-**itrice** *f.*)

trasmigr-are [A I] *intr.* (*aux.* essere, avere) to migrate; to transmigrate; to emigrate. (-**amento** *m.* -**ante** *part. adj.*) -**ato** *part. adj.* migrated, passed; spirito -ato in altro corpo, spirit passed into a different body. -**azione** *f.* transmigration, transformation; metempsychosis.

trasmiss-i·bile *adj.* transmissible; transferable; (finan.) negotiable; titoli -ibili, transferable bonds. (-**ibilità** *f.*) -**ione** *f.* transmission; (leg.) -ione per successione, transmission by descent, passing by inheritance; (eng.) transmission; broadcast(ing); -ione del giornale radio, news broadcast; (naut.) onda di -ione, backwash; albero di -ione, propeller shaft. -**ivo** *adj.* transmitting, transferring. -**ore** *m.* transmitter; (leg.) transferor; *adj.* transmitting. (-**ora** *f.*)

trasmittente *adj.* transmitting; *n.f.* transmitter.

trasmod-are [A I] *intr.* (*aux.* avere) to go to excess; to overstep proper bounds; to exaggerate; -a nel bere, he drinks too much. -**amento** *m.* going to excess. -**anza** *f.* excess. -**ato** *adj.* immoderate; excessive. -**atamente** *adv.* immoderately, excessively; exceedingly. (-**atore** *m.* -**atrice** *f.*)

trasmut-are [A I] *tr.* to transmute, to transform; to change over, to transfer; †to translate; *rfl.* to be transformed; to change. -**a·bile** *adj.* transmutable. -**ato** *part. adj.* transformed; changed. (-**atore** *m.* -**atrice** *f.*) -**azione** *f.* transmutation, change; transformation; transfer, passing; †translation. -**évole** *adj.* transmutable.

†**trasnaturare** *intr., rfl.* to degenerate.

trasogn-are [A 5 c] *intr.* (*aux.* avere) to daydream; to be lost in reverie; mi par di —, I seem to be dreaming, I can hardly believe my eyes. -**amento** *m.* daydreaming; reverie, amazement. -**ato** *part. adj.* dreamy, daydreaming; half-asleep, only half-awake; lost in reverie; amazed, bewildered; mi guardò con occhi -ati, he looked at me with a far-away look in his eyes.

†**trasordinare** *tr.* to disorder.

†**trasoriere** *m.* See **tesoriere**.

traspadano *adj.* relating to the north bank of the Po; *n.m.* the region north of the Po.

traspar-ire [D 3] *intr.* (essere) to shine through, to appear (through) to be transparent; dai suoi occhi -iva la felicità, happiness shone from (in) his eyes; il suo viso non lasciava — alcuna emozione, his face betrayed no emotion; to be apparent, to be obvious. -**ente** *part. adj.* apparent, clear; transparent, diaphanous; un velo -entissimo, a very thin veil; *n.m.* illuminated screen; transparency (picture); back-projection shot; sun-blind. -**enza** *f.* transparence, transparency; mettere a -enze, to place against the light (so that light shines through); obviousness. (-**ito** *part. adj.*)

traspir-are [A I] *intr.* (*aux.* essere) (physiol.) to transpire; (bot.) to transpire; (fig.) (*aux.* essere) to leak out, to become known, to be manifested; -ò che, it transpired that. -**a·bile** *adj.* liable to ooze out. (-**ato** *part. adj.*) -**azione** *f.* (physiol.) transpiration.

†**traspo·nere** *vb.* See **trasporre**.

trasponimento *m.* transposition.

trasporre [B 21] *tr.* to transpose; to transfer, to move; to transplant; (mus.) to transpose.

trasport-are [A I] *tr.* to transport; to convey; to carry; to transfer; lasciarsi — dall'ira, to be carried away by anger, to fly into a rage; il vento -ò la nave sulle coste d'Algeria, the wind drove the ship on to the Algerian coast; la capitale fu -ata da Firenze a Roma, the capital was transferred from Florence to Rome; to translate; (leg.) to transmit; to convey; to assign; to transfer; (mus.) to transpose; *rfl.* to go, to betake oneself; -arsi col pensiero, to go back in thought. -**a·bile** *adj.* transportable, movable; translatable. -**amento** *m.* transport(ation); conveying; transposition. -**ato** *part. adj.* transported, conveyed, transferred; -ato dall'ira, in a (transport of) rage. -**atore** *m.* carrier, transporter; (eng.) conveyor; -atore a nastro, conveyor belt; *adj.* (mus.) strumento -atore, transposing instrument. (-**atrice** *f.*) -**azione** *f.* see **trasporto**.

trasporto *m.* transport; conveyance; carriage; transfer; una nave —, a troopship, a transport; (comm.) — di partite, accounts transfer; transfer of entries; carriage of goods; — marittimo, carriage by sea; franco di —, carriage prepaid; spese di —, carriage, freight charges; contratto di — marittimo, affreightment; (cinem.) — del film, film feed; (typ.) — di dieci righe, carrying over of ten lines to the following page; (mus.) transposition; (art) transfer; -o funebre, funeral; (fig.) rapture; joy; un — d'ira, a transport of rage; zeal; studia con molto —, he studies with great enthusiasm; un — per, a passion for; †apocop. *part.* of **trasportare**.

traspos-itore *m.* (mus.) transposing instrument. -**izione** *f.* transposition; (gramm.) change in word-order, hyperbaton; (mus.) transposition.

tras·posto, -posto *part.* of **trasporre**, q.v.; *adj.* transposed; removed.

trassato *m.* (finan.). See **trattario**, under **tratta**.

trassin-are [A I] *tr.* to mishandle; to ill-treat; — l'usura, to practise usury; †to torment. **-amento** *m.* ill-usage, mishandling. (**-ato** *part. adj.*)

trasso *m.* (miner.) trass.

Trastever-e *pr.n.m.* region of Rome on the west bank of the Tiber. (**-ino** *adj.*)

trastiberino *adj.* relating to the region on the west bank of the Tiber.

trasto *m.* (techn.) plank, etc. to separate blocks of stone etc., when stacked; (naut.) ropemaker's trestle; crossbench of a gondola; †thwart; †fore and aft bridge in a galley.

tra·stol-a *f.* trick; deception. **-ogi·a** *f.* (joc.) (the science of) trickery.

†**trastornare** *vb.* and derivs. See **frastornare**.

trastull-are [A I] *tr.* to amuse; to beguile; *rfl.* (*prep.* di) to amuse oneself; -arsi di uno, to amuse oneself at someone's expense, to make fun of someone; to toy (with); to trifle (with). **-a** *adj.* (in the phrase) pascer di erba -a, to put off with vain promises. **-amento** *m.* amusement, trifling. (**-ato** *part. adj.* amused. **-atore** *m.* **-atrice** *f.*) †**-evole** *adj.* playful. **-ini** *m.pl.* roasted and salted seeds of melon or pumpkin. **-o** *m.* play; toy; game; amusement; sport; fun; (fig.) sport, plaything; compagno di -i, playfellow, playmate; laughing-stock; butt. **-one** *adj., n.m.* 'play-boy', idler (*f.* **-ona**).

trasud-are [A I] *intr.* (*aux.* avere) to sweat, to perspire; (fig.) to sweat; (*aux.* essere) to ooze out; *tr.* to ooze. **-amento** *m.* transuding; sweating; oozing. **-ato** *part. adj.* sweated; *n.m.* (med.) transudate. **-azione** *f.* transudation; sweating; oozing.

trasuman-are [A I] *intr.* (*aux.* essere), *rfl.* to become more than human, to transcend the limit of the mortal existence of humans. (**-ato** *part. adj.* **-azione** *f.*)

trasvers-o *adj.* transverse; oblique; †perverse. **-ale** *adj.* transverse, transversal, crossing; oblique; (anat.) transverse; (leg.) transverse; linea -ale, collateral line of relationship; parenti -ali, collateral kin; *n.f.* (geom.) transversal. **-almente** *adv.* transversely; crosswise.

†**trasviare** *vb.* and derivs. See **traviare**.

trasvol-are [A I] *tr.* to fly across; to traverse in flight; (fig.) to pass over quickly; *intr.* (*aux.* avere; *prep.* su) to fly over; -ò su questo argomento, he passed quickly over this subject. **-ata** *f.* flight; -ata atlantica, flight across the Atlantic. (**-ato** *part. adj.*) **-atore** *m.* flyer; *adj.* flying. (**-atrice** *f.*)

tra tra *onom.* imitative of screeching or strident noise.

tratt·a *f.* pull, tug; drawing of lots, etc., draw; distance, stretch; (rlwy.) section; (comm.) draft; bill; — a data fissa, draft on a fixed date; valore attuale di una —, present value of a bill; — a vista, cash order, sight draft; demand draft; girare una —, to endorse a draft; — domiciliata, addressed draft; — documentale, draft with documents attached; — scaduta, overdue draft; spiccare una —, to draw a bill; cambiale —, bill of exchange; onorare una —, to take up a bill; ho spiccato — su di voi per dieci sterline, I have drawn upon you for ten pounds; interval, period; train; throng; export permit; — dei negri, slave trade; — delle bianche, white slave traffic. **-a·rio** *m.* (finan.) drawee.

tratt-are [A I] *tr.* to treat; to handle; to employ; to work; to ply; to deal with; to deal in; to discuss; to treat (in view of a treaty); — di, to treat as, to address as; lo -ò di ladro, he called him a thief; to have relations with; — il pennello, to handle the brush, i.e. to be a painter; — il ferro, to treat (work on, work in) iron; to provide food; in quella pensione -ano bene, in that boarding-house the food is good; ci -ano a polli, they give us chicken; come ti -a l'inverno?, how are you standing the winter? (how is the winter treating you?); *intr.* (*aux.* avere; *prep.* di) to deal (with); to negotiate; to treat (of); to speak (of); to write (of); to expound; to interpret; *rfl.* to eat, to live; si -a da principe, he lives like a prince; -arsela bene, to do oneself well; *impers.* to be a question of, to have to do with; si -a di una grossa somma di denaro, it is a matter (question) of a large sum of money; di che si -a?, what is the matter?; si -ava del capitano, it was the captain, *or* it turned out to be, who was it but, the captain. **-a·bile** *adj.* tractable; manageable; easy to work; that can be dealt with; (med.) amenable. (**-abilità** *f.*) **-abilmente** *adv.* tractably; †tangibly, palpably. **-amento** *m.* treatment, usage; reception; entertainment; salary, emoluments; allowance of food,

table; ci fu -amento in casa del mio amico, there was a reception at my friend's house; tutto -amento, board and lodging; dinner; supper; treating (to drink, etc.); -amento della persona, personal cleanliness, toilet; (mining) -amento del minerale, ore dressing; (mil.) field allowance; (med.) treatment; therapy; (chem.) treatment, processing; (comm.) treatment; -amento di favore, special consideration; negotiation, treating (with someone). **-a·rio** *m.* (comm.) drawee. **-atino** *m. dim.* little treatise. **-atista** *m.* writer of treatises. **-ativa** *f.* (usu. *pl.*) negotiation(s); sono a -ative per vendere la casa, they are treating for the sale of the house; (comm.) dealings; negotiations; -ative in corso, pending negotiations; entrare in -ative, to enter into negotiations. **-ato** *part. adj.* negotiated; dealt with; received; *n.m.* treatise; tract; treaty; agreement; convention; (leg.) -ato di diritto, law book, legal treatise; -ato di pace, peace treaty; capitoli di un -ato, terms or conditions of a treaty; -ato secreto, secret treaty; -ato internazionale, international treaty; firma del -ato, signature of a treaty; testo del -ato, the contents of a treaty; -ato di Versailles, Treaty of Versailles; -ato commerciale, commercial treaty. **-atore** *m.* negotiator; instigator; treatise writer, exponent (of theories, ideas). (**-atrice** *f.*) **-azione** *f.* treatment (of a subject, doctrine, etc.); (comm.) handling; negotiation; management; -azione degli affari, business dealings; business management; (leg.) -azione della causa, pleading of the case.

tratteggi-are [A 3 c] *tr.* (art) to draw (in outline), to sketch, to delineate; to cross-hatch; (sculp.) to work marble with a claw-tool; (fig.) to describe, to delineate; to describe graphically. **-amento** *m.* outlining; sketching. **-ato** *part. adj.* delineated; linea -ata, a dotted line. **-atura** *f.* (art) outlining; cross-hatching.

tratteggio *m.* outlining; sketching; marks, short strokes; sketch, outline.

tratten-ere [B 32] *tr.* to keep; to hold; to hold back; to restrain; to detain; to keep waiting; to entertain; to amuse; — il respiro, to hold one's breath; — le lagrime, to restrain one's tears; *rfl.* to stay, to remain, to stop; to restrain oneself; si -ne per circa un' ora nel giardino, he stayed in the garden for about an hour; non potei -ermi dal ridere, I couldn't help laughing; †-ersi con alcuno, to live with someone. **-imento** *m.* detention; delay; stay; sojourn; party; 'treat', entertainment; (mil.) guerra di -imento, delaying action, holding war. **-uta** *f.* deduction; -uta sullo stipendio, pay deduction(s), stopped pay. **-uto** *part. adj.* stopped, detained, kept back, kept; nave -uta dai ghiacci, ice-bound ship.

tratt-o *part.* of **trarre**, q.v.; *adj.* led, pulled, drawn; tràttone, except; *n.m.* stroke; line, dash; trait, feature; gesture, manner, bearing; pull, tug; twitch; touch; distance; (provb.) dal detto al fatto c'è un gran —, easier said than done, *or* there's many a slip 'twixt cup and lip; stretch (of road, etc.); mi accompagnò per un bel — (di strada), he accompanied me a good part of the way; reach (of river); space; period of time; moment, instant; difference; reference, relation; passage (in a book); — d'unione, hyphen; (art) disegnato a -i, a larghi -i, drawn in outline; dare il — alla bilancia, to turn the scale; un — di spirito, a witticism, a joke; — geniale, stroke of genius; (naut.) distance, spacing; — di mare, stretch of sea; — di gomena, cable's length (200 metres); (liturg.) Tract; (mus.) Tract (part of the plain-chant proper of the Mass); *adv. phrs.* tratto tratto, di tratto in tratto, now and then, from time to time; tutto d'un —, all at once, suddenly; in un —, in an instant; a -i, from time to time; anzi —, first of all. **-ino** *m.* hyphen.

trattora *f.* (text.) cocoon reeler.

tratt-ore *m.* tractor; — a cingoli, caterpillar tractor; silk-spinner; innkeeper; restaurant-keeper; restaurant. **-ori·a** *f.* restaurant; inn; eating-house. **-rice** *f.* tractor; (motor.) lorry with a trailer; any vehicle which tows another.

trattura *f.* (silkb.) reeling.

tratturo *m.* (geog.) sheep-track.

traudire [D 15] *tr.* to hear only part of (e.g. a conversation); to mishear.

tra·um-a *m.* (med.) trauma; — psichico, psychical trauma, emotional shock. **-a·tico** *adj.* traumatic; †*n.m.* healing ointment. **-atismo** *m.* (med.) traumatism. **-atologi·a** *f* (med.) traumatology.

travagli-are [A 4] *tr.* to trouble, to torment, to harass; to afflict; to shake, to disturb; to overwork (a horse, etc.); *intr.* (*aux.* avere) to toil; to labour; *rfl.* to be troubled, tormented, upset; to take trouble, to strive. **-ato** *part. adj.* tormented; troubled; agitated;

travagli-are (*cont.*)
tempo -ato, rough weather. **-atamẹnte** *adv.* laboriously; distressfully.

trava·gli-o *m.* toil, labour; trouble; pain; travail; distress; torment; uneasiness; aver — di stomaco, to feel sick; (vet.) 'crush' (to restrain a horse during veterinary operations). **-ọso** *adj.* (poet.) toilsome; troublesome; †laborious. **-osamẹnte** *adv.* (poet.) with toil and trouble.

†**travalcare** *intr.* (equestr.) to canter with the hind legs and trot with the fore.

travalic-are [A 2 s] *tr.* to cross; to traverse; (fig.) to pass; — il comando, to disregard the order. (**-ato** *part. adj.*)

travamẹnto *m.* See **trav-ata, -atura.**

travaṣ-are [A 1] *tr.* to pour off; to decant; to transfer from one vessel to another; (cinem., etc.) to dub. **-amẹnto** *m.* pouring off, decanting; -amento sanguigno, bleeding; blood-letting. **-ato** *part. adj.* poured off; decanted. (**-atọre** *m.* **-atrice** *f.*)

travaṣo *m.* pouring off, decanting; transferring; instilling; *Il Travaso delle idee*, title of a humorous weekly paper founded in Rome in 1899.

travat-a *f.* (archit.) beams; framework. **-o** *adj.* shored-up, strengthened with beams. **-ura** *f.* beams; framework; truss.

trav-e *f.* beam; rafter; girder; d'ogni fuscello fare una —, to make a mountain out of a molehill; le vive -i, trees; (mil. hist.) heavy beam supporting a ram. **-ẹtta** *f. dim.* (sewing) whipping to form a raised edge.

traved-ẹre [B 1] *tr.* to catch a glimpse of; to see dimly or indistinctly; *intr.* (*aux.* avere) to be mistaken (in seeing); mi pareva lui, ma forse ho -uto, I thought I saw him, but perhaps I was mistaken. **-imẹnto** *m.* mistake in seeing; illusion. (**-uto** *part. adj.*)

travẹggole *f. pl.* illusion(s), distorted vision; avere le —, to mistake one thing for another.

travers-a *f.* cross-bar; cross-piece; cross-head; (rlwy.) sleeper; barrier across a road; (sport) goal cross-bar (e.g. soccer); (naut.) beam, ship's beam; cross-trees; intermediate frame; battledore; (mil.) traverse; defensive work protecting a flank or echelon; cross-street, side-turning; draw-sheet; band across a woman's dress; (archit.) palisade forming a dam across a stream; (mus.) see under **traverso**; (herald.) bendlet sinister; †crossroad; †untimely event, setback. **-are** [A 1] *tr.* to cross; to place across; -are la via a uno, to stand in someone's way, to bar the way (also fig.); †(naut.) -are l'àncora, to balance a close stowing anchor before securing it horizontally. **-ata** *f.* crossing, sea-crossing, passage. **-ato** *part. adj.* crossed; cavallo ben -ato, heavy draught-horse. **-i·a** *f.* (naut.) wind or gale particularly dangerous to ships entering or secured in a harbour; (fig.) mishap, misfortune, accident, trial; trying experience, annoyance. **-iera** *f.* cross-bar, cross-piece; (naut.) any form of transverse beam or spar, most frequently cross-members of the foretop or gun-director tower. **-iere** *m.* (naut.) apron of a boat, breasthook; small fishing-vessel (Charente); *adj.* (naut.) vento -iere, see **traversia**; (mus.) flauto -iere, see under **traverso**. **-ina** *f. dim.* small cross-bar; railway sleeper. **-ino** *m.* (naut.) securing line, bow wire, stern wire; cat tackle for catting the anchor; stud in a link of chain cable.

travers-o *adj.* transverse, cross; oblique; colpo -o, back-handed blow; una via -a, a side turning; (fig.) per vie -e, by underhand methods; (mus.) flauto -o, flute, concert flute, transverse flute, German flute (also *n.m.*); wrong; untoward; una parola -a, a cross word; adverse; mare -o, rough sea; (Tusc., fam.) broad-shouldered, squarely built; †perverse; *n.m.* breadth; al -o di, abreast of; sul -o, across the breadth; (naut.) beam, direction at right angles to the keel; -o del timone, rudder yoke; -i delle bitte, battledore on the bitts; vento di -o, beam wind; *adv. phrs.* di -o, askew, awry; amiss; wrong; askance; tutto mi va di -o, everything goes contrary with me; (of food) andare a -o, to go down the wrong way. **-ọne** *m.* heavy cross-bar (esp. in cart); (naut.) -oni dei ponti, deck-beams; cross pass (soccer); †*adv.* (in) -one, obliquely, crosswise.

travertino *m.* (miner.) travertine, calc-sinter.

travest-ire [D 1] *tr.* (*prep.* da) to disguise; (fig.) to travesty, burlesque; to misrepresent, to transform; *rfl.* to disguise oneself (as); (of actors) to make up (as). **-imẹnto** *m.* disguise; alteration; travesty, parody; transformation. **-ito** *part. adj.* (*prep.* da) disguised (as); dressed up, made up (as); (fig.) travestied; *Eneide -ita*, title of a parody of the *Aeneid* by G. B. Lalli. (**-itọre** *m.* **-itrice** *f.* **-itura** *f.*)

travèt *m. indecl.* (Piedm.) see **Travetto.**

Travẹtto *pr. n. m.* the name of the protagonist in the comedy *Le miserie di monsù Travèt* by V. Bersezio (1862); (fig.) an impoverished and insignificant clerk.

travi-are [A 4] *tr.* to mislead, to lead astray; to pervert; *intr.* (*aux.* avere) to stray (also fig.); to deviate; *rfl.* to go astray; to stray. **-amẹnto** *m.* straying, going astray; perversion; aberration; depravation; †digression. **-ata** *f.* courtesan, 'lost woman', one who has gone astray; *La Traviata*, title of Verdi's opera founded on Dumas' *La Dame aux Camélias*. **-ato** *part. adj.* misled; perverted. **-atọre** *m.* misleader, corrupter; *adj.* misleading, corruptive. (**-atrice** *f.*)

travicell-a *f.* joist, small beam; rafter. **-o** *m.* joist, small beam; contare i -i, to count the joists, (fig., joc.) to lie in bed, to be lazy; Il Re Travicello, King Log.

†**travirare** *intr.* (naut.) to veer too far; (of ship's side) to curve.

traviṣ-are [A 1] *tr.* to distort, to misrepresent; to alter; to falsify; to disguise; to conceal. (**-amẹnto** *m.*) **-ato** *part. adj.* distorted; misrepresented; (archit.) elaborately carved. †**-o** *m.* mask, disguise.

†**travito** *m.* palisaded enclosure.

travolare [A 1] and derivs. See **trasvolare.**

travol·g-ere [C 5] *tr.* to sweep away, to carry away; to overwhelm; to overcome; to overturn; to upset; to throw into confusion; — gli occhi, to roll one's eyes; to involve. **-ente** *part. adj.* overwhelming. **-imẹnto** *m.* overturning; overthrow; confusion.

†**travoltare** *vb.* and derivs. See **travolgere.**

travolto *part.* of **travolgere,** q.v.; *adj.* overturned; overwhelmed; upside-down; knocked down; †upset; †confused.

trazione *f.* traction; — a vapore, steam traction; (techn.) resistenza alla —, (ultimate) tensile strength.

trẹ *card. num.* three; — volte tanto, three times (thrice) as much; erano in numero di —, they were three (in number); regola del —, rule of three; non bisogna essere — volte buono, one must not be too good; (joc., in reply to the question 'Perchè?') perchè due non fanno —, ask me no questions and I'll tell you no lies; *excl.* e —!, ditto for the third time!; *n.m.* il —, the third (of the month); le —, three o'clock. **-al·beri** *m. indecl.* (naut.) three-master.

trẹbbia *f.* (agric.) threshing-flail; (hist.) ancient instrument of torture; (poet.) threshing.

trebbian-a *f.* (agric.) kind of white grape. **-o** *m.* a white wine of Romagna; also the grape.

trebbi-are [A 4 c] *tr.* (agric.) to thresh; †to torment. (**-ato** *part. adj.*) **-atọre** *m.* thresher. **-atrice** *f.* threshing-box, threshing-machine. **-atura** *f.* threshing; threshing-time; cost of threshing.

†**treb·bio** *m.* harrow.

trẹcci-a[1] *f.* tress; plait, pigtail; — di cipolle, string of onions; plaited covering for wine-flasks; (text.) plaited work; (naut.) sennet, grommet. **-a·io, -ai(u)olo** *m.*, **-a·ia, -ai(u)ola** *f.* straw-plait worker. **-ẹtta** *f. dim.* (archit.) cable moulding. **-uola** *f.* (naut.) log line. **-(u)olo** *m.* plaited cord; *pl.* (paperm.) chain lines (watermark).

trẹccia[2] *f.* team of horses or oxen used to tread corn on the threshing-floor.

†**trẹc·c-olo** *m.*, †**-ola** *f.* costermonger, vendor of foodstuffs.

trecent-o *card. num.* three hundred; *n.m.* il — a.C., the fourth century B.C.; il — d.C., the fourth century A.D.; il —, the fourteenth century. **-ẹsco** *adj.* (*m. pl.* **-ẹschi**) fourteenth-century. **-e·ṣimo, -ẹṣimo** *ord. num., adj.* three-hundredth; *n.m.* three-hundredth (part). **-ista** *m.* fourteenth-century writer or artist; scholar specializing in fourteenth-century studies. **-i·stico** *adj.* (of the) fourteenth century, of the Trecento. **-ocinque** *m. indecl.* (mil.) 305-millimetre gun, one of the heavier calibre much used in the 1914–18 war both on land and at sea.

†**trede·cimo** *ord. num., adj.* See **tredicesimo,** under **tredici.**

trẹdic-i *card. num.* thirteen; *n. f. pl.* le —, one o'clock (in the afternoon). **-enne** *adj.* thirteen years old; *n.m., f.* boy, girl, of thirteen. **-eṣimẹṣe** *m.* extra payment of one month's salary or basic wages which the Italian employees and workmen are entitled to receive on 24 December. (NOTE: this is not to be confused with 'gratifica natalizia', which is a Christmas box and is optional, whereas the 'tredicesimese' is a legal right.) **-e·ṣimo, -ẹṣimo** *adj.* thirteenth; *n.m.* a thirteenth (part). **-ina** *f.* a baker's dozen. **-ista** *m.* (sport) person achieving the maximum score of thirteen points in Italian football pools.

trefo·glie *m.* (herald.) trefoil.

†**trefo·glio** *m.* See **trifoglio**.

trẹfolo *m.* strand of rope; strand of steel cable.

tregenda *f.* horde (of witches, demons, etc.); crowd, host.

†**tregge·a** *f.* sweetmeats, small 'confetti', q.v.

treggi·a *f.* sledge; drag; (joc.) carriage. **-ata** *f.* drag-load. †**-atore** *m.* sledge-driver.

tregua, (Tusc.) **trẹgua** *f.* truce; respite; rest.

trelingag·gio *m.* See **trilingaggio**.

trem-are [A I] *intr.* (*aux.* avere) to tremble; to shake; to quake; to quiver; to shiver; la voce gli -ò per l'emozione, his voice shook with emotion; -ava tutto del freddo, he was shivering all over with cold; †to be afraid. **-acuore** *m.* palpitation; trepidation; anxiety, agitation. **-a·glio** *m.* see **tramaglio**. **-ante** *part. adj.* trembling; shaking, shaky; tremulous; quivering; palpitating; *n.m.pl.* (rel.) Quakers. **-arella** *f.* nervous anxiety; trembling; (slang) blue funk; avere la **-arella**, to be shaking in one's shoes.

tremebọndo *adj.* trembling; full of trepidation; (poet.) quivering, shimmering.

tremend-o *adj.* awful, fearful, to be feared; terrible; tremendous; dreadful. **-amẹnte** *adv.* tremendously, awfully.

trementina *f.* turpentine; (industr.) — artificiale, white spirit.

tremerella *f.* See **tremarella**.

†**tremeste** *m.* (agric.) corn that takes three months to ripen.

tre-mila *card. num.* three thousand. **-millẹsimo** *ord. num., adj., n.m.* three-thousandth.

tremit-o *m.* trembling; shake; quiver; c'era un — nella sua voce, his voice was trembling. **-ìo** *m.* continual trembling.

†**tremo** *m.* See **tremito**.

tre·mola *f.* (ichth.) electric ray, *Torpedo* spp.

tremol-are [A I S] *intr.* (*aux.* avere) to tremble; to quiver; (mus.) to sing (or play) with a quavering voice (or sound); to quaver, to sing (or play) with a vibrato; *tr.* (mus.) — la voce, to make the voice quaver; *n.m.* trembling; shimmering, rippling. **-amẹnto** *m.* trembling; quivering; tremulousness. **-ante** *part. adj.* trembling; quivering; *n.m.* (mus.) tremulant; fine feather made of glass or wire, worn for ornament. **-ìo** *m.* constant trembling, quivering; quaking. **-ite** *f.* (miner.) tremolite, grammatite.

tre·mol-o *adj.* quivering; trembling; tremulous; *n.m.* (mus.) tremolo, vibrato; tremulant. **-ino** *m.* (bot.) aspen *Populus tremula*.

tremọre *m.* trembling; shivering; tremor; shaking; vibration.

trem(u)oto *m.* (pop. for **terremoto**) earthquake; (fig.) whirlwind; commotion. **-ìo** *m.* noise; row; commotion.

tre·mula *f.* (bot.). See **tremolino**, under **tremolo**.

tremuloterapi·a *f.* (med.) vibration treatment.

trenag·gio *m.* (mining) haulage.

trenato *adj.* trained (e.g. of an athlete); in training.

tren-o¹ *f.* (rlwy.) train; — rapido, express; — diretto, through train; — direttissimo, express through train stopping only at main stations; — accelerato, stopping train; — omnibus, slow stopper; — merci, goods train; retinue, train; manner, way (of life); pace, rate; routine; (eng.) — di rulli, roller train; (mil.) artillery train; — blindato, armoured train; (phys.) — di onde, wave train. **-ino** *m.* train of light railway; tram; model train, toy train.

tren-o² *m.* lamentation; threnody; (Bibl.) i Treni, the Lamentations of Jeremiah. **-ode** *f.* (mus.) hired female mourner, threnodist. **-odi·a** *f.* (mus.) threnody, funeral song, epicedium.

trent-a, (Tusc.) **trẹnt-a** *card. num., adj. indecl., n.m.* thirty; i — denari, the thirty pieces of silver; (cards) — e quaranta, 'trente-et-quarante'. **-aduẹ·simo, -aduẹsimo** *ord. num., adj., n.m.* thirty-second. **-amila** *n.m., adj.* thirty thousand. (**-amille·simo, -amillẹsimo**.) **-enne** *adj.* thirty years old. **-en·nio** *m.* period of thirty years. **-ẹsimo, -ẹsimo** *ord. num., adj., n.m.* thirtieth; (liturg.) trental (cf. **trigesimo**). **-ina** *f.* period of about thirty years; ha passato la **-ina**, he is in his thirties. †**-ino** *m.* (Florent.) coin of 30 centesimi. **-ottino** *m.* an old Papal coin equiv. to ten baiocchi. **-uno** *card. num.* thirty-one; sometimes used for the year 1831, a year of revolutionary disturbances in Italy.

Trent-o *pr.n.m.* (geog.) Trent; (hist.) il Concilio di —, the Council of Trent (1545–63). **-ino** *adj.* (geog.) of, relating to Trent(o); *n.m.* (geog.) Trentino.

trepesti·o *m.* (Tusc., pop.) sound of trampling; il — di soldati, the tramp tramp of soldiers marching.

tre·pid-o *adj.* trembling; anxious; timorous; fluttering; con — cuore, with a beating heart. **-amẹnte** *adv.* with fear and trembling; anxiously. **-ante** *part. adj.* anxious; trembling. **-antemẹnte** *adv.*

with trepidation, anxiously. **-anza** *f.* trepidation; flurry, flutter; anxiety. **-are** [A I S] *intr.* (*aux.* avere) to be anxious; to tremble; to be in a flutter; *tr.* to fear. **-ato** *part. adj.* feared; dreaded. **-azione** *f.* see **trepidanza**. **-ẹzza** *f.* anxiety; distress; fear. **-ità** *f.* see **trepidanza**.

†**treppello** *m.* See **drappello**.

†**treppiare** *tr.* to trample.

trep-piede, -piedi, -piè *m. indecl.* tripod; trivet; three-legged stool; (joc.) fare il —, to have triplets.

treppọnte *m.* triangular drill bit.

treppọnti *m. indecl.* (naut.) warship with three rows of guns, on three levels of bridges.

trequarti *m. sing. indecl.* (rugby) three-quarters, back; — centro, centre three-quarter; (surg.; vet.) trecar; †three-quarter length dress or coat.

†**trereme** *f.* See **trireme**.

tresc-a *f.* intrigue, liaison; — amorosa, love-affair; dance accompanied by mime. **-are** [A 2 c] *intr.* (*aux.* avere; *prep.* con) to dance the 'tresca'; to have dealings (with); to have an understanding (with), to have sexual intercourse (with). **-ọne** *m.* (Tusc.) name of a country dance, danced in couples with leaping and hand-clapping.

Trespiano *pr.n.m.* (geog.) name of a district near Florence where there is a cemetery; (fig.) andare a —, to die.

†**tre·spide** *m.* See **trespolo**.

trespino *m.* (bot.) barberry, *Berberis*.

trẹspolo *m.* trestle; support; (sculp.) modelling table; (joc.) rickety old carriage.

tressett-e, -i *m. indecl.* (cards) three sevens (a game in which the holder of three sevens wins).

treto *m.* (bot.) capsule dehiscing by pores.

†**tretticare** *intr.* to totter; to vacillate.

†**treviere** *m.* (naut.) sailmaker in a ship.

trevigian-o *adj.* of, relating to, Treviso; *n.m.* native of Treviso; district round Treviso. (**-a** *f.*)

Treviri *pr.n.f.* (geog.) Trier, Trèves.

trẹvo *m.* (naut.) course, lowest square sail on fore- and mainmasts.

†**trezza** *f.* See **treccia¹**.

tri- *pref.* triple, threefold.

triac-a *f.* (pharm.) theriac; *adj. f.* vite —, vine treated, in planting, with theriac.

triacanto *m.* (bot.) honey locust, *Gleditsia triacanthos*.

tr·iade *f.* (mus.) triad, common chord; (rel.) a triad of deities; (theol.) the Christian Trinity; triad; three inseparable companions.

triale *m.* (gramm.) number indicating three persons, trinal; †group of three.

trian·gol-o *m.* triangle; — rettangolo, right-angled triangle; cappello a —, tricorn, cocked-hat; (electr.) collegamento a —, delta connexion; (astron.) Triangulum; (mus.) triangle; *pl.* (mil. hist.) tridents used as obstacles. **-are** *adj.* triangular; (radio) antenna **-are**, triatic aerial; (eng.) filettature **-are**, V-thread; (anat.) triangularis (both of the mouth and of the sternum); *n.m.* (naut.) gripe, canvas-covered swordmat used for securing a seaboat; — nautico, — di posizione, spherical triangle; (embroidery) cross-stitch. **-arità** *f.* triangularity. **-ato** *adj.* triangular, three-cornered; (herald.) barry indented, point in point. **-azione** *f.* triangulation.

†**tri-are¹** *tr.* to select, to sift. †**-ato** *part. adj.* select choice.

†**triare²** *tr.* (paint.) to mash (colours).

tria·rio *m.* (Rom. hist.) *triarius* (usu. *pl., triarii*).

trias·sico *adj.* (geol.) Triassic.

tri·bad-e *f.* tribade. **-ịsmo** *m.* tribadism, Lesbianism.

†**tribaldare** *tr.* to cheat.

triba·sico *adj.* (chem.) tribasic.

trib·bi-a *f.* flail; threshing. **-are** [A 4] *tr.* to thresh; to break (up); to beat; **-are** un lavoro, to spoil a job. (**-ato** *part. adj.*) **-atura** *f.* threshing. †**-o** *m.* threshing apparatus.

†**tribo** *m.* See **tribù**.

tribol-are [A I S] *tr.* to trouble; to torment; to afflict; to vex, to worry; *intr.* (*aux.* avere) to toil, to labour; to suffer; finir di —, to end one's sufferings, to die; — a camminare, to walk with difficulty. **-amẹnto** *m.* trouble, suffering. **-ato** *part. adj.* afflicted; oppressed; distressed, tormented. **-atamẹnte** *adv.* with toil and trouble. (**-atọre** *m.* **-atrice** *f.*) **-azione** *f.* tribulation, trouble; suffering; torment.

tri·bolo[1] *m.* (bot.) *Tribulus terrestris*; bramble; *pl.* (mil.) see **triangolo**; (herald.) caltrop.

tri·bolo[2] *m.* trouble, trial, suffering, tribulation.

tribordo *m.* (naut.). See **dritta**.

tri·braco *m.* (prosod.) tribrach.

tribù *f. indecl.* tribe; le dodici —, the twelve tribes (of Israel).

†**tribuire** *vb.* and derivs. See **attribuire**.

†**tribulare** *vb.* and derivs. See **tribolare**.

tribule *adj.* of the same tribe.

tribun-a *f.* (Rom. antiq.) tribunal; (archit.) apse; dome; vault; tribune, rostrum, platform; gallery; (organ) loft; — parlamentare, parliament hall (chamber); — riservata alla stampa, press gallery; — delle rappresentanze diplomatiche, distinguished strangers' gallery; stand (e.g. on a football-ground); — centrale, grandstand.

tribunal-e *m.* (leg.) tribunal; court; palazzo del —, law courts; chiamare in —, to summon; — supremo, supreme court; — civile, civil court or court of law; — militare, military court, court martial; — penale, criminal court; — di commercio, Commercial Court; presidente del —, presiding judge, chairman of bench; — falli-mentare, Bankruptcy Court; — d'arbitrato, arbitration tribunal, court of arbitration; — delle acque pubbliche, Court of Public Waters; — per i minorenni, Juvenile Court; sedute del —, law sittings; (pol. hist.) — Speciale, Special Tribunal (set up by the Fascist Regime to dispose of political opponents); (rel.) — di penitenza, confessional; (eccl. hist.) — del Sant'Ufficio, tribunal of the Holy Office; — dell'Aia, Hague Court (of international justice). **-esco** *adj.* (*m.pl.* **-eschi**) (derog.) relating to a court, legal. **-mente** *adv.* in court; legally.

tribun-o *m.* (Rom. hist.) tribune; — della plebe, tribune of the people. **-ato** *m.* (Rom. hist.) tribunate. **-esco** *adj.* (*m.pl.* **-eschi**) of a tribune; superbia -esca, tribune's haughtiness; declamazioni -esche, rantings of a demagogue. **-izio** *adj.* of, relating to, a tribune or a magistrate.

tribut-o *m.* tribute; tax; (fig.) debt; pagare il — alla natura, to pay one's debt to nature, i.e. to die; pagare il — alla patria, to do one's duty to one's country (military service); (euphem.) — mensile, monthly period; (leg.) tax, duty; *adj.* (Rom. hist.) arranged in tribes; comizi -i, *comitia tributa*. **-are** [A 1] *tr.* to render (homage), to pay (tribute), to give, to offer, to bestow. **-ario** *adj.* tributary; fiume -ario, tributary (river); concerning taxation; riforma -aria, tax reform; (finan.) sistema -ario, system of taxation. **-ato** *part. adj.* bestowed, offered, paid, etc.

†**tricamerato** *adj.* three-roomed.

tricche tracche *onomat.* See **tric trac**.

tricheco *m.* (zool.) walrus, *Odobenus rosmarus*.

trichi·asi *f.* (med.) trichiasis.

trich-ina *f.* (zool.) *Trichinella spiralis*, a nematode parasite of man. **-inosco·pio** *adj.* esame -inoscopio, inspection of pork to see whether it is infected with the nematode *T. spiralis*. **-inosi** *f.* (vet.; med.) trichinosis.

triciclo *m.* tricycle.

†**trici·nio**, †**tricinium** *m.* (mus.) tricinium.

trici·pite *adj.* three-headed; *n.m.* (anat.) triceps.

tricli·nio *m.* (class. antiq.) triclinium; †dining-hall, dining-room.

triclino *adj.* (cryst.) triclinic.

tricloroetilene *m.* (chem.) trichlorethylene.

trico-ce·falo *m.* (zool.) *Trichocephalus dispar*, a nematode intestinal parasite of man; (med.) trichocephalus. **-cefalosi** *f.* (med.) tricho-cephaliasis. **-fiti·asi** *f.* (med.) ringworm, trichophytosis. **-fizi·a** *f.* ringworm.

trico·foro *adj.* (zool.) ciliated.

tricologi·a *f.* study of hair, trichology.

tricolor-e *adj.* tricoloured, of three colours; *n.m.* tricolour (esp. the Italian flag). **-ato** *adj.* tricoloured.

tricoma *m.* (med.) trichoma, plica; (bot.) trichome.

tricoptilosi *f.* (med.) trichoptilosis.

tri-corde *adj.* three-stringed. **-cordo** *m.* (mus.) three-stringed pan-doura. **-corne** *adj.* three-horned. **-corno** *m.* three-cornered hat, tricorn (esp. as worn by priests and carabinieri); (geog.) Monte Tricorno, Triglay.

tricosi *f.* (med.) trichosis.

tricotomi·a *f.* trichotomy.

tricresilfosfato *m.* (chem.; motor.) tricresyl phosphate.

tricrom-a *f.* (mus.) demisemiquaver. **-i·a** *f.* three-colour printing.

tric trac *onom.* tap, tap, tapping; clatter; the game of backgammon.

†**tricu·bito** *m.* measure of three cubits.

tricu·spid-e *adj.* tricuspid, three-pointed; (anat.) tricuspid; valvola —, tricuspid valve. **-ale** *adj.* tricuspid. **-ato** *adj.* shaped with three points.

tri·dace *m.* (pharm.) lactucarium; French lactucarium, thridace.

tridimensionale *adj.* (geom.) three-dimensional.

trident-e *m.* trident; hayfork. **-ato** *adj.* armed with a trident; tri-dentate. **-iere**, **-iero** *adj.* epithet of Neptune, armed with a trident.

tridentin-o *adj.* (geog.) of, relating to, Trent or the Trentino; Venezia -a, Trentino and Alto Adige; (hist.) concilio —, Council of Trent.

†**tri·dere** *vb.* and derivs. See **intridere**.

tridimite *f.* (miner.) tridymite.

tri·du-o *m.* period of three days; (liturg.) triduum. **-ano** *adj.* triduan, three-day.

†**tridura** *f.* See **tritura**, under **tritume**.

triedro *m.* (geom.) trihedron; *adj.* trihedral.

†**triegua** *f.* See **tregua**.

†**trie·mito** *m.* See **tremito**.

†**triemo** *m.* fear, timor.

trienn-e *adj.* three years old; of three years' duration. **-ale** *adj.* triennial; of three years; *n.f.* festival or event held every three years.

trien·nio *m.* period of three years.

trier-a *f.* (naut. hist.) trireme. †**-arca**, †**-arco** *m.* trierarch, captain of one or more triremes. **-archi·a** *f.* (Gk. antiq.) trierarchy.

triete·r-ico, **-ide** *adj.* (Gk. antiq.) triennial, trieteric (festival).

†**trieva** *f.* See **tregua**.

tri-fase *adj.* (electr.) three-phase. **-fa·sico** *adj.* (electr.) three-phase.

trifa·uce *adj.* (poet.) three-throated.

†**tri·fera** *f.* an Arabic medical preparation.

tri·fido *adj.* threefold, trifid, divided into three parts; three-pointed; asta trifida di Nettuno, Neptune's trident.

trifillina *f.* (miner.) triphylite, lithiophyllite.

trifillo *m.* (bot.). See **trifoglio**.

trifla·uto *m.* (mus.) triple flute (ancient Greek music).

trifo·gli-o *m.* (bot.) trefoil, name of various clovers, medicks, etc. **-a·io** *m.* clover-field. **-ato** *adj.* trifoliate(d); (herald.) croce -ata, cross botonny, cross trefly.

tri·fol-a *f.* (dial. Piedm.) truffle. **-ato** *adj.* served with truffles.

tri·fora *adj. f.* (archit.) having three lights; *n.f.* window with three lights.

triforc-are [A 2] *rfl.* to form three forks, to divide into three. **-ato** *part. adj.* forming three forks, divided into three. **-uto** *adj.* three-pronged.

trifo·rio *m.* (archit.) triforium.

triforme *adj.* triform, appearing in three different forms.

†**triga** *f.* three-horse chariot.

tri·gam-o *adj.* trigamous, thrice-married; *n.m.* trigamist. **-i·a** *f.* trigamy.

trigant-e, **-o** *m.* (naut. Ven.) backboard transom.

trige·mino *adj.* triple; parto —, birth of triplets; *n.m.* triplet; *adj.* (anat.) trigeminal; *n.m.* (anat.) trigeminal nerve.

†**trigena·rio** *adj.* See **trentenne**.

trige·sim-a *f.* (liturg.) month's mind (requiem mass thirty days after death or burial). **-o** *ord. num.*, *adj.* thirtieth; (liturg.) trental.

†**trig·ghia** *f.* (ichth.). See **triglia**.

trigla *f.* See **cappone**.

tri·glia *f.* (ichth.) red mullet; — di scoglio, — maggiore, *Mullus surmuletus*; — di fango, — minore, — d'alga, *M. barbatus*; far l'occhio di — a, to make sheep's eyes at.

tri·glifo *m.* (archit.) triglyph.

triglo·chide *f.* (ichth.) *Carcharias ferox*, a kind of shark.

tri·gone *m.* (ichth.) sting ray; — nero, — bruno, *Dasyatis brucco*; — altavela, *Pteroplatea altavela*.

tri·gon-o *adj.* trigonal; *n.m.* (astrol.) trigon; trine; (anat.) trigone; (mus.) trigonon (ancient Greek music). **-ocefali·a** *f.* (anat.) trigonocephaly. **-ocefa·lico** *adj.* trigonocephalic. **-ometri·a** *f.* (math.) trigonometry. **-ome·trico** *adj.* trigonometrical. (**-ome-tricamente** *adv.*)

trila·tera *f.* (zool.) *Donax trunculus*, an edible marine bivalve.

tri-la·tero, **-laterale** *adj.* trilateral. **-li·neo**, **-lineare** *adj.* trilinear.

trilingag·gio *m.* (naut.) lashings; action preventers; — di battaglia, — di combattimento, overhead nettings.

trilingue *adj.* trilingual.

trilione *m.* trillion; (Amer. usage) a million millions.

trill-o *m.* trill; ringing (e.g. of electric bell); (mus.) trill, shake. **-are** [A 1] *intr.* (*aux.* avere) to trill; to vibrate, to shake. (**-ato** *part. adj.*) **-eggiare** [A 3 c] *intr.* (*aux.* avere) to trill. **-io** *m.* ringing.

trilobite *f.* (palaeont.) trilobite.

trilobo *m.* (archit.) trefoil; *adj.* (archit.) trefoiled, three-lobed.

trilogia *f.* trilogy.

trilustre *adj.* fifteen years old; fifteen-year-old.

Trimalcione *pr.n.m.* (Lat. lit.) Trimalchio (in Petronius); (fig.) glutton, gormandizer.

trimembre *adj.* three-limbed.

trimestr-e *m.* quarter, three months; (school) term; quarter's rent, salary, etc. **-ale** *adj.* quarterly. **-almente** *adv.* every quarter.

tri·metro *m.* (Gk. prosod.) trimeter (iambic or trochaic).

trimotore *adj.* (aeron.) three-engined; *n.m.* three-engined aircraft.

trimpell-are [A 1] *intr.* (*aux.* avere) to stagger; to strum hesitatingly (on guitar, etc.); to dally; — nel manico, to play fast and loose. **-ino** *m.* one who hums and haws. **-io** *m.* continual or frequent strumming.

Trimurti *pr.n.f.* (Ind. rel.) the Trimurti, the Hindu Triad of Brahma, Vishnu and Siva.

trin-a *f.* lace. **-a·ia** *f.* lace-maker; vendor of lace. **-ame** *m.* lace-work, lace-goods. **-are** [A 1] *tr.* to trim with lace. **-ato** *part. adj.* trimmed with lace; lacelike; carta **-ata**, paper-lace, paper cut out to resemble lace. **-ellatore** *m.* device attached to a sewing-machine for sewing on lace or other trimming.

Trina·cri-a *pr.n.f.* (poet.) Sicily. **-o** *adj.* (poet.) Sicilian.

trinamente *adv.* See under **trino**.

trinato[1] *adj.* See under **trina**.

trinato[2] *adj.* See under **trino**.

trinca *f.* (naut.) lashing (hemp, wire or chain).

trinc-are[1] [A 2] *tr.* to lash, to secure, to haul taut; **-a!**, belay! **-arino** *m.* (naut.) longitudinal of a deck corresponding to or forming part of the scuppers. **-ata** *f.* (naut.) act of lashing. **-atura** *f.* (naut.) lashing; effect of lashing; the point where a lashing is passed; †breeching, guntackle, stormlashing.

trinc-are[2] [A 2] *tr.* to drink greedily; to toss off; to swill. **-ata** *f.* draught, deep drink. **-ato** *part. adj.* drunk; (fig.) deep, crafty. **-atore** *m.* drinker. (**-atrice** *f.*) **-one** *m.* heavy drinker. (**-ona** *f.*)

trincarello *m.* (techn.) filter, strainer.

trinc-era, -e·a *f.* (mil.) trench; guerra di —, trench warfare; (rlwy.) cutting. **-eramento** *m.* trenching; entrenchment. **-erare** [A 1] *tr.* to entrench; (mil.) to entrench; *rfl.* to entrench oneself; (fig.) to take refuge. **-erato** *part. adj.* entrenched, fortified. **-erone** *m.* (mil.) long, deep trench.

trincett-o *m.* (shoem.) leather-knife. **-ata** *f.* cut with a leather-knife.

trinchett-o *m.* (naut.) foremast; †foresail; muro il —!, aft foresheet! **-ina** *f.* (naut.) jib; **-ina** di fortuna, running jib. †**-ino** *m.* (naut.) forecastle of a galley.

trinci-are [A 3] *tr.* to cut up, to carve; to mince, to hash; — la paglia, to cut chaff; — l'aria, to beat the air; — giudizi, to express hasty judgements; — capriole, to cut capers; — reverenze, to make a series of bows or nods; — i panni addosso a uno, to speak ill of someone. **-aforaggi** *m. indecl.* (agric.) fodder-cutter. **-afo·glia** *m.* see **trinciaradici**. **-amento** *m.* cutting up; carving. **-ante** *part. adj.* cutting, sharp; *n.m.* carving-knife; carver. **-apa·glia** *m. indecl.* reaping-hook; hay-cutter. **-aradici, -arape** *m. indecl.* turnip-cutter, slicing-knife. **-ata** *f.* cut; slice. **-ato** *part. adj.* cut up; sliced; minced; foraggio **-ato**, chaff; (bot.) truncate; (archit.) closely carved (of ornament); hatched; (herald.) per bend; *n.m.* cut tobacco (for the pipe). **-atoio** *m.* (agric.) cutting-shed (where turnips, etc. are cut up). **-atore** *m.* carver; scandalmonger. **-atrice** *f.* chaff-cutter (machine); carver; scandalmonger. **-atura** *f.* carving; chaff-cutting; cutting up, slicing, etc.; slices; chaff.

trinciera *f.* See **trincera**.

trin·cio *m.* cut; tear.

trinellatore *m.* See under **trina**.

Tri·nita *pr.n.m.* (Florent.) il ponte di Santa Trinita, Trinity bridge; †see **trinità**.

trini·tà *f.* (theol.) Trinity. NOTE: the old alternative pronunciation **tri·nita** survives here and there in Tuscany, and is obligatory for the church and bridge in Florence; Santissima —, Trinity Sunday; (geog.) la —, Trinidad. **-ta·rio** *adj., n.m.* (eccl.) Trinitarian; (priest) of the order for the redemption of captives; †(eccl. hist.) (person) holding heretical views on the Trinity.

trinitro-fenolo *m.* (chem.) trinitrophenol. **-toluene** *m.* (chem.) trinitrotoluene, T.N.T.

trin-o *adj.* triple; (theol.) trine, threefold; Dio Uno e —, God who is One and Three, the Triune God; (astrol.) trine; *n.m.* (numism.) coin of Perugia, fifteenth century, bearing the gryphon, equiv. to 2 denari. **-amente** *adv.* trebly. **-ato** *adj.* (naut.) having three guns.

trino·mi-o *m.* (math.) trinomial. **-ale** *adj.* (math.) trinomial.

trinu·zia *f.* woman who has been married three times.

trio *m.* (mus.) trio (in both senses, viz. three-part composition or contrasting minuet).

triocco *m.* (†-a *f.*) feasting, junketing.

tri·odo *m.* (radio) triode.

trionf-o *m.* triumph; victory; glory; portare in —, to bear in triumph, to carry shoulder-high; (Rom. hist.) triumph; — da tavola, centre-stand for a table, epergne; (cards) trump. **-ale** *adj.* triumphal; magnificent; (Rom. hist.) uomo **-ale**, one who has celebrated a triumph. (**-almente** *adv.*) **-ante** *part. adj.* triumphant; victorious; successful; exultant; (theol.) chiesa **-ante**, Church Triumphant; *n.m.* blessed (spirit). **-are** [A 1 c] *intr.* (*aux.* avere) to triumph; to be victorious; to be triumphant; to be blessed (in heaven); **-are** di, to triumph over, to exult; to enjoy oneself (e.g. at table); to receive honours; (of colours) to stand out, to be striking; (of countryside) to be fertile and prosperous; (of foodstuffs) to soar in price; *tr.* to overcome; to dominate. **-ato** *part. adj.* conquered, overcome, subjugated; battaglie **-ate**, victorious battles, battles won. **-atore** *m.* triumphant hero, general, etc.; happy winner. (**-atrice** *f.*)

Trioni *pr.n.m.pl.* (astron.) Triones, the Great Bear, Plough, King Charles's Wain.

trios·sido *m.* (chem.) trioxide.

triotto *m.* (ichth.) *Leuciscus rutilus*, a freshwater fish similar to the dace.

tripalmitina *f.* (chem.) tripalmitin, glycerol tripalmitate.

tripanosom-a *m.* (biol.) trypanosome. **-i·asi** *f.* (med.) trypanosomiasis, sleeping-sickness.

tripart-ire [D 1] *tr.* to divide into three. **-ito** *part. adj.* tripartite; (pol. hist.) Il Patto **-ito**, the Alliance between Germany, Italy and Japan during the Second World War. (**-itamente** *adv.*) **-izione** *f.* tripartition, division into three parts; (math.) division by three.

triplano *m.* triplane.

tri·plic-e *adj.* threefold, treble, triple; triplicate; (hist.) la — Alleanza, the Triple Alliance between Germany, Austria and Italy (1882–1915). **-emente** *adv.* trebly. **-ista** *m.* supporter of the Triple Alliance. **-ità** *f.* triplicity.

tripl-o *adj.* triple; con forze **-e**, with threefold strength; *n.m.* three times as much; nove è il — di tre, nine is three times, the square of, three. **-a** *f.* (mus.) triple time, triple measure. **-etta** *f.*, **-ettina.** *f.* (mus.) three-eight time; **-etta** quadrupla, three-four time. **-icare** [A 2 s] *tr.* to treble; to triplicate. (**-icato** *part. adj.*)

tri·pod-e *m.* tripod. **-i·a** *f.* (class. prosod.) tripody.

tripolare *adj.* (electr.) three-pole.

Tri·pol-i[1], †-o *pr.n.m.* (geog.) Tripoli (N. Africa); — di Soria, Tripoli (Syria). **-ita·nia** *pr.n.f.* (geog.) Tripolitania. **-itano** *adj.* Tripolitan.

tri·poli[2] *m. indecl.* (miner.) tripoli, infusorial earth, kieselguhr.

tri·polo *m.* (miner.). See **tripoli[2]**.

tripp-a *f.* tripe; paunch, fat belly; (fam.) a — innanzi, haughtily, with exaggerated gravity; (tan.) pelt. **-a·io, -aiuolo, -aro** *m.* tripe-seller; cats' meat man. **-are** [A 1] *tr.* (cul.) to cook and serve like tripe (with cheese and butter). (**-ato** *part. adj.*) **-eri·a** *f.* tripe-shop. **-etta** *f. dim.* see **pancetta**; dried cod or stock-fish; a paunchy person.

tripsina *f.* (chem.) trypsin.

tripu·di-o *m.* exaltation; jumping for joy; jubilation; (Rom. antiq.) *tripudium*. **-amento** *m.* exultation; jumping for joy; revelry. **-are** [A 1] *intr.* (*aux.* avere) to exult; to jump for joy; to kick up one's heels. (**-atore** *m.* **-atrice** *f.*)

triregno *m.* (eccl.) papal tiara, *triregnum*.

trireme *f.* trireme.

tris *m. indecl.* (cards) three of a kind (at poker).

Trisacramentari *pr.n.m.pl.* (eccl. hist.) Trisacramentarians.

trisa·gio *adj.* (rel.) thrice holy; *n.m.* (liturg.) Trisagion.

tris-arca·volo *m.* great-great-great-grandfather; remote ancestor. **-a·volo** *m.* great-great-grandfather; ancestor. (**-a·vola** *f.*)

trisezione *f.* (math.) trisection.

trisil·l-abo *m.* trisyllable. **-a·bico** *adj.* trisyllabic.

triṣm-o *m.*, **-a** *m.* (med.) trismus.

Trissottino *pr.n.m.* Trissotin, in Molière's *Femmes savantes*.

Tristano *pr.n.m.* Tristram, Tristan; — **e Isotta**, Tristram and Iseult, Tristan and Isolde.

trist-e *adj.* sad, sorrowful, grieved, woeful; dreary, gloomy, dismal; bleak, depressing. **-emẹnte** *adv.* sadly, sorrowfully. **-ẹzza** *f.* sadness, sorrow; gloominess.

trist-o *adj.* bad; wicked, evil; sorry, wretched; mean; deplorable; gloomy; **fare una -a figura**, to cut a poor figure; *n.m.* wicked person, rogue; wickedness; roguery. †**-ore** *m.* sadness, melancholy. **-amẹnte** *adv.* wickedly; wretchedly. **-i·zia** *f.* wickedness; wretchedness; wicked deed.

trisul·co *adj.* (*m.pl.* **-chi**) three-pointed; forked; **lingua -ca**, forked tongue (of serpents); **folgori -che**, forked lightning.

trit-are [A I] *tr.* to mince, to hash; to pound; to rub down; (fig., art) to treat in too much detail, to over-refine; *rfl.* to be broken, to break, into little pieces; to be ground down. **-acarne** *m. indecl.* mincer. **-amẹnto** *m.* mincing; pounding; threshing, breaking down; (in the stomach) digestion. **-ato** *part. adj.* minced, hashed; pounded; **carne -ata**, minced meat. (**-atọre** *m.* **-atrice** *f.*) **-atura** *f.* mincing; hashing; grinding. **-atutto** *m. indecl.* mincer for general kitchen use.

trite-iṣmo *m.* (theol.) Tritheism. **-ista** *m.* (theol.) Tritheist.

tritell-o *m.* fine bran, pollard; small grain; pea (of coal). **-ọso** *adj.* containing bran.

†**tri·tico** *m.* corn; frumenty.

triti-onato *m.* (chem.) trithionate. **-o·nico** *adj.* (chem.) trithionic.

trit-o *adj.* minced, hashed; pounded; beaten; rubbed down; fine; **terra -a**, dust; **paglia -a**, chaff; (fig.) trite, commonplace; mincing, finicking; **vesti -e**, worn clothing; **via -a**, beaten track; **notizie -e**, stale news; **cose -e e ritrite**, things everybody knows; (art) over-refined, too detailed. **-amẹnte** *adv.* minutely, in great detail. **-ino** *adj.* finely powdered; (miner.) **-ino di carbone**, pea coal.

tri·tol-o¹ *m.* (Tusc., fam.) little bit; scrap; crumb; **non sapere —**, not to know anything. **-are** [A I s] *tr.* to crush; to pound.

trito·lo² *m.* (chem.) T.N.T., trinitrotoluene.

Tritọne *pr.n.m.* (myth.) Triton; **Fontana del —**, the Triton Fountain in Rome, Piazza Barberini; (zool.) *Tritonium nodiferum*, a large marine gastropod, whose shell can be blown like a trumpet, and is used for calling sheep and cattle; newt; **— comune, — cristato**, *Triturus cristatus*; **— italiano**, *T. italicus*; **— punteggiato**, *T. vulgaris*; **— alpestre**, *T. alpestris*.

tri·tono *m.* (mus.) tritone.

tritteri·gio *m.* (ichth.) *Tripterygium caponero*.

trit·tico *m.* (paint.) triptych.

trittọngo *m.* triphthong.

trit-ume *m.* (usu. *pl.*) bits, scraps; crumbs; (art) excessive detail and ornament. **-ura** *f.* mincing; reducing to little bits; scraps; finicking details. **-ura·bile** *adj.* susceptible to trituration. **-uramẹnto** *m.* trituration. **-urare** [A I] *tr.* to triturate, to pound, to grind to fine particles. **-urazione** *f.* trituration. **-uzzare** [A I] *tr.* to triturate, to grind very fine.

trium·vir-o *m.* (Rom. hist., fig.) triumvir. **-ale** *adj.* triumviral. **-ato** *m.* triumvirate (in Rom. hist., used especially of the groupings of 60 B.C. and 43 B.C.; (mod. Ital. hist.) triumvirate of Mazzini, Saffi e Armellini in 1849); (fig.) any influential group of three people.

trivalente *adj.* (chem.) trivalent.

trivell-a *f.* auger; borer; drill. **-are** [A I] *tr.* to bore; to drill; (fig.) **un pensiero mi -a il cervello**, a thought keeps nagging at my mind; *intr.* (*aux.* avere) (of water) to swirl, to eddy. **-ato** *part. adj.* **stoccate -ate**, piercing thrusts. **-atura** *f.* boring, drilling; shavings, sawdust, etc. (from boring). **-azione** *f.* boring, drilling; (mining) **scarpa di -azione**, spudding shoe. **-o** *m.* brace and bit; gimlet; small drill. †**-otta** *f.* (naut.) lighter; pile lighter; screw lighter.

Tri·via *pr.n.f.* (myth.) Trivia, Hecate or Diana as goddess of crossroads.

tri·vi-o¹ *m.* place where three roads meet; low quarter; **gente da —**, low people; **modi da —**, coarse, vulgar manners. **-ale** *adj.* low, vulgar, coarse; commonplace, humdrum. (**-almẹnte** *adv.*) **-alità** *f.* vulgarity, coarseness; coarse expression.

tri·vio² *m.* (hist.) trivium.

troca·ico *adj.* trochaic.

trocantere *m.* (anat.) trochanter.

†**troc·cola** *f.* clapper.

troche·o *m.* (prosod.) trochee; †(mil.) lever.

tro·chilo *m.* (archit.) trochilus or scotia (moulding).

troc·isco *m.* (pharm.) lozenge.

troc·le-a *f.* (anat.) trochlea; †pulley-frame. **-are** *adj.* (anat.) trochlear; *n.m.pl.* **i -ari**, the trochlear nerves.

troc-o *m.* (zool.) top shell, *Trochus* and related genera. **-ocefali·a** *f.* (med.) trococephalia, trococephaly. **-ocefa·lico** *adj.* (med.) trococephalic.

trofe·o *m.* trophy; (archit.) column, arch, etc. adorned with trophies of victory; (mil.) trophies of war, booty; (fig.) victory; fruits of victory.

tro·f-ico *adj.* (biol.) trophic. **-iṣmo** *m.* (med.) trophism, nutrition. **-ologi·a** *f.* (med.) trophology, the science of nutrition. **-oneuroṣi** *f.* (med.) trophoneurosis. **-oneuro·tico** *adj.* (med.) trophoneurotic. **-onu·cleo** *m.* (biol.) trophonucleus. **-oterapi·a** *f.* (med.) trophotherapy, dietetics. **-otropiṣmo** *m.* (med.) trophotropism, trophotaxis.

trofoblasto *m.* (med.) trophoblast.

†**tro·gli-o** *m.* stutterer. †**-are** *intr.* to stutter.

troglod-ita *m.* troglodyte, cave-dweller; (fig.) uncouth, primitive person; (zool.) gorilla. **-i·tico** *adj.* troglodytic(al). (**-itiṣmo** *m.*)

tro·gol-o *m.* trough, water-trough, feeding-trough; (ichth.) **— d'incubazione**, a trough used for keeping fish eggs after artificial fertilization; (techn.) trough, vat. **-ẹtto** *m. dim.* pig-trough. **-ọne** *m.* filthy person (also fig.). (**-ọna** *f.*)

tro·i-a¹ *f.* sow; (vulg.) prostitute. **-a·io** *m.* (Tusc., pop.) filth; filthy place. **-ata** *f.* filth; filthy behaviour; bad work; †ribald company. **-eri·a** see **troiata**. **-ẹtta** *f. dim.* young sow. **-ẹtto** *m. dim.* tub. **-ọne** *m. augm.* filthy person; swine, pig. **-ume** *m.* filth.

Tro·i-a² *n.m. adj.* Troy. **-ano** *adj.* Trojan; *n.m.* Trojan; (colloq.) **al tempo dei Troiani**, in the remote past, long, long ago; (vet.) horse with long ears which it twitches constantly. (**-ana** *f.*)

tro·ica, tro·ika *f.* troika, Russian carriage or sleigh, drawn by three horses abreast.

Tro·ilo *pr.n.m.* Troilus.

trolle, trolley *m. indecl.* (electr. eng.) trolley, current collector.

tromb-a *f.* (mus.) trumpet; **— da tirarsi**, slide-trumpet; (mil.) bugle; trumpet; gunport; embrasure; rocket tube; triton's horn (shell); (motor.) horn; **— acustica**, ear trumpet; (elephant's) trunk; pump siphon (for drawing off wine); water-spout; the leg of a boot; **— delle scale**, well of the staircase; (fig.) public auction; spy; (anat.) **-e falloppiane**, (anat.) Fallopian tubes; (meteor.) tornado; (naut.) **— marina**, waterspout; (mus.) marine trumpet; **suonare la —**, to play the trumpet, (joc.) to snore, etc.; (fig.) **la — epica**, epic poetry; **— a vento**, windsail, windcowl; **— di sentina**, pump, bilge pump; **— d'incendio**, fire pump; **— da mano**, hand pump, cask pump; **— ingorgata, — ingranata, — ostruïta**, choked pump; **avviare la —, caricare la —**, to prime the pump; **alla —!, man the pump!**. **-a·io** *m.* plumber. **-are** [A I c] *tr.* to draw off wine with a siphon; (pop.) to reject (a candidate); †to sell by auction. **-ata** *f.* trumpeting, boasting; water drawn up by a water-spout. **-ato** *part. adj.* (pop.) not elected; failed. †**-atore** *m.* trumpeter. **-atura** *f.* drawing off wine; (pop.) rejection, failure. **-ẹtta** *f.* (mus.) small trumpet, trump; bugle; toy trumpet; *m. indecl.* bugler, trumpeter; (ichth.) **pesce -etta**, trumpet fish, *Centriscus scolopax*; *pl.* (cul.) form of 'pasta'. **-ettare** [A I c] *tr.*, *intr.* (*aux.* avere) to trumpet; to boast. (**-ettata** *f.*) **-ettato** *part. adj.* trumpeted, noised abroad; sold by auction. **-ettatọre** *m.* trumpeter. (**-ettatrice** *f.*) **-ettiere** *m.* (mus.; mil.) bugler; (poet.) trumpeter; (orn.) trumpeter bullfinch, *Bucanetes githagineus*. **-ettina** *f. dim.* little toy trumpet. **-ettino** *m. dim.* (mil.) boy trumpeter. **-ẹtto** *m.* (mil.) bugle; bugler. **-iere** *m.* plumber. **-ino** *m.* (naut.) safety valve steam-pipe; silent exhaust; *pl.* (cul.) sort of 'pasta' made with honey, and fried. **-o** *m.* (vet.) haematoma of neck. **-oncino** *m.* (mus.) primitive organ reed-stop; *pl.* (bot.) Lady tulip, *Tulipa clusiana*. **-ọne** *m.* (mus.) trombone; (bot.) daffodil, name of *Narcissus pseudo-narcissus* and of cultivated tulips; blunderbuss; *pl.* large riding-boots.

trombina *f.* (physiol.) plasmase.

trọmbo¹ *m.* See under **tromba**.

trọmb-o² *m.* (med.) blood clot. **-oṣi** *f.* (med.) thrombosis.

trompẹto *m.* (ichth.) tunny.

trona *m.* (miner.) trona.

tronc-are [A2c] *tr.* to cut off; to truncate; to crop, to break off, to interrupt, to cut short; to break, to break in two; to clip (a word); to weaken. **-a·bile** *adj.* that can be truncated. **-amento** *m.* cutting off, cutting short; interruption; (*gramm.*) apocope; elision. **-ativo** *adj.* cutting, serving to cut off; fragile, breakable. **-ato** *part. adj.* cut off; truncated; amputated; unfinished, imperfect; (*herald.*) per fess; couped in chief; (*herald.*) -ato in lambello, dovetailed; -ato, -ato semipartito, per fess, the base per pale. (**-atore** *m.*) **-atrice** *f.* (*eng.*) cropper. **-atura** *f.* truncation; cutting (off); (*gramm.*) apocope; (*eng.*) cropping; (*foundry*) sprueing.

tron-chese *m.* cutting nippers; — a molla con taglio laterale, netting nippers. **-chesino** *m.* cutting pliers, nippers. **-chetto** *m.* wire cutters, nippers; (*shoem.*) Derby boot. **-chevole** *adj.* that can be cut short.

tron-co (*m.pl.* **-chi**) apocop. *part.* of **troncare**, q.v.; *adj.* mutilated; (*geom.*) truncated; (*prosod., etc.*) parola -ca, word accented on the last syllable; verso —, line (of verse) ending in a 'parola tronca'; (*naut.*) alberi -chi, lowermasts (after topmasts have been housed); *n.m.* trunk; (*fig.*) unfinished condition; arrestarsi in —, to stop short; lasciare in —, to leave (something) unfinished; esser licenziato in —, to be summarily dismissed; (*rlwy.*) trunk line; lineage, stock; (*sculp.*) statue without arms or legs, torso; (*archit.*) — del piedistallo, dado of the pedestal; (*math.*) truncated figure, frustum; — di cono, truncated cone; (*vet.*) — della coda, root of the tail of a horse; (*naut.*) mast; trunks (ventilation pipes). **-cone** *m. augm.* stump; trunk (of the body); colonna a -cone, broken, truncated, column.

troneggiare [A3c] *intr.* (*aux.* avere) to sit (as) on a throne; to reign supreme; to tower; to stand out, to dominate.

tronfi-are [A4c] *intr.* (*aux.* avere) (of a peacock, etc.) to spread its feathers; to strut; (of pigeons) to pout.

tronfi-o *adj.* pompous (of voice); puffed up, conceited; gonfio e —, as proud as a peacock. **-ezza** *f.* arrogance; conceit. **-one** *m.* conceited person; one who struts proudly.

trono[1] *m.* throne; salire al —, to ascend the throne; *pl.* (*theol.*) Thrones.

†**tron-o**[2] *m.* see **tuono**. †**-iera** *f.* (*mil.*) gun-post, embrasure for a gun. †**trope·a** *f.* whirlwind with hail.

trope·olo *m.* (*bot.*) garden nasturtium, *Tropaeolum majus*.

tro·pic-o *m.* (*astron.*) tropic; solstitial point; (*geog.*) tropic; *adj.* tropical. **-ale** *adj.* tropical.

trop-o *m.* (*rhet.*) trope; metaphor; (*mus.*) trope: (i) transposed mode in ancient Greek music, (ii) words inserted into a plain-chant melisma, (iii) stylized cadence in Gregorian music; (*theatr. hist.*) trope. **-a·rio** (*mus.*) troparion, troper. **-ismo** *m.* tropism. **-ologi·a** *f.* tropology; parable. **-olo·gico** *adj.* tropological; moral. (**-ologicamente** *adv.*) **-opa·usa** *f.* (*meteor.*) tropopause. **-osfera** *f.* (*meteor.*) troposphere.

troppo *adv.* too; too much; much too much, far too much; pur —, unfortunately, only too well; †much, very; *adj., prn.* too much; *pl.* too many; quattro sono troppi, four are too many; togliere il — e il vano, to take away all that is superfluous or useless; *adj. phr.* di —, superfluous.

troppopieno *m. indecl.* overflow.

†**tro·scia** *f.* pit for curing hides; dirty pool; channel left by water.

trot-a *f.* (*ichth.*) trout. (**-ella** *f. dim.*) **-ino** *m.* (*vet.*) strawberry roan.

trott-are [A1] *intr.* (*aux.* avere) (*equestr.*) to trot; (*fig.*) to trot along, to walk fast. **-a·bile** *adj.* (of a road) suitable for trotting. **-apiano** *m.* slowcoach. **-ata** *f.* (*equestr.*) trot; (*fig.*) quick walking. (**-atore** *m.* **-atora** *f.* **-atrice** *f.*) **-erellare** [A1] *intr.* (*aux.* avere) to trot along, to jog along; (of child) to toddle. **-erello** *m.* jog-trot.

trotto *m.* (*equestr.*) trot; — all'inglese, rising to the trot; scuola di —, riding-school; (*fig.*) è stato il — dell'asino, he soon got tired.

trot·tol-a *f.* top, spinning top; whip-top; (*zool.*) top shell, *Trochus* spp.; (*fig., fam.*) girare come una —, to 'buzz round', to be very busy; (*joc.*) lively little girl. **-are** [A1s] *intr.* (*aux.* avere) to spin, to whirl round; to toddle about. **-ino** *m.* toddler, small child.

trov-are [A1] *tr.* to find; to find out; to discover; — il tempo, to find time, to spare the time; to catch; se ti -o a far questo un'altra volta, if I catch you doing that again; to think, to consider, to feel; il cliente -a che non è il caso di..., the customer thinks there is no point in...; — da ridire su qualche cosa, to find fault with something; — marito, to get a husband; — un posto, to get a job; andare a — qualcuno, to go and see someone; ogni sabato mi veniva a —, he used to come and see me every Saturday; to

run into, to encounter, to meet with; ha -ato un ostacolo, he met with an obstacle; to strike; ha -ato la morte, he met his death; — pane per i propri denti, to come to grips with a task worthy of one's powers; (*comm.*) — il costo, to cost; *rfl.* to be, to feel; to happen to be; -arsi in buone condizioni finanziarie, to be well off; -arsi in cattive acque, to be badly off; -arsi come a casa propria, to feel at home; mi -ai nel mezzo di una folla, I found myself in the middle of a crowd; to be situated. **-a·bile** *adj.* discoverable. **-adore** *m.* (*lit. hist.*) troubadour. **-ado·rico** *adj.* relating to, of, the troubadours; (*mus.*) l'arte -adorica, the art of the troubadours. **-ante** *part. adj.*; *n.m.* (*geol.*) erratic. **-arobe** *m. indecl.* (*theatr.*) property-man; costumier. **-ata** *f.* discovery; invention, contrivance; trick, expedient; lucky find; 'brain wave'. **-atello** *m.* foundling. **-ato** *part. adj.* found, discovered; experienced, felt; ben -ato, well said, witty, clever, appropriate; (*provb.*) se non è vero è ben -ato, if it is not true it's a good story; cosa -ata non è rubata, finding is keeping; (*poet.*) composed, invented; *n.m.* invention; discovery; fiction: contrivance, trick. **-atore** *m.* finder; inventor; troubadour; *Il Trovatore*, title of an opera by Verdi; (*joc.*) picker-up of unconsidered trifles; scavenger. (**-atrice** *f.*) **-(i)ero** *m.* (*lit. hist.; mus.*) trouvère.

trozza *f.* (*naut.*) sling, yardsling, spectacle plate.

†**trozzo**[1] *m.* group; — di gente armata, band of armed men.

†**trozzo**[2] *m.* alley, lane.

trucc-are [A2] *tr.* to cheat; to rig; (*theatr.*) to make up; *rfl.* (*theatr., etc.*) to make (oneself) up; to disguise oneself. **-ato** *part. adj.* cheated; tricked; made-up; wearing make-up. **-atura** *f.* trick, fake; (*theatr.*) make-up; disguise. **-one** *m.* swindler; (*pop.*) matrimonial agent. (**-ona** *f.*)

trucchiare [A4] *intr.* (*aux.* avere) (of a horse) to rub the forelegs together.

truc-co[1] *m.* (*usu. pl.* **-chi**) a kind of bagatelle played on a table like an elongated billiard-table, but with more pockets (eight balls and one smaller ball are used).

truc-co[2] *m.* (*pl.* **-chi**) (*theatr., etc.*) make-up; cassetta del —, make-up box; disguise; trick; deceit; fare un buon —, to do a good stroke of business; cheat; sono tutti -chi, they are all cheats.

truc-co[3] *m.*, **-one** *m.* See under **truccare**.

truc-e *adj.* fierce; threatening; grim; cruel; savage. **-emente** *adv.* cruelly; savagely.

tru·ci-a *f.* raggedness; poverty; wretchedness. **-ante** *adj.* ragged.

trucid-are [A1s] *tr.* to slay, to slaughter; to murder; to cut up. (**-ato** *part. adj.* **-atore** *m.* **-atrice** *f.*)

tru·cio *adj.* ragged; shabby; poverty-stricken.

truciol-are [A1s] *tr.* to reduce (wood, etc.) to shavings; to chip; †to shear, to clip; *intr.* (*aux.* avere) to make chips or shavings (of wood, etc.). (**-ato** *part. adj.*)

tru·ciolo *m.* (wood-)shaving; curl; chip; scatola di —, match-wood box.

truculent-o, †**-e** *adj.* threatening, grim, truculent; (of sea) stormy.

truff-a *f.* swindle, swindling; cheating; fraud; — all'americana, confidence trick; (*leg.*) deceit; fraud; swindling; †poor quality material or goods. **-are** [A1] *tr.* to get by swindling; to cheat; gli ha -ato un migliaio di lire, he cheated him of a thousand lire or so; (*leg.*) to cheat; to defraud; to deceive; to swindle. **-ato** *part. adj.* cheated, swindled. **-atore** *m.* (*leg.*) cheat; deceiver; defrauder; swindler; (*Scot.*) barrator. (**-atrice** *f.*) **-eri·a** *f.* cheat(ing); swindle; trick; fraud.

Truffaldino *pr.n.m.* name of a character who swindles and cheats in the *Commedia dell'Arte*.

trufolare [A1s] and derivs. See **intrufolare**.

truismo *m.* truism.

trulla *f.* (*Rom. antiq.*) *trulla*; wine-ladle; cup; (*bldg.*) trowel.

trullo[1] *m.* (*geog.*, Apulia) one-roomed house of drystone with conical roof; (*mil. hist.*) a sort of catapult.

trull-o[2] *m.* silly; *n.m.* simpleton, nincompoop. **-ag·gine** *f.* silliness, stupidity; silly thing. **-eri·a** *f.* silliness.

†**trull-o**[3] *m.* fart. †**-are** *intr.* to fart.

†**trunc-o** *m.* see **tronco**. †**-are** *vb.* and derivs. see **troncare**.

truo·golo *m.* See **trogolo**.

†**truono** *m.* See **tuono**.

truppa *f.* troop; band, group; in —, in a troup; *pl.* (*mil.*) troops; regiment; army; militia; rank and file; -e di assalto, storm troops; -e aereoportate, airborne troops; uomini di —, other ranks.

†**truppello** *m.* See **drappello**.

truschino *m.* (techn.) cutting gauge.

†trutilare *intr.* to whistle (of thrushes).

tu *prn. 2nd pers. sing.* thou; you; dare del —, 'tutoyer', to use the familiar form of address; amico di —, intimate friend; a — per —, intimately; trovarsi a — per — con, to come very close to; stare a — per — con, to be intimate with, *or* to stand one's ground with, not to be daunted by; also used impersonally when narrating something of general application, e.g.: — vai all'ufficio tasse e ti dicono…, you go to the income-tax office and they tell you….

tuba[1] *f.* (mus.) tuba, bass tuba, †trumpet; †voice; (joc.) ha una — che sı sente da lontano un miglio, he has a vocal organ you can hear a mile off; — acustica, ear-trumpet; top hat, silk hat; (anat.) Fallopian tube.

tuba[2] *f.* (mus.). See **catuba**.

tub-are [A I] *intr.* (*aux.* avere) (of pigeons, doves) to coo; (of owls) to hoot; (fig.) to bill and coo. **-atore** *m.* trumpeter; (hist.) town crier of Ancona.

tubatura *f.* See under **tubo**.

tuber·col-o *m.* (anat.; med.) tubercle; (bot.) root-tubercle. **-are** *adj.* (med.) tubercular; tisi -are, tuberculosis. **-osa·rio** *m.* sanatorium for tubercular patients. **-osi** *f.* tuberculosis.

tu·ber-o *m.*, **†-a** *f.* bulb, corm; tuber. **-etto** *m. dim.* see **tubercolo**. **-osa** *f.* (bot.) tuberose, *Polianthes tuberosa.* **-osità** *f.* (bot.) tuberosity; tuber. **-oso** *adj.* tuberous; pimply; tuberous.

Tubinga *pr.n.f.* (geog.) Tübingen.

tub-o *m.* pipe; tube; — del gas, gas pipe; — di scarico, exhaust pipe; (bot.) — pollinico, pollen tube; (naut.) tube; — dell'albero portaelica, shaft tube; — anima, inner tube of a gun; — di lancio, torpedo tube; — laterale, beam tube; — poppiero, stern tube; — di sfogo, breathing tube, vent. **-atura** *f.* piping, (system of) pipes. **-azione** *f.* piping, pipes. **-etto** *m. dim.* thin pipe; (paint.) paint-tube; tube (e.g. of toothpaste); -etto deformabile, collapsible tube. **-iera** *f.* radiator; pipes of a radiator, cylindrical water-heater, geyser, etc. **-olare** *adj.* tubular; tube-shaped; furnished with pipes; caldaia -olare, tubular boiler. **-olatura**, **-ulatura** *f.* (naut.; eng.) system of pipes; -olatura d'acqua dolce, freshwater system; -olatura d'allagamento e d'incendio, fire and bilge system; -olatura di sentina, pumping system.

tucano[1] *m.* (orn.) toucan, *Rhamphastidae* spp.

tucano[2] *pr.n.m.* (astron.) Tucana.

tucùl *m. indecl.* conical hut (in Abyssinia).

tuello *m.* (vet.) quick (of the hoof of a horse).

tufa·ceo *adj.* See under **tufo**.

tuf-are [A I] *intr.* (*aux.* essere), *rfl.* to snuggle. **-ato** *part. adj.* stuffy.

tuff *onom.* puff; bump; splash.

tuff-are [A I] *tr.* to plunge; to dip; (naut.) *intr.* (*aux.* essere) see **attuffare**; (aeron.) to dive, to dive down; *rfl.* to plunge; to dive; to sink; -arsi nel sonno, to sink into sleep. **-amento** *m.* plunging; diving; immersing. **-ata** *f.* plunge, dive. **-ato** *part. adj.* dipped; sunk; panni -ati nella tinta, clothes dipped in dye; candela -ata, dip (cheap candle); (mus.) nota -ata, stopped note (on French horn). **-atore** *m.* diver, plunger. (*-atrice f.*) **-atura** *f.* plunging, diving; dipping. **-etto** *m.* (orn.) dabchick, little grebe, *Podiceps ruficollis.* **-ettone** *m.* a name given popularly to various diving birds. **-o** *m.* dip, plunge; plump; sudden heavy shower; throb, sudden emotion; sentii un -o al cuore, my heart gave a sudden leap; dare un -o, to make a mistake, to 'drop a brick'; battere il -o, to lose credit; fare un gran -o, to come to grief; dare un -o nello scimunito, to do something silly; (sport) dive; tuffi, diving; -o alla rondine, swallow dive; -o a serpentina, corkscrew dive; (football) -o all'angolo, flying dive made by goalkeeper when stopping a ball. **-olino** *m.* (orn.) see **tuffetto**.

tuf-o *m.* (geol.) tufa, tuff. **-a·ceo** *adj.* tufaceous. **-igno** *adj.* tufaceous. **-oso** *adj.* tufaceous.

tuga *f.* (naut.) superstructure, deckhouse; wheelhouse; †stern cabin; †— di prora, forecastle.

tugu·rio *m.* hovel; hut; dog-kennel.

tu·ia *f.* (bot.) arbor vitae, *Thuja.*

tularemi·a *f.* (med.) deer-fly fever.

tu·lio *m.* (chem.) Thulium.

tulip-ano *m.* (bot.) tulip, *Tulipa*; young fop; (tulip-shaped) lampshade; (mil.) belling of a gun; bell-mouth; tulip of a spiked gun. **-anista** *m.* grower of tulips. **-i·fero** *m.* (bot.) tulip tree, *Liriodendron tulipiferum.*

tulle *m.* (text.) tulle.

Tul·li-o *pr.n.m.* Tully (M. Tullius Cicero). **-ano** *adj., n.m.* Ciceronian.

tumarca *m.* (mil. hist.) platoon captain.

tume-fare [B 14] *rfl.* (med.) to tumefy, to swell. **-fatto** *part. adj.* swollen, tumid. **-fazione** *f.* swelling, tumefaction.

tu·mid-o *adj.* swollen, tumid, inflated; turgid. (**-amente** *adv.*) **-ezza** *f.* tumidity, inflation; turgidness. **-ità** *f.* swelling, tumidity.

tu·molo *m.* and derivs. See **tumulo**.

tumor-e *m.* (med.) tumour.

tu·mul-o *m.* tumulus; grave; barrow; cairn; catafalque; sand-hill (on seashore). **-are** [A I S] *tr.* to bury, to inter; *adj.* tumular. **-ato** *part. adj.* buried. **-azione** *f.* burial, interment. **-eto** *m.* (geog., Latium) dune formed of volcanic dust.

tumult-o *m.* tumult, uproar; turmoil; riot; fare —, to run riot; disturbance; (leg.) — popolare, civil commotion; riot. **-uante** *part. adj.* riotous; tumultuous; *n.m.* rioter. **-uare** [A 6] *intr.* (*aux.* avere) to riot, to start a riot or tumult; to be in uproar; (of the stomach) to be upset. **-ua·rio** *adj.* tumultuous; riotous. **-uariamente** *adv.* tumultuously; riotously. **-uoso** *adj.* tumultuous; riotous; noisy. **-uosamente** *adv.* tumultuously; riotously.

tungst-ato *m.* (chem.) tungstate. **-eno** *m.* (chem.; metall.) tungsten.

tung·stico *adj.* (chem.) tungstic, wolframic.

tu·nic-a *f.* long tunic; (eccl.) la santa —, the Holy Coat (at Treves); (anat.) tunica; (bot.) tunic; (fig.) binding of a book. **-ato** *adj.* wearing a tunic; (bot.) tunicated.

Tu·n-işi *pr.n.f.* (geog.) Tunis. **-işi·a** *pr.n.f.* (geog.) Tunisia. **-işino** *adj., n.m.* relating to inhabitant or native of Tunis; (text.) Tunisian fillet lace.

tun·nel *m. indecl.* tunnel.

tunstato *m.* and derivs. See **tungstato**.

tu-o *poss. adj. m. sing.* thy; your; *poss. prn.* thine; yours; (subjective or objective in meaning, e.g.:) il — amore, the love you bear, *or*, the love of you; la -a, yours, your letter, etc.; dalla -a, on your part; delle -e!, the things you do!; *n.m.* il —, your property; *pl.* i tuoi, your people.

tuon-o *m.* thunder; roar; †thunderbolt, lightning. **-are** [A I] *intr.* (*aux.* avere; *impers. aux.* essere) to thunder; to roar.

tuorlo *m.* See **torlo**.

tup·pete *onom.* bump; bang.

tura *f.* See under **turare**.

tur-are [A I] *tr.* to stop, to stop up; to plug; to cork; to bung; — un dente, to fill a tooth; — con cemento, to fill in with cement; — la bocca a qualcuno, to silence someone; (provb.) chi non -a bucolin -a bucone, a stitch in time saves nine; *rfl.* (acc. of prn. 'si') -arsi in casa, to stay at home, to shut oneself up; (dat. of prn. 'si') -arsi gli orecchi, to block one's ears. **-a** *f.* bung; stopper; dam; (naut.) -a galleggiante, coffer dam. **-abuchi** *m.* stop-gap. **-ac·ciolo** *m.* cork; stopper; provvisto di -acciolo, corked. **-afalle** *m. indecl.* (naut.) shot stopper (large wooden cones in various sizes kept handy for sealing shot holes in destroyers, etc.). **-amento** *m.* stopping (up), corking; obstruction. **-ata** *f.* stopping up; shutter; barrier. **-ato** *part. adj.* corked, stopped up; covered up, muffled (up); †reserved, discreet. **-o** *m.* bung, stopper; cork.

turba *f.* disorderly crowd, mob, rabble; tumult; (fig.) disturbance; (med.) disorder, upset complaint.

turbante[1] *m.* turban; Turk's head (knot).

turbante[2] *part.* of **turbare**, q.v.

turb-are [A I] *tr.* to trouble; to disturb; to confuse; — lo stomaco, to upset the stomach; to upset; to agitate; (leg.) — il possesso di, to disturb the quiet enjoyment of; *rfl.* to become agitated; to become uneasy; to be perturbed; to be upset; si -ò assai, he got very upset; to be deeply moved (e.g. with wonder, admiration). **-abile** *adj.* easily disturbed or perturbed. (**-abilità** *f.*) **-amento** *m.* perturbation, agitation; uneasiness; excitement; confusion, commotion. **-ante** *part. adj.* disturbing, perturbing, upsetting. **-ativa** *f.* (leg.) disturbance; obstruction; annoyance. **-ativo** *adj.* troublesome; disturbing. **-ato** *part. adj.* troubled; uneasy; agitated, disturbed, perturbed; (of sky, weather) overcast, gloomy. **-atamente** *adv.* uneasily; excitedly; confusedly. **-atore** *m.* disturber; agitator. (**-atrice** *f.*) **-azione** *f.* disturbance; confusion; upsetting; (med.) disorder.

†tur·bico *m.* See **turbine**.

†tur·bido *adj.* and derivs. See **torbido**.

turbina *f.* (eng.) turbine; — a vapore, steam turbine.

tur·bin-e *m.* whirlwind; gale; hurricane; — di polvere, whirl of dust. **-are** [A I s] *intr.* (*aux.* avere) to whirl; to eddy. **-ato** *part. adj.* spiral, winding spirally. **-azione** *f.* whirl; whirling. **-ìo** *m.* continual whirling, eddying; turmoil; storm; restless throng. **-oso** *adj.* whirling, eddying; stormy; tumultuous. (**-osamente** *adv.*)

turbo *adj.* turbid, troubled; gloomy; stormy; *n.m.* trouble; disturbance.

turbo-alternatore *m.* (electr.) turbo-alternator. **-elica** *f.* turboprop; (aeron.) motore a -elica, turboprop engine. **-generatore** *m.* (electr.) turbogenerator. **-getto** *m.* (aeron.) motore a -getto, turbojet engine. **-motore** *m.* (eng.) turbine engine. **-nave** *f.* turbine steamship. **-pompa** *f.* (eng.) turbine pump. **-propulsore** *m.* turboprop. **-reattore** *m.* (aeron.) turbojet. **-soffiante** *m.* (eng.) turboblower.

turbolen-to *adj.* turbulent, unruly; restless; boisterous; stormy; acque -te, troubled waters; *n.m.* restless, unruly person; agitator. **-tamente** *adv.* turbulently, restlessly. **-za** *f.* turbulence, disorder; rioting; agitation, disturbance; (techn.) turbulence.

turbulento *m.* (tan.) drum.

turcasso *m.* quiver; †tweezer case.

Turch-i·a *pr.n.f.* (geog.) Turkey. **-eggiare** [A 3 c] *intr.* (*aux.* avere) to favour or imitate the Turks. **-esa** *f.* see **turchesia**. **-esco** *adj.* (*m.pl.* -eschi) (derog.) Turkish, Turk-like.

turch-ese *f.* (miner.) turquoise. **-ineggiare** [A 3 c] *intr.* (*aux.* avere) to be bluish; to be rather dark blue. **-inetto** *adj. dim.* bluish; *n.m.* (laundress's) blue; indigo; prussian blue. **-inic·cio** *adj.* bluish. **-ino** *adj.* and *n.m.* deep blue, dark blue; farne delle -ine, to be up to all sorts of tricks.

turcimanno *m.* (derog.) dragoman, interpreter.

turc-o *adj.* (*m.pl.* **turchi**) Turkish; (bot.) grano —, maize, corn, *Zea mays*; *n.m.* Turk; the Turkish language, Turkish; fumare come un —, to smoke like a chimney; bestemmiare come un —, to swear like a trooper; parlare —, to speak Turkish, or 'to speak Greek', to speak Double-Dutch; *adv. phr.* alla -a, in the Turkish manner; sedere alla -a, to sit cross-legged; (vet.) ferri alla -a, half-shoe. (**-a** *f.*) **-o·filo** *adj., n.m.* Turcophil. **-o·fobo** *adj., n.m.* Turcophobe. **-omanno** *m.* (hist.) Turcoman.

Turenna *pr.n.f.* (geog.) Touraine.

†**turfa** *f.* See **torba**.

turg-enza *f.* (med.) swelling, turgescence; congestion. **-escente** *adj.* turgescent, turgid, swollen. **-escenza** *f.* turgescence, swelling.

†**tur·gere** *intr.* to swell, to be tumescent.

tur·gid-o *adj.* swollen; (fig.) turgid, pompous, bombastic, inflated. **-amente** *adv.* turgidly, pompously, bombastically. **-ezza** *f.*, **-ità** *f.* swelling; turgidity; pompousness.

turgore *m.* turgidity; swelling.

Turgo·via *pr.n.f.* (geog.) Thurgau.

tur-i·bolo *m.* censer, thurible. **-ifera·rio** *m.* (liturg.) thurifer; (fig.) flatterer. **-i·fero** *adj.* (bot.) incense-yielding. **-ificati** *m.pl.* (eccl. hist.) *turificati*, Christians who under persecution burned incense to the gods. **-ificazione** *f.* (rel.) censing.

Turin·gia *pr.n.f.* (geog.) Thuringia.

tur-ismo *m.* tourism, the tourist industry; touring. **-ista** *m., f.* tourist. **-i·stico** *adj.* relating to tourism; of, for, relating to tourists.

turlupin-are [A I] *tr.* to fool, to swindle, to cheat. (**-ato** *part. adj.*) **-atore** *m.* swindler, cheat; dishonest politician. (**-atrice** *f.*) **-atura** *f.* swindling, cheating; dishonesty.

†**turma** *f.* See **torma**.

turno *m.* turn; rotation; medico di —, doctor on duty; shift; tabaccheria, farmacia, di —, tobacconist's, chemist's, open on alternate Sundays or feast days; — di notte, night shift; cedere il proprio — di parlare, to forgo one's turn to speak.

turo *m.* See under **turare**.

turoniano *adj.* (geol.) Turonian.

turp-e, †**-o** *adj.* abject, base; mean; filthy; indecent, obscene. (**-emente** *adv.*) **-ilo·quio** *m.* coarse language; filthy conversation; (leg.) obscene language. **-itu·dine** *f.* turpitude, baseness; obscenity.

turri·bolo *m.* See **turibolo**.

turrito *adj.* turreted; many-towered.

tussah *f. indecl.* (ent.) farfalla —, tussah moth, *Antherea paphia*; (text.) tussore silk.

tussilag·gine *f.* (bot.) coltsfoot, *Tussilago farfara*.

tuta *f.* overalls (of workman, racing-driver, etc.); boiler-suit.

tuta·nia *f.* (metall.) tutania.

†**tutare** *tr.* to defend.

tutel-a *f.* (leg.) tutelage; (leg.) guardianship; — dei minori, guardianship of infants; protection; — del nome, protection of name; (rel.) patronage, protection (of a saint); (fig.) protection; defence; a — di, in defence of. **-are** [A I] *tr.* to protect; to defend; (leg.) to be, to act as, the guardian of; to protect; *adj.* tutelar(y); angelo -are, guardian angel; (leg.) giudice -are, tutelary judge (of wards of Court and persons under disability); Master in Lunacy; leggi -ari, protective legislation. (**-ato** *part. adj.*)

tu·tolo *m.* (agric.) core of maize cob, corn-cob.

tut-ore *m.* (leg.) guardian; (Scot.) tutor; protector. **-o·rio** *adj.* tutelar; tutorial; autorità -oria, superior (supervisory) authority. **-ora, -rice** *f.* (woman) guardian.

tutt-o *prn. sing.* all, the whole; the lot; everything; anything; sapere far di —, to be able to turn one's hand to anything; (provb.) non è tutt'oro quello che riluce, all is not gold that glitters; — quanto, the whole lot; il —, the total, the sum, the whole thing; *pl.* all, everybody, everyone; -i se n'andarono, they all went away; voi -i, all of you; egli conosce -i, he knows everybody; -i e singoli, every single one; *adj.* all, the whole (of); every; any; full; only, sole; di — cuore, con — il cuore, with all one's heart; Tutti i Santi, All Saints' Day; — il giorno, all day long; -a notte, all night, all through the night; -a Roma, all Rome; -a Italia, the whole of Italy; tutt'e due, both; tutti e tre, all three; tutto tutto, every bit; *adv.* all, entirely, wholly; è — famiglia, he is wholly devoted to his family; che bella fotografia! è -a lui, what a good photograph! it's exactly like him; essere — muscoli, to be all muscle; — pulito, all clean; — solo, all alone; è tutt'uno, it's all the same, it makes no difference; very; thoroughly; fully; quite; — sveglio, wide awake; — nudo, stark naked; — dritto, bolt upright; *adv. phrs.* a -a prima, at the very first, at first sight; — d'un tratto, all of a sudden; all at once; del —, quite; sei stanco? Del —!, are you tired? Not at all!; a tutt'oggi, up to the present; in — e per —, in all respects, completely; tutt'altro, quite different, quite otherwise; tutt'altro che, anything but; fare di —, to do everything in one's power; con — questo, nevertheless; — uno con, the same as; con — che, although; da per — (*usu.* **dappertutto**), everywhere; (herald.) sopra il —, sopra il — del —, over all; (mus.) tutti; full orchestra, organ or chorus; full passage (contrasted with *concertino*, q.v., in a *concerto grosso*, q.v.). **-asanta** *adj., n.f.* Most Holy (said of the B.V.M.). **-avi·a** *adv.* still; yet; nevertheless, all the same; †-avia che, at the same time as, all the time that; although. **-avolta** *adv.* continuously; nevertheless. **-is·simo** *adj. superl.* (fam.) absolutely all. **-ochè** *conj.* though, although. †**-odì** *adv.* all day; always; continually. **-ofare** *f. indecl.* (colloq.) *bonne à tout faire*, maid-of-all-work. **-ora** *adv.* yet, still; continually.

tu·zia *f.* (miner.) tutty.

tuzior-ismo *m.* (moral theol.) Tutiorism (opposed to Laxism). **-ista** *m.* Tutiorist.

tzigan-o *adj., n.m.* gipsy, esp. of Hungary. (**-a** *f.*)

u¹ *f.*, *m.* the letter U; the vowel U; the sound U; (eng.; bldg.) ferro ad U, channel iron.

†**u²** *conj.* or.

†**u'³** *adv.* where.

uà (onom.) wa! wa! (sound of a baby crying).

uadi *m. indecl.* (geog.) wadi, wady (dry bed of river or stream in N. Africa).

ubara *f.* (orn.) houbara bustard, *Chlamydotis undulata*.

ubb-i·a *f.* superstition, superstitious fear; delusion, prejudice, fad, whim; timidity; avere delle -ie, to be full of fads. **-ioso** *adj.* superstitious; full of foolish fears.

ubbidien-te *adj.* obedient; docile; biddable; essere — ai genitori, to obey one's parents; cavallo —, well-trained horse. **-temente** *adv.* obediently; docilely. **-za** *f.* obedience; submission; compliance; -za cieca, blind obedience; -za passiva, passive obedience; per -za, out of obedience; ridurre all'-za, to reduce to obedience, to tame; fare l'-za, to do what one is told to do; stare a -za, to be submissive; (leg.) -za alle leggi, compliance with the law; (eccl.) see **obbedienza**

ubbid-ire [D 2] *intr.* (*aux.* avere; *prep.* a) to obey; to pay heed; to do as one is told; to show respect; to respond, to be responsive;

ubbid-ire (*cont.*)

— a Roma, to be subject to Rome; *tr.* to obey; to carry out, to fulfil, to execute. **-ito** *part. adj.* obeyed; fulfilled; carried out. (**-itore** *m.* **-itrice** *f.*)

ubbioso *adj.* See under **ubbia**.

†**ubbligare** *vb.* and derivs. See **obbligare**.

ubbriaco *adj.* and derivs. See **ubriaco**.

u·bere *adj.* (poet.). See **ubertoso**, under **ubertà**.

ubero[1] *adj.* (vet.) roan, including black roan (colour of a horse).

†**u·ber-o**[2] *m.*, †**-a** *f.* breast; udder. **-i·fero** *adj.* having breasts; having udders; (fig.) copious, abundant; eloquent.

uber·rimo *adj. superl.* abundant, copious (cf. **ubere**).

ubert-à *f.* fertility, fecundity; abundance; prosperity, thriving aspect. **-osità** *f.* fertileness; fruitfulness. **-oso** *adj.* fertile; fecund; fruitful; abundant, copious.

Uberto *pr.n.m.* Hubert.

ubi *adv.* (Latin) where; l'— consistam, the wherewithal; trovare l'— consistam, to find solid ground.

ubic-are [A 2 s] *tr.* to place, to position, to post; to locate; to site. **-ato** *part. adj.* located, situated; placed, posted; sited. **-atore** *m.* (radar) locator. **-azione** *f.* position, situation, location; whereabouts; local position; situation; emplacement; ubication; (bldg.) siting.

ubiero *adj.* (vet.). See **ubero**.

†**ubino** *m.* small swift steed.

ubiquisti *m.pl.* (eccl. hist.) Ubiquists.

ubiquit-à *f.* ubiquity; ubiquitousness; (theol.) the normal doctrine of God's ubiquity; (eccl. hist.) the special Eucharistic doctrine of Lutheran Ubiquitarians; (pop.) bilocation, as attributed esp. to St Anthony of Padua. **-ari** *m.pl.* (eccl. hist.) Ubiquitarians.

†**uboè** *m.* (mus.). See **oboe**.

ubria-co *adj.* (*m.pl.* **-chi**) drunk, intoxicated; tipsy; — fradicio, — marcio, dead-drunk; (fig.) inebriated; — di gioia, beside oneself with joy; (ichth.) cappone —, *Trigla lineata*, rock gurnard; *n.m.* drunken man, drunk; drunkard. **-ca** *f.* drunken woman. **-care** [A 2] *tr.* to make drunk, to intoxicate; (fig.) to inebriate; *abs.* birra che -a, beer that goes to one's head; *rfl.* to get drunk; to become intoxicated; to booze, to tipple; (fig.) to become inebriated; to lose one's head, to have one's head turned. **-cato** *part. adj.* intoxicated; (fig.) inebriated; in an exalted state, 'lit up'. (**-catore** *m.* **-catrice** *f.*) **-catura** *f.* drunkenness; prendere una -catura, to get drunk; binge. **-chezza** *f.* drunkenness. **-cone** *m.* drunkard.

ucase *m.* ukase; (fig.) peremptory order.

uccell-o *m.* bird; (fig.) fool, simpleton; — di bosco, fugitive from justice; — di Giove, eagle; — di Giunone, peacock; — della Madonna, — di S. Maria, kingfisher; — di mal augurio, bird of ill omen; — del paradiso, bird of Paradise; — delle tempeste, storm petrel, *Hydrobates pelagicus*; — delle tempeste codaforcuta, Leach's petrel, *Oceanodroma leucorrhoa*; — mosca, humming bird; vispo come un —, gay as a bird; a volo di —, from a bird's-eye view; (provb.) gli -i appaiono co' loro pari, birds of a feather flock together. **-a·bile** *adj.* snarable; (fig.) gullible. †**-ac·cio** *m.* simpleton. **-agione** *f.* bird-catching; the total of birds caught. **-a·ia** *f.* quantity of birds; place for, or act of, bird-catching; (fig.) trick. **-a·io** *m.* bird-seller. **-ame** *m.* birds caught (collectively). **-amento** *m.* act of bird-catching; (fig.) trickery. **-anda** *f.* site for bird-catching. **-are** [A 1] *intr.* (*aux.* avere) to catch birds; (fig.) to make fun of; -are a una cosa, to try to get something; -are alle cime, to snap-shoot, to fire at a head appearing out of a trench. **-atoio** *m.* site for bird-catching. **-atore** *m.* bird-catcher. **-atura** *f.* art, practice, of bird-catching. **-iera** *f.* aviary, bird-cage.

†**ucchiello** *m.* See **occhiello**.

ucci·d-ere [C 3] *tr.* to kill; to murder; to do to death; to slay; (fig.) to stifle; *rfl.* to commit suicide; to kill oneself; to be killed; to risk one's life; *recip. rfl.* to kill each other. **-ente** *part. adj.* deadly; killing; *n.m.* killer. †**-imento** *m.* killing; slaughter. (**-itore** *m.* **-itrice** *f.*)

uc·cio *adj.* (pop.) bad, poor, rotten; questo vino è proprio —, this wine is awful; uccio uccio, absolutely terrible.

uccis-ione *f.* killing; slaying; (sport) l'—, the kill; murder; commettere —, to commit murder; (mil.) slaughter. **-o** *part.* of **uccidere**, q.v.; *adj.* killed; dead; slain; *n.m.* dead man; victim; gli -i, the slain. **-ore** *m.* murderer; killer. (**-ora** *f.*)

Ucra·ina *pr.n.f.* (geog.) Ukraine.

U·din-e *pr.n.f.* (geog.) Udine. **-ese** *adj.* (geog.) relating to or characteristic of Udine; *n.m., f.* native or inhabitant of Udine.

ud-ire [D 15] *tr.* to hear; -ite?, can you hear?; to listen to; to pay heed to; to attend to; -ite!, listen!; Dio -ì le sue preghiere, God heard his prayers (and granted them); non ne voler —, not to allow mention of it; to understand; se ben odo, if I understand aright; to sit under, to attend the lectures of; (leg.) — i testimoni, to hear evidence; — l'imputato, to hear the accused; *n.m.* hearing; sottile —, keen hearing, good hearing; esser privo dell'—, to be deaf; (leg.) hearing. **-ente** *part. adj.* hearing; listening. **-i·bile** *adj.* audible. **-ibilità** *f.* audibility; soglia di -ibilità, audibility threshold. **-ienza** *f.* audience, admission to a presence; interview; concedere un'-ienza, to grant an audience; dare -ienza a, to listen to; (leg.) hearing; sitting; le -ienze sono pubbliche, sittings are public; in pubblica -ienza, in open Court; -ienza a porte chiuse, a hearing in Chambers (C.C.P.), trial *in camera* (C.P.P.); ruolo di -ienza, cause list (C.C.P.), calendar (C.P.P.). **-ita** *f.* hearing; per -ita, on hearsay; (leg.) testimone d'-ita, ear-witness; thing heard. **-itivo** *adj.* auditive; auditory. **-ito** *part. adj.* heard; per -ito dire, by hearsay; *n.m.* hearing, sense of hearing; perdere l'-ito, to lose one's hearing. **-itorato** *m.* status of listener. **-itore** *m.* listener; student entitled to attend lectures but not to sit for examinations; (leg.) -itore giudiziario, magistrate (of lowest rank in establishment of Italian judicature); (eccl.) -itore del papa, *Auditor Papae*; -itore generale, Auditor General; -itore della Ruota, Auditor of the Rota; (mil.) head of a standing military tribunal; provost; *pl.* audience. (**-itrice** *f.*) **-ito·rio** *m.* audience, listeners; *adj.* (anat.) auditory. **-izione** *f.* hearing; audition; (leg.) hearing; (mus.) see **audizione**.

udo·m-etro *m.* (meteor.) pluviometer, rain-gauge. **-e·trico** *adj.* pluviometric.

†**udore** *m.* See **odore**.

uffa *excl.* ouff!; phew!

uffi·ci-o *m.* office; place of business, place of work; study, workroom; department; ore di —, orario di —, office-hours; — postale, post-office; duty; — di madre, duty as a mother; badare al suo —, to do one's duty; far bene il suo —, to function well; service; i buoni uffici di, the good offices of; post, position, office; accettare l'—, to accept office; rimanere in —, to stay in office; — di presidenza, general committee; (liturg.) l'— (divino), the (Divine) office; l'— della Madonna, the Little Office; dir l'—, to say (one's) office; (eccl.) Sant'—, Holy Office; uffici della Camera dei Deputati, committees of the House or Legislative Assembly; d'—, ex officio, in discharge of duty, in virtue of office; — del bollo, stamp office; — pubblico, public office; — del registro, registry office; — principale, head office; (leg.) avvocato d'—, solicitor or counsel designated under Legal Aid Rules (C.C.P.); abbandono di —, desertion of public post (C.P.); procedimento d'—, public prosecution (instituted by competent authority) (C.P.); (naut.; aeron.) — presagi, meteorological office. **-ale** *adj.* official; formal; authorized; authenticated; (leg.) official; nella carica -ale, in an official capacity; *n.m.* official; officer; representative; functionary; (mil.) officer; la mensa degli -ali, officers' mess; -ale di complemento, reserve officer; (naut.) -ale alle artiglierie, gunnery officer; -ale ammiraglio, flag officer; -ale delle armi subacquee, torpedo officer; -ale in comando di guardia, deputy company officer; -ale del C.E.M.M. (Corpo Equipaggi della Marina Militare), branch officer (until 1955, Warrant Officer, i.e. promoted from the ranks, not from lower ratings who, if qualified, became sub-lieutenants); -ale d'ispezione, officer of the day; -ale di coperta, deck officer (merchant navy); -ale commissario, pay-master; -ale di guardia, officer of the watch; -ali naviganti, seagoing officers; -ale di rotta, navigating officer; (leg.) Gazzetta -ale, Official Gazette; pubblico -ale, public official (C.P.); -ale giudiziario, bailiff, tipstaff (C.C.P.); -ale dello stato civile, Registrar (of births, deaths and marriages) (C.C.). **-almente** *adv.* officially; formally; solemnly; (leg.) ex officio, in the course of duty. **-aletto** *m.* (mil.) sub-lieutenant, second-lieutenant. **-alità** *f.* official character; formality, body of officials; (mil.) officer strength in a unit. **-ante** *part. adj.* officiating; (liturg.) sacerdote -ante, officiating priest. **-are** [A 3] *intr.* (*aux.* avere) to officiate; to function; (liturg.) to officiate; *tr.* to approach (in order to ask a favour of), to solicit; (liturg.) -are una chiesa, to serve a church, to hold services in it. **-ato** *part. adj.* solicited, approached; (liturg.) chiesa -ata, church where services are held; chiesa bene

uffici-o (*cont.*)
-ata, church where ceremonies are done well, 'liturgical' church; chiesa non -ata, church no longer used for services. **-atore** *m.* functionary; person officiating; (litur.) officiant. (**-atrice** *f.*) **-atura** *f.* officiating; functioning; function; (litur.) the holding of services in a church; the celebration of divine worship. **-olo** *m.* (litur.) Little Office. **-osità** *f.* courtesy; obligingness. **-oso** *adj.* courteous; obliging; semi-official; informal; unofficial; bugia -osa, white lie; nella carica -osa, in an unofficial capacity. **-osamente** *adv.* informally; unofficially; obligingly.

Uffizi *pr.n.m.pl.* (art) galleria degli —, the most famous picture-gallery in Florence, housed in the Palazzo degli — (former public offices).

uffi-zio *m.* and derivs. see **ufficio**; (eccl.) Sant'—, Holy Office, Inquisition.

ufo *adv. phr.* a —, free, gratis; mangiare a —, to scrounge a meal.

ugello *m.* (eng.) nozzle, tuyère; (metall.) — allargato, splayed tuyère (of furnace).

ug·gi-a *f.* gloom; deep shade; shadow; lack of sunlight; (fig.) ennui, boredom, tedium; annoyance; dislike, aversion; mettere l'— a, to cause annoyance to; avere l'—, to be in a bad mood; avere in —, to have a dislike for; prendere in —, to take a dislike to; †pain. **-osità** *f.* unpleasantness; distastefulness; dislike. **-oso** *adj.* displeasing; annoying; tiresome; troublesome; vexatious; dull, boring; gloomy; shadowy; tempo -oso, dull weather. (**-osamente** *adv.*)

uggiol-are [A 1 s] *intr.* (*aux.* avere) to howl; to whine. (**-amento** *m.*) **-io** *m.* (*pl.* -ii) howling; whining; continuous howling or whining.

ugg-ire [D 2] *tr.* (Tusc.) to cast shadow on; to bore; to displease; *rfl.* to suffer boredom, to be bored. **-ito** *part. adj.* bored, displeased.

Ugigi *pr.n.m.* (geog.) Ujiji.

u·gioli *adv. phr.* (Florence) tra — e barugioli, what with one thing and another.

ugna *f.* (poet.; pop.). See **unghia**; (carp.) mitre.

ugn-are [A 6] *tr.* (eng.) to chamfer, to bevel. (**-ato** *part. adj.*) **-atura** *f.* chamfer, bevel; chamfering, bevelling. **-ella** *f.* (eng.) fine gauge; (vet.) chestnut (on a horse's leg). **-etto** *m.* (eng.) chaser. **-olo** *adj.* (vet.) sure-footed (of a horse).

Ugo, Ugone *pr.n.m.* Hugo, Hugh.

u·gola *f.* (anat.) uvula; (mus.) che —!, what an organ! (of a powerful singer); avere l'— d'oro, to have a golden voice; (joc.) bagnare l'—, to wet one's whistle.

ugonott-o *pr.n.m.* (rel. hist.) Huguenot. **-ismo** *m.* (rel. hist.) Huguenot beliefs, French Calvinism.

uguagli-are [A 4] *tr.* to equalize; to make equal; to make even; to even up; to be equal to; to compare, to speak of in the same breath; (techn.) to level, to smooth; *rfl.* (*prep.* a) to be equal (to); to consider oneself equal (to). **-amento** *m.* equalizing, equalization. **-anza** *f.* equality; parity; evenness. **-ato** *part. adj.* equalized; compared; even. **-atore** *m.* equalizer; *adj.* equalizing; levelling. (**-atrice** *f.*)

ugual-e *adj.* equal; identical; same; similar; sono d'ugual grandezza, they're the same height; like; non ha l'—, there's nobody like him; è l'—, it's all the same; per me torna —, it's all the same to me; essere — a sè stesso, to be consistent; — al campione, up to standard; even, regular; smooth; even-tempered; *n.m.* equal; mi tratta come un suo —, he treats me like an equal; i nostri -i, our equals. **-mente** *adv.* equally; all the same, nevertheless, notwithstanding. **-ità** *f.* equality; parity.

†**uguanno** *adv.* (Lat. 'hoc anno') this year.

uh, uhi *excl.* alas!; alack!; woe is me!; ah!; oh!

uhm *excl.* hum!; h'm!

uistiti *f.* (zool.) marmoset.

ulalgi·a *f.* (med.) ulalgia, sore gums.

†**ulamo** *m.* crowd; herd.

ul·cer-a *f.* (med.; vet.) ulcer; (fig.) canker, gnawing pain, wound. **-are** [A 1 s] *tr.* to ulcerate; *intr.* (*aux.* essere), *rfl.* to be, to become, ulcerated. **-ativo** *adj.* ulcerative. **-ato** *part. adj.* ulcerated. **-azione** *f.* ulceration. **-iforme** *adj.* (med.) ulceriform, ulceroid. **-o·ide** *adj.* (med.) ulceroid, ulceriform. **-oso** *adj.* ulcerous; (fig.) coscienza -osa, very guilty conscience.

†**ulcire** *tr.* to avenge.

ulema *m.* (Moslem rel.) ulema.

ulescina *f.* (chem.) ulexine, cytisine.

uli·gin-e *f.* moisture, dampness, damp. **-oso** *adj.* moist, damp.

†**ulire** *intr.* to be fragrant, to give forth fragrance.

Ulisse *pr.n.m.* (myth.) Ulysses.

ulite *f.* (med.) gingivitis.

uliv-a *f.* (bot.) olive, fruit of *Olea europaea*; (techn.) chisel, graving tool (see also **oliva** and derivs.). **-aceo** *adj.* olive-hued. **-ale** *adj.*, **-are** *adj.* olive-shaped. **-ato** *m.* (bot.) land planted with olive trees. **-ella** *f.* (bldg.) lewis, hoist. **-eta** *f.*, **-eto** *m.* (bot.) plantation of olive trees. **-o** *m.* (bot.) olive tree, *Olea europaea*; olive-branch; (litur.) domenica degli -i (dell'-o), Palm Sunday (olive being a liturgical alternative to palm); -o benedetto, blessed 'palm' (received in church on Palm Sunday and·kept in the house, often over one's bed, till the next year); (fig.) ramoscello d'-o, olive-branch, peace-overture.

†**ullo** *prn.*, *adj.* any.

Ulma *pr.n.f.* (geog.) Ulm.

ul·m-ico *adj.* (chem.) humic. **-ato** *m.* (chem.) humate. **-ina** *f.* (chem.) humin.

uln-a *f.* (anat.) ulna. **-are** *adj.* ulnar, cubital.

ulno-car·pico *adj.* (anat.) ulnocarpal. **-metacar·pico** *adj.* (anat.) ulnometacarpal. **-radiale** *adj.* (anat.) ulnoradial.

ulorragi·a *f.* (med.) ulorrhagia, bleeding from the gums.

ulo·trico *adj.* (anthrop.) ulotrichous, having woolly hair.

ulterior-e *adj.* further; subsequent; second; fare -i ricerche, to search further, to make further inquiries; (geog.) Gallia —, Transalpine Gaul. **-mente** *adv.* further on; later on; subsequently; besides; indagare -mente la questione, to look further into the matter.

ul·tim-o *adj.* last; final; extreme; final; newest, latest; utmost; ultimate; in — luogo, finally; dare l'-a mano a, to put the finishing touch to; arrivare —, to come in last, to arrive last; l'— supplizio, death; non —, last but not least, among the first; questa è l'-a!, that's the last time you play that trick!; top, topmost; l'— piano, the top floor; deliberare in -a istanza, to give a final ruling; (leg.) -a volontà, last will; gli atti di -a volontà, testamentary instruments; l'— erede, the last heir; *n.m.* the last one; gli -i saranno i primi, the last shall be first; essere l'— della classe, to be bottom of one's class; *adv. phr.* all'—, in the end; in —, at the end, at last, in the end, eventually; per —, after everyone else; sull'—, towards the end. **-amente** *adv.* of late, lately, latterly, in recent times; romanzo -amente uscito, novel just out; at last, in the end, at the end, finally, eventually. **-are** [A 1 s] *tr.* to terminate, to complete, to finish, to bring to an end; to close; (comm.) -are un affare, to settle a bargain; †*intr.* to draw to a close; †*n.m.* ending, close; in sull'-are del giorno, towards evening. **-ato** *part. adj.* completed, complete; published, 'out'. **-a·tum** *m. indecl.* ultimatum; dare un -atum, to send an ultimatum. **-azione** *f.* completion, finishing, termination. **-oge·nito** *adj.*, *n.m.* last born; youngest.

ult-o *adj.* (poet.) vindicated, revenged; punished. **-ore** *m.* vindicator; *adj.* avenging, vindicating; punishing. (**-rice** *f.*)

ultra- *pref.* ultra —; super. **-accelerante** *m.* (rubber industr.) fast accelerator. **-brachice·falo** *adj.* (anthrop.) ultra-brachycephalic. **-condensatore** *m.* (opt.) ultra-condenser. **-corto** *adj.* (radio) onda -corta, ultra-short wave, V.H.F. wave. **-democra·tico** *adj.* ultra-democratic. **-ffondato** *adj.* (geog.) overdeepened. **-filtrazione** *f.* (scient.) ultra-filtration. **-filtro** *m.* (scient.) ultra-filter. **-mi·crobo** *m.* ultramicrobe. **-micro·metro** *m.* (eng.) ultra-micrometer. **-microsco·pico** *adj.* ultra-microscopic. **-microsco·pio** *m.* ultra-microscope. **-montano** *adj.* ultramontane. **-potente** *adj.* super-charged. **-ra·pido** *adj.* fast; (photog., of lens) ultrarapid. **-rosso** *adj.* infra-red. **-sensi·bile** *adj.* ultra-sensitive. **-so·nico** *adj.* (phys.) supersonic. **-sonoro** *adj.* (phys.) supersonic. **-suono** *m.* (phys.) ultra-sound. **-vigoroso** *adj.* (photog.) ultra-hard. **-violetto** *adj.* (phys.) ultra-violet, uveal. **-virus** *m. indecl.* ultra-virus.

ultro·ne-o *adj.* voluntary; spontaneous. (**-amente** *adv.*)

u·lul-a *f.* (orn.) hawk owl, *Surnia ulula*. **-are** [A 1 s] *intr.* (*aux.* avere) to howl; to hoot; to moan (of wind, sea, etc.); (mus.) to wail, to howl. **-ato** *m.* howl, howling; hooting; moaning (of wind, sea).

u·lul-o *m.* howl, howling. **-one** *m. augm.* loud howling; various frogs and toads producing a loud croaking.

ulva *f.* (bot.) sea-lettuce, *Ulva*.

†**ulzione** *f.* revenge, vengeance.

um *excl.* hum!; h'm! (cf. **uhm**).

uman-o *adj.* human; natural; humane; mundane, worldly; courteous, gracious; genial; -e lettere, *belles-lettres*, humanities, literature; rispetto —, human respect, *or* exaggerated fear of other people's opinion; (mus.) voce -a, see under **voce**; *n.m.* human being; humaneness; avere dell'—, to be humane; *pl.* human beings; gli -i, the human race. **-aménte** *adv.* humanly; humanely; genially, courteously; civilly; in a civilized manner. **-are** [A I] *tr.* to make human, to humanize; to render humane; *rfl.* (theol.) to be incarnate, to be made man; (fig.) to become humanized, to become humane. **-ato** *part. adj.* (theol.) incarnate, made man; *La nascita del Verbo -ato, The Birth of the Word Made Flesh* (a Nativity play at Naples); (fig.) humanized; rendered humane. **-azióne** *f.* (theol.) Incarnation; anthropomorphism. **-ęsimo** *m.* (lit. hist.; philos.) humanism. **-ismo** *m.* see **umanesimo**. **-ista** *m., f.* humanist, classicist; scholar; student enrolled in the faculty of arts, arts student. **-i·stico** *adj.* humanistic; relating to humanism. **-ità** *f.* humanity; mankind; human nature; humaneness; human kindness; humane studies, humanistic studies; civilization, culture. **-ita·rio** *adj.* humanitarian; philanthropic; (rel.) humanitarian; also *n.m.* **-itarismo** *m.* humanitarianism. **-iżżare** [A I] *tr.* to humanize; to civilize. **-iżżato** *part. adj.* humanized; civilized; latte -izzato, humanized milk. †**-o·ide** *adj.* sub-human.

†**um-ato** *adj.* buried, interred. **-azione** *f.* burial, interment.

†**tumbè** *excl., interr.* well?

umbella *f.* (bot.). See **ombrella**.

umbilic-o *m.* (anat.) umbilicus; navel; (fig.) centre, heart; Foligno è l'— d'Italia, Foligno is the very centre of Italy; (bot.) — di Venere, pennywort, navelwort, *Umbilicus rupestris*. **-ale** *adj.* (anat.) umbilical; cordone -ale, umbilical cord. **-ato** *adj.* (mil. hist.) scudo -ato, centre-bossed shield; (bot.) umbilicate.

umbo *m.* (anat.) umbilicus.

umbòn-e *m.* (mil. hist.) centre portion of a round shield having a point in the middle; (zool.) umbo (of a shell). **-ato** *adj.* scudo -ato, shield as above.

umbra·tile *adj.* (poet.) shady; dark, shrouded; imaginary, illusory.

Um·br·ia *pr.n.f.* (geog.) Umbria. **-o** *adj., n.m.* Umbrian. (**-a** *f.*)

umbrina *f.* (ichth.). See **ombrina**.

u·mer-o *m.* (anat.) see **omero**. **-ale** *adj.* (anat.) (liturg.) velo -ale, humeral veil (also *n.m.*).

umett-are [A I C] *tr.* to moisten, to damp, to wet. **-aménto** *m.* moistening, damping, wetting. **-ante** *part. adj.* moistening. **-ativo** *adj.* moisture-producing. **-ato** *part. adj.* moistened; (poet.) occhi -ati, eyes moist with tears. **-atóre** *m.* (paperm.) damping rolls. (**-azióne** *f.*)

u·mico *adj.* and derivs. See **ulmico**.

u·mid-o *adj.* damp; wet; moist; occhi -i di pianto, eyes moist with tears; tempo —, damp weather; humid; watery; liquid; bollo a —, rubber stamp; (chem.) analisi per via -a, wet-way analysis, (metall.) wet assay; (med.) tosse -a, loose cough; (poet.) gregge -a, fish; *n.m.* damp, wet, moisture; humidity; (cul.) stew, stewed meat; in —, cooked in casserole, casseroled. †**-erboso** *adj.* marshy. **-ęzza** *f.* dampness, moisture. **-ic·cio** *adj.* rather damp; clammy; la sua mano -iccia, his clammy hand; stanza -iccia, damp room. **-ificare** [A 2s] *tr.* (phys.) to humidify, to moisten. **-ificatóre** *m.* (air conditioning) humidifier. **-ificazióne** *f.* (phys.) humidification. **-ino** *adj. dim.* not quite dry, still rather damp (e.g. of laundry). **-ità** *f.* dampness; moisture, humidity. **-ito** *adj.* damp; moistened. **-óre** *m.* humidity. †**-oso** *adj.* see **umido**.

umi-fero *adj.* (agric.) rich in humus.

u·mil-e *adj.* humble, lowly; self-effacing; unpretentious; submissive; meek, modest, simple; di -i natali, of humble origin; humbling, humiliating; servizi -i, menial tasks; (rhet.) stile —, plain style; †low-lying. **-ménte**, †**-emente** *adv.* humbly; with humility; meekly.

umili-are [A 4] *tr.* to humiliate; to humble; to mortify; to lower; — la fronte, to bow one's head; to present humbly; -iamo alla maestà della Regina questa nostra richiesta, we humbly present our request to the Queen's Majesty; *rfl.* to humiliate oneself; to humble oneself; to lower oneself; to ask pardon; (fig., poet.) to slope, to decline. (**-aménto** *m.*) **-ante** *part. adj.* humiliating; humbling, mortifying. †**-anza** *f.* humility. **-ativo** *adj.* humiliating. **-ato** *part. adj.* humiliated; humbled; downcast, dejected; *n.m.pl.* (eccl. hist.) Humiliati; *f.pl.* (eccl.) 'Blassoni' nuns. (**-atóre** *m.* **-atrice** *f.*) **-azióne** *f.* humiliation; submission; humbling, abasement. †**-e·vole** *adj.* submissive.

†**umilire** *rfl.* to humiliate oneself, to be humble.

†**umil·limo** *adj. superl.* of **umile**, q.v.

umiltà *f.* humility; humbleness; simplicity, modesty; lowliness; submission; submissiveness; finta —, false modesty; (theol.) humility.

umo *m.* humus.

umọr-e *m.* moisture; liquid; sap; secretion; temperament; di buon —, good-humoured; cattivo —, ill-temper; l'— della bestia, the nature of the beast; caprice, whim, humour; tendency, trend, mode, fashion; vivacity, wit; di bell'—, witty; humour; humorousness; (physiol.) gli -i del corpo, the body's humours. **-ale** *adj.* (physiol.) humoral. **-ismo** *m.* humour, humorousness; sense of humour; joke; -ismo di bassa lega, vulgar joke. **-ista** *m., f.* humorist. **-i·stico** *adj.* humorous; amusing; funny; comic; facetious; giornale -istico, comic paper.

un, una *indef. art. m., f.* See under **uno**.

una *adv.* in accord.

una·nim-e *adj.* unanimous; concordant; per voto —, by unanimous vote. **-eménte** *adv.* unanimously; in complete agreement. **-ità** *f.* unanimity; eletto all'-ità, unanimously elected; deliberazione all'-ità, unanimous resolution; approvato all'-ità, carried unanimously.

†**u·ncia** *f.* See **oncia**.

unciale *adj.* (of script) uncial.

†**u·ncic-o** *m.* see **uncino**. †**-are** *vb.* and derivs. see **uncinare**.

unciforme *adj.* (anat.) unciform, hook-shaped.

uncinare [A I] and derivs. See under **uncino**.

uncin-o *m.* hook; a —, hook-shaped, hooked; mani a —, thieving hands; (fig.) pretext, excuse; attaccare l'—, to find an excuse; tirare con gli -i, to force an argument; *pl.* bad handwriting, scribbling. **-are** [A I] *tr.* to hook; (naut.) to grapple (enemy); to hook up (cable); (fig.) to steal, to 'hook'; *rfl.* to become hook-shaped; *recip. rfl.* to grapple with each other, to fight tooth and nail. **-ato** *part. adj.* hooked, hook-shaped; croce -ata, swastika; (anat.) unciform; (herald.) croce -ata, fylfot, swastika, cross cramponnée. **-ętto** *m. dim.* crochet-needle; lavoro ad -etto, *or* all'-etto, crochet work, crocheting; lavorare all'-etto, to crochet; (techn.) hook on a knitting-machine. **-uto** *adj.* hooked; (fig.) rapacious.

†**und-ante** *adj.* undulating. †**-azione** *f.* undulating, undulation.

†**unde**[1] *adv.* See **dunque**.

†**unde**[2] *adv.* See **onde**.

undec-ile·nico *adj.* (chem.) undecylenic, 9-hendecenoic. **-i·lico** *adj.* (chem.) undecyl; acido -ilico, undecylic acid, hendecenoic acid.

unde·cimo *ord. num.* See **undicesimo**, under **undici**.

un·dic-i *card. num. indecl.* eleven; l'—, the figure eleven; l'— del mese, the eleventh of the month; sono le —, it's eleven o'clock; alle —, at eleven (o'clock); all'età di — anni, at eleven (years of age); *n.m.* (sport) an eleven, a side of eleven, team. **-en·ne** *adj.* eleven years old; *n.m., f.* eleven-year-old. **-e·simo** *ord. num.* eleventh; un -esimo, an eleventh (part). **-imila** *card. num.* eleven thousand. †**-isil·labo** *adj.* (prosod.) hendecasyllabic; *n.m.* hendecasyllable.

†**undoso** *adj.* See **ondoso**.

†**undunque** *adv.* See **ovunque**.

un·g-aro *adj.* (geog.; hist.) Hungarian; *n.m.* Hungarian; (numism.) gold Hungarian coin, hungar; gold coin formerly current in Modena. **-a·rico** *adj.* (hist.) Hungarian; esercito -arico, Hungarian army; impero austro-ungarico, Austro-Hungarian Empire.

ungella *f.* (vet.) see **ungula**; †iris (of the eye).

un·g-ere [C 5] *tr.* to grease; to smear; (liturg.) to anoint (e.g. in confirmation, extreme unction, consecration of altar); (eng.) to grease, to oil, to lubricate; (fig.) to 'butter up', to flatter; to soothe, to allay; — la palma a, to oil the palm of, to bribe; — le ruote, to pull strings; aver che —, to have work to do; — il dente, to eat, to scrounge a meal; *abs.* to be greasy; non -e e non macchia gli indumenti, is non-greasy and does not stain clothing; *rfl.* to rub oneself with oil; to get a spot of oil on or e's clothes. **-iménto** *m.* oiling; greasing; †softening, mitigation **-itóre** *m.* greaser; (eng.) lubricator, greaser. (**-itóra** *f.* **-itrice** *f.*) **-itura** *f.* oiling; greasing; (eng.) greasing, oiling, lubrication.

Ungher-i·a *pr.n.f.* (geog.) Hungary. **-ése** *adj.* Hungarian; *n.m.* Hungarian (language); *m., f.* Hungarian, inhabitant or native of Hungary.

un·ghero *adj.* ancient Hungarian; *n.m.* (numism.) see **ungaro**.

un·ghi-a *f.* nail; le -e delle mani, finger-nails; le -e dei piedi, toe-nails; tagliarsi le -e, to cut one's nails; spazzolino per le -e, nail-brush; — incarnita, ingrowing nail; essere carne e — con, to be hand in glove with; claw; talon; mettere fuori le -e, to put one's claws out; cadere nelle -e di, to fall into the clutches of; allungare le -e, to be rapacious, to grab, to be on the make; avere nelle -e, to have got one's claws into; (fig.) strip, tiniest bit, thin slice, slither; (zool.) nail or claw of an animal, esp. the hoof of an ungulate; (tan.) shank; (eng.) taglio ad —, bevel cut, chamfer cut; (naut.) butt of a plank or ship's side plate; — dell'ancora, peak or bill of an anchor. **-ata** *f.* scratch; graze; claw-mark. **-ato** *adj.* furnished with nails; clawed; (zool.) ungulate; (herald.) hooved; armed. **-ella** *f.* (vet.) cataract (see also **ungula**). **-ello** *m. dim.* of **unghia**; sharp claw; cat's claw; (of a cat) mettere gli -elli, to put its claws out. **-ẹtta** *f.* cross-cut chisel. **-olo** *m.* cat's claw; (tan.) shank. **-one** *m. augm.* of **unghia**; talon; (zool.) hoof. **-uto** *adj.* (fig.) rapacious, predatory.

ungi-mẹnto *m.*, **-tọre** *m.* See under **ungere**.

†**unguanno** *adv.* this year.

†**ungue** *f.* See **unghia**.

ungue-ale *adj.* (anat.) ungual, unguinal. **-ato** *adj.* (anat.) unguiculate

unguent-o *m.* unguent, ointment; — refrigerante, soothing ointment; (fig.) balm; remedy; dare dell'— a, to flatter; — di maggio, spring air (which cures chilblains); (joc.) — di zecca, money. †**-a·io** *m.* vendor of ointments; maker of ointments. **-are** [A 1] *tr.* to smear with ointment, to apply ointment to; †*rfl.* to perfume oneself. **-a·rio** *adj.* pertaining to unguents; vaso -ario, ointment jar; (bot.) ghianda -aria, myrobalon; *n.m.* maker or vendor of ointment. **-ato** *part. adj.* anointed with unguents; perfumed. †**-iere** *m.* see **unguentario**. **-i·fero** *adj.* ointment-producing.

un·gul-a *f.* (zool.) nail, hoof; (geom.) segment. **-ati** *m.pl.* (zool.) ungulates.

uniassiale *adj.* (scient.) uniaxial, mono-axial, monaxial.

uni·bil-e *adj.*, **-ità** *f.* See under **unire**.

unicabozimale *m.* (naut.) dinghy.

uni-cameralismo *m.* (pol.) single chamber system. **-cellulare** *adj.* (scient.) unicellular, single-celled. **-colọre** *adj.* of one colour, single-toned, one-hued, monochrome.

u·nic-o *adj.* only; sole; single; figlio —, only son, only child; one; unique; above comparison; atto —, one-act play; numero —, special number, publication which is not one of a series; (leg.) testo —, Consolidation Act; — azionista, sole shareholder (C.C.). **-amẹnte** *adv.* only; solely; uniquely.

unicorn-e *adj.* (anat.) unicornous, unicorn. **-o** *m.* (myth.) unicorn; (astron.) the constellation of the Unicorn.

unific-are [A 2 s] *tr.* to unify; to unite; to make one; to consolidate; to amalgamate; to standardize; (leg.) — i codici, to consolidate different codes of laws; — il diritto privato, to unify private law; — la legislazione, to consolidate the Acts or statutes; — le società, to amalgamate companies; — i prestiti, to consolidate loans; (econ.) — i debiti dello stato, to consolidate the National Debt. (**-a·bile** *adj.*) **-ativo** *adj.* unifying; standardizing. **-ato** *part. adj.* unified; united; made one; standardized; standard; (comm.) debito -ato, unified (loan) stock. **-atọre** *m.* uniter; (hist.) gli -atori d'Italia, those who brought about the Unification of Italy; standardizer; *adj.* unifying, uniting; centralizing; standardizing. (**-atrice** *f.*) **-azione** *f.* amalgamation; consolidation; centralization; (comm.) -azione delle società, amalgamation of companies; (techn.) standardization; unification; union; (hist.) l'Unificazione, the Unification (of Italy).

uniform-e *adj.* uniform; even; regular; — di dimensioni, of uniform size; unbroken; monotonous, same; — a, in keeping with; *n.f.* uniform; portare un'—, to wear uniform; regimentals; in grande —, in full dress. **-emẹnte** *adv.* uniformly; evenly, regularly. **-are** [A 1 c] *tr.* to render uniform; to standardize; to bring into line; -are a, to adopt to, to adjust to; *rfl.* to become uniform; -arsi a, to comply with; (of wind) to blow steadily, to be constant. (**-ato** *part. adj.*) **-azione** *f.* standardization; equalizing. **-ità** *f.* uniformity; conformity; identity; evenness, regularity; monotony, sameness.

†**unige·neo** *adj.* of the same nature.

unige·nere *adj.* (gramm.) single-gender.

unige·nito *m.* only son; *adj.* (theol.) only-begotten; *n.m.* il divino —, the only-begotten Son of God.

unilaterale *adj.* one-sided; unilateral; (leg.) atto —, Deed Poll; unilateral act or instrument.

uniloculare *adj.* (med.) unilocular.

unimetallismo *m.* (finan.) monometallism.

uninominale *adj.* (pol.) single-member; scrutinio —, voting for a single candidate; collegio —, single-member constituency.

union-e *f.* union; unity; society; league, association; group; concord, concordat; agreement; (mus.) coupler (of organ); (techn.) joint, jointing; (geog.) — Sudafricana, Union of S. Africa; — Sovietica, Soviet Union; — delle Repubbliche Socialiste Sovietiche, Union of Soviet Socialist Republics, U.S.S.R.; (leg.) — di cause, consolidation of actions (C.C.P.); una — di terra, an accretion (C.C.); (theol.) — ipostatica, Hypostatic Union; (paint.) harmony of lights and colours; blending; (comm.) contratto d'—, creditors' bill; in — alla Vostra (lettera), enclosed with your letter; (equit.) collection, the technique of getting a horse collected for a jump, etc. **-ista** *m.* (pol.) Unionist, adherent of policy of unity.

uni·par-o *adj.* (zool.) uniparous. **-a** *f.* (med.) unipara.

unipolar-e *adj.* (electr.) unipolar, homopolar, single-poled. **-ità** *f.* (electr.) unipolarity.

un-ire [D 2] *tr.* to unite; to unify; to join together; — ad una lettera, to enclose in a letter; — in matrimonio, to join in matrimony; to link; to bring together; — a, to add to; — il pregio dell'utilità con quello dell'eleganza, to combine usefulness with elegance; to fuse; to harmonize; (equit.) to collect; *rfl.* to unite, to become united; (*prep.* a) to join; molti si -irono a loro, many people joined them; to become a member of; to become part of; *recip. rfl.* to join, to be joined, to become joined, together; -irsi in matrimonio, to be joined in matrimony, (leg.) to intermarry; -irsi in società, to form a society. **-i·bile** *adj.* capable of being united; attachable. **-ibilità** *f.* unitability; attachableness. **-imẹnto** *m.* uniting. **-ito** *part. adj.* see separate entry.

unisessuale *adj.* (biol.) dioecious, unisexual.

unisi·l·labo *m.* monosyllable. **-la·bico** *adj.* monosyllabic.

uni·son-o *adj.* (mus.) unisonant; (fig.) agreeing; — a, in agreement with; *n.m.* (mus.) unison; canone all'—, canon at the unison; (fig.) unison, concord, harmony, agreement; essere all'—, to be in full accord; approvato all'—, unanimously approved. †**-anza** *f.* (mus.) unison. †**-are** *tr.* (mus.) to bring into unison.

†**unita** *f.* uniting; union.

unit-à *f.* unity; union; unitedness; oneness; concord; — d'azione, unity of action; le tre —, the three unities (in the construction of tragedy); (theol.) — di Dio, Divine Unity; unit; (leg.) la minima — culturale, the smallest farm acreage able to support a family (C.C.); (electr.) unit; (math.) unit; unity, one; (mil.) unit; regiment, corps, etc.; *pr.n.f.* title of a Communist daily paper. **-a·rio** *adj.* unitarian; (rel.) Unitarian; (leg.) avere una destinazione -aria, to serve a common purpose (C.C.); (econ.) prezzo -ario, average price; sistema -ario, unitary system; *n.m.* unitarian, advocate of unitarian policy or principles; (rel.) Unitarian.

unit-o *part.* of **unire**, q.v.; *adj.* united; joined; assembled; joint; — ad una lettera, enclosed in a letter; qui —, enclosed herewith; entire; compact; close-knit; even, regular; unvaried; superficie -a, unbroken surface; stile —, even style; tinta -a, even colour; moto —, regular movement; harmonious; in agreement; animi -i, minds that are at one; (text.) plain, all one colour; (eccl.) chiese orientali -e, churches of Eastern rites in communion with the Holy See, 'Uniate' Eastern Churches; (equit.) trotto —, collected trot, canter; (geog.) Regno Unito, United Kingdom; Stati Uniti, U.S.A., United States (of America). **-amẹnte** *adv.* together; unitedly; conjointly. **-ẹzza** *f.* compactness; firmness (of texture); uniformity, evenness (of colour); -ezza di stile, regularity of style. **-itọre** *m.* uniter; *adj.* uniting. (**-itrice** *f.*) **-itura** *f.* uniting, union; oneness; point of union. **-ivo** *adj.* uniting, unifying; (gramm.) le congiunzioni -ive, the conjunctive conjunctions (as opposed to disjunctive); copulative.

universit-à *f.* university (usu. '— degli Studi'); andare all'—, to go to a university; †all the inhabitants of a city, province, or kingdom; †all humanity, all mankind; †universality. **-a·rio** *adj.* pertaining to a university, of a university; laurea -aria, university degree; vita -aria, university life; studente -ario, university student; *n.m.* university teacher, academic, university man.

univers-o *m.* universe; whole world; all mankind; creation, cosmos; *adj.* universal; whole, entire; l'— mondo, the whole world.

univers-o (*cont.*)

(**-amẹnte** *adv.*) **-ale** *adj.* universal; storia -ale, universal history, history of mankind; common; widespread; very usual; suffragio -ale, universal suffrage; all-round, all-purposes; ingegno -ale, versatile mind, many-sided ability; (philos.) idea -ale, universal idea; (theol.) giudizio -ale, general judgement; Last Judgement; risurrezione -ale, general resurrection; (med.) paralisi -ale, total paralysis; (leg.) erede -ale, universal heir, sole next-of-kin, sole residuary legatee; †uomo -ale, man who knows everything, person with encyclopaedic knowledge; *n.m.* totality; full complement; the people at large; in -ale, nell'-ale, on the whole, all in all, †universally; accetto all'-ale, acceptable to all; (philos.) universal; †map of the world. **-almẹnte** *adv.* universally; throughout the world; by everybody, generally. **-aleggiare** [A 3 c] *tr.* to render universal, to make general. **-alità** *f.* universality; entirety; †universal knowledge; (leg.) una -alità di mobili, an aggregation of personal property (C.C.). **-alizzare** [A I] *tr.* to make universal, to make general; to make accessible to all. (**-alizzato** *part. adj.*)

uni·vọc-o *adj.* univocal, having only one meaning; not equivocal, unambiguous. (**-amẹnte** *adv.*) **-aziọne** *f.* unambiguousness.

†**un-iziọne** *f.* union. †**-izzare** *tr.* to unify.

Unn-o *pr.n.m.* (hist.) Hun. **-ico** *adj.* relating to the Huns.

un-o 1. *indef. art. m.*, **-a** *f.* (contracted to **un** before a masculine noun beginning with a vowel or before a consonant other than **z** or impure **s**) A, AN; one; un cento, about a hundred; un quattro o cinque, four or five; un Michelangelo, a (veritable) Michelangelo; gli venne un appetito!, he developed a terrific appetite; (herald.) dell'uno nell'altro, dall'uno all'altro, counterchanged. 2. *card. num.* ONE; one single; the number one, the figure one; tre -i, three ones; un asino numero —, a prodigious ass; ad — ad —, one by one, one after the other; dieci contro —, ten to one; all'-a, at one o'clock; camminare per —, to walk in single file; †(gramm.) numero dell'—, singular; (fig.) numero —, tip-top, A 1, foremost, excellent; in —, together; unity; totality; rimanere nella via -a, never to get any 'forrader'. 3. *indef. prn.* ONE; someone; — di campagna, a man from the country; l'un l'altro, each other; gli -i gli altri, one another; nè l'—nè l'altro, neither; — compensando l'altro, averaging one with the other. 4. *adj.* UNITED, one; siamo -i di lingua, di fede e d'armi, we are united under one language, one faith, one army; sono tutt'—, they're great friends; è tutt'—, it's identical, *or* it's all one, it doesn't matter. †**-o·culo**, †**-oculo** *adj.* one-eyed.

†**unqu-a**, †**-e**, †**-anche**, †**-anco**, †**-ema·i** *adv.* ever; never.

untare [A I] and derivs. See under **unto**.

unt-o *part.* of **ungere**, q.v.; *adj.* greasy; oily; dirty; — e bisunto, all greasy, very oily; (fig.) bocca -a, oily tongue; anointed; *n.m.* (Bibl.) l'Unto del Signore, the Lord's Anointed; grease; lard; dare l'— a, to grease (see also under fig.); macchie d'—, grease spots; l'— della carne, fat of meat; (fig.) flattery; dare dell'— a, to 'butter up'. **-are** [A I] *tr.* to grease; to oil; (fig.) -are la mano a, to grease the palm of. **-ata** *f.* greasing; oiling; dare un'-ata a, to give a touch of grease to; (fig.) flattery, 'buttering up'. (**-ato** *part. adj.* **-atọre** *m.* **-atrice** *f.*) **-atura** *f.* thorough greasing or oiling. **-ọre** *m.* greaser; (hist.) gli -ori, people suspected in Milan in the seventeenth century of spreading the plague by smearing a poisonous substance on walls (see A. Manzoni, *I Promessi Sposi*, and *Storia della Colonna Infame*). (**-rice** *f.*) **-orello** *m. dim.* see untore. †**-o·rio** *m.* unguent; (class. antiq.) *unctorium*, the anointing room in a bath. **-ume** *m.* dripping; lard; grease; fat; dirt, filth. **-uosità** *f.* greasiness; oiliness; (fig.) unctuousness. **-uọso** *adj.* greasy; oily; (fig.) unctuous; sanctimonious; modi -uosi, unctuous behaviour. **-ura** *f.* greasing; oiling.

unziọne *f.* greasing; (med.) application of ointment; (liturg.) anointing, unction; — estrema, Extreme Unction.

†**tuo'** *m.* See **uopo**.

uo·m-o *m.* (*pl.* **uọ·mini**) man; grown man, adult; person; human being; — economico, economic man; a memoria d'—, in human memory; gli -ini, men, mankind; l'— qualunque, l'— medio, the man in the street, the common man; un — da nulla, a nonentity; un pover'—, a poor man, an unfortunate wretch; un — povero, a man who is poor; un — fatto, a grown-up man; portarsi da —, to behave manfully; a tutt'—, with all one's might and main; da — a —, as man to man; servant, manservant; workman, hand, labourer; (mil.) soldier; quattro -ini e un caporale, four men and a corporal; (naut.) nostr'—, see **nostromo**; — in mare!, man

overboard!; — rana, frogman; — morto, dead man, (fig.) hat-stand, †(naut.) bollard; — di chiesa, ecclesiastic, churchman; †*impers. prn.* one.

uopo *m.* need; necessity; essere —, essere d'—, to be necessary; avere —, avere d'—, to have need (of); all'—, in case of necessity, if need be; benefit, advantage.

uọṣa *f.* legging; *pl.* hose, leggings; tights; thigh-boots.

uọv-o *m.* (*pl.f.* **-a**) egg; (biol.) egg; (zool.) — di mare, *Microcosmus sulcatus*, an edible tunicate; guscio d'—, eggshell; deporre le -a, to lay eggs; schiacciare -a, to crack eggs; la chiara d'—, white of egg; il tuorlo d'—, yolk of egg; — fresco, — da bere, egg eaten raw; — della giornata, new-laid egg; — in camicia, — affogato, poached egg; — in padella, — affrittellato, fried egg; — all'ostrica, egg yolk eaten raw with a few drops of lemon juice and a pinch of salt, 'prairie oyster'; -a al burro, -a nel tegamino, eggs cooked in butter in the oven in a baking-dish; -a sode, hard-boiled eggs; -a impazzate, -a strapazzate, scrambled eggs; sbattere le -a, frullare le -a, to beat eggs; (provb.) meglio un — oggi che una gallina domani, a bird in the hand is worth two in the bush; trovare il pel nell'—, to find fault with the smallest detail, to be finiking; essere come bere un —, to be as easy as falling off a log, to be 'a piece of cake'; rompere le -a nel paniere a, to put a spoke in the wheel of; accomodare le -a nel panierino, to feather one's nest; (rel.) — benedetto, — di Pasqua, egg blessed by priest for Easter, Easter egg; Pasqua d'—, Easter.

uo·volo *m.* (bot.) ovule.

upas *f. indecl.* (bot.) arrow poison, obtained from the upas tree (*Antiaris toxicaria*); (chem.) upas.

u·pupa *f.* (orn.) hoopoe, *Upupa epops*.

u·rac-o *m.* (anat.) urachus. **-ale** *adj.* (anat.) urachal. **-ile** *adj.* (pharm.) uracil.

uragan-o *m.* (naut.; meteor.) hurricane (Beaufort scale 12); (fig.) storm; — d'applausi, thunderous applause, a storm of clapping. **-ọso** *adj.* hurricane-like; pertaining to a hurricane; nubi -ose, hurricane clouds.

Urali *pr.n.m.pl.* (geog.) Urals, Ural mountains.

uramile *m.* (chem.) uramil, dialuramide.

uran-go *m.* (*pl.* **-ghi**) (zool.) orang-utan.

Ura·nia *pr.n.f.* (myth.; astron.) Urania.

ura·nico *adj.* (chem.) uranic.

uran-ile *m.* (chem.) uranyl. **-i·lico** *adj.* (chem.) uranyl.

uraninite *f.* (miner.) uraninite, pitchblende.

ura·n-io *m.* (chem.) uranium. **-ato** *m.* uranate. **-iṣmo** *m.* (med.) uranism. **-ite** *f.* (med.) uranitis.

Urano *pr.n.m.* (myth.; astron.) Uranus, Heaven.

urano-grafi·a *f.* (astron.) uranography. **-gra·fico** *adj.* (astron.) uranographical. **-mani·a** *f.* (psych.) uranomania, religious mania. **-metri·a** *f.* (astron.) uranometry. **-me·trico** *adj.* (astron.) uranometrical. **-pla·stica** *f.* (surg.) uranisoplasty. **-rrafi·a** *f.* (surg.) uraniscorrhaphy. **-schiṣi** *f.* (med.) uraniscochasma, uranoschisis, cleft palate. **-scopi·a** *f.* uranoscopy, astronomical observation. **-sco·pio** *m.* telescope. **-steopla·stica** *f.* (med.) uraniscosteoplasty.

urano·scopo *m.* astronomical observer, stargazer; (ichth.) stargazer, *Uranoscopus scaber*.

ura·o *m.* (miner.) urao, trona.

ura·tico *adj.* (med.) uratic.

urat-o *m.* (chem.) urate. **-o·liṣi** *f.* (med.) uratolysis. **-oli·tico** *adj.* (med.) uratolytic. **-oma** *m.* (med.) uratoma, tophus. **-uri·a** *f.* (med.) uraturia.

urban-o[1] *adj.* urban, city; polizia -a, city police; vigile —, city policeman; nettezza -a, refuse collection in a city; (leg.) pretura -a, magistrates' or police court; county courts; court of Petty Session; urbane, polite; civilized; cultured. **-amẹnte** *adv.* urbanely; politely, civilly. **-e·ṣimo**, **-ẹṣimo**, **-iṣmo** *m.* urbanism; growth of towns; tendency of population to settle in cities. **-i·stica** *f.* town planning. **-ità** *f.* urbanity, urbaneness; civility; politeness, courtesy.

Urban-o[2] *pr.n.m.* Urban. **-iste** *f.pl.* (eccl.) Urbanist nuns (Poor Clares).

urbe *f.* (Lat.) city; l'Urbe, Rome, the Eternal City; (eccl.) Urbi et Orbi, *Urbi et Orbi*, to Rome and the world (used sometimes of papal decrees so promulgated, more usu. of papal blessing so given); (colloq.) noto urbi et orbi, known to one and all, greatly renowned.

urceolato *adj.* (archit.) bulging, like an oil jar.

ure·a *f.* (chem.) urea, carbamide. **-aṣi** *f.* (chem.) urase. **-ide** *f.* (chem.) ureide. **-ometri·a** *f.* (med.) ureametry, ureometry. **-ome·trico** *adj.* ureametrical, ureometrical. **-o·metro** *m.* (med.) ureameter, ureometer.

†**urec·chio** *m.* See orecchio.

ure·dine *f.* (bot.) rust fungus.

ur-emi·a *f.* (med.) uraemia. **-e·mico** *adj.* (med.) uraemic.

urente *adj.* (med.) burning, feverish; (poet.) burning; fevered.

uretano *m.* (chem.) urethane.

uret-ere *m.* (anat.) ureter. **-erale** *adj.* (anat.) ureteral. **-erovescicale** *adj.* (med.) ureterovesical. **-ra** *f.* (anat.) urethra. **-rale** *adj.* (anat.) urethral. **-rite** *f.* (med.) urethritis. **-roscopi·a** *f.* (med.) urethroscopy. **-rosco·pico** *adj.* (med.) urethroscopic. **-rosco·pio** *m.* (med.) urethroscope. **-rotomi·a** *f.* (surg.) urethrotomy.

urgen-te *adj.* urgent; pressing; immediate; caso —, urgent case; *n.m.* express telegram. **-temẹnte** *adv.* urgently. **-za** *f.* urgency; urgent need; emergency; d'-za, urgent, urgently, in an emergency; promptness, speed; con la massima -za, with the utmost speed; soccorsi d'-za, first-aid; (leg.) chiedere l'-za, to ask that a matter be treated as urgent; applicare la procedura di -za, to apply the 'urgent' procedure; provvedimenti d'-za, Interim Orders (in urgent matters) (C.C.P.); (Parliament) dichiarare l'-za di un disegno di legge, to declare a Bill proper for the short procedure (I.C.). **-zare** [A I] *tr.* (comm.) to speed up, to expedite.

ur·gere [def.] *tr.* to urge; to press; to incite; *intr.* (no compound tenses) to be urgent; urge che tu ci sia, it is vital that you should be there; to be pressing; urgono aiuti, help is urgently needed.

ui *f. indecl.* houri, huri.

u·ria *f.* (orn.) guillemot, *Uria aalge*; — nera, black guillemot, *Cepphus grylle*.

u·ric-o *adj.* (chem.) uric. **-emi·a** *f.* (med.) uricacidaemia. **-e·mico** *adj.* (med.) uricacidaemic. **-o·liṣi** *f.* (med.) uricolysis.

†**urin-a** *f.* and derivs. see orina. **-are** *vb.* and derivs. see orinare.

urin-i·fero *adj.* (anat.) uriniferous. **-i·paro** *adj.* (anat.) producing urine.

url-are [A I] *intr.* (aux. avere) to howl; to shriek; to bawl; to shout, to yell, to bawl; — a, to shout at, to scold. **-amẹnto** *m.* howl. **-ante** *part. adj.* howling. **-ata** *f.* howl; yell; hoots of derision. **-ato** *adj.* howled down, derided. (**-atore** *m.* **-atrice** *f.*) **-io** *m.* (*pl.* **-ii**) prolonged howling; frequent howling.

url-o *m.* (*pl.* **-i** *m.*) howl (of an animal); howling (of the wind); (*pl.* **-a** *f.*) shout, yell (of a human); shriek; gettare un —, to give a yell; perdere l'—, to lose one's voice. **-ọne** *m.* shouter, yeller; (zool.) howling monkey, *Mycetes* spp.

urna *f.* urn; — cineraria, funeral urn; ballot-box; uscire vittorioso dalle urne, to be elected; disertare le urne, not to vote; il responso delle urne, the result of an election; (poet.) tomb.

urnin·gio *m.* urning, homosexual.

uro *m.* (zool.) auroch, *Bos primigenius*.

ur-obilina *f.* (chem.) urobilin. **-ocele** *m.* (med.) urocele. **-ociste**, **-ocisti**, **-ocite** *f.* (med.) urocyst. **-ocromo** *m.* (physiol.) urochrome. **-oeritrina** *f.* (med.) uroerythrin. **-oliti·aṣi** *f.* (med.) urolithiasis. **-olito** *m.* (med.) urinary calculus, urolith. **-oluteina** *f.* (physiol.) urolutein. **-o·metro** *m.* (med.) urinometer. **-oscopi·a** *f.* (med.) uroscopy. **-otropina** *f.* (chem.) urotropin, hexamethylene tetramine.

urodeli *m.pl.* (zool.) urodeles (newts, salamanders).

ur-ologi·a *f.* (med.) urology. **-olo·gico** *adj.* (med.) urological. **-o·logo** *m.* (*pl.* **-o·loghi**) (med.) urologist.

urọne *adj.*, *n.m.* (ethn.) Huron, Huronian.

uroniano *adj.* (geol.) Huronian.

uropati·a *f.* (med.) uropathy.

uropi·gio *m.* (orn.) uropygium (rump of bird.)

uropoieṣi *f.* (med.) ureapoiesis.

urotropina *f.* (chem.) hexamethylenetetramine, urotropine.

urrà, urrah *excl.* hurrah!; hooray!; ip, ip —!, hip, hip, hurrah!; *n.m. indecl.* a shout 'hurrah!'; un triplice —, three cheers; un formidabile —, terrific cheering.

†**ursac·chio** *m.* See orsacchio.

ursọne *m.* (zool.) porcupine, *Hystrix* spp.

urta *f.* See under urtare.

urt-are [A I] *tr.* to jolt; to hurtle; to bump against; to stumble against; to collide with; to shove, to push; to strike; mi -a i nervi, it gets on my nerves; *intr.* (aux. avere, *prep.* in) to run up against; — in uno scoglio, to bump into a rock; (fig.) — in una difficoltà,

to come up against a difficulty; *recip. rfl.* to jostle one another, to push and shove; to collide; to clash; to quarrel. **-a** *f.* dislike; prendere in — a qualcuno, to take a dislike to someone; avere in — a, to dislike, to have a grudge against. **-acchiare** [A 3] *tr.* to brush against, to jostle slightly. **-amẹnto** *m.* jostling; bumping; shoving. **-ante** *part. adj.* jostling; (fig.) brusque; irritating, annoying (also *n.m.*). **-ata** *f.* push, shove; jolt; bump. **-ato** *part. adj.* jostled; pushed about; irritated; shocked; annoyed; -ato contro, antagonized towards. **-atọre** *m.* jostler; rough, clumsy individual; (poet.) Nettuno -atore, Neptune the earth-shaker. (**-atrice** *f.*) **-atura** *f.* shove, push; bump; bumping; jostling.

urt-o *m.* push; shove; knock; clash; collision; (rlwy.) crash; (naut.) collision; ramming; blow; touching bottom; (mil.) contact; l'— dell'attacco, the brunt of the attack; (eng.) impact; — di caduta, drop impact; (fig.) — di nervi, irritation; — d'idee, clash of ideas; — d'interessi, conflict of interests; essere in — con, to be on bad terms with, to be at loggerheads with; *apocop. part.*, *adj.* see urtato. **-elli** *m.pl.* soft padding on a saddle. **-icchiare** [A 4] *tr.* to jostle slightly, to jerk. **-onata** *f.* violent push. **-ọne** *m.* *augm.* of **urto**; violent push.

urubu *m. indecl.* (orn.) turkey vulture, *Cathartes aura*.

uṣ-are [A I] *tr.* to use; to make use of; to handle; — minacce, to use threats; — modi gentili, to behave politely; — pietà, to be compassionate; — la massima cura, to exercise the greatest care; — vino, to have the habit of drinking wine; non -a mai medicine, he never takes medicine; to show, to display, m'ha -ato tante premure, he has shown me great courtesy; to practise; — carità, to practise charity, to be charitable; — la cortesia di, to be so kind as to; — cortesia a, to be courteous to; to wear out; to use up; *intr.* (aux. avere) to be accustomed to; in quel paese -ano fare così, it is the custom in that country; -a alzarsi presto al mattino, he is accustomed to rise early in the morning; to be the custom, to be in fashion (cf. *impers.*); quest'anno -ano le sottane strette, tight skirts are the fashion this year; questo non -a più, this is out of fashion; to behave; (provb.) quel che s'-a, non fa scusa, custom is no excuse; to keep company; — con cattivi compagni, to keep bad company; †— con donne, to have sexual intercourse with women; (*prep.* di) to avail oneself of, to make use of; — di un diritto, to avail oneself of a right; *impers.* to be customary; incontrandosi -a salutare, it is customary to greet one another on meeting; †to be the custom to go. **-a·bile** *adj.* usable; fit for use; current. **-ante** *part. adj.* using; †*n.m.* see utente. **-anza** *f.* usage; custom; avere -anza, to be accustomed, to have the habit; (provb.) tanti paesi, tante -anze, *autres pays*, *autres mœurs*; paese che vai, — che trovi, when in Rome, do as the Romans do; (leg.) usance; custom. **-ato** *part. adj.* used; employed; worn out; second-hand; customary, usual; le cortesie -atemi, the courtesy shown me; trained, accustomed; -ato alle armi, trained to arms; *n.m.* custom; più dell'-ato, più che l'-ato, more than is customary; secondo l'-ato, as is usual, in the usual way. **-atamẹnte** *adv.* usually; commonly. (**-atore** *m.* **-atrice** *f.*) †**-e·vole** *adj.* customary.

†**uṣatto** *m. dim.* of uosa, q.v.; leather boot; riding boot; pouch, container, pocket; truss.

uṣbergo *m.* hauberk, coat of mail; (fig.) defence, protection.

uscente *part.* of uscire, q.v.

usc-ẹtto *m. dim.* of uscio, q.v.; wicket-gate. **-ino** *m. dim.* of uscio.

u·sci-o *m.* door; a — a —, from door to door, from house to house; stare sull'—, to stand in the doorway; l'— di strada, the front door, the street door; exit; prendere l'—, to take oneself off; opening, outlet; entrance; (poet.) threshold; (provb.) è come dire all'—, you might as well talk to the wall; essere a — e bottega, to be cheek by jowl, to be as thick as thieves; non si trovano a ogni —, they're not to be found on every hedgerow; avere il male, il malanno e l'— addosso, to be up to the eyes in trouble; trovarsi tra l'— e il muro, to have one's back to the wall; il peggior passo è quello dell'—, the first step is the most difficult. †**-a·ia** *f.* door. **-ale** *m.* glass door; †threshold; †portière. **-ata** *f.* slam of a door, dare un'-ata sul muso a uno, to slam the door in somebody's face. **-ere** *m.* usher; door-keeper; -ere di campagna, high bailiff; (leg.) usher; bailiff; tipstaff; mandare gli -eri, to issue a warrant of distress, to put the bailiffs in; atto di -ere, duty of an usher; -ere giudiziario, sheriff's officer, Court bailiff, tipstaff. **-olare** [A I S] *intr.* (aux. avere) to listen at keyholes. **-olino**, **-(u)olo** *dim.* of uscio; wicket, wicket-gate; (provb.) sole a -uoli,

usci-o (*cont.*)

acqua a bigonciuoli, when the sun peeps from behind clouds, rain is coming.

usc-ire [D 16] *intr.* (*aux.* essere) to go out; to come out; fare —, to let out; -ite!, get out!; — a passeggio, to go out for a walk; -iamo un po'!, let's go for a little walk; — di casa, to leave the house; — dalla porta, to go out by the door; — per la finestra, to get out through the window; — del letto, to get up, to get out of bed; — di collegio, to leave school; to come through; — illeso e salvo, to come through unscathed; — vincitore, to come off victorious, to come out top; — di mano a, to escape from, to fall from one's hand, to be the work of, to come forth from the hands of; — di mente a, to slip one's memory; mi è -ito di mente, I forgot all about it; — di vita, to depart this life; — di carica, to end a term of office; — dal seminato, to digress; — di guai, to get over difficulties; — dal ginepraio, to be out of the wood; — di sè, to be beside oneself; — di cervello, to go off one's head; (of flowers) to come out, to bud; (of the sun) to come out, to break through; to originate, to issue; — di buona famiglia, to be of good family; di dove è -ito quello lì?, where did that chap spring from?; to come out, to be issued; — alla luce, to be published; to come to light; to be finished; to end, to terminate; una parola che esce in consonante, a word ending in a consonant; to burst out, to act precipitately; — a sclamare, to exclaim suddenly; — fuori con una proposta, to come out with a suggestion; to result; to be got out (of); di questa materia non ci esce un vestito, you won't get a dress out of this material, there's not enough material to make a dress; (naut.) — dalla portata del cannone, to pass out of range; — in rado, to go to outer anchorage; — dal bacino, — dalla darsena, to undock; — fuori ai pennoni, to go out to the yard-arms; — in mare, to put out to sea; †— con la miccia in mano, to sail ready for action; (archit.) to project; *rfl.* -irsene, to get out of it, to get rid of it, to get through somehow. **-ente** *part. adj.* (of an official, etc.) retiring, retiring from office, out-going; ending; vocabolo -ente in vocale, word ending in a vowel; (herald.) leone -ente, demi-lion issuant. **-imento** *m.* leaving; issuing; exit; impedire l'-imento, to block up an outlet. **-ita** *f.* exit; way out, egress; vietata l'-ita, no exit; -ita di sicurezza, emergency exit; giornata di -ita, day off; outcome, upshot; issuing forth, departure; end; ending, termination; statement, remark, *bon mot*; emergence (e.g. from egg); — dell'ago, withdrawal of the needle (in injections); (mil.) sally; exit, escape route; (techn.) outlet; (mus.) -ita di tono, modulation, change of key; (soccer) coming out of goal (of goalkeeper); (rugby) -ita laterale, touch; (telev.) monitore di -ita, actual monitor; (comm.) expenditure; l'-ita supera l'entrata, expenditure exceeds income; -ita al noleggiatore, dispatch money; dichiarazione d'-ita, declaration outwards; diritti d'-ita, export duty; entrata ed -ita, income and expenditure; buon'-ita, goodwill (of business), premium (to outgoing tenant, etc.); permesso d'-ita, clearance permit. **-ito** *part. adj.* out; gone out; issued; published; descended (from), sprung (from).

Uscocchi *pr.n.m.pl.* Uskok, Serbo-Croat refugees who settled in Albania, Croatia and Dalmatia; pirates in the Adriatic who fought against the Turks.

usignuolo *m.* (orn.) nightingale, *Luscinia megarhyncos*; — d'Africa, rufous warbler, *Agrobates galactotes*; — di fiume, Cetti's warbler, *Cettia cetti*; — maggiore, thrush nightingale, *Luscinia luscinia*.

usitat-o *adj.* frequently used, in common use; employed; frequented; usual; all'ora -a, at the usual hour; *n.m.* constant use. (**-amente** *adv.*)

us-o *adj.* accustomed; — a, in the habit of, inured to; *n.m.* use; fare — di, to use; fare — di vino, to drink wine; fare — di medicine, to take medicine; ad — di, for the use of; purpose; a che — serve?, what's it for; fuori d'—, old-fashioned, no longer current; fuori —, unserviceable, out of use; dell'—, in use, current; usage; — esterno, external use; custom, habit; fashion; style; a —, all'—, customary; parla a — contadino, he speaks peasant-fashion, like a peasant; un'azionaccia a — Giovanni, a nasty trick of the kind that John goes in for; avere per —, to be usual; practice; conosco il francese ma mi manca l'—, I know French but I'm a bit rusty; fare — del diritto di voto, to exercise the right to vote; *pl.* conventions; (naut.) -i di mare, -i marittimi, maritime practice; (leg.) custom (one of the sources of 'diritto', C.C.); usage; -i e costumi, usages and customs; -i civici, civic customs; user; diritto d'—,

right of user; il non —, non-user (C.C.); use; — illegittimo di cadavere, unlawful use of cadaver (C.P.); (finan.) a —, in token, in lieu of; (comm.) cambiale ad —, bill payable at usance; interesse ad —, usual interest; — e consumo, wear and tear; ad — e consumo di, for the greater convenience of; — di commercio, trade custom.

usofrutto *m.* See usufrutto, under usuario.

usolare [A I S] and derivs. See usciolare, under uscio.

†usoliere *m.* belt; braces.

us·saro *m.* (mil.) hussar.

us·sero *m.* (pop. Tusc.). See ussaro.

Ussita *pr.n.m.* (rel. hist.) Hussite.

†usso *m.* gipsy.

ussoricida *m.* and deriv. See uxoricida.

usta *f.* scent (of hounds).

ustion-e *f.* (surg.) cauterization; (med.) burn. **-are** [A I C] *tr.* (med.) to cauterize.

†usto¹ *m.* (naut.) double length of mooring cable; port cable.

ust-o² *adj.* burnt; (chem.) calcined; magnesia -a, calcined magnesia. **-o·rio** *adj.* specchio -orio, burning-glass. **-rina** *f.* (Gk. and Rom. antiq.) crematorium. **-ulazione** *f.* (chem.) drying over a flame.

ustol-are [A I S] *intr.* (*aux.* avere) to whine, to beg; †to long, to feel ardent desire. **-one** *m.* whining beggar.

usual-e *adj.* usual; customary; common, ordinary; nel modo —, in the usual way; alle condizioni -i, on the usual terms; †convenient to use. **-mente** *adv.* usually; commonly; ordinarily. **-ità** *f.* usualness, customariness; commonness.

usu-a·rio *m.* (leg.) user (enjoyer of use). **-capione** *f.* (leg.) acquisition of ownership by long use or enjoyment; acquisition of property by prescription; usucaption. **-capire** [D I] *tr.* (leg.) to acquire by prescription; to acquire title by uninterrupted possession. **-catto** *adj.* (leg.) acquired by adverse possession for prescribed period. **-fruire** [D 2] *intr.* (*aux.* avere; *prep.* di) to benefit; to take advantage (of); (leg.) to enjoy; to have an interest in. **-fruito** *part. adj.* benefited. **†-fruttare**, **†-fruttuare** *tr.* to benefit from, to have the benefit of; to exhaust; to exploit; to have sexual intercourse with. **-frutto** *m.* (leg.) usufruct (strictly: right of temporary possession, use or enjoyment of the advantages of property belonging to another so far as may be had without causing damage or prejudice to it); life or lesser interest; tenancy for life; -frutto legale, legal interest of parent, during infancy, in property of infant (C.C.). **-fruttua·rio** *adj.* (leg.) usufructuary; relating to usufruct; *n.m.* usufructuary; tenant for life.

usur-a¹ *f.* usury; high interest; prestare ad —, to lend at interest; excessive profit; (fig.) ad —, in full measure; (leg.) usury (C.P.); †benefit received for use of money or a thing lent. **-a·io** *m.* usurer; miser, skinflint. **-a·rio** *adj.* pertaining to usury; (leg.) interessi -ari, usurious interest (C.C.). (**-eggiamento** *m.*) **-eggiare** [A 3 C] *intr.* (*aux.* avere) to practise usury; to lend at high interest. **-eggiato** *part. adj.* gained by usury. **†-iare** *tr.* to lend at usury. **†-iere**, **†iero** *m.* usurer.

usur-a² *f.* wear, wear and tear; indumenti resistenti all'—, hard-wearing clothes; (techn.) fretting. **-are** [A I] to use up, to wear out.

usurp-are [A I] *tr.* to usurp; to occupy by fraud; (leg.) to encroach upon; to trespass upon (land); — una decorazione, to wear a decoration to which one has no right (C.P.); to supplant; to intrude on; to use; — un vocabolo, to use a word (in a certain arbitrary sense); — la faccia di filantropo, to put on a benevolent expression. **-amento** *m.* usurping, usurpation. **-ativo** *adj.* usurping; (fig.) presumptuous, preposterous. (**-ativamente** *adv.*) **-ato** *part. adj.* usurped; illicitly held; used; vocabolo -ato in senso metaforico, word used in a metaphorical sense; †usual. **-atore** *m.* usurper. (**-atrice** *f.*) **-ato·rio** *adj.* (*m.pl.* -atorii) usurping. **-azione** *f.* usurpation; (leg.) intrusion; encroachment; -azione di una funzione pubblica, usurpation of public office (C.P.).

ut *m. indecl.* (mus.) do (i.e. first degree of scale), doh, ut; the note C; the key of C.

†utello *m.* small glazed earthenware oil-jar.

uten·sil-e *m.* utensil; implement; tool; -i di corredo, borsa -i, tool kit, set of tools; — meccanico, power tool; (eng.) macchina —, machine tool. **-eri·a** *f.* (eng.) tooling; set of tools; tool store.

uten·te *m.* user; consumer; gli -ti del gas, gas consumers; (telephone) subscriber; (leg.) beneficiary; tenant. **-za** *f.* (leg.) right of use; usage.

u·ter-o *m.* (anat.) womb, uterus; (fig.) bosom; heart. **-o-addominale** *adj.* (anat.; med.) utero-abdominal. **-ocervicale** *adj.* (anat.) utero-cervical. **-ino** *adj.* uterine; (leg.) born of one mother, uterine; fratelli -ini, brothers born of one mother but of different fathers, half-brothers. **-o-ova·rico** *adj.* (anat.) utero-ovarian. **-otuba·rico** *adj.* (anat.) uterotubal.

u·til-e *adj.* useful; serviceable; effective; usable; profitable; helpful; un rimedio — alla dissenteria, a remedy good for dysentery; (provb.) tutti sono -i e nessuno è necessario, nobody is indispensable; superficie —, working area, working top; carico —, payload; (pol.) — idiota, fellow-traveller (in sense of being favourable towards Communism); (leg.) tempo —, due time, time allowed; il termine — per iscriversi, the last day for registration; — versione, conversion to one's own use; *n.m.* profit; utility; usefulness; benefit; advantage; (econ.) interest; profit; gain; — lordo, gross profit; — netto, net profit; — sociale, profit available for distribution; partecipare agli -i, to share in the profits. **-mente** *adv.* usefully; profitably; passare il tempo -mente, to spend the time usefully. **-ità** *f.* utility; usefulness; essere di grande -ità, to be very useful; riuscire d'-ità, to prove useful; profit; benefit; advantage; ne ebbe poca -ità, he didn't get much use out of it; (leg.) espropriazione per -ità pubblica, compulsory acquisition for public purposes (C.C.); †interest, profit, gain. **-ita·rio** *adj.* (philos.) utilitarian; for everyday use; automobile -itaria, utility car, a run-about, cheap non-luxury but efficient car; *n.m.* (philos.) Utilitarian. **-itarismo** *m.* (philos.) Utilitarianism. **-itarista** *m.* (philos.) Utilitarian. **-itari·stico** *adj.* (philos.) Utilitaristic. **-izzare** [A 1] *tr.* to utilize; to turn to account; to convert to one's use. **-izza·bile** *adj.* utilizable; adaptable. (-izzato *part. adj.*) **-izzazione** *f.* utilization; using, use.

†**utonno** *m.* See **autunno**.

Utop-i·a *pr.n.f.* Utopia; unrealizable aspiration. **-ista** *m.*, *f.* Utopian; impractical dreamer; idealist; *adj.* Utopian. **-i·stico** *adj.* Utopian; impracticable.

†**tutr-e, -icello** *m.* See **otre**.

utroque (Lat.) (leg.) dottore in — iure, U.J.D., doctor of civil and canon law.

†**tutte** *m. indecl.* (mus.). See **ut**.

uum *excl.* See **uhm**.

uv-a *f.* grapes; un chicco d'—, a grape; un grappolo d'—, a bunch of grapes; un po' d'—, some grapes; — acerba, sour grapes (also fig.); (bot.) — di volpe, herb paris, *Paris quadrifolia*; — fragola, fox grape, *Vitis labrusca*; — marina, sea-grape, *Ephedra distachya*; — orsina, bear-berry, *Arctostaphylos uva-ursi*; — spina, gooseberry, *Ribes grossularia*; — passa, — secca, raisins; zucchero d'—, grape sugar, glucose; — fragola, — americana, a very sweet kind of grape. **-a·ceo** *adj.* relating to grapes; grape-coloured. **-ag·gio** *m.* grapes of different kinds; wine made from these. **-i·fero** *adj.* (agric.) grape-bearing.

u·ve-a *f.* (anat.) uvea. **-ale** *adj.* (anat.) uveal.

u·vola *f.* See **uvola**.

u·vula *f.* (anat.) uvula.

uxori-cida *m.* (leg.) uxoricide; wife-killer. **-ci·dio** *m.* uxoricide, wife-killing (C.P.).

uzza *f.* keen, pungent atmosphere with a light breeze; sharpness in the air; tang.

uzz-o *m.* bulge, belly (of a cask); (techn.) bilge; dar — a, to shape (a cask). **-ato** *adj.* bulging, bellied (or like a cask).

uz·zol-o *m.* (colloq., Tusc.) whim, fancy; caprice; craze; bee in one's bonnet; mi è venuto l'— di, I've developed a craze for. **-ire** [D 2] see **inuzzolire**.

v *m., f.* (pron. **vu**, colloq. **vi**) the letter V; the consonant V; (aeron.) formazione a V, wedge formation; (eng.; aeron.) incastratura a V, fishmouth splice.

va'[1] *excl.* see!; look!

va'[2] *imp.* of **andare**, q.v.

va bene *excl.* all right! (cf. **andare**).

vac-are [A 2] *intr.* (aux. essere) (of a post, position, office, etc.) to be vacant; to be unoccupied; to be empty; -ava il posto, the post was vacant; to fall vacant, to become vacant; (eccl.) to be vacant; (of a person) to be free, to have nothing to do; — a, to be free to devote oneself to; — agli studi, to concentrate on one's work,

to give oneself up to one's studies; †to come to an end; †— di, to be lacking in, to lack; †— da, to cease; *tr.* (leg.) to vacate. **-a·bile** *adj.* able to be vacated; liable to be vacated; ufficio -abile, office that can be vacated; *adj.* (eccl. hist.) vacabile, due to fall vacant (of certain temporary offices in the Apostolic Chancery). **-abilisti** *m.pl.* (eccl. hist.) candidates for a vacant chancery office or benefice. **-ante** *adj.* empty, vacant, unoccupied; (of post, throne, benefice, etc.) unoccupied; (leg.) vacant; beneficio -ante, vacant benefice or living; eredità -ante, vacant succession; (naut., Neapol.) bastimento -ante, ship in ballast; †meaningless, empty, vacant; †useless, futile; †attending. †**-anteri·a** *f.* uselessness, superfluousness. **-anza** *f.* vacancy; coprire una -anza, to fill a vacancy; state of vacancy, emptiness; vacation, holiday; fare -anza, to take a holiday, to be absent from work; andare in -anza, to go on holiday; domani è -anza, tomorrow is a holiday; giorno di -anza, a day's holiday; mezza -anza, half-holiday; *pl.* holidays, school holidays, university vacation; parliamentary recess; essere in -anze, to be on holiday; -anze estive, summer holidays; -anze natalizie, -anze di Natale, Christmas holidays; -anze di Pasqua, -anze pasquali, Easter holidays; (eccl.) vacancy. **-ato** *part. adj.* empty, unoccupied, vacant. **-azione** *f.* period of paid work (usu. two hours) performed by a professional (e.g. chartered accountant); il perito ha fatto due -azioni, the expert did four hours' work; †vacation; end, ending, dying out; intermission, cessation; rest; (leg.) period of professional attendance; attendance fee; la -azione della legge, pendency of Act of Parliament, between enactment and entry into force.

vacc-a *f.* cow; — da latte, milch cow; — seccaticcia, dry cow, cow not in milk; latte di —, cow's milk; burro di —, butter made from cow's milk; the meat of the cow, beef; hai venduto la —?, said to someone who suddenly appears to be well off; (colloq.) idle person, lazy-bones, slacker; coward; (vulg.) slut, slattern, woman of low repute; hag, deformed or disfigured woman; (tan.) cowhide; lingua di —, silversmith's anvil; (zool.) — di mare, sea hare, *Aplysia* sp.; (ichth.) — marina, pesce —, devil fish, *Mobula mobula*; (silkb.) silkworm that will not pupate. **-a·io, -aro** *m.* cowman, cowherd; (naut.) nodo (di) -aio, carrick bend (used when ropes are required to pass round a capstan). **-areccia** *f.* herd of cows; (Apulia) dairy farm.

vaccherella *f.* heifer; (ichth.) see 'vacca marina', under **vacca**.

vaccheri·a *f.* cow-house, cowshed, dairy; dairy farm.

vacchetta *f. dim.* of **vacca**, q.v.; little cow; cowhide; (tan.) kip; (eccl.) parish register; (mil.) register, ledger; (Merchant Navy) daily expense book; †(naut.) parcelling of a rope; small galley having twenty oars; (ichth.) see 'vacca marina', under **vacca**.

vaccin-a *f.* cattle; cow flesh; cow dung. **-ara** *adv. phr.* (cul.) coda alla -ara, oxtail stewed in wine.

vaccin-are [A 1] *tr.* (med.) to vaccinate; farsi —, to get vaccinated. **-ato** *part. adj.* vaccinated. **-atore** *m.* vaccinator. **-azione** *f.* vaccination.

vaccino *adj.* bovine; relating to cattle; *n.m.* (med.) lymph, vaccine; (vet.) see 'vaiuolo bovino', under **vaiuolo**.

vacill-are [A 1] *intr.* (aux. avere) to reel; to totter, to wobble; ebbe una vertigine e -ò, he became dizzy and lost his balance; vecchio che -a, a doddering old man; (of a flame or light) to flicker; (fig.) to hesitate, to be unsteady, to waver; to vacillate; il trono già -ava, the throne by now was tottering; to be unstable; (of the mental powers, the will, the memory, faith, etc.) to be uncertain; la memoria dei vecchi spesso -a, the memory of old people is often shaky; -are nella fede, to waver in one's faith. **-amento** *m.* tottering; vacillating; flickering. **-ante** *part. adj.* tottering; andatura -ante, unsteady gait; fede -ante, wavering faith; barlume -ante, flickering light. **-anza** *f.* hesitation. †**-ato** *adj.* uncertain, irresolute. **-azione** *f.* vacillation; perplexity; hesitation. †**-ità** *f.* ambiguity, doubt. **-o** *adj.* vacillating; unstable.

va·cu-o *adj.* (fig.) empty, vacant; una mente -a, a blank mind; — di dottrina, lacking in learning; promesse -e, empty promises; speranze -e, vain hopes; dissertazione -a, empty, inane dissertation; free; momenti -i, spare moments; *n.m.* (phys.; philos.) vacuum; (fig.) emptiness (cf. **vuoto**). †**-are** *tr.* to empty; to evacuate. †**-ato** *part. adj.* emptied; devoid, empty. **-ità** *f.* vacuity, emptiness; vanity, inanity; la -ità della sua mente, the inanity of his mind; (comm.) vacuity. **-olo** *m.* (cyt.) vacuole.

vada *f.* stake (at play); share (cf. **andare**).

†**vadare** *vb.* and derivs. See **guadare**.

vade-mecum *m. indecl.* vademecum, handbook; (leg.) certified cheque.

†**va·dere** *vb.* and derivs. See **andare**.

vadimo·nio *m.* promise.

†**vado**[1] *m.* See **guado**.

†**vado**[2] *m.* help, assistance.

va-e-vieni *m. indecl.* coming and going; (naut.) endless line used with a dinghy to allow landing from a ship.

†**vafro** *adj.* astute; alert.

vagabond-o *adj.* vagabond, wandering, vagrant, casual; una vita -a, a wandering life; una gente -a, a vagrant, or homeless people; pecore -e dall'ovile, sheep wandering from the fold; (fig.) errant; affetti -i, straying affections; lazy; loafing; un marito —, an idle husband; *n.m.* vagabond, rover, tramp; loafer, idler; fare il —, to be a tramp, *or* to waste one's time, to be idle; (leg.) vagrant. -**ag·gine** *f.* vagabondage, state of vagabondage. -**ag·gio** *m.* vagrancy; darsi al -aggio, to take to the roads; estirpare, combattere, reprimere il -aggio, to put down vagrancy; *n.m.* wandering; i -aggi d'un artista, d'un esule, the wanderings of an artist, of an exile. (act of) wandering, rambling; digressing. -**are** [A 1] *intr.* (*aux.* avere) to wander, to stray, to ramble; to go out for a short walk; mi piace -are nelle campagne, I like wandering about the countryside; to be a tramp; scacciato di casa, si mise a -are, driven from home, he became a tramp; (fig.) to wander; -are col pensiero, to let one's thoughts wander; to be lazy, to do no work. -**eggiare** [A 3 c] *intr.* (*aux.* avere) to loaf, to lounge, to be lazy. -**eri·a** *f.* vagabondage, idleness.

†**vagabundo** *adj., n.m.* See **vagabondo**.

vagantivo *m.* (hist.) a right of hunting and reed collecting that existed in the Veneto.

vag-are [A 2] *intr.* (*aux.* avere) to wander, to ramble; to rove; — per l'Italia, to wander about Italy; — con la fantasia, to let one's fancy roam; to digress, to stray from the point; (of an epidemic) to spread; (of clouds) to drift; (of a breeze) to blow gently here and there; le api che -ano sui fiori, bees hovering among the flowers; l'occhio -a sugli oggetti, the eye wanders over objects; †*tr.* to roam over. †-**a·bile** *adj.* wandering, errant; fugitive. -**amento** *m.* wandering, roaming, straying. -**ante** *part. adj.* wandering, roaming, straying; (euphem.) donna -ante, street-walker, prostitute; (hist.) clerici -anti, *vagantes*, wandering scholars. -**atore** *m.* wanderer. (-**atrice** *f.*) -**azione** *f.* wandering; raccontare le sue -azioni per il mondo, to relate one's wanderings through the world; †diversion, distraction, amusement.

vagell-are [A 1] *intr.* (*aux.* avere) to rave; to be delirious; (fig.) to talk wildly, to make wild suggestions. -**amento** *m.* wild, incoherent mutterings; -amenti d'infermo, ravings of a sick person.

vagell-o *m.* boiler, vat; (techn.) dyer's vat; a dye made of woad and indigo. -**a·io** *m.* dyer. -**ino** *m. dim.* (techn.) small copper dyeing pan.

vaghegg-iare [A 3 c] *tr.* to gaze upon fondly, to look at with love; la mamma -iava il bimbo dormiente, the mother gazed lovingly at her sleeping babe; — le bellezze della natura, to admire the beauties of nature; to look amorously at; to woo, to court; to desire; to covet; — una speranza, to cherish a hope; to long for, to hope for, to aspire to, to anticipate with pleasure; -ava un villino quieto, he pictured to himself a quiet cottage; -ò un seggio in parlamento, he hoped to get into parliament; *rfl.* to admire oneself; -iarsi allo specchio, to admire oneself in the mirror. †-**eri·a** *f.* ogling; wooing. -**iamento** *m.* gaze of admiration; flirtatious look; aspiration, hopeful longing. -**iato** *part. adj.* cherished; longed for, desired; gazed upon with love. -**iatore** *m.* admirer, wooer, beau, lover. -**iatrice** *f.* admirer. -**ino** *m.* young gallant; ladies' man, flirt; fop, dandy; fare il -ino, to flirt. -**ina** *f.* coquette, flirt. -**ione** *m.* (joc.) admirer, suitor, one who makes sheep's eyes at a woman.

vaghezza *f.* vagueness, indetermination; beauty, charm, grace; che — di fiori!, what beautiful flowers!; sono una —, they are a joy to look at; adornment, decoration; pleasure, delight; prendere — a, to take delight in; wish, desire; gli venne — di cantare, he felt an urge to sing; (mus.) †ornament, grace.

vagin-a *f.* (anat.) vagina; (zool.) razor shell, *Solen vagina*; †sheath, scabbard. -**alite** *f.* (med.) vaginalitis. -**ite** *f.* (med.) vaginitis.

vag-ire [D 2] *intr.* (*aux.* avere) (of a baby) to cry, to whimper; (of newly born kid or lamb) to bleat; (of an art or civilization) — in culla, to be in its cradle, in its infancy. †-**imento** *m.* whimpering; bleating. -**io** *m.* (*pl.* -ii) see **vagito**. -**ito** *m.* infant's cry; bleat; (fig.) i primi -iti della letteratura, the earliest beginnings of literature.

va·glia[1] *f.* merit, worth, ability; pittore di gran —, a painter of great merit; †efficacy; †value; †*adv. phr.* di —, valiantly.

va·glia[2] *m. indecl.* money order; — postale, — telegrafico, postal, telegraphic, money order; — bancario, bank draft; — cambiario, note of hand; promissory note; — internazionale, foreign money order; tassa per l'emissione del —, poundage.

vagli-are [A 4] *tr.* to sift; to winnow; (fig.) to scrutinize, to examine closely; a -arla bene, on close examination; -are una proposta, to examine, to weigh, a proposal; †to choose; †to reject; *rfl.* to shake, to twist, to contort oneself. -**ata** *f.* sifting; winnowing. -**ato** *part. adj.* sifted; examined, scrutinized; tested. -**atura** *f.* sifting; winnowing; material sifted, siftings; (techn.) sifting, screening, riddling; -atura scossa, vanning.

va·gli-o *m.* sieve; riddle; passare al —, to sift, to sieve; (fig.) è un —, it is riddled with holes; portar l'acqua col —, to perform a useless task; examination, scrutiny; non resiste al —, it does not bear examination; fare un —, to make a considered choice; (techn.) screen, sieve, riddle; — a scossa, vibrating screen; — rotante, revolving screen. -**a·io** *m.* maker or seller of sieves. -**atrice** *f.* (techn.) sifting machine, mechanical screen.

vag-o *adj.* (*m.pl.* **vaghi**) wandering, straying; drifting; vague, uncertain; una risposta molto -a, a very vague reply; somiglianza -a, a slight resemblance; wanton, fickle; — di, desirous of, fond of, longing for; è — di mal fare, he likes to do evil; far — di sè, to charm, to attract; (poet.) charming, lovely, pleasing; una donna -a, a beautiful woman; un modo di dire —, a pleasing turn of phrase; *n.m.* lover; favourite; best-beloved; charm, beauty; il — dei begli occhi, the charm of her beautiful eyes; vagueness; cadere nel —, to fall into vagueness; (med.) vagus. -**amente** *adv.* vaguely; prettily, charmingly. -**olare** [A 1 s] *intr.* (*aux.* avere) to wander about; (of birds) to fly about; (of mists) to drift. †-**olino** *m.* weakling.

vag-one *m.* railway truck; railway carriage; — letti, sleeping-car; — ristorante, restaurant car; — merci, goods waggon. -**oncino** *m.* small truck used in mines and quarries, tub.

†**vainella** *f.* (naut.) hem of a sail.

vaini·gl-ia *f.* (bot.) vanilla (pod of *Vanilla fragrans*); common heliotrope, *Heliotropium arborescens*. -**iato** *adj.* flavoured with vanilla. -**ina** *f.* vanilla essence.

va·i-o *m.* (zool.) squirrel, and its fur used especially on the robes of certain dignitaries; (herald.) vair; gran —, vair; gran — in palo, vair in pale; *adj.* piebald, white with black patches; dark grey; il —, the colour dark grey; purplish black (of ripening grapes); †**troba** *f.*, a robe made of vair. †-**a·io** *m.* maker and seller of garments made of vair. -**ano** *m.* (bot.) a kind of grape which turns purplish grey; the wine from this grape. -**are** [A 4] *intr.* (*aux.* avere) (of grapes) to turn a purplish grey hue. †-**eggiare** *intr.* to darken, to grow dark grey; to darken in patches. -**etto** *adj. dim.* resembling vair.

vaiol-are [A 1] *intr.* (*aux.* essere, avere) to darken (of ripening olives, grapes, etc.). -**ato** *part. adj.* (of the surface of a stone) scabbed, encrusted; blotched; stained; streaked; (metall.) pitted. (-**atura** *f.*)

vairone *m.* (ichth.) *Squalius muticellus*, a kind of chub.

vai(u)olo *m.* (med.) smallpox; — spurio, chickenpox; (vet.) pox in any species; — bovino, cow pox; — ovino, sheep pox; (bot.) disease of peach leaves caused by *Exoascus deformans*; (orn.) disease of the eyes in pigeons.

Valac-chi-a *pr.n.f.* (geog.) Wallachia. -**co** *adj.* Wallach; Wallachian; *n.m.* Wallachian; Wallachian language.

Valalla *pr.n.m.* Valhalla.

valanga *f.* avalanche; snow-slip; landslide; (fig.) flood, avalanche, vast heap.

Valchi·ri-a *pr.n.f.* Valkyria; le -e, the Valkyrie.

Valchiusa *pr.n.f.* (geog.) Vaucluse.

Valdemaro *pr.n.m.* (hist.) Waldemar; Valdemar.

valdese *adj., n.m., f.* (rel.) Waldensian; *pl.* Waldensians, Waldenses, Vaudois.

valdostano *m., adj.* inhabitant of the Valley of Aosta.

val-e *excl. sing.* farewell; *n.m.* farewell greeting; l'ultimo —, the last farewell. -**ete** *excl. pl.* fare-ye-well.

†**valeg·gio** *m.* power, strength.

Valenza¹ *pr.n.f.* (geog.) Valencia (Spain); Valence (France); (techn.) terra di —, a refractory earth.

valenza² *f.* See under **valere**.

val·ere [B 34] *intr.* (*aux.* essere, avere) to be worth; val molto e costa poco, it is worth a lot but it costs little; il vino buono -e moltissimo, good wine is very expensive; -e cento lire, it is worth a hundred lire; (provb.) -e più un asino vivo che un dottore morto, (a warning against overwork); -e tant'oro quanto pesa, he is worth his weight in gold; dare una cosa per quel che -e, to sell something for what it's worth; to yield, to afford a profit of; podere che può — un milione di lire annue, farm affording a profit of a million lira a year; to be of worth, to be of value; uomo che -e molto, man of great worth; (non) -e la pena, it is (not) worth while; — nel dipingere, to be good at painting; to have merit as a painter; la moneta -e secondo le condizioni del mercato, the value of money depends on the state of the market; to be valid, to be in force, to count; la scommessa non -e, the bet is off; questa partita non -e, this game does not count; to be valid; la legge -e ancora, the law is still in force; (typ.) -e, *stet*; to apply (e.g. of a condition); far — i propri diritti, to get one's rights recognized; non saper fare — le proprie ragioni, to fail to do oneself justice; per quanto -e il biglietto?, for how long is the ticket valid?; farsi —, to make oneself felt; to avail, to be of use; contro la forza la ragione non -e, right is powerless against might; -ga il vero, it must be admitted; to mean, to correspond to; -e a dire, that is to say, it amounts to saying; to be equal to; uno -e l'altro, one is as good (as bad) as the other; nessuno -eva lui, no one was equal to him; la seminiminima -e due crome, a crotchet equals two quavers; to merit, to deserve; beneficare persone che non lo -gono, to benefit people who are not worth it, who do not deserve it; to suffice; -e a proteggerci, it is enough to protect us; -e, it is meet, it is fitting; tanto -e per noi andar via, we had better go away; val meglio tacere, it is better to be silent; *rfl.* (*prep.* di) to make use (of), to avail oneself (of); si è valso di me come mediatore, he used me as a mediator; mi -go di quest'occasione, I take this opportunity. **-ente** *adj.* able, clever; talented; skilful; un -ent'uomo, a splendid man; una donna -ente, a magnificent, admirable woman. (**-entemente** *adv.*) **-enteri·a** *f.* prowess, ability. †**-entezza** *f.* valour, gallantry; valiant deed. †**-enti·gia** *f.* valour. **-enti·a** *f.* skill, skilfulness, ability, prowess. **-entinite** *f.* (miner.) valentinite, white antimony. **-entuomo** *m.* man of merit, outstanding man; good man, honest man. **-enza** *f.* value, merit, virtue, prowess; value, worth, price; (chem.) valency. **-en·zia** *f.* (leg.) the value or price of anything.

valerian·a *f.* valerian; — minore, — silvestre, *Valeriana officinalis*; — maggiore, hortense, *V. phu*; — pisana, spur valerian, *Centranthus ruber*; radice di —, valerian rhizome. **-ato** *m.* (chem.) valerianate.

valeria·nico *adj.* (chem.) valerianic, *n*-valeric.

Vale·şia *pr.n.f.* (geog.) Valois.

valęte *excl.* see under **vale**.

valetu·din·e *f.* constitution, health. **-a·rio** *m.* valetudinarian.

valęvol·e *adj.* valid; scusa —, valid excuse; biglietto — fino a domani, ticket valid until tomorrow; efficacious; helpful, useful. **-mente** *adv.* validly, with validity; efficaciously.

valì *m. indecl.* vali, the civil governor of a Turkish province.

valic·are [A 2 s] *tr.* to cross; to ford; to climb over; to surmount; †to surpass; †to omit; not to mention. **-a·bile** *adj.* that can be crossed, traversable; fordable; surmountable. (**-abilità** *f.*) **-a·toio** *m.* stepping-stone; plank or tree trunk serving as a bridge.

va·li·co *m.* (*pl.* **-chi**) ford, way, passage, crossing-place; mountain pass; railway tunnel; †step, stride; †place where birds rise or game runs.

va·lid·o *adj.* able; strong, robust; le sue membra sono sempre -e, his limbs have not lost their power; — a sostener le fatiche, able to withstand fatigue; un'arma -a, a powerful weapon; una serratura -a, a secure lock; valid, good, acceptable; un argomento -a, a valid argument; una ricevuta -a, a valid receipt; dichiarare -a una candidatura, to declare a candidature receivable; (leg.) good; valid; atto —, valid deed; una causa -a di un contratto, good consideration for a contract. **-amente** *adv.* strongly, robustly; validly. **-are** [A 1 s] *tr.* to validate, to confirm, to ratify. **-ato** *adj.* made valid. **-azione** *f.* (leg.) validation. **-ità** *f.* strength, force, power; validity.

vali·g·ia *f.* (*pl.* **-ie**, **-e**) suitcase; small portmanteau; attaché case; — diplomatica, diplomatic bag; fare le -ie, to pack one's bag; (mil.) cavalryman's kitbag. †**-e** *f.* saddlebag; purse; †post, mail; †(fig.) aver la —, to be round-shouldered, to be a hunchback. **-eri·a** *f.* saddler's shop, shop where all leather goods, trunks, suitcases, etc. are sold; factory where trunks and suitcases are made. **-ętta** *f. dim.* small suitcase, attaché case. **-ia·io** *m.* saddler; one who makes and sells leather harness, suitcases and other leather goods. **-iona** *f.*, **-ione** *m. augm.* very large suitcase. **-iotta** *f.*, **-iotto** *m.* fairly large suitcase.

†**val-imento** *m.* valour; strength; prowess; value, price; (mus.) value. †**-itore**, **-idore** *m.*, **-itrice** *f.* help, helper, helpmeet.

vall-are¹ [A 1] *tr.* (mil. hist.) to surround with trenches, earthworks, etc.; to fortify (a camp). **-ata** *f.* (mil.) defence of banks and ditches. (**-ato** *part. adj.*)

vallare² *adj.* (Rom. antiq.) of a rampart or vallum; corona —, *corona vallaris*, vallar crown.

vallata¹ *f.* See under **vallare¹**.

vallata² *f.* (geog.) wide valley; dale, vale; plain.

vall-e¹ *f.* (when forming part of *pr.n.* the final syllable is often dropped, e.g. la Val d'Aosta, the valley of Aosta; sometimes it contracts into a single word, e.g. il Valdarno, the Arno valley; la Valtellina, the Valtelline valley; per -i e monti, up hill and down dale; — di lacrime, vale of tears; la — di Giosafàt, the valley of Jehoshaphat, (colloq.) place where people of all nations and conditions are assembled; a —, downstream; il Tevere a — di Roma, the Tiber below Rome; scendere a —, to run downhill; precipitare a —, to rush downwards; (naut., Adriatic) bight on a buoy; lagoon; fishery; *pl.* dikes dividing up the eel-fishing ponds in certain Adriatic lagoons; marshes, marshland; (bot.) giglio delle -i, lily-of-the-valley, *Convallaria majalis*; †(geog.) basin. †**-ame** *m.* distance between two valleys; (fig.) space, gap. **-e·a** *f.* valley, vale. **-e·cola** *f. dim.*, **-icella** *f. dim.* small valley; dell. **-icoltura** *f.* fish hatchery in lagoons, etc. **-igiano** *m.* valley dweller. **-ivo** *adj.* (of ground) low-lying; marshy. **-onata** *f.* wide valley, vale. **-oncello** *m. dim.* small ravine, gully. **-one** *m. augm.* deep valley; deep inlet. †**-oso** *adj.* full of vales, all hills and dales.

Vallęse *pr.n.f.* (geog.) Valais.

Valle·şia *pr.n.f.* (geog.) Vaud (in Switzerland).

vallętto *m.* valet; page; groom; (mil. hist.) — d'arme, equerry, esquire, arms-bearer to a knight; (watchm.) valet.

vall-icoltura *f.*, **-igiano** *m.*, **-ivo** *adj.* See under **valle**.

vallo *m.* (mil.) revetment; trench; buttressed fortifications; camp surrounded by trenches; main enclosure; parade ground in a fort; (geog.) stretch of stagnant water, narrow inlet, marshy area; (Rom. antiq.) vallum; Vallo d'Adriano, Hadrian's Wall.

vallombrosano *adj., n.m.* (eccl.) Vallumbrosan (monk).

Vallone¹ *pr.n.m.* (geog.) Walloon; Walloon language; *adj.* Walloon.

vallone² *m. augm.* See under **valle**.

vallone·a *f.* nut gall; (bot.) Vallonia oak, *Quercus aegilops*; (tan.) Vallonia.

†**valloso** *adj.* See under **valle**.

valor-e *m.* worth, value; anello di gran —, a very valuable ring; validity, use; argomenti di gran —, sound, valid arguments; questa scusa non ha —, this excuse does not hold good; mettere in —, to put in circulation, to put to good use, to make the most of, to turn to account, to put into force; meaning, significance; il — preciso di una parola, the exact meaning, the exact force of a word; la sua proposta ha acquistato il — d'una promessa, his proposal is now as good as a promise; aggettivo con — d'avverbio, adjective used adverbially; merit; scienziato, pittore di —, scientist, painter, of merit; è un —, he is a very gifted man, (iron.) he's a fine one!; virtue; — umano, human goodness; courage, bravery, endurance; — militare, military valour; medaglia al — civile, medal awarded to a civilian for heroic conduct; importance; non ho capito il — della notizia, I did not understand how important the news was; power; il primo —, the prime mover, i.e. God; *pl.* valuables; values; rovesciamento dei -i umani, reversal of human values; (leg.; comm.; finan.) value; — commerciale, market value; — reale, real or intrinsic value; — nominale, face or nominal value; — imponibile, assessable, taxable value; — venale, cash price; — ricevuto, value received; — assegnato, amount to be collected on delivery; campione senza —, free sample; -i (pubblici), stock; shares, bonds, securities; corso dei -i, quotations of securities; dazio al —, *ad valorem* duty; secondo il —,

valor-e (*cont.*)

according to the value; pacco —, parcel securities; — locativo, letting (hence rateable) value; — assicurato, insured value; — di rinunzia, surrender value; — di riscatto, — convertibile, convertible value; — capitale, capitalized value; — nominativo, inscribed stock; — lordo, gross value; — del mercato, market value; aggregato di -i capitali, omnium, aggregate value of stocks; — mobiliari, debentures, bonds; -i ordinari, ordinary shares; — attuale, — effettivo, actual value, present value; senza —, valueless; oggetti di —, valuables; competenza per il — della causa, jurisdiction up to amount involved in action (C.C.P.); — di bollo, stamps (C.P.); (philos.) teoria dei -i, value-theory; (mus.) il — d'una nota, the value, length, duration of a note; (math.) value, magnitude. †**-are** *vb.* and derivs. see **avvalorare**. †**-i·a** *f.* prowess; valiant deeds. **-izzare** [A I] *tr.* to utilize, to put to use, to improve; to make valuable. **-izzazione** *f.* utilization; improvement. **-oso** *adj.* talented, skilful, clever, outstanding; brave, courageous, valiant; †strong, hardy; †costly. **-osamente** *adv.* skilfully, cleverly; bravely, courageously.

vals-ente *m.* cash value; price; lo vendette e si tenne il —, he sold it and kept the money; capital, substance, wealth. †**-uta** *f.* see **valuta**.

†**valura** *f.* See **valore**.

valut-a *f.* value, price; perla di gran —, pearl of great price; money, currency; sum; (comm. finan.) — intesa, agreed currency, agreed sum; in — locale, in local currency; — avuta, value received; — in conto, value in account; — di conto, money of account; — in contanti, cash value; — alla pari, par value; — sotto la pari, below par value; — cartacea, paper money; — ricevuta, value or money received; — estera, foreign currency; — fissa, fixed rate; — corrente, current value, current money; controllo della —, exchange control; effective date; — primo gennaio, interest to run from January 1. **-abile** *adj.* calculable, capable of being valued. **-are** [A I] *tr.* to value, to appraise, to estimate the value of; -are i danni, to estimate the (cost of) damages; il quadro fu -ato troppo, the painting was overvalued; to estimate, to judge; -arono che ci volessero due anni, they estimated that it would take two years; to take into account; to value, to esteem highly; -ava l'onore più che la stessa vita, he valued his honour more than life itself; (leg.) -are le prove, to weigh evidence (C.C.P.); (comm.) to estimate; to appraise; to assess. **-ario** *adj.* (admin.) relating to currency. **-ativo** *adj.* (admin.) relating to valuation. **-ato** *part. adj.* valued, appraised, estimated. **-azione** *f.* valuation, estimation, appraisal; -azione dei danni, assessment of damages; criterio per la -azione dei danni, measure of damages; (leg.) -azione delle prove, appreciation of evidence (C.C.P.); (comm.) estimate; appraisal; assessment.

valva *f.* (zool.) a shell valve of a mollusc, etc.; (bot.) valve.

valvassino *m.* (hist.) vassal or tenant of a vavasour.

valvassore *m.* (hist.) vavasour.

val·vol-a *f.* (techn.) valve; -e in testa, overhead valves; fuse; è saltata una —, a fuse has blown; (anat.) valve. **-ame** *m.* valve fittings. **-are** *adj.* valvular. **-ato** *adj.* (eng.) pistone -ato, sucker, bucket.

valzer *m. indecl.* waltz; suonare un —, to play a waltz; fare un giro di —, to dance a waltz.

vamp-a *f.* blaze, heat, fiery glow; (of the sun) burning heat; gust of hot air; flush, deep glow; mi sentii salire le -e in viso, I felt my face burning; flare, flash; fuoco a —, flare light; (Tusc.) extreme poverty. **-are** [A I] and derivs. see **avvampare**. **-ata** *f.* gust of heat; una -ata d'aria calda, a rush of hot air; burst (of sounds). **-eggiare** [A 3 c] *intr.* (*aux.* avere) to blaze, to flame, to glow; to send off gusts of heat.

vampiro *m.* (zool.) vampire bat; (myth.) vampire; (fig.) vampire, extortionate or possessive person, usurer.

vampo *m.* sudden blaze, flame, flash, flare; flush; menar —, to flare up, to lose one's temper; burning heat, blaze, glow.

vana·d-io *m.* (chem.) vanadium. **-inite** *f.* (miner.) vanadinite.

vanaglo·ri-a *f.* vainglory; self-love; arrogance, boastfulness; conceit, vanity. **-are** [A 4] *intr.* (*aux.* avere) to revel in self-glory, to be full of oneself, to be conceited, to be puffed up with pride; *rfl.* to boast, to brag, to vaunt; che cos'ha da -arsi?, what has he got to boast about?; si -ava di essere buon pianista, he boasted that he was a good pianist. **-oso** *adj.* vainglorious; boastful, conceited; pretentious; puffed up. (**-osamente** *adv.*)

†**vanare** *vb.* and derivs. See **vaneggiare**.

---

van·d-alo *m.* (hist.) Vandal; (fig.) vandal, one who commits vandalism. **-a·lico** *adj.* vandalic, given to vandalism. (**-alicamente** *adv.*) **-alismo** *m.* vandalism.

Vandé-a *pr.n.f.* (geog.) La Vendée. **-ano** *adj.*, *n.m.* Vendéen; (fig.) bitter revolutionary. (**-ana** *f.*)

†**vaneare** *vb.* and derivs. See **vaneggiare**.

†**vaneg·gi-a** *f.*, †**-o** *m.* See **maneggia**.

vaneggi-are [A 3 c] *intr.* (*aux.* avere) to rave, to talk deliriously; to be wandering in one's mind; to be delirious; †to be empty; to yawn, to lie open; †to move, to stir, to toss; †to prove ineffective, to come to nothing; †*tr.* to render vain or useless; to dream, to conjure up in delirious raving; †*rfl.* -arsi di, to pride oneself on. **-amento** *m.* raving, delirious talk; wandering of the mind; wild imagination; i -amenti d'infermo, a sick man's ravings. **-atore** *m.* delirious person; impractical idealist, daydreamer; (fig.) è -atore!, he's a raving lunatic!, *or* he's always full of wild, impractical schemes. (**-atrice** *f.*)

vanescente *adj.* fading, evanescent; disappearing, vanishing.

vane·s-io *adj.* fatuous and conceited, foppish, vain, pretentious; *n.m.* fop; conceited fool. **-iata** *f.* conceit; vanity, foppishness; è una delle sue -iate, it is one of his silly pretentions *or* affectations.

vanessa *f.* (ent.) tortoiseshell, red-admiral and similar butterflies; — maggiore, peacock butterfly, *Nymphalis io*; — antiopa, Camberwell beauty, *N. antiopa*.

vang-a *f.* spade; — manritta, right-handed spade; — mancina, left-handed spade; andare a —, to find the ground soft for digging, (fig.) to find the going easy; la — ha la punta d'oro, the spade is tipped with gold, gold is earned by spade-work; seminare sulla —, to sow on roughly dug ground. **-are** [A 2] *tr.* to dig, to turn up the ground, to spade; — fondo, to dig deep; — acqua, to tire oneself for nothing. **-ata** *f.* soil that has been turned up with a spade; spit, thrust of a spade, dig; digging; sarà meglio che diamo prima alla terra una -ata, it will be best if we dig the ground up first. **-ato** *part. adj.* (of soil, ground) dug, turned over with a spade (also *n.m.*). **-atore** *m.* digger; è un buon -atore, he is good at digging, he is handy with a spade. (**-atrice** *f.*) **-atura** *f.* digging; non mi piace la -atura, I do not like digging. **-one** *m. augm.* large spade.

Vang-elo *m.* (rel.) Gospel; sermon (on the gospel of the day); essere ordinato al —, to be ordained deacon; (fig.) questo è —!, gospel truth!; il — dei socialisti, the gospel of the socialists; giurare sul —, to swear on the Bible. **-e·lico** *adj.*, **-elista** *m.* see **evang-e·lico**, **-elista**. **-elizzare** [A I] and derivs. see **evangelizzare**.

vangheggia *f.* blade of a spade; (Tusc.) a small ploughshare.

vanghett-are [A I c] *tr.* to dig lightly, to dig the surface of, to dig with a trowel or small light spade. (**-ato** *part. adj.*)

vanghetto *m. dim.* small light spade, gardening trowel.

†**vanghile** *m.* See **vangile**.

vangile *m.* foot-rest of a spade.

vangone *m. augm.* See under **vanga**.

vanguar·dia *f.* See under **avanguardia**.

vani·gl-ia *f.* see **vainiglia**; (bot.) — d'inverno, winter heliotrope, *Petasites fragrans*. **-iato** *adj.* flavoured with vanilla. **-ione** *m.* (bot.) see 'vaniglia d'inverno'.

vanilo·quio *m.* futile talk, idle talk, mere words; random talk; twaddle; non voglio più ascoltare i suoi vaniloqui, I don't want to listen to any more of his twaddle; wandering talk, raving.

vanire [D 2] *intr.* (*aux.* essere) to vanish, to disappear, to fade from view (cf. **svanire**).

vanit-à *f.* vanity, emptiness, fruitlessness, futility; l'infinita — del tutto (Leopardi), the infinite vanity of everything; frivolousness, worthlessness; andar dietro alle —, to indulge in frivolous pursuits; personal vanity, conceit. **-oso** *adj.* frivolous, light-headed; vain, conceited. (**-osamente** *adv.*)

vanno *m.* (poet.) feather; *pl.* wings (of eagle or other large bird); pinions.

van-o *adj.* empty, hollow; noce -a, empty nutshell; unreal, unsubstantial; fantasma —, vain apparition; (fig.) i beni di quaggiù sono -i, the goods of this world are an illusion; groundless, false, deceptive; -e speranze, vain hopes; un nome —, a mere name; useless, ineffectual; (of prayers, threats, tears, promises, etc.) of no avail, unavailing; è — il pregarlo, it is of no avail to ask him; le sue ricerche sono riuscite -e, his researches bore no fruit; pelo —, down on a boy's face; uovo —, unfertilized egg; frivolous, light-headed; conversazioni -e, idle conversations;

van-o (*cont.*)

libro —, futile book; vain, conceited; anxious about one's looks; †città -a d'abitanti, uninhabited city; *n.m.* empty space, void; nel — dell'aria, in the empty air; il — della campana, the hollow of a bell; room; appartamento di dieci -i, ten-roomed flat; in —, in vain; togliere il troppo e il —, to cut out what is superfluous and useless; (archit.) embrasure; window-opening, opening of doorway or arch; — dell'ascensore, lift-shaft; il — delle scale, the well of the staircase. **-amẹnte** *adv.* deceptively, falsely, without grounds; in vain, to no avail; vainly, conceitedly. **-erello** *adj.* rather vain; è -erello, he tends to be a bit vain; *n.m.* fop. **-ẹzza** *f.* see **vanità**.

van-porto *m.*, **-posto** *m.*, *f.* See **avamporto, avamposto**, under **avambecco**.

vanscoperta *f.* See **avanscoperta**, under **avancarica**.

vantạg·g-io *m.* advantage; gain; superiority; precedence; andare tutto a — di uno, to be all to one's advantage; prendere il — su, to get the better of; avere un'ora di —, to have an hour in hand, an hour to spare, to be an hour ahead of schedule; (mil.) advantage, superiority; — del numero, superiority of numbers; avere — nel mirare, to have the range, i.e. to outrange; spendere la propria vita al — del prossimo, to devote one's life to the service of others; extra, something thrown in; derivare — di, to profit by, to gain by; a mio —, to my gain; a — di chi?, to whose advantage?, *or* on whose behalf?; parlare con — di qualcuno, to speak favourably of someone; (on a shoe) patch, reinforcement; (sport) start; dare a uno dieci passi di —, to give someone a start of ten paces; (tennis) van, vantage; (typ.) galley; (comm.) *pl.* profits; *adv.* more, extra; dieci grammi —, ten grammes over; *adv. phr.* (Tusc.) di —, too much, over, extra; dieci grammi di —, ten grammes over; qualche copia di —, some extra copies; da —, more; per —, in addition, extra; *adj. phr.* †di —, superior; †a —, above, crowning; †strada a —, a street sloping down; †*adv. phr.* a —, more and more, increasingly. **-iare** [A 3] *tr.* to surpass, to exceed, to overcome; to favour; (Tusc.) -iare uno in qualche cosa, to allow a person a reduction in the price of something; *rfl.* (*prep.* di) to benefit (by), to profit (by); to gain advantage, to progress, to make headway; -iarsi nei propri interessi, to advance one's own interests; (in fighting) to get the upper hand. **-iato** *part. adj.* increased, extra large; un metro -iato, over a metre, a full metre with some to spare; vestito -iato, roomy garment; (finan.) moneta -iata, oversized, overweight coin; †superior. **-ino** *m.* extra, something over; me lo diede per -ino, he gave it me as an extra. **-iọso** *adj.* advantageous; (of conditions) favourable. **-iosamẹnte** *adv.* advantageously; favourably.

vant-are [A I] *tr.* to vaunt; to boast of; — un successo, to boast of a success; — i propri meriti, to blow one's own trumpet; (fig.) la campagna può — molte bellezze, the countryside boasts of many beauty spots; to boast about; — i propri figli, to boast about one's children; to praise; — i meriti d'altrui, to sing other people's praises; (leg.) — un diritto, to set up a claim; — un credito presso, to pretend (falsely) to have a claim upon; *rfl.* to boast; -arsi di origini modeste, to claim humble origins; me ne -o, I am proud of it; si -a d'aver ammazzato un leone, he boasts that he has killed a lion; si -a di ammazzare un leone, he boasts that he is capable of killing a lion; (provb.) chi si -a si spianta, pride goes before a fall. (**-amẹnto** *m.*) **-ato** *part. adj.* boasted, flaunted; bragged about. **-atore** *m.* boaster, braggart. (**-atrice** *f.*) **-aziọne** *f.* boast, boastfulness; lo dice per -azione, he says it to show off. **-eggiare** [A 3 c] *intr.* (*aux.* avere) to boast, to brag. **-erị·a** *f.* boasting, bragging; boastfulness. †**-ẹvole** *adj.* boasting, boastful.

vanticuore *m.* (naut.) angle iron, breasthook.

vanto *m.* boast; vaunt; menar —, to brag; darsi — di, to pride oneself on, to boast of; virtue; il — della costanza, the virtue of constancy; credit, glory; dare il — di qualcosa a uno, to give the credit for something to someone; (iron.) che bel —!, a fine thing!; honour, reputation; riportare il —, to take all the honours; avere il — sopra, to have a better reputation than; aspirare al — di poeta, to aspire to the name of poet; (hist.) challenge.

vanume *m.* (agric.) part of wheat or other grain which dries without fully ripening; (fig.) vanities, vain things.

†**vanura** *f.* vanity.

van·vera *adv. phr.* a —, at random, haphazardly; parlare a —, to babble on, to talk nonsense.

†**va·pido** *adj.* vapid; weak, inert.

vapọr-e *m.* steam, vapour; steamboat, steamer; manzo a —, steamed beef; bagni a —, vapour baths; l'aria è piena di -i, the air is very damp; a tutto —, at full speed; *pl.* mist; i -i del vino, the fumes of wine; -i mefitici, pestilential exhalations; †fine veiling; *pl.* (med. hist.) 'the vapours'. **-a·bile** *adj.* vaporable, vaporizable. (**-abilità** *f.*) **-a·io** *m.* (joc.) engine-driver. **-ale** *adj.* vaporous. (**-ante** *part. adj.*) **-are** [A I c] *intr.* (*aux.* avere) to evaporate; to give off vapour, to exhale vapour; to steam; to appear mistily, as in a mist. **-ativo** *adj.* vaporable, vaporizable. **-aziọne** *f.* evaporation; fumigation. **-ẹtto** *m.*, **-ino** *m.*, **-uc·cio** *m.* (naut.) small steamer; ferry. **-iera** *f.* steam-engine, locomotive. **-iẓzare** [A I] *intr.* (*aux.* essere) to vaporize. **-iẓzato** *part. adj.* vaporized. **-iẓzatore** *m.* vaporizer, pulverizer, atomizer, spray. (**-iẓzatrice** *f.*) **-iẓzaziọne** *f.* vaporizing; (phys.) vaporization; (text.) decatizing. **-osità** *f.* vaporousness; (text.) airy texture. **-ọso** *adj.* vaporous; (of clothes) gauzy, flimsy, transparent; (of style, speech, etc.) vague, indeterminate, illogical.

†**vappa** *f.* senseless thing; nonsense.

†**vaquatt-o** *m.* hypocrite; sneak; dissembler. †**-ù** *m.* person of great power and authority.

vara *f.* barra (Spanish measurement equiv. to three feet).

varagno *m.*, **vara·gnolo** *m.* (ichth.) weever fish; — bianco, *Trachinus draco*; — nero, *T. araneus*; — pagano, *T. radiatus*.

varano *m.* See **vaiano**, under **vaio**.

var-are [A I] *tr.* (naut.) to launch; — a secco, to slip, to dry dock; *rfl.* -arsi in terra, -arsi in spiaggia, to beach, to go aground; (fig.) to launch; — una legge, to have an act passed; — un libro, to launch a book; — una commedia, to have a play put on, to present a play; (comm.) — un affare, to float a business. (**-amẹnto** *m.* **-ato** *part. adj.*)

varc-are [A 2] *tr.* to cross, to pass; — la frontiera, to cross over the frontier; — i limiti, to overstep the bounds; (in age) — la sessantina, to pass the sixty mark. **-a·bile** *adj.* (of mountains, territory, etc.) capable of being crossed. **-ato** *part. adj.* crossed; (of time) passed.

var-co *m.* (*pl.* **-chi**) narrow way, passage, opening; aprirsi un —, to force a way, to force an opening; ford; mountain pass; (mil.) affrontare il nemico al —, to hold the pass; (fig.) aspettare uno al —, to lie in wait for someone, to wait to catch someone out.

vardosso *m.* See **bardosso**.

vare·a *f.* (naut.) peak; truck.

varẹcchi *m.pl.* (bot.) kelp.

varechina *f.* household disinfectant and bleaching agent.

Varẹs-e *pr.n.f.* (geog.) Varese. **-ino** *adj.* of (Lake) Varese. (**-ina** *f.*)

vari-are [A 4] *tr.* to change; to vary, to alter; — un passo d'uno scritto, to rewrite a passage; to vary, to change frequently; — le letture, to vary one's reading; — la pena secondo il delitto, to make the punishment fit the crime; *intr.* (*aux.* avere, essere) to vary, to have a change; che bisogno c'è di —?, why do anything different?; (iron.) tanto per —!, just for a change!; (with *prep.* 'di') to vary; — di pensiero, to have a changeable opinion; — di colore, to change colour; to change, to grow different; da allora il mondo è -ato, the world has changed since then; non ha -ato punto di fisonomia, his face has not changed a bit; to differ; da paese a paese i costumi -ano, customs differ from country to country; (with *prep.* 'da') to differ from; †— da, not to follow, to depart from. **-a·bile** *adj.* (of wind, weather, etc.) variable, changeable; (in a barometer) change; (of a person) temperamental, moody; essere d'umor -abile, to be temperamental; (of parts of speech) variable; (math.) variable. **-abilità** *f.* variability, changeability. **-amẹnto** *m.* variation, varying. **-ante** *part. adj.* varying, different; una lezione -ante, a different reading, an alternative reading; *n.f.* variant (in the text or MS. of an author); variation; different form; difference. (**-antemẹnte** *adv.*) †**-anza** *f.* variation; (gramm.) aver -anza, to be variable. **-ato** *part. adj.* varied; (of ground) uneven; changed, altered; il tuo animo è -ato, your feelings have changed; †inconstant, unfaithful. **-atamẹnte** *adv.* with variation, with variety; varyingly. **-atore** *m.* one who varies; (eng.) variator; -atore di coppia, torque converter; (electr.) -atore di fase, phase transformer; -atore di frequenza, frequency changer. **-aziọne** *f.* variation; varying; far continue -azioni nei proponimenti, to make continual changes in the arrangements; una -azione di domestici, a change of servants; (eng.) con -azione continua, infinitely variable; (mus.) variation; †variety.

†**varicare** vb. and derivs. See **varcare**.

varic-e f. (med.) varix; varicosity. **-ọso** adj. (med.) varicose; vene -ose, varicose veins.

varicella f. (med.) chicken-pox, varicella.

variegato adj. variegated.

va·r·io adj. various; per -ie ragioni, for various reasons; several; lo vidi -ie volte, I saw him several times; varied; un uomo d'in-gegno —, a man of many parts; essere d'umore —, to be of uncertain temper; il mondo è bello perchè è —, the world is beautiful because it has variety; versatile; of different colours; occhi -i, eyes of different colours; chioma -ia, greying hair; n.m. variety; mi piace il —, I like variety; pl. various people; scrivere a -i, to write to various people; †diverse, different. **-iamẹnte** adv. variously, in various ways. **-ieggiare** [A 3 C] intr. (aux. avere) to vary, to keep changing. **-iętà** f. variety; la -ietà toglie sazietà, variety is the spice of life; (theatr.) variety; teatro di -ietà, music-hall; kind, species; una -ietà di scimmia, a variety of monkey; diversity; -ietà tra una cosa e un'altra, difference between one thìng and another; multiplicity; una -ietà di modi, a variety of ways; differing quality; -ietà di terreno, varieties of soil; (paint.) variety (within a composition); †inconstancy, changeableness; †variant; †adv. phr. a -ietà, with variety, variously, varyingly. **-iforme** adj. having various forms. **-iolato** adj. pockmarked, pitted (of the skin, and fig. of rocks and other surfaces). **-iolingue** adj. speaking various languages. **-iolite** f. (miner.) variolite, variolitic rock. **-io·metro** m. (aeron.) rate-of-climb indicator; (eng.) variometer. **-iopinto** adj. many-coloured; variegated; speckled.

varo¹ m. (naut.) launching; — trasversale, broadside launch.

Varo² pr.n.m. (geog.) the river Var.

†**varo³** adj. See **vario**.

†**varole** f.pl. (med.) pockmarks.

varọne m. (ichth.). See **vairone**.

varroc·chio m. (mil. hist.) capstan.

Varrọne pr.n.m. Varro.

Varsa·vi·a pr.n.f. (geog.) Warsaw. (**-ano** adj.)

varvassọr-e, -o m. See **valvassore**.

vaṣ-a·io, -aro m. potter. †**-ame** m. pottery (collectively).

vas-ca f. basin; pond; — da bagno, bath, bath-tub; — per nuoto, swimming-pool; tank; watering-trough; (geog.) reservoir, basin; (tan.) pit; — da calce, lime-pit; (naut.) tank; — del condensa-tore, hot well; — subacquea di addestramento, submarine escape tank, training tank. **-chẹtta** f. dim. small basin; bulb, cistern (for mercury in a barometer); (motor.) -chetta del carburatore, float chamber.

vascello m. (naut.) ship; full-rigged ship; — latino, lateen-rigged ship; — quadro, square-rigged ship; — in giolito, boat rolling in the trough of the sea; — geloso, a handy ship; — di linea, ship of the line; capitano di —, port captain; tenente di —, lieutenant in the Navy (executive); (colloq.) tubby person; (dial. Lomb.) kind of tub or barrel.

va·scol-o m. (anat.; bot.) vasculum. **-are** adj. (bot.; anat.) vascular; sistema -are, vascular system; (bot.) tessuto -are, vascular tissue.

vaṣelina f. vaseline, petrolatum, petroleum jelly.

vaṣell-o m. dim. of **vaso**, q.v.; (theol.) — dello Spirito Santo, vessel of the Holy Ghost (St Paul); †see **vascello**. **-a·io** m. potter. **-ame** m. crockery, china, dishes; plate. †**-amenta** m.pl., †**-amento** m. quantity of pottery or earthenware. **-ẹtto** m. dim. little dish; small jar, pot; -etto per conserve, jam pot. **-iere** m. potter.

vaṣeri·a f. garden pottery, tubs, flower-pots, etc.

vaṣ-o m. vase, vessel; portar -i a Samo, to take coals to Newcastle; vase-full; un — di fiori, a vase of flowers; un — da fiori, a flower-vase, a flower-pot; (Bibl.) — d'elezione, chosen vessel (esp. St Paul); (liturg.) -i sacri, sacred vessels; jar, pot; — da notte, chamber, chamber-pot; potful; tub, barrel, vat; -i di cantina, wine-barrels; (Gk. myth.) il — di Pandora, Pandora's box; cubic-space of an interior; il — della sala del teatro è troppo grande, e la voce si perde, the body of the theatre is too big, and the voice does not carry; (anat.) vessel; -i sanguigni, blood vessels; -i linfatici, lymph vessels; †(naut.) ship, galleon; — di bevanda, mess tub for wine ration; culo di —, overhand knot at the end of a rope; see **invasatura**; (astron.) the constellation Crater; (bot.) vessel; (archit.) space, room; body of a capital, of the Corinthian or Composite Order. **-ẹtto** m. dim. small jar. †**-ina** f. (dial. Tusc.)

pedestal or stand for a vase of flowers. **-olino** m. (naut., Viareggio) weatherboard. **-omotọre** adj., **-omoto·rio** adj. (med.) vasomotor.

†**vassag·gio** m. See **vassallo**.

vassall-o m. vassal, feudal tenant; feudatory; subject, servant; (fig.) ci tratta come tanti -i, he treats us like so many slaves; †scullion; †rascal; adj. vassal, dependent; stati -i, satellite states. **-ag·gio** m. (leg.) vassalage; tenure at will; subjection, dependence; vassals; aveva d'intorno il suo -aggio, he was surrounded by his vassals; †service; †power, ascendancy. **-a·tico** adj. of a vassal, belonging to a vassal. **-ẹsco** adj. (m.pl. -ẹschi) pertaining to a vassal, after the fashion of vassals.

vassọi-o m. tray; pen-tray; — da tè, tea-tray; (bldg.) mortarboard, hod; (eng.) — raccoglitore dell'olio, oil-drip tray; (found.) — per anime, core plate. **-ata** f. trayful.

†**vastare¹** vb. and derivs. See **bastare**.

†**vastare²** vb. and derivs. See **devastare**.

vast-o adj. large; spacious; wide; ample; un — salone, a spacious drawing-room; erudizione molto -a, very extensive learning; idee troppo -e, overambitious plans; -a mortalità, widespread mor-tality; le donne formano una delle più -e frazioni del pubblico lettore, women form one of the biggest sections of the reading public; — oceano, boundless ocean; vast; una mente -a, a pro-digious mind; una -a impresa, a vast undertaking. **-amẹnte** adv. widely. **-ẹzza** f. amplitude. **-ità** f. great size; spaciousness; -ità di dottrina, breadth of knowledge; vastness.

vate m. prophet, soothsayer, seer; poet, bard.

Vatican-o pr.n.m. Vatican; adj. relating to the Vatican. **-ista** m. (eccl. hist.) Vaticanist.

vati-cinare [A I] tr. to prophesy, to foretell, to predict. (**-cinato** part. adj.) **-cinatọre** m. soothsayer, prophet. (**-cinatrice** f.) **-cinaziọne** f. vaticination, prophecy, divination, solemn or inspired pre-diction. **-ci·nio** m. prophecy; science of prophecy, science of divination.

†**vati-ci·nio** m. See **vaticinatore**, under **vaticinare**.

vattelappẹsca excl. who knows?; my guess is as good as yours.

va·uda f. (geog., Piedmont) infertile, leached region.

vaudeville m. indecl. (pron. as Fr.) vaudeville; vaudeville song.

vavọrna f. (bot.) wayfaring tree, *Viburnum lantana*.

ve¹ pers. prn. you, to you; form of pers. pron. **vi** used before oblique cases of pronouns, i.e. before ne, lo, li, la, le; — lo dissi, I told you so; chi — ne parlò?, who told you about it?

ve² adv. there; form of adv. **ivi**, or **vi** used before oblique cases of pronouns, i.e. before ne, lo, li, la, le; — n'erano venti, there were twenty of them; non voglio rivedervelo, I do not want to see him there again; il libro era nel salotto, chi — lo portò?, the book was in the sitting-room, who took it there?

've adv. (poet.). See **ove**.

ve', veh excl. look!; see!; (following a threat, a warning, an expression of thanks, etc. to give emphasis); attenti, —!, look out!; grazie, —!, oh thank you!

vẹcchio¹ m. (zool.) monk-seal, *Monachus monachus*, the only seal living in the Mediterranean.

vec·ch·io² adj. old, aged; più — di Noè, as old as the hills; (fig., of person) una volpe -ia, a cunning old fox; of long standing; -i amici, old friends; la sua -ia malattia, his old illness; son — del mestiere, I have been a long time in the trade; notizia -ia, stale news; former, previous; i -i tempi, the old days; il governo —, the old régime; il — Adamo, the old Adam; old, worn-out, discarded; scarpe -ie, cast-off shoes; rami -i, dead branches; (of cheese, wine, etc.) old, matured; — grano, last year's grain; (joc.) great, huge, enormous; ho una -ia fame, I am terribly hungry; n.m. old man; i -i, old people or the ancients, our ancestors; ospizio dei -i, old people's home; i miei -i, my (old) parents, my people; il —, the elder (of two men bearing the same name); Catone il —, Cato the Elder; anything old, old things, old stuff; levare via il —, to remove what is old; quality and appearance of age; l'abito ha già perso il —, the coat no longer looks old. **-ia** f. old woman; (colloq.) la mia -ia, my old woman. **-ia·ia** f. old age; morì di -iaia, he died of old age; pensare alla -iaia, to look to one's old age; rispettare la -iaia, to respect the aged; pensioni per la -iaia, old age pensions; old things, old customs; out-of-date things. **-iardo** m. old man; (derog.) silly old man; horrible old man; (Ven. hist.) elder. **-iata** f. old man's escapade; ancient, out-of-date custom. **-iarello, -ierello, -ierellino** adj. poor old; n.m. poor old man. **-ierella** f. dim. poor old woman, poor old

vecchi-o (*cont.*)

lady. **-ietto** *adj. dim.* ageing, elderly, approaching old age; *n.m.* brisk, lively old man. (**-ietta** *f.*) **-iezza** *f.* (of people) old age; sino all'ultima **-iezza**, right into extreme old age; the aged, old people; non vuol dar retta alla **-iezza**, he will not listen to old people's advice; (of things) the quality and appearance of age; lo riconobbi dalla **-iezza** dei suoi abiti, I recognized him by his old clothes. **-ino** *adj. dim.* rather old; (as a term of endearment) una cara **-ina**, a dear little old lady; (derog.) storielle un po' **-ine**, chestnuts, stories everyone has heard before; (of a boy or young man) avere il **-ino**, to look like a little old man. **-ione** *m. augm.* old gentleman, venerable old man; *pl.* chestnuts dried in their shells and cooked in wine; raw dried chestnuts. **-iotto** *adj.* ageing, approaching old age; *n.m.* flourishing old man. (**-iotta** *f.*) †**-itu·dine** *f.* see **vecchiezza**. **-iume** *m.* old things, old stuff; trash, rubbish; old customs; dead branches and foliage.

vecci-a *f.* (bot.) vetch, *Vicia sativa.* **-arini** *m.pl.* milk vetch, *Astragalus glycyphyllos* and *Coronilla* spp. **-ola** *f.* bitter vetch, *Vicia ervilia.* **-one** *m.* narrow-leaved everlasting pea, *Lathyrus silvestris.* **-oso** *adj.* (of grain) containing much vetch seed.

vec·cio *m.* (ichth.) gudgeon, *Gobius fluviatilis.*

vec-e[1] *f.* place, stead; in mia —, instead of me; in quella —, instead; in —, see **invece**; (leg.) in sua —, in his place, acting for him; (poet.) change, vicissitude; con — assidua, with never-ending change; *pl.* functions, business; adempiere le **-i** d'uno, to act as substitute for some one; fare le **-i** di direttore, to act as manager.

vece[2] *pref.* See **vice**[2].

†**vecorde** *adj.* senseless; out of one's senses.

V-eda *pr.n.m.* Veda; i —, the Vedas. **-e·dico** *adj.* Vedic.

ved·ere [B 35] *tr.* to see; lo vidi povero e malato, when I saw him he was poor and ill; **-emmo** abbattere la casa, we saw the house pulled down; (fig.) — Dio, (of the dead) to be in heaven; — la luce, to be born, to see the light of day; — le stelle, to see stars; **-i** Napoli e poi muori, see Naples and die; lo **-o** e non lo **-o**, it will be gone in a minute, (of money lent) I shall never see that again, (of a person) he seems hardly to be there, he is on his last legs; la **-remo**, lo **-remo!**, mi **-rete!**, we'll see!, you had better look out!; far —, to show; dare a —, to show; dava a — di essere stanco, he showed that he was tired; to look at; **-i** questo libro, look at this book; non lo può —, he can't bear the sight of him; to read; non ho visto tutto questo libro, I have not read the whole of this book; to notice; si **-e** che è matto, one can see he is mad; bisogna — se dice sul serio, we must see if he means it seriously; to try; — di, to see if one can; **-ete** di contentarlo, see if you can make him happy; **-i** di venire, try to come, see if you can come; non prometto niente, ma **-rò**, I don't promise anything, but I'll see what I can do; to consider, to decide; **-i** tu che cosa si deve fare, decide for yourself what should be done; questo è da —, la **-remo**, we'll see about this; to regard, to form a judgement; — bene, to think well of, to regard favourably; — male, to dislike, to think little of, to regard with disfavour; essere ben visto da tutti, to be popular with everyone; — di buon occhio (di mal occhio), to regard favourably (unfavourably); tentate, ma io la **-o** male, try, but I don't like the look of it; to imagine, to see in one's mind; — con la fantasia, to picture to oneself; non — l'ora (di), to long for the time (when); non **-o** l'ora di rivederti, I am longing to see you again; — un sogno, to have a dream; — uno in sogno, to dream of someone; non è contento se non mi **-e** morto, he won't be happy until he sees me dead; to meet, to visit, to go to see; voglio — il mio avvocato, I must see my lawyer; fatevi — di quando in quando, come and see us from time to time; to take care; bisogna — che tutto vada bene, we must see to it that all goes well; to witness; il mondo ha **-uto** l'eroismo dei nostri, the world has witnessed the heroism of our men; to realize, to understand; non **-o** come sia possibile, I don't see how it could be possible; to penetrate deeply into, to know thoroughly; fare —, to explain, to show; farla — a uno, to show someone what's what, to show someone where he gets off; to appreciate, to see the worth of; nei pericoli si **-e** l'uomo, the true man is seen in times of danger; aver che (da) — (with *prep.* 'con' or 'in'), to have relation to, to have something to do with; in questo non ci ho che —, I have nothing to do with this; i miei quadri non hanno nulla da — con i suoi, my pictures are nothing like his; *intr.* (*aux.* avere) to see; — doppio, to see double; (fig.) non — più in là del naso, to see

no further than the end of one's nose; (poker) **-o**, 'see you'; stare a —, to wait and see; (iron., of something considered absurd) sta (stare) a — che, of course, no doubt; state a — che non potrò spendere il mio tempo come voglio!, I suppose I have no right to do what I like with my own time!; **-remo!**, we'll see!; **-rai**, (as a reassurance) you'll see; **-iamo!**, now!, let's see!, let us try!; **-rò** io, I will see to it; se **-este!**, if you had only seen!; **-i**, io farei così, look, this is what I would do; **-i** tu, io non c'entro, you see about it, it isn't my business; — per credere, it must be seen to be believed; **-erci**, to be able to see; non ci si **-e** più, it is no longer possible, it has grown too dark, to see; ce n'è tanto poco, che non ci si **-e**, there is hardly even enough to see; non **-erci** più dalla fame, to be ravenously hungry; non ci vide più, he could no longer see reason; *rfl.* (acc. of *prn.* 'si') **-ersi** nello specchio, to see oneself in the mirror; si vide abbandonato da tutti, he saw he was abandoned by all; **-ersi** venir meno, to feel faint, to feel oneself fainting; in quella casa non mi ci posso —, I cannot see (imagine) myself, I cannot bear to be, in that house; guarda chi si **-e!**, look who's here!; (dat. of *prn.* 'si') **-ersela**, to sort it out for yourselves; *recip. rfl.* to see one another; to meet; ci **-iamo** di rado, we seldom see each other; ci **-iamo!**, see you again soon!; ci siam visti, it's all over, we are done for; non ci siam visti, (enjoining secrecy) don't breathe a word; *impers.* si **-e** che, it is evident that, it looks as if; si **-e** che è matto, he must be mad; si **-e** che ha perso il treno, he must have missed the train; non si **-eva** anima viva, there was not a soul to be seen; *n.m.* sight; perdere il —, to lose one's sight; fare un bellissimo —, to make a wonderful sight; il — certe cose fa ribrezzo, some things are repulsive to see; a suo —, in his opinion; dal — al non —, in the twinkling of an eye. **-ente** *part. adj.* see also **veggente**; †*n.m.* sight; †prophet, seer. †**-e·vole** *adj.* see **vedibile**. **-i·bile** *adj.* visible. †**-imento** *m.* sight, vision; appearance; supernatural vision. **-itivo** *adj.* able to see. **-itore** *m.* spectator, person who sees; †sentry; †inspector; †customs official. **-itura** *f.* customs examination.

vedett-a *f.* (mil.) look-out post; look-out; sentry; stare in — di, stare alle **-e** di, to be on the look-out for, to be on the alert, to be on the *qui vive*; (fig.) bisogna stare alle **-e**, we must be on our guard, we must be on the look-out; (naut.) look-out vessel; exploring ship; look-out; mastheadsman; — alla riva!, man aloft!; — al salvagente, lifebuoy sentry; — del cinema, filmstar; — del teatro, famous actor, star.

vedov-o *adj.* deprived, bereaved, despoiled, stripped, desolated, emptied; una città **-a** di genti, a city emptied of its people; un regno —, a kingdom bereft of its ruler; un albero —, a tree stripped of its leaves; **-i** solchi, land untilled or neglected; una vita **-a**, a bereaved life; (liturg.) altare —, bare altar (as stripped in triduum of Holy Week); †see **vedovile**; *n.m.* widower; relict; rimaner —, to be left a widower. **-a** *f.* widow; relict; far **-a**, to widow; pensione alla **-a**, widow's pension; (joc.) figlio unico di madre **-a**, the last of its kind, the only one left; (bot.) fior della **-a**, scabious, *Scabiosa*; (hist.) la **-a**, the guillotine. †**-ag·gio** *m.* widowed state, widowhood, widowerhood. †**-ale** *adj.* see **vedovile**. **-anza** *f.* widowhood, bereavement, deprivation; (eccl.) bereaved state of church or diocese on death of parish priest or bishop. **-are** [A 1 s] *tr.* to widow, to bereave, to deprive, to despoil; l'inverno **-a** le piante delle foglie, winter strips the trees of their leaves; *rfl.* to be deprived; *intr.* (*aux.* avere) to live a life of widowhood, to live a life of bereavement. †**-a·ria** *f.* widowhood. †**-a·tico** *m.* widowed state. **-ato** *part. adj.* widowed; bereaved. **-ella** *f. dim.* little widow; (bot.) **-elle** celesti, *Globularia vulgaris* and *G. cordifolia.* **-ezza** *f.* see **vedovanza**. **-ile** *adj.* of or pertaining to a widow or widower; essere in abito **-ile**, to be in full mourning, †to wear widow's weeds; *n.m.* widow's pension; dower; widow's weeds, mourning. **-ina** *f.* (bot.) *Scabiosa atropurpurea.* †**-ità** *f.* widowed state, widowhood.

vedretta *f.* (geog.) old snow; small glacier.

vedut-a *f.* view; lieto della mia —, delighted to see me; testimone di —, eyewitness; affermare di —, to bear witness that; una bella —, a beautiful view; impedire la —, to block the view; (of postcard, engraving, painting, etc.) view; ho comprato delle **-e** di Roma, I have bought some views of Rome; aspect; mi piace questa — del duomo, I like the view of the cathedral from here; (art) le **-e** di una statua, the (several) aspects of a statue; appearance; (fig.) view, opinion; un uomo di larghe **-e**, a man with a broad outlook, a man of wide views; (leg.) outlook, prospect

vedut-a (*cont.*)

(one kind of 'finestra'); opening in wall giving view over neighbouring property (as distinguished from 'luce', opening admitting light and air without view) (C.C.). †**-amente** *adv.* visibly. **-ina** *f.* (art) vignette; small print or painting.

veduto *part.* of **vedere**, q.v.; *adj.* seen, perceived; — di buon occhio, ben —, esteemed, favourably regarded; — di mal occhio, mal —, hated, disliked; far —, to show; †*n.m.* view, sight; †di —, on sight.

veem-ente *adj.* vehement; intense. **-entemente** *adv.* vehemently; intensely. **-enza** *f.* vehemence; impetus; ardour. †**-en·zia** *f.* see **veemenza**.

Vega *pr.n.f.* (astron.) Vega.

vegeta·bile *adj.* vegetable; †*n.m.* vegetables; plant.

vegetale *adj.* See under **vegeto**.

ve·get-o *adj.* vigorous, strong, thriving, flourishing, luxuriant; vivo e —, alive and kicking, hale and hearty. **-ale** *adj.* vegetal, vegetable; regno -ale, vegetable kingdom; *n.m.* vegetable life; plant, vegetable; vegetable substance. **-ante** *part. adj.* thriving, flourishing; vegetating. **-are** [A I s] *intr.* (*aux.* avere) to vegetate, to grow; piante che -ano sotto diversi climi, plants that grow in different climates; (fig., of person) to vegetate. **-arianismo** *m.* vegetarianism. **-ariano** *adj., n.m.* vegetarian. **-ativa** *f.* power of vegetable growth. **-ativo** *adj.* vegetative; of vegetation; (fig.) una vita -ativa, a vegetable life; (philos.) potenza -ativa, vegetative principle. **-azione** *f.* vegetation; -azione tropicale, tropical vegetation; growth; ritardare la -azione d'una pianta, to delay the growth of a plant; -azione spontanea, natural, wild vegetation. **-ominerale** *adj.* (chem.) acqua -ominerale, solution of basic lead acetate.

vegg-ente *adj.* seeing; *n.m.* seer, prophet, soothsayer; *f.* clairvoyante. **-enza** *f.* clear-sightedness, lucidity of thought; gift of divination; clairvoyance.

†**veg·ghia** *f.* and derivs. See **veglia** and **vegliare**.

†**veg·gia** *f.* barrel, cask, vat, tub.

†**veggiare** *vb.* and derivs. See **vegliare**.

†**veg·gi-o** *m.* small hand brazier. †**-one** *m.* bed-warmer, warming-pan.

vegli-a¹ *f.* wakefulness, watchfulness, vigil; essere tra la — e il sonno, to be half asleep; lunghe -e, long watches; ore di —, hours of vigil; late night (spent in study, recreation, etc.); stare a — sino a tarda notte, to have a late night, to stay up late; far — insieme, to spend an evening together; party, dance; tener —, to give a party, to give a dance, to entertain in the evening; cose da raccontarsi a —, tall stories, after-dinner stories; †(naut.) dangerous submerged rock; night watchman; gavitello alla —, a buoy that is watching, i.e. on the surface; àncora alla —, anchor ready for letting go. **-one** *m. augm.* party; ball; andare al -one, to go to a party.

ve·glia² *f.* See under **veglio¹**.

vegliard-o *m.* venerable old man. (**-a** *f.*)

vegli-are [A 4 c] *intr.* (*aux.* avere) to be awake, to be wakeful, to watch, to be watchful; to be up; to stay up late; — fino a mezzanotte, to stay up until midnight; to be on the look-out, to be on the alert, to take care; — nel preparare una cosa, to take care in the preparation of something; — su, to watch over, to take care of; *tr.* — un ammalato, to watch by an invalid's bed during the night; — gli interessi di A, to watch A's interests; (naut.) -a!, stand by!; †— e non —, said of blinder or rock visible at some state of tide or weather; †(of laws, decrees, etc.) to be in force. (**-amento** *m.* **-ante** *part. adj.*) **-ato** *part. adj.* (of time) spent in wakefulness; (of person) watched over; cared for. †**-atore** *m.* watcher, one who watches late; one who keeps late hours; guest at an evening party. **-atrice** *f.* night nurse. †**-evole** *adj.* vigilant, watchful; wakeful; attentive; solicitous.

ve·gli-o¹ *adj.* (poet.) old; il tempo —, ancient time; *n.m.* old man; il Veglio della Montagna, the Old Man of the Mountain. **-a** *f.* (poet.) old woman.

†**ve·glio²** *m.* See **vello¹**.

veglione *m.* See under **veglia²**.

vegn-ente *adj.* next, coming; il lunedì —, this coming Monday; following, subsequent; flourishing, promising, coming on well. †**-enza** *f.* coming; yieldingness; need.

vegro *m.* (bot.) blackthorn, *Prunus spinosa*.

veh *excl.* look!; see!

vei·colo *m.* vehicle; conveyance; medium, conveyer; (chem.) vehicle, medium, solvent.

†**vei·culo** *m.* See **veicolo**.

†**vel** *adv. phr.* a un — circa, more or less, almost, nearly; †un — circa a secento, round about six hundred.

vȩl-a *f.* (naut.) sail, canvas; ship; senza veder —, without sighting a ship; — aurica, fore and aft sail (spanker, etc.); -e basse, lower sails, courses; — imbrogliata, sail brailed up; -e inferite, sails laced or hooked by runners; — latina, lateen sail; — di maestra, mainsail; — quadra, square sail; -e sferite, sails that are unlaced and lowered; -e al soleggio, †-e a secco, sails drying; — serrata, furled sail; — sfondata, — sgratilata, — sralingata, sail that has blown out; — spiegata, spread sail; — squarciata, split sail; -e di strallo, -e di straglio, staysails; -e di taglio, fore and aft sails, lugsails; -e tannate, dyed sails; -e a tarchia, sprit sails; -e triangolari, lateen sails; forza di -e, spread of sail; — di ricambio, — di rispetto, — di riserva, spare sail; (fig.) far forza di -e e di remi, to use all one's powers; a gonfie -e, successfully, prosperously; raccoglier le -e, to stop, to finish, to shut up shop; calar le -e, to sober down, to settle down to adult life, to relinquish one's youthful pleasures; volgere la — secondo il vento, to trim one's sail according to the wind; (archit.) muro a —, wall one brick-width thick (NOT 'one-brick wall', which is a brick-length thick), also called 'muro di testa'; volta a —, cap-like vault, resting on arches; curtain; theatre curtain; (aeron.) volo a —, dynamic soaring. **-acciere** *m.* (naut.) three-masted vessel, square on the fore and lateen-rigged on main and mizzen. **-accino** *m.* (naut.) fore top gallant sail. **-ac·cio** *m.* (naut.) main top gallant sail. †**-ada** *f.* man's tail-coat, morning coat. **-a·io** *m.* (naut.) sailmaker; caviglia da -aio, marline spike. **-ata** *f.* (naut.) a run under sail. **-ato** *adj.* (poet.) having sails.

velame¹ *m.* (naut.) a suit of sails; ship's outfit (cf. **vela**).

velame² *m.* veil; covering; sotto — di, under pretext of; il — dell'allegoria, the veil of allegory (cf. **velo**).

†**velare¹** *adj.* pertaining to sails; sail-like.

velare² *adj.* (phon.) velar.

vel-are³ [A I] *tr.* to veil, to cover with a veil; (fig.) to cover, to hide; — la verità, to conceal the truth; to disguise; -ano il loro vizio sotto oneste apparenze, their vice is concealed by a show of their apparent respectability; to darken, to obscure; nubi che -ano il sole, clouds obscuring the sun; (paint.) to paint very lightly over a surface similarly coloured and already dry; †to ornament; *rfl.* to veil oneself; to conceal oneself, to hide oneself; (of eyes) to grow misty; (of voice) to thicken; le si -arono gli occhi di lagrime, her eyes were dimmed with tears; (eccl.) to take the veil. **-a·bile** *adj.* disguisable; capable of being veiled. **-amento** *m.* veiling; pretext, excuse; appearance, semblance, guise; (eccl.) taking (or giving) of the veil. **-a·rio** *m.* (Rom. antiq.) *velarium*, theatre-awning; curtain; veil, disguise. **-ata** *f.* nun, one who has taken the veil. **-atino** *m.* (photog.) vignetter. **-ato** *part. adj.* veiled; low, husky; concealed, hidden; zucchero -ato, icing sugar. **-atamente** *adv.* secretly. **-atis·simo** *superl. adj.* donna -atissima, woman heavily veiled; calza -atissima, superfine mesh stocking. (**-atore** *m.* **-atrice** *f.*)

velata¹ *f.* See under **vela**.

velata² *f.* See under **velare**.

velato¹ *adj.* See under **vela**.

velato² *part.* See under **velare**.

velatura¹ *f.* veiling; una — di zucchero, a light dusting of sugar; una — d'argento, a thin coating of silver; blur, mistiness; (photog.) clouding; (paint.) very thin wash of colour over paint already dry.

velatura² *f.* (naut.) construction and furnishing with sails; provision or outfit of sails; type of sails; quantity of sails; trim of the sails; rig; — latina, lateen rig; — quadra, square rig.

veleggi-are [A 3 c] *intr.* (*aux.* avere) to sail; — su tutti gli oceani, to sail over all the oceans; (naut.) to sail; to make short trips under sail; — alla latina, to sail under lateen rig; — di bolina, to sail close hauled; — di buon braccio, to sail seven points from the wind; (aeron.) to glide; *tr.* — i mari, to sail the seas; to provide with sails. **-amento** *m.* sailing. **-ata** *f.* sail, sailing trip; fare una -ata, to go for a sail; (naut.) fast and continuous run under sail; short cruising with a fresh and favourable wind; pleasure cruise. **-ato** *part. adj.* (naut.) fitted with sail; -ato a quadra, fitted with square sail; -ato a due antenne, carrying two yards. **-atore** *m. adj.*

veleggi-are (*cont.*)
(naut.) of a sailing vessel that goes well under sail; (aeron.) glider. (**-atrice** *f.*)

veleggio *m.* sailing.

veleni·fero *adj.* See under **veleno**.

velen-o *m.* poison; venom; (fig.) il tabacco è un lento —, tobacco is a slow poison; quel medicamento è un —, that medicine is poisonous stuff; poisonous smell; love-potion, love-philtre; amaro come il —, as bitter as gall; hatred, malice, loathing; una lingua che schizza —, a venomous tongue; sputar —, to pour out one's loathing, to give vent to hatred; avere del — contro di uno, to have one's knife into someone, to hate someone like poison; far —, to act viciously, to do grievous harm; che gli faccia —!, curse him!, blast his eyes!; masticar —, to contain one's hatred, to repress an outburst of hatred; (of conversation, thought, epigram, etc.) malice, venom; spargere il —, to spread pernicious ideas; avere il miele sulla bocca e il — nel cuore, to be as sweet as honey outwardly while feeling hatred in ones heart; il — sta nella coda, the sting is in the tail. †**-are** *vb.* and derivs. see **avvelenare**. **-i·fero** *adj.* poisonous, venomous. **-osità** *f.* venomousness, poison; malevolence, malice; perfidy; corruption; hatred, spite. **-oso** *adj.* poisonous; poisoned, venomous; malicious, malevolent, pernicious, vicious; bitter, furious, enraged, rabid; una malattia **-osa**, a pestiferous, malignant disease. **-osamente** *adv.* poisonously.

veleri·a[1] *f.* (naut.) art of sail-making; sail-maker's yard; sail draft.

veleri·a[2] *f.* veiling; wedding veils.

veletta[1] *f. dim.* of **velo**, q.v.; hat veil.

velett-a[2] *f. dim.* of **vela**, q.v.; †(naut.) look-out, watch; stare alla **-e**, to keep watch. †**-are** *tr.*, *intr.* to keep watch, to observe; correre **-ando**, to patrol.

veletto *m. dim.* of **velo**, q.v.

ve·lia *f.* (orn.) shrike.

velico *adj.* (naut.) referring to sails; gala, competizione velica, sailing regatta; sistema —, complex of sails on a particular mast; superficie velica, sail area; di equilibrio —, well-balanced.

†**veliera** *f.* head ornament of gold or silver worn to support veils.

velier-e, -o *m.* (naut.) sailing-ship; sailing-boat; windjammer; buon —, fast and safe sailing-vessel; — con motore ausiliario, sailing-ship with auxiliary motors.

†**velificare** *intr.* (*aux.* avere) to sail; to cruise under sail.

velina[1] *f. dim.* of **vela**, q.v.; tissue-paper (cf. **velino**).

†**velina**[2] *f.* marsh, marshy area, expanse of stagnant water.

velin-o *adj.* carta **-a**, tissue-paper, air-mail paper; foglio —, sheet of tissue-paper.

ve·liti *m.pl.* (Rom. antiq.) *velites* (light-armed troops); (mil. hist.) militia under Napoleon in Italy (1805); *adj.* armi —, light weapons, sidearms. †**-are** *adj.* (of weapons) light.

veli·volo *adj.* (poet., of a ship) with sails flying, winged; (of the sea) skimmed by sailing-ships; (also *n.m.*) aeroplane; glider.

†**velle** *m.* will, wish.

velleit-à *f.* velleity; empty wish, foolish aspiration; ha la — di diventare ministro, he has the ridiculous hope that he may become a minister. **-a·rio** *adj.* showing velleity, weak-willed.

†**vel·lere** *vb.* and derivs. See **svellere**.

vellic-are [A 2 S] *tr.* to pinch; to sting; to tickle; to titillate, to stimulate; — la fantasia, to excite the imagination. **-aménto** *m.* pinching; tickling; titillating. **-ante** *part. adj.* stinging; stimulating. (**-ato** *part. adj.*) **-azione** *f.* pinch, pinching; tickling; titillation, stimulation, excitement; prickling, itching.

vell-o[1] *m.* furry or woolly skin of animal; (of sheep) fleece; (of lion, tiger, etc.) skin, coat; (Gk. myth.) — d'oro, Golden Fleece; tuft of wool, flock of wool. **-oso** *adj.* fleecy, shaggy; hairy; (text.) cotone **-oso**, hairy cotton, (bot.) *Gossypium hirsutum*.

†**vello**[2] *excl.* (expressing scorn) look at him!, see him!

vellut-o *m.* velvet; — di seta, silk velvet; — di cotone, velveteen; sofà di —, plush-covered sofa; — a grosse coste, corduroy; velvet dress or suit; smooth soft surface; (of hair, hand, skin, etc.) sembra un —, it is like velvet; capelli che sono —, hair as soft as silk; (fig.) pugno di ferro e guanto di —, an iron hand in a velvet glove; †di —, of superlative quality; †giocare sul —, to gamble when one has already pocketed some winnings; *adj.* shaggy, hairy. **-are** [A 1] *tr.* (tan.) to buff, to fluff. **-ato** *adj.* velvety, like velvet; nero **-ato**, velvety black; carta **-ata**, wallpaper with a velvet finish; *n.m.* damask velvet. **-atura** *f.* velvety quality; velvety surface, fine nap. **-ina** *f.* (cul.) soup made with ground cereals;

a kind of face-powder. **-ino** *m.* velvet ribbon; very fine velvet; (bot.) *Aristolochia rotunda*; *adj.* (bot.) velutinous.

velma *f.* (geog., Ven.) muddy island in lagoon awash at high tide, muddy shoal.

velo *m.* veil, hat-veil; mourning-veil, mourning-band; — nuziale, wedding-veil; (eccl.) prendere il —, to take the veil, to become a nun; deporre, lasciare, il —, to leave one's convent, to return to the world; (liturg.) — da spalla, umerale, humeral veil; — del calice, chalice veil; (Bibl.) the veil of the Temple; veiling; fine transparent material; muslin, gauze, voile, georgette, tulle; wire gauze of a sieve; covering, cloth; (fig.) stendiamo un — su queste miserie, let us draw a veil over these troubles; (rel.; poet.) the body; il corpo è come un — dell'anima, the body is the garment of the soul; il mortal —, 'this fleshly dress', 'this mortal coil'; appearance, mask; sotto il — della pietà, under the guise of piety; illusion; le cadde il — dagli occhi, the scales fell from her eyes; l'amore paterno gli fa —, paternal love prevents him from seeing clearly; obstruction; il — dell'ignoranza, the barrier of ignorance; far —, to hide, to obscure; le nuvole fanno — al sole, the clouds are hiding the sun; la passione fa — alla mente, passion clouds the mind; mettersi il — innanzi agli occhi, to turn a blind eye; a fine layer; un — di nebbia, a fine veil of mist; un — d'acqua, a sheet of water; (paint.) dare un — di colore, to paint lightly over a surface already painted; (bot.) volva, veil; tunic; (anat.) — palatino, palatine veil, *velum palatinum*; †(naut.) see **vela**.

veloc-e *adj.* swift, fast, rapid, quick, speedy; ingegno —, swift intelligence; più — del pensiero, quick as lightning; *n.m.* (mil.) light infantryman. **-emente** *adv.* swiftly, fast, rapidly, quickly, speedily. **-i·pede** *adj.* swift-footed; *n.m.* bicycle, velocipede; penny-farthing bicycle. **-ipedista** *m.* cyclist. **-ipedi·stico** *adj.* relating to cycling or velocipedes. **-ista** *m.* (sport) sprinter. **-ità** *f.* velocity, speed, rapidity, swiftness; una **-ità** di trenta chilometri all'ora, a speed of thirty kilometres an hour; **-ità** massima, maximum velocity; spedir le merci a piccola **-ità**, to send the goods by goods train; spedir le merci a grande **-ità**, to send goods by a quicker rate than 'piccola velocità' (not as fast as by express train). †**-itare** *tr.* to increase the speed of; *rfl.* to gain speed.

velo·dromo *m.* cycling-stadium, cycle-track.

veltr-o *m.* (zool.) greyhound. (**-a** *f.*)

†**vembr-o** *m.* see **membro**. **-uto** *adj.* see **membruto**.

vemen-te *adj.* see **veemente**. **-za** *f.* see **veemenza**, under **veemente**.

ven-a *f.* (anat.) vein; — cava, vena cava; — porta, portal vein; (bot.) vein; (Rom. antiq.) tagliare, segare, le **-e**, to open one's veins (a fashionable form of suicide); (fig.) non ha sangue nelle **-e**, he's soft, he's got no guts; a pensarci si sentì bollire il sangue nelle **-e**, it made his blood boil to think of it; non le rimase sangue nelle **-e**, her heart failed her, her courage failed her; spring of water; acqua di —, spring water; allacciar le **-e**, to connect natural streams in order to direct their flow for useful purposes; (mining) lode, vein; (fig.) ha trovato una — d'oro, he has discovered a goldmine; (fig.) streak, vein, gift, talent, knack; una — d'umorismo, a streak of humour; ha la — poetica, he has a gift for poetry; gli manca la —, he hasn't the gift, he hasn't the knack; disposition, humour; di buona —, in good part, cheerfully, willingly; far qualcosa di —, to do something readily, with alacrity; essere in — di scherzare, to be in a joking mood; luck; oggi non sono in —, today I don't feel in the mood, this is not my good day; (of wine) full-bodiedness, richness; (of wine) essere sulla —, to be at its best; *pl.* (in marble, stone, etc.) veins, veinings; (in wood) grain; seguire le **-e**, to follow the grain, to go with the grain; †quality; †temper; †state, condition; †humour, disposition.

†**venagione** *f.* venery; venison; game.

venal-e *adj.* venal; marketable; prezzo —, sale price; †piazza —, market square; (fig.) venal, mercenary, grasping, open to bribes. (**-mente** *adv.*) **-ità** *f.* venality, corruptibility.

ven-are [A 1] *tr.* to vein, to cover as with veins; *rfl.* to be veined; *intr.* (*aux.* essere) to become veined. (**-amento** *m.*) **-ato** *part. adj.* (of stone, marble, rock) veined; (fig.) **-ato** di malinconia, tinged with melancholy; †edged, trimmed, piped. **-atura** *f.* veining; †piping, narrow trimming or edging.

†**venat-ore** *m.* hunter, huntsman. †**-rice** *f.* huntress.

venato·rio *adj.* pertaining to hunting; la stagione venatoria, the hunting season; l'arte venatoria, the art of hunting.

†**venazione** *f.* See **venagione**.

†**vencido** *adj.* pliable, supple, yielding.

†**vendag·gio** *m.* sale; selling.

†**vendemia** *f.* See **vendemmia.**

vendemmi·a *f.* grape-harvest, grape-gathering, wine-harvest; vintage-time, vintage; †grain-harvest; †olive-gathering, olive-harvest; †gain, booty, prize. **-a·bile** *adj.* ripe for harvesting. **-ale** *adj.* of the grape-harvest; autumnal; *n.m.* see **Vendemmiaio.** **-are** [A 4 C] *tr.* to reap, to gather, to harvest; to plunder, to despoil; *intr.* (*aux.* avere) to gather grapes, to take part in the grape-harvest; to profit handsomely, to make ill-gotten gains, to seize all; †to gather honey. (**-ante** *part. adj.* **-ato** *part. adj.*) **-atore** *m.* grape-gatherer, vintager. **-atrice** *f.* woman grape-gatherer; *f.* (astron.) Vindemiatrix, ∈ *Virginis.*

Vendemmia·io *pr.n.m.* Vendémiaire (French revolutionary month, 22 September to 21 October).

vend-ere [B 1] *tr.* to sell; to sell up; — all'asta, to sell by auction; — a contanti, to sell for cash; — a credito, to sell on credit; — all'ingrosso, to sell wholesale; — al minuto, to sell by retail; — a peso, to sell by weight; — a metro, to sell by the metre; — sotto costo, to sell below cost price; — monete, to change money, to change currency; — per —, to sell without profit; — fumo, to sell a false story; (leg.) see 'fumo -uto' below; to put up for sale; si -e, for sale; to betray, to prostitute, to surrender for private gain; — parole, to give fair words; — i suoi favori, to sell one's favours; — la patria, to betray one's country; — documenti segreti, to traffic in secret documents; (fig.) — cara la propria vita, to sell one's life dear(ly), to put up a strong resistance; — la pelle dell'orso prima d'averlo preso, to count one's chickens before they are hatched; averne da —, to have some to spare, to have more than one needs; ce n'è da —, there is more than enough; avete ragione da —, you have an extremely strong case; sa — la sua merce, he knows how to blow his own trumpet; tu non me ne -i, you won't make me believe that; — la camicia, — l'anima, — l'osso del collo, to pawn one's shirt; *rfl.* to hire oneself out; to prostitute oneself, to betray oneself, to sell oneself; -ersi anima e corpo, to sell oneself body and soul; to sell at, to cost; un pollo si -e 400 lire al kg., chicken costs 400 lire the kilo; *intr.* (*aux.* avere) to be a shopkeeper, to have a business; si mise a —, he set up shop, he set up business; to sell up. †**-enda** *f.* unit of weight corresponding to a kilogram. **-erec·cio** *adj.* saleable; venal, mercenary, corruptible. †**-eri·a** *f.* buying and selling, traffic of business, marketing. **-i·bile** *adj.* saleable; for sale, on sale; (of person) corruptible. **-ibub·bole** *m. indecl.* gossip, story-teller, chatterbox. **-icchiare** [A 4] *tr.* to sell on a small scale, to dabble in business. **-ifrot·tole** *m.*, **-ifumo** *m. indecl.* cheat, swindler, humbug, charlatan. **-imento** *m.* sale, selling. **-iparole** *m. indecl.* chatterbox, gossip. †**-ispaghi** *m.* cord and rope merchant. **-ucchiare** [A 4] see **vendicchiare.** **-uto** *part. adj.* sold; (fig.) è un'anima -uta, he is a lost soul; corrupt, unscrupulous, mercenary; scrivere con una penna -uta, to debase one's pen for profit; un giornale -uto, a corrupt newspaper (leg.) fumo -uto, the crime of pretending fraudulently, for gain, to have influence with a public servant; *n.m.*, one who takes bribes (used esp. as term of abuse for football referees).

vendetta *f.* feud, vendetta; — del sangue, blood-feud; vengeance, revenge; prender —, to take revenge; gridar —, to cry vengeance; far la — di, to avenge; affidò la sua — al figlio, he entrusted his son with the task of avenging him; ricever —, to be revenged, to gain vengeance; punishment, chastisement; giusta —, just vengeance, just retribution; fare — a, to make amends to; la — di Dio non piomba in fretta, the mills of God grind slowly; (theol.) giorno della —, the Day of Wrath.

vendic-are [A 2 S] *tr.* to avenge; — un insulto, to avenge an insult; — un amico, to avenge a friend; to vindicate; — l'onore, to vindicate one's honour; to pay for, to compensate for; *rfl.* to avenge oneself; to be revenged; -arsi d'un'ingiuria, to avenge an insult; -arsi di qualcuno, to take revenge on someone; -arsi coi nemici, to take revenge against the enemy; to regain, to redeem; -arsi la libertà, to regain one's liberty. **-a·bile** *adj.* to be avenged; capable of being avenged. †**-abilmente** *adv.* revengefully; vindictively. **-amento** *m.* avenging, taking revenge; revenge. **-ante** *part. adj.* avenging, revengeful; *n.m.*, *f.* avenger. †**-anza** *f.* vengeance, revenge. **-ativo** *adj.* vengeful, revengeful; vindictive. **-ativamente** *adv.* revengefully; vindictively. **-atore** *m.* avenger; vindicator. (**-atrice** *f.*) †**-azione** *f.* avenging; revenge.

vendichevole *adj.* vengeful, revengeful; vindictive.

†**ven·dico** *apocop. part.* of **vendicare**, q.v.

vendit-a *f.* sale; in —, on sale, for sale; essere in —, to be for sale; mandare in —, mettere in —, to put on sale; — all'asta, auction sale, public auction; — a rate, hire purchase; — all'ingrosso, wholesale; — al minuto, — al dettaglio, retail; (leg.) — giudiziale, sale by order of the court; condizioni di —, conditions of sale; — forzata, compulsory sale (by way of execution); mandato di —, sale warrant (C.C.); — di fumo, see above, 'fumo venduto' under **vendere**); (comm.) contratto di compra e —, contract for sale of goods; conveyance; — sulla banchina, sale ex quay; su campione, sale by sample; sale by private treaty; prezzo di —, selling price; — sotto costo, under sale (at below cost price); — all'estero sotto costo, dumping; — franco a bordo, F.O.B. sale; conto di —, account sales, sale note; bando di —, notice of sale; — per netto, net sale; — a contanti, cash sale; contratto e —, bargain and sale; — a credito, credit sale; — per descrizione, sale by description; — di prodotti, sale of produce; spese di —, selling costs; aver buona —, (of goods) to sell well; c'è molta — di stoffe leggiere, light materials are selling very well; la — aumenta, business is increasing; shop; — di pane, baker's shop; aprire una —, to open a shop, to set up shop; (hist.) — dei Carbonari, lodge, secret meeting-place of the Carbonari; group of Carbonari belonging to one particular meeting-place. **-ore** *m.* seller, vendor; **-ore** ambulante, hawker, pedlar; **-ore** all'ingrosso, wholesale dealer; **-ore** al minuto, retailer; **-ore** di carboni, coal-merchant; (fig.) **-ore** di fumo, humbug, swindler, charlatan; (comm.) eccedenza di **-ori**, sellers over, more sellers than buyers; (leg.) vendor, vender, seller; azioni dei **-ori**, vendors' shares; diritti di **-ore**, seller's rights; **-ore** e compratore, vendor and purchaser (C.C.). (**-ora** *f.* **-rice** *f.*) †**-ura** *f.* sale, selling.

†**vendizione** *f.* (leg.) vendition.

-vendol-o *m. suff.* -vendor. **-a** *f. suff.* woman vendor.

venefi·cio *m.* (leg.) poisoning; fu imputato di —, he was accused of poisoning; causa di —, cause of poisoning.

vene·fico poisonous; (fig.) clima —, unhealthy climate; propaganda venefica, pernicious propaganda; †*n.m.* sorcerer, wizard.

†**venenare** *vb.* and derivs. See **avvelenare.**

vener-a·bile *adj.*, †**-agione** *f.* **-ando** *adj.*, etc. see under **venerare.**

vener-are [A 1 S] to venerate, to revere, to reverence, to honour; to worship. **-a·bile** *adj.* venerable; (eccl.) Venerable (used of holy persons not yet beatified and also of certain church institutions, e.g. the English College in Rome); (Masonic) Worshipful (Master of a lodge); *n.m.* (liturg.) the Blessed Sacrament. **-abilmente** *adv.* venerably. **-abilità** *f.* venerableness. †**-agione** *f.* veneration, venerating. **-amento** *m.* veneration, reverence; worship; **-amento** degl'idoli, idolatry. **-ando** *adj.* venerable, worthy of reverence. **-ante** *part. adj.* venerating; atto **-ante**, act of veneration, act of reverence. †**-anza** *f.* see **venerazione.** **-ato** *part. adj.* venerated, revered, reverenced, honoured; worshipped; di **-ata** memoria, of hallowed memory. (**-atore** *m.* **atrice** *f.*) **-azione** *f.* veneration, reverence; avere in **-azione**, to venerate, to hold in veneration; worship, adoration, cult. †**-e·vole** *adj.* venerable.

venerdì *pr.n.m.* Friday; il — santo, Good Friday; non mangio carne il —, I don't eat meat on Fridays; non avere tutti i suoi —, to have a screw loose, to be a bit lacking; gli manca un —, he isn't quite all there; — gnocolàr, the Friday of the Carnival festivities in Verona.

Ve·ner-e *pr.n.f.* Venus; (Gk. and Rom. art) — Anadiomene, Aphrodite Anadyomene, Venus rising from the sea; — callipige, the callipygian Aphrodite (Venus); — capitolina, the Capitoline Venus; (in Plato, not in historical cults) — celeste, the Heavenly Aphrodite, intellectual love; — terrestre, the Earthly Aphrodite, physical love; (art) statue or painting of Venus; bella come una —, as beautiful as a goddess; beauty, grace, elegance, loveliness; le -i del suo stile, the elegances of his style; lust, desire, passion, sensuality, carnality; essere dedito ai piaceri di —, to be given over to the pleasures of Venus, to be engrossed in the pursuit of sensual pleasure; sacrificare a —, to pay tribute to Venus; — vaga, wanton lust; — di marciapiede, streetwalker, prostitute; sentire il tocco di —, to feel the call of passion; (astron.) Venus; (hist.) astro di —, alchemist's term for copper; (chem.) vetriolo di —, blue vitriol; acetato di —, verdigris; (zool.) — chione, *Meretrix chione*; — gallina, *Chamelea gallina*; — incrocicchiata, *Amigdala decussata*; — tartufo, *Venus verrucosa*, various edible bivalves. **-ina** *f. dim.* small statue of Venus.

vene·re-o *adj.* pertaining to Venus; le grazie -e, the beauties of Venus; sensual, lascivious, lustful; piacere —, carnal pleasure; (med.) venereal; morbo —, venereal disease. **-aménte** *adv.* sensually, carnally; conoscere -amente, to have carnal knowledge of.

Ve·neto¹ *pr.n.m.* (geog.) il —, Venetia.

ve·neto² *adj.*, of or belonging to Venetia; (hist.) regno Lombardo —, Lombardo-Venetian Kingdom (Austrian possession, 1815–59); *n.m.* Veneto dialect.

Vene·zi-a *pr.n.f.* (geog.) Venice; (hist.) la Repubblica di —, the Venetian republic; Venetia; le tre -e, the three Venetias, i.e. Veneto, Venezia Tridentina, and Venezia Giulia. **-ano** *n.m.* Venetian; Venetian dialect; *adj.* Venetian; alla -ana, in the Venetian manner; lampioncini alla -ana, Chinese lanterns; pavimento alla -ana, marble floor; vogare alla -ana, to row in a standing position; ricamo -ano, embroidery in the style of Venetian lace. **-ana** *f.* Venetian woman; (cul.) soft bun; small milk roll.

†vengiare *vb.* and derivs. See **vendicare**.

ve·ni-a *f.* indulgence, pardon; chieder —, to ask pardon; con vostra — devo partire, with your permission I must leave; †supplication, request, earnest entreaty, prostration. **-ale** *adj.* venial, worthy of indulgence, pardonable; (theol.) peccato -ale, venial sin. **-alménte** *adv.* venially, pardonably. **-alità** *f.* veniality.

veni-ente *part. adj.*, *n.m.*, *f.* of venire, q.v. **-ménto** *m.* see under venire.

ven-ire [D 17] *intr.* (*aux.* essere). **1.** To COME; verrò a Roma, I shall come to Rome; -ga a Roma, come to Rome; — a piedi, to come on foot; — in scena, to come on the scene; vieni e vedi, come and see; -ite a tavola, come and have your lunch, come and have your dinner; viemmi ad aprire, come and let me in; un andare e —, a coming and going; chi va e chi viene, they come and go; un vai e vieni, a coming and going, a backward and forward movement; segare il marmo con un va e vieni regolare, to saw marble with a regular backward and forward movement; far — una cosa, to order something, to have something sent; far — uno, to send for someone; — dietro a uno, to come up behind someone; — contro a uno, to come towards someone; — fuori, to come out; — dentro, to come inside; — su, to come up; — qui, to come here; non — quaggiù!, don't come down here!; di dove vieni?, where do you come from?; — giù, to fall; -iva giù la pioggia, the rain was falling; — a, — per, to come with the purpose of; -ne a chiedermi un piacere, he came to ask me a favour; viene per aiutarti, he is coming to help you; — per, to come for the purpose of obtaining; — per aiuto, to come for help; to approach, to apply; mi -ne con le buone, he approached me nicely; venirsene, to come away; con che te ne vieni?, come off it!; con che se ne viene!, he can't get away with that one, he can't make me believe that! **2.** To MOVE, to pass, to proceed; — dietro a tutti, to follow on behind everyone else; — in città dalla campagna, to move from the country into the town; -ne a dire, he proceeded to say; — alle prese, to come to blows, to have words, to have a tiff; — alle prese con, to come to grips with; — alle mani, to come to blows; — alle parole, to have words; — alle brutte, to have violent words; — a questione, to have a tiff, to have a hostile discussion; — a battaglia, to proceed to battle; to enter hostilities; — a patti, to come to terms; — al fatto, to come to the point; — ad altro, to move on to something else; ora -go a te, now I come to your point, now I come on to you; -iamo a noi, let us take *our* problem; to return; — a casa, to come back home; -ite presto!, come back soon! **3.** To ARRIVE; -nero a un fiume, they arrived at a river; — a galla, to come to the surface; -uto il treno, the train has arrived; -ne il giorno, the day arrived, came the day; aspettare che -ga il giorno, to wait for daybreak; — alla verità, to arrive at the truth; -ne a notizia del mio arrivo, the news of my arrival reached him; — agli orecchi di, to come to the ears of; — in, to come into, to fall into; — in dispregio, to fall into disfavour; — in odio a uno, to incur someone's hatred; — in fama, to become famous; — in basso stato, to fall to a low position; — in palese, to become known; — in chiaro d'una cosa, to get clear about something; — a capo di, to complete, to finish; — alle strette, to come to the point, to touch on the heart of the matter; ai ferri corti, to come to grips ('venire alle strette' can also mean this); — al mondo, — alla luce, to be born; quelli che verranno dopo di noi,

those that shall come after us; -ne sull'uscio, he appeared in the doorway; mi -ne davanti, he stood before me; -ne in tavola un dolce squisito, an exquisite sweet appeared; — fuori, (of books) to appear, to come out, to be published; to reach; la strada viene sino qui, the road reaches this far. **4.** To DERIVE, to originate; è tutta roba che viene dall'Inghilterra, it is all stuff imported from England; ne -iva un gran puzzo, it gave off a horrible smell; ho gradito il dono perchè mi vien da te, I accepted the present because it was from you; i guadagni che gli -gono dalla professione, the money he earns in his profession; — da una buona famiglia, — di buona famiglia, to come of a good family; — da una delle migliori università, to be a graduate of one of the foremost universities; — dalla gavetta, to rise from the ranks; di qui viene che le cose nostre vanno male, this is the source of our ill-fortune. **5.** To HAPPEN, to arise, to befall, to occur; quando viene l'occasione, when the occasion arises; son cose di là da —, it will be a long time before such things take place; tutto il male non viene per nuocere, it's an ill-wind that blows nobody any good; ora viene il buono, the good time is coming now; dopo la pioggia viene il bel tempo, after rain comes fine weather; che ti -ga il ben di Dio!, God's blessing on you!; le -ne questo caso, this circumstance befell her; -ne che un giorno..., it happened that one day...; se non -gono disgrazie, if nothing dreadful happens; verrà una carestia, a famine will come; — in taglio, — a proposito, to happen at the right time, to fit in appropriately; far —, to cause, to provoke; questi cibi fanno — la nausea, this food makes one sick; dire quel che gli viene sulla lingua, to say the first thing that comes into one's head; gli viene naturale, it comes naturally to him; mi -ne da ridere, I was seized with the impulse to laugh; mi -ne in mente, it occurred to me; gli è -uto questo capriccio, he has got hold of this notion; (of a date) to fall; il Natale scorso -ne di domenica, last year Christmas fell on a Sunday; la Pasqua viene presto quest'anno, Easter falls early this year; (of numbers in a draw) to be drawn, to turn up; è -uto il tre, the three has been drawn; (mus.) musica sonata come viene, improvised music. **6.** To GROW, to develop, to progress; nei climi freddi non viene il grano, corn will not grow in cold climates; — su bene, to come on well; il bambino vien proprio benino, the little boy is really coming on splendidly; il tuo ricamo vien bene, your embroidery is coming on nicely; — male, to make slow progress; to grow worse; le -ne male la febbre, her fever took a turn for the worse. **7.** To DEVELOP, to form; — agli occhi, (of tears) to spring to the eyes; far — l'acquolina in bocca, to make one's mouth water; un foruncolo gli -ne al collo, a boil formed on his neck; gli è -uta la paura, he was seized with fear. **8.** To BECOME, to turn; — sazio, to grow sated; -ne desideroso di vederla, he became desirous of seeing her; — nonno, to become a grandfather; — scuro, to darken; — rosso, to turn red; — in uggia, to grow distasteful; ora il cinema mi è -uto in uggia, I can't stick the cinema now; — a noia, to become tedious; le è -uto a noia, she has grown tired of him; — in uso, to come into use; — di moda, to come into fashion, to become fashionable; — meno, to faint; — meno alla parola data, to fall short of one's word, to break one's word; — meno al proprio dovere, to fail in one's duty. **9.** To RESULT, to add up to, to come out; ho fatto la somma, e mi viene quarantadue, I have added it up and make it forty-two; quanto viene il conto?, what does the bill come to?; quel che viene viene, cost what it may; viene a cento lire il fiasco, it costs a hundred lire the bottle; viene a dire che sono un ladro, it is as good as saying that I am a thief; il problema non gli viene, he cannot solve the problem; mi -ne bene, I succeeded, I managed to do it; lo feci, ma non mi -ne bene, I did it, but had little success; mi -ne male, I couldn't do it, I didn't succeed. **10.** To BE ABOUT TO COME; viene l'inverno, the winter is coming; il mese che viene, next month. **11.** To BE SENT, to be directed, to be addressed; questa lettera viene a voi, this letter is addressed to you; mi è -uto un giornale, a paper came for me; questa viene a te, there's one in the eye for you; to belong; ti si darà quel che ti si viene, you will be given as much as is your due. **12.** To APPEAR; — sull'orizzonte, to appear on the horizon; — fuori, to emerge. **13.** To GIVE WAY, to give, to yield; se tiri forte, vedrai che viene, if you pull hard you'll find it will come; — via, to come unstuck, to come away; cuoio che viene, supple leather; (naut.) to alter course; — a dritta, to sail to starboard; — alla banda, to put her hard over; — a tiro, to come in range; — di fianco, to come

ven·ire (*cont*)

into a beam wind; — al traverso a, to come abeam of (another ship); — al vento, to come up into the wind; non -ite al vento!, no higher! (into the wind); donde -ite e dove andate?, whence do you come and where are you bound? **14.** Syntactical Uses: (i) *As an aux. in a Passive Construction:* per questo viene ammirata, she is admired for this; -ne eletto re, he was elected king; — fatto, to happen; mi -ne fatto d'incontrarlo, I happened to meet him; gli -ne fatto come voleva, he succeeded in his wish; mi -ne fatto di coglierlo, I managed to catch him; — detto, (of words) to escape, to slip out; mi -ne detto che, I let it slip out that, *or* I was told that. (ii) *With a ger. expressing gradual fulfilment of an action:* si viene accorgendo, he gradually begins to notice; lo -go leggendo con comodo, I am reading it at my leisure. -ente, -iente *part. adj.* coming; il giorno -iente, the next day; lunedì -iente, next Monday; *n.m., f.* comer; si faceva incontro ai -ienti, he went to meet them as they came. -imento *m.* arrival, coming; †event. †-itic·cio *adj.* adventitious; gente -iticcia, rabble, mob. -uto *part. adj.* come; arrived; returned; grown; happened; appeared; resolved; ben -uto!, welcome!; dare il ben -uto a, to welcome; i nuovi -uti, the new arrivals; essere il primo -uto, to be the first comer, to be first in the field; non essere il primo -uto, to be someone, not to be a nobody.

venosino *adj.* (Rom. antiq.) of Venusia; il poeta —, Horace.

venoso *adj.* veined; venous; (anat.) sangue -oso,

†vense·i *card. num.* See ventisei, under venti.

venta·gl-ia *f.* (mil. hist.) face-piece of a helmet; mouth-piece of a gun-mask. -ia·io, -iaro *m.* see under ventaglio. -ia [A4] *rfl.* see under ventaglio. -ina *f.* (bot.) lady's mantle, *Alchemilla.*

venta·gli-o *m.* fan; — di carta, paper fan; — giapponese, Japanese fan: agitare il —, to fan oneself, to use a fan; a —, a forma di —, fan-shaped, fan-wise; coda a —, fan-tail; (of roads) dipartirsi a —, to branch out fan-wise; (mil.) a —, fanned out; (aeron.) segnalatore a —, fan-marker; (zool.) scallop, *Pecten jacobaeus.* -a·io, -aro *m.* fan-maker, one who makes, sells and mends fans. -are [A4] *rfl.* to fan oneself.

ventame *m.* (naut.) fly of a flag; †leech of a sail.

vent-are [A1] *intr.* (*aux.* avere) (of wind, hurricane, etc.) to blow, to blow hard; *impers.* (poet.) to be windy. (-amento *m.*) -ante *part. adj.* blowing; lato -ante, fly (of a flag). -ata *f.* gust of wind, rush of wind; (fig.) una -ata di follia, a wave of madness; una -ata di patriottismo, a wave of patriotism. -azione *f.* blowing, blast.

ventar(u)ola *f.* weathercock; fan; fire-fan; ventilator; (fig.) chatterbox, feather-brain; fickle person.

ventata *f.* See under ventare.

†venta·volo *m.* north wind.

†venteggiare *intr.* (*aux.* avere) to blow (of wind).

vent-i *card. num.* twenty; un —, about twenty; abita al —, he lives at number twenty; arriverò il —, I shall arrive on the twentieth; le —, eight p.m.; (fig.) several; te l'ho detto — volte, I have told you twenty times; a few; disse — parole e se ne andò, he said a couple of words and went away; †dare il — a, to burn; †tenere il —, reggere il —, to be a go-between. -enne *adj., n.m., f.* twenty-year-old. -en·nio *m.* period of twenty years. -e·simo, -ęsimo *ord. num.* twentieth; twentieth part (Note: 'ventesimo' is sometimes compounded with other ordinal numbers, e.g. -esimo primo, *or* -esimoprimo, -esimo secondo, -esimo terzo, but such numbers are more often rendered thus: ventunesimo, ventiduesimo, ventitreesimo, etc.). -icinque *card. num.* twenty-five; (fig.) a few. -icinquenne *adj., n.m., f.* twenty-five-year-old; (also -icinquennale *adj.*) of twenty-five years' duration; renewable every twenty-five years. -icinquen·nio *m.* period of twenty-five years; twenty-fifth anniversary. -icinquina *f.* set, group or batch of (about) twenty-five. -idue *card. num.* twenty-two. (-idue·simo, -iduęsimo *ord. num.*) -imila *card. num.* twenty thousand. -imille·simo, -imillęsimo *ord. num.* twenty-thousandth; twenty-thousandth part. -ina *f.* set, group or batch of (about) twenty, score; ha toccato la -ina, he is over twenty. -ino *m.* (numism.) piece of money worth twenty centesimi. -inove *card. num.* twenty-nine. -inovennale *adj.* of twenty-nine years' duration. (-inove·simo, -inovęsimo *ord. num.*) -iquattro *card. num.* twenty-four; -iquattr'ore, twenty-four hours; (rel.) le -iquattr'ore, the evening Angelus (cf. **ora**); son sonate le -iquattr'ore, it's finished, it's all over; le -iquattr'ore, (in secular modern usage) midnight, †sunset; biglietto delle -iquattro, notice

sent to persons under police observation warning them to be in by midnight. (-iquattre·şimo, -iquattręşimo *ord. num.*) -ise·i *card. num.* twenty-six. (-isee·simo, -iseeşimo *ord. num.*) -isette *card. num.* twenty-seven; il -isette, pay-day (day on which State employees are paid); lo fa solo per il -isette, he's only doing it for the money. (-isette·şimo, -isetteşimo *ord. num.*) -itre *card. num.* twenty-three; (eccl.) le -itrè, an hour before sundown (cf. **ora**); essere alle -itrè, essere alle -itrè e tre quarti, to be on one's last legs, to have reached the last stages of old age; portare il cappello sulle -itrè, to wear one's hat cocked slightly on one side, at a rakish angle. (-itree·şimo *ord. num.*) -otto *card. num.* twenty-eight. (-otte·şimo *ord. num.*) -uno *card. num.* twenty-one; -un cavalli, twenty-one horses; -un bei cavalli, twenty-one fine horses; i -un cavalli, the twenty-one horses; (naut.) -un colpi di cannone, royal salute (guns).

venticello *m. dim.* of vento, q.v.

ventiera *f.* (mil.) mask or shield over an entrance or view slit.

ventilabro *m.* winnowing-fan; (mus.) pallet (valve admitting wind to organ-pipe).

ventil-are [A1 s] *tr.* to winnow; — una proposta, to examine a proposal; to discuss aloud; to consider (silently); taceva, -ando il progetto, he was silent, thinking over the suggestion); to air, to ventilate; — le ali, to fly; — il viso, to fan one's face; to expose to the wind; *intr.* (*aux.* avere) to blow, to be windy; (of a flag, wings, etc.) to flap, to flutter; to discuss; -ò di ricorrere al governo, there was talk of appealing to the government; *rfl.* to blow about in the wind, to flutter; to be ventilated. (-amento *m.* -ante *part. adj.*) -ato *part. adj.* aired, blown about; cooled by the wind; examined, discussed; †blown away, carried off by the wind; †destroyed. -atore *m.* ventilator; fan; (naut.) -atore a sacco, canvas cowl, ventilator. -azione *f.* ventilation; blowing, movement of air; winnowing; sifting, examination (of project, etc.); (naut.) manica di -azione, windcowl, (aeron.) windsock.

vent-o *m.* wind; -i costanti, -i alisei, trade-winds; -i etesii, Etesian winds; — favorevole, favourable wind; — contrario, contrary wind; tira (il) —, the wind blows; è mutato —, the wind has changed; avere il — in faccia, to have the wind against one; — di nord, north wind; — imbrifero, — d'acqua, rain-bearing wind; nodo di —, whirlwind, hurricane; rosa dei -i, compass-card; acqua a —, wind-driven rain; mulino a —, windmill; giacca a —, wind-cheater, anorak; torcia a —, link, wind-resisting torch of pitch and tow; (tan.) mettere al —, to set out, to strike out; mettitrice a —, setting out machine; (naut.) i trenta due -i, the pointing of the compass used to indicate wind direction; — dominante, prevailing wind; — forte, moderate gale (Beaufort scale 7); — fresco, strong breeze (B.s. 6); — maneggevole, suitable wind for all purposes; — teso, fresh breeze, fresh wind (B.s. 5); — abborracciato, wind that is easing; buon —, steady breeze; — afoso, hot, damp wind; (naut.) al —, windward; — al giardinetto, — per area, quartering wind; paterazzo al —, weather shroud; dare, levare le vele al —, to spread sail in the wind, to set sail, to set out on a voyage; — al traverso, beam wind; — di traversia, wind blowing into the entrance of a port; †— da viaggio, soldiers' wind (favourable for going and returning); con — largo, quartering wind; stretto al —, close to the wind, close hauled; prendere il — davanti, pigliare il — a prora, di rovescio, to be taken aback; (fig.) pigliare il —, to lose the thread of one's discourse; essere sotto —, avere il vento in poppa, to be to leeward; rubare, togliere il — a, to take the wind from (another vessel); venire al —, to come up into the wind; il — rinfresca, the wind freshens; il — cambia, the wind shifts; il — favorisce, the wind favours; il — rifiuta, il — rinfaccia, the wind heads; il — gira, the wind veers or backs; guarda il —!, watch your course!; -i del pesce, cringler for the crowsfoot of an awning or a sail; eyelets at the ends of a hammock; — obliquo, oblique wind; — stretto, wind before the beam; — largo, wind abaft the beam; salto di —, squall putting the sails aback; (fig.) avere il — in poppa, to be in fortune's way; fatiche buttate al —, wasted effort; parlare al —, to speak to a brick wall; volare come il —, to fly like the wind; tirare calci al —, (of hanged person) to swing; che buon —?, che buon — ti porta?, what good fortune brings you here?; navigare secondo il — che tira, essere bandiera da ogni —, voltarsi a tutti i -i, to be a turncoat, to swim with the tide; spirava cattivo — per noi, it was an awkward time for us,

vent-o (*cont.*)

we were going through a difficult period; piuma al —, turncoat, fickle person; spargere ai quattro -i, to spread (news) far and wide; restar con le mani pieni di —, to have one's hopes defeated; pascer di —, to delude with empty promises; secondo che spira il —, according to which way the wind blows; far — a, to make off with; gli hanno fatto — a quanto aveva in casa, they have made off with everything he had in the house; air; farsi —, to fan oneself; pallone a —, inflatable ball, balloon; schioppo a —, air-gun; pigliar —, (of water-pipes) to have an air-lock; (mus.) strumenti a —, wind-instruments, the wind (i.e. brass and wood-wind); pompa a —, wind pump; *pl.* air-bubbles (in casting); (med.) flatulence, wind; breath; spirit; un — di fronda, a spirit of rebellion; vanity; le grandezze umane sono un —, human greatness is as a puff of smoke; *pl.* tent-ropes, guy-ropes. **-ipio·volo** *m.* a wind charged with rain.

ven·tol-a *f.* fire-fan; winnowing-fan; small firescreen with handle; wall-bracket; (eng.) impeller; (joc.) orecchie a —, enormous ears; che -e!, what huge ears!; (archit.) muro a —, partition; party-wall. †**-a·io** *m.* see **ventilabro**. **-ana** *f.* (bot.) *Cynosurus echinatus*. **-are** [A I] *tr.* to ventilate, to air; to shake, to wave in the wind; to winnow; *intr.* (*aux.* avere) to be windy, to blow; to flutter, to wave. **-ato** *part. adj.* aired, ventilated; flapped; winnowed. †**-ato·io** *m.* see **ventilabro**. (**-atóre** *m.* **-atrice** *f.*) **-atura** *f.* airing, ventilating; winnowing. **-azione** *f.* ventilation.

ventosa *f.* (zool.) sucker, of an octopus, etc.

ventoso[1] *pr.n.m.* Ventose, the sixth month of the French Revolutionary calendar (19 February to 20 March).

ventos-o[2] *adj.* windy, exposed to the wind; bombastic, conceited, puffed up; (med.) flatulent; †(poet.) swift as the wind. **-aménte** *adv.* emptily, vainly. **-ità** *f.* (med.) flatulence; (fig.) conceit, vanity; bombast.

ventotto *card. num.* See under **venti**.

ventr-e *m.* belly, abdomen; paunch; womb; mal di —, stomach-ache; bowels; muovere il —, to move the bowels; aprire il —, to open the bowels; — inferiore, lower abdomen; (colloq.) stomach; che —!, what an appetite!; non pensare che al —, to think only of one's stomach; empire la gola, il — e le budelle, to cram the stomach, to stuff oneself full; dedito al —, greedy, gluttonous; — a terra, at full gallop; (aeron.) face (of propeller blade); (vet.) — di serpe, a horse with a yellowish or white belly; bulge, swelling, curve; — di un vaso, curve of a vase; (of cask) bilge; (of river) swell; interior, inside, hollow; — d'una caverna, hollow of a cave; il — della terra, the womb of the earth; (anat.) — del muscolo, muscle belly; (mil.) barrel of a gun; (archit.) entasis; (naut.) — della vela, belly of a sail; sag of badly stowed sail, etc.; (acoustics) loop, antinode; (metall.) belly (of blast furnace); †— medio, chest. **-ac·cio** *m. pejor.* glutton. **-ai·a** *f.* big belly; 'pluck', butchers' term for the guts of a slaughtered animal. †**-aiuola** *f.* tripe-woman, woman who washed out and sold the intestines of slaughtered animals. **-ale** *adj.* (anat.) ventral. **-ata** *f.* blow or kick in the stomach; bellyful; †unborn child, weight of pregnancy. **-ésca** *f.* tripe; the belly of tunny; stuffed pig's stomach; †belt for carrying money. †**-ic·chio** *m.* see **ventriglio**. **-icello** *m. dim.* of **ventre**; ventricle. **-icino** *m.* (vet.) the abomasum or fourth stomach of a sheep used to make junket. **-icolare** *adj.* (med.) ventricular; gastric. **-i·colo** *m.* (anat.) ventricle; †stomach. **-iera** *f.* purse worn at the waist attached to belt; body-belt; (naut.) scantlings of a launching cradle; (surg.) abdominal belt, abdominal support. **-i·glio** *m.* (orn.) gizzard, stomach; (anat.) ventricle. **-ilo·quio** *m.* ventriloquy, ventriloquism. **-i·loquo** *m.* ventriloquist; *adj.* ventriloquous. **-ina** *f.* (vet.) colic in cattle, sheep or horses. **-ino** *m.* tummy, little paunch; (naut.) gripe, canvas-covered rope or sword-matting used for securing a sea-boat. **-oc·cio** *m.* (vet.) see **ventricino**. **-one** *m. augm.* big belly; fat fellow, person with large paunch; glutton, great eater.

ventrilo·quio *m.* See under **.ventre**

vent-uno *card. num.* **-une·simo** *ord. num.* See under **venti**.

ventur-a *f.* fortune, future; far la —, dar la —, predire la —, to foretell the future, to tell fortunes; augurare la buona — a uno, to wish someone good luck; good luck, good fortune; essere l'amico della —, to be smiled upon by fortune; per mia — lo riconobbi, luckily I recognized him; luck, chance; la mala —, ill luck; per —, by chance, stare alla —, andare alla —, mettersi alla —, to trust to luck; la — di Dio, providence; alla —, at

random, *or* at one's risk, at a venture; (comm.) prestito alla grossa —, bottomry bond; (mil. hist.) soldato di —, soldier of fortune. **-iere, -iero** *m.* (mil. hist.) volunteer; militiaman; fencible; Home Guard; (fig.) adventurer, free lance; *adj.* having no permanent or stable occupation. **-ina** *f.* (miner.) see **avventurina**. **-o** *adj.* next, coming, future; il mese -o, next month; le generazioni -e, future generations; l'ira -a, the wrath to come; i -i, posterity; lunedì —, next Monday. **-one** *m.* (orn.) variety of finch. **-oso** *adj.* fortunate, lucky; happy. **-osaménte** *adv.* fortunately, luckily.

venust-à *f.* beauty, grace, loveliness; (of style) grace, beauty, distinction. †**-are** *tr.* to render beautiful. **-o** *adj.* beautiful, graceful, charming, lovely; uno stile -o, a graceful style.

venuta *f.* arrival, coming; alla — di, on the arrival of; alla mia —, when I arrived; (mil.) approaches to a bridge, gateway or pass; ceremonial route; †way, street.

vepr-e *m.* (bot.) blackthorn, *Prunus spinosa*; copse, brushwood; (herald.) créquier. **-a·io** *m.* thorny place, thorny ground; bramble-bush, brake.

†**ver** *prep.* See **verso**.[3]

vera[1] *f.* (S. Italy, admin.) authentic signature.

vera[2] *f.* (N. Italy) wedding-ring; †metallic circle; †parapet round the top of a well.

Vera[3] *pr.n.f.* Vera.

verac-e *adj.* true, real; figlio —, legitimate son; truthful, veracious, sincere; testimone —, faithful witness. **-eménte** *adv.* truthfully. **-ità** *f.* veracity; truthfulness.

veranda *f.* verandah, veranda.

veratro *m.* (bot.) hellebore, *Veratrum*.

verbal-e *adj.* verbal, oral; contratto —, verbal contract; ordine —, spoken command; literal; traduzione —, word for word translation; (gramm.) verbal; aggettivi -i, participles; processo —, minute, minutes (of a meeting); Nota —, diplomatic communication written in third person and unsigned, *Note Verbale*; (leg.) contratto —, parole contract (C.C.); processo — di costatazione, Circumstantial Police Report (C.P.); *n.m.* minutes; libro dei -i, minute-book; mettere a —, to enter in the minutes; (leg.) record (of trial, etc.); note; minute; written report; — di accertamento, Police report of officially ascertained fact(s) (C.P.). **-ménte** *adv.* aloud, verbally, orally; literally, word for word. **-ista** *m.., f.* verbatim reporter. **-iẓẓare** [A I] *tr.* to verbalize; (leg.) to make a report on, of; to include in a report (C.P.); (admin.) to minute, to put on record.

verbena *f.* (bot.) vervain, *Verbena officinalis*; †see **vermena**.

†**verberare** *tr.* to shake, to beat (of wind).

verb-o *m.* word; non dire —, to say not a word, to be silent; a — a —, word for word; (theol.) il — di Dio, the Word of God; il — umanato, the Word Incarnate; (eccl.) Suore del — incarnato, Sisters of the Incarnate Word; main point, essential point, essence; verb; — sostantivo, verbal noun. †**-ica·usa** *f.* see **verbigrazia**. †**-igra·zia** *adv.* for instance, for example; per —, for example. **-osità** *f.* verbosity. **-oso** *adj.* verbose, loquacious, wordy. **-osaménte** *adv.* verbosely, loquaciously, wordily.

†**ver·cio** *adj.* See **guercio**.

†**verdadero** *adj.* See **veritiero**, under **verità**.

verd-e *adj.* green; — bottiglia, bottle-green; — bandiera, bright green; — barriera, green belt; — oliva, olive green; (of complexion) green, livid; — d'invidia, green with envy; angry, livid with anger; unripe, immature, bitter, sour; (of wood, vegetables, etc.) green, full of sap, fresh, juicy; young; i -i anni, the years of youth; flourishing, thriving, vigorous; vivo e —, alive and kicking; (of words, usage) prevalent, current; ridere —, to force a hollow laugh; (herald.) vert; †età —, spring; †star sempre —, to be inflexible, to be firm, unyielding; *n.m.* green; vestirsi di —, to dress in green; greenery, foliage; siepe di —, evergreen hedge; green vegetables, greens, green stuff; green fodder; mettere le bestie al —, to put animals out to grass; essere al —, to be broke, to be penniless, to be at the end of one's resources (cf. under **candela**); ridursi al —, to lose all one's money; avere del —, to be full of vigour. **-ac·chia** *f.* (bot.) name of two greenish kinds of plum and pear. **-ac·chio** *adj.* pale green. **-ac·cio** *m. pejor.* ugly green; (paint.) verdaccio, used in fresco painting and composed of dark ochre, lime-white and cinabrese (as explained by Cennino Cennini: *Il libro dell'Arte*, cap. 67). †**-ante** *adj.* green. **-astro** *adj.* greenish; *n.m.* greenish hue. **-azzurro** *adj.* greenish blue, sea-green; *n.m.* greenish-blue hue, haze or tone. **-e·a** *f.*

verd-e (*cont.*)

(agric.) name of kind of grape; the wine made from it. **-ebruno** *adj.* dark green; *n.m.* dark green colour. **-echiaro** *adj.* light green; *n.m.* light green hue; (agric.) a kind of fig. **-ecupo** *adj.* dark green; *n.m.* dark green colour. **-ega·io** *adj.* clear green; *n.m.* clear green tone. **-egiallo** *adj.* greenish yellow, apple-green (also *n.m.*). (**-eggiamento** *m.* **-eggiante** *part. adj.*) **-eggiare** [A 3 C] *intr.* (*aux.* avere) to turn green, to begin to be green; to be green; to be greenish; to flourish, to thrive; †*tr.* to turn green. **-egi·glio** *adj.*, *n.m.* (paint.) a bright green prepared from irises. **-emare** *adj.* sea-green, aquamarine (also *n.m.*). †**-emezzo** *adj.* half-ripe; half-cooked, half-raw. **-eporro** *adj.*, *n.m.* bright green, emerald green, leek-green. **-erame** *m.* (chem.) verdigris. †**-ero·gnolo** *adj.* greenish, tending towards green. **-esca** *f.* (ichth.) blue shark, *Carcharias glaucus.* **-escuro** *adj.*, *n.m.* dark green. **-eterra** *adj.*, *n.m.* (paint.) terre verte, a green paint used in fresco painting. **-etto** *adj. dim.* greenish; Saxon green; (of white wine) sharp; *n.m.* (paint.) a mineral green derived from Austria. **-ezza** *f.* greenness; greenery, verdure. **-ibruno** *adj.*, *n.m.* see **-ebruno.** †**-icare** *intr.* see **verdeggiare.** **-ic·chio** *m.* white wine from the Marche. **-ic·cio** *adj.* greenish, glaucous. **-igno** *adj.* greenish. **-ino** *adj.* delicate green; (agric.) a kind of fig. †**-ire** *intr.* see **verdeggiare.** †**-oc·cio** *adj.* deep green. **-ognolo** *adj.* greenish; pale green; tending towards green. **-olino** *adj.* slightly green; *n.m.* a green liqueur; (agric.) a kind of grape. **-one** *adj. augm.* deep green; *n.m.* deep green colour; (orn.) green linnet. †**-ore** *m.* see **verdezza.**

verdetto¹ *m.* (leg.) verdict; il capogiurato legge il **—**, the foreman of the jury reads the verdict; (fig.) considered opinion, judgement, consensus of views.

verdetto² *adj. dim.* See under **verde.**

verdiano *adj.* (mus.) of, relating to or characteristic of, Giuseppe Verdi.

†**verdicente** *adj.* truthful.

†**verdugale** *m.* a kind of crinoline.

†**verdugo** *m.* quadrangular blade of a swordstick.

verdume *m.* green foliage, greenery; green fodder; (iron.) super-abundance of green; mi spiace quel **—**, I don't like all that green.

verdura *f.* green foliage; greenery; verdure; grass, green pasture; green vegetables; minestra con **—**, vegetable soup.

†**vere** *m.* spring.

vere-condo *adj.* bashful, shy, diffident; modest, chaste. **-condamente** *adv.* bashfully, shyly; modestly. **-condia** *f.* bashfulness; modesty, chastity; shame, embarrassment.

vereda·rio *m.* (Rom. antiq.) *veredarius*, letter-carrier.

ver-ga *f.* small branch; twig; tremare a **— a —**, to shake like a leaf; (fig.) offsprlng, descendant; rod, stick, switch; **— di disciplina**, cane; (Rom. antiq.) fascio di **-ghe**, *fasces*, bundle of rods; staff; sceptre; wand, verge; (fig.) symbol of discipline; gemere sotto la **—** d'un tiranno, to groan beneath the yoke of a tyrant; (eccl.) **—** pastorale, pastoral staff, crosier; lance; rod of pendulum; (of metal, especially of gold) bar; ingot; stripe, line, dash, streak; (naut.) **— secca**, bare pole, i.e. without sail; (anat.) penis; (bot.) **—** d'oro, golden rod, *Solidago virgaurea*; (ent.) **—** d'oro, *Polyommatus virgaurea*, one of the 'blue' butterflies. **-gadoro** *m.* (class. myth.) he of the golden wand, Hermes, Mercury. **-ga·io**, **-garo** *m.* farmer entrusted with the care of sheep in winter, usually in charge of several flocks belonging to various owners. **-gare** [A 2] *tr.* to flog, to cane; to mark with streaks or stripes; to draw lines on, to rule lines on; to write; **-gare una lettera**, to write a letter; to jot down; *rfl.* (of ripening chestnuts, fruit, etc.) to become streaky, to have dark streaks. **-gata** *f.* stroke of a cane; una buona dose di **-gate**, a good thrashing. **-gatino** *m.* striped cloth. **-gato** *adj.* thrashed, flogged; striped; written; (paperm.) carta **-ata**, laid, i.e. ruled; *n.m.* striped cloth. **-gatura** *f.* flogging; writing; jotting down; (paperm.) laid wires. **-gella** *f.* small rod; (metall.) rod, bar; (bldg.) reinforcing rod (for concrete); (paperm.) laid wire; carta a **-gella**, laid, i.e. ruled, paper. **-gello** *m.* notched twig with birdlime in the notches; essere in sul **-gello**, to be in great danger.

ver-g-ere [C 4] *intr.* (*aux.* essere) to bend, to turn; to converge. (**-ente** *part. adj.*) **-enza** *f.* tendency, propensity, inclination.

vergheggia-re [A 3] *tr.* to thrash, to flog, to cane; **—** un tappeto, to beat a carpet. **-ato** *part. adj.* beaten, thrashed, flogged; wealed, marked with stripes; striped; affected with dry rot. **-atore** *m.* one who thrashes; mattress-maker. (**-atrice** *f.*)

verghett-a *f. dim.* of **verga**, q.v.; twig, small stick; (herald.) pallet. **-ato** *adj.* (herald.) paly.

Vergi·lie *pr.n.f.pl.* (astron.) Pleiades.

†**Vergi·lio** *pr.n.m.* See **Virgilio**.

vergillo *m.* See **vergello**, under **verga**.

vergin-e *f.* virgin; maiden, girl; (Rom. antiq.) **— del tempio di Vesta**, Vestal Virgin; (lit.) le caste **-i**, the Muses; (rel.) la **—**, the Blessed Virgin, the Madonna, the Virgin Mary; *excl.* santissima **—**, good heavens!; *pl.* (lit.) le (sacre) **-i**, cloistered virgins, nuns; (astron.) Virgo; *m.* virgin, male virgin; *adj.* virgin, pure, chaste, unstained, unspotted; untouched; terra **—**, virgin soil; caso **—**, case that has not yet been examined; sentire a caso **—**, to hear with an open mind; asta fino ad estinzione di candela **—**, see under **candela**; (of any commodity in its natural state) new, un-mixed, untreated; cera **—**, unbleached wax; vino **—**, wine removed from the vat before fermentation is complete; untarnished, un-contaminated; **—** d'ogni reo pensiero, untouched by any evil thought; (cinem.) film **—**, unexposed film, stock; (naut.) rigging deadeye or single block; **—** doppia, double deadeye or block; (geog.) Isole **-i**, Virgin Islands. **-ale** *adj.* virginal; chaste, pure; free, devoid. (**-almente** *adv.*) **-ella**, **-etta** *f. dim.* little virgin; maiden, girl. **-ina** *f. dim.* little maid; (rel.) small shrine to the Madonna. †**-eo** *adj.* see **virgineo.** **-ità** *f.* virginity; maidenhood; (fig.) rifare la **-ità** a uno, to clear some one's name. **-ona** *f. augm.* (derog.) old maid.

vergogn-a *f.* shame; aver perduta la **—**, to have lost all sense of shame; che **—**!, shame on you!; aver **—** di, to be ashamed of; shameful deed, cause of shame; la **—**, le **-e**, the pudenda; disgrace, dishonour; vivere con **—**, to lead a shameful life; far **—** a uno, to bring shame on someone; essere la **—** della famiglia, to be the black sheep of the family; modesty, diffidence; avere **—** di recitare, to be too shy to recite; confusion, embarrassment; look of confusion, blush; food or drink left unfinished as a gesture of politeness. **-are** [A 1] *rfl.*, *intr.* (*aux.* essere) to be ashamed, to feel shame; vergògnati!, you ought to be ashamed of yourself!; (with *prep.* 'di') to be ashamed of; **-arsi per altrui**, to be ashamed for others; non **-arsi**, to be impudent, to be bare-faced; to blush; to redden; (of cherries) to turn red; to be shy, to be diffident; to hesitate; (without *rfl. prn.* after *vb.* denoting cause) lo feci **-are**, I made him ashamed; †*tr.* to disgrace, to shame. **-ato** *part. adj.* shamed, put to shame; disgraced. †**-e·vole** *adj.* shameful. **-osa** *f.* (bot.) sensitive plant, *Mimosa pudica.* **-oso** *adj.* ashamed; modest, bashful, shy; shameful, dishonourable, disgraceful. (**-osamente** *adv.*)

vergol-a *f. dim.* of **verga**, q.v.; small twig or rod; thread; narrow stripe; silk twist; seta a **—**, silk twist; (naut.) a boat that is crank or easily capsized. **-amento** *m.* striping, streaking. **-ato** *adj.* striped, streaked.

verg-one *m.* large twig, rod, cane; large stripe; twig smeared with birdlime. **-uc·cia** *f.* small twig; small stripe.

†**vericida** *m.* liar.

veri·dic-o *adj.* truthful, veracious, trustworthy. (**-amente** *adv.*) **-ità** *f.* truthfulness, veracity.

veri·fica *f.* (leg.; comm.) attestation; audit; examination; check; (act of) checking; inspection; proof; audit; fare **—** dei libri, to audit the books; **—** dei conti, auditing of accounts; salvo vista e **—**, on approval; commissione per la **—** dei conti, auditing committee; commissione per la **—** dei poteri, credentials com-mittee; (leg.) proof; examination; attestation; **—** dei crediti, proof of debts; **—** dell'opera compiuta, inspection of completed work(s); **—** del passivo, official ascertainment of net deficiency (C.C.).

verific-are [A 2 s] *tr.* to verify, to ascertain, to check, to prove; **— se**, to find out whether; (leg.; comm.) to attest; to audit; to inspect; to tally; to verify; **— a mastro**, to check the postings; *rfl.* to happen, to come to pass; to come true, to be realized; to be proved. **-a·bile** *adj.* verifiable. **-ato** *part. adj.* verified; (leg.) copia **-ata**, attested copy; telegramma **-ato**, collated telegram. (**-atore** *m.* **-atrice** *f.*) **-azione** *f.* verification; realization; inspection, examination; (leg.) **-azione** di un testamento, probate; **-azione** dello stato passivo, ascertainment of final statement of affairs (C.C.); istanza di **-azione**, summons to put document(s) to proof (C.C.P.); (comm.) bilancio di **-azione**, trial balance.

†**verilo·quio** *m.* narration of the truth.

verina *f.* kink; punch for making a preliminary hole (e.g. for a nail); (naut.) cable hook rope.

verisimigliante *adj.* and derivs. See **verosimigliante**, under **vero**.

verisi·mile *adj.* and derivs. See **verosimile**, under **vero**.

ver-iṣmo *m.* (lit. hist.) realism, the Italian realist movement in literature in the nineteenth and early twentieth centuries; (fig.) realism; parlare con crudo —, to speak in crudely realistic terms. **-ista** *m., f.* realist; member of the Italian literary movement of 'verismo'. **-i·stico** *adj.* relating to or characteristic of the Italian literary realist school.

verit-à *f.* truth; verity; truthfulness; la pura —, the plain truth; dire la —, to tell the truth; una — fondamentale, a fundamental truth; non dire la —, to tell lies; (of a clock) not to keep good time, not to tell the right time; la — si fa strada, truth will out; la — è nel vino, *in vino veritas*; è la bocca della —, he is the very soul of truth; essere in luogo di —, to have passed on to the next life; per —, in —, really, truly, in fact; justice, right; un uomo della —, a man of integrity. **†-a·bile, †-e·vole, †-iere** *adj.* see **veritiero**. **-iero** *adj.* truthful, veracious, trustworthy; true, real; loyal; sincere; *n.m.* truthful man; trustworthy and loyal person; true blue.

verla *f.* (orn.). See **averla**.

verm-e *m.* (zool.) worm; (pop.) grub; maggot; weevil; chrysalis; (fig.) vile creature; nudo come un —, without a shirt to one's back; (of envy, ambition, jealousy, etc.) sting, gnawing; il — della coscienza, the sting of remorse; avere il —, to be in love; (vet.) mal del —, ringworm; (zool.) — dei legni, shipworm, *Teredo navalis*; *pl.* (techn.) thread of female screw. **-ica·io** *m.* mass of worms; place infested with worms. **-icella·io** *m.* maker and vendor of vermicelli. **-icelli** *m.pl.* (ent.) vermicelli; (zool.) -icelli di mare, egg masses of the sea hare, *Aplysia* sp.; (cul.) vermicelli. **-iciat·tolo** *m.* (zool.) small worm, maggot or grub. **-icciuolo** *m.* (zool.) small worm, maggot or grub; -icciuolo della seta, silkworm. **-icolare** *adj.* vermicular, wormlike; (anat.) appendice -icolare, vermiform appendix; *n.f.* (bot.) *Sedum hispanicum*. **-icolato** *adj.* (archit.) covered with mosaic. **-iforme** *adj.* vermiform. **-i·fugo** *adj.* (med.) vermifugal; *n.m.* vermifuge. **-ilingui** *m.pl.* (zool.) chameleons.

vermena *f.* young branch or shoot, twig.

vermi·gli-o *adj.* brilliant red, carmine, vermilion; *n.m.* vermilion colour; (ent.) cochineal insect, *Dactylopius coccus*; also the similar *Kermes ilicis*. **-ẹzza** *f.* vermilion colour. **-ọne** *m.* (chem.; miner.) vermilion, chinese red.

ver·min-e *m.* (zool.) parasitic intestinal worm; †silkworm. **-a·ia** *f.* vermin (collectively; used also fig.). **-azione** *f.* infestation with tapeworms, etc. **-oso** *adj.* infested with parasitic worms; verminous; worm-eaten; full of worms; afflicted with worms.

†vermo *m.* See **verme**.

†vermocane *m.* (vet.) a horse disease; ti venga il —!, a pox on you!; maggot.

vermoc·chio *m.* (ent.) a silkworm in its cocoon.

vermu·t *m.* vermouth.

†verna *m.* slave or servant born and brought up in a household.

vernac·cia *f.* name of a sweet white wine (e.g. as made in Sardinia and in the region of San Gimignano); (in Perugia) a red wine.

verna·colo *m.* vernacular; dialect; †native of the same household or district; *adj.* vernacular; dialectal; †born and brought up in the same household or district.

†vernadì *m.* See **venerdì**.

vernaiolo *m.* (agric., Tusc.) peasant who passes the winter at home instead of in the Maremma.

vernale *adj.* wintry; †relating to spring, vernal.

†vern-are *intr.* to pass the winter; to hibernate; to suffer cold; to be winter-cold; *impers.* to be winter; quando -a, when it is winter; to be stormy weather; to be spring, to bloom; (of birds) to sing. **†-ante** *part. adj.* relating to spring, of the spring, agnelli -anti, spring lambs; spring-like, blooming, turning green. **†-ata** *f.*, **†-ato** *m.* duration of winter, wintry season, wintertime.

vernazione *f.* (bot.) vernation, arrangement of leaves in bud.

vernerẹccio *adj.* wintry, winter; †stormy; †rainy.

†vernicale *m.* (naut., Venice) communal feeding-platter used in galleys; (Neap.) cup; dish.

†vernicare *vb.* and derivs. See **verniciare**, under **vernice**.

vernic-e *f.* varnish; polish; glaze; paint; una mano di —, a coat of paint; — per mobili, French polish; sandarac; scarpe di —, patent leather shoes; (art) glaze, enamel; ingredients of glaze for pottery; (fig.) polish, veneer; ha una — di buona educazione, he has a

veneer of good manners; 'varnishing day', preliminary private showing of an exhibition (esp. of painting); (colloq., derog.) cosmetics; †litter, refuse, dust-heap. **-iare** [A 3] *tr.* to varnish; to paint; to glaze; to polish; *rfl.* (fig.) to paint one's face. **-iato** *part. adj.* varnished; painted; glazed; polished; cuoio -iato, patent leather. (**-iatọre** *m.* **-iatrice** *f.*) **-iatura** *f.* varnishing; polishing; painting; glazing; outward appearance, veneer.

verniero *m.* vernier.

vern-o¹ *m.* (poet.) see **inverno**. **†-ile** *adj.* relating to winter; wintry. **-ino** *adj.* winter; available in winter, in season in winter. **†-itic·cio** *adj.* relating to winter; wintry; in season in winter.

verno² *adj.* vernal, of spring.

vẹr-o *adj.* true; è —?, is that so?; non sei stanco, è —?, you aren't tired, are you?; non è —?, n'è —?, isn't that so?; parla italiano, non è —?, you speak Italian, don't you?; com'è — ch'io son qui, as true as I stand here; fosse —!, if only that were true!; ma se è —!, but it's true!; -a seta, genuine silk; veritable; una -a menzogna, a downright lie; avere per —, to know for a truth; è stato per lui un — padre, he has been a real father to him; è suo padre —, he is his real father; convincing, true to life; un ritratto assai —, a very lifelike portrait; correct, exact; la parola -a, the right word; l'ora -a, the right time by the sun; possible; non parrebbe —!, it doesn't seem possible!; *n.m.* truth; la luce del —, the light of truth; salvo il —, if I'm not mistaken; valga il —, see under **valere**; a dire il —, a dir —, per —, in —, in truth, truth to tell; da —, see **davvero**; o —, see **ovvero**; (of clocks, scales, etc.) dire il —, to be accurate; (of limbs, senses) to be reliable; le gambe non mi dicono più il —, I can no longer trust my legs; (in literature, art, etc.) reality, life; ritrarre dal —, to draw from life; grande il —, life-size; un terzo del —, a third of life-size; *pl.* (poet.) truths, truth; †*adv.* truly; really. **-amẹnte** *adv.* truly; truthfully; really. **-osimigliante** *adj.* probable, likely; lifelike. **-osimiglianza** *f.* probability; verisimilitude. **-osi·mile** *adj.* probable, likely; lifelike; *n.m.* likelihood; un racconto che non ha del -osimile, an unlikely tale; verisimilitude. **-osimilmẹnte** *adv.* in a probable or likely way.

†Verola *pr.n.f.* name of an imaginary being; ogre.

Verọn-a *pr.n.f.* (geog.) Verona. **-ẹse** *adj.* Veronese, of Verona; *n.m.* Veronese, man from, of, Verona; il Veronese, the painter Paolo Caliari (1528–88); district round Verona; *f.* Veronese woman or girl.

veronale *m.* (med.) barbital, barbitone, veronal.

verọne *m.* balcony (covered or open); loggia; porch at the top of an outside staircase, giving access to the upper floor of a house in the country.

veronẹse *adj.* See under **Verona**.

vero·nica¹ *f.* (bot.) speedwell, *Veronica*.

Vero·nica² *pr.n.f.* Veronica; (rel.) 'vernicle', the kerchief or 'veil' of Veronica at St Peter's, Rome.

vero-simigliante *adj.*, **-simiglianza** *f.*, **-si·mile** *adj.* See under **vero**.

verre *m.* See **verro**.

†verrett-a *f.* spear; lance; javelin. **†-one** *m.* (mil. hist.) large dart shot by a balister.

verr-icello *m.* (eng.) winch, windlass; (naut.) cargo winch; capstan; †small dart. **-ina** *f.* (eng.; carpen.) auger. **-inare** [A I] *tr.* to bore (with an auger).

verrino *m.* (bot.) poisonous fungus, *Boletus mutabilis*.

verro *m.* boar; (bot.) *B. luridus* (fungus).

verruc-a *f.* (med.) verruca, wart; — senile, acanthokeratodermia seborrhoica. **-oso** *adj.* warty, wart-ridden, covered with warts.

†verruto *m.* (mil. hist.) a kind of dart.

versa *f.* wicker fish-trap, similar to a lobster pot.

Versa·glia *pr.n.f.* (geog.) Versailles.

vers-are [A I] *tr.* to pour; to pour out; -ami da bere, pour me a drink; (fig.) — i propri dolori in seno ad uno, to pour out one's troubles on somebody's shoulder; to ladle; to spill, to upset; to shed (tears, blood); to spend, to dissipate; chi non ha non ne -a, what you haven't got you can't spend; (finan.) — alla banca, to pay into the bank; — come caparra, to put down as a deposit; — a mezzo assegno, to pay by cheque; (joc.) to versify; *intr.* (*aux.* avere) to spill; to leak, to overflow; la pentola -a, the saucepan is boiling over; (fig.) to give away (a secret), to blab; to have to do with; la difficoltà -a in questo, the difficulty lies here; (with *prep.* su) to deal with, to treat of, to speak of; to live, to be; — in misere condizioni, to live in wretched conditions; — in pericolo

vers-are (*cont.*)
di vita, to be in danger of death; *rfl.* to spill, to be spilt, to leak; to flow, to run; -arsi in mare, (of river) to flow into the sea; -arsi in qualcuno, to confide in someone; -arsi con tutto l'animo in una cosa, to throw oneself into something heart and soul. -amento *m.* pouring; spilling; shedding; spending; (finan.) payment; distinta del -amento, paying-in slip; -amento rateale, payment of instalment; -amento in anticipo, payment in advance; -amento parziale, part-payment. -ante *part. adj.* pouring; spilling; *n.m.* (geog.) versant, slope; watershed; (finan.) payer, depositor. -a·tile *adj.* versatile; changeable, unstable; reversible. -atilità *f.* versatility; changeableness. -ato *part. adj.* poured; spilt; shed; spent; deposited; -ato in, versed in, proficient in; able, skilled; (comm.) capitale interamente -ato, called, fully paid up capital; capitale non -ato, uncalled capital. (-atore *m.* -atrice *f.*)

verseggi-are [A 3 c] *intr.* (*aux.* avere) to versify, to write verse; *tr.* to turn into verse. -a·bile *adj.* capable of being rendered into verse. -amento *m.* versification; writing of verse. -ato *part. adj.* versified, done into rhyme. -atore *m.* versifier. (-atrice *f.*) -atura *f.* versification; versifying; writing of verse.

verselato *m.* (ichth.). See **verzelato**.

versicolore *adj.* of changing hue, iridescent.

versiera *f.* the wife of the devil; fare il diavolo e la —, to play the very devil; non aver paura né di diavoli né di versiere, to fear nobody; she-devil, hobgoblin, evil spirit; (fig.) ugly old woman, old witch.

versific-are [A 2 s] *tr.* to versify, to put into verse. -ato *part. adj.* versified, put into verse; †*n.m.* composition in verse; verse rendering. (-atrice *f.*) -ato·rio *adj.* (*m.pl.* -atorii) of or relating to versification; l'arte -atoria, the art of versification. -azione *f.* versification; versifying; writing of verses.

versione *f.* translation; version; unseen.

versipelle *adj.* cunning, crafty, two-faced; *n.m.* rogue, crafty fellow.

vers-o[1] *m.* line (of writing); (lit.) verse (as against prose and sometimes as against poetry); line (of verse); mezzo —, half-line; — piano, the normal Italian hendecasyllabic line, with an accent on the last syllable but one (e.g. 'Nel mezzo del cammin di nostra vita'); — sdrucciolo, a twelve-syllable line with an accent on the last syllable but two (e.g. 'Parlando andava per non parer fievole', *Inf.* XXIV, 64); — tronco, a ten-syllable line with an accent on the last syllable (e.g. 'E con Rachele, per cui tanto fè', *Inf.* IV, 60); -i rimati, rhymed, rhyming, verse; -i sciolti, blank verse; -i barbari, the 'barbaric' verse in which Carducci adapted Latin or Greek quantitative rhythms to Italian accentual rhythms; commedia in -i, verse comedy; mi piacciono i suoi -i, I like his verses, his poems; †stanza of a *canzone*; (Bibl.) verse; sound, noise, note; il — del gatto, the sound made by a cat; song (of birds); intonation, cadence, peculiar sound; rifare il — a uno, to mimic someone; peculiar gesture; direction, way; da ogni —, from all directions; piallare il legno contro il suo —, to plane wood against the grain; inclination, aptitude; preferisco pigliarlo per il suo —, I prefer to take him as I find him; andare a — a, to get on well with, to humour, to please, to be to the liking of; fare per — suo, to go one's own way; senza —, without shape, without head or tail; dare — a, to arrange, to adjust; in questi -i, in these parts, in this region; tone, spirit; rispondere a —, to reply in the same vein; mutar —, to change one's tone; meaning, value; pigliar parole per il loro —, to take words in their right sense; manner, way, possibility; non ci fu — di persuaderlo, there was no way of persuading him; per un —, in one way, for one reason; ora per un — ora per un altro, in one way and another; per ogni —, in any case; a —, of the right kind; una ragazza a —, a nice girl; a modo e a —, thoroughly; †inscription on a tomb. -ac·cio *m. pejor.* poor, ill-sounding verse; grimace; ugly noise; screech. -aiuolo *m.* inferior poet, poetaster. -etto *m. dim.* little verse; little song; brief line (of writing); grimace; (Bibl.) verse; (liturg.) versicle. †-i·colo *m.* (prosod.) short line; small unit in verse, e.g. a *terzina*. -iliberista *m.* (lit. crit.) free verse writer; *vers-libriste*. -isciolta·io *m.* (lit. crit.; derog.) blank verse writer †-o·rio *adj.* turning in all directions; l'ago -orio, the needle of the compass.

verso[2] *m.* reverse (of coin); verso (of book leaf); *adj.* turned, changed; vice -a, on the other hand.

verso[3] *prep.* towards; guardare — il mare, to face the sea; — est, eastwards; (usu. with *prep.* 'di' before *pers. prn.*) — di me, towards me; (fig.) poco pietoso — i debitori, not very lenient to his debtors; — di, in comparison with; about; — la metà del mese, about the middle of the month; — dove?, whereabouts?; vengono di — Siena, they come from somewhere near Siena; (comm.) against; — pagamento, against payment.

versoio *m.* (agric.) mould-board.

versta *f.* (Russian) verst (3500 ft., almost two-thirds of a mile).

versuro *m.* (geog., Tusc.) unit of land-holding of 25–30 ha. in long-settled land.

†**vers-uto** *adj.* astute, cunning; sly; subtle. †-u·zia *f.* astuteness, cunning; slyness; subtlety.

verta *f.* the bag part of a casting-net; knapsack.

†**vert-à**, †-ade *f.* See **verità**.

ver·tebr-a *f.* (anat.) vertebra. -ale *adj.* (anat.) vertebral; colonna -ale, spinal column. -ato *adj.*, *n.m.* (zool.) vertebrate.

†**vertempo** *m.* spring; springtime.

ver·t-ere [B 1 def.] *intr.* (only found in *3rd pers. sing.* of indicative tenses) to regard, to concern, to be about; la questione -e su questo, the question turns on this; la controversia -e tra lui e i contadini, the dispute lies between him and the peasants; †*impers.* to matter, to be important. -ente *part. adj.* (leg.) in dispute; pending; undecided; †l'anno -ente, the current year. -enza *f.* difference, dispute, controversy; (leg.) action; matter in dispute.

vertical-e *adj.* vertical; pianoforte -ale, upright piano; (math.) vertical; *n.f.* vertical line, perpendicular; (gymn.) vertical pole; *pl.* (in crossword puzzles) 'down'. -mente *adv.* vertically. (-alità *f.*)

ver·tice *m.* vertex; summit, top; zenith; (fig.) al — della gloria, at the height of glory.

verticill-o *m.* (bot.) whorl. -ato *adj.* (bot.) whorled.

verticità *f.* (phys.) polarity.

verticoso *adj.* eddying (cf. **vorticoso**).

verti·gin-e *f.* (med.) vertigo; dizziness, giddiness; loss of balance; (vet.) gid, 'staggers' in sheep; sturdy, turnsick; (fig.) ha le -i, it has turned his head; revolution (of earth, stars, etc.). -oso *adj.* vertiginous, dizzy, giddy; altezze -ose, giddy heights; subject to vertigo; speedily revolving; (of speed) breakneck.

†**vertoso** *adj.* truthful, veracious.

†**vert-ù** *f.* see **virtù**. †-udioso *adj.* see **virtuoso**, under **virtù**.

veru·colo *m.* (art) a style of encaustic painting.

veruno *adj.* (in neg. context) any; senza veruna ragione, without any reason; *prn.* (in neg. context) anybody; non c'è stato —, nobody has been; non offesi mai —, I never offended anybody (cf. **nessuno**).

†**veruto** *m.* See **verruto**.

verve *f.* (pron. as Fr.) verve, vivacity, vigour.

very *m. indecl.* (pron. as Eng.) Very light.

verza[1] *f.* See **sverza**.

verza[2] *f.* (bot.) Savoy cabbage, *Brassica oleracea* var. *sabauda*.

verzelato *m.* (ichth.) *Mugil saliens*, a kind of grey mullet.

verzellina *f.* (bot.) groundsel, *Senecio vulgaris*.

verzicare [A 2 s] *intr.* (*aux.* avere) to turn green; to grow, to thrive; †*tr.* to turn green, to cause to grow green.

verzi·cola *f.* sequence of three in game of cards or gambling.

verz-iere *m.* orchard; kitchen garden; fruit and vegetable market. -ino *m.* (bot.) sappan-wood, *Caesalpinia sappan*; (paint.) crimson; †red ink. †-ire *intr.* to grow green; to thrive, to flourish.

verz-otto *m.* (bot.) drumhead cabbage, *Brassica oleracea* var. *capitata*. †-ume *m.* see **verdume**, under **verde**. -ura *f.* verdure, green foliage, greenery; green; greens; †grass; †grassy slope; †vitality.

†**vesa·nia** *f.* madness.

vesci-a *f.* (bot.) puff-ball, *Lycoperdon bovista*; (fig.) chatter, gossip; sapere tutte le -e, to know all the gossip; far la —, (of polenta) to swell up in cooking; silent discharge of wind. -a·ia *f.* gossip, chatterer.

vescic-a *f.* (anat.) bladder; — biliare, gall bladder; (med.) blister, vesicle; — di strutto, — di lardo, pig's bladder cleaned and dried, used for keeping lard in; (ichth.) — natatoria, swim bladder of fishes; (fig.) swollen-headed person; emptiness, vanity; far —, to fail, to misfire; (chem.) distillation flask; (techn.) air bubble (in glass, metal, etc.), blister (in paint); (metall.) gap in welded or soldered joint. -ante *m.* (med.) blister-paper; blister ointment; (ent.) cantharid beetle; (fig.) irritating person, pest, plague. †-are *tr.* to cause to blister, to raise blisters on. -a·ria *f.* (bot.) bladder

vescic-a (*cont.*)
senna, *Colutea arborescens*. **-ọna** *f.*, **-ọne** *m. augm.* large bladder; (vet.) -one articolare, puffy joint (e.g. bog spavin); -one tendineo, windgall (see also **muletta**); (derog.) pompous, puffed-up person.

vescichẹtta, *f. dim.* of **vescica**, q.v.; small bladder; blister.

vesci·col-a *f.* (med.; anat.) vesicle; (anat.) -e polmonari, pulmonary alveoli; -e seminali, seminal vesicles. **-are** *adj.* (med.; anat.) vesicular.

ve·scola *f.* (zool.) lugworm, *Arenicola* spp.

vẹscov-o *m.* (eccl.) bishop; †non-Christian high priest or the like; †overseer; (ichth.) pesce —, *Dasybatus violaceus*, a kind of sting ray. **-ado** *m.* bishop's palace. **-ato** *m.* (eccl.) episcopate; status of bishop; bishop's tenure of office; diocese, bishopric; diocesan curia. **-ile** *adj.* episcopal; anello -ile, bishop's ring. **-ilmẹnte** *adv.* as, like, a bishop; pontifically.

Vesevo *pr.n.m.* (poet.). See **Vesuvio**.

Vesfa·lia *pr.n.f.* (geog.). See **Vestfalia**.

Veso *pr.n.m.* (geog.) Monte —, Monviso.

vesp-a *f.* (ent.) wasp; (fig.) avere un vitino di —, to have a wasp waist; molesto come una —, waspish; (neol.) a make of motor-scooter, Vespa. **-a·io** *m.* wasps' nest; (fig.) suscitare un -aio, to stir up a hornet's nest; (archit.) vaults; (bldg.) loose stone foundation; †a kind of jewelled ornament. **†-aioso** *adj.* spongy, honeycombed. **-a·ria** *f.* (bot.) bee orchid, *Ophrys apifera*. **-ẹto** *m.* wasps' nest. **-ina** *f.* (ent.) -ina delle galle, gall wasp.

Vespaṣiano *pr.n.m.* Vespasian; (joc.) (monumento di) Vespasiano, public urinal.

†vespe *f.* See **vespa**.

†ve·spera *f.* See **vespero**.

ve·sper-o *m.* the evening star; west wind; †evening; *pr.n.m.* Vesper, Hesperus (cf. **vespro**). **†-ale** *adj.* evening. **†-are** *intr.* to draw towards evening. **-ọne** *m.* (liturg.) solemn Vespers. **-ti·lio**, **-tillo** *m.* (zool.) bat, of the genus *Vespertilio*. **-tino** *adj.* evening, of the evening; l'ora -tina, the evening hour.

vesp-ẹto *m.*, **-ina** *f.* See under **vespa**.

†vespistrello *m.*, **†vespritello** *m.* (zool.). See **vespertilio** and **pipistrello**.

vespro *m.* evening; evening star; (liturg.; often *pl.*) Vespers; primi, secondi, -i, First, Second, Vespers; cantare il — (e la compieta) a uno, to give someone a piece of one's mind; vesper-bell; (hist.) Vespri Siciliani, the Sicilian Vespers (of 1282); (fig.) un — siciliano, a massacre; far cantare il — siciliano a, to massacre.

vess-are [A I] *tr.* to vex, to molest, to harass; to oppress, to ill-treat, to torment. **-ato** *part. adj.* vexed; harassed; oppressed; questione -ata, vexed question. (**-atọre** *m.* **-atrice** *f.*) **-atọ·rio** *adj.* (*m.pl.* **-atọrii**) vexing, tormenting. **-aziọne** *f.* molestation, oppression, torment.

vessica *f.* and derivs. See **vescica**.

vessill-o *m.* flag; standard; ensign; — tricolore, tricolor; (Rom. antiq.) *vexillum*. **-a·rio** *m.* (*pl.* -arii) (Rom. antiq.) *vexillarius*, ensign; the oldest class of veterans. **-aziọne** *f.* (Rom. antiq.) *vexillatio*. **-i·fero** *m.* standard-bearer, flag-bearer.

Vest-a¹ *pr.n.f.* (Rom. myth.) (the goddess) Vesta. **-ale** *f.* (Rom. antiq.) Vestal; (fig.) maidenly person, chaste woman; (joc.) whole-hearted defender of some cause; -ali del positivismo, priestesses of positivism; (iron.) loose woman.

vesta² *f.* husk on grain and other cereals; †see **veste**.

vesta·glia *f.* See under **veste**.

vest-e *f.* dress, attire, clothing; article of clothing, garment; — di camera, dressing-gown; *pl.* -i, clothes; -i estive, summer clothes; far la — secondo il panno, to cut one's coat according to one's cloth; (woman's) dress, frock, gown; petticoat; — da camera, dressing-gown, robe; (eccl.) — talare, cassock; — cardinalizia, cardinal's dress; (eccl.) cloak worn by members of religious guilds; (rel.) the body, 'this muddy vesture of decay'; (fig.) la fiorita — dei prati, the meadows' flowery robe; in — elegante, elegantly got up or produced; nobili pensieri in nobile —, noble thoughts clothed in noble words; piccoli pensieri in piccole -i, little thoughts in swaddling clothes; aspect, appearance; traditore in — d'amico, traitor disguised as a friend; quality, capacity; vengo in — di rappresentante, I am here as a representative; right; con qual — dovrò agire così?, what pretext shall I have for doing this?; straw casing of a wine-bottle. **-a·glia** *f.* dressing-gown; house-coat, peignoir; négligée.

Vestfa·lia *pr.n.f.* (geog.) Westphalia.

vestia·r-io *m.* clothing, clothes; wardrobe (contents of); outfit; capo di —, article of clothing; spende molto nel —, she spends a lot on clothes; (theatr.) wardrobe. **-ista** *m.* theatrical outfitter; costumier.

vesti·bolo *m.* vestibule, entrance-hall; foyer (of a theatre); (archit.) portico, vestibule, (of a temple) pronaos; (anat.) vestibule, vestibulum.

†vesti·bulo *m.* See **vestibolo**.

†vesti·gia *f.* See **vestigio**.

vesti·g-io *m.* (*pl.* **-i** *m.*, **-ia** *f.*) trace, vestige; footprint, track; *pl.* footprints; remains; -i dell'antichità, relics of antiquity; †memory; †example; †*pl.* armour.

vest-ire [D I] *tr.* to dress; — una bambola, to dress a doll; to put on (clothing); — la flanella, to wear flannel; — le armi, to arm oneself; — la divisa militare, to put on military uniform, to become a soldier; (eccl.) — l'abito religioso, to take the religious habit, to be clothed (as monk or nun); to clothe; — gl'ignudi, to clothe the naked; to cover; l'edera -e la muraglia, the wall is covered with ivy; l'unghia -e l'estremità del dito, the nail covers the finger-tip; — i fiaschi, to cover wine-bottles with straw casing; to decorate, to adorn; spogliar un altare per -irne un altro, to rob Peter to pay Paul; -e i suoi concetti con eloquenza, he clothes his ideas with eloquent phrases; *intr.* (*aux.* avere) to dress; — da donna, to dress as a woman; — di rosso, to wear red; — da lavoro, da fatica, to dress working-clothes; saper —, to know how to dress; to fit; calzoni che -ono bene, well-fitting trousers; *rfl.* to dress, to get dressed; -irsi da festa, to put on one's Sunday best; -irsi da un gran sarto, to have one's clothes made by a good tailor; (of trees) -irsi di foglie, to be covered with leaves; (theol.) Dio -ì umana carne, Dio si -ì di carne, God took human flesh upon him, God clothed himself in flesh; *n.m.* dress; nel — deve spendere poco, he surely does not spend much on clothes; è sempre elegante nel —, he is always smartly dressed. (**-icciuola** *f. pejor.*) **-imẹnto** *m.* (*pl.* **-imẹnti** *m.*, **-imẹnta** *f.*) clothing, clothes; outfit, wardrobe; -imento di lino, underclothes; (eccl.) clothing (with religious habit); (liturg.) -imenti sacerdotali, vestments. **-ito** *part. adj.* dressed; -ito di velluto, dressed in velvet; bianco -ito, dressed in white; ben -ito, well-dressed; nascer -ito, to be born with a silver spoon in one's mouth; un asino calzato e -ito, a complete and utter fool; covered, clothed, clad; -ito a due pezzi, dressed in blazer and trousers, or in sports jacket and flannels; riso -ito, unhusked rice; un riso -ito, a forced smile; (herald.) vetu, a lozenge throughout; vested; *n.m.* suit, outfit; farsi il -ito nuovo, to have a new suit made; coat; dress; -ito da sera, evening dress (for man or woman); -ito d'estate, summer frock; *pl.* clothes. **-itọre** *m.* one who makes the straw casing for wine bottles. **-itura** *f.* dressing; clothes; -itura alla moda, fashionable clothes; investiture; straw casing on bottles. **-iziọne** *f.* dressing; (eccl.) clothing (with the religious habit). **†-ura** *f.* see **vestitura**. **†-uto** *part. adj.* see **vestito**.

Vesu·vi-o *pr.n.m.* (geog.) Vesuvius. **-anite** *f.* (miner.) vesuvianite, idocrase. **-ano** *adj.* of or relating to Vesuvius.

veterano *adj. m.* (mil.) veteran; ex-serviceman; (fig.) un — dell'insegnamento, an old hand at teaching; Società dei veterani e reduci, equiv. to Old Comrades' Association.

veterin-a·rio *adj.* veterinary; medico —, veterinary surgeon; *n.m.* veterinary surgeon; (iron.) inferior doctor, 'horse-doctor'. **-a·ria** *f.* veterinary science. **†-o** *adj.* relating to draught horses or other animals used for pulling.

veto *m.* veto; mettere il — a, to put a veto on; diritto di —, right of veto; opporre un — a, to veto.

vetr-a·io *m.* glass-maker; glass-blower; glass-manufacturer; glazier; glass-dealer. **-ai(u)olo** *m.* glass-blower. **-ame** *m.* glassware. **-a·rio** *adj.* pertaining to glass-making; industria -aria, glass manufacture. **-ata** *f.* glass window; glass door, glass front (to cupboard, book-case, etc.); glass partition; glass wall (of greenhouse); stained glass window; *pl.* (joc.) spectacles. **-atina** *f.* glass door (of a shop). **-ato** *adj.* glazed; made of glass; containing glass; carta -ata, glass-paper; *n.m.* thin layer of slippery ice. **-eri·a** *f.* glass-works, glass-factory; glass-furnace; *pl.* glassware. **-iata** *f.* see **invetriata**.

vẹtrice *f.* (bot.) common osier, *Salix viminalis*; — bianca, *S. alba*; — rossa, *S. purpurea*.

vẹtr-o *m.* glass; — ghiacciato, frosted glass; — arrotato, cut glass; carta —, glass-paper; lastra di —, — di finestra, window-pane;

vetr-o (*cont.*)
pane of glass; glass part of mirror; lens (of spectacles); (watchm.) crystal; article of glassware; tumbler, glass; dar nel —, to drink freely; (art) object made of glass; — di Murano, coloured glassware made at Murano in the Venetian lagoon; stained-glass window; picture painted on glass; — solubile, water-glass. **-iera** *f.* see vetrata. **-ifica·bile** *adj.* **-ificare** [A 2 s] *tr.* to vitrify; *rfl., intr.* (*aux.* essere) to be vitrified, to turn into glass. (**-ificato** *part. adj.* **-ificazione** *f.*) **-igno** *adj.* glassy. **-ina** *f.* glaze, glass-case, show-case; shop window; glass-fronted cupboard. **-inista** *m., f.* window-dresser. **-ino** *adj.* of glass; glassy; brittle; barba -ina, bristly, stubbly beard; *n.m.* small piece of glass; -ino di microscopio, microscope slide. **-i(u)ola** *f.* (bot.) see vetriuolo. **-ioleggiare** [A 3 c] *tr.* to vitriolize, to injure by throwing vitriol. **-io·lico** *adj.* vitriolic. **-i(u)olo** *m.* (chem.) vitriol; (bot.) yellow vetchling, *Lathyrus aphaca*; *adj.* glassy; brittle. **-ocromi·a** *f.* (art) painting on glass. **-ofani·a** *f.* (art) transfer, transparent coloured sheet for sticking on glass. **-one** *m. augm.* large piece of glass; †(mil.) thick glass used for primitive type of hand grenade. **-oso** *adj.* glassy, vitreous. (**-osità** *f.*)

vett-a¹ *f.* top, peak, summit; topmost branch; little branch; tremare come una —, to tremble like a leaf; swingle of a flail; †(naut.) hauling part. **-aiuolo** *adj.* growing at the end of a branch.

†**vetta²** *f.* head-band.

†**vettigale** *adj.* relating to tribute; *n.m.* tribute, tax.

†**vettina** *f.* pot of glazed earthenware.

vetto·nica *f.* (bot.) betony, *Stachys officinalis* (cf. **bettonica**).

vettor-e *adj.* (math.) vectorial; *n.m.* (phys.) vector; (comm.) common carrier; (naut.) travel or shipping agency or agent; emigration organizer or guide; patente di — di emigrazione, emigration licence granted to a company, agent or master. **-iale** *adj.* pertaining to transport; (phys.) vectorial.

vettova·gli-a *f.* (usu. *pl.*) provisions, food, victuals; stores; -e a bordo, ship's stores. **-amento** *m.* provisioning, victualling. **-are** [A 4] *tr.* to provision. (**-ato** *part. adj.*)

†**vettu-a·glia**, †**-va·glia** *f.* See vettovaglia.

vettur-a *f.* conveyance, transport; hire of transport; charge for hire of transport; a —, for hire; avere a —, to hire; bestie da —, hired animals (esp. horses and mules); carriage-load; (of cabman) fare una —, to drive a fare; (of fare) far —, to ride in a hired vehicle; cab, fly, carriage; taxi; ci si va in —, let's take a taxi; — di piazza, cab off the rank; — ferroviaria, railway carriage; in —!, take your seats!; — da corsa, racing-car; (colloq.) — di ritorno, said of a feeble joke capping a good one; driver; (leg.) lettera di —, bill of lading; carriage-note; way-bill (C.C.). **-ale** *m.* carter; (mil.) man employed with the baggage train, i.e. supply and transport. **-eggiare** [A 3 c] *intr.* (*aux.* avere) to drive a cart, to carry goods by cart. **-etta** *f.* small car; corsa di -ette, small-car race.

vetturino¹ *adj.* (bot.) erba vetturina, *Tribulus terrester*.

vetturino² *m.* driver; coachman; cabman, cabby; bestemmiare come un —, to swear like a trooper (cf. **vettura**).

†**vetust-ate**, †**-ade** *f.* See vetustà, under vetusto.

vetust-o *adj.* ancient, very old; aged. **-à** *f.* antiquity, old age.

†**vezzato** *adj.* sharp, alert, cunning.

vezzeggi-are [A 3 c] *tr.* to fondle, to cherish; to pet, to coax, to pamper; *intr.* (*aux.* avere) to flirt; *rfl.* to pamper oneself; -arsi nello specchio, to admire oneself in the glass. (**-amento** *m.* **-ante** *part. adj.*) **-ativo** *adj.* fondling, coaxing; (gramm.) denoting term of endearment; *n.m.* diminutive form of nouns and adjectives, terminating usually in suffix -ino, -ina, implying a sense of endearment, prettiness or charm; pet-name. (**-ato** *part. adj.*)

vezz-o *m.* habit; pet habit, trick; affectation; caress, endearment; far -i a un bambino, to fondle a child; mio —!, my love!, my pet!; necklace; toy, plaything; *pl.* charms. **-oso** *adj.* pretty, graceful, charming; sweet; flattering; fare il -oso, to philander, to play the gallant; affected. **-osamente** *adv.* sweetly, prettily; flatteringly; allevare -osamente, to pamper, to bring up soft.

vi¹ *pers. prn., acc., dat.* (before **lo, la, li, le, ne** it becomes **ve**) you; to you.

vi² *adv.* there (before **lo, la, li, le, ne** it becomes **ve**); non vi è anima viva, there is not a soul to be seen; to it, of it, about it; non volevo pensarvi, I didn't want to think about it; quando vi si applica, when he gets down to it.

via¹ *f.* 1. ROAD; street; tutte le vie conducono a Roma, all roads lead to Rome; una — romana, a Roman road; dall'altra parte della —, on the other side of the road; — maestra, main road; (Bibl., fig.) — di Damasco, the road to Damascus; abitiamo nella stessa —, we live in the same street; la prima — a destra, the first street on the right. 2. WAY; route; direction; qual'è la — più corta per la stazione?, which is the shortest way to the station?; vieni per questa —, come this way; mettersi in —, to set off; mettere uno per la —, to show someone the way; tra —, on the way; in — per, on the way to; seguire la — di Napoli, to travel in the direction of Naples; (geog.) la — di lizza, slip-way, skid; (astron.) la — lattea, the milky way; (leg.) foglio di —, travel document, way-bill (C.C.), (road-traffic) temporary pass or permit, (mil.) route order; foglio di — obbligatorio, travel order (C.P.; cf. **foglio**), (mil.) pass, travel warrant. 3. PATH, course, way; la — della virtù, the path of virtue; la — battuta, the beaten track; una — cieca, a blind alley; ha scelto la — degli impieghi, he has gone in for clerical work; — di mezzo, middle course; essere una — di mezzo fra, to be half way between, to be a mixture of two things; — crucis, way of the Cross, (liturg.) Stations of the Cross; (fig.) fu per me una vera — crucis, I found it an agonizing experience. 4. PASSAGE, opening, outlet; dare la — a, to make way for, to let out, to set free, to give utterance to; dare la — a un animale, to put an animal out to grass; (anat.) tract; vie respiratorie, respiratory tract. 5. COURSE, progress, process; in —, under way, on the way; in — di guarigione, in process of healing. 6. REGION, part, side; da questa —, from hereabouts; fuori —, out of the way, remote; parente per — di donna, related on the female side. 7. MEANS; method; vie traverse, underhand means; non c'è — di persuaderlo, there is no way of persuading him; per — diplomatica, through diplomatic channels; per — breve, informally, without going through official channels; ricorrere alle -e legali, to have recourse to legal action; (chem.) analisi per — secca, dry-way analysis, (metall.) dry assay. 8. CAUSE, reason; per — di, on account of, because of; per — che, because; in — di, as; in — di contrapposto, by way of contrast; (admin.) in — provvisoria, provisionally.

via² *adv.* 1. away; andar —, to go away; prese il cappello e —, he took his hat and off he went; dar —, to give away; portar —, to carry off; — col vento, gone with the wind; — come uno saetta, off like a shot. 2. on, onwards; e così —, e così — dicendo, and so on; via via, on and on; via via che, as soon as, as fast as. 3. (math.) quattro — quattro, four times four. 4. *excl.* via!, go away!, be off! *or* yes! come on!; no, —!, here, stop it!; non c'è male, —, sono contento, it's all right, really, I'm quite happy; se si contentasse di poche lire, —!, it would be all right if one didn't mind being poor!; well, all right then!; here!; look!; listen!; see here!; ma —!, now look here!, nonsense!.

via³ *m. indecl.* starting signal; dare il —, to give the signal to start; dare il — a una discussione, to open a discussion; dare il — ai lavori, to begin work, operations.

viabilità *f.* state of the roads, suitability of roads for traffic; road system; (med.) viability; (leg.) infrazioni inerenti alla —, road-traffic offences (C.P.).

viadotto *m.* viaduct; (mil.) protected passage.

viag·g-io *m.* journey; — d'andata, outward journey; — di ritorno, return journey; mettersi in —, to set out on a journey; trip; l'ha fatto in tre -i, he did it in three journeys; voyage; — di piacere, tour; buon —!, *bon voyage!*, have a good journey, never mind!, it doesn't matter!; l'estremo —, (of death) the last journey; travel; *I Viaggi di Gulliver*, *Gulliver's Travels*; libri di —, travel books; (fig.) path, way; andar per il suo —, to go one's own way; fare un — e due servizi, to kill two birds with one stone; †path, way, course. **-iante** *part. adj.* travelling; redattore -iante, travelling correspondent (of newspaper); personale -iante, travelling personnel (of railway staff). **-iare** [A 3] *intr.* (*aux.* avere) to travel; -iare come i bauli, to learn nothing from one's travels; -iare col cavallo di San Francesco, to travel on Shank's pony; aver -iato molto, to be much travelled; (comm.) to travel; -ia per una ditta di Milano, he travels for a Milanese firm; -ia in pellami, he travels in skins; (of goods) -iare a rischio del destinatario, to be carried at buyer's risk; *tr.* to journey through; ha -iato l'Italia da un capo all'altro, he has travelled all over Italy from one end to the other. (**-iato** *part. adj.*) **iatore** *m.* traveller; passenger; treno -iatori, passenger train; commesso -iatore, commercial traveller;

viagg·io (*cont.*)

albergo dei ~iatori, commercial hotel; explorer; (orn.) piccione ~iatore, homing pigeon. (~iatrice *f.*)

viale[1] *m.* avenue; shady path; — della rimembranza, avenue with trees dedicated to the memory of men fallen in the 1915–1918 and 1940–1945 wars.

viale[2] *adj.* (Rom. myth.) lari viali, *Lares viales*, guardian deities of roads and travellers.

†vianda *f.* See **vivanda**.

viandante *m.* traveller, wayfarer; passer-by; tramp.

†viarec·cio *adj.* portable, transportable.

†viatanto *adv.* nevertheless, notwithstanding.

via·tico *m.* provisions for a journey; (rel.) Viaticum, Holy Communion for the dying; †journey.

†viatore *m.* traveller.

viato·r·io *adj.* pertaining to journey; tessera ~ia, travelling ticket; †transitory, ephemeral.

via-va·i *m. indecl.* bustling, coming and going; backward and forward movement. **~vieni** *m. indecl.* upward and downward movement.

vi·bice *m.* (med.) weal; *pl.* (med.) striae.

vibr·are [A I] *tr.* to shake, to brandish; to lash; (of an animal) — la coda, to lash its tail; (of a horse) — la criniera, to toss its mane; to hurl, to fling, to throw; to deal, to strike (a blow); *intr.* (*aux.* avere) to resound; (of a bell) to ring; to reverberate; (of light) to quiver, to gleam; to vibrate; to thrill; *rfl.* to shake, to tremble. **~a·fono** *m.* (mus.) vibraphone. **~amento** *m.* vibrating. **~ante** *part. adj.* vibrating; trembling; vibrant; forceful, vigorous. **~atezza** *f.* vigour, forcefulness (of style). **~a·tile** *adj.* vibrating; pulsating; vibratile; (anat.) epitelio ~atile, ciliary epithelium. **~ato** *part. adj.* shaken, flung, hurled; forceful, vigorous; (mus.) vibrato, tremolo. (~**atore** *m.* ~**atrice** *f.*) **~ato·rio** *adj.* (*m.pl.* ~atorii) vibratory. **~azione** *f.* vibration; (fig.) thrill, sensation. **~ione** *m.* parasite, leech, sinecurist, exploiter of public funds. **~isse** *f.pl.* (zool.) vibrissae, whiskers. **~o·grafo** *m.* vibrograph. **~osco·pio** *m.* vibroscope.

vic·a·rio *adj.* vicarious; substituted; *n.m.* deputy, representative; (hist.) — imperiale, imperial vicar; (eccl.) — di Cristo, Vicar of Christ, the Pope; cardinale —, cardinal-vicar; — apostolico, vicar-apostolic; — generale, del vescovo, vicar-general; — capitolare, vicar-capitular; — foraneo, vicar-forane, dean (of parochial district); — parrocchiale, curate; padre —, father vicar. **~a·ria** *f.* madre ~aria, mother vicaress; vicariate; (eccl.) vicaress; deputy's wife; (joc.) talkative woman. **~ariale** *adj.* vicarial. **~ariato** *m.* office of vicar, vicariate.

vice[1] *f.* stead, place; per —, as substitute; — versa, on the other hand, *or* else, otherwise, *or* on the contrary, *or* (less usu.) vice versa; †in — di, instead of.

vice[2] *pref.* vice-, deputy. **~ammira·glio** *m.* see Ammiraglio di Squadra, under **ammiraglio**; †second in command of the galleys. **~biblioteca·rio** *m.* assistant librarian. **~camarlingo** *m.* vice-treasurer. **~cancelliere** *m.* vice-chancellor. **~caso** *m.* (gramm.) preposition before a noun, having the force conveyed by a Latin case-ending (usu. 'a', 'di', and 'da'). **~comitale** *adj.* of a viscount. **~commissa·rio** *m.* deputy chief of police. **~compare** *m.* person standing proxy for a godfather. **~conservatore** *m.* assistant custodian. **~consolare** *adj.* vice-consular. **~consolato** *m.* vice-consulate. **~con·sole** *m.* vice-consul. †**~conte** *m.* See visconte. **~curato** *m.* (eccl.) curate. **~decano** *m.* (eccl.) sub-dean. **~dio** *m.* (derog.) God's Vicar, the Pope. **~direttore** *m.* deputy director, assistant manager; assistant headmaster; assistant editor; ~direttore generale, deputy director general. **~do·mino** *m.* (eccl. hist.) vicedominus. **~gerente** *m.* vicegerent; (eccl.) vicegerent, *vicegerens*. **~gerenza** *f.* vice-gerency. **~governatore** *m.* vice-governor. **~imperatore** *m.* governor of a country ruling in the name of the emperor. **~ispettore** *m.* assistant inspector. **~legato** *m.* deputy or vice-legate; (eccl.) ~legato apostolico, papal vice-legate. **~legazione** *f.* vice-legation. **~madre** *f.* foster-mother. †**~nome** *m.* (gramm.) pronoun. **~opera·io** *m.* (eccl.) assistant superintendent of a church fabric. **~padre** *m.* foster-father. **~par·roco** *m.* (eccl.) assistant priest, (senior) curate. **~prefetto** *m.* sub-prefect, deputy prefect (of a province); deputy headmaster. **~presidente** *m.* vice-chairman, vice-president. **~presidenza** *f.* vice-presidency; vice-chairmanship. **~pretore** *m.* (leg.) assistant magistrate. **~priore** *m.* (eccl.) sub-prior, vice-prior. **~pronome** *m.* (gramm.) pronominal particle. **~questore** *m.* (leg.) deputy superintendent of police. **~questura** *f.* (leg.) office of the

deputy superintendent of police. **~rè** *m.* viceroy. **~reale** *adj.* viceregal. **~reame** *m.* that part of a kingdom which is governed by a viceroy. **~reggente** *m.* vice-regent. **~regina** *f.* viceroy's lady, viceroy's wife. **~rettorato** *m.* office of the vice-chancellor; vice-chancellorship. **~rettore** *m.* vice-chancellor. **~sca·mbio** *m.* (joc.) substitute, proxy. **~segreta·rio** *m.* assistant secretary. (~**segretariato** *m.*)

vicend·a *f.* vicissitude; event, happening; adventure; affair; alternation, alternate succession; turn; a —, in turn, by turns; la — dei buoi al giogo, the time during which the oxen are yoked; (agric.) rotation of crops. **~evole** *adj.* reciprocal, mutual. **~evolmente** *adv.* mutually, reciprocally; in turn, by turns. **~evolezza** *f.* reciprocity; alternation; exchange.

vic·ennale *adj.* recurring every twenty years. **~en·nio** *m.* period of twenty years.

vicentin·o *adj.* of Vicenza; *n.m.* native of Vicenza. (~**a** *f.*)

viceversa *adv.* See 'vice versa', under **vice**[1].

vichiano *adj.* (philos.) relating to G. B. Vico.

Vichingo *m. adj.* Vicking.

vicin·o *adj.* near, close; neighbouring; eravamo ~i a casa, we were near home; le ~e campagne, the neighbouring countryside; un parente dei più ~i, a very close relative; at hand, imminent; la pioggia è ~a, rain is on the way; la fine è ~a, the end is near; la casa è qui ~a, the house is near here (cf. under *adv.*); il vino è — alla fine, the wine is nearly finished; essere — a finire, to be about to finish; like, similar; idee ~e alle mie, ideas approaching my own; *n.m.* neighbour; eravamo ~i di casa, we were neighbours; †citizen; *adv.* near, nearby; la casa è qui —, the house is near here (cf. under *adj.*); da —, closely; osservare da —, to observe at close quarters; *prep.* near, close to, beside; (usu. with *prep.* a; rarely with *prep.* di) una villa — a Milano, a house near Milan; siedi — a me, sit next to me. **~ale** *adj.* strada ~ale, by-road, by-way, country road between villages. **~ame** *m.* (derog.) neighbours. **~ante** *m., f.* neighbour. **~anza** *f.* nearness, closeness, proximity; in ~anza della città, close to the city; neighbourhood, vicinity; mettere tutta la ~anza a rumore, to set the whole neighbourhood by the ears; *pl.* surroundings; nelle ~anze di Firenze, in the neighbourhood of Florence; affinity, similarity. **~are** [A I] *intr.* (*aux.* avere; *prep.* con) to be a neighbour, to live near; ~a con loro, he is a neighbour of theirs; †*rfl.* ben ~arsi, to be a good and peaceable neighbour. **~ata** *f.* see **vicinato**. **~ato** *m.* vicinity, neighbourhood; essere in rapporti di buon ~ato, to be good neighbours; people of the neighbourhood. †**~iore** *adj.* nearer. **~ità** *f.* proximity, closeness; likeness, affinity.

vicissitu·din·e *f.* vicissitude; *pl.* events; circumstances; changes. †**~evolmente** *adv.* reciprocally.

†vicitare *vb.* and derivs. See **visitare**.

Vico[1] *pr.n.m.* abbrev. of Ludovico, q.v.

†**vico**[2] *m.* lane, alley; village, hamlet; region.

vi·colo *m.* lane, alley; — cieco, blind alley.

†**vidanda** *f.* See **vivanda**.

vi·deo *adj. indecl.* (telev.) video; segnale —, video signal.

vidim·are [A I S] (leg.) to authenticate; to certify; to visa. **~ato** *part. adj.* (leg.) authenticated; examined and found correct; viséd. **~azione** *f.* (leg.) certification; authentication; (of a passport) visa, stamping.

†**vidovile** *adj.* and derivs. See under **vedova**.

vie *adv.* See under **via**.

viella, vielle *f.* (mus.) fiddle, vielle; hurdy-gurdy.

Vienn·a *pr.n.f.* (geog.) Vienna (Austria); Vienne (France); **~ese** *adj.* Viennese; *n.m., f.* Viennese.

viepiù, vieppiù *adv.* much more (cf. under **via**).

†**viera** *f.* See **ghiera**.

viet·are [A I] *tr.* to forbid, to prohibit; m'è ~ato di dirlo, I am not allowed to say; il medico gli ~ò il fumare, the doctor forbade him to smoke; (fig.) to prevent; nulla ~a che tu le scriva, there is nothing to stop you writing to her; †to deny; †to avoid, to flee; †to condemn; †to refuse. **~a·bile** *adj.* avoidable; non ~abile, unavoidable, inevitable. (~**abilità** *f.*) **~amento** *m.* prohibition. **~ativo** *adj.* prohibitive. (~**atore** *m.* ~**atrice** *f.*) **~ato** *part. adj.* forbidden, prohibited; ~ato fumare, no smoking; ~ato sputare, do not spit; (traffic sign) direzione ~ata, no entry; ~ata l'affissione, stick no bills.

viet·o *adj.* stale, rancid; sa di —, it tastes rancid; (fig.) faccia ~a, sickly face; antiquated, disused, old-fashioned; forme ~e, obsolete forms; usanze -e, antiquated customs; *n.m.* rancid taste, stale taste; prendere il —, to turn rancid, to go off. **-ume** *m.* old stuff.

†**vige·cuplo** *adj.* twentyfold.

vi·g·ere [B I def.] *intr.* (no *past part.*) to flourish, to thrive; (of laws) to be in force; (of customs) to prevail, to be in use. **-ente** *part. adj.* in force; having effect; (leg.) leggi -enti, laws in force; le leggi -enti, the law of the land (I.C.).

vige·ṣim·o *ord. num.* twentieth; — primo, twenty-first; — secondo, twenty-second, etc. **-anona** *f.* (mus.) twenty-ninth (mutation-stop of organ). **-aseconda** *f.* (mus.) twenty-second (mutation-stop of organ); flautino alla -aseconda, sopranino recorder. **-asesta** *f.* (mus.) twenty-sixth (mutation-stop of organ).

vigil·are [A I s] *tr.* to watch over, to keep an eye on; to keep watch over, to keep under observation; lo fecero —, they had him watched; to oversee, to supervise; *intr.* (*aux.* avere) to be awake, to be wakeful; to be on the alert, to be attentive, to be on the look-out; to pay attention, to be careful; — che siano eseguiti gli ordini, to take good care that orders are carried out. **-ambu-liṣmo** *m.* (med.) vigilambulism. **-ante** *part. adj.* watchful; wakeful; vigilant, attentive; *n.m.pl.* watchmen, guards. **-antemente** *adv.* vigilantly. **-anza** *f.* care, supervision, attention; watchfulness, vigilance; inspection, close observation; squadre di -anza, (strike) pickets; commissione di -anza, superintending committee, (U.S.) vigilance committee; committee of inspection; -anza speciale, special inspection; maintenance of a telegraphic or telephonic line; squadra di —, strike picket; (leg.) -anza sull'esecuzione delle pene, supervision of carrying-out of punishments; -anza speciale della polizia, police supervision (esp. of infants and persons of unsound mind (C.P.)); (herald.) vigilance. **-ato** *part. adj.* watched over, guarded; (leg.) libertà -ata, liberty under (police) supervision (C.P.); *n.m.* (leg.) person under police supervision (C.P.P.). (**-atore** *m.* **-atrice** *f.* **-azione** *f.*)

vi·gil·e *adj.* wakeful, watchful; alert; *n.m.* — urbano, local or city policeman; corpo dei -i del (al) fuoco, fire brigade; (Rom. antiq.) *vigiles*, firemen, watchmen.

vigi·l·ia *f.* vigil, watch; lunghe -ie passate in studi, long nights spent in study; fra il sonno e la —, between sleeping and waking; (hist.) — d'armi, all-night vigil kept by one about to be made a knight; (liturg.) vigil (eve, day before); fasting or abstinence on eve of feast; la Vigilia di Natale, Christmas Eve; eve, day before; (fig.) sono -ie di brutte feste, there are worse things to come; alla — del fallimento, on the brink of bankruptcy; (mil.) watchman; length of sentry duty; (Rom. antiq.) watch (division of the night and of night duty); *pl.* watchmen, sentinels; (joc.) far delle -ie non comandate, to starve, to have nothing to eat; †psalms recited at night while keeping watch by a dead person. †**-o** *m.* vigil; keeping vigil.

vigintivirato *m.* (Rom. antiq.) viginitivirate.

vi·glia *f.* (bot.) belvedere, *Kochia scoparia.*

vigli·acco *adj.* vile, ignoble, low, mean; cowardly; *n.m.* bully; coward; -acchi!, vile scum! **-accamente** *adv.* vilely, ignobly; in a cowardly way. **-accheri·a** *f.* meanness, vileness; cowardice; act of meanness; act of cowardice.

†**vigli·are** *tr.* (agric.) to separate (vetch, straw, etc.) from grain by means of a brush or besom; (fig.) to winnow out, to select. †**-a·volo** *m.* stalks, etc. separated from the grain.

†**viglietto** *m.* See **biglietto**.

vign·a *f.* vine; vineyard; piece of land planted principally with vines; — andante, vineyard planted solely with vines; (fig.) non è terreno da piantar —, it's no use trying to deceive him, it's not safe to rely on that; questa — non fa uva, there's nothing to be got out of him; (rel.) la — del signore, di Cristo, the Lord's vineyard, Christ's vineyard, the Church, (joc.) land of plenty; source of great wealth, 'goldmine'; trovare la — di Cristo, to strike lucky; (Rom. hist.) *vinea*, screen used by mining parties in sieges. **-a·io** *m.* vine-dresser; †vineyard. **-aiuolo, -arolo, -aruolo** *m.* vine-dresser. **-aruola** *pr.n.f.* (astron.) see **vendemmiatrice**. **-are** [A 5] *tr.* to grow vines; †to dupe, to mock. †**-ata** *f.* vineyard; pleasure garden. **-ato** *part. adj.* planted with vines. †**-azzo** *m.* vine; vineyard. **-eto** *m.* vineyard. **-uola** *f. dim.* little vineyard; †pleasure, pastime; comfort, ease; the tool of someone (for evil or shameful purposes). †**-uolo** *m.* withy for tying up vine-branches.

vignett·a *f.* (art; photog.) vignette; sketch; cartoon. **-ista** *m.* cartoonist; illustrator.

vigọgna *f.* (zool.) vicuna, *Lama vicugna*; cloth made from vicuna wool.

vigọr·e *m.* vigour, strength; cibo che mette —, health-giving food; (of wine) potency; (of soil) richness, fertility; — dell'ingegno, intellectual power; stile pieno di —, vigorous style; (of laws, treaties, etc.) force, efficacy, validity; entrare in —, to come into force; essere in —, (of theories) to be current, to be in favour; mettere in — le disposizioni di una convenzione, to implement the provisions of a convention; †per — di, by virtue of. †**-are**, †**-ire** *tr.* to invigorate; *intr.*, *rfl.* to become invigorated. †**-ato** *part. adj.* invigorated; strengthened. **-eggiare** [A 3 c] *intr.* (*aux.* avere) to thrive, to be vigorous; to grow vigorous; (fig.) to do well. (**-eggiante** *part. adj.*) †**-ezza** *f.* see **vigoria**. **-i·a** *f.* vigour, strength, force. **-ioso** *adj.* see **vigoroso**. **-osità** *f.* vigorousness. **-ọso** *adj.* vigorous, strong; powerful; brave, daring; (photog.) carta -osa, hard paper. **-osamente** *adv.* vigorously, with vigour.

vilaiet *pr.n.m.* vilayet (Turkish province ruled by a Vali).

vil·e *adj.* (abbrev. to **vil** before certain nouns) cheap; a prezzo —, cheaply; comprar —, to buy cheaply; il vino era —, wine was cheap; metallo —, cheap metal; (iron.) il vil metallo, filthy lucre; al vil prezzo di due lire, for the mere sum of two lire; low, humble, mean, modest; insignificant; di nascita —, of low birth; depressed; stato d'animo —, miserable state of mind; cowardly; mean-spirited; fearful; contemptible, mean, despicable, ignoble; tenere a —, to despise, to hold in contempt; una menzogna —, a contemptible lie; (comm.) — prezzo, underprice; vendere a prezzo —, to undersell; danaro a — interesse, cheap money, loans at cheap interest; *n.m.* coward; un'azione da —, a cowardly action. **-mente** *adv.* vilely; in a cowardly way; contemptibly, ignobly, despicably. †**-anza** *f.* see **viltà**. †**-are** *vb.* and derivs. see **avvilire**. †**-esco** *adj.* of little worth, of no account. **-ẹzza** *f.* cheapness; meanness, low estate; cowardice; contemptibility.

†**vi·lia** *f.* See **vigilia**.

vilific·are [A 2 s] *tr.* to debase; to lower; to humiliate; to defame; to degrade; to dishonour, to disgrace; to scorn, to contemn, to despise; *rfl.* to humiliate oneself, to degrade oneself. **-amẹnto** *m.* scorn, contempt. **-ativo** *adj.* humiliating, degrading, debasing. **-ato** *part. adj.* vilified; scorned. (**-atore** *m.* **-atrice** *f.*)

†**vi·lio** *adj.* cheap.

†**vilipendenza** *f.* See **vilipendio**, under **vilipendere**.

vil·ipen·dere [C I] *tr.* to despise, to scorn, to hold in contempt; to humiliate, to defame, to disgrace, to dishonour; to revile, to vilify; — pubblicamente, to defame publicly, to hold up to public scorn, publicly to cast scorn upon (C.P.). **-ipen·dio** *m.* contempt, scorn; humiliation, disgrace; (leg.) public defamation (criminal offence of which publicity is one element); disparagement, revilement, vilification; act of holding up to public scorn; -ipendio alla bandiera, public insult to the flag (C.P.). †**-ipensione** *f.* see **vilipendio**. †**-ipenso** *part.* of **vilipendere**. **-ipẹso** *part. adj.* humiliated, defamed, disgraced, dishonoured; scorned, despised. †**-ire** *tr.* to despise. †**-ità** *f.*, **-itanza** *f.* see **viltà**.

vill·a *f.* country-house, country-seat; sono andati in —, they are at their place in the country; large town-house with garden; public garden, park; countryside; uomo della —, uomo di —, peasant; village; †city; †andare in — colla brigata, to go out of one's mind; †mandare qualcuno in —, to send someone away. **-eggiare** [A 3 c] *intr.* (*aux.* avere) to stay in the country; to spend the summer in the country. **-eggiamẹnto** *m.* country holiday. **-eggiante** *part. adj.* on holiday, away in the country; *n.m.* holiday-maker. **-eggiatura** *f.* country holiday; andare in -eggiatura, to go for one's summer holiday; holiday place. **-erẹccio** *adj.* rural, rustic; la quiete -ereccia, the quiet of the country; (ent.) farfalla -ereccia, *Arctia villica*, kind of tiger moth. †**-eresco** *adj.*, †**-esco** *adj.* countrified, rustic. †**-essa** *f.* a large and splendid villa. **-ẹtta** *f. dim.* small villa; little rustic dwelling. **-ino** *m.* small country-house; villa, town house; suburban house with small garden.

Villaco *pr.n.f.* (geog.) Villach.

Villafranca *pr.n.f.* (geog.) Villefranche (France); Villafranca (Italy).

villag·gio *m.* village; di —, village-like, simple, countrified; vita di —, village life.

villancico *m.* (Span. lit. and mus.) *villancico*.

villan·o *m.* countryman, peasant, rustic; — nato e calzato, countryman born and bred; — rifatto, parvenu, *nouveau riche*; boor, lout, ill-mannered person; †a kind of rustic garment; *adj.* rustic; peasant; low born, of humble birth; loutish, boorish, rude, coarse,

villan-o (*cont.*)
ill-bred, ill-mannered, crude; insulting; brutal, cruel; una morte -a, a cruel death; †ugly, repellent. (**-a** *f.*) **-aménte** *adv.* coarsely; offensively; crudely, roughly; loutishly; cruelly, brutally; rudely. **-ata** *f.* crude, unpleasant action; boorish action; piece of incivility. †**-eggiare** *tr.* to treat ill, to abuse; *intr.* to behave ill. **-ella** *f.* peasant girl; la bella **-ella**, name given by Michelangelo to the Church of San Miniato, Florence; (prosod.) *villanella*, pastoral verse form of the sixteenth century; (mus.) villanella, rustic partsong. **-ęsco** *adj.* (*m.pl.* **-ęschi**) rustic; peasant; rough, coarse; ill-bred, loutish; cruel. (**-escaménte** *adv.*) **-i-a** *f.* crude, unpleasant behaviour; bad manners; injury; abuse; offence; insulting language; vomitare **-ie**, to pour out abuse; †dishonesty; †wrong, injustice, injury. **-zóne** *m.* lout, boor, bumpkin.

villarsite *f.* (miner.) villarsite.

†**vill-ata** *f.* village. †**-a·tico** *adj.* rustic, village-like.

villeggiare [A 3 c] and derivs. See under **villa**.

vil·lico *m.* villager, countryman, peasant; †steward, bailiff; †farm-bailiff.

vill-o *m.* (bot.) root hair; (anat.) villus. **-óso** *adj.* villous; hairy, downy. **-osità** *f.* hairiness.

villotta *f.* (mus.). See **villanella**, under **villano**.

†**vilpistrello** *m.* (zool.). See **pipistrello**.

viltà *f.* cheapness; meanness; lowness; cowardice; meanness of spirit; cowardly action.

viluc·chio *m.* (bot.) bindweed, *Convolvulus arvensis*; — rosso, *C. athaeoides*; — saettino, black bindweed, *Polygonum convolvulus*.

†**vilume** *m.* volume; confused mass; long, rambling discourse; vile rabble.

†**viluppare** *vb.* and derivs. See **avviluppare**.

vilupp-o *m.* entanglement, tangle; (fig.) bundle; muddle, confusion. **-óne** *m.* *augm.* great confusion; †intriguer. †**-óso** *adj.* tangled; intricate, difficult.

†**vim-e** *m.* (bot.) see **vimine**; (fig.) tie, bond. †**-are** *tr.* to tie, to bind.

vi·min-e *m.* (bot.) osier, especially *Salix purpurea* and *S. viminalis*; cesto di **-i**, wicker basket. **-ata** *f.* osier-work; wicker-work. **-e·o** *adj.* made of osiers.

vina *f.* (mus.) vina (kind of Indian guitar).

vin-ac·cia *f.* dregs of pressed grapes (stalks, pips and skins); (fig.) la — va in fondo, there is no time to lose. **-acciuolo** *m.* grape-pip; raisin-stone. †**-agro** *m.* vinegar. **-a·io** *m.* wine-seller; vintner, wine-merchant. †**-ale** *adj.* relating to wine. **-a·lie** *f.pl.* (Rom. antiq.) *vinalia*, wine feasts in April and August. **-arello** *m.* thin wine. **-a·rio** *adj.* of wine, relating to wine; cella **-aria**, cellar. **-ato** *adj.* wine-coloured; *m.* (chem.) vinate. **-attiere** *m.* wine-seller.

vincastr-o *m.*, **-a** *f.* staff, rod, cane, switch; withe; shepherd's crook; †punishment, scourge.

Vincenzo *pr.n.m.* Vincent.

Vincęsla·o *pr.n.m.* Wenceslas.

vin·c-ere [c 5] *tr.* to conquer, to vanquish, to overcome; — una città, to seize a city; (fig.) to master, non ti far — dall'ira, don't let your anger get the better of you; per lo stile nessun libro — questo, no one can beat this book for style; to win; — una scommessa, to win a bet; — una lite, to win a lawsuit; — una partita, to win a game; **-erla**, to win; con me non la **-e** di sicuro, he certainly won't get the better of me; to outdo, to excel, to surpass; — alcuno in dottrina, to outshine someone in learning; vinse tutti nel concorso, he beat everybody in the competition; to prevail over; — la mano, to break loose, to run wild; to win over; le preghiere lo vinsero, he was won over by entreaties; to gain; — un premio, to win a prize; gli vinsi 2000 lire alle carte, I won 2000 lire off him at cards; *intr.* (*aux.* avere) to win; to be victorious; to win a vote; *rfl.* to master oneself; to control oneself. **-ente** *part. adj.* winning; la parte **-ente**, the winning side; rimase **-ente**, he finished up by winning; *n.m.* winner; winning (horse); puntare su un cavallo **-ente**, to back a horse to win. **-enzine** *f.pl.* (eccl.) Sisters of Charity. †**-e·vole** *adj.* easy to overcome, easily defeated; non **-evole**, invincible. **-i·bile** *adj.* conquerable, vanquishable, vincible. **-iménto** *m.* conquering, victory. **-iperdi** *m.* game in which the loser of the game is the winner of the stake. **-ipremi** *m. indecl. victor ludorum.* **-itóre** *m.* winner; victor; conqueror; esser **-itore** delle proprie passioni, to rule one's passions. (**-itrice** *f.*) †**-iuto** *part.* of **vincere** (cf. **vinto**).

vincetos·sico *m.* (bot.) swallow-wort, *Vincetoxicum officinale*.

vinchęto *m.* osier-bed.

vinciano *adj.* concerning. or characteristic of, Leonardo da Vinci.

vincibosco *m.* (bot.) perfoliate honeysuckle, *Lonicera caprifolium*.

vin·cido *adj.* soft, flexible, pliable; flabby.

†**vinci-gl-ia** *f.*, **-io** *m.* See **vinco**[1].

†**vincire** *tr.* to bind, to tie up; to surround, to encircle; to bind together.

vin·cita *f.* winnings; gain; fare una — di mille lire, to win 1000 lire.

vin-co[1] *m.* (*pl.* **-chi**) osier, withy; †bond, tie.

vin-co[2] *adj.* (*m.pl.* **-chi**) soft, flexible, pliable; flabby; (of bread) stale. **-cóne** *m.* flabby dried chestnut.

vin·col-o *m.* tie; bond; (fig.) — matrimoniale, bond of wedlock; i **-i** del sangue, ties of blood; relationship; knot; (leg.) — contrattuale, contractual obligation; libero da ogni —, free from encumbrances; — matrimoniale, *vinculum matrimonii*; sotto il — del giuramento, under the obligation of an oath, on oath; — ipotecario, charge by way of mortgage; restraint; restriction; restrictive covenant; restrictive clause (C.C.); *pl.* chains, bonds, fetters. **-are** [A I s] *tr.* (fig.) to tie, to bind; la coscienza mi **-a** a tacere, I am bound by my conscience not to speak; (leg.) to tie up; to entail; to charge (by way of mortgage or lien); to encumber; to impose a restraint or restrictive covenant or clause upon; (comm.) to place (funds) on fixed deposit; (fig.) to impede, to hinder; i vestiti troppo stretti **-ano** i movimenti, too tight clothing restricts one's movements; *rfl.* to bind oneself. **-ato** *part. adj.* bound, tied; fettered; restricted, impeded; (leg.) encumbered; subject to restraint or restriction; charged (by way of mortgage); tied up; terreno **-ato**, entailed land subject to restriction upon user (C.C.); (comm.) cartelle di credito **-ate**, debenture stock; in conto **-ato**, (money) on deposit; deposito **-ato**, entailed consignment; magazzino **-ato**, bonded warehouse.

vin·dice *adj.* avenging, vengeful; *n.m.* avenger.

vi·nico *adj.* (chem.) vinic.

vin·nola *f.* (mus.) quilisma (plain-chant ornament).

vin-o *m.* wine (made from grapes); mezzo —, wine made from grape skins and water; — vergine, unfermented wine; — sincero, pure wine (made by natural process); — artefatto, wine produced by artificial process; è —, it is real wine; — caldo, *vin brûlé*, wine made from grapes, drunk hot, with herbs, etc. added; — di palma, wine made from the wine-palm; — di mele, cider; nota dei **-i**, wine-list; dir pane al pane e — al —, to call a spade a spade; dire pane un giorno e un altro —, to say one thing one day and another the next; (provb.) buon — non vuole frasca, good wine needs no bush; (fig.) alcoholic drink; effects of drink, intoxication; trarre il — di testa, to clear one's head, to sober up; smaltire il —, to sleep off the effects of drink. **-ello** *m.* wine of low alcoholic content. **-ętta** *f.* (mus.) song of the wine-harvesters. **-i·colo** *adj.* wine-producing; concerned with the production of wine. **-i·fero** *adj.* (of region, country, etc.) vine-growing; wine-producing. **-ificatóre** *m.* wine manufacturer. **-ificazióne** *f.* wine-making. **-olento** *adj.* given to drink; drunken. (**-olenza** *f.*) **-omele** *m.* (Gk. antiq.) a kind of mead. **-óne** *m.* heady wine. (**-osità** *f.*) **-óso** *adj.* vinous; winey, tasting of wine; colore **-oso**, wine colour; given to drink; flowing with wine. **-u·colo** *m. dim.* weak wine.

†**vinta** *f.* victory.

vinto *part.* of **vincere**, q.v.; *adj.* beaten, conquered, vanquished, defeated; darsi per —, to give up, to give in; darla vinta (a), to give in (to), to spoil, to indulge; volerla vinta, to want one's own way; won over, persuaded; overcome, worn out; won (of battle, cause, game, money, etc.); *n.m.* loser.

†**vinza·glio** *m.* See **guinzaglio**.

viol-a[1] *f.* (mus.) viola; viol; — bastarda, lyra viol; — pomposa, a kind of large viola (eighteenth century), a small violoncello (in music of J. S. Bach); — tenore, tenor viol; — da braccio, treble viol; — d'amore, viola d'amore; — da gamba, bass viol; — da orbo, hurdy-gurdy; — da spalla, tenor viol; — di bordone, — di fagotto, viola paradon, baryton. **-ętta** *f. dim.* (mus.) small viola; †viol without frets. **-ista** *m.*, *f.* viola-player, violist; viol-player.

viol-a[2] *f.* (bot.) violet, *Viola*; — a mazzetti, sweet-william, *Dianthus barbatus*; — ciocca, stock, gilliflower, *Matthiola incana*; — ciocca gialla, wallflower, *Cheiranthus cheiri*; — del pensiero, — di tre colori, pansy, *Viola tricolor*; — farfalla, *V. calcarata*; — mammola, *V. hirta* and *V. odorata*; — matronale, dame's violet,

viol-a (*cont.*)
Hesperis matronalis; — senza odore, dog violet (name of unscented wild violets); — tricolore, pansy, *Viola tricolor*; *f.pl.* tales, fibs, gossip; *adj.*, *n.m.* violet, the colour violet. **-a·ceo** *adj.* violet; purple; (liturg.) paramenti -acei, purple (violet) vestments; (eccl.) abito -aceo, violet dress (of prelates). **-a·io** *m.* place planted with violets. **-ana** *f.* (miner.) violane. **-ato** *adj.* violet, violet-coloured; made with violet juice.

viol-are [A I s] to violate; to pollute, to contaminate; to spoil; to profane; to corrupt; to break, to infringe (faith, a vow, an oath, the law, etc.); to trespass into, to break into; — una tomba, to break into a tomb; — il segreto postale, to open somebody else's correspondence; to profane, to desecrate. (**-a·bile** *adj.* **-amento** *m.*) **-ato** *part. adj.* violated; contaminated; corrupted; broken; damaged; profaned. **-atore** *m.* violator; -atore di fede, one who breaks faith; -atore di sepolcri, one who breaks into graves, resurrectionist. (**-atrice** *f.*) **-azione** *f.* violation; profanation; (leg.) -azione della legge, breach of the law; -azione di proprietà, trespass; -azione di un contratto, breach of contract (C.C.); -azione di domicilio, violation of the sanctity of the home (I.C.); illegal entry upon private enclosed premises; breaking and entering; housebreaking; -azione del dovere, criminal breach of duty; -azione della libertà personale, violation of, interference with, personal liberty; -azione della segretezza della corrispondenza, breach of secrecy of mails; -azione di sepolcro, profanation of grave (C.P.).

violato[1] *adj.* See under **viola**.

violato[2] *part.* of **violare**, q.v.

†**violente** *adj.* See **violento**.

violentemente *adv.* violently; by force; with violence.

violent-o *adj.* violent; colpo —, violent blow; morte -a, violent death; parole -e, high words; febbre -a, high fever; (leg.) atto di libidine -a, indecent assault (C.P.); *n.m.* violent man. **-amento** *m.* use of violence, forcing; doing of violence, outraging. **-are** [A I] *tr.* to force, to use violence on; to do violence to; to outrage. **-ato** *part. adj.* (**-atore** *m.* **-atrice** *f.*)

violenza *f.* violence; force; ricorrere alla —, to have recourse to violence; far — a se stesso, to do oneself a violence; con dolce —, with gentle force; vehemence; (leg.) duress (C.C.); force; violence; (leg.) atto di —, act of violence; assault; — carnale, carnal knowledge had by force or threat of force (C.P.); †violation, profanation.

viol-etta[1] *f.* (bot.) hairy violet, *Viola hirta*; scent of violets. **-etto** *adj.* violet-coloured; *n.m.* a kind of snuff. **-ina** *f.* (bot.) -ina selvatica, red campion, *Melandrium rubrum*; (med.) †dire della -ina, to grumble, to grouse.

Violetta[2] *pr.n.f.* Violet.

violetta[3] *f. dim.* See under **viola**[1].

viol-ina·io *m.* (mus.) violin-maker. **-inac·cio** *m.* (mus.) wretched fiddle. **-inata** *f.* (mus.) violin-piece, piece for strings; passage for strings. **-inismo** *m.* (mus.) violin-playing, violinism. **-inista** *m.*, *f.* (mus.) violinist. **-ini·stico** *adj.* (mus.) violinistic; la scuola -inistica italiana, the Italian school of violin-playing (or -writing). **-ino** *m.* (mus.) violin; -ino piccolo, small violin, kit-fiddle; -ino primo, -ino secondo, first, second violin; chiave di -ino, treble clef (G clef on second line), French violin clef (G clef on first line); -ino da spalla, first violin, leader (because, being seated on the left side of the platform, he turns his shoulder to the conductor); (fig.) chief assistant, chief supporter; (joc.) un -ino, a ham; *pl.* (joc.) hard-working pupils who sit in the front row of a class, saps, swots. **-inuc·cio** *m.* (mus.) violin of poor quality. **-i·stico** *adj.* (mus.) pertaining to the viol or violin. **-oncellista** *m.*, *f.* (mus.) violoncellist, 'cellist. **-oncello** *m.* (mus.) violoncello, 'cello. **-one** *m.* (mus.) double-bass viol.

viot·tol-a *f.* country lane; narrow country pathway, footpath. **-o** *m.* footpath, track; esser fuori del -o, to be off the track.

vi·per-a *f.* (zool.) viper, adder and various related poisonous snakes; (fig.) poisonous person; ha una lingua da —, he's got a viper's tongue; scaldarsi la — in seno, to cherish a snake in one's bosom; †(naut.) type of rig used in Venice. **-a·io** *m.* viper catcher; nest of vipers. **-ato** *adj.* fed upon vipers. **-ina** *f.* (bot.) see 'erba viperina'. **-ino** *adj.* viperine; (fig.) viperous, poisonous; (bot.) erba -ina, black salsify, *Scorzonera hispanica*.

vipe·reo *adj.* viperous.

vipistrello *m.* See **pipistrello**.

virag·gio *m.* (photog.) toning.

vir-a·gine, -ago *f.* brave woman; heroine; strong, or strong-minded, girl or woman; virago; termagant, shrew.

vir-are *intr.* (*aux.* avere) (naut.) to go about; — di bordo, to change tack; pronti a — di bordo!, ready about!; abbriva per —!, bear up! (preparatory to tacking); *tr.* (naut.) to heave in on a capstan; — all'argano, to heave in; † — l'àncora, to weigh; — a picco, to heave (the cable) till the anchor is 'up and down', i.e. underfoot; -a!, heave!, heave in!; -a forte!, heave away!; (fig.) to turn about; to veer; (photog.) to tone. †**-adore** *m.* (naut.) messenger, rope used for weighing when the cable was too thick to be brought to the capstan. **-amento** *m.*, **-ata** *f.* (naut.) heaving in on capstan; evolution of going about; -amento di bordo in poppa, act of tacking or heaving; -amento di bordo, change of tack; (aeron.) turn; bend; -ata in cabrata, climbing turn; -ata in planato, gliding turn.

virente *adj.* (poet.) green, growing green; fresh.

virg-a *f.* (mus.) virga (a kind of note in plain-chant); †rood (cf. **verga**). **-apastoris** *m.* (bot.) name of various thistle-like plants.

Virgi·li-o *pr.n.m.* Virgil. **-ano** *adj.* Virgilian.

virginale *adj.* maidenly; virgin; virginal; *n.m.* (mus.) virginal, virginals.

†**virgine** *f.* See **vergine**.

virgi·neo *adj.* maidenly; virginal.

Virgi·nia *pr.n.f.* Virginia; (geog.) Virginia; *m.*, *f.* Virginia cigar; Virginia tobacco.

†**virginità** *f.* See **verginità**, under **vergine**.

vir·gol-a *f.* comma; punto e —, semicolon; (fig.) punto e virgola!, stop a minute!; stare a punto e —, to stick to the letter, to take no licence; far una cosa a punto e —, to do something with extreme precision; (fig.) non s'è allontonato una — dall'originale, he hasn't strayed one jot from the original; una mezza —, one tiniest little bit; guardare a tutte le -e, to pay attention to the least detail; doppie -e, inverted commas; (math.) point; tre — due, three point two. **-are** [A I s] *tr.* to mark the commas; to put in inverted commas; to punctuate; **-ato** *part. adj.* marked with commas; punctuated; put in inverted commas; *n.m.* the passage (or phrase) in inverted commas. **-atura** *f.* marking with commas; marking with inverted commas; passage (or phrase) in inverted commas. **-eggiare** [A 3 c] and derivs. see **virgolare**. **-ettare** [A I c] *tr.* to mark with inverted commas, to put in quotes. **-ette** *f.pl.* inverted commas, quotation marks.

†**vir·gula** *f.* wisp (of smoke or incense).

virgulto *m.* young shoot; offshoot.

†**vi·rid-e** *adj.* green; turning green. †**-a·rio** *m.* garden. †**-escenza** *f.* greenness. †**-ezza** *f.*, †**-ità** *f.* greenness, freshness.

viridina *f.* (chem.) viridine, jervine, barytine.

viril-e *adj.* virile; male; (anat.) membro —, penis, *membrum virile*; manly; adult, full-grown; (Rom. antiq.) toga —, *toga virilis*; strong, brave, courageous, purposeful; uno stile —, a vigorous style; †(leg.) porzione —, equal share of deceased's estate. **-mente** *adv.* virilely; in a manly way; vigorously; boldly. **-ità** *f.* manhood; virility; manliness; courage, firmness of purpose; -ità d'animo, strength of mind.

†**viripotente** *adj.* (leg.) ripe for marriage.

†**viro** *m.* a man, a grown man, an adult male human being; an august man.

viro-fissag·gio *m.* (photog.) fixing and toning.

virola *f.* (watchm.) collet.

†**Virtemberga** *pr.n.f.* (geog.) Württemberg.

virt-ù *f.* virtue; amare la —, to love virtue; la — dell'abnegazione, the virtue of self-sacrifice; fare di necessità —, to make a virtue of necessity; le — civili, the civil virtues; un fiore di —, a paragon of virtue; (philos.) le — cardinali, the cardinal (natural) virtues; (theol.) le — teologali, the theological (supernatural) virtues; (theol.) le Virtù, the Virtues as an order of angels; virtuous person or persons; perseguitare la —, to persecute the virtuous; potency; power; strength; la — dell'esempio, the power of example; non ho la — di infondergli un po' d'intelligenza, I have no means of driving any intelligence into him; la divina —, the divine power, the power of God; strength, valour, courage; — militare, military valour; aver la — sufficiente per sopportare il male, to have sufficient courage to bear pain; resoluteness; (in Machiavelli) ruthlessness and determination combined with exceptional ability to conceive and carry through a plan of action; merit, worth;

virt·ù (*cont.*)
la — d'un cavallo, the merits of a horse; aptitude; talent, ability; una ragazza piena di —, a very talented girl; faculty; la — visiva, the visual faculty; property; le — medicinali delle erbe, the medicinal properties of herbs; la — delle stelle, the influence of the stars; means; per — di, through, through the power of, by virtue of, by means of; per — delle preghiere, by virtue of prayer; in — di, by reason of; in — di questa legge, by virtue of this law; †in —, potentially; †far — —, to perform miracles; †military valour; †morire di —, to die valiantly. **-uale** *adj.* virtual, potential; (opt.) immagine -uale, virtual image; †relating to virtue; †powerful, effective. **-ualmente** *adv.* potentially; virtually, effectively. **-ualità** *f.* virtuality, potentiality. †**-ude** *f.* see **virtù.** †**-udioso** *adj.* see **virtuoso.** †**-udire** *intr.* to grow in strength and valour. **-uoso** *adj.* virtuous; menare una vita -uosa, to lead a virtuous life; having good properties, having healing properties; erbe -uose, medicinal herbs; †valorous; †effective; †useful; †miraculous; †parola -uosa, word of power, magic formula; *n.m.* virtuous person; skilled writer or artist; (mus.) virtuoso, brilliant performer or singer. **-uosamente** *adv.* virtuously; ably, with skill, with virtuosity, expertly. **-uosistico** *adj.* (mus.) virtuosic, brilliant. **-uosità** *f.* virtuosity, technical skill; (mus.) virtuosity, brilliance. †**-ute** *f.* see **virtù.**

virulen·to *adj.* virulent; (fig.) bitter, rancorous, malignant. **-tamente** *adv.* virulently; (fig.) bitterly. **-za** *f.* virulence.

virus *m. indecl.* (med.) virus.

visac·cio *m. pejor.* of **viso,** q.v.

†**visag·gio** *m.* See **viso.**

†**visa·glia** *f.* See **avvisaglia.**

†**visare** *tr.* to see.

vis-à-vis *adv.* (pron. as Fr.) opposite; la famiglia —, the family opposite; *n.m.* vis-à-vis, person opposite (at table, in a dance, etc.); sofa for two, sociable, *vis-à-vis*; kind of carriage with four seats.

vi·scer-e *m.* (*pop. pl.* **vi·scere** or **vi·sceri,** *f., scient. pl.* **vi·sceri** *m.*) internal organ; (anat.) i -i, the viscera; (fig.) bowels, heart, feelings; non aver —, to have no heart; — mie!, heart of my heart!; womb; il frutto delle sue —, the fruit of her womb; le — della terra, the bowels of the earth; le — dell'argomento, the gist of the argument; the substantial core or intimate centre of anything; †— della città, citizens. **-ale** *adj.* (anat.) visceral. †**-are** [A I] *tr.* see **sviscerare.** †**-oso** *adj.* ardent, passionate; heartfelt.

vi·schi-o *m.* (bot.) mistletoe, *Viscum album*; — guercino, *Loranthus europaeus*; bird-lime; (fig.) sticky substance; trap. **-osi·metro** *m.* viscometer. **-osità** *f.* stickiness, viscous quality. **-oso** *adj.* sticky, viscous.

vi·scid-o *adj.* viscid, viscous, glutinous, sticky; slimy; clammy. **-ezza** *f.*, **-ità** *f.* viscidity, stickiness. **-ume** *m.* viscous matter; sticky stuff; stickiness, nastiness, messiness.

viscina *f.* (chem.) viscin.

vi·sciol-a *f.* (bot.) sour cherry, fruit of the **visciolo,** q.v.; wild cherry jam. **-ata** *f.* drink prepared from wild cherries. **-ato** *m.* Kirschwasser, liqueur prepared from wild cherries. **-o** *m.* (bot.) sour cherry tree, *Prunus cerasus*.

visco *m.* and derivs. See **vischio.**

viscont-e *m.* viscount. **-ado** *m.*, **-ea** *f.*, **-eri·a** *f.* viscountcy. **-e·o** *adj.* pertaining to the Visconti of Milan. **-essa** viscountess.

viscosio *m.* (text.) viscose.

viscoso *adj.* and derivs. See **vischioso,** under **vischio.**

visdo·min-e, -o *m.* (eccl. hist.) *vicedominus.* **-ato** *m.* status of *vicedominus.*

vis·etto, -ettino *m. dim.* of **viso,** q.v.

vis·i·bile *adj.* visible; perceptible; evident, manifest; accessible, available; il direttore è — dalle quattro alle cinque, the director is available between four and five; (scient.) apparent; (astron.) orizzonte —, apparent horizon. **-ibilmente** *adv.* visibly. **-ibi·lio** *m.* great number; un -ibilio di gente, a great number of people; andare in -ibilio, to go into ecstasies, to go into raptures. **-ibilità** *f.* visibility.

visiera *f.* visor, vizor; (fig.) a — alzata, boldly, fearlessly; abbassar la —, to throw caution to the winds; fencing-mask; peak of a cap.

visigoto *m.* Visigoth; *adj.* Visigothic.

vision-e *f.* vision, sight, eyesight; (admin.) prender — di, to have a sight of, to look over, to take notice of; dar — di, to give a

sight of, to show, to give notice of; (cinem.) in prima —, first showing of a film (in any one particular town); le prime -i nelle città chiave, the first release of a film in principal cities; (philos.) — intellettiva, intellectual vision; — della mente, mental vision, perspicacity, intelligence; vision, apparition; (rel.) vision; — beatifica, Beatific Vision; fantasy, image, mental picture. **-a·rio** *adj., n.m.* visionary.

vis·ir *m. indecl.* vizier. **-irato** *m.* vizierate, office of vizier.

vi·sit-a *f.* visit; call; biglietto di —, visiting-card; fare una — ai monumenti, to go sight-seeing; doctor's visit; examination by a doctor; — di ufficio, official medical examination; (mil. slang.) marcar —, to attend sick parade; passar la —, to undergo medical examination; examination, inspection; — sanitaria, sanitary inspection; — doganale, customs examination; (leg.) — domiciliare, inspection of premises; — peritale, survey; (naut.) visit and search (right of a ship in time of war); — di un bastimento in mare, stopping and search of a ship at sea; — di corpo, senior officers' calls; — di quadrato, officers' wardroom courtesy call; (eccl.) — pastorale, santa —, (bishop's) visitation of diocese, etc.; — d'una chiesa, visit to a church; — dei sepolcri, visit to the Altar of Repose in different churches (on Maundy Thursday or Good Friday); Congregazione della Sacra —, Congregation of Apostolic Visitation; (rel.) — del Signore, visitation of God, affliction; — della Madonna a Santa Elisabetta, Visitation, the visit of the Virgin Mary to St Elizabeth (which was of three months); (joc.) la — di santa Elisabetta, a very long visit; visitor; c'è una — in salotto, there's a visitor in the drawing-room. **-andine** *f.pl.* (eccl.) Visitation nuns, Visitandines.

visit-are [A I S] *tr.* to visit, to call upon, to pay a visit to; — gl'infermi, to visit the sick; to visit regularly, to frequent; to look at; — i musei, to look round the museums; — un paese straniero, to tour a foreign country; — una nave, to look over a ship; (naut.) — una nave in arrivo, to rummage; to examine; to examine medically; il medico è venuto ma non l'ha -ato, the doctor came but did not examine him; to inspect, to make an official inspection of; (eccl.) (of a bishop) — la diocesi, to visit his diocese; to visit, to chastise; la sventura lo ha -ato, misfortune has overtaken him; (rel.) il Signore vi ha -ato, God has indeed visited you, has afflicted you; *intr.* (*aux.* avere) to visit, to call on one's neighbours, to maintain social intercourse. (**-ante** *part. adj.* **-ato** *part. adj.*) **-atore** *m.* visitor; inspector; (eccl.) -atore apostolico, Visitor Apostolic. (**-atrice** *f.*) **-azione** *f.* visitation; (rel.) Visitation (of the Virgin Mary to St Elizabeth); (eccl.) Order of the Visitation.

visivo *adj.* See under **viso¹** *m.*

vis-o¹ *m.* face; guardare alcuno in —, to look somebody in the face; accendersi in —, to blush; dire a uno una cosa sul —, to tell something to his face; — a —, face to face; (fig.) a — aperto, openly, fearlessly; gettar sul — a uno, to throw in someone's face; rosso in —, flushed; allungare il —, to pout, *or* to grow thin in the face; aver — da, to dare, to have the face to; non ha mai visto denari in —, he doesn't even know what money is; non guardare in — a nessuno, not to look anyone in the face, to be shifty; expression; l'aria del —, the expression; cambiar —, to change one's expression; far buon — a, to welcome, to accept gratefully, to look favourably upon; far buon — a cattivo gioco, to put a good face on it, to make the best of a bad job; far mal —, to sulk, to be sullen; appearance, aspect; piatto di buon —, special dish made in honour of a guest; lavare il — a una stanza, to clean a room; †look, glance, regard; †sight; †mind, intellect. **-ivo** *adj.* visual, of vision; facoltà -iva, visual faculty, vision; campo -ivo, field of vision; (phys.) raggi -ivi, visible rays.

†**viso²** *m.* See **avviso.**

†**viso³** *part.* of **vedere,** q.v.

visone *m.* (zool.) mink, *Mustela vison.*

viso·rio *adj.* (anat.) optic; nervo —, optic nerve.

†**vispistrello** *m.* See **pipistrello.**

visp-o *adj.* brisk, lively, vivacious, sprightly; mi fa piacere che ti vedo —, I'm glad to see you looking so sprightly; un vecchietto ancora —, a gay old dog. **-ezza** *f.* briskness; sprightliness.

vissuto *part.* of **vivere,** q.v.; *adj.* lived; mal —, of evil life.

vist-a *f.* faculty of seeing, sight, avere la — buona, to have good eyesight; avere la — lunga, to be long-sighted, (fig.) to have great foresight; ogni creata —, every human eye; fin dove arriva la —, as far as the eye can see; seconda —, foresight, second sight;

vist-a (*cont.*)

view, sight, act of looking; saziare la —, to grow tired of looking; sfuggire alla —, to escape notice, to pass unobserved; impedire la —, to block the view; alla — di, at the sight of; perdere di —, to lose sight of; guardare a —, to keep an eye on; a — di tutti, within sight of all; alla —, by sight; dare una — a un libro, to glance over a book; stare alle -e, to be on the alert; a — d'occhio, visibly; essere in —, to be in sight; (fig.) c'è una crisi in —, a crisis is imminent; essere in — d'un luogo, to be within sight of a place; testimone di —, eyewitness; tradurre Omero a prima —, to translate Homer at sight; punto di —, angle, point of view; spectacle, view, prospect, sight; fare bella —, to make a beautiful sight; (fig.) essere in —, to be in evidence, to be in the public eye; (fig.) consideration; avere in —, to have in view; in — di, in view of; tenere in —, to bear in mind, to keep in view; ci avrà le sue -e, he'll have his own ideas on the subject; appearance, likeness; dar — di, to appear to, to seem to; far — di, fare le -e di, to pretend to; far gran — di, to make a great show of; mettere una cosa in buona —, to put something in a good light; appearance of beauty; cosa troppo vista, perde grazia e —, familiarity breeds contempt; sample; dammene un pochino per —, give me a little to see what it's like; window, opening; †(leg.) see **veduta**; (leg.; comm.) a —, at sight, on demand; a otto giorni —, eight days after sight (C.C.).

vistare [A I] *tr.* See under **visto**.

vist-o *part.* of **vedere**, q.v.; *adj.* seen; bene —, well-liked, popular; mal —, ill-liked; considered; — che, considering; †sharp, alert, far-seeing; *n.m.* visa; authorizing signature. -**are** [A I] *tr.* to visé. -**osità** *f.* showiness, gaudiness; garishness. -**oso** *adj.* striking, conspicuous; gaudy, showy, garish; ostentatious; magnificent; una somma -osa, a considerable sum of money. -**osamente** *adv.* strikingly; showily.

Vi·stola *pr.n.f.* (geog.) the river Vistula.

visual-e *adj.* visual; relating to sight; *n.f.* view, prospect; una magnifica —, a most wonderful view. -**mente** *adv.* visually.

vit-a *f.* 1. life; — materiale, physical life; — intellettuale, intellectual life; darei la — piuttosto di tradirlo, I would rather die than betray him; dare la — a, to give birth to, to bring to life; dare alla —, to give birth to; venire alla —, to be born; essere in —, to be alive; uscir di —, to die; rendere alla —, rendere la — a, to restore to life; dovere la — a, to owe one's life to; togliersi la —, to take one's life; assicurazione sulla —, life-insurance; pericolo di —, danger of death; ne va la —, si tratta di — o di morte, it's a matter of life and death; sotto pena della —, on pain of death; avere alla —, to have at one, to have attacking one; ne avevo quattro alla —, there were four of them at me; — mia!, dearest heart!, light of my life!; o la borsa o la —!, your money or your life!; (theol.) il libro della —, the book of life; vigour, life, power to live; mancar della —, to lack vigour; se Dio mi dà —, if I live; finchè c'è —, c'è speranza, while there's life there's hope; source of life; l'aria è la nostra —, air is the source of life, gli abbonati sono la — del giornale, a paper is kept going by its subscribers; liveliness, animation; una commedia senza —, a spiritless play; dar — alla compagnia, to liven up, to bring a bit of life into, the party; lifetime, span of life; in — di, during the lifetime of; in — non era stato gran che di buono, in life he had never been anything very wonderful; duration of life; membro a —, life-member; per la —, a —, for life; condannato a —, condemned for life; per la — (adjectival phrase), consummate, out and out, of the first water; un bugiardo per la —, a born liar; — di un libro, span of a book's popularity; (leg.) — naturale durante, during the lifetime; life; aspettazione di —, expectation of life; living person; quante -e costa la guerra!, how many lives are lost in war!; non v'è traccia di —, there is no sign of life; living, livelihood, sustenance; il costo della —, the cost of living; mendicar la —, to beg one's bread; living, existence; gli agi della —, life's comforts; fare —, to live, to make one's home; fa — da sè, he lives alone; un sistema di —, a rule of life; behaviour, way of life; mutar —, to change one's ways; darsi alla mala —, to go to the bad; fare una — indipendente, to lead an independent life; la — monastica, the monastic life; (iron.) time; passar la — negli studi, to spend all one's time in study; activities, doings; — sociale, social life; — privata, private life; written life-story, biography; — di sè stesso, autobiography; (rel.) —, morte e miracoli d'un santo, the life, death and miracles of a saint; (fig.) saper —, morte

e miracoli d'un altro, to know all about somebody else's business; fame; aver — fra i posteri, to be known to posterity, to 'live'. 2. waist; ci tiene ad aver la — snella, she is anxious to have a slim waist-line; ritto sulla —, bolt upright; abito lungo di —, long-waisted garment; stature, figure; blouse; andare in bella —, to go out without a coat. -**accia** *f. pejor.* wretched existence. -**ai(u)olo** *m. bon viveur*, pleasure-lover. -**ina** *f. dim.* tiny, slender waist; camisole, bodice; andare in -ina, to go out without a coat.

vitalb-a *f.* (bot.) travellers' joy, old man's beard, *Clematis vitalba*; — paonazza, *C. viticella*; — piccola, *C. flammula*. -**ino** *m.* (bot.) *C. recta*.

vit-ale *adj.* vital, life-giving; spirito —, life-giving spirit; essential, necessary; cosa —, essential, necessity; important, crucial; questione —, vital question; living, alive; membra -ali, living limbs; vivo e —, alive and healthy (of a child born in the normal way); †*n.m.* vitality, life. -**almente** *adv.* vitally. -**alismo** *m.* (philos.) vitalism. -**alità** *f.* vitality, energy, vital force; un'istituzione che ha poca -alità, an organization lacking in driving force; vital importance; viability; (demog.; insurance) tavole di -alità, life-table. -**aliziare** [A4] *tr.* (finan.) to turn into an annuity. -**ali·zio** *adj.* life-long; socio, membro, -alizio, life-member; (leg.) pensione -alizia, life-pension; debito -alizio, the state's liability to provide for pensioners; costituzione di rendita -alizia, establishment of life-annuity; *n.m.* life-annuity; fare un -alizio, to invest in purchase of, to buy, a life-annuity; -alizio gratuito, voluntary life-annuity (C.C.).

vitamina *f.* (biol.) vitamin.

vitando *adj.* (of person) to be avoided; (canon law) scomunicato —, a *vitandus*.

†**vitare**[1] *tr.* to flee; to avoid (cf. **evitare**).

†**vitare**[2] *tr.* to forbid, to prohibit (cf. **vietare**).

vit-e[1] *f.* (bot.) grapevine, *Vitis vinifera*; — bianca, white or red bryony, *Bryonia dioica*; — del Canadà, virginia creeper, ampelopsis, *Parthenocissus tricuspidata*; — d'orso, cowberry, *Vaccinium vitis-idaea*; — nera, black bryony, *Tamus communis*; — selvatica, wild vine, *Vitis vinifera* var. *silvestris*; (joc.) il sugo della —, wine. -**ame** *m.* a number of vines.

vit-e[2] *f.* screw; screw thread; girare la — a, to screw up; (aeron.) — orrizontale, wing-over; — piana, flat spin; a —, screw-shaped, *or* screwed on, held in place by screws; (sport) turn, twist (in diving). -**asse** *m.* (watchm.) screw-axle. -**ina** *f. dim.* small screw.

vitell-o *m.* (zool.) calf; — della tigre, tiger cub; (zool.) — marino, seal; (zool.) yolk (of an egg); (vet.) aver gamba di —, 'tied in below the knee'; calf-leather; (cul.) veal; costoletta di —, veal cutlet; il — d'oro, the Golden Calf; (fig.) adorare il — d'oro, to worship money. -**a** *f.* female calf, heifer. †-**aio** *m.* (calf-)leather worker. -**ina** *f.* (chem.) vitellin, ovovitellin; young calf; pretty little calf. -**ino** *adj.* of calves; yellow like the yolk of egg; *n.m.* young calf; calf-leather; (techn.) -ino abortivo, unborn calfskin. -**one** *m. augm.* of **vitello**; (butcher.) carne di -one, meat of young steer (not full grown).

†**vite·vole** *adj.* vital; life-restoring.

vitic·ci·o *m.* (bot.) tendril; traveller's joy, *Clematis vitalba*; (archit.) spiral or scroll-like ornament (esp. on Corinthian capital); — d'oro, gold filigree. -**ato** *adj.* (bot.) bearing tendrils.

vit-i·colo *adj.* (of district) vine-growing; viticultural, concerning vine-growing. -**icoltura**, -**icultura** *f.* viticulture, vine-growing. -**icultore** *m.* viticulturist, expert on vine-growing. -**i·fero** *adj.* (of district) vine-growing; viticultural, concerning vine-growing. -**iforme** *adj.* vine-shaped; (techn.) cotone -iforme, vine cotton.

vitigno *m.* (bot.) — americano, fox grape vine, *Vitis labrusca*.

vitili·gine *f.* (med.) vitiligo.

†**vitiperare** *vb.* and derivs. See **vituperare**.

vito *m.* (mus.) lively Andalusian dance in triple time; (med.) ballo di San —, St Vitus's dance, chorea.

vitone *m.* (mil.) breech block of a rifle; obturator cylinder (usu. having an interrupted thread).

†**vitoperare** *vb.* and derivs. See **vituperare**.

†**vitor·zolo** *m.* See **bitorzolo**.

vi·tr-eo *adj.* vitreous, glassy; occhi -ei, glassy eyes; (anat.) umore —, vitreous, vitreous humour. -**ificare** [A2s] and derivs. see **vetrificare**, under **vetro**. -**iolare** [A I] *tr.* (agric.) to spray with copper sulphate. -**iolo** *m.* and derivs. see **vetriolo**.

†**vitta** *f.* bandeau; headband.

vit·tim-a *f.* victim; sacrificial victim; sacrifice; (fig.) — d'un intrigo, victim of an intrigue; essere — del dovere, to suffer on behalf of duty; (iron.) povera —!, you poor old thing!, poor you! †**-are** *tr.* to offer up as a sacrificial victim; *intr.* to offer sacrifices. **-a·rio** *m.* sacrificial slaughterer; dealer in sacrificial animals. †**-ato** *adj.* offered up as a sacrificial victim. **-azione** *f.* victimization; sacrifice. **-ismo** *m.* (psych.) persecution complex. **-izzare** [A I] *tr.* to victimize.

vitto¹ *m.* food, nutriment, sustenance; fare; il — è molto caro, food prices are very high; — da poveri, simple fare; — vegetariano, vegetarian food; — vegetale, vegetable foods; tutto —, normal diet; mezzo —, invalid diet; — e alloggio, board and lodging.

†**vitt-o²** *part.* of vincere (cf. **vinto**). †**-ore** *m.* victor. (†**-rice** *f.*)

Vit·tore *pr.n m.* Victor.

vitto·ri-a¹ *f.* victory; guadagnarsi la —, to win a victory; avere la — in mano, to be sure of victory; disperare della —, to despair of winning; — di Pirro, Pyrrhic victory; (fig.) — su se stesso, victory over oneself; (Rom. myth.) Victory as a divinity, Victoria; (sculpt.) statue of Victory as a winged goddess; victoria (carriage); (bot.) — regia, victoria regia, royal water lily, *Victoria amazonica.* †**-ale** *adj.* relating to victory; inno -ale, hymn of victory. †**-are** *intr.* to win, to conquer; to obtain victory. **-ato** *adj.* (Rom. antiq.) 'victoriate', bearing the figure of a Victory; *n.m. victoriatus* (coin). †**-eggiante** *adj.* triumphant. **-oso** *adj.* victorious. (**-osamente** *adv.*)

Vitto·ri-a² *pr.n.f.* Victoria; (astron.) Victoria; (geog.) Victoria; Lago —, Lake Victoria. **-ano** *adj.* Victorian.

Vitto·rio *pr.n.m.* Victor.

vittoru-gheggiare [A 3 c] *intr.* (*aux.* avere) (lit. hist.) to imitate the style of Victor Hugo. **-ghiano** *adj.* Hugoesque, in the style of Victor Hugo.

†**vittua·glia** *f.*, †**vittua·ria** *f.* See **vettovaglia**.

vituli·na *f.* (zool.) seal.

†**vi·tulo** *m.* See **vitello**.

vituper-are [A I s] *tr.* to vituperate; to execrate; to bring shame upon; to shame, to disgrace, to dishonour; †to reproach, to blame; †to besmirch; *rfl.* to disgrace oneself, to bring shame upon oneself; †to become foul; †to injure oneself. **-a·bile** *adj.* vituperable, worthy to be vituperated (cf. **vituperevole**). **-ando** *adj.* despicable, ignominious, contemptible. **-ativo** *adj.* vituperative. **-ato** *part. adj.* vituperated; shamed, disgraced, put to shame; vituperable, despicable. (**-atore** *m.* **-atrice** *f.*) **-azione** *f.* vituperation; execration; shame, infamy, disgrace, dishonour. **-evole** *adj.* shameful, despicable, contemptible; ignominious. **-evolmente** *adv.* shamefully; contemptibly.

vitupe·r-io *m.* vituperation; execration; abuse; reproach; disgrace, shame, dishonour; sei il — della famiglia, you're a disgrace to the family. **-oso** *adj.* vituperative; abusive; defamatory; shameful, despicable, contemptible, ignominious. **-osamente** *adv.* vituperatively; shamefully; contemptibly; ignominiously.

viuzza *f. dim.* of **via**, q.v.; lane; alley; narrow street.

viva *excl.* hurrah!; hurray!; bravo!; gridare —, to cheer; three cheers for..., hurrah for...; — il re!; long live the King!; ma — Dio!, by God! (*pl.* **vivano**); *n.m.* un —, a cheer, a hurrah.

vivacchiare [A 4] *intr.* (*aux.* avere) to be hard up; to live from hand to mouth; to get along somehow, to rub along.

vivac-e *adj.* flourishing, thriving, full of life; terra —, fertile soil; long-lived, lasting; (bot.) perennial; intense, strong, untiring; vivid; luce —, brilliant light; vivacious, lively; sharp, keen, quick; parole -i, sharp words; agitated, animated; restless; (mus.) lively, quicker than allegro and slower than presto; †brightly coloured; †flushed; *n.m.* lively, vivacious person; †living creature. **-emente** *adv.* vivaciously; vividly. †**-ezza** *f.* see **vivacità**. **-ità** *f.* vitality; intensity; brightness; vivacity, liveliness; quickness, keenness; alertness; agitation, excitement; restlessness.

vivaddi·o *excl.* good heavens!; by Jove!; rather!

viva·gno *m.* selvedge, selvage; edge, border.

viva·io *m.* vivarium; warren; game-preserve; fish-rearing tank or pond; keep-net for live fish; (bot.) nursery.

vivand-a *f.* food, dish; -e saporite, tasty dishes; le prime -e, the first course; (rel.) mistica —, spiritual food, the Eucharist; food supplies, victuals. †**-are** *intr.* to eat; to eat a great deal. **-etta** *f.* tit-bit, dainty morsel. **-iere** *m.* sutler; canteen-keeper. **-iera** *f.* sutler's wife; vivandière.

vi·v-ere [C 16] *intr.* (*aux.* essere, vivere) to live; to be alive; pianta che -e bene, plant that grows well; visse nel Trecento, he lived in the fourteenth century; to dwell, to have one's habitation; — a Roma, to live in Rome; chi può — con quello lì?, who could bear to live with him?; to lead one's life, to spend one's time; — sempre in casa, to spend all one's time at home; to comport oneself, to behave; — saggiamente, to live wisely; — come un santo, to lead a saintly life; to carry on, to keep going; (in answer to the question 'come sta?', how are you?) si -e, grazie, bearing up, thank you; to feed, to sustain oneself; — di carne, to live on meat; — di ricordi, to live on memories; to maintain oneself; -e del suo lavoro, he lives on his earnings; hanno tanto da —, they have enough to live on; — alla giornata, to live from hand to mouth; to live fully, to enjoy life; ma ti par —, cotesto?, do you call this living?; lasciar —, to live in peace; lasciatemi —, leave me alone; — e lasciar —, to live and let live; to be, to stay, to remain; — sicuro che, to rest assured that; to be in existence; società che -e da tanti anni, society which has existed for so many years; to thrive, to flourish; far — l'industria, to make industry flourish; il ricordo di lui -rà perenne, his memory will live for ever; to devote one's life; — per i figli, to live for one's children; (typ.) -e!, *stet!*; *tr.* to lead, to live (a life); — una misera vita, to lead a wretched life; to experience; in quei giorni -evo una vita beata, in those days I was living a life of blissful happiness; *n.m.* life; il — dei Cinesi, the Chinese way of life; il — in campagna, life in the country; living; il — costa carissimo, the cost of living is very high; *pl.* foodstuffs, victuals, provisions; (comm.) deposito -eri, victualling yard; -eri di bordo, ship's stores. **-ente** *part. adj.* living; lingue -enti, living languages; †in suo -ente, during his lifetime; †al suo -ente, for the whole of his lifetime; (theol.) Dio -ente, the living God; *n.m.* living person; i -enti, the living; mal -ente, evil-doer, person of evil habits.

viverra *f.* (zool.) civet cat, *Viverra civetta.*

viveur *m. indecl.* (pron. as Fr.) bon viveur, pleasure-lover.

†**vive·vole** *adj.* vivid, keen, penetrating.

vi·vid-o *adj.* lively, vigorous; thriving; bright, vivid; -a luce, brilliant light; (poet.) life-giving.

viv-o *adj.* alive, living, live; — e verde, flourishing, alive and kicking; prendere gli uccelli -i, to catch birds alive; esser sepolto —, to be buried alive; più morto che —, more dead than alive; è ancora —, he is still alive; (fig.) mangiar —, to glare fiercely at, to kill with looks; se l'è rimangiato —, he fairly slew him, he gave him a good dressing down; (theol.) anima -a, soul in (a state of) grace; qui non c'è anima -a, there's not a soul here; persona ancora -a nel ricordo, person whose memory still lives; farsi —, to give news of oneself; non si fece più —, he didn't put in an appearance again, *or* he didn't come to see us again; lingua -a, living language; uso —, common parlance; lifelike; ritratto —, living portrait; thriving, strong; pianta -a, sturdy plant; siepe -a, quickset hedge; sharp; taglio —, sharp cut; spigolo —, sharp jutting corner; erta -a, sheer slope; (mil.) angolo —, salient; occhi -i, bright eyes; brisk, vigorous; vivacious; bambino troppo —, restless child; discussione -a, animated discussion; excitable, quick to flare up; indole un po' -a, rather touchy disposition; active, busy; commercio —, brisk business; (mech.) forza -a, kinetic energy; (fig.) le forze -e d'un paese, the active thinking population of a country; a -a forza, di -a forza, by main force; keen, intense, deeply felt; acute; dolore —, acute pain; gratitudine -a, deep gratitude; pianto —, heartfelt weeping; una -a impressione, a vivid impression; una -a necessità, a very real necessity; di — cuore, with heartfelt sincerity; vigorous, enduring, inexhaustible; fiamma -a, undying flame; tener — il discorso, to keep the conversation going; fonte -a, unending source, *or* fountain of fresh spring water; strong; calor —, burning heat; fresh, bright, pure; aria -a, fresh air; acqua -a, fresh spring water; colore —, vivid colour; carni -e, fresh complexion; a -a voce, aloud, by word of mouth; il rumore si fece più —, the noise grew louder, *or* the rumour grew; (mil.) effective; la forza -a d'un battaglione, the effective strength of a unit; (chem.; miner.) calce -a, quicklime; argento —, quicksilver, mercury; pietra -a, living rock; (leg.; comm.) spesa -a, necessary cost; spese -e, out-of-pockets; denaro —, ready money; (naut.) opere -e, hull (submerged portion); (theol.) opere -e, living works, deeds done in charity; *n.m.* living person; i -i e i morti, the living and the dead; living flesh; toccare sul —, tagliare fino al —, to cut to the quick; (fig.) heart, centre; penetrare nel — dell'argomento, to get to the root of the question; si pentì nel — del cuore, he repented from the bottom of his heart; (vet.) — del

viv-o (*cont.*)

piede del cavallo, 'quick' of the hoof of a horse; (art) life; al —, to the life; lifelike; grande quanto il —, lifesize; (archit.) — della colonna, shaft of the column; (radio) trasmissione dal —, 'live' broadcast, or telebroadcast; (mil.) breech; †(naut.) hull below the waterline; †— dell'acqua, spring tides. (**-aménte** *adv.*) **-acchiare** [A4] *intr.* (*aux.* avere) to make a poor living, to scrape along. **-ẹzza** *f.* liveliness, vivacity, briskness; vigour, animation; vividness, éclat, brightness; freshness. †**-icombu·rio** *m.* death by burning alive. **-ificaménto** *m.* vivifying. **-ificante** *part. adj.* vivifying; life-giving; restoring, enlivening; encouraging. **-ificare** [A2s] *tr.* to vivify, to quicken; to endue with life; to revive, to restore, to give new life to, to enliven; (fig.) mi sentii -ificato da quelle parole, those words gave me fresh heart; †*intr.* to live, to have life. **-ificativo** *adj.* life-giving; restorative. (**-ificatóre** *m.* **-ificatrice** *f.*) **-ificazióne** *f.* vivification; bringing to life. **-i·fico** *adj.* live-giving. †**-imento** *m.* livelihood; victuals. **-i·paro** (biol.) viviparous. †**-i·scere** *intr.* to revive, to come to life. **-isettóre** *m.* vivisector. **-isezióne** *f.* vivisection; far la -isezione di, to vivisect; (fig.) extensive examination, extensive research. **-ucchiare** [A4] *intr.* (*aux.* avere) see vivacchiare. †**-uto** *part.* of **vivere** (cf. **vissuto**).

†**viv-ola** *f.*, †**-uola** *f.* See **viola**[1].

vi·vole *f.pl.* (vet.) swollen parotid glands (horses).

†**vivolino** *adj.* violet-hued.

†**vivor-e** *m.*, **-oso** *adj.* See **vigor-e**, **-oso**.

†**vivo·rio** *m.* See **avorio**.

vi·z-io *m.* vice; il — del giuoco, the vice of gambling; ingolfarsi nei -i, to plunge into vice; il lupo perde il pelo ma non il —, the leopard will not change his spots; (theol.) i sette -i capitali, the seven deadly (capital) sins; bad habit; cavallo che ha il — di tirar calci, horse with the nasty habit of kicking; unpleasant habit; ha il — di lavarsi poco, he has an unpleasant way of not washing; pigliare un —, to get into a habit; fault, defect; il tessuto ha un — qui, there is a fault in the material here; weakness; (med.) (leg.) vice; defect; — occulto, hidden defect (C.C.); — totale di mente, insanity; — parziale di mente, diminished responsibility (C.P.); (comm.) — d'imballaggio, defective packing; — di forma, di procedura, error of form, of procedure; — di logica, logical flaw; — tipografico, printer's error. **-iare** [A4] *tr.* to vitiate, to render defective; to taint, to infect; to deprave, to corrupt; to lead into bad habits, to spoil; -iare i figliuoli, to spoil one's children; to invalidate (a contract, an agreement, etc.); to detract from; to spoil; questo difetto -ia la statua, this fault spoils the statue; †to deflower; *rfl.* to become spoiled; to become infected. **-iato** *part. adj.* vitiated, spoilt; un bimbo -iato, a spoilt child; infected, tainted; defective, spoilt, damaged; testo -iato, faulty text; invalidated, made null; †astute; †violated, deflowered. (**-iataménte** *adv.*) **-iatóre** *m.* one who spoils or corrupts; *adj.* tending to spoil or corrupt. (**-iatrice** *f.*) **-iatura** *f.* vitiating; spoiling; defect, fault, flaw; weakness, infirmity. **-iosàg·gine** *f.* depravity; viciousness. **-iosità** *f.* viciousness, corruption; defectiveness, faultiness; erroneousness; infectedness. **-ioso** *adj.* vicious; circolo -ioso, vicious circle; corrupt; depraved, having bad habits; faulty, defective; erroneous, full of mistakes; unhealthy, infected. (**-iosaménte** *adv.*)

vizzo *adj.* faded; withered; flabby; guancia vizza, withered cheek; fiori vizzi, faded flowers.

vobulazióne *f.* (electron.) wobbulation.

voca·bol-o *m.* word; l'origine d'un —, the origin of a word; -i scientifici, scientific terms; a rigor di —, strictly speaking; name; †district. **-a·rio** *m.* dictionary; lexicon; -ario tascabile, pocket dictionary; -ario dantesco, dictionary of words used by Dante; -ario latino, Latin dictionary; vocabulary, range of words; il -ario scientifico aumenta continuamente, the scientific vocabulary is increasing all the time; (fig.) nel suo -ario non c'è la parola paura, he doesn't know the meaning of fear. **-arista** *m.* lexicographer. **-iera** *f.* (Alfieri) Monna Vocaboliera, name for a pedantic woman. †**-ista** *m.* see **vocabolario**. **-ista·rio** *m.* compiler of a dictionary, lexicographer.

†**voca·bulo** *m.* See **vocabolo**.

voc-ale *adj.* vocal; (anat.) corde -ali, vocal cords; (mus.) vocal; musica —, vocal music, music for voices; accademia —, school of singing; (poet.) musical, full of harmony; *n.f.* vowel; vowel-sound. **-alménte** *adv.* vocally, orally, aloud; intendersi -almente,

to come to an understanding by talking things over. **-a·lico** *adj.* vocal, having a vowel character; vocalic; suoni -alici, vowel-sounds. **-alismo** *m.* vocalism, vowelism, system of vowels. **-alis·simo** *superl. adj.* very loud, resounding. **-alizzare** [A1] *tr.* (ling.) to vowelize; to render vocalic; (phon.) to vocalize; *intr.* (*aux.* avere) (mus.) to vocalize, to sing many notes to one vowel. (**-alizzato** *part. adj.*) **-alizzazióne** *f.* (ling.) vowelization; (phon.; mus.) vocalization. **-alizzo** *m.* (mus.) solfeggio, vocalize, vocal exercise.

†**voc-are** *tr.* to name, to call; to invoke, to call upon; *intr.* to call; *rfl.* to be called, to be named; to call oneself. †**-ato** *part. adj.* named, called.

vocativo *adj.* (gramm.) vocative; caso —, vocative case.

vocazión-e *f.* vocation, calling; non averci —, to have no vocation for it; (rel.) vocation (esp. to the priesthood or the religious life). **-ale** *adj.* vocational.

vóc-e *f.* voice; muovere la —, to start to speak; ad alta —, aloud; gridare ad alta —, to cry out in a loud voice; a —, a viva —, by word of mouth; sotto —, in an undertone; parlare a bassa —, to speak in a low voice; dar — ai propri sentimenti, to voice one's feelings; con tutta la — che aveva in corpo, at the top of his voice; nessuna — si levò a difenderlo, no voice was raised in his defence; (fig.) la — della coscienza, the voice of conscience; la — del sangue, the call of kinship; — di popolo, — di Dio, the voice of the people is the voice of God; — pubblica, public opinion; voice, cry (of animal); — dell'usignuolo, nightingale's song; noise, sound; (mus.) voice; part; sound; — affogata, muffled voice; — angelica, vox angelica (organ-stop); — bianca, treble-voice, voice of castrato; -i bianche, upper voices; — fessa, cracked voice; — finta, falsetto voice; — formata, well-produced voice; — di gola, throaty voice; — pastosa, mellow voice; — di petto, chest voice; — di testa, head-voice; — corale, vox humana (organ-stop); — umana, undulating flue stop characteristic of Italian classical organ (rarely used with the same meaning as '— corale', q.v.); sotto —, very soft (abbrev. s.v.); non aver —, to be out of voice; essere in —, to be in good voice; mottetto a tre -i, motet for three voices, three-part motet; la — del violino, del flauto, etc., the sound of the violin, flute, etc.; messa di —, see **messa**[2]; tone (interval); accent; con — supplichevole, in an imploring tone of voice; vote; ebbe tre -i sole, he only had three votes; aver — in capitolo, to have a say in the matter; a una —, unanimously; — attiva, right to vote; — passiva, qualification for being elected; reputation; essere in cattiva —, to have a bad name; aver — di ladro, to be reputed to be a thief; di gran —, of much fame; rumour; corre — che, rumour has it that; — di guerra, rumour of war; darsi la —, to send the word round; word, speech; — di comando, word of command; dare sulla — a, to contradict; (naut.) — di comando, verbal order; comandare a —, to give spoken or shouted orders; dare la —, to shout the executive order; saluto alla —, cheer; alla —!, still!, as you were!; word, term; -i antiquate, obsolete words; -i dell'uso militare, military terms; — sdrucciola, word accented on the antepenult; voice (of verb); — attiva, active voice; le -i principali d'un verbo, the principal parts of a verb; (in a dictionary or encyclopaedia) heading; lo troverai sotto questa —, you will find it under this heading; (comm.) item; -i di tariffa doganale, schedules of goods subject to customs duty. **-iare** [A3] *intr.* (*aux.* avere) to shout, to bawl; to gossip, to rumour; *n.m.* si sentiva un gran -iare, a great noise of shouting was heard; si fa un gran -iare dei nuovi ospiti, there is a lot of talk going on about the new guests. (**-iatóre** *m.* **-iatrice** *f.*) **-iferante** *part. adj.* vociferating. **-iferare** [A1s] *intr.* (*aux.* avere) to vociferate; (of birds) to chirp loudly, to clamour; to gossip to rumour; si -ifera che, it is rumoured that. **-iferato** *part. adj.* vociferated; rumoured. (**-iferatóre** *m.* **-iferatrice** *f.*) **-iferazióne** *f.* vociferation; clamour; rumour. **-io** *m.* (*pl.* -ii) noise of voices; clamour. **-ióne** *m.* loud voice; loud talker. (**-ióna** *f.*) †**-itare** *intr.* to call out; to vociferate.

†**vo·colo** *adj.* blind.

vodka *f.* vodka.

vòga,[1] **voga** *f.* fashion, vogue; essere in —, to be in vogue, to be in fashion, to be popular; acquistar —, to become fashionable; favour; mood, disposition; non sono in — di farlo, I am not in the mood to do it.

vog-a[2] *f.* (naut.) rowing; stroke; mezza —, short stroke; — gagliarda, hard, sustained rowing; — lunga, long stroke; — in piedi, fisher-

vog-a (*cont.*)
man's standing stroke (gondolier, etc.); — di punta, arrangement where alternate thwarts are manned (port and starboard); a —, under oars; allungare la —, to lengthen the stroke; regolare, dare la —, to give the stroke; serrare la —, to quicken the stroke; praticare la —, to go in for rowing; a — sinistra!, give way port!; — reale, stroke in which rowers stand and pause before falling back on the thwarts; — unita!, — assieme!, — insieme!, keep the stroke together!; (fig.) alacrity; mettersi con — al lavoro, to set to work with a will. **-are** [A 2] *intr.* (*aux.* avere) (naut.) to row, to proceed under oars; (fig.) to work hard; (of web-footed birds) to swim; †*rfl.* to proceed swiftly, to fly. **-amento** *m.* rowing. **-ante** *part. adj.* rowing. **-ata** *f.* oar-stroke. **-ato** *part. adj.* (of boat) rowed. **-atore** *m.* rower, oarsman. **-atura** *f.* rowing. †**-avanti!** (naut. comm.) give way together!

vo·gli-a *f.* (*pl.* **voglie**) wish; aver — di dormire, to want to go to sleep; non avere — di scherzare, to have no wish to joke; avere altra —, to wish otherwise; fancy; avrei — d'un buon pranzetto, I should love a nice dinner; mi vien — di..., I am seized by a fancy to...; mi mette — di..., it makes me want to...; craving, longing, desire; cavarsi una —, to satisfy a longing; le umane voglie, human desires; will; far le voglie d'un altro, to do the will of another; a mia —, at my pleasure; andare a sua —, to go one's own way; ragazzi senza — di studiare, boys without the will to study; contro —, against one's will; willingness, alacrity; di —, willingly; di mala —, unwillingly, reluctantly; mood, humour; sentirsi di buona —, to feel in a good mood; darsi buona —, to have a good time, to enjoy oneself; (pop.) birthmark (formerly said to occur as the result of unsatisfied craving on the part of the expectant mother); crumb, morsel; †(naut.) buona —, volunteer in a galley; (fig.) buona —, idle person. †**-ente** *part. adj.* wishful of, wanting to. **-enza** *f.* wish, desire, will. †**-e·vole** *adj.* lustful; desiring. **-oloso** *adj.* capricious, full of childish wishes. **-osità** *f.* capriciousness; desirousness. **-oso** *adj.* capricious; desirous, longing; *n.m.* è un gran -oso, he's always wanting something; †willing, ready, eager. (**-osamente** *adv.*) **-uzza** *f.* caprice, foolish wish.

voi *pers. pron.* (*2nd pers. pl.*) you; — altri, you others, you people; — altri inglesi, you English; eccomi a —, here I am at your service; (*2nd pers. sing.*) you (the use of **voi** as a form of address to one person is now intermediate between the formal **lei** and the intimate **tu**; in business letters it is used when addressing a firm or a corporation; in archaic usage it was the only formal mode of address before the **lei** form was taken over from Spanish); dare del — a, to address as 'voi'; †a —!, come on!, come along! †**vo·ia** *f.* See **voglia**.

voivoda *m.* (hist., S.E. Europe, Transylvania) vaivode, voivode.

volà *f.* flounce.

volapük *m.* volapük (a proposed international language).

vol-are [A I C] *intr.* (*aux.* essere, avere) to fly; — su, to fly over; — alto, to fly high; sarebbe come — senz'ali, it's an impossibility; credere che gli asini -ino, to be very gullible, to believe anything; — al cielo, to go to heaven; (aeron.) — a quota di, — a motore spento, to fly with engine switched off; volere o —, there's no getting away from it; — in minute schegge, to fly into small splinters; to be hurled, to be flung; gli schiaffi -avano, insults were flying; (of feathers, leaves, dust, etc.) to fly about, to blow about; il vento gli fece — via il cappello, the wind blew his hat away; to hurry, to move quickly; un treno che -a, a very fast train; la notizia -ava, the news spread rapidly; a te -a il mio pensiero, my thoughts fly to you; -ano i giorni, the days fly past. †**-a·gio** *adj.* see **volubile**. **-amento** *m.* flight. **-anda** *f.* flywheel; dust (from a mill). **-ano** *m.* (sport) shuttlecock; (eng.) flywheel; stabilizer; -ano per movimento alternativo, reciprocating wheel. **-ante** *part. adj.* flying; foglio -ante, fly-sheet; sedia -ante, sedan-chair; cervo -ante, paper kite; (ent.) see under **cervo**; compagnia -ante, (mil.) emergency unit ready for instant duty; colonna -ante, flying column; squadra -ante, flying platoon; ponte -ante, bridge of boats; (naut.) portable; temporary; jury; candeliere -ante, staunchion which can be unshipped; bozza -ante, temporary stopper; (aeron.) piatto -ante, flying-saucer; †vela -ante, flying-jib; †unstable, volatile; *n.m.* (motor.) steering-wheel; stare al -ante, to be at the wheel; (eng.) handwheel; flywheel, (motor.; aeron.) avviatore a -ante, inertia starter; flounce, frill. **-antino** *m.* tame pigeon; (eng.) handwheel, control

wheel; printed leaflet; pamphlet; handbill. **-astro** *adj.* able to fly. **-ata** *f.* flight; journey by air; una -ata da Torino a Palermo, a flight from Turin to Palermo; una -ata d'uccelli, a flight of birds; (fig.) rapid promotion; una -ata lirica, a flight of lyricism; di -ata, quickly, rapidly, in an instant; pariglia di -ata, pair of horses, oxen, etc., not attached to the shaft (in a team of more than one pair); (sport) sprint (cycle-racing); di -ata, on the volley (tennis, etc.); (mil.) fore-end, muzzle, chase of a gun; tirare di -ata, to fire at extreme or maximum elevation; trajectory; (mus.) run, passage. †**-ate·vole** *adj.* see **volatile**. **-a·tica** *f.* (med.) rash, eruption. †**-a·tico** *adj.* †pesce -atico, flying-fish; †dragone -atico, winged dragon. **-a·tile** *adj.* able to fly; winged; volatile, flighty, fickle, inconstant; (chem.) volatile; (fig.) scienza -atile, knowledge quickly forgotten; *n.m.* bird, winged creature. **-atilità** *f.* volatility. **-atilizzare** [A I] *tr.* (chem.) to volatilize; *rfl.* to volatilize; to evaporate. **-atilizzatore** *m.* (chem.) vaporizer. **-atilizzazione** *f.* (chem.) volatilization, vaporization. **-atina** *f.* (mus.) little run. **-atio** *adj.* volatile. **-ativo** *adj.* (chem.) volatile. **-atizzare** [A I] *tr., intr.* (*aux.* avere) (chem.) to volatilize, to vaporize. **-atizzazione** *f.* (chem.) vaporization. **-ato** *part. adj.* thrown, hurled, flung; ingiurie -ate da una parte e dall'altra, insults hurled from all directions; †*n.m.* flying, flight. **-atoio** *adj.* able to fly; winged; rapid, swift. **-atore** *m.* flyer, flier; un cavallo -atore, a flier; (mil. hist.) light infantryman. **-azzo** *m.* flourish.

volent-e *part.* of **volere**, q.v.; *adj.* willing; — o nolente, willy-nilly; -i i genitori, with one's parents' consent; desirous; — compire il suo dovere, anxious to do his duty; l'uomo, essere intelligente e —, man, a being endowed with intelligence and will. **-eroso** *adj.* willing, keen, eager; †capricious; †desirous; †*n.m.* volunteer. (**-erosamente** *adv.*) **-ieri** *adv.* willingly, with pleasure; mal -ieri, reluctantly, unwillingly, with a bad grace; viaggiar -ieri, to like travelling, to enjoy travelling; bere -ieri, to be too fond of drink; easily, readily; spesso e -ieri, only too often. †**-iermente** *adv.*, †**-iero** *adv.* see **volentieri**.

vol-ere [B 36] *tr.* to want; — tutto a suo modo, to want everything one's own way; — una per moglie, to want to marry someone; vuole un po' di pane?, would you like a little bread?; voglio che sappia, I'd like you to know; non voglio nessuno, I want nobody; i genitori lo -lero prete, his parents wanted him to be a priest; vuol farsi frate, si vuol far frate, he wants to become a monk; (in compound tenses, usu. with the *aux.* required by the verb in *infin.*) ha -uto parlare, he wanted to speak; è -uto partire, he wanted to leave; to long for; — la sua casa, to long for home; to will; accada quel che vuole, come what will; il destino vuole così, destiny will have it so; Dio -esse che fosse ancor vivo!, would to God he were still alive!; to like, to wish; se vuoi, if you like; come vuoi, as you wish; dica quello che vuole (with *infin.* of 'dire' understood), say what you like; volendo, si potrebbe ottenerne, we could get some if we wanted to; (in the conditional) vorrei un po' d'attenzione, I should like a little attention; quanto vorrei vederla!, how I should love to see her!; vorrei morir se non è così, on my life it is true; (iron.) vorrei vedere che non pagasse!, I'd like to see him not pay up!; to be willing, to be pleased to; vuole farmi il piacere di, will you please do me the favour of; vogliate venire con me, please come with me; -ete tacere!, will you be quiet!; to insist on; non vogliate farlo!, don't do it; mi -le leggere la sua poesia, he insisted on reading me, he would read me, his poem; to permit; verrò se vuole mio padre, I shall come if my father allows me; to prefer; chi la vuole cotta, chi la vuole cruda, it's all according to taste; to expect; -ete altro?, isn't that enough?; che -ete, what do you expect?; cosa vogliono da un povero diavolo, what do they expect of a poor devil; to deserve; l'ha -uto, he asked for it; to intend; voglio sbrigar tutto domani, I mean to finish it all off tomorrow; non -endo, senza —, involuntarily, unintentionally; to wish to see; il direttore vi vuole, the manager wants to see you; to accept; non lo vogliono tra loro, they won't have him among them(selves); nessuno vuole questa moneta, nobody will accept this coin; to like; i cavalli vogliono poco la paglia, horses don't like straw very much; voglia o non voglia, willy-nilly; to hold, to insist, to maintain; vogliono che ne sia l'autore, he is alleged to be the author; (math.) to carry; sette e sette quattordici e — uno, seven and seven are fourteen and carry one; to demand, to ask (a price); quanto ne -ete di queste pere?, how much do you want for these pears?; to demand, to require, to need; l'educazione dei figli vuole molta

vol-ere (*cont.*)

diligenza, much care must be taken over the upbringing of one's children; verbo che vuole il dativo, verb taking the dative case; la legge vuole che si faccia così, the law demands that we do this; -erci, to be needed, to be necessary; quanta stoffa ci vuole per un vestito?, how much material will a dress take?; ci vorrebbe un uomo ardito, it would take a bold man; ci vuole altro!, it needs something more than that!, non ci vorrebbe altro che..., it would be too bad if...; -ercene, to take some doing; ce n'è voluto, c'è voluto del bello e del buono, it took some doing; non -ercene con alcuno, to refuse to have anything to do with someone; — bene a, to love; le -eva un bene matto, he loved her madly; — male a, to detest, to hate; lo -evano morto, they hated him bitterly, they wished him dead; — dire, to matter, to mean; non vuole dire, it doesn't matter; che cosa vuol dire?, what does it mean?; mille lire non vogliono dire niente per lui, a thousand lire mean nothing to him; questo vuol dire molto contro di lui, this says a great deal against him; voglio dire, vogliam dire, that is to say; -evo ben dire!, I was going to say!, I told you so!; -erla con uno, to have a grudge against someone; (in *3rd pers. indic.* as an equivalent of 'dovere') to require; si vuole andar adagio, one must go gently; vuole essere trattata con prudenza, it must be carefully handled; vuol essere una faccenda seria, it must be a serious business; non —, to refuse; il dolore non vuole passare, the pain refuses to go; non mi -evo persuadere, I refused to believe; (as an *aux.* followed by an *infin.*) to be about to; to try to; vuol piovere, it looks like rain; *intr.* (*aux.* avere) to will; l'uomo pensa e vuole, man thinks and wills; Dio non voglia!, God forbid!; chi vuole, può, where there's a will there's a way; neanche a —, not possibly; o voglio, or rather, or better still; vuoi...vuoi, whether...or, as...as; scrive bene vuoi in prosa vuoi in poesia, he writes as well in prose as in poetry; *n.m.* il —, the will; a tuo —, at your will; — libero, free will; buon —, goodwill; di buon —, willingly; il — dire che l'Italia mancò al patto è un errore, those who make out that Italy broke the agreement are wrong. **-uto** *part. adj.* desired, longed-for.

†**vole·vole** *adj.* See **volatile**.

†**volgano** *adj.* popular, common.

volgar-e[1] *adj.* vulgar; coarse; uneducated, unrefined; mean; trivial; common; low; plebeian; modi -i, low-class habits; popular, current, vulgar; pregiudizi -i, popular prejudices; (ling.) latino —, Vulgar Latin; vernacular; Era —, Christian era; (lit.) poesia —, vernacular poetry; *n.m.* vernacular; in —, in Italian (not Latin); in buon —, in good plain speaking; parlance; †rumour; †proverb, saw, saying. **-mente** *adv.* vulgarly, coarsely, commonly; proverbially; commonly, popularly. †**-e·simo** *m.* see **volgarismo**. **-ismo** *m.* vulgarism. **-ità** *f.* vulgarity, coarseness; dire una -ità, to use a vulgar expression. **-izzamento** *m.* translation into the vernacular. **-izzare** [A 1] *tr.* to translate into the vernacular; to popularize, to present in popular form, to vulgarize. **-izzato** *part. adj.* translated into the vernacular; popularized. **-izzatore** *m.* one who translates into the vernacular; one who spreads or circulates (a belief, a view, etc.). (**-izzatrice** *f.*) **-izzazione** *f.* translation into the vernacular; spreading, diffusion, propagation; il nostro scopo è la -izzazione di certe norme igieniche, our aim is to teach the general public a certain standard of hygiene.

†**volgare**[2] *vb.* and derivs. See **divulgare**.

Volgata *pr.n.f.* (Bibl.) the Vulgate; commonly known text of a work; la — della *Divina Commedia*, the Crusca edition (1595) of the *Divine Comedy*; la — della Tavola Rotonda, the Arthurian Prose Vulgate.

volgato *adj.* well-known, popular, common, widespread.

vol·g-ere [C 5] *tr.* to turn; — sottosopra, to overturn, to turn upside-down; — il dorso a, to turn one's back on; — parole a, to address; — una cantonata, to turn a corner; — nell'animo, to turn over in one's mind, to think out; — un libro, to turn the pages of a book; (fig.) — il freno, to hold the reins; to change; — bandiera, to change sides, to change one's opinion; — ad altro uso, to put to another use; to revolve; — una ruota, to turn a wheel; — un sasso, to roll a stone; to encircle, to surround, to enwrap; to wind round; to direct; — i passi, to turn one's steps; — la sua ira contro, to direct one's wrath against; to make to turn; — il nemico in fuga, to drive back the enemy; — in italiano, to put into Italian; *intr.* (*aux.* essere, avere) (of a road, a wheel, etc.) to turn; — da, to turn from; (of time) to roll on, to pass; volsero

alcuni mesi, a few months rolled by; — a, to tend towards, to verge on, to approach; lo spettacolo -eva alla fine, the show was drawing to a close; -e al verde, it is almost green; il sole -e al tramonto, the sun has almost set; (archit.) to arch (over), to form a vault; *rfl.* to turn; (of the earth, the heavens, etc.) to revolve; -ersi all'amico, to turn to one's friend; to be turned towards, to face; -ersi a destra, to turn (to the) right; to turn round; -ersi dall'altra parte, to turn the other way round; to apply oneself; to devote oneself; -ersi allo studio, to turn to study; to change; il tempo si -e al brutto, the weather is breaking up; (of wine) to go sour. **-ente** *part. adj.* turning; verging on; changing; current; la settimana -ente, the current week. †**-e·vole** *adj.* turning; revolving. †**-iarrosti** *m.* turnspit. **-i·bile** *adj.* that can be turned. **-imento** *m.* turning; revolution; -imento della fortuna, change of fortune, vicissitude. †**-ito·io** *m.* twist, wrapping; turn lathe; bond, fetter; *adj.* turning. (**-itore** *m.* **-itrice** *f.*)

volgo *m.* crowd, multitude; il — degli scienziati, the common run of scientists; common people, common herd, plebs, lower classes.

vol·golo *m.* bundle.

volicchiare [A 4] *intr.* (*aux.* essere) to flutter; to flit.

volit-are [A 1 s] *intr.* (*aux.* avere) to flit; (poet.) to fly hither and thither. **-ante** *part. adj.* flitting. **-anti** *m.pl.* (zool.) bats.

volitivo *adj.* volitive, volitional; la facoltà volitiva, the faculty of will; wilful, self-willed, headstrong; *n.m.* è un —, he is a man of strong will.

†**vo·lito** *m.* flight; in —, flying, on the wing, in flight.

volizione *f.* volition; atto di —, act of the will.

†**vol·lere** *vb.* and derivs. See **volgere**.

†**vollienza** *f.* See **voglia**.

vol-o[1] *m.* flight; passare a —, passare di —, librarsi a —, alzarsi a —, to fly, to soar; pigliare il —, spiccare il —, prendere il —, to take flight, to rise in the air; (fig.) prendere il —, to escape, to make off, to elope, to take flight, to disappear, to be stolen; in —, upwards; vedere a — d'uccello, to get a bird's-eye view of; dare il — a, to set free, to let out of a cage; far fare un — a una cosa, to throw something away; flying; — basso, low-flying; colpire un uccello a —, to shoot a bird on the wing; power of flight; atto al —, able to fly; privare un uccello del —, to clip the wings of a bird; — abbassato, with the wing-tips turned downwards; — spiegato, with the wing-tips upwards; di primo —, newly fledged; (fig.) speed, swiftness; fare un —, dare un —, to race, to run; in un —, in a second; a —, immediately; in passing; afferrar un'occasione a —, to seize an opportunity on the spot; a —, di —, in a trice; il cavallo passò la barriera di —, the horse cleared the fence like a bird; toccare a —, to touch lightly on; leggere di —, to skim through; rapid promotion; la sua carriera è stata un —, he has risen to great heights in his career; (aeron.) flight; assistente di —, air-hostess; — a vela, gliding; — strumentale, blind flying; (herald.) vol, a pair of wings joined; — all'antico, two wings addorsed.

Volo[2] *pr.n.m.* (geog.) Volos.

volont-à *f.* will; uomo senza —, man with no will-power; libera —, free will; willingness; ha la — di studiare, he is willing to study; con —, di —, willingly; desire, wish, will, pleasure; a mia —, at my will; a —, at will; contro la mia —, against my will; la — di Dio, the will of God; essere di una sola —, to share a desire, to be of one mind; l'estrema — d'un estinto, the last wishes of a dying person (cf. leg. use below); la — di sapere, the longing to find out; una — bestiale, a bestial desire; disposition; buona —, goodwill; mala —, ill will; consent; senza la — dei genitori, against the will of one's parents; (leg.) gli atti di ultima —, testamentary instruments; le ultime —, Last Will; (comm.) a —, at option; pane a —, bread included without extra charge; †faction, sect. **-ariato** *m.* (admin.) unpaid apprenticeship; (mil.) voluntary service before call-up. **-a·rio** *adj.* spontaneous; moto -ario del cuore, spontaneous impulse of the heart; self-willed, impulsive, headstrong; intentional; voluntary; morte -aria, suicide; (comm.) liquidazione -aria, voluntary liquidation; (leg.) comparizione -aria, voluntary appearance; giuramento -ario, voluntary oath; †pigliare soldo -ario, to go for a soldier, to enlist; †willing, eager; *n.m.* (mil.) volunteer; -ario di guerra, volunteer (for the duration of hostilities); unpaid official; voluntary worker. **-ariamente** *adv.* spontaneously; voluntarily. **-arismo** *m.* (philos.) voluntarism. †**-arioso** *adj.* willing; desirous. **-eroso** *adj.* and derivs. see **volenteroso**, under **volente**. †**-ieri** *adv.* see **volentieri**. †**-iero** *adj.* see **volontario**.

volp-e *f.* (zool.) fox; la — e l'uva, the fox and the grapes; caccia alla —, fox-hunting; (fig.) cunning person; vecchia —, old fox, cunning fellow; fox fur; mal della —, laziness; (naut. hist.) quartermaster's tally board used for noting passing of time; *pl.* frame of a lattice mast; (bot.) rust-fungus; (zool.) — polare, Arctic fox; (ichth.) — di mare, pesce —, thresher shark, *Alopias vulpinus* (also, in some dialects, rockling, *Onos tricirratus*); (vet.) naso di —, a horse with a reddish nose. **-a·ia** *f.* fox's den; (fig.) squalid hovel. **-are** [A 1] *intr.* (*aux.* essere) (bot.) to become infected with rust. **-ato** *part. adj.* (bot.) infected with rust. **-eggiare** [A 3 c] *intr.* (*aux.* avere) to be foxy, to be wily; to use cunning. **-igno** *adj.* vulpine, fox-like; foxy, cunning. **-ina** *f.* (ichth.) grey mullet, *Mugil cephalus.* **-inite** *f.* (miner.) vulpinite. **-ino** *adj.* vulpine, fox-like, fox-coloured; crafty, cunning, foxy, wily; deceitful; malicious. †**-o** *adj.* see volpino. **-one** *m. augm.* of **volpe**; (fig.) old fox, cunning and fraudulent person; (comm.) stag.

volsuto *part.* (pop.) of **volere**, q.v.

volt *m. indecl.* (electr.). See **volta³**.

volt-a¹ *f.* **1.** TURN, twist; due -e della chiave, two turns of the key; (aeron.) gran —, looping-the-loop; (naut.) turn; hitch; knot; — semplice, hitch; — doppia, two round turns; — incrociata, riding turn; — di gomena, see 'volta delle catene'; — con mezzo parato, half hitch; — rotonda, round turn; — tonda, round turn; — volante, slip hitch; — di un cavo, kink; — delle catene, turns in a ship's cable when moored without a swivel; dare — a, to turn up; fare la — a, to brace up (a yard); levare —, to cast off turns; prendere, pigliare —, to take turns (on a bollard, etc.); leva —!, let go!; piglia —!, turn up!; —!, secure! **2.** TURNING ROUND; dar —, to turn, to turn one's back, to turn about; dar — al cavallo, to turn a horse round; tornare in —, to turn back; girare in —, to turn about; dar — nel letto, to turn over in bed; a — di corriere, by return of post, (fig.) without delay; flight; dar (di) —, to flee, mettere in —, to put to flight; turning (of path or road); turning upside-down; dar la — a un vaso, to upturn a vase; *pl.* twistings, turnings; le -e d'un fiume, the meanderings of a river; le -e d'un leone, the pacing up and down of a lion; stare sulle -e, to manœuvre, to act shrewdly; (naut.) stare sulle -e, to tack; (prosod.) *volta*, division of the stanza in *canzone* or *ballata.* **3.** TURN, trip, spin; fare una —, to take a trip, to go for a spin; menare in —, to spin out (a discussion), to shilly-shally. **4.** DIRECTION; alla — di Roma, in the direction of Rome; alla nostra —, in our direction, towards us; dar — a, to turn towards. **5.** CHANGE; meglio — che stravolta, it is better to alter one's plans than fail; change for the worse; vino che dà la —, wine that is turning sour; il successo gli ha dato — al cervello, success has turned his head; dar di —, to lose one's head. **6.** ALTERNATION, turn; viene la tua —, your turn is coming; è la — che non si scherza, it is time to stop joking. **7.** TIME; alle -e, certe -e, qualche —, tal —, sometimes; ancora una —, again, once more; una —, once; due -e, twice; c'era una —, once upon a time there was; — per —, each time, every time; a — a —, from time to time; una — o l'altra, sooner or later; tutto in una —, all at once; spesse -e, often; una —, una buona —, una — per sempre, once and for all; smettila una —, for heaven's sake stop it; una —, sta' zitto, do be quiet; una — tanto, just this once; tutta —, however; uno per —, uno alla —, one at a time; dieci -e dieci, ten times ten; una — che, since, now that; una — che l'ha ammesso, now that he has admitted it.

volta² *f.* (archit.) vault; — a botte, barrel vault; — reale, vault built with large bricks laid edgeways; underground vault; roof; (anat.) — del palato, palatal arch; (zool.) — archenterica, archenteron roof; (naut.) — di poppa, poop; run down of an aircraft-carrier (i.e. curved deck at the stern); (mil.) — di torre, protective arches over quarters, batteries, etc.

volt-a³ *m.* (electr.) volt. **-ag·gio** *m.* voltage. NOTE: the word is not so widely used as the English 'voltage', which is usually 'tensione' in Italian. 'Voltaggio' means the 'tensione' expressed in volts. The difference is rather like that between 'distance' and 'mileage'. **-a·ico** *adj.* (electr.) voltaic. **-aismo** *m.* (electr.) Volta effect. **-a·metro** *m.* (electr.) coulometer, voltameter.

voltafac·cia *m. indecl.* See under **voltare**.

volt-are [A 1] *tr.* to turn; to turn over; to revolve; to roll over; — sotto sopra, to turn upside-down; — le spalle, to turn one's back; — un canto, to turn a corner; to change; — discorso, to

change the subject; — in ridicolo, to turn to ridicule; — mantello, — bandiera, — casacca, — gabbana, to change sides, to rebel; to transfer; to translate; to turn round, to reverse; to turn inside-out; to bend; to direct; to turn aside, to lead off, to deflect; to change (in character and ideas); (archit.) to vault; to cover with a vault; *intr.* (*aux.* avere) to turn; to turn round; to go back; to take a turning; to bend; — a, to turn towards, to face, to look towards; — a destra, to turn right; — largo ai canti, to allow plenty of room when turning corners, (fig.) to act cautiously when in difficulties; †to measure in circumference; — trenta miglia, to measure thirty miles round; to change; (of sun and moon) to sink, to set; (of wine) to turn sour; la nostra fortuna comincia a —, our luck is beginning to turn; *rfl.* to turn; to turn round; to turn back; to roll; to change; il levante s'è -ato in tramontana, the wind has changed from east to north; to change one's mind; -arsi a tutti i venti, to be easily swayed; -arsi a, to apply oneself, to turn to; non sapeva da che parte -arsi, he did not know which way to turn; -arsi contro, to turn against, to rebel against; fare una cosa senza -arsi nè in qua nè in là, to do something with the utmost indifference; -arsi e rivoltarsi nel letto, to toss and turn in bed; (mus.) volti subito (abbrev. v.s.), turn over quickly. **-a·bile** *adj.* capable of being turned; inconstant, easily swayed. †**-acatene** *m. indecl.* (naut.) mooring swivel. **-afac·cia** *m.* turning round; *volte-face*, complete change of front. **-agabbana** *m. indecl.* turncoat. **-ama·schio** *m.* (techn.) wrench. **-amento** *m.* turning; †(naut.) prolonged beating of the seas. **-asto·maco** *m.* repugnance experienced by the stomach; nauseating object, object causing the stomach to retch. **-ata** *f.* turn; una -ata di spalle, a turn of the shoulders; in una -ata d'occhi, in the twinkling of an eye; turning, bend; curve; corner; †address, speech apostrophizing someone. **-a·tile** *adj.* see **voltabile**. **-ato** *part. adj.* turned; naso -ato all'insù, snub nose, tip-tilted nose; vaulted. **-azione** *f.* turning, act of turning.

volt-eggiare [A 3 c] *intr.* (*aux.* avere) to turn about, to twist about; to shuffle, to wriggle; to wind, to meander; to flit, to flutter; to flap; to hesitate, to hover, to hover round; †(naut.) to sail; to sail frequently; to sail back and forth; to beat the seas; (sport) to vault; (equit.) to vault (into the saddle); *tr.* to navigate; — l'Africa, to sail round the coast of Africa. **-eggiamento** *m.* turning, twisting; winding, meandering, tortuousness; fluttering, hovering. **-eggiatore** *m.* one who turns about; one who flutters or hovers; vaulter; tumbler; trick-rider; (mil. hist.) skirmisher; *pl.* Napoleonic troops; †(naut.) phantom ship. (**-eggiatrice** *f.*) **-eggio** *m.* (equit.) trick-riding; (equit.; gymn.) vault.

Volterr-a *pr.n.f.* (geog.) Volterra. **-ano** *adj.* of, relating to, Volterra; *n.m.* inhabitant or native of Volterra. **-ana** *f.* woman or girl of Volterra; (archit.) vault built with bricks laid flat, as at Volterra; kind of hollow brick or tile used in building small vaults.

volterrian-o *adj.* (lit. hist.) Voltairian; (fig.) sceptical, critical; derisive; †(joc.) (of a coat) turned inside-out. **-ismo** *m.* Voltairianism.

†**voltigliola** *f.* (naut.) forecastle railing.

voltimetri·a *f.* (archit.) measurement of vaults.

volti·metro *m.* See **voltametro**, under **volta³**.

volto¹ *m.* face, countenance; look, expression; aver — da, to have the face to; a — aperto, openly; — Santo (Santo —), the Holy Face, usual name of the ancient crucifix at Lucca and also of that at Borgo San Sepolcro.

volto² *part.* of **volgere**, q.v.; naso — all'insù, tip-tilted nose; †colore —, strong colour.

volto³ *m.* (archit.) arch, arcade, vault (cf. **volta**).

voltoio¹ *m.* lower part of a horse's reins.

†**volto·io²** *m.* See **avvoltoio**.

voltol-are [A 1 s] *tr.* to roll, to turn over, to roll along; *rfl.* to roll; to roll over; to turn over; to roll along; to wallow. (**-amento** *m.* **-ato** *part. adj.*) **-one**, **-oni** *adv.* rolling about; tumbling down.

voltur-a *f.* turning; turning over; bend; (leg.; comm.) assignment; transfer; clearance; per —, by transfer; far la —, to transfer; — di debiti, debt clearance; †uprising, revolt; †rendering, version, translation. **-are** [A 1] *tr.* (leg.; comm.) to assign; to transfer; to clear. (**-ato** *part. adj.*)

volturno¹ *m.* east-north-east wind.

Volturno² *pr.n.m.* (geog.) the Volturno (river).

volu·bil-e *adj.* inconstant; unstable; variable; fickle, changeable; ever-changing; turning; rotating, revolving; twisting; (bot.)

volubil-e (*cont.*)
twining; (poet.) flowing, fluent; *n.m.* (bot.) twining stem; (mus.) turn; quilisma. (**-mente** *adv.*) **-ità** *f.* inconstancy; instability; variability, fickleness, changeability; ability to revolve, to rotate; †volubleness, volubility, rapidity of speech.

vol-ume *m.* bulk, solid content; il — di una sfera, the volume of a sphere; mass, quantity; un — di fiamme, a mass of flames; -umi di fumo, volumes of smoke; volume, fullness of tone; scroll of papyrus; volume; opera in dieci -umi, work in ten volumes; (comm.) bulk; †(astron.) heavenly sphere; †orbit; †entanglement, confusion. **-umeno·metro** *m.* (phys.) volumenometer. **-ume·trico** *adj.* volumetric. **-u·metro** *m.* pyknometer. **-uminosità** *f.* voluminosity, voluminousness. **-uminoso** *adj.* voluminous, bulky, massive, huge; opera -uminosa, voluminous work.

†**voluntà** *f.* and derivs. See **volontà**.

volut-a *f.* (archit.) volute; a —, voluted; scroll-shaped; coil; volution, spiral turn; whorl of spiral shell; (zool.) *Voluta* spp., large gastropods resembling whelks. †**-o** *m.* see **voluta**. **-abro** *m.* wallowing-place for pigs; (fig.) immerso nell'-abro dell'ozio, wallowing in idleness.

volutt-à *f.* delight; pleasure; voluptuousness; sensual enjoyment. †**-a·rio** *adj., n.m.* see **voluttuario**. **-ua·rio** *adj.* voluptuary; pleasure-loving; pleasure-seeking; unnecessary; spese -uarie, non-essential expenses, luxury spending. **-uoso** *adj.* voluptuous; pleasure-loving. **-uosamente** *adv.* voluptuously; sensuously; with great enjoyment; lusciously.

volv-a *f.* (bot.) volva. **-oce** *m.* (bot.) *Volvox*.

volv·v-olo, **-ulo** *m.* (med.) volvulus.

vombato *m.* (zool.) wombat, *Phascolomys* spp.

vo·mer-e[1], **-o** *m.* ploughshare; (naut.) sweep; minesweep; (anat.) vomer, nasal septum. **-a·ia** *f.* front part of a plough to which the coulter fits. †**-ale** *m.* coulter.

†**vo·mere**[2] see **vomitare**.

vomit-are [A I S] *tr., intr.* (aux. avere) to vomit; sentirsi venir da —, to feel one is going to be sick; una cosa che fa —, a nauseating thing; (fig.) to vomit, to belch forth; (of the sea) to wash ashore; — bestemmie, to pour out curses. **-amento** *m.* vomiting. **-ativo** *adj.* vomitory, vomitive. (**-atore** *m.* **-atrice** *f.*) **-ato·rio** *m.* (*pl.* -atorii) (med.) emetic. **-ivo** *adj., n.m.* emetic.

vo·mit-o *m.* vomit; vomiting; mi faceva venir —, it made me feel sick, it turned my stomach; (fig.) tornare al —, to return to bad habits; far —, to nauseate, to sicken. **-o·rio** *m.* (med.) emetic; (Rom. antiq.) *vomitorium*, gangway in theatres, etc. **-urazione** *f.* (med.) regurgitation.

†**vomuto** *part.* of **vomere**[2], q.v.

von·gola *f.* (zool.) *Amigdala decussata*, an edible bivalve; also other similar species.

vorac-e *adj.* voracious; insatiable; ravenous, ravening; avid; ravaging, devastating. **-emente** *adv.* voraciously; insatiably; ravenously; avidly. **-ità** *f.* voracity; avidity; la -ità del tempo, the ravages of time.

†**vorag·gine** *f.* See **voragine**.

vor-a·gine *f.* whirlpool; gulf; abyss; chasm; gorge; hollow; (fig.) bottomless pit; gap; situation in which financial demands cannot be met; insatiable eater. **-aginoso** *adj.* full of whirlpools, full of chasms; forming a whirlpool; forming an abyss, chasm, gulf, etc. **-ago** *f.* (poet.) see **voragine**.

†**vorare** *vb.* and derivs. see **divorare**.

vor·tic-e *m.* vortex; whirlpool; whirlwind; (fig.) tumult, turmoil; whirl, whirling; gettarsi nel — della danza, to throw oneself into the whirling stream of the dance; il — della vita, the maelstrom of life. **-oso** *adj.* vortical; whirling; tumultuous; full of whirlwinds; full of whirlpools.

vortiginoso *adj.* vertiginous, whirling.

†**vosco** *prn.* with you; known among you.

Vosgi *pr.n.m.pl.* (geog.) Vosges.

†**vosignori·a** *f.* See **vossignoria**.

vossignori·a *f.* your lordship; your ladyship; (pop.) sir; madam.

†**vosso**, †**vosto** *poss. adj., prn.* See **vostro**.

vostr-o *poss. adj.* 2nd pers. pl. your; un — amico, a friend of yours; la -a mercè, thanks to you; tutto —, yours ever; -a eccellenza, Your Excellency; il — Ariosto, your beloved Ariosto; *poss. prn.* yours; your property, your belongings; i -i, your people, your family; your followers; your friends; una delle -e, one of your tricks; dite la -a, you tell your story.

vot-are[1] [A I] and derivs. see **vuotare**. **-aborse** *adj. indecl.* expensive; *n.m. indecl.* squanderer, spendthrift; expensive item, great expense. **-acan·teri** *adj. indecl.* menial; *n.m., f. indecl.* menial servant; skivvy. **-acapo** *m. indecl.* bore, tedious person. **-acase** *adj. indecl.* extravagant, prodigal; *n.m.* spendthrift. **-acassette** *m. indecl.* postman clearing boxes. **-acessi** *m. indecl.* cesspool emptier. **-ag·gine** *f.* emptiness; vacuity, empty-headedness, inability to think; ho una -aggine, my mind is a blank; discorso che è una -aggine, empty-headed talk. †**-agione** *f.* emptying; evacuation of the bowels. **-ama·dia** *m. indecl.* prodigious eater. **-ame** *m.* emptiness; empty things, empties; (joc.) pieno di -ame, full of nothing, empty. **-amento** *m.* emptying; evacuation. **-apentole** *m. indecl.* (joc.) dinner-time. **-apolla·i** *m. indecl. adj.* poultry-thief. **-apozzi** *m. indecl.* well cleaner. **-ascodelle** *m. indecl.* glutton; *adj.* gluttonous. **-ata** *f.* emptying; turning out; cleaning out; evacuation. **-ato** *part. adj.* emptied. (**-atore** *m.* **-atrice** *f.*) **-atura** *f.* emptying; turning out.

vot-are[2] [A I] *tr.* to vote; — una proposta, to vote in favour of a proposal; to devote, to dedicate, to consecrate; to make a vow of; — un tempio ad Apollo, to vow a temple to Apollo; (rel.) -are la verginità a, to make a vow of virginity to; *intr.* (aux. avere) to vote; il diritto di —, the right to vote; — per, to vote for; — per alzata di mani, to vote by show of hands; — per divisione, to take a separate vote; preghiera di — per..., vote for...; — contro, to vote against; *rfl.* to offer oneself, to devote oneself; -arsi alla scienza, to dedicate oneself to science; -arsi alla morte, to risk one's life; to entrust oneself; -arsi agli dei, to commend oneself to the gods. **-ante** *part. adj.* voting; *n.m.* voter. **-ato** *part. adj.* voted for, carried; vowed, dedicated, devoted, consecrated; doomed; -ato alla distruzione, doomed to destruction; è -ato alla morte, he's as good as dead. **-atore** *m.* voter. (**-atrice** *f.*) **-azione** *f.* vote; voting; -azione segreta, secret ballot; -azione per alzata di mano, vote by show of hands; -azione per appello nominale, vote by roll-call; astenersi dalla -azione, to abstain from voting; dichiarare aperta la -azione, to open the voting; passare alla -azione, to proceed to a vote; porre in -azione, to put to the vote; venire alla -azione, to come to the vote; il giorno della -azione, polling day.

votazza *f.* scoop; ladle; bailer.

votezza *f.* emptiness; vacuity (cf. **vuoto**).

vot-o[1] *m.* vow; emettere —, to take a vow; mancare al —, to break a vow; fare un — di, to make a vow to; -i di marinari, vows made by sailors in time of danger never to go to sea again, i.e. empty vows; (eccl.) -i religiosi, semplici, solenni, religious, simple, solemn, vows; votive offering; votive tablet, picture, statue, etc.; prayer, solemn wish, desire; questo è il nostro —, this is our earnest wish; vote; mettere ai -i, to put to the vote; — palese, open vote; scheda di —, voting-paper, ballot paper; — consultivo, advisory vote (which does not count, as opposed to) — deliberativo, effective vote (which does); indicatore del —, vote-indicator; (finan.) con — deliberativo, with a right to vote; azione con — limitato, share with limited voting rights; azione a — plurimo, share with multiple voting rights; con — consultivo, without a right to vote; emettere un — preponderante, to give a casting vote; rettificare il proprio —, to change one's vote; ritornare su un —, to go back upon a vote; — per alzata e seduta, rising vote; (at school, etc.) mark; pieni -i, full marks; avere buoni -i negli esami, to get good marks in the exams. †**-ire** *vb.* and derivs. see **votare**. **-ivo** *adj.* votive; offerta -iva, votive offering.

voto[2] *adj.* (poet.). See **vuoto**.

†**voto**[3] *part.* of **votare**[1], q.v.

vox angelica, voxumana (mus.). See **voce**.

†**vui** *pers. prn.* See **voi**.

Vulc-ano[1] *pr.n.m.* (Rom. myth.) Vulcan. **-anale**, **-a·nio** *adj.* relating to Vulcan.

vulc-ano[2] *m.* volcano; — spento, extinct volcano; (fig.) essere sopra un —, to be on the edge of a volcano; essere un —, avere la testa come un —, to be given to flashes of imagination, to be seething with ideas. **-a·nico** *adj.* volcanic; (fig.) fiery, impetuous; testa -anica, person with impetuous ideas. **-anismo** *m.* (geol.) vulcanism; plutonism. **-anite** *f.* ebonite, vulcanite, hard rubber. **-anizzare** [A I] (techn.) to vulcanize, to cure (rubber). (**-anizzato** *part. adj.*) **-anizzazione** *f.* vulcanization; -anizzazione a freddo, cold cure. **-anologi·a** *f.* vulcanology. **-anolo·gico** *adj.* vulcanological. **-ano·logo** *m.* vulcanologist.

vulgano *m.* (mus.) a trumpet of tenor register (used in Monteverdi's 'Orfeo').

†**vulgare** *adj.* and derivs. See **volgare**.

vulgata *f.* See **volgata**.

vulgo[1] *m.* See **volgo**.

vulgo[2] *adv.* Lat. (joc.) commonly, vulgarly, in vulgar language.

vulner-are [A I S] *tr.* to wound; to hurt; to violate; to offend; — la legge, to offend against the law. -a·bile *adj.* vulnerable; punto -abile, weak point. -abilità *f.* vulnerability; (naut.) vulnerability, i.e. deficiency in armour against attack on certain bearings and ranges. -a·ria *f.* (bot.) kidney-vetch, *Anthyllis vulneraria*. -a·rio *adj.* healing, having healing properties. -ato *part. adj.* wounded; offended; (of law, principle, etc.) violated, outraged.

†**vul·t-ore, -ure, -uro** *m.* See **avvoltoio**.

vulv-a *f.* (anat.) vulva. -a·ria *f.* stinking goosefoot, *Chenopodium vulvaria*. -a·rio *adj.* (anat.) vulvar. -ite *f.* (med.) vulvitis.

vuot-are [A I] *tr.* to empty; to turn out, to clear out; to strip; to rifle; — la casa, (of burglars) to carry off everything in the house; — le tasche a uno, to clean someone out, to strip someone of all his money; — il sacco, to have one's say, to 'spill the beans'; — l'arcione, to fall from the saddle; (naut.) — il bacino, to pump out a dock; — la sentina, to dry out the bilges; — la zavorra; to unballast; *rfl.* to empty; to be emptied; la sala si -a, the room is emptying; mi sono -ato il capo, my mind has become a complete blank. -ato *part. adj.* emptied; cleaned out. -atura *f.* emptying.

vuot-o *adj.* empty; mezzo —, half-empty; hollow; vacant, unoccupied; free; deserted; unpeopled; (of an animal) unladen; a mani -e, empty-handed; rimanere a mani -e, to have one's hopes dashed, to be disillusioned; sentirsi il capo —, to be unable to think; avere il cuore —, to have no heart; a corpo —, on an empty stomach; — di, lacking in, empty of; parole -e di senso, senseless words; empty, vain; meaningless, inane; aimless, silly, empty-headed, unthinking, futile; free; — di cure, carefree; (herald.) voided; *n.m.* empty space, qui c'è un —, here is an empty place; (archit.) misurare — per pieno, to reckon the extent of a wall as if it were full (i.e. without openings); (naut.) — per pieno, dead freight; i.e. payment due to a ship for incomplete filling of a hold; empty bottle, empty container; rispedire i -i, to send back the empties; lasciare un —, to leave a gap; ha lasciato un gran — fra noi, we feel his loss very much; a —, in vain, vainly, to no effect; andare a —, to fail, to come to nothing; (mus.) suonare a —, to play silently; (phys.) vacuum; (radio) valvola a — spinto, hard valve; (aeron.) — d'aria, air pocket; (eng.) absence of load; a —, no-load; marciare a —, to idle; (philos.) vacuum, void; (comm.) — di cassa, cash deficit; un assegno a —, worthless cheque, (colloq.) stumer; emptiness, vanity, silliness, inanity, futility; il — di quel libro, the inanity of that book. (-amẹnte *adv.*) -o·metro *m.* (phys.) vacuum-metre, vacuum gauge.

†**vuovo** *m.* See **uovo**.

vuovolo *m.* See **ovolo**.

w *m.* (pron. **doppio vu**) the letter W; (written W) monogram for viva!, q.v. under **vivere**.

wafer *m. indecl.* (pron. as Eng.) biscuit, wafer.

wagner-iano *adj.* (mus.) Wagnerian. -ịsmo *m.* (mus.) Wagnerism.

water-closet *m. indecl.* (pron. as Eng.) lavatory.

watt *m. indecl.* (pron. **vat**) (electr.) watt; — ora (electr.) watt-hour; kilo —, 1000 watts. -i·metro *m.* (electr.) watt-meter.

wealdiano *adj.* (geol.) Wealden.

wernerite *f.* (miner.) wernerite.

western *m. indecl.* (cinem.) western.

whewellite *f.* (miner.) whewellite.

willemite *f.* (miner.) willemite.

witherite *f.* (miner.) witherite.

wolfra·m-io *m.* (chem.) wolfram, tungsten. -ite *f.* (miner.) wolframite, peanut ore.

wollastonite *f.* (miner.) wollastonite, tabular spar.

wulfenite *f.* (miner.) wulfenite.

wurstel *m. indecl.* a small sausage.

wurzite *f.* (miner.) wurzite.

x *m., f.* (pron. **ics**) the letter X; gambe a —, crooked legs, knock-knees; un — qualsiasi, Tom, Dick or Harry; *f.* (math.) una —, an unknown; raggi X, X-rays.

xantofilla *f.* (chem.) xanthophyll, lutein.

xantoma *m.* (med.) xanthoma.

xantopsi·a *f.* (med.) xanthopsia.

xeno *m.* (chem.) xenon.

†**xenodo·chio** *m.* hostel for foreigners.

xen-ofobi·a *f.* hatred of foreigners, xenophobia. -o·fobo *m.* enemy of foreigners, hater of foreigners, xenophobe; *adj.* hostile to foreigners.

Xeres *pr.n.m.* (geog.) Jerez de la Frontera; sherry.

xero·fite *f.* (bot.) xerophyte.

xerofor·mio *m.* (pharm.) xeroform, bismuth tribromophenate.

xifo·id-e *adj.* xiphoid, ensiform; *n.f.* (anat.) xiphoid cartilage. -e·o *adj.* (anat.) xiphoid. -ite *f.* (med.) xiphoiditis.

xilema *m.* (bot.) xylem.

xilene *m.* (chem.) xylene.

xilo·fago *m.* (ent.) xylophagous, wood-eating.

xilo·fon-o *m.*, **-ista** *m.* (mus.) See **silofon-o, -ista**.

xil-ografi·a *f.* (art of) wood-engraving; woodcut. -ogra·fico *adj.* pertaining to wood-engraving. -o·grafo *m.* wood-engraver.

xilo·ide *adj.* (miner.) xyloid.

xilolite *f.* wood chipboard, hardboard.

xilolo *m.* (chem.) xylene.

xilologi·a *f.* See **silologia**.

xiloteca *f.* See **siloteca**.

y *f., m.* (pron. **ipsilon**, but generally called 'i greco') the letter Y; a —, in the form of a Y.

yacht *m. indecl.* (pron. as Eng.) (naut.) yacht; uno — a vela con motore ausiliario, a sailing yacht with auxiliary motor; — a vapore, steam yacht; — bimotore, twin screw yacht; — d'alto mare, seagoing yacht; — da corsa, — da regata, racing yacht; — da crociera, a cruising yacht; — armato a goletta, schooner-rigged yacht.

yama·maī *adj. indecl.* (ent.) farfalla —, Japanese oak silk moth.

yankee *m. indecl.* (pron. as Eng.; derog.) American.

yataga·n *m. indecl.* yataghan, Turkish sword.

yoga *m. indecl.* lo —, yoga.

yoghurt *m. indecl.* yoghourt.

yole *f.* See **iole**.

yprite *f.* (mil.) yperite, mustard gas.

yucca *f.* See **iucca**.

yuta *f.* See **iuta**.

z *f.* (pron. **zeta**) the letter Z; the consonant Z; — dolce, voiced Z (as in **zeta**); — aspra, unvoiced Z (as in **zio**); dall'A alla —, from A to Z; essere A e —, to be the beginning and the end, to be alpha and omega; non distinguere l'acca dalla —, to be unable to read; gambe a —, crooked legs.

za[1] *excl.* (onom.) swish!

†**za**[2] *adv.* See **qua**.

†**zaba** *f.* (mil. hist.) kind of armour.

zabaglione *m.* See **zabaione**.

zabaione *m.* sweet made of beaten-up egg yolks, sugar, and Marsala wine; egg flip; (fig.) medley, muddle, confusion, mix-up.

†**zabattiero** *m.* See **ciabattiere**, under **ciabatta**.

†**zaccarale** *m.* wringer; press.

zac·cher-a *f.* splash of mud; mud-spot; dried dung on goats and sheep; (fig.) trifle, bagatelle; *pl.* (Florence) a bit of extra money made on the side. -one *m.* slovenly person; mud-bespattered individual. (-ọna *f.*) -oso *adj.* spattered with mud.

zaf, zaffe, zaf·fete *excl.* (onom.) swish!

zafardare [A I] and derivs. See **inzafardare**.

zaff-are [A I] *tr.* to plug, to bung, to stop up; †to arrest, to seize. -amẹnto *m.* plugging, stopping up. -ata *f.* whiff (of foul air), stench; spurt, splash; -ata di fumo, belch of smoke; angry words, recriminations. -atura *f.* plugging, stopping up.

†**zaf·fera** *f.* blue paint based on cobalt.

zafferan-o *m.* (bot.) saffron; — coltivato, saffron crocus, *Crocus sativus*; — bastardo, meadow saffron, naked ladies, autumn

zafferan-o (*cont.*)

crocus, *Colchicum autumnale*; — falso, — saracinesco, safflower, *Carthamus tinctorius*; — selvatico, saffron, *Crocus vernus*; di —, saffron-coloured; viso di —, yellow face, sallow face; (orn.) lesser black-backed gull, *Larus fuscus*. **-ato** *adj.* flavoured with saffron; saffron-coloured. **-ino** *adj.* saffron-coloured. **~one** *m.* (bot.) safflower, *Carthamus tinctorius*.

†zaffe·tica *f.* corruption of **assa fetida**, q.v., under **fetido**.

zaffirina *f.* (zool.) *Sapphirina gemma*, a luminous pelagic copepod.

zaffiro *m.* sapphire.

zaffo *m.* wooden plug, bung; (joc.) little runt; (mil.) oakum wad used for cleaning the bore of a gun; †police-spy.

zaffrone *m.* (bot.). See **zafferanone**, under **zafferano**.

zaga·gli·a *f.* assegai; (native) spear; (mil. hist.) spear, lance; (archaeol.) bone point. **-ata** *f.* thrust with an assegai; thrust with a spear.

†zaganella *f.* mockery, scorn, derision; kind of rope.

za·gara *f.* (bot., Sicil. dial.) orange blossom.

Zagra·bia *pr.n.f.* (geog.) Zagreb, Agram.

zagrino *m.* (ichth.) *Etmopterus spinax*, a kind of dogfish, from whose liver a medicinal oil, similar to cod-liver oil, is prepared; the same name, or variants of it, is also applied to *Centrophorus granulosus*, a related dogfish, whose liver also yields oil, and whose skin provides a kind of shagreen used as sandpaper by cabinet makers.

†za·ina *f.* cradle.

za·ino[1] *m.* (mil.) knapsack, kit-bag, pack; fare lo —, to pack one's kit; school-bag, satchel; shepherd's goat-skin purse.

za·ino[2] *adj.* (vet.) dark chestnut colour of a horse.

zamaru·golo *m.* (zool.) pelican's foot shell, *Aporrhais pes-pelicani*.

†zamarra *f.* See **zimarra**.

†zambecco *m.* (naut.). See **sciabello**.

zamberlucco *m.* long Turkish coat.

†zambra *f.* room, little room.

†zambracca *f.* kitchen wench; loose woman.

zambu·ca *f.*, **-co**, **-cco** *m.* (naut.). See **sambucco**.

zambuco *m.* (bot.). See **sambuco**.

zamp-a *f.* paw; claw; leg (of an animal, bird or insect); foot (of an animal); (joc.) foot of a human being; hoof; ~e di gallina, 'crows-feet' (wrinkles near the eyes); (tan.) shank; (cul.) shin; ~e di maiale, pig's trotters; claw-foot (of a table, etc.); (joc.) hand, 'paw'; giù le ~e!, hands off!; leccare le ~e a uno, to flatter someone, to fawn on someone, to lick someone's boots; (naut.) — d'oca, crowsfoot; †palm (of an anchor); †crowsfoot on a sheet. **-are** [A I] *intr.* (aux. avere) to paw the ground; to lash out (with paw or hoof); to stamp. **-ata** *f.* blow with a paw; kick; hoof-mark, claw-mark, footprint; (mus.) skirl; (fig.) ungracious action, surly behaviour; *gaffe*; dare una -ata, to 'put one's foot in it'. **-eggiare** [A 3 c] *intr.* (aux. avere) (of horses) to paw the ground impatiently; (of cattle, when ploughing) to walk unevenly. **-ettare** [A I c] *intr.* (aux. avere) to toddle; to totter. **-etto** *m. dim.* of **zampa**; -etto di lepre, hare's foot (used as a duster); (Rome. S. Ital.) peasant wearing cloth and leather puttees instead of shoes. **-icare** [A 2 s] *intr.* (aux. avere) see **ciampicare**. **-ino** *m. dim.* of **zampa**; (provb.) tanto va la gatta al lardo che ci lascia lo -ino, be sure your sins will find you out; (fig.) mettere lo -ino in, to stick one's nose in, to interfere in, to have a finger in; (bot.) Norway spruce, *Picea abies*. **-one** *m. augm.* of **zampa**; (cul.) skin of a pig's foot stuffed with sausage meat; -one di Modena, the same, stewed with lentils.

zampill-are [A I] *intr.* (aux. essere, avere) to gush forth, to spurt, to squirt; to spring; *tr.* to cause to spurt. **-ante** *part. adj.* (of water) gushing, springing; fontana -ante, leaping fountain. **-io** *m.* continual spurting. **-o** *m.* jet, spurt, gush; fountain.

zampogn-a *f.* (mus.) rustic bagpipe. **-are** [A 5] *intr.* (aux. avere) (mus.) to pipe. **-aro** *m.* (mus.) piper. **-etta** *f. dim.* (mus.) little pipe.

zan-a *f.* (Tusc.) basket; cradle, Moses basket; basketful; recess, depression; pond, pool (of stagnant water); (archit.) niche; †deception, trick; †appiccare ~e, to put the blame on other people. **-a·io**, **-aro** *m.* (Tusc.) basket-maker. **†-ai(u)olo** *m.* hired man who brought food in baskets and was sometimes employed as cook. **-ata** *f.* (Tusc.) basketful; una -ata di pere, a basket of pears.

zanc-a *f.* (naut.) steering oar; (Ven.) leeboard; †leg; shin; end; shaft. **†-ato** *adj.* folded back at one end.

†zanco *m.* See **fianco**.

†zandado *m.* See **zendado**.

zanfarda *f.* immoral woman.

zan·gol-a *f.* churn. **-are** [A I s] *tr., intr.* (aux. avere) to churn.

zangone *m.* (naut.) scantlings near bow or stern.

zann-a *f.* fang; tusk; dar di — a, to fang, to sink one's fangs into; mostrare le ~e, to snarl; (techn.) bone, burnisher, boning tool. **-are** [A I] *tr.* to fang; (techn.) to burnish, to bone. **-ata** *f.* bite, savaging; scar from fangs. **-ato** *part. adj.* bitten, savaged; (techn.) burnished, boned. **-uto** *adj.* with fangs, fanged; (of a person) with ugly teeth, with protruding teeth.

Zann-i *pr.n.m.* (dial. Bergamo) Johnny, Jack (abbrev. of **Giovanni**); (theatr.) clown; zany. **-ata** *f.* clowning; farce. **-eri·a** *f.* clowning; buffoonery. **-esco** *adj.* (*m.pl.* **-eschi**) jesting, comic.

†zano *m.* See **zaino**.

zanzar-a *f.* (ent.) gnat, mosquito; — comune, gnat, *Culex pipiens*; (joc.) irritating individual; voce di —, thin, piping voice; avere una — nella testa, to have a bee in one's bonnet. **-iera** *f.*, **-iere** *m.* mosquito-net. **-ino** *m.* (joc.) instrument which makes a buzzing sound. **-one** *m.* (ent.) mosquito, *Anopheles* spp.

†zanzaverata *f.* sauce; ointment.

†zan·zero *m.* dissolute young man.

zappa *f.* mattock; — meccanica, sap; (mil.) entrenching tool; — coperta, covered sap; — volante, fast dug sap; (fig.) darsi la — sui piedi, to defeat one's ends; (provb.) al villano la — in mano, every man to his trade; †number 7; †essere alle due ~e, to be 77 years old.

zapp-are [A I] *tr., intr.* (aux. avere) to dig with a mattock; (provb.) sto coi frati e -o l'orto, I am quietly minding my own business; (of horses) to paw the ground, to stamp; (fig.) -are i denari, to have money to burn; -are il pianoforte, to bang the piano, i.e. to play with too heavy a touch. **-amento** *m.* digging. **-ata** *f.* digging; blow with a mattock; amount dug; dare una -ata a, to dig, to turn over, to dig round. **-aterra** *m. indecl.* farm-labourer; clod-hopper. **-ato** *part. adj.* hoed; dug; turned; orto -ato di fresco, garden of which the soil has been freshly turned. **-atore** *m.* hoer; digger; agricultural labourer; (mil.) sapper. **-atura** *f.* hoeing; digging; ground dug; loosened soil.

zappata[1] *f.* See under **zappa**.

Zappata[2] *pr.n.m.* an imaginary friar mentioned in the proverbial saying, 'Padre — che predicava bene e razzolava male'; fare come Padre —, to contradict oneself, not to practise what one preaches.

zappett-a *f. dim.* of **zappa**; hoe; pick. **-are** [A I c] *tr.* to hoe; to dig lightly; *abs.* to do a little digging. **-ina** *f. dim.* light hoe.

zappon-e *m. augm.* of **zappa**; heavy mattock. **-are** [A I c] *tr., intr.* (aux. avere) to dig with a 'zappone'.

zaptiè *m. indecl.* native soldier of the former Italian colony of Eritrea.

Zar *pr.n.m.* (hist.) Tsar. **-e·vic** *pr.n.m.* Tsarevitch. **-ina** *pr.n.f.* Tsarina.

zar-a *f.* hazard, chance; game of chance played with three dice; a low point in the game; mettersi a —, to take a risk, to expose oneself to risk. †**-o** *m.* see **zara**. †**-oso** *adj.* hazardous, risky.

Zaragoza, Zaragozza *pr.n.f.* (geog.) Saragossa.

zarzuela *f.* (theatr.) comedy or farce with music and spoken dialogue (a Spanish form of comic opera).

zatta *f.* (bot.) a kind of melon; (naut.) barge, dumb lighter.

zat·ter-a *f.* (naut.) raft; lighter; — bersaglio, torpedo float; ponte di ~e, pontoon bridge; — di salvataggio, life raft; (Tusc.) ferry. **-iere** *m.* lighterman. **-ino** *m. dim.* float; Balsa raft.

zavorr-a *f.* (naut.) ballast; nave in —, ship in ballast (i.e. without cargo); paleggiare bene la —, to distribute ballast correctly; (fig.) unnecessary trimmings and accessories. **-a·i** *m.pl.* (naut.) ballast labourers. **-amento** *m.* (naut.) ballasting. **-ante** *part. adj.* ballasting; *n.m.* (naut.) ballast barge. **-are** [A I] *tr.* (naut.) to ballast. **-a·tico** *m.* (naut.) ballast dues. **-ato** *part. adj.* (naut.) ballasted. **-atura** *f.* (naut.) act or effect of ballasting.

†zazze-are *intr.* to stroll, to wander about. †**-ato** *adj.* andare -ato, to go strolling about.

zaz·zer-a *f.* long hair (in men), hair worn down to the shoulders (e.g. Garibaldi); portare la —, to wear one's hair long (of a man); page-boy style of hair; (neol.) of women's hair) page-boy bob; (of a lion) mane; (fig.) colla —, antiquated, 'out of the Ark'; (paperm.) deckle-edge. **-ato** *adj.* (of a man) long-haired. **-one** *m.* long hair, shock of hair; man with long hair; (derog.) an old-fashioned looking elderly person. **-uto** *adj.* (of a man) with long hair; (of a plant) leafy.

†**zeba** *f.* goat; kid.

zebbare [A I] (Tusc.). See **inzeppare**.

Zebed-e·o *pr.n.m.* (Bibl.) Zebedee. **-e·i** *pr.n.m.pl.* the sons of Zebedee, James and John; (joc.) testicles.

zebr-a *f.* (zool.) zebra. **-ata.** *f* (motor.) zebra-crossing. **-ato** *m.* a horse or ass with traces of stripes on its coat; *adj.* striped; (motor.) passaggio pedonale -ato, zebra-crossing. **-atura** *f.* stripes; striped effect; cracks and lines in ceilings and walls; (motor.) -atura con strisce inclinate, traffic island; -atura con strisce parallele, pedestrian-crossing.

zebù *m. indecl.* (zool.) zebu.

zecc-a¹ *f.* (zool.) tick. **-aiuola, -aruola** *f.* (ent.) mole cricket, *Gryllotalpa*.

zecc-a² *f.* mint (for money); (fig.) nuovo di —, brand new; (joc.) unguento di —, money, 'palm-oil'; (bot.) name of several umbelliferous plants. †**-are** *tr.* to coin, to mint.

zecchiere *m.* superintendent at a mint; coiner.

zecchinẹtta *f.* (cards) lansquenet, a game of German origin formerly called 'lanzichinetto'.

zecchino *m.* (numism.) small coin; (Tusc.) — gigliato, florin; sequin; (Ven.) gold coin (value about half a sovereign); oro di —, purest gold; non devi prendere tutto per oro di —, all is not gold that glisters; giallo come l'oro di —, golden-yellow.

zẹccol-a *f.* bur; trifle, bagatelle; petty detail. **-o** *m.* tangle of wool; tangle of straw.

zedoa·ria *f.* (bot.) zedoary, *Curcuma zedoaria*.

zẹ·f(f)iro *m.* zephyr; light breeze; prospero —, favourable wind, (fig.) good fortune; (text.) light cloth of wool and cotton; (joc.) icy blast; *pl.* (Tusc.) gossips.

zegrino *m.* (ichth.). See **zagrino**.

zeida *f.* (chem.) zein.

zelamina *f.* (geol.) (miner.) calamine, smithsonite.

Zelanda *pr.n.f.* (geog.) Zealand; la Nuova —, New Zealand.

zẹl-o *m.* zeal; fervour; ardour. **-ante** *adj.* zealous; fervent; ardent; conscientious; overzealous; anxious to please; non troppo -ante, somewhat indifferent; non troppo -ante della sua bellezza, not very particular about her looks; -ante di, anxious about, concerned about; *n.m.* zealot; fare lo -ante, to be overzealous. **-antemẹnte** *adv.* zealously; fervently. **-anteri·a** *f.* excess of zeal; zealotry. **-are** [A I] *intr.* (*aux.* avere) to be zealous; to be a fervent supporter; *tr.* to champion. **-ato** *part. adj.* zealous. **-atọre** *m.* zealot. (**-atrice** *f.*) **-ọso** *adj.* zealous. †**-ote** *adj.* zealous; *n.m.* zealot.

†**zemb-o**, †**-uto** *adj.* distorted; deformed; hunchbacked.

zendado *m.* sendal, a kind of silken material; head-dress or head-covering of fine silk.

zendavesta *m.* (Zoroastrian rel.) Zend-Avesta.

†**zendoluto** *adj.* hairy; fringed.

zẹ·nit *m. indecl.* (astron.) (geog.) zenith; (fig.) zenith, acme, highest point. **-ale** *adj.* zenithal; cerchio -ale, vertical circle; (astron.) distanza -ale, zenith distance.

†**zentano** *m.* See **zendado**.

†**zenzeri·a** *f.* mixture, medley; confusion.

zen·zero *m.* (bot.) ginger, rootstock of *Zingiber officinale*.

zẹo-lite *f.* (miner.) zeolite. **-sco·pio** *m.* (phys.) ebullioscope.

zẹpp-a *f.* wedge; bung; metterci una —, to wedge; (in writing) padding; repetitive section; poor excuse; mettere delle -e, to put a spanner in the works, *or* to stir up discord; mettere -e tra marito e moglie, to come between husband and wife; a form of the game of charades, in which a letter is introduced in a given word thus forming a new one (e.g. **libro**, **lib-e-ro**). **-are** [A I c] and derivs. see **inzeppare**.

zẹppo¹ *adj.* full; crammed; packed; full to bursting point; *adv.* pieno —, packed tight, packed like sardines.

†**zeppo²** *m.* alms-box.

Zerbin-o¹ *pr.n.m.* Zerbino, a character in Ariosto's *Orlando Furioso*; (fig.) dandy, coxcomb, beau. **-eri·a** *f.* dandified elegance. **-ẹsco** *adj.* (*m.pl.* -ẹschi) dandified. (**-escamẹnte** *adv.*) **-otto** *m.* dandy, fop.

zerbino² *m.* door-mat.

zerbino³ *m.* plug, bung.

†**zerbo** *m.* fare —, to fight.

zerene *f.* (ent.) currant moth, *Abraxas grossulariata*.

zeriba *f.* stockade.

zero¹ *m.* zero; nought (as in telephone numbers); (fig.) nil; uno —,

a mere nothing; spaccare lo —, to account for every halfpenny; (mil.) sparare a —, to fire with zero degree of elevation.

zero² *m.* (ichth.) sand-smelt, *Atherina hepsetus*.

zerolo *m.* (ichth.). See **zerro**.

zerro *m.* (ichth.) — coronato, — della corona, *Spicara alcedo*, — di scoglio, *S. vulgaris*, edible marine fish.

zeta *m.*, *f.* (*pl.* zeta, zete) name of the letter Z; the letter Z, q.v.

†**zetano** *m.* a heavy silken material.

zetẹ·tico *adj.* (philos.) zetetic, investigative (method, dialogue).

zẹ·ugma, †**zẹ·uma** *m.* (rhet.) zeugma.

Ze·us *pr.n.m.* (myth.) Zeus.

†**zevadera**, †**zevedera** *f.* (naut.) square sail on the bowsprit.

zẹzzio *m.* whistling, whirring; scolding.

†**zezzo** *adj.* last; *adv. phr.* al da —, at last (also **sezzo**).

†**zezzolo** *m.* nipple.

zi *excl.* pst!

zi·a *f.* aunt; grande —, great-aunt; stepmother; (colloq.) house-maid's-knee. **-ẹtta** *f. dim.* auntie.

†**ziano** *m.* See **zio**.

zibaldọne *m.* medley, miscellany; notebook; commonplace book; record of day-to-day thoughts, jottings; lo — del Leopardi, the Leopardi notebooks.

zibellino *m.* (zool.) sable, *Mustela zibellina*; sable fur, sable skin; *adj.* of sable.

zibẹ(t)t-o *m.* (zool.) musk rat, musquash, *Ondatra zibethica*. **-ato** *adj.* musky, musk-scented.

zibibbo *m.* a kind of sweet grape, sold also as raisins.

ziẹsco *adj.* See under **zio**.

ziẹtta *f. dim.* See under **zia**.

†**zifera**, †**zifra** *f.* See **cifra**.

ziffe *excl.* (onom.) swish!; zip!

zi·fio *m.* (zool.) *Ziphius* spp., a kind of dolphin.

zifọne *m.* See **sifone**.

zigano *m.*, *adj.* Hungarian gipsy, tzigane.

zigare [A 2] *intr.* (*aux.* avere) (of a rabbit) to squeak; to squeak like a rabbit.

zigarella *f.* (ichth.) *Coris julis*, rainbow wrasse.

zi·garo *m.* See **sigaro**.

zigena, zighena *f.* (ent.) burnet moth; *Zygaena* spp.

zighe-zaghe *m.* (Tusc.). See **zigzag**.

zig-odat·tile *adj.* (orn.) zygodactylous. **-omorfo** *adj.* (bot.) zygomorphic. **-ote** *f.* (biol.) zygote.

zi·golo *m.* (orn.) bunting; — boschereccio, rustic bunting, *Emberiza rustica*; — delle nevi, snow bunting, *Plectrophenax nivalis*; — giallo, yellow bunting, *Emberiza citrinella*; — minore, little bunting; *E. pusilla*; — muciatto, rock bunting, *E. cia*; — nero, cirl bunting, *E. cirlus*; — testanera, black-headed bunting, *E. melanocephala*.

zi·gom-a, **-o** *m.* (anat.) zygoma, cheek-bone. **-a·tico** *adj.* (anat.) zygomatic.

zigrin-are [A I] *tr.* (tan.) to grain, to board, to pebble; (eng.) to knurl. **-ato** *adj.* (tan.) grained, boarded, pebbled; (eng.) knurled. **-atura** *f.* (tan.) graining, etc.; (eng.) knurling; knurl.

zigrino *m.* See **zagrino**.

zigzag *m. indecl.* zigzag; *adv. phr.* a —, zigzag; camminare a —, to walk zigzag; *pl.* (mil.) trenches built in a zigzag; (ent.) gipsy moth, *Lymantria dispar*; (paperm.) piegato a —, lapped in and in. **-are** [A 2] *intr.* (*aux.* avere) to zigzag.

zimarra *f.* robe; dressing-gown; priest's cassock.

zim·balon *m.* (mus.) cimbalom, dulcimer.

zimbẹll-o *m.* (orn.) bird used as decoy; (fig.) attraction; bribe; object of ridicule; essere lo —, servire di —, to be the butt; †little sack stuffed with padding or ashes used by boys in mock battles. **-are** [A I] *tr.* to lure (esp. birds); *intr.* (*aux.* avere) to flirt, to be flirtatious; to be alluring. **-atọra** *f.* flirt. **-atọre** *m.* allurer, enticer. (**-atrice** *f.*)

zimbro *m.* (bot.) arolla pine, *Pinus cembra*.

zi·mico *adj.* (chem.) zymotic, pertaining to fermentation.

†**zimino** *m.* food consisting mainly of vegetables for use on days of abstinence; in —, cooked with vegetables in casserole.

zimmoca *f.* (zool.) *Hippospongia equina*, a Mediterranean species of sponge, of inferior quality.

zim-ologi·a *f.* zymology. **-oma** *m.* zymoma. **-osi** *f.* zymosis. **-osi·metro** *m.* zymometer. **-otecni·a** *f.* zymotechnics. **-otec·nico** *adj.* zymotechnic. **-o·tico** *adj.* zymotic.

zinale *m.* (N. Ital.) apron.

zinc-o *m.* (chem.; metall.) zinc; — commerciale, spelter; bianco di —, zinc white; (typ.) block, cliché. **-are** [A 2] *tr.* to galvanize; to cover with zinc. **-ato** *part. adj.* galvanized; zinc-covered. **-ografi·a** *f.* engraving on zinc; factory in which zinc-engravings are made. **-o·grafo** *m.* zinc-engraver; (typ.) block-maker. **-otipi·a** *f.* zincotype, zincotyping.

zin·gar-o *m.* gipsy; una vita da —, a gipsy life; (mus.) musica degli -i ungheresi, Hungarian gipsy music; (paint.) lo —, nickname of Antonio Solario, of Abruzzi (d. 1455). **-ęsca** *f.* (mus.) gipsy song. **-ęsco** *adj.* (*m.pl.* **-ęschi**) gipsy, gipsy-like; wandering.

zingo *m.* (pop.). See **zinco**.

zingọne *m.* (bot.) sucker; stub of cut branch.

zinn-a *f.* nipple. **†-are** *tr.* to suck; to suckle.

zin·nia *f.* (bot.) *Zinnia*.

zinẓa·nia *f.* (bot.). See **zizzania**.

†zinzibo *m.* See **zenzero**.

zinzi·lio *m.* snuff.

zinẓilulare [A 1 S] *intr.* (*aux.* avere) to twitter (like a swallow).

zinzin-o *m.* little bit; pinch; drop, drip; crumb, morsel, speck; bere a —, to take little sips. **†-are** *intr.* to take little sips.

zinzolino *m.* See **zinzino**.

zi-o *m.* uncle; lo — Arturo, uncle Arthur; — cugino, first cousin once removed; (joc.) — d'America, rich relative who leaves one an inheritance; *excl.* (euphem. for **dio**) Good Lord!; per —!, by golly! **-ęsco** *adj.* (*m.pl.* **-ęschi**) (joc.) avuncular.

zip *m. indecl.* zip-fastener.

zi·pol-o *m.* spigot. **-are** [A 1 S] *tr.* to fasten with a spigot.

zirc-ọne *m.* (miner.) zircon, hyacinth, jargon. **-oni·a** *f.* (chem.) zirconia, zirconium oxide. **-o·nio** *m.* (chem.) zirconium.

zirl-ìo, -o *m.* trilling; trill; gli -ii d'allodole, the trilling of larks; whistling (of thrushes). **-are** [A 1] *intr.* (*aux.* avere) to trill.

ziro *m.* pitcher, jar; oil-jar; water-jar (esp. those found in Etruscan tombs).

ziro ziro *onom.* (mus.) diddle diddle (imitating fiddle-playing).

†zita *f.* See **zitella**.

zitell-a *f.* spinster; unmarried woman; old maid; **†**maid, young girl. **-ismo** *m.* soured or spinsterish outlook. **-ọna** *f.* old maid. **-ọne** *m.* old bachelor.

ziti *m.pl.* (cul.) a kind of macaroni.

†zit-o¹ *m.* (Gk. antiq.) *zuthos*, beer as known to the Greeks through travel in Egypt or the North. **†-ogala** *f.* beer and milk. **†-otecni·a** *f.* brewing.

†zito² *m.* boy; young man; bachelor; *adj.* pure, chaste.

zitt-ire [D 2] *intr.* (*aux.* avere) to hiss; to whisper; non —!, sh!, not a murmur!; to be silent; *tr.* to hiss, to boo. **-ito** *part. adj.* la commedia venne -ita, the play was hissed.

zitto¹ *adj.* quiet; silent; star —, to keep quiet, not to say a word, to be discreet; stai —!, sh!, be quiet!; zitto!, be quiet!, hold your tongue!; zitto zitto, as quiet as a mouse; *adv. phr.* alla zitta, quietly; secretly; without a word.

zitto² *m.* whisper; murmur; non si sentiva uno —, not a sound was heard, you could have heard a pin drop.

zizza¹ *f.* (zool.). See 'cocciola zizza', under **cocciola**.

zizza² *f.* (pop., vulg.) breast; nipple; teat.

ziẓẓa·nia *f.* (bot.) darnel, *Lolium temulentum*; (Bibl.) tare, cockle; (pop.) weed; zizzania, wild rice, *Zizania aquatica*; (fig.) discord; dissension; seminare —, to sow dissension.

ziẓẓol-a *f.* (Tusc.) see **giuggiola**; (fig.) blow, misfortune; *excl.* che —!, what a blow! **-o** *m.* (bot.) see **giuggiolo**.

zoan-to *m.* (zool.) sea anemone. **-tropi·a** *f.* (med.) zoanthropy.

zoarco *m.* mahout.

†zocco *m.* (archit.). See **zoccolo**.

zoc·col-o *m.* clog; sabot, wooden shoe; hoof; clod; sod; turf; (fig.) ne'er-do-well, good-for-nothing; (cul.) frittata con gli -i, mixed grill with thick pieces of ham; (archit.) plinth, socle; (eng.) base, pedestal; (brake) shoe; (bldg.) wainscot; skirting board; (radio) base (of valve), socket; (geog.) — continentale, continental slope. **-a·io** *m.* maker or vendor of wooden shoes. **-ante** *part. adj.* wearing clogs; *n.m.,* person wearing clogs; (eccl.) *m.* Observant (friar). **-are** [A 1 S] *intr.* (*aux.* avere) to go in clogs; to clatter along in clogs. **-ata** *f.* stamp with a clog; kick with a clog.

zodi·a-co *m.* (*pl.* **-chi**) (astron.) zodiac. **-cale** *adj.* (astron.) zodiacal.

zo-e·pica *f.* (lit.) epic, long poem, with animals as characters (e.g. Leopardi's *Paralipomeni*). **-foro** *m.* (archit.) z(o)ophorus, frieze.

-iatri·a *f.* see **zooiatria**. **-idiofili·a** *f.* (bot.) animal pollination. **-iero** *m.* (bot.) *Anagyris foetida*.

zo·ilo *m.* severe and carping critic (from Zoilus, the adverse critic of Homer).

zoịṣite *f.* (miner.) zoisite, thulite.

zọlf-o *m.* sulphur. **-aia** *f.* see **zolfara**. **-anello** *m.* large match with a blob of sulphur below the striking head to make it burn well out of doors; lucifer, sulphur-match. **-ara** *f.* sulphur-mine. **-are** [A 1 C] *tr.* to sulphur. **-atara** *f.* see **zolfara**. **-atura** *f.* sulphuration. **-ina** *f.* (bot.) a kind of everlasting flower. **†-ina·io** *m.* match-seller. **-ino** *adj.* sulphurous; coated with sulphur; sulphur-coloured; *n.m.* sulphur-match; (fig.) spitfire; (bot.) a kind of everlasting flower. **-orato** *adj.* sulphured; (industr.) sulphurized.

zọliano *adj.* (lit. hist.) pertaining to the novelist, Émile Zola (1840–1903); written in the style of Zola.

zoll-a *f.* clod; sod; turf; upturned soil; piece of cultivated land; glebe; aver delle -e, to have a bit of land; — di zucchero, lump of sugar; — di pane, crust of bread. **-ata** *f.* blow with a clod of earth. **-ętta** *f. dim.* lump of sugar; zucchero in -ette, lump sugar. **-ọso** *adj.* (of soil) full of clods.

zomb-are [A 1] *tr.* (Tusc., dial.) to thump; to trounce, to belabour. **-ata** *f.* thump. **-atura** *f.* trouncing. **†-olare** *vb.* see **zombare**.

zomp-are [A 1] *intr.* (*aux.* avere) (dial. Rome, S. Ital.) to leap; to jump; to romp. **-ata** *f.* leap; jump; romp; duel with knives.

zompo *m.* (dial. Rome, S. Ital.) jump.

zon-a *f.* zone; area; — verde, green belt; belt; girdle; (med.) shingles; (mil.) — militare, military zone; — di guerra, war zone; — di fuoco, fire zone, fire sector; (leg.) — franca, free zone; — di esclusiva, area of sole agency; (cards) in —, vulnerable (at bridge). **-ale** *adj.* zonal. **†-are** *tr.* to encircle; to girdle. **-ato** *adj.* divided into zones; **†**encircled; girdled. **-iẓẓare** [A 1] *tr.* (admin.) to zone. (**-iẓẓato** *part. adj.*) **-iẓẓazione** *f.* (admin.) zoning.

zonzella *f.* green-winged orchis, *Orchis morio*.

zọnzo *adv. phr.* a —, round and about, here and there; andare a —, to wander about, to saunter, to stroll; to loaf, to loiter.

zo·o *m. indecl.* zoo, zoological gardens.

zo-ocore *f.pl.* (bot.) plant adapted to animal distribution. **-ocori·a** *f.* (bot.) animal distribution. **-ofili·a** *f.* love of animals. **-o·filo** *adj.* devoted to the welfare of animals; società -ofila, society for the protection of animals. **-o·fito** *m.* (zool.) zoophyte (sea anemones, corals, sponges, etc.). **-ofobi·a** *f.* aversion to animals. **-ofo·rico** *adj.* (archit.) adorned with a zoophorus or frieze. **-oge·nico** *adj.* (geol.) zoogenic. **-ogẹnico** *adj.* (geol.) zoogenic. **-ogọmmito** *adj.* (biol.) mucoid. **-oiatri·a** *f.* veterinary surgery. **-oiatro** *m.* veterinarian, veterinary surgeon. **-olatri·a** *f.* worship of animals. **-olito** *m.* (geol.) fossil. **-ologi·a** *f.* zoology. **-olo·gico** *adj.* zoological. **-o·logo** *m.* zoologist. **-onomi·a** *f.* zoology. **-o·noṣi** *f.* zoonosis. **-opedi·a** *f.* training of animals. **-oprofilat·tico** *adj.* (vet.) zooprophylactic, pertaining to veterinary medicine. **-ospora** *f.* zoospore. **-otec·nica** *f.* animal husbandry. **-otoca** *f. Lacerta vivipara*, viviparous lizard. **-otomi·a** *f.* zootomy, animal dissection.

zoppeggiare [A 3 c]. See under **zoppo**.

zoppic-are [A 2 S] *intr.* (*aux.* avere) to limp; to be lame; to walk with a limp; to wobble, to be unsteady, to be shaky; (naut.) to be laggard (of a vessel that is slow and unhandy); (fig.) to vacillate, to waver; un verso che -a, a halting line of verse; (of arguments) not to hold water, not to stand up to examination. **-amẹnto** *m.* limping; lameness. **-ante** *part. adj.* limping; lame; unsteady; wobbly; rickety; uncertain, hesitant; uno scolare -ante in latino, a pupil who is weak in Latin; versi -anti, halting verses. **-atura** *f.* lameness. **-ọne, -ọni** *adv.* limpingly; haltingly; shakily; unsteadily; andar -oni, to limp.

zopp-o *adj.* lame; limping; halt; unsteady, shaky; wobbling, tottering; (of speech) halting, hesitant; weak, ineffectual; defective; una sedia -a, a rickety chair; (fig.) tornare a piè —, to return empty-handed, to return having accomplished nothing; *n.m.* cripple; limping man; lame man; *pl.* gli -i, the lame and the halt; (provb.) chi pratica lo — impara a zoppicare, evil communications corrupt good manners; *pr.n.m.* (astron.) Sirius, Dog star. **-a** *f.* (mus.) dance with a syncopated rhythm; contrappunto alla -a, a fourth-species counterpoint (i.e. with syncopations). **-ag·gine** *f.* lameness. **-eggiare** [A 3 c] *intr.* (*aux.* avere) to limp a bit, to have a slight limp; (fig.) to be rather underhand, not to go quite straight. **-i·a** *f.* (vet.) lameness. **-ina** *f.* (vet.) foot rot (of sheep and cattle) (also 'zoppina lombarda').

zop·polo *m.* (naut.) a kind of dug-out boat used for fishing in the Adriatic.

zo·ster *m.* (med.) herpes zoster, shingles.

zostere *m.* (naut.) rubbing strake; (archit.) band.

zo·ti·co *adj.* boorish; rough; uncouth; loutish; rough; churlish; panno —, coarse cloth; terreno —, hard soil. (**-camente** *adv.*) **-cag·gine** *f.* boorishness; coarseness; uncouth behaviour. **-chęzza** *f.* roughness; lack of polish. **-cone** *m.* boor, lout, oaf.

zot·tol-o *m.*, **-ina** *f.* (zool.) *Sepiola rondeletii*, a kind of cuttlefish.

zozz-a *f.* drink compounded of brandy and rum, sometimes flavoured with aniseed; rough spirituous liquor; (colloq.) person of no account, unimportant individual; trifle; lowering storm, threatening clouds. **-a·io** *m.* vendor of rough spirits.

zuav-o *m.* (mil.) zouave; (hist.) gli zuavi pontifici, the Papal guard; *adj.* pertaining to the zouaves; pantaloni alla -a, full knee-breeches. **-a** *f.* zouave jacket (women's fashion, nineteenth century).

zucc-a *f.* gourd; pumpkin; (slang) head, top-knot, pate; grattarsi la —, to scratch one's pate; in —, bareheaded; uomo di — secca, man without an ounce of brains; una — vuota, a blockhead; non avere sale in —, to be devoid of common sense; (chem.) distillation flask, retort. **-a·io** *adj.* pertaining to pumpkins, pumpkin-like. **-ai(u)ola** *f.* (ent.) mole cricket, *Gryllotalpa*. **-aiolo** *m.* a variety of early fig. **-ata** *f.* (colloq.) butt with the head; knock on the head; fare alle -ate con, to butt against, to knock one's head against. **-onag·gine** *f.* pigheadedness. **-one** *m.* *augm.* of **zucca**; large head; stupid individual; pigheaded fool; (sculpt.) name given to a bust of Niccolò da Uzzano, by Donatello.

zuc·cher-o *m.* sugar; canna da —, sugar cane; — in pezzi, — in zollette, lump sugar; — in polvere, granulated sugar; — a velo, icing sugar; — candito, candy sugar; — di barbabietole, beet sugar; pane di —, sugar-loaf; — d'orzo, barley sugar; — bruciato, caramel; raffineria di —, sugar refinery; — filato, candy floss; a pan di —, conical, sugar-loaf; (fig.) dolce come lo —, as sweet as honey, charming, delightful; è un vero —, he's a perfect angel; he's a lamb; carta da —, paper in which sugar is wrapped; colore carta da —, blue-grey. **-ag·gio** *m.* (wine-making) addition of sugar to must. **-are** [A I s] see **inzuccherare**. **-ato** *part. adj.* sugared; sugary; (iron.) honeyed. **-iera** *f.* sugar-basin. **-iere** *m.* sugar-manufacturer. **-iero** *adj.* pertaining to sugar-manufacturing; l'industria -iera, the sugar industry. **-i·fero** *adj.* sugar-producing; yielding sugar. **-ifi·cio** *m.* sugar factory, sugar refinery, sugar

works. **-i·fluo** *adj.* flowing with sugar; sugary. **-ino** *adj.* sugary; sweet; *n.m.* sweet-meat. **-oso** *adj.* sugary; sweet; sickly; (fig.) honeyed.

zucchętta *f. dim.* of **zucca**, q.v.

zucchętto *m.* (eccl.) skull-cap; (zool.) *Ilia nucleus*, a kind of crab.

zucchino *m. dim.* of **zucca**, q.v.; dwarf vegetable marrow; squash (cf. Fr. *courgette*).

Zucco *pr.n.m.* (geog.) Zucco, near Palermo; wine from Zucco.

zuccotto *m.* (Tusc.) skull-cap (cf. **zuchetto**).

zuffa *f.* scuffle, scrimmage; (mil.) engagement; encounter; affray; mêlée; fierce but short action.

zuf·folo *m.* See **zufolo**.

zufol-are [A I s] *intr.* (*aux.* avere) to whistle; to hiss; mi -ano le orecchie, my ears are buzzing, there is a singing in my ears; to whisper; to carry tales, to be an informer; (mus.) to pipe, to whistle; *tr.* to whisper about, to inform about. **-amento** *m.* (mus.) piping, whistling; †(archit.) to build on piles; buzzing, buzz. **-ata** *f.* whistle, whistling. (**-ato** *part. adj.*) **-atore** *m.* whistler; (fig.) gossip, trouble-maker. **-io** *m.* (*pl.* **-ii**) incessant whistling, prolonged whistling; constant buzzing; tittle-tattle.

zu·folo *m.* (mus.) tin whistle; flageolet; chanter; (fig.) informer, spy; simpleton.

†**zug·fol-o** *m.* sweet fritter; simpleton; rimanere uno —, to be made a fool of. †**-olino** *m.* simpleton.

Zulù *m. indecl.* Zulu; (fig.) boor, lout; (geog.) il paese degli —, Zululand.

zum *onom.* boom (of the big bass-drum).

zum·mene *onom.* (Tusc.) boom! boom! boom! (cf. **zum**).

zupp-a *f.* soup; sop; pap; far la — nel vino, to dip bread in one's wine; — inglese, tipsy cake, trifle pudding; — di verdura, vegetable soup; — di lenticchie, lentil soup; (fig.) confusion, mess, mix-up; trouble, scolding; se non è — è pan bagnato, it's six of one and half-dozen of the other, they're one and the same thing. **-are** [A I] *tr.* to dip (bread, etc.); to moisten; to soak; -are i piedi nell'acqua, to get one's feet wet; to plunge. **-ata** *f.* dipping, dip. **-ato** *part. adj.* soaked; soaking wet. **-iera** *f.* soup-tureen. **-o** *adj.* soaked; wet; -o d'acqua, wet through; -o fradicio, soaking wet, drenched.

Zurigo *pr.n.f.* (geog.) Zürich.

zurl-are [A I] *intr.* (*aux.* avere) to romp; to frolic; to be skittish. **-o** *m.* romping; horse-play; frolic; skittish behaviour.

zurro *m.* gaiety, vivacity.

zuzzerellon-e, **zuzzurellon-e** *m.* (Tusc., joc.) rollicking person, great baby of a man, 'a boy at heart'. **-a** *f.* tomboy, romping girl.

ABBREVIATIONS IN COMMON USE
IN ITALIAN

A. autore – author; (title) Altezza – Highness; (electr.) ampère; (theatr.) atto – act; (rlwy.) automotrice – diesel-propelled rail-car.

AA. autori – authors; (motor.) Assistenza Automobilistica – ACI (q.v.) organization for assisting motorists; (mil.) Arma Aeronautica – (Italian) Air Force.

ab. abitanti – population; (eccl.) abate – abbé.

abbr. abbreviazione – abbreviation.

a.c. anno corrente – current year; (typ.) a capo – new paragraph.

a.C. avanti Cristo – before Christ, B.C.

a.c. (comm.) assegno circolare – banker's cheque.

Acc. accademia – academy; (rlwy.) accelerato – slow train (i.e. faster than a 'treno omnibus').

A.C.D.G. Associazione Cristiana dei Giovani: *see* Y.M.C.A.

ACI Azione Cattolica Italiana – Catholic Action Party; Automobile Club d'Italia – Italian Automobile Club.

ACLI Associazioni Cristiane dei Lavoratori Italiani – Christian Workers' (welfare) Societies.

A.D. Anno Domini.

ag. agosto – August.

AG (car registration plates) Agrigento.

agg. (gramm.) aggettivo – adjective.

AGIP Azienda Generale Italiana dei Petroli – National Italian Oil Company.

AL (car registration plates) Alessandria (Piedmont).

ALITALIA Aerolinee Italiane Internazionali – Italian Air Lines.

a.m. antemeridiano – before midday, a.m.

AMIG Associazione Mutilati e Invalidi di Guerra – Association of Disabled Servicemen.

AN (car registration plates) Ancona.

ANA Associazione Nazionale Alpini – National Association of former members of Alpine Regiments.

ANAS Azienda Nazionale Autonoma della Strada – National Road Board.

ANB Associazione Nazionale Bersaglieri – National Association of former members of Bersaglieri Regiments.

ANC Associazione Nazionale Combattenti – Ex-Soldiers' Association.

ANSA Agenzia Nazionale Stampa Associata – Italian News Agency.

ant. antemeridiano – a.m.

AO (car registration plates) Aosta.

AP (car registration plates) Ascoli Piceno.

apr. aprile – April.

AQ (car registration plates) Aquila.

AR (car registration plates) Arezzo.

A.R. Altezza Reale – Royal Highness.

AA.RR. Altezze Reali – Royal Highnesses; (rlwy.) (biglietti d') andata e ritorno – return tickets.

ARAR Azienda Rilievo e Alienazione Residuati – Organization for the Resale of Army Surplus Stores.

Arc. (eccl.) arcivescovo – archbishop.

arch. architetto – architect.

art. (gramm.) articolo – article.

A.S. Altezza Serenissima – Serene Highness.

ASCI Associazione Scoutistica Cattolica Italiana – Catholic Boy Scouts.

AT (car registration plates) Asti; (telegrams) a – to.

A.T. Antico Testamento – Old Testament.

AUT (telegrams) o – or.

a.v. (in bibliogr. references) ad vocem – s.v.

AV (car registration plates) Avellino.

AVIS Associazione Volontari Italiani del Sangue – Association of Voluntary Italian Blood-donors.

avv. avvocato – solicitor or barrister; (gramm.) avverbio – adverb.

B. (eccl.) Beato – Blessed.

BA (car registration plates) Bari.

B.A. Belle Arti – Fine Arts.

bar. (title) barone – baron.

B.F. (mil.) Bassa Forza – Other Ranks.

BG (car registration plates) Bergamo.

BL (car registration plates) Belluno.

B.M. Buona Memoria – of blessed memory.

BN (car registration plates) Benevento.

BO (car registration plates) Bologna.

BR (car registration plates) Brindisi.

BS (car registration plates) Brescia.

B.U. Bollettino Ufficiale – Official Bulletin.

B.V. (eccl.) Beata Vergine – the Blessed Virgin Mary.

BZ (car registration plates) Bolzano.

c. (manuscripts) carta – folio; (books) capitolo – chapter; (leg.) codice – code; (eccl.) (after names of saints) confessore – confessor; (comm.) conto – account; (typ.) corpo – type-size (*e.g.* c. 8 = 8-point).

C.A. (electr.) corrente alternata – alternating current.

CA (car registration plates) Cagliari.

CAI Club Alpino Italiano – Italian Alpine Club.

cap. (mil.) caporale – corporal.

Cap. (mil.) capitano – captain.

CAR (mil.) Centro Addestramento Reclute – Recruit Training Centre.

Card. (eccl.) cardinale; (gramm.) cardinale (number).

cav. cavaliere (decoration, corresponding approximately to O.B.E.).

CB (car registration plates) Campobasso.

CC Carabinieri (Italian gendarmerie).

c.c., c/c (comm.) conto corrente – current account.

C.C. (leg.) codice civile – civil code; (electr.) corrente continua – direct current; (comm.) Camera di Commercio – Chamber of Commerce; Corpo consolare – Consular Corps.

CCI Camera di Commercio Internazionale – International Chamber of Commerce.

C.Co. (leg.) Codice di Commercio – Commercial Code.

c.c.p. (comm.) conto corrente postale – current postal account.

C.C.p. Codice di procedura civile, Code of Civil Procedure.

C.D. Corpo Diplomatico – Diplomatic Corps; (comm.) Consigliere Delegato – Managing Director.

C.d.A. (mil.) Corpo d'Armata – Army Corps.

c.d.d. (math.) come dovevasi dimostrare – Q.E.D., quod erat demonstrandum, which was to be demonstrated.

C.d.G. (eccl.) Compagnia di Gesù – Society of Jesus (Jesuits).

C.d.L. Camera del Lavoro – Trade Union H.Q.

C.d.R. Cassa di Risparmio – Savings Bank.

CE (car registration plates) Caserta.

C.E. Comitato Esecutivo – Executive Committee.

ced. (comm.) cedola – (dividend or interest) coupon.

C.E.R.N. Consiglio Europeo per le Ricerche Nucleari – European Council for Nuclear Research.

cfr. confronta – cf.

C.G. Console Generale – Consul-General.

C.G.I.L. Confederazione Generale Italiana di Lavoro – Federation of Italian Trade Unions with extreme-left-wing political trend, cf. C.I.S.L., C.I.S.Na.L., U.I.L.

CH (car registration plates) Chieti.

chiar.mo chiarissimo – form of address used when writing to distinguished persons.

Cia Compagnia – Company.

C.I.O. Comitato Internazionale Olimpico – International Olympics Committee.

C.I.P. Comitato Interministeriale dei Prezzi – Interdepartmental Committee on Prices.

C.I.S.L. Confederazione Italiana Sindacati Liberi – Federation of Italian Trade Unions, officially non-party, but with moderate Socialist–Christian Democrat trend; cf. C.G.I.L., C.I.S.Na.L., U.I.L.

C.I.S.Na.L. Confederazione Italiana Sindacati Nazionali Liberi – Federation of Italian Trade Unions with right-wing tendency.

CIT Compagnia Italiana Turismo – Italian Travel Agency.

CITOM Compagnia Italiana Trasporto Olii Minerali, Italian Oil Transport Company.

CL (car registration plates) Caltanissetta.

CLN Comitato di Liberazione Nazionale – organizers of Resistance Movement during Second World War.

c.m. corrente mese – inst.

C.M. Circolare Ministeriale – Ministerial Circular.

CN (car registration plates) Cuneo.

CNR Consiglio Nazionale delle Ricerche – National Research Council.

CO (car registration plates) Como.

cod. codice – code, codex.

Col. (mil.) Colonel.

com. (mil. and naval) comandante – commanding officer.

comm. commendatore – decoration, corresponding approximately to C.B.E.

cond. (gramm.) condizionale – conditional.

cong. (gramm.) congiunzione – conjunction.

compar. (gramm.) comparativo – comparative.

CONI Comitato Olimpionico Nazionale Italiano – Italian Olympic Games Committee (also controls football pools).

cons. consigliere – member of a municipal council or of a board of directors.

corr. corrente – current.

cors. (typ.) corsivo – italic.

c.p. cartolina postale – postcard.

C.P. Casella Postale – (Private) Post Box; Consiglio Provinciale – District Council; (leg.) Codice Penale – Penal Code.

C.P.p. Codice di Procedura Penale, Code of Criminal Procedure.

CR (car registration plates) Cremona.

CRAL Circolo Ricreativo Assistenza Lavoratori – Recreational Clubs organized by National Assistance Board.

C.R.I. Croce Rossa Italiana – Italian Red Cross.

CS (car registration plates) Cosenza.

C.S. Codice della Strada – Highway Code.

c.s. come sopra – as above.

C.S. di C. Centro Sperimentale di Cinematografia – Experimental Film Studios, Rome.

c.ssa contessa – countess.

CT (car registration plates) Catania.

cte conte – count (title).

cto (comm.) conto – account.

C.V. cavallo vapore – H.P.

C.X. (Venice) Consiglio de Dieci – Council of Ten.

CZ (car registration plates) Catanzaro.

d. don – (eccl.) rev.; also used as courtesy title for members of the nobility; (bibliogr.) data – date.

D (rlwy.) diretto – fast train; (typ.) Didot.

d.c. (mus.) da capo; (typ.) new para.

d.C. dopo Cristo – after Christ, A.D.

D.C. Democrazia Cristiana – Christian Democrat Party.

DD (rlwy.) direttissimo – express train.

DDT Dicloro-Difenil-Tricloruroetano – insecticide.

dev., dev.mo devotissimo – (in letters) your truly.

D.G. Direzione Generale – Managing Director's Office.

dic. (or 10bre) dicembre – December.

dis. disegno – drawing, design.

D.L. Decreto Legge – decree promulgating a law.

doc. documenti – documents.

dott. or **dr.** doctor (of medicine, etc.); first university degree, corresponding approximately to B.A.

D.P.R. Decreto del Presidente della Repubblica – Decree of President of the Republic.

E (geog.) est – East.

E.A. Ente autonomo – Independent Committee.

ECA Ente Comunale di Assistenza (formerly Congregazione di Carità) – Municipal Public Assistance Board.

ecc. eccetera – etc.

Ecc. Eccellenza – Excellency (ambassador, minister, etc.); Lordship (bishop).

ed. edito, editore – edited by, editor, publisher.

EE Escursionisti Esteri (temporary registration plate for foreign cars).

EFTA Associazione europea di libero scambio – European Free Trade Association (cf. Z.C.L.).

Eg. (or **Egr.**) **Sig.** Egregio Signore – (in addresses) Mr.

EI (car registration plates) Esercito Italiano – Italian Army.

Em. (eccl.) Eminenza – Eminence.

EN (car registration plates) Enna (Sicily).

ENAL Ente Nazionale Assistenza Lavoratori – National Association for Assistance to Workers.

ENAPI Ente Nazionale per l'Artigianato e le Piccole Industrie – National Association of Artisans and Owners of Small Factories.

ENI Ente Nazionale Idrocarburi – National Hydrocarbon Corporation.

ENIC Ente Nazionale Industrie Cinematografiche – National Association of Film Producers.

ENIT Ente Nazionale Industrie Turistiche – National Institution for the Promotion of Tourist Industry.

ENPI Ente Nazionale per la Prevenzione degli Infortuni – National Institution for the Prevention of Accidents.

E.P.T. Ente Provinciale per il turismo – Provincial Board for promotion of Tourist Industry.

es. esempio – example.

E.V. Era Volgare – Anno Domini; Eccellenza Vostra – Your Excellency.

f., ff. (mus.) forte, fortissimo.

fatt. (comm.) fattura – invoice.

f.c. (boxing) fuori combattimento – knockout.

f.co. franco – free.

f.c.t. (boxing) fuori combattimento tecnico – technical knockout.

FE (car registration plates) Ferrara.

febb. febbraio – February.

fem. (gramm.) femminile – feminine.

FERT motto of the House of Savoy and of the Order of the Annunziata, traditionally supposed to denote 'Fortitudo Eius Rhodum Tenuit' (its valour saved the island of Rhodes), but other interpretations have been suggested.

FF.SS. Ferrovie dello Stato – Italian State Railways.

FG (car registration plates) Foggia.

FGC Federazione Giovanile Comunista – Association of Young Communists.

FI (car registration plates) Firenze – Florence.

F.I.A. Federazione Internazionale dell'Automobile – International Automobile Federation.

FIDAL Federazione Italiana di Atletica Leggera – Italian Light Athletics Association.

F.I.E. Fondazione Figli Italiani all'Estero – Foundation of Sons of Italy abroad.

FIFA Federazione Internazionale Football Association.

F.I.G.C. Federazione Italiana Gioco Calcio – Italian Football Association.

FILM Federazione Italiana Lavoratori del Mare – Italian Seamen's Union.

FIP Federazione Italiana Pallacanestro – Italian Basketball Association.

FIR Federazione Italiana Rugby – Italian Rugby Association.

FIS Federazione Italiana Scherma – Italian Fencing Association; Fédération Internationale de Ski.

FISI Federazione Italiana Sports Invernali – Italian Winter Sports Association.

FIT Federazione Italiana Tennis – Italian Lawn Tennis Association.

FITAV Federazione Italiana Tiro a Volo – Italian Pigeon-Shooting Association.

FO (car registration plates) Forlì.

fob (comm.) franco a bordo – free on board.

F.P.I. Federazione Pugilistica Italiana – Italian Boxing Association.

fr. (comm.) franco – French or Swiss franc.

FR (car registration plates) Frosinone.

F.S. Ferrovie dello Stato – Italian State Railways.

f.to (comm.) firmato – signed.

FUCI Federazione Universitaria Cattolica Italiana – Italian Catholic University Association.

g. giorno – day; (med.) grani – grains.
G.A. Giunta Amministrativa – Municipal Council.
G.B. (name) Giovanni Battista; (geog.) Gran Bretagna.
G.C. (eccl.) Gesù Cristo – Jesus Christ; (decoration) Gran Croce – Grand Cross.
G.D. Granduca – Grand Duke.
G.d.F. Guardia di Finanza – Revenue Guard.
GE (car registration plates) Genova.
GEI Giovani Esploratori Italiani – Italian Boy Scouts.
Gen. (mil.) Generale.
genn. gennaio – January.
G.G. (name) Gian Giacomo.
G.I.A.C. Gioventù Italiana di Azione Cattolica – Catholic Youth Association.
giugn., giu. giugno – June.
G.M. (mil.) Genio Militare – Corps of Engineers; (Masonic title) Gran Maestro – Grand Master.
G.N. Genio Navale – Engineer Branch of Italian Navy.
GO (car registration plates) Gorizia.
G.P. (sport) Gran Premio – Grand Prix.
G.P.A. Giunta Provinciale Amministrativa – County Council.
gr. grammo – gramme.
GR (car registration plates) Grosseto.
GR.EST Gruppo Estivo – Church organization which arranges games, etc., for children during summer holidays.
Gr. Uff. (decoration) Grande Ufficiale – corresponds approximately to K.B.E.
G.U. Gazzetta Ufficiale – Official Gazette.
G.V. (rlwy.) Grande Velocità – express goods service.

I (car registration plates) Italia.
ICE Istituto Nazionale per il Commercio Estero – National Institute for Foreign Trade.
I.C.S. Istituto Centrale di Statistica – National Statistics Office.
I.G.E. Imposta Generale Entrate – turnover tax, generally 3% charged on all invoices, unless goods are intended for export.
I.G.M. Istituto Geografico Militare – Military Survey Office.
Ill., Ill.mo Illustre, Illustrissimo – courtesy forms of address.
IM (car registration plates) Imperia.
IMEO Istituto Italiano per il Medio ed Estremo Oriente – Italian Near and Far East Association.
INA Istituto Nazionale Assicurazioni – National Insurance Service.
INA Casa Department of INA which finances building of houses for the working classes.
INAM Istituto Nazionale Assicurazione Malattie – National Health Insurance Service.
INCIS Istituto Nazionale Case per gli Impiegati di Stato – Institute for providing houses for Civil Servants.
INE Istituto Nazionale per l'Esportazione – National Export Institute.
ing. ingegnere – engineer.
INPI Istituto Nazionale per la Prevenzione degli Infortuni – National Institution for the Prevention of Accidents.
int. (comm.) interessi – interest.
INT Istituto Nazionale Trasporti – National Transport Institute.
I.R. Imperiale Regio – Imperial and Royal.
IRI Istituto Nazionale per la Ricostruzione Industriale – National Institute for the Reconstruction of Industry.
ISPI Istituto per gli Studi di Politica Internazionale.
I.T.C. Compagnia Italiana Cavi Telegrafici Sottomarini (Italcable) – Italian Cable Company.

kg. chilogramma – kilogram – latitude..
km. chilometro – kilometre.
mk/h chilometri all'ora – kilometres per hour.
kmq. chilometro quadrato – square kilometre.

lat. latitudine – latitude.
LE (car registration plates) Lecce.
LI (car registration plates) Livorno (Leghorn).
Lit. (comm.) Lire Italiane – Italian lire.
lit. (measure of capacity) litro – litre.
LL.AA Loro Altezze – Their Highnesses.
LL.EE Loro Eccellenze – Their Excellencies.

LL.PP Lavori Pubblici – (Ministry of) Public Works.
LL.MM Loro Maestà – Their Majesties.
L.N.I. Lega Navale Italiana.
long. longitudine – longitude.
L.st. (comm.) Lire sterline – pounds sterling (usu. written £ not £ in Italian).
LT (car registration plates) Latina.
lu., lugl. luglio – July.
LU (car registration plates) Lucca.

m. metro – metre; (comm.) mio – my; morto – died.
M.A.E. Ministero degli Affari Esteri – Ministry of Foreign Affairs.
magg. maggio – May.
Magg. (mil.) Maggiore – Major.
marz. marzo – March.
MAS (naval) Motoscafo Antisommergibile – MTB.
masc. (gramm.) maschile – masculine.
MC (car registration plates) Macerata.
M.C. (eccl.) Minore Conventuale; (hist.) Maggior Consiglio – Grand Council.
m.c.d. (math.) massimo comune divisore – highest common factor.
m.c.m. (math.) minimo comune multiplo – lowest common multiple.
m.coli (typ.) maiuscoli – caps.
m.coletti (typ.) maiuscoletti – small caps.
ME (car registration plates) Messina.
M.E. (hist.) Medio Evo – Middle Ages.
M.E.C. Mercato Europeo Comune, European Common Market.
M.F.E. Movimento Federalista Europeo.
MI (car registration plates) Milano.
min. (typ.) minuscoli – lower-case letters.
mitt. (on envelopes) mittente – sender.
M.L. (name) Maria Luisa.
M.M. Marina Militare – Italian Navy (formerly known as R.M., q.v.).
MN (car registration plates) Mantova.
Mn. Motonave – Motor Vessel.
Mo. Maestro.
MO (car registration plates) Modena.
M.O. Minori Osservanti.
mons. (eccl.) monsignore.
M.P. (hist.) manu propria (in documents, after king's signature).
mq. metro quadrato – square metre.
M.R. Molto Reverendo (a courteous variant of 'Reverendo') – Reverend.
ms. or MS. manoscritto – manuscript.
MS (car registration plates) Massa.
M.S. Mutuo Soccorso – Mutual Aid.
M.S.I. Movimento Sociale Italiano – neo-Fascist Party.
mss. manoscritti – manuscripts.
MT (car registration plates) Matera.
Mv. Motoveliero – sailing-boat or fishing-boat with auxiliary motor.

n. nota – note; nato – born.
no. numero – number.
N Nord – North.
NA (car registration plates) Naples.
NATO (pronounced as in Italian) North Atlantic Treaty Organization.
N.B. nota bene.
N.D. (eccl.) Nostra Donna – Our Lady; (title) Nobil Donna – member of a noble family.
D.d.A. Nota dell'autore – author's note.
N.d.D. Nota della Direzione – note by the editor (of a newspaper).
N.d.E. Nota dell'editore – publisher's or editor's note.
N.d.R. Nota della redazione – editor's note (newspapers).
N.d.T. Nota del Traduttore – translator's note.
NE (geog.) Nord-est – North-east, NE.
N.H. Nobil Uomo (Homo) – member of a noble family.
N.N. Nescio nomen – (on birth certificates, etc.) name (of father) unknown.
NNE (geog.) Nord-nord-est – North-north-east, NNE.
NNO (geog.) Nord-nord-ovest – North-north-west, NNW.

NO (geog.) Nord-ovest – North-west, NW.

nob. nobile – nobleman.

nov. (or **9bre**) novembre – November.

ns. (comm.) nostro – our.

N.S. (eccl.) Nostro Signore – Our Lord.

N.S.G.C. (eccl.) Nostro Signore Gesù Cristo – Our Lord Jesus Christ.

N.T. Nuovo Testamento – New Testament.

NU (car registration plates) Nuoro (Sardinia).

N.U. Nettezza Urbana – Municipal service for collecting rubbish, cleaning streets, etc.

O Ovest (cf. W) – West.

obb.mo obbligatissimo – your obedient servant.

O.C.S. (decoration) Ordine Civile di Savoia.

O.d.G. (mil.) Ordine del Giorno, dispatches; (pol.) parliamentary motion; (admin.) agenda; order of the day, resolution.

O.F.M. Ordine dei Frati Minori.

O.M.S. (decoration) Ordine Militare di Savoia.

on. onorevole – honourable (prefixed to names of members of the Chamber of Deputies).

ONO (geog.) Ovest-nord-ovest – West-north-west, WNW.

ONU Organizzazione Nazioni Unite – United Nations Organization (UNO).

OO.PP Opere Pubbliche – Public Works.

O.P. Ordine dei Predicatori (i.e. Dominicans).

OSO (geog.) Ovest-sud-ovest – West-south-west, WSW.

O.S.SS.A. (decoration) Ordine Supremo della Santissima Annunziata.

ott. (or **8bre**) ottobre – October.

OVRA (hist.) Opera Volontaria per la Repressione dell'Antifascismo – Fascist Secret Police.

p., pp. (mus.) piano, pianissimo.

p. pagina – page; (eccl.) padre – Father.

p.a. per auguri – used on visiting cards to express congratulations, birthday wishes, etc.

PA (car registration plates) Palermo.

pag. pagina – page.

pagg. pagine – pages.

par. paragrafo – paragraph.

pass. passim.

p.c. per condoglianza – used on visiting cards to express condolence; per cortesia – please.

PC (car registration plates) Piacenza.

P.C.A. Pontificia Commissione di Assistenza.

p.c.c. per copia conforme – certified true copy.

P.C.I. Partito Comunista Italiano – Italian Communist Party.

PD (car registration plates) Padova.

P.D.C. Partito della Democrazia Cristiana (cf. D.C.).

P.D.I. Partito Democratico Italiano – new name (1960) of Monarchist Party in Italy (cf. P.N.M.).

P.D.O. (eccl.) Prete dell'Oratorio.

PE (car registration plates) Pescara.

p.es. per esempio – for example.

p.f. (comm.) prossimo futuro – prox.

PG (car registration plates) Perugia.

P.G. (leg.) Procuratore Generale – Attorney General; (eccl.) Padre Generale.

PI (car registration plates) Pisa.

P.I. Pubblica Istruzione – (Ministry of) Public Education.

P.L. (name) Pier Luigi.

P.L.I. Partito Liberale Italiano – Italian Liberal Party.

p.m. pomeridiano – after midday, p.m.

P.M. Pontifex Maximus; (leg.) Pubblico Ministero – Public Prosecutor.

P.M.P. Partito Monarchico Popolare – Popular Monarchist Party.

P.N. (after names of rlwy. stations) Porta Nuova.

P.N.F. (hist.) Partito Nazionale Fascista – National Fascist Party.

P.N.M. Partito Nazionale Monarchico – National Monarchist Party (now P.D.I., q.v.).

pp. pagine – pages.

p.p. (comm.) per procura – by proxy; per pro, through… for…; prossimo passato – ult.

PP. (comm.) porto pagato – carriage paid; (eccl.) Padri – Fathers.

P.P., P.P.I. (on packages) posa piano – handle with care; (hist.) Partito Popolare founded in 1919 by Don Sturzo, reformed in 1943 as P.D.C., q.v.

PR (car registration plates) Parma.

p.r. (on visiting cards) per ringraziamento – with thanks.

PRA Pubblico Registro Automobilistico – office where cars and other motor vehicles are registered and numbers allotted.

P.R.I. Partito Repubblicano Italiano.

prof. Professore – Professor.

PS (car registration plates) Pesaro.

PS. Post-scriptum.

P.S. Publica Sicurezza – Police.

P.S.D.I. Partito Socialista Democratico Italiano – right-wing Socialist Party.

P.S.I. Partito Socialista Italiano – left-wing Socialist Party.

PT (car registration plates) Pistoia.

P.T. Poste e Telegrafi – Post and Telegraph Service.

P.T.P. Posto telefonico pubblico – public telephone.

P.T.T. Poste, Telegrafi e Telefoni – Post, Telegraph and Telephone Services.

PV (car registration plates) Pavia.

p.v. (comm.) prossimo venturo – prox.

P.V. (rlwy.) Piccola Velocità – ordinary goods service.

PZ (car registration plates) Potenza.

q. quadrato – square.

q.e.d. quod erat demonstrandum.

r. (bibliogr.) recto.

R. (rlwy.) rapido – express train; (eccl.) Rev(erend).

RA (car registration plates) Ravenna.

rag. ragioniere – accountant.

RAI Radio Audizioni Italiane – Italian Broadcasting Corporation, formerly EIAR.

rc (math.) radice cubica – cube root.

RC (car registration plates) Reggio Calabria.

R.C. Rotary Club.

R.D. (hist.) Regio Decreto – Royal Decree.

R.D.L. (hist.) Regio Decreto Legge – Law promulgated by Royal Decree.

RE (car registration plates) Reggio Emilia.

Rev.mo *see* R.mo.

RG (car registration plates) Ragusa (Sicily).

R.I. Repubblica Italiana, Republic of Italy.

RI (car registration plates) Rieti.

ric. ricevuta – received, receipt.

R.M. Ricchezza Mobile – (tax on) income; (hist.) Regia Marina – Royal (Italian) Navy, now Marina Militare, M.M., q.v.

R.mo, Rev.mo Reverendissimo – Most Reverend, Right Rev(erend), Very Rev(erend).

R.N. Riserva Navale – Naval Reserve; Regia Nave – Royal Ship (cf. H.M.S.).

RO (car registration plates) Rovigo.

RR.CC. (hist.) Reali Carabinieri, now CC, q.v.

RP (post) risposta pagata – reply paid.

R.S.I. (hist.) Repubblica Sociale Italiana (also known as Repubblica di Salò), founded by Mussolini after his escape from the Gran Sasso (1943–5).

RSM (car registration plates) Repubblica di San Marino.

R.T. Radiotelegrafia – wireless; radiotelegrafista – wireless operator; radiotelegrafo – wireless telegraph.

s. san, santo, santa – St (before names of saints); (mus.) solo, soli.

S. San, Santo, Santa – St (before names of churches and places); (geog.) Sud – South.

SA (car registration plates) Salerno.

S.A. Sua Altezza – His (or Her) Highness; (comm.) Società Anonima – Limited Company.

S.A.R. Sua Altezza Reale – His (or Her) Royal Highness.

S.a.r.l. Società a responsabilità limitata – (private) limited company.

s.b.f. salvo buon fine – under usual reserve (formula used when acknowledging receipt of cheques).

S.C. (on restaurant menus) Secondo consumo – according to amount eaten; (comm.) Sede Centrale – Head Office.

S.C.V. Stato della Città del Vaticano – Vatican City; (joc.) Se Cristo vedesse – If Christ could only see it!

S.D.N. (hist.) Società delle Nazioni – League of Nations.

s.d. (bibliogr.) senza data – no date.

s.d.l. (bibliogr.) senza data o luogo – no date or place of publication.

SE (geog.) Sud-est – South-east, SE.

S.E. Sua Eccellenza – His Excellency; (eccl.) His Grace; His Lordship.

S.E.A.T. Società Elenchi Ufficiali Abbonati al Telefono – Official Telephone Directory Company.

Sec. secolo – century.

S.E. & O. (comm.) Salvo errori ed omissioni – E. & O.E.

seg. seguente – following.

S.Em. (eccl.) Sua Eminenza – His Eminence.

Sen. Senatore – Senator.

Serg. (mil.) Sergente – Sergeant.

SET Società Esercizi Telefoni – Telephone Company.

SETAF Southern European Task Forces – Nato Powers H.Q. in Italy.

sett. (or **7bre**) settembre – September.

sfr (post) sotto fascia raccomandata – registered printed matter; franco svizzero – Swiss franc.

sfs (post) sotto fascia semplice – unregistered printed matter.

S.G. (on restaurant menus) Secondo grandezza – according to size of portion; (title) Sua Grazia – His Grace.

SI (car registration plates) Siena.

SIA Servizio Informazioni Aeronautiche – (Italian) Air Intelligence.

S.I.A.E. Società Italiana Autori ed Editori – Italian Authors' and Publishers' Association.

Sig. Signore – Mr.

Sig.a, Sig.ra Signora – Mrs.

Sigg. Signori – Messrs.

Sig.na Signorina – Miss.

SIM Servizio Informazioni Militari – (Italian) Military Intelligence.

SIN Servizio Informazioni Navali – (Italian) Naval Intelligence.

SISAL Sport Italiana Società a responsabilità limitata – original founders of football pools in Italy, now administered by CONI (q.v.).

s.l.m. sul livello del mare – above sea level.

S.M. Sua Maestà – His (or Her) Majesty; (mil.) Stato Maggiore – Staff; (naut.) submarine (also S.M.G.).

S.M.G. (mil.) Stato Maggiore Generale – General Staff; (naut.) sommergibile – submarine.

S.M.O.M. Sovrano Militare Ordine di Malta – Sovereign Military Order of Malta (Knights of Malta).

S.N.D.A. Società Nazionale Dante Alighieri.

SO (car registration plates) Sondrio.

sost. (gramm.) sostantivo – substantive.

sp. specie – species.

SP (car registration plates) Spezia.

S.P. (eccl.) Santo Padre – His Holiness (the Pope).

SPA Società Protettrice degli Animali – (Italian) Society for the Protection of Animals.

S.p.a. Società per azioni – Limited Company.

S.P.E. (mil.) Servizio Permanente Effettivo – Service in regular army qualifying for pension.

sped. (on envelopes) spedisce – sender.

Spett. Spettabile – (in letters addressed to firms) Messrs.

s.p.m. sua propria mano – personal for addressee.

S.P.Q.R. Senatus Populusque Romanus – still used on proclamations, etc. by Rome City Council.

S.Q. (on bill of fare) secondo quantità – price according to quantity consumed.

SR (car registration plates) Siracusa.

S.R.C. Santa Romana Chiesa – Holy Roman Church.

S.R.I. Sacro Romano Impero – Holy Roman Empire.

s.r.l. società a responsabilità limitata – (private) limited company.

SS (car registration plates) Sassari.

S.S. (eccl.) Sua Santità – His Holiness; Santa Sede – Holy See.

SS. Piroscafo – Steamship; (eccl.) Santi – Saints; Santissim-o, -a, Blessed.

SS.A. Santissima Annunziata – Order of the Holy Annunciation.

SSE (geog.) Sud-sud-est – South-south-east, SSE.

SS.M.e L. Santi Maurizio e Lazzaro – Order of knighthood.

SSO (geog.) Sud-sud-ovest – South-south-west, SSW.

SS.PP. (eccl.) Santi Padri – Holy Fathers (esp. the 'Fathers of the Church').

S.Ten. (mil.) Sottotenente – 2nd Lieutenant – Sub-Lieutenant.

STET Società Torinese Esercizio Telefoni – Turin Telephone Co.

STIPEL Società Telefonica Interregionale Piemonte e Lombardia – Company controlling telephone services in Piedmont and Lombardy.

S.T.V. Società Tiro a Volo – Pigeon-Shooting Association.

S.U.C.A.I.N.I. Sezione Universitarii Club Alpino Italiano – Italian Universities Alpine Club.

succ. successori – successors.

SV (car registration plates) Savona.

s.v. (bibliogr.) sub voce.

S.V. Signoria Vostra – Your Lordship but also used in official communications to ordinary citizens.

S.V.P. Südtiroler Volkspartei – Party of the Germany-speaking minority in Alto Adige; s'il vous plaît – please.

T. (mus.) tutti; or trillo – trill (more usually TR).

TA (car registration plates) Taranto.

tbc. (med.) tuberculosi – tuberculosis.

tang. (math.) tangente – tangent.

T.C.I. Touring Club Italiano – Italian Touring Club.

TE (car registration plates) Teramo.

T.E. (rlwy.) Trazione elettrica – electrified line.

TELVE Società Telefoni delle Venezie – Company controlling telephone services in the Three Venetias.

Ten. (mil.) Tenente – Lieutenant.

TETI Telefoni del Tirreno – Company controlling telephone services along the Tyrrhenian Coast.

TIMO (Società) Telefoni Italiani Medio-Orientali – Company controlling telephone services in Central and Eastern Italy.

tit. titolare – owner; titolo – title, share certificate.

TN (car registration plates) Trento.

TO (car registration plates) Torino.

tom. (bibliogr.) tomo – volume.

TOTIP Totalizzatore Ippico – Company controlling totalizators on racecourses and also pools on the same lines as football pools.

TP (car registration plates) Trapani.

tr. traduzione – translation; (mus.) trillo – trill.

Tr. (comm.) tratta – bill of exchange.

TR (car registration plates) Terni.

TS (car registration plates) Trieste.

T.S.F. Telegrafo senza fili – wireless.

T.U. (leg.) Testo Unico – Consolidation Act.

TV (car registration plates) Treviso.

T.V. Televisione.

U.C. (mil.) Ufficiale di Complemento – Territorial Army Officer.

U.C.D.G. Unione Cristiana delle Giovani – Italian branch of the Y.W.C.A.

UD (car registration plates) Udine.

U.D.I. Unione Donne Italiana – Association of Italian Women.

UFAC Unione Femminile di Azione Cattolica – Catholic Women's Association.

U.I. Utile Idiota – useful idiot (said of well-known personages who lend their names to a political party).

U.I.L. Ufficio Internazionale del Lavoro – International Labour Office; Unione Italiana del Lavoro – Italian Federation of Trade Unions with moderate Socialist and Republican trend (cf. C.I.G.L., C.I.S.L., C.I.S.Na.L.).

U.R.S.S. Unione Repubbliche Socialisti Sovietiche – U.S.S.R.

u.s. (comm.) ultimo scorso – ult.

U.T.E. Ufficio Tecnico Erariale, Inland Revenue Surveyors' Office.

v. vedi – see; (bibliogr.) verso – verse, verso.

VA (car registration plates) Varese.

val. (comm.) valuta – value; currency; foreign exchange; effective date.

VC (car registration plates) Vercelli.

V.C. Vice-Console – Vice-Consul; Valore Civile – used after decorations awarded for non-military services (cf. V.M.).

VE (car registration plates) Venice.

V.E. Vostra Eccellenza – Your Excellency; (eccl.) Your Grace; Your Lordship; (name) Vittorio Emanuele.

V.Em. Vostra Eminenza – Your Eminence.

ver. (comm.) versamento – payment, remittance.

V.E.R.D.I. Vittorio Emanuele Re d'Italia – (hist.) slogan of Italian patriots during Risorgimento; now name of a monarchist students' association.

VF Vigili di Fuoco – Fire Brigade.

VI (car registration plates) Vicenza.

V.M. Vostra Maestà – Your Majesty; Valore Militare – used after military decorations, cf. V.C.

vol. (bibliogr.) volume – volume.

VR (car registration plates) Verona.

vs. (comm.) vostro – your.

V.S. Vostra Signoria – cf. S.V.; (mus.) volti subito, turn over quickly.

VT (car registration plates) Viterbo.

VV usually written W) viva!, long live!

W West – often used instead of O (Ovest).

W.C. Water-Closet.

WL Wagon Lits, Carrozza con letti – sleeping-car.

X Mas Decima Flottiglia Mas (q.v.) – Naval unit which during 1939–45 War controlled 'secret weapons' such as human torpedoes, frogmen, etc. Subsequently expanded to include Commando units (Battaglioni San Marco).

Y.C.I. Yacht Club Italia – Italian Yacht Club.

Y.C.N. Yacht Club Napoli – Neapolitan Yacht Club.

Y.M.C.A. Associazione Cristiana dei Giovani, Young Men's Christian Association (initials as English, to distinguish it from U.C.D.G., q.v.).

ZA (international motoring) Union of South Africa.

Z.C.L. Zona di Commercio Libero – European Free Trade Area (cf. EFTA).

THE VERB SCHEME

In the following pages the user will find a complete survey of Italian conjugation by means of which any verb occurring in the body of the dictionary may be conjugated or its various forms recognized. Care has been taken to include models of every type of conjugation, including anomalies presenting only minor orthographical and other variations, since it is on such points that the user is most likely to seek assistance. The scheme also serves as a comprehensive guide to the Italian verb in general, and includes forms which are obsolete, pedantic or poetic (distinguished by an appropriate indication in each case) as well as those which are in current use.[1]

METHOD OF REFERENCE

Every infinitive in current use included in the Italian word-list of the dictionary is followed by a reference in square brackets which consists of one of the upper-case letters A, B, C, or D, followed by a figure, to which may be added one or more of the lower-case letters, s, d, c, a, etc. For example: **andare** [A8]; **danneggiare** [A3c].

The verbs have been grouped into four main categories, lettered A, B, C, D. Group A comprises the true -*are* verbs and corresponds to what grammarians term the First Conjugation, except that 'fare' and its compounds are not included in it. Group D comprises the -*ire* verbs and corresponds to what some grammarians term the Third and others the Fourth Conjugation. Groups B and C comprise the -*ere* verbs, which have been subdivided arbitrarily according to how much of the conjugation it is necessary to give in full; they correspond to what some grammarians term the Second, and others the Second and Third Conjugation.

INDICATION OF STRESS

The lower-case letters s. d. and c serve to indicate verbs in which the stress or tonic accent differs from that of the model in certain forms of the present indicative and subjunctive and in the imperative. The lower-case letter 's' (=stress), placed after an upper-case letter and a figure, indicates that the stress falls on the antepenultimate syllable in certain finite forms of the verb. For instance, the verb **abdicare** is given as follows: **abdicare** [A2s]. The indication A2 signifies that the verb is conjugated like the A2 models, **peccare** and **pagare**; the lower-case letter 's' signifies that in the relevant persons of the present indicative and subjunctive and of the imperative, the stress falls on the antepenultimate syllable, for example: **ab·dico, ab·dichi, ab·dica**, etc. If the stressed vowel in question is 'e' or 'o', it is necessary to indicate whether it is open or close in pronunciation. If the vowel is close, a lower-case 'c' (=close) is included in the reference. For instance, the indication [A2sc] given after the verb **convocare** conveys that in the relevant tenses the tonic or stressed syllable is the antepenultimate and that the vowel in question is close, for example: **convoco, convochi, convoca**, etc. If no lower-case 'c' is included in the reference, the pronunciation of the stressed vowel is open.

In cases of diphthongization of the stressed vowel (i.e. the change of e to ie and of o to uo), a lower-case letter 'd' is included in the reference. (For an instance of such verbs, see paradigm of **muovere**, p. 895). In other cases in which stress falls on the first of two vowels, the vowel in question appears in the reference (in lower-case). For instance, the verb **augurare** has the reference [A1sa]. This indicates that in the relevant tenses the stress is on the vowel 'a' of the antepenultimate syllable, for example: **a·uguro, a·uguri, a·ugura,** etc.

USE OF THE PARADIGM OR MODEL

It will be found that some paradigms represent unique verbs, whereas others serve as models for many others. When it is desired to conjugate a verb from a model to which reference is made, *remove as* *much from the end of the infinitive of the verb in question as is identical with the infinitive of the example* and build up the tenses on this basis. For instance, the verb **crescere** has the reference [B9c]. On reference to the verb scheme it will be found that the model for B9 is **conoscere**. Removing from the end of the infinitive of **crescere** as much as is identical with **conoscere**, we are left with the syllable **cre-**, corresponding to the syllables **cono-** of the model. If it is desired to know, for instance, the 3rd person plural past definite of **crescere**, reference to the paradigm shows that the form for **conoscere** is: **connobbero**. Replacing **cre-** for **cono-**, we obtain the form **crebbero**. The lower-case letter 'c' contained in the reference for **crescere** (as for **conoscere**) shows that the stressed vowel has the close pronunciation.

GROUP A

[A1]   **mandare**

INDICATIVE

Present:

mando (†mande)	mandiamo (†mandamo)
mandi	mandate
manda	man·dano (†man·dono)

Imperfect:

mandavo (†mandava)[2]	mandavamo
mandavi	mandavate
mandava	manda·vano

Past definite:

manda·i	mandammo
mandasti	mandaste
mandò (†mandòe)	manda·rono (†mandaro, †mandar, †mandarno, †mando·rono, †mandonno)

Future:

manderò (†manderòe, †manderaggio, †mandarò)	manderęmo
mandera·i	manderęte
manderà (†manderàe)	manderanno

Conditional:

mandere·i (†manderebbi, †manderi·a)	manderęmmo
manderesti	manderęste
manderebbe (†manderi·a)	mandereb·bero (†manderi·ano, †mandereb·bono)

SUBJUNCTIVE

Present:

mandi (†mande)	mandiamo
mandi (†mande)	mandiate
mandi (†mande)	man·dino

---

[1] A reference list of the principal verbs constructed with a preposition before an infinitive will be found at the end of this verb scheme.

[2] This form was in current use up to the end of the nineteenth century.

Imperfect:

mandassi (†mandasse)	mandas·simo
mandassi (†mandasse)	mandaste
mandasse (†mandassi)	mandas·sero (†mandas·sino, †mandas·seno, †mandas·sono)

IMPERATIVE

—	mandiamo
manda	mandate
mandi	man·dino

Gerund: mandando
Present participle: mandante
Past participle: mandato

[A I s]   **evitare**

e·vito	evitiamo
e·viti	evitate
e·vita	e·vitano

Present subjunctive:

e·viti	evitiamo
e·viti	evitiate
e·viti	e·vitino

Imperative:

—	evitiamo
e·vita	evitate
e·viti	e·vitino

All other tenses as A I.

[A2] The verbs of this group are conjugated exactly as those in group A I except that adjustments have to be made in the spelling to show that the 'hard' sound of *c* or *g* at the end of the stem is retained throughout the conjugation. This means that *h* is inserted in such verbs wherever the termination begins with *e* or *i*. In the following examples only those tenses are given in which these adjustments are necessary.[1] All other tenses are conjugated as in A I in every detail.

peccare	**pagare**

INDICATIVE

Present:

pecco	pago
pecchi	paghi
pecca	paga
pecchiamo	paghiamo
peccate	pagate
pec·cano	pa·gano

Future:

peccherò	pagherò
pecchera·i	paghera·i
peccherà	pagherà
peccherẹmo	pagherẹmo
peccherẹte	pagherẹte
peccheranno	pagheranno

Conditional:

pecchere·i	paghere·i
peccherẹsti	pagherẹsti
peccherebbe	pagherebbe
peccherẹmmo	pagherẹmmo
peccherẹste	pagherẹste
pecchereb·bero	paghereb·bero

SUBJUNCTIVE

Present:

pecchi	pǝghi
pecchi	paghi
pecchi	paghi
pecchiamo	paghiamo
pecchiate	paghiate
pec·chino	pa·ghino

IMPERATIVE

—	—
pecca	paga
pecchi	paghi
pecchiamo	paghiamo
peccate	pagate
pec·chino	pa·ghino

[A2 s]   **abdicare**

Present indicative:

ab·dico	abdichiamo
ab·dichi	abdicate
ab·dica	ab·dicano

Present subjunctive:

ab·dichi	abdichiamo
ab·dichi	abdichiate
ab·dichi	ab·dichino

Imperative:

—	abdichiamo
ab·dica	abdicate
ab·dichi	ab·dichino

All other tenses as A2.

[A2 s a]   **augurare**

Present indicative:

a·uguro	auguriamo
a·uguri	augurate
a·ugura	a·ugurano

Present subjunctive:

a·uguri	auguriamo
a·uguri	auguriate
a·uguri	a·ugurino

Imperative:

—	auguriamo
a·ugura	augurate
a·uguri	a·ugurino

All other tenses as A I.

[A3] This group comprises verbs having a stem ending in a 'soft' *c* or *g*. This is denoted in the infinitive (i.e. before *a*) by *ci* or *gi*. These verbs are conjugated exactly as those of group A I except that before terminations beginning with *e* or *i* the orthographical *i* is omitted because it is no longer necessary to show the 'softness' of the *c* or *g*. In the examples only those tenses are given in which these adjustments are necessary.[1] All other tenses are conjugated as in A I in every detail.

scacciare	**mangiare**

INDICATIVE

Present:

scaccio	mangio
scacci	mangi
scaccia	mangia
scacciamo	mangiamo
scacciate	mangiate
scac·ciano	man·giano

Future:

scaccerò	mangerò
scaccera·i	mangera·i
scaccerà	mangerà
scaccerẹmo	mangerẹmo
scaccerẹte	mangerẹte
scacceranno	mangeranno

Conditional:

scaccere·i	mangere·i
scaccerẹsti	mangerẹsti
scaccerebbe	mangerebbe
scaccerẹmmo	mangerẹmmo
scaccerẹste	mangerẹste
scaccereb·bero	mangereb·bero

[1] Only the modern terminations are given. For obsolete and poetic forms, etc., see the paradigm for group A I.

SUBJUNCTIVE

Present:

scacci	mangi
scacci	mangi
scacci	mangi
scacciamo	mangiamo
scacciate	mangiate
scac·cino	man·gino

IMPERATIVE

—	—
scaccia	mangia
scacci	mangi
scacciamo	mangiamo
scacciate	mangiate
scac·cino	man·gino

[A4] This group comprises verbs having a stem ending in *i* preceded by a consonant other than *c* or *g*, or by a vowel. Such verbs are conjugated as in A I except that the *i* is omitted before terminations beginning with *i*. In the example, only those tenses are given in which these adjustments are necessary.[1] All other tenses are conjugated as in A I in every detail.

invidiare   abbaiare

INDICATIVE

Present:

invi·dio	abba·io
invidi	abba·i
invi·dia	abba·ia
invidiamo	abbaiamo
invidiate	abbaiate
invi·diano	abba·iano

SUBJUNCTIVE

Present:

invidi	abba·i
invidi	abba·i
invidi	abba·i
invidiamo	abbaiamo
invidiate	abbaiate
invi·dino	abba·ino

IMPERATIVE

—	—
invi·dia	abba·ia
invidi	abba·i
invidiamo	abbaiamo
invidiate	abbaiate
invi·dino	abba·ino

[A5] This group comprises verbs having a stem ending in *-gnare*. Such verbs are conjugated as in A I except that two forms are permissible in certain tenses. In the example only those tenses are given in which such variation is permissible. All other tenses are conjugated as in A I in every detail.

regnare

INDICATIVE

Present:

rẹgno	regniamo *or* regnamo[2]
rẹgni	regnate
rẹgna	rẹgnano

SUBJUNCTIVE

Present:

rẹgni	regniamo *or* regnamo[2]
rẹgni	regniate *or* regnate[2]
rẹgni	rẹgnino

IMPERATIVE

—	regniamo *or* regnamo[2]
rẹgna	regnate
rẹgni	rẹgnino

[A6] This group comprises verbs having a stem ending in *-uare* or *-eare*. Such verbs are conjugated as A I except that two forms are permissible in certain tenses. In the example only those tenses are given in which such variation is permissible. All other tenses are conjugated as in A I in every detail.

continuare   creare

INDICATIVE

Present:

conti·nuo	creo
conti·nui	crei
conti·nua	crea
continuiamo *or* continuamo[3]	creiamo *or* creamo
continuate	create
conti·nuano	cre·ano

IMPERATIVE

conti·nua	crea
conti·nui	crei
continuiamo *or* continuamo[3]	creiamo *or* creamo[3]
continuate	create
conti·nuino	cre·ino

[A7]   andare

INDICATIVE

Present:

vado, vo	andiamo
vai	andate
va	vanno

Imperfect:
andavo, *etc.* as A I

Past definite:
anda·i, *etc.* as A I

Future:

andrò (†anderò)	andrẹmo (†anderemo)
andra·i (†anderai)	andrẹte (†anderete)
andrà (†anderà)	andranno (†anderanno)

Conditional:

andre·i	andrẹmmo
andrẹsti	andrẹste
andrebbe	andreb·bero

SUBJUNCTIVE

Present:

vada	andiamo
vada	andiate
vada	va·dano

Imperfect: as A I

IMPERATIVE

—	andiamo
va (vai, va')	andate
vada	va·dano

Gerund: andando
Present participle: andante
Past participle: andato

[A8]   dare

INDICATIVE

Present:

do	diamo
da·i	date
da, dà	danno, dànno

---

[1] Only the modern terminations are given. For obsolete and poetic forms, etc., see the paradigm for group A I.

[2] The first of these forms is preferred in present-day usage.

[3] The first of these forms is preferred in present-day usage, but some grammarians consider such verbs defective in these forms and recommend their avoidance by means of an impersonal construction, e.g. 'noi si continua'.

Imperfect:

davo	davamo
davi	davate
dava	da·vano

Past definite:

detti, diedi	dęmmo
dęsti	dęste
dette, diede	det·tero, die·dero (†diero)

Future:

darò (†drò)	daręmo (†dremo)
dara·i (†drai)	daręte (†drete)
darà (†drà)	daranno (†dranno)

Conditional:

dare·i	daręmmo
daręsti	daręste
darebbe	dareb·bero

SUBJUNCTIVE

Present:

dia	diamo
dia	diate
dia	di·ano, di·eno

Imperfect:

dęssi	dęmmo
dęssi	dęste
dęsse	dęssero

IMPERATIVE

—	diamo
da (dai, da')	date
dia	di·ano, di·eno

Gerund: dando
Present participle: dante
Past participle: dato

[A9]   **stare**

INDICATIVE

Present:

sto	stiamo
stai	state
sta	stanno

Imperfect:

stavo	stavamo
stavi	stavate
stava	sta·vano

Past definite:

stetti	stęmmo
stęsti	stęste
stette	stet·tero

Future:

starò	staręmo
stara·i	staręte
starà	staranno

Conditional:

stare·i	staręmmo
staręsti	staręste
starebbe	stareb·bero

SUBJUNCTIVE

Present:

sti·a	stiamo
sti·a	stiate
sti·a	sti·ano

Imperfect:

stęssi	stęssimo
stęssi	stęste
stęsse	stęssero

IMPERATIVE

—	stiamo
sta (stai, sta')	state
stia	sti·ano

Gerund: stando
Past participle: stato

GROUP B

[B1]   **temęre**   **vęndere**

Although these verbs may be said to fall into two classes in that the stress occurs on a different syllable in the infinitive (temęre, vęndere), this is the only place in the whole conjugation where such a difference in stress occurs. Such verbs have therefore been classed together, the marking of the infinitive as it occurs in the body of the dictionary being sufficient indication regarding the position of the stress on the infinitive itself.

INDICATIVE

Present:

tęmo	vęndo
tęmi	vęndi
tęme	vęnde
temiamo (†tememo)	vendiamo (†vendemo)
temęte	vendęte
tęmono	vęndono (†vendano)

Imperfect:

temęvo (temęva,[1] †temea, †temia)	vendęvo (vendęva,[1] †vendea, †vendia)
temęvi	vendęvi
temęva (†temea, †temia)	vendęva (†vendea, †vendia)
temevamo (†temavamo)	vendevamo (†vendavamo)
temevate (†temavate)	vendevate (†vendavate)
temęvano (†teme·ano, †temi·ano, †temi·eno)	vendęvano (†vende·ano, †vendi·ano, †vendi·eno)

Past definite:

temęi, temetti (†temèo)	vendęi, vendetti
temęsti	vendęsti
temè, temette	vendè, vendette
temęmmo	vendęmmo
temęste	vendęste
temęrono, temet·tero (†temero, †temer, †temerno, †temenno)	vendęrono, vendet·tero (†vendero, †vender, †venderno, †vendenno)

Future:

temerò (†temeròe, †temerag·gio)	venderò (†venderoe, †venderag·gio)
temera·i	vendera·i
temerà (†temeràe)	venderà (†venderàe)
temeręmo	venderęmo
temeręte	venderęte
temeranno	venderanno

Conditional:

temere·i (†temerebbi, †temeria)	vendere·i (†venderebbi, †venderia)
temeręsti (†temereste)	venderęsti (†vendereste)
temerebbe (†temerìa)	venderebbe (†venderìa)
temeręmmo	venderęmmo
temeręste	venderęste
temereb·bero (†temeri·ano, †temereb·bono)	vendereb·bero (†venderi·ano, †vendereb·bono)

---

[1] This form was in current use up to the end of the nineteenth century.

SUBJUNCTIVE

Present:

tẹma	vẹnda
tẹma	vẹnda
tẹma	vẹnda
temiamo	vendiamo
temiate	vendiate
tẹmano	vẹndano

Imperfect:

temẹssi	vendẹssi
temẹssi	vendẹssi
temẹsse	vendẹsse
temẹssimo	vendẹssimo
temẹste	vendẹste
temẹssero	vendẹssero

IMPERATIVE

—	—
tẹmi	vẹndi
tẹma	vẹnda
temiamo	vendiamo
temẹte	vendẹte
tẹmano	vẹndano

Gerund: temendo vendendo
Present participle: temente vendente
Past participle: temuto venduto

[B2] **addurre**

Present:

adduco	adduciamo
adduci	adducẹte
adduce	addu·cono

Imperfect: adducẹvo, *etc.*
Past definite:

addussi	adducẹmmo
adducẹsti	adducẹste
addusse	addus·sero

Future: addurrò, *etc.*
Conditional: addurrei, *etc.*

SUBJUNCTIVE

Present:

adduca	adduciamo
adduca	adduciate
adduca	addu·cano

Imperfect: adducẹssi, *etc.*

IMPERATIVE

—	adduciamo
adduci	adducẹte
adduca	addu·cano

Gerund: adducendo
Present participle: adducente
Past participle: addọtto

[B3] **avẹre**

INDICATIVE

Present:

ho (†ag·gio, †abbo)	abbiamo (†avemo)
hai	avẹte
ha (†ave)	hanno

Imperfect: avẹvo, *etc.*
Past definite:

ebbi	avẹmmo
avẹsti	avẹste
ebbe	eb·bero (†eb·bono)

Future: avrò, *etc.* (†averò, †arò, *etc.*)
Conditional:

avre·i (†avria)	avrẹmmo
avrẹsti	avrẹste
avrebbe (†avria, †arebbe)	avreb·bero (†avri·ano, †areb·bono, †areb·bano)

SUBJUNCTIVE

Present:

ab·bia (†ag·gia, †abbi)	abbiamo
ab·bia (†ag·gia, †abbi)	abbiate
ab·bia (†ag·gia, †abbi)	ab·biano (†ag·giano, †ab·bino)

Imperfect: avẹssi *etc.*

IMPERATIVE

—	abbiamo
abbi	abbiate
abbia	ab·biano

Gerund: avendo (†abbiendo)
Present participle: avente (†abbiente)[1]
Past participle: avuto

[B4] **bẹre** or **bevẹre**

INDICATIVE

Present:

bẹvo	beviamo
bẹvi	bevẹte
bẹve	bẹvono

Imperfect: bevẹvo, *etc.*
Past definite:

bẹvvi, bevetti	bevẹmmo
bevẹsti	bevẹste
bẹvve, bevette	bẹvvero, bevet·tero

Future: beverò, *etc.*
Conditional: bevere·i, *etc.*

SUBJUNCTIVE

Present:

bẹva	beviamo
bẹva	beviate
bẹva	bẹvano

Imperfect: bevẹssi, *etc.*

IMPERATIVE

—	beviamo
bẹvi	bevẹte
bẹva	bẹvano

Gerund: bevendo
Present participle: bevente
Past participle: bevuto

[B5] **cadẹre**

As B1, except past definite, future and conditional as follows:

Past definite:

caddi	cadẹmmo
cadẹsti	cadẹste
cadde	cad·dero

Future: cadrò, *etc.*
Conditional: cadre·i, *etc.*

[B6] **chiẹdere**

INDICATIVE

Present:

chiẹdo (†chieggo)	chiediamo
chiẹdi	chiedẹte
chiẹde	chiẹdono (†chieggono)

Past definite:

chiẹsi	chiedẹmmo
chiedẹsti	chiedẹste
chiẹse	chiẹsero

Past participle: chiẹsto

Other tenses and forms as for B1.

[1] As a participial adjective, 'abbiente', meaning 'well-to-do', is not obsolete.

[B7]   **co·gliere (corre. cor)**

INDICATIVE

Present:

colgo	cogliamo
cogli	coglięte
co·glie	col·gono

Imperfect: coglięvo, *etc.*
Past definite:

colsi	coglięmmo
coglięsti	coglięste
colse	col·sero

Future: coglierò, *etc.*
Conditional: cogliere·i, *etc.*

SUBJUNCTIVE

Present:

colga	cogliamo
colga	cogliate
colga	col·gano

Imperfect: coglięssi, *etc.*

IMPERATIVE

—	cogliamo
cogli (co')	coglięte
colga	col·gano

Gerund: cogliendo
Present participle: cogliente
Past participle: colto

[B8]   **cọmpiere**

See D6.

[B9]   **conọscere**

INDICATIVE

Present:

conọsco	conosciamo
conọsci	conoscęte
conọsce	conọscono

Imperfect: conoscęvo, *etc.*
Past definite:

conọbbi	conoscęmmo
conoscęsti	conoscęste
conọbbe	conọbbero

Future: conoscerò, *etc.*
Conditional: conoscere·i, *etc.*

SUBJUNCTIVE

Present:

conọsca	conosciamo
conọsca	conosciate
conọsca	conọscano

Imperfect: conoscęssi, *etc.*

IMPERATIVE

—	conosciamo
conọsci	conoscęte
conọsca	conọscano

Gerund: conoscendo
Present participle: conoscente
Past participle: conosciuto

[B10]   **dire (†di·cere)**

INDICATIVE

Present:

dico	diciamo
dicⁱ	dite
dice	di·cono

Imperfect: dicęvo, *etc.*
Past definite:

dissi	dicęmmo
dicęsti	dicęste
disse	dis·sero

Future: dirò, *etc.* (†dicerò, *etc.*)
Conditional: dire·i, *etc.*

SUBJUNCTIVE

Present:

dica	diciamo
dica	diciate
dica	di·cano

Imperfect: dicęssi, *etc.*

IMPERATIVE

—	diciamo
di' (†di)	dite
dica	di·cano

Gerund: dicendo
Present participle: dicente
Past participle: dętto

[B11]   **dolęre**

INDICATIVE

Present:

dolgo	dogliamo
duoli	dolęte
duole	dol·gono

Imperfect: dolęvo, *etc.*
Past definite:

dolsi	dolęmmo
dolęsti	dolęste
dolse	dol·sero

Future: dorrò, *etc.*
Conditional: dorre·i, *etc.*

SUBJUNCTIVE

Present:

dolga	dogliamo
dolga	dogliate
dolga	dol·gano

Imperfect: dolęssi, *etc.*

IMPERATIVE

—	dogliamo
duoli	dolęte
dolga	dol·gano

Gerund: dolendo
Present participle: dolente
Past participle: doluto

[B12]   **dovęre**

INDICATIVE

Present:

devo, debbo (deg·gio)	dobbiamo
devi (†dei)	dovęte
deve (†debbe, †dee)	de·vono, deb·bono (†denno)

Imperfect: dovęvo, *etc.*
Past definite:

dovęi, dovetti	dovęmmo
dovęsti	dovęste
dovę, dovette	dovet·tero

Future: dovrò, *etc.*
Conditional: dovre·i, *etc.*

SUBJUNCTIVE

Present:

debba (deva, deg·gia)	dobbiamo
debba (deva, deg·gia)	dobbiate
debba (deva, deg·gia)	deb·bano (de·vano)

Imperfect: dovęssi, *etc.*

Gerund: dovendo
Past participle: dovuto

[B13]   **es·sere**

INDICATIVE

Present:
sọno[1]   siamo (†semo)
sei (†siei)   sięte (†sete)
è   sọno[1] (†enno)

Imperfect:
ero (era)[2]   eravamo (†eramo, †savamo)
eri   eravate (†erate, †savate)
era   e·rano

Past definite:
fui   fummo
fọsti (†fusti)   fọste (†fuste)
fu (†fue)   fu·rono (†furo, furno, foro, fur)

Future:
sarò   sarẹmo
sarai   sarẹte
sarà (†fia, †fie)   saranno (†fi·ano, †fi·eno)

Conditional:
sare·i, *etc.*   sarẹmmo
sarẹsti   sarẹste
sarebbe[3] (sarìa, fora)   sareb·bero[3] (†sari·ano)

SUBJUNCTIVE

Present:
sia (†sie)   siamo
sia (†sie)   siate
sia (†sie)   si·ano (†si·eno, †fi·**eno**)

Imperfect:
fọssi (†fussi)   fọssimo (†fus·simo)
fọssi (†fussi)   fọste (†fuste)
fọsse (†fusse)   fọssero (†fus·sero)

IMPERATIVE

—   siamo
sii, si'   siate
sia   si·ano

Gerund: essendo (†sendo)
Present participle: None
Past participle: stato (†suto)

[B14]   **fare (†fa·cere)**

INDICATIVE

Present:
faccio, fo   facciamo
fai   fate
fa   fanno

Imperfect: facẹvo, *etc.*
Past definite:
fẹci   facẹmmo
facẹsti (†festi)   facẹste
fẹce   fẹcero (†fer, †fe·ciono)

Future: farò, *etc.*
Conditional: fare·i, *etc.*

SUBJUNCTIVE

Present:
faccia   facciamo
faccia   facciate
faccia   fac·ciano

Imperfect:
facẹssi   facẹssimo
facẹssi   facẹste
facẹsse   facẹssero

IMPERATIVE

—   facciamo
fa (fai, fa')   fate
faccia   fac·ciano

Gerund: facendo
Present participle: facente
Past participle: fatto

[B15]   **giacẹre**

INDICATIVE

Present:
giaccio   giaciamo
giaci   giacẹte
giace   gia·ciono

Imperfect: giacẹvo, *etc.*
Past definite:
giacqui   giacẹmmo
giacẹsti   giacẹste
giacque   giac·quero

Future: giacerò, *etc.*
Conditional: giacere·i, *etc.*

SUBJUNCTIVE

Present:
giacia   giaciamo
giacia   giaciate
giacia   gia·ciano

Imperfect: giacẹssi, *etc.*

IMPERATIVE

—   giaciamo
giaci   giacẹte
giacia   gia·ciano

Gerund: giacendo
Present participle: giacente
Past participle: giaciuto

[B16]   **godẹre**

As B1, except that future and conditional may be godrò, godre·i, *etc.*, as well as goderò, godere·i, *etc.*

[B17]   **mẹscere**

As B1 except for alternative in the Present Indicative, as follows:

INDICATIVE

Present:
mẹscio, mẹsco   mesciamo
mẹsci   mescẹte
mẹsce   mẹscono

[B18]   **na·scere**

INDICATIVE

Present:
nasco   nasciamo
nasci   nascẹte
nasce   na·scono

Imperfect: nascẹvo, *etc.*
Past definite:
nacqui   nascẹmmo
nascẹsti   nascẹste
nacque   nac·quero

Future: nascerò, *etc.*
Conditional: nascere·i, *etc.*

---

[1] In Rome the pronunciation preferred is 'sono' (with an open *o*).
[2] This form was in current use up to the end of the nineteenth century.
[3] In Rome, the pronunciation preferred is sarẹbbe, sarẹbbero.

SUBJUNCTIVE

Present:

nasca	nasciamo
nasca	nasciate
nasca	na·scano

Imperfect: nascęssi, *etc.*

IMPERATIVE

—	nasciamo
nasci	nascęte
nasca	na·scano

Gerund: nascendo
Present participle: nascente
Past participle: nato (†nasciuto)

[B19] **parẹre**

INDICATIVE

Present:

pa·io	paia·mo
pari	parẹte
pare	pa·iono

Imperfect: parẹvo, *etc.*
Past definite:

parvi	parẹmmo
parẹsti	parẹste
parve	par·vero

Future: parrò, *etc.*
Conditional: parre·i, *etc.*

SUBJUNCTIVE

Present:

pa·ia	paiamo
pa·ia	paiate
pa·ia	pa·iano

Imperfect: parẹssi, *etc.*
Gerund: parendo
Past participle: parso

[B20] **piacẹre**

This is conjugated like B15 except for slight differences (-cc- for -c-) in present indicative and subjunctive.

Present indicative:

piaccio	piacciamo
piaci	piacẹte
piace	piac·ciono

Present subjunctive:

piaccia	piacciamo
piaccia	piaciate
piaccia	piac·ciano

[B21] **pọrre**

INDICATIVE

Present:

pọngo	poniamo
pọni	ponęte
pọne	pọngono

Imperfect: ponẹvo, *etc.*
Past definite:

pọsi	ponẹmmo
ponẹsti	ponẹste
pọse	pọsero

Future: porrò, *etc.*
Conditional: porre·i, *etc.*

SUBJUNCTIVE

Present:

pọnga	poniamo
pọnga	poniate
pọnga	pọngano

Imperfect: ponęssi, *etc.*

IMPERATIVE

—	poniamo
pọni (pon)	ponęte
pọnga	pọngano

Gerund: ponendo
Present participle: ponente
Past participle: pọsto

[B22] **potẹre**

Present:

posso	possiamo
puo·i	potẹte
può (†puote)	pos·sono (†ponno)

Imperfect: potẹvo, *etc.*
Past definite:

potẹi	potẹmmo
potẹsti	potẹste
potẹ	potẹrono

Future: potrò, *etc.*
Conditional: potre·i, *etc.*

SUBJUNCTIVE

Present:

possa	possiamo
possa	possiate
possa	pos·sano

Imperfect: potẹssi, *etc.*
Gerund: potendo
Present participle: None
  [potente, possente, *adjs.* meaning 'powerful']
Past participle: potuto

[B23] **prevedẹre**

As B35, except future and conditional as follows:

Future: prevederò, *etc.*
Conditional: prevedere·i, *etc.*

[B24] **riavẹre**

As B3, but note present indicative forms.

Present indicative:

riò	riabbiamo
ria·i	riavẹte
rià	rianno

[B25] **rimanẹre**

Except for infinitive, like B21.

[B26] **sapẹre**

INDICATIVE

Present:

so	sappiamo
sai	sapẹte
sa	sanno

Imperfect: sapẹvo, *etc.*
Past definite:

seppi	sapẹmmo
sapẹsti	sapẹste
seppe	sep·pero

Future: saprò, *etc.*
Conditional: sapre·i, *etc.*

SUBJUNCTIVE

Present:

sap·pia	sappiamo
sap·pia	sappiate
sap·pia	sap·piano

Imperfect: sapẹssi, *etc.*

892

IMPERATIVE

—	sappiamo
sa	sapẹte
sap·pia	sap·piano

Gerund: sapendo
Present participle: sapiente
Past participle: saputo

[B27] **scẹgliere (†scerre)**

INDICATIVE

Present:

scẹlgo	scegliamo
scẹgli	scegliẹte
scẹglie	scẹlgono

Imperfect: scegliẹvo, *etc.*
Past definite:

scẹlsi	scegliẹmmo
scegliẹsti	scegliẹste
scẹlse	scẹlsero

Future: sceglierò, *etc.* (†scerrò, *etc.*)
Conditional: scegliere·i, *etc.* (†scerrei, *etc.*)

SUBJUNCTIVE

Present:

scẹlga	scegliamo
scẹlga	scegliate
scẹlga	scẹlgano

Imperfect: scegliẹssi, *etc.*

IMPERATIVE

—	scegliamo
scẹgli	scegliẹte
scẹlga	scẹlgano

Gerund: scegliendo
Present participle: None
Past participle: scẹlto

[B28] **sedẹre**

INDICATIVE

Present:

siedo, (seggo, †seg·gio)	sediamo
siedi	sedẹte
siede	sie·dono (seg·gono)

Imperfect: sedẹvo, *etc.*
Past definite: sedẹi *or* sedetti, *etc.*
Future: sederò, *etc.*
Conditional: sedere·i, *etc.*

SUBJUNCTIVE

Present:

sieda, segga	sediamo
sieda, segga	sediate
sieda, segga	sie·dano, seg·gano

Imperfect: sedẹssi, *etc.*

IMPERATIVE

—	sediamo
siedi	sedẹte
sieda, segga	sie·dano, seg·gano

Gerund: sedendo
Present participle: sedente
Past participle: seduto

[B29] **soddisfare**

INDICATIVE

Present: As A1 or B14

All other tenses: as B14

[B30] **solẹre**

INDICATIVE

Present:

soglio	sogliamo
suoli	solẹte
suole	so·gliono

Imperfect: solẹvo, *etc.*
Past definite: solẹi, *etc.*
Future: solerò, *etc.*
Conditional: solere·i, *etc.*

SUBJUNCTIVE

Present:

soglia	sogliamo
soglia	sogliate
soglia	so·gliano

Imperfect: solẹssi, *etc.*
Gerund: solendo
Past participle: so·lito

[B31] **ṣvel·lere (ṣverre)**

INDICATIVE

Present:

ṣvello, ṣvelgo	ṣvelliamo
ṣvelli, ṣvelgi	ṣvellẹte
ṣvelle, ṣvelge	ṣvel·lono, ṣvel·gono

Imperfect: ṣvellẹvo, *etc. or* ṣvelgẹvo, *etc.*
Past definite:

ṣvelsi	ṣvelgẹmmo
ṣvellẹsti, svelgẹsti	ṣvellẹste, svelgẹste
ṣvelse	ṣvel·sero

Future: ṣvellerò, *etc. or* ṣvelgerò, *etc.*
Conditional: ṣvellere·i, *etc. or* ṣvelgere·i, *etc.*
Gerund: ṣvellendo
Past participle: ṣvelto

[B32] **tenẹre**

INDICATIVE

Present:

tengo	teniamo
tieni	tenẹte
tiene	ten·gono

Imperfect: tenẹvo, *etc.*
Past definite:

tẹnni	tenẹmmo
tenẹsti	tenẹste
tẹnne	tẹnnero

Future: terrò, *etc.*
Conditional: terre·i, *etc.*

SUBJUNCTIVE

Present:

tenga	teniamo
tenga	teniate
tenga	ten·gano

Imperfect: tenẹssi, *etc.*

IMPERATIVE

—	teniamo
tieni	tenẹte
tenga	ten·gano

Gerund: tenendo
Present participle: tenente
Past participle: tenuto

[B33] **trarre**

INDICATIVE

Present:

traggo	traiamo, tragghiamo
trai	traẹte
trae	trag·gono

Imperfect: traẹvo, *etc.*
Past definite:

trassi	traẹmmo
traẹsti	traẹste
trasse	tras·sero

Future: trarrò, *etc.*
Conditional: trarre·i, *etc.*

SUBJUNCTIVE

Present:

tragga	traiamo, tragghiamo
tragga	traiate
tragga	trag·gano

Imperfect: traẹssi, *etc.*

IMPERATIVE

—	traiamo
trai	traẹte
tragga	trag·gano

Gerund: traendo
Present participle: traente
Past participle: tratto

[B34] **valẹre**

INDICATIVE

Present:

valgo	valiamo, vagliamo
vali	valẹte
vale	val·gono

Imperfect: valẹvo, *etc.*
Past definite:

valsi	valẹmmo
valẹsti	valẹste
valse	val·sero

Future: varrò, *etc.*
Conditional: varre·i, *etc.*

SUBJUNCTIVE

Present:

valga	valiamo
valga	valiate
valga	val·gano

Imperfect: valẹssi, *etc.*

IMPERATIVE

—	valiamo
vali	valẹte
valga	val·gano

Gerund: valendo
Present participle: valente
Past participle: valuto, valso

[B35] **vedẹre**

INDICATIVE

Present:

vẹdo (vẹggo, veg·gio)	vediamo (veggiamo)
vẹdi	vedẹte
vẹde	vẹdono (vẹggono)

Imperfect: vedẹvo, *etc.*
Past definite:

vidi	vedẹmmo
vedẹsti	vedẹste
vide	vi·dero

Future: vedrò, *etc.*
Conditional: vedre·i, *etc.*

SUBJUNCTIVE

Present:

vẹda (vẹgga, veg·gia)	vediamo
vẹda (vẹgga, veg·gia)	vediate
vẹda (vẹgga, veg·gia)	vẹdano (vẹggano)

Imperfect: vedẹssi, *etc.*

IMPERATIVE

—	vediamo
vẹdi	vedẹte
vẹda	vẹdano

Gerund: vedendo
Present participle: vedente, veggente
Past participle: veduto, visto

[B36] **volẹre**

INDICATIVE

Present:

voglio, vo' (†vuo, †vuo')	vogliamo
vuoi (†vuogli, †vui)	volẹte
vuole	vogliono

Imperfect: volẹvo, *etc.*
Past definite:

volli (†volsi)	volẹmmo
volẹsti	volẹste
volle (†volse)	vol·lero (†vol·sero)

Future: vorrò, *etc.*
Conditional: vorre·i, *etc.*

SUBJUNCTIVE

As B30

Gerund: volendo
Present participle: volente
Past participle: voluto (†volsuto)

GROUP C

The verbs given under the letter c. sometimes known as strong verbs, all belong to the -*ere* conjugation. They are conjugated like B I except for the past participle and the first person singular and third person singular and plural of the past definite. The full conjugation of 'prendere' is here given as an example showing where the irregular forms occur.

[C I] **pren·dere**

Present:

prendo	prendiamo
prendi	prendẹte
prende	pren·dono

Imperfect:

prendẹvo	prendevamo
prendẹvi	prendevate
prendẹva	prendẹvano

Past definite:

prẹsi	prendẹmmo
prendẹsti	prendẹste
prẹse	prẹsero

Future:

prenderò	prenderẹmo
prendera·i	prenderẹte
prenderà	prenderanno

Conditional:

prendere·i	prenderẹmmo
prenderẹsti	prenderẹste
prenderebbe	prendereb·bero

SUBJUNCTIVE

Present:

prenda	prendiamo
prenda	prendiate
prenda	pren·dano

Imperfect:

prendẹssi	prendẹssimo
prendẹssi	prendẹste
prendẹsse	prendẹssero

IMPERATIVE

—	prendiamo
prendi	prendęte
prenda	pren·dano

Gerund: prendendo
Present participle: prendente
Past participle: pręso

It will be seen from the above that it is sufficient to know the first person singular of the past definite (pręsi) in order to be able to form the third person singular and plural (pręse, pręsero). As the same applies to all verbs of group c, it is only necessary for the infinitive, first person singular past definite and the past participle to be listed in order to give sufficient data for the whole conjugation.

	Infinitive	1st pers. sing. past def.	Past participle
c1	pren·dere	pręsi	pręso
	contundere	contuși	contușo
c2	fondere	fuși	fușo
c3	ri·dere	risi	riso
	ar·dere	arsi	arso
	persuadęre	persuași	persuașo
c4	emer·gere	emersi	emerso
	spar·gere	sparsi	sparso
c5	sor·gere	sorsi	sorto
	assur·gere	assursi	assurto
	pun·gere	punsi	punto
	tor·cere	torsi	torto
	vin·cere	vinsi	vinto
	vol·gere	volsi	volto
	correre	corsi	corso
c6	distin·guere	distinsi	distinto
c7	spęgnere	spensi	spento
c8	assu·mere	assunsi	assunto
c9	redi·mere	redensi	redento
c10	strin·gere	strinsi	stretto
c11	rispondere	risposi	risposto
c12	frig·gere	frissi	fritto
	leg·gere	lessi	letto
	strug·gere	strussi	strutto
	scri·vere	scrissi	scritto
c13	diri·gere	diressi	diretto
c14	invol·gere	involsi	involto, involuto
	assol·vere	assolvetti, assolvei, assolsi	assolto, assoluto
	asciol·vere	asciolsi	asciolto
c15d	cuo·cere	cossi	cotto
	muo·vere	mossi	mosso
c16	vivere	vissi	vissuto
c17	prefig·gere	prefissi	prefisso
c18	oppri·mere	oppressi	oppresso
c19	inflet·tere	inflessi	inflesso
	conce·dere	concessi	concesso
	discu·tere	discussi	discusso
c19d	scuo·tere	scossi	scosso
c20	męttere	misi	męsso
c21	scin·dere	scindetti	scisso
	fen·dere	fendetti	fesso
c22	succe·dere	succedetti, successi	succeduto, successo
c23	espel·lere	espulsi	espulso
c24	resi·stere	resistei, resistetti	resistito
c25	span·dere	spandetti	spanto
c26	rompere	ruppi	rotto
c27	pio·vere	piovvi	piovuto
c28	per·dere	perdette, persi	perduto, perso
c29	cer·nere	cernei, cernetti	cernito
c30	contes·sere	contessei	contessuto, contesto
c31	riful·gere	rifulsi	rifulso
c32	redi·gere	redigei	redatto

Diphthongization of verbs of Group C

In the example which follows, only those tenses are given in which diphthongization occurs. In all other tenses, such verbs are conjugated as c1 in every detail.

[c15d] **muo·vere**

INDICATIVE

Present:

muovo	moviamo
muovi	movęte
muove	muovono

SUBJUNCTIVE

Present:

muova	moviamo
muova	moviate
muova	muovano

IMPERATIVE

—	moviamo
muovi	movęte
muova	muovano

GROUP D

[D1] **servire**

INDICATIVE

Present:

servo	serviamo (†servimo)
servi	servite
serve	ser·vono (†servano)

Imperfect:

servivo (serviva,[1] †servi·a)	servivamo
servivi	servivate
serviva	servi·vano (†servi·ano, †servi·eno)

Past definite:

servii	servimmo
servisti	serviste
servì (†servi·o, †servitte)	servi·rono (†serviro. †servir, †servirno, †servinno)

Future:

servirò (†serviròe, †servirag·gio)	servięmo
servira·i	serviręte
servirà (†serviràe)	serviranno

Conditional:

servire·i (†servirebbi, †serviri·a)	servięmmo
servięsti (†servireste)	servięste
servirebbe (†serviri·a)	servireb·bero (†serviri·ano. †serviri·eno, †servireb·bono)

SUBJUNCTIVE

Present:

serva (†servi)	serviamo
serva (†servi)	serviate
serva (†servi)	ser·vano (†ser·vino)

Imperfect:

servissi	servis·simo
servissi	serviste
servisse (†servissi)	servis·sero (†servis·sino, †servis·seno, †servis·sono

IMPERATIVE

—	serviamo
servi	servite
serva	ser·vano

Gerund: servendo
Present participle: serviente (the present participle is usually wanting in verbs of D group, though *adjs.* servente, divertente, etc., exist)
Past participle: servito

---

[1] This form was in current use up to the end of the nineteenth century.

[D 2]   finire

As D I except in the present indicative and subjunctive and in the imperative:

Present indicative:

finisco	finiamo (†finimo)
finisci	finite
finisce	fini·scono (†finiscano)

Present subjunctive:

finisca (†finischi)	finiamo
finisca (†finischi)	finiate
finisca (†finischi)	fini·scano (†fini·schino)

IMPERATIVE

—	finiamo
finisci	finite
finisca	fini·scano

[D 3]   apparire

INDICATIVE

Present:

appa·io, apparisco	appaiamo
appari, apparisci	apparite
appare, apparisce	appa·iono, appari·scono

Imperfect: apparivo, *etc.*

Past definite:

apparii, apparvi, apparsi	apparimmo
apparisti	appariste
apparì, apparve, apparse	apparirono, apparvero, appar·sero

Future: apparirò, *etc.*
Conditional: apparire·i, *etc.*

SUBJUNCTIVE

Present:

appa·ia, apparisca	appaiamo
appa·ia, apparisca	appariate
appa·ia, apparisca	appa·iano, appari·scano

Imperfect: apparissi, *etc.*

IMPERATIVE

—	appaiamo
appari, apparisce	apparite
appaia, apparisca	appa·iano, appariscano

Gerund: apparendo
Past participle: apparito, apparso

[D 4]   assalire

INDICATIVE

Present:

assalgo	assalghiamo
assali	assalite
assale	assal·gono

Past definite:

assalsi, assalii	assalimmo
assalisti	assaliste
assalse, assalì	assali·rono, assal·sero

SUBJUNCTIVE

Present:

assalga	assalghiamo
assalga	assalghiate
assalga	assal·gano

IMPERATIVE

—	assalghiamo
assali	assalite
assalga	assal·gano

All other tenses as D I.

[D 5]   comparire

INDICATIVE

Present:

comparisco, compaio	compariamo
comparisci	comparite
comparisce, compare	compari·scono, compa·iono

Imperfect: comparivo, *etc.*
Past definite:

comparii, comparsi, comparvi	comparimmo
comparisti	compariste
comparì, comparse, comparve	compar·vero

[N.B. The three forms in the singular of this tense are used for different meanings, viz. comparì = he made a good appearance; comparse = he appeared in court; comparve = he made his appearance.]

SUBJUNCTIVE

Present:

comparisca, compa·ia	compariamo
comparisca, compa·ia	compariate
comparisca, compa·ia	compa·iano

IMPERATIVE

—	compariamo
comparisci	comparite
comparisca, compa·ia	compa·iano

Past participle: comparso

Other tenses as for D I.

[D 6]   compire *or* compiere

INDICATIVE

Present:

compio, compisco	compiamo
compi, compisci	compite
compie, compisce	compiono, compi·scono

SUBJUNCTIVE

Present:

compia, compisca	compiamo
compia, compisca	compiate
compia, compisca	compiano, compiscano

Imperfect: compissi, *etc. or* compiessi, *etc.*

IMPERATIVE

—	compiamo
compisci, compi	compite
compisca, compia	compiscano, compiano

Past participle: compito, compiuto

Other tenses as D I.

[D 7]   convertire

As D I, but past participle converso besides convertito.

[D 8]   coprire

Past definite:

coprii, copersi	coprimmo
copristi	copriste
coprì, coperse	copri·rono, coper·sero

Past participle: coperto

Other tenses as D I.

[D 9]   costruire

As D 2, except that alternative form of past definite is costrussi, etc. and alternative past participle is costrutto.

[D10] disparire

Present indicative:

disparisco	—
disparisci	disparite
disparisce	dispari·scono

Past definite:

disparii, disparvi	disparimmo
disparisti	dispariste
disparve	dispar·vero

Other tenses as D2.

[D11] empire *or* ẹmpiere

Present indicative:

ẹmpio	empiamo
ẹmpi	empite
ẹmpie	ẹmpiono

Present subjunctive:

ẹmpia	empiamo
ẹmpia	empiate
ẹmpia	ẹmpiano

Past participle: empito, empiuto

Other tenses as D1.

[D12] morire

INDICATIVE

Present:

m(u)o·io	moriamo
m(u)ori	morite
m(u)ore	m(u)o·iono

SUBJUNCTIVE

Present:

m(u)oia (†mora, †muora)	moriamo
m(u)oia (†mora, †muora)	moriate
m(u)oia (†mora, †muora)	m(u)o·iano

IMPERATIVE

—	moriamo
m(u)ori	morite
m(u)oia	m(u)o·iano

Past participle: morto

Other tenses as D1.

[D13] salire

INDICATIVE

Present:

salgo	saliamo
sali	salite
sale	sal·gono

SUBJUNCTIVE

Present:

salga	saliamo
salga	saliate
salga	sal·gano

IMPERATIVE

—	saliamo
sali	salite
salga	sal·gano

Other tenses as D1.

[D14] sparire

Past definite:

sparii, sparvi	sparimmo
sparisti, sparvisti	spariste
sparì, sparve	spari·rono, spar·vero

Other tenses as D2.

[D15] udire

INDICATIVE

Present:

odo	udiamo
odi	udite
ode	o·dono

Imperfect: udivo, *etc.*
Past definite: udii, *etc.*
Future: ud(i)rò, *etc.*
Conditional: ud(i)re·i, *etc.*

SUBJUNCTIVE

Present:

oda	udiamo
oda	udite
oda	o·dano

Imperfect: udissi, *etc.*

IMPERATIVE

—	udiamo
odi	udite
oda	o·dano

Gerund: udendo
Past participle: udito

[D16] uscire

INDICATIVE

Present:

esco	usciamo (†esciamo)
esci	uscite (†escite)
esce	e·scono

SUBJUNCTIVE

Present:

esca	usciamo
esca	usciate
esca	e·scano

IMPERATIVE

—	usciamo
esci	uscite
esca	e·scano

Other tenses as D1.

[D17] venire

INDICATIVE

Present:

vengo	veniamo
vieni	venite
viene	ven·gono

Imperfect: venivo, *etc.*
Past definite:

venni	venimmo
venisti	veniste
venne	ven·nero

Future: verrò, *etc.*
Conditional: verre·i, *etc.*

SUBJUNCTIVE

Present:

venga	veniamo
venga	veniate
venga	ven·gano

Imperfect: venissi, *etc.*

IMPERATIVE

—	veniamo
vieni	venite
venga	ven·gano

Gerund: venendo
Present participle: veniente, vegnente
Past participle: venuto

DEFECTIVE VERBS

calere   exists only as *infin.* and in *impers.* cale

consu·mere   as C8, but used only in *1st, 3rd pers. sing., 3rd pers. pl.* of *past def.* and in *past part.*

controver·tere   as B1, but *pres. indic.* and *pres. subj.* only.

conver·gere   as B1, but lacks *past part.*

delin·quere   as B1, but lacks *past part.*

diri·mere   as B1 but lacks *past part.*

discer·nere   as B1, but rare except in *infin. pres. indic., pres. subj., imperf.*

erompere   as C26, but lacks *past part.*

gire   poet., chiefly found in *3rd pers. sing. imperf.* giva; *past part.* gito.

investire   as D1, but lacks *pres. part.*

ire   exists only as *infin.* and *past part.* ito.

le·dere   as C3, but chiefly in *3rd pers. sing.* in simple tenses.

lucere   *3rd pers. sing., pl. pres. indic.* luce, lucono; *imperf.* luceva, lucevano.

molcere   as B1 but chiefly in *3rd pers. sing.* in simple tenses; lacks *past part.*

pentire   as D1, but lacks *pres. part.*

pru·dere   as B1, but lacks *pres. part., past part.*

rilu·cere   as C1, but lacks *pres. part., past part.*

stri·dere   as B1, but lacks *past part.*

ur·gere   as B1, but lacks *past def.* and *past part.*

ver·tere   as B1, but chiefly in *3rd pers. sing.* of simple tenses; lacks *past part.*

vi·gere   as B1, but chiefly in *3rd pers. sing.* of simple tenses; lacks *past part.*

REFERENCE LIST OF PRINCIPAL VERBS SHOWING PREPOSITIONS COMMONLY USED IN CONSTRUCTION WITH AN INFINITIVE[1]

abituare	a	figurare	di	procurare	di
accettare	di	fingere	di	proibire	di
affrettare	a	finire	di	promettere	di
agognare	a	forzare	a	proporre	di
aiutare	a	giustificare	di	provare	a
ammonire	di	guardare	di	rassegnare	a
ardire	(di)	imparare	a	ricordare	di
arrischiare	a	impedire	di	ricusare	di
aspettare	a, per	impegnare	a, di	rinunziare	a
autorizzare	a	imprendere	a	riuscire	a
avvezzare	a	incitare	a	scongiurare	di
avviare	a	inclinare	a	scusare	di
badare	a, di *di*	incoraggiare	a	sdegnare	di
bramare	a, di *di*	indugiare	a	sedurre	a
cercare	di	indurre	a	seguire	a
cessare	a, di	insegnare	a	seguitare	a
cominciare	a	intendere	di	sembrare	(di)
concedere	di	invitare	a	servire	a
conchiudere	di	mancare	di	sfidare	a
condannare	a	meravigliare	di	sforzare	a, di
condurre	a	meritare	di	smaniare	di
consentire	a, di	mettere	a	smettere	di
consigliare	a, di	muovere	a	sollecitare	a
continuare	a	obbligare	a, di	sopportare	di
contribuire	a	occupare	a	sperare	(di)
costringere	a	offrire	di	spingere	a
credere	di	ordinare	di	spronare	a
dare	a	ostinare	a	stabilire	di
degnare	di	parere	(di)	stentare	a
deliberare	di	penare	a	stimolare	a
desiderare	(di)	pensare	a, di ✗	suggerire	di
determinare	a	pentire	di	supplicare	a, di
dichiarare	di	permettere	di	tardare	a
dimenticare	di	persistere	a	temere	di
disperare	di	persuadere	a, di	tentare	a, di
disporre	a	pervenire	a	tornare	a
divertire	a	preferire	(di)	valere	a
domandare	di	prendere	a	vantare	di
eccitare	a	preparare	a	vergognare	a *di*
esercitare	a	presumere	di	vietare	a
esitare	a	pretendere	di		
esortare	a	principiare	a		

[1] This list is intended only for ready reference. For more detailed guidance the user should consult the relevant entry in the Dictionary. Brackets round a preposition indicate that its use is optional.

✗ *a with person, di with verb*

THE CAMBRIDGE

Italian

Dictionary

GENERAL EDITOR:
BARBARA REYNOLDS

VOLUME 1:
Italian-English

CAMBRIDGE UNIVERSITY PRESS